Mirá Paris
Phantom of Museum

Galaxia Cosmic Princess 1991

For Information call... 1-800-441-0455

TREBY

IMAGE SIZE 40" X 29.5"

© LONDON CONTEMPORARY ART 1993

"AEGEAN LEGEND I"

Announcing the release of a new serigraph.

Regular Edition on Arches 100% Rag Paper.

Deluxe Embellished Edition on linen.

London Contemporary Art
PUBLISHERS OF ORIGINAL PRINTS

729 Pinecrest Prospect Heights IL 60070 USA. Tel: 708 459 3990 Fax: 708 459 3997 Toll Free: 1 800 366 2788

SEE US AT ARTEXPO CALIFORNIA BOOTH #540, 548

ROY FAIRCHILD

A PASSION FOR BEAUTY

IMAGE SIZE 38" X 29" © LONDON CONTEMPORARY ART 1993

"WRITING ON WALLS"

Announcing the release of a serigraph hand printed in 63 colours

For further information on the artist contact:

LONDON CONTEMPORARY ART

PUBLISHERS OF ORIGINAL PRINTS

729 Pinecrest Prospect Heights IL 60070 USA. Tel: 708 459 3990 Fax: 708 459 3997 Toll Free: 1 800 366 2788

In every decade a new artist emerges who captures the imagination of the world.

IMAGE SIZE 25" X 51"

© LONDON CONTEMPORARY ART 1993

TARKAY

"RIVE GAUCHE"

Announcing a new serigraph. Signed and numbered by the artist.

For further information on the artist contact:

LONDON CONTEMPORARY ART
PUBLISHERS OF ORIGINAL PRINTS

729 Pinecrest Prospect Heights IL 60070 USA. Tel: 708 459 3990 Fax: 708 459 3997 Toll Free: 1 800 366 2788

ALI GOLKAR

IMAGE SIZE 38" X 26"

© ALI GOLKAR 1993

LCA

LONDON CONTEMPORARY ART

PUBLISHERS OF ORIGINAL PRINTS

729 Pinecrest Prospect Heights IL 60070 USA. Tel: 708 459 3990 Fax: 708 459 3997 Toll Free: 1 800 366 2788

MAIMON

"BUS STOP CAFÉ"

Serigraph on Westwind Paper; Image size: 25.2" x 35.63"

Maimon

EXCLUSIVELY PUBLISHED AND DISTRIBUTED BY

B & R
INTERNATIONAL ART, LTD.

5641 Circle View Drive, Bonsall, CA 92003 (619)945-5581, Fax # (619) 945-7827

MAIMON

"CORINA"

Height : 17.25"; 1992

EXCLUSIVELY PUBLISHED AND DISTRIBUTED BY

B&R
INTERNATIONAL ART, LTD.

5641 Circle View Drive, Bonsall, CA 92003　　　　Fax # (619) 945-7827, (619)945-5581

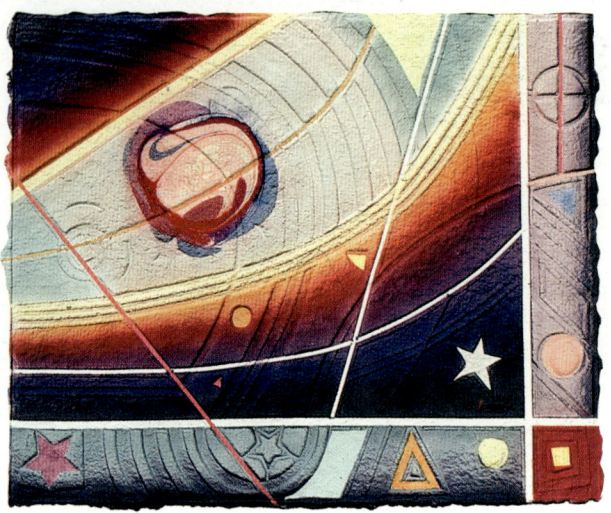

STARDUST 32" x 40"

FLASH POINT 32" x 40"

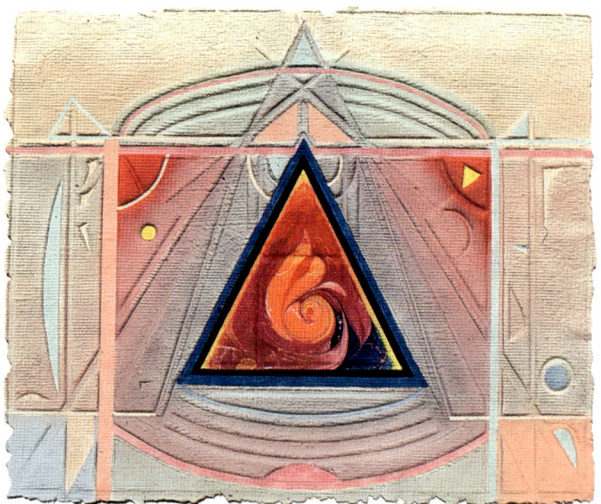

ETERNAL FLAME 32" x 40"

ANOTHER CHANNEL 32" x 40"

Multiples on artist-made paper
Embossed and hand colored
Edition size: 30, 5 A/P's
Paper size: 32" x 40"
Note: Some variation in color might occur.

44 Horton Lane, New Canaan, CT 06840
Phone: 203 972-0137
FAX: 203 972-3182

© 1993 M. Tomchuk. All rights reserved.

HARBOR 32" x 40"

"Apple Blossom"   25"x19"   950 Ed.

Nina Petrovna Bondarenko

KIEV, UKRAINE, C.I.S.

Offset Lithographs
from batik on silk crepe de chine

"Cherry Orchard"   16"x27"   950 Ed.

Seattle Design Center
5701-6th Avenue South
Suite 325
Seattle, Washington 98108

(206) 763-9527
Fax (206) 763-7053

Femme au Fauteuil Rouge
22 x 29 inches

Femme Assise Pres d'une Fenetre
22 x 29 inches

Portrait de'Homme Barbu
21 x 28 inches

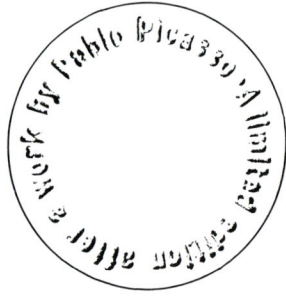

To ensure authenticity, each of the 500 limited edition Lithographs is numbered and signed by Marina Picasso, and is stamped with the embossed seal of the estate and the chromist.

Limited Edition Lithographs

Pablo Picasso, the pre-eminent 20th Century artist, was a genius whose works have been appreciated by hundreds of millions throughout this century.

The estate of Picasso authorized the printing of 500 and only 500 each of a select group of images from their private collection. The lithographic plates of these images will never again be available.

Can you see Your Profit in Our Art?

Though it takes a master's eye to create a great work of art, it is not hard to see how you can create a profit with one.

At RO GALLERY our aim is to make you successful! You'll find select works of art offered to you at strictly trade prices!

Our stock and trade can be your bread and butter with signed and numbered lithographs and seriographs by artists such as:

Ali	Bearden	Cottingham	Guetary	Kacere	Lindner	Oppenheim	Soto
Anuszkiewicz	Beauchamp	Davis	Hall	Katz	Matta	Picasso	Soyer
Appel	Calder	D'Archangelo	Impiglia	Kooning	Max	Ramos	Shuzimi
Arman	Cesar	Francis	Inukai	Kruschenick	Morris	Rotella	Ting
Azuz	Chryssa	Goings	Johnson	Lautrec	Mucha	Rosenquist	Yokoi
Barooshian	Corneille	Grooms	Judd	Lawrence	McCall	Schaare	and more!

- AFRICAN AMERICAN • ABSTRACT • ART DECO
- ANIMALS AND WILDLIFE • EROTICA • FLORAL • FANTASY
- GENRE/LANDSCAPES • INDIAN • POP • REALISM • RELIGIOUS
- SEASCAPES • SPORTS • TRAVEL POSTERS • POSTERS
- WESTERN AND MORE!

With this selection at our prices, fast sales and high turnover are practically guaranteed!

With high margins *and* volume how can you not SEE YOUR PROFIT IN OUR ART?

The Source For Limited Edition Images
47-15 36th Street Long Island City, NY 11101

By Appointment
(718) 937-0901   FAX 718-937-1206

International Resources for Fine and Decorative Art

Art @ Taipei

March 3-7, 1994
Jacob Javits Center
New York City, New York

April 2-6, 1994
World Trade Center
Taipei, Taiwan, R.O.C.

September 8-11, 1994
Los Angeles Convention Center
Los Angeles, California

October 6-9, 1994
Merchandise Mart ExpoCenter
Chicago, Illinois

Exhibiting Information: 216-826-2885
(toll-free: 800-827-7170); fax: 216-826-2801

Attendee Information: 218-723-9130
(toll-free: 800-331-5706); fax 218-723-9122

Produced and Managed by Advanstar Expositions, 7500 Old Oak Boulevard, Cleveland, Ohio 44130 USA

DODSWORTH

A contemporary journey through the art of the ancient world

IMAGE SIZE 37" X 26"

© LONDON CONTEMPORARY ART 1993

"ALTAMARA I"

Announcing the release of a series of
carborundum etchings based on Prehistoric Art.

LONDON CONTEMPORARY ART

PUBLISHERS OF ORIGINAL PRINTS

729 Pinecrest Prospect Heights IL 60070 USA. Tel: 708 459 3990 Fax: 708 459 3997 Toll Free: 1 800 366 2788

QUAN SUN

IMAGE SIZE 37" X 26" © LONDON CONTEMPORARY ART 1993

"THE BRIDE"

London Contemporary Art are pleased to announce their association with Quan Sun. Sun's first serigraph will be released in March 1993.

LONDON CONTEMPORARY ART
PUBLISHERS OF ORIGINAL PRINTS

729 Pinecrest Prospect Heights IL 60070 USA. Tel: 708 459 3990 Fax: 708 459 3997 Toll Free: 1 800 366 2788

G.H. Rothe

Master of the Mezzotint

G.H. Rothe Gallery

26364 Carmel Rancho Lane
Carmel, California 93923
(Adjacent to The Barnyard)

(408) 626-1338
Fax (408) 624-0499

G.H. Rothe Gallery
Lincoln btwn 7th & Ocean
P.O. Box 4837
Carmel, CA 93921
(408) 624-9377

G.H. Rothe Gallery
Doubletree Hotel
Lobby
Monterey, CA 93940
(408) 655-1313

L.E.C.
Print Artists

BALTHUS

JOHN BIGGERS

HENRI CARTIER-BRESSON

ELIZABETH CATLETT

FRANCESCO CLEMENTE

WILLEM DE KOONING

JOHN HEJDUK

ROBERTO JUAREZ

ELLSWORTH KELLY

YURI KUPER

TADAAKI KUWAYAMA

JACOB LAWRENCE

ROBERT MAPPLETHORPE

ROBERT MOTHERWELL

HANK O'NEAL

SEAN SCULLY

SETSUKA

AARON SISKIND

NEIL WELLIVER

THE LIMITED EDITIONS CLUB
39 East 72nd Street, New York, NY 10021   Telephone: (212) 737-7600   Telefax: (212) 249-3939

F.B.I. CRACKS DOWN ON ART FORGERY!

AUTHENTICATE AND PROTECT YOUR ART

WHO MAY APPLY

Artists, Publishers, Galleries, Collectors, Investors and Museums. Membership Applications Available on Request.

Benefits and Privileges of Becoming a Member of The International Museum and Artists Registration Association

Each piece of art registered with IMARA is permanently recorded in the Archives. Complete documentation and current retail values of the artist's works are available for every inquiry from the highly computerized resources of IMARA. This makes information immediately available for insurance claims and current market values of the artist's works as provided to us for investors, art patrons, galleries, museums, universities or other institutions.

APPLY FOR MEMBERSHIP NOW

Application for membership in IMARA is open to all professional artists meeting the necessary requirements and sponsored by a board member, artist member or approved Gallery or Museum without regard to race, color or creed. We believe in equality for all deserving artists. Selection is made solely on the basis of the artist's work and qualifications and application.

Additional information or questions can be answered by your sponsor or by writing direct to:

International Museum and Artists Registration Association
1000 Connecticut Ave., Suite #9
Washington, D.C. 20036

TABLE OF CONTENTS

Editor's Comments XIII
Artist Index ....III–XI
New Artist Index ....XII–XIII
Auction Index 1117
Fine Art Appraisers Index 1117
Gallery Index 1118–1147
Print Publishers Index 1108–1111
Printers/Print Workshop Index 1112–1117
Print Club Index 1117
Printworld Abbreviations (General) 1148–1149
Printworld Abbreviations (Paper) 1150–1151
Artist Biographical Application Form 1152
Print Documentation Form 1153

Printworld directory of contemporary
    prints & prices.—1982—
    — Bala Cynwyd, PA: Printworld, Inc.,
    v.: ill.; 28 cm.

1st ed (1982)
2nd ed (1983/84)
3rd ed (1985/86)
4th ed (1988/89)
5th ed (1991/92)
6th ed (1994)
ISSN 0734-2721

1. Prints - 20th Century — Catalogs.
2. Printmakers - Directories.

NE 491.P77   Dewey -769.92′2
Library of Congress   82-644944

1982   - ISBN-0-943606-00-4
1983/84 - ISBN-0-943606-01-2
1985/86 - ISBN-0-943606-02-0
1988/89 - ISBN-0-943606-03-0
         ISSN-0734-2721
         SAN-0240-7515
1991/92 - ISBN-0-943606-04-7 (Paper)
1991/92 - ISBN-0-943606-05-5 (Cloth)
1994   - ISBN-0-943606-06-3 (Cloth)

ON THE COVER

Front Cover: Sam Francis - Untitled - Lithograph, 1992

Back Cover: Sam Francis - Untitled - Etching, 1992

Our thanks to Sam Francis for permission to reproduce these two images

---

Copyright © January 1994 by Printworld International, Inc

All rights reserved. Any reproduction of the directory, in whole or in any part, without written permission of the publisher, is prohibited. The Printworld Directory of Contemporary Prints & Prices 1994 was printed and bound in the United States of America.

The publishers disclaim any liability to any party for any loss or damage caused by omissions or errors in the fifth edition of The Printworld Directory of Contemporary Prints & Prices 1994 whether such omissions or errors result from negligence, accident, or any cause.

For information, please write:
PRINTWORLD INTERNATIONAL, INC.
Post Office Box 1957
West Chester, PA 19380
(610) 431-6654 / (610) 649-5140
800-788-9101—Book orders only
(610) 431-6653—FAX

ARTIST INDEX

Abeles, Sigmund	1
Abakanowicz, Magdalena	1–2
Abrahami, Elie	2
Abrahams, Ivor	2
Abramowicz, Janet	3
Abrams, Jane Eldora	3
Acconci, Vito	3–4
Adams, Clinton	4–5
Adami, Valerio	5
Adams, Mark	6
Adams, Pat	6–7
Africano, Nicholas	7
Agam, Yaacov	7–13
Agudelo-Botero, Orlando	14–16
Albright, Ivan Le Lorraine	17
Albers, Josef	17–18
Albers, Anni	18
Albuquerque, Lita	19
Alechinsky, Pierre	19–20
Alexander, John	20
Alexander, Peter	21
Allan, William George	21
Allen, Terry	22
Allison, Dan	22–25
Allner, Walter	25–26
Almayda, Joseph	26
Alpert, George	26
Amar, Joseph	26
Altman, Harold	27–31
Alvar (Sunol)	31–32
Amen, Irving	32
Amft, Robert	32
Amenoff, Gregory	33
Amos, Emma	33
Amrhein, Joe	34
Anastasi, William	34
Anderson, Bruce	34
Anderson, Curtis	34
Anderson, Doug	34–35
Anderson, Ivan Delos	35
Anderson, Jeremy	35
Anderson, Laurie	35
Anderson, Leslie	35
Anderson, Othello	213
Anderson, Sally	36
Anderson, Robert	36
Andoe, Joe	36–37
Andrew, David Neville	37
Angel, Felix	37
Anguiano, Raul	38
Anker, Suzanne C	38
Ansell, Michael	39
Antin, Eleanor	39
Antonakos, Stephen	39
Antreasian, Garo Zareh	39–40
Antrim, Craig Keith	41
Anuszkiewicz, Richard	41
Aponovich, James	41
Appel, Karel	42–43
Applebroog, Ida	44
Aquino, Edmundo	44
Arakawa (Shusaku)	44–45
Archer, Cynthia	46
Argimon, Daniel	46
Arman (Armand Fernandez)	46–47
Arneson, Robert	47
Arons, Joyce	47–48
Arnoldi, Charles Arthur	48
Artschwager, Richard	48–49
Asano, Kyoko	50
Asaro, John	50–51
Ashbraugh, Dennis John	51
Askin, Walter	52
Asmar, Alice	52–53
Asoma, Tadashi	53
Atirnomis (Rita Simon)	53–54
Atkinson, Conrad	54
Attersee, Christian Ludwig	54
Attridge, Tom	55
Attie, Dotty	55
Audette, Anna Held	55–56
Auerbach, Frank	56
Austen, David	56
Avati, Mario	57
Avedisian, Edward	57
Avery, Eric	57
Axton, John	57
Aycock, Alice	58
Azaceta, Luis Cruz	58–59
Azoulay, Guillaume A	59–61
Azuz, David	61–62
Baber, Alice	62
Bacon, Bruce	63
Bacon, Francis	63
Back, John	64
Badalamenti, Fred	64
Baechler, Donald	64–65
Baeder, John	65–66
Baer, Jo	66
Baggett, William	66
Bailey, William	67
Baj, Enrico	68
Baker, Richard	66
Baldessari, John	68–69
Balet, Jan	69–71
Ballagh, Robert	67
Balog, Michael	67
Baltz, Lewis	71
Bannard, Walter Darby	71
Barber, Philip Judd	71
Barceló, Miguel	72
Bark, Jared	72
Barker, Laurence	72
Barnet, Will	73–74
Barnett, Helmut	72
Barooshian, Martin	74–75
Barr, David John	75
Barry, Robert Thomas	75
Barsch, Wulf E	75–76
Barth, Charles	76–77
Barth, Frances	77
Bartek, Tom	77–78
Bartlett, Jennifer	78–79
Baselitz, Georg	79–80
Baskin, Leonard	80–83
Basquiat, Jean-Michel	84
Battle, Georgette	84
Baum, Don	84
Baumgarten, Lothar	84–85
Baxter, Iain	85
Baxter, Robert	85–86
Bayer, Herbert	86–87
Baynard, Ed	87–88
Bazinet, Jane	88
Beal, Jack	89
Beament, Tib	89
Beall, Dennis Ray	90
Bearce, Jeana Dale	91
Bearden, Romare	90–91
Beattie, Drew	92
Beaumont, Mona	92
Bechara, Tony	92
Bechtle, Robert Alan	92–93
Becker, David	93
Beckman, William George	93–94
Beerman, John	94
Behnke, Leigh	94
Behnken, William	94
Bell, Larry	94–95
Bellegarde, Claude	95
Bellmer, Hans	95
Benaim, Ricardo	95
Bender, Gretchen	96
Benes, Barton Lidice	96
Benglis, Lynda	96–97
Bengston, Billy Al	97–98
Benjamin, Karl Stanley	98
Benny, Paul	98
Berea, Dimitrie	98–99
Berg, Siri	99
Berg, Tom	99
Berger, Jason	100
Berger, Nicholas	100
Berlin, Daniel	100
Berman, Ariane R	101
Berman, Wallace	101
Berman, Zeke	101
Bernstein, Judith	101–102
Bernstein, Richard	102
Berry, Ray	102
Berthois-Rigal, Bernard	102
Berthot, Jake	103
Besser, Arne Charles	103
Bevan, Tony	103
Beyer, Steven J	103
Beuys, Joseph	104–107
Bezombes, Roger	107–108
Bhavsar, Natvar Prahladji	108
Biberman, Edward	108
Biferie, Dan	108–109
Bill, Max	109
Binder, Erwin	109
Bird, Jim	109–110
Birmelin, Robert A	110
Blackwell, Tom	110
Blagden, Allen	111
Blair, Dike	111
Blais, Jean-Charles	111
Blake, Peter	111–112
Blatas, Arbit	114
Bleach, Bruce R	112–113
Bleckner, Ross	113
Bleiberg, Gertrude T	114
Blizzard, Alan	114–115
Block, Gay	115
Bluhm, Norman	115
Blum, Andrea	116
Bochner, Mel	116
Bodnar, Peter	116–117
Boers, Marianne	117
Bogarin, Rafael	117
Bohrod, Aaron	117–118
Boilauges, Fernand	118
Bolotin, Jay	118
Bolotowsky, Ilya	118
Boltanski, Christian	119
Boni, Paolo	119
Bonk, Keiko	120
Bonnefoit, Alain	120
Bontecou, Lee	120
Booth, George Warren	120
Borofsky, Jonathan	121–122
Borris, Marshall	122
Bosman, Richard	122–125
Botello, Angel	125–126
Botero, Fernando	126
Botti, Italo	126
Boulanger, Graciela Rodo	127–129
Bowler, Joseph, Jr	126
Bourgeois, Louise	129
Bowes, David	129
Bowling, Katherine	130
Boxer, Stanley Robert	130–131
Boyden, Frank	131
Brach, Paul Henry	131–132
Bradford, Howard	132
Bradford, Katherine	132
Bradshaw, Dove	133
Brady, Carolyn	132–133

ARTIST INDEX CONTINUED

Bragg, Charles	133–134	Caporael, Suzanne	168	Condak, Cliff	214
Bragg, Charles Lynn	134	Carabba, Leonilde	169	Condo, George	215
Bramson, Phyllis	135	Carcan, René	169	Connelly, Chuck	215
Branstetter, Gwendolyn	135	Card, Greg S	169	Conner, Ann	215–216
Bratt, Byron H	135–136	Card, Royden	170	Conner, Lois	216
Braun, Jorge Tarallo	136	Cardillo, Rimer	170–171	Conover, Robert Fremont	216–217
Braunecker, Andre	136	Carlson, Cynthia	171	Cook, Beryl	217–218
Brauntuch, Troy	136	Carnwath, Squeak	171–172	Cook, Gordon	217
Brennan, Fanny	136–137	Caro, Anthony	172	Cook, Howard	218–219
Breverman, Harvey	137–138	Carreiro, Joel	172	Cooper, Ann T	219
Brice, William	138	Carrino, David	173	Cooper, Marve H	219
Briggs, Lamar	138	Carroll, Lawrence	173	Cooper, Ron	220
Brodsky, Alexander & Utkin, Ilya	139	Carruthers, Roy	173	Cooper, Ruffin, Jr	220
Brodsky, Stan	139	Carsman, Jon	174	Cooper, Wayne	220–221
Brody, Arthur William	139	Carson, Karen	174	Copley, William Nelson	221
Broodthaers, Marcel	140	Carswell, Rodney	174–175	Cormenzana, Enric	221
Brooks, James	140	Carter, Clarence Holbrook	175	Corneille (Cornelis Van Beverloo)	221–222
Brosen, Frederick	141	Carter, James	175–176	Cornell, Joseph	222
Brosk, Jeffrey Owen	140	Carulla, Ramon	176	Corning, Merv	222–223
Brown, Charlotte	141	Casas, Fernando Rodriguez	176	Capron, Carlotta	223
Brown, Christopher	142	Case, Richard	177	Costa, Iza	223–224
Brown, James	143	Casebere, James Edward	177	Costan, Chris	226
Brown, Joan	143–144	Cassigneul, Jean-Pierre	177	Cottingham, Robert	224–225
Brown, Larry	142	Castel, Moshe	177–178	Cowan, Don Kellogg	226
Brown, Louise Freshman	141	Castellon, Federico	178	Cowin, Jack	226
Brown, Pamela Wedd	144	Castillo, Jorge	179–180	Cragg, Tony	226–227
Brown, Roger	144	Castro, Giovanni	181	Cramer, George	228
Brown, Theophilus	144–145	Caulfield, Patrick	180–181	Crawford, Neelon	227
Browning, Colleen	145	Celmins, Vija	181–182	Crile, Susan	228
Bruni, Bruno	145	Cenedella, Robert	182	Crouch, Don	229
Bruns, Carol	146	Cespedes, Mario	182	Crutchfield, William	229
Brüs, Günter	146	Cetin, Anton	183	Csoka, Stephen	229–230
Brusca, Jack	146	Chagall, Marc	184–187	Cucchi, Enzo	230–231
Bruskin, Grisha	147	Chadwick, Nancy	213	Cuevas, Jose Luis	231–232
Bryce, Mark Adams	146	Challenger, Michael	187	Cumming, Robert H	232–233
Buck, John E	147–149	Chamberlain, John	187–188	Cunningham, Merce (Mercier)	233
Buckels, Jim	150–151	Chard, Daniel	188	Cunningham, Robert	233
Buckley, Stephen	151	Charlesworth, Sarah E	188	Curran, Darryl Joseph	233–234
Buffet, Bernard	152	Chase, Louisa	189–190	Cyphers, Peggy K	234
Bukovnik, Gary	152–153	Chemeche, George	201	D'Amico, Larry	234
Bull, Fran	149	Chemiakin, Mihail	190	D'Arcangelo, Allan	234–235
Bulley, Hugh	153	Cheng, Emily	183	Daggett, Noel	235
Bumbeck, David	154	Chermayeff, Ivan	191	Dali, Salvadore	239A–239B
Burchfield, Jerry	154	Chernow, Ann	191–192	Dallmann, Daniel Forbes	235–236
Burden, Chris	154–155	Chi, Chen	192	Damon, Betty	236
Buren, Daniel	155	Chia, Sandro	192–193	Danby, Ken	236
Burkert, Robert	155	Chicago, Judy	194	Daphnis, Nassos	236–237
Burford, Byron Leslie	155	Chillida, Eduardo	194–195	Darboven, Hanne	237
Burkhardt, Hans Gustav	156	Chinn, Yuey Yuey	196	Dash, Robert (Warren)	237
Burko, Diane	156	Chiriani, Richard	196	Dass, Dean Allan	237–238
Burle-Marx, Roberto	156–157	Christenberry, William	196	Dater, Judy	238
Burman, Sakti	157	Christensen, Dan	197	David, Michael	238–239
Burns, Jerome	158	Christensen, Ronald Julius	197	Davies, Jordan	239
Burr, Ruth Basler	157	Christo (Javacheff)	198–199	Davies, Theodore Peter	239
Burri, Alberto	157	Chryssa (Verdea)	200	Davila, Carlos	240
Burroughs, William	158	Chwast, Seymour	197	Davis, Brad	240–241
Bury, Pol	158–159	Ciarrochi, Ray	200	Davis, Douglas Matthew	241
Butler, James D	159	Civale, Biagio A	200–201	Davis, Gene	241–242
Büttner, Werner	160	Clark, Michael Vinson	201	Davis, Ronald	242–243
Button, John	160	Clavé, Antonio	206	Daze (Chris Ellis)	243
Byron, Michael	160	Clement, Kathleen	204	De Camp, Michael	243
Cadmus, Paul	160–161	Clemente, Francesco	202–204	De Cointet, Guy	243–244
Cady, Dennis Vern	161	Clerk, Pierre	205	De Forest, Roy	244
Cady, Samuel Lincoln	161–162	Close, Chuck	206–207	De Groat, George Hugh	244–245
Cage, John	162–163	Closson, Nanci Blair	205	De Jong, Thom	245
Calderaro, Al	163	Cobo, Chema	205	De Kooning, Elaine	245
Calder, Alexander	164–165	Coe, Sue	207	De Kooning, Willem	245–246
Calle, Paul	165	Coffin, Edward	207	De Lama, Alberto	246–247
Camacho, Jorge	166	Cohen, Bernard	208	De Maria, Nicola	247
Camberoque, Jean	166	Cohen, Bruce	208	De Maria, Walter	247–248
Campanile, Dario	166	Coignard, James	210–211	De Mattos, Hick	248
Campano, Miguel Angel	166	Cole, Max	208–209	De Mejo, Oscar	248
Campbell, Nancy	166–167	Colescott, Robert	209	De Palma, Brett	249
Campbell, Steven	167	Colescott, Warrington	209	De Saint-Alban, Michel	249
Canogar, Rafael	167	Collin, Pierre	214	De Saint-Phalle, Niki	249
Cantieni, Graham	168	Conaway, James D	214	De Woody, James	249–250
Capobianco, Domenick	168	Concha, Jerry	214	Deacon, Richard	250

ARTIST INDEX CONTINUED

Dean, Peter	250–251
Debonne, Jeannette	251
Deem, George	251
Dehn, Adolf Arthur	251–252
Dehner, Dorothy	252
Delacroix, Michel	253–255
Delamonica, Roberto	256
Delap, Tony	256
Delaunay, Sonia	256–257
Delval, Robert	255
Delvaux, Paul	258–259
Delos, Kate	257
Denby, Jillian	257
Denes, Agnes	259
Dennis, Donna Frances	260
Denny, Robyn	257
Denton, Pat	260–261
Dergalis, George	261
Derrier, Jean Paul	257
Desmazieres, Erik	261
Deutsch, Richard	261–262
Di Cerbo, Michael	262
Di Giorgio, Joseph	262
Diamond, Jessica	263
Diamond, Martha	263
Di Suvero, Mark	264
Diao, David	264
Dibbets, Jan	265
Dickson, Jane	265
Diebenkorn, Richard	266–268
Dike, Philip	269
Dill, Laddie John	269
Dill, Leslie	270
Dine, Jim	270-277B
Dirube, Rolando Lopez	278
Disler, Martin	278
Divola, John Manford	279
Dix, Otto	279
Dmitrienko	279
Dokoupil, Jiri Georg	280
Dona, Lydia	280
Donnangelo, David Michael	280–281
Dorazio, Piero	281
Dove, Toni	281
Downes, Rackstraw	281–282
Downing, Holly	279
Doyle, Joe	282
Drake, James	282–283
Driesbach, David Fraiser	283
Drum, Sydney Maria	283–284
Du Niko, W	284
Dubasky, Valentina	284
Dubuffet, Jean	285–286
Duff, John Ewing	284
Duffy, Michael	286
Dumontier, Francoise	286
Dunham, Carroll	286–287
Dunlop, David A	287
Duron, Jorge	287–288
Dwyer, Nancy	288
Earle, Eyvind	288–290
Echo, Alex	290
Eckart, Christian	290
Eckstein, Ruth	290–291
Edell, Nancy	291
Edlich, Stephen	291
Eggleston, William	292
Elias, Sheila	292
Elias, Susan	292
Ellenshaw, Peter	292
Ellis, Robert M	293
Ellis, Stephen	293
Engel, Nissan	293–294
Ensrud, E Wayne	294
Epstein, Yale	295
Eriksen, Gary L	295
Eriksson, Ulf	295–296
Erlebacher, Martha Mayer	296
Ernst, Jimmy	296–297
Ernst, Max	297
Erté (Romain De Tirtoff)	297–302
Escher, Maurits Cornelis	302–303
Ess, Barbara	302
Essig, Joseph	302
Estes, Richard	304
Everts, Connor	304
Eyre, Ivan	303
Faden, Lawrence Steven	305
Fairchild-Woodard, Roy	306–307
Falkenstein, Claire	305
Farnsworth, Donald	305
Faulconer, Mary (Fullerton)	305
Faulkner, Frank	305
Fazzino, Charles	308–309
Federle, Helmut	309
Fehlau, Fred	309
Feinberg, Elen	310
Feinberg, Jean	310
Feinstein, Rochelle H	310–311
Feito, Luis	311
Feldman, Aline	311
Feldman, Franklin	311
Feltus, Alan Evan	312
Ferguson, Max	312
Fernandez, Agustin	312–313
Fernandez, Roberto	313
Fernandez, Rudy M, Jr	313
Ferrer, Rafael	314–315
Fetting, Rainer	315
Feuerman, Carole Jean	313
Fichter, Robert W	315
Fine, Jud	316
Fini, Leonor	316–317
Fink, Aaron	317
Fink, Larry (Laurence B)	317
Finocchiaro, Pino	317
Fischl, Eric	318–319
Fish, Janet	320
Fisher, Joel A	319
Fisher, Vernon	321–322
Fitzgerald, Astrid	320–321
Fitzpatrick, Tony	322
Flack, Audrey	322–323
Flanagan, Barry	323–324
Flanery, Gail	324
Flavin, Dan	324–325
Flora, James	325
Flood, Edward C	321
Florsheim, Richard A	325–326
Folon, Jean Michel	326–327
Ford, James	327
Förg, Günther	327
Forrester, Patricia Tobacco	328
Forsman, Chuck (Charles Stanley)	328
Foulger, Richard F	328–329
Fox, Terry	329
Frank, Mary	329
Francis, Sam	330–333
Frankenthaler, Helen	334–335
Franzheim, Elizabeth	336
Freckelton, Sondra	336–337
Freed, David	337–338
Freed, Hermine	338
Freilicher, Jane	339
Freimark, Bob	339–342
Frelaunt, Jean	337
Freud, Lucian	343
Friedeberg, Pedro	338
Friedlaender, Johnny	343–344
Friedlander, Lee	338
Frings, Dennis	345
Frink, Elisabeth	345–347
Fuerst, Shirley	347
Fulton, Hamish	347
Fumagalli, Barbara	348
Funakoshi, Katsura	349
Gabin, George Joseph	349
Gabino, Amadeo	350
Gafgen, Wolfgang	349
Gaines, Charles	349
Gaitis, Yannis	350
Gainsky, Norman	350
Gallagher, Cynthia	351
Gallagher, Michael R	351
Gallegos, Margaret W	351
Gallo, Frank	351–352
Gandolfi, Diana Gonzalez	352
Gantz, Ann Cushing	352–353
Gantz, Jeanne Alice	353
Garabedian, Charles	354
Garache, Claude	354
Garces, Carme	355
Gardner, Joan A	355
Garet, Jedd	355–356
Garthwaite, Ernest P	353
Gastini, Marco	356
Gechtoff, Sonia	356
Geisert, Arthur Frederick	356–357
Gellis, Sandy	357
General Idea	357
Genoves, Juan	357–358
Gentilli, Jeremy	358
Gerbarg, Darcy	358
Gersovitz, Sarah Valerie, RCA	358–359
Gertsch, Franz	360
Getz, Ilse	359
Gianakos, Cristos	360–361
Gianakos, Steve	361
Gibson, Ralph H	359
Giegerich, Jill	361
Gifford, J Nebraska	362
Gilhooly, David James, III	362
Gill, Lunda Hoyle	362–363
Gillespie, Gregory Joseph	363
Gimblett, Max (Maxwell)	363
Gilliam, Sam	364–365
Ginzburg, Yankel	366
Giordano, Joseph	363
Gipe, Lawrence	365
Girona, Maria	367
Girouard, Tina	367
Glankoff, Sam	367
Glarner, Fritz	368
Glick, John P	368
Glier, Mike	368
Goell, Abby Jane	368–369
Goff, Lloyd	367
Gold, E J	369–373
Goldberg, Glenn	374
Goldberg, Michael	374–375
Golden, Libby	375
Golden, Rolland Harve	375
Goldman, Jane E	375–376
Goldstein, Daniel Joshua	376–377
Goldstein, Jack	376
Goldyne, Joseph	377
Golkar, Ali	379
Golub, Leon	378–379
González-Torres, Félix	377
Goode, Joe (Jose Bueno)	380–381
Goodman, Ken (Kenneth Hunt)	379
Goodman, Sidney	379
Gorchov, Ron	381
Gordon, P S	381
Gordon, Russell Talbert	381–382
Gordy, Robert	382
Gore, Arnold S	382

ARTIST INDEX CONTINUED

Görg, Jürgen	383
Gorman, R C	383–386
Gormley, Antony	386
Gornik, April	387
Gorny, Anthony-Petr	387
Gottlieb, Adolph	388
Gradus, Ari	389
Graham, Robert	389–390
Gramberg, Liliana	390
Granitz, Judith Ann	390
Granne, Regina	390–391
Grass, Günter	391
Grass, Peter	391
Graupe-Pillard, Grace	391–392
Graves, Michael	392
Graves, Nancy Stephenson	392
Green, Alan	393
Green, Denise G	393
Green, Jasha	393
Green, Martin Leonard	393–394
Greenberg, Richard	394
Greenblat, Rodney Alan	394
Greene, Milton	394–395
Greenfield-Sanders, Timothy	395
Gregor, Harold	305
Gregory-Goodrum, Ellna Kay	395
Gregory, Michael	396
Greve, Gerrit	396
Grey, Alex V	396
Grillo, John	396
Groedel, Burt	397
Groff, James	397
Grooms, Red	398–400
Groover, Jan	397
Grosch, Laura	401
Gross, Chaim	401–402
Gross, Freidrich	402
Grossman, Nancy	402
Grosz, George	307
Grove, Kathy	402
Gruau, Rene	402–403
Grubb, David	403–404
Gruen, John	404
Guastella, Dennis	404
Guccione, Bob	404
Guerrero, Raul	405
Guetary, Helene	405
Guinovart, Josép	405–406
Gunderson, Karen	406
Guston, Philip	407
Gutkin, Peter	408
Guzak, Karen	408
Gwathmey, Robert	408–409
Haacke, Hans	409
Haas, Richard John	409–412
Haass, Terry	412
Hackman, Vida	412–413
Haddelsey, Vincent	413
Hafftka, Michael	413
Hagan, Frederick	413
Hagin, Nancy	413–414
Hagstrum, Katherine	414
Halaby, Samia Asaad	414–415
Halberstadt, Ernst	415
Hall, Susan	416
Haller, Emanuel	415
Halley, Peter	417
Halsey, Brian Elliott	417–418
Hamaguchi, Yozo	419
Hambleton, Mary	419–420
Hamilton, Richard	420–422
Hammerman, Pat Jo	422
Hammersley, Frederick	422
Hammond, Harmony	422–423
Hanks, Steve	415
Hanley, Jack	423

Hanna, Boyd Everett	423–424
Hara, Keiko	424
Harden, Marvin	424
Harden, Richard C	425
Hardy, DeWitt (Clarion)	425
Hare, David	425
Haring, Keith	426–427
Harmon, Paul	427–428
Harrill, James	428
Harrison, Helen Mayer	428–429
Harrison, Newton A	429
Hart, Gordon	429
Hartigan, Grace	430
Hartung, Hans	430
Harvey, Donald	431
Hasen, Burt Stanly	431
Hashmi, Zarina	431
Hasted, Michael	431–432
Havard, James	432
Hayter, Stanley William	432–433
Hayward, James	433
Heard, Peter	433
Hebald, Milton Elting	434
Heeks, Willy	434–435
Heilmann, Mary	435
Heindorff, Michael	435–436
Heizer, Michael	436–437
Helander, Bruce	437
Held, Al	437–438
Heller, Jules	438
Helmuts, Inars	438–439
Henderson, Edward	439
Hendon, Cham	439
Hepworth, Barbara	439–440
Herfield, Phyllis	440
Herman, Alan	440
Herman, Roger	440
Hermel, Michel	440–441
Hernandez-Cruz, Luis	441
Heron, Patrick	441
Hershey, Nona	441–442
Heyboer, Anton	442
Heyman, Lawrence	442
Heywood, J C	443
Hibel, Edna	443–444
Highstein, Jene	444–445
Hill, Charles Christopher	445
Hill, Clinton J	445–446
Hill, Darrell	446
Himmelfarb, John	446–447
Hinman, Charles B	447–448
Hios, Theo	448
Hirsch, Joseph	448–449
Hirtzel, Sue	449
Hisachika, T	449
Hitch, Stewart	450
Hitzler, Franz	450
Hoare, Tyler James	450
Hobbs, Robert Dean	450–451
Hockney, David	451–459
Hodgkin, Howard	460–461
Hofflander, Jack	461
Hofmann, Douglas William	461–462
Hoie, Claus	462
Holden, Barry	462
Holland, Tom	462–463
Hollander, Gino	463
Holtzman, Chuck	463
Honda, Kazuhisa	466
Hopkins, Budd	466
Horan, Steve	466–467
Hornak, Ian John	467
Horowitz, Larry	467
Hourian, Mohammad	464–465
House, Gordon	465
Houshiary, Shirazeh	467
Howard, David	467–468

Howard, Linda	468
Howell, Frank	468
Howey, Nicholas	468–469
Hoyland, John	469–470
Hubbard, John	470
Hubler, Julius	470–471
Hudson, Robert H	471
Huggins, Victor, Jr	471
Hull, Richard	472
Hultberg, John	472
Humphrey, David Aiken	472–473
Humphrey, Margo	213
Humphrey, Ralph	213
Hundertwasser, Friedensreich	473–474
Hunt, Bryan	475
Hunt, Diane	475
Hunt, Richard Howard	475–476
Hunter, Mel	476
Hurd, Peter	476–477
Hurson, Michael	477
Hutchinson, Claudia Jane	477–478
Hutchinson, Peter Arthur	478
Huttinger, Peter	478
Hwang, Kyu-Baik	478–479
Iannone, Dorothy	479
Icart, Louis	479–480
Ida, Shoichi	481–482
Ihara, Yasuo	480
Immendorff, Jörg	483
Impiglia, Giancarlo	483
Indiana, Robert	483–484
Innerst, Mark	484–485
Inukai, Kyohei	485
Israel, Margaret	486
Itatani, Michiko	485
Jablonsky, Carol	486–488
Jacklin, Bill	489
Jackson, Herb	489–490
Jackson, Jett	490
Jackson, Oliver Lee	490
Jacobs, Jim	490–491
Jacobshagen, Keith	491
Jacobson, Arthur	492
Jacquette, Yvonne	492–493
Jacquot, Pierre	494
Jaffe, Lee	491
Jaidinger, Judith C	493
James, Christopher P	494
James, Geoffrey	494
Jannetti, Tony	494–495
Janopoulos, Vailios	495
Janowitz, Joel	495
Jansen, Angela Bing	496
Janz, Robert	496
Jaudon, Valerie	496–497
Jaworska, Dansk	497
Jefferds, Vince	497
Jefferson, Jack	497
Jelinek, Hans	497–498
Jenkins, Paul	498
Jennis, Stevan	498–499
Jensen, Alfred	499
Jiang (Tie-Feng)	500–501
Jilg, Michael Florian	499–500
Jimenez, Luis Alfonso, Jr	501
Johns, Jasper	504–508
Johnson, Lester	502–503
Johnson, Tom	508–509
Johnston, Thomson Alix	501–502
Jonas, Joan	509
Jones, Allen	503
Jones, Ronald Warren	510
Jonson, Jim	510
Juarez, Roberto	510–511
Judd, Donald Clarence	512–513

ARTIST INDEX CONTINUED

Julian, Peter	511
Juszczyk, James Joseph	513
Kabakov, Ilya	513
Kacere, John C	513–514
Kadishman, Menashe	514
Kahn, Erika	514
Kahn, Wolf	514–515
Kaiser, Raffi	515
Kaiser, S Burkett	515–516
Kalina, Richard	516
Kaminsky, Jack Allan	516
Kane, Bob	516
Kane, Bob Paul	517
Kanovitz, Howard	517
Kaplan, Sandra	517
Kapoor, Anish	518
Kapp, David	519
Kaprov, Susan	518
Kardon, Dennis	519
Karwelis, Donald C	519
Karwoski, Richard C	520
Kass, Deborah	520
Kassel, Barbara	518–519
Kassoy, Bernard	520–521
Kasten, Karl Albert	521
Katz, Alex	522–524
Kauffman, Robert Craig	525
Kaye, Mildred Elaine	526–527
Kearns, Jerry	528
Keefer, Peter	525
Keister, Steve	528
Kelley, Mike	528
Kelly, Daniel	529
Kelly, Ellsworth	529–533
Kelso, David William	534
Kendrick, Mel	534
Kent, Douglas	533
Kent, Jane	535
Kentridge, William	534
Keramea, Zoe	535
Kepets, Hugh	536–537
Kern, Haim	535
Kernan, Catherine	537
Kerne, Barbara Davis	537–538
Kerrigan, Maurie	538
Ketchum, Robert Glenn	538–539
Kidder, Harvey	539
Kiecol, Hubert	539
Kiland, Lance	540
Kilar, Stephen	540
Killip, Chris	539
King, Mark	540–542
King, Tony	543
Kingman, Dong M	543
Kinnee, Sandy (Floyd)	543
Kipniss, Robert	544
Kirby, Kent Bruce	544
Kirschner, Ernst Ludwig	544–545
Kisch, Gloria	545
Kitaj, R B	546–547
Klabunde, Charles S	547–548
Klapheck, Konrad	548
Klarwein, Mati	548
Kleemann, Ron	548–549
Klein, Fritz	549
Klein, Lynn (Ellen)	549
Kleinman, Art	549–550
Kleinrock, Sybil	550
Knigin, Michael Jay	550–551
Knoebel, Imi	551
Knutsson, Anders	551–552
Koehler, Henry	552
Kogan, Deborah Ray	552
Kogelnik, Kiki	552
Kogler, Peter	553
Kohl, Barbara	553
Kohlmeyer, Ida	553–554
Kolar, Jiri	554
Kolosvary, Eva & Paul	555–556
Komar & Melamid	554–555
Komoski, Bill	556
Koons, Jeff	556
Koppelman, Chaim	557
Koren, Edward B	557
Koscianski, Leonard J	557–558
Kossoff, Leon	558
Kostabi, Mark	558–559
Kosuth, Joseph	559
Kounellis, Jannis	560
Koursaros, Harry	559
Kozloff, Joyce	560–561
Kozo	561
Kramer, Mireille	561
Kramer, Steve	561
Krasin, Kate	562
Krasner, Lee	562
Kravjansky, Mikulas	562–563
Kreneck, Lynwood	564
Kruger, Barbara	564
Krushenick, Nicholas	564–565
Kruskamp, Janet	565
Krut, Ansel Jonathan	565
Kudo, Muramasa	566
Kuhler, Otto August	565
Kuhn, Audrey Grendahl	567
Kunc, Karen	566
Kunstler, Morton	567
Kuopus, Clinton	567
Kurlander, Honey W	567–568
Kushner, Robert Ellis	568–570
La Noue, Terence	570
La Plant, Mimi	570–571
Labriola, Jochen	571
Labrot, Syl	571
Lack, Stephen	571
Laemmle, Cheryl	572
Lagorio, Irene R	572
Lainere, Barbara	572
Lalande, Jacques	572–573
Laliberté, Norman	573
Lam, Wilfredo	574
Landau, Jacob	574
Landon, Edward August	575
Landry, Richard	577
Lane, Lois	576
Lane, Rosemary Louise	576–577
Lanier, Doris	577–578
Lanigan-Schmidt, Thomas	575
Lansner, Fay	575
Lanyon, Ellen	578
Lapinski, Tadeusz	578–579
Lapointe, Frank	579
Larmee, Kevin	579
Larson, Edward	579
Larson, Philip Seely	580
Lasansky, Mauricio L	580–581
Lasch, Pat	581
Laster, Paul	581
Lasuchin, Michael	581–582
Lau, Rex	582
Laufer, Susan	582
Lauridsen, Hanne H7L	583
Lavier, Bertrand	583
Lawrence, Jacob	583
Lawrence, Sandra	584
Lazarof, Eleanore Berman	584
Lazuka, Robert	585
LeRoy, Harold M	584
Le Va, Barry	585
Leaf, June	585–586
Lebadang	586–588
Ledan, Fanch	588–589
Lee, Catherine	589
Lee, Li Lin	590
Leeson, Tom	590
Lehrer, Leonard	590
Leighton-Jones, Barry	591
Leighton, Daniel	590
Lekakis, Kostas	591
Lemieux, Annette Rose	591
Leon, Dennis	591–592
Leone & MacDonald	591
Leong, James Chan	592
Lere, Mark	592
Lerner, Leslie	592
Leslie, Alfred	593
Lethbridge, Julian	593
Letitia, Joseph	593
Levi, Josef	594
Levine, Erik	594
Levine, Jack	595
Levine, Les	594–595
Levine, Marion Lerner	596
Levine, Tom	596
Levine, Sherrie	597
Levinson, Mon	597
Levy, Benjamin	597–598
Lew, Douglas	598
Lew, Jeffrey	598
Lew, Weyman	598
Lewis, Martin	599
Lewis, Stanley	599–600
LeWitt, Sol	600–603
Liashkov, Peter	603
Lichtenberg, Manes	603
Lichtenstein, Gary	604
Lichtenstein, Roy	605–608
Lieberman, Louis (Karl)	604
Ligare, David	608
Ligon, Glenn	608
Lim, John	609
Limont, Naomi	609
Lindner, Richard	610
Lindquist, Evan	610–611
Lindroth, Linda Hammer	612
Lipschitz, Jacques	612
Lipton, Seymour	612
Lissitsky, Lazar El	612–613
Lobdell, Frank	613
Lobe, Robert	614
Lobello, Peter	614
Lockhart, David	609
Loewy, Raymond	614
Lombardi, Gina	614–615
Long, Richard	615
Longo, Robert	616
Longobardi, Nino	617
Lord, Andrew	617
Lorenz, Lee	617
Lorber, Stephen Neil	618
Loring, John	619
Lostutter, Robert	619
Lotan, Yona	617
Lovejoy, Margot	619
Lowe, Marvin	620
Lowney, Bruce Stark	620–621
Lozowick, Louis	621
Luce, Charles	622
Lucero, Michael (Lewis)	622
Lucioni, Luigi	622–623
Luongo, Aldo	624–625
Lüpertz, Markus	623
Lutes, James (Jim)	623
Luyten, Mark	626
Macaray, Lawrence	626–627
Macaulay, David	627
Maccombie, Turi Spear	627
Macconnel, Kim	627

ARTIST INDEX CONTINUED

MacCoy, Guy	630
MacDougall, Anne	630
Macs, Yan	630
Maimon, Isaac	628–629
Maki, Sheila	631–632
Makos, Christopher	630
Maltzman, Stanley	632
Man Ray (Emmanuel Radinski)	633
Mansen, Matthias	632
Manessier, Alfred	634
Mangold, Robert Peter	634
Mangold, Sylvia Plimack	635
Manville, Elsie	636
Manzavrakos, Michael	636–637
Mapplethorpe, Robert	639
Maraldo, Ushanna	637
Maranz, Leo	637
Marca-Relli, Conrad	639
Marcel	640
Marclay, Christian	640
Marcus, Marcia	640
Marden, Brice	641
Mardon, Allan	642
Margerin, Jacques	642
Marini, Marino	641A–641B
Marioni, Tom	643
Marisol, Escobar	643–644
Markle, Robert	644
Markman, Ronald	644
Martin, Agnes Bernice	644
Martin, Fred	644–645
Martin, Kenneth	645
Martin, Knox	645
Martin, Michael	645
Martin, Stefan	646
Marx, Marcia	646
Masi, Oliviero	646
Massie, Lorna	647
Masson, André	648
Masterfield, Maxine	647
Mateu, Julia	648
Matta, Roberto Sebastian	648–649
Matthews, Wanda Miller	649–650
Max, Peter	650–657
Maxwell, Paul	657
Maxwell, William	658
Mayes, Steven Lee	658–659
Mazonowicz, Douglas	659
Mazur, Michael	659–660
McCafferty, Jay David	660
McCain, James	660
McCall, Ann	660–661
McCarthy, Rick	661
Mccombs, Bruce	661–663
McCormick, Harry	663
McCoy, Ann	663–664
McDowell, Mark	664
McGarrell, James	664–665
McGraw, Deloss	665
McKim, William Wind	665
McKnight, Thomas	666–670
McLean, Richard	670
McNeil, George	670–671
McVicker, J Jay	671–672
Meader, Jonathan	672
Meisel, Susan Pear	672–673
Mendelson, Haim	673
Mendieta, Ana	673–674
Merkin, Richard Marshall	674
Merz, Mario	674
Mesches, Arnold	674–675
Metzker, Ray K	675
Meyerowitz, Joel	675
Michals, Duane	676
Mielko, Tom	676
Milder, Jay	676
Millei, John	675
Miller, Frances St Clair	676–677
Miller, Henry	678–679
Miller, Kathryn	677
Miller, Richard Kidwell	679–680
Miller, Robert (Buck)	677
Miller, Steve	680
Mills, Richard K	680–681
Milton, Peter Winslow	682–683
Minter, Marilyn	681
Mintz, Harry	681
Mirá Paris	683–688
Miró, Joan	689–694
Misrach, Richard Laurence	695
Mitchell, Jessica	695
Mitchell, Joan	695–696
Mitchell, Margaretta K	696
Miyamoto, Wayne Akira	696–697
Miyasaki, George Joji	697
Mock, Richard Basil	698–699
Modeen-Watkinson, Mary K	699
Mogensen, Paul	697
Mohitz, Philippe	699
Moix, Santiago	699–700
Mominee, John	700
Mondino, Aldo	700
Monory, Jacques	700
Montesinos, Vicky	700–701
Moon, Mick	701
Moore, Henry	702–705
Moore, Wayland D	705–706
Morales, Armando	706
Morcos, Maher N	706
Morellet, Francois	707
Morgan, Barbara Brooks	701
Morinoue, Hiroki	707
Morley, Malcolm	707–708
Morper, Daniel	708
Morris, Robert	708–709
Morris, Robin	709–710
Mortensen, Gordon	710–711
Moses, Ed	711–712
Moskowitz, Ira	712
Moskowitz, Robert S	712–713
Moss, Joe (Francis)	713
Moss, P Buckley	713
Motherwell, Robert	714–720
Moti, Kaiko	721–722
Motoi, Oi	722
Mouly, Marcel	723
Moylan, Donna	723
Müeller, Otto	723–724
Muizule, Malda	713
Mullen, Philip Edward	724
Mullican, Matt	725
Mumford, Daphne	725
Muranaka, Hideo	725–726
Murata, Hiroshi	726
Murray, Elizabeth	726–727
Myers, Frances	727–728
Myers, Joyce Stillman	728
Naar, Jon	728
Nagy, Peter	728
Nakashima, Thomas Vincent	729
Nakazato, Hitoshi	729
Naponic, Anthony (George)	729
Nares, James	730
Narkiewicz, Paul	729
Narotzky, Norman	730–731
Natkin, Robert	731
Nauman, Bruce	732–733
Nawara, Jim	733
Nawara, Lucille Procter	734
Nechvatal, Dennis	734
Nechvatal, Joseph	735
Neel, Alice	735
Neill, Joe	731
Neiman, LeRoy	736–739
Nelson, Joan	740
Nelson, Roger Laux	740
Nemec, Nancy	740
Nesbitt, Ilse Buchert	740–741
Nesbitt, Lowell (Blair)	741–742
Nessim, Barbara	742
Neuhaus, Ervin	742
Nevelson, Louise	743–744
Newman, Barnett	744
Newman, Donald	744–745
Newman, Libby	745
Newman, John	745
Newsome, Victor	735
Nice, Don	746
Nierman, Leonardo M	747
Nieto, John W	53B
Nind, Jean	747–748
Nipper, Anne E	748
Nissen, Brian	748
Nitsch, Hermann	748
Noland, Kenneth	749
Norman, Irving	748
Novoa, Gustavo	749–750
Noyer, Denis Paul	750
Noyer, Philippe	750–751
Nugent, Bob L	751–752
O'Connell, Edward E	752
O'Donnell, Hugh	752–753
Obel, Nils	753
Obler, Geri	753
Ocepek, Louis (David)	753–754
Oehlen, Albert	754
Ogloff, Alec	754
Oji, Helen	754
Okada, Kenzo	754–755
Oku (Shigeo Okumura)	755
Oldenburg, Claes	756–758
Oliphant, Patrick	759
Olitski, Jules	759
Oliveira, Nathan	759–760
Oppenheim, Dennis A	760
Oropallo, Deborah	760–761
Orozco, José Clemente	761
Orr, Eric	761
Ortega, Jose	755
Ortwed, Kirsten	764
Osbourne, Elizabeth	762
Ossorio, Alfonso A	762
Osze, Andrew	761
Ostendarp, Carl	762
Ott, Jerry	762–763
Ott, Sabina	763
Otterness, Tom	763
Outin, Julien	763
Owen, Frank (Franklin Charles)	764
Ox, Jack	764
Oxman, Katja	765
Pagés, Pierre	765
Paiement, Alain	765
Paik, Nam June	766
Pakowski, Wojciech	766
Palestine, Charlemagne	766
Paladino, Mimmo	767
Palazuelo, Pablo	767–768
Paley, Joan R	768
Palomer, Pilar	768
Paolini, Giulio	769
Papart, Max	770–773
Parker, Bill	769
Parker, J Whiteman	769
Parker, Kingsley	769
Parker, Olivia	773
Parry, Marian	773–774
Partenheimer, Jürgen	769
Paschke, Edward F (Ed)	774

ARTIST INDEX CONTINUED

Pasmore, Victor	774–776
Passa, Mayeu	776
Passuntino, Peter Zaccaria	776
Patrick, Lorna	777
Patterson, Clayton	777
Patterson, William Joseph	777–778
Pattison, Abbott	778
Peak, Elizabeth Jayne	778
Pearlstein, Philip	778–780
Pearson, Hency C	780
Pekarsky, Mel (Melvin Hirsch)	780–781
Pellettieri, Michael Joseph	781
Penck, A R (Ralf Winkler)	782–783
Pepper, Beverly	783
Pereznieto, Fernando	781–782
Pergola, Linnea	783–784
Perlmutter, Jack	784
Peterdi, Gabor F	785
Peters, Jürgen	776
Petersen, Martin	785
Petersen, Robert	785–786
Peterson, Robert	786
Petheo, Bela	786
Peticov, Antonio	786–787
Petrie, Sylvia Spencer	787
Petrov, Dimitre	787
Pfahl, John	787
Pfaff, Judy	788
Pfrang, Erwin	788
Phelan, Ellen Denise	788–789
Phillips, Frederick	789
Phillips, Jay C	789–790
Phillips, Matt	790
Phillips, Tom	790–791
Picasso, Pablo	792–795
Piccillo, Joseph	791
Pindell, Howardena Doreen	796
Pistoletto, Michelangelo	796
Pittman, Lari	796–797
Plattner, Phyllis	797
Pletka, Paul	791
Plossu, Bernard	797
Plotkin, Linda	797–798
Plunkett, Edward	798
Poehlmann, Joanna	798–799
Pogany, Miklos	799
Poliakoff, Serge	799
Polke, Sigmar	800
Poleskie, Steve (Stephen Francis)	800
Poloukhine, Olga	801
Ponce De Leon, Michael	801
Pond, Clayton	801–802
Poons, Lawrence	802
Porter, Bern	802
Porter, David	802–803
Porter, Fairfield	803
Porter, Katherine	803
Porter, Lilliana	803–804
Portnow, Marjorie Anne	804
Posillico, Leo	804
Possati, Concetto	805
Pozzati, Rudy O	805
Pozzi, Lucio	805
Prentice, David Ramage	806
Preston, David	806
Preuss, Roger	806–807
Price, Joe	807–808
Price, Ken	808
Priest, Terri	808–809
Prince, Richard Edmund	809
Provisor, Janis	810
Purcell, Charles Roy	809
Puryear, Martin	810–811
Putterman, Florence	812
Pylant, Carol	811
Quaytman, Harvey	812
Quijada, Robert	812–813
Quinn, William	813
Rabinovitch, William A	813
Raetz, Markus	814
Raffael, Joseph	814–815
Rainer, Arnulf	815
Rakovan, Lawrence Francis	815–816
Rammellzee	816
Ramos, Melvin John (Mel)	816–817
Ranalli, Daniel	817
Rand, Archie	817
Rasmussen, Keith	817–818
Rattner, Abraham	818
Raucher, Hava	818–819
Rauschenberg, Robert	820–827
Raymond, Lilo	819
Rayner, Gordon	819
Rebbeck, Lester James, Jr	819
Rebeyrolle, Paul	827
Reckling, Genevieve	828
Reich, Steve	828
Reindorf, Samuel	828
Reine, Charlotte	828–830
Reinhardt, Ad F	830
Renouf, Edda	830
Retivat, Annie	830–831
Richardson, Brent	831
Richardson, Jean	831–832
Richardson, Roland	833–834
Richardson, Sam	833
Richmond, Jim	834
Richmond, Rebekah	834
Richter, Gerhard	835
Richter, Scott	834–835
Rifka, Judy	836
Riley, Bridget	835–836
Riopelle, Jean-Paul	836–837
Rios, Susan	838–839
Ripps, Rodney	839
Riss, Murray	839
Rivard, J B	840
Rivers, Larry	840–841
Rizzi, James	842–846
Rizzie, Dan	846–847
Robbins, David	837
Robbins, Michael	847
Robinson, Charlotte	847
Rocamora, Jaume	848
Rockburne, Dorothea	848
Rockwell, Norman	848–852
Rodrigo, Angel Pascual	852
Rodriguez, Oscar	852–853
Rogers, P J	853
Rollins, Tim + Kos*	853
Romano, Clare Camille	854
Romero, Frank	854
Romero, Juan	854–855
Romney, Barbara	855
Ronald, William	855
Rosamond, Christine	855
Rosas, Mel	856
Rosen, Kay	856
Rosenblum, Jay	856
Rosenhouse, Irwin	856–857
Rosenquist, James	858–862
Ross, Charles	857
Roth, David	857
Roth, Dieter	862–863
Roth, Sylvia	863
Rothe, G H	864–870
Rothenberg, Susan	871–872
Rotterdam, Paul	863
Rovegno, Jeanne	872
Rowland, Frank	872–873
Rowland, Mark	873
Rozman, Joseph John	873–874
Rubin, Michael	870
Rubinfien, Leo H	874
Ruby, Janet	857
Ruby, Laura	874
Ruff, Thomas	875
Ruppersberg, Allen	875
Ruscha, Edward	875–878
Ruttenberg, Janet	878
Ryman, Robert	878–879
Saar, Betye	879
Saari, Peter	879
Sabelis, Huibert	879–880
Sacilotto, Deli	880
Saff, Donald Jay	881
Saito, Kaoru	881
Salinas, Baruj	881–882
Salle, David	882–883
Salomoni, Tito	883
Saltz, Jerome	884
Samaras, Lucas	884–885
Sandback, Fred	885
Sandell, Scott	886–887
Sandlin, David	885
Santlofer, Jonathan	887
Saret, Alan	887
Sargent, J McNeil	888
Sargent, Robert	888
Sassone, Marco M	888–889
Saul, Peter	889–890
Saunders, David C	890
Saunders, Raymond Jennings	890–891
Saura, Antonio	891
Savage, Naomi	891
Savage, Roger, RCA	891–892
Savitz, Frieda	892–893
Sawai, Noboru	893
Scanga, Italo	893–896
Scanlon, Marcia	896
Schapiro, Miriam	896
Scharf, Kenny	896–897
Scharf, William	897
Schary, Emanuel	897
Schiffleger, Carol	897–898
Schlump, John Otto	898
Schnabel, Julian	899
Schneeman, George	898
Schneemann, Carolee	899–900
Schnurnberger, Lynn	900
Scholder, Fritz	900–901
Scholder, Laurence	901
Schrag, Karl	902
Schreiber, Georges	902
Schreiber, Ilse	901
Schurr, Jerry	902–903
Schuselka, Elfi	903
Schuyff, Peter	903
Schwartz, Barbara Ann	904
Schwartz, Daniel	904
Schwiering, Conrad	904
Scott, Michael L	904
Scully, Sean	905
Sculthorpe, Peter	906
Seager, Sarah	907
Seabourn, Bert D	907–908
Seborovski, Carole	906
Secunda, Arthur	908–909
Segal, George	909–910
Sehring, Adolf	910
Seltzer, Joanne Lynn	910
Seltzer, Phyllis	911
Sepyo, James	910
Serra, Richard	912–913
Serra-Badue, Daniel	914
Serrier	913
Sesma, Raymundo	913

ARTIST INDEX CONTINUED

Shaffer, Richard	914–915
Shahn, Ben	915
Shapiro, David (1916)	915–916
Shapiro, David (1944)	916–917
Shapiro, Dee	917
Shapiro, Joel	918–919
Sharir, David	913
Sharp, Anne	919
Shatter, Susan	919
Shaw, Cameron	920
Shaw, Richard Blake	920
Shea, Judith	920
Shechter, Laura J	921
Shedletsky, Stuart	921
Sheets, Millard Owen	921
Sherman, Cindy	922
Sherman, Z Charlotte	922–923
Sherrod, Philip Lawrence	923
Shersher, Zinovy	926
Shields, Alan J	924–926
Shimomura, Roger Yutaka	927
Shiraga, Sharon	917
Shizume, Mori	921
Shorr, Harriet	927
Showell, Kenneth	927
Shukman, Solomon	927–928
Shuptrine, Hubert	928
Sicilia, Jose Maria	928–929
Siebner, Herbert, RCA	929
Sigler, Hollis	930–931
Sikora, Zdzislaw R	929–930
Siler, Todd (Lael)	931
Simbari, Nicola	931–932
Simmons, Laurie	933
Simpson, Lorna	933
Singer, Clifford	933
Singer, Michael	934
Sirica, John Clemente	934
Sivard, Robert Paul	934
Slavin, Arlene	934–935
Slaymaker, Martha	935
Slettehaugh, Thomas Chester	935–936
Sloan, Jeanette Pasin	936–937
Smith, Cary	937
Smith, Gary Douglas	937–938
Smith, Kiki	938
Smith, Leslie	938–939
Smith, Jaune Quick-To-See	939
Smith, Michael A	939–940
Smith, Moishe	940
Smith, Philip	942
Smith, Richard	940–941
Smith, Rupert Jason	941
Smythe, Ned	942
Snyder, Joan	942
Snyder, Randall	942
Solano, Susana	942–943
Solien, T L	943
Solombre, Jean	943–944
Sonfist, Alan	944
Sonnier, Keith	944
Sorman, Steven	944–947
Sorokin, Janet	947
Soto, Jesus Raphael	947–948
Soulages, Pierre	948
Soviak, Harry	948
Soyer, Raphael	948–950
Spandorfer, Merle Sue	950
Spanfeller, Jim	950
Spark, Michelle	950
Sparling, Cinda	951
Spear, Chip	953
Spector, Buzz (Franklin Mac)	951
Spence, Andrew	952
Spero, Nancy	951
Spiegelman, Art	952
Spruance, Benton Murdock	952–953
Stack, Gael Z	953
Stackhouse, Robert	954–955
Stacy, Donald L	955
Stadler, Anselm	955
Stamos, Theodoros S	955–956
Stanczak, Julian	956
Stanley, Robert	956–957
Stanuga, Ted	957
Stark, Larry	957
Starn, Doug & Mike	957–958
Starr, Jeff	958
Stayton, Janet	958
Steckel, Anita	959
Steinberg, Saul	959
Steiner, Michael	959
Steir, Pat	960–961
Stella, Frank	962–967
Stephan, Gary	968
Stephany, Jaromir	968
Stern, Bert	969
Stevens, May	961
Stevens, Peter	967
Stevovich, Andrew Vlastimir	969
Stewart, Norman	969–970
Stewart, Paul L	970
Stinnett, Hester A	958
Stoianovich, Marcelle	970
Stolpe, Daniel O	971–973
Stoltenberg, Donald	973
Stone, Todd	973–974
Stonehouse, Fred	974
Storer, Inez	974
Storey, David	975
Stowers, Hal	975
Strand, Paul	975–976
Strickland, Thomas J	976
Strider, Marjorie Virginia	976
Stroh, Earl	976–977
Strong, Brett-Livingstone	977
Struwer, Ardy	970
Stuart, Michelle	977
Sturges, Jock	978
Sturman, Sally Mara	978
Sturman, Eugene	978
Sugarman, George	978–979
Sullivan, Bill	979
Sullivan, Jim	979–980
Sultan, Altoon	980
Sultan, Donald K	980–982
Summers, Carol	982
Summy, Anne Tunis	982–983
Sumner, George	983
Sungur, Barbara Zeigler	983
Supplee, Sarah	984
Sutherland, Graham	984
Sutton, Sharon E	984
Sverdlove, Zolita	984–985
Swain, Robert	985
Sznajderman, Marius	985–986
Taggart, William John	986
Tahedl, Ernestine	986–987
Takal, Peter	987
Takara, Seikichi	988
Takis	988
Talasnik, Stephen	988–989
Talmor, Raya	989
Tamasauskas, Otis	989
Tamayo, Rufino	990
Tanning, Dorothea	291
Tapies, Antoni	992–993
Tarkay, Itzchak	994–995
Tarlow, Philip	990–991
Tarnower, Jain	991
Tatafiore, Ernesto	991
Tavenner, Patricia	991
Taylor, Al C	991
Taylor, Ann	996
Taylor, Elyse	996
Taylor, N Wayne	996
Taylor, Prentiss	997
Taylor, Sydney	997
Teichman, Mary	997–998
Tepper, Irvin	998
Teraoka, Masami	998
Tetherow, Michael	998
Theimer, Ivan	999
Thek, Paul	999
Theobald, Gillian Lee	999
Thiebaud, Wayne	1000–1001
Thomas, Larry W	1002
Thomas, Lew	1002
Thomas, Steffen Wolfgang	1002–1003
Thompson, Richard Earl, Sr	1003
Thorne, Joan	1003
Thursz, Frederic Matys	1003
Tice, George Andrew	1003
Tillyer, William	1004
Tilson, Joe	1004–1006
Ting, Shao Kuang	1008–1009
Ting, Walasse	1006–1007
Tinkelman, Murray	1007
Titus-Carmel, Gérard	1007
Tobey, Mark	1010
Tobias, Robert Paul	1010–1011
Tobiasse, Theo	1011–1014
Tomchuk, Marjorie	1015
Tompkins, Betty	1016
Tooker, George Clair, Jr	1016
Torpor, Roland	1016
Torlen, Michael Arnold	1017
Torreano, John	1017
Torres, Francesc	1017
Treaster, Richard A	1017–1018
Treby, Janet	995
Tripp, Jan Peter	1018
Trova, Ernest Tino	1018–1019
Trowbridge, David	1020
True, David	1019
Trupp, Barbara Lee	1020
Tsiaras, Philip	1020
Tubis, Seymour	1020–1021
Tuchman, Ellen Francis	1021
Tuckman, William G	1021
Tucker, William G	1021
Turner, Alan	1021–1022
Turner, Janet E	1022
Turrell, James	1022–1023
Tuttle, Richard	1023
Twaddle, Randy	1023–1024
Twombly, Cy	1024–1025
Tworkov, Jack	1025
Ubac, Raoul	1026
Uecker, Günther	1026
Uglow, Alan	1026
Umlauf, Karl	1027
Upton, Richard Thomas	1026
Urquhart, Tony	1027
Utenkov, Demian	1027–1028
Uttech, Thomas	1028
Uzilevsky, Marcus	1028–1030
Vadala, Angelo	1030
Vaisman, Meyer	1030
Valdes, Manolo	1030–1031
Valerio, James Robert	1031
Valesco, Frances	1031
Vallei, Bhun	1032
Van Alstine, John	1032–1033
Van Elk, Ger	1033
Van Hoesen, Beth	1033–1034
Van Hoeydonck, Paul	1034
Van-Pitterson, Lloyd	1034
Van Horn, Dana Carl	1034

ARTIST INDEX CONTINUED

Van Velde, Bram	1034–1036
Van Vliet, Claire	1036
Van Wieringen, Jan Pieter	1037
Vasarely, Victor	1037–1039
Vavra, Robert	1040
Vedova, Emilio	1040–1041
Velickovic, Vladimir	1041
Venet, Bernar P	1041
Ventresca, Michael	1041
Vicente, Esteban	1042
Vickrey, Robert Remsen	1042
Viera, Ricardo	1042–1043
Vigil, Veloy	1043
Vinn, Vello	1044
Vital, Not	1044
Vo-Dinh, Mai	1045
Volkin, Hilda Appel	1045
Von Huene Stephan	1045
Waddell, Theodore	1046
Wahle, Frank	1045
Waldman, Paul	1046
Waldum, Paul	1046
Walker, Clay	1047
Walmsley, William Aubrey	1047
Walters, Ernest	1047
Warhol, Andy	1048–1052
Wasserman, Burton	1052–1053
Watanabe, Ryo	1053
Watanabe, Sol	1053
Wayne, June	1053–1055
Weatherford, Mary	1056
Weaver, Robert (John)	1055
Webb, Doug	1056
Webster, Stokely	1056–1057
Weddige, Emil	1057
Wedman, Neil	1057
Weedman, Kenneth Russell	1057–1058
Weege, William	1058
Wegman, William	1059–1060
Weidenaar, Reynold Henry	1060
Weil, Robert	1058
Weil, Susan	1060–1061
Weiner, Lawrence Charles	1061
Weisberg, Ruth Ellen	1061–1062
Weiss, Clemens	1062
Welden, Daniel W	1062
Welling, James	1063
Welliver, Neil G	1063
Wells, C J	1064
Wells, Lynton	1063
Wenniger, Mary Ann	1064
Wessel, Fred W	1064
Wesselmann, Tom	1066–1067
West, Doug	1065
Westermann, H C	1064–1065
Wharton, David W	1068
Whipple, Barbara	1068–1069
Whitaker, Eileen Monaghan	1065
Whitaker, Frederic	1069
White, C J	1069
White, Ray Charles	1072
White, Susan Dorothea	1070–1071
Whitney, Guy	1065
Wholey, Mark	1072
Wilde, John	1069
Wilder, Chris	1071
Wiley, William T	1072–1074
Wilke, Hannah	1074
Wilke, Ulfert	1075
Will, John A	1075
Williams, Diane	1075
Williams, Guy	1075
Willing, Victor	1076
Willis, Jay Stewart	1076
Willis, Thornton	1076
Wilson, Charles Banks	1076–1077
Wilson, Donald Roller	1077
Wilson, Gahan	1077
Wilson, Robert	1077–1078
Wilson, York	1078
Winnewisser, Rolf	1078
Winters, Robin	1079
Winters, Terry	1079–1080
Wirsum, Karl	1080
Wirth, Peter	1075
Witt, Nancy Camden	1081
Woelffer, Emerson	1081
Wojnarowicz, David	1082
Wong Moo-Chew	1082
Wonner, Paul (John)	1081
Woodman, Betty	1084
Wool, Christopher	1082–1083
Wootton, Frank	1083
Worthen, Amy N	1083
Wörsel, Troels	1085
Wortzel, Adrianne	1084–1085
Wou-ki, Zao-Ki	1085–1086
Wray, Dick	1086
Wright, David Orr	1086–1087
Wujcik, Theo	1087
Wunderlich, Paul	1087–1088
Wyeth, Henriette	1088
Wyeth, Jamie	1088
Yamagata, Hiro	1088–1090
Yao, C J	1090
Yarber, Robert	1090
Yarbrough, Leila Kepert	1091–1092
Yaskil, Amos	1092
Yeros, Dimitris	1092–1093
Yokoi, Tomoe	1093
Youkeles, Anne	1093
Young, Michael	1093–1094
Young, Nancy J	1094
Young, Robert	1094–1095
Youngerman, Jack	1095
Yrisarry, Mario	1095
Yunkers, Adja	1095–1096
Yust, David E	1096–1097
Yvaral	1097
Zacharias, Athos	1098
Zago, Tino (Agostino C)	1098
Zakanitch, Robert S	1098–1099
Zaloudek, Duane	1099
Zambrelli, Marco	1100
Zelt, Martha	1099
Zirker, Joseph	1100
Zorn, Anders Leonard	1100
Zox, Larry	1100–1101
Zu Ming Ho	1101
Zucker, Joseph	1102
Zucker, Murray Harvey	1102–1103
Zupanc, Terri	1101
Zwack, Michael	1103
Zwick, Rosemary	1103
Zuñiga, Francisco	1103–1107

Collectors! Art Dealers!
Quality Prints at Very Special Prices!
Call Toll-FREE — (800) 788-9101

- Agam
- Calder
- Haring
- Motherwell
- Rosenquist
- Rauschenberg
- Ting
- Vasarely
- Warhol

Avantgarde Art Associates (800) 788-9101

NEW ARTIST INDEX

Abakanowicz, Magdalena	1–2	Ernst, Max	297	Lissitsky, Lazar El	612–613
Agudelo-Botero, Orlando	14–16	Escher, Maurits Cornelis	302–303	Lobe, Robert	614
Albright, Ivan Le Lorraine	17	Ess, Barbara	302	Lorenz, Lee	621
Allison, Dan	22–25			Lozowick, Louis	621
Amen, Irving	32	Fabian, Gisela	304A–304B	Lucioni, Luigi	662–623
Amos, Emma	33	Fairchild-Woodard, Roy	306–307	Lutes, James (Jim)	623
Andoe, Joe	36–37	Fehlau, Fred	309		
Aponovich, James	41	Ferguson, Max	312	Macaulay, David	627
Argimon, Daniel	46	Fine, Jud	316	Makos, Christopher	630
Ashbaugh, Dennis John	51	Fitzpatrick, Tony	322	Mansen, Matthias	632
Asoma, Tadashi	53	Freed, Hermine	338	Manzavrakos, Michael	636–637
		Frelaunt, Jean	337	Marclay, Christian	640
Baker, Richard	66	Funakoshi, Katsura	349	Markman, Ronald	644
Barker, Laurence	72			Mendieta, Ana	673–674
Baum, Don	84	Gabino, Amadeo	349	Miller, Henry	678–679
Benes, Barton Lidice	96	Gafgen, Wolfgang	349	Mominee, John	700
Berman, Wallace	101	Garces, Carme	355	Morellet, Francois	707
Berthot, Jake	103	Gillespie, Gregory Joseph	363	Morinoue, Hiroki	707
Bevan, Tony	103	Gipe, Lawrence	365	Morper, Daniel	708
Bolotin, Jay	118	Girona, Maria	367	Moskowitz, Ira	712
Botanski, Christian	119	Golkar, Ali	379	Moylan, Donna	723
Booth, George Warren	120	Gormley, Antony	386	Mueller, Otto	723–724
Bowling, Katherine	130	Grass, Peter	391	Mullican, Matt	725
Bradford, Katherine	132	Gregory, Michael	396	Mumford, Daphne	725
Bradshaw, Dove	133	Grey, Alex	396		
Brennen, Fanny	136–137	Grosz, George	307	Naar, Jon	728
Brosen, Frederick	141	Grove, Kathy	402	Nechvatal, Dennis	734
Brown, Charlotte	141	Guastella, Dennis	404	Newman, Barnett	744
Brown, Louise Freshman	141	Guccioni, Bob	404	Nieto, John W	53B
Brown, Pamela Wedd	144	Gwathmey, Robert	408–409		
Brushkin, Grisha	147			Oliphant, Patrick	759
Buckels, Jim	150–151	Hammersley, Frederick	422	Orozco, Jose Clemente	761
Bumbeck, David	154	Harrison, Helen Mayer	428–429	Ossorio, Alfonso	762
Burle-Marx, Roberto	156–157	Harrison, Newton A	429	Ostendarp, Carl	762
Burns, Jerome	158	Hartigan, Grace	430	Ott, Sabina	763
Burroughs, William	158	Heilmann, Mary	435	Owen, Frank (Franklin Charles)	764
Butler, James D	159	Henderson, Edward	439		
		Hendon, Cham	439	Pakowski, Wojciech	766
Camacho, Jorge	166	Heyboer, Anton	442	Passa, Mayeu	776
Campano, Miguel Angel	166	Highstein, Jene	444–445	Petersen, Martin	785
Canogar, Rafael	167	Hisachika, T	449	Pfrang, Erwin	788
Carnwath, Squeak	171–172	Holzman, Chuck	463	Phillips, Frederick	789
Carreiro, Joel	172	Hourian, Mohammad	464–465	Pletka, Paul	791
Carroll, Lawrence	173	Houshiary, Shirazeh	467	Poliakoff, Serge	799
Chemiakin, Mihail	190	Howey, Nicholas	468–469	Polke, Sigmar	800
Christenberry, William	196			Portnow, Marjorie Anne	804
Civale, Biagio A	200–201	Jacklin, Bill	489	Preston, David	806
Cormenza, Enric	221	Jones, Ronald Warren	510	Pylant, Carol	811
Costa, Iza	223–224				
Cowin, Jack	226	Kabakov, Ilya	513	Ramos, Jose Carlos	819A–819B
Cramer, George	228	Kaiser, S Burkett	515–516	Richardson, Sam	833
Crutchfield, William	229	Kalina, Richard	516	Richter, Scott	834–835
Csoka, Stephen	229–230	Kass, Deborah	520	Robbins, David	837
Cyphers, Peggy K	234	Kent, Jane	535	Rodrigo, Angel Pascual	852
		Kentridge, William	534	Rollins, Tim + Kos*	853
Damon, Betty	236	Keramea, Zoe	535	Romero, Frank	854
Darboven, Hanne	237	Kiecol, Hubert	539	Ronald, William	855
Davis, Douglas Matthew	241	Kirschner, Ernst Ludwig	544–545	Rosen, Kay	856
Daze (Chris Ellis)	243	Kogler, Peter	553	Roth, Sylvia	863
De Maria, Nicola	247	Kominski, Bill	556	Rovegno, Jean	872
De Palma, Brett	249	Koren, Edward B	557	Ruff, Thomas	875
Dehn, Adolf Arthur	251–252	Kozo	561	Ruttenberg, Janet	878
Delval, Robert	255	Kuhler, Otto August	565		
Delvaux, Paul	258–259	Kunc, Karen	566	Saar, Betye	879
Desmazieres, Erik	261	Kuopus, Clinton	567	Saari, Peter	879
Diamond, Jessica	263			Scott, Michael	904
Dike, Philip	269	Lane, Lois	576	Sculthorpe, Peter	906
Dill, Leslie	270	Laster, Paul	581	Seager, Sarah	907
Dix, Otto	279	Lazuka, Robert	585	Shaw, Cameron	920
Dunlop, David A	287	Lemieux, Annette Rose	591	Siler, Todd (Lael)	931
Dwyer, Nancy	288	Leone & MacDonald	591	Simpson, Lorna	933
		Letheridge, Julian	593	Smith, Cary	937
Echo, Alex	290	Levine, Erik	594	Smith, Kiki	938
Eckhart, Christian	290	Levine, Tom	596	Smith, Leslie	938–939
Engle, Nissan	293–294	Lewis, Martin	599	Smith, Philip	942
Ernst, Jimmy	296–297	Ligon, Glenn	608	Solano, Susana	942–943

NEW ARTIST INDEX CONTINUED

Spector, Buzz (Franklin Mac)	951	Tarkay, Itzchak	994–995	Walmsley, William Audrey	1047
Spruance, Benton Murdock	952–953	Taylor, Al C	991	Weatherford, Mary	1056
Stevens, May	961	Taylor, Prentiss	997	Weidenaar, Reynold Henry	1060
Stevens, Peter	967	Tetherow, Michael	998	Weisberg, Ruth Ellen	1061–1062
Stevovich, Andre Vlastimir	969	Thek, Paul	999	Weiss, Clemens	1062
Stonehouse, Fred	974	Thursz, Frederic Matys	1003	White, Ray Charles	1072
Struwer, Ardy	970	Treby, Janet	995	White, Susan Dorothea	1070–1071
Sturges, Jock	978	Tuchman, Ellen Frances	1021	Wilder, Chris	1071
Supplee, Sarah	984			Wilke, Hannah	1074
Sutherland, Graham	984	Uecker, Günther	1026	Wool, Christopher	1082–1083
Sverdlove, Zolita	984–985				
		Valdes, Manolo	1030–1031	Zaloudek, Duane	1099
Talasnik, Stephen	988–989	Van Wieringen, Ian Pieter	1037	Zambrelli, Marco	1100
Talmor, Raya	989			Zorn, Anders Leonard	1100
Tanning, Dorothea	990	Wahle, Frank	1045		

LIBRARIES · COLLECTORS · ART DEALERS

BACK ISSUES OF

The Printworld Directory
Are Still Available!

Printworld International, Inc

PO Box 1957

West Chester, PA 19380

TEL (610) 431-6654 • FAX (610) 431-6653

EDITOR'S COMMENTS

This seems like the right time to answer the most frequently asked questions about **THE PRINTWORLD DIRECTORY OF CONTEMPORARY PRINTS & PRICES.** So here goes!

Q—How can an artist apply to be considered as a candidate for inclusion in the directory?

A—Anyone can apply if they think their credentials are appropriate. Print publishers and galleries may also submit their artists. Forms are located in the back of the directory... a biographical form and a documentation form. We add 300 new artists to each new edition.

Q—Do artists pay to be listed in the directory?

A—No! However, there is a nominal first-time fee to be entered into our system.

Q—How are the artists selected to participate in the directory?

A—A panel assesses the nominees and makes that decision. Some of the credentials include their awards, education, recent exhibitions, where their works are collected, where they teach, etc.

Q—How do you gather the information in the directory?

A—We contact print publishers, galleries and artists.

Q—How do you determine the prices in the secondary and primary markets?

A—The prices are established by the print publishers, galleries and artists in both markets. However, in the case of older and very rare prints, we consult the auction market, use the highest price paid for a particular print and add the fee that the buyer paid for the print to the auction price.

Q—How do galleries get listed on the artist's page?

A—There is a nominal fee for each listing.

Q—How do people list galleries, print workshops, print publishers, appraisers, etc, in the indexes in the back of the directory?

A—There is a charge for these listings of $10. per line.

Q—Do you include posters in the directory?

A—Only signed and numbered posters in small editions are listed.

Q—Are only American artists included?

A—No! Artists from every corner of the earth are included.

Q—Why are some very wonderful artists excluded because they do very large editions?

A—It was an arbitrary decision to list only small editions. The directory would be ten times larger if we didn't limited the prints listed to signed, numbered and limited editions. Initially, we didn't list any editions over 300. Recently, we have expanded the edition number to 500 to accommodate galleries and art dealers.

Q—Who uses the directory?

A—THE PRINTWORLD DIRECTORY is a source book for art dealers, galleries, collectors, appraisers, decorators, architects, banks, curators, librarians, and many`others.

I hope this has been helpful. If your questions have not been answered, please write to us.

Selma Smith, Editor

The Printworld Directory is accepting new applications for the seventh edition. Approximately 300 new artists will be accepted. Please use the two forms provided in the back section of this directory to submit biographical data and documentation of prints. Edition number of each print must not exceed 500 and the retail price must be $100 or more.

The print market has become very selective. For the first time since we published the first edition of The Printworld Directory in 1982, the prices of prints have been greatly reduced and greatly increased for the same artists by the most reputable and established print publishers. Check the fifth edition to understand the movement.

SIGMUND ABELES

BORN: New York, NY; November 6, 1934
EDUCATION: Pratt Inst, NY; Univ of South Carolina, BA, 1955; Art Students League; Skowhegan Sch, ME; Brooklyn Mus Sch, NY; Columbia Univ, NY, MFA, 1957
TEACHING: Instr, Swain Sch of Design, New Bedford, MA, 1961–64; Instr, Wellesley Col, MA, 1964–69; Instr, Boston Univ, MA, 1969–70; Prof Emeritus, Univ of New Hampshire, Durham, NH, 1970–1987
AWARDS: Nat Inst of Arts and Letters Award, 1965; Sabbatical Grant, Nat Coun Arts and Humanities, 1966; Grant for Graphics, Louis Comfort Tiffany Foundation, 1967; Nat Inst of Arts & Letters, NY, 1983; Purchase Prize, Hassam/Speicher Mem, NY, 1983; Am Jewish Committee ACAP Seminar to Israel, 1981; Richard Florsheim Art Found Grant, 1991
RECENT EXHIB: Retrosp, Univ Art Galleries, Univ of New Hampshire, Durham, NH, 1988; Barridoff Galleries, Portland, ME, 1990; New Orleans Mus of Art, LA, 1990; Retrosp, Northeast Col, Henniker, NH, 1991; Retrosp, McKissick Mus, Columbia, SC, 1992; Retrosp, Cheekwood Mus, Nashville, TN, 1992; Retrosp, Fitchburg Mus, MA, 1993; Retrosp, Boston Public Library, MA, 1993
COLLECTIONS: Mus of Mod Art, NY; Mus Arte, Ponce, Puerto Rico; Philadelphia Mus of Art, PA; Boston Mus of Fine Arts, MA; British Mus, London, England; Brooklyn Mus of Art, NY; Cleveland Mus of Art, OH; Mint Mus, Charlotte, NC; Victoria & Albert Mus, London, England; Smithsonian Inst, Wash, DC
PRINTERS: Paul Maguire, Boston, MA (PM); Flat Rock Press, Boston, MA (FRP); Pat Sulgalski, Cranbrook Hills, MI (PS); Dellas Henke (DH); Plucked Chicken Press, Chicago, IL (PCP); Impressions Gallery, Boston, MA (IG) (OB); Herb Fox, Merrimac, MA (HF); Fox Graphics, Merrimac, MA (FG)
PUBLISHERS: Associated American Artists (AAA); The Lakeside Press, Lakeside, MI (LP); Limited Edition Press, CA (LEP); Plucked Chicken Press, Chicago, IL (PCP); Davidson Galleries, Seattle, WA (DG); Univ of Massachusetts Print Workshop (UMPW); Impressions Gallery, Boston, MA (IG) (OB); Robert Townsend, Georgetown, MA (RT); Herbert A Fox, Merrimac, MA (HF); Fox Graphics, Merrimac, MA (FG); Artist (ART)
GALLERIES: Fox Graphics, Merrimac, MA; Portfolio Gallery, Columbia, SC; O'Farrell Gallery, Brunswick, ME; Mast Cove Gallery, Kennebunkport, ME

Sigmund Abeles
Embracing Couple
Courtesy the Artist

MAILING ADDRESS: 1 W 64th St, #7-B, New York, NY 10023

TITLE	PUBLISHER	PRINTER	DATE	MEDIUM	DIMENSION (PAPER SIZE) IN INCHES	TYPE OF PAPER	EDITION NUMBER	NO. OF COLORS	ORIGINAL OPENING PRICE	CURRENT RETAIL PRICE
SOLD OUT EDITIONS (RARE):										
Head of a Girl	AAA	PM	1970	DPT	12 DIA	AP	250	1	60	350
Self-Portrait Saddles	LP	PM	1973	LC	30 X 23	R/BFK	50	1	150	850
Tiger Lily	LP	PM	1978	LC	16 X 22	R/BFK/G	50	4	150	700
A Domestic Pair	ART/FG		1978	LB	36 X 48	AP	20	1	300	1500
Paul / Printer	LP	PM/LP	1978	LC	30 X 23	R/BFK	50	1	125	400
Print Dealer and his Lamp	PCP	PCP	1979	LC	23 X 15	R/BFK	50	3	150	350
Cock of the Roost	AAA	DH	1981	DPT	9 X 9	ROMA	250	1	100	300
Hugging Herself	UMPW	DH	1981	DPT	14 X 13	ROMA	20	1	125	350
Niki	UMPW	DH	1981	DPT	14 X 13	ROMA	20	1	125	300
My Rolling Mare	IG	RT/IG	1981	DPT	13 X 17	R/BFK	125	1	100	600
The Pensioner	UMPW	DH	1981	EB	23 X 30	R/BFK	40	1	200	1000
Light Slip	UMPW	DH	1981	DPT	14 X 13	ROMA	20	1	125	400
Peck's Nanny	ART	RT	1982	LB	23 X 30	R/BFK	30	1	185	500
Sig's Pup	ART	RT	1982	LB	15 X 22	R/BFK	30	1	150	500
Carl's Cow	ART	RT	1982	LB	22 X 15	R/BFK	30	1	150	250
Choices	ART	RS	1983	LB	36 X 36	R/BFK	28	1	275	750
CURRENT EDITIONS:										
Conundrum	ART	PM/FRP	1986	LB	30 X 22	AP/CR	50	1	400	500
Embracing Couple	ART	HF/FG	1993	LB	30 X 22	RP/G	30	1	400	400
Shabbat with Max	ART	RT	1993	DPT	14 X 17	R/BFK/G	30	1	350	350

MAGDALENA ABAKANOWICZ

BORN: Falenty, Poland; 1930
EDUCATION: Academy of Fine Arts, Warsaw, Poland, 1950–54
AWARDS: Grand Prix, Sao Paulo Biennale, Brazil, 1965
RECENT EXHIB: Biuro Wystaw Artystycznych i Muzeum Chemitex-Stilon, Gorzow Weilkopolski, Poland, 1988; Mucsarnok, Budapest, Hungary, 1988; Laumeier Sculpture Park, St. Louis, MO 1988; Stadtische Galerie im Stadelschen Kinstinstitut, Frankfurt, Germany, 1989; Richard Gray Gallery, Chicago, IL, 1990; Marlborough Fine Art, London, England, 1990; Marlborough Fine Art, Tokyo, Japan, 1991; Mus of Mod Art, Shiga, Japan, 1991; Art Tower Mito, Japan, 1991; Hiroshima City Mus of Contemp Art, Japan, 1991; Muzeum Sztuki, Lodz, Poland, 1991; Muzeum Narodowe Wroclaw, Poland, 1991; Walker Art Center, Minneapolis, MN, 1992; Nelson-Atkins Mus, Kansas City, MO, 1992; Marlborough Fine Art, NY, 1989,92; Inst for Contemp Art, PS 1, NY, 1993

The retail prices of the 100,000 limited edition prints quoted in this directory are subject to change. Print publishers, artists and galleries were the direct sources for these quotations. Prices in the secondary market listed as "Sold Out Editions (Rare)" indicate that the publisher has a limited supply of that print or that the print is difficult to locate in the galleries.

MAGDALENA ABAKANOWICZ CONTINUED

COLLECTIONS: Mus of Mod Art, NY; Metropolitan Mus of Art, NY; Mus of Contemp Art, Chicago, IL; Stedelijk Mus, Amsterdam, The Netherlands; Portland Art Mus, OR; Los Angeles County Art Mus, CA; Malmo Mus, Sweden; Fullerton Univ, Los Angeles, CA; Hirshhorn Mus, Wash, DC; Israel Mus, Jerusalem, Israel; Art Inst of Chicago, IL; Art Gallery of Western Australia, Perth, Australia; Australian Nat Gallery, Canberra, Australia; DeCordova Mus, Lincoln, MA; Denver Art Mus, CO; Detroit Inst of Arts, MI; Kyoto Nat Mus of Mod Art, Japan; Univ of Oslo, Norway; Walker Art Center, Minneapolis, MN; Wellesley Col, MA; Power Inst of Fine Arts, Univ of Sydney, Australia; Centre Georges Pompidou, Mus Nat d'Art Mod, Paris, France; Centralne Mus Hitorii Wlokiennictwa, Lodz, Poland; City of Elblag, Poland; Fonds Regional d'Art Contemporain, Rhone-Alpes, France; Frans Halsmuseum, Haarlem, The Netherlands; Palais des Congres, Biel, Switzerland; Mus des Beaux-Arts, La Chaux-de-Fonds, Switzerland; Sidney Lewis Coll, Richmond, VA; Stadtische Kunsthalle, Mannheim, Germany; Mus Cantonal des Beaux-Arts, Lausanne, Switzerland; Mus Espanol de Arte Contemporaneo, Madrid, Spain; Mus de Arte Moderna, Sao Paulo, Brazil; Mus Bellerive, Zurich, Switzerland; Mus am Ostwall, Dortmund, Germany; Nat Mus, Stockholm, Sweden; Rohsska Konstslojdmuseet, Goteborg, Sweden; Museo Rufina Tamayo, Mexico City, Mexico; Caracas Mus of Mod Art, Venezuela; Mus Narodowe, Warsaw, Poland; Mus of Mod Art, Seoul, Korea
PUBLISHERS: Marlborough Gallery, NY (MG)
GALLERIES: Marlborough Galleries, New York, NY & London, England & Tokyo, Japan; Richard Grey Gallery, Chicago, IL; Dorothy Goldeen Gallery, Santa Monica, CA; Jacques Baruch Gallery, Chicago, IL

TITLE	PUBLISHER	PRINTER	DATE	MEDIUM	DIMENSION (PAPER SIZE) IN INCHES	TYPE OF PAPER	EDITION NUMBER	NO. OF COLORS	ORIGINAL OPENING PRICE	CURRENT RETAIL PRICE
CURRENT EDITIONS:										
Faces	MG		1984	LB	30 X 23	SOM	10	1		8000
Faces (Color Trial Proofs)	MG		1984	LB/HC	30 X 23	SOM		Varies		9000
Katarsis (Set of 6)	MG		1985	LB	22 X 30 EA	SOM		1 EA		18000 SET
Untitled	MG		1987	LB		SOM		1		3000

ELIE ABRAHAMI

BORN: Iran; 1941
EDUCATION: Studied at the Beaux-Arts, Tel Aviv, Israel, 1964–68
AWARDS: Premier Rix de Peinture, Mus D'art Jif, Paris, France, 1971; Premiere Biennale Int de Gravure, Monaco, 1971
COLLECTIONS: Mus of Mod Art, NY; Guggenheim Mus, NY; Mus of Jerusalem, Israel; Bibliotheque Nationale, Paris, France; City of Paris Mus, France; Nat Fine Arts Mus, Paris, France; Tel Aviv Mus, Israel; New York Public Library, NY
PRINTERS: Editions Press, San Francisco, CA (EP)
PUBLISHERS: Editions Press, San Francisco, CA (EP)
GALLERIES: Walton-Gilbert Galleries, San Francisco, CA

TITLE	PUBLISHER	PRINTER	DATE	MEDIUM	DIMENSION (PAPER SIZE) IN INCHES	TYPE OF PAPER	EDITION NUMBER	NO. OF COLORS	ORIGINAL OPENING PRICE	CURRENT RETAIL PRICE
SOLD OUT EDITIONS (RARE):										
Couple	EP	EP	1981	LC	30 X 22	AC/W	100	8	400	600
Theatre	EP	EP	1981	LC	30 X 22	AC/W	100	9	400	600
Chess	EP	EP	1981	LC	30 X 22	AC/W	100	10	400	600
Musician	EP	EP	1981	LC	30 X 22	AC/W	100	9	400	600

IVOR ABRAHAMS

BORN: Wigan, Lancashire, England; 1935
EDUCATION: St Martin's Sch of Art, 1952–54; Camberwell Sch of Art, London, England, 1954–57
TEACHING: Birmingham Col of Art; Coventry Col of Art; Hull Col of Art; Goldsmith Col of Art, England
COLLECTIONS: Nat Gallery of Australia, Sydney, Australia; Victoria & Albert Mus, London, England; Arts Council of Great Britain, London, England; Rice Univ, Houston, TX; Tate Gallery, London, England; Fort Lauderdale Mus, FL; Minneapolis Inst of Art, MN; Williams Col Mus of Art, Williamstown, MA; Mus of Mod Art, NY
PRINTERS: Advanced Graphics Ltd, London, England (AG); Alan Cox (AC); J C Editions (JCE)
PUBLISHERS: Bernard Jacobson Ltd, London, England (BJL)
GALLERIES: Bernard Jacobson Ltd, London, England

TITLE	PUBLISHER	PRINTER	DATE	MEDIUM	DIMENSION (PAPER SIZE) IN INCHES	TYPE OF PAPER	EDITION NUMBER	NO. OF COLORS	ORIGINAL OPENING PRICE	CURRENT RETAIL PRICE
SOLD OUT EDITIONS (RARE):										
Sundial I (Summer)	BJL	AG	1975	SP	40 X 48	JG	95		1000	2500
Sundial II (Winter)	BJL	AG	1975	SP	40 X 48	JG	95		1000	2500
Pathways (Set of 6)	BJL	AC	1975	LC	24 X 24	SP	55		2000 SET	7500 SET
Monuments (Set of 3)	BJL	AG	1978	SP	41 X 28	JG	100	6	1500 SET	4500 SET
CURRENT EDITIONS:										
Stone Bench	BJL	AC	1975	LC	24 X 25	SP	70	7	400	750
Edgar Allen Poe (Set of 20)	BJL	AG	1976	SP	20 X 14	CR/HMP	100	10–20	7000 SET	12000 SET
Domain at Arnheim II	BJL	AG	1976	SP	21 X 15	CR/HMP	93	20	400	750
Poussin Fountain (Set of 4)	BJL	JCE	1976	EC	19 X 15	SP	20	2	1600 SET	3000 SET
Works Past (Set of 6)	BJL	JCE	1976	EC	19 X 15	SP	20	2	2400 SET	4500 SET
Hedges (Set of 2)	BJL	AG	1977	SP	56 X 40	CR/HMP	100	20–30	1100 SET	3600 SET
Oxford Gardens (Set of 10)	BJL	AG	1977	SP	11 X 15	CR/HMP	250	5–7	1500 SET	3600 SET
Soft-ground etchings (Set of 3)	BJL	JCE	1979	EB	25 X 20	AP	25	1	500 EA	750 EA
Femme du Midi (Set of 6)	BJL	JCE	1979	EC	28 X 22	AP	33	5	3000 SET	4500 SET
Burke Portfolio (Set of 15)	BJL	AC	1979	LC	24 X 19	JG	100	7	4000 SET	7500 SET
Untitled (diptych)	BJL	AC	1980	LC	40 X 27	AT	50	7	1200 SET	3500 SET
Untitled (Pair)	BJL	AC	1982	PO	11 X 9 EA		10 EA		1200 SET	2500 SET

JANET ABRAMOWICZ

BORN: New York, NY
EDUCATION: Art Students League, with Morris Kantor; Columbia Univ, Acad delle Belle Arge, Bologna, Italy, BFA, MFA, with Giorgio Morandi
TEACHING: Lectr, Painting, Printing & Drawing, Fine Arts Dept, Fogg Art Mus, Harvard Univ, Cambridge, MA, 1971 to present
AWARDS: MacDowell Colony Fel, 1976,76; Senior Fulbright Fel, Japan, 1978–79; Japanese Found, 1979–80: Fulbright Travelling Grant, Italy, 1988–89; Rockefeller Found Study Center, Bellagio, Italy, 1989; Am Coun Learned Soc Fel, 1990–91
RECENT EXHIB: British Int Invitational Print Biennale, London, England, 1990–91
COLLECTIONS: Metropolitan Mus of Art, NY; Mus of Mod Art, Kyoto, Japan; New York Public Library, NY; Ohara Mus, Kurashiki, Japan; Contemp Art, Mus d'Arte Mod, Bologna, Italy; Mus d'Arte Mod, La Spezia, Italy
PRINTERS: Antonio Sannino, Rome, Italy (AS)
PUBLISHERS: Artist (ART)
GALLERIES: Tokyo Nanten Shi Gallery, Tokyo, Japan
MAILING ADDRESS: 30 W 15th St, #8, New York, NY 10011

TITLE	PUBLISHER	PRINTER	DATE	MEDIUM	DIMENSION (PAPER SIZE) IN INCHES	TYPE OF PAPER	EDITION NUMBER	NO. OF COLORS	ORIGINAL OPENING PRICE	CURRENT RETAIL PRICE
CURRENT EDITIONS:										
Roman Sites (Series of 20)	ART	AS	1988–89	I/CON/CC	16 X 20 EA	FAB	1 EA	Varies	2200/ 3200 EA	2200/ 3200 EA

JANE ELDORA ABRAMS

BORN: Eau Claire, WI; January 2, 1940
EDUCATION: Univ of Wisconsin-Stout, Menomonie, WI, BS, 1962, MS, 1967; Indiana Univ, Bloomington, IN, MFA, 1971
AWARDS: Texas Tech Univ Mus, Lubbock, TX, 1973; Ford Found Grant, 1979; Univ of New Mexico, Albuquerque, NM, 1971–74,76,79–80
TEACHING: Univ of Wisconsin-Stout, Menomonie, WI, 1967–69; Indiana Univ, Bloomington, IN, Printmaking, Summer, 1976; Univ of New Mexico, Albuquerque, NM, 1971 to present
COLLECTIONS: Indiana Univ Mus of Fine Arts, Bloomington, IN; Univ of Illinois, Macomb, IL; Potsdam Univ, NY; Univ of Dallas, TX; Texas Tech Univ, Lubbock, TX; Minot State Univ, ND; Mus of New Mexico, Santa Fe, NM; Univ of New Mexico, Mus of Fine Arts, Albuquerque, NM; East Carolina Univ, Greenville, NC; Louisiana State Univ, Baton Rouge, LA; Univ of Louisville, KY; Albuquerque Mus of Art & History, NM
PRINTERS: Tamarind Institute, Albuquerque, NM (TI); Robert Arber (RA); Richard Newlin (RN); Bruce Porter (BP); Judith Solodkin (JS); David Keister, Bloomington, IN (DK); David Calkins, Bloomington, IN (DC); Echo Press, Bloomington, IN (EPr)
PUBLISHERS: Tayler Gallery, Taos, NM (TG); Two Tulip Press, Albuquerque, NM (TTP); Tamarind Institute, Albuquerque, NM (TI); Echo Press, Bloomington, IN (EPr)
GALLERIES: Diane Villani, New York, NY; Tamarind Institute, Albuquerque, NM; Kron-Reck Gallery, Albuquerque, NM; Kendall Rackshaw Gallery, Albuquerque, NM; Echo Press, Bloomington, IN
MAILING ADDRESS: 7811 Guadalupe Trail NW, Albuquerque, NM 87101; c/o Department of Art, University of New Mexico, Albuquerque, NM 87131

TITLE	PUBLISHER	PRINTER	DATE	MEDIUM	DIMENSION (PAPER SIZE) IN INCHES	TYPE OF PAPER	EDITION NUMBER	NO. OF COLORS	ORIGINAL OPENING PRICE	CURRENT RETAIL PRICE
SOLD OUT EDITIONS (RARE):										
Not According to Code I	TTP	ART	1980–81	I/CCT	14 X 12	B/G WIN	12	3	225	400
CURRENT EDITIONS:										
Not According to Code II	TTP	ART	1980–81	I/CCT	14 X 12	B/G WIN	12	3	225	300
Not According to Code III	TTP	ART	1980–81	I/CCT	14 X 12	B/G WIN	12	3	225	300
Not According to Code IV	TTP	ART	1980–81	I/CCT	14 X 12	B/G WIN	12	3	225	300
Not According to Code V	TTP	ART	1980–81	ENG/PH	14 X 12	B/G WIN	12	3	225	300
Cosmic Laugh	TTP	ART	1982	EC	15 X 20	AP/W	10	3	275	350
Cosmic Bad Dog	TTP	ART	1982	EC	15 X 20	AP/W	11	3	275	350
Sky Mice	TTP	ART	1982	EC	15 X 20	AP/W	9	3	275	350
Cosmic Strum	TTP	ART	1982	EC	15 X 20	AP/W	10	3	275	350
Ranchos de Albuquerque II,III	EPr	DK/DC/EPr	1991	MON/PAS	26 X 20 EA	R/BFK/W	1 EA	Varies	800 EA	1000 EA
Tzompantli I,II	EPr	DK/DC/EPr	1991	MON/PAS	26 X 20 EA	R/BFK/W	1 EA	Varies	800 EA	1000 EA

VITO ACCONCI

BORN: New York, NY; January 24, 1940
EDUCATION: Holy Cross Col, BA; State Univ of Iowa, Iowa City, IA, MFA
TEACHING: Sch of Visual Arts, NY, 1968–71; California Inst of Art, CA, 1976
RECENT EXHIB: International Monument Gallery, NY, 1987; La Jolla Mus of Contemp Art, CA, 1987; Neuberger Mus, Purchase, NY, 1987–88; Laumeier Sculpture Park, St Louis, MO, 1988; Mus of Mod Art, NY, 1988; East Carolina Univ, Gray Art Gallery, Greenville, NC, 1989; Grants Pass Mus, OR, 1989; Landfall Press, Inc, NY, 1990; Univ of South Florida/Graphicstudio, Tampa, FL, 1992; Univ of Maryland, Baltimore County, Fine Arts Gallery, Baltimore, MD, 1992; Laumeier Sculpture Park, St Louis, MO, 1992; William Paterson Col, Ben Shahn Gallery, Wayne, NJ, 1989,92; Univ of Akron, Emily H Davis Gallery, OH, 1992; Ohio Univ, Seigfred Gallery, Athens, OH, 1992; Cleveland Inst of Art, Reinberger Gallery, Athens, OH, 1992; Contemp Arts Mus, Houston, TX, 1992; Muhlenberg Col, Frank Martin Art Gallery, Allentown, PA, 1989,92

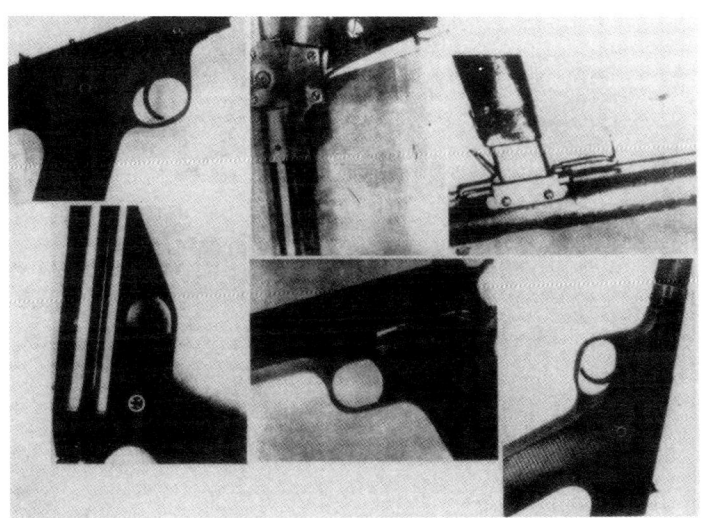

Vito Acconci
Bite the Bullet . . .
Courtesy Crown Point Press

VITO ACCONCI CONTINUED

COLLECTIONS: Mus of Mod Art, NY; Mus of Mod Art, Paris, France; Los Angeles County Mus, CA; Williams Col, Williamstown, MA
PRINTERS: Crown Point Press, San Francisco, CA (CPP); D Simmelelink, Oakland, CA Landfall Press Inc, Chicago, IL (LPI); Jack Lemon, Chicago, IL (JL); Patrik Lindhardt, Tampa, FL; Graphicstudio II, Tampa, FL (GII); George Holzer (GH); Deli Sacilotto (DS); John Silvon (JS); David Yaeger (DY); Maurice Sanchez, NY (MS); Derriére L'Etoile Studio, NY (DES)
PUBLISHERS: Crown Point Press, San Francisco, CA (CPP); Landfall Press Inc, Chicago, IL (LPI); Graphicstudio II, Tampa, FL (GII); Art Issue Editions, Inc, NY (AIE)
GALLERIES: Crown Point Press, New York, NY & San Francisco, CA; Rhona Hoffman Gallery, Chicago, IL; Barbara Gladstone Gallery, New York, NY; James Corcoran Gallery, Santa Monica, CA; Landfall Press, Inc, Chicago, IL; Mattress Factory, Pittsburgh, PA
MAILING ADDRESS: 39 Pearl Street, Brooklyn, NY 11201

TITLE	PUBLISHER	PRINTER	DATE	MEDIUM	DIMENSION (PAPER SIZE) IN INCHES	TYPE OF PAPER	EDITION NUMBER	NO. OF COLORS	ORIGINAL OPENING PRICE	CURRENT RETAIL PRICE
SOLD OUT EDITIONS (RARE):										
Touchtone	ART	ART	1972	LC	29 X 20	AP	50		200	2000
Bite the Bullet: Slow Guns for Quick Sale (To Be Etched on Your American Mind)	CPP	DS/CPP	1977	EB	30 X 42	R/BFK	25	1	500	2500
Stones for a Wall (Set of 10)	LPI	JL/LPI	1979	LC	30 X 23 EA	HMP	10 EA	1–2 EA	2000 SET	5000 SET
Three Flags for One Space and Six Regions (6 Parts)	CPP	CPP	1979–81	EB	24 X 32 EA 72 x 64 TOT		25 EA	1 EA	3000 SET	10000 SET
CURRENT EDITIONS:										
Why Don't You Come Up and See Mine Sometime? Or, Sex for Sale	CPP	DS/CPP	1977	PH/E	30 X 42	R/BFK	25	1	500	2000
The Selling of Five Americans and a Place for One World Citizen	CPP	DS/CPP	1977	PH/E	30 X 42	STP	35	2	400	2000
20 Ft Ladder for any Size Wall (8 Parts)	CPP	CPP	1979–80		31 X 43 EA 244 X 43 TOT		15 EA		2000 SET	5500 SET
2 Wings for Wall and Person (12 Parts)	CPP	CPP	1979–81	EB	26 X 41 EA 53 X 24'4" TOT		10 EA	1 EA	4000 SET	5500 SET
Red Mask/Purple Mask/End Mask (3 Parts)	GII	PL/GII	1983	EC/EMB	8 X 7 EA	AC	30 EA	3 EA	750 SET	2000 SET
Building-Blocks for a Doorway (Dipt) (Soft Ground & Hard Ground)	GII	GH/DS/JS/DY	1983–85	A/EC/PH	93 X 48 EA	AC	8 EA	5 EA	10000 SET	12000 SET
Thou Shalt Not Commit Adultery (from Ten Commandments Suite)	AIE	MS/DES	1987	LC	24 X 18	DIEU	84	5	500	2000

CLINTON ADAMS

BORN: Glendale, CA; December 11, 1918
EDUCATION: Univ of California, Los Angeles, CA, BEd, 1940, MA, 1942
TEACHING: Asst Prof, Painting & Lithography, Univ of California, Los Angeles, CA, 1946–54; Chmn, Art Dept, Univ of Kentucky, Lexington, KY, 1954–57; Chmn, Art Dept, Univ of Florida, Gainesville, FL, 1957–60; Dean, Col of Fine Arts, Univ of New Mexico, Albuquerque, NM, 1961–76, Prof, Art, 1961 to present
AWARDS: Nat Council of Art Administrators, Art Administrator of the Year, 1982; State of New Mexico, Governor's Award, 1985
RECENT EXHIB: California State Univ Art Gallery, Northridge, CA, 1988; Tobey C. Moss Gallery, Los Angeles, CA, 1989; Univ of New Mexico, Albuquerque, NM, 1987,92
COLLECTIONS: Mus of Mod Art, NY; Brooklyn Mus of Art, NY; Art Inst of Chicago, IL; Los Angeles County Mus, CA; Albuquerque Mus, NM; Australian Nat Gallery, Canberra, Australia; Amon Carter Mus, Fort Worth, TX; La Jolla Mus of Contemp Art, CA; Nat Mus of Am Art, Smithsonian Inst, Wash, DC; New York Public Library, NY; Phoenix Art Mus, AZ; Victoria and Albert Mus, London, England; Achenbach Found of Graphic Art Inst, San Francisco, CA
PRINTERS: Randy Gibbs, Albuquerque, NM (RG); Wayne Kline, Albuquerque, NM (WK); Artist (ART); Maria Schleiner, Albuquerque, NM (MS); Tamarind Inst, Albuquerque, NM (TI)
PUBLISHERS: Tamarind Inst, Albuquerque, NM
GALLERIES: Tamarind Inst, Albuquerque, NM; Tobey C Moss Gallery, Los Angeles, CA; Richard Levy Gallery, Albuquerque, NM; Janus Gallery, Santa Fe, NM

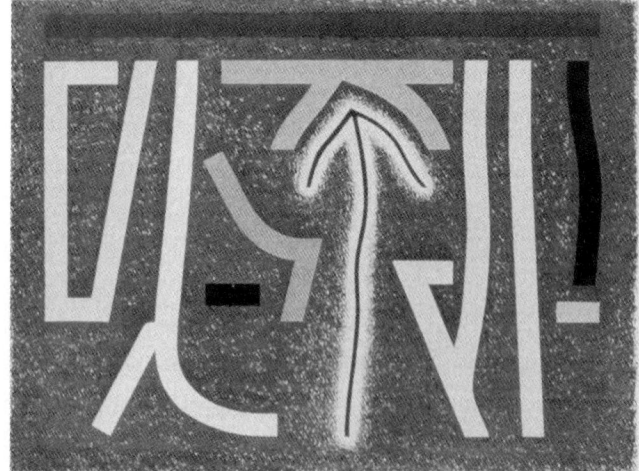

Clinton Adams
Pavane for Nine Colors
Courtesy Tamarind Institute

MAILING ADDRESS: 1917 Morningside Drive, NE, Albuquerque, NM 87110

TITLE	PUBLISHER	PRINTER	DATE	MEDIUM	DIMENSION (PAPER SIZE) IN INCHES	TYPE OF PAPER	EDITION NUMBER	NO. OF COLORS	ORIGINAL OPENING PRICE	CURRENT RETAIL PRICE
SOLD OUT EDITIONS (RARE):										
Second Hand Store I,II			1953	LC	8 X 14 EA	AP	37 EA			500 EA
Window Series I,II,III			1960	LC	15 X 11 EA	AP	20 EA			500 EA
Requiem, November			1963	LC	30 X 22 EA	AP	20 EA			500 EA

CLINTON ADAMS CONTINUED

TITLE	PUBLISHER	PRINTER	DATE	MEDIUM	DIMENSION (PAPER SIZE) IN INCHES	TYPE OF PAPER	EDITION NUMBER	NO. OF COLORS	ORIGINAL OPENING PRICE	CURRENT RETAIL PRICE
CURRENT EDITIONS:										
Fugue for Nine Colors	TI	ART/WK/TI	1983	LC	18 X 24	R/BFK	20	8	200	400
Pavane for Nine Colors	TI	ART/RG/TI	1983	LC	18 X 24	R/BFK	25	7	200	400
Costa Brava	TI	ART/MS/TI	1988	LC	20 X 30	GE	25	4	400	600

VALERIO ADAMI

BORN: Bologna, Italy; 1935
RECENT EXHIB: Marisa del Re Gallery, NY, 1992
COLLECTIONS: Mus of Mod Art, NY; Tokyo Mus, Japan; Mus de Arte Mod, Mexico, City, Mexico; Israel Mus, Jerusalem, Israel
PRINTERS: Maeght Editeur, Paris, France (ME); Galerie Maeght Lelong, Paris, France (ML)

PUBLISHERS: Maeght Editions, Paris, France (ME); Editions Press, San Francisco, CA (EP); Transworld Art, Inc, NY (TAI); Martin Lawrence Limited Editions, Van Nuys, CA (MLLE); Galerie Maeght Lelong, Paris, France (ML)
GALLERIES: Spaightwood Galleries, Madison, WI; Marisa del Re Gallery, New York, NY; Martin Lawrence Galleries, Escondido, CA & Newport Beach, CA & Palm Springs, CA & Redondo Beach, CA & Santa Clara, CA & Sherman Oaks, CA & Thousand Oaks, CA & West Los Angeles, CA & Los Angeles, CA & Short Hills, NJ & Soho, NY & Phila, PA; Galerie Thomas R Monahan, Chicago, IL

TITLE	PUBLISHER	PRINTER	DATE	MEDIUM	DIMENSION (PAPER SIZE) IN INCHES	TYPE OF PAPER	EDITION NUMBER	NO. OF COLORS	ORIGINAL OPENING PRICE	CURRENT RETAIL PRICE
SOLD OUT EDITIONS (RARE):										
On the Moon	TAI	ART	1971	LC	20 X 23	AP	90		135	850
Homage to Israel	TAI	ART	1971	LC	20 X 23	AP	90		135	850
Nostalgia	ME	ME	1978	EC	36 X 25	AP	75		800 FF	8000 FF
Les-Blessures de Staline	ME	ME	1978	EC	30 X 36	AP	75		800 FF	8000 FF
Disegno di un Paesaggio	ME	ME	1978	EC	36 X 25	AP	75		800 FF	8000 FF
Collecting Nostalgia	ME	ME	1978	EC	35 X 25	AP	75		800 FF	8000 FF
Ritratti Con Espressione	ME	ME	1978	EC	30 X 42	AP	75		800 FF	8000 FF
Etude Pour les Courts de Tennis	ME	ME	1978	LC	16 X 27	AP	200		500 FF	5000 FF
Pelouse Interdite	ME	ME	1978	LC	22 X 30	AP	75		500 FF	5500 FF
La Vie Simple d'un Homme Genial	ME	ME	1978	LC	21 X 30	AP	75		500 FF	5500 FF
Monsieur Untel	ME	ME	1978	LC	22 X 30	AP	75		500 FF	5500 FF
Chiron Enseignant la Lyre a Achille	ME	ME	1979	LC	42 X 30	AP	75		800 FF	10000FF
Prelude	EP	EP	1979	SP	30 X 40	AS/W	60	6	450	900
Caprichos Americano	EP	EP	1979	SP	30 X 40	AS/W	60	6	450	900
Homer	EP	EP	1979	SP	42 X 25	STP/W	75	7	450	900
Le Mariage	ME	ME	1979	LC	42 X 30	AP	75	7	450	1000
Catullo	EP	EP	1979	SP	30 X 40	AS/W	60	6	450	1000
Personage	EP	EP	1980	SP	73 X 54 cm	AS/W	125	7	450	1000
Melancolie	ME	ME	1980	LC	53 X 68 cm	AP	75		900 FF	8000 FF
La Charrette	ME	ME	1980	LC	38 X 56 cm	AP	75		900 FF	8000 FF
Pandora's Box	ME	ME	1980	LC	66 X 25 cm	AP	75		1100 FF	8000 FF
Achille	ME	ME	1980	LC	155 X 535 cm	AP	125		1200 FF	8000 FF
Catullo—Voyage en Italie	ME	ME	1980	LC	73 X 54 cm	AP	60		1200 FF	8000 FF
Le Mariage	ME	ME	1980	LC	105 X 65 cm	AP	60		1200 FF	8000 FF
Kiss of the Moon	ME	ME	1980	LC	66 X 46 cm	AP	75		1200 FF	8000 FF
Affiche Avant la Lettre Roland Garros	ME	ME	1980	LC	87 X 66 cm	AP	50	4	400	1250
Affiche n°182 Avant la Lettre	ME	ME	1980	LC	81 X 60 cm	AP	150	3	400	1250
Affiche Avant la Lettre Caen	ME	ME	1980	LC	130 X 83 cm	AP	100	4	400	1250
Naissance de la Peinture	ME	ME	1980	LC	66 X 85 cm	AP	75	4	400	1250
Odalisque	MLLE	ME	1981	LC	56 X 76 cm	AP	75	12	450	1250
Song of Myself	MLLE	ME	1981	LC	56 X 76 cm	AP	75	9	450	1250
Le Talon d'Achille	MLLE	ME	1981	LC	26 X 33 cm	AP	75	5	450	1250
Le Gardien de Phare	ME	ME	1981	LC	66 X 85 cm	AP	100	5	1800 FF	5000 FF
Clair de Lune	ME	ME	1981	LC	66 X 84 cm	AP	100	5	1800 FF	5000 FF
Paysage de Ruines	ME	ME	1981	LC	67 X 85 cm	AP	100	4	1800 FF	5000 FF
Mon Atelier en Italie	ML	ML	1982	LC	107 X 74 cm	AP	100	5	1800 FF	5000 FF
Crépuscule	MLLE	ML	1982	LC	26 X 33	AP	75	5	450	1250
Le Peintre aux Lunettes	ML	ML	1982	LC	66 X 84 cm	AP	100	5	1800 FF	5000 FF
Etoile du Matin	ML	ML	1982	LC	91 X 65 cm	AP	100	4	1800 FF	5000 FF
Stèle	ML	ML	1982	LC	55 X 42 cm	AP	100	3	900 FF	3500 FF
Pastorale	ML	ML	1982	LC	96 X 66 cm	AP	75	4	2000 FF	6000 FF
Paysage Gothique	MLLE	ML	1982	LC	26 X 33	AP	75	5	450	850
Orphée	ML	ML	1982	LC	84 X 66 cm	AP	100	5	1800 FF	5000 FF
Angélus	ML	ML	1982	LC	94 X 65 cm	AP	100	6	1800 FF	5000 FF
Tete de Femme	ML	ML	1982	LC	60 X 57 cm	AP	150	5	1300 FF	5000 FF
Thorvaldsen	ML	ML	1982	LC	94 X 66 cm	AP	75	5	2000 FF	6000 FF
La Mort de Marat	ML	ML	1983	LC	91 X 65 cm	AP	100	5	1800 FF	5000 FF
Still Life	ML	ML	1983	LC	104 X 76 cm	AP	75	5	2200 FF	5000 FF
La Feville de Vigne	ML	ML	1983	LC	92 X 66 cm	AP	100	5	1800 FF	5000 FF
Picasso et la Femme Neoclassique	ML	ML	1983	LC	85 X 67 cm	AP	100	6	1800 FF	5000 FF
L'urne	ML	ML	1983	LC	91 X 66 cm	AP	100	5	1800 FF	5000 FF
L'enlèvement d'Europe	ML	ML	1983	EC	103 X 75 cm	AP	75	5	2600 FF	6000 FF
Vers le Soteilque se Lève	ML	ML	1983	EC	86 X 63 cm	RP	75	5	2400 FF	6000 FF
Carte de Visite	ML	ML	1983	LC	50 X 40 cm	AP	75	5	900 FF	4500 FF

MARK ADAMS

BORN: Fort Plain, NY; Oct 27, 1925
EDUCATION: Syracuse Univ, NY with Hans Hofmann
TEACHING: Am Acad, Rome, Italy, 1963; San Francisco Art Inst, CA, 1961,72; Univ of California, Davis, CA, 1978
RECENT EXHIB: John Berggruen Gallery, San Francisco, CA, 1987; Palo Alto Cult Center, CA, 1989
COLLECTIONS: Dallas Mus of Fine Arts, TX
PRINTERS: Trillium Graphics, San Francisco, CA (TG); Shark's Lithography, Boulder, CO (SL); Bud Shark, Boulder, CO (BS); Katherine Lincoln Press, San Francisco, CA (KLP); RE Townsend, Boston, MA (RT); Timothy Berry, San Francisco, CA (TB); Teaberry Press, San Francisco, CA (TP)
PUBLISHERS: John Berggruen Gallery, San Francisco, CA (JBG); Ed Hill Editions, El Paso, TX (EHE); Graphic Arts Council, Achenbach Foundation, San Francisco, CA (GAC); Artist (ART)
GALLERIES: John Berggruen Gallery, San Francisco, CA; Jane Haslem Salon, Wash, DC; First Impressions/Barbara Linhard Gallery, Carmel, CA; Ed Hill Gallery, El Paso, TX
MAILING ADDRESS: 4627 Briar Cliff Rd, Baltimore, MD 21229

TITLE	PUBLISHER	PRINTER	DATE	MEDIUM	DIMENSION (PAPER SIZE) IN INCHES	TYPE OF PAPER	EDITION NUMBER	NO. OF COLORS	ORIGINAL OPENING PRICE	CURRENT RETAIL PRICE
CURRENT EDITIONS:										
Pale Orange Begonia	JBG	BS/SL	1979	LC	13 X 17	A/W	80	5	400	1500
Pink Poppy	JBG	KLP	1980	AC	11 X 9	A/W	50	6	450	1000
Rose in Jar	JBG	KLP	1981	AC	14 X 16	A/W	50	7	600	1800
Glass of Water	EHE	TG	1981	LC	20 X 22	A/W	100	11	625	1800
Water Jar (State II)	ART/GAC	RT/TB/TP	1984	AC	24 X 23	R/BFK	100	2	600	2000
Ivory Rose			1989	EB/A		R/BFK	112		1000	1000

PAT ADAMS

BORN: Stockton, CA; July 8, 1928
EDUCATION: Col of Arts and Crafts, Oakland, CA, 1945; Univ of California, Berkeley, CA, BA, 1949; Brooklyn Mus Art Sch, NY, 1950–51
TEACHING: Vis Prof, Yale Univ, New Haven, CT, Fall, 1983; Bennington Col, VT, 1964 to present
AWARDS: Fullbright Fel, France, 1956–57; College Art Association Distinguished Teaching of Art Award, 1984; Am Acad & Inst of Arts & Letters Award, Painting, 1986; Childe Hassam Purchase Awards, 1980,89; Nat Endowment for the Arts Awards, 1968,76,80,84,87,89
RECENT EXHIB: Trisolini Gallery, Ohio Univ, Athens, OH, 1987; Berkshire Mus, Pittsfield, MA, 1988–89; Zabriskie Gallery, NY, 1990
COLLECTIONS: Philadelphia Mus of Art, PA; Whitney Mus of Am Art, NY; Hirshhorn Mus, Wash, DC; Univ of VT, Burlington, VT; Fleming Mus, VT; Montclair Mus, NJ; Univ of CA, Berkeley, CA; Middlebury Col, VT; Univ of Michigan, Ann Arbor, MI; Williams Col, Williamstown, MA; Univ of North Carolina, Greensboro, NC; Yale Art Gallery, New Haven, CT; Brooklyn Mus, NY; Berkshire Mus, Pittsfield, MA
PRINTERS: Athens Print Workshop, Ohio Univ, Athens, OH (APW); Yong Soon Min (YSM); David Keister (DK); Artist (ART); Patricia Branstead, NY (PB); Riverhouse Editions, Clark, CO (REd)
PUBLISHERS: Solo Press, NY (SP); Rutgers Univ, NJ (RU); Bennington Col, VT (BC); Ox-Bow Press (O-BP); Athens Print Workshop, Ohio Univ, Athens, OH (APW); Artist (ART); Riverhouse Editions, Clark, CO (REd)
GALLERIES: Zabriskie Gallery, New York, NY; Ox-Bow Press, Bennington Col, Bennington, VT; Van Straaten Gallery, Chicago, IL
MAILING ADDRESS: 370 Elm, Bennington, VT 05201

Pat Adams
And All the Times
Courtesy Riverhouse Editions

The retail prices of the 100,000 limited edition prints quoted in this directory are subject to change. Print publishers, artists and galleries were the direct sources for these quotations. Prices in the secondary market listed as "Sold Out Editions (Rare)" indicate that the publisher has a limited supply of that print or that the print is difficult to locate in the galleries.

PAT ADAMS CONTINUED

TITLE	PUBLISHER	PRINTER	DATE	MEDIUM	DIMENSION (PAPER SIZE) IN INCHES	TYPE OF PAPER	EDITION NUMBER	NO. OF COLORS	ORIGINAL OPENING PRICE	CURRENT RETAIL PRICE
CURRENT EDITIONS:										
Rutgers' Contemporary Art Series	RU	ART	1978	LC	30 X 23	AP	50	4	200	300
Endless Rocking	BC	ART	1979	PO/C/MM	18 X 23	AP	150	12	150	400
Fair, Fair	O-BP	ART	1981	LC/MM	26 X 18	AC	60	15	500	600
Seraph's Disc	APW/ART	APW/YSM/DK	1984	LC/I/STEN/CO	24 X 35	AP/W	43	7	800	900
And All the Time	REd	PB/REd	1989	EC	25 X 38	SAK	40	5	900	900

NICHOLAS AFRICANO

BORN: Kankakee, IL; 1948
EDUCATION: Illinois State Univ, BA, 1970; MA, 1974; MFA, 1975
RECENT EXHIB: Illinois State Univ, Normal, IL, 1987,89; Dart Gallery, Chicago, IL, 1989; Michael H Lord Gallery, Chicago, IL, 1992
PRINTERS: Aeropress, NY (A); Patricia Branstead, NY (PB); Steven Andersen, Minneapolis, MN (SA); Philip Barker, Minneapolis, MN (PhB); Vermillion Editions, Ltd, Minneapolis, MN (VEL)
PUBLISHERS: Barbara Gladstone Editions, NY (BGE); Vermillion Editions, Ltd, Minneapolis, MN (VEL)
GALLERIES: Holly Solomon Editions, New York, NY; Dart Gallery, Chicago, IL; Vermillion Editions, Ltd, Minneapolis, MN; Michael H Lord Gallery, Chicago, IL; Montgomery Glasoe Fine Art, Minneapolis, MN; Jan Weiner Gallery, Kansas City, MO
MAILING ADDRESS: 705 N School Rd, Normal, IL 61761

TITLE	PUBLISHER	PRINTER	DATE	MEDIUM	DIMENSION (PAPER SIZE) IN INCHES	TYPE OF PAPER	EDITION NUMBER	NO. OF COLORS	ORIGINAL OPENING PRICE	CURRENT RETAIL PRICE
CURRENT EDITIONS:										
The Shadow (Set of 4)	BGE	PB/A	1979	EC	11 X 14 EA	HMP	45 EA	4 EA	1500 SET	3000 SET
Flesh, Armor	VEL	SA/PhB/VEL	1986	LC/SP/CO	40 X 30 EA	AP	46 EA	5 EA	1200 EA	1800 EA
Lilacs & Smoke (Series of Monotypes)	VEL	ART/VEL	1987	MON	18 X 22 EA	HMP	1 EA		2000 EA	2500 EA
					26 X 20 EA	HMP	1 EA		2500 EA	3000 EA
					29 X 37 EA	HMP	1 EA		4500 EA	5000 EA
					40 X 31 EA	HMP	1 EA		6000 EA	6500 EA
Noble, Sincere, Hopeless (Series of Monotypes)	VEL	ART/VEL	1987	MON	18 X 22 EA	HMP	1 EA		2000 EA	2500 EA
					26 X 20 EA	HMP	1 EA		2500 EA	3000 EA
					29 X 37 EA	HMP	1 EA		4500 EA	5000 EA
					40 X 31 EA	HMP	1 EA		6000 EA	6500 EA

YAACOV AGAM

BORN: Rishon Le Zion, Israel; 1928
EDUCATION: Bezalel Sch of Art, Jerusalem, Israel; Atelier d'Art Abstrait, Paris, France, 1951
TEACHING: Harvard Univ, Cambridge, MA, 1968
AWARDS: First Prize, Biennial, Sao Paulo, 1963; Chevalier de l'Ordre des Arts and Letters, 1974; Medal of the Council of Europe, 1977
RECENT EXHIB: Mus of Holography, NY, 1989
COLLECTIONS: Julliard Sch, NY; Hirshhorn Mus, Wash, DC; Mus of Mod Art, NY; Mus of Mod Art, Paris, France; Stedelijk Mus, Amsterdam, The Netherlands; Elysee Palace, Paris, France
PRINTERS: Meissner Editions, Gutenbergring, Germany (ME); Joseph Burns, NY (JB); Rowland Studio, Chicago, IL (RS); Chicago Serigraphic Workshop, Chicago, IL (CSW); C Graphics, Chicago, IL (CG); Caza Press, Paris, France (CP); Atelier Arcay, Paris, France (AA); Atelier Mayeux, Abasson, France (AM); Artist (ART); La Poligrafa, Barcelona, Spain (LP); Diverse Dimensions Art, Ltd, Scarsdale, NY (DDA); BLD Limited, NY (BLD)
PUBLISHERS: Contemporary Art Masters, NY (CAM); Transworld Art, Inc, NY (TAI); Abrams Original Editions, NY (AOE); Circle Fine Art, Chicago, IL (CFA); Chicago Serigraphic Workshop, Chicago, IL (CSW); Martin Lawrence Limited Editions, Van Nuys, CA (MLLE); Gallery West Editions, Los Angeles, CA (GWE); Zimmerman Editions, Baltimore, MD (ZE); Metropolitan Art Associates, Huntington, NY (MAA); Ediciones Poligrafa, Barcelona, Spain (EdP); Diverse Dimensions Art, Ltd, Scarsdale, NY (DDA); BLD Limited, NY (BLD)
GALLERIES: Martin Lawrence Galleries, Sherman Oaks, CA & West Los Angeles, CA & Newport Beach, CA & Palm Springs, CA & Santa Clara, CA & Redondo Beach, CA & Thousand Oaks, CA & Escondido, CA & Phila, PA & Short Hills, NY & Soho, NY; Saper Galleries, East Lansing, MI; Gallery Yakir, Huntington Woods, MI; Short Hills Gallery, Short Hills, NJ; Nathan Silberberg Fine Arts, New York, NY; TR's Gallery, New York, NY; Laura Paul Galleries, Columbus, OH; Gallery Louis, York, PA; Owl Gallery, San Francisco, CA; The Hang-Up, Sarasota, FL; Fernette's Gallery of Art, Des Moines, IA; Charles Barry International, Rockville, MD; Circle Galleries, San Diego, CA & San Francisco, CA & Northbrook, IL & Pittsburgh, PA & Houston, TX & Soho, New York & Scottsdale, AZ & Beverly Hills, CA & Costa Mesa, CA & Sherman Oaks, CA & Palm Beach, FL & Honolulu, HI & New Orleans, LA & Las Vegas, NV & Seattle, WA; Gallery West, Los Angeles, CA; ISART, Israeli Art Gallery, Westhills, CA

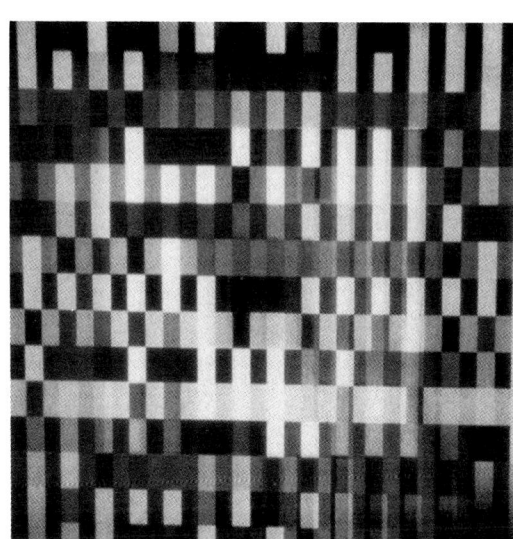

Yaacov Agam
Bing Bang: Creation of Time
Courtesy Diverse Dimensions Art

The print market has become very selective. For the first time since we published the first edition of The Printworld Directory in 1982, the prices of prints have been greatly reduced and greatly increased for the same artists by the most reputable and established print publishers. Check the fifth edition to understand the movement.

YAACOV AGAM CONTINUED

TITLE	PUBLISHER	PRINTER	DATE	MEDIUM	DIMENSION (PAPER SIZE) IN INCHES	TYPE OF PAPER	EDITION NUMBER	NO. OF COLORS	ORIGINAL OPENING PRICE	CURRENT RETAIL PRICE
SOLD OUT EDITIONS (RARE):										
Etoile de David	TAI	ART	1971	SP	31 X 31	BUT	100		400	2000
Spring	TAI	CP	1971	SP/PO	22 X 28	AP	150		400	1200
Summer	TAI	CP	1971	SP/PO	22 X 28	AP	150		400	1200
Winter	TAI	CP	1971	SP/PO	22 X 28	AP	150		400	1200
Blue Star	TAI	CP	1971	SP/PO	28 X 22	AP	150		400	1200
Daliah	TAI	CP	1971	SP/PO	28 X 22	AP	150		400	1200
Prayer	TAI	CP	1971	SP/PO	32 X 25	AP	150		400	1200
Time Change Suite (Set of 5)	CFA	AA	1971	SP	7 X 26 EA	AP	180 EA		1250 SET	2700 SET
Life Suite (Set of 5)	CFA	AA	1971	SP	28 X 9 EA	AP	180 EA		1500 SET	3500 SET
Espace Agam Suite I (Set of 5)	CFA	AA	1971	SP	53 X 20 EA	AP	144 EA		2500 SET	6200 SET
Espace Agam Suite II (Set of 5)	CFA	AA	1971	SP	53 X 20 EA	AP	144 EA		2500 SET	6200 SET
Midnight Flower Suite (Set of 6)	CFA	AA	1972	SP	29 X 30 EA	AP	180 EA		3500 SET	10000 SET
One and Another Suite (Set of 6)	CFA	AA	1972	SP	37 X 25 EA	AP	180 EA		3500 SET	7200 SET
Double Metamorphisis II (Set of 5)	CFA	AA	1972	SP	36 X 50 EA	AP	180 EA		3800 SET	9000 SET
Peace and War (Set of 2)	CFA	AA	1972	SP	29 X 9 EA	AP	198 EA		950 SET	2100 SET
End to End Suite (Set of 5)	CFA	AA	1972	SP	30 X 30 EA	AP	180 EA		2500 SET	5225 SET
Becoming (Standard Agamograph) (Framed)	DDA	DDA	1972	MULT	23 X 24	AP	99		1500	10000
Many Fields (Standard Agamograph) (Framed)	DDA	DDA	1972	MULT	23 X 24	AP	99		1500	10000
Star Suite (Standard Agamograph) (Framed) (Set of 4):										
Star of Love	DDA	DDA	1973	MULT	23 X 24	AP	99		1500	10000
Star of Light	DDA	DDA	1973	MULT	23 X 24	AP	99		1500	10000
Star of David	DDA	DDA	1973	MULT	23 X 24	AP	99		1500	10000
Hidden Star	DDA	DDA	1973	MULT	23 X 24	AP	99		1500	10000
Forever (Standard Agamograph) (Framed)	DDA	DDA	1973	MULT	23 X 24	AP	99		1500	10000
After (Standard Agamograph) (Framed)	DDA	DDA	1973	MULT	23 X 24	AP	99		1500	10000
Homage A J S Bach (Set of 3)	CFA	AA	1973	SP	19 X 40 EA	AP	200 EA		2000 SET	4500 SET
Homage A GB (Set of 5)	CFA	AA	1973	SP	25 X 35 EA	AP	200 EA		2000 SET	5000 SET
Bird's Eye View	CFA	AA	1974	SP	30 X 41	AP	180		750	2000
Before Time and Space	CFA	AA	1974	SP	30 X 41	AP	99		900	2500
Before the Big Boom	CFA	AA	1974	SP	30 X 41	AP	99		900	2300
Homage A Tantra	CFA	AA	1974	SP	30 X 41	AP	150		5000	13000
The Big Bang (Set of 6)	CFA	AA	1974	SP	30 X 41	AP	200 EA		2350 SET	5000 SET
The Rainbow Outer Space	CFA	AA	1974	SP	30 X 41	AP	99		950	2400
Visual Orchestration (Standard Agamograph) (Framed)	DDA	DDA	1974	MULT	23 X 24	AP	99		1800	10000
See See (Standard Agamograph) (Framed)	DDA	DDA	1974	MULT	23 X 24	AP	99		1800	10000
Fusion V (Standard Agamograph) (Framed)	DDA	DDA	1974	MULT	23 X 24	AP	99		1800	10000
Agam Suite, Agam Suite, Agam (Port of 3 w/Text):									1200 SET	3000 SET
Forme Couleur	TAI	AA	1974	SP	31 X 31	AP	200		400	950
Forme Lignes	TAI	AA	1974	SP	31 X 31	AP	200		400	950
Rhythme-Ligne Forme	TAI	AA	1974	SP	31 X 31	AP	200		400	950
Love Star of David (Sterling Silver)	TAI	AM	1975	MS	7 X 6 X 6	SIL	27			POR
Love Star of David (Gold)	TAI	AM	1975	MS	7 X 6 X 6	GOLD	27			POR
Birth of a Flag	TAI	AA	1975	MS/SP	26 X 20 X 2	PLEX	175	1	1800	3000
Spring	CAM	AA	1976	SP	25 X 39	AP	144		450	2200
Summer	CAM	AA	1976	SP	25 X 39	AP	144		450	2200
Noon	CAM	AA	1976	SP	25 X 39	AP	144		450	2200
Evening	CAM	AA	1976	SP	25 X 39	AP	144		450	2200
Galaxy Suite (Set of 3):										
Hidden Galaxy	CFA	AA	1976	SP	14 X 14	AP	99		1000	2200
Hidden Path	CFA	AA	1976	SP	14 X 15	AP	99		1000	2200
Outer Galaxy	CFA	AA	1976	SP	14 X 14	AP	99		1000	2200
Union (Standard Agamograph) (Framed)	DDA	DDA	1976	MULT	23 X 24	AP	99		1500	10000
Space Agam A (Standard Agamograph) (Framed)	DDA	DDA	1976	MULT	23 X 24	AP	99		1500	10000
Space Agam B (Standard Agamograph) (Framed)	DDA	DDA	1976	MULT	23 X 24	AP	99		1500	10000
Fond Marin (Standard Agamograph) (Framed)	DDA	DDA	1976	MULT	23 X 24	AP	99		1500	10000
Chad Gadya (Standard Agamograph) (Framed)	DDA	DDA	1976	MULT	23 X 24	AP	99		1500	10000
Birmingham (Standard Agamograph) (Framed)	DDA	DDA	1976	MULT	23 X 24	AP	99		1500	10000
Night	CAM	AA	1976	SP	32 X 31	AP	144		450	2500

YAACOV AGAM CONTINUED

TITLE	PUBLISHER	PRINTER	DATE	MEDIUM	DIMENSION (PAPER SIZE) IN INCHES	TYPE OF PAPER	EDITION NUMBER	NO. OF COLORS	ORIGINAL OPENING PRICE	CURRENT RETAIL PRICE
SOLD OUT EDITIONS (RARE):										
Festival	CAM	AA	1976	SP	32 X 31	AP	33		450	2500
Midnight Flower (Standard Agamograph) (Framed)	DDA	DDA	1977	MULT	23 X 24	AP	99		1800	10000
Fusion Plastique (Standard Agamograph) (Framed)	DDA	DDA	1977	MULT	23 X 24	AP	99		1800	10000
Fleur du Midi (Standard Agamograph) (Framed)	DDA	DDA	1977	MULT	23 X 24	AP	99		1800	10000
Double Movement (Standard Agamograph) (Framed)	DDA	DDA	1977	MULT	23 X 24	AP	99		1800	10000
Triple Movement (Standard Agamograph) (Framed)	DDA	DDA	1977	MULT	23 X 24	AP	99		1800	10000
Cycle (Standard Agamograph) (Framed)	DDA	DDA	1977	MULT	23 X 24	AP	99		1800	10000
Counterpoint (Standard Agamograph) (Framed)	DDA	DDA	1977	MULT	23 X 24	AP	99		1800	10000
Begin the Begin (Standard Agamograph) (Framed)	DDA	DDA	1977	MULT	23 X 24	AP	99		1800	10000
Mardi Gras (Standard Agamograph) (Framed)	DDA	DDA	1978	MULT	23 X 24	AP	99		2000	10000
Springtime (Standard Agamograph) (Framed)	DDA	DDA	1978	MULT	23 X 24	AP	99		2000	10000
Autumn (Standard Agamograph) (Framed)	DDA	DDA	1978	MULT	23 X 24	AP	99		2000	10000
Transformable Dialogue (Set of 3):									2700 SET	7000 SET
Transformable Dialogue I	TAI	AA	1978	MS/SP	20 X 21 X 1		99		1000	2500
Transformable Dialogue II	TAI	AA	1978	MS/SP	20 X 21 X 1		99		1000	2500
Transformable Dialogue III	TAI	AA	1978	MS/SP	20 X 21 X 1		99		1000	2500
Time Change Suite (Set of 5)	MLLE	A/P/FR	1978	SP	7 X 26 EA	AP	180 EA	54 EA	1200 SET	3500 SET
3 in 1 Blue/Black/Red	MLLE	ART	1978	SP	26 X 23	AP	75	36	2400	4500
One & Another (Set of 6)	MLLE	A/P/FR	1979	SP	28 X 40 EA	AP	180 EA	27 EA	7000 SET	8500 SET
One & Another (Deluxe) (Set of 6)	MLLE	A/P/FR	1979	SP	28 X 40 EA	AP	90 EA	27 EA	8000 SET	9500 SET
18 Peace Stars (Deluxe)	MLLE	ART	1979	LC	27 X 19	AP	63	12	500	2000
18 Peace Stars (Regular)	MLLE	ART	1979	LC	27 X 19	AP	180	12	400	1800
Star of Peace	CFA	AA	1979	LC	30 X 22	AP	99	4	500	2500
+ − X 9	MLLE	A/P/FR	1980	SP	8 X 28	AP	180	36	1800	4000
+ − X 9	MLLE	A/P/FR	1980	SP	28 X 67	AP	54	36	1500	2700
3 X 3 Interplay Gold (Sculpture)	MLLE	A/P/FR	1980	MULT	14 HT	AP	36	1	5400	8500
3 X 3 Interplay Silver (Sculpture)	MLLE	A/P/FR	1980	MULT	14 HT	AP	99	1	4500	7500
Memory	MLLE	A/P/FR	1980	MULT	16 X 16	AP	180/BLK	36	900	2500
Memory	MLLE	A/P/FR	1980	MULT	16 X 16	AP	99/SIL	36	900	2700
Recollection	MLLE	A/P/FR	1980	MULT	16 X 16	AP	180/BLK	36	900	2500
Recollection	MLLE	A/P/FR	1980	MULT	16 X 16	AP	99/SIL	36	900	2700
Magic Rainbow I	CFA/CSW	CSW	1980	SP	41 X 48	MIR/R	180	14	3250	5100
Magic Rainbow II	CFA/CSW	CBE/CSW	1980	SP/EMB	22 X 26	MIR/R	180	13	975	2300
Magic Rainbow III (Silver)	CFA/CSW	CSW	1980	SP	22 X 25	MIR/R	63	14	1100	2300
Magic Rainbow IV (Gold)	CFA/CSW	CSW	1980	SP	22 X 25	MIR/R	37	14	1100	2300
Magic Rainbow V (Small)	CFA/CSW	CBE/CSW	1980	SP/EMB	18 X 21	MIR/R	180	7	750	2200
Magic Rainbow VI (Silver)	CFA/CSW	CSW	1980	SP	18 X 21	MIR/R	99	8	1100	2200
Magic Rainbow VII (Gold)	CFA/CSW	CSW	1980	SP	18 X 21	MIR/R	99	8	1100	2250
Magic Rainbow VIII	CFA/CSW	CSW	1980	SP	41 X 48	MIR/R	99	15	3500	4300
Magic Rainbow IX	CFA/CSW	CSW	1980	SP	41 X 48	MIR/R	99	15	3500	4300
Cosmic Relationship Gold (Mirror)	MLLE	A/P/FR	1980	MULT	30 X 38	AP	99	18	1200	2700
Cosmic Relationship Silver (Mirror)	MLLE	A/P/FR	1980	MULT	30 X 38	AP	99	18	1200	2700
Infinity	MLLE	ART	1980	SP	31 X 31	AP	180	17	750	1250
Agamscope Deluxe (Signed)	MLLE	ART	1980	MULT	2 X 8	AP	270		500	650
Festival	MLLE	ART	1980	SP	47 X 31	AP	45	90	2300	4200
Triple Galaxy (Regular)	MLLE	ART	1980	SP	29 X 29	AP	180	5	600	1100
Triple Galaxy (Deluxe)	MLLE	ART	1980	SP	29 X 29	AP	99	5	700	1350
Tapestry	MLLE	ART	1980	SP		AP	180	24	2400	3200
Homage to Johann Sebastian Bach, I, II, III (Set of 3)	AOE	ME	1980	SP	17 X 38 EA	HMP	99 EA		1800 SET	5000 SET
Homage to Johann Sebastian Bach (Deluxe Print)	AOE	ME	1980	SP	64 X 48	HMP	54	24	750 EA / 1500	1800 EA / 3200
Day Night (Polymorph)	DDA	DDA	1980	MULT	23 X 24	HMP	99		2200	18000
Magic Rain (Polymorph)	DDA	DDA	1980	MULT	23 X 24	HMP	99		2200	18000
Split Space #1 (Gold)	CFA	CSW	1982	SP/CO	25 X 30	CSW	270		1150	2500
Split Space #2 (Silver)	CFA	CSW	1982	SP/CO	25 X 30	CSW/R	90		1250	2800
Square Wave #1 (Gold)	CFA	RS	1982	SP	24 X 27	CSW/R	180		1300	2200
Square Wave #2 (Silver)	CFA	CSW	1982	SP	24 X 27	CSW/R	90		1400	2200
Metamorphosis	MLLE	A/P/FR	1982	SP	12 X 16	AP	180		2000	2700
Metamorphosis (Deluxe)	MLLE	A/P/FR	1982	SP	12 X 16	AP	99		2000	3200
Night Rainbow (Gold)	CFA	CSW	1983	SP	41 X 48	CSW/R	50		3900	4350
Night Rainbow (Silver)	CFA	CSW	1983	SP	41 X 48	CSW/R	50		3900	4350

YAACOV AGAM CONTINUED

TITLE	PUBLISHER	PRINTER	DATE	MEDIUM	DIMENSION (PAPER SIZE) IN INCHES	TYPE OF PAPER	EDITION NUMBER	NO. OF COLORS	ORIGINAL OPENING PRICE	CURRENT RETAIL PRICE
SOLD OUT EDITIONS (RARE):										
Sparkling Night Rainbow (Gold)	CFA	CSW	1984	SP	21 X 25	CSW/R	270		1300	2300
Sparkling Night Rainbow (Silver)	CFA	CSW	1984	SP	21 X 25	CSW/R	72		1500	2500
Image Aquatic Prismagraph (Color Serigraph with 8 Transparent Prisms)	DDA	DDA	1990	SP		AP	99	48	5000	7400
CURRENT EDITIONS:										
Sea Suite (Standard Agamograph) (Framed) (Set of 5):										
Sea Rhythm	DDA	DDA	1978	MULT	23 X 24	AP	99		2200	5000
Underseascape	DDA	DDA	1978	MULT	23 X 24	AP	99		2200	5000
Sea Fathom	DDA	DDA	1978	MULT	23 X 24	AP	99		2200	5000
Sea Light	DDA	DDA	1978	MULT	23 X 24	AP	99		2200	5000
Straight Wave	DDA	DDA	1978	MULT	23 X 24	AP	99		2200	5000
Magic Rain Suite (Standard Agamograph) (Framed) (Set of 6):										
Magic Rain	DDA	DDA	1978	MULT	23 X 24	AP	99		2200	5000
Magic Rain Dawn	DDA	DDA	1978	MULT	23 X 24	AP	99		2200	5000
Magic Rain Cloud	DDA	DDA	1978	MULT	23 X 24	AP	99		2200	5000
Magic Rain Dusk	DDA	DDA	1978	MULT	23 X 24	AP	99		2200	5000
Magic Rain Rain	DDA	DDA	1978	MULT	23 X 24	AP	99		2200	5000
Magic Night Rain	DDA	DDA	1978	MULT	23 X 24	AP	99		2200	5000
Magic Rainbow	DDA	DDA	1978	MULT	23 X 24	AP	99		2200	5000
Vertical Midnight Suite (Standard Agamograph) (Framed) (Set of 6):										
Midnight Light	DDA	DDA	1979	MULT	23 X 24	AP	99		2200	3600
Galaxy	DDA	DDA	1979	MULT	23 X 24	AP	99		2200	3600
Vertical Midnight #3	DDA	DDA	1979	MULT	23 X 24	AP	99		2200	3600
Vertical Midnight #4	DDA	DDA	1979	MULT	23 X 24	AP	99		2200	3600
Light Night	DDA	DDA	1979	MULT	23 X 24	AP	99		2200	3600
White Night	DDA	DDA	1979	MULT	23 X 24	AP	99		2200	3600
Metamorphosis Suite (Standard Agamograph) (Framed) (Set of 6):										
Metamorphosis	DDA	DDA	1979	MULT	23 X 24	AP	99		2200	5000
Double Meta	DDA	DDA	1979	MULT	23 X 24	AP	99		2200	5000
Metaphor	DDA	DDA	1979	MULT	23 X 24	AP	99		2200	5000
Inter Image	DDA	DDA	1979	MULT	23 X 24	AP	99		2200	5000
Poly Meta	DDA	DDA	1979	MULT	23 X 24	AP	99		2200	5000
Image Maze	DDA	DDA	1979	MULT	23 X 24	AP	99		2200	5000
Liberty Suite (Standard Agamograph) (Framed) (Set of 6):										
Liberty #1–#6	DDA	DDA	1980	MULT	23 X 24 EA	AP	99 EA		2200 EA	3600 EA
Festival Suite (Standard Agamograph) (Framed) (Set of 6):										
Festival 1	DDA	DDA	1980	MULT	23 X 24	AP	99		2200	5000
Festival 2	DDA	DDA	1980	MULT	23 X 24	AP	99		2200	5000
World of Color	DDA	DDA	1980	MULT	23 X 24	AP	99		2200	5000
Cosmic Festival	DDA	DDA	1980	MULT	23 X 24	AP	99		2200	5000
Expanding Galaxy	DDA	DDA	1980	MULT	23 X 24	AP	99		2200	5000
Day/Night Festival	DDA	DDA	1980	MULT	23 X 24	AP	99		2200	5000
Counterpoint	MLLE	A/P/FR	1981	SP	30 X 37	AP	99	18	1200	3200
Holograph I, Homage to Einstein	AOE	JB	1981	MULT	8 X 10	HMP	250		2400	3200
Holograph I, (Holograph)	MLLE	ART	1981	MULT		AP	250	6	1800	3200
Imagic	CAM	AA	1981	SP		AP	225	60	1250	3200
Rhythm Mirror	MLLE	TS	1981	SP	28 X 28	AP	180		750	1200
Rhythm Mirror (Deluxe)	MLLE	TS	1981	SP	28 X 28	AP	99		900	1500
Image of the World Suite (Standard Agamograph) (Framed) (Set of 11):										
Invisible Rainbow	DDA	DDA	1981	MULT	23 X 24	AP	99		2200	3600
Festive Rainbow	DDA	DDA	1981	MULT	23 X 24	AP	99		2200	3600
Swirling Rainbow	DDA	DDA	1981	MULT	23 X 24	AP	99		2200	3600
Message of Peace Rainbow	DDA	DDA	1981	MULT	23 X 24	AP	99		2200	3600
Day Night Rainbow	DDA	DDA	1981	MULT	23 X 24	AP	99		2200	3600
Undersea Rainbow	DDA	DDA	1981	MULT	23 X 24	AP	99		2200	3600
Rainbow Fantasy	DDA	DDA	1981	MULT	23 X 24	AP	99		2200	3600
Cosmic Rainbow	DDA	DDA	1981	MULT	23 X 24	AP	99		2200	3600
World Rainbow	DDA	DDA	1981	MULT	23 X 24	AP	99		2200	3600
Universal Rainbow	DDA	DDA	1981	MULT	23 X 24	AP	99		2200	3600
Infinite Rainbow	DDA	DDA	1981	MULT	23 X 24	AP	99		2200	3600
Triple Galaxy Suite (Standard Agamograph) (Framed)										
Triple Galaxy B	DDA	DDA	1982	MULT	23 X 24	AP	99		2200	5000
Counterpoint Suite (Standard Agamograph) (Framed) (Set of 6):										
Counterpoint X 12	DDA	DDA	1982	MULT	23 X 24	AP	99		2200	3600
Infinite Search	DDA	DDA	1982	MULT	23 X 24	AP	99		2200	3600

YAACOV AGAM CONTINUED

TITLE	PUBLISHER	PRINTER	DATE	MEDIUM	DIMENSION (PAPER SIZE) IN INCHES	TYPE OF PAPER	EDITION NUMBER	NO. OF COLORS	ORIGINAL OPENING PRICE	CURRENT RETAIL PRICE
CURRENT EDITIONS:										
Visual Integrity	DDA	DDA	1982	MULT	23 X 24	AP	99		2200	3600
Integrated Space	DDA	DDA	1982	MULT	23 X 24	AP	99		2200	2700
Expanded Vision	DDA	DDA	1982	MULT	23 X 24	AP	99		2200	2200
Visual Choreography	DDA	DDA	1982	MULT	23 X 24	AP	99		2200	3600
Synthesis/Antithesis (Standard Agamograph) (Framed)	DDA	DDA	1982	MULT	23 X 24	AP	99		2200	5000
New Landscape	CFA	RS	1982	SP	24 X 27	CSW/R	270		1300	1450
Night Rainbow	CFA	CSW	1982	SP	41 X 48	CSW/R	270		3500	4000
Light Wave Form in Elaboration	AOE	JB	1982	HOL	8 X 10	HMP	250		2400	3200
Double Metamorphosis II (Set of 5)	MLLE	ART	1982	SP	36 X 50	AP	180	54	5400 SET	9500 SET
Hope	CFA	RS	1983	LC/SP	23 X 26	AP	270		800	1550
Magic Raindrops I	CFA	RS	1984	LC/SP	36 X 42	AP	270		1500	3100
Magic Raindrops II	CFA	RS	1984	SP	30 X 35	AP	180		1800	3650
Nines	CFA	CSW	1984	CP	40 X 40	AP	99		2800	3600
Triple Galaxy (Standard Agamograph) (Framed):										
Triple Galaxy A	DDA	DDA	1985	MULT	23 X 24	AP	99		2200	5000
Mexico Suite (Standard Agamograph) (Framed) (Set of 9):										
Mehico	DDA	DDA	1985	MULT	23 X 24	AP	99		2200	3600
Yucatan	DDA	DDA	1985	MULT	23 X 24	AP	99		2200	3600
Acapulco	DDA	DDA	1985	MULT	23 X 24	AP	99		2200	3600
Chapultepec	DDA	DDA	1985	MULT	23 X 24	AP	99		2200	3600
Cuernavaca	DDA	DDA	1985	MULT	23 X 24	AP	99		2200	3600
El Dorado	DDA	DDA	1985	MULT	23 X 24	AP	99		2200	3600
Meridia	DDA	DDA	1985	MULT	23 X 24	AP	99		2200	3600
Zenetia	DDA	DDA	1985	MULT	23 X 24	AP	99		2200	3600
Cozumel	DDA	DDA	1985	MULT	23 X 24	AP	99		2200	3600
Rhythm Horizontal Suite (Standard Agamograph) (Framed) (Set of 3):										
Good Times	DDA	DDA	1985	MULT	23 X 24	AP	99		2200	3600
Hot Times	DDA	DDA	1985	MULT	23 X 24	AP	99		2200	3600
Moods	DDA	DDA	1985	MULT	23 X 24	AP	99		2200	3600
Five Phases	EdP	LP	1985	SP					1000	2000
Simple	EdP	LP	1985	SP	42 X 27	HMP	99		800	1500
Dally to Eternal Suite (Standard Agamograph) (Framed) (Set of 5):										
Infinite Reach	DDA	DDA	1985	MULT	23 X 24	AP	99		2200	3600
New Dimensions	DDA	DDA	1985	MULT	23 X 24	AP	99		2200	3600
Now and Then	DDA	DDA	1985	MULT	23 X 24	AP	99		2200	3600
Passage	DDA	DDA	1985	MULT	23 X 24	AP	99		2200	3600
Presence	DDA	DDA	1985	MULT	23 X 24	AP	99		2200	3600
Day to Day Suite (Standard Agamograph) (Framed):										
Here & There	DDA	DDA	1985	MULT	23 X 24	AP	99		2200	3600
Never Before Suite (Standard Agamograph) (Framed) (Set of 5):										
Emerging	DDA	DDA	1985	MULT	23 X 24	AP	99		2200	3600
Gathering	DDA	DDA	1985	MULT	23 X 24	AP	99		2200	3600
Memories	DDA	DDA	1985	MULT	23 X 24	AP	99		2200	3600
Mirage	DDA	DDA	1985	MULT	23 X 24	AP	99		2200	3600
Never Ever	DDA	DDA	1985	MULT	23 X 24	AP	99		2200	3600
Lines and Forms (Set of 4)	MLLE	ART	1986	LC	11 X 14 EA	AP	317 EA		1400 SET	1500 SET
New Star Suite (Standard Agamograph) (Framed) (Set of 5):										
Rainbow Star	DDA	DDA	1988	MULT	23 X 24	AP	99		2200	3600
Memorial Star	DDA	DDA	1988	MULT	23 X 24	AP	99		2200	3600
Eternal Star	DDA	DDA	1988	MULT	23 X 24	AP	99		2200	3600
Galaxy Star	DDA	DDA	1988	MULT	23 X 24	AP	99		2200	3600
Blessing Star	DDA	DDA	1988	MULT	23 X 24	AP	99		2200	3600
Petite Secret Suite (Standard Agamograph) (Framed) (Set of 3):										
Petite Secret in Light	DDA	DDA	1989	MULT	23 X 24	AP	99		2200	3600
Petite Secret Out of Dark	DDA	DDA	1989	MULT	23 X 24	AP	99		2200	3600
Intimate Petite Secret	DDA	DDA	1989	MULT	23 X 24	AP	99		2200	3600
Nouvel Suite (Standard Agamograph) (Framed) (Set of 3):										
New Year's Eve	DDA	DDA	1989	MULT	23 X 24	AP	99		2200	3600
New Year's Air	DDA	DDA	1989	MULT	23 X 24	AP	99		2200	2700
New Year's Day	DDA	DDA	1989	MULT	23 X 24	AP	99		2200	3600
Memoire Suite (Standard Agamograph) (Framed) (Set of 3):										
Step of Time Remembrance	DDA	DDA	1989	MULT	23 X 24	AP	99		2200	3600

YAACOV AGAM CONTINUED

Yaacov Agam
Celebration Masquerade
Courtesy Diverse Dimensions Art

Yaacov Agam
Hommage a Picasso
Courtesy Diverse Dimensions Art

TITLE	PUBLISHER	PRINTER	DATE	MEDIUM	DIMENSION (PAPER SIZE) IN INCHES	TYPE OF PAPER	EDITION NUMBER	NO. OF COLORS	ORIGINAL OPENING PRICE	CURRENT RETAIL PRICE
CURRENT EDITIONS:										
Step of Time History	DDA	DDA	1989	MULT	23 X 24	AP	99		2200	3600
Step of Time Memoire	DDA	DDA	1989	MULT	23 X 24	AP	99		2200	3600
Celebration Mystery (Large Agamograph) (Framed):										
Celebration Mystery	DDA	DDA	1990	MULT	33 X 35	AP	99		4000	5500
Petite Secret Suite (Standard Agamograph) (Framed) (Set of 5):										
Petite Secret Romance	DDA	DDA	1990	MULT	23 X 24	AP	99		2200	3600
Petite Secret Midnight	DDA	DDA	1990	MULT	23 X 24	AP	99		2200	2200
Petite Secret Revelation	DDA	DDA	1990	MULT	23 X 24	AP	99		2200	2200
Petite Secret in Shadow	DDA	DDA	1990	MULT	23 X 24	AP	99		2200	2200
Petite Secret Confidente	DDA	DDA	1990	MULT	23 X 24	AP	99		2200	2200
Mexico Suite (Standard Agamograph) (Framed) (Set of 4):										
Yucatan Magic	DDA	DDA	1990	MULT	23 X 24	AP	99		2200	2200
Yucatan Mystery	DDA	DDA	1990	MULT	23 X 24	AP	99		2200	3600
Yucatan Holiness	DDA	DDA	1990	MULT	23 X 24	AP	99		2200	2200
Yucatan Monument	DDA	DDA	1990	MULT	23 X 24	AP	99		2200	2200
Rencouture Suite (Standard Agamograph) (Framed):										
Hommage a Picasso	DDA	DDA	1990	MULT	23 X 24	AP	99		2200	2200
Seasons Suite (Standard Agamograph) (Framed):										
Happy Marriage	DDA	DDA	1990	MULT	23 X 24	AP	99		3600	3600
Celebration Suite (Standard Agamograph) (Framed) (Set of 3):										
Celebration Festivity	DDA	DDA	1990	MULT	23 X 24	AP	99		2200	3600
Celebration Masquerade	DDA	DDA	1990	MULT	23 X 24	AP	99		2200	3600
Celebration Carnival	DDA	DDA	1990	MULT	23 X 24	AP	99		2200	3600
Big Bang Suite (Standard Agamograph) (Framed) (Set of 8):										
Double Rainbow	DDA	DDA	1991	MULT	23 X 24	AP	99		2200	2200
Time Origin	DDA	DDA	1991	MULT	23 X 24	AP	99		2200	2200
Out of Black Hole	DDA	DDA	1991	MULT	23 X 24	AP	99		2200	2200
Constellation	DDA	DDA	1991	MULT	23 X 24	AP	99		2200	2200
Infinite Dimension	DDA	DDA	1991	MULT	23 X 24	AP	99		2200	2200
Hidden Black Hole	DDA	DDA	1991	MULT	23 X 24	AP	99		2200	2200
Rainbow	DDA	DDA	1991	MULT	23 X 24	AP	99		2200	2200
In Blue Space	DDA	DDA	1991	MULT	23 X 24	AP	99		2200	2200

The retail prices of the 100,000 limited edition prints quoted in this directory are subject to change. Print publishers, artists and galleries were the direct sources for these quotations. Prices in the secondary market listed as "Sold Out Editions (Rare)" indicate that the publisher has a limited supply of that print or that the print is difficult to locate in the galleries.

YAACOV AGAM CONTINUED

TITLE	PUBLISHER	PRINTER	DATE	MEDIUM	DIMENSION (PAPER SIZE) IN INCHES	TYPE OF PAPER	EDITION NUMBER	NO. OF COLORS	ORIGINAL OPENING PRICE	CURRENT RETAIL PRICE
CURRENT EDITIONS:										
Telfila Suite (Standard Agamograph) (Framed) (Set of 4):										
In Deep Prayer	DDA	DDA	1991	MULT	23 X 24	AP	99		2200	2200
Visual Prayer	DDA	DDA	1991	MULT	23 X 24	AP	99		2200	2200
Intense Prayer	DDA	DDA	1991	MULT	23 X 24	AP	99		2200	2200
Silent Prayer	DDA	DDA	1991	MULT	23 X 24	AP	99		2200	2200
Nouvelle Suite (Large Agamograph) (Framed):										
New Year Night	DDA	DDA	1991	MULT	33 X 35	AP	99		4000	4400
Step of Time Suite (Large Agamograph) (Framed):										
Invaded Space	DDA	DDA	1991	MULT	33 X 35	AP	99		4000	4400
Intimate Secret Suite (Large Agamograph) (Framed):										
Sweet Secret	DDA	DDA	1991	MULT	33 X 35	AP	99		4000	4400
Love Secret	DDA	DDA	1991	MULT	33 X 35	AP	99		4000	4400
Tefila Suite (Large Agamograph) (Framed):										
Prayer for Hope	DDA	DDA	1991	MULT	33 X 35	AP	99		4000	4400
Rythme Blanc Noir Suite (Large Agamograph) (Framed):										
Expanded Spaces	DDA	DDA	1991	MULT	33 X 35	AP	99		4000	4400
Big Bang Suite (Large Agamograph) (Framed):										
Timescape	DDA	DDA	1991	MULT	33 X 35	AP	99		4000	4400
Black Hole Vision	DDA	DDA	1991	MULT	33 X 35	AP	99		4000	4400
Creation of Time	DDA	DDA	1991	MULT	33 X 35	AP	99		4000	4400
Rythme Blanc Noir Suite (Standard Agamograph) (Framed) (Set of 4):										
End And	DDA	DDA	1991	MULT	23 X 24	AP	99		2200	2200
In and Out	DDA	DDA	1991	MULT	23 X 24	AP	99		2200	2200
Color and Space	DDA	DDA	1991	MULT	23 X 24	AP	99		2200	2200
Multiple Space	DDA	DDA	1991	MULT	23 X 24	AP	99		2200	2200
Night Lights Prismagraph (Color Serigraph with 8 Transparent Prisms)	DDA	DDA	1991	SP/MULT	23 X 24	AP	99	21	3000	3600
Big Bang Albums (Color Serigraphs—Each with a Transparent Overlay) (Set of 6)	DDA	DDA	1991	SP		AP	99 EA		5000 SET	5000 SET
Galaxy Suite (Large Agamograph) (Framed):										
External Galaxy	DDA	DDA	1992	MULT	33 X 35	AP	99		3800	4400
Galaxy Suite (Standard Agamograph) (Framed) (Set of 5):										
Hidden Galaxy	DDA	DDA	1992	MULT	23 X 24	AP	99		3000	3600
Hidden Path	DDA	DDA	1992	MULT	23 X 24	AP	99		3000	3600
Outer Galaxy	DDA	DDA	1992	MULT	23 X 24	AP	99		3000	3600
Overtime Victory	DDA	DDA	1992	MULT	23 X 24	AP	99		2200	2700
Midnight Path	DDA	DDA	1992	MULT	23 X 24	AP	99		2200	2700
Fasination (Prismagraph—16 Prisms) (Framed)	DDA	DDA	1993	MULT	27 X 36	Prisms	99		3800	4500
Midnight Rainbow (Prismagraph—16 Prisms) (Framed)	DDA	DDA	1993	MULT	30 X 34	Prisms	99		3800	4500
Color in a Moving Space (2 Movable Serigraphic Panels) (Framed)	DDA	DDA	1993	MULT	21 X 25	Prisms	99		3000	3600
Mezzuzah (Crystal Edition—Serigraph with Star Crystal Cover—Sterling Silver Back) (Includes Stand)	DDA	DDA	1993	MULT		Prisms	99		500	500
La Gamme d'Agam Series (Agamographs) (Framed):										
The First La Gamme	DDA	DDA	1993	MULT	23 X 24	Prisms	99		2200	2200
The Second La Gamme	DDA	DDA	1993	MULT	23 X 24	Prisms	99		2200	2200
The Third La Gamme	DDA	DDA	1993	MULT	23 X 24	Prisms	99		2200	2200
Birth of the Star Series (Agamographs) (Framed):										
The First Star	DDA	DDA	1993	MULT	23 X 24	Prisms	99		2200	2200
The Second Star	DDA	DDA	1993	MULT	23 X 24	Prisms	99		2200	2200
The Third Star	DDA	DDA	1993	MULT	23 X 24	Prisms	99		2200	2200
The Fourth Star	DDA	DDA	1993	MULT	23 X 24	Prisms	99		2200	2200
The Fifth Star	DDA	DDA	1993	MULT	23 X 24	Prisms	99		2200	2200
Becoming Series (Agamographs) (Framed):										
The First Becoming	DDA	DDA	1993	MULT	23 X 24	Prisms	99		2200	2200

ORLANDO AGUDELO-BOTERO

BORN: Colombia, South America; August 26, 1946
EDUCATION: Self-Taught
TEACHING: Library of Congress, Wash, DC
RECENT EXHIB: Cogswell Gallery, Vail, CO, 1987; Laura Paul Gallery, Cincinnati, OH, 1987,88; Joan Bowers Fine Ars, Ltd, Kalamazoo, MI, 1988; Jacqueline Westbrook Gallery, La Jolla, CA, 1988; Sherrel Gallery, Los Angeles, CA, 1989; Engman International, Laguna Beach, CA, 1989,90; International Gallery Invitational, Chicago, IL, 1990,91; DagenBela Galeria, San Antonio, TX, 1991; Univ of Texas, San Antonio Art Mus, TX, 1991; New World Sch of the Arts Gallery, Miami-Dade Com Col, Miami, FL, 1991; Fine Arts Mus of Long Island, Hempstead, NY, 1991; Art Forum Gallery, Tokyo, Japan, 1992; Art Asia, Hong Kong, 1992; Patricia Judith Art Gallery, Ltd, Boca Raton, FL, 1987,88,90,92; Meisner SoHo, NY, 1991;93; BlumHelman Gallery, NY, 1993
PRINTERS: J Owen Studio (JOS); Aztlan Editions (AzEd); Bluestone Editions, Anaheim, CA (BlEd); Wieman-Hinte Studios, Los Angeles, CA (W-HS); Arion Press, San Francisco, CA (AP); Clearwater Printing, Inc (CPI); Yasha Fine Art (YFA)
PUBLISHERS: Engman International, Laguna Hills, CA (EI)
GALLERIES: Engman International, Laguna Beach, CA; Contemporary Fine Arts, La Jolla, CA; Lekae Galleries, Palm Desert, CA; Images Fine Art, Yountville, CA; Butters Gallery, Portland, OR; Dagenbela Galleria, San Antonio, TX; Joan Bowers Fine Arts, Sagatuck, MI; Long Wharf Fine Arts, Newport, RI; Renjeau Galleries, Natick, MA & Concord, MA; Meisner SoHo, NY; Lavon Art Galleries, East Brunswick, NJ & Freehold NJ; Patricia Judith Art Gallery, Boca Raton, FL; Windsor Gallery, Dania, FL; BlumHelman Gallery, New York, NY
MAILING ADDRESS: c/o Engman International, 23182 Alcalde Drive, #J, Laguna Hills, CA 92653

**Orlando Agudello-Botero
Latinoamerica**
Courtesy Engman Limited

TITLE	PUBLISHER	PRINTER	DATE	MEDIUM	DIMENSION (PAPER SIZE) IN INCHES	TYPE OF PAPER	EDITION NUMBER	NO. OF COLORS	ORIGINAL OPENING PRICE	CURRENT RETAIL PRICE
SOLD OUT EDITIONS (RARE):										
Tribute to America	EI	JOS	1981	SP/HC	30 X 42	STP	100	22	275	4500
The Muse of Self-Expression	EI	BlEd	1984	LC/HC	23 X 30	RICE 100		8	550	4000
Silent Passions	EI	AzEd	1985	SP	38 X 38	STP	100	300	900	4800
Candor	EI	BlEd	1985	AC/HC	24 X 30	STP	100	8	600	4600
Growth	EI	AzEd	1985	SP/HC	29 X 41	STP	100	26	600	2400
Hereñcia	EI	AzEd	1986	SP	38 X 38	STP	100	34	800	2500
Hermitana	EI	AzEd	1986	SP	38 X 38	STP	100	24	800	2500
Onyx (with Goldleaf)	EI	W-HS	1986	SP/HC	38 X 38	Act	1000	22	1200	6000
Prophecies (with Gold Leaf, Silver Leaf, Copper Leaf & Collage of Sheet Music)	EI	W-HS	1987	SP/CO	38 X 38	Act	100	28	1600	6000
Zarzuela de al Media Noche (Midnight Operetta)	EI	W-HS	1987	SP	29 X 37	Act	100	18	1000	2500
Rainy Days	EI	W-HS	1987	SP	26 X 34	Act	100	22	1000	2500
Euterpe-The Muse of Music	EI	W-HS	1987	SP	29 X 37	STP	100	22	1000	2400
Lyrical Expressions (with Gold Leaf & Silver Leaf (Set of 3):									3600 SET	8400 SET
Momento	EI	W-HS	1987	SP	28 X 38	Act	100	23	150	2800
Grand Oriente	EI	W-HS	1987	SP	28 X 38	Act	100	23	1500	2800
Vendimia (Vintage)	EI	W-HS	1987	SP	28 X 38	Act	100	23	1500	2800
Resplandor	EI	W-HS	1987	SP	28 X 38	Act	100		1500	2400
Resoluto	EI	W-HS	1987	SP	28 X 38	Act	100		1500	2600
CURRENT EDITIONS:										
Apolo	EI	W-HS	1988	SP/EMB/GL/HC	24 X 32	AC	100		1400	2800
Guardian	EI	W-HS	1988	SP/EMB/GL/HC	22 X 30	AC	100		2500	4200
Ingenio	EI	W-HS	1988	SP/EMB/GL/HC	31 X 46	AC	100		1400	4500
Minerva	EI	W-HS	1988	SP/EMB/GL/SL	22 X 30	RICE	100		1500	4000
Poeta	EI	W-HS	1988	SP/EMB/GL/HC	22 X 30	AC	100		2200	4200
Purisima	EI	W-HS	1988	SP/EMB/GL/HC	36 X 48	AC	100		2000	4500
Royal Dawn	EI	W-HS	1988	SP/GL/HC	27 X 38	AC	100		1400	3000
Solitude and Passion	EI	W-HS	1988	SP/GL/HC	27 X 36	AC	100		1400	3000

ORLANDO AGUDELO-BOTERO CONTINUED

TITLE	PUBLISHER	PRINTER	DATE	MEDIUM	DIMENSION (PAPER SIZE) IN INCHES	TYPE OF PAPER	EDITION NUMBER	NO. OF COLORS	ORIGINAL OPENING PRICE	CURRENT RETAIL PRICE
CURRENT EDITIONS:										
Arco Iris	EI	W-HS	1989	SP/EMB/GL/HC	22 X 31	AC	50		1600	5000
Comunion	EI	CPI	1989	SP/EMB/HC	20 X 41	AC	50		1800	3400
Dos Personas I,II	EI	CPI	1989	SP/EMB/HC	29 X 41 EA	AC	50 EA		1800 EA	4400 EA
Espiritu	EI	CPI	1989	SP/EMB/HC	27 X 39	AC	50		1600	4000
Fortaleza	EI	W-HS	1989	SP/EMB/GL/HC	22 X 31	AC	50		1600	5000
I (Torn Edges)	EI	CPI	1989	SP/HC	29 X 41	AC	50		2200	4200
Maria Eugenia	EI	W-HS	1989	SP/EMB/GL/HC	22 X 31	AC	50		1600	5000
Orfeo (Collage of Sheet Music)	EI	CPI	1989	SP/EMB/CO	29 X 41	AP	50		1800	4500
Pintor	EI	CPI	1989	SP/EMB/HC	27 X 39	AC	50		1600	5500
Poesia	EI	CPI	1989	SP/EMB/HC	27 X 39	AC	50		1600	3500
Serenata de la Luna	EI	AP	1989	SP/EMB/GL/HC	40 X 40	AC	100		1800	5000
The Offering	EI	W-HS	1989	MM	32 X 48	AC	18		6000	10000
Destino	EI	AP	1990	SP/EMB/HC	39 X 58	AC	30		4000	9500
Dusk of an Era (Torn Edges)	EI	CPI	1990	SP/HC	40 X 60	AC	90		2200	8000
Esencia (Torn Edges)	EI	CPI	1990	SP/HC	24 X 36	AC	90		2200	3000
Eva (Torn Edges)	EI	AP	1990	SP/EMB/HC	36 X 48	R/100	90		2500	4200
Galanteria (Torn Edges)	EI	CPI	1990	SP/HC	29 X 41	AC	50		2200	3800
Madona Negra	EI	CPI	1990	SP/EMB/HC	39 X 59	AC	30		3500	7000
Paz	EI	CPI	1990	SP/HC	40 X 54	AP	90		3200	4500
Percepciones (Torn Edges)	EI	CPI	1990	SP/HC	29 X 41	AP	50		2200	4200
Reflejo (Torn Edges)	EI	AP	1990	SP/EMB/HC	50 X 75	AC	30		7000	9000
Adoracion (Torn Edges)	EI	YFA	1991	SP	31 X 46	AP	90		2800	4000
Autoretratos (Torn Edges)	EI	YFA	1991	SP/HC	22 X 30	FAB	50		2800	3400
Esperando La Rondalla (Torn Edges)	EI	YFA	1991	SP/HC	20 X 30	R/100	90		2500	3500
Estratos (Torn Edges)	EI	YFA	1991	SP/HC	35 X 35	R/100	90		2800	3400

Orlando Agudelo-Botero
An Angel Llamado Maria del Pilar
Courtesy Engman Limited

ORLANDO AGUDELO-BOTERO CONTINUED

Orlando Agudelo-Botero
La Familia IV: The Gifted Child
Courtesy Engman Limited

Orlando Agudelo-Botero
Mentor (Benevolence)
Courtesy Engman Limited

TITLE	PUBLISHER	PRINTER	DATE	MEDIUM	DIMENSION (PAPER SIZE) IN INCHES	TYPE OF PAPER	EDITION NUMBER	NO. OF COLORS	ORIGINAL OPENING PRICE	CURRENT RETAIL PRICE
CURRENT EDITIONS:										
Gris Uno (Torn Edges)	EI	YFA	1991	SP/HC	22 X 30	FAB	50		2800	3400
La Familia IV: The Gifted Child (Torn Edges)	EI	YFA	1991	SP/HC	31 X 46	AC	90		2800	4500
Luz (Torn Edges)	EI	YFA	1991	SP/HC	31 X 46	AP	90		2500	5000
Origen	EI	YFA	1991	SP/HC	22 X 30	FAB	50		2800	3400
Privilegio: Don Natural (Torn Edges)	EI	YFA	1991	SP	30 X 58	AP	75		4000	5500
Un Angel Llamado Maria del Pilar (Torn Edges)	EI	YFA	1991	SP/HC	20 X 30	R/100	90		2500	4000
Accion de Gracias (Torn Edges)	EI	YFA	1992	SP/HC	50 X 50	LANA	50		3500	5000
Humanidad (Quote Handwritten-English) (Torn Edges)	EI	YFA	1992	SP/CO	38 X 38	AC	30		2600	3500
Humanidad (Quote Handwritten-Spanish) (Torn Edges)	EI	YFA	1992	SP/CO	38 X 38	AC	30		2600	3500
Inquietos Luceros (Torn Edges)	EI	YFA	1992	SP/HC	36 X 54	R/100	90		3000	4000
Light (Torn Edges)	EI	YFA	1992	SP/HC	50 X 50	R/100	50		3500	5000
Mentor, Benevolence (Torn Edges)	EI	YFA	1992	SP/HC	24 X 59	AP	30		4000	6000
Movimento Perpetuo (Torn Edges)	EI	YFA	1992	SP/HC	23 X 32	LANA	46		2600	3200
Celebration of Life (with Sewn Rope)	EI	YFA	1993	SP/HC	35 X 35	AP	50		2800	3400
Latinoamerica (Torn Edges)	EI	YFA	1993	SP/HC	20 X 28	AP	50		2500	3000
Solidoa (Torn Edges)	EI	YFA	1993	SP/HC	38 X 52	LANA	30		4000	5000

The retail prices of the 100,000 limited edition prints quoted in this directory are subject to change. Print publishers, artists and galleries were the direct sources for these quotations. Prices in the secondary market listed as "Sold Out Editions (Rare)" indicate that the publisher has a limited supply of that print or that the print is difficult to locate in the galleries.

The print market has become very selective. For the first time since we published the first edition of The Printworld Directory in 1982, the prices of prints have been greatly reduced and greatly increased for the same artists by the most reputable and established print publishers. Check the fifth edition to understand the movement.

IVAN LE LORRAINE ALBRIGHT

BORN: North Harvey, IL; (1897–1983)
EDUCATION: Northwestern Univ, Evanston, IL, 1915–16; Univ of Illinois, Champaign, IL, 1916–17; Ecole Regionale Beaux Arts, Nantes, France, 1919; Art Inst of Chicago, IL, 1920–23, PhD, Fine Arts, Pennsylvania Acad of Fine Arts, Phila, PA, 1923; Nat Acad of Design, NY, 1924; Mundelein Col, LHD, 1969; Lake Forest Col, IL, PhD, Fine Arts, 1972; Columbia Col, LHD, 1974
RECENT EXHIB: Col of DuPage, William E Gahlberg Arts Center Gallery, Glen Ellyn, IL, 1992
COLLECTIONS: Metropolitan Mus of Art, NY; Mus of Mod Art, NY; Solomon R Guggenheim Mus, NY; Whitney Mus of Am Art, NY; Nat Gallery of Fine Arts, Wash, DC
PRINTERS: American Atelier, NY (AA)
PUBLISHERS: Associated American Artists, NY (AAA)
GALLERIES: Kennedy Gallery, New York, NY; Associated American Artists, New York, NY

TITLE	PUBLISHER	PRINTER	DATE	MEDIUM	DIMENSION (PAPER SIZE) IN INCHES	TYPE OF PAPER	EDITION NUMBER	NO. OF COLORS	ORIGINAL OPENING PRICE	CURRENT RETAIL PRICE
SOLD OUT EDITIONS (RARE):										
Fleeting Time, Thou Hast Left	AAA	AA	1945	LB	14 X 10	WOVE	250	1	100	3000
Self Portrait, 55 East	AAA	AA	1947	LB	14 X 10	WOVE	250	1	100	3000
Follow Me	AAA	AA	1948	LB	14 X 9	WOVE	250	1	100	1200
Showcase Doll	AAA	AA	1954	LB	17 X 26	AP	44	1	250	8500

JOSEF ALBERS

BORN: Boltrop, Westphalia, Germany; (1888–1976)
EDUCATION: Royal Art Sch, Berlin, Germany, 1913–15; Sch of Applied Art, Essen, Germany, 1916–19; Acad of Fine Arts, Munich, Germany, 1919–20; Bauhaus, Weimar, Germany, 1920–23
AWARDS: Corcoran Gallery, William A Clark Prize, Wash, DC, 1954; Ada S Garrett Prize, Chicago Inst of Art, IL, 1954; Ford Found Fel, 1959; Philadelphia Mus of Art, PA, Citation, 1962; Am Inst of Graphic Art, Medal of the Year, 1964; Carnegie Inst, Pittsburgh, PA, 1967; Minnesota Col of Art & Design, 1969; Royal Society, 1971; Maryland Inst, 1972; Pratt Inst, NY, 1975
RECENT EXHIB: Block Gallery, Northwestern Univ, Evanston, IL, 1987; Des Moines Art Mus, IA, 1987; Allen Mem Art Mus, Oberlin, OH, 1987–88; Denver Mus of Art, CO, 1988; Mus of Mod Art, NY, 1988; Denver Art Mus, CO, 1988; Montreal Mus of Fine Arts, Canada, 1989; Arkansas State Univ, Fine Arts Gallery, AR, 1989; Fairleigh Dickinson Univ, Phyllis Rothman Gallery, Madison, NJ, 1989,92; Asheville Art Mus, NC, 1992; Bakersfield Mus, CA, 1992; Mattatuck Mus, Waterbury, CT, 1992; Midwest Mus of Am Art, Elkhart, IN, 1992; Lincoln Center, Fine Arts Prints, Avery Fisher Hall, NY, 1992
COLLECTIONS: Stedelijk Mus, Amsterdam, Holland; Mus of Mod Art, NY; Baltimore Mus of Art, MD; Bennington Col, VT; Brown Univ, Providence, RI; Albright-Knox Art Gallery, Buffalo, NY; Carnegie Inst, Pittsburgh, PA; Chicago Inst of Art, IL; Corcoran Art Gallery, Wash, DC; Detroit Inst of Art, MI; Wadsworth Atheneum, Hartford, CT; Whitney Mus of Am Art, NY; Yale Univ, New Haven, CT; Harvard Univ, Cambridge, MA; Denver Mus of Art, CO; San Francisco Mus of Art, CA; Smith College, MA; Smithsonian Inst, Wash, DC
PRINTERS: Yale University Press, New Haven, CT & New London, CT (YUP); Biltmore Press, Asheville, NC (BP); Reinhard Schumann, Hickory, NC (RS); Ives-Sillman, New Haven, CT (IS);Tamarind Lithography Workshop, Los Angeles, CA (TI); Artist (ART); Ken Tyler, NY (KT); C Hanley, NY (CH); B Fiske Workshop (BFW); Gemini GEL, Los Angeles, CA (GEM)

Josef Albers
Multiplex D
Courtesy Biltmore Press

PUBLISHERS: Ives-Sillman, New Haven, CT (IS); Tamarind Lithography, Los Angeles, CA (TI); Artist (ART); Yale University Press, New Haven, CT & New London, CT (YUP); Tyler Graphics, Ltd, Bedford Village, NY (TGL); Gemini GEL, Los Angeles, CA (GEM)
GALLERIES: Sidney Janis Gallery, New York, NY; Randall Beck Gallery, Boston, MA; Tyler Graphics, Ltd, Mount Kisco, NY; Prakapas Gallery, La Jolla, CA; Reger Galleries, Tinton Falls, NJ; Thomas Erben Gallery, Inc, New York, NY; Constance Kamens Fine Art, New York, NY

Miller (M)—Tyler (T)

TITLE	PUBLISHER	PRINTER	DATE	MEDIUM	DIMENSION (PAPER SIZE) IN INCHES	TYPE OF PAPER	EDITION NUMBER	NO. OF COLORS	ORIGINAL OPENING PRICE	CURRENT RETAIL PRICE
SOLD OUT EDITIONS (RARE):										
Multiplex D (M–77)		BP	1948	WB	9 X 12	WOVE	30	1	50	3500
Segments	ART	ART	1934	LB	9 X 11	SP	25	1	25	6000
Graphic Tectonics Series: Seclusion (from Set of 8) (M-57f)	ART	RS	1942	LB	12 X 13	AP	30	1	50	6000
Fenced (M-69)	ART	BP	1944	LI	10 X 12	R/100	30	1	50	4500
Interaction of Color Portfolio	YUP	YUP	1963				45 EA		500 SET	5000 SET
Midnight + Noon Series:										
Midnight + Noon II	TI	TI	1964	LB	16 X 16	AP	20	1	75	2500
Midnight + Noon V	TI	TI	1964	LC	16 X 16	AP	20	1	75	2500
Midnight + Noon VII	TI	TI	1964	LC	16 X 16	AP	20	1	75	2500
Homage to the Square—Soft Edge—Hard Edge (Set of 10)	IS	IS	1964	SP	17 X 17 EA	R/BFK	250 EA		1000 SET	7500 SET
Ten Variants (Set of 10)	IS	IS	1966	SP	17 X 17 EA	R/BFK	200 EA		1500 SET	15000 SET
White Line Square I (Yellow)	GEM	GEM	1966	LC	21 X 21	AP	125	3	150	1000
White Line Square II (Light Gap)	GEM	GEM	1966	LC	21 X 21	AP	125	3	150	1000

JOSEF ALBERS CONTINUED

TITLE	PUBLISHER	PRINTER	DATE	MEDIUM	DIMENSION (PAPER SIZE) IN INCHES	TYPE OF PAPER	EDITION NUMBER	NO. OF COLORS	ORIGINAL OPENING PRICE	CURRENT RETAIL PRICE
CURRENT EDITIONS:										
White Line Square III (Blue/Green)	GEM	GEM	1966	LC	21 X 21	AP	125	3	150	1000
White Line Square V (Warm Gray/Dark Gray)	GEM	GEM	1966	LC	21 X 21	AP	125	3	150	1000
White Line Square VI (Orange)	GEM	GEM	1966	LC	21 X 21	AP	125	3	150	1000
White Line Square VII (Yellow/Gray)	GEM	GEM	1966	LC	21 X 21	AP	125	3	150	1500
White Line Square VIII (Umber/Gray)	GEM	GEM	1966	LC	21 X 21	AP	125	3	150	1000
White Line Square IX (Gray/Black)	GEM	GEM	1966	LC	21 X 21	AP	125	3	150	1000
White Line Square X (Yellow/Ochre)	GEM	GEM	1966	LC	21 X 21	AP	125	3	150	1500
White Line Square XI (Magenta)	GEM	GEM	1966	LC	21 X 21	AP	125	3	150	1000
White Line Square XIII (Blue)	GEM	GEM	1966	LC	21 X 21	AP	125	3	150	1000
White Line Square XIV (Sand/Warm Gray)	GEM	GEM	1966	LC	21 X 21	AP	125	3	150	1500
White Line Square XVI (Ochre/Brown)	GEM	GEM	1966	LC	21 X 21	AP	125	3	150	1500
White Line Square XVII (Citron)	GEM	GEM	1966	LC	21 X 21	AP	125	3	150	1500
Embossed Linear Construction I-A	GEM	GEM	1969	EMB	20 X 26	AP/WA	100		200	1500
Embossed Linear Construction I-B	GEM	GEM	1969	EMB	20 X 26	AP/WA	100		200	1500
Embossed Linear Construction I-C	GEM	GEM	1969	EMB	20 X 26	AP/WA	100		200	1500
Embossed Linear Construction I-D	GEM	GEM	1969	EMB	20 X 26	AP/WA	100	AP	200	1500
Embossed Linear Construction II-A	GEM	GEM	1969	EMB	20 X 26	AP/WA	100	AP	200	1500
Embossed Linear Construction II-D	GEM	GEM	1969	EMB	20 X 26	AP/WA	100	AP	200	1500
White Embossings on Gray, I-X	GEM	GEM	1971	LI/EMB	26 X 20 EA	RLP	125 EA	1 EA	250 EA	5000 EA
IS-J	IS	IS	1973	SP	30 X 40	R/BFK	100		200	1000
IS-J	IS	IS	1973	SP	30 X 40	R/BFK	100		200	1000
Mitered Squares (Set of 12)	TGL	KT/CH/BFW	1976	SP	19 X 19	AP88	36	3	8000 SET	12000 SET
Never Before (Set of 12) (T-58-69)	TGL	KT/CH/BFN	1976	SP	19 X 20 EA	AP88	46 EA		8000 SET	12000 SET

ANNI ALBERS

BORN: Berlin, Germany; June 12, 1899; US Citizen
EDUCATION: Bauhaus Weiman, Germany
TEACHING: Black Mountain Col, 1933–49; Asst Prof, Art, Black Mountain Col, 1933–49; Maryland Col of Art, Hon PhD, 1972; York Univ, Toronto, Canada, Hon PhD, 1973; Philadelphia Col of Art, PA, Hon PhD, 1976; Univ of Hartford, CT, Hon PhD, 1978
AWARDS: Medal, Am Inst of Arch, 1961; Citation, Philadelphia Col of Art, PA, 1962; Tamarind Lithography Workshop Fel, Los Angeles, CA, 1964

COLLECTIONS: Metropolitan Mus of Art, NY; Mus of Mod Art, NY; Monmouth Art Mus, NJ; Univ of California, Riverside, CA; Art Inst of Chicago, IL; Victoria and Albert Mus, London, England; Baltimore Mus of Art, MD
PRINTERS: B Fiske Workshop (BFW); Tyler Graphics, Ltd, Mount Kisco, NY (TGL)
PUBLISHERS: Tyler Graphics Ltd, Mount Kisco, NY (TGL); Gemini GEL, Los Angeles, CA (GEM)
GALLERIES: Alice Simsar Gallery, Ann Arbor, MI
MAILING ADDRESS: 808 Birchwood Dr, Orange, CT 06477

TITLE	PUBLISHER	PRINTER	DATE	MEDIUM	DIMENSION (PAPER SIZE) IN INCHES	TYPE OF PAPER	EDITION NUMBER	NO. OF COLORS	ORIGINAL OPENING PRICE	CURRENT RETAIL PRICE
SOLD OUT EDITIONS (RARE):										
TR I	TGL	TGL	1970	LC	22 X 23	ARJ	44	3	200	500
TR II	TGL	BFW	1970	LC	22 X 24	ARJ	45	3	200	500
TR III	TGL	BFW	1970	SP/EMB	17 X 19	WL/HMP	60	1	200	500
Triangulated Intaglio IV (Red)	TGL	TGL	1976	AB	24 X 20	AC	20	1	300	600
Triangulated Intaglio V (Blue/Black)	TGL	TGL	1976	AC	24 X 20	AC	20	2	300	600
CURRENT EDITIONS:										
Triangulated Intaglios (Set of 6):										
Triangulated Intaglio I (Black)	TGL	BFW	1976	EB/A	24 X 20	AC	20	1	200	500
Triangulated Intaglio II (Black)	TGL	BFW	1976	AB	24 X 20	AC	20	1	250	600
Triangulated Intaglio III (Black)	TGL	BFW	1976	EB/A	24 X 20	AC	20	1	250	600
Triangulated Intaglio VI (Black)	TGL	BFW	1976	EB/A	24 X 20	AC	20	1	200	500
Mountainous I–VI (Set of 6):	TGL	BFW	1978	EMB	23 X 21	TGL/MHP	20	1	1600 SET	2800 SET
									300 EA	500 EA
Second Movement (Set of 6):	TGL								2400 SET	3500 SET
Second Movement I (Black)	TGL	TGL	1978	EB	28 X 28	AC	20	1	450	600
Second Movement II (Gray/Orange)	TGL	TGL	1978	EC	30 X 30	AC	20	2	450	600
Second Movement III (Blue/Black)	TGL	TGL	1978	EC	31 X 25	AC	20	2	450	600
Second Movement IV (Brown/Black)	TGL	TGL	1978	EC	28 X 28	AC	20	2	450	600
Second Movement V (Gray/Black)	TGL	TGL	1978	EC	28 X 28	AC	20	2	450	600
Second Movement VI	TGL	TGL	1978	EC	28 X 28	AC	20	2	450	600

The Printworld Directory is accepting new applications for the seventh edition. Approximately 300 new artists will be accepted. Please use the two forms provided in the back section of this directory to submit biographical data and documentation of prints. Edition number of each print must not exceed 500 and the retail price must be $100 or more.

LITA ALBUQUERQUE

BORN: Santa Monica, CA; January 3, 1946
EDUCATION: Univ of California, Los Angeles, CA, BFA, Cum Laude, 1968; Otis Art Inst, Los Angeles, CA, 1971
TEACHING: California State Univ, Los Angeles, CA, Drawing & Painting, 1975–77; Univ of California, Santa Barbara, CA, Painting & Drawing, Grad Seminar, 1977; Art Center Col of Design, Pasadena, CA, Painting Workshop, 1979,80; Claremont Grad Sch, CA, 1980; California State Univ, Bakersfield, CA, Seminar, 1981; California State Univ, San Diego, CA, Seminar, 1981; California State Univ, Long Beach, CA, Workshop, 1981; Art Center Col of Design, Pasadena, CA, Fine Arts Seminar, 1982; Vis Artist, Chicago Art Inst, IL, 1984; Arizona State Univ, Tucson, AZ, Seminar, 1984; San Francisco Art Inst, CA, Winter Conf on Women & Grad Seminar, 1985; Marin Headlands Art Center, Sausalito, CA, Grad Seminar, 1985; Idyllwild Sch of Music & Arts, CA, Workshop, 1986,87; Otis/Parson, Los Angeles, CA, Sculpture, 1982,83,84,85,86,87; Grad Advisor, Art Center Col of Design, Pasadena, CA, 1988
AWARDS: Nat Endowment for the Arts Fel Grants, 1975,83,84; Palm Springs Mus of Art, CA, Woman of the Year in the Visual Arts Grant, 1985
RECENT EXHIB: Richard Green Gallery, Los Angeles, CA, 1988; Los Angeles Fellows of Contemp Art, CA, 1989
COLLECTIONS: Los Angeles County Mus of Art, CA; Newport Harbor Art Mus, Newport Beach, CA; Palm Springs Desert Mus, CA
PRINTERS: Francesco Siqueiros, Los Angeles, CA (FS); Robert Dansby, Los Angeles, CA (RD); Cirrus Editions Workshop, Los Angeles, CA (CEW)
PUBLISHERS: Cirrus Editions, Ltd, Los Angeles, CA (CEL)
GALLERIES: Cirrus Gallery, Los Angeles, CA; Sharon Truax Fine Art, Venice, CA; Richard Green Gallery, Santa Monica, CA; The Works Gallery, Long Beach, CA
MAILING ADDRESS: c/o Otis Parsons Sch of Design, 2401 Wilshire Blvd, Los Angeles, CA 90057

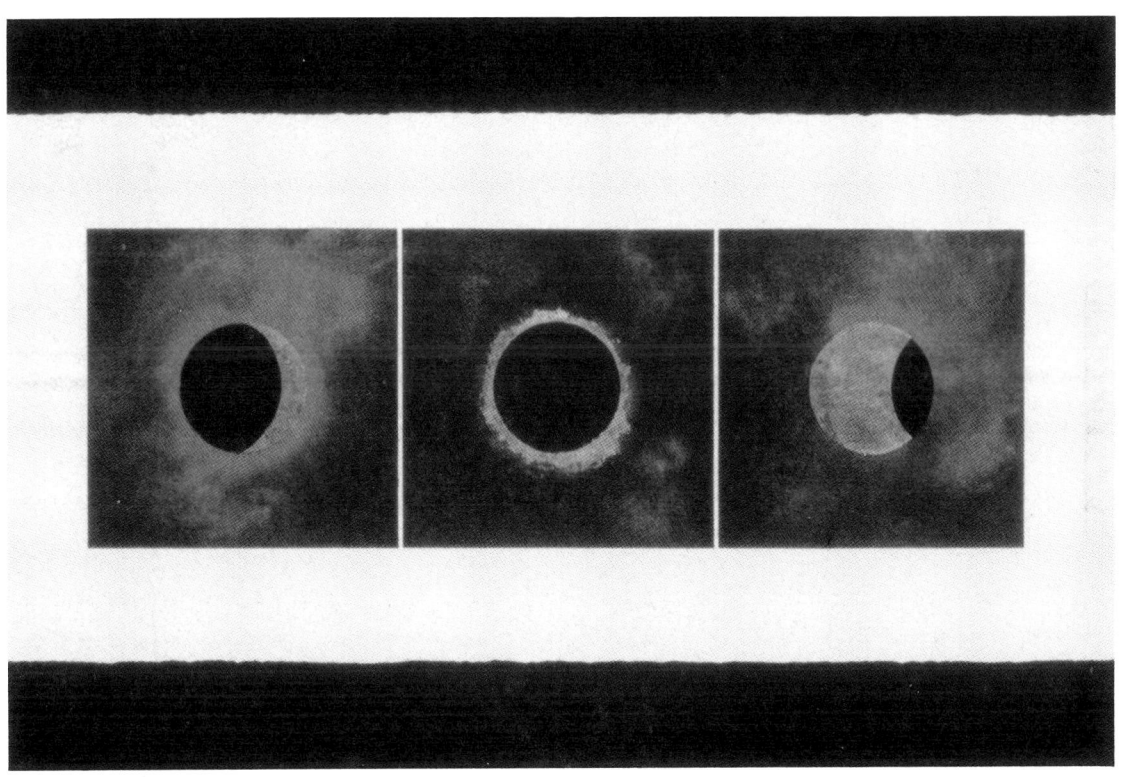

Lita Albuquerque
Solar Eclipse
Courtesy Cirrus Editions, Ltd

TITLE	PUBLISHER	PRINTER	DATE	MEDIUM	DIMENSION (PAPER SIZE) IN INCHES	TYPE OF PAPER	EDITION NUMBER	NO. OF COLORS	ORIGINAL OPENING PRICE	CURRENT RETAIL PRICE
CURRENT EDITIONS:										
Night Time Signatures	CEL	FS/RD/CEW	1988	LC/MON	20 X 53 EA	AP88	1 EA		1500 EA	1800 EA
100 Breaths	CEL	FS/RD/CEW	1989	LC/MON	19 X 51 EA	AP88	1 EA		1500 EA	1800 EA
The Edge (501c)	CEL	FS/RD/CEW	1992	LC/GL	28 X 60	COV	40	2	1000	1500
Solar Oscillation (502c)	CEL	FS/RD/CEW	1992	LC/GL	28 X 60	COV	40	2	1000	1500
Solar Geometry (503c)	CEL	FS/RD/CEW	1992	LC/GL	28 X 60	COV	40	2	1000	1500
Solar Eclipse (504c)	CEL	FS/RD/CEW	1992	LC/GL	28 X 60	COV	40	2	1000	1500

PIERRE ALECHINSKY

BORN: Brussels, Belgium; 1927
EDUCATION: Ecole Nat Superieure de Arch et des Arts Decoratifs, Brussels, Belgium, 1944–47; Atelier 17, Paris, France, 1952
AWARDS: Andrew Mellon Prize, 1977
RECENT EXHIB: Galerie Lelong, NY, 1987; André Emmerich Gallery, NY, 1990; Retrops, Musee de la Marine, Paris, France, 1992
COLLECTIONS: Stedelijk Mus, Amsterdam, Netherlands; Mus of Contemp Art, Houston, TX; Inst of Contemp Arts, London, England; Jewish Mus, NY; Carnegie Inst, Pittsburgh, PA; Galerie Nabis, Tokyo, Japan; Georges Pompidou Center, Paris, France; Mus Nat d'Art Mod, Paris, France
PRINTERS: Clot, Bramsen et Georges, Paris, France (CBG); Arts de Metiers Graphics, Paris, France (AMG); Maeght Editeur, Paris, France (ME); Artist (ART)

PIERRE ALECHINSKY CONTINUED

PUBLISHERS: Maeght Editions, NY, Paris, France; Transworld Art, Inc, (TAI); Abrams Original Editions, NY (AOE); London Arts, Inc, Detroit, MI (LAI)
GALLERIES: Galerie Lelong, New York, NY & Paris, France & Zürich, Switzerland; Spaightwood Gallery, Madison, WI; Michael J McDonnell, Santa Rosa, CA; American-European Art Assoc, Inc, New York, NY; André Emmerich Gallery, New York, NY; BenedicteSaxe Gallery/Maeght Editions, Beverly Hills, CA

TITLE	PUBLISHER	PRINTER	DATE	MEDIUM	DIMENSION (PAPER SIZE) IN INCHES	TYPE OF PAPER	EDITION NUMBER	NO. OF COLORS	ORIGINAL OPENING PRICE	CURRENT RETAIL PRICE
SOLD OUT EDITIONS (RARE):										
Une Pierre Deux Passages			1966	LC	20 X 25	AP	45		100	4000
Man on the Moon	TAI	CBG	1970	LC	20 X 26	AP	100		135	1000
Gnomes et Gnose			1974	LC	21 X 29	AP	150		200	4000
CURRENT EDITIONS:										
Central Park	TAI	CBG	1975	LC	20 X 26	AP	175	9	350	1200
Invisible Flying Objects	LAI	ART	1978	LC	26 X 19	AP	125	8	400	1200
Paris Flying Objects	LAI	ART	1978	LC	26 X 19	AP	125	9	400	1200
Spacial Objects	LAI	ART	1978	LC	26 X 19	AP	125	6	400	1200
Unidentified Flying Objects	LAI	ART	1978	LC	26 X 19	AP	125	6	400	1200
Rue Serpente (with Signed Book)	AOE	AMG	1978	LC	12 X 9	AP	100		200	1200
Chemin de Ronde	AOE	AMG	1978	LC	26 X 19	AP	150		200	1200
Disque Bleu	AOE	AMG	1978	LC	26 X 19	AP	75		300	1200
Between Four Fires	ME	ME	1979	EC	21 X 40	AP	60		1500 FF	3500 FF
In the Process of Disappearing	ME	ME	1979	EC	23 X 31	AP	50		1500 FF	3500 FF
1815	ME	ME	1979	EC	24 X 31	AP	60		1500 FF	3500 FF
Union House	ME	ME	1979	EC	16 X 10	AP	30		1000 FF	2000 FF
Starving Fireman	ME	ME	1979	EC	18 X 16	AP	30		1000 FF	2000 FF
Covering Motion	ME	ME	1979	EC	67 X 35	AP	35		3000 FF	9500 FF
Negative Aura	ME	ME	1979	EC	67 X 35	AP	35		3000 FF	9500 FF
New Island	ME	ME	1979	EC	67 X 35	AP	35		3000 FF	9500 FF
Defeated Because Stronger	ME	ME	1979	EC	67 X 34	AP	35		3000 FF	9500 FF
Blurred Ephemerids	ME	ME	1979	EC	67 X 35	AP	35		3000 FF	9500 FF
Case Par Case	ME	ME	1980	E/A	67 X 35	AP	35		3000 FF	9500 FF
Female Sphinx Questioning Herself	ME	ME	1980	EC	67 X 35	AP	35		3000 FF	9500 FF
Mineral Order	ME	ME	1980	EC	24 X 36	AP	99		1500 FF	3000 FF
Tilt-Yard	ME	ME	1980	EC	36 X 25	AP	99		1500 FF	3000 FF
The Businesses	ME	ME	1980	EC	18 X 12	AP	99		3000 FF	9500 FF
The Studios of the Marais	ME	ME	1980	EC	18 X 12	AP	99		2000 FF	6000 FF
Schisms (Set of 4)	ME	ME	1980	LC	13 X 10	AP	150		1500 FF	3000 FF
Treated Papers (Set of 6)	ME	ME	1980	LC	26 X 21	AP	99		2000 FF	9500 FF
With Michael Portal	ME	ME	1980	LC	15 X 13	AP	90		500 FF	1500 FF
Still Water	ME	ME	1980	LC	26 X 19	AP	60		500 FF	1500 FF
Experience without Experience	ME	ME	1980	LC	25 X 18	AP	99		2000 FF	10000 FF
Sous le Mental (with Appel)	ME	ME	1981	EC	30 X 21 cm	AP	75	2	1500 FF	2500 FF
Sur la Tête (with Appel)	ME	ME	1981	EC	30 X 21 cm	AP	75	2	1500 FF	2500 FF
Hors de Soi (with Appel)	ME	ME	1981	EC	30 X 21 cm	AP	75	2	1500 FF	2500 FF
Hors Saison			1988	I	74 X 37	AP	70		4500	8000

JOHN ALEXANDER

BORN: Beaumont, TX; October 26, 1945
EDUCATION: Lamar Univ, Beaumont, TX, BA; Southern Methodist Univ, Dallas, TX, MFA
TEACHING: Asst Prof, Art, Univ of Houston, 1971 to present
RECENT EXHIB: Contemp Arts Center, Cincinnati, OH, 1988,92; Texas A & M Univ, College Station, TX, 1988,92; Marlborough Gallery, NY, 1990,92
COLLECTIONS: Contemp Arts Mus, Houston, TX; Mus of Fine Arts, Amarillo, TX; Mus of Fine Arts, Beaumont, TX; Southern Methodist Univ, Dallas, TX
PUBLISHERS: Marlborough Graphics, NY (MG)
GALLERIES: Marlborough Gallery, New York, NY; Zolla/Lieberman Gallery, Chicago, IL; Jan Turner Gallery, Los Angeles, CA; Peregrine Press Gallery, Dallas, TX
MAILING ADDRESS: c/o Peregrine Press Gallery, 2604 Main St, Dallas, TX 75226

TITLE	PUBLISHER	PRINTER	DATE	MEDIUM	DIMENSION (PAPER SIZE) IN INCHES	TYPE OF PAPER	EDITION NUMBER	NO. OF COLORS	ORIGINAL OPENING PRICE	CURRENT RETAIL PRICE
SOLD OUT EDITIONS (RARE):										
Feast Fit for a King	MG		1986	LB/CC	24 X 26	AC	30	1	900	2000
CURRENT EDITIONS:										
Feeding the Monkeys at Ma Maison	MG		1986	LB/CC	26 X 18	AC	25	1	800	1200
The Great Ape	MG		1986	LB/CC	21 X 18	AC	30	1	800	1200
Madonna and Child	MG		1986	LB/CC	12 X 9	AC	30	1	600	900
Queen for a Day	MG		1986	LB	38 X 28	AC	30	1	800	2000
Parrots	MG		1989	WC/HC	37 X 30	SOM	60	Varies	1500	1500
Untitled (Set of 4):									2500 SET	2500 SET
Honky Tonk Moon	MG		1990	EB/A/HC	26 X 29	R/BFK	35	Varies	700	700
Chauncey's Garden	MG		1990	EB/A/HC	26 X 29	R/BFK	35	Varies	700	700
Sabine Pass	MG		1990	EB/A/HC	26 X 29	R/BFK	35	Varies	700	700
Heart of Darkness	MG		1990	EB/A/HC	26 X 29	R/BFK	35	Varies	700	700

PETER ALEXANDER

BORN: Los Angeles, CA; February 27, 1939
EDUCATION: Pennsylvania State Univ, Univ Park, PA, 1957–60; Univ of London, England, 1960–62; Univ of California, Berkely, CA, 1962–63; Univ of Southern California, Los Angeles, CA, 1963–64; Univ of California, BA, 1965, MFA, 1968
AWARDS: Nat Endowment for the Arts Fel, 1980
RECENT EXHIB: Jan Turner Gallery, Los Angeles, CA, 1987
COLLECTIONS: Walker Art Center, Minneapolis, MN; Mus of Mod Art, NY; Minneapolis Inst of Art, MN; Joslyn Art Mus, Omaha, NE; Los Angeles County Mus of Art, CA
PRINTERS: Lloyd Baggs (LB); John Roberts (JR); Ed Hamilton (EH); Richard Hammond, Los Angeles, CA (RH); Francesco Siqueiros, Los Angeles, CA (FS); Christopher Bonfatti (CB); Cirrus Editions Workshop, Los Angeles, CA (CEW); Robert S Gingras (RG); Centrum Press, Port Townsend, WA (CP); Timothy Berry (TB); La Poligrafa, Barcelona, Spain (LP)
PUBLISHERS: Cirrus Editions, Ltd, Los Angeles, CA (CE); Centrum Press, Port Townsend, WA (CP); Editions Poligrafa, Barcelona, Spain (EdP)
GALLERIES: James Corcoran Gallery, Santa Monica, CA; David Stuart Galleries, Los Angeles, CA; Sharon Truax Fine Art, Venice, CA; Charles Whitchurch Fine Arts, Huntington Beach, CA; Galeria Joan Prats, New York, NY & Barcelona, Spain; Brian Gross Fine Art, San Francisco, CA; Works Gallery, Long Beach, CA; Deanna Miller Fine Arts, Pasadena, CA

Peter Alexander
Caspar
Courtesy Cirrus Editions, Ltd

TITLE	PUBLISHER	PRINTER	DATE	MEDIUM	DIMENSION (PAPER SIZE) IN INCHES	TYPE OF PAPER	EDITION NUMBER	NO. OF COLORS	ORIGINAL OPENING PRICE	CURRENT RETAIL PRICE
CURRENT EDITIONS:										
Anacin I	CE	CEW	1972	LC/OFF	11 X 13	ChC	74	5	50	125
Anacin II	CE	CEW	1972	LC/OFF	11 X 13	ChC	79	5	50	125
Golden Arches	CE	CEW	1972	LC/OFF	11 X 13	ChC	85	5	50	125
Monument Valley	CE	CEW	1972	LC/OFF	11 X 13	ChC	87	5	50	125
Huh	CE	LB/JR/CEW	1975	LC/SP	27 X 34	R/RO	50	5	150	3000
Cuervo	CE	CEW	1975	LC	23 X 30	R/RO	100	Multi	200	850
Chula Vista I	CE	EH/CEW	1981	LC	31 X 35	AP88	30	2	400	850
Chula Vista II	CE	EH/CEW	1981	LC	31 X 35	AP88	30	2	400	850
Chula Vista Cirrus	CE	CB/CEW	1982	LC/HC	30 X 35	AP88	20	3	1400	2500
Gooeyduck	CP	TB/CEW	1982	EB/A	23 X 26	R/BFK	50	3	400	1000
Baloo	CP	TB/CEW	1982	EB/A	17 X 19	R/BFK	50	1	400	1000
Santa Cruz Cirrus	CE	CEW	1983	MON	30 X 36 EA	AC	1 EA		2400 EA	4000 EA
Panocha Cirrus	CE	CEW	1983	MON	21 X 28 EA	AC	1 EA		1800 EA	2800 EA
Dorado	CE	CEW	1983	LC	15 X 17	AP88	300		250	600
Caspar	CE	RG/CEW	1984	LC	30 X 36	AC	50	5	850	3000
Cayucos	CE	RG/CEW	1984	LC	30 X 36	AC	50	5	850	3000
Teacake	CE	RG/CEW	1985	LC	28 X 30	AP88	30		500	850
Riccoso (Dipt)	CE	RH/FS/CEW	1987	LC	31 X 66 EA	AP88	40	8	1500	3500

WILLIAM GEORGE ALLAN

BORN: Everett, Wash; March 28, 1936
EDUCATION: San Francisco Art Inst, CA BFA
TEACHING: Univ of California, Davis, CA, 1965–67; Univ of California, Berkeley, CA, 1969; California State Univ, Sacramento, CA, 1968 to present
RECENT EXHIB: Redding Mus, CA, 1992; Paule Anglim Gallery, San Francisco, CA, 1987,89,92
COLLECTIONS: Santa Barbara Art Mus, CA; San Francisco Mus of Art, CA; Fort Worth Art Center, TX; Philadelphia Mus of Art, PA; Whitney Mus of Am Art, NY; Mus of Mod Art, NY
PRINTERS: Landfall Press, Inc, Chicago, IL (LPI); David Keister (DK); Timothy Berry (TB)
PUBLISHERS: Landfall Press, Inc, Chicago, IL (LPI)
GALLERIES: Odyssia Gallery, New York, NY; Village Galleries, Lahaina, HI; Landfall Press Inc, Chicago, IL; Paule Anglim Gallery, San Francisco, CA; Hanson Fuller Gallery, San Francisco, CA
MAILING ADDRESS: Art Dept, California State University, 6000 Junior St, Sacramento, CA 95819

TITLE	PUBLISHER	PRINTER	DATE	MEDIUM	DIMENSION (PAPER SIZE) IN INCHES	TYPE OF PAPER	EDITION NUMBER	NO. OF COLORS	ORIGINAL OPENING PRICE	CURRENT RETAIL PRICE
SOLD OUT EDITIONS (RARE)										
Trout	LPI	DK/LPI	1973	LC	23 X 22	AP/CR	50	1	100	350
Tamales	LPI	TB/LPI	1975	AC	9 X 10	TWP	50	2	100	600
Bodega Bay	LPI	LPI	1976	AC	15 X 20	JBG	35	2	100	750

The retail prices of the 100,000 limited edition prints quoted in this directory are subject to change. Print publishers, artists and galleries were the direct sources for these quotations. Prices in the secondary market listed as "Sold Out Editions (Rare)" indicate that the publisher has a limited supply of that print or that the print is difficult to locate in the galleries.

The Printworld Directory is accepting new applications for the seventh edition. Approximately 300 new artists will be accepted. Please use the two forms provided in the back section of this directory to submit biographical data and documentation of prints. Edition number of each print must not exceed 500 and the retail price must be $100 or more.

TERRY ALLEN

BORN: Wichita, KS; May 1943
EDUCATION: Chouinard Art Inst, Los Angeles, CA, BFA, 1966
TEACHING: Fresno State Col, CA, 1971-72
AWARDS: Guggenheim Fel, NY, 1986
RECENT EXHIB: San Francisco Art Inst, Emanuel Walter & Atholl McBean Galleries, 1989, Cuestra Col Art Gallery, San Luis Obispo, CA, 1989; Florida State Univ Mus Gallery, Tallahassee, FL, 1989; Contemp Mus, Honolulu, HI, 1989; Cuestra Col Art Gallery, San Luis Obispo, CA, 1989,92; Florida State Univ. Mus, Tallahassee, FL, 1989,92; Fresno Metropolitan Mus, CA, 1992; John Weber Gallery, NY, 1992; Moody Gallery, Houston, TX, 1992; Gallery Paule Anglim, San Francisco, CA, 1992-93
COLLECTIONS: Am Fed of the Arts, NY; Stanford Univ Mus, CA; La Jolla Mus of Contemp Art, CA; Alberta Col of Art, Alberta, Can
PRINTERS: Cirrus Editions Workshop, Los Angeles, CA (CEW); Landfall Press, Inc, Chicago, IL (LPI); Jack Lemon, Chicago, IL (JL); David Keister (DK); Fred Gude (FG); Ron Wyffels (RW); Ernest F DeSoto, San Francisco, CA (EDS); Ernest F DeSoto Workshop, San Francisco, CA (EDSW); Bill Lagattuta (BL); Mark Attwood (MA); Cole Rogers (CR); Tamarind Inst, Albuquerque, NM (TI); Bud Shark, Boulder, CO (BS); Shark's Inc, Boulder, CO (SI)
PUBLISHERS: Cirrus Editions, Los Angeles, CA (CE); Landfall Press, Inc, Chicago, IL (LPI); Fresno Arts Center, CA (FAC); Hanson Gallery, Sausalito, CA (HG);Tamarind Inst, Albuquerque, NM (TI)
GALLERIES: Cirrus Editions Ltd, Los Angeles, CA; Ernest DeSoto Workshop, San Francisco, CA; Gallery Paule Anglim, San Francisco, CA; L A Louver Galleries, Venice, CA; Landfall Press, Inc, Chicago, IL; Moody Gallery, Houston, TX; John Weber Gallery, New York, NY; Tamarind Institute, Albuquerque, NM; Morgan Gallery, Kansas City, MO; Shark's, Inc, Boulder, CO

TITLE	PUBLISHER	PRINTER	DATE	MEDIUM	DIMENSION (PAPER SIZE) IN INCHES	TYPE OF PAPER	EDITION NUMBER	NO. OF COLORS	ORIGINAL OPENING PRICE	CURRENT RETAIL PRICE
SOLD OUT EDITIONS (RARE):										
Yellow Mans Revenge	LPI	RW/LPI	1974	LC/CO	23 X 30	AP/W	25	6	150	1800
Texas Goes to Europe	LPI	DK/LPI	1974	LC	23 X 29	AP/W	35	17	150	1500
Them Ol' Love Songs (Pink Version)	LPI	JL/LPI	1981	LC	21 X 15	AP/W	20	2	200	700
Them Ol' Love Songs (Yellow)	LPI	JL/LPI	1981	LC	21 X 15	AP/W	10	2	300	1000
Juarez Suite (Set of 6):									600 SET	2500 SET
Pillow in Mountains	LPI	JL/LPI	1976	LC	13 X 13	R/BFK	50	5	100	450
Room with Horns	LPI	JL/LPI	1976	LC	13 X 113	R/BFK	50	5	100	450
Bed with Heart	LPI	JL/LPI	1976	LC	13 X 13	R/BFK	50	5	100	450
Bed with Ditch	LPI	JL/LPI	1976	LC	13 X 13	R/BFK	50	5	100	450
Ditch with Heart	LPI	JL/LPI	1976	LC	13 X 13	R/BFK	50	5	100	450
Pillow in the Mountains II	LPI	JL/LPI	1976	LC	13 X 13	R/BFK	50	5	100	450
CURRENT EDITIONS:										
Pintos on Parade	CE	CEW	1970	LC	23 X 29	AP	50		150	850
Pintos to Paradise	CE	CEW	1970	LC	23 X 29	AP	50		150	850
Debris Suite (Set of 4):									1600 SET	1800 SET
Debris from the Text—R	LPI	FG/LPS	1981	LC	30 X 24	HMP	32	9	400	450
Debris from the Text—I	LPI	JL/LPI	1981	LC	30 X 24	HMP	32	5	400	450
Debris from the Text—G	LPI	JL/LPI	1981	LC	30 X 24	HMP	32	5	400	450
Debris from the Text—N	LPI	FG/LPI	1981	LC	30 X 24	HMP	32	9	400	450
Angel Whispers	LPI	JL/LPI	1981	LC	22 X 30	R/BFK	30	4	600	800
China Sky over New Mexico	HG/FAC	EDS/EDSW	1985	LC	22 X 30	AP/W	75	7	700	1200
Palabros Malos	LPI	JL/LPI	1989	LC	39 X 30	SOM	35		1200	1200
Positions on the Desert (with Kent Hall) (Set of 6)	TI	BL/MA/CR/TI	1990	LB	30 X 39	SOM/CR	30 EA		6000 SET	6000 SET
Monotypes	SI	BS/SI	1991	MON	45 X 30 EA	HMP	Varies		4500 EA	4500 EA
Heads Lips across the Near Frontier (with William T Wiley)	SI	BS/SI	1991	LC	30 X 42	SOM			3500	3500

DAN ALLISON

BIRTH: Houston, TX; 1953
EDUCATION: Sam Houston State Univ, Huntsville, TX, 1978
AWARDS: Selection Award, Philadelphia Print Club, PA, 1985; Grand Prix Award, Ljubljana, Yugoslavia, 1987; Lecture Tour & Workshop Travel Fel, Eastern Europe, U S Information Service, Wash, DC, 1989
RECENT EXHIB: Mus of Mod Art, Ljubljana, Yugoslavia, 1989; Mod Art Mus, Ft Worth, TX, 1992; Laguna Gloria Mus, Austin, TX, 1992; Charles Cowles Gallery, NY, 1992
COLLECTIONS: Mod Art Mus, Ft. Worth, TX; Mus of Mod Art, Belgrade, Yugoslavia; Albuquerque Mus, NM; Elvehjem Mus of Art, Madison, WI; Univ of Texas, Austin, TX; Prince of Spain Coll, Palace Mus, Madrid, Spain
PRINTERS: Artist (ART); Flat Bed Graphics, Austin, TX (FBG)
PUBLISHERS: Artist (ART); Flat Bed Graphics, Austin, TX (FBG)
GALLERIES: William Campbell Contemporary Art, Ft Worth, TX; Chemers Gallery, Tustin, CA; Malton Gallery, Cincinnati, OH; Wilhelmi/Holland Gallery, Corpus Christi, TX; Tercera Gallery, Los Gatos, CA; McNair Gallery, Telluride, CO; Broden Gallery, Madison, WI; Charles Whitchurch Gallery, Huntington Beach, CA; Beverly Gordon Gallery, Dallas, TX
MAILING ADDRESS: 1107 E Freeway, Houston, TX 77002

TITLE	PUBLISHER	PRINTER	DATE	MEDIUM	DIMENSION (PAPER SIZE) IN INCHES	TYPE OF PAPER	EDITION NUMBER	NO. OF COLORS	ORIGINAL OPENING PRICE	CURRENT RETAIL PRICE
SOLD OUT EDITIONS (RARE):										
Wishing You were Here	ART	ART	1979	AC	9 X 12	GCP	34	3	80	350
Angel	ART	ART	1979	AC	7 X 7	GCP	40	3	80	175
High Wire Desire	ART	ART	1979	AC	27 X 27	GCP	12	3	80	400
High Chair	ART	ART	1979	AC	6 X 6	GCP	28	3	75	500
Harlequin	ART	ART	1979	AC	14 X 21	GCP	40	3	100	875
Curtain Call	ART	ART	1979	AC	5 X 5	GCP	16	3	50	425
Christmas on Broadway	ART	ART	1979	AC	27 X 27	GCP	15	3	125	800
Cowgirl Boots	ART	ART	1979	AC	7 X 7	GCP	40	3	80	450
Cowgirl Art	ART	ART	1979	AC	7 X 9	GCP	40	3	75	450
Texas in Your Window	ART	ART	1979	AC	6 X 9	GCP	40	3	75	350
Some Things You Left Behind (Storyboard)	ART	ART	1979	AC	22 X 27	GCP	12	3	200	3000

DAN ALLISON CONTINUED

Dan Allison
Electric Blue
Courtesy the Artist

TITLE	PUBLISHER	PRINTER	DATE	MEDIUM	DIMENSION (PAPER SIZE) IN INCHES	TYPE OF PAPER	EDITION NUMBER	NO. OF COLORS	ORIGINAL OPENING PRICE	CURRENT RETAIL PRICE
SOLD OUT EDITIONS (RARE):										
Some Call It Home	ART	ART	1979	AC	23 X 35	GCP	24	3	250	1500
Sail Away	ART	ART	1979	AC	8 X 10	GCP	50	3	60	250
Magritte Dreams Amarillo	ART	ART	1979	AC	6 X 6	GCP	40	3	75	450
In the Theatre	ART	ART	1979	AC	10 X 8	GCP	10	3	40	400
In the Big Top, #2	ART	ART	1979	AC	22 X 27	GCP	12	3	70	800
Your Place or Mine	ART	ART	1979	AC	16 X 20	GCP	17	3	85	600
Your Laundry on My Line	ART	ART	1979	AC	6 X 9	GCP	40	3	75	250
Some Things You Left Behind	ART	ART	1979	AC	6 X 6	GCP	40	3	75	250
Sitting Pretty	ART	ART	1979	AC	22 X 28	GCP	30	3	175	1250
What Cha Say	ART	ART	1979	AC	19 X 15	GCP	35	3	90	500
The Catch	ART	ART	1979	AC	7 X 9	GCP	12	3	90	800
Hungry on the Trail	ART	ART	1979	AC	9 X 9	GCP	40	3	75	175
In My Little Town	ART	ART	1979	AC	15 X 20	GCP	20	3	70	650
In the Big Top	ART	ART	1979	AC	27 X 22	GCP	12	3	70	600
Angel's Scrapbook	ART	ART	1980	AC	23 X 35	GCP	35	3	350	2500
Apple Target	ART	ART	1980	AC	6 X 9	GCP	36	3	80	275
Hop Along Katy	ART	ART	1980	AC	7 X 9	GCP	35	3	80	175
Your Pretty Things	ART	ART	1980	AC	5 X 7	GCP	30	3	80	200
Trail into Oz	ART	ART	1980	AC	22 X 27	GCP	30	3	175	1650
Blue Rider	ART	ART	1980	AC	7 X 7	GCP	20	3	80	425
May Tag	ART	ART	1980	AC	5 X 7	GCP	32	3	80	300
Headress	ART	ART	1980	AC	17 X 23	GCP	33	3	350	600
Head	ART	ART	1980	AC	9 X 9	GCP	34	3	80	250
Honey's Glasses	ART	ART	1980	AC	9 X 9	GCP	28	3	80	175
Honey Buns	ART	ART	1980	AC	9 X 9	GCP	28	3	75	250
St Sebastian in New York	ART	ART	1980	AC	16 X 12	GCP	40	3	125	600
When Heaven and Nature Sing	ART	ART	1980	AC	23 X 35	GCP	17	3	300	1250
William Wolf	ART	ART	1980	AC	6 X 9	GCP	26	3	80	175
Lullaby	ART	ART	1980	AC	23 X 17	GCP	33	3	175	900
Serenade	ART	ART	1980	AC	7 X 7	GCP	26	3	80	450
Stick Horses	ART	ART	1980	AC	9 X 9	GCP	32	3	80	250
Joseph's Robe	ART	ART	1982	AC	23 X 17	GCP	35	3	250	850
Amerikans Suite (Set of 4)	ART	ART	1982	AC	23 X 17 EA	GCP	40 EA	3 EA	150 EA	500 EA
The Dance	ART	ART	1982	AC	23 X 35	GCP	38	3	600	2400
Hocus Pocus	ART	ART	1982	AC	24 X 36	GCP	35	3	600	1400
Withered Rose	ART	ART	1982	AC	9 X 11	GCP	12	3	100	300
Cactus Attackus	ART	ART	1982	AC	23 X 35	GCP	35	3	800	1200

DAN ALLISON CONTINUED

TITLE	PUBLISHER	PRINTER	DATE	MEDIUM	DIMENSION (PAPER SIZE) IN INCHES	TYPE OF PAPER	EDITION NUMBER	NO. OF COLORS	ORIGINAL OPENING PRICE	CURRENT RETAIL PRICE
SOLD OUT EDITIONS (RARE):										
Yesterday Evening	ART	ART	1982	AC	17 X 23	GCP	40	3	300	1250
Skizophrenia	ART	ART	1983	AC	17 X 23	GCP	46	3	400	850
Single Nude	ART	ART	1983	AC	23 X 18	GCP	10	3	400	950
Nest	ART	ART	1983	AC	3 X 5	GCP	37	3	75	250
Parade	ART	ART	1983	AC	23 X 35	GCP	35	3	600	1600
At Sunset	ART	ART	1983	AC	6 X 6	GCP	44	3	175	225
Beat	ART	ART	1983	AC	23 X 17	GCP	35	3	250	600
A Bird for Ya'	ART	ART	1983	AC	23 X 18	GCP	25	3	250	450
Black Chair	ART	ART	1983	AC	23 X 17	GCP	35	3	250	600
Splash 'N' Dash	ART	ART	1983	AC	6 X 6	GCP	45	3	200	400
Son of Attackus	ART	ART	1983	AC	5 X 9	GCP	47	3	100	350
Annunciation	ART	ART	1983	AC	6 X 8	GCP	50	3	150	250
Picture Book	ART	ART	1983	AC	23 X 35	GCP	12	3	350	2000
Rain Coat	ART	ART	1983	AC	23 X 17	GCP	37	3	300	750
Mexitech	ART	ART	1983	AC	8 X 6	GCP	45	3	175	400
The Get-Together	ART	ART	1983	AC	16 X 20	GCP	12	3	350	650
Meanwhile	ART	ART	1983	AC	24 X 36	GCP	47	3	500	800
Little Red Ryder	ART	ART	1983	AC	11 X 12	GCP	33	3	300	600
Los Amerikanskies	ART	ART	1983	AC	23 X 29	GCP	60	3	375	750
Today's Girl	ART	ART	1984	AC	23 X 17	GCP	30	3	400	600
Tolkenee Trail	ART	ART	1984	AC	17 X 23	GCP	40	3	300	1250
Merlin's Garden	ART	ART	1984	AC	23 X 18	GCP	37	3	600	900
Chi Sci Fi	ART	ART	1984	AC	28 X 29	GCP	30	3	1500	2500
Madonna of Canon George Vanderpaile	ART	ART	1984	AC	21 X 27	GCP	40	3	600	2400
Senderos del Corazon	ART	ART	1985	AC	15 X 29	GCP	65	3	325	750
Ritual	ART	ART	1985	AC	17 X 23	GCP	55	3	350	950
Spinners	ART	ART	1985	AC	15 X 28	GCP	42	3	375	1400
Heart and Soul	ART	ART	1985	AC	28 X 39	GCP	29	3	1200	2500
La La Land	ART	ART	1985	AC	28 X 39	GCP	33	3	1200	2500
Rosita	ART	ART	1986	COL	10 X 16	R/BFK	30	3	250	300
Sticky Business	ART	ART	1986	COL	15 X 15	R/BFK	30	3	200	400
Sunset Lake	ART	ART	1986	COL	29 X 41	R/BFK	6	3	900	1200
Out of the Clear Blue	ART	ART	1986	COL	30 X 24	R/BFK	30	3	600	1050
One Fell Swoop	ART	ART	1986	COL	29 X 42	R/BFK	3	3	1200	1800
Ju Ju Buana Jim	ART	ART	1986	AC	28 X 39	GCP	30	3	800	1600
Icarus and the Orange Tree	ART	ART	1986	COL	29 X 41	R/BFK	9	3	800	1800
Between Heaven and Earth (Trip)	ART	ART	1986	COL	32 X 82	R/BFK	12	3	4500	4500
Huf der Kanta	ART	ART	1986	AC	28 X 38	GCP	10	3	800	1250
Astroville	ART	ART	1986	AC	28 X 21	GCP	38	3	250	550
Deep Green	ART	ART	1986	AC	28 X 38	GCP	34	3	800	1400
St Billy Bob	ART	ART	1986	AC	14 X 13	GCP	50	3	300	850
Mother's Little Daughters	ART	ART	1986	AC	22 X 27	GCP	65	3	175	1200
Mr Tornado Head	ART	ART	1986	AC	11 X 9	GCP	35	3	175	200
Rosas del Fuego	ART	ART	1987	AC	8 X 12	GCP	65	3	175	450
The Starter House	ART	ART	1987	AC	23 X 30	GCP	65	3	600	1650
Together Once . . . We're Dreaming	ART	ART	1987	AC	23 X 29	GCP	65	3	600	1250
Beatrice	ART	ART	1987	COL	29 X 29	R/BFK	12	3	700	1250
East of Eden	ART	ART	1987	COL	66 X 66	R/BFK	5	3	3600	7200
Birdland	ART	ART	1987	COL	29 X 29	R/BFK	12	3	400	1250
Into the Night	ART	ART	1987	COL	42 X 69	R/BFK	7	3	2400	2800
King of the Mountain	ART	ART	1987	MON	29 X 29	R/BFK	1	3	800	1000
Red Sky at Morning	ART	ART	1987	COL	15 X 15	R/BFK	10	3	400	900
A Lovely Farewell	ART	ART	1987	COL	16 X 19	R/BFK	30	3	300	750
Bubba	ART	ART	1987	COL	30 X 42	R/BFK	25	3	1000	1450
Evening Through My Window	ART	ART	1987	COL	30 X 41	R/BFK	9	3	1600	1800
El Rey	ART	ART	1987	MON	29 X 29	R/BFK	1	3	800	1600
Cactus Dan was a Big Chicken	ART	ART	1987	COL	30 X 41	R/BFK	12	3	800	1250
The Magic Pool	ART	ART	1987	COL	30 X 42	R/BFK	25	3	1200	1800
Time	ART	ART	1987	COL	29 X 29	R/BFK	25	3	800	1450
Target	ART	ART	1987	COL	29 X 29	R/BFK	6	3	800	1250
Corazon del Fuego	ART	ART	1987	COL	29 X 29	R/BFK	16	3	800	1600
Raisin' Hell	ART	ART	1988	COL	84 X 161	R/BFK	3	3	8200	10400
Open All Night	ART	ART	1988	COL	66 X 66	R/BFK	5	3	3600	7200
Standard Issue	ART	ART	1988	COL	65 X 135	R/BFK	7	3	6400	9600
West of Eden	ART	ART	1988	COL	66 X 66	R/BFK	5	3	3600	5400
The Demise of Dr X	ART	ART	1988	COL	65 X 98	R/BFK	5	3	5200	6400
Big Chief America	ART	ART	1989	COL	86 X 66	R/BFK	9	3	3000	6000
Electric Blue	ART	ART	1989	COL	23 X 35	R/BFK	35	3	800	1200
Good Morning Little Schoolgirl	ART	ART	1989	COL	71 X 98	R/BFK	5	3	5800	5800
Infinity	ART	ART	1989	COL	32 X 22	R/BFK	35	3	800	800
Mona Missle	ART	ART	1989	COL	66 X 88	R/BFK	7	3	6450	7200
Somewhere Over Georgia	ART	ART	1989	COL	23 X 35	R/BFK	10	3	800	800

DAN ALLISON CONTINUED

TITLE	PUBLISHER	PRINTER	DATE	MEDIUM	DIMENSION (PAPER SIZE) IN INCHES	TYPE OF PAPER	EDITION NUMBER	NO. OF COLORS	ORIGINAL OPENING PRICE	CURRENT RETAIL PRICE
SOLD OUT EDITIONS (RARE):										
Dino	ART	ART	1989	COL	23 X 35	R/BFK	5	3	800	1200
CURRENT EDITIONS:										
Puppets in Bondage	ART	ART	1977	AC	9 X 9	GCP	20	3	50	450
Dorothy and Toto	ART	ART	1979	AC	9 X 12	GCP	10	3	60	250
X's	ART	ART	1979	AC	6 X 9	GCP	40	3	75	400
Rosetta	ART	ART	1979	AC	14 X 21	GCP	40	3	100	650
Stalking Through	ART	ART	1979	AC	14 X 13	GCP	40	3	75	250
Witching Way	ART	ART	1979	AC	17 X 23	GCP	40	3	50	350
In and Out	ART	ART	1979	AC	27 X 21	GCP	40	3	300	450
Wounded Fruit	ART	ART	1980	AC	15 X 19	GCP	40	3	125	550
Rose and the Wolf	ART	ART	1980	AC	7 X 7	GCP	38	3	80	175
Rosey	ART	ART	1980	AC	7 X 7	GCP	40	3	80	175
Range Rider	ART	ART	1980	AC	7 X 7	GCP	29	3	80	375
Technique	ART	ART	1980	AC	17 X 23	GCP	30	3	300	650
Angel and the Wolf	ART	ART	1980	AC	6 X 7	GCP	36	3	80	175
Guiding Light	ART	ART	1980	AC	7 X 7	GCP	35	3	80	175
Angel	ART	ART	1980	AC	21 X 27	GCP	40	3	125	500
Art	ART	ART	1983	AC	11 X 9	GCP	44	3	150	350
Totem	ART	ART	1983	AC	23 X 17	GCP	54	3	250	350
Attack on Rainbow Valley	ART	ART	1983	AC	23 X 35	GCP	53	3	400	700
Rocky	ART	ART	1983	AC	4 X 6	GCP	43	3	75	100
Los Gringos Flamingos	ART	ART	1983	AC	23 X 29	GCP	60	3	375	750
Mona Madonna Neona	ART	ART	1983	AC	23 X 18	GCP	30	3	250	450
Venus of the Canyon	ART	ART	1983	AC	11 X 7	GCP	47	3	150	300
Mr Honeykins	ART	ART	1985	AC	29 X 23	GCP	65	3	300	475
Ms Babykakes	ART	ART	1985	AC	29 X 23	GCP	65	3	300	475
Salvadora	ART	ART	1985	AC	29 X 39	GCP	37	3	500	750
Hot Kitty Pepper	ART	FBG	1985	AC	28 X 33	GCP	42	3	450	825
Amigo del Diablo	ART	ART	1985	AC	28 X 39	GCP	33	3	600	900
Kid Twister	ART	ART	1986	AC	11 X 9	GCP	35	3	50	175
Mr. Bill's Place	ART	ART	1986	AC	28 X 21	GCP	38	3	250	650
Watuzee	ART	ART	1986	AC	27 X 23	GCP	30	3	450	650
The Lucky Birds of Huntsville	ART	ART	1987	COL	15 X 15	R/BFK	30	3	200	400
Dancing in the Shadows	ART	ART	1987	AC	23 X 28	GCP	65	3	600	800
Exotica	ART	ART	1987	COL	29 X 23	R/BFK	30	3	350	750
Bigger Toys	ART	ART	1987	COL	42 X 92	R/BFK	7	3	3200	4200
The Ascension of the Innocents	ART	ART	1988	COL	88 X 65	R/BFK	5	3	4300	7200
Angel	ART	ART	1988	COL	45 X 33	R/BFK	7	3	1600	1800
The Ascension	ART	ART	1988	COL	85 X 163	R/BFK	3	3	8200	16000
Between Heaven and Earth, #2	ART	ART	1989	COL	33 X 83	R/BFK	35	3	1800	1800
Dino and the Colasaurus	ART	ART	1989	COL	56 X 35	R/BFK	5	3	1200	1800
Venus	ART	ART	1989	COL	23 X 35	R/BFK	35	3	600	800
Big Chief America (Small)	ART	ART	1990	COL	41 X 31	R/BFK	50	3	800	900
Soul Man Suite (set of 6):										
Ground Zero	ART	ART	1990	COL	23 X 23	R/BFK	60	3	900	900
Inside Out	ART	ART	1990	COL	23 X 23	R/BFK	60	3	900	900
Pathfinder	ART	ART	1990	COL	23 X 23	R/BFK	60	3	900	900
The Shadow	ART	ART	1990	COL	23 X 23	R/BFK	60	3	900	900
Mortal Coil	ART	ART	1990	COL	23 X 23	R/BFK	60	3	900	900
Touching Soul	ART	ART	1990	COL	23 X 23	R/BFK	60	3	900	900
Fire Suite (Set of 5):										
Magritte, Magritte	ART	ART	1991	AC	18 X 15	GCP	30	3	400	550
Hey Darlin'	ART	ART	1991	AC	18 X 15	GCP	30	3	400	550
Cliff Hanger	ART	ART	1991	AC	18 X 15	GCP	30	3	400	550
William Tell	ART	ART	1991	AC	18 X 15	GCP	30	3	400	550
Reverend Art	ART	ART	1991	AC	18 X 15	GCP	30	3	400	550
Garden Suite (Set of 3):										
The Fire	ART	ART	1991	AC	25 X 21	GCP	35	3	800	800
The Weight	ART	ART	1991	AC	25 X 21	GCP	35	3	800	800
The Garden	ART	ART	1991	AC	25 X 21	GCP	35	3	800	800
Earth Angel	ART	ART	1991	COL	19 X 19	R/BFK	50	3	500	500
Cowboy	ART	ART	1991	COL	31 X 32	R/BFK	15	3	1200	1200
Glass Book Suite (Set of 3):										
Sandbox	FBG	FBG	1992	COL	47 X 52	R/BFK	7	3	1600	1600
Vantage	FBG	FBG	1992	COL	47 X 52	R/BFK	7	3	1600	1600
Viewpoint	FBG	FBG	1992	COL	47 X 52	R/BFK	7	3	1600	1600

WALTER ALLNER

BORN: Dessau, Germany; January 2, 1909
EDUCATION: Bauhaus-Dessau with Josef Albers, V Kandinsky, Paul Klee
TEACHING: Parsons Sch of Design, NY, 1974 to present, Vis Critic, Yale Univ, New Haven, CT
COLLECTIONS: Bauhaus-Archiv Mus, Berlin, Germany
PUBLISHERS: Bank Street Atelier, NY (BSA); Ives-Sillman, New Haven, CT (IS); Edition Domberger, Stuttgart, Germany (ED); McCoy Ltd (M)
MAILING ADDRESS: 110 Riverside Drive, New York, NY 10024

WALTER ALLNER CONTINUED

TITLE	PUBLISHER	PRINTER	DATE	MEDIUM	DIMENSION (PAPER SIZE) IN INCHES	TYPE OF PAPER	EDITION NUMBER	NO. OF COLORS	ORIGINAL OPENING PRICE	CURRENT RETAIL PRICE
CURRENT EDITIONS:										
Diagonios 70–61–M	BSA	BSA	1970	LC	22 X 23		100	7	100	250
Diagonios 71–106–1	IS	IS	1972	SP	30 X 20		100	7	125	350
Diagonios 72–112–2	ED	ED	1973	SP	20 X 20		75	5	125	350
Diagonios 76–119–4	M	M	1978	SP	20 X 20		100	2	150	300
Diagonios 76–119–6	M	M	1978	SP	20 X 20		100	2	150	300
Diagonios 75–136–3	M	M	1978	SP	20 X 20		100	4	185	300
Diagonios 75–136–6	M	M	1978	SP	20 X 20		100	4	185	300

JOSEPH ALMYDA

EDUCATION: Florida State Univ, Tallahassee, FL, BA, 1949; Chicago Art Inst, IL, 1950; Florida State Univ, Tallahassee, FL, MA, 1955
AWARDS: Art in Res, Wurlitzer Found, Taos, NM, 1985–86
COLLECTIONS: El Paso Mus of Art, TX; High Mus, Atlanta, GA; Fort Lauderdale Mus, FL; M D Anderson Library, Houston, TX; Texas A & M Univ, Bryan, TX
PRINTERS: Craig Corwall (CC); Rodney Hamon (RH); Beth Lovendusky (BL); Tamarind Inst, Albuquerque, NM
PUBLISHERS: Tamarind Inst Publications, Albuquerque, NM (TI)
GALLERIES: Tamarind Inst, Albuquerque, NM; Novus Gallery, Inc, Atlanta, GA

Joseph Almyda
Fleur du Mal II
Courtesy Tamarind Institute

TITLE	PUBLISHER	PRINTER	DATE	MEDIUM	DIMENSION (PAPER SIZE) IN INCHES	TYPE OF PAPER	EDITION NUMBER	NO. OF COLORS	ORIGINAL OPENING PRICE	CURRENT RETAIL PRICE
CURRENT EDITIONS:										
Fleur du Mal Series:										
Fleur du Mal I	TI	CC/TI	1987	LC	24 X 33	SOM/W	30	8	400	600
Fleur du Mal II	TI	RH/TI	1987	LC	24 X 33	SOM/W	30	6	400	600
Fleur du Mal III	TI	BL/TI	1987	LC	24 X 33	CD	30	5	400	600

GEORGE ALPERT

BORN: New York, NY; April 3, 1922
EDUCATION: New York Univ, NY; North Carolina State Col, Raleigh, NC; Stanford Univ, CA; Univ of California, Berkeley, Ca; Inst of Seven Arts, NY
TEACHING: Prof, New Sch for Social Research, NY, 1974–79
PUBLISHERS: C G Rein Publishers, St Paul, MN (CGR)
GALLERIES: C G Rein Galleries, Scottsdale, AZ & Santa Fe, NM & Houston, TX, & Minneapolis, MN; Udinotti Gallery, San Francisco, CA
MAILING ADDRESS: 5702 N 55th Place, Paradise Valley, AZ 85253

TITLE	PUBLISHER	PRINTER	DATE	MEDIUM	DIMENSION (PAPER SIZE) IN INCHES	TYPE OF PAPER	EDITION NUMBER	NO. OF COLORS	ORIGINAL OPENING PRICE	CURRENT RETAIL PRICE
CURRENT EDITIONS:										
Skyline	CGR		1985	SP	30 X 30	AP	200		250	400

JOSEPH AMAR

BORN: Casablanca, Morocco; 1954
EDUCATION: Ontario Col of Art, Canada, BFA, 1977
AWARDS: Canada Council Grant, 1978
RECENT EXHIB: Bess Cutler Gallery, NY, 1989; Virginia Commonwealth Univ, Anderson Gallery, Richmond, VA, 1989; Lorence • Monk Gallery, NY, 1990; Fay Gold Gallery, Atlanta, GA, 1991
COLLECTIONS: Virginia Commonwealth Univ, Anderson Gallery, Richmond, VA
PUBLISHERS: John Szoke Graphics, Inc, NY (JSG)
PRINTERS: Sabina Klein Studios, NY (SKS)
GALLERIES: Bess Cutler Gallery, New York, NY; Stux Gallery, New York, NY

TITLE	PUBLISHER	PRINTER	DATE	MEDIUM	DIMENSION (PAPER SIZE) IN INCHES	TYPE OF PAPER	EDITION NUMBER	NO. OF COLORS	ORIGINAL OPENING PRICE	CURRENT RETAIL PRICE
CURRENT EDITIONS:										
Grey Bar	JSG	SKS	1986	EB/DPT	37 X 30	R/BFK	45		500	850

HAROLD ALTMAN

BORN: New York, NY; April 20, 1924
EDUCATION: Art Students League, NY, 1941–42; Cooper Union Sch, NY, 1941–47; New Sch for Social Res, NY, 1947–49; Acad Grande Chaumiere, Paris, France, 1949–52; Black Mountain Col, SC
TEACHING: Univ of North Carolina, Greensboro, NC, 1954–56; Univ of Wisconsin, Milwaukee, WI, 1956–62; Pennsylvania State Univ, University Park, PA, 1962–76
AWARDS: Guggenheim Fel, 1960,61; Nat Arts & Letters Award, 1963; Fulbright Fel, France, 1964–65
RECENT EXHIB: Art Inst for the Permian Basin, Odessa, TX, 1989
COLLECTIONS: Metropolitan Mus, NY; Mus of Mod Art, NY; Whitney Mus of Am Art, NY; Art Inst of Chicago, IL; Boston Mus of Fine Arts, MA; Cleveland Mus, OH; Los Angeles County Mus, CA; Stedelijk Mus, Schiedam, The Netherlands; Kunstmuseum, Basel, Switzerland; Victoria & Albert Mus, London, England; Royal Mus of Fine Arts, Copenhagen, Denmark; Malmo Mus, Sweden; Nat Gallery of Art, Wash, DC; Philadelphia Mus, PA; Albright-Knox Art Gallery, Buffalo, NY; Walker Art Ctr, Minneapolis, MN

PRINTERS: Georges Le Blac, Paris, France (GLB); Mourlot, Paris, France (M); LeMont Editions, Lemont, PA (LME)
PUBLISHERS: Circle Art Galleries, Chicago, IL (CAG); LeMont Editions, Lemont, PA (LME); Merrill Chase Galleries, Chicago, IL (MCG); Associated American Artists, NY (AAA)
GALLERIES: Georgetown Gallery of Art, Wash, DC; Art Collector Gallery, Gainesville, FL; Benjamin-Beattie Fine Arts, Chicago, IL; Tower Park Gallery, Peoria Heights, IL; Merrill Chase Galleries, Chicago, IL; Editions Limited Gallery, Indianapolis, IN; Thronja Original Art, Springfield, MA; J Todd Galleries, Wellesley, MA; Saper Galleries, East Lansing, MI; Summa Galleries, New York, NY & Brooklyn, NY; Newmark Gallery, New York, NY; Uptown Gallery, New York, NY; Landing Gallery of Woodbury, Inc, Woodbury, NY; Renaissance Gallery, Pittsburgh, PA & Mount Lebanon, PA; JRS Fine Art, Providence, RI; Gallerie International, Dallas, TX; American Art, Tacoma, WA; Fanny Garver Gallery, Madison, WI; R Michelson Gallery, Amherst, MA; Artists Showcase, International, Hartsdale, NY; Morningstar Gallery, New York, NY; Multiple Impressions, New York, NY; Art Works, Bealsburg, PA; Post Gallery, Houston, TX
MAILING ADDRESS: P O Box 777, Lemont, PA 16851

TITLE	PUBLISHER	PRINTER	DATE	MEDIUM	DIMENSION (PAPER SIZE) IN INCHES	TYPE OF PAPER	EDITION NUMBER	NO. OF COLORS	ORIGINAL OPENING PRICE	CURRENT RETAIL PRICE
SOLD OUT EDITIONS (RARE):										
Two Trees	ART	DAG	1973	LC	21 X 30	AP	150	4	120	1500
Luxembourg, November	ART	ART	1976	LC	18 X 27	AP	185	5	175	1000
Street	AAA	ART	1977	LC	18 X 12	AP	200		185	850
Walking Man	MCG	ART	1980	EC	14 X 20	AP	275	6	450	800
Shadow 1980	ART	GLB	1980	EC	12 X 9	AP	55	4	165	485
Two Trees II	CAG	DAG	1980	LC	21 X 30	AP	185		300	800
Waiting, 1981	ART	ART	1981	LC	17 X 26	AP	285		350	585
Walking Figures, Luxembourg, 1981	ART	ART	1981	LC	26 X 17	AP	285		350	1250
Anna	ART	ART	1981	LC	17 X 26	AP	285		350	585
Balustrade	ART	ART	1981	LC	18 X 26	AP	285		350	900
Children, Parc Montsouris	ART	ART	1981	LC	20 X 14	AP	285		300	450
Destinations	ART	ART	1981	LC	14 X 20	AP	285		300	450
Flowers, Luxembourg	ART	ART	1981	LC	14 X 20	AP	285		300	585
Hyde Park	ART	ART	1981	LC	18 X 26	AP	285		350	685
Leaves, Luxembourg	ART	ART	1981	LC	14 X 20	AP	285		300	1750
Luxembourg, November 1981	ART	ART	1981	LC	14 X 20	AP	285	6	300	2500
Man and Woman, Luxembourg	ART	ART	1981	LC	14 X 20	AP	285		300	525
Market, Late Afternoon	ART	ART	1981	LC	20 X 31	AP	285		400	685
Market, Rue Mouffetard	ART	ART	1981	LC	26 X 17	AP	285		350	685
Seated Man, 1981	ART	ART	1981	LC	17 X 26	AP	285		350	685
Seated People, Parc Montsouris	ART	ART	1981	LC	17 X 26	AP	285		350	685
Sunny Day, Luxembourg	ART	ART	1981	LC	18 X 26	AP	285		350	850
Three Walking Figures	ART	ART	1981	LC	14 X 20	AP	285		300	485
Walking Woman	ART	ART	1981	LC	17 X 26	AP	285		350	585
December Snow	LME	GLB	1982	EC	12 X 8	AP	200	5	165	485
Conversation, 1982	LME	GLB	1982	EC	12 X 8	AP	200	6	165	185
Park, 1982	LME	GLB	1982	EC	9 X 6	AP	200	6	140	250
Prominade	LME	GLB	1982	EC	8 X 8	AP	200	5	165	350
Two Women, 1982	LME	GLB	1982	EC	8 X 6	AP	200	6	140	185
Walking Couple, 1982	LME	GLB	1982	EC	12 X 9	AP	200	5	165	185
Autumn, 1982 (Set of 4)	LME	ART/LID	1982	LC	9 X 12 EA	AP	285 EA	6 EA	400 SET	1250 SET
Benches, 1982	LME	ART/LID	1982	LC	14 X 20	AP	285	6	330	2500
December Afternoon	LME	ART/LID	1982	LC	18 X 26	AP	285	6	385	585
Fifty-Eight Pigeons	LME	ART/LID	1982	LC	18 X 26	AP	285	6	385	750
Fruit Stand	LME	ART/LID	1982	LC	14 X 20	AP	285	6	330	485
Hyde Park, 1982	LME	ART/LID	1982	LC	18 X 26	AP	285	6	385	650
Late Afternoon	LME	ART/LID	1982	LC	18 X 26	AP	285	7	385	585
October, 1982 (Set of 4)	LME	ART/LID	1982	LC	9 X 12 EA	AP	285 EA	6 EA	400 SET	1200 SET
Parc Montsouris, 1982 (Set of 4)	LME	ART/LID	1982	LC	9 X 12 EA	AP	285 EA		400 SET	1500 SET
Pigeons, Luxembourg, 1982	LME	ART/LID	1982	LC	25 X 17	AP	285	7	385	585
Rue Mouffetard	LME	ART/LID	1982	LC	18 X 26	AP	285	7	385	650
September, 1982 (Set of 4)	LME	ART/LID	1982	LC	13 X 9 EA	AP	285	7	400 SET	850 SET
Shadows	LME	ART/LID	1982	LC	14 X 20	AP	285	6	330	2500
Stand	LME	ART/LID	1982	LC	20 X 31	AP	285	6	450	800
Street Market	LME	ART/LID	1982	LC	26 X 18	AP	285	6	385	585
Sunlit Path, 1982	LME	ART/LID	1982	LC	18 X 25	AP	285	6	385	585
The Awning	LME	ART/LID	1982	LC	14 X 20	AP	285	6	330	585
The Red Dress	LME	ART/LID	1982	LC	27 X 18	AP	285	7	385	550
Cart	LME	ART/LID	1983	EC	9 X 12	AP	200		185	250
Conversation, 1983	LME	ART/LID	1983	EC	9 X 6	AP	165		125	175
December, 1983	LME	ART/LID	1983	EC	12 X 9	AP	200		185	250
February, 1983	LME	ART/LID	1983	EC	8 X 6	AP	200		125	200
Park, 1983	LME	ART/LID	1983	EC	8 X 6	AP	200		125	200
Path, 1983	LME	ART/LID	1983	EC	8 X 6	AP	200		125	200

HAROLD ALTMAN CONTINUED

TITLE	PUBLISHER	PRINTER	DATE	MEDIUM	DIMENSION (PAPER SIZE) IN INCHES	TYPE OF PAPER	EDITION NUMBER	NO. OF COLORS	ORIGINAL OPENING PRICE	CURRENT RETAIL PRICE
SOLD OUT EDITIONS (RARE):										
Rue Rambuteau	LME	ART/LID	1983	EC	9 X 12	AP	200		185	285
The Bench	LME	ART/LID	1983	EC	6 X 8	AP	200		185	225
The White Hat	LME	ART/LID	1983	EC	8 X 6	AP	200		125	175
Two Umbrellas	LME	ART/LID	1983	EC	10 X 13	AP	200		185	600
Winter, 1983	LME	ART/LID	1983	EC	6 X 9	AP	200		185	250
Afternoon Shadows, 1983	LME	ART/LID	1983	LC	26 X 18	AP	285		385	550
Balustrade, 1983	LME	ART/LID	1983	LC	18 X 26	AP	285		385	550
Benches, 1983	LME	ART/LID	1983	LC	18 X 26	AP	285		385	525
Fall, 1983 (Set of 4)	LME	ART/LID	1983	LC	9 X 13 EA	AP	285 EA		485 SET	2500 SET
Jardin du Luxembourg, 1983	LME	ART/LID	1983	LC	18 X 26	AP	285		385	2500
Le Grand Bassin Luxemburg	LME	ART/LID	1983	LC	18 X 26	AP	285		385	650
Luxembourg, 1983 (Set of 4)	LME	ART/LID	1983	LC	9 X 13 EA	AP	285 EA		485 SET	1200 SET
Market Rue de Buci	LME	ART/LID	1983	LC	18 X 26	AP	285		385	650
Monceau, 1983 (Set of 4)	LME	ART/LID	1983	LC	13 X 9 EA	AP	285 EA		485 SET	3000 Set
November, 1983 (Set of 4)	LME	ART/LID	1983	LC	9 X 13 EA	AP	285 EA		485 SET	950 SET
November Day	LME	ART/LID	1983	LC	18 X 27	AP	285		485	585
Parc Monceau, 1983	LME	ART/LID	1983	LC	18 X 26	AP	285		485	585
Promenade, 1983	LME	ART/LID	1983	LC	17 X 20	AP	285		485	525
Seated People Monceau	LME	ART/LID	1983	LC	18 X 26	AP	285		485	950
Shopper, 1983	LME	ART/LID	1983	LC	18 X 25	AP	285		485	650
The Strollers	LME	ART/LID	1983	LC	18 X 25	AP	285		485	585
Two Market Women	LME	ART/LID	1983	LC	18 X 26	AP	285		485	485
Two Seated Women, 1983	LME	ART/LID	1983	LC	17 X 20	AP	285		485	485
December Snow, 1984	LME	ART/LID	1984	EC	12 X 8	AP	200		165	325
February, 1984	LME	ART/LID	1984	EC	9 X 12	AP	165		165	250
Figures in the Snow	LME	ART/LID	1984	EC	12 X 9	AP	200		165	250
Walking Figures, 1984	LME	ART/LID	1984	EC	12 X 9	AP	200		165	185
Walking Man, 1984	LME	ART/LID	1984	EC	9 X 12	AP	200		165	600
April	LME	ART/LID	1984	LC	18 X 25	AP	285		385	2500
Autumn Riders	LME	ART/LID	1984	LC	18 X 25	AP	285		385	2500
Bridle Path	LME	ART/LID	1984	LC	25 X 18	AP	285		385	2500
Central Park (Set of 4)	LME	ART/LID	1984	LC	13 X 9 EA	AP	285 EA		550 SET	2800 SET
Evening Walk	LME	ART/LID	1984	LC	26 X 18	AP	285		385	650
Family	LME	ART/LID	1984	LC	18 X 26	AP	285		385	585
Jardin du Luxembourg, 1984	LME	ART/LID	1984	LC	18 X 24	AP	285		385	650
Marronnier	LME	ART/LID	1984	LC	25 X 18	AP	285		385	500
November, 1984 (Set of 4)	LME	ART/LID	1984	LC	8 X 7 EA	AP	285 EA		550 SET	950 SET
October, 1984 (Set of 4)	LME	ART/LID	1984	LC	9 X 13 EA	AP	285 EA		550 SET	1200 SET
Parc Monceau, 1984	LME	ART/LID	1984	LC	26 X 18	AP	285		385	685
Park Figures, 1984 (Set of 4)	LME	ART/LID	1984	LC	13 X 9 EA	AP	285 EA		550 SET	1200 SET
Path, Central Park	LME	ART/LID	1984	LC	18 X 25	AP	285		385	585
Red Leaves	LME	ART/LID	1984	LC	18 X 25	AP	285		385	650
Rue Mouffetard, 1984 (Set of 4)	LME	ART/LID	1984	LC	9 X 13 EA	AP	285 EA		550 SET	1200 SET
Sailboats	LME	ART/LID	1984	LC	18 X 25	AP	285		385	2500
September, 1984 (Set of 4)	LME	ART/LID	1984	LC	8 X 7 EA	AP	285 EA		550 SET	750 SET
Shadows, 1984	LME	ART/LID	1984	LC	16 X 21	AP	285		325	650
Trio, 1984	LME	ART/LID	1984	LC	18 X 25	AP	285		385	750
February, 1985	LME	ART/LID	1985	EC	12 X 9	AP	200		185	275
Snow, 1985	LME	ART/LID	1985	EC	12 X 9	AP	200		185	275
The Umbrella	LME	ART/LID	1985	EC	12 X 9	AP	200		185	350
Walking Man, 1985	LME	ART/LID	1985	EC	12 X 9	AP	200		185	500
Allee de l'Observatoire	LME	ART/LID	1985	LC	16 X 24	AP	285		440	585
April, 1985	LME	ART/LID	1985	LC	18 X 26	AP	285		440	550
Autumn Parc Montsouris, 1985	LME	ART/LID	1985	LC	17 X 24	AP	285		440	3000
Benches Parc Montsouris, 1985	LME	ART/LID	1985	LC	17 X 24	AP	285		440	650
Bridle Path, 1985	LME	ART/LID	1985	LC	26 X 18	AP	285		440	650
Central Park I,II,III,IV, 1985 (Set of 4)	LME	ART/LID	1985	LC	9 X 12 EA	AP	285 EA		650 SET	1250 SET
Central Park, South	LME	ART/LID	1985	LC	24 X 17	AP	285		440	1200
December I,II,III,IV, 1985 (Set of 4)	LME	ART/LID	1985	LC	9 X 12 EA	AP	285 EA		650 SET	850 SET
Dubonnet	LME	ART/LID	1985	LC	18 X 26	AP	285		440	550
Early April Central Park	LME	ART/LID	1985	LC	18 X 26	AP	285		440	650
Fall I,II,III,IV,1985	LME	ART/LID	1985	LC	13 X 9 EA	AP	285 EA		650 SET	1500 SET
January Jardin du Luxembourg	LME	ART/LID	1985	LC	16 X 24	AP	285		440	2500
Jessie	LME	ART/LID	1985	LC	17 X 25	AP	285		440	550
Joggers	LME	ART/LID	1985	LC	18 X 24	AP	285		440	900
Late Afternoon, 1985	LME	ART/LID	1985	LC	18 X 26	AP	285		440	550
Picnic Central Park	LME	ART/LID	1985	LC	17 X 24	AP	285		440	1200
Sailboats, 1985	LME	ART/LID	1985	LC	18 X 24	AP	285		440	2500
Seated Figures Central Park	LME	ART/LID	1985	LC	18 X 26	AP	285		440	440
Seesaws	LME	ART/LID	1985	LC	17 X 23	AP	285		440	650
Snow Central Park	LME	ART/LID	1985	LC	18 X 24	AP	285		440	2500
Sunday Central Park	LME	ART/LID	1985	LC	18 X 26	AP	285		440	585

HAROLD ALTMAN CONTINUED

TITLE	PUBLISHER	PRINTER	DATE	MEDIUM	DIMENSION (PAPER SIZE) IN INCHES	TYPE OF PAPER	EDITION NUMBER	NO. OF COLORS	ORIGINAL OPENING PRICE	CURRENT RETAIL PRICE
SOLD OUT EDITIONS (RARE):										
The Bench, 1985	LME	ART/LID	1985	LC	18 X 24	AP	285		440	585
The Sheepmeadow	LME	ART/LID	1985	LC	16 X 24	AP	285		440	2500
Walking Figures, 1985	LME	ART/LID	1985	LC	16 X 2	AP	285		440	585
Autumn Riders, 1986	LME	ART/LID	1986	LC	17 X 25	AP	285		485	900
Benches, 1986	LME	ART/LID	1986	LC	17 X 24	AP	285		485	600
Blossoms and Buildings	LME	ART/LID	1986	LC	18 X 25	AP	285		485	5000
Bridle Path I,II,III,IV,1986 (Set of 4)	LME	ART/LID	1986	LC	9 X 13 EA	AP	285 EA		625 SET	950 SET
Fall, 1986	LME	ART/LID	1986	LC	17 X 25	AP	285		485	685
Family, 1986	LME	ART/LID	1986	LC	18 X 24	AP	285		485	550
Jessie, 1986	LME	ART/LID	1986	LC	16 X 24	AP	285		485	550
Jogging, Central Park I,II,III,IV (Set of 4)	LME	ART/LID	1986	LC	9 X 13 EA	AP	285 EA		625 SET	950 SET
March, 1986	LME	ART/LID	1986	LC	17 X 25	AP	285		485	650
October, 1986	LME	ART/LID	1986	LC	16 X 22	AP	285		485	585
Picnic, 1986	LME	ART/LID	1986	LC	24 X 17	AP	285		485	650
Pigeons, 1986	LME	ART/LID	1986	LC	26 X 17	AP	285		485	1100
Reflections	LME	ART/LID	1986	LC	18 X 24	AP	285		485	585
Spring, 1986	LME	ART/LID	1986	LC	17 X 24	AP	285		485	650
Sunday Afternoon	LME	ART/LID	1986	LC	17 X 23	AP	285		485	550
Sunday Afternoon, Luxembourg	LME	ART/LID	1986	LC	16 X 24	AP	285		485	585
The Gallop	LME	ART/LID	1986	LC	18 X 24	AP	285		485	1500
The Tree, 1986	LME	ART/LID	1986	LC	17 X 25	AP	285		485	650
Trio, 1986	LME	ART/LID	1986	LC	16 X 24	AP	285		485	650
Two Riders	LME	ART/LID	1986	LC	26 X 18	AP	285		485	550
Winding Path, 1986	LME	ART/LID	1986	LC	17 X 24	AP	285		485	1200
Autumn, 1987	LME	ART/LID	1987	LC	25 X 18	AP	285		525	525
Bridle Path, 1987	LME	ART/LID	1987	LC	17 X 25	AP	285		585	685
Central Park, 1987	LME	ART/LID	1987	LC	19 X 25	AP	285		1500	1500
Conversation, 1987	LME	ART/LID	1987	LC	25 X 18	AP	285		585	585
Early Spring	LME	ART/LID	1987	LC	18 X 25	AP	285		525	525
Four Seasons, 1987 (Horizontal) (Set of 4)	LME	ART/LID	1987	LC	13 X 18 EA	AP	285 EA		1500 SET	1500 SET
Four Seasons, 1987 (Vertical) (Set of 4)	LME	ART/LID	1987	LC	18 X 13 EA	AP	285 EA		1500 SET	1500 SET
Great Tree	LME	ART/LID	1987	LC	18 X 26	AP	285		585	685
January, 1987 (Set of 4)	LME	ART/LID	1987	LC	13 X 18 EA	AP	285 EA		1250 SET	1250 SET
Jardin au Luxembourg, 1987	LME	ART/LID	1987	LC	17 X 25 EA	AP	285		525	525
Late Afternoon, 1987	LME	ART/LID	1987	LC	25 X 19	AP	285		525	525
Lovers	LME	ART/LID	1987	LC	19 X 25	AP	285		585	650
Quiet Afternoon	LME	ART/LID	1987	LC	18 X 25	AP	285		525	525
Reader, 1987	LME	ART/LID	1987	LC	18 X 25	AP	285		1500	2500
San Francisco Bay	LME	ART/LID	1987	LC	18 X 26	AP	285		750	750
Shaded Path	LME	ART/LID	1987	LC	18 X 25	AP	285		2500	2500
Spring Blossoms	LME	ART/LID	1987	LC	25 X 18	AP	285		1500	1500
Three Seated People	LME	ART/LID	1987	LC	16 X 24	AP	285		750	750
Trio, 1987	LME	ART/LID	1987	LC	24 X 17	AP	285		585	650
Walking Woman, 1987	LME	ART/LID	1987	LC	19 X 24	AP	285		525	525
Winter Walk	LME	ART/LID	1987	LC	24 X 18	AP	285		685	900
Yellow Tree	LME	ART/LID	1987	LC	17 X 24	AP	285		685	900
Afternoon, 1988	LME	ART/LID	1988	LC	17 X 23	AP	285		585	585
April	LME	ART/LID	1988	LC	17 X 24	AP	285		685	785
Autumn, 1988	LME	ART/LID	1988	LC	24 X 16	AP	285		900	1200
Benches, 1988	LME	ART/LID	1988	LC	16 X 25	AP	285		585	585
California	LME	ART/LID	1988	LC	32 X 23	AP	285		1200	1200
Central Park, 1988 (Set of 4)	LME	ART/LID	1988	LC	13 X 9 EA	AP	285 EA		1200 SET	1200 SET
Conversation, 1988	LME	ART/LID	1988	LC	13 X 9	AP	285		200	200
Couple, 1988	LME	ART/LID	1988	LC	9 X 13	AP	285		325	325
Elm	LME	ART/LID	1988	LC	13 X 9	AP	285		200	200
Fall Morning	LME	ART/LID	1988	LC	31 X 23	AP	285		1200	1200
Four Seasons I, 1988 (Set of 4)	LME	ART/LID	1988	LC	13 X 18 EA	AP	285 EA		1500 SET	1500 SET
Four Seasons, II 1988 (Set of 4)	LME	ART/LID	1988	LC	13 X 18 EA	AP	285 EA		1500 SET	1500 SET
Mother and Child	LME	ART/LID	1988	LC	9 X 13	AP	285		325	325
My Street	LME	ART/LID	1988	LC	18 X 26	AP	285		1200	1200
Parc Monceau, 1988	LME	ART/LID	1988	LC	33 X 23	AP	285		1200	1200
Reader, 1988	LME	ART/LID	1988	LC	26 X 18	AP	285		685	685
Sailboats, 1988	LME	ART/LID	1988	LC	26 X 18	AP	285		900	900
Shaded Path, 1988	LME	ART/LID	1988	LC	18 X 25	AP	285		900	2500
Sledding	LME	ART/LID	1988	LC	19 X 25	AP	285		585	585
Spring Walk	LME	ART/LID	1988	LC	22 X 33	AP	285		1500	1500
Sunday, 1988	LME	ART/LID	1988	LC	17 X 24	AP	285		685	685
Trio, 1988	LME	ART/LID	1988	LC	19 X 26	AP	285		785	785
Umbrella, 1988	LME	ART/LID	1988	LC	17 X 25	AP	285		585	585
Berry Street	LME	ART/LID	1989	LC	17 X 24	AP	285		850	850
Blossoms and Buildings, 1989	LME	ART/LID	1989	LC	17 X 24	AP	285		850	850

HAROLD ALTMAN CONTINUED

TITLE	PUBLISHER	PRINTER	DATE	MEDIUM	DIMENSION (PAPER SIZE) IN INCHES	TYPE OF PAPER	EDITION NUMBER	NO. OF COLORS	ORIGINAL OPENING PRICE	CURRENT RETAIL PRICE
SOLD OUT EDITIONS (RARE):										
Bow Bridge	LME	ART/LID	1989	LC	16 X 23	AP	285		1200	1200
Bridle Path, 1989	LME	ART/LID	1989	LC	17 X 26	AP	285		750	750
Central Park, 1989	LME	ART/LID	1989	LC	23 X 17	AP	285		650	650
Church in Lemont	LME	ART/LID	1989	LC	20 X 24	AP	285		1200	2500
Couple, 1989	LME	ART/LID	1989	LC	13 X 9	AP	285		850	850
Couples Suite (Set of 2):									750 SET	850 SET
Flowered Path	LME	ART/LID	1989	LC	13 X 9	AP	285		375	450
Yellow Dress	LME	ART/LID	1989	LC	13 X 9	AP	285		375	450
Fall, 1989	LME	ART/LID	1989	LC	17 X 24	AP	285		450	450
Family, 1989	LME	ART/LID	1989	LC		AP	285		685	685
Family Suite (Set of 2):									650 SET	650 SET
Family Walk	LME	ART/LID	1989	LC	13 X 9	AP	285		325	325
The Hill	LME	ART/LID	1989	LC	13 X 9	AP	285		325	325
Four Seasons Suite I, 1989 (Set of 4)	LME	ART/LID	1989	LC	18 X 13 EA	AP	285 EA		1700 SET	1700 SET
Four Seasons Suite II, 1989 (Set of 4)	LME	ART/LID	1989	LC	13 X 9 EA	AP	285 EA		1200 SET	1200 SET
Harry's House	LME	ART/LID	1989	LC	18 X 25	AP	285		685	685
Le Jardin du Luxembourg, 1989	LME	ART/LID	1989	LC	18 X 25	AP	285		650	650
Meeting, 1989	LME	ART/LID	1989	LC	16 X 23	AP	285		750	750
Morning Walk	LME	ART/LID	1989	LC	17 X 24	AP	285		750	750
Path Suite (Set of 2):									650 SET	650 SET
Conversation, 1989	LME	ART/LID	1989	LC	9 X 13	AP	285		325	325
Path, 1989	LME	ART/LID	1989	LC	9 X 13	AP	285		325	325
Road to Lemont	LME	ART/LID	1989	LC	18 X 23	AP	285		650	650
Shaded Path, 1989	LME	ART/LID	1989	LC	18 X 25	AP	285		685	685
Siesta	LME	ART/LID	1989	LC	16 X 23	AP	285		850	850
Spring Blossoms Suite (Set of 2):									650 SET	650 SET
April Blossoms	LME	ART/LID	1989	LC	9 X 13	AP	385		325	325
Resting Couple	LME	ART/LID	1989	LC	9 X 13	AP	385		325	325
Summer Afternoon	LME	ART/LID	1989	LC	18 X 25	AP	385		650	650
Sunday Afternoon, 1989	LME	ART/LID	1989	LC	16 X 23	AP	385		650	650
Three Riders	LME	ART/LID	1989	LC	18 X 13	AP	385		450	450
Walking Woman, 1989	LME	ART/LID	1989	LC	16 X 23	AP	385		685	685
CURRENT EDITIONS:										
Bridge	LME	ART/LID	1990	LC	16 X 24	AP	285		850	1750
Bridle Path, 1990 (Set of 2)	LME	ART/LID	1990	LC	9 X 13 EA	AP	285 EA		650 SET	650 SET
Central Park, 1990 (Set of 4)	LME	ART/LID	1990	LC	13 X 18 EA	AP	285 EA		1700 SET	1700 SET
Children	LME	ART/LID	1990	LC	16 X 24	AP	285		685	685
Couple, 1990	LME	ART/LID	1990	LC	16 X 24	AP	285		685	685
Couple, Central Park	LME	ART/LID	1990	LC	17 X 24	AP	285		650	650
Family, 1990	LME	ART/LID	1990	LC	17 X 24	AP	285		1200	1200
First Snow	LME	ART/LID	1990	LC	17 X 24	AP	285		750	750
Friends	LME	ART/LID	1990	LC	16 X 25	AP	285		650	750
Great Tree, 1990	LME	ART/LID	1990	LC	24 X 16	AP	285		650	650
Jardin du Luxembourg, 1990	LME	ART/LID	1990	LC	18 X 25	AP	285		685	685
Orchard Road	LME	ART/LID	1990	LC	18 X 25	AP	285		650	650
Parc Monceau, 1990	LME	ART/LID	1990	LC	17 X 25	AP	285		650	650
Pasture (Set of 2)	LME	ART/LID	1990	LC	9 X 13 EA	AP	285 EA		650 SET	685 SET
Paths, 1990 (Set of 2)	LME	ART/LID	1990	LC	13 X 9 EA	AP	285 EA		650 SET	650 SET
Pennsylvania	LME	ART/LID	1990	LC	18 X 25	AP	285		650	650
Promenade Heian Garden	LME	ART/LID	1990	LC	16 X 24	AP	285		650	650
Rider, 1990	LME	ART/LID	1990	LC	17 X 24	AP	285		650	650
Sailboats, 1990	LME	ART/LID	1990	LC	21 X 27	AP	285		650	1200
Shadows Luxembourg	LME	ART/LID	1990	LC	17 X 25	AP	285		650	650
Shinjuku Gyoen Garden	LME	ART/LID	1990	LC	16 X 24	AP	285		650	650
Slab Cabin Hill	LME	ART/LID	1990	LC	18 X 24	AP	285		650	650
Spring, 1990	LME	ART/LID	1990	LC	16 X 25	AP	285		685	685
Tusseyville	LME	ART/LID	1990	LC	17 X 24	AP	285		650	650
Walk, 1990	LME	ART/LID	1990	LC	16 X 24	AP	285		685	685
Butchart Garden	LME	ART/LID	1992	LC	23 X 30	AP	285		900	900
Central Park 1992 (Set of 2)	LME	ART/LID	1992	LC	9 X 13 EA	AP	285 EA		685 SET	685 SET
Center County, PA	LME	ART/LID	1992	LC	22 X 30	AP	285		685	685
Converation 1992	LME	ART/LID	1992	LC	22 X 30	AP	285		685	685
Deerfield	LME	ART/LID	1992	LC	23 X 30	AP	285		660	650
Elms 1992	LME	ART/LID	1992	LC	25 X 18	AP	285		650	650
Giverny	LME	ART/LID	1992	LC	22 X 30	AP	285		650	650
Golden Gate Park, 1992	LME	ART/LID	1992	LC	22 X 30	AP	285		650	650
Golf (Set of 4)	LME	ART/LID	1992	LC	18 X 24 EA	AP	285 EA		1700 SET	1700 SET
Halloween Pumpkins	LME	ART/LID	1992	LC	22 X 30	AP	285		650	650
Japanese Garden, Portland	LME	ART/LID	1992	LC	22 X 30	AP	285		685	685
Jardin du Luxembourg, 1992	LME	ART/LID	1992	LC	22 X 30	AP	285		685	685
Jessie's Ball Game	LME	ART/LID	1992	LC	22 X 30	AP	285		650	650
Minnie	LME	ART/LID	1992	LC	22 X 30	AP	285		650	650
Mt Nittany	LME	ART/LID	1992	LC	22 X 30	AP	285		685	685

HAROLD ALTMAN CONTINUED

TITLE	PUBLISHER	PRINTER	DATE	MEDIUM	DIMENSION (PAPER SIZE) IN INCHES	TYPE OF PAPER	EDITION NUMBER	NO. OF COLORS	ORIGINAL OPENING PRICE	CURRENT RETAIL PRICE
CURRENT EDITIONS:										
Paradise, Butchart Garden	LME	ART/LID	1992	LC	23 X 30	AP	285		650	650
Parc Monceau, 1992	LME	ART/LID	1992	LC	22 X 30	AP	285		685	685
Red Cabin	LME	ART/LID	1992	LC	22 X 30	AP	285		650	650
Reflection, 1992 (Set of 2)	LME	ART/LID	1992	LC	13 X 9 EA	AP	285 EA		750 SET	750 SET
Snow, Central Park, 1992	LME	ART/LID	1992	LC	30 X 22	AP	285		650	650
Spring I,II, 1992	LME	ART/LID	1992	LC	24 X 18 EA	AP	285 EA		425 EA	425 EA
Toftrees	LME	ART/LID	1992	LC	22 X 30	AP	285		750	750
Trio, Lemont	LME	ART/LID	1992	LC	22 X 30	AP	285		685	685
Two Women, 1992	LME	ART/LID	1992	LC	22 X 30	AP	285		650	650

ALVAR (SUNOL)

BORN: Montgat, Spain; 1935
EDUCATION: Escuela Superior de Bellas Artes de San Jorge, 1952–56
COLLECTIONS: Musée Hyacenthe Rigaud, Perignon, France; Utah Mus of Fine Arts, Salt Lake City, UT; Mus of Mod Art, Barcelona, Spain; Wichita Art Mus, KS
PRINTERS: Imprimerie Artistique Bellini, Paris, France (IAB); Lithografias Artisticas, Barcelona, Spain (LA); Taller Artesanal Vincente Aznar, Barcelona, Spain (TAVA)
PUBLISHERS: Circle Gallery, Ltd, Chicago, IL (CGL); FKH Editions, Inc, NY (FKH); Circle Fine Arts Corp, Chicago, IL (CFA); Edmund Newman, Swampscott, MA (EN)
GALLERIES: Gallery Studio 53, New York, NY; Nuance Galleries, Tampa, FL; Shirley Fox Galleries, Atlanta, GA; Fernette's Gallery of Art, Des Moines, IA; Nan Miller Gallery, Rochester, NY; Circle Galleries, Chicago, IL & New York, NY & Northbrook, IL & Pittsburgh, PA & Houston, TX & Scottsdale, AZ & Beverly Hills, CA & Costa Mesa, CA & San Francisco, CA & San Diego, CA & Sherman Oaks, CA & Palm Beach, CA & Honolulu, HI & New Orleans, LA & Las Vegas, NV & Seattle, WA; Saper Gallery, East Lansing, MI; Atlas Galleries, Inc, Chicago, IL; Bryant Galleries, New Orleans, LA & Birmingham, AL & Jackson, MS

Alvar (Sunol)
Le Peintre et sa Realite
Courtesy Edmund Newman, Inc

TITLE	PUBLISHER	PRINTER	DATE	MEDIUM	DIMENSION (PAPER SIZE) IN INCHES	TYPE OF PAPER	EDITION NUMBER	NO. OF COLORS	ORIGINAL OPENING PRICE	CURRENT RETAIL PRICE
SOLD OUT EDITIONS (RARE):										
Bullfighter	CGL	P/FR	1970	LC	20 X 26	AP	150	3	65	700
Woman with Guitar	CGL	P/FR	1970	LC	20 X 26	AP	150	5	65	700
Les Musicians	CGL	P/FR	1970	LC	22 X 30	AP	200		95	700
La Tour Terelle	CGL	P/FR	1970	LC	22 X 30	AP	200		95	700
Violinist	CGL	IAB	1970	LC	30 X 22	AP	200		95	600
Pink Flute	CGL	IAB	1972	EC	16 X 13	AP	150	3	65	600
Blue Flute	CGL	IAB	1972	EC	13 X 17	AP	150	2	65	600
Guitarist	CGL	IAB	1972	EC	16 X 13	AP	150	2	65	600
Interieur Reve	FKH	IAB	1972	EC	16 X 13	AP	150	2	65	600
La Muse et Les Reveuses	FKH	IAB	1974	LC	36 X 28	AP	225		175	2500
Sonate Rouge	FKH	IAB	1974	LC	40 X 29	AP	225		200	2500
Le Miracle Quotidien	RKH	IAB	1974	LC	40 X 29	AP	225		200	2500
Le Chevalet (AP)	EN	LA	1974	LC	40 X 29	AP	225		175	2500
Le Chevalet (JP)	EN	LA	1981	LC/EMB	18 X 26	AP	275		500	1800
La Caresse (AP)	EN	LA	1981	LC/EMB	18 X 26	JP	75		540	2000
La Caresse (JP)	EN	LA	1981	LC/EMB	18 X 26	AP	275		500	1800
L'Inspiration (AP)	EN	LA	1981	LC/EMB	18 X 26	JP	75		540	2000
L'Inspiration (JP)	EN	LA	1981	LC/EMB	18 X 26	AP	275		500	1800
Reverie	EN	LA	1981	LC/EMB	18 X 26	JP	75		540	2000
Le Peintre et sa Realite (AP)	EN	LA	1981	LC/EMB	18 X 26	AP	275		500	1350
Le Peintre et sa Realite (JP)	EN	LA	1981	LC/EMB	18 X 26	AP	275		500	1500
L'Oiseau sur la Table	EN	LA	1981	LC/EMB	18 X 26	AP	275		500	1000

ALVAR (SUNOL) CONTINUED

TITLE	PUBLISHER	PRINTER	DATE	MEDIUM	DIMENSION (PAPER SIZE) IN INCHES	TYPE OF PAPER	EDITION NUMBER	NO. OF COLORS	ORIGINAL OPENING PRICE	CURRENT RETAIL PRICE
SOLD OUT EDITIONS (RARE):										
Suite Biblique (Set of 5):									2500 SET	8500 SET
The Seventh Day	EN	LA	1981	LC/EMB	32 X 25	AP	275		500	1800
Ruth Gleaning Wheat	EN	LA	1981	LC/EMB	32 X 25	AP	275		500	1800
David Plays His Harp	EN	LA	1981	LC/EMB	32 X 25	AP	275		500	1800
Esther at the Banquet	EN	LA	1981	LC/EMB	32 X 25	AP	275		500	1800
Susanna and the Elders	EN	LA	1981	LC/EMB	32 X 25	AP	275		500	1800
Suite Biblique (Deluxe) (Set of 5):									2700 SET	9000 SET
The Seventh Day	EN	LA	1981	LC/EMB	32 X 25	JP	75		550	1850
Ruth Gleaning Wheat	EN	LA	1981	LC/EMB	32 X 25	JP	75		550	1850
David Plays His Harp	EN	LA	1981	LC/EMB	32 X 25	JP	75		550	1850
Esther at the Banquet	EN	LA	1981	LC/EMB	32 X 25	JP	75		550	1850
Susanna and the Elders	EN	LA	1981	LC/EMB	32 X 25	JP	75		550	1850
Carmen Suite (Set of 5):									2700 SET	6000 SET
Couplets	EN	LA	1982	LC/EMB	21 X 28	AP	275		600	1300
Chanson Boheme	EN	LA	1982	LC/EMB	21 X 28	AP	275		600	1300
Chez Lillias Pastia	EN	LA	1982	LC/EMB	21 X 28	AP	275		600	1300
Duo Final	EN	LA	1982	LC/EMB	21 X 28	AP	275		600	1300
Trio	EN	LA	1982	LC/EMB	21 X 28	AP	275		600	1300
Carmen Suite (Deluxe) (Set of 5):									2900 SET	6500 SET
Couplets	EN	LA	1982	LC/EMB	21 X 28	JP	75		650	1350
Chanson Boheme	EN	LA	1982	LC/EMB	21 X 28	JP	75		650	1350
Chez Lillias Pastia	EN	LA	1982	LC/EMB	21 X 28	JP	75		650	1350
Duo Final	EN	LA	1982	LC/EMB	21 X 28	JP	75		650	1350
Trio	EN	LA	1982	LC/EMB	21 X 28	JP	75		650	1350
Le Cartes	EN	LA	1982	LC/EMB	21 X 28	AP	275		600	1300
Le Cartes	EN	LA	1982	LC/EMB	21 X 28	JP	75		650	1350
Deux Villages (Set of 2)	EN	LA	1983	LC/EMB	20 X 26 EA	AP	125 EA		1500 SET	3000 SET
Deux Villages (Set of 2)	EN	LA	1983	LC/EMB	20 X 26 EA	JP	90 EA		1550 SET	3000 SET
CURRENT EDITIONS:										
La Nature Humaine	EN	TAVA	1987	LC/EMB		AP	275 EA		4000 SET	5000 SET
La Nature Humaine	EN	TAVA	1987	LC/EMB		JP	90 EA		4250 SET	5500 SET

IRVING AMEN

BORN: New York, NY; July 25, 1918
EDUCATION: Pratt Inst, Scholar, NY, 1932–39; Independent Study, Paris, France, 1950, Italy, 1953
TEACHING: Instr, Art, Pratt Inst, NY; Univ of Notre Dame, South Bend, IN
AWARDS: Directors Prize, Audubon Artists, NY
COLLECTIONS: Mus of Mod Art, NY; Metropolitan Mus of Art, NY; Butler Inst of Am Art, Youngstown, OH; Victoria & Albert Mus, London, England; Smithsonian Inst, Wash, DC; Bibliotheque Nat, Paris, France; Albertina Mus, Vienna, Austria
PRINTERS: Artist (ART)
PUBLISHERS: Artist (ART)
GALLERIES: Hillel Jewish Student Center, Cincinnati, OH
MAILING ADDRESS: 90 SW 12th Terrace, Boca Raton, FL 33486

TITLE	PUBLISHER	PRINTER	DATE	MEDIUM	DIMENSION (PAPER SIZE) IN INCHES	TYPE OF PAPER	EDITION NUMBER	NO. OF COLORS	ORIGINAL OPENING PRICE	CURRENT RETAIL PRICE
SOLD OUT EDITIONS (RARE):										
Trick or Treat—Holloween	ART	ART	1964	WG		AP	50		50	300
Bull Fight #1	ART	ART	1968	EC	12 X 18	AP	200		75	350

ROBERT AMFT

BORN: Chicago, IL; December 7, 1916
EDUCATION: Grad Art Inst, 1941; Oxbow Sch, Saugatuck, MI
TEACHING: Ray-Vogue Sch, Chicago, IL, 1948; New Orleans Acad, LA, 1949
AWARDS: Hallmark Award, 1952; Butler Inst, Purchase Prize, 1958; New Horizons Award, 1975; Renaissance Prize, Chicago, IL, 1975
COLLECTIONS: Butler Inst of Art, Youngstown, OH; Chicago Inst of Art, IL
PRINTERS: Artist (ART)
PUBLISHERS: Artist (ART)
GALLERIES: Joy Horwich, Chicago, IL; Carl Hammer Gallery, Chicago, IL; Miriam Perlman, Flint, MI
MAILING ADDRESS: 7340 North Ridge, Chicago, IL 80845

TITLE	PUBLISHER	PRINTER	DATE	MEDIUM	DIMENSION (PAPER SIZE) IN INCHES	TYPE OF PAPER	EDITION NUMBER	NO. OF COLORS	ORIGINAL OPENING PRICE	CURRENT RETAIL PRICE
CURRENT EDITIONS:										
Trout	ART	ART	1979	WC	23 X 30	AP	30	2	200	300
The Cat	ART	ART	1978	WC	23 X 30	AP	30	2	200	300
Double Gorilla	ART	ART	1978	WC	23 X 30	AP	25	3	200	300

The retail prices of the 100,000 limited edition prints quoted in this directory are subject to change. Print publishers, artists and galleries were the direct sources for these quotations. Prices in the secondary market listed as "Sold Out Editions (Rare)" indicate that the publisher has a limited supply of that print or that the print is difficult to locate in the galleries.

GREGORY AMENOFF

BORN: St. Charles, IL; September 16, 1948
EDUCATION: Beloit Col, WI, BA
AWARDS: Creative Artists Prog Service Award, 1981;Nat Endowment for the Arts Fel, 1980,81,89
RECENT EXHIB: Hirschl & Adler Modern, NY, 1987; Stephen Wirtz Gallery, San Francisco, CA, 1989; Phoenix Art Mus, AZ, 1989; Butler Inst of Am Art, Youngstown, OH, 1989; Hirschl & Adler Modern, NY, 1990; Univ of Florida Mus, Gainesville, FL, 1992; DeCordova Mus, Lincoln, MA, 1992; Gerald Peters Gallery, Santa Fe, NM 1991; Victoria Munroe Gallery, NY, 1992
COLLECTIONS: Metropolitan Mus of Art, NY; Mus of Mod Art, NY; Whitney Mus of Am Art, NY; Mus of Fine Arts, Boston, MA; Neuberger Mus, State Univ of New York, Purchase, NY; Rose Art Mus, Brandeis Univ, Waltham, MA; Albright-Knox Art Gallery, Buffalo, NY; Phoenix Art Mus, AZ
PRINTERS: Chip Elwell, NY (CE); Maurice Sanchez, NY (MS); Dwight Pogue, NY (DP); Derriére L'Etoile Studios, NY (DES); Smith Col, Northampton, MA (SC); Will Foo, San Francisco, CA (WF); Andrew Saftel, San Francisco, CA (AS); John Stemmer, San Francisco, CA (JS); Experimental Workshop, San Francisco, CA (EW); Bill Weege, Madison, WI (BW); Andrew Rubin, Madison, WI (AR); Tandem Press, University of Wisconsin, Madison, WI (TanPr)
PUBLISHERS: Diane Villani Editions, NY (DVE); Experimental Workshop, San Francisco, CA (EW); Tandem Press, University of Wisconsin, Madison, WI (TanPr)
GALLERIES: Betsy Rosenfield Gallery, Chicago, IL; Diane Villani Editions, New York, NY; Hirschl & Adler Modern, New York, NY; Experimental Workshop, San Francisco, CA; Riva Yares Gallery, Scottsdale, AZ, & Santa Fe, NM; Stephen Wirtz Gallery, San Francisco, CA; James Corcoran Gallery, Santa Monica, CA; Flanders Graphics, Minneapolis, MN; Davis/McClain Gallery, Houston, TX; Gerald Peters Gallery, Santa Fe, NM; Victoria Munroe Gallery, New York, NY; Betsy Senior Contemporary Prints, New York, NY; Fabric Workshop, Phila, PA
MAILING ADDRESS: 533 Canal Street, New York, NY 10013

Gregory Amenoff
Spine
Courtesy Tandem Press

TITLE	PUBLISHER	PRINTER	DATE	MEDIUM	DIMENSION (PAPER SIZE) IN INCHES	TYPE OF PAPER	EDITION NUMBER	NO. OF COLORS	ORIGINAL OPENING PRICE	CURRENT RETAIL PRICE
SOLD OUT EDITIONS (RARE):										
In the Fifth Season	DVE	CE	1983	WC	41 X 37	SEK	25	10	900	3000
Untitled	DVE	CE	1984	WC	36 X 34	SEK	30	9	900	3000
Chamber	DVE	CE	1984	WC	38 X 43	SUZ	35	18	1200	3000
CURRENT EDITIONS:										
Haven	DVE	MS/DES	1986	LC/OFF	22 X 30	AP	40	3	500	600
Crux	ART	MS/DP/SC/DES	1986	LC/MON	38 X 30	R/BFK/AC	23	Varies	1200	3000
Final Hours	DVE	MS/DP/SC/DES	1986	LC	37 X 39	AP	40		900	1800
El Santuario de Chimayo	DVE	MS/DP/SC/DES	1986	LC	37 X 39	AP	40		900	1800
Gnarl	EW	WF/AS/JS/EW	1987	WC	49 X 43	R/BFK	35	22	1800	3500
Urania	DVE	WF/AS/JS/EW	1988	WC	37 X 48	SUZ	35	13	1500	1800
Mnemosyne	DVE	WF/AS/JS/EW	1988	WC	37 X 48	SUZ	35	11	1500	2000
El Rito Group, Nos 1-5	TanPr	BW/AR/TanPr	1990	MON	75 X 60 EA	AC	1 EA	Varies	4000 EA	4000 EA
Spine	TanPr	BW/AR/TanPr	1990	WC	41 X 37	SUZ	40	8	1600	1600
Veil	TanPr	BW/AR/TanPr	1990	WC	38 X 37	SUZ	40	8	1600	1600
Island in the Moon I,II,III (Set of 3)	TanPr	BW/AR/TanPr	1990	MON	24 X 24 EA	SUZ	40 EA	2 EA	1000 SET	1000 SET

EMMA AMOS

BORN: Atlanta, GA; March 16, 1938
EDUCATION: Antioch Col, Yellow Springs, OH, BA, 1958; London Central Art Sch, London, England, BFA, 1959; New York Univ, NY, MA, 1966
TEACHING: Assoc Prof, Fine Art, Mason Gross Sch of Arts, Rutgers Univ, NJ, 1980; Skowkegan Sch of Painting & Sculpture, ME, 1987
AWARDS: Nat Endowment Fel, Drawing, 1983; New York Found Fel, Painting, 1989; New York Council on the Arts Award, 1989
RECENT EXHIB: Williams Col Mus, Williamstown, MA, 1989; Mus of Mod Art, NY, 1988,90; New York State Mus, Trenton, NJ, 1990; Newark Mus, NJ, 1990; Mus of Contemp Hispanic Art, NY, 1990

COLLECTIONS: New Jersey State Mus, Trenton, NJ; Newark Mus, NJ; Minnesota Mus of Art, Minneapolis, MN; Schomburg Coll, NY
PRINTERS: Paul Wong, NY (PW); Dieu Donne Press, NY (DDP); Kathy Caraccio, NY (KC)
PUBLISHERS: Artist (ART)
GALLERIES: Associated American Artists, New York, NY; Nancy Stein Gallery, New York, NY; Wendell Street Gallery, Cambridge, MA; McIntosh Gallery, Atlanta, GA; Zimmerman/Saturn Gallery, Nashville, TN
MAILING ADDRESS: 21 Bond St, New York, NY 10012

TITLE	PUBLISHER	PRINTER	DATE	MEDIUM	DIMENSION (PAPER SIZE) IN INCHES	TYPE OF PAPER	EDITION NUMBER	NO. OF COLORS	ORIGINAL OPENING PRICE	CURRENT RETAIL PRICE
CURRENT EDITIONS:										
Sambos Tigers	ART	PW/DDP	1984	MULT	15 X 140 EA	PP/FABRIC	1 EA		2000	2500
Cheetah	ART	KC	1984	MULT	15 X 30	PP/FABRIC	20		200	300

JOE AMRHEIN

RECENT EXHIB: Turske Whitney Gallery, Los Angeles, CA, 1988; Turske & Turske, Zürich, Switzerland, 1989
PRINTERS: Toby Michel, Los Angeles, CA (TM); Angeles Press, Los Angeles, CA (AP)
PUBLISHERS: Artist (ART)
GALLERIES: Turske Whitney Gallery, Los Angeles, CA; Turske & Turske, Zürich, Switzerland

TITLE	PUBLISHER	PRINTER	DATE	MEDIUM	DIMENSION (PAPER SIZE) IN INCHES	TYPE OF PAPER	EDITION NUMBER	NO. OF COLORS	ORIGINAL OPENING PRICE	CURRENT RETAIL PRICE
CURRENT EDITIONS:										
Kiss (Construction)	ART	TM/AP	1987	LC	40 X 32	AP	30	6	575	750

WILLIAM ANASTASI

BORN: Philadelphia, PA; August 11, 1933
EDUCATION: Univ of Pennsylvania, Phila, PA, 1953–58
TEACHING: Sch of Visual Arts, NY, 1968–87; Lectr, Yale Univ, New Haven, CT, 1991
AWARDS: Am Acad of Arts & Letters, NY, 1982
RECENT EXHIB: Ball State Univ, Muncie, IN, 1991; Art Inst of Chicago, IL, 1991
COLLECTIONS: Mus of Mod Art, NY; Metropolitan Art Mus, NY; Brooklyn Mus, NY; Walker Art Inst, Minneapolis, MN; Phoenix Mus of Art, AZ; George Mus of Art, Athens, GA; Univ of North Carolina, Greenboro, NC; Des Moines Art Inst, IA; Philadelphia Art Mus, PA; Mus of Contemp Art, Los Angeles, CA; Chicago Art Inst, IL; Moderna Museet, Stockholm, Sweden
PRINTERS: Sue Evans, NY (SE); Evans Editions, NY (EEd)
PUBLISHERS: Evans Editions, NY (EEd)
GALLERIES: Sandra Gering Gallery, New York, NY; Anders Tornberg Gallery, Lund, Sweden; Mattress Factory, Pittsburgh, PA; David Lawrence Editions, Beverly Hills, CA
MAILING ADDRESS: 924 West End Ave, New York, NY 10025

TITLE	PUBLISHER	PRINTER	DATE	MEDIUM	DIMENSION (PAPER SIZE) IN INCHES	TYPE OF PAPER	EDITION NUMBER	NO. OF COLORS	ORIGINAL OPENING PRICE	CURRENT RETAIL PRICE
CURRENT EDITIONS:										
Subway Etchings (Set of 10)	EEd	SE/EEd	1992	EB	20 X 21 EA	R/BFK	30 EA	1 EA	3500 SET	3500 SET

BRUCE ANDERSON

BORN: Minneapolis, MN; 1945
EDUCATION: Minneapolis Sch of Art, MN; Atelier 63, Haarlem, Holland
PRINTERS: Vermillion Editions Ltd, Minneapolis, MN (VEL); Agnes Story, Minneapolis, MN (AS); Michael Reid, Minneapolis, MN (MR)
PUBLISHERS: Vermillion, Minneapolis, MN (VEL)
GALLERIES: Jentra Fine Art Gallery, Freehold, NJ; Bockley Galleries, Minneapolis, MN; Works Gallery, Phila, PA; Rare Findings, Denver, CO

TITLE	PUBLISHER	PRINTER	DATE	MEDIUM	DIMENSION (PAPER SIZE) IN INCHES	TYPE OF PAPER	EDITION NUMBER	NO. OF COLORS	ORIGINAL OPENING PRICE	CURRENT RETAIL PRICE
CURRENT EDITIONS:										
Conversation	VEL	AS/MR/VEL	1981	LC/SP/I/HC	23 X 30	R/BFK	20	14	500	750

CURTIS ANDERSON

PRINTERS: Jon Goodman, Hadley, MA (JG); Felix Harlan, NY (FH); Carol Weaver, NY (CW); Rudolf Klein, Cologne, Germany (RK); Karl-Heinz Neumann, Cologne, Germany (KHN)
PUBLISHERS: Baron/Boisanté Editions, NY (B/BEd)
GALLERIES: Baron/Boisanté Editions, New York, NY; Paul Kasmin Gallery, New York, NY

TITLE	PUBLISHER	PRINTER	DATE	MEDIUM	DIMENSION (PAPER SIZE) IN INCHES	TYPE OF PAPER	EDITION NUMBER	NO. OF COLORS	ORIGINAL OPENING PRICE	CURRENT RETAIL PRICE
CURRENT EDITIONS:										
Der 7 Grad (Set of 7)	B/BEd	JG/FH/CW	1989	PH/G	11 X 15 EA	SOM	24 EA		3500 SET	4000 SET
The Perfect Cocoon (The Golden Andrgyne) (Goldplated Silver)	B/BEd	RK	1991	MULT	7 X 4 X 4	Silver/Gold	24		3500	4000
Linen (A Porcelain Deathmask of Napoleon Bonaparte Placed on a Stainless Steel Disc)	B/BEd	KHN	1991	MULT	7 X 14	Steel	12		3500	4000

DOUG ANDERSON

BORN: Syracuse, NY; 1954
EDUCATION: Sch of Mus of Fine Arts, Tufts Univ, Medford, MA 1979
AWARDS: Massachusetts County Arts Fel, 1982; Engelhard Award, 1986; Nat Endowment for the Arts Fel, 1987
RECENT EXHIB: Brockton Art Mus, MA, 1987; Kicken Pauseback, Cologne, Germany, 1990; Mayor Rowan Gallery, London, England, 1990
PRINTERS: Michael Berdan, Boston, MA (MB); Mulberry Press, Boston, MA (MulP)
PUBLISHERS: Mulberry Press, Boston, MA (MulP)
GALLERIES: Stux Galleries, New York, NY; Phyllis Kind Gallery, Chicago, IL & New York, NY; Glass Gallery, Bethesda, MD; Barbara Krakow Gallery, Boston, MA
MAILING ADDRESS: c/o Stux Gallery, 155 Spring St, New York, NY 10012

The Printworld Directory is accepting new applications for the seventh edition. Approximately 300 new artists will be accepted. Please use the two forms provided in the back section of this directory to submit biographical data and documentation of prints. Edition number of each print must not exceed 500 and the retail price must be $100 or more.

DOUG ANDERSON CONTINUED

TITLE	PUBLISHER	PRINTER	DATE	MEDIUM	DIMENSION (PAPER SIZE) IN INCHES	TYPE OF PAPER	EDITION NUMBER	NO. OF COLORS	ORIGINAL OPENING PRICE	CURRENT RETAIL PRICE
CURRENT EDITIONS:										
Met a Stranger on a Train #1,#2,#3	MulP	MB/MulP	1986	WC	38 X 28 EA	HANGA	30 EA		500 EA	750 EA

IVAN DELOS ANDERSON

BORN: Yankton, SD; February 13, 1915
EDUCATION: Yankton Col, SD, BA, 1937

COLLECTIONS: Mus of Mod Art, NY; Los Angeles County Mus of Art, CA; Cody Mus, WY
PRINTERS: Guy Maccoy, Canoga Park, CA (Deceased)
PUBLISHERS: Artist (ART)
MAILING ADDRESS: 1060 Flamingo Rd, Laguna Beach, CA 92651

TITLE	PUBLISHER	PRINTER	DATE	MEDIUM	DIMENSION (PAPER SIZE) IN INCHES	TYPE OF PAPER	EDITION NUMBER	NO. OF COLORS	ORIGINAL OPENING PRICE	CURRENT RETAIL PRICE
CURRENT EDITIONS:										
Secrets	ART	GM	1975	SP	24 X 20	AP	200	47	65	1000
Madonna & Child	ART	GM	1976	SP	30 X 23	AP	225	44	65	300
Beach Buddies	ART	GM	1977	SP	20 X 24	AP	200	60	65	300
Boy with Stick	ART	GM	1977	SP	30 X 20	AP	200	44	65	300
Baby Brown Eyes	ART	GM	1978	SP	20 X 24	AP	225	45	65	300
Pinkie	ART	GM	1978	SP	30 X 24	AP	300	48	65	300

JEREMY ANDERSON

BORN: Bloomington, IL, October 28, 1938
EDUCATION: Univ of Arizona, MFA, 1967
AWARDS: Mercyhurst Purchase Prize, 1965

PRINTERS: Edward Hamilton, Los Angeles, CA (EH)
PUBLISHERS: Cirrus Editions Los Angeles, CA (CE); Edward Hamilton (EH)
GALLERIES: Cirrus Editions Ltd, Los Angeles, CA; Braunstein/Quay Gallery, San Francisco, CA

TITLE	PUBLISHER	PRINTER	DATE	MEDIUM	DIMENSION (PAPER SIZE) IN INCHES	TYPE OF PAPER	EDITION NUMBER	NO. OF COLORS	ORIGINAL OPENING PRICE	CURRENT RETAIL PRICE
CURRENT EDITIONS:										
Sun Lawn II, III	CE/EH	EH	1972	LC	23 X 29 EA	AP	30 EA	4 EA	125 EA	550 EA

LAURIE ANDERSON

BORN: Chicago, IL; 1947
EDUCATION: Barnard Col, NY, 1969; Columbia Univ, NY, MFA, 1972
TEACHING: Instr, Art History, City Col of New York, NY, 1973–75
AWARDS: Grants, New York State Coun, 1975,77; Nat Endowment for the Arts, 1977,79; Guggenheim Fel, 1983

RECENT EXHIB: William Paterson Col, Ben Shahn Galleries, Wayne, NJ, 1989,92
COLLECTIONS: William Paterson Col, Ben Shahn Galleries, Wayne, NJ
PRINTERS: Bud Shark, Boulder, CO (BS); Shark's Lithography Ltd, Boulder, CO (SLL)
PUBLISHERS: Shark's Lithography Ltd, Boulder, CO (SLL)
GALLERIES: Shark's, Inc, Boulder, CO
MAILING ADDRESS: c/o Original Artists, 129 W 69th St, New York, NY 10023

TITLE	PUBLISHER	PRINTER	DATE	MEDIUM	DIMENSION (PAPER SIZE) IN INCHES	TYPE OF PAPER	EDITION NUMBER	NO. OF COLORS	ORIGINAL OPENING PRICE	CURRENT RETAIL PRICE
SOLD OUT EDITIONS (RARE):										
Mount Daly/US 4	SLL/ART	BS/SLL	1982	LC	22 X 30	AC/W	50	7	750	900

LESLIE ANDERSON

BORN: Anoka, MN; August 26, 1953
EDUCATION: Ruskin Sch of Drawing, Oxford Univ, England; Minneapolis Col of Art & Design, MN
RECENT EXHIB: Artemesia Gallery, Chicago, IL, 1992

PRINTERS: Land Mark Editions, Minneapolis, MN (LME)
PUBLISHERS: C G Rein Publishers, St. Paul, MN (CGR)
GALLERIES: C G Rein Galleries, Scottsdale, AZ & Santa Fe, NM & Houston TX & Minneapolis, MN; Artemesia Gallery, Chicago, IL
MAILING ADDRESS: 2035 E 7th Ave, North St Paul, MN 55109

TITLE	PUBLISHER	PRINTER	DATE	MEDIUM	DIMENSION (PAPER SIZE) IN INCHES	TYPE OF PAPER	EDITION NUMBER	NO. OF COLORS	ORIGINAL OPENING PRICE	CURRENT RETAIL PRICE
CURRENT EDITIONS:										
Checkers	CGR	LME	1982	LC	28 X 24		80	6	300	400
The Second Floor (Arches)	CGR	LME	1983	LC	21 X 21	AP/W	40	7	300	375
The Second Floor (Japan)	CGR	LME	1983	LC	21 X 21	JP	40	7	325	400
Midnight	CGR	LME	1983	LC	28 X 18		80	7	350	400

The retail prices of the 100,000 limited edition prints quoted in this directory are subject to change. Print publishers, artists and galleries were the direct sources for these quotations. Prices in the secondary market listed as "Sold Out Editions (Rare)" indicate that the publisher has a limited supply of that print or that the print is difficult to locate in the galleries.

SALLY ANDERSON

BORN: Rockford, IL; February 5, 1942
EDUCATION: Inst Allende, San Miguel Allende, Mexico, 1962; Beloit Col, WI, BA, 1964; Univ of Wisconsin, Madison, WI, 1967

PRINTERS: Naravisa Press, Albuquerque, NM (NP)
PUBLISHERS: C G Rein Publishers, St. Paul, MN (CGR)
GALLERIES: Works Gallery, II, Southampton, NY; C G Rein Galleries Scottsdale AZ & Santa Fe, NM & Houston, TX & Minneapolis, MN
MAILING ADDRESS: 7522 Bear Canyon Rd, Albuquerque, NM 87119

TITLE	PUBLISHER	PRINTER	DATE	MEDIUM	DIMENSION (PAPER SIZE) IN INCHES	TYPE OF PAPER	EDITION NUMBER	NO. OF COLORS	ORIGINAL OPENING PRICE	CURRENT RETAIL PRICE
SOLD OUT EDITIONS (RARE):										
Lily	CGR	NP	1982	LC	29 X 29	AP/B	50	8	300	500
Lily	CGR	NP	1982	LC	29 X 29	R/BFK/G	50	8	300	400
CURRENT EDITIONS:										
Cornflower	CGR	NP	1983	LC	34 X 28	R/BFK	100	8	350	475
Rose	CGR	NP	1983	LC	28 X 36	R/BFK	100	10	400	475
Deer Park	CGR	NP	1983	LC	31 X 30	R/BFK	100	9	300	450
Blue Rose	CGR	NP	1983	LC	28 X 38	R/BFK	100	10	350	475
Iris	CGR	NP	1983	LC	28 X 31	R/BFK	100		390	475

ROBERT ANDERSON

BORN: Orange, NJ; November 9, 1945
EDUCATION: NJ Inst of Tech, 1964–66; State Univ, Brockport, CT, BS, 1969; Pratt Inst, NY, MFA, 1972
TEACHING: Newark Mus Arts Workshop, NJ 1976–79; County Col of Morris, NJ, 1978–79
AWARDS: Grand Prize, Silvermine Guild, 1972; New Jersey State Fel, 1976–77; Nat Endowment for the Arts Fel, 1985–86
RECENT EXHIB: Pyramid Art Center, Rochester, NY, 1988; Eastern Washington Univ, Cheney, PA, 1988; St Tammany Art Assoc, Covington, LA, 1989
COLLECTIONS: Morris Mus, Morristown, NJ; Univ of Massachusetts, Amherst, MA; State Univ of Brockport, NY; Bloomfield Col, NJ
PRINTERS: Artist (ART)
PUBLISHERS: Stefanotti, NY (S); Collector's Group, FL (CG); Evergreen Pub, NJ (EP); Fine Arts Acquisitions (FAA); Channel Fine Arts, NY (ChFA); Circle Fine Art, Chicago, IL (CFA)
GALLERIES: Littlejohn-Sternau Gallery, New York, NY; Wetherholt Gallery, Wash, DC; Space Gallery, Los Angeles, CA; Circle Galleries, Scottsdale, AZ & Beverly Hills, CA & Costa Mesa, CA & San Diego, CA & San Francisco, CA & Sherman Oaks, CA & Honolulu, HI & Palm Beach, FL & Chicago, IL & Northbrook, IL & New Orleans, LA & Las Vegas, NV & Pittsburgh, PA & Houston, TX & Seattle, WA; Ro Gallery Image Makers, New York, NY
MAILING ADDRESS: 37 Glenfield Rd, Bloomfield, NJ 07003

TITLE	PUBLISHER	PRINTER	DATE	MEDIUM	DIMENSION (PAPER SIZE) IN INCHES	TYPE OF PAPER	EDITION NUMBER	NO. OF COLORS	ORIGINAL OPENING PRICE	CURRENT RETAIL PRICE
CURRENT EDITIONS:										
King's Masque	EP	ART	1980	LC	16 X 20	AP	250	4	125	400
Jack of Hearts	CG	ART	1980	LC	16 X 20	AP	250	4	125	400
Wisteria	FAA	ART	1980	LC	16 X 20	AP	250	5	125	400
Robin's Summer Dream	FAA	ART	1980	LC	16 X 20	AP	250	4	125	400
Alliance Band Revue	FAA	ART	1980	LC	16 X 20	AP	250	4	125	400
Summer Queen	CG	ART	1980	LC	16 X 20	AP	250	5	125	400
Hopelessly Watching	CG	ART	1980	LC	16 X 20	AP	250	4	125	400
On the Amazon	CG	ART	1980	LC	16 X 20	AP	250	4	125	400
Easier to Change the Past	ChFA	ART	1980	LC	16 X 20	AP	250	4	125	400
Heartkeepers	EP	ART	1980	MEZ	16 X 20	AP	250	4	125	400
Startled Silence	EP	ART	1981	LC	16 X 20	AP	250	6	125	400
Stars and Stripes	CFA	ART	1984	LC	25 X 26	AP	300		250	450

JOE ANDOE

BORN: Tulsa, OK; 1955
EDUCATION: Univ of Oklahoma, Norman, OK, MFA, 1981
RECENT EXHIB: Tom Cugliani Gallery, NY, 1988; Michael Kohn Gallery, Los Angeles, CA, 1989; Dart Gallery, Chicago, IL, 1988,89; Univ of Oklahoma Mus of Art, Norman, OK, 1990; Greenberg Gallery, St. Louis, MO, 1990; Galerie Daniel Templon, Paris, Fance, 1990; Yodo Gallery, Japan, 1991; BlumHelman Gallery, NY, 1989,90,91; Univ of Colorado, Colorado Springs, CO, 1992
COLLECTIONS: Metropolitan Mus of Art, NY; Oklahoma Mus of Art, Norman, OK
PRINTERS: Joe Wilfer, NY (JW); Ruth Lingen, NY (RL); Spring Street Workshop, NY (SprSW); Maurice Payne, NY (MP)
PUBLISHERS: Spring Street Workshop, NY (SprSW); Metropolitan Mus of Art, Mezzanine Gallery, New York, NY; Lococo-Mulder, Inc, St Louis, MO (L-M)
GALLERIES: Pace Prints, New York, NY; Lemberg Gallery, Birmingham, MI; A/D, New York, NY; BlumHelman Gallery, New York, NY; Jonathan Novak Contemporary Art, Los Angeles, CA

TITLE	PUBLISHER	PRINTER	DATE	MEDIUM	DIMENSION (PAPER SIZE) IN INCHES	TYPE OF PAPER	EDITION NUMBER	NO. OF COLORS	ORIGINAL OPENING PRICE	CURRENT RETAIL PRICE
CURRENT EDITIONS:										
Untitled (Set of 5)	SprSW	JW/RL/SprSW	1990	EB/A	20 X 22 EA	OKP	50 EA		4500 SET / 1000 EA	4500 SET / 1000 EA
Untitled (Set of 5)	SprSW	JW/RL/SprSW	1990	EB/A	17 X 22 EA	OKP	50 EA		5000 SET / 1200 EA	5000 SET / 1200 EA
Untitled Series	SprSW	JW/RL/SprSW	1990	MON	20 X 24 EA	OKP	1 EA		2500 EA	2500 EA
Untitled (Flower)	SprSW	JW/RL/SprSW	1991	EB/CC	25 X 29	OKP	35	1	900	900
Galilee	SprSW	JW/RL/SprSW	1991	EB	22 X 28	OKP	35	1	900	900
Untitled (Horse)	SprSW	JW/RL/SprSW	1991	EB	17 X 22	OKP	15	1	700	700
Tower	SprSW	JW/RL/SprSW	1991	EB/A	22 X 28	OKP	35	1	700	700

JOE ANDOE CONTINUED

TITLE	PUBLISHER	PRINTER	DATE	MEDIUM	DIMENSION (PAPER SIZE) IN INCHES	TYPE OF PAPER	EDITION NUMBER	NO. OF COLORS	ORIGINAL OPENING PRICE	CURRENT RETAIL PRICE
CURRENT EDITIONS:										
Untitled (Red Ducks) (Set of 3)	SprSW	JW/RL/SprSW	1991	STR	18 X 21 EA	OKP	30 EA		1500 SET	1500 SET
									600 EA	600 EA
Untitled (Swans) (Set of 3)	SprSW	JW/RL/SprSW	1991	EB/A	18 X 18 EA	OKP	50 EA		2000 SET	2000 SET
									750 EA	750 EA
Untitled (Ducks) (Set of 3)	SprSW	JW/RL/SprSW	1991	EB/A	21 X 24 EA	OKP	25 EA		1500 SET	1500 SET
									600 EA	600 EA
Untitled (Chicks) (Set of 3)	SprSW	JW/RL/SprSW	1991	EB/A	18 X 18 EA	OKP	18 EA		1000 SET	1000 SET
									400 EA	400 EA
Untitled (Telephone Poles) (Set of 3)	SprSW	JW/RL/SprSW	1992	EB/A	14 X 15 EA	OKP	20 EA		1200 SET	1200 SET
									450 EA	450 EA
Untitled (Poppy)	SprSW	JW/RL/SprSW	1992	EB	29 X 23	OKP	30	1	750	750
Set of Three:									1500 SET	1500 SET
Horn	MMA	MP	1992–93	AB	19 X 21	SOM	50	1	575	575
Horse	MMA	MP	1992–93	AB	19 X 21	SOM	50	1	575	575
Swan	MMA	MP	1992–93	AB	19 X 21	SOM	50	1	575	575
Untitled Portfolio (Set of 6):									3600 SET	3600 SET
Candle	L-M	MP	1993	AB	19 X 20		35	1	700	700
Falling Tree	L-M	MP	1993	AB	19 X 20		35	1	700	700
Moon	L-M	MP	1993	AB	19 X 20		35	1	700	700
Pussy Willow	L-M	MP	1993	AB	19 X 20		35	1	700	700
Rose	L-M	MP	1993	AB	19 X 20		35	1	700	700
Tulip	L-M	MP	1993	AB	19 X 20		35	1	700	700

FELIX ANGEL

BORN: Medellin, Columbia; 1949
EDUCATION: Inst of Fine Arts, Bogota, Colombia; Nat Univ of Colombia, Bogota, Colombia
COLLECTIONS: Mus of Mod Art of Latin Am, Wash, DC; Interamerican Development Bank, Wash, DC; Museo de Arte Moderno de Medellin, Francisco Antonio Zea, Colombia; Bando de America, Managua, Nicaragua; Museo de Arte de la Universidad Nacional, Bogota, Colombia; Biblioteca Publica Piloto de Medellin, Colombia
PRINTERS: Editions Press, San Francisco, CA (EP)
PUBLISHERS: Editions Press, San Francisco, CA (EP); Moss Gallery, San Francisco, CA (MG)
GALLERIES: Moss Gallery, San Francisco, CA

TITLE	PUBLISHER	PRINTER	DATE	MEDIUM	DIMENSION (PAPER SIZE) IN INCHES	TYPE OF PAPER	EDITION NUMBER	NO. OF COLORS	ORIGINAL OPENING PRICE	CURRENT RETAIL PRICE
SOLD OUT EDITIONS (RARE):										
Caballo de Aminta	EP/MG	EP	1982	LC	23 X 32	AC/W	70	3	350	800

DAVID NEVILLE ANDREW

BORN: Redruth, England; April 19, 1934
EDUCATION: Falmouth Sch of Art, England, 1954; Slade Sch of Fine Art, London, England, 1958
TEACHING: Bournemouth Col of Art, England; Portsmouth Polytechnic Sch. England; Queen's Univ, Kingston, Canada, presently
AWARDS: Purchase Award, Print & Drawing Prize, Council of Canada, 1976; Purchase, Award, Soc of Canadian Artists, 1977; Gold Medal, Acad Italia della Art & del Lavoro, 1980
COLLECTIONS: Kettles Yard Mus, Cambridge Univ, England; Univ of Alberta, Red Deer, Canada; Queen's Univ, Kingston, Canada; Burnaby Art Gallery, Canada
PRINTERS: Artist (ART)
PUBLISHERS: Artist (ART)
GALLERIES: Mira Godard Gallery, Toronto, Canada, ON
MAILING ADDRESS: c/o Department of Art, Queen's Univ, Kingston, Canada K7L 3N6

TITLE	PUBLISHER	PRINTER	DATE	MEDIUM	DIMENSION (PAPER SIZE) IN INCHES	TYPE OF PAPER	EDITION NUMBER	NO. OF COLORS	ORIGINAL OPENING PRICE	CURRENT RETAIL PRICE
SOLD OUT EDITIONS (RARE):										
Torrey Canyon, Version I	ART	ART	1970	EC	26 X 30	AP	25	10	100	500
Composition in Greys	ART	ART	1972	EC	15 X 12	AP	10	5	75	400
Houses & Trees	ART	ART	1974	SP	29 X 26	AP	25	3	50	300
Vestiges	ART	ART	1976	MM	25 X 27	AP	30	7	350	500
Concerning Transformation	ART	ART	1977	MM	25 X 34	AP	30	10	400	550
Departing	ART	ART	1977	MM	30 X 25	AP	30	8	350	450
Something Missing, Versions I, II	ART	ART	1977	MM	24 X 28 EA	AP	30 EA	10 EA	300 EA	450 EA
Only a Beautiful Picture	ART	ART	1978	SP	24 X 29	AP	30	10	300	450
Silent Thoughts	ART	ART	1979	SP	26 X 29	AP	30	20	350	500
Ephemera from an Ancient World	ARt	ART	1979	MM	25 X 34	AP	30	5	400	550
Just a Quick Note	ART	ART	1979	MM	30 X 24	AP	30	20	400	550
. . . and then when Separation, Version II, III	ART	ART	1980	SP	29 X 26 EA	AP	30 EA	7/10 EA	350 EA	500 EA
Family Reflections, Version II	ART	ART	1980	SP	28 X 31	AP	30	10	350	500
Rememberance of Things Past, Version II	ART	ART	1981	SP	28 X 37	AP	30	7	350	500

RAUL ANGUIANO

BORN: Guadalajara, Mexico; February 26, 1915
EDUCATION: Escuela Libre de Pintura, Guadalajara, Mex; Art Student's League, NY
TEACHING: Inst Nat de Bellas Artes, Mex; Univ Nat Autonoma, Mex
COLLECTIONS: Museo de Arte Moderno, Mexico City, Mex; Mus of Mod Art, NY; Palm Springs Desert Mus, CA; Museos Reales de Arte e Historia, Brussels, Belgium; Mus of Mod Art, San Francisco, CA; Arch of Monumental Art Mus, Lund, Sweden
PRINTERS: Taller de Kyron Ediciones Graficas Limitadas, SA, Mexico (TKE); La Poligrafa, Barcelona, Spain (LP); Artist (ART)
PUBLISHERS: Ocean Works, Medical Lake, WA (OW); Tallero Graphica Popular, Mexico City, Mex (TGP); Henri Duprest, Paris, France (HD); Leo Acosta, Mex (LA); Leo Burnette (LB); Lacouriere & Frelaut, Paris, France (L/F); Rotten Gallery (RG); Ediciones Graficas Coyoacan, Cruz Verde, Mexico (EGC); Ediciones Poligrafa, SA, Barcelona, Spain (EdP); Artist (ART)
GALLERIES: Salon de la Plastica Mexcana, Havre, Mex; Ediciones Graficas Coyoacan, Cruz Verde, Mexico; Galeria Joan Prats, New York, NY & Barcelona, Spain; B Lewin Galleries, Palm Springs, CA
MAILING ADDRESS: Francisco Sosa 114, Coyoacan, 04000, Mexico, DF, Mexico

TITLE	PUBLISHER	PRINTER	DATE	MEDIUM	DIMENSION (PAPER SIZE) IN INCHES	TYPE OF PAPER	EDITION NUMBER	NO. OF COLORS	ORIGINAL OPENING PRICE	CURRENT RETAIL PRICE
SOLD OUT EDITIONS (RARE):										
Carnival	TGP	ART	1939	LB	14 X 11	AP	30	1	15	500
Dichos Populares (Album of 6)	TGP	ART	1939	LB	16 X 12	AP	20	1	15	3500 SET
Muchacha con Manzana	LB	ART	1976	LC	20 X 28	AP	180	3	200	1000
Madre Huichola	ART	ART	1977	WB	12 X 8	AP	50	1	250	300
Llanto	HD	ART	1979	LB	25 X 20	AP	45	1	700	800
Llanto	ART	ART	1979	WB	12 X 12	AP	50	1	250	300
Carrera de Caballos	HD	ART	1979	LC	13 X 19	AP	40	3	400	500
Mascara Africana	HD	ART	1979	LC	19 X 13	AP	40	3	400	500
Mujer con Trubante	LA	ART	1980	LC	28 X 20	AP	150	3	600	700
Mujer en Hamaca	LA	ART	1980	LC	20 X 28	AP	100	3	600	700
Leda y el Cisne I	L/F	ART	1980	EB	13 X 15	AP	30	1	600	700
Leda y el Cisne II	L/F	ART	1980	EB	13 X 15	AP	30	1	400	500
Leda y el Cisne III	L/F	ART	1980	EB	12 X 7	AP	30	1	400	500
Orchida Nocturna	L/A	ART	1981	LC	23 X 17	AP	30	3	400	500
Mujer con Rebozo Blanco	OW	ART	1981	LC	30 X 23	AP	20	3	700	800
Dios Olmeco	ART	ART	1981	W	12 X 6	AP	20	2	300	400
Rebozo Blanco	EGC	TKE	1983	LC	31 X 23	AP	100	5	400	800
Set of Four Lithographs:									1600 SET	2000 SET
Lola	EdP	LP	1983	LC	29 X 22	AP	100	4	400	550
Muchacha de Oaxaca	EdP	LP	1983	LC	29 x 22	AP	100	4	400	550
Alfarera de Pehuantepec	EdP	LP	1983	LC	29 x 22	AP	100	4	400	550
Peinando a la Niña	EdP	LP	1983	LC	29 x 22	AP	100	4	400	550

SUZANNE C ANKER

BORN: Brooklyn, NY; August 6, 1946
EDUCATION: Brooklyn Col, NY, BA; Univ of Colorado, Boulder, CO, MFA
TEACHING: Asst Prof, Experimental Printmaking, Washington Univ, St Louis, MO, 1976–78; New York Univ, NY, presently
AWARDS: New York State Council on the Arts Award, Sculpture, 1989
COLLECTIONS: St Louis Mus, MO; Denver Art Mus, CO; Williams Col, Williamstown, MA; Santa Barbara Mus, CA; Santa Cruz County Mus, CA
PRINTERS: Landfall Press, Inc, Chicago, IL; Bud Shark, Boulder, CO (BS); Shark's, Inc, Boulder, CO (SI); Artist (ART); Jonathan Higgins, NY (JH); New York Univ, NY (NYU); Marjorie Van Dyke, NY (MVD); Printmaking Workshop, NY (PW)
PUBLISHERS: Landfall Press, Inc, Chicago, IL (LPI); Shark's, Inc, Boulder, CO (SI); Artist (ART); Mia Feroleto, NY (MF)
GALLERIES: Landfall Press, Inc, Chicago, IL; Solo Gallery, New York, NY
MAILING ADDRESS: 101 Wooster St, New York, NY 10012

TITLE	PUBLISHER	PRINTER	DATE	MEDIUM	DIMENSION (PAPER SIZE) IN INCHES	TYPE OF PAPER	EDITION NUMBER	NO. OF COLORS	ORIGINAL OPENING PRICE	CURRENT RETAIL PRICE
SOLD OUT EDITIONS (RARE):										
Dust Runners	ART	BS/SLL	1978	LC/HC	22 X 30	AP/W	32	3+	250	500
Satin Spar	SLL	BS/SLL	1979	LC/CO	22 X 30	AP/BL	13	2	450	750
Diamond Arbor (Spinner)	SLL	BS/SLL	1979	LB	22 X 30	R/BFK-NEWS/G	13	1	450	750
Lodestone	SLL	BS/SLL	1979	LB/CO	22 X 30	AC/BL	13	1	450	750
Push Bar	SLL	BS/SLL	1979	LC	22 X 30	AC/W	13	4	450	750
CURRENT EDITIONS:										
Desire's Muse	LPI	JL/LPI	1985	CP	29 X 29 X 2	HMP	10	12	900	1000
Blue Moon	ART	ART/DR	1985	CP	29 X 39 X 2	HMP	1 EA	Varies	1250 EA	1500 EA
Red Hot	ART	ART/DR	1985	CP	29 X 39 X 2	HMP	1 EA	Varies	1250 EA	1500 EA
Hot Rocks	ART	ART/DR	1985	CP	29 X 39 X 2	HMP	1 EA	Varies	1250 EA	1500 EA
If (Ever After)	ART	DR/RPMS	1986	CP/GRA	29 X 29 X 1	HMP	10	1	700	800
Wild Focus (Series of 20)	MF	MVD/PW	1990	PH/E/MON	18 X 22 EA	R/BFK/G	1 EA	Varies	1200 EA	1200 EA
Gene Pool	ART	JH/NYU	1991	LC/MON/CC	30 X 20 EA	AC-W/AP-BL	17 EA	Varies	700 EA	800 EA

The retail prices of the 100,000 limited edition prints quoted in this directory are subject to change. Print publishers, artists and galleries were the direct sources for these quotations. Prices in the secondary market listed as "Sold Out Editions (Rare)" indicate that the publisher has a limited supply of that print or that the print is difficult to locate in the galleries.

MICHAEL ANSELL

BORN: Jersey City, NJ; June 28, 1948
EDUCATION: Visual Communications, American University, Wash, DC, BA, 1970
COLLECTIONS: Midwest Mus of Contemp Art, Elkhart, IN
PRINTERS: Editions Press, San Francisco, CA (EP)
PUBLISHERS: Editions Press, San Francisco, CA (EP)
GALLERIES: Walton Gilbert Galleries, San Francisco, CA; J Rosenthal Fine Arts, Chicago, IL

TITLE	PUBLISHER	PRINTER	DATE	MEDIUM	DIMENSION (PAPER SIZE) IN INCHES	TYPE OF PAPER	EDITION NUMBER	NO. OF COLORS	ORIGINAL OPENING PRICE	CURRENT RETAIL PRICE
CURRENT EDITIONS:										
The In-Laws Come to Visit	EP	EP	1984	SP	24 X 36	AP	75	15	375	750

ELEANOR ANTIN

BORN: New York, NY; February 27, 1935
EDUCATION: City Col of New York, NY, BA
TEACHING: Univ of California, Irvine, CA, 1974–75; Asst Prof, Visual Arts, Univ of California, San Diego, CA, 1975–77
AWARDS: Nat Endowment for the Arts, Fel, 1979
RECENT EXHIB: Inst of Contemp Art, Los Angeles, CA, 1989
PRINTERS: Black Stone Press (BSP)
PUBLISHERS: Ronald Feldman Fine Arts, NY (RF)
GALLERIES: Ronald Feldman Fine Art, New York, NY; Tortue Gallery, Santa Monica, CA
MAILING ADDRESS: P O Box 1147, Del Mar, CA 92014

TITLE	PUBLISHER	PRINTER	DATE	MEDIUM	DIMENSION (PAPER SIZE) IN INCHES	TYPE OF PAPER	EDITION NUMBER	NO. OF COLORS	ORIGINAL OPENING PRICE	CURRENT RETAIL PRICE
CURRENT EDITIONS:										
Ballets for Diaghilev (Set of 18)	RF	BSP	1980	PH	14 X 11 EA	BP	5		10000	15000
Recollections of My Life with Diaghilev	RF	BSP	1980	PH	14 X 11 EA	BP	18		2000	3000

STEPHEN ANTONAKOS

BORN: Greece; November 1, 1926; US Citizen
EDUCATION: Brooklyn Community Col, NY
TEACHING: Brooklyn Mus Sch, NY
AWARDS: New York State Creative Artists Public Service Program, 1972; Nat Endowment for the Arts, 1973
RECENT EXHIB: Bali Miller Gallery, NY, 1988; Ileana Tounta Contemp Art Center, Athens, Greece, 1989; Fairleigh Dickinson Univ, Phyllis Rothman Gallery, Madison, NJ, 1989,92
COLLECTIONS: Guggenheim Mus, NY; Whitney Mus of Am Art, NY; Mus of Mod Art, NY; Milwaukee Art Center, WI; La Jolla Mus, CA; Aldrich Mus of Contemp Art, Ridgefield, CT; Newark Mus, NJ; Brandeis Mus, Waltham, MA; Wadsworth Atheneum, Hartford, CT; Univ of Utah, Salt Lake City, UT; Univ of Maine, Orono, ME; Univ of North Carolina, Greensboro, NC; Phoenix Art Mus, AZ; Milwaukee Inst of Art, WI
PRINTERS David Leach (DL); Wright State Univ, Dayton, OH (WSU); Julie D'Amario, NY (JD); Bill Hall, NY (BH); Printmaking Workshop, NY (PW)
PUBLISHERS: Artist (ART)
GALLERIES: John Weber Gallery, New York, NY; Ianuzzi Gallery, Scottsdale, AZ
MAILING ADDRESS: 435 W Broadway, New York, NY 10012

Stephen Antonakos
The Purple Square
Courtesy the Artist

TITLE	PUBLISHER	PRINTER	DATE	MEDIUM	DIMENSION (PAPER SIZE) IN INCHES	TYPE OF PAPER	EDITION NUMBER	NO. OF COLORS	ORIGINAL OPENING PRICE	CURRENT RETAIL PRICE
CURRENT EDITIONS:										
Incomplete Square	ART	SL/WSU	1975	SP	22 X 21	R/BFK	30	1	150	600
The Purple Square	ART	JD/BH/PW	1985	A/REL/WG	30 X 22	R/BFK	5		700	900

GARO ZAREH ANTREASIAN

BORN: Indianapolis, IN; February 16, 1922
EDUCATION: Herron Sch of Art, Indianapolis, IN, BFA, 1948; Art Students League, NY; Atelier 17, NY, with Stanley William Hayter, 1948–49
TEACHING: Herron Sch of Art, Indianapolis, IN, 1948–50, 1961–64; Technical Dir, Tamarind Lithography Workshop, Inc, Los Angeles, CA, 1960–61; Prof, Dept of Art, Univ of New Mexico, Albuquerque, NM, 1964 to present; Technical Dir, Tamarind Inst, Univ of New Mexico, Albuquerque, NM, 1970–72; Chmn, Dept of Art, Univ of New Mexico, Albuquerque, NM, 1981–84
AWARDS: Honorary Doctor of Fine Arts, Indiana/Purdue Universities, 1972; Senior Grant for Visual Artists, Nat Endowment for the Arts, 1982–83; Western States Print Invitational, Portland Art Mus, OR, 1985; Vis Lectr, Fulbright Award, Sao Paulo, Brazil, 1985
RECENT EXHIB: Coos Art Mus, Coos Bay, OR, 1989; Univ of New Mexico Art Mus, Albuquerque, NM, 1989,92
COLLECTIONS: Brooklyn Mus, NY; Art Inst of Chicago, IL; Guggenheim Mus, NY; Los Angeles County Mus, CA; Metropolitan Mus, NY; Mus of Mod Art, NY; Philadelphia Art Mus, PA; Mus of Fine Arts, Boston, MA

GARO ZAREH ANTREASIAN CONTINUED

PRINTERS: Jim Kraft, Albuquerque, NM (JK); Unified Arts, Albuquerque, NM (UA); John Sommers, Albuquerque, NM (JS); San Juan Studio, Albuquerque, NM (SJS); Bud Shark, Boulder, CO (BS); Matthew Christie, Boulder, CO (MC); Shark's Lithography, Ltd, Boulder, CO (SLL); Bill Weege, Madison, WI (BW); Andrew Rubin, Madison, WI (AR); Tandem Press, Univ of Wisconsin, Madison, WI (TanPr)
PUBLISHERS: Tamarind Inst, Albuquerque, NM (TI); Artist (ART); Shark's Lithography, Ltd, Boulder, CO (SLL); Tandem Press, Univ of Wisconsin, Madison, WI (TanPr)
GALLERIES: Robischon Gallery, Denver, CO; Alice Simsar Gallery, Ann Arbor, MI; Rettig y Martinez Gallery, Santa Fe, NM; Malton Gallery, Cincinnati, OH; Tamarind Inst, Albuquerque, NM; Babcock Galleries, New York, NY; Louis Newman Gallery, Beverly Hills, CA
MAILING ADDRESS: 7711 Hermanson Place, NE, Albuquerque, NM 87110

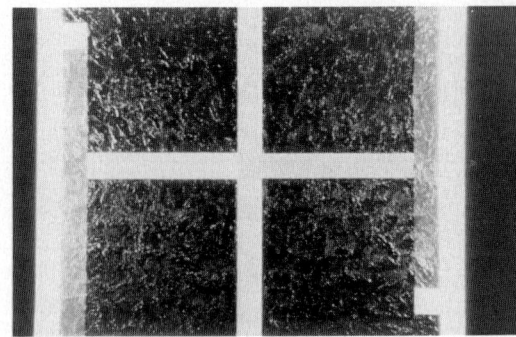

Garo Zareh Antreasian
Crossover I
Courtesy Shark's, Inc

Garo Zareh Antreasian
Crossover II
Courtesy the Shark's, Inc

Garo Zareh Antreasian
Untitled
Courtesy Tandem Press

TITLE	PUBLISHER	PRINTER	DATE	MEDIUM	DIMENSION (PAPER SIZE) IN INCHES	TYPE OF PAPER	EDITION NUMBER	NO. OF COLORS	ORIGINAL OPENING PRICE	CURRENT RETAIL PRICE
SOLD OUT EDITIONS (RARE):										
Magic City	ART		1954	LC	11 X 8	AP	16		75	350
Zenagir: Red (Pierced)	ART	JK/UA	1983	SP	38 X 46	AP88	8	6	950	1000
Tamam (Pierced)	TI	JC/TI	1985	LC/CC		AC/B	75	3	500	900
CURRENT EDITIONS:										
Ramagir A	ART	JK/UA	1983	SP/EM13	35 X 39	AP88	8	9	950	1000
Mohagir A	ART	JK/UA	1983	SP/EM13	37 X 49	AP88	8	9	950	1000
Mamigon	ART	JK/UA	1983	SP/EM13	40 X 38	AP88	16	7	950	1000
Malatya I	ART	AT/UA	1984	SP	34 X 25	AP88	10	2	600	700
Malatya II	ART	AT/UA	1984	SP	34 X 25	AP88	10	2	600	700
Malatya III	ART	AT/UA	1984	SP/PO	34 X 25	AP88	12	2/9	750	850
Yaman III	ART	AT/UA	1984	SP/PO	34 X 25	AP88	12	2/5	750	850
Bebek II	ART	AT/UA	1984	SP/PO	34 X 25	AP88	12	2/6	750	850
Mihrab	ART	MB/TI	1984	LB/CC	26 X 19	AC	12	1	550	650
Ayasofya I	ART	MB/TI	1984	LB/CC	26 X 19	AC	12	1	550	650
Galata II	ART	LPA/TI	1984	LB/CC	26 X 19	AC	12	1	550	650
Untitled	TanPr	BW/AR/TanPr	1987	LC	21 X 31	AC/W	50	2	750	1000
Crossover I,II	SLL	BS/MC/SLL	1989	LC	35 X 38 EA	R/BFK	25 EA	7/8 EA	1200 EA	1200 EA
Zervos	SLL	BS/MC/SLL	1989	MON	48 X 32 EA	AC/W	1 EA	Varies	2250 EA	2250 EA
Boulder Cut	SLL	BS/MC/SLL	1989	MON	48 X 32 EA	AC/W	1 EA	Varies	2250 EA	2250 EA

CRAIG KEITH ANTRIM

BORN: Pasadena, CA; September 6, 1942
EDUCATION: Univ of California, Santa Barbara, CA, BA with honors, 1965; Claremont Grad Sch, MFA, 1970
AWARDS: Ford Found Fel, 1963–65; California State Fel, Claremont Grad Sch, 1969–70
TEACHING: Asst Prof, Drawing, Design & Painting, Scripps Col, Claremont Grad Sch, CA, 1974–76; Instr, Painting & Drawing, Loyola Marymount Univ, Los Angeles, CA, 1983–85; Instr, Painting, Otis-Parsons Art Inst, Los Angeles, CA, 1986 to present
RECENT EXHIB: Los Angeles County Mus of Art, CA, 1986–87; Mus of Contemp Art, Chicago, IL, 1987; Gemeentemuseum, The Hague, The Netherlands, 1987
COLLECTIONS: Mus of Mod Art, NY; San Francisco Mus of Mod Art, CA; Corcoran Gallery of Art, Wash, DC; Univ of California, Los Angeles, CA
PRINTERS: Katherine Lincoln Press, San Francisco, CA (KLP)
PUBLISHERS: Katherine Lincoln Press, San Francisco, CA (KLP); Artist (ART)
GALLERIES: Ruth Bachofner Gallery, Santa Monica, CA; John Thomas Gallery, Santa Monica, CA; Magnolia Editions, Oakland, CA; Works Gallery, Long Beach, CA
MAILING ADDRESS: 1129 N La Brea Ave, Inglewood, CA 90302

TITLE	PUBLISHER	PRINTER	DATE	MEDIUM	DIMENSION (PAPER SIZE) IN INCHES	TYPE OF PAPER	EDITION NUMBER	NO. OF COLORS	ORIGINAL OPENING PRICE	CURRENT RETAIL PRICE
CURRENT EDITIONS:										
Talisman Suite, I, II, III (Set of 3)	ART	KLP	1983	EC	22 X 30	R/BFK/W	40	3	750 SET 250 EA	1200 SET 500 EA
Touchstone	ART	KLP	1983	EC/COL	22 X 30	R/BFK/W	30	3	250	500
Silver Sentence	ART/KLP	KLP	1984	COL	22 X 30	R/BFK/G	10	2	250	500
Solstice	ART/KLP	KLP	1984	COL	22 X 30	R/BFK/CR	10	2	250	500

RICHARD ANUSZKIEWICZ

BORN: Erie, PA; May 23, 1930
EDUCATION: Cleveland Inst of Art, BFA, 1953; Yale Univ, New Haven, CT, 1955; Kent State Univ, OH, BS Ed, 1956
TEACHING: Dartmouth Col, Hanover, NH, 1967; Univ of Wisconsin, 1968; Cornell Univ, Ithaca, NY, 1968; Kent State Univ, OH, 1968
AWARDS: Silvermine Guild, Philosophers Stone Prize, 1963, First Prize, 1964; Flint Inst, First Prize, PP, 1966
RECENT EXHIB: Solomon R Guggenheim Mus, NY, 1987; Richard Green Gallery, NY, 1988; Cleveland Inst of Art, OH, 1989; Arkansas State Univ, Fine Arts Gallery, State University, AR, 1989; Harman-Meek Gallery, Gallery of Fine Art, Fort Meyers, FL, 1989; Univ of Florida, Samuel P Harn Mus, Gainesville, Fl, 1990; Univ of South Florida, Graphicstudio, Tampa, FL, 1989,92
COLLECTIONS: Corcoran Gallery of Art, Wash, DC; Fogg Mus, Harvard Univ, Cambridge, MA; Hirshhorn Mus, Wash, DC; Mus of Mod Art, NY; Whitney Mus of Am Art, NY; Art Inst, Akron, OH; Chicago Art Inst, IL; Albright-Knox Mus, Buffalo, NY; Cleveland Mus of Art, OH; Butler Inst, Youngstown, OH; Allentown Art Mus, PA
PRINTERS: New York Inst of Technology, Old Westbury, NY (NYI); Norman Lassiter, NY (NL); Steve Maiorano, NY (SM); Editions Lassiter-Meisel, NY (ELM); American Atelier, NY (AA)
PUBLISHERS: Transworld Art, Inc, NY; Abrams Original Editions, NY (AOE); Arnerne Art, Inc, NY (AAI); Edward Weston NY (EWE); Circle Fine Art, Chicago, IL (CFA)
GALLERIES: Graphics Gallery, San Francisco, CA; Hokin Galleries, Palm Beach, FL & Bay Harbor Islands, FL; Harmon-Meek Gallery, Naples, FL; Corbino Galleries, Sarasota, FL; Charles Foley Gallery, Columbus, OH; Langman Gallery, Jenkintown, PA; Harcourts Modern & Contemporary Art, San Francisco, CA; Foster Harmon Galleries of American Art, Sarasota, FL; Topaz Editions, Inc, Tampa, FL; ACA Galleries, New York, NY; Eva J Pape Fine Arts, New York, NY; Ro Gallery Image Makers, Inc, New York, NY; Circle Galleries, Scottsdale, AZ & Beverly Hills, CA & Costa Mesa, CA & San Diego, CA & San Francisco, CA& Sherman Oaks, CA & Palm Beach, FL & Honolulu, HI & Chicago, IL & Northbrook, IL & New Orleans, LA & Las Vegas, NV & New York, NY & Pittsburgh, PA & Houston, TX & Seattle, WA

TITLE	PUBLISHER	PRINTER	DATE	MEDIUM	DIMENSION (PAPER SIZE) IN INCHES	TYPE OF PAPER	EDITION NUMBER	NO. OF COLORS	ORIGINAL OPENING PRICE	CURRENT RETAIL PRICE
SOLD OUT EDITIONS (RARE):										
Sequential (Set of 10)	SE	SE	1972	SP	28 X 21 EA	AP	200 EA		1000 SET	5000 SET
Reflections II-Red Line	EWE		1976	SP	64 X 45	AP	88		2500	5000
Reflections II-Green Line	EWE		1976	SP	64 X 45	AP	88		2500	5000
Reflections IV-Red	EWE		1976	SP	79 X 45	AP	88		2500	5000
Reflections IV-Grey	EWE		1976	SP	79 X 45	AP	88		2500	5000
New Glory	TAI	NL/SM	1976	SP	26 X 20	LEN	175	5	300	850
Soft Lime, with Signed Book	AOE	NL/SM	1976	SP	48 X 36	LEN	75	8	500	1000
Splendor of Orange	AOE	NL/ELM	1978	SP	33 X 33	LEN	100	3	350	850
Triangulated Green	PA	NL/ELM	1978	SP/MP	48 X 84	MP	50	3	2500	3000
Triangulated Orange	PA	NL/ELM	1978	SP/MP	48 X 84	MP	50	3	2500	3000
Red to Blue Portal	PA	NL/ELM	1978	SP/MP	48 X 84	MP	50	3	2500	3000
Blue to Red Portal	PA	NL/ELM	1978	SP/MP	48 X 84	MP	50	3	2500	3000
Reflections VII, Red Line	AAI		1979	SP/HC	65 X 47				4000	5000
Autumn V	CFA	AA	1980	EB	32 X 32	AP	95	1	450	850
Midnight V	CFA	AA	1980	EB	32 X 32	AP	95	1	450	850
Spring V	CFA	AA	1980	EB	32 X 32	AP	95	1	450	850

JAMES APONOVICH

BORN: Nashua, NH; May 8, 1948
EDUCATION: Univ of New Hampshire, Durham, NH; Rivier Col, Nashua, NH
TEACHING: Univ of New Hampshire, Durham, NH, 1987; Studio Sch of Drawing, Nashua, NH, 1991 to present
AWARDS: Pollack-Krasner Award, 1989
RECENT EXHIB: Louis Newman Gallery, Beverly Hills, CA, 1992; Peter Tatischeff, Inc, NY, 1993; Gerald Peters Gallery, Santa Fe, NM, 1993; Midtown-Payson Gallery, NY, 1993
COLLECTIONS: Mus of Fine Arts, Boston, MA; Art Inst of Chicago, IL; Arkansas Art Center, Little Rock, AR; DeCordova Mus, Lincoln, MA; Currier Gallery of Art, Manchester, NH; Cardigan Mountain Sch, Canaan, NH; Performing Arts Center, Manchester, NH; Chapel Art Center, Saint Anselm Col, Manchester, NH
PRINTERS: Herbert A Fox, Merrimac, MA (HF); Merrimac Editions, Merrimac, MA (MEd)
PUBLISHERS: Artist (ART); Fox Graphics, Merrimac, MA (FG); Merrimac Editions, Merrimac, MA (MEd)
GALLERIES: Gerald Peters Gallery, Santa Fe, NM; Midtown-Payson Gallery, New York, NY; Louis Newman Gallery, Beverly Hills, CA; Peter Tatischeff, Inc, New York, NY
MAILING ADDRESS: c/o Fox Graphics/Merrimac Editions, 4 Mechanic St, Merrimac, MA 01860

JAMES APONOVICH CONTINUED

TITLE	PUBLISHER	PRINTER	DATE	MEDIUM	DIMENSION (PAPER SIZE) IN INCHES	TYPE OF PAPER	EDITION NUMBER	NO. OF COLORS	ORIGINAL OPENING PRICE	CURRENT RETAIL PRICE
CURRENT EDITIONS:										
Apples	ART	HF/MEd	1989	LC	29 X 31	AP	100	16	500	1900
Peaches	ART	HF/MEd	1989	LC	32 X 29	AP	100	15	500	900
Oranges	ART	HF/MEd	1989	LC	32 X 29	AP	100	15	500	900
Beets	ART/FG/MEd	HF/MEd	1993	LC	30 X 40	AP	100	17	1500	1500

KAREL APPEL

BORN: Amsterdam, Holland; April 25, 1921
EDUCATION: Acad of Art, Amsterdam, The Netherlands, 1940–43
RECENT EXHIB: Marisa del Re, NY, 1987; Avanti Galleries, Inc, NY, 1990; Gallery Urban, NY, 1990; Univ of Maryland, Baltimore County, Catonsville, MD, 1992; Andre Emmerich Gallery, NY, 1992
COLLECTIONS: Mus of Mod Art, NY; Guggenheim Mus, NY; Mus Nat d'Art Mod, Paris, France; Stedelijk Mus, Amsterdam, The Netherlands; Baltimore Mus, MD; Mus of Fine Arts, Boston, MA; Albright-Knox Mus, Buffalo, NY; Chicago Inst of Art, IL; Detroit Inst of Art, MI; Tate Gallery, London, England; Walker Art Ctr, Minneapolis, MN; Vassar Col Mus, Poughkeepsie, NY; Toronto Art Gallery, Canada; Mus of Fine Art, Montreal, Canada
PRINTERS: Mourlot, Paris, France (M); Editions Press, San Francisco, CA (EP); Maeght Editions, Paris, France (ME); Atelier Nouveau, Paris, France (AN); Sienna Studios, NY (SIS); Joseph Kleineman, NY (JK); Perrin, Paris, France (P); Arte, Paris, France (ARTE); T Davis, San Francisco, CA (TD); M Sebastian, San Francisco, CA (MS); Jorge Dumas, NY (JD); Michael Caza, Francoville, France (MC); ABCD Editions, Paris, France (ABCD); La Poligrafa, Barcelona, Spain, SA (LP)
PUBLISHERS: Maeght Editions, Paris, France (ME); Editions Press, San Francisco, CA (EP); Transworld Arts, Inc, NY (TAI); Abrams Original Editions, NY (AOE); London Arts Inc, Detroit, MI (LAI); Post Oak Fine Art, Houston, TX (POFA); Metropolitan Art Associates, Huntington, NY (MAA); Circle Gallery, Ltd, Chicago, IL (CGL); ABCD Editions, Paris, France (ABCD); Ediciones Poligrafa, Barcelona, Spain, SA (EdP)
GALLERIES: Marisa del Re Gallery, New York, NY; David Anderson Gallery, Buffalo, NY; American-European Art Assoc, Inc, New York, NY; Short Hills Art Gallery, Short Hills, NJ; Jack Rutberg Fine Art, Los Angeles, CA; Michael Campbell Fine Art, Scottsdale, AZ; Stephen Gill Gallery, New York, NY; Jane Kahan Gallery, New York, NY; Alexander Kahan Fine Arts, New York, NY; Michelle Rosenfeld Fine Arts, New York, NY; Argus Fine Arts, Eugene, OR; Circle Galleries, San Diego, CA & San Francisco, CA & Northbrook, IL & Houston, TX & Pittsburgh, PA & Soho, NY & Chicago, IL & Scottsdale, AZ & Beverly Hills, CA & Costa Mesa, CA & Sherman Oaks, CA & Palm Beach, FL & Honolulu, HI & New Orleans, LA & Las Vegas, NV & Seattle, WA; Avanti Galleries, Inc, New York, NY; Gallery Urban, New York, NY & Paris, France & Tokyo, Japan; Metropolitan Art Gallery, Los Angeles, CA; Walton-Gilbert Galleries, San Francisco, CA; Galleria Maray, Allendale, NJ; Anderson Gallery, Brooklyn, NY; Bonnier Gallery, New York, NY; Thomas Erben Gallery, Inc, New York, NY; Andre Emmerich Gallery, New York, NY; Ro Gallery Image Makers, Inc, New York, NY

TITLE	PUBLISHER	PRINTER	DATE	MEDIUM	DIMENSION (PAPER SIZE) IN INCHES	TYPE OF PAPER	EDITION NUMBER	NO. OF COLORS	ORIGINAL OPENING PRICE	CURRENT RETAIL PRICE
SOLD OUT EDITIONS (RARE):										
Black Face	LAI		1969	LC	22 X 30	AP	75		125	6000
Deux Personages	LAI		1969	LC	22 X 30	AP	75		125	6000
Grand Tete	LAI		1969	LC	30 X 21	AP	100		125	6000
Homme Souriant	LAI		1969	LC	30 X 22	AP	75		125	6000
Happy Face	LAI		1969	LC	30 X 22	AP	75		125	6000
L'Hibour Rouge	LAI		1969	LC	30 X 22	AP	75		125	6000
Le Grande Torture	LAI		1969	LC	22 X 30	AP	75		125	6000
Le Chat	LAI		1969	LC	25 X 35	AP	100		325	3500
Le Cheval	LAI		1969	LC	30 X 22	AP	75		125	6000
Le Coup de Pied	LAI		1969	LC	30 X 22	AP	75		125	6000
Le Coup de Rouge	LAI		1969	LC	22 X 30	AP	75		125	6000
Looking Like Green	LAI		1969	LC	32 X 23	AP	100		250	6000
Personnage Volant	LAI		1969	LC	30 X 22	AP	75		250	6000
Personnage a la Cravatt	LAI		1969	LC	30 X 22	AP	75		125	6000
Personnage	LAI		1969	LC	30 X 22	AP	75		125	6000
Personnage & Oiseau	LAI		1969	LC	22 X 30	AP	75		125	6000
Tete de Femme	LAI		1969	LC	30 X 22	AP	100		125	6000
Bear	LAI		1970	LC	15 X 11	AP	300		125	4500
Dancing in the Spring	LAI		1970	LC	28 X 41	AP	100		325	6000
Dancing Man	LAI		1970	LC	32 X 23	AP	100		250	6000
Dream Colored Head	LAI		1970	LC	26 X 40	AP	100		325	6000
L'Oiseau	LAI		1970	SP	26 X 40	AP	90		350	6000
Monkey	LAI		1970	LC	15 X 11	AP	300		125	4500
Monstor	LAI		1970	LC	15 X 11	AP	300		125	4500
Mouse	LAI		1970	LC	15 X 11	AP	300		125	4500
Personage de Profil	LAI		1970	LC	30 X 21	AP	75		250	6000
Personage de Face	LAI		1970	LC	30 X 22	AP	100		125	6000
Red Face	LAI		1970	LC	32 X 23	AP	100		250	6000
Sourire	LAI		1970	LC	25 X 35	AP	100		250	6000
Yellow Face	LAI		1970	LC	32 X 23	AP	100		250	6000
Looking Around	LAI	EP	1971	LC	30 X 23	AP	100	8	250	7500
Love You So Much	LAI	EP	1971	LC	28 X 40	AP	100	8	250	7500
Three Figures	LAI	FP	1971	LC	26 X 40	AP	100	8	300	7500
Pink Nose Pussy	LAI	EP	1971	LC	25 X 35	AP	100	8	200	6000
Blue Eyed Creature	LAI	EP	1971	LC	25 X 35	AP	100		200	6000
Blue Faced Beast	LAI	EP	1971	LC	25 X 35	AP	100		250	6000
Blue Mask	LAI	EP	1971	LC	28 X 42	AP	100		300	5000
Cat with Yellow Eyes	LAI	EP	1971	LC	25 X 32	AP	100		200	6000
Child with His Pretend Animal	LAI	EP	1971	LC	28 X 41	AP	100		300	5000
Donkey	LAI	EP	1971	LC	28 X 40	AP	100		250	5000

KAREL APPEL CONTINUED

TITLE	PUBLISHER	PRINTER	DATE	MEDIUM	DIMENSION (PAPER SIZE) IN INCHES	TYPE OF PAPER	EDITION NUMBER	NO. OF COLORS	ORIGINAL OPENING PRICE	CURRENT RETAIL PRICE
SOLD OUT EDITIONS (RARE):										
Head One a One Wheel Wagon	LAI	EP	1971	LC	28 X 42	AP	100		300	5000
Head Pieces	LAI	EP	1971	LC	28 X 41	AP	100		300	5000
Head Like Clouds	LAI	EP	1971	LC	28 X 42	AP	100		300	5000
I am an Animal	LAI	EP	1971	LC	28 X 40	AP	100		325	5000
Mouse with Big Ears	LAI	EP	1971	LC	33 X 23	AP	100		250	5000
Red Cat	LAI	EP	1971	LC	28 X 40	AP	100		325	5000
Red Tail	LAI	EP	1971	LC	25 X 35	AP	100		200	6000
Tete	LAI	EP	1971	LC	25 X 35	AP	100		200	6000
Walking Alone	LAI	EP	1971	LC	40 X 26	AP	100		325	6000
Affiche avant Lettre	LAI	EP	1973	LC	31 X 24	AP	110		300	4500
Waiting For the Second Kiss	EP	EP	1974	LC/CO	27 X 34	CD	120	9	500	6000
Boy Jumping on a Blue Hat	EP	EP	1974	LC/CO	27 X 34	GE	120	8	500	6000
Come Back Pussy Cat	EP	EP	1974	LC/CO	27 X 34	CD	120	10	500	6000
Woman with Golden Eye	EP	EP	1974	LC/CO	27 X 34	R/BFK	120	11	500	6000
Sunshine People (Set of 10):										
Sunshine Face	LAI	EP	1974	LC	28 X 40	GE	110	8	450	5000
Colorful People	LAI	EP	1974	LC	28 X 41	AP	110		750	5000
Flower Hand	LAI	EP	1974	LC	28 X 41	AP	110		750	5000
Moving in the Wind	LAI	EP	1974	LC	28 X 41	AP	110		750	5000
Nothing to Do	LAI	EP	1974	LC	28 X 41	AP	110		750	5000
Smiling in the Sun	LAI	EP	1974	LC	28 X 41	AP	110		750	5000
Sun Flower Girls	LAI	EP	1974	LC	28 X 41	AP	110		750	5000
Sunny Beach Life	LAI	EP	1974	LC	28 X 41	AP	110		750	5000
Sunny Parrot in Landscape	LAI	EP	1974	LC	28 X 41	AP	110		750	5000
Sunshine Face	LAI	EP	1974	LC	28 X 41	AP	110		750	5000
Twins Maybe	LAI	EP	1974	LC	28 X 41	AP	110		750	5000
The Face (Yellow Plate)	ME	ARTE	1975	A/CAR	37 X 31	AP	50		450	5000
The Face (Blue Plate)	ME	ARTE	1975	A/CAR	37 X 31	AP	50		450	5000
The Face (Red Plate)	ME	ARTE	1975	A/CAR	37 X 31	AP	50		450	5000
The Face (Green Plate)	ME	ARTE	1975	A/CAR	37 X 31	AP	50		450	5000
The Face (Dark Yellow Plate)	ME	ARTE	1975	A/CAR	37 X 31	AP	50		450	5000
Seeing Eyes	TAI	M	1975	LC	26 X 20	AP	175	8	450	1500
Night Face in Broadway 5 Times	ME	ME	1975	EB/A	31 X 37	AP	50	8	600	3500
Homage a Mourlot	TAI	M	1976	LC	30 X 22	AP	125	8	450	3500
Flying Flower Passion	EP	TD/MS/EP	1977	LC	30 X 40	R/BFK	125	10	750	5000
The Kiss	EP	TD/EP	1977	LC	30 X 40	R/BFK	125	10	750	5000
Singing Hands Luke	EP	TD/EP	1977	LC	30 X 40	R/BFK	125	10	750	5000
Blue Kiss, Red Rose	LAI	EP	1978	SP	38 X 25	R/BFK	125	7	500	5000
Encounter in Yellow Fields	POFA	AN	1978	LC	21 X 30	SOM	160	8	500	5000
Floating Flower Passion	LAI	EP	1978	SP	38 X 26	R/BFK	125	8	500	3500
Gilt Edge Singing Hands	LAI	EP	1978	SP	41 X 30	R/BFK	125	5	500	3500
Cats (Set of 17)	LAI	P	1978	LC	22 X 30 EA	AP	125		17500 SET	30000 SET
I Pagliacci (Metropolitan Opera II)	CGL	MC	1978	LC	30 X 22	AP	250		500	3100
Black Eyed Animal	LAI	JK	1978	LC	20 X 26	SOM	175	8	450	3500
Mask Face	LAI	JK	1978	LC	22 X 30	SOM	175	8	500	3500
Moving in The Night	LAI	JK	1978	LC	22 X 30	SOM	175	9	500	3500
Philosophical Cat	POFA	AN	1978	LC	30 X 41	SOM	175	8	500	3500
Summer Couple	LAI	JK	1978	LC	22 X 30	AP	160	8	500	3500
Indigo Blue Singing Hands	LAI	EP	1978	SP	41 X 40	R/BFK	125	6	500	4000
Kool Luke Singing Hands	LAI	EP	1978	SP	41 X 30	R/BFK	125	5	500	4000
Putting Green Kiss	LAI	EP	1978	SP	30 X 41	R/BFK	125	6	500	4000
The Red Cap Singing Hands	LAI	EP	1978	SP	41 X 30	R/BFK	125	6	500	4000
Silvered Kiss	LAI	EP	1978	SP	30 X 41	R/BFK	125	7	500	4000
Sky Blue Kiss	LAI	EP	1978	SP	30 X 41	R/BFK	125	7	500	4000
With my Pussycat	LAI	JK	1978	LC	22 X 30	SOM	175	9	500	3500
Circus Volumes I, II, III (Set of 10)	ABCD	ABCD	1978	WC	30 X 22 EA	AP	130 EA		10000 SET	22000 SET
Street Kittens	AOE	SS	1979	LC/EMB	25 X 33	R/100	100	12	500	3500
Laughing Frog and all His Friends	EP	EP	1979	SP	41 X 72	AC/W	50	11	3500	6000
Sleepy Bird	LAI	JK	1979	LC	21 X 30	SOM	175	14	600	3500
Lying in Colors	LAI	JK	1979	LC	21 X 30	SOM	175	14	600	3500
Walking in Colors	LAI	JK	1979	LC	22 X 30	SOM	175	14	600	3500
Faces Together	MAA	SIS	1980	LC	30 X 22	AP	160		450	3500
Landscape Head	MAA	SIS	1980	LC	30 X 22	AP	160		450	3500
Loving Heads	MAA	SIS	1980	LC	30 X 22	AP	160		450	3500
Personnage in Blue	LAI	JK	1980	LC	29 X 22	SOM	175	15	600	3500
Dancing Girl	LAI	JK	1980	LC	29 X 22	SOM	175	14	600	3500
Blue Boy	LAI	JK	1980	LC	29 X 22	SOM	175	14	600	3500
Personnage in Red	LAI	JK	1980	LC	29 X 22	SOM	175	14	600	3500
Face	LAI	JK	1980	LC	21 X 30	SOM	175	14	600	3500
Ten by Appel (Set of 10)	LAI	JD	1981	LC	21 X 32 EA	SOM	175 EA	15 EA	10000 SET	40000 SET
CURRENT EDITIONS:										
Set of Five Etchings (Set of 5)	EdP	LP	1988	EC	30 X 22 EA	LP			5000 SET	10000 SET
									1000 EA	2000 EA

IDA APPLEBROOG

BORN: Bronx, NY; November 11, 1929
EDUCATION: New York State Inst of Applied Arts & Science, NY, 1950; Art Inst of Chicago, IL, 1965–68
TEACHING: Asst Instr, Painting, Art Inst of Chicago, IL, 1962–66; Instr, Painting & Sculpture, Univ of California, San Diego, CA 1973–74
AWARDS: Creative Artists Public Service Prog Fel, 1983; Nat Endowment for the Arts Grants, 1980,85; New York Found for the Arts Grants, 1986,90
RECENT EXHIB: Documenta 8, Kassel, Germany, 1987; Chrysler Mus, Norfolk, VA, 1987,89; Ronald Feldman Fine Arts, NY, 1987,89; Contemp Arts Mus, Houston, TX, 1988,90; Gallery Paule Anglim, San Francisco, CA, 1993
COLLECTIONS: Mus of Mod Art, NY; Metropolitan Mus of Art, NY; Solomon R Guggenheim Mus, NY; Denver Mus of Art, CO; Wadsworth Atheneum, Hartford, CT
PRINTERS: Judith Solodkin, NY (JS); Solo Press, NY (SP)
PUBLISHERS: Solo Press, NY (SP); Ronald Feldman Fine Arts, NY (RFFA)
GALLERIES: Ronald Feldman Fine Arts, New York, NY; Solo Gallery, New York, NY; Gallery Paule Anglim, San Francisco, CA
MAILING ADDRESS: 491 Broadway, New York, NY 10012

TITLE	PUBLISHER	PRINTER	DATE	MEDIUM	DIMENSION (PAPER SIZE) IN INCHES	TYPE OF PAPER	EDITION NUMBER	NO. OF COLORS	ORIGINAL OPENING PRICE	CURRENT RETAIL PRICE
CURRENT EDITIONS:										
Promise I Won't Die? (with Color Washes)	SP/RFFA	JS/SP	1987	LC/LI/WA/CO	36 X 48	AP/SEIK	45		3500	7500
Gulf + Western Plaza	SP/RFFA	JS/SP	1987	LC/HC	32 X 23	AC	45		1500	4000
"I will go before Thee, and Make the Crooked . . .	SP/RFFA	JS/SP	1989	LC	21 X 37	AC	81		1800	2500

EDMUNDO AQUINO

BORN: Zimatlan, Oaxaca, Mexico; June 30, 1939
EDUCATION: Nat Sch of Plastic Arts, Mexico City, Mexico, 1958–62; Ecole Nat Superieure des BeauxArts, Paris, France, 1967–69; Slade Sch of Fine Arts, London, England, 1970
TEACHING: Nat Sch of Plastic Arts, Mexico City, Mexico, 1963; Sch of Fine Arts, Oaxaca, Mexico, 1964–67
AWARDS: DAAD Fel, West Berlin, Germany, 1986
COLLECTIONS: Bibliotheque Nat, Paris, France; Mus of Mod Art of Latin America, Wash, DC; Museo de Arte Moderno, Mexico; Panamerican Graphic Art Coll, Reforma, Mexico; Mexican Mus, San Francisco, CA; Univ of Massachusetts, Amherst, MA
PRINTERS: Ernest F. DeSoto Workshop, San Francisco, CA (DSW); Raúl Soruco, Mexico City, Mexico (RS); Ediciones Multiarte, SA, Mexico City, Mexico (EdMult)
PUBLISHERS: Galeria de Arte Mexicano, Milan, Mexico (GAM); Ernest F. DeSoto Workshop, San Francisco, CA (DSW); Galeria Proteus, Estocolmo, Mexico (GP)(OB); Luis Remba, Ediart, SA, Tlalnepantla, Mexico (LR); Artist (ART); Raúl Soruco, Mexico City, Mexico (RS); Ediciones Multiarte, SA, Mexico City, Mexico (EdMult)
GALLERIES: Alfonso Rubio Art Gallery, Monterrey, Mexico; Carmen Llewellyn, New Orleans, LA; AliArte, SA, Mexico City, Mexico; Galeria JLS, Mexico City, Mexico
MAILING ADDRESS: Calle Ave Maria, 60–1, Coyoacan 04000, Mexico DF, Mexico

TITLE	PUBLISHER	PRINTER	DATE	MEDIUM	DIMENSION (PAPER SIZE) IN INCHES	TYPE OF PAPER	EDITION NUMBER	NO. OF COLORS	ORIGINAL OPENING PRICE	CURRENT RETAIL PRICE
SOLD OUT EDITIONS (RARE):										
Santero de Fiesta	GAM	PR WKSP	1978	E/AC	30 X 22	AP	25	3	140	400
CURRENT EDITIONS:										
Callejón del Desollado	LR	PR WKSP	1973	LC	30 X 22	FAB	99	4	140	300
Contradicciones del Espía	LR	PR WKSP	1973	LC	30 X 22	FAB	99	4	140	300
Invierno en Chartres	ART	PR WKSP	1974	SP	28 X 40	FAB	45	12	150	350
Intento Fallido	ART	PR WKSP	1974	SP	40 X 28	FAB	40	5	150	350
Entrespejos	ART	PR WKSP	1978	MEZ	13 X 13	FAB	50	1	60	150
Venus	GP	DSW	1981	LC	30 X 22	AP	100	4	400	450
Tenor	GP	DSW	1981	LC	30 X 22	AP	100	4	400	450
Los Mimos	GP	DSW	1981	LC	22 X 30	AP	100	4	400	450
Cazador de Mariposas	GP	DSW	1981	LC	22 X 30	AP	100	4	400	450
El Pescador	DSW	DSW	1981	LC	30 X 22	AP	100	4	400	450
Obelisco I–IV (Set of 4)	RS	RS	1987	LC	32 X 20 EA	Alpha	25 EA	3 EA	250 EA	400 EA
Paradiso Suite (Set of 6)	EdMult	EdMult	1991	SP	20 X 16 EA	AP	100 EA	9–10 EA	830 SET	1000 SET
									140 EA	170 EA

ARAKAWA (SHUSAKU)

BORN: Nagoya City Japan; July 6, 1936
EDUCATION: Univ of Tokyo, Japan, 1954–58; Col of Art, Boston, MA
AWARDS: DAAD Fel, W Berlin, Germany, 1972
RECENT EXHIB: van Straaten Gallery, Chicago, IL, 1987; Seibu Mus, Tokyo, Japan, 1987; Seibu Mus, Karuizawa, Japan, 1988; Univ of Hartford, Joseloff Gallery, West Hartford, CT, 1992; Univ of South Florida, Graphicstudio, Tampa, FL, 1992
COLLECTIONS: Mus of Mod Art, NY; Stedelijk Mus, Eindhoven, Netherlands; Basel Mus, Switzerland, Walker Art Center, Minneapolis, MN; Japan Nat Mus, Tokyo, Japan; Dayton Art Inst, OH; Hupestahl Mus, Germany; Metropolitan Mus of Art, NY; Solomon R Guggenheim Mus, NY; Seibu Mus, Tokyo, Japan
PRINTERS: Styria Studios, NY (SS); Patricia Branstead, NY (PB); Aeropress, NY (A); Gelb (G); Handworks, NY (H); Maurel Studio, NY (MS); Maeght Editeur, Paris, France (ME); Artist (ART)
PUBLISHERS: Multiples, NY (M); Abrams Original Editions, NY (AOE); Editions Schellmann & Klüser, Munich, West Germany (SK); Maeght Editions, Paris, France (ME); Artist (ART)
GALLERIES: Ronald Feldman Fine Arts, Inc, New York, NY; Gloria Luria Gallery, Bay Harbor Islands, FL; Dorothy Rosenthal Gallery, Chicago, IL; Marvin Ross Friedman & Co, Miami, FL; Peter M David Gallery, Minneapolis, MN; Virginia Lust Gallery, New York, NY
MAILING ADDRESS: 124 W Houston St, New York, NY 10012

TITLE	PUBLISHER	PRINTER	DATE	MEDIUM	DIMENSION (PAPER SIZE) IN INCHES	TYPE OF PAPER	EDITION NUMBER	NO. OF COLORS	ORIGINAL OPENING PRICE	CURRENT RETAIL PRICE
SOLD OUT EDITIONS (RARE):										
The Old Story (Explosion)	M	MS	1967	SP	35 X 27	AP	100		300	2500
La Gioconda			1970–71	SP	40 X 30	AP	100		400	4000

ARAKAWA (SHUSAKU) CONTINUED

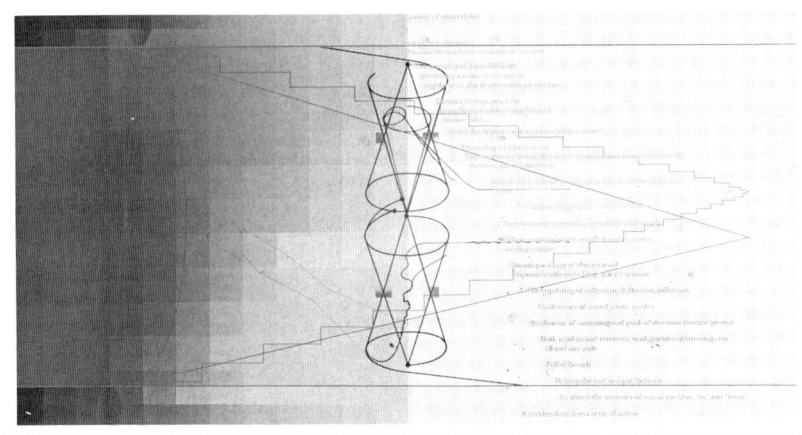

Arakawa (Shusaku)
Hypostalizing Distance
Courtesy Ronald Feldman Fine Art

TITLE	PUBLISHER	PRINTER	DATE	MEDIUM	DIMENSION (PAPER SIZE) IN INCHES	TYPE OF PAPER	EDITION NUMBER	NO. OF COLORS	ORIGINAL OPENING PRICE	CURRENT RETAIL PRICE
SOLD OUT EDITIONS (RARE):										
Evening of Which	M/ART	SS	1974	LC/SP	31 X 62	AP	60	Multi	900	6000
Iris Field	M	SS	1974	LC/SP/EMB	30 X 42	R/BFK	60	Multi	800	5000
Redolence	M	SS	1974	LC/SP/EMB	30 X 42	AP	60	Multi	800	5000
That in Which Series:										
That in Which #1	M	PB/A	1979	LC/SP	31 X 59	AP	25		1850	4500
That in Which #2	M	PB/A	1979	LC/SP	31 X 59	AP	25		1850	4500
That in Which #3	M	PB/A	1979	LC/SP	31 X 59	AP	25		1950	4500
A Forgettance (Exhaustion Exhumed) (Diptych)	M	PB/A	1974–75	LC	31 X 77 EA	AP	60	88	1750	4000
And/or In Profile	M	PB/A	1975	LC	31 X 42	AP	60	2	900	3500
Test Mirror	M	PB/A	1975	LC/SP/EMP	30 X 42	AP	100		900	3500
The Signified or if . . . (Set of 7)	M	PB/A	1975–76	EC/A/PH	30 X 42 EA	AP/B	60	3/3/12/4 3/9/11	6000 SET 900 EA	20000 SET 3000 EA
Flash Gravity	M	H/MS	1977	LC/SP/EMB	42 X 61	R/BFK	50	22	1600	6000
Out of Which	M	H/MS	1979	LC/SP	29 X 48	AP	35		1850	4500
In Voice/In and Around	M	H/MS	1979	LC/SP	30 X 45	AP	40		1850	4500
Blankless Tone	M	H/MS	1979	LC/SP	29 X 48	AP	35		1850	4500
In a Restrained Quantum	M	H/MS	1979	LC/SP	35 X 35	AP	40		1850	4500
Color Samples (Set of 3)	M	H/MS	1979	LC/SP	30 X 24 EA	AP	30/30/35		900 EA	3500 EA
Point Blank Series:										
Point Blank #1	M	H/MS	1979	LC/SP	31 X 59	AP	25		1850	4500
Point Blank #2	M	H/MS	1979	LC/SP	31 X 59	AP	28		1850	4500
Point Blank #3	M	H/MS	1979	LC/SP	31 X 59	AP	38		1850	4500
A Forgettance (Exhaustion Exhumed) (Diptych)	M	PB/A	1974–75	LC	31 X 77 EA	AP	60	88	1750	4000
And/or In Profile	M	PB/A	1975	LC	31 X 42	AP	60	2	900	3500
Test Mirror	M	PB/A	1975	LC/SP/EMP	30 X 42	AP	100		900	3500
The Signified or if . . . (Set of 7)	M	PB/A	1975–76	EC/A/PH	30 X 42 EA	AP/B	60	3/3/12/4 3/9/11	6000 SET 900 EA	20000 SET 3000 EA
Flash Gravity	M	H/MS	1977	LC/SP/EMB	42 X 61	R/BFK	50	22	1600	6000
Out of Which	M		1979	LC/SP	29 X 48	AP	35		1850	4500
In Voice/In and Around	M		1979	LC/SP	30 X 45	AP	40		1850	4500
Blankless Tone	M		1979	LC/SP	29 X 48	AP	35		1850	4500
In a Restrained Quantum	M		1979	LC/SP	35 X 35	AP	40		1850	4500
Color Samples (Set of 3)	M		1979	LC/SP	30 X 24 EA	AP	30/30/35		900 EA	3500 EA
Point Blank Series:										
Point Blank #1	M		1979	LC/SP	31 X 59	AP	25		1850	4500
Point Blank #2	M		1979	LC/SP	31 X 59	AP	28		1850	4500
Point Blank #3	M		1979	LC/SP	31 X 59	AP	38		1850	4500
Tomb of Chance	ART	ART	1974–80	LC	29 X 68	AP	46		3200	5000
Texture of Point Blank	ART	ART	1979–80	LC	35 X 60	AP	38		3200	5000
Texture of Point Blank, No. 2	ART	ART	1979–80	LC	35 X 60	AP	45		3200	5000
Hypostalizing Distance and/or Embodying Weight/the Call of . . .	ART	ART	1980	LC	36 X 64	AP	48		3200	5000
Within a Region of Blank	ART	ART	1980	LC	36 X 64	AP	48		3200	5000
Distance of Forming/Model/by Model/the	ART	ART	1980	LC	36 X 64	AP	48		3200	5000
Degrees of Blank	ART	ART	1981	LC/SP/EMB	38 X 66	AP	38		3200	5000
Outside Blank	ME	ME	1981	LC	38 X 5 cm	VC	100		4000 FF	10000 FF
Weight Without Place, No. 1	ART	ART	1981	LC/SP	37 X 68	AP	55	29	3250	5000
Weight Without Place, No. 2	ART	ART	1981	LC/SP/EMB	38 X 66	AP	45	12	3250	5000
Is As It: Blind Intensions (Set of 9)	SK	ART	1982–83	E/A/I/SG/REL	22 X 30	AC	55	Multi	10800 SET 1200 EA	20000 SET 2500 EA
Pregunta III (Painted Wooden Objects)	M	ART	1983	MULT	38 X 10	WOOD	6		2500	6000

CYNTHIA ARCHER

BORN: New Martinsville, WVA; March 28, 1953
EDUCATION: Goucher Col, Towson, MD, BA, 1975; West Virginia Univ, Morgantown, WVA, MFA, 1978
TEACHING: Instr, Printmaking, Bradley Univ, Peoria, IL, 1987
AWARDS: Purchase Award, Huntington Art Galleries, WVA, 1977; Governor's Award, Charleston, WVA, 1979; Merit Award, Beverly Art Center, Chicago, IL, 1982
RECENT EXHIB: Malton Gallery, Cincinnati, OH, 1987
COLLECTIONS: Nat Art Gallery, Wellington, New Zealand; Portland Art Mus, OR; Illinois State Mus, Springfield, IL; Mus of Art & Archeology, Univ of Missouri, Columbia, MO; Univ of Colorado, Boulder, CO; Frostburg State Col, MD; Huntington Art Galleries, WVA; Northwestern Univ, Evanston, IL
PUBLISHERS: Plucked Chicken Press, Evanston, IL (PCP)
PRINTERS: Plucked Chicken Press, Evanston, IL (PCP); Artist (ART)
GALLERIES: Lakeside Studios, Lakeside, MI; Campanile Galleries, Chicago, IL; Charlotte Brauer Fine Art, Munster, IL
MAILING ADDRESS: c/o Plucked Chicken Press, 1604 Greenleaf, Evanston, IL 60202

TITLE	PUBLISHER	PRINTER	DATE	MEDIUM	DIMENSION (PAPER SIZE) IN INCHES	TYPE OF PAPER	EDITION NUMBER	NO. OF COLORS	ORIGINAL OPENING PRICE	CURRENT RETAIL PRICE
CURRENT EDITIONS:										
Lydian Cypher	PCP	ART/WP/PCP	1985	MULT	40 X 30	R/BFK			400	450

DANIEL ARGIMON

BORN: Barcelona, Spain; 1929
RECENT EXHIB: Galerie Joan Oliver, Palma de Mallorca, Spain, 1987; Galeria Nomen, Barcelona, Spain, 1987; Galeria Ambit, Barcelona, Spain, 1987; Galerie Cuenca, Ulm, Germany, 1988; Franz Spiegel Buch, GmbH, Ulm, Germany, 1988; Galerie Baumgarten, Freiburg, Germany, 1988; Museo Montsia, Amposta, Tarragona, Spain, 1988
PRINTERS: La Poligrafa, SA, Barcelona, Spain (LP)
PUBLISHERS: Ediciones Poligrafa, SA, Barcelona, Spain (EdP)
GALLERIES: Galeria Joan Prats, New York, NY & Barcelona, Spain

TITLE	PUBLISHER	PRINTER	DATE	MEDIUM	DIMENSION (PAPER SIZE) IN INCHES	TYPE OF PAPER	EDITION NUMBER	NO. OF COLORS	ORIGINAL OPENING PRICE	CURRENT RETAIL PRICE
CURRENT EDITIONS:										
Set of Five Etchings:									1200 SET	1600 SET
Brotxa	EdP	LP	1977	EC	22 X 30	GP	75	4	250	350
Paleta	EdP	LP	1977	EC	22 X 30	GP	75	4	250	350
Rosset	EdP	LP	1977	EC	22 X 30	GP	75	4	250	350
Serra	EdP	LP	1977	EC	22 X 30	GP	75	4	250	350
Aixa	EdP	LP	1977	EC	22 X 30	GP	75	4	250	350

ARMAN (ARMAND FERNANDEZ)

BORN: Nice, France; November 17, 1928; U S Citizen
EDUCATION: Ecole Nat d'Art Decoratif, Nice, France, 1946–49; Ecole du Louvre, Paris, France, 1949–51
TEACHING: Instr, Univ of California, Los Angeles, CA, 1967–68
AWARDS: L'Order de Merit, Paris France, 1972; Commandeur des Arts et Letters, Paris, France, 1984
RECENT EXHIB: Mus Beaux Arts, Nimes, France, 1988; Retrosp, Pavillion Werd, Zürich, Switzerland, 1988; Arkansas State Univ, Fine Arts Gallery, State Univ, AR, 1989; Mayor Gallery, London, England, 1989; Galerie Heinz Holtmann, Cologne, Germany, 1991; Marisa del Re, NY, 1992; Brooklyn Mus, NY, 1992
COLLECTIONS: Mus of Mod Art, NY; Metropolitan Mus, NY; Stedelijk Mus, Einhoven, Netherlands, Albright-Knox Mus, Buffalo, NY; Walker Art Center, Minneapolis, NM; Mus of Contemp Art, Chicago, IL; Hirshhorn Mus, Wash, DC; Peggy Guggenheim Coll, Venice, Italy; Mus of Mod Art, Paris, France; Galleria d'Arte Mod, Rome, Italy; Louisiana Mus, Denmark; Mus of Mod Art, Stockholm, Sweden
PRINTERS: Alexander Heinrici, NY (AH); Studio Heinrici, NY (SH); Atelier Badet, Paris, France (AB); Artist (ART)
PUBLISHERS: London Arts, Inc, Detroit, MI (LAI); Contemporary Art Masters, NY (CAM); Abrams Original Editions, NY (AOE); Prestige Art Ltd, Mamaroneck, NY (PA); Edition Schellmann, Munich, Germany & NY (ES); John Gibson, NY (JG)
GALLERIES: London Arts Gallery, Detroit, MI; Riva Yares Gallery, Scottsdale, AZ & Santa Fe, NM; Wenger Gallery, Los Angeles, CA; Marvin Ross Friedman & Co, Miami FL; Marisa del Re Gallery, New York, NY; Mayor Gallery, London, England; John Gibson Gallery, New York, NY; Galerie Heinz Holtmann, Cologne, Germany; Wenger Gallery, Los Angeles, CA; Rembla Gallery, Mixografia Workshop, Santa Monica, CA; Freites-Revilla Gallery, Boca Raton, FL; Gloria Luria Gallery, Bay Harbor Islands, FL; J Rosenthal Fine Arts, Chicago, IL; A/D Gallery New York, NY; Karen Amiel Modern & Contemporary Art, New York, NY; Artes Magnus, New York, NY; Thomas Erben Gallery, New York, NY; Locks Gallery, Phila, PA; Phyllis Hattis Fine Arts, New York, NY; Ro Gallery Image Makers, Inc, New York, NY; Edition Schellmann, New York, NY
MAILING ADDRESS: 430 Washington St, New York, NY 10013

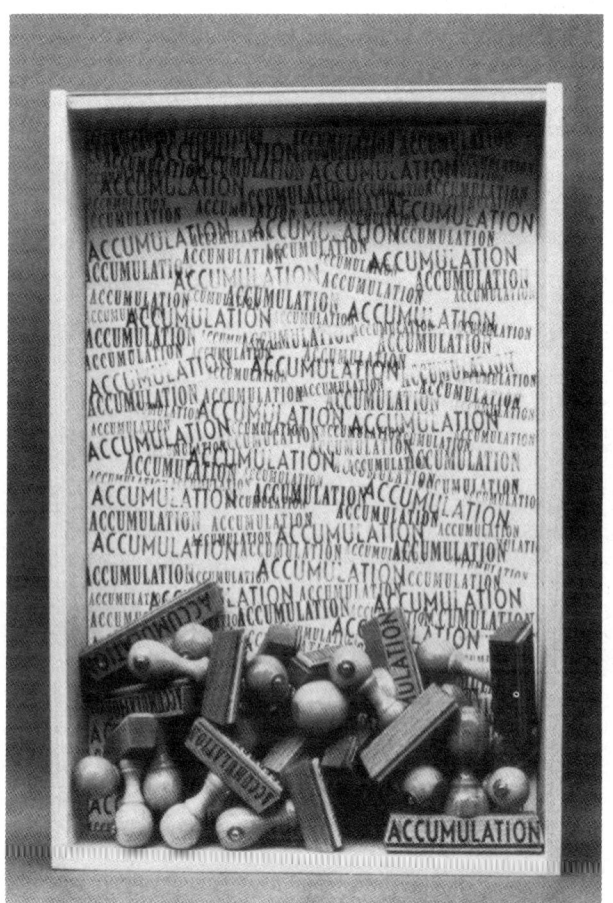

Arman (Armand Fernandez)
Accumulation
Courtesy Edition Schellmann

ARMAN CONTINUED

TITLE	PUBLISHER	PRINTER	DATE	MEDIUM	DIMENSION (PAPER SIZE) IN INCHES	TYPE OF PAPER	EDITION NUMBER	NO. OF COLORS	ORIGINAL OPENING PRICE	CURRENT RETAIL PRICE
SOLD OUT EDITIONS (RARE):										
Accumulation (Stamped Print and Rubber Stamps in Natural Wood Box with Plexiglas)	ES/JG	ART	1973	MULT	18 X 12 X 3	Wood	100		1500	7500
CURRENT EDITIONS:										
Romantic Suite Set (A–F):	PA	AB	1976	LC	24 X 37 EA	AP	100 EA	9 EA	500 EA	750 EA
Grey Mood	LAI	AH/SH	1978	SP	30 X 23	AP	150	4	275	750
Intermission	LAI	AH/SH	1978	SP	30 X 23	AP	150	4	275	750
Romanticism in Gold	LAI	AH/SH	1978	SP	29 X 22	AP	150	4	275	750

ROBERT ARNESON

BORN: Benicia; CA; (1930–1992)
EDUCATION: California Col of Arts & Crafts, Oakland, CA, BA, 1954; Mills Col, Oakland, CA, MFA, 1958
TEACHING: Mills Col, Oakland, CA, 1960-62; Univ of California, Davis, CA, 1962 to present
RECENT EXHIB: Portland Art Mus, OR, 1986–87; Everson Art Mus, Syracuse, NY, 1988; Mus of Mod Art, NY, 1987–88; Palm Springs Desert Mus, CA, 1989; Redding Mus & Art Center, CA, 1989; Richmond Art Center, CA, 1989; Frumkin/Adams Gallery, NY, 1990, 92; Univ of California, Richard L Nelson Gallery, Davis, CA; Palm Springs Desert Mus, CA, 1992; Palo Alto Cultural Center, CA, 1992; Miami-Dade Com Col, Miami, FL, 1992; Moravian Col, Payne Col, Bethlehem, PA, 1992; James Madison Univ, Sawhill Gallery, Harrisonburg, VA, 1992; Univ of Wisconsin, Carlsten Art Gallery, Stevens Point, WI, 1992
COLLECTIONS: Oakland Art Mus, CA; Santa Barbara Mus of Art, CA; Univ of California Mus, Berkeley, CA; Nat Mus of Mod Art, Kyoto, Japan; San Francisco Mus of Mod Art, CA

PRINTERS: Landfall Press, Inc, Chicago, IL (LPI); Jack Lemon, Chicago, IL (JL); Timothy Berry, Chicago, IL (TB); David Keister, Chicago, IL (DK); Mary McDonald, Chicago, IL (MM); Wil Foo (WF); John Stemmer (JS); Experimental Workshop, San Francisco, CA (EW)
PUBLISHERS: Landfall Press, Inc, Chicago, IL (LPI); Experimental Workshop, San Francisco, CA (EW)
GALLERIES: Frumkin/Adams Gallery, New York, NY; Fuller Gross Gallery, San Francisco, CA; Dorothy Goldeen Gallery, Santa Monica, CA; Fendrick Gallery, Wash, DC; Ochi Galleries, Boise, ID & Sun Valley, ID; Kass/Meridian Gallery, Chicago, IL; Klein Gallery, Chicago, IL; Flanders Contemp Art, Minneapolis, MN; Stremmel Gallery, Reno, NV; Charles Cowles Gallery, New York, NY; Garner Tullis, New York, NY; Experimental Workshop, San Francisco, CA; Riva Yares Galleries, Scottsdale, AZ & Santa Fe, NM; Struve Gallery, Chicago, IL; John Natsoulas Gallery, Davis, CA; John Berggruen Gallery, San Francisco, CA; Magnolia Editions, Oakland, CA; Brian Gross Fine Art, San Francisco, CA; Dorothy Goldeen Gallery, Santa Monica, CA
MAILING ADDRESS: c/o Art Dept, University of California, David, CA 95616

TITLE	PUBLISHER	PRINTER	DATE	MEDIUM	DIMENSION (PAPER SIZE) IN INCHES	TYPE OF PAPER	EDITION NUMBER	NO. OF COLORS	ORIGINAL OPENING PRICE	CURRENT RETAIL PRICE
SOLD OUT EDITIONS (RARE):										
Untitled	LPI	DK	1975	LC	23 X 30	AC/W	38	7	250	1200
Rock Cup	LPI	TB/LPI	1977	SG/EB	11 X 12	AP/W	10	1	200	600
Nuclear War Head	EW	WF/JS/EW	1983	WB	42 X 56	R/BFK	10	1	1200	2000
Five Guys (Set of 4)	EW	WF/JS/EW	1983	WC	31 X 25 EA	HMP	25 EA	2 EA	1200 SET	3600 SET
									300 EA	900 EA
CURRENT EDITIONS:										
Brick Suite (Set of 4 Plus 1 Ceramic Brick Multiple):									700 SET	2000 SET
New Brick/Old Stone	LPI	JL/LPI	1976	LC	16 X 17	AP/W	50	4	175	500
Moby Brick	LPI	JL/LPI	1976	LC	16 X 17	AP/W	50	4	175	500
Broken Brick	LPI	TB/LPI	1976	SG/AB	16 X 17	AP/W	50	1	175	500
California Brick	LPI	TB/LPI	1976	SG/AB	16 X 17	AP/W	50	1	175	500
Angle Brick	LPI	TB/LPI	1979	SG/EC	11 X 15	AP/W	20	3	200	300
Flat Brick	LPI	TB/LPI	1979	SG/EC	11 X 15	AP/W	20	3	200	300
Up against It	LPI	MM/LPI	1980	LC	40 X 30	AP/W	35	6	600	1200
Pic	LPI	MM/LPI	1980	LC	40 X 30	AP/W	35	4	500	1500
A Hollow Jesture	LPI	JL/LPI	1980	LC	40 X 30	AP/W	35	5	600	1500
Squint	LPI	JL/LPI	1981	LC	40 X 30	AP/W	35	6	750	1500
Son of Sam	LPI	JL/LPI	1981	LC	28 X 38	AP/W	35	4	600	1200
General Nuke	LPI	JL/LPI	1986	LC/HC	36 X 28	R/BFK/GRAY	25	9	600	1200
The Colonel is at it Again	LPI	JL/LPI	1986	LC/HC	40 X 30	AP/W	26	9	900	1500
Rembrandt J	EW	EW	1986–87	CP/HC	55 X 42 X 12	HMP				

JOYCE ARONS

BORN: April 3, 1948

EDUCATION: Moore Col of Art, Phila, PA, BFA, 1970; Hoffberger Sch of Painting, Md Inst of Art, MFA, 1973
PRINTERS: J K Fine Art, NY (JK); Fine Creations, NY (FC)
PUBLISHERS: Transworld Art, Inc, NY (TAI)

TITLE	PUBLISHER	PRINTER	DATE	MEDIUM	DIMENSION (PAPER SIZE) IN INCHES	TYPE OF PAPER	EDITION NUMBER	NO. OF COLORS	ORIGINAL OPENING PRICE	CURRENT RETAIL PRICE
SOLD OUT EDITIONS (RARE):										
Ford	TAI	JK	1979	LB	30 X 22	EX/100	250	1	200	250
Frame 46	TAI	JK	1979	SP	29 X 23	RG/100	250	4	200	250
Rides	TAI	JK	1979	SP	23 X 29	RG/100	250	4	200	250

JOYCE ARONS CONTINUED

TITLE	PUBLISHER	PRINTER	DATE	MEDIUM	DIMENSION (PAPER SIZE) IN INCHES	TYPE OF PAPER	EDITION NUMBER	NO. OF COLORS	ORIGINAL OPENING PRICE	CURRENT RETAIL PRICE
SOLD OUT EDITIONS (RARE):										
Moths	TAI	JK	1979	SP	29 X 23	RG/100	250	4	200	250
Dandelion	TAI	JK	1979	LC	22 X 30	EX/100	250	2	200	250
Fly $3	TAI	JK	1979	SP	29 X 23	RG/100	250	6	200	250
Fairchild	TAI	JK	1979	LC	21 X 28	RG/100	250	6	200	250
ABC	TAI	JK	1979	LC	29 X 23	RG/100	250	8	200	250

CHARLES ARTHUR ARNOLDI

BORN: Dayton, OH; April 10, 1946
EDUCATION: Chouinard Art Sch, Los Angeles, CA 1968
AWARDS: Wittowsky Award, Art Inst of Chicago, IL, 1972; John Simon Guggenheim Found Fel, NY, 1975; Nat Endowment for the Arts Fel, Wash, DC, 1974,82; Maestro Fel, California Arts Council, 1982
RECENT EXHIB: Charles Cowles Gallery, NY, 1987; Texas Gallery, Houston, TX, 1987; Asahi Shimbun Gallery, Tokyo, Japan, 1987; James Corcoran Gallery, Los Angeles, CA, 1987; Univ of Missouri, Kansas City, MO, 1987; Kansas City Gallery of Art, MO, 1987; Sena Galleries West, Santa Fe, NM, 1987,88; Metropolitan Mus of Art, NY, 1988; Pamela Auchincloss Gallery, NY, 1989; Garner Tullis Gallery, NY, 1990; Arthur Roger Gallery, New Orleans, LA, 1990; Michael Dunev Gallery, San Francisco, CA, 1990; Malmgran Gallery, Goteborg, Sweden, 1990; Flanders Contemp Art, Minneapolis, MN; Sena Galleries West, Santa Fe, NM, 1990; Gallery Kuranuki, Osaka, Japan, 1991; Fred Hoffman Gallery, Santa Monica, CA, 1991; Ochi Gallery, Ketchum, ID, 1991; Klein Art Works, Chicago, IL, 1992
COLLECTIONS: Los Angeles County Art Mus, CA; Mus of Mod Art, NY; Art Inst of Chicago, IL; Metropolitan Mus of Art, NY; San Francisco Mus of Mod Art, CA
PRINTERS: Landfall Press, Inc, Chicago, IL (LPI); Jack Lemon, Chicago, IL (JL); Centrum Press, Port Townsend, WA (CP); New City Editions, NY (NCE); Artist (ART)
PUBLISHERS: Landfall Press, Inc, Chicago, IL (LPI); Centrum Press, Port Townsend, WA (CP); Timothy Berry (TB); Joel Stearns (JS); New City Editions, Venice, CA (NCE)
GALLERIES: The Texas Gallery, Houston, TX; Garner Tullis Workshop, Santa Barbara, CA; New City Editions, Venice, CA; Charles Cowles Gallery, New York, NY; Flanders Contemporary Art, Minneapolis, MN; Arthur Roger Gallery, New Orleans, LA; Michael Dunev Gallery, San Francisco, CA; Malmgran Gallery, Goteborg, Sweden; Gallery Kuranuki, Osaka, Japan; Fred Hoffman Gallery, Santa Monica, CA; Ochi Gallery, Sun Valley, ID & Boise, ID; Klein Art Works, Chicago, IL; Charles Whitchurch Gallery, Huntington Beach, CA; The Works Gallery, Long Beach, CA; Brian Gross Fine Art, San Francisco, CA; Kass/Meridian Gallery, Chicago, IL; Stremmel Gallery, Reno, NV; Sena Galleries, Santa Fe, NM; Herbert Palmer Gallery, Los Angeles, CA
MAILING ADDRESS: 721 Hampton Dr, Venice, CA 90291

Charles Arthur Arnoldi
Night Repair
Courtesy Landfall Press, Inc

TITLE	PUBLISHER	PRINTER	DATE	MEDIUM	DIMENSION (PAPER SIZE) IN INCHES	TYPE OF PAPER	EDITION NUMBER	NO. OF COLORS	ORIGINAL OPENING PRICE	CURRENT RETAIL PRICE
SOLD OUT EDITIONS (RARE):										
For Decisions and Revisions	LPI	JL/LPI	1982	LC	24 X 30	AP/W	50	8	600	2000
Night Repair	LPI	JL/LPI	1982	LC	32 X 27	R/BFK	25	3	450	1750
Untitled	CP	TB/CP	1982	EB/A	17 X 23	R/BFK	50	3	400	1300
Untitled	CP	TB/CP	1982	EB/A	15 X 17	R/BFK	50	2	400	1300
Untitled #2	NCE	JS/NCE	1983	WB/REL	24 X 37	RICE	45		500	3000
Untitled #4	NCE	JS/NCE	1983	WB	48 X 37	AC	70		500	6000
Series of 46 Wood-Relief Monoprints:										
20 Monoprints	NCE	ART	1985	WB/MON	67 X 56 EA	HMP	1 EA		5750	10000
26 Monoprints	NCE	ART	1985	WB/MON	90 X 74 EA	HMP	1 EA		10000	20000

RICHARD ARTSCHWAGER

BORN: Washington, DC; December 26, 1923
EDUCATION: Cornell Univ, Ithaca, NY, BA
AWARDS: Nat Endowment for the Arts Fel, 1971
RECENT EXHIB: Whitney Mus of American Art, NY, 1988; Palacio de Velásquez, Madrid, Spain, 1989; Mus Nat d'Art Mod, Paris, France, 1989; Städtische Kunsthalle, Düsseldorf, West Germany, 1989; Columbia Univ, Wallach Art Gallery, NY, 1989; Leo Castelli Gallery, NY, 1989; Kent Gallery, NY, 1989; Fairleigh Dickinson Univ, Phyllis Rothman Gallery, Madison, NJ, 1989,92; Mary Boone Gallery, NY, 1993
COLLECTIONS: Mus of Mod Art, NY; Whitney Mus of Am Art, NY; Detroit Inst of Art, MI, Kunstmus, Basle, Switzerland; Wallraf-Richartz Mus, Cologne, Germany; Rotterdam Mus, Holland; Chicago Art Inst, IL; Tate Gallery, London, England
PRINTERS: Sally Mara Sturman, NY (SMS); Kevin Auster, NY (KA); Branstead Studio, NY (BS); Aeropress, NY (A); Patricia Branstead, NY (PB); A Kirk (AK)
PUBLISHERS: Multiples, NY (M); Brooke Alexander, Inc, NY (BAI)
GALLERIES: Daniel Weinberg, Santa Monica, CA; Donald Young Gallery, Seattle, WA; Susanne Hilberry Gallery, Birmingham, MI; Leo Castelli Graphics, New York, NY; Judith Goldberg Gallery, New York, NY; Kent Fine Art, New York, NY; Jan Krugier Gallery, New York, NY; Marian Goodman Gallery, New York, NY; Pence Fine Art, Inc, Los Angeles, CA; Goodman/Tinnon Fine Art, San Francisco, CA; Mary Boone Gallery, New York, NY; Bonnier Gallery, New York, NY; Locks Gallery, Phila, PA
MAILING ADDRESS: 158 S Oxford St, Brooklyn, NY 11217–1604

RICHARD ARTSCHWAGER CONTINUED

TITLE	PUBLISHER	PRINTER	DATE	MEDIUM	DIMENSION (PAPER SIZE) IN INCHES	TYPE OF PAPER	EDITION NUMBER	NO. OF COLORS	ORIGINAL OPENING PRICE	CURRENT RETAIL PRICE
SOLD OUT EDITIONS (RARE):										
Untitled (Wooden Box with Five Drawers)	M		1971	MULT	13 X 15 X 13	WOOD	50			10000
Untitled (Two-Part Object in the Form of Quotation Marks-Painted on Wood & Formica)	M		1980	MULT	13 X 10 X 2	WOOD/FOR	50			POR
Untitled	M	PB/A	1981	EB	29 X 35	AC	20	1	500	3500
Untitled	M	PB/A	1981	EB	30 X 32	AC	20	1	450	3500
Cactus Scape II	M	PB/A	1981	EB	32 X 37	AC	20	1	450	3500
Door (Formica, Hardware, Wood)	BAI		1987	MM	18 X 25 X 5		25		8000	12000
Fractal	BAI		1987	MM	17 X 17 X 6		25		8000	10000
Hair Blp (Ruberized Horsehair)	BAI		1989	MM	½ X 7 X 13		25		1000	1500
Bookends (Formica on Wood)	BAI		1990	MM	7 X 7 X 4		50		4000	5000
CURRENT EDITIONS:										
Interior #1 (Two Plants)	M	PB/A	1977	EB	24 X 21	AC	45	1	350	1500
Interior #2 (Woodgrain)	M	AK/A	1977	DPT/E/Z	23 X 19	AC	45	1	300	1400
Interior #3	M	AK/A	1977	DPT/E/Z	24 X 19	AC	35	1	300	1400
Mount St Helen's	M	PB/A	1981	EB	24 X 21	AC	20	1	350	2500
Cactus Scape I	M	PB/A	1981	EB	34 X 29	AC	20	1	400	3000
Set of 3:									18000 SET	18500 SET
Building Riddled with Listening Devises (Alpha)	M	PB/A	1990	EB/SG/A/BUR/DPT	33 X 35	AC	60		6000	6000
Building Riddled with Listening Devises (Beta)	M	PB/A	1990	EB/SG/A/BUR/DPT	33 X 35	AC	60		6000	6000
Horizon	M	PB/A	1990	EB/SG/A/BUR/DPT	35 X 48	AC	60		6000	6000
Four Approximate Objects (Mahogany, Formica, Brass Chrome, Painted Brass & Flocking)	BAI		1970–91	MM	4 X 15 X 14		30		12000	12000
Cherokee	M	SMS/KA/BS	1991	AC/SG/DPT/SB	39 X 51	R/BFK	60	2	2500	2500
Corner (Painted Wood, Formica & Chrome Plated Steel)	BAI		1991–92	MM	36 X 15 X 5		30		6000	6000

Richard Artschwager
Cherokee
Courtesy Multiples, Inc

KYOKO ASANO

BORN: Tokyo, Japan; December 23, 1933
EDUCATION: Mt San Antonio Col, Walnut, CA, AA, 1969; California State Univ, Fullerton, CA, BA, 1971, MA, 1972; Claremont Grad Sch, MFA, 1978
RECENT EXHIB: West Hills Col, Coalinga, CA, 1987; Cirrus Gallery, Los Angeles, CA, 1988,92
COLLECTIONS: Mt San Antonio Col, Walnut, CA; Scripps Inst of Oceanography, La Jolla, CA
PRINTERS: Richard Hammond, Los Angeles, CA (RH); Francesco Sequeiros, Los Angeles, CA (FS); Cirrus Editions Workshop, Los Angeles, CA (CEW)
PUBLISHERS: Cirrus Editions, Ltd, Los Angeles, CA (CEL)
GALLERIES: Cirrus Gallery, Los Angeles, CA; Art Angles Gallery, Orange, CA

TITLE	PUBLISHER	PRINTER	DATE	MEDIUM	DIMENSION (PAPER SIZE) IN INCHES	TYPE OF PAPER	EDITION NUMBER	NO. OF COLORS	ORIGINAL OPENING PRICE	CURRENT RETAIL PRICE
CURRENT EDITIONS:										
Leaves & Wishbone	CEL	RH/FS/CEW	1985	LC	36 X 54	AP88	50	7	800	850
Sea	CEL	RH/FS/CEW	1987	LC	30 X 30	COV	62	6	550	650

JOHN ASARO

BORN: San Diego, CA
EDUCATION: Art Center Col of Design, Los Angeles, CA; Art Students League, NY; Los Angeles, Inst of Arch, CA
AWARDS: Award of Excellence, New York Art Directors Club, 1968; Watercolor Award, Riverside, CA, 1981; Major Award, Am Watercolor Show, 1985
COLLECTIONS: Smithsonian Inst, Wash, DC
PRINTERS: Marco Fine Arts Studio, Gardenia, CA (MFAS)
PUBLISHERS: Marco Fine Arts Gardena, CA (MFA)
GALLERIES: Gillis Enterprises, Cincinnati, OH; Hoitt Limited, San Francisco, CA; Coppersmith, Wandesha, WI; Jane Anthony Gallery, Newtown, PA; Aspen Mountain Gallery, Aspen, CO; Promenade, Santa Monica, CA; Red Door Fine Art, Detroit, MI; White Oak, St Edina, MN; Kahn Galleries, Kauai, HI; Theodores, Salinas, CA; Upstairs Gallery, Huntington Beach, CA; Hogg Interiors, Inc, Destin, FL; Grycner Studio/Galley Taos, Taos, Taos, NM; Artists Showcase Internationale, Hartsdale, NY; Premier Gallery, Fredericksburg, VA
MAILING ADDRESS: 1633 W 135th St, Gardena, CA 90249

John Asaro
Special Love
Courtesy Marco Fine Arts

TITLE	PUBLISHER	PRINTER	DATE	MEDIUM	DIMENSION (PAPER SIZE) IN INCHES	TYPE OF PAPER	EDITION NUMBER	NO. OF COLORS	ORIGINAL OPENING PRICE	CURRENT RETAIL PRICE
SOLD OUT EDITIONS (RARE):										
Second Summer	MFA	MFAS	1989	SP	32 X 25	WWP	295	95	500	4000
Summer Breeze	MFA	MFAS	1989	SP	28 X 38	WWP	295	85	500	4000
First Encounter	MFA	MFAS	1989	SP	28 X 35	WWP	295	90	600	4000
Warm Embrace	MFA	MFAS	1989	SP	52 X 38	WWP	125	105	1400	8000
Gladiolas	MFA	MFAS	1990	SP	32 X 29	WWP	195	151	750	4000
Sunday Afternoon	MFA	MFAS	1990	SP	28 X 36	WWP	195	125	750	4000
Still Life with Child	MFA	MFAS	1990	SP	31 X 24	WWP	295	125	750	4000
Mediterranean Breeze	MFA	MFAS	1990	SP	34 X 40	WWP	195	130	1000	4000
Mother's Love	MFA	MFAS	1990	SP	36 X 26	WWP	195	140	750	4000
Summer Holiday	MFA	MFAS	1990	SP	31 X 28	WWP	295	118	700	1900
Amber	MFA	MFAS	1990	SP	27 X 37	WWP	195	140	750	1900
Sisters	MFA	MFAS	1991	SP		WWP	195			4000
Warming Up	MFA	MFAS	1991	SP		WWP	195			1100
Bernadette & Ginger	MFA	MFAS	1991	SP	24 X 30	WWP	195			4000
Special Love	MFA	MFAS	1992	SP	24 X 32	WWP	195			4000
Beach at Coronado	MFA	MFAS	1992	SP		WWP	195			2500
Hawaiian Ginger	MFA	MFAS	1992	SP	25 X 31	WWP	195		1100	1100
Porcelain Ginger	MFA	MFAS	1992	SP	20 X 30	WWP	195		4000	4000
Harmony in White	MFA	MFAS	1992	SP	26 X 28	WWP	195		4000	4000

JOHN ASARO CONTINUED

TITLE	PUBLISHER	PRINTER	DATE	MEDIUM	DIMENSION (PAPER SIZE) IN INCHES	TYPE OF PAPER	EDITION NUMBER	NO. OF COLORS	ORIGINAL OPENING PRICE	CURRENT RETAIL PRICE
CURRENT EDITIONS:										
The Bathers	MFA	MFAS	1991	SP		WWP	195			5000
Mother's Care	MFA	MFAS	1991	SP		WWP	195		1000	1000
Santa Maria Suite (Set of 2):									1100 SET	1100 SET
Sunrise	MFA	MFAS	1992	SP		WWP	195			
Sunset	MFA	MFAS	1992	SP		WWP	195		600	600
Playing Dress-Up	MFA	MFAS	1992	SP		WWP	195		600	600

John Asaro
**Santa Maria della Salute:
Sunrise**
Courtesy Marco Fine Arts

John Asaro
**Santa Maria della Salute:
Sunset**
Courtesy Marco Fine Arts

DENNIS JOHN ASHBAUGH

BORN: Red Oak, IA; October 25, 1946
EDUCATION: Orange Coast Col, Costa Mesa, CA, AA, 1966; California State Col, Fullerton, CA, BA, 1968, MA, 1969
AWARDS: Creative Artists Public Service Program, New York Council of the Arts, 1975; Guggenheim Found Fel, 1976
RECENT EXHIB: Marisa del Re Gallery, NY, 1993
COLLECTIONS: Toledo Art Mus, OH; Seattle Art Mus, WA; Miami Art Center, FL
PRINTERS: Peter Pettengill, Hinsdale, NY (PP); Wingate Studio, Hinsdale, NY (WinSt)
PUBLISHERS: Kevin Begos Publishing, NY (KBP)
GALLERIES: Paul Kasmin Gallery, New York, NY; Margulies Taplin Gallery, Boca Raton, FL; Marisa del Re Gallery, New York, NY
MAILING ADDRESS: c/o Paul Kasmin Gallery, 580 Broadway, New York, NY 10012

TITLE	PUBLISHER	PRINTER	DATE	MEDIUM	DIMENSION (PAPER SIZE) IN INCHES	TYPE OF PAPER	EDITION NUMBER	NO. OF COLORS	ORIGINAL OPENING PRICE	CURRENT RETAIL PRICE
CURRENT EDITIONS:										
Genetic Portraits (set of 6)	KBP	PP/WS	1992	EB/A/SB/CAR	26 X 27 EA	MAG	50 EA	1 EA	3000 EA	3500 SET

ALICE ASMAR

BORN: Flint, MI
EDUCATION: Lewis & Clark Col, Portland, OR, BA, Magna Cum Laude, 1946–49; Univ of Washington, Seattle, WA, MFA, 1950–51; Univ of Washington, Seattle, WA, Teaching Certificate, 1954; Ecole Nationale Superieure des Beaux-Arts, paris, France, 1958–59
TEACHING: Instr, St Helen's Hall, Portland, OR, 1949–50; Asst Prof, Lewis & Clark Col, Portland, OR, 1955–58; Instr, Santa Monica City Col, 1964–66; Instr, Descanso Gardens, La Canada, CA, 1988; McGroarty Arts Center, Cultural Affairs Dept, Los Angeles, CA, 1988–90
AWARDS: Award, Seattle Art Mus, WA, 1952; Award, Art Inst of Chicago Art Sch, IL, 1957; Harriet H Wooley Grant, Paris, France, 1959; MacDowell Colony Fel, 1964; Best in Professional Class, Irrespective of Medium, 1964; First Prize, IPA Exhibit, Wash, DC, 1967; Award, Drawing & Mixed Media, California Mus of Science & Industry, 1976; Award, Academia Italia, 1985; Distinguished Alumni Award, Lewis & Clark Col, Portland, OR, 1986; Purchase Award, Westwood Exhib, CA, 1986; Purchase Award, Alan Casden Exhib, Westwood, CA, 1987; Award, 2000 Notable Women, CA, 1989; Honorary Member, Nat League of Am Pen Women, Wash, DC, 1991
RECENT EXHIB: Brea Cultural Center, CA, 1987; California State Capitol, Sacramento, CA, 1987; Senior Eye Gallery, Long Beach, CA, 1988; Nat Congress of Art & Design, Salt Lake City, UT, 1988; McGroarty Arts Center, Tujunga, CA, 1989; Highland Hall, Northridge, CA, 1991; Small Wilderness Area Preservation, Montrose, CA, 1991; Beaux-Arts Soc, Portland, OR, 1991; Main Street Gallery, Hillsboro, OR, 1991; Abbott Hall Gallery, William Temple House, Portland, OR, 1992
COLLECTIONS: Smithsonian Mus, Kistler Coll, Wash, DC; Huntington Hartford Mus, NY; Roswell Mus & Art Center, Roswell, NM; Southwest Mus, Los Angeles, CA; Huntington Beach Cultural Center, CA; Mus of Humour, Gabrova, Bulgaria; Portland Art Mus, OR; Nat Art Mus, Gabrova, Bulgaria
PRINTERS: Lynton Kistler, Los Angeles, CA (LK); Richard Royce, NY (RR); Atelier Royce, NY (AR); Al Mably, Burbank, CA (AM); Francis Fine Arts Lithography, Northridge, CA (FFAL); Color West, Burbank, CA (CW); Ted Kowalke (TK); Esther Kowalke (EK); Digital Imaging, CA (DI)
PUBLISHERS: Atelier Royce, NY (AR); American Graphics, NY (AG); Artists Profusions, NY (AP); Collier Publishing Company, Los Angeles, CA (CPC); Artist (ART); San Francisco Center for Visual Studies, CA (SFCVS); Les Editions Arts et Images de Monde, Paris, France (LEAIM); Dreamscape Productions, Ltd, Burnaby, BC, Canada (DPL)
GALLERIES: Circle Galleries, San Diego, CA & San Francisco, CA & Northbrook, IL & Houston, TX & Pittsburgh, PA & Soho, NY & Chicago, IL; Sachs Gallery, Los Angeles, CA; Dukow Gallery, Toluca Lake, CA; The Jade Corner, Portland, OR; Gloria's Gallery, Scottsdale, AZ; Asmar Art Gallery, Burbank, CA; The Gallery, Kokomo, IN; Design Unlimited, Melbourne, FL; Dora Prokope Haslett, Portland, OR (Artist Rep)
MAILING ADDRESS: P O Box 1963, Burbank, CA 91507; 1125 N Screenland Dr, Burbank, CA 91505

TITLE	PUBLISHER	PRINTER	DATE	MEDIUM	DIMENSION (PAPER SIZE) IN INCHES	TYPE OF PAPER	EDITION NUMBER	NO. OF COLORS	ORIGINAL OPENING PRICE	CURRENT RETAIL PRICE
SOLD OUT EDITIONS (RARE):										
Set of Four:									250 SET	1150 SET
Palace of Governors-Santa Fe	ART	LK	1971	LB	20 X 26	R/BFK/W	200	1	75	300
Brownie & Apache from Pecos	ART	LK	1971	LB	20 X 26	R/BFK/W	200	1	75	300
Navahos Watching the Dance at Shiprock	ART	LK	1971	LC	20 X 26	R/BFK/W	200	2	75	300
Eagle Dancer, Laguna Pueblo	ART	LK	1971	LC	20 X 26	R/BFK/W	200	2	75	300
Mushroom & Zuni-Hopi Jewelry	ART	RR/AR	1975	EC/A/EMB/SL	24 X 36	GE	12	9	400	2500
Zuni Shalako Dancers	ART	RR/AR	1975	EC/A/EMB/SL	40 X 22	GE	17	12	450	2500
Elizabeth the Queen	CPC	AM	1977	LC	20 X 26	STP	200	4	100	300
Rose of Mystery	CPC	AM	1977	LC	20 X 26	STP/W	200	3	125	300
Rainbow Dancer	AG	FFAL	1980	LC	22 X 30	R/BFK	150	17	300	900
Shalako Dancers	AP	FFAL	1980	LC	22 X 30	R/BFK	75	15	300	900
Harvest Dancers	AP	FFAL	1980	LC	22 X 30	R/BFK	100	14	300	800
Taos Corn Dancers	AP	FFAL	1980	LC	22 X 30	R/BFK	90	18	300	900
Zuni Rain Dancers	AP	FFAL	1980	LC	22 X 30	R/BFK	100	15	300	900
Mystic Rose	AP	FFAL	1980	LC	22 X 30	R/BFK	115	25	300	900
Joy of the Eternal Now	AG	FFAL	1980	LC	22 X 30	R/BFK	105	17	300	900
Only the Dreamer Can Choose the Dream	AG	FFAL	1980	LC	22 X 30	R/BFK	110	16	300	900
The Golden Apple	AG	FFAL	1980	LC	22 X 30	AP/B	125	7	350	800
Scheherazade & Star of David	AP	FFAL	1980	LC	22 X 30	AP/B	130	7	350	800
Bouquet	DPL	TK/EK/CW	1991	LUMA	24 X 30	KODAK	20	24	130	1000
Oregon Coast	DPL	TK/EK/CW	1991	LUMA	24 X 30	KODAK	20	15	140	1000
Sunday at Descanso Gardens	DPL	TK/EK/CW	1991	LUMA	24 x 30	KODAK	20	27	140	900
Governor Abel Sanchez, San Ildefonso Pueblo	DPL	TK/EK/CW	1991	LUMA	24 X 30	KODAK	20	22	150	1800
Coast (Dendrobium)	DPL	TK/EK/CW	1991	LUMA	24 X 30	KODAK	20	19	135	800
Dusk (Iris)	DPL	TK/EK/CW	1991	LUMA	24 X 30	KODAK	20	13	135	700
Moonlight & One Indian Vase	DPL	TK/EK/CW	1991	LUMA	24 X 30	KODAK	20	17	130	1200
Ann Taliman, Santa Clara Pueblo	DPL	TK/EK/CW	1991	LUMA	24 X 30	KODAK	20	31	125	1800
CURRENT EDITIONS:										
Nesting Doves	ART	DI	1993–94	LC	8 X 10	LIM/100	600		100	200
The Beach	ART	DI	1993–94	LC	8 X 10	LIM/100	600		100	200
Moonlight & Indian Cannon Beach & Indian Pottery	ART	DI	1993–94	LC	8 X 10	LIM/100	600		100	200
Bouquet	ART	DI	1993–94	LC	8 X 8	LIM/100	600		100	200
Cob Cactus & Fireball	ART	DI	1993–94	LC	8 X 10	LIM/100	600		100	200
Agave Sunset	ART	DI	1993–94	LC	7 X 12	LIM/100	600		100	200
Ocotillo Sunset	ART	DI	1993–94	LC	8 X 10	LIM/100	600		100	200
Totem Cockatoo	ART	DI	1993–94	LC/HC	16 X 12	R/BFK	12		500	900
Opera Fantasy	ART	DI	1993–94	LC/HC	14 X 11	R/BFK	12		500	900
Dreams	ART	DI	1993–94	LC/HC	8 X 6	R/BFK	12		300	500
Point de L'Arcoest, Brittany	ART	DI	1993–94	PH	10 X 5	R/BFK	12		150	250
Violet Orchid	ART	DI	1993–94	PH	8 X 10	R/BFK	12		150	250

The retail prices of the 100,000 limited edition prints quoted in this directory are subject to change. Print publishers, artists and galleries were the direct sources for these quotations. Prices in the secondary market listed as "Sold Out Editions (Rare)" indicate that the publisher has a limited supply of that print or that the print is difficult to locate in the galleries.

ALICE ASMAR CONTINUED

Alice Asmar
Ocotillo Cactus
Courtesy the Artist

Alice Asmar
Moonlight and One Indian
Courtesy the Artist

Alice Asmar
Agave-Sunset (Century Plant)
Courtesy the Artist

Alice Asmar
Cannon Beach & Indian Pottery
Courtesy the Artist

WALTER ASKIN

BORN: Pasadena, CA; September 12, 1929
EDUCATION: Univ of California, Berkeley, CA, BA, MA; Ruskin Sch of Drawing and Fine Art, Oxford Univ, England
TEACHING: Prof, Art, California State Univ, Los Angeles, CA, 1956 to present; Adjunct Prof, Art, Arizona State Univ, Tempe, AZ, 1987 to present
AWARDS: Print Purchase Award, California State Univ, San Diego, CA, 1968; Phelan Award, San Francisco Mus of Art, CA, 1969; Pasadena Arts Council, CA, 1970
RECENT EXHIB: Florida State Univ, Tallahassee, FL, 1988; Lizardi/Harp Gallery, Pasadena, CA, 1988; Valley Col, Van Nuys, CA, 1989; Arizona State Univ, Tempe, AZ, 1990
COLLECTIONS: Hellenic Am Union, Athens, Greece; Mus of Contemp Art, Chicago, IL; Tate Gallery, London, England; Nat Coll of Fine Arts, Wash, DC; Oxford Mus of Mod Art, England; Hawaiian State Found of Culture and Art, Honolulu, HI; San Francisco Mus of Art, CA; Kunstlerhaus, Vienna, Austria; Phoenix Art Mus, AZ; Grunwald Center for the Graphic Arts, Univ of California, Los Angeles, CA; Zentralinstitute für Kunstgeschichte, Munich, Germany
PRINTERS: Black Dolphin Press, Long Beach, CA (BDP); Cynthia Osbourne, Long Beach, CA (CO); California State Univ, Long Beach, CA (CSU); Dan Britton, Tempe, AZ (DB); Wayne Kimball, Tempe, AZ (WK); Arizona State Univ, Tempe, AZ (ASU); Conner Everts, Bloomfield Hills, MI (CE); Cranbrook Press, Bloomfield Hills, MI (CRP); Chris Pater, London, England (C)); Kelpra Studio, London, England (KS); John Sommers, Albuquerque, NM (JS); Tamarind Inst, Albuquerque, NM (TI); Sette Press, Tempe, AZ (SP); Joseph Segura, Tempe, AZ (JS); Lisa Sette, Tempe, AZ (LS); Mark Klett, Tempe, AZ (MK); John Risseeuw, Tempe, AZ (JR); Jill Livermore, Tempe, AZ (JL); William Lagatutta, Albuquerque, NM (WL)
PUBLISHERS: Black Dolphin Press, California State Univ, Long Beach, CA (BDP); Arizona State Univ, Tempe, AZ (ASU); Cranbrook Press, Bloomfield Hills, MI (CRP); Sette Publishing Co, Tempe, AZ (SPC); Tamarind Inst, Albuquerque, NM (TI)
GALLERIES: Sette Gallery, Tempe, AZ; Lizardi/Harp Gallery, Pasadena, CA; Lightside Gallery, Santa Fe, NM
MAILING ADDRESS: P.O. Box 50381, Pasadena, CA 91105-0381

TITLE	PUBLISHER	PRINTER	DATE	MEDIUM	DIMENSION (PAPER SIZE) IN INCHES	TYPE OF PAPER	EDITION NUMBER	NO. OF COLORS	ORIGINAL OPENING PRICE	CURRENT RETAIL PRICE
SOLD OUT EDITIONS (RARE):										
Brueghel Britannia	KS	KS/CP	1970	SP	40 X 28	JBG	75	5	90	500
Ned's Noggin	SPIN	SPIN	1982	I	30 X 22	AP	10	2	250	300
The Purple Pelf	ACD	ACD	1982	LC	16 X 16	AP	10	2	250	325
Saints Preserve	ACD	ACD	1982	AC	10 X 18	AP	12	17	200	375
Lum's Luggage	BOD	BOD	1982	AC	30 X 22	AP	10	4	250	325
CURRENT EDITIONS:										
Voices	BDP	BDP	1978	LC	30 X 22	AP	17	3	200	300
Double Cross	CRP	CRP	1978	LC/SP	30 X 22	AP	17	3	175	300
Yellow Nocturne	CRP	CRP	1978	LC/SP	30 X 22	AP	17	3	175	300
Tuesday's Song I	ASU	ASU	1979	LC	30 X 22	AP	30	3	225	300
Desert Songs	ASU	ASU	1979	LC	30 X 22	AP	30	3	225	300
The Dancer	ASU	ASU	1979	LB	16 X 20	AP	8	1	100	200
A Briefer History of the Greeks	ASU	JS/JR	1983	LC/HST	11 X 14	RP/G	30	3	275	275
Studio Tours: Repulsive Romps Through the Field of Contemporary Art	ASU	JS/MK/JR	1983	PH/HST	11 X 14	AC	30	2	275	275
Serene Totems	SPC	JS/LS/SP	1983	LC	22 X 30	AP	15	5	400	400
Sette	SPC	JS/LS/SP	1983	LC	22 X 30	RP	17	5	400	400
The Trophy Room	SPC	JL/SP	1985	LC	22 X 30	RP/W	30	3	400	400
Vessels & Vessels	SPC	JL/SP	1985	LC	22 X 30	RP/W	30	3	400	400
Selected Ancient Monuments	SPC	JL/SP	1985	LC	22 X 30	RP/W	30	3	400	400
The Collector	TI	TI	1989	LC	22 X 30		20	4	400	400
Memory Park	TI	TI	1989	LC	22 X 30		20	3	400	400
Mr Mesa (30-Year Suite)	TI	TI	1989	L	12 X 12		30	1		
The Solution to World Conflict	TI	TI	1989	LC	16 X 14		15	2	175	175

TADASHI ASOMA

BORN: Iwatsuki, Japan; April 28, 1923
EDUCATION: Saitama Teachers Col, Urawa, MS; Govt Scholar, Bijitsu Gakko, Tokyo, Japan; Govt Scholar, Grand Chaumiere, Paris, 1956, Art Students League, NY
TEACHING: Instr, Art Ed, Iwatsuki Jr High Sch, Japan, 1950–64
AWARDS: Second Prize, Saitama Bijitsu Ten, 1955; Second Prize, Nat Exhib of Professional Art, 1968; Best of Show, Putnam Art Council, Mahopac, NY, 1982
COLLECTIONS: Andrew Dickson White Mus, Ithaca, NY; San Diego Mus of Art, CA; Nelson Mus, Kansas City, MO; Tokyo Central Mus, Japan; Foundry Sch Mus
PRINTERS: Robert Schmid Studio, NY (RSS)
PUBLISHERS: John Szoke Graphics, Inc, NY (JSG)
GALLERIES: John Szoke Graphics, Inc, New York, NY; David Findlay Galleries, New York, NY

Tadashi Asoma
Water Lilies
Courtesy John Szoke Graphics, Inc

The Printworld Directory is accepting new applications for the seventh edition. Approximately 300 new artists will be accepted. Please use the two forms provided in the back section of this directory to submit biographical data and documentation of prints. Edition number of each print must not exceed 500 and the retail price must be $100 or more.

TADASHI ASOMA CONTINUED

TITLE	PUBLISHER	PRINTER	DATE	MEDIUM	DIMENSION (PAPER SIZE) IN INCHES	TYPE OF PAPER	EDITION NUMBER	NO. OF COLORS	ORIGINAL OPENING PRICE	CURRENT RETAIL PRICE
CURRENT EDITIONS:										
Seven Lakes	JSG	RSS	1989	SP	13 X 18	R/BFK	400		400	500
Reflection	JSG	RSS	1990	SP	25 X 32	R/BFK	200		850	950
Cascading Leaves	JSG	RSS	1992	SP	20 X 28	R/BFK	120		850	850
Early Autumn	JSG	RSS	1992	SP	25 X 31	R/BFK	200		850	850
The End of Summer	JSG	RSS	1992	SP	29 X 38	R/BFK	150		850	850
Glory of Fall	JSG	RSS	1992	SP	23 X 31	R/BFK	120		850	850
Water Lilies	JSG	RSS	1992	SP	27 X 29	R/BFK	120	38	650	650
Red Leaves	JSG	RSS	1993	SP	10 X 13	R/BFK	175	35+	325	325
Distance	JSG	RSS	1993	SP	13 X 16	R/BFK	175	35+	375	375

JOHN W NIETO

BORN: Denver, CO; August 6, 1936
EDUCATION: Pan Am Univ, Edinburg, TX, 1955–56; Southern Methodist Univ, Dallas, TX, 1957–59; Dallas Mus of Fine Arts, TX
TEACHING: Art, North Texas State Univ, Denton, TX, 1964–65; Southern Methodist Univ, Dallas, TX, 1974–75
AWARDS: Blue Ribbon Award, Heard Mus, Phoenix, AZ, 1981
RECENT EXHIB: Axis Gallery, Tokyo, Japan, 1989; Retrosp, Utah Mus of Fine Arts, Salt Lake City, UT, 1993; Ventana Fine Art Gallery, Santa Fe, NM, 1991,92,93; J Cacciola Gallery, NY, 1991,92,93

COLLECTIONS: Heard Mus, Phoenix, AZ; Smithsonian Inst, Wash, DC; New Mexico Mus of Fine Arts, Santa Fe, NM; Marine Corp Mus, Wash, DC; Southern Methodist Univ, Dallas, TX; Reagan Library, CA
PRINTERS: Marco Fine Arts, Gardena, CA (MFA)
PUBLISHERS: Marco Fine Arts, Gardena, CA (MFA)
GALLERIES: J Cacciola Gallery, New York, NY; Ventana Fine Art Gallery, Santa Fe, NM; Kneeland Gallery, Las Vegas, NV; Santa Fe Gallery, Madison, WI; Grycner Studio, Taos, NM
MAILING ADDRESS: c/o Marco Fine Arts, 1633 W 135th St, Gardena, CA 90249

John W Nieto
Eagle
Courtesy Marco Fine Arts

John W Nieto
Chief
Courtesy Marco Fine Arts

TITLE	PUBLISHER	PRINTER	DATE	MEDIUM	DIMENSION (PAPER SIZE) IN INCHES	TYPE OF PAPER	EDITION NUMBER	NO. OF COLORS	ORIGINAL OPENING PRICE	CURRENT RETAIL PRICE
SOLD OUT EDITIONS (RARE):										
Coyote (Black)	MFA	MFA	1991	SP	23 X 30	WWP	195		1200	3500
Coyote (White)	MFA	MFA	1991	SP	23 X 30	WWP	195		1000	3500
Custer Suite (Set of 5)	MFA	MFA	1993	SP	10 X 12 EA	COV	195		1500 SET	1800 SET
CURRENT EDITIONS:										
Chief	MFA	MFA	1991	SP	24 X 30	WWP	195		1000	1000
Fancy Dancer	MFA	MFA	1992	SP	35 X 44	COV	195		4000	4000
Eagle	MFA	MFA	1992	SP	24 X 30	COV	195		1000	1000
Buffalo Medicine for the 90's	MFA	MFA	1993	SP	33 X 26	COV	195		1100	1100

ATIRNOMIS (RITA SIMON)

BORN: New York, NY; June 26, 1938
EDUCATION: Cornell Univ, Ithaca, NY, Sch of Arch, BFA; Acad of Rome, Italy
COLLECTIONS: Hirshhorn Mus, Wash, DC; Cornell Univ, Ithaca, NY; Pale Univ Art Coll; Housatonic State Col Mus, CT
PRINTERS: Alexander Heinrici, NY (AH); Studio Heinrici, Ltd, NY (SH)
PUBLISHERS: London Arts, Inc, Detroit, MI (LAI)
GALLERIES: London Arts Gallery, Detroit, MI

TITLE	PUBLISHER	PRINTER	DATE	MEDIUM	DIMENSION (PAPER SIZE) IN INCHES	TYPE OF PAPER	EDITION NUMBER	NO. OF COLORS	ORIGINAL OPENING PRICE	CURRENT RETAIL PRICE
SOLD OUT EDITIONS (RARE):										
Ariadne	LAI	AH/SH	1979	SP	34 X 26	SOM	300	10	150	200
Spacescape	LAI	AH/SH	1979	SP	32 X 24	SOM	300	11	150	200
Chance Encounter	LAI	AH/SH	1979	SP	40 X 21	SOM	300	6	150	200
Reflected Landscape	LAI	AH/SH	1979	SP	32 X 26	SOM	300	5	150	200
Visionary Landscape	LAI	AH/SH	1979	SP	40 X 26	SOM	300	11	150	200

CONRAD ATKINSON

BORN: Cambria, England; June 15, 1940
EDUCATION: Liverpool Col of Art, NDD, ATD, 1961; Royal Acad Sch of Art, London, England, Cert, RAS, Honors, 1965; Manchester Col of Art, England, AFD, 1967
TEACHING: Lectr, Fine Art, Slade Sch of Fine Art, London, England, 1975–78
AWARDS: Churchill Fel, 1972; Art in Res, Lewisham, England, 1984–85; Art in Res, Edinburgh Univ, Scotland, 1986
COLLECTIONS: Tate Gallery of Art, London, England; Victoria & Albert Mus, London, England; British Mus of Art, London, England; Mus of Mod Art, NY; Australian Nat Gallery, Canberra, Australia, Power Inst, Sydney, Australia
PRINTERS: Judith Solodkin, NY (JS); Solo Press, NY (SP)
PUBLISHERS: Solo Press, NY (SP); Ronald Feldman Fine Arts, NY (RFFA)
GALLERIES: Ronald Feldman Fine Arts, New York, NY; Solo Gallery, New York, NY
MAILING ADDRESS: 172 Erlanger Rd, London, SE 14, England

TITLE	PUBLISHER	PRINTER	DATE	MEDIUM	DIMENSION (PAPER SIZE) IN INCHES	TYPE OF PAPER	EDITION NUMBER	NO. OF COLORS	ORIGINAL OPENING PRICE	CURRENT RETAIL PRICE
CURRENT EDITIONS:										
Objects of Desire (Set of 3):									1500 SET	3600 SET
Aesthetics	RFFA	JS/SP	1990	PH/E/A/HC	42 X 30	R/BFK	40	Varies	550	1250
Passion/Postmodern	RFFA	JS/SP	1990	PH/E/A/HC	42 X 30	R/BFK	40	Varies	550	1250
Fantasy/Desire	RFFA	JS/SP	1990	PH/E/A/HC	42 X 30	R/BFK	40	Varies	550	1250
Baseball Series (Set of 3):									1500 SET	2000 SET
Baseball: El Salvador	RFFA	JS/SP	1990	EB/HC	20 X 20	R/BFK	40		600	800
Baseball: Imagine	RFFA	JS/SP	1990	EB/HC	23 X 24	R/BFK	40		600	800
Baseball: Poetry/Thompson	RFFA	JS/SP	1990	EB/HC	21 X 23	R/BFK	40		600	800
Untitled (Telephone)	SP	JS/SP	1990	MON	13 X 11 EA	AC	6 EA		400 EA	500 EA
Untitled (Telephone/Artists)	SP	JS/SP	1990	MON	13 X 11 EA	AC	3 EA		400 EA	500 EA
Le Monde	RFFA	JS/SP	1990	EB/HC	12 X 15	R/BFK		Varies	600	800
Western Capitalism Collapsing...	RFFA	JS/SP	1990	LB	30 X 20	AC	20	1	650	800
I was Walking	RFFA	JS/SP	1990	LB	30 X 22	AC	20	1	650	800
Strike at Brannans	RFFA		1972	SP	30 X 22	AP	75		100	1200
Ulster	RFFA		1974	PH/SP	40 X 30	AP	30		100	1200
Untitled (Set of 12):										
The Right to Bear Arms	RFFA	DS/DE	1982	EB	11 X 13	R/BFK		1	250	1000
The Camouflaged Palette	RFFA	DS/DE	1982	EB	11 X 13	R/BFK		1	250	1000
The Artist's Palette	RFFA	DS/DE	1982	EB	14 X 14	R/BFK		1	250	1000
The Artist's Palette	RFFA	DS/DE	1982	EB	11 X 13	R/BFK		1	250	1000
Overkill	RFFA	DS/DE	1982	EB	12 X 13	R/BFK		1	250	1000
The Land, The Law, The Dream	RFFA	DS/DE	1982	EB	14 X 14	R/BFK		1	250	1000
A Modern Aesthetic	RFFA	DS/DE	1982	EB	11 X 13	R/BFK		1	250	1000
The Man Who Exploded	RFFA	DS/DE	1982	EB	12 X 13	R/BFK		1	250	1000
Aboringal Australian Hand	RFFA	DS/DE	1982	EB	20 X 14	R/BFK		1	250	1000
The Wall Street Journal	RFFA	LBW	1985	SP/HC	30 X 22	AC	50	Varies	350	1500
Thanks Portfolio (Set of 4)	RFFA	LBW	1988	SP	44 X 30 EA	Paper/Felt	40 EA		2500 SET	4500 SET

CHRISTIAN LUDWIG ATTERSEE

BORN: Vienna, Austria; 1941
EDUCATION: Akademie für Angewandte Kunste, 1957–63
PRINTERS: Christopher Novotny Steindruck, Werkstat, Vienna, Austria (VNS)
PUBLISHERS: Galerie Heike Curtze, Dusseldorf, Germany & Vienna, Austria (GHC); Maximilian Verlag Sabine Kunst, Munich, Germany (MVSK)
GALLERIES: Margarete Roeder Gallery, New York, NY

TITLE	PUBLISHER	PRINTER	DATE	MEDIUM	DIMENSION (PAPER SIZE) IN INCHES	TYPE OF PAPER	EDITION NUMBER	NO. OF COLORS	ORIGINAL OPENING PRICE	CURRENT RETAIL PRICE
CURRENT EDITIONS:										
Attersee (Set of 5)	GHC/MVSK	CNS	1988–89	LC	30 X 22 EA	R/BFK	35 EA		4500 SET	5000 SET

The retail prices of the 100,000 limited edition prints quoted in this directory are subject to change. Print publishers, artists and galleries were the direct sources for these quotations. Prices in the secondary market listed as "Sold Out Editions (Rare)" indicate that the publisher has a limited supply of that print or that the print is difficult to locate in the galleries.

TOM ATTRIDGE

BORN: St Paul, MN; April 8, 1939
EDUCATION: Minneapolis Col of Art & Design, MN, BFA, Sculpture; Academy 63, Haarlem, The Netherlands
TEACHING: Wayne Univ, Detroit, MI; Minneapolis Col of Art & Design, MN
AWARDS: Ford Found Purchase Award; Prince Bernard Funds Grant, The Netherlands
COLLECTIONS: Minneapolis Inst of Art, MN; Grey Gallery, New York Univ, NY
PRINTERS: Vermillion Editions Ltd, Inc, Minneapolis, MN (VEL)
PUBLISHERS: Vermillion Editions Ltd, Inc, Minneapolis, MN (VEL)
GALLERIES: Dolly Fiterman Gallery, Minneapolis, MN; Vermillion Editions, Ltd, Minneapolis, MN
MAILING ADDRESS: 1699 Marshall Ave, St Paul, MN 55104

TITLE	PUBLISHER	PRINTER	DATE	MEDIUM	DIMENSION (PAPER SIZE) IN INCHES	TYPE OF PAPER	EDITION NUMBER	NO. OF COLORS	ORIGINAL OPENING PRICE	CURRENT RETAIL PRICE
CURRENT EDITIONS:										
Cubist Messenger	VEL	VEL	1984	LC/SP	58 X 32	AP/ROL	10	4	250	500
Inner City Lovers	VEL	VEL	1984	LC	18 X 25	JAP/D	18	3	150	250
Court Order	VEL	VEL	1984	LB	21 X 30	KUR/HW	10	1	175	250
Court Order	VEL	VEL	1984	LC	16 X 26	AP	25	7	175	350

DOTTY ATTIE

BORN: Pennsauken, NJ; March 20, 1938
EDUCATION: Philadelphia Col of Art, PA, BFA, 1959; Brooklyn Mus Art Sch, NY, 1960; Art Students League, NY, 1967
TEACHING: New York Univ, NY, 1977; Manhattanville Col, NY, 1977
AWARDS: Beckmann Fel, NY, 1960; Creative Artists Public Service Grant, New York Council of the Arts, 1973–74, 76–77; Nat Endowment for the Arts Grant, 1975–76 & 1983–84
RECENT EXHIB: PPOW, NY, 1988, 92
COLLECTIONS: Allen Mem Art Mus, Oberlin Col, OH; Univ of Massachusetts, Amherst, MA; Fairleigh Dickinson Univ, Rutherford, NY; Smith Col Mus, Northampton, MA; Mus of Kansas, Lawrence, KS
PRINTERS: Arnold Samet, NY (AS); Judith Solodkin, NY (JS); Solo Press, NY (SP); Bill Lagattuta, Albuquerque, NM (BL); Tamarind Inst, Albuquerque, NM (TI)
PUBLISHERS: Solo Press, NY (SP); Artist (ART); Tamarind Inst, Albuquerque, NM (TI)
GALLERIES: PPOW, New York, NY; Solo Gallery, New York, NY; Mary Ryan Gallery, New York, NY; Betsy Senior Contempory Prints, New York, NY
MAILING ADDRESS: 334 E 22nd St, New York, NY 10010

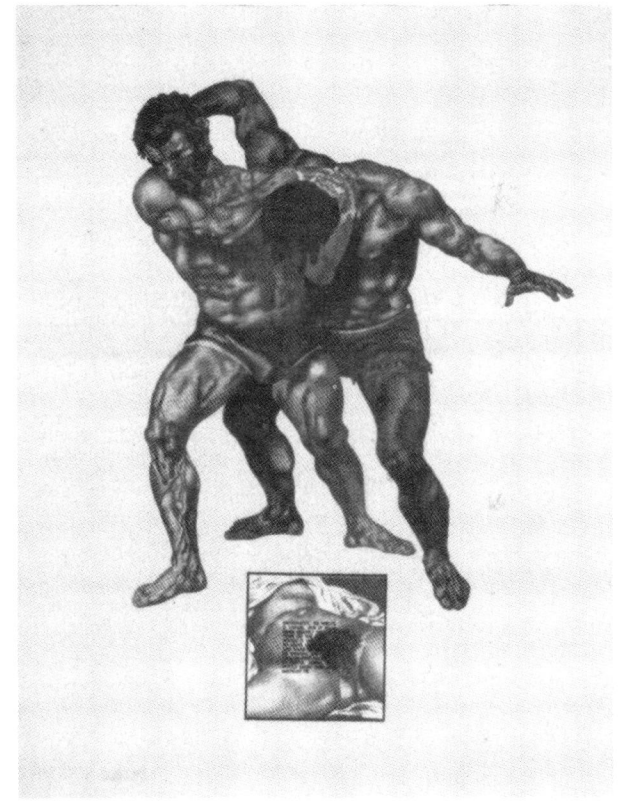

Dotty Attie
Exile
Courtesy Tamarind Institute

TITLE	PUBLISHER	PRINTER	DATE	MEDIUM	DIMENSION (PAPER SIZE) IN INCHES	TYPE OF PAPER	EDITION NUMBER	NO. OF COLORS	ORIGINAL OPENING PRICE	CURRENT RETAIL PRICE
CURRENT EDITIONS:										
Mothers Kisses Narrative (26 Parts)	SP	JS/SP	1982	LC	36 X 27	R/BFK	25		950 SET	2000 SET
The Store/One Night (with 22 Framed Details)	ART	AS/JS/SP	1986	LC/HC	30 X 25 (Central) 7 X 6 (Details)	R/BFK	8		1400 SET	2500 SET
Exile	TI	BL/TI	1993	LC	28 X 22	Mylar/AP-B/GE	22	5	1000	1000

ANNA HELD AUDETTE

BORN: New York, NY; July 16, 1938
EDUCATION: Smith Col, Northampton, MA, BA, 1960; New York Univ, NY, 1960–61; Yale Univ, New Haven, CT, BFA, 1962, MFA, 1964
TEACHING: Southern Connecticut State Univ, New Haven, CT, 1964 to present
AWARDS: Louis Comfort Tiffany Found Fel, 1965; Purchase Prize, Nat Prints & Drawing Comp, Mount Holyoke Col, MA, 1976
COLLECTIONS: Metropolitan Mus, NY; Nat Gallery, Wash, DC; Yale Univ, New Haven, CT; Univ of Vermont, Burlington, VT; Univ of Southern Illinois, Edwardsville, IL; Rijksmuseum, Amsterdam, Netherlands; Museo de Arte de Ponce, Puerto Rico; Furman Univ, Greenville, SC; Kalamazoo Inst of Art, MI; Lessing Rosenwald Coll, Phila, PA; Fitzwilliam Mus, Cambridge, England
PRINTERS: Aeropress, NY (A); Patricia Branstead, NY (PB); Alan Robinson, Easthampton, MA (AR); Chelonidae Press, Easthampton, MA (CP); Charles March, Jefferson City, MO (CM); The Deckle Edge Workshop, Inc, Jefferson City, MO (DEW); Nelson Wagner Lithography Workshop, Southern Illinois Univ, Edwardsville, IL (NWLW)
PUBLISHERS: Barbara Gladstone Editions, NY (BGE); Diane Villani Editions, NY (DVE); Artist (ART)
GALLERIES: Munson Gallery, New Haven, CT
MAILING ADDRESS: 24 Everit St, New Haven, CT 06511

ANNA HELD AUDETTE CONTINUED

TITLE	PUBLISHER	PRINTER	DATE	MEDIUM	DIMENSION (PAPER SIZE) IN INCHES	TYPE OF PAPER	EDITION NUMBER	NO. OF COLORS	ORIGINAL OPENING PRICE	CURRENT RETAIL PRICE
SOLD OUT EDITIONS (RARE):										
Under Glass	BGE/DVE	PB/A	1979	EB	38 X 47	R/BFK	35	1	300	750
CURRENT EDITIONS:										
The Last Temple	ART	NWLW	1979	LC	38 X 27	R/BFK	12	2	250	450
Conservatory I	BGE	CM/DEW	1980	EB	47 X 35	R/BFK	10	1	375	750
Conservatory II	BGE	AR/CP	1982	EB	46 X 35	R/BFK	35	1	375	750

FRANK AUERBACH

BORN: Berlin, Germany; April 29, 1931
EDUCATION: St. Martin's Sch of Art, London, England, 1948–52; Royal Col of Art, London, England, 1952–55
RECENT EXHIB: Yale Univ, Yale Center for British Art, New Haven, CT, 1992
COLLECTIONS: Metropolitan Mus of Art, NY; Mus of Mod Art, NY; Los Angeles County Mus, CA; Nat Gallery of Australia, Canberra, Australia; Tate Gallery, London, England; Mus of Mod Art, Bahia, Brazil; Chrysler Mus, Provincetown, MA; Scottish Nat Gallery of Mod Art, Edinburgh, Scotland
PRINTERS: Palm Tree Studios (PTS)
PUBLISHERS: Bernard Jacobson, Ltd, London, England (BJL); Marlborough Graphics, Inc, NY (MG)
GALLERIES: Marlborough Gallery, New York, NY
MAILING ADDRESS: 39 Old Bond St, London, W1X 4BY, England

TITLE	PUBLISHER	PRINTER	DATE	MEDIUM	DIMENSION (PAPER SIZE) IN INCHES	TYPE OF PAPER	EDITION NUMBER	NO. OF COLORS	ORIGINAL OPENING PRICE	CURRENT RETAIL PRICE
SOLD OUT EDITIONS (RARE):										
Six Drypoints of the Nude (Set of 6)			1954	DPT	10 X 8 EA	WOVE	12 EA	1 EA	300 SET	65000 SET
Gerda Boehm Suite (Set of 6):									900 SET	5000 SET
Joe Tilson	BJL	PTS	1980	EC	16 X 14	AP	50	1–2	150	800
R B Kitaj	BJL	PTS	1980	EC	16 X 14	AP	50	1–2	150	1000
Lucien Freud	BJL	PTS	1980	EC	16 X 14	AP	50	1–2	150	1000
Gerda Boehm	BJL	PTS	1980	EC	16 X 14	AP	50	1–2	150	800
Julia	BJL	PTS	1980	EC	16 X 14	AP	50	1–2	150	800
Leon Kossoff	BJL	PTS	1980	EC	16 X 14	AP	50	1–2	150	1000
Seven Portraits (Julia, David, Catherine, Jym, Michael, Geoffrey, Jake) (Set of 7)	MG		1989–90	EB	10 X 9 EA	SOM	50 EA	1 EA	20000 SET	22000 SET

DAVID AUSTEN

BORN: Harlow, Essex, England; 1960
EDUCATION: Maidstone Col of Art, England, 1968–81; Royal Col of Art, London, England, 1982–85
RECENT EXHIB: Serpentine Gallery, London, England, 1987; Castle Mus, Nottingham, England, 1989; Frith Street Gallery, London, England, 1990; Stephen Solovy Fine Art, Chicago, IL, 1991; Anthony Reynolds Gallery, London, England, 1988,91; Cirrus Gallery, Los Angeles, CA, 1989,91
PRINTERS: Cirrus Editions Workshop, Los Angeles, CA (CEW)
PUBLISHERS: Cirrus Editions, Ltd, Los Angeles, CA (CEL)
GALLERIES: Cirrus Gallery, Los Angeles, CA; Anthony Reynolds Gallery, London, England; Stephen Solovy Fine Art, Chicago, IL; Serpentine Gallery, London, England; Frith Street Gallery, London, England

David Austen
Untitled, 442c
Courtesy Cirrus Editions, Ltd

TITLE	PUBLISHER	PRINTER	DATE	MEDIUM	DIMENSION (PAPER SIZE) IN INCHES	TYPE OF PAPER	EDITION NUMBER	NO. OF COLORS	ORIGINAL OPENING PRICE	CURRENT RETAIL PRICE
CURRENT EDITIONS:										
Untitled (440 c)	CEL	CEW	1990	LC	32 X 28	AP88	45		650	750
Untitled (442 c)	CEL	CEW	1990	LC	32 X 28	AP88	45		650	750
Untitled (443 c)	CEL	CEW	1990	LC	32 X 28	AP88	45		650	750
Untitled (444 c)	CEL	CEW	1990	LC	32 X 28	AP88	45		650	750
Untitled (445 c)	CEL	CEW	1990	LC	32 X 28	AP88	45		650	750
Untitled (446 c)	CEL	CEW	1990	LC	32 X 28	AP88	45		650	750

MARIO AVATI

BORN: Monaco; 1921
EDUCATION: Ecole des Beaux-Arts, Paris, France; Ecole des Arts Decoraifis, Paris, France Gold Medal, President of the Italian Republic, Rome, Italy, 1969

COLLECTIONS: Louvre Mus, Paris, France; Metropolitan Mus of Art, NY; Philadelphia Art Mus, PA
GALLERIES: River Gallery, Irvington-On-Hudson, NY; Michael Ward Gallery, New York, NY; MiraMar Gallery, Sarasota, FL; Newmark Gallery, New York, NY

TITLE	PUBLISHER	PRINTER	DATE	MEDIUM	DIMENSION (PAPER SIZE) IN INCHES	TYPE OF PAPER	EDITION NUMBER	NO. OF COLORS	ORIGINAL OPENING PRICE	CURRENT RETAIL PRICE
CURRENT EDITIONS:										
Le Dessus de Marble	ART	ART	1979	MEZ	15 X 18	AP	85	1	300	600

EDWARD AVEDISIAN

BORN: Lowell, MA; 1936
EDUCATION: Boston Mus Sch of Art, MA
TEACHING: Univ of Kansas, Lawrence, KS, 1969; Sch of Visual Arts, NY, 1969–70; Univ of California, Irvine, CA, 1972; Univ of Louisiana, Ruston, LA, 1973
AWARDS: Guggenheim Found Fel, 1967; Nat Council of the Arts Award, 1968

RECENT EXHIB: Belian Art Center, Gallery of Fine Art, Troy, MI, 1989,92
COLLECTIONS: Guggenheim Mus, NY; Whitney Mus of Am Art, NY, Metropolitan Mus of Art, NY; Los Angeles County Mus of Art, CA; Pasadena Mus of Art, CA; Wadsworth Atheneum, Hartford, CT; Minneapolis Inst of Art, MN; Chrysler Mus, Norfolk, VA; State Univ of New York, Purchase, NY; Aldrich Mus of Contemp Art, Ridgefield, CT
PUBLISHERS: Brooke Alexander, Inc, NY (BAI)
GALLERIES: Brooke Alexander, Inc, New York, NY
MAILING ADDRESS: 26 Warren St, Hudson, NY 12534

TITLE	PUBLISHER	PRINTER	DATE	MEDIUM	DIMENSION (PAPER SIZE) IN INCHES	TYPE OF PAPER	EDITION NUMBER	NO. OF COLORS	ORIGINAL OPENING PRICE	CURRENT RETAIL PRICE
SOLD OUT EDITIONS (RARE):										
Blush House	BAI		1969	LC	30 X 22		100		100	500
Cleo, Fur Queen	BAI		1969	LC	22 X 30		100		100	500
Green Gold	BAI		1969	LC	22 X 30		100		100	500
Tide Light	BAI		1969	LC	22 X 30		100		100	500

ERIC AVERY

BORN: Milwaukee, WI; 1948
EDUCATION: Univ of Arizona, Tucson, AZ, BA, 1970; Univ of Texas Medical Branch, Galveston, TX, MD, 1974
RECENT EXHIB: Peregrine Press, Dallas, TX, 1987; Mus of Fine Arts, Boston, MA, 1992
COLLECTIONS: New York Public Library, NY; Dallas Mus, TX; Corpus Christi Inst of Medical Humanities, Galveston, TX; Menil Coll, Houston, TX; Artistas Plasticas Assoc Sandinista de Trabajadores de la Cultura, Managua, Nicaragua; Library of Congress, Wash, DC
PRINTERS: Artist (ART)
PUBLISHERS: Artist (ART)
GALLERIES: Mary Ryan Gallery, New York, NY; Brody's Gallery, Wash, DC; Tamarind Inst, Albuquerque, NM; Print Club, Phila, PA; Peregrine Gallery, Dallas, TX; W A Graham Gallery, Houston, TX
MAILING ADDRESS: c/o Mary Ryan Gallery, 24 W 57th St, New York, NY 10019

TITLE	PUBLISHER	PRINTER	DATE	MEDIUM	DIMENSION (PAPER SIZE) IN INCHES	TYPE OF PAPER	EDITION NUMBER	NO. OF COLORS	ORIGINAL OPENING PRICE	CURRENT RETAIL PRICE
CURRENT EDITIONS:										
New World Order	ART	ART	1992	WB	30 X 21	SUGI	50	1	600	800

JOHN AXTON

BORN: Carmi, IL
EDUCATION: Southern Illinois Univ, Carbondale, IL
COLLECTIONS: McNay Art Inst, San Antonio, TX

PRINTERS: Shark's Lithography Ltd, Boulder, CO (SLL); Bud Shark, Boulder, CO (BS)
PUBLISHERS: John Szoke Graphics, NY (JSG)
GALLERIES: John Szoke Graphics, New York, NY; Ventana Fine Art, Santa Fe, NM; J Cacciola Galleries, New York, NY

TITLE	PUBLISHER	PRINTER	DATE	MEDIUM	DIMENSION (PAPER SIZE) IN INCHES	TYPE OF PAPER	EDITION NUMBER	NO. OF COLORS	ORIGINAL OPENING PRICE	CURRENT RETAIL PRICE
SOLD OUT EDITIONS (RARE):										
Last Buffalo	JSG	BS/SLL	1982	LC	30 X 22	R/BFK	150	5	450	1000
Drum Maker	JSG	BS/SLL	1983	LC	26 X 34	R/BFK	115	5	500	1000
Silent Passage	JSG	BS/SLL	1983	LC	22 X 31	R/BFK	100	5	450	1000
Taos Echoes	JSG	BS/SLL	1983	LC	22 X 30	R/BFK	150	5	400	600
Boundary Line	JSG	BS/SLL	1984	LC	30 X 40	R/BFK	150	5	550	1000
Chamisa Winds	JSG	BS/SLL	1984	LC	16 X 36	R/BFK	100	5	400	1000
Hacienda Dream	JSG	BS/SLL	1984	LC	30 X 22	R/BFK	115	5	400	600
Deer Dancer	JSG	BS/SLL	1985	LC	30 X 40	R/BFK	100	5	500	900
Rio Grande Rainbow	JSG	BS/SLL	1985	LC	40 X 30	R/BFK	45	5	600	900

The Printworld Directory is accepting new applications for the seventh edition. Approximately 300 new artists will be accepted. Please use the two forms provided in the back section of this directory to submit biographical data and documentation of prints. Edition number of each print must not exceed 500 and the retail price must be $100 or more.

ALICE AYCOCK

BORN: Harrisburg, PA; November 20, 1946
EDUCATION: Douglass Col, New Brunswick, NY, 1964–68; BA; Hunter Col, NY, 1968–71, MA
TEACHING: Art in Res, Williams Col, Williamstown, MA, 1974; Instr, Sculpture, Sch of Visual Arts, NY, 1979–82; Assoc Prof, Hunter Col, NY 1982–85
AWARDS: Nat Endowment for the Arts Grants, 1975,80; Creative Artist Public Service Grant, 1976; City Univ of New York Research Grant, NY, 1983
RECENT EXHIB: John Weber Gallery, NY, 1988; Hudson River Mus, Yonkers, NY, 1988; Freedman Gallery, Albright Col, Reading, PA, 1988; Indianapolis Center for Contemp Art, Heron Gallery, IN, 1989; Storm King Art Center, Mountainville, NY, 1990, 92; Western Washington Univ, Western Gallery, Bellingham, WA 1992
COLLECTIONS: Mus of Mod Art, NY; Williams Col, Williamstown, MA; Amherst Col, MA; Whitney Mus of Am Art, NY; Solomon R Guggenheim Mus, NY; Walker Art Center, Minneapolis, MN; Kunstmuseum, Basel, Switzerland; Museum Ludwig Köln, Germany; Mus of Contemp Art, Chicago, IL; Australian Nat Gallery, Australia; Philadelphia Mus of Art, PA
PRINTERS: Palm Press, Tampa, FL (PP); Atelier Black Box, Chicago, IL (ABB); John W. Roberts, Chicago, IL (JWR); Bill Weege, Madison, WI (BW); Andrew Rubin, Madison, WI (AR); Tandem Press, Univ of Wisconsin, Madison, WI (TanPr)
PUBLISHERS: Graphicstudio II, Tampa, FL (GSII); Klein Gallery, Chicago, IL (K); Lawrence Oliver Gallery, Philadelphia, PA (LOG); Artist (ART); Tandem Press, Univ of Wisconsin, Madison, WI (TanPr)
GALLERIES: John Weber Gallery, New York, NY
MAILING ADDRESS: 142 Greene St, New York, NY 10012

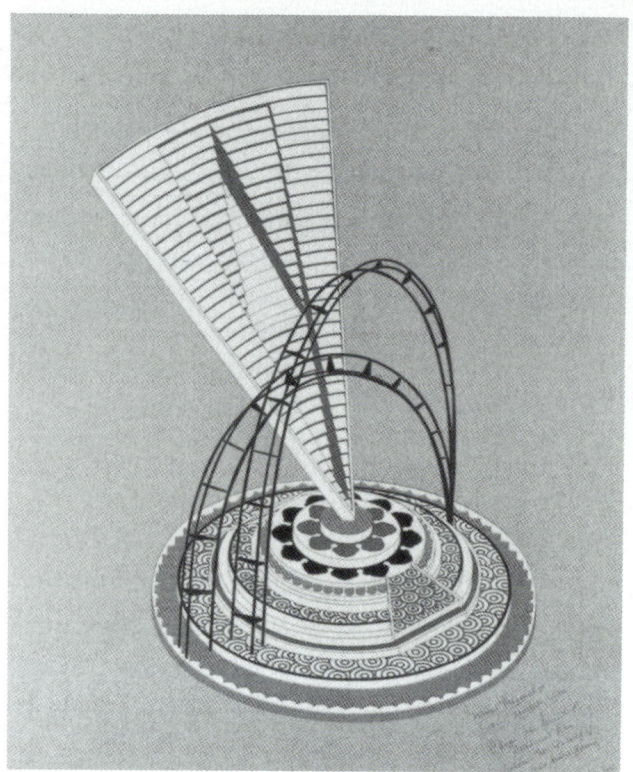

Alice Aycock
Miami Proposal III
Courtesy Tandem Press

TITLE	PUBLISHER	PRINTER	DATE	MEDIUM	DIMENSION (PAPER SIZE) IN INCHES	TYPE OF PAPER	EDITION NUMBER	NO. OF COLORS	ORIGINAL OPENING PRICE	CURRENT RETAIL PRICE
SOLD OUT EDITIONS (RARE):										
How to Catch and Manufacture Ghosts-Collected Ghost Stories:										
From the Workhouse-A	GSII	PP	1981	RH/E/HC	29 X 39	STP	30		1000	2500
From the Workhouse-B	GSII	PP	1981	RH/E/HC	29 X 39	R/BFK	15		1000	2500
Preliminary Study for a Theory of Universal Causality (Time/Creation Machines)	LOG	PP	1982	RH/E/HC	29 X 39	R/BFK	60		1000	2500
The Theory of Universal Causality Series:										
The Theory of Twilight	KG/ART	ABB/JWR	1983	SP	18 X 24	R/BFK/G	35	13	550	1000
The Glance of Eternity	KG/ART	ABB/JWR	1983	SP	18 X 24	R/BFK/G	35	7	550	1000
Miami Proposal I (Steel, Concrete, Water) Above-The Wheely Whirly Steps/Below-Island of the Assembly Place	TanPr TanPr	TanPr TanPr	1990 1990	SP SP	29 X 22 29 X 22	RP/T AP/BL	40 10	4 4	850 950	1500 2000
Miami Proposal II (Steel, Concrete, Water) Above-The Twin Big Wheel/Below-The Island of the Rose Apple Tree (detail)	TanPr	TanPr	1990	SP	29 X 22	RP/T	40	4	850	1500
Miami Proposal III (Steel, Concrete, Water) Above-The Cyclone Tunnel/Below-The Island of the Four Cardinal Points	TanPr TanPr	BW/AR/TanPr BW/AR/TanPr	1990 1990	SP SP	29 X 22 29 X 22	RP/T AP/BL	40 10	4 4	850 950	1500 2000
Miami Proposal IV (Steel, Concrete, Water) Above-The Descent and Redescent Artk/Below- The Island of the Moons and Suns	TanPr TanPr	BW/AR/TanPr BW/AR/TanPr	1990 1990	SP SP	29 X 22 29 X 22	RP/T AP/BL	40 10	4 4	850 950	1500 2000

LUIS CRUZ AZACETA

BORN: Marianao, Cuba; April 5, 1942; US Citizen
EDUCATION: Sch of Visual Arts, NY, with Leon Golub, Frank Roth & Michael Loew, Certificate, 1969
TEACHING: Vis Art, Univ of California, Davis, CA; Vis Art, Louisiana State Univ, Baton Rouge, LA; Vis Art, Univ of California, Berkeley, CA; Vis Art, Cooper Union, NY
AWARDS: Nat Endowment for the Arts Awards, 1980–81, 85–86; Guggenheim Mem Found Grant, NY, 1985–86; New York Found Arts Grant, NY, 1985–86

The retail prices of the 100,000 limited edition prints quoted in this directory are subject to change. Print publishers, artists and galleries were the direct sources for these quotations. Prices in the secondary market listed as "Sold Out Editions (Rare)" indicate that the publisher has a limited supply of that print or that the print is difficult to locate in the galleries.

LUIS CRUZ AZACETA CONTINUED

RECENT EXHIB: Metropolitan Mus of Art, NY, 1987; Mus of Mod Art, NY, 1988; Kunst Statan, Sankt Peter, Cologne, West Germany, 1988; Redding Mus, CA, 1989; Opus Gallery, Miami, FL, 1990; Univ of Minnesota, Duluth Tweed Mus, MN, 1992; Miami-Dade Com Col, FL, 1992; Frumkin/Adams Gallery, NY, 1988,92,93; Galeria Ramis F Barquet, Monterrey, Mexico, 1992,93
COLLECTIONS: Metropolitan mus of Art, NY; Mus of Mod Art, NY; Virginia Mus of Fine Arts, Richmond, VA; Rhode Island Sch of Design, Providence, RI; Delaware Art Mus, Wilmington, DE
PRINTERS: Sette Publishing Company, Tempe, AZ (SPC)
PUBLISHERS: Sette Publishing Company, Tempe, AZ (SPC)
GALLERIES: Frumkin/Adams Gallery, New York, NY; Gallery Paule Anglim, San Francisco, CA; Sette Gallery, Scottsdale, AZ; Arch Gallery, New York, NY; Opus Gallery, Miami, FL; Galeria Ramis F Barquet, Monterrey, Mexico; Galeria Botello II, Hato Rey, PR
MAILING ADDRESS: 1729 Greene Ave, Ridgewood, NY 11385

TITLE	PUBLISHER	PRINTER	DATE	MEDIUM	DIMENSION (PAPER SIZE) IN INCHES	TYPE OF PAPER	EDITION NUMBER	NO. OF COLORS	ORIGINAL OPENING PRICE	CURRENT RETAIL PRICE
CURRENT EDITIONS:										
The Scream	SPC	SPC	1987	LC	49 X 36	AC	50		750	1200

GUILLAUME A AZOULAY

BORN: Casablanca, Morocco; February 8, 1949
COLLECTIONS: Wichita Art Mus, KS; Mussee de Louvre, Cabinet des Dessins, Paris, France; Bibliotheque Nat, Paris, France; Nelson Gallery, Atkins Mus, Kansas City, MO; Monterey Peninsula Mus, CA; Mus of Native Am Cultures, Spokane, WA
PRINTERS: Spectrum Press, NY (SP); Bluestone Editions (BE); Watermark Editions, Hoodsport, WA (WE); Joel Stearns (JS); Martin-John Graphics, Denver, CO (M-JG); Pascal Giraudon (PG)
PUBLISHERS: S M Gupta (SMG); Ondine Enterprises (OnE); American Design, NY (AD); Provenance, Inc, Los Angeles, CA (PI); Metro Gallery, Rochester, NY (MG); Solomon Fima Fine Art, Los Angeles, CA (SFFA)
GALLERIES: Swahn Fine Arts, San Diego, CA; Lake Gallery, Inc, Tahoe City, CA; Gallery One at Second Avenue, Denver, CO; Renaissance Gallery, Pittsburgh, PA; Professional Fine Arts Services, New York, NY
MAILING ADDRESS: Saddle Bow, Bell Canyon, CA 91307

TITLE	PUBLISHER	PRINTER	DATE	MEDIUM	DIMENSION (PAPER SIZE) IN INCHES	TYPE OF PAPER	EDITION NUMBER	NO. OF COLORS	ORIGINAL OPENING PRICE	CURRENT RETAIL PRICE
SOLD OUT EDITIONS (RARE):										
Arabesques	SMG	JS	1977	EB	22 X 30	STP	300	1	125	5000
Harvest Moon	SMG	JS	1977	EB	22 X 30	STP	100	4	100	5000
IL Etait une Fois	SMG	JS	1977	EB	22 X 30	AP	300	1	100	7500
Kaftan and Jellabieh	SMG	JS	1977	EB	22 X 30	STP	100	4	100	7000
la Conversation	SMG	JS	1977	EB	22 X 30	STP	300	1	125	3500
Mere Afrique	SMG	JS	1977	EB	22 X 30	AP	300	1	125	2500
Noir et Blanc	SMG	JS	1977	EB	22 X 30	STP	100	2	100	5000
Ondine	SMG	JS	1977	EB	22 X 30	STP	180	1	125	7500
On the Beach	SMG	JS	1977	EB	22 X 30	STP	250	1	100	2000
Pebbles	SMG	JS	1977	EB	22 X 30	STP	100	1	100	4200
Pégase	SMG	JS	1977	EB	22 X 30	STP	300	1	125	3000
Romain	SMG	JS	1977	EB	22 X 30	STP	100	1	100	4000
Silhouettes	SMG	JS	1977	EB	22 X 30	AP	300	1	125	2500
Three Figures	SMG	JS	1977	EB	22 X 30	STP	100	1	125	4000
Titan	SMG	JS	1977	EB	22 X 30	STP	100	1	100	4000
Camarque, State II	SMG	JS	1977	EB	22 X 30	STP	75	1	100	15000
Torso	OnE	SP	1978	EB	22 X 30	AP	300	1	125	2500
Libre	OnE	SP	1978	EB	22 X 30	STP	300	1	125	2500
Cello	OnE	SP	1978	EB	22 X 30	STP	300	1	125	3000
Printemps	OnE	SP	1978	EB	22 X 30	STP	300	1	125	2500
Cote Pile	OnE	SP	1979	EB	22 X 30	STP	300	1	100	2500
Basic	OnE	SP	1979	EB	22 X 30	STP	300	1	100	2500
Galina	OnE	SP	1979	EB	22 X 30	STP	300	1	125	3200
Pas de Deux	OnE	SP	1979	EB	22 X 30	STP	300	1	100	2500
Etude	OnE	SP	1979	EB	22 X 30	STP	300	1	125	1800
Home Assis	OnE	SP	1979	EB	22 X 30	STP	300	1	125	1800
Recontre	OnE	SP	1979	EB	22 X 30	STP	300	1	125	2000
Whisper	OnE	SP	1979	EB	22 X 30	STP	300	1	125	3800
Set of 5:									800 SET	6000 SET
Dance in the Making	OnE	SP	1980	EB	22 X 30	STP	300	1	160	1500
Dramatique	OnE	SP	1980	EB	22 X 30	STP	300	1	160	1500
Soubresaut	OnE	SP	1980	EB	22 X 30	STP	300	1	160	1500
Retire	OnE	SP	1980	EB	22 X 30	STP	300	1	160	1500
Variation	OnE	SP	1980	EB	22 X 30	STP	300	1	160	1500
La Jumet pour Stuart	AD	BE	1980	EB	22 X 30	STP	300	1	300	1800
La Chute	AD	SP	1980	EB	22 X 30	STP	300	1	400	2500
Le Chevaux (Set of 3):									900 SET	6000 SET
Colere	OnE	SP	1980	EB	22 X 30	STP	300	1	300	2200
Quatre Chevaux	OnE	SP	1980	EB	22 X 30	STP	300	1	300	2200
Les Chevaux	OnE	SP	1980	EB	22 X 30	STP	300	1	300	2200
Monegasque	AD	SD	1980	SP	22 X 32	STP	300	Multi	500	900
Maureque	AD	SD	1980	SP	22 X 32	STP	300	Multi	300	900
Chasse	AD	SP	1980	EB	22 X 30	STP	300	1	200	2000

The print market has become very selective. For the first time since we published the first edition of The Printworld Directory in 1982, the prices of prints have been greatly reduced and greatly increased for the same artists by the most reputable and established print publishers. Check the fifth edition to understand the movement.

GUILLAME A AZOULAY CONTINUED

TITLE	PUBLISHER	PRINTER	DATE	MEDIUM	DIMENSION (PAPER SIZE) IN INCHES	TYPE OF PAPER	EDITION NUMBER	NO. OF COLORS	ORIGINAL OPENING PRICE	CURRENT RETAIL PRICE
SOLD OUT EDITIONS (RARE):										
Les Arlequinades (Set of 3):									900 SET	8000 SET
L'Assassinat	OnE	SP	1980	EB	22 X 30	STP	300	1	300	2200
Le Baiser	OnE	SP	1980	EB	22 X 30	STP	300	1	300	2200
Au Bord de L'Eau	OnE	SP	1980	EB	22 X 30	STP	300	1	300	2200
Images, I–IV	AD	SP	1981	EB	20 X 30 EA	STP	300 EA	1 EA	1600 EA	5000 EA
Contraction	AD	SP	1981	EB	18 X 24	STP	300	1	500	1500
Arnaud	AD	SP	1981	EB	22 X 30	AP	300	1	500	1800
Epuise	AD	SP	1981	EB	30 X 22	AP	300	1	400	4200
Embuscade	AD	SP	1981	EB	22 X 30	STP	300	1	400	3500
La Bete	AD	SP	1981	EB	22 X 30	STP	300	1	500	7000
Home	AD	WE	1982	EB	19 X 15	STP	300	1	300	1400
Le Mouvement	AD	SP	1982	EB	22 X 30	STP	300	1	500	2000
Shahrit	AD	WE	1982	EB	22 X 30	STP	300	1	500	4000
Deux Bisons	AD	SP	1982	EB	22 X 30	STP	300	1	400	2500
Variations on a Theme:									1000 SET	4000 SET
The Fall	AD	SP	1982	EB	15 X 19	STP	300	1	350	1500
The Missing Bra	AD	SP	1982	EB	15 X 19	STP	300	1	350	1500
Stepping Out	AD	SP	1982	EB	15 X 19	STP	300	1	350	1500
Willows	AD	SP	1982	EB	22 X 30	STP	300	1	1500	7000
Souk	AD	SP	1982	EB	22 X 30	STP	300	1	500	2000
Blesse'	AD	SP	1982	EB	22 X 30	STP	300	1	500	2000
Murmure	AD	WE	1982	SP	19 X 22	STP	300	14	500	1500
Twin Spires	AD	WE	1983	SP	22 X 30	STP	300	Multi	500	1000
Run for the Roses	AD	SP	1983	EB	22 X 30	STP	300	1	500	1800
Preakness	AD	SP	1983	EB	22 X 30	STP	300	1	500	2000
Compagnon des Mauvais Jours	AD	WE	1983	SP	18 X 24	STP	300	1	500	1000
Belmont	AD	SP	1983	SP	22 X 30	STP	300	1	500	1800
Full Field	AD	WE	1983	SP	22 X 30	STP	300	Multi	500	2500
Blue Horse	AD	WE	1983	SP	22 X 30	STP	300	Multi	600	2000
Homage to C Dellepiane	AD	WE	1983	SP	22 X 30	STP	300	17	500	1800
Derby	AD	SP	1983	EB	22 X 30	STP	300	1	500	3200
Dejeuner	AD	BE	1983	EB	14 X 16	STP	300	1	500	3500
Last Furlong	AD	SP	1983	EB	22 X 30	STP	300	1	500	2500
Fugue	AD	BE	1984	EB	26 X 22	STP	230	1	500	2000
Monsieur Hamilton	AD	BE	1984	EB	22 X 26	STP	300	1	500	1200
Suite (Set of 2):										
State I	AD	BE	1984	EB	22 X 26	JAP	300	1	700	2700
State II	AD	BE	1984	EB	22 X 26	STP	230	1	500	1800
Fantasia	AD	WE	1984	SP	20 X 28	STP	230	Multi	600	2800
Rires et Sourires	AD	BE	1984	EB	22 X 26	STP	120	1	600	1500
Allegro	AD	BE	1984	EB	11 X 13	STP	300	1	250	600
Joy of Thora (Set of 3)	AD	BE	1984	EB	22 X 26 EA	STP	300 EA	1 EA	1500 SET	3500 SET
Suite of Three:									750 SET	1800 SET
Purpurea Autres Saules	AD	BE	1984	EB	11 X 13	STP	300	1	250	650
Gracilistyla Autres Saules	AD	BE	1984	EB	11 X 13	STP	300	1	250	650
Matsudana Autres Saules	AD	BE	1984	EB	11 X 13	STP	300	1	250	650
Le Vacher	AD	BE	1984	EB	11 X 13	STP	300	1	250	650
L'Indian	AD	BE	1984	EB	11 X 13	STP	300	1	250	650
Hamilton Encore	AD	BE	1984	EB	22 X 26	STP	230	1	500	900
Danse du Bison	AD	BE	1985	EB	22 X 36	STP	230	1	600	1000
Les Cariatides (Set of 2)	AD	BE	1985	EB	22 X 26 EA	STP	230 EA	1 EA	600 SET	1500 SET
Manipulateur	AD	WE	1985	EB	30 X 22	STP	230	1	600	900
Passo di Due	AD	BE	1985	EB	22 X 26	STP	230	1	600	900
Regain	OnE	BE	1985	EB	22 X 26	STP	230	1	500	900
La Mere et Son Fils	AD	M-JG	1985–86	SP	23 X 30	COV	230	Multi	500	900
Chai (Set of 3):									1500 SET	2500 SET
Dixhuit Chevaux I	AD	M-JG	1985–86	SP	19 X 23	COV	230	Multi	500	900
Dixhuit Chevaux II	AD	M-JG	1985–86	SP	19 X 23	COV	230	Multi	500	900
Dixhuit Chevaux III	AD	M-JG	1985–86	SP	19 X 23	COV	230	Multi	500	900
Twilight	PI	M-JG	1986	SP	29 X 36	STP	225	Multi	600	900
Rue de L'Horloge	PI	WE	1986	SP	28 X 36	STP	225	Multi	600	900
Exodus	PI	M-JG	1986	SP	29 X 36	STP	225	Multi	600	900
Sagittaire (B&W)	MG/SFFA	PG	1988	EB	22 X 30	AP	35	1	900	1500
Sagittaire (Color)	MG/SFFA	PG	1988	EB/HC	22 X 30	AP	65		1200	1800
Sagittaire (Gold Leaf)	MG/SFFA	PG	1988	EB/GL	22 X 30	AP	75		1500	2100
Sagittaire (Remark)	MG/SFFA	PG	1988	REM	22 X 30	AP	35		1800	3500
Behest Palace	MG	PG	1989	EB	25 X 36	AP	10	1	9500	18000
King of Hearts	MG/SFFA	STS	1990	SP	36 X 36	COV	100	15	1750	2500
CURRENT EDITIONS:										
Taurus (Black & White)	MG/SFFA	PG	1989	EB	22 X 30	AP	35		900	1500
Taurus (Color)	MG/SFFA	PG	1989	EB/HC	22 X 30	AP	65		1200	1800
Taurus (Gold Leaf)	MG/SFFA	PG	1989	EB/GL	22 X 30	AP	75		1500	2100
Taurus (Remark)	MG/SFFA	PG	1989	REM	22 X 30	AP	35		1800	3500

GUILLAME A AZOULAY CONTINUED

TITLE	PUBLISHER	PRINTER	DATE	MEDIUM	DIMENSION (PAPER SIZE) IN INCHES	TYPE OF PAPER	EDITION NUMBER	NO. OF COLORS	ORIGINAL OPENING PRICE	CURRENT RETAIL PRICE
CURRENT EDITIONS:										
Aquarius (Black & White)	MG/SFFA	PG	1989	EB	22 X 30	AP	35		900	1500
Aquarius (Color)	MG/SFFA	PG	1989	EB/HC	22 X 30	AP	65		1200	1800
Aquarius (Gold Leaf)	MG/SFFA	PG	1989	EB/GL	22 X 30	AP	75		1500	2100
Aquarius (Remark)	MG/SFFA	PG	1989	REM	22 X 30	AP	35		1800	3500
Leo (Black & White)	MG/SFFA	PG	1989	EB	22 X 30	AP	35		900	1500
Leo (Color)	MG/SFFA	PG	1989	EB/HC	22 X 30	AP	65		1200	1800
Leo (Gold Leaf)	MG/SFFA	PG	1989	EB/GL	22 X 30	AP	75		1500	2100
Leo (Remark)	MG/SFFA	PG	1989	REM	22 X 30	AP	35		1800	3500
Scorpio (Black & White)	MG/SFFA	PG	1989	EB	22 X 30	AP	35		900	1500
Scorpio (Color)	MG/SFFA	PG	1989	EB/HC	22 X 30	AP	65		1200	1800
Scorpio (Gold Leaf)	MG/SFFA	PG	1989	EB/GL	22 X 30	AP	75		1500	2100
Scorpio (Remark)	MG/SFFA	PG	1989	REM	22 X 30	AP	35		1800	3500
Gemini (Black & White)	MG/SFFA	PG	1990	EB	22 X 30	AP	35		900	1500
Gemini (Color)	MG/SFFA	PG	1990	EB/HC	22 X 30	AP	65		1200	1800
Gemini (Gold Leaf)	MG/SFFA	PG	1990	EB/GL	22 X 30	AP	75		1500	2100
Gemini (Remark)	MG/SFFA	PG	1990	REM	22 X 30	AP	35		1800	3500
Virgo (Black & White)	MG/SFFA	PG	1990	EB	22 X 30	AP	35		900	1500
Virgo (Color)	MG/SFFA	PG	1990	EB/HC	22 X 30	AP	65		1200	1800
Virgo (Gold Leaf)	MG/SFFA	PG	1990	EB/GL	22 X 30	AP	75		1500	2100
Virgo (Remark)	MG/SFFA	PG	1990	REM	22 X 30	AP	35		1800	3500
Aries (Black & White)	MG/SFFA	PG	1991	EB	22 X 30	AP	35		900	900
Aries (Color)	MG/SFFA	PG	1991	EB/HC	22 X 30	AP	65		1200	1200
Aries (Gold Leaf)	MG/SFFA	PG	1991	EB/GL	22 X 30	AP	75		1500	1500
Aries (Remark)	MG/SFFA	PG	1991	REM	22 X 30	AP	35		1800	2500
Cancer (Black & White)	MG/SFFA	PG	1991	EB	22 X 30	AP	35		900	900
Cancer (Color)	MG/SFFA	PG	1991	EB/HC	22 X 30	AP	65		1200	1200
Cancer (Gold Leaf)	MG/SFFA	PG	1991	EB/GL	22 X 30	AP	75		1500	1500
Cancer (Remark)	MG/SFFA	PG	1991	REM	22 X 30	AP	35		1800	1800
Capricorn (Black & White)	MG/SFFA	PG	1992	EB	22 X 30	AP	35		900	900
Capricorn (Color)	MG/SFFA	PG	1992	EB/HC	22 X 30	AP	65		1200	1200
Capricorn (Gold Leaf)	MG/SFFA	PG	1992	EB/GL	22 X 30	AP	75		1500	1500
Capricorn (Remark)	MG/SFFA	PG	1992	REM	22 X 30	AP	35		1800	2500
Libra (Black & White)	MG/SFFA	PG	1992	EB	22 X 30	AP	35		900	900
Libra (Color)	MG/SFFA	PG	1992	EB/HC	22 X 30	AP	65		1200	1200
Libra (Gold Leaf)	MG/SFFA	PG	1992	EB/GL	22 X 30	AP	75		1500	1500
Libra (Remark)	MG/SFFA	PG	1992	REM	22 X 30	AP	35		1800	2500
Pisces (Black & White)	MG/SFFA	PG	1992	EB	22 X 30	AP	35		900	900
Pisces (Color)	MG/SFFA	PG	1992	EB/HC	22 X 30	AP	65		1200	1200
Pisces (Gold Leaf)	MG/SFFA	PG	1992	EB/GL	22 X 30	AP	75		1500	1500
Pisces (Remark)	MG/SFFA	PG	1992	REM	22 X 30	AP	35		1800	2500

DAVID AZUZ

BORN: Tel Aviv, Israel; 1942
EDUCATION: Acad of Joseph Schwartzman, Israel, 1951–55; Anvi Acad, Tel Aviv, Israel, 1955–58; Grand Chaumiere & Acad des Beaux Arts, Paris, France, 1958–63

PRINTERS: Artist (ART)
PUBLISHERS: Jackie Fine Arts, Inc, NY (JFA)
GALLERIES: Soufer Gallery, New York, NY; Galerie René Drouet, Paris, France; Ro Gallery Image Makers, Inc, New York, NY
MAILING ADDRESS: 47, Av de la Motte Picquet, 75015, Paris, France

TITLE	PUBLISHER	PRINTER	DATE	MEDIUM	DIMENSION (PAPER SIZE) IN INCHES	TYPE OF PAPER	EDITION NUMBER	NO. OF COLORS	ORIGINAL OPENING PRICE	CURRENT RETAIL PRICE
SOLD OUT EDITIONS (RARE):										
Bistro Booth	JFA	ART	1979	SP	19 X 25	AP	200	29	350	450
Gray Lady Red, Bar	JFA	ART	1979	LC	19 X 25	AP	200	14	350	450
Dome of Montparnasse	JFA	ART	1979	SP	19 X 25	AP	200	30	350	450
Market in Napoli	JFA	ART	1979	LC	19 X 25	AP	200	12	350	450
Martinique	JFA	ART	1979	SP	19 X 25	AP	200	26	350	450
The Select Montparnasse	JFA	ART	1979	SP	19 X 25	AP	200	28	350	450
Women of Guadeloupe	JFA	ART	1979	SP	19 X 25	AP	200	32	350	450
Cafe La Ronde a Montparnasse	JFA	ART	1979	SP	19 X 25	AP	200	33	350	450
CURRENT EDITIONS:										
Marche Daquerre	JFA	ART	1979	SP	19 X 25	AP	200	32	350	450
Tropical Flowers	JFA	ART	1979	SP	20 X 25	AP	200	28	350	450
Coupole Bar Montparnasse, Paris	JFA	ART	1979	LC	19 X 25	AP	200	15	350	450
Italian Waiter	JFA	ART	1979	SP	19 X 25	AP	200	21	350	450
Waiter in Cafe Margolin	JFA	ART	1979	SP	19 X 25	AP	200	28	350	450
Dome Montparnasse, Paris	JFA	ART	1979	SP	19 X 25	AP	200	22	350	450
La Guadeloupe	JFA	ART	1979	SP	19 X 25	AP	200	24	350	450
Solitude	JFA	ART	1979	SP	19 X 25	AP	200	36	350	450
Le Bistro	JFA	ART	1979	SP	18 X 24	AP	200	18	350	450

DAVID AZUZ CONTINUED

TITLE	PUBLISHER	PRINTER	DATE	MEDIUM	DIMENSION (PAPER SIZE) IN INCHES	TYPE OF PAPER	EDITION NUMBER	NO. OF COLORS	ORIGINAL OPENING PRICE	CURRENT RETAIL PRICE
CURRENT EDITIONS:										
Market in the Virgin Islands	JFA	ART	1979	SP	19 X 25	AP	200	24	350	450
The Billiard Room	JFA	ART	1979	SP	19 X 25	AP	200	35	350	450
Open Air Market	JFA	ART	1979	SP	19 X 25	AP	200	30	350	450
Bartender in Green	JFA	ART	1979	LC	19 X 25	AP	200	19	350	450
Yeshiva Boy	JFA	ART	1979	SP	19 X 25	AP	200	31	350	450
Dreaming in Montparnasse Cafe, Paris	JFA	ART	1980	SP	19 X 25	AP	200	15	350	450

ALICE BABER

BORN: Charleston, IL; (1928–1982)
EDUCATION: Indiana Univ, Bloomington, IN, BFA, 1950; Fountainbleau, France, MFA
TEACHING: Univ of Minnesota, Duluth, MN, 1970–71; Univ of California, Santa Barbara, CA, 1971; State Univ of New York, Purchase, NY, 1972–73; Sch of Visual Arts, NY, 1974–76; Univ of California, Berkeley, CA, 1976; Sch for Social Res, NY, 1975–77
RECENT EXHIB: Bicentennial Art Center & Mus, Paris, IL, 1989; Helander Gallery, Palm Beach, FL, 1991; Eastern Illinois Univ, Tarble Arts Center, Charleston, IL, 1989,92
COLLECTIONS: Metropolitan Mus of Art, NY; Whitney Mus of Am Art, NY; Mus of Mod Art, NY; Guggenheim Mus, NY; Corcoran Gallery, Wash, DC; San Francisco Mus of Art, CA; Nat Coll of Fine Arts, Wash, DC
PRINTERS: La Poligrafa, Barcelona, Spain (LP); Tamarind Institute, Albuquerque, NM (TI); Brynn Jensen (BJ); Timothy P Sheesley (TPS); Catherine Kisch Kuhn (CK)
PUBLISHERS: Mourlot, Paris, France (MP); Tamarind Institute, Albuquerque, NM (TI); Ediciones Poligrafa, Barcelona, Spain (EdP)
GALLERIES: Lillian Heidenberg Gallery, New York, NY; Galeria Joan Prats, New York, NY & Barcelona, Spain, & Paris, France; Tamarind Institute, Albuquerque, NM; Frances Aronson Gallery, Atlanta, GA; Eva Cohon Gallery, Highland Park, IL

Alice Baber
Ancestor of the Wind
Courtesy Tamarind Institute

TITLE	PUBLISHER	PRINTER	DATE	MEDIUM	DIMENSION (PAPER SIZE) IN INCHES	TYPE OF PAPER	EDITION NUMBER	NO. OF COLORS	ORIGINAL OPENING PRICE	CURRENT RETAIL PRICE
SOLD OUT EDITIONS (RARE):										
Catalonian Diary:										
Transformation (Set of 5):	EdP	LP	1979	LC	30 X 22	GP	75		1100 SET	2000 SET
The Texture of the Mountain becomes a Wing	EdP	LP	1979	LC	30 X 22	GP	75	5	250	450
The Space between the Mountains becomes a Dance	EdP	LP	1979	LC	30 X 22	GP	75	5	250	450
The Wing of the Mountain Turns to Light	EdP	LP	1979	LC	30 X 22	GP	75	5	250	450
The Shadow of the Mountain becomes the Light	EdP	LP	1979	LC	30 X 22	GP	75	5	250	450
The Wing of the Mountain Dances to the Piper	EdP	LP	1979	LC	30 X 22	GP	75	5	250	450
Ceremony: Rock and Dancing Yellow	TI	BJ/TI	1979	LC	26 X 19	ARJ	12	3	200	800
Preparation of the Fetish:										
Air, Light, Sun, Rain	TI	TPS/TI	1979	LC	26 X 19	ARJ	40	5	200	800
Appearance of the Wind Tree Light	TI	BJ/TI	1979	LC	31 X 23	AC/B	10	4	250	550
Ancestor of the Wind	TI	BJ/TI	1979	LB	31 X 23	AC/W	10	1	250	550
Presentation of the Ancestors of the Wind (State II)	TI	BJ/TI	1979	LC	31 X 23	AC/W	8	3	250	800
Dance of the Ancestors of the Tree	TI	BJ/TI	1979	LC	31 X 23	AC/W	8	3	250	800
Ceremony of the Dancing Jaguar	TI	CK/TI	1979	LC	20 X 26	AC/W	40	4	200	800
Center of the Wind	TI	CK/TI	1979	LC	23 X 31	AC/W	20	3	250	800
Spiral of the Wind Dance	TI	CK/TI	1979	LC	23 X 31	AC/W	15	4	250	800
Transformation of the Fetish:										
Water, Jaguar, Wind	TI	TPS/TI	1979	LC	23 X 31	ARJ	12	2	250	800
Road to the Ceremony of the Blue Dance	TI	TPS/TI	1979	LC	31 X 23	AC/BL	20	3	250	800
Mountain Road to the Mask	TI	TPS/TI	1979	LC	23 X 31	AC/BL	20	3	250	800

BRUCE BACON

BORN: New York, NY; 1935
EDUCATION: Rhode Island Sch of Design, Providence, RI
TEACHING: Sch of the Visual Arts, NY
PRINTERS: Artist (ART)
PUBLISHERS: Fred Dorfman, Inc, NY (FDI)
GALLERIES: Fred Dorfman Gallery, New York, NY

TITLE	PUBLISHER	PRINTER	DATE	MEDIUM	DIMENSION (PAPER SIZE) IN INCHES	TYPE OF PAPER	EDITION NUMBER	NO. OF COLORS	ORIGINAL OPENING PRICE	CURRENT RETAIL PRICE
CURRENT EDITIONS:										
Gliders With Attachments	FDI	ART	1979	LC	24 X 30	AP	140	7	150	350
Ten Flappers	FDI	ART	1979	LC	24 X 30	AP	140	7	150	350

FRANCIS BACON

BORN: Dublin, Ireland; (1909–1992)
EDUCATION: Self-Taught
RECENT EXHIB: Marlborough Gallery, NY, 1987; Galerie Lelong, Paris, France, 1987; Retrosp, Galerie Ernst Beyeler, Basel, Switzerland, 1987; Scottish Nat Gallery of Mod Art, Edinburgh, Scotland, 1989; Mus of Mod Art, NY, 1990; Marlborough Gallery, Madrid, Spain, 1992; Marlborough Gallery, NY, 1990,92,93
COLLECTIONS: Mus of Mod Art, NY; Guggenheim Mus, NY; Carnegie Inst, Pittsburgh, PA
PRINTERS: Maeght Lelong, Paris, France (ML); La Poligrafa, SA, Barcelona, Spain (LP); Ediciones de la Différence, Paris, France (EdD); Centre Nat d'Art Contemporain, Paris, France (CNAC); A Manaranthe Lithography (AML); Arte, Paris, France (Arte); Arts-Litho, Paris, France (AL)
PUBLISHERS: Maeght Lelong, Paris, France (ML); Ediciones Poligrafa, SA, Barcelona, Spain (EdP); Galerie Lelong, Paris, France (GL); Metropolitan Mus of Art, NY (MMA); Arte, Paris, France (ARTE); Arts Litho, Paris, France (AL); Marlborough Graphics, NY (MG)
GALLERIES: Galerie Lelong, New York, NY & Paris, France & Zürich, Switzerland; Marlborough Galleries, New York, NY & London, England; Waddington Galleries, London, England; Galeria Joan Prats, New York, NY & Barcelona, Spain; Nathan Silberberg Fine Arts, New York, NY; Galerie Ernst Beyeler, Basel, Switzerland; Charles Whitchurch Fine Arts, Huntington Beach, CA; Andrew Dierken Fine Art, Los Angeles, CA; Barbara Gillman Gallery, Miami, FL; Arras Galleries, New York, NY; Claude Bernard Gallery, New York, NY; R K Goldman Contemporary, Los Angeles, CA; Ehrenkranz Fine Arts, Chevy Chase, MD; TwoSixtyOne Art, New York, NY; Professional Arts Services, Inc, New York, NY

  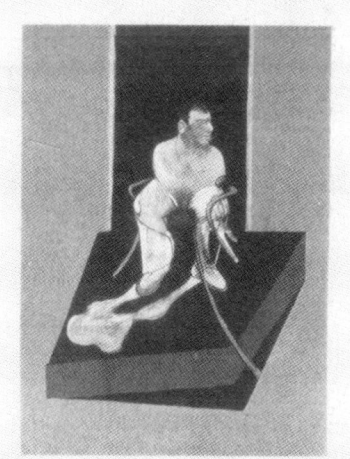

Francis Bacon
Triptych
Courtesy Ediciones Poligrafa

TITLE	PUBLISHER	PRINTER	DATE	MEDIUM	DIMENSION (PAPER SIZE) IN INCHES	TYPE OF PAPER	EDITION NUMBER	NO. OF COLORS	ORIGINAL OPENING PRICE	CURRENT RETAIL PRICE
SOLD OUT EDITIONS (RARE):										
Study for Bullfight No 1	CNAC	Arte	1971	LC	50 X 45	AP	150		3500	16000
Metropolitan Museum Poster	MMA	AML	1975	LC	45 X 34	AP	200		600	4500
Three Studies for a Self Portrait (Set of 3)	EdD	AL	1979	LC	19 X 41 EA	AP	25 EA		3500 SET	15000 SET
Triptych Studies of the Human Body (Set of 3)	MG		1979	LC	40 X 26 EA	AP	250 EA		3500 SET	15000 SET
Triptych Inspired by Orestia of Aeschylus (Set of 3)	EdD	AL	1979	LC	21 X 41 EA	AP	25 EA		3500 SET	8500 SET
Etude de Corps Humain	ML	ML	1983	LB	88 X 61 cm	AP	180		25000 FF	80000 FF
Seated Figure	EdP	LP	1983	MM/CAR	40 X 28	GP	99	1	7500	15000
Set of Three (Trip)	EdP	LP	1987	EC	26 X 19 EA	AP	99		15000 SET	25000 SET
Three Studies of the Male Back (Trip)	GL		1987		32 X 22 EA		99 EA		10000 SET	15000 SET
Study for Portrait of John Edwards	GL		1987		27 X 20		180		3500	6500

The retail prices of the 100,000 limited edition prints quoted in this directory are subject to change. Print publishers, artists and galleries were the direct sources for these quotations. Prices in the secondary market listed as "Sold Out Editions (Rare)" indicate that the publisher has a limited supply of that print or that the print is difficult to locate in the galleries.

FRED BADALAMENTI

BORN: Long Island, NY; June 25, 1935
EDUCATION: Pratt Inst, NY; 1953–55; State Univ New York Col, New Paltz, NY, BA, 1958–61; Brooklyn Col, NY, MFA, 1967; Studied with Philip Pearlstein
TEACHING: Assoc Prof, Drawing & Painting, Brooklyn Col, NY, 1967 to present, Dept Chmn, Grad Art, 1972 to present; Vis Assoc Prof, Drawing & Painting, State Univ of New York, Stony Brook, NY, 1977–78 & Summer, 1980,81,83
COLLECTIONS: Brooklyn Col, NY; State Univ of New York, Stony Brook, NY
PRINTERS: Welden Press, Sag Harbor, NY (WP)
PUBLISHERS: Welden Press, Sag Harbor, NY (WP)
GALLERIES: First Street Gallery, New York, NY
MAILING ADDRESS: 182 Lower Sheep Pasture Rd, Setauket, NY 11733

TITLE	PUBLISHER	PRINTER	DATE	MEDIUM	DIMENSION (PAPER SIZE) IN INCHES	TYPE OF PAPER	EDITION NUMBER	NO. OF COLORS	ORIGINAL OPENING PRICE	CURRENT RETAIL PRICE
CURRENT EDITIONS:										
Memento Mori	WP	WP	1979	LB	21 X 26	AP	36	1	110	300
Studio Study I-V	WP	WP	1980	LB	10 X 11 EA	AP	36 EA	1 EA	70 EA	200 EA

JOHN BACK

PRINTERS: Artist (ART)
PUBLISHERS: Essentials Editions, NY (EE)

TITLE	PUBLISHER	PRINTER	DATE	MEDIUM	DIMENSION (PAPER SIZE) IN INCHES	TYPE OF PAPER	EDITION NUMBER	NO. OF COLORS	ORIGINAL OPENING PRICE	CURRENT RETAIL PRICE
CURRENT EDITIONS:										
Smaller than Small and Bigger than Big	EE	ART	1982–86	PH	20 X 16	AP	40		400	500

DONALD BAECHLER

BORN: Hartford, CT; 1956
EDUCATION: Maryland Inst, Col of Art, Baltimore, MD, 1974–77; Cooper Union, NY, 1977–78; Staatliche Hochschule fuer Bildende Kuenste, Frankfurt, Germany, 1978–79
RECENT EXHIB: Whitney Mus of Am Art, NY, 1989; Paul Kasmin Gallery, NY, 1989; Tony Shafrazi Gallery, NY, 1989; Illinois State Univ, Univ Galleries, Normal, IL, 1989; Baron/Boisante Editions, NY, 1990
COLLECTIONS: Mus of Mod Art, NY; Metropolitan Mus of Art, NY; Philadelphia Mus of Art, PA; Centre Pompidou, Paris, France; William Alan Mus, Oberlin, OH
PRINTERS: Larry B Wright Art Productions, NY (LBW); Chip Elwell, NY (CE); Andrew Bovell, NY (AB); Mark Baron, Riverdale, NY (MB); Donna Shulman, Brooklyn, NY (DS); Downstairs Editions, Brooklyn, NY (DE); Ruth Lingen, NY (RL); Joe Wilfer, NY (JW); Spring Street Workshop, NY (SpSW); Alexander Heinrici, NY (AH); Heinrici Studios, NY (HS); Felix Harlan, NY (FH); Carol Weaver, NY (CW); Nicole Ouellette, NY (NO); Michael Wodkowski, NY (MW); Harlan & Weaver Intaglio, NY (HWI); Edition Works, Tokyo, Japan, (EdW)
PUBLISHERS: Delano Greenridge Editions, NY (DGE); Barbara Gladstone Gallery, NY (BGG); Tony Shafrazi Gallery, NY (TSG); Mark Baron, Riverdale, NY (MB); Baron/Boisante Editions, NY (B/B); Spring Street Workshop, NY (SpSW); Edition Works, Tokyo, Japan (EdW); AC&T Corporation, Tokyo, Japan, (ACTC)
GALLERIES: Tony Shafrazi Gallery, New York, NY; Pat Hearn Gallery, New York, NY; Mokotoff Asian Arts, New York, NY; Montenay del Sol Gallery, Paris, France; Castelli Graphics, New York, NY; Greenberg Gallery Annex, St Louis, MO; Pace Prints, New York, NY; Goodman/Tinnon Fine Art, San Francisco, CA; Baron/Boisante Gallery, New York, NY; Paul Krasmin Gallery, New York, NY; John Post Lee Gallery, New York, NY; Turner Fine Art, New York, NY

Donald Baechler
Conversation
Courtesy AC & T Corporation

MAILING ADDRESS: c/o Tony Shafrazi Gallery, 163 Mercer St, New York, NY 10012

TITLE	PUBLISHER	PRINTER	DATE	MEDIUM	DIMENSION (PAPER SIZE) IN INCHES	TYPE OF PAPER	EDITION NUMBER	NO. OF COLORS	ORIGINAL OPENING PRICE	CURRENT RETAIL PRICE
SOLD OUT EDITIONS (RARE):										
Donald Baechler (Set of 6)	DGE	LBW	1984	SP/HC	24 X 24 EA	STP	30 EA		1200 SET	10000 SET
Five Woodcuts (Set of 5)	BGG/TSG	CE/AB	1985	WC	26 X 26 EA	KOZO	20 EA	3 EA	2000 SET	12000 SET
Objects (Set of 8)	MB	DS/DE	1986	AC	20 X 14 EA	FAB	12 EA		2400 SET	15000 SET
Subjects (Set of 5)	MB	DS/DE	1986	AC	20 X 14 EA	FAB	12 EA		1500 SET	10000 SET
Increments (Set of 5)	MB	DS/DE	1987	EB/A/SG/SB	36 X 28 EA	FAB	17 EA		4000 SET	18000 SET
The Assistants (Set of 9)	B/B	DS/DE	1988	A/SB/LG	17 X 14 EA	FAB	19 EA		3600 SET	12000 SET

DONALD BAECHLER CONTINUED

TITLE	PUBLISHER	PRINTER	DATE	MEDIUM	DIMENSION (PAPER SIZE) IN INCHES	TYPE OF PAPER	EDITION NUMBER	NO. OF COLORS	ORIGINAL OPENING PRICE	CURRENT RETAIL PRICE
CURRENT EDITIONS:										
Composition with Guitar	SpSW	JW/SpSW	1988	STEN/WC	35 X 35	HMP	22		3500	4500
Composition with Suitcase	SpSW	JW/SpSW	1988	STEN/WC	35 X 35	HMP	22		3500	4500
Tree	SpSW	JW/SpSW	1988	STEN/WC	35 X 35	HMP	22		3500	4500
Flowers and Trees (for Klaus Wittmann) (Set of 6)	SpSW	JW/SpSW	1990	EB/REL/CC	26 X 20 EA	HMP	50 EA		5000 SET 1200 EA	5000 SET 1200 EA
Onion Eater I-V (Set of 5)	TSG	AH/HS	1991	SP	30 X 30	KOZO	50 EA	21 EA	10000 SET	10000 SET
Owls (Set of 7)	B/B	FH/CW/NO/ MW/HWI	1992	EB/A	25 X 19 EA	SOM/S	24 EA	1 EA	5600 SET	5600 SET
Fruits (Set of 5)	EdW	EdW	1990	LC	35 X 28 EA	HMP	35 EA		10000 SET	10000 SET
Conversation	ACTC		1990	WC	59 X 58	JP	30		3500	4000

JOHN BAEDER

BORN: South Bend, IN; December 24, 1938
EDUCATION: Auburn Univ, AL, BA, 1960; Emory Univ, Atlanta, GA; Georgia State Univ, Atlanta, GA
COLLECTIONS: Whitney Mus of Am Art, NY; Denver Art Mus, CO; Detroit Inst of Arts, MI; Rhode Island Sch of Design, Providence, RI; Yale Univ, New Haven, CT; Cooper-Hewitt Mus, NY; High Mus, Atlanta, GA; Mus of Mod Art, NY
PRINTERS: Donn Steward, Halesite, NY (DS); Norman Lassiter, NY (NL); Lassiter-Meisel, NY (LM); Muhammad Khalil, NY (MK); JB Editions, NY (JBE); Timothy Berry (TB); Teaberry Press, Oakland, CA (TP); Alexander Heinrici, NY (AH); Studio Heinrici, Ltd, NY (SH)
PUBLISHERS: London Arts, Inc, Detroit, MI (LAI); Abrams Original Editions, NY (AOE); Madeleine-Claude Jobrick, NY (M-CJ); Donn Steward, Halesite, NY (DS); J B Editions, NY (JBE); Muhammad Khalil, NY (MK); Morgan Gallery, Kansas City, KS (MG)
GALLERIES: OK Harris Works of Art, New York, NY; Thomas Segal Gallery, Boston, MA; Morgan Gallery, Kansas City, MO; Cumberland Gallery, Nashville, TN; Helander Gallery, Palm Beach, FL; Modernism, San Francisco, CA; Ro Gallery Image Makers, Inc, New York, NY

John Baeder
Lisi's Pittsfield Diner
Courtesy London Arts, Inc

John Baeder
Blue Beacon
Courtesy London Arts, Inc

TITLE	PUBLISHER	PRINTER	DATE	MEDIUM	DIMENSION (PAPER SIZE) IN INCHES	TYPE OF PAPER	EDITION NUMBER	NO. OF COLORS	ORIGINAL OPENING PRICE	CURRENT RETAIL PRICE
SOLD OUT EDITIONS (RARE):										
American Grille	LPI	LPI	1975	LB	18 X 24	AP	50	2	250	1000
Empire Diner	M-CJ		1975	PA/E/MEZ	18 X 24	AP	100	1	200	1000
CURRENT EDITIONS:										
Embassy Diner	DS	DS	1976	EB	20 X 22	AP	40	1	250	1000
White Manna Hamburgers	LAI	NL/EL-M	1978	E/MEZ	22 X 30	AP	200	1	500	1000
Interior Curly's Diner	LAI	NL/EL-M	1978	E/MEZ	22 X 30	AP	200	1	500	1000
Boulevard Diner	LAI	NL/EL-M	1978	E/MEZ	22 X 30	AP	200	1	500	1000
Buddy's Truck Stop	LAI	NL/EL-M	1978	E/MEZ	22 X 30	AP	200	1	500	1000
Mickey's	LAI	NL/EL-M	1979	E/MEZ	22 X 30	AP	200	1	500	1000
Trailer with House	LAI	NL/EL-M	1979	E/MEZ	22 X 30	AP	200	1	500	1000
Wally's Diner	LAI	NL/EL-M	1979	E/MEZ	22 X 30	AP	200	1	500	1000
Lithographs	LAI	NL/EL-M	1979	E/MEZ	22 X 30	AP	200	1	500	1000
Chateau Diner	LAI	NL/EL-M	1979	E/MEZ	22 X 30	AP	200	1	500	1000
Tumble Inn Diner	LAI	NL/EL-M	1979	E/MEZ	22 X 30	AP	200	1	500	1000
Diner	MK	NL/EL-M	1980	EC	22 X 30	AP	35	7	500	1000
Casey's Diner	LAI	NL/EL-M	1980	SP	22 X 30	SOM	250	34	500	1000
Royal Diner	LAI	NL/EL-M	1980	SP	22 X 30	SOM	250	35	500	1000
Yankee Clipper	LAI	NL/EL-M	1980	SP	22 X 30	SOM	250	34	500	1000
C & C Restaurant	LAI	NL/EL-M	1980	SP	22 X 30	SOM	250	34	500	1000
Pappy's Diner	LAI	NL/EL-M	1980	SP	22 X 30	SOM	250	32	500	1000
Chicken-Chops	LAI	NL/EL-M	1980	SP	22 X 30	SOM	250	35	500	1000
Blue Beacon	LAI	NL/EL-M	1980	SP	22 X 30	SOM	250	32	500	1000
O'Conners Diner	LAI	NL/EL-M	1980	SP	22 X 30	SOM	250	35	500	1000
Lisi's Pittsfield Diner	LAI	NL/EL-M	1980	SP	22 X 30	SOM	250	35	500	1000
White Castle	LAI	AH/SH	1980	SP	22 X 25	SOM	250	35	500	1000
White Palace	LAI	AH/SH	1980	SP	22 X 27	SOM	250	32	500	1000

JOHN BAEDER CONTINUED

TITLE	PUBLISHER	PRINTER	DATE	MEDIUM	DIMENSION (PAPER SIZE) IN INCHES	TYPE OF PAPER	EDITION NUMBER	NO. OF COLORS	ORIGINAL OPENING PRICE	CURRENT RETAIL PRICE
CURRENT EDITIONS:										
Mary's Diner	LAI	AH/SH	1980	SP	22 X 30	SOM	250	30	500	500
Yankee Clipper	LAI	NL/EL-M	1980	SP	22 X 30	SOM	250	30	500	500
Vista-Mar Inn	LAI	NL/EL-M	1980	SP	22 X 30	SOM	250	38	500	500
Empire Diner	JBE	JBE	1981	PH/LC/SP	22 X 30	AP	175	11	375	600
Market Street Cafe	WSP	WSP	1981	G/CO	22 X 30	AP	200	2	500	600
Morgan's	MG	TB/TP	1983	A/E/SG	23 X 30	R/BFK	50	3	600	750

JO BAER

BORN: Seattle, WA; August 7, 1929
EDUCATION: Univ of Washington; New Sch of Soc Research, NY
TEACHING: Sch of Visual Arts, NY, 1969–70
AWARDS: Nat Council of Arts Award, 1968–69
RECENT EXHIB: Neuberger Mus, State Univ of New York, Purchase, NY, 1986–87; La Couleur Seule, Mus St Pierre, Lyon, France, 1988
COLLECTIONS: Mus of Mod Art, NY; Guggenheim Mus, NY; Kolnischer Kunstverein, Koln, West Germany; Albright-Knox Art Gallery, Buffalo, NY; Nat Mus, Canberra, Australia; Whitney Mus of Am Art, NY; Norton Simon Mus, Pasadena, CA
PRINTERS: Maurel Studios, NY (MS)
PUBLISHERS: Brooke Alexander, Inc, NY (BAI)
GALLERIES: Brooke Alexander, Inc, New York, NY; John Weber Gallery, New York, NY; Lisson Gallery, London, England; Flynn Gallery, New York, NY; Rhona Hoffman Gallery, Chicago, IL
MAILING ADDRESS: c/o Flynn Gallery, 113 Crosby St, New York, NY 10012

TITLE	PUBLISHER	PRINTER	DATE	MEDIUM	DIMENSION (PAPER SIZE) IN INCHES	TYPE OF PAPER	EDITION NUMBER	NO. OF COLORS	ORIGINAL OPENING PRICE	CURRENT RETAIL PRICE
CURRENT EDITIONS:										
Cadmos Thicket	BAI	MS	1973	I/HC/OIL	40 X 30	JBG	30		400	1500
Cardinations (Set of 9)	BAI	MS	1974	SP	28 X 21	JBG	75		1000 SET / 125 EA	450 SET / 500 EA

WILLIAM BAGGETT

BORN: Montgomery, AL; 1946
EDUCATION: Auburn Univ, Grad Studies
TEACHING: Dept of Art, Chmn, Univ of Southern Mississippi, 1983 to present
AWARDS: Award, Alumni Professorship, Auburn Univ, Birmingham, AL, Scholarly & Creative Achievement, 1982; Nat Endowment for the Arts, 1983; First Place, Design Competition, Southeastern Theatre Conf, Atlanta, GA, 1988
PUBLISHERS: Nahan Editions, New Orleans, LA (NE)
GALLERIES: Nahan Editions, New Orleans, LA & New York, NY & Tokyo, Japan

TITLE	PUBLISHER	PRINTER	DATE	MEDIUM	DIMENSION (PAPER SIZE) IN INCHES	TYPE OF PAPER	EDITION NUMBER	NO. OF COLORS	ORIGINAL OPENING PRICE	CURRENT RETAIL PRICE
CURRENT EDITIONS:										
Experimentation	NE		1982	LC	24 X 32	AP	125	5	300	400
Holiday Fantasy	NE		1982	LC	20 X 35	AP	285	6	300	400
Reflex	NE		1982	LC	24 X 32	AP	125	6	300	400
Summer House	NE		1982	LC	21 X 30	AP	285	4	200	275
Tradition	NE		1982	LC	19 X 24	AP	125	5	250	350
Travel Fantasy	NE		1982	LC	20 X 35	AP	285	3	250	350
Ultimate Dream	NE		1982	LC	24 X 32	AP	125	5	300	400

RICHARD BAKER

BORN: Baltimore, MA; 1959
EDUCATION: Maryland Inst, Col of Art, Baltimore, MD, 1977–1979; Sch of Mus of Fine Arts, Boston, MA, 1979–81
TEACHING: Vis Artist, Norwich Sch of Art, Norwich, England, 1956
AWARDS: Fine Arts Work Center Fel, Provincetown, MA, 1989–92; New England Found for the Arts Grant, 1992
RECENT EXHIB: Provincetown Group Gallery, MA, 1988,89,90,91; Universal Fine Objects, Provincetown, MA, 1991; Washburn Gallery, NY, 1991,92
COLLECTIONS: Mus of Fine Arts, Boston, MA
PRINTERS: Cirrus Editions Workshop, Los Angeles, CA (CEW)
PUBLISHERS: Cirrus Editions, Ltd, Los Angeles, CA (CE)
GALLERIES: Cirrus Gallery, Los Angeles, CA; Washburn Gallery, New York, NY

TITLE	PUBLISHER	PRINTER	DATE	MEDIUM	DIMENSION (PAPER SIZE) IN INCHES	TYPE OF PAPER	EDITION NUMBER	NO. OF COLORS	ORIGINAL OPENING PRICE	CURRENT RETAIL PRICE
CURRENT EDITIONS:										
Few-Flowered Shooting Star (505c)	CE	CEW	1992	LC	24 X 24	R/BFK	50		850	850
Fire Poppy (506c)	CE	CEW	1992	LC	24 X 24	R/BFK	50		850	850
Bladder Sage (507c)	CE	CEW	1992	LC	24 X 24	R/BFK	50		850	850

The retail prices of the 100,000 limited edition prints quoted in this directory are subject to change. Print publishers, artists and galleries were the direct sources for these quotations. Prices in the secondary market listed as "Sold Out Editions (Rare)" indicate that the publisher has a limited supply of that print or that the print is difficult to locate in the galleries.

The Printworld Directory is accepting new applications for the seventh edition. Approximately 300 new artists will be accepted. Please use the two forms provided in the back section of this directory to submit biographical data and documentation of prints. Edition number of each print must not exceed 500 and the retail price must be $100 or more.

WILLIAM BAILEY

BORN: Council Bluffs, IA; November 17, 1930
EDUCATION: Yale Univ, New Haven, CT, BFA, 1955; MFA, 1957; with Joseph Albers
TEACHING: Prof, Fine Arts, Indiana University, Bloomington, IN, 1962–69; Prof, Art, Yale Univ, New Haven, CT, 1969–78; Dean, Sch of Art, 1974–75; Kingman Brewster Prof, 1978 to present
AWARDS: Guggenheim Found Fel, NY, Painting, 1965; Isram Merrill Found Grant, 1979–80
RECENT EXHIB: John Berggruen Gallery, San Francisco, CA, 1988; Robert Schoelkoph Gallery, NY, 1991; Andre Emmerich Gallery, NY, 1992
COLLECTIONS: Whitney Mus of Am Art, NY; St Louis Mus, MO; Pennsylvania Acad of Fine Art, Phila, PA; Yale Univ, New Haven, CT; Joseph Hirshhorn Mus, Wash, DC; Duke Univ, Durham, NC; Indiana Univ, Bloomington, IN; J B Speed Art Mus, Louisville, KY; Univ of Massachusetts, Boston, MA; Michigan State Univ, East Lansing, MI; Univ of North Carolina, Greensboro, NC; Univ of New Mexico, Albuquerque, NM; Kalamazoo Inst, MI Jeryl Parker Editions, New Paltz, NY
PRINTERS: Solo Press, Ny (SP); Jennifer Melby, NY (JM); Jeryl Parker Editions, New Paltz, NY (JPE)
PUBLISHERS: Steven Miles Kossak, NY (SMK); Parasol Press, NY (PaP)
GALLERIES: John Berggruen Gallery, San Francisco, CA; Andre Emmerich Gallery, New York, NY; Thomas Smith Fine Art, Fort Wayne, IN
MAILING ADDRESS: 344 Willow, New Haven, CT 06511

William Bailey
Untitled Still Life
Courtesy Associated American Artists

TITLE	PUBLISHER	PRINTER	DATE	MEDIUM	DIMENSION (PAPER SIZE) IN INCHES	TYPE OF PAPER	EDITION NUMBER	NO. OF COLORS	ORIGINAL OPENING PRICE	CURRENT RETAIL PRICE
SOLD OUT EDITIONS (RARE):										
Untitled (Set of 2)	PaP	JM	1982	EB/A	28 X 22	WOVE	50		800	4500
CURRENT EDITIONS:										
6 Dry Points	PaP	CPP	1974	DPT	24 X 20 EA	AP	23 EA	23 EA	2500 SET	7500 SET
Untitled #3	SMK	SP	1976	LB	26 X 34	R/BFK	100	1	400	1200
Untitled #4	SMK	SP	1976	LB	20 X 25	R/BFK	50	1	275	1200
Still Life #6	SMK	SP	1982	LB	25 X 21	R/BFK	50	1	850	1500
Untitled Still Life	PaP	JM	1982	EB/A	28 X 22	R/BFK	50		800	2500
Still Life	PaP	JPE	1987	AB/CC	26 X 21	GAMPI/SOMS-S	50	1	1000	1800

ROBERT BALLAGH

BORN: Dublin, Ireland; 1943
EDUCATION: Self-Taught
PRINTERS: Process Printers, Dublin, Ireland (PrPr)
PUBLISHERS: Circuit Arts, Ltd, Dublin, Ireland (CA)
GALLERIES: David Hendriks Gallery, Dublin, Ireland

TITLE	PUBLISHER	PRINTER	DATE	MEDIUM	DIMENSION (PAPER SIZE) IN INCHES	TYPE OF PAPER	EDITION NUMBER	NO. OF COLORS	ORIGINAL OPENING PRICE	CURRENT RETAIL PRICE
SOLD OUT EDITIONS (RARE):										
The Silicon Suite (Set of 3)	CA	PrPr	1986		24 X 38 EA		286 EA		£2500 SET	£5000 SET

MICHAEL BALOG

BORN: San Francisco, CA; April 30, 1946
EDUCATION: Ventura Col, CA, 1966–67; Chouinard Art Sch, Los Angeles, CA, with Stephan Von Huene, 1959
COLLECTIONS: Iowa Univ Mus of Art, Iowa City, IA; Herbert Distel Mus, Bern, Switzerland; Wichita Art Mus, KS; Joslyn Art Mus, Omaha, NE
PRINTERS: David Trowbridge (DT); Perry Tymeson (PT); Cirrus Editions Workshop, Los Angeles, CA (CEW)
PUBLISHERS: Cirrus Editions, Ltd, Los Angeles, CA (CE)
GALLERIES: Cirrus Editions, Ltd, Los Angeles, CA; Film in the Cities Gallery, St Paul, MN
MAILING ADDRESS: 142 Greene St, New York, NY 10012

TITLE	PUBLISHER	PRINTER	DATE	MEDIUM	DIMENSION (PAPER SIZE) IN INCHES	TYPE OF PAPER	EDITION NUMBER	NO. OF COLORS	ORIGINAL OPENING PRICE	CURRENT RETAIL PRICE
CURRENT EDITIONS:										
Constriction	CE	DT/CEW	1972	LC	23 X 30	AP	50	1	100	250
Coercion	CE	DT/CEW	1972	LC	23 X 30	AP	50	3	100	250
Untitled (Set of 5):									150 SET	250 SET
The Club Manager	CE	PT/CEW	1974	LC	10 X 8	CP	35	3	XXX	XXX
You Girls Look So Nice	CE	PT/CEW	1974	LC	10 X 8	CP	35	3	XXX	XXX
It's What I've Always Dreamed of	CE	PT/CEW	1974	LC	10 X 8	CP	35	3	XXX	XXX
A Moment Alone	CE	PT/CEW	1974	LC	10 X 8	CP	35	5	XXX	XXX
Among the First Nighters	CE	PT/CEW	1974	LC	10 X 8	CP	35	5	XXX	XXX

ENRICO BAJ

BORN: Italy; 1924
PRINTERS: Alexander Heinrici, NY (AH); Studio Heinrici, NY (SH); Schwartz (Sch); Rosi & Bellasich, Italy (T/B); Coopo (Coop)

PUBLISHERS: Studio Heinrici, NY (SH); Rousseau (Rou); Soleil Noir (SN)
GALLERIES: Arras Gallery, New York, NY; Fred Dorfman Gallery, New York, NY; Virginia Lust Gallery, New York, NY

Jean Petit (P)

TITLE	PUBLISHER	PRINTER	DATE	MEDIUM	DIMENSION (PAPER SIZE) IN INCHES	TYPE OF PAPER	EDITION NUMBER	NO. OF COLORS	ORIGINAL OPENING PRICE	CURRENT RETAIL PRICE
SOLD OUT EDITIONS (RARE):										
Lady Jane Grey, Queen of England for Nine Days			1965	AC	10 X 14	R/BFK			75	600
I Like Sex (Set of 5)			1965	SP	14 X 14 EA	AP			400 SET	2000 SET
Figure			1965	EC/A	10 X 8	R/BFK	100		75	500
Meccano		T/B	1966	SP	7 X 21	AP	74		80	1200
Le General			1967	LC	27 X 21	AP			100	800
Femme en Pleurs (P-23)			1969	EC	19 X 15	R/BFK	100		125	2000
Danseuse (P-239)			1969	EC	19 X 15	R/BFK	100		125	600
Bacchanale			1970	EB/A	20 X 28	R/BFK	60		125	600
Grand Nu National			1970	AC/CO	24 X 19	R/BFK			125	1800
Premio (on Embroidered Fabric)			1970	SP	23 X 17	Fabric	50		200	1500
M Fall (P-302)			1970	SP	16 X 13	AP	100		120	600
Do Baj by Yourself (P-26)			1971	SP	28 X 23	AP	1200		100	400
Matilde di Canossa (P-33)			1971	SP	28 X 23	AP	1100		100	400
La Prophetesse Deborah			1972	SP	30 X 24	AP	250		100	750
CURRENT EDITIONS:										
After Seeing Series:										
After Seeing Van Gogh	AH	AH/SH	1973	LC/CO	38 X 29	AP	250	14	250	900
After Seeing Chagall	AH	AH/SH	1973	LC/CO	38 X 29	AP	250	14	250	900
After Seeing Picasso	AH	AH/SH	1973	CL/CO	38 X 29	AP	250	14	250	900
After Seeing Seurat	AH	AH/SH	1973	LC/CO	38 X 29	AP	250	14	250	900
Il Paradiso Perduto (Set of 40)			1986	EB	23 X 17 EA	R/BFK	100 EA		2500 SET	3800 SET

JOHN BALDESSARI

BORN: National City, CA; June 17, 1931
EDUCATION: San Diego State Col, CA, BA, 1953, MA, 1957; Univ of California, Berkeley, CA, 1954–55; Univ of California, Los Angeles, CA, 1955; Otis Art Inst, Los Angeles, CA, 1957–59
TEACHING: Instr, San Diego Fine Arts Sch, CA, 1953–54; Instr, San Diego State Col, CA, 1956, 1959–61; Instr, Southwestern Col, Chula, CA, 1962–68; Asst Prof, Art, Univ of California, San Diego, CA, 1968–70; Prof, La Jolla Univ, CA, 1966–70; Prof, Art, Hunter Col, NY, 1971; Prof, Art, California Inst of Arts, Valencia, CA, 1970 to present
AWARDS: Nat Endowment for the Arts Grants, 1973–75; Solomon R Guggenheim Fel, 1986
RECENT EXHIB: Cirrus Editions Gallery, Los Angeles, CA, 1990; Crown Point Press, NY, 1991; Newport Harbor Art Mus, Newport Beach, CA, 1989,92; Brooke Alexander Editions, Inc, NY, 1993
COLLECTIONS: Mus of Mod Art, NY; Basel Mus of Art, Switzerland; Los Angeles County Mus of Art, CA; Inst of Mod Art, Eindhoven, Holland; La Jolla Mus, CA; Carnegie Inst, Pittsburgh, PA
PRINTERS: Harry Westlund, Los Angeles, CA (HW); Cirrus Editions Workshop, Los Angeles, CA (CEW); Aeropress, NY (A); Patricia Branstead, NY (PB); Peter Kneybühler, Zürich, Switzerland (PK); Sally Mara Sturman, NY (SMS); Mark Sofield, NY (MS); Francisco Siqueiros, Los Angeles, CA (FS); Robert Danby, Los Angeles, CA (RD); Richard Hammond, Los Angeles, CA (RH); Maurice Sánchez, NY (MS); Linda Gray, NY (LG); James Miller, NY (JM); Joe Petruzzelli, NY (JP); Derriére L'Etoile Studios, NY (DES); Crown Point Press, San Francisco, CA (CPP)
PUBLISHERS: Cirrus Editions Ltd, Los Angeles, CA (CEL); Multiples, NY (M); Peter Blum Edition, NY (PBE); Brooke Alexander, Inc, NY (BAI); Arion Press, San Francisco, CA (AP); Crown Point Press, San Francisco, CA (CPP)
GALLERIES: Cirrus Editions, Ltd, Los Angeles, CA; Marian Goodman Gallery, New York, NY; Peter Blum Edition, New York, NY; Deson-Saunders Gallery, Chicago, IL; Margo Leavin Gallery, Los Angeles, CA; Arion Press, San Francisco, CA; Lawrence Mangel Gallery, Phila, PA; Brooke Alexander, Editions, New York, NY; Gemini GEL, Los Angeles, CA; Crown Point Press, San Francisco, CA & New York, NY; Christopher Grimes Gallery, Santa Monica, CA; Katie Block Fine Art, Boston, MA; Moira James Gallery, Green Valley, NV; Richard Levy Gallery, Albuquerque, NM; Carol Evans Fine Arts, Brooklyn, NY; Jim Kempner Fine Art, New York, NY
MAILING ADDRESS: 2001½ Main St, Santa Monica, CA 90405-1021

TITLE	PUBLISHER	PRINTER	DATE	MEDIUM	DIMENSION (PAPER SIZE) IN INCHES	TYPE OF PAPER	EDITION NUMBER	NO. OF COLORS	ORIGINAL OPENING PRICE	CURRENT RETAIL PRICE
SOLD OUT EDITIONS (RARE):										
Five Pickles (with Fingerprints) in the Shape of a Hand	M	PB/A	1975	PHC/CO	23 X 31	AP	60	3	300	1800
Raw Prints (Set of 6)	CE	HW/CEW	1976	LC	19 X 25 EA	AP	50 EA	3 EA	900 SET	9000 SET
									150 EA	1500 EA
Black Dice (Set of 9)	PBE	PK	1982	EB/A	17 X 20 EA	AP	35 EA	3 EA	2500 SET	6000 SET
(T)here (Set of 10):									5000 SET	14000 SET
Horse	M	SMS/MS	1986	PH/A/DPT/SB/SG	20 X 30	R/BFK	35	5	500	1500
Bat	M	SMS/MS	1986	PH/A/DPT/SB/SG	20 X 26	R/BFK	35	3	500	1500
Man in Boat	M	SMS/MS	1986	PH/A/DPT/SB/SG	20 X 28	R/BFK	35	1	500	1500
Man on Beach	M	SMS/MS	1986	PH/A/DPT/SB/SG	20 X 21	R/BFK	35	2	500	1500

JOHN BALDESSARI CONTINUED

TITLE	PUBLISHER	PRINTER	DATE	MEDIUM	DIMENSION (PAPER SIZE) IN INCHES	TYPE OF PAPER	EDITION NUMBER	NO. OF COLORS	ORIGINAL OPENING PRICE	CURRENT RETAIL PRICE
SOLD OUT EDITIONS (RARE):										
Diver	M	SMS/MS	1986	PH/A/DPT/SB/SG	20 X 20	R/BFK	35	4	500	1500
Guns (folded)	M	SMS/MS	1986	PH/A/DPT/SB/SG	20 X 38	R/BFK	35	1	500	1500
Circles	M	SMS/MS	1986	PH/A/DPT/SB/SG	20 X 26	R/BFK	35	3	500	1500
Cavalry	M	SMS/MS	1986	PH/A/DPT/SB/SG	22 X 30	R/BFK	35	3	500	1500
Octopus	M	SMS/MS	1986	PH/A/DPT/SB/SG	22 X 30	R/BFK	35	3	500	1500
Hands (Embossed)	M	SMS/MS	1986	PH/A/DPT/SB/SG	20 X 29	R/BFK	35	3	500	1500
Hegel's Cellar (Set of 10):									10000 SET	16000 SET
Two Figures (one with Shadow)	M	SMS/MS	1986	PH/A/SL	21 X 20	R/BFK	35		1200	2000
Kiss, Hair, Hands	M	SMS/MS	1986	PH/A/SL/DPT	20 X 29	R/BFK	35		1200	2000
Seeds	M	SMS/MS	1986	PH/A/SG	26 X 20	R/BFK	35		1200	2000
Two Boats	M	SMS/MS	1986	PH/A	20 X 27	R/BFK	35		1200	2000
Three Colors (with Horse Ascending) (with Sanding)	M	SMS/MS	1986	PH/A/SB	28 X 20	R/BFK	35		1200	2000
Calvary	M	SMS/MS	1986	PH/A	28 X 20	R/BFK	35		1200	2000
Boat (with Figure Standing)	M	SMS/MS	1986	PH/A	28 X 20	R/BFK	35		1200	2000
Large Door	M	SMS/MS	1986	PH/A/SB	20 X 38	R/BFK	35		1200	2000
Leg, Straw, Diver	M	SMS/MS	1986	PH/A/SB	26 X 20	R/BFK	35		1200	2000
Deer and Octopus	M	SMS/MS	1986	PH/A/SB	30 X 22	R/BFK	35		1200	2000
Person and Ladder (Red)/Hose/Smoke	CPP	CPP	1991	PH/A/SB	36 X 27	SOM	25	1	3000	3200
CURRENT EDITIONS:										
The Fallen Easel (9 Parts) (Printed on Metal)	CE/M	FS/RD/CEW	1987	LC/SP	74 X 95 TOT	AP88/METAL	35		6000	8500
Juggler's Hand (with Diver)	CE	FS/RD/CEW	1988	LC	55 X 27	AP88	60		2000	6500
Studio	CE	FS/RD/CEW	1988	LC	30 X 39	AP88	150		1800	3500
A Suite of Five Lithographs for Tristam Shandy (Set of 5)	AP		1988	LC		THS	50 EA		2500 SET	20000 SET
Aligned Trumpeteering	BAI		1988	LC	25 X 27	AP	50		750	1200
Object (with Flaw)	CE	FS/RD/CEW	1989	LC	52 X 109	AP88/SOM/PLEX	35		6000	20000
Falling Star	BAI		1989-90	PH/AC	63 X 21	SOM	45		3500	6000
Helmsman (with Various Fires)(Trip)	BAI	PB/A	1989-90	PH/AC	98 X 55	SOM	45		7000	7000
Paradise	BAI	PB/A	1989-90	PH/AC	28 X 54	SOM	45		5000	5000
Rollercoaster	BAI	PB/A	1989-90	PH/AC	39 X 68	SOM	45		7500	7500
Two Hands (with Distant Figure)	BAI	PB/A	1989-90	PH/AC	53 X 35	SOM	45		6000	6000
Two Sets (One with Bench	BAI	PB/A	1989-90	PH/AC	48 X 30	SOM	45		5000	5000
Life's Balance (with Money)	BAI	PB/A	1989-90	PH/AC	51 X 43	SOM	45		6000	6000
Love and Work	BAI		1991	PH/AC	26 X 12	SOM	60		1200	1200
Six Colorful Gags (Male)	CPP	CPP	1991	PH/AC/SB	47 X 54	SOM	25		3500	3500
Person with Conscience (Green)/Animals Quiescent	CPP	CPP	1991	PH/AC/SB	36 X 27	SOM	25		2000	2000
Hand and Chin (with Entwined Hands)	CPP	CPP	1991	PH/AB/SP	33 X 22	SOM	25	1	1500	1500
Six Rooms (Set of 6)	BAI	MS/LG/JM/JP/DES	1993	LB	21 X 18 EA	SEN	150 EA		1500 SET	1500 SET

JAN BALET

BORN: Bremen, Germany; 1913
PRINTERS: Wolfenberger (W); American Atelier, NY (AA)
PUBLISHERS: Senans (S); Circle Fine Art, Chicago, IL (CFA); Artist (ART)

GALLERIES: Circle Galleries, San Diego, CA & San Francisco, CA & Pittsburgh, PA & New York, NY & Chicago, IL & Scottsdale, AZ & Beverly Hills, CA & Costa Mesa, CA & Sherman Oaks, CA & Palm Beach, FL & Honolulu, HI & New Orleans, LA & Las Vegas, NV & Seattle, WA & Houston, TX; Owl Gallery, San Francisco, CA; Walton Street Gallery, Chicago, IL; Art Works, State College, PA

TITLE	PUBLISHER	PRINTER	DATE	MEDIUM	DIMENSION (PAPER SIZE) IN INCHES	TYPE OF PAPER	EDITION NUMBER	NO. OF COLORS	ORIGINAL OPENING PRICE	CURRENT RETAIL PRICE
SOLD OUT EDITIONS (RARE):										
Fourteenth of July	S	M-H	1977	CC	20 X 24	R/BFK	200	17	140	800
Picnic	S	M-H	1978	LC	20 X 17	R/BFK	300	17	160	800
Time for Beer	S	M-H	1979	LC	20 X 24	R/BFK	300	17	160	800
Tarzan	CFA	AA	1981	LC	18 X 25	R/BFK	300		160	600
Badminton	CFA	AA	1981	LC	20 X 25	R/BFK	300		250	600
Croquet	CFA	AA	1981	LC	20 X 25	R/BFK	300		250	700
Honeymoon	CFA	AA	1981	LC	22 X 30	R/BFK	300	15	250	800
Prohibition	CFA	AA	1981	LC	26 X 20	R/BFK	150		250	800

JAN BALET CONTINUED

TITLE	PUBLISHER	PRINTER	DATE	MEDIUM	DIMENSION (PAPER SIZE) IN INCHES	TYPE OF PAPER	EDITION NUMBER	NO. OF COLORS	ORIGINAL OPENING PRICE	CURRENT RETAIL PRICE
SOLD OUT EDITIONS (RARE):										
Isolde	CFA	AA	1981	LC	18 X 25	R/BFK	300		200	650
Winter	CFA	AA	1981	LC	14 X 17	R/BFK	200		250	800
Summer	CFA	AA	1981	LC	14 X 17	R/BFK	200		250	800
Summer Cat	CFA	AA	1981	LC	25 X 31	R/BFK	200		250	1300
Castle Cat, State I (Grey)	CFA	AA	1981	LC	28 X 21	R/BFK	100	1	250	550
Castle Cat, State II (Brown)	CFA	AA	1981	LC	28 X 21	R/BFK	100	1	250	550
Castle Cat, State III (Blue)	CFA	AA	1981	LC	28 X 21	R/BFK	100	1	250	550
Birth of Time	CFA	AA	1981	LC	32 X 24	R/BFK	140		300	900
Winter in Normandy	CFA	AA	1981	LC	23 X 31	R/BFK	300		250	1000
In Search of Happiness	CFA	AA	1981	LC	22 X 30	R/BFK	300		250	1550
Three Beach Fleas	CFA	AA	1981	LC	22 X 23	R/BFK	300		250	1100
Fantastic Number	CFA	AA	1981	LC	26 X 20	R/BFK	300		250	700
Quai de Bercy	CFA	AA	1981	LC	21 X 26	R/BFK	300		250	950
Union Pacific	CFA	AA	1981	LC	21 X 24	R/BFK	300		250	2200
Grand Hotel	ART	W	1981	LC	22 X 30	R/BFK	300	16	250	2200
Ladies Matinee	CFA	AA	1981	LC	20 X 25	R/BFK	300		250	800
Le Pecheur	CFA	AA	1982	LC	22 X 30	R/BFK	300		300	700
Quincaillerie & Metaux	CFA	AA	1982	LC	22 X 30	R/BFK	300		300	600
Orpheus Ascending	CFA	AA	1982	LC	30 X 22	R/BFK	300		300	1525
Market Day in Normandy	CFA	AA	1982	LC	29 X 32	R/BFK	300		300	1400
Senator	CFA	AA	1982	LC	30 X 22	R/BFK	300		300	1000
Adam & Eve (with Timepiece)	CFA	AA	1982	LC	24 X 18	R/BFK	60		500	1450
Suite of Six Proverbs (Set of 6):									1500 SET	2800 SET
Cold Hands, Warm Heart	CFA	AA	1983	LC	17 X 21	R/BFK	200		250	600
Out of Sight, Out of Mind	CFA	AA	1983	LC	17 X 21	R/BFK	200		250	600
Small Gifts Preserve Friends	CFA	AA	1983	LC	17 X 21	R/BFK	200		250	600
All's Well that Ends Well	CFA	AA	1983	LC	17 X 21	R/BFK	200		250	600
Birds of a Feather, Flock Together	CFA	AA	1983	LC	17 X 21	R/BFK	200		250	600
Absence Makes the Heart Grow Fonder	CFA	AA	1983	LC	17 X 21	R/BFK	200		250	600
Coca Cola	CFA	AA	1983	LC	25 X 20	R/BFK	300		250	800
Picnic	CFA	AA	1983	LC	22 X 30	R/BFK	300		600	1400
An Elevating Experience	CFA	AA	1984	LC	30 X 22	R/BFK	300		700	900
In Search of Happiness	ART	W	1984	LC	22 X 30	R/BFK	300	16	250	1550
Herald Tribune	CFA	AA	1984	LC	25 X 20	R/BFK	300		250	1100
Nouvelle Cuisine	CFA		1989	EC	15 X 21	R/BFK	100		500	1050
You and Your Stinking Cigar	CFA		1987	EC	15 X 21	R/BFK	100		500	750
CURRENT EDITIONS:										
Brother Dougherty	CFA	AA	1981	LC	20 X 25	R/BFK	300		250	700
Debit de la Marine	CFA	AA	1981	LC	20 X 25	R/BFK	300		250	650
Cafe de la Belle Etoile	CFA	AA	1981	LC	20 X 25	R/BFK	300		250	650
Suite of 8 Mini Lithos	ART	W	1981	LC	3 X 3 EA	R/BFK	300 EA	11 EA	320 SET	1500 SET
Famous Lovers	ART	W	1982	LC	9 X 7	R/BFK	300	10	220	500
Two Cafes	ART	W	1982	LC	14 X 18	R/BFK	300	14	260	600
Joe's Bar	CFA	AA	1983	LC	20 X 26	R/BFK	300		375	900
Cigar Factory	CFA	AA	1983	LC	20 X 26	R/BFK	300		375	650
Amusement Park	CFA	AA	1983	LC	22 X 30	R/BFK	300		425	900
Rites of Spring	CFA	AA	1984	LC	22 X 30	R/BFK	300		400	900
Pains (Bread)	CFA	AA	1985	LC	22 X 30	R/BFK	300		450	1000
By the Sea; By the Sea	CFA	AA	1985	LC	22 X 30	R/BFK	300		450	825
Summertime	CFA	AA	1985	LC	20 X 24	R/BFK	300		450	550
Who Says You Can't Change Your Mind?	CFA	AA	1985	LC	22 X 30	R/BFK	300		450	1400
Fancy People	CFA	AA	1986	LC	24 X 19	R/BFK	300		500	1200
Paradise Junction	CFA	AA	1986	LC	25 X 32	R/BFK	300		500	1100
Cafe de Paris	CFA	AA	1986	LC	25 X 32	R/BFK	300		800	875
Busy, Busy	CFA	AA	1986	LC	22 X 30	R/BFK	300		800	1200
Osteria Italiana	CFA	AA	1987	LC	22 X 30	AP	300		800	850
Childhood Memory	CFA	AA	1987	LC	22 X 30	AP	300		800	850
Once Upon a Clara	CFA	AA	1987	EC	15 X 21	AP	100		600	750
Butterfly Collector	CFA	AA	1988	LC	24 X 32	AP	300		700	850
Second Honeymoon	CFA	AA	1988	LC	22 X 30	AP	300		700	850
Song of the Sea	CFA		1988	EC	15 X 10	R/BFK	100		500	550
3 Times 8 Makes 8	CFA		1988	EC	15 X 21	R/BFK	100		600	1000
Mutual Feelings	CFA		1988	EC	15 X 10	R/BFK	100		425	475
A Man of Feeling	CFA		1988	EC	15 X 10	R/BFK	100		425	475
Navel Engagement	CFA		1988	EC	15 X 10	R/BFK	100		500	550
Body Contact	CFA		1988	EC	15 X 10	R/BFK	100		425	475
Moonlight Sonata	CFA		1988	EC	15 X 21	R/BFK	100		600	750
Trumpet Muse	CFA		1988	EC	15 X 10	R/BFK	100		500	550
Lady Chatterley's Chauffer	CFA	AA	1989	LC	22 X 30	R/BFK	300		800	925
Bang, Bang Big Shot	CFA	AA	1989	LC	22 X 30	R/BFK	300		850	850
Tandem d'Amour	CFA	AA	1989	LC	25 X 32	R/BFK	300		800	800

JAN BALET CONTINUED

TITLE	PUBLISHER	PRINTER	DATE	MEDIUM	DIMENSION (PAPER SIZE) IN INCHES	TYPE OF PAPER	EDITION NUMBER	NO. OF COLORS	ORIGINAL OPENING PRICE	CURRENT RETAIL PRICE
CURRENT EDITIONS:										
Love Makes You Blind	CFA	AA	1989	LC	22 X 30	R/BFK	300		800	800
Just Married	CFA		1989	EC	15 X 21	R/BFK	100		700	750
Winter in Venice	CFA	AA	1990	LC	25 X 34	R/BFK	300		800	1050
Caught Lovers	CFA	AA	1990	LC	25 X 34	R/BFK	300		800	800

LEWIS BALTZ

BORN: Newport Beach, CA; September 12, 1945
EDUCATION: San Francisco Art Inst, CA, BFA, 1969; Claremont Grad Sch, CA, MFA, 1971
TEACHING: Vis Lectr, Univ of California, Davis, CA, Fall, 1981; Vis Art, Univ of California, Santa Cruz, CA, Spring, 1982; Vis Art, Rhode Island Sch of Design, Providence, RI, 1983; Vis Prof, Univ of California, Riverside, CA, 1984; Art in Res, Univ of Nevada, Reno, NV, Summer, 1986
AWARDS: Nat Endowment for the Arts Fel Grant, Photography, 1973, Ind Fel, 1976; Guggenheim Mem Found Fel, Photography, 1980; US-UK Bicentennial Exchange Fel, 1980
RECENT EXHIB: Univ of Nevada, Inst of Fine Art, Donna Beam Fine Art Gallery, Las Vegas, NV, 1989; Castelli Graphics, NY, 1989; Cuesta Col Art Gallery, San Luis Obispo, CA, 1989,92; Germans Van Eck, NY, 1992
COLLECTIONS: Mus of Mod Art, NY; Art Inst of Chicago, IL; George Eastman House, Rochester, NY; Bibliotheque Nat, Paris, France; La Jolla Mus of Contemp Art, CA; Baltimore Art Mus, MD; Mus of Fine Arts, Houston, TX; Corcoran Gallery of Art, Wash, DC; Seattle Art Mus, WA
PRINTERS: Artist (ART)
PUBLISHERS: Eaton/Shoen Gallery, San Francisco, CA (E/S); Castelli Graphics, NY (CG)
GALLERIES: Eaton Gallery, San Francisco, CA; Castelli Graphics, New York, NY; Stephen Wirtz Gallery, San Francisco, CA; Ursula Gropper Associates, Sausalito, CA; Germans Van Eck, New York, NY
MAILING ADDRESS: PO Box 42, Sausalito, CA 94965

TITLE	PUBLISHER	PRINTER	DATE	MEDIUM	DIMENSION (PAPER SIZE) IN INCHES	TYPE OF PAPER	EDITION NUMBER	NO. OF COLORS	ORIGINAL OPENING PRICE	CURRENT RETAIL PRICE
SOLD OUT EDITIONS (RARE):										
The New Industrial Park Near Irvine, California (Set of 51)	CG	ART	1974	PH	6 X 9 EA	MB	21 EA		3000 SET	7500 SET
CURRENT EDITIONS:										
Near Reno (Gelatin-Silver Prints) (Set of 14)	E/S	ART	1986	PH	8 X 10 EA	MB	15 EA		5500 SET	7500 SET

WALTER DARBY BANNARD

BORN: New Haven, CT; 1934
EDUCATION: Princeton Univ, NJ, BA
TEACHING: Prof, Grad Sch, Sch of Visual Arts, NY, 1984 to present
AWARDS: Nat Found of Arts Award, 1968–69; Solomon R Guggenheim Fel, 1968–69; Francis J Greenberger Found Award, 1986
RECENT EXHIB: Greenberg/Wilson Gallery, NY, 1990; Stamford Mus, Leonhardt Galleries, CT, 1992; Miami-Dade Com Col, FL, 1992; Trenton City Mus, NJ, 1992
COLLECTIONS: Mus of Mod Art, NY; Guggenheim Mus, NY; Whitney Mus of Am Art, NY; Boston Mus of Fine Art, MA; Baltimore Mus of Art, MD; Albright-Knox Gallery, Buffalo, NY; Cleveland Mus of Art, OH; Harvard Univ, Cambridge, MA; Nat Gallery, Melbourne, Australia; Brandeis Univ, Waltham, MA; Aldrich Mus of Contemp Art, Ridgefield, CT; Oberlin Col, OH; Honolulu Acad, HI; Mus of Fine Arts, Houston, TX
PRINTERS: John Campione, NY (JC)
PUBLISHERS: Prestige Art Ltd, Mamaroneck, NY (PA)
GALLERIES: Jayne H Baum Gallery, New York, NY; M Knoedler & Co, New York, NY; Images Gallery, Toledo, OH; Alan Brown Gallery, Hartsdale, NY; Greenberg/Wilson Gallery, New York, NY; R H Love Galleries, Chicago, IL; Ann Jaffe Gallery, Bay Harbor Islands, FL
MAILING ADDRESS: P O Box 296, Rocky Hill, NJ 08553

TITLE	PUBLISHER	PRINTER	DATE	MEDIUM	DIMENSION (PAPER SIZE) IN INCHES	TYPE OF PAPER	EDITION NUMBER	NO. OF COLORS	ORIGINAL OPENING PRICE	CURRENT RETAIL PRICE
SOLD OUT EDITIONS (RARE):										
Jacaranda	PA	JC	1980	SP	35 X 24	AC	100	6	350	500
Siciliand Magician	PA	JC	1980	SP	35 X 24	AC	100	6	350	500
Stone Pond	PA	JC	1980	SP	35 X 24	AC	100	6	350	500
Black Hound Night	PA	JC	1980	SP	35 X 24	AC	100	6	350	500

PHILIP JUDD BARBER

BORN: Cleveland, OH; September 27, 1951
EDUCATION: Ohio Univ, Athens, OH, BS, 1973; BFA, 1977
AWARDS: Purchase Award, Purdue Univ, West Lafayette, IN, 1984; First Place, Art Center of Minnesota, Minneapolis, MN, 1985
COLLECTIONS: Purdue Univ, West Lafayette, IN; Minneapolis Inst of Art, MN; Frans, Masereel Centrum, Kasterlee, Belgium
PRINTERS: Artist (ART)
PUBLISHERS: Vermillion Editions Ltd, Minneapolis, MN (VEL)
GALLERIES: Vermillion Editions Ltd, Minneapolis, MN
MAILING ADDRESS: 121 15th St, West, #3, Minneapolis, MN 55403-23

TITLE	PUBLISHER	PRINTER	DATE	MEDIUM	DIMENSION (PAPER SIZE) IN INCHES	TYPE OF PAPER	EDITION NUMBER	NO. OF COLORS	ORIGINAL OPENING PRICE	CURRENT RETAIL PRICE
CURRENT EDITIONS:										
Mr Arithmatic	VEL	ART	1984	LC/SP/EB/DPT	7 X 9	R/BRK	10	4	100	350

MIGUEL BARCELÓ

RECENT EXHIB: Leo Castelli Gallery, NY, 1987; Gallery Bruno Bischofberger, Zürich, Switzerland, 1988,93
PRINTERS: Atelier Pasnic, Paris, France (APas); Patrice Forest, Paris, France (PF); Items Editions, Paris, France (IEd)
PUBLISHERS: Editions F B, Paris, France (EdFB); Items Editions, Paris, France (IEd)

GALLERIES: Castelli Graphics, New York, NY; Figura, Inc, New York, NY; Thomas Segal Gallery, Boston, MA; Gallery Bruno Bischofberger, Zürich, Switzerland; Flanders Graphics, Minneapolis, MN; Rick Jones Modern Art, St Louis, MO; Bonnier Gallery, New York, NY

TITLE	PUBLISHER	PRINTER	DATE	MEDIUM	DIMENSION (PAPER SIZE) IN INCHES	TYPE OF PAPER	EDITION NUMBER	NO. OF COLORS	ORIGINAL OPENING PRICE	CURRENT RETAIL PRICE
CURRENT EDITIONS:										
Tres Bodegónes (Two with Collage) (Set of 3)	EdFB	APas	1986	EC/CO	25 X 36 EA	AP	40 EA		650 EA	800 EA
El Ball de la Carne	IEd	PF/IEd	1992	LC	82 X 52	AP	16		SF125000	SF125000

JARED BARK

BORN: May 5, 1944
EDUCATION: Stanford Univ, CA, 1966
PRINTERS: Derriere l'Etoile Studios, NY (DES)
PUBLISHERS: Holly Solomon Editions, NY (HSE)
GALLERIES: Holly Solomon Editions, Ltd, New York, NY

TITLE	PUBLISHER	PRINTER	DATE	MEDIUM	DIMENSION (PAPER SIZE) IN INCHES	TYPE OF PAPER	EDITION NUMBER	NO. OF COLORS	ORIGINAL OPENING PRICE	CURRENT RETAIL PRICE
SOLD OUT EDITIONS (RARE):										
Stick Man	HSE	DES	1976	PH	19 X 22	RAG			500	900
CURRENT EDITIONS:										
House on Fire, State I	HSE	DES	1981	LC	37 X 32	AP	40	4	500 EA	600 EA
House on Fire, State II	HSE	DES	1981	LC	37 X 32	AP	20	3	500 EA	600 EA
House on Fire, State III	HSE	DES	1981	LC	37 X 32	AP	20	3	500 EA	600 EA

LAURENCE BARKER

BORN: Houston, TX; November 20, 1930
EDUCATION: Principia Col, Elsah, IL, BA; Cranbrook Acad of Art, Bloomfield Hills, MI, MFA; Atelier 17, Paris, France with Stanley William Hayter; Hand Papermaking Seminar, with Douglass Howell, Westbury, NY
TEACHING: Miami Univ, Oxford, OH; Cranbrook Acad of Art, Bloomfield Hills, MI; Vis Artist, Cleveland Inst of Art, OH; Barcelona Paper Workshop, Barcelona, Spain

COLLECTIONS: Brooklyn Mus, NY; Cleveland Mus of Art, OH; Dayton Art Inst, OH; Cincinnati Art Mus, OH; Bibliotheque Nat, Paris, France; Detroit Inst of Art, MI; Smithsonian Inst, Wash, DC; Biblioteca Nacional, Madrid, Spain; Chicago Art Inst, IL; Library of Congress, Wash, DC
PRINTERS: La Poligrafa, SA, Barcelona, Spain (LP); Artist (ART)
PUBLISHERS: Ediciones Poligrafa, SA, Barcelona, Spain (EdP)
GALLERIES: Galleri Miguel de Agustin, Helsingborg, Sweden; Galeri Papierkunst, Cologne, Germany; Galeria Joan Prats, New York, NY & Barcelona, Spain; Stewart & Stewart, Bloomfield Hills, MI
MAILING ADDRESS: Granduxer 5, #1-7B, 08021 Barcelona, Spain

TITLE	PUBLISHER	PRINTER	DATE	MEDIUM	DIMENSION (PAPER SIZE) IN INCHES	TYPE OF PAPER	EDITION NUMBER	NO. OF COLORS	ORIGINAL OPENING PRICE	CURRENT RETAIL PRICE
CURRENT EDITIONS:										
Series of Five Prints:									750 SET	1800 SET
Cornerpiece 2	EdP	LP	1975	MM	30 X 22	BAK	75	4	180	400
Black Fourth	EdP	LP	1975	MM	22 X 30	BAK	75	4	180	400
Cornerpiece 4	EdP	LP	1975	MM	30 X 22	BAK	75	5	180	400
Starboard List/One	EdP	LP	1975	MM	30 X 22	BAK	75	5	180	400
Peconic Fold	EdP	LP	1975	MM	30 X 22	BAK	75	5	180	400
Hidden Twenty I, II	S-S	ART	1991	EB/POL	41 X 27 EA	HMP	30 EA	1 EA	1500 EA	1500 EA
Network Café	S-S	ART	1991	EB/POL	41 X 27	HMP	30	1	1500	1500
Black Diode	S-S	ART	1991	EB/POL	41 X 27	HMP	30	1	1500	1500

HELMUT BARNETT

BORN: Stuttgart, West Germany; February 16, 1946; U S Citizen
EDUCATION: Univ of Texas, Austin, TX, BA, German, 1969-73; BFA, Studio Art, 1973

AWARDS: SPAR Nat Merit Award, Shreveport, LA
COLLECTIONS: Univ of Texas, Austin, TX
PRINTERS: Artist (ART)
PUBLISHERS: Kathleen Behbehani Fine Arts, Inc, Houston, TX (KB)
GALLERIES: James Gallery, Houston, TX

TITLE	PUBLISHER	PRINTER	DATE	MEDIUM	DIMENSION (PAPER SIZE) IN INCHES	TYPE OF PAPER	EDITION NUMBER	NO. OF COLORS	ORIGINAL OPENING PRICE	CURRENT RETAIL PRICE
CURRENT EDITIONS:										
#1	KB	ART	1982	SP	23 X 29	RGP	40	4	200	350
#2	KB	ART	1982	SP	22 X 30	STP	50	6	200	350
#3	KB	ART	1982	SP	22 X 30	STP	45	7	200	350
#4	KB	ART	1982	SP	22 X 30	STP	45	10	200	350
#5	KB	ART	1982	SP	22 X 30	STP	40	16	200	350
Between Acts	KB	ART	1983	SP	29 X 23	RG/100	65	19	200	300

WILL BARNET

BORN: Beverly, MA; May 25, 1911
EDUCATION: Boston Mus Art Sch, MA, 1927–30; Art Students League, NY, 1930–33
TEACHING: Montana State Col, Summer, 1951; Vis Art Critic, Yale Univ, New Haven, CT, 1952,53; Instr, Univ of Ohio, Athens, OH, 1954–56; Instr, Univ of Minnesota, Duluth, MN, 1958; Instr, Univ of Washington, St Louis, MO, 1963; Instr, Des Moines Art Center, IA, 1965; Distinguished Vis Prof, Art, Pennsylvania State Univ, University Park, PA, 1965–66; Vis Prof, Cornell Univ, Ithaca, NY, 1968–69; Instr, Art Students League, NY, 1936 to present; Cooper Union Art Sch, NY, 1945–65, Prof, 1965 to present; Instr, Pennsylvania Acad of Fine Arts, Phila, PA, 1967 to present
AWARDS: Purchase Prize, Corcoran Gallery, Wash, DC, 1968; Walter Lippincott Prize, Pennsylvania Acad of Fine Arts Award, Phila, PA, 1968; Benjamin Altman Prize, Nat Acad of Design, NY, 1977
RECENT EXHIB: Kennedy Galleries, NY, 1987; Coos Art Mus, Coos Bay, OR, 1989; Greater Lafayette Mus of Art, IL, 1989; Sioux City Art Center, IA, 1989; Meridian Mus of Art, MS, 1989,92; St Mary's Col of Maryland, Dwight Frederick Boyden Gallery, St Mary City, MO, 1992; Bakersfield Mus of Art, CA, 1992; Southeast Arkansas Arts & Services Center, Pine Bluff, AR, 1992; Arkansas Arts Center, Little Rock, AR, 1992; Terry Dintenfass Gallery, NY, 1992
COLLECTIONS: Metropolitan Mus, NY; Whitney Mus of Am Art, NY; Guggenheim Mus, NY; Brooklyn Mus, NY; Boston Mus of Fine Arts, MA; Cincinnati Art Mus, OH
PRINTERS: American Atelier, NY (AA); Styria Studio, NY (SS); Fine Creations, Inc, NY (NY); Clot Bramsen et Georges, Paris, France (CBG); Artist (ART)
PUBLISHERS: Circle Gallery, Ltd, Chicago, IL (CG); Circle Fine Art Corp, Chicago, IL (CFA); Transworld Art, Inc, NY (TAI); Associated American Artists, NY (AAA); Abrams Original Editions, NY (AOE); Styria Studio, NY; Artist (ART)
GALLERIES: Hirschl & Adler Modern Galleries, New York, NY; Kennedy Graphics, New York, NY; Associated American Artists, New York, NY; Scherer Gallery, Marlboro, NJ; Foster Harmon Galleries of American Art, Sarasota, FL; Valhalla Gallery, Wichita, KS; River Gallery, Irvington-on-Hudson, NY; Sylvan Cole Gallery, New York, NY; A Clean Well-Lighted Place, New York, NY; Morningstar Gallery, New York, NY; Styria Studio, New York, NY; Jupiter Fine Arts, Jupiter, FL; Harmon-Meek Gallery, Naples, FL; Benjamin-Beattie Fine Arts, Chicago, IL; Swearington Gallery, Louisville, KY; O'Farrell Gallery, Brunswick, ME; Charles Barry International, Rockville, MD; Troy Art Gallery, Royal Oak, MI; Kornbluth Gallery, Fair Lawn, NJ; River Gallery, Irvington-on-Hudson, NY; Sylvan Cole Gallery, New York, NY; Circle Galleries, San Diego, CA & San Francisco, CA & Northbrook, IL & Houston, TX & Pittsburgh, PA & Soho, NY & Chicago, IL; Bingham Kurts Gallery, Memphis, TN; Robley Gallery, Roslyn, NY; Morningstar Gallery, New York, NY; Harmon-Meek Third Street Gallery, Harbor Springs, MI; Terry Dintenfass Gallery, New York, NY
MAILING ADDRESS: 15 Gramercy Park, New York, NY 10003

Will Barnet
Circe
Courtesy the Artist

Will Barnet
Reclining Woman
Courtesy Circle Fine Art

TITLE	PUBLISHER	PRINTER	DATE	MEDIUM	DIMENSION (PAPER SIZE) IN INCHES	TYPE OF PAPER	EDITION NUMBER	NO. OF COLORS	ORIGINAL OPENING PRICE	CURRENT RETAIL PRICE
SOLD OUT EDITIONS (RARE):										
Dialogue in Green	CG	CBG	1970	LC	25 X 39	AP	200	4	175	5000
Woman with White Cat	CG	CBG	1971	SP	26 X 22	AP	200	3	175	5000
Girl at Piano	CG	FC	1973	SP	41 X 30	AP	200	4	250	3100
Atlanta	ART	ART	1974	SP/LC	41 X 25	AP	200	10	400	5000
Woman and the Sea	ART	ART	1974	LC	21 X 29	AP	75	12	400	5000
Summer (Silent Season)	CG	AA	1974	LC	32 X 24	R/BFK	200	16	250	3000
Dawn	TAI	AA	1975	LC	26 X 20	MAG	175	21	400	5000
Summer Idyll	CG	FC	1976	SP	36 X 44	Len/100	300	3	450	5000
The Reader	AAA	AA	1979	LC	22 X 38	AP	250	3	600	4800
Circe	TAI	SS	1979	LC	27 DIA	R/BFK	300	17	700	5000
Circe (Deluxe)	TAI	SS	1979	LC	27 DIA	R/BFK	175	17	750	5500
Paean	TAI	FC	1979	SP	21 X 24	AP	300	15	750	5000
The Caller	CFA	AA	1979	SP/LC	46 X 21	R/BFK	300		450	5000
The Blue Bicycle	CFA	FC	1979	SP	32 X 30	AP	300	5	450	3000
Madama Butterfly	CFA	AA	1980	LC	24 X 37	AP	300	3	750	4000
Meditation and Minou	CFA/ADE	SS	1980	SP/LC	28 X 34	AP	150	3	750	3000
The Bannister	CFA	AA	1981	LC	36 X 25	AP	300	2	1100	2600
The Bannister (Deluxe)	CFA	AA	1981	LC	36 X 25	SOM/T	125	2	1200	2750
Reclining Woman	CFA	AA	1981	LC	33 X 41	AP	300	2	1300	3250

WILL BARNET CONTINUED

TITLE	PUBLISHER	PRINTER	DATE	MEDIUM	DIMENSION (PAPER SIZE) IN INCHES	TYPE OF PAPER	EDITION NUMBER	NO. OF COLORS	ORIGINAL OPENING PRICE	CURRENT RETAIL PRICE
SOLD OUT EDITIONS (RARE):										
Stairway to the Sea	SS	SS	1981	SP/LC	42 X 36	AP	300	23	1000	5000
Woman and Cat Play	AAA	FC	1982	AC	18 X 15	AP	112		1200	5000
Peter Grimes	CFA	AA	1983	LC	30 X 22	AP	250		1100	2300
CURRENT EDITIONS:										
Circe II	AAA	FC	1980	SP	18 DIA	R/BFK	150		750	4500
Totem	AAA	FC	1982	SP	41 X 15	R/BFK	112			5000
Images of Children 1937–1940 (Set of 8):									3000 SET	7500 SET
Images of Children (4)	AAA	FC	1982	WC	10 X 11 EA	R/BFK	60 EA		300 EA	1000 EA
Images of Children (4)	AAA	FC	1982	EC	14 DIA EA	R/BFK	60 EA		500 EA	1200 EA
Persephone	AAA	FC	1982	SP	35 X 17	AP	250	2	750	4500
Stairway to the Sea	SS	SS	1982–84	SP/LC	39 X 36	AP	300		1200	5000

MARTIN BAROOSHIAN

BORN: Chelsea, MA; December 18, 1929
EDUCATION: Mus of Fine Arts Sch, Boston, MA, 1952,55; Tufts Univ, Boston, MA, BS Ed, 1953; Boston Univ, MA, 1958, Art History, 1958; Studied with S W Hayter, Paris, France
TEACHING: Instr, Printmaking Workshop, Pratt Inst, NY, 1960–69
AWARDS: Albert H Whitlin Traveling Fel, Europe, 1952; New York State Grant, Study in India, 1972; Nat Acad of Design, Print Award, 1974
RECENT EXHIB: Firehouse Gallery, Nassau Comm Col, NY, 1993
COLLECTIONS: Mus of Mod Art, NY; Mus of Mod Art, Yerevan, USSR; Metropolitan Mus of Art, NY; Brooklyn Mus, NY; Lincoln Center Mus of Performing Arts, NY; Boston Mus of Fine Arts, MA; Nat Gallery of Mod Art, New Delhi, India; Montreal Art Mus, Canada; Heckscher Mus, NY; La Jolla Mus of Art, CA; Portland Mus, ME; Boston Public Library, MA
PRINTERS: Artist (ART)
PUBLISHERS: AGE International Ltd (AGEI); Rose Art Inc (RAI); Fine Art Assoc (FAA); Hayes Art (HA); Houston Fine Arts (HFA); HMK (HMK); Artist (ART); Ro Gallery, NY (RG)
GALLERIES: Ro Gallery Image Makers, Inc, New York, NY
MAILING ADDRESS: 17 West Drive, Kings Park, NY 11754-3814

Martin Barooshian
Venus Rising
Courtesy the Artist

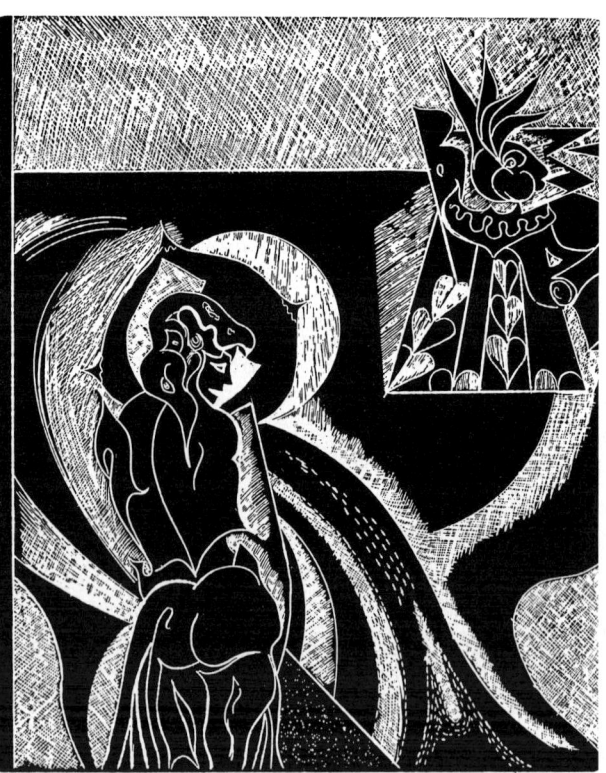

Martin Barooshian
Alice: Who Stole the Tarts?
Courtesy the Artist

TITLE	PUBLISHER	PRINTER	DATE	MEDIUM	DIMENSION (PAPER SIZE) IN INCHES	TYPE OF PAPER	EDITION NUMBER	NO. OF COLORS	ORIGINAL OPENING PRICE	CURRENT RETAIL PRICE
SOLD OUT EDITIONS (RARE):										
Man Myth And Magic (Set of 15)	HMK	ART	1975	I/EB	11 X 15 EA	AP	75	6	900 SET	2000 SET
Natural History Suite (Set of 16)	HMK	ART	1976	I/EB	11 X 15 EA	AP	60	6	1000 SET	2500 SET
Flight	OPCG	ART	1978	I/EB	12 X 24	AP	48	8	175	500
Flamingoes	OPCG	ART	1979	I/EB	16 X 19	AP	120	7	98	400
Zodiac	FAA	ART	1979	I/EB	18 X 20	AP	175	7	175	400

MARTIN BAROOSHIAN CONTINUED

TITLE	PUBLISHER	PRINTER	DATE	MEDIUM	DIMENSION (PAPER SIZE) IN INCHES	TYPE OF PAPER	EDITION NUMBER	NO. OF COLORS	ORIGINAL OPENING PRICE	CURRENT RETAIL PRICE
SOLD OUT EDITIONS (RARE):										
Twelve Zodiac Signs	FAA	ART	1980	I/EB	18 X 20	AP	20	7	175	400
Eagle	FAA	ART	1980	I/EB	15 X 17	AP	175	11	175	400
Pelicans	AGEI	ART	1980	I/EB	17 X 15	AP	175	8	150	400
Summer Olympics	HA	ART	1980	I/EB	15 X 12	AP	175	8	150	400
Owl	RAI	ART	1980	I/EB	15 X 17	AP	175	8	125	400
Beethoven	ART	ART	1980	I/EB	15 X 17	AP	60	3	125	400
Mother Goose	HFA	ART	1981	I/EB	22 X 18	AP	88	8	175	400
CURRENT EDITIONS:										
10 X 11 Suite (Set of 10)	RG	ART	1993	I/EC	10 X 11 EA	R/100	30 EA	Multi	1250 SET	1250 SET
12 X 15 Suite (Set of 8)	RG	ART	1993	I/EC	12 X 15 EA	R/100	30 EA	Multi	1400 SET	1400 SET
Football Suite (Set of 5)	RG	ART	1993	I/EC	18 X 22 EA	R/100	30 EA	Multi	1125 SET	1125 SET

DAVID JOHN BARR

BORN: Detroit, MI; October 10, 1939
EDUCATION: Wayne State Univ, NE, BFA, MA
AWARDS: Michigan Found of the Arts Award, 1977; Concerned Citizens Art Award, 1988
COLLECTIONS: Macomb Col, Warren, MI; Detroit Inst of Art, MI; Wayne State Univ, NE; Portland Art Mus, OR; Ft Lauderdale Mus, FL
PRINTERS: Plucked Chicken Press, Chicago, IL (PCP); Artist (ART)
PUBLISHERS: Donald Morris Gallery, Birmingham, MI (DMG); Artist (ART)
GALLERIES: Donald Morris Gallery, Birmingham, MI; Richard Gray Gallery, Chicago, IL
MAILING ADDRESS: 22600 Napier, Novi, MI 48374

TITLE	PUBLISHER	PRINTER	DATE	MEDIUM	DIMENSION (PAPER SIZE) IN INCHES	TYPE OF PAPER	EDITION NUMBER	NO. OF COLORS	ORIGINAL OPENING PRICE	CURRENT RETAIL PRICE
CURRENT EDITIONS:										
The Four Corners Project (Set of 4)	DMG	PCP	1981	LC	24 X 27	AP	50	8	1200 SET	2500 SET
Sunsweep	ART	PCP	1985	LC	24 X 28	AP	50	4	300	400
Arctic Arc	ART	ART	1986	SP	26 X 30	AP	25	4	300	400

ROBERT THOMAS BARRY

BORN: New York, NY; March 9, 1936
EDUCATION: Hunter Col, NY, BFA, 1957, MA, 1963
TEACHING: Asst Prof, Hunter Col, 1969–77; Guest Art, California Inst of Art, 1971,76; Rhode Island Sch of Design, Providence, RI, 1974
AWARDS: Nat Endowment for the Arts Fel, 1976
RECENT EXHIB: Leo Castelli Gallery, NY, 1990; Holly Solomon Gallery, NY, 1991; Renaissance Society Mus, Chicago, IL, 1992
COLLECTIONS: Stedelijk Mus, Amsterdam, The Netherlands; Van Abbe Mus, Einhoven, The Netherlands; Kunstmuseum, Basel, Switzerland; Wallraf-Richartz Mus, Cologne, Germany; Wadsworth Atheneum, Hartford, CT; Centre Georges Pompidou, Paris, France
PRINTERS: John Silvon (JS); Ekkeland Götze, Munich, Germany (EG)
PUBLISHERS: Crown Point Press, San Francisco, CA (CPP); Wassermann Galerie, Cologne, Germany (WasG)
GALLERIES: Leo Castelli Gallery, New York, NY; Crown Point Press, New York, NY & San Francisco, CA; Holly Solomon Galllery, New York, NY; Michael Ingbar Gallery, New York, NY; Wassermann Galerie, Cologne, Germany; Brenda Edelson Gallery, Baltimore, MD
MAILING ADDRESS: 1091 Emerson Ave, Teaneck, NJ 07666

TITLE	PUBLISHER	PRINTER	DATE	MEDIUM	DIMENSION (PAPER SIZE) IN INCHES	TYPE OF PAPER	EDITION NUMBER	NO. OF COLORS	ORIGINAL OPENING PRICE	CURRENT RETAIL PRICE
CURRENT EDITIONS:										
Suite Six (Set of 6)	CPP	JS	1978	EB	19 X 26 EA	AS	25	1	1000 SET	4000 SET
Five (Set of 5)	CPP	JS	1978	EB	26 X 26 (4) 26 X 33 (1)	AS	25	1	1000 SET	4000 SET
Untitled	CPP	JS	1978	EB	26 X 33	AS	10	1	400	1500
Diptych (2 Sheets)	WasG	EG	1991	SP	20 X 20 EA	R/BFK	50 EA		1125 SET	1550 SET

WULF E BARSCH

BORN: Reudnitz, Germany; August 27, 1943; US Citizen
EDUCATION: Werkkunstschule, Hannover, Germany, BFA, 1968; Brigham Young Univ, Salt Lake City, UT, MA, 1970; MFA, 1971
TEACHING: Brigham Young Univ, Salt Lake City, UT, 1974 to present
AWARDS: California Col of Arts & Crafts, World Print Comp, 1973; Rome Prize, Guerin Fel, Am Acad in Rome, Italy, 1975–76; 1979; Western States Art Found Fel, 1980
RECENT EXHIB: Nora Eccles Harrison Mus of Art, Logan, UT, 1988; Gremillion Fine Arts, Houston, TX, 1987,88; River Center Gallery, Memphis, TN, 1988
COLLECTIONS: Oakland Mus of Art, CA; Utah Mus of Fine Art, Salt Lake City, UT; San Francisco Mus of Art, CA; California Col of Arts & Crafts, Oakland, CA; States Senate, Hamburg, Germany; Brooklyn Mus, NY; Brigham Young Univ, Salt Lake City, UT
PRINTERS: Tamarind Inst, Albuquerque NM (TI); Nata Visa Press, Albuquerque, NM (NVP); Carawan Intalio Studio, Provo, UT (CIS); Artist (ART); Brian Haberman (BH); Russell Craig (RC)
PUBLISHERS: Tamarind Inst, Albuquerque, NM (TI); Artist (ART)
GALLERIES: Gremillion & Company, Houston, TX; Dieter Brusberg, Hannover, Germany; Dolores Chase Fine Art, Salt Lake City, UT; Tamarind Institute, Albuquerque, NM; Trinity Gallery, Atlanta, GA; Naravisa Press, Santa Fe, NM
MAILING ADDRESS: P O Box 354, Boulder, UT 84716

WULF E BARSCH CONTINUED

TITLE	PUBLISHER	PRINTER	DATE	MEDIUM	DIMENSION (PAPER SIZE) IN INCHES	TYPE OF PAPER	EDITION NUMBER	NO. OF COLORS	ORIGINAL OPENING PRICE	CURRENT RETAIL PRICE
SOLD OUT EDITIONS (RARE):										
Oberbayern	ART	TI	1977	LC	19 X 25	AP	10	3	175	800
Villa Aurelia	ART	TI	1979	LC	19 X 25	AP	25	4	210	500
Cumorah	ART	TI	1980	LC	19 X 25	AP	25	5	280	550
Herr Ich Bin Nicht Wurdig	ART	ART	1981	LC	29 X 41	AP	14	4	350	550
Italian Journey	ART	CS	1982	EC	19 X 25	AP	7	4	350	500
The Journey	ART	ART	1982	LC	30 X 42	AP	7	5	350	500
Am Duat	ART	NVP	1982	LC	19 X 25	R/BFK	25	4	350	500
Amduat	ART	ART	1982	LC	19 X 25	AP	25	5	350	500
Abaton	ART	NVP	1982	LC	19 X 25	R/BFK	25	3	350	500
On My Way Home	ART	ART	1984	LC	19 X 25	AP	14	5	350	500
CURRENT EDITIONS:										
On My Way to Maranello	ART	TI	1979	LC	19 X 25	AP	25	2	210	400
Birnen	ART	TI	1979	LC	19 X 25	AP	25	4	210	400
Ramah	ART	TI	1980	LC/MON	19 X 25	AP	10	7	280	500
CBC IV	ART	ART	1982	LC	19 X 25	AP	25	5	280	400
Two Falcons	ART	ART	1982	LC	19 X 25	AP	25	4	280	400
Two Falcons	ART	NVP	1982	LC	19 X 25	R/BFK	25	4	280	400
Stone	ART	ART	1982	LC	19 X 25	AP	14	4	350	400
Innudation	ART	ART	1983	LB	22 X 30	AP	25	1	280	300
Mesha	ART	ART	1983	LC	19 X 25	AP	25	4	280	300
Khartoom	ART	ART	1983	LC	19 X 25	AP	12	4	280	300
Indio	ART	ART	1984	LC	19 X 25	AP	14	5	350	400
The Farm	TI	ART	1984	LC	24 X 32	GE	14	4	350	400
The Center	TI	RC/TI	1984	LC	32 X 24	GE/KIT	30	6	350	400
The Sentinel	TI	RC/TI	1984	LC	23 X 30	GE	25	6	350	400

CHARLES BARTH

BORN: Chicago IL; November 27, 1942
EDUCATION: Chicago Teachers Col, IL, BS Ed, 1960–63; IL Inst of Tech, MS, 1964–66; Illinois State Univ, Ed D in Art, 1974–78
TEACHING: Instr, Art, Lincoln Univ, Jefferson City, MO, 1969–72; Prof, Mount Mercy Col, Cedar Rapids, IA 1972 to present
AWARDS: Benton Spruance Mem Purchase Award, The Print Club, Phila, PA 1969; Friends of Art Award, Davenport Munic Gallery, IA, 1977; Best in Show, Octagon Art Center, Ames, IA, 1978; Printmaking Award, Philbrook Art Center, Tulsa, OK 1979; Purchase Awards, Fort Hays State Univ, KS 1982,83; First Place Award, Print Comp, Artlink Contemp Artspace, Fort Wayne, IN, 1985; First Place Award, Printmaking Mussavi Gallery, NY 1985; Purchase Award, Nat Print Exhib, Trenton State Col, NJ, 1986; First Place in Printmaking, Artist's Soc of Int Art Achievement Award Exhib, San Francisco, CA, 1987; Purchase Award, Graphic Chemical and Ink Col, Print Club, Phila, PA 1988; Special Purchase Awards, Hunterdon Art Center, Clinton, NY, 1981, 88
RECENT EXHIB: Fort Hays State Univ, KS, 1988
COLLECTIONS: Art Inst of Chicago, IL; Philadelphia Mus of Art, PA; Univ of Wisconsin, Platteville, WI; Cedar Rapids Mus, IA; Hunterdon Art Center, Clinton, NJ; Minot State Col, ND; Chattahoochee Valley Art Assn, LaGrange, GA; Oklahoma Art Center, Oklahoma City, OK; Chicago Historical Soc, IL; Columbia Art League, MO
PRINTERS: Artist (ART)
PUBLISHERS: Artist (ART)
GALLERIES: Miriam Perlman, Inc, Chicago, IL; Chicago Center for the Print, IL; Des Moines Art Center, Sales & Rental Gallery, IA; Print Club, Phila, PA
MAILING ADDRESS: 1307 Elmhurst Dr, NE, Cedar Rapids, IA 52402

Charles Barth
Side Show
Courtesy the Artist

TITLE	PUBLISHER	PRINTER	DATE	MEDIUM	DIMENSION (PAPER SIZE) IN INCHES	TYPE OF PAPER	EDITION NUMBER	NO. OF COLORS	ORIGINAL OPENING PRICE	CURRENT RETAIL PRICE
SOLD OUT EDITIONS (RARE):										
Side Show	ART	ART	1977	I	18 X 24	AP	15	3	60	175
Lights of Broadway	ART	ART	1978	I	16 X 24	AP	15	3	60	175
Maya Daze	ART	ART	1984	I	22 X 30	R/BFK	15	3	150	150
Diego and Frida	ART	ART	1984	I	22 X 30	R/BFK	15	3	150	150
CURRENT EDITONS:										
Card Sharks	ART	ART	1977	I	18 X 24	AP	15	3	50	175
Disco Dan and Debbie Dancer	ART	ART	1978	I	18 X 24	AP	15	3	60	175
Double Bubble Man	ART	ART	1978	I	18 X 24	AP	15	3	60	175
King Tut and His Toots	ART	ART	1978	I	18 X 24	AP	15	3	60	175
Shall We Dance?	ART	ART	1979	I	16 X 24	AP	15	3	60	175
20,000 Leagues Beneath the Disco Floor	ART	ART	1979	I	18 X 24	AP	15	3	60	175
Midnight Round-Up	ART	ART	1980	I	18 X 24	AP	15	3	60	175

CHARLES BARTH CONTINUED

TITLE	PUBLISHER	PRINTER	DATE	MEDIUM	DIMENSION (PAPER SIZE) IN INCHES	TYPE OF PAPER	EDITION NUMBER	NO. OF COLORS	ORIGINAL OPENING PRICE	CURRENT RETAIL PRICE
CURRENT EDITIONS:										
Whatsa Matta You?	ART	ART	1980	I	18 X 24	AP	15	3	60	175
Beach Party at the Black Lagoon	ART	ART	1981	I	22 X 30	R/BFK	15	3	80	200
California Dreamers	ART	ART	1981	I	22 X 30	R/BFK	15	3	80	200
Arnie and His Bride	ART	ART	1982	I	22 X 30	R/BFK	15	3	100	200
Hurray for Hollywood	ART	ART	1982	I	22 X 30	R/BFK	15	3	100	200
Jack Pott and His Bride	ART	ART	1983	I	22 X 30	R/BFK	15	3	100	200
Al E Gator and His Bride	ART	ART	1983	I	22 X 30	R/BFK	15	3	100	200
Alfredo and His Bride	ART	ART	1984	I	22 X 30	R/BFK	15	3	150	150
Michael and Angela	ART	ART	1984	I	22 X 30	R/BFK	15	3	150	150
Arnold and His Bride	ART	ART	1985	I	22 X 30	R/BFK	15	3	150	150
Dance Macabre	ART	ART	1985	I	22 X 30	R/BFK	15	3	150	150
Dia de Los Muertos	ART	ART	1985	I	22 X 30	R/BFK	15	3	150	150
Mexican Baroque	ART	ART	1985	I	22 X 30	R/BFK	15	3	150	150
Mexican Hat Dance	ART	ART	1985	I	22 X 30	R/BFK	15	3	150	150
Aztec Warriors	ART	ART	1986	I	22 X 30	R/BFK	15	3	150	150
My Maya	ART	ART	1987	I	22 X 30	R/BFK	15	3	150	200
Tree of Life	ART	ART	1988	I	22 X 30	R/BFK	15	3	150	200
San Miguel	ART	ART	1989	I	22 X 30	R/BFK	15	3	150	200

FRANCES BARTH

BORN: New York, NY; July 31, 1946
EDUCATION: Hunter Col, NY, BFA, MFA, Painting
AWARDS: Creative Artists Public Service Grant, NY, 1973; Guggenheim Found Grant, NY, 1977; Nat Endowment for the Arts Grants, 1974,82
RECENT EXHIB: Waterworks Visual Arts Center, Salisbury, NC, 1989; Tomoko Liguori Gallery, NY, 1988,89; Jan Cicero Gallery, Chicago, IL, 1990
COLLECTIONS: Whitney Mus of Am Art, NY; Mus of Mod Art, NY; Metropolitan Mus of Art, NY; Albright-Knox Art Gallery, Buffalo, NY; Dallas Mus of Fine Art, TX; Herbert F. Johnson Mus, Cornell Univ, Ithaca, NY
PRINTERS: Kathy Caraccio, NY (KC); Jennifer Melby, NY (JM); Artist (ART)
PUBLISHERS: 724 Prints, NY (724P); Orion Editions, NY (OE); Matsumera Editions, NY (MatEd); New York Assoc for the Blind, NY (NYAB); Artist (ART)
GALLERIES: Jan Cicero Gallery, Chicago, IL; Tomoko Liguori Gallery, New York, NY; André Zarre Gallery, New York, NY; Susan Caldwell & Company, New York, NY
MAILING ADDRESS: 99 Vandam St, New York, NY 10013

Frances Barth
Landscape
Courtesy Tomoko Liguori Gallery

TITLE	PUBLISHER	PRINTER	DATE	MEDIUM	DIMENSION (PAPER SIZE) IN INCHES	TYPE OF PAPER	EDITION NUMBER	NO. OF COLORS	ORIGINAL OPENING PRICE	CURRENT RETAIL PRICE
SOLD OUT EDITIONS (RARE):										
Untitled	724P	ART	1981	LC	24 X 23	AP	50		300	450
Untitled	OE	ART	1986	AC	30 X 36	AP	50		575	700
CURRENT EDITIONS:										
A Russian Abecedary (Book with Hand-Colored Etchings, Drypoint & Engravings)	ART	JM	1980	EB/HC/ DPT/ENG	15 X 21 EA	SOM	20 EA	Multi	5000 SET	15000 SET
Goro	NYAB	JM	1981	EB/HC/ DPT/EMB	23 X 28	LIN	250	7	300	900
Landscape	MatEd	KC	1989	LI	23 X 28	RdL	35	6	600	650

TOM BARTEK

BORN: Omaha, NE; July 25, 1932
EDUCATION: Creighton Univ, Omaha, NE, 1950–53; Cooper Union Art Sch, NY, with Robert Gwathmey, 1955–56
TEACHING: Joslyn Art Mus, Omaha, NE, 1962–64; Instr, Col of St Mary, Omaha, NE, 1964–66; Assoc Prof, Creighton Univ, Omaha, NE, 1966–74
AWARDS: Honorable Mentions, Joslyn Art Mus, Omaha, NE, 1962,64,66; Honorable Mention, Nelson Atkins Mus, Kansas City, MO, 1978; Purchase Award, Anderson Fine Arts Center, IN, 1985

TOM BARTEK CONTINUED

COLLECTIONS: Joslyn Art Mus, Omaha, NE; Wichita Art Mus, KS; Neville Public Mus, Green Bay, WI; UENO-JUKO Educational Found, Tokyo, Japan; Burpee Art Mus, Rockford, IL; California Col of Arts & Crafts, San Francisco, CA; Nebraska Art Coll, Kearney, NE; Sioux City Art Center, IA; Albrecht Art Mus, St Joseph, MO; Hastings Col, NE; Bowles Fine Arts Center, Iola, KS; Harry S Truman Mem Library, Independance, MO; John F Kennedy Mem Library, Cambridge; Inst Mexicano-Norteamericano de Relaciones Culturales, Mexico City, Mexico
PRINTERS: Martin Perkins (MP); Gene Chaves (GC); Ethan Bartek, Denver, CO (EB); Jesse Bartek, Omaha, NE (JB); Jack Bartek, Springfield, NE (JaB); Artist (ART)
PUBLISHERS: Artist (ART)
GALLERIES: Haymarket Art Gallery, Lincoln, NE
MAILING ADDRESS: 1314 S 9th St, Omaha, NE 68108

TITLE	PUBLISHER	PRINTER	DATE	MEDIUM	DIMENSION (PAPER SIZE) IN INCHES	TYPE OF PAPER	EDITION NUMBER	NO. OF COLORS	ORIGINAL OPENING PRICE	CURRENT RETAIL PRICE
CURRENT EDITIONS:										
December Window... Cranberries, Pecans, etc	ART	ART/JB	1982	SP	20 X 26	LEN/100	290	10	100	150
May Sunlight (Irises & Potatoes)	ART	ART/JB	1983	SP	20 X 26	LEN/100	270	9	100	150
Spring Cedars	ART	ART/JB	1983	SP	22 X 30	LEN/100	170	11	130	175
Fall Crossing	ART	ART/JB	1983	SP	22 X 30	LEN/100	180	12	130	175
Summer Morning	ART	ART/JB	1984	SP	22 X 30	LEN/100	170	10	130	175
Winter Sunlight	ART	ART/JB	1984	SP	22 X 30	LEN/100	170	8	150	175
Dark Window	ART	ART/JB	1985	SP	28 X 26	LEN/100	140	11	150	200
Passage of Ecstasy	ART	ART/JB	1985	SP	28 X 26	LEN/100	140	11	150	200
Poem-Souvenir	ART	ART/JB	1985	SP	32 X 26	LEN/100	120	8	175	200

JENNIFER BARTLETT

BORN: Long Beach, CA; March 14, 1941
EDUCATION: Mills Col, CA, BA, 1963; Yale Univ, New Haven, CT, BFA, 1964; MFA, 1965; Studied with Jack Tworkov, James Rosenquist, Al Held & Jim Dine
AWARDS: Creative Artists Public Service Fel, 1974; Lucus Vis Award, Carleton Col, Northfield, MN, 1979; Brandeis Univ Creative Arts Award, Waltham, MA, 1983; Am Acad of Arts & Letters Award, 1983; Harris Prize, Art Inst of Chicago, IL, 1976,86; M V Kohnstamm Award, Art Inst of Chicago, IL, 1986; Am Inst of Architects Award, 1987
RECENT EXHIB: Philadelphia Mus of Art, PA, 1988; Fort Wayne Mus of Art, IN, 1988; La Jolla Mus of Contemp Art, CA, 1988–89; Univ of Nevada, Inst for Fine Art, Donna Beam Fine Art Gallery, Las Vegas, NV, 1989; Sonoma State Univ, Rohnert Park, CA, 1992; Lincoln Center, Fine Art Prints, Avery Fisher Hall, NY, 1992; Paula Cooper Gallery, NY, 1987,90,92,93; John Berggruen Gallery, San Francisco, CA, 1990,93
COLLECTIONS: Mus of Mod Art, NY; Metropolitan Mus of Art, NY; Whitney Mus of Am Art, NY; Philadelphia Mus of Art, PA; Walker Art Center, Minneapolis, MN
PRINTERS: Simca Print Artists, NY (SPA); Patricia Branstead, NY (PB); Branstead Studios, NY (BS); Aeropress, NY (A); Simon Draper, NY (SD); Felix Harlan, NY (FH); Yong Soon Min, NY (YSM); Catherine Tirr, NY (CT); Carol Weaver, NY (CW); Artist (ART)
PUBLISHERS: Brooke Alexander, Inc, NY (BA); Simca Print Artists, NY (SPA); Paula Cooper, NY (PC); Multiples, NY (M); Harry N Abrams, Inc, NY (HNA); Artist (ART); Parasol Press, Ltd, NY (PaP); Creative Works Editions, Osaka, Japan (CWE)
GALLERIES: Brooke Alexander, Inc, New York, NY; Paula Cooper Gallery, New York, NY; Marian Goodman, New York, NY; Gloria Luria Gallery, Bay Harbor Islands, FL; Margo Leavin Gallery, Los Angeles, CA; Heath Gallery, Atlanta, GA; Barbara Krakow Gallery, Boston, MA; R K Goldman Contemporary, Los Angeles, CA; A Clean, Well-Lighted Place, New York, NY; Ruth O'Hara Fine Art, New York, NY; John Berggruen Gallery, San Francisco, CA; Van Straaten Gallery, Chicago, IL; Lemberg Gallery, Birmingham, MI; S Clara BB Galleries, Cleveland, OH; Brett Mitchell Collection, Cleveland, OH
MAILING ADDRESS: c/o Paula Cooper Gallery, 155 Wooster St, New York, NY 10012

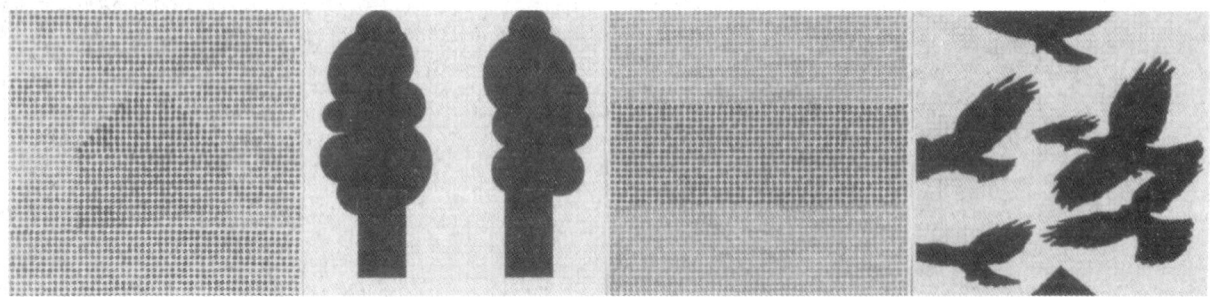

Jennifer Bartlett
From Rhapsody: House, Tree, Beach, Birds
Courtesy the Artist

TITLE	PUBLISHER	PRINTER	DATE	MEDIUM	DIMENSION (PAPER SIZE) IN INCHES	TYPE OF PAPER	EDITION NUMBER	NO. OF COLORS	ORIGINAL OPENING PRICE	CURRENT RETAIL PRICE
SOLD OUT EDITIONS (RARE):										
Day and Night, #1, #2, #3 (Set of 3)	M	PB/A	1978	EB/DPT	31 X 21 EA	AP	35 EA		500 SET	25000 SET
Graceland Mansion (Set of 5)	BAI	PB/A	1978	DPT/A/SP	24 X 24 EA	AP	40 EA		3000 SET	40000 SET
Untitled (Graceland Woodcut) (Series of 5) State I	BAI	PB/A	1979–80	WC	28 X 28 EA	AP	20 EA		3000 SET	40000 SET
Untitled (Graceland Woodcut) (Series of 3) State II	BAI	PB/A	1979–80	WC	32 X 32 EA	AP	20 EA		2000 SET	25000 SET
At Sea, Japan	SPA/ART	SPA	1980	WC/SP	23 X 101 TOT	HMP	58 EA		5000 SET	50000 SET

JENNIFER BARTLETT CONTINUED

TITLE	PUBLISHER	PRINTER	DATE	MEDIUM	DIMENSION (PAPER SIZE) IN INCHES	TYPE OF PAPER	EDITION NUMBER	NO. OF COLORS	ORIGINAL OPENING PRICE	CURRENT RETAIL PRICE
SOLD OUT EDITIONS (RARE):					23 X 17 EA					
In the Garden #190 (Dipt)	SPA/ART	SPA/ART	1982	WB	17 X 23 EA	HMP	52 EA		1500 SET	10000 SET
In the Garden #40 (4 Parts)	SPA/ART	SPA/ART	1983	WB/SP	25 X 30 EA	JAP/HMP	68 EA		2800 SET	15000 SET
In the Garden #116	SPA/ART	SPA/ART	1983	SP	29 X 38	AP	100		1000	10000 SET
Shadow (4 Parts)	M/PC	SD/FH/YSM/ CT/CW	1984	EB/A	30 X 20 EA	FAB	60 EA		7500 SET	18000 SET
Set of 4:									1600 SET	7500 SET
House	HNA	PB/A	1985	A/SL/PHE	12 X 12	THS	100		400	2000
Trees	HNA	PB/A	1985	A/SL/PHE	12 X 12	THS	100		400	2000
Beach	HNA	PB/A	1985	A/SL/PHE	12 X 12	THS	100		400	2000
Birds	HNA	PB/A	1985	A/SL/PHE	12 X 12	THS	100		400	2000
From Rhapsody (3 Sheets)	PaP		1987	EB/A/PHE		R/BFK	100		2500	6000
CURRENT EDITIONS:										
The Four Seasons: Autumn	SPA/ART	SPA	1990	SP	33 X 35	HOSHO	60	62	2500	2500
The Elements: Air, Earth, Fire & Water (Set of 4)	CWE	PB/BS	1992	EB/A/SG	33 X 33 EA	R/BFK	80 EA	25–32 EA	14000 SET	14000 SET

GEORG BASELITZ

BORN: Deutschbaselitz, Saxony, Germany; 1938
EDUCATION: Hochschule for Bildende Kunste, Berlin, Germany, 1957–64
RECENT EXHIB: Toledo Mus of Art, OH, 1988; Anthony d'Offay Gallery, London, England, 1990; Runhel-Hue-Williams, Ltd, London, England, 1990; Grob Gallery, London, England, 1990; Pace Gallery, NY, 1990,92; Matthew Marks Gallery, NY, 1992; Michael Werner Gallery, NY, 1992; Brooke Alexander, Inc, NY, 1987,91,92
COLLECTIONS: Stadtisches Kunstmuseum, Bonn, West Germany; Toledo Mus of Art, OH
PRINTERS: Patricia Branstead, NY (BP); Aeropress, NY (A); Artist (ART); Maximilian Verlag, Munich, Germany, (MV); Niels Borch Jensen, Copenhagen, Denmark (NBJ)
PUBLISHERS: Multiples, Inc, NY (M); Edition Heiner Friedrich, Munich, Germany (EHF); Achenbach Art Edition, Düsseldorf, Germany (AAE); Maximilian Verlag, Munich, Germany (MV)
GALLERIES: Marian Goodman, New York, NY; Fay Gold Gallery, Atlanta, GA; Alpha Gallery, Boston, MA; Brody's Gallery, Wash, DC; Brooke Alexander, Inc, New York, NY; Mary Boone Gallery, New York, NY; Galerie Thaddaeus Ropac, Salzburg, Austria; Flanders Graphics, Minneapolis, MN; David Nolan Gallery, New York, NY; Margarete Roeder Gallery & Editions, New York, NY; Anthony d'Offay Gallery, London, England; Runhel-Hue-Williams, Ltd, London, England; Grob Gallery, London, England; Pace Gallery, New York, NY; Michael Werner Gallery, New York, NY; Matthew Marks Gallery, New York, NY; Goodman/Tinnon Fine Art, San Francisco, CA; Anthony Meier Fine Arts, San Francisco, CA; Stephen Solovy Fine Art, Chicago, IL; Thomas Erben Gallery, Inc, New York, NY; Hirschl & Adler Modern, New York, NY; Susan Sheehan Gallery, Inc, New York, NY; Eugene Binder Gallery, Dallas, TX

Jahn (J); Gohr (G)

Georg Baselitz
#7 (from Suite 45)
Courtesy Achenbach Art Edition

TITLE	PUBLISHER	PRINTER	DATE	MEDIUM	DIMENSION (PAPER SIZE) IN INCHES	TYPE OF PAPER	EDITION NUMBER	NO. OF COLORS	ORIGINAL OPENING PRICE	CURRENT RETAIL PRICE
SOLD OUT EDITIONS (RARE):										
Rebell (J-27)	EHF	ART	1965	EB/A/DPT	13 X 9	AP	60		50	8000
Birken (J-101)	EHF	ART	1968	EB/DPT/CC	14 X 19	AP	52	1	100	5000
Dreibeiniger AKT (G-9h)			1979	LI	80 X 59	R/BFK	10	1	1200	35000
Adler, Baume, Frau im Fenster (Eagle, Trees, Woman in Window) (Set of 9)	M	PB/A	1981	DPT/A	12 X 20 EA	R/BFK	20 EA		2600 SET	20000 SET
Flaschen (Bottles) (Set of 5)	M	PB/A	1981	DPT	31 X 22 EA	R/BFK	20 EA		1450 SET	12000 SET
Strassenbild (Street Scene) (Set of 30)	M	PB/A	1981	EB/A/LI	26 X 20 EA	R/BFK	20 EA		1450 SET	15000 SET

GEORG BASELITZ CONTINUED

TITLE	PUBLISHER	PRINTER	DATE	MEDIUM	DIMENSION (PAPER SIZE) IN INCHES	TYPE OF PAPER	EDITION NUMBER	NO. OF COLORS	ORIGINAL OPENING PRICE	CURRENT RETAIL PRICE
SOLD OUT EDITIONS (RARE):										
Landschaften (Landscapes) (Set of 4)	M	PB/A	1981	EB/DPT/LI	31 X 23 EA	R/BFK	20 EA		1450 SET	10000 SET
Trinker (J-386)	MV	MV	1981	LI	32 X 23	R/BFK	50		1000	5000
Trommler (Printed in Brown) (J-417)			1982	LI	79 X 59	R/BFK	10	1	1500	35000
Kopf			1984	WC	26 X 20	LAID	10		2000	5000
Head	MV/SK	ART	1985	LI	87 X 60	R/BFK	10	1	8000	15000
Suite 45	AAE	ART	1990	LI	100 X 70 cm	AC	35 EA	21	35000 SET	40000 SET
Untitled (Series of 22 Intaglias)	MV	NBJ	1991-92	IC	30 X 22 EA	SOM/S	30 EA		1900/ 2500 EA	1900/ 2500 EA

LEONARD BASKIN

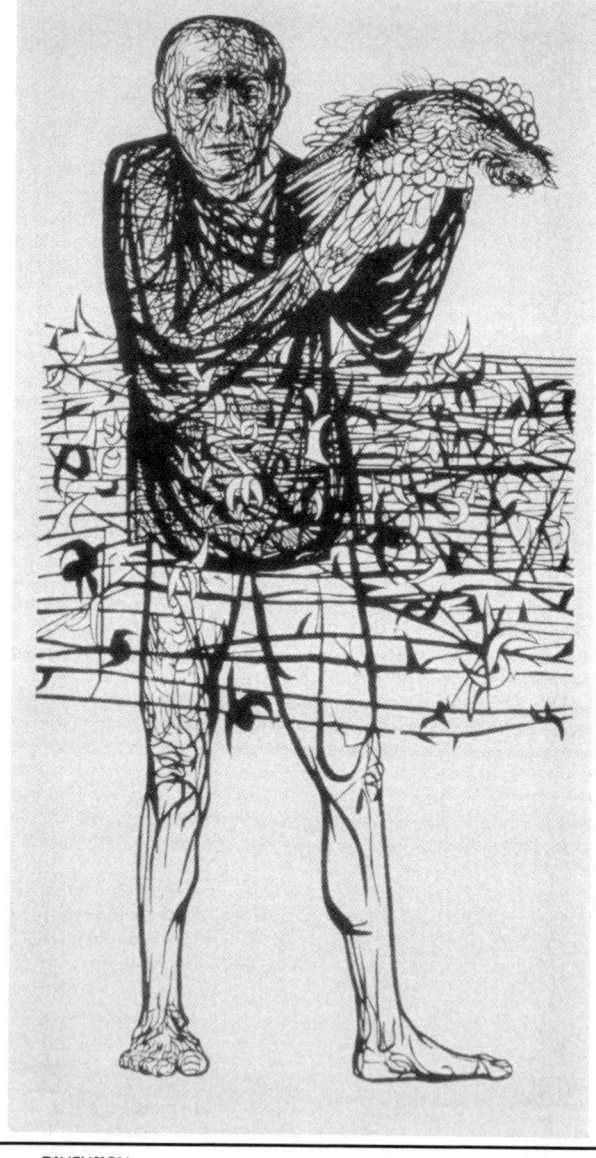

**Leonard Baskin
Man of Peace**
Courtesy the Artist

BORN: New Brunswick, NJ; August 15, 1922
EDUCATION: New York Univ, 1939–41; Yale Sch of Fine Arts, New Haven, CT, 1941–43; New Sch for Soc Research, NY, BA, 1949; DFA, 1966; Acad de la Grand Chaumiere, France, 1950; Acad di Belle Arte, Florence, Italy, 1951; Clark Univ, MA, LHD, 1966; Univ of Massachusetts, DFA, 1968
TEACHING: Smith Col, Northampton, MA, 1953–74; Vis Prof, Art, Hamshire Col, Amherst, MA, 1984
AWARDS: Tiffany Found Fel, 1947; Print Club of Philadelphia, PA; Print Prize, Brooklyn Mus Annual, NY; Guggenheim Fel, 1953; Art Inst of Chicago, IL, Mather Prize; Medal, Am Inst of Graphic Artists, 1965; Nat Inst of Arts and Letters Award, 1969; Gold Medal, Graphics, Skowhegan Sch, ME, 1973; Gold Medal, Nat Acad of Design, 1989
RECENT EXHIB: Hunter Mus of Art, Chattanooga, TN, 1989; Univ of Tennessee, Chattanooga, TN, 1992; Southeast Arkansas Arts & Sciences Center, Pine Bluff, AR, 1992; Midtown Payson Gallery, NY, 1992
COLLECTIONS: Pennsylvania Acad of Fine Arts, Phila, PA; Mus of Fine Arts, Boston, MA; Mus of Mod Art, NY; Whitney Mus of Am Art, NY; Metropolitan Mus of Art, NY; Brooklyn Mus of Art, NY; Fogg Mus, Cambridge, MA; Albright-Knox Art Gallery, Buffalo, NY; Art Inst of Chicago, IL; Princeton Univ, NJ; Brandeis Univ, Waltham, MA; Detroit Inst of Art, MI; Univ of Delaware, Wilmington, DE; St Lawrence Univ, Canton, NY; Mississippi Mus, Jackson, MS; Univ of Massachusetts, Amherst, MA; Nat Gallery of Art, Wash, DC
PRINTERS: Herb Fox, Boston, MA (HF); Malord Press, NY (MP); American Atelier, NY (AA); Gehanna Press (GP)
PUBLISHERS: Kennedy Graphics, Inc, NY (KG); Horn Editions, NY (HE); Associated American Artists, NY (AAA)
GALLERIES: Kennedy Graphics, New York, NY; Topaz Universal Burbank, CA; R Michelson Galleries, Northampton, MA; Midtown Payson Gallery, New York, NY; Bowles-Sorokko Gallery, Beverly Hills, CA & San Francisco, CA & Soho, NY; Bishop Galleries, Scottsdale, AZ & Allenspark, CO; Ella Lerner Gallery, Lenox, MA; Cove Gallery, Wellfleet, MA; R Michelson Galleries, Northampton, MA; Galerie Cujas, San Diego, CA; Georgetown Gallery of Art, Wash, DC
MAILING ADDRESS: Leeds, MA 01053

Fern & O'Sullivan (F&O)

TITLE	PUBLISHER	PRINTER	DATE	MEDIUM	DIMENSION (PAPER SIZE) IN INCHES	TYPE OF PAPER	EDITION NUMBER	NO. OF COLORS	ORIGINAL OPENING PRICE	CURRENT RETAIL PRICE
SOLD OUT EDITIONS (RARE):										
Yeat's Easter (F&O 217)	ART	ART	1916	WB	10 X 10		40	1	10	1500
Mourning Woman (F&O-#78)	ART	ART	1950	WB	32 X 9	AP	50	1	50	950
Son Carrying Father (F&O-#82)	ART	ART	1950	WB	46 X 14	AP		1	50	2000
Castle Street (F&O-#88)	ART	ART	1950	WB	46 X 14	AP		1	50	2000
Ant (F&O-#93)	ART	ART	1951	LI	2 X 2	AP		1	25	200
Bacon's Boar (F&O-#97)	ART	ART	1951	LI	2 X 4	AP		1	25	200
Bull (F&O-#102)	ART	ART	1951	LI	4 X 7	AP		1	25	200
Insects (F&O-#109)	ART	ART	1951	LI	3 X 3	AP		1	25	200
Owls (F&O-#114)	ART	ART	1951	LI	3 X 3	AP		1	25	200
Peacock (F&O-#115)	ART	ART	1951	LI	3 X 3	AP		1	25	xxx
Live Poultry (F&O-#125)	ART	ART	1951	WB	23 X 34	AP		1	60	xxx
Porcupine (F&O-#129)	ART	ART	1951	WB	26 X 21	AP		1	50	xxx
Self Portrait (F&O-#137)	ART	ART	1951	WB	21 X 18	AP		1	50	2000

LEONARD BASKIN CONTINUED

TITLE	PUBLISHER	PRINTER	DATE	MEDIUM	DIMENSION (PAPER SIZE) IN INCHES	TYPE OF PAPER	EDITION NUMBER	NO. OF COLORS	ORIGINAL OPENING PRICE	CURRENT RETAIL PRICE
SOLD OUT EDITIONS (RARE):										
Hanging Woman-Ex-Libris for Moly and Bill Esty (F&O-#164)	ART	ART	1952	WB	3 X 1	AP		1	25	200
Little Florentino	ART	ART	1952	WB/ENG	2 X 4	AP		1	30	275
Dead Tailor (F&O-#162)	ART	ART	1952	WB	43 X 12	AP	50	1	50	1200
Man and the City (F&O-#179)	ART	ART	1952	WB/ENG	2 X 4	AP		1	30	275
Man of Peace (F&O-#180)	ART	ART	1952	WB	60 X 31	AP			80	3000
Portrait of an Irishman, Sean O'Casey (F&O-#190)	ART	ART	1952	WB	26 X 20	AP	15		80	1200
Self Portrait as a Priest (F&O-#193)	ART	ART	1952	WB	21 X 10	AP		1	50	1200
Man with Sculpture of Woman	ART	ART	1952	WB	37 X 23	AP			100	2500
Man with Dog (F&O-#221)	ART	ART	1953	WB	36 X 10	AP		1	60	1600
Still Life, New Year's Greeting (F&O-#227)	ART	ART	1953	WB/ENG	2 X 3	AP		1	30	200
A Poem Called the Tunning of Elynour Rummynge (F&O-#234)	ART	ART	1953	WB/ENG	6 X 2	AP	118	1	30	300
View of Worcester/View in Worcester (F&O-#240)	ART	ART	1953	WB/ENG	10 X 9	AP	20		50	190
Ex-Libris for Samuel D Lockshin (F&O-#245)	ART	ART	1954	WB/ENG	3 X 2				25	175
Projected Ex-Libris for CG (F&O-#246)	ART	ART	1954	WB/ENG	2 X 3				25	200
Hydrogen Man (F&O-#249)	KG	ART	1954	WB	62 X 31	JP	125	1	100	2500
The Hanged Man	ART	ART	1955	WB	67 X 23	JP			100	3000
The Poet Laureate (F&O-#257)			1955	WB	23 X 48	AP			100	3500
The Strabismic Jew (F&O-#259)	ART	ART	1955	WB	41 X 22	AP			100	1000
Blake, a Fragment (F&O-#264)	ART	ART	1956	WB/ENG	1 X 2	AP			35	150
Blake, an Imagined Death Mask (F&O-#267)	ART	ART	1956	WB/ENG/HC	3 X 2	AP			50	600
Edward Calvert Preparing to Sacrifice a Lamb (F&O-#271)	ART	ART	1956	WB/ENG	2 X 1	AP			40	400
Francis Finch (F&O-#272)	ART	ART	1956	WB/ENG	1 X 1	AP			40	125
Samuel Palmer (F&O-#273)	ART	ART	1956	WB/ENG	2 X 2	AP			50	150
Samuel Palmer When He First Met William Blake (F&O-#276)	ART	ART	1956	WB/ENG	1 X 1	AP			40	150
Mark for Richard Warren-Owl and Pomegranate (Two prints with text) (F&O-#286)	ART	GP	1956	WB/ENG					40	100
Hyman	ART	GP	1956		48 X 23				125	2500
Six Poems from White Buildings (F&O-#294)	ART	ART	1957	WB/ENG	8 X 3	AP	1000	1	50	500
Field (F&O-#302)	ART	ART	1957	WB/ENG	5 X 4	AP		1	50	150
For Flaubert's St Julien the Hospitaller the Ascension (F&O-#303)	ART	ART	1957	WB/ENG	6 X 2	AP		1	50	400
For Flaubert's St Julien the Hospitaller Stag (F&O-#306)	ART	ART	1957	WB/ENG	3 X 3	AP		1	50	300
Thistle (F&O-#314)	ART	ART	1957	WB/ENG	5 X 3	AP	125	2	75	250
Thistle (F&O-#314)	ART	ART	1957	WB/ENG	5 X 3	AP		1	50	125
Crow (F&O-#316)	ART	ART	1958	WB/ENG	8 DIA	AP	50	1	60	600
Love Me, Love My Dog	ART	GP	1958	WB/ENG	7 X 6	AP		1	60	600
Torment	ART	GP	1958	WB	13 X 23	AP		1	150	2500
The Seven Deadly Sins (Set of 7):										
Avarice (F&O-#355)	ART	ART	1958	WB/ENG	3 DIA	AP	600	1	50	500
Envy (F&O-#356)	ART	ART	1958	WB/ENG	3 DIA	AP	600	1	50	500
Gluttony (F&O-#357)	ART	ART	1958	WB/ENG	3 DIA	AP	600	1	50	500
Lust (F&O-#358)	ART	ART	1958	WB/ENG	2 DIA	AP	600	1	50	500
Pride (F&O-#359)	ART	ART	1958	WB/ENG	4 DIA	AP	600	1	50	600
Sloth (F&O-#360)	ART	ART	1958	WB/ENG	3 DIA	AP	600	1	50	500
Wrath (F&O-#361)	ART	ART	1958	WB/ENG	2 DIA	AP	600	1	50	500
Death of the Poet Laureate			1959	WB/ENG	12 DIA	AP		1	75	2000
Angel of Death (F&O-#369)	ART	ART	1959	WB	62 X 31	AP		1	125	2000
Death Among the Thistles (F&O-#379)	ART	ART	1959	WB/ENG	6 X 9	AP			75	2000
New Year's Greeting (F&O-#390)	ART	ART	1960	WB/ENG	4 X 3	AP		1	60	500
Etchings of Ten Favorite Artists	ART	ART	1962	EB/HC	18 X 15 EA	R/BFK	50 EA	1 EA	500 SET	2000 SET
Bird Man (F&O-#421)	ART	ART	1962	WB/ENG	8 X 5	R/BFK		1	75	450
Leonard Baskin-AET	ART	GP	1962	WB	32 X 24	R/BFK		1	125	1200
The Great Bird Man (F&O-#447)	ART	ART	1963	WB	61 X 31	R/BFK		1	150	2500
Rembrandt (F&O-#455)	ART	ART	1963	EB/HC	14 X 18	AP	50	1	100	4000
Velasquez (F&O-#458)	ART	ART	1963	WB	20 X 13	AP	50		100	900
Velasquez (F&O-#458)	ART	ART	1963	WB/HC	20 X 13 EA	AP	1 EA		150 EA	1500 EA
Ernst Barlach	ART	GP	1963	EB	17 X 15	AP	1		175	1200
Francisco de Goya	ART	GP	1963	EB	17 X 15	AP		1	175	1200
William Blake	ART	GP	1963	EB	17 X 15	AP		1	175	1200

LEONARD BASKIN CONTINUED

TITLE	PUBLISHER	PRINTER	DATE	MEDIUM	DIMENSION (PAPER SIZE) IN INCHES	TYPE OF PAPER	EDITION NUMBER	NO. OF COLORS	ORIGINAL OPENING PRICE	CURRENT RETAIL PRICE
SOLD OUT EDITIONS (RARE):										
The Cry (Igas)	ART	ART	1964	WB	15 X 12	AP	400		75	650
New Year's Greeting (F&O-#480)	ART	ART	1964	WB/ENG	3 X 3	AP		1	60	200
Edvard Munch	ART	GP	1964	EB	12 X 18	AP		1	100	1200
Adolf Von Menzel	ART	GP	1964	EB	18 X 17	AP		1	100	1200
Thomas Eakins (F&O-#484)	ART	ART	1965	WB	32 X 24	AP		1	100	4000
Thomas Eakins (50th Anniversary of His Death) (F&O-#496)	ART	ART	1966	WB/ENG	2 X 2	AP	500	1	50	200
Joseph Conrad (F&O-#494)	ART	ART	1966	WB	5 X 3	AP	1100	1	75	250
Icarus	ART	GP	1967	WC	32 X 22	AP		2	150	1500
The Sheriff	ART	GP	1967	WB	18 X 18	AP		1	100	800
Mummy	ART	GP	1968	EB	28 X 18	AP		1	125	1000
Death Mask (from Figures of Dead Men) (F&O-#733)	ART	ART	1968	WC	7 X 6	AP	200	2	75	4000
View of Deer Isle (F&O-#516)	ART	ART	1968	EB/HC	9 X 12	AP	100	Varies	100	800
Betrayal (F&O-#518)	ART	ART	1969	WB	32 X 22	AP		1	125	100
Euripides (F&O-#524)	ART	ART	1969	EB	12 X 7	AP	200	1	75	600
Ram's Skull (F&O-#525)	ART	ART	1969	EB	6 X 7	AP	200	1	75	600
Theseus (Self Portrait, Age 46) (F&O-#530)	ART	ART	1969	EB/HC	12 X 7	AP	200	Varies	100	1200
Corot (F&O-#525)	ART	ART	1969	WB/ENG	7 X 5	AP	525	1	100	500
Pictor Ignotus (F&O-#546)	ART	ART	1969	WB/ENG	4 X 4	AP		1	75	250
Monticelli (F&O-#552)	ART	ART	1969	EB/HC	18 X 18	AP		Varies	200	2000
Camille Corot (from Laus Pictorum) (F&O-#538)	ART	ART	1969	WB/ENG	7 X 5	AP	525	1	100	1000
Pig (Pig is Forbidden to thee)	ART	ART	1969	EB	18 X 24	AP	120	1	125	2500
George Minne (F&O-#545)	ART	ART	1969	WB/ENG	6 X 4	AP		1	75	400
Birdman	ART	GP	1969	EB	18 X 23	AP		1	125	1200
Géricault	ART	GP	1969	EB	17 X 24	AP		1	125	1800
Agonized	ART	GP	1969	WB	30 X 23	AP		1	150	2000
Distention	ART	GP	1969	EB	36 X 14	AP		1	150	2000
Great Teasel	ART	GP	1969	EB	28 X 22	AP		1	125	1000
J F Millet & T H Rousseau	ART	GP	1969	WB/ENG	6 X 7	AP		1	75	600
J De Gheyn (F&O-#562)	ART	ART	1970	WB	23 X 14	AP		1	100	900
Baskin's Iris (F&O-#578)	ART	ART	1970	EB/HC	18 X 12	R/BFK	130	Varies	100	2500
Teasel (F&O-#579)	ART	ART	1970	EB/HC	18 X 12	R/BFK	130	Varies	100	2000
Thistle and Yellow Flower (F&O-#580)	ART	ART	1970	EB/HC	18 X 12	R/BFK	130	Varies	100	2000
Thistle and Blue Flower (F&O-#581)	ART	ART	1970	EB/HC	18 X 12	R/BFK	130	Varies	100	2000
Aaron (F&O-#593)	ART	ART	1970	EB	13 X 8	R/BFK	550	1	100	600
Iris for Lisa	KG	ART	1970	EB	30 X 22	R/BFK	130	1	100	2000
Moby Dick Portfolio (Set of 8)	KG	ART	1970	LB/LC	17 X 12 EA	R/BFK	200 EA		1800 SET	7500 SET
Dudley Randall Braadside	ART	ART	1970	LC/OFF	19 X 6	R/BFK			75	1200
Titus Andronicus Portfolio (Set of 12)	KG	ART	1970	EB	20 X 14 EA	JP	550 EA	1 EA	2000 SET	12000 SET
Othello (Set of 10)	KG	ART	1973	WB	20 X 30 EA	JP	600 EA	1 EA	2000 SET	12000 SET
Safari	AAA	AA	1973	LB	26 X 16	AP	160	1	250	1800
Leonard Baskin at 51 (F&O-#618)	ART	ART	1973	WB	32 X 23	AP	100	1	250	1200
Chief Wets It—Assinnboine (F&O-#609)	ART	ART	1972	LB/HC	33 X 22	R/BFK	160	Varies	800	2000
Hidatsa Medicine Man (F&O-#610)	ART	ART	1972	LB/HC	29 X 25	R/BFK	160	Varies	800	2000
Sharp Nose—Arapaho (F&O-#612)	ART	ART	1972	LB/HC	32 X 21	R/BFK	160	Varies	800	2000
Wolf Robe—Cheyenne (F&O-#617)	ART	ART	1972	LB/HC	32 X 21	R/BFK	160	Varies	800	2000
Leonard Baskin at 51 (F&O-#618)	ART	ART	1973	WB	32 X 23	R/BFK	6		1000	2000
High Bear—Sioux (F&O-#620)	ART	ART	1973	LC	36 X 24	R/BFK	100	5	1000	1800
Othello by William Shakespeare (Set of 10):										
The Accused Desdemona (F&O-#624)	ART	ART	1973	WB	13 X 7	JP	400		75	600
The Bard (F&O-#625)	ART	ART	1973	WB	13 X 7	JP	400		75	700
Desdemona (F&O-#626)	ART	ART	1973	WB	13 X 7	JP	400		75	600
Emilia (F&O-#627)	ART	ART	1973	WB	13 X 7	JP	400		75	600
Grieving Othello (F&O-#628)	ART	ART	1973	WB	13 X 7	JP	400		75	600
The Handkerchief (F&O-#629)	ART	ART	1973	WB	13 X 7	JP	400		75	600
Iago (Portrait and Profile) (F&O-#630)	ART	ART	1973	WB	13 X 7	JP	400		75	600
Iago (Portrait) (F&O-#631)	ART	ART	1973	WB	13 X 7	JP	400		75	600
Othello (F&O-#632)	ART	ART	1973	WB	13 X 7	JP	400		75	600
Othello Young (F&O-#633)	ART	ART	1973	WB	13 X 7	JP	400		75	600
At the Bureau (F&O-#636)	ART	ART	1974	LC		AP	100	5		2000
Cheyenne Woman in the Robes of a Secret Society (F&O-#638)	KG	ART	1974	LC	29 X 41	R/BFK	100	4	1000	6000
Crazy Horse (F&O-#640)	KG	ART	1974	LC	41 X 29	R/BFK	100	10	1000	6000

LEONARD BASKIN CONTINUED

Leonard Baskin
Death Among the Thistles
Courtesy the Artist

Leonard Baskin
Yeat's Easter
Courtesy the Artist

TITLE	PUBLISHER	PRINTER	DATE	MEDIUM	DIMENSION (PAPER SIZE) IN INCHES	TYPE OF PAPER	EDITION NUMBER	NO. OF COLORS	ORIGINAL OPENING PRICE	CURRENT RETAIL PRICE
SOLD OUT EDITIONS (RARE):										
Crow Scout—White Man Runs Him (F&O-#641)	KG	ART	1974	LC	41 X 29	R/BFK	100	10	1000	6000
Indian Faces (F&O-#642)			1974	LC/HC	25 X 34	R/BFK	100		1200	3500
Red Cloud—Sioux (F&O-#653)	ART	ART	1974	LC	34 X 24	R/BFK	100	5	1000	2000
Noah	KG	MP	1975	LC	42 X 30	AP	100	9	550	2000
Rachel	KG	MP	1976	LC	42 X 30	AP	100	6	550	2000
Sarah (F&O-#66)	KG	MP	1976	LC	42 X 30	AP	100	5	550	2000
Jacob (F&O-#665)	KG	MP	1976	LC	42 X 30	AP	100	7	550	2000
Marsyas	ART	ART	1976	EB	35 X 18	AP	1	1	450	3500
Self Portrait, Age 55	ART	ART	1977	LB	14 X 12	AP		1	350	1500
Cave Bird	KG/HE	MP	1978	EB/ENG	30 X 20	AP	125	1	450	2000
Crow	KG/HE	MP	1978	EB	20 X 17	FH	150	1	400	2000
Embattled Youth	KG/HE	MP	1978	EB/ENG	29 X 30	AP	125	1	450	2000
Oracular Sybil	KG/HE	MP	1978	EB	20 X 15	AP	125	2	375	2000
Yom Kippur Angel	KG/HE	MP	1978	EB/A	42 X 30	R/BFK	150	1	800	2200
Lessons In the Future	KG/HE	MP	1978	EC	6 X 6	AP	125	2	110	1500
De Hooghe's Sibyl	KG/HE	MP	1978	EC	6 X 6	AP	125	2	110	1500
Woman with Downcast Eyes	KG/HE	MP	1978	ENG/AB	20 X 15	AP	125	1	375	2000
Yom Kippur	KG	HF	1982	LC	21 X 15	AP	30	5	500	2000
Augustus St Gaudens	KG	HF	1982	LC	21 X 15	AP	30	5	500	2000
Self Portrait	KG	HF	1982	LC	21 X 15	AP	30	6	500	2000
Medea	KG	HF	1982	LC	21 X 15	AP	30	6	500	2000
Medea with Birds	KG	HF	1982	LC	21 X 15	AP	30	5	500	2000
Crow Ikon	KG	HF	1982	LC	48 X 37	AP	50	3	750	2200
Tyranus	ART	ART	1982	WC	72 X 38	AP		2	1200	3500
Bee Fly (F&O-#691)	ART	ART	1983	EC	4 X 6	R/BFK	15	2	400	600
Grasshoppers Mating (F&O-#692)	ART	ART	1983	EB/HC	3 X 4	R/BFK	15	Varies	450	800
Praying Mantis (F&O-#697)	ART	ART	1983	EB/HC	3 X 5	R/BFK	15	Varies	450	800
Cave Cricket (F&O-#703)	ART	ART	1983	EB/HC	3 X 5	R/BFK	15	Varies	450	800
Eugene O'Neil (F&O-#739)	ART	ART	1983	LC	8 X 5	R/BFK	200	1	200	350
Death of a Salesman (Set of 5)	ART	ART	1984	EB	7 X 5 EA	R/BFK	1500 EA	1 EA	1000 SET	3000 SET
CURRENT EDITIONS:										
Untitled Shrunken Head (Red Ink)	ART	ART	1985	EC/HC	7 X 5	R/BFK	50	1	450	800
Untitled Shrunken Head (Black Ink)	ART	ART	1985	EB	7 X 5	R/BFK	50	1	450	800
Untitled Shrunken Head (Green Ink)	ART	ART	1985	EC/HC	5 X 4	R/BFK	50	1	450	800
Untitled Shrunken Head (Blue Ink)	ART	ART	1985	EC/HC	5 X 6	R/BFK	50	1	400	700
J Q A Ward	ART	ART	1985	MON	5 X 4 EA	R/BFK	1 EA		500 EA	1000 EA
Saint Gaudens	ART	ART	1985	MON	5 X 4 EA	R/BFK	1 EA		500 EA	1000 EA
Untitled-Man with Hat	ART	ART	1985	MON	5 X 4 EA	R/BFK	1 EA	Varies	500 EA	1000 EA
Elie Nadelman	ART	ART	1985	MON	5 X 4 EA	R/BFK	1 EA	Varies	500 EA	1000 EA
Iris's (Set of 3)										
Blue Iris	ART	ART	1988	EC		R/BFK	35	1	600	800
Pink Iris	ART	ART	1988	EC		R/BFK	35	1	600	800
Purple Iris	ART	ART	1988	EC		R/BFK	35	1	600	800
Blindfolded Man	ART	ART	1988	WB		R/BFK			500	700
Iris (Full Bloom)	ART	ART	1989	EC	5 X 5	R/BFK		2	575	650
Iris (Full Bloom, Part Stem)	ART	ART	1989	EC	5 X 4	R/BFK		3	600	675
Iris (Among Many Stems)	ART	ART	1989	EC	5 X 5	R/BFK		4	750	850

JEAN-MICHEL BASQUIAT

RECENT EXHIB: William Paterson Col, Ben Shahn Gallery, Wayne, NJ, 1987; Galerie Fabien Boulakia, Paris, France, 1990; Whitney Mus of Am Art, NY, 1992–93
PRINTERS: Joel Stearns, Venice, CA (JS); New City Editions, Venice, CA (NCE); Jo Wananabe, NY (JW)
PUBLISHERS: Larry Gagosian Gallery, Los Angeles, CA (LG); New City Editions, Venice, CA (NCE); Annina Nosei Gallery, NY (ANG)
GALLERIES: Editions Schellmann, New York, NY; Galerie Thaddaeus Ropac, Salzburg, Austria; Lillian Heidenberg, New York, NY; Constance Kamens Fine Art, Inc, New York, NY; Edward Tyler Nahem Fine Art, New York, NY; Schlesinger Gallery, New York, NY; Tony Shafrazi Gallery, New York, NY; Annina Nosei Gallery, New York, NY; Gagosian Gallery, New York, NY; New City Editions, Venice, CA; Galerie Fabien Boulakia, Paris, France; Fay Gold Gallery, Atlanta, GA; Barbara Braathen Gallery, New York, NY; Robert Miller Gallery, New York, NY; Enrico Navarra Gallery, New York, NY

TITLE	PUBLISHER	PRINTER	DATE	MEDIUM	DIMENSION (PAPER SIZE) IN INCHES	TYPE OF PAPER	EDITION NUMBER	NO. OF COLORS	ORIGINAL OPENING PRICE	CURRENT RETAIL PRICE
SOLD OUT EDITIONS (RARE):										
Anatomy (Set of 18)	ANG		1982	SP/PH	30 X 22 EA	STP	18 EA		2500 SET	30000 SET
Back of the Neck (Hand-Rolled Print)	LG/NCE	JS/NCE	1983	SP/HC	53 X 102	STP	24	Varies	2000	40000

GEORGETTE BATTLE

BORN: Hackensack, NJ; 1942
COLLECTIONS: Brooklyn Mus, NY; Israel Mus, Jerusalem, Israel
PRINTERS: John Nichols, NY (JN); Artist (ART)
PUBLISHERS: Fred Dorfman, Inc, NY (FDI)
GALLERIES: Fred Dorfman, New York, NY; Gallery Yvon Lambert, Paris, France

TITLE	PUBLISHER	PRINTER	DATE	MEDIUM	DIMENSION (PAPER SIZE) IN INCHES	TYPE OF PAPER	EDITION NUMBER	NO. OF COLORS	ORIGINAL OPENING PRICE	CURRENT RETAIL PRICE
SOLD OUT EDITIONS (RARE):										
New York Profiles	FDI	ART	1974	SP	29 X 23	AP	150	7	150 EA	400 EA
CURRENT EDITIONS:										
Ruby Red	FDI	ART	1979	SP/MM	26 X 40	AP	125	4	200	500
Ultra Silver	FDI	ART	1979	SP/MM	26 X 40	AP	125	4	200	500
Collage Elements I-IV	FDI	JN	1981	SP	43 X 29 EA	SOM	125 EA	14 EA	300 EA	600 EA
Surface Element I, II, III	FDI	ART	1982	LC	44 X 30 EA	R/BFK	40 EA	14	300 EA	500 EA

DON BAUM

BORN: Escanaba, MI; June 2, 1922
EDUCATION: Univ of Chicago, IL, BA, 1946; Art Inst of Chicago, IL, Hon PhD, Fine Arts, 1984
TEACHING: Instr, Painting, Hyde Park Art Center, Chicago, IL, 1955-65; Faculty Mem, Art Dept, Roosevelt Univ, Chicago, IL, 1948–84; Grad Sch, Art Inst of Chicago, IL, 1988–92
AWARDS: Pauline Palmer Prize, Chicago, IL, 1984; Nat Endowment for the Arts, Visual Arts Fel, 1984; Sidney Yates Arts Advocacy Award, Illinois Arts Alliance, 1989
RECENT EXHIB: Madison Art Center, WI, 1988–89; Rockford Col Art Gallery, IL, 1989; Siena Art Gallery, Adrian, MI, 1990; Art Center of Battle Creek, MI, 1989,92; Betsy Rosenfield Gallery, Chicago, IL, 1987,89,92
COLLECTIONS: Illinois State Mus, Springfield, IL; Krannert Mus, Univ of Illinois, Champaign, IL; Milwaukee, WI
PRINTERS: Jack Lemon, Chicago, IL (JL); Landfall Press, Inc, Chicago, IL (LPI)
PUBLISHERS: Landfall Press, Inc, Chicago, IL (LPI)
GALLERIES: Betsy Rosenfield Gallery, Chicago, IL; Landfall Press, Chicago, IL; Quartet Editions, New York, NY
MAILING ADDRESS: c/o Betsy Rosenfield Gallery, 212 W Superior St, Chicago, IL 60610

TITLE	PUBLISHER	PRINTER	DATE	MEDIUM	DIMENSION (PAPER SIZE) IN INCHES	TYPE OF PAPER	EDITION NUMBER	NO. OF COLORS	ORIGINAL OPENING PRICE	CURRENT RETAIL PRICE
CURRENT EDITIONS:										
Domus (6 Panels)	LPI	JL/LPI	1992	MULT	17 X 9 X 14	AP	100		200	200

LOTHAR BAUMGARTEN

BORN: Rheinsberg, Germany; 1944
RECENT EXHIB: Leo Castelli Gallery, NY, 1990; Solomon R Guggenheim Mus, NY, 1992–93
COLLECTIONS: Rheinishes Landesmuseum, Bonn, West Germany
PRINTERS: Patricia Branstead, NY (PB); Aeropress, NY (A)
PUBLISHERS: Multiples, NY (M); Carnegie Mus, Pittsburgh, PA (CM)
GALLERIES: Marian Goodman Gallery, New York, NY

TITLE	PUBLISHER	PRINTER	DATE	MEDIUM	DIMENSION (PAPER SIZE) IN INCHES	TYPE OF PAPER	EDITION NUMBER	NO. OF COLORS	ORIGINAL OPENING PRICE	CURRENT RETAIL PRICE
SOLD OUT EDITIONS (RARE):										
Mato Grosso	M	PB/A	1983	DT	5 X 8	AC	30		300	3600
Fish	ART	PB/A	1985	SP	31 X 45	R/BFK	35		850	4500
CURRENT EDITIONS:										
Land of the Spotted Eagle	M	PB/A	1983	LC/OFF	24 X 33	AC	80		300	2500
Red Cloud (Printed in Two Parts)	M		1983	LP	20 X 26 EA	AC	30 EA	2 EA	600 SET	1500
Metalle	ART	PB/A	1985	SP	29 X 41	R/BFK	35		850	3600
Aquator	ART	PB/A	1985	SP	29 X 41	R/BFK	35		850	3600
Shaiprabowe	ART	PB/A	1985	SP	31 X 45	R/BFK	35		850	3600

LOTHAR BAUMGARTEN CONTINUED

TITLE	PUBLISHER	PRINTER	DATE	MEDIUM	DIMENSION (PAPER SIZE) IN INCHES	TYPE OF PAPER	EDITION NUMBER	NO. OF COLORS	ORIGINAL OPENING PRICE	CURRENT RETAIL PRICE
CURRENT EDITIONS:										
Von Aroma der Namen (Set of 6):									4500 SET	10000 SET
Quaruba	M	PB/A	1985	COL/SP	33 X 24	AC	40		750	2000
Jacaranda	M	PB/A	1985	COL/SP	33 X 24	AC	40		750	2000
Platano	M	PB/A	1985	COL/SP	33 X 24	AC	40		750	2000
Acapu	M	PB/A	1985	COL/SP	33 X 24	AC	40		750	2000
Pijiguao	M	PB/A	1985	COL/SP	33 X 24	AC	40		750	2000
Algarobo	M	PB/A	1985	COL/SP	33 X 24	AC	40		750	2000
Carnegie Museum Poster	CM		1987	LC/OFF/HC	36 X 50	AP	50		750	1500

IAIN BAXTER

BORN: Middlesborough, England; November 16, 1936; Canadian Citizen
EDUCATION: Univ of Idaho, Moscow, ID, BS, 1959, M Ed, 1962; Washington State Univ, Pullman, WA, MFA, 1964
TEACHING: Art Ed Dept, Univ of British Columbia, Can, 1965–66; Asst Prof, Fine Arts, Simon Frazer Univ Visual Arts Dept, York Univ, Can, 1964–66, Assoc Prof, 1972–73
AWARDS: Japanese Govt Foreign Scholarship, 1961; Canadian Centennial Award, Printmaking, 1967; Prize, Canadian Artists, Ont, Can, 1969,72; Senior Canadian Council Grant, 1971
COLLECTIONS: Nat Gallery of Canada, Ottawa, Canada; Montreal Mus of Fine Arts, Canada; Mus of Mod Art, NY; Canadian Council Art Bank; Univ of British Columbia, Canada
PRINTERS: Nancy Anello (NA); Crown Point Press, San Francisco, CA (CPP)
PUBLISHERS: Crown Point Press, San Francisco, CA (CPP)
GALLERIES: Crown Point Press, New York, NY & San Francisco, CA

Iain Baxter
Reflected San Francisco Beauty Spots
Courtesy Crown Point Press

TITLE	PUBLISHER	PRINTER	DATE	MEDIUM	DIMENSION (PAPER SIZE) IN INCHES	TYPE OF PAPER	EDITION NUMBER	NO. OF COLORS	ORIGINAL OPENING PRICE	CURRENT RETAIL PRICE
CURRENT EDITIONS:										
Reflected San Francisco Beauty Spots (Set of 4)	CPP	NA/CPP	1979	PH/EB/A	35 X 30 EA	R/BFK	20	3	600 SET 200 EA	1000 SET 200 EA
Color/Language Participatory Etching	CPP	NA/CPP	1979	EC/SG	21 X 16	R/BFK	15	4	150	650

ROBERT BAXTER

BORN: Milwaukee, WI; November 30, 1933
EDUCATION: Univ of Wisconsin, Madison, WI, BS, 1952–56, MS, 1958–59, MFA, Painting, with John Wilde, 1959–60
TEACHING: Prof, Art, San Diego State Univ, CA, 1962–75
AWARDS: Grant, Painting, Norfolk Mus of Arts & Science, 1963, San Diego State Univ Found Grant, 1970; Louis Comfort Tiffany Grant, Painting, Italy, 1972
RECENT EXHIB: San Francisco Mus of Mod Art, CA, 1987; Portland Mus, ME, 1987
COLLECTIONS: Whitney Mus of Am Art, NY; Fogg Mus, Harvard Univ, Cambridge, MA; California Palace of the Legion of Honor, San Francisco, CA; de Saissett Mus, Univ of Santa Clara, CA; San Jose Mus, CA; Inst Nazionale per la Grafica, Rome, Italy; Hirshhorn Mus, Wash, DC; Vatican Pinicoteca, Rome, Italy; Milwaukee Art Mus, WI; San Francisco Mus of Mod Art, CA; Phoenix Mus, AZ; Gruenwald Center for the Graphic Arts, Univ of California, Los Angeles, CA; San Diego Mus, CA; Univ of North Carolina, Greensboro, NC; Wichita Falls Mus, TX; Foothill Col, Los Altos, CA; Art Inst of Chicago, IL
PRINTERS: Angelo Gabanini, Rome, Italy (AG); Evelyn Lincoln, San Francisco, CA (EL); Brian Shure, San Francisco, CA (BS); Editions Press, San Francisco, CA (EP); Ernest DeSoto, San Francisco, CA (EDS); Desoto Workshop, San Francisco, CA (DSW)
PUBLISHERS: Woodside Editions, Los Altos Hills, CA (WE); Editions Press, San Francisco, CA (EP); Perimeter Gallery, Chicago, IL (PER); Artist (ART)
GALLERIES: Perimeter Gallery, Chicago, IL; Kennedy Gallery, New York, NY; Martin Sumers, New York, NY; Fitch-Febvrel, New York, NY; Thackrey Robinson, San Francisco, CA; Munson Gallery, Chatham, MA

TITLE	PUBLISHER	PRINTER	DATE	MEDIUM	DIMENSION (PAPER SIZE) IN INCHES	TYPE OF PAPER	EDITION NUMBER	NO. OF COLORS	ORIGINAL OPENING PRICE	CURRENT RETAIL PRICE
SOLD OUT EDITIONS (RARE):										
Interior	ART	AG	1977	EB	14 X 20	AP/CC	100	1	200	1200
Ironing	ART	AG	1978	EB	14 X 20	AP/CC	100	1	200	1200
A Checkered History	ART	AG	1979	EB	9 X 18	AP/CC	43	1	300	1200

ROBERT BAXTER CONTINUED

TITLE	PUBLISHER	PRINTER	DATE	MEDIUM	DIMENSION (PAPER SIZE) IN INCHES	TYPE OF PAPER	EDITION NUMBER	NO. OF COLORS	ORIGINAL OPENING PRICE	CURRENT RETAIL PRICE
SOLD OUT EDITIONS (RARE):										
Roman Girl	ART	AG	1980	ENG	2 X 4	AP/CC	100	1	100	800
Still Life	ART	AG	1980	EB/ENG	7 X 8	AP/CC	100	1	100	1000
Piazza San Trovaso	ART	AG	1980	EB/ENG	18 X 27	AP/CC	150	1	300	1350
Seamstress I	EP	EL/EP	1984	LC	13 X 18	FAB	60	3	450	800
CURRENT EDITIONS:										
Folding Linen	WE	AG	1981	EB/ENG	14 X 20	FAB/CC	170	1	300	1250
The Seamstress	WE	AG	1981	EB/ENG	14 X 20	AP/CC	170	1	300	850
Intervallo	WE	AG	1981	EB/ENG	14 X 20	AP/CC	170	1	585	1250
Intervallo II	WE	AG	1982	EB/ENG	14 X 20	AP/CC	170	1	585	1000
Folding Linen II	WE	AG	1982	EB/ENG	14 X 20	AP/CC	170	1	585	900
La Stiratrice	EP	BS/EP	1985	LC	22 X 26	AP	120	2	800	900
Folding Linen III	EP	BS/EP	1985	LC	23 X 32	AP	75	2	800	900
Folding Linen IV	EP	BS/EP	1985	LC	22 X 28	AC/W	75	4	800	900
Intervallo	EP	BS/EP	1985	LC	23 X 28	R/BFK	100	2	800	900
Sensa Titolo I	EP	EP	1985	LC	7 X 9	AC/W	120	2	150	500
Sensa Titolo II,III	EP	EP	1985	LC	7 X 9 EA	AC/W	150 EA	2 EA	150 EA	500 EA
Natura Morte	EP	EP	1985	LC	7 X 9	AC/W	150	2	150	500
Cutting Collars	PER	EDS/DSW	1986	LC	23 X 30	AP	120	3	800	900

HERBERT BAYER

BORN: Haag, Austria; (1900–1985)
EDUCATION: Real-Gym, Linz, Austria, 1919; Painting with Vassily Kandinsky, 1921; Bauhaus, Dessau, Austria, 1921–23
TEACHING: Master, Bauhaus, Dessau, Austria, 1925–28
AWARDS: Aspen Inst for Humanistic Studies, 1965; Ambassador's Award for Excellence, London, England, 1968; Gold Medal Award, Am Inst of Graphic Arts, 1970
RECENT EXHIB: Univ of Tennessee, UTC Art Gallery, Chattanooga, TN, 1989
COLLECTIONS: Mus of Mod Art, NY; San Francisco Mus of Art, CA; Guggenheim Mus of Art, NY; Staatsgemaldesammulungen, Munich, Germany; Denver Art Must, CO; Aldrich Mus of Contemp Art, Ridgefield, CT; Bauhaus Archiv, Berlin, Germany; Busch-Reisinger Mus, Cambridge, MA; Colorado Springs Fine Arts Center, CO; Dusseldorf Mus, Germany; Folkwang Mus, Essen, Germany; Fort Worth Art Center, TX; Hudson River Mus, Yonkers, NY; Joslyn Art Mus, Omaha, NE; Univ of Michigan, Ann Arbor, MI; Mus of Mod Art, Rome, Italy; Roswell Mus, NM; Mus Oldenburg, Germany; Oklahoma Art Center, OK; Evansville Mus of Arts and Sciences, IN; Fogg Mus, Harvard Univ, Cambridge, MA
PRINTERS: Kelpra Studio, London, England (KS); Styria Studio, NY (SS); Maurel Studio, NY (MS); Domberger, KG (DOM); Wolfesnberger (WOLF); Editions Press, San Francisco, CA (EP)
PUBLISHERS: Marlborough Gallery, Inc, NY (MG); Editions Press, San Francisco, CA (EP); Editions Limited, Pittsfield, MA (EL); Patricia Moore, Aspen, CO (PM)
GALLERIES: Marlborough Gallery, Inc, New York, NY; Walton-Gilbert Galleries, San Francisco, CA; Galerie Thomas, Munich, Germany; Charles J Pollyea & Associates, Beverly Hills, CA; Mixografia Gallery, Santa Monica, CA; Turner/Krull Gallery, Los Angeles, CA; Charles J Pollyea & Associates, Beverly Hills, CA

TITLE	PUBLISHER	PRINTER	DATE	MEDIUM	DIMENSION (PAPER SIZE) IN INCHES	TYPE OF PAPER	EDITION NUMBER	NO. OF COLORS	ORIGINAL OPENING PRICE	CURRENT RETAIL PRICE
SOLD OUT EDITIONS (RARE):										
Al-Agsa II	EP	EP	1979	LC	29 X 22	AC/W	150	6	450	2000
Spiral and Free Curve	EP	EP	1979	LC	22 X 33	HMP	60	10	450	1500
CURRENT EDITIONS:										
Blue Moon	MG	KS	1961	SP	30 X 30	AP	50		125	1500
Green Star	MG	KS	1962	SP	30 X 30	AP	48		125	1500
Disc with Blue Center	MG	KS	1968	SP	30 X 30	AP	70		150	1500
Luminous Center	MG	KS	1968	SP	30 X 30	AP	70		150	1500
Striped Twists	MG	KS	1968	SP	30 X 30	AP	70		150	1500
Square with Three Corners	MG	KS	1968	SP	30 X 30	AP	70		150	1500
Chromatic Triangulation I	MG	KS	1968	SP	30 X 30	AP	70		150	1500
Four Seasons	MG	KS	1969	SP	30 X 30	AP	70		150	1500
One Reversed	MG	KS	1969	SP	30 X 30	AP	70		150	1500
Birthday Picture I	MG	KS	1970	SP	30 X 30	AP	75		180	1500
Birthday Picture II	MG	KS	1970	SP	30 X 30	AP	75		180	1500
Chromatic Intersection	MG	KS	1970	SP	30 X 30	AP	75		180	1500
Chromatic Triangulation I, II	MG	KS	1970	SP	30 X 30	AP	75		200	1500
Complimentary and Gold	MG	KS	1970	SP	30 X 30	AP	75		200	1500
Four Segmented Circles	MG	KS	1970	SP	30 X 30	AP	75		200	1500
Yellow Center	MG	KS	1970	SP	30 X 30	AP	75		200	1500
At Dusk	MG	SS	1973	SP	30 X 30	AP	50		250	1200
Divided into Sections	MG	SS	1973	LC/SP	30 X 30	AP	50		250	1200
Four Warped Corner	MG	SS	1973	SP	30 X 30	AP	50		250	1200
Free Arrangements of 4 Equal Parts	MG	SS	1973	SP	30 X 30	AP	50		250	1200
New Nucleus	MG	SS	1973	SP	30 X 30	AP	50		250	1200
Red Transparency	MG	WOLF	1973	LC	32 X 32	AP	75		250	1200
Two Sinking Spheres	MG	SS	1973	SP	32 X 32	AP	50		250	1200
Curve from Two Progressions	MG	KS	1974	SP	32 X 32	AP	50		300	1200
Deep Gate	MG	KS	1974	SP	32 X 32	AP	50		300	1200
Spiral Motions	MG	MS	1974	SP	32 X 32	AP	50		300	1200
Standing Oblong II	MG	DOM	1974	SP	32 X 32	AP	50		300	1200
Stratum	MG	MS	1974	SP	32 X 32	AP	50		300	1200

HERBERT BAYER CONTINUED

TITLE	PUBLISHER	PRINTER	DATE	MEDIUM	DIMENSION (PAPER SIZE) IN INCHES	TYPE OF PAPER	EDITION NUMBER	NO. OF COLORS	ORIGINAL OPENING PRICE	CURRENT RETAIL PRICE
CURRENT EDITIONS:										
Triangulated Square	MG	MS	1974	SP	32 X 32	AP	50		300	1200
Twin Gyration	MG	MS	1974	SP	32 X 32	AP	50		300	1200
Eclyptic	MG	DOM	1975	SP	32 X 32	AP	50		300	1000
Into the Dark	MG	DOM	1975	SP	32 X 32	AP	50		300	1000
Progressions with a Curve	MG	DOM	1975	SP	32 X 32	AP	50		300	1000
Standing Curve	MG	DOM	1975	SP	32 X 32	AP	50		300	1000
Tanger 4	MG	DOM	1975	SP	32 X 32	AP	50		300	1000
Three Floating Segments	MG	DOM	1975	SP	32 X 32	AP	50		300	1000
Two Curves from Colored Progressions (Red)	MG	DOM	1975	SP	32 X 32	AP	50		300	1000
Two Curves from Colored Progressions (Blue)	MG	DOM	1975	SP	32 X 32	AP	50		300	1000
Two Curves from Colored Progressions (Soft Red)	MG	DOM	1975	SP	32 X 32	AP	50		300	1000
Two Triangulated Squares	MG	DOM	1975	SP	32 X 32	AP	50		300	1000
Weightless Blue	MG	DOM	1975	SP	32 X 32	AP	50		300	1000
Mosiak	EL/PM	DOM	1980	SP	24 X 32	AP	175	15	300	1000

ED BAYNARD

BORN: Washington, DC; September 5, 1940
RECENT EXHIB: Elaine Horwitch Galleries, Scottsdale, AZ, 1987; Associated Am Artists, NY, 1988,90; Marcuse Pfeifer Gallery, NY, 1990
COLLECTIONS: Mus of Mod Art, NY; Whitney Mus of Am Art, NY; Philadelphia Mus of Art, PA; Inst of Contemp Art, Univ of Pennsylvania, Phila, PA; Wadsworth Atheneum, Hartford, CT; Walker Art Center, Minneapolis, MN; High Mus, Atlanta, GA; San Francisco Mus of Mod Art, CA
PRINTERS: Maurice Payne, NY (MP); Jennifer Melby, NY, (JM); Adan Spilka, NY (AS); Shelia Marbain, NY (SM); Maurel Studio, NY (MS); Mountain Shadow Studio, Highland, NY (MSS); Tyler Graphics, Ltd, Mount Kisco, NY (TGL); Artist (ART); Smith Andersen Editions, Palo Alto, CA (SAE)
PUBLISHERS: Barbara Gladstone Editions, NY (BGE); Tyler Graphics, Ltd, Mount Kisco, NY (TGL); Multiples, NY (M); Mountain Shadow Studio, Highland, NY (MSS); Smith Andersen Editions, Palo Alto, CA (SAE)
GALLERIES: Marian Goodman Gallery, New York, NY; Erika Meyerovich Gallery, San Francisco, CA; Sylvia Cordish Fine Art, Baltimore, MD; Tyler Graphics, Ltd, Mount Kisco, NY; Associated American Artists, New York, NY; Judith Goldberg Fine Art, New York, NY; Green Gallery, Miami, FL; Gallery 30, Burlingame, CA
MAILING ADDRESS: 69 Bostock Road, Shokan, NY 12481-9727

Ed Baynard
The Lilies
Courtesy Tyler Graphics, Ltd

Ed Baynard
The Sunflower
Courtesy Tyler Graphics, Ltd

TITLE	PUBLISHER	PRINTER	DATE	MEDIUM	DIMENSION (PAPER SIZE) IN INCHES	TYPE OF PAPER	EDITION NUMBER	NO. OF COLORS	ORIGINAL OPENING PRICE	CURRENT RETAIL PRICE
SOLD OUT EDITIONS (RARE):										
Le Premier Fois	M	ART/MS	1977	PO	29 X 41	AP	25	5	500	6000
Marigold	M	MS	1977	PO	29 X 41	AP	16	6	550	6000
Pines	M	ART/SM	1977	PO	29 X 41	AP	12	3	400	6000
Wave	M	SM/MS	1977	PO	29 X 41	AP	9	2	400	6000
The Fog's Pavan	M	SM/MS	1977	SP	40 X 60	STP	38	5	500	2500
Right as Rain	M	SM/MS	1977	SP	40 X 57	STP	39	13	600	2500
Flower's (Set of 7)	BGE	AS	1979	EC	23 X 19 EA	THS	24 EA		2300 SET	10000 SET

ED BAYNARD CONTINUED

TITLE	PUBLISHER	PRINTER	DATE	MEDIUM	DIMENSION (PAPER SIZE) IN INCHES	TYPE OF PAPER	EDITION NUMBER	NO. OF COLORS	ORIGINAL OPENING PRICE	CURRENT RETAIL PRICE
SOLD OUT EDITIONS (RARE):										
The Lillies	TGL	ART/TGL	1980	LC/HC	58 X 41	AWP	12	Varies	2500	6000
The Sunflower	TGL	ART/TGL	1980	LC/HC	58 X 41	AAWP	12	Varies	2500	6000
The Roses	TGL	ART/TGL	1980	LC/HC	40 X 42	AWP	12	Varies	2000	5000
Pomegranate Red Orchid	BGE	AS	1980	AC	30 X 42	AP/500	60	5	800	5000
Vermillion Clair Orchid	BGE	MP	1980	AC	30 X 42	AP/500	60	5	800	5000
The Blue Tulips	TGL	TGL	1980	WC	30 X 42	OKP	70	15	1200	4000
The China Pot	TGL	TGL	1980	WC	42 X 30	OKP	70	27	1200	3000
A Dark Pot with Roses	TGL	TGL	1980	WC	42 X 30	OKP	70	35	1200	1200
The Dragonfly Vase	TGL	TGL	1980	WC	30 X 42	OKP	70	21	1200	3000
The Print Scarf	TGL	TGL	1980	WC	30 X 42	OKP	70	29	1200	3000
A Quarter Moon	TGL	TGL	1980	WC	42 X 30	OKP	70	25	1200	3000
A Still Life with Orchid	TGL	TGL	1980	WC	30 X 42	OKP	70	21	1200	4000
The Tulip Pitcher	TGL	TGL	1980	WC	42 X 30	OKP	70	16	1200	2400
Two-Faced Orchid	BGE	MP/JM	1981	AC/SB	30 X 41	AP/500	60	5	1200	4000
Untitled	MSS	MSS	1983	EB/HC	36 X 38	AP/WA	12	Varies	1500	3000
CURRENT EDITIONS:										
Series of Color Monotypes:					23 X 33 EA to				1500/	1800/
Single Sheets	TGL	TGL	1987	MON	48 X 31 EA	HMP/TGL	1 EA		2500 EA	3000 EA
Diptychs	TGL	TGL	1987	MON	57 X 33 EA to 57 X 36 EA	HMP/TGL	1 EA		3000 EA	4500 EA
The London Quartet Series:										
Westbourne Grove	TGL	TGL	1988	LC/A/WC	33 X 28	AC/W	60	31	1800	2000
Notting Hill Gate	TGL	TGL	1988	LC/A/WC	33 X 28	AC/W	60	30	1800	2000
Blenheim Crescent	TGL	TGL	1988	LC/A/WC	33 X 28	AC/W	59	40	2500	2800
Pembridge Gardens	TGL	TGL	1988	LC/A/WC	33 X 28	AC/W	58	26	2500	2800
Anemonies	SAE	SAE	1991	MON/CC	23 X 29	AP/JP	1 EA	Varies	2000	2000

JANE BAZINET

BORN: Basile, LA; February 7, 1945
EDUCATION: Arizona State Univ, Tempe, AZ; San Francisco State Univ, CA; Phoenix Col, AZ; Putney Col, London, England
AWARDS: Award, Jennings Art Mus, LA; Award, Phoenix Art Mus, AZ; Award, Grady Gammadge, AZ
RECENT EXHIB: Aida Gallery, Cairo, Egypt, 1987; Raul Gutierrez Gallery, San Antonio, TX, 1987; Jack Meier Gallery, Houston, TX, 1987
COLLECTIONS: Phoenix Art Mus, AZ; Jennings Art Mus, LA
PRINTERS: Nepenthe, Houston, TX (NEP); Prints Inkorp, Houston, TX (PI); Dynaprint, Inc, Hollywood, FL (Dyn)
PUBLISHERS: Bazinet Editions, Kingwood, TX (BE); Collectors Art Plus, Lauderhill, FL (CAP); B J Seger Fine Arts, Deerfield Beach, FL (BJS)
GALLERIES: B J Seger Fine Arts, Deerfield Beach, FL; Jack Meier Gallery, Houston, TX; Heritage Galleries, Lafayette, LA
MAILING ADDRESS: 1400 NW 9th Ave, #C-21 Boca Raton, FL 33486

TITLE	PUBLISHER	PRINTER	DATE	MEDIUM	DIMENSION (PAPER SIZE) IN INCHES	TYPE OF PAPER	EDITION NUMBER	NO. OF COLORS	ORIGINAL OPENING PRICE	CURRENT RETAIL PRICE
SOLD OUT EDITIONS (RARE):										
Elegance of Blackberry	BE	NEP	1982	SP	30 X 40	R/100	50	13	375	900
Rainbow Frill	BE	NEP	1982	SP	22 X 30	R/100	100	10	250	900
Dancers Ascent	BE	NEP	1982	SP	30 X 40	R/100	75	16	375	900
Aft and Fro	BE	NEP	1984	SP	30 X 40	R/100	75	16	375	1000
Wind Rose	CAP	PI	1986	SP	38 X 50	LEN	275	14	750	2000
Primrose Fantasy	BJS	PI	1987	SP	38 X 50	LEN	275	18	750	2000
Elegance of Blackberry II	BJS	PI	1987	SP	30 X 40	LEN	275	16	500	900
Meadow Breeze	CAP	DYN	1987	SP	38 X 50	COV	275	16	750	800
Le Femmes du Bazinet (Set of 4)	JBFA	PI	1987	SP	16 X 22 EA	LEN	275 EA		900 EA	1000 EA
Le Jardin	JBFA	PI	1987	SP	38 X 50	LEN	275		1000	1800
Ballet Visions (Dipt)	JBFA	PI	1988	SP	22 X 30 EA	LEN	275 EA	16 EA	750 SET	1400 SET
Coral Mist (Trip)	JBFA	PI	1988	SP	24 X 36 EA	LEN	275 EA	18 EA	1200 SET	2100 SET
Lady Mead	BJS	PI	1988	SP	13 X 19	LEN	350	25	125	350
Painted Cloak	BJS	PI	1988	SP	13 X 19	LEN	350	25	125	350
Le Chat	BJS	PI	1989	SP	13 X 19	LEN	350	25	125	350
Misty Rose	BJS	PI	1990	SP	38 X 50	LEN	275	26	750	1800
Balaeric Breeze	BJS	PI	1990	SP	38 X 50	LEN	275	26	750	2000
CURRENT EDITIONS:										
Sonata	BJS	PI	1989	SP	13 X 19	LEN	350	25	125	350
Les Chat	BJS	PI	1991	SP	38 X 50	LEN	275	28	750	1400
Printemps	HR	PI	1992	SP	38 X 50	LEN	250	24	750	900
Trois Dame	HR	PI	1992	SP	38 X 50	LEN	250	26	750	900
Meadow Breeze	BS	PI	1992	SP	38 X 50	LEN			650	800
Arches Noires	BS	Far	1992	SP	38 X 50	LEN	300	36	650	750

The retail prices of the 100,000 limited edition prints quoted in this directory are subject to change. Print publishers, artists and galleries were the direct sources for these quotations. Prices in the secondary market listed as "Sold Out Editions (Rare)" indicate that the publisher has a limited supply of that print or that the print is difficult to locate in the galleries.

JACK BEAL

BORN: Richmond, VA; June 25, 1931
EDUCATION: William and Mary Col, Norfolk, VA and Polytech Inst, 1950–53; Art Inst of Chicago, IL, 1953–56
AWARDS: Wild Award, Art Inst of Chicago, IL, 1972; Nat Endowment for the Arts Fel, 1972
RECENT EXHIB: Jesse Besser Mus, Alpena, MI, 1992; Frumkin/Adams Gallery, NY, 1993
COLLECTIONS: Mus of Mod Art, NY; Whitney Mus of Am Art, NY; Art Inst of Chicago, IL; Delaware Art Mus, Wilmington, DE; Philadelphia Mus of Art, PA; Walker Art Center, Minneapolis, MN; San Francisco Mus of Art, CA; Univ of Notre Dame, South Bend, IN; Neuberger Mus, Purchase, NY; Wake Forest Col, Winston-Salem, NC; Univ of Vermont, Burlington, VT; Univ of North Carolina, Charlotte, NC; Nat Gallery of Art, Wash, DC
PRINTERS: Shorewood-Bank Street Atelier, NY (S-BSA); Paul Narkiewicz, NY (PN); W Weegee (WW); Shenanigan Press (SP); Chip Elwell, NY (CE)
PUBLISHERS: Brooke Alexander, Editions NY (BAE); Center for Constitutional Rights, NY (CCR); Shenanigan Press (SP); Allan Frumkin Gallery, NY (AFG)
GALLERIES: Brooke Alexander, Inc, New York, NY; Frumkin/Adams Gallery, New York, NY; Thomas Segal Gallery, Boston, MA; Alice Simsar Gallery, Ann Arbor, MI; Martha Tepper Contemporary Fine Arts, West Newton, MA
MAILING ADDRESS: 83-A Delhi Stage, HC 64, Oneonta, NY 13820–9117

TITLE	PUBLISHER	PRINTER	DATE	MEDIUM	DIMENSION (PAPER SIZE) IN INCHES	TYPE OF PAPER	EDITION NUMBER	NO. OF COLORS	ORIGINAL OPENING PRICE	CURRENT RETAIL PRICE
SOLD OUT EDITIONS: (RARE)										
Frogs and Toads	CCR	S-BSA	1971	LB	18 X 24	AP	150	1	150	1500
Oysters, Wine and Lemon	BAI		1974	LC	20 X 24	AC	91		250	1800
Blacksmith	BAI		1977	SP	26 X 20	AC	20		150	500
Rowboat (4 Panels) (Folding Screen)	BAI/SP	WW/SP	1977	SP	70 X 94	AG	24		3500	10000
CURRENT EDITIONS:										
Doyle's Glove	BAI	S-BSA	1969	LC	20 X 21	AP	100		225	750
Spotted Salamander (29 Examples)	BAI		1973	LB	11 X 14 EA	AP	1 EA		300 EA	1200 EA
Self Portrait	BAI		1974–75	LC	30 X 23	AC	52		150	2500
Lobster	BAI	PN	1975	LC	20 X 25	AC	90	6	450	1500
Brook Trout	BAI/AFG	PN	1976	LB	25 X 31	AP	32	1	400	1200
Blue Crab	BAI	CE	1977	LI	17 X 24	UMB	52	4	175	500
Crab, Black State	BAI	CE	1977	LI	17 X 24	UMB	25	1	125	350
Trillium	BAI	CE	1977	LI	19 X 16	UMB	50	4	275	1200
Trout	BAI/AFG	PN	1976–77	LC	25 X 31	AP	102	9	450	1500
Colonist	BAI		1977	SP	26 X 20	AC	38		150	500
Cornucopia	BAI		1962–77	WC	15 X 16	AC	20		125	350
Self Portrait	BAI		1963–77	WC	15 X 13	AC	20		125	400
Woman with a Fan	BAI		1964–77	LI	16 X 14	AP	200		100	300
Caviar	BAI		1978	EB/AC	19 X 15	R/BFK	50		400	1200
Kiddo	BAI		1978	LI	25 X 30	AC	27	1	250	750
Still Life I	BAI		1978	LC	19 X 24	AC	75		500	1800
Still Life II	BAI		1979	LC	23 X 30	AC	60		400	1200
Chicago	BAI		1979	LC	31 X 40	AC	90		750	1500
Garden	BAI		1978–80	LI	25 X 30	AC	74		500	1000
Buds	BAI		1980	LC	31 X 41	AC	80		750	1800
Wisconsin Still Life	BAI		1980	LC	22 X 28	AC	100		450	750
Wisconsin Still Life (Printed in Black)	BAI		1980	LB	22 X 28	AB	50		250	450

TIB BEAMENT

BORN: Montreal, Canada; February 17, 1941
EDUCATION: Fettes Col, Edinburgh, Scotland, 1951–59; Ecole Beaux-Arts, Monteal, Can, 1959–63; Sir George Williams Univ, Can, MA; Studied printmaking in France
TEACHING: McGill Univ, Montreal, Can, 1973; Concordia Univ, Montreal, Can, 1975
AWARDS: Bronfman Purchase Prize, 1963; Italian Govt Scholarship, 1963–64; Anaconda Merit Award, 1965; Quebec Govt Exhib Grant, 1973; Elizabeth T Greenshields Found Grants, 1971,75
COLLECTIONS: Montreal Mus of Fine Arts, Can; Mus de Quebec, Can; Mus of Mod Art, NY; Chicago Inst of Art, IL; Phila Art Mus, PA; Stedelijk Mus, Amsterdam, Holland; Tate Gallery, London, England; Rio de Janeiro Mus, Brazil; Nat Gallery of Art, Ottawa, Can; Art Gallery of Ontario, Toronto, Can
PRINTERS: Donna Miro, Montreal, Can (DM); Artist (ART)
PUBLISHERS: Merritt Publishing, Toronto, Can (MP); La Guilde Graphique, Montreal, Can (LGG); Artist (ART)
GALLERIES: Walter Klinkhoff Gallery, Montreal, Canada; Roberts Gallery, Toronto, Canada; Robertson Galleries, Ottawa, Canada
MAILING ADDRESS: R R #1, Ayers Cliff, PQ Canada J0B 1C0

TITLE	PUBLISHER	PRINTER	DATE	MEDIUM	DIMENSION (PAPER SIZE) IN INCHES	TYPE OF PAPER	EDITION NUMBER	NO. OF COLORS	ORIGINAL OPENING PRICE	CURRENT RETAIL PRICE
SOLD OUT EDITIONS (RARE):										
Late Summer	MP	ART	1978	LC	16 X 24	AP	100	4	200	400
CURRENT EDITIONS:										
Speckled Owl with Monocle	ART	ART	1975	LC	28 X 36	AP	50	1	200	300
Passenger Bumble-Bee	LGG	ART	1976	SP	18 X 12	AP	75	5	100	200
Three-Seater Deluxe Butterfly	LGG	ART	1976	SP	13 X 15	AP	75	4	100	200
First Leaves of Spring	LGG	ART	1976	SP	18 X 12	AP	100	4	225	300
Flight Plans	ART	ART	1977	SP	24 X 24	AP	45	5	125	200
Abandoned Farm	MP	ART	1980	LC	18 X 24	AP	100	4	225	300
Farm/Black Eyed Susan	MP	DM	1981	LC	18 X 24	AP	100	6	225	300
Lighthouse on Barnacles	MP	DM	1981	LC	26 X 18	AP	100	5	225	300
Talisman II	ART	DM	1981	LC	30 X 22	AP	50	5	350	400
Talisman IV	ART	DM	1982	LC	29 X 22	AP	100	4	375	450
. . . and what-is-it?	ART	DM	1982	LC	20 X 22	AP	20	7	400	450

DENNIS RAY BEALL

BORN: Chickasha, OK; March 13, 1929
EDUCATION: Oklahoma City Univ, OK, 1950–51; San Francisco State Univ, CA, BA, 1957, MA, 1958
TEACHING: San Francisco Art Inst, CA, 1964; Univ of Wisconsin, Madison, WI, 1967; San Francisco Univ, CA, 1965 to present
RECENT EXHIB: Univ of Montana, Missoula, MT, 1987–88
COLLECTIONS: Oklahoma Art Center, Oklahoma City, OK; Oakland Art Mus, CA; Victoria & Albert Mus, London, England; San Francisco Mus of Mod Art, CA; Achenbach Found for Graphics Arts, San Francisco, CA; Roanoke Art Center, VA; Fresno Art Center, CA; Wichita Art Mus, KS; Philadelphia Mus, PA; Mus of Mod Art, NY; Ohio Univ, Athens, OH; Southern Illinois Univ, Carbondale, IL; Albion Col, MI; Bard Col, Bard-on-Hudson, NY; Chicago State Col, CA; San Jose State Univ, CA; Univ of Alberta, Edmonton, Canada; Univ of Nevada, Reno, NV; Arizona State Univ, Tempe, AZ; Univ of Wisconsin, Madison, WI; Mills Col, Oakland, CA; Mesa Com Col, AZ; Univ of Oklahoma, Norman, OK; Texas Christian Univ, Ft Worth, TX; Baylor Univ, Waco, TX; Ohio State Univ, Columbus, OH; San Diego State Univ, CA; De Anza Col, Cupertino, CA; Hayward State Col, CA; Philadelphia Free Library, PA; Starr King Sch of the Ministry, Berkeley, CA
PRINTERS: James Reed, CA (JR); Karl Folsom, Sausalito, CA (KF); Chukar Press, Daly City, CA (CP); Artist (ART)
PUBLISHERS: Milestone Graphics, CA (MG); Flyway Publications, Sausalito, CA (FP); Chukar Press, Daly City, CA (CP)
GALLERIES: Los Robles Galleries, Palo Alto, CA
MAILING ADDRESS: c/o Doelger Art Center, 200 Northgate Ave, #11–A, Daly City, CA 94015

TITLE	PUBLISHER	PRINTER	DATE	MEDIUM	DIMENSION (PAPER SIZE) IN INCHES	TYPE OF PAPER	EDITION NUMBER	NO. OF COLORS	ORIGINAL OPENING PRICE	CURRENT RETAIL PRICE
SOLD OUT EDITIONS (RARE):										
Eclipse	MG	JR	1977	LC/ENG	15 X 22	R/BFK	18	2	175	500
CURRENT EDITIONS:										
Set of Six Titles:									750 SET	1200 SET
Myth and Prophecy	FP	ART/KF	1975	SP	22 X 29	R/BFK	20	14	175	250
Dreams of Adventure	FP	ART/KF	1975	SP	22 X 29	R/BFK	20	14	175	250
Trophies	FP	ART/KF	1975	SP	22 X 29	R/BFK	20	14	175	250
The Biggest TV	FP	ART/KF	1975	SP	22 X 29	R/BFK	20	14	175	250
The Biggest Tire	FP	ART/KF	1975	SP	22 X 29	R/BFK	20	14	175	250
Oscar	FP	ART/KF	1975	SP	22 X 29	R/BFK	20	14	175	250
Where Have You Been?	FP	KF	1975	EB	22 X 29	GE	30	1	350	400
Where Are You Going?	FP	KF	1975	EB	22 X 29	GE	30	1	350	400
AT-6	CP	ART	1976	EB	22 X 28	GE	35	1	350	400
Aero Landscape I,II	CP	ART	1976	EB	22 X 30 EA	GE	20 EA	1 EA	300 EA	350 EA
Aero Spacescape	CP	ART	1977	EB	22 X 29	AC	15	1	350	400
Moonbirds	CP	ART	1977	EB	21 X 15	GE	35	1	300	350
Night Piece	CP	ART	1978	EB	22 X 28	GE	35	1	400	450
Encounters	CP	ART	1978	EB	15 X 20	GE	35	1	300	350
Old Red	CP	ART	1978	EB	28 X 22	GE	20	1	350	400
Encounters II	CP	ART	1983	EC	15 X 19	GE	35	3	400	450
Harriers	CP	ART	1984	EC	20 X 24	GE	35	4	400	450
Day of the Iguana	CP	ART	1985	EB	22 X 20	GE	35	1	300	350
Day of the Eagle	CP	ART	1985	EB	20 X 24	GE	35	1	300	350
Duster	CP	ART	1985	EB	22 X 28	GE	35	1	400	450
Ghost Birds	CP	ART	1985	EC	15 X 21	GE	35	2	300	350
Cloud Birds	CP	ART	1985	EB	22 X 24	GE	35	1	400	450
Birds	CP	ART	1986	EB	22 X 29	AC	25	1	300	350

ROMARE BEARDEN

BORN: Charlotte, NC; (1914–1988)
EDUCATION: New York Univ, NY, BS, 1935; Art Students League, NY, 1936–37; Columbia Univ, NY, 1943; Sorbonne, Paris, France, 1950–51
TEACHING: Williams Col, Williamstown, MA, 1969; Yale Univ, New Haven, CT, 1980
AWARDS: Am Artists Arts and Letters Painting Award, 1966; Guggenheim Found Fel, 1969; Ford Found Grant, 1973; Nat Arts Medal, 1987
RECENT EXHIB: Coos Art Mus, Coos Bay, OR, 1989; ACA Galleries, NY, 1989; Nat Acad of Sciences, Wash, DC, 1989,92; Southeast Arkansas Arts & Sciences Center, Pine Bluff, AR, 1992; Minnesota Mus of Art, St Paul, MN, 1992; Asheville Art Mus, NC, 1992; Hickory Mus of Art, NC, 1992; Cleveland Inst of Art, Reinberger Gallery, OH, 1992; Afro-American Historical & Cultural Mus, Phila, PA, 1992; South Carolina State Col, I P Stanback Mus, Orangeburg, SC, 1992; Fisk Univ, Carl Van Vechten Gallery of Fine Arts, Nashville, TN, 1992; Nat Mus of Am Art, Smithsonian Inst, Wash, DC, 1992
COLLECTIONS: Mus of Mod Art, NY; Metropolitan Mus of Art; Whitney Mus of Am Art, NY; Philadelphia Mus of Art, PA; Boston Mus of Fine Art, MA; St Louis Art Mus, MO; Princeton Univ, NJ; Newark Mus, NJ; Rochester Mem Art Gallery, NY; High Mus, Atlanta, GA; Flint Inst of Arts, MI; Akron Art Mus, OH; Madison Art Center, WI; Albright-Knox Art Gallery, Buffalo, NY
PRINTERS: Atelier Ettinger, NY (AE); Printmaking Workshop, NY (PW); Shorewood-Bank Street Atelier, NY (S/BSA); Joseph Kleinman (JK); George J Goodstadt, NY (GG); Mohammad Khalil, NY (MK); Ives-Sillman, New Haven CT (IS)

Romare Bearden
Prevalence of Ritual
Courtesy Ives-Stillman

ROMARE BEARDEN CONTINUED

PUBLISHERS: Transworld Art, Inc, NY (TAI); London Arts, Inc, Detroit, MI (LAI); Abrams Original Editions, NY (AOE); Post Oak Fine Art Distributors, Houston, TX (POFA); J K Fine Arts, NY (JKFA); Ives Sillman, New Haven, CT (IS)
GALLERIES: Sheldon Ross Gallery, Birmingham, MI; Jerald Melberg Gallery, Charlotte, NC; Malcolm Brown Gallery, Shaker Heights, OH; Concept Gallery, Pittsburgh, PA; McIntosh Gallery, Atlanta, GA; Heritage Gallery, Los Angeles, CA; G R N'Namdi Gallery, Birmingham, MI; Alan Brown Gallery, Hartsdale, NY; ACA Galleries/Contemporary, New York, NY; Sid Deutsch Gallery, New York, NY; June Kelly Gallery, New York, NY; Jo Aarons Gallery, Rhinebeck, NY; International Images, Inc, New York, NY; Wendell Street Gallery, Cambridge, MA; Alitash Kebede Fine Arts, Los Angeles, CA; Ro Gallery Image Makers, Inc, New York, NY

TITLE	PUBLISHER	PRINTER	DATE	MEDIUM	DIMENSION (PAPER SIZE) IN INCHES	TYPE OF PAPER	EDITION NUMBER	NO. OF COLORS	ORIGINAL OPENING PRICE	CURRENT RETAIL PRICE
SOLD OUT EDITIONS (RARE):										
Dreams of Exile (With Signed Book)	AOE	GG	1973	SP	28 X 22	AP	100		250	8000
Prevalence of Ritual (Set of 5)	IS	IS	1974	SP	36 X 29 EA	AP	100 EA		2000 SET	20000 SET
The Train (Deluxe Edition)	TAI	PW	1975	EC/HC	22 X 30	FAB	25		700	7000
The Train	TAI	PW	1975	EC/HC	22 X 30	AP	125		300	8000
The Family (Deluxe Edition)	TAI	PW	1975	EB/A/PH	19 X 26	HMB	50	8	400	7000
The Family	TAI	PW	1975	EB/A/PH	19 X 26	AP	175	8	400	7000
Conjunction	TAI	AE	1979	LC	28 X 21	AP	300		350	2000
Three Women	TAI	AE	1979	LC	28 X 21	AP	300		350	2000
Pilate	TAI	AE	1979	LC	28 X 21	AP	300		350	2000
Firebirds	TAI	AE	1979	LC	28 X 21	AP	300		350	2000
Mecklenberg Series:										
The Conversation	LAI	JK	1979	LC	28 X 22	SOM	175	14	600	4500
The Lantern	LAI	JK	1979	LC	22 X 28	SOM	175	13	600	4500
Morning	LAI	JK	1979	LC	19 X 25	SOM	175	14	600	4500
Mecklenberg Autumn	LAI	JK	1980	LC	21 X 27	AP	175	11	600	4500
Falling Star	LAI	JK	1980	LC	28 X 22	AP	175	12	600	4500
Open Door	LAI	JK	1980	LC	23 X 17	SOM	175		600	4500
Mother and Child	TAI	S/BSK	1980	LC	18 X 24	AP	150		500	4500
Quilting Time	POFA	JK	1981	LC	29 X 22	SOM	175	12	600	4500
The Open Door	POFA	JK	1981	LC	29 X 22	SOM	175	12	600	4500
Sunday Morning at Avila	JKFA	MK	1981	EC	30 X 22	R/BFK	100	5	1200	4500
Jamming at the Savoy	JKFA	MK	1981–82	EC	22 X 30	R/BFK	180	9	1000	4500
Mother and Child	TAI	AE	1982						600	4500

JEANA DALE BEARCE

BORN: St. Louis, MO; October 3, 1929
EDUCATION: Washington Univ, St Louis, MO, BFA, 1951; New Mexico Highlands Univ, Las Vegas, NM, MA, 1954; Independent Study, Italy, France & India
TEACHING: Instr, Drawing, Painting & Printmaking, Univ of Maine, Portland, ME, 1965–66, Asst Prof, 1966–70, Assoc Prof, 1970–81; Prof, Univ of Southern Maine, 1981 to present
AWARDS: Fannie Cook Award; McMillian Award; Fulbright Fel; Putzell Purchase Prize, St Louis City Art Mus, MO, 1952; Purchase Prize, Sarasota Art Assn, FL, 1958; State of Maine, 1964; Sabbatical & Research Awards, India, 1980–81,85
COLLECTIONS: St. Louis Mus of Art, MO; Sarasota Art Found, FL; US Educational Found, New Delhi, India; Bowdoin Col Mus of Art, Brunswick, ME; Brooklyn Mus of Art, NY; Cornell Univ, Ithaca, NY
PRINTERS: Impressions Workshop, Boston, MA (IW) (OB); Artist (ART)
PUBLISHERS: Impressions Workshop, Boston, MA (IW) (OB); Artist (ART)
GALLERIES: Barridorf Galleries, Portland, ME
MAILING ADDRESS: 327 Maine St, Brunswick, ME 04011

TITLE	PUBLISHER	PRINTER	DATE	MEDIUM	DIMENSION (PAPER SIZE) IN INCHES	TYPE OF PAPER	EDITION NUMBER	NO. OF COLORS	ORIGINAL OPENING PRICE	CURRENT RETAIL PRICE
SOLD OUT EDITIONS (RARE):										
Good Mouser I	IW	IW	1965	ENG	4 X 9	AP/B	25		60	250
Flying Cranes	IW	IW	1965	WC	11 X 19	RICE	25		60	300
Mystique of the Forest	ART	ART	1968	I	18 X 24	R/BFK	12		90	350
The Lady (Set of 4)	ART	ART	1970	EC	18 X 24	R/BFK	15		90	400
Stonehouse Series I	ART	ART	1972	EC	9 X 12	R/BFK	15		150	450
CURRENT EDITIONS:										
Woman Series	ART	ART	1972	EC	12 X 18	DE	25		500	550
Barrier Series	ART	ART	1974	EC	18 X 24	DE	25		500	650
Growth Series	ART	ART	1978	EC	9 X 12	R/BFK	25			
Doll Series	ART	ART	1980	EC	18 X 24	R/BFK	25		100	250
Reflections in a Bar Room Window	ART	ART	1981	EC	18 X 24	R/BFK	25		250	300
Reflections, Russia	ART	ART	1981	CO	12 X 32	R/BFK	20		150	200
Reflections, Paris	ART	ART	1982	EC	9 X 18	R/BFK	15		150	200
Maine Islands	ART	ART	1982	EC	18 X 20	R/BFK	25		150	200
Lion and Lamb Series	ART	ART	1982	EC	18 X 24	DE	25		200	250
The Animal	ART	ART	1983	I/WC	15 X 22	R/BFK	12	7	300	350
The Animal II	ART	ART	1984	I/CC	18 X 24	R/BFK	13	5	300	350
Volcano (Group of 4)	ART	ART	1984	I	44 X 54	R/BFK	13	12	600	650

The retail prices of the 100,000 limited edition prints quoted in this directory are subject to change. Print publishers, artists and galleries were the direct sources for these quotations. Prices in the secondary market listed as "Sold Out Editions (Rare)" indicate that the publisher has a limited supply of that print or that the print is difficult to locate in the galleries.

DREW BEATTIE

BORN: Atlanta, GA; April 24, 1952
EDUCATION: Univ of North Carolina, Chapel Hill, NC, BFA. Phi Beta Kappa, 1970–74; Drake Univ, Florence, Italy, 1972–74; Skowhegan Sch of Painting & Sculpture, ME, 1976; Sch of Mus of Fine Arts, Tufts Univ, Boston, MA & Medford, MA, MFA, 1975–78
TEACHING: Teaching Assoc, Tufts Univ, Medford, MA, 1975–76; Assoc Instr, Tufts Univ, Medford, MA, 1976–78; Asst Prof, Scripps Col, Claremont, CA, 1978–80; Asst Prof, Claremont Grad Sch, CA, 1978–80; Vis Artist, Sun Valley Center for the Arts & Humanities, ID, 1981; Instr, Evergreen Valley Col, San Jose, CA, 1981; Vis Lectr, Univ of California, Berkeley, CA, 1982–83; Vis Lectr, Univ of California, Davis, CA, 1983,84,85
AWARDS: William Meade Prince Scholarship, Mus of Fine Arts, Boston, MA, 1976; Purchase Prize, Painting, Skowhegan Sch of Painting & Sculpture, ME, 1976; Louise L. Jones Scholarship, Atlanta Arts Alliance, GA, 1977; Dana Pond Prize, Sch of Mus of Fine Arts, Boston, MA, 1978; Eureka Fel, Painting, Mortimer Fleishhacker Found, San Francisco, CA, 1987
RECENT EXHIB: Fay Gold Gallery, Atlanta, GA, 1989
COLLECTIONS: Claremont Col, CA; Marion Koogler McNay Mus, San Antonio, TX; Jane Voorhees Zimmerli Mus, Rutgers, New Brunswick, NJ; Skowhegan Sch, ME
PRINTERS: David Kelso, Oakland, CA (DK); Made in California, Oakland, CA (MIC)
PUBLISHERS: Made in California, Oakland, CA (MIC)
GALLERIES: Gallery Paule Anglim, San Francisco; Fay Gold Gallery, Atlanta, GA

TITLE	PUBLISHER	PRINTER	DATE	MEDIUM	DIMENSION (PAPER SIZE) IN INCHES	TYPE OF PAPER	EDITION NUMBER	NO. OF COLORS	ORIGINAL OPENING PRICE	CURRENT RETAIL PRICE
CURRENT EDITIONS:										
Bridge of Sighs	MIC	DK/MIC	1986	DPT/HG/SG/A	18 X 33	RP/HWT/B	70	1	275	400

MONA BEAUMONT

BORN: Paris, France; January 1, 1932; US Citizen
EDUCATION: Univ of California, Berkeley, BA, MA; Harvard Grad Sch, Cambridge, MA; Hans Hofmann Studios, NY
AWARDS: Purchase Award, US Artist Tour of Asia, 1963; Grey Found Award, Wash, DC; Bulart Art Found Award, San Francisco, CA; San Francisco Art Festival Award; Ackerman Award, SFWAA, 1968
COLLECTIONS: Honolulu Acad of Art, HI; Oakland Mus of Art, CA; City, County, San Francisco, CA; Hoover Found, San Francisco, CA; Grey Found, Wash, DC; Bulart Found, San Francisco, CA
PRINTERS: Artist (ART)
PUBLISHERS: Artist (ART)
GALLERIES: William Sawyer Gallery, San Francisco, CA; Galerie Zodiaque-Perroy, Geneva, Switzerland; Galerie Alexandre Monnet, Brussels, Belgium
MAILING ADDRESS: 1087 Upper Happy Valley Rd, Lafayette, CA 94549

TITLE	PUBLISHER	PRINTER	DATE	MEDIUM	DIMENSION (PAPER SIZE) IN INCHES	TYPE OF PAPER	EDITION NUMBER	NO. OF COLORS	ORIGINAL OPENING PRICE	CURRENT RETAIL PRICE
CURRENT EDITIONS:										
Screen Project #1	ART	ART	1980	SP	22 X 30	R/BFK	50	2	300	300
Screen Project #2	ART	ART	1980	SP	22 X 30	R/BFK	50	2	300	300
Cornered (from Sculpture Series)	ART	ART	1984	SP	30 X 22	R/BFK	50	3	350	350
Joined (from Sculpture Series)	ART	ART	1984	SP	30 X 22	R/BFK	50	3	350	350
Expanding (from Sculpture Series)	ART	ART	1984	SP	30 X 22	R/BFK	50	2	300	300
The Sacrifice of Isaac	ART	ART	1985	SP	30 X 22	R/BFK	50	5	600	600
Passage	ART	ART	1988	LB	22 X 30	R/BFK	30	1	400	600
Design for a Tree	ART	ART	1989	LB/PH	22 X 30	AP	30	1	400	600
Family Outing	ART	ART	1989	LB/PH	22 X 30	AP	30	1	400	600

TONY BECHARA

PRINTERS: American Atelier, NY (AA)
PUBLISHERS: Circle Fine Art, Chicago, IL (CFA)
GALLERIES: Circle Galleries, San Diego, CA & San Francisco, CA & Northbrook, IL & Pittsburgh, PA & Houston, TX & Soho, NY & Chicago, IL & Scottsdale, AZ & Beverly Hills, CA & Costa Mesa, CA & Sherman Oaks, CA & Palm Beach, FL & Honolulu, HI & New Orleans, LA & Las Vegas, NV & Seattle, WA; Ro Gallery Image Makers, Inc, New York, NY

TITLE	PUBLISHER	PRINTER	DATE	MEDIUM	DIMENSION (PAPER SIZE) IN INCHES	TYPE OF PAPER	EDITION NUMBER	NO. OF COLORS	ORIGINAL OPENING PRICE	CURRENT RETAIL PRICE
SOLD OUT EDITIONS (RARE):										
151 Colors	CFA	AA	1978	SP	30 X 23	AP	250		150	325
Comb 21	CFA	AA	1978	SP	22 X 30	AP	250		150	250
Nocturne II	CFA	AA	1978	SP	30 X 22	AP	250		150	250
Pyram	CFA	AA	1978	SP	22 X 30	AP	250		150	250
Sixes	CFA	AA	1978	SP	23 X 30	AP	250		150	250

ROBERT ALAN BECHTLE

BORN: San Francisco, CA; May 14, 1932
EDUCATION: California Col of Arts and Crafts, CA, BA, MFA; Univ of California, Berkeley, CA
TEACHING: Vis Art, Univ of California, Davis, CA, 1966–68; Prof, Printmaking, California Col of Arts and Crafts, 1957 to present; San Francisco State Univ, CA, 1968 to present
AWARDS: James S Phelan Award, Painting, 1965; Nat Endowment for the Arts Grant, 1977,82; Guggenheim Found Fel, Painting, 1985
RECENT EXHIB: San Francisco Mus of Mos Art, CA, 1992; OK Harris Gallery, NY, 1992
COLLECTIONS: Mus of Mod Art, NY; Whitney Mus of Am Art, NY; Oakland Mus, CA; Mus of Mod Art, San Francisco, CA; Nat Coll of Fine Arts, Wash, DC; Lowe Art Mus, Univ of Miami, FL; Library of Congress, Wash, DC; Arts Council of Great Britain; Achenbach Found for Graphic Arts; Neue Galerie der Stadt, Aachen, Germany; Guggenheim Mus, NY; Univ of California Art Mus, Berkeley, CA

ROBERT ALAN BECHTLE CONTINUED

PRINTERS: Nuristani Press (NP); Lilah Toland (LT); Peter Pettengill (PP); June Lambla (JL); Crown Point Press, Oakland, CA (CPP); Don Farnsworth Press, San Francisco, CA (DFP); Sun Shumei, Beijing, China (SS); Rong Bao Zhai Studio, Beijing, China (RBZ); Brian Shure, San Francisco, CA (BS); Julie Goldman, San Francisco, CA (JG)

PUBLISHERS: John Berggruen, San Francisco, Ca (JB); London Arts, Inc, Detroit, MI (LAI); Crown Point Press, Oakland, CA (CPP)
GALLERIES: O K Harris, New York, NY; Crown Point Press, New York, NY & San Francisco, CA; John Berggruen Gallery, San Francisco, CA; Graystone, San Francisco, CA; Gallery Paule Anglim, San Francisco, CA
MAILING ADDRESS: c/o Dept of Art, San Francisco State Univ, 1600 Holloway Ave, San Francisco, CA 94132

TITLE	PUBLISHER	PRINTER	DATE	MEDIUM	DIMENSION (PAPER SIZE) IN INCHES	TYPE OF PAPER	EDITION NUMBER	NO. OF COLORS	ORIGINAL OPENING PRICE	CURRENT RETAIL PRICE
SOLD OUT EDITIONS (RARE):										
Four Chevies	JB	NP	1973	LC	13 X 17	R/BFK	60		720 SET	3000 SET
'64 Impala	JB	NP	1973	LC	13 X 17	R/BFK	60		180	1000
'71 Caprice	JB	NP	1973	LC	13 X 17	R/BFK	60		180	1000
'62 Impala	JB	NP	1973	LC	13 X 17	R/BFK	60		180	1000
Oakland Blue Ghia	LAI	DFP	1978	SP	23 X 28	AP	250	5	425	900
Station Wagon	LAI	DFP	1978	SP	23 X 28	AP	250	9	425	900
Berkeley Buick	LAI	DFP	1979	SP	23 X 28	AP	250	6	425	900
Sunset Street (Soft Ground)	CPP	LT/PP/JL	1982	EC/SG	22 X 30	SOM	50	5	750	2500
Sunset Intersection (Triptych on Single Sheet)	CPP	LT/PP/CPP	1983	EC/SG	32 X 60	EXV	35		1500	5000
Potrero Houses-Pennsylvania Avenue	CPP	SS/BS/SG/CPP	1989	WC	27 X 26	AC/B/SILK	45		650	1200
CURRENT EDITIONS:										
Sunset Tercel	CPP	BS/PP/CPP	1987	EC	21 X 22	SOM/W	15		300	650
34th Avenue	CPP	BS/PP/CPP	1987	EC/SG	31 X 34	SOM/W	50		1000	1500
Sunset Cadillac	CPP	BS/PP/CPP	1987	EC	20 X 24	SOM/W	25	3	500	650
Albany Monte Carlo	CPP	CPP	1990	WC/CC	26 X 26	SILK/RAG/AC	50		650	750
Rockridge House	CPP	CPP	1993	MON/WA	21 X 25 EA	AC	1 EA	Varies	3500 EA	3500 EA
Potrero Honda	CPP	CPP	1993	MON/WA	22 X 25 EA	AC	1 EA	Varies	3500 EA	3500 EA
Potrero VW	CPP	CPP	1993	MON/WA	22 X 25 EA	AC	1 EA	Varies	3500 EA	3500 EA
Near Ocean View	CPP	CPP	1993	MON/WA	17 X 15 EA	AC	1 EA	Varies	1800 EA	1800 EA
Path Near Ocean View	CPP	CPP	1993	MON/WA	19 X 24 EA	AC	1 EA	Varies	2200 EA	2200 EA
Figure Studies	CPP	CPP	1993	MON/WA	18 X 18 EA	AC	1 EA	Varies	1800 EA	1800 EA
20th and Texas	CPP	CPP	1993	MON/WA	19 X 21 EA	AC	1 EA	Varies	2200 EA	2200 EA
20th and Mississippi	CPP	CPP	1993	MON/WA	23 X 27 EA	AC	1 EA	Varies	3500 EA	3500 EA

DAVID BECKER

BORN: Milwaukee, WI; August 16, 1937
EDUCATION: Layton Sch of Art, Milwaukee, WI, 1956–58; Univ of Wisconsin, Milwaukee, WI, BS, 1961; Univ of Illinois, Urbana, IL, MFA 1965
TEACHING: Prof, Art, Wayne State Univ, MI, 1965–85; Vis Prof, Printmaking, Univ of Wisconsin, Madison, WI, 1978–79; Vis Art, Utah State Univ, Logan, UT, Summer, 1981; Prof, Art, Univ of Wisconsin, Madison, WI, 1985–87, Prof, 1987–present
AWARDS: Philadelphia Print Club, PA; Purchase Award, Library of Congress, Wash, DC; Award, Silvermine Guild of Artists; Purchase Award, Hunterdon Art Center, 30th Nat Print Exhib, 1986; Award, Nat Acad of Design, Loggie Prize, 1987; Cannon Prize, 1990; Univ of Wisconsin-Madison Acad Sch, Research Grants, 1986–87,88–89, 90–92,92–93
RECENT EXHIB: Jane Haslem Gallery, Wash, DC, 1990; Davidson Galleries, Seattle, WA, 1993
COLLECTIONS: Portland Mus, OR; Brooklyn Mus, NY; Art Inst of Chicago, IL; Alberta Col of Art, Canada; Butler Inst of Am Art, Youngstown, OH; Library of Congress, Wash, DC; Mus de Arte Mod, Cali, Colombia; Art Inst of Chicago, IL; Detroit Inst of Art, MI; Nat Mus of Am Art, Wash, DC; Rose Art Mus, Brandeis Univ, Waltham, MA; Bradley Univ, Peoria, IL; Elvehjem Mus, Univ of Wisconsin-Madison, WI; Clark Col, Dubuque, IA, Davidson Col, NC; Minot Art Assoc, ND; Silvermine Guild of Arts, New Canaan, CT; Univ of Colorado, Boulder, CO; New York Public Library, NY
PRINTERS: Artist (ART)
PUBLISHERS: John Szoke Graphics, NY (JSG); Artist (ART)
GALLERIES: Szoke Graphics, New York, NY; Fanny Garver, Madison, WI; Jane Haslem Gallery, Wash, DC; Davidson Galleries, Seattle, WA
MAILING ADDRESS: 2512 Lunde Lane, Mount Horeb, WI 53572

TITLE	PUBLISHER	PRINTER	DATE	MEDIUM	DIMENSION (PAPER SIZE) IN INCHES	TYPE OF PAPER	EDITION NUMBER	NO. OF COLORS	ORIGINAL OPENING PRICE	CURRENT RETAIL PRICE
CURRENT EDITIONS:										
Last Day	ART	ART	1980	EB		R/BFK	139	1	225	300
Monument	ART	ART	1980	EB		R/BFK	100	1	500	600

WILLIAM GEORGE BECKMAN

BORN: Maynard, MN; October 19, 1942
EDUCATION: St Cloud Univ, BA, MN, BA, 1966; Univ of Iowa, Iowa City, IA, 1968, MFA. 1969
RECENT EXHIB: Stiebel Modern, NY, 1992; Forum Gallery, NY, 1993
COLLECTIONS: Art Inst of Chicago, IL; Rose Art Mus, Brandeis Mus, Waltham, MA; Hirshhorn Mus, Wash, DC; Des Moines Art Center, IA; Mus of Mod Art, Vienna, Austria; Whitney Mus of Am Art, NY; Carnegie Inst, Pittsburgh, PA
PRINTERS: Jack Lemon, Chicago, IL (JL); Landfall Press, Inc, Chicago, IL (LPI)
PUBLISHERS: Landfall Press, Inc, Chicago, IL (LPI)
GALLERIES: Landfall Press, Inc, Chicago; Frumkin/Adams Gallery, New York, NY; Stiebel Modern, New York, NY; Forum Gallery, New York, NY; Quartet Editions, New York, NY

WILLIAM GEORGE BECKMAN CONTINUED

TITLE	PUBLISHER	PRINTER	DATE	MEDIUM	DIMENSION (PAPER SIZE) IN INCHES	TYPE OF PAPER	EDITION NUMBER	NO. OF COLORS	ORIGINAL OPENING PRICE	CURRENT RETAIL PRICE
CURRENT EDITIONS:										
Self Portrait ¾ View	LPI	JL/LPI	1989	LC	48 X 37	AC	10	1	2400	2400
Self Portrait with Black Shirt	LPI	JL/LPI	1989	LC	42 X 34	AC	5	1	2000	2000

JOHN BEERMAN

BORN: Greensboro, NC; 1958
EDUCATION: Showhegan Sch of Painting & Sculpture, ME, 1980; Rhode Island Sch of Design, Providence, RI, 1982
AWARDS: Scholarship, Skowhegan Sch of Painting & Sculpture, ME, 1980; Yaddo Fel, Visual Arts, Painting, Saratoga Springs, NY, 1984; Prize, Jane Voorhees Zimmerli Art Mus, Rutgers Univ, New Brunswick, NJ, 1986; Nat Science Found Grant, Travel & Painting, Antartica, 1992
RECENT EXHIB: Hudson River Mus, Yonkers, NY, 1987; Hiram Butler Gallery, Houston, TX, 1990; Lorence-Monk Gallery, NY, 1990,91; North Carolina Mus of Art, Raleigh, NC, 1991; Peden Gallery II, Raleigh, NC, 1992; Jerald Melberg Gallery, Charlotte, NC, 1992; Van Straaten Gallery, Chicago, IL, 1993
COLLECTIONS: Brooklyn Mus, NY; Metropolitan Mus of Art, NY; Walker Art Center, Minneapolis, MN; Weatherspoon Art Gallery, Univ of North Carolina, Greensboro, NC; Portland Mus, ME; Center for Contemp Art, Cleveland, OH; Farnsworth Mus, Rockland, ME; Bowdoin Col, Brunswick ME; Mus of Fine Arts, Houston, TX
PRINTERS: Sue Mallozzi, NY (SM); Johanna Hesse, NY (JH); Hudson River Editions, South Nyack, NY (HRE); Sylvia Roth, South Nyack, NY (SR); Mary Seibert, Nyack, NY (MS)
PUBLISHERS: Rutgers Archives for Printmaking Studies, New Brunswick, NJ (RAPS); Artist (ART); Hudson River Editions, South Nyack, NY (HRE); Riverhouse Editions, Clark, CO (REd)
GALLERIES: Dart Gallery, Chicago, IL; Vinalhaven Press, Vinalhaven, ME; Tamarind Inst, Albuquerque, NM; Hudson River Editions, South Nyack, NY; Peden Gallery II, Raleigh, NC; MiraMar Gallery, Sarasota, FL; L Bartman Fine Arts, Chicago, IL; Van Straaten Gallery, Chicago, IL

TITLE	PUBLISHER	PRINTER	DATE	MEDIUM	DIMENSION (PAPER SIZE) IN INCHES	TYPE OF PAPER	EDITION NUMBER	NO. OF COLORS	ORIGINAL OPENING PRICE	CURRENT RETAIL PRICE
CURRENT EDITIONS:										
The Stone's Silent Witness	RAPS	SM/JH/HRE	1986	EC	31 X 42	GE	60		900	1200
Resolute Resonance (Series of 15 Variant Etchings with Monotype)	HRE/ART	SR/HRE	1987	EB/MON	22 X 30 EA	GE	1 EA		1200 EA	1500 EA
Untitled (with Gold Leaf)	HRE/ART	SR/MS/HRE	1989	EB/SB/A	15 X 21	GE	36		450	1000
Untitled (with Gold Leaf)	HRE/ART	SR/MS/HRE	1989	EB/SB/A	21 X 27	GE	36		450	1000

LEIGH BEHNKE

BORN: Hartford, CT; December 22, 1946
EDUCATION: Pratt Inst, NY, BFA, 1969; New York Univ, NY, MA, 1976
TEACHING: Painting, Sch of Visual Arts, NY, 1979 to present
COLLECTIONS: Currier Mus, Manchester, NH
RECENT EXHIB: Nat Acad of Sciences, Wash, DC, 1992
PRINTERS: Handworks, NY (HAN); Sheila Marbain, NY (SM); Frank Versaggi, NY (FV)
PUBLISHERS: Diane Villani Editions, NY (DVE)
GALLERIES: Magnuson Gallery, Boston, MA; Roger Ramsay, Chicago, IL; Diane Villani Editions, New York, NY; Fischbach Gallery, New York, NY
MAILING ADDRESS: Department of Fine Arts, School of Visual Arts, 543 Broadway, #3, New York, NY 10012

TITLE	PUBLISHER	PRINTER	DATE	MEDIUM	DIMENSION (PAPER SIZE) IN INCHES	TYPE OF PAPER	EDITION NUMBER	NO. OF COLORS	ORIGINAL OPENING PRICE	CURRENT RETAIL PRICE
CURRENT EDITIONS:										
Light Study with Mirror #1	DVE	HAN/SM/FV	1981	SP/LC/PO	25 X 35	AC/W	50	7	500	500
Light Study with Mirror #2 (Roman Numerals I–X)	DVE	HAN/SM/FV	1981	LB	25 X 35	RP/G	10	1	300	300

WILLIAM BEHNKEN

BORN: New York, NY; 1943
EDUCATION: City Col of New York, NY, MA, BA
COLLECTIONS: Chrysler Mus, Norfolk, VA
PRINTERS: George C Miller & Son, NY (GCM)
PUBLISHERS: Orion Editions, NY (OE)
GALLERIES: Orion Editions, New York, NY

TITLE	PUBLISHER	PRINTER	DATE	MEDIUM	DIMENSION (PAPER SIZE) IN INCHES	TYPE OF PAPER	EDITION NUMBER	NO. OF COLORS	ORIGINAL OPENING PRICE	CURRENT RETAIL PRICE
CURRENT EDITIONS										
Night	OE	GCM	1980	LC	23 X 27	AP	85	4	250	350

LARRY BELL

BORN: Chicago, IL; Dec 9, 1939
EDUCATION: Chouinard Art Inst, Los Angeles, CA, 1957–59
TEACHING: Instr, Sculpture, Univ of South Florida, Tampa, FL, 1970; Instr, Univ of California, Berkeley, CA, 1971; Instr, Univ of California, Irvine, CA, 1970–73; Instr, Southern California Inst of Architecture, Santa Monica, CA, 1988; Instr, Taos Inst of Arts, NM, 1989–90
AWARDS: Copley Found, 1962; Guggenheim Mus Fel, 1970; Nat Endowment for the Arts, 1975
RECENT EXHIB: Laguna Art Mus, Laguna Beach, CA, 1989; Schmidt-Bingham Gallery, NY, 1990; Sena Galleries West, Santa Fe, NM, 1990; Galerie Rolf Ricke, Cologne, Germany, 1990
COLLECTIONS: Nat Coll of Fine Arts, Wash, DC; Mus of Mod Art, NY; Whitney Mus of Am Art, NY; Tate Gallery, London, England; Gallery New South Wales, Australia

LARRY BELL CONTINUED

PRINTERS: Aeropress, NY (A); Patricia Branstead, NY (PB); Gemini GEL, Los Angeles, CA (GEM)
PUBLISHERS: Multiples, NY (M); Gemini GEL, Los Angeles, CA (GEM)
GALLERIES: Marian Goodman, New York, NY; Tally Richards Galleries, Taos, NM; L A Louver, Venice, CA; The New Gallery, Houston, TX; Sena Galleries West, Santa Fe, NM; Charles Whitchurch Fine Arts, Huntington, CA; Art Source, Los Angeles, CA; Schmidt-Bingham Gallery, New York, NY; The Works Gallery, Long Beach, CA; Kiyo Higashi Gallery, Los Angeles, CA
MAILING ADDRESS: PO Box 1778, Taos, NM 87571

TITLE	PUBLISHER	PRINTER	DATE	MEDIUM	DIMENSION (PAPER SIZE) IN INCHES	TYPE OF PAPER	EDITION NUMBER	NO. OF COLORS	ORIGINAL OPENING PRICE	CURRENT RETAIL PRICE
CURRENT EDITIONS:										
Taos	M	PB/A	1981	LC/OFF	35 X 24	AP	75		350	350
EL-25	M	PB/A	1981	LC/OFF	33 X 22	AP	75		350	350
Assembled Reliefs (Unique Watercolor and Vapor Drawings on Hand Cast Paper)	GEM	GEM	1987	WA/DRAW	20 X 16 EA	HMP	1 EA	Varies	2000 EA	2000 EA
Assembled Reliefs (Unique Watercolor and Vapor Drawings on Hand Cast Paper)	GEM	GEM	1988	WA/DRAW	30 X 22 EA	HMP	1 EA	Varies	3500 EA	3500 EA
Mirage Constructions (Unique Paper and Mixed Media Works on Canvas	GEM	GEM	1988	MM	30 X 22 EA	CAN	1 EA	Varies	4500 EA	4500 EA
Mirage Constructions (Unique Paper and Mixed Media Works on Canvas)	GEM	GEM	1988	MM	40 X 28 EA	CAN	1 EA	Varies	5500 EA	5500 EA

CLAUDE BELLEGARDE

BORN: Paris, France; 1927
TEACHING: Sorbonne Univ, Paris, France
AWARDS: Lissone Prize, 1959, 1961; First Prize for France, San Marino Biennial, 1965
COLLECTIONS: Tate Gallery, London, England; Guggenheim Mus, NY; Fairleigh Dickinson Univ, Rutherford, NJ
PRINTERS: Makor Press, NY (MaP)
PUBLISHERS: Post Oak Fine Art, Houston, TX (POFA)
GALLERIES: Galeries D'Art International, Chicago, IL; Michael H Lord Gallery, Milwaukee, WI

TITLE	PUBLISHER	PRINTER	DATE	MEDIUM	DIMENSION (PAPER SIZE) IN INCHES	TYPE OF PAPER	EDITION NUMBER	NO. OF COLORS	ORIGINAL OPENING PRICE	CURRENT RETAIL PRICE
CURRENT EDITIONS:										
Pan	POFA	MaP	1982	LC	12 X 30	AP	200	6	500	600
Apia	POFA	MaP	1982	LC	12 X 30	AP	200	6	500	600

HANS BELLMER

BORN: Katowice, Upper Silesia; (1902–1975)
EDUCATION: Technical Sch of Art, Berlin, Germany, 1923
PRINTERS: Mourlot, Paris, France (M)
PUBLISHERS: Transworld Art Inc, NY (TAI); Contemporary Art Masters, NY (CAM)
GALLERIES: Virginia Lust Gallery, New York, NY; Galerie Cujas, San Diego, CA

TITLE	PUBLISHER	PRINTER	DATE	MEDIUM	DIMENSION (PAPER SIZE) IN INCHES	TYPE OF PAPER	EDITION NUMBER	NO. OF COLORS	ORIGINAL OPENING PRICE	CURRENT RETAIL PRICE
CURRENT EDITIONS:										
Les Bas Rayes	TAI	M	1974	LC	26 X 20	AP	175	4	550	900
Etreintes	TAI	M	1974	LC	28 X 22	AP	150		550	900
Games of the Doll	CAM	M	1974	EC	22 X 30	AP	25		800	1800
Two Eggs	CAM	M	1974	EC	20 X 26	AP	75		600	1000
Blue Eye	CAM	M	1974	EC	15 X 22	AP	99		600	1200
The Girl in the Street	CAM	M	1974	EC	15 X 20	AP	99		600	900
Pudic Rose	CAM	M	1974	EC	15 X 22	AP	99		600	1200

RICARDO BENAIM

BORN: Caracas, Venezuela; 1949
EDUCATION: Graphics Design, Caracas, Venezuela, BA
TEACHING: Pratt Graphic Center, NY
PRINTERS: Artist (ART)
PUBLISHERS: John Szoke Graphics, Inc, NY (JSG)
GALLERIES: Szoke Graphics, New York, NY; A Clean, Well-Lighted Place, New York, NY; Reece Galleries, New York, NY

TITLE	PUBLISHER	PRINTER	DATE	MEDIUM	DIMENSION (PAPER SIZE) IN INCHES	TYPE OF PAPER	EDITION NUMBER	NO. OF COLORS	ORIGINAL OPENING PRICE	CURRENT RETAIL PRICE
CURRENT EDITIONS:										
Beethoven Sonata: Pathétique	JSG	ART	1984	EMB/CO	31 X 23	HMP	50	7	350	400
Beethoven Sonata: Appassionata	JSG	ART	1984	EMB/CO	31 X 23	HMP	50	7	350	400

The Printworld Directory is accepting new applications for the seventh edition. Approximately 300 new artists will be accepted. Please use the two forms provided in the back section of this directory to submit biographical data and documentation of prints. Edition number of each print must not exceed 500 and the retail price must be $100 or more.

GRETCHEN BENDER

BORN: Seaford, DE; 1951
EDUCATION: Univ of North Carolina, Chapel Hill, NC, BFA, 1972
RECENT EXHIB: Cleveland State Univ Art Gallery, OH, 1989
PRINTERS: Maurice Sanchez, NY (MS); Derriére L'Etoile Studio, NY (DES); Judith Solodkin, NY (JS); Solo Press, NY (SP); Stephanie Serena, NY (StSer); Artist (ART)
PUBLISHERS: Art Issue Editions, Inc, NY (AIE); Serena + Warren, NY (S/W)
COLLECTIONS: Georges Pompidou Center, Paris, France
GALLERIES: Nature Morte, New York, NY; CEPA Galleries, Buffalo, NY; Margo Leavin Gallery, Los Angeles, CA; Otis Parsons Gallery, Los Angeles, CA; Metro Pictures, New York, NY; Robbin Lockett Gallery, Chicago, IL

TITLE	PUBLISHER	PRINTER	DATE	MEDIUM	DIMENSION (PAPER SIZE) IN INCHES	TYPE OF PAPER	EDITION NUMBER	NO. OF COLORS	ORIGINAL OPENING PRICE	CURRENT RETAIL PRICE
CURRENT EDITIONS:										
Thou Shalt Not Take the Name of God in Vain	AIE	JS/SP	1987	LC	24 X 19	DIEU	84	5	500	1800
Untitled (Entertainment Cocoon Series) (Laminated Thermal Transfer Print) (Dipt)	S/W	ART/StSer	1992	THERM	36 X 47	PLEX	35		2100	2100

BARTON LIDICE BENES

BORN: New Jersey; November 16, 1942
EDUCATION: Pratt Inst, NY, Painting, 1960–61, with Walter Murch; Beaux Arts, Avignon France, Graphics, 1968; Atleier Jean D'Orcier, Le Barroux, France, 1968
COLLECTIONS: Princeton Univ, NJ; Univ of Iowa Mus, Iowa City, IA; Nat Gallery of Art, Canberra, Australia; Art Inst of Chicago, IL; Albuquerque Mus of Art, NM; Bibliotheque Nat, Paris, France
PRINTERS: Sarah Amos, Albuquerque, NM (SA); Anne Marie Allen, Albuquerque, NM (AMA); Tamarind Inst, Albuquerque, NM (TI)
PUBLISHERS: Tamarind Inst, Albuquerque, NM (TI); Brooke Alexander, Inc, NY (BAI)
GALLERIES: Hokin Kaufman Gallery, Chicago, IL; Federal Reserve Board Art Gallery, Wash, DC; Tamarind Institute, Albuquerque, NM; Barbara Fendrick Gallery, New York, NY; Betsy Senior Contemporary Prints, New York, NY
MAILING ADDRESS: 463 West St, #956-H, New York, NY 10014

TITLE	PUBLISHER	PRINTER	DATE	MEDIUM	DIMENSION (PAPER SIZE) IN INCHES	TYPE OF PAPER	EDITION NUMBER	NO. OF COLORS	ORIGINAL OPENING PRICE	CURRENT RETAIL PRICE
CURRENT EDITIONS:										
Money Matters (Set of 4)	BAI		1983	LC	14 X 14	HMP	40 EA		1800 SET	6000 SET
Money Suite (Set of 4):										
Butterflies	BAI		1983	LC/CO	14 X 14	HMP	40		500	1800
Midas Touch	BAI		1983	LC/CO	14 X 14	HMP	40		500	1800
Paintbrush	BAI		1983	LC/CO	14 X 14	HMP	40		500	1800
Purse	BAI		1983	LC/CO	14 X 14	HMP	40		500	1800
Graffitti Letters from My Aunt Evelyn (Set of 8 with Object)	TI	SA/AMA/TI	1992	LC	12 X 12 EA	AP/SOM	20 EA		2125 SET	2125 SET

LYNDA BENGLIS

BORN: Lake Charles, LA; October 25, 1941
EDUCATION: Yale Norfolk Sch, CT, 1963; Newcomb Col, Tulane Univ, New Orleans, LA; BFA, 1964; Brooklyn Mus Art Sch, NY, 1965
TEACHING: Vis Prof, California Inst of Arts, 1974, 76; Vis Prof, Princeton Univ, NJ, 1975; Vis Art, Kent State Univ, OH, 1977; Skohegan Sch of Painting & Sculpture, ME, 1979; Asst Prof, Hunter Col, NY, 1972–73, Prof, 1980–81; Univ of Arizona, Tucson, AZ, 1981,82; Sch of Visual Arts, Fine Arts Workshop, 1982–83, 1985–87
AWARDS: Solomon R Guggenheim Fel, 1975; Art Park Grant, 1976; Australian Art Council Award, 1976; Nat Endowment for the Arts Grant, 1979
RECENT EXHIB: Margo Leavin Gallery, Los Angeles, CA, 1987; Mus of Mod Art, NY, 1986–87; Albright-Knox Art Gallery, Buffalo, NY, 1987; Sena Galleries West, Santa Fe, NM, 1990; Paula Cooper Gallery, NY, 1987,90; High Mus, Atlanta, GA, 1991; San Jose Mus, CA, 1992; Corcoran Gallery of Art, Wash, DC, 1992; Alexandria Mus of Art, LA, 1989,92; Univ of Maine, Orono Mus of Art, ME, 1989,92; William Patterson Col, Ben Shahn Gallery, Wayne, ME, 1989,92; Guild Hall Mus, East Hampton, NY, 1992; Bridge Center for Contemp Art, El Paso, TX, 1992
COLLECTIONS: Guggenheim Mus, NY; Mus of Mod Art, NY; Nat Gallery, Canberra, Australia; Walker Art Ctr, Minneapolis, MN; Milwaukee Art Ctr, WI; Whitney Mus of Am Art, NY; Hokkaido Mus of Mod Art, Sapporo, Japan

Lynda Benglis
Tandem Press Series
Courtesy Tandem Press

LYNDA BENGLIS CONTINUED

PRINTERS: A Lynn Forgach, NY (ALF); Exeter Press, NY (ExPr); Jack Lemon, Landfall Press, Inc, Chicago, IL (JL); Fred Gude, Chicago, IL (FG); Artist (ART); Julio Juristo, Tampa, FL (JJ); Topaz Editions, Tampa, FL (TE); Garner Tullis Workshop, San Francisco, CA (GTW); Judith Solodkin, NY (JS); Solo Press, NY (SP); Bill Weege, Madison, WI (BW); Andrew Rubin, Madison, WI (AR); Tandem Press, Univ of Wisconsin, Madison, WI (TanPr); Patricia Branstead, NY (PB); Riverhouse Editions, Clark, CO (REd)
PUBLISHERS: Fabric Workshop, Phila, PA (FW); Inst for Art & Urban Resources, NY (IAUR); Landfall Press, Inc, Chicago, IL (LPI); Topaz Editions, Inc, Tampa, FL (TE); Paula Cooper Gallery, NY (PC); Brooke, Alexander, Inc, NY (BAI); Garner Tullis, NY (GT); Solo Press, NY (SP); Tandem Press, Univ of Wisconsin, Madison, WI (TanPr); Riverhouse Editions, Clark, CO (REd)
GALLERIES: Paula Cooper Gallery, New York, NY; Brooke Alexander, Inc, New York, NY; Arthur Roger Gallery, New Orleans, LA; Dart Gallery, Chicago, IL; Heath Gallery, Atlanta, GA; Texas Gallery, Houston, TX; Margo Leavin Gallery, Los Angeles, CA; Susanne Hilberry Gallery, Birmingham, MI; Tilden-Foley Gallery, New Orleans, LA; Landfall Press, Inc, Chicago, IL; Charles Cowles Gallery, New York, NY; Res Nova Gallery, New York, NY; Garner Tullis Gallery, New York, NY; Topaz Editions, Inc, Tampa, FL; Sena Galleries, Santa Fe, NM; Solo Gallery, New York, NY; Van Straaten Gallery, Chicago, IL; Quartet Editions, New York, NY
MAILING ADDRESS: 222 Bowery St, New York, NY 10012

TITLE	PUBLISHER	PRINTER	DATE	MEDIUM	DIMENSION (PAPER SIZE) IN INCHES	TYPE OF PAPER	EDITION NUMBER	NO. OF COLORS	ORIGINAL OPENING PRICE	CURRENT RETAIL PRICE
SOLD OUT EDITIONS (RARE):										
Untitled	LPI	JL/FG	1979	LC	22 X 30	AP/W	100	4	400	650
Lagniappe II	PC	ALF/ExPr	1979	CP/HC	38 X 14 X 8	HMP	16	Varies	1500	4000
Aquanots, with Paint & Pigment (33 Examples)	BAI		1980	MULT/CP	Varies	HMP	1 EA		2000/ 3500 EA	4000 EA
Ceramic Knot	BAI		1983	MULT	18 X 12 X 8	CER	8		2500	6000
CURRENT EDITIONS:										
Gujurat	IAUR	ALF/EP	1980	MULT/HC	31 X 19 X 9	CP	10		2000	4000
Indian Pants	FW	FW	1980	MULT	41 X 17	FABRIC	9	3	400	900
Torso	TE	TE	1982	MULT	32 X 12 X 5	CER/BR/LUS	12	1	2500	6000
Paladium Wave	TE	TE	1984	MULT	14 X 18 X 16	CER/PAL/LUS	24	1	4000	5000
The Windy City Series	LPI	ART/LPI	1987	MON	50 X 36 EA	HMP	1 EA	Varies	2800 EA	3000 EA
Tandem Press Series (81 Monoprints)	TanPr	BW/AR/TanPr	1988	MON/CO/HC	39 X 25 EA	SEK	1 EA	Varies	2000 EA	2500 EA
Oscar Skilo	TanPr	BW/AR/TanPr	1988	REL	39 X 25	SEK	20		650	750
Dual Natures (Large) (Set of 2):									6000 SET	6000 SET
Dual Natures (Large) (Gold Leaf on Terra Cotta Hand Tinted Paper)	SP	JS/SP	1990	LC	47 X 31	HMP	20		3200	3200
Dual Natures (Large) (Gold Leaf on Blue Hand Tinted Paper)	SP	JS/SP	1990	LC	47 X 31	HMP	20		3200	3200
Dual Natures (Small) (Set of 4):									5000 SET	5000 SET
Dual Natures (Small) (Gold Leaf on Black Hand Tinted Paper)	SP	JS/SP	1990	LC	32 X 24	HMP	25		1500	1500
Dual Natures (Small) (Gold Leaf on Yellow Hand Tinted Paper)	SP	JS/SP	1990	LC	32 X 24	HMP	25		1500	1500
Dual Natures (Unique) (Gold Leaf on Hand Tinted Paper)	SP	JS/SP	1990	LC/CO	44 X 30 EA	HMP	1 EA		2500 EA	2500 EA
Dual Natures (Unique) (Gold Leaf on Chiyogami Paper)	SP	JS/SP	1990	LC/CO	18 X 15 EA	CHI	1 EA		2000 EA	2000 EA
Untitled #1, #2	REd	PB/REd	1992	EC	29 X 53 EA	R/BFK	35 EA	1–2 EA	550 EA	550 EA
Untitled #3	REd	PB/REd	1992	EB	48 X 53	R/BFK	35	1	750	750

BILLY AL BENGSTON

BORN: Dodge City, KS; June 7, 1934
EDUCATION: Los Angeles City Col, CA, 1953–54; Los Angeles State Col of Arts & Crafts, San Francisco, CA, 1955–56; Los Angeles County Art Inst, CA, 1956–57
AWARDS: Nat Found Arts Grant, 1967; Guggenheim Found Fel, 1975; Tamarind Fel, 1968,82
RECENT EXHIB: Thomas Babeor Gallery, La Jolla, CA, 1987; James Corcoran Gallery, Santa Monica, CA, 1987,88; Newport Harbor Mus, Newport Beach, CA, 1989; Contemp Art Mus, Houston, TX, 1988; Oakland Mus, CA, 1988; Los Angeles County Mus of Art, CA, 1988–89; Contemp Arts Center, Honolulu, HI, 1989; Thomas Babeor Gallery, La Jolla, CA, 1989
COLLECTIONS: Mus of Mod Art, NY; Art Inst, Chicago, IL; Whitney Mus of Am Art, NY; Guggenheim Mus, NY; Los Angeles County Mus, CA; Mus of Contemp Art, Houston, TX; Ft Worth Art Ctr Mus, TX; San Francisco Mus of Mod Art, CA; Pasadena Art Mus, CA
PRINTERS: Tamarind Inst, Albuquerque, NM (TI); Lynne P Allen (LPA); Wayne Kline (WK); Catherine Kirsch Kuhn (CKK); Barbara Telleen (BT); Ernest DeSoto Workshop, San Francisco, CA (EDSW); Craig Cornwall (CC); Rodney Hamon (RH); Unified Arts, Albuquerque, NM (UA)
PUBLISHERS: Brooke Alexander, Inc, NY (BAI); Tamarind Inst, Albuquerque, NM (TI); Karl Bornstein, Inc, Santa Monica, CA (KB)
GALLERIES: Brooke Alexander, Inc, New York, NY; James Corcoran Gallery, Santa Monica, CA; Cirrus Gallery, Los Angeles, CA; Linda Farris Gallery, Seattle, WA; Thomas Babeor Gallery, La Jolla, CA; Acquavella Contemp Art, New York, NY; Texas Gallery, Houston, TX; Smith Andersen Gallery, Palo Alto, CA; J Rosenthal Fine Art, Chicago, IL; Garner Tullis, New York, NY; Tamarind Inst, Albuquerque, NM; The Works Gallery, Long Beach, CA; Deanna Miller Fine Art, Pacific Palisades, CA
MAILING ADDRESS: 811 Hampton Drive, Venice, CA 90291

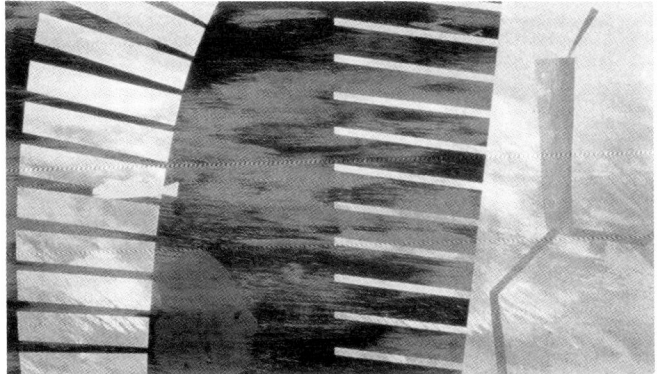

Billy Al Bengston
Noche Corrida
Courtesy Tamarind Institute

BILLY AL BENGSTON CONTINUED

TITLE	PUBLISHER	PRINTER	DATE	MEDIUM	DIMENSION (PAPER SIZE) IN INCHES	TYPE OF PAPER	EDITION NUMBER	NO. OF COLORS	ORIGINAL OPENING PRICE	CURRENT RETAIL PRICE
SOLD OUT EDITIONS (RARE):										
Turkey Dracula Edition	BAI		1975	LC/WA/HC	22 X 33		30		300	1800
Punk Chino	TI	LPA/TI	1982–83	LC/LAM/REL	24 X 20	CD	25	4	600	1000
Punk Indio (State of Punk Chino)	TI	LPA/TI	1982–83	LC/LAM/REL	24 X 20	CD	23	6	600	1000
Agua a la Mañana	TI	WK/TI	1982–83	LC	23 X 22	JGW	25	11	600	1000
Agua a la Noche (State of Agua a la Mañana)	TI	WK/TI	1982–83	LC	23 X 22	AP/BL	25	11	600	1000
Mañana Corrida	TI	CKK/TI	1982–83	LC/CO	25 X 48	AP/W	25	10	950	1250
Noche Corrida	TI	CKK/TI	1982–83	LC/CO	25 X 48	AP/W-AP/BL	25	9	950	1250
Pescado Cabeza Negra	TI	BT/TI	1982–83	LC	24 X 14	AP/B	20	3	450	900
Lanai Draculas	KB	EDSW	1983	LC/H-Cut	40 X 28	AP	100	8	500	900
CURRENT EDITIONS:										
Polvadera, State I	TI	CC/TI	1987	LC	14 X 16	ARJ	20	7	300	450
Polvadera, State II	TI	CC/TI	1987	LC	14 X 16	AP/BL	20	6	300	450
Trementina, State I	TI	RH/TI	1987	LC	14 X 34	ARJ	20	9	400	600
Trementina, State II	TI/RH/TI		1987	LC	14 X 34	AP/BL	20	9	400	600
Chilili	TI	RH/TI	1987	LC	25 X 37	TI	20	3	500	800
Oscura	TI	RH/CC/UA/TI	1987	LC	41 X 30	AP/BL	15	2	500	800

KARL STANLEY BENJAMIN

BORN: Chicago, IL; December 29, 1925
EDUCATION: Northwestern Univ; Univ of Redlands, CA, BA, 1949; Claremont Graduate Sch, Claremont, CA, MA, 1960
TEACHING: Prof, Art, Pomona Col, CA at present
AWARDS: Art Endowment for the Arts Grant, 1983–84
RECENT EXHIB: Retrosp, Redding Mus, 1989; Retrosp, Shasta Col, 1989; Retrosp, Univ of Pacific, 1989–90; Retrosp, California State Univ, Northridge, CA, 1990
COLLECTIONS: Whitney Mus of Am Art, NY; Los Angeles County Mus, CA; San Francisco Mus of Art, CA; Wadsworth Atheneum, Hartford, CT; Seattle Mus of Mod Art, WA; Univ of Art Mus, Berkeley, CA; La Jolla Mus of Art, CA; Santa Barbara Mus of Art, CA; Utah Mus of Fine Arts; Nat Coll of Fine Arts, Wash, DC; Univ of New Mexico, Albuquerque, NM; Denver Art Mus, CO; Portland Art Mus, OR; Henry Gallery, Univ of Washington, Seattle, WA
PRINTERS: Artist (ART)
PUBLISHERS: Artist (ART)
GALLERIES: Moderism, San Francisco, CA; Francine Seders Gallery, Seattle, WA; Vorpal Gallery, San Francisco, CA; Soma Fine Art, San Francisco, CA; Baum Gallery, San Francisco, CA; Ruth Bachofner Gallery, Santa Monica, CA
MAILING ADDRESS: 675 W Eighth St, Claremont, CA 91711

TITLE	PUBLISHER	PRINTER	DATE	MEDIUM	DIMENSION (PAPER SIZE) IN INCHES	TYPE OF PAPER	EDITION NUMBER	NO. OF COLORS	ORIGINAL OPENING PRICE	CURRENT RETAIL PRICE
CURRENT EDITIONS:										
Red Field-Diagonal	ART	ART	1976	SP	20 X 20	AP88	35	3	150	250
Red-Orange Field-Diagonal	ART	ART	1976	SP	20 X 20	AP88	35	3	150	250
Green Field-Diagonal	ART	ART	1976	SP	20 X 20	AP88	35	3	150	250
Violet Field-Diagonal	ART	ART	1976	SP	20 X 20	AP88	35	3	150	250
Red Diamond	ART	ART	1976	SP	19 X 19	AP88	35	2	150	250
Orange Diamond	ART	ART	1976	SP	19 X 19	AP88	35	2	150	250
Blue Diamond	ART	ART	1976	SP	19 X 19	AP88	35	2	150	250
Green Diamond	ART	ART	1976	SP	19 X 19	AP88	35	2	150	250
V S Grey Field	ART	ART	1979	SP	25 X 33	AP88	50	4	400	450
V S Blue Field	ART	ART	1979	SP	25 X 33	AP88	50	4	400	450
V S Magenta Field	ART	ART	1979	SP	25 X 33	AP88	50	4	400	450

PAUL BENNY

RECENT EXHIB: PPOW Show, NY, 1987
PRINTERS: Donna Shulman, Brooklyn, NY (DS); Downtown Editions, Brooklyn, NY (DEd); Sylvia Roth, South Nyack, NY (SR); Hudson River Editions, South Nyack, NY (HRE)
PUBLISHERS: Rutgers Archives, New Brunswick, NJ (RA); Zimmerli Art Mus, New Brunswick, NJ (ZAM)

TITLE	PUBLISHER	PRINTER	DATE	MEDIUM	DIMENSION (PAPER SIZE) IN INCHES	TYPE OF PAPER	EDITION NUMBER	NO. OF COLORS	ORIGINAL OPENING PRICE	CURRENT RETAIL PRICE
CURRENT EDITIONS:										
Untitled	RA/ZAM	DS/DE	1987	EB/DPT/A	31 X 42	GE	65	Varies	800	1000

DIMITRIE BEREA

BORN: Bacau, Rumania; (1908–1975)
EDUCATION: Sch of Architecture, Budapest, Hungary; Acad des Beaux Arts, Rome, Italy
PRINTERS: American Atelier, NY (AA)
PUBLISHERS: Circle Fine Art, Chicago, IL (CFA)
GALLERIES: Circle Galleries, San Diego, CA & San Francisco, CA & Northbrook, IL & Pittsburgh, PA & Houston, TX & Soho, NY & Chicago, IL & Scottsdale, AZ & Beverly Hills, CA & Costa Mesa, CA & Sherman Oaks, CA & Palm Beach, FL & Honolulu, HI & New Orleans, LA & Las Vegas, NV & Seattle, WA; Ergane Gallery, New York, NY

DIMITRIE BEREA CONTINUED

TITLE	PUBLISHER	PRINTER	DATE	MEDIUM	DIMENSION (PAPER SIZE) IN INCHES	TYPE OF PAPER	EDITION NUMBER	NO. OF COLORS	ORIGINAL OPENING PRICE	CURRENT RETAIL PRICE
SOLD OUT EDITIONS (RARE):										
Ships	CFA	AA	1978	LC	22 X 30	AP	200	50		200
Face	CFA	AA	1978	LC	27 X 20	AP	200	50		200
Face/Japon	CFA	AA	1978	LC	27 X 20	JP	10	50		225
Girl at Window	CFA	AA	1979	LC	26 X 20	AP	250	50		200
Girl at Window/Japon	CFA	AA	1979	LC	26 X 20	JP	25	50		225
Flower Terrace	CFA	AA	1980	COL	34 X 27	AP	200	50		200
Le Vase des Fleurs	CFA	AA	1980	COL	34 X 27	AP	200	50		200
Pont des Arts	CFA	AA	1980	COL	28 X 33	AP	200	50		200
Interieur aux Fleurs	CFA	AA	1980	COL	27 X 33	AP	200	50		200
Door to the Garden	CFA	AA	1980	COL	34 X 27	AP	200	50		200
Large Window with Flowers	CFA	AA	1980	COL	27 X 33	AP	200	50		200

SIRI BERG

BORN: Stockholm, Sweden; September 14, 1921; US Citizen
EDUCATION: Inst of Art and Architecture, Univ of Brussels, Belgium, BA; Victoria Col, Prague, Czechoslovakia; Pratt Graphics Center, Brooklyn, NY
TEACHING: Instr, City Univ of New York, 1970–74; Instr, Col of New Rochelle, NY, 1974–82; Parsons Sch of Design, NY, 1977–82
AWARDS: New York State Council of the Arts Grant, 1978
RECENT EXHIB: Elaine Benson Gallery, Bridgehampton, NY, 1990; Galerie Konstrucktiv Tendens, Stockholm, Sweden, 1992; Elaine Benson Gallery, Bridgehampton, NY, 1992
COLLECTIONS: Herbert F Johnson Mus, Cornell Univ, Ithaca, NY; Solomon R Guggenheim Mus, NY
PRINTERS: Sue Kleinman, NY (SK); Artist (ART)
PUBLISHERS: Orion Editions, NY (OE); American Scandanavian Found, NY (ASF); Artist (ART)
GALLERIES: Orion Editions, New York, NY; Belanthi Gallery, Brooklyn, NY; Elaine Benson Gallery, Bridgehampton, NY; Galerie Konstruktiv Tendrens, Stockholm, Sweden; Jean Lumbard Fine Arts, New York, NY
MAILING ADDRESS: 93 Mercer St, #6–F, New York, NY 10012

TITLE	PUBLISHER	PRINTER	DATE	MEDIUM	DIMENSION (PAPER SIZE) IN INCHES	TYPE OF PAPER	EDITION NUMBER	NO. OF COLORS	ORIGINAL OPENING PRICE	CURRENT RETAIL PRICE
CURRENT EDITIONS:										
La Ronde—Shadow Series III	OE	SK	1980	C/EMB	30 X 50	R/BFK	50	14	375	600
La Ronde—Sets I,II	ART	SK	1980	C/EMB	25 X 25 EA	R/BFK	50 EA	10 EA	250 EA	300 EA
La Ronde—Triptych I,II,III,IV	ART	SK	1980	C/EMB	22 X 30 EA	R/BFK	50 EA	5 EA	250 EA	300 EA
La Ronde—Triptych V	ART	SK	1980	EMB	22 X 30	R/BFK	50		225	300
White Holes	ART	SK	1980	EMB	16 X 21	R/BFK	50		175	250
25 Times	ART	SK	1980	EMB	16 X 21	R/BFK	50		175	250
Tablets	ART	SK	1980	EMB	16 X 21	R/BFK	50		175	250
La Ronde-Trio	ASF	ART	1981	C/EMB	19 X 30	R/BFK	10		225	300
Der Reigen	ART	SK	1981	C/EMB	30 X 44	R/BFK	50	5	350	400

TOM BERG

BORN: Cheyenne, WY; February 10, 1943
EDUCATION: Univ of Wyoming, Laramie, WY, BA, 1966, MA, 1969, MFA, 1972
TEACHING: Instr, Art, Point Park Col, Pittsburgh, PA, 1969–71; Vis Lectr, Painting, Univ of Wyoming, Laramie, WY, Summer, 1977; Univ of Oklahoma, Norman, OK, 1989
AWARDS: Visual Arts Fel, Wyoming Western States Art Found, Denver, CO, 1976–77
RECENT EXHIB: Wade Gallery, Los Angeles, CA, 1988; Linda Durham Gallery, Santa Fe, NM, 1987,89; Univ of Oklahoma Rt Mus, Norman, OK, 1989
COLLECTIONS: Kansas City Art Inst, MO; El Paso Mus of Art, TX; Mus of New Mexico, Santa Fe, NM; Univ of Wyoming, Laramie, WY; Univ of Texas, Austin, TX
PRINTERS: Bill Lagattuta (BL); Eileen Foti (EF); Tamarind Inst, Albuquerque, NM (TI)
PUBLISHERS: Tamarind Inst Publications, Albuquerque, NM (TI)
GALLERIES: Wade Gallery, Los ANgeles, CA; Robischon Gallery, Denver, CO; Linda Durham Gallery, Santa Fe, NM; Tamarind Inst, Albuquerque, NM; Janus Gallery, Santa Fe, NM; J Cacciola Galleries, New York, NY
MAILING ADDRESS: Rt 1, P O Box 171–A, Santa Fe, NM 87501

TITLE	PUBLISHER	PRINTER	DATE	MEDIUM	DIMENSION (PAPER SIZE) IN INCHES	TYPE OF PAPER	EDITION NUMBER	NO. OF COLORS	ORIGINAL OPENING PRICE	CURRENT RETAIL PRICE
CURRENT EDITIONS:										
Dark Adirondack	TI	EF/TI	1988	LC/CC	22 X 22	R/BFK/SEK	20	2	300	400
Sunny Pair	TI	EF/TI	1988	LC/CC	22 X 30	AP/CGP	35	6	450	500
White Solo, State I	TI	BL/TI	1988	LC/CC	22 X 18	AP/KIT	15	2	250	350
White Solo, State II	TI	BL/TI	1988	LC	22 X 18	RP/CGP	15	2	250	500
Duet	TI	BL/TI	1988	LC	22 X 30	AP/W	20	5	400	500

The retail prices of the 100,000 limited edition prints quoted in this directory are subject to change. Print publishers, artists and galleries were the direct sources for these quotations. Prices in the secondary market listed as "Sold Out Editions (Rare)" indicate that the publisher has a limited supply of that print or that the print is difficult to locate in the galleries.

The print market has become very selective. For the first time since we published the first edition of The Printworld Directory in 1982, the prices of prints have been greatly reduced and greatly increased for the same artists by the most reputable and established print publishers. Check the fifth edition to understand the movement.

JASON BERGER

BORN: Malden, MA; January 22, 1924
EDUCATION: Sch of Mus of Fine Arts, Boston, MA, 1942–43, 1946–49; Studied in Paris with Ossip Zadkine, Paris, France, 1950–52
TEACHING: Boston Mus Sch, MA; Wellesley Col, MA; Mt Holyoke Sch, MA; State Univ of New York, Buffalo, NY; Boston Univ, MA; Art Inst of Boston, MA
AWARDS: Boston Mus Sch, Page Traveling Scholarship, MA; Grand Prize, Boston Arts Festival, MA; Boston Mus Sch, Clarissa Barttett Traveling Scholarship, MA; First Prize, Boston Arts Festival, MA; State Univ of New York, Buffalo, NY, Faculty Research Fel
RECENT EXHIB: Alon Gallery, Brookline, MA, 1989; Fitchburg Mus of Art, MA, 1990
COLLECTIONS: Mus of Mod Art, NY; Guggenheim Mus, NY; Smith Col, Northampton, MA; Brandeis Univ, Waltham, MA; Rockefeller Medical Center, NY
PRINTERS: Herb Fox, Merrimac, MA (HF); Herb Fox Graphic Workshop, Merrimac, MA (HFGW)
PUBLISHERS: Alon Gallery, Brookline, MA (AG)
GALLERIES: Alon Gallery, Brookline, MA; Art Store, Charleston, WVA
MAILING ADDRESS: 1665-A Beacon St, Brookline, MA 02146

TITLE	PUBLISHER	PRINTER	DATE	MEDIUM	DIMENSION (PAPER SIZE) IN INCHES	TYPE OF PAPER	EDITION NUMBER	NO. OF COLORS	ORIGINAL OPENING PRICE	CURRENT RETAIL PRICE
CURRENT EDITIONS:										
Places (Set of 5)	AG	HF/HFGW	1990	WC	16 X 20 EA	RICE	25 EA	2 EA	1400 SET	1400 SET

NICHOLAS BERGER

BORN: New York, NY; 1949
EDUCATION: Alfred Univ, NY, MFA, 1975
PRINTERS: American Atelier, NY (AA)
PUBLISHERS: Circle Fine Art, Chicago, IL (CFA)
GALLERIES: Circle Galleries, San Diego, CA & San Francisco, CA & Northbrook, IL & Pittsburgh, PA & Houston, TX & Soho, NY & Chicago, IL & Scottsdale, AZ & Beverly Hills, CA & Costa Mesa, CA & Sherman Oaks, CA & Palm Beach, FL & Honolulu, HI & New Orleans, LA & Las Vegas, NV & Seattle, WA

TITLE	PUBLISHER	PRINTER	DATE	MEDIUM	DIMENSION (PAPER SIZE) IN INCHES	TYPE OF PAPER	EDITION NUMBER	NO. OF COLORS	ORIGINAL OPENING PRICE	CURRENT RETAIL PRICE
SOLD OUT EDITIONS (RARE):										
Early Winter	CFA	AA	1980	LC	25 X 18	AP	300		100	200
Fading Light	CFA	AA	1980	LC	16 X 28	AP	300		100	200

DANIEL BERLIN

BORN: 1954
EDUCATION: Illinois State Univ, Normal, IL, BS, Painting, & BS, Psychology, with Honors, 1972–76; Maropa Inst, Poetics, 1978–80; Univ of Colorado, Boulder, CO, MFA, Painting, with Honors, 1980–83
AWARDS: Doctorial Fel, Grad Sch, 1981–82; Kennedy Center Comm, Denver, CO, 1982; Anderson Ranch Arts Center, Snowmass, CO, Painting Res, Summer, 1983; MacDowell Colony Fel, 1987
RECENT EXHIB: Henry Street Arts Center, NY, 1987; Kent Gallery, NY, 1992
PRINTERS: Bud Shark, Boulder, CO (BS); Matthew Christie, Boulder, CO (MC); Shark's, Inc, Boulder, CO (SI)
PUBLISHERS: Shark's Inc, Boulder, CO (SI)
GALLERIES: Shark's, Inc, Boulder, CO; Quartet Editions, New York, NY; Kent Gallery, New York, NY

TITLE	PUBLISHER	PRINTER	DATE	MEDIUM	DIMENSION (PAPER SIZE) IN INCHES	TYPE OF PAPER	EDITION NUMBER	NO. OF COLORS	ORIGINAL OPENING PRICE	CURRENT RETAIL PRICE
CURRENT EDITIONS:										
A-P (Shaped)	SI	BS/MC/SI	1987	MON	29 X 37 EA	HMP	1 EA	Varies	850 EA	1000 EA
Marpa Mountain I–IV	SI	BS/MC/SI	1987	MON	30 X 43 EA	HMP	1 EA	Varies	850 EA	1000 EA
Mountain! Mountain!	SI	BS/MC/SI	1987	MON	30 X 43 EA	HMP	1 EA	Varies	850 EA	1000 EA
Little Heart	SI	BS/MC/SI	1987	MON	33 X 30 EA	HMP	1 EA	Varies	850 EA	1000 EA
Four Green Balls (Shaped)	SI	BS/MC/SI	1987	MON	33 X 30 EA	HMP	1 EA	Varies	850 EA	1000 EA
Masculus I (Shaped)	SI	BS/MC/SI	1987	MON	32 X 30 EA	HMP	1 EA	Varies	850 EA	1000 EA
Masculus II (Shaped)	SI	BS/MC/SI	1987	MON	31 X 29 EA	HMP	1 EA	Varies	850 EA	1000 EA
Single Act (Shaped)	SI	BS/MC/SI	1988	MON	30 X 30 EA	HMP	1 EA	Varies	850 EA	1000 EA
Green, I Assume (Shaped)	SI	BS/MC/SI	1988	MON	30 X 31 EA	HMP	1 EA	Varies	850 EA	1000 EA
Untitled (Shaped)	SI	BS/MC/SI	1988	MON	32 X 30 EA	HMP	1 EA	Varies	850 EA	1000 EA
Red Cross (Shaped)	SI	BS/MC/SI	1988	MON	33 X 30 EA	HMP	1 EA	Varies	850 EA	1000 EA
Dervish (Shaped)	SI	BS/MC/SI	1988	MON	31 X 30 EA	HMP	1 EA	Varies	850 EA	1000 EA
Southwest Float	SI	BS/MC/SI	1988	MON	43 X 30 EA	HMP	1 EA	Varies	850 EA	1000 EA
Squirm	SI	BS/MC/SI	1988	MON	43 X 30 EA	HMP	1 EA	Varies	850 EA	1000 EA
Cluster	SI	BS/MC/SI	1988	MON	43 X 30 EA	HMP	1 EA	Varies	850 EA	1000 EA
Coterie	SI	BS/MC/SI	1988	MON	43 X 30 EA	HMP	1 EA	Varies	850 EA	1000 EA
Whose Afraid . . .	SI	BS/MC/SI	1988	MON	43 X 30 EA	HMP	1 EA	Varies	850 EA	1000 EA
Trumpet Mind	SI	BS/MC/SI	1989	MON	30 X 25 EA	HMP	1 EA	Varies	850 EA	1000 EA
Inside Sentry	SI	BS/MC/SI	1989	MON	30 X 25 EA	HMP	1 EA	Varies	850 EA	1000 EA
Sound Operator	SI	BS/MC/SI	1989	MON	30 X 26 EA	HMP	1 EA	Varies	850 EA	1000 EA
Black Ink	SI	BS/MC/SI	1989	MON	30 X 43 EA	HMP	1 EA	Varies	850 EA	1000 EA
(Head) Hands & Feet	SI	BS/MC/SI	1989	MON	30 X 43 EA	HMP	1 EA	Varies	850 EA	1000 EA
Aqueous Wagner	SI	BS/MC/SI	1989	MON	30 X 43 EA	HMP	1 EA	Varies	850 EA	1000 EA
Wagner Vein	SI	BS/MC/SI	1989	MON	30 X 43 EA	HMP	1 EA	Varies	850 EA	1000 EA
Tenacious Terma	SI	BS/MC/SI	1989	MON	30 X 43 EA	HMP	1 EA	Varies	850 EA	1000 EA
Animated Terma	SI	BS/MC/SI	1989	MON	30 X 43 EA	HMP	1 EA	Varies	850 EA	1000 EA
Now It is Allowable II	SI	BS/MC/SI	1989	MON	30 X 43 EA	HMP	1 EA	Varies	850 EA	1000 EA
"I" Series	SI	BS/MC/SI	1990	MON/CO	29 X 22 EA	HMP	1 EA	Varies	1000 EA	1000 EA
1992 Series	SI	BS/MC/SI	1990	MON/CO	42 X 29 EA	HMP	1 EA	Varies	1000 EA	1000 EA

ARIANE R BERMAN

BORN: Danzig, Poland; March 27, 1937; US Citizen
EDUCATION: Hunter Col, NY, BFA, 1959; Yale Univ, New Haven, CT, MFA, 1959–62; Ecole Beaux-Arts, Paris, France, 1962–63; Studied with Stanley William Hayter & Jacques Desjobert
AWARDS: Catherine L Wolf Arts Club, Gold Medal, 1973; Philadelphia Art Alliance, Gold Medal & Purchase Prize, 1973
COLLECTIONS: Metropolitan Mus of Art, NY; Wustum Mus of Fine Arts, WI; Purdue Univ, IN; Philadelphia Art Alliance, PA; Philadelphia Mus of Art, PA
PUBLISHERS: Circle Fine Art, Inc, Chicago, IL (CFA); Galleria d'Arte Helioart, Rome, Italy (GH); Fine Arts 260 (FA); Associated American Artists, NY (AAA)
GALLERIES: Associated American Artists, New York, NY
MAILING ADDRESS: 161 W 54th St, New York, NY 10019

TITLE	PUBLISHER	PRINTER	DATE	MEDIUM	DIMENSION (PAPER SIZE) IN INCHES	TYPE OF PAPER	EDITION NUMBER	NO. OF COLORS	ORIGINAL OPENING PRICE	CURRENT RETAIL PRICE
SOLD OUT EDITIONS (RARE):										
Instamatic I: Tourists	AAA		1973	SP	22 X 28		40	10	150	500
CURRENT EDITIONS:										
Justaposition II	AAA		1973	SP	27 X 31		50	3	125	350
Spring Gardens	CFA		1975	SP	44 X 33		250	14	100	400
Garden Party	AAA		1976	SP	17 X 24		50	9	120	300
Dreams of Summer	AAA		1977	SP	18 X 28		50	9	120	300
Wicker Chair	AAA		1980	SP	23 X 23		125	9	175	300
Terrace	AAA		1980	SP	22 X 34		125	12	250	400

WALLACE BERMAN

PRINTERS: Gemini GEL, Los Angeles, CA (GEM)
PUBLISHERS: Gemini GEL, Los Angeles, CA (GEM)
GALLERIES: Gemini GEL, Los Angeles, CA

TITLE	PUBLISHER	PRINTER	DATE	MEDIUM	DIMENSION (PAPER SIZE) IN INCHES	TYPE OF PAPER	EDITION NUMBER	NO. OF COLORS	ORIGINAL OPENING PRICE	CURRENT RETAIL PRICE
SOLD OUT EDITIONS (RARE):										
Radio/Aether (Boxed Set of 13)	GEM	GEM	1966–74	LC/OFF	13 X 13 EA	AP	50 EA		900 SET	2500 SET

ZEKE BERMAN

RECENT EXHIB: Friends of Photography, Ansel Adams Center, San Francisco, CA, 1992

PRINTERS: Artist (ART)
PUBLISHERS: Artist (ART)
GALLERIES: Robert Klein Gallery, Boston, MA; Lieberman & Saul Gallery, New York, NY; Jones Troyer Fitzpatrick Gallery, Wash, DC

TITLE	PUBLISHER	PRINTER	DATE	MEDIUM	DIMENSION (PAPER SIZE) IN INCHES	TYPE OF PAPER	EDITION NUMBER	NO. OF COLORS	ORIGINAL OPENING PRICE	CURRENT RETAIL PRICE
CURRENT EDITIONS:										
Table Study	ART	ART	1983	PH	16 X 20		25	1	450	500

JUDITH BERNSTEIN

BORN: Newark, NJ; October 14, 1942
EDUCATION: Pennsylvania State Univ, BS, MS, 1964; Yale Univ, BFA, MFA, Sch of Art and Architecture, 1967
TEACHING: Pratt Inst, NY; Sch of Visual Arts, NY; Rutgers Univ, NJ; Asst Prof, Fine Arts, State Univ of New York, Stony Brook, NY, 1974; Asst Prof, Fine Arts, State Univ of New York, Purchase, NY, 1978 to present
AWARDS: Elizabeth Canfield Hicks Mem Scholarship, Yale Univ, 1964–67; Nat Endowment for the Arts, Ind Artist's Fellowship Grants, 1974–75, 1985,86; New York Found for the Arts, 1988
COLLECTIONS: Mus of Mod Art, NY; Univ of Colorado Mus, Boulder, CO; Colgate Univ, Hamilton, NY; Kronhausen Coll, Lund, Sweden; Brooklyn Mus, NY; Yale Art Mus, New Haven, CT
PRINTERS: Solo Press, NY (SP); Paula Crane (PC); Artist (ART)
PUBLISHERS: Solo Press, NY (SP); Horizontal Editions, NY (HE)
GALLERIES: Associated American Artists, New York, NY; Pace Editions, New York, NY
MAILING ADDRESS: P O Box 145, Knickerbocker Station, New York, NY 10002-0145

TITLE	PUBLISHER	PRINTER	DATE	MEDIUM	DIMENSION (PAPER SIZE) IN INCHES	TYPE OF PAPER	EDITION NUMBER	NO. OF COLORS	ORIGINAL OPENING PRICE	CURRENT RETAIL PRICE
SOLD OUT EDITIONS (RARE):										
Flocked II	HE		1976	SP	22 X 30	AP	1	1	200	900
Flocked Horizontal/Black	HE		1976	SP	22 X 30	AP	75	1	125	600
Flocked Horizontal/Red	HE		1976	SP	22 X 30	AP	75	1	125	600
Flocked Horizontal/Deep Red	HE		1976	SP	22 X 30	AP	75	1	125	600
Two on a Page/Silver	HE		1976	SP	22 X 30	AP	30	4	125	600
Two on a Page/Gold	HE		1976	SP	22 X 30	AP	1	4	125	850
Two on a Page/Copper	HE		1976	SP	22 X 30	AP	35	2	125	600
Two on a Page/Copper I	HE		1976	SP	22 X 30	AP	7	4	125	600
Two on a Page/Blue	HE		1976	SP	22 X 30	AP	35	4	125	600
Two on a Page/Flocked	HE		1976	SP	22 X 30	AP	75	2	125	600
Two on a Page/Flocked I	HE		1976	SP	22 X 30	AP	1	2	200	850
Etched Horizontal	HE		1976	EB	22 X 30	AP	20	1	125	600

JUDITH BERNSTEIN CONTINUED

TITLE	PUBLISHER	PRINTER	DATE	MEDIUM	DIMENSION (PAPER SIZE) IN INCHES	TYPE OF PAPER	EDITION NUMBER	NO. OF COLORS	ORIGINAL OPENING PRICE	CURRENT RETAIL PRICE
SOLD OUT EDITIONS (RARE):										
Horizontal	HE		1976	LB	22 X 30	AP	25	1	140	500
CURRENT EDITIONS:										
Big Horizontal	SP	JS/SP	1976	LB	30 X 42	AP	40	1	175	750
Metaphorical Series, #1–#10	HE	ART	1982–83	I	30 X 22	AP	25	1	2000 SET	5000 SET
									225 EA	600 EA

RICHARD BERNSTEIN

BORN: New York, NY; 1942
EDUCATION: Pratt Inst, NY; Columbia Univ, NY
COLLECTIONS Metropolitan Mus of Art, NY; Mus of Mod Art, NY; Corcoran Gallery of Art, Wash, DC; Columbia Univ, NY; Pratt Inst, NY; Stedelijk Mus, Amsterdam, Holland; Kennedy Coll, Drew Univ, Madison, NY
PRINTERS: Alexander Heinrici, NY (AH); Studio Heinrici, NY (SH)
PUBLISHERS: London Arts, Inc, Detroit, MI (LAI); Gimpel & Weitzenhoffer Ltd, NY (GWL)
GALLERIES: Gimpel & Weitzenhoffer Gallery, New York, NY; Rempire Fine Art Gallery, New York, NY; B Z Wagman Art, Inc, St Louis, MO; Ro Gallery Image Makers, Inc, New York, NY

TITLE	PUBLISHER	PRINTER	DATE	MEDIUM	DIMENSION (PAPER SIZE) IN INCHES	TYPE OF PAPER	EDITION NUMBER	NO. OF COLORS	ORIGINAL OPENING PRICE	CURRENT RETAIL PRICE
SOLD OUT EDITIONS (RARE):										
Warhil Wall	GWL	HS	1973	SP	28 X 33	NAJ	100	4	100	200
CURRENT EDITIONS:										
Diamond	LAI	AH/SH	1978	SP	26 X 30	SOM	200	8	150	150
Ruby	LAI	AH/SH	1978	SP	26 X 30	SOM	200	8	150	150

RAY BERRY

PRINTERS: Mohammad Khalil, NY; MOK, Inc, NY (MOK)
PUBLISHERS: This History, Brooklyn, NY (TH)

TITLE	PUBLISHER	PRINTER	DATE	MEDIUM	DIMENSION (PAPER SIZE) IN INCHES	TYPE OF PAPER	EDITION NUMBER	NO. OF COLORS	ORIGINAL OPENING PRICE	CURRENT RETAIL PRICE
CURRENT EDITIONS:										
Life Boat	TH	MK/MOK	1985	EB	20 X 26	AP	20	1	300	400

BERNARD BERTHOIS-RIGAL

BORN: Paris, France; 1927
EDUCATION: Self-Taught
COLLECTIONS: Mus of Mod Art, Paris, France; Ingres Mus, Montaubon, France
PRINTERS: Atelier Dutrou, Paris, France (DUT); Atelier Joban, Paris, France (JOB); Atelier Pasnic, Paris, France (APas)
PUBLISHERS: Nahan Editions, New Orleans, LA (NE)
GALLERIES: Nahan Galleries, New Orleans, LA & New York, NY & Tokyo, Japan; Alphonse Chave Gallery, Vence, France; Le Scribe Gallery, Montauban, France; Galerie Francoise, Saavebruck, Germany & Munich, Germany; Graphica Gallery, Tokyo, Japan; Seine Gallery, Paris, France; Galerie Protée, Paris, France

TITLE	PUBLISHER	PRINTER	DATE	MEDIUM	DIMENSION (PAPER SIZE) IN INCHES	TYPE OF PAPER	EDITION NUMBER	NO. OF COLORS	ORIGINAL OPENING PRICE	CURRENT RETAIL PRICE
CURRENT EDITIONS:										
Mysterious Energy	NE	DUT	1986	CAR/CO	18 X 22	HMP	125	6	300	300
Par un Chemin Detourne	NE	DUT	1987	CAR/GRA	27 X 20	HMP	125	8	300	375
La Triple Alliance	NE	DUT	1987	CAR/GRA	27 X 20	HMP	95	4	375	375
L'Arbre qui Reve	NE	DUT	1987	CAR/GRA	27 X 20	HMP	95	4	375	375
A Peaceful Region	NE	DUT	1987	AC	26 X 20	AC	85	8	450	450
Inner Worlds	NE	JOB	1987	LC	19 X 26	AC	150	5	300	300
Ils Sont Lá (Set of 3)	NE	JOB	1988	LC	21 X 15 EA	AC	15 EA	5 EA	900 SET	900 SET
Les Tirailles	NE	DUT	1988	AC	30 X 23	AC	125	6	475	475
Chez les Fugaces	NE	DUT	1989	AC	30 X 23	AC	125	7	475	475
Le Fondation	NE	DUT	1989	AC	29 X 39	AC	125	4	600	600
Le Bustrophedon	NE	DUT	1989	AC	29 X 39	AC	125	4	600	600
La Redemption du Bustrophedon	NE	DUT	1990	EB/A	29 X 39	AC	95	4	650	650
La Nef de Lysimaque aux River du Bustrophedon	NE	DUT	1990	EB/A	29 X 39	AC	95	4	650	650
Un Bustre et Quelque Ophedons Lysimaque et la Convoitisedea des Ophedons	NE	DUT	1990	EB/A	29 X 39	AC	95	4	650	650
	NE	DUT	1990	AC	29 X 39	AC	95	4	650	650
Another World	NE	JOB	1990	LC	24 X 35	AP	135		450	450
Mystical World I, II	NE	JOB	1990	LC	25 X 19 EA	AP	135 EA		300 EA	300 EA
Ancient Secrets	NE	APas	1991	SP	30 X 49	AP	225		1150	1150
Games of Life	NE	APas	1991	SP	29 X 29	AP	175		750	750
Yin and Yang	NE	APas	1991	SP	29 X 30	AP	175		750	750

JAKE BERTHOT

BORN: Niagara Falls, NY, March 30, 1939
EDUCATION: New Sch of Socials Resources, NY; Self-Taught
TEACHINGS: Instr, Yale Univ, New Haven, CT, 1982
AWARDS: Guggenheim Found Fel; Nat Endowment for the Arts Fel; Am Acad & Inst of Arts & Letters, 1992
RECENT EXHIB: Rose Art Mus, Brandeis Univ, Waltham, MA, 1988; Lannan Mus, Lake Worth, FL, 1988–89; David McKee Gallery, NY, 1989,92
COLLECTIONS: Mus of Mod Art, NY; Solomon R Guggenheim Mus, NY; Whitney Mus of Am Art, NY; Philadelphia Mus of Art, PA; Baltimore Mus, MD; Virginia Mus of Fine Arts, Richmond, VA; Fogg Art Mus, Cambridge, MA; Dallas Mus of Fine Art, TX
PRINTERS: Doris Simmelink, Marina Del Rey, CA (DS); Simmelink/Sukimoto Editions, Marina Del Rey, CA (S/SE)
PUBLISHERS: Simmelink/Sukimoto Editions, Marina Del Rey, CA (S/SE)
GALLERIES: David McKee Gallery, New York, NY; Betsy Senior Contemporary Prints, New York, NY; Nielsen Gallery, Boston, MA; Hope Weiss Fine Art, Los Angeles, CA; CompassRose, Ltd, Chicago, IL

TITLE	PUBLISHER	PRINTER	DATE	MEDIUM	DIMENSION (PAPER SIZE) IN INCHES	TYPE OF PAPER	EDITION NUMBER	NO. OF COLORS	ORIGINAL OPENING PRICE	CURRENT RETAIL PRICE
CURRENT EDITIONS:										
Untitled #7	S/SE	DS/S/SE	1989	EB	30 X 23	AP/WA	35	1	900	900

ARNE CHARLES BESSER

BORN: Hinsdale, IL; May 11, 1935
EDUCATION: Univ of New Mexico, Albuquerque, NM, 1953–54,56,58; Art Center Sch, Los Angeles, CA, with John Audobon Tyler and Lorser Freidelsson
AWARDS: Butler Inst of Am Art, Youngstown, OH, Medal of Merit, 1975
COLLECTIONS: Smithsonian Inst, Wash, DC; Butler Inst of Am Art, Youngstown, OH
PRINTERS: Alexander Heinrici, NY (AH); Studio Heinrici, NY (SH)
PUBLISHERS: London Arts Inc, Detroit, MI (LAI)
GALLERIES: Louis K Meisel Gallery, New York, NY
MAILING ADDRESS: c/o Louis K Meisel Gallery, 141 Prince St, New York, NY 10012

TITLE	PUBLISHER	PRINTER	DATE	MEDIUM	DIMENSION (PAPER SIZE) IN INCHES	TYPE OF PAPER	EDITION NUMBER	NO. OF COLORS	ORIGINAL OPENING PRICE	CURRENT RETAIL PRICE
CURRENT EDITIONS:										
Circus Triad	LAI	AH/SH	1980	SP	26 X 22	SOM	250	33	450	750
The Street Below	LAI	AH/SH	1980	SP	28 X 22	SOM	250	32	450	750
The Candy Kitchen	LAI	AH/SH	1980	SP	26 X 22	SOM	250	32	450	750

TONY BEVAN

BORN: England; 1951
PUBLISHERS: Ronald Feldman Fine Arts, NY (RFFA)
GALLERIES: Ronald Feldman Fine Arts, New York, NY; L A Louver, Inc, Venice, CA & New York, NY

TITLE	PUBLISHER	PRINTER	DATE	MEDIUM	DIMENSION (PAPER SIZE) IN INCHES	TYPE OF PAPER	EDITION NUMBER	NO. OF COLORS	ORIGINAL OPENING PRICE	CURRENT RETAIL PRICE
CURRENT EDITIONS:										
Black Water			1985	WC	48 X 33	WOVE	30			2200
Girl Friends			1985	LB	32 X 48	WOVE	30	1		2200
Untitled (Special Edition Unbound Book of Offset Lithographs & Color Woodcut in Portfolio Case)	RFFA		1988	LC/OFF WC	18 X 13 EA 15 X 11	AP	100			900

STEVEN J BEYER

BORN: Minneapolis, MN; August 27, 1951
EDUCATION: Macalester Col, St Paul, MN, BA, 1973
TEACHING: Univ of Iowa, Iowa City, IA, 1979–81; Minneapolis Col of Art & Design, MN, 1981–82
AWARDS: Guggenheim Fel 1978; McKnight Found Fel 1982; Bush Found Fel, 1982; Nat Endowment for the Arts Fel, 1981,88
RECENT EXHIB: Pennsylvania Acad of Fine Arts, Phila, PA, 1988; Diane Brown Gallery, NY, 1988
COLLECTIONS: Whitney Mus of Am Art, NY; Walker Art Center, Minneapolis, MN; Northern Illinois Univ, DeKalb, IL; Newport Harbor Art Mus, Newport Beach, CA; Minneapolis Inst of Art, MN; Madison Art Center, WI
PRINTERS: Vermillion Editions Ltd, Minneapolis, MN (VEL)
PUBLISHERS: Landfall Press, Inc, Chicago, IL (LPI); Vermillion Editions, Minneapolis, MN (V); Bird Island Publishing, Inc, Minneapolis, MN (BIPI); Artist (ART)
GALLERIES: Glen Hanson Gallery, Minneapolis, MN
MAILING ADDRESS: c/o Tyler School of Art, Beech & Penrose Ave, Phila, PA 19126

TITLE	PUBLISHER	PRINTER	DATE	MEDIUM	DIMENSION (PAPER SIZE) IN INCHES	TYPE OF PAPER	EDITION NUMBER	NO. OF COLORS	ORIGINAL OPENING PRICE	CURRENT RETAIL PRICE
CURRENT EDITIONS:										
White Cross	VEL	VEL	1977	DPT	14 X 42	ACW	79	1	200	900
Untitled	BIPI	VEL	1978	LC	30 X 41	R/BFK	50	4	175	600
Untitled	ART	VEL	1979–80	LC	23 X 30	ACW	35	2	200	600
Four Member Family System	ART	VEL	1979–80	DPT	48 X 42	ACW	30	1	600	1200
Dissolution	VEL	VEL	1980	MON/E	56 X 36	ACW	10	1	800	1500
Dissolution	VEL	VEL	1980	MON/E	56 X 36	ACW	10	2	800	1500
Six Questions	VEL	VEL	1981	MULT/SS	3 X 48 X 1	ACW	8		800	1500

JOSEPH BEUYS

BORN: Kleve, Germany; (1921–1986)
EDUCATION: Kunstakademie, Düsseldorf, West Germany, 1947–52
RECENT EXHIB: Dia Art Found, NY, 1987; Temple Univ, Tyler Gallery, Phila, PA, 1987; John Gibson Gallery, NY, 1989; Galeria Alfonso Alcalea, Barcelona, Spain, 1989; Arnold Herstand & Company, NY, 1990; Anthony d'Offay Gallery, London, England, 1990; East Carolina Univ, Wellington B Gray Gallery, Greenville, NC, 1992
PRINTERS: Editions Schellmann & Klüser, Munich, Germany (SK); John Nichols, NY (JN); Nenad Bozic, NY (NB); Arnold Brooks, NY (AB); Fritz Getlinger, Kleve, Germany (FG); Matthiew Press, Zurich, Switzerland (MP); Ute Klphaus, Wuppertal, Germany (UK); Grafos-Verlag, Vaduz, Switzerland (GV)
PUBLISHERS: Editions Schellmann & Klüser, Munich, Germany (ESK); Edition Staeck, Heidelberg, Germany (ES); Multiples, Inc, NY (M); Edition Tangente (ET); Edizione Modern Art Agency (EMA); Strother/Elwood Art Editions, Brooklyn, NY (SEAE); John Gibson, NY (JG); Edition Schellmann, Munich, Germany & NY; Edition Galerie Heiner Friedrich, Munich, Germany (EGHF); Vice Verstand, Remscheid, Germany (VV); Galerie Art Intermedia, Cologne, Germany (GAI); Galerie Bernd Klüser, Munich, Germany (GBK); Matthieu Press, Zürich, Switzerland (MP); Piccolo Museo Edizioni Novoli, Italy (PMEN); Edizioni Lucrezia de Domizio, Pescara, Italy (ELD); Grefos-Verlag, Vaduz, Switzerland; Ronald Feldman Fine Arts, NY (RFFA)
GALLERIES: Marian Goodman, New York, NY; Edition Schellmann, New York, NY; Ronald Feldman Fine Arts, New York, NY; Tavelli Gallery, Aspen, CO; Massimo Audiello, New York, NY; Tossan-Tossan Gallery, New York, NY; Editions Ilene Kurtz, New York, NY; Nicola Jacobs Gallery, London, England; Sperone Westwater, New York, NY; Mary Boone Gallery, New York, NY; Luhring-Augustine Gallery, New York, NY; John Gibson Gallery, New York, NY; Galeria Alfonso Alcalea, Barcelona, Spain; Hirsch & Adler Modern, New York, NY; David Nolan Gallery, New York, NY; Davis/McClain Gallery, Houston, TX; Heath Gallery, Atlanta, GA; Arnold Herstand & Company, New York, NY; Anthony d'Offay Gallery, London, England; Primavera Gallery, Huntington, NY; Thomas Erban Gallery, Inc, New York, NY; Michael Lowe Gallery, Cincinnati, OH; Locks Gallery, Phila, PA; Lawrence Mangel Gallery, Phila, Pa; Davis/McClain Gallery, Houston, TX; Pat Kery Fine Arts, New York, NY; Carol Evans Fine Arts, New York, NY; Schwartz Art Gallery, New York, NY

Schellmann (S)

Joseph Beuys
Elch (Elk)
Courtesy Edition Schellmann

TITLE	PUBLISHER	PRINTER	DATE	MEDIUM	DIMENSION (PAPER SIZE) IN INCHES	TYPE OF PAPER	EDITION NUMBER	NO. OF COLORS	ORIGINAL OPENING PRICE	CURRENT RETAIL PRICE
SOLD OUT EDITIONS (RARE):										
Intuition (Wooden Box with Pencil Line)	VV		1968		12 X 0 X 2				500	10000
Vaccuum—Mass	GAI		1970	PH/E	31 X 41	LINEN	100		100	18000
Celtic + ~ (Set of 10 Photographs)	ES		1971	PH/B	16 X 20 EA		100		500 SET	35000 SET
Fingernagelabdruck aus Geharteter Butter (Fingernail Impression of Hardened Butter in Plastic Box Mounted on Perforated Grey Cardboard)	ES		1971	SP	10 X 8	AP	150		100	5500

JOSEPH BEUYS CONTINUED

TITLE	PUBLISHER	PRINTER	DATE	MEDIUM	DIMENSION (PAPER SIZE) IN INCHES	TYPE OF PAPER	EDITION NUMBER	NO. OF COLORS	ORIGINAL OPENING PRICE	CURRENT RETAIL PRICE
SOLD OUT EDITIONS (RARE):										
Celtic Im			1971	LC	17 X 21	AP	100			5000
Print I,II	ES		1971	LC/OFF/SP	32 X 23 EA	AP			100 EA	5000 EA
Sonnenscheibe (Sun Disc)	ES		1972	MULT	15 X 15 X 2		77			9000
La Rivoluzione Siamo Noi (S-47)	ET/EMA	ET/EMA	1972	LC/OFF	75 X 39	FOIL	180		350	25000
Ohne die Rose (Rose for Diplomacy)			1972	SP	23 X 32	AP	80		200	12000
Folien	ES		1973	SP/HC	18 X 18	VINYL	100		175	6000
Sonnenscheibe	ES		1973	SP/CO	18 X 14 X 2		77		175	6000
Erdtelephon (Earth Telephone)	ES		1973	SP/CO	39 X 24	FELT	100		250	8000
Das Schweigen	ES		1973	SP	10 X 17 X 17		50		300	12000
Iphigenie	M		1973	SP	17 X 22	MYLAR	20		250	6000
Holzschnitte			1973–74	SP	20 X 26		50		200	6000
Spur I Series (Set of 9):									15000 SET	48000 SET
Spur I-a	SK		1974	SP	29 X 21	AP	98		200	5000
Spur I-b	SK		1974	SP	29 X 21	AP	98		200	5000
Spur I-c	SK		1974	SP	29 X 21	AP	98		200	5000
Spur I-d	SK		1974	SP	29 X 21	AP	98		200	5000
Spur I-e	SK		1974	SP	29 X 21	AP	98		200	5500
Spur I-f	SK		1974	SP	29 X 21	AP	98		200	5000
Spur I-g	SK		1974	SP	29 X 21	AP	98		200	5500
Spur I-h	SK		1974	SP	29 X 21	AP	98		200	5000
Spur I-i	SK		1974	SP	29 X 21	AP	98		200	5000
Fahne (Flag)	ES		1974	MULT	17 X 14 X 2		12		300	6000
Incontro con Beuys (S-127)	ELD		1974	SP	31 X 26	AP	150		300	4500
Musik als Grün (Music as Green) (Green Painted Violin)	ES		1974	MULT	8 X 24 X 4		24		350	12000
Telephone S— (Telephone S—) (Two Tin Cans, One with Symbols in Brown Paint, 180 CMS, String & Paper Tag)	ES		1974	MULT	80 X 4 X 4		24		350	12000
Zwei Weibliche Torsos (Two Female Torsos)	ES/GV	MP	1975	LC/COL	21 X 30	RdB	75		400	5500
Elch (Elk)	ES/GV	MP	1975	LC/COL	21 X 30	RdB	75		400	5000
Mirror Piece			1975	SP	8 X 5	AP	100		300	3500
Aurora Borealis (Icelandic Postcard with Handwritten Gulo Mounted on Grey Board)	ESK		1975	SP	28 X 20	AP	9		300	5000
Zeichnungen Zu Leonardo Codices Madrid—A			1975	SP	9 X 13	AP	100		150	5000
Zeichnungen Zu Leonardo Codices Madrid—B			1975	SP	15 X 12	AP	100		200	5500
Initiation Gauloise	ESK	MP	1976	LC	26 X 34	BD/W	185		300	6500
Pointing Version 1–90 (Oil Paint & Butter on Rag Paper with Torn Hole) (90 Variants))	ESK		1976	MULT	30 X 22 EA	R/BFK	1 EA		300 EA	6000 EA
La Zappa			1977	MULT	35 X 5 X 3		35		600	9000
Spur II Series (Set of 9):									2400 SET	45000 SET
Spur II-f	ES		1977	SP	22 X 31	AP	98		300	5000
Spur II-g	ES		1977	SP	22 X 31	AP	98		300	5000
Spur II-h	ES		1977	SP	22 X 31	AP	98		300	5000
Spur II-i	ES		1977	SP	22 X 31	AP	98		300	5000
Letter from London	ES		1977	SP	36 X 47	AP	115		400	5500
5 Lithographien:										
5 Lithographien a	ES		1977	LC	22 X 31	R/BFK	60		300	5500
5 Lithographien b	ES		1977	LC	22 X 31	R/BFK	60		300	5500
5 Lithographien c	ES		1977	LC	22 X 31	R/BFK	60		300	5500
5 Lithographien d	ES		1977	LC	22 X 31	R/BFK	60		300	5500
5 Lithographien e	ES		1977	LC	22 X 31	R/BFK	60		300	5500
Minneapolis Fragments (Set of 6)	ESK	KI	1977	SP	25 X 35 EA	RP/W	1 EA	1 EA	1500 SET	30000 SET
Zeige deine Wunde (Show Your Wound)	ESK	UK	1977	PH	43 X 32 X 2		28 EA		600	12000
Letter from London	MP	MP		LC	47 X 35	AP			400	25000
Flug des Adlers ins Tal und Zurück	ESK	MP	1977	LC	44 X 8	AP	120		350	6000
;Aus dem Leben der Bienen (:from Life of the Bees)	ESK	MP	1978	LC	22 X 30	R/BFK	90		350	6000
Geruchsplastik	ESK	MP	1978	SP	14 X 4	AP	30		450	4500
Greta Garbo und des Filzlappen	ESK	MP	1979	SP	26 X 38	AP	40		450	7500
Im Kopf und im Topf	ESK	MP	1979	SP	40 X 28	AP	100		450	7500
Hasenblut (Hare's Blood)	ESK	MP	1971–79	LC	25 X 18	SchD	45		500	7500
Rot Loch Lampe	ESK	MP	1976–79	LC	40 X 26	R/BFK	34		600	7500
Gletscher, Schwamm Totenbett	ESK	MP	1979	LC	40 X 28	R/BFK	75		600	6000
Hirschkuh	ESK	MP	1979	LC	22 X 30	AP	180		500	12000
Sandzeichnungen	ESK	MP	1979	LC	25 X 17	AP	250		500	7500

JOSEPH BEUYS CONTINUED

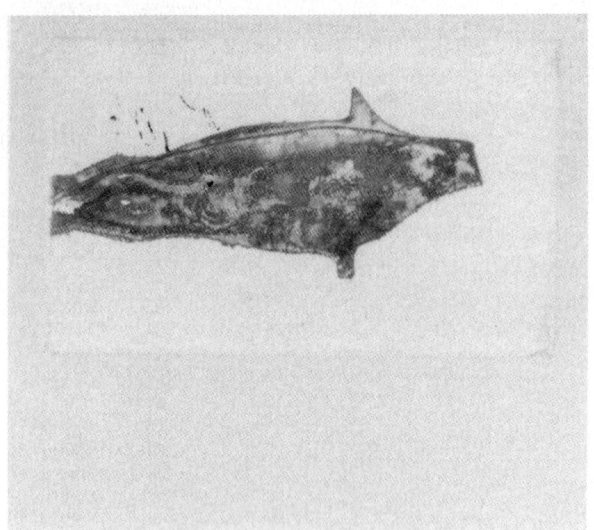

Joseph Beuys
Sea Angeles Seal II
Courtesy Grafos Verlag

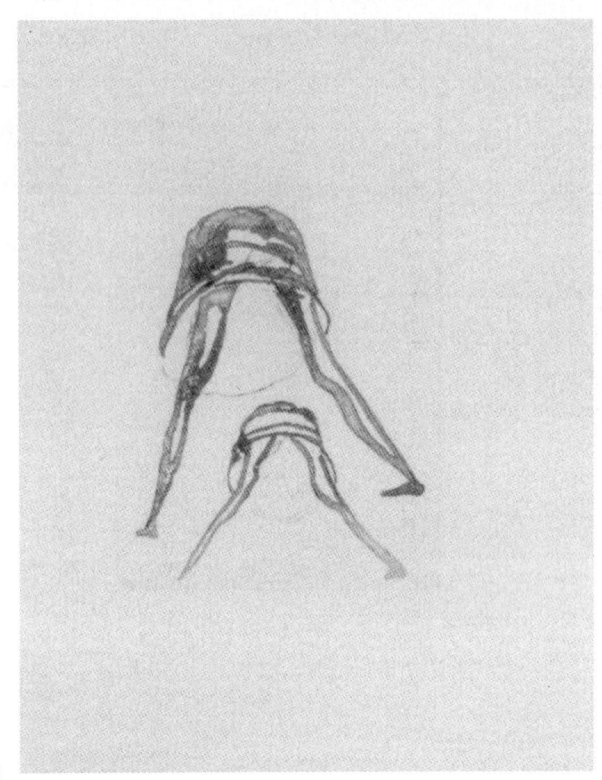

Joseph Beuys
Tranen: Petticoat
Courtesy Grafos Verlag

TITLE	PUBLISHER	PRINTER	DATE	MEDIUM	DIMENSION (PAPER SIZE) IN INCHES	TYPE OF PAPER	EDITION NUMBER	NO. OF COLORS	ORIGINAL OPENING PRICE	CURRENT RETAIL PRICE
SOLD OUT EDITIONS (RARE):										
Transsibirische Bahn (Transsiberian Rail) (16 mm in Black & White, Sound, 22 Minutes—in Metal Tin with Railway Labels)	ESK/EGHF	MP	1980	PH/B	1 X 16 DIA		45		500	15000
Der Motor	ESK	MP	1980	LC	28 X 39	R/BFK	230		500	5000
Suite Schwurhand (Set of 28):									15000 SET	35000 SET
Eiszeit	ESK	MP	1980	LC	13 X 10	R/BFK	75		400	3500
Eiszeit	ESK	MP	1980	LC	30 X 22	R/BFK	75		750	5500
Materie	ESK	MP	1980	LC	13 X 10	R/BFK	75		400	3500
Materie	ESK	MP	1980	LC	30 X 22	R/BFK	75		750	5500
Frau Rennt Weg mit Gehim	ESK	MP	1980	LC	13 X 10	R/BFK	75		400	3500
Frau Rennt Weg mit Gehim	ESK	MP	1980	LC	30 X 22	R/BFK	75		750	5500
Skulptur aus Gold	ESK	MP	1980	LC	13 X 10	R/BFK	75		400	3500
Skulptur aus Gold	ESK	MP	1980	LC	30 X 22	R/BFK	75		750	5500
Schwurhand	ESK	MP	1980	LC	13 X 10	R/BFK	75		400	3500
Schwurhand	ESK	MP	1980	LC	30 X 22	R/BFK	75		750	5500
Kalb mit Kinder	ESK	MP	1980	LC	13 X 10	R/BFK	75		400	3500
Kalb mit Kinder	ESK	MP	1980	LC	30 X 22	R/BFK	75		750	5500
Hirsch	ESK	MP	1980	LC	13 X 10	R/BFK	75		400	3500
Hirsch	ESK	MP	1980	LC	30 X 22	R/BFK	75		750	5500
Mit Fettgefullte Skulptur	ESK	MP	1980	LC	13 X 10	R/BFK	75		400	3500
Mit Fettgefullte Skulptur	ESK	MP	1980	LC	30 X 22	R/BFK	75		750	5500
Vogel	ESK	MP	1980	LC	13 X 10	R/BFK	75		400	3500
Vogel	ESK	MP	1980	LC	30 X 22	R/BFK	75		750	5500
Foetus	ESK	MP	1980	LC	13 X 10	R/BFK	75		400	3500
Foetus	ESK	MP	1980	LC	30 X 22	R/BFK	75		750	5500
Scrolls	ESK	MP	1980	LC	13 X 10	R/BFK	75		400	3500
Scrolls	ESK	MP	1980	LC	30 X 22	R/BFK	75		750	5500
Lumen	ESK	MP	1980	LC	13 X 10	R/BFK	75		400	3500
Lumen	ESK	MP	1980	LC	30 X 22	R/BFK	75		750	5500
Zelt und Lichtstrahl	ESK	MP	1980	LC	13 X 10	R/BFK	75		400	4000
Zelt und Lichtstrahl	ESK	MP	1980	LC	30 X 22	R/BFK	75		750	7500
Blitz und Bienenkonigin	ESK	MP	1980	LC	13 X 10	R/BFK	75		400	4000
Blitz und Bienenkonigin	ESK	MP	1980	LC	30 X 22	R/BFK	75		750	7500
Hirsch und Hut	ESK		1980	LC	15 X 11	R/BFK	100		400	4000
Triptychon (Triptych) (Set of 3):									2800 SET	18000 SET
Geschnatter Unterhalb der Hütte (Quacking Underneath the Hut)	ESK	MP	1981	LC	30 X 22	BD/W	90		1000	6000
Sternbild des Bärer (Constellation of the Bear)	ESK	MP	1981	LC	30 X 22	BD/W	90		1000	6000

JOSEPH BEUYS CONTINUED

TITLE	PUBLISHER	PRINTER	DATE	MEDIUM	DIMENSION (PAPER SIZE) IN INCHES	TYPE OF PAPER	EDITION NUMBER	NO. OF COLORS	ORIGINAL OPENING PRICE	CURRENT RETAIL PRICE
SOLD OUT EDITIONS (RARE):										
Junger Elch über dem Haus des Alten Müllers (Young Elk above the Old Miller's House)	ESK	MP	1981	LC	30 X 22	BD/W	90		1000	6000
L'Arte e una Zanzara			1981	LC	32 X 24	R/BFK				
Kleve 1950–1961 (Set of 37 Black & White Photographs of Joseph Beuy's Studio with 1 Original Drawing or Collage)	ESK	FG	1981	PH/B	16 X 12 EA		20 EA	1 EA		POR
Robbe	ESK	MP	1981	LC	39 X 24	AP	150		1000	5000
Difesa della Natura (Clavicembalo) (S-290)	RFFA		1981	SP	40 X 27	AP	300	1	500	3500
Zirkulationszeit Suite (Set of 21) Suite Circulation Time: Sea Angels	GV	GV	1982	EB/A/LB		R/BFK/W	75 EA	2 EA	10000 SET	75000 SET
Seal II (S-306)	GV	GV	1983	EB/A	3 X 6	R/BFK/W	75	2	500	4000
Collezione di Grafica (Set of 8)	PME			PH/EC	20 X 14 EA	R/BFK/W	100 EA		2000 SET	15000 SET
Creativity-Capital (S-365)	SEAE	NB/AB/JN	1983	EC	11 X 28	R/BFK/W	120	3	200	7500
Tranen: Petticoat (S-397)	GV	GV	1985	EC	7 X 5	AP	75	1	400	3000
Seal (S-276)	RFFA		1981–83	LC	39 X 24	AP	150		1200	7500
Iphigenie/Titus Andronicus	ESK		1985	EC	28 X 22 X 2		45		3500	12000
Brustwarze (Nipple)	ESK		1985	MULT	1 X 1		25			POR
Cuprum 0.3% Unguentum Metallicum Praeparatum, 1978–86 (Beeswax Sculpture) (with Embossing)	ES/GBK		1978–86							

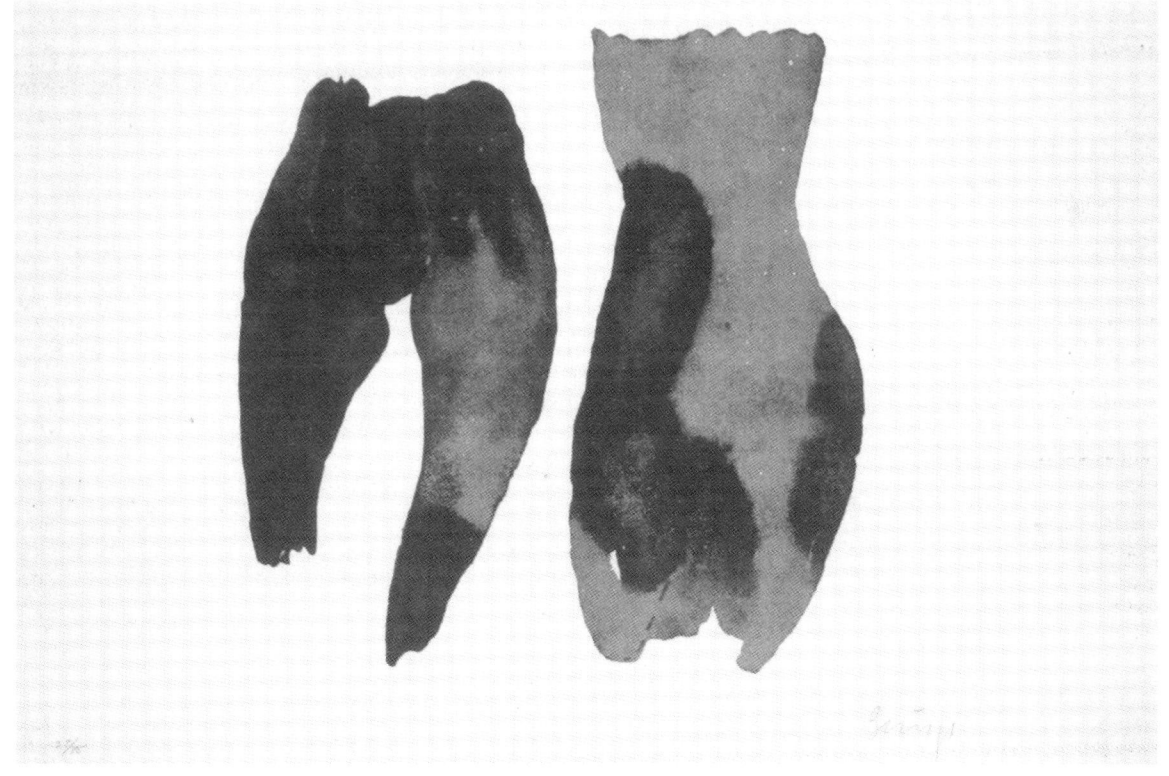

Joseph Beuys
Zwei Weibliche Torsos
(Two Female Torsos)
Courtesy Edition Schellmann

ROGER BEZOMBES

BORN: Paris, France; 1913
COLLECTIONS: Musée Nat d'Art Moderne, Paris, France; Bibliotheque Nat, Paris, France; Musée des Beaux Arts, Dijon, France
PRINTERS: American Atelier, NY (AA)
PUBLISHERS: Circle Fine Art, Chicago, IL (CFA)
GALLERIES: Circle Galleries, San Diego, CA & San Francisco, CA & Northbrook, IL & Pittsburgh, PA & Houston, TX & Soho, NY & Chicago, IL & Scottsdale, AZ & Beverly Hills, CA & Costa Mesa, CA & Sherman Oaks, CA & Palm Beach, FL & Honolulu, HI & New Orleans, LA & Las Vegas, NV & Seattle, WA

ROGER BEZOMBES CONTINUED

TITLE	PUBLISHER	PRINTER	DATE	MEDIUM	DIMENSION (PAPER SIZE) IN INCHES	TYPE OF PAPER	EDITION NUMBER	NO. OF COLORS	ORIGINAL OPENING PRICE	CURRENT RETAIL PRICE
SOLD OUT EDITIONS (RARE):										
Tapis Persan	CFA	AA	1978	LC	23 X 30	AP	150		100	350
Petit Côte d'Azur	CFA	AA	1978	LC	26 X 19	AP	150		100	275
Ti Fee Fee	CFA	AA	1978	LC	30 X 23	AP	150		100	250
Pierre de Reve	CFA	AA	1978	LC	32 X 24	AP	150		100	300
Le Poisson Rouge	CFA	AA	1978	LC	30 X 21	AP	150		100	325
CURRENT EDITIONS:										
Composition	CFA	AA	1979	LC	30 X 22	AP	150		125	300
Poisson Verte	CFA	AA	1979	LC	29 X 20	AP	150		125	250
Yellow Rose	CFA	AA	1979	LC	30 X 23	AP	150		125	350
Lumiére Noire	CFA	AA	1979	LC	32 X 24	AP	150		125	350

NATVAR PRAHLADJI BHAVSAR

BORN: Gothava, India; April 7, 1934
EDUCATION: Bombay State Higher Art Exam, India, AM, 1958; Govt Dipl, Art, 1959; Gujarat Univ, India, BA, 1960; Univ of Pennsylvannia, MFA, 1965
COLLECTIONS: Whitney Mus of Am Art, NY; Metropolitan Mus of Art, NY; Massachusetts Inst of Tech, Cambridge, MA; Boston Mus of Fine Arts, MA; Australian Nat Gallery, Canberra, Australia
PRINTERS: Artist (ART)
PUBLISHERS: Marlborough Gallery, London, England (MG)
GALLERIES: Marlborough Gallery, New York, NY; Gloria Luria Gallery, Bay Harbor Islands, FL; Dumont-Landis Fine Art, New Brunswick, NJ
MAILING ADDRESS: 131 Greene St, New York, NY 10012

TITLE	PUBLISHER	PRINTER	DATE	MEDIUM	DIMENSION (PAPER SIZE) IN INCHES	TYPE OF PAPER	EDITION NUMBER	NO. OF COLORS	ORIGINAL OPENING PRICE	CURRENT RETAIL PRICE
CURRENT EDITIONS:										
Neighbor Blue	MG	ART	1968	SP		AP	20		75	150
Purple Extent	MG	ART	1968	SP		AP	20		75	175
Red Extent	MG	ART	1968	SP		AP	20		75	150
Astaka	MG	ART	1969	SP		AP	20		75	150
Chatura	MG	ART	1969	SP		AP	20		75	150
Panchaka	MG	ART	1969	SP		AP	20		75	150
Sastaka	MG	ART	1969	SP		AP	20		75	175

EDWARD BIBERMAN

BORN: Philadelphia, PA; (1904–1987)
EDUCATION: Univ of Pennsylvania, Phila, PA, BS, 1924; Pennsylvania Acad of Fine Arts, Phila, PA, 1924–26
TEACHING: Sch of Design, Los Angeles, CA, 1938–50; Univ of California, Los Angeles, CA, Irvine, CA, & San Diego, CA, 1967 to present
COLLECTIONS: Los Angeles County Mus, Los Angeles, CA; Palm Springs Desert Mus, CA; Butler Inst of Am Art, Youngstown, OH; Brandeis Univ, Waltham, MA; Pennsylvania Acad of Fine Arts Mus, Phila, PA; Mus of Fine Arts, Houston, TX; De Saisset Mus, Santa Clara, CA; Tupperware Mus, Orlando, FL; Stanford Univ Library, Palo Alto, CA; Smithsonian Inst, Wash, DC
PRINTERS: Artist (ART)
PUBLISHERS: Artist (ART)

TITLE	PUBLISHER	PRINTER	DATE	MEDIUM	DIMENSION (PAPER SIZE) IN INCHES	TYPE OF PAPER	EDITION NUMBER	NO. OF COLORS	ORIGINAL OPENING PRICE	CURRENT RETAIL PRICE
CURRENT EDITIONS:										
The Yellow Doorway	ART	ART	1957	SP	20 X 32	AP	225	12	50	1500
Cypress Trunks & Sand	ART	ART	1962	SP	18 X 43	AP	220	7	65	1800
Grieving Woman No 2	ART	ART	1965	SP	36 X 24	RICE	50	3	75	2000
Gulls-Low Tide	ART	ART	1968	SP	24 X 36	RICE	100	8	85	2000
Flight at Dawn	ART	ART	1970	SP	38 X 25	RICE	44	6	100	2000
October Sun	ART	ART	1970	SP	23 X 35	AP	100	8	85	2000
Sunrise, Sunset	ART	ART	1975	SP	25 X 39	AP	100	6	100	2000
Four & Twenty Blackbirds	ART	ART	1978	SP	26 X 40	AP	100	9	125	2000
Homage to the Archaic Smile	ART	ART	1980	SP	18 X 24	RICE	45	5	150	1500
30's L A Facade	ART	ART	1982	SP	19 X 26	CAN	100	6	100	1500

DAN BIFERIE

BORN: Miami, FL; December 17, 1950
EDUCATION: Ohio Univ, Athens, OH, BFA, 1972; MFA 1974; Daytona Beach Community Col, FL
TEACHING: Instr, Photography, Daytona Beach Community Col, FL, 1975 to present
AWARDS: Halifax Cultural Arts Award, 1979
RECENT EXHIB: Polk Mus of Art, Lakeland, FL, 1987
COLLECTIONS: Baltimore Mus of Art, MD; High Mus, Atlanta, GA; Loch Haven Art Center, Orlando, FL; Middle Tennessee State Univ, Murfreesborough, TN; Stetson Univ, Deland, FL; Mint Mus, NC; Santa Barbara Mus of Art, CA; California Mus of Photography; New Orleans Mus of Art, LA; Bibliotheque Nat, Paris, France
PRINTERS: Artist (ART)
PUBLISHERS: Phantasy, Santa Barbara Mus of Art, CA (P); SE Printing and Publishing Company (SEP); Florida Light, Loch Haven Art Center, FL (FL); Artist (ART)
MAILING ADDRESS: 22 Virginia Ave, Deland, FL 32724; Daytona Beach Community College, P O Box 1111, Daytona Beach, FL 32015

DAN BIFERIE CONTINUED

TITLE	PUBLISHER	PRINTER	DATE	MEDIUM	DIMENSION (PAPER SIZE) IN INCHES	TYPE OF PAPER	EDITION NUMBER	NO. OF COLORS	ORIGINAL OPENING PRICE	CURRENT RETAIL PRICE
CURRENT EDITIONS:										
Lightscapes	ART	ART	1984	PH	8 X 10		20	1	135	200
Lightscapes	ART	ART	1984	PH	11 X 14		10	1	250	300
A Few People (Portraits)	ART	ART	1984	PH	8 X 10		20	1	135	200
A Few People (Portraits)	ART	ART	1984	PH	11 X 14		10	1	250	300
Triptych Series	ART	ART	1984	PH	6 X 13		10	1	250	300

MAX BILL

BORN: Winterthur, Switzerland, 1908
EDUCATION: Kunstgewerbeschule, Zurich, Switzerland, 1924–27; Bauhaus, Dessau, Germany, 1927–29

PRINTERS: Kroll Workshop, Munich, Germany (K)
PUBLISHERS: Kennedy Gallery, NY (KG); Marlborough Gallery, London, England (MG)
GALLERIES: Kennedy Gallery, New York, NY; Marlborough Gallery, New York, NY; Herbert Palmer Gallery, Los Angeles, CA

TITLE	PUBLISHER	PRINTER	DATE	MEDIUM	DIMENSION (PAPER SIZE) IN INCHES	TYPE OF PAPER	EDITION NUMBER	NO. OF COLORS	ORIGINAL OPENING PRICE	CURRENT RETAIL PRICE
SOLD OUT EDITIONS (RARE):										
Color Composition			1967	SP	17 X 17	AP	30	5	100	1200
System of Four Equal Colors			1968	SP	8 X 8	AP	66	4	100	1500
CURRENT EDITIONS:										
Solid Circles	KG	K	1971	SP	30 X 22	R/BFK/W	200	5	200	300
Edition Olympia	KG	K	1972	SP	40 X 25	R/500	200	9	200	750
Untitled	MG	K	1972	LC	34 X 24	AP	75		100	300
Four Color in Rotation and Reflection	MG	K	1973	LC	24 X 20	AP	50		100	350

ERWIN BINDER

BORN: Philadelphia, PA; January 24, 1934
EDUCATION: Temple Univ, Phila, PA, 1951; Otis Art Inst, Los Angeles, CA, 1962
RECENT EXHIB: Butler Inst of Am Art, Youngstown, OH, 1991; Jansen-Perez Gallery, Los Angeles, CA, 1992

COLLECTIONS: Butler Inst of Am Art, Youngstown, OH; Univ of Judaism, Los Angeles, CA; Palm Springs Desert Mus, CA; Hebrew Univ, Jerusalem, Israel;
PUBLISHERS: Topaz Universal, Inc, Burbank, CA (TUI)
PRINTERS: Topaz Universal, Inc, Burbank, CA (TUI)
GALLERIES: Heritage Gallery, Los Angeles, CA; Jansen-Perez Gallery, Los Angeles, CA
MAILING ADDRESS: c/o Topaz Universal, 4632 West Magnolia Blvd, Burbank, CA 91505

TITLE	PUBLISHER	PRINTER	DATE	MEDIUM	DIMENSION (PAPER SIZE) IN INCHES	TYPE OF PAPER	EDITION NUMBER	NO. OF COLORS	ORIGINAL OPENING PRICE	CURRENT RETAIL PRICE
SOLD OUT EDITIONS (RARE):										
The Thinker	TUI	TUI	1981	CP	25 X 25 X 5	HMP	75	0	950	2000
CURRENT EDITIONS:										
Moon Goddess	TUI	TUI	1981	CP	26 X 20 X 4	HMP	75	0	850	1800
Breeze of the North	TUI	TUI	1982	CP	38 X 25 X 5	HMP	100	0	1250	3000
Fertility Goddess	TUI	TUI	1982	CP	46 X 35 X 8	HMP	75	0	2600	4500
Maize Goddess	TUI	TUI	1982	CP	32 X 26 X 7	HMP	35	0	1800	3000
Seekers of Life	TUI	TUI	1983	CP	27 X 23 X 5	HMP	35	0	1500	2400
Venus	TUI	TUI	1984	CP	36 X 25 X 5	HMP	35	0	1500	2500
Tears Beyond Reach	TUI	TUI	1985	CP	25 X 39 X 3	HMP	35	0	1800	2500
Rite of Dawn	TUI	TUI	1986	CP	39 X 55 X 7	HMP	30	0	3750	5500
Shy Patricia	TUI	TUI	1992	CP	12 X 12 X 2	HMP	99	1	500	500
Fertility Icon	TUI	TUI	1992	CP	13 X 16 X 3	HMP	99	1	600	600

JIM BIRD

BORN: Bloxwich, England; November 9, 1937
EDUCATION: Wolverhampton Col of Art, England
TEACHING: Univ of Wisconsin, Madison, WI; Carnegie-Mellon Univ, Pittsburgh, PA
RECENT EXHIB: Galeria Joan Prats, Barcelona, Spain, 1989; River Gallery, Westport, CT, 1989; Karl Bornstein Gallery, Santa Monica, CA, 1989
PRINTERS: La Poligrafa, Barcelona, Spain (LP)

PUBLISHERS: Ediciones Poligrafa, SA, Barcelona, Spain (EdP)
GALLERIES: Spaightwood Galleries, Madison, WI; Galeria Joan Prats, New York, NY & Barcelona, Spain; Sala Pelaires, Palma de Mallorca, Spain; Redfern Gallery, London, England; River Gallery, Westport, CT; Lucy Berman Gallery, Palo Alto, CA; Esther Saks Gallery, Chicago, IL; Bryant Galleries, New Orleans, LA & Birmingham, AL & Atlanta, GA & Jackson, MS; Flanders Contemporary Art, Minneapolis, MN; Charlotte Jackson Fine Art, Santa Fe, NM; Concept Art Gallery, Pittsburgh, PA
MAILING ADDRESS: Es Moli Nou, S'Esgleyeta, Palma de Mallorca, Spain

---

The retail prices of the 100,000 limited edition prints quoted in this directory are subject to change. Print publishers, artists and galleries were the direct sources for these quotations. Prices in the secondary market listed as "Sold Out Editions (Rare)" indicate that the publisher has a limited supply of that print or that the print is difficult to locate in the galleries.

JIM BIRD CONTINUED

TITLE	PUBLISHER	PRINTER	DATE	MEDIUM	DIMENSION (PAPER SIZE) IN INCHES	TYPE OF PAPER	EDITION NUMBER	NO. OF COLORS	ORIGINAL OPENING PRICE	CURRENT RETAIL PRICE
SOLD OUT EDITIONS (RARE):										
Reflections, I–XV (Set of 15)	EdP	LP	1970	LC	27 X 27	GP	75		1400 SET	4000 SET
									120 EA	300 EA
Lithographs BL I–X (Set of 10)	EdP	LP	1977	LC	25 X 25	GP	75		1300 SET	2700 SET
									140 EA	300 EA
JPI Lithographs, I–X (Set of 10)	EdP	LP	1980	LC	30 X 22	GP	75		1400 SET	2700 SET
									150 EA	300 EA
Lithographs Bird I–V (Set of 5)	EdP	LP	1981	LC	22 X 30	GP	50		1200 SET	2000 SET
									220 EA	450 EA
Lithographs JB, I–IV (Set of 6)	EdP	LP	1982	LC	22 X 30	GP	60		1200 SET	2500 SET
									220 EA	450 EA
AL Lithographs (Set of 2):									250 SET	550 SET
Chicago	EdP	LP	1982	LC	22 X 22	GP	99		140 EA	300 EA
Barcelona	EdP	LP	1982	LC	30 X 22	GP	99		140 EA	300 EA
Lithographs Jim, I–V (Set of 5)	EdP	LP	1983	LC	22 X 30	GP	60		1000 SET	2000 SET
									220 EA	450 EA

ROBERT A BIRMELIN

BORN: Newark, NJ; November 7, 1933
EDUCATION: Cooper Union Art Sch, NY; Yale Univ, New Haven, CT, BFA, MFA
TEACHING: Prof, Art, Queens Col, NY, 1964 to present
AWARDS: Am Acad Fel, Rome, Italy, 1961–64; Purchase Award, Childe Hassam, Nat Inst of Arts & Letters, NY, 1981; Nat Endowment for the Arts Fel, 1982
RECENT EXHIB: Univ of Richmond, Marsh Gallery, VA, 1989
COLLECTIONS: Mus of Mod Art, NY; Metropolitan Mus of Art, NY; Hirshhorn Mus, Wash, DC; Smithsonian Inst, Wash, DC; Mus of Contemp Art, Nagaoka, Japan
PRINTERS: David Keister, Bloomington, IN; David Calkins, Bloomington, IN (OC); Echo Press, Bloomington, IN (EPr)
PUBLISHERS: Echo Press, Bloomington, IN (EPr)
GALLERIES: Claude Bernard Gallery, New York, NY; Echo Press, Bloomington, IN
MAILING ADDRESS: 176 Highwood Ave, Leonia, NJ 07605

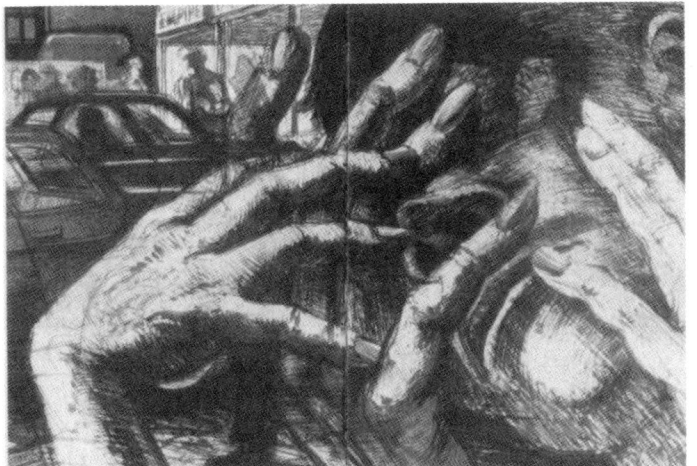

**Robert A Birmelin
The Walking Dream**
Courtesy Echo Press

TITLE	PUBLISHER	PRINTER	DATE	MEDIUM	DIMENSION (PAPER SIZE) IN INCHES	TYPE OF PAPER	EDITION NUMBER	NO. OF COLORS	ORIGINAL OPENING PRICE	CURRENT RETAIL PRICE
CURRENT EDITIONS:										
The Walking Dream	EPr	DK/DC/EPr	1988	LC	36 X 52	AP/W	30		1100	1100
The 20 Dollar Bill	EPr	DK/DC/EPr	1988–89	LC	22 X 30	AP/W	30		700	700

TOM BLACKWELL

BORN: Chicago, IL; March 9, 1938
COLLECTIONS: Guggenheim Mus, NY; Mus of Mod Art, NY; Elvehjem Mus, Univ of Wisconsin, Madison, WI; Smithsonian Inst, Wash, DC; San Francisco Mus of Mod Art, CA; Museé d'Art Contemporain, Montreal, Canada; Nat Gallery of Victoria, Melbourne, Australia

PRINTERS: Editions Lassiter-Meisel, NY (ELM)
PUBLISHERS: London Arts Inc, Detroit, MI (LAI); Lakeco Properties (LP); Bramlett Petroleum (BP); Glenn Interests (GI)
GALLERIES: Louis K Meisel Gallery, New York, NY; Karin Demorest/Creative Directions, Tucson, AZ; Herbert A Starr Gallery, New York, NY; Ro Gallery Image Makers, Inc, New York, NY

TITLE	PUBLISHER	PRINTER	DATE	MEDIUM	DIMENSION (PAPER SIZE) IN INCHES	TYPE OF PAPER	EDITION NUMBER	NO. OF COLORS	ORIGINAL OPENING PRICE	CURRENT RETAIL PRICE
CURRENT EDITIONS:										
1–610 North	LAI	ELM	1980	SP	22 X 30	SOM	250	11	450	1000
Battleship Texas	LAI	ELM	1980	SP	22 X 30	SOM	250	21	450	1000
Charles Jourdan Galloria	LAI	ELM	1980	SP	22 X 30	SOM	300	22	450	1000
Red, White and Blue Mustang	LP	ELM	1980	SP	22 X 30	SOM	250	11	450	1000
Bypass	BP	ELM	1980	SP	22 X 30	SOM	250	12	450	1000
Oil Rig	GI	ELM	1980	SP	22 X 30	SOM	250	10	450	1000

The print market has become very selective. For the first time since we published the first edition of The Printworld Directory in 1982, the prices of prints have been greatly reduced and greatly increased for the same artists by the most reputable and established print publishers. Check the fifth edition to understand the movement.

ALLEN BLAGDEN

BORN: New York, NY; February 21, 1938
EDUCATION: Cornell Univ, Ithaca, NY, BFA; New York State Univ, New Paltz, NY, MFA
TEACHING: Instr, Painting, Hotchkiss Sch, 1968–69; Art in Res, Cornell Univ, Ithaca, NY, 1982
AWARDS: Allied Artist Award, 1963; Century Assoc Medal; Nat Acad of Design Award, 1971
COLLECTIONS: Berkshire Mus, Pittsfield, MA; Peabody Mus, New Haven, CT; New Britain Mus of Am Art, CT; Adirondack Mus, Blue Mountain Lake, NY; Leigh Yankey Woodson Mus, Wausau, WI
PRINTERS: Handworks, NY (HW); Tony Kirk, NY (TK)
PUBLISHERS: Kennedy Galleries, NY (KG); Artist (ART)
GALLERIES: Kennedy Galleries, New York, NY; Foster Harmon Galleries of American Art, Sarasota, FL; Mongerson-Wunderlich Gallery, Chicago, IL
MAILING ADDRESS: Dark Hollow Rd, Salisbury, CT 06068

TITLE	PUBLISHER	PRINTER	DATE	MEDIUM	DIMENSION (PAPER SIZE) IN INCHES	TYPE OF PAPER	EDITION NUMBER	NO. OF COLORS	ORIGINAL OPENING PRICE	CURRENT RETAIL PRICE
CURRENT EDITIONS:										
Hornbill I,II	KG	HW	1980	LC/HC	35 X 25 EA	AP	60 EA	6 EA	1000 EA	1200 EA
Seated Lady	KG	HW	1981	HC/E/A/DPT	24 X 22	FAB	25	1	600	700
Seated Lady	KG	HW	1981	EB/A/DPT	24 X 22	FAB	15	2	1000	1100
West Side Clam	ART	TK	1984	EB	30 X 36	FAB	50	1	500	600

DIKE BLAIR

BORN: New Castle, PA; August 2, 1952
EDUCATION: Univ of Colorado, Boulder, CO, 1971–75; Skowhegan Sch of Painting & Sculpture, ME, 1974; Whitney Mus of Independent Study Program, 1976; Sch of Art Inst of Chicago, IL, MFA, 1977
RECENT EXHIB: Whitney Mus, Fairfield County, NY, 1987
PRINTERS: Richard Finch, Normal, IL (RF); Normal Editions Workshop, Illinois State Univ, IL (NEW)
PUBLISHERS: Getler/Pall/Saper Gallery, NY (GPS); Artist (ART)
GALLERIES: Jack Tilton Gallery, New York, NY; Texas Gallery, Houston, TX
MAILING ADDRESS: 235 E 11th St, New York, NY 10003

TITLE	PUBLISHER	PRINTER	DATE	MEDIUM	DIMENSION (PAPER SIZE) IN INCHES	TYPE OF PAPER	EDITION NUMBER	NO. OF COLORS	ORIGINAL OPENING PRICE	CURRENT RETAIL PRICE
CURRENT EDITIONS:										
Lotus and Robot	ART/GPS	RF/NEW	1984	LB/EMB	37 X 8	CD	24	1	250	350

JEAN-CHARLES BLAIS

RECENT EXHIB: Cavaliero Fine Arts, NY, 1991
PRINTERS: Peter Kneubuhler, Zurich, Switzerland (PK); Artist (ART)
PUBLISHERS: Galerie Buchmann, Basel, Switzerland (GB); Edition Schellmann, NY (ES)
GALLERIES: Galerie Buchmann, Basel, Switzerland; Nicola Jacobs Gallery, London, England, Castelli Graphics, New York, NY; Garner Tullis, New York, NY; BenedicteSaxe Gallery, Maeght Editions, Beverly Hills, CA; Enrico Navarra Gallery, New York, NY; Edition Schellmann, New York, NY & Cologne, Germany

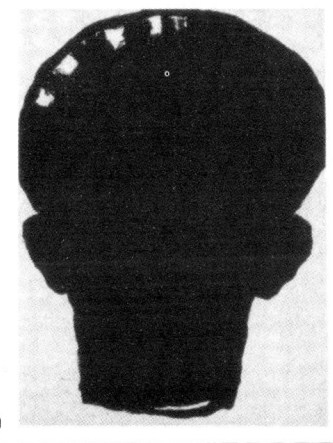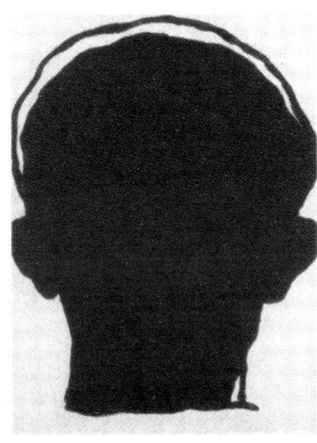

Jean-Charles Blais
Mo Re No
Courtesy Edition Schellmann

TITLE	PUBLISHER	PRINTER	DATE	MEDIUM	DIMENSION (PAPER SIZE) IN INCHES	TYPE OF PAPER	EDITION NUMBER	NO. OF COLORS	ORIGINAL OPENING PRICE	CURRENT RETAIL PRICE
CURRENT EDITIONS:										
Catastrophe (Set of 6):	GB	ART	1984	E/LIN	26 X 20 EA	R/100	25 EA		1200 SET	2500 SET
Trois Nuits	GB	PK	1985	EB/A	29 X 20	AP/250	25		300	500
Mo Re No (Set of 5)	ES		1990	AB/SL	26 X 20 EA	AC	25 EA		3500 SET	4000 SET

PETER BLAKE

BORN: Dartford, England; June 22, 1932
EDUCATION: Gravesend Sch of Art, England, 1946–51; Royal Col of Art, London, England, 1956–57
TEACHING: Royal Col of Art, London, England
AWARDS: Leverhulme Research Award, England; Guggenheim Painting Award, NY
COLLECTIONS: Mus of Mod Art, NY; Baltimore Mus, Baltimore, MD; Tate Gallery of Art, London, England; Arts Council of Great Britain, London, England; Wallraf-Richartz Mus, Cologne, Germany; Boymans-Van Beuningen, Rotterdam, Netherlands
PRINTERS: Chris Prater (CP), Kelpra Studio, London, England (KS); Cliff White, London, England (CW); White Ink, London, England (WI); Aldo Crommelynck, Paris, France (AC); Atelier Crommelynck, Paris, France (AC)
PUBLISHERS: Waddington Graphics, London, England (WG)
GALLERIES: Waddington Graphics, London, England; Claude Bernard Gallery, New York, NY

The retail prices of the 100,000 limited edition prints quoted in this directory are subject to change. Print publishers, artists and galleries were the direct sources for these quotations. Prices in the secondary market listed as "Sold Out Editions (Rare)" indicate that the publisher has a limited supply of that print or that the print is difficult to locate in the galleries.

PETER BLAKE CONTINUED

TITLE	PUBLISHER	PRINTER	DATE	MEDIUM	DIMENSION (PAPER SIZE) IN INCHES	TYPE OF PAPER	EDITION NUMBER	NO. OF COLORS	ORIGINAL OPENING PRICE	CURRENT RETAIL PRICE
SOLD OUT EDITIONS (RARE):										
French Postcards (Set of 6)	WG	CP/KS	1969	SP	17 x 11 EA	AP	75 EA		750 SET	4500 SET
Alice in Wonderland (Set of 8):									800 SET	18000 SET
Ant the Two Knights Sat . . .	WG	CP/KS	1970	SP	10 x 7	AP	100		125	2500
And to Show You I'm Not . . .	WG	CP/KS	1970	SP	10 X 7	AP	100		125	2500
But It isn't Old . . .	WG	CP/KS	1970	SP	10 X 7	AP	100		125	2500
It isn't Manners	WG	CP/KS	1970	SP	10 X 7	AP	100		125	2500
Just at This Moment . . .	WG	CP/KS	1970	SP	10 X 7	AP	100		125	2500
King's Messenger . . .	WG	CP/KS	1970	SP	10 X 7	AP	100		125	2500
So Alice Picked Him Up	WG	CP/KS	1970	SP	10 X 7	AP	100		125	2500
Well, This is Grand	WG	CP/KS	1970	SP	10 X 7	AP	100		125	2500
The Wrestlers (Set of 5):									900 SET	7000 SET
Ebony Tarzan	WG	CP/KS	1972	SP	18 X 12	AP	125	1	225	1500
Penny Black	WG	CP/KS	1972	SP	18 X 12	AP	125	1	225	1500
Pretty Boy Michelangelo	WG	CP/KS	1972	SP	18 X 12	AP	125	1	225	1500
Red Power	WG	CP/KS	1972	SP	18 X 12	AP	125	1	225	1500
The Tuareg	WG	CP/KS	1972	SP	18 X 12	AP	125	1	225	1500
Costume Life Drawing	WG	CP/KS	1972	SP	31 X 22	AP	125	1	135	3000
Girl in a Poppy Field	WG	CP/KS	1974	SP	16 X 11	AP	125		150	1800
Side Show (Set of 5)	WG	CW/WI	1974–78	W/ENG	11 X 9 EA	R/BFK	100 EA	1 EA	1800 SET	6000 SET
James Joyce in Paris (Set of 9):									3000 SET	8000 SET
James Joyce	WG	AC/AC	1983–84	EB	13 X 10	R/BFK	75	1	525	1200
James Stephens, Joyce and John Sullivan in Paris	WG	AC/AC	1983–84	EB/A	10 X 13	R/BFK	75		525	1200
Joyce and Sylvia Beach in Paris	WG	AC/AC	1983–84	EB	13 X 10	R/BFK	75	1	450	1000
Ford Madox Ford, Joyce, Ezra Pound and John Quinn, Paris 1923	WG	AC/AC	1983–84	EB	10 X 13	R/BFK	75	1	450	1000
Joyce in the 1920's	WG	AC/AC	1983–84	EB	13 X 10	R/BFK	75	1	525	1200
Joyce in Brancusi (Figurative)	WG	AC/AC	1983–84	EB	13 X 10	R/BFK	75	1	260	750
Joyce by Brancusi (Abstract)	WG	AC/AC	1983–84	EB	13 X 10	R/BFK	75	1	225	750
Joyce's Dance by Desmond Harmsworth	WG	AC/AC	1983–84	EB	13 X 10	R/BFK	75	1	225	750
Joyce and his Friends by F Scott Fitzgerald	WG	AC/AC	1983–84	EB	13 X 10	R/BFK	75	1	260	750
Tattooed Lady (Black State)	WG		1985	SP	48 X 32	AC	25	1	500	1000
Tattooed Lady (Colored State)	WG		1985	SP	48 X 32	AC	5		900	1800
Untitled (RCA)	WG		1987	SP	8 X 8	AC	48		300	500
CURRENT EDITIONS:										
A is for Alphabet	WG		1990	SP	39 X 30	AC	95		1500	1500
B is for Boxer	WG		1990	SP	39 X 30	AC	95		1500	1500
C is for Clowning	WG		1990	SP	39 X 30	AC	95		1500	1500
E is for Everly Brothers	WG		1991	SP	39 X 30	AC	95		1500	1500
H is for Heart	WG		1991	SP	30 X 30	AC	95		1500	1500
R is for Babe Rainbow	WG		1991	SP	39 X 30	AC	95		1500	1500
S is for Sumo	WG		1991	SP	39 X 30	AC	95		1500	1500
X is for Xylophonist	WG		1991	SP	39 X 30	AC	95		1500	1500

BRUCE R BLEACH

BORN: Monticello, NY; March 12, 1950
EDUCATION: Orange County Comm Col, CA, AA, 1970; Univ of Hartford Art Sch, CT, BFA, 1972; State Univ of New York, New Paltz, NY, MFA, 1974
TEACHING: New Paltz, NY, Printmaking, 1973–74; Rochambeau Sch, Etching, White Plains, NY, 1978–80
AWARDS: Knickerbocker Exhibition, NY, Director's Award for Graphics, 1975; Hastings Drawing Award, NY, 1978
RECENT EXHIB: Fred Dorfman Gallery, NY, 1987; Syd Entel Gallery, Tampa, FL, 1988; Art Farms Gallery, Redbank, NJ, 1989
COLLECTIONS: Hudson River Mus, NY; Taiwan Provincial Mus, Taiwan; Nat Mus of History, NY
PRINTERS: Printmakers Workshop, NY (PW); Atelier Ettinger, NY (AE); Blackburn Studio (BS); Lori Moss Studio (LSM); Joanne Bleach, NY (JB); Artist (ART)
PUBLISHERS: Fred Dorfman, Inc, NY (FDI)
GALLERIES: Fred Dorfman Gallery, New York, NY; C S Schulte Gallery, NJ; Haines Gallery, San Francisco, CA; Art Forms, Red Bank, NJ
MAILING ADDRESS: 123 Wilmot Circle, Scarsdale, NY 10583

TITLE	PUBLISHER	PRINTER	DATE	MEDIUM	DIMENSION (PAPER SIZE) IN INCHES	TYPE OF PAPER	EDITION NUMBER	NO. OF COLORS	ORIGINAL OPENING PRICE	CURRENT RETAIL PRICE
SOLD OUT EDITIONS (RARE):										
Aztec	FDI	LMS	1976	EC	40 X 30	AP	125	6	225	700
Blade Series I, II	FDI	PW	1977	EC	41 X 30 EA	AP/W	85 EA	6 EA	200 EA	700 EA
Parallel	FDI	PW	1977	EC	30 X 41	AP/W	100	8	200	700
Breakthrough	FDI	ART	1977	EC	35 X 30	AP	85	8	150	700
Bands	FDI	ART	1977	EC	35 X 30	AP	125	9	170	700
A Scopic Sighting I	FDI	PW	1977	EC	30 X 41	AP/B	85	6	200	1000
A Scopic Sighting II	FDI	ART	1978	EC	30 X 40	AP	100	10	200	850
Black Parallel	FDI	ART	1978	EC	30 X 40	AP	100	9	225	850

BRUCE R BLEACH CONTINUED

TITLE	PUBLISHER	PRINTER	DATE	MEDIUM	DIMENSION (PAPER SIZE) IN INCHES	TYPE OF PAPER	EDITION NUMBER	NO. OF COLORS	ORIGINAL OPENING PRICE	CURRENT RETAIL PRICE
SOLD OUT EDITIONS (RARE):										
Perched	FDI	ART	1978	LC	40 X 30	AP/B	150	9	225	850
Transient Peak	FDI	PW	1979	EC	21 X 26	AP	85	5	125	600
Arielle	FDI	BS	1980	EC	15 X 13	AP	125	7	50	300
Gemini	FDI	BS	1980	EC	15 X 13	AP	125	7	50	300
Journey I, II	FDI	ART	1980	EC	42 X 29 EA	AP	200 EA	10 EA	200 EA	500 EA
Bavar Series	FDI	ART/JB	1985	EC	35 X 30 EA	AP/W	75 EA	8 EA	700 EA	1200 EA
CURRENT EDITIONS:										
AutoBio Found & Founded	FDI	PW	1978	EC	36 X 30 EA	AP/BL	85 EA	5 EA	240 EA	850 EA
Day; Night Windows II	FDI	AE	1979	LC	42 X 29	AP	275	7	200	600
Linear Dance I, II	FDI	ART	1981	EC	36 X 29 EA	R/BFK	120 EA	7 EA	525 EA	600 EA
Linear Flight I, II	FDI	ART	1981	AC	33 X 27 EA	AP	120 EA	4 EA	525 EA	700 EA
Windows of Winter	FDI	ART	1981	EC	30 X 45	R/BFK	275	6	250	700
Spacial Passing	FDI	ART	1981	AC	40 X 58	AP	100	7	700	1200
Tapa I-IV	FDI	ART/JB	1982	EC	36 X 30 EA	R/BFK/G	60 EA	4 EA	300 EA	700 EA
Divisions I, II	FDI	ART/JB	1984	EC	30 X 40 EA	R/BFK/G	60 EA	8 EA	350 EA	600 EA
Orient I, II	FDI	ART/JB	1984	EC	30 X 40 EA	AP/W	60 EA	8 EA	350 EA	600 EA
Wrap Series	FDI	ART/JB	1985	EC	35 X 30 EA	AP/W	75 EA	8 EA	700 EA	1200 EA
Spacial Passing (Dipt)	FDI	ART	1985	A/HC/MON	40 X 57	AP	100		1200	1350
Division Study	FDI	ART	1985	EC/REL/EMB	27 X 39	AP/G	1 EA		500 EA	600 EA
Ecco (with Gold Leaf)	FDI	ART	1986	EB/REL/EMB	32 X 54	AP	75		750	850
Trax	FDI	ART	1986	MON/EMB	30 X 53 EA	AP	1 EA		950	1000
Trax (on Handmade Colored Paper)	FDI	ART	1986	MON/EMB	30 X 53 EA	HMP/C	1 EA		750	850
HMP	FDI	ART	1986	MON/EMB/REL	24 X 24 EA	HMP/G	1 EA		300	400
Atlantic Narrows	FDI	ART	1986	MON/EMB/REL	19 X 64 EA	HMP	1 EA		1000 EA	1200 EA
Segmentations (with Drawing)	FDI	ART	1986	MM	34 X 23 EA	CP	1 EA		1200 EA	1350 EA
Lune Demi I, II, III	FDI	ART	1986	EB/REL	37 X 30 EA	R/BFK	100 EA		1200 SET	1250 SET
Illume Series	FDI	ART	1987	MON/EB/CO/HC	24 X 52 EA	R/BFK	1 EA		800 EA	900 EA
Waftage Series	FDI	ART	1987	MON/PAS/WA/HC	64 X 20 EA	HMP	1 EA		1000 EA	1200 EA
Illume Field	FDI	ART	1987	MON/CO	30 X 44 EA	HMP	1 EA		700 EA	800 EA

ROSS BLECKNER

BORN: New York, NY; 1949
EDUCATION: New York Univ, NY, BA, 1973; California Inst of Arts, Valencia, CA, MFA, 1976
RECENT EXHIB: Carnegie Inst Art Mus, Pittsburgh, PA, 1988; Milwaukee Art Mus, WI, 1989; Contemp Art Mus, Houston, TX, 1989; Perry Rubenstein Gallery, NY, 1990; Tony Shafrazi Gallery, NY, 1990; Mus Haus Lange, Krefeld, Germany, 1990; Galeria Soledad Lorenzo, Madrid, Spain, 1990; Helander Wetterling Gallery, Stockholm, Sweden, 1990; Kunsthalle, Zurich, Switzerland, 1990; Kolnscher Kunstverein, Cologne, Germany, 1991; Moderna Museet, Stockholm, Sweden, 1991; Museo de Arte Contemp de Monterrey, Mexico, 1991; Cleveland Center for Contemp Art, Cincinnati, OH, 1992; Sena Gallery, Santa Fe, NM, 1992; Guild Hall, East Hampton, NY, 1993
COLLECTIONS: Joslyn Art Mus, Omaha, NE; J B Speed Art Mus, Louisville, KY
PRINTERS: Artist (ART)
PUBLISHERS: Lincoln Center, NY (LC); List Art Posters & Prints, NY (LAPP)
GALLERIES: Mary Boone Gallery, New York, NY; Fred Hoffman Gallery, Santa Monica, CA; Thomas Smith Fine Art, Fort Wayne, IN; Flanders Contemp Art, Minneapolis, MN; Sena Gallery, Santa Fe, NM; Rubenstein/Diacono Gallery, New York, NY; Davis/McClain Gallery, Houston, TX
MAILING ADDRESS: c/o Mary Boone Gallery, 417 West Broadway, New York, NY 10012

Ross Bleckner
Untitled
Courtesy Lincoln Center

TITLE	PUBLISHER	PRINTER	DATE	MEDIUM	DIMENSION (PAPER SIZE) IN INCHES	TYPE OF PAPER	EDITION NUMBER	NO. OF COLORS	ORIGINAL OPENING PRICE	CURRENT RETAIL PRICE
CURRENT EDITIONS:										
Untitled	LC/LAPP		1987	SP	35 X 29	AP	72		1800	3500
5749 (For the Jewish New Year)	LC/LAPP		1988	LC	30 X 22	AP	72		1200	1500

ARBIT BLATAS

BORN: Kaunas, Lithuania
COLLECTIONS: Mus of Mod Art, NY; Metropolitan Mus of Art, NY; Whitney Mus of Am Art, NY; Carnegie Inst of Art, Pittsburgh, PA; Jeu de Paume, Paris, France; Orangerie, Paris, France; Musee de Grenoble, France; Musee de Ceret, France; Musee des Beaux Arts, Lausanne, Switzerland; Nat Mus of Wales, Cardiff, Wales
PRINTERS: Atelier Ettinger, NY (AE)
PUBLISHERS: Transworld Art Inc, NY (TAI); Associated American Artists, NY (AAA)
GALLERIES: Associated American Artists, New York, NY; Ro Gallery Image Makers, Inc, New York, NY

TITLE	PUBLISHER	PRINTER	DATE	MEDIUM	DIMENSION (PAPER SIZE) IN INCHES	TYPE OF PAPER	EDITION NUMBER	NO. OF COLORS	ORIGINAL OPENING PRICE	CURRENT RETAIL PRICE
SOLD OUT EDITIONS (RARE):										
Zizi	AAA		1967	LB	20 X 15 X 9		200		50	800
Mime	AAA		1967	LC	18 X 8 X ¼		200		50	800
CURRENT EDITIONS:										
Redentore from Venice	TAI	AE	1980	LC	24 X 31	AP	175		350	500
Campo Bandiera Elmoro	TAI	AE	1980	LC	24 X 29	AP	175		350	500
San Trovaso-Venice	TAI	AE	1980	LC	24 X 30	AP	175		350	500

GERTRUDE T BLEIBERG

BORN: New York, NY; 1921
EDUCATION: Univ of California, Los Angeles, CA, B Ed, 1941; Univ of Southern California, Grad Sch, Business Adm, 1942; San Francisco Art Inst, CA, BFA, 1975, MFA, 1977
AWARDS: Lifetime Achievement Award, Women's Caucus for Art, South Bay Chapter, Northern California Region, 1992
RECENT EXHIB: Ek'ynose Contemporian, Bordeaux, France, 1987; Judah Magnes Mus, Berkeley, CA, 1987; Galerie EK y Mose Contemp, Bordeaux, France, 1986–88; Elizabeth S Fine Mus Palo Alto, CA, 1988; Branner Spangenberg Fine Arts, Palo Alto, CA, 1989; Palo Alto Cultural Center, CA, 1989; Jennifer Pauls Gallery, Sacramento, CA, 1990; Branner Spangenberg Gallery, Palo Alto, CA, 1991
COLLECTIONS: San Francisco Mus of Mod Art, CA; San Jose Mus, CA; Brooklyn Mus, NY; Santa Cruz County Art Mus, CA; Jane Voorhees Zimmerle Mus, Rutgers Univ, New Brunswick, NJ
PRINTERS: David Kelso, Oakland, CA (DK); Made in California, Oakland, CA (MIC)
PUBLISHERS: Made in California, Oakland, CA (MIC)
GALLERIES: Jennifer Pauls Gallery, Sacramento, CA; Mary Jean Place Fine Art, Palo Alto, CA; Made in California, Oakland, CA; Branner Spangenberg Contemporary Art, Davis, CA
MAILING ADDRESS: c/o Made in California, 3246 Ettie St, #16, Oakland, CA 94608

TITLE	PUBLISHER	PRINTER	DATE	MEDIUM	DIMENSION (PAPER SIZE) IN INCHES	TYPE OF PAPER	EDITION NUMBER	NO. OF COLORS	ORIGINAL OPENING PRICE	CURRENT RETAIL PRICE
CURRENT EDITIONS:										
Annie is Just Thirteen	MIC	DK/MIC	1982	EC/A/SG/SB	22 X 15	R/BFK/W	24	3	225	400
Naomi Tap Dances	MIC	DK/MIC	1982	EC/A/SG/HG/SB	22 X 15	R/BFK/W	24	3	200	375
Sarah Loves Ballet	MIC	DK/MIC	1982	AB	22 X 15	R/BFK/W	24	1	150	375
Mostly Shoes (Set of 10):									1200 SET	2000 SET
Don Tells Me Stories	MIC	DK/MIC	1982	EC	15 X 11	R/BFK/W	24		225	350
Dennis' Shoes	MIC	DK/MIC	1982	EB	15 X 11	R/BFK/W	24	1	150	225
My Shoes	MIC	DK/MIC	1982	EB	15 X 12	R/BFK/W	24	1	150	225
Retired	MIC	DK/MIC	1982	EB	15 X 11	R/BFK/W	24	1	150	225
My Brown Bag	MIC	DK/MIC	1982	EB	15 X 11	R/BFK/W	24	1	125	200
David's Boots	MIC	DK/MIC	1982	EC	15 X 11	R/BFK/W	24	2	200	275
Naomi's Thongs	MIC	DK/MIC	1982	EB	15 X 11	R/BFK/W	24	1	200	275
Vicki and Alan	MIC	DK/MIC	1982	EB	15 X 11	R/BFK/W	24	1	150	225
Norm and Joel	MIC	DK/MIC	1982	EC	15 X 11	R/BFK/W	24	2	200	275
Diana	MIC	DK/MIC	1982	EB	15 X 11	R/BFK/W	24	1	200	275
The Wedding (Set of 8):									1350 SET	2500 SET
The Bride's Cuff	MIC	DK/MIC	1982	AB	30 X 23	R/BFK/W	24	1	190	275
Waiting for the Bride	MIC	DK/MIC	1982	AB	30 X 23	R/BFK/W	24	1	190	400
It Just Rained a Little	MIC	DK/MIC	1982	AB	30 X 23	R/BFK/W	24	1	190	400
Sisters—at the Reception	MIC	DK/MIC	1982	AB	30 X 23	R/BFK/W	24	1	190	550
The Bridesmaid's Shoes	MIC	DK/MIC	1982	AB	30 X 23	R/BFK/W	24	1	190	450
The Cake was Lousy!	MIC	DK/MIC	1982	AB	30 X 23	R/BFK/W	24	1	190	400
The Marriage Canapy	MIC	DK/MIC	1982	AB	30 X 23	R/BFK/W	24	1	190	400
Satin Ribbons in the Breeze	MIC	DK/MIC	1982	AB	30 X 23	R/BFK/W	24	1	190	400
In the Garden, State I	MIC	DK/MIC	1986	EB/HG	16 X 19	JWP/W	10	1	175	225
Mary's Barn, State I	MIC	DK/MIC	1986	EB/HG	16 X 19	JWP/W	10	1	175	225
Edgewood, State I	MIC	DK/MIC	1988	EB/HG	23 X 30	RdL	10	1	300	400
Silver Pond	MIC	DK/MIC	1991	AB	23 X 30	R/BFK/W	24	1	400	475

ALAN BLIZZARD

BORN: Boston, MA; March 25, 1939
EDUCATION: Massachusetts Col of Art, Boston, MA; Univ of Arizona, Tucson, AZ, MA; Univ of Iowa, Iowa City, IA, MFA
TEACHING: Univ of Iowa, Iowa City, IA; Univ of Oklahoma, Norman, OK; Univ of California, Los Angeles, CA; Scripps Col, Claremont, CA; Claremont Grad Sch, CA
RECENT EXHIB: Chrysalis Gallery, Claremont, CA, 1987
COLLECTIONS: Metropolitan Mus of Art, NY; Art Inst of Chicago, IL; Denver Art Mus, CO; Brooklyn Mus, NY; La Jolla Mus of Art, CA; Nat Gallery, Wash, DC; Ashland Col, OH; Scripps Col, Claremont, CA; Claremont Grad Sch, CA; Univ of Iowa, Iowa City, IA; Univ of California, Los Angeles, CA; Pomona Col, CA
PRINTERS: Ocean Works Limited Editions, Medical Lake, WA (OW); Artist (ART)

ALAN BLIZZARD CONTINUED

PUBLISHERS: New Garde Editions, Seal Beach, CA (NE)
GALLERIES: Maurice-Heyman Fine Arts, Westlake Village, CA; Downtown Art Show Space, Los Angeles, CA

MAILING ADDRESS: Dept of Art, Scripps Col, 10th & Columbia, Claremont, CA 91711

TITLE	PUBLISHER	PRINTER	DATE	MEDIUM	DIMENSION (PAPER SIZE) IN INCHES	TYPE OF PAPER	EDITION NUMBER	NO. OF COLORS	ORIGINAL OPENING PRICE	CURRENT RETAIL PRICE
SOLD OUT EDITIONS (RARE):										
Enter Laughing	NE	ART	1971	EB	21 X 28	R/BFK	20	1	200	400
Man Tipping Hat	NE	ART	1972	LB	23 X 15	AP	10	1	200	500
Orator with Flag	NE	ART	1973	I	21 X 14	R/BFK	15	1	200	500
The Agitator	NE	ART	1974	EB	19 X 16	R/BFK	20	1	200	600
Seated Man in a Landscape	NE	ART	1975	LB	20 X 18	AP	10	1	200	600
CURRENT EDITIONS:										
Green Hero	NE	ART	1976	WC	17 X 22	RICE	20	2	200	600
Gray Hero	NE	ART	1977	WB	24 X 19	RICE	20	1	200	600
Blue Hero	NE	ART	1978	LC	17 X 15	R/BFK	100	3	175	500
Hurrah Seurat	NE	ART	1979	WC	40 X 28	AP	23	8	375	700
The Truth of the Matter	NE	ART	1980	LC	20 X 28	AP	50	2	400	650
Broken Arrow	NE	OW	1982	LC	22 X 18	R/100	42	3	400	700
Compliments of the Artist	NE	OW	1985	LC	22 X 18	R/100	44	4	400	700

GAY BLOCK

BORN: Houston, TX; March 5, 1942
EDUCATION: Sophie Newcomb Col, New Orleans, LA, 1959–61, Univ of Houston, TX, 1971–72
TEACHING: Vis Art, Photography, Univ of Houston, TX, 1979–80, 1982–83; Instr, California Inst of Arts, CA, 1987
AWARDS: Nat Endowment for the Arts Photography Fel Grant, 1978; Nat Endowment for the Arts Survey Grant to Women & their Work, 1981
COLLECTIONS: Mus of Fine Arts, Houston, TX; Fort Worth Art Mus, TX; Portland Mus of Art, ME; Center for Creative Photography, Tucson, AZ; Cronin Gallery, Houston, TX (CG)
GALLERIES: Graham Gallery, Houston, TX
MAILING ADDRESS: 2341 Sunset Blvd, Houston, TX 77005

TITLE	PUBLISHER	PRINTER	DATE	MEDIUM	DIMENSION (PAPER SIZE) IN INCHES	TYPE OF PAPER	EDITION NUMBER	NO. OF COLORS	ORIGINAL OPENING PRICE	CURRENT RETAIL PRICE
CURRENT EDITIONS:										
Mothers & Daughters	ART	ART	1976	PH	20 X 16	AP		1	300	350
Mother & Me	ART	ART	1977	PH	20 X 16	AP		1	300	350
Simeon & Alla	ART	ART	1977	PH	20 X 16	AP		1	300	350

NORMAN BLUHM

BORN: Chicago, IL; March 28, 1920
EDUCATION: Illinois Inst of Tech, Chicago, IL; Studied with Mies Van der Ruhe
RECENT EXHIB: Hamilton Col, Clinton, NY, 1987; Allentown Mus, PA, 1987; Ball State Univ, Muncie, IN, 1987; Arkansas Art Center, Little Rock, AR, 1987; Manny Silverman Gallery, Los Angeles, CA, 1990
COLLECTIONS: Dallas Mus of Art, TX; Dayton Art Mus, OH; Mus of Mod Art, NY; Whitney Mus of Am Art, NY; Corcoran Gallery of Art, Wash, DC; Albright-Knox Art Gallery, Buffalo, NY
PRINTERS: Jon Cone, East Topsham, VT (JC); Eric Great-Rex (EGR); Cone Editions, East Topsham, VT (CEd)
PUBLISHERS: Cone Editions, East Topsham, VT (CEd)
GALLERIES: Washburn Gallery, New York, NY; Manny Silverman Gallery, Los Angeles, CA; Zolla/Lieberman Gallery, Chicago, IL; David Anderson Gallery, Buffalo, NY; Martha Henry Fine Arts, New York, NY; Edward Tyler Nahem Fine Art, New York, NY; Raydon Gallery, New York, NY; Vanderwoude/Tananbaum Gallery, New York, NY; Cone Editions, East Topsham, VT

TITLE	PUBLISHER	PRINTER	DATE	MEDIUM	DIMENSION (PAPER SIZE) IN INCHES	TYPE OF PAPER	EDITION NUMBER	NO. OF COLORS	ORIGINAL OPENING PRICE	CURRENT RETAIL PRICE
CURRENT EDITIONS:										
Series of Eight Painted Collages—Poem Prints (with John Yau):										
Chicago 1920 (Trip)	CEd	JC/EGR/CEd	1987	SP	40 X 75	R/BFK	35	18	2000	3000
Private Eye (Trip)	CEd	JC/EGR/CEd	1987	SP	40 X 75	R/BFK	35	18	2000	3000
Song of the Concubine (Trip)	CEd	JC/EGR/CEd	1987	SP	40 X 75	R/BFK	35	16	2000	3000
Sam Spade Haiku	CEd	JC/EGR/CEd	1987	SP	34 X 60	R/BFK	35	7	1500	2000
Sam Spade Haiku #1	CEd	JC/EGR/CEd	1987	SP	34 X 60	R/BFK	35	9	1500	2000
Sam Spade Haiku #4	CEd	JC/EGR/CEd	1987	SP	34 X 60	R/BFK	35	6	1500	2000
Sam Spade (Trip)	CEd	JC/EGR/CEd	1987	SP	40 X 75	R/BFK	35	24	2000	3000
Hymns and Hers	CEd	JC/EGR/CEd	1987	SP	32 X 57	KIN/ROL	35	6	1500	2000
8 Beefy Babes	CEd	JC/EGR/CEd	1987	SP	36 X 25 EA	AP88	20 EA	5–7 EA	1000 EA	1500 EA
Beefy Babes I–VIII (Series of 8 Painted Collages Combining Cut and Assembled Screenprints with Acrylic Paint)	CEd	JC/EGR/CEd	1987	SP/CO	40 X 32 EA	AP88	1 EA	Varies	2000 EA	3000 EA

ANDREA BLUM

BORN: New York, NY; April 6, 1950
EDUCATION: Univ of Denver, CO; Boston Mus of Fine Arts, MA, BFA, 1973; Sch of Art, Chicago Art Inst, IL, MFA, 1976
TEACHING: Vis Art & Lectr, Univ of Iowa, Iowa City, IA, 1977; Vis Art, Kalamazoo Inst of Art, MI, 1977; Vis Art, Univ of Illinois, Chicago, IL, 1977; Visa Art, Univ of Hartford, CT, 1978; Vis Art, Univ of Northern Iowa, Cedar Falls, IA, 1979; Vis Art, Univ of Chicago, IL, 1979; Vis Art, Art Inst of Chicago, IL, 1981
AWARDS: Individual Grants, Nat Endowment for the Arts, 1976, 78
COLLECTIONS: Art Inst of Chicago, IL; Univ of Iowa Mus, Iowa City, IA; Nat Coll of Fine Arts, Wash, DC
PRINTERS: Artist (ART)
PUBLISHERS: Art Matters, Boulder, CO (AM)
GALLERIES: Vanguard Gallery, Phila, PA
MAILING ADDRESS: 322 Seventh Ave, 2nd FL, New York, NY 10001

TITLE	PUBLISHER	PRINTER	DATE	MEDIUM	DIMENSION (PAPER SIZE) IN INCHES	TYPE OF PAPER	EDITION NUMBER	NO. OF COLORS	ORIGINAL OPENING PRICE	CURRENT RETAIL PRICE
CURRENT EDITIONS:										
Untitled	AM	ART	1983	LB	41 X 29	AC	20	1	400	500
Untitled	AM	ART	1983	LB/HC	41 X 29	AC	5	Varies	500	600

MEL BOCHNER

BORN: Pittsburgh, PA; 1940
EDUCATION: Carnegie Inst, Pittsburgh, PA, BFA, 1962
TEACHING: Instr, Sch of Visual Arts, NY, 1965
AWARDS: Am Acad of Inst of Arts & Letters, NY, 1990
RECENT EXHIB: Gallery Monterey, Paris, France, 1987; David Nolan Gallery, NY, 1988; Althea Viafora Gallery, NY, 1988; Centro de Arte Reina, Sofia Madrid, Spain, 1988; Carnegie-Mellon Univ Art Gallery, Pittsburgh, PA, 1989; David Nolan Gallery, NY, 1990; Lincoln Center, Fine Art Prints, Avery Fisher Hall, NY, 1992
COLLECTIONS: Los Angeles Mus of Art, CA; Mus of Mod Art, Paris, France; Whitney Mus of Am Art, NY
PRINTERS: Simca Print Artists, NY (SPA); Orlando Condeso, NY (OC); Maurice Payne, NY (MP); Vinalhaven Press, Vinalhaven, ME (VP); Keiji Shinohara, Malden, MA (KS); James Miller, NY (JM); Lucy Gray, NY (LG); Joe Petruzelli, NY (JP); Maurice Sanchez, NY (MS); Derriére L'Etoile Studios, NY (DES)
PUBLISHERS: Simca Print Artists, NY (SPA); Vinalhaven Press, Vinalhaven, ME (VP); Fred Jahn, Munich, Germany (FJ); David Nolan Gallery, NY (DNG); Editions Ilene Kurtz, NY (EIK); Parasol Press, Ltd, NY (PaP); Arion Press, San Francisco, CA (AP); Diane Villani Editions, NY (DVE)
GALLERIES: Sonnabend Gallery, New York, NY; Dolly Fiterman Gallery, Minneapolis, MN; Janet Steinberg Gallery, San Francisco, CA; David Nolan Gallery, New York, NY; Greene Gallery, Miami, FL; Cava Gallery, Phila, PA; J J Brookings Gallery, San Jose, CA; Roger Ramsay Gallery, Chicago, IL; Editions Ilene Kurtz, New York, NY; SteinGladstone Gallery, New York, NY; Diane Villani Editions, New York, NY; Vinalhaven Press, Vinalhaven, ME; L Bartman Fine Arts, Chicago, IL
MAILING ADDRESS: c/o Sonnabend Gallery, 420 W Broadway, New York, NY 10012

TITLE	PUBLISHER	PRINTER	DATE	MEDIUM	DIMENSION (PAPER SIZE) IN INCHES	TYPE OF PAPER	EDITION NUMBER	NO. OF COLORS	ORIGINAL OPENING PRICE	CURRENT RETAIL PRICE
SOLD OUT EDITIONS (RARE):										
Set of Three:										
Three Plus Four			1973	I	17 X 19	AP	25	1	250	3000
Four Plus Three			1973	I	17 X 19	AP	25	1	250	3000
Five Plus Three			1973	I	17 X 19	AP	25	1	250	3000
Apices (Set of 3)			1974	AC		AP			700 SET	10000 SET
QED (Set of 4)			1974	AC	26 X 37 EA	AP	25 EA		900 SET	12000 SET
Rules of Inference			1974	I	29 X 38	AP	35	1	300	3500
Ten to 10			1978	LB	25 X 35	AP	35	1	300	3500
Range	SPA	SPA	1979	SP	25 X 36	AP	40	3	400	3000
On/Over/Under	SPA	SPA	1979	SP	25 X 20	AP	43	2	350	2500
White Island	VP	OC/MP/VP	1985	EB/A	37 X 30	R/BFK	30	1	800	3000
Iron Point	VP	OC/MP/VP	1985	AB	22 X 30	AP	20	1	600	1200
Prelude I (4 Sheets)			1988	LB	15 X 11 EA	AP	10 EA	1 EA	2000 SET	3500 SET
Untitled (Exploding Cube)			1989	AC	34 X 47	AP	32		1200	3500
CURRENT EDITIONS:										
Quartet Series:										
First Quartet	PaP	MP	1988	AC	39 X 39	AP/WA	15	2	1000	2500
Second Quartet	PaP	MP	1988	AC	49 X 38	AP/WA	15	2	1000	2500
Third Quartet	PaP	MP	1988	AC	49 X 38	AP/WA	15	2	1000	2500
Fourth Quartet	PaP	MP	1988	AC	48 X 39	AP/WA	15	2	1000	2500
Untitled (Dipt)	FJ/DNG	MP	1989	AB/SL	33 X 47	SOM	32	1	2500	3500
Floating World (Set of 5)	EIK	KS	1990	WC	14 X 18 EA	KOZO	40 EA		8000 SET	10000 SET
Four Color Quartets (Set of 4)	DVE	MS/JM/JP/LG/DES	1990	LC	35 X 35 EA to 45 X 45 EA	CAN	35 EA		10000 SET 3000 EA	10000 SET 3000 EA

PETER BODNAR

BORN: Andrejova, Czechoslovakia; November 27, 1928; U S Citizen
EDUCATION: Flint Inst of Art, MI, 1941–44; Western Michigan Univ, Kalamazoo, MI, BS, 1951; Michigan State Univ, East Lansing, MI, MA, 1956
TEACHING: Asst Prof, Art, State Univ of New York, Plattsburgh, NY, 1956–58; Asst Prof, Art, Univ of Florida, Gainesville, FL, 1960–62; Prof, Painting, Univ of Illinois, Urbana-Champaign, IL, 1962 to present
AWARDS: Tamarind Lithography Workshop, Inc, Grant, 1964; Univ of Illinois Fel, Center for Advanced Study, Urbana-Champaign, IL, 1967–68; Nat Endowment for the Arts Fel, 1975–76
COLLECTIONS: Univ of Southern California, Los Angeles, CA; Illinois State Mus, Springfield, IL; Delgado Mus, New Orleans, LA
PRINTERS: Marcia Brown, Albuquerque, NM (MB); Randy Gibbs, Albuquerque, NM (RG); Tamarind Inst, Albuquerque, NM (TI)
PUBLISHERS: Tamarind Inst, Albuquerque, NM (TI)
MAILING ADDRESS: c/o Dept of Art, Univ of Illinois, Urbana-Champaign, IL 61801

PETER BODNAR CONTINUED

TITLE	PUBLISHER	PRINTER	DATE	MEDIUM	DIMENSION (PAPER SIZE) IN INCHES	TYPE OF PAPER	EDITION NUMBER	NO. OF COLORS	ORIGINAL OPENING PRICE	CURRENT RETAIL PRICE
CURRENT EDITIONS:										
Untitled	TI	MB/TI	1983	LC	13 X 12	AP/W	20	3	100	150
Untitled I–IV	TI	RG/TI	1983	LC	8 X 10 EA	AP/W	15 EA	2 EA	75 EA	100 EA
Untitled I–IV	TI	MB/TI	1983	LC	8 X 10 EA	AP/W	22 EA	2 EA	75 EA	100 EA

MARIANNE BOERS

BORN: Modesto, CA; (1945–1984)
EDUCATION: Immaculate Heart Col, Los Angeles, CA, 1963; San Francisco State Univ, CA, BFA, 1971; MFA, 1975
TEACHING: Vis Art, Univ of California, Davis, CA, 1976,78; Vis Art, California Col of Arts & Crafts, Oakland, CA, 1980; Vis Art, Chabot Col, Hayward, CA, 1980–81
COLLECTIONS: San Francisco Mus of Mod Art, CA; Oakland Mus, CA; Yale Univ Art Mus, New Haven, CT; Boise Gallery of Art, ID
PRINTERS: Katherine Lincoln Press, San Francisco, CA (KLP); Jennifer Cole (JC); Katie Kahn (KK)
PUBLISHERS: Katherine Lincoln Press, San Francisco, CA (KLP); Ed Hill Editions, El Paso, TX (EHE); Artist (ART)
GALLERIES: Ed Hill Gallery, El Paso, TX; John Berggruen Gallery, San Francisco, CA
MAILING ADDRESS: 1242 Alabama St, San Francisco, CA 94110

TITLE	PUBLISHER	PRINTER	DATE	MEDIUM	DIMENSION (PAPER SIZE) IN INCHES	TYPE OF PAPER	EDITION NUMBER	NO. OF COLORS	ORIGINAL OPENING PRICE	CURRENT RETAIL PRICE
SOLD OUT EDITIONS (RARE):										
Dark Bench	KLP/ART	JC/KK/KLP	1983	EC/DPH/SB	22 X 30	R/BFK	40	5	400	600
Perrier Bottles	EHE	KLP	1983	EC/A	23 X 30	R/BFK	100	5	400	600
Perrier	EHE/ART	KLP	1984	EC	22 X 30	R/BFK	100	5	400	600

RAFAEL BOGARIN

BORN: El Tigre, Venezuela; January 20, 1946
EDUCATION: Cristobal Rojas, Caracas, Venezuela, BA, 1966; Pratt Graphics Center, NY, 1970–71, with Michael Ponce de Leon; Blackburn Workshop, NY, 1971–73
AWARDS: Roma Prize, Salon de Arte, Venezaland, Italian Govt, 1968
COLLECTIONS: Mus of Fine Arts, Caracas, Venezuela; Corcoran Gallery of Art, Wash, DC; Mus of Mod Art, NY
PRINTERS: Artist (ART)
PUBLISHERS: Fedelé Fine Arts, NY (FFA); Circle Fine Art, Chicago, IL (CFA)
GALLERIES: Circle Galleries, San Diego, CA & San Francisco, CA & Northbrook, IL & Pittsburgh, PA & Houston, TX & Soho, NY & Chicago, IL & Scottsdale, AZ & Beverly Hills, CA & Costa Mesa, CA & Sherman Oaks, CA & Palm Beach, FL & Honolulu, HI & New Orleans, LA & Las Vegas & Seattle, WA
MAILING ADDRESS: 14 West 17th St, 5th Fl, New York, NY 10011

TITLE	PUBLISHER	PRINTER	DATE	MEDIUM	DIMENSION (PAPER SIZE) IN INCHES	TYPE OF PAPER	EDITION NUMBER	NO. OF COLORS	ORIGINAL OPENING PRICE	CURRENT RETAIL PRICE
SOLD OUT EDITIONS (RARE):										
Jupiter IV, VI, VII	FFA	ART	1978	SP	29 X 23 EA	AP	295 EA		150 EA	300 EA
RB-1	FFA	ART	1978	SP	30 X 40	AP	10		200	750
RB-2 (Trip)	FFA	ART	1978	SP	40 X 90	AP	10		350	2500
RB-3	FFA	ART	1978	SP	30 X 40	AP	10		200	750
RB-4	FFA	ART	1978	SP	30 X 40	AP	10		200	750
RB-5	FFA	ART	1978	SP	30 X 40	AP	10		200	750
RB-6	FFA	ART	1979	SP	20 X 26	AP	50		125	500
RB-7	FFA	ART	1979	SP	40 X 30	AP	10		200	750
RB-8	FFA	ART	1979	SP	20 X 26	AP	50		125	500
RB-9	FFA	ART	1979	SP	26 X 20	AP	50		125	500
RB-10	FFA	ART	1979	SP	26 X 20	AP	50		125	500
RB-11 (Trip)	FFA	ART	1980	SP	40 X 90	AP	9		600	2500
RB-12	FFA	ART	1980	SP	40 X 30	AP	10		200	750
RB-13	FFA	ART	1980	SP	22 X 28	AP	50		125	500
New Color	FFA	ART	1980	SP	20 X 26	AP	50		500	4000
CURRENT EDITIONS:										
Jupiter III, V	CFA	ART	1978	SP	29 X 23 EA	AP	295 EA		150 EA	325 EA

AARON BOHROD

BORN: Chicago, IL; 1907
EDUCATION: Sch of Art Inst, Chicago, IL; Art Students League, NY, with John Sloan
TEACHING: Art in Res, Southern Illinois Univ, Carbondale, IL, 1941–42; Artist in Res, Univ of Wisconsin, Madison, WI, 1948–73
AWARDS: Guggenheim Fel (2); Clark Prize & Silver Medal, Corcoran Gallery of Art, Wash, DC; Prize, Metropolitan Mus of Art, NY; First Logan Prizes, Art Inst of Chicago, IL, 1937,45; Wisconsin Acad of Art & Science Fel, 1982
RECENT EXHIB: Brown County Art Guild, Nashville, IN, 1989; Trova Found, Clayton, MO, 1989; Oshkosh Public Mus, WI, 1992
COLLECTIONS: Whitney Mus of Am Art, NY; Metropolitan Mus, NY; Pennsylvania Acad of Fine Art, Phila, PA; Philadelphia Mus, Phila, PA; Mus of Fine Arts, Boston, MA; Art Inst of Chicago, IL; Corcoran Gallery of Art, Wash, DC; Philippines Mus of Art, Manilla, The Philippines
PRINTERS: Artist (ART); American Atelier, NY (AA)
PUBLISHERS: Associated American Artists, NY (AAA); Circle Fine Art, Chicago, IL (CFA)

AARON BOHROD CONTINUED

GALLERIES: Oehlschlaeger Galleries, Sarasota, FL; Harmon-Meek Gallery, Naples, FL; Circle Galleries, San Diego, CA & San Francisco, CA & Northbrook, IL & Pittsburgh, PA & Houston, TX & Soho, NY & Chicago, IL & Scottsdale, AZ & Beverly Hills, CA & Costa Mesa, CA & Sherman Oaks, CA & Palm Beach, CA & Honolulu, HI & New Orleans, LA & Las Vegas, NV & Seattle, WA; Harmon-Meek Third Street Gallery, Harbor Springs, MI; Charlotte Brauer Fine Art, Munster, IN
MAILING ADDRESS: 4811 Tonyawatha Trail, Madison, WI 53716

TITLE	PUBLISHER	PRINTER	DATE	MEDIUM	DIMENSION (PAPER SIZE) IN INCHES	TYPE OF PAPER	EDITION NUMBER	NO. OF COLORS	ORIGINAL OPENING PRICE	CURRENT RETAIL PRICE
SOLD OUT EDITIONS (RARE):										
Farm Ruins	AAA	ART	1933	LB	13 X 14	WOVE	25	1	25	500
New Orleans Street	AAA	ART	1935	LB	10 X 14	WOVE	100	1	35	500
Pennsylvania Highway			1944	LB	9 X 14	WOVE	250	1	50	500
Street in Noumea	AAA	ART	1945	LB	9 X 13	WOVE	100	1	50	350
Sun Over Montparnasse	AAA	ART	1945	LB	12 X 9	WOVE	100	1	50	500
Reflections In Shop Window		ART	1948	LB	9 X 13	WOVE	100	1	50	300
Toys		ART		LB	10 X 13	WOVE	100	1	50	300
Red Horse	CFA	AA	1978	LC	22 X 30		200		100	300

FERNAND BOILAUGES

BORN: Lillie, France; 1902
PRINTERS: American Atelier, NY (AA)
PUBLISHERS: Circle Fine Art, Chicago, IL (CFA)
GALLERIES: Circle Galleries, San Diego, CA & San Francisco, CA & Northbrook, IL & Pittsburgh, PA & Houston, TX & Soho, NY & Chicago, IL & Scottsdale, AZ & Beverly Hills, CA & Costa Mesa, CA & Sherman Oaks, CA & Palm Beach, CA & Honolulu, HI & New Orleans, LA & Las Vegas, NV & Seattle, WA

TITLE	PUBLISHER	PRINTER	DATE	MEDIUM	DIMENSION (PAPER SIZE) IN INCHES	TYPE OF PAPER	EDITION NUMBER	NO. OF COLORS	ORIGINAL OPENING PRICE	CURRENT RETAIL PRICE
SOLD OUT EDITIONS (RARE):										
Restaurant Faison Doré	CFA	AA		LC	19 X 26	AP	225		100	425
Restaurant/Japon	CFA	AA		LC	19 X 26	AP	25		125	450
Boat	CFA	AA		LC	20 X 26	AP	250		100	425
Boat/Japon	CFA	AA		LC	20 X 26	AP	25		125	450

JAY BOLOTIN

PRINTERS: Georgia Nold, Cincinnati, OH (GN); Julie Crossen, Cincinnati, OH (JC); Mark Patsfall Graphics, Cincinnati, OH (MPGr)
PUBLISHERS: Mark Patsfall Graphics, Cincinnati, OH (MPGr)
GALLERIES: Carl Solway Gallery, Cincinnati, OH

TITLE	PUBLISHER	PRINTER	DATE	MEDIUM	DIMENSION (PAPER SIZE) IN INCHES	TYPE OF PAPER	EDITION NUMBER	NO. OF COLORS	ORIGINAL OPENING PRICE	CURRENT RETAIL PRICE
CURRENT EDITIONS:										
Limbus Fatuo'rum	MPGr	GN/JC/MPGr	1992	WC	51 X 75	AP	25	12	2500	2500

ILYA BOLOTOWSKY

BORN: Petrograd, Russia; 1907–1984; US Citizen
EDUCATION: Col of St Joseph, Istanbul, Turkey; Nat Acad of Design, NY, 1924–30
TEACHING: Univ of Wyoming, Laramie, WY, 1948–57; Brooklyn Col, NY, 1954–55; Hunter Col, NY, 1954–56, 1963–64; State Univ of New York, New Paltz, NY, 1957–65; Long Island Univ, Brooklyn, NY, 1965–71; Queens Col, Flushing, NY 1973
AWARDS: Nat Acad of Design, NY, Drawing/Printing, 1924,25; Louis C Tiffany Grant, 1930,31; Yaddo Fel, 1935; Guggenheim Found Fel 1941; Nat Inst of Arts & Letters, NY 1971
RECENT EXHIB: Phillips Collection, Wash, DC, 1992; Lincoln Center, Fine Arts Prints, Avery Fisher Hall, NY, 1992
COLLECTIONS: Mus of Mod Art, NY; Metropolitan Mus of Art, NY; Brandeis Univ, Waltham, MA; Brooklyn Mus, NY; Albright-Knox Art Gallery, Buffalo, NY; Hirshhorn Mus, Wash, DC; Univ of Iowa, Iowa City, IA; Univ of Michigan, Ann Arbor, MI; Univ of Nebraska, Omaha, NE; Univ of New Mexico, Albuquerque, NM; Chrysler Mus, Norfolk, VA; Univ of North Carolina, Greensboro, NC; Philadelphia Mus; PA; Phillips Gallery, Wash, DC; North Carolina Mus, Raleigh, NC; Univ of Vermont, Burlington, VT; Aldrich Mus of Contemp Art, Ridgefield, CT; State Univ of New York, New Paltz, NY
PRINTERS: Gerald Johnson, NY (GJ)
PUBLISHERS: London Arts Inc, Detroit, MI (LAI)
GALLERIES: Washburn Gallery, New York, NY; Leila Taghinia-Milani, New York, NY; Beth Urdang Fine Art, Boston, MA; River Gallery, Irvington-on-Hudson, NY; Gallery at Lincoln Center, New York, NY; Sid Deutsch Gallery, New York, NY

TITLE	PUBLISHER	PRINTER	DATE	MEDIUM	DIMENSION (PAPER SIZE) IN INCHES	TYPE OF PAPER	EDITION NUMBER	NO. OF COLORS	ORIGINAL OPENING PRICE	CURRENT RETAIL PRICE
CURRENT EDITIONS:										
Suite of Four Screenprints	LAI	GJ	1979	SP	22 X 33	R/BFK	225	4 EA	2000 SET	3000 SET
									500 EA	750 EA

The retail prices of the 100,000 limited edition prints quoted in this directory are subject to change. Print publishers, artists and galleries were the direct sources for these quotations. Prices in the secondary market listed as "Sold Out Editions (Rare)" indicate that the publisher has a limited supply of that print or that the print is difficult to locate in the galleries.

CHRISTIAN BOLTANSKI

BORN: Paris, France; 1944
RECENT EXHIB: Shoshana Wayne Gallery, Santa Monica, CA, 1989; The Power Plant, Toronto, Canada, 1989; Marian Goodman Gallery, NY, 1990; Ghislaine Hussenot Galerie, Paris, France, 1991; Lisson Gallery, London, England, 1991; Contemp Arts Mus, Houston, TX, 1992
PRINTERS: Daria Sywaulak, San Francisco, CA (DS); Lothar Osterburg, San Francisco, CA (LO); Crown Point Press, San Francisco, CA (CPP)
PUBLISHERS: Crown Point Press, San Francisco, CA (CPP)
GALLERIES: Crown Point Press, San Francisco, CA & New York, NY; Marian Goodman Gallery, New York, NY; Mattress Factory, Pittsburgh, PA; Fay Gold Gallery, Atlanta, GA; Andrew Dierken Fine Art, Los Angeles, CA; Ghislaine Hussenot Galerie, Paris, France; Lisson Gallery, London, England; Shoshana Wayne Gallery, Santa Monica, CA

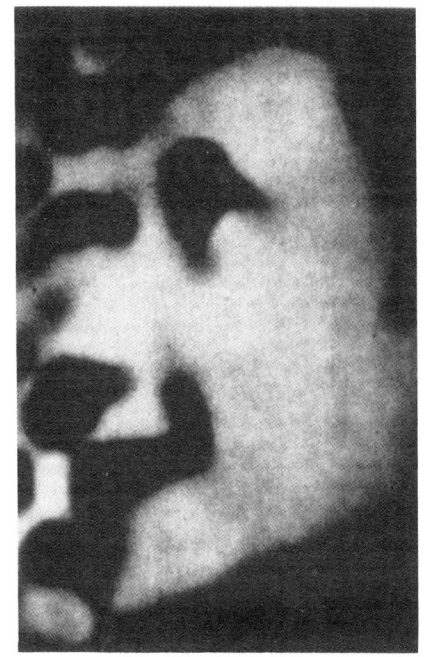

**Christian Boltanski
Gymnasium Chases**
Courtesy Crown Point Press

TITLE	PUBLISHER	PRINTER	DATE	MEDIUM	DIMENSION (PAPER SIZE) IN INCHES	TYPE OF PAPER	EDITION NUMBER	NO. OF COLORS	ORIGINAL OPENING PRICE	CURRENT RETAIL PRICE
CURRENT EDITIONS:										
Gymnasium Chases (Set of 24)	CPP	DS/LO/CPP	1991	PH/G	23 X 17 EA	SOM/S	15 EA	1 EA	18000 SET	18000 SET

PAOLO BONI

BORN: Florence, Italy; 1926
EDUCATION: Liceo Artistico, Florence, Italy
COLLECTIONS: Metropolitan Mus, NY; Mus of Mod Art, NY; Philadelphia Mus of Art, PA; Picasso Mus, Antibes, France; Mus of Modern Art, Paris, France; Yale Univ, New Haven, CT; Biblioteque Nacional, Madrid, Spain; Mus of Haifa, Israel; Princeton Univ, NJ; Balitmore Mus of Art, MD; Albright-Knox Art Gallery; Buffalo, NY; Brooklyn Mus, NY; Mus of Honolulu, Hawaii; Nat Gallery of Art, Wash, DC; Fogg Mus, Harvard Univ, Cambridge, MA; Cleveland Mus of Art, OH; Art Inst of Chicago, IL; Davison Art Center, Middlebury, CT; La Jolla Mus, CA; Mus Cantini, Marseille, France; Mus of Contemp Art, Montreal, Can; Mus of Beaux Arts, Nantes, France; Univ of Oregon, Eugene, OR; Univ of Iowa, Iowa City, IA; Bibliotheque Nat, Paris, France; New York Public Library; Achenbach Foundation, San Francisco, CA; Robert McDougal Art Gallery, Christ Church, New Zealand; Library of Congress, Wash, DC
PRINTERS: Sebastian Pagnier, Paris, France (SP); Morsang (MOR); Chave, Paris, France (CH)
PUBLISHERS: Transworld Art, Inc, NY (TAI); Nahan Editions, Inc, New Orleans, LA (NE)
GALLERIES: Nahan Galleries, New Orleans, LA & New York, NY & Tokyo, Japan

TITLE	PUBLISHER	PRINTER	DATE	MEDIUM	DIMENSION (PAPER SIZE) IN INCHES	TYPE OF PAPER	EDITION NUMBER	NO. OF COLORS	ORIGINAL OPENING PRICE	CURRENT RETAIL PRICE
SOLD OUT EDITIONS (RARE):										
Reve	TAI	SP	1980	GRS	30 X 22	AP	50		225	400
Passage	TAI	SP	1980	GRS	30 X 22	AP	50		225	400
Le Voyant	TAI	SP	1980	GRS	30 X 22	AP	50		225	400
L'Abre de Vie	TAI	SP	1980	GRS	30 X 22	AP	50		225	400
Archipelago	NE	SP	1980	GRS/EB	22 X 29	AP	60		250	550
Letterland	NE	SP	1980	GRS/FR	29 X 22	AP	60		250	500
Silent Valley	NE	SP	1980	GRS/EB	22 X 29	AP	60		250	500
Movement	NE	SP	1980	GRS/EB	29 X 22	AP	60		250	500
Memories	NE	SP	1980	GRS/EB	25 X 36	HMP	50		300	600
Frolic	NE	SP	1980	GRS/EB	36 X 25	HMP	50		300	600
Homage to Music and Composer Series:										
Cantata (Bach)	NE	MOR	1981	GRS/EB	19 X 19	HMP	50		300	650
Cantata (Bach) (Deluxe)	NE	MOR	1981	GRS/EB	19 X 19	HMP	25		350	750
Homage to Wagner	NE	MOR	1981	GRS/EB	19 X 19	HMP	50		300	650
Homage to Wagner (Deluxe)	NE	MOR	1981	GRS/EB	19 X 19	HMP	25		350	750
A Musical Fragment	NE	MOR	1981	GRS/EB	19 X 19	HMP	50		300	700
A Musical Fragment (Deluxe)	NE	MOR	1981	GRS/EB	19 X 19	HMP	25		350	850
Mozart (Deluxe)	NE	MOR	1981	GRS/EB	19 X 19	HMP	25		350	850
Prelude (Ravel (Deluxe)	NE	MOR	1981	GRS/EB	19 X 19	HMP	25		350	850
Chopin	NE	MOR	1981	GRS/EB	19 X 19	HMP	50		300	650
Chopin (Deluxe)	NE	MOR	1981	GRS/EB	19 X 19	HMP	25		350	750
Mozart	NE	MOR	1981	GRS/EB	19 X 19	HMP	50		300	700
Prelude (Ravel)	NE	MOR	1981	GRS/EB	19 X 19	HMP	50		300	700
Third World	NE	CH	1982	LC	23 X 30	AP	150		150	400
Transport	NE	CH	1982	LC	23 X 30	AP	150		150	400

KEIKO BONK

PUBLISHERS: Felix Harlan, NY (FH); Carol Weaver, NY (CW); Artist (ART)
PRINTERS: Felix Harlan, NY (FH); Carol Weaver, NY (CW)

TITLE	PUBLISHER	PRINTER	DATE	MEDIUM	DIMENSION (PAPER SIZE) IN INCHES	TYPE OF PAPER	EDITION NUMBER	NO. OF COLORS	ORIGINAL OPENING PRICE	CURRENT RETAIL PRICE
CURRENT EDITIONS:										
Blind Love	ART/FH/CW	FH/CW	1985	AB/DPT	16 X 25	SOM	50	1	150	200

ALAIN BONNEFOIT

BORN: Paris, France; 1937
EDUCATION: Ecoles des Beaux Arts, Paris, France; Ecole des Beaux Arts, Brussels, Belgium
PRINTERS: American Atelier, NY (AA)

PUBLISHERS: Circle Fine Art, Chicago, IL (CFA)
GALLERIES: Circle Galleries, San Diego, CA & San Francisco, CA & Northbrook, IL & Pittsburgh, PA & Houston, TX & Soho, NY & Chicago, IL & Scottsdale, AZ & Beverly Hills, CA & Costa Mesa, CA & Sherman Oaks, CA & Palm Beach, CA & Honolulu, HI & New Orleans, LA & Seattle, WA; Chetkin Gallery, Red Bank, NJ; New Riverside Gallery, Red Bank, NJ

TITLE	PUBLISHER	PRINTER	DATE	MEDIUM	DIMENSION (PAPER SIZE) IN INCHES	TYPE OF PAPER	EDITION NUMBER	NO. OF COLORS	ORIGINAL OPENING PRICE	CURRENT RETAIL PRICE
SOLD OUT EDITIONS (RARE):										
Nude	CFA	AA	1975	LC	26 X 20	AP	200		100	450
Nude with Yellow Hair	CFA	AA	1978	LC	30 X 21	AP	175		175	450
Response	CFA	AA	1978	LC	27 X 38	AP	250		150	850
Marlena	CFA	AA	1978	LC	38 X 27	AP	250		125	450
Odalisque	CFA	AA	1979	LC	27 X 35	AP	250		125	450
Nude with Red Robe	CFA	AA	1979	LC	38 X 27	AP	250		150	450
Genevieve	CFA	AA	1979	LC	30 X 22	AP	250		150	400
Black Negligee	CFA	AA	1979	LC	30 X 21	AP	250		150	450
Siameese	CFA	AA	1979	LC	22 X 30	AP	250		150	500
Reverie	CFA	AA	1979	LC	25 X 32	AP	250		150	450
CURRENT EDITIONS:										
Melancolie	CFA	AA	1980	LC	30 X 22	AP	250		150	450
Nu Pensif	CFA	AA	1980	LC	34 X 22	AP	250		150	450
Nu Avec Dentelle	CFA	AA	1980	LC	24 X 29	AP	250		150	450

LEE BONTECOU

BORN: Providence, RI; 1931
EDUCATION: Art Students League, NY, 1952–55
AWARDS: Fulbright Fel, Rome, Italy, 1957–58; Tiffany Grant, 1959

PRINTERS: Universal Limited Art Editions, West Islip, NY (ULAE); James V Smith, NY (JS); Thomas Cox, NY (TC)
PUBLISHERS: Universal Limited Art Editions, West Islip, NY (ULAE)
GALLERIES: Texann Ivy Fine Arts, Orlando, FL
MAILING ADDRESS: 147 Wooster St, New York, NY 10012

TITLE	PUBLISHER	PRINTER	DATE	MEDIUM	DIMENSION (PAPER SIZE) IN INCHES	TYPE OF PAPER	EDITION NUMBER	NO. OF COLORS	ORIGINAL OPENING PRICE	CURRENT RETAIL PRICE
CURRENT EDITIONS:										
Untitled (6th Stone II)	ULAE	ULAE	1964	LC	25 X 20	AP	14		300	2500
Untitled	ULAE	ULAE	1964	LC	36 X 44	AP	6		300	3000
12th Stone	ULAE	ULAE	1966–70	LC	21 X 27	AP	21		300	1500
Fifteenth Stone	ULAE	ULAE	1980	LC	22 X 18	AP	19		500	1500

GEORGE WARREN BOOTH

BORN: Omaha, NE; July 6, 1917
EDUCATION: Ohio Univ, Athens, OH, AB, MA, with L C Mitchell; Chouinard Sch of Art, with Pruett Carter; John Huntington Polytech, with Ralf Stoll
TEACHING: Instr, Photog, Ohio Univ, Athens, OH, 1941–42

AWARDS: Gold Medal, Art Director's Club, NY, 1954; Kerwin A. Fulton Medal, Art Director's Club, NY, 1954; Grand Award, Outdoor Advertising Assn of America, NY, 1954
PRINTERS: Judith Solodkin, NY (JS); Solo Press, NY (SP)
PUBLISHERS: Solo Press, NY (SP)
GALLERIES: Beresford Galleries, Potomac, MD; Sporting Gallery, Middleburg, VA
MAILING ADDRESS: 1771 SW 55th Rd, Ocala, FL 32674

TITLE	PUBLISHER	PRINTER	DATE	MEDIUM	DIMENSION (PAPER SIZE) IN INCHES	TYPE OF PAPER	EDITION NUMBER	NO. OF COLORS	ORIGINAL OPENING PRICE	CURRENT RETAIL PRICE
CURRENT EDITIONS:										
Bloomingdale's	SP	JS/SP	1982	LC	18 X 17	SOM	50		150	250
Maw Maw and the Family	SP	JS/SP	1982	LC/HC	20 X 30	SOM	80	Varies	250	350

The retail prices of the 100,000 limited edition prints quoted in this directory are subject to change. Print publishers, artists and galleries were the direct sources for these quotations. Prices in the secondary market listed as "Sold Out Editions (Rare)" indicate that the publisher has a limited supply of that print or that the print is difficult to locate in the galleries.

JONATHAN BOROFSKY

BORN: Boston, MA; 1942
EDUCATION: Carnegie Mellon Univ, Pittsburgh, PA, 1964; Ecole de Fontainbleau, Paris, France, 1964; Yale Sch of Art & Arch, New Haven, CT, 1966
TEACHING: Instr, Sch of Visual Arts, NY, 1969–77; Instr, California Inst of Arts, Valencia, CA, 1977–80
RECENT EXHIB: Nelson-Atkins Mus of Art, Kansas City, MO, 1988; Mus of Mod Art, NY, 1988; Philadelphia Mus of Art, PA, 1988; Milwaukee Art Mus, WI, 1988; Univ of Florida, Gainesville, FL, 1992; Remba Gallery, Santa Monica, CA, 1993; Paula Cooper Gallery, NY, 1988,90,93
PRINTERS: H M Büchi, Basel, Switzerland, Screenprints (HMB); Robert Aull, Los Angeles, CA (RA); Leslie Sutcliffe, Los Angeles, CA, NY (LS); Simca Print Artists, NY (SPA); Artist (ART); James Reid, Los Angeles, CA (JR); Gemini GEL, Los Angeles, CA (GEM)
PUBLISHERS: Gemini GEL, Los Angeles, CA (GEM); Simca Print Artists, NY (SPA) Peter Blum Edition, NY (PBE); Artist (ART)
GALLERIES: Paula Cooper Gallery, New York, NY; Harcus Gallery, Boston, MA; Asher/Faure Gallery, Los Angeles, CA; Leila Taghinia-Milani, New York, NY; Mokotoff Gallery, New York, NY; Gemini GEL, Los Angeles, CA; Gemini GEL at Joni Weyl, New York, NY; Joni Moisant Weyl, Los Angeles, CA; Cynthia Drennon Fine Arts Resources, Los Angeles, CA; Richard Green Gallery, Los Angeles, CA; Ochi Galleries, Boise, ID & Sun Valley, ID; Sylvia Cordish Fine Art, Baltimore, MD; Rembla Gallery/Mixografia Workshop, Santa Monica, CA
MAILING ADDRESS: c/o Paula Cooper Gallery, 155 Wooster St, New York, NY 10012

TITLE	PUBLISHER	PRINTER	DATE	MEDIUM	DIMENSION (PAPER SIZE) IN INCHES	TYPE OF PAPER	EDITION NUMBER	NO. OF COLORS	ORIGINAL OPENING PRICE	CURRENT RETAIL PRICE
SOLD OUT EDITIONS (RARE):										
2,740,475 (Set of 13) (6 Etchings, 7 Screenprints)	PBE	RA/LS/HMB	1982	EC/SP	30 X 22	AP	50		2800 SET	20000 SET
I Dreamed I Was Having My Photograph Taken . . . (with Airbrushed Drawing by Artist)	GEM	GEM	1983	SP	78 X 98	AC	10	Varies	3500	6000
Space Head	GEM	GEM	1983	LB/SP	55 X 31	AC	25		1500	3000
Flying Man with Briefcase No (28169) (Painted Gatorfoam) (Number Changes)	GEM	GEM	1983	MULT	95 X 25 X 1		9		12000	20000
CURRENT EDITIONS:										
Split Head with Hammering Man at 2,688,099	ART	ART	1979–80	LB	30 X 22	AP	18	1	450	2500
Untitled at 2,466,159	ART/SPA	SPA	1976–80	SP	50 X 36	STP	36		950	4000
Molecule Men	GEM	GEM	1982	SP	97 X 80	AP88	24		2500	4500
People Running	GEM	GEM	1982	LB	40 X 76	EXP	30	1	1500	3500
Self Portrait	GEM	GEM	1982	LB	40 X 30	AC	23	1	1000	3500
In Search of the Truth	GEM	GEM	1982	LB	48 X 34	AC	40	1	800	3500
I Dreamed I was Having My Photograph Taken with a Group of People, Suddenly, I Began to Rise Up and Fly Around the Room. Half Way Around, I Tried to Get Out the Door. When I Couldn't Get Out, I Continued to Fly Around the Room Until I Landed and Sat Down Next to My Mother who Said I had Done a Good Job!	GEM	GEM	1983	SP	78 X 98	AC	10	4	2500	5000
Subway Dream (with Programmed Electronic Dimmer/Incandescent Lamp)	GEM	GEM	1983	SP	77 X 64	AC	11	2	1800	4000
Subway Dream	GEM	GEM	1983	SP	77 X 64	AC	9	2	2200	4000
Subway Dream	GEM	GEM	1983	SP	77 X 64	AC	6	2	1700	3000
All is One, All is One (2 Panels)	GEM	GEM	1983	SP	17 X 86 (Top) 14 X 83 (Bottom)	AC	37	5	1700	3500
Molecule Men (Lexan Cut-Out)	GEM	GEM	1983	MULT	87 X 72 X 3/8		15		7000	12000
Molecule Men (1/4 Aluminum, Shot-Peened and Sandblasted)	GEM	GEM	1983	MULT	87 X 70 X 9	ALUM	15		13000	20000
El Salvador Stamp (Screen Printed Aluminum)	GEM	GEM	1983	MULT	60 X 86 X 3/16	ALUM	9		5000	8000
What is Dragging Me	GEM	GEM	1986	SP	31 X 23	AC	100	1	700	2000
Berlin Dream Stamp	GEM	GEM	1986	PH	13 X 20	KOD/RC	100	1	300	2000
Numbered Money (A Sheet of US Currency that has been Encased between 2 Sheets of Plexiglas on which Numbers have been Screened with Green Ink; Should be Installed from the ceiling by Chain so that Work can be Viewed from Both Sides)	GEM	GEM	1986	SP	26 X 22		35	2	900	2000
Male Aggression (Black Version)	GEM	GEM	1986	SP	43 X 46	AC	53	1	1000	2000
Male Aggression (Pink Version)	GEM	GEM	1986	SP	43 X 46	AC	28	1	1000	2000
Male Aggression (Red Version)	GEM	GEM	1986	SP	43 X 46	AC	19	1	1000	2000
Berlin Dream (Black Version) (Red Numbers—Written with Prisma-Color Stick)	GEM	GEM	1986	PH/C	22 X 32	AC	41	1	900	2000

JONATHAN BOROFSKY CONTINUED

TITLE	PUBLISHER	PRINTER	DATE	MEDIUM	DIMENSION (PAPER SIZE) IN INCHES	TYPE OF PAPER	EDITION NUMBER	NO. OF COLORS	ORIGINAL OPENING PRICE	CURRENT RETAIL PRICE
CURRENT EDITIONS:										
Foot Prints (Black, with 3-Dimensional Ink that Puffs Out from the Surface) (Set of 2):										
Right Foot Print	GEM	GEM	1986	SP	69 X 47	AC	35	2	1800	3000
Left Foot Print	GEM	GEM	1986	SP	69 X 47	AC	35	2	1800	3000
Half Foot (Purple)	GEM	GEM	1986	EC	38 X 26	AC	35	1	1200	2000
Berlin Dream with Steel Window Frame (Torch Cut, Rusted Metal Frame Casing)	GEM	GEM	1986	LC	34 X 41	AP88	30	2	2800	3500
Berlin Dream (Closeup) at No_____ (Number Changes with Each Print) (Black—on Mirrored Plexiglas)	GEM	GEM	1986	SP/HC	57 X 77	AP88	8	1	7500	12000
Foot Print in Copper (Photo Etched Copper Plate—weighs 150 lbs—to be placed on Floor—coated for indoor or outdoor Placement)	GEM	GEM	1986		64 X 28	COP	18		6000	12000
I Dreamed I Found a Red Ruby (Red Acrylic Sculpture—Electronic Light & Motor-Revolves in Circular Motion)	GEM	GEM	1986	MULT	23 X 23 X 23		35		6000	8500
Berlin Dream Lamp (Printed on Mylar—Electrical Light Fixture) (Black)	GEM	GEM	1986	MULT	24 X 8		25		3500	5500
Dancing Clown at No—(Number Changes with Each Unique Work) (Series of 30)	GEM	GEM	1986	SP/CO/HC	94 X 65 EA		1 EA	Varies	9000 EA	15000 EA
Flowers at No 2984220 (G-1279) (Series of 73)	GEM	GEM	1986	SP	47 X 39 EA	AC			3000 EA	10500 EA
Art is for the Spirt	GEM	SB/JR/GEM	1989	SP	47 X 38	AC	85		2500	4500
Art is for the Spirit, State I	GEM	SB/JR/GEM	1989	SP	47 X 38	AC	50		2500	4500
I Dreamed I Could Fly at No_____ (Maroon)	GEM	SB/JR/GEM	1989	LC	50 X 40	AC	20	1	2000	3500
I Dreamed I Could Fly at No_____ (Green)	GEM	SB/JR/GEM	1989	LC	50 X 40	AC	20	1	2000	3500
I Dreamed I Could Fly at No_____ (Orange)	GEM	SB/JR/GEM	1989	LC	50 X 40	AC	20	1	2000	3500
I Dreamed I Could Fly at No_____ (Blue)	GEM	SB/JR/GEM	1989	LC	50 X 40	AC	20	1	2000	3500
I Dreamed I Could Fly at No_____ (Yellow)	GEM	SB/JR/GEM	1989	LC	50 X 40	AC	20	1	2000	3500
Picasso Dream	GEM	SB/JR/GEM	1989	LC/SP	54 X 35	AC	25		1200	1800
Cross Head	GEM	SB/JR/GEM	1990	SP/EB	52 X 40	R/BFK	25		1200	2000
White Horse (With Gold Leaf)	GEM	SB/JR/GEM	1990	LC	38 X 32	AC	35		800	1500
Picasso Dream Fractured (Framed) (5 Sheets)	GEM	SB/JR/GEM	1991	LC/SP	56 X 40	AC/B	35		2000	2500

MARSHALL BORRIS

BORN: New York, NY; 1946
EDUCATION: Univ of Toledo, OH; California Col of Arts and Crafts, Valencia, CA
TEACHING: Stamford Mus, CT; California Col of Arts and Crafts, Valencia, CA
COLLECTIONS: Stamford Mus, CT; New Mus of Mod Art, Oakland, CA; Toledo Mus of Art, OH; Igor Mead Gallery, San Francisco, CA
PRINTERS: Artist (ART)
PUBLISHERS: Fred Dorfman Gallery, Inc, NY (FDI)
GALLERIES: Fred Dorfman Gallery, New York, NY

TITLE	PUBLISHER	PRINTER	DATE	MEDIUM	DIMENSION (PAPER SIZE) IN INCHES	TYPE OF PAPER	EDITION NUMBER	NO. OF COLORS	ORIGINAL OPENING PRICE	CURRENT RETAIL PRICE
CURRENT EDITIONS:										
Dos Equis	FDI	ART	1979	LC	24 X 34	AP	275	3	125	300
Ha Ha	FDI	ART	1979	LC	21 X 28	AP	275	2	125	300

RICHARD BOSMAN

BORN: Madras, India; 1944
EDUCATION: Byam Shaw Sch of Painting & Drawing, London, England, 1964–69; New York Studio Sch, NY, 1969–71; Skowhegan Sch of Painting & Sculpture, ME, 1970
TEACHING: Instr, New York Studio Sch, NY, 1972; Skowhegan Sch of Painting & Sculpture, ME, 1982; Sch of Visual Arts, NY, 1982–84
RECENT EXHIB: Diane Villani Editions, NY, 1990; John Berggruen Gallery, San Francisco, CA, 1990; Brooke Alexander, Inc, NY, 1990; Patrick & Beatrice Haggerty Mus of Art, Milwaukee, WI, 1990; Cleveland Center for Contemp Art, OH, 1992

RICHARD BOSMAN CONTINUED

COLLECTIONS: Albright-Knox Art Gallery, Buffalo, NY; ARCO Center for the Visual Art, Los Angeles, CA; Australian Nat Gallery, Canberra, Australia; Brooklyn Mus, NY; Fogg Art Mus, Harvard Univ, Cambridge, MA; Metropolitan Mus of Art, NY; Lannan Found, Palm Beach, FL; Mus of Mod Art, NY; Nat Mus of Am Art, Wash, DC; Philadelphia Mus of Art, PA; Toledo Mus of Fine Art, OH; Weatherspoon Art Gallery, Univ of North Carolina, Greensboro, NC; Yale Univ, New Haven, CT
PRINTERS: Experimental Workshop, San Francisco, CA (EW); John Stemmer (JS); Wilbert Foo (WF); X Press, NY (XP); Alan Koslin (AK); Chip Elwell, NY (CE); Ted Warner, NY (TW); Chris Erickson, Aspen, CO (CE); Anderson Ranch, Aspen, CO (AR); Maurice Sanchez, NY (MS); Lucy Gray, NY (LG); Joe Petruzelli, NY (JP); James Miller, NY (JM); Derriére L'Etoile Studio, NY (DES); Joe Wilfer, NY (JW); Ruth Lingen, NY (RL); Spring Street Workshop, NY (SSW); Patricia Branstead, NY (PB); Branstead Studios, NY (BS); Bill Weege, Madison, WI (BW); Andrew Rubin, Madison, WI (AR); Tandem Press, Univ of Wisconsin, Madison, WI (TanPr); Aldo Crommelynck, NY (AC); Atelier Crommelynck, NY (AtC)
PUBLISHERS: Brooke Alexander, Inc, NY (BAI); Experimental Workshop, San Francisco, CA (EW); Anderson Ranch, Aspen, CO (AR); Spring Street Workshop, NY (SSW); Diane Villani Editions, NY (DVE); Art Issue Editions, Inc, NY (AIE); Artist (ART); Derriére L'Etoile Studios, NY (DES); Hartford Art Sch, CT (HAS); Aldo Crommelynck, NY (AC); Tandem Press, Univ of Wisconsin, Madison, WI (TanPr); Riverhouse Editions, Clark, CO (REd); Olive Press, NY (OPr)
GALLERIES: Brooke Alexander, Inc, New York, NY; Dart Gallery, Chicago, IL; Fay Gold Gallery, Atlanta, GA; Signet Arts, St Louis, MO; Associated American Artists, New York, NY; Asher/Faure Gallery, Los Angeles, CA; Montenay del Sol, Paris, France; John Berggruen Gallery, San Francisco, CA; Pace Prints, New York, NY; Diane Villani Editions, New York, NY; Arion Press, San Francisco, CA; Flanders Graphics, Minneapolis, MN; Betsy Senior Contemporary Prints, New York, NY; Experimental Workshop, San Francisco, CA; Dean Jensen Gallery, Milwaukee, WI; Signet Arts, St Louis, MO; Van Straaten Gallery, Chicago, IL
MAILING ADDRESS: 285 Hudson St, New York, NY 10013

Richard Bosman
Bullrider
Courtesy Van Straaten Gallery

TITLE	PUBLISHER	PRINTER	DATE	MEDIUM	DIMENSION (PAPER SIZE) IN INCHES	TYPE OF PAPER	EDITION NUMBER	NO. OF COLORS	ORIGINAL OPENING PRICE	CURRENT RETAIL PRICE
SOLD OUT EDITIONS (RARE):										
Mutiny	BAI	CE	1980-81	WC	19 X 25	JEP	36		300	4500
Man Overboard	BAI	CE	1981	WC	27 X 17	JEP	8		300	4500
Man Overboard	BAI	CE	1981	WB	28 X 19	JEP	17	1	250	3500
Polar Bear	BAI	CE	1981	WC	30 X 26	JEP	14		300	4000
Suicide	BAI	CE	1981	WC	13 X 28	JEP	42		250	2500
South Seas Kiss	BAI	CE	1981	WC	16 X 25	JEP	31	21	300	3500
Drowning Man	BAI	CE	1981	WC	48 X 30	JEP	47		750	5000
Drowning Man, State II	BAI	CE	1981	WC	48 X 30	OKP	30	13	750	5000
South Seas Kiss	BAI	CE	1981	WB	20 X 24	JEP	17	1	200	1800
Car Crash (Color State)	BAI	CE	1981-82	WC	37 X 50	JEP	60		750	1500
Car Crash (Gray State)	BAI	CE	1981-82	WC	35 X 48	JEP	60		750	1500
Lobster Pot	BAI	CE	1982	WC	14 X 13	SEK	10		350	1500
Spider	BAI	CE	1982	WC	17 X 13	SEK	10		350	1500
The Fight	BAI	CE	1982	WC	28 X 51	SEK	36	1	600	1500
Leap	BAI	CE	1982	WC	33 X 17	DD/DPA	35	2	350	900
Adversaries	BAI	CE/TW	1982	WB	30 X 20	RAG	42	1	500	4500
Survivor	BAI	CE/TW	1983	WC	38 X 26	KOZO	10	2	650	4500
Revenge of the Cat (Diptych)	BAI	AK/XP	1983	EB/SL	31 X 44	THS	40	1	600	1500
Forced Entry	BAI	AK/XP	1983	EB/SL	28 X 20	B/HMP	20	1	300	900
Attacker	BAI	CE	1983	WC	33 X 30	HANGA	48	7	650	1500
Double Trouble	BAI	CE	1983	WB	29 X 35	HANGA	43	1	600	2500
Nightmare (with Acrylic)	BAI	CE	1983	EB/SG/HC	23 X 30	HANGA	20	Varies	350	900
Life Raft	BAI	CE	1983-84	EC	22 X 30	HANGA	40		750	2000
Adrift	BAI	CE	1984	PO	27 X 22	HANGA	25		900	1800
Ashore	BAI	CE	1984	PO	27 X 22	HANGA	25		900	1800
The Rescue	EW	JS/WF/EW	1984	WC	38 X 50	R/BFK	49	8	1500	4500
Night Visitor	EW	JS/WF/EW	1984	WC	25 X 25	R/LIN	42	1	600	2500
Falling Man	EW	JS/WF/EW	1984	WB	61 X 42	HIR	32	1	1000	3500
Falling Man	EW	JS/WF/EW	1984	WC	61 X 42	HIR	32	4	1500	4000
Meteorman	ART/AR	CE/AR	1985	LB	34 X 25	MUL	28	1	750	2500
Full Moon	EW	WF/JS/EW	1986	WC	35 X 46	R/BFK	35	3	1800	3500
The Wave	EW	WF/JS/EW	1987	WC	30 X 38	R/BFK	35	10	1800	3500
CURRENT EDITIONS:										
Thou Shalt Not Covet Thy Neighbor's Goods (from Ten Commandments Suite)	AIE	MS/DES	1987	LC	24 X 19	DIEU	84	5	500	1200

RICHARD BOSMAN CONTINUED

Richard Bosman
Ocean Breeze
Courtesy Van Straaten Gallery

Richard Bosman
The Cast
Courtesy Van Straaten Gallery

TITLE	PUBLISHER	PRINTER	DATE	MEDIUM	DIMENSION (PAPER SIZE) IN INCHES	TYPE OF PAPER	EDITION NUMBER	NO. OF COLORS	ORIGINAL OPENING PRICE	CURRENT RETAIL PRICE
CURRENT EDITIONS:										
White Caps	BAI/SSW	JW/RL/SSW	1987	WC	24 X 33	KOZO	36	3	500	1200
Untitled (Study for Estuary)	DVE		1987	WC	16 X 23	KOZO	25		500	1500
Estuary	DVE		1987	WC	42 X 38	SUK	35		1500	3500
Rapids	DVE		1987	WC	42 X 38	SUK	35		1500	3000
Buried at Sea	SSW	SSW	1987	LI	23 X 30	SUK	35	1	500	900
Sunset	SSW	SSW	1987	LI	34 X 26	SUK	40	1	600	3000
Adrift I	AC	AC/AtC	1988	SG/SB	24 X 29	SUK	50	1	800	1000
Adrift II	AC	AC/AtC	1988	SB	24 X 29	SUK	50	1	800	1000
Poison	DVE		1988	WC	18 X 12	SUK	50		500	1200
Fog Bank	AC	BW/AR/AC/AtC	1988	SB/AB	31 X 23	SUK	50	1	800	1000
Awash	TanPr	BW/AR/TanPr	1988	WC/PO	37 X 23	KOZO	30		1500	1750
Flood	TanPr	BW/AR/TanPr	1988	WC	18 X 25	TAB	18		1800	2000
Volcano	BAI	BW/AR/AC/AtC	1989	WC	44 X 30	SUK	45		1500	2500
Whirlabout	TanPr	TanPr	1989	SP	27 X 17	MASA	46	7	900	900
Lightning	ART/DES/HAS	MS/LG/JP/JM/DES	1990	LC	47 X 31	R/BFK	34	2	1500	1800
Moonrise	ART/DES/HAS	MS/LG/JP/JM/DES	1990	LC	31 X 35	R/BFK	40	2	1250	1500
Moonlight, State II	ART/DES/HAS	MS/LG/JP/JM/DES	1990	LC	31 X 35	R/BFK	10	2	2000	2200
Homeward Bound	DVE	PB/BS	1990	EC	25 X 25	SOM	30		1000	1200
Night Sky	DVE	PB/BS	1990	EC	44 X 30	SOM	35		1800	2000
High Tide/Low Tide	EW	WF/JS/EW	1990	WC	43 X 32	SOM	40	7	1800	2500
Maelstrom	TanPr	TanPr	1990	WC	41 X 27	SUZ	30	2	2000	2000
Jetty	BAI	PB/BS	1991	WC	22 X 54	R/BFK	45		2000	2000
Nightscape	BAI	PB/BS/BW/AR	1992	EC	25 X 55	R/BFK	41	3	2000	2000
Night Light	TanPr	BW/AR/TanPr	1992	EC	18 X 32	AC/W	40	5	1250	1250
Canis Major/Minor	TanPr	BW/AR/TanPr	1992	EC	26 X 15	AC/W	40	2	750	750
Night Lace	TanPr	BW/AR/TanPr	1992	EC/CAR	27 X 19	AC/W	40	2	1250	1250
Water Towers	SSW	SSW	1992	WC	25 X 32	AC/W	30		1000	1000
Night Haul	SSW/OPr	SSW	1992	WC	25 X 34	AC/W	35		1200	1200

RICHARD BOSMAN CONTINUED

TITLE	PUBLISHER	PRINTER	DATE	MEDIUM	DIMENSION (PAPER SIZE) IN INCHES	TYPE OF PAPER	EDITION NUMBER	NO. OF COLORS	ORIGINAL OPENING PRICE	CURRENT RETAIL PRICE
CURRENT EDITIONS:										
Bullrider	REd	REd	1992	EC	28 X 23		20		950	950
Moonrise	REd	REd	1992	EC	28 X 23		20		950	950
Sunset	REd	REd	1992	EC	28 X 23		20		950	950
The Cast	REd	REd	1992	EC	28 X 23		35		1200	1200

Richard Bosman
Winter
Courtesy Van Straaten Gallery

ANGEL BOTELLO

BORN: Spain; (1913–1986)
EDUCATION: Academia San Fernando, Madrid, Spain; Ecole des Beaux Arts, Paris, France
RECENT EXHIB: Hokin Gallery, Palm Beach, FL, 1987
COLLECTIONS: George Washington Univ, Wash, DC; Kennedy Art Center, Wash, DC; Hakone Art Mus, Japan; Fresno Art Inst, CA;
PRINTERS: Jobin Grapholith, Paris, France (JG)
PUBLISHERS: Nahan Editions, New Orleans, LA (NE); Artist (ART)
GALLERIES: Galeria Botello I, San Juan, PR; Galeria Botello II, Hato Rey, PR; Hokin Galleries, Palm Beach, FL & Bay Harbor Islands, FL; Nahan Editions, New York, NY & & New Orleans, LA & Tokyo, Japan; Daruma Gallery, Cedarhurst, NY; Landsman Gallery, Magnolia, NJ
MAILING ADDRESS: c/o Galeria Botello, 208 Cristo St, San Juan, PR 00901

TITLE	PUBLISHER	PRINTER	DATE	MEDIUM	DIMENSION (PAPER SIZE) IN INCHES	TYPE OF PAPER	EDITION NUMBER	NO. OF COLORS	ORIGINAL OPENING PRICE	CURRENT RETAIL PRICE
SOLD OUT EDITIONS (RARE):										
Small Girl with Flowers	ART	JG	1980	LI	20 X 26	AP	100		225	1000
Maternidad	ART	JG	1980	LI	17 X 24	AP	100		550	1500
Mother and Child	ART	JG	1980	LI	20 X 25	AP	50		675	2500
Mother and Daughter I	ART	JG	1980	LI	20 X 26	AP	50		550	2000
Mother and Daughter II	ART	JG	1980	LI	24 X 31	AP	50		675	2500
Girl Combing Hair	ART	JG	1980	LI	20 X 35	AP	100		450	2000
Children with Balloons	ART	JG	1980	LI	26 X 30	AP	100		775	3000
Girl with Flowers	ART	JG	1980	LI	26 X 35	AP	50		775	3000
Young Boy	ART	JG	1980	LI	18 X 22	AP	50		350	1500
Young Girl	ART	JG	1980	LI	18 X 22	AP	50		275	1000
Anne Frank	ART	JG	1980	LI	16 X 24	AP	50		300	1200
Roscandose la Oreja	ART	JG	1980	LI	15 X 21	AP	50		300	1200
The Wink	ART	JG	1980	LI	20 X 26	AP	100		550	2000
Reading	ART	JG	1980	LI	31 X 28	AP	100		675	2500
Soledad	ART	JG	1980	LI	20 X 28	AP	50		225	900
Tirando la Cola	ART	JG	1980	LI	28 X 20	AP	100		225	900
Alimentando la Vaca	ART	JG	1980	LI	28 X 20	AP	100		225	900
Seated Girl	ART	JG	1980	LI	25 X 32	AP	100		350	1500
Family II	ART	JG	1980	LI	22 X 29	AP	50		550	2000
Three Girls	ART	JG	1980	LI	27 X 30	AP	50		775	3000
Girl with a Dream	NE	JG	1980	LC	24 X 36	AP	150	13	275	1000
Girl with Little Bird	NE	JG	1980	LC	13 X 24	AP	150	14	275	1000
Girl with Flowers	NE	JG	1980	LC	21 X 30	AP	150		250	1000
Girl Playing Violin	NE	JG	1980	LC	17 X 23	AP	150		250	1000

ANGEL BOTELLO CONTINUED

TITLE	PUBLISHER	PRINTER	DATE	MEDIUM	DIMENSION (PAPER SIZE) IN INCHES	TYPE OF PAPER	EDITION NUMBER	NO. OF COLORS	ORIGINAL OPENING PRICE	CURRENT RETAIL PRICE
CURRENT EDITIONS:										
Girl Playing Piano	NE	JG	1980	LC	17 X 23	AP	150		250	1000
Checker Game	NE	JG	1980	LC	21 X 30	AP	150		250	1000

FERNANDO BOTERO

BORN: Medellin, Colombia; 1932
EDUCATION: Acad San Fernando, Spain, 1953; Prado Mus, Madrid, Spain, 1954; Mus of Florence, Italy, Art History with Robert Longhi
RECENT EXHIB: Marlborough Gallery, NY, 1990; Found Pierre Gianadda, Martigny, Switzerland, 1990; Galeria El Museo, Bogata, Colombia, 1992
COLLECTIONS: Mud d'Arte Mod del Vatican, Rome, Italy; Mus de Arte Contemp, Madrid, Spain, Mus de Arte Mod, Bogata, Colombia; Mus of Mod Art, NY; Guggenheim Mus, NY; Atheneum Taidemuseo, Helsinki, Finland; Museo de Bellas Artes, Caracas, Venezuela; Smithsonian Inst, Wash, DC; Metropolitan Mus of Art, NY
PUBLISHERS: Editions de la Différence, Paris, France (EdD)
GALLERIES: Marlborough Gallery, New York, NY; Ianuzzi Gallery, Scottsdale, AZ; Andrew Dierken Fine Art, Los Angeles, CA; R K Goldman & Co, Los Angeles, CA; Jonathan Novak Fine Art, Los Angeles,CA; George Belcher Gallery, San Francisco, CA; Hokin Gallery, Bay Harbor Islands, FL & Palm Beach, FL; Gary Nader Fine Arts, Coconut Grove, FL; Marta Gutierrez Fine Arts, Key Biscayne, FL; Claude Bernard Gallery, New York, NY; James Goodman Gallery, New York, NY; Nohra Haime Gallery, New York, NY; Lillian Heidenberg Gallery, New York, NY; Mary-Anne Martin Fine Art, New York, NY; Posner Gallery, Milwaukee, WI; Irving Galleries, Palm Beach, FL; Phyllis Needlman Gallery, Chicago, IL; Stein Bartlow Gallery, Ltd, Chicago, IL; Elkan Gallery, Inc, New York, NY; Pat Kery Fine Art, New York, NY; Weintraub Gallery, New York, NY; De Ville Galleries, Los Angeles, CA; Freites-Revilla Gallery, Boca Raton, FL; Magidson Fine Art, Inc, Aspen, CO; Richard Arregui Fine Art, Coral Gables, FL; Professional Fine Arts Services, Inc, New York, NY
MAILING ADDRESS: c/o Marlborough Fine Arts, 40 W 57th St, New York, NY 10019

TITLE	PUBLISHER	PRINTER	DATE	MEDIUM	DIMENSION (PAPER SIZE) IN INCHES	TYPE OF PAPER	EDITION NUMBER	NO. OF COLORS	ORIGINAL OPENING PRICE	CURRENT RETAIL PRICE
CURRENT EDITIONS:										
Woman	EdD		1984	LC	16 X 13	AP	226		1800	8000
Mujer Ante El Espejo	EdD		1985	LC	16 X 13	AP	150		2200	10000
Mujer Fumando	EdD		1985	LC	16 X 13	AP	150		2200	10000

ITALO BOTTI

BORN: New York, NY; 1923
EDUCATION: Brooklyn Acad of Fine Art; Leonardi Da Vinci Sch of Art, Italy, Art Students League, NY
TEACHING: Art Students League, NY; City Col of New York, NY; Sch of the Art Inst of Chicago, IL
RECENT EXHIB: Grove Street Galleries, Evanston, IL, 1989
PRINTERS: American Atelier, NY (AA)
PUBLISHERS: Circle Fine Art, Chicago, IL (CFA)
GALLERIES: Grove Street Galleries, Evanston, IL; Brubaker Gallery, Sarasota, FL; Circle Galleries, San Diego, CA & San Francisco, CA & Northbrook, IL & Pittsburgh, PA & Houston, TX & Soho, NY & Chicago, IL & Scottsdale, AZ & Beverly Hills, CA & Costa Mesa, CA & Sherman Oaks, CA & Palm Beach FL & Honolulu, HI & Chicago, IL & New Orleans, LA & Las Vegas, NV & Seattle, WA

TITLE	PUBLISHER	PRINTER	DATE	MEDIUM	DIMENSION (PAPER SIZE) IN INCHES	TYPE OF PAPER	EDITION NUMBER	NO. OF COLORS	ORIGINAL OPENING PRICE	CURRENT RETAIL PRICE
SOLD OUT EDITIONS (RARE):										
Summer Day in the Park	CFA	AA	1978	SP	34 X 34	AP	300		150	500
Sails and Sand	CFA	AA	1978	SP	34 X 34	AP	300		150	500
Spring Bouquet	CFA	AA	1978	SP	36 X 36	AP	300		150	500
Sunlit Sails	CFA	AA	1978	SP	30 X 42	AP	300		150	550

JOSEPH BOWLER, JR

BORN: Forest Hills, NY; September 4, 1928
EDUCATION: Charles E Cooper Studios, NY; Art Students League, NY
TEACHING: Instr, Painting, Parsons Sch of Design, NY, 1968–72; Instr, Syracuse Univ, NY, 1980 to present
AWARDS: Artist of the Year, Artists Guild, NY, 1967
COLLECTIONS: Hartford Mus, CT
PRINTERS: American Atelier, NY (AA)
PUBLISHERS: Circle Fine Art, Chicago, IL (CFA)
GALLERIES: Circle Galleries, San Diego, CA & San Francisco, CA & Northbrook, IL & Pittsburgh, PA & Houston, TX & Soho, NY & Chicago, IL & Scottsdale, AZ & Beverly Hills, CA & Costa Mesa, CA & Sherman Oaks, CA & Palm Beach, FL & Honolulu, HI & New Orleans, LA & Las Vegas, NV & Seattle, WA
MAILING ADDRESS: 9 Baynard Cove Rd, Hilton Head Island, SC 29928

TITLE	PUBLISHER	PRINTER	DATE	MEDIUM	DIMENSION (PAPER SIZE) IN INCHES	TYPE OF PAPER	EDITION NUMBER	NO. OF COLORS	ORIGINAL OPENING PRICE	CURRENT RETAIL PRICE
SOLD OUT EDITIONS (RARE):										
Girl with Flowers	CFA	AA	1976	LC	26 X 20		250		50	150
Nude	CFA	AA	1976	EC	30 X 22		150		75	175
CURRENT EDITIONS:										
Two Girls	CFA	AA	1978	LC	25 X 18		250		50	150
Girl with Mirror	CFA	AA	1978	LC	28 X 19		300		50	150

GRACIELA RODO BOULANGER

BORN: La Paz, Bolivia; 1935
EDUCATION: Sch of Fine Arts, La Paz, Bolivia; Santiago, Chili, Atelier Friedlaender, Paris, France
AWARDS: UN International Peace Medal, 1980
COLLECTIONS: Mus of Mod Art, La Paz, Bolivia; Mod Art Center, Zurich, Switzerland; Gallery H, Buenos Aires, Argentina; United Nations General Assembly, NY
PRINTERS: Atelier Desjobert, Paris, France (AD); Imprimerie Capelle, Paris, France (IC); Atelier Robert, Paris, France (AR); Arts Litho, Paris, France (AL); Atelier LeBlanc, Paris, France (ALB); Imprimerie Matthieu, Paris, France (IM); Imprimerie Michael Bon, Paris, France (IMB); Atelier Mourlot, Paris, France (AM); Atelier Martinez, Paris, France (AMa); Artist (ART)
PUBLISHERS: Lublin Graphics, Greenwich, CT (LG); Transworld Art Inc, NY (TAI); Orangerie Publishing, Paris, France (OP)
GALLERIES: Brewster Gallery, New York, NY; Fernette's Gallery of Art, Des Moines, IA; Centurion Galleries, Chicago, IL; Petrini Art Gallery, Rocky Hill, CT; Art Gallery, Studio 53, New York, NY; Rolly-Michaux Gallery, Boston, MA; Argus Fine Arts, Eugene, OR; Tribeca Gallery, New York, NY

Graciela Rodo Boulanger
Fille a Cheval
Courtesy the Artist

TITLE	PUBLISHER	PRINTER	DATE	MEDIUM	DIMENSION (PAPER SIZE) IN INCHES	TYPE OF PAPER	EDITION NUMBER	NO. OF COLORS	ORIGINAL OPENING PRICE	CURRENT RETAIL PRICE
SOLD OUT EDITIONS (RARE):										
La Course	OP		1971	EC	66 X 49 cm	AP	100		300	1500
Fille a Cheval	OP		1971	EC	49 X 64 cm	AP	100		300	1500
Hide and Seek	LG	AR	1972	EC	19 X 26	AP	105	14	160	2000
Le Zebre	LG	AR	1973	EC	19 X 26	AP	105	15	80	1500
To Each His Own	LG	AL	1979	LC	17 X 27	AP/JP	150/150	16	400	1800
CURRENT EDITIONS:										
Un Chat pour Deux	LG	ALB	1972	EC	26 X 20	AP/JP	100/30		250	1600
Couple a L'Oiseau	LG	ALB	1972	EC	26 X 20	AP/JP	100/30		150	1500
Petits Musiciens Suite	LG	ALB	1972	EC	26 X 20 EA	AP/JP	100/30		800 SET	8700 SET
L'Oranger	LG	ALB	1972	EC	26 X 20	AP/JP	100/30		200	1950
La Jongleuse	LG	ALB	1972	EC	26 X 20	AP/JP	100/30		100	1800
Fillette au Velo	LG	ALB	1972	EC	26 X 20	AP/JP	100/30		200	1700
Enfant au Ballon	LG	ALB	1972	EC	26 X 20	AP/JP	100/30		100	1500
Les Enfants Endormis	LG	ALB	1972	EC	26 X 20	AP/JP	100/30		200	1950
Le Chat Blanc	LG	ALB	1972	EC	26 X 20	AP/JP	100/30		180	1850
Les Violoncellistes	LG	ALB	1972	EC	26 X 20	AP/JP	100/30		275	2000
La Vache Orange	LG	ALB	1972	EC	26 X 20	AP/JP	100/30		275	1850
Cercle de Jeu	LG	ALB	1973	EC	26 X 20	AP/JP	100/30		275	1500
Promenade en Bicyclette	LG	ALB	1974	EC	26 X 20	AP/JP	100/30		300	2100
Exercises	LG	ALB	1974	EC	26 X 20	AP/JP	100/30		300	1850
Petit Chef d'Orchestre	LG	ALB	1972	EC	26 X 20	AP/JP	100/30		120	1500
Joueurs de Ballon	LG	IC	1975	EC	26 X 20	AP/JP	100/150		275	1500
Enfant Revant	LG	IC	1975	EC	26 X 20	AP/JP	100/150		500	2100
Enfant et Chevre	LG	IC	1975	EC	26 X 20	AP/JP	100/150		500	2150
Le Chat	LG	IC	1975	EC	26 X 20	AP/JP	100/150		500	2500
L'Oiseau Indifferent	LG	IC	1975	EC	26 X 20	AP/JP	100/150		500	2500
Rencontre a Chaval	LG	IC	1975	EC		AP/JP	100/50		500	2400
Sur le Toro	LG	IC	1975	EC	25 X 32	AP/JP	100/50		500	2400
Le Boeuf Tranquille	LG	IC	1975	LC	25 X 32	AP/JP	100/50		500	2500
Le Dimanche Main	TAI	AM	1976	EC	26 X 20	AP	175	7	450	1000
Orchestra	LG	IM	1976	LC	26 X 20	AP/JP	200/100		350	2000
Tambours et Trompettes	LG	IM	1976	LC	25 X 32 cm	AP/JP	200/100		350	2200
Tennis	LG	IM	1976	LC	25 X 32 cm	AP/JP	200/100		350	2200
Corde a Sauter	LG	IMB	1977	EC	25 X 32 cm	AP/JP	200/100		500	2200
Boid de Vincennes	LG	IMB	1977	EC	26 X 20	AP/JP	200/100		500	2400
Balancelles	LG	IMB	1977	EC	26 X 20	AP/JP	200/100		500	2000
Jardin du Luxembourg	LG	IC	1977	EC	26 X 20	AP/JP	200/100		500	2000
Zodiac Suite (Set of 13)	OP			MM	76 X 57 cm EA	AP	200 EA		1800 SET	10000 SET
Trapezes	LG	IC	1977	EC	26 X 20	AP/JP	150/50		500	2400
Julieta au Zoo	LG	IC	1977	EC	26 X 20	AP/JP	150/50		500	2500
Los Domingos de Julieta I	LG	IC	1977	EC	26 X 20	AP/JP			3000	15500
Seule a Venise	LG	IMB	1977	EC	26 X 20	AP/JP	150/50		500	2400
Le Trio de Juliette	LG	IMB	1977	EC	26 X 20	AP/JP	150/50		500	2500
Tennis Court	LG	IMB	1977	EC	26 X 20	AP/JP	150/50		500	3000
Le Ceri-Volant	LG	IC	1977	EC	26 X 20	AP/JP	150/50		500	2500

GRACIELA RODO BOULANGER CONTINUED

TITLE	PUBLISHER	PRINTER	DATE	MEDIUM	DIMENSION (PAPER SIZE) IN INCHES	TYPE OF PAPER	EDITION NUMBER	NO. OF COLORS	ORIGINAL OPENING PRICE	CURRENT RETAIL PRICE
CURRENT EDITIONS:										
En Attendant Juliette	LG	IC	1977	EC	26 X 20	AP/JP	150/50		500	2500
Ballon et Soleil	LG	IC	1977	EC	26 X 20	AP/JP	150/50		500	2500
Los Domingos de Julietta II	LG	AD	1977	EC	26 X 20	AP/JP	150/50		3200	17500
Deux Personnages	LG	AD	1977	LC	13 X 9	AP/JP	200/100		160	800
Taureau	LG	AD	1977	LC	13 X 9	AP/JP	200/100		160	800
Festival	LG	AD	1977	LC	26 X 20	AP/JP	200/100		300	1500
Balancoire	LG	AD	1978	LC	26 X 20	AP/JP	200/100		300	1200
Boy on Bull	LG	AD	1978	LC	13 X 9	AP/JP	200/100		400	800
Girl on Bull	LG	AD	1978	LC	13 X 9	AP/JP	200/100		400	800
Droleries	LG	AL	1978	LC	26 X 20	AP/JP	200/100		600	1500
Rigolo	LG	AL	1978	LC	26 X 20	AP/JP	200/100		600	1500
Les Inseperables	LG	AL	1978	LC	26 X 20	AP/JP	200/100		600	1500
Droles de Zebres (Trip)	LG	AL	1978	LC	26 X 20	AP/JP			1200	4500
The Year of the Child	LG	AL	1979	LC	26 X 20	AP/JP	200/100		350	1500
De Branche en Branche	LG	AD	1979	LC	26 X 20	AP/JP	200/100		350	1500
Un Elephant pour Kris	LG	AL	1979	LC	26 X 20	AP/JP	200/100		450	2000
Un Papillon pour Aniko	LG	AL	1979	LC	26 X 20	AP/JP	200/100		600	1500
Un Koala pour Sandra	LG	AL	1979	LC	26 X 20	AP/JP	200/100		600	1500
Un Coq pour Tatiana	LG	AL	1979	LC	26 X 20	AP/JP	200/100		600	1350
Un Paon pour Sophie	LG	AL	1979	LC	26 X 20	AP/JP	200/100		600	1500
Un Puma pour Josquin & Matthieu	LG	AL	1979	LC	26 X 20	AP/JP	200/100		600	1500
Un pour Chacun	LG	AL	1979	LC	26 X 20	AP/JP	200/100		600	1300
Chacun le Sien Suite	LG	AL	1979	LC	26 X 20 EA	AP/JP	200/100		5000 SET	10650 SET
Jump Rope	LG	AD	1980	LC	26 X 20	AP/JP		15	650	1200
Hopscotch	LG	AD	1980	LC	26 X 20	AP/JP	200/100		650	1100
Jeu de Ballon	LG	AD	1980	LC	26 X 20	AP/JP	200/100	14	800	1100
La Pousette	LG	AD	1980	LC	26 X 20	AP/JP	200/100	14	800	1100
Promenade en Bicyclette	LG	AD	1980	LC	26 X 20	AP/JP	200/100	16	1500	2500
Trois Chevaux	LG	AD	1980	LC	25 X 32 cm	AP/JP	200/100	15	950	1500
Trois Girafes	LG	AD	1980	LC	25 X 32 cm	AP/JP			950	2000
Trois Rhinoceros	LG	AD	1980	LC	25 X 32 cm	AP/JP	200/100	16	950	2000
Trois Cheameaux	LG	AD	1980	LC	25 X 32 cm	AP/JP	200/100	15	950	1500
Trois Elephants	LG	AD	1980	LC	25 X 32 cm	AP/JP	200/100		950	2000
Trois Vaches	LG	AD	1980	LC	25 X 32 cm	AP/JP	200/100		950	2000
Troit Partout Suite	LG	AD	1980	LC	25 X 32 cm EA	AP/JP			4000 SET	12500 SET
Serenade	LG	AD	1981	LC	26 X 20	AP/JP	200/100	15	700	1500
Le Petite Rat	LG	AD	1981	LC	26 X 20	AP/JP	200/100	15	800	1500
Entre Acte	LG	AD	1981	LC	26 X 20	AP/JP	200/100		800	1250
Pas de Quatre	LG	AD	1981	LC	26 X 20	AP/JP	200/100		800	1250
Reverence	LG	AD	1981	LC	26 X 20	AP/JP	200/100		800	1300
En Troisieme	LG	AD	1981	LC	26 X 20	AP/JP	200/100		800	1250
Apres le Danse	LG	AD	1981	LC	26 X 20	AP/JP	200/100		800	1300
Toutes sur Scene	LG	AD	1981	LC	26 X 20	AP/JP	200/100		800	1300
Les Petits Rats Suite	LG	AD	1981	LC	26 X 20 EA	AP/JP	200/100		6500 SET	11000 SET
The Babysitter	LG	AD	1983	LC	26 X 20	AP/JP	200/100	17	800	1200
Au Repos	LG	AD	1983	LC	26 X 20	AP/JP	200/100	17	800	1000
Tricycle	LG	AD	1983	LC	26 X 20	AP/JP	200/100		800	1000
Football	LG	AD	1983	LC	26 X 20	AP/JP	200/100		800	1000
L'Oiseau Jaune	LG	AD	1983	LC	26 X 20	AP/JP	200/100		800	1000
Encore	LG	AL	1984	LC	26 X 20	AP/JP	250/50		800	1000
Musician Jaune	LG	AL	1985	LC	26 X 20	AP/JP	250/50	17	800	1000
Polo I, II, III	LG	AMa	1986	EC	23 X 31 EA	AP	250 EA		1500 EA	1600 EA
La Infanta y Su Gato	LG	AMa	1987	EC	37 X 25	CYP	250		1500	2500
Juego de Domingo	LG	AMa	1987	EC	30 X 22	COLP	250		1500	2000
Les Musicians	LG	AL	1987	LC		AP	500		1500	1600
Bicyclette	LG	AMa	1987	EC		AP	200		550	800
Trapeze	LG	AMa	1987	EC		AP	200		550	800
Footballeur	LG	AMa	1987	EC		AP	200		550	800
Violoniste	LG	AMa	1987	EC		AP	200		550	1000
Trottinette	LG		1987	EC		AP	200		550	800
Villes Lointaines Suite	LG	AMa	1987	EC		AP	200		2500 SET	4800 SET
The Magic Flute	LG	AL	1987	LC	40 X 28	AP	300		1750	2500
La Danse	LG	ART/AL	1988	LC	26 X 19	AP/CGP/LP	100/100/100		600	600
La Musique	LG	ART/AL	1988	LC	26 X 19	AP/CGP/LP	100/100/100		600	600
Meditation	LG		1988	SCULP	13¼"H	Bronze	99		5000	6750
Portrait de la Mariée	LG	AMa	1988	EC	39 X 27	R/BFK	175		1800	2000
Concert a Trois	LG		1988	SCULP	12"H	Bronze	75		6250	6250
Mezzo Forte	LG		1988	SCULP	10½"H	Bronze	75		6500	6500
Violoncelliste	LG		1988	SCULP	13½"H	Bronze	99		6000	6000
Voyage Imaginaire I, II	LG	AMa	1989	EC	29 X 29 EA	RP	200 EA		1700 EA	2000 EA
Rondeau Bleu	LG	AMa	1989	LC		RP	300		1500	1800
Rondeau Rouge	LG	AMa	1989	LC		RP	300		1500	1800

GRACIELA RODO BOULANGER CONTINUED

TITLE	PUBLISHER	PRINTER	DATE	MEDIUM	DIMENSION (PAPER SIZE) IN INCHES	TYPE OF PAPER	EDITION NUMBER	NO. OF COLORS	ORIGINAL OPENING PRICE	CURRENT RETAIL PRICE
CURRENT EDITIONS:										
Spring	LG	AMa	1989	EC		AP	250		1100	1250
Summer	LG	AMa	1989	EC		AP	250		1100	1250
Autumn	LG	AMa	1989	EC		AP	250		1100	1250
Winter	LG	AMa	1989	EC		AP	250		1100	1250
Chien et Chat I,II	LG	AMa	1990	EC		AP	200 EA		1700 EA	2000 EA
Scherzo	LG	AMa	1990	LC		AP/JP	200/100		1300	1300
Andante	LG	AMa	1990	LC		AP/JP	200/100		1300	1300
Allegro	LG	AMa	1990	LC		AP/JP	200/100		1300	1300
Largo	LG	AMa	1990	LC		AP/JP	200/100		1300	1300
Adagio	LG	AMa	1990	LC		AP/JP	200/100		1300	1300
La Fenetre	LG	AMa	1991	EC		AP	200		1500	1500
Ouverture	LG	AMa	1991	EC		AP	200		1500	1500

LOUISE BOURGEOIS

BORN: Paris France; December 25, 1911; US Citizen
EDUCATION: Lycee Fenelon, Paris, France, Baccalaureate, 1932; Sorbonne, Paris, France, 1932–35; Ecole du Louvre, Paris, France, 1936–37; Acad Beaux-Arts, Paris, France, 1936–38; Acad Grande Chaumiére, Paris, France, 1937–38; Atelier Fernand Leger, Paris, France, 1938
TEACHING: Instr, Sculpture, Pratt Inst, NY, 1964–65; Instr, Sculpture, Brooklyn Col, NY, 1963,68; Instr, Cooper Union, NY, 1978–79
AWARDS: Distinguished Sculpture Award, Sculpture Center NY 1990; Int Sculpture Center Award, First Recipient, Wash, DC, 1991; Grand Prix Nat Sculpture Award, French Ministry of Culture, Paris, France, 1991
RECENT EXHIB: Laguna Gloria Art Mus, Austin, TX, 1988; Carl Schlosberg Fine Arts, Sherman Oaks, CA, 1988; Mus Ludwig, Cologne, Germany, 1989; Whitney Mus of Am Art, NY, 1989; Kroller-Muller Mus, Otterlo, The Netherlands, 1989; Milwaukee Art Mus, WI, 1990; Mus of Fine Arts, Boston, MA, 1990; Robert Miller Gallery, NY, 1991; Solomon R Guggenheim Mus, NY, 1992; Mus of Mod Art, NY, 1992; Parrish Art Mus, Southampton, NY, 1992; Florida Int Univ Art Mus, Miami, FL, 1992; Univ of Washington, Henry Art Gallery, Seattle, WA, 1992
COLLECTIONS: Mus of Mod Art, NY; Whitney Mus of Am Art, NY; Metropolitan Mus of Art, NY; New York Univ, NY; Albright-Knox Art Gallery, Buffalo, NY; Denver Art Mus, CO; Musee d'Art Moderne, Paris, France; Storm King Art Center, Mountainville, NY

PRINTERS: Atelier Piero Crommelynck, Paris, France (APC); Harlan & Weaver Intaglio, NY (H-WI)
PUBLISHERS: Galerie Lelong, Paris, France (GL); Peter Blum Edition, NY (PBE)
GALLERIES: Galerie Lelong, New York, NY & Paris, France; Peter Blum Edition, New York, NY; Robert Miller Gallery, New York, NY; Rhona Hoffman Gallery, Chicago, IL; Tavelli Williams Gallery, Aspen, CO; Ginny Williams Gallery, Denver, CO
MAILING ADDRESS: 347 W 20th St, New York, NY 10011

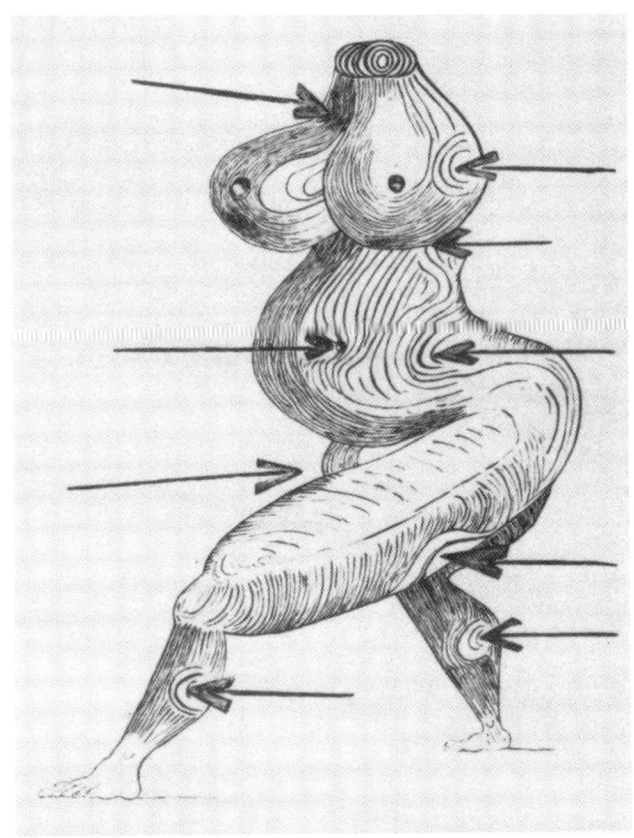

Louise Bourgeois
Sainte Sebastienne
Courtesy Peter Blum Edition

TITLE	PUBLISHER	PRINTER	DATE	MEDIUM	DIMENSION (PAPER SIZE) IN INCHES	TYPE OF PAPER	EDITION NUMBER	NO. OF COLORS	ORIGINAL OPENING PRICE	CURRENT RETAIL PRICE
CURRENT EDITIONS:										
Spirales, 1947	GL	APC	1990	EB	10 X 13	AP	50	1	1400	1400
Album Quarantania, 1947 (Set of 9)	GL	APC	1990	EB	10 X 13 EA	AP	50 EA	1 EA	10000 SET	10000 SET
Sainte Sebastienne	PBE	H-WI	1992	DPT	48 X 37	SOM/S	50	1	5500	5500
Stamp of Memories-I	PBE	H-WI	1993	DPT/ENG/REL	26 X 17	SOM/S	30	1	3200	3200

DAVID BOWES

RECENT EXHIB: Vrej Baghoomian, Inc, NY, 1989,90
PRINTERS: Centre Genevais de la Gravure Contemporan, Geneva, Switzerland (CGGC)
PUBLISHERS: Galerie Eric Franck, Geneva, Switzerland (GEF)
GALLERIES: Galerie Eric Franck, Geneva, Switzerland

TITLE	PUBLISHER	PRINTER	DATE	MEDIUM	DIMENSION (PAPER SIZE) IN INCHES	TYPE OF PAPER	EDITION NUMBER	NO. OF COLORS	ORIGINAL OPENING PRICE	CURRENT RETAIL PRICE
CURRENT EDITIONS:										
Look Back in Wonder	GEF	CGGC	1985	LB	30 X 22	AP	30	1	400	600

KATHERINE BOWLING

BORN: Washington, DC; 1955
EDUCATION: Virginia Commonwealth Univ, Richmond, VA, BFA, 1978
AWARDS: Nat Endowment for the Arts Grant, 1991
RECENT EXHIB: Albright-Knox Members Gallery, Buffalo, NY, 1988; Rosa Esman Gallery, NY, 1987,89; BlumHelman Gallery, Los Angeles, CA, 1990; BlumHelman Gallery, NY, 1990,91
COLLECTIONS: Metropolitan Mus of Art, NY
PRINTERS: Greg Burnet (GB); Riverhouse Editions, Clark, CO (REd)
PUBLISHERS: Riverhouse Editions, Clark, CO (REd)
GALLERIES: BlumHelman Gallery, New York, NY

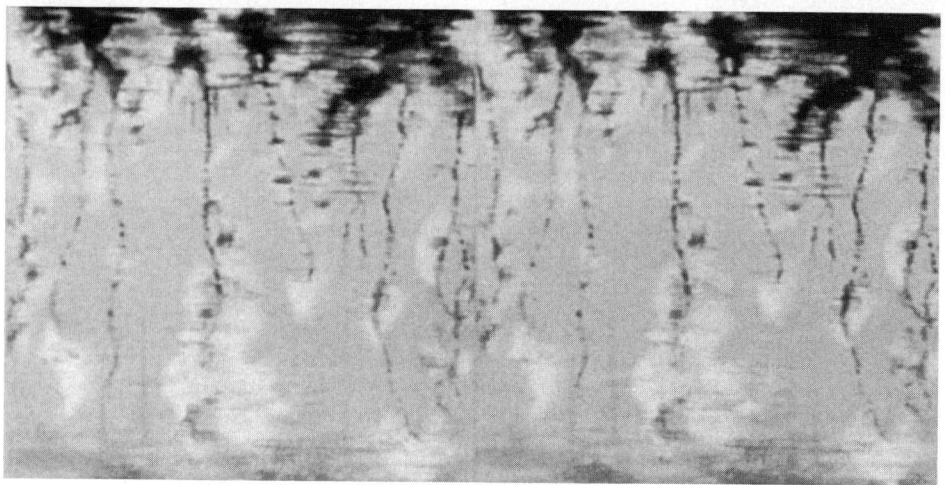

Katherine Bowling
Double Reflection
Courtesy Van Straaten Gallery

TITLE	PUBLISHER	PRINTER	DATE	MEDIUM	DIMENSION (PAPER SIZE) IN INCHES	TYPE OF PAPER	EDITION NUMBER	NO. OF COLORS	ORIGINAL OPENING PRICE	CURRENT RETAIL PRICE
CURRENT EDITIONS:										
Winter	REd	GB/REd	1992	EC	15 X 15	WHP	30	2	350	350
Blue Sky	REd	GB/REd	1992	EC	15 X 15	WHP	30	3	350	350
Forest	REd	GB/REd	1992	EC	15 X 15	WHP	30	4	350	350
Pond	REd	GB/REd	1992	EC	15 X 15	WHP	30	4	350	350
Double Reflection	REd	GB/REd	1992	EC	25 X 33	RP/MdG	40	4	600	600

STANLEY ROBERT BOXER

BORN: New York, NY; June 26, 1926
EDUCATION: Brooklyn Col, NY; Art Students League, NY
TEACHING: Instr, Vermont Sch of Art, 1986
AWARDS: John S Guggenheim Mem Found Fel, 1975; Visual Artist Fel Grant, 1989
RECENT EXHIB: Tibor de Nagy Gallery, NY, 1987; Hokin Gallery, Palm Beach, FL, 1987,88; Retrosp, Associated Am Artists, NY, 1990; Posner Gallery, Milwaukee, WI, 1990; Hokin Gallery, Palm Beach, 1990; Andre Emmerich Gallery, NY, 1990; Galerie Wentzel, Cologne, Germany, 1990; Meredith Long & Co, Houston, TX, 1990; Dorsky Gallery, NY, 1991
COLLECTIONS: Mus of Mod Art, NY; Boston Mus of Fine Art, MA; Guggenheim Mus, NY; Houston Mus of Fine Art, TX; Cornell Univ, Johnson Mus, NY; Albright-Knox Art Gallery, Buffalo, NY; Santa Barbara Mus, CA; Ball State Univ, Muncie, IN; Des Moines Art Center, IA; Wichita Mus of Fine Arts, KS; Rose Art Mus, Brandeis Univ, Waltham, MA; Univ of Massachusetts, Boston, MA; William Jewell Col, Liberty, MO; Walker Art Center, Minneapolis, MN; Everson Mus, Syracuse, NY; Solomon R. Guggenheim Mus, NY; Whitney Mus of Am Art, NY; Dayton Art Inst, OH; Columbia Mus, Texas, SC; Corcoran Gallery of Art, Wash, DC; Hirshhorn Mus, Wash, DC; Birla Mus, India; Edmonton Art Gallery, Can; Mus of the Twentieth Century, Vienna, Austria; Milwaukee Art Center, WI
PRINTERS: P Saunders, NY (PS); Ken Tyler, NY (KT); Tyler Graphics Ltd, Mount Kisco, NY (TGL); Garner Tullis Workshop, Santa Barbara, CA (GTW); Artist (ART); Patrick Surgalski, Palo Alto, CA (PS); Smith Andersen Editions, Palo Alto, CA (SAE); Catherine Mosley, NY (CM); Janice Stemmerman, NY, (JS); David Keister, Bloomington, IN (DK); David Calkins, Bloomington, IN (DC); Echo Press, Bloomington, IN (EPr)
PUBLISHERS: Tyler Graphics Ltd, Mount Kisco, NY (TGL); Garner Tullis Workshop, Santa Barbara, CA (GTW); Lucy Berman Modern Graphics, Palo Alto, CA (LBM); Smith/Andersen Editions, Palo Alto, CA (SAE); Associated Am Artists, NY (AAA); Echo Press, Bloomington, IN (EPr)
GALLERIES: André Emmerich Gallery, New York, NY; Aronson Gallery, Atlanta, GA; Hokin Gallery, Bay Harbor Islands, FL & Palm Beach, FL; Hokin Kaufman Gallery, Chicago, IL, Thomas Segal Gallery, Boston, MA; Salander O'Reilly Galleries, New York, NY; Jerald Melberg Gallery, Charlotte, NC; Meredith Long & Co, Houston, TX; Garner Tullis Workshop Santa Barbara, CA; Ruth Bachofner Gallery, Santa Monica, CA; Associated American Artists, New York, NY; Smith/Andersen Gallery, Palo Alto, CA; Dorsky Gallery, New York, NY; Echo Press, Bloomington, IN; Levinson Kane Gallery, Boston, MA; Cone Editions Press, East Topsham, VT; Remba Gallery/Mixografia Workshop, Santa Monica, CA; Tyler Graphics, Ltd, Mount Kisco, NY
MAILING ADDRESS: 37 E 18th St, New York, NY 10012

TITLE	PUBLISHER	PRINTER	DATE	MEDIUM	DIMENSION (PAPER SIZE) IN INCHES	TYPE OF PAPER	EDITION NUMBER	NO. OF COLORS	ORIGINAL OPENING PRICE	CURRENT RETAIL PRICE
CURRENT EDITIONS:										
Ring of Dust in Bloom (Set of 12):									5000 SET	10000 SET
Gatheringforsomereason	TGL	ART/TGL	1976	EB/A/WA	20 X 24	HMP	28	20	500	1000
Obliquequestionofaturtle	TGL	ART/TGL	1976	EB/A/WA	26 X 24	HMP	28	20	500	1000

STANLEY ROBERT BOXER CONTINUED

TITLE	PUBLISHER	PRINTER	DATE	MEDIUM	DIMENSION (PAPER SIZE) IN INCHES	TYPE OF PAPER	EDITION NUMBER	NO. OF COLORS	ORIGINAL OPENING PRICE	CURRENT RETAIL PRICE
CURRENT EDITIONS:										
Fegbowlofplay	TGL	ART/TGL	1976	EB/A/WA	26 X 24	HMP	28	20	500	1000
Askanceglancelongingly	TGL	ART/TGL	1976	EB/A/WA	26 X 24	HMP	28	20	500	1000
Curiousstalking	TGL	ART/TGL	1976	EB/A/WA	26 X 24	HMP	28	20	500	1000
Pauseofnoconcern	TGL	ART/TGL	1976	EB/A/WA	26 X 24	HMP	28	20	500	1000
Strangetalkwithfriend	TGL	ART/TGL	1976	EB/A/WA	26 X 24	HMP	28	20	500	1000
Oddconverversationatnoon	TGL	ART/TGL	1976	EB/A/WA	26 X 24	HMP	28	20	500	1000
Amissinamist	TGL	ART/TGL	1976	EB/A/WA	26 X 24	HMP	28	20	500	1000
Argumentofnoavail	TGL	ART/TGL	1976	EB/A/WA	26 X 24	HMP	28	20	500	1000
Buddingwithoutpast	TGL	ART/TGL	1976	EB/A/WA	26 X 24	HMP	28	20	500	1000
Conversationofslydiscussants	TGL	ART/TGL	1976	EB/A/WA	26 X 24	HMP	28	20	500	1000
Spawnofcloverwithcuriousoccupants	TGL	TGL	1977	EB/A/WA	24 X 24	HMP	45	20	450	1000
Cleavedsummerautumnalglance	TGL	ART/PS/TGL	1977	EB/A/WA	23 X 31	HMP	34	30	450	1000
Carnival of Animals (Set of 14):									6000 SET	14000 SET
Introduction, Royal Prance of the Lion	TGL	ART/TGL	1979	EC/A/WA	23 X 26	TGL/HMP	20	20	475	1000
Chicken and Cock	TGL	ART/TGL	1979	EC/A/WA	23 X 26	TGL/HMP	20	20	475	1000
Jackass Free	TGL	ART/TGL	1979	EC/A/WA	23 X 26	TGL/HMP	20	20	475	1000
Turtle	TGL	ART/TGL	1979	EC/A/WA	23 X 26	TGL/HMP	20	20	475	1000
Elephants	TGL	ART/TGL	1979	EC/A/WA	23 X 26	TGL/HMP	20	20	475	1000
Kangaroos	TGL	ART/TGL	1979	EC/A/WA	23 X 26	TGL/HMP	20	20	475	1000
Aquarium	TGL	ART/TGL	1979	EC/A/WA	23 X 26	TGL/HMP	20	20	475	1000
Personnages with Long Ears	TGL	ART/TGL	1979	EC/A/WA	23 X 26	TGL/HMP	20	20	475	1000
Cockatoo in the Depths of the Woods	TGL	ART/TGL	1979	EC/A/WA	23 X 26	TGL/HMP	20	20	475	1000
Birds Soaring	TGL	ART/TGL	1979	EC/A/WA	23 X 26	TGL/HMP	20	20	475	1000
Pianist	TGL	ART/TGL	1979	EC/A/WA	23 X 26	TGL/HMP	20	20	475	1000
Fossils	TGL	ART/TGL	1979	EC/A/WA	23 X 26	TGL/HMP	20	20	475	1000
Swan	TGL	ART/TGL	1979	EC/A/WA	23 X 26	TGL/HMP	20	20	475	750
Mapnowhere (Unique Print) (with Oil Pastel)	EPr	EPr	1984	LC/HC	29 X 41	AP88	1	1	2000	3500
Finale	TGL	ART/TGL	1979	EC/A/WA	23 X 26	TGL/HMP	20	20	475	750
Marbleman (Alcamo) (Set of 10)	LBM/SAE	PS/SAE	1987	EC/A	19 X 15 EA	Varies	14 EA		6500 SET	7000 SET
Marks of Passion	AAA/SAE	CM/JS	1989	CAR/AC	24 X 18	GE	30		1800	2000
Anoglalawander	EPr	DK/DC/EPr	1989-90	LC	37 X 25	AC/W	20	21	1000	1000
Charmatbloomington	EPr	DK/DC/EPr	1989-90	LC/WC/PAS	38 X 26	AC/W	20	16	1000	1000
Dakotaheats	EPr	DK/DC/EPr	1989-90	LC	37 X 28	AC/W	20	12	1000	1000
Freizeofamarbleman	EPr	DK/DC/EPr	1989-90	LC/WC	11 X 60	AC/W	30	10	1000	1200
Thepassionmottled	EPr	DK/DC/EPr	1989-90	LC/WC	30 X 37	AC/W	20	14	1000	1000

FRANK BOYDEN

PRINTERS: North Light Editions, Portland, OR (NLE); Artist (ART)
PUBLISHERS: Artist (ART)
GALLERIES: Mariposa Gallery, Albuquerque, NM; Dawson Gallery, Rochester, NY; Lawrence Gallery,, Sheridan, OR; Sunbird Gallery, Bend, OR

TITLE	PUBLISHER	PRINTER	DATE	MEDIUM	DIMENSION (PAPER SIZE) IN INCHES	TYPE OF PAPER	EDITION NUMBER	NO. OF COLORS	ORIGINAL OPENING PRICE	CURRENT RETAIL PRICE
CURRENT EDITIONS:										
Changes (Set of 10)	ART	NLE	1983	LB	13 X 17 EA	R/BFK/AP	45 EA	1 EA	1600 SET	3000 SET

PAUL HENRY BRACH

BORN: New York, NY; March 13, 1924
EDUCATION: Iowa State Univ, Ames, IA, BFA, 1948; MFA, 1949
TEACHING: Univ of Missouri, Columbia, MO, 1949–1951; New Sch for Social Research, NY, 1952-55; New York Univ, NY, 1954–56; Parsons Sch of Design, NY, 1956–67; Chmn, Cooper Union, NY, 1960–62; 1978–80; Cornell Univ, Ithaca, NY, 1965–67; Chmn, Art Dept, Univ of California, San Diego, CA, 1967–69; Dean, Sch of Art, California Inst of Arts, Valencia, CA, 1969–75; Chmn, Dir, Arts, Lincoln Center Campus, Fordham Univ, 1975–79

RECENT EXHIB: Fairleigh Dickinson Univ, Phyllis Rothman Gallery, Madison, NJ, 1992
COLLECTIONS: Mus of Mod Art, NY; Whitney Mus of Am Art, NY; St Louis Art Mus, MO; Los Angeles County Mus, CA; Smith Col, Northampton, MA
PRINTERS: Frank Versaggi, NY (FV); Sheila Marbain, NY (SM); Kathleen Caraccio, NY (KC); Paul Narkiewicz, NY (PN)
PUBLISHERS: Orion Editions, NY (OE)
GALLERIES: Bernice Steinbaum Gallery, New York, NY; Orion Editions, New York, NY; Vered Gallery, East Hampton, NY; Landsman Gallery, Magnolia, NJ
MAILING ADDRESS: 393 W Broadway, New York, NY 10012

TITLE	PUBLISHER	PRINTER	DATE	MEDIUM	DIMENSION (PAPER SIZE) IN INCHES	TYPE OF PAPER	EDITION NUMBER	NO. OF COLORS	ORIGINAL OPENING PRICE	CURRENT RETAIL PRICE
SOLD OUT EDITIONS (RARE):										
Navajo I	OE	FV/SM	1979	LC	24 X 29	AP	50	15	300	500

PAUL HENRY BRACH CONTINUED

TITLE	PUBLISHER	PRINTER	DATE	MEDIUM	DIMENSION (PAPER SIZE) IN INCHES	TYPE OF PAPER	EDITION NUMBER	NO. OF COLORS	ORIGINAL OPENING PRICE	CURRENT RETAIL PRICE
CURRENT EDITIONS:										
Rimrock I,II,III (with Metal Foil)	OE	KC	1980	AC	24 X 28 EA	AP	50 EA	3 EA	350 EA	400 EA
Rimrock IV (with Metal Foil)	OE	KC	1980	AC	24 X 28	AP	50	3	350	450
Blue Mesa (with Metal Foil)	OE	PN	1983	LC	23 X 32	AP	33	5	450	550
Manifest Destiny I (with Stencil)	OE		1986–87	EC/STEN	27 X 39		100	9	700	750
Arc of the Sky	OE		1988–89	EC/DPT	30 X 40		40	2	900	950

HOWARD BRADFORD

BORN: Toronto, ON, Canada; July 14, 1919; US Citizen
EDUCATION: Chouinard Art Inst, Los Angeles, CA; Jepson Art Inst, Los Angeles, CA
TEACHING: Instr, Jepson Art Inst, Los Angeles, CA, 1949–51; Vis Art, Univ of Wisconsin, Madison, WI, 1957; Instr, Univ of Salt Lake City, UT, 1959
AWARDS: Library of Congress, 1951; Dallas Mus of Fine Arts, 1953; Guggenheim Fel, Creative Printmaking, 1960

COLLECTIONS: Dallas Mus of Fine Arts, TX; Los Angeles County Mus, CA; Mus of Mod Art, NY; San Diego Mus, CA; Boston Mus of Fine Arts, MA; New York Public Library, NY; Crocker Art Gallery, Sacramento, CA; Philadelphia Mus of Fine Arts, PA; Metropolitan Mus of Art, NY; Bibliotheque Nat, Paris, France; Victoria & Albert Mus, London, England
PRINTERS: Artist (ART)
PUBLISHERS: Graphics Arts Unlimited, NY (GAU); Artist (ART)
GALLERIES: Young Gallery, Los Gatos, CA
MAILING ADDRESS: 684 Alice St, Monterey, CA 93940

TITLE	PUBLISHER	PRINTER	DATE	MEDIUM	DIMENSION (PAPER SIZE) IN INCHES	TYPE OF PAPER	EDITION NUMBER	NO. OF COLORS	ORIGINAL OPENING PRICE	CURRENT RETAIL PRICE
CURRENT EDITIONS:										
Early Morning	GAU	ART	1981	SP	23 X 33	TWC	50	7	150	200
Birch Silhouettes	GAU	ART	1981	SP	23 X 33	TWC	50	15	150	200
Lavender Arrangement I, II, III	GAU	ART	1982	SP	20 X 18 EA	TWC	10 EA	6 EA	90 EA	150 EA
Autumn Twilight	GAU	ART	1982	SP	23 X 33	TWC	40	15	110	150
Desert Floor	GAU	ART	1982	SP	23 X 33	TWC	40	10	110	150
Lavender Floral I	ART	ART	1983	SP	20 X 17	TWC	18	9	100	150
Lavender Floral II	ART	ART	1983	SP	20 X 17	TWC	20	9	100	150
Lavender Floral III	ART	ART	1983	SP	20 X 17	TWC	17	9	100	150

KATHERINE BRADFORD

PRINTERS: Tandem Press, Madison, WI (TanPr)
PUBLISHERS: Tandem Press, Madison, WI (TanPr)
GALLERIES: Zolla/Lieberman Gallery, Chicago, IL; Victoria Munroe Fine Art, Ltd, New York, NY

TITLE	PUBLISHER	PRINTER	DATE	MEDIUM	DIMENSION (PAPER SIZE) IN INCHES	TYPE OF PAPER	EDITION NUMBER	NO. OF COLORS	ORIGINAL OPENING PRICE	CURRENT RETAIL PRICE
CURRENT EDITIONS:										
Untitled #1–#9	TanPr	TanPr	1993	MON	32 X 26 EA	AC	1 EA	Varies	1500 EA	1500 EA

CAROLYN BRADY

BORN: Chickasha, OK; May 22, 1937
EDUCATION: Oklahoma State Univ, Stillwater, OK, 1955–58; Univ of Oklahoma, BFA, Norman, OK, 1958–59, MFA, 1959–61
TEACHING: Univ of Missouri, St Louis, MO, 1974
RECENT EXHIB: Univ of Oklahoma Mus of Art, Norman, OK, 1989; Nancy Hoffman Gallery, NY, 1993
COLLECTIONS: Delaware Art Mus, Wilmington, DE; Indiana Univ Mus, Bloomington, IN; Mint Mus, Charlotte, NC; St Louis Art Mus, MO; J B Speed Mus, Louisville, KY; Springfield Art Mus, MO; Univ of Rochester, NY; Marion Koogler McNay Art Inst, San Antonio, TX; Oklahoma Art Ctr, Oklahoma City, OK; Metropolitan Art Mus, NY; Worcester Art Mus, MA

PRINTERS: Maurice Payne Studios, NY (MP); Judith Solodkin, NY (JS); Solo Press, NY (SP); Lynne Allen, Albuquerque, NM (LA); Marcia Brown, Albuquerque, NM (MB); Tamarind Inst, Albuquerque, NM (TI)
PUBLISHERS: Barbara Gladstone Editions, NY (BGE); 724 Prints, NY (724P); Solo Press, NY (SP); Tamarind Inst, Albuquerque, NM (TI)
GALLERIES: Barbara Gladstone Gallery, New York, NY; Nancy Hoffman Gallery, New York, NY; Solo Gallery, New York, NY; Mary Singer Gallery, Wash, DC; Steven Scott Gallery, Baltimore, MO; MI; Tamarind Inst, Albuquerque, NM; Topaz Editions, Inc, Tampa, FL; Nancy Singer Gallery, St Louis, MO
MAILING ADDRESS: c/o Nancy Hoffman Gallery, 429 W Broadway, New York, NY 10012

TITLE	PUBLISHER	PRINTER	DATE	MEDIUM	DIMENSION (PAPER SIZE) IN INCHES	TYPE OF PAPER	EDITION NUMBER	NO. OF COLORS	ORIGINAL OPENING PRICE	CURRENT RETAIL PRICE
SOLD OUT EDITIONS: (RARE)										
Green Lamp, Red Table	724P	MP	1985	EC/A	22 X 30	R/BFK			800	1500
CURRENT EDITIONS:										
Anthurium	BGE	MP	1980	AC	27 X 30	AP	36		600	900
Blue and Yellow	SP	JS/SP	1983	AC	29 X 37	AP	45		1000	1800
Green Wallpaper—Tulips and Daffodils	724P	MP	1983	AC	30 X 36	AP	45	9	1300	1750
Anemones on Red Table	724P	MP	1983	AC	35 X 30	R/BFK	50	8	1000	1750
White Plate on Morning Glories	TI	LA/TI	1984	LB	22 X 30	JEP	30	1	600	900
White Plate on Pink Grid	TI	LA/TI	1984	LC	23 X 32	GE	40	5	600	1200

CAROLYN BRADY CONTINUED

TITLE	PUBLISHER	PRINTER	DATE	MEDIUM	DIMENSION (PAPER SIZE) IN INCHES	TYPE OF PAPER	EDITION NUMBER	NO. OF COLORS	ORIGINAL OPENING PRICE	CURRENT RETAIL PRICE
CURRENT EDITIONS:										
White Plate on Umber	TI	MB/TI	1984	LC	22 X 30	GE	40	7	600	1200
Single Iris	SP	JS/SP	1985	EC	30 X 22	R/BFK	20		700	900
Double Iris	SP	JS/SP	1985	EC	36 X 30	R/BFK	45		800	1200

DOVE BRADSHAW

BORN: New York, NY; September 24, 1949
EDUCATION: Boston Mus Sch of Fine Arts, MA, BFA, 1973
TEACHING: Instr, Sch of Visual Arts, NY, 1975–81
AWARDS: Nat Endowment for the Arts, 1975; Pollock-Krasner Award, 1985
RECENT EXHIB: Syracuse Univ, NY, 1988; Mus of Mod Art, NY, 1990; Mattress Factory, Pittsburgh, PA, 1990
COLLECTIONS: Metropolitan Mus of Art, NY; Mus of Mod Art, NY; Whitney Mus of Am Art, NY; Brooklyn Mus, NY; Getty Mus, Santa Monica, CA; Philadelphia Mus of Art, PA; Muestra Int de Arte Grafico, Bilbao, Spain; Piccolo Mus Novoli, Italy; Kunstmuseum, Desseldorf, Germany; Art Inst of Chicago, IL; Le Centre Georges Pompidou, Paris, France
PRINTERS: Sue Evans, NY (SE); Evans Editions, NY (EEd); Renaissance Press, NH (RPr)
PUBLISHERS: Evans Editions, NY (EEd); Renaissance Press, NH (RPr)
GALLERIES: Sandra Gering Gallery, New York, NY
MAILING ADDRESS: 640 Riverside Dr, New York, NY 10031

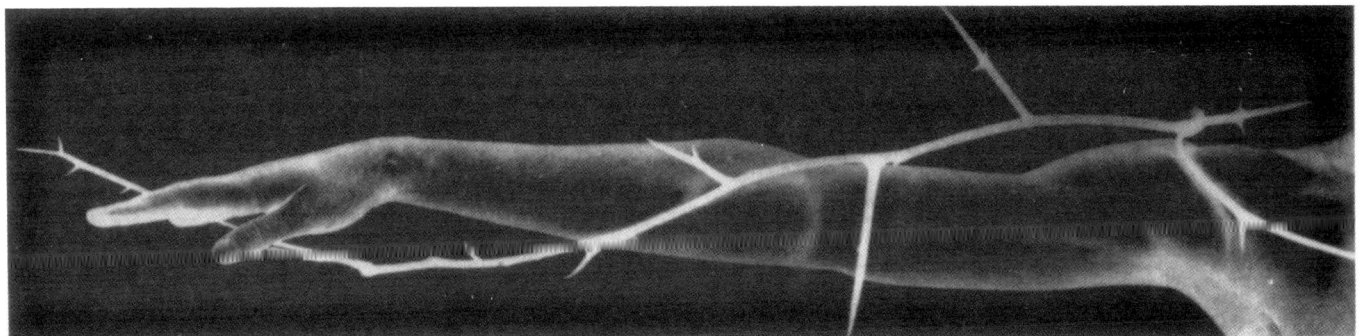

Dove Bradshaw
Untitled
Courtesy the Artist

TITLE	PUBLISHER	PRINTER	DATE	MEDIUM	DIMENSION (PAPER SIZE) IN INCHES	TYPE OF PAPER	EDITION NUMBER	NO. OF COLORS	ORIGINAL OPENING PRICE	CURRENT RETAIL PRICE
CURRENT EDITIONS:										
Untitled	EEd/RPr	SE/EEd/RPr	1992	PH/G	8 X 29	SOM/S	12		800	800

CHARLES BRAGG

BORN: St Louis, MO; March 13, 1931
EDUCATION: Music & Art High Sch, NY; Art Students League, NY
AWARDS: Gold Medal, Art Guild of Chicago, IL
COLLECTIONS: Pushkin Mus, Moscow, Russia; Dayton Art Mus, OH
PRINTERS: First Impressions, Los Angeles, CA (FI)
PUBLISHERS: Martin Lawrence Limited Editions, Van Nuys, CA (MLLE)
GALLERIES: Martin Lawrence Galleries, Sherman Oaks, CA & Los Angeles, CA & Newport Beach, CA & Short Hills, NJ & Phila, PA & Palm Springs, CA & Redondo Beach, CA & Escondido, CA & Thousand Oaks, CA & West Los Angeles, CA & Santa Clara, CA; P C Hart Gallery, Jupiter, FL; Saper Galleries, East Lansing, MI; Dyansen Corp, New York, NY

TITLE	PUBLISHER	PRINTER	DATE	MEDIUM	DIMENSION (PAPER SIZE) IN INCHES	TYPE OF PAPER	EDITION NUMBER	NO. OF COLORS	ORIGINAL OPENING PRICE	CURRENT RETAIL PRICE
SOLD OUT EDITIONS (RARE):										
Angels of Mercy	MLLE	FI	1980	EB	11 X 13	R/BFK	300	1	200	1050
Antique Ambulance	MLLE	FI	1980	EB	12 X 16	R/BFK	340	1	200	800
Closing Argument	MLLE	FI	1980	EB	14 X 18	R/BFK	340	1	250	1200
Consultation	MLLE	FI	1980	EB	11 X 14	R/BFK	310	1	200	1050
Divorce Lawyer	MLLE	FI	1980	EB	12 X 14	R/BFK	305	1	200	1200
Doyle the Mohel	MLLE	FI	1980	EB	8 X 8	R/BFK	301	1	200	775
Exhibit A	MLLE	FI	1980	EB	9 X 11	R/BFK	296	1	200	800
J'Accuse	MLLE	FI	1981	EB	11 X 14	R/BFK	301	1	200	900
Objection Overruled	MLLE	FI	1982	EB	11 X 11	R/BFK	315	1	200	1050
Orthodonist	MLLE	FI	1982	EB	12 X 14	R/BFK	316	1	200	1050
Out-of-Court Settlement II	MLLE	FI	1982	EB	11 X 13	R/BFK	335	1	200	1050
Psychologist	MLLE	FI	1982	EB	10 X 12	R/BFK	316	1	200	1050
Plastic Surgeon	MLLE	FI	1982	EB	9 X 10	R/BFK	311	1	200	900
Recovery Room	MLLE	FI	1983	EB	12 X 15	R/BFK	300	1	200	750
Researcher	MLLE	FI	1983	EB	11 X 13	R/BFK	310	1	200	900
Urologist	MLLE	FI	1983	EB	12 X 14	R/BFK	311	1	200	1050
Veterinarian	MLLE	FI	1983	EB	14 X 18	R/BFK	351	1	250	1050

CHARLES BRAGG CONTINUED

TITLE	PUBLISHER	PRINTER	DATE	MEDIUM	DIMENSION (PAPER SIZE) IN INCHES	TYPE OF PAPER	EDITION NUMBER	NO. OF COLORS	ORIGINAL OPENING PRICE	CURRENT RETAIL PRICE
SOLD OUT EDITIONS (RARE):										
Charlie's Bar (Set of 3):									750 SET	2200 SET
Happy Hour	MLLE	FI	1984	EB	13 X 22	R/BFK	370	1	250	925
Last Call	MLLE	FI	1984	EB	13 X 17	R/BFK	370	1	250	725
Honeymooners	MLLE	FI	1984	EB	13 X 16	R/BFK	370	1	250	725
Manny, Moe & Jacques	MLLE	FI	1984	EB/HC	13 X 13	R/BFK	400	1	250	725
The Professionals (Set of 3):									800 SET	2200 SET
The Stockbrokers	MLLE	FI	1984	EB	14 X 30	R/BFK	370	1	350	925
The Banker	MLLE	FI	1984	EB	13 X 16	R/BFK	370	1	250	725
The Real Estate Broker	MLLE	FI	1984	EB	13 X 16	R/BFK	370	1	250	725
On the House	MLLE	FI	1985	LB	16 X 22	R/BFK	370	1	350	1100
X-Ray 1898	MLLE	FI	1985	LB	12 X 16	R/BFK	310	1	350	900
CURRENT EDITIONS:										
Aclu	MLLE	FI	1980	EB	9 X 10	R/BFK	246	1	200	800
Anesthesiologist	MLLE	FI	1980	EB	11 X 13	R/BFK	321	1	200	1050
Brain Surgeon	MLLE	FI	1980	EB	11 X 13	R/BFK	306	1	200	1050
Cross Examination	MLLE	FI	1980	EB	14 X 12	R/BFK	315	1	200	900
Defense Rests	MLLE	FI	1980	EB	12 X 20	R/BFK	340	1	250	800
The Dentist	MLLE	FI	1980	EB	14 X 16	R/BFK	375	1	200	1050
GP	MLLE	FI	1980	EB	11 X 14	R/BFK	275	1	200	1050
Gynecologist	MLLE	FI	1980	EB	9 X 11	R/BFK	315	1	200	1050
Neurologist	MLLE	FI	1980	EB	12 X 14	R/BFK	375	1	200	1050
Night Court	MLLE	FI	1980	EB	12 X 14	R/BFK	296	1	200	1100
Her Honor	MLLE	FI	1981	EB	12 X 15	R/BFK	340	1	200	775
Night Nurse	MLLE	FI	1981	EB	9 X 8	R/BFK	295	1	200	750
Nolo Contendre	MLLE	FI	1981	EB	11 X 13	R/BFK	300	1	200	900
Objection Sustained	MLLE	FI	1981	EB	12 X 15	R/BFK	305	1	200	1050
Out-of-Court Settlement I	MLLE	FI	1981	EB	11 X 13	R/BFK	305	1	200	1200
Pediatrician	MLLE	FI	1981	EB	11 X 13	R/BFK	315	1	200	1050
Process Server	MLLE	FI	1982	EB	14 X 12	R/BFK	340	1	200	1050
Psychiatrist	MLLE	FI	1982	EB	12 X 16	R/BFK	340	1	200	700
Recess	MLLE	FI	1982	EB	9 X 11	R/BFK	306	1	200	900
Small Claims Court	MLLE	FI	1982	EB	14 X 16	R/BFK	340	1	200	1050
Stress Test	MLLE	FI	1983	EB	11 X 15	R/BFK	300		200	700
Surgeon	MLLE	FI	1983	EB	12 X 15	R/BFK	308	1	200	1100
Tort	MLLE	FI	1983	EB	12 X 14	R/BFK	305	1	200	950
Traffic Court	MLLE	FI	1983	EB	18 X 24	R/BFK	340	1	200	950
Transplant	MLLE	FI	1983	EB	10 X 15	R/BFK	350	1	200	800
Witness	MLLE	FI	1983	EB	10 X 12	R/BFK	290	1	200	950
Your Witness	MLLE	FI	1983	EB	12 X 16	R/BFK	340	1	200	1200
The Archaeologist	MLLE	FI	1984	EB	11 X 13	R/BFK	330	1	250	750
Court of Appeals	MLLE	FI	1985	LB	14 X 22	R/BFK	370	1	350	2000
1870–1910	MLLE	FI	1985	LB	14 X 18	R/BFK	165	1	250	750
Jurisprudence III (Set of 3):									800 SET	2500 SET
Steinem Court	MLLE	FI	1986	EB	18 X 28	R/BFK	340	1	350	900
Yippie/Yuppie	MLLE	FI	1986	EB	18 X 15	R/BFK	340	1	300	900
Justice Department	MLLE	FI	1986	EB	15 X 18	R/BFK	340	1	300	900

CHARLES LYNN BRAGG

BORN: Detroit, MI; January 22, 1952
EDUCATION: California Inst of Arts, Valencia, CA; Los Angeles City Col, CA; Univ of California, Los Angeles, CA; Pierce Col, Los Angeles, CA
COLLECTIONS: Heal the Bay Gallery Mus, Santa Monica, CA
PRINTERS: Arellanes Company, San Rafael, CA (AC); Overland Printers (OP)
PUBLISHERS: Hasson Publishing, Newport Beach, CA (HaP); Blinder Fine Arts, Santa Monica, CA (BFA)

GALLERIES: Promenade Gallery, Santa Monica, CA; Art Images, Long Beach, CA; Ocean Avenue Gallery, Santa Monica, CA; Art Dimensions, Century City, CA; Galerie des Champs Elysees, Paris, France; Brana Enterprises, Brentwood, CA; Palos Verdes Art & Design, Palos Verdes, CA; Art Moods, Atlanta, GA; Art City, Los Angeles, CA; Art Forum, Honolulu, HI; Emporium Enterprises, Dallas, TX; Nan Miller Gallery, Rochester, NY; Rejeau Galleries, Natick, MA; Silver K Gallery, Melbourne, Australia; Studio 53, New York, NY; Triangle Galleries, San Francisco, CA

TITLE	PUBLISHER	PRINTER	DATE	MEDIUM	DIMENSION (PAPER SIZE) IN INCHES	TYPE OF PAPER	EDITION NUMBER	NO. OF COLORS	ORIGINAL OPENING PRICE	CURRENT RETAIL PRICE
CURRENT EDITIONS:										
Riviera: Approaching the 18th	BFA	AS	1989	SP	34 X 42	COV	495	64	550	750

The Printworld Directory is accepting new applications for the seventh edition. Approximately 300 new artists will be accepted. Please use the two forms provided in the back section of this directory to submit biographical data and documentation of prints. Edition number of each print must not exceed 500 and the retail price must be $100 or more.

The print market has become very selective. For the first time since we published the first edition of The Printworld Directory in 1982, the prices of prints have been greatly reduced and greatly increased for the same artists by the most reputable and established print publishers. Check the fifth edition to understand the movement.

PHYLLIS BRAMSON

BORN: Madison, WI; February 20, 1941
EDUCATION: Yale Univ, New Haven, CT, Summer, 1962; Univ of Illinois, Urbana, IL, BFA, 1963; Univ of Wisconsin, Madison, WI, MA, 1964; Sch of Art Inst of Chicago, IL, MFA, 1973
TEACHING: Instr, Drawing & Painting, Columbia Col, Chicago, IL, 1972 to present; Instr. Drawing & Painting, Columbia Col, Chicago, IL, 1972–82; Via Art, Univ of Illinois, Chicago, IL, 1975; Vis Art, Univ of Iowa, Iowa City, IA, 1979; Vis Art, Univ of Chicago, IL, 1980; Vis Art, Art Inst of Chicago, IL, 1981; Vis Art, Indiana State Univ, 1981; Vis Art, Univ of Wisconsin, 1983; Vis Art, Univ of Colorado, Boulder, CO, 1986; Vis Art, Univ of Nebraska, 1986
AWARDS: Yale/Norfolk Art Scholarship, New Haven, CT, 1962; Nat Endowment for the Arts Fel, 1976; Louis Comfort Tiffany Grant, 1980; Pauline Palmer Prize, Art Inst of Chicago, IL, 1980; Illinois Arts Council Fel Grant, 1981; Nat Endowment for the Arts Fel Grant, 1983
RECENT EXHIB: G W Einstein Company, Inc, NY, 1991; State of Illinois Art Gallery, Chicago, IL, 1989,92; Col of DuPage, William E Gahlberg Arts Center Gallery, Glen Ellyn, IL, 1992; Bradley Univ, Heuserast Gallery, Hartmann Center Gallery, Peoria, IL, 1992; Douglass Col Library, New Brunswick, NJ, 1992; Illinois State Mus, Springfield, IL, 1992
COLLECTIONS: Univ of Wisconsin, Madison, WI; Illinois State Univ, IL; Oberlin Col Mus, OH; Mus of Contemp Art, Chicago, IL; Art Inst of Chicago, IL; Madison Art Center, IL; Indiana State Univ, Turman Gallery, Terre Haute, IN
PRINTERS: Mark Genrich, Chicago, IL; (MG); Landfall Press Inc, Chicago, IL (LPI); Bud Shark, Boulder, CO (BS); Matthew Christie, Boulder, CO (MC); Shark's Inc, Boulder, CO (SI)

Phyllis Bramson
Spring
Courtesy Shark's, Inc

PUBLISHERS: Landfall Press Inc, Chicago, IL (LPI); Shark's, Inc, Boulder, CO (SI)
GALLERIES: Dart Gallery, Chicago, IL; Landfall Press Inc, Chicago, IL; Brody's Gallery, Wash, DC; G W Einstein Gallery, New York, NY; Printworks Gallery, Chicago, IL; Quarter Editions, New York, NY
MAILING ADDRESS: 1423 Blackthorn Drive, Glenview, IL 60025–2009

TITLE	PUBLISHER	PRINTER	DATE	MEDIUM	DIMENSION (PAPER SIZE) IN INCHES	TYPE OF PAPER	EDITION NUMBER	NO. OF COLORS	ORIGINAL OPENING PRICE	CURRENT RETAIL PRICE
SOLD OUT EDITIONS (RARE):										
A Flash of Spiritual Meaning	LPI	JL/LPI	1981	LC	42 X 26	AP/W	30	9	350	1200
The Eroticism of Seeing	LPI	JL/LPI	1981	LC	42 X 26	AP/W	30	9	350	1200
CURRENT EDITIONS:										
Psychology of Fire, #1, #2 (Dipt)	LPI	MG/LPI	1983	WC	24 X 32 EA	AP/W	25 EA	5 EA	450 EA	1500 EA
Shaking Still			1985	EC	27 X 37	AP/W	30		350	600
The Savage Garden			1990	MON		AP/W	1 EA	Varies	1500 EA	1800 EA
Fall, Winter, Spring, Summer	SI	BS/MC/SI	1992	MON/CO	30 X 44 EA	AP/W	1 EA	Varies	2000 EA	2000 EA

GWENDOLYN BRANSTETTER

BORN: Beeville, Bee County, TX; October 7, 1924
EDUCATION: Texas Tech Univ, TX, 1949–50
TEACHING: Instr, Refugio County Mus, Adults, 1986 to present, Children, 1987 to present
RECENT EXHIB: Refugio County Mus, TX, 1988
PRINTERS: Robert K Jones, NY (RKJ)
PUBLISHERS: Post Oak Fine Art Distributors, Houston, TX (POFA)
MAILING ADDRESS: P O Box 143, 1004 Douglas St, Refugio, TX 78377–0143

TITLE	PUBLISHER	PRINTER	DATE	MEDIUM	DIMENSION (PAPER SIZE) IN INCHES	TYPE OF PAPER	EDITION NUMBER	NO. OF COLORS	ORIGINAL OPENING PRICE	CURRENT RETAIL PRICE
CURRENT EDITIONS:										
Dust on the Desert	POFA	RKJ	1982	SP	23 X 30	SOM	200	22	175	300
Watering Hole	POFA	RKJ	1982	SP	23 X 30	SOM	200	22	175	300
Fence Riders	POFA	RKJ	1982	SP	23 X 30	SOM	200	22	175	300
Rounding Up the Herd	POFA	RKJ	1982	SP	23 X 30	SOM	200	22	175	300
Storm Brewing	POFA	RKJ	1982	SP	22 X 27	AP	200	22	175	300

BYRON H BRATT

BORN: Everett, WA; 1952
EDUCATION: Western Washington State Univ, Bellingham, WA; Univ of Washington, Seattle, WA
AWARDS: Purchase Prize, Pratt Graphics Center, NY; Purchase Prize, Oregon Arts Commission; Purchase Prize, Library of Congress, Wash, DC
COLLECTIONS: Smithsonian Inst, Wash, DC; Pratt Graphics Center, NY
PRINTERS: Eldindean Press, Elmhurst NY (EldP); First Impressions Workshop, NY (FIW); Artist (ART)
PUBLISHERS: John Szoke Graphics, NY (JSG)
GALLERIES: Stone Press Gallery, Seattle, WA; Summa Gallery, Brooklyn, NY; Waterworks Gallery, Friday Harbor, WA
MAILING ADDRESS: 2907 Hewett, Everett, WA 98201

TITLE	PUBLISHER	PRINTER	DATE	MEDIUM	DIMENSION (PAPER SIZE) IN INCHES	TYPE OF PAPER	EDITION NUMBER	NO. OF COLORS	ORIGINAL OPENING PRICE	CURRENT RETAIL PRICE
SOLD OUT EDITIONS (RARE):										
Royal Jelly	JSG	EldP	1983	MEZ/HC	11 X 8	AC	150	6	190	250
Storm Window	JSG	EldP	1983	MEZ/HC	12 X 18	AC	100	8	300	350
Irisi Goddess of the Rainbow	JSG	EldP	1984	MEZ/HC	12 X 18	AC	100	10	235	300

BYRON H BRATT CONTINUED

TITLE	PUBLISHER	PRINTER	DATE	MEDIUM	DIMENSION (PAPER SIZE) IN INCHES	TYPE OF PAPER	EDITION NUMBER	NO. OF COLORS	ORIGINAL OPENING PRICE	CURRENT RETAIL PRICE
CURRENT EDITIONS:										
The Red Herring	JSG	ART/EldP	1985	MEZ/DPT/HC	15 X 19	R/BFK	15	6	200	400
The Four Seasons	JSG	ART/EldP	1986	MEZ/HC	18 X 30	R/BFK	100	6	250	300
With Open Arms	JSG	EldP	1986	MEZ/HC	15 X 12	R/BFK	100	Varies	250	300

JORGE TARALLO BRAUN

PRINTERS: American Atelier, NY (AA)

PUBLISHERS: Circle Fine Art, Chicago, IL (CFA)
GALLERIES: Circle Galleries, Pittsburgh, PA & Houston, TX & Chicago, IL & Soho, NY & Northbrook, IL & Scottsdale, AZ & Beverly Hills, CA & Costa Mesa, CA & Sherman Oaks, CA & Palm Beach, CA & Honolulu, HI & New Orleans, LA & Las Vegas, NV & Seattle, WA

TITLE	PUBLISHER	PRINTER	DATE	MEDIUM	DIMENSION (PAPER SIZE) IN INCHES	TYPE OF PAPER	EDITION NUMBER	NO. OF COLORS	ORIGINAL OPENING PRICE	CURRENT RETAIL PRICE
CURRENT EDITION:										
Full Dress Indian	CFA	AA	1985	LC	27 X 21	AP	300		100	250

TROY BRAUNTUCH

BORN: Jersey City, NJ; 1954
EDUCATION: California Inst of the Arts, Valencia, CA, BFA, 1973
RECENT EXHIB: Kent Gallery, NY, 1989

PRINTERS: Sheila Marbain, NY (SM); Frank Versaggi, NY (FV); Handworks/Maurel Studios, NY (H/MS)
PUBLISHERS: Editions Schellmann & Klüser, Munich, West Germany (SK)
GALLERIES: Editions Schellmann, New York, NY; Mary Boone Gallery, New York, NY; Pace Prints, New York, NY; Jan Baum Gallery, Los Angeles, CA; Kent Gallery, New York, NY

TITLE	PUBLISHER	PRINTER	DATE	MEDIUM	DIMENSION (PAPER SIZE) IN INCHES	TYPE OF PAPER	EDITION NUMBER	NO. OF COLORS	ORIGINAL OPENING PRICE	CURRENT RETAIL PRICE
CURRENT EDITIONS:										
Untitled (Set of 2)	SK	SM/FV/H/MS	1983	LC/SP	47 X 32 EA	AC	45 EA	5	1200 SET	1200 SET
									500 EA	600 EA

ANDRÉ BRAUNECKER

PRINTERS: American Atelier, NY (AA)
PUBLISHERS: Circle Fine Art, Chicago, IL (CFA)

GALLERIES: Circle Galleries, Chicago, IL & Northbrook, IL & Pittsburgh, PA & Houston, TX & Soho, NY & Scottsdale, AZ & Beverly Hills, CA & Costa Mesa, CA & Sherman Oaks, CA & Palm Beach, FL & Honolulu, HI & New Orleans, LA & Las Vegas, NV & Seattle, WA

TITLE	PUBLISHER	PRINTER	DATE	MEDIUM	DIMENSION (PAPER SIZE) IN INCHES	TYPE OF PAPER	EDITION NUMBER	NO. OF COLORS	ORIGINAL OPENING PRICE	CURRENT RETAIL PRICE
SOLD OUT EDITIONS (RARE):										
Face	CFA	AA	1984	LC	20 X 26	AP	200		100	200
Woman with Child	CFA	AA	1984	LC	19 X 26	AP	200		100	200
Blue Bird	CFA	AA	1984	LC	19 X 26	AP	200		100	200

FANNY BRENNAN

PRINTERS: Joseph Kleineman, NY (JK); Maureen Turci, NY (MT); J K Fine Arts, NY (JKFA)

PUBLISHERS: Chalk & Vermilion Fine Arts, Greenwich, CT (CVFA)
GALLERIES: Coe Kerr Gallery, New York, NY
MAILING ADDRESS: c/o Chalk & Vermilion Fine Arts, 200 Greenwich Ave, Greenwich, CT 06830

TITLE	PUBLISHER	PRINTER	DATE	MEDIUM	DIMENSION (PAPER SIZE) IN INCHES	TYPE OF PAPER	EDITION NUMBER	NO. OF COLORS	ORIGINAL OPENING PRICE	CURRENT RETAIL PRICE
CURRENT EDITIONS:										
La Premiere Edition (Set of 6):									550 SET	550 SET
Beach to Sky	CVFA	JKFA	1992	LC	6 X 7	AC	300		100	100
Chateau	CVFA	JKFA	1992	LC	6 X 7	AC	300		100	100
Christmas Tree	CVFA	JKFA	1992	LC	6 X 7	AC	300		100	100
Forest	CVFA	JKFA	1992	LC	6 X 7	AC	300		100	100
Mont St Michel	CVFA	JKFA	1992	LC	6 X 7	AC	300		100	100
Tagged Tree	CVFA	JKFA	1992	LC	6 X 7	AC	300		100	100
Folio II (Set of 6):									550 SET	550 SET
Aqueduct	CVFA	JKFA	1992	LC	6 X 7	AC	300		100	100
Big Horn	CVFA	JKFA	1992	LC	6 X 7	AC	300		100	100
Falling Ribbon	CVFA	JKFA	1992	LC	6 X 7	AC	300		100	100
Mountain Lift	CVFA	JKFA	1992	LC	6 X 7	AC	300		100	100

FANNY BRENNAN CONTINUED

TITLE	PUBLISHER	PRINTER	DATE	MEDIUM	DIMENSION (PAPER SIZE) IN INCHES	TYPE OF PAPER	EDITION NUMBER	NO. OF COLORS	ORIGINAL OPENING PRICE	CURRENT RETAIL PRICE
CURRENT EDITIONS:										
Pink House	CVFA	JKFA	1992	LC	6 X 7	AC	300		100	100
The Visitor	CVFA	JKFA	1992	LC	6 X 7	AC	300		100	100

HARVEY BREVERMAN

BORN: Pittsburgh, PA; January 7, 1934
EDUCATION: Carnegie-Mellon Univ, BFA, 1956; Ohio Univ, MFA, 1960
TEACHING: Art in Res, State Acad of Fine Arts, Amsterdam, Holland, 1965–66; Illinois State Univ, 1969; Ruskin Sch of Art, Oxford Univ, England, 1974,77; State Univ of New York, Buffalo, NY, 1961 to present
AWARDS: Tiffany Found Grant, 1962; Netherlands Government Grant, 1965; Graphics Prizes: 3rd British Int Print Biennale, 1972 & 2nd Norwegian Int Print Biennale, 1974; Nat Endowment for the Arts Fel, 1974–75, 1980–81; Mini Print Int de Cadaques, Spain, 1988
RECENT EXHIB: Gadatsy Gallery, Toronto, Can, 1987; Miami Univ Art Mus, Oxford, OH 1987; Mus of Fine Arts, Houston, TX, 1988; Mem Art Gallery, Rochester, NY, 1988; Contemp Arts Center, Cincinnati, OH, 1988; Albright-Knox Art Gallery, Buffalo, NY, 1989; Babcock Galleries, NY, 1990,91
COLLECTIONS: Albright-Knox Art Gallery, Buffalo, NY; Butler Inst of Am Art, Youngstown, OH; Israel Mus, Jerusalem, Israel; Nat Coll of Fine Arts, Wash, DC; British Mus, London, England; Mus of Mod Art, NY; Whitney Mus of Am Art, NY; Baltimore Mus of Art, MD; Philadelphia Mus of Art, PA
PRINTERS: Impressions Workshop, Inc, Boston, MA (IW); Robert Marx (RM); John Hutcheson (JH); Tom Tracy (TT); Tom Gordon (TG); Michael Morin (MM); Jennifer Hilton (JeH); Michael Morin, Buffalo, NY (MM); Celtic Press, Buffalo, NY (CP); Paul Martyka (PMar); Robert Aull (RA); Carol Luick (CL); Mike Crouse (MC); Jim Catalano (JCa); Jonathan Clemens (JC); Paul Maguire, Inc, Lake Oswego, OR (PM); Herb Fox, Merrimac MA (HF); Fox Editions, Merrimac, MA (FE); Artist (ART); Donald Robertt (DR); Alan Friedman (AF); Flat Rock Press, Portland, OR (FRP)
PUBLISHERS: Lakeside Studio, Lakeside, MI (LS); Ohio Northern Univ Printshop, Ada, Ohio (ONUP); Univ of West Virginia Printshop, Morgantown, W VA (UWVP); Celtic Press, Buffalo, NY (CP); Univ of Michigan Print Shop, Ann Arbor, MI (UMPS); Lake Placid Workshop, NY (LPW); Artist (ART); Arizona State Univ, Tempe, AZ (ASU)
GALLERIES: Lakeside Studio, Lakeside, MI; Babcock Galleries, New York, NY; Wenniger Graphics Gallery, Boston, MA: Gadatsy Gallery, Port Dover, ON, Canada
MAILING ADDRESS: 76 Smallwood Drive, Buffalo, NY 14226

TITLE	PUBLISHER	PRINTER	DATE	MEDIUM	DIMENSION (PAPER SIZE) IN INCHES	TYPE OF PAPER	EDITION NUMBER	NO. OF COLORS	ORIGINAL OPENING PRICE	CURRENT RETAIL PRICE
SOLD OUT EDITIONS (RARE):										
Manipulator	ART	ART	1965	I	30 X 22	R/BFK	20	1	90	475
Figure with Medallion	ART	ART	1965	I	32 X 25	GCP	15	1	100	700
Dubious Honor III	ART	ART	1965	I	30 X 20	R/BFK	20	1	90	475
Newcomer and the Honors	ART	ART	1965	I	23 X 35	R/BFK	20	1	150	1200
Figure with Tallis XII	ART	ART	1967	I	26 X 25	R/BFK	25	1	75	500
Dutch Interior	ART	ART	1967	I	22 X 27	R/BFK	25	1	150	700
Dutchman II	ART	ART	1967	I	23 TON	R/HWT	25	2	100	700
Dutchman IV	ART	ART	1967	I	22 TON	R/HWT	30	2	100	700
Dutchman V	ART	ART	1968	I	22 X 28	MUR	25	2	100	700
Brooding Figure	ART	ART	1968	I	23 TON	MUR/T	25	3	150	700
Discourse	IW	HF/JW	1970	I	25 X 22	R/HWT	35	1	135	700
Seated Figure in Red	ART	RA/AF	1975	IC	13 X 15	R/BFK	25	3	85	150
Study of Peter Redgrove	LPW	JCa	1977	SP	22 X 30	AP/B	16	4	125	250
Sinclair (Hitchings)	LS	PM	1981	LC	22 X 15	AC/B	50	3	100	175
CURRENT EDITIONS										
View of Acre	ART	ART	1967	I	22 X 30	AC/B	30	1	90	350
Dubious Honor with Illuminations	IW	HF	1970	LC	16 X 26	AP/B	30	2	150	300
Two Men	ART	CL/IW	1970	I	23 TON	R/HWT	40	1	100	300
Dispution	IN	PM/JH	1971	LC	27 X 16	R/BFK	30	3	135	850
Cynic	IW	PM/JH	1971	LC	27 X 18	GE	35	4	135	500
Time Sequence-Honig	ONUP	DR	1971	LB	35 X 25	R/BFK	10	1	150	750
Study of Michael Rothenstein	LS	JC/LS	1973	LC	25 X 18	AC/W	75	5	135	185
Study of Leslie Fiedler	ART	RA	1973	I	23 X 31	AC/W	25	1	150	250
Study of Mischa Schnieder II	ART	ART	1973	I/SP	25 X 25	MUR/T	15	2	150	250
Study of Creeley	ART	RA	1974	I	23 X 31	R/HWT/T	20	1	150	250
Seated Figure in Profile	ART	RA	1975	I	13 X 15	R/BFK	40	1	75	110
Standing Figure in Profile (Ruthenstein)	ART	RA	1975	I	12 X 15	AC/B	50	1	75	110
English Poet-Ruthven Todd	LS	HF	1977	LC	22 X 30	AP/B	16	4	125	300
Literary Critic-Dwight MacDonald	LS	HF	1977	LC	22 X 30	AP/B	50	4	135	300
The Draftsman	ART	TT	1977	LC	22 X 30	AP/B	25	4	125	375
Schneider with Fragments	LPW	JCa	1977	SP	50 X 38	AE	10	5	450	600
Hamberg with Fragments	LPW	JCa	1977	SP	50 X 38	AE	10	5	450	600
The Lithographer	LPW	HF	1978	LC	22 X 30	RP/G	12	3	150	300
The Painter Kamrowski	UMPS	MC	1979	LC	23 X 34	AP/B	34	3	165	250
The Etcher Cassara	UMPS	PMar	1980	IC	19 X 24	R/BFK	35	2	165	250
Paul (Maguire)	LS	PM	1980	LC	26 X 20	RP/G	50	1	150	200
Self-Portrait 1980	LS	PM	1981	LC	15 X 22	AP/B	50	3	150	185
Cartesian Composite	ONUP	TG	1981	LC	22 X 30	RP/B	10	1	185	300

The retail prices of the 100,000 limited edition prints quoted in this directory are subject to change. Print publishers, artists and galleries were the direct sources for these quotations. Prices in the secondary market listed as "Sold Out Editions (Rare)" indicate that the publisher has a limited supply of that print or that the print is difficult to locate in the galleries.

HARVEY BREVERMAN CONTINUED

TITLE	PUBLISHER	PRINTER	DATE	MEDIUM	DIMENSION (PAPER SIZE) IN INCHES	TYPE OF PAPER	EDITION NUMBER	NO. OF COLORS	ORIGINAL OPENING PRICE	CURRENT RETAIL PRICE
CURRENT EDITIONS:										
Cartesian Interior	ART	JeH	1982	LC	27 X 20	RP/G	18	4	285	400
Barth-Fiedler-Etc	UWVP	MM	1982	I	12 X 24	RP/HNT	18	1	250	275
Edwin Dickinson	CP	MM/CP	1983	I	22 X 21	AC/B	20	1	125	150
The Transfer Press	ART	PM	1983	LB	22 X 30	AP/B	10	1	125	150
Double Beckett	ART	PM	1985	LC	22 X 30	RP/T	20	5	300	375
The Etcher Morin	ART/CP	MM	1986	IC	22 X 30	AP/B	20	2	250	375
Michel Serres	ART	PM	1986	LC	22 X 30	AC/W	20	4	300	300
Collaboration	FRP	PM	1987	LB	15 X 22	R/BFK/G	10	1	125	150
Robert Duncan	ART	ART	1988	I	15 X 11	AC/B	30	1	60	85
Krishna Reddy	ART	ART	1988	I	15 X 11	AC/B	30	1	60	85
Samuel Beckett	ART	ART	1991	I	11 X 10	AC/B	25	1	60	85
Alan Ginsberg	ART	ART	1991	I	11 X 10	AC/B	25	1	60	85
Robbe-Grillet	ART	ART	1992	I	11 X 10	AC/B	25	1	70	70
J M Coetzee	ART	ART	1992	I	11 X 10	AC/B	25	1	70	70
The Humanist	ASU	ART	1992	I	11 X 14	AC/B	33	1	100	100

WILLIAM BRICE

BORN: New York, NY; April 23, 1921
EDUCATION: Art Student's League, NY; Chouinard Art Inst, Los Angeles, CA
TEACHING: Jepson Art Inst, Los Angeles, CA; Univ of California, Los Angeles, CA, 1953 to present
RECENT EXHIB: L A Louver, Venice, CA, 1989; Los Angeles County Mus, CA, 1990
COLLECTIONS: Mus of Mod Art, NY; Metropolitan Mus, NY; Whitney Mus of Am Art, NY; Art Inst of Chicago, IL; Los Angeles County Mus, CA; Santa Barbara, Mus, CA; Wichita Art Mus, KS; Univ of Nebraska, Lincoln, NE; Phillips Acad, Andover, MA: Utica Col, Ithaca, NY; Hirshhorn Mus, Wash, DC
PUBLISHERS: Crown Point Press, San Francisco, CA(CPP)
PRINTERS: Hidekatsu Takada, Oakland, CA (HT); Pam Paulson, San Francisco, CA (PP); Lawrence Hamlin, San Francisco, CA (LH); Crown Point Press, San Francisco, CA (CPP)
GALLERIES: Robert Miller Gallery, New York, NY; L A Louver Gallery, Venice, CA; Crown Point Press, New York, NY; & San Francisco, CA; Richard Levy Gallery, Albuquerque, NM; Tamarind Institute, Albuquerque, NM
MAILING ADDRESS: 427 Beloit St, Los Angeles, CA 90049

TITLE	PUBLISHER	PRINTER	DATE	MEDIUM	DIMENSION (PAPER SIZE) IN INCHES	TYPE OF PAPER	EDITION NUMBER	NO. OF COLORS	ORIGINAL OPENING PRICE	CURRENT RETAIL PRICE
SOLD OUT EDITIONS (RARE):										
Untitled Suite (Set of 3)									1200 SET	1500 SET
Untitled #1 (Gray Rock)	CPP	HT/CPP	1985	I/AC	12 X 15	SOM	25	1	450	550
Untitled #2 (Three Elements)	CPP	HT/CPP	1985	I/AC	12 X 15	SOM	25	1	450	550
Untitled #3 (Sepia Rock)	CPP	HT/CPP	1985	I/AC	12 X 15	SOM	25	1	450	550
Untitled #4 (Pattern)	CPP	HT/CPP	1985	I/AC	16 X 16	SOM	25	1	550	750
Untitled #5 (Ivory Field)	CPP	HT/CPP	1985	I/AC	30 X 44	SOM	25	1	1800	2200
Untitled #6 (Gray Field)	CPP	HT/CPP	1985	I/AC	31 X 44	SOM	25	1	1800	2200
Kyoto	CPP	CPP	1987	WC	41 X 28	SOM	100	7	800	800
CURRENT EDITIONS:										
Untitled #7	CPP	PP/LH/CPP	1990	EB/A/HG	15 X 12	SOM/S	15	1	300	350
Untitled #8 (Color)	CPP	PP/LH/CPP	1990	EB/HG/SG	12 X 15	SOM/S	25		450	600
Untitled #9 (Color)	CPP	PP/LH/CPP	1990	EB/A/SG/SB	12 X 15	SOM/S	25		450	600
Untitled #10	CPP	PP/LH/CPP	1990	EB/A/SG	38 X 30	SOM/TEX	15	1	650	700
Untitled #11 (Color)	CPP	PP/LH/CPP	1990	EB/A/SB	38 X 30	SOM/TEX	25		900	900
Untitled #12 (Color)	CPP	PP/LH/CPP	1990	EB/A/SB	21 X 19	SOM/S	25	1	600	650
Untitled #13	CPP	PP/LH/CPP	1990	EB/SG/SB	21 X 19	SOM/S	15	1	450	500

LAMAR BRIGGS

BORN: Lafayette, LA; 1935
EDUCATION: Univ of Southwestern Louisiana, Lafayette, LA, 1953; Univ of Houston, TX, 1958; Art Center of Los Angeles, CA, 1959; Colorado Inst of Art, Denver, CO, 1960; Independent Study, Antibes, France, 1966
AWARDS: Ford Found Award, Mus of Fine Arts, Houston, TX, 1962–63; Annual Purchase Award, Beaumont Art Mus, TX, 1964
RECENT EXHIB: Joanne Lyon Gallery, Aspen, CO, 1987; Neville-Sargent Gallery, Chicago, IL, 1987; Odette Gilbert Gallery, London, England, 1988; Lisa Dubins Gallery, Los Angeles, CA, 1988; Marilyn Butler Fine Art, Scottsdale, AZ, 1987,88; Moody Gallery, Houston, TX, 1987,88
COLLECTIONS: Univ of Houston, TX; Denver Art Mus, CO; Laguna Gloria Art Mus, Austin, TX; Aspen Art Mus, CO; Mint Mus, Charlotte, NC; Univ of Southern Louisiana, LA
PRINTERS: Atelier Dumas, NY (AD); Jorge Dumas, NY (JD); Kathleen Caraccio, NY (KC)
PUBLISHERS: London Arts Inc, Detroit, MI (LAI)
GALLERIES: Moody Gallery, Houston, TX; Robert L Kidd Associates, Birmingham, MI; Malcolm Brown Gallery, Shaker Heights, OH; Susan Duval Gallery, Aspen, CO; Galerie Martin, Boca Raton, FL; Martin Lawrence Galleies, Newport Beach, CA

TITLE	PUBLISHER	PRINTER	DATE	MEDIUM	DIMENSION (PAPER SIZE) IN INCHES	TYPE OF PAPER	EDITION NUMBER	NO. OF COLORS	ORIGINAL OPENING PRICE	CURRENT RETAIL PRICE
CURRENT EDITIONS:										
Bird Landscape	LAI	JD/AD	1978	LC	21 X 29	SOM	200	8	350	600

ALEXANDER BRODSKY & ILYA UTKIN

BORN: Moscow, Russia; 1955
EDUCATION: Moscow Architecture Inst, Russia, 1978
AWARDS: Second Prize, OISTT Competition, Paris, France, 1978; First Prize, Central Glass Competition, Crystal Palace, Tokyo, Japan, 1982; Third Prize, Shinkenchiku Competition, Tokyo, Japan, 1983; Second Prize, Shinkenchiku Competition, Tokyo, Japan, 1985; Second Prize, Central Glass Competition, Tokyo, Japan, 1984,86; First Prize, Architecture, NY, 1988
RECENT EXHIB: Ronald Feldman Fine Arts, NY, 1990; Linda Farris Gallery, Seattle, WA, 1990; Pittsburgh Center for the Arts, PA, 1991; Tacoma Art Mus, WA, 1991; Gallery 72, Omaha, NE, 1991; San Diego State Univ Mus, CA, 1989,91; Univ of Arizona Mus, Tucson, AZ, 1992; Wellington City Art Gallery, New Zealand, Australia, 1992

COLLECTIONS: Mus of Mod Art, NY; Pushkin State Mus of Fine Arts, Moscow, Russia; Des Moines Art Center, IA; Inst of Contemp Art, Boston, MA; Univ of Arizona Art Mus, Tucson, AZ; San Diego Mus of Contemp Art, CA; San Diego State Univ Art Gallery, CA; Hirshhorn Mus, Wash, DC
PRINTERS: Kathy Carracio, NY (KC); John Wagner, NY (JW); K Carracio Studios, NY (KCS)
PUBLISHERS: Ronald Feldman Fine Arts, NY (RFFA)
GALLERIES: Ronald Feldman Fine Arts, New York, NY; Linda Farris Gallery, Seattle, WA; Gwenda Jay Gallery, Chicago, IL
MAILING ADDRESS: c/o Ronald Feldman Fine Arts, 31 Mercer St, New York, NY 10013

TITLE	PUBLISHER	PRINTER	DATE	MEDIUM	DIMENSION (PAPER SIZE) IN INCHES	TYPE OF PAPER	EDITION NUMBER	NO. OF COLORS	ORIGINAL OPENING PRICE	CURRENT RETAIL PRICE
CURRENT EDITIONS:										
Projects (Set of 35)	RFFA	KC/JW/KCS	1981–90	EB	42 X 31 EA (25) Various (10)	AP	30 EA	1 EA	75000 SET	75000 SET
Twelfth Street Pedestrian Bride, City of Tacoma	RFFA	KC/JW/KCS	1991	EB	36 X 60	AP	40	1	7500	7500

STAN BRODSKY

BORN: New York, NY; March 23, 1925
EDUCATION: Univ of Missouri, Kansas City, MO, Bachelor of Journalism, 1949; Univ of Iowa, Iowa City, IA, MFA, 1950; Columbia Univ, NY, Doctorate in Art Educ, 1959
TEACHING: Univ of Delaware, Newark, DE, 1957–59; C W Post, Long Island Univ, Brooklyn, NY, 1960–91
AWARDS: First Prize, Delaware Art Center, Wilmington, DE, 1958; Second Prize, Heckscher Mus, Huntington, NY, 1968; Second Prize, North Shore Art Assn, Manhasset, NY, 1970; MacDowell Colony Fel, Peterboro, NH, 1971; Virginia Center for Creative Art Fel, Sweetbriar, VA, 1985,86,89; Yaddo Fel, Sarasota Springs, NY, 1987,88; Trustees Award, Long Island Univ, NY, 1992

RECENT EXHIB: Benton Gallery, Southampton, NY, 1987,88; Munic Gallery, Regensberg, Germany, 1988; June Kelly Gallery, NY, 1988,89; Retrosp, Heckscher Mus, Huntington, NY, 1991; June Kelly Gallery, NY, 1991; Hopkins Gallery, Wellfleet, MA, 1992
COLLECTIONS: Heckscher Mus, Huntington, NY; Guild Hall, Easthampton, NY; Parrish Mus, Southampton, NY; New York Univ, NY; Univ of Delaware, Newark, DE
PUBLISHERS: Welden Press, Sag Harbor, NY (WP)
PRINTERS: Dan Welden, Sag Harbor, NY (DW); Welden Press, Sag Harbor, NY (WP); Joanne Guidice, NY (JG); Rick Mills, NY (RM); C W Post Center, Long Island Univ, Brookville, NY (CWP)
GALLERIES: June Kelly Gallery, New York, NY; Gallery North, Setauket, NY
MAILING ADDRESS: 7 Glen-Na-Little Trail, Huntington, NY 11743

TITLE	PUBLISHER	PRINTER	DATE	MEDIUM	DIMENSION (PAPER SIZE) IN INCHES	TYPE OF PAPER	EDITION NUMBER	NO. OF COLORS	ORIGINAL OPENING PRICE	CURRENT RETAIL PRICE
CURRENT EDITIONS:										
Passages	WP	WP	1980	LB	24 X 20	R/BFK	26		175	350
Passages	WP	WP	1980	HC/LC/WA	24 X 20	R/BFK	26		275	400
Tide Drift	WP	WP	1980	LB	9 X 11	R/BFK	10		100	250
Vigil		JG/CWP	1989	LB	17 X 24	R/BFK	24	1	200	200

ARTHUR WILLIAM BRODY

BORN: New York, NY; March 2, 1943
EDUCATION: Harvey Mudd Col, BS, 1965; Claremont Grad Sch, CA, MFA, 1967
TEACHING: Asst Prof, Ripon Col, Ripon, WI, 1970–75; Instr, Univ of Alaska, Fairbanks, AK, 1967–69, Asst Prof to Assoc Prof, 1977–84, Prof, 1984 to present
AWARDS: Achievement Award, Riverside Art Assn, Riverside, CA, 1966; NE Wisconsin Annual, Greenbay, WI, Merit Award, 1971, First Prize, 1974; Print Award, All Alaska Juried Show, 1980
COLLECTIONS: Southern Illinois Univ, Carbondale, IL; St Lawrence Univ, Canton, NY; Neville Mus, Greenbay, WI; Art Bank, State of Alaska, Anchorage, AK; Historical and Fine Arts Mus, Anchorage, AK; Univ of Alaska, Fairbanks, AK
PRINTERS: Artist (ART)
PUBLISHERS: Artist (ART)
GALLERIES: The Gathering, Ketchikan, AK; Steven King, Lincoln, MA
MAILING ADDRESS: SR 10276, Fairbanks, AK 99701; Dept of Art, Univ of Alaska, Fairbanks, AK 99201

TITLE	PUBLISHER	PRINTER	DATE	MEDIUM	DIMENSION (PAPER SIZE) IN INCHES	TYPE OF PAPER	EDITION NUMBER	NO. OF COLORS	ORIGINAL OPENING PRICE	CURRENT RETAIL PRICE
CURRENT EDITIONS:										
What Can I Say	ART	ART	1975	I	24 X 24	MUR	25	1	100	200
Touch	ART	ART	1976	WC	24 X 36	GORU	50	5	150	250
Land/Cut	ART	ART	1976	WC	24 X 36	GORU	50	5	150	250
Comfortably Hot	ART	ART	1980	MEZ	22 X 24	R/BFK	20	4	200	250
Soft	ART	ART	1980	WC	24 X 36	JAP/E	50	9	175	250
Knock Not	ART	ART	1981	WC	24 X 36	JAP/E	50	4	175	250
Kisses	ART	ART	1981	WB	30 X 60	R/BFK	25	1	200	300
Run in the Woods	ART	ART	1982	WC	30 X 60	OKP	10	4	300	450
Run Alone	ART	ART	1982	WC	30 X 60	OKP	25	4	300	450
The Space	ART	ART	1982	WC	30 X 60	OKP	25	4	300	450

MARCEL BROODTHAERS

BORN: (1924–1976)
RECENT EXHIB: Galerie Michael Werner, Cologne, West Germany, 1987; Mary Boone Gallery, NY, 1989; Michael Werner Gallery, NY, 1991

PUBLISHERS: Galerie Heiner Friedrich, Munich, Germany (GHF); Galerie Yvon Lambert, Paris, France (GYL); Multiples, NY (M)
GALLERIES: Marian Goodman Gallery, New York, NY; Mary Boone Gallery, New York, NY; Galerie Michael Werner, Cologne, Germany; Michael Werner Gallery, New York, NY

Jamar (J); Werner (W)

TITLE	PUBLISHER	PRINTER	DATE	MEDIUM	DIMENSION (PAPER SIZE) IN INCHES	TYPE OF PAPER	EDITION NUMBER	NO. OF COLORS	ORIGINAL OPENING PRICE	CURRENT RETAIL PRICE
SOLD OUT EDITIONS (RARE):										
La Soupe de Daguerre	M			PH/C/CO	20 X 21	AC			1500	13000
Comedie	M			PH/C	25 X 18	AC			1200	9000
Ein Eisenbahnuberfall (J-11) (W-11)	GHF		1972	LC/OFF	31 X 20	AP	100		500	9000
Comment Va Le Memoire et La Fontaine (J-17) (W-16)	GYL		1973	LC/OFF	26 X 17	AP	100		500	9000
CURRENT EDITIONS:										
Museum I, II (Set of 2)	M		1972	SP	33 X 23 EA	AC	100 EA		1000 SET	12000 SET
Das Recht (Set of 2)	M		1972	SP	24 X 17 / 24 X 27	AC / AC	120 EA		1000 SET	12000 SET
Poeme-Change-Exchange-Wechsel	M		1973	SP	41 X 28	AC	100		1200	10000
Comedie	M				25 X 18				1200	9000
Les Animaux de la Ferme (Set of 2)	M		1974	LC/OFF	33 X 23 EA	AP	100 EA		800 SET	12000 SET
Portraits (16 Portraits with 1 Self-Portrait) (Set of 17)	M		1983	PH	20 X 16 EA		50 EA		2000 SET	4500 SET

JAMES BROOKS

BORN: St Louis, MO; (1906–1992)
EDUCATION: Southern Methodist Univ, Dallas, TX; Art Students League, NY
AWARDS: Carnegie Int Prize, 1952; Art Inst of Chicago, Purchase Prizes, 1957,61; Ford Found Fel, 1962; Guggenheim Fel, NY, 1967–68
COLLECTIONS: Mus of Mod Art, NY; Metropolitan Mus of Art, NY; Solomon R Guggenheim Mus, NY; Tate Gallery, London, England; Brooklyn Mus, NY

PRINTERS: American Atelier, NY (AA)
PUBLISHERS: Transworld Art Inc, NY (TAI)
GALLERIES: Elaine Benson Gallery, Bridgehampton, NY; Manny Silverman Gallery, Los Angeles, CA; David Anderson Gallery, Buffalo, NY; Vered Gallery, New York, NY; Berry-Hill Galleries, Inc, New York, NY; Edward Tyler Nahem Fine Art, New York, NY; Argus Fine Arts, Eugene, OR; Benjamin-Beattie Fine Arts, Chicago, IL
MAILING ADDRESS: 128 Neck Path, The Springs, East Hampton, NY 11937

TITLE	PUBLISHER	PRINTER	DATE	MEDIUM	DIMENSION (PAPER SIZE) IN INCHES	TYPE OF PAPER	EDITION NUMBER	NO. OF COLORS	ORIGINAL OPENING PRICE	CURRENT RETAIL PRICE
CURRENT EDITIONS:										
Eastern	TAI	AA	1981	LC	30 X 22	SOM	150	1	350	500

JEFFREY OWEN BROSK

BORN: New York, NY; February 15, 1947
EDUCATION: Univ of Pennsylvania, BA, BS, 1970; Massachusetts Inst of Tech, Cambridge, Inst of Tech, Cambridge, MA, MA, 1976
COLLECTIONS: Mercy Col, Dobbs Ferry, NY
PRINTERS: Bud Shark, Boulder, CO (BS); Ron Trujillo, Boulder, CO (RT); Matthew Christie, Boulder, CO (MC); Mark Villarreal, Boulder, CO (MV);
PUBLISHERS: Shark's, Inc, Boulder, CO (SI)
GALLERIES: Shark's Inc, Boulder, CO; Max Hutchinson Gallery, New York, NY; Stephen Rosenberg Gallery, New York, NY; Quartet Editions, New York, NY
MAILING ADDRESS: 135 Spring St, New York, NY 10012

Jeffrey Owen Brosk
Dakota Ridge
Courtesy Shark's Inc

TITLE	PUBLISHER	PRINTER	DATE	MEDIUM	DIMENSION (PAPER SIZE) IN INCHES	TYPE OF PAPER	EDITION NUMBER	NO. OF COLORS	ORIGINAL OPENING PRICE	CURRENT RETAIL PRICE
SOLD OUT EDITIONS (RARE):										
*Dakota Ridge	SI	BS/RT/RC/SI	1989	LC/CO	22 X 33 X 2	R/BFK	25	5	1200	1600
Shadow Dance	SI	BS/RT/RC/SI	1992	LC/WC	26 X 50 X 3	R/BFK	20	2	1400	1600

*(Each Print has been cut, folded, assembled and mounted in a plexiglas frame—total size is 27 X 39 X 4)

FREDERICK BROSEN

BORN: New York, NY
COLLECTIONS: Metropolitan Mus of Art, NY; Hood Mus, Hanover, NH; New York Historical Soc, NY; Knoxville Mus of Art, TN; Rockefeller Found, NY
PRINTERS: Atelier Ettinger, NY (AE)
PUBLISHERS: John Szoke Graphics, Inc, NY (JSG)
GALLERIES: John Szoke Graphics, New York, NY; Schmidt Bingham Gallery, New York, NY

Frederick Brosen
Brooklyn Bridge
Courtesy John Szoke Graphics, Inc

TITLE	PUBLISHER	PRINTER	DATE	MEDIUM	DIMENSION (PAPER SIZE) IN INCHES	TYPE OF PAPER	EDITION NUMBER	NO. OF COLORS	ORIGINAL OPENING PRICE	CURRENT RETAIL PRICE
CURRENT EDITIONS:										
Brooklyn Bridge	JSG	AE	1992	LC	23 X 34	AP	150	8	650	650

CHARLOTTE BROWN

PRINTERS: Virginia Commonwealth Univ Workshop, Richmond, VA (VCU)
PUBLISHERS: Virginia Commonwealth Univ, Richmond, VA (VCU)
GALLERIES: Joy Horwich Gallery, Chicago, IL; Shippee Gallery, New York, NY

TITLE	PUBLISHER	PRINTER	DATE	MEDIUM	DIMENSION (PAPER SIZE) IN INCHES	TYPE OF PAPER	EDITION NUMBER	NO. OF COLORS	ORIGINAL OPENING PRICE	CURRENT RETAIL PRICE
SOLD OUT EDITIONS (RARE):										
*China Song	VCU	VCU	1983	PH/LC/SP/CO	24 X 28	FABRIC	9		600	1000
**Red River Rose	VCU	VCU	1983	PH/LC/SP/CO	25 X 28	RICE	9		600	1000

*(Printed on Non-Woven Fabric)
**(Collage Printed on Rice Paper)

LOUISE FRESHMAN BROWN

PRINTERS: Judith Solodkin, NY (JS); Solo Press, NY (SP)
PUBLISHERS: Solo Press, NY (SP)
GALLERIES: Solo Impressions, New York, NY

TITLE	PUBLISHER	PRINTER	DATE	MEDIUM	DIMENSION (PAPER SIZE) IN INCHES	TYPE OF PAPER	EDITION NUMBER	NO. OF COLORS	ORIGINAL OPENING PRICE	CURRENT RETAIL PRICE
CURRENT EDITIONS:										
Untitled	SP	JS/SP	1984	LB	15 X 12	AP		1	150	200

The retail prices of the 100,000 limited edition prints quoted in this directory are subject to change. Print publishers, artists and galleries were the direct sources for these quotations. Prices in the secondary market listed as "Sold Out Editions (Rare)" indicate that the publisher has a limited supply of that print or that the print is difficult to locate in the galleries.

CHRISTOPHER BROWN

BORN: Camp Lejeune, NC; 1951
EDUCATION: Univ of Illinois, Urbana, Champaign, IL, BA, 1972, BFA, 1973; Univ of California, Davis, CA, 1976
AWARDS: Nat Endowment for the Arts, Special Projects Grant, Art Criticism, 1981; Univ of California, Berkeley, Regents' Junior Faculty Fel, 1984; Mortimer Fleishhacker Found, Eureka Fel, 1985; Nat Endowment for the Arts Grant, Painting, 1987; Am Acad & Inst of Arts & Letters Award, 1988
RECENT EXHIB: Newport Harbor Art Mus, CA, 1987; Contemp Arts Center, Cincinnati, OH, 1987; Univ of Texas, Arlington, TX, 1988; Univ of Santa Clara, de Saisset Mus, CA, 1988; Richmond Art Center, VA, 1989; Gallery Paule Anglim, San Francisco, CA, 1987,90; Shea & Beker Gallery, NY, 1990; Edward Thorp Gallery, NY, 1992; Linda Farris Gallery, Seattle, WA, 1992; Campbell-Thiebaud Gallery, San Francisco, CA, 1993
COLLECTIONS: Univ of California, Berkeley, CA, Walker Art Center, Minneapolis, MN; New York Public Library, NY; Redding Mus, CA; New York Univ, Grey Art Gallery, NY; San Francisco Mus of Mod Art, CA; Sheldon Mem Art Gallery, Lincoln, NE
PRINTERS: Bill Lagattuta, Albuquerque, NM (BL); Tamarind Inst, Albuquerque, MN (TI); Artist (ART); Crown Point Press, San Francisco, CA (CPP)
PUBLISHERS: Tamarind Inst, Albuquerque, NM (TI); Crown Point Press, San Francisco, CA (CPP)
GALLERIES: Gallery Paule Anglim, San Francisco, CA; Zolla/Lieberman Gallery, Chicago, IL; Tamarind Inst, Albuquerque, NM; Experimental Workshop, San Francisco, CA; Crown Point Press, San Francisco, CA & New York, NY; Richard Levy Gallery, Albuquerque, NM; Susan Caldwell & Company, New York, NY; Betsy Senior Contemporary Prints, New York, NY; Schmidt/Dean Gallery, Phila, PA; L Bartman Fine Arts, Chicago, IL; Campbell-Thiebaud Gallery, San Francisco, CA

Christopher Brown
Station
Courtesy Crown Point Press

TITLE	PUBLISHER	PRINTER	DATE	MEDIUM	DIMENSION (PAPER SIZE) IN INCHES	TYPE OF PAPER	EDITION NUMBER	NO. OF COLORS	ORIGINAL OPENING PRICE	CURRENT RETAIL PRICE
CURRENT EDITIONS:										
Yellow Light (Hand drawing with Brush, Ink & Pastel Crayon)	TI	ART/BL	1988	MON/HC	41 X 30 EA	AP/W	1 EA	Multi	2000 EA	2000 EA
Coursing the Yangtze	TI	ART/BL	1988	MON/WC	39 X 30 EA	AP/W	1 EA	Multi	2000 EA	2000 EA
Ming Light	TI	ART/BL	1988	MON/WC	42 X 30 EA	AP/W	1 EA	Multi	2000 EA	2000 EA
Under the Flag	CPP	CPP	1991	EB/A/SB	42 X 41	AP/W	25		1500	1500
Seventy-Nine Men	CPP	CPP	1991	EB/SG	42 X 41	AP/W	25	1	1500	1500
Forty Flakes	CPP	CPP	1991	EB/A/SG	42 X 41	AP/W	50	1	2000	3000
Crowd at the Base of a Monument	CPP	CPP	1991	EB/SG	42 X 41	AP/W	25	1	1500	1800
Station	CPP	CPP	1993	EB/A/SG/SB	31 X 30	AP/W	65		2500	2500
1929	CPP	CPP	1993	EB/A/SG/SB	18 X 17	SOM	35		1000	1000
Eighty-Second Street	CPP	PP/PB/CPP	1993	EB/A/SG/SB	18 X 17	SOM	25		1000	1000
Malaga	CPP	PP/PB/CPP	1993	EB/A/SG/SB	18 X 17	SOM	35	1	1000	1000
Flight (Red)	CPP	PP/PB/CPP	1993	EB/A/SG/SB	18 X 17	SOM	10	1	1000	1000
Flight (Blue)	CPP	PP/PB/CPP	1993	EB/A/SG/SB	18 X 17	SOM	10	1	1000	1000

LARRY BROWN

BORN: New Brunswick, NJ; June 1, 1942
EDUCATION: Washington State Univ, Pullman, WA, BA, 1967; Univ of Arizona, Tucson, AZ, MFA, 1970
TEACHING: Vis Art, Painting, Montana State Univ, Boseman, MT, 1978; Vis Art, Painting, Iowa State Univ, Ames, IA, 1982; North Texas State Univ, Denton, TX, 1985; Vis Art, Painting, Ohio State Univ, Columbus, OH, 1983,86; Vis Art, Painting, Rutgers Univ, New Brunswick, NJ, 1987; Vis Art, Painting, State Univ of New York, Stony Brook, NY, 1987; Vis Art, Painting, New Mexico State Univ, Albuquerque, NM, 1988; Vis Art, Painting, Arizona State Univ, Tempe, AZ, 1988; Vis Art, Painting, Syracuse Univ, NY, 1988
AWARDS: Nat Endowment for the Arts Fel, 1979-80
RECENT EXHIB: Galerie Ninety-Nine, Bay Harbor Islands, FL, 1987; Elliot Smith Gallery, St Louis, MO, 1988; Ivory/Kimpton Gallery, San Francisco, CA, 1988; G H Dalsheimer Gallery, Baltimore, MD, 1988; Carnegie Mus of Art, Pittsburgh, PA, 1988; Edward Thorden Gallery, Gothenburg, Sweden, 1989; Frank Morton Art Gallery, Muhlenberg Col, Allentown, PA, 1989; Carlo Lamagna Gallery, NY, 1987,89
COLLECTIONS: Indianapolis Mus, IN; Minnesota Mus, Minneapolis, MN; Portland Mus, ME; St Lawrence Univ, Canton, NY; Univ of Wisconsin, Madison, WI; Walker Art Center, Minneapolis, MN
PRINTERS: Bill Lagattuta, Albuquerque, NM (BL); Anya Szykitka, Albuquerque, NM (AS); Artist (ART); Tamarind Inst, Albuquerque, NM (TI)
PUBLISHERS: Tamarind Inst, Albuquerque, NM (TI); Artist (ART)
GALLERIES: Signet Arts, St Louis, MO; Tamarind Inst, Albuquerque, NM; Elliot Smith Gallery, St Louis, MO; Edward Thorden Gallery, Gothenburg, Sweden; Ann Jaffe Gallery, Bay Harbor Islands, FL; Morgan Gallery, Kansas City, MO; Richard Levy Gallery, Albuquerque, NM; Helander Gallery, New York, NY; Brenda Kroos Gallery, Cleveland, OH
MAILING ADDRESS: 54 Franklin St, #4-R, New York, NY 10013

TITLE	PUBLISHER	PRINTER	DATE	MEDIUM	DIMENSION (PAPER SIZE) IN INCHES	TYPE OF PAPER	EDITION NUMBER	NO. OF COLORS	ORIGINAL OPENING PRICE	CURRENT RETAIL PRICE
CURRENT EDITIONS:										
Veil of Delhi	TI	ART/BL/TI	1989	LC	26 X 19	SOM/S	20	6	300	400
Saturn Time	TI	ART/AS/TI	1989	LC	26 X 19	MAG	20	5	300	400
Born in Paris	TI	ART/AS/TI	1989	LC	26 X 19	R/BFK	20	5	300	400
Red Rain	TI	ART/BL/TI	1989	LC	26 X 19	SOM/W	20	6	300	400
Dieties and Mortals	TI	ART/JS/TI	1989	LC	26 X 19	ARJ	20	5	600	750
Untitled: LB–04–IV	ART	ART	1989	MON	31 X 24 EA	ARS	1 EA	Varies	1500 EA	1800 EA

JAMES BROWN

BORN: Los Angeles, CA; 1951
EDUCATION: Immaculate Heart Col, Hollywood, CA, 1970–72; Ecole Superieure Des Beaux Arts, Paris, France, 1973–75; Immaculate Heart Col, Hollywood, CA, BFA, 1975; Inst Michaelangelo, Florence, Italy, 1979
RECENT EXHIB: Maloney Gallery, Santa Monica, CA, 1987; Leo Castelli Graphics, NY, 1989; Tony Shafrazi Gallery, NY, 1989; Greenberg Gallery, St Louis, MO, 1987; Thomas Segal Gallery, Boston, MA, 1987; Anders Tornberg Gallery, Sweden, 1987; Maloney Gallery, Santa Monica, CA, 1987; Galerie Maeght Lelong, Paris, France, 1987; Galerie Thaddaeus Ropac, Salzburg, Austria, 1987; Galerie Catherine Issert, St Paul de Vence, France, 1987; Galerie Lucio Amelio, Naples, Italy, 1987; Heland & Wetterling Gallery, Stockholm, Sweden, 1988; Leo Castelli Gallery, NY, 1989; Tony Shafrazi Gallery, NY, 1989; Galerie Lelong, NY, 1990; Stephen Haller Gallery, NY, 1992; Leo Castelli Gallery, NY, 1992; Sena Gallery, Santa Fe, NM, 1992; Galeria der Brücke, Buenos Aires, Argentina, 1993
PRINTERS: Alan Koslin, NY (AK); X Press, NY (XP); Joe Wilfer, NY (JW); Spring Street Workshop, NY (SpSW); Atelier Franck Bordas, Paris, France (AFB); James Miller, NY (JM); Jennifer Di Joseph, NY (JDJ); Adrienne Yarme, NY (AY); Derriére L'Etoile Studios, NY (DES); Alexander Heinrici, NY (AH); Heinrici Studio, NY (HS)
PUBLISHERS: Pace Editions, NY (PE); Spring Street Workshop, NY (SpSW); Galerie Lelong, Paris, France (GL); Castelli Graphics, NY (CG); Derriére L'Etoile Studios, NY (DES); Lococo-Mulder, Inc, St Louis, MO (L-M)
GALLERIES: Pace Prints, New York, NY; Atelier Galerie Fontaine, Inc, PQ, Canada; Leo Castelli Graphics, New York, NY; Tony Shafrazi Gallery, New York, NY; Greenberg Gallery Annex, St Louis, MO; Nohra Haime Gallery, New York, NY; Heland & Wetterling Gallery, Stockholm, Sweden; Galerie Thaddaeus Ropac, Salzburg, Austria; Catherine Issert, St Paul de Vence, France; Galerie Lucio Amelio, Naples, Italy; Galerie Lelong, New York, NY & Paris, France; Sena Gallery, Santa Fe, NM; Hine Editions/Limestone Press, San Francisco, CA; Lemberg Gallery, Birmingham, MI; Richard Green Gallery, Santa Monica, CA; Margulies Taplin Gallery, Boca Raton, FL; Stephen Haller Fine Art, New York, NY; Figura, Inc, New York, NY; Rick Jones Modern & Contemporary, St Louis, MO; Daniel Acosta Art Source, Inc, New York, NY; Galeria der Brücke, Buenos Aires, Argentina

James Brown
Fifteen American Indians VII
Courtesy Galerie Lelong

MAILING ADDRESS: 117–54 29th St, Cambria Heights, NY 11411

TITLE	PUBLISHER	PRINTER	DATE	MEDIUM	DIMENSION (PAPER SIZE) IN INCHES	TYPE OF PAPER	EDITION NUMBER	NO. OF COLORS	ORIGINAL OPENING PRICE	CURRENT RETAIL PRICE
CURRENT EDITIONS:										
Untitled #1–#7 (Set of 7)	PE	AK/XP	1986	EB/DPT/WA/HC	30 X 22 EA	SOM	15 EA	Varies	7500 SET 1200 EA	40000 SET 6500 EA
Untitled #1–#7 (Set of 7)	SpSW	JW/SpSW	1986	WB	19 X 23 EA	SEK	27 EA	1 EA	5000 SET 750 EA	6500 SET 1200 EA
Untitled #1–#5 (Set of 5)	PE	AK/XP	1985–88	WC	27 X 23 EA	SEK	7 EA		5000 SET 750 EA	6500 SET 500 EA
Untitled (Brown Ink Heads) (Set of 4)	SpSW	JW/SpSW	1985/88	EB/HG/REL	29 X 25 EA	AC	35 EA	1 EA	3500 SET 1000 EA	4500 SET 1200 EA
Untitled (Stella Maris) (Set of 4)	SpSW	JW/SpSW	1988	EB/HG/REL	30 X 30 EA	GE	15 EA	1 EA	2500 SET 750 EA	2500 SET 750 EA
Self Portrait Suite I-XXV (Set of 25)	SpSW	JW/SpSW	1988	LC	24 X 18 EA	GE	35 EA		750 EA	1200 EA
Untitled (Set of 5)	SpSW	MH/SpSW	1985–89	WC/CC	27 X 23 EA	AC/W	7 EA		1350 EA	1500 EA
The Five Sorrowful Mysteries (Set of 5)	SpSW	MH/SpSW	1989	EB	31 X 26 EA	AC/W	35 EA	1 EA	6500 SET 1350 EA	8000 SET 1750 EA
Fifteen American Indians I-XV (Set of 15)	GL	AFB	1990	LB/CO	29 X 22 EA	LarP	25 EA		1200 EA	1200 EA
Salt Suite (Violet) (Four Lithographs & One Monoprint) (Set of 5)	CG/DES	JM/JDJ/AY/DES	1990	LB (4) MON (1)	31 X 23 EA	JWP	15 EA	1 EA	5200 SET	5200 SET
White Square	GL	AFB	1990	LB/LI/CO	41 X 30	AP	30	1	3000	3000
Moroccan Woman	L-M	AH/HS	1993	SP	24 X 18	MB	75	18	1500	1500
The Moroccan I-VI (Set of 6)	L-M	AH/HS	1993	SP	41 X 33 EA	MB	75 EA	11-14EA	12000 SET 2200 EA	12000 SET 2200 EA

JOAN BROWN

BORN: (1938–1990)
EDUCATION: San Francisco Art Inst, CA, with Elmer Bischoff
RECENT EXHIB: Frumkin/Adams Gallery, NY, 1991; Oakland Mus, CA, 1992; Redding Mus, CA, 1992; Univ of California Mus, Santa Barbara, CA, 1992
TEACHING: Univ of California, Berkeley, CA
AWARDS: Nat Endowment for the Arts Fel; Guggenheim Fel
PRINTERS: Marcia Brown, Albuquerque, NM (MB); Lynne Allen, Albuquerque, NM (LA); Tamarind Inst, Albuquerque, NM (TI)
PUBLISHERS: Tamarind Inst, Albuquerque, NM (TI)
GALLERIES: Brian Gross Gallery, San Francisco, CA; Frumkin/Adams Gallery, New York, NY; Tamarind Inst, Albuquerque, NM; John Natsoulas Gallery, Davis, CA; Magnolia Editions, Oakland, CA

JOAN BROWN CONTINUED

TITLE	PUBLISHER	PRINTER	DATE	MEDIUM	DIMENSION (PAPER SIZE) IN INCHES	TYPE OF PAPER	EDITION NUMBER	NO. OF COLORS	ORIGINAL OPENING PRICE	CURRENT RETAIL PRICE
CURRENT EDITIONS:										
Adolescent Cat	TI	LA/TI	1983	LC	30 X 23	R/BFK	40	4	600	1500
Donald, State I	TI	MB/TI	1983	LC	30 X 22	R/BFK	38	5	600	1500
Donald, State II	TI	MB/TI	1983	LC	30 X 22	AP		1	600	1200
Leela	TI	LA/TI	1983	LC	41 X 30	GE	36	5	800	1600

PAMELA WEDD BROWN

BORN: France; November 21, 1928
EDUCATION: Academie Julian, Paris, France, 1946–51; Ecole des Beaux Arts, Paris, France, 1946–51; Studio of Motoi Oi, Tokyo, Japan, 1957–59; Studied with Sarah Baker, Joy Luke & Constance Costigan, Wash, DC, 1966–80
AWARDS: First Prize, Drawing, Academie Julian, Paris, France, 1947; Honorable Mention, Miniature Painters, Sculptors & Gravers Soc, 1983; Outstanding Artist of the Year, Woman's Nat Democratic Club, 1987,88; Honorable Mention, Artists' Equity Awards, 1992 (Patricia Tobacco Forrester, Juror)
RECENT EXHIB: Washington Printmakers Gallery, Wash, DC, 1989; Studio Gallery, Wash, DC, 1988,90,91
COLLECTIONS: Nat Mus of Am History, Wash, DC; Nat Mus of Women in the Arts, Wash, DC; Nat Inst of Health, Wash, DC; Christopher Newport Col, Newport News, VA; Library of Congress, Wash, DC
PRINTERS: Artist (ART)
PUBLISHERS: Artist (ART)
GALLERIES: Studio Gallery, Wash, DC
MAILING ADDRESS: 3500 Macomb St, NW, Washington, DC 20016

TITLE	PUBLISHER	PRINTER	DATE	MEDIUM	DIMENSION (PAPER SIZE) IN INCHES	TYPE OF PAPER	EDITION NUMBER	NO. OF COLORS	ORIGINAL OPENING PRICE	CURRENT RETAIL PRICE
CURRENT EDITIONS:										
Roman Pears	ART	ART	1989	WC	13 X 17	AC	10	3	125	150
Cave Dwellers #1, #2	ART	ART	1991	MON	19 X 26 EA	MUL	1 EA	3 EA	400 EA	400 EA
(Wood Plates, Stencils & Stylus)										
Set of :										
March of the Curanderos	ART	ART	1991	MON	19 X 26 EA	MUL	1 EA	3+	400 EA	400 EA
Return of the Curanderos	ART	ART	1991	MON	19 X 26 EA	MUL	1 EA	3+	400 EA	400 EA
Marching by the Mesa	ART	ART	1991	MON	19 X 26 EA	MUL	1 EA	3+	400 EA	400 EA
Ritual March	ART	ART	1991	MON	19 X 26 EA	MUL	1 EA	3+	400 EA	400 EA

ROGER BROWN

BORN: Hamilton, AL; December 10, 1941
EDUCATION: American Acad of Art, Chicago, IL; Art Inst of Chicago, IL
RECENT EXHIB: Retrosp, Hirshhorn Mus, Wash, DC, 1987; Univ of Oklahoma Mus, Norman, OK, 1987; Beaver Col, Glenside, PA, 1987; La Jolla Mus of Contemp Art, CA, 1987–88; Lowe Art Mus, Univ of Miami, Coral Gables, FL, 1988; Des Moines Art Center, IA, 1988; Hirshhorn Mus, Wash, DC, 1987,88; Evanston Art Center for the Visual Arts, IL, 1989; Phyllis Kind Gallery, NY, 1987,88,89,92
PRINTERS: Landfall Press, Inc, Chicago, IL (LPI); Jack Lemon, Chicago, IL (JL); Styria Studio, NY (SS)
PUBLISHERS: Opera Guild, Chicago, IL (OG); Styria Studio, NY (SS); Landfall Press, Inc, Chicago, IL (LPI)
GALLERIES: Phyllis Kind Gallery, Chicago, IL & New York, NY; Styria Studio, New York, NY; Asher/Faure Gallery, Los Angeles, CA; Helander Gallery, Palm Beach, FL; Fendrick Gallery, Wash, DC; Lakeside Studio, Lakeside, MI; Landfall Press, Inc, Chicago, IL; R H Love Galleries, Chicago, IL; Dean Jensen Gallery, Milwaukee, WI
MAILING ADDRESS: c/o Phyllis Kind Gallery, 213 W Superior, Chicago, IL 60610

TITLE	PUBLISHER	PRINTER	DATE	MEDIUM	DIMENSION (PAPER SIZE) IN INCHES	TYPE OF PAPER	EDITION NUMBER	NO. OF COLORS	ORIGINAL OPENING PRICE	CURRENT RETAIL PRICE
SOLD OUT EDITIONS (RARE):										
Cosi Fan Tutte	OG	JL/LPI	1979	LC	30 X 22	AP/W	75	7	400	900
CURRENT EDITIONS:										
Cathedrals of Space	SS	SS	1983	LC/SP	46 X 36	AP88	65	9	800	1800
Sketchbook-1982 (Bound Book of Lithographs with Collage)	SS	SS	1984	LB/CO	11 X 9 EA	AP88	50 EA	1 EA	2200	2800
One Share Art Stock	LPI	JL/LPI	1989	LC	22 X 30	AP/W	50		800	800
Fear No Evil	LPI	JL/LPI	1991	LB	36 X 36	AP/W	50	1	1200	1200
Honky Tonk Man	LPI	JL/LPI	1991	LC	40 X 40	AP/W	75		2000	2000
Museum of What's Happening Now	LPI	JL/LPI	1991	LC	16 X 20	AP/W	100		500	500

THEOPHILUS BROWN

BORN: Moline, IL; April 7, 1919
EDUCATION: Yale Univ, New Haven, CT, BA, 1941; Studied with Ozenfant, NY, 1948; Studied with Leger, Paris, France, 1949; Univ of California, Berkeley, CA, MFA, 1952
TEACHING: Univ of California, Berkeley, CA, 1954–56; San Francisco Art Inst, CA, 1955–57; Univ of Kansas, Lawrence, KS, 1967; Stanford Univ, CA, 1967; Univ of California, Davis, CA, 1956–60, 1975–76; Instr, Univ of California, Berkeley, CA, 1954–56; Instr, San Francisco Art Inst, CA, 1955–57; Instr, Univ of Kansas, Lawrence, KS, 1967; Instr, Stanford Univ, CA, 1967; Instr, Univ of California, Davis, CA, 1956–60, 1975–76
RECENT EXHIB: Harcourts Mod & Contemp Art, San Francisco, CA, 1992; Tatischeff Gallery, NY, 1992
COLLECTIONS: San Francisco Mus of Mod Art, CA; Univ of Kansas Art Mus, Lawrence, KS; Minneapolis Art Inst, MN; Oakland Art Mus, CA; Santa Barbara Mus of Art, CA; M H de Young Mem Mus, San Francisco, CA; Palace of the Legion of Honor, San Francisco, CA; Univ of New Mexico, Albuquerque, NM; Metropolitan Mus of Art, NY; J B Speed Art Mus, Louisville, KY; Sheldon Mus, Univ of Nebraska, Lincoln, NE
PRINTERS: Editions Press, San Francisco, CA (EP); Stephen Thomas, San Francisco, CA (ST); Brian Shure, San Francisco, CA (BS); David Kelso, Oakland, CA (DK); Made in California, Oakland, CA (MIC)

THEOPHILUS BROWN CONTINUED

PUBLISHERS: Editions Press, San Francisco, CA (EP); Made in California, Oakland, CA (MIC)
GALLERIES: John Berggruen Gallery, San Francisco, CA; Made in California, Oakland, CA; Harcourts Modern & Contemporary Art, San Francisco, CA
MAILING ADDRESS: 468 Jersey St, San Francisco, CA 94114

TITLE	PUBLISHER	PRINTER	DATE	MEDIUM	DIMENSION (PAPER SIZE) IN INCHES	TYPE OF PAPER	EDITION NUMBER	NO. OF COLORS	ORIGINAL OPENING PRICE	CURRENT RETAIL PRICE
SOLD OUT EDITIONS (RARE):										
Double Portrait	EP	EP	1983	LB	18 X 24	AC/W	12	1	350	500
CURRENT EDITIONS:										
Two Artists Drawing Seated Model	EP	EP	1983	LC	21 X 25	AC/W&B	16	2	350	400
Seated Figure in Striped Jacket, Dark Background	EP	EP	1983	LC	18 X 13	AC/W	15	2	350	400
Seated Model with Chin Resting on Hand	EP	EP	1983	LC	18 X 13	AC/W	29	2	450	500
Untitled (Rhino and Elephant)	MIC	DK/MIC	1984	EB/A/HG/SB/DPT	11 X 15	R/BFK	40	3	250	300
Untitled (Seated Woman) (with Burnishing)	MIC	DK/MIC	1984	EB/A/HG/ENG	15 X 11	R/BFK	17	1	150	300
Self-Portrait	MIC	DK/MIC	1984	DPT	15 X 11	R/BFK	12	1	125	250
Twenty Etchings (One Hand-Colored Etching with Each Edition) (Set of 20)	EP	BS/ST/EP	1984/85	I		SOM/S	20 EA		4800 SET	7500 SET

COLLEEN BROWNING

BORN: Fermoy, County Cork, Ireland; May 18, 1929; US Citizen
EDUCATION: Slade Sch, Univ of London, England
TEACHING: Instr, Painting & Drawing, City Col of New York, NY, 1962–76; Instr, Nat Acad of Design, NY, 1979–81
RECENT EXHIB: Charles B Goddard Center for Visual & Performing Arts, Ardmore, OK, 1989,92
COLLECTIONS: Detroit Inst of Arts, MI; Corcoran Mus, Wash, DC; Univ of Miami, Coral Gables, FL; Univ of Rochester, NY; Butler Inst of Am Art, Youngstown, OH; Williams Col, Williamstown, MA; Wichita Mus of Art, KS; New York State Mus, Albany, NY; Randolph Macon Woman's Col, VA; Milwaukee Art Center, WI; St Louis Art Mus, MO; Columbia Mus, SC
PUBLISHERS: Kennedy Graphics Inc, NY (KG)
GALLERIES: Kennedy Galleries, New York, NY; Harmon-Meek Gallery, Naples, FL; ACA Galleries, New York, NY
MAILING ADDRESS: 100 La Salle St, New York, NY 10027

TITLE	PUBLISHER	PRINTER	DATE	MEDIUM	DIMENSION (PAPER SIZE) IN INCHES	TYPE OF PAPER	EDITION NUMBER	NO. OF COLORS	ORIGINAL OPENING PRICE	CURRENT RETAIL PRICE
CURRENT EDITIONS:										
The Veils	KG		1969	LC	32 X 25	AP	100	12	200	500
Fifty-Ninth Street Subway	KG		1970	LC	26 X 38	AP	100	3	200	500
Girl in Purple and Blue	KG		1971	LC	30 X 22	AP	100	5	200	500
Luna	KG		1971	LC	23 X 30	AP	100	8	200	500
Odalisque	KG		1971	LC	21 X 26	AP	100	3	200	500
Revolving Door	KG		1971	LC	24 X 36	AP	100	9	200	500
Window	KG		1971	LC	36 X 24	AP	100	4	200	500
The Gymnast	KG		1974	LC	40 X 25	AP	100	3	250	600

BRUNO BRUNI

BORN: Pesaro, Italy, 1935
EDUCATION: Pesaro Inst of Art, Italy; State Univ of Art, Hamburg, Germany
AWARDS: Senefelder Prize, Lithography, 1977; Lichtwark Prize, Scholarship, City of Hamburg, Germany
COLLECTIONS: Kumamoto Public Mus, Japan; Fukuoka City Mus, Japan; Mus of Hamburg, Germany
PRINTERS: Atelier Matthieu, Geneva, Switzerland (AM)
PUBLISHERS: John Szoke Graphics, NY (JSG)
GALLERIES: Now & Then Gallery, East Meadow, NY; Southwest Gallery, Dallas, TX; Art Gallery-Studio 53, New York, NY; Fernette's Gallery, Des Moines, IA; Summa Gallery, New York, NY & Brooklyn, NY; Newmark Gallery, New York, NY; John Szoke Graphics, Inc, New York, NY

TITLE	PUBLISHER	PRINTER	DATE	MEDIUM	DIMENSION (PAPER SIZE) IN INCHES	TYPE OF PAPER	EDITION NUMBER	NO. OF COLORS	ORIGINAL OPENING PRICE	CURRENT RETAIL PRICE
SOLD OUT EDITIONS (RARE):										
I Promissi Sposi	JSG	AM	1982	LC	32 X 24	R/BFK	150	5	600	1800
CURRENT EDITIONS:										
Abbraccio	JSG	AM	1982	LC	40 X 28	R/BFK	250		800	1000
Arrivederci	JSG	AM	1982	LC	40 X 28	R/BFK	250		800	1000
Ballet with Cynthia (Set of 4)	JSG	AM	1983	LC	32 X 24	R/B	200	6	1800 SET	3000 SET
Carnevale di Venezia	JSG	AM	1983	LC	40 X 29	R/BFK	150	5	550	750

The print market has become very selective. For the first time since we published the first edition of The Printworld Directory in 1982, the prices of prints have been greatly reduced and greatly increased for the same artists by the most reputable and established print publishers. Check the fifth edition to understand the movement.

CAROL BRUNS

BORN: Des Moines, IA; September 18, 1943
EDUCATION: New York Univ, NY, BS, Fine Arts, 1965; Art Students League, NY, 1966; La Grande Chaumiere, Paris, France, 1968; Drake Univ, Art Ed, Des Moines, IA, 1972

PRINTERS: Kathleen Caraccio, NY, NY (KC)
PUBLISHERS: Orion Editions, NY (OE)
GALLERIES: Orion Editions, New York, NY;
MAILING ADDRESS: 134 Greene St, New York, NY 10012

TITLE	PUBLISHER	PRINTER	DATE	MEDIUM	DIMENSION (PAPER SIZE) IN INCHES	TYPE OF PAPER	EDITION NUMBER	NO. OF COLORS	ORIGINAL OPENING PRICE	CURRENT RETAIL PRICE
SOLD OUT EDITIONS (RARE):										
Riddle of Strange Fruit (Brown)	OE	KC	1980	AC	22 X 30	AP	14	11	250	450
Cleared to Land (Green)	OE	KC	1980	AC	22 X 30	AP	24	11	250	450

GÜNTER BRÜS

BORN: Ardning, Austria; 1938
EDUCATION: Sch of Arts & Crafts, Graz, Austria, 1953–57; Acad of Applied Arts; Vienna, Austria, 1957–60
COLLECTIONS: Kunsthalle, Bremen, West Germany; Kunstmuseum, Lucerne, Switzerland

PRINTERS: Crown Point Press, San Francisco, CA (CPP); Peter Kneubühler, Zürich, Switzerland (PK)
PUBLISHERS: Crown Point Press, San Francisco, CA (CPP); Heike Curtze, Düsseldorf, Germany & Vienna, Austria (HC): Maximilian Verlag Sabine Knust, Munich, Germany (MVSK)
GALLERIES: Crown Point Press, New York, NY & San Francisco, CA; Margarete Roeder Fine Art, New York, NY; Editions Ilene Kurtz, New York, N; Schmidt/Dean Gallery, Phila, PA

TITLE	PUBLISHER	PRINTER	DATE	MEDIUM	DIMENSION (PAPER SIZE) IN INCHES	TYPE OF PAPER	EDITION NUMBER	NO. OF COLORS	ORIGINAL OPENING PRICE	CURRENT RETAIL PRICE
SOLD OUT EDITIONS (RARE):										
Grosse Erdangst (Set of 3):	CPP	CPP	1982	EC	30 X 44 EA	HMP	5 EA		2200 SET	5500 SET
Grosse Erdangst I	CPP	CPP	1982	EB/A/DPT/SB	30 X 44	HMP	5		850	2000
Grosse Erdangst II	CPP	CPP	1982	EC	30 X 44	HMP	15		850	2000
Grosse Erdangst III	CPP	CPP	1982	EC	30 X 44	HMP	15		850	2000
CURRENT EDITIONS:										
The Diamond Cutter	CPP	CPP	1982	EC	21 X 15	HMP	25		350	350
Vertiefung durch Bewölkung (Collaboration with Arnulf Rainer) (Set of 5)	HC/MVSK	PK	1985	EB	22 X 16 EA	AP/B	50 EA	1 EA	3000 SET	4000 SET

JACK BRUSCA

BORN: New York, NY; November 18, 1939
EDUCATION: Univ of New Hampshire; Sch of Visual Arts, NY, with Alex Gottlieb, Alex Katz, Joe Tilson, and Helen Frankenthaller
TEACHING: PUC Univ, Rio de Janeiro, Brazil
COLLECTIONS: Aldrich Mus of Contemp Art, Ridgefield, CT; Rhode Island Sch of Design, Providence, RI; Powers Gallery, Univ of Sydney, Australia; Albright-Knox Art Gallery, Buffalo, NY; Cleveland Mus of Art, OH; Whitney Mus of Am Art, NY

PRINTERS: Alexander Heinrici, NY (AH); Studio Heinrici, NY (SH); American Atelier, NY (AA)
PUBLISHERS: London Arts, Inc, Detroit, MI (LAI); Circle Fine Art, NY (CFA)
GALLERIES: Galeria Bonino, New York, NY; Circle Galleries, Scottsdale, AZ & Beverly Hills, CA & Costa Mesa, CA & San Diego, CA & San Francisco, CA & Sherman Oaks, CA & Palm Beach, FL & Honolulu, HI & Chicago, IL & Northbrook, IL & New Orleans, LA & Las Vegas, NV & New York, NY & Pittsburgh, PA & Houston, TX & Seattle, WA; Ro Gallery Image Makers, Inc, New York, NY
MAILING ADDRESS: 109 W 26th St, New York, NY 10001

TITLE	PUBLISHER	PRINTER	DATE	MEDIUM	DIMENSION (PAPER SIZE) IN INCHES	TYPE OF PAPER	EDITION NUMBER	NO. OF COLORS	ORIGINAL OPENING PRICE	CURRENT RETAIL PRICE
SOLD OUT EDITIONS (RARE):										
America	LAI	AH/SH	1978	SP	26 X 34	SOM	200	8	175	300
Galaxy	LAI	AH/SH	1978	LC	28 X 26	SOM	200	6	175	300
Girl with Beach Ball	LAI	AH/SH	1978	SP	27 X 26	SOM	200	10	300	300
Globe Flower	LAI	AH/SH	1978	SP	27 X 26	SOM	200	7	175	300
Sounds of Summer	LAI	AH/SH	1978	SP	26 X 26	SOM	200	6	175	300
Whisper Theme: A Trilogy	LAI	AH/SH	1978	SP	24 X 24	SOM	200	6	175	300
Revolution	CFA	AA	1980	SP	30 X 26	SOM	200		175	300

MARK ADAMS BRYCE

BORN: San Francisco, CA; July 4, 1953
EDUCATION: Philadelphia Col of Art, PA, 1970–72; Pennsylvania Acad of Fine Arts, Phila, PA, 1970–74

AWARDS: New Jersey State Mus, Trenton, NJ, 1974; Charles Smith Endowment Prize, Woodmere Art Gallery, PA, 1981
PRINTERS: Chen Lee, Phila, PA (CL)
PUBLISHERS: Artist (ART)
GALLERIES: Marion Locks Gallery, Phila, PA; Somerville Manning Gallery, Greenville, DE

TITLE	PUBLISHER	PRINTER	DATE	MEDIUM	DIMENSION (PAPER SIZE) IN INCHES	TYPE OF PAPER	EDITION NUMBER	NO. OF COLORS	ORIGINAL OPENING PRICE	CURRENT RETAIL PRICE
CURRENT EDITIONS										
Environmental Water Series I	ART	CL	1976	LB/HC	8 X 12	R/BFK	10	Multi	125	200
Gladiolia	ART	CL	1981	LB/HC	22 X 30	R/BFK	50	Multi	200	300
3 Tulips	ART	CL	1981	LB/HC	22 X 30	R/BFK	20	Multi	200	300

GRISHA BRUSKIN

BORN: Moscow, Russia; 1945
EDUCATION: Graduated, Moscow Textile Inst, Russia, 1968
RECENT EXHIB: Marlborough Gallery, NY, 1990; Hokin Gallery, Palm Beach, FL, 1991
COLLECTIONS: Mus of Mod Art, NY; Art Inst of Chicago, IL; Mus Ludwig, Cologne, Germany; Kunsthalle Emden, Emden, Germany; Jewish Mus, NY
PRINTERS: Randy Hemminghaus, ME (RH); Johnathon Higgins, ME (JH); Vinalhaven Press, ME (VP)
PUBLISHERS: Marlborough Graphics, NY (MG); Vinalhaven Press, ME (VP)
GALLERIES: Marlborough Gallery, New York, NY & London, England

Grisha Bruskin
Anghel
Courtesy Vinalhaven Press

Grisha Bruskin
Glaza
Courtesy Vinalhaven Press

TITLE	PUBLISHER	PRINTER	DATE	MEDIUM	DIMENSION (PAPER SIZE) IN INCHES	TYPE OF PAPER	EDITION NUMBER	NO. OF COLORS	ORIGINAL OPENING PRICE	CURRENT RETAIL PRICE
CURRENT EDITIONS:										
Untitled	MG		1988	LC	40 X 30	AC	100		1800	2000
Notes A, B, C, D, (Set of 4)	MG		1991	SP	34 X 27 EA	SOM	75 EA		6500 SET	6500 SET
									1800 EA	1800 EA
Lexika (Set of 5)	MG/VP	RH/JH/VP	1992	EB/A	16 X 14 EA	R/BFK	24 EA		4000 SET	4000 SET

JOHN E BUCK

BORN: Ames, Iowa; February 14, 1946
EDUCATION: Kansas City Art Inst & Sch of Design, Kansas City, KS, BFA, 1968; Skowhegan Sch of Sculpture & Painting, ME, Summer, 1971; Univ of California, Davis, CA, MFA, 1972
TEACHING: Instr, Humbolt State Univ, Arcata, CA, 1973–74; Instr, Montana State Univ, Bozeman, MT, 1976–83
AWARDS: Nat Endowment for the Arts Fel, 1980
RECENT EXHIB: Yellowstone Art Center, Billings, MT, 1989; Volcano Art Center, HI, 1989; Evanston Art Center, IL, 1989; Allene Lapides Gallery, Santa Fe, NM, 1991,92
PRINTERS: Jack Lemon Chicago, IL (JL); Mark Genrich, Chicago, IL (MG); Landfall Press Inc, Chicago, IL (LPI); Bud Shark, Boulder, CO (BS); Barbara Shark, Boulder, CO (BaS); Jean Pless, Boulder, CO (JP); Shark's Inc, Boulder, CO (SI); Experimental Workshop, San Francisco, CA (EW); Artist (ART); Hiroki Morinue, Boulder, CO (HM); Roseanne Colachis, Boudler, CO (RC); Lisa Merrin, Boulder, CO (LM); Aleta Braun, Boulder, CO (AB); Ron Irujillo, Boulder, CO (RT); Bill Weege, Madison, WI (BW); Andrew Rubin, Madison, WI (AR); Tandem Press, Univ of Wisconsin, Madison, WI (TanPr)
PUBLISHERS: Landfall Press Inc, Chicago, IL (LPI); Shark's Inc, Boulder, CO (SI); Experimental Workshop, San Francisco, CA (EW); Artist (ART); Tandem Press, Univ of Wisconsin, Madison, WI (TanPr)
GALLERIES: Morgan Gallery, Kansas City, MO; Thomas Segal Gallery, Boston, MA; Zolla/Lieberman Gallery, Chicago, IL; Asher/Faure Gallery, Los Angeles, CA; Landfall Press, Chicago, IL; Experimental Workshop, San Francisco, CA; John Berggruen Gallery, San Francisco, CA; Robischon Gallery, Denver, CO; Helander Gallery, Palm Beach, FL; Phyllis Kind Gallery, New York, NY; Shark's Inc, Boulder, CO; Styria Studio, New York, NY; Allene Lapides Gallery, Santa Fe, NM; John Berggruen Gallery, San Francisco, CA; Ann Jaffe Gallery, Bay Harbor Islands, FL; Mark Masuoka Gallery, Las Vegas, NV; MIA Gallery, Seattle, WA; Anne Reed Gallery, Chicago, IL; Eve Mannes Gallery, Atlanta, GA; Quartet Editions, New York, NY
MAILING ADDRESS: 1129 Cottonwood Rd, Bozeman, MT 59715

John E Buck
Great Falls
Courtesy Shark's Inc

JOHN E BUCK CONTINUED

John E Buck
The Times
Courtesy Shark's, Inc

John E Buck
Green River
Courtesy Landfall Press, Inc

John E Buck
The Night Sky (Polyphemus)
Courtesy Shark's, Inc

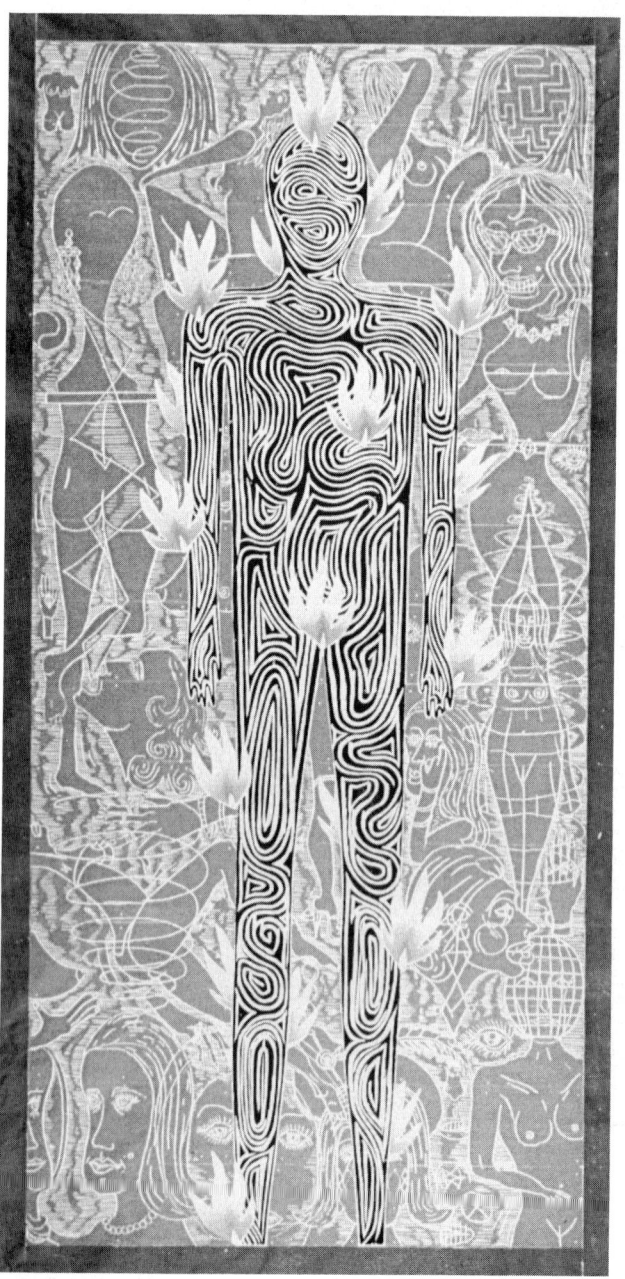

John E Buck
Tattoo
Courtesy Shark's, Inc

JOHN E BUCK CONTINUED

TITLE	PUBLISHER	PRINTER	DATE	MEDIUM	DIMENSION (PAPER SIZE) IN INCHES	TYPE OF PAPER	EDITION NUMBER	NO. OF COLORS	ORIGINAL OPENING PRICE	CURRENT RETAIL PRICE
SOLD OUT EDITIONS (RARE):										
Les Grand Eclipse	LPI	DH/LPI	1982	WC	75 X 38	SUZ	20	3	450	3500
Beirut	SI	BS/BaS/JP	1983	WC	63 X 37	SUZ	30	2	650	3000
Equator	LPI	MG/LPI	1984	WB	36 X 27	OKP	20	1	300	800
Tropic of Capricorn	LPI	MG/LPI	1984	WB	37 X 61	OKP	10	1	500	2500
Tropic of Cancer	LPI	MG/LPI	1984	WB	37 X 61	OKP	10	1	500	2500
Green River	LPI	JL/LPI	1984	WC	43 X 60	SUZ	20	3	850	2000
Avenue of the Americas	LPI	MG/LPI	1984	WC	50 X 34	SUZ	20	2	750	1200
Jihad	SI/ART	BS/SI	1984	LC	45 X 30	R/BFK	20	3	750	850
Father and Son	SI	BS/SI	1985	WB	83 X 37	SUZ	30	1	1500	2800
Red Jesus	SI	BS/SI	1985	WB	74 X 37	SUZ	30	1	1200	2800
Capetown	SI	BS/SI	1987	WB	74 X 37	SUZ	15	1	1500	2500
Crossroads	SI	BS/SI	1987	WB	74 X 37	SUZ	15	2	1800	2500
Prisoner	SI	BS/SI	1987	WB	74 X 37	SUZ	15	1	1500	2500
Basket	SI	BS/SI	1987	WB	74 X 37	SUZ	15	2	1500	2500
CURRENT EDITIONS:										
East/West (Dipt)	SI	BS/SI	1988	WC	74 X 74	SUZ	15	2	3800	5000
Green Fruit	SI	HM/BS/BAS/RC/ RT/MC/SI	1989	WC	32 X 37	SUZ	20		2000	2200
Trails Plowed Under	SI	BS/BAS/ART/SI	1989	WB	64 X 37	SUZ	15	1	2400	2400
Mountain Home	LPI	MG/LPI	1989	WC	43 X 60	SUZ	10	3	1800	1800
Roundup (Trip)	SI	BS/BAS/HM/RC/ LM/AB/RT/SI	1990	WC	29 X 38 EA	SUZ	15 EA		3200	3400
The Shillelagh Tree	SI	BS/BAS/RC/LM/ AB/SI	1990	WC	54 X 37	SUZ	15		2400	2600
The Language of the Times	TanPr	BW/AR/TanPr	1990	WC/DPT	80 X 53	SUZ	36	7	3000	3000
Seeing Things (Rain)	SI	BS/SI	1990	WC	37 X 44	SUZ	40	12	2000	2000
Seeing Things (Shade Tree)	SI	BS/SI	1990	WC	44 X 37	SUZ	40	21	2000	2000
The Times	SI	BS/SI	1991	WC	54 X 36	SUZ	15		2000	2600
Fire Weed	LPI	JL/LPI	1991	WC/D	67 X 40	SUZ	25		2000	2000
A Common Tongue	SI	BS/SI	1991	WC	62 X 37	SUZ	15		2600	2600
The Big City	SI	BS/SI	1991	WC	45 X 36	SUZ	15		2200	2200
Great Falls	SI	BS/SI	1991	WC	84 X 66	SUZ	15		4000	4000
The Night Sky (Polyphemus)	SI	BS/SI	1992	WC	38 X 30	SUZ	15		2200	2200
The Night Sky (Luna)	SI	BS/SI	1992	WC	38 X 30	SUZ	15		2200	2200
Tattoo	SI	BS/SI	1992	WC/CC	74 X 37	SUZ	15		2600	2600

FRAN BULL

BORN: Orange, NJ; 1938
EDUCATION: Bennington Col, VT, 1960
COLLECTIONS: Speed Art Mus, Louisville, KY
PRINTERS: Alexander Heinrici, NY (AH); Studio Heinrici, Ltd, NY (SH); Editions Lassiter-Meisel, NY (ELM)

PUBLISHERS: London Arts, Inc, Detroit, MI (LAI); Post Oak Fine Art Distributor, Houston, TX (PAFA); Olympia Petroleum (OP); Joan Scruby Grieco (JSG)
GALLERIES: Seraphim Fine Art Gallery, Englewood, NY; Morgan Gallery, Kansas City, MO
MAILING ADDRESS: P.O. Box 442, Alpine, NJ 07620

TITLE	PUBLISHER	PRINTER	DATE	MEDIUM	DIMENSION (PAPER SIZE) IN INCHES	TYPE OF PAPER	EDITION NUMBER	NO. OF COLORS	ORIGINAL OPENING PRICE	CURRENT RETAIL PRICE
CURRENT EDITIONS										
Zebras (Seeming Inversion)	LAI	AH/SH	1978	LC	28 X 36	AP	160	11	400	750
Sky Day Suite	LAI	AH/SH	1979	SP	20 X 29	SOM	250	28	400	750
Zoo Bear	LAI	ELM	1980	SP	22 X 30	SOM	250	32	400	750
Two Storks	LAI	AH/SH	1980	SP	22 X 30	SOM	250	18	400	750
Storks at Water	LAI	AH/SH	1980	SP	22 X 30	SOM	250	33	400	750
Lion Dipstyck	LAI	ELM	1980	SP	22 X 30	SOM	250	31	400	750
Horses of the Camarque	LAI	ELM	1980	SP	22 X 30	SOM	250	34	400	750
Three Egrets	OP	AH/SH	1980	SP	22 X 30	SOM	250	18	400	750
Winged Narcissus	JSG	ELM	1981	SP	30 X 22	SOM	250	25	400	750
Fire Bellied Toads	POFA	ELM	1981	SP	22 X 30	SOM	250	17	400	750
French Seaport	POFA	ELM	1981	SP	30 X 22	SOM	250	18	400	750
Two Horses	POFA	ELM	1981	SP	30 X 22	SOM	250	18	400	750
Two Zebras	POFA	ELM	1981	SP	30 X 22	SOM	250	18	400	750
Reflected Bridge	POFA	ELM	1981	SP	22 X 30	SOM	250	18	400	750
Pelicans I, II	POFA	AH/SH	1982	SP	22 X 30 EA	SOM	250 EA	18 EA	400 EA	750 EA

The retail prices of the 100,000 limited edition prints quoted in this directory are subject to change. Print publishers, artists and galleries were the direct sources for these quotations. Prices in the secondary market listed as "Sold Out Editions (Rare)" indicate that the publisher has a limited supply of that print or that the print is difficult to locate in the galleries.

The Printworld Directory is accepting new applications for the seventh edition. Approximately 300 new artists will be accepted. Please use the two forms provided in the back section of this directory to submit biographical data and documentation of prints. Edition number of each print must not exceed 500 and the retail price must be $100 or more.

JIM BUCKELS

BORN: Boone, IA; June 9, 1948
EDUCATION: Univ of Northern Iowa, Cedar Falls, IA, 1972-76
AWARDS: Art Director's Awards, IA, 1979-85; Am Illustration Annual Awards, 1982-85
PRINTERS: Joseph Kleineman, NY (JK); Maureen Turci, NY (MT); J K Fine Arts, NY (JKFA); Robert Duty, Jersey City, NY (RD); Stanley Rosenberg, Jersey City, NJ (SR); David Griswald, Jersey City, NJ (DG); Chameleon Editions, Jersey City, NJ (ChEd)
PUBLISHERS: Newbury Fine Arts, Boston, MA (NFA)

GALLERIES: Newbury Fine Arts, Boston, MA; Sierra Gallery, Reno, NV; Atlas Galleries, Chicago, IL; P & C Art, Wash, DC; Devecchis Gallery, Phila, PA; Summa Galleries, New York & Brooklyn, NY; Carol Condit Gallery, New York, NY; Central Park Gallery, Kansas City, MO; Corner House Gallery, Cedar Rapids, IA; Heartland Gallery, Des Moines, IA; Greenwich Village Gallery, Camp Hill, PA; Gallery of Art, Independence, MI; James Bond Gallery, Los Gatos, CA; Thomas Charles Gallery, Las Vegas, NV; Artworks of Main Street, Voorhees, NJ; Johnson Art Gallery, San Luis Obispo, CA
MAILING ADDRESS: c/o Newbury Fine Arts, 29 Newbury St, Boston, MA 02116

TITLE	PUBLISHER	PRINTER	DATE	MEDIUM	DIMENSION (PAPER SIZE) IN INCHES	TYPE OF PAPER	EDITION NUMBER	NO. OF COLORS	ORIGINAL OPENING PRICE	CURRENT RETAIL PRICE
SOLD OUT EDITIONS (RARE):										
Seven Sisters Road	NFA	JK/MT/JKFA	1988	LC	27 X 27	AP	300		400	2500
Druid Point	NFA	JK/MT/JKFA	1988	LC	27 X 27	AP	300		400	6500
Guardino Segretto	NFA	JK/MT/JKFA	1988	LC	36 X 26	AP	300		450	2400
Trouble at Walnut Ridge	NFA	JK/MT/JKFA	1989	LC	27 X 39	AP	300		650	1600
The Seventh Tori	NFA	JK/MT/JKFA	1989	LC	39 X 26	AP	300		750	1800
Phaedra's Vigil	NFA	JK/MT/JKFA	1989	LC	33 X 22	AP	300		600	2400
Jupiter and Calisto	NFA	RD/SR/DG/ChEd	1989	SP	36 X 35	COV/320	300		700	2200
Blue Ruin	NFA	RD/SR/DG/ChEd	1990	SP	35 X 35	COV/320	300		775	3800
Princes Kept the View	NFA	JK/MT/JKFA	1990	LC	27 X 31	AP	300		800	5800
Scylla and Charybdis	NFA	RD/SR/DG/ChEd	1990	SP	35 X 39	COV/320	300		800	1400
Boston Public Garden	NFA	JK/MT/JKFA	1990	LC	32 X 24	AP	300		750	1000
Boston Public Garden	NFA	JK/MT/JKFA	1990	LC	32 X 24	JP	300		750	1000
New Order	NFA	RD/SR/DG/ChEd	1990	SP	36 X 35	COV/320	300		850	2000
The Huntress	NFA	RD/SR/DG/ChEd	1991	SP	22 X 22	COV/320	300		800	1600
Son et Lumiere (Boxed Portfolio)	NFA	RD/SR/DG/ChEd	1991	SP	22 X 22	COV/320	300		800	1200
Le Duex Cheval	NFA	RD/SR/DG/ChEd	1991	SP	29 X 28	COV/320	300		800	1800
Morning on the Cher	NFA	RD/SR/DG/ChEd	1991	SP	29 X 28	COV/320	300		800	1200
El Camino Monterey	NFA	RD/SR/DG/ChEd	1992	SP	28 X 36	COV/320	300		850	1600
CURRENT EDITIONS:										
The San Remo	NFA	RD/SR/DG/ChEd	1990	SP	40 X 26	COV/320	300		850	1300
Winterset Farm	NFA	RD/SR/DG/ChEd	1992	SP	28 X 37	COV/320	300		850	1050
Villa Capulet	NFA	RD/SR/DG/ChEd	1992	SP	28 X 34	COV/320	300		850	1050
Glen Eyrie	NFA	RD/SR/DG/ChEd	1993	SP	17 X 21	COV/320	300		500	600
Fleeting Hour	NFA	RD/SR/DG/ChEd	1993	SP	17 X 21	COV/320	300		500	500

Jim Buckels
The Huntress
Courtesy Newbury Fine Arts

Jim Buckels
Fleeting Hour
Courtesy Newbury Fine Arts

Jim Buckels
El Camino Monterey
Courtesy Newbury Fine Arts

Jim Buckels
Glen Eyrie
Courtesy Newbury Fine Arts

Jim Buckels
Winterset Farm
Courtesy Newbury Fine Arts

STEPHEN BUCKLEY

BORN: Leicester, England; 1944
EDUCATION: Univ of Newcastle-Upon-Tyne, England, 1962–67; Univ of Reading, England, 1967–69
TEACHING: Canterbury Col of Art, England; Leeds Col of Art, England; Chelsea Sch of Art, London, England; Art in Res, Kind's Col, Cambridge, England
AWARDS: John Moores Exhib, Walker Art Gallery, Liverpool, England, 1974; Chichester Nat Art Exhib, Hampshire, England, 1975; Tolly Cobbold Exhib, London, England, 1977
COLLECTIONS: The Tate Gallery, London, England; Metropolitan Art Mus, NY; Nat Art Gallery, New Zealand; Australian Nat Gallery, Canberra, Australia
PRINTERS: Chris Prater, London, England (CP); Kelpra Studio, London, England (KS); Alan Cox, London, England (AC); Sky Editions, London, England (SE)
PUBLISHERS: Waddington Graphics, London, England (WG)
GALLERIES: Waddington Graphics, London, England; Brooke Alexander, Inc, New York, NY

TITLE	PUBLISHER	PRINTER	DATE	MEDIUM	DIMENSION (PAPER SIZE) IN INCHES	TYPE OF PAPER	EDITION NUMBER	NO. OF COLORS	ORIGINAL OPENING PRICE	CURRENT RETAIL PRICE
SOLD OUT EDITIONS (RARE):										
Beanpole I, II	WG	CP/KS	1981	MON	32 X 46 EA	AC	1 EA	Varies	300 EA	3000 EA
Jesmond	WG	CP/KS	1982	SP	31 X 45	AC	70		400	1000
Les Flon-Flons	WG	CP/KS	1982	SP	31 X 40	AC	70		400	1000
Album	WG	CP/KS	1982	SP	43 X 31	AC	70		400	1000
Bamboo Too	WG	CP/KS	1983	MON	32 X 46 EA	AC	1 EA	Varies	600 EA	3000 EA
Belt	WG	AC/SE	1983	LC	21 X 16	AC	25		450	650
Byker I	WG	CP/KS	1983	MON	31 X 40 EA	AC	1 EA	Varies	600 EA	2500 EA
Byker II	WG	CP/KS	1983	MON	30 X 40 EA	AC	1 EA	Varies	600 EA	2500 EA
Caught	WG	CP/KS	1983	MON	39 X 25 EA	AC	1 EA	Varies	600 EA	2500 EA
Chung	WG	AC/SE	1983	LC	28 X 28	AC	35		450	650
Cricket	WG	AC/SE	1983	LC	14 X 19	AC	25		450	550
Drub	WG	CP/KS	1983	MON	39 X 26 EA	AC	1 EA	Varies	600 EA	2000 EA
Fahey	WG	CP/KS	1983	MON	37 X 25 EA	AC	1 EA	Varies	600 EA	2000 EA
Fornasari III	WG	CP/KS	1983	MON	40 X 30 EA	AC	1 EA	Varies	600 EA	3500 EA
Held	WG	CP/KS	1983	MON	39 X 26 EA	AC	1 EA	Varies	600 EA	2000 EA
Le Lendemain	WG	AC/SE	1983	LC	42 X 30	AC	45		450	1000
Orpheum II	WG	CP/KS	1983	MON	30 X 36 EA	AC	1 EA	Varies	600 EA	2500 EA
Pang	WG	AC/SE	1983	LC	19 X 12	AC	25		450	650
Pitch	WG	CP/KS	1983	MON	39 X 26 EA	AC	1 EA	Varies	600 EA	2750 EA
Pots and Pans	WG	AC/SE	1983	LC	23 X 17	AC	25		450	650
Redpath	WG	CP/KS	1983	MON	39 X 32 EA	AC	1 EA	Varies	600 EA	3000 EA
Spry	WG	CP/KS	1983	MON	32 X 47 EA	AC	1 EA	Varies	600 EA	2000 EA
Terrol	WG	CP/KS	1983	MON	31 X 40 EA	AC	1 EA	Varies	600 EA	2000 EA
Tokyo Joe	WG	AC/SE	1983	LC	42 X 30	AC	45		450	1000
Tony's Restaurant	WG	CP/KS	1983	MON	27 X 32 EA	AC	1 EA	Varies	600 EA	2500 EA
Pyon Yang I	WG	CP/KS	1983	MON	31 X 40 EA	AC	1 EA	Varies	600 EA	2000 EA
Pyon Yang II	WG	CP/KS	1983	MON	32 X 45 EA	AC	1 EA	Varies	600 EA	1800 EA
Pyon Yang III	WG	CP/KS	1983	MON	25 X 32 EA	AC	1 EA	Varies	600 EA	2500 EA
Going on III	WG	CP/KS	1984	MON	31 X 88 EA	AC	1 EA	Varies	800 EA	5000 EA

BERNARD BUFFET

BORN: Paris, France; 1928
RECENT EXHIB: Buschlen-Mowatt Gallery, Vancouver, Canada, 1990; Galerie Dir Carlton, Cannes, France, 1990
PRINTERS: Atelier Mourlot, Paris, France (AM); Atelier Lacouriér et Frelaunt, Paris, France (ALF)
PUBLISHERS: Beyeler Gallery, Basel, Switzerland (BG); A C Mazo & Co, Paris, France (ACM); Crewzevevault, Paris, France (CREUZ); Editions David et Garnier, Paris, France (EDG); Joseph Foret, Paris, France (JF); Editions Lacoriere, Paris, France (EL); Editions Maurice Barnier, Paris, France (EMG); Artist (ART); Les Peintres Témoins de Leur Temps, Paris, France (LPTLT)
GALLERIES: R K Goldman & Company, Los Angeles, CA; Royal Art Gallery, New Orleans, LA; Turner Fine Art, New York, NY; Ruth O'Hara Fine Art, New York, NY; Noble House, Los Angeles, CA; Galleria Maray, Allendale, NJ; Galerie Lareuse, Wash, DC; Galerie Mourlot, Boston, MA; Galerie Tamenga, New York, NY

Sorlier (S)—Mourlot (M)

Bernard Buffet
Sunflowers and Melons
Courtesy Avantgarde Art Associates

TITLE	PUBLISHER	PRINTER	DATE	MEDIUM	DIMENSION (PAPER SIZE) IN INCHES	TYPE OF PAPER	EDITION NUMBER	NO. OF COLORS	ORIGINAL OPENING PRICE	CURRENT RETAIL PRICE
SOLD OUT EDITIONS (RARE):										
Le Pacifiste	BG	ALF	1953	LC	26 X 20	AP	220		50	3500
Port Breton (R-7)	CREUZ	ALF	1954	DPT	20 X 28	AP	100	1	50	3500
Sun Flowers and Melons	BG	ALF	1955	LC	19 X 26	AP	125		75	4500
La Rue	CREUZ	ALF	1955	DPT	22 X 27	RP/WOVE	125	1	75	4500
Book with 18 Drypoints (R-309–326)	JF	ALF	1958	DPT	16 X 13 EA	AP	281 EA	1 EA	800 SET	2500 SET
La Phare (R-17)	EL	ALF	1958	DPT	20 X 25	WOVE	75	1	100	3500
UNO	ART	ALF	1959	DPT	21 X 27	WOVE	200		100	10000
La Place des Vosges (from Abum Paris) (S-32)	LPTLT		1962	LC	21 X 23	AP	150		150	5000
La Route (M-32)	LPTLT		1962	LC	26 X 20	AP	250		150	7500
Insecte	ART	ALF	1964	DPT	19 X 25	WOVE	100		125	3500
Album, New York (Set of 10) (S53-S-62)	ACM	AM	1964	LC	29 X 21 EA	AP	150 EA		1000 SET	12000 SET
New York I-IV (Set of 4)	ACM		1964	LC	27 X 19 EA	AP	150 EA		500 SET	22000 SET
New York VIII	ACM		1964	LC	24 X 20	AP	150		150	20000
Canal a Soissons (R-46)	EL/EDG	ALF	1964	DPT	20 X 25	WOVE	100	1	150	5000
La Guepe (S-44)	EDG		1964	LC		WOVE	100	1	150	3000
Hyacinths			1966	LC	14 X 11	AP	50		100	4500
A Small Beach			1967	LC	14 X 21	AP	125		100	1500
Clown with Red Nose and . . .			1968	LC	15 X 12	AP	125		100	1500
Man Cirque (Set of 44) (S-140-185)	AM	AM	1968	LC	28 X 20 EA	AP	120 EA		3500 SET	140000 SET
Sacre Coeur	GDG		1968	DPT	25 X 20	RP	100		150	5000
Sacre Coeur	GDG		1969	LC	26 X 21	AP/WOVE	175		125	6000
Geranium	EMG		1976	LC	26 X 19	AP/WOVE	150		125	4000
Chateau de Cartes	EMG		1979	LC	13 X 9	JP	150		200	2500

GARY BUKOVNIK

BORN: Cleveland, OH; April 10, 1947
EDUCATION: Cleveland Inst of Art, OH
AWARDS: George Bunker Award, The Print Club, 1981; Am Soc of Mus Publications, Award of Merit, 1982; Award of Merit, Arts Comm of San Francisco, CA, 1988
RECENT EXHIB: Young Gallery, Saratoga, CA, 1988; Concept Art Gallery, Pittsburgh, PA, 1988; Galerie Kutter, Luxembourg, Germany, 1988; Gallery 460, Green Point, Australia, 1989; Staempfli Gallery, NY, 1989; Mary Bell Galleries, Chicago, IL 1990; Lisa Kurts Gallery, Memphis, TN, 1990; Concept Art Gallery, Pittsburgh, PA, 1990; Robley Gallery, Roslyn, NY 1990; Mary Bell Galleries, Chicago, IL, 1990; Ansorena, Madrid, Spain, 1991; Bingham Kurts Gallery, Memphis, TN, 1990,91; Chicago Botanic Garden, IL, 1991; de Saisset Mus, Santa Clara Univ, CA, 1991; Galerie Kutter, Luxembourg, Germany, 1991; Staempfli Gallery, NY, 1991; Garden Center of Greater Cleveland, OH, 1992; Concept Art Gallery, Pittsburgh, PA, 1990,92
COLLECTIONS: Metropolitan Mus of Art, NY; Mus of Fine Arts, Boston, MA; Oakland Mus, CA; San Francisco Mus of Mod Art, CA; Univ of California, Berkeley, CA; Fine Arts Mus of San Francisco, CA; Art Inst of Chicago, IL; Brooklyn Mus, NY; Hunt Inst for Botanical Documentation, Carnegie Mellon Univ, Pittsburgh, PA; Art Gallery of Hamilton, Ontario, Canada; Atlanta Botanical Garden, Atlanta, GA; Smithsonian Inst, Wash, DC; Library of Congress, Wash, DC; Fine Arts Mus of San Francisco, CA; de Saisset Mus, Santa Clara Univ, CA
PRINTERS: Trillium Graphics, San Francisco, CA (TG); Katherine Lincoln Press, San Francisco, CA (KLP)
PUBLISHERS: Erickson & Elins Fine Art, San Francisco, CA (EEFA); Artist (ART); Metropolitan Opera Guild, NY (MOG)
GALLERIES: Concept Art Gallery, Pittsburgh, PA; Galerie Kutter, Luxembourg, Germany; Gallery 460, Greenpoint, Australia; Irving Galleries, Palm Beach, FL; Bingham Kurts Gallery, Memphis, TN; Mary Bell Galleries, Chicago, IL; Robley Gallery, Roslyn, NY; Staempfli Gallery, New York, NY; Young Gallery, Sarasota, OH; Staempfli Gallery, New York, NY; Erickson & Elins Gallery, San Francisco, CA; Ansorena, Madrid, Spain; Steven Scott Gallery, Baltimore, MD
MAILING ADDRESS: 1179 Howard St, San Francisco, CA 94103

GARY BUKOVNIK CONTINUED

TITLE	PUBLISHER	PRINTER	DATE	MEDIUM	DIMENSION (PAPER SIZE) IN INCHES	TYPE OF PAPER	EDITION NUMBER	NO. OF COLORS	ORIGINAL OPENING PRICE	CURRENT RETAIL PRICE
SOLD OUT EDITIONS (RARE):										
Cosmos	ART	KLP	1980	EC	30 X 23	R/BFK	100	4	300	800
Peonies	ART	KLP	1980	EC	30 X 23	R/BFK	100	3	300	800
Pink Lilies	ART	KLP	1980	EC	30 X 23	R/BFK	100	3	300	850
Rhododendron	ART	TG	1980	LC	35 X 27	AP/W	100	5	300	650
Gloxinia	ART	TG	1980	LC	35 X 27	AP/W	100	6	300	650
Begonia	ART	TG	1980	LC	35 X 27	AP/W	100	7	300	750
Amaryllis	ART	KLP	1981	EC	30 X 23	R/BFK	100	4	350	900
Freesia in a Red Vase	ART	KLP	1981	EC	30 X 23	R/BFK	100	5	350	800
Vase of Tulips	ART	KLP	1981	DPT	30 X 21	BFK/TOR	25	1	150	500
Gloxinia in a Pot	ART	KLP	1981	DPT	26 X 22	BFK/TOR	25	1	175	450
Spotted Lilies	ART	TG	1981	LC	30 X 42	AP	100	8	400	800
Easter Lilies	ART	TG	1981	LC	40 X 30	AP/W	100	6	450	700
Pink Lilies	ART	TG	1982	LC	40 X 30	AP/W	100	7	450	800
Anemones	ART	KLP	1982	EC	30 X 23	R/BFK	100	3	400	750
Iris	ART	TG	1983	LC	30 X 39	AP/W	100	9	500	800
Tiger Lily II	ART	TG	1983	LC	30 X 40	AP/W	100	9	500	800
Rhododendron II	ART	TG	1984	LC	41 X 30	AP/W	100	8	500	700
Peonies II	ART	TG	1984	LC	35 X 14	AP/W	100	12	500	750
Japanese Magnolia, Variation I (Dipt)	ART/TG	TG	1984	LC	41 X 59	AP/W	100	9	900 SET	1200 SET
Japanese Magnolia, Variation II (Dipt)	ART/TG	TG	1984	LC	41 X 59	AP/W	100	10	900 SET	1200 SET
California Still Life #1	EEFA	TG	1985	LC	30 X 41	AP/W	100	12	500	1400
Anticipation (Dipt)	EEFA	TG	1985	LC	30 X 80	AP/W	98	9	900 SET	1700 SET
Daybreak (Dipt)	EEFA	TG	1985	LC	30 X 83	AP/W	98	16	925 SET	1800 SET
Still Life for Fantin Latour	EEFA	TG	1985	LC	30 X 40	AP/W	98	11	500	800
San Francisco Still Life #23	EEFA	TG	1986	LC	39 X 27	DSA	143	15	550	800
Golden Gate Park #14	EEFA	TG	1987	LC	36 X 54	AP/W	225	20	800	1800
Camellia	EEFA	TG	1988	LC	21 X 18	AP/W	134	17	225	350
California Still Life #28	EEFA	TG	1988	LC	39 X 53	AP/W	225	24	800	1800
Bowl of Tulips	EEFA	TG	1989	LC	32 X 38	COV/W	200	24	675	1200
Hybrid Lilies	MOG	TG	1991	LC	32 X 53	WWR	150	19	600	1500
CURRENT EDITIONS:										
Daisy Mum	ART	TG	1980	LC	35 X 27	AP/W	100	7	300	650
Calla Lily I, II	ART	TG	1980	LC	35 X 14 EA	AP/W	100 EA	5 EA	200 EA	300 EA
Freesia	ART	KLP	1981	EB/SG	26 X 19	ROMA/TOR	25	1	150	250
Iris	ART	KLP	1981	DPT/SG	26 X 16	BFK/TOR	25	1	150	250
Parrot Tulips	ART	KLP	1981	DPT	26 X 19	ROMA	25	1	100	200
Lilacs	ART	KLP	1981	DPT	20 X 30	BFK/TOR	25	1	150	300
Camellias	ART	KLP	1981	DPT	26 X 19	ROMA	25	1	100	300
Eucalyptus	EEFA	TG	1987	LC	40 X 30	AP/W	143	14	500	750
Atlanta Symphony Posters (Signed)	ASO	TG	1988	LC	40 X 30	AP/W	50	4	250	300
Cyclamen	EEFA	TG	1988	LC	21 X 18	AP/W	225	12	250	275
Set of Three:									1200 SET	1200 SET
Reflective Begonia	EEFA	TG	1988	LC	20 X 29	AP/W	225	13	475	500
Iris	EEFA	TG	1988	LC	20 X 29	AP/W	225	13	475	575
Six Camellias after an Unknown Japanese Artist	EEFA	TG	1988	LC	20 X 29	AP/W	225	13	475	500
San Francisco Still Life #37	EEFA	TG	1990	LC	41 X 16	AC/W	200	18	500	600
Sunflowers	EEFA	TG	1990	LC	39 X 22	AC/W	200	19	600	600
Still Life with Musical Instruments	EEFA	TG	1990	LC	30 X 42	SOM/S	194	16	875	950
California Still Life #51	EEFA	TG	1990	LC	31 X 23	SOM	194	17	500	575
Still Life for Betty	EEFA	TG	1991	LC	26 X 30	SOM/S	197	12	500	550
Nasturtiums	EEFA	TG	1991	LC	25 X 17	SOM/S	197	13	350	350
California Poppies	EEFA	TG	1991	LC	23 X 15	SOM/S	197	13	300	300
Iridescent Tulips	EEFA	TG	1991	LC	35 X 54	AC/W	197	13	950	1000
Composition in Pink & Green	EEFA	TG	1991	LC	26 X 17	SOM/S	194	17	350	350
Infrequent Gladiolus	EEFA	TR	1991	LC	51 X 39	AC/W	190	19	925	950

HUGH BULLEY

BORN: London, England
EDUCATION: Central Sch of Art and Design, London, England; Art Workers Guild, 1963
COLLECTIONS: Nat Portrait Gallery, London, England
PRINTERS: Atelier Ettinger, NY (AE)
PUBLISHERS: Transworld Art Inc, NY (TAI)

TITLE	PUBLISHER	PRINTER	DATE	MEDIUM	DIMENSION (PAPER SIZE) IN INCHES	TYPE OF PAPER	EDITION NUMBER	NO. OF COLORS	ORIGINAL OPENING PRICE	CURRENT RETAIL PRICE
CURRENT EDITIONS:										
Flowers in a Vase	TAI	AE	1980	LC	29 X 21	AP	250		250	300
Flowers in a Vase	TAI	AE	1980	LC	29 X 21	JP	50		300	350
Lillies	TAI	AE	1980	LC	21 X 29	AP	250		250	300
Lillies	TAI	AE	1980	LC	21 X 29	JP	50		300	350

DAVID BUMBECK

BORN: Framingham, MA; May 15, 1940
EDUCATION: Rhode Island Sch of Design, Providence, RI, BFA, 1962; Syracuse Univ, NY, MFA, 1966, with Robert Marx
TEACHING: Instr, Painting & Printmaking, Massachusetts Col of Art, Boston, MA, 1966–68; Prof, Printmaking, Middlebury Col, VT, 1968 to present
AWARDS: Purchase Award, Everson Mus, NY, 1966; David Berger Mem Award, Boston Printmakers Nat Exhib, 1968; Dartmouth Col Regional Purchase Award, Hanover, NH, 1973; Purchase Award, Society of Am Graphic Artists, NY, 1979
RECENT EXHIB: Northern Arizona Univ Art Mus, Flagstaff, AR, 1992
COLLECTIONS: Metropolitan Mus of Art, NY; Brooklyn Mus, NY; Univ of Pennsylvania, Phila, PA; Rochester Mem Gallery, NY; Everson Mus, Syracuse, NY; Boston Public Library, Wiggin Coll, MA; New York Public Library, NY; Georgia State Mus, Atlanta, GA; Library of Congress, Wash, DC
PRINTERS: Artist (ART)
PUBLISHERS: Artist (ART)
GALLERIES: Mary Ryan Gallery, New York, NY; Chicago Center for the Print, Chicago, IL; Oxford Gallery, Rochester, NY
MAILING ADDRESS: Drew Lane, RD #3, Middlebury, VT 05753

TITLE	PUBLISHER	PRINTER	DATE	MEDIUM	DIMENSION (PAPER SIZE) IN INCHES	TYPE OF PAPER	EDITION NUMBER	NO. OF COLORS	ORIGINAL OPENING PRICE	CURRENT RETAIL PRICE
SOLD OUT EDITIONS (RARE):										
In Twilight	ART	ART	1978	EB	19 X 22	AP	65	1	200	500
The Lake	ART	ART	1987	EB/A/ENG	12 X 10	AP	80	1	250	400

JERRY BURCHFIELD

BORN: Chicago, IL; July 28, 1947
EDUCATION: California State Univ, Photo-Communications, Fullerton, CA, 1971; California State Univ, Fullerton, CA, MA, Art, 1972
TEACHING: Instr & Lectr, Photography, California State Univ, Fullerton, CA, 1978–87; Instr, Orange Coast Col, CA, 1981–87; Instr, Saddleback Col, Mission Viejo, CA, 1979 to present; Cyprus Col Cyprus, CA, 1988 to present
AWARDS: Photoworks, CA, Photography, 1979; Purchase Award Photo National; Nat Endowment for the Arts Photographers Fel, 1981
COLLECTIONS: Los Angeles Center for Photographic Studies, CA; Eastern Wash Univ, Cheney, WA; Bellevue Art Mus, WA; Bibliotheque Nat, Paris, France; Denver Art Mus, CO; St Louis Mus of Art, MO; Minneapolis Inst of Arts, MN; Los Angeles County Mus, CA; Minneapolis, Inst of Arts, MN
RECENT EXHIB: Min Gallery, Tokyo, Japan, 1988; Long Beach Mus, CA, 1989
PRINTERS: Artist (ART)
PUBLISHERS: BC Space Gallery (BCS); Amphoto, (A); Susan Spiritus Gallery (SSG); Los Angeles Center for Photographic Studies, CA (CPS)
GALLERIES: G Ray Hawkins Gallery, Los Angeles, CA; Susan Spiritus Gallery, Newport Beach, CA; Kicken Gallery, Cologne, Germany; Sandy Carson Gallery, Denver, CO; Merging One Gallery, Santa Monica, CA
MAILING ADDRESS: 6 Meade St, Irvine, CA 92720-2623

TITLE	PUBLISHER	PRINTER	DATE	MEDIUM	DIMENSION (PAPER SIZE) IN INCHES	TYPE OF PAPER	EDITION NUMBER	NO. OF COLORS	ORIGINAL OPENING PRICE	CURRENT RETAIL PRICE
SOLD OUT EDITIONS (RARE):										
Self Appraisal Series	BCS	ART	1976	PH/C	11 X 14	CIBA	5		125	600
Details-Leaf Series #1434	BCS	ART	1979	PH/C	16 X 20	CIBA	35		250	500
Considering Painting #1	BCS	ART	1978	PH/C	11 X 14	CIBA	60		250	600
CURRENT EDITIONS:										
Pleasure Beach Revisited (21 Images)	BCS	ART	1977–78	PH/C	11 X 14 EA	CIBA	15 EA		125 EA	300 EA
Details-Leaf Series (50 Images)	BCS	ART	1976–79	PH/C	16 X 20 EA	CIBA	25 EA		100 EA	350 EA
Night Walking (100 Images)	BCS	ART	1977–80	PH/C	11 X 14 EA	CIBA	25 EA		125 EA	250 EA
Night Walking (100 Images)	BCS	ART	1977–80	PH/C	16 X 20 EA	CIBA	25 EA		200 EA	350 EA
Details-Snow Series (35 Images)	BCS	ART	1979	PH/C	16 X 20 EA	CIBA	25 EA		250 EA	350 EA
Details-Ash Series (15 Images)	BCS	ART	1980	PH/C	16 X 20 EA	CIBA	25 EA		250 EA	350 EA
Fading Away (39 Images)	BCS	ART	1980	PH/C	11 X 14 EA	CIBA	25 EA		200 EA	250
Negative Editions (Series of 5)	BCS	ART	1981	PH/C	11 X 14 EA		5 EA		500 EA	600 EA
Second Degree (50 Images)	BCS	ART	1981–82	PH/C	38 X 48 EA	CIBA	1 EA		800 EA	900 EA
66 Days-The Daily News (66 Images)	BCS	ART	1982	PH/C	11 X 14 EA	CIBA	25 EA		200 EA	300 EA

CHRIS BURDEN

BORN: Boston, MA; April 11, 1946
EDUCATION: Pomona Col, BRA, 1969; Univ of California, Irvine, CA, MFA, 1971
TEACHING: Instr, Avant-Guard Art, La Verne Col, 1973–74; Vis Art, Fresno State Univ, 1974; Instr, San Francisco Art Inst, CA, 1978; Univ of California, Los Angeles, CA, 1978 to present
AWARDS: New Talent Award, Los Angeles County Mus, CA, 1973; Nat Endowment for Arts Grants 1974,76,80; John Simon Guggenheim Fel, 1978
RECENT EXHIB: Newport Harbor Mus, Newport Beach, CA, 1988; Christine Burgin Gallery, NY, 1989; Whitney Mus of Am Art, NY, 1989; Jurgen Becker Gallery, Hamburg, Germany, 1990; Daniel Buchholz Gallery, Cologne, Germany, 1990; Rosa Felsen Gallery, Los Angeles, CA, 1990; Whitechapel Art Gallery, London, England, 1990; Wexner Center of Visual Arts, Columbus, OH, 1990–91; Lannan Found, Los Angeles, CA, 1992; Newport Harbor Art Mus, Newport Beach, CA 1992
COLLECTIONS: Mus of Mod Art, NY; Long Beach Arts Mus, CA; Art Mus of South Texas, Corpus Christi, TX; La Jolla Mus of Contemp Art, CA; Magasin Konsthall, Stockholm, Sweden
PRINTERS: Hidekatsu Takada (HT); Peter Pettengil (PP); Perry Tymeson (PT); John Slivon (JS); Crown Point Press, San Francisco, CA (CPP)
PUBLISHERS: Cirrus Editions, Los Angeles, CA (CE); Crown Point Press, San Francisco, CA (CPP)
GALLERIES: Cirrus Editions, Los Angeles, CA; Ronald Feldman Fine Arts, New York, NY; Crown Point Press, New York, NY & San Francisco; Rosamund Felsen Gallery, Los Angeles, CA; Christine Burgin Gallery, New York, NY; Kent Fine Art, New York, NY; David Lawrence Editions, Beverly Hills, CA; Fred Hoffman Gallery, Santa Monica, CA; Josh Baer Gallery, New York, NY; Donald Young Gallery, Seattle, WA; Michael Lowe Gallery, Cincinnati, OH
MAILING ADDRESS: c/o Kent Fine Art, Inc, 41 E 57th St, New York, NY 10022

CHRIS BURDEN CONTINUED

TITLE	PUBLISHER	PRINTER	DATE	MEDIUM	DIMENSION (PAPER SIZE) IN INCHES	TYPE OF PAPER	EDITION NUMBER	NO. OF COLORS	ORIGINAL OPENING PRICE	CURRENT RETAIL PRICE
SOLD OUT EDITIONS (RARE):										
Diecimila (Printed en verso)	CPP	JS/CPP	1977	PH/EC	10 X 14	R/BFK	35	14	700	3500
The Atomic Alphabet	CPP	HT/PP	1980	EB/HC	57 X 39	AP88	20	2	1200	8500
CURRENT EDITIONS:										
Untitled	CE	PT	1974	LC/HC	16 X 20	CP	50	2	275	2000

DANIEL BUREN

BORN: Boulogne, France; 1938
RECENT EXHIB: Daniel Templon Gallery, Paris, France, 1987; Renaissance Soc, Univ of Chicago, IL 1989,92; Univ of Massachusetts, Amherst, MA, 1992; John Weber Gallery, NY, 1987,93
COLLECTIONS: Art Inst of Chicago, IL; Detroit Inst of Arts, MI
PRINTERS: Crown Point Press, San Francisco, CA (CPP); Gemini GEL, Los Angeles, CA (GEM)
PUBLISHERS: Crown Point Press, San Francisco, CA (CPP); Gemini GEL, Los Angeles, CA (GEM)
GALLERIES: Hayward Gallery, London, England; John Weber Gallery, New York, NY; Crown Point Press, San Francisco, CA & New York, NY; Daniel Templon Gallery, Paris, France; Gemini GEL, Los Angeles, CA; Barbara Krakow Gallery, Boston, MA; Bobbie Greenfield Fine Art, Inc, Venice, CA

TITLE	PUBLISHER	PRINTER	DATE	MEDIUM	DIMENSION (PAPER SIZE) IN INCHES	TYPE OF PAPER	EDITION NUMBER	NO. OF COLORS	ORIGINAL OPENING PRICE	CURRENT RETAIL PRICE
CURRENT EDITIONS:										
Framed/Exploded/Defaced (25 Individually Framed Fragments) (No Proofs)	CPP	CPP	1979	EB	8 X 8 EA	R/BFK	46		3000 SET	20000 SET
Five Out of Eleven (10 Panels)	GEM	GEM	1989	LC	98 X 209 TOT	HMP	55	1 EA	15000	20000
The Missing Square (4 Panels)	GEM	GEM	1989	LC	97 X 97 TOT	HMP	55	1 EA	8000	10000
SOLD OUT EDITIONS (RARE):										
The Rotating Square—In and Out of the Frame (4 Panels)	GEM	GEM	1989	LC	97 X 97 TOT	HMP	36	2 EA	15000	20000

ROBERT BURKERT

BORN: Racine, WI; August 20, 1930
EDUCATION: Wustum Art Center, Racine, WI; Univ of Wisconsin, Madison, WI, BS, MS, 1948–55
TEACHING: Univ of WI, Milwaukee, WI, 1956 to present
RECENT EXHIB: Charles A Wustum Mus of Fine Arts, Milwaukee, WI, 1987,88
COLLECTIONS: Nat Coll of Fine Arts, Wash, DC; Tate Gallery, London, England; Metropolitan Mus of Art, NY; Fogg Mus, Cambridge, MA; Boston Mus of Fine Arts, MA
PRINTERS: Artist (ART)
PUBLISHERS: Judith Posner and Associates, Milwaukee, WI (JP); Associated American Artists, NY (AAA)
GALLERIES: Associated American Artists, New York, NY; Rubiner Gallery, West Bloomfield, MI; Bradley Galleries, Milwaukee, WI; Judith Posner Gallery, Milwaukee, WI
MAILING ADDRESS: 3228 N Marietta Ave, Milwaukee, WI 53211

TITLE	PUBLISHER	PRINTER	DATE	MEDIUM	DIMENSION (PAPER SIZE) IN INCHES	TYPE OF PAPER	EDITION NUMBER	NO. OF COLORS	ORIGINAL OPENING PRICE	CURRENT RETAIL PRICE
SOLD OUT EDITIONS (RARE):										
Autumn Sail	JP	ART	1973	SP	19 X 31	AP	100	9	200	500
Wild Apples	JP	ART	1973	SP	19 X 32	AP	100	7	200	500
CURRENT EDITIONS:										
Winter Ravine	AAA	ART	1974	SP	18 X 26	AP	100		200	400

BYRON LESLIE BURFORD

BORN: Jackson, MS; July 12,1920
EDUCATION: Univ of Iowa, Iowa City, IA, BFA, MFA
TEACHING: Prof, Painting, Univ of Iowa, Iowa City, IA, 1947-86, Emeritus, 1986 to present
AWARDS: Guggenheim Found Fel, 1960-61; Ford Found Awards,1961,62,64; Nat Inst of Arts & Letters Grants, 1967,72,75; Midwest Arts Nat Endowment Regional Fel, 1988
COLLECTIONS: Worcester Art Mus, MA; Walker Art Center, Minneapolis, MN; Nelson-Atlkins Gallery, Kansas City, MO; Sheldon Art Mus, Lincoln, NE; High Mus of Art, Atlanta, GA
PRINTERS: Artist (ART); Jeffrey Sippel (JS); Conrad Schwable (CS); Bill Lagattuta (BL); Toby Michel (TM); Tamarind Inst, Albuquerque, NM (TI)
PUBLISHERS: Tamarind Inst, Albuquerque, NM (TI)
GALLERIES: Carega Foxley Leach Gallery, Wash, DC; Gallery 72, Omaha, NE; Babcock Galleries, New York, NY
MAILING ADDRESS: 113 S Johnson, Iowa City, IA 52240

TITLE	PUBLISHER	PRINTER	DATE	MEDIUM	DIMENSION (PAPER SIZE) IN INCHES	TYPE OF PAPER	EDITION NUMBER	NO. OF COLORS	ORIGINAL OPENING PRICE	CURRENT RETAIL PRICE
SOLD OUT EDITIONS (RARE):										
Roly Boly	TI	JS/TI	1978	LC	43 X 54	R/BFK/G	20	3	125	400
Soldier with Gas Mask	TI	BL/TI	1978	LC	33 X 40	R/BFK/G	20	4	125	400
A Novel Bicycle Race	TI	TM/TI	1978	LC	36 X 36	R/BFK/G	20	3	125	400
May You Always Hold Sacred The Art of Magic	TI	CS/TI	1978	LC	43 X 54	R/BFK/G	20	4	125	400
Memories of Greenville	TI	CS/TI	1978	LC	79 X 64	AP	30	6	125	300
Two Snake Ladies	TI	BL/TI	1978	LC	90 X 67	AP	35	2	125	300
Blanket Courtmartial of a Female Spy	TI	JS/TI	1978	LC	43 X 33	AP	40	4	125	175
Kaden with 60 Bears	TI	BL/TI	1978	LC	70 X 57	AP	20	3	125	400
Dumont #1	TI	JS/TI	1978	LC	67 X 56	R/BFK/G	17	3	125	400

HANS GUSTAV BURKHARDT

BORN: Basel, Switzerland; December 20, 1904; US Citizen
EDUCATION: Cooper Union, NY, 1925–28; Grand Central Sch of Art, NY, 1928–29; Studied with Arshile Gorky, 1929–36
TEACHING: Prof, Painting and Drawing, Univ of Southern CA, 1959–60; Univ of CA, Los Angeles, CA, 1961–63; Long Beach State Col, CA; CA State Univ, Northridge, CA, 1963–73; Emer Prof, 1973 to present
AWARDS: Am Acad & Inst of Arts & Letters Award, 1992
RECENT EXHIB: Jack Rutberg Fine Arts, Los Angeles, CA, 1990,92; Muhlenberg Col, Frank Martin Art Gallery, Allentown, PA, 1992
COLLECTIONS: Santa Barbara Mus of Art, CA; Pasadena Art Mus, CA; Los Angeles County Mus of Art, CA; Corcoran Gallery of Art, Wash, DC; Hirshhorn Mus, Wash, DC; Guggenheim Mus, NY; Oakland Mus, CA; Columbia Mus of Art, SC; Joslyn Art Mus, Omaha, NE; Moderna Museet, Stockholm, Sweden; Kunstmuseum, Basel, Switzerland
PRINTERS: Artist (ART)
PUBLISHERS: Artist (ART); Jack Rutberg Fine Arts, Los Angeles, CA (JR)
GALLERIES: Jack Rutberg Fine Arts, Los Angeles, CA; Robert Schoelkopf Gallery, New York, NY
MAILING ADDRESS: 1914 Jewett Drive, Los Angeles, CA 90046

TITLE	PUBLISHER	PRINTER	DATE	MEDIUM	DIMENSION (PAPER SIZE) IN INCHES	TYPE OF PAPER	EDITION NUMBER	NO. OF COLORS	ORIGINAL OPENING PRICE	CURRENT RETAIL PRICE
SOLD OUT EDITIONS (RARE):										
After the Bomb	ART	ART	1948	LC	10 X 14	WOVE	6		30	1500
Journey into the Unknown	JR	ART	1969	LI/C	20 X 26	AP	25		200	1000
Models Mourning	JR	ART	1973	LI	25 X 19	AP	12		200	1000
From Here to Eternity	JR	ART	1974	LC	11 X 14	AP	25		250	1000
Las Vegas	JR	ART	1975	LI/C	18 X 24	AP	8		250	1000
Hommage to Mark Tobey	JR	ART	1976–78	LI/C	24 X 18	AP	14		350	1200
Adam and Eve	JR	ART	1977	LI	16 X 17	AP	14		300	1200
City Abstraction	JR	ART	1979	LI/C	24 X 18	AP	8		500	1200
Sex Pistols (Graffiti Series)	JR	ART	1982	LI/C	20 X 16	AP	8		700	1200

DIANE BURKO

BORN: New York, NY; September 24, 1945
EDUCATION: Skidmore Col, Saratoga Springs, NY, BS, Art; Grad Sch of Fine Arts, Univ of Pennsylvania, Phila, PA, MFA
TEACHING: Vis Prof, Princeton Univ, NJ, Spring, 1985; Prof, Community Col of Philadelphia, PA, 1969 to present
AWARDS: Vis Fel, Tamarind Inst, Albuquerque, NM, 1980,82; Nat Endowment for the Arts, 1985–86; Ind Artists Grants, Pennsylvania Council for the Arts, 1981,89
COLLECTIONS: Philadelphia Mus of Art, PA; DeCordova Mus, Lincoln, MA; Univ of New Mexico, Albuquerque, NM; Reading Public Mus, PA; Pennsylvania Acad of Fine Arts, Phila, PA; Rutgers Univ, Camden, NJ
PRINTERS: Tamarind Inst, Albuquerque, NM (TI); Brynn Jensen (BJ); Kate Leavitt (KL); Lynne D Allen (LDA); Catherine Kirsch Kuhn (CKK); Print Research Facility, Arizona State Univ, Tempe, AZ (PRF/ASU); Joseph Segura, Tempe, AZ (JS); Corridor Press, Cheltenham, PA (CP); Tim Sheesely, Phila, PA (TS)
PUBLISHERS: Tamarind Inst, Albuquerque, NM (TI); Print Research Facility, Arizona State Univ, Tempe, AZ (PRF/ASU); Corridor Press, Cheltenham, PA (CP)
GALLERIES: Marian Locks Gallery, Phila, PA; Tamarind Institute, Albuquerque, NM
MAILING ADDRESS: 510 South 46th St, Phila, PA 19143

TITLE	PUBLISHER	PRINTER	DATE	MEDIUM	DIMENSION (PAPER SIZE) IN INCHES	TYPE OF PAPER	EDITION NUMBER	NO. OF COLORS	ORIGINAL OPENING PRICE	CURRENT RETAIL PRICE
CURRENT EDITIONS:										
Yavapai Point #2-Revisited	TI	KL/CKK/TI	1980	LC	57 X 77 cm	GE	40	7	350	600
Red Rocks Park-Revisited	TI	BJ/CKK/TI	1981	LC	76 X 52 cm	AP/W	40	9	350	600
Delaware River #1	PRF/ASU	JMS	1982	LC	25 X 31	GE	25	7	350	600
Delaware River #2	TI	LDA/TI	1982	LC	57 X 76 cm	GE	50	10	350	600
Delaware River #3	TI	CKK/TI	1982	LC	57 X 76 cm	GE	50	9	350	600
Point Sur	CP	TS/CP	1985	LC	23 X 30	AC	30	6	350	500

ROBERTO BURLE-MARX

BORN: Sao Paolo; Brazil, August 4, 1909
EDUCATION: Sch of Fine Arts, Rio de Janeiro, Brazil
AWARDS: Fine Arts Medal, Am Inst of Architects, NY, 1965; Honorary Mem, Am Acad & Inst of Arts & Letters, NY, 1979; Honorary Mem, Inst of Landscape Architects of Canada, 1980; Honorary Doctorate, Royal Col of Art, London, England, 1982; Grande Gold Medal, Soc of Architecture of Paris, France, 1982; Albert P and Blanche Y Greensfelder Award, Missouri Botanical Garden, 1983; Medal Award, Am Soc of Landscape Architects, 1985
COLLECTIONS: Mus of Mod Art, NY; Rio Mus of Fine Arts, Rio de Janeiro, Brazil; Sao Paulo Mus, Brazil; Mus of Buenos Aires, Argentina; Landscape Architecture Found, Wash, DC; Brazilian-American Inst, Wash, DC; Fort Lauderdale Mus, FL
RECENT EXHIB: Roslyn Sailor Gallery, Margate City, NY, 1987
PUBLISHERS: Brandywine Gallery, Ltd, Wilmington, DE (BGL)
GALLERIES: Roslyn Sailor Gallery, Margate City, NJ; H M Glickenstein, Willow Grove, PA

TITLE	PUBLISHER	PRINTER	DATE	MEDIUM	DIMENSION (PAPER SIZE) IN INCHES	TYPE OF PAPER	EDITION NUMBER	NO. OF COLORS	ORIGINAL OPENING PRICE	CURRENT RETAIL PRICE
SOLD OUT EDITIONS (RARE):										
Sepetiba	ART	ART	1985	LC	22 X 32	FAB	100	4	250	900
Erotica	ART	ART	1985	LB	22 X 32	FAB	36	1	200	900
Erotica I	ART	ART	1985	LB	22 X 32	FAB	36	1	200	900
Erotica II	ART	ART	1985	LB	22 X 32	FAB	40	1	200	900
CURRENT EDITIONS:										
Set of Twelve:									4400 SET	6500 SET
Stravazavia	BGL	ART	1986	LC	22 X 32	FAB	50	4	385	625
Stravazavia I	BGL	ART	1986	LC	22 X 32	FAB	50	4	385	625
Pauliceia	BGL	ART	1986	LC	22 X 32	FAB	50	4	385	575

ROBERTO BURLE-MARX CONTINUED

TITLE	PUBLISHER	PRINTER	DATE	MEDIUM	DIMENSION (PAPER SIZE) IN INCHES	TYPE OF PAPER	EDITION NUMBER	NO. OF COLORS	ORIGINAL OPENING PRICE	CURRENT RETAIL PRICE
CURRENT EDITIONS:										
Pauliceia I	BGL	ART	1986	LC	22 X 32	FAB	50	4	385	575
Mutamba	BGL	ART	1986	LC	22 X 32	FAB	50	4	385	525
Mutamba I	BGL	ART	1986	LC	22 X 32	FAB	50	4	385	525
Carnivalia	BGL	ART	1986	LC	22 X 32	FAB	50	4	385	525
Carnivalia I	BGL	ART	1986	LC	22 X 32	FAB	50	4	385	525
Irere	BGL	ART	1986	LC	22 X 32	FAB	50	4	385	550
Irere I	BGL	ART	1986	LC	22 X 32	FAB	50	4	385	550
Florestela	BGL	ART	1986	LC	22 X 32	FAB	50	4	385	575
Florestela I	BGL	ART	1986	LC	22 X 32	FAB	50	4	385	575
Ciclonia 0,I,II,III (Set of 4)	ART	ART	1986	LC	22 X 32 EA	FAB	50 EA	4 EA	500 EA	750 EA
Mistelia 0,I,II,III (Set of 4)	ART	ART	1986	LC	22 X 32 EA	FAB	60 EA	4 EA	650 EA	750 EA

SAKTI BURMAN

BORN: Calcutta, India; 1935
EDUCATION: Ecole des Beaux Arts, Paris, France
COLLECTIONS: Nat Art Gallery, Wellington, New Zealand; Musée d'Art Moderne, Paris, France; Nat Gallery of Mod Art, New Delhi, India; Allahbad Mus, India

PRINTERS: American Atelier, NY (AA)
PUBLISHERS: Circle Fine Art, Chicago, IL (CFA)
GALLERIES: Circle Galleries, San Diego, CA & San Francisco CA & Northbrook, IL & Pittsburgh, PA & Houston, TX & Soho, NY & Chicago, IL & Scottsdale, AZ & Beverly Hills, CA & Costa Mesa, CA & Sherman Oaks, CA & Palm Beach, FL & Honolulu, HI & New Orleans, LA & Las Vegas, NV & SEattle, WA

TITLE	PUBLISHER	PRINTER	DATE	MEDIUM	DIMENSION (PAPER SIZE) IN INCHES	TYPE OF PAPER	EDITION NUMBER	NO. OF COLORS	ORIGINAL OPENING PRICE	CURRENT RETAIL PRICE
SOLD OUT EDITIONS (RARE):										
Cirque	CFA	AA	1978	LC	20 X 26	AP	200		50	200
Acrobat	CFA	AA	1978	LC	20 X 26	AP	200		50	200

RUTH BASLER BURR

BORN: Chicago, IL; February 12, 1932
EDUCATION: Glendale Col, CA; Pierce Col, Canoga Park, CA; Univ of California, Los Angeles, CA; Laguna Beach Sch of Art, CA
TEACHING: Pasadena City Col, CA, 1975–80
RECENT EXHIB: Watercolor Gallery, Laguna Beach, CA, 1990
COLLECTIONS: California Inst of Tech, Pasadena, CA; Univ of California Medical Center, Los Angeles, CA

PRINTERS: Ultra Color, Canoga Park, IL (UC)
PUBLISHERS: New York Graphics, Greenwich, CT (NYG); Creative Distribution, San Juan Capistrano, CA (CD); Burr Studio, San Juan Capistrano, CA (BS)
GALLERIES: Watercolor Gallery, Laguna Beach, CA; Back Door Gallery, Rancho Mirage, CA; Larry Dotson Gallery, Lahaina, HI; Lees Gallery, Riverside, CA
MAILING ADDRESS: 27071 Glenar, FF Lane, San Juan Capistrano, CA 92675

TITLE	PUBLISHER	PRINTER	DATE	MEDIUM	DIMENSION (PAPER SIZE) IN INCHES	TYPE OF PAPER	EDITION NUMBER	NO. OF COLORS	ORIGINAL OPENING PRICE	CURRENT RETAIL PRICE
CURRENT EDITIONS:										
Prime Time	CD/BS	UC	1988	LC	34 X 25	R/100	498	5	150	150
Labuna Brisas	CD/BS	UC	1988	LC	34 X 25	R/100	498	5	150	250
High Country Meadow	CD/BS	UC	1988	LC	34 X 26	R/100	500	5	150	150
English Cottage	CD/BS	UC	1988	LC	34 X 25	R/100	500	5	150	150
Peonies	CD/BS	UC	1988	LC	34 X 25	R/100	500	5	150	150
Celebration	CD/BS	UC	1988	LC	34 X 25	R/100	500	5	150	150
California Coast	CD/BS	UC	1989	LC	34 X 25	R/100	500	5	150	150
Bird's Eye View	CD/BS	UC	1990	LC	34 X 25	R/100	500	5	150	150
California Riviera	CD/BS	UC	1990	LC	34 X 25	R/100	500	5	150	150

ALBERTO BURRI

BORN: Citta di Castello, Italy; 1915
EDUCATION: Univ of Perugia, Italy; 1934–40
RECENT EXHIB: Murray & Isabella Rayburn Found, NY, 1992

PRINTERS: 2 RC Workshop, Rome, Italy (2RC); Mixografia, Santa Monica, CA (MIX)
PUBLISHERS: 2 RC, Rome, Italy (2RC); Mixografia, Santa Monica, CA (MIX)
GALLERIES: Remba Gallery/Mixografia Workshop, Santa Monica, CA; Salvatore Ala Gallery, New York, NY

TITLE	PUBLISHER	PRINTER	DATE	MEDIUM	DIMENSION (PAPER SIZE) IN INCHES	TYPE OF PAPER	EDITION NUMBER	NO. OF COLORS	ORIGINAL OPENING PRICE	CURRENT RETAIL PRICE
CURRENT EDITIONS:										
Cretti (Set of 8)	2RC	2RC	1972	EB	27 X 38 EA	FAB	90 EA	1 EA	1050 EA	20000 EA
Mixoblack (Set of 10)	MIX	MIX	1989	MIX	27 X 39 EA	HMP	30 EA		600000 SET	600000 SET

JEROME BURNS

BORN: Brooklyn, NY; March 26, 1919
EDUCATION: Art Students League, NY, 1936-39; Hans Hofmann Sch, NY, 1942; Brooklyn Mus Art Sch, NY, 1949
TEACHING: Instr, Brooklyn Mus Art Sch, Drawing, Paint, Composition, 1961-62
AWARDS: Samuel F B Morse Medal, Am Nat Acad, 1963; Tesser Mem Award, Audubon Artists, 1964; Director's Award, Nat Society of Painters in Casein & Acrylic, 1966; Memory of Ada Award, 1978
COLLECTIONS: Oklahoma Mus, Oklahoma City, OK; C W Post Col Mus, Long Island Univ, NY; Metropolitan Mus of Art, NY
PRINTERS: Bruce Cleveland, Brooklyn, NY (BC); Cleveland Editions, Brooklyn, NY (ClEd)
PUBLISHERS: Cleveland Editions, Brooklyn, NY (ClEd)
GALLERIES: Cleveland Editions, Brooklyn, NY
MAILING ADDRESS: 248 Garfield Place, Brooklyn, NY 11215

Jerome Burns
Where I Live
Courtesy Cleveland Editions

Jerome Burns
177 Books
Courtesy Cleveland Editions

TITLE	PUBLISHER	PRINTER	DATE	MEDIUM	DIMENSION (PAPER SIZE) IN INCHES	TYPE OF PAPER	EDITION NUMBER	NO. OF COLORS	ORIGINAL OPENING PRICE	CURRENT RETAIL PRICE
CURRENT EDITIONS:										
Cat's Cradle	ClEd	BC/ClEd	1992	EB/A	17 X 23	R/BFK	30	1	175	175
One Hundred Seventy Seven Books	ClEd	BC/ClEd	1992	EB/SPG	17 X 22	AP	30	1	175	175
Where I Live	ClEd	BC/ClEd	1992	EB/A	17 X 23	R/BFK	30	1	175	175

WILLIAM S BURROUGHS

RECENT EXHIB: Claremont Grad Sch, East & West Galleries, CA, 1992; Univ of Missouri, Kansas City, MO, 1992; Gagosian Gallery, NY, 1993
PRINTERS: Jean-Paul Russell, Durham, PA (JPR); Durham Press, Durham, PA (DurPr)
PUBLISHERS: Lococo-Mulder, St. Louis, MO (L-M)
GALLERIES: Gagosian Gallery, New York, NY; Tony Shafrazi Gallery, New York, NY; Earl McGrath Gallery, Los Angeles, CA; 65 Thompson Street Gallery, New York, NY

TITLE	PUBLISHER	PRINTER	DATE	MEDIUM	DIMENSION (PAPER SIZE) IN INCHES	TYPE OF PAPER	EDITION NUMBER	NO. OF COLORS	ORIGINAL OPENING PRICE	CURRENT RETAIL PRICE
CURRENT EDITIONS:										
The Seven Deadly Sins (7 Screenprint, Shotgun-Woodblock Images with 7 Screen Print Text) (Set of 14):									12000 SET	12000 SET
Anger	L-M	JPR/DurPr	1991	SP/WB	45 X 31	MB	90	4/1	2000	2000
Avarice	L-M	JPR/DurPr	1991	SP/WB	45 X 31	MB	90	5/1	2000	2000
Envy	L-M	JPR/DurPr	1991	SP/WB	45 X 31	MB	90	4/1	2000	2000
Gluttony	L-M	JPR/DurPr	1991	SP/WB	45 X 31	MB	90	4/1	2000	2000
Lust	L-M	JPR/DurPr	1991	SP/WB	45 X 31	MB	90	5/1	2000	2000
Pride	L-M	JPR/DurPr	1991	SP/WB	45 X 31	MB	90	4/1	2000	2000
Sloth	L-M	JPR/DurPr	1991	SP/WB	45 X 31	MB	90	4/1	2000	2000
X-Ray Man	L-M	JPR/DurPr	1992	SP	11 X 8	MB	178	2	250	300

POL BURY

BORN: Haine-Saint Pierre, Belgium, 1922
EDUCATION: Acad des Beaux-Arts, Mons, Belgium, 1938–39
PRINTERS: Maeght Editions, Paris, France (ME); Galerie Maeght Lelong, Paris, France (ML)
RECENT EXHIB: Arnold Herstand Gallery, NY, 1991
PUBLISHERS: Maeght Editions, Paris, France (ME); Galerie Maeght Lelong, Paris, France (ML)
GALLERIES: Galerie Lelong, Paris, France & Zürich, Switzerland & New York, NY; Lefebre Gallery, New York, NY; Arnold Herstand Gallery, New York, NY

POL BURY CONTINUED

TITLE	PUBLISHER	PRINTER	DATE	MEDIUM	DIMENSION (PAPER SIZE) IN INCHES	TYPE OF PAPER	EDITION NUMBER	NO. OF COLORS	ORIGINAL OPENING PRICE	CURRENT RETAIL PRICE
SOLD OUT EDITIONS (RARE):										
Tiges et Cercle	ME	ME	1975	M/MOB	29 X 30	AP	40		1300 FF	10000 FF
Entrelaces I	ME	ME	1975	M/MOB	23 X 31	AP	30		1300 FF	10000 FF
Entrelaces II	ME	ME	1975	M/MOB	23 X 31	AP	80		1300 FF	10000 FF
Cercle Eclate	ME	ME	1976	EB	48 X 32	AP	65		1300 FF	15000 FF
Disque et Triangle Eclatés	ME	ME	1976	EB	32 X 48	AP	50		1300 FF	15000 FF
Octogone Duvert	ME	ME	1976	EB	32 X 48	AP	60		1300 FF	15000 FF
Cercle au Carre Eclate	ME	ME	1976	EB	48 X 32	AP	65		1300 FF	15000 FF
Disque Elargei	ME	ME	1976	EB	48 X 32	AP	75		1300 FF	15000 FF
Trois Disques Deux Carres en Equilbre	ME	ME	1976	EB	48 X 32	AP	75		1300 FF	15000 FF
Disque Eclate (Jaune)	ME	ME	1976	EB	48 X 32	AP	65		1300 FF	15000 FF
Disque Carre (Bleu Jaune)	ME	ME	1976	EB	24 X 16	AP	50		500 FF	8500 FF
Cercle sur une Bente (Bleu Orange)	ME	ME	1977	EB	20 X 26	AP	50		800 FF	8500 FF
Cercle sur une Bente (Bleu Jaune)	ME	ME	1977	EB	20 X 26	AP	50		800 FF	8500 FF
Cercle sur une Angle Aigu (Bleu Orange)	ME	ME	1977	EB	20 X 26	AP	50		800 FF	8500 FF
Disque Triangle Losange (Bleu Jaune)	ME	ME	1978	EB	32 X 24	R/BFK	50		1000 FF	10000 FF
Losange Disque Triangle (Bleu Rouge)	ME	ME	1978	EB	32 X 24	R/BFK	50		1000 FF	10000 FF
Losange Disque Triangle (Bleu Brun)	ME	ME	1978	EB	32 X 23	R/BFK	50		1000 FF	10000 FF
Cercle sur un Angle Aigu (Blue Jaune)	ME	ME	1978	EB	20 X 26	R/BFK	50		800 FF	8500 FF
40 Batons entre Deux	ME	ME	1978	EB	20 X 25	R/BFK	75		1500 FF	15000 FF
14 Cercles, 6 Carres, 2 Losanges, 3 Triangles Soulignes	ME	ME	1978	EB	20 X 26	R/BFK	75		1500 FF	15000 FF
28 Disques entre Deux	ME	ME	1978	EB	26 X 18	R/BFK	75		1500 FF	15000 FF
40 Barres et un Cercle sur 2 Traverses	ME	ME	1978	EB	26 X 20	R/BFK	75		1500 FF	15000 FF
Cercle Dechire	ME	ME	1978	EB	20 X 26	R/BFK	75		1500 FF	15000 FF
11 Cercles sur un Carre	ME	ME	1978	EB	20 X 26	R/BFK	75		1500 FF	15000 FF
12 Batons en Eventail sur un Disque	ME	ME	1978	EB	26 X 20	R/BFK	75		1500 FF	15000 FF
Carre Disque et Batons Encadres	ME	ME	1979	EB	26 X 20	R/BFK	75		1500 FF	15000 FF
10 Losanges Descendan sur un Disque	ME	ME	1979	EB	26 X 20	R/BFK	75		1500 FF	15000 FF
Petit Cercle entre 9 et 1 Carres	ME	ME	1979	EB	26 X 20	R/BFK	75		1500 FF	15000 FF
2 Rectangles Arrondis	ME	ME	1979	EB	26 X 20	R/BFK	75		1500 FF	15000 FF
19 Disques entre 2 Obliques	ME	ME	1979	EB	26 X 20	R/BFK	75		1500 FF	15000 FF
13 Carres sur 5 Cercles	ME	ME	1979	EB	26 X 20	R/BFK	75		1500 FF	15000 FF
10 Triangles sur un Cercle	ME	ME	1979	EB	26 X 20	R/BFK	75		1500 FF	15000 FF
19 Rectangles, 18 Disques Superposes	ME	ME	1979	EB	26 X 20	R/BFK	75		1500 FF	15000 FF
13 Carres Diminues sur un Cercle	ME	ME	1979	EB	26 X 20	R/BFK	75		1500 FF	15000 FF
24 Disques entre Deux	ME	ME	1979	EB	26 X 20	R/BFK	75		1500 FF	15000 FF
14 Carres en Eventail	ME	ME	1979	EB	26 X 20	R/BFK	75		1500 FF	15000 FF
2 Groupes de Barres Vers la Droite et un Disque	ME	ME	1979	EB	26 X 19	R/BFK	75		1500 FF	15000 FF
Groupe de Barres Surplombant un Petit	ME	ME	1980	EB	26 X 20	R/BFK	75		1500 FF	15000 FF
3 Groupes de Barres Tournantes	ME	ME	1980	EB	26 X 20	R/BFK	75		1500 FF	15000 FF
Horizontale Avec Disques et Barres	ME	ME	1980	EC	26 X 20	R/BFK	75		1500 FF	15000 FF
Mondrian Composition 23 Ramolissements	ME	ME	1981	LC	56 X 76 cm	AP	75	4	1200 FF	10000 FF

JAMES D BUTLER

BORN: Ft Dodge, IA; August 30, 1945
EDUCATION: Omaha Univ, NE, BS, 1967; Univ of Nebraska, Lincoln, NE, MFA, 1970
TEACHING: Asst Prof, Southern Illinois, Edwardsville, IL, 1970–76; Assoc Prof, Illinois State Univ, Normal, IL, 1976–81, Prof, 1981 to present
AWARDS: Robert Cooke Endowment Award, 1971; First Place, Fine Art of Printmaking, Lexington, KY, Nat Soc of Arts & Letters, 1971; Nat Endowment for the Arts, 1975–76,79

RECENT EXHIB: Eastern Illinois Univ, Tarble Arts Center, Charleston, IL, 1992; Lakeview Mus of Arts & Sciences, Peoria, IL, 1992
COLLECTIONS: British Mus, London, England; Brooklyn Mus, NY; Smithsonian Inst, Wash, DC; Library of Congress, Wash, DC
PRINTERS: Richard Finch Studio, Normal, IL (RFS)
PUBLISHERS: John Szoke Graphics, Inc, NY (JSG)
GALLERIES: Associated American Artists, NY; Struve Gallery, Chicago, IL; Linda McAdoo Galleries, Santa Fe, NM; John Szoke Graphics, Inc, New York, NY
MAILING ADDRESS: c/o Department of Art, Illinois State University, Normal, IL 61761

TITLE	PUBLISHER	PRINTER	DATE	MEDIUM	DIMENSION (PAPER SIZE) IN INCHES	TYPE OF PAPER	EDITION NUMBER	NO. OF COLORS	ORIGINAL OPENING PRICE	CURRENT RETAIL PRICE
CURRENT EDITIONS:										
Midsummer Landscape	JSG	RFS	1989	LC	28 X 38	AC	100	4	650	700

WERNER BÜTTNER

PRINTERS: Hobusch Printing, Hamburg, Germany (HP)
PUBLISHERS: Edition Julie Sylvester, NY (EJS)
GALLERIES: Julie Sylvester Gallery, New York, NY

TITLE	PUBLISHER	PRINTER	DATE	MEDIUM	DIMENSION (PAPER SIZE) IN INCHES	TYPE OF PAPER	EDITION NUMBER	NO. OF COLORS	ORIGINAL OPENING PRICE	CURRENT RETAIL PRICE
CURRENT EDITIONS:										
Widows One Two	EJS	HP	1988	LIN/RS	26 X 32	FRP	20		400	500
Widows One Two	EJS	HP	1988	LIN/RS	26 X 32	FRP	20		400	500

JOHN BUTTON

BORN: San Francisco, CA; (1929–1982)
EDUCATION: Univ of California, Berkeley, CA; California Sch of Fine Arts, San Francisco, CA
TEACHING: Skowhegan Sch, ME, 1964,65; Sch of Vis Arts, NY, 1965–70, 70–73, 74; Cornell Univ, Ithaca, NY, 1967–68; Swarthmore Col, PA, 1969–70

COLLECTIONS: Mus of Mod Art, NY; Hirshhorn Mus, Wash, DC; Columbia Univ, NY; Univ of North Carolina, Chapel Hill, NC
PRINTERS: Solo Press, NY (SP)
PUBLISHERS: 724 Prints, NY (724P)
GALLERIES: Fischbach Gallery, New York, NY

TITLE	PUBLISHER	PRINTER	DATE	MEDIUM	DIMENSION (PAPER SIZE) IN INCHES	TYPE OF PAPER	EDITION NUMBER	NO. OF COLORS	ORIGINAL OPENING PRICE	CURRENT RETAIL PRICE
CURRENT EDITIONS:										
N Y U Housing	724P	SP	1978	LC	23 X 30	R/BFK	50	6	350	500

MICHAEL BYRON

BORN: Providence, RI: August 1954
EDUCATION: Kansas City Art Inst, MO, BFA, 1976; Nova Scotia Col of Art & Design, Canada, MFA,1981
RECENT EXHIB: Mario Diacono Gallery, Boston, MA 1987; Galerie Barbara Farber, Ansterdam, The Netherlands, 1987; Bernd Kluser Gallery, Munich, Germany, 1987; Aldrich Mus of Contemp Art, Ridgefield, CT, 1987; Galerie Borgman-Capitain, Kohn, Germany, 1987; Luhring, Augustine & Hodes Gallery, NY, 1988; Lawrence Oliver Gallery, Phila, PA, 1989; Phyllis Kind Gallery, Chicago, IL, 1989; Baron/Boisante Gallery, NY, 1989; Randolph Street Gallery, Chicago, IL, 1989; Witte de With Gallery, Paris, France, 1992; Maryland Inst, Col of Art, Decker & Meyerhoff Gallery, Baltimore, MD, 1992
PRINTERS: Donna Shulman, Brooklyn, NY (DS); Downstairs Editions, Brooklyn, NY (DEd); Maurice Sanchez, NY (MS); Derriére L'Etoile Studios, NY (DES); David Keister, Bloomington, IN (DK); David Calkins, Bloomington, IN (DC); Echo Press, Bloomington, IN (EPr); Crown Press, San Francisco, CA (CPP)
PUBLISHERS: Echo Press, Bloomington, IN (EPr); Mark Baron, Riverdale, NY (MB); Edition Julie Sylvester, NY (EJS)
GALLERIES: Galerie Barbara Farber, Amsterdam, The Netherlands; Mario Diacono Gallery, Boston, MA; Bernd Kluser Gallery, Munich, Germany; Galerie Borgman-Capitain, Cologne, Germany; Phyllis Kind Galleries, New York, NY & Chicago, IL; Lawrence Mangel Gallery, Phila, PA; Echo Press, Bloomington, IN; Downstairs Editions, Brooklyn, NY; Baron/Boisante Gallery, New York, NY; Luhring, Augustine Gallery, New York, NY; Witte de With Gallery, Paris, France; Merrill Chase Galleries, Chicago, IL
MAILING ADDRESS: c/o Luhring, Augustine Gallery, 130 Prince St, New York, NY 10012

TITLE	PUBLISHER	PRINTER	DATE	MEDIUM	DIMENSION (PAPER SIZE) IN INCHES	TYPE OF PAPER	EDITION NUMBER	NO. OF COLORS	ORIGINAL OPENING PRICE	CURRENT RETAIL PRICE
CURRENT EDITIONS										
Players (Set of 6)	MB	DS/DE	1986	EB/A	19 X 15 EA	GE	12 EA		1400 SET	4000 SET
For the People of Mexico	EPr	DK/DC/EPr	1988	LC/EB/CO	29 X 51	AP/R-BFK	20	8	1100	2100
Who Remembers Adam	EPr	DK/DC/EPr	1988	LC/EB/CO	29 X 51	AP88/R-BFK	20	13	1100	2100
Faust Suite (Set of 7)	EJS	MS/DES	1988	MON/CC	21 X 25 EA	HMP	1 EA		1000 EA	2500 EA
Often Seen But Seldom. . . .			1991		40 X 30	HMP	20		1500	1800

PAUL CADMUS

BORN: New York, NY; December 17, 1904
EDUCATION: Nat Acad of Design, NY, 1919–26; Art Students League, NY, 1928
AWARDS: Flora Mayer Witkowsky Prize, Art Inst of Chicago, IL, 1945; Nat Inst of Arts & Letters Grant, 1961; Purchase Prize, Norfolk Mus of Arts & Science, VA, 1967
RECENT EXHIB: Midtown Galleries, NY, 1990; Bridge Center for Contemp Art, El Paso, TX, 1992; Midtown Payson Gallery, NY, 1992; Louis Newman Gallery, Beverly Hills, CA, 1992
COLLECTIONS: Mus of Mod Art, NY; Whitney Mus of Am Art, NY; Metropolitan Mus, NY; Brooklyn Mus, NY; Art Inst of Chicago, IL; Philadelphia Mus, PA; Los Angeles County Mus, CA; Mus of Fine Arts, Boston, MA; Nat Mus of Am Art, Smithsonian Inst, Wash, DC; Wadsworth Atheneum, Hartford, CT; Fogg Art Mus, Harvard Univ, Cambridge, MA
PUBLISHERS: The Print Cabinet, Ridgefield, CT (PC); Imago Imprint, Inc, NY (II); Midtown Galleries, NY (MG)
PRINTERS: Richard Waller (RW); Suzan Steinbrock, NY (SS); Cheryl Pelavin, NY (CP); Gordon Kluge, NY (GK); George C Miller & Sons, NY (GCM)
GALLERIES: Harbor Gallery, New York, NY; Button Gallery, Saugatuck, MI; Rosenfeld Fine Arts, New York, NY; Michael Rosenfeld Gallery, New York, NY; Images Gallery, Toledo, OH; Midtown Payson Gallery, New York, NY; Louis Newman Gallery, Beverly Hills, CA
MAILING ADDRESS: P.O. Box 1255, Weston, CT 06883

PAUL CADMUS CONTINUED

TITLE	PUBLISHER	PRINTER	DATE	MEDIUM	DIMENSION (PAPER SIZE) IN INCHES	TYPE OF PAPER	EDITION NUMBER	NO. OF COLORS	ORIGINAL OPENING PRICE	CURRENT RETAIL PRICE
SOLD OUT EDITIONS (RARE):										
The Fleet's In (J-79)	ART	ART	1934	EB	7 X 14	LAID	50	1	25	5000
Stewart's	ART	ART	1934	EB	8 X 12	LAID	50	1	25	4000
Coney Island	ART	ART	1935	EB	9 X 10	LAID	50		25	9500
Shore Leave	ART	ART	1935	EB	11 X 12	LAID/CR	50		25	9500
Horseplay	ART	ART	1935	EB	9 X 5	LAID	50		25	3000
Mobile	ART	ART	1953	SP	17 X 19	WOVE	75		60	4000
Dancers Resting	MG	GK	1974	LC	25 X 18	RP/W	40	5	600	3000
Suite of 12 Etchings:										
The Fleets in ! (1934)	PC	RW	1979	EB	8 X 14	GE	35		300	1500
YMCA Locker Room (1934)	PC	RW	1979	EB	7 X 13	GE	35		300	1500
Mother and Child (1934)	PC	RW	1979	EB	5 X 4	GE	35		250	800
Stewarts (1934)	PC	RW	1979	EB	8 X 12	GE	35		300	1200
Shore Leave (1935)	PC	RW	1979	EB	10 X 12	GE	35		350	9500
Horseplay (1935)	PC	RW	1979	EB	9 X 5	GE	35		300	3000
Coney Island (1935)	PC	RW	1979	EB	9 X 10	GE	35		300	9500
Polo Spill (1938)	PC	RW	1979	EB	7 X 10	GE	35		300	900
Two Boys on a Beach #1 (1938)	PC	RW	1979	EB	5 X 7	GE	35		200	1200
Youth with a Kite (1941)	PC	RW	1979	EB	11 X 5	GE	35		300	800
Arabesque (1947)	PC	RW	1979	EB	7 X 7	GE	35		200	1200
The Bath (1953)	PC	RW	1979	EB	7 X 8	GE	35		200	2000
Waiting for Rehearsal	II	SS/CP	1984	EB/HG	15 X 19	HMP	175		600	1000
CURRENT EDITIONS:										
Nudo #1, #2, #3, State I	MG	GCM	1984	EB	14 X 18 EA	HMP	100 EA		1000 SET / 400 EA	2100 SET / 750 EA
Nudo #1, #2, #3, State II	MG	GCM	1984	EB	14 X 18 EA	HMP	30 EA		2000 SET / 900 EA	4000 SET / 1500 EA
Teddo	MG	GCM	1985	LB	9 X 11	R/BFK/W	200	1	400	600
Teddo	II	SS/CP	1985	LC	6 X 7	HMP	200		600	900

Johnson (J)

DENNIS VERN CADY

BORN: Portland, OR; November 10, 1944
EDUCATION: Portland State Univ, OR; Brooklyn Mus Art Sch, NY; Pratt Inst Graphic Center, NY; Empire State Col, NY, BS, 1974–77
TEACHING: Oregon Arts Council, Portland, OR; Portland State Univ, OR; Brooklyn Mus Sch, NY; Gilbert Sch, Brooklyn, NY; The Printshop, NY
AWARDS: Nat Scholastics Award, NY, 1962; Max Beckmann Mem Grant, 1969; America the Beautiful Fund Grant, 1971
COLLECTIONS: Univ of Toronto, Canada; South Street Seaport Mus, NY
PRINTERS: South Street Seaport Mus, NY (SSSM); Artist (ART)
PUBLISHERS: Artist (ART)
GALLERIES: Orion Editions, New York, NY; Ellen Sragow Gallery, New York, NY; Jayne H Baum Gallery, New York, NY
MAILING ADDRESS: 45 Orchard St, New York, NY 10002

TITLE	PUBLISHER	PRINTER	DATE	MEDIUM	DIMENSION (PAPER SIZE) IN INCHES	TYPE OF PAPER	EDITION NUMBER	NO. OF COLORS	ORIGINAL OPENING PRICE	CURRENT RETAIL PRICE
CURRENT EDITIONS:										
City Mass I	ART	ART	1978	SP	22 X 27	R/BFK	10	5	150	400
City Mass III	ART	ART	1978	SP	22 X 27	R/BFK	10	7	150	400
City Mass IV	ART	ART	1978	SP	22 X 27	R/BFK	8	6	150	250
City Mass V	ART	ART	1978	SP	22 X 27	R/BFK	9	4	150	400
City Mass VII	ART	ART	1978	SP	22 X 27	R/BFK	12	6	150	400
City Mass VIII	ART	ART	1978	SP	22 X 27	R/BFK	10	5	150	400
Roof Top II	ART	ART	1978	SP	22 X 27	R/BFK	10	8	150	400
Roof Top IV	ART	ART	1978	SP	22 X 27	R/BFK	9	6	150	400
Winter	ART	ART	1978	SP	22 X 27	R/BFK	10	7	150	400
Morning	ART	ART	1978	SP	22 X 27	R/BFK	10	5	150	400
City Impression	ART	ART	1978	SP	22 X 27	R/BFK	10	6	150	400
Wall Street Blue Prints	ART	ART/SSSM	1984	LT	7 X 14 EA	MO	45 EA	1 EA	700 SET	1000 SET

SAMUEL LINCOLN CADY

BORN: Boothbay Harbor, Maine; July 21, 1943
EDUCATION: Univ of New Hampshire, Durham, NH BA, 1961–65; Indiana Univ, Bloomington, IN, MFA, 1965–67
TEACHING: Instr, Painting, Printmaking, Univ of New Hampshire, Durham, NH, 1968–69; Art in Res, Illinois State Univ, Normal, IL, 1981; Instr, Grad Workshop, Sch of Visual Arts, NY, 1984 to present
RECENT EXHIB: Addison Gallery of Am Art, Andover, MA, 1987; Fujii Gallery, Tokyo, Japan, 1988; Gwenda Joy Gallery, Chicago, IL, 1989
COLLECTIONS: Addison Gallery of Am Art, Andover, MA
PRINTERS: John Nichols, NY (JN)
PUBLISHERS: Holly Solomon Editions, Ltd, NY (HSE); John Nichols, NY (JN)
GALLERIES: Holly Solomon Editions, Ltd, New York, NY; John Nichols Gallery, New York, NY; Howard Yezerski Gallery, Boston, MA
MAILING ADDRESS: P.O. Box 51, 58 Deerhill Rd, Cornwall, NY 12520

SAMUEL LINCOLN CADY CONTINUED

TITLE	PUBLISHER	PRINTER	DATE	MEDIUM	DIMENSION (PAPER SIZE) IN INCHES	TYPE OF PAPER	EDITION NUMBER	NO. OF COLORS	ORIGINAL OPENING PRICE	CURRENT RETAIL PRICE
SOLD OUT EDITIONS (RARE):										
Single Scull	HSE	JN	1981	SP	39 X 29	R/BFK/W	40	37	500	2000
Dinghy	HSE	JN	1981	SP	39 X 29	R/BFK/W	40	35	500	2000
Kayak	HSE	JN	1981	SP	39 X 29	R/BFK/W	40	25	500	1800
Highway Fragment-Three Levels	HSE/JN	JN	1985	SP	39 X 29	TR/HMP	65	18	650	1000

JOHN CAGE

BORN: Los Angeles, CA; September 5, (1912–1992)
AWARDS: Guggenheim Fel, NY; Nat Acad of Arts and Letters Award; Grand Honor, Int Biennial, Exhib of Prints, Tokyo, Japan, 1979; Skowhegan Sch of Painting & Sculpture Award, ME, 1990
RECENT EXHIB: Virginia Mus of Fine Arts, Richmond, VA, 1988; Crown Point Press, NY & San Francisco, CA, 1989; The Philips Coll, Wash, DC, 1989; Cooper Union, Arthur A Houghton Gallery, NY, 1992; Roanoke Mus of Fine Arts, VA, 1992
COLLECTIONS: Metropolitan Mus of Art, NY; Mus of Mod Art, NY; Stedelijk Mus, Amsterdam, The Netherlands; San Francisco Mus of Mod Art, CA; Mus of Fine Arts, Houston, TX; Virginia Mus of Fine Art, Richmond, VA
PRINTERS: Stephen Thomas (ST); Lilah Toland (LT); Renée Bott (RB); Marcia Bartholme (MB); Peter Pettengill, San Francisco, CA (PP); Crown Point Press, San Francisco, CA (CPP); Paula Paulson (PP); Lawrence J Hamlin (LJH); Nancy Aneloo (NA); Daria Sywalak (DS); Paul Mullowney, San Francisco, CA (PM); Lothar Osterburg, San Francisco, CA (LO)
PUBLISHERS: Crown Point Press, San Francisco, CA (CPP)
GALLERIES: Crown Point Press, New York, NY & San Francisco, CA; L A Louver Gallery, Venice, CA; Margarete Roeder Fine Art, New York, NY; Jeffrey Fuller Fine Art, Phila, PA; Carl Solway Gallery, Cincinnati, OH; BlumHelman Gallery, New York, NY; Topaz Editions, Inc, Tampa, FL; Stephen Solovy Fine Arts, Chicago, IL; Schmidt/Dean Gallery, Phila, PA; Mattress Factory, Pittsburgh, PA

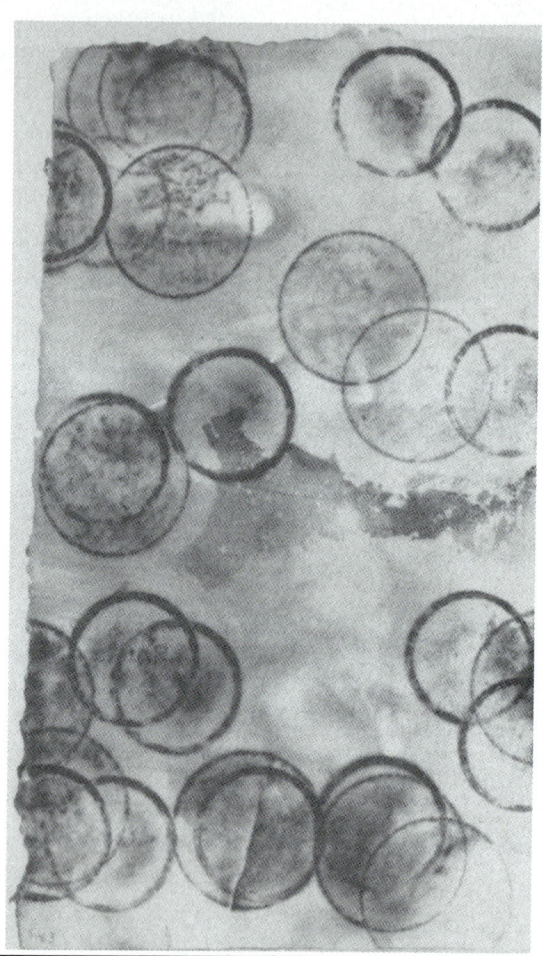

John Cage
Fire #3
Courtesy Crown Point Press

TITLE	PUBLISHER	PRINTER	DATE	MEDIUM	DIMENSION (PAPER SIZE) IN INCHES	TYPE OF PAPER	EDITION NUMBER	NO. OF COLORS	ORIGINAL OPENING PRICE	CURRENT RETAIL PRICE
SOLD OUT EDITIONS (RARE):										
Signals (25 Related Images, Each Unique)	CPP	ST/CPP	1978	EC	13 X 20 EA	UMB	25 EA		1500 EA	8000 EA
17 Drawings by Thoreau	CPP	ST/CPP	1978	EC	24 X 36 EA	HOD	25 EA	18 EA	800 EA	7000 EA
Seven Day Diary (Set of 7)	CPP	ST/CPP	1978	EC	12 X 17 EA	RHW/B	25 EA	7 EA	1000 SET	8000 SET
Score without Parts	CPP	ST/CPP	1978	EC	22 X 30		25		500	5000
Weather-ed	CPP	LT/MB/CPP	1983	PH/EC	27 X 16	SAM/SAT	25		750	3000
Global Village, 37–48 (Diptych) (Smoked Paper)	CPP	PH/LJH/NA/CPP	1989	AC	38 X 26	FAB/BR	15		1500	5000
9 Stones 2 (Smoked Paper)	CPP	PH/LJH/NA/CPP	1989	AC/SB	23 X 18	WP/W	20		1000	4500
10 Stones 2 (Smoked Paper)	CPP	PH/LJH/NA/CPP	1989	AC/SB	23 X 18	WP/W	20		1000	4500
11 Stones (Smoked Paper)	CPP	PH/LJH/NA/CPP	1989	AC/SB	23 X 18	WP/W	20		1000	4500
CURRENT EDITIONS:										
Changes and Disappearances (35 Related Images)	CPP	LT/CPP	1979–81	EC	12 X 22 EA	TRHN/G	35 EA		1200 EA	8000 EA
On the Surface (35 Related Images)	CPP	LT/CPP	1980–82	EC	19 X 25 EA	F/HM	35 EA		1200 EA	6000 EA
Déreau (38 Related Images)	CPP	LT/PS/MB/CPP	1982	EB/A	19 X 25 EA	JAP	38 EA	2 EA	2000 EA	8000 EA
Where R-Ryoanji (Set of 4):	CPP	LT/MB/CPP	1983	DPT	9 X 23 EA	JW/HMP C 1920	25 EA	1 EA	1500 SET 400 EA	10000 SET 3000 EA
(R³), R³ (Set of 2):	CPP	LT/MB/CPP	1983	DPT	9 X 23 EA	JW/HMP C 1920	25 EA	1 EA	750 SET 400 EA	5000 SET 3000 EA
HV (Horizontal-Vertical)	CPP	LT/MB/CPP	1983	MON	19 X 12 EA	JW/HMP	35 EA	1 EA	900 EA	2500 EA
HV (Horizontal-Vertical)	CPP	CPP	1983	MON	12 X 19 EA	SAM/SAT	35 EA	1 EA	900 EA	2500 EA
Fire (Series of 16)	CPP	PP/CPP	1985	MON	20 X 11 EA	GAMPI	1 EA	1 EA	1000 EA	3500 EA

JOHN CAGE CONTINUED

TITLE	PUBLISHER	PRINTER	DATE	MEDIUM	DIMENSION (PAPER SIZE) IN INCHES	TYPE OF PAPER	EDITION NUMBER	NO. OF COLORS	ORIGINAL OPENING PRICE	CURRENT RETAIL PRICE
CURRENT EDITIONS:										
Ryoku (Set of 13)	CPP	PP/CPP	1985	DPT	18 X 24 EA	GAMPI	1 EA	10 EA	6500 SET 600 EA	40000 SET 4000 EA
Mesotics: Earth, Air, Fire, Water	CPP	PP/CPP	1985	MON/CO	44 X 30 EA	GAMPI	9 EA	1 EA	2250 EA	4500 EA
Eninka (Series of 50)	CPP	CPP	1986	MON	24 X 19 EA	GAMPI	50 EA	1 EA	1100 EA	4500 EA
Déka (Series of 35)	CPP	MB/RB/CPP	1987	MON	16 X 19 EA	HANGA	1 EA	1 EA	650 EA	2500 EA
Variations (Series of 44)	CPP	MB/RB/CPP	1987	MON	9 X 11 EA	HANGA	1 EA	1 EA	550 EA	2000 EA
Where There is Where There (Series of 38)	CPP	MB/RB/CPP	1987–89	MON	23 X 30 EA	HANGA	48 EA	1 EA	1000 EA	4000 EA
Where There is Where There—Urban Landscape (48 Related Images)	CPP	RB/DS/CPP	1987–89	AC/DPT	22 X 30 EA	FAB/BR	1 EA		1200 EA	4000 EA
Global Village, 1–36 (Diptych) (Smoked Paper)	CPP	RB/DS/CPP	1989	AC	38 X 26	FAB/BR	15		1500	5000
Empty Fire (Smoked Paper)	CPP	PH/LJH/NA/CPP	1989	AC	18 X 23	WP/W	25		1000	1800
9 Stones (Smoked Paper)	CPP	PH/LJH/NA/CPP	1989	AC/SB	18 X 23	WP/W	20		1000	4500
10 Stones (Smoked Paper)	CPP	PH/LJH/NA/CPP	1989	AC/SB	18 X 23	WP/W	25		1000	4500
11 Stones 2 (Smoked Paper)	CPP	PH/LJH/NA/CPP	1989	AC/SB	18 X 23	WP/W	20		1000	4500
Dramatic Fire (Smoked Paper)	CPP	PH/NA/CPP	1989	AB/SB	18 X 23	WP/W	20	1	1200	4500
75 Stones (Smoked Paper)	CPP	PH/NA/CPP	1989	AB/SB	54 X 41	WP/W	25	1	1200	10000
The Missing Stone (Smoked Paper)	CPP	PH/NA/CPP	1989	AB/SB	54 X 41	WP/W	25	1	1200	10000
Smoke Weather Stone Weather (Smoked Paper)	CPP	PM/LJ/LO/CPP	1991	AB/SB/SL/SG	15 X 25	MIT	37	1	2200	4500
Without Horizon (Smoked Paper)	CPP	PP/PM/CPP	1992	I	8 X 9	HMP	57	Varies	1000	2500
Variations III	CPP	PP/PM/CPP	1992	MON	18 X 19 EA	HMP	1 EA	Varies	4000 EA	4000 EA
HV2 (Series of 15)	CPP	PP/PM/CPP	1992	EC	12 X 15 EA	HMP	45 EA		3500	3500

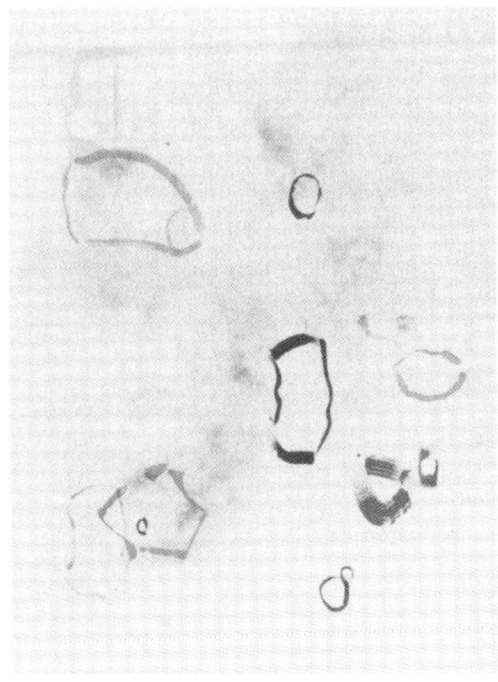

John Cage
The Missing Stone
Courtesy Crown Point Press

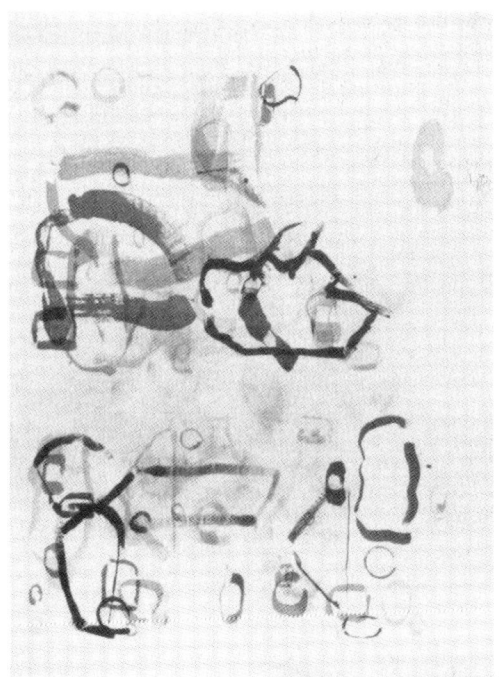

John Cage
75 Stones
Courtesy Crown Point Press

AL CALDERARO

BORN: Passaic, NJ; 1950

EDUCATION: Fairleigh Dickinson Univ, Rutherford, NJ, BA, 1971; Virginia Commonwealth Univ, Richmond, VA 1972–74
PRINTERS: Larry B Wright Art Productions, NY (LBW)
PUBLISHERS: Concord Contemporary Art, NY (CCA)
GALLERIES: Concord Contemporary Art Gallery, New York, NY

TITLE	PUBLISHER	PRINTER	DATE	MEDIUM	DIMENSION (PAPER SIZE) IN INCHES	TYPE OF PAPER	EDITION NUMBER	NO. OF COLORS	ORIGINAL OPENING PRICE	CURRENT RETAIL PRICE
CURRENT EDITIONS:										
A Real Pussycat	CCA	LBW	1982	SP	38 X 34	LEN/100	50	6	250	450

ALEXANDER CALDER

BORN: Philadelphia, PA; (1898–1976)
RECENT EXHIB: Retrosp, Galerie Linssen, Cologne, West Germany, 1987; State Univ of New York, Neuberger Mus, Purchase, NY, 1990,92; Univ of Rochester Mem Art Gallery, NY, 1990,92; Storm King Art Center, Mountainville, NY, 1987,90,92; Stamford Mus, Leonhardt Gallery, CT, 1992; Mattatuck Mus, Waterbury, CT, 1992; Midwest Mus of Am Art, Elkhart, IN, 1992; Fort Wayne Mus of Art, IN, 1992; Berkshire Mus, Pittsfield, MA, 1992; Mus of FIne Arts, Springfield, MA 1990,92; Michigan State Univ, Kresge Art Mus, East Lansing, MI, 1987,90,92
COLLECTIONS: Stedelijk Mus, Amsterdam, The Netherlands; Art Inst of Chicago, IL; Mus of Fine Art, Dallas, TX; Wadsworth Atheneum, Hartford, CT; Honolulu Acad, HI; Mus of Mod Art, NY; Whitney Mus of Am Art, NY; Nat Mus of Art, Stockholm, Sweden; PA Acad of Fine Arts, Phila, PA; Washington Univ, St Louis, MO; Yale Univ, New Haven, CT; Smith Col, Northampton, MA; Metropolitan Mus of Art, NY; Montreal Mus of Art, Can; Toronto Mus of Art, Can; Philadelphia Mus of Art, PA; Mus of Western Art, Moscow, Russia
PRINTERS: Atelier Mourlot, Paris, France (AM); Shorewood-Bank Street Atelier, NY (SBSA); Maeght Editions, Paris, France (ME); Arte, Paris, France (ARTE); American Atelier, NY (AA)
PUBLISHERS: Maeght Editions, Paris, France (ME); Transworld Art, Inc, NY (TAI); Kennedy Graphics, Inc, NY (KG); Associated American Artists, NY (AAA); Editions of the Difference, Paris, France (ED); Circle Fine Art, Chicago, IL (CFA); Alba Editions, Inc, NY (AE)
GALLERIES: Jack Rutberg Fine Arts, Los Angeles, CA; Andrew Dierken Fine Art, Los Angeles, CA; R K Goldman Contemporary, Los Angeles, CA; Jonathan Novak Contemporary Art, Los Angeles, CA; Herbert Palmer Gallery, Los Angeles, CA; John Berggruen Gallery, San Francisco, CA; Harcourts Modern & Contemporary Art, San Francisco, CA; Galerie Lareuse, Wash, DC; Foster Harmon Galleries of American Art, Sarasota, FL; Richard Gray Gallery, Chicago, IL; Rolly-Micheau Galleries, Boston, MA; Donald Morris Gallery, Birmingham, MI; John C Stoller & Company, Minneapolis, MN; Greenberg Gallery, St Louis, MO; Scherer Gallery, Marlboro, NJ; Gerald Peters Gallery, Santa Fe, NM; Brewster Gallery, New York, NY; Sigrid Freundorfer Fine Art, New York, NY; James Goodman Gallery, New York, NY; Nohra Haime Gallery, New York, NY; Arnold Herstand & Company, New York, NY; Alexander Kahan Fine Arts, New York, NY; Jane Kahan Gallery, New York, NY; Jan Krugier Gallery, New York, NY; M-13 Gallery, New York, NY; Edward Tyler Nahem Fine Art, New York, NY; O'Hara Gallery, New York, NY; Solomon & Company, New York, NY; Turner Fine Art, New York, NY; Weintraub Gallery, New York, NY; Kennedy Graphics, New York, NY; Associated American Artists, New York, NY; Galerie Linssen, Cologne, West Germany; BenedicteSaxe Gallery, Beverly Hills, CA; Gallery Mourlot, Boston, MA; Connecticut Fine Arts, Westport, CT; Rachel Adler Gallery, New York, NY; James Goodman Gallery, New York, NY; Gallery Urban, New York, NY; SImon/Neuman Gallery, New York, NY; Pat Kery Fine Arts, New York, NY; Professional Fine Arts, New York, NY

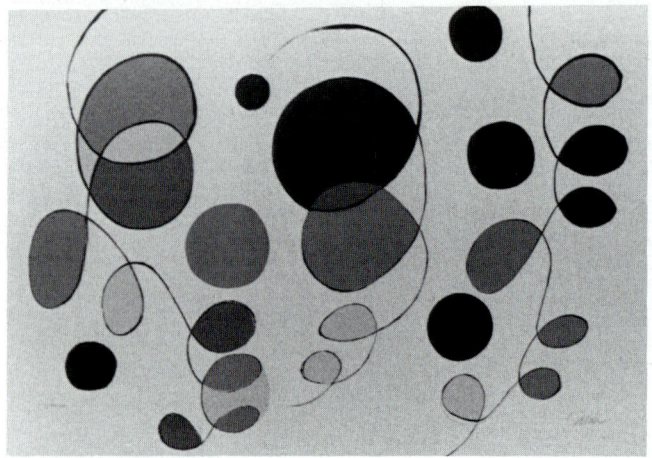

Alexander Calder
Coupeaux de Couleurs
Courtesy Avantgarde Art Associates

Alexander Calder
Lettres
Courtesy Avantgarde Art Associates

TITLE	PUBLISHER	PRINTER	DATE	MEDIUM	DIMENSION (PAPER SIZE) IN INCHES	TYPE OF PAPER	EDITION NUMBER	NO. OF COLORS	ORIGINAL OPENING PRICE	CURRENT RETAIL PRICE
SOLD OUT EDITIONS (RARE):										
Un Drole de Poisson	ME	ME	1965	LC	20 X 26	AP	90		200	4500
Far West	ME	ME	1967	LC	30 X 44	AP	90		300	5000
Le Chevalier	ME	ME	1968	LC	25 X 35	AP	90		300	5000
Spirals	KG	AM	1968	LC	26 X 20	AP	125	7	500	2500
Circles	KG	AM	1969	LC	26 X 20	AP	125	7	500	2500
Blue	KG	AM	1969	LC	22 X 29	AP	125	9	500	2500
Inspiration	KG	AM	1969	LC	27 X 21	AP	125	6	500	2500
Bulles d'Air	ME	ME	1969	LC	23 X 31	AP	75		300	4500
Serpent Parmi Les Etoiles	ME	ME	1969	LC	29 X 43	AP	75		300	4500
Red Nose	ME	ME	1969	LC	29 X 43	AP	75		300	4500
Pyramid Rouge	ME	ME	1969	LC	15 X 20	AP	75		200	3000
Papause	ME	ME	1969	LC	30 X 44	CMP	75		500	5000
Coupeaux de Couleurs	ME	ME	1969	LC	30 X 44	CMP	75		500	5000
Galatic System	KG	AM	1969	LC	20 X 28	CMP	100	5	500	2500
Fetes (Set of 7)	ME	ME	1971	EC		WOVE	200			
Carrefour	ME	ME	1971	LC	26 X 19	AP	75		300	3500
Les Rubans	ME	ME	1971	LC	31 X 20	AP	75		500	3000
Carnival in Rio	TAI	AM	1971	LC	30 X 44	AP	20		600	5000
Creation	TAI	AM	1971	LC	30 X 44	AP	20		600	5000
Temptation of the Butterfly	TAI	AM	1971	LC	30 X 44	AP	20		600	5000
Champ Jaune	ME	ME	1972	LC	22 X 29	AP	75		600	3500
Deux Serpents	ME	AM	1972	LC	22 X 26	AP	75		600	3500
Flamme Interieure	ME	ME	1972	LC	15 X 21	AP	75		300	3000
Hope of the Volubilis	ED	ARTE	1973	LC	20 X 28	AP	150		250	3500

ALEXANDER CALDER CONTINUED

TITLE	PUBLISHER	PRINTER	DATE	MEDIUM	DIMENSION (PAPER SIZE) IN INCHES	TYPE OF PAPER	EDITION NUMBER	NO. OF COLORS	ORIGINAL OPENING PRICE	CURRENT RETAIL PRICE
SOLD OUT EDITIONS (RARE):										
The Blues	ED	ARTE	1973	LC	20 X 28	AP	150		150	3500
Nostalgic Flight	ED	ARTE	1973	LC	20 X 28	AP	150		250	3500
Bubbles	ED	ARTE	1973	LC	30 X 44	AP	50		650	5000
Tank Traps	ED	ARTE	1973	LC	30 X 44	AP	95		650	5000
Curliques	ED	ARTE	1973	LC	30 X 44	AP	150		650	5000
Boomerang	TAI	AM	1974	LC	44 X 30	AP	125		500	5000
Lettres	ME	ME	1974	LC	30 X 44	AP	75		500	5000
Red & Blue Wave	ME	ME	1974	SP	45 X 31	AP	120		500	3500
Bateau Noir	AAA	ME	1975	LC	23 X 31	AP	100	5	475	3500
Flat World	ME	ME	1975	LC	29 X 42	AP	100		600	3500
Grey Oval	ME	ME	1975	LC	29 X 42	AP	100		600	3500
146 AV	ME	ME	1975	LC	22 X 31	AP	150		550	3000
Un Patriote	ME	ME	1975	LC	16 X 22	AP	75		300	3000
Mama Citron	ME	ME	1975	LC	18 X 22	AP	75		300	3000
Triangles Rouges	ME	ME	1975	LC	19 X 26	AP	90		400	3000
Le Inquietude	ME	ME	1975	LC	27 X 39	AP	125		700	3500
Affiche Artig	ME	ME	1975	LC	20 X 27	AP	150		400	3000
Homage to the Sun	ME	ME	1975	LC	27 X 39	AP	150		500	3000
Santa Claus Suite (Set of 9)	ME	ME	1975	LC	15 X 21	AP	175		3000 SET	20000 SET
Birds in Flight			1975	LC	27 X 37	AP	125		600	3000
La Bete			1975	LC	27 X 37	AP	150		600	3000
Landscape	TAI	AM	1975	LC	30 X 44	AP	150		500	4000
Our Unfinished Revolution (Set of 10)	AE	AM	1976	LC	30 X 22 EA	AP	175 EA		3000 SET	10000 SET
Blue Sun	TAI	SBSA	1976	LC	18 X 24	AP	250		500	3000
Mes Etoffes	ME	ME	1976	LC	21 X 28	AP	150		600	3000
Lollipops	ME	ME	1976	LC	26 X 39	AP	125		700	3500
Dark Pyramids	ME	ME	1976	LC	21 X 28	AP	125		600	3000
Candycane	ME	ME	1976	LC	21 X 28	AP	150		700	3500
Red And Blue Wave	ME	ME	1976	LC	31 X 45	AP	120		800	3500
Universe	ME	ME	1976	LC	29 X 43	AP	150		800	3500
Joys of the Neophyte	ME	ME	1976	LC	29 X 21	AP	150		400	3000
Curliques	ME	ME	1976	LC	30 X 43	AP	150		800	3500
La Pierre and Les Spirals			1976	LC	28 X 40	AP	150		800	3500
Poisson Rouge et Poisson Blanc	ME	ME	1976	LC	23 X 31	AP	150		600	3500
Soucoupes Dans Le Noir	ME	ME	1976	LC	43 X 29	AP	75		800	3500
Circle	ME	ME	1976	LC	43 X 29	AP	75		800	3500
Les Vagues Vagues	ME	ME	1976	LC	23 X 31	AP	75		800	3500
Deux Spirales	ME	ME	1976	LC	30 X 43	AP	75		800	3500
Une Famille de La Bas	ME	ME	1976	LC	21 X 30	AP	75		800	3500
Les Folles de Sanche	ME	ME	1976	LC	21 X 30	AP	75		800	3500
Les Tetards	ME	ME	1976	LC	31 X 23	AP	75		800	3500
Autres Tetards	ME	ME	1976	LC	23 X 31	AP	75		800	3500
Zebre Jaune et Zebre Noir	ME	ME	1976	LC	31 X 23	AP	75		800	3500
Ciel d'Orage	ME	ME	1976	LC	31 X 23	AP	150		600	3000
Soleil Sur Les Vagues	ME	ME	1976	LC	23 X 31	AP	150		600	3500
Flies in The Spider Web	TAI	AM	1976	LC	20 X 26	AP	175	4	1000	3000
Number Nine	CFA	AA	1976	TAP	55 X 82	AP	100		1800	8500
Zebra	CFA	AA	1976	TAP	55 X 82	AP	100		1800	8500

PAUL CALLE

BORN: New York, NY; March 3, 1928
EDUCATION: Pratt Inst, NY
AWARDS: Contemp Achievement Medal, Pratt Inst, NY, 1970
COLLECTIONS: Phoenix Art Mus, AZ; Nat Portrait Gallery, Wash, DC; Pacific Northwest Indian Center, Spokane, WA
PRINTERS: American Atelier, NY (AA)
PUBLISHERS: Circle Fine Art, Chicago, IL (CFA)
GALLERIES: Circle Galleries, San Diego, CA & San Francisco, CA & Northbrook, IL & Pittsburgh, PA & Houston, TX & Soho, NY & Chicago, IL & Scottsdale, AZ & Beverly Hills, CA & Costa Mesa, AZ & Sherman Oaks, CA & Palm Beach, FL & Honolulu, HI & New Orleans, La & Las Vegas, NV & Seattle, WA
MAILING ADDRESS: 149 Little Hill Dr, Stamford, CT 06905

TITLE	PUBLISHER	PRINTER	DATE	MEDIUM	DIMENSION (PAPER SIZE) IN INCHES	TYPE OF PAPER	EDITION NUMBER	NO. OF COLORS	ORIGINAL OPENING PRICE	CURRENT RETAIL PRICE
SOLD OUT EDITIONS (RARE):										
Waiting	CFA	AA	1975	LC	34 X 24	AP	300		125	400

The retail prices of the 100,000 limited edition prints quoted in this directory are subject to change. Print publishers, artists and galleries were the direct sources for these quotations. Prices in the secondary market listed as "Sold Out Editions (Rare)" indicate that the publisher has a limited supply of that print or that the print is difficult to locate in the galleries.

The Printworld Directory is accepting new applications for the seventh edition. Approximately 300 new artists will be accepted. Please use the two forms provided in the back section of this directory to submit biographical data and documentation of prints. Edition number of each print must not exceed 500 and the retail price must be $100 or more.

JORGE CAMACHO

BORN: Havana, Cuba, 1934
EDUCATION: Studied with André Breton, Paris, France, 1961–63
PRINTERS: La Poligrafa, SA, Barcelona, Spain (LP)
PUBLISHERS: Ediciones Poligrafa, Barcelona, Spain (EdP)
GALLERIES: Galeria Joan Prats, New York, NY & Barcelona, Spain

TITLE	PUBLISHER	PRINTER	DATE	MEDIUM	DIMENSION (PAPER SIZE) IN INCHES	TYPE OF PAPER	EDITION NUMBER	NO. OF COLORS	ORIGINAL OPENING PRICE	CURRENT RETAIL PRICE
CURRENT EDITIONS:										
Cenizas Suite (Set of 10)	EdP	LP	1974	LC	22 X 30 EA	GP	75 EA	5 EA	1500 SET	2500 SET
Cenizas Suite (Color Variants)									180 EA	280 EA
(Set of 10)	EdP	LP	1974	LC	22 X 30 EA	GP	XXV EA	5 EA	1800 SET	3000 SET
Lithograph A L Joan Prats	EdP	LP	1979	LC	30 X 22	GP	99	3	180	280

JEAN CAMBEROQUE

BORN: Paris, France, 1917
PRINTERS: American Atelier, NY (AA)
PUBLISHERS: Circle Fine Art, Chicago, IL (CFA)
GALLERIES: Rodi Karkazis Gallery, Chicago, IL; Circle Galleries, San Diego, CA & San Francisco, CA & Northbrook, IL & Pittsburgh, PA & Houston, TX & Soho, NY & Chicago, IL & Scottsdale, AZ & Beverly Hills, CA & Costa Mesa, CA & Sherman Oaks, CA & Palm Beach, FL & Honolulu, HI & New Orleans, LA & Las Vegas, NV & Seattle, WA

TITLE	PUBLISHER	PRINTER	DATE	MEDIUM	DIMENSION (PAPER SIZE) IN INCHES	TYPE OF PAPER	EDITION NUMBER	NO. OF COLORS	ORIGINAL OPENING PRICE	CURRENT RETAIL PRICE
CURRENT EDITIONS:										
Fisherman	CFA	AA	1980	LC	20 X 26	AP	200		50	175

DARIO CAMPANILE

BORN: Rome, Italy; April 21, 1948
EDUCATION: Edmondo de Amicis, Industrial Design, Rome, Italy, 1968
AWARDS: Silver Cup, Minstry of Public Ed, Rome, Italy, 1971; Silver Medal, Palace of Rome, Italy, 1971
COLLECTIONS: Univ of Southern California, Los Angeles, CA; Pratt Inst, NY; Ministry of Defense, Rome, Italy
PRINTERS: Artist (ART)
PUBLISHERS: David Lawrence Editions, Beverly Hills, CA (DLE)
GALLERIES: David Lawrence Editions, Beverly Hills, CA

TITLE	PUBLISHER	PRINTER	DATE	MEDIUM	DIMENSION (PAPER SIZE) IN INCHES	TYPE OF PAPER	EDITION NUMBER	NO. OF COLORS	ORIGINAL OPENING PRICE	CURRENT RETAIL PRICE
CURRENT EDITIONS:										
Christina	DLE	ART	1984	CPM	39 X 43 X 2	CP	300	1	400	800
Morning Dream	DLE	ART	1984	CPM	37 X 40 X 3	CP	300	1	400	600
Donna Giovane	DLE	ART	1984	CPM	35 X 22 X 1	CP	300	1	250	500
Torsos	DLE	ART	1984	CPM/HC	28 X 38	CP	50	4	750	900
Agro Dolce	DLE	ART	1984	CPM	30 X 40 X 3	CP	150	1	500	750
Sulla Spiagglia at 5 PM	DLE	ART	1984	CPM	36 X 86 X 4	CP	150	1	600	1200
Il Cavallo	DLE	ART	1985	CPM	32 X 32 X 2	CP	250	1	400	600
Menage at Four	DLE	ART	1985	CPM	29 X 39 X 3	CP	50	4	1000	1200
Dieci Visi	DLE	ART	1985	CPM	30 X 40 X 2	CP	50	4	1000	1200

MIGUEL ANGEL CAMPANO

PRINTERS: Edicion T, Barcelona, Spain (EdT)
PUBLISHERS: Edicions T, Barcelona, Spain (EdT)

TITLE	PUBLISHER	PRINTER	DATE	MEDIUM	DIMENSION (PAPER SIZE) IN INCHES	TYPE OF PAPER	EDITION NUMBER	NO. OF COLORS	ORIGINAL OPENING PRICE	CURRENT RETAIL PRICE
CURRENT EDITIONS:										
M A Campano III	EdT	EdT	1992	AB	29 X 75	HMP	12	1	SF 2950	SF 2950

NANCY CAMPBELL

BORN: Syracuse, NY; May 28, 1952
EDUCATION: Syracuse Univ, NY, BFA, 1974; Univ of Michigan, Ann Arbor, MI, MFA, 1976
TEACHING: Asst Prof, Art, Oberlin Col, OH, 1979–80; Vis Lectr, Univ of Hartford Art Sch, West Hartford, CT, 1980–81; Assoc Prof, Art, Mount Holyoke Col, South Hadley, MA, 1981 to present
AWARDS: Purchase Award, Univ of Dallas, Irving, TX, 1985; Award, Nat Exhib, Mus of Fine Arts, Springfield, MA, 1985; Stewart M Egnal Prize, Int Comp, Print Club, Phila, PA, 1986; Found Patron Award, Inst Comp, Print Club, Phila, PA, 1987; Special Commendation Award, Brockton Art Mus, MA, 1988; Juror's Merit Award, Nat Print & Drawing Exhib, Bradley Univ, Peoria, IL, 1989; Award, Valley Women Artists Annual Exhib, Northampton Center for the Arts, MA, 1990; Juror's Commendation, Boston Printmakers, North Am Print Exhib, DeCordova Mus, Lincoln, MA, 1991; Awards, Springfield Art League, Nat Exhib, Mus of Fine Arts, Springfield, MA, 1990,91

NANCY CAMPBELL CONTINUED

RECENT EXHIB: Haggerty Art Gallery, Univ of Dallas, Irving, TX, 1990; Hampshire Col, Amherst, MA, 1990; Alice Simsar Gallery, Ann Arbor, MI, 1990
COLLECTIONS: Philadelphia Art Mus, PA; Library of Congress, Wash, DC; Worcester Art Mus, MA; Syracuse Univ, NY; Mount Holyoke Col Art Mus, South Hadley, MA; Illinois State Univ, Normal, IL; Lamar Univ, Beaumont, TX; Nova Scotia Col of Art & Design, Halifax, NS, Canada; Univ of Connecticut, Storrs, CT; Univ of Dallas, TX; Univ of Hartford, West Hartford, CT: Univ of Massachusetts, Amherst, MA; Univ of Massachusetts, Boston, MA; Univ of New Hampshire, Durham, NH; Univ of Vermont, Burlington, VT; Univ of Rhode Island, Kingston, RI
PRINTERS: Artist (ART); Norman Stewart, Bloomfield Hills, MI (NS); Joe Keenan, Bloomfield Hills, MI (JK); Stewart & Stewart, Bloomfield Hills, MI (S–S)
PUBLISHERS: Artist (ART); Stewart & Stewart, Bloomfield Hills, MI (S–S)
GALLERIES: Stewart & Stewart, Birmingham, MI; Mary Ryan Gallery, New York, NY; Alice Simsar Gallery, Ann Arbor, MI
MAILING ADDRESS: 369 Middle St, Amherst, MA 01002

TITLE	PUBLISHER	PRINTER	DATE	MEDIUM	DIMENSION (PAPER SIZE) IN INCHES	TYPE OF PAPER	EDITION NUMBER	NO. OF COLORS	ORIGINAL OPENING PRICE	CURRENT RETAIL PRICE
CURRENT EDITIONS:										
Wara	ART	ART	1988	SP/LC	21 X 26	R/BFK/T	20	30	500	750
Tsubasa	S–S	NS/JK/S–S	1988	SP	21 X 26	R/BFK/W	64	21	400	750
Tatsu	ART	ART	1989	SP/LC	23 X 60	R/BFK/W	20	30	500	750
Kiwa	ART	ART	1990	SP/LC	18 X 17	R/BFK/W	60		500	750
Igai	ART	ART	1991	SP/LC	29 X 19	R/BFK/W	18	25	600	600

STEVEN CAMPBELL

BORN: Glasgow, Scotland; March 19, 1954
EDUCATION: Glasgow Sch of Art, Scotland, 1978–82
AWARDS: Fulbright Scholarship, 1982
RECENT EXHIB: Marlborough Fine Art, London, England, 1987
COLLECTIONS: High Mus of Art, Atlanta, GA; Sidney & Frances Lewis Foundation, Richmond, VA
PRINTERS: Chip Elwell, NY (CE); Jane Kent, NY (JK); Sally Sturman, NY (SS)
PUBLISHERS: Barbara Toll Fine Arts, Inc, NY (BTFA); Jane Kent, NY (JK); Jeffrey Rian, NY (JR)
GALLERIES: Barbara Toll Fine Arts, Inc, New York, NY; Rhona Hoffman Gallery, Chicago, IL; Dart Gallery, Chicago, IL; Galerie Six Freidrich, Munich, Germany; Marlborough Fine Art, London, England & New York, NY
MAILING ADDRESS: 248 Lafayette Street, New York, NY 10012

TITLE	PUBLISHER	PRINTER	DATE	MEDIUM	DIMENSION (PAPER SIZE) IN INCHES	TYPE OF PAPER	EDITION NUMBER	NO. OF COLORS	ORIGINAL OPENING PRICE	CURRENT RETAIL PRICE
SOLD OUT EDITIONS (RARE):										
The Hiker said, "Death, You Shall Not Take the Child" (Dipt)	BTFA	CE	1983	WB	102 X 100	SEK	15	1	800	2000
Gesturing Hiker	BTFA	CE	1984	WB	66 X 52	SEK	20	1	600	1200
Tragic Hikers	BTFA	CE	1983–85	WB	101 X 102	SEK	5	1	2500	3500
Age of Reason	JK/JR	JK/SS	1985	A/SL/PHG	41 X 29	R/BFK	42	11	600	1000

RAFAEL CANOGAR

PRINTERS: La Poligrafa, SA, Barcelona, Spain (LP)
PUBLISHERS: Ediciones Poligrafa, SA, Barcelona, Spain (EdP)
GALLERIES: Galeria Juan Prats, New York, NY & Barcelona Spain

TITLE	PUBLISHER	PRINTER	DATE	MEDIUM	DIMENSION (PAPER SIZE) IN INCHES	TYPE OF PAPER	EDITION NUMBER	NO. OF COLORS	ORIGINAL OPENING PRICE	CURRENT RETAIL PRICE
SOLD OUT EDITIONS (RARE):										
Series of 5 Lithographs (Set of 5):									1250 SET	3500 SET
La Manifestacion	EdP	LP	1972	LC	22 X 30	GP	75		350	700
Los Solados Musicas	EdP	LP	1972	LC	22 X 30	GP	75		350	700
El Juego de la Guerra	EdP	LP	1972	LC	22 X 30	GP	75		350	700
El Abrazo	EdP	LP	1972	LC	22 X 30	GP	75		350	700
Estudio para un Monumento	EdP	LP	1972	LC	22 X 30	GP	75		350	700
CURRENT EDITIONS:										
Series of 5 Lithographs (Set of 5)	EdP	LP	1972	LC	22 X 30 EA	GP	XXV EA		1500 SET	3500 SET
				LC					400 EA	750 EA
Series of 15 Lithographs (Set of 15):									5000 SET	9000 SET
Composicion con Manos	EdP	LP	1975	LC	22 X 30	GP	75	3	350	700
Figura Sentada	EdP	LP	1975	LC	22 X 30	GP	75	3	350	700
Ei Caminante	EdP	LP	1975	LC	22 X 30	GP	75	3	350	700
Figura Ciega	EdP	LP	1975	LC	22 X 30	GP	75	3	350	700
El Pensador	EdP	LP	1975	LC	22 X 30	GP	75	3	350	700
Composición con Tres Figuras	EdP	LP	1975	LC	22 X 30	GP	75	3	350	700
Estudio para un Momento	EdP	LP	1975	LC	22 X 30	GP	75	3	350	700
Composción	EdP	LP	1975	LC	22 X 30	GP	75	3	350	700
Figura en Paisaje	EdP	LP	1975	LC	22 X 30	GP	75	3	350	700
Estudio para una Bandera	EdP	LP	1975	LC	22 X 30	GP	75	3	350	700
Composición con Perro	EdP	LP	1975	LC	22 X 30	GP	75	3	350	700
Composición con Cabeza	EdP	LP	1975	LC	22 X 30	GP	75	3	350	700
Figura Sobre la Hierba	EdP	LP	1975	LC	22 X 30	GP	75	3	350	700
Paisaje Humano	EdP	LP	1975	LC	22 X 30	GP	75	3	350	700
Humenaje a Goya	EdP	LP	1975	LC	22 X 30	GP	75	3	350	700

GRAHAM CANTIENI

BORN: Albury, Australia; August 26, 1938; Canadian Citizen
EDUCATION: Royal Melbourne Teachers Col, Australia; Royal Melbourne Inst of Tech, Australia; Univ of Melbourne, Australia
TEACHING: Wesley Col, Perth, Australia, 1967–68; Ateliers d'Animation Cult, Sherbrooke, Can, 1969–76; Univ of Sherbrooke, Can, 1974–76

COLLECTIONS: Mus D'Art Contemp, Montreal, Can; Mus d'Art de Jolloitte, Can; Univ Sherbrooke, Can, Swan Hill Art Gallery, Victoria, Australia; Univ de Montreal, Can
PUBLISHERS: Editions Suistral (ES); Atelier Cahiers, Montreal, Canada (AC)
PRINTERS: Artist (ART)
GALLERIES: Galerie L'Aquatinte, Montral, Canada
MAILING ADDRESS: 425 London, Sherbrooke, Quebec, Canada J1H 3M8

TITLE	PUBLISHER	PRINTER	DATE	MEDIUM	DIMENSION (PAPER SIZE) IN INCHES	TYPE OF PAPER	EDITION NUMBER	NO. OF COLORS	ORIGINAL OPENING PRICE	CURRENT RETAIL PRICE
SOLD OUT EDITIONS (RARE):										
Les Trois Muses	GLA	ART	1976	LB	10 X 8	AP	10	1	120	300
Firenze	GLA	ART	1976	LB	18 X 26	AP	30	1	140	350
Parergon 1	AC	ART	1980	EB	12 X 8	AP	30	1	100	250
Parergon 2	AC	ART	1980	EB	12 X 8	AP	4	1	100	250
CURRENT EDITIONS:										
Sorciere (Set of 6)	ES	ART	1975–76	SP	16 X 15 EA	AP	20 EA	5 EA	200 SET	600 SET
Homage A Kandinsky (Set of 14)	ES	ART	1976	SP	16 X 12 EA	AP	20 EA	1 EA	400 SET	1000 SET

DOMENICK CAPOBIANCO

BORN: St Louis, MO; December 22, 1928
EDUCATION: Washington Univ, St Louis, MO, BFA, 1958; Skowhegan Sch of Painting & Sculpture, ME, 1958,59
TEACHING: Instr, Painting, Univ of Washington, St Louis, MO, 1957–58; Lectr, Art Dept, Univ of North Carolina, Greensboro, NC, 1967; Asst Prof & Chmn of Art Dept, Rutgers Univ, Neward, NJ, 1967 to present
AWARDS: Secor Award Scholarship, Washington Univ, St Louis, MO, 1956,57; Skowhegan Scholarship, Washington Univ, St Louis, MO, 1958; Skowhegan Scholarship, Skowhegan Sch of Painting & Sculpture, ME, 1959; Walter Gutman Found Award, 1963,66; Cassandra Found Award, 1967; Creative Artists Public Service Grant, 1976; Faculty Acad Study Prog Grant, Rutgers Univ, Newark, NJ, 1979; Guggenheim Fel, 1984–85

COLLECTIONS: Univ of Dallas, TX; Mus of Mos Art, Skopje, Yugoslavia; Mus of Mod Art, Ljubljana, Yugoslavia Graphische Sammlung Albertina, Vienna, Austria; Nat Mus of Krakow, Poland; Weatherspoon Mus, Univ of North Carolina, NC; Acad des Beaux-Arts, Ljublijana, Yugoslavia; Newark Public Library, NJ
PRINTERS: Joe Watanabe, NY (JW); Elfi Schuselka, NY (ES); Studio 13, NY (S-13)
PUBLISHERS: Studio 13, NY (S-13)
GALLERIES: Condeso/Lawler Gallery, New York, NY; Lumley Cazalet Ltd, London, England; Studio 13, New York, NY
MAILING ADDRESS: c/o Studio 13, 133 Eldridge St, New York, NY 10002

TITLE	PUBLISHER	PRINTER	DATE	MEDIUM	DIMENSION (PAPER SIZE) IN INCHES	TYPE OF PAPER	EDITION NUMBER	NO. OF COLORS	ORIGINAL OPENING PRICE	CURRENT RETAIL PRICE
SOLD OUT EDITIONS (RARE):										
B.A.L.L.&S.	S-13	ES	1976	LC/SP	22 X 30	R/BFK	50	16	175	500
CURRENT EDITIONS:										
Wall	S-13	ES/S-13	1979	LC/SP	22 X 30	R/BFK	50	7	225	500
Target-Six Color Try	S-13	ES/S-13	1980	LC/SP	22 X 30	R/BFK	50	10	200	400
'A' for Ascension	S-13	JW/S-13	1982	SP	22 X 30	R/BFK	40	7	225	400
'D' for Dance	S-13	JW/S-13	1982	SP	22 X 30	R/BFK	40	7	225	400
Flame	S-13	ES	1986	SP	22 X 30	AC/BL	12	1	150	375
Tower in Dis	S-13	ES	1986	SP	22 X 30	AC/BL	12	1	150	375
Resurrection	S-13	ES	1986	SP	22 X 30	AC/BL	12	1	150	375
Fallen Tower	S-13	ES	1989	LC/SP	22 X 30	AC	12	12	325	375
Mountain + Sun (Set of 2)	S-13	ES	1989	LC/SP	22 X 30	R/BFK	12	10	600 SET	650 SET
Yanked I, II	S-13	ES	1989–92	LC/SP/HC	22 X 30	R/BFK	12 EA	13 EA	325 EA	375 EA
Double Zapped	S-13	ES	1989–92	LC/SP/HC	22 X 30	R/BFK	12	13	325	375
Studies for a Madonna	S-13	ES	1992	LC/HC	22 X 30	R/BFK	12	3	375	375

SUZANNE CAPORAEL

RECENT EXHIB: John Berggruen Gallery, San Francisco, CA, 1989; Richard Green Gallery, Santa Monica, CA, 1991; Stephen Wirtz Gallery, San Francisco, CA, 1992
PRINTERS: Sette Publishing Company, Tempe, AZ (SPC); Wilbert Foo, San Francisco, CA (WF); Barry Russakis, San Francisco, CA (BR); John Stemmer, San Francisco, CA (JS); Charles Thomas, San Francisco, CA (CT); Experimental Workshop, San Francisco, CA (EW)
PUBLISHERS: Sette Publishing Company, Scottsdale, AZ (SPC); Experimental Workshop, San Francisco, CA (EW)
GALLERIES: John Berggruen Gallery, San Francisco, CA; Betsy Senior Contemporary Prints, New York, NY; Lisa Sette Gallery, Scottsdale, AZ; Harcus Gallery, Boston, MA; Richard Green Gallery, Santa Monica, CA; Stephen Wirtz Gallery, San Francisco, CA; Katie Block Fine Art, Boston, MA; Sette & Segura Publishing Company, Scottsdale, AZ

TITLE	PUBLISHER	PRINTER	DATE	MEDIUM	DIMENSION (PAPER SIZE) IN INCHES	TYPE OF PAPER	EDITION NUMBER	NO. OF COLORS	ORIGINAL OPENING PRICE	CURRENT RETAIL PRICE
CURRENT EDITIONS:										
Not You Again	SPC	SPC	1988	WC	50 X 44	AC	36		1200	2000
Seeing Things (Shade Tree)	EW	WF/BR/JS/CT/EW	1990	WC	43 X 36	R/BFK/W	40	21	1500	2000
Untitled	EW	WF/BR/JS/EW	1990	MON	20 X 56 EA	R/BFK/W	1 EA	Varies	3000 EA	3000 EA
Untitled	EW	WF/BR/JS/EW	1990	MON	11 X 20 EA	R/BFK/W	1 EA	Varies	1500 EA	1500 EA

LEONILDE CARABBA

BORN: Milan, Italy; November 28, 1938
EDUCATION: International Lyceum, Milan, Italy
AWARDS: First Prize, Graphics, Termoli, Italy, 1969; First Prize, Graphics, Knokke-Heist, The Netherlands, 1976
COLLECTIONS: Mus di Citta', Bolivar, Venezuela; Maison de la Culture, Namur, Belgium; Oud Hospital Mus, Aalst, Belgium; Mod Art Mus, Asyla, Maroc; Museo di Montecatini, Italy; Pinacoteca di Bari, Italy
PRINTERS: Soma Fine Art Press, San Francisco, CA (SOMA)
PUBLISHERS: Casa Editrice Carabba, Bolinas, CA (CEC)
GALLERIES: Soma Fine Art Press, San Francisco, CA
MAILING ADDRESS: c/o Soma Fine Art Press, 665 Third, #225, San Francisco, CA 94107

Leonilde Carabba
The Hercules Pillars or I am my Own Door
Courtesy the Artist

TITLE	PUBLISHER	PRINTER	DATE	MEDIUM	DIMENSION (PAPER SIZE) IN INCHES	TYPE OF PAPER	EDITION NUMBER	NO. OF COLORS	ORIGINAL OPENING PRICE	CURRENT RETAIL PRICE
CURRENT EDITIONS:										
Aaron of the Mountain	CEC	SOMA	1985	SP	22 X 30	SOM	100	12	200	600
The Servant of the Timeless Beauty	CEC	SOMA	1985	SP	22 X 30	SOM	100	7	200	600
The Alchemical Fire of Transformation	CEC	SOMA	1985	SP	22 X 30	SOM	100	14	200	600
The Hercules Pillars or I am My Own Door	CEC	SOMA	1985	SP	22 X 30	SOM	100	15	200	600

RENÉ CARCAN

BORN: Brussels, Belgium; June 25, 1925
EDUCATION: Royal Acad of the Beaux-Arts, Brussels, Belgium
PRINTERS: Atelier Georges Leblanc, Paris, France (AGL)
PUBLISHERS: Horn Editions, NY (HE); Galleri Kunsi-Invest, Oslo, Norway (GKI)
GALLERIES: Multiple Impressions, New York, NY; J-Michael Galleries, Edina, MN; Tower Park Gallery, Peoria Heights, IL

TITLE	PUBLISHER	PRINTER	DATE	MEDIUM	DIMENSION (PAPER SIZE) IN INCHES	TYPE OF PAPER	EDITION NUMBER	NO. OF COLORS	ORIGINAL OPENING PRICE	CURRENT RETAIL PRICE
SOLD OUT EDITIONS (RARE):										
Seasons in Brabant (Set of 4)									1260 SET	2000 SET
Printemps	HE	AGL	1980	EB/A	24 X 20	AP	99		350	600
Eté	HE	AGL	1980	EB/A	24 X 20	AP	99		350	600
Automne	HE	AGL	1980	EB/A	24 X 20	AP	99		350	600
Hiver	HE	AGL	1980	EB/A	24 X 20	AP	99		350	600
L'Homme et le Soleil (Set of 7)	HE	AGL	1982	EB/A	7 X 9 EA	AP	99 EA		180 EA	350 EA
Set of 5	GKI		1985	EB/A	38 X 29 cm	AP/W	166 EA		1875 SET	2000 SET

GREG S CARD

BORN: Los Angeles, CA; August 28, 1945
AWARDS: Contemp Art County Award, Los Angeles, CA; Mus of Art, 1969; Purchase Award, Southern Illinois Univ, Carbondale, IL, 1971; Nat Endowment for the Arts Fellowship, 1975
COLLECTIONS: White House, Wash, DC; New Mexico Mus of Art
PRINTERS: Cirrus Editions Workshop, Los Angeles, CA (CEW); Artist (ART)
PUBLISHERS: Cirrus Editions, Ltd, Los Angeles, CA (CE); Artist (ART)
GALLERIES: Cirrus Gallery, Los Angeles, CA; Koplin Gallery, Los Angeles, CA
MAILING ADDRESS: 534 S Broadway, 6th Fl, Los Angeles, CA 90012

TITLE	PUBLISHER	PRINTER	DATE	MEDIUM	DIMENSION (PAPER SIZE) IN INCHES	TYPE OF PAPER	EDITION NUMBER	NO. OF COLORS	ORIGINAL OPENING PRICE	CURRENT RETAIL PRICE
SOLD OUT EDITIONS (RARE):										
Non-Active Single Silver	ART	ART	1975	X/HC	19 X 28	RP	20	6	35	500
CURRENT EDITIONS:										
Light is the Color, Infinity the Number	CE	CEW	1972	LC	13 X 21	RP	55	1	150	350
+ + −	CE	CEW	1972	SP/PLEX	26 X 26	PLEX	21	Multi	250	650

ROYDEN CARD

BORN: Cardston, Alberta, Canada, August 2, 1952; US Citizen
EDUCATION: Brigham Young Univ, Provo, UT, BFA, Painting, 1976, MFA, Printmaking, 1979
TEACHING: Instr, Printmaking, Brigham Young Univ, Provo, UT, 1980–86
AWARDS: Utah Arts Council, Cash Award, 1984; Utah Arts Council, Purchase Awards, 1985,87
RECENT EXHIB: John Szoke Graphics, NY, 1987; Nora Eccles Harrison Mus of Art, Logan, UT, 1988; Hunterdon Art Mus, Clinton, NJ, 1988

COLLECTIONS: Brigham Young Univ Mus, Provo, UT; Smithsonian Inst Library, Wash, DC; Utah State Coll of Fine Art, Salt Lake City, UT; Latter-Day Saints Mus of History & Art, Salt Lake City, UT; Springville Mus of Art, UT; Smithsonian Inst Library, Wash, DC
PRINTERS: Artist (ART)
PUBLISHERS: Artist (ART)
GALLERIES: Annex Galleries, Santa Rosa, CA; Phillips Gallery, Salt Lake City, UT
MAILING ADDRESS: 559 South 1150 West, Orem, UT 84058

TITLE	PUBLISHER	PRINTER	DATE	MEDIUM	DIMENSION (PAPER SIZE) IN INCHES	TYPE OF PAPER	EDITION NUMBER	NO. OF COLORS	ORIGINAL OPENING PRICE	CURRENT RETAIL PRICE
SOLD OUT EDITIONS (RARE):										
Bentwood Chairs	ART	ART	1980	WB	19 X 24	AP	24	1	60	150
Still Life	ART	ART	1980	WB	19 X 24	AP	24	1	60	150
Tables	ART	ART	1980	WB	26 X 19	AP	24	1	60	150
Buttes	ART	ART	1983	WB	20 X 26	AP	16	1	100	150
East Window	ART	ART	1983	WB	18 X 21	AP	20	1	100	250
Last Great Hiding Place	ART	ART	1983	WB	18 X 21	AP	20	1	80	150
Red Deseret	ART	ART	1983	WC	13 X 13	KIT	14	1	80	150
East Wall	ART	ART	1984	WC	14 X 16	KIT	24	1	100	150
Jenni's Bookshelf	ART	ART	1984	WC	21 X 18	KIT	24	1	100	150

RIMER CARDILLO

BORN: Montevideo, Uruguay; August 17, 1944
EDUCATION: Nat Sch of Fine Arts, Uraguay, MFA, 1968; Weissenssee Sch of Art & Architecture, Berlin, Germany, 1970; Leipzig Sch of Graphic Arts, Leipzig, Germany, 1971
TEACHING: Print Workshops, Southern Dakota Univ, Vermillion, SC, 1983; Print Workshops, Southern Illinois Univ, Carbondale, IL, 1982,84
AWARDS: First Prize, Nat Graphic Assn, Uraguay, 1969; Award of Excellence, Int Miniature Print Exhib, Seoul, Korea, 1980; Purchase Award, Int Miniature Prize Comp, Pratt Inst, NY, 1980; Fourth Prize, Int Mezzotint Comp, The Print Club, Phila, PA, 1984; New Jersey Council on the Arts Fel, 1984; New York Found for the Arts Fel, 1985; Purchase Award, Rockford Int, Rockford, IL, 1985
RECENT EXHIB: Opus Gallery, Miami, FL, 1989; Atlanta Col of Art, Robert M Woodruff Art Center Gallery, GA, 1992; Linda Moore Gallery, San Diego, CA, 1992
COLLECTIONS: Albion Col, MI; Albright-Knox Art Gallery, Buffalo, NY; Art Mus, Porto Alegre, Brazil; Cabinet des Estampes, Bibliothèque Nat, Paris, France; California Col of Arts & Crafts, Oakland, CA; Chicago Art Inst, IL; Cincinnati Art Mus, OH; Inst de Cultura Puertorriqueña, San Juan, PR; Inst Nacional de Bellas Artes, México City, México; Mus Circulante, Asunción, Paraguay; Mus de Arte Americano, Cuzco, Perú; Mus de Arte Contemporáneo, Caracas, Venezuela; Mus de Arte Moderno, Cali, Columbia; Mus de Bellas Artes, Bogatá, Colombia; Mus de Bellas Artes, Santiago, Chile; Mus del Grabado, Buenos Aires, Argentina; Mus Nacional de Artes Plásticas, Montevideo, Uruguay; Mus of Contemp Graphic Arts, Fredrikstad, Norway; Mus of Mod Art, NY; New York Public Library; Prints Cabinet of Berlin, Germany; Skopje Mus of Contemp Art, Yugoslavia; Southern Illinois Univ, Carbondale, IL
PUBLISHERS: HMK Fine Arts, NY (HMK); Contempo Arts Ltd, Winston Salem, NC (CAL); Southern Illinois Univ Art Dept, Carbondale, IL (SIU); AGPA Editions, Caracas, Venezuela (AGPA); South Dakota Univ Art Dept, Brookings, SD (SDU); Artist (ART)
PRINTERS: Southern Illinois Univ Workshop, Carbondale, IL (SIU); South Dakota Univ Workshop, Brookings, SD (SDU); Artist (ART)
GALLERIES: Galeriá Latina, Montevideo, Uruguay; Galeriá Vermeer, Buenos Aires, Argentina; Wenniger Graphics, Boston, MA; Galeriá Sur, P del Este, Uruguay; Atlantic Gallery, New York, NY; Cretum Art Ab, Huddinge, Sweden; Opus Gallery, Miami, FL; Linda Moore Gallery, San Diego, CA; Art Spectrum Gallery, New York, NY; Opus Gallery, Miami, FL
MAILING ADDRESS: 508 W 53rd St, 3rd FL, New York, NY 10019

Rimer Cardillo
Wood Box II
Courtesy the Artist

TITLE	PUBLISHER	PRINTER	DATE	MEDIUM	DIMENSION (PAPER SIZE) IN INCHES	TYPE OF PAPER	EDITION NUMBER	NO. OF COLORS	ORIGINAL OPENING PRICE	CURRENT RETAIL PRICE
SOLD OUT EDITIONS (RARE):										
Mariposa de la Quinta	HMK	ART	1980	EC/ENG/EMB	30 X 22	AP	99	9	200	500
Mariposa de San Francisco	HMK	ART	1980	EC/ENG/EMB	30 X 22	AP	99	7	200	500

RIMER CARDILLO CONTINUED

TITLE	PUBLISHER	PRINTER	DATE	MEDIUM	DIMENSION (PAPER SIZE) IN INCHES	TYPE OF PAPER	EDITION NUMBER	NO. OF COLORS	ORIGINAL OPENING PRICE	CURRENT RETAIL PRICE
SOLD OUT EDITIONS (RARE):										
Polilla de Primavera	HMK	ART	1980	EC/ENG/EMB	30 X 22	AP	99	8	200	500
Mariposa del Espinillo	HMK	ART	1980	EC/ENG/EMB	30 X 22	AP	99	9	200	500
Mariposa de Piedras Blancas	CAL	ART	1980	EC/ENG/EMB	30 X 22	AP	75	10	200	500
Pomona's Butterfly	HMK	ART	1981	EC/ENG/EMB	30 X 22	AP	150	8	200	500
Ann Arbor's Butterfly	HMK	ART	1981	EC/ENG/EMB	30 X 22	AP	150	9	200	500
Makanda's Butterfly	HMK	ART	1981	EC/ENG/ENB	30 X 22	AP	150	8	200	500
Coronilla's Butterfly	HMK	ART	1981	EC/ENG/EMB	30 X 22	AP	150	9	200	500
Wasp Dabber and Barogue	SIU	SIU	1981	A/MEZ	30 X 22	AP	30	6	400	600
Angelotes de Los Claustros	AGPA	ART	1982	EC/ENG/EMB	30 X 22	AP	150	8	400	600
Wasp	SDU	SDU	1982	EC/ENG/EMB	30 X 22	AP	30	8	400	600
CURRENT EDITIONS:										
Ritual Box	ART	ART	1983	MEZ/CC	30 X 22	SOM	45	2	450	600
Black Box	ART	ART	1983	MEZ	30 X 22	SOM	30	2	400	500
Papillon Gris	ART	ART	1983/84	EC/ENG/EMB	30 X 22	SOM	150	12	350	600
Papillon Ciel Bleu	ART	ART	1983/84	EC/ENG/EMB	30 X 22	SOM	150	12	350	600
Papillon de Lune	ART	ART	1983/84	EC/ENG/EMB	30 X 22	SOM	150	12	350	600
Fleur au Lac	ART	ART	1983/84	EC/ENG/EMB	30 X 22	SOM	150	12	350	600
Coquillage sur Plage	ART	ART	1985	REL	30 X 22	SOM	150	10	450	600
Coquillage Muraille	ART	ART	1985	REL	30 X 22	SOM	150	10	450	600
Coquillage Empreinte	ART	ART	1985	REL	30 X 22	SOM	150	10	450	600
Coquillage de Mer	ART	ART	1985	REL	30 X 22	SOM	150	10	450	600
Wood Box I	ART	ART	1985	WC/A	22 X 30	AP	30	2	400	500
Wood Box II	ART	ART	1985	WC/A	30 X 22	AP	30	8	490	600
Wood Box III	ART	ART	1985	WC/A/MEZ	30 X 22	AP	30	4	400	500
Found Totem	ART	ART	1985	WC/MEZ	22 X 30	R/BFK	30	3	490	600
Long Box	ART	ART	1986	COL/WC/HC	22 X 30	SOM	30	5	450	600

CYNTHIA CARLSON

BORN: Chicago, IL; April 15, 1942
EDUCATION: Sch of Art Inst of Chicago, IL, BFA, 1965; Pratt Inst, Brooklyn, NY, MFA, 1967
TEACHING: Assoc Prof, Art, Phila Col of Art, PA, 1967–81; Prof, Art, Philadelphia Col of Art, PA, 1981–86; Assoc Prof, Queens Col, City Univ of New York, NY, 1986 to present
AWARDS: New York State Council for the Arts, NY, 1978; Nat Endowment for the Arts, 1975,78,80,87; PSC-CUNY Res Award, 1988; New York Found for the Arts Grant, Graphic Award, NY, 1990
RECENT EXHIB: Albright Col, Freedman Gallery, Reading, PA, 1989
COLLECTIONS: Virginia Mus of Fine Art, Richmond, VA; Philadelphia Mus of Art, PA; Metropolitan Mus of Art, NY; Guggenheim Mus, NY; Albright-Knox Art Gallery, Buffalo, NY
PRINTERS: Exeter Press (EX)
PUBLISHERS: 724 Prints, NY (724P)
GALLERIES: Wenger Gallery, Los Angeles, CA; More Gallery, Phila, PA
MAILING ADDRESS: 139 W 19th St, New York, NY 10011

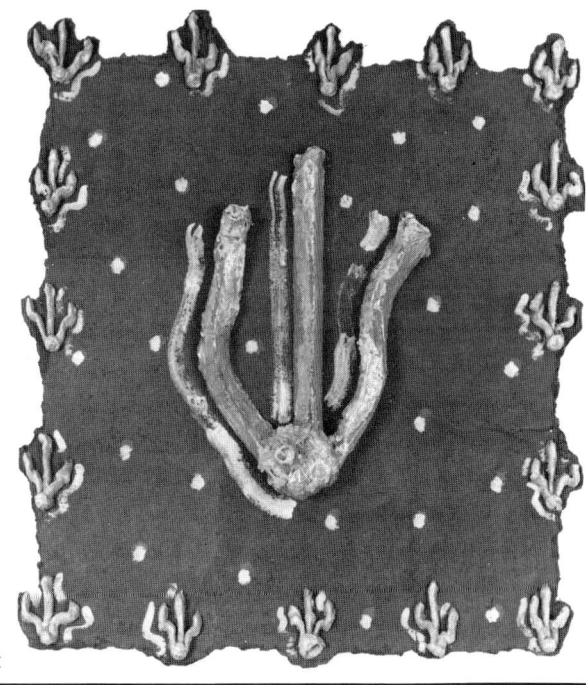

Cynthia Carlson
Fleur-De-Lis
Courtesy the Artist

TITLE	PUBLISHER	PRINTER	DATE	MEDIUM	DIMENSION (PAPER SIZE) IN INCHES	TYPE OF PAPER	EDITION NUMBER	NO. OF COLORS	ORIGINAL OPENING PRICE	CURRENT RETAIL PRICE
SOLD OUT EDITIONS (RARE):										
Point	724P	EX	1981	HM/CR	21 X 21 X 4	CP/100	15	6	1400	1600
Fleur de Lis	724P	EX	1981	HM/CR	32 X 36 X 3	CP/100	15	7	1400	1600
Loop	724P	EX	1981	HM/CR	25 X 28 X 4	CP/100	15	7	1400	1600

SQUEAK CARNWATH

BORN: Abington, PA; May 24, 1947
EDUCATION: Goddard Col, Plainsfield, VT, 1969–70; California Col of Arts & Crafts, Oakland, CA, MFA, 1977
TEACHING: Guest Instr, Studio Art, Univ of California, Berkeley, 1982–83; Prof, Univ of California, Davis, CA, 1984 to present
AWARDS: Nat Endowment for the Arts Grants, 1980; Soc Encouragement Contemp Art Award, 1980; Alice Baber Art Award, 1990; John Berggruen Gallery, Duerassi Artists Residence Fel, 1992
COLLECTIONS: Oakland Mus of Art, CA; San Francisco Mus of Mod Art, CA

SQUEAK CARNWATH CONTINUED

PRINTERS: Experimental Workshop, San Francisco, CA (EW)
PUBLISHERS: Experimental Workshop, San Francisco, CA (EW)
GALLERIES: Betsy Senior Contemporary Prints, New York, NY; Dorothy Goldeen Gallery, Santa Monica, CA; John Berggruen Gallery, San Francisco, CA

TITLE	PUBLISHER	PRINTER	DATE	MEDIUM	DIMENSION (PAPER SIZE) IN INCHES	TYPE OF PAPER	EDITION NUMBER	NO. OF COLORS	ORIGINAL OPENING PRICE	CURRENT RETAIL PRICE
CURRENT EDITIONS:										
Look See	EW	EW	1991	WC	30 X 30	R/BFK	40	7	1500	1500

ANTHONY CARO

BORN: London, England; March 8, 1924
EDUCATION: Charterhouse Sch, Cambridge, England; Christ's Col, Cambridge, England; Regent Street Polytechnic Art Sch, London, England; Royal Acad Sch, London, England
RECENT EXHIB: Richard Gray Gallery, Chicago, IL, 1989; Brown Univ, David Winton Bell Gallery, Providence, RI, 1992; Western Washington Univ, Bellingham, WA, 1992
COLLECTIONS: Mus of Mod Art, NY; Tate Gallery, London, England
PRINTERS: Tyler Graphics, Ltd, Mount Kisco, NY (TGL)
PUBLISHERS: Tyler Graphics, Ltd, Mount Kisco, NY (TGL)
GALLERIES: Richard Gray Gallery, Chicago, IL; Harcus Gallery, Boston, MA; Douglas Drake Gallery, New York, NY; Andre Emmerich Gallery, New York, NY; Tyler Graphics, Ltd, Mount Kisco, NY; O'Farrell Gallery, Brunswick, ME; Pat Kery Fine Arts, New York, NY; Meredith Long & Company, Houston, TX; G Grimaldis Gallery, Baltimore, MD; Ameringer & Award Fine Art, Inc, New York, NY
MAILING ADDRESS: 111 Frognal, Hampstead, London NW3, England

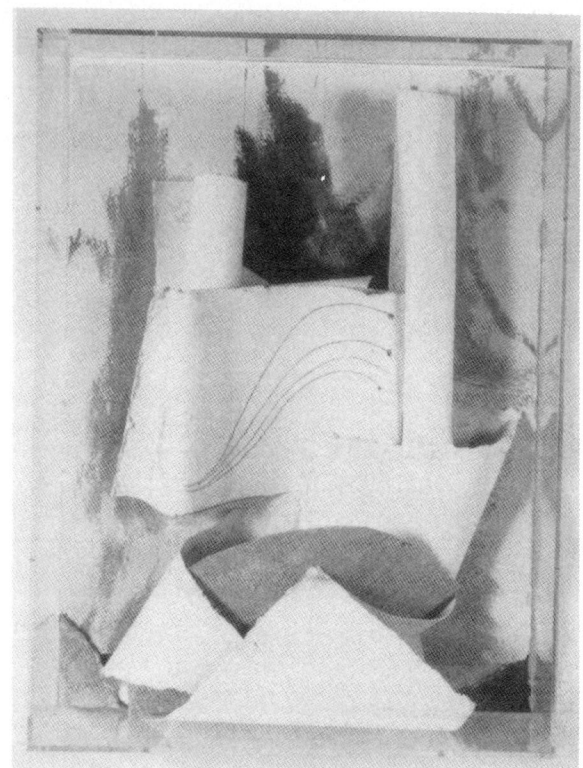

Anthony Caro
Paper Sculptures: Violin
Courtesy Tyler Graphics, Ltd

TITLE	PUBLISHER	PRINTER	DATE	MEDIUM	DIMENSION (PAPER SIZE) IN INCHES	TYPE OF PAPER	EDITION NUMBER	NO. OF COLORS	ORIGINAL OPENING PRICE	CURRENT RETAIL PRICE
SOLD OUT EDITIONS (RARE):										
Paper Sculptures	TGL	TGL	1982	MULT	11 X 8 X 5 EA	HMP/TGL	1 EA	Varies	3500 EA	5000 EA
Paper Sculptures	TGL	TGL	1982	MULT	19 X 20 X 10 EA	HMP/TGL	1 EA	Varies	4500 EA	6000 EA
Paper Sculptures	TGL	TGL	1982	MULT	29 X 38 X 18 EA	HMP/TGL	1 EA	Varies	5000 EA	6500 EA
Paper Sculptures: Violin (Contained in Plexiglas Box) (T-729)	TGL	TGL	1982	MULT	33 X 25 X 6 EA	Tycore Panel	1 EA	Varies	5000 EA	7000 EA

Tyler (T)

JOEL CARREIRO

EDUCATION: Cornell Univ, Ithaca, NY, BFA, 1971; Studied Hand Papermaking with Dieu Donne Press, New Sch, NY, 1979; Hunter Col, City Univ of New York, NY, MFA, 1982
TEACHING: Vis Artist, Ithaca Col, NY, 1984; Vis Artist Prog, New York Found for the Arts, NY, 1984,85; Artist in Res, Daniel Webster Sch, New Rochelle, NY, 1985–86; Asst Prof, Hunter Col, City Univ of New York, NY, 1986 to present
AWARDS: Six Week Sch, Haystack Sch of Arts & Crafts, Deer Isle, ME, 1969; Charles Sands Mem Award, Cornell Univ, Ithaca, NY, 1971; Ind Artist Project Grant, New York State Council on the Arts, NY, 1982; Jurors' Award, Rotunda Gallery, Brooklyn, NY, 1985; Honorable Mention, Pindar Gallery, NY, 1988; Yaddo Fel, Sarasota Springs, NY, 1989
RECENT EXHIB: Alternative Mus, NY, 1987; Finkelstein Library, Spring Valley, NY, 1992
PRINTERS: Sylvia Roth, South Nyack, NY (SR); Mary Siebert, South Nyack NY (MS); Hudson River Editions, South Nyack, NY (HRE)
PUBLISHERS: Hudson River Editions, South Nyack, NY (HRE)
GALLERIES: Hudson River Editions, South Nyack, NY
MAILING ADDRESS: c/o Hudson River Editions, 288 Piermont Ave, South Nyack, NY 10960

TITLE	PUBLISHER	PRINTER	DATE	MEDIUM	DIMENSION (PAPER SIZE) IN INCHES	TYPE OF PAPER	EDITION NUMBER	NO. OF COLORS	ORIGINAL OPENING PRICE	CURRENT RETAIL PRICE
CURRENT EDITIONS:										
Untitled	HRE	SR/MS/HRE	1992	HT	30 X 22 EA	GE	1 EA	Varies	600 EA	600 EA

DAVID CARRINO

BORN: New York, NY; 1959
EDUCATION: Sch of Visual Arts, NY, BFA, 1981
RECENT EXHIB: Rooseum, Malmo, Sweden, 1988; 121 Gallery, Antwerp, Belgium, 1988; Alex Stales Gallery, Barcelona, Spain, 1989
PRINTERS: Randy Hemminghaus, Vinalhaven, ME (RH); Vinalhaven Press, Vinalhaven, ME (VP); Joe Wilfer, NY (JW); Ruth Lingen, NY (RL); Spring Street Workshop, NY (SprSW)
PUBLISHERS: Vinalhaven Press, Vinalhaven, ME (VP); Spring Street Workshop, NY (SprSW)
GALLERIES: Tony Shafrazi Gallery, New York, NY; Pace Prints, New York, NY; 121 Gallery, Antwerp, Belgium; Alex Stales Gallery, Barcelona, Spain
MAILING ADDRESS: c/o Tony Shafrazi Gallery, 130 Prince St, New York, NY 10012

TITLE	PUBLISHER	PRINTER	DATE	MEDIUM	DIMENSION (PAPER SIZE) IN INCHES	TYPE OF PAPER	EDITION NUMBER	NO. OF COLORS	ORIGINAL OPENING PRICE	CURRENT RETAIL PRICE
CURRENT EDITIONS:										
Grand Amphitheatre: According to Horizon	VP	RH/VP	1989	PH/EB	22 X 42 X 1	R/BFK	10		3200	4000
A List of Needs (Set of 6):									2000 SET	2000 SET
Always	SprSW	JW/RL/SprSW	1990	REL/C	24 X 19	OKP	25	5	400	400
Faithfully	SprSW	JW/RL/SprSW	1990	REL/C	24 X 19	OKP	25	5	400	400
May I	SprSW	JW/RL/SprSW	1990	REL/C	24 X 19	OKP	25	5	400	400
Please	SprSW	JW/RL/SprSW	1990	REL/C	24 X 19	OKP	25	5	400	400
Sincerely	SprSW	JW/RL/SprSW	1990	REL/C	24 X 19	OKP	25	5	400	400
Truly	SprSW	JW/RL/SprSW	1990	REL/C	24 X 19	OKP	25	5	400	400

LAWRENCE CARROLL

BORN: Melbourne, Australia; 1954
EDUCATION: Moorpark Col, CA, 1972–75; Art Center Col of Design, Pasadena, CA, 1976–80; Otis Art Inst, Los Angeles, CA, 1980
RECENT EXHIB: Galerie Ryzaart Varisella, Frankfurt, Germany, 1989; Konrad Fischer Galerie, Dusseldorf, Germany, 1990; Stux Gallery, NY, 1988,89,93
PRINTERS: Julie D'Amario, NY (JDA); Bill Hall, NY (BH); Kathy Kuehn, NY (KK); Spring Street Workshop, NY (SprSW)
PUBLISHERS: Spring Street Workshop, NY (SprSW)
GALLERIES: Pace Prints, New York, NY; Stux Gallery, New York, NY

TITLE	PUBLISHER	PRINTER	DATE	MEDIUM	DIMENSION (PAPER SIZE) IN INCHES	TYPE OF PAPER	EDITION NUMBER	NO. OF COLORS	ORIGINAL OPENING PRICE	CURRENT RETAIL PRICE
CURRENT EDITIONS:										
Portfolio of Three Hand-Colored Etchings:									1000 SET	1000 SET
Father	SprSW	JDA/BH/KK/SprSW	1991	EB/HC	32 X 25	R-BFK/AC	35		400	400
For Rory	SprSW	JDA/BH/KK/SprSW	1991	EB/HC	32 X 25	R-BFK/AC	35		400	400
For Those Who See	SprSW	JDA/BH/KK/SprSW	1991	EB/HC	32 X 25	R-BFK/AC	35		400	400

ROY CARRUTHERS

BORN: Port Elizabeth, South Africa; Dec 14, 1938
EDUCATION: Technical Col of Art Sch, Port Elizabeth, South Africa, 1956
TEACHING: Sch of Visual Arts, NY, 1975
AWARDS: Am Inst of Graphic Art, 1973; Gold Medal Soc of Illustrators, 1973
COLLECTIONS: Ulrich Mus, Wichita State Univ, Wichita, KS; Weatherspoon Art Gallery, Univ of North Carolina, Greensboro, NC; Univ of Wyoming, Laramie, WY; Ponce Mus, Ponce, Puerto Rico
PUBLISHERS: Editions Press, San Francisco, CA (EP)
GALLERIES: ACA Galleries, New York, NY; Helander Gallery, Palm Beach, FL; Martin Lawrence Galleries, Sherman Oaks, CA & West Los Angeles, CA & Newport Beach, CA & Palm Springs, CA & Santa Clara, CA & Redondo Beach, CA & Thousand Oaks, CA & Escondido, CA & Phila, PA & Short Hills, NJ & Soho, NY & Los Angeles, CA; Walton Gilbert Gallery, San Francisco, CA
MAILING ADDRESS: 13 Center Rd, Old Greenwich, CT 06870

TITLE	PUBLISHER	PRINTER	DATE	MEDIUM	DIMENSION (PAPER SIZE) IN INCHES	TYPE OF PAPER	EDITION NUMBER	NO. OF COLORS	ORIGINAL OPENING PRICE	CURRENT RETAIL PRICE
SOLD OUT EDITIONS (RARE):										
Still Life with Safety Razor	EP	EP	1981	LC	30 X 22	AC/W	75	12	475	1200
Standing Man, Seated Woman, Both Smoking	EP	EP	1981	LC	30 X 22	AC/W	75	9	475	1200
Seated Figure	EP	EP	1981	LC	30 X 22	AC/W	75	23	475	1200
Left Handed Bureaucrat/State I	EP	EP	1981	LB	42 X 29	AC/W	30	1	650	1500
Left Handed Bureaucrat/State II	EP	EP	1981	LC	42 X 29	AC/W	30	1	650	1500
Studies Series:										
Study #1–#4	EP	EP	1981	LB/CO	9 X 6 EA	AC/W	30 EA	1 EA	150 EA	500 EA
Common Objects Suite (Set of 6)	EP	EP	1982	E/CO	9 X 6 EA	TC/FR	20 EA	1 EA	900 SET	2500 SET
Woman with Remarque	EP	EP	1982	LC/CO	52 X 19	HMP	60	9	725	2000
Still Life Diptych	EP	EP	1982	LC	60 X 42	AC/W	40	8	1400	2500
Five Figures with Ties, State I	EP	EP	1983	LB	40 X 29	AC/W	30	1	725	2000
Five Figures with Ties, State II	EP	EP	1983	LB	40 X 29	AC/B	30	1	725	2000
Sleeping Woman	EP	EP	1983	LC	29 X 34	AC/B	60	9	800	2000
Tying Shoes	EP	EP	1983	LC	21 X 15	TR/WF	60	11	650	1500
South Paw	EP	EP	1983	LC	21 X 15	TR/WF	60	8	650	1500
The Doll House	EP	EP	1983	LC	21 X 15	TR/WF	60	10	650	1500

JON CARSMAN

BORN: Wilkes Barre, PA; 1944
EDUCATION: Wilkes Col, Wilkesboro, NC; New York Univ, NY, MA, 1967
COLLECTIONS: Metropolitan Mus of Art, NY; Cleveland Mus of Art, OH; Nueberger Mus, Purchase, NY; Brooklyn Mus, NY; Newark Mus, NJ; Minneapolis Art Inst, MN; Akron Art Inst, OH; Fort Worth Art Mus, TX; San Francisco Mus of Mod Art, CA; Corcoran Gallery, Wash, DC; Huntsville Mus, AL; Oklahoma Art Center, Oklahoma City, OK
PRINTERS: Alpha Omega (AO); Marie Deluth, NY (MD)
PUBLISHERS: London Arts, Inc, Detroit, MI (LAI); Post Oak Art Distributors, Houston, TX (POFA); Frank Fedele Fine Arts Inc, NY (FF); Museum Editions, NY (ME)
GALLERIES: Images Gallery, Toledo, OH; De Graaf Fine Art, Chicago, Il; Robert Kidd Gallery, Birmingham, MI; ACA Contemporary Gallery, New York, NY; Ro Gallery Image Makers, Inc, New York, NY

TITLE	PUBLISHER	PRINTER	DATE	MEDIUM	DIMENSION (PAPER SIZE) IN INCHES	TYPE OF PAPER	EDITION NUMBER	NO. OF COLORS	ORIGINAL OPENING PRICE	CURRENT RETAIL PRICE
SOLD-OUT EDITIONS (RARE):										
Cannas	LAI	ART	1978	SP	35 X 24	AP	175	13	275	650
Faded Glory	LAI	ART	1978	AP/SP	35 X 24	AP	175	10	275	650
Summer Solace	POFA	AO	1981	SP	22 X 30	AP	175	9	275	650
Sunflowers	ME	MD	1984	SP	34 X 25	AP	80		500	600
Floral Bursts	ME	MD	1984	SP	34 X 25	AP	80		500	600

KAREN CARSON

BORN: Corvallis, OR; 1943
EDUCATION: Univ of Oregon, Eugene, OR; Claremont Grad Sch CA; Univ of California, Los Angeles, CA
TEACHING: Instr, Painting and Drawing, California State Col, Northridge, CA
AWARDS: Purchase Prize, 8th Annual Southern California Exhib, Long Beach, CA, 1970; Purchase Prize, Southern Illinois Univ, Carbondale, IL 1971
PRINTERS: Mary Sundstrom (MS); Perry Tymeson (PT); Cirrus Editions Workshop, Los Angeles, CA (CEW)
PUBLISHERS: Cirrus Editions, Ltd, Los Angeles, CA (CE)
GALLERIES: Cirrus Editions, Ltd, Los Angeles, CA; Rosamund Felsen Gallery, Los Angeles, CA

TITLE	PUBLISHER	PRINTER	DATE	MEDIUM	DIMENSION (PAPER SIZE) IN INCHES	TYPE OF PAPER	EDITION NUMBER	NO. OF COLORS	ORIGINAL OPENING PRICE	CURRENT RETAIL PRICE
CURRENT EDITIONS:										
Offence Spread	CE	MS/CEW	1973	LC	18 X 25	AP	30	1	100	200
Holy Virgin Mattress	CE	PT/CEW	1974	LC	18 X 26	AP	50	3	150	500
Untitled (Set of 3)	CE	CEW	1987	LC	35 X 49 EA	R/BFK	40 EA		2700 SET / 900 EA	2850 SET / 950 EA

RODNEY CARSWELL

BORN: Carmel, CA; December 15, 1946
EDUCATION: Univ of New Mexico, Albuquerque, NM, BFA, 1968; Univ of Colorado, Boulder, CO, 1972
TEACHING: Asst Prof, Painting & Drawing, Univ of Illinois, Chicago, IL, 1983 to present
AWARDS: Viewler Award, Art Inst of Chicago, IL, 1973; Purchase Award, Illinois State Mus, Chicago, IL, 1973; Purchase Award, Evansville Mus, IN, 1974; Illinois Arts Council, Chicago, IL, Artist Fel, 1985; Nat Endowment for the Arts Award, 1987
RECENT EXHIB: Terra Mus of Am Art, Chicago, IL, 1987; Roy Boyd Galleries, Chicago, IL & Los Angeles, CA, 1987–88
COLLECTIONS: Univ of New Mexico, Albuquerque, NM; Univ of Colorado, Boulder, CO; Illinois State Univ, Springfield, IL; Evansville Mus of Art, IN; Art Inst of Chicago, IL
PRINTERS: Bud Shark, Boulder, CO (BS); Ron Trujillo, Boulder, CO (RT); Shark's Lithography, Ltd, Boulder, CO (SLL)
PUBLISHERS: Shark's Lithography, Ltd, Boulder, CO (SLL)
GALLERIES: Roy Boyd Galleries, Chicago, IL & Santa Monica, CA; Linda Durham Gallery, Santa Fe, NM; Robischon Gallery, Denver, CO
MAILING ADDRESS: Dept of Art, Design M-C 036, University of Illinois, P O Box 4348, Chicago, IL 60680

Rodney Carswell
Cross in Red with 2 Grays
Courtesy Shark's, Inc

The retail prices of the 100,000 limited edition prints quoted in this directory are subject to change. Print publishers, artists and galleries were the direct sources for these quotations. Prices in the secondary market listed as "Sold Out Editions (Rare)" indicate that the publisher has a limited supply of that print or that the print is difficult to locate in the galleries.

RODNEY CARSWELL CONTINUED

TITLE	PUBLISHER	PRINTER	DATE	MEDIUM	DIMENSION (PAPER SIZE) IN INCHES	TYPE OF PAPER	EDITION NUMBER	NO. OF COLORS	ORIGINAL OPENING PRICE	CURRENT RETAIL PRICE
CURRENT EDITIONS:										
Cross in Red with 2 Grays	SLL	BS/RT/SLL	1990	LC/WC	48 X 32	R/BFK		18	1200	1500

CLARENCE HOLBROOK CARTER

BORN: Portsmouth, OH; March 26, 1904
EDUCATION: Cleveland Sch of Art, 1923–27; Studied with Hans Hofmann, Capri, Italy, Summer, 1927
TEACHING: Instr, Cleveland Mus of Art, OH, 1930–37; Instr, Carnegie Inst of Art, Pittsburgh, PA, 1938–44; Instr, Univ of Iowa, Iowa City, IA, 1970; Prof, Printmaking & Drawing, Carnegie Mellon Univ, Pittsburgh, PA, 1963 to present
AWARDS: Butler Inst of Am Art, Youngstown, OH, 1937,40,43,46; Carnegie Inst of Art, Pittsburgh, PA, 1941,43,44
RECENT EXHIB: New Jersey State Mus, Trenton, NJ, 1987; Retrosp, Gimpel & Weitzenhoffer Gallery, NY, 1988; Moravian Col, Payne Gallery, Bethlehem, PA, 1989,92
COLLECTIONS: Mus of Mod Art, NY; Metropolitan Mus of Art, NY; Whitney Mus of Am Art, NY; Brooklyn Mus, NY; Newark Mus, NJ; Philadelphia Mus of Art, PA; Montclair Mus, NJ; New Jersey State Mus, Trenton, NJ; Corcoran Gallery of Art, Wash, DC; Nat Gallery of Art, Wash, DC; Cleveland Mus of Art, OH; Victoria & Albert Mus, London, England; Baukunst Mus, Cologne, Germany; Boysman-Van Beuningen, Rotterdam, Holland
PRINTERS: Artist (ART); American Atelier, NY (AA); Alexander Heinrici, NY (AH); Studio Heinrici, Ltd, NY (SH)
PUBLISHERS: Associated Am Artists, NY (AAA); Artist (ART); London Arts, Inc, Detroit, MI (LAI)
GALLERIES: Gimpel & Weitzenhoffer Gallery, New York, NY; Hirschl & Adler Modern, New York, NY; Foster Harmon Galleries of American Art, Sarasota, FL; Princeton Gallery of Fine Art, NJ; Associated American Artists, New York, NY; Harmon-Meek Gallery, Naples, FL; Tomlin-Acheson Fine Arts, Santa Monica, CA; Sid Deutsch Gallery, New York, NY; Janet Marqusee Fine Arts, New York, NY; Ro Gallery Image Makers, Inc, New York, NY
MAILING ADDRESS: 251 Shire Rd, Milford, NJ 08848

TITLE	PUBLISHER	PRINTER	DATE	MEDIUM	DIMENSION (PAPER SIZE) IN INCHES	TYPE OF PAPER	EDITION NUMBER	NO. OF COLORS	ORIGINAL OPENING PRICE	CURRENT RETAIL PRICE
SOLD OUT EDITIONS (RARE):										
Nude #1	ART	ART	1931	AC	7 X 8	WOVE			25	1200
The Picking of Grapes	ART	ART	1931	EB/A	2 X 5	WOVE	37		20	650
Capri Olive Trees	ART	ART	1932	EB/A	7 X 8	WOVE			25	750
Abandoned Power	ART	ART	1935	EB	6 X 9	WOVE		1	20	350
Jane Reed and Dora Hunt	AAA	AA	1950	LC	10 X 13	AP	250		100	950
Burning Bush	LAI	AH/SH	1978	SP	40 X 26	AP	200	4	150	400
Tulip	LAI	AH/SH	1978	SP	35 X 26	AP	200	4	150	400

JAMES CARTER

BORN: Port Chester, NY; 1948
COLLECTIONS: Yale Univ, New Haven, CT; Bruce Mus, Greenwich, CT; City of Miami, FL
PUBLISHERS: Lublin Graphics, Greenwich, CT (LG)
PRINTERS: Cone Editions, Port Chester, NY (CEd)
GALLERIES: Summa Gallery, Brooklyn, NY; Zenith Gallery, Wash, DC; J Todd Galleries, Wellesley, MA; Southwest Gallery, Dallas, TX; Lublin Collection Fine Art Gallery, New York, NY

TITLE	PUBLISHER	PRINTER	DATE	MEDIUM	DIMENSION (PAPER SIZE) IN INCHES	TYPE OF PAPER	EDITION NUMBER	NO. OF COLORS	ORIGINAL OPENING PRICE	CURRENT RETAIL PRICE
SOLD OUT EDITIONS (RARE):										
Still Life	LG	CEd	1983	SP	28 X 22	AP	270		225	350
Glass	LG	CEd	1983	SP	19 X 19	AP	270		175	250
Pleasure Principle	LG	CEd	1983	SP	28 X 22	AP	270		225	350
Thought	LG	CEd	1984	SP	28 X 22	AP	270		225	350
Iris	LG	CEd	1984	SP	28 X 22	AP	270		225	400
Face to Face	LG	CEd	1984	SP	30 X 22	AP	270		225	350
Siren's Song	LG	CEd	1984	SP	26 X 20	AP	295		250	450
Indian Summer	LG	CEd	1984	SP	30 X 22	AP	295		400	500
Wedding Vase	LG	CEd	1985	SP	30 X 22	AP	295		400	500
Playhouse	LG	CEd	1985	SP	30 X 22	AP	295		400	500
Wind Up	LG	CEd	1986	SP	16 X 19	AP	300		300	300
Toymaker Suite	LG	CEd	1986	SP	16 X 19 EA	AP	300 EA		1150 SET	1150 SET
Electric Rhino	LG	CEd	1986	SP	16 X 19	AP	300		300	300
Toy Cows	LG	CEd	1986	SP	16 X 19	AP	300		300	300
Zebra	LG	CEd	1986	SP	16 X 19	AP	300		300	300
Simple Magic	LG	CEd	1986	SP	23 X 30	AP	300		500	500
Music Box Triptych (Set of 3):									1200 SET	1200 SET
Music Box #1	LG	CEd	1987	LC	20 X 20	AP	300		400	400
Music Box #2	LG	CEd	1987	LC	20 X 20	AP	300		400	400
Music Box #3	LG	CEd	1987	LC	20 X 20	AP	300		400	400
Two Eggs	LG	CEd	1988	LC	20 X 25	AP	300		500	500
Weather Vane	LG	CEd	1988	LC	20 X 25	AP	300		500	500
CURRENT EDITIONS:										
Eggscape	LG	CEd	1989	LC	40 X 30	AP	300		1000	1000
Deluxe Book with 4 Lithographs	LG	CEd	1989	LC	8 X 11	AP	300		1000	1000
American Buffalo	LG	CEd	1990	LC	16 X 12	AP	300		225	225
Music	LG	CEd	1990	LC	16 X 12	AP	300		225	225

JAMES CARTER CONTINUED

TITLE	PUBLISHER	PRINTER	DATE	MEDIUM	DIMENSION (PAPER SIZE) IN INCHES	TYPE OF PAPER	EDITION NUMBER	NO. OF COLORS	ORIGINAL OPENING PRICE	CURRENT RETAIL PRICE
CURRENT EDITIONS:										
Still Life	LG	CEd	1991	LC	16 X 12	AP	300		225	225
Wet Paint	LG	CEd	1991	LC	16 X 12	AP	300		225	225
Shield	LG	CEd	1992	LC	30 X 24	AP	300		700	700

RAMON CARULLA

BORN: Havana, Cuba; December 7, 1938
EDUCATION: Self-Taught
TEACHING: Vis Lectr, Cranbrook Acad of Art, Bloomfield Hills, MI, 1983; Vis Lectr, Wayne State Univ, Detroit, MI, 1983; Vis Lectr, Cleveland State Univ, OH, 1985
AWARDS: Cintas Fel Grant, 1973–74, 1979–80; Silvia Daro Dawidowicz Award, Metropolitan Mus & Arts Center, Coral Gables, FL 1982; First Prize, Latin Am Graphic Art Biennale, San Juan, PR, 1983
RECENT EXHIB: Bacardi Gallery, Miami, FL, 1988; Joy Moos Gallery, Bar Harbor Island, FL, 1988; Le Jeunns Auhordi Grand Palais, Paris, France, 1988; Cabinet Room, The Capitol, Tallahassee, FL, 1991; Hollywood Art & Cultural Center, FL, 1991–92
COLLECTIONS: Detroit Inst of Art, MI; Cincinnati Art Mus, OH; Museo Tamayo, Mexico City, Mexico; Mus of Fine Arts, Montreal, Canada, Mus of Mod Art of Latin Am, Wash, DC; Lowe Art Mus, Coral Gables, FL; Norton Gallery of Art, West Palm Beach, FL
PRINTERS: Robert Blackburn Print Workshop, NY (RBPW); Claudio Juarez (CJ); Claudio Juarez Workshop, NY (CJW); Artist (ART)
PUBLISHERS: Schweyer-Galdo Editions, Detroit, MI (SGE); Claudio Juarez Workshop, NY (CJW); Artist (ART)
GALLERIES: Barbara Scott Gallery, Bay Harbor Islands, FL; Arte Fino, Charlotte, NC; The American Collection, Coral Gables, FL
MAILING ADDRESS: 4735 NW 184th Terrace, Miami, FL 33055

Ramon Carulla
Imaginary Portrait of a Politician
Courtesy the Artist

TITLE	PUBLISHER	PRINTER	DATE	MEDIUM	DIMENSION (PAPER SIZE) IN INCHES	TYPE OF PAPER	EDITION NUMBER	NO. OF COLORS	ORIGINAL OPENING PRICE	CURRENT RETAIL PRICE
SOLD OUT EDITIONS (RARE):										
Image I	ART	ART	1977	EB	11 X 14	AP	10	1	125	300
Double Imagery	ART	ART	1978	COL	22 X 30	AP	5	3	150	500
CURRENT EDITIONS:										
The Art Critics	SGE	ART/CJW	1983	EB/A/HC	22 X 30	AP	10	Varies	500	500
Confrontation	SGE	ART/CJW	1983	EB/A/HC	22 X 30	AP	10	Varies	500	500
Imaginary Portrait of a Feeling	CJW	CJ/CJW	1988	EB/DPT/HC	25 X 19	AP	10	4	450	450
The Last Chance	CJW	CJ/CJW	1988	EB/DPT/HC	25 X 19	AP	10	1	450	450
The Political Scenes	ART	ART	1991–92	EB/DPT	25 X 19	AP	10	1	450	450

FERNANDO RODRIGUEZ CASAS

BORN: Cochabamba, Bolivia; March 25, 1946
EDUCATION: Colorado Col, Colorado Springs, CO, BA, 1968–70; Rice Univ, Houston, TX, MA, 1970–72, PhD, 1973–78
TEACHING: Univ of Bolivia, San Andres, Bolivia
COLLECTIONS: Mus of Mod Art, La Paz, Bolivia; Pinacoteca Nat, Mus, Cochabamba, Bolivia; Mus of Fine Arts, Houston, TX
PRINTERS: Artist (ART)
PUBLISHERS: Eidos Fine Art, Inc, Houston, TX (EFA)
GALLERIES: Brewster Gallery, New York, NY; Gremillion & Company Fine Art, Inc, Houston, TX; Robert Berman Galleries, Inc, Hot Springs, AR
MAILING ADDRESS: 22214 Meadow Sweet, Houston, TX 77355

TITLE	PUBLISHER	PRINTER	DATE	MEDIUM	DIMENSION (PAPER SIZE) IN INCHES	TYPE OF PAPER	EDITION NUMBER	NO. OF COLORS	ORIGINAL OPENING PRICE	CURRENT RETAIL PRICE
SOLD OUT EDITIONS (RARE):										
Early Morning, Late Afternoon	EFA	ART	1979	LB	23 X 34	AP	99	1	150	500
Spying on Oneself	EFA	ART	1979	LB	23 X 29	AP	99	1	150	300
The Measure of All Things	EFA	ART	1979	LC	24 X 36	AP	99	5	250	400
The Rothko Chapel	EFA	ART	1980	LC	24 X 32	AP	99	5	250	400
The Polar Eye	EFA	ART	1980	LC	24 X 36	AP	99	5	250	400
The Myth of Grabriela	EFA	ART	1980	LB	24 X 35	AP	99	1	150	300

RICHARD CASE

BORN: Colorado
EDUCATION: Chouinard Inst of Art, Los Angeles CA
PRINTERS: American Atelier, NY (AA)
PUBLISHERS: Circle Fine Art, Chicago, IL (CFA)

GALLERIES: Circle Galleries, San Diego, CA & San Francisco, CA & Northbrook, IL & Pittsburgh, PA & Houston, TX & Soho, NY & Chicago, IL & Scottsdale, AZ & Beverly Hills, CA & Costa Mesa, CA & Sherman Oaks, CA & Palm Beach, FL & Honolulu, HI & New Orleans, LA & Las Vegas, NV & Seattle, WA

TITLE	PUBLISHER	PRINTER	DATE	MEDIUM	DIMENSION (PAPER SIZE) IN INCHES	TYPE OF PAPER	EDITION NUMBER	NO. OF COLORS	ORIGINAL OPENING PRICE	CURRENT RETAIL PRICE
SOLD OUT EDITIONS (RARE):										
Returning to Sea	CFA	AA	1980	LC	20 X 26	AP	85		35	125
Divided Light from Dark	CFA	AA	1980	LC	20 X 26	AP	85		35	125

JAMES EDWARD CASEBERE

BORN: Lansing, MI; September 17, 1953
EDUCATION: Michigan State Univ, East Lansing, MI, 1971–72; Minneapolis Col of Art & Design, MN, BFA, 1976; Whitney Mus, Independent Study Program, NY, 1977; California Inst of the Arts, Valencia, CA, MFA, 1979
TEACHING: Asst Prof, Photography, Rockland Comm Col, NY, 1985 to present
AWARDS: Nat Endowment for the Arts, Visual Artists Fel, 1982,85; Grant, 1986; New York State Council on the Arts Grant, 1989

RECENT EXHIB: Baltimore Mus of Art, MD, 1987; Mus of Living Art, NY, 1988; Univ of South Florida, Graphicstudio, Tampa, FL, 1992; Michael Klein, Inc, NY, 1990,93
COLLECTIONS: Neuberger Mus, State of New York, Purchase, NY; Allen Mem Mus, Oberlin Col, OH; Houston Mus of Fine Arts, TX
PRINTERS: Artist (ART)
PUBLISHERS: Artist (ART)
GALLERIES: Sonnabend Gallery, New York, NY; Diane Brown Gallery, New York, NY; Michael Klein, Inc, New York, NY
MAILING ADDRESS: 175 Ludlow St, Store, New York, NY 10002

TITLE	PUBLISHER	PRINTER	DATE	MEDIUM	DIMENSION (PAPER SIZE) IN INCHES	TYPE OF PAPER	EDITION NUMBER	NO. OF COLORS	ORIGINAL OPENING PRICE	CURRENT RETAIL PRICE
SOLD OUT EDITIONS (RARE):										
Boats	ART	ART	1980	PH	16 X 20	AgB	7	1	500	1000
Deserthouse with Cactus	ART	ART	1980	PH	16 X 20	AgB	7	1	500	1000
CURRENT EDITIONS:										
Courtroom	ART	ART	1980	PH	16 X 20	AgB	7	1	500	800
Three Planes	ART	ART	1981	PH	16 X 20	AgB	7	1	500	800
Back Porch 2	ART	ART	1981	PH	16 X 20	AgB	7	1	500	800
Shooting Gallery	ART	ART	1981	PH	16 X 20	AgB	7	1	500	800
Sutpens Cave	ART	ART	1982	PH	16 X 20	AgB	7	1	500	800
Kitchen Table	ART	ART	1982	PH	16 X 20	AgB	7	1	500	800
Groceries	ART	ART	1982	PH	16 X 20	AgB	7	1	500	800
Subdivision Close-Up	ART	ART	1982	PH	16 X 20	AgB	7	1	500	800
Stone House	ART	ART	1983–84	PH	30 X 24	AgB	7	1	950	1200
Lighthouse	ART	ART	1983–84	PH	30 X 24	AgB	7	1	950	1200
Cottenmill	ART	ART	1983–84	PH	30 X 24	AgB	7	1	950	1200
Street with Pots	ART	ART	1983–84	PH	30 X 24	AgB	7	1	950	1200
Waterfall	ART	ART	1983–84	PH	30 X 24	AgB	7	1	950	1200
Utility Room	ART	ART	1983–84	PH	24 X 30	AgB	7	1	950	1200
Garage	ART	ART	1983–84	PH	24 X 30	AgB	7	1	950	1200
Water Toys	ART	ART	1983–84	PH	24 X 30	AgB	7	1	950	1200
Stairwell	ART	ART	1983–84	PH	24 X 30	AgB	7	1	950	1200

JEAN-PIERRE CASSIGNEUL

BORN: Paris, France; 1935
EDUCATION: Ecole des Beaux Arts, Paris, France
PRINTERS: American Atelier, NY (AA)
PUBLISHERS: Circle Fine Arts, Chicago, IL (CFA)

GALLERIES: William Haber Gallery, New York, NY; Circle Galleries, San Diego, CA & San Francisco, CA & Northbrook, IL & Pittsburgh, PA & Houston, TX & Soho, NY & Chicago, IL & Scottsdale, AZ & Beverly Hills, CA & Costa Mesa, CA & Sherman Oaks, CA & Palm Beach, FL & Honolulu, HI & New Orleans, LA & Las Vegas, NV & Seattle, WA; Jones Gallery, La Jolla, CA; Robert Dana Gallery, San Francisco, CA; Art Works, Bealsburg, PA

TITLE	PUBLISHER	PRINTER	DATE	MEDIUM	DIMENSION (PAPER SIZE) IN INCHES	TYPE OF PAPER	EDITION NUMBER	NO. OF COLORS	ORIGINAL OPENING PRICE	CURRENT RETAIL PRICE
SOLD OUT EDITIONS (RARE):										
Woman against Trellis	CFA	AA	1978	LC	26 X 20	AP	130		150	2900
Woman with Fur	CFA	AA	1978	LC	26 X 20	AP	130		150	2900
Woman in Olive Dress	CFA	AA	1978	LC	26 X 20	AP	130		150	2900
Woman in Yellow Cloche	CFA	AA	1978	LC	30 X 24	AP	130		150	2900

MOSHE CASTEL

BORN: Jerusalem, Israel; 1909
EDUCATION: Bezalel Acad of Art, Jerusalem, Israel; Acad Julien, Paris, France.
AWARDS: Grand Prize, Biennale de Sao Paulo, Brazil, 1959
RECENT EXHIB: Marcos Salade Arte, Madrid, Spain, 1992; S J Jacques Soussana Graphics, Jerusalem, Israel, 1992

MOSHE CASTEL CONTINUED

COLLECTIONS: Mus of Mod Art, NY; Tate Gallery, London, England; Boston Mus of Fine Arts, MA; Houston Mus of Fine Arts, TX; Phoenix Art Mus, AZ; Fogg Art Mus, Cambridge, MA; Baltimore Mus of Art, MD; Musee D'Art Moderne de Sao Paulo, Brazil; Mus of Tel-Aviv, Israel
PRINTERS: Joseph Kleineman, NY (JK); Jorge Dumas, NY (JD)
PUBLISHERS: Post Oak Fine Art Distributors, Houston, TX (POFA); London Arts Inc, Detroit, MI (LAI)
GALLERIES: Nathan Silberberg Fine Arts, New York, NY
MAILING ADDRESS: 11 Akiva Arie, Tel Aviv 62154, Israel

TITLE	PUBLISHER	PRINTER	DATE	MEDIUM	DIMENSION (PAPER SIZE) IN INCHES	TYPE OF PAPER	EDITION NUMBER	NO. OF COLORS	ORIGINAL OPENING PRICE	CURRENT RETAIL PRICE
CURRENT EDITIONS:										
King Solomon Mines	LAI	JK	1979	LC	26 X 29	SOM	150	14	300	600
The Ritual	LAI	JD	1979	LC	28 X 21	SOM	150	13	300	600
Stone of the Temple	LAI	JK	1980	LC	29 X 22	SOM	150	13	300	600
Prophesy	LAI	JK	1980	LC	29 X 22	SOM	150	13	300	600
Above Jerusalem	LAI	JK	1980	LC	30 X 22	SOM	150	12	300	600
Prayer	LAI	JK	1980	LC	22 X 28	SOM	150	14	300	600
Secret Writing	LAI	JK	1980	LC	29 X 22	SOM	150	12	300	600
Soaring Letters	LAI	JK	1980	LC	22 X 29	SOM	150	20	300	600
Stone & Script	LAI	JK	1980	LC	22 X 29	SOM	150	12	300	600
Judean Hills Manuscript	POFA	JD	1980	LC	27 X 24	SOM	150	13	300	600
Hallelujah to Peace	POFA	JK	1981	LC	21 X 30	SOM	150	12	300	600
Scrolls	POFA	JK	1981	LC	28 X 21	SOM	150	12	300	600
Shofar at the Lion's Gate	POFA	JK	1981	LC	28 X 21	SOM	150	13	300	600
Book of Moses	POFA	JK	1981	LC	21 X 30	SOM	150	14	300	600

FEDERICO CASTELLON

BORN: Almeria, Spain; (1914–1971)
TEACHING: Columbia Univ, NY; Pratt Inst, Brooklyn, NY
AWARDS: Guggenheim Fel (2); Am Acad of Arts & Letters; Pennsylvania Acad of Fine Arts, Eyre Medal, Phila, PA; Art Inst of Chicago, Logan Prize, IL
RECENT EXHIB: Print Club of Albany, Inc, NY, 1989,92
COLLECTIONS: Metropolitan Mus, NY; Whitney Mus of Am Art, NY; Brooklyn Mus, NY; Art Inst of Chicago, IL; Pennsylvania Acad of Fine Arts, Phila, PA
PRINTERS: American Atelier, NY (AA)
PUBLISHERS: Circle Fine Arts, Chicago, IL (CFA)
GALLERIES: Parkerson Gallery, Houston, TX; Circle Galleries, San Diego, CA & San Francisco, CA & Northbrook, IL & Pittsburgh, PA & Houston, TX & Soho, NY & Chicago, IL & Scottsdale, AZ & Beverly Hills, CA & Costa Mesa, CA & Sherman Oaks, CA & Palm Beach, CA & Honolulu, HI & New Orleans, LA & Las Vegas, NV & Seattle, WA

TITLE	PUBLISHER	PRINTER	DATE	MEDIUM	DIMENSION (PAPER SIZE) IN INCHES	TYPE OF PAPER	EDITION NUMBER	NO. OF COLORS	ORIGINAL OPENING PRICE	CURRENT RETAIL PRICE
SOLD OUT EDITIONS (RARE):										
Gordian Knot	AAG		1936	LB	9 X 14	R/100		1	30	250
Landscape in Spain	AAG		1937	LB	10 X 14	R/100		1	35	250
By the Ark	AAA	AA	1941	LB	9 X 12	AP	250	1	100	950
Artist and Model	AAA	AA	1942	EB/A/DPT	5 X 4	AP	50	1	75	250
Mexican Couple	AAA	AA	1942	EB	8 X 8	AP	50	1	75	450
Road in Arizona	AAA	AA	1942	LB	10 X 14	AP	50	1	100	350
Taos Tryst	AAA	AA	1942	EB	8 X 12	AP	50	1	100	800
Visiting Day	AAA	AA	1942	EB	9 X 6	AP	50	1	100	450
Diana and Acteon	AAA	AA	1942	EB	6 X 9	AP	50	1	75	300
Bus Ride	AAA	AA	1946	EB	8 X 12	AP	250	1	75	250
The Family	AAA	AA	1946	EB	8 X 12	AP	250	1	75	250
The Groom	AAA	AA	1946	LB	10 X 13	AP	250	1	75	350
Kumming Bus	AAA	AA	1946	LB	8 X 12	AP	200	1	75	250
Peasant Family	AAA	AA	1946	EB	8 X 12	AP	250		75	250
Studio Trial(Nudes)	AAA	AA	1947	EB	8 X 12	AP	50	1	75	200
The Studio	AAA	AA	1947	EB	8 X 12	AP	50	1	75	300
Trio	AAA	AA	1947	EB/A	11 X 9	AP	40		100	700
Woman Threading a Needle	AAA	AA	1947	EB/A	11 X 9	AP	50		100	700
Heads of Two Women	AAA	AA	1948	LB	8 X 12	AP	50	1	75	350
Lady of the Ravens	AAA	AA	1948	EB	11 X 9	AP	20		100	450
Portrait of the Artist	AAA	AA	1948	EB	9 X 12	AP	50	1	75	800
Portrait of the Gene	AAA	AA	1948	EB	10 X 11	AP	100	1	75	350
Gengalese Sisters	AAA	AA	1949	LB	10 X 13	AP	150	1	100	350
Gladiator and the Tourist	AAA	AA	1950	EB	15 X 12	AP	100	1	125	450
Roman Urchins	AAA	AA	1952	EB/A	16 X 12	AP	200	1	125	600
Rome, Yesterday, Today and Tomorrow			1967	EB/A	12 X 7	AP	100	1	125	350
Tightrope Walker	CFA	AA	1969	LC	30 X 22	AP	160		50	600
Family Portrait	CFA	AA	1969	LC	26 X 20	AP	200		50	550
Blessed are the Meek	CFA	AA	1969	LC	30 X 22	AP	200		50	500
Erotic Alphabet (with Peter Poone)			1970	ED		AP	50	1	130	1200

The Printworld Directory is accepting new applications for the seventh edition. Approximately 300 new artists will be accepted. Please use the two forms provided in the back section of this directory to submit biographical data and documentation of prints. Edition number of each print must not exceed 500 and the retail price must be $100 or more.

JORGE CASTILLO

BORN: Pontevedra, Spain; 1933
EDUCATION: Escuela de Bellas Artes, Buenos Aires, Argentina; Contemp Engraving Center, Buenos Aires, Argentina
AWARDS: Government of Berlin Grant, Germany, 1969; Int Drawing Prize, Darmstadt, Germany, 1974
RECENT EXHIB: Marlborough Gallery, NY, 1992

COLLECTIONS: Carnegie Inst, Pittsburgh, PA; Mus of Mod Art, Vienna, Austria; Mus of Mod Art, Lausanne, Switzerland; Mus of Mod Art, Edinburgh, Scotland
PRINTERS: La Poligrafa, SA, Barcelona, Spain (LP)
PUBLISHERS: Ediciones Poligrafa, SA, Barcelona, Spain (EdP)
GALLERIES: Galeria Joan Prats, New York, NY & Barcelona, Spain; Adams-Middleton Gallery, Dallas, TX; Marlborough Gallery, New York, NY

TITLE	PUBLISHER	PRINTER	DATE	MEDIUM	DIMENSION (PAPER SIZE) IN INCHES	TYPE OF PAPER	EDITION NUMBER	NO. OF COLORS	ORIGINAL OPENING PRICE	CURRENT RETAIL PRICE
SOLD OUT EDITIONS (RARE):										
Polychrome Etchings Suite (Set of 5):									1100 SET	5000 SET
Los Niños de la Noche	EdP	LP	1973	EC	22 X 25	GP	75	3	250	1100
El Caminante	EdP	LP	1973	EC	22 X 25	GP	75	2	250	1100
El Poeta	EdP	LP	1973	EC	22 X 25	GP	75	3	250	1100
Jardin de Otoño	EdP	LP	1973	EC	22 X 25	GP	75	3	250	1100
Los Pensamientos	EdP	LP	1973	EC	22 X 25	GP	75	3	250	1100
Color Variants (Set of 5)	EdP	LP	1973	EC	22 X 25 EA	GP	75 EA		1200 SET	5500 SET
									280 EA	1200 EA
Polychrome Etchings (Set of 12):									2800 SET	15000 SET
Jardin de Noche	EdP	LP	1974	EC	22 X 30	GP	75		300	1300
Taggio en Raset	EdP	LP	1974	EC	22 X 30	GP	75		300	1300
Palomares Hoy	EdP	LP	1974	EC	22 X 30	GP	75		300	1300
Agua Amarga	EdP	LP	1974	EC	22 X 30	GP	75		300	1300
Jardin de Invierno	EdP	LP	1974	EC	22 X 30	GP	75		300	1300
Muchacha Sobre el Diván	EdP	LP	1974	EC	22 X 30	GP	75		300	1300
La Espera	EdP	LP	1974	EC	22 X 30	GP	75		300	1300
Marienza y Metello	EdP	LP	1974	EC	22 X 30	GP	75		300	1300
Tiergarten	EdP	LP	1974	EC	40 X 28	GP	75		300	1300
El Domingo	EdP	LP	1974	EC	40 X 28	GP	75		300	1500
Paseo por el Jardin Botánico	EdP	LP	1974	EC	40 X 28	GP	75		300	1500
Retrato de la Familia Castillo	EdP	LP	1974	EC	40 X 28	GP	75		300	1500
Color Variations on the Same 12 Above (Set of 12)									2800 SET	17000 SET
Variants 1–8	EdP	LP	1974	EC	22 X 30 EA	GP	75 EA		320 EA	500 EA
Variants 9–12	EdP	LP	1974	EC	40 X 28 EA	GP	75 EA		350 EA	700 EA
Series of 13 Polychrome Etchings (Set of 13):									3000 SET	18000 SET
Baile Vampiresco	EdP	LP	1978	EC	28 X 40	GP	75		350	1400
Habitación	EdP	LP	1978	EC	28 X 40	GP	75		350	1400
El Nadador	EdP	LP	1978	EC	28 X 40	GP	75		350	1400
Dos Mujeres	EdP	LP	1978	EC	28 X 40	GP	75		350	1400
Olga en el Campo	EdP	LP	1978	EC	28 X 40	GP	75		350	1400
Siluetas	EdP	LP	1978	EC	28 X 40	GP	75		350	1400
Don Ramón	EdP	LP	1978	EC	28 X 40	GP	75		350	1400
Escena Campestre	EdP	LP	1978	EC	28 X 40	GP	75		350	1400
La Vision de un Niño	EdP	LP	1978	EC	22 X 30	GP	75		320	1300
Bambino Pipistelli	EdP	LP	1978	EC	22 X 30	GP	75		320	1300
El Jardinero	EdP	LP	1978	EC	22 X 30	GP	75		320	1300
Marienza	EdP	LP	1978	EC	22 X 40	GP	75		350	1400
Marienza Recortada	EdP	LP	1978	EC	22 X 40	GP	75		350	1400
Two Color Lithographs (Set of 12):										
Batiburrillo	EdP	LP	1978	LC	22 X 30	GP	75		280	1000
Ruth en el Parque	EdP	LP	1978	LC	22 X 30	GP	75		280	1000
El Rey de los Paganos (Set of 17):									3500 SET	18000 SET
El Rey de los Paganos 1	EdP	LP	1978	EC	22 X 26	GP	75		250	1100
El Rey de los Paganos 2	EdP	LP	1978	EC	22 X 26	GP	75		250	1100
El Rey de los Paganos 3	EdP	LP	1978	EC	22 X 26	GP	75		250	1100
El Rey de los Paganos 4	EdP	LP	1978	EC	22 X 26	GP	75		250	1100
El Rey de los Paganos 5	EdP	LP	1978	EC	22 X 26	GP	75		250	1100
El Rey de los Paganos 6	EdP	LP	1978	EC	22 X 26	GP	75		250	1100
El Rey de los Paganos 7	EdP	LP	1978	EC	22 X 26	GP	75		250	1100
El Rey de los Paganos 8	EdP	LP	1978	EC	22 X 26	GP	75		250	1100
El Rey de los Paganos 9	EdP	LP	1978	EC	22 X 26	GP	75		250	1100
El Rey de los Paganos 10	EdP	LP	1978	EC	22 X 26	GP	75		250	1100
El Rey de los Paganos 11	EdP	LP	1978	EC	22 X 26	GP	75		250	1100
El Rey de los Paganos 12	EdP	LP	1978	EC	22 X 26	GP	75		250	1100
El Rey de los Paganos 13	EdP	LP	1978	EC	22 X 26	GP	75		250	500
El Rey de los Paganos 14	EdP	LP	1978	EC	22 X 26	GP	75		250	500
El Rey de los Paganos 15	EdP	LP	1978	EC	22 X 26	GP	75		250	500
El Rey de los Paganos 16	EdP	LP	1978	EC	22 X 26	GP	75		250	500
El Rey de los Paganos 17	EdP	LP	1978	EC	22 X 26	GP	75		250	500
El Rey de los Paganos (Set of 12):										
El Rey de los Paganos 1	EdP	LP	1978	LB	22 X 26	GP	75		250	900
El Rey de los Paganos 2	EdP	LP	1978	LB	22 X 26	GP	75		250	900
Tauromaquia Suite (Set of 10)	EdP	LP		EC	22 X 30 EA	AP	80 EA		5000 SET	13000 SET
									550 EA	1400 EA

JORGE CASTILLO CONTINUED

TITLE	PUBLISHER	PRINTER	DATE	MEDIUM	DIMENSION (PAPER SIZE) IN INCHES	TYPE OF PAPER	EDITION NUMBER	NO. OF COLORS	ORIGINAL OPENING PRICE	CURRENT RETAIL PRICE
CURRENT EDITIONS:										
Barcelona Suite (Set of 3):									800 SET	1000 SET
Barcelona I, III	EdP	LP	1981	LC	30 X 22 EA	GP	99 EA		300 EA	350 EA
Barcelona II	EdP	LP	1981	LC	30 X 22	GP	99		350	400

PATRICK CAULFIELD

BORN: London, England; 1936
EDUCATION: Chelsea Sch of Art, London, England, 1956–59; Royal Col of Art, London, England, 1959–63
TEACHING: Chelsea Sch of Art, London, England
COLLECTIONS: Victoria and Albert Mus, London, England; British Council of Art, London, England; Nat Gallery of Australia; Dallas Mus of Fine Arts, Dallas, TX; Tate Gallery of Art, London, England; Kunsthalle, Biefeld, Germany

PRINTERS: Chis Prater (CP); Kelpra Studio, London, England (KS); Petersburg Press, London, England (PP)
PUBLISHERS: Waddington Graphics, London, England (WG); Petersburg Press, London, England (PP)
GALLERIES: Waddington Graphics, London, England; Petersburg Press, New York, NY & London, England

TITLE	PUBLISHER	PRINTER	DATE	MEDIUM	DIMENSION (PAPER SIZE) IN INCHES	TYPE OF PAPER	EDITION NUMBER	NO. OF COLORS	ORIGINAL OPENING PRICE	CURRENT RETAIL PRICE
SOLD OUT EDITIONS (RARE):										
Set of Five:										
Bathroom Mirror	WG	CP/KS	1968	SP	28 X 37	AP	75		100	1800
Cafe Sign	WG	CP/KS	1968	SP	28 X 37	AP	75		100	1800
Crucifix	WG	CP/KS	1968	SP	28 X 37	AP	75		100	1200
Found Objects	WG	CP/KS	1968	SP	28 X 37	AP	75		100	1200
Loudspeaker	WG	CP/KS	1968	SP	28 X 37	AP	75		100	1200
Set of Five:										
Lampshade	WG	CP/KS	1969	SP	14 X 12	AP	75		75	800
Small Window	WG	CP/KS	1969	SP	14 X 12	AP	75		75	800
Two Jugs	WG	CP/KS	1969	SP	14 X 12	AP	75		75	800
Wine Glasses	WG	CP/KS	1969	SP	14 X 12	AP	75		75	800
Portrait of a Frenchman	WG	CP/KS	1971	SP	25 X 21	AP	75		100	2500
Interior Suite (Set of 4):										
Interior: Morning	WG	CP/KS	1971	SP	28 X 23	AP	100		125	1200
Interior: Noon	WG	CP/KS	1971	SP	28 X 23	AP	100		125	1200
Interior: Evening	WG	CP/KS	1971	SP	28 X 23	AP	100		125	1200
Interior: Night	WG	CP/KS	1971	SP	28 X 23	AP	100		125	1200
Small Window at Night	WG	CP/KS	1971	SP	34 X 26	AP	72		125	1200
Vase on Display	WG	CP/KS	1971	SP	26 X 22	AP	100		125	1800
Napkins and Onions	WG	CP/KS	1972	SP	34 X 26	AP	72		180	1500
Fig Branch	WG	CP/KS	1972	SP	40 X 30	AP	72		180	2200
Pipe	WG	CP/KS	1972		34 X 26	AP	72		180	1500
Coat Stand	WG	CP/KS	1973	SP	22 X 31	AP	72		180	1800
Curtain and Bottle	WG	CP/KS	1973	SP	22 X 31	AP	72		180	1800
Paris Separates	WG	CP/KS	1973	SP	22 X 31	AP	72		180	1800
Pipe and Jug	WG	CP/KS	1973	SP	29 X 37	AP	72		180	2000
Tulips	WG	CP/KS	1973	SP	22 X 31	AP	72		180	1800
Spider Plant	WG	CP/KS	1973	SP	22 X 31	AP	72		180	1800
Jar	WG	CP/KS	1974	SP	35 X 28	AP	70		180	1500
Jug	WG	CP/KS	1974	SP	35 X 28	AP	70		180	1500
Garden with Pines	WG	CP/KS	1975	SP	31 X 41	AP	70		180	2500
Lamp and Pines	WG	CP/KS	1975	SP	31 X 41	AP	70		180	2500
Signature Pots	WG	CP/KS	1975	SP	31 X 41	AP	70		180	1800
Terracotta Vase	WG	CP/KS	1975	SP	31 X 41	AP	70		180	1800
Rosé Bottle	WG	CP/KS	1975	SP	31 X 41	AP	70		180	2200
Evening Menu	WG	CP/KS	1975	SP	31 X 41	AP	70		180	2500
Lamp and Pines	WG	CP/KS	1975	SP	31 X 41	AP	70		180	2200
Glazed Earthenware	WG	CP/KS	1976	SP	31 X 41	AP	76		270	3500
Still Life Ingredients	WG	CP/KS	1976	SP	28 X 28	AP	76		220	3000
White Pot	WG	CP/KS	1976	SP	39 X 31	AP	76		270	2500
Pipe in Bowl	WG	CP/KS	1976	SP	16 X 16	AP	76		270	1500
Bananas with Leaves	WG	CP/KS	1977	SP	29 X 35	AP	75		270	1800
Three Sausages	WG	CP/KS	1978	SP	29 X 36	AP	75		270	1200
Sausage	WG	CP/KS	1978	SP	29 X 36	AP	75		270	1200
Picnic Set	WG	CP/KS	1978	SP	30 X 30	AP	100		270	3000
Big Sausage	WG	CP/KS	1978	SP	35 X 30	AP	75		270	1500
Cigar	WG	CP/KS	1978	SP	23 X 24	AP	75		270	1200
Fruit & Bowl	WG	CP/KS	1979	SP	33 X 24	AP	100		360	2200
Cream Glazed Pot	WG	CP/KS	1979	SP	33 X 24	AP	100		360	2800
Plant Pot	WG	CP/KS	1979	SP	33 X 24	AP	100		360	2000
Ridged Jar	WG	CP/KS	1980	SP	33 X 24	AP	40		360	2000
Fern Pot	WG	CP/KS	1980	SP	33 X 24	AP	65		360	1800
Ridged Jar	WG	CP/KS	1980	SP	33 X 24	AP	40		360	1500

PATRICK CAULFIELD CONTINUED

TITLE	PUBLISHER	PRINTER	DATE	MEDIUM	DIMENSION (PAPER SIZE) IN INCHES	TYPE OF PAPER	EDITION NUMBER	NO. OF COLORS	ORIGINAL OPENING PRICE	CURRENT RETAIL PRICE
SOLD OUT EDITIONS (RARE):										
Pink Jug	WG	CP/KS	1981	SP	39 X 32	AP	80	4	500	2000
Grey Pipe	WG	CP/KS	1981	SP	29 X 29	AP	75	3	400	1500
Water Jug	WG	CP/KS	1982	SP	40 X 31	AP	80		540	1800
Brown Jug	WG	CP/KS	1982	SP	40 X 31	AP	80		540	1800
Pitcher	WG	CP/KS	1982	SP	41 X 31	AP	80		540	1800
Large Jug	WG	CP/KS	1983	SP	46 X 33	AP	80		600	1800
Vessel	WG	CP/KS	1987	SP	37 X 26	AP	35		800	1800
Wall Plate Suite (Set of 4):										
Wall Plate: Screen	WG	CP/KS	1987	SP	41 X 30	AP	50		800	1200
Wall Plate: Stones	WG	CP/KS	1987	SP	41 X 30	AP	50		800	1200
Wall Plate: Stucco	WG	CP/KS	1987	AP	41 X 30	AP	50		800	1200
Wall Plate: Highlights	WG	CP/KS	1987	SP	41 X 30	AP	50		800	1200
CURRENT EDITIONS:										
Coal Fire	WG	CP/KS	1989	SP	14 X 12	AP	75		600	800
Arita Flask	WG	CP/KS	1990	SP	43 X 32	AP	45		1200	1500
Arita Flask (Black)	WG	CP/KS	1990	SP	43 X 32	AP	45	1	1200	1500
Lamp & Lung Ch'uan Ware	WG	CP/KS	1990	SP	43 X 32	AP	45		1200	1500
Lamp & Kuan Ware	WG	CP/KS	1990	SP	43 X 32	AP	45		1200	1500
Lung Ch'uan Ware-Lamp	WG	CP/KS	1990	SP	43 X 32	AP	45		1200	1500
Lung Ch'uan Ware-Window	WG	CP/KS	1990	SP	43 X 32	AP	45		1200	1500
Sun Ware Jar	WG	CP/KS	1990	SP	43 X 32	AP	45		1200	1500

GIOVANNI CASTRO

BORN: Colombia; June 16, 1946
EDUCATION: Anthropoly, BA
TEACHING: Javeriana Univ, Bogotá, Colombia
AWARDS: First Prize, Latin Am Primitive Art, Pamplona, Colombia
COLLECTIONS: Univ of Miami, Coral Gables, FL; Mus of Science, Miami, FL
PRINTERS: Atelier Ettinger, Inc, NY (AE)
PUBLISHERS: Annuaire de L'Art International, Paris France (AAI); Artist (ART)
MAILING ADDRESS: 999 Bayshore Drive, #1102, Miami, FL 33131-2931

TITLE	PUBLISHER	PRINTER	DATE	MEDIUM	DIMENSION (PAPER SIZE) IN INCHES	TYPE OF PAPER	EDITION NUMBER	NO. OF COLORS	ORIGINAL OPENING PRICE	CURRENT RETAIL PRICE
CURRENT EDITIONS:										
Colombian Landscape	ART	AE	1985	LC	25 X 35	AP	300	14	200	250

VIJA CELMINS

BORN: Riga, Latvia; 1939
EDUCATION: Univ of California, Los Angeles, CA, MFA, 1965
TEACHING: Univ of California, Irvine, CA
AWARDS: Wolcott Award for travel in Europe, 1962; UCLA Acad Fellowships, 1962–65; Cassandra Foundation Award, 1968; Nat Endowment for the Arts, 1970–71
RECENT EXHIB: Indianapolis Center for Contemp Art, Herron Gallery, IN, 1989; Newport Harbor Art Mus, CA, 1989,92; Univ of Washington, Henry Art Gallery, Seattle, WA, 1992; David McKee Gallery, NY, 1992
COLLECTIONS: Mus of Mod Art, NY; Fort Worth Art Center Mus, Dallas, TX; Los Angeles Co Mus of Art
PRINTERS: Lloyd Baggs (LB); Cirrus Editions Workshop, Los Angeles, CA (CEW); Gemini GEL, Los Angeles, CA (GEM); Leslie Miller, NY (LM); Grenfell Press, NY (GrPr)
PUBLISHERS: Cirrus Editions, Los Angeles, CA (CE); Gemini GEL, Los Angeles, CA (GEM); Grenfell Press, NY (GrPr)
GALLERIES: Cirrus Editions, Ltd, Los Angeles, CA; David McKee Gallery, New York, NY; Gemini GEL, Los Angeles, CA; Richard Levy Gallery, Albuquerque, NM

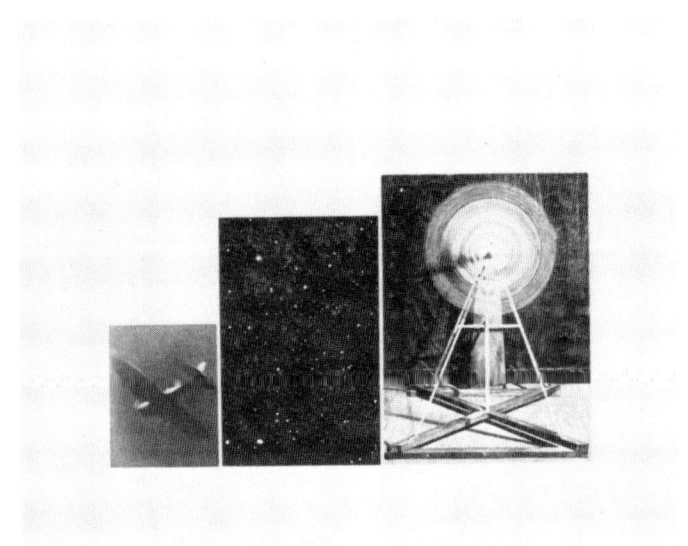

Vija Celmins
Concentric Bearings D
Courtesy Gemini GEL

The retail prices of the 100,000 limited edition prints quoted in this directory are subject to change. Print publishers, artists and galleries were the direct sources for these quotations. Prices in the secondary market listed as "Sold Out Editions (Rare)" indicate that the publisher has a limited supply of that print or that the print is difficult to locate in the galleries.

The print market has become very selective. For the first time since we published the first edition of The Printworld Directory in 1982, the prices of prints have been greatly reduced and greatly increased for the same artists by the most reputable and established print publishers. Check the fifth edition to understand the movement.

VIJA CELMINS CONTINUED

TITLE	PUBLISHER	PRINTER	DATE	MEDIUM	DIMENSION (PAPER SIZE) IN INCHES	TYPE OF PAPER	EDITION NUMBER	NO. OF COLORS	ORIGINAL OPENING PRICE	CURRENT RETAIL PRICE
SOLD OUT EDITIONS (RARE):										
Untitled (Desert)	CE	LB/CEW	1971	LB	22 X 29	AP/W	65	3	175	8000
Untitled (Ocean)	CE	LB/CEW	1972	LB	39 X 46 R/BFK	65	2	200		15000
Untitled (Desert, Ocean Sky, Galaxy) (Set of 4)	CE	LB/CEW	1975	LB	17 X 20	TW/HMP	75	3	1200 SET 300 EA	24000 SET 6000 EA
Constellation-Uccello	GEM	GEM	1983	EC/A	27 X 23	R/BFK	49	4	1000	4500
Strata	GEM	GEM	1983	MEZ	30 X 35	R/BFK	37		1200	4500
Alliance	GEM	GEM	1983	A/MEZ/DPT	24 X 19	R/BFK	48		1000	4500
Drypoint-Ocean Surface	GEM	GEM	1983	DPT	26 X 20	R/BFK	75	1	1200	3500
Jupiter Moon-Constellation	GEM	GEM	1983	EC/MEZ	24 X 19	R/BFK	48	3	850	3500
December 1984	GEM	GEM	1985	MEZ	30 X 23	R/BFK	25	1	1000	7000
Concentric Bearings A	GEM	GEM	1985	PH/A/DPT	24 X 18	R/BFK	34	2	850	4200
Concentric Bearings B	GEM	GEM	1985	A/DPT/MEZ	18 X 15	R/BFK	35	2	650	4200
Concentric Bearings C	GEM	GEM	1985	A/DPT/MEZ	20 X 20	R/BFK	34	3	750	5000
Concentric Bearings D	GEM	GEM	1985	PH/A/DPT/MEZ	18 X 23	R/BFK	34	3	1000	4200
Drypoint-Ocean Surface, State II	GEM	GEM	1985	DPT	24 X 19	R/BFK	55	1	1000	3500
Ocean Surface	GrPr	LM/GrPr	1992	WB	20 X 16	WP/1953	50	1	1500	1500

ROBERT CENEDELLA

BORN: Milford, MA; 1940
EDUCATION: Art Students League, NY; Studied with George Grosz
RECENT EXHIB: Martin Lawrence Gallery, Soho, NY, 1987; Realist Gallery, Santa Fe, NM, 1987; Center for Contemporary Arts, Santa Fe, NM, 1987
PRINTERS: Alexander Heinrici, NY (AH); Studio Heinrici, NY (SH); Michael Knigin, NY (MK); Avin Ferrin, NY (AF); Cinderella Press, NY (CP); Sienna Studio, NY (SiS); Robinson Lithography, NY (RL); Artist (ART)
PUBLISHERS: Martin Lawrence Limited Editions, Van Nuys, CA (MLLE); Cinderella Press, NY (CP); Chait Editions, NJ (CEI); Art Equity, Inc, Toronto, Canada (AEI); Baldwin International Graphics, NY (BIG)
GALLERIES: Martin Lawrence Galleries, Sherman Oaks, CA & Los Angeles, CA & Newport Beach, CA & West Los Angeles, CA & Short Hills, NJ & Phila, PA & Santa Monica, CA & Soho, New York, NY; Ernesto Mavans Gallery, Santa Fe, NM; Trianon Gallery, Paris, France

TITLE	PUBLISHER	PRINTER	DATE	MEDIUM	DIMENSION (PAPER SIZE) IN INCHES	TYPE OF PAPER	EDITION NUMBER	NO. OF COLORS	ORIGINAL OPENING PRICE	CURRENT RETAIL PRICE
SOLD OUT EDITIONS (RARE):										
Tall Barn	CP	ART	1971	LB	26 X 20	AP	100	1	50	350
The Cross	CP	ART	1971	LB	27 X 19	AP	75	1	50	350
The Family	CP	MK	1975	LB	25 X 20	AP	20	1	50	350
Man with Credentials	CP	MK	1977	LB	25 X 20	AP	75	1	50	350
Broome Street Bar	BIG	SiS	1979	LC	23 X 26	AP	116	11	200	650
Broome Street Bar (Deluxe Edition)	BIG	SiS	1979	LC	23 X 26	AP	61	11	300	850
The Symphony	CEI	SiS	1980	LC	29 X 26	AP	175	12	250	550
Second Avenue	AEI	SiS	1981	LC	27 X 22	AP	205	11	250	550
The Giants	BIG	SiS	1981	LC	22 X 30	AP	175	11	200	800
Unpopular Decision	BIG	SiS	1981	LC	25 X 29	AP	300	14	150	500
Loose Ball Foul	AEI	AF	1981	LC	22 X 28	AP	205	9	250	550
The Giants (Deluxe Edition)	BIG	SiS	1981	LC	22 X 30	AP	100	HC	300	700
Day Break	BIG	SiS	1982	LC	22 X 30	AP	110	10	250	650
59th Street Station	BIG	SiS	1982	LC	18 X 28	AP	150	12	200	750
Free Gifts	MLLE	AH/SH	1984	SP	32 X 35	SE	275	62	550	900
Balcony	MLLE	AH/SH	1984	SP	46 X 26	SE	275	51	550	900
Santa Fe Rider	BIG	CP	1982	LC	35 X 25	AP	150	11	250	800
Happy Hour (Limited Edition Poster)	BIG	RL	1986	SP	38 X 25	AP	50	8	100	250
60 Million Sold (Limited Edition Poster)	BIG	RL	1986	SP	38 X 25	AP	50	8	100	250
2001 A Stock Odyssey	BIG	AH/SH	1987	SP	40 X 38	LEN	250	52	450	900

MARIO CESPEDES

BORN: La Paz, Bolivia; 1942
PRINTERS: American Serigraph, Los Angeles, CA (AS)
PUBLISHERS: American Fine Art Editions, North Hollywood, CA (AFAE); Blinder Fine Arts, Inc, Santa Monica, CA (BFA)
GALLERIES: Art Moods, Atlanta, GA; Art City, Los Angeles, CA; Art Forum, Honolulu, HI; Billy Hork Galleries, Chicago, IL; Bromberg Fine Art, Columbia, MD; Court Gallery, Cincinnati, OH; Emporium Enterprises, Dallas, TX; Galerie Maxis, Canyon Country, CA; Grossman Galerie, Franklin, MI; Hoitts Gallery, San Francisco, CA; Laurence Galleries, Santa Rosa, CA; Marson Galleries, Baltimore, MD; Mary Roberts Gallery, Honolulu, HI; Metropolis Gallery, Boston, MA; Nan Miller Gallery, Rochester, NY; Park Place Gallery, St Louis, MO; Portland Place Gallery, Norwalk, CT; Rejeau Galleries, Natick, MA; Revann Galleries, Atlantic City, NJ; Sherman Gallery, Manhattan, CA; Silver K Gallery, Melbourne, Australia; Studio 53, New York, NY; Uptown Galleries, Fresno, CA; Warwick Gallery, Warwick, RI; Westbelt Gallery, Wayne, NJ

TITLE	PUBLISHER	PRINTER	DATE	MEDIUM	DIMENSION (PAPER SIZE) IN INCHES	TYPE OF PAPER	EDITION NUMBER	NO. OF COLORS	ORIGINAL OPENING PRICE	CURRENT RETAIL PRICE
CURRENT EDITIONS:										
Fiesta del Sol	BFA	AS		SP	34 X 41	COV	510	86	550	600

ANTON CETIN

BORN: Bojana, Croatia, Yugoslavia; September 18, 1936
EDUCATION: Sch of Applied Art, Zagreb, Yugoslavia, 1954–59; Acad of Fine Arts, Zagreb, Yugoslavia, 1959–64
AWARDS: Artist of the Year, Toronto, Canada, 1986
RECENT EXHIB: Del Bello Gallery, Toronto, Can, 1987; Beverly Gordon Gallery, Dallas, TX, 1987; Pfarrzentrum Stiftsgasoe, Bonn, Germany, 1987; Nat Univ Library, Croatia, 1988; Gallery Dubrava, Dubrovnik, Croatia, 1989; Del Bello Gallery, Toronto, ON, Canada, 1990; Oberhausmusem, Passau, Germany, 1990; Nat Library of Canada, Ottawa, Canada, 1990; Sony Plaza Art Gallery, Tokyo, Japan, 1991
COLLECTIONS: Canadian Cultural Centre, Paris, France; Art Gallery of Hamilton, ON, Canada; Univ of Michigan, Dearborn, MI; Nat Library of Canada, Ottawa, Canada; Nat Library of France, Paris, France; Mus of Arts & Crafts, Zagreb, Croatia; Mus & Gallery Center, Zagreb, Croatia; Vatican, Rome, Italy; Oberhausmuseum, Passau, Germany; Princeton Univ, NJ
PRINTERS: Arts-Litho, Paris, France (AL); Artist (ART)
PUBLISHERS: Original Print Collectors Group, NY (OPCG); Artist (ART)
GALLERIES: Galeria Juan Martin, Mexico City, Mexico; Sony Plaza International Fine Art, Tokyo, Japan; Beverly Gordon Fine Art Gallery, Dallas, TX
MAILING ADDRESS: 37 Hanna Ave, #13A, Toronto, ON, Canada M6K 1W9

TITLE	PUBLISHER	PRINTER	DATE	MEDIUM	DIMENSION (PAPER SIZE) IN INCHES	TYPE OF PAPER	EDITION NUMBER	NO. OF COLORS	ORIGINAL OPENING PRICE	CURRENT RETAIL PRICE
SOLD OUT EDITIONS (RARE):										
Eve Series, 1977, No 1	ART	ART	1977	LC	30 X 23	AP	100	4	150	1000
Eve Series, 1977, No 2	ART	ART	1977	LC	30 X 23	AP	75	4	150	1000
Eve Series, 1977, No, 3	ART	ART	1977	LC	30 X 23	AP	100	5	150	1000
Eve Series, 1977, No 4	ART	ART	1977	LC	30 X 23	AP	100	4	150	1000
Eve Series, 1977, No 5	ART	ART	1977	LC	30 X 23	AP	100	3	150	1000
Eve Series, 1977, No 6	ART	ART	1977	LC	23 X 30	AP	100	5	150	1000
Eve Series, 1977, No 7	ART	ART	1977	LC	30 X 23	AP	100	6	150	1000
Eve Series, 1977, No 8	ART	ART	1977	LC	30 X 25	AP	100	2	150	1000
Eve Series, 1977, No 9	ART	ART	1977	LC	23 X 30	AP	100	5	150	1000
Eve	OPCG	ART	1980	EB/A	22 X 15	AP	150	7	225	750
Mystery in Green	ART	AL	1981	LC	30 X 22	AP	200	6	375	800
Eve with Red Hair	ART	AL	1981	LC	30 X 22	AP	150	5	350	800
Forever	ART	AL	1981	LC	30 X 22	AP	150	5	350	800
I Carry My Past Along	ART	AL	1981	LC	30 X 22	AP	150	7	400	800
Prayer	ART	AL	1981	LC	30 X 22	AP	150	6	350	800
Awaiting I	ART	AL	1981	LC	30 X 22	AP	150	5	350	800
Awaiting II	ART	AL	1981	LC	30 X 22	AP	150	5	350	800
Remembrance	ART	AL	1981	LC	22 X 30	AP	150	6	375	800
Contemplation I	ART	AL	1981	LC	22 X 30	AP	150	8	400	800
Contemplation II	ART	AL	1981	LC	22 X 30	AP	150	6	400	800
Eve and the Flower-Bird Series No 1–No 12	ART	AL	1983	LC	9 X 8 EA	AP	50 EA	7	110 EA	500 EA
CURRENT EDITIONS										
Croatian Indian Eve I,II,III	ART	ART	1988	EC/A	15 X 11 EA	R/BFK	50 EA	2 EA	250 EA	400 EA
Eve and Bird	ART	ART	1990	EC/A	15 X 11	R/BFK	50	4	350	500
Eve and Flower-Bird with Space Architecture I,II	ART	ART	1990	EC/A	13 X 15 EA	R/BFK	50 EA	4 EA	350 EA	500 EA
Eve and Flower-Bird with Space Architecture III	ART	ART	1990	EC/A	16 X 13	R/BFK	50	6	350	500
Eve	ART	ART	1990	EC/A/REL	16 X 14	R/BFK	75	2	350	500
Window	ART	ART	1991	EC/A	14 X 17	R/BFK	75	4	350	500
In Space	ART	ART	1991	EC/A	18 X 13	R/BFK	75	4	350	500
In Harmony	ART	ART	1991	EC/A	18 X 13	R/BFK	50	7	500	600
Reminiscence I,II	ART	ART	1991	EC/A	18 X 13 EA	R/BFK	75 EA	4/6	400 EA	500 EA
Acquaintance	ART	ART	1991	EC/A/WC	15 X 16	R/BFK	75	5	500	600
Surprise	ART	ART	1991	EC/A/WC	15 X 16	R/BFK	75	7	500	600
Caring	ART	ART	1991	EC/A/WC	15 X 16	R/BFK	75	8	500	600
Window to Another Dimension	ART	ART	1991	EC/A/WA	15 X 18	R/BFK	75	8	500	600
Because of You	ART	ART	1991	EC/A	18 X 13	R/BFK	75	6	500	600

EMILY CHENG

BORN: New York, NY; 1953
EDUCATION: Rhode Island Sch of Design, Providence, RI, BFA, Painting, 1975; New York Studio Sch, NY, 1977–79
AWARDS: Nat Endowment for the Arts Fel, 1982–83
RECENT EXHIB: Lang & O'Hara Gallery, NY, 1987,88,90
PRINTERS: Jon Cone, East Topsham, VT (JC); Cone Editions, East Topsham, VT (CEd); Artist (ART)
PUBLISHERS: Cone Editions, East Topsham, VT (CEd); Artist (ART)
GALLERIES: Jonathan O'Hara Gallery, New York, NY; M-13 Gallery, New York, NY; Cone Editions, East Topsham, VT; David Beitzel Gallery, New York, NY; Pelavin Editions, New York, NY
MAILING ADDRESS: c/o Lang & O'Hara Gallery, 41 E 57th St, New York, NY 10022–1908

TITLE	PUBLISHER	PRINTER	DATE	MEDIUM	DIMENSION (PAPER SIZE) IN INCHES	TYPE OF PAPER	EDITION NUMBER	NO. OF COLORS	ORIGINAL OPENING PRICE	CURRENT RETAIL PRICE
CURRENT EDITIONS:										
Etching (with Roulette and Burnishing)	CEd	JC/CEd	1987	EB	16 X 20	RP/HWT	20	1	250	350
Untitled (Series of 36 Monoprints)	CEd/ART	ART/CEd	1991	MON	26 X 30 EA to 36 X 24 EA	LANA	1 EA	Varies	1000 EA	1000 EA

MARC CHAGALL

BORN: Vitebsk, Russia; (1887-1985)
EDUCATION: Vitebsk, Russia, 1907; St Petersburg, Russia, 1907-10; Paris, France, 1910-14
TEACHING: Vitebsk Acad, Russia, 1919-20
AWARDS: Carnegie Prize, Pittsburgh, PA, 1939
PRINTERS: Atelier Mourlot, Paris, France (AM); Maeght Editeur, Paris, France (ME); Arte, Paris, France (ARTE); Maeght Lelong, Paris, France (ML); Louis Fort, Paris, France (LF)
PUBLISHERS: Editions Albert Morance Paris, France (EAM); Kornfeld (K); Paul Cassirer, Berlin, Germany (PC); Tériade, Paris, France (TER); Verve Publishing, Paris, France (VP); Léon Amiel, Paris, France (LA); Galerie Cramer, Geneva, Switzerland (GC); Maeght Editions, Paris, France (ME); Transworld Art, Inc, NY (TAI); Maeght Lelong, Paris, France (ML); Paul Morand/Ouvert la Nuit, Paris, France (PM/OLN); Vollard, Paris, France (VOL); Musées Nat, Paris, France (MN)

GALLERIES: Erika Meyerovich Gallery, San Francisco, CA; Horoshak Contemp Art, Sunnyvale, CA; Charles Whitchurch Fine Arts, Huntington Beach, CA; Glabman Ring Gallery, Los Angeles, CA; R K Goldman & Company, Los Angeles, CA; Jack Rutberg Fine Arts, Los Angeles, CA; Smith/Andersen Gallery, Palo Alto, CA; Centurion Galleries, Chicago, IL; Merrill Chase Galleries, Chicago, IL; Stephen Galleries, Minneapolis, MN; Gallery of the Masters, St Louis, MO; Brewster Gallery, New York, NY; Peter Findlay Gallery, New York, NY; Galerie Select, Ltd, New York, NY; Hilde Gerst Gallery, New York, NY; Studio 53, New York, NY; Weintraub Gallery, New York, NY; Contemporary Gallery, Dallas, TX; Spaightwood Galleries, Madison, WI; Masters Portfolio, Chicago, IL; Ana Izax Gallerie, Los Angeles, CA; Benedicte-Saxe Gallery/Maeght Editions, Beverly Hills, CA; Professional Fine Arts Services, Inc, New York, NY

Kornfeld (K); Paul Cassirer (PC); Mourlot (M); Cramer (C); Vollard (V); Sorlier (S)

TITLE	PUBLISHER	PRINTER	DATE	MEDIUM	DIMENSION (PAPER SIZE) IN INCHES	TYPE OF PAPER	EDITION NUMBER	NO. OF COLORS	ORIGINAL OPENING PRICE	CURRENT RETAIL PRICE
SOLD OUT EDITIONS (RARE):										
Bella	EAM		1922	EB/DPT	9 X 11	LAID	100	1	35	6500
Self-Portrait	PC		1922	EB/DPT	10 X 9	LAID	110	1	35	15000
Self-Portrait	PC		1922	EB/DPT	11 X 9	LAID	100	1	35	15000
Le Vieux Juif			1922	EB	5 X 4	LAID	110	1	35	9000
Die Liebenden (K-25)	PC		1922	EB/DPT	11 X 9	JP	110	1	35	20000
Bearded Man Seated with Violin Under His Arm (M-11)	AM	AM	1922-23	LC	6 X 10	LAID	35		50	8000
Man with Book (M-15)	AM	AM	1922-23	LC	11 X 14	LAID	100		50	8000
Chévre et Violon (K-34)	AM	AM	1922-23	WB		LAID	20	1	50	8500
Mein Leben Series:										
Mein Leben: Der Rabbi (K-21)	PC		1923	EB/DPT	18 X 14	LAID	110	1	50	10000
Mein Leben: Haus in Peskowatik (K-8)	PC		1923	EB/DPT	14 X 18	LAID/CR	110	1	50	15000
Mein Leben-Ein alter Jude (K-13)	PC		1923	EB/DPT	10 X 8	LAID	110	1	50	10000
Mein Leben: Selbstbildnis (K-17)	PC		1923	EB/DPT	11 X 9	LAID	110	1	50	10000
Mein Leben: Der Musiker (K-23)	PC		1923	EB/DPT	17 X 14	LAID	110	1	50	15000
Mein Leben: Der Spazierung (K-26)	PC		1923	EB/DPT	10 X 8	LAID/CR	110	1	50	15000
Akt mit Fächer (K-39)	LPPGI	LF	1924	EB/DPT	9 X 11	LAID	100	1	75	20000
Der Akrobat mit der Geige (Dark Brown) (K-40)	VOL	LF	1924	EC/DPT	16 X 13	WOVE	150	1	50	12000
Bella	PC		1924	EB/DPT	9 X 5	LAID	100	1	50	18000
Ouvert la Nuit-Seine und Eiffelturm (K-74)	PM/OLN		1926-27	EB/A/DPT	6 X 4	LAID	120		50	12000
Le Lion et el Moucheron			1927	EB	10 X 10	LAID	200	1	50	3500
Abraham et les Trois Anges (V-205)			1935	EB	12 X 9	LAID	50	1	50	3500
Eiffelturm (K-85/a)			1943	EB/MON	11 X 8	WOVE	20	Varies	125	15000
Le Offrande			1944-45	EB	10 X 7	AP	80	1	75	15000
Das Geschenk (K-96)			1944-45	EB/WA/GOU/HC	10 X 7	AP	50		100	60000
The Blue Fish (M-198)			1947	LC	10 X 17	AP	90		100	6500
Four Tales from Arabian Nights: Then the Old Woman Mounted on the Ifrits Back...(M-42)			1948	LC	15 X 11	AP	111	7	100	40000
Four Tales from Arabian Nights: Abdullah Got the Net Ashore (M-43)	PB	AC	1948	LC	15 X 11	AP	90		100	15000
Abdullah Discovered Before Him Mountains of Water (M-44)	PB	AC	1948	LC	15 X 11	AP	90		100	15000
Couple en Ocre (M-59)			1952	LC	25 X 20	AP	100		500	12000
Bonjour sur Paris (M-71)	AM	AM	1952	LC	19 X 26	AP	75		500	35000
Fables de la Fontaine	ARTE	ARTE	1953	EB	10 X 13	AP	200	1	600	18000
Derriére le Miroir (Set of 11) (M-93-103)	ME	ME	1954	LC	15 X 11 EA	AP	2500 EA		3000 SET	20000 SET
Eiffel Tower with Donkey (M-97)	ME	ME	1954	LC	16 X 11	AP	75		600	12000
Quai aux Fleurs (M-99)	ME	ME	1954	LC	15 X 11	AP	75		600	12000
La Bastille (M-111)	ME	ME	1954	LC	20 X 26	AP	75		800	50000
Poster for City of Venice			1954	LC	25 X 20	AP			850	20000
Abraham und Sarah (M-122)	AM	AM	1956	LC	14 X 10	AP			600	8000
The Bible Suite (Set of 105):									10000 SET	100000 SET
La Descente Vers Sodome-#8	TER		1956	EB/HC		MONT	100		100	3000
Les Tenebres sur L'Egypte-#31	TER		1956	EB/HC		MONT	100		100	3000
Rebecca a la Fontaine-#12	TER		1956	EB/HC		MONT	100		100	3000
Moise Sauve des Faux-#26	TER		1956	EB/HC		MONT	100		100	3000
Repas de la Paque #32	TER		1956	EB/HC		MONT	100		100	3000
Sortie de L'Egypte #33	TER		1956	EB/HC		MONT	100		100	3000
Moise Recontre dans le Desert son Frere Aaron...#28	TER		1956	EB/HC		MONT	100		100	3000
Moise Recoit les Table de la Loi #37	TER		1956	EB/HC		MONT	100		100	3000
Mort de Moise-#41	TER		1956	EB/HC		MONT	100		100	3000

MARC CHAGALL CONTINUED

TITLE	PUBLISHER	PRINTER	DATE	MEDIUM	DIMENSION (PAPER SIZE) IN INCHES	TYPE OF PAPER	EDITION NUMBER	NO. OF COLORS	ORIGINAL OPENING PRICE	CURRENT RETAIL PRICE
SOLD OUT EDITIONS (RARE):										
Fin d'Absalom #72	TER		1956	EB/HC		MONT	100		100	3000
La Reine de Seba #80	TER		1956	EB/HC		MONT	100		100	4500
Moses (M-114)	AM	AM	1956	LC	25 X 26	AP	50		800	18000
Daphnis et Chloe (M-228)	VP	AM	1956	LC	13 X 9	AP	75		800	10000
The Concert (M-176)	ME	ME	1957	LC	15 X 22	AP	90		800	6000
The Red Rooster (M-203)	ME	ME	1957	LC	10 X 15	AP	90		800	6000
Les Amoureaux (M-194,195)			1957	LC	9 X 8 EA	AP				
Le Coq sur Paris (M-223)			1958	LC	24 X 18	AP	125		1000	25000
De Mauvais Sujets			1958	EC	15 X 11	AP			1000	7500
Ile Saint-Louis (M-225)			1959	LC	20 X 26	AP	75		1200	20000
The Blue Dream	ME	ME	1959	LC	15 X 10	AP	75		1500	15000
Couple with Bird	ME	ME	1959	LC	13 X 20	AP	75		1000	8500
Self-Portrait					13 X 10	AP	40	5	800	18000
Home in My Village	VP	AM	1960	LC	19 X 13	AP	50		1000	12000
Rachel Hides Her Father's Household Gods (M-242)	VP	AM	1960	LC	14 X 11	AP	50		800	20000
Rahab and the Spies of Jericho (M-244)	VP	AM	1960	LC	15 X 11	AP	50		800	20000
L'Offrande	ARTE	ARTE	1960	LB	10 X 13	AP	100	1	1250	12000
Ahasver Vertriebt Vashti (M-251)			1960	LC	14 X 10	AP				
Dessins pour la Bible:										
Adam et Eva Chassés du Paradis Terrestre (M-237)			1960	LC	14 X 10	AP			1250	5000
Adam et Eva et le Fruit Défendu			1960	LC	14 X 10	AP			1250	5000
Agar dans le Désert			1960	LC	14 X 10	AP			1250	5000
Assuérus Chasse Vasthi (M-252)			1960	LC	14 X 10	AP			1250	5000
Le Couple devant l'Arbre (M-292)			1960	LB	12 X 10	AP	40	1	1250	5000
Daphnis et Chloe (Frontispiece) (M-328)	VP	AM	1961	LC	17 X 26	AP	60		4500	93000
Daphnis et Chloe Suite:										
Daphnis et Chloe Beside the Fountain (M-313)	TER		1961	LC	21 X 15	AP	60		1500	38000
Chloe's Judgement (M-315)	TER		1961	LC	17 X 25	AP	60		1500	40000
Chloe's Kiss (M-316)	TER		1961	LC	17 X 13	AP	60		1500	30000
The Nymphs Cave (M-321)	TER		1961	LC	17 X 25	AP	60		1500	20000
Philetas's Lesson (M-323)	TER		1961	LC	22 X 15	AP	60		1500	50000
Pan's Bouquet (M-331)	TER		1961	LC	17 X 13	AP	60		1500	30000
The Orchard (M-341)	TER		1961	LC	17 X 25	AP	60		1500	100000
Hymen (M-349)	TER		1961	LC	17 X 25	AP	60	10	1500	50000
Bay of Angels (M-350)	AM	AM	1962	LC	31 X 23	AP	50		2000	90000
La Baie (the Bay) (M-356)	AM	AM	1962	LC	15 X 23	AP	75		1500	20000
Acrobats at Play			1963	LC		R/BFK	50		1800	6000
Large Bouquet (M-384)	AM		1963	LC	27 X 20	R/BFK	50	8	1800	75000
Paravant (Set of 4) (M-390)	GC		1963	LC		AP	100 EA		4500 SET	30000 SET
The White Clown (M-411)			1964	LB	16 X 11	R/BFK	75	1	1800	5000
Circus Girl Rider (M-419)			1964	LC	25 X 21	AP	50		2000	30000
Woman by the Window (M-420)			1964	LC	25 X 20	AP	50		2000	20000
Basket of Fruit & Pineapples			1964	LC	30 X 22	AP	50		2000	40000
The Black Moon (M-438)	AM	AM	1965	LC	23 X 19	AP	50		1800	8500
The Blue Pirouette (M-471)	AM	AM	1966	LC	14 X 11	AP	50		1500	8500
The Story of Exodus (Set of 24) (M-444-467)	LA		1966	LC	20 X 15	AP	285		5000 SET	60000 SET
The Circus (Set of 38) (M-490-527):	VP	AM	1967	LC(23)	17 X 13 EA	AP	250 EA		10000 SET	300000 SET
				LB(15)	17 X 13 EA					
				DIPT(3)	26 X 17 EA					
The Circus (Set of 38):									20000 SET	350000 SET
Green Clown (M-505)	VP	AM	1967	LC	17 X 13	AP/WOVE	14		1600	25000
Acrobat and Goat (M-515)	VP	AM	1967	LC	17 X 13	AP/WOVE	14		1600	20000
Center Ring (M-517)	VP	AM	1967	LC	17 X 26	AP/WOVE	14		1600	50000
La Baie des Anges	VP	AM	1967	LC	15 X 18	AP/WOVE	50		1500	30000
Acrobate et Violoniste (C-64)			1968	EB/A	14 X 16	AP/WOVE	50		1600	10000
Dawn at St Paul	AM	AM	1968	LC	29 X 22	AP/WOVE	50		2000	45000
Peasant with a Bouquet	AM	AM	1968	LC			50		1600	18000
Garden of Pomona (M-541)			1968	LC	24 X 17	AP/WOVE	50	6	1600	55500
The Blue Bird (S-41)			1968	LC	22 X 17	AP/WOVE	200		1600	8000
The Big Peasant (M-549)	AM	AM	1968	LC	23 X 18	AP/WOVE	50		2000	12000
Peasant with a Violin (M-551)			1968	LC	12 X 9	AP/WOVE	50		1600	10000
Vision of Moses (M-554-A)	AM	AM	1968	LC	23 X 30	AP/WOVE	75		2000	25000
Chasing the Bluebird (M-594)	AM	AM	1969	LC	24 X 21	AP/WOVE	75		2000	25000
Fairyland (M-576)	AM	AM	1969	LC	19 X 22	AP/WOVE	50		1600	10000
Chagall Lithographs Volume III:										
Composition (M-577A)	AM	AM	1969	LC	13 X 10	AP/WOVE	75	2	1600	10000
Baou de St Jeannet II (M-585)	AM	AM	1969	LC	20 X 17	AP/WOVE	50		1600	7500

MARC CHAGALL CONTINUED

TITLE	PUBLISHER	PRINTER	DATE	MEDIUM	DIMENSION (PAPER SIZE) IN INCHES	TYPE OF PAPER	EDITION NUMBER	NO. OF COLORS	ORIGINAL OPENING PRICE	CURRENT RETAIL PRICE
SOLD OUT EDITIONS (RARE):										
Yellow Rooster	AM	AM	1969	AC	18 X 11		75		1800	12000
A Sequestered Garden	AM	AM	1969	LC	30 X 21	AP			1800	12000
Twentieth Century	AM	AM	1969	LC		AP			1800	12000
Paris of Dream	AM	AM	1969	LC	40 X 31	AP			1800	60000
Light of the Circus	AM	AM	1969	LC	26 X 20	AP				
Chasing the Bluebird (M-594)	ME	ME	1969	LC	24 X 21	AP	75		1800	50000
Bouquet Clair (M-610)	AM	AM	1970	LC		AP	50		2000	20000
Au-Dessus de Paris (M-614)	AM	AM	1970	LC	20 X 25	AP	50		1800	12000
Married Couple in the Studio (M-621)	AM	AM	1970	LC	26 X 20		50	4	1800	10000
The Open Window (M-637)	AM	AM	1971	LC	28 X 21			2	2000	10000
Pantomime (M-649A)	ME	ME	1972	LC	15 X 12	AP/WOVE	50		2000	10000
The Little Horse (M-681)	ME	ME	1972	LC	22 X 16	AP/WOVE	50		2000	10000
The Things He Says Without Speaking Series:										
#2-The Eiffel Tower	ME	ARTE	1972	EC		AP	25	7	2250	20000
#4-The Lovers	ME	ARTE	1972	EC		AP	25	7	2250	20000
#5-At Home	ME	ARTE	1972	EC		AP	25	7	2250	20000
#7-Before the Window	ME	ARTE	1972	EC		AP	25	7	2250	20000
The Dance (M-652)	ME	ME	1972	LC	16 X 12	AP	50		1800	10000
Day in May (M-654)	ME	ME	1972	LC	25 X 15	AP	50		2250	10000
Blue Profile	ME	ME	1972	LC	29 X 22	AP	50		2250	20000
Near St Jeannet	ME	ME	1972	LC	13 X 10	AP			800	2500
Hexerei (M-678)	AM	AM	1972	LB	25 X 20	LAID	50	1	1500	12000
The Blue Studio	ME	ME	1973	LC	25 X 22	AP	50		2250	12500
Circus Riders	ME	ME	1973	LB	26 X 19	AP	50		2250	8500
Bacchantin (M-690)	AM	AM	1973	LC	19 X 24	AP	50		2250	10000
David (M-700)	MN	ME	1973	LC	4 X 5	AP	150		2000	6000
The Green Horse	ME	ME	1973	LC	22 X 16		50		2000	10000
Red and Yellow Bouquet (M-711)	AM	AM	1974	LC	25 X 19	AP/WOVE	50		2000	30000
The Red Acrobat (M-717)	AM	AM	1974	LC	27 X 21	AP/WOVE	50		2000	30000
L'Artiste: Théme Biblique			1974	LC	15 X 23	AP/WOVE	50		2000	18000
Ares et Aphrodite (from L'Odyssee) (M-772)	AM	AM	1974	LC	17 X 13	AP/WOVE	250		850	8000
The Orange Tree			1975	LC	26 X 19	AP/WOVE	50		3000	18000
Le Peintre	ME	ME	1975	LB	66 X 48 cm	JP	50	1	2500	10000
Roses et Mimosas	TAI	AM	1975	LC	33 X 26	AP	50		7500	30000
Les Arums (M-748)	AM	AM	1975	LC	27 X 22	AP	50		3500	4000
Les Affiches de Chagall	D-V	CS	1975	LC	13 X 10	AP				
Nu et la Tour Eiffel-Celui...	AM	AM	1976	EB/A	16 X 12	R/BFK	205	4	800	3500
Le Arc de Triomphe (M-840)	AM	AM	1976	LC	32 X 23	AP	50		7500	20000
Double Portrait au Chevalet	AM	AM	1976	LC	22 X 17	AP	50		5000	20000
Studio Light	AM	AM	1976	LC	29 X 22	AP	50		6000	35000
Bouquet aux Amoureux (M-842)	ME		1976	LC	25 X 19	AP	50		3500	25000
Small Bouquet of Lilies (M-909)	AM	AM	1977	LC	16 X 12	AP	50		2500	10000
Le Chevalet (S-926)	ME	ME	1978	LB	13 X 10	AP	50		5000	20000
L'Arbre Fleuri	ME	ME	1978	LC	20 X 16	AP	50		6500	20000
The Interior (M-931)			1978	LC	13 X 10	AP	50		5000	10000
La Bénédiction de Jacob	ME	ME	1979	LC	58 X 46 cm	JP	50	6	6000	20000
La Peintre á la tour Eiffel	ME	ME	1979	LC	59 X 46 cm	JP	50	4	6000	20000
Acrobate sur fond Vert	ME	ME	1979	LC	50 X 38 cm	AP	50	12	6000	20000
Soleil au Cheval Rouge	ME	ME	1979	LC	46 X 58 cm	AP	50	10	6000	20000
Le Roi David	ME	ME	1979	LC	60 X 45 cm	JP	50	5	6000	20000
Moses and the Tablets	AM	AM	1979	LC	26 X 19	AP	50		6500	20000
The Wedding of Bethsabee	AM	AM	1979	LC	26 X 19	AP	50		6000	20000
The Lovers	AM	AM	1979	LB	26 X 19	AP	50	1	5000	18000
Jacobs and the Angels	AM	AM	1979	LC	26 X 19	AP	50		6500	20000
Abraham et les trois Anges (M-948)	AM	AM	1979	LC	15 X 13	AP	50		4000	8000
Le Dimanche (M-98)	AM	AM	1979	LC	28 X 25	AP	50		5000	9000
Couple et Anges (C-104)			1980	DPT	13 X 11	AP	1	50	1500	3500
Couple at Dusk (M-972)	ME	ME	1980	LC	37 X 24	AP	50		6500	25000
Les Clowns Musicien (M-978)	ME	ME	1980	LC	38 X 24	AP	50		6500	35000
The Blue Painter	ME	ME	1980	LC	21 X 14	AP	50		5000	15000
Vue Sur Notre-Dame	ME	ME	1980	LC	120 X 80 cm	AP	50	20	6500	30000
Dans le Ciel de l'Opera	ME	ME	1980	LC	120 X 80 cm	AP	50	20	6500	30000
L'Ame du Cirque	ME	ME	1980	LC	80 X 120 cm	AP	50	15	6500	30000
La Parade	ME	ME	1980	LC	120 X 80 cm	AP	50	15	6500	30000
Creation	ME	ME	1980	LC	120 X 80 cm	AP	50	15	6500	30000
Les Lilas	ME	ME	1980	LC	120 X 80 cm	AP	50	10	6500	30000
Les Clowns Musiciens	ME	ME	1980	LC	120 X 80 cm	AP	50	10	6500	30000
Les Deux Rives	ME	ME	1980	LC	37 X 24	AP	50	10	6500	30000
Maternite Rouge	ME	ME	1980	LC	120 X 80 cm	AP	50	20	6500	30000
Le Bouquet Rose	ME	ME	1980	LC	120 X 80 cm	AP	50	15	6500	30000
La Joie	ME	ME	1980	LC	120 X 80 cm	AP	50	20	6500	30000

MARC CHAGALL CONTINUED

TITLE	PUBLISHER	PRINTER	DATE	MEDIUM	DIMENSION (PAPER SIZE) IN INCHES	TYPE OF PAPER	EDITION NUMBER	NO. OF COLORS	ORIGINAL OPENING PRICE	CURRENT RETAIL PRICE
SOLD OUT EDITIONS (RARE):										
Les Amoureux á l'Isba	ME	ME	1980	LC	80 X 120 cm	AP	50	12	6500	30000
L'Envolée Magique	ME	ME	1980	LC	120 X 80 cm	AP	50	15	6500	30000
Le Couple au Crepuscule	ME	ME	1980	LC	120 X 80 cm	AP	50	15	6500	30000
The Green Tree with Lovers (M-959)	AM	AM	1980	LC	22 X 15	AP	50		6000	30000
Le Couple au Cheval Bleu	ME	ME	1981	LC	38 X 28 cm	AP	50	4	5000	15000
Paris on Holiday (M-997)	AM	AM	1982	LC	10 X 21	AP	50		5000	12000
Painter with Hat (M-1010)	AM	AM	1983	LC	18 X 12	AP	50		5000	12000
The Sky (M-1034)	AM	AM	1984	LC	24 X 19	AP	50		7500	20000
The Green Branch	AM	AM	1984	LC	33 X 24	AP	50		7500	20000
Maternity	AM	AM	1984	LC		AP	50		5000	13500
The Blue Clown (S-1032)	AM	AM	1984	LC	25 X 19	AP	50		5000	25000
Bouquets with a Blue Sky (M-1024)	AM	AM	1984	LC	13 X 10	AP	50		3500	9000

MICHAEL CHALLENGER

BORN: England; 1939
EDUCATION: Goldsmiths Col of Art, London, England, 1960–64; Slade Sch of Art, London, England, 1964–66
TEACHING: Slade Sch of Art, London, England, 1966–67; Chesterfield Col of Art, England, 1967–68; Goldsmiths Col, London, England, 1968
AWARDS: Sainsbury Award, London, England, 1966
COLLECTIONS: Duke Univ, Durham, NC; Univ of Maine, Orono, ME; Bowdoin Col, Brunswick, ME; Boston Col, MA; Georgia State Col, MA; Bucknell Univ, Lewisburg, PA; Wayne State Col, NE; Victoria & Albert Mus, London, England; California State Col, Los Angeles, CA; Villanova Univ, PA; Slade Sch of Art, London, England; Arts Council of Great Britain
PRINTERS: Vistec Graphics, Rochester, NY (VG)
PUBLISHERS: London Arts Inc, Detroit, MI (LAI); Post Oak Fine Art, Houston, TX (POFA)
GALLERIES: London Arts, Inc, Detroit, MI

TITLE	PUBLISHER	PRINTER	DATE	MEDIUM	DIMENSION (PAPER SIZE) IN INCHES	TYPE OF PAPER	EDITION NUMBER	NO. OF COLORS	ORIGINAL OPENING PRICE	CURRENT RETAIL PRICE
CURRENT EDITIONS:										
Whichcup	LAI	VG	1979	SP	25 X 29	SOM	300	11	250	350
Heaven Forbid	LAI	VG	1979	SP	25 X 29	SOM	300	12	250	350
C²	LAI	VG	1979	SP	25 X 29	SOM	300	12	250	350
Ends and Bends	LAI	VG	1979	SP	25 X 30	SOM	300	14	250	350
Full Volume	POFA	VG	1979	SP	29 X 23	SOM	300	15	250	350

JOHN CHAMBERLAIN

BORN: Rochester, IN; April, 16, 1927
EDUCATION: Art Inst of Chicago, IL, 1950–52; Black Mountain Col, NC, 1955–56
AWARDS: Guggenheim Fels, 1966,67; Creative Arts Awards, Brandeis Univ, Waltham, MA, 1984; Am Acad of Inst of Arts & Letters, NY, 1990; Skowhegan Sch of Painting & Sculpture Award, ME, Sculpture, 1993
RECENT EXHIB: Xavier Fourcade, Inc, NY, 1987; Pace Gallery, NY, 1989; Indianapolis Center for Contemp Art, Herron Gallery, IN, 1989; Chinati Found, Marfa, TX, 1989; Waddington Galleries, London, England, 1990; Karsten Greve Gallery, Cologne, Germany, 1991; Laura Carpenter Fine Art, Santa Fe, NM, 1992; Governors State Univ, Nathan Manilow Sculpture Park, University Park, IL, 1989,92; Chinati Found, Marfa, TX, 1992; Bradley Univ, Heuser Art Center Gallery, Hartmann Center Gallery, Peoria, IL, 1992
COLLECTIONS: Mus of Mod Art, NY; Albright-Knox Art Gallery, Buffalo, NY; Los Angeles County Mus of Art, CA; Univ of North Carolina, Greensboro, NC
PRINTERS: Topaz Editions, Tampa, FL (TE); Hudson River Editions, Garnerville, NY (HRE); Gemini GEL, Los Angeles, CA (GEM); Mark Doffy, Sarasota, FL (MD); Ten Coconut, Sarasota, FL (TC); Spring Street Workshop, NY (SpSW)
PUBLISHERS: London Arts, Inc, Detroit, MI (LAI); Topaz Editions, Tampa, FL (TE); Hudson River Editions, Garnerville, NY (HRE); Gemini GEL, Los Angeles, CA (GEM); Ten Coconut, Sarasota, FL (TC); Artist (ART); Pace Editions, NY (PE)
GALLERIES: Pace Prints, New York, NY; James Corcoran Gallery, Santa Monica, CA; Robert Kidd Gallery, Birmingham, MI; Margo Leavin Gallery, Los Angeles, CA; Marian Goodman Gallery, New York, NY; Helander Gallery, Palm Beach, FL; Stephen A Solovy Fine Arts, Chicago, IL; Beth Urdang Fine Art, Boston, MA; Lennon & Weinberg, New York, NY; Lawrence Mangel Gallery, Phila, PA; Waddington Galleries, London, England; Karsten Greve Gallery, Cologne, Germany; Laura Carpenter Fine Art, Santa Fe, NM; Jonathan Novak Contemporary Art, Los Angeles, CA; Daniel Weinberg Gallery, Santa Monica, CA; John C Stoller & Company, Minneapolis, MN; Hudson River Editions, South Nyack, NY
MAILING ADDRESS: c/o Pace Gallery, 32 E 57th St, New York, NY 10022

TITLE	PUBLISHER	PRINTER	DATE	MEDIUM	DIMENSION (PAPER SIZE) IN INCHES	TYPE OF PAPER	EDITION NUMBER	NO. OF COLORS	ORIGINAL OPENING PRICE	CURRENT RETAIL PRICE
SOLD OUT EDITIONS (RARE):										
Flashback I,II,III,IV,V	LAI		1979	SP	28 X 20 EA	AP	175 EA	7 EA	600 EA	800 EA
Untitled I,II,III	TE	TE	1977	LC	32 X 24 EA	AP	27 EA	6 EA	400 EA	800 EA
Le Mole I, II, III (Molded Polyester Resin)	GEM	TE	1978	LC	24 X 33 EA	AP	56 EA	27 EA	600 EA	800 EA
The French Couple (Set of 2)	ART/HRE	HRE	1982	EC	20 X 18 EA	GE	25 EA	3 EA	800 SET	800 SET
Untitled	ART/HRE	HRE	1982	EB	20 X 18	GE	25	1	250	600
Relief Monoprints (Set of 5):									3500 SET	3750 SET
After "Daddy-O-Springs"	M	ART	1983	REL/MON	32 X 27 EA	AC	27 EA		700 EA	900 EA
After "And His Hair was Perfect"	M	ART	1983	REL/MON	31 X 27 EA	AC	27 EA		700 EA	900 EA

The print market has become very selective. For the first time since we published the first edition of The Printworld Directory in 1982, the prices of prints have been greatly reduced and greatly increased for the same artists by the most reputable and established print publishers. Check the fifth edition to understand the movement.

JOHN CHAMBERLAIN CONTINUED

TITLE	PUBLISHER	PRINTER	DATE	MEDIUM	DIMENSION (PAPER SIZE) IN INCHES	TYPE OF PAPER	EDITION NUMBER	NO. OF COLORS	ORIGINAL OPENING PRICE	CURRENT RETAIL PRICE
SOLD OUT EDITIONS (RARE):										
After "Three Cornered Desire"	M	ART	1983	REL/MON	27 X 37 EA	AC	27 EA		700 EA	900 EA
After "Broke Purple"	M	ART	1983	REL/MON	27 X 27 EA	AC	27 EA		700 EA	900 EA
After "Chick Meat"	M	ART	1983	REL/MON	27 X 27 EA	AC	27 EA		700 EA	900 EA
Gondolas	TC	MD/TC	1984	MON	20 X 28 EA	AP	1 EA		1000 EA	1200 EA
Melon Collie Gondola Series (Set of 3)	PE	SpSW	1991	EB	14 X 28 EA	R/BFK	18 EA	1 EA	2700 SET 1000 EA	2700 SET 1000 EA
Alphabet Series II (Set of 9)	PE	SpSW	1991	EB	15 X 15 EA	R/BFK	18 EA	1 EA	5000 SET	5000 SET
Detail Series	PE	SpSW	1991	MON	18 X 18 EA	AC	1 EA	Varies	3600 EA	3600 EA
Me (One-Nine) (Set of 9)	PE	SpSW	1992	EB	14 X 14 EA	R/BFK	18 EA	1 EA	700 EA	700 EA
Conversations with Myself (Letterpress and Relief Print Book with Loose Etching)	PE	SpSW	1992	EB	6 X 6 X 2	AP	108		500	500
The Estate of Lucy Series	PE	SpSW	1992	MON	9 X 31 EA	AC	1 EA	Varies	4000 EA	4000 EA
The Estate of the Dude Series	PE	SpSW	1992	MON	31 X 63 EA	AC	1 EA	Varies	12500 EA	12500 EA

DANIEL CHARD

BORN: Cande Camden, NJ; 1938
EDUCATION: Univ of South Dakota, Vermillion, SD, BFA, 1961; Columbia Univ, NY, EdD, 1975
TEACHING: Prof, Art, Glassboro State Col, NJ, 1968 to present
RECENT EXHIB: OK Harris Works of Art, NY, 1987; Tortue Gallery, Santa Monica, CA, 1988; OK South, Bay Harbor Islands, FL, 1988; Moravian Col, Payne Gallery, Bethlehem, PA, 1989,92
PRINTERS: Artist (ART)
PUBLISHERS: Orion Editions, NY (OE)
GALLERIES: OK South Works of Art, Bay Harbor Islands, FL; Orion Editions Gallery, New York, NY

TITLE	PUBLISHER	PRINTER	DATE	MEDIUM	DIMENSION (PAPER SIZE) IN INCHES	TYPE OF PAPER	EDITION NUMBER	NO. OF COLORS	ORIGINAL OPENING PRICE	CURRENT RETAIL PRICE
CURRENT EDITIONS:										
Cheney	OE	ART	1983	SP	10 X 26	AC	175	17	300	450
Toward Benson	OE	ART	1984	SP	10 X 26	AC	250	17	350	450
Turning Field	OE	ART	1984	SP	25 X 42	AC	175	22	400	850
Bird's Eye	OE	ART	1988	SP	23 X 40	AC	175	25	600	750
Twin Vistas	OE	ART	1988	SP	25 X 34	AC	175	43	600	750
Tetons	OE	ART	1989	SP	29 X 36	AC	175		850	850

SARAH E CHARLESWORTH

BORN: East Orange, NJ; March 29, 1947
EDUCATION: Barnard Col, NY, BA, 1969
TEACHING: Instr, Photography, New York Univ, NY, 1983 to present
AWARDS: Creative Artists Public Service Fel, 1977; Nat Endowment for the Arts Fel, 1980,83
RECENT EXHIB: International with Monument Gallery, NY, 1987; Editions Ilene Kurtz, NY, 1989; Queens Mus of Art, New York City Bldg, NY, 1992; Jay Gorney Mod Art, NY, 1993
COLLECTIONS: Allen Mem Art Mus, Oberlin, OH; Stedelikj Van Abbemuseum, Eindhoven, The Netherlands; Univ of California, Mus of Photography, Riverside, CA
PRINTERS: Maurice Sanchez, NY (MS); James Miller, NY (JM); Joe Petrocelli, NY (JP); Derriére L'Etoile Studios, NY (DES)
PUBLISHERS: Editions Ilene Kurtz, NY (EIK)
GALLERIES: Editions Ilene Kurtz, New York, NY; Tony Shafrazi Gallery, New York, NY; Feature, Chicago, IL; Margo Leavin Gallery, Los Angeles, CA; Jay Gorney Modern Art, New York, NY
MAILING ADDRESS: 31 Great Jones St, New York, NY 10003

Sarah E. Charlesworth
Dress MacCleod
Courtesy Editions Ilene Kurtz

TITLE	PUBLISHER	PRINTER	DATE	MEDIUM	DIMENSION (PAPER SIZE) IN INCHES	TYPE OF PAPER	EDITION NUMBER	NO. OF COLORS	ORIGINAL OPENING PRICE	CURRENT RETAIL PRICE
CURRENT EDITIONS:										
Untitled (Fabric Box) (Set of 3):									1500 SET	2500 SET
Black Steward	EIK	MS/JM/JP/DES	1986	LC	32 X 24	RCP	60		500	850
Dress MacCleod	EIK	MS/JM/JP/DES	1986	LC	32 X 24	RCP	60		500	850
MacGregor	EIK	MS/JM/JP/DES	1986	LC	32 X 24	RCP	60		500	850

LOUISA CHASE

BORN: Panama City, Panama; March 18, 1951; US Citizen
EDUCATION: Syracuse Univ, NY, BFA, 1973; Yale Univ Sch of Art, New Haven, CT, MFA, 1975
TEACHING: Instr, Rhode Island Sch of Design, Providence, RI, 1975–79; Instr, Painting, Sch of Visual Arts, NY, 1980–82
AWARDS: Creative Artists Public Service Grant, 1979–80; Nat Endowment for the Arts Grants, 1978–79, 1982–83
RECENT EXHIB: Wellesley Col, MA, 1987; Texas Gallery, Houston, TX, 1987; Metropolitan Mus of Art, NY, 1988; Brooke Alexander, Inc, NY, 1989; Newport Harbor Art Mus, Newport Beach, CA, 1992; Albrecht-Kemper Mus of Art, St Joseph, MO, 1992; Lincoln Center, Fine Art Prints, NY, 1992
COLLECTIONS: Mus of Mod Art, NY; Whitney Mus of Am Art, NY; Metropolitan Mus of Art, NY; Corcoran Gallery of Art, Wash, DC; Denver Art Mus, CO; Portland Mus of Art, ME; Univ of Massachusetts, Worcester, MA; Albright-Knox Art Gallery, Buffalo, NY; Inst of Contemp Art, Boston, MA
PRINTERS: Chip Elwell, NY (CE); Simpson Press, NY (S); Aeropress, NY (A); Patricia Branstead (PB); Sally Mara Sturman, NY (SMS); Jane Kent, NY (JK); Experimental Workshop, San Fracisco, CA (EW); Maurice Sanchez, NY (MS); James Miller, NY (JM); Derriére L'Etoile Studios, NY (DES); Heather Hoover (HH); Bill Lagattuta (BL); Peter Pettengill, Hinsdale, NY (PP); Wingate Studio, Hinsdale, NY (WS); Tamarind Inst, Albuquerque, NM (TI); Bill Weege, Madison, WI (BW); Andrew Rubin, Madison, WI (AR); Tandem Press, Univ of Wisconsin, Madison, WI (TanPr)
PUBLISHERS: Diane Villani Editions, New York, NY (DVE); Aeropress, NY (A); Simpson, NY (S); Experimental Workshop, San Francisco, CA (EW); Derriére L'Etoile Studios, NY (DES); Tamarind Inst, Albuquerque, NM (TI); Smith College, Northampton, MA (SC); Artist (ART); Brooke Alexander, Inc, NY (BAI); Tandem Press, Univ of Wisconsin, Madison, WI (TanPr)
GALLERIES: Roger Ramsay, Chicago, IL; Diane Villani Editions, New York, NY; Harcus Gallery, Boston, MA; van Straaten Gallery, Chicago, IL; Signet Arts, St. Louis, MO; Robert Miller Gallery, New York, NY; Texas Gallery, Houston, TX; Paul Cava Gallery, Phila, PA; Thomas Smith Fine Art, Fort Wayne, IN; Barbara Krakow Gallery, Boston, MA; Flanders Contemporary Art, Minneapolis, MN; Betsy Rosenfield Gallery, Chicago, IL; Tavelli Williams Gallery, Aspen, CO; Tamarind Inst, Albuquerque, NM; Brooke Alexander, Inc, New York, NY; Nohra Haime Gallery, New York, NY; Topaz Editions, Tampa, FL; Betsy Rosenfield Gallery, Chicago, IL; Richard Levy Gallery, Albuquerque, NM; Vinalhaven Press, Vinalhaven, ME
MAILING ADDRESS: 185 Lafayette St. New York, NY 10013–3219

Louisa Chase
Sleepwalker
Courtesy Tandem Press

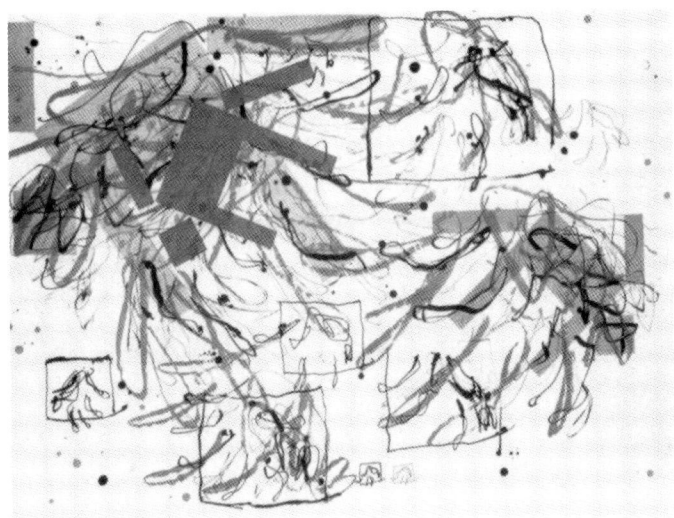

Louisa Chase
Icarus
Courtesy Tandem Press

TITLE	PUBLISHER	PRINTER	DATE	MEDIUM	DIMENSION (PAPER SIZE) IN INCHES	TYPE OF PAPER	EDITION NUMBER	NO. OF COLORS	ORIGINAL OPENING PRICE	CURRENT RETAIL PRICE
SOLD OUT EDITIONS (RARE):										
Cave	DVE/S	CE	1981	WB	36 X 48	OKP	15	1	600	3000
Squall	DVE/S	PB/A	1981	WB	39 X 48	OKP	20	1	600	3000
Dawn	DVE	CE	1982	WC	30 X 53	SEK	20	6	900	3000
Dusk	DVE	CE	1982	WC	30 X 53	SEK	20	6	900	3000
Cloudburst	DVE	CE	1982	WC	29 X 29	OKP	25	5	600	3000
Daybreak State I (Pink)	DVE	CE	1982	WC	29 X 53	SEK	20		900	3500
Daybreak State II (Grey)	DVE	CE	1982	WC	30 X 53	SEK	20		900	3500
Chasm	DVE	CE	1982	WC	26 X 30	KOZO	30	4	650	3000
Red Sea	DVE	CE	1982	WC/WA	33 X 39	DPA	25		800	3500
Thicket	DVE	CE	1983	WB	30 X 36	DPA	10	1	500	3000
Thicket	DVE	CE	1983	WC	38 X 44	DPA	25		800	3000
Untitled	DVE	SMS	1988	EB/A	30 X 33	R/BFK	25		1000	2000
CURRENT EDITIONS:										
Black Sea	DVE	CE	1983	WB	30 X 36	DPA	10	1	500	3000
Untitled (Set of 6)	DVE	SMS/JK	1984	EB/A/DPT/SB	11 X 11 EA		30 EA		1200 SET	2500 SET
Untitled (Feet)	DVE	SMS	1984	EB/A/DPT/SB	12 X 12	AC/W	25	1	500	500
Untitled (Hands)	DVE	SMS	1984	EB/A/DPT/SB	12 X 12	AC/W	25	1	500	500
Untitled (Fire)	DVE	SMS	1984	EB/A/DPT/SB	19 X 20	AC/W	30	3	600	700
Untitled (Water)	DVE	SMS	1984	EB/A/DPT/SB	19 X 15	AC/W	30	3	600	700
Fire	DVE	SMS	1984	EB/A/DPT/SB	33 X 32	AC/W	15	3	900	1500
Water	DVE	SMS	1984	EB/A/DPT/SB	34 X 28	AC/W	15	3	900	1500
Woods	DVE	SMS	1984	EB/A/DPT/SB	33 X 28	AC/W	15	3	900	1500
Untitled Small/Large (Series of 14)	EW	EW	1985	MON	21 X 19 (8) EA 31 X 25 (6) EA	R/BFK	1 EA	Varies		

LOUISA CHASE CONTINUED

TITLE	PUBLISHER	PRINTER	DATE	MEDIUM	DIMENSION (PAPER SIZE) IN INCHES	TYPE OF PAPER	EDITION NUMBER	NO. OF COLORS	ORIGINAL OPENING PRICE	CURRENT RETAIL PRICE
CURRENT EDITIONS:										
Untitled (Pink)	DVE	SMS	1985	LI	12 X 12	R/BFK	15		300	500
Untitled (Blue)	DVE	SMS	1985	LI	12 X 12	R/BFK	15		300	500
Untitled (Yellow)	DVE	SMS	1985	LI	12 X 12	R/BFK	15		300	500
Woods	DVE	SMS	1985	EB/A	22 X 23	R/BFK	15		700	800
Nightfall	DVE	SMS	1985	EB/A	25 X 23	R/BFK	15		700	800
Untitled	DVE	SMS	1985	EB/A	17 X 15	R/BFK	15		600	600
Untitled	DVE	SMS	1985	EB/A	12 X 12	R/BFK	15		450	450
Spooks	DVE	SMS	1986–87	LC	30 X 45	RNP/G	40		1200	1200
Red Mountain	ART/DES	MS/JM/DES	1986–87	LC	45 X 30	R/BFK/G	40	3	1200	1200
Untitled	DVE	SMS	1988	EB/A	27 X 23	R/BFK	25		1000	1200
Untitled	DVE	SMS	1988	EB/A	23 X	R/BFK	25		1000	1200
Untitled (Mountains)	TI	HH/BL/TI	1988	LC	24 X 39	SEK	35	5	800	800
Untitled	TI	HH/BL/TI	1988	LC	22 X 28	R/BFK	24	5	600	600
Untitled (Set of 3):										
Hands	DVE	JM	1990	AB/SG/SL/SL/CC	36 X 51	SOM	30	2–3	2500	2500
Head	DVE	JM	1990	AB/SG/SL/SL/CC	36 X 51	SOM	30	2–3	2500	2500
Feet	DVE	JM	1990	AB/SG/SL/SL/CC	51 X 36	SOM	30	2–3	2500	2500
Baby, Baby	BAI		1991	EB/SL/SG/SB/LIN	29 X 32	SOM	35	1	1200	1200
Oedipus	BAI		1991	EB/SL/SG/SB/LIN	33 X 28	SOM	35	1	1200	1200
Sleepwalker	TanPr	BW/AR/TanPr	1991	LC/REL	30 X 40	AC/W	40	5	1500	1500
Headstand	TanPr	BW/AR/TanPr	1991	LC/REL	30 X 40	AC/W	40	5	1500	1500
Icarus	TanPr	BW/AR/TanPr	1991	LC/REL	30 X 40	AC/W	40	5	1500	1500

MIHAIL CHEMIAKIN

BORN: Moscow, Russia; 1943
EDUCATION: Ecole de Peinture Repine, Moscow, Russia, 1957-59
AWARDS: First Prize, Concours Nichido, Paris, France, 1975
PRINTERS: Grapholith, Paris, France (GRAPH)
PUBLISHERS: Alliance Art Publishing, Hayward, WI (AAP)
GALLERIES: Bowles-Sorokko Galleries, Beverly Hills, CA & San Francisco, CA & Soho, NY; Sloane Gallery of Art, Denver, CO

TITLE	PUBLISHER	PRINTER	DATE	MEDIUM	DIMENSION (PAPER SIZE) IN INCHES	TYPE OF PAPER	EDITION NUMBER	NO. OF COLORS	ORIGINAL OPENING PRICE	CURRENT RETAIL PRICE
SOLD OUT EDITIONS (RARE):										
Les Baladins			1977	LC	30 X 21	AP			100	500
Composition Allegorique				LC	22 X 30	AP			100	600
Formes				LC	30 X 22	AP			100	600
Le Masque				LC	21 X 30	AP			100	500
Le Rére des Fruits				LC	28 X 20	AP			100	500
Russian Lovers (Female)				LC	29 X 20	AP			100	750
Russian Lovers (Male)				LC	29 X 20	AP			100	750
Russian Couple				LB	24 X 17	AP	225	1	75	600
Three Faces of Nyjinsky				LC	36 X 26	AP	225		100	750
CURRENT EDITIONS:										
Carnival at St. Petersburg (Set of 3):									600 SET	6000 SET
Famille	AAP	GRAPH	1977	LC	18 X 20	AP	225	10	250	3200
Mauve Harlequin	AAP	GRAPH	1977	LC	18 X 20	AP	225	8	250	3200
Fez Rouge	AAP	GRAPH	1977	LC	18 X 20	AP	225	8	250	3200
Carnival at St. Petersburg (Set of 3):									950 SET	6500 SET
Famille	AAP	GRAPH	1977	LC	18 X 20	JP	75	10	350	5500
Mauve Harlequin	AAP	GRAPH	1977	LC	18 X 20	JP	75	8	350	3500
Fez Rouge	AAP	GRAPH	1977	LC	18 X 20	JP	75	8	350	3500
Carnival in St. Petersburg (Set of 5):									SET	10000 SET
Magician	AAP	GRAPH	1988	LC	30 X 21	AP	250	10		5250
Gendarme with Black Hat	AAP	GRAPH	1988	LC	30 X 21	AP	250	10		5250
Mirror Image	AAP	GRAPH	1988	LC	30 X 21	AP	250	6		5250
Harlequin Right	AAP	GRAPH	1988	LC	30 X 21	AP	250	8		5250
Harlequin Left	AAP	GRAPH	1988	LC	30 X 21	AP	250	12		5250
Carnival in St. Petersburg (Set of 5):										10500 SET
Magician	AAP	GRAPH	1988	LC	30 X 21	JP	75	10		5500
Gendarme with Black Hat	AAP	GRAPH	1988	LC	30 X 21	JP	75	10		5500
Mirror Image	AAP	GRAPH	1988	LC	30 X 21	JP	75	6		5500
Harlequin Right	AAP	GRAPH	1988	LC	30 X 21	JP	75	8		5500
Harlequin Left	AAP	GRAPH	1988	LC	30 X 21	JP	75	12		5500

The retail prices of the 100,000 limited edition prints quoted in this directory are subject to change. Print publishers, artists and galleries were the direct sources for these quotations. Prices in the secondary market listed as "Sold Out Editions (Rare)" indicate that the publisher has a limited supply of that print or that the print is difficult to locate in the galleries.

IVAN CHERMAYEFF

BORN: London, England; June 6, 1932; U S Citizen
EDUCATION: Harvard Univ, Cambridge, MA, 1950–52; Inst of Design, Illinois Inst of Tech, Moholy-Nagy Scholar, 1952–54; Yale Univ Sch of Design, New Haven, CT, BFA, 1955
TEACHING: Instr, Design, Brooklyn Col, NY, 1956–57; Instr, Design, Sch of Visual Arts, NY, 1959–65; Andrew Carnegie Prof, Design, Cooper Univ, NY; Joyce C Hall, Distinguished Prof, Kansas City Art Inst, MO

AWARDS: Industrial Arts Medal, Am Inst of Architects, 1967; President's Fel Award, Rhode Island Sch of Design, Providene Providence, RI, 1981; Yale Arts Medal, New Haven, CT, 1985
PRINTERS: Serigrafia Limited, NY (SER)
PUBLISHERS: Serigrafia Limited, NY (SER)
MAILING ADDRESS: 15 E 26th St, New York, NY 10010

TITLE	PUBLISHER	PRINTER	DATE	MEDIUM	DIMENSION (PAPER SIZE) IN INCHES	TYPE OF PAPER	EDITION NUMBER	NO. OF COLORS	ORIGINAL OPENING PRICE	CURRENT RETAIL PRICE
CURRENT EDITIONS:										
Innocent Japanese Person	SER	SER	1990	SP	21 X 29	AC	125	15	750	850
Smoker	SER	SER	1990	SP	21 X 29	AC	125		750	850

ANN CHERNOW

BORN: New York, NY; February 1, 1936
EDUCATION: Syracuse Univ, NY, MA, Painting, 1953–55; New York Univ, NY, 1966–69
TEACHING: Mus of Mod Art, NY, 1966–71; Silvermine Guild & Col of Art, NY, 1968–80; Head, Art Dept, Norwalk Com Col, 1981 to present
AWARDS: Fel, Painting, State of Connecticut, 1980–81; Purchase Award, Lithography, Hudson River Mus, NY, 1987; Award, Lithography, Philadelphia Print Club, PA, 1988; Award, Etching, Albany Print Club, NY, 1990; Purchase Award, Univ of Mississippi, University, MS, Nat Works on Paper, 1990
RECENT EXHIB: UFO Gallery, Provincetown, MA, 1988; Munson Gallery, New Haven, CT, 1988; Uptown Gallery, NY, 1989; Stanford Mus, Leonhardt Galleries, CT, 1992
COLLECTIONS: Elvehjem Mus of Art, Madison, WI; Rose Art Mus, Brandeis Univ, Waltham, MA; New York Public Library, NY; Nat Mus of Women in the Arts, Wash, DC; Rutgers Univ, Newark, NJ; Utah Mus of Fine Arts, Salt Lake City, UT; Mattatuck Mus of Art, CT; Hofstra Univ, Hempstead, NY; Stamford Mus, CT; Univ of Arizona, Tucson, AZ; Bruce Mus, Greenwich, CT; Mus of Contemp Art, Skopje, Yugoslavia; Lehigh Univ, Bethlehem, PA; St Mary's of Maryland Coll, MD; Bicentennial Coll, Town of Westport, CT
PRINTERS: Miguel Herrera, NY (MH); Lone Town Press, Redding, CT (LTP); Sophie Acheson (SA); Mauro Guiffreda, NY (MG); Joe Petruzelli, NY (JP); Jon Cone, East Topsham, VT (JC); Milestone Press (MP); Old Lyme Art Works, CT (OLAW); Silvermine Press, New Canaan, CT (SilP); Michael Edge, NY (ME (ME); Sirocco Press, NY (SirPr); Deli Sacilotto, NY (DS)
PUBLISHERS: Connecticut Fine Arts, Westport, CT (ConFA); Old Lyme Art Works, CT (OB) (OLAW); Collectors Press, Greenwich, CT (OB) (CPr)
GALLERIES: Connecticut Fine Arts Gallery, Westport, CT; Uptown Gallery, New York, NY; Virginia Lust Gallery, New York, NY; Universal Fine Objects Gallery, Providence, MA
MAILING ADDRESS: c/o Connecticut Fine Arts, 2 Gorham Ave, Westport, CT 06880

TITLE	PUBLISHER	PRINTER	DATE	MEDIUM	DIMENSION (PAPER SIZE) IN INCHES	TYPE OF PAPER	EDITION NUMBER	NO. OF COLORS	ORIGINAL OPENING PRICE	CURRENT RETAIL PRICE
SOLD OUT EDITIONS (RARE):										
Les Amies	ConFA	ME	1976	SP	26 X 30	DOM	75	5	150	400
One Flew Out of the Cuckoo's Nest	ConFA	ME	1976	SP	24 X 22	DOM	75	5	150	300
There, I've Said It Again I	ConFA	SilPr	1978	LB	30 X 22	AP/B	7	1	200	500
There, I've Said It Again II	ConFA	SilPr	1978	LB	30 X 22	AP	20	1	200	300
Tenderly	ConFA	SilPr	1978	LB		AP/B	14	1	85	200
Subjects and Objects (Set of 8)	ConFA	SA	1978	EB	15 X 11 EA	AP	12 EA	1 EA	800 SET 150 EA	1500 SET 200 EA
Music Makes Me	ConFA	SilPr	1978	LB		AP/B	11	1	85	200
Emmaline	ConFA	SA	1978	AB	7 X 5	AP/B	6	1	150	500
No, No, A Thousand Times No (Dipt)	ConFA	SilPr	1979	LB	24 X 18	AP/GE	6	1	200	400
Annie's Soda Fountain #1	ConFA	SilPr	1979	LB	18 X 26	AP	11	1	150	500
Annie's Soda Fountain #2	ConFA	JP	1980	LC	20 X 30	AP	60	3	200	500
By the Sea	ConFA	JP	1980	LC	22 X 30	AP/B	60	4	300	500
Coffee and a Roll	ConFA	JP	1980	LC	22 X 30	AP	30		200	300
Queen Aminatare	ConFA	MP	1982	LC	18 X 24	AP	6	3	200	400
Let Em Eat Cake	ConFA	DS	1982	EB/GRA/HC	8 X 10	AP	6	Varies	150	350
Dial 227-1743	ConFA	MG	1986	LB	20 X 16	AP	175	1	150	300
The Cafeteria	ConFA	JC	1987	DPT/GRA/HC	12 X 24	AP	11	1	450	600
CURRENT EDITIONS:										
Star Series:										
Casseopaiea	ConFA	SirPr	1976–77	SP	30 X 20	CoP	50	2	200	400
Gemini	ConFA	SirPr	1976–77	SP	30 X 20	CoP	50	2	200	400
Ursa Major	ConFA	SirPr	1976–77	SP	30 X 20	CoP	50	2	200	400
Cygnus	ConFA	SirPr	1976–77	SP	30 X 20	CoP	50	2	200	400
Hercules	ConFA	SirPr	1976–77	SP	30 X 20	CoP	50	2	200	400
Welcome to My Dreams	ConFA	SilPr	1978	LB	18 X 24	AP	10	1	200	300
Always True to You in My Fashion	ConFA	SilPr	1979	LB	18 X 24	AP	20	1	200	200
I Get Along without You Very Well	ConFA	JP	1979	LB	30 X 22	AP	75	1	200	200
The Heart is Quicker than the Eye	ConFA	MP	1980	LB	18 X 24	AP	50	1	200	300
On the Atchison, Topeka & Santa Fe	ConFA	MP	1980	LB	18 X 24	AP	60	1	200	300
Three on a Match	ConFA	DS	1980	EB/GRA	11 X 15	AP	30	1	150	250
In the Still of the Night	ConFA	JP	1980	LB	22 X 30	AP	75	2	200	400
Two Cents Plain	ConFA	MP	1981	LB	18 X 24	AP	50	1	200	300
Three Little Girls	ConFA	DS	1982	EB/GRA/HC	7 X 9	AP	10	Varies	150	350
Yesterdays	ConFA	SA	1983	EB/HC	17 X 16	AP	25	Varies	200	350
Paper Moon	ConFA	SA	1983	EB/HC	17 X 16	AP	12	Varies	200	350

ANN CHERNOW CONTINUED

TITLE	PUBLISHER	PRINTER	DATE	MEDIUM	DIMENSION (PAPER SIZE) IN INCHES	TYPE OF PAPER	EDITION NUMBER	NO. OF COLORS	ORIGINAL OPENING PRICE	CURRENT RETAIL PRICE
CURRENT EDITIONS:										
Hooray for Hollywood	ConFA	SA	1984	LB	30 X 22	AP	37	1	200	200
The Letter	ConFA	SA	1984	LB	22 X 30	AP	32	1	200	300
Legacy	ConFA	OLAW	1985	LC	26 X 38	SOM	50	2	325	400
Music, Music, Music	ConFA	JP	1985	LC	22 X 30	AP	43	3	300	300
Ten Cents a Dance	ConFA	MG	1986	LB	25 X 35	AP	68	1	300	300
Beach I, II	ConFA	MG	1986	LB	27 X 19 EA	AP	55 EA	1 EA	350 SET 200 EA	350 SET 200 EA
Shuffle off to Buffalo	ConFA	LTP	1987	LB	22 X 29	SOM/W	55 EA	1 EA	300	400
Can You Spell Schenectady?	ConFA	LTP	1988	LC	23 X 30	AP/B	47	1	400	400
Fair and Warmer	ConFA	LTP	1989	LC	23 X 30	R/BFK/CR	48	1	400	400
Time after Time	ConFA	MG	1989	LC/HC	22 X 30	AP	56	Varies	350	400
Orders	ConFA	SA	1989	EB/HC	8 X 6		8	Varies	250	350
Seems Like Old Times	ConFA	LTP	1990	LB	24 X 30	SOM	28	1	400	400
Suite of Etchings (Set of 9):									1500 SET	1500 SET
Apples and Stripes	ConFA	SA	1990	EB/DPT/HC	4 X 2	AP	5	Varies	200	200
Interlude	ConFA	SA	1990	EB/DPT/HC	4 X 2	AP	5	Varies	200	200
Conversation	ConFA	SA	1990	EB/DPT/HC	4 X 2	AP	5	Varies	200	200
Sore Feet	ConFA	SA	1990	EB/DPT/HC	4 X 2	AP	5	Varies	200	200
Checks and Balances	ConFA	SA	1990	EB/DPT/HC	4 X 2	AP	5	Varies	200	200
Par	ConFA	SA	1990	EB/DPT/HC	4 X 2	AP	5	Varies	200	200
Coctails for Two	ConFA	SA	1990	EB/DPT/HC	4 X 2	AP	5	Varies	200	200
Boa	ConFA	SA	1990	EB/DPT/HC	4 X 2	AP	5	Varies	200	200
The Flowered Dress	ConFA	SA	1990	EB/DPT/HC	4 X 2	AP	5	Varies	200	200
Reverie (Set of 10)	ConFA	MH	1990	EB/HC	15 X 11 EA	FolAn	20	Varies	500 SET	500 SET

CHEN CHI

BORN: Wu-sih, China; May 2, 1912
TEACHING: Inst, Watercolor, St Johns Univ, Shanghai, China, 1942–46; Vis Prof, Watercolor, Pennsylvania State Univ, University Park, PA, 1959–60; Art in Res, Ogden City Schools, UT, 1967
AWARDS: Nat Inst of Arts & Letters Grant for Creative Work in Art, 1960; Samuel Finley Breese Mose Medal, 1961; Nat Acad of Design, 1969; Gold Medal, Am Watercolor Soc, Benjamin West Clinedirst Fel, 1976; Edmund Greacen, Nat Art Honor Award; Award, Nat Acad of Design 1982
COLLECTIONS: Metropolitan Mus, NY; Pennsylvania Acad of Fine Arts, Phila, PA; Butler Inst of Am Art, Youngstown, OH; Fort Worth Art Mus, TX; Charles & Emma Frye Art Mus, Seattle, WA
RECENT EXHIB: Butler Inst of Am Art, Youngstown, OH, 1990
PRINTERS: The American Atelier, NY (AA)
PUBLISHERS: Circle Gallery, Ltd, Chicago, IL (CGL)
GALLERIES: Grand Central Galleries, New York, NY; Hartley Hills Gallery, Gallery, Carmel by the Sea, CA; Circle Galleries, San Diego, CA & San Francisco, CA & Northbrook, IL & Pittsburgh, PA & Houston, TX & Soho, NY & Chicago, IL & Scottsdale, AZ & Beverly Hills, CA & Costa Mesa, CA & Sherman Oaks, CA & Palm Beach, FL & Honolulu, HI & New Orleans, LA & Las Vegas, NV & Seattle, WA
MAILING ADDRESS: 23 Washington Square, North, New York, NY 10011

TITLE	PUBLISHER	PRINTER	DATE	MEDIUM	DIMENSION (PAPER SIZE) IN INCHES	TYPE OF PAPER	EDITION NUMBER	NO. OF COLORS	ORIGINAL OPENING PRICE	CURRENT RETAIL PRICE
SOLD OUT EDITIONS (RARE):										
Spring	CGL	AA	1976	LC	22 X 29	AP	300	11	175	900
Summer	CGL	AA	1976	LC	21 X 30	AP	30	13	160	900
CURRENT EDITIONS:										
Spring Blossom	CGL	AA	1982	LC	52 X 26	AP	300	3	475	1100
Spring Blossom (Deluxe)	CGL	AA	1982	LC	52 X 26	HMP	100	3	550	1200
Autumn Forest	CGL	AA	1982	LC	52 X 26	AP	300	3	475	1100
Autumn Forest (Deluxe)	CGL	AA	1982	LC	52 X 26	HMP	100	3	550	1200

SANDRO CHIA

BORN: Florence, Italy; 1946
RECENT EXHIB: Daniel Templon Gallery, Paris, France, 1988; Sperone Westwater Gallery, NY, 1987,90; Yoshimitsu Hijikata Gallery, Nagoya, Japan, 1990; Palazzo Medici, Florence, Italy, 1992; Univ of Florida, Graphicstudio, Tampa, FL, 1992; Galerie Thaddeus Ropac, Paris, France, 1993
PRINTERS: Aeropress, NY (A); Patricia Branstead, NY (PB); Stamperia d'Arte Grafica Studio, Rome, Italy (SGS); Editions Schellmann & Klüser, Munich, Germany & New York, NY (SK); Felix Harlan, NY (FH); Carol Weaver, NY (CW); Francesco Copello, NY (FC); Michael Caza, Francoville, France (MC); Harlan-Weaver, NY (HW); Sarah Feigenbaum, NY (SF); Michele Pisa, NY (MP); Susan Steinbrock, NY (SS); American Atelier, NY (AA)
PUBLISHERS: Metropolitan Museum of Art Limited Editions, NY (MMA); Peter Blum Edition, NY (PBE); Editions Schellmann & Klüser, NY & Cologne, Germany (ESK); Raymond Foye Editions, NY (RFE); Circle Fine Art, Ltd, Chicago, IL (CFA)
GALLERIES: James Corcoran Gallery, Santa Monica, CA; Sperone Westwater Gallery, New York, NY; Metropolitan Mus of Art, New York, NY; Brody's Gallery, Wash, DC; Harcus Gallery, Boston, MA; Magnuson Gallery, Boston, MA; Editions Schellmann Gallery, New York, NY & Munich, Germany; Barbara Krakow Gallery, Boston, MA; Nicola Jacobs Gallery, London, England; Thaddaus Ropac Galerie, Salzburg, Austria; Daniel Templon Gallery, Paris, France; Walton Street Gallery, Chicago, IL; Signet Arts, St Louis, MO; Dorsky Gallery, New York, NY; Figura, Inc, New York, NY; Nohra Haime Gallery, New York, NY; Lillian Heidenberg Gallery, New York, NY; Schlesinger Gallery, New York, NY; Circle Galleries, Chicago, IL & New York, NY & Pittsburgh, PA & Houston, TX & Northbrook, IL & San Diego, CA; Zoe Gallery, Boston, MA; Signet Arts, St Louis, MO; Bonnier Gallery, New York, NY; Galerie Thaddeus Ropac, Paris, France
MAILING ADDRESS: 521 W 23rd St, New York, NY 10011

SANDRO CHIA CONTINUED

Sandro Chia
Two Boys on a Raft
Courtesy Edition Schellmann

Sandro Chia
Boy and His Double
Courtesy Edition Schellmann

TITLE	PUBLISHER	PRINTER	DATE	MEDIUM	DIMENSION (PAPER SIZE) IN INCHES	TYPE OF PAPER	EDITION NUMBER	NO. OF COLORS	ORIGINAL OPENING PRICE	CURRENT RETAIL PRICE
SOLD OUT EDITIONS (RARE):										
Il Trovatore	CFA	AA	1976	LC	30 X 22	AP	250	8	500	2600
Manuale de Aprile	PBE	A/PB	1981	EB/A/DPT	30 X 22	AP/B	50	1	2200 SET	10000 SET
(April Mannval (Set of 5):										
L'Artificio (The Artifice)										
alla Torre (to the Tower)										
Circa L'Imprendible										
(About the Unseizable)										
L'Anima-Buona (A Good Soul)										
E Gli Eroi alla Finestra										
(And the Horses at the Window)										
Children's Holiday (6 Panels)	CFA	AA	1984	LC	77 X 71	SOM/W	75	50	4500	24000
Ragazzo Coraggioso										
(Courageous Boy)	MMA	SGS	1982	EB/A/DPT	20 X 14	FAB	40	1	500	2500
Two Boys on a Raft	ESK	SS/CW/HW	1982	EB/A/CC	23 X 27	SOM	30	3	1500	2500
Mechanical Figures I,II (Set of 2)	ESK	FH/CW/HW	1983	PH/EC/DPT/CC	30 X 23	SOM/CR	15	2	1000	4500
Figure Looking Out	ESK	SF/MP	1983	EB/CC	30 X 22	STP/W	25	1	1000	2500
Man and Vegetation	ESK	FH/CW/HW	1983	EB/DPT	32 X 23	PP/HMP	15	1	1000	3000
Man and Vegetation	ESK	FH/CW/HW	1983	EB/SG	48 X 32	AC	25	1	1000	3500
Boy and his Double	ESK	FH/CW/HW	1983	EB/SG	48 X 32	AC/W	25	1	1000	4000
Sandro Chia/Gregory Corso:										
Five Etchings (Set of 5)	RFE	FC	1986	EC	40 X 30 EA	FAB	70 EA	2 EA	6000 SET	13500 SET
Father and Son Song	RFE	FC	1987	WC	06 X 71	FAB	12		10000	25000
Explorers Suite	CFA	AA	1989	LC		SOM/W	75 EA			10700 SET
Man with Dog	CFA	AA	1989	LC	34 X 24	SOM/W	75		1200	3750
Portrait	CFA	AA	1989	LC	33 X 24	SOM/W	75	23	1200	3750
Torso	CFA	AA	1989	LC	36 X 20	SOM/W	75	20	1200	3500
Sentimental Figure	CFA	AA	1989	LC	33 X 24	SOM/W	75	14	1200	2750
Topo	CFA	AA	1989	LC	34 X 21	SOM/W	75	12	1200	2750
Alchemist's Accident	CFA	AA	1990	LC	29 X 25	SOM/W	75	13	1200	3500
Mosquito Hunter	CFA	AA	1990	LC	31 X 26	SOM/W	75	17	1200	5200
Interior with Dog	CFA	AA	1990	LC	29 X 25	SOM/W	75	17	1200	3000
Dancing Figures	CFA	AA	1990	LC	34 X 25	SOM/W	75	17	1200	2750
Lonely Explorer	CFA	AA	1990	LC	29 X 26	SOM/W	75	14	1200	3500
Southern Comfort	CFA	AA	1990	LC	29 X 26	SOM/W	75	16	1200	3300
Bread and Wine	CFA	AA	1991	LC	29 X 25	SOM/W	75		1500	3400
Outdoor Scene	CFA	AA	1991	LC	39 X 25	SOM/W	75		1500	3150
Water Bearer	CFA	AA	1991	LC	31 X 25	SOM/W	75		1500	3600

The retail prices of the 100,000 limited edition prints quoted in this directory are subject to change. Print publishers, artists and galleries were the direct sources for these quotations. Prices in the secondary market listed as "Sold Out Editions (Rare)" indicate that the publisher has a limited supply of that print or that the print is difficult to locate in the galleries.

JUDY CHICAGO

BORN: Chicago, IL; July 20, 1939
EDUCATION: Univ of California, Los Angeles, CA, BA, 1962; MA, 1964
TEACHING: Instr, Feminist Studio Workshop, 1973–74; Asst Prof, California State Univ, 1969–71
AWARDS: Ind Art Grant, 1976; Service to the Field Grant, 1977; Nat Endowment for the Arts, 1984
RECENT EXHIB: Nat Mus of Women in the Arts, Wash, DC, 1989,92; Florida State Univ Gallery, Tallahassee, Fl, 1992; Univ of Wisconsin, Carlsten Art Gallery, Stevens Point, WI, 1992
PRINTERS: Mary Sundstrom (MS); Cirrus Editions Workshop, Los Angeles, CA (CEW); Jim Kraft, Albuquerque, NM (JK); Unified Arts, Albuquerque, NM (AU)
PUBLISHERS: Cirrus Editions, Ltd, Los Angeles, CA (CE); ACA Galleries, NY (ACA)
GALLERIES: Cirrus Editions, Ltd, Los Angeles, CA; ACA Galleries, New York, NY; Wallace Wentworth Galleries, Wash, DC

TITLE	PUBLISHER	PRINTER	DATE	MEDIUM	DIMENSION (PAPER SIZE) IN INCHES	TYPE OF PAPER	EDITION NUMBER	NO. OF COLORS	ORIGINAL OPENING PRICE	CURRENT RETAIL PRICE
CURRENT EDITIONS:										
Mary, Queen of Scots	CE	MS/CEW	1973	LC	25 X 25	CP	40	Multi	250	1200
The Birth Project (Set of 5):									4000 SET	7000 SET
Guided by the Goddess	ACA	JK/UA	1985	SP	30 X 40	R/BFK/G	75	16	900	1500
Earth Birth	ACA	JK/UA	1985	SP	30 X 40	AP/B	75	10	900	1500
Birth Tear/Tear	ACA	JK/UA	1985	SP	30 X 40	STP/W	75	24	900	1500
Birth Trinity	ACA	JK/UA	1985	SP	30 X 40	STP/W	75	22	900	1500
The Creation	ACA	JK/UA	1985	SP	30 X 40	AP/B	75	45	900	1500

EDUARDO CHILLIDA

BORN: San Sebastian, Spain; 1924
EDUCATION: Univ of Madrid, Spain, 1943–47
AWARDS: First Prize, Venice Int Biennale, Venice, Italy, 1958; Kandinsky Prize, 1960; Wilhelm-Lehmbruck Prize, 1966; Nordhein-Westfalen Prize, 1966; Andrew W Mellon Prize, 1978
RECENT EXHIB: Galeria Joan Prats, Barcelona, Spain, 1987; Sidney Janis Gallery, NY, 1990
COLLECTIONS: Carnegie Inst, Pittsburgh, PA; Nat Gallery of Art, Wash, DC; Stedelijk Mus, Amsterdam, Netherlands; Künsthalle, Basel, Switzerland; Mus des Beaux-Arts, Zürich, Switzerland; Neue Pinakothek, Munich, Germany; Mus of f Fine Arts, Houston, TX; Stäatlische Künsthalle, Baden-Baden, Germany; Konstsalongen Samlaren, Stockholm, Sweden
PRINTERS: Maeght Editeur, Paris, France (ME); La Poligrafa, Barcelona, Spain (LP)
PUBLISHERS: Maeght Editions, Paris, France (ME); Ediciones Poligrafa, SA, Barcelona, Spain (EdP)
GALLERIES: Galerie Lelong, New York, NY & Paris, France & Zürich, Switzerland; Galeria Joan Prats, New York, NY & Barcelona, Spain; Tasende Gallery, La Jolla, CA; Mary-Anne Martin Gallery, New York, NY; Adams-Middleton Gallery, Dallas, TX; Sidney Janis Gallery, New York, NY; BenedicteSaxe Gallery, Maeght Editions, Beverly Hills, CA; Nancy Singer Gallery, St Louis, MO

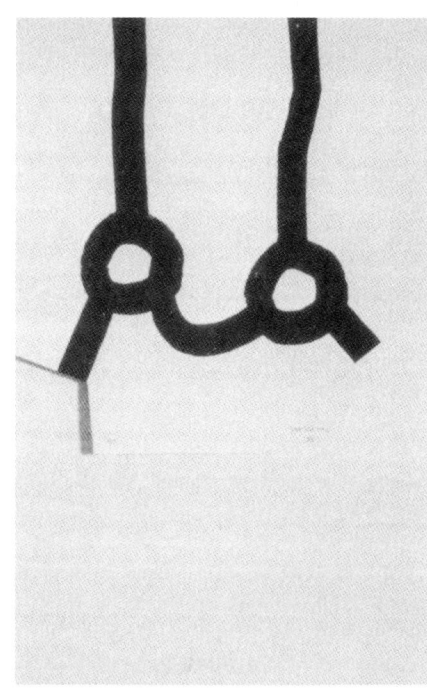

Eduardo Chillida
A L Joan Prats
Courtesy Ediciones Poligrafa, SA

TITLE	PUBLISHER	PRINTER	DATE	MEDIUM	DIMENSION (PAPER SIZE) IN INCHES	TYPE OF PAPER	EDITION NUMBER	NO. OF COLORS	ORIGINAL OPENING PRICE	CURRENT RETAIL PRICE
SOLD OUT EDITIONS (RARE):										
Eldu	ME	ME	1971	EB	9 X 5	AP	60	1	50	1500
Main IX	ME	ME	1973	EC	20 X 15	AP	50		100	1500
Main XI	ME	ME	1973	EC	16 X 20	AP	50		100	1500
Main XII	ME	ME	1973	EC	19 X 15	AP	50		100	1500
Suzmur	ME	ME	1974	EC	15 X 12	AP	50		125	1500
Enda II	ME	ME	1974	EC	26 X 20	AP	50		150	1500
Enda III	ME	ME	1974	EC	26 X 20	AP	50		150	1500
Enda IV	ME	ME	1974	EC	24 X 16	AP	50		125	1500
Bois III	EdP	LP	1974	WB	13 X 10	RBP	75	1	300	1500
Homentage a Joan Prats	EdP	LP	1975	WB	19 X 21	LFP	100	1	400	1800
Enda VII	ME	ME	1976	EC	10 X 10	AP	50		100	1000
Esku XIV	ME	ME	1976	EC	30 X 23	AP	30		400	2000
Esku XV	ME	ME	1976	EC	30 X 22	AP	50		400	2000
Esku XVI	ME	ME	1976	EC	24 X 20	AP	30		400	2000
Esku XVII	ME	ME	1977	EB/DPT	30 X 22	AP	50	1	300	2000
Esku XXIII	ME	ME	1977	AB	24 X 18	AP	50	1	300	1500
Esku XXIV	ME	ME	1977	EC	21 X 14	AP	50		300	1500
Esku XXV	ME	ME	1977	EC	24 X 18	AP	50		450	1500
Ze V	ME	ME	1977	EC	16 X 23	AP	50		500	1500

EDUARDO CHILLIDA CONTINUED

TITLE	PUBLISHER	PRINTER	DATE	MEDIUM	DIMENSION (PAPER SIZE) IN INCHES	TYPE OF PAPER	EDITION NUMBER	NO. OF COLORS	ORIGINAL OPENING PRICE	CURRENT RETAIL PRICE
SOLD OUT EDITIONS (RARE):										
Leku IV	ME	ME	1977	EC	29 X 41	AP	50		400	2000
Aundi I	ME	ME	1977	EC	47 X 63	AP	50		400	2000
Adikaitz	ME	ME	1977	EC	26 X 21	AP	50		400	1500
Main II	ME	ME	1977	EC	19 X 15	AP	50		500	1200
Kate III	ME	ME	1977	EC	26 X 20	AP	50		400	1500
Egitura	ME	ME	1977	EC	42 X 30	AP	50		400	2000
Burni Bizitu II	ME	ME	1977	EC	27 X 23	AP	50		400	1500
Luze	ME	ME	1977	EC	20 X 17	AP	50		400	1200
Irtezin	ME	ME	1977	EC	13 X 12	AP	50		125	1000
Txerto	ME	ME	1977	EC	26 X 20	AP	50		250	1500
Bidegin	ME	ME	1977	EC	30 X 22	AP	50		300	1800
Itzaure	ME	ME	1977	EC	25 X 20	AP	50		250	1800
Zur II	ME	ME	1977	EC	15 X 12	AP	50		150	800
Zur III	ME	ME	1977	EC	15 X 12	AP	50		150	1000
Atzapar	ME	ME	1977	EC	31 X 24	AP	50		300	1500
Zeartu I	ME	ME	1977	EC	31 X 24	AP	50		300	1500
Zeartu II	ME	ME	1977	EC	36 X 31	AP	50		300	1500
Zeartu III	ME	ME	1977	EC	24 X 24	AP	50		350	1500
Zeartu IV	ME	ME	1977	EC	31 X 24	AP	50		300	1500
Zeartu VI	ME	ME	1977	EC	30 X 24	AP	50		300	1500
Bi Esku	ME	ME	1978	EC	16 X 12	AP	50		300	1000
Gogai	ME	ME	1978	EC	19 X 16	AP	50		150	1000
Barenean	ME	ME	1978	EC	18 X 14	AP	50		150	1000
Ernemindu	ME	ME	1978	EC	21 X 16	AP	50		150	1000
Evzkadi I	ME	ME	1978	EC	54 X 38	AP	50		350	2000
Evzkadi II	ME	ME	1978	EC	54 X 38	AP	50		350	2000
Evzkadi III	ME	ME	1978	EC	54 X 38	AP	50		350	2000
Evzkadi VI	ME	ME	1978	EC	55 X 37	AP	50		350	2000
Main VIII	ME	ME	1978	EC	19 X 16	AP	50		250	1000
Bi Esku II	ME	ME	1978	EC	30 X 23	AP	25		300	1500
Euzkadi IV	ME	ME	1978	EC	63 X 46	AP	50		450	2000
Gudari Txiki	ME	ME	1979	EC	19 X 15	AP	50		250	1500
Zur IV	ME	ME	1979	EC	9 X 9	AP	50		125	800
Homenaje a Guillen II	ME	ME	1979	EC	17 X 13	AP	50		250	900
Emparantza II	ME	ME	1981	EB	20 X 25	R/BFK	50	1	300	1000
Emparantza III	ME	ME	1981	EB	26 X 20	R/BFK	50	1	300	1000
Emparantza IV	ME	ME	1981	EB	26 X 20	R/BFK	50	1	300	1000
Ozendu	ME	ME	1981	EB	26 X 20	R/BFK	50	1	300	1000
Bidearte I	ME	ME	1981	EB	30 X 21	R/BFK	45	1	350	1000
Bidearte II	ME	ME	1981	EB	30 X 21	R/BFK	45	1	350	1000
Emparantza V	ML	ML	1982	EB	30 X 21	R/BFK	50	1	350	1000
Bi Esku III	ML	ML	1982	EB	10 X 10	MDL	50	1	200	800
Emparantza I	ML	ML	1982	EB	30 X 21	R/BFK	50	1	350	1200
Bideak	ML	ML	1982	EB	29 X 21	R/BFK	50	1	350	1200
Esku XVIII	ML	ML	1982	EB	21 X 17	LFP	50	1	300	1200
Esku XX	ML	ML	1982	EB	11 X 8	AP	50	1	200	1000
Esku XXI	ML	ML	1982	EB	21 X 15	R/BFK	50	1	300	1200
Esku XXVI	ML	ML	1982	EB	26 X 20	R/BFK	50	1	350	1200
Homenaje a Rosalio de Castro	ML	ML	1982	EB	26 X 20	R/BFK	50	1	350	1200
Homenaje a Gabriel Aresti	ML	ML	1982	EB	26 X 20	R/BFK	50	1	350	1200
Zalantzan Egon	ML	ML	1983	EB	8 X 5	AUV	50	1	200	800
Hildokatu III	ML	ML	1983	EB	46 X 31	AP	50	1	450	2000
Gogortasun Bat	ML	ML	1983	EB	6 X 8	AUV	30	1	250	800
Gogortasun Bi	ML	ML	1983	EB	5 X 8	AUV	20	1	250	800
Irudin	ML	ML	1984	EB	8 X 5	AP	50	1	250	1200
CURRENT EDITIONS:										
Lithograph AL Joan Prats (On Special Brown Paper)	EdP	LP	1987	LC	30 X 20	Brown	99	1	900	1000
Bikaina VII	EdP	LP	1987	EB	30 X 21	RP	50	1	1000	1200
Bikaina VI, VIII, IX, X	EdP	LP	1987	EB	26 X 20 EA	RP	50 EA	1 EA	900 EA	1000 EA
Bikaina XVI	EdP	LP	1988	EB	38 X 26	JP	50	1	2500	2800
Aizatu III	EdP	LP	1987	EB	56 X 38	AP	50	1	2500	7000
Agri I	EdP	LP	1988	EB/ENG	8 X 5	AP	50	1	500	1500
Agri II	EdP	LP	1988	ENG	8 X 5	AP	50	1	500	1650
Agri III	EdP	LP	1988	ENG	8 X 5	AP	50	1	500	1500
Agri VI	EdP	LP	1988	EB	37 X 27	RP	50	1	2500	2800
Bidearte II	EdP	LP	1988	EB/DPT/CC	9 X 5	AP	45	1	500	1800
Zabaldu	EdP	LP	1988	EB	5 X 8	AP	50	1	500	1650
Hommage a Luis Bergareche	EdP	LP	1990	I	63 X 48	AP	50	1	12000	15000

The print market has become very selective. For the first time since we published the first edition of The Printworld Directory in 1982, the prices of prints have been greatly reduced and greatly increased for the same artists by the most reputable and established print publishers. Check the fifth edition to understand the movement.

YUEN YUEY CHINN

BORN: Canton, China; December 24, 1922
EDUCATION: Columbia Univ, NY, MFA, 1954
TEACHING: Am Center for Students & Artists, Paris, France, 1968–69; Brooklyn Col, NY, 1975 to present
AWARDS: Brevoort Eickmeyer, 1952–53; Fulbright Award, Italy, 1954–55; John Hay Whitney, 1956–57
COLLECTIONS: Nat Col of Fine Arts, Wash, DC; Fogg Art Mus, Cambridge, MA; Columbia Univ, NY; Wadsworth Atheneum Mus, Hartford, CT
PRINTERS: Artist (ART)
PUBLISHERS: Artist (ART)
GALLERIES: Galerie Karl Flinker, Paris France; Franz Bader, Wash, DC
MAILING ADDRESS: 80 N Moore St, Apt #15-J, New York, NY 10013

TITLE	PUBLISHER	PRINTER	DATE	MEDIUM	DIMENSION (PAPER SIZE) IN INCHES	TYPE OF PAPER	EDITION NUMBER	NO. OF COLORS	ORIGINAL OPENING PRICE	CURRENT RETAIL PRICE
SOLD OUT EDITIONS (RARE):										
Movement	ART	ART	1956	WC	7 X 23	MUL	20	3	40	400
Kites	ART	ART	1956	WC	7 X 24	MUL	20	3	40	400
Two Figures	ART	ART	1957	WC	11 X 19	MUL	20	2	40	400
Tao Scripts	ART	ART	1957	WB	9 X 23	MUL	20	1	40	400
CURRENT EDITIONS:										
Paris in Winter	ART	ART	1982	WC	11 X 12	MUL	50	1	200	200
Unknown Place	ART	ART	1984	WC	16 X 20	MUL	50	Multi	500	500

RICHARD CHIRIANI

BORN: Staten Island, NY; 1942
EDUCATION: Art Students League, NY, 1963; Pratt Inst, NY, BFA, 1964; Brooklyn Col, NY, MFA, 1967
AWARDS: Art Students League Scholarship, NY, 1962; Pratt Inst Painting Scholarship, 1968; Ingram Merrill Found Award, 1982–1983
COLLECTIONS: Metropolitan Mus of Art, NY; Brooklyn Col, NY; Kansas City Art Inst, MO
PRINTERS: Brand X, NY (BX)
PUBLISHERS: Orion Editions Inc, NY (OE)
GALLERIES: Orion Editions, New York, NY

TITLE	PUBLISHER	PRINTER	DATE	MEDIUM	DIMENSION (PAPER SIZE) IN INCHES	TYPE OF PAPER	EDITION NUMBER	NO. OF COLORS	ORIGINAL OPENING PRICE	CURRENT RETAIL PRICE
CURRENT EDITIONS:										
Untitled (Shells)	OE	BX	1983	SP	30 X 39	AP	50	9	350	500
Schoharie Marsh Spring	OE	BX	1984	SP	30 X 45	AP	125	39	650	850
View from the Triboro Bridge	OE	BX	1985	SP	28 X 51	AP	150	55	700	850
View from East Hill	OE	BX	1988	SP	35 X 47	AP	175	46	800	950
Winter Ravine	OE	BX	1989	SP	42 X 31	AP	175	36	950	950

WILLIAM CHRISTENBERRY

BORN: Tuscaloosa, AL; November 5, 1936
EDUCATION: Univ of Alabama, Tuscaloosa, AL, BFA, 1958, MA, 1959
TEACHING: Assoc Prof, Art, Corcoran Sch of Art, Wash, DC, 1968–74, Prof, 1974 to present
AWARDS: Nat Endowment for the Arts Fel, 1976; Lyndhurst Found Prize, 1982,83,84; Guggenheim Found Fel, 1984
RECENT EXHIB: Univ of Alabama, Moody Gallery of Art, Tuscaloosa, AL, 1992; Univ of Mississippi, University, MS, 1992; Yellowstone Art Center, Billings, MT, 1992; Roanoke Mus of Fine Arts, VA, 1992
COLLECTIONS: Corcoran Gallery of Art, Wash, DC; Mus of Mod Art, NY
PRINTERS: Wayne Kline, Atlanta, GA (WK); William Holton, Atlanta, GA (WH); Rolling Stone Press, Atlanta, GA (RSP)
PUBLISHERS: Rolling Stone Press, Atlanta, GA (RSP)
GALLERIES: Middendorf Gallery, Wash, DC; Nancy Drysdale Gallery, Wash, DC; Heath Gallery, Inc, Atlanta, GA; Pace/MacGill Gallery, New York, NY; Moody Gallery, Houston, TX; Morgan Gallery, Kansas City, MO
MAILING ADDRESS: c/o Middendorf Gallery, 2009 Columbia Rd, NW, Wash, DC 20009

William Christenberry
Brute
Courtesy Rolling Stone Press

TITLE	PUBLISHER	PRINTER	DATE	MEDIUM	DIMENSION (PAPER SIZE) IN INCHES	TYPE OF PAPER	EDITION NUMBER	NO. OF COLORS	ORIGINAL OPENING PRICE	CURRENT RETAIL PRICE
CURRENT EDITIONS:										
Lithographs Suite (Set of 5):									5000 SET	5000 SET
Ghost Image	RSP	WK/WH/RSP	1991	LB	22 X 18	R/BFK	40	1	750	750
Brute	RSP	WK/WH/RSP	1991	LB	34 X 26	R/BFK	40	1	1250	1250
Dream of Fear	RSP	WK/WH/RSP	1991	LB	34 X 26	R/BFK	40	1	1250	1250
Pointed Female	RSP	WK/WH/RSP	1991	LB	34 X 26	R/BFK	40	1	1250	1250
Pointed Male	RSP	WK/WH/RSP	1991	LB	34 X 26	R/BFK	40	1	1250	1250

DAN CHRISTENSEN

BORN: Lexington, NE; 1942
EDUCATION: Kansas City Art Inst, KS, BFA, 1964
TEACHING: Instr, Sch of Visual Arts, NY, 1978–82
AWARDS: Nat Endowment for the Arts Grant, 1968; Guggenheim Found Fel; Theodoran Award, 1969
COLLECTIONS: Mus of Mod Art, NY; Metropolitan Mus, NY; Hirshhorn Mus, Wash, DC; St Louis Mus, MO; Denver Mus, CO; Solomon R Guggenheim Mus, NY; Whitney Mus of Am Art, NY; Ludwig Coll, Wallraf-Richartz Mus, Cologne, West Germany
PRINTERS: Landfall Press Inc, Chicago, IL (LPI); Jack Lemon, Chicago, IL (JL); Jerry Raidiger, Chicago, IL (JR); Charles Cardinale (CC)
PUBLISHERS: Landfall Press Inc, Chicago, IL (LPI), Prestige Art Ltd, Mamaroneck, NY (PA)
GALLERIES: Andre Emmerich Gallery, Inc, New York, NY; Landfall Press, Inc, Chicago, IL & New York, NY; Harcus Gallery, Boston, MA; Salander-O'Reilly Galleries, New York, NY; Sandy Carson Gallery, Denver, CO; Gloria Luria Gallery, Bar Harbor Islands, FL; Meredith Long Gallery, Houston, TX; Alan Brown Gallery, Hartsdale, NY; Vered Gallery, New York, NY; C S Schulte Galleries, South Orange, NJ; Douglas Drake Gallery, New York, NY; Robley Gallery, Roslyn, NY; Salander-O'Reilly Gallery, New York, NY; Ro Gallery Image Makers, Inc, New York, NY
MAILING ADDRESS: 16 Waverly Place, New York, NY 10003

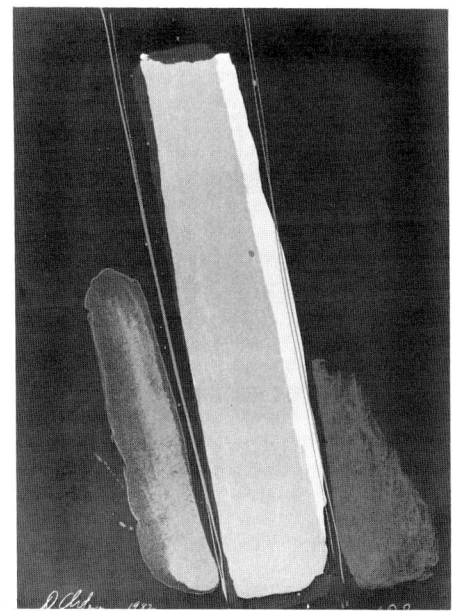

Dan Christensen
Galina Territory #1
Courtesy Landfall Press, Inc

TITLE	PUBLISHER	PRINTER	DATE	MEDIUM	DIMENSION (PAPER SIZE) IN INCHES	TYPE OF PAPER	EDITION NUMBER	NO. OF COLORS	ORIGINAL OPENING PRICE	CURRENT RETAIL PRICE
SOLD OUT EDITIONS (RARE):										
Untitled	LPI	JR/JL	1972	LC	50 X 26	ARJ	75	8	150	800
CC-#1, #2, #3, #4	PA	CC	1980	SP	36 X 25 EA	AC	100 EA	5 EA	350 EA	350 EA
Galina Territory #1	LPI	JL/LPI	1982	LC/PO	42 X 31	GE/BL	20	6	950	1000
Galina Territory #2	LPI	JL/LPI	1982	LC/PO	42 X 31	GE/BL	20	5	950	1000
Galina Territory #3	LPI	JL/LPI	1982	LC/PO	42 X 31	GE/BL	20	5	950	1000
Color Monoprints #17B, #19B, #30B	LPI	LPI	1986	MON	32 X 23	AC	1 EA	Varies	600	600
Color Monoprints #4, #5, #7	LPI	LPI	1986	MON	40 X 30	AC	1 EA	Varies	900	900

RONALD JULIUS CHRISTENSEN

PRINTERS: American Atelier, NY (AA)
PUBLISHERS: Circle Fine Art, Chicago, IL (CFA)
GALLERIES: Frances Aronson Gallery, Atlanta, GA; Harmon-Meek Gallery, Naples, FL; Circle Galleries, San Diego, CA & San Francisco, CA & Northbrook, IL & Pittsburgh, PA & Houston, TX & Soho, NY & Chicago, IL & Scottsdale, AZ & Beverly Hills, CA & Costa Mesa, CA & Sherman Oaks, CA & Palm Beach, FL & Honolulu, HI & New Orleans, LA & Las Vegas, NV & Seattle, WA

TITLE	PUBLISHER	PRINTER	DATE	MEDIUM	DIMENSION (PAPER SIZE) IN INCHES	TYPE OF PAPER	EDITION NUMBER	NO. OF COLORS	ORIGINAL OPENING PRICE	CURRENT RETAIL PRICE
SOLD OUT EDITIONS (RARE):										
Field of Poppies	CFA	AA	1976	SP	27 X 35	AP	300		75	275

SEYMOUR CHWAST

BORN: New York, NY; August 18, 1931
EDUCATION: Cooper Union, NY
TEACHING: Instr, Design, Cooper Union, NY, 1975 to present
AWARDS: St Gardens Medal, Cooper Union, NY; Art Director's Club, Hall of France, 1983
RECENT EXHIB: Jack Gallery, NY, 1987
COLLECTIONS: Mus of Mod Art, NY; Cooper-Hewitt Mus, NY; Smithsonian Inst, Wash, DC; Israeli Mus, Jerusalem, Israel; Gutenberg Mus, Mainz, Germany
PRINTERS: Serigrafia Limited, NY (SER)
PUBLISHERS: Serigrafia Limited, NY (SER)
GALLERIES: Ro Gallery Image Makers, Inc, New York, NY
MAILING ADDRESS: c/o Push Pin Group, Inc, 215 Park Ave, South, New York, NY 10003

TITLE	PUBLISHER	PRINTER	DATE	MEDIUM	DIMENSION (PAPER SIZE) IN INCHES	TYPE OF PAPER	EDITION NUMBER	NO. OF COLORS	ORIGINAL OPENING PRICE	CURRENT RETAIL PRICE
CURRENT EDITIONS:										
"O" Series:										
Groucho	SER	SER	1989	SP	28 X 41	R/BFK	200	17	750	850
Garbo	SER	SER	1989	SP	28 X 41	R/BFK	200	16	750	850
Satchmo	SER	SER	1989	SP	28 X 41	R/BFK	200	21	750	850
Pablo	SER	SER	1989	SP	28 X 41	R/BFK	200	16	750	850

The retail prices of the 100,000 limited edition prints quoted in this directory are subject to change. Print publishers, artists and galleries were the direct sources for these quotations. Prices in the secondary market listed as "Sold Out Editions (Rare)" indicate that the publisher has a limited supply of that print or that the print is difficult to locate in the galleries.

CHRISTO (JAVACHEFF)

BORN: Gabrovo, Bulgaria; June 13, 1935
EDUCATION: Fine Arts Acad of Sofia, Bulgaria, 1952–56, Burian Theatre, Prague, Czechoslovakia, 1956; Vienna Fine Arts Acad, Austria, 1957
RECENT EXHIB: Southern Plains Indian Mus, Anadarko, OK, 1989; Evanston Art Center, Center for the Visual Arts, IL, 1989; New Gallery, Bemis Found, Omaha, NE, 1989; Santa Clara Univ, De Saisset Mus, CA, 1992; Rocky Mountain Col of Art, Philip J Steele Gallery, Denver CO, 1992; Miami-Dade Com Col, FL, 1992; Galerie Alex Lachman, Berlin, Germany, 1992
COLLECTIONS: Mus of Mod Art, NY; Whitney Mus of Am Art, NY; Stedelijk Mus, Amsterdam, Netherlands; Tate Gallery, London, England; Albright-Knox Art Gallery, Buffalo, NY; Victoria & Albert Mus, London, England; Hara Mus of Contemp Art, Tokyo, Japan; Seibu Mus, Tokyo, Japan; Nat Galerie, Berlin, Germany
PRINTERS: Hans-Peter Haas, Stuttgart, Germany (HPH); Edition Domberger KG, Stuttgart, Germany (DOM); Karl Maurer, Munich, Germany (KM); Matthiew AG, Düsseldorf, Germany (MAG); David Keister, Chicago, IL (DK); Donald Holman, Chicago, IL (DH); Timothy Berry, Chicago, IL (TB); Jack Lemon, Chicago, IL (JL); Landfall Press Inc, Chicago, IL (LPI); La Poligrafa, Barcelona, Spain (LP)
PUBLISHERS: Galerie der Spiegel, Cologne, Germany (GDS); Verlag Gerd Hatje, Stuttgart, Germany (VGH); Edition Schellmann, Munich, Germany (ES); Landfall Press Inc, Chicago, IL (LPI); Abrams Original Editions, NY (AOE); Editions Schellmann and Klüser, Munich, Germany (ESK); Torsten Lilja, Stockholm, Sweden (TL); Makoto Ohaka, Tokyo, Japan (MO); Yoshiako Tono, Tokyo, Japan (YT); Yoich Yamamoto, Tokyo, Japan (YY); Nantenshi Gallery, Tokyo, Japan (NG); Artist (ART); Hans Möller, Düsseldorf, Germany; Ediciones Poligrafa, Barcelona, Spain (EdP); Torsten Lilja, Stockholm, Sweden (TL)
GALLERIES: Editions Schellmann, New York, NY & Munich, Germany; Landfall Press Inc, Chicago, IL; Marvin Ross Friedman & Co, Miami, FL; Galeria Joan Prats, Barcelona, Spain & New York, NY; John Gibson Gallery, New York, NY; Hill Gallery, Birmingham, MI; Deson-Saunders Gallery, Chicago, IL; Graystone, San Francisco, CA; Arnold Herstand & Co, New York, NY; Greenberg Gallery, St Louis, MO; Nohra Haime Gallery, New York, NY; Nathan Silberberg Fine Arts, New York, NY; Uptown Gallery, New York, NY; Nantenshi Gallery, Tokyo, Japan; Hanson Galleries, Beverly Hills, CA & La Jolla, CA; Herbert Palmer Gallery, Los Angeles, CA; Margaret Lipworth Fine Art, Boca Raton, FL; J Rosenthal Fine Arts, Chicago, IL; Donald Morris Gallery, Birmingham, MI; Galleria Maray, Allendale, NJ; Laura Carpenter Fine Arts, Albuquerque, NM; Bonnier Gallery, New York, NY; Douglas Drake Gallery, New York, NY; Reinhold-Brown Gallery, New York, NY; Peltz Gallery, Milwaukee, WI; Galerie Alex Lachman, Berlin, Germany

Christo (Javacheff)
Wrapped Book—Modern Art
Courtesy Landfall Press, Inc

Schellmann (S)

TITLE	PUBLISHER	PRINTER	DATE	MEDIUM	DIMENSION (PAPER SIZE) IN INCHES	TYPE OF PAPER	EDITION NUMBER	NO. OF COLORS	ORIGINAL OPENING PRICE	CURRENT RETAIL PRICE
SOLD OUT EDITIONS (RARE):										
Der Spiegel Magazine Empaqueté (S-1)			1963		310 X 120 MM	AP	130		50	20000
5600 Cubic Meter Package			1968	COL/CO	32 X 24	AP	90		100	3500
Monuments (Set of 10) (S12–22)	GDS		1968	SP	29 X 25 X 3	EABrB	100 EA		1500 SET	40000 SET
Set of 5 Prints:									600 SET	30000 SET
Whitney Museum Wrapped	LPI	JR/DH/LPI	1971	LC/CO	22 X 28 EA	ARJ	100	7	125	8000
Museum of Modern Art (front)	LPI	JR/DH/LPI	1971	LC/CO	22 X 28 EA	R/BFK	100	3	125	8000
Museum of Modern Art (rear)	LPI	JR/LPI	1971	LC/PH	22 X 28 EA	R/BFK	100	6	125	8000
Times Square (front)	LPI	JR/DH/LPI	1971	LC	22 X 28 EA	ARJ	100	5	125	8000
Times Square (rear)	LPI	JR/DH/LPI	1971	LC	22 X 28 EA	R/BFK	100	2	125	8000
Museum of Contemporary Art Chicago	LPI	OK/LPI	1972	LC	42 X 32	ARJ	60	9	500	9000
Ten Million Oil Drums Wall			1972	SP	28 X 22	ARJ	70		500	3000
Lower Manhattan Wrapped Building 20 Exchange Place, Project for New York	AOE	JL/LPI	1973	LC/OFF/SP	28 X 22	AC/MB	100		200	8000
Wrapped Venus, Villa Borghese, 1963	LPI	TB/JL/LPI	1975	LC/EC/CO	28 X 22	TWP	50	3	400	9000
Wrapped Armchair	AOE	MAG	1977	LC	22 X 28	RP	100		400	8000
Red Store Front	ESK/VGH	HPH	1977	SP/CO	28 X 22	BD/W	110		400	7500
Wrapped Modern Art Book (Wrapped by the Artist in Pliofilm and Twine)	AOE	JL/LPI	1978	MULT	11 X 10 X 2	AC/W	120		750	8000
Yellow Storefront	AOE	JL/LPI	1980	LC/CO	32 X 23	AP/W	100	6	400	5000
Pink Storefront (S-105)	YY/NG	JL/LPI	1980	LC/CO	22 X 18	AP/W	100	8	400	5000
Two Lower Manhattan Wrapped Buildings, Project for New York (S-106)	EdP	LP	1980	LC/CO	28 X 22	AC/MB	99		1200	15000
Package on Handtruck Project	AOE	JL/LPI	1981	LC/CO	28 X 22	AC/W	100	4	1200	6000

CHRISTO (JAVACHEFF) CONTINUED

TITLE	PUBLISHER	PRINTER	DATE	MEDIUM	DIMENSION (PAPER SIZE) IN INCHES	TYPE OF PAPER	EDITION NUMBER	NO. OF COLORS	ORIGINAL OPENING PRICE	CURRENT RETAIL PRICE
SOLD OUT EDITIONS (RARE):										
Puerta de Alcala, Wrapped Project for Madrid (with Fabric, Thread, City Map & Photographs) (S-107)	EdP	LP	1981	LC/CO	28 X 22	AC/MB	99		1500	8500
Wrapped Floors, Project for Haus Lange Museum, Krefeld (with Brown Wrapping Paper, Hand Painted Cloth & Staples) (S-110)	ESK	JL/LPI	1983	LC/CO	23 X 28	AC/MB	100	4	1500	10000
Wrapped Walkways (Project for St Stephen's Green Park in Dublin) (S-111)	ESK	JL/LPI	1983	LC/CO	28 X 44	AC/MB	100	7	1800	15000
Package on Carozza (Project for a Beringerri Tanento, South Italy, 1971) (S-112)	LPI	JL/LPI	1984	LC/CO	22 X 28	AC/MB	100	4	1500	10000
Lower Manhattan Wrapped Building Project for #2 Broadway New York City, 1964–84)	TL	JL/LPI	1984	LC/CO	22 X 28	AC/MB	110	5	1500	20000
Wrapped Automobile (Project for Volvo 122-S Sport Sedan, 1981-84) (S-113)	ESK/ART	JL/LPI	1984	LC/CO	22 X 28	R/BFK-MB	100	3	1500	15000
Five Urban Projects (Set of 5):									18000 SET	25000 SET
Curtains for La Rotonda (Project for Milan)	ES	DOM/KM	1985	CO	14 X 11	AP	100		4000	5000
Lower Manhattan Wrapped Building (Project for New York)	ES	DOM/KM	1985	CO	14 X 11	AP	100		4000	5000
Mein Kölner Dom (Wrapped Project for Cologne)	ES	DOM/KM	1985	CO	14 X 11	AP	100		4000	5000
Wrapped Trees (Project for the Avenue des Champs-Elysées)	ES	DOM/KM	1985	CO	14 X 11	AP	100		4000	5000
Ponte S Angelo, Wrapped (Project for Rome)	ES	DOM/KM	1985	CO	14 X 11	AP	100		4000	5000
Ericson Display Monitor . . .			1985	LC/CO	28 X 23	AP/W	100		5000	8000
Surrounded Islands			1985	LB/OFF/CO	31 X 24	AP/W	100		3500	6000
Wrapped Telephone			1985	LC/CO	38 X 23	AP/W	100		3500	8000
Mastabe Project for . . .			1986	LC/CO	28 X 23	AP/W	100		5000	8000
CURRENT EDITIONS:										
Surrounded Islands (Two-Part Print):										
Part I—Photograph Mounted on Rag Paper with Collotype	ES	DOM	1987	SP/COL/PH/CO	15 X 16	FAB	125		6000	8000
Part II—Collotype & Silkscreen with Collage of Map, Pink Woven Polypropylene Fabric & Masking Tape	ES	DOM	1987	SP/COL/PH/CO	15 X 16	FAB	125		6000	8000
Wrapped Trees, Project for the Avenue des Champs-Elysées, Paris	TL	JL/LPI	1987	LC/CO	28 X 22	AC/MB	200		2000	20000
Wrapped Statues (Project for the Glyptothek-Munchen, West Germany) (25 Impressions)	LPI	JL/LPI	1988	SP/PH/CO	35 X 27 EA	AP/W	1 EA		2500	12000
Wrapped Payphone (New York Payphone Wrapped in Heavy Fabric & Polyethylene & Rope)	ES	ART	1988	MULT	23 X 10 X 9	AP/W	30		20000	28000
Wrapped Road Sign	ES	ART	1988	LC/CO	28 X 22	AP/W	150		10000	12000
Wrapped Statues	LPI	JL/LPI	1988	SP/OFF	35 X 27	AP/W	600		2500	2500
Arc de Triomphe, Wrapped (Project for Paris)	TL	JL/LPI	1989	LC	28 X 22	AC/MB	150		7500	20000
Ponte Sant Angelo, Wrapped (Project for Rome)	TL	JL/LPI	1989	LC	28 X 22	AC/MB	150		7500	20000
Package on a Table	TL	JL/LPI	1989	LC/CO	32 X 24	AC/FABRIC	100		7500	10000
Pont Sant' Angelo, Wrapped . . .	TL	JL/LPI	1989	LC/CO	30 X 22	AC	20	5	12000	16000
Pont Sant' Angelo, Wrapped . . .	TL	JL/LPI	1989	LC/CO	30 X 22	AC	150		7500	9500
Lower Manhattan Project	LPI	JL/LPI	1990	LC/CO	40 X 26	AC/MB	125		12500	15000
Lower Manhattan Wrapped . . .	LPI	JL/LPI	1990	LC/CO	40 X 26	AC/MB	125		15000	22000
Wrapped Arm Chair	LPI	JL/LPI	1990	LC/CO	25 X 35	AC/MB	100		6000	7000
Wrapped Building, Allied Chemical	LPI	JL/LPI	1991	LC/CO	39 X 25	AC/MB	125		7500	7500
Orange Store Front	LPI	JL/LPI	1991	LC/CO	28 X 31	AC/MB	100		7500	7500
The Umbrellas Project (Unnumbered)	LPI	JL/LPI	1991	LC/OFF/CO	28 X 40	AC/MB	600		1500	1500
Times Square, Late Afternoon			1991	LC/CO			125		12000	12000
Wrapped Allied Chemical . . .			1991	LC/SP/COL/CHAR			125		12000	12000

CHRYSSA (VERDEA)

BORN: Athens, Greece; 1933; US Citizen
EDUCATION: Acad Grant Chaumiere, Paris, France, 1953–54; California Sch of Fine Art, Los Angeles, CA, 1954–55
RECENT EXHIB: Leo Castelli Gallery, NY, 1988,90
COLLECTIONS: Mus of Mod Art, NY; Whitney Mus of Am Art, NY; Guggenheim Mus, NY; Albright-Knox Art Gallery, Buffalo, NY; Walker Art Center, Minneapolis, MN; Tate Gallery of Art, London, England; Mus Boymans Van Bueningen, Rotterdam, Netherlands; Metropolitan Mus of Art, NY
PRINTERS: Broadway Maintenance Corp, Long Island City, NY (BMC); Seri Arts, NY (SA); American Atelier, NY(AA)
PUBLISHERS: Parasol Press, NY (PaP); Abrams Original Editions, NY (AOE); Prestige Art Ltd, Mamaroneck, NY (PA); Circle Fine Art, Chicago, IL (CFA)
GALLERIES: Alan Brown Gallery, Hartsdale, NY; Jayne Baum Gallery, New York, NY; Judith Posner Gallery, Milwaukee, WI; Leo Castelli Gallery, New York, NY; Graphics Gallery, San Francisco, CA; Virginia Lust Gallery, New York, NY; Circle Galleries, Scottsdale, AZ & Beverly Hills, CA & Costa Mesa, CA & San Diego, CA & San Francisco, CA & Sherman Oaks, CA & Palm Beach, FL & Honolulu, HI & Chicago, IL & Northbrook, IL & New Orleans, LA & Las Vegas, NV & New York, NY & Pittsburgh, PA & Houston, TX & Seattle, WA
MAILING ADDRESS: c/o Albright-Knox Art Gallery, 1285 Elmwood Ave, Buffalo, NY 14222

TITLE	PUBLISHER	PRINTER	DATE	MEDIUM	DIMENSION (PAPER SIZE) IN INCHES	TYPE OF PAPER	EDITION NUMBER	NO. OF COLORS	ORIGINAL OPENING PRICE	CURRENT RETAIL PRICE
CURRENT EDITIONS:										
Reflection	AOE	SA	1972	SP	48 X 28	AP	75		250	1000
Greek Theme (Neon Multiple)	AOE	BMC	1978	MULT	16 X 12 X 9		37		1200	3000
Gates to Time Square (Set of 20)	PA	SS	1978	SP	40 X 30 EA	HMP	100 EA	4–7 EA	8000 SET	20000 SET
									400 EA	1000 EA
Untitled Suite (Set of 6)	PA	AH/SH	1980	SP	36 X 32 EA	AP	100 EA		2700 SET	7000 SET
					32 X 36 EA				450 EA	1000 EA
Oriental Series (Set of 12):									2000 SET	8400 SET
I (Yellow with White & Gray)	CFA	AA	1980	LC	30 X 40	AP	150		200	800
II (Blue with Blue & Gold)	CFA	AA	1980	LC	30 X 40	AP	150		200	800
III (Light Yellow with White)	CFA	AA	1980	LC	30 X 40	AP	150		200	800
IV (Blue with Blue, Red, Green & Black)	CFA	AA	1980	LC	30 X 40	AP	150		200	800
V (Dark Gray with Gray & Black)	CFA	AA	1980	LC	30 X 40	AP	150		200	800
VI (Dark Gray with Small Gray & Black)	CFA	AA	1980	LC	30 X 40	AP	150		200	800
VII (Black with Blue)	CFA	AA	1980	LC	30 X 40	AP	150		200	800
VII (Green with Green & Blue)	CFA	AA	1980	LC	30 X 40	AP	150		200	800
IX (Red with Orange & Gray)	CFA	AA	1980	LC	30 X 40	AP	150		200	800
X (Red with Red, Orange & Gray)	CFA	AA	1980	LC	30 X 40	AP	150		200	800
XI (Black with Gray)	CFA	AA	1980	LC	30 X 40	AP	150		200	800
XII (Green with Green, Blue & Gray)	CFA	AA	1980	LC	30 X 40	AP	150		200	800

RAY CIARROCHI

BORN: Chicago, IL; August 23, 1933
EDUCATION: Chicago Acad of Fine Arts, IL; Washington Univ, 1956–59, BFA; Boston Univ, MA, 1959–61, MFA
TEACHING: Parsons Sch of Design, NY, 1966–71; Maryland Inst, Baltimore, MD, 1971–72; Brooklyn Col, NY, 1972–76; Pratt Inst, NY, 1972; Baruch Col, NY, 1977; Columbia Univ, NY, 1969,71,76
AWARDS: Fulbright Fel, Florence, Italy, 1963–64; Louis Comfort Tiffany Grant, 1967; Ingram Merrill Found Awards, 1977,82
RECENT EXHIB: Katharina Rich Perlow Gallery, NY, 1993
COLLECTIONS: Brooklyn Mus, NY; Univ of Massachusetts, Amherst, MA; Columbus Mus, OH
PRINTERS: Atelier Ettinger, NY (AE); Artist (ART)
PUBLISHERS: John Szoke Graphics, Inc., NY (JSG); Artist (ART)
GALLERIES: Fischbach Gallery, New York, NY; John Szoke Graphics, New York, NY; Katharine Rich Perlow Gallery, New York, NY
MAILING ADDRESS: 55 Bethune St, D-1004, New York, NY 10014

TITLE	PUBLISHER	PRINTER	DATE	MEDIUM	DIMENSION (PAPER SIZE) IN INCHES	TYPE OF PAPER	EDITION NUMBER	NO. OF COLORS	ORIGINAL OPENING PRICE	CURRENT RETAIL PRICE
CURRENT EDITIONS:										
Manhattan Spring Morning	ART	ART	1982	MON	19 X 27	JO	1 EA		1200	1350
Manhattan Morning Dream	ART	ART	1982	MON	19 X 27	JO	1 EA		1200	1350
Manhattan Sunset Light	ART	ART	1982	MON	19 X 27	JO	1 EA		1200	1350
Manhattan January	ART	ART	1982	MON	19 X 27	JO	1 EA		1200	1350
Manhattan Summer	ART	ART	1982	MON	19 X 27	JO	1 EA		1200	1350
Island	ART	ART	1982	MON	28 X 39	JO	1 EA		1500	1650
Hemlock Pond	ART	ART	1982	MON	28 X 39	JO	1 EA		1500	1650
Inlet	ART	ART	1982	MON	28 X 39	JO	1 EA		1500	2250
Manhattan June	ART	ART	1982	MON	19 X 27	JO	1 EA		1500	1800
Delaware	ART	ART	1983	MON	28 X 39	JO	1 EA		1500	2250
Southerly View	JSG	AE	1985	LC	28 X 38	AP	85	10	400	600

BIAGIO A CIVALE

BORN: Rome, Italy; August 11, 1935
EDUCATION: Acad Grande Chaumiere, Paris, France, 1953–55; Fine Arts Acad, Rome, Italy, Diploma, Art Education, 1958; State Univ of New York, NY, 1984; New York Univ, NY, 1983–90
TEACHING: Instr, Art Education, Roosevelt High Sch, Yonkers, NY, 1979,80
AWARDS: Third Place, Sea Heritage Marine Art, Southport, NY, 1988
COLLECTIONS: Mus of Mod Art, Stockholm Sweden; Mod Sacred Art Gallery, Montecatini Mus, Florence, Italy; Argenton-Sur-Creuse Mus, France; Mus Espanol Art Contemp, Madrid, Spain; Gabinette Naz Stampe, Rome, Italy

BIAGIO A CIVALE CONTINUED

PRINTERS: Artist (ART)
PUBLISHERS: Artist (ART)

GALLERIES: Castillon Fine Arts, New York, NY; Noel Fine Art Gallery, Bronxville, NY
MAILING ADDRESS: 311 Lee Ave, Yonkers, NY 10705

TITLE	PUBLISHER	PRINTER	DATE	MEDIUM	DIMENSION (PAPER SIZE) IN INCHES	TYPE OF PAPER	EDITION NUMBER	NO. OF COLORS	ORIGINAL OPENING PRICE	CURRENT RETAIL PRICE
SOLD OUT EDITIONS (RARE):										
Along the Seine River	ART	ART	1950	WC	8 X 10	AP	33		50	250
Bandit (The Hunter)	ART	ART	1950	WC	12 X 10	AP	33		50	250
Bandit (Tower)	ART	ART	1950	WC	6 X 4	AP	33		50	250
The Bridge	ART	ART	1950	LC	9 X 6	AP	33		50	250
Drinker	ART	ART	1950	WC	6 X 4	AP	33		50	200
Einstein	ART	ART	1950	WC	6 X 3	AP	33		50	200
Fisherman, Houses in ...	ART	ART	1950	WC	12 X 10	AP	33		50	200
Fisherman, River	ART	ART	1950	WC	10 X 13	AP	33		50	200
Houses in the Country	ART	ART	1950	LC	10 X 8	AP	33		50	200
In Zadkin's Studio	ART	ART	1950	LC	10 X 6	AP	33		50	200
Lamp Fixture at the Academy	ART	ART	1950	WC	12 X 10	AP	33		50	200
Man in the Night	ART	ART	1950	WC	6 X 4	AP	33		50	200
Pieta	ART	ART	1950	WC	8 X 10	AP	33		50	200
Relaxed, on the Beach	ART	ART	1950	WC	2 X 5	AP	33		50	200
Sandman on Arno River	ART	ART	1950	WC	10 X 8	AP	33		50	200
Spanish Portrait	ART	ART	1950	WC	6 X 4	AP	33		50	200
Stars over the Roofs	ART	ART	1950	WC	5 X 5	AP	33		50	200
Bottles, Glasses & Candle	ART	ART	1960	LC	9 X 6	AP	33		80	250
Clochard	ART	ART	1960	LC	10 X 5	AP	33		80	200
Houses at Elmas	ART	ART	1960	LC	6 X 9	AP	33		80	200
Little Boat	ART	ART	1960	LC	6 X 4	AP	33		80	200
Man with Thoughts	ART	ART	1960	LC	11 X 8	AP	33		80	200
Man, along the River	ART	ART	1960	WC	10 X 7	AP	33		80	200
Man, Woman with Basket	ART	ART	1960	LC	8 X 10	AP	33		80	200
Three Fisherman at Bari	ART	ART	1960	LC	8 X 6	AP	33		80	200
Three Venuses	ART	ART	1960	LC	8 X 6	AP	33		80	200
Two Figures	ART	ART	1960	WC	6 X 7	AP	33		80	200
Big Head	ART	ART	1970	WC	6 X 4	AP	33		100	250
Communion	ART	ART	1970	LC	6 X 6	AP	33		100	250
Face	ART	ART	1970	WC	9 X 5	AP	33		100	250
Family	ART	ART	1970	WC	5 X 10	AP	33		100	250
Fisherman, Houses	ART	ART	1970	WC	14 X 13	AP	33		100	250
Houses	ART	ART	1970	WC	8 X 6	AP	33		100	250
Man and Landscape	ART	ART	1970	LC	12 X 16	AP	33		100	250
Man Leaning Against Tree	ART	ART	1970	WC	6 X 4	AP	33		100	250
Man with Gondola	ART	ART	1970	WC	4 X 6	AP	33		100	250
Table Nude	ART	ART	1970	WC	6 X 4	AP	33		100	250
Peddle of Necklaces	ART	ART	1970	LC	14 X 13	AP	33		100	250
Profile	ART	ART	1970	WC	6 X 4	AP	33		100	250
Venice	ART	ART	1970	WC	8 X 8	AP	33		100	250
Wizzard	ART	ART	1970	WC	6 X 4	AP	33		100	250
Boats at La Rochelle	ART	ART	1980	LC	12 X 12	AP	33		150	250
Children in Lebanon	ART	ART	1980	LC	23 X 18	AP	33		150	250
House Plant	ART	ART	1980	WC	16 X 10	AP	33		150	200
Lighthouse	ART	ART	1980	LC	13 X 7	AP	33		150	200
Nocturne	ART	ART	1980	LC	12 X 12	AP	33		150	200
Old Mexican Woman	ART	ART	1980	LC	23 X 18	AP	33		150	250
Pontevecchio, Man with Pipe	ART	ART	1980	WC	9 X 8	AP	33		150	200
Red Bridge under Snow	ART	ART	1980	WC	6 X 6	AP	33		150	200

MICHAEL VINSON CLARK

BORN: Texas; November 20, 1946
EDUCATION: Pratt Inst, Brooklyn, NY, 1965–66
AWARDS: Purchase Award, Nat Drawing Soc, Philadelphia Mus of Art, PA, 1970; Purchase Award, Painting, Friends of the Corcoran, Wash, DC, 1977
COLLECTIONS: Nat Gallery of Fine Art, Wash, DC; Phillips Mem Coll, Wash, DC; Corcoran Gallery of Art, Wash, DC; Everson Mus of Art, Syracuse, NY; Philadelphia Mus of Art, PA; Cooper-Hewitt Mus of Design, NY; George Washington Univ, Wash, DC
PRINTERS: John Nichols, NY (JN)
PUBLISHERS: Davidson Press, Wash, DC (DP) (OB); John Nichols, NY (JN)
GALLERIES: Sander Gallery, New York, NY; John Nichols Gallery, New York, NY; Kathleen Ewing Gallery, Wash, DC; Martha Tepper Contemp Fine Arts, West Newton, MA; Barbara Gillman Gallery, Miami, FL; David Adamson Gallery, Wash, DC
MAILING ADDRESS: 220 East 60th Street, #6H, New York, NY 10022

TITLE	PUBLISHER	PRINTER	DATE	MEDIUM	DIMENSION (PAPER SIZE) IN INCHES	TYPE OF PAPER	EDITION NUMBER	NO. OF COLORS	ORIGINAL OPENING PRICE	CURRENT RETAIL PRICE
CURRENT EDITIONS:										
Washington Windows I, II	DP/JN	JN	1982	SP	30 X 45 EA	R/BFK/B	85 EA	14 EA	400 EA	650 EA
Elizabeth Street, Little Italy I, II	DP/JN	JN	1983	SP	30 X 44 EA	R/BFK/B	85 EA	17/20EA	400 EA	500 EA
Pavilion at the Old Post Office	EC	JN	1983	SP	30 X 28	R/BFK/B	200	10	400	500
L A Windows	DP/JN	JN	1984	SP	30 X 44	R/BFK/B	85	15	400	500

FRANCESCO CLEMENTE

BORN: Naples, Italy; 1952
RECENT EXHIB: Mus of Mod Art, NY, 1986-87; Albright-Knox Art Gallery, Buffalo, NY, 1987; Mus of Contemp Art, Los Angeles, CA, 1987, Gallery Bruno Bischofberger, Zürich, Switzerland, 1987; Los Angeles County Mus, CA, 1987; Minneapolis Mus of Art, Saint Paul, MN, 1987-88; Winnipeg Art Gallery, Manitoba, Can, 1988; Columbia Univ, Wallach Art Gallery, NY, 1989; Dia Art Found, NY, 1989; Anthony d'Offay Gallery, London, England, 1989; Sperone Westwater Gallery, NY, 1990; Philadelphia Mus of Art, PA, 1990; Wadsworth Atheneum, Hartford, CT, 1991; San Francisco Mus of Mod Art, CA, 1991; Virginia Mus of Fine Arts, Richmond, VA, 1991; Crown Point Press, San Francisco, CA & NY, 1991; Galerie Beyeler, Basel, Switzerland, 1991; Gagosian Gallery, NY, 1991; Perry Rubenstein Gallery, NY, 1992; Gallery Bruno Bischofberger, Zurich, Switzerland, 1992; Univ of Colorado, Colorado Springs, CO, 1992; Anthony d'Offay Gallery, London, England, 1993
COLLECTIONS: Stedelijk Mus, Amsterdam, Holland
PRINTERS: Hidekatsu Takada (HT); Peter Pettengill (PP); Marcia Bartholme (MB); Crown Point Press, San Francisco, CA (CCP); Francois Lafranca, Locarno, Switzerland (FL); Patricia Branstead, NY (PB); Aeropress, NY (A); Sheila Marbain, NY (SM); Frank Versaggi, NY (FV); John Hutcheson, Hoboken, NJ (JH); Tadashi Toda, Kyoto, Japan (TT); 2 RC, Rome, Italy (2RC); Petersburg Press, Inc, London, England (PP); Maurice Payne, NY (MP); Handworks, NY (HW); Valter Rossi, Rome, Italy (VR); Vigna Antoniniana, Rome, Italy (VA); Brian Shure, CA (BS); Reneé Bott, CA (RB); Paul Mullowney, CA (PM); Linda Geary, CA (LG); Aldo Crommelynck, NY (AC); Atelier Crommelynck, NY (AtC); Maurice Payne, NY (MP); Wellington Studios, London, England (WellSt)
PUBLISHERS: Crown Point Press, San Francisco, CA (CPP); Peter Blum Edition, NY (PBE); Multiples, NY (M); Editions Schellmann & Klüser, Munich, Germany (SK); Editions Schellmann, Munich, Germany & NY (ES); Petersburg Press, Inc, London, England (PP); Raymond Foye Editions, NY (RFE); Galerie Bernd Klüser, Munich, Germany (GBK); Brooke Alexander, Inc, NY (BAI); Aldo Crommelynck, NY (AC); Lococo-Mulder, St Louis, MO (L-M); 2 RC Editions, Rome, Italy (2RC)
GALLERIES: Sperone Westwater, New York, NY; Marian Goodman, New York, NY; Crown Point Press, New York, NY & San Francisco, CA; James Corcoran Gallery, Santa Monica, CA; Baumgartner Galleries, Wash, DC; Harcus Gallery, Boston, MA; Magnuson Gallery, Boston, MA; Elizabeth Leach, Portland, OR; Editions Schellmann, New York, NY; Nancy Singer Gallery, St Louis, MO; Paul Cava Gallery, Phila, PA; Brody's Gallery, Wash, DC; Flanders Contemp Art, Minneapolis, MN; Galeria Quintana, Bogota, Colombia; Petersburg Press, Inc, New York, NY & London, England; Gallery Bruno Bischofberger, Zürich, Switzerland; Andrew Dierken Fine Art, Los Angeles, CA; Signet Arts, St Louis, MO; Figura, Inc, New York, NY; Anthony d'Offay Gallery, London, England; Galerie Beyeler, Basil, Switzerland; Brooke Alexander Gallery, New York, NY; Takada Fine Arts, San Francisco, CA; Katie Block Fine Art, Boston, MA; Montgomery Glasoe Fine Art, Minneapolis, MN; Galdy Galleries, New York, NY; Matthew Marks Gallery, New York, NY; Rubenstein/Diacono Gallery, New York, NY; Hine Editions/Limestone Press, San Francisco, CA; Gagosian Gallery, New York, NY
MAILING ADDRESS: 684 Broadway, New York, NY 10012

Francesco Clemente
Telemone No 2
Courtesy Crown Point Press

TITLE	PUBLISHER	PRINTER	DATE	MEDIUM	DIMENSION (PAPER SIZE) IN INCHES	TYPE OF PAPER	EDITION NUMBER	NO. OF COLORS	ORIGINAL OPENING PRICE	CURRENT RETAIL PRICE
SOLD OUT EDITIONS (RARE):										
Circuit	CPP	HT/PP/CPP	1981	EB	22 X 15	S	10	1	300	750
Still Life	CPP	HT/PP/CPP	1981	EB	23 X 15	S	15	1	30	750
Tondo	CPP	HT/PP/CPP	1981	EC	17 DIA	DF/HMP	25	1	300	2500
Not St Girolamo	CPP	HT/PP/CPP	1981	EC	63 X 25	AP/88/HMP	25	9	750	6500
Self Portrait #1 (India)	CPP	HT/PP/CPP	1981	EB	16 X 21	AP/S	10	1	350	2000
Self Portrait #2 (Teeth)	CPP	HT/PP/CPP	1981	EB	16 X 21	AP/S	10	1	350	2000
Self Portrait #3 (Pincers)	CPP	HT/PP/CPP	1981	EB	16 X 21	AP/S	10	1	400	2000
Self Portrait #4 (Snake)	CPP	HT/PP/CPP	1981	EB	16 X 21	AP/S	10	1	400	2000
Self Portrait #5 (Scowl)	CPP	HT/PP/CPP	1981	EB	16 X 21	AP/S	10	1	400	2000
Self Portrait #6 (Stoplight)	CPP	HT/PP/CPP	1981	EB	16 X 21	AP/S	10	1	400	2000
Telemone #1	CPP	HT/PP/CPP	1981	EB	63 X 25	DF/HMP	25	1	750	6500
Telemone #2	CPP	HT/PP/CPP	1981	EB	63 X 25	DF/HMP	25	1	750	6500

FRANCESCO CLEMENTE CONTINUED

TITLE	PUBLISHER	PRINTER	DATE	MEDIUM	DIMENSION (PAPER SIZE) IN INCHES	TYPE OF PAPER	EDITION NUMBER	NO. OF COLORS	ORIGINAL OPENING PRICE	CURRENT RETAIL PRICE
SOLD OUT EDITIONS (RARE):										
Knots	CPP	HT/PP/CPP	1981	EC	25 X 24	DF/HMP	25	1	400	2000
Screen	CPP	HT/PP/CPP	1981	EB	11 X 23	DF/HMP	25	1	350	2500
Fragment	CPP	HT/PP/CPP	1981	EB	15 X 18	AP88	25	1	150	650
Landscape #1 (Vines)	CPP	HT/PP/CPP	1981	EB	22 X 15	S	10	1	300	750
Landscape #2 (Lily Pads)	CPP	HT/PP/CPP	1981	EB	22 X 15	S	10	1	300	750
Landscape #3 (Tree & Rock)	CPP	HT/PP/CPP	1981	EB	22 X 15	S	10	1	300	750
Seascape	CPP	HT/PP/CPP	1981	EB	25 X 19	DF/HMP	10	1	450	1000
Music	CPP	HT/PP/CPP	1981	EB	23 X 15	S	10	1	300	750
This Side Up	CPP	HT/PP/CPP	1981	EB	29 X 48	AP88	25	1	350	2500
Yes or No	CPP	HT/PP/CPP	1982	AC	30 X 44	S	15	1	900	3500
The Twins	CPP	HT/PP/CPP	1982	AC	30 X 44	S	15	1	900	3500
Morning (MMA–48)	CPP	TT/CPP	1982	WC	17 X 23	KOZO	100	45	650	6500
I (MMA–50)	CPP	TT/CPP	1982	WC	17 X 23	KOZO	100	45	650	6500
Febbra Alta Portfolio (Set of 8)	PBE	FL	1982	WC	26 X 21 EA	HMP	35 EA	1 EA	3500 SET	12000 SET
Untitled	CPP	CPP	1984	WC	17 X 23	KOZO	200	14	1000	8500
CURRENT EDITIONS:										
Untitled (2 part woodcut)	M	PB/A	1982	WC	15 X 42	HMP	25	1	900	3500
Peso (Printed on Both Sides of Paper)	ESK	SM/FV/HW	1983	LC	55 X 34	JAP	50	2	1000	3000
Untitled (Pairs)	ESK	JH	1984	LC	42 X 30	AP88	25	6	800	4000
Untitled (Head)	ESK	JH	1984	LC	42 X 30	AP88	25	5	1000	4000
Untitled	CPP	CPP	1985	AC/SB/SG/HS	41 X 65	AP88	35		5800	10000
Untitled	ES	2RC	1986	EB/A/SG/SB	51 X 61	FAB	40		4800	12000
Conversion to Her	ES	VR/VA	1986	EB/A/SG	52 X 62	FAB	40		4800	8000
Faith and Hope (Set of 2)	ES	VR/VA	1986	EB/A/SG	18 X 25 EA	FAB	40 EA		3500 SET	4500 SET
Riconciliazione (with Gold Leaf) (from Joseph Beuys)	ES/GBK	VR/VA	1986	EB/A	24 X 32	FAB	90		1000	3500
The Departure of the Argonaut (50 Lithographs Bound in Book)	PP	PP	1986	LC	26 X 39 EA	OKP	200		9000	15000
Untitled A (Trip)	PP	PP	1986	LC	27 X 119	OKP	100		4800	8000
Untitled B (Trip)	PP	PP	1986	LC	26 X 80	OKP	100		3750	7500
Untitled (Set of 5)	RFE	MP	1987	EB/SG	26 X 20	JBG	50	1	4000 SET	8500 SET
The Two Flames (with Silk Brocade Borders)	CPP	CPP	1987	WC	10 X 6	HMP	100		750	950
Conception	2 RC	2 RC	1988	EB/A	34 X 25	HMP		55	3500	10000
Untitled (Set of 6)									4000 SET	4000 SET
Bestiary	AC	AtC	1989	EB/A	22 X 16	COV	55		750	750
Everything I Know	AC	AtC	1989	EB/A	22 X 16	COV	55		750	750
Architecture	AC	AtC	1989	EB/A	22 X 16	COV	55		750	750
Pessimist Rose	AC	AtC	1989	EB/A	22 X 16	COV	55		750	750
Religious Activity	AC	AtC	1989	EB/A	22 X 16	COV	55		750	750
St Vincent	AC	AtC	1989	EB/A	22 X 16	COV	55		750	750
Platonic Love	AC	AtC	1989	EB/A	32 X 21	COV	55		1500	1500

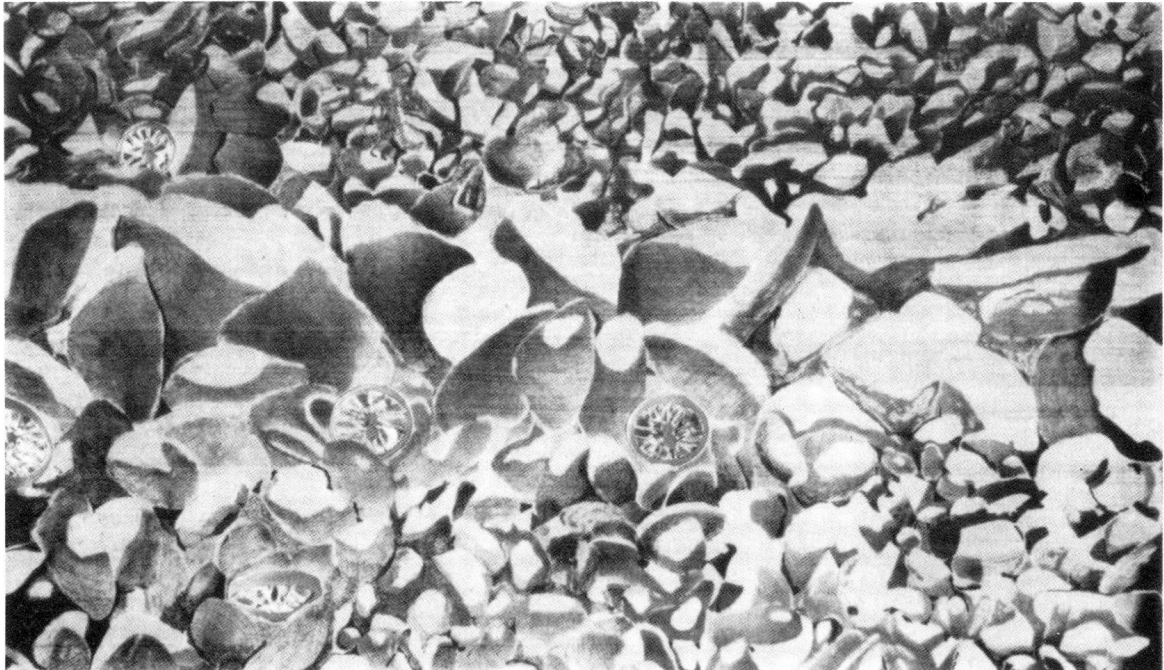

Francesco Clemente
Untitled, 1985
Courtesy Crown Point Press

FRANCESCO CLEMENTE CONTINUED

TITLE	PUBLISHER	PRINTER	DATE	MEDIUM	DIMENSION (PAPER SIZE) IN INCHES	TYPE OF PAPER	EDITION NUMBER	NO. OF COLORS	ORIGINAL OPENING PRICE	CURRENT RETAIL PRICE
CURRENT EDITIONS:										
Self-Portrait	CPP	CPP	1990	WC	29 X 22	HMP	120	16	5000	6500
Poetry Project Poster (with Allen Ginsberg)	BAI		1990	LC/OFF	22 X 29	AP	500		175	175
Sigilli (Set of 8):									8000 SET	8000 SET
Seed	CPP	CPP	1991	EB/A/SB	25 X 24		25		1250	1250
Order and Disorder	CPP	CPP	1991	EB/A/SB	25 X 24		25		1250	1250
Birth	APP	CPP	1991	EB/A/SB	25 X 24		25		1500	1500
Three Worlds	CPP	CPP	1991	EB/A/SB	25 X 24		25		1250	1250
Time	CPP	CPP	1991	EB/A/SB	25 X 24		25		1250	1250
Mother of Letters	CPP	CPP	1991	EB/A/SB	25 X 24		25		1250	1250
Witness	CPP	CPP	1991	EB/A/SB	25 X 24		25		1250	1250
Crucible	CPP	CPP	1991	EB/A/SB	25 X 24		25		1250	1250
Perusa (Set of 3):	CPP	CPP	1991	EB/A/SB/STEN	45 X 53 EA		21 EA		6500 SET	6500 SET
Fathers	CPP	CPP	1991	EB/A/SB/STEN	45 X 53		21		2500	2500
Mothers	CPP	CPP	1991	EB/A/SB/STEN	45 X 53		21		2500	2500
Seeds	CPP	CPP	1991	EB/A/SB/STEN	45 X 53		21		3000	3000
Frieze	CPP	CPP	1991	EB/A/HG/SL	17 X 168		10		5000	5000
9 Black Muses Twice (Set of 9)	CPP	CPP	1991	EB/A/SG	25 X 21 EA		4 EA		18000 SET	18000 SET
Sigilli (Set of 8):									8000 SET	8000 SET
Birth	CPP	BS/RB/LG/PM/CPP	1991	EB/A/SP/	25 X 24	SOM/T	25	1	1250	1250
Crucible	CPP	BS/RB/LG/PM/CPP	1991	EB/A/SP/	25 X 24	SOM/T	25	1	1250	1250
Mother of Letters	CPP	BS/RB/LG/PM/CPP	1991	EB/A/SP/	25 X 24	SOM/T	25	1	1250	1250
Order & Disorder	CPP	BS/RB/LG/PM/CPP	1991	EB/A/SP/	25 X 24	SOM/T	25	1	1250	1250
Seed	CPP	BS/RB/LG/PM/CPP	1991	EB/A/SP/	25 X 24	SOM/T	25	1	1250	1250
Three Worlds	CPP	BS/RB/LG/PM/CPP	1991	EB/A/SP/	25 X 24	SOM/T	25	1	1250	1250
Time	CPP	BS/RB/LG/PM/CPP	1991	EB/A/SP/	25 X 24	SOM/T	25	1	1250	1250
Witness	CPP	BS/RB/LG/PM/CPP	1991	EB/A/SP/	25 X 24	SOM/T	25	1	1250	1250
Geography (Set of 4): North, East, South, West	L-M	MP/WellSt	1992	EC/SG	28 X 25 EA	TRP/B	60	2 EA	10000 SET 3000 EA	10000 SET 3000 EA

KATHLEEN CLEMENT

BORN: Ord, NE; May 28, 1928
EDUCATION: Univ of Nebraska, Lincoln, NE, BA, 1950; American Univ, Wash, DC, 1977–79; Mus Studies, Paris, France, 1980
AWARDS: Prize in Graphics, Nebraska Reg Compt, 1948; Purchase Prize, House of Humour & Satire, Bulgaria, 1989
RECENT EXHIB: Nat Mus of Anthropology, Mexico, 1988; Nat Mus of Fine Arts, Mexico, 1988; Gallery Bella Vista, Mexico City, Mexico, 1989; Margolis Gallery, Vail, CO, 1989; Rafael Matos Gallery, Mexico City, Mexico, 1989; Mus of Fine Arts, Toluca, Mexico, 1992
COLLECTIONS: Mus of Mod Art, Mexico City, Mexico; Nat Exhib Sala, Buenos Aires, Argentina; North Am Cultural Inst, Mexico City, Mexico; Inst Isedro Fabela, Mexico City, Mexico
PRINTERS: Artist (ART); Enrique Cattaneo, Mexico City, Mexico (EC)
PUBLISHERS: Artist (ART); Enrique Cattaneo, Mexico City, Mexico (EC)
GALLERIES: Margolis Gallery, Vail, CO; Rafael Matos Gallery, Mexico City, Mexico
MAILING ADDRESS: Tulipan 359, Col El Toro Z 20, Mexico 10610 DF Mexico

TITLE	PUBLISHER	PRINTER	DATE	MEDIUM	DIMENSION (PAPER SIZE) IN INCHES	TYPE OF PAPER	EDITION NUMBER	NO. OF COLORS	ORIGINAL OPENING PRICE	CURRENT RETAIL PRICE
SOLD OUT EDITIONS (RARE):										
Frog I	ART	ART	1979	MON	30 X 25 EA	R/100	1 EA	1 EA	300 EA	700 EA
Frog II	ART	ART	1981	MON	15 X 25 EA	R/100	1 EA	1 EA	400 EA	500 EA
Nude I,II	ART	ART	1981	MON	15 X 25 EA	R/100	1 EA	1 EA	400 EA	500 EA
Still Life I	ART	ART	1982	MON	30 X 25 EA	R/100	1 EA	1 EA	700 EA	700 EA
CURRENT EDITIONS:										
Paisaje	ART	ART	1983	MON	8 X 12 EA	HMP	1 EA	1 EA	200 EA	200 EA
Flores	ART	ART	1984	MON	17 X 17 EA	HMP	1 EA	1 EA	500 EA	500 EA
Retrato de Leonora	ART	ART	1984	MON	17 X 17 EA	HMP	1 EA	1 EA	500 EA	500 EA
La Cabeza I,II	ART	ART	1984	MON	17 X 17 EA	HMP	1 EA	1 EA	500 EA	500 EA
Behind the Looking Glass	ART	ART	1989	MON	15 X 25 EA	RAG/100	1 EA	6 EA	700 EA	700 EA
Behind the Mirror	EC	EC	1992	SP	27 X 27	HMP	200	6	150	150
Flower Landscape	EC	EC	1992	SP	28 X 20	HMP	200	6	150	150

GEORGE CHEMECHE

BORN: Baghdad, Iraq; May 11, 1934, US Citizen
EDUCATION: Avni Sch of Fine Arts, Tel Aviv, Israel, 1956–59; Ecole de Beaux-Arts, Paris, France, 1960–63
AWARDS: Am-Israeli Cultural Found Award, 1960
COLLECTIONS: Israel Mus, Jerusalem, Israel; Newark Mus, NJ; Fogg Art Mus, Boston, MA; Solomon R Guggenheim Mus, NY; Denver Art Mus, CO; San Francisco Mus of Mod Art, CA; Herbert F Johnson Mus of Art, Cornell Univ, Ithaca, NY

PRINTERS: American Atelier, NY (AA)
PUBLISHERS: Circle Fine Art, Chicago, IL (CFA)
GALLERIES: Circle Galleries, Chicago, IL & New York, NY & Scottsdale, AZ & Beverly Hills, CA & Costa Mesa, CA & Sn Diego, CA & San Francisco, CA & Sherman Oaks, CA & Palm Beach, FL & Honolulu, HI & New Orleans, LA & Northbrook, IL & Las Vegas, NV & Pittsburgh, PA & Houston, TX & Seattle, WA; Lillian Heidenburg Gallery, New York, NY
MAILING ADDRESS: 222 W 23rd St, New York, NY 10011

TITLE	PUBLISHER	PRINTER	DATE	MEDIUM	DIMENSION (PAPER SIZE) IN INCHES	TYPE OF PAPER	EDITION NUMBER	NO. OF COLORS	ORIGINAL OPENING PRICE	CURRENT RETAIL PRICE
CURRENT EDITIONS:										
Divided Landscape	CFA	AA	1980	SP	28 X 39	AP	250		125	300

PIERRE CLERK

BORN: Atlanta, GA; April 26, 1928
EDUCATION: McGill Univ, Montreal, Can; Loyola Col, Montreal, Can; Montreal Mus of Fine Arts, Can; Acad Julian, Paris, France; Acad delle Belle Arti, Florence, Italy
AWARDS: Canadian Council Awards, 1971,72; Tamarind Fel, Albuquerque, NM, 1972; US Info Service Exhib Grant, 1977; Municipal Art Soc Grant, 1977; US State Dept Travel Grant, 1977–78

COLLECTIONS: Mus of Mod Art, NY; Guggenheim Mus, NY; Whitney Mus of Am Art, NY; Nat Gallery of Canada; Montreal Mus of Fine Arts, Can; Rose Art Mus, Brandeis Univ, Waltham, MA; Glasgow Art Mus, Scotland; New Mexico Univ, Albuquerque, NM; Queens Col, NY; State Univ of New York, Purchase, NY
PRINTERS: Vistec Graphics, Rochester, NY (VG)
PUBLISHERS: London Arts Inc, Detroit, MI (LAI)
GALLERIES: Jean Lumbard Fine Arts, New York, NY
MAILING ADDRESS: 70 Grand St, New York, NY 10013

TITLE	PUBLISHER	PRINTER	DATE	MEDIUM	DIMENSION (PAPER SIZE) IN INCHES	TYPE OF PAPER	EDITION NUMBER	NO. OF COLORS	ORIGINAL OPENING PRICE	CURRENT RETAIL PRICE
CURRENT EDITIONS										
Africa Suite #9	LAI	VG	1980	SP	20 X 30	SOM	200	4	275	300

NANCI BLAIR CLOSSON

BORN: Durham, NC; September 5, 1943
EDUCATION: Purdue Univ, West Lafayette, IN, BA, 1965; Univ of Arizona, with Maurice Grossman 1984–86
AWARDS: High Winds Medal, Am Watercolor Soc, 1984; Century Award, Rocky Mountain Nat, 1984

COLLECTIONS: Springfield Art Mus, MO; Indiana Univ, Bloomington IN; Southwest Forest Industries, Phoenix, AZ
PRINTERS: Sette Publishing Co, Tempe, AZ (SPC)
PUBLISHERS: C G Rein Publishers, St Paul, MN (CGR)
GALLERIES: C G Rein Galleries, Scottsdale, AZ & Santa Fe, NM & Houston, TX & Minneapolis, MN; Gallery 22, Bloomfield, MI
MAILING ADDRESS: 646 E 5th St, Tucson, AZ 85705-7923

TITLE	PUBLISHER	PRINTER	DATE	MEDIUM	DIMENSION (PAPER SIZE) IN INCHES	TYPE OF PAPER	EDITION NUMBER	NO. OF COLORS	ORIGINAL OPENING PRICE	CURRENT RETAIL PRICE
CURRENT EDITIONS:										
Cold Blue	CGR	SPC	1982	LC	30 X 40	AP	100	5	300	400
Descent	CGR	SPC	1983	LC	30 X 40	AP	100	7	300	450
Tlaquepaque	CGR	SPC	1983	LC	38 X 28	AP	100	6	300	400

CHEMA COBO

RECENT EXHIB: Charles Cowles Gallery, NY, 1989,92
PRINTERS: 3 K Workshop, Rome, Italy (3KW);
PUBLISHERS: Il Ponte, Rome, Italy, (IP);

GALLERIES: Metropolitan Mezzanine Gallery, New York, NY; Charles Cowles Gallery, New York, NY; Sette Gallery, Scottsdale, AZ; Sette & Segura Publishing Company, Tempe, AZ; Zolla/Lieberman Gallery, Chicago, IL; Signet Arts, St Louis, MO; Terry Dintenfass Gallery, New York, NY

TITLE	PUBLISHER	PRINTER	DATE	MEDIUM	DIMENSION (PAPER SIZE) IN INCHES	TYPE OF PAPER	EDITION NUMBER	NO. OF COLORS	ORIGINAL OPENING PRICE	CURRENT RETAIL PRICE
SOLD OUT EDITIONS (RARE):										
Transito (Set of 5)	IP	3KW	1985	AB/SG/DPT	18 X 14	SIC	60	1	1000	1500

The retail prices of the 100,000 limited edition prints quoted in this directory are subject to change. Print publishers, artists and galleries were the direct sources for these quotations. Prices in the secondary market listed as "Sold Out Editions (Rare)" indicate that the publisher has a limited supply of that print or that the print is difficult to locate in the galleries.

The Printworld Directory is accepting new applications for the seventh edition. Approximately 300 new artists will be accepted. Please use the two forms provided in the back section of this directory to submit biographical data and documentation of prints. Edition number of each print must not exceed 500 and the retail price must be $100 or more.

ANTONIO CLAVÉ

BORN: Barcelona, Spain; 1913
EDUCATION: Escuela de Bellas Artes, Barcelona, Spain
COLLECTIONS: Tate Gallery, London, England; Mus of Fine Arts, Boston, MA; Musée Nat d'Art Moderne, Petit Palais, Paris, France; Mus of Mod Art, Tokyo, Japan; Musée Picasso, Antibes, France
PRINTERS: Maurice Rousseau, Monaco (MR)

PUBLISHERS: Circle Fine Art, Chicago, IL (CFA)
GALLERIES: Nathan Silberberg Fine Arts, New York, NY; Circle Galleries, San Diego, CA & San Francisco, CA & Northbrook, IL & Pittsburgh, PA & Houston, TX & Soho, NY & Chicago, IL & Scottsdale, AZ & Beverly Hills, CA & Costa Mesa, CA & Sherman Oaks, CA & Palm Beach, FL & Honolulu, HI & New Orleans, LA & Las Vegas, NV & Seattle, WA; Yoshii Gallery, New York, NY

TITLE	PUBLISHER	PRINTER	DATE	MEDIUM	DIMENSION (PAPER SIZE) IN INCHES	TYPE OF PAPER	EDITION NUMBER	NO. OF COLORS	ORIGINAL OPENING PRICE	CURRENT RETAIL PRICE
SOLD OUT EDITIONS (RARE):										
Landscape			1975	LC	42 X 30	AP	50		300	2000
Avec des Etoiles			1975	LC/CAR	30 X 22	AP	75		250	2000
Carmen (Metropolitan Opera I)	CFA	MR	1978	I/MEZ	30 X 22	AP/W	250		350	2300
Aimée			1990	EB/CAR	30 X 22	AP/W	75		1500	2000

CHUCK CLOSE

BORN: Monroe, WA; July 5, 1940
EDUCATION: Univ of Washington, Seattle, WA, BA, 1958–60; BFA, 1962; Yale Univ Summer Sch, Norfolk, CT, Music & Art, 1961; Yale Univ, Sch of Art & Arch, New Haven, CT, MFA, 1964; Acad of Fine Arts, Vienna, Austria, 1964–65
TEACHING: Instr, Univ of Massachusetts Sch of Art, Amherst, MA, 1965–67; Instr, Sch of Visual Arts, NY, 1967–71; Instr, New York Univ, NY, 1970–73
AWARDS: Fulbright Fel Grant, 1964–65; Nat Endowment for the Arts Grant, 1973
RECENT EXHIB: Aldrich Mus of Contemp Art, Ridgefield, CT, 1987; Pace Editions, NY, 1987,88; Indianapolis Center for Contemp Art, Herron Gallery, IN, 1989; Univ of Missouri, Kansas City, MO, 1989; Lannan Found, Los Angeles, CA, 1991; Tampa Mus of Art, FL, 1992; Univ of Southwestern Louisiana, Lafayette, LA, 1992; Art Director's Club Gallery, NY, 1992; Pace Gallery, NY, 1993
COLLECTIONS: Mus of Mod Art, NY; Whitney Mus of Am Art, NY; Walker Art Center, Minneapolis, MN; Neue Gallerie, Aachen, Germany; Nat Art Gallery, ON, Can; Mus of Contemp Art, Utrecht, Holland; Oberlin Col, OH
PRINTERS: Vermillion Editions, Ltd, Minneapolis, MN (VEL); Joe Wilfer (JW); Patrick Foy, Tampa, FL (PF); Deli Sacilotto, Tampa, FL (DS); Graphicstudio, Univ of South Florida, Tampa, FL (GS); Tadashi Toda, Kyoto, Japan (TT); Shunzo Matsuda, Kyoto, Japan (SM); Hidekatsu Takada, Kyoto, Japan (HT); Crown Point Press, San Francisco, CA (CPP); Kathy Kuehn, NY (KK); Ruth Lingen, NY (RL); Joe Wilfer, NY (JN); Spring Street Workshop, NY (SpSW); Aldo Crommelynck, NY (AC); Atelier Crommelynck, NY (AtC)
PUBLISHERS: Pace Editions, NY (PE); Graphicstudio, Univ of South Florida, Tampa, FL (GS); Crown Point Press, San Francisco, CA (CPP); Aldo Crommelynck, NY (AC); Spring Street Workshop, NY (SpSW)
GALLERIES: Pace Prints, New York, NY; John C. Stoller & Co, Minneapolis, MN; Greenberg Gallery, St Louis, MO; Michael H Lord Gallery, Milwaukee, WI; Crown Point Press, New York, NY & San Francisco, CA; Opus Art Studios, Miami, FL; Pace/MacGill Gallery, New York, NY; Lemberg Gallery, Birmingham, MI; Barbara Gillman Gallery, Miami, FL; Janet Levitt Fine Art, San Francisco, CA; Margulies Taplin Gallery, Wash, DC
MAILING ADDRESS: 271 Central Park, West, New York, NY 10024

Chuck Close
Self-Portrait/White Ink
Courtesy Pace Editions, Inc

TITLE	PUBLISHER	PRINTER	DATE	MEDIUM	DIMENSION (PAPER SIZE) IN INCHES	TYPE OF PAPER	EDITION NUMBER	NO. OF COLORS	ORIGINAL OPENING PRICE	CURRENT RETAIL PRICE
SOLD OUT EDITIONS (RARE):										
Keith/4 Times	PE	CPP	1975	LC	31 X 88		50		2000	20000
Self Portrait	PE	CPP	1977	EB/A	54 X 41	WPP	35		2500	15000
Self Portrait—Black Ink	PE	CPP	1977	EB/A	55 X 41	WP	35		2500	15000
Self Portrait—White Ink	PE	CPP	1978	EB/A	54 X 41	C/425	35		2500	12500
Phil/Fingerprint	PE	VEL	1981	LB	50 X 38	HMP	36	1	3000	10000
Keith Series:										
Keith I	PE	JW/ART	1981	EB/A	36 X 27	HMP/G	20		2500	6500
Keith II	PE	JW/ART	1981	EB/A	35 X 27	HMP/W	20		2500	6500
Keith III	PE	JW/ART	1981	EB/A	35 X 27	HMP/BL	20		2500	6500
Keith IV	PE	JW/ART	1981	FR/A	35 X 27	HMP/G	20		2500	6500
Keith V	PE	JW/ART	1981	EB/A	33 X 26	HMP/G	20		2500	12500
Phil/Manipulated	PE	JW/ART	1982	EB/A	70 X 54	HMP/G	20		10000	30000
Phil Series:										
Phil I	PE	JW/ART	1982	HMP	69 X 54	HMP/W	15	1	6500	25000
Phil II	PE	JW/ART	1982	HMP	69 X 54	HMP/G	15	1	6500	25000
Phil III	PE	JW/ART	1982	HMP	69 X 54	HMP/BL	15	1	6500	25000

CHUCK CLOSE CONTINUED

TITLE	PUBLISHER	PRINTER	DATE	MEDIUM	DIMENSION (PAPER SIZE) IN INCHES	TYPE OF PAPER	EDITION NUMBER	NO. OF COLORS	ORIGINAL OPENING PRICE	CURRENT RETAIL PRICE
SOLD OUT EDITIONS (RARE):										
Robert Series:										
Robert I	PE	JW/ART	1982	HMP	25 X 19	HMP/W	20	1	1000	4000
Robert II	PE	JW/ART	1982	HMP	30 X 22	HMP/W	20	1	1000	4500
Self Portrait (Manipulated)	PE	JW/ART	1982	HMP	39 X 29	HMP/G	25	1	3000	20000
Robert (Manipulated)	PE	JW/ART	1982	HMP	34 X 26	HMP/G	25	1	3000	10000
Georgia	PE	JW/ART	1984	MULT	56 X 44	HMP	35		6500	17500
Georgia Fingerprint, State II	PE	PF/DS/GS	1985	EC	30 X 22	HMP	35		3000	3000
Leslie/Fingerprint	PE/GA	PF/DS/GS	1986	EC/TE	54 X 41	AP/WP/1114	45		5000	6500
Emily/Fingerprint	PE/GA	PF/DS/GS	1986	EC/TE	54 X 41	AP/WP/1114	45		5000	6500
Marta/Fingerprint	PE/GA	PF/DS/GS	1986	EC/TE	54 X 41	AP/WP/1114	45		5000	8500
Leslie	CPP	TT/SM/HT/CPP	1986	WC	30 X 25	KOZO	150	19	2000	4000
CURRENT EDITIONS:										
Self Portrait (172-29)	AC	AC/AtC	1988	AB/SB	21 X 16	HAHN	50	1	2500	6500
Susan (172-30)	PE	AC/AtC	1988	PO	28 X 22	HMP	50	1	3000	7500
Arne (172-31)	AC	AC/AtC	1988	AC/SB	30 X 22	HAHN	35		2500	3000
Lucas (172-35)	SpSW	KK/RL/JW/SpSW	1988	LI	30 X 22	HAHN	50	1	2500	5000
Janet (172-36)	SpSW	KK/RL/JW/SpSW	1988	LI	30 X 22	HAHN	50	1	2500	3500
Lucas	PE	KK/RL/JW/SpSW	1988-90	LI/C	30 X 22	GAS/GE	50	7	6500	7000
Lucas/Book (Accordian Fold Letterpress Book)	PE		1990	LP	11 X 62	AP	100		1500	1500
John	PE	SpSW	1990	EB	30 X 23	R/BFK	40		3500	3500
John II	PE	SpSW	1990	EC	30 X 23	R/BFK	40		4500	4500
Alex	PE	KS	1991	WC	28 X 23	HANGA	75	95	4000	4000
Self Portrait	PE	SpSW	1992	EB	20 X 16	R/BFK	70	1	1500	1500
Alex	PE	KS	1992	WC	28 X 23	HANGA	75	165	4000	5000

SUE COE

BORN: London, England
RECENT EXHIB: Gallery Paule Anglim, San Francisco, CA, 1987; Zilkha Gallery, Wesleyan Univ, Middleton, CT, 1987; Houston Mus of Contemp Art, TX, 1987; Univ Gallery of Fine Art, Ohio State Univ, Columbus, OH, 1988; San Francisco Art Inst, CA, 1988; Kansas City Art Inst, Charlotte Crosby Kemper Gallery, MO, 1989; Virginia Commonwealth Univ, Anderson Gallery, Richmond, VA, 1989,92

PRINTERS: Steve Murray, NY (SM); Jo Watanabe, Brooklyn, NY (JW); Frances Thiel, Houston, TX (FT)
PUBLISHERS: Artist (ART); Sally Baker, NY (SB); Fawbush Editions, NY (FE); Sarah Blaffer Gallery, Univ of Houston, TX (SBG)
GALLERIES: PPOW Gallery, New York, NY; Barbara Gladstone Gallery, New York, NY; Gallery Paule Anglim, San Francisco, CA; Brody's Gallery, Wash, DC; Fawbush Gallery, New York, NY; Paul McCarron Fine Prints, New York, NY
MAILING ADDRESS: c/o Gallery St Etienne, 24 W 57th St, New York, NY 10019

TITLE	PUBLISHER	PRINTER	DATE	MEDIUM	DIMENSION (PAPER SIZE) IN INCHES	TYPE OF PAPER	EDITION NUMBER	NO. OF COLORS	ORIGINAL OPENING PRICE	CURRENT RETAIL PRICE
CURRENT EDITIONS:										
Untitled (Set of 7)	ART	SM	1984	PH/EB	12 X 18 EA	AP	250 EA	1 EA	450 SET	600 SET
The Landlord	ART	SM	1985	PH/EB	18 X 12	R/100	250	1	100	250
The Tenant	ART	SM	1985	PH/EB	18 X 12	R/100	250	1	100	250
Nicaragua	ART	SM	1987	EB	17 X 11	AP	87	1	200	350
Meat and Pork for Your Fork	ART/SBG	FT/SBG	1987	LB	30 X 22	AC/B-R/BFK	50	1	450	600
Large Hog Hoist	SB/FE	JW	1989	PH/A/SP	42 X 31	R/BFK	50	1	1000	1200

EDWARD COFFIN

PRINTERS: Artist (ART)
PUBLISHERS: Orion Editions, NY (OE)
GALLERIES: Orion Editions, NY

TITLE	PUBLISHER	PRINTER	DATE	MEDIUM	DIMENSION (PAPER SIZE) IN INCHES	TYPE OF PAPER	EDITION NUMBER	NO. OF COLORS	ORIGINAL OPENING PRICE	CURRENT RETAIL PRICE
SOLD OUT EDITIONS (RARE):										
David Lloyd Series I, II	OE	ART	1980	COL/HC	28 X 37 EA	AP	15 EA	Varies	275 EA 400	EA
David Lloyd Series III	OE	ART	1980	COL/HC	37 X 27	AP	15	Varies	300	425
David Lloyd Series V	OE	ART	1980	COL/HC	28 X 37	AP	15	Varies	275	400
David Lloyd Series VI	OE	ART	1980	COL/HC	26 X 38	AP	15	Varies	275	400
Structure Series I, II, III	OE	ART	1981	COL/HC	30 X 42 EA	AP	15 EA	Varies	300 EA	425 EA
Seat, States I, II	OE	ART	1983	COL/HC	30 X 42 EA	AP	15 EA	Varies	300 EA	425 EA
Sri Lanka, I, II, III, IV	OE	ART	1984	COL/HC	30 X 42 EA	AP	35 EA	Varies	400 EA	550 EA

The print market has become very selective. For the first time since we published the first edition of The Printworld Directory in 1982, the prices of prints have been greatly reduced and greatly increased for the same artists by the most reputable and established print publishers. Check the fifth edition to understand the movement.

BERNARD COHEN

BORN: London, England, 1933
EDUCATION: St Martin's Sch of Art, London, England, 1950–51; Slade Sch of Fine Art, London, England, 1951–54
RECENT EXHIB: John Berggruen Gallery, San Francisco, CA, 1988; Waddington Galleries, London, England, 1990,92
PRINTERS: Kelpra Studio, London, England (KS); Chris Prater, London, England (CP); Bud Shark, Boulder, CO (BS); Ron Trujillo, Boulder, CO (RT); Shark's Inc, Boulder, CO (SI); Matthew Christie, Boulder, CO (MC)
PUBLISHERS: Waddington Galleries, London, England (WG); Art Matters, Boulder, CO (AM); Shark's Inc, Boulder, CO (SI)
GALLERIES: Waddington Galleries, London, England; Shark's, Inc, Boulder, CO; John Berggruen Gallery, San Francisco, CA

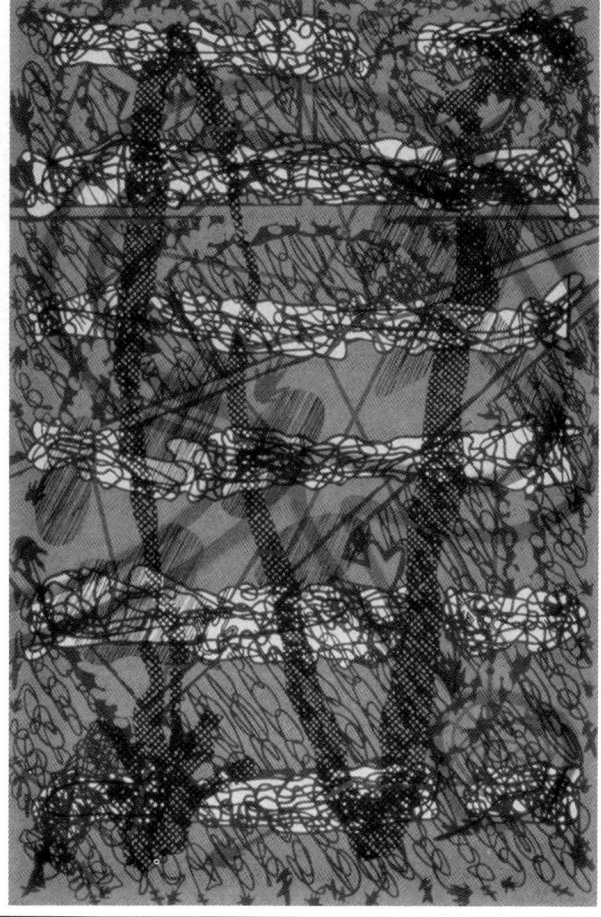

Bernard Cohen
In the Distance
Courtesy Shark's, Inc

TITLE	PUBLISHER	PRINTER	DATE	MEDIUM	DIMENSION (PAPER SIZE) IN INCHES	TYPE OF PAPER	EDITION NUMBER	NO. OF COLORS	ORIGINAL OPENING PRICE	CURRENT RETAIL PRICE
SOLD OUT EDITIONS (RARE):										
Concerning the Meal	WG	CP/KS	1980	EC	36 X 27	AP	60		200	900
The Party	AM		1981	LC	16 x 18	AP	50		200	800
The Trace	WG	CP/KS	1981	EC	36 X 27	AP	60		250	900
The Trace (Small Version)	AM		1981	LC	15 X 11	AP	30		200	500
Imitations	WG	CP/KS	1981	EC	36 X 27	AP	60		250	900
Things Seen	WG	CP/KS	1981	EC	36 X 27	AP	60		250	900
CURRENT EDITIONS:										
Imitating Shadows (Four Panels)	SI	BS/SI	1989	LC	20 X 20 EA 40 X 40 TOTAL	R/BFK/W	25 EA	11 EA	2500 SET	2500 SET
In the Distance	SI	BS/MC/SI	1990	LC	48 X 32	R/BFK/W	25	9	2500	2500

BRUCE COHEN

BORN: Santa Monica, CA; 1953
EDUCATION: Univ of California, Los Angeles, CA; Univ of California, Berkeley, CA; Univ of California, Santa Barbara, CA, 1975
RECENT EXHIB: Asher/Faure Gallery, Los Angeles, CA; Ruth Siegel Contemp Art, NY, 1987
COLLECTIONS: Solomon R Guggenheim Mus, NY; Frederick R Weisman Found, Baltimore, MD
PRINTERS: Richard Hammond, Los Angeles, CA (RH); Francesco Siqueiros, Los Angeles, CA (FS); Cirrus Editions Workshop, Los Angeles, CA (CEW)
PUBLISHERS: Cirrus Editions, Ltd, Los Angeles, CA (CE)
GALLERIES: Cirrus Editions Gallery, Los Angeles, CA; Asher/Faure Gallery, Los Angeles, CA; van Straaten Gallery, Chicago, IL; John Berggruen Gallery, San Francisco, CA

TITLE	PUBLISHER	PRINTER	DATE	MEDIUM	DIMENSION (PAPER SIZE) IN INCHES	TYPE OF PAPER	EDITION NUMBER	NO. OF COLORS	ORIGINAL OPENING PRICE	CURRENT RETAIL PRICE
CURRENT EDITIONS:										
Untitled (407C)	CE	RH/FS/CEW	1987	LB	40 X 40	AP88	40	1	950	1200
Untitled (410C)	CE	RH/FS/CEW	1987	LB	50 X 37	AP88	43	1	950	1200

MAX COLE

BORN: Hodgeman County, Kansas; February 14, 1937
EDUCATION: Univ of Arizona, Tucson, AZ, MFA, 1964
TEACHING: Asst Prof, Painting, Pasadena City Col, CA, 1967–79; Adj Assoc Prof, Columbia Univ, NY, 1985 to present
AWARDS: Purchase Award, St Paul Art Center, 1965; May Lieberman Award, Frye Mus of Art, Seattle, WA, 1966; Purchase Award, Laguna Beach Art Assn, CA, 1969; Nat Endowment for the Arts Fel, 1983; Pollock-Krasner Fel, 1986; Res Fel, Indo-US Submission 1988
RECENT EXHIB: Zabriskie Gallery, NY, 1987; Galerie Helene Grubair, Miami, FL 1988; Haines Gallery, San Francisco, CA, 1988; Galerie Schroder Monchengladbach, Germany, 1990

MAX COLE CONTINUED

COLLECTIONS: Los Angeles County Mus of Art, CA; Santa Barbara Mus of Art, CA; La Jolla Mus of Contemp Art, CA; Louisiana Mus, Denmark; Nat Gallery of Mod Art, New Delhi, India; Mus of New Mexico, Albuquerque, NM; Utah Mus, Salt Lake City, UT; Dallas Mus, TX; Everson Mus, Syracuse, NY; St Paul Art Center, MN; Newport Harbor Art Mus, Newport Beach, CA

PRINTERS: Leslie Sutcliff, Los Angeles, CA (LS); Robert Aull, Los Angeles, CA (RA)
PUBLISHERS: L A Louver Publications, Venice, CA (LAL)
GALLERIES: L A Louver Gallery, Venice, CA; Louis K Meisel Gallery, New York, NY; Zabriskie Gallery, New York, NY; Haines Gallery, San Francisco, CA; Kiyo Higashi Gallery, Los Angeles, CA
MAILING ADDRESS: 195 E Third St, New York, NY 10009

TITLE	PUBLISHER	PRINTER	DATE	MEDIUM	DIMENSION (PAPER SIZE) IN INCHES	TYPE OF PAPER	EDITION NUMBER	NO. OF COLORS	ORIGINAL OPENING PRICE	CURRENT RETAIL PRICE
CURRENT EDITIONS:										
Los Angeles Series (Set of 5):									2000 SET	3500 SET
Los Angeles Series #1	LAL	LS/RA	1980	E/I/REL	23 X 22	R/BFK/W	50	3	350	600
Los Angeles Series #2	LAL	LS/RA	1980	E/I/REL	23 X 22	R/BFK/W	50	3	350	600
Los Angeles Series #1	LAL	LS/RA	1981	E/I/REL	22 X 28	R/BFK/W	50	3	500	700
Los Angeles Series #2	LAL	LS/RA	1981	E/I/REL	22 X 28	R/BFK/G	50	4	500	800
Los Angeles Series #3	LAL	LS/RA	1981	E/I/REL	22 X 28	R/BFK/W	50	2	500	800

ROBERT H COLESCOTT

BORN: Oakland, CA; August, 26, 1925
EDUCATION: Univ of California, Berkeley, CA, AB, MA, with Atelier Fernand Leger, Paris, France
TEACHING: Assoc Prof, Drawing & Art Ed, Portland State Univ, OR, 1957–66; Assoc Prof, Painting, Am Univ, Cairo, Egypt, 1966–67; Prof, Art, California State Col, Stanislaus, CA, 1970–74; Lectr, Univ of California, Berkeley, CA, 1974–79; Instr, San Francisco Art Inst, CA, 1979–83; Prof, Art, 1983 to present
AWARDS: Nat Endowment for the Arts Grants, Creative Painting, 1976, 80,83; Guggenheim Found Fel, 1985
RECENT EXHIB: Rena Bransten Gallery, San Francisco, CA, 1987; Illinois State Univ, Normal, IL, 1989; New Mus of Contemp Art, NY, 1989; Contemp Arts Mus, Houston, TX, 1989; Marsh Gallery, Univ of Richmond, VA, 1989; Linda Cathcart Gallery, Santa Monica, CA, 1990; Overholland Mus, Amsterdam, The Netherlands, 1990; Delaware Art Mus, Wilmington, DE, 1992; Univ of Texas, UTA Center for Research in Contemp Art, Arlington, TX, 1992
COLLECTIONS: Metropolitan Mus of Art, NY; Seattle Art Mus, WA; Portland Art Mus, OR; San Francisco Mus of Mod Art, CA; Delaware Art Mus, Wilmington, DE
PRINTERS: Bill Lagatutta, Albuquerque, NM (BL); Eric Katter, Albuquerque, NM (EK); Anya K Szykitka, Albuquerque, NM (AKS); Artist (ART); Tamarind Inst, Albuquerque, NM (TI)
PUBLISHERS: Tamarind Inst, Albuquerque, NM (TI)
GALLERIES: Semaphore Gallery, New York, NY; Tamarind Inst, Albuquerque, NM; Phyllis Kind Galleries, Chicago, IL & New York, NY; Laura Russo Gallery, Portland, OR; Rena Bransten Gallery, San Francisco, CA; Linda Cathcart Gallery, Santa Monica, CA; Howard Yezerski Gallery, Boston, MA
MAILING ADDRESS: Art Dept, University of Arizona, Tucson, AZ 85719

TITLE	PUBLISHER	PRINTER	DATE	MEDIUM	DIMENSION (PAPER SIZE) IN INCHES	TYPE OF PAPER	EDITION NUMBER	NO. OF COLORS	ORIGINAL OPENING PRICE	CURRENT RETAIL PRICE
CURRENT EDITIONS:										
Lock and Key, State I	TI	EK/BL/TI	1989	LC	107 X 76 cm	SOM/CR	20	9	1000	1000
Lock and Key, State II	TI		1989	LC	107 X 76 cm	SOM/CR	20	9	1000	1000
Some Thoughts on Inter-Racial Sex (Set of 8)	TI	BL/TI	1989	LB	42 X 32 cm EA	SEK/AP	15 EA	1 EA	500 EA	600 EA
Fried Chicken and Fantasy	TI	BL/TI	1989	LB	61 X 76 cm	SEK/JP	15	1	450	450
Of Time and Place	TI	AKS/BL/TI	1989	LC	108 X 77 cm	GE	20	9	1000	1000

WARRINGTON COLESCOTT

BORN: Oakland, CA; March 7, 1921
EDUCATION: Univ of California, Berkeley, CA, BA, MA; Acad Grande Chaumiere, Paris, France; Slade Sch of Art, Univ Col, London, England
TEACHING: Prof, Art, Univ of Wisconsin, Madison, WI, 1949–78; Leo Steppart, Chmn, 1979–84, Prof, Emeritus, Dept of Art, 1986
AWARDS: Solomon R Guggenheim Fel, 1963, Nat Endowment Fel, 1976,79,83–84
RECENT EXHIB: Tampa Mus of Art, FL, 1987; Perimeter Gallery, Chicago, IL, 1988; Milwaukee Art Mus, WI, 1988; Retrosp, Elvehjem Mus of Art, Madison, WI, 1988–89; Nelson-Atkins Mus of Art, Kansas City, MO, 1989; Oklahoma State Univ, Gardiner Art Gallery, Stillwater, OK, 1992
COLLECTIONS: Metropolitan Mus of Art, NY; Mus of Mod Art, NY; Brooklyn Mus, NY; Art Inst of Chicago, IL; Carnegie Mus, Pittsburgh, PA
PRINTERS: Smith Anderson Editions, Palo Alto, CA (SAE)
PUBLISHERS: Smith Anderson Editions, Palo Alto, CA (SAE)
GALLERIES: Garver Gallery, Madison, WI; Perimeter Gallery, Chicago, IL; Smith Anderson Gallery, Palo Alto, CA; Peltz Gallery, Milwaukee, WI
MAILING ADDRESS: Route 1, Hollandale, WI 53544

TITLE	PUBLISHER	PRINTER	DATE	MEDIUM	DIMENSION (PAPER SIZE) IN INCHES	TYPE OF PAPER	EDITION NUMBER	NO. OF COLORS	ORIGINAL OPENING PRICE	CURRENT RETAIL PRICE
SOLD OUT EDITIONS (RARE):										
Bridge Across the Arno			1953	SP	15 X 12	RED	25		50	1500
Dillinger: The Battle			1964	EC/DPT	19 X 28		20		125	750
Wild West: Home on the Range			1969	SP	24 X 19	AP	75		100	300
CURRENT EDITIONS:										
Life and Times of Prof Dr Freud (Series of 15)	SAE	SAE	1989	DPT	46 X 32 EA	R/BFK	1 EA	1 EA	1800/ 2500 EA	1800/ 2500 EA

The retail prices of the 100,000 limited edition prints quoted in this directory are subject to change. Print publishers, artists and galleries were the direct sources for these quotations. Prices in the secondary market listed as "Sold Out Editions (Rare)" indicate that the publisher has a limited supply of that print or that the print is difficult to locate in the galleries.

JAMES COIGNARD

BORN: Tours, France; September 15, 1925
EDUCATION: L'Ecole des arts Decoratifs, Nice, France
RECENT EXHIB: First Impressions Gallery, Toronto, Canada, 1988; Nahan Galleries, NY, 1988,90
COLLECTIONS: Whitney Mus of Am Art, NY; Univ of Pennsylvania, Phila, PA; Mus of Mod Art, San Francisco, CA; Mus of San Diego, CA; Dublin Mus, Ireland; Bibliotheque Nat, Paris, France; Mus de Saint-Denis, Paris, France; Mus of New Mexico, Santa Fe, NM; British Mus, London, England; Mus of Israel, Jerusalem, Israel; Phoenix Art Mus, AZ; Syracuse Univ, NY; Univ of Alabama, Huntsville, AL; Lincoln Univ, Oxford, PA; Rutgers Univ, New Brunswick, NJ; South African Nat Gallery, Capetown, South Africa; Mus de Dimona, Israel; Mus Nat de Luxembourg, Germany; High Art Mus, Atlanta, GA; Delgado Art Mus, New Orleans, LA; Yale Univ, New Haven, CT
PRINTERS: Atelier Pasnic, Paris, France (APas); Fequet-Baudier, Paris, France (FB)
PUBLISHERS: Transworld Art, Inc, NY (TAI); Nahan Editions, New Orleans, LA (NE)
GALLERIES: Hahn Gallery, Phila, PA; Concept Art Gallery, Pittsburgh, PA; Gallery 22, Bloomfield Hills, MI; Graphic Art Collection, Hallandale, FL; Patricia Judith Gallery, Boca Raton, FL; Boody Fine Arts, St Louis, MO; Nahan Galleries, New Orleans, LA & New York, NY & Tokyo, Japan; Tower Park Gallery, Peoria Heights, IL; Stephen Gill Gallery, New York, NY; Galerie Internationale, Bloomfield Hills, MI

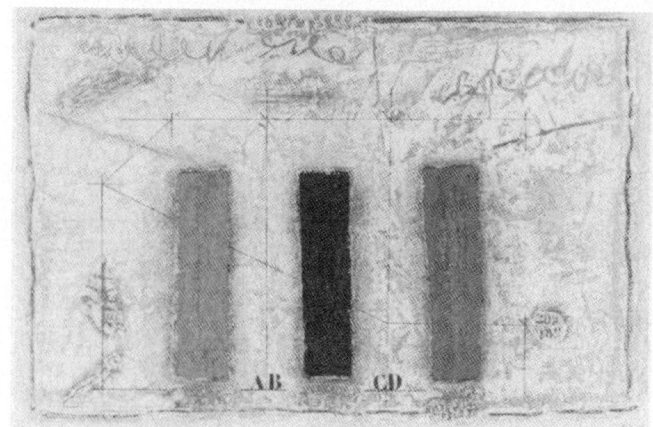

James Coignard
Trois Espaces Rouge, Noir, Bleue
Courtesy Nahan Editions, Inc

TITLE	PUBLISHER	PRINTER	DATE	MEDIUM	DIMENSION (PAPER SIZE) IN INCHES	TYPE OF PAPER	EDITION NUMBER	NO. OF COLORS	ORIGINAL OPENING PRICE	CURRENT RETAIL PRICE
SOLD OUT EDITIONS (RARE):										
Ecriture-Ecretues (Set of 3)	NE	APas	1978	CAR/PO	16 X 21 EA	HMP	75 EA		550 SET	2500 SET
Deux Profils Justaposes et Ecritures	TAI	ART	1978	EB/SE/CR/RP	23 X 35	RP	75	9	300	5500
Otages en Lumiere	TAI	ART	1978	EB/SE/CR/RP	31 X 23	RP	75	9	300	5500
L'Observateur 8 et Otage	TAI	ART	1978	EB/SE/CR/RP	30 X 23	RP	75	8	300	5500
Les Jumeaux-Otages Sur Rouge	TAI	ART	1978	EB/SE/CR/RP	30 X 23	RP	75	8	300	5500
Deux Mannequins-Otages	TAI	ART	1979	EB/SE/CR/RP	30 X 24	RP	75	9	300	5500
Profil et Overture Rouge	TAI	ART	1979	EB/SE/CR/RP	23 X 35	RP	75	9	300	5500
Triangles et Otage en Rouge	TAI	APas	1980	EB/HC	33 X 23	ML	75	Varies	300	5500
Personage et Agression Verticale	TAI	APas	1980	EB/HC	30 X 22	ML	75	Varies	300	5500
Verticalite	TAI	APas	1980	EB/HC	30 X 22	ML	75		300	4500
Profile Blanc en Blocage 5	TAI	APas	1980	EB/HC	22 X 30	ML	75		300	4500
Horizontales Ludiques	TAI	APas	1981	EB/CO/HC	22 X 30	ML	75		400	4500
Quatre Espaces Pre Occupes	TAI	APas	1981	EB/CO/HC	22 X 30	ML	75		400	4500
Surface Equivoque	TAI	APas	1981	EB/CO/HC	30 X 22	ML	75		400	4500
Itineraire Multiples	TAI	APas	1981	EB/CO/HC	30 X 22	ML	75		400	4500
Architectures: Integration de Bleu	TAI	APas	1981	EB/A/HC	26 X 39	ML	55		650	4500
Architectures: Structure Ouverte	TAI	APas	1981	EB/A/HC	39 X 26	ML	55		650	4500
Song of Broad Ave Portfolio	TAI	FB	1982	EB/CO/HC	30 X 23 EA	ML	95 EA		2400 SET	8500 SET
Habitat	TAI	FB	1982	EB/CO/HC	30 X 23	ML	95		425	4500
Structure Contestée	TAI	FB	1982	EB/CO/HC	30 X 23	ML	95		425	4500
Report d'Horizontalite	TAI	FB	1982	EB/CO/HC	30 X 23	ML	95		425	4500
Axial du Bleu	TAI	FB	1982	EB/CO/HC	30 X 23	ML	95		425	4500
Elaboration Partielle	TAI	FB	1982	EB/CO/HC	30 X 23	ML	95		425	4500
Les Axes Divergents	TAI	FB	1982	EB/CO/HC	30 X 23	ML	95		425	4500
Univers Encastres	TAI	APas	1982	EB/CO/HC	22 X 30	ML	75		425	4500
Etude de Verticalites	TAI	APas	1982	EB/CO/HC	22 X 18	ML	95		280	4000
Recherche d'Integration et Rouge	TAI	APas	1982	EB/CO/HC	22 X 30	ML	75		425	4000
Structure d'un Espace Bleu	TAI	APas	1982	EB/CO/HC	26 X 40	ML	75		650	5000
Amenagements d'Equilibre Naturel	TAI	APas	1982	EB/CO/HC	26 X 40	ML	75		650	5000
Geometries Autour d'un Prealable	TAI	APas	1982	EB/CO/HC	17 X 22	ML	95		280	4000
Espaces Corriges	TAI	APas	1982	EB/CO/HC	22 X 17	ML	95		280	4000
Blocage du Bleu	TAI	APas	1983	EB/A/CO/HC	40 X 60	HMP	40		1250	5500
Geometrics Autour d'un Prealable	TAI	APas	1983	EB/A/CO/HC	18 X 22	ML	95		280	4000
Dyptique I Blockage Bleu	TAI	APas	1983	EB/A/CO/HC	30 X 22	ML	95		425	4500
Dyptique II Blockage Bleu	TAI	APas	1983	EB/A/CO/HC	30 X 22	ML	95		425	4500
Rouge en Axe AB	TAI	APas	1983	EB/A/CO/HC	22 X 18	ML	95		280	4000
Blues en Axe AB	TAI	APas	1983	EB/A/CO/HC	22 X 18	ML	95		280	4000
Deux Rouges en Nomenclature	NE	APas	1984	CAR/PO	40 X 26	HMP	75		550	4000
Trois Espaces Rouge, Noir, Bleur	NE	APas	1985	CAR/PO	59 X 39	DUCH	60		1500	6000
Resolution Triangulaire	NE	APas	1985	CAR/PO	59 X 39	DUCH	60		1500	6000
Les Integrations (Set of 3)	NE	APas	1985	CAR/PO	26 X 20 EA	DUCH	75 EA		1200 SET	6000 SET
Les Penetrantes (Set of 4)	NE	APas	1985	CAR/PO	22 X 18 EA	HMP	75 EA		850 SET	5000 SET
Deux Bleus en Axe AB	NE	APas	1985	CAR/PO	27 X 20	HMP	75		275	3000
Penetration Architecturale	NE	APas	1985	CAR/PO	26 X 20	DUCH	75		425	3000
Grand Diagonal Rouge	NE	APas	1985	CAR/PO	59 X 39	HMP	60		1200	5000
Symetrie Blanche	NE	APas	1985	CAR/PO	40 X 26	DUCH	75		750	4500
Rouge Determinante	NE	APas	1985	CAR/PO	40 X 26	DUCH	75		750	4500
Quatre Ouvertures en Biege et Vert	NE	APas	1985	CAR/PO	40 X 26	HMP	75		600	3500
Team	NE	APas	1986	CAR/PO	26 X 20	DUCH	75		450	2000
Le Buste	NE	APas	1986	CAR/PO	39 X 29	DUCH	75		900	3500

JAMES COIGNARD CONTINUED

TITLE	PUBLISHER	PRINTER	DATE	MEDIUM	DIMENSION (PAPER SIZE) IN INCHES	TYPE OF PAPER	EDITION NUMBER	NO. OF COLORS	ORIGINAL OPENING PRICE	CURRENT RETAIL PRICE
SOLD OUT EDITIONS (RARE):										
Recherche Lineaire (Trip)	NE	APas	1986	CAR/PO	26 X 20 EA	DUCH	75 EA		1000 SET	5000 SET
Etude Reflective	NE	APas	1986	CAR/PO	26 X 20	DUCH	45		425	2500
Le Grand Circle Rouge	NE	APas	1986	CAR/PO	59 X 39	DUCH	60		1500	6000
Les Blancs Contraires	NE	APas	1986	CAR/PO	40 X 29	DUCH	75		750	4500
Horizontal Violette	NE	APas	1987	CAR/PO	29 X 39	DUCH	75		950	4000
Tension Jaune	NE	APas	1987	CAR/PO	26 X 20	DUCH	95		600	3000
Double Verticale Bleue	NE	APas	1987	CAR/PO	26 X 20	DUCH	95		600	3000
Dynamic Horizontal	NE	APas	1987	CAR/PO	39 X 59	DUCH	80		1800	6000
Equilibre Triangulaire	NE	APas	1987	CAR	59 X 39	DUCH	80		2400	5800
Verticalite Violette	NE	APas	1987	CAR	39 X 29	DUCH	95		1400	4000
Rouges Antiques	NE	APas	1987	CAR	29 X 39	DUCH	95		1400	4000
Rouge Limite	NE	APas	1988	CAR	27 X 20	DUCH	95		750	3200
Etude Masse Bleue	NE	APas	1988	CAR	27 X 20	DUCH	95		750	2500
Etude Masse Rouge	NE	APas	1988	CAR	27 X 20	DUCH	95		750	2500
Verticalite Rouge	NE	APas	1988	CAR	39 X 59	DUCH	85		2800	6000
Tension en AB	NE	APas	1988	CAR	29 X 39	DUCH	95		1800	5000
Determination d'un Axe	NE	APas	1988	CAR	29 X 39	DUCH	95		1800	3500
Rupture	NE	APas	1988	CAR	39 X 28	DUCH	95		1200	3500
Deux Noir en Stratification	NE	APas	1988	CAR	39 X 29	DUCH	95		1800	3500
Noir et Rouge	NE	APas	1989	CAR	59 X 39	DUCH	85		2000	5000
Espace Dynamique Bleu	NE	APas	1989	CAR	20 X 26	DUCH	95		700	2000
Dynamique en Brun	NE	APas	1989	CAR	29 X 30	DUCH	95		1200	3500
Directional II	NE	APas	1989	CAR	26 X 20	DUCH	95		700	2000
Preoccupation Double (Dipt)	NE	APas	1989	CAR	39 X 60	DUCH	95		1800	6000
Les Positionements-Rouge	NE	APas	1989	CAR	26 X 20	DUCH	95		900	2000
CURRENT EDITIONS:										
Presence	NE	APas	1986	CAR/PO	39 X 29	DUCH	75		900	2500
Tension Derivee (Trip)	NE	APas	1987	CAR/PO	26 X 20 EA	DUCH	85 EA		1500 SET	2400 SET
Grand Angulaire Vert (Dipt)	NE	APas	1987	CAR/PO	26 X 20	DUCH	85 EA		1000 SET	2700 SET
Bleu Tension Horizontale (Dipt)	NE	APas	1988	CAR	29 X 68	DUCH	85		2400	5000
Actions Complementaires (Trip)	NE	APas	1988	CAR	26 X 18	DUCH	85		1800	5000
Concentration d'un Bleu	NE	APas	1988	CAR	59 X 39	DUCH	80		2200	4000
Blocage Rouge	NE	APas	1989	CAR	39 X 29	DUCH	95		1200	2200
Designation	NE	APas	1989	CAR	39 X 29	DUCH	95		1200	1800
Directional I	NE	APas	1989	CAR	39 X 59	DUCH	85		2000	3200
Vecteur Rouge	NE	APas	1989	CAR	20 X 26	DUCH	95		700	2000
Difraction	NE	APas	1989	CAR	39 X 29	DUCH	95		1250	2700
Les Positionements-Gris	NE	APas	1989	CAR	26 X 20	DUCH	95		900	1800
Lumiere	NE	APas	1990	CAR	20 X 26	DUCH	95		800	1200
Bleus Syncopes	NE	APas	1990	CAR	39 X 29	DUCH	95		1600	2400
Communication	NE	APas	1990	CAR	29 X 39	DUCH	95		1800	1800
Attente	NE	APas	1990	CAR	50 X 39	DUCH	85		2500	2500
Architecture	NE	APas	1991	CAR	39 X 29	DUCH	85		2000	2500
Introduction sur Bleu	NE	APas	1991	CAR	49 X 39	DUCH	85		3000	3000
Forme Noire	NE	APas	1991	CAR	49 X 39	DUCH	85		3000	3000
Riposte	NE	APas	1991	CAR	27 X 20	DUCH	95		1200	1400
Face Minerale (Dipt)	NE	APas	1991	CAR	26 X 20 EA	DUCH	95		2400	2400
Chuté sur Rouge	NE	APas	1991	CAR	30 X 22	DUCH	95		1400	1800

James Coignard
Directional II
Courtesy Nahan Editions, Inc

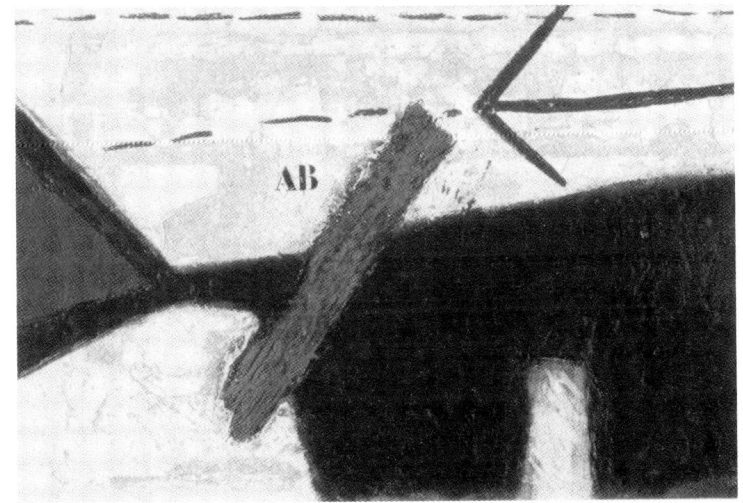

James Coignard
Directional
Courtesy Nahan Editions, Inc

JAMES COIGNARD CONTINUED

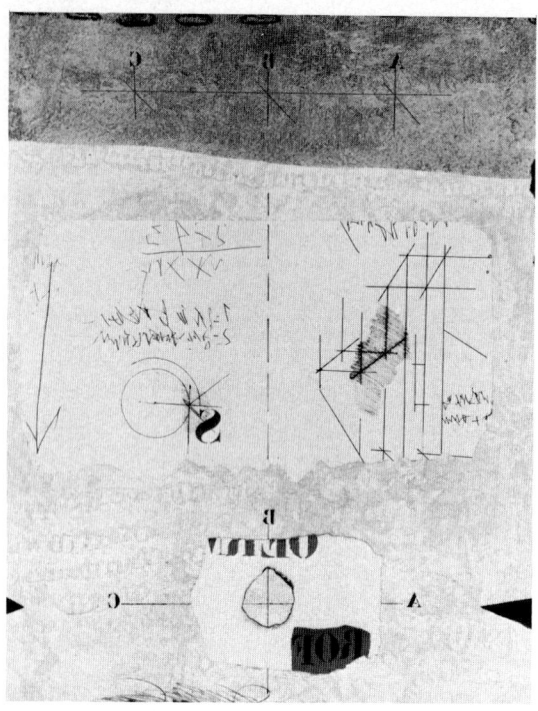

James Coignard
Report d'Horizontalite
Courtesy Transworld Art, Inc

James Coignard
Les Blancs Contraries
Courtesy Nahan Editions, Inc

James Coignard
Profile Blanc en Blocage S
Courtesy Transworld Art, Inc

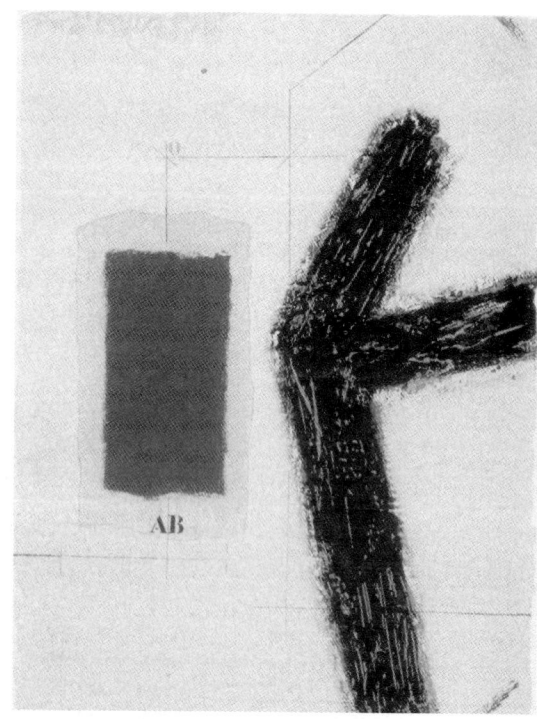

James Coignard
Dyptique II Blocage Rouge
Courtesy Transworld Art, Inc

The print market has become very selective. For the first time since we published the first edition of The Printworld Directory in 1982, the prices of prints have been greatly reduced and greatly increased for the same artists by the most reputable and established print publishers. Check the fifth edition to understand the movement.

OTHELLO ANDERSON

PRINTERS: Fred Gude (FG); Landfall Press, Inc, Chicago, IL (LPI)

PUBLISHERS: Landfall Press, Inc, Chicago, IL (LPI)
GALLERIES: Landfall Press, Inc, Chicago, IL; Quartet Editions, New York, NY

TITLE	PUBLISHER	PRINTER	DATE	MEDIUM	DIMENSION (PAPER SIZE) IN INCHES	TYPE OF PAPER	EDITION NUMBER	NO. OF COLORS	ORIGINAL OPENING PRICE	CURRENT RETAIL PRICE
CURRENT EDITIONS:										
Event Horizon, Exit-Entry	LPI	FG/LPI	1980	LC	22 X 30	AP/W	100	2	125	300

NANCY CHADWICK

BORN: Houston, TX; March 3, 1953
EDUCATION: Phillips Acad, Studio Arts Prog, Andover, MA, 1968; Temple Univ, Rome, Italy, Film Prog, 1973; Univ of Wisconsin, Madison, WI, BA, 1975; Cornish Inst of Allied Arts, Visual Arts Prog, Seattle, WA, 1978

PRINTERS: Artist (ART)
PUBLISHERS: Gremillion & Co, Houston, TX (G); Artist (ART)
GALLERIES: Glass Gallery, New York, NY

TITLE	PUBLISHER	PRINTER	DATE	MEDIUM	DIMENSION (PAPER SIZE) IN INCHES	TYPE OF PAPER	EDITION NUMBER	NO. OF COLORS	ORIGINAL OPENING PRICE	CURRENT RETAIL PRICE
CURRENT EDITIONS:										
Earth/Sky	ART/GC	ART	1981	LC/WC	16 X 19	IT	5	2	100	350
Reserved Air Space	ART/GC	ART	1981	I/WC	18 X 15	VGZ	5	3	100	350
Complete Circuit	ART/GC	ART	1981	WC	19 X 21	AC/BL	10	3	125	400
Wave with Rain	ART/GC	ART	1981	WC	12 X 24	TOR	5	3	100	400
Spring	ART/GC	ART	1981	WC	12 X 24	TOR	5	3	100	400
Memorial Park	ART/GC	ART	1981	WC	25 X 19	YO #25	5	4	100	400
Alaska One	ART/GC	ART	1981	WC	22 X 30	INO	15	2	125	450
Alaska Two	ART/GC	ART	1982	WC	30 X 22	INO	15	2	125	450
Hour of the Snake	ART/GC	ART	1982	WC	30 X 22	TOR	15	5	125	450
Open Heart	ART/GC	ART	1982	WC	17 X 24	YO #4	15	1	100	200
Heart Over Water	ART	ART	1982	WC	17 X 23	YO #4	15	1	200	300

MARGO HUMPHREY

BORN: 1942
COLLECTIONS: San Francisco Mus of Mod Art, CA
PRINTERS: Brian Haberman, Albuquerque, NM (BH); Lynne D Allen, Albuquerque, NM (LDA); Tom Pruitt, Albuquerque, NM (TP); Tamarind Inst, Albuquerque, NM (TI)

PUBLISHERS: Tamarind Inst, Albuquerque, NM (TI)
GALLERIES: Tamarind Inst, Albuquerque, NM; Brody's Gallery, Wash, DC; McIntosh Gallery, Atlanta, GA; McKee Gallery, New York, NY

TITLE	PUBLISHER	PRINTER	DATE	MEDIUM	DIMENSION (PAPER SIZE) IN INCHES	TYPE OF PAPER	EDITION NUMBER	NO. OF COLORS	ORIGINAL OPENING PRICE	CURRENT RETAIL PRICE
CURRENT EDITIONS:										
The Night Kiss	TI	TP/TI	1985	LC	22 X 30	AP/W	40	10	400	650
The Lady & the Tiger	TI	BH/LDA/TI	1985	LC	22 X 30	AP/W	40	4	400	650

RALPH HUMPHREY

BORN: Youngstown, OH; April 4, 1932
EDUCATION: Youngstown Univ, OH, 1951–52; 1954–56
TEACHING: Instr, Art Students League, NY; Harley House, NY, 1959–60; Bennington Col, VT, 1961–63; New Sch for Social Res, NY; Prof. Art, Hunter Col, NY, 1966 to present
RECENT EXHIB: Univ of California, Mandeville Gallery, San Diego, CA, 1988; Butler Inst of Am Art, Youngstown, OH, 1988; Mary Boone Gallery, NY, 1990

COLLECTIONS: Bennington, Col, VT; Rose Art Mus, Brandeis Univ, Waltham, MA; Wadsworth, Atheneum, Hartford, CT; Mus of Mod Art, NY; Univ of North Carolina, Greensboro, NC; Australian Nat Gallery, Canberra, Australia; Philadelphia Mus of Art, PA; San Francisco Mus of Mod Art, CA
PRINTERS: Aeropress, NY (A); Patricia Branstead, NY (PB)
PUBLISHERS: Parasol Press, NY (PaP)
GALLERIES: Rhona Hoffman Gallery, Chicago, IL; Martina Hamilton Gallery, New York, NY; Nielsen Gallery, Boston, MA; Mary Boone Gallery, New York, NY; Daniel Weinberg Gallery, Santa Monica, CA; Locks Gallery, Phila, PA; Sorrentino/Mayer Fine Art, New York, NY & Great Neck, NY

TITLE	PUBLISHER	PRINTER	DATE	MEDIUM	DIMENSION (PAPER SIZE) IN INCHES	TYPE OF PAPER	EDITION NUMBER	NO. OF COLORS	ORIGINAL OPENING PRICE	CURRENT RETAIL PRICE
SOLD OUT EDITIONS (RARE):										
Neighbors (Series of 4)	PaP	A/PB	1980	AC	22 X 25 EA	R/BFK	40 EA		700 EA	2000 EA

The Printworld Directory is accepting new applications for the seventh edition. Approximately 300 new artists will be accepted. Please use the two forms provided in the back section of this directory to submit biographical data and documentation of prints. Edition number of each print must not exceed 500 and the retail price must be $100 or more.

PIERRE COLLIN

PRINTERS: Atelier Lacouriére et Frélaut, Paris, France (ALF); Atelier Juan Barbara, Barcelona, Spain (AJB)
PUBLISHERS: Artist (ART)
GALLERIES: Brody's Gallery, Wash, DC; Galerie Lacouriére, Paris, France

TITLE	PUBLISHER	PRINTER	DATE	MEDIUM	DIMENSION (PAPER SIZE) IN INCHES	TYPE OF PAPER	EDITION NUMBER	NO. OF COLORS	ORIGINAL OPENING PRICE	CURRENT RETAIL PRICE
SOLD OUT EDITIONS (RARE):										
Le Réveil II (The Awakening II)	ART	AJB	1983	EB/DPT	79 X 39	AP	10	1	1600	2200
Au Lavebo I (At the Sink I)	ART	ALF	1984	EB/DPT	79 X 39	AP	10	1	1600	2200
CURRENT EDITIONS:										
Atelier Lacouriére II (Trip)	ART	ALF	1985–87	EB	49 X 176	AP	10	1	3000	6500

JAMES D CONAWAY

BORN: Granite City, IL; October 9, 1932
EDUCATION: Southern Illinois Univ, Carbondale, IL, BA; Univ of Iowa, Iowa City, IA, MA, MFA
TEACHING: Asst Prof, Univ of Wisconsin, Stevens Point, WI; Prof, Painting & Drawing, Anoka Ramsey Col, Minneapolis, MN, presently; Prof, Painting, Hamline Univ, St Paul, MN, presently
AWARDS: Purchase Award, Davenport Municipal Art Gallery, IA, 1963; Waterloo Municipal Art Galleries, IA, 1965; Donors Prize, Walker Art Center, Minneapolis, MN, 1966
PUBLISHERS: C G Rein Publishers, St Paul, MN (CGR); Artist (ART)
PRINTERS: Land Mark Editions, Minneapolis, MN (LME); Sette Publishing Company, Tempe, AZ (SPC)
GALLERIES: C G Rein Galleries, Scottsdale, AZ & Santa Fe, NM & Houston, TX & Minneapolis, MN; Suzanne Kohn Gallery, St Paul, MN & Minneapolis, MN; Wilhelm Gallery, Scottsdale, AZ; Lisa Dubins Gallery, Los Angeles, CA; Harris Gallery, Houston, TX; Stephanie Dorn Gallery, Chicago, IL
MAILING ADDRESS: 2758 Benjamin St, Minneapolis, MN 55418

TITLE	PUBLISHER	PRINTER	DATE	MEDIUM	DIMENSION (PAPER SIZE) IN INCHES	TYPE OF PAPER	EDITION NUMBER	NO. OF COLORS	ORIGINAL OPENING PRICE	CURRENT RETAIL PRICE
CURRENT EDITIONS:										
Vermillion Cliffs (Dipt)	CGR	LME	1983	LC	38 X 25 EA	OKP	100 EA		600 SET	950 SET
Jemez Springs	CGR	LME	1983	LC	26 X 35	HANGA	100		300	350
Upper Havasu	CGR	LME	1984	LC	24 X 30	HANGA	100		300	350
City Park Series	CGR	SPC	1986	LC	30 X 42	R/BFK/W	100		450	375
River City	CGR	SPC	1986	LC	30 X 42	R/BFK/W	100		450	375
Lakeside Confluence	ART	LME	1990	LC	24 X 33	HANGA	50	5	500	500
Aerial Confluence	ART	LME	1990	LC	24 X 33	HANGA	50	5	500	500

JERRY CONCHA

BORN: Sacramento, CA; 1935
EDUCATION: San Francisco Art Inst, CA, BFA, 1970
AWARDS: Artist of the Year Award, Oakland Mus, CA, 1983
COLLECTIONS: San Francisco Mus of Mod Art, CA; De Saisset Art Mus, Univ of Santa Clara, CA; Seattle Art Mus, WA
PUBLISHERS: Ernest De Soto Workshop, San Francisco, CA (EDSW)
PRINTERS: Ernest F De Soto, San Francisco, CA (EDS); Ernest De Soto Workshop, San Francisco, CA (EDSW)
GALLERIES: Allrich Gallery, San Francisco, CA; Ernest De Soto Workshop, San Francisco, CA

TITLE	PUBLISHER	PRINTER	DATE	MEDIUM	DIMENSION (PAPER SIZE) IN INCHES	TYPE OF PAPER	EDITION NUMBER	NO. OF COLORS	ORIGINAL OPENING PRICE	CURRENT RETAIL PRICE
CURRENT EDITIONS:										
Curandero II	EDSW	EDS/EDSW	1979	LC	22 X 30	AP/W	75	8	400	700
Untitled (Regular)	EDSW	EDS/EDSW	1981	LC	30 X 23	AP/W	80	9	400	600
Untitled (DeLuxe)	EDSW	EDS/EDSW	1981	LC	30 X 23	HMP	21	9	500	700
Ahote	EDSW	EDS/EDSW	1982	LC	30 X 23	AP/W	90	10	500	600
Untitled	EDSW	EDS/EDSW	1986	LC	30 X 22	AP/W	80	9	750	850

CLIFF CONDAK

BORN: Havervill, MA; 1930
EDUCATION: Inst of Applied Arts & Sciences, NY, 1951; Brooklyn Mus, NY; Mus of Fine Arts, Salzburg, Austria, 1952–53; Art Students League, NY, 1953–54; The New Sch, NY, 1956–57; L'Accademenia Delle Belle Art, Florence, Italy, 1957–58; Independent Study, Mexico, 1962; Pratt Inst, Brooklyn, NY; Mus of Mod Art Sch, NY
TEACHING: Sch of Visual Arts, NY; Pratt Inst, NY; Parsons Sch of Design, NY
COLLECTIONS: Allentown Art Mus, PA; Muhlenberg Col, PA
PRINTERS: Atelier Ettinger, NY (AE)
PUBLISHERS: Fred Dorfman, Inc, NY (FDI)
GALLERIES: OK Harris, New York, NY; Fred Dorfman, New York, NY; Cordier & Ekstrom, New York, NY

TITLE	PUBLISHER	PRINTER	DATE	MEDIUM	DIMENSION (PAPER SIZE) IN INCHES	TYPE OF PAPER	EDITION NUMBER	NO. OF COLORS	ORIGINAL OPENING PRICE	CURRENT RETAIL PRICE
SOLD OUT EDITIONS (RARE):										
Jiggs & Annie A Study of Truman Capote	FDI	AE	1979	LC	28 X 33	AP	150	6	150	300
Walking	FDI	AE	1979	LC	34 X 28	AP	150	6	150	300
Banafish	FDI	AE	1981	LC	24 X 30	AP	175	6	250	400

GEORGE CONDO

BORN: New Hampshire; 1957
RECENT EXHIB: Gallery Bruno Bischofberger, Zürich, Switzerland, 1987; Akira Ikeda Gallery, Nagoya, Japan, 1987; Monika Sprueth Galerie, Cologne, West Germany, 1987–88; Pace Gallery, NY, 1988; Vrej Baghoomian, Inc, NY, 1988; Waddington Galleries, London, England, 1989; Daniel Templon Gallery, Paris, France, 1990

PRINTERS: Aldo Crommelynk, NY (AC); Atelier Crommelynk, NY (AtC)
PUBLISHERS: Aldo Crommelynk, NY (AC)
GALLERIES: Pace Prints, New York, NY; Waddington Galleries, London, England; Monika Sprueth Galerie, Cologne, West Germany; Gallery Bruno Bischofberger, Zürich, Switzerland; Akira Ikeda Gallery, Nagoya, Japan; Daniel Templon Gallery, Paris, France

TITLE	PUBLISHER	PRINTER	DATE	MEDIUM	DIMENSION (PAPER SIZE) IN INCHES	TYPE OF PAPER	EDITION NUMBER	NO. OF COLORS	ORIGINAL OPENING PRICE	CURRENT RETAIL PRICE
CURRENT EDITIONS:										
Untitled (169-1) (Set of 4)	AC	AC/AtC	1989	EB	13 X 10 EA	HAHN	55 EA	1 EA	1500 SET	1500 SET
Untitled (169-2) (Set of 7)	AC	AC/AtC	1989	EB	18 X 15 EA	HAHN	55 EA	1 EA	4000 SET	4000 SET
Untitled (Landscape) (169-3)	AC	AC/AtC	1989	EB	28 X 19	HAHN	55	1	850	850
Untitled (Portrait) (169-4)	AC	AC/AtC	1989	EB	27 X 19	HAHN	55	1	850	850
Table (169-5)	AC	AC/AtC	1989	EB	25 X 31	HAHN	55	1	1200	1200
Clown (169-6)	AC	AC/AtC	1989	EB/A	25 X 21	HAHN	55	1	1800	1800

CHUCK CONNELLY

BORN: Pittsburgh, PA; 1955
EDUCATION: Tyler Sch of Art, Temple Univ, Phila, PA, BFA, 1977
RECENT EXHIB: Galleria La Planita, Rome, Italy, 1987; Annina Nosei Gallery, NY, 1987; Thomas Segal Gallery, Boston, MA, 1988; Lennon, Weinberg, Inc, NY, 1989,90,92
PRINTERS: Joe Fawbush Editions, NY (JFE); Mohammad Omer Khalil, Brooklyn, NY (MOK)

PUBLISHERS: Joe Fawbush Editions, NY (JFE); This History, Brooklyn, NY (TH); Artist (ART)
GALLERIES: Joe Fawbush Editions, New York, NY; Annina Nosei Gallery, New York, NY; Edward Tyler Nahem Fine Art, New York, NY; Lennon Weinberg, Inc, New York, NY; Daniel Newburg Gallery, New York, NY; Locks Gallery, Phila, PA
MAILING ADDRESS: c/o Lennon Weinberg Gallery, 580 Broadway, 2nd Floor, New York, Ny 10012

TITLE	PUBLISHER	PRINTER	DATE	MEDIUM	DIMENSION (PAPER SIZE) IN INCHES	TYPE OF PAPER	EDITION NUMBER	NO. OF COLORS	ORIGINAL OPENING PRICE	CURRENT RETAIL PRICE
SOLD OUT EDITIONS (RARE):										
Untitled	ART/JFE	JFE	1983	LI	17 X 22	HOS	5	1	250	400
Untitled	TH	MOK	1985	EB	20 X 26	AC	20	1	400	500
Untitled	TH	MOK	1986	EB/SG	43 X 30	AP	16	1	600	750

ANN CONNER

BORN: Wilmington, NC; August 11, 1948
EDUCATION: Salem Col, Winston-Salem, NC, 1970; Univ of North Carolina, Chapel Hill, NC, MACT, Painting, 1972, Painting, MFA, 1975
TEACHING: Assoc Prof, Art, Univ of North Carolina, Wilmington, NC, 1972 to present
AWARDS: Asolo Italy, Scholarship, Salem Col, Winston-Salem, NC, 1970; Hofstra Univ, Hempstead, NY, 1970; Title III Fel, Univ of North Carolina, Chapel Hill, NC, 1974; Arts Council Emerging Artists Grant, 1991; Research & Development Grant, Univ of North Carolina, Wilmington, NC 1974,80,86,89,90,92
RECENT EXHIB: Brody's Gallery, Wash, DC, 1987; Danville Mus of Fine Arts, VA, 1988; Kanagawa Perfectural Gallery, Kanagawa-ken, Japan, 1988,89; John Szoke Graphics, NY, 1990; Hanes Art Gallery, Univ of North Carolina, Chapel Hill, NC, 1991; Central Slovak Gallery, Banska Bystricia, Czechoslovakia, 1991; California Legion of Honor, Lincoln Park, San Francisco, CA, 1991; Lilly Library Gallery, Duke Univ, Durham, NC, 1992; Wenniger Graphics, Boston, MA, 1992
COLLECTIONS: North Carolina Mus, Raleigh, NC; Amon Carter Mus, Ft Worth, TX; Duke Univ Medical Center, Durham, NC; Southern Graphics Center, Oxford, MI; Nat Gallery of Art, Wash, DC; Library of Congress, Wash, DC; North Carolina Mus of Art, Raleigh, NC
PRINTERS: Solo Press, NY (SP); Artist (ART); Vicki Sclafani (VS); Cappy Kuhn (CK); Mark Abrahamson (MA); Winstone Press, Inc, Mocksville, NC (WPI)
PUBLISHERS: John Szoke Graphics, Inc, NY (JSG); Orion Editions, NY (OE); Artist (ART); Winstone Press, Inc, Mocksville, NC (WPI)
GALLERIES: Corporate Art Directions, New York, NY; John Szoke Graphics, New York, NY; Wenniger Graphics, Boston, MA; L Bartman Fine Arts, Chicago, IL; Raleigh Contemporary Galleries, Raleigh, NC
MAILING ADDRESS: 329 Stradleigh Rd, Wilmington, NC 28403

TITLE	PUBLISHER	PRINTER	DATE	MEDIUM	DIMENSION (PAPER SIZE) IN INCHES	TYPE OF PAPER	EDITION NUMBER	NO. OF COLORS	ORIGINAL OPENING PRICE	CURRENT RETAIL PRICE
SOLD EDITIONS (RARE):										
Vermillion I	ART	ART	1982	WC	38 X 25	KOZO	14	9	250	500
Coral	ART	ART	1983	WC	38 X 25	KOZO	10	6	350	500
CURRENT EDITIONS:										
Lily Pond	ART	ART	1982	WC	38 X 25	KOZO	12	5	300	350
Vermillion II	ART	ART	1982	WC	38 X 25	KOZO	13	4	250	350
Royal	ART	ART	1982	WC	38 X 25	KOZO	11	4	250	350
Carmine I	ART	ART	1982	WC	38 X 25	KOZO	15	4	250	350
Carmine II	ART	ART	1982	WC	38 X 25	KOZO	10	4	250	350
Amethyst I	ART	ART	1982	WC	38 X 25	KOZO	26	5	250	350
Russet	ART	ART	1983	WC	38 X 24	OKP	10	6	300	350
Milori	ART	ART	1983	WC	35 X 23	CHIRI	10	6	300	350
Jaune I,II	ART	ART	1983	WC	38 X 24 EA	OKP/CHIRI	11 EA	6 EA	300 EA	350 EA
Amethyst II	ART	ART	1983	WC	38 X 25	KOZO	20	7	300	350
Viridian	ART	ART	1983	WC	35 X 23	CHIRI	23	6	300	350
Azure	ART	ART	1983	WC	38 X 24	OKP	15	8	300	350

ANN CONNER CONTINUED

TITLE	PUBLISHER	PRINTER	DATE	MEDIUM	DIMENSION (PAPER SIZE) IN INCHES	TYPE OF PAPER	EDITION NUMBER	NO. OF COLORS	ORIGINAL OPENING PRICE	CURRENT RETAIL PRICE
CURRENT EDITIONS:										
Spectrum I,II	JSG	VS	1984	WC	24 X 29 EA	MUL	25 EA	5 EA	450 EA	500 EA
Cadmium	ART	ART	1984	WC	38 X 24	OKP	15	8	350	350
Cadmium II	ART	ART	1984	WC	38 X 24	OKP	13	12	350	350
Flora	ART	ART	1985	WC	38 X 25	KOZO	7	4	400	450
Minoan	ART	ART	1985	WC	27 X 27	CHIRI	13	5	450	450
Fleur	ART	ART	1985	WC	25 X 25	KOZO	10	8	400	450
Reef	ART	ART	1985	WC	27 X 27	KOZO	17	4	450	450
Coral Sea	ART	ART	1986	KOZO	37 X 51	KOZO	10	2	750	750
Minoan Lion	ART	ART	1986	WC	39 X 27	CHIRI	9	5	450	450
Throne Room	ART	ART	1986	WC	39 X 27	CHIRI	9	5	450	450
Teatro I,II	OE	ART	1987	WC/LI	27 X 41 EA	GUT	15 EA	3 EA	500 EA	550 EA
Sacra Conversazione	OE	ART	1987	WC/LI	27 X 41	GUT	25	4	500	550
Crane Beach	ART	ART	1988	WC	27 X 41	GUT	7	6	500	500
Elbow Beach	ART	ART	1988	WC	27 X 41	GUT	7	6	500	500
Jumby Bay	ART	ART	1988	WC	27 X 41	GUT	8	7	500	500
Objects 1,3,5,6,7	ART	ART	1989	WC	27 X 41 EA	GUT	6 EA	4 EA	500 EA	500 EA
Objects 2	ART	ART	1989	WC	27 X 41	GUT	5	4	500	500
Objects 4	ART	ART	1989	WC	27 X 41	GUT	7	4	500	500
Milan	ART	ART	1990	WB	39 X 25	HANGA	10	1	300	500
Peruzzi	ART	ART	1990	WB	39 X 25	HANGA	10	1	300	500
Rocher du Diamant	ART	ART	1990	WC	42 X 27	SOM/S	6	6	500	500
Anse Mitan	ART	ART	1990	WC	42 X 27	CP/W	9	5	500	500
Trois-Ilets	ART	ART	1990	WC	42 X 27	AP/W	7	6	500	500
Uffizi	ART	ART	1990	WB	39 X 25	HANGA	10	1	300	500
Kapalua Screen	ART/WPI	ART/CK/MA	1991	LC/WB	43 X 27	RP/CR	7	3	500	500
Wailea Screen	ART/WPI	ART/MA	1991	LC/WB	43 X 27	RP/CR	8	3	500	500
Wailea Screen	ART/WPI	ART/MA	1991	LC/WB	43 X 27	RP/CR	8	3	500	500
Waikoloa Screen	ART/WPI	ART/MA	1991	LC/WB	43 X 27	RP/CR	15	3	500	300
Wetlants I,III	ART	ART/MA	1992	LC/WB	42 X 27 EA	RP/W	7 EA	3 EA	450 EA	450 EA
Wetlands II,IV	ART	ART/MA	1992	LC/WB	42 X 27 EA	RP/W	8 EA	3 EA	450 EA	450 EA

LOIS CONNER

EDUCATION: Pratt Inst, NY, Photog, BFA, 1973–75; Yale Univ, New Haven, CT, Photog, MFA, 1979–81
AWARDS: Pratt Inst Research Grant, NY, 1975; Nat Endowment for the Arts Fel, 1979; New York State Council on the Arts Fel, NY, 1983; Guggenheim Fel, NY, 1984
TEACHING: Instr, Jersey City State Col, NJ, 1977–80; Instr, Pratt Inst, NY, 1981; Instr, Louisiana State Univ, Baton Rouge, LA, Fall, 1983; Instr, Stanford Univ, Palo Alto, CA, Summer, 1984; Prof, New Sch for Social Research, NY, 1982–88; Prof, Cooper Union Sch for the Arts, NY, 1987 to present; Prof, Sch of Visual Arts, NY, 1987 to present; Prof, Fordham Univ, NY, 1987 to present
RECENT EXHIB: Ewing Gallery, Wash, DC, 1988; Baker Col of Art, KS, 1988; Photographers Gallery, London, England, 1988; Canton Mus of Art, China, 1988; Cleveland Mus of Art, OH, 1988; St Olaf Col, MN, 1988; Texas Christian Univ, Fort Worth, TX, 1988; Texas Christian Univ, Brown-Lupton and Moudy Galleries, Fort Worth, TX, 1988; Marcuse Pfeifer Gallery, NY, 1988; Robert Koch Gallery, San Francisco, CA, 1987,89; Krannert Art Mus, Univ of Illinois, IL, 1990; Nat Centre for Photog, Bombay, India, 1990
COLLECTIONS: Detroit Inst of the Arts, MI; Mus of Mod Art, NY; Metropolitan Mus of Art, NY; New Orleans Mus of Art, LA; Smithsonian, Nat Mus of Am Art, Wash, DC; Victoria & Albert Mus, London, England; Toledo Art Mus, OH; Yale Univ Art Gallery, New Haven, CT; Vassar Col Art Gallery, NY; Nat Gallery of Victoria, Australia; Bibliotheque Nat, Paris, France; Canadian Centre for Architecture, Ottawa, Canada; Chinese Photographers Assn, Canton, China; Hallmark Photographic Coll, KS
PRINTERS: Thomas Platt Palmer, Newport RI (TPP)
PUBLISHERS: Marcuse Pfeifer Gallery, NY (MPG)
GALLERIES: Robert Koch Gallery, San Francisco, CA; Kathleen Ewing Gallery, Wash, DC; Laurence Miller Gallery, New York, NY; Harcourts Modern & Contemporary Art, San Francisco, CA
MAILING ADDRESS: 36 Gramercy Park, East, #4-E, New York, NY 10003

TITLE	PUBLISHER	PRINTER	DATE	MEDIUM	DIMENSION (PAPER SIZE) IN INCHES	TYPE OF PAPER	EDITION NUMBER	NO. OF COLORS	ORIGINAL OPENING PRICE	CURRENT RETAIL PRICE
CURRENT EDITIONS:										
The River Flows into the Heavens (Set of 18)	MPG	TPP	1988	PH	15 X 24 EA	SOM/S	55 EA		3600 SET 400 EA	3600 SET 400 EA

ROBERT FREMONT CONOVER

BORN: Trenton, NJ; July 3, 1920
EDUCATION: Philadelphia Mus Sch, PA (PCA), 1938–42; Art Students League, NY, 1945–48; Brooklyn Mus Sch, NY, 1948–50
AWARDS: Purchase Prize, Brooklyn Mus, NY, 1954; MacDowell Colony Fel, 1958; Purchase Prize, Soc of Am Graphic Artists, 1967; Purchase Prize, Philadelphia Print Club, PA, 1967; New York State Fel, 1976; Creative Artists Public Service Award, 1976; Vera List Award, Ed of Twenty Nation Acad, 1982,84
TEACHING: Brooklyn Mus Sch, NY, 1961–72; New Sch for Social Research, NY, 1957 to present; Neward Sch of Fine Industrial Art, NJ, 1967 to present
COLLECTIONS: Mus of Mod Art, NY; Whitney Mus of Am Art, NY; Cooper Hewitt Mus, NY; Brooklyn Mus, NY; New York Public Library, NY; Australian Nat Gallery, Canberra, Australia; Detroit Inst of Art, MI; New York Public Library; Smithsonian Mus, Wash, DC
PRINTERS: Artist (ART)
PUBLISHERS: Artist (ART)
GALLERIES: Associated American Artists, New York, NY
MAILING ADDRESS: 162 E 33rd St, New York, NY 10016

ROBERT FREMONT CONOVER CONTINUED

TITLE	PUBLISHER	PRINTER	DATE	MEDIUM	DIMENSION (PAPER SIZE) IN INCHES	TYPE OF PAPER	EDITION NUMBER	NO. OF COLORS	ORIGINAL OPENING PRICE	CURRENT RETAIL PRICE
CURRENT EDITIONS:										
New Amsterdam Theatre-42 Street	ART	ART	1977	EB	20 X 34	AC/B	40	1	200	400
Octagon House-Irvington-on-Hudson	ART	ART	1979	EB	20 X 27	RP/G	50	1	200	400
Old Lord and Taylor Store	ART	ART	1981	EB	20 X 36	AC/B	40	1	250	400
Coney Island Board	ART	ART	1981	EB	20 X 28	AC/W	50	1	200	300
Collapse of Pier 51	ART	ART	1981	EB	28 X 40	AC/W	50	1	300	500
Demolition of Helen Hayes Theatre	PG	ART	1983	EB	14 X 21	AC/W	60	1	100	300
32nd Street and 5th Avenue	ART	ART	1984	EB	21 X 35	AC/W	50	1	250	400
Abandoned Hospital-Roosevelt Island	ART	ART	1985	EB	24 X 30	RP/G	40	1	250	350

GORDON COOK

BORN: Chicago, IL; (1927–1985)
EDUCATION: Illinois Wesleyan Univ, Bloomington, IL, BFA, 1950; Am Acad of Art, Chicago, IL, 1948–49; Art Inst of Chicago Art Sch, IL; State Univ of Iowa, Iowa City, IA, 1950,51
TEACHING: Instr, San Francisco Art Inst, CA, 1960–71; Instr, Printmaking & Drawing, Sacramento State Col, CA, 1970–71; Instr, Printmaking, Acad of Art Col, San Francisco, CA, 1971–73; Instr, Drawing, Printmaking & Painting, Univ of California, Davis, CA, 1975; Univ of California, Santa Cruz, CA, 1975
RECENT EXHIB: Univ of Nebraska, Sheldon Mem Art Gallery, Lincoln, NE, 1989
COLLECTIONS: San Francisco Mus, CA; Oakland Mus, CA; Pasadena Mus, CA; Mills Col, Oakland, CA; Achenbach Found, San Francisco, CA
PUBLISHERS: Made in California, Oakland, CA (MIC)
PRINTERS: David Kelso, Oakland, CA (DK); Forum Gallery, New York, NY; Smith Andersen Gallery, Palo Alto, CA; Pamela Auchincloss
GALLERIES: Charles Campbell Gallery, San Francisco, CA; Forum Gallery, New York, NY; Smith Andersen Gallery, Palo Alto, CA; Pamela Auchincloss Gallery, Santa Barbara, CA

Gordon Cook
Point Richmond, San Francisco Bay
Courtesy Limestone Press

TITLE	PUBLISHER	PRINTER	DATE	MEDIUM	DIMENSION (PAPER SIZE) IN INCHES	TYPE OF PAPER	EDITION NUMBER	NO. OF COLORS	ORIGINAL OPENING PRICE	CURRENT RETAIL PRICE
SOLD OUT EDITIONS (RARE):										
Untitled (Port Richmond Gas Tower)	MIC	DK/MIC	1983	AC/SG	22 X 15	JWP/W	34	8	450	1200
Untitled (Near Terminous)	MIC	DK/MIC	1984	AC/ENG/HC	23 X 22	R/BFK/W	50	8	350	1200
Untitled (Amish Doll) (with Scraping, Burnishing & Roulette)	MIC	DK/MIC	1985	EB/A/HG/SG	18 X 15	R/BFK/W	50	8	550	1000
Delta (Posthumously Printed, Estate Stamped) (Set of 5)	MIC	DK/MIC	1985	EB/A/ENG/HC	11 X 10 EA	RdB/W	40 EA		1775 SET 375 EA	2500 SET 600 EA
Untitled (Stick Figure with Arms Out) (Proofing and Printing Completed Posthumously, Estate Stamped)	MIC	DK/MIC	1985	AC/HC	17 X 15	JWP/W	40		600	1000
Untitled (Stick Figure with White Dickey) (Proofing and Printing Completed Posthumously, Estate Stamped)	MIC	DK/MIC	1985	AC/HC	17 X 15	JWP/W	40		600	1000

BERYL COOK

BORN: 1926
EDUCATION: Self Taught
PRINTERS: Chelsea Art Press, London, England (CAP); American Atelier, NY (AA); Har-EL Printers, Tel Aviv, Israel (HE); J K Fine Art Editions, NY (JKFA); Renaissance Print Studio, Tel Aviv, Israel (RPS)
PUBLISHERS: Flanagan Graphics, Linwood, NJ (FG)
GALLERIES: Circle Galleries, San Diego, CA & San Francisco, CA & Northbrook, IL & Pittsburgh, PA & Houston, TX & Soho, NY & Chicago, IL & Scottsdale, AZ & Beverly Hills, CA & Costa Mesa, CA & Sherman Oaks, CA & Palm Beach, FL & Honolulu, HI & New Orleans, LA & Las Vegas, NV & Seattle, WA; Art Insights, New York, NY; Jane Anthony Gallery, Newtown, PA; Barucci Galleries, St Louis, MO; Central Square Gallery, Linwood, NJ; Framagraphic, Vancouver, BC, Canada; Madaline Michaels Gallery, Kula, Maui, HI; One World Gallery, Las Vegas, NV; Renjeau Gallery, Natick, MA; Royce Gallery, Denver, CO; Steve Stein Gallery, Sherman Oaks, CA; Carol Lawrence Gallery, Beverly Hills, CA; Syd Entel Gallery, Safty Harbor, FL; Art Spectrum, North Miami, FL

The retail prices of the 100,000 limited edition prints quoted in this directory are subject to change. Print publishers, artists and galleries were the direct sources for these quotations. Prices in the secondary market listed as "Sold Out Editions (Rare)" indicate that the publisher has a limited supply of that print or that the print is difficult to locate in the galleries.

The Printworld Directory is accepting new applications for the seventh edition. Approximately 300 new artists will be accepted. Please use the two forms provided in the back section of this directory to submit biographical data and documentation of prints. Edition number of each print must not exceed 500 and the retail price must be $100 or more.

BERYL COOK CONTINUED

TITLE	PUBLISHER	PRINTER	DATE	MEDIUM	DIMENSION (PAPER SIZE) IN INCHES	TYPE OF PAPER	EDITION NUMBER	NO. OF COLORS	ORIGINAL OPENING PRICE	CURRENT RETAIL PRICE
SOLD OUT EDITIONS (RARE):										
Women Running	FG	CAP	1985	SP	30 X 24	AP	275	65	500	3000
Tango	FG	CAP	1985	SP	22 X 34	AP	275	60	500	2500
Russian Tea Room	FG	CAP	1986	SP	18 X 23	AP	300	57	500	1000
Bar and Barbara	FG	AA	1986	LC	16 X 15	AP	300	16	500	1100
Dancing Class	FG	HE	1986	SP	22 X 22	FAB	300	55	600	1500
A Bathroom	FG	CAP	1987	SP	27 X 14	AP	300	35	550	1500
Lunch in the Gardens	FG	HE	1987	SP	17 X 24	FAB	300	55	600	800
Dustbinmen	FG	CAP	1987	SP	24 X 26	AP	300	60	800	1000
Jackpot	FG	CAP	1988	SP	30 X 11	AP	300	55	650	1500
Taxi	FG	JKFA	1988	LC	19 X 25	AP	300	25	750	2500
Big Olives and Little Olives	FG	JKFA	1988	LC	27 X 27	AP	300	25	850	3000
My Fur Coat	FG	CAP	1989	SP	21 X 21	AP	250		750	1500
Bryant Park	FG	CAP	1986	SP	19 X 23	AP	300	55	650	800
Panto Dame	FG	JK	1987	LC	27 X 21	AP	300	25	650	700
Nathans	FG	CAP	1988	SP	32 X 25	AP	300	55	750	850
Tennis	FG	JKFA	1988	LC	31 X 25	AP	300	25	900	1200
Dancing on the QE2	FG	CAP	1988	SP	30 X 27	AP	300	55	900	900
Twins	FG	JKFA	1989	LC	24 X 24	AP	300	55	900	950
Chartiers	FG	CAP	1989	SP	32 X 22	AP	300	55	850	850
Coctails for three	FG	CAP	1989	SP	29 X 16	AP	300	55	550	550
A Bird in the Hand	FG	CAP	1989	LC	26 X 21	AP	300	20	750	750
Gare du Nord	FG	JKFA	1990	SP	28 X 17	FAB	300	50	750	850
The Baron Entertains	FG	CAP	1990	SP	26 X 17	FAB	300	50	750	850
Percy at the Fridge	FG	CAP	1990	LC	22 X 17	FAB	300	25	650	750
Ladies Night	FG	CAP	1991	SP	27 X 28	AP	300	55	750	950
Girls in a Taxi	FG	CAP	1992	SP	24 X 31	AP	300	55	750	875
The Manipulators	FG	RPS	1993	SP	25 X 31	AP	300	64	750	750

HOWARD NORTON COOK

BORN: Springfield, MA; (1901–1980)
EDUCATION: Art Students League, NY
AWARDS: Guggenheim Fel Awards, 1931–32, 34–35; Gold Medal, Arch, 1937; Dallas Mus of Fine Arts, TX, 1958; New Mexico Award, Albuquerque, NM, 1958; Samuel F B Morse Gold Medal, Nat Acad of Design, 1963; Oklahoma Art Center, Oklahoma City, OK
RECENT EXHIB: Roswell Mus, NM, 1992
COLLECTIONS: Mus of Mod Art, NY; Metropolitan Mus of Art, NY; Oklahoma Art Center, Oklahoma City, OK; Whitney Mus of Am Art, NY; Santa Barbara Mus, CA; de Young Mem Mus, CA; Philadelphia Mus of Art, PA; Minneapolis Inst of Art, MN; Denver Art Mus, CO; Dartmouth Col, Hanover, NH
PRINTERS: Artist (ART)
PUBLISHERS: Artist (ART); AAG Editions, NY (AAF); Associated Am Artists, NY (AAA)
GALLERIES: Bethesda Art Gallery, Glen Echo, MD; Ernesto Mayans Gallery, Santa Fe, NM; Mission Gallery, Taos, NM; Susan Sheehan Gallery, New York, NY; Wiggins Fine Art, Santa Fe, NM; Harbor Gallery, New York, NY

TITLE	PUBLISHER	PRINTER	DATE	MEDIUM	DIMENSION (PAPER SIZE) IN INCHES	TYPE OF PAPER	EDITION NUMBER	NO. OF COLORS	ORIGINAL OPENING PRICE	CURRENT RETAIL PRICE
SOLD OUT EDITIONS (RARE):										
Boat Building (25 Printed)	ART	ART	1926	WC	17 X 9	WOVE	50		35	1000
Governor's Palace (50 Printed)	ART	ART	1926	WC	8 X 8	WOVE	75		20	1800
Snow and Dobe (40 Printed)	ART	ART	1926	LB	12 X 9	WOVE	50	1	25	1500
District School House (25 Printed)	ART	ART	1926	WC	17 X 13	WOVE	50		60	1500
Grand Canyon	ART	ART	1927	WC	12 X 15	WOVE	35		60	2500
Hopi House (40 Printed)	ART	ART	1927	WC	8 X 8	WOVE	50		60	900
Morning Smokes, Taos (50 Printed)	ART	ART	1927	WC	8 X 8	WOVE	75		60	1000
Sage and Cactus	ART	ART	1927	WC	12 X 10	WOVE	50		60	1200
Taos Indian (Fat John) (40 Printed)	ART	ART	1927	WC	12 X 10	WOVE	50		60	1000
The Dictator (25 Printed)	ART	ART	1928	WC	12 X 8	WOVE	50		60	6000
Downtown, New York (25 Printed)	ART	ART	1928	EB	9 X 6	WOVE	50	1	40	2500
New England Valley (35 Printed)	ART	ART	1928	EB	12 X 10	WOVE	50	1	40	1500
Rubber Center (25 Printed)	ART	ART	1928	WC	10 X 13	WOVE	50		60	3000
Towers (NYC)	ART	ART	1928	EB	7 X 5	WOVE	50		40	2000
The Village	ART	ART	1928	EC	7 X 12	WOVE	50		60	1000
Self Portrait, Paris	ART	ART	1929	LC/CC	11 X 10	WOVE	40		75	1200
Tunisia	ART	ART	1929	LB	8 X 13	WOVE	50	1	50	1200
Aristocracy (30 Printed)	ART	ART	1930	LB	8 X 14	WOVE	75	1	25	1000
Chrysler Building (50 Printed)	ART	ART	1930	WE	10 X 7	WOVE	75		50	6500
Edison Plant (35 Printed)	ART	ART	1930	LB	14 X 10	WOVE	75	1	25	1500
Engine Room (35 Printed)	ART	ART	1930	LB	10 X 12	WOVE	75	1	25	3500
Harbor Skyline (40 Printed)	ART	ART	1930	EB/A	10 X 12	WOVE	50		50	9000
New England City (35 Printed)	ART	ART	1930	EB	7 X 10	WOVE	50	1	35	1800
The New Yorker (35 Printed)	ART	ART	1930	WC	18 X 19	WOVE	50		50	8000
Paris Street	ART	ART	1930	WE	6 X 4	WOVE	100		50	900
Queensboro Bridge (40 Printed)	ART	ART	1930	EB	11 X 7	WOVE	50		35	7500
Studio Bed	ART	ART	1930	EB/A	7 X 11	WOVE	30		50	1000
Times Square Sector (35 Printed)	ART	ART	1930	EB	12 X 10	WOVE	75	1	50	12500

HOWARD NORTON COOK CONTINUED

TITLE	PUBLISHER	PRINTER	DATE	MEDIUM	DIMENSION (PAPER SIZE) IN INCHES	TYPE OF PAPER	EDITION NUMBER	NO. OF COLORS	ORIGINAL OPENING PRICE	CURRENT RETAIL PRICE
SOLD OUT EDITIONS (RARE):										
Bremen #1 (30 Printed)	ART	ART	1931	WE	9 X 6	WOVE	75		50	3500
Country Store (with Drawing)	ART	ART	1931	EB/DRAW	6 X 9	WOVE		1	60	6000
Financial District	ART	ART	1931	LB	14 X 10	WOVE	75	1	35	6500
George Washington Bridge	ART	ART	1931	LB	14 X 10	WOVE	50	1	35	5000
Montparnasse Street (25 Printed)	ART	ART	1931	EB	5 X 10	WOVE	50	1	40	2000
New England Church	ART	ART	1931	WE	12 X 9	WOVE	50		50	1000
New York Night	ART	ART	1931	LB	18 X 14	WOve	75	1	75	8000
New York Night (City Night) (35 Printed)	ART	ART	1931	LB	10 X 12	WOVE	75	1	40	9000
Self Portrait	ART	ART	1931	WC	4 X 3	WOVE	50		40	900
Soaring New York	ART	ART	1931	EB/A/SG	9 X 12	WOVE	25		50	6500
West Side, New York (30 Printed)	ART	ART	1931	EB/A	7 X 13	WOVE	50		50	7500
The Cocoanut Palm	ART	ART	1932	WE	10 X 8	WOVE	50		60	1200
Mexican Interior	ART	ART	1933	EB	16 X 11	WOVE	50	1	60	3000
Mexican Landscape	ART	ART	1933	EB/A	9 X 12	WOVE	30		75	1000
Old Woman of Taxco	ART	ART	1933	EB/A/REL	12 X 9	WOVE	27		75	1200
Little Dolphin	AAG	ART	1936	LC	12 X 8	WOVE			50	350
Southern Mountaineer	AAG	ART	1936	EB/A	12 X 9	WOVE	20		60	1000
Southern Pioneers	AAG	ART	1936	EB/SG	13 X 10	WOVE	20	1	60	1000
Longhorns	AAG	ART	1937	LC	9 X 15	WOVE	25		60	1500
Looking Up Broadway	AAG	ART	1937	LC	13 X 9	WOVE	200		50	2500
Rosanna	AAA	ART	1939	LC	12 X 8	AP	250		50	500
Mexican Family	AAA	ART	1940	LC	10 X 13	AP	250		75	500
Desert Tree	AAA	ART	1941	EB/A	9 X 12	AP	250		75	800
Eagle Dance	AAA	ART	1942	WE	10 X 8	AP	200		85	900
Bougainville Barracks Bags	AAA	ART	1945	LC	12 X 16	AP			75	600
Exodus	AAA	ART	1946	EB/A/SG/REL	10 X 14	AP	30		100	900
Tio Vivo #1	AAA	ART	1949	LB	17 X 13	AP	30		100	900
Tio Vivo #2	AAA	ART	1949	LB	11 X 14	AP	10		100	1200

ANN T COOPER

BORN: New Orleans, LA; 1936
EDUCATION: Newcomb Col, Tulane Univ, New Orleans, LA
COLLECTIONS: Eastern Illinois Univ, Charleston, IL; New Orleans Mus, LA; Beaumont Mus, TX
PRINTERS: Tom Jones Graphics, Greensboro, NC (TJG) OB; Frank Rowland Workshop, Libertyville, IL (FRW)

PUBLISHERS: London Arts Inc, Detroit, MI (LAI); Circle Gallery, Ltd, Chicago, IL (CGL)
GALLERIES: Circle Galleries, Chicago, IL & New York, NY & Scottsdale, AZ & Beverly Hills, CA & Costa Mesa, CA & San Diego, CA & San Francisco, CA & Sherman Oaks, CA & Palm Beach, FL & Honolulu, HI & Northbrook, IL & New Orleans, LA & Las Vegas, NV & Pittsburgh, PA & Houston, TX & Seattle, WA

TITLE	PUBLISHER	PRINTER	DATE	MEDIUM	DIMENSION (PAPER SIZE) IN INCHES	TYPE OF PAPER	EDITION NUMBER	NO. OF COLORS	ORIGINAL OPENING PRICE	CURRENT RETAIL PRICE
CURRENT EDITIONS:										
Particular Parrots	CGL	FRW	1976	SP	24 X 28	TT	275	4	100	300
Falling Leaves	LAI	TJG	1980	SP	22 X 30	SOM	250	17	175	300
Lilies	LAI	TJG	1980	SP	30 X 22	SOM	300	4	100	300
Marsh Birds	LAI	TJG	1980	SP	30 X 22	SOM	300	4	100	300
Primavera	LAI	TJG	1980	SP	30 X 22	SOM	300	4	100	300
Spring Lilies	LAI	TJG	1980	SP	30 X 22	SOM	300	4	100	300
Sunflowers	LAI	TJG	1980	SP	30 X 22	SOM	300	4	100	300

MARVE H COOPER

BORN: Bronx, NY; January 1, 1939
EDUCATION: Caton Rose Inst, NY, 1954; Cooper Union, NY, 1959; Pratt Inst, Brooklyn, NY; Queens Col, NY

TEACHING: Instr, Painting, Queens Col, NY, 1967; Lectr, Art, Sch of Fine Arts, Boston, MA, 1968
AWARDS: First Prize & Hon Mention, Art Assn of Newport, Drury, RI, 1968; First Prize, Prints, South County Art Assn, RI, 1969
PUBLISHERS: Tide Ltd, Scarsdale, NY (TL)
GALLERIES: Marian Locks Gallery, Phila, PA; Asuna Gallery, Wash, DC
MAILING ADDRESS: 251 Snuff Mill Rd, Saunderstown, RI 02874-3013

TITLE	PUBLISHER	PRINTER	DATE	MEDIUM	DIMENSION (PAPER SIZE) IN INCHES	TYPE OF PAPER	EDITION NUMBER	NO. OF COLORS	ORIGINAL OPENING PRICE	CURRENT RETAIL PRICE
SOLD OUT EDITIONS (RARE):										
House of Clowns	TL	ART	1981	SP	39 X 27		200		300	500
The Master's Toys	TL	ART	1981	SP	27 X 39		200		300	500

The retail prices of the 100,000 limited edition prints quoted in this directory are subject to change. Print publishers, artists and galleries were the direct sources for these quotations. Prices in the secondary market listed as "Sold Out Editions (Rare)" indicate that the publisher has a limited supply of that print or that the print is difficult to locate in the galleries.

RON COOPER

BORN: New York, NY; (1943–1985)
EDUCATION: Chouinard Art Inst, Los Angeles, CA, 1963–65
AWARDS: Los Angeles County Mus of Art, CA, Purchase Prize, 1968; Nat Endowment Arts Award, 1970; Theodoran Purchase Award, Guggenheim Mus, NY, 1971
COLLECTIONS: Chicago Art Inst, IL; Guggenheim Mus, NY; Kaiser Wilhelm Mus, Krefeld, West Germany; Stedelijk Mus, Amsterdam, Netherlands; Whitney Mus of Am Art, NY
PRINTERS: Cirrus Editions Workshop, Los Angeles, CA (CEW); David Ordaz, Los Angeles, CA (DO)
PUBLISHERS: Cirrus Editions, Los Angeles, CA (CE)
GALLERIES: Cirrus Editions, Ltd, Los Angeles, CA; Neil G. Ovsey Gallery, Los Angeles, CA; Philip Bareiss Gallery, Taos, NM
MAILING ADDRESS: P.O. Box 667, Ranchos de Taos, NM 87557

TITLE	PUBLISHER	PRINTER	DATE	MEDIUM	DIMENSION (PAPER SIZE) IN INCHES	TYPE OF PAPER	EDITION NUMBER	NO. OF COLORS	ORIGINAL OPENING PRICE	CURRENT RETAIL PRICE
SOLD OUT EDITIONS (RARE):										
Tri-Axial Rotation of a Floating Volume of Light	CE	CEW	1972	LC	23 X 30	AP	50	3	200	650
Untitled (300 C)	CE	DO/CEW	1981	LB	10 X 38	AP88	60	1	450	500

RUFFIN COOPER JR

BORN: Washington, DC; January 4, 1942
EDUCATION: Univ of Houston, TX, 1960–61; Boston Univ, MA, BFA, 1961–64
AWARDS: New York Art Director's Club, Merit Award, 1982; Worlitzer Found Grant, Taos, NM, 1989
RECENT EXHIB: European Photos, De Saisset Mus, Santa Clara, CA, 1988; Firenze Gray Hawkins, Los Angeles, CA, 1988
COLLECTIONS: New Orleans Mus of Art, LA; Brooklyn Mus, NY; Bibliotheque Nat, Paris, France
PRINTERS: Michael Wilder, Venice, CA (MW); Frank Bonfiglio, San Francisco, CA (FB); Imperial Color Labs, San Francisco, CA (ICL)
PUBLISHERS: A-I, Houston, TX (A-I); Artist (ART)
GALLERIES: Weston Gallery, Carmel, CA; O K Harris, New York, NY; Sandy Carson Gallery, Denver, CO; Middendorf Gallery, Wash, DC; G Ray Hawkins Gallery, Los Angeles, CA; Elaine Horwitch Galleries, Scottsdale, AZ & Santa Fe, NM
MAILING ADDRESS: 285 Chestnut St, San Francisco, CA 94133

TITLE	PUBLISHER	PRINTER	DATE	MEDIUM	DIMENSION (PAPER SIZE) IN INCHES	TYPE OF PAPER	EDITION NUMBER	NO. OF COLORS	ORIGINAL OPENING PRICE	CURRENT RETAIL PRICE
SOLD OUT EDITIONS (RARE):										
Las Trampas Church Series	ART	FB/ICL	1973	PH/C	48 X 48 EA	T-C	40 EA	Multi	550 EA	800 EA
Church at Rancho de Taos	ART	FB/ICL	1973	PH/DT	22 X 30	T-C	75	Multi	350	600
Statue of Liberty Series	A-I	FB/ICL	1979	PH/C	33 X 48 EA	T-C	100 EA	Multi	450 EA	800 EA
Golden Gate Series	A-I	FB/ICL	1979	PH/C	33 X 48 EA	T-C	20 EA	Multi	450 EA	800 EA
Personal Portfolio (Set of 10)	ART	MW	1982	PH/C	20 X 30 EA	CIBA	40 EA	Multi	3000 SET	3500 SET
									350 EA	500 EA

WAYNE COOPER

BORN: DePew, OK; 1942
EDUCATION: Valparaiso Univ, IN
AWARDS: Best in Show, Twas Bay Show, Gilcrease Mus, Tulsa, OK, 1969; First Place, Oils, Southern Shores, Gary, IN, 1970; First Place, Watercolors, Ft Wayne Mus, IN, 1975; Best in Show, Nat Small Painting Show, Miniatures, Albuquerque, NM, 1990
COLLECTIONS: Purdue Univ, Lafayette, IN; Thomas Gilcrease Inst of Am History & Art, Tulsa, OK; Art Inst of Chicago, IL; Ft Wayne Mus, IN
PRINTERS: American Atelier, NY (AA)
PUBLISHERS: Circle Fine Art, Chicago, IL (CFA)
GALLERIES: Circle Galleries, San Diego, CA & San Francisco, CA & Northbrook, IL & Pittsburgh, PA & Houston, TX & Soho, NY & Chicago, IL & Scottsdale, AZ & Beverly Hills, CA & Costa Mesa, CA & Sherman Oaks, CA & Palm Beach, FL & Honolulu, HI & New Orleans, LA & Las Vegas, NV & Seattle, WA
MAILING ADDRESS: P O Box 361, Hebrion, IN 46347

TITLE	PUBLISHER	PRINTER	DATE	MEDIUM	DIMENSION (PAPER SIZE) IN INCHES	TYPE OF PAPER	EDITION NUMBER	NO. OF COLORS	ORIGINAL OPENING PRICE	CURRENT RETAIL PRICE
SOLD OUT EDITIONS (RARE):										
Tuesday	CFA	AA	1975	LC	22 X 30	AP	300		75	400
Bossy's House	CFA	AA	1975	LC	18 X 28	AP	300		75	400
Brunch	CFA	AA	1975	LC	19 X 26	AP	300		75	175
Papa Leon	CFA	AA	1975	LC	26 X 18	AP	300		75	125
Seven Seas	CFA	AA	1976	LC	24 X 34	AP	300		75	175
December Nine	CFA	AA	1976	LC	20 X 27	AP	300		75	175
Enjoy	CFA	AA	1977	LC	24 X 34	AP	300		75	350
Red Fork	CFA	AA	1977	LC	12 X 17	AP	300		75	200
Blue Ridge	CFA	AA	1977	LC	23 X 16	AP	300		75	200
Stream	CFA	AA	1977	LC	24 X 33	AP	300		75	200
Willow Slew	CFA	AA	1977	LC	21 X 27	AP	300		75	250
Cooper's Rainbow	CFA	AA	1977	LC	20 X 28	AP	300		75	200
Spring Road	CFA	AA	1978	LC	21 X 29	AP	300		75	200
Spring Road (Rives Journal)	CFA	AA	1978	LC	21 X 29	AP	35		75	250
The Second Snow	CFA	AA	1978	LC	27 X 21	AP	300		75	150
North	CFA	AA	1978	LC	25 X 28	AP	300		75	175
One Bull	CFA	AA	1978	LC	32 X 24	AP	300		75	125
Rambling Fence	CFA	AA	1978	LC	22 X 27	AP	300		75	125
Vanishing Images Portfolio (Set of 4):									750 SET	1000 SET
Tobacco Road	CFA	AA	1979	LC	25 X 35	AP	300		200	300
Will Creek	CFA	AA	1979	LC	25 X 35	AP	300		200	300
Stone Valley	CFA	AA	1979	LC	25 X 35	AP	300		200	300
Crow Hollow	CFA	AA	1979	LC	25 X 35	AP	300		200	300

WAYNE COOPER CONTINUED

TITLE	PUBLISHER	PRINTER	DATE	MEDIUM	DIMENSION (PAPER SIZE) IN INCHES	TYPE OF PAPER	EDITION NUMBER	NO. OF COLORS	ORIGINAL OPENING PRICE	CURRENT RETAIL PRICE
SOLD OUT EDITIONS (RARE):										
By the Sea	CFA	AA	1979	LC	24 X 35	AP	350		100	150
Evening Mist	CFA	AA	1979	LC	21 X 28	AP	350		100	150

WILLIAM NELSON COPLEY

BORN: New York, NY; January 24, 1919
EDUCATION: Yale Univ, New Haven, CT, 1942; Philips Acad, Andover, MA
COLLECTIONS: Mus of Art, Paris, France; Mus of Mod Art, NY; Tate Gallery, London, England; Whitney Mus of Am Art, NY; Chicago Art Inst, IL; Los Angeles County Mus, CA; Nagoka Mus, Tokyo, Japan; Phila Mus of Art, PA; Pasadena Mus, CA; Princeton Mus, NJ; Oberlin Col, OH; Louvre Mus, Paris, France
PRINTERS: Alexander Heinricci, NY (AH); Studio Heinricci, NY (SH)
PUBLISHERS: London Arts, Inc, Detroit, MI (LAI)
GALLERIES: Phyllis Kind Gallery, New York, NY & Chicago, IL
MAILING ADDRESS: c/o Phyllis Kind Gallery, 136 Greene St, New York, NY 10012

TITLE	PUBLISHER	PRINTER	DATE	MEDIUM	DIMENSION (PAPER SIZE) IN INCHES	TYPE OF PAPER	EDITION NUMBER	NO. OF COLORS	ORIGINAL OPENING PRICE	CURRENT RETAIL PRICE
SOLD OUT EDITIONS (RARE):										
Baby Bonnett	LAI	AH/SH	1978	SP	33 X 26	SOM	200	3	150	200
Baby Buggy	LAI	AH/SH	1978	SP	33 X 26	SOM	200	7	150	200

ENRIC CORMENZANA

BORN: Barcelona, Spain; 1948
EDUCATION: Escuela Massana, Barcelona, Spain; Escola de Belles Arts de Sant Jordi, Spain; Architectural Sch of Barcelona, Spain
AWARDS: First Millenary of the Found of Santa Maria de de L'Estany, 1970; Bronze Medal, Salon Nacional de Mayo, Barcelona, Spain, 1971
PRINTERS: La Poligrafa, SA, Barcelona, Spain (LP)
PUBLISHERS: Ediciones Poligrafa, SA, Barcelona, Spain (EdP)
GALLERIES: Galeria Joan Prats, New York, NY & Barcelona, Spain

TITLE	PUBLISHER	PRINTER	DATE	MEDIUM	DIMENSION (PAPER SIZE) IN INCHES	TYPE OF PAPER	EDITION NUMBER	NO. OF COLORS	ORIGINAL OPENING PRICE	CURRENT RETAIL PRICE
CURRENT EDITIONS:										
Set of 6 Lithographs:									350 SET	1200 SET
Gos	EdP	LP	1974	LB	22 X 30	GP	75	1	100	220
Personatges II	EdP	LP	1974	LB	22 X 30	GP	75	1	100	220
Personatges III	EdP	LP	1974	LB	22 X 30	GP	75	1	100	220
Personatges IV	EdP	LP	1974	LB	22 X 30	GP	75	1	100	220
Personatges V	EdP	LP	1974	LB	22 X 30	GP	75	1	100	220
Personatges VI	EdP	LP	1974	LB	22 X 30	GP	75	1	100	220
Jocs a Pel Suite (Set of 10)	EdP	LP	1976	LC	22 X 30 EA	GP	75 EA	5 EA	900 SET	2500 SET
									100 EA	280 EA
Pas de Dansa Suite (Set of 7)	EdP	LP	1981	LC	45 X 32 EA	GP	99 EA	3 EA	1100 SET	1400 SET
									120 EA	220 EA
Migjorn Suite (Set of 3)	EdP	LP	1981	LC	30 X 22 EA	GP	75 EA	3 EA	500 SET	800 SET
Walpurga Suite (Set of 5)	Ed	LP	1982	LC	22 X 30 EA	GP	75 EA	2-3 EA	800 SET	1300 SET
									180 EA	280 EA
3 AL Lithographs (Set of 3):									500 SET	800 SET
Tel Aviv	EdP	LP	1982	LC	28 X 22	GP	99	5	180	280
Zaragoza	Edp	LP	1982	LC	30 X 22	GP	99	3	180	280
Barcelona	EdP	LP	1982	LC	30 X 22	GP	99	3	180	280

CORNEILLE (CORNELIS VAN BEVERLOO)

BORN: Liege, France; 1922
EDUCATION: Rijksakademie, Amsterdam, Netherlands, 1940–43; Atelier 17, Paris, France, 1953
AWARDS: First Honorable Mention, Carnegie Inst, Pittsburgh, PA, 1956
RECENT EXHIB: Three Continents Gallery, NY, 1987; Seattle Art Mus, WA, 1988; Spencer Mus of Art, Lawrence, KS, 1988; Mus of Mod Art, NY, 1988; Nelson-Atkins Mus of Art, Kansas City, MO, 1989
COLLECTIONS: Brooklyn Mus, NY; Mus Centre Pompidou, Paris, France; Mus Des Beaux Arts, Brussels, Belgium; Mus of Mod Art, Paris, France; Stedelijk Mus, Amsterdam, Holland; Louisiana Mus, Germany; Berlin Mus, Germany; Grand Rapids Mus of Art, MI; Brooklyn Mus, NY; Nelson-Atkins Mus of Art, Kansas City, MO; Dayton Art Inst, OH; Newark Mus, NJ
PRINTERS: Joseph Kleineman, NY (JK); Jorge Dumas, Atelier Dumas, NY (JD/AD); Michel Casse, Paris, France (MC)
PUBLISHERS: London Arts, Inc, Detroit, MI (LAI); Post Oak Fine Arts Distributor, Houston, TX (POFA); Transworld Art, Inc NY (TAI)
GALLERIES: Branchville Soho Gallery, Ridgefield, CT; Three Continents Gallery, New York, NY; Ro Gallery Image Makers, Inc, New York, NY

The Printworld Directory is accepting new applications for the seventh edition. Approximately 300 new artists will be accepted. Please use the two forms provided in the back section of this directory to submit biographical data and documentation of prints. Edition number of each print must not exceed 500 and the retail price must be $100 or more.

CORNEILLE (CORNELIS VAN BEVERLOO) CONTINUED

TITLE	PUBLISHER	PRINTER	DATE	MEDIUM	DIMENSION (PAPER SIZE) IN INCHES	TYPE OF PAPER	EDITION NUMBER	NO. OF COLORS	ORIGINAL OPENING PRICE	CURRENT RETAIL PRICE
SOLD OUT EDITIONS (RARE):										
Jeux d'Été			1960	LC	25 X 20	AP	210		75	1000
Green Woman	TAI	MC	1972	LC	26 X 20	AP	200		150	1000
Starry Night	TAI	MC	1972	LC	26 X 20	AP	200		150	1000
La Tour, la Nuit, le Jour	POFA	JK	1978	HC/LC	20 X 26	SOM	250	10	400	1000
Volupté	LAI	JK	1978	HC/LC	20 X 26	SOM	300	12	400	1000
Complicite	LAI	JD/AD	1979	HC/LC	20 X 26	SOM	250	12	400	1000
Conversation	LAI	JD/AD	1979	LC	20 X 26	SOM	250	13	400	1000
Le Bouquet de Fleurs	LAI	JD/AD	1979	LC	20 X 26	SOM	250	14	400	1800
Les Amies	LAI	JK	1979	LC	20 X 26	SOM	250	12	400	1000
La Chambre Enluminee	LAI	JD/AD	1980	LC	20 X 26	SOM	250	12	400	1000
La Papier Peint	LAI	JD/AD	1980	LC	20 X 26	SOM	250	14	400	1000
Le Divan Bleu	LAI	JD/AD	1980	LC	20 X 26	SOM	250	13	400	1000
Les Deux Amies	POFA	JD/AD	1980	LC	20 X 26	SOM	250	13	400	1000
Ivresse	LAI	JK	1981	LC	20 X 26	SOM	200	12	400	1000
L'Arbre a'Oiseau	LAI	JK	1981	LC	21 X 26	SOM	200	12	400	1000
L'Arbre Extatique	LAI	JK	1981	LC	26 X 20	SOM	200	12	400	1000
L'Ete Exalte	LAI	JK	1981	LC	26 X 20	SOM	200	12	400	1000
Le Voyage de L'Oiseau	LAI	JK	1981	LC	20 X 26	SOM	250	12	400	1000
Portrait Imaginaire	LAI	JK	1981	LC	20 X 26	SOM	200	12	400	1000
Nu a la Rose	POFA	JK	1981	LC	20 X 23	SOM	200	10	400	1000
Sous les Palmiers	POFA	JK	1981	LC	20 X 23	SOM	200	11	400	1000
Overture Sur L'ete	POFA	JK	1981	LC	20 X 23	SOM	200	12	400	1000
Nu Rouge a L'Oiseau	POFA	JK	1981	LC	20 X 23	SOM	200	10	400	1000
Femme et L'Oiseau d'Ete	POFA	JK	1981	LC	23 X 20	SOM	200	10	400	1000
Image d'Un Ete	POFA	JK	1981	LC	23 X 20	SOM	200	10	400	1000

JOSEPH CORNELL

BORN: Nyacki, NY; (1903–1972)
AWARDS: William & Noma Copley Found Grant, 1954; Ada S Garrett Prize, Art Inst of Chicago, IL, 1959; Am Artists Arts & Letters Award, 1968
RECENT EXHIB: Karsten Greve Gallery, Cologne, West Germany, 1988; Thomas Babeor Gallery, La Jolla, CA, 1989; Pace Gallery, NY, 1989; Richard Gray Gallery, Chicago, IL, 1989,90; Nat Mus of AM Art, Smithsonian Inst, Wash, DC, 1989,92; Hudson River Mus of Westchester, Yonkers, NY, 1992
COLLECTIONS: Mus of Mod Art, NY; Whitney Mus of Am Art, NY; Boston Mus of Fine Arts, MA; Mus of Art, Pasadena, CA
PUBLISHERS: Brooke Alexander, Inc, NY (BAI)
GALLERIES: Brooke Alexander, Inc, New York, NY; James Corcoran Gallery, Santa Monica, CA; Jack Rutberg Fine Arts, Los Angeles, CA; John Berggruen Gallery, San Francisco, CA; ACA Contemporary Gallery, New York, NY; Thomas Babeor Gallery, La Jolla, CA; Richard Gray Gallery, Chicago, IL; Karsten Greve Gallery, Cologne, West Germany; Karen Amiel Modern & Contemporary Art, New York, NY; Marcia Blum Gallery, Old Westbury, NY; Jeffrey Fuller Fine Art, Phila, PA; Davis/McClain Gallery, Houston, TX; Enrico Navarra Gallery, New York, NY; Linda R Silverman Fine Art, Inc, New York, NY

TITLE	PUBLISHER	PRINTER	DATE	MEDIUM	DIMENSION (PAPER SIZE) IN INCHES	TYPE OF PAPER	EDITION NUMBER	NO. OF COLORS	ORIGINAL OPENING PRICE	CURRENT RETAIL PRICE
SOLD OUT EDITIONS (RARE):										
Hotel du Nord	BAI		1972	SP	21 X 16	WOVE	125		200	3500
CURRENT EDITIONS:										
Untitled (Derby Hat)	BAI		1972	HG	20 X 16	AP	125		200	2500
Untitled (How to Make a Rainbow)	BAI		1972	SP/STEN	20 X 16	AP	125		200	2500
Untitled (Landscape with Figure)	BAI		1972	HG	20 X 16	AP	125		200	1800

MERV CORNING

BORN: Santa Ana, CA; 1926
AWARDS: Dillon Lauritzen Mem Award, Art Directors Club, Los Angeles, CA
COLLECTIONS: Smithsonian Inst, Wash, DC
PRINTERS: American Atelier, NY (AA)
PUBLISHERS: Circle Fine Art, Chicago, IL (CFA)
GALLERIES: Conacher Galleries, San Francisco, CA; Circle Galleries, San Diego, CA & San Francisco, CA & Northbrook, IL & Pittsburgh, PA & Houston, TX & Soho, NY & Chicago, IL & Scottsdale, AZ & Beverly Hills, CA & Costa Mesa, CA & Sherman Oaks, CA & Palm Beach, FL & Honolulu, HI & New Orleans, LA & Las Vegas, NV & Seattle, WA

TITLE	PUBLISHER	PRINTER	DATE	MEDIUM	DIMENSION (PAPER SIZE) IN INCHES	TYPE OF PAPER	EDITION NUMBER	NO. OF COLORS	ORIGINAL OPENING PRICE	CURRENT RETAIL PRICE
SOLD OUT EDITIONS (RARE):										
Captain Eddie	CFA	AA	1976	LC	25 X 22	AP	300		75	425
The Red Baron	CFA	AA	1976	LC	23 X 22	AP	300		75	700
Marine Corsair	CFA	AA	1976	LC	33 X 24	AP	300		80	1200
Arlington House	CFA	AA	1976	LC	28 X 22	AP	300		75	1300
Santa Marguerita	CFA	AA	1976	LC	31 X 24	AP	300		80	900
Santa Marguerita (Rives Journal)	CFA	AA	1976	LC	31 X 24	RP	30		80	1000
Green River	CFA	AA	1976	LC	21 X 28	AP	300		75	475
Green River (Rives Journal)	CFA	AA	1976	LC	21 X 28	RP	30		75	575

MERV CORNING CONTINUED

TITLE	PUBLISHER	PRINTER	DATE	MEDIUM	DIMENSION (PAPER SIZE) IN INCHES	TYPE OF PAPER	EDITION NUMBER	NO. OF COLORS	ORIGINAL OPENING PRICE	CURRENT RETAIL PRICE
SOLD OUT EDITIONS (RARE):										
Miramar House	CFA	AA	1976	LC	24 X 29	AP	300		75	500
Miramar House (Rives BFK)	CFA	AA	1976	LC	24 X 29	R/BFK	60		75	600
Cabins	CFA	AA	1976	LC	22 X 28	AP	300		75	425
Cabins (Rives Journal)	CFA	AA	1976	LC	22 X 28	RP	30		75	550
Miramar Nocturn	CFA	AA	1977	LC	24 X 29	AP	100		75	500
Old Bale Mill	CFA	AA	1977	LC	24 X 30	AP	300		75	550
Joya	CFA	AA	1977	LC	22 X 25	AP	300		75	525
Down in the Road	CFA	AA	1977	LC	21 X 24	AP	300		75	425
Pensive	CFA	AA	1978	LC	21 X 28	AP	300		100	350
Toy Sailors	CFA	AA	1978	LC	27 X 22	AP	300		100	600
Man without Fear	CFA	AA	1978	LC	26 X 24	AP	300		100	1550
Figueroa House	CFA	AA	1978	LC	26 X 28	AP	300		100	850
Ancient Warrior	CFA	AA	1978	LC	22 X 27	AP	300		100	1550
Ancient Warrior (BFK Buff)	CFA	AA	1978	LC	22 X 27	R/BFK/B	50		100	1650
CURRENT EDITIONS:										
Flying Fool	CFA	AA	1976	LC	26 X 22	AP	300		50	300
Set Backs	CFA	AA	1976	LC	24 X 30	AP	300		50	275
Old Pro	CFA	AA	1976	LC	25 X 17	AP	300		50	275
On the Line	CFA	AA	1976	LC	18 X 23	AP	300		50	300
Black Flight	CFA	AA	1977	LC	26 X 22	AP	300		50	375
High Country	CFA	AA	1977	LC	21 X 27	AP	300		75	375
Chaperone	CFA	AA	1977	LC	29 X 24	AP	300		75	475
Lost Hills Ranch	CFA	AA	1978	LC	22 X 30	AP	300		100	475
Rain Pool	CFA	AA	1978	LC	21 X 27	AP	300		100	525
Rain Pool (BFK Buff)	CFA	AA	1978	LC	21 X 27	R/BFK/B	50		100	550
The Great Airplanes (1914–1918) (Set of 4):									1000 SET	1850 SET
Red Knight of Germany (Baron von Richthofen)	CFA	AA	1982	LC	21 X 26	AP	300		300	500
Arizona Balloon Buster (Frank Luke, Jr)	CFA	AA	1982	LC	21 X 26	AP	300		300	500
Boy Legend (Georges Guynemer)	CFA	AA	1982	LC	21 X 26	AP	300		300	500
King of the Air Fighters (Edward Mannock)	CFA	AA	1982	LC	21 X 26	AP	300		300	500
The Great Airplanes (1914–1918) (Deluxe) (Set of 4)	CFA	AA	1982	LC	21 X 26 EA	AP	100 EA		1200 SET	2300 SET

CARLOTTA CORPRON

BORN: Blue Earth, MN; December 9, 1901
EDUCATION: Eastern Michigan Univ, Ypsilanti, MI, BA, 1925; Teachers Col, Columbia Univ, NY, MA, 1926
TEACHING: Instr, Univ of Cincinnati, OH, 1928-35; Prof, Photography, Texas Women's Univ, Denton, TX, 1935-68
RECENT EXHIB: Amon Carter Mus, Fort Worth, TX, 1987
COLLECTIONS: Mus of Mod Art, NY; New Orleans Mus of Art, LA; Mus of Creative Photography, AZ
PRINTERS: Artist (ART)
PUBLISHERS: Artist (ART)
GALLERIES: Virginia Lust Gallery, New York, NY

TITLE	PUBLISHER	PRINTER	DATE	MEDIUM	DIMENSION (PAPER SIZE) IN INCHES	TYPE OF PAPER	EDITION NUMBER	NO. OF COLORS	ORIGINAL OPENING PRICE	CURRENT RETAIL PRICE
CURRENT EDITIONS:										
Light Follows Form	ART	ART	1946	PH					100	1250

IZA COSTA

BORN: Anicuns, Goias, Brazil; 1942
EDUCATION: Sch of Fine Arts, Goiania, Brazil; Univ of Mexico; Studied with Siqueiros
AWARDS: Best Artists of the Year, Goiania, Brazil, 1981; Special Medal, Int Salon of Ireland, Dublin, Ireland, 1982; Third Prize, Int Salon, Drawing, Barcelona, Spain, 1982; First Prize, Nat Art Salon, Goiania, Brazil, 1984; Best Three Artists of Goias, Goiania, Brazil, 1987
RECENT EXHIB: Roslyn Sailor Gallery, Margate City, NY, 1987
COLLECTIONS: Mus Municipal de Goiania, Brazil; Mus de Arte Moderna de Sao Paulo, Brazil; Mus de San Carlos, Mexico; Mus da Escola de Belas Artes do Peru, Lima, Peru
GALLERIES: Roslyn Sailor Gallery, Margate City, NJ

TITLE	PUBLISHER	PRINTER	DATE	MEDIUM	DIMENSION (PAPER SIZE) IN INCHES	TYPE OF PAPER	EDITION NUMBER	NO. OF COLORS	ORIGINAL OPENING PRICE	CURRENT RETAIL PRICE
CURRENT EDITIONS:										
Andarilho do Sertao	ART	ART	1986	WC	49 X 36	HMP	10	4	400	500
Porta-Bandeira	ART	ART	1986	WC	49 X 36	HMP	10	5	400	500
Bumba-Meu-Boi	ART	ART	1986	WC	36 X 49	HMP	10	3	400	500
Rendeira do Crivo	ART	ART	1986	WC	36 X 49	HMP	10	4	400	500
Tribo Dos Jivauari	ART	ART	1986	WC	49 X 36	HMP	10	5	400	500

IZA COSTA CONTINUED

TITLE	PUBLISHER	PRINTER	DATE	MEDIUM	DIMENSION (PAPER SIZE) IN INCHES	TYPE OF PAPER	EDITION NUMBER	NO. OF COLORS	ORIGINAL OPENING PRICE	CURRENT RETAIL PRICE
CURRENT EDITIONS:										
Lemanja Rainha du Mar	ART	ART	1986	WC	36 X 49	HMP	10	4	400	500
Jaburus	ART	ART	1987	WC	36 X 24	HMP	10	5	450	550
Borbelatas	ART	ART	1987	WC	24 X 36	HMP	10	5	450	550
Azul e Amarela	ART	ART	1987	WC	24 X 36	HMP	10	5	450	550
Arars	ART	ART	1987	WC	36 X 24	HMP	10	4	450	550
Beija-Flor	ART	ART	1987	WC	36 X 24	HMP	10	4	450	550
Tartarugas	ART	ART	1987	WC	24 X 36	HMP	10	5	450	550
Gafanhotos	ART	ART	1987	WC	24 X 36	HMP	10	4	450	550
Peixes I	ART	ART	1987	WC	24 X 36	HMP	10	4	450	550
Tucano	ART	ART	1987	WC	36 X 24	HMP	10	5	450	550
Abellas	ART	ART	1987	WC	24 X 36	HMP	10	4	450	550

ROBERT COTTINGHAM

BORN: Brooklyn, New York; September 26, 1935
EDUCATION: Pratt Inst, NY, 1959–64
TEACHING: Art Center, Col of Design, Los Angeles, CA, 1969–70; Artist in Res, Wesleyan Univ, Middletown, CT, 1987–89
AWARDS: Nat Endowment for the Arts Fel, 1974–75; Artist of the Year Award, Fairfield Chamber of Commerce, CT, 1988
RECENT EXHIB: Print Retrosp, Hunter Mus, Chattanooga, TN, 1986–87; Print Retrosp, Nelson-Atkins Mus, Kansas City, MO, 1987; Print Retrosp, Spiva Art Center, Joplin, MO, 1987; Print Retrosp, Mus of Art, Univ of Oklahoma, Norman, OK, 1987; Print Retrosp, Cedar Rapids, Mus, IA, 1987; Print Retrosp, Davidson Art Center, Middleton, CT, 1988; Print Retrosp, Wesleyan Univ, Middleton, CT, 1988; Bucknell Univ, Lewisburg, PA, 1988; Fendrich Gallery, Wash, DC, 1988–89; Muscarella Mus, William & Mary Col, Williamsburg, VA, 1989; Tampa Mus of Art, FL, 1989; Roger Ramsey Gallery, Chicago, IL,, 1988,90; Herbert F Johnson Mus, Cornell Univ, Ithaca, NY, 1990; Marisa Del Rey
COLLECTIONS: Whitney Mus of Am Art, NY; Hirshhorn Mus, Wash, DC; Honolulu Acad, HI; Indianapolis Mus, IN; Syracuse Univ, NY; Mus of Art, Toledo, OH; Abilene Christian Univ, TX; Ackland Art Mus, Univ of North Carolina, Chapel Hill, NC; Arkansas Arts Center, Little Rock, AR; Arts Council of Great Britain, London, England; Baltimore Mus, MD; Birmingham Mus, AL; Boymans-von-Beuningen, Rotterdam, Netherlands; Carnegie Inst, Pittsburgh, PA; Cincinnati Art Mus, OH; Cleveland Mus, OH; Columbus Mus, OH; Cornell Univ, Herbert J Johnson Mus, Ithaca, NY; Currier Gallery of Art, Manchester, NH; Dartmouth Col, Hood Mus, Hanover, NH; Davenport Art Gallery, IA; Davidson Art Center, Wesleyan Univ, Middleton, CT; Delaware Art Mus, Wilmington, DE; Detroit Inst of Arts, MI; Fogg Art Mus, Harvard Univ, Cambridge, MA; Guggenheim Mus, NY; Hamburg Mus, Germany; High Mus, Atlanta, GA; Hirshhorn Mus, Smithsonian Inst, Wash, DC; Honolulu Acad of Arts, HI; Hopkins Center Art Gallery, Dartmouth Col, Hanover, NH; Illinois State Univ, Normal, IL; Indianapolis Mus, IN; La Jolla Mus of Contemp Art, CA; Long Beach Mus, CA; Ludwig Coll, Germany; Madison Art Center, WI; Metropolitan Mus of Art, NY; Mus of the City of New York, NY; Mus of Fine Arts, Springfield, MA; Mus of Mod Art, NY; Nat Mus of Am Art, Smithsonian Inst, Wash, DC; New Britain Mus of Am Art, CT; New Orleans Mus, LA; Philadelphia Mus, PA; Princeton Univ of Art Mus, NJ; Reynolda House Mus of Am Art, Winston-Salem, NC; Rhode Island Sch of Design, Providence, RI; Rutgers Univ, Camden, NJ; St Louis Mus, MO; Smith Col Mus, Northampton, MA; Springfield Art Mus, MO; Syracuse Univ, Joe & Emily Lowe Art Gallery, NY; Univ of Iowa Mus, Iowa City, IA; Univ of Kansas, Spencer Mus, Lawrence, KS; Univ of Utah Mus, Salt Lake City, UT; Univ of Virginia, Charlottesville, VA; Utrecht Mus, Netherlands; Virginia Mus of Fine Arts, Richmond, VA; Whitney Mus of Am Art, NY; Wichita Art Mus, KS; Williams Col Mus, Williamstown, MA; Yale Univ Art Gallery, New Haven, CT
PRINTERS: Landfall Press, Inc, Chicago, IL (LPI); Jack Lemon, Chicago, IL (JL); Timothy Berry, Chicago, IL (TB); Fred Gude, Chicago, IL (FG); David Kelsler, Chicago, IL (DK); Thomas Minkler, Chicago, IL (TM); Jerry Raidiger, Chicago, IL (JR); Chip Elwell, NY (CE); Thomas Cvikota (TC); Laura Holland (LH); David Panosh (DP); Gregory Grenon (GG); Ron Wyffels (RW); Carol Plummer (CP); Lowell Farlow (LF); Ted Carter (TC); Herbert Fox, Merrimac, MA (HF); Fox Graphics, Merrimac, MA (FG); Myra R Burks, Portland, OR (MB); Vicki Vanderslice, Portland, OR (VV); Randy Folkman, Redding, CT (RF); Lonetown Press, Redding, CT (LP); Joe Petruzzelli, NY (JP); Deli Sacilotto, NY (DS); Atelier Editions, NY (AEd); Chip Elwell, NY (CE); Sienna Studios, NY (SiS); Felix Harlan, NY (FH); Carol Weave, NY (CW); Harlan-Weaver Intaglio, NY (H-WI); Karl Hecksher, Brooklyn, NY (KH); Artist (ART); Andy Rubin, Madison, WI (AR); Tandem Press, Madison, WI (TanPr)

Robert Cottingham
Rolling Stock Series No 7, for Jim
Courtesy Tandem Press

ROBERT COTTINGHAM CONTINUED

PUBLISHERS: Landfall Press, Inc, Chicago, IL (LPI); North Light Editions, Portland, OR (NLE); Signet Arts, St Louis, MO (SA); John Gentleman (Jackie Fine Arts), NY (JG); Alex M Steinbergh, (Jackie Fine Arts), NY (AMS); Fox Graphics, Merrimac, MA (FG); Artist (ART); Tandem Press, Madison, WI (TanPr)
GALLERIES: Thomas Segal Gallery, Boston, MA; Signet Arts, St Louis, MO; Modernism, San Francisco, CA; Brenda Kroos Gallery, Cleveland, OH; Gimpel & Weitzenhoffer Gallery, New York, NY; O K Harris, New York, NY; Barbara Fendrick Gallery, New York, NY; Landfall Press, Inc, Chicago, IL; Louis K Meisel Gallery, New York, NY; Roger Ramsay Gallery, Chicago, IL; Marisa del Re, New York, NY; Harcourts Modern & Contemporary Art, San Francisco, CA; Martin Lawrence Gallery, New York, NY; Farber Fine Arts, Secauscus NJ; Ro Gallery Image Makers, New York, NY
MAILING ADDRESS: 16 Blackman Rd, P O Box 604, Newtown, CT 06470

TITLE	PUBLISHER	PRINTER	DATE	MEDIUM	DIMENSION (PAPER SIZE) IN INCHES	TYPE OF PAPER	EDITION NUMBER	NO. OF COLORS	ORIGINAL OPENING PRICE	CURRENT RETAIL PRICE
SOLD OUT EDITIONS (RARE):										
Orph	SHI	SHI	1972	LC	24 X 34	AC/W	300	7	200	700
Fox	LPI	DK/TM/LPI	1973	LC	23 X 23	ARJ	100	24	300	1000
Hot	LPI	JL/JR/TM/LPI	1973	LC	23 X 23	ARJ	100	17	300	1000
Dr Gibson	LPI	JL/DK/LPI	1974	LC	36 X 36	ARJ	50	20	500	2000
Ice	LPI	TB/LPI	1975	EB/A/SG	30 X 22	DE	50	1	300	750
FW	LPI	TB/CP/LPI	1975	EB/A	28 X 22	TWP/JAP	50	1	300	1200
Everybody's Bookshop—Everybody's Books	SSC-K	JL/DK/LPI	1975	LC	23 X 18	ARJ	200	2	200	800
Tattoo	LPI	JL/DK/LPI	1975	LC	36 X 36	RP	50	21	900	1500
Champagne	LPI	JL/LPI	1975	LB	11 X 9	CAN	300	1		
Women-Girls	FA/NAM	FG/TC/LPI	1978	LC	17 X 17	AC/W	101	3		
Cottingham Suite (Set of 4):										
Carl's	LPI	TB/LPI	1980	EB/A	17 X 18	AP	50	1	400	1500
Star	LPI	TB/LPI	1980	EB/A	17 X 18	AP	50	1	400	1500
Hamburger	LPI	JL/FG/LPI	1980	LC	17 X 18	R/BFK	50	26	600	750
Black Girl	LPI	JL/LPI	1980	LC	17 X 18	R/BFK	50	32	600	950
CURRENT EDITIONS:										
Cold Beer	RHH	DS/AEd	1980	LC/OFF	20 X 20	AC/W	150	2	600	1000
Cold Beer	ART	DS/AEd	1980	LB/OFF/AC	20 X 20	AC/W	XIII	Varies	300	650
The Spot	NLE	MB/VV/NLE	1982	LC	27 X 19	AP/W	46	8	1000	1500
Candy	SA	CE	1984	PO	26 X 25	AP/W	40	39	1200	1200
Star	ART/FG	HF/FG	1984	LC	22 X 22	AC	50	8	750	900
Barrera-Rosa (Framed) (Set of 3)	SP/LPI	JL/LPI	1986	LC	23 X 46 EA	AP/W	29 EA	24	1500 SET	6000 SET
O	ART	FH/CW/H/WI	1986	AC/SB	22 X 17	SOM/S	50	3	375	800
Starr	LPI	JL/LPI	1988	LC	23 X 30	SOM	50	12	900	1200
Santa Fe I	LPI	JL/LPI	1988	WC	35 X 35	AP/W	48	25	2500	2800
Santa Fe II	SA	KH/ART	1989	WC/HC	35 X 35	KOZO	23	20	2000	2250
C & O	LPI	JL/LPI	1989	LC	30 X 38	SOM/S	50	9	1200	1500
Rolling Stock Series, No 7, for Jim	TanPr	AR/TanPr	1991	EC/COL/MON	83 X 38 EA	AC/W	40 EA	16 EA	4000 EA	4000 EA
Rolling Stock Series, No 22, for Bill	TanPr	AR/TanPr	1992	EB/COL	48 X 68		40	25	4000	5000

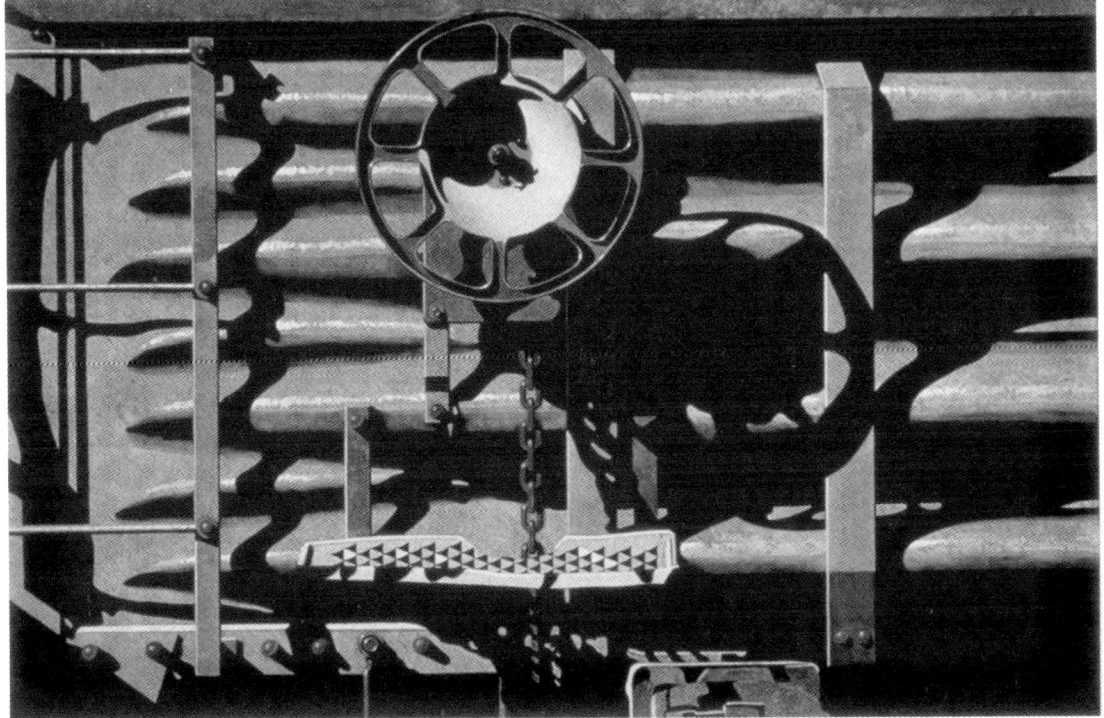

Robert Cottingham
Rolling Stock Series, No 22, for Bill
Courtesy Tandem Press

CHRIS COSTAN

BORN: Chicago, IL; September 18, 1950
EDUCATION: Univ of Illinois, Chicago, IL, BA, 1973; Univ of Wisconsin, Madison, WI, MA, 1974, MFA, 1975
RECENT EXHIB: Peter Miller Gallery, Chicago, IL, 1987; Avenue B Gallery, NY, 1987; Germans Van Eck Gallery, NY, 1988
AWARDS: C A T Laboratory Prog Grant, Just Above Midtown, NY
COLLECTIONS: Elvehjiem Art Mus, Madison, WI; Art Inst of Chicago, IL; Madison Art Center, WI; Univ of Illinois, Chicago, IL; Univ of Wisconsin, Madison WI; Grand Rapids Mus, MI; Miami-Dade Com Col, FL
PRINTERS: The Printmaking Workshop, NY (PW); Bob Blackburn, NY (BB); Holly Sears, NY (HS); Cheryl Pelavin, NY (CP); Pelavin Editions, NY (PeEd)
PUBLISHERS: Avenue B Gallery, NY (ABG); Pelavin Editions, NY (PeEd)
GALLERIES: Peter Miller Gallery, Chicago, IL; Pelavin Editions, New York, NY; Germans Van Eck Gallery, New York, NY

TITLE	PUBLISHER	PRINTER	DATE	MEDIUM	DIMENSION (PAPER SIZE) IN INCHES	TYPE OF PAPER	EDITION NUMBER	NO. OF COLORS	ORIGINAL OPENING PRICE	CURRENT RETAIL PRICE
CURRENT EDITIONS:										
You're Just a Pack of Cards	ABG	HS/PW	1986	LC	48 X 32	R/BFK/W	75	5	350	750
Announcement	PeEd	CP/PeEd	1989	AC	22 X 30	R/BFK	35	4	1200	1500

DON KELLOGG COWAN

BORN: January 8, 1947
EDUCATION: Northwestern Univ, Evanston, IL, BS, Math; Northwestern Univ, Evanston, IL, Masters in Computer Science
COLLECTIONS: Medical Sch, Ohio Univ, Athens, OH
PUBLISHERS: John Szoke Graphics, Inc, NY (JSG)
PRINTERS: Cleveland Editions, Brooklyn, NY (ClEd)
GALLERIES: John Szoke Graphics, Inc, New York, NY

TITLE	PUBLISHER	PRINTER	DATE	MEDIUM	DIMENSION (PAPER SIZE) IN INCHES	TYPE OF PAPER	EDITION NUMBER	NO. OF COLORS	ORIGINAL OPENING PRICE	CURRENT RETAIL PRICE
SOLD OUT EDITIONS (RARE):										
Terrain I, II, III	JSG	ClEd	1986	EC/HC	30 X 42 EA	AP	75 EA	Varies	250 EA	400 EA
CURRENT EDITIONS:										
Terrain IV, V, VI, VII (Set of 4)	JSG	ClEd	1986	EC/HC	30 X 42 EA	AP	125 EA	Varies	1000 SET	1350 SET
									300 EA	400 EA

JACK COWIN

PRINTERS: Jack Lemon, Chicago, IL (JL); Landfall Press, Inc, Chicago, IL (LPI)
PUBLISHERS: Landfall Press, Inc, Chicago, IL (LPI)
GALLERIES: Landfall Press, Inc, Chicago, IL; Quartet Editions, New York, NY

TITLE	PUBLISHER	PRINTER	DATE	MEDIUM	DIMENSION (PAPER SIZE) IN INCHES	TYPE OF PAPER	EDITION NUMBER	NO. OF COLORS	ORIGINAL OPENING PRICE	CURRENT RETAIL PRICE
CURRENT EDITIONS:										
Hen-Rainbow Trout	LPI	JL/LPI	1983	LC	28 X 40	AC	50	5	450	450
Spring Run	LPI	JL/LPI	1985	LC	23 X 28	AC	20	4	250	250
Future Considerations	LPI	JL/LPI	1985	LC	18 X 24	AC	75	4	350	500
Rainbow Suite (Set of	LPI	JL/LPI	1987	LC(2) EB/HC(2) PH/G(1)	14 X 15 EA	AC	25 EA	Varies	1500 SET	1500 SET
Tarpon	LPI	JL/LPI	1990	LC	25 X 34	AC	24		400	400

TONY CRAGG

BORN: Liverpool, England; 1949
EDUCATION: Found Course, Gloucestershire Col of Art, Cheltenham, England, 1968; Wimbledon Sch of Art, England, 1969–72; Royal Col of Art, London, England, Sculpture, 1973–77
TEACHING: Art in Res, Headlands, Center for the Arts, Sausalito, CA, 1988
AWARDS: Turner Prize, Tate Gallery, London, England, 1988
RECENT EXHIB: Antonio Tucci Russo Gallery, Torino, Italy, 1987; Hayward Gallery, London, England, 1987; Galeria Foksal, Waszawa, Tokyo, 1988; Galerie Marga Paz, Madrid, Spain, 1988; Galerie Buchman, Basel, Switzerland, 1988; Galerie Crousel-Robelin, Paris, France, 1988; Nishimurz Gallery, Tokyo; Japan, 1989; Galerie de Expeditie, Amsterdam, The Netherlands, 1989; Galeria Atlantica, Portugal, Spain, 1989; Lisson Gallery, London, England, 1989; Munson-Williams-Proctor Inst, Mus of Art, Utica, NY, 1989; Crown Point Press, NY, 1990; Runhel-Hue-Williams, Ltd, London, England, 1990; Marian Goodman Gallery, NY, 1987,89,90; Newport Harbor Art Mus, RI, 1990; Donald Young Gallery, Chicago, IL, 1990; Marisa Del Re Gallery, NY, 1990; Corcoran Gallery of Art, Wash, DC, 1991; Power Plant, Toronto, Canada, 1991; Contemp Art Mus, Houston, TX, 1991–92

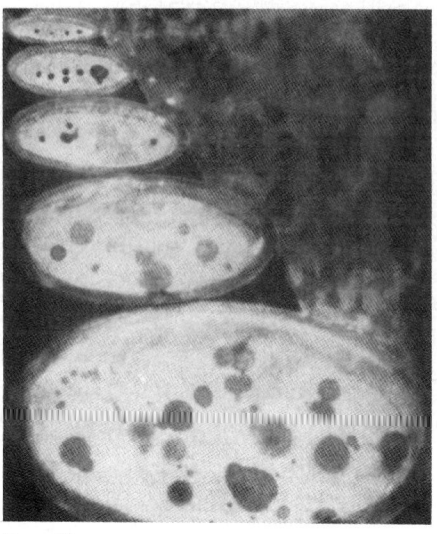

Tony Cragg
14 from Die Erste Ara
Courtesy Galerie Bernd Klüser

TONY CRAGG CONTINUED

COLLECTIONS: Tate Gallery, London, England; Albertina Mus, Vienna, Austria; Mus of Mod Art, NY; Trisolini Gallery, Ohio Univ, Athens, OH; Georgia Mus of Art, Athens, GA; New York Public Library, NY; Brooklyn Mus, NY; La Jolla Mus of Contemp Art, CA; Palais des Beaux-Arts, Brussels, Belgium; Mus d'Art Mod de la Ville de Paris, Paris, France
PRINTERS: Mark Cullen, San Francisco, CA (MC); Lawrence Hamlin, San Francisco, CA (LH); Pamela Paulson, San Francisco, CA (PP); Crown Point Press, San Francisco, CA (CPP); Paul Mullowney, San Francisco, CA (PM); Lothar Osterburg, San Francisco, CA (LO); Daria Sywulak, San Francisco, CA (DS)

PUBLISHERS: Crown Point Press, San Francisco, CA (CPP)
GALLERIES: Crown Point Press, New York, NY & San Francisco, CA; Lisson Gallery, London, England; Galerie Atlantica, Portugal, Spain; Nishimurz Gallery, Tokyo, Japan; Galerie Buchman, Basel, Switzerland; Galerie Marga Paz, Madrid, Spain; Hayward Gallery, London, England; Marian Goodman Gallery, New York, NY; Donald Young Gallery, Seattle, WA; Runhel-Hue-Williams, Ltd, London, England; Marisa del Re, New York, NY; R K Goldman Contemporary, Los Angeles, CA; Gallery Paule Anglim, San Francisco, CA; Fred Hoffman Gallery, Santa Monica, CA; Laura Carpenter Fine Art, Santa Monica, CA
MAILING ADDRESS: Wuppertal, West Germany

TITLE	PUBLISHER	PRINTER	DATE	MEDIUM	DIMENSION (PAPER SIZE) IN INCHES	TYPE OF PAPER	EDITION NUMBER	NO. OF COLORS	ORIGINAL OPENING PRICE	CURRENT RETAIL PRICE
SOLD OUT EDITIONS (RARE):										
Laboratory Still Life, #1, State II	CPP	MC/LH/PP/CPP	1988	AC	23 X 24	SOM	30		2200	3500
Laboratory Still Life #2, State I	CPP	MC/LH/PP/CPP	1988	AB	21 X 44	SOM	30	1	2200	4500
Laboratory Still Life #2, State 2	CPP	MC/LH/PP/CPP	1988	AC	21 X 44	SOM	30		2200	5000
Laboratory Still Life #3	CPP	MC/LH/PP/CPP	1988	AB	23 X 24	SOM	20	1	2200	3000
Six Bottles State II	CPP	MC/LH/PP/CPP	1988	AC	17 X 22	SOM	25		1500	1200
CURRENT EDITIONS:										
Laboratory Still Life, #1, State I	CPP	MC/LH/PP/CPP	1988	AB	23 X 24	SOM	30	1	2200	3000
Laboratory Still Life #4	CPP	MC/LH/PP/CPP	1988	AB	30 X 30	SOM	40	1	2200	3500
Balloon	CPP	MC/LH/PP/CPP	1988	AB	25 X 22	SOM	35	1	750	750
Exhaust	CPP	MC/LH/PP/CPP	1988	AB	25 X 22	SOM	35	1	750	750
Container I, II, III	CPP	MC/LH/PP/CPP	1988	AC	22 X 24 EA	SOM	15 EA		750 EA	750 EA
Container Out of Control	CPP	MC/LH/PP/CPP	1988	EB/SB	18 X 23	SOM	15	1	750	750
Figures I–XI (Set of 11)	CPP	MC/LH/PP/CPP	1988	EC/SG	19 X 16 EA	SOM	10 EA		9500 SET	10000 SET
Landscape	CPP	MC/LH/PP/CPP	1988	EB/AB	23 X 20	SOM	15	1	850	850
Six Bottles, State I	CPP	MC/LH/PP/CPP	1988	EB/AB	17 X 22	SOM	25	1	1000	1000
Six Bottles, Large, State I	CPP	MC/LH/PP/CPP	1988	EB/AB	30 X 39	SOM	25	1	2500	3000
Six Bottles, Large, State II	CPP	MC/LH/PP/CPP	1988	AC	30 X 39	SOM	25		2500	4000
Set of Five Aquatint Etchings:									3000 SET	3000 SET
Horns I, II	CPP	MC/LH/PP/CPP	1988	AC	23 X 24 EA	SOM	15 EA		850 EA	850 EA
Spores	CPP	MC/LH/PP/CPP	1988	AC	23 X 24	SOM	15		850	850
Vessels	CPP	MC/LH/PP/CPP	1988	AC	23 X 24	SOM	15		850	850
Untitled	CPP	MC/LH/PP/CPP	1988	AC	23 X 24	SOM	15		850	850
Two Bottles, State I	CPP	MC/LH/PP/CPP	1988	AB	17 X 15	SOM	25	1	850	850
Two Bottles, State II	CPP	MC/LH/PP/CPP	1988	AC	17 X 15	SOM	25		950	950
Suburbs I, II	CPP	LH/PM/LO/ DS/CPP	1990	AC/SB	28 X 26 EA	SOM	35 EA		1500 EA	1800 EA
Suburbs I–V (Softground Series)	CPP	LH/PM/LO/ DS/CPP	1990	I/A/SG	20 X 17 EA	SOM	20 EA	3 EA	3000 SET 650 EA	3000 SET 650 EA
Suburbs I–V (Spitbite Series)	CPP	LH/PM/LO/ DS/CPP	1990	I/A/SB	20 X 17 EA	SOM	20 EA	3 EA	3000 SET 650 EA	3000 SET 650 EA
Test Tubes I	CPP	CPP	1990	AC/SB/DPT	17 X 16	SOM	10		700	700
Test Tubes II–VI	CPP	CPP	1990	AC/SB/DPT	17 X 16 EA	SOM	15 EA		700 EA	700 EA
Branching Line	CPP	CPP	1990	EB/HG	26 X 25	SOM	15	1	850	850
Cannisters I, II, III	CPP	CPP	1990	AC/EB/SB	15 X 13	SOM	15		600 EA	600 EA
Fruit Juice Bottles I, States, I, II	CPP	CPP	1990	AC/EB/SB	22 X 24 EA	SOM	25 EA		1000 EA	1000 EA
Fruit Juice Bottles II, States, I, II	CPP	CPP	1990	AC/EB/SB	22 X 24 EA	SOM	25 EA		1000 EA	1000 EA
Fruit Juice Bottles III, States, I, II	CPP	CPP	1990	AC/EB/SB	22 X 24 EA	SOM	25 EA		1000 EA	1000 EA
Fruit Juice Bottles IV, States, I, II	CPP	CPP	1990	AC/EB/SB	22 X 24 EA	SOM	25 EA		1000 EA	1000 EA
Breathers, States I, II	CPP	CPP	1990	AB/SG	17 X 16 EA	SOM	15 EA	1 EA	550 EA	550 EA
Chalices, States I, II	CPP	CPP	1990	AB/SG	17 X 16 EA	SOM	15 EA	1 EA	550 EA	550 EA
Listeners, States I, II	CPP	CPP	1990	AB/SG	17 X 16 EA	SOM	15 EA	1 EA	550 EA	550 EA
Untitled, States I, II	CPP	CPP	1990	AB/SG	17 X 16 EA	SOM	15 EA	1 EA	550 EA	550 EA
Meandering River I	CPP	CPP	1990	AB/SG	13 X 11	SOM	15	1	750	750
Meandering River II	CPP	CPP	1990	AB/SG/SL	20 X 17	SOM	15	1	900	900
Meandering River III	CPP	CPP	1990	EC/SG	29 X 36	SOM	20		1100	1100
Die Erste Ara (Set of 14)	GBK	JVB	1991	AB	21 X 16 EA	HAHN	18 EA	1 EA	DM16500 SET	DM16500 SET

NEELON CRAWFORD

PUBLISHERS: Artist (ART)
PRINTERS: Sally Sturman, NY (SS); Deli Sacilotto, NY (DS)

GALLERIES: Perimeter Gallery, Chicago, IL; Jayne H Baum Gallery, New York, NY; Witkin Gallery, New York, NY

TITLE	PUBLISHER	PRINTER	DATE	MEDIUM	DIMENSION (PAPER SIZE) IN INCHES	TYPE OF PAPER	EDITION NUMBER	NO. OF COLORS	ORIGINAL OPENING PRICE	CURRENT RETAIL PRICE
SOLD OUT EDITIONS (RARE):										
Pratt and Whitney R-4360	ART	SS/DS	1984	PH/GR	23 X 30	R/BFK	15	1	600	850

GEORGE CRAMER

BORN: Spring Arbor, MI; 1938
EDUCATION: Univ of Michigan, Ann Arbor, MI, BS, 1968; Univ of Wisconsin, Madison, WI, MFA, 1970
RECENT EXHIB: Spaightwood Gallery, Madison, WI, 1987; Western Illinois Univ, Macomb, IL, 1991
COLLECTIONS: Elvehjem Mus of Art, Univ of Wisconsin, Madison, WI; Central Michigan Univ, Mt Pleasant, WI; Kohler Art Center, Sheboygan, WI; Madison Art Center, WI; Anderson Fine Arts Center, IN
PRINTERS: Bill Weege, Madison, WI (BW); Andrew Rubin, Madison, WI (AR); Tandem Press, University of Wisconsin, Madison, WI (TanPr)
PUBLISHERS: Tandem Press, University of Wisconsin, Madison, WI (TanPr)
GALLERIES: Peltz Gallery, Milwaukee, WI

George Cramer
Neo Harmony (Monotype)
Courtesy Tandem Press

TITLE	PUBLISHER	PRINTER	DATE	MEDIUM	DIMENSION (PAPER SIZE) IN INCHES	TYPE OF PAPER	EDITION NUMBER	NO. OF COLORS	ORIGINAL OPENING PRICE	CURRENT RETAIL PRICE
CURRENT EDITIONS:										
Monotypes (16 Unique Prints)	TanPr	BW/AR/TanPr	1992	MON	Varies	AC/W	1 EA	Varies	850/3500	850/3500

SUSAN CRILE

BORN: Cleveland, OH; 1942
EDUCATION: Bennington Col, VT, 1961–62, 64–65; New York Univ, 1962–64; Hunter Col, 1971–72
TEACHING: Instr, Princeton Univ, NJ, 1974–76; Sarah Lawrence Col, Bronxville, NY, 1976–78; Sch of Visual Arts, NY, 1976 to present
AWARDS: Ingram Merrill Found Grant, 1972; Nat Endowment for the Arts Fel, 1982
COLLECTIONS: Phillips Col, Wash, DC; Hirshhorn Mus, Wash, DC; Brooklyn Mus, NY; Albright-Knox Art Gallery, Buffalo, NY; Carnegie Inst of Art Pittsburgh, PA; Metropolitan Mus, NY; Solomon R Guggenheim Mus, NY; Smithsonian Inst, Wash DC
PRINTERS: Condeso & Brokopp Studios (CBS); Sharks Lithography Ltd, Boulder, CO (SLL); Bud Shark, Boulder, CO (BS); Orlando Condeso, NY (OC); Susan Volker (SV); Dan Waller (DW); Vinalhaven Press, Vinalhaven, ME (VP); Norman Stewart, Bloomfield Hills, MI (NS); Joe Keenan, Bloomfield Hills, MI (JK); Wing Lake Studio, Bloomfield Hills, MI (WLS); Catherine Kuhn, Albuquerque, MN (CK); Melissa Katzman Braggins, Albuquerque, NM (MKB); Tamarind Inst, Albuquerque, NM (TI); Corey Stewart, Bloomfield Hills, MI (CS); Stewart & Stewart, Bloomfield Hills, MI (S-S)
PUBLISHERS: 724 Prints, NY (724P); Graham Modern, NY (GM); Vinalhaven Press, Vinalhaven, ME (VP); Stewart & Stewart, Bloomfield Hills, MI (S-S); Tamarind Inst, Albuquerque, NM (TI)
GALLERIES: Sandy Carson Gallery, Denver, CO, van Straaten Gallery, Chicago, IL; Nina Freudenheim Gallery, Buffalo, NY; Rubiner Gallery, West Bloomfield, MI; Graham Modern, New York, NY; Tamarind Inst, Albuquerque, NM
MAILING ADDRESS: 168 W 86th St, New York, NY 10024

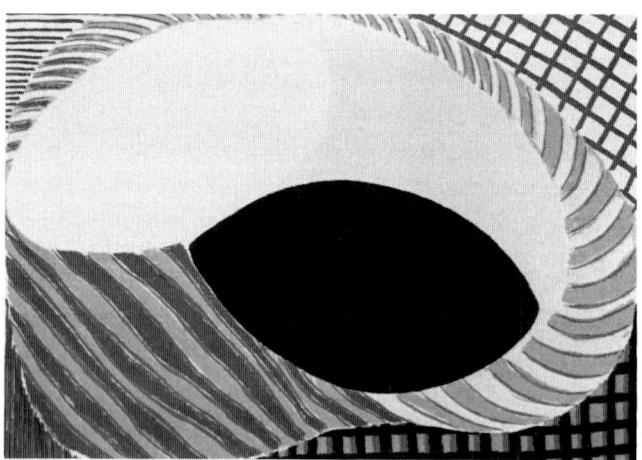

Susan Crile
Echo
Courtesy Stewart & Stewart

TITLE	PUBLISHER	PRINTER	DATE	MEDIUM	DIMENSION (PAPER SIZE) IN INCHES	TYPE OF PAPER	EDITION NUMBER	NO. OF COLORS	ORIGINAL OPENING PRICE	CURRENT RETAIL PRICE
SOLD OUT EDITIONS (RARE):										
Triple Twist #1	724P	OC/CBS	1979	AC	18 X 24	R/BFK	40	16	325	1800
Triple Twist #2, #3	724P	OC/CBS	1979	AC	18 X 24 EA	R/BFK	40	17	325	1800
Triple Twist #3	724P	OC/CBS	1979	AC	18 X 24	R/BFK	40	17	325	1800
Expansion	724P	SLL	1981	LC	25 X 42	R/BFK	50	8	900	2500
Transparent Solid	724P	SLL	1981	LC	24 X 25	R/BFK	50	10	700	2000
Buskirk Junction	724P	OC/CBS	1982	WC	30 X 36	SUZ	35	3	600	2200
Renvers of Two Tracks	724P	OC/CBS	1982	WC	24 X 36	GTP	35	7	850	2200
Back and Forth	TI	CK/MBK/TI	1982	LC	24 X 36	AP/W	40	9	350	1500
CURRENT EDITIONS:										
Thoroughfare	GM/VP	OC/DW/SV/VP	1986	EB/A	24 X 54	AC	30	1	900	3000
Oculus	S-S	NS/JK/WLS	1988	SP	29 X 21	R/BFK/W	69	15	750	1750
Echo	S-S	NS/JK/WLS	1989	SP	22 X 30	R/BFK/W	62	11	900	1250
Palio	S-S	NS/JK/WLS	1989	SP	29 X 41	R/BFK/W	38	4	900	1500
Ragtime	VP	VP	1989	SP	34 X 25	SEK	25	8	1200	2000
Osage's Copperhead	S-S	NS/JK/S-S	1991	SP	22 X 30	R/BFK	3	1	850	850
Osage's Command	S-S	NS/JK/S-S	1991	SP	22 X 30	R/BFK/W	60	5	850	850
Racer	S-S	NS/JK/CS/S-S	1991	SP	41 X 29	R/BFK/W	36	8	1500	1800

DON CROUCH

BORN: Carlsbad, New Mexico; 1940
EDUCATION: Univ of Iowa, Iowa City, IA, MFA
TEACHING: Western Illinois Univ, Macomb, IL
COLLECTIONS: Cleveland Mus of Art, OH; Illinois State Mus, Springfield, IL; Tyler Mus of Art, TX; Scottsdale Center for the Arts, AZ; Arkansas Art Center, Little Rock, AR
PRINTERS: American Atelier, NY (AA)
PUBLISHERS: Circle Fine Art, Chicago, IL (CFA)
GALLERIES: Circle Galleries, San Diego, CA & San Francisco, CA & Northbrook, IL & Pittsburgh, PA & Houston, TX & Soho, NY & Chicago, IL & Scottsdale, AZ & Beverly Hills, CA & Costa Mesa, CA & Sherman Oaks, CA & Palm Beach, FL & Honolulu, HI & New Orleans, LA & Las Vegas, NV & Seattle, WA

TITLE	PUBLISHER	PRINTER	DATE	MEDIUM	DIMENSION (PAPER SIZE) IN INCHES	TYPE OF PAPER	EDITION NUMBER	NO. OF COLORS	ORIGINAL OPENING PRICE	CURRENT RETAIL PRICE
CURRENT EDITIONS:										
Hawk Dancer	CFA	AA	1978	SP	40 X 26	AP	275		125	300

WILLIAM CRUTCHFIELD

BORN: Indianapolis, IN; January 21, 1932
EDUCATION: Herron Art Sch, Indiana Univ, Indianapolis, IN, 1956; Tulane Univ, New Orleans, LA
AWARDS: Mary Milliken Award, Indiana Univ, Indianapolis, IN, 1956; Fulbright Fel, 1961
COLLECTIONS: Mus of Mod Art, NY; Art Inst of Chicago, IL; Cleveland Mus, OH; Philadelphia Mus of Art, PA; Amon Carter Mus of Western Art, Forth Worth, TX; Atlanta Mem Art Center, Atlanta, GA; Brooklyn Mus, NY; Fort Lauderdale Mus, FL; Harvard Univ, Cambridge MA; Indianapolis Mus, IN; La Jolla Mus, CA; Los Angeles County Mus, CA; Nat Mus of Australia, Canberra, Australia; New Jersey State Mus, Trenton Mus, NJ; New Orleans Mus, LA; Pasadena Art Mus, CA; Rhode Island Sch of Design, Providence, RI; Sheldon Swope Gallery of Art, Terre Haute, IN; Tate Gallery, London, England; Univ of Texas, Austin, TX; Wichita Art Mus, KS; Wabash Col, Crawfordsville, IN; Grunwald Graphic Arts Found, Univ of California, Los Angeles, CA
PRINTERS: Tyler Graphics Workshop, Mt. Kisco, NY (TGL); Gemini GEL, Los Angeles, CA (GEM); Ed Hamilton (EH); Jeff Wasserman (JW)
PUBLISHERS: Tyler Graphics Ltd, Mt. Kisco, NY (TGL); Gemini GEL, Los Angeles, CA (GEM); Barbara Crutchfield, San Pedro, CA (BC)
GALLERIES: Barbara Crutchfield, San Pedro, CA; Gemini GEL, Los Angeles, CA; Tyler Graphics, Ltd, Mount Kisco, NY
MAILING ADDRESS: P.O. Box 591, San Pedro, CA 90733

TITLE	PUBLISHER	PRINTER	DATE	MEDIUM	DIMENSION (PAPER SIZE) IN INCHES	TYPE OF PAPER	EDITION NUMBER	NO. OF COLORS	ORIGINAL OPENING PRICE	CURRENT RETAIL PRICE
SOLD OUT EDITIONS (RARE):										
Edwin G Robinson	GEM	GEM	1972	LC	20 X 17	AP	18	1	200	600
Ira Gershwin	GEM	GEM	1972	LC	20 X 17	AP	20	1	200	600
CURRENT EDITIONS:										
At the Falls (from Vistas Series)	GEM	GEM	1967	LC/HC/WA	17 X 31	AP	30	Varies	100	1200
Brown Pelican	GEM	GEM	1971	LC	20 X 25	AP	28	1	150	600
Five Trains and Zeppelin Island (Set of 6):										
Zeppelin Island (Sold Out)	TGL	TGL	1977-78		37½ X 56¼	AP88	32	11	600	1500
Trestle Trains	TGL	TGL	1977-78	LC	39 5/16 X 55¼	AP88	48	11	600	1000
Elevated Smoke	TGL	TGL	1977-78	LC	38 7/8 X 53¼	AP88	48	8	600	1000
Burial at Sea	TGL	TGL	1977-78	LC	29 1/8 X 53 1/8	AP88	48	7	600	1000
Diamond Express	TGL	TGL	1977-78	LC	39 1/8 X 49½	AP88	48	10	600	1200
Cubie Smoke	TGL	TGL	1977-78	LC	39 1/8 X 49½	AP88	48	9	600	1000
Train of Thought	BC	EH/JW	1984	LC/SP	29½ X 22	AP88	40	6	600	700
Sunset	BC	EH/JW	1984	LC/SP	29 3/8 X 37¾	R/BFK	30	10	1000	1000
Up in Smoke	BC	EH	1985	LC	30 X 22	AP88	35	8	600	700
The Duchamp Flamingo I	BC	EH	1985	LC	39 X 21½	AP88	30	8	800	800
The Duchamp Flamingo II	BC	EH	1985	LC	29 X 21½	AP/BL	12	8	1000	1000
Arles Express	BC	EH	1985	LC	22 X 30	AP88	43	8	600	700

STEPHEN CSOKA

BORN: Gardony, Hungary; (1887–1989)
EDUCATION: Royal Acad of Art, Budapest, Hungary
TEACHING: Instr, Hunter Col, NY; Instr, Parsons Sch of Design, NY; Instr, City Col of New York, NY; Instr, Nat Acad of Design, NY; Instr, Fashion Inst of Tech, NY
COLLECTIONS: British Mus, London, England; Metropolitan Mus of Art, NY; Brooklyn Mus, NY; Mus of Budapest, Hungary; Georgia Mus, Athens, GA; New York Public Library, NY; Dayton Mus of Art, OH; Columbus Mus, OH; Peabody Mus, Cambridge, MA; Hunter Col, NY; City Col, NY; Reading Public Mus, PA; Princeton Print Club, NJ; Carnegie Inst, Pittsburgh, PA; Norfolk Mus, CT; Library of Congress, Wash, DC
PRINTERS: Artist (ART); American Atelier, NY (AA)
PUBLISHERS: Artist (ART); Associated American Artists, NY (AAA)
GALLERIES: Associated American Artists, New York, NY

TITLE	PUBLISHER	PRINTER	DATE	MEDIUM	DIMENSION (PAPER SIZE) IN INCHES	TYPE OF PAPER	EDITION NUMBER	NO. OF COLORS	ORIGINAL OPENING PRICE	CURRENT RETAIL PRICE
SOLD OUT EDITIONS (RARE):										
Artist and Model	ART	ART	1927	EB	7 X 6	WOVE	50	1	60	250
Flight	ART	ART	1928	EB	12 X 15	WOVE	50	1	75	800
Hungarian Landscape	ART	ART	1928	EB	8 X 11	WOVE	50	1	75	600
Patato Pickers	ART	ART	1928	EB	10 X 12	WOVE	30	1	75	900
Drinking Workman	ART	ART	1929	EB	12 X 9	WOVE	75	1	85	600
Landscape	ART	ART	1929	EB	3 X 4	WOVE	100	1	50	300
Peasant	ART	ART	1929	EB	4 X 4	WOVE	75	1	50	400

STEPHEN CSOKA CONTINUED

TITLE	PUBLISHER	PRINTER	DATE	MEDIUM	DIMENSION (PAPER SIZE) IN INCHES	TYPE OF PAPER	EDITION NUMBER	NO. OF COLORS	ORIGINAL OPENING PRICE	CURRENT RETAIL PRICE
SOLD OUT EDITIONS (RARE):										
Village Market	ART	ART	1929	EB	3 X 4	WOVE	50	1	50	350
Endless is the Way Leading Home	ART	ART	1931	EB	13 X 17	WOVE	50	1	100	750
Brooklyn Landscape	ART	ART	1940	EB	8 X 11	WOVE		1	100	250
Long Island Farm	ART	ART	1943	EB	5 X 7	WOVE	50	1	50	500
Country Bath	ART	ART	1943	EB	6 X 4	WOVE	50	1	50	500
Composition	ART	ART	1945	EB	4 X 6	WOVE	50	1	50	600
Farm Crisis	ART	ART	1947	EB	3 X 4	AP	100	1	75	350
Fatherless	ART	ART	1947	EB	11 X 9	AP	0	1	100	950
Pasture	ART	ART	1947	EB	9 X 11	AP	50	1	100	500
Carnival	ART	ART	1948	EB	9 X 11	AP	75	1	100	550
Meet the Gang	ART	ART	1950	EB	18 X 15	AP	12	1	150	1500
Approaching the Storm	ART	ART	1951	EB	12 X 16	AP	30	1	150	1500
Sketchbook Plate	AAA	AA	1981	EB	8 X 8	AP	30	1	200	600
Spirited Horses	AAA	AA	1981	EB	2 X 4	AP	50	1	100	500
Goodbye to Summer	AAA	AA	1981	EB	8 X 10	AP	50	1	125	200
Seated Nude	AAA	AA	1981	EB	3 X 2	AP	50	1	75	300

ENZO CUCCHI

BORN: Ancona, Italy; 1950
RECENT EXHIB: Galerie Bruno Bischofberger, Zürich, Switzerland, 1988; Murray & Isabella Rayburn Found, NY, 1992; Nathan Silberberg Gallery, NY, 1992; BlumHelman Gallery, NY, 1992
COLLECTIONS: Mus of Mod Art, NY
PRINTERS: 2 RC Stamperia d'Arte, Rome, Italy (2RC); Luciano Bougiovanni, Ancona, Italy (LB); Valter Rossi, Rome, Italy (VR); Eleanora Rossi, Rome, Italy (ER); Vigna Antoniniana Stamperia d'Arte, Rome, Italy (VA)

PUBLISHERS: Peter Blum Edition, NY (PBE); Edition Schellmann, NY & Munich, Germany (ES); Eleanora Rossi, Rome, Italy (ER); Galerie Bernd Klüser, Munich, Germany (GBK; 2 RC, Rome, Italy (2RC); Nathan Silverberg Gallery, NY (NSG)
GALLERIES: Sperone Westwater Gallery, New York, NY; Pace Editions, New York, NY; Editions Schellmann, New York, NY; Peter Blum Edition, New York, NY; James Corcoran Gallery, Santa Monica, CA; Mary Ryan Gallery, New York, NY; Gallery Bruno Bischofberger, Zürich, Switzerland; Figura, Inc, New York, NY; Marlborough Gallery, New York, NY & London, England; Tossan-Tossan Gallery, New York, NY; Nathan Silberberg Gallery, New York, NY; BlumHelman Gallery, New York, NY

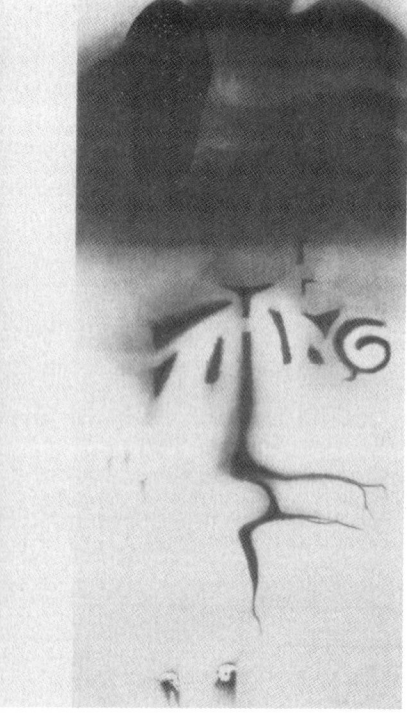

Enzo Cucchi
La Lupa di Roma
Courtesy 2 RC Editions

The retail prices of the 100,000 limited edition prints quoted in this directory are subject to change. Print publishers, artists and galleries were the direct sources for these quotations. Prices in the secondary market listed as "Sold Out Editions (Rare)" indicate that the publisher has a limited supply of that print or that the print is difficult to locate in the galleries.

ENZO CUCCHI CONTINUED

TITLE	PUBLISHER	PRINTER	DATE	MEDIUM	DIMENSION (PAPER SIZE) IN INCHES	TYPE OF PAPER	EDITION NUMBER	NO. OF COLORS	ORIGINAL OPENING PRICE	CURRENT RETAIL PRICE
SOLD OUT EDITIONS (RARE):										
Martire delle Tempeste	2RC	2RC	1981	EB/A	20 X 31	FAB	50		600	3000
Montagne in Guerra	2RC	2RC	1981	EB/A	25 X 31	FAB	50		600	3000
Immagine Feroce (Set of 5):	PBE	2RC	1981	LB	25 X 19	FAB	50 EA	1 EA	1850 SET	15000 SET
Al Buio Sul Marc Adriatico (Darkness Over the Adreiatic)										
Immagine Minore Marchigiana (Minor Image of the Marche)										
IL Santo di Loreto (The Saint of Loreto)										
Tutti Pesci Devono Andare Piano (All Fish Must Go Slowly)										
Tutte le Montagne Sono Sante (All the Mountains are Holy)										
Un'Immagine Oscura...	PBE	VR/VA/2RC	1982	EC	47 X 69	FAB	30		1800	5500
CURRENT EDITIONS:										
La Mano di Pietra	ESK/GBK	LB	1982	EB/A	34 X 24	FAB	50	1	750	5500
IL Respiro del Cavallo	ESK/GBK	LB	1982	EB/A	24 X 33	FAB	50	1	750	5500
La Lupa di Roma (Trip) (S-17-19)	PBE/ES/GBK	ER/VR/2RC	1984–85	EB/A/SP/ DPT/EMB	77 X 34	FAB	45	12	12800 SET	16000 SET
L'Elefante di Giotto	PBE	VR/2RC	1986	AB/DPT	55 X 101	FAB	45		9000	12000
Sparire I, II	2RC	2RC	1988	EB/A/SP	31 X 119	FAB	45 EA	5 EA	9000 EA	15000 EA
La Dono	2RC	VA/2RC	1992	AC/DPT/EMB	54 X 98 Oval	FAB	60	2	12000	12000
Senza Titolo	2RC	VA/2RC	1992	EB/A/DPT	39 X 11	FAB	60	1	5000	5000
Particular	NSG		1992	EB/A/EMB/ DPT	27 X 38					

JOSE LUIS CUEVAS

BORN: Mexico City, Mexico; 1933; February 26, 1934
EDUCATION: Mexico City Col, Mexico, 1948
TEACHING: Res Art, Philadelphia Mus Sch of Art, PA, 1957; Lectr, Art, San Jose Col, CA, 1970; Instr, Fullerton Col, CA, 1975; Instr, Washington State Univ, Seattle, WA, 1975
AWARDS: First Prize, Drawing, Biennial, Sao Paulo, Brazil, 1959; First Prize, Mostra Bianco e Nero, 1962; Award of Excellence, Art Director's Club, Phila, PA, 1983
RECENT EXHIB: Mus de Grabado Latinoamericano, Inst of Puerto Rican Culture, Old San Juan, PR, 1989; Edison Com Col, Gallery of Fine Art, Fort Meyers, NJ, 1992
COLLECTIONS: Mus of Mod Art, NY; Solomon R Guggenheim Mus, NY; Brooklyn Mus, NY; Mus of Albi & Lyons, France
PRINTERS: La Poligrafa, Barcelona, Spain (LP); Ernest F De Soto, San Francisco, CA (EDS); Ernest De Soto Workshop, San Francisco, CA (EDSW); Atelier Ettinger, NY (AE)
PUBLISHERS: Ediciones Poligrafa, Barcelona, Spain (EdP); Ernest De Soto Workshop, San Francisco, CA (EDSW); Eleanor Ettinger, Inc, NY (EEI); International Images, Kimball Hill, Putney, VT (InIm)
GALLERIES: Galeria Joan Prats, Barcelona, Spain & New York, NY; Tasende Gallery, La Jolla, CA; Lewin Galleries, Palm Springs, CA; Ernest De Soto Workshop, San Francisco, CA; Graphics Gallery, San Francisco, CA; Marisa del Re Gallery, New York, NY; Eleanor Ettinger, Inc, New York, NY; Galeria Palomas, Old San Juan, PR; Grace Borgenicht Gallery, New York, NY; Carmen Llewellyn Gallery, New Orleans, LA; Brewster Gallery, New York, NY; Gerhard Wurzer Gallery, Houston, TX; John Berggruen Gallery, San Francisco, CA; Kimberly Gallery, Wash, DC; Downtown Gallery, New Orleans, LA; International Images, Inc, New York, NY; TwoSixtyOne Art, New York, NY; Bond Street Gallery, Oakland, CA; Galerie Cujas, San Diego, CA; Harcourts Modern & Contemporary Art, San Francisco, CA; Stein Bartlow Gallery, Ltd, Chicago, IL; Carmichael & Carmichael Fine Art, St Paul, MN; Ernesto Mayans Gallery, Santa Fe, NM; Rettig y Martinez Gallery, Santa Fe, NM; Professional Fine Arts Services, Inc, New York, NY
MAILING ADDRESS: c/o Tasende Gallery, 820 Prospect St, La Jolla, CA 92037

TITLE	PUBLISHER	PRINTER	DATE	MEDIUM	DIMENSION (PAPER SIZE) IN INCHES	TYPE OF PAPER	EDITION NUMBER	NO. OF COLORS	ORIGINAL OPENING PRICE	CURRENT RETAIL PRICE
SOLD OUT EDITIONS (RARE):										
Music is a Higher...	ART	ART	1966	LC	22 X 30	AP	100		100	2000
Condicion Humana I	ART	ART	1969	LC	22 X 9	AP	100		75	800
Tower of Babel	ART	ART	1972	LC	30 X 22	AP	150		150	2000
CURRENT EDITIONS:										
Set of 14 Etchings:									9800 SET	12000 SET
Viaje a Marruecos	EdP	LP	1981	EC	30 X 22	GP	100		550	1000
Aurorretrato en Blanes	EdP	LP	1981	EC	30 X 22	GP	100		550	1000
La Familia del Marino	EdP	LP	1981	EC	30 X 22	GP	100		550	1000
El Cuarto Amarillo	EdP	LP	1981	EC	30 X 22	GP	100		550	1000
Pescadores de Blanes	EdP	LP	1981	EC	30 X 22	GP	100		550	1000
Barrio Chino I	EdP	LP	1981	EC	30 X 22	GP	100		550	1000
Barrio Chino II	EdP	LP	1981	EC	30 X 22	GP	100		550	1000
Autorretrato en la Barceloneta	EdP	LP	1981	EC	30 X 22	GP	100		550	1000
Carrer d'Avinyó	EdP	LP	1981	EC	30 X 22	GP	100		550	1000
Desperdicios de Guerra	EdP	LP	1981	EC	30 X 22	GP	100		550	1000
Autorretrato con Pareja	EdP	LP	1981	EC	30 X 22	GP	100		550	1000
Pareya en el Mar	EdP	LP	1981	EC	30 X 22	GP	100		550	1000
Carte de Blanes	EdP	LP	1981	EC	30 X 22	GP	100		550	1000
Travestistas	EdP	LP	1981	EC	30 X 22	GP	100		550	1000

The print market has become very selective. For the first time since we published the first edition of The Printworld Directory in 1982, the prices of prints have been greatly reduced and greatly increased for the same artists by the most reputable and established print publishers. Check the fifth edition to understand the movement.

JOSE LUIS CUEVAS CONTINUED

TITLE	PUBLISHER	PRINTER	DATE	MEDIUM	DIMENSION (PAPER SIZE) IN INCHES	TYPE OF PAPER	EDITION NUMBER	NO. OF COLORS	ORIGINAL OPENING PRICE	CURRENT RETAIL PRICE
CURRENT EDITIONS:										
Set of 8 Etchings:									400 SET	5500 SET
Holofernes	EdP	LP	1982	EC	22 X 15	GP	15		550	700
Autorretrato con Prostituta	EdP	LP	1982	EC	22 X 15	GP	15		550	700
Autorretrato	EdP	LP	1982	EC	22 X 15	GP	15		550	700
Prostituta	EdP	LP	1982	EC	22 X 15	GP	15		550	700
Prostitutas	EdP	LP	1982	EC	22 X 15	GP	15		550	700
Figura Siniestra	EdP	LP	1982	EC	22 X 15	GP	15		550	700
Corte de Cabello	EdP	LP	1982	EC	22 X 15	GP	15		550	700
Doble Autorretrato	EdP	LP	1982	EC	22 X 15	GP	15		550	700
Lithograph al Joan Prats	EdP	LP	1982	LC	30 X 22	GP	99		500	600
Papeles de Salazar	EDSW	EDS/EDSW	1984	EB/A	24 X 34	AP/W	100	5	800	1200
Tranquil Reflections	EEI	AE		LC/MULT		AP	280		800	1000
Fragments of a Rose	EEI	AE		LC/MULT		AP	280		800	1000
Four Profiles			1986	LC		AP	280		800	1000
Self Portrait in Room #523			1986	LC		AP	280		800	1000
Self Portrait with Profiles			1986	LC		AP	280		800	1000
Two Heads			1986	LC		AP	280		800	1000
Intolerance Suite (Set of 6):										
Marquez de Sade	Inlm		1989	EB/A	35 X 55	R/BFK	50			

ROBERT H CUMMING

BORN: Worcester, MA; October 7, 1943
EDUCATION: Massachusetts Col of Art, Boston, MA, BA, 1965; Univ of Illinois, Champaign-Urbana, IL, MFA, 1967; Art in Res, Gracie Mansion, NY, 1988–89
TEACHING: Instr, Painting, Drawing, Univ of Wisconsin, Milwaukee, WI, 1967–70; Lectr, Photography, Univ of California, Los Angeles, CA, 1974 to present
AWARDS: Frank Logan Prize, Chicago, Art Inst, IL, 1969; Guggenheim Fel, 1980; Nat Endowment for the Arts Awards, Wash, DC, 1972,74,83
RECENT EXHIB: California State Univ, Long Beach, CA, 1988; Univ of Missouri, Kansas City, MO, 1989; Mus of Contemp Art, San Diego, CA, 1992; Muhlenberg Col, Frank Martin Gallery, PA, 1992; Print Club, Phila, PA, 1992; San Diego Mus of Contemp Art, CA, 1993; Boston Mus of Fine Arts, MA, 1993; Houston Contemp Art Mus, TX, 1994; Contemp Mus, Honolulu, HI, 1994
COLLECTIONS: Univ of New Mexico, Albuquerque, NM; San Diego State Col, CA; Walker Art Center, Minneapolis, MN; Corcoran Gallery of Art, Wash, DC; Univ of California, Santa Barbara, CA; Art Inst of Chicago, IL; Mus of Fine Arts, Houston, TX; California State Univ, Long Beach, CA
PRINTERS: Richard Hammond, Los Angeles, CA (RH); David Udoff, Los Angeles, CA (DU); Cirrus Editions Workshop, Los Angeles, CA (CEW); Vermillion Editions, Ltd, Minneapolis, MN (VEL); James Miller, NY (JM); Maurice Sanchez, NY (MS); Derriére L'Etoile Studio, NY (DES); Mary Pat Opatz, Minneapolis, MN (MPO); Susan Steinbrock, Minneapolis, MN (SS); Steven Andersoon, Minneapolis, MN (SA); Vermillion Editions, Ltd, Minneapolis, MN (VEL); Chris Erickson (CE); Vinalhaven Press, Vinalhaven, ME (VP); Hecksher, Brooklyn, NY (KH); Artist (ART); Michael Harrison (MH); Brendan O'Malley (BO); Brenda Zlamany (BZ); Peter Suchecki (PS)
PUBLISHERS: Castelli Graphics NY (CG); Cirrus Editions, Ltd, Los Angeles, CA (CE); Derriére L'Etoile Studio, NY (DES); Vermillion Editions, Ltd, Minneapolis, MN (VEL); Vinalhaven Press, Vinalhaven, ME (VP); Signet Arts, St Louis, MO (SA); Artist (ART)
GALLERIES: John Gibson Gallery, New York, NY; Castelli Graphics, New York, NY; Cirrus Gallery, Los Angeles, CA; van Straaten Gallery, Chicago, IL; Vermillion Editions, Ltd, Minneapolis, MN

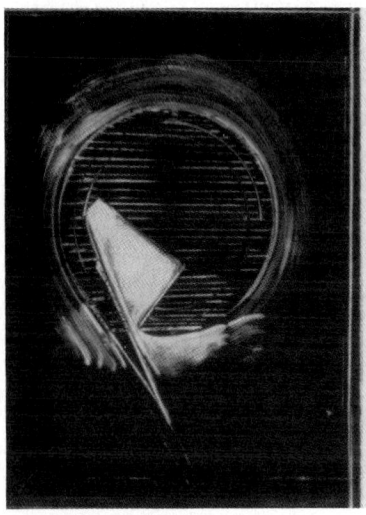  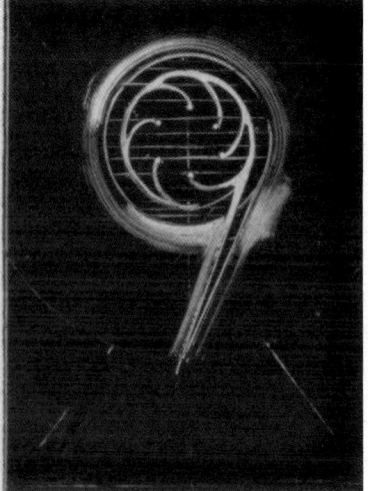

Robert H Cumming
Comma Series—Monotypes
Courtesy the Artist

ROBERT H CUMMING CONTINUED

TITLE	PUBLISHER	PRINTER	DATE	MEDIUM	DIMENSION (PAPER SIZE) IN INCHES	TYPE OF PAPER	EDITION NUMBER	NO. OF COLORS	ORIGINAL OPENING PRICE	CURRENT RETAIL PRICE
SOLD OUT EDITIONS (RARE):										
Studio Still Lifes (Set of 25)	ART	ART	1977	PH	11 X 14 EA	AB	25 EA		2500 SET	7500 SET
CURRENT EDITIONS:										
One Frame Step	CE/CG/DES	RH/DU/CEW	1985	LC/SP	39 X 38	AC/W	65	6	800	1100
Two Frame Arc	CE/CG/DES	RH/DU/CEW	1985	LC/SP	39 X 38	AC/W	65	6	800	1100
Apex Oculus	VEL	VEL	1986	LC	40 X 30	AC	65		1500	1800
Berlin Brazil	CG/DES	MS/JM/DES	1986	LC/SP	48 X 37	AC	65		1500	1800
The First Three Minutues, Etc (Series of 9)	VEL	MPO/SS/SA/VEL	1987	DPT/HC	14 X 13 EA	HMP	24 EA	Varies	2500 SET	5500 SET
Untitled (Cup)	VP	CE/VP	1987	MON	29 X 38 EA	AP	1 EA	4 EA	2500 EA	2800 EA
Odessa	VP	CE/VP	1988	WC	46 X 36	MINO	18	3	1500	1800
Santa Fe	SA	KH	1988	WC	35 X 35	KOZO/HMP	48	25	1800	2000
Small Chemistry	VP	CE/VP	1989	WC	13 X 15	MINO	30	4	600	750
Arcadia Suite (Set of 4)	VP/ART	MH/BO/BZ/VP	1991	EB	15 X 11 EA	AP	30 EA	1 EA	1000 SET	1000 SET
Palette Pedestal I, II	VP	PS/BZ/VP	1991	EB/A	37 X 27 EA	R/BFK	25 EA		1800 EA	1800 EA

MERCE (MERCIER) CUNNINGHAM

BORN: Centralia, WA; April 16, 1919
EDUCATION: Washington, Univ, Wash, DC, 1936–37; Cornish Sch, Seattle, WA, 1937; Mills Col, Oakland, CA, 1938; Bennington Col, Sch of Dance, Oakland, CA, 1939
AWARDS: Guggenheim Fel Awards, 1954,59; New York Dance & Performance Award, NY, 1986; Algur H Meadows Award, Southern Methodist Univ, Dallas, TX, Excellence in the Arts Award, 1987; Legion of Honor Award, Paris, France, 1989
RECENT EXHIB: Tampa Mus of Art, FL, 1992
PRINTERS: Patricia Branstead, NY (PB); Aeropress, NY (A)
PUBLISHERS: Multiples, Inc, NY (M); Castelli Graphics, NY (CG)
GALLERIES: Castelli Graphics, New York, NY; Marian Goodman Gallery, New York, NY; Margarete Roeder Gallery, New York, NY

TITLE	PUBLISHER	PRINTER	DATE	MEDIUM	DIMENSION (PAPER SIZE) IN INCHES	TYPE OF PAPER	EDITION NUMBER	NO. OF COLORS	ORIGINAL OPENING PRICE	CURRENT RETAIL PRICE
SOLD OUT EDITIONS (RARE):										
Merce Cunningham Portfolio (Prints Recording Collaborations with Merce Cunningham & Dance Company with Text by Calvin Tomkins (Set of 7)	M/CG	PB/A	1975	LC		AP	100 EA		1800 SET	6000 SET

ROBERT CUNNINGHAM

PRINTERS: American Atelier, NY (AA); Karl Hecksher, Brooklyn, NY (KH)
PUBLISHERS: Circle Fine Arts, Chicago, IL (CFA); Signet Arts, St Louis, MO (SA)
GALLERIES: Circle Galleries, San Diego, CA & San Francisco, CA & Northbrook, IL & Houston, TX & Pittsburgh, PA & Soho, NY & Chicago, IL & Scottsdale, AZ & Beverly Hills, CA & Costa Mesa, CA & Sherman Oaks, CA & Palm Beach, FL & Honolulu, HI & New Orleans, LA & Las Vegas, NV & Seattle, WA

TITLE	PUBLISHER	PRINTER	DATE	MEDIUM	DIMENSION (PAPER SIZE) IN INCHES	TYPE OF PAPER	EDITION NUMBER	NO. OF COLORS	ORIGINAL OPENING PRICE	CURRENT RETAIL PRICE
SOLD OUT EDITIONS (RARE):										
Twin Coves	CFA	AA	1984	SP	31 X 26	AP	275		400	600
Thundering Hooves	CFA	AA	1984	SP	30 X 32	AP	250		400	600
CURRENT EDITIONS:										
Santa Fe	SA	KH	1988	WC	35 X 35	KOZO/HMP	48	25	1800	2000

DARRYL JOSEPH CURRAN

BORN: Santa Barbara, CA; October 19, 1935
EDUCATION: Univ of California, Los Angeles, BA, 1960, MA, 1964
TEACHING: Vis Art, Photography, Sch of Art, Inst of Chicago, IL, Spring, 1975; California State Univ, Fullerton, CA, 1967 to present; Univ of California, Los Angeles, CA, Ext, Sch, 1971 to present
AWARDS: John D Phelan Award, San Francisco, CA, 1971; Nat Endowment for the Arts Fel, Photography, 1980; California Mus, Photography Award, Career Achievement, Los Angeles, CA, 1986
COLLECTIONS: Mus of Mod Art, NY; Fogg Art Mus, Cambridge, MA; Univ of Arizona, Tucson, AZ; Grunwald Center for the Graphics Arts, Univ of California, Los Angeles, CA; Center for Creative Photography, Univ of Arizona, Tucson, AZ; Royal Photographic Soc, Bath, England; Oakland Mus, CA; Minneapolis Inst of Arts, MN
PRINTERS: Unified Artists, Albuquerque, NM (UA); Artist (ART)
PUBLISHERS: Artist (ART)
GALLERIES: G Ray Hawkins Gallery, Los Angeles, CA; Visual Studies Workshop, Rochester, NY; Jeffrey Fuller Fine Arts, Phila, PA
MAILING ADDRESS: 10537 Dunleer Dr, Los Angeles, CA 90064

The retail prices of the 100,000 limited edition prints quoted in this directory are subject to change. Print publishers, artists and galleries were the direct sources for these quotations. Prices in the secondary market listed as "Sold Out Editions (Rare)" indicate that the publisher has a limited supply of that print or that the print is difficult to locate in the galleries.

DARRYL JOSEPH CURRAN CONTINUED

TITLE	PUBLISHER	PRINTER	DATE	MEDIUM	DIMENSION (PAPER SIZE) IN INCHES	TYPE OF PAPER	EDITION NUMBER	NO. OF COLORS	ORIGINAL OPENING PRICE	CURRENT RETAIL PRICE
CURRENT EDITIONS:										
RWF's Birthday	ART	UA	1979	SP	28 X 22	AP	10	5	350	600
Lone Star Stars	ART	UA	1979	SP	22 X 28	AP	10	5	350	600
Screen Play	ART	ART	1981	PH/DT	20 X 16	KOD	10	3	350	600
Classic Diagonal	ART	ART	1981	PH/DT	20 X 16	KOD	10	3	350	600
Backyard Seascape	ART	ART	1981	PH/DT	16 X 20	KOD	10	3	350	600
Chair/Landscape	ART	ART	1981	PH/DT	16 X 20	KOD	10	3	350	600
Moon Indigo	ART	ART	1981	PH/DT	20 X 16	KOD	10	3	350	600
SPE/Quaker State	ART	ART	1981	PH/DT	20 X 16	KOD	10	3	350	600
Tilted Screen	ART	ART	1981	PH/DT	20 X 16	KOD	10	3	350	600
Palm/Screen	ART	ART	1981	PH/DT	20 X 16	KOD	10	3	350	600

PEGGY K CYPHERS

BORN: Baltimore, MD; April 19, 1954
EDUCATION: Maryland Inst, Col of Art, Baltimore, MD; Towson State Univ, BFA, 1977; Pratt Inst, NY, MFA, 1979
TEACHING: Instr, Painting & Drawing, Parson Sch of Design, NY, 1988; Instr, Pratt Inst. NY, 1989; Instr, New York Univ, NY, 1990
AWARDS: Ford Found Award, 1979; Igor Found Grant, 1988; Nat Endowment for the Arts Fel, 1989–90
RECENT EXHIB: Baltimore Mus of Art, MD, 1988; Hudson River Mus, NY, 1988; Mincher/Wilcox Gallery, San Francisco, CA, 1989; Baruch Col, NY, 1990; Betsy Rosenfield Gallery, Chicago, IL, 1990; E M Donahue Gallery, NY, 1988,90
COLLECTIONS: Mus of Mod Art, NY; Aldrich Mus of Contemp Art, CT
PRINTERS: Judith Solodkin, NY (JS); Solo Press, NY (SP)
PUBLISHERS: Solo Press, NY (SP)
GALLERIES: Betsy Rosenfield Gallery, Chicago, IL; E M Donahue Gallery, New York, NY; Solo Gallery, New York, NY
MAILING ADDRESS: c/o E M Donahue Gallery, 560 Broadway, #304 New York, NY 10012

TITLE	PUBLISHER	PRINTER	DATE	MEDIUM	DIMENSION (PAPER SIZE) IN INCHES	TYPE OF PAPER	EDITION NUMBER	NO. OF COLORS	ORIGINAL OPENING PRICE	CURRENT RETAIL PRICE
CURRENT EDITIONS:										
Biomorphic Impressions	SP	JS/SP	1990	LC/MON/CO/HC	48 X 15	HMP	12	Varies	2500	2500
Primal Paradise	SP	JS/SP	1991	LC/CAR/HC	42 X 15	HMP	36	Varies	1500	1500

LARRY D'AMICO

EDUCATION: Sch of Visual Arts, NY; Silvermine Col of Art, CT; San Francisco Art Inst, CA; State Univ of New York, Purchase, NY, BFA
COLLECTIONS: Pace Univ, NY
PRINTERS: Jon Cone, East Topsham, VT (JC); Cone Editions, East Topsham, VT (CEd)
PUBLISHERS: Cone Editions, East Topsham, VT (CEd); John Szoke Graphics, NY (JSG)
GALLERIES: Jean Lumbard Fine Arts, New York, NY; Windmueller Fine Arts, Scarsdale, NY; Cone Editions, East Topsham, VT; Artworkers Fine Art, Old Greenwich, CT; Kendall Art Gallery, Wellfleet, MA; John Szoke Graphics, New York, NY

TITLE	PUBLISHER	PRINTER	DATE	MEDIUM	DIMENSION (PAPER SIZE) IN INCHES	TYPE OF PAPER	EDITION NUMBER	NO. OF COLORS	ORIGINAL OPENING PRICE	CURRENT RETAIL PRICE
CURRENT EDITIONS:										
River Road	CEd	JC/CEd	1983	SP	22 X 30	R/BFK	75	17	300	400
Hazy Light	CEd	JC/CEd	1984	SP	20 X 25	R/BFK	75	12	300	350
Road to an Open Field	CEd	JC/CEd	1985	SP	20 X 25	R/BFK	75	13	300	350
Evening Glow on the Hudson	CEd	JC/CEd	1985	SP	20 X 25	R/BFK	75	12	300	350
Untitled	CEd	JC/CEd	1986	SP	20 X 25	R/BFK	200	13	300	350
Fire Road	JSG	JC/CEd	1990	SP	30 X 22	R/BFK	150	12	500	500

ALLAN D'ARCANGELO

BORN: Buffalo, NY; June 16, 1930
EDUCATION: Univ of Buffalo, NY, BA, 1948–52; Mexico City Col, Mexico, 1957–59; City Col of New York, NY, 1955
TEACHING: Instr, Painting, Sch of Visual Arts, NY, 1963–68; Instr, Painting, Cornell Univ, Ithaca, NY, 1968; Instr, Painting, Syracuse Univ, Ithaca, NY, 1971; Instr, Painting, Univ of Wisconsin, 1972; Instr, Painting, Univ of Alabama, Birmingham, 1972; Prof, Art & Grad Fac, Brooklyn Col, NY, 1973 to present; Grad Fac, Sch of Visual Art, 1983 to present
AWARDS: Aspen Inst of Humanistic Studies, 1965,67; Nat Inst of Arts and Letters Award, 1970; John Simon Guggenheim Fol, 1987–88
RECENT EXHIB: Odakyu Grand Gallery, Tokyo, Japan, 1987; Univ Art Mus, Berkeley, CA, 1987
COLLECTIONS: Mus of Mod Art, NY; Guggeneim Mus, NY; Whitney Mus of Am Art, NY; Albright-Knox Mus, Buffalo, NY; Charles Burchfield Center, Buffalo, NY; Gemeente Mus, The Hague, Holland; Wallraf-Richartz Mus, Cologne, Germany; Wadsworth Atheneum, Hartford, CT; Hirshhorn Mus, Wash, DC
PRINTERS: Alexander Heinrici, NY (AH); Studio Heinrici, Ltd, NY (SH); Artist (ART)
PUBLISHERS: Marlborough Graphics, NY (MG); Editions Domberger, Stuttgart, West Germany (ED); Ghigraphics, Inc (GI); Jackie Fine Arts, NY (JFA); Editions Rue de Louve, Paris, France (ERL); London Arts, Inc, Detroit, MI (LAI)
GALLERIES: Fischbach Gallery, New York, NY; Marlborough Graphics, New York, NY; Dolly Fiterman Gallery, Minneapolis, MN; Jaffe Baker Gallery, Boca Raton, FL
MAILING ADDRESS: PO Box 33, Kenoza Lake, NY 12750

The Printworld Directory is accepting new applications for the seventh edition. Approximately 300 new artists will be accepted. Please use the two forms provided in the back section of this directory to submit biographical data and documentation of prints. Edition number of each print must not exceed 500 and the retail price must be $100 or more.

ALLAN D'ARCANGELO CONTINUED

TITLE	PUBLISHER	PRINTER	DATE	MEDIUM	DIMENSION (PAPER SIZE) IN INCHES	TYPE OF PAPER	EDITION NUMBER	NO. OF COLORS	ORIGINAL OPENING PRICE	CURRENT RETAIL PRICE
SOLD OUT EDITIONS (RARE):										
In Memorium	ART	ART	1939	EB	15 X 12	WOVE	150	1	50	6500
Arrow	FG	ART	1965	SP	18 X 18	AP	50	2	150	1200
Highway	FG	ART	1965	SP	18 X 20	AP	30	3	200	1250
Landscape	FG	ART	1966	LC	24 X 24	AP	30	3	200	1250
Untitled	FG	ART	1966	LC	20 X 20	AP	25	3	200	1250
Constellation L'Homme Dieu	FG	ART	1972	LB	18 X 18	AP	75	1	200	1000
Pegasus	FG	AH/SH	1975	SP	8 X 10	AP	60	4	100	1250
CURRENT EDITIONS:										
Water Tower Suite	MG	AH/SH	1974	SP	36 X 28 EA	STP	100 EA	5 EA	225 EA	1000 EA
Red Line Landscape	LAI	AH/SH	1978	LC/SP	26 X 34	STP	30	6	750	1250
Mr & Mrs Moby Dick	LAI	AH/SH	1978	SP	30 X 26	STP	150	5	300	1000
Resonance	LAI	AH/SH	1978	SP	30 X 26	STP	150	5	300	1000
U S Highway #1	LAI	AH/SH	1978	SP	26 X 31	STP	150	5	300	1000
Left Turn	LAI	AH/SH	1979	SP	34 X 26	STP	175	5	300	1000
Rail & Bridge	GI	AH/SH	1979	SP	40 X 28	STP	175	6	600	1000
Pike	GI	AH/SH	1979	SP	40 X 28	STP	175	6	600	1000
Curve	GI	AH/SH	1979	SP	40 X 28	STP	175	4	600	1000
Steel and Shadow	GI	AH/SH	1979	SP	40 X 28	STP	175	4	600	1000
Web I	JFA	AH/SH	1979	SP	30 X 37	STP	200	12	750	1000
Morning Star	JFA	AH/SH	1980	SP	10 X 41	STP	175	4	1100	1500
The Holy Family	JFA	AH/SH	1980	SP	20 X 32	STP	175	5	750	1000
Smoke Dream	JFA	AH/SH	1980	SP	30 X 32	STP	175	8	750	1000
Morning Star	ERL	AH/SH	1980	SP	14 X 47	STP	250	5	500	1000

NOËL DAGGETT

BORN: Phoenix, AZ, December 25, 1925
EDUCATION: California Sch of Fine Arts, San Francisco, CA, 1941; Chicago Art Inst, IL, 1950–53; Art Ctr Col of Design, Los Angeles, CA, 1958–60; The New Sch, NY, 1960–61

AWARDS: Emily Lowe Award, 1962
PRINTERS: The American Atelier, NY (AA)
PUBLISHERS: Jackie Fine Arts, NY (JFA); Original Fine Arts, NY (OFA); Triton Press, NY (TP); Donald Art Co, Port Chester, NY (DAO)
GALLERIES: Peter Rose Gallery, New York, NY; Merrill Chase Galleries, Chicago, IL; Ro Gallery Image Makers, Inc, New York, NY
MAILING ADDRESS: 35 W 9th St, New York, NY 10011

TITLE	PUBLISHER	PRINTER	DATE	MEDIUM	DIMENSION (PAPER SIZE) IN INCHES	TYPE OF PAPER	EDITION NUMBER	NO. OF COLORS	ORIGINAL OPENING PRICE	CURRENT RETAIL PRICE
SOLD OUT EDITIONS (RARE):										
The Messenger	JFA	AA	1980	LC	20 X 16	R/100	300	16	150	300
Race to the Station	JFA	AA	1980	LC	20 X 24	R/100	300	16	150	250
Forest Sounds	JFA	AA	1980	LC	17 X 20	R/100	300	14	150	250
We Shall Not Talk of War	JFA	AA	1980	LC	19 X 25	R/100	300	12	150	250
Bring Back the Buffalo	JFA	AA	1980	COL	19 X 24	R/100	300	12	150	200
Let's Move Em	JFA	AA	1980	COL	18 X 27	R/100	300	12	150	200
Half Way to Lamy	JFA	AA	1980	COL	18 X 22	R/100	300	12	150	250
Blackfoot Hunting Party	JFA	AA	1980	COL	19 X 25	R/100	300	12	150	250
The Only Sound was Moonlight	JFA	AA	1980	COL	19 X 26	R/100	300	12	150	250
Mustangs on the Run	JFA	AA	1981	LC	20 X 24	R/100	300	14	150	250
Roll Your Own	JFA	AA	1981	LC	20 X 24	R/100	300	14	150	250
Last of the Strays	JFA	AA	1981	LC	20 X 27	R/100	300	14	150	200
Trackers Moon	JFA	AA	1981	LC	17 X 26	R/100	300	14	150	200
A Twig Snapped	JFA	AA	1981	LC	19 X 23	R/100	300	14	150	200
Last to Arrive	JFA	AA	1981	LC	19 X 23	R/100	300	12	150	200
A Long Rifle Waits	JFA	AA	1981	COL	17 X 16	R/100	300	12	150	200
A Last Look Back	JFA	AA	1981	LC	18 X 25	R/100	300	14	150	200
Shattered Silence	JFA	AA	1982	LC	17 X 26	R/100	300	16	150	250
Prize Rack	JFA	AA	1982	LC	18 X 23	R/100	300	12	150	200
High Country Chill	JFA	AA	1982	LC	17 X 26	R/100	300	14	150	200
Pay Dirt	JFA	AA	1982	LC	20 X 25	R/100	300	14	150	200
A Helping Nose	JFA	AA	1982	LC	19 X 26	R/100	300	14	150	200
Hunters Success	OFA	AA	1982	LC	19 X 26	R/100	175	16	325	500
Approach of a Rider	JFA	AA	1983	LC	19 X 23	R/100	300	16	150	200
Chance Encounter	OFA	AA	1983	LC	19 X 26	R/100	175	16	325	500

DANIEL FORBES DALLMANN

BORN: St. Paul, MN; March 21, 1942
EDUCATION: St Cloud State Univ, MN, BS, 1965; Univ of Iowa, Iowa City, IA, MA, 1968, MFA 1969
TEACHING: Prof, Drawing & Printmaking, Tyler Sch of Art, Phila, PA, 1969 to present

AWARDS: Visual Arts Fel, Pennsylvania Council of the Arts, 1987
RECENT EXHIB: Robert Schoelkopf Gallery, NY, 1987; The Cols, Geneva, NY, 1988; Albright Col, Reading, PA, 1988; Nat Acad of Design, NY, 1988
COLLECTIONS: Art Inst of Chicago, IL; Cleveland Mus, OH; Nat Mus of Am Art, Wash, DC; Neuberger Mus, Purchase, NY; Philadelphia Mus, PA; Yale Univ, New Haven, CT; Am Embassy, Tokyo, Japan

DANIEL FORBES DALLMANN CONTINUED

PUBLISHERS: John Szoke Graphics, Inc, NY (JSG)
PRINTERS: Corridor Press, Phila, PA (CorPr)
GALLERIES: Robert Schoelkopf Gallery, New York, NY; John Szoke Graphics, Inc, New York, NY; Tatischeff & Company, New York, NY
MAILING ADDRESS: 205 Oakland Place, North Wales, PA 19454

TITLE	PUBLISHER	PRINTER	DATE	MEDIUM	DIMENSION (PAPER SIZE) IN INCHES	TYPE OF PAPER	EDITION NUMBER	NO. OF COLORS	ORIGINAL OPENING PRICE	CURRENT RETAIL PRICE
CURRENT EDITIONS:										
Landscape	JSG	CorPr	1986	LC	23 X 30	AP	85		500	600

BETTY DAMON

PRINTERS: Judith Solodkin, NY (JS); Solo Press, NY (SP)
PUBLISHERS: Solo Press, NY (SP)
GALLERIES: Solo Impressions Gallery, New York, NY

TITLE	PUBLISHER	PRINTER	DATE	MEDIUM	DIMENSION (PAPER SIZE) IN INCHES	TYPE OF PAPER	EDITION NUMBER	NO. OF COLORS	ORIGINAL OPENING PRICE	CURRENT RETAIL PRICE
CURRENT EDITIONS:										
Untitled	SP	JS/SP	1983	LC	21 X 30	AP	30		350	600

KEN DANBY

BORN: Sault Ste Marie, ON, Canada; 1940
EDUCATION: Ontario Col of Art, Toronto, ON, Canada, 1957–60
AWARDS: Award, Best Painting, Jessie Dow Award, Montreal, Can, 1964; Award, Drawing, Hadassah Exhib, Toronto, ON, Can, 1965; Ontario Arts Council Editions Award, Art Gallery of Brant, Brantford, ON, Can, 1976; Appointment, Canada Council, 1985
RECENT EXHIB: Gallery Moos, NY, 1989
COLLECTIONS: Mus of Mod Art, NY; Art Inst of Chicago, IL; Univ of California, Berkeley, CA; Indianapolis Mus of Fine Arts, IN; Nat Gallery of Canada, Ottawa, Can; Montreal Mus of Fine Arts, Montreal, Can; Saskatoon Art Centre, Sask; Art Gallery of Vancouver, BC, Can; Mendel Art Gallery, Saskatoon, Sask; Norman MacKenzie Art Gallery, Regina, Sask; Art Gallery of Hamilton, ON, Can; Bradford City Art Gallery, Yorkshire, England; Univ of Guelph, ON, Can; Oklahoma Art Centre, Oklahoma City, OK; Univ of British Columbia, BC, Can; Kitchener-Waterloo Art Gallery, ON, Can; Simon Frazer Univ, Vancouver, BC, Can
PUBLISHERS: Gallery Moos, Ltd, Toronto, ON, Can (GM)
PRINTERS: Danby Studios, Toronto, ON, Can (DS)
GALLERIES: Gallery Moos, Ltd, Toronto, ON, Canada & Miami, FL
MAILING ADDRESS: c/o Gallery Moos, Ltd, 136 Yorkville Ave, Toronto, ON, Canada M5R 1G2

TITLE	PUBLISHER	PRINTER	DATE	MEDIUM	DIMENSION (PAPER SIZE) IN INCHES	TYPE OF PAPER	EDITION NUMBER	NO. OF COLORS	ORIGINAL OPENING PRICE	CURRENT RETAIL PRICE
SOLD OUT EDITIONS (RARE):										
Under the Arch	GM	DS	1972	SP	16 X 22	AP	100	17	200	3800
In the Shade	GM	DS	1972	SP	18 X 24	AP	100	24	200	3200
White Stallion	GM	DS	1978	SP	18 X 24	AP	100	32	625	3200
CURRENT EDITIONS:										
Below the Dam	GM	DS	1982	SP	18 X 24	SOM/WL	100	29	950	1500
The Swans	GM	DS	1983	SP	18 X 24	SOM/WL	100	34	950	150
English Saddle	GM	DS	1985	LB	23 X 18	SOM/WL	100	1	550	750

NASSOS DAPHNIS

BORN: Krockeai, Greece; July 23, 1914; US Citizen
TEACHING: Horace Mann Sch, NY
AWARDS: Ford Found Grant, 1962; Nat Found of the Arts, 1966; Nat Endowment for the Arts Grant, 1971; Guggenheim Mem Found Fel, 1977
RECENT EXHIB: Leo Castelli Gallery, NY, 1990
COLLECTIONS: Mus of Mod Art, NY; Whitney Mus of Am Art, NY; Guggenheim Mus, NY; Albright-Knox Art Gallery, Buffalo, NY; Pittsburgh Mus of Art, PA; Hirshhorn Mus, Wash, DC; Chrysler Mus, Norfolk, VA; Everson Mus, Syracuse, NY; Carnegie Inst, Pittsburgh, PA
PRINTERS: Gerald Marks (GM); John Nichols, NY (JN)
PUBLISHERS: Castelli Graphics, NY (CG); Dana Art Management Corp, Laverock, NY (DAM); Prestige Art, Ltd, Mamaroneck, NY (PA)
GALLERIES: John Nichols Gallery, New York, NY; Judith Posner Gallery, Milwaukee, WI; Alan Brown Gallery, Hartsdale, NY; Leo Castelli Gallery, New York, NY; Andre Zarre Gallery, New York, NY
MAILING ADDRESS: 362 West Broadway, New York, NY 10013

TITLE	PUBLISHER	PRINTER	DATE	MEDIUM	DIMENSION (PAPER SIZE) IN INCHES	TYPE OF PAPER	EDITION NUMBER	NO. OF COLORS	ORIGINAL OPENING PRICE	CURRENT RETAIL PRICE
SOLD OUT EDITIONS (RARE):										
SS 1-70	CG	GM	1970	SP	30 X 30	AP	60	6	350	1000
SS 2-70	CG	GM	1970	SP	30 X 30	AP	60	6	350	1000
SS 3-70	CG	GM	1970	SP	30 X 30	AP	60	6	350	1000
SS 4-70	CG	GM	1970	SP	30 X 30	AP	60	6	350	1000
SS 5-70	CG	GM	1970	SP	30 X 30	AP	60	6	350	1000
CURRENT EDITIONS:										
SS 1-78	DAM	JN	1978	SP	32 X 50	INV	120	3	600	800
SS 2-78	DAM	JN	1978	SP	32 X 50	INV	120	3	600	800
SS 3-78	DAM	JN	1978	SP	32 X 50	INV	120	3	600	800
SS 4-78	DAM	JN	1978	SP	32 X 50	INV	120	3	600	800
SS 5-78	DAM	JN	1978	SP	32 X 50	INV	120	3	600	800

NASSOS DAPHNIS CONTINUED

TITLE	PUBLISHER	PRINTER	DATE	MEDIUM	DIMENSION (PAPER SIZE) IN INCHES	TYPE OF PAPER	EDITION NUMBER	NO. OF COLORS	ORIGINAL OPENING PRICE	CURRENT RETAIL PRICE
CURRENT EDITIONS:										
SS 6-78	DAM	JN	1978	SP	32 X 50	INV	120	3	600	800
SS 19-78	DAM	JN	1978	SP	32 X 50	INV	120	3	600	800
SS 7-78	DAM	JN	1978	SP	32 X 41	INV	120	3	500	650
SS 8-78	DAM	JN	1978	SP	32 X 41	INV	120	3	500	650
SS 9-78	DAM	JN	1978	SP	32 X 41	INV	120	3	500	650
SS 10-78	DAM	JN	1978	SP	32 X 41	INV	120	3	500	650
SS 11-78	DAM	JN	1978	SP	32 X 41	INV	120	3	500	650
SS 12-78	DAM	JN	1978	SP	32 X 41	INV	120	3	500	650
SS 14-78	DAM	JN	1978	SP	32 X 35	INV	120	3	500	650
SS 17-78	DAM	JN	1978	SP	35 X 35	INV	120	3	500	650
Untitled Suite a	PA	JN	1980	SP	38 X 33	R/BFK	100	2	400	450
Untitled Suite b	PA	JN	1980	SP	38 X 33	R/BFK	100	2	400	450
Untitled Suite c	PA	JN	1980	SP	38 X 33	R/BFK	100	2	400	450
SS-1-82	JN	JN	1982	SP	36 X 30	R/BFK	120	4	500	800
SS-1A-82	JN	JN	1982	SP	36 X 30	R/BFK	120	4	500	800

HANNE DARBOVEN

BORN: Munich, Germany; April 29, 1941
EDUCATION: Hochscule for Bildende Kunst, Hamburg, Germany
RECENT EXHIB: Leo Castelli Gallery, NY, 1993
COLLECTIONS: Stedelijk Mus, Amsterdam, The Netherlands; Kaiser Wilhelm Mus, Krefeld, Germany
PRINTERS: Thomas Sanmann, Hamburg, Germany (TS); Domberger Studio, Stuttgart, Germany (DOM)
PUBLISHERS: Editions Schellmann, Munich, Germany (ES); Helga Maria Klosterfelde Gesellschraft Kunst, Hamburg, Germany
GALLERIES: Editions Schellmann, New York, NY & Munich, Germany; Castelli Gallery, New York, NY; Texann Ivy Fine Arts, Orlando, FL
MAILING ADDRESS: c/o Leo Castelli Gallery, 420 W Broadway, New York, NY 10012

TITLE	PUBLISHER	PRINTER	DATE	MEDIUM	DIMENSION (PAPER SIZE) IN INCHES	TYPE OF PAPER	EDITION NUMBER	NO. OF COLORS	ORIGINAL OPENING PRICE	CURRENT RETAIL PRICE
CURRENT EDITIONS:										
Astra			1982	LB	17 X 24	AP	100	1	150	500
Misikzimmer			1985	LB	28 X 20	AP	100	1	175	600
Untitled (Post) (Set of 2)	HMKGK	TS	1992	CO	11 X 9 EA	AP	30 EA	Varies	750 SET	750 SET
Geigensolo (Violin Solo) (Miniature Violin with Card Polis: Burg Berg Staat and Sheet of Music Vilin Solo)	ES	DOM	1992		40 X 13 X 13		28		4000	4000
Chants (Chords)	ES	DOM	1990	SP/CO	61 X 105	AP	33		5400	5400
Chants (Melody)	ES	DOM	1990		61 X 210	AP	33		8000	8000

ROBERT DASH (WARREN)

BORN: New York, NY; June 8, 1934
EDUCATION: Univ of NM, Anthropology and English, BA
TEACHING: Southampton, Col, NY, 1970,75
RECENT EXHIB: Fort Wayne Mus, IN, 1988
COLLECTIONS: Mus of Mod Art, Munich, West Germany; NY Univ, NY; Brooklyn Mus, NY; Yale Univ, New Haven, CT; Weatherspoon Art Gallery, Greensboro, NC; Philadelphia Mus of Art, PA; Carnegie Mus, Pittsburgh, PA; Hirshhorn Mus, Wash, DC; Parrish Mus, Southhampton, NY; Joslyn Art Mus, Omaha, NE; Heckscher Mus, Huntington, NY
PRINTERS: Artist (ART)
PUBLISHERS: Arnold Hoffman Screen Print Workshop (AH); Dan Welden Graphics, Deer Park, NY (WG); Transworld Art Inc, NY (TAI); Artist (ART)
GALLERIES: Hirschl and Adler Contemporaries, New York, NY; C Grimaldis Gallery, Baltimore, MD; Elaine Benson Gallery, Bridgehampton, NY
MAILING ADDRESS: Sagg Main, Sagaponack, NY 11962

TITLE	PUBLISHER	PRINTER	DATE	MEDIUM	DIMENSION (PAPER SIZE) IN INCHES	TYPE OF PAPER	EDITION NUMBER	NO. OF COLORS	ORIGINAL OPENING PRICE	CURRENT RETAIL PRICE
CURRENT EDITIONS:										
Garden (Set of 6)	ART	ART	1971	LB	40 X 25 EA	AP	200 EA	1	300 EA	350 EA
Sagg	ART	ART	1973	LB	40 X 25	AP	40	1	400	450
Reverse	WG	ART	1977	LB	30 X 20	AP	30	1	400	450
Sunday Morning	AH	ART	1979	SP	33 X 26	AP	65	19	300	350
October Brunch	WG	ART	1980	SP	33 X 26	AP	65	12	200	350
Sagaponack	TAI	ART	1982	SP					450	500

DEAN ALLAN DASS

BORN: Hampton, IA; November 16, 1955
EDUCATION: Univ of Northern Iowa, Cedar Falls, IA, BA, 1978; Tyler Sch of Art, Temple Univ, Phila, PA, MFA, 1980
TEACHING: Instr, Printmaking & Drawing, Kutztown Univ, PA, 1983–84; Asst Prof, Univ of Virginia, Charlottesville, VA, 1985 to present
AWARDS: Purchase Award, Univ of South Dakota, Vermillion, SD, 1979; Purchase Award, Charlotte Printmakers Soc, NC, 1983; Artist's Fel, Pennsylvania Council of the Arts, 1985
RECENT EXHIB: Thomson Gallery, Minneapolis, MN, 1987; Fayerweather Galley, Gallery, Charlottesville, VA, 1987; Dolan/Maxwell Gallery, NY, 1989; Danville Mus, VA, 1991; 1708 East Main Gallery, Richmond, CA, 1991; Schmidt/Dean Gallery, Phila, PA, 1992
COLLECTIONS: Brooklyn Mus, NY; Kansas Univ, Lawrence, KS; Univ of Dallas, Irving, TX; Nat Coll of Poland, Krakow, Poland; Philadelphia Art Mus, PA; Walker Art Center, Minneapolis, MN; Kansas State Univ, Manhattan KS; Davidson Col, NC; Temple Univ, Phila, PA; Univ of Northern Iowa, Cedar Falls, IA; Virginia Mus of Fine Art, Richmond, VA

DEAN ALLAN DASS CONTINUED

PRINTERS: Artist (ART); Heather Hoover, Albuquerque, NM (HH); Bill Lagattuta, Albuquerque, NM (BL); Tamarind Inst, Albuquerque, NM (TI)
PUBLISHERS: Artist (ART); Tamarind Inst, Albuquerque, NM (TI)
GALLERIES: Hodges Taylor Gallery, Charlotte, NC; Olson/Larsen Gallery, Des Moines, IA; Thomson Gallery, Minneapolis, MN; Tamarind Inst, Albuquerque, NM; Schmidt/Dean Gallery, Phila, PA
MAILING ADDRESS: c/o University of Virginia, 2601 Jefferson, Park Circle, Charlottesville, VA 22903

TITLE	PUBLISHER	PRINTER	DATE	MEDIUM	DIMENSION (PAPER SIZE) IN INCHES	TYPE OF PAPER	EDITION NUMBER	NO. OF COLORS	ORIGINAL OPENING PRICE	CURRENT RETAIL PRICE
CURRENT EDITIONS:										
Death Zone (with Gouache and Dry Pigments)	ART	ART	1984	I/CO/CC/CT/DPT	14 X 12	SEK/IND		Varies	375	900
The Moon Feeds the Twin Brothers	ART	ART	1984	I/GRA/CC/DPT	18 X 21	KIT/GE		Varies	475	900
Within-Without	ART	ART	1985–86	I/GOU/DPT	25 X 31	SEK	10	Varies	1200	1800
Outpost	ART	ART	1986	PEN/CT/GOU	25 X 34	SEK	10	Varies	1200	1800
Wicce (Monoprint Series) (Part I)	TI	HH/BL/TI	1988	MON/GO/LC/CO	34 X 46	JP	1 EA	Varies	1200 EA	1500 EA
Wicce (Monoprint Series) (Part II)	TI	HH/BL/TI	1988	MON/GO/LC/CO	37 X 55	JP	1 EA	Varies	1800 EA	2000 EA

JUDY DATER

BORN: Hollywood, CA; June 21, 1941
EDUCATION: Univ of California, Los Angeles, CA, 1959–62; San Francisco State Univ, CA, BA, 1963, MA, 1966
TEACHING: Instr, Photography, San Francisco Art Inst, CA, 1974–78
AWARDS: Dorothea Lange Award, Oakland Mus, CA, 1974; Nat Endowment for the Arts Fel, 1976; J S Guggenhiem Mem Found Fel, NY, 1978
RECENT EXHIB: Toledo Mus of Art, OH, 1988; Albin O Kuhn Gallery, Baltimore, MD, 1988; Spectrum Gallery, Fresno, CA, 1989; Silver Eye Gallery, Pittsburgh, PA, 1989; Sonoma State Univ, CA, 1990; Jane Baum Gallery, NY, 1990; Whitney Mus of Am Art, NY, 1990; Univ of Colorado, Colorado Springs, CO, 1992
COLLECTIONS: San Francisco Mus of Mod Art, CA; Boston Mus of Fine Arts, MA; Mus of Mod Art, NY; Center for Creative Photography, Tucson, AZ; Toledo Mus of Art, OH
PRINTERS: Anderson Ranch Arts Center, Snowmass, CO (AR); Matthew Christie (MC); Marsha Immerman (MI); Witkin-Berley Ltd, NY (WBL)
PUBLISHERS: Anderson Ranch Arts Center, Snowmass, CO (AR); Witkin-Berley Ltd, NY (WBL)
GALLERIES: Anderson Ranch Arts Center, Snowmass, CO; Silver Image Gallery, Seattle, WA; Halsted Gallery, Birmingham, MI; Kathleen Ewing Gallery, Wash, DC; Camera Obscura Gallery, Denver, CO; Witkin Gallery, New York, NY; Collected Images, Berkeley, CA; Photographer's Gallery of Palo Alto, CA; Scheinbaum & Russek Gallery, Albuquerque, NM; Collected Images, Berkeley, CA; Witkin Gallery, New York, NY
MAILING ADDRESS: c/o Photographer's Gallery, 540 Ramona St, Palo Alto, CA 94301

TITLE	PUBLISHER	PRINTER	DATE	MEDIUM	DIMENSION (PAPER SIZE) IN INCHES	TYPE OF PAPER	EDITION NUMBER	NO. OF COLORS	ORIGINAL OPENING PRICE	CURRENT RETAIL PRICE
SOLD OUT EDITIONS (RARE):										
Ten Photographs/Joyce Goldstein	WBL	ART	1974	PH	16 X 20 EA		25 EA		950 SET	2000 SET
CURRENT EDITIONS:										
4th of July 1984, States I, II, III (Set of 3)	AR	MC/MI/AR	1984	LC/PH/MP	30 X 22 EA	AP/BL	10 EA		1000 SET	1500 SET
									400 EA	500 EA

MICHAEL DAVID

BORN: Reno, NV; 1954
EDUCATION: Parsons Sch of Design, NY, BFA, 1976
TEACHING: Vis Prof, Advanced Painting, Princeton Univ, NJ, 1982
AWARDS: Edward Albee Found Grants, Montauk, NY, 1980,81,82; Am Acad & Inst of Arts & Letters Award, NY, 1982; Yaddo Fel, Saratoga Springs, NY; Meet the Composer Grant, NY, 1982; Nat Endowment for the Arts Fel, 1983; Guggenheim Fel, NY, 1984
RECENT EXHIB: Inst of Fine Arts, Boston, MA, 1992; Knoedler Gallery, NY, 1992
PRINTERS: Joe Wilfer, NY (JW); Ruth Lingen, NY (RL); Spring Street Workshop, NY (SprSW); Experimental Workshop, San Francisco, CA (EW); Alan Holoubek, NY (AH); Rebecca Lax, NY (RebL); Solo Press, NY (SP)
PUBLISHERS: Spring Street Workshop, NY (SprSW); Experimental Workshop, San Francisco, CA (EW); Metropolitan Mus of Art, NY (MMA); Solo Press, NY (SP)
GALLERIES: Knoedler & Company, New York, NY; Pace Prints, New York, NY; Greenberg Gallery, St Louis, MO; American House, Tenafly, NJ; Meredith Long & Company, Houston, TX; CompassRose Gallery, Chicago, IL; Mezzanine Gallery, Metropolitan Museum of Art, New York, NY; Solo Press, New York, NY; Walter/White Fine Arts, Carmel, CA; Margulies Taplin Gallery, Boca Raton, FL

TITLE	PUBLISHER	PRINTER	DATE	MEDIUM	DIMENSION (PAPER SIZE) IN INCHES	TYPE OF PAPER	EDITION NUMBER	NO. OF COLORS	ORIGINAL OPENING PRICE	CURRENT RETAIL PRICE
CURRENT EDITIONS:										
Untitled (Set of 9)	EW	EW	1985	MON	12 X 17	Linen	1 EA	Varies	800 EA	3000 EA
Meridian I-IV	SprSW	JW/RL/SprSW	1987	REL/PO	28 X 34 EA	CP	15 EA	4 EA	2000 SET	5000 SET
									600 EA	2000 EA
White Golem (183–1)	SprSW	JW/RL/SprSW	1988	WC	24 X 22	SOM	10		900	1000
Golem	MMA	JW/RL/SprSW	1988	WC	25 X 22	SOM	35	6	800	2500
Lingen (183–2)	SprSW	JW/RL/SprSW	1988	LI/PO/SG	21 X 24	AC	12		500	750
Between Sex & Logic (183–4)	SprSW	JW/RL/SprSW	1988	EB/A/HC	30 X 41	R/BFK	15		900	2000
Black Golem (183–6)	SprSW	JW/RL/SprSW	1988	WC	24 X 22	SOM	10		1000	1000
Echo Park (183–5)	SprSW	JW/RL/SprSW	1989	LC/REL/HC	28 X 22	R/BFK	35		1000	1000

MICHAEL DAVID CONTINUED

TITLE	PUBLISHER	PRINTER	DATE	MEDIUM	DIMENSION (PAPER SIZE) IN INCHES	TYPE OF PAPER	EDITION NUMBER	NO. OF COLORS	ORIGINAL OPENING PRICE	CURRENT RETAIL PRICE
SOLD OUT EDITIONS (RARE):										
Georgia Monoprint AP-4	SP	AH/RebL/SP	1991	MON/CO	21 X 21	AP/SEK	1		1500	2000
Georgia Monoprint AP-5	SP	AH/RebL/SP	1991	MON/CO	21 X 21	AP/SEK	1		1500	2000
CURRENT EDITIONS:										
Georgia Series (Small) (Set of 3)	SP	AH/RebL/SP	1991	LC/WC/CO/HC	21 X 21 EA	AP/SEK	30 EA	Varies	3500 SET 1400 EA	3500 SET 1400 EA
Georgia Series (Large) (Set of 3)	SP	AH/RebL/SP	1991	LC/WC/CO/HC	46 X 35 EA	AP/SEK	50 EA	Varies	8000 SET 3000 EA	8000 SET 3000 EA
Georgia Monoprint AP-1	SP	AH/RebL/SP	1991	MON/CO	35 X 35	AP/SEK	1		3500	3500
Georgia Monoprint AP-2	SP	AH/RebL/SP	1991	MON/CO	37 X 37	AP/SEK	1		3500	3500
Georgia Monoprint AP-3	SP	AH/RebL/SP	1991	MON/CO	33 X 33	AP/SEK	1		3500	3500
Georgia Monoprint AP-6	SP	AH/RebL/SP	1991	MON/CO	35 X 35	AP/SEK	1		3500	3500
Georgia Monoprint AP-7	SP	AH/RebL/SP	1991	MON/CO	14 X 14	AP/SEK	1		900	900
Georgia Monoprint AP-8	SP	AH/RebL/SP	1991	MON/CO	21 X 21	AP/SEK	1		1500	1500

JORDAN DAVIES

BORN: Chicago, IL; 1941
EDUCATION: Art Inst of Chicago, IL, MFA, 1959–66
AWARDS: Logan Prize and Medal, AIC, 1965; Nat Endowment Fel, 1971
COLLECTIONS: Art Inst of Chicago, IL
PRINTERS: Jerry Raidiger (JR); Bill Cons (BC); Landfall Press, Inc, Chicago, IL (LPI); Jennifer Melby, NY (JM)
PUBLISHERS: Orion Editions, NY (OE); Landfall Press, Inc, Chicago, IL (LPI)
GALLERIES: Orion Editions, New York, NY; Landfall Press, Inc, Chicago, IL

TITLE	PUBLISHER	PRINTER	DATE	MEDIUM	DIMENSION (PAPER SIZE) IN INCHES	TYPE OF PAPER	EDITION NUMBER	NO. OF COLORS	ORIGINAL OPENING PRICE	CURRENT RETAIL PRICE
SOLD OUT EDITIONS (RARE):										
Untitled	LPI	JR/BC/LPI	1971	LC	34 X 34	ARJ	50	5	200	750
Untitled	OE	JM	1980	EC	30 X 23	AP	25	4	250	350

THEODORE PETER DAVIES

BORN: Brooklyn, NY; October 9, 1928
EDUCATION: New York Univ, BS; Sch of Mod Photography, NY, 1952; Art Students League, NY, with George Grosz & Harry Sternberg, 1957–60
AWARDS: John Sloan Merit Scholar, NY, 1960; Creative Artists Public Service Fel, 1973–74; Guild Hall Awards Exhib, Guild Hall Mus, East Hampton, LI, NY, 1983
COLLECTIONS: Mus of Mod Art, NY; Art Students League, NY; Philadelphia Mus of Art, PA; Lessing J Rosenwald Coll, Nat Gallery of Art, Wash, DC; Queens Mus, NY; Guild Hall Mus, East Hampton, NY
PRINTERS: Artist (ART)
PUBLISHERS: Artist (ART)
GALLERIES: Associated American Artists, New York, NY; John Szoke Graphics, New York, NY
MAILING ADDRESS: 87–38 Santiago St, Hollis NY 11423

TITLE	PUBLISHER	PRINTER	DATE	MEDIUM	DIMENSION (PAPER SIZE) IN INCHES	TYPE OF PAPER	EDITION NUMBER	NO. OF COLORS	ORIGINAL OPENING PRICE	CURRENT RETAIL PRICE
SOLD OUT EDITIONS (RARE):										
O'Rourkes, O'Rourkes	ART	ART	1958	WC	23 X 15	RICE	40	2	35	200
Cathedral	ART	ART	1958	WC	22 X 33	RICE	50	4	50	350
PS 66	ART	ART	1962	WC	32 X 28	RICE	52	6	100	350
CURRENT EDITIONS:										
New York Exchange	ART	ART	1968	WC	20 X 30	RICE	250	2	75	200
Broadway at Bowling Green	ART	ART	1968	WC	28 X 23	RICE	250	2	75	200
Wall Street	ART	ART	1968	WC	22 X 28	RICE	250	2	75	200
Automobiles (Alphabet Series)	AAA	ART	1969	SP	19 X 26	AP	50	6	75	200
Cigarettes (Alphabet Series)	AAA	ART	1969	SP	19 X 26	AP	50	6	75	200
Drugs (Alphabet Series)	AAA	ART	1971	SP	19 X 26	AP	50	6	75	200
Electronics (Alphabet Series)	AAA	ART	1971	SP	19 X 26	AP	50	6	75	200
Food (Alphabet Series)	AAA	ART	1971	SP	19 X 26	AP	50	6	75	200
Graves (Alphabet Series)	AAA	ART	1971	SP	19 X 26	AP	50	6	75	200
Houses (Alphabet Series)	AAA	ART	1972	SP	19 X 26	AP	50	6	75	200
Instruments (Alphabet Series)	AAA	ART	1972	SP	19 X 26	AP	50	6	75	200
Junk (Alphabet Series)	AAA	ART	1974	SP	19 X 26	AP	50	6	75	200
Pollution (Alphabet Series)	ART	ART	1976	SP	19 X 26	RP	50	7	75	200
Queues (Alphabet Series)	AAA	ART	1976	SP	19 X 26	AP	50	5	75	200
Roads (Alphabet Series)	AAA	ART	1976	SP	19 X 26	RP	50	6	75	200
Television (Alphabet Series)	ART	ART	1976	SP	19 X 26	RP	50	5	75	200
Vehicles (Alphabet Series)	ART	ART	1976	SP	19 X 26	RP	50	5	75	200
Windows (Alphabet Series)	AAA	ART	1976	SP	19 X 26	AP	50	6	75	200
X Rays (Alphabet Series)	ART	ART	1976	SP	19 X 26	RP	50	6	75	200
Yards (Alphabet Series)	ART	ART	1976	SP	19 X 26	RP	50	5	75	200
Zoo (Alphabet Series)	ART	ART	1976	SP	19 X 26	RP	50	7	75	200
Library	ART	ART	1982	WC/SP	28 X 33	RICE	100	3+	150	200

SALVADOR DALI

BORN: Figueras, Spain; (1904–1989)
EDUCATION: Sch of Fine Arts, Madrid, Spain, 1921–26
AWARDS: Huntington Hartford Found Award, 1957
RECENT EXHIB: Masur Mus of Art, Monroe, LA, 1989; Delta State Univ, Cleveland, MS, 1989; Connell Found For the Fine Arts, East Haven, CT, 1989; Salvador Dali Mus, St Petersburg, FL, 1989,92; Munson-Williams-Proctor Mus of Art, Utica, NY, 1992; Michigan State Univ, Kresge Art Mus, East Lansing, MI, 1989,92;
PRINTERS: Paris, France (P/FR); Atelier Rigal, Paris, France (AR); Porter-Winer, NY (PW); American Atelier, NY (AA); Léon Amiel, NY (LA); Artist (ART)
PUBLISHERS: Transworld Art, Inc, NY (TAI); Atelir Rigal, Paris, France (AR); Edward Weston Editions, Northridge, CA (EWE); Martin Lawrence Limited Editions, Van Nuys, CA (MLLE); Lawrence Ross Publishers, Beverly Hills, CA (LRP); A Skira, Geneva, Switzerland (AS); Sherwood Publishers, NY (SPI); Jacques David, NY (JS); Circle Fine Art, Chicago, IL (CFA); Artist (ART)
GALLERIES: Knoedler & Co, New York, NY; Hanson Galleries, New Orleans, LA & Carmel, CA & Los Angeles, CA & San Francisco, CA; La Galeria, Kansas City, MO; Lake Gallery, Incline Village, NV; J Richards Gallery, Englewood, NJ; Davlyn Gallery, New York, NY; Randi's Art Gallery, Canoga Park, CA; Jack Rutberg Fine Arts, Los Angeles, CA; Lake Gallery, Tahoe City, CA; Brenner Gallery, Boca Raton, FL; Shirley Fox Galleries, Atlanta, GA; Merrill Chase Galleries, Chicago, IL; DiLaurenti Gallery, Ltd, New York, NY; Fine Art Unlimited, St Petersburg, FL; Rodi Karkazis Gallery, Chicago, IL; Gallery One at Second Avenue, Denver, CO; Jason McCoy, Inc, New York, NY; Mendelson Gallery, Pittsburgh, PA; Hensley Gallery, Alexandria, VA; Gallery G Fine Arts, Wichita, KS; Casell Galleries, New Orleans, LA; The Hang-Up, Sarasota, FL; Martin Lawrence Galleries, Sherman Oaks, CA & Los Angeles, CA & Newport Beach, CA & Short Hills, NJ & Phila, PA & Palm Springs, CA & Escondido, CA & Redondo Beach, CA & Escondido, CA & Thousand Oaks, CA & West Los Angeles, CA & Santa Clara, CA; The Masters Portfolio, Chicago, IL; Modern Realism Gallery, Dallas, TX; Downtown Gallery, New Orleans, LA; Royal Art Gallery, New Orleans, LA; Ella Lerner Gallery, Lenox, MA; Saper Galleries, East Lansing, MI; Short Hills Art Gallery, Short Hills, NJ; Stephen Gill Gallery, New York, NY; R K Goldman & Company, Los Angeles, CA; Edward Weston Fine Arts, Northridge, CA; Apropos Art Gallery, Ft Lauderdale, FL; John Denton Gallery, Hiawassee, GA; Arnold Herstand & Company, New York, NY; Professional Fine Arts Services, Inc, New York, NY

TITLE	PUBLISHER	PRINTER	DATE	MEDIUM	DIMENSION (PAPER SIZE) IN INCHES	TYPE OF PAPER	EDITION NUMBER	NO. OF COLORS	ORIGINAL OPENING PRICE	CURRENT RETAIL PRICE
SOLD OUT EDITIONS (RARE):										
The Grasshopper's Child	ART	ART	1934	EB	15 X 12	R/100	100	1	25	12000
St. George and the Dragon	ART	ART	1946	EB	18 X 11	R/100	260	1	50	12000
Washington Square, NY (Brown Ink)	ART	ART	1964	EC	17 X 24	AP	125	1	350	1800
Nu de Dos-Sanguine			1967	EC	12 X 9	AP	50	1	250	3500
Embrace			1968	EB	13 X 9	AP	140	1	200	3000
Aliyah (Set of 25)	SPI		1968	LC	20 X 26 EA	AP	275 EA		1000 SET	15000 SET
Song of Songs	LA	JD	1971	ENG/C	23 X 15 EA	AP	250 EA		1000 SET	13500 SET
Homage a Cranach	TAI	AR	1971	LB/EB	30 X 22	AP	175		150	3500
Homage a Cranach	TAI	AR	1971	LB/EB	30 X 22	JP	40		175	4000
Twelve Tribes of Israel (Set of 13): Frontispiece, Simeon, Reuben, Judah, Asher, Issachar, Dan, Gad, Zebulin, Naphtali, Joseph, Benjamin, Levi	TAI	AR	1973	EB/HC	19 X 25	R/BFK	195		2000 SET	18000 SET
André Malraux: Roi je t'Attends a' Babylone (on Parchment) (Set of 12)	AS		1973	DPT		PARCH	150		2500 SET	18000 SET
After 50 Years of Surrealism (Set of 12):									2000 SET	35000 SET
Flung Out Like a Fag-end by the Big Wigs	TAI	AR	1974	EB/HC	26 X 20	R/BFK	195		200	5000
Gala's Godly Back	TAI	AR	1974	EB/HC	26 X 20	R/BFK	195		200	4000
Picasso: A Ticket for Glory	TAI	AR	1974	EB/HC	26 X 20	R/BFK	195		200	4000
The Laurels of Happiness	TAI	AR	1974	EB/HC	26 X 20	R/BFK	195		200	4000
The Curse Overthrown	TAI	AR	1974	EB/HC	26 X 20	R/BFK	195		200	4000
The Great Inquisitor Expels the Saviour	TAI	AR	1974	EB/HC	26 X 20	R/BFK	195		200	4000
Freud with a Snail Head	TAI	AR	1974	EB/HC	26 X 20	R/BFK	195		200	4000
A Shattering Entrance upon the American Stage	TAI	AR	1974	EB/HC	26 X 20	R/BFK	195		200	4000
God, Time, Space and the Pope	TAI	AR	1974	EB/HC	26 X 20	R/BFK	195		200	4000
The Divine Love of Gala	TAI	AR	1974	EB/HC	26 X 20	R/BFK	195		200	4000
Gala's Castle	TAI	AR	1974	EB/HC	26 X 20	R/BFK	195		200	4000
The Museum of Genius and Fancy	TAI	AR	1974	EB/HC	26 X 20	R/BFK	195		200	4000
La Jungle Humaine	MLLE	P/FR	1974	LC	20 X 26	AP	250	20	2400	6500
The Glory That was Spain's	TAI	AR	1975	EB/HC	26 X 20	AP	175	7	500	3200
Melting Watch Suite	MLLE	P/FR	1976	LC	22 X 30	AP	250	14	600	3200
Timeless Statue	MLLE	P/FR	1976	LC	22 X 30	AP	250	14	600	3200
Stillness of Time & Desert Jewels	MLLE	P/FR	1976	LC	22 X 30	AP	250	14	600	3200
Dali's Pieta American	LRP	P/FR	1976	LC	19 X 26	AP	250	14	750	4500
Dali's Pieta European	LRP	P/FR	1976	LC	19 X 26	AP	175	14	750	4500
Les Animaux (Falde la Fontaine Suite)	AR	AR	1976	DPT/EB	30 X 23	AP	300		300	3200
La Cour du Lyon (Fables de la Fountaine Suite)	AR	AR	1976	DPT/EB	23 X 30	AP	300		300	3200
Le Senge et le Leonard (Fables de la Fountaine Suite)	AR	AR	1976	DPT/EB	23 X 30	AP	300		300	3200
Coche et la Mouche (Fables de la Fountaine Suite)	AR	AR	1976	DPT/EB	30 X 23	AP	300		300	3200
Aliyah	EWE	P/FR	1976	LC	27 X 22	AP	300		300	3200
Summer and Winter	CFA	AA	1976	EB/LC	25 X 36	AP	300		1200	4500
Lady Blue	MLLE	P/FR	1977	LC	22 X 30	AP	250	16	900	5500
Lincoln in Dalivision	MLLE	P/FR	1977	I/EB/LC	22 X 30	AP	350	18	750	15000
European Edition	MLLE	P/FR	1977	I/EB/LC	22 X 30	AP	350	18	750	15000

SALVADOR DALI CONTINUED

TITLE	PUBLISHER	PRINTER	DATE	MEDIUM	DIMENSION (PAPER SIZE) IN INCHES	TYPE OF PAPER	EDITION NUMBER	NO. OF COLORS	ORIGINAL OPENING PRICE	CURRENT RETAIL PRICE
SOLD OUT EDITIONS (RARE):										
International Edition	MLLE	P/FR	1977	I/EB/LC	22 X 30	AP	200	18	750	15000
German Edition	MLLE	P/FR	1977	I/EB/LC	22 X 30	AP	125	18	750	15000
Dali's Dreams	MLLE	P/FR	1978	LC	22 X 30	AP	250	14	50	4500
International Edition	MLLE	P/FR	1978	LC	22 X 30	AP	150	14	750	4500
Dali's Inferno	MLLE	P/FR	1978	LC	22 X 30	AP	250	16	750	4500
International Edition	MLLE	P/FR	1978	LC	22 X 30	AP	150	16	750	4500
The Kingdom	LRP	P/FR	1978	LC	22 X 30	AP	350	14	900	4500
International Edition	LRP	P/FR	1978	LC	22 X 30	AP	350	14	900	4500
The Kingdom, International Edition	LRP	P/FR	1978	LC	22 X 30	JP	100	14	1000	4500
Dreams of a Horseman	MLLE	P/FR	1979	LC	22 X 30	AP	250	12	750	4000
Dreams of a Horseman	MLLE	P/FR	1979	LC	22 X 30	AP	150	12	750	4000
Dreams of a Horseman	MLLE	P/FR	1979	LC	22 X 30	JP	100	12	900	4500
L'Adventure Medicale (Set of 2)	MLLE	P/FR	1979	LC	22 X 30 EA	AP	350 EA	18 EA	1800 SET	9500 SET
International Edition (Set of 2)	MLLE	P/FR	1979	LC	22 X 30 EA	AP	350 EA	18 EA	1800 SET	9500 SET
L'Adventure Medicale	MLLE	P/FR	1979	LC	22 X 30	AP	150	18	2000	7500
Golden Calf	MLLE	P/FR	1979	LC	22 X 30	AP	250	16	750	4000
International Edition	MLLE	P/FR	1979	LC	22 X 30	AP	150	16	750	4000
Golden Calf	MLLE	P/FR	1979	LC	22 X 30	AP	100	16	900	4000
Dali's Paradise	MLLE	P/FR	1979	LC	22 X 30	AP	250	16	600	3500
International Edition	MLLE	P/FR	1979	LC	22 X 30	AP	200	16	600	3500
Prince of Cups	MLLE	P/FR	1979	LC	22 X 30	AP	250	12	750	3500
International Edition	MLLE	MLG	1979	LC	22 X 30	AP	150	12	750	3500
Prince of Cups	MLLE	P/FR	1979	LC	22 X 30	JP	150	12	900	3500
Dali's Renaissance	LRP	P/FR	1979	LC	22 X 30	AP	250	18	750	4500
International Edition	LRP	P/FR	1979	LC	22 X 30	AP	150	18	750	4500
Dali's Renaissance	LRP	P/FR	1979	LC	22 X 30	JP	100	18	900	4500
Knights of the Round Table (Set of 12)	MLLE	P/FR	1979	LC	19 X 25 EA	AP	350 EA	18 EA	3600 SET	8500 SET
Lincoln in Dalivision:										
Bas Relief Bronze (American Edition)	MLLE	NY	1979	EB/REL	28 X 20	AP	195	1	3900	20000
Bas Bronze (International Edition)	MLLE	NY	1979	EB/REL	28 X 20	AP	195	1	3900	20000
Silver American Edition)	MLLE	NY	1979	EB/REL	28 X 20	AP	175	1	4900	20000
Silver International Edition)	MLLE	NY	1979	EB/REL	28 X 20	AP	175	1	4900	20000
Gold American Edition)	MLLE	NY	1979	EB/REL	28 X 20	AP	160	1	5900	20000
Gold International Edition)	MLLE	NY	1979	EB/REL	28 X 20	AP	160	1	5900	20000
Gold-HC's	MLLE	NY	1979	EB/REL	28 X 20	AP	125	1	5900	20000
Gold-Designated for Museums	MLLE	NY	1979	EB/REL	28 X 20	AP	125	1	5900	20000
Platinum-American Edition)	MLLE	NY	1979	EB/REL	28 X 20	AP	95	1	6900	20000
Platinum-International Edition)	MLLE	NY	1979	EB/REL	28 X 20	AP	95	1	6900	20000
Platinum HC's	MLLE	NY	1979	EB/REL	28 X 20	AP	65	1	6900	20000
Cave V	CFA	AA	1980	SP	31 X 26	AP	175		500	4000
American Madonna	CFA	AA	1980	SP	47 X 36	AP	150		500	4500
Icarus	CFA	AA	1980	SP	47 X 41	AP	150		500	4500
Dalian Prophecy	CFA	AA	1980	DPT/PO	22 X 30	AP	250		800	4000
Diamond Head	MLLE	P/FR	1980	LC	22 X 30	AP	350	20	900	4500
Diamond Head	MLLE	P/FR	1980	LC	22 X 30	JP	150	20	1000	5000
Bronze-American Edition	MLLE	NY	1980	EB/REL	28 X 20	AP	215	1	3500	7500
Bronze-American Edition	MLLE	NY	1980	EB/REL	28 X 20	AP	215	1	3500	7500
Silver-International Edition	MLLE	NY	1980	EB/REL	28 X 20	AP	175	1	4500	8500
Silver-International Edition	MLLE	NY	1980	EB/REL	28 X 20	AP	175	1	4500	8500
Gold-American Edition	MLLE	NY	1980	EB/REL	28 X 20	AP	160	1	5500	10000
Gold-American Edition	MLLE	NY	1980	EB/REL	28 X 20	AP	160	1	5500	10000
Gold HC's	MLLE	NY	1980	EB/REL	28 X 20	AP	125	1	5500	10000
Gold-Designated Museums	MLLE	NY	1980	EB/REL	28 X 20	AP	125	1	5500	10000
Platinum-American Edition	MLLE	NY	1980	FB/REL	28 X 20	AP	75	1	6500	12000
Platinum-International Edition	MLLE	NY	1980	EB/REL	28 X 20	AP	75	1	6500	12000
Gold AP's	MLLE	NY	1980	EB/REL	28 X 20	AP	65	1	6500	10000
Dali Retrospective Vol I	MLLE	P/FR	1980	LC	22 X 30	AP	350	14	900	4500
International Edition	MLLE	P/FR	1980	LC	22 X 30	AP	350	14	900	4500
Dali Retrospective Vol II	MLLE	P/FR	1980	LC	22 X 30	AP	350	14	900	4500
Enchanted Hawaii	MLLE	P/FR	1980	LC	22 X 30	AP	250	12	750	4500
International Edition	MLLE	P/FR	1980	LC	22 X 30	AP	150	12	750	4500
Enchanted Hawaii	MLLE	P/FR	1980	LC	22 X 30	JP	100	12	900	5000
International Edition	MLLE	P/FR	1980	LC	22 X 30	AP	350	14	900	4500
Dali Retrospective Vol III	MLLE	P/FR	1980	LC	22 X 30	AP	350	14	900	4500
International Edition	MLLE	P/FR	1980	LC	22 X 30	AP	350	14	900	4500
Dali Retrospective Vol IV	MLLE	P/FR	1980	LC	22 X 30	AP	350	14	900	4500
International Edition	MLLE	P/FR	1980	LC	22 X 30	AP	350	14	900	4500
Les Mysteres e L'Alchimiste	MLLE	P/FR	1980	LC	22 X 30	JP	350	18	900	4500
International Edition	MLLE	P/FR	1980	LC	22 X 30	AP	350	18	900	4500
Les Mysteres de L'Alchimiste	MLLE	P/FR	1980	LC	22 X 30	JP	150	18	1000	4500
The Quest	LRP	PW	1982	AC	22 X 30	AP	300	6	900	3500
The Quest	LRP	PW	1982	AC	22 X 30	JP	150	6	1000	4000

CARLOS DAVILA

BORN: Lima, Peru; February 1, 1935
EDUCATION: Nat Sch of Fine Arts, Lima, Peru; Pratt Graphics, NY
AWARDS: First Award, Soc of Hebraica Nat Comp, NY, 1964; First Award, Jovenes Artistas, Univ of San Marcos, Lima, Peru, 1967; First Award, Adela Investment Mus Arte, 1968
COLLECTIONS: Mus Arte, Lima, Peru; Mus of Modern Art, Miami, FL; Univ of San Marcos, Lima, Peru; Mint Mus of Art, Charlotte, NC
PRINTERS: Artist (ART)
PUBLISHERS: Fred Dorfman, Inc, NY (FDI)
GALLERIES: Miller Gallery, Cincinnati, OH; Rubiner Gallery, West Bloomfield, MI; Jenetra Fine Art Gallery, Freehold, NY

TITLE	PUBLISHER	PRINTER	DATE	MEDIUM	DIMENSION (PAPER SIZE) IN INCHES	TYPE OF PAPER	EDITION NUMBER	NO. OF COLORS	ORIGINAL OPENING PRICE	CURRENT RETAIL PRICE
SOLD OUT EDITIONS (RARE):										
Seascape I	FDI	ART	1978	EC	34 X 26	AP	125	8	200	750
Landscape I	FDI	ART	1978	EC	34 X 26	AP	125	8	200	750
Mountain of Serenity	FDI	ART	1979	EC	34 X 26	AP	125	8	200	750
Poem I, II	FDI	ART	1979	EC	34 X 26 EA	DE	125 EA	8 EA	200 EA	750 EA
Lyric III, IV	FDI	ART	1980	EC	22 X 17 EA	DE	150 EA	8 EA	100 EA	750 EA
Spectrum I, II	FDI	ART	1980	EC	34 X 26	DE	125 EA	8	200 EA	750 EA
Lyric I, II	FDI	ART	1980	EC	22 X 17 EA	DE	150 EA	8 EA	100 EA	750 EA
Fossil Series	FDI	ART	1982	EC	25 X 18 EA	AC	99 EA	11 EA	200 EA	750 EA
Cosmos, I, II, III	FDI	ART	1982	EC	25 X 18 EA	AC	99 EA	11 EA	200 EA	750 EA
Galaxy	FDI	ART	1982	EC	25 X 18	AC	99	11	200	750
Firebird Series	FDI	ART	1986	MON/COL	35 X 25 EA	AC/W	1 EA		500 EA	900 EA
Primavera Series	FDI	ART	1986	MON/HC	42 X 30	AC/W	1 EA		900 EA	1500 EA

BRAD DAVIS

BORN: Duluth, Minnesota; April 24, 1942
EDUCATION: St Olaf Col, 1961; Univ of Chicago, IL, 1962; Art Inst of Chicago, IL, 1962–63; Univ of Minnesota, MN, BA, 1964– 66; Hunter Col, NY, 1968–70
AWARDS: First Prize & Jury Award, Minneapolis Inst of Art, MN, 1965; Second Prize & Purchase Prize, Walker Art Inst, Minneapolis, MN, 1966
RECENT EXHIB: San Antonio Art Inst, TX, 1992
COLLECTIONS: Univ of Minnesota, Minneapolis, MN; Walker Art Center, Minneapolis, MN; Whitney Mus of Am Art, NY; Neue Galerie, Sammlung Ludwig, Aachen, West Germany; Mus of Mod Art, NY; Saarbracken Mus, West Germany
PRINTERS: Solo Press, NY (SP); Sally Mara Sturman, NY (SMS); Chip Elwell, NY (CE); Brand X, NY (BX); Bud Shark, Boulder, CO (BS); Shark's Lithography, Ltd, Boulder, CO (SLL); Vermillion Editions, Ltd, Minneapolis, MN (VEL); Berghoff-Cowden Studio, Tampa, FL (B-CS)
PUBLISHERS: Holly Solomon Editions, NY (HSE); Fabric Workshop, Phila, PA (FW); Crystal Springs Press, NY (CSP); Diane Villani Editions, NY (DVE); Shark's Lithography, Ltd, Boulder, CO (SLL); Vermillion Editions, Ltd, Minneapolis, MN (VEL); Berghoff-Cowden Editions, Tampa, FL (B-CEd)
GALLERIES: Holly Solomon Editions, Ltd, New York, NY; Diane Villani Editions, New York, NY; van Straaten Gallery, Chicago, IL; Roger Ramsay Gallery, Chicago, IL; McIntosh/Drysdale Gallery, Houston, TX; Shark's Inc, Boulder, CO; Tavelli Gallery, Aspen, CO; Vermillion Editions, Ltd, Minneapolis, MN
MAILING ADDRESS: P O Box 473, Carbondale, CO 81623

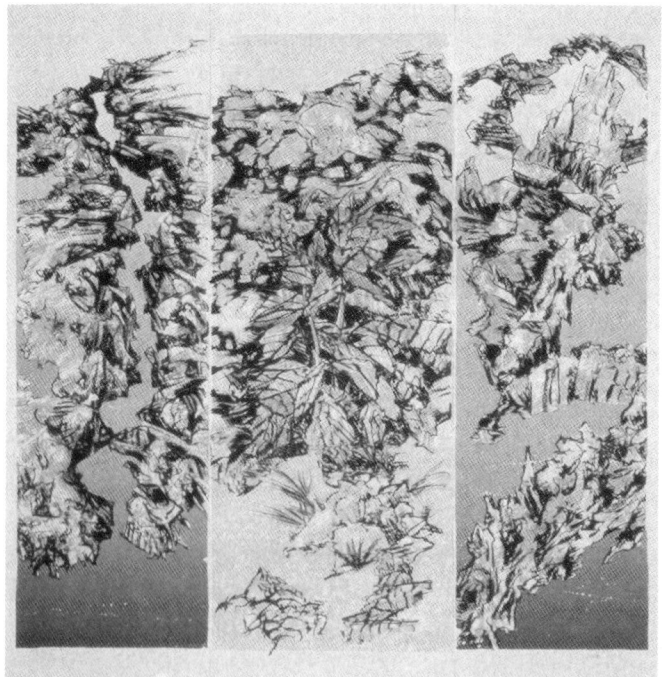

Brad Davis
City of Refuge
Courtesy Shark's, Inc

TITLE	PUBLISHER	PRINTER	DATE	MEDIUM	DIMENSION (PAPER SIZE) IN INCHES	TYPE OF PAPER	EDITION NUMBER	NO. OF COLORS	ORIGINAL OPENING PRICE	CURRENT RETAIL PRICE
SOLD OUT EDITIONS (RARE):										
Dog and Partridges	DVE	SMS	1982	PH/ENG	41 X 30	AC/W	30		800	3000
CURRENT EDITIONS:										
Dog and Bird I	HSE	SP	1980	WC	76 X 39	SRP/W	21	2	600	1500
Dog and Bird I	HSE	SP	1980	W/HC	76 X 39	SRP/W	10	2	2500	5000
Untitled	FW	FW	1980	SP/SI/HP	80 X 31	TAP	5		3000	5000
Untitled	FW	FW	1980	SP/SI/HP	78 X 50	TAP	4		4000	6000
Untitled	FW	FW	1980	SP/SI/HP	96 X 66	TAP	6		6000	8000
Fox and Hare	HSE	SP	1981	LC	19 X 54	AP/W	36	3	600	2200
Dog and Bird II	HSE	SP	1981	WC	76 X 39	SRP/W	28	2	600	2800
Dog and Bird III	HSE	SP	1981	WC	76 X 39	SRP/W	28	2	600	2800
Eight Dog Portraits (Set of 8)	CSP	SMS	1981	EB	26 X 20 EA	R/BFK	40 EA	1 EA	1500 SET	10000 SET
Long Branch	DVE	CE/BX	1983	WC/SP/PO	36 X 72	SEK	40	6	1200	5000
Three Junipers	VEL	VEL	1985	LC/SP	40 X 30	AC			800	3000
Piñon	SLL	BS/SLL	1987	LC/CC	35 X 35	SUK-R/BFK	20	6	1200	1400
City of Refuge (Trip)	SLL	BS/SLL	1991	LC	44 X 45	SUK	25		2000	2000
Monotypes, 1991	SLL	BS/SLL	1991	MON	Varies	SUK	1 EA	Varies	3500 EA	3500 EA

BRAD DAVIS CONTINUED

TITLE	PUBLISHER	PRINTER	DATE	MEDIUM	DIMENSION (PAPER SIZE) IN INCHES	TYPE OF PAPER	EDITION NUMBER	NO. OF COLORS	ORIGINAL OPENING PRICE	CURRENT RETAIL PRICE
CURRENT EDITIONS:										
Quince	B-CEd	B-CS	1992	SP	32 X 49	LEN	25	5	1800	1800
Rock and Bamboo Diptych (Dipt)	B-CEd	B-CS	1992	SP	38 X 50	LEN	30	11	2200	2200
Rock and Bamboo Diptych (Dipt)	B-CEd	B-CS	1992	SP	37 X 49	JP	6	11	2200	2200
Chair in the Garden	B-CEd	B-CS	1992	SP	20 X 26	HMP	15	1	800	800
Periwinkle Fan (Color Variants)	B-CEd	B-CS	1992	SP	15 X 22 EA	CRP	40 EA	1 EA	800 EA	800 EA
Bamboo & Landscape Diptych (Dipt)	B-CEd	B-CS	1992	SP	20 X 26	CRP	25	8	1200	1200
Rock Diptych (Dipt)	B-CEd	B-CS	1992	SP	38 X 50	LEN	30	10	2200	2200
Rock Diptych (Dipt)	B-CEd	B-CS	1992	SP	37 X 4	JP	6	10	2200	2200
Rock	B-CEd	B-CS	1992	SP	22 X 50	LEN	30	10	1800	1800

DOUGLAS MATTHEW DAVIS

BORN: Washington, DC; April 11, 1933
EDUCATION: Abbott Art Sch, Wash, DC; American Univ, Wash, DC, BA, 1956; Rutgers Univ, Camden, NJ, MA, 1958
TEACHING: Vis Artist, Corcoran Art Sch, Wash, DC, 1970,71; Instr, State Univ of New York, Buffalo, NY, 1973; Art Critic in Res, New York Univ, NY, 1975; Regents Lectr, Univ of California, San Diego, CA, 1976; Instr, Advanced Video & Performance Int Network Arts, New York State Univ, Purchase, NY, 1976; Instr, Columbia Univ, NY, 1988-90; Vis Prof, Artcener Col, Pasadena, CA, 1988–90; Vis Prof, Art & Design, Univ of California, Los Angeles, CA, 1990–91; Instr, Philadelphia Col of Art, PA, 1976 to present

AWARDS: New York Council of the Arts Grant for Creative Work, Mixed Media, 1970; Nat Endowment for the Arts Grants, 1970,75; Chairman's Grant, Nat Endowment for the Arts, 1981; Nat Public Radio Award, 1983; Intermedia Arts Prize, Boston, MA, 1988; Trust for Mutual Understanding Award, 1989; Rockefeller Found Grant, 1990
COLLECTIONS: Metropolitan Mus of Art, NY; Wadsworth Atheneum, Hartford, CT; Hirshhorn Mus of Art, Wash, DC; Walker Art Center, Minneapolis, MN; Dahlem Mus, Berlin, German; Ludwig Mus, Cologne, Germany
PUBLISHERS: Ronald Feldman Fine Arts, NY (RFFA)
GALLERIES: Ronald Feldman Fine Arts, New York, NY
MAILING ADDRESS: 80 Wooster St, New York, NY 10012

TITLE	PUBLISHER	PRINTER	DATE	MEDIUM	DIMENSION (PAPER SIZE) IN INCHES	TYPE OF PAPER	EDITION NUMBER	NO. OF COLORS	ORIGINAL OPENING PRICE	CURRENT RETAIL PRICE
CURRENT EDITIONS:										
Keep Time (Set of 6):									1500 SET	5000 SET
Handing	RFFA		1976	PH/ENG/HC	30 X 22	R/BFK	25	1	300	1200
The Florence Tapes	RFFA		1976	PH/ENG	30 X 22	R/BFK	25	1	300	1200
Three Silent & Secret Acts	RFFA		1976	LB/DEB	30 X 22	R/BFK	25	1	300	1200
Reading Marx	RFFA		1976	PH/ENG	30 X 22	R/BFK	25	1	300	1200
Reading Brecht	RFFA		1976	PH/OFF/BL	30 X 22	R/BFK	25	1	300	1200
Multi-Image (with Rubber Stamp)	RFFA		1976	PH/ENG/EB/EMB	30 X 22	R/BFK	25	1	300	1200
Seven Thoughts	RFFA		1977–78	SP/LC	30 X 22	R/BFK	10	1	350	1200
Three-Man Song with Father and Foot	RFFA		1989	I/REL/PH	22 X 30	R/BFK	29	1	1200	1500

GENE DAVIS

BORN: Washington, DC; (1920–1985)
EDUCATION: Univ of Maryland, College Park, MD
TEACHING: American Univ, Wash, DC, 1968–70; Corcoran Gallery Art Sch, Wash, DC, 1967 to present
AWARDS: Bronze Medal for Painting, Corcoran Gallery, Wash, DC, 1965; Nat Endowment for the Arts Fel, 1967; Guggenheim Fel, NY, 1974–75
RECENT EXHIB: Charles Cowles Gallery, NY, 1989,90,91; Kornblatt Gallery, Wash, DC, 1991; Fort Wayne Mus, IN, 1992
COLLECTIONS: Metropolitan Mus of Art, NY; Guggenheim Mus, NY; Mus of Mod Art, NY; Whitney Mus of Am Art, NY; Tate Gallery, London, England; Corcoran Gallery of Art, Wash, DC; Rose Art Mus, Brandeis Univ, Waltham, MA; Des Moines Art Mus, IA; Nat Coll of Fine Arts, Wash, DC; Yale Univ, New Haven, CT; San Francisco Mus of Mod Art, CA; Phillips Coll, Wash, DC; Hirshhorn Mus, Wash, DC; J B Speed Art Mus, Louisville, KY; Massachusetts Inst of Art, Cambridge, MA; Denver Art Mus, CO; Milwaukee Art Center, WI; McNay Art Inst, San Antonio, TX; Dallas Mus of Fine Arts, TX; Philadelphia Mus of Art, PA
PRINTERS: Alpha Omega, Detroit, MI (AO); Fine Creations, NY (FC); A Moskowitz (AM); Movex Ltd (ML); Bob Roberts, London, England (BR); Petersburg Press, London, England (PP)
PUBLISHERS: London Arts, Inc, Detroit, MI (LAI); Pace Editions, NY (PE); Petersburg Press, London, England (PP); Post Oak Fine Arts Distributor, Houston, TX (POFA); Dale R Collins (DRC); Roger S Geibel (RSG); Dr Morris & Dr Morris (M/M); Paul Rosenthal (PR)
GALLERIES: Pace Prints, New York, NY; L A Louver, Venice, CA; David Adamson Gallery, Wash, DC; Middendorf Gallery, Wash, DC; Hokin Gallery, Bay Harbor Islands, FL & Palm Beach, FL; Charles Cowles Gallery, New York, NY; Kornblatt Gallery, Wash, DC

TITLE	PUBLISHER	PRINTER	DATE	MEDIUM	DIMENSION (PAPER SIZE) IN INCHES	TYPE OF PAPER	EDITION NUMBER	NO. OF COLORS	ORIGINAL OPENING PRICE	CURRENT RETAIL PRICE
SOLD OUT EDITIONS (RARE):										
Series I, on Canvas, Lam to Board (Set of 6)									500 SET	3000 SET
No's 1–3	PP	BR/PP	1969	SP	33 X 20	AP	150		100 EA	800 EA
No's 4–6	PP	BR/PP	1969	SP	35 X 33	AP	150		100 EA	800 EA

The retail prices of the 100,000 limited edition prints quoted in this directory are subject to change. Print publishers, artists and galleries were the direct sources for these quotations. Prices in the secondary market listed as "Sold Out Editions (Rare)" indicate that the publisher has a limited supply of that print or that the print is difficult to locate in the galleries.

GENE DAVIS CONTINUED

TITLE	PUBLISHER	PRINTER	DATE	MEDIUM	DIMENSION (PAPER SIZE) IN INCHES	TYPE OF PAPER	EDITION NUMBER	NO. OF COLORS	ORIGINAL OPENING PRICE	CURRENT RETAIL PRICE
SOLD OUT EDITIONS (RARE):										
Series II on Canvas, Lam to Board									500 SET	3000 SET
No's 1–3	PP	BR/PP	1969	SP	33 X 20 EA	AP	150 EA		100 EA	800 EA
No's 4–6	PP	BR/PP	1969	SP	35 X 33 EA	AP	150 EA		100 EA	800 EA
Yankee Doodles	HKL		1972	SP		AP	144		150	1200
Ten Lithographs (Set of 10):										
Three Acres	PP	BR/PP	1973	LC	30 X 40	AP	75		150	1000
Cold Turkey	PP	BR/PP	1973	LC	30 X 40	AP	75		150	1000
Narcissus	PP	BR/PP	1973	LC	30 X 40	AP	75		150	1000
Prince Igor	PP	BR/PP	1973	LC	30 X 40	AP	75		150	1000
Tightrope	PP	BR/PP	1973	LC	30 X 40	AP	75		150	1000
Albatros	PP	BR/PP	1973	LC	30 X 40	AP	75		150	1000
Checkmate	PP	BR/PP	1973	LC	40 X 30	AP	75		150	1000
Witch Doctor	PP	BR/PP	1973	LC	40 X 30	AP	75		150	1000
Home Run	PP	BR/PP	1973	LC	30 X 40	AP	75		150	1000
Ferris Wheel	PP	BR/PP	1973	LC	30 X 40	AP	75		150	1000
Yoyo	PP	BR/PP	1973	LC/OFF	30 X 40	HMP	75		225	1000
Black Watch I,II,III,IV	PE	FC	1974	SP	72 X 45 EA	AP	150 EA		250 EA	1000 EA
Davy's Locker	PE	AM/ML	1977	SP/HSTE	38 X 42	LEN	100	8	250	1000
Royal Canoe	PE	AM/ML	1977	SP	32 X 38	LEN	100	9	250	1000
Green Giant	LAI	AO	1979	LC	26 X 29	AP	250	3	500	1000
Tom Thumb	LAI	AO	1979	SP	25 X 23	AP	250	4	500	1000
Lilac	LAI	AO	1979	SP	22 X 30	AP	250	3	500	1000
Royal Curtain	LAI	AO	1980	SP	30 X 21	AP	250	7	500	1000
Banjo	DRC	AO	1981	LC	22 X 29	AP	250	4	500	1000
Adam's Rib	POFA	AO	1981	LC	20 X 27	AP	250	4	500	1000
Ferris Wheel	POFA	AO	1981	LC	20 X 27	AP	250	4	500	1000
Carousel	RSG	AO	1981	LC	17 X 24	AP	250	4	450	1000
Sonata	M/M-PR	AO	1981	LC	21 X 29	AP	250	3	500	1000

RONALD DAVIS

BORN: Santa Monica, CA; June 29, 1937
EDUCATION: San Francisco Art Inst, CA, 1960–64
AWARDS: Nat Endowment for the Arts Fel, 1968
RECENT EXHIB: BlumHelman Gallery, NY, 1987; The Art Show, NY, 1989; John Berggruen Gallery, San Francisco, CA, 1989; Newport Harbor Art Mus, Newport Beach, CA, 1989; Palm Springs Desert Mus, CA, 1989,92
COLLECTIONS: Los Angeles County Art Mus, CA; Mus of Mod Art, NY; Tate Gallery of Art, London, England; Albright-Knox Art Gallery, Buffalo, NY; San Francisco Art Mus, CA
PRINTERS: Betty Fiske, NY (BF); Tyler Graphics, Ltd, Mount Kisco, NY (TGL); Dan Freeman, Los Angeles, CA (DF); Anthony Zepeda, Los Angeles, CA (AZ); Ron Bigelow, Los Angeles, CA (RB); Serge Lozingot, Los Angeles, CA (SL); B Thomason, Los Angeles, CA (BT); Gemini GEL, Los Angeles, CA (GEM)
PUBLISHERS: Tyler Graphics, Ltd, Mt Kisco, NY (TGL); Gemini GEL, Los Angeles, CA (GEM)
GALLERIES: Asher/Faure, Los Angeles, CA; John Berggruen Gallery, San Francisco, CA; Patricia Heesy Gallery, New York, NY; BlumHelman Gallery, New York, NY; David Lawrence Editions, Beverly Hills, CA; Charles Whitchurch Fine Arts, Huntington Beach, CA; Jonathan Novak, Los Angeles, CA; Ochi Galleries, Boise, ID & Sun Valley, ID; Gemini GEL, Los Angeles, CA; Joni Moisant Weyl, Los Angeles, CA; Philip Bareiss Contemporary Gallery, Taos, NM
MAILING ADDRESS: P O Box 276, Arroyo Hondo, NM 87513-0276

TITLE	PUBLISHER	PRINTER	DATE	MEDIUM	DIMENSION (PAPER SIZE) IN INCHES	TYPE OF PAPER	EDITION NUMBER	NO. OF COLORS	ORIGINAL OPENING PRICE	CURRENT RETAIL PRICE
SOLD OUT EDITIONS (RARE):										
Cube Series (Each Mounted on Plastic with Mylar Overlay) (Set of 3):										
Cube I (MOMA-267)	TGL	TGL	1971	PH/OFF	30 X 40	SDW	100	5	250	4500
Cube II (MOMA-268)	TGL	TGL	1971	PH/OFF	30 X 40	SDW	114	5	250	4500
Cube III (MOMA-269)	TGL	TGL	1971	PH/OFF	30 X 40	SDW	125	5	250	4500
Rectangle Series (Set of 5):										
Four Circle (MOMA-360)	GEM	GEM	1972	LC/SP	30 X 39	AC	70	6	250	3000
Two Circle (MOMA-361)	GEM	GEM	1972	LC/SP/EMB	20 X 41	AC	75	8	250	3000
Two Bar (MOMA-364)	GEM	GEM	1972	LC/SP/EMB	20 X 39	AC	70	14	300	3000
Triangle Slice (MOMA-365)	TGL	TGL	1972	LC/SP/EMB	19 X 41	AC	75	12	300	3000
Single Divider (MOMA-362)	TGL	TGL	1972	LC/SP/EMB	20 X 42	AC	66	11	200	3000
Six Frame (MOMA-526)	TGL	TGL	1974	SP	29 X 42	ARJ	50	8	300	1800
Six Prong-Color Notation	GEM	GEM	1974	SP	16 X 42	AP	25		300	1500
Six Prong-Perspective Line	GEM	GEM	1974	SP	16 X 42	AP	29		300	1500
Six Prong-Grey	GEM	GEM	1974	SP	16 X 42	AP	23		300	1500
Black Vent Beam (G-666)	GEM	DF/AZ/RB/ SL/BT/GEM	1975	LC	25 X 36	AP	23	5	300	1250
Pinwheel, Diamond & Stripe	TGL	TGL	1975	EB/A/DPT	20 X 24	HMP	42	3	400	2000
Bent Beam	TGL	BF/TGL	1975	EB/A/DPT	20 X 24	HMP	44	2	250	3000
Upright Slab	TGL	TGL	1975	EB/A/DPT	24 X 20	HMP	38	3	250	3000
Arch	TGL	TGL	1975	EB/A/DPT	20 X 24	HMP	32	3	250	3000
Big Open Box	TGL	TGL	1975	EB/A/DPT	20 X 24	HMP	39	4	400	3500
Arc Arch	TGL	TGL	1975	LC/SP	32 X 42	TGL/HMP	50	29	400	5000
Twin Wave	TGL	TGL	1979	LC/SP	32 X 42	TGL/HMP	50	34	400	5000
Wide Wave	TGL	TGL	1979	LC/SP	32 X 42	TGL/HMP	50	30	400	5000

RONALD DAVIS CONTINUED

TITLE	PUBLISHER	PRINTER	DATE	MEDIUM	DIMENSION (PAPER SIZE) IN INCHES	TYPE OF PAPER	EDITION NUMBER	NO. OF COLORS	ORIGINAL OPENING PRICE	CURRENT RETAIL PRICE
SOLD OUT EDITIONS (RARE):										
Invert Span	TGL	TGL	1979	LC/SP	32 X 42	TGL/HMP	50	34	400	5000
Tilt	GEM	GEM	1981	EB/A/ENG	30 X 18	AP	31		800	1500
Rotation—Tilt, Black State	GEM	GEM	1981	EB/A/ENG	34 X 24	AP	20		700	1500
Drypoint Beta	GEM	GEM	1981	DPT	14 X 9	AP	18		300	700
Drypoint Gamma	GEM	GEM	1981	DPT	14 X 9	AP	18		300	700
Drypoint Delta	GEM	GEM	1981	DPT	14 X 9	AP	18		300	700
Drypoint Epsilon	GEM	GEM	1981	DPT	14 X 9	AP	18		300	700
Drypoint Zeta	GEM	GEM	1981	DPT	14 X 9	AP	18		300	700
Drypoint Eta	GEM	GEM	1981	DPT	14 X 9	AP	18		300	700
Drypoint Theta	GEM	GEM	1981	DPT	14 X 9	AP	18		300	750
Drypoint Iota	GEM	GEM	1981	DPT	14 X 9	AP	18		300	700
Drypoint Kappa	GEM	GEM	1981	DPT	14 X 9	AP	18		300	700
Drypoint Lambda	GEM	GEM	1981	DPT	14 X 9	AP	18		300	700
Drypoint Mu	GEM	GEM	1981	DPT	14 X 9	AP	18		300	700
Drypoint Nu	GEM	GEM	1981	DPT	14 X 9	AP	18		300	700
Brick	GEM	GEM	1983	LC	43 X 32	AC	40	6	600	1800
Block	GEM	GEM	1983	LC	45 X 36	AC	39	7	600	1800
Green Disc	GEM	GEM	1983	LC	34 X 47	AC	45	5	600	1000
Black Disc	GEM	GEM	1983	LC	34 X 47	AC	21	4	600	650
Yellow Brick	GEM	GEM	1983	LC	43 X 34	AC	23	3	600	800
Red Brick	GEM	GEM	1983	LC	43 X 34	AC	23	3	600	800
Disc Slab	GEM	GEM	1983	LC	32 X 44	AC	40	3	600	950
Disc Slab, Black State	GEM	GEM	1983	LC	32 X 44	AC	22	3	600	600
Samson's Lizard	GEM	GEM	1983	PHG/AB/HC	39 X 28	AC	37	1	500	800
Tri-Box and Grid	GEM	GEM	1983	EC	22 X 18	AC	35	1	450	450
Pyramid and Cube	GEM	GEM	1983	EB	44 X 34	AC	33	4	600	900
Nebula One	GEM	GEM	1983	AC	47 X 34	AC	30	1	600	700
Copper Block	GEM	GEM	1983	AC/CO	48 X 34	AC	31	1	600	1500
Yellow Slab	GEM	GEM	1983	AC/MEZ	48 X 34	AC	29	2	600	1800
Red Slab	GEM	GEM	1983	AC/MEZ	48 X 34	AC	33	2	600	1800
Nebula Two	GEM	GEM	1983	AC	33 X 47	AC	25	1	600	700

DAZE (CHRIS ELLIS)

RECENT EXHIB: Bronx Mus, NY, 1987

COLLECTIONS: Mus of Mod Art, NY; Neue Galerie-Sammlung Ludwig, Aachen, Germany; Dannheiser Found, NY; Raimund Thomas Coll, Munich, Germany; Yaki Kornblit Coll, Amsterdam, The Netherlands
PRINTERS: Judith Solodkin, NY (JS); Solo Press, NY (SP)
PUBLISHERS: Solo Press, NY (SP)
GALLERIES: Solo Press, New York, NY

TITLE	PUBLISHER	PRINTER	DATE	MEDIUM	DIMENSION (PAPER SIZE) IN INCHES	TYPE OF PAPER	EDITION NUMBER	NO. OF COLORS	ORIGINAL OPENING PRICE	CURRENT RETAIL PRICE
CURRENT EDITIONS:										
Special Express	SP	JS/SP	1985	LC	28 X 35	SOM	45		500	800
Self Portrait/Portrait (with Grace Graupe-Pillard)	SP	JS/SP	1987	LC/PAS	31 X 47	SOM	20		1200	1500

MICHAEL DE CAMP

BORN: New York; 1928
EDUCATION: Princeton Univ, NJ

COLLECTIONS: Mus of Mod Art, NY; Mus of Mod Art, Rio de Janiero, Brazil
PRINTERS: Stuart Photo, NY (SP)
PUBLISHERS: Fred Dorfman, Inc, NY (FDI)
GALLERIES: Soma Fine Arts, San Francisco, CA; Fred Dorfman Gallery, New York, NY

TITLE	PUBLISHER	PRINTER	DATE	MEDIUM	DIMENSION (PAPER SIZE) IN INCHES	TYPE OF PAPER	EDITION NUMBER	NO. OF COLORS	ORIGINAL OPENING PRICE	CURRENT RETAIL PRICE
CURRENT EDITIONS:										
Room By The Sea	FDI	SP	1980	PH/C	15 X 22	KEP	55		200	800
View of The Sea	FDI	SP	1980	PH/C	15 X 22	KEP	55		200	500
The Cloud	FDI	SP	1980	PH/C	15 X 22	KEP	55		200	500
Door To . . .	FDI	SP	1981	PH/C	15 X 22	KEP	60		300	450
The Alchemist	FDI	SP	1981	PH/C	15 X 22	KEP	60		300	450

GUY DE COINTET

BORN: Paris, France; 1940
TEACHING: Otis Art Inst, Los Angeles, CA, 1975–77

PRINTERS: Jan Aman (JA); Cirrus Editions Workshop, Los Angeles, CA (CEW)
PUBLISHERS: Cirrus Editions Ltd, Los Angeles, CA (CE)
GALLERIES: Cirrus Editions, Ltd, Los Angeles, CA; Barbara Braathen, New York, NY
MAILING ADDRESS: 1489 W Washington Blvd, Los Angeles, CA 90013

GUY DE COINTET CONTINUED

TITLE	PUBLISHER	PRINTER	DATE	MEDIUM	DIMENSION (PAPER SIZE) IN INCHES	TYPE OF PAPER	EDITION NUMBER	NO. OF COLORS	ORIGINAL OPENING PRICE	CURRENT RETAIL PRICE
CURRENT EDITIONS:										
A Page from My Intimate Journal	CE	JA/CEW	1974	SP	23 X 30	AP	50	1	150	300

ROY DE FOREST

BORN: North Platte, NE; February 11, 1930
EDUCATION: A A Yakima Junior Col, WA, 1950; California Sch of Fine Arts, Valencia, CA, 1950–52; San Francisco State Col, CA, BA, 1952–53, MA, 1956–58
TEACHING: Instr, California Col of Arts & Crafts, Oakland, CA, 1964–65; Asst Prof to Assoc Prof, Univ of California, Davis, CA, 1965–82
AWARDS: Neallie Sullivan Award, San Francisco Art Assn, CA, 1964; Purchase Award, La Jolla Art Mus, CA, 1965; Nat Endowment for the Arts, 1972
RECENT EXHIB: Schmidt Bingham Gallery, NY, 1987; Pittsburgh Art Center of the Arts, PA, 1987; Rhode Island Sch of Design, Providence, RI; Darthea Speyer Gallery, 1987; Struve Gallery, Chicago, IL, 1988; Lew Allen/Butler Fine Art, Santa Fe, NM, 1990; Univ of California, Davis, CA, 1992; Redding Mus & Art Center, CA, 1989,92; Stanford Univ Mus, CA, 1992
COLLECTIONS: Art Inst of Chicago, IL; Crocker Art Mus, Sacramento, CA; Whitney Mus of Am Art, NY; San Francisco Mus of Mod Art, CA; Brooklyn Mus, NY; Centre Georges Pompidou, Paris, France; Philadelphia Art Mus, PA; Joslyn Art Mus, Omaha, NE
PRINTERS: Jerry Raidiger, Chicago, IL (JR); Landfall Press Inc, Chicago, IL (LPI); Ernest De Soto Workshop, San Francisco, CA (EDSW); Ernest F De Soto, San Francisco, CA (EDS); Sette Publishing Company, Tempe, AZ (SPC); Lynne Allen, Albuquerque, NM (LA); Russell Craig, Albuquerque, NM (RC); Tom Pruitt, Albuquerque, NM (TP); Tamarind Inst, Albuquerque, NM
PUBLISHERS: Allan Frumkin Inc, NY (AFI); Tamarind Inst, Albuquerque, NM (TI); Ernest De Soto Workshop, San Francisco, CA (EDSW); Sette Publishing Company, Tempe, AZ (SPC)
GALLERIES: Gallery K, Wash, DC; Ernest DeSoto Workshop, San Francisco, CA; Tamarind Inst, Albuquerque, NM; Sette Publishing Company, Tempe, AZ; Struve Gallery, Chicago, IL; Garner Tullis Workshop, Santa Monica, CA; Experimental Workshop, San Francisco, CA; Dorothy Goldeen Gallery, Santa Monica, CA; Tamarind Inst, Albuquerque, NM; LewAllen Fine Art, Santa Fe, NM; Frumkin/Adams Gallery, New York, NY; MIA Gallery, Seattle, WA; Fulcrum Gallery, New York, NY; Lisa Sette Gallery, Scottsdale, AZ; John Natsoulas Gallery, Davis, CA; John Berggruen Gallery, San Francisco, CA; Brian Gross Fine Art, San Francisco, CA; Dorothy Goldeen Gallery, Santa Monica, CA; Naravisa Press, Santa Fe, NM
MAILING ADDRESS: PO Box 47, Port Costa, CA 94569

Roy De Forest
Untitled (Mutants)
Courtesy Tamarind Institute

TITLE	PUBLISHER	PRINTER	DATE	MEDIUM	DIMENSION (PAPER SIZE) IN INCHES	TYPE OF PAPER	EDITION NUMBER	NO. OF COLORS	ORIGINAL OPENING PRICE	CURRENT RETAIL PRICE
SOLD OUT EDITIONS (RARE):										
Untitled	AFI	JR/LPI	1972	LC	22 X 30	AP/W	30	4	300	1500
Untitled	TI	TI	1978	LC	22 X 30	AP/W	100		400	1200
Untitled (Cowboy/Kangroo)			1978	LC	30 X 41	AP/W	30		500	6000
CURRENT EDITIONS:										
Untitled	TI	TI	1980	LC	22 X 30	AP/W	100		400	800
Untitled	EDSW	EDS/EDSW	1983	LC	25 X 30	AP/W	100	5	500	1000
Beware of the Night Dog (State I)	TI	LA/TI	1985	LC	27 X 39	GE	38	4	450	800
Beware of the Night Dog (State II)	TI	LA/TI	1985	LC/CC	27 X 39	AP/BL	24	6	450	800
Untitled (Campfire)	TI	RC/TP/TI	1985	LC	27 X 40	GE	33	6	450	800
Untitled (Reflection)	TI	LA/TI	1985	LC	27 X 38	AP/B	32	7	450	800
Untitled (Mutants)	TI	LA/TP/TI	1985	LC	22 X 30	GE	26	7	450	450
Bigfoot (State II)	SPC	SPC	1985–86	LC/HC	33 X 45	R/BFK		Varies	1500	2000
Untitled (with Hand-Decorated Frame)	SPC	SPC	1986	LC/HC	33 X 45	R/BFK/G	50	Varies	1200	1800
Bigfoot 2	SPC	SPC	1986	LC/HC	26 X 38	R/BFK/G	20	Varies	1200	1800

GEORGE HUGH DE GROAT

BORN: Newark, NJ; January 7, 1917
EDUCATION: Newark Sch of Fine Arts, NJ, 1934–38; Newark Prep Col, NJ, BA, 1938–40; Detroit Soc of the Arts, IL, 1954–56
TEACHING: Instr, Painting, California State Col San Diego, CA, 1966–67; Instr, Painting, Col of Design, Pasadena, CA, 1966–69; Instr, Painting, Col of Design, Los Angeles, CA, 1968–71; Instr, Life Drawing & Painting, Otis Art Inst, Los Angeles, CA, 1968–78
AWARDS: First Prize, Long Beach Mus of Art, CA, 1966; McBride Award, Pasadena Art Mus, CA, 1969; Ford Found Grant, Color Field Painting, 1977
COLLECTIONS: Monterey Peninsula Mus, CA; Downey Mus of Art, CA
PRINTERS: Artist (ART)
PUBLISHERS: Fireside Gallery, Carmel, CA (FG); Phyllis Lucas Gallery, NY (PLG); Associated American Artists, NY (AAA)
GALLERIES: Phyllis Lucas Gallery, New York, NY; Montera Gallery, Carmel, CA
MAILING ADDRESS: P O Box 306, Carmel Valley, CA 93924

The retail prices of the 100,000 limited edition prints quoted in this directory are subject to change. Print publishers, artists and galleries were the direct sources for these quotations. Prices in the secondary market listed as "Sold Out Editions (Rare)" indicate that the publisher has a limited supply of that print or that the print is difficult to locate in the galleries.

GEORGE HUGH DE GROAT CONTINUED

TITLE	PUBLISHER	PRINTER	DATE	MEDIUM	DIMENSION (PAPER SIZE) IN INCHES	TYPE OF PAPER	EDITION NUMBER	NO. OF COLORS	ORIGINAL OPENING PRICE	CURRENT RETAIL PRICE
SOLD OUT EDITIONS (RARE):										
The Quest	FG	ART	1975	AC	18 X 12	AP	25	1	100	300
Shadow of Illusion	PLG	ART	1975	AC	11 X 9	AP	25	2	150	350
The Red Archer	FG	ART	1976	AC	18 X 13	AP	20	3	125	350
Emergence	FG	ART	1976	AC	16 X 12	AP	25	3	125	350
Acrobats	PLG	ART	1977	AC	12 X 16	AP	20	3	125	350
CURRENT EDITIONS:										
Don Quixote de La Mancha	FC	ART	1975	WC	18 X 13	AP	50	3	250	300
Ixion's Dream	FG	ART	1976	AC	20 X 15	AP	25	1	150	200
Seated Archer	FG	ART	1977	AC	18 X 13	AP	25	1	150	200
Images of Freedom	FG	ART	1977	AC	14 X 16	AP	25	3	225	400
Emperor's New Clothes	FG	ART	1978	AC	16 X 12	AP	10	5	225	400
California Oak	AAA	ART	1978	AC	16 X 12	AP	20	5	200	400
The Musician's Dream	AAA	ART	1979	AC	18 X 12	AP	20	5	150	400
The Color of Music	AAA	ART	1979	AC	12 X 7	AP	20	6	125	350
Opus 27	AAA	ART	1979	AC	12 X 7	AP	20	6	125	350
Challenge	AAA	ART	1979	AC	12 X 8	AP	20	5	125	300
Midnight Dream	FG	ART	1980	AC	18 X 12	AP	20	6	225	400

THOM DE JONG

BORN: Amsterdam, Holland; 1940
EDUCATION: Univ of Amsterdam, Holland; Art Students League, NY
COLLECTIONS: Mus of Mod Art, NY; Stedelijk Mus, Amsterdam, Holland
PRINTERS: Artist (ART)
PUBLISHERS: Fred Dorfman, Inc, NY (FDI); Edward Weston Editions Ltd, NY & Northridge, CA (EDE)
GALLERIES: Judith Posner, Milwaukee, WI; Wenninger Graphics, Boston, MA; Jean Lumbard Fine Arts, New York, NY; A Clean Well-Lighted Place, New York, NY

TITLE	PUBLISHER	PRINTER	DATE	MEDIUM	DIMENSION (PAPER SIZE) IN INCHES	TYPE OF PAPER	EDITION NUMBER	NO. OF COLORS	ORIGINAL OPENING PRICE	CURRENT RETAIL PRICE
CURRENT EDITIONS:										
Sculling	FDI	ART	1981	EC	20 X 30	SOM	100	7	175	300
Making Waves	FDI	ART	1981	EC	20 X 30	SOM	100	7	175	300
Ocean Chase	FDI	ART	1981	EC	20 X 30	SOM	100	7	175	300
The Harbor	FDI	ART	1981	EC	20 X 30	SOM	100	7	175	300

ELAINE DE KOONING

BORN: New York, NY; (1920–1989)
EDUCATION: Moore Col of Art, Phila, PA, DFA, Western Col for Women, DFA
TEACHING: Prof, Painting, Yale Univ Grad Sch, New Haven, CT, 1967–68; Mellon Chair, Painting, Carnegie-Mellon Univ, Pittsburgh, PA, 1969–70; Wagner Col, Staten Island, NY, 1971; Parsons Sch of Fine Art, NY, 1974–76; Empire State Col, Urban Studies Center, NY, 1974–76; Artist-in-Res, Brandeis Univ, Waltham, MA, 1975; Rice Univ, Houston, TX, 1976; Vis Prof, Cooper Union, NY, 1976; Prof, Art, Univ of Georgia, Athens, GA, 1976–79
RECENT EXHIB: New York State Mus, NY, 1987; Univ of California, Richard L Nelson Gallery, Davis, CA, 1989; Heckscher Mus, Huntington, NY, 1992
COLLECTIONS: Mus of Mod Art, NY; New York Univ, NY; Elmira Col, NY; Greenville Mus, SC; Drew Univ, Madison, NJ
PRINTERS: J Sommers (JS); M Dietrick (MD); Tamarind Inst, Albuquerque, NM (TI); Crown Point Press, San Francisco, CA (CPP)
PUBLISHERS: Tamarind Inst, Albuquerque, NM (TI); Crown Point Press, San Francisco, CA (CPP)
GALLERIES: Vared Gallery, East Hampton, NY; Elaine Benson Gallery, Bridgehampton, NY; C Grimaldis Gallery, Baltimore, MD; Crown Point Press, San Francisco, CA & New York, NY; Wenger Gallery, Los Angeles, CA; Paul Holoweski Gallery, Royal Oak, MI; Kornbluth Gallery, Fair Lawn, NJ; Fischbach Gallery, New York, NY

TITLE	PUBLISHER	PRINTER	DATE	MEDIUM	DIMENSION (PAPER SIZE) IN INCHES	TYPE OF PAPER	EDITION NUMBER	NO. OF COLORS	ORIGINAL OPENING PRICE	CURRENT RETAIL PRICE
SOLD OUT EDITIONS (RARE):										
Jardin de Luxembourg I	TI	JS/MD/TI	1977	LC/HC	76 X 56 cm	GE	70	8	750	2500
Les Eyzies	CPP	CPP	1985	AC	30 X 44	AC	35		2000	6500
Pech-Merle	CPP	CPP	1985	AC	16 X 16	AC	35		600	1800
CURRENT EDITIONS:										
Torchlight Cave Drawings (Set of 8)	CPP	CPP	1985	AC	20 X 26 EA	AC	25 EA		2400 SET	7500 SET
									500 EA	1500 EA

WILLEM DE KOONING

BORN: (1904–1988)
EDUCATION: Acad voor Beeldende Kunsten ed Tech Wetenschappen, Amsterdam, Holland, 1916–24
RECENT EXHIB: Karsten Greve Gallery, Paris, France, 1990; Salander-O'Reilly Galleries, NY, 1990; Montclair Art Mus, NJ, 1992; Albright-Knox Art Gallery, Buffalo, NY, 1989,92; Nassau County Mus of Fine Art, Roslyn Harbor, NY, 1992; State Univ of New York, Neuberger Mus, Purchase, NY, 1989,92; C & M Gallery, NY, 1993; Pace Gallery, NY, 1993

WILLEM DE KOONING CONTINUED

COLLECTIONS: Mus of Mod Art, NY; Metropolitan Mus of Art, NY; Whitney Mus of Am Art, NY; Brooklyn Mus, NY; Baltimore Mus of Art, MD; Albright-Knox Gallery, Buffalo, NY; Chicago Inst of Art, IL; Carnegie Inst of Art, Pittsburgh, PA; Univ of North Carolina, Greensboro, NC; Washington Univ, St Louis, MO; Philips Gallery, Wash, DC; Vassar Col, Poughkeepsie, NY; Walker Art Ctr, Minneapolis, MN
PRINTERS: Gemini GEL, Los Angeles, CA (GEM); Edicions de la Difference, Paris, France (EdD); Irwin Hollander, NY (IH); Hollander Workshop, NY (HW); American Atelier, NY (AA); Styria Studio, NY (SS); Trestle, NY (Tres)
PUBLISHERS: Styria Studio, NY (SS); Gemini GEL, Los Angeles, CA (GEM); Edicions de la Difference, Paris, France (EdD); Morris Gallery, NY (MG); Rainbow Art Found, NY (RAF)
GALLERIES: Richard Gray Gallery, Chicago, IL; Annette Couch Fine Arts, Los Angeles, CA; Marvin Ross Friedman & Co, Miami, FL; Janie C Lee Gallery, Houston, TX; Solomon & Co Fine Art, New York, NY; Barbara Krakow Gallery, Boston, MA; Ellen Sragow Gallery, New York, NY; Kass/Meridian Gallery, Chicago, IL; Galerie Lelong, New York, NY & Paris, France & Zürich, Switzerland; Margo Leavin Gallery, Los Angeles, CA; James Corcoran Gallery, Santa Monica, CA; Stephen A Solovy Fine Arts, Chicago, IL; Flanders Modern, Minneapolis, MN; Greenberg Gallery, St Louis, MO; Vered Gallery, East Hampton, NY; Gagosian Gallery, New York, NY; James Goodman Gallery, New York, NY; Sidney Janis Gallery, New York, NY; Jan Krugier Gallery, New York, NY; Janie C Lee Master Drawings, New York, NY; Lennon/Weinberg Gallery, New York, NY; Edward Tyler Nahem Fine Art, New York, NY; International Images, New York, NY; Karsten Greve Gallery, Paris, France; Charles Whitchurch Gallery, Huntington Beach, CA; Noble House, Los Angeles, CA; Metropolitan Art Gallery, Los Angeles, CA; Tavelli Williams Gallery, Aspen, CO; Moira James Gallery, Green Valley, NV; Stephen Solovy Fine Art, Chicago, IL; Flanders Modern, Minneapolis, MN; Gottheiner Fine Arts, Ltd, St Louis, MO; Dranoff Fine Art, New York, NY; Matthew Marks Gallery, New York, NY; Anthony Ralph Gallery, New York, NY; Salander O'Reilly Galleries, New York, NY; Stux Modern, New York, NY; Turner Fine Art, New York, NY; TwoSixtyOne Art, New York, NY; Yoshii Gallery, New York, NY; Ron Hall Gallery, Dallas, TX; Ro Gallery Image Makers, Inc, New York, NY; C & M Gallery, New York, NY

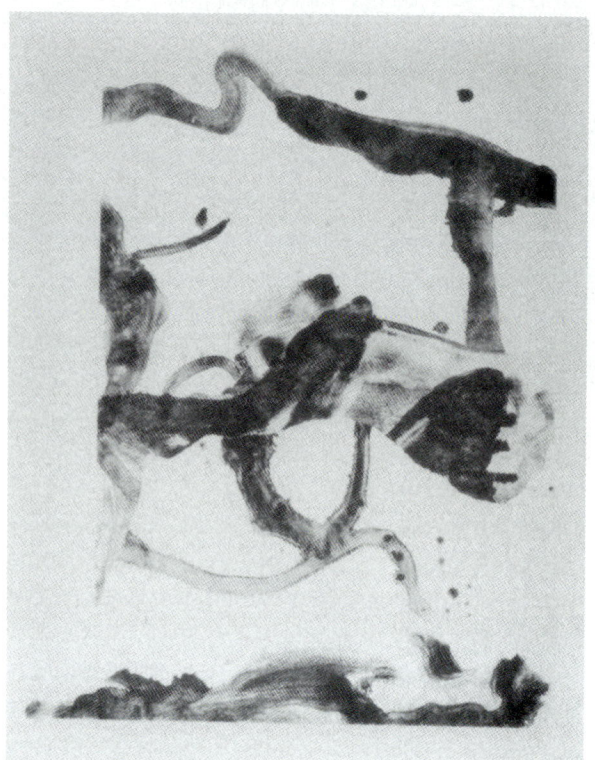

Willem De Kooning
Souvenir of Montauk
Courtesy Avantgarde Art Associates

TITLE	PUBLISHER	PRINTER	DATE	MEDIUM	DIMENSION (PAPER SIZE) IN INCHES	TYPE OF PAPER	EDITION NUMBER	NO. OF COLORS	ORIGINAL OPENING PRICE	CURRENT RETAIL PRICE
SOLD OUT EDITIONS (RARE):										
Revenge	MG		1955-60	EB/A	12 X 14	WOVE	50		100	8000
Untitled			1967	LB	23 X 14	AP	7	1	100	4500
Souvenir of Mantauk		IH/HW	1970	LB	34 X 27	ARA	43	1	300	8000
Love to Wakuko		IH/HW	1970	LB	40 X 25	ARA	58	1	300	8000
Wah Kee Spare Ribs		IH/HW	1970	LB	42 X 31	CD	57	1	300	12000
Woman at Clearwater Beach		IH/HW	1970	LB	24 X 32	AP	44	1	300	10000
Stingray		IH/HW	1970	LC	52 X 37	SUZ	48	1	500	12000
Landing Place	GEM	GEM	1970	LC	28 X 37	ARA	54	1	500	12000
Woman with Corset and Long Hair	GEM	GEM	1970	LC	37 X 30	AP	61	1	300	12000
Big		IH/HW	1970	LC	32 X 24	AP	10		500	12000
Clam Digger		IH/HW	1970	LB	41 X 29	AP	34	1	400	7500
Landscape at Stanton Street	GEM	GEM	1971	LC	30 X 22	AP	60		350	12000
The Preacher		IH/HW	1971	LB	25 X 19	AP	60	1	300	12000
Untitled	GEM	GEM	1972	SCULP	6 X 11 X 2	Metal	100		1500	30000
The Man and the Big Blond (Painted on Dansk)	RAF	AA	1972	LC	26 X 30	DP	150		500	27000
Two Women	SS	SS	1973	LC	14 X 11	AC	100		300	5000
Untitled (Set of 4)	GEM	GEM	1986	LC	28 X 32 EA	AC	100 EA		10000 SET	75000 SET
Untitled (Set of 4)	EdD	EdD	1987	LC	28 X 25 EA	WOVE	100 EA		7500 SET	60000 SET
Frank O'Hara Suite (Exhibition) (Set of 17)	LEC	Tres	1988	LC	38 X 24 EA	TRP	60 EA		8000 EA	12500 EA
CURRENT EDITIONS:										
Frank O'Hara Suite (Portfolio Edition) (Set of 17)	LEC	Tres	1988	LC	27 X 24 EA	TRP	60 EA		8000 EA	13500 EA
Signed Book (Set of 17)	LEC	Tres	1988	LC					5000	15000

ALBERTO DE LAMA

BORN: Havana, Cuba
EDUCATION: De La Salle Sch, Havana, Cuba, Havana Univ; Am Acad of Art, Chicago, IL; Northeastern Illinois Univ, Chicago, IL, MFA
TEACHING: Am Acad of Art, 1969-75
AWARDS: Diamond Medal, Palette and Chisel, Chicago, IL, 1970, 71; Gold Medal, Palette and Chisel, 1972, 75; First Prize, Harriet Bittery Mem Award, 1976
PRINTERS: Artist (ART)
PUBLISHERS: de Lama Gallery, Chicago, IL (dLG)
GALLERIES: de Lama Gallery, Chicago, IL
MAILING ADDRESS: 3005 Horation St, Tampa, FL 33609

ALBERTO DE LAMA CONTINUED

TITLE	PUBLISHER	PRINTER	DATE	MEDIUM	DIMENSION (PAPER SIZE) IN INCHES	TYPE OF PAPER	EDITION NUMBER	NO. OF COLORS	ORIGINAL OPENING PRICE	CURRENT RETAIL PRICE
SOLD OUT EDITIONS (RARE):										
Nude	dLG	ART	1978	EB	8 X 4	ST	25	1	75	350
Newspaper Stand	dLG	ART	1978	AB	8 X 6	ST	35	1	70	300
Flowers	dLG	ART	1979	EB	5 X 7	ST	43	1	55	300
Landscape	dLG	ART	1980	EB	5 X 7	ST	50	1	80	350
Mountains	dLG	ART	1980	EB	9 X 4	ST	60	1	60	350
CURRENT EDITIONS:										
En Su Burrito	dLG	ART	1980	WB	9 X 6	R	50	1	75	250
El Arriero	dLG	ART	1980	AB	4 X 8	MUR	75	1	75	250
Flower Vendor	dLG	ART	1980	AB	8 X 4	ST	35	1	45	200
The Big Red Machine	dLG	ART	1980	EB	18 X 24	ST	120	1	200	350
Grape Vendor	dLG	ART	1980	EB	24 X 17	ST	80	1	120	250
Chippewa Elder	dLG	ART	1980	EB	6 X 7	ST	85	1	80	200
Wisconsin Barn	dLG	ART	1980	EB	5 X 7	ST	80	1	70	200
Wausau Farm	dLG	ART	1980	EB	4 X 8	ST	85	1	65	200

NICOLA DE MARIA

BORN: Foglianise, Italy; 1954
COLLECTIONS: Kunsthalle, Basel, Switzerland
PRINTERS: Atleier Franck Bordas, Paris, France (AFB)
PUBLISHERS: Galerie Lelong, New York, NY & Paris, France (GL)
GALLERIES: Laura Carpenter Fine Art, Santa Fe, NM; Galerie Lelong, New York, NY & Paris, France; Nohra Haime Gallery, New York, NY

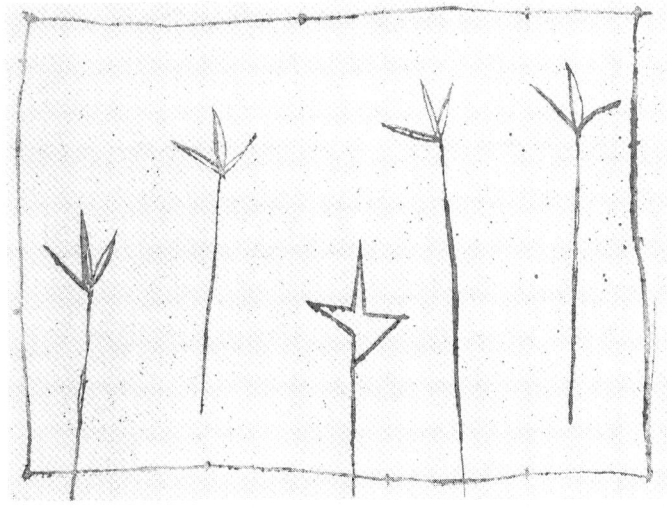

Nicola De Maria
Regno dei Fiore &
Sentimenti Invernali Dipinti
Courtesy Galerie Lelong

TITLE	PUBLISHER	PRINTER	DATE	MEDIUM	DIMENSION (PAPER SIZE) IN INCHES	TYPE OF PAPER	EDITION NUMBER	NO. OF COLORS	ORIGINAL OPENING PRICE	CURRENT RETAIL PRICE
CURRENT EDITIONS:										
Regno dei Fiori & Sentiment: Invernali Dipinti	GL	AFB	1991	LB	47 X 63	FAB	27	1	1700	1700
Soave Regno dei Fiori	GL	AFB	1991	LC/HC	47 X 63	FAB	18	Varies	4700	4700

WALTER DE MARIA

BORN: Albany, CA; October 1, 1935
EDUCATION: Univ of California, Berkeley, CA, MA, 1959
AWARDS: John Simon Guggenheim Fel, 1969–70; Mather Sculpture Prize, Art Inst of Chicago, IL, 1976
RECENT EXHIB: 65 Thompson Street Gallery, NY, 1989; Moderna Museet, Stockholm, Sweden, 1989; Munson-Williams-Proctor Inst, Utica, NY, 1989; DIA Art Found, NY, 1989,90; Gagosian Gallery, NY, 1989,92
COLLECTIONS: Mus of Mod Art, NY; Whitney Mus of Am Art, NY; Kunstmuseum, Basil, Switzerland; Mus Boymans-von Beuingen, Rotterdam, The Netherlands
PUBLISHERS: Artist (ART)
PRINTERS: Artist (ART)
GALLERIES: Gagosian Gallery, New York, NY; 65 Thompson Street Gallery, New York, NY; Galerie Lelong, New York, & Paris, France & Zürich, Switzerland; Lennon/Weinberg Gallery, New York, NY
MAILING ADDRESS: 421 E Sixth St, New York, NY 10009

The retail prices of the 100,000 limited edition prints quoted in this directory are subject to change. Print publishers, artists and galleries were the direct sources for these quotations. Prices in the secondary market listed as "Sold Out Editions (Rare)" indicate that the publisher has a limited supply of that print or that the print is difficult to locate in the galleries.

WALTER DE MARIA CONTINUED

TITLE	PUBLISHER	PRINTER	DATE	MEDIUM	DIMENSION (PAPER SIZE) IN INCHES	TYPE OF PAPER	EDITION NUMBER	NO. OF COLORS	ORIGINAL OPENING PRICE	CURRENT RETAIL PRICE
CURRENT EDITIONS:										
Pure Polygon Series (Boxed Series of 7 Drawings)	ART	ART	1975–86	DRAW	36 X 36	AE	21		16000	20000

NICK DE MATTIES

BORN: Honolulu, HI; October 19, 1939
EDUCATION: Long Beach State Col, CA, BA, 1964; Inst of Design, Chicago, IL, with Misch Kohn, MS, 1967
TEACHING: Instr, Printmaking & Drawing, San Diego State Col, Ca, 1967–69; Asst Prof, Mount St Mary's Col, CA, 1969–70; Vis Prof, Printing, Univ of Oregon, Eugene, OR, 1972; Instr, Albion Col, MI, 1973–74; Asst Prof, Printmaking & Drawing Arizona State Univ, Tempe, AZ, 1974–76; Assoc Prof, 1977 to present
AWARDS: Jurors Award, Phoenix Art Mus, AZ, 1977; Purchase Award, Nat Print & Drawing Exhib, Peoria, IL, 1977; Award, Oklahoma Art Center, Oklahoma City, OK, 1977; Award, Scottsdale Center for the Arts, AZ, 1977; Western State Arts Found Fel, 1979; Award, Texas Fine Arts Assn, Austin, TX, 1984; Award of Distinction, Tucson Mus of Art, AZ, Ivan Karp, Juror, 1984–85; Laguna Gloria Mus, Austin, TX, 1984,85; Collier Gallery, Scottsdale, AZ, 1986; Tucson Mus, AZ, 1988
COLLECTIONS: Los Angeles County Mus, CA; Brooklyn Mus, NY; Phoenix Art Mus, AZ; Portland Art Mus, OR; Cabinet des Estampes, Bibliotheque Nat, Paris, France; San Francisco Mus of Mod Art, CA; Univ of Houston, TX; Arizona State Univ, Tempe, AZ; Univ of Chicago, IL; San Diego State Univ, CA; Univ of Oregon, Eugene, OR; Univ of Arizona, Tucson, AZ; Houghton Col, NY; State Univ of New York, Buffalo, NY; Brown Univ, Providence, RI; Univ of Iowa, Iowa City, IA; Albion Col, MI; Bradley Univ Sch of Art, Peoria, IL; Oklahoma Art Center, Oklahoma City, OK
PRINTERS: Chantal Guillemin, Phoenix, AZ (CG); Sylvia Robertson, Phoenix, AZ (SR); Artist (ART)
PUBLISHERS: Artist (ART)
GALLERIES: Collier Gallery, Scottsdale, AZ; The Studio, Phoenix, AZ
MAILING ADDRESS: 233 N 10th St, Phoenix, AZ 85006

TITLE	PUBLISHER	PRINTER	DATE	MEDIUM	DIMENSION (PAPER SIZE) IN INCHES	TYPE OF PAPER	EDITION NUMBER	NO. OF COLORS	ORIGINAL OPENING PRICE	CURRENT RETAIL PRICE
CURRENT EDITIONS:										
Night Time	ART	ART	1977	I/CC	22 X 30	AP/B	25	7	250	800
The Shadow	ART	ART	1977	I/CC	22 X 30	AC	30	5	250	700
The Dream	ART	ART	1977	I/CC	22 X 30	AP/W	30	5	250	700
Steps #1	ART	ART	1977	I/CC	22 X 30	AP/W	75	5	125	400
Steps #2	ART	ART	1977	I/CC	22 X 30	AP/W	40	4	250	1250
H–H	ART	ART/SR/CG	1977	I/CC	22 X 30	RP/G	40	9	250	700
h	ART	ART/SR/CG	1977–78	I/CC	22 X 30	RP/G	40	5	250	700
Ear	ART	ART/CG	1978	I/CC	22 X 30	AC	40		250	1250
Pilot	ART	ART/CG	1978	I/CC	22 X 30	AC	30	7	250	700
Ball	ART	ART/CG	1978	I/CC	22 X 30	AP/W	40	6	250	800
Fence	ART	ART/CG	1978	I/CC	22 X 30	RP/G	35	5	250	700
Eyes	ART	ART/CG	1978	I/CC	22 X 30	R/BFK	40	5	250	800
Diver	ART	ART/CG	1978	I/CC	22 X 30	AC	30	7	250	700
Scout	ART	ART/SR	1978	I/CC	22 X 30	AP/W	35	6	250	700
Fate	ART	ART/SR/CG	1978	I/CC	22 X 30	AP/W	25	7	250	700
Kitt Peak	ART	ART/SR/CG	1978	I/CC	22 X 30	AC	40	4	250	800
Chains	ART	ART/CG	1978	I/CC	22 X 30	AC	40	5	250	700
The Walk	ART	ART/CG	1978	I/CC	22 X 30	AC	30	5	250	700
A–Z	ART	ART/SR/CG	1978	I/CC	22 X 30	AP/B	30	4	250	700
Apple	ART	ART/CG	1978	I/CC	22 X 30	AC	30	8	250	700
Dawn	ART	ART/CG	1978	I/CC	22 X 30	AC	40	6	250	700
Myth	ART	ART/SR/CG	1978	I/CC	22 X 30	AP/W	40	6	250	700

OSCAR DE MEJO

BORN: Trieste, Italy; (1911–1992); U S Citizen
COLLECTIONS: Musee de L'Art Naif, Nice, France; Fraunces Tavern Mus, NY; Bayly Art Mus, Charlottesville, VA
PRINTERS: Artist (ART); Har-El Printers, Jaffa, Israel (HarEl)
PUBLISHERS: Nahan Editions, New Orleans, LA (NE)
GALLERIES: Nahan Galleries, New Orleans, LA & New York, NY & Tokyo, Japan; Contini Galeria de Arte, Caracas, Venezuela; Pocket Gallery, London, England

TITLE	PUBLISHER	PRINTER	DATE	MEDIUM	DIMENSION (PAPER SIZE) IN INCHES	TYPE OF PAPER	EDITION NUMBER	NO. OF COLORS	ORIGINAL OPENING PRICE	CURRENT RETAIL PRICE
CURRENT EDITIONS:										
Bouquet	NE	ART	1987	LC/HC	15 X 22	AP	45	6	350	400
Roseland	NE	ART	1987	LC/HC	22 X 15	AP	45	5	350	400
One-Two-Three	NE	ART	1987	LC/HC	22 X 15	AP	45	6	350	400
Two Ladies	NE	ART	1988	LC/HC	15 X 22	AP	45	6	350	400
Rainbow (of Birds)	NE	HarEl	1989	SP	26 X 21	AP	275	12	300	300
Creation	NE	HarEl	1989	SP	26 X 21	AP	275	8	300	300

The retail prices of the 100,000 limited edition prints quoted in this directory are subject to change. Print publishers, artists and galleries were the direct sources for these quotations. Prices in the secondary market listed as "Sold Out Editions (Rare)" indicate that the publisher has a limited supply of that print or that the print is difficult to locate in the galleries.

The Printworld Directory is accepting new applications for the seventh edition. Approximately 300 new artists will be accepted. Please use the two forms provided in the back section of this directory to submit biographical data and documentation of prints. Edition number of each print must not exceed 500 and the retail price must be $100 or more.

BRETT DE PALMA

BORN: Lexington, KY; June 19, 1949
EDUCATION: Peabody Col, Nashville, TN, BA, 1970; Boston Sch of Mus & Fine Arts, MA, MFA, 1972; Tufts Univ, Medford, MA, MFA, 1973
TEACHING: Vis Fel, Painting, Princeton, NJ, 1989 to present; Lectr, Painting, Sch of Visual Arts, NY, 1989 to present
AWARDS: Nat Endowment for the Arts Grant, 1987
RECENT EXHIB: Univ of Massachusetts, Amherst, MA, 1987; Anders Tornberg Gallery, Lund, Sweden, 1988; Fawbush Editions, NY, 1988,89; Philippe Briet Gallery, NY, 1989; Colleen Greco Gallery, NY, 1990; Tennessee State Mus, Nashville, TN, 1990; Jacob Karpio San Juan Costa Rica, 1990; Indiana Univ, Bloomington, IN, 1990; Ft Wayne Mus, IN, 1990; Tennessee Art Comm, Nashville, TN, 1990; Robert Thomson Gallery, Minneapolis, MN, 1990
COLLECTIONS: Kunsthalle, Malmo, Sweden; Tennessee State Mus, Nashville, TN; Smithsonian Inst, Wash, DC
PRINTERS: David Keister, Bloomington, IN (DK); David Calkins, Bloomington, IN (DC); Echo Press, Bloomington, IN (EPr)
PUBLISHERS: Echo Press, Bloomington, IN (EPr)
GALLERIES: Robert Thomson Gallery, Minneapolis, MN; Philippe Briet Gallery, New York, NY; Fawbush Editions, New York, NY; Echo Press, Bloomington, IN
MAILING ADDRESS: 262 Mott St, New York, NY 10012

Brett De Palma
Four Corners of the World
Courtesy Echo Press

TITLE	PUBLISHER	PRINTER	DATE	MEDIUM	DIMENSION (PAPER SIZE) IN INCHES	TYPE OF PAPER	EDITION NUMBER	NO. OF COLORS	ORIGINAL OPENING PRICE	CURRENT RETAIL PRICE
CURRENT EDITIONS:										
Four Corners of the World (4 Parts)	EPr	DK/DC/EPr	1988	LC/EB/A/SL/LI/WC	52 X 41	AC & CRP	25	6	2000	2500
Trotters	EPr	DK/DC/EPr	1988	MON	24 X 31 EA	AC/W	1 EA	Varies	650 EA	750 EA
Chinese Vase with Head	EPr	DK/DC/EPr	1988	MON	42 X 30 EA	AC/W	1 EA		750 EA	900 EA

MICHEL DE SAINT-ALBAN

BORN: Paris, France
COLLECTIONS: Houston Com Col, TX

TITLE	PUBLISHER	PRINTER	DATE	MEDIUM	DIMENSION (PAPER SIZE) IN INCHES	TYPE OF PAPER	EDITION NUMBER	NO. OF COLORS	ORIGINAL OPENING PRICE	CURRENT RETAIL PRICE
CURRENT EDITIONS:										
Coin de Peche	POFA	SER	1982	SP	29 X 35	R/100	200	28	240	350
Tournus	POFA	SER	1982	SP	29 X 35	R/100	200	28	240	350
Barque Sur la Saone	POFA	SER	1982	SP	29 X 35	R/100	200	28	240	350
Fermeture Anneulle	POFA	JK	1982	LC	22 X 29	SOM	200	12	240	350
L'Epine	POFA	JK	1982	LC	22 X 29	SOM	200	12	240	350
Le Loir	POFA	JK	1982	LC	22 X 29	SOM	200	12	240	350

NIKI DE SAINT-PHALLE

RECENT EXHiB: Nassau County Mus of Fine Art, Roslyn Harbor, NY, 1989; Gimpel & Weitzenhoffer Gallery, NY, 1990; Galerie Wild, Frankfurt, Germany, 1992

PRINTERS: Lichtenstein Publishers, NY (LP)
PUBLISHERS: Lichtenstein Publishers, NY (LP)
GALLERIES: Hokin Galleries, Bay Harbor Islands, FL & Palm Beach, FL; Gimpel & Weitzenhoffer Gallery, NY; Gimpel Fils Gallery, London, England; Merryman Collection, Stanford, CA; Galerie Wild, Frankfurt, Germany

TITLE	PUBLISHER	PRINTER	DATE	MEDIUM	DIMENSION (PAPER SIZE) IN INCHES	TYPE OF PAPER	EDITION NUMBER	NO. OF COLORS	ORIGINAL OPENING PRICE	CURRENT RETAIL PRICE
CURRENT EDITIONS:										
Nana Power Series I, II, III, IV	LP	LP	1974	SP		AP	115 EA		175 EA	850 EA

JAMES DE WOODY

BORN: Texas; May 31, 1945
EDUCATION: Tulane Univ, New Orleans, LA, BA, 1967; Pratt Inst, NY, MFA, 1972

TEACHING: Philadelphia Col of Art, PA, 1975–77; New York Univ, NY 1978–81
COLLECTIONS: New York Univ, NY

JAMES DE WOODY CONTINUED

PRINTERS: Roni Henning, NY (RH); Ted Warner, NY (TW); Artist (ART); Judith Solodkin, NY (JS); Solo Press, NY (SP)
PUBLISHERS: Orion Editions, NY (OE); Artist (ART); Solo Press, NY (SP)
GALLERIES: Orion Editions, New York, NY; Arthur Roger Gallery, New Orleans, LA; Andrea Marquit Fine Art, New York, NY; Mary Ryan Gallery, New York, NY; Piestrosana Gallery, New York, NY; More Gallery, Phila, PA; Associated American Artists, New York, NY
MAILING ADDRESS: 146 Franklin St, New York, NY 10013

TITLE	PUBLISHER	PRINTER	DATE	MEDIUM	DIMENSION (PAPER SIZE) IN INCHES	TYPE OF PAPER	EDITION NUMBER	NO. OF COLORS	ORIGINAL OPENING PRICE	CURRENT RETAIL PRICE
CURRENT EDITIONS:										
Untitled	OE	RH	1979	STEN	22 X 31		50	7	200	500
Lehigh-Starett	ART	TW	1985	WC	21 X 21	AC	50	3	400	600
Remaisnil	ART	ART	1989	PO/C	39 X 38	AC	6	3	950	1200
Ten Images of the City (Set of 10):									4000 SET	6000 SET
10th Avenue At 32nd STreet	SP	JS/SP	1987	PO/ACRYLIC	24 X 24	AC	30		600	750
3rd Avenue at 53rd Street	SP	JS/SP	1987	PO/ACRYLIC	24 X 24	AC	30		600	800
53rd Street at Lexington Avenue	SP	JS/SP	1987	PO/ACRYLIC	24 X 24	AC	30		600	750
53rd Street at 3rd Avenue	SP	JS/SP	1987	PO/ACRYLIC	24 X 24	AC	30		600	750
55th Street at Madison Avenue	SP	JS/SP	1987	PO/ACRYLIC	24 X 24	AC	30		600	750
90th Street at East End Avenue	SP	JS/SP	1987	PO/ACRYLIC	24 X 24	AC	30		600	750
First Avenue at 24th Street	SP	JS/SP	1987	PO/ACRYLIC	24 X 24	AC	30		600	750
Lexington at 48th Street	SP	JS/SP	1987	PO/ACRYLIC	24 X 24	AC	30		600	750
Park Avenue at 79th Street	SP	JS/SP	1987	PO/ACRYLIC	24 X 24	AC	30		600	750
West Broadway at Walker Street	SP	JS/SP	1987	PO/ACRYLIC	24 X 24	AC	30		600	750

RICHARD DEACON

BORN: Bangor, Wales; 1949
EDUCATION: Somerset Col of Art, Taunton, Wales, 1968-69; St Martin's Col of Art, London, England, 1969-72; Royal Col of Art, London, England,1974-77; Chelsea Sch of Art,London, England, 1977-78
AWARDS: Turner Prize, Sculpture, London, England, 1987
RECENT EXHIB: Hirshhorn Mus, Wash, DC,1987; Lisson Gallery, London, England, 1987; Kunstmuseum, Luzern, Switzerland, 1987; Fundacion Caja de Pensiones, Madrid, Spain, 1987; Mus van Hedendaagse Kunst, Antwerp, Belgium, 1987; Mus of Contemp Art, Los Angeles, CA, 1988; Art Gallery of Ontario, Toronto, Canada, 1988; Carnegie Mus of Art, Pittsburgh, PA, 1988; Ecoles des Beaux Arts de Macon, Paris, France, 1988; Tate Gallery, London, England, 1988; Musee de'Art Mod de la Ville de Paris, Paris, France, 1989; Whitechapel Art Gallery, London, England, 1989-90; Kunstnerner, Oslo, Norway, 1990; Marian Goodman Gallery, NY, 1990; Donald Young Gallery, Chicago, IL, 1989
PRINTERS: Peter Kneubühler, Zürich, Switzerland (PK)
PUBLISHERS: Margarete Roeder Editions,NY (MRE)
GALLERIES: Margarete Roeder Gallery, New York, NY; Marian Goodman Gallery, New York, NY; Whitechapel Art Gallery, London, England; Donald Young Gallery, Seattle, WA

TITLE	PUBLISHER	PRINTER	DATE	MEDIUM	DIMENSION (PAPER SIZE) IN INCHES	TYPE OF PAPER	EDITION NUMBER	NO. OF COLORS	ORIGINAL OPENING PRICE	CURRENT RETAIL PRICE
CURRENT EDITIONS:										
Muzot (Set of 4)	MRE	PK	1987	EB	25 X 25 EA	R/BFK	25 EA	1 EA	4000 SET	5000 SET
Untitled	MRE	PK	1987	EB/REL	22 X 15	R/BFK	25	1	750	1000

PETER DEAN

BORN: Berlin, MT; July 9, 1939
EDUCATION: Cornell Univ, Ithaca, NY; Univ of Wisconsin, Madison, WI, BA; Pratt Graphic Art Center, NY
AWARDS: Creative Artists Public Service Grant, NY, 1975–1976; Nat Endowment for the Arts Fel, 1981
RECENT EXHIB: San Antonio Art Inst, TX, 1988; Koplin Gallery, Los Angeles, CA, 1987,89; North Dakota Mus of Art, Grand Forks, ND, 1989; Retrosp, Alternative Mus, NY, 1990; Clark Gallery, Lincoln, MA, 1989,92; Alternative Mus, NY, 1992; R H Love Contemporary, Chicago, IL, 1992
COLLECTIONS: Mus of Mod Art, NY; Brooklyn Mus, NY; Los Angeles County Mus, Los Angeles, CA; Nat Call of Art, Wash, DC; Art Inst of Chicago, IL; Madison Art Center, WI
PRINTERS: Landfall Press Inc, Chicago, IL (LPI); Jack Lemon, Chicago, IL (JL); Barbara Spies, Chicago, IL (BS)
PUBLISHERS: Landfall Press Inc. , Chicago, IL (LPI)
GALLERIES: Landfall Press Inc, Chicago, IL & New York, NY; Jerald Melberg Gallery, Charlotte, NC; Heath Gallery, Atlanta, GA; Darthea Speyer Gallery, Paris, France; Alexandre Monett Gallery, Brussels, Belgium; Allan Stone Gallery, New York, NY; Struve Gallery, Chicago, IL; Osuna Gallery, Wash, DC; Koplin Gallery, Los Angeles, CA; Snyderman Gallery, Phila, PA; Koplin Gallery, Los Angeles, CA; Read Stremmel Gallery, San Antonio, TX; Shahin Requicha Gallery, Manhattan Beach, CA; Bienville Gallery, New Orleans, LA; R H Love Contemporary, Chicago, IL; Gasperi Gallery, New Orleans, LA

Peter Dean
Hear No Evil
Courtesy Landfall Press, Inc

PETER DEAN CONTINUED

TITLE	PUBLISHER	PRINTER	DATE	MEDIUM	DIMENSION (PAPER SIZE) IN INCHES	TYPE OF PAPER	EDITION NUMBER	NO. OF COLORS	ORIGINAL OPENING PRICE	CURRENT RETAIL PRICE
SOLD OUT EDITIONS (RARE):										
Summer Interior	LPI	JL/BS/LPI	1983	LC	24 X 38	AP/W	25	4	450	650
The Hypnotist	LPI	JL/LPI	1983	SP	26 X 38	R/BFK	25	5	450	650
Hear No Evil	LPI	JL/LPI	1983	LC	26 X 34	AP/W	25	2	450	650

JEANNETTE DEBONNE

BORN: Huntington Park, CA; December 2, 1937
EDUCATION: Univ of California, Los Angeles, CA, BA, 1959
RECENT EXHIB: Retrospective Gallery, La Jolla, CA, 1989

PRINTERS: Palo Verde Press, Palm Springs, CA (PVP)
PUBLISHERS: Palo Verde Press, Palm Springs, CA (PVP)
GALLERIES: Mokotoff Gallery, New York, NY; Aaron Aubrey Contemporary Fine Art, Santa Monica, CA
MAILING ADDRESS: 653 Commercial Rd, #3, Palm Springs, CA 92262

TITLE	PUBLISHER	PRINTER	DATE	MEDIUM	DIMENSION (PAPER SIZE) IN INCHES	TYPE OF PAPER	EDITION NUMBER	NO. OF COLORS	ORIGINAL OPENING PRICE	CURRENT RETAIL PRICE
CURRENT EDITIONS:										
Catalunya Suite (with Gold Leaf) (Series of 50)	PVP	PVP	1985	MON/HC	22 X 30 EA	R/BFK	1 EA	4 EA	300 EA	400 EA
Spirit Window Suite (Series of 24)	PVP	PVP	1986	MON	30 X 23 EA	RdL	1 EA	8 EA	350 EA	400 EA
Spirit Window Suite (Series of 8)	PVP	PVP	1986	MON	30 X 22 EA	AC	1 EA	8 EA	350 EA	400 EA
Spirit Window Suite (Series of 6)	PVP	PVP	1986	MON	27 X 21 EA	COL/W	1 EA	8 EA	300 EA	350 EA
Spirit Window Suite (Series of 6)	PVP	PVP	1986	MON	27 X 21 EA	COL/CR	1 EA	8 EA	300 EA	350 EA
Spirit Window Suite (Series of 6)	PVP	PVP	1986	MON	44 X 30 EA	R-BFK/CR	1 EA	8 EA	550 EA	600 EA
Spirit Window Suite (Series of 6)	PVP	PVP	1986	MON	40 X 30 EA	AC	1 EA	8 EA	550 EA	600 EA
Spirit Window Suite (Series of 6)	PVP	PVP	1986	MON	31 X 23 EA	RdB	1 EA	8 EA	350 EA	400 EA

GEORGE DEEM

BORN: Vincennes, IN; August 18, 1932
EDUCATION: Art Inst of Chicago Sch, IL, BFA, 1958
TEACHING: Instr, Sch of Visual Arts, NY, 1965–66; Instr, Painting, Leicester Polytechnic, London, England, 1966–67; Instr, Painting, Univ of Pennsylvania, Phila, PA, 1967–68
RECENT EXHIB: Indianapolis Center for Contemp Art, IN, 1988,90

COLLECTIONS: Indianapolis Art Mus, IN; Ludwig Coll, Neue Galerie Aachen, West Germany; Evansville Mus of Arts & Sciences, IN; Albright-Knox Art Gallery, Buffalo, NY; Allen Mem Art Mus, Oberlin Col, OH
PRINTERS: Sienna Studios, NY (SS); Jorge Dumas, NY (JD)
PUBLISHERS: Jackie Fine Art, NY (JFA)
GALLERIES: Allan Stone Gallery, New York, NY; Nancy Hoffman Gallery, New York, NY; Merida Gallery, Inc, Farmington, KY
MAILING ADDRESS: 10 W 18th St, New York, NY 10011

TITLE	PUBLISHER	PRINTER	DATE	MEDIUM	DIMENSION (PAPER SIZE) IN INCHES	TYPE OF PAPER	EDITION NUMBER	NO. OF COLORS	ORIGINAL OPENING PRICE	CURRENT RETAIL PRICE
CURRENT EDITIONS:										
Random House	JFA	JD	1980	LC	16 X 25	AC	300	6	200	250
Milk	JFA	SS	1980	LC	19 X 26	AC	300	5	200	250
Hands off Mayakousky	JFA	JD	1980	LC	19 X 17	AC	300	8	200	250
Dutch Painting on Vermeer's Easel	JFA	JD	1980	LC	21 X 19	AC	300	6	200	250
Composition in Red and Black (Vermeer, Rubins)	JFA	SS	1980	LC	26 X 19	AC	300	4	200	250
George Washington, George Washington	JFA	SS	1980	LC	21 X 17	AC	300	6	200	250

ADOLF ARTHUR DEHN

BORN: Waterville, MN; (1895–1968)
EDUCATION: Minneapolis Inst, MN; Art Students League, NY
AWARDS: Philadelphia Art Alliance, PA, 1936; Philadelphia Print Club, PA, 1939; Guggenheim Found Fel, 1939,51; Library of Congress, Pennell Purchase Prize Award, 1946
RECENT EXHIB: Barnard's Mill Art Mus, Glen Rose, TX, 1992; State Historical Society of Missouri, Columbia, MO, 1992

COLLECTIONS: Museum of Mod Art, NY; Metropolitan Mus of Art, NY; Whitney Mus of Am Art, NY; Brooklyn Mus, NY; Mus of Fine Art, Boston, MA; Art Inst of Chicago, IL; Cleveland Mus of Art, OH; Cincinnati Mus of Art, OI I; Minneapolis Inst, MN; Newark Mus, NJ; Herron Mus, Indianapolis, IN; Lehigh Univ, Bethlehem, PA
PRINTERS: Artist (ART); George Miller, NY (GM)
PUBLISHERS: Artist (ART); Associated American Artists, NY (AAA)
GALLERIES: Harmon-Meek Gallery, Naples, FL; Harmon-Meek Third Street Gallery, Harbor Springs, MI; Touchstone Gallery, Wash, DC; Susan Teller Gallery, New York, NY; Sande Garcia Fine Arts, Miami, FL

TITLE	PUBLISHER	PRINTER	DATE	MEDIUM	DIMENSION (PAPER SIZE) IN INCHES	TYPE OF PAPER	EDITION NUMBER	NO. OF COLORS	ORIGINAL OPENING PRICE	CURRENT RETAIL PRICE
SOLD OUT EDITIONS (RARE):										
Clowns	ART	ART	1928	LC	9 X 13	WOVE	25		25	500
Paris Lithographs (Set of 10)	ART	ART	1928	LC	9 X 13 EA	WOVE	50 EA		200 SET	7500 SET
Sisters at the Palace	ART	ART	1928	LC/CC	9 X 13	WOVE	25		25	650
Dog's Life	ART	ART	1930	LC	10 X 14		20		35	1500
Central Park	ART	ART	1931	LC	8 X 13	WOVE	20		35	1000

ADOLPH A DEHN CONTINUED

TITLE	PUBLISHER	PRINTER	DATE	MEDIUM	DIMENSION (PAPER SIZE) IN INCHES	TYPE OF PAPER	EDITION NUMBER	NO. OF COLORS	ORIGINAL OPENING PRICE	CURRENT RETAIL PRICE
SOLD OUT EDITIONS (RARE):										
Snow in the Mountains	ART	ART	1931	LC	9 X 12	WOVE	25		35	250
We Nordics	ART	ART	1931	LC/CC	14 X 11	WOVE	25		35	2500
26 Men and a Girl	ART	ART	1932	LC/CC	9 X 15	WOVE	20		35	800
Broadway Parade	AAA	GM	1934	LC		WOVE	100		50	700
Minnesota Farm	AAA	GM	1935	LC		WOVE	100		50	500
Minnesota Farmyard	AAA	GM	1935	LC		WOVE	100		50	400
Innocence in Venice	AAA	GM	1937	LC	9 X 13	WOVE	100		60	250
Peaceful Cove	AAA	AA	1938	LC	8 X 13	WOVE	161		60	250
Threshing	AAA	AA	1938	LC	8 X 13	WOVE	160		60	200
Threshing Scene	AAA	AA	1938	LC	10 X 13	WOVE	162		60	350
The Great God Pan	AAA	AA	1939	LC	10 X 14	WOVE	30		75	1000
Colorado Sunflowers	AAA	AA	1941	LC	10 X 14	WOVE			80	450
Circus	AAA	AA	1942	LC	13 X 17	WOVE	50		80	1200
Boulder Dam I	AAA	AA	1942	LC	15 X 21	WOVE	35		80	1000
Black Mountain	AAA	AA	1942	LC	13 X 17	WOVE			80	450
Fishing in Colorado	AAA	AA	1944	LB	9 X 13	WOVE	250	1	75	400
Before the Fall		AA	1945	LC	13 X 18	WOVE	50		80	750
Mademoiselle Fifi		AA	1945	LB	15 X 11	WOVE			60	350
Boulder Dam II		AA	1946	LC	15 X 21	WOVE	25		80	900
Venezuelan Village	AAA	AA	1946	LB	9 X 13	WOVE	250	1	75	150
Women in the Rockies	AAA	AA	1946	LB	9 X 13	WOVE	250	1	75	150
Women are all Alike	AAA	AA	1946	LC	17 X 13	WOVE	30		100	1000
Central Park Lake and . . .	AAA	AA	1947	LC	9 X 13	WOVE	30		100	1000
Farm in Summer	AAA	AA	1947	LB	4 X 5	WOVE	250	1	80	300
A Fine Day on the Farm	AAA	AA	1947	LB	9 X 13	WOVE	250	1	80	150
Black Mountain	AAA	AA	1947	LB	13 X 17	WOVE	250	1	80	350
Lake in Central Park	AAA	AA	1947	LB	9 X 13	WOVE	250	1	80	800
The Lake	AAA	AA	1949	LB	10 X 13	WOVE	250	1	90	300
Mountain in Autumn	AAA	AA	1949	LC	13 X 17	WOVE	30		120	800
North Country Lake	AAA	AA	1949	LC	10 X 14	WOVE	250		100	650
Lake Country	AAA	AA	1949	LB	9 X 13	WOVE	250	1	100	175
Market in Haiti	AAA	AA	1952	LB	10 X 14	WOVE	250	1	115	450
Nice Summer Day	AAA	AA	1954	LB	10 X 14	WOVE	250	1	125	150
Summer Day	AAA	AA	1954	LB	10 X 14	WOVE	250	1	125	250
October Sunday	AAA	AA	1955	LC	10 X 14	WOVE			135	800
King of India	AAA	AA	1960	LC	14 X 18	AP	25		150	1800
Country Night	AAA	AA	1963	LC	18 X 14	AP	200		150	650
Migration Upwards	AAA	AA	1963	LC	18 X 14	AP	20		150	650
Proud Bull	AAA	AA	1963	LC	18 X 14	AP	20		150	350
Central Park Winter	AAA	AA	1965	LC	15 X 21	AP	150	3	200	700

DOROTHY DEHNER

BORN: Cleveland, OH; December 23, 1901
EDUCATION: Univ of California, Los Angeles, CA; Skidmore Col, NY, BS; Art Students League, NY; Atelier 17, NY; Hon Degree, Skidmore Col, NY, 1982; Hon Degree, Womans Art Degree, 1983
AWARDS: Art in Res, Tamarind Lithography Inst, Albuquerque, NM, 1970–71; Yaddo Found Fel, 1971
RECENT EXHIB: State Univ of New York, New Paltz, NY, 1990; Phillips Coll, Wash, DC, 1990; Muhlenberg Col, Frank Martin Art Gallery, Allentown, PA, 1990; Twinning Gallery, NY, 1990; Malcolm Brown Gallery, Cleveland, OH, 1990; Muhlenberg Col, Frank Martin Art Gallery, Allentown, PA, 1992
COLLECTIONS: Metropolitan Mus of Art, NY; Mus of Mod Art, NY; Seattle Art Mus, WA; Minneapolis Art Mus, MN; Cleveland Mus, OH
PRINTERS: Artist (ART); Teller 8 (T-8)
PUBLISHERS: Artist (ART)
GALLERIES: Twining Gallery, New York, NY; Susan Teller Gallery, New York, NY; Associated American Artists, New York, NY; Malcolm Brown Gallery, Cleveland, OH
MAILING ADDRESS: 33 Fifth Ave, New York, NY 10003

Dorothy Dehner
Bird Machine #2
Courtesy Associated American Artists

TITLE	PUBLISHER	PRINTER	DATE	MEDIUM	DIMENSION (PAPER SIZE) IN INCHES	TYPE OF PAPER	EDITION NUMBER	NO. OF COLORS	ORIGINAL OPENING PRICE	CURRENT RETAIL PRICE
SOLD OUT EDITIONS (RARE):										
Bird Machine #2	ART	ART/T-8	1953	EB	8 X 14	R/100	20	1	50	2000
The Maiden Aunts	ART	ART/T-8	1953	EB/A/ENG	6 X 7	R/100	20	1	50	500
Ancestors	ART	ART/T-8	1954	ENG	2 X 9	HMP	25	1	50	500

MICHEL DELACROIX

BORN: Paris, France; 1933
EDUCATION: Lycee Louis-Le-Grand, France
AWARDS: Prix Pro Arte, Morges, Switzerland, 1973; Grand Prix des Amateurs d'Art, Paris, France, 1975; Prix de la Cotes D'Azure Cannes, 1976; Premier Prix des Sept Collines, Rome, Italy, 1976
RECENT EXHIB: Martin Lawrence Gallery, Short Hills, NJ, 1991
PRINTERS: Arts Litho, Paris, France (AL); Mourlot Imprimeurs, Paris, France (MI); Art Estampe, Paris, France (AEs); ChromaComp, Inc, NY (CCI); Chameleon Editions (ChEd); Hue Art Studio, Inc (HAS); Noblet Serigraphie, Inc, NY (NSI)
PUBLISHERS: Lublin Graphics, Greenwich, CT (LG); Circle Gallery, Ltd, Chicago, IL (CGL); Axelle Fine Art Co, NY (AFA); Chalk & Vermilion Fine Art, Greenwich, CT (CVFA)
GALLERIES: Studio 53 Art Gallery, New York, NY; Todd Galleries, Wellesley, MA; Daruma Gallery, Cedarhurst, NY; J-Michael Gallery, Edina, MN; Gallery One at Second Avenue, Denver, CO; Allyson Louis Gallery, Bethesda, MD; Charles Berry International, Bethesda, MD; Artists Showcase International, Hartsdale, NY; Lublin Collection Fine Art Gallery, New York, NY; Gallerie International, Dallas, TX; Circle Galleries, San Diego, CA & San Francisco, CA & Northbrook, IL & Pittsburgh, PA & Houston, TX & Soho, NY & Chicago, IL & Scottsdale, AZ & Beverly Hills, CA & Costa Mesa, CA & Sherman Oaks, CA & Palm Beach, FL & Honolulu, HI & New Orleans, LA & Las Vegas, NV & Seattle, WA; Gallery 121 International, New York, NY

Michel Delacroix
Autobus
Courtesy Lublin Graphics, Inc

TITLE	PUBLISHER	PRINTER	DATE	MEDIUM	DIMENSION (PAPER SIZE) IN INCHES	TYPE OF PAPER	EDITION NUMBER	NO. OF COLORS	ORIGINAL OPENING PRICE	CURRENT RETAIL PRICE
SOLD OUT EDITIONS (RARE):										
Chez Marcel	CGL	MI	1972	LC	24 X 30	AP	200	3	65	2300
Rue de Grenelle	LG	AL	1973	LC	26 X 20	AP/JP	150/100		75	2300
The Parade	CGL	MI	1974	LC	33 X 28	AP	200	4	135	2300
Moulin Rouge	LG	AL	1974	LC	26 X 20	AP/JP	150/100		75	2300
Cafe le Marsouin	LG	AL	1974	LC	26 X 20	AP/JP	150/100		80	2100
Le Defile	LG	AL	1974	LC	26 X 20	AP/JP	150/100		80	1400
Au Petit Marin	LG	AL	1974	LC	26 X 20	AP/JP	150/100	15	80	2100
Au Coin de la Rue	LG	AL	1975	LC	26 X 20	AP/JP	150/100		80	1400
A la Bonne Galette	LG	AL	1975	LC	26 X 20	AP	250		100	1500
Bord de la Seine	LG	AL	1975	LC	26 X 20	AP/JP	150/100		120	3500
Jours Heureux	LG	AL	1975	LC	26 X 20	AP/JP	150/100		120	1350
Place Furstenburg	LG	AL	1975	LC	26 X 20	AP/JP	150/100		120	4000
Au Petit Mousse	LG	AL	1975	LC	25 X 32 cm	AP	250		120	1350
Ballon Rouge	LG	AL	1975	LC	25 X 32 cm	AP	250		150	1800
Les Halles	LG	AL	1976	LC	26 X 20	AP/JP	150/100		120	3500
Au Gant d'Or	LG	AL	1976	LC	26 X 20	AP/JP	150/100		150	1350
L'Alsacienne	LG	AL	1976	LC	26 X 20	AP/JP	150/100		150	1350
Chez Camille	LG	AL	1976	LC	25 X 32 cm	AP	250		170	2300
Moulin de la Galette	LG	AL	1976	LC	26 X 32 cm	AP	250		170	1600
Vieux Paris	LG	AL	1976	LC	25 X 32 cm	AP/JP	150/100		170	2100
Marchand de Glaces	LG	AL	1976	LC	25 X 32 cm	AP/JP	150/100		170	1600
Soir d'Hiver	LG	AL	1976	LC	26 X 20	AP/JP	150/100		170	2850
Le Mariage	LG	AL	1976	LC	25 X 32 cm	AP/JP	150/100		170	2300
Liberte	LG	AL	1976	LC	25 X 32 cm	AP/JP	150/100		170	2300
Hotel de la Comete	LG	AL	1976	LC	26 X 20	AP/JP	150/100		170	1800
Pantheon	LG	AL	1976	LC	26 X 20	AP	250		170	1500
Aux Deux Amis	LG	AL	1977	LC	26 X 20	AP/JP	150/100		170	1500
Bonheur du Jour	LG	AL	1977	LC	26 X 20	AP/JP	150/100		180	2300
Marchande de Pommes de Terre	LG	AL	1977	LC	26 X 20	AP	250		170	1350
Arche de Noe	LG	AL	1977	LC	26 X 20	AP/JP	150/100		170	1350
Le Phaeton	LG	AL	1977	LC	26 X 20	AP/JP	150/100		180	1350
Chez Berthe	LG	AL	1977	LC	26 X 20	AP/JP	150/100		180	1350
Grande Hotel du Midi	LG	AL	1977	LC	26 X 20	AP/JP	150/100		180	1350
Eiffel Tower	LG	AL	1977	LC	32 X 22	AP	250		200	3500
Pere Tranquille	LG	AL	1977	LC	25 X 32 cm	AP/JP	150/100		180	1500
Le Cirque	LG	AL	1977	LC	25 X 32 cm	AP/JP	150/100		200	1500
Transport Parisien	LG	AL	1977	LC	25 X 32 cm	AP/JP	150/100		200	1500
Aux Mariniers	LG	AL	1977	LC	26 X 20	AP/JP	150/100		250	4200
Maison de M Martin	LG	AL	1978	LC	25 X 32 cm	AP/JP	150/100		250	1800
Le Marche	LG	AL	1978	LC	26 X 20	AP/JP	150/100		250	1800
Hotel Bellevue	LG	AL	1978	LC	25 X 32 cm	AP/JP	150/100		250	1500
Place des Vosges	LG	AL	1978	LC	25 X 32 cm	AP/JP	150/100	14	250	2600
A la Victoire	LG	AL	1978	LC	25 X 32 cm	AP/JP	150/100		250	1350
Soir d'Ete	LG	AL	1978	LC	26 X 20	AP/JP	150/100		250	1950
Carrousel	LG	AL	1978	LC	25 X 32 cm	AP/JP	150/100		300	1950
Rendezvous des Macons	LG	AL	1978	LC	25 X 32 cm	AP/JP	150/100		300	1500
Hotel Medicis	LG	AL	1978	LC	25 X 32 cm	AP/JP	150/100		300	1350
Moulin de la Galette en Ete	LG	AL	1978	LC	25 X 32 cm	AP/JP	150/100		300	1600

MICHEL DELACROIX CONTINUED

TITLE	PUBLISHER	PRINTER	DATE	MEDIUM	DIMENSION (PAPER SIZE) IN INCHES	TYPE OF PAPER	EDITION NUMBER	NO. OF COLORS	ORIGINAL OPENING PRICE	CURRENT RETAIL PRICE
SOLD OUT EDITIONS (RARE):										
Marchand de Sapins	LG	AL	1978	LC	25 X 32 cm	AP/JP	150/100		350	2300
Le Defile (Grande Taille)	LG	AL	1978	LC	25 X 32 cm	AP/JP	150/100		400	1350
L'Arret d'Omnibus	LG	AL	1978	LC	26 X 20	AP/JP	150/100		400	1400
Le Ramoneur	LG	AL	1978	LC	13 X 9	AP/JP	200/100		150	750
Drapeau pour Tous	LG	AL	1978	LC	13 X 9	AP/JP	200/100		150	750
L'Herboriste	LG	AL	1978	LC	26 X 20	AP/JP	150/150		400	750
La Bonne Rencontre	LG	AL	1978	LC	26 X 20	AP/JP	150/150		400	1350
Bord de la Seine Sous la Neige	LG	AL	1979	LC	25 X 32 cm	AP/JP	150/150		600	4200
Hommage a Rousseau	LG	AL	1979	LC	26 X 20	AP/JP	150/150		600	2700
A la Manille	LG	AL	1979	LC	25 X 32 cm	AP/JP	150/150		600	1350
Kiosque	LG	AL	1979	LC	25 X 32 cm	AP/JP	150/150		600	2700
Au Bon Vivant	LG	AL	1979	LC	26 X 20	AP/JP	150/150		600	1600
Sortie d'Ecole	LG	AL	1979	LC	25 X 32 cm	AP/JP	150/150		700	1600
Mt Vernon	LG	AL	1979	LC	22 X 23	AP/JP	150/150	16	700	1950
Place Contrescarpe	LG	AL	1979	LC	25 X 32 cm	AP/JP	150/125		700	1800
Place de la Bastille	LG	AL	1979	LC	25 X 32 cm	AP/JP	150/125		700	1800
Place Furstenburg	LG	AL	1979	LC	25 X 32 cm	AP/JP	150/125	12	700	4200
Place de l'Opera	LG	AL	1979	LC	25 X 32 cm	AP/JP	150/125		700	2300
Place de la Concorde	LG	AL	1979	LC	19 X 23	AP/JP	150/125	15	700	1800
CURRENT EDITIONS:										
Place Dauphine	LG	AL	1979	LC	25 X 32 cm	AP/JP	150/125		700	4200
Places de Paris Suite	LG	AL	1979	LC	25 X 32 cm	AP/JP			5000 SET	12000 SET
Metropolitan	LG	AL	1980	LC	19 X 24	AP/JP	150/150	16	700	1800
Guignol	LG	AL	1980	LC	19 X 24	AP/JP	150/150	19	700	1600
Nuit de Decembre	LG	AL	1980	LC	25 X 32 cm	AP/JP	150/150		800	4200
Moulin de Montmartre	LG	AL	1980	LC	19 X 24	AP/JP	150/150	16	700	1500
Fleche de Notre Dame	LG	AL	1980	LC	20 X 24	AP/JP	150/150	16	800	4200
Les Heures du Jour Suite	LG	AL	1981	LC	25 X 32 cm	AP/JP	150/125		4000 SET	9500 SET
Moulin Rouge	LG	AL	1981	LC	20 X 24	AP/JP	150/125	16	800	5000
Quai de la Seine au Matin	LG	AL	1981	LC	20 X 26	AP/JP	150/125	15	800	1600
Dejeuner au Restaurant	LG	AL	1981	LC	20 X 24	AP/JP	150/125	15	800	1600
Lever du Soleil	LG	AL	1981	LC	25 X 32 cm	AP/JP	150/150	15	800	1350
Crepuscule	LG	AL	1981	LC	25 X 32 cm	AP/JP	150/150		800	1750
Passage Cloute	LG	AL	1981	LC	25 X 32 cm	AP/JP	150/150		800	1400
Tour Eiffel la Nuit	LG	AL	1981	LC	18 X 24	AP/JP	150/150	16	500	950
Colleur d'Affiches	LG	AL	1981	LC	18 X 24	AP/JP	150/150	15	450	1500
Marchand de Quatre Saisons	LG	AL	1981	LC	18 X 24	AP/JP	150/150	17	500	950
Allumeur de Reverbere	LG	AL	1981	LC	18 X 24	AP/JP	150/150	16	450	950
Notre Dame au Crepuscule	LG	AL	1981	LC	18 X 24	AP/JP	150/150		450	950
Chauds les Marrons	LG	AL	1981	LC	18 X 24	AP/JP	150/150		500	1500
Aux Deux Magots	LG	AL	1982	LC	26 X 20	AP/JP	150/150		800	1800
Au Moulin de Paris	LG	AL	1982	LC	18 X 24	AP/JP	150/150		450	900
Sur les Toits	LG	AL	1982	LC	18 X 24	AP/JP	150/150		400	900
Le Remorqueur	LG	AL	1982	LC	18 X 24	AP/JP	150/150		500	900
La Bal du 14 Juillet	LG	AL	1982	LC	18 X 24	AP/JP	150/150		500	1500
Le Defile du 14 Juillet	LG	AL	1982	LC	18 X 24	AP/JP	150/150		450	650
Le Marchand de Farine	LG	AL	1982	LC	18 X 24	AP/JP	150/150		500	900
Marchand de Vin	LG	AL	1982	LC	18 X 24	AP/JP	150/150		450	900
Carrousel	LG	AL	1983	LC	18 X 24	AP/JP	150/150		500	950
Homme Sandwich	LG	AL	1983	LC	18 X 24	AP/JP	150/150		500	950
Atelier du Peintre	LG	AL	1983	LC	18 X 24	AP/JP	150/150		450	650
Paris Suite with Watercolor	LG	AL	1983	LC					11000 SET	20000 SET
Paris Suite without Watercolor	LG	AL	1983	LC					7800 SET	13500 SET
Cerceau de Reves	LG	AL	1983	LC	18 X 24	AP/JP	150/150		450	700
L'Artiste	LG	AL	1984	LC	26 X 20	AP/JP	150/150		600	2100
La Manege	LG	AL	1984	LC	25 X 32 cm	AP/JP	150/150		800	2300
Autobus	LG	AL	1984	LC	26 X 20	AP/JP	150/150		600	2100
Chez Joseph	LG	AL	1984	LC	26 X 20	AP/JP	150/150		600	1350
Neige, Neige, Neige	LG	AL	1984	LC	26 X 20	AP/JP	150/150		600	1050
Petite Balade	LG	AL	1984	LC	26 X 20	AP/JP	150/150		600	1050
La Tourelle	LG	AL	1984	LC	26 X 20	AP/JP	150/150		600	1050
Le Grande Bal	LG	AL	1985	LC	25 X 32 cm	AP/JP	150/150		1000	2100
Antoinette	LG	AL	1985	LC	25 X 32 cm	AP/JP	150/150		1000	2800
Le Canal St Martin	LG	AL	1985	LC	19 X 24	AP/JP	150/150		1000	2000
Le Grand Sapin	LG	AL	1985	LC	25 X 32 cm	AP/JP	150/150		1000	1800
Parfumerie Guerlain	LG	AL	1986	LC	26 X 20	AP/JP	150/150		1000	2100
L'Aubade	LG	AL	1986	LC	20 X 24	AP/JP	150/150		1000	1400
Harvard 350th Celebration (Set of 4)	LG	AL	1986	LC	25 X 32 cm	AP/JP	250/100		7500 SET	8000 SET
Quai des Orfevres	LG	AL	1986	LC	25 X 32 cm	AP/JP	150/150		1000	3200
Boules de Neige	LG	AL	1986	LC	26 X 20	AP/JP	150/150		800	1800
Souvenirs de Paris	LG	AL	1987	LC		AP	500		1500	2100
Jardin des Tuileries sous la Neige	LG	AL	1987	LC		AP/JP	150/150		1200	3200

MICHEL DELACROIX CONTINUED

TITLE	PUBLISHER	PRINTER	DATE	MEDIUM	DIMENSION (PAPER SIZE) IN INCHES	TYPE OF PAPER	EDITION NUMBER	NO. OF COLORS	ORIGINAL OPENING PRICE	CURRENT RETAIL PRICE
CURRENT EDITIONS:										
Six Chateaux de la Loire Suite (Set of 6):									9000 SET	15500 SET
Azay-le-Rideau	LG	AL	1987	LC		AP/JP	150/150		1500	4200
Chambord	LG	AL	1987	LC		AP/JP	150/150		1500	4200
Chenonceaux	LG	AL	1987	LC		AP/JP	150/150		1500	2700
Cheverny	LG	AL	1987	LC		AP/JP	150/150		1500	2000
Blois	LG	AL	1987	LC		AP/JP	150/150		1500	1800
Amboise	LG	AL	1987	LC		AP/JP	150/150		1500	1800
Chasse a Courre Suite (Set of 4):									6000 SET	7000 SET
La Sortie du Chenil	LG	AL	1988	LC		AP/JP	150/150		1500	2500
Le Rendez-vous	LG	AL	1988	LC		AP/JP	150/150		1500	2500
Le Debucher	LG	AL	1988	LC		AP/JP	150/150		1500	1800
Les Honneurs	LG	AL	1988	LC		AP/JP	150/150		1500	2100
Le Marche de Noel en Alsace	LG	AL	1988	LC		AP/JP	150/150		1500	3200
Le Canal St Martin En Automne	CVFA/AFA	AES	1989	LC	31 X 35	AP/B	461	26	1500	2500
La Belle de Jour	CVFA/AFA	AES	1989	LC	31 X 35	AP/B	471	26	1500	3000
Cosi Fan Tutte	CVFA	CCI	1989	SP	31 X 35	COV	495	64	1500	3800
Moulin Rouge Sous la Neige	CVFA	HAS	1989	SP	38 X 45	COV	495		1750	4500
Arc de Triomphe	CVFA	AES	1989	LC	31 X 35	AP/B	495	26	1500	2600
Tour Eiffel le Soir au Ciel Nuageux	CVFA	CCI	1989	SP	30 X 35	COV	495	64	1500	2800
Joyeux Noel	CVFA	AES	1989	LC	31 X 35	AP/RP	495	26	1500	2600
Sept Heures du Matin	CVFA	AES	1989	LC	30 X 22	AP/RP	495	26	950	1500
Town & Country Suite (Set of 4):									1850 SET	2500 SET
Dans le Parc de Gennevilliers	CVFA	AES	1990	LC	19 X 15	AP/RP	495		550	750
Promenade Sans-Soucis	CVFA	AES	1990	LC	19 X 15	AP/RP	495		550	750
L'Octroi	CVFA	AES	1990	LC	19 X 15	AP/RP	495		550	750
Neige en Normandie	CVFA	AES	1990	LC	19 X 15	AP/RP	495		550	750
Grand Hotel	CVFA	AES	1990	LC	30 X 22	AP/RP	495		1500	2000
Vue de Paris de L'Ile de la Cite	CVFA	AES	1990	LC	18 X 44	AP/RP	495		1850	2500
Vive le Cirque	CVFA	HAS	1990	SP	31 X 38	WWP	495		1750	2300
Soir de Mai	CVFA	AES	1990	LC	22 X 30	AP/RP	495		1350	1800
Les Joies du Sport Suite (Set of 4):									7000 SET	8000 SET
Arrivee du Tour de France sur les Champs-Elysees	CVFA	ChEd	1990	SP	30 X 36	COV	495		1950	2600
Golf a Saint-Cloud	CVFA	ChEd	1990	SP	30 X 36	COV	495		1950	2575
Polo a Bagatelle	CVFA	ChEd	1990	SP	30 X 36	COV	495		1950	2425
Regates a Enghien	CVFA	ChEd	1990	SP	30 X 36	COV	495		1950	2400
Coup d'Oeil sur le Pont-Neuf	CVFA	CCI	1990	SP	37 X 45	COV	495		1825	2300
Le Chateau de Chantilly	CVFA	AES	1990	LC	22 X 30	AP/RP	495		2250	2800
Le Chevet de Notre Dame la Nuit	CVFA	ChEd	1990	SP	31 X 36	COV	495		3250	3900
L'Abbaye de Paray-Le-Monial	CVFA	AES	1990	LC	22 X 30	AP/RP	495		1550	2100
Temps de Noel dans la Campagne	CVFA	AES	1990	LC	23 X 31	AP/RP	495		1550	2100
Place de la Bastille le Soir	CVFA	AES	1990	LC	22 X 30	AP/RP	495		1125	1550
Paysages Inspires au Bord de L'Eau Suite (Set of 4)	CVFA	AES	1991	LC	22 X 26	AP/RP	495 EA		3550 SET	4000 SET
Matin Calme	CVFA	AES	1991	LC	23 X 26	RP	495		750	925
Noel Approche dans le Vieux Paris	CVFA	AES	1991	LC	26 X 30	RP	495		1125	1350
La Villa Rossini a Passy	CVFA	NSI	1991	SP	25 X 28	COV	495		950	1150
Les Toits de Paris sous la Neige	CVFA	NSI	1991	SP	26 X 30	COV	495		1350	1700
Grand Lapin Agile sous la Neige	CVFA	AES	1991	LC	23 X 26	AP/RP	495		1025	1600
Neige, Fumeé, Charbon	CVFA	NSI	1993	SP	26 X 30	COV	495		1000	1600
Bord de Seine á l'Aube	CVFA	AES	1993	LC	20 X 17	AP/RP	495		650	750

ROBERT DELVAL

EDUCATION: Self-Taught
PUBLISHERS: C G Rein Galleries, St Paul, MN (CGR)
GALLERIES: C G Rein Galleries, Santa Fe, NM & Houston, TX & Scottsdale, AZ & Minneapolis, MN

TITLE	PUBLISHER	PRINTER	DATE	MEDIUM	DIMENSION (PAPER SIZE) IN INCHES	TYPE OF PAPER	EDITION NUMBER	NO. OF COLORS	ORIGINAL OPENING PRICE	CURRENT RETAIL PRICE
SOLD OUT EDITIONS (RARE):										
La Soupiere Bleue	CGR		1987	LC	17 X 17	AP	175		150	200
CURRENT EDITIONS:										
Laurence (Blue Lady)	CGR		1987	LC	16 X 13	AP	175		200	250
Honfleur	CGR		1987	LC	19 X 27	AP	150		375	450
St Tropez	CGR		1987	LC	26 X 18	AP	150		475	525

The retail prices of the 100,000 limited edition prints quoted in this directory are subject to change. Print publishers, artists and galleries were the direct sources for these quotations. Prices in the secondary market listed as "Sold Out Editions (Rare)" indicate that the publisher has a limited supply of that print or that the print is difficult to locate in the galleries.

The Printworld Directory is accepting new applications for the seventh edition. Approximately 300 new artists will be accepted. Please use the two forms provided in the back section of this directory to submit biographical data and documentation of prints. Edition number of each print must not exceed 500 and the retail price must be $100 or more.

ROBERTO DELAMONICA

BORN: Ponta Pora, State of Mato Grosso, Brazil; 1933
EDUCATION: Sao Paulo & Rio de Janeiro, Brazil
TEACHING: Prof, Art Students League, NY; Instr, Graphics, Mus of Mod Art, NY; Instr, Rio de Janeiro, Brazil; Instr, Nat Sch of Fine Arts, Lima, Peru; Catholic Univ, Santiago; Sch of Fine Arts, Valparaiso, Chile; Minneapolis Graphics Center, MN; Pratt Graphics Center, NY; Prof, Art Students League, NY presently
AWARDS: Guggenheim Fel, 1965
COLLECTIONS: Rio de Janeiro Mus of Mod Art, Brazil; Nat Sch of Fine Arts, Lima, Peru; Mus of Mod Art, NY; Metropolitan Mus, NY; Brooklyn Mus, NY; Smithsonian Mus, Wash, DC; Stedelijk Mus, Amsterdam, The Netherlands; Nat Mus, Warsaw, USSR; Mus of Fine Art, Lodz, Poland
PRINTERS: American Atelier, NY (AA)
PUBLISHERS: Circle Fine Art, Chicago, IL (CFA)
GALLERIES: Circle Galleries, San Diego, CA & San Francisco, CA & Scottsdale, AZ & Beverly Hills, CA & Costa Mesa, CA & Sherman Oaks, CA & Palm Beach, FL & Honolulu, HI & New Orleans, LA & Las Vegas, NV & Seattle, WA & Northbrook, IL & Houston, TX & Pittsburgh, PA & Soho, NY & Chicago, IL
MAILING ADDRESS: Dept of Art, Art Students League, 215 W 57th St, New York, NY 10019

TITLE	PUBLISHER	PRINTER	DATE	MEDIUM	DIMENSION (PAPER SIZE) IN INCHES	TYPE OF PAPER	EDITION NUMBER	NO. OF COLORS	ORIGINAL OPENING PRICE	CURRENT RETAIL PRICE
SOLD OUT EDITIONS (RARE):										
Sorceress	CFA	AA	1976	EC	31 X 21	AP	100		75	200
Introvert	CFA	AA	1976	EC	31 X 21	AP	100		75	200
Outer Limits	CFA	AA	1976	EC	31 X 21	AP	100		75	200
Opus 22	CFA	AA	1976	EC	31 X 21	AP	100		75	200
Still Life	CFA	AA	1976	EC	31 X 21	AP	100		75	200
Let it Be	CFA	AA	1976	EC	31 X 21	AP	100		75	200

TONY DELAP

BORN: Oakland, CA; November 4, 1927
EDUCATION: California Col of Arts and Crafts, Oakland, CA; Prof, Fine Arts, Claremont Grad Sch, CA to present
TEACHING: Lect, Univ of California, Davis, CA 1963–64; Univ of California, Irvine, CA, 1965
AWARDS: Nealie Sullivan Award, San Francisco Art Inst, 1964; Am Fed of Arts Grant, 1966; Ford Found Grant, 1966; Mus in Res Prog, Haverford, PA, 1966; Purchase Prize, Long Beach Mus of Art, 1969; First Prize, Sculpture, Los Angeles Dept of Airports, CA, 1976
RECENT EXHIB: Jan Turner Gallery, Los Angeles, CA, 1987; Thomas Babeor Gallery, La Jolla, CA, 1989
COLLECTIONS: Whitney Mus of Am Art, NY; Walker Art Inst, Minneapolis, MN; San Francisco Mus of Art, CA; Mus of Mod Art, NY; Tate Gallery, London, England
PRINTERS: William Law, Los Angeles, CA (WL); Cirrus Edition Workshop, Los Angeles, CA (CEW)
PUBLISHERS: Cirrus Editions, Los Angeles, CA (CE); Newport Harbor Art Mus, CA (NHAM)
GALLERIES: Cirrus Editions Gallery, Los Angeles, CA; John Berggruen Gallery, San Francisco, CA; Sette & Segura Publishing, Tempe, AZ; Jan Turner Gallery, Los Angeles, CA; Modernism, San Francisco, CA; J J Brookings Gallery, San Jose, CA; Thomas Babeor Gallery, La Jolla, CA; The Works Gallery, Long Beach, CA; Wenger Gallery, Los Angeles, CA; Allene Lapides Gallery, Santa Monica, CA

TITLE	PUBLISHER	PRINTER	DATE	MEDIUM	DIMENSION (PAPER SIZE) IN INCHES	TYPE OF PAPER	EDITION NUMBER	NO. OF COLORS	ORIGINAL OPENING PRICE	CURRENT RETAIL PRICE
SOLD OUT EDITIONS (RARE):										
Karnac Series I–IV (Set of 4)	CE	WL/CEW	1972	LC	19 X 19	AC/W	50	3	600 SET / 150 EA	3000 SET / 750 EA
Untitled	CE	WL/CEW	1973	SP	10 X 15	AC/W	20	3	200	500
Florine, Child of the Air	NHAM	WL/CEW	1977	LC	21 X 21	AC/W	78	3	250	600

SONIA DELAUNAY

BORN: (1885–1979)
PRINTERS: Damease, Paris, France (DAM)
PUBLISHERS: Damease, Paris, France (DAM)
GALLERIES: Andre Zarre Gallery, New York, NY; Rolly-Michaux Galleries, New York, NY & Boston, MA; Rachel Adler Gallery, New York, NY; Jane Kahan Gallery, New York, NY; Thomas Segal Gallery, Boston, MA; Gala Art Gallery, Palm Beach, FL; Mary Singer Gallery, Wash, DC; Nancy Singer Gallery, St Louis, MO; Professional Fine Art Services, Inc, New York, NY

TITLE	PUBLISHER	PRINTER	DATE	MEDIUM	DIMENSION (PAPER SIZE) IN INCHES	TYPE OF PAPER	EDITION NUMBER	NO. OF COLORS	ORIGINAL OPENING PRICE	CURRENT RETAIL PRICE
SOLD OUT EDITIONS (RARE):										
Abstract Composition	DAM	DAM	1962	EB/A	19 X 16	AP	125		75	2000
Composition with Rectangles	DAM	DAM	1962	EB	20 X 16	AP	125	1	50	1500
Composition with Incomplete	DAM	DAM	1962	SP	21 X 19	AP	75		75	1500
Composition-Black Square	DAM	DAM	1969	LC	21 X 15	RP	100		150	1800
Composition #1	DAM	DAM	1970	EB/A	20 X 16	WOVE	125	5	200	2500
Composition #2	DAM	DAM	1970	EB/A	20 X 16	WOVE	125	8	200	3000
Composition #3	DAM	DAM	1970	EC	20 X 16	AP	75		200	1500
Composition #4	DAM	DAM	1970	EB/A	19 X 16	AP	125		200	1800
Composition-Black Arches	DAM	DAM	1970	EB/A	20 X 16	AP/BL	125		200	1800
Composition-Blue Corners	DAM	DAM	1970	EB/A	20 X 16	AP	125		200	1800
Rayonnist Composition	DAM	DAM	1970	EC	16 X 14	AP	100		200	2200
Untitled	DAM	DAM	1970	EC	20 X 16	AP	125		200	1800
Composition Horizontale	DAM	DAM	1971	LC	22 X 30	AP	125		225	2500
With Myself Series: (Set of 3)										
(A) Study on the Square	DAM	DAM	1971	EC	22 X 30	AP	75	7	225	2500
(B) Study on the Triangle	DAM	DAM	1971	EC	22 X 30	AP	75	7	225	2500
(C) Study on the Circle	DAM	DAM	1971	EC	22 X 30	AP	75	7	225	2500

SONIA DELAUNAY CONTINUED

TITLE	PUBLISHER	PRINTER	DATE	MEDIUM	DIMENSION (PAPER SIZE) IN INCHES	TYPE OF PAPER	EDITION NUMBER	NO. OF COLORS	ORIGINAL OPENING PRICE	CURRENT RETAIL PRICE
SOLD OUT EDITIONS (RARE):										
L'Oeil	DAM	DAM	1974	LC	30 X 22	AP	125		250	3000
Yellow Rhythm	DAM	DAM	1976	LC	30 X 22	AP	100		250	3000
Rhythm in Color	DAM	DAM	1976	LC	30 X 22	AP	100		250	2500

KATE DELOS

RECENT EXHIB: Richmond Art Center, VA, 1987
PRINTERS: Jill Livermore, San Francisco, CA (JL); Limestone Press, San Francisco, CA (LPr; Artist (ART)
PUBLISHERS: Eaton/Shoen Gallery, San Francisco, CA (E/S); Limestone Press, San Francisco, CA (LP)
GALLERIES: Hine Editions/Limestone Press, San Francisco, CA
MAILING ADDRESS: Limestone Press, 357 Tehama, San Francisco, CA 94103

TITLE	PUBLISHER	PRINTER	DATE	MEDIUM	DIMENSION (PAPER SIZE) IN INCHES	TYPE OF PAPER	EDITION NUMBER	NO. OF COLORS	ORIGINAL OPENING PRICE	CURRENT RETAIL PRICE
CURRENT EDITIONS:										
Imago, Four States (Three Prints with One Unique Monotype) (Set of 4)	E/S-LP	JL/ART/LP	1987	LC/EC/MON	26 X 20 EA	R/BFK	10 EA		2000 SET	2500 SET

JILLIAN DENBY

BORN: New York, NY
AWARDS: Nat Endowment for the Arts Fel, 1976,80
PRINTERS: Maurel Studios, NY (MS)
PUBLISHERS: Barbara Gladstone Editions, NY (BGE)
GALLERIES: Barbara Gladstone Gallery, New York, NY

TITLE	PUBLISHER	PRINTER	DATE	MEDIUM	DIMENSION (PAPER SIZE) IN INCHES	TYPE OF PAPER	EDITION NUMBER	NO. OF COLORS	ORIGINAL OPENING PRICE	CURRENT RETAIL PRICE
SOLD OUT EDITIONS (RARE):										
Juniper Swamp	BGE	MS	1980	SP	27 X 33	AC	85	25	400	500

ROBYN DENNY

BORN: Abinger, Surrey, England; 1930
EDUCATION: St Martin's Sch of Art, London, England; Royal Col of Art, London, England
COLLECTIONS: Mus of Mod Art, NY; Walker Art Center, Minneapolis, MN; Tate Gallery, London, England; Victoria & Albert Mus, London, England; Arts Council of Great Britain; British Council; Walker Art Gallery, Liverpool, England; Ulster Mus, Belfast, Ireland; Nat Gallery of Scotland, Edinburgh, Scotland
PRINTERS: Kelpra Studio, London, England (KS); Ian Lawson (IL); Advanced Graphics (AG); J C Editions (JCE); Alan Cox (AC)
PUBLISHERS: Bernard Jacobson, Ltd, London, England (BJL)
GALLERIES: Bernard Jacobson Gallery, London, England

TITLE	PUBLISHER	PRINTER	DATE	MEDIUM	DIMENSION (PAPER SIZE) IN INCHES	TYPE OF PAPER	EDITION NUMBER	NO. OF COLORS	ORIGINAL OPENING PRICE	CURRENT RETAIL PRICE
SOLD OUT EDITIONS (RARE):										
The Heavenly Suite (Set of 5)	BJL	KS	1971	SC	32 X 30 EA	JG	65 EA	8 EA	1500 SET	5000 SET
The Night Suite (Set of 5)	BJL	KS	1972	SC	31 X 24 EA	JG	70 EA	7 EA	1500 SET	5000 SET
Portraits (Set of 10)	BJL	IL	1973	LC	33 X 23 EA	SP	30 EA	3 EA	2000 SET	4000 SET
From Nature (Set of 5)	BJL	KS	1973	SC	54 X 40 EA	JG	60 EA	3 EA	400 EA	1500 EA
Mirrors (Set of 6)	BJL	AG	1974	3-DSC	25 X 18 EA	JG	40 EA	6 EA	300 EA	1000 EA
Thomas Set (Set of 6)	BJL	AG	1975	SC	36 X 25 EA	JG	100 EA	4 EA	600 SET	2500 SET
Graffiti (Set of 25)	BJL	JCE	1977	EB/A	27 X 23 EA	AP	10–5 EA	3–4 EA	8000 SET	15000 SET
Four Quarters (Set of 16)	BJL	AG	1977	SP	36 X 57 EA	JG	10 EA	7 EA	8000 SET	15000 SET
Generations (Set of 24)	BJL	JCE	1978	EC	21 X 28 EA	SP	35 EA	3–4 EA	300 EA	1500 EA
Autographs (Set of 5)	BJL	AC	1981	LC	41 X 30 EA	R/BFK	35 EA	4 EA	3500 SET	5000 SET
									750 EA	1500 EA

JEAN PAUL DERRIER

PRINTERS: American Atelier, NY (AA)
PUBLISHERS: Circle Fine Art, Chicago, IL (CFA)
GALLERIES: Circle Galleries, San Diego, CA & San Francisco, CA & Northbrook, IL & Pittsburgh, PA & Houston, TX & Soho, NY & Chicago, IL & Scottsdale, AZ & Beverly Hills, CA & Costa Mesa, CA & Sherman Oaks, CA & Palm Beach, FL & Honolulu, HI & New Orleans, LA & Las Vegas, NV & Seattle, WA

TITLE	PUBLISHER	PRINTER	DATE	MEDIUM	DIMENSION (PAPER SIZE) IN INCHES	TYPE OF PAPER	EDITION NUMBER	NO. OF COLORS	ORIGINAL OPENING PRICE	CURRENT RETAIL PRICE
SOLD OUT EDITIONS (RARE):										
La Place	CFA	AA	1980	LC	15 X 21	AP	300		50	175
L'Avenue des Ameriques	CFA	AA	1980	LC	15 X 21	AP	300		50	200

PAUL DELVAUX

BORN: Antheit, Belgium; 1897
EDUCATION: Acad of Fine Arts, Brussels, Belgium, 1920–24
COLLECTIONS: San Francisco Mus of Mod Art, CA; Neuberger Mus, State Univ of New York, Purchase, NY; Univ of Arizona, Tucson, AZ

PRINTERS: La Bateau La Voir, Paris, France (LBLV); Atelier Lacouriére, Paris, France (AL)
PUBLISHERS: La Bateau La Voir, Paris, France (LBLV); Galerie Le Bateau Lavoir, Paris, France (GLBL); Soleil Noir, Paris, France (SN); Rizzoli, NY (RIZ)
GALLERIES: R K Goldman & Company, Chicago, IL; Elkon Gallery, Inc, New York, NY

Jacob (J)

Paul Delvaux
The Garden
Courtesy Sotheby's

TITLE	PUBLISHER	PRINTER	DATE	MEDIUM	DIMENSION (PAPER SIZE) IN INCHES	TYPE OF PAPER	EDITION NUMBER	NO. OF COLORS	ORIGINAL OPENING PRICE	CURRENT RETAIL PRICE
SOLD OUT EDITIONS (RARE):										
Half Length Portrait of a Woman (J-2)	LBLV	LBLV	1960	LB	6 X 5	JP	50	1	500	3500
Tender Night (J-4)		AL	1960	EB	12 X 8	R/BFK	65	1	500	1500
Le Contre			1965	LB	25 X 20	AP	65	1	600	6000
Les Trois Femmes			1965	LB	22 X 29	AP	75	1	600	4500
The Rivals (J-5)	LBLV	LBLV	1966	LC	26 X 20	AP	75		800	15000
Near the Sea	LBLV	LBLV	1966	LC	25 X 19	AP	75		800	6000
Anne Lost in Thought (J-7)	LBLV	LBLV	1966	LC	26 X 20	AP	75		800	15000
The Secret (J-9)	LBLV	LBLV	1966	LB	26 X 20	AP	75	1	600	5500
The Mirrors (J-10)	LBLV	LBLV	1966	LB	20 X 27	AP	50	1	600	9000
Mauve Curtains (J-14)	LBLV	LBLV	1967	LC	15 X 11	AP	100		800	5000
Mauve Curtains (J-15)	LBLV	LBLV	1967	LC/HC	15 X 11	AP	XXX	Varies	1000	6000
Three Women (J-14)	LBLV	LBLV	1967	LB	21 X 29	AP	50	1	700	6000
Sunday Dress (J-18)	LBLV	LBLV	1967	LC	25 X 20	AP	75		800	15000
The Fan (J-20)	LBLV	LBLV	1968	LB	30 X 21	AP	75	1	700	4500
The Fan (J-21)	LBLV	LBLV	1968	LC	30 X 21	AP	75		800	7500
The Ends of the Earth (J-23)	LBLV	LBLV	1968	LC	21 X 30	AP	75		800	12500
Stained Glass Window (Le Vitrail) (J-26)	GLBL	AL	1969	EB/HC	16 X 11	AP	XX		1000	2500
Hat with Flowers II (J-36)	GLBL		1969	LC	12 X 9	AP	75		800	5500
Dance (J-38)	LBLV	LBLV	1969	LC	12 X 10	AP	75		800	6000
Phryne (J-40)			1969	LC	12 X 10	AP	75		800	4000
Pompeian Woman (J-41)	LBLV	LBLV	1970	LB	16 X 12	WOVE/CR	50	1	900	5000
The Garden (J-47)	LBLV	LBLV	1971	LB	22 X 30	AP	50	1	1000	12000
The Station (J-51)	LBLV	LBLV	1971	LB	23 X 31	AP	75	1	1000	8000
Seven Dialogues with Paul Delvaux (J-80)	SN		1971	EB	6 X 5	R/BFK	150	1	600	1500
The Garden (J-47)			1971	LB	22 X 30	AP	50	1	900	12000
The Garden (J-48)			1971	LC	22 X 30	AP	75		1000	22000
Femme a' la Boule			1971	LB	20 X 12	AP	75		900	5000
The Lover (J-50)			1971	LB	20 X 26	AP	75		900	4000
The Station (J-51)			1971	LB	23 X 31	AP	75	1	900	7000
Le Tramway (J-55)			1971	LB	13 X 28	AP	75	1	900	4500
The Clairvoyant (J-69)	GLBL		1974	LB	1 X 1	AP	50	1	500	5000
The Empress (J-71)			1974	LB	39 X 28	AP	50	1	900	5500
The Empress (J-72)			1974	LC	39 X 28	AP	75		1000	6500

PAUL DELVAUX CONTINUED

TITLE	PUBLISHER	PRINTER	DATE	MEDIUM	DIMENSION (PAPER SIZE) IN INCHES	TYPE OF PAPER	EDITION NUMBER	NO. OF COLORS	ORIGINAL OPENING PRICE	CURRENT RETAIL PRICE
SOLD OUT EDITIONS (RARE):										
Nus dans la Forét (J-77)			1974	EB	12 X 9	AP	50	1	800	2500
Night (J-91)	GLBL		1975	LB	12 X 10	AP	100	1	900	6000
Le Reflect (J-92)	RIZ	LBLV	1975	LB	13 X 10	AP	100	1	900	6000
The Speech (J-93)	LBLV	LBLV	1975		13 X 10	WOVE	100	1	900	3500
Paiolive	GLBL		1975	LC	23 X 31	AP	100	1	1000	20000
Woman with Stool (J-94)	LBLV	LBLV	1975	LB	20 X 15	AP	100	1	900	5500
Nais Unclothed	GLBL		1975	LB	13 X 4	AP	90	1	800	2500
Stone & Stiletto (J-84)	GLBL		1975	LB	13 X 26	AP	40	1	900	3500
Le Diner			1976	LB	13 X 24	AP		1	900	3500
Four Mysterious Ladies	LBLV	LBLV	1982	SP		JP	75		1650	6000
The Lady Sitting at the Train Station	LBLV	LBLV	1982	SP		JP	75		1650	6000
Anglica Sitting	LBLV	LBLV	1982	SP		JP	75		1650	6000

AGNES DENES

BORN: Budapest, Hungary; May, 1938; US Citizen
EDUCATION: New Sch for Social Research, NY, 1959–63; City Col, NY, 1961–62; Columbia Univ, NY, 1964–66
TEACHING: Inst for Visual Arts, NY, 1974–79
AWARDS: N L Robinson Fel, 1964–65; DAAD Fel, Berliner Kunstleroprogramm, 1978; Creative Artists Public Service Grants, 1972,74,80; Berthe Von Moschzisker Prize, Int Print Comp, Print Club of Philadelphia, PA, 1980; Nat Endowment for the Arts Fel, 1974–75,81; Ann and Donald McPhail Award, Int Print Comp, Print Club of Philadelphia, PA, 1982; Hassam & Speicher Fund Purchase Award, 1985; Purchase Award, Am Acad of Arts & Letters, 1985; Eugene McDermott Achievement Award, Massachusetts Inst of Technology, MA, 1990
RECENT EXHIB: Kolnischer Kunstverein, Cologne, West Germany, 1987; New Orleans Mus of Art, LA, 1989; Cincinnati Art Mus, 1989; Denver Art Mus, CO, 1989; Retrosp, Herbert F Johnson Mus, Ithaca, NY, 1991
COLLECTIONS: Mus of Modern Art, NY; Whitney Mus of Am Art, NY; Nat Coll of Fine Arts, Wash, DC; Allen Mem Art Mus, Oberlin, OH; Israel Mus, Jerusalem, Israel; Elvehjem Art Mus, Univ of Wisconsin, Madison, WI; Moderna Museet, Stockholm, Sweden; Philadelphia Mus of Art, PA
PRINTERS: Fox Graphics, Boston, MA (FG); Herb Fox, Boston, MA (HF); Donn Steward, NY (DS); Nova Scotia Col Workshop, Can (NSCW); John Hutcheson, NY (JH); Palisades Press, Jersey City, NJ (PalP)
PUBLISHERS: Pace Editions, NY (PE); Elise Meyer, Inc, NY (EM); Jill Epstein, NY (JE); Donn Steward, NY (DS); Editions 99, NY (E99); Greenfield and Associates, Phila, PA (GAA): Metropolitan Museum of Art, Mezzanine Gallery, NY (MMA); Artist (ART)
GALLERIES: Pace Prints, New York, NY; Germans Van Eck Gallery, New York, NY; Galleriet, Lund, Sweden; Mezzanine Gallery, Metropolitan Museum of Art, New York, NY; Dranoff Fine Art, New York, NY
MAILING ADDRESS: 595 Broadway, New York, NY 10012

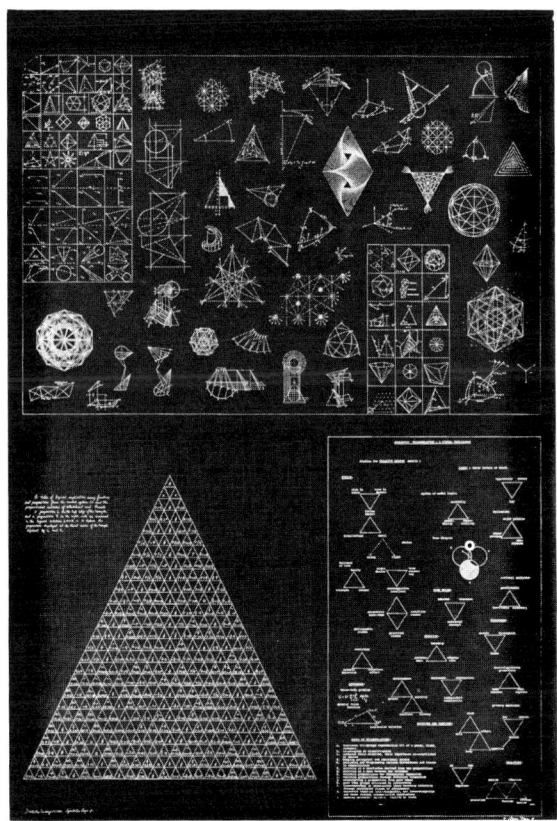

Agnes Denes
Dialectric Triangulation: A Visual Philosophy
Courtesy the Artist

TITLE	PUBLISHER	PRINTER	DATE	MEDIUM	DIMENSION (PAPER SIZE) IN INCHES	TYPE OF PAPER	EDITION NUMBER	NO. OF COLORS	ORIGINAL OPENING PRICE	CURRENT RETAIL PRICE
SOLD OUT EDITIONS (RARE):										
Study of Distortion-Isometric Systems in Isotropic Space-Map Projections (Set of 9)	E99	NSCW	1974				25			8500 SET
4000 Years-If the Mind	ART/DS	DS	1976	EC	30 X 22		42	2		1200
Map Projection: The Snail II	PE	HF	1978	LC	29 X 36	R/BFK	50	3	400	1000
Probability Pyramid	PE	HF	1978	LC	30 X 41	R/BFK	40		450	1200
Probability Pyramid II	PE	HF	1981	LB	30 X 41	R/BFK	75	1	500	1000
The Reflection	ART/JE	JF/FG	1981	LC	35 X 25		75	3	750	1200
Dialectic Triangulation: A Visual Philosophy (with Metallic Powder)	GAA	FG/HF	1983	LC	37 X 26	MOR	75	2	950	1200
Map Projections: the Cube	MMA	JH/PalP	1986	LC	37 X 26	MOR	50		500	800

The retail prices of the 100,000 limited edition prints quoted in this directory are subject to change. Print publishers, artists and galleries were the direct sources for these quotations. Prices in the secondary market listed as "Sold Out Editions (Rare)" indicate that the publisher has a limited supply of that print or that the print is difficult to locate in the galleries.

The Printworld Directory is accepting new applications for the seventh edition. Approximately 300 new artists will be accepted. Please use the two forms provided in the back section of this directory to submit biographical data and documentation of prints. Edition number of each print must not exceed 500 and the retail price must be $100 or more.

DONNA FRANCES DENNIS

BORN: Springfield, OH; October 16, 1942
EDUCATION: Carelton Col, Northfield, MN, BA, 1964; Art Students League, NY, 1966
TEACHING: Skowhegan Sch of Art, ME, 1982; Boston Mus Sch, MA, 1983; Princeton Univ, NJ; 1984; State Univ of New York, Purchase, NY, 1984,85; Instr, Skowhegan Sch of Art, ME, 1982; Instr, Sch of Visual Arts, NY, 1983; Instr, Princeton Univ, NJ, 1984; Instr, State Univ of New York, Purchase, NY, 1984–88; Sch of Visual Arts, NY, 1983–89; Assoc Prof, State Univ of New York, Purchase, NY, 1990 to present
AWARDS: John Simon Guggenheim Found Fel, 1979; Nat Endowment for the Arts, 1977,80; Creative Artist Public Service Grant, 1975,82; Am Acad & Inst of Arts & Letters Art Award, NY, 1984; New York Found for the Arts Award, NY, 1985; New York State Council for the Arts Fel, 1985; Award for Excellence, Design, Art Comm, NY, 1987; Bard Award of Merit, Architecture & Urban Design, City Club, NY, 1989; Comm Service Award for Excellence, Urban Design, Parks Council of New York, 1989; Distinguished Achievement Award, Carleton Col & Carleton Alumni Assn, 1989
RECENT EXHIB: Brooklyn Mus, NY, 1987; Delaware Art Mus, Wilmington, DE, 1988; Madison Art Center, WI, 1989; Muhlenberg Col, Frank Martin Art Gallery, Allentown, PA, 1989; Univ of Massachusetts, Amherst, MA, 1992
COLLECTIONS: Geneva Art Mus, Switzerland; Neue Galerie-Sammlung Ludwig Aachen, W Germany; Walker Art Center, Minneapolis, MN
PRINTERS: Carlton College Print Workshop, Northfield, MN (CCPW); Maurice Sanchez, NY (MS); James Miller, NY (JM); Derriére L'Etoile Studio, NY (DES); Steve Andersen, Minneapolis, MN (SA); Vermillion Editions, Ltd, Minneapolis, MN (VEL); Eric Greatrex, NY (EG); Neuberger Mus, SUNY, Purchase, NY (NM); Artist (ART); Bud Shark, Boulder, CO (BS); Shark's Lithography Ltd, Boulder, CO (SLL)
PUBLISHERS: Carlton College Print Workshop, Northfield, MN (CCPW); John Campione, NY (JC); Vermillion Editions, Ltd, Minneapolis, MN (VEL); Neuberger Mus, State Univ of New York, Purchase, NY (NM); Mano Editions, NY (MaEd); Artist (ART); Shark's Lithography, Ltd, Boulder, CO (SLL)
GALLERIES: Adler Gallery, Los Angeles, CA; Patricia Hamilton, Art Agent, New York, NY; John Szoke Graphics, New York, NY; Shark's, Inc, Boulder, CO
MAILING ADDRESS: 131 Duane St, New York, NY 10013

Donna Dennis
Night Roof
Courtesy Shark's, Inc

Donna Frances Dennis
Deep Station
Courtesy Shark's, Inc

TITLE	PUBLISHER	PRINTER	DATE	MEDIUM	DIMENSION (PAPER SIZE) IN INCHES	TYPE OF PAPER	EDITION NUMBER	NO. OF COLORS	ORIGINAL OPENING PRICE	CURRENT RETAIL PRICE
SOLD OUT EDITIONS (RARE):										
False Favella	JC	ART	1972	LC	20 X 16	AP	75	3	300	1000
Porch Front	ART	ART	1975	EB	10 X 9	AP	5	1	200	1000
Tunnel Tower	CCPW	CCPW	1979	LC	22 X 30	HMP	20		500	1000
Two Buildings	CCPW	CCPW	1979	LB/HC	22 X 30	HMP	20	1	750	1000
Night Roof	SLL	BS/SLL	1988	LC/3D	19 X 20 X 13	HMP	18		800	1500
CURRENT EDITIONS:										
Two Towers	ART	MS/DES	1982–83	LB/HC	19 X 15	AP	45	1	400	1000
Mad River Tunnel: Entrance and Exit	VEL	SA/VEL	1985–86	LC	20 X 17	R/BFK	48	16	1200	1400
Deep Station	MaEd	MS/JM/DES	1987	LC/HC	27 X 36	AP	55	3	1000	1500
1989 Monotypes (Large)	SLL	BS/SLL	1989	MON	30 X 45 EA	SUZ	1 EA	Varies	2400 EA	2400 EA
1989 Monotypes (Small)	SLL	BS/SLL	1989	MON	22 X 30	SUZ	1 EA	Varies	1800 EA	1800 EA

PAT DENTON

BORN: Scottsbluff, NE; July 20, 1943
EDUCATION: Univ of Kansas, Lawrence, KS, 1961; Univ of Denver, CO, 1962
AWARDS: First Prize, Graphics, New Mexico Art League, 1972; Ida Becker Mem Award, Catherine L Wolfe Art Club, NY, 1974; Best of Show, Wind River Nat, Dubois, WY, 1982; Pauline Mintz Award, Audubon, NJ, 1987; Rocky Mountain Nat, Watermedia, Foothills Art Center, Denver, CO, 1983,86,87; Brown Williamson Award, Georgia Watercolor Soc, 1988; Best of Show & Juror's Choice, Colorado Artists' Assn, 1988
RECENT EXHIB: West Nebraska Art Center, 1990
COLLECTIONS: West Texas Mus of Art, Lubbock, TX
PRINTERS: Tewel's Printing and Lithograph, Denver, CO (TPL)
PUBLISHERS: Printage Arts, Denver, CO (PA)
GALLERIES: Saxon Mountain Gallery, Georgetown, CO; I Barrett Galleries, Toledo, OH
MAILING ADDRESS: 2948 Pierson Way, Lakewood, CO 80215

The print market has become very selective. For the first time since we published the first edition of The Printworld Directory in 1982, the prices of prints have been greatly reduced and greatly increased for the same artists by the most reputable and established print publishers. Check the fifth edition to understand the movement.

PAT DENTON CONTINUED

TITLE	PUBLISHER	PRINTER	DATE	MEDIUM	DIMENSION (PAPER SIZE) IN INCHES	TYPE OF PAPER	EDITION NUMBER	NO. OF COLORS	ORIGINAL OPENING PRICE	CURRENT RETAIL PRICE
CURRENT EDITIONS:										
Wings of the Wind	PA	TPL	1982	LC	16 X 21	R/100	500	4	70	250
While the Dew..	PA	TPL	1982	LC	16 X 21	R/100	500	4	70	250
Look Again	PA	TPL	1982	LC	16 X 20	R/100	500	4	70	250

GEORGE DERGALIS

BORN: Athens, Greece, August 31, 1928; US Citizen
EDUCATION: Acad delle Belle Arti, Rome, Italy, 1946–51, MFA; Mus Sch of Fine Arts, Boston, MA, 1956–58, MFA
TEACHING: Instr, Mus Sch of Fine Arts, Boston, MA, 1961–70; Instr, DeCordova Mus Sch, MA, 1961 to present
AWARDS: Prix de Rome, Italy, 1951; James William Paige Fel, 1959; Gold Medal, Acad Italia delle Arti, Lavoro, Italy, 1980
RECENT EXHIB: Boston Public Library, MA, 1988; Danforth Mus, Framingham, MA, 1988,90
COLLECTIONS: Univ of Michigan, Ann Arbor, MI; Camara de Comercio, Medellin, Colombia, SA; Mus de Zea, Medellin, Colombia, SA; DeCordova Mus, Lincoln, MA; Camara de Comercio, Medellin, Columbia; Mus de Arte, Medellin, Colombia
PRINTERS: Artist (ART)
PUBLISHERS: Artist (ART)
MAILING ADDRESS: 72 Oxbow Rd, Wayland, MA 01778

TITLE	PUBLISHER	PRINTER	DATE	MEDIUM	DIMENSION (PAPER SIZE) IN INCHES	TYPE OF PAPER	EDITION NUMBER	NO. OF COLORS	ORIGINAL OPENING PRICE	CURRENT RETAIL PRICE
SOLD OUT EDITIONS (RARE):										
Conversing Priests	ART	ART	1962	LB	20 X 30	STP	250	1	30	700
Face of Viet Nam (Set of 20)	ART	ART	1968	LB	10 X 12	STP	100	1	50	850
Climax	ART	ART	1973	LB	19 X 22	STP	160	1		600
The Bridge	ART	ART	1974	EB	12 X 13	STP	50	1	150	550
Boston Skyline	ART	ART	1974	EB	4 X 26	STP	50	1	150	500
Filograph I	ART	ART	1980	MM	12 X 15	STP	150		125	450
Filograph II	ART	ART	1980	MM	14 X 19	STP	150		225	550
Filograph V	ART	ART	1980	MM	22 X 25	STP	150		300	650
Filograph VI	ART	ART	1980	MM	12 X 9	STP	150		100	450
CURRENT EDITIONS:										
Filograph III	ART	ART	1980	MM	8 X 22	STP	150		200	500
Filograph IV	ART	ART	1980	MM	15 X 22	STP	150		250	550
Filograph VII	ART	ART	1980	MM	30 X 40	STP	150		550	900
Filograph VIII	ART	ART	1980	MM	10 X 15	STP	150		125	500
Filograph IX	ART	ART	1980	MM	9 X 40	STP	150		350	650
Filograph X	ART	ART	1980	MM	14 X 19	STP	150		225	550
Filograph XI	ART	ART	1980	MM	8 X 22	STP	150		200	600
Everlasting	ART	ART	1981	MM	29 X 37	STP	15		600	1100
Figures	ART	ART	1981	MM	29 X 37	STP	15		750	1300
The Victor	ART	ART	1981	MM	29 X 37	STP	15		1000	1600
Colombiana	ART	ART	1981	MM	29 X 37	STP	15		1200	2300
Fantasy	ART	ART	1983	LB	21 X 27	STP	300	1	1200	2300
Harmony	ART	ART	1984	EMB	29 X 37	STP	2	1	1500	2600
Technotron	ART	ART	1985	EMB	29 X 37	STP	2	1	2500	2600

ERIK DESMAZIERES

BORN: Paris, France; 1948
PRINTERS: René Tazé, Paris, France (RT); Francois Baudequin, Paris France (FB); Atelier René Tazé, Paris, France
PUBLISHERS: Artist (ART); Graphic Arts Council, Achenbach Found, San Francisco, CA (GAC/AF)
GALLERIES: Fitch-Febvrel Gallery, New York, NY; Edith Caldwell Gallery, San Francisco, CA; Gerhard Wurzer Gallery, Houston, TX

TITLE	PUBLISHER	PRINTER	DATE	MEDIUM	DIMENSION (PAPER SIZE) IN INCHES	TYPE OF PAPER	EDITION NUMBER	NO. OF COLORS	ORIGINAL OPENING PRICE	CURRENT RETAIL PRICE
SOLD OUT EDITIONS (RARE):										
La Grand Bataille	ART	RT/AtRT	1978	EB	20 X 28	R/BFK	90	1	150	2000
CURRENT EDITIONS:										
L'Atelier de Louis Icart	ART	RT/AtRT	1980	EB/A	23 X 16	R/BFK	90	1	200	2000
Le Vent Souffle ou il Veut	GAC/AF	RT/FB/AtRT	1989	EB/A	17 X 23	HAHN	90	2	350	1000
Atelier René Tazé VI	ART	RT/AtRT	1993	EB/A/ROU	28 X 43	R/BFK	90	1	1200	1200

RICHARD DEUTSCH

BORN: Chicago, IL; 1953
EDUCATION: Sch of Art Inst of Chicago, IL, BFA, 1977; Univ of Chicago, IL, MFA, 1982
TEACHING: Indiana Univ, Gary, Indiana, 1981
AWARDS: Ox-Bow Summer Workshop Grant, 1978
PRINTERS: Will Petersen, Chicago, IL (WP); Plucked Chicken Press, Chicago, IL (PCP)
PUBLISHERS: Balkin Editions, Chicago, IL (BE)
GALLERIES: Gump's Gallery, San Francisco, CA; Dorothy Weiss Gallery, San Francisco, CA; Allrich Gallery, San Francisco, CA

RICHARD DEUTSCH CONTINUED

TITLE	PUBLISHER	PRINTER	DATE	MEDIUM	DIMENSION (PAPER SIZE) IN INCHES	TYPE OF PAPER	EDITION NUMBER	NO. OF COLORS	ORIGINAL OPENING PRICE	CURRENT RETAIL PRICE
SOLD OUT EDITIONS (RARE):										
Untitled	BE	WP/PCP	1981	LC	28 X 22	AP/B	50	7	200	550

MICHAEL DI CERBO

BORN: Paterson, NJ; November 6, 1947
EDUCATION: Pratt Inst, Brooklyn, NY, BFA, 1971; MFA, 1973
TEACHING: Brooklyn Col, NY, 1974–75; Soho Graphics Arts Workshop, NY, 1980–83; Seton Hall Univ, South Orange, NJ, 1992
AWARDS: Purchase Award, Nat Print Exhib, Trenton State Col, 1980; Boston Printmakers Award, De Cordova Mus, Lincoln, MA, 1986; Andres-Nelson-Whitehead Award, 1987; Res Grant, Palenville Interarts Colony Award, 1987; Purchase Award, SAGA Nat Award, NY, 1989
RECENT EXHIB: Lumen-Winter Gallery, New Rochelle, NY, 1991
COLLECTIONS: Brooklyn Mus, NY; New Jersey State Mus, Trenton, NJ; Columbia Univ, NY; Pratt Inst, NY; Victoria & Albert Mus, London, England; The Sidney Lewis Found, Richmond, VA; Detroit Art Inst, MI; New York Public Library, NY; Portland Mus, OR; Kanagawa Prefectural Gallery, Yokohama, Japan; Hanoi Nat Mus of Fine Arts, Vietnam; Newark Public Library, NJ; Univ of Oklahoma, Oklahoma City, OK; Arkansas State Univ, Fayetteville, AR
PRINTERS: Sue Press, NY (SP); Water Street Press, Brooklyn, NY (WS); Brent Wright, NY (BW); Sue Kleinman, NY (SK); Xavier Rivera, NY (XR); Artist (ART); Soho Graphic Arts Workshop, NY (SGAW)
PUBLISHERS: Bruce Teleky Editions, NY (BTE); Polizzi Graphics, Brooklyn, NY (PG); Contemp Masterworks Corp, NY (CMC); Soho Graphic Arts Workshop, NY (SGAW)
GALLERIES: Weyhe Gallery, New York, NY; Corporate Art Directions, New York, NY; Polizzi Gallery, Brooklyn, NY; Bruce Teleky Editions, New York, NY
MAILING ADDRESS: 277 W 10th St, #5A, New York, NY 10014

Michael Di Cerbo
Nocturne
Courtesy the Artist

TITLE	PUBLISHER	PRINTER	DATE	MEDIUM	DIMENSION (PAPER SIZE) IN INCHES	TYPE OF PAPER	EDITION NUMBER	NO. OF COLORS	ORIGINAL OPENING PRICE	CURRENT RETAIL PRICE
SOLD OUT EDITIONS (RARE):										
Pinnacles	BTE	XR/SGAW	1987	I	11 X 15	R/BFK/CR	80	1	120	135
Noctrune	BTE	XR/SGAW	1987	I	16 X 22	R/BFK/CR	80	1	120	160
Peaks	BTE	XR/SGAW	1990	I	16 X 12	R/BFK/CR	80	1	120	135
Gap	BTE	XR/SGAW	1990	I	15 X 11	R/BFK/CR	80	1	130	145
Cliffs	BTE	XR/SGAW	1990	I	13 X 16	R/BFK/T	80	1	130	145
Towers	BTE	XR/SGAW	1990	I	15 X 17	R/BFK/G	80	1	130	145
Nocturnale	BTE	XR/SGAW	1990	I	17 X 14	R/BFK/G	80	1	130	145
Night Fog	BTE	XR/SGAW	1992	I	22 X 15	R/BFK/T	80	1	160	160
Structulite	BTE	XR/SGAW	1992	I	36 X 30	R/BFK/T	80	1	420	420

JOSEPH J DI GIORGIO

BORN: Brooklyn, NY; January 1, 1931
EDUCATION: Cooper Union, NY, BFA, 1958
TEACHING: Instr, Drawing, New York Univ, NY, 1980
AWARDS: Virginia Center for Creative Artists Fel, 1982, 84
RECENT EXHIB: Santa Clara Univ, De Saisset Mus, CA, 1989
PRINTERS: Artist (ART)
PUBLISHERS: Orion Editions, NY (OE)
GALLERIES: Nina Freidenheim Gallery, New York, NY; Michael Walls Gallery, New York, NY; Orion Editions, New York, NY
MAILING ADDRESS: 269 Bowery, New York, NY 10002

TITLE	PUBLISHER	PRINTER	DATE	MEDIUM	DIMENSION (PAPER SIZE) IN INCHES	TYPE OF PAPER	EDITION NUMBER	NO. OF COLORS	ORIGINAL OPENING PRICE	CURRENT RETAIL PRICE
CURRENT EDITIONS:										
Hudson Series (Set of 2):									1000 SET	1500 SET
Hudson Series I	OE	ART	1985	SP	44 X 30	AC	125	19	500	750
Hudson Series II	OE	ART	1985	SP	44 X 30	AC	125	25	500	750

The print market has become very selective. For the first time since we published the first edition of The Printworld Directory in 1982, the prices of prints have been greatly reduced and greatly increased for the same artists by the most reputable and established print publishers. Check the fifth edition to understand the movement.

JESSICA DIAMOND

BORN: June 6, 1957
EDUCATION: Sch of Visual Art, NY, BFA, 1979; Columbia Univ, NY, MFA, 1981
RECENT EXHIB: Rosamund Felsen Gallery, Los Angeles, CA, 1990; Fahnemann, Berlin, Germany, 1991; Jablonka Galerie, Cologne, Germany, 1991; Autospace Annex, San Francisco, CA, 1991; American Fine Arts Company, NY, 1989–90,92
PRINTERS: Jack Lemon, Chicago, IL (JL); Landfall Press, Inc, Chicago, IL (LPI)
PUBLISHERS: Landfall Press, Inc, Chicago, IL (LPI)
GALLERIES: Rosamund Felsen Gallery, Los Angeles, CA; American Fine Arts Company, New York, NY; Real Art Ways, Hartford, CT; Landfall Press, Chicago, IL; Quartet Editions, New York, NY; Jablonka Galerie, Cologne, Germany; Galerie Fahnemann, Berlin, Germany
MAILING ADDRESS: c/o American Fine Arts Company, 40 Wooster St, New York, NY 10013

TITLE	PUBLISHER	PRINTER	DATE	MEDIUM	DIMENSION (PAPER SIZE) IN INCHES	TYPE OF PAPER	EDITION NUMBER	NO. OF COLORS	ORIGINAL OPENING PRICE	CURRENT RETAIL PRICE
CURRENT EDITIONS:										
Commemorative Gold Pieces (Set of 15)	LPI	JL/LPI	1990	LC/EMB	10 X 9 EA	R/BFK	25 EA	1 EA	4000 SET	4000 SET

MARTHA DIAMOND

BORN: New York, NY; 1944
EDUCATION: Art Students League, NY, 1962; Carleton Col, Northfield, MN, 1964; Alliance Francaise, Paris, France, 1965; New York Univ, MA, 1969
TEACHING: Guggenheim Mus, NY, 1971–75; Skowhegan Sch of Painting & Sculpture, ME, 1977; Tyler Sch of Art, Temple Univ, Phila, PA, 1979
AWARDS: New York State Council on the Arts Fel, Painting, 1985
RECENT EXHIB: Robert Miller Gallery, NY, 1990
COLLECTIONS: Mus of Mod Art, NY; Whitney Mus of Am Art, NY; Larry Aldrich Mus, Ridgefield, CT; Lehigh Univ, PA; Harpur Col, Binghampton, NY; Australian Nat Gallery, Canberra, Australia
PRINTERS: Vermillion Editions Ltd, Minneapolis, MN (VEL); Simca Print Artists, NY (SPA); Betty Winkler, NY (BW); Yama Press, NY (YP)
PUBLISHERS: Brooke Alexander Editions, NY (BAI); Vermillion Editions, Ltd, Minneapolis, MN (VEL); Diane Villani Editions, NY (DVE); Simca Print Artists, NY (SPA); Yama Press, NY (YP); Artist (ART); Orion Editions, NY (OE)
GALLERIES: Brooke Alexander, Inc, New York, NY; Vermillion Editions, Minneapolis, MN; Robert Miller Gallery, New York, NY; Mary Ryan Gallery, New York, NY

**Martha Diamond
Untitled (Monotype)**
Courtesy Brooke Alexander, Inc

TITLE	PUBLISHER	PRINTER	DATE	MEDIUM	DIMENSION (PAPER SIZE) IN INCHES	TYPE OF PAPER	EDITION NUMBER	NO. OF COLORS	ORIGINAL OPENING PRICE	CURRENT RETAIL PRICE
SOLD OUT EDITIONS (RARE):										
Citadel	BAI	SPA	1978	LI	26 X 34	AP	17		250	500
Cityscape/Domicile	BAI	SPA	1978	LI	10 X 10	AP	15		125	400
Domicile	BAI	SPA	1978	LI	10 X 11	AP	10		125	400
Hogan	BAI	SPA	1978	LI	25 X 27	AP	24		250	500
Landscape/Domicile	BAI	SPA	1978	LI	31 X 23	AP	15		250	500
Rise	BAI	SPA	1978	LI	23 X 31	AP	24		250	500
Shore	BAI	SPA	1979	LI/C	30 X 20	AP	10		300	500
American Dance Festival Poster	BAI	SPA	1981	LC/OFF	36 X 25	AP	150		125	400
City Suite	BAI	SPA	1982	LC	36 X 28	R/BFK	20		400	600
CURRENT EDITIONS:										
Manhatten Suite (Set of 5):									1200 SET	1200 SET
Windows	ART/SPA	SPA	1985	SP	23 X 20	Varies	36		300	400
Construction	ART/SPA	SPA	1985	SP	23 X 20	Varies	36		300	400
Cornice	ART/SPA	SPA	1985	SP	23 X 20	Varies	36		300	400
High Rise	ART/SPA	SPA	1985	SP	23 X 20	Varies	36		300	400
Pediment	ART/SPA	SPA	1985	SP	23 X 20	Varies	36		300	400
Intersection	VEL	VEL	1986	AC/SP	32 X 24	AC	36	2	850	850
Midday	DVE		1986	LC	26 X 22	R/BFK	45		600	900
Battery Park City	VEL	VEL	1985	AC/SP	41 X 29	AC	36		600	950
Shifting View	ART/YP	BW/YP	1988	CAR	26 X 28	R/BFK/T	20	3	650	800
Winds	ART/YP	BW/YP	1988	CAR	26 X 28	SOM	20	4	650	800
Towers	OE		1988		47 X 37				900	1000

The retail prices of the 100,000 limited edition prints quoted in this directory are subject to change. Print publishers, artists and galleries were the direct sources for these quotations. Prices in the secondary market listed as "Sold Out Editions (Rare)" indicate that the publisher has a limited supply of that print or that the print is difficult to locate in the galleries.

MARK DI SUVERO

BORN: Shanghai, China; September 18, 1933
EDUCATION: San Francisco City Col, CA, 1953–54; Univ of California, Santa Barbara, CA, 1954–55; Univ of California, Berkeley, CA, MA, 1956
AWARDS: Longview Found Grant; Walter K Gutman Found Grant; Art Inst of Chicago, IL, 1963; Nat Endowment for the Arts Grant; Brandeis Univ Creative Arts Award; Skowhegan Sch Award, ME
RECENT EXHIB: Governor's State Univ, Nathan Manilow Gallery, IL, 1989,92; Western Washington Univ, Bellingham, WA, 1992; Art Center/Col of Design, Pasadena, CA, 1989,92; Storm King Art Center, Mountainville, NY, 1992; Fort Wayne Mus, IN, 1992; Gagosian Gallery, NY, 1993; John Berggruen Gallery, San Francisco, CA, 1993
COLLECTIONS: Wadsworth Atheneum, Hartford, CT; New York Univ, NY; Chicago Inst of Art, IL; Mus of Fine Art, Dallas, TX; Toronto Mus of Art, Can; Hirshhorn Mus, Wash, DC; MIT, Cambridge, MA; Whitney Mus of Am Art, NY; Storm King Art Center, MA; Western Washington State Col, WA; Univ of Iowa; Walker Art Center, Minneapolis, MN
PRINTERS: Ken Farley, Los Angeles, CA (KF); Kyle Militzer, Los Angeles, CA (KM); Gemini GEL, Los Angeles, CA (GEM)
PUBLISHERS: Tyler Graphics Ltd, Bedford Village, NY (TGL); Gemini GEL, Los Angeles, CA (GEM)
GALLERIES: John Berggruen Gallery, San Francisco, CA; Hill Gallery, Birmingham, MI; Elizabeth Leach Gallery, Portland, OR; Makler Gallery, Phila, PA; Janie C Lee Gallery, Houston, TX; Harcourts Contemporary Gallery, San Francisco, CA; Tasende Gallery, La Jolla, CA; Gemini GEL, Los Angeles, CA; Manny Silverman Gallery, Los Angeles, CA; Adams-Middleton Gallery, Dallas, TX; L A Louver, Inc, Venice, CA; Klein Art Works, Chicago, IL; Hill Gallery, Birmingham, MI; Oil & Steel Gallery, Long Island City, NY; Argus Fine Arts, Eugene, OR; Tyler Graphics, Ltd, Mount Kisco, NY; Gagosian Gallery, New York, NY
MAILING ADDRESS: 3030 Vernon Blvd, P O Box 2218, Long Island City, NY 11102

TITLE	PUBLISHER	PRINTER	DATE	MEDIUM	DIMENSION (PAPER SIZE) IN INCHES	TYPE OF PAPER	EDITION NUMBER	NO. OF COLORS	ORIGINAL OPENING PRICE	CURRENT RETAIL PRICE
SOLD OUT EDITIONS (RARE):										
Untitled (5 Torch-cut Pieces of 2" Steel)	TGL	TGL	1972	KS	10 X 8 X 2	HMP	250		500	5000
CURRENT EDITIONS:										
Jak	TGL	TGL	1976	LC/SP	41 X 29	AC	100	2	600	4500
Afterstudy for Marianne Moore	TGL	KT/JH/RB	1976	LC	39 X 52	R/BFK	25	2	750	4500
For Rilke	TGL	KT/JH/RB	1976	LC	48 X 32	AC	26	1	450	4500
Centering	TGL	KT/JH/RB	1976	LC	43 X 62	AP88	10	2	950	4500
Centering (State)	TGL	KT/JH/RB	1976	LC	43 X 62	AP88	10	2	1500	4500
Tetra	TGL	KT/JH/RB	1976	LC	51 X 40	R/BFK	20	1	550	1500
Delivered Word (5 Torch-Cut Pieces of 2" Steel Plate)	GEM	GEM	1981	MULT	10 X 8 X 2	STEAL	75		1200	2700
Moon Dog (5 Saw-Cut Pieces of 5/8" Nickel-Plated Aluminum)	GEM	GEM	1981	MULT	5/8 X 18 X 12	ALUM	75		1800	4000
Rising (For Walt Whitman) (5 Saw-Cut Pieces of 5/8" Shot-Peened; Copper-Plated Aluminum)	GEM	GEM	1981	MULT	5/8 X 21 X 18	ALUM	50		1800	4000
Stainless (6 Saw-Cut Pieces of 1/2" Copper-Plate Aluminum)	GEM	GEM	1981	MULT	1/2 X 26 X 16	ALUM	75		1500	3500
Longing (4 Saw-Cut Pieces of 5/8" Nickel-Plated Aluminum)	GEM	GEM	1981	MULT	5/8 X 27 X 22	ALUM	75		1800	4000
Santana Wind	GEM	KF/KM/GEM	1991	EB/A/DPT/SL	19 X 22	R/BFK	30		1000	1000

DAVID DIAO

BORN: Sichuan, China; August 7, 1943; U S Citizen
EDUCATION: Kenyon Col, Gambier, OH, AB, 1964
TEACHING: Instr, Independent Study Prog, Whitney Mus, NY, 1970 to present
AWARDS: Guggenheim Fel, 1973–74; Creative Artists Public Service Award, 1978; Nat Endowment for the Arts Grant, 1980,87
COLLECTIONS: Whitney Mus of Am Art, NY; San Francisco Mus of Mod Art, CA; Art Gallery of Ontario, Toronto, Canada; Virginia Mus of Art, Richmond, VA
RECENT EXHIB: Whitney Mus of Am Art, NY, 1987; Aldrich Mus of Contemp Art, Ridgefield, CT, 1987; Los Angeles County Mus of Art, CA, 1987; Galeria Westersingal 8, Rotterdam, The Netherlands, 1988; Postmasters Gallery, NY, 1988,89; Musee d'Art Moderne, Saint Etienne, France, 1989; Galerie Joseph Dutertre, Rennes, France, 1989; Whitney Mus of Am Art, NY, 1989; Provincial Mus, voor Moderne Kunst, Oostende, Belgium, 1990; Het Kruithuis, Mus voor Hedendaagse' Kunst, Hertogenbosch, The Netherlands, 1990; Claire Burrus Gallery, Paris, France, 1990; Lawrence Oliver Gallery, Phila, PA, 1990
PRINTERS: Catherine Mosley, NY (CM); Spring Street Workshop, NY (SpSW)
PUBLISHERS: Spring Street Workshop, NY (SpSW)
GALLERIES: Pace Prints, New York, NY; Jack Shainman Gallery, New York, NY; Postmasters, New York, NY
MAILING ADDRESS: 72 Franklin St, New York, NY 10013

TITLE	PUBLISHER	PRINTER	DATE	MEDIUM	DIMENSION (PAPER SIZE) IN INCHES	TYPE OF PAPER	EDITION NUMBER	NO. OF COLORS	ORIGINAL OPENING PRICE	CURRENT RETAIL PRICE
CURRENT EDITIONS:										
Untitled (Red and Black)	SpSW	CM/SpSW	1987	EB/A	24 X 28	HAHN	30	3	800	1200
Untitled (China in Russian)	SpSW	CM/SpSW	1987	EB/A	22 X 24	HAHN	30	3	800	1200
Untitled (Black Image)	SpSW	CM/SpSW	1988	EB/A	25 X 25	HAHN	30		900	1200
Liberation	SpSW	CM/SpSW	1989	EB/A	34 X 25	HAHN	30		1200	1200
Untitled (Berg)	SpSW	CM/SpSW	1989	EB/A	22 X 30	HAHN	10		1000	1000

The print market has become very selective. For the first time since we published the first edition of The Printworld Directory in 1982, the prices of prints have been greatly reduced and greatly increased for the same artists by the most reputable and established print publishers. Check the fifth edition to understand the movement.

JAN DIBBETS

BORN: Weert, Netherlands; May 9, 1941
RECENT EXHIB: Retrosp, Guggenheim Mus, NY, 1987; Walker Art Center, Minneapolis, MN, 1988; Detroit Inst of Art, MI, 1988; Norton Gallery, West Palm Beach, FL, 1988; Stedelijk van Abbemuseum, Eindhoven, The Netherlands, 1989
PRINTERS: Aeropress, NY (A); Patricia Branstead, NY (PB); Rento Brattinga, Amsterdam, The Netherlands (RB); Steendrukkerij, Amsterdam, The Netherlands (ST)
PUBLISHERS: Multiples, NY (M); Castelli Graphics, NY (CG); Waddington Graphics, London, England (WG)
GALLERIES: Marian Goodman Gallery, New York, NY; Waddington Gallery, London, England
MAILING ADDRESS: Boer Haaveplane #6, Amsterdam, Netherlands

TITLE	PUBLISHER	PRINTER	DATE	MEDIUM	DIMENSION (PAPER SIZE) IN INCHES	TYPE OF PAPER	EDITION NUMBER	NO. OF COLORS	ORIGINAL OPENING PRICE	CURRENT RETAIL PRICE
SOLD OUT EDITIONS (RARE):										
Untitled	M	PB/A	1975	PHC/CO	20 X 24	AP	60		750	3500
Untitled I, II, III (Set of 3)	M	PB/A	1981	LB/PH/CO	30 X 30 DIA	AP	30 EA		3000 SET	9000 SET
									1000 EA	3500 EA
CURRENT EDITIONS:										
Untitled (Land, Sea) (Set of 2)	M/CG	PB/A	1975	PHC/CO	29 X 39 EA	AP	50 EA		900 SET	5000 SET
									500 EA	2500 EA
Four Courts/Dublin A & B (Set of 2)	M	RB	1983	LC/PH/CO	29 X 32 EA	RAG/B	25 EA		3000 SET	9000 SET
Untitled (Set of 2)	WG	RB/ST	1985	LC/PH/CO	40 X 46 EA	RMB	28 EA		3600 SET	10000 SET
Round Lutheran Church (2 Sheets)	WG	RB/ST	1985	LC	40 X 46	RMB	28		3600 SET	10500 SET
Wayzata	WG	RB/ST	1990	SP/CO	35 X 35	RMB	25		9000 SET	10000 SET
Three Cupolas A,B,C (Series of 3)	WG	RB/ST	1990	SP/PH/CO	35 X 35	RMB	25		25000 SET	28000 SET

JANE DICKSON

BORN: Chicago, IL; May 18, 1952
EDUCATION: Sch of Boston Mus of Fine Arts, MA, Dipl, 1976; Harvard Univ, BA, MA (Magna Cum Laude), 1976
RECENT EXHIB: Dart Gallery, Chicago, IL, 1987; Brooklyn Mus, NY, 1986–87; Walker Art Center, MN, 1986–87; Carnegie Inst, Pittsburgh, PA, 1986–87; Brooke Alexander, Inc, NY, 1987,90; Illinois State Univ, Normal, IL, 1992
COLLECTIONS: Metropolitan Mus, NY; Mus of Mod Art, NY; Brooklyn Mus, NY; Art Inst of Chicago, IL; Mt Holyoke Col, South Hadley, MA; Toledo Mus, OH; Victoria and Albert Mus, London, England; Wake Forest Univ, Winston-Salem, NC
PRINTERS: Judity Solodkin, NY (JS); Solo Press, NY (SP); Gregory Burnet, NY (GB); Maurice Payne, NY (MP); IME Studios, NY (IME); Maurice Sanchez, NY (MS); Derriére L'Etoile Studios, NY (DES)
PUBLISHERS: Solo Press, NY (SP); Joe Fawbush Editions, NY (JFE); Maurice Payne, NY (MP); Art Issue Editions, NY (AIE); Mount Holyoke Col, South Hadley, MA (MHC); Brooke Alexander, Inc, NY (BAI); Artist (ART); Derriére L'Etoile Studios, NY (DES)
GALLERIES: Joe Fawbush Editions, New York, NY; Barbara Krakow Gallery, Boston, MA; Brooke Alexander, Inc, New York, NY; Asher/Faure Gallery, Los Angeles, CA; Castelli Gallery, New York NY; Dart Gallery, Chicago, IL; Betsy Rosenfield Gallery, Chicago, IL; A Clean, Well-Lighted Place, New York, NY
MAILING ADDRESS: 276 W 43rd St, New York, NY 10036

TITLE	PUBLISHER	PRINTER	DATE	MEDIUM	DIMENSION (PAPER SIZE) IN INCHES	TYPE OF PAPER	EDITION NUMBER	NO. OF COLORS	ORIGINAL OPENING PRICE	CURRENT RETAIL PRICE
CURRENT EDITIONS:										
Hotel	SP/JBE	JS/SP	1984	MON	30 X 15 EA	GE	1 EA	Varies	500 EA	1500 EA
Woman in Stairway (Series of Monotypes)	SP/JBE	JS/SP	1984	MON	30 X 15 EA	GE/BL	1 EA	Varies	500 EA	1500 EA
Set of 3 Aquatints:									1500 SET	4000 SET
Mother and Child	MP	GB/MP	1985	AC	36 X 23	R/BFK	45	2	600	1500
Stairwell	MP	GB/MP	1985	AC	36 X 23	R/BFK	45	2	600	1500
White Haired Girl	MP	GB/MP	1985	AC	36 X 23	R/BFK	45	2	600	1500
Kiss	JFE	MP	1985	AB/CAR	18 X 15	R/BFK	25	1	450	600
Smoker	JFE	MP	1985	AB/CAR	15 X 18	R/BFK	25	1	450	600
The Crash Series (Series of 25–30)	JFE	MP	1986	MON/CC	26 X 38 EA	JP/R-BFK	1 EA	Varies	1600 EA	2500 EA
Yo-Yo Ride	JFE	MP	1986	EB/CAR	30 X 44	R/BFK	30	1	800	1200
Yo-Yo Ride	JFE	MP	1986	EC/CAR	18 X 23	HMP	13		475	600
Thou Shalt Not Steal (from Ten Commandments Suite)	AIE	JS/SP	1987	LC	24 X 19	DIEU	04	5	500	1200
Blue Dust	JFE	MP	1988	EC/CAR	16 X 28	SOM	14		750	900
Midnight Special	AIE/JFE	MP	1988	EC/CAR	24 X 43	R/BFK	35	1	1000	1500
Keep Moving I	AIE/JFE/MHC	MP	1988	AB	30 X 23	SOM	20	1	900	1200
Keep Moving II	AIE/JFE/MHC	MP	1988	AC	30 X 23	SOM	50	2	900	1200
Herald I, II, III	ART/DES	MS/DES	1990	MON	34 X 25 EA	R/BFK	5 EA	4 EA	1500 EA	1500 EA
Revelers I, II, III, IV	ART/DES	MS/DES	1990	MON	34 X 25 EA	R/BFK	1 EA	2 EA	1200 EA	1200 EA
Revelers (Series of 6 Aquatints):										
Big Bottle	BAI	MP/IME	1991	AB	32 X 31	SOM	25	1	900	900
Couple Looking Back	BAI	MP/IME	1991	AB	32 X 31	SOM	25	1	900	900
Fat Girl	BAI	MP/IME	1991	AB	32 X 31	SOM	25	1	900	900
Horsing Around	BAI	MP/IME	1991	AB	32 X 31	SOM	25	1	900	900
Tooting Her Own Horn	BAI	MP/IME	1991	AB	32 X 31	SOM	25	1	900	900
Umbrella Man	BAI	MP/IME	1991	AB	32 X 31	SOM	25	1	900	900

The retail prices of the 100,000 limited edition prints quoted in this directory are subject to change. Print publishers, artists and galleries were the direct sources for these quotations. Prices in the secondary market listed as "Sold Out Editions (Rare)" indicate that the publisher has a limited supply of that print or that the print is difficult to locate in the galleries.

RICHARD DIEBENKORN

BORN: Portland, Oregon; (1922–1993)
EDUCATION: Stanford Univ, CA, 1940–43; Univ of California, Berkeley, CA, 1943–44; California Fine Arts, CA, 1946; Stanford Univ, CA, BA, 1949; Univ of New Mexico, MA, 1952
TEACHING: Instr, Univ of Illinois, Chicago, IL, 1952–53; Instr, California Col of Arts & Crafts, Valencia, CA, 1955–57; Instr, San Francisco Art Inst, CA, 1959–63; Stanford Univ, CA, 1963–64; Prof, Art, Univ of California, Los Angeles, CA, 1966–73
AWARDS: Albert M Bender Fel, 1946; Rosenberg Traveling Fel, 1959; Gold Medal, Pennsylvania Acad of Fine Arts, Phila, PA, 1968; Skowhegan Medal, Painting, Skowhegan Sch of Art, ME, 1979; Edwin MacDowell Medal, 1978; Am Acad & Inst of Arts & Letters, NY, 1986; California Governor's Award for the Arts, 1990
RECENT EXHIB: Pamela Auchincloss Gallery, NY, 1988; Crown Point Press, NY, 1988; Mus of Mod Art, NY, 1988–89; Associated American Artists, NY, 1989; Phillips Collection, Wash, DC, 1989; Yellowstone Art Center, Billings, MT, 1989; Univ of Nebraska, Sheldon Mem Art Gallery, Lincoln, NE, 1989; State Univ of New York, Neuberger Mus, Purchase, NY, 1989; Pennsylvania Acad of Fine Arts, Phila, PA, 1989; Newport Harbor Art Mus, Newport Beach, CA, 1989; Fundacion Juan March, Madrid, Spain, 1992; Frankfuter Kunstverein, Frankfurt, Germany, 1992; Crown Point Press, San Francisco, CA, 1992; Knoedler & Co, NY, 1992; Whitechapel Art Gallery, London, England, 1991,92; Los Angeles Mus of Contemp Art, CA, 1992; Gagosian Gallery, NY, 1992,93; San Francisco Mus of Mod Art, CA, 1992–93
COLLECTIONS: Albertina Mus, Vienna, Austria; Albright-Knox Art Gallery, Buffalo, NY; Arkansas Art Center, Little Rock, AR; Art Gallery of Toronto, Canada; Art Inst of Chicago, IL; Baltimore Mus, MD; Brooklyn Mus, NY; California Palace of the Legion of Honor, San Francisco, CA; Carnegie Inst, Pittsburgh, PA; Chrysler Mus, Norfolk, VA; Cincinnati Art Mus, OH; Cleveland Mus, OH; Colorado Springs Fine Art Center, CO; Corcoran Gallery of Art, Wash, DC; Des Moines Art Center, IA; J Paul Getty Mus, Malibu, CA; Grand Rapids Art Mus, MI; Solomon Guggenheim Mus, NY; Hirshhorn Mus, Smithsonian Inst, Wash, DC; Los Angeles County Mus, CA; Metropolitan Mus of Art, NY; Mus of Fine Arts, Houston, TX; Nelson Gallery, Atkins Mus, Kansas City, MO; Neuberger Mus, State Univ of New York, Purchase, NY; North Carolina Mus, Raleigh, NC; Norton Simon Mus, Pasadena, CA; Oakland Mus, CA; Philips Coll, Wash, DC; Phoenix Art Mus, AZ; Royal Ontario Mus, Toronto, Canada; Santa Barbara Mus, CA; Smith Col Mus, Northampton, MA; Stanford Univ Mus, CA; Univ of California Art Mus, Berkeley, CA; Univ of Iowa Mus, Iowa City, IA; Univ of Michigan Mus, Ann Arbor, MI; Univ of Nebraska Art Galleries, Lincoln, NE; Univ of New Mexico, Alberquerque, NM; Univ Art Gallery, State Univ of New York, Albany, NY; Whitney Mus of Am Art, NY; Witte Mem Mus, San Antonio, TX; William Benton Mus, Univ of Connecticut, Storrs, CT; Fort Worth Art Mus, TX
PRINTERS: Tamarind Inst, Albuquerque, NM (TI); Joe Zirker, San Francisco, CA (JZ); Original Press, San Francisco, CA (OPr); John Slivon

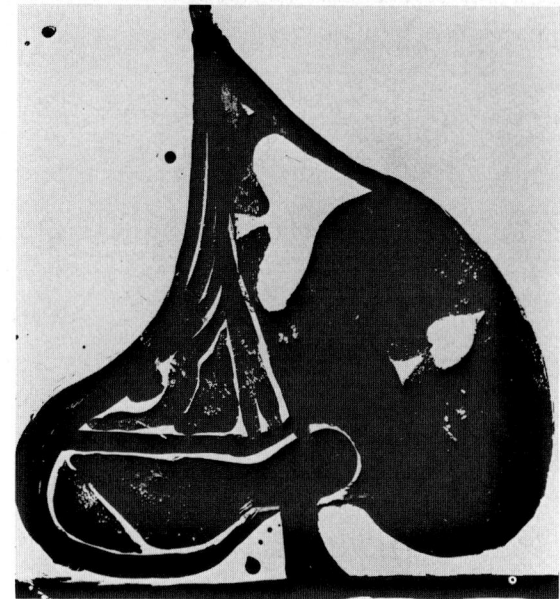

Richard Diebenkorn
Sugar Lift Spade
Courtesy Crown Point Press

(JS); Stephen Thomas (ST); Lilah Toland (LT); David Kelso (DK); Hidekatsu Takada (HT); Nancy Anello (NA); Marcia Bartholme (MB); Renée Bott (RB); Lawrence Hamlin (LH); Artist (ART); Brian Shure (BS); Pamela Paulson (PP); Crown Point Press, San Francisco, CA (CPP); Paul Singdahlsen (PS); Gemini GEL, Los Angeles, CA (GEM)
PUBLISHERS: Tamarind Inst, Albuquerque, NM (TI); Original Press, San Francisco, CA; Crown Point Press, San Francisco, CA (CPP); Gemini GEL, Los Angeles, CA (GEM)
GALLERIES: Crown Point Press, New York, NY & San Francisco, CA; M Knoedler & Co, New York, NY; Magnuson Gallery, Boston, MA; Flanders Contemporary Art, Minneapolis, MN; BlumHelman Gallery, New York, NY; Marisa del Re Gallery, New York, NY; Nancy Singer Gallery, St Louis, MO; Elizabeth Leach Gallery, Portland, OR; Associated American Artists, New York, NY; Gallery 30, San Mateo, CA; Graphics Gallery, San Francisco, CA; Jeffrey Fuller Fine Art, Phila, PA; Thomas Babeor Gallery, La Jolla, CA; Graystone, San Francisco, CA; Greg Kucera Gallery, Seattle, WA; Leslie Freely Fine Art, New York, NY; Contemporary Gallery, Dallas, TX; Pamela Auchincloss Gallery, New York, NY; Charles Whitchurch Fine Arts, Huntington Beach, CA; Andrew Dierken Fine Art, Los Angeles, CA; Gemini GEL, Los Angeles, CA; R K Goldman Contemporary, Los Angeles, CA; Smith Andersen Gallery, Palo Alto, CA; Hank Baum Gallery, San Francisco, CA; John Berggruen Gallery, San Francisco, CA; Harcourts Modern & Contemporary, San Francisco, CA;

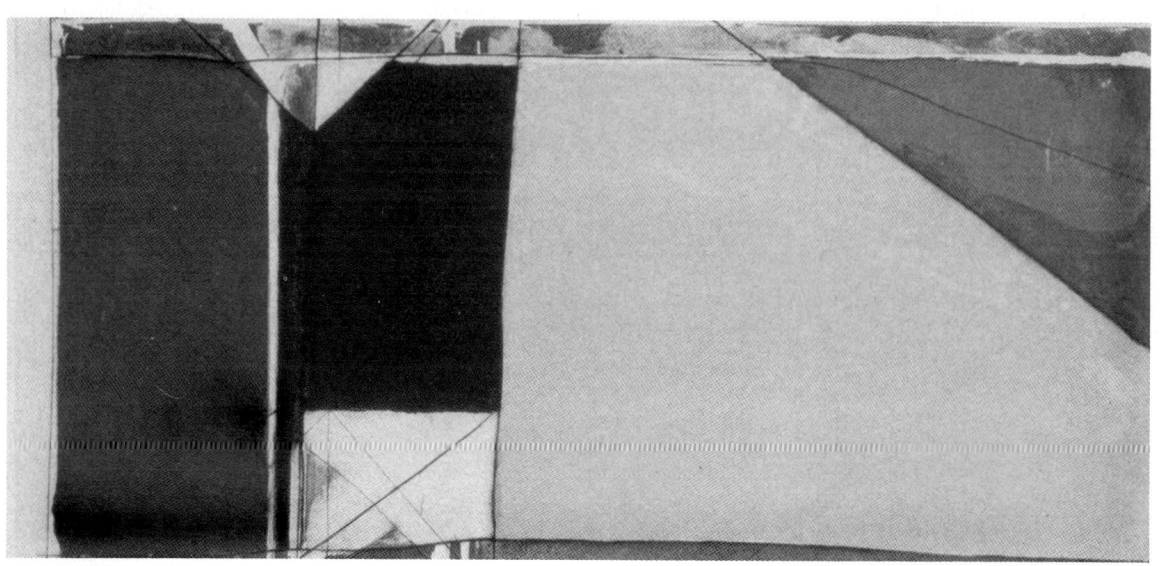

Richard Diebenkorn
Folsom Street Variations III (Primaries)
Courtesy Crown Point Press

RICHARD DIEBENKORN CONTINUED

GALLERIES: Golden Gallery, Chestnut Hill, MA; Thomson Gallery, Minneapolis, MN; Greenberg Gallery Gallery, St Louis, MO; Scherer Gallery, Marlboro, NJ; Takada Fine Arts, San Francisco, CA; J J Brookings Gallery, San Jose, CA; James Corcoran Gallery, Santa Monica, CA; Opus Art Gallery, Miami, FL; Ochi Galleries, Boise, ID & Sun Valley, ID; Thomas Smith Fine Art, Fort Wayne, IN; Nohra Haime Gallery, New York, NY; Mary Ryan Gallery, New York, NY; Garner Tullis Gallery, New York, NY; Elizabeth Paul Gallery, Cincinnati, OH; Gagosian Gallery, New York, NY

Guillemin (G); Gemini (GEM)

TITLE	PUBLISHER	PRINTER	DATE	MEDIUM	DIMENSION (PAPER SIZE) IN INCHES	TYPE OF PAPER	EDITION NUMBER	NO. OF COLORS	ORIGINAL OPENING PRICE	CURRENT RETAIL PRICE
SOLD OUT EDITIONS (RARE):										
Woman—Head & Arms			1961	LC	18 X 16	AP	20		75	8500
Reclining Figure II	TI	TI	1962	LC	20 X 15	RP	20		100	15000
41 Etchings & Drypoints (Set of 41)			1964	EB	6 X 9 EA	R/BFK	25 EA	1 EA	1800 SET	20000 SET
									50 EA	6000 EA
Woman Standing			1964–65	DPT	18 X 15	R/BFK	25	1	100	3000
Seated Woman with Drinking Cup	OPr	JZ/OPr	1965	LC	28 X 21	R/BFK	100		100	3000
Seated Woman in Striped Dress	OPr	JZ/OPr	1965	LC	27 X 20	R/BFK	100		100	8500
Seated Woman on Sofa	OPr	JZ/OPr	1965	LC	24 X 17	R/BFK	100		100	8500
Seated Woman in Armchair	OPr	JZ/OPr	1965	LB	25 X 17	R/BFK	100	1	100	5000
Seated Nude	OPr	JZ/OPr	1965	LC	26 X 20	R/BFK	100		100	3000
Woman Seated at Table			1967	LC	30 X 22	AP	75		150	13000
Untitled (Spade and Club)	CPP	CPP	1977	AB	23 X 15	BE-R/BFK	5	1	1500	6000
Nine Drypoints and Etchings (Set of 9)	CPP	JS/ST/CPP	1977	EB/DPT	30 X 22 EA	BE/R/BFK	25 EA	1 EA	6500 SET	35000 SET
Aquatint with Drypoint Halo	CPP	LT/DK/CPP	1978	EB/A/DPT	36 X 26 EA	R/HW/B	35	1	2000	5500
Five Aquatints with Drypoint (Set of 5) (G-5)	CPP	LT/DK/CPP	1978	EB/A/DPT	19 X 13 EA	R/HW/B	35 EA	1 EA	7000 SET	18000 SET
Six Soft-Ground Etchings (Set of 6)	CPP	LT/DK/CPP	1978	EB/SG	40 X 26 EA	R/HW/B	35 EA	1 EA	9000 SET	30000 SET
									1200 EA	5000 EA
Small Red	CPP	CPP	1980	EB/AC	27 X 19	R/HW/B	35	1	4000	15000
Small Thin	CPP	CPP	1980	EB/A	27 X 14	R/HW/B	35	1	2500	12000
Construct (Drypoint)	CPP	CPP	1980	DBT	19 X 27	R/HW/B	35	1	2500	5500
Construct (Grid)	CPP	CPP	1980	EB/A	27 X 19	R/HW/B	35	1	2500	6500
Construct (Red)	CPP	CPP	1980	EB/A	28 X 20	R/HW/B	35		2000	6000
Large Bright Blue	CPP	CPP	1980	EB/A/SG	40 X 26	R/HW/B	35	8	7500	45000
Four Small Prints (Set of 4):									5000 SET	10000 SET
Self-Portrait	CPP	CPP	1980	DPT	19 X 13	AP/W	35	1	1400 EA	2500 EA
Isosoles Triangle	CPP	CPP	1980	DPT	19 X 13	AP/W	35	1	1400 EA	2500 EA
Two Right Triangles, One in Another	CPP	CPP	1980	DPT/ROU	19 X 13	AP/W	35	1	1400 EA	2500 EA
Irregular Grid-Drypoint	CPP	CPP	1980	EB/A	19 X 13	AP/W	35	1	1400 EA	2500 EA
Large Light Blue	CPP	CPP	1980	EB/A	40 X 26	R/HW/B	35	8	7500	45000
Blue Loop	CPP	CPP	1980	EB/A	30 X 23	R/HW/B	35	7	4000	20000
Clubs and Spades (Set of 8):										100000 SET
Black Club	CPP	CPP	1981	EB/A	31 X 22	AP/S	35	1	2200	10000
Tri-Color	CPP	NA/LT/HT/CPP	1981	EB/A	31 X 22	AP/S	35		3500	16000
Tri-Color II	CPP	NA/LT/HT/CPP	1981	EB/AC	38 X 31	AP/S	35		4000	18000
Spreading Spade	CPP	NA/LT/HT/CPP	1981	EB/AC	37 X 31	AP/S	35		5000	25000
Combination	CPP	NA/LT/HT/CPP	1981	EB/A	31 X 22	AP/S	40		5000	22000
Blue Club	CPP	NA/LT/HT/CPP	1981	EB/AC	38 X 31	AP/S	35		3500	20000
Oakland Image	CPP	NA/LT/HT/CPP	1981	EB/SG	22 X 30	AP/S	35	1	1400	2500
Card Game	CPP	NA/LT/HT/CPP	1981	EB/SG	22 X 30	AP/S	35	1	1400	2500
Four Softgrounds (Set of 4):									4000 SET	18000 SET
Two-Way	CPP	LT/HT/CPP	1982	EB/SG	40 X 27	RP/H/W	35	1	1200	5000
Softground Y	CPP	LT/HT/CPP	1982	EB/SG	40 X 27	RP/H/W	35	1	1200	5000
Softground Cross	CPP	LT/HT/MB/CPP	1982	EB/SG	40 X 27	RP/H/W	35	1	1200	5000
Softground Splay	CPP	LT/HT/MB/CPP	1982	EB/SG	27 X 40	RP/H/W	35	1	1200	5000
Blue Surround	CPP	CPP	1982	A/DPT	35 X 26	R/BFK	35		4000	35000
Clubs-Blue Ground	CPP	LT/CPP	1982	EB/A	33 X 26	R/BFK	35		2800	22000
Two-Way II	CPP	CPP	1982	EB/A	37 X 27	R/BFK	40		2800	22000
Five Spades (Set of 5):									5000 SET	18000 SET
Green Tree Spade	CPP	LT/HT/PS/CPP	1982	EB/AC	19 X 23	RP/H/W	35	4	1000	6500
Tri-Color Spade	CPP	LT/HT/PS/CPP	1982	EB/AC	26 X 20	RP/H/W	50	4	1000	6500
Eiffelspade	CPP	LT/HT/PS/CPP	1982	EB/A	24 X 19	WP/ART	50	1	600	2500
Spade Drypoint	CPP	LT/HT/PS/CPP	1982	DPT	23 X 18	WP/ART	50	1	600	2500
Sugarlift Spade	CPP	LT/CPP	1982	EB/A	33 X 27	R/BFK	35	1	1000	3200
Ochre	CPP	TT/SPS/CPP	1983	WBP	27 X 38	MIT	200	12	2800	28000
Blue	CPP	TT/SPS/CPP	1984	WC	42 X 27	MIT	200	11	3800	35000
M (G-1192)	GEM	GEM	1985	LC	30 X 22	AP88	60		1000	9000
Center Square	CPP	MB/RB/LH/CPP	1985	EB/A	26 X 20	R/BFK/HW	25	1	1500	6000
Indigo Horizontal	CPP	MB/RB/LH/CPP	1985	EB/A	36 X 49	R/BFK	50	1	7500	45000

The print market has become very selective. For the first time since we published the first edition of The Printworld Directory in 1982, the prices of prints have been greatly reduced and greatly increased for the same artists by the most reputable and established print publishers. Check the fifth edition to understand the movement.

RICHARD DIEBENKORN CONTINUED

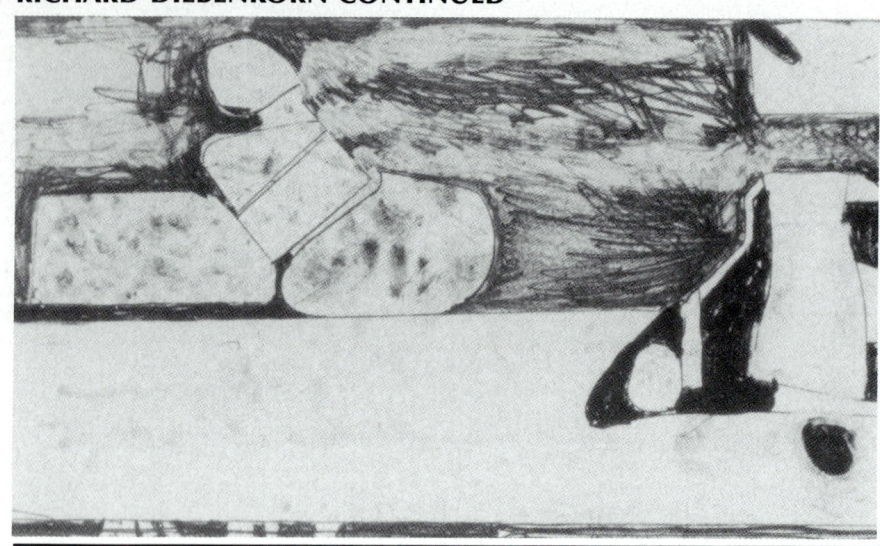

Richard Diebenkorn
Blue Softground
Courtesy Crown Point Press

TITLE	PUBLISHER	PRINTER	DATE	MEDIUM	DIMENSION (PAPER SIZE) IN INCHES	TYPE OF PAPER	EDITION NUMBER	NO. OF COLORS	ORIGINAL OPENING PRICE	CURRENT RETAIL PRICE
SOLD OUT EDITIONS (RARE):										
Twelve	GEM	GEM	1985	LC	44 X 34	AP88	50	14	5500	60000
Greyland	GEM	GEM	1985	LC	44 X 34	AS	40	5	5000	55000
Serge	GEM	GEM	1985	LC	44 X 34	AP88	26	4	3000	35000
Black & Grey (Gem-1197)	GEM	GEM	1985	LC	44 X 34	AP88	42	3	2500	12000
Trip on the Ground	GEM	GEM	1985	LC	37 X 25	HMP	33	2	2000	13500
Scrabbling	GEM	GEM	1985	LC	34 X 25	HMP	47	3	2000	13500
Green	CPP	CPP	1986	EC/A/DPT	54 X 42	SOM	60		9000	100000
X	CPP	CPP	1986	EB	19 X 13	HMP	50	1	700	2200
Y	CPP	MB/NA/CPP	1986	DPT	19 X 13	HMP	50	1	700	2200
Folsom Street Variations (Set of 3):									15000 SET	42000 SET
Folsom Street Variations I (Black)	CPP	MB/NA/CPP	1986	AC/DPT	26 X 33	R/BFK/HWT	60		5000	10000
Folsom Street Variations II (Gray)	CPP	MB/NA/CPP	1986	AC/DPT	26 X 40	R/BFK/HWT	60		5000	18000
Folsom Street Variations III (Primaries)	CPP	MB/NA/CPP	1986	AC/DPT	26 X 40	R/BFK/HWT	60		5000	22000
Red-Yellow-Blue	CPP	CPP	1986	EB/AC	26 X 40	R/BFK	60		5000	22000
Double X	CPP	ART/TT/CPP	1987	WB	23 X 17	MIT	50	1	1800	4000
CJD	CPP	RB/BS/PP/CPP	1990	DPT	17 X 14	R/BFK/HWT/W	15	1	1250	2800
Domino I	CPP	CPP	1990	EB/DPT/SG/HG	21X 16	R/BFK	35		1800	3200
Domino II	CPP	CPP	1990	EB/DPT/SG/HG	27 X 21	R/BFK	35		1800	3500
Passage I	CPP	CPP	1990	EB/AC/DPT/HG	30 X 20	R/BFK	35		2800	4000
Passage II	CPP	CPP	1990	EB/AC	23 X 20	R/BFK	25		1800	3000
Tulips	CPP	RB/BS/CPP	1989	SG	17 X 13	RP/HWT/W	25		950	2200
Reading	CPP	BS/PP/CPP	1990	SG	15 X 16	RP/HWT/W	15		1250	3000
Window	CPP	RB/BS/PP	1990	SG/SL/A	17 X 14	RP/HWT/W	35		1000	2200
Ne Comprend Pas	CPP	CPP	1990	EB/A/SL/SB	15 X 15	R/BFK	25	1	1000	2200
Oui	CPP	CPP	1990	EB/A/DPT	14 X 13	R/BFK	25	1	1200	2200
Touched Red	CPP	CPP	1991	EB/A/SB/SG/DPT	36 X 27	RP/HWT/W	85	16	12500	22000
CURRENT EDITIONS:										
White Club	CPP	NA/LT/HT	1981	EB/A	38 X 31	AP/S	22	1	3000	12000
Blue Softground	CPP	CPP	1985	EC/SG	26 X 36	AP88	35		2500	8500
Blue with Red	CPP	TT/SM/CPP	1987	WC	38 X 26	KOZO	200	12	10500	23000
Flotsam	CPP	RB/BS/PP/CPP	1991	EB/A/DPT	34 X 27	RP/HWT/B	85	1	3500	3500
The Barbarian	CPP	CPP	1992	A/SCRA/BUR/DPT	34 X 27	AC	15	1	3500	3500
The Barbarian's Garden—Threatened (Aquatint Reversal)	CPP	CPP	1992	A/SCRA/BUR/DPT	34 X 27	AC	15	1	3500	3500
High Green, Version I	CPP	CPP	1992	AC/SB/DPT/SG/HG/SL	53 X 34	AC	65		30000	36000
High Green, Version II	CPP	CPP	1992	AC/SB/DPT/SG/HG/SL	53 X 34	AC	65		30000	33000

The retail prices of the 100,000 limited edition prints quoted in this directory are subject to change. Print publishers, artists and galleries were the direct sources for these quotations. Prices in the secondary market listed as "Sold Out Editions (Rare)" indicate that the publisher has a limited supply of that print or that the print is difficult to locate in the galleries.

The Printworld Directory is accepting new applications for the seventh edition. Approximately 300 new artists will be accepted. Please use the two forms provided in the back section of this directory to submit biographical data and documentation of prints. Edition number of each print must not exceed 500 and the retail price must be $100 or more.

PHILIP DIKE

BORN: Redlands, CA; (1906–1990)
EDUCATION: Chouinard Art Inst, Los Angeles, CA, with Chamberlain; Art Students League, NY; American Acad, Fountainbleau, Paris, France
AWARDS: Pasadena Art Inst, CA, 1933; Butler Inst of AM Art, Youngstown, OH, 1959; Am Watercolor Society of New York, NY, 1965; John Ernst Award, 1965; British Nat Watercolor Society, London, England, 1962; Nat Acad of Design, NY, 1950,58,63; California Nat Watercolor Society, Los Angeles, CA, 1931,35,39,45,52,53,56,57,65; Brugger Prize, 1966; Purchase Award, Springfield Mus, MA, 1967
COLLECTIONS: Metropolitan Mus of Art, NY; Santa Barbara Art Mus, CA; Wood Mus, Montpelier, VT; Scripps Col, Claremont, CA
PRINTERS: Artist (ART)
PUBLISHERS: Artist (ART)

TITLE	PUBLISHER	PRINTER	DATE	MEDIUM	DIMENSION (PAPER SIZE) IN INCHES	TYPE OF PAPER	EDITION NUMBER	NO. OF COLORS	ORIGINAL OPENING PRICE	CURRENT RETAIL PRICE
SOLD OUT EDITIONS (RARE):										
Fishing Wharf	ART	ART	1949	LB	10 X 14	AP	20	1	75	500
Return of the Swallows	ART	ART	1949	LB	6 X 9	AP	80	1	50	300

LADDIE JOHN DILL

BORN: Long Beach, CA; September 14, 1943
EDUCATION: Inst of the Arts, Valencia, CA, BFA, 1968
TEACHING: Lectr, Painting, Univ of California, Los Angeles, CA, 1975 to present
AWARDS: Guggenheim Fel, 1980; Nat Endowment for the Arts, 1975, 82
RECENT EXHIB: Thomas Babeor Gallery, La Jolla, CA, 1987; Fuller Goldeen Gallery, San Francisco, CA, 1987; Sena Galleries West, Santa Fe, NM, 1990
COLLECTIONS: Los Angeles County Mus, Los Angeles, CA; Norton Simon Mus, Pasadena, CA; San Francisco Mus of Mod Art, CA; Smithsonian Inst, Wash, DC; Mus of Mod Art, NY; Oakland Mus of Art, OH; Chicago Art Inst, IL; Long Beach Mus of Art, CA
PRINTERS: Landfall Press Inc, Chicago, IL (LPI); Jack Lemon, Chicago, IL (JL); Timothy Berry, Chicago, IL (TB); Milan Milojevic, Chicago, IL (MM); Art Casting Studio (ACS); Black Dolphin Workshop, Long Beach, CA (BDW); A Goldman, CA (AG); R Skalak, CA (RS); 3 EP Ltd, Palo Alto, CA (3EP); Centrum Press, Port Townsend, WA (CP); Cirrus Editions Workshop, Los Angeles, CA (CEW); Richard Hammond, Los Angeles, CA (RH); Francesco Siqueiros, Los Angeles, CA (FS); La Poligrafa, SA, Barcelona, Spain (LP)
PUBLISHERS: Landfall Press Inc, Chicago, IL (LPI); Black Dolphin Workshop, Long Beach, CA (BDW); 3 EP Ltd, Palo Alto, CA (3EP); Centrum Press, Port Townsend, WA (CP); Cirrus Editions Ltd, Los Angeles, CA (CE); Ediciones Poligrafa, SA, Barceona, Spain (EdP)
GALLERIES: James Corcoran Gallery, Los Angeles, CA; Patricia Heesy, New York, NY; Signet Arts, St Louis, MO; Landfall Press, Chicago, IL; Zolla/Lieberman Gallery, Chicago, IL; Linda Farris Gallery, Seattle, WA; Ianuzzi Gallery, Scottsdale, AZ; Thomas Babeor Gallery, La Jolla, CA; Charles Cowles Gallery, New York, NY; Cirrus Editions, Ltd, Los Angeles, CA; Irene Drori Graphics, Los Angeles, CA; Charles Whitchurch, Huntington Beach, CA; Mixografia Gallery, Santa Monica, CA; Site 311, Pacific Grove, CA; Smith Andersen Gallery, Palo Alto, CA; Annex Gallery, San Diego, CA; Ochi Galleries, Boise, ID & Sun Valley, ID; Stremmel Gallery, Reno, NV; Kornbluth Gallery, Fair Lawn, NJ; Sena International, Santa Fe, NM; Judy Youens Gallery, Houston, TX; Galeria Joan Prats, New York, NY & Barcelona, Spain; The Works Gallery, Long Beach, CA; Winged Horse Gallerie, Las Vegas, NV
MAILING ADDRESS: 1625 Electric Ave, Venice, CA 90291

TITLE	PUBLISHER	PRINTER	DATE	MEDIUM	DIMENSION (PAPER SIZE) IN INCHES	TYPE OF PAPER	EDITION NUMBER	NO. OF COLORS	ORIGINAL OPENING PRICE	CURRENT RETAIL PRICE
SOLD OUT EDITIONS (RARE):										
Untitled (Red)	BDW	AG/RS/BDW	1976	COL	18 X 21	AC/W	10	1	300	500
Untitled (Black)	BDW	AG/RS/BDW	1976	COL	18 X 21	AC/W	10	1	300	500
Untitled	BDW	AG/RS/BDW	1976	COL	24 X 31	AC/W	26	1	300	600
Untitled	LPI	JL/LPI	1978	LC	35 X 48	ARP	25	6	500	800
Portal Series (Set of 4):										
Portal #1	LPI	JL/LPI	1978	LC	21 X 40	AP/W	20	3	400	600
Portal #2	LPI	JL/LPI	1978	LC	34 X 26	AP/W	20	6	400	600
Portal #3	LPI	JL/LPI	1978	LC	28 X 48	AP/W	20	5	400	600
Portal #4	LPI	MM/LPI	1978	LC	18 X 26	AP/W	20	2	250	400
Ashland Series:										
Ashland Series #1	LPI	TB/LPI	1980	SG/A	22 X 30	R/BFK	35	3	400	600
Ashland Series #2	LPI	TB/LPI	1980	SG/A	22 X 30	R/BFK	35	3	400	600
Ashland Series #3	LPI	TB/LPI	1980	SG/A	22 X 30	R/BFK	35	3	400	600
Ashland Series #4	LPI	TB/LPI	1980	SG/A	22 X 30	R/BFK	35	3	400	600
Arial Landscape I	EdP	LP	1980	EB		AP/W			400	900
Set of 2 Lithographs	EdP	LP	1980	LC		AP/W			400 EA	800 EA
Stage Left	LPI	JL/LPI	1981	LC	21 X 46	ARJ	35	6	550	800
Stage Whispers	LPI	JL/LPI	1981	LC	21 X 46	ARJ	35	5	550	750
Stage Fright	LPI	JL/LPI	1981	LC	16 X 28	ARJ	35	5	350	500
Stage Struck	LPI	JL/LPI	1981	LC	16 X 28	ARJ	35	3	350	500
Buffalo Portal	LPI	ASC	1982	BR	18 X 24	BR	6		3000	3500
Sioux Portal	LPI	ASC	1982	BR	18 X 24	BR	6		3000	3500
Untitled	CP	TB	1982	EB/A	16 X 26	R/BFK	50	3	400	800
Untitled Monotype Series (Set of 3):										
Untitled	3EP	3EP	1982	MON	30 X 60 EA	HMP	1 EA	Varies	800	2000 EA
Untitled	3EP	3EP	1982	MON	27 X 55 EA	HMP	1 EA	Varies	800 EA	2000 EA
Untitled	3EP	3EP	1982	MON	36 X 37 EA	HMP	1 EA	1	600 EA	2000 EA
Untitled Monotype Series (Set of 2):										
Untitled	3EP	3EP	1983	MON	33 X 35 EA	HMP	1 EA	Varies	800 EA	1500 EA
Untitled	3EP	3EP	1983	MON	17 X 27 EA	HMP	1 EA	Varies	600 EA	1200 EA
Untitled Monotype	3EP	3EP	1983	MON	30 X 38 EA	HMP	1 EA	Varies	800 EA	1800 EA
Untitled Monotype	3EP	3EP	1984	MON	23 X 23 EA	HMP	1 EA	Varies	600 EA	1200 EA
Untitled Cast Paper	3EP	3EP	1984	MON	30 X 48 EA	CP	1 EA	Varies	1500 EA	4500 EA
CURRENT EDITIONS:										
Untitled (368c)	CE	CEW	1984	LC/WC	13 X 27	ARJ	275		250	300
Untitled (382w)	CE	RH/FS/CEW	1985	LC/WC	29 X 56	AP88	35	4	850	1000

LESLEY DILL

PRINTERS: Judith Solodkin, NY (JS); Solo Press, NY (SP); Jack Lemon, Chicago, IL (JL); Landfall Press, Inc, Chicago, IL (LPI)
PUBLISHERS: Solo Press, NY (SP); Landfall Press, Inc, Chicago, IL (LPI)
GALLERIES: Ann Jaffe Gallery, Bay Harbor Islands, FL; Sandler Hudson Gallery, Atlanta, GA; Gracie Mansion Fine Art, New York, NY; Philippe Staib Gallery, New York, NY; Solo Gallery, New York, NY; Landfall Press, Inc, Chicago, IL; Quartet Editions, New York, NY

TITLE	PUBLISHER	PRINTER	DATE	MEDIUM	DIMENSION (PAPER SIZE) IN INCHES	TYPE OF PAPER	EDITION NUMBER	NO. OF COLORS	ORIGINAL OPENING PRICE	CURRENT RETAIL PRICE
CURRENT EDITIONS:										
The Poetic Body (Set of 4):									2600 SET	2600 SET
Poem Eyes	SP	JS/SP	1992	LC/LP/CO	18 X 13	AC	20		700	700
Poem Gloves	SP	JS/SP	1992	LC/LP/CO	18 X 13	AC	20		700	700
Poem Ears	SP	JS/SP	1992	LC/LP/CO	18 X 13	AC	20		700	700
Poem Dress of Circulation	SP	JS/SP	1992	LC/LP/CO	18 X 13	AC	20		700	700
Red Poem Suit	LPI	JL/LPI	1992	LC/WC	31 X 51	AC	20		1200	1200

JIM DINE

BORN: Cincinnati, OH; June 16, 1935
EDUCATION: Univ of Cincinnati, OH; Boston Mus Sch, MA; Ohio Univ, Athens, OH, BFA, 1958
TEACHING: Vis Prof, Oberlin Col, OH, 1965; Vis Prof, Cornell Univ, Ithaca, NY, 1967; Art in Res, Williams Col, Williamstown, MA, 1976
AWARDS: Norman Harris Silver Medal & Prize, Chicago Inst of Art, IL, 1964
RECENT EXHIB: Walker Art Center, Minneapolis, MN, 1987; Williams Col Mus, Williamstown, MA, 1987; Penson Gallery, NY, 1988; Waddington Galleries, London, England, 1989; Associated Am Artists, NY, 1989; Miami Univ Art Mus, Oxford, OH, 1989; Galerie 1900–2000, Paris, France, 1989; Pace Prints, NY, Retrosp, 1990; Nelson-Atkins Mus of Art, Kansas City, MO, 1990; Argus Gallery, Portland, OR, 1990; BlumHelman Gallery, Santa Monica, CA, 1990; Galeria Enrico Navarra, Paris, France, 1990; Martin-Gropius-Bau, Berlin, Germany, 1990; James Goodman Gallery, NY, 1990; Galleria Isy Brachot, Brussels, Belgium, 1990; Fairfield Univ, CT, 1990; Galeria Kaj Forsblom, Helsinki, Finland, 1990; Lowe Art Mus, Univ of Miami, FL, 1990; Isetan Mus, Tokyo, Japan, 1990–91; Kintetsu Mus of Art, Osaka, Japan, 1990–91; Pace Gallery, NY, 1991; Pace Prints, NY, 1992; Pace Downtown, NY, 1992; Newport Harbor Art Mus, Newport Beach, CA, 1989,92; Center for the Fine Arts, Miami, FL, 1992; Univ of South Florida, Graphicstudio/USF, Tampa, FL, 1992; Contemporary Arts Center, Cincinnati, OH, 1989,92; Southern Alleghenies Mus, Loretto, PA, 1992; Univ of Washington, Henry Art Gallery, Seattle, WA, 1989,92; Associated Am Artists, NY, 1993
COLLECTIONS: Mus of Mod Art, NY; Whitney Mus of Am Art, NY; Guggenheim Mus, NY; Tate Gallery, London, England; Stedelijk Mus, Amsterdam, Netherlands; Albright-Knox Art Gallery, Buffalo, NY; Brandeis Mus, Waltham, MA; Mus of Fine Arts, Dallas, TX; Jewish Mus, NY; Ball State Univ, Muncie, IN; Oberlin Col, OH; Mus of Art, Toronto, Canada; Centre Pompidou, Paris, France; Western Australia Art Gallery, Perth, Australia
PRINTERS: Univ of Hartford, CT (UH); Landfall Press Inc, Chicago IL (LPI); Deli Sacilotto (DS); Patrick Foy, Tampa, FL (PF); Graphicstudio, Univ of Florida, Tampa, FL (GS/USF); K Ronn (KR); J Berman (JB); A Rosenberg (AR); M Friedman (MF); S Hennesey (SH); J Jurista (JJ); A Brooks (AB); Maurice Sanchez, NY (MS); Burston Graphics (BG); Petersburg Press, London, England (PP); Palm Press, Tampa, FL (P); William Law, Los Angeles, CA (WL); Wroeth (WR); Donald Saff (DS); T Kettner (TK); R Durham (RD); Mitchell Friedman Workshop (MFW); Williams Col, MA (WC); R E Townsend, Boston, MA (RT); Experimental Printmaking, San Francisco, CA (EP); Angeles Press, Los Angeles CA (AP); Universal Limited Art Editions, West Islip, NY (ULAE); Aldo Crommelynck, Paris, France (AC); Atelier Crommelynck, Paris, France (AtC); Artist (ART); Tamarind Inst, Albuquerque, NM (TI); Irwin Hollander, NY (IH); Arion Press, San Francisco, CA (ArPr); Angeles Press, Los Angeles, CA (AP); Niels Borch Jensen, Copenhagen, Denmark (NBJ); Luigi Berardinelli, Verona, Italy (LB); Marco Berardinelli, Verona, Italy (MB); Stamperia d'Arte, Verona, Italy (SdA)
PUBLISHERS: Pace Editions, Inc, NY (PE); Petersburg Press, Ltd, London, England (PP); Pyramid Arts Ltd (PAL); Univ of South Florida, Tampa, FL (USF); Waddington Graphics, London, England (WC); Aldo Crommelynck, Paris, France (AC); Artist (ART); Tamarind Inst, Albuquerque, NM (TI); Original Editions, NY (OEd); Universal Limited Art Editions, West Islip, NY (ULAE)
GALLERIES: Harcourts Modern & Contemporary, San Francisco, CA; Hokin Galleries, Bay Harbor Islands, FL & Palm Beach, FL; Richard Gray Gallery, Chicago, IL; van Straaten Gallery, Chicago, IL; Barbara Krakow Gallery, Boston, MA; Magnuson Gallery, Boston, MA; Nancy Singer Gallery, St Louis, MO; Claude Bernard Gallery, New York, NY; Edward Tyler Nahem Fine Art, New York, NY; Pace Prints, New York, NY; Nan Miller Gallery, Rochester, NY; Charles Foley Gallery, Columbus, OH; Contemporary Gallery, Dallas, TX; Janie C Lee Gallery, Houston, TX & New York, NY; Greg Kucera Gallery, Seattle, WA; Posner Gallery, Milwaukee, WI; Lemberg Gallery, Birmingham, MI; Waddington & Gorce, Inc, Montreal, Canada; Evelyn Aimis Fine Art, Toronto, Canada; Baudoin Lebon Gallery, Paris, France; Andrew Dierken Fine Art, Los Angeles, CA; R K Goldman Contemporary, Los Angeles, CA; Marilyn Pink Fine Arts, Ltd, Los Angeles, CA; Morgan Gallery, Boston, MA; Barbara Gillman Gallery, Miami, FL; Frances Aronson Gallery, Atlanta, GA; Landfall Press, Chicago, IL; Golden Gallery, Chestnut Hill, MA; Horoshak Contemporary Art, Sunnyvale, CA; Elizabeth Paul Galleries, Cincinnati, OH & Columbus, OH; Michael H Lord Gallery, Milwaukee, WI; Signet Arts, St Louis, MO; Nohra Haimes Gallery, New York, NY; Jim Kempner Fine Art, New York, NY; Magidson Fine Arts, New York, NY; L'Imagerie, Encino, CA; Metropolitan Art Gallery, Los Angeles, CA; Herbert Palmer Gallery, Los Angeles, CA; Arion Press, San Francisco, CA; John Berggruen Gallery, San Francisco, CA; Erika Meyrovich Gallery, San Francisco, CA; Richard Green Graphics, Santa Monica, CA; Park Granada Editions, Tarzana, CA; William Turner Gallery, Venice, CA; Margulies Taplin Gallery, Boca Raton, FL; Kass/Meridian Gallery, Chicago, IL; Randall Beck Gallery, Boston, MA; John Denton Gallery, Hiawassee, GA; Peter M David, Minneapolis, MN; Dolly Fiterman Fine Arts, Minneapolis, NM; Moira James Gallery, Green Valley, NV; DEL Fine Art Galleries, Santa Fe, NM; Greenhut Galleries, Albany, NY; Associated American Artists, New York, NY; Posner Gallery, Milwaukee, WI; Fenton Fine Arts, Fort Worth, TX; Quartet Editions, New York, NY

Williams College (WC)—D'Oench & Feinberg (DO/F)

TITLE	PUBLISHER	PRINTER	DATE	MEDIUM	DIMENSION (PAPER SIZE) IN INCHES	TYPE OF PAPER	EDITION NUMBER	NO. OF COLORS	ORIGINAL OPENING PRICE	CURRENT RETAIL PRICE
SOLD OUT EDITIONS (RARE):										
The End of the Crash	PP	PP	1960	LC	40 X 26	HMP	32		200	12000
Crash Series (Set of 5)	PP	PP	1960	LB	30 X 22 EA	HMP	33 EA		600 SET	5000 SET
Colored Pal	ULAE	ULAE	1963	LC	32 X 23	HMP	23		150	8500
Double Apple Palette with Gingham	ULAE	ULAE	1965	LC/CO	24 X 28	HMP	23		200	8500
Flesh Palette in a Landscape	PP	PP	1965	LC	26 X 20	HMP	22		150	10000
Awl	PP	PP	1965	SP	24 X 20	HMP	50		200	1000
Throat	OEd	PP	1965	SP	30 X 24	HMP	200		200	1000
Calico	PP	PP	1965	SP	40 X 30	HMP	200		200	1000
Kenneth Koch Poem	PP	PP	1966	LC	37 X 24	HMP	31		300	3500

JIM DINE CONTINUED

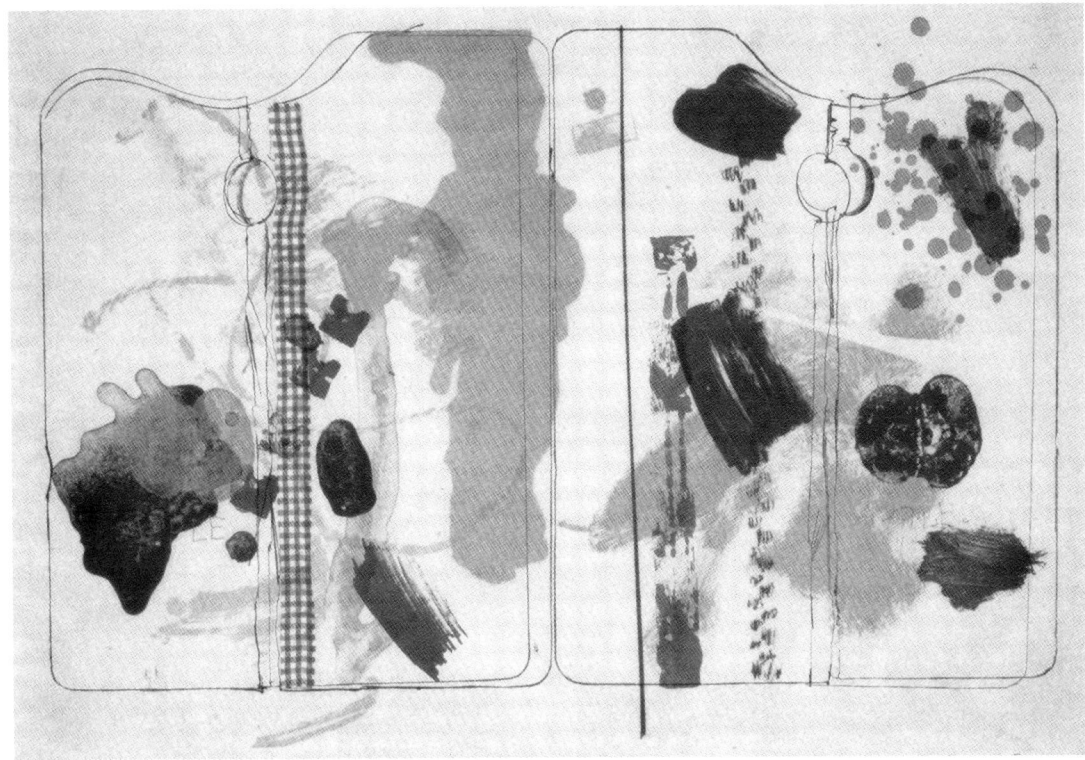

Jim Dine
Double Apple Palette with Gingham
Courtesy Universal Limited Art Editions

TITLE	PUBLISHER	PRINTER	DATE	MEDIUM	DIMENSION (PAPER SIZE) IN INCHES	TYPE OF PAPER	EDITION NUMBER	NO. OF COLORS	ORIGINAL OPENING PRICE	CURRENT RETAIL PRICE
SOLD OUT EDITIONS (RARE):										
Silver Star	PP	IH/PP	1966	LB	30 X 22	R/BFK	60	1	200	2000
Drag-Johnson and Mao	PP	PP	1967	EC	34 X 48	HMP	53		399	5000
Wall	PP	PP	1967	EC	31 X 22	HMP	120		300	2000
Bleeding Heart with Ribbons	PP	PP	1968	WC/CO/SP	20 X 15	HMP	48		500	8000
									2000 SET	10000 SET
The Picture of Dorian Gray (Book with 12 Loose Color Lithographs)										
Edition A (Bound in Red Velvet-6 Wove Lithographs)	PP	PP	1968	LC	18 X 12 EA	AP	200		100	3500
Edition B (Bound in Green Velvet-4 Loose Etchings)	PP	PP	1968	EC	18 X 12 EA	AP	200		100	600
Editions C (Bound in Printed Snakeskin (6 Loose Lithographs, 4 Etchings Plus Multiple)	PP	PP	1968	LC/MULT	18 X 12 EA	AP	100		200	10000
Dorian Gray with Rainbow Scarf	PP	PP	1968	LC	18 X 12	AP	200/100		xxx	xxx
Hose Lamp	PP	PP	1968	LC	18 X 12	AP	200/100		xxx	xxx
Basil in Black Leather Suit	PP	PP	1968	LC	18 X 12	AP	200/100		xxx	xxx
Dorian Gray in Multi-Coloured Vinyl Striped Cape	PP	PP	1968	LC	18 X 12	AP	200/100		xxx	1200
Sibyl in Her Dressing Room	PP	PP	1968	LC	18 X 12	AP	200/100		xxx	xxx
Red Piano	PP	PP	1968	LC	18 X 12	AP	200/100		xxx	xxx
Red Design for Satin Heart	PP	PP	1968	EC	18 X 12	AP	200/100		xxx	xxx
Study for the Rings on Dorian Gray's Hand	PP	PP	1968	EC	18 X 12	AP	200/100		xxx	xxx
Dorian Gray at the Opium Den	PP	PP	1968	EC	18 X 12	AP	200/100		xxx	xxx
Imprint from Dorian Gray's Stomach	PP	PP	1968	EC	18 X 12	AP	200/100		xxx	xxx
Cincinnati Series (Set of 4):										
Cincinnati I	PP	PP	1969	LB	28 X 40	HMP	75	1	200	2500
Cincinnati II	PP	PP	1969	LB	28 X 40	HMP	75	1	200	2500
Cincinnati III	PP	PP	1969	LC	30 X 45	HMP	75	1	200	2500
Cincinnati IV	PP	PP	1969	LB	29 X 41	HMP	75	1	200	2500
Photos and Etchings (with Lee Friedlander) (Set of 16)	PP	PP	1969	EC/PH	18 X 30 EA		75 EA		1600 SET	15000 SET
Vegetables (Set of 8)	PP	PP	1969	LB/CO	18 X 15 EA	WSHP	96 EA		800 SET	7500 SET
Landscape Screen (5-Panel Folding Screen) (Screen printed on Linen)	PP	PP	1969	SP	73 X 92	LIN	30		2500	30000
Four Palettes (Set of 4):										
Palette I—Silkscreen	PP	PP	1969	SP	28 X 20	FAB	75		500	3000
Palette II—Color Lithograph with Collage	PP	PP	1969	LC/CO	28 X 20	FAB	75		500	3500

JIM DINE CONTINUED

TITLE	PUBLISHER	PRINTER	DATE	MEDIUM	DIMENSION (PAPER SIZE) IN INCHES	TYPE OF PAPER	EDITION NUMBER	NO. OF COLORS	ORIGINAL OPENING PRICE	CURRENT RETAIL PRICE
SOLD OUT EDITIONS (RARE):										
Palette III—Color Etching	PP	PP	1969	EC	28 X 20	FAB	75		500	3000
Palette IV—Multiple	PP	PP	1969	MULT	28 X 20		75		600	3500
Self Portrait: The Landscape	PP	PP	1969	LC	53 X 38	HMP	75		600	30000
Photographs and Etchings (with Lee Friedlander) (Set of 16)	PP	PP	1969	EC/PH	18 X 30 EA	HMP	75 EA		1500 SET	30000 SET
Red Bathrobe	PP	PP	1969	LC	53 X 38	HMP	35		600	25000
Eleven Hearts	PP	PP	1969	EC/HC	14 X 21	HMP	50		400	9500
Night Portrait	PP	PP	1969	LC	53 X 38	HMP	21		600	12000
A Pure Self Portrait	PP	PP	1969	LC	53 X 38	HMP	3		600	9500
Pliers	PP	PP	1969	LB	20 X 25	FAB	21	1	500	4500
Oo La La (with Ron Padgett) (Set of 15)	PP	PP	1970	LC	18 X 27 EA	HMP	75 EA		3000 SET	6500 SET
Tools	PP	PP	1970	LC	40 X 55	HMP	63		400	3000
Tools—The Rainbow	PP	PP	1970	LC/CO/HC	40 X 55	HMP	11		400	15000
Six Hearts	PP	PP	1970	LC/CO/HC	30 X 22	HMP	79		400	8000
Dutch Hearts (Set of 8)	PP	PP	1970	LC/CO	17 X 20	WSHP	85	1	2500 SET	50000 SET
Hammers	PP	PP	1970	LC	26 X 16 EA	HMP	53 EA		600	2500
Bathrobe	PP	PP	1970	LC	31 X 22	HMP	150		400	4000
Hands	PP	PP	1970	LC	31 X 22	HMP	150		400	4000
Ties	PP	PP	1970	LC/HC	31 X 22	HMP	150		400	4000
The Poet Assassinated	PP	PP	1970	EB/HC	27 X 21	HMP	75	Varies	400	3500
The Realistic Poet Assassinated	PP	PP	1970	EB/HC	27 X 21	HMP	75		400	5000
A Girl and Her Dog I	PP	PP	1970	EC/A	35 X 28	HMP	75		300	4500
The World (for Anne Waldman) (WC-38)	PP	PP	1971	LC/SP/CO	30 X 40	HMP	100	Varies	450	28000
Four Kinds of Pubic Hair	PP	PP	1971	EB	23 X 16	HMP	50	1	300	3500
Paintbrush	PP	PP	1971	EB	35 X 28	HMP	75		300	4000
Black Heart	PP	PP	1971	LB	30 X 40	HMP	55	1	400	2000
The World	PP	PP	1971	LB	40 X 30	HMP	1		500	25000
Self Portraits (Set of 9)	PP	PP	1971	DPT	17 X 14 EA	HMP	25 EA		2500 SET	20000 SET
Sledgehammer and Axe	PP	PP	1971	LC	56 X 40	HMP	80		450	2500
Picabia Series:										
Picabia I (Cheer)	PP	PP	1971	LB/CO	53 X 35	HMP	75	1	500	4000
Picabia II (Forgot)	PP	PP	1971	LB/CO	53 X 35	HMP	75	1	500	4000
Picabia III (Groans)	PP	PP	1971	LB/CO	53 X 35	HMP	75	1	500	4000
Self Portraits (Set of 9)	PP	PP	1971	DPT	17 X 14 EA	HMP	25 EA	1 EA	5000 SET	20000 SET
Etching, Self Portrait (Primary Colors) (3 Etchings in Red, Yellow and Blue) (WC-57)	PP	PP	1969–72	EC	22 X 30 EA	HMP	75 EA	3 EA	350 EA	9000 EA
Scissors	PP	PP	1972	DPT	30 X 22	HMP	10	1	500	2000
Two Hearts (the Donut) (Two Sheets)	ULAE	ULAE	1972	LC		R/BFK-JWP	17		400	20000
The Tomato	PP	PP	1972	EC/SP	30 X 40	HMP	75		400	6500
Gustave Flaubert	PP	PP	1972	EC	31 X 22	HMP	25		350	2000
Bolt Cutters, State I	PP	PP	1972	EC	40 X 30	HMP	75		500	4000
Morning Glory (2 Prints Mounted)	PP	PP	1972	EC/LC	8 X 10 EA	HMP	47 EA		400	2800
Rimbaud Historia	PP	PP	1972	LC/SP/EC/HC	30 X 22	HMP	80		350	5500
Blue Haircut	PP	PP	1972	EC/PH/OFF	35 X 28	HMP	75		400	4000
Brown Haircut	PP	PP	1972	EC/PH/OFF	35 X 28	HMP	75		400	4000
Silhouette Black Boots on Brown Paper	PP	PP	1972	LB	30 X 22	CWCP/T	100	1	350	4000
Five Paintbrushes, State I	PP	PP	1972	EC	30 X 40	MUR	75		600	20000
Self Portrait Head, State I	PP	PP	1972	EC	31 X 22	HMP	10		450	2400
Thirty Bones of My Body (Set of 30)	PP	PP	1972	DPT	30 X 22 EA	HMP	10 EA	1 EA	4500 SET	50000 SET
Oil Can	PP	PP	1972	EC	41 X 30	HMP	75		450	3000
Braid, State I	PP	PP	1972	EB	42 X 32	HMP	46		600	10000
Braid, State II	PP	PP	1973	EB	38 X 25	HMP	50		600	14500
Rimbaud Alchemy, on Japanese Paper	PP	PP	1973	EB	20 X 16	HMP	45	1	600	2000
Rimbaud, the Coffee Exporter	PP	PP	1973	EB	26 X 20	HMP	29	1	600	2000
Rimbaud at Harrar in 1883	PP	PP	1973	EB	17 X 14	HMP	25	1	600	2000
Rimbaud Wounded in Brussels	PP	PP	1973	EB	20 X 15	HMP	30	1	600	2000
Rimbaud, Cool Impudence on His Part	PP	PP	1973	EB	20 X 15	HMP	45	1	600	3000
Five Paintbrushes Series:										
Five Paintbrushes, State II	PP	PP	1973	EC	30 X 37	MUR	20		600	12500
Five Paintbrushes, State III	PP	PP	1973	EC	20 X 27	MUR	28		600	12500
Five Paintbrushes, State IV	PP	PP	1973	EC	30 X 35	MUR	15		600	12500
Five Paintbrushes, State V	PP	PP	1973	EC	30 X 37	MUR	19		600	12500
Five Paintbrushes, State VI	PP	PP	1973	EC	27 X 39	MUR	25	2	600	12500
Shoe Series:										
Shoe, State I	PP	PP	1973	EC	42 X 30	HMP	19		600	3500
Shoe, State II	PP	PP	1973	EC	24 X 29	HMP	36		600	3500
Shoe, State II	PP	PP	1973	EC	22 X 30	HMP	15		600	3500

JIM DINE CONTINUED

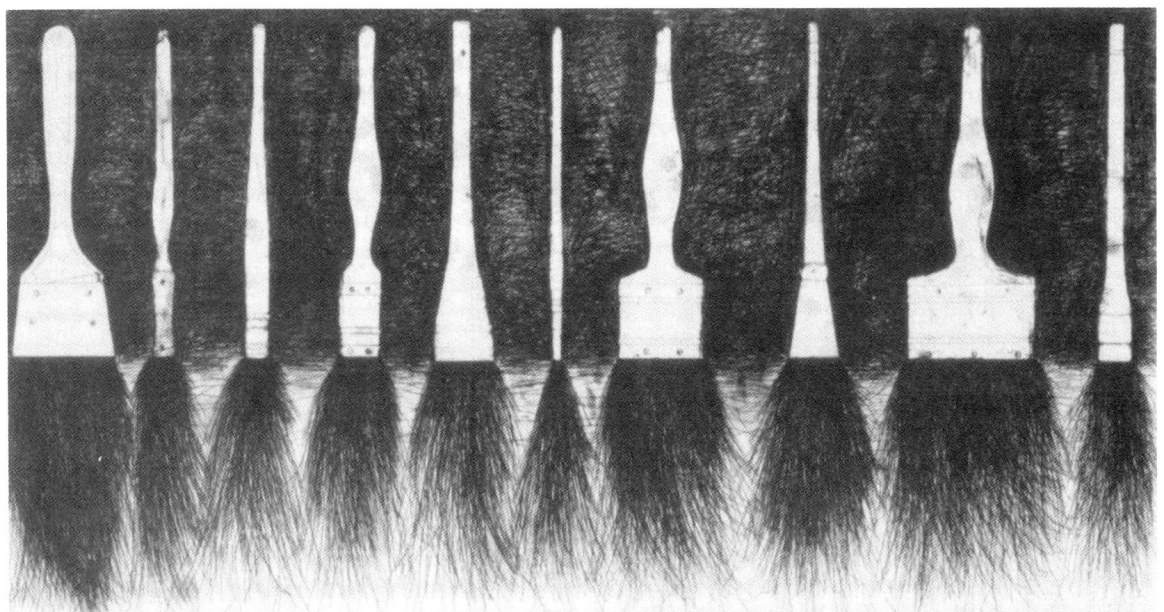

Jim Dine
Five Paintbrushes, State V
Courtesy Petersburg Press, Ltd

TITLE	PUBLISHER	PRINTER	DATE	MEDIUM	DIMENSION (PAPER SIZE) IN INCHES	TYPE OF PAPER	EDITION NUMBER	NO. OF COLORS	ORIGINAL OPENING PRICE	CURRENT RETAIL PRICE
SOLD OUT EDITIONS (RARE):										
Spoon	PP	PP	1973	EC	22 X 30	HMP	10		600	4000
Self Portrait Head Series:										
Self Portrait Head, State II	PP	PP	1973	EC	26 X 20	HMP	10		600	2000
Self Portrait Head, State III	PP	PP	1973	EC	26 X 20	HMP	15		600	2000
Ten Winter Tools (Set of 10)	PP	PP	1973	LC/WA/HC	28 X 21 EA	RdB	100 EA		3500 SET	18000 SET
Big Red Wrench in a . . .	PP	PP	1973	LC	30 X 22	RdB	120		500	3000
Wrench	PP	PP	1973	LC			10		750	4500
Black Beard	PP	PP	1973	EB	21 X 20	HMP	50	1	200	9000
Red Beard	PP	PP	1973	EC	21 X 20	JGP	50	1	200	9000
Tinsnip	PP	PP	1973	EB/LC	18 X 24	AC/W	34	2	200	3000
Four German Brushes	PP	PP	1973	EC	31 X 22 EA	HMP	75		200	10000
Bolt Cutters, State II	PP	PP	1973	EC	42 X 31	HMP	45		200	9000
Heads of Nancy	PP	PP	1973	EC	30 X 22	HMP	10		200	2500
Bid Red Wrenchina Landscape	PP	PP	1973	LC	30 X 22	HMP	120		200	5500
Wall Chart I	PP	PP/LPI	1974	LC	48 X 35	R/BFK	75	4	900	8000
Wall Chart II	PP	PP/LPI	1974	LC	48 X 35	R/BFK	75	3	900	8000
Wall Chart III	PP	PP/LPI	1974	LC	48 X 35	R/BFK	14	4	1200	3000
Wall Chart IV	PP	PP/LPI	1974	LC	48 X 35	R/BFK	14	3	1200	4000
Self Portrait in a Ski Hat, State I	PP	PP	1974	EB/HC	26 X 20	HMP	20	Varies	650	3500
Self Portrait in a Ski Hat (Surrounded by Tulips), State II	PP	PP	1974	EB	26 X 20	HMP	30	1	650	2000
Self Portrait in a Ski Hat (Tulips), State III	PP	PP	1974	EB	26 X 20	HMP	30	1	650	2000
Self Portrait in a Ski Hat (Obliterated by Tulips) State IV	PP	PP	1974	EB	28 X 20	HMP	40	1	650	3000
Self Portrait in a Flat Cap (Winter), State I	PP	PP	1974	EB	31 X 24	HMP	30	1	650	2000
Self Portrait in a Flat Cap (the Green Cap), State II	PP	PP	1974	EB	26 X 20	HMP	28	1	650	2000
Self Portrait in a Flat Cap (Baboon), State III	PP	PP	1974	EB	26 X 20	HMP	35	1	650	2000
Self Portrait in a Flat Cap (Weeds), State IV	PP	PP	1974	EB	26 X 20	HMP	38	1	650	2000
Lithographs of the Sculpture: the Plant becomes a Fan (Set of 5)	PP	PP	1974	LC/SP	36 X 24 EA	HMP	80 EA		2500 SET	5000 SET
Souvenir	PP	PP	1974	EB	23 X 18	HMP	75	1	500	5500
The Red Bandana	PE	LPI	1974	LC	48 X 36	JLP/R	50	2	500	5000
Piranesi's 24 Colored Marks	PP	PP	1974	EB/HC	27 X 24	HMP	30	Varies	650	4500
Black and White Bathrobe	PP	PP	1975	LB	36 X 24	HMP	80	1	600	3500
Self Portraits (the Dartmouth Portraits), State I (Set of 9)	PP	PP	1975	DPT	20 X 15 EA	HMP	25 EA	1 EA	3500 SET	20000 SET
Pink Chinese Scissors	PP	PP	1976	EB/HC	42 X 30	HMP	30	Varies	1000	7000
Piranesi's 24 Coloured Marks	PP	PP	1976	EB/HC	39 X 27	HMP	30	Varies	1000	10000

JIM DINE CONTINUED

TITLE	PUBLISHER	PRINTER	DATE	MEDIUM	DIMENSION (PAPER SIZE) IN INCHES	TYPE OF PAPER	EDITION NUMBER	NO. OF COLORS	ORIGINAL OPENING PRICE	CURRENT RETAIL PRICE
SOLD OUT EDITIONS (RARE):										
Red Etching Robe	PE	MF/WR	1976	EC/HG	43 X 30	CD	36	2	1000	25000
Two Robes (Ferns, Acid & Water)	PE	MF/ART	1976	EB/DPT	43 X 30	CD	15	1	1000	15000
A Robe with 13 Kinds of Oil Paint	PE	MF/WC	1976	EC	43 X 30	CD	10	14	1000	25000
Asian Woman, Pregnant and Grieving	PE	WC	1976	EB/HC	43 X 30	CD	23	4	750	4500
Black and White Flowers	PE	MF/ART	1976	EB/HC	39 X 27	FAB	50	1	750	5000
Black and White Flowers	AAA	DS	1977	EB/WA/HC	29 X 30	AC	30	Varies	2500	15000
The Brown Coat	PE	MF/PE	1976	EB/HC	42 X 23	R/BFK	50	2	750	4000
Dark Blue Self Portrait with White Crayon	PE	ME/PE	1976	EB/HC	30 X 22	R/BFK	11	3	1000	5000
Eight Sheets from an Undefined Novel (Set of 8):									18000 SET	100000 SET
A Fancy Lady	PAL	MF/DS/TK	1976	EB/HC	31 X 42	GE	30	Multi	1700	15000
A Nurse	PAL	MF/DS/TK	1976	EB/HC	31 X 42	GE	30	Multi	2300	15000
Cher Maitre	PAL	MF/DS/TK	1976	EB/HC	31 X 42	GE	30	Multi	1400	15000
The Cellist	PAL	MF/DS/TK	1976	EB/HC	31 X 42	GE	30	Multi	2500	15000
The Die Maker	PAL	MF/DS/TK	1976	EB/HC	31 X 42	GE	30	Multi	2000	15000
Russian Poetess	PAL	DS/TK/RD	1976	EB/HC	31 X 42	GE	30	Multi	3000	15000
A Sulfi Baker	PAL	MF/DS/TK	1976	EB/HC	31 X 42	GE	30	Multi	2500	15000
The Swimmer	PAL	MF/DS/TK	1976	EB/HC	31 X 42	GE	30	Multi	2800	15000
Saw	PAL	MF/MFW	1976	EB/HC	32 X 23	CP	30	1	1000	5000
Two Figures Linked by Pre-Verbal Feelings	PAL	MF/RD	1976	EB/DPT	31 X 42	GE/MIT	30	Multi	1400	2500
Warm Drypoint Robe	PE	MF/ART	1976	EC	42 X 30	CD	6	2	900	20000
Paris Smiles Portfolio (Set of 4):									3500 SET	25000 SET
Paris Smiles	AC	MF/ART/AtC	1976	EB/DPT/SL/SG	35 X 25	CD	45		900	2000
Paris Smiles in Darkness	AC	MF/ART/AtC	1976	EB/DPT/SL/SG	35 X 25	CD	45		900	2000
Drypoint Eiffel Tower (DO/F-6)	AC	MF/ART/AtC	1976	EB/DPT/SL/SG	35 X 25	CD	45		900	2000
Retroussage Eiffel Tower	AC	MF/ART/AtC	1976	EB/DPT/SL/SG	35 X 25	CD	45	1	900	2000
Multicolored Robe	PE	MF/ART	1977	LC	41 X 29	CD	10		900	35000
Spray Painted Robe	PE	MF/ART	1977	LC/OFF/EB/HC	41 X 29	AP/B	27	3	900	25000
Black and White Robe	PE	MF/ART	1977	LC	42 X 29	CD	12		900	3000
Untitled (Robe)	PE	MF/ART	1977	LC	41 X 29	CD	100		900	8500
Hand Colored Flowers, State I	PE	MF/MFW	1977	EB/HC	42 X 32	CD	50		900	8500
Self-Portrait	AAA	DS	1977	LB	41 X 29	AP/BL	100		1800	4000
Black and White Flowers	PE	MF/MFW	1977	EB	29 X 27	R/BFK	50	1	900	6000
Black and White Flowers	AAA	DS	1977	EB/WA/HC	29 X 30	AC	30	Varies	2500	15000
The Brown Coat	PE	MF/MFW	1977	LC	42 X 30	R/BFK	50	1	900	5000
Temple of Flora (Set of 9):									9500 SET	40000 SET
Amarylis	PE	CR	1977-78	EB/HC	39 X 28	CD	30	Varies	1200	4500
Anemones	PE	CR	1977-78	EB/HC	39 X 28	CD	30	Varies	1200	4500
Anthurium	PE	CR	1977-78	EB/HC	39 X 28	CD	30	Varies	1200	4500
Strelitzia	PE	AC/AtC	1977-78	EB/HC	39 X 28	CD	30	Varies	1200	4500
Iris	PE	AC/AtC	1977-78	EB/HC	39 X 28	CD	30	Varies	1200	4500
Superb Lilies	PE	AC/AtC	1977-78	EB/HC	39 X 28	CD	30	Varies	1200	4500
Tropical Succulents	PE	AC/AtC	1977-78	EB/HC	39 X 28	CD	30	Varies	1200	4500
Yellow Calla Lilies	PE	AC/AtC	1977-78	EB/HC	39 X 28	CD	30	Varies	1200	4500
Tulips	PE	AC/AtC	1977-78	EB/HC	39 X 28	CD	30	Varies	1200	4500
The Pine in a Storm of Aquatint	PE	AC/AtC	1978	EB/A/DPT	66 X 40	R/BFK	45	1	1500	10000
Self-Portrait Series:										
Self-Portrait with Glasses in Sepia	PE	AC/AtC	1978	EC	25 X 20	R/BFK	10		800	2000
Self-Portrait (Blue Tint)	PE	AC/AtC	1978	EC	26 X 20	R/BFK	15		800	2000
Self-Portrait on J D Paper	PE	AC/AtC	1978	EC	26 X 20	R/BFK	23		800	4500
Harvard Self-Portrait without Glasses, State IV	PE	AC/AtC	1978	EC	30 X 21	R/BFK	9		800	2000
Roses	PE	AC/AtC	1978	DPT	24 X 20	R/BFK	40	1	800	4000
Harvard Self Portrait	PE	AC/AtC	1978	EC/MON	12 X 9	R/BFK	5	Varies	1200	3500
Men and Plants	PE	AC/AtC	1978	EB	40 X 30	R/BFK	40	1	900	3500
Red Ochre Flowers	PE	AC/AtC	1978	EC	39 X 28	R/BFK	45		1000	4000
Nancy Outside in July, State IV	AC	AC/AtC	1978	EC	42 X 30	R/BFK	15		1200	5500
Nancy Outside in July I	AC	AC/AtC	1978	EC	35 X 24	R/BFK	60		1200	2500
Nancy Outside in July III	AC	AC/AtC	1978	EC/AC/DPT	41 X 30	R/BFK	60		1200	4000
Nancy Outside in July V	AC	AC/AtC	1978	EC	36 X 24	R/BFK	25		1200	3000
Nancy Outside in July VI (Flowers of the Holy Land)	AC	AC/AtC	1979	EC/HC	35 X 25	R/BFK	25		1200	9500
Rachel Cohen's Flags	PE	BG	1979	EB/A/HC	17 X 134	R/BFK	13		1000	10000
Self-Portrait in Grey	PE	BG	1979	EC	40 X 23	R/BFK	6		1200	2500
Unique, Hand-Painted Self-Portrait	PE	BG	1979	EC	30 X 22	R/BFK	35	4	1500	6000
Unique, Hand-Painted Self-Portrait (with Crayon & Pastel)	PE	BG	1979	EB/HC	30 X 23	R/BFK	4	Varies	1200	5000

JIM DINE CONTINUED

Jim Dine
Nancy Outside in July III
Courtesy Pace Editions, Inc

Jim Dine
Temple of Flora: Iris
Courtesy Pace Editions, Inc

TITLE	PUBLISHER	PRINTER	DATE	MEDIUM	DIMENSION (PAPER SIZE) IN INCHES	TYPE OF PAPER	EDITION NUMBER	NO. OF COLORS	ORIGINAL OPENING PRICE	CURRENT RETAIL PRICE
SOLD OUT EDITIONS (RARE):										
Akmatova, the Russian Poetess	PE	BG	1979	EC	30 X 22	R/BFK	35	4	1500	7500
Summer (A Swimmer), State II	PE	BG	1979	GB/HC	30 X 32	R/BFK	35	4	1500	5000
The Leaning Man, State II	PE	BG	1979	EC/HC	30 X 22	R/BFK	35	4	1200	2500
Jerusalem Plant Series:										
Jerusalem Plant, State I	PE	BG	1979	DPT	41 X 29	R/G	4		1000	2000
Jerusalem Plant, State II	PE	BG	1979	DPT/HC	41 X 29	R/G	8	3	1000	3000
Jerusalem Plant, State III	PE	BG	1979	DPT/HC	41 X 22	R/G	3		1000	4000
The Cellist against Blue, State II	PE	BG	1979	EC/HC	30 X 32	R/BFK	35	4	1500	2500
Self Portrait as a Diemaker	PE	BG	1979	EB/HC	30 X 32	R/BFK	35	4	1500	2500
Our Nurse at Home, State II	PE	BG	1979	EC/HC	30 X 32	R/BFK	35	4	1500	2500
A Little Girl	PE	BG	1979	EC/HC	30 X 22	R/BFK	35	4	1500	2500
Etching Lesson, State II	PE	BG	1979	EC/HC	30 X 22	R/BFK	35	4	1500	2500
Nancy in Jerusalem	PE	BG	1979	EB/HC	29 X 25	R/BFK	4		1000	2000
Nancy in Jerusalem, State II	PE	BG	1979	LC/HC	41 X 29	R/BFK	15		1000	2500
Nancy in Jerusalem (Through the Window)	PE	BG	1979	EB/LC	41 X 29	R/BFK	12		500	2500
Nancy in Jerusalem	PE	BG	1979	LC	41 X 29	R/N	12		500	3000
Hand-Painted Head of Nancy (with Crayon & Oil Paint)	PE	BG	1979	LC/HC/CC	30 X 23	A/HWC	8		800	6500
Me in Horn-Rimmed Glasses	PE	BG	1979	LC/HC	26 X 30	C/R	8		1200	2500
Self Portrait	PE	BG	1979	EB/HC	41 X 29	R/BFK	6		1200	3000
Handpainted Portrait on Thin Fabriano	PE	BG	1979	EB/HC	30 X 23	FAB	6		1200	5000
A Dark Portrait	PE	BG	1979	EB/HC	25 X 18	FAB	3		1200	2500
A Robe against the Desert Sky	PE	BG	1979	LB/SP	42 X 30	R/BFK	17		2000	15000
Self-Portrait, Hand-Painted in Paris	PE	MF/ART	1979	EB/HC	18 X 15	R/BFK	25		1200	3000
A Magenta Robe, A Rose Robe (Dipt)	PE	MF/ART	1979	A/HC/SL/HC	59 X 41	R/BFK	16 EA	2 EA	2000	20000
The Yellow Robe	PE	LPI	1980	LB	50 X 35	A/K	40		2500	20000
Red and Black Diptych Rose	PE	MS/JB	1980	LC	37 X 29 EA	R/N	20 EA		2500 SET	15000 SET
Strelitzia with Monotype	PE	MF/ART	1980	EB/MON/HC	35 X 24	CD	17		2500	6000
Green Etched Strelitzia	PE	MS/JB	1980	EB	35 X 24	R/BFK	10	1	2500	3500
Green-Gold Strelitzia	PE	MS/JB	1980	EB	41 X 28	R/BFK	3	1	2500	4500
A Well-Painted Strelitzia	PE	MS/JB	1980	EC/HC	35 X 24	R/BFK	33		2500	5000
Pink Strelitzia	PE	JB	1980	EB	35 X 24	R/BFK	12	3	2000	3500
White Strelitzia	PE	JB	1980	EC	35 X 24	R/BFK	18		1500	3500
Winter (Robe)	PE	AR/KR	1980	EC	43 X 30	R/BFK	40		1200	7500
Nancy Outside in July VII	CR		1980	EC/HWA	36 X 25	R/BFK	25		2000	4000
Nancy Outside in July X: Young and Blue	AC	AR/KR	1980	EC	30 X 22	R/BFK	25		2000	3500

JIM DINE CONTINUED

TITLE	PUBLISHER	PRINTER	DATE	MEDIUM	DIMENSION (PAPER SIZE) IN INCHES	TYPE OF PAPER	EDITION NUMBER	NO. OF COLORS	ORIGINAL OPENING PRICE	CURRENT RETAIL PRICE
SOLD OUT EDITIONS (RARE):										
Nancy Outside in July XI:										
Red Sweater in Paris	AC	AR/KR	1980	EC/AC	30 X 22	R/BFK	25		2000	5000
A Robe in a Furnace	PE	AR/KR	1980	EC	43 X 30	CD	31	3	2000	9500
Printing Outdoors (Robe)	PE	AR/KR	1980	EB/HC	41 X 30	CD	40		2000	9500
Flowered Robe with Sky	PE	MS/AB	1980	EB/HC	38 X 30	R/BFK	31		2000	18000
Nancy Outside in July XII:										
Green Leaves	PE	SH/P	1981	EC	42 X 25	R/BFK	30		2000	6000
Nancy Outside in July XIV:										
Wrestling with Spirits	AC	AC/AtC	1981	EB	36 X 25	R/BFK	30	1	2000	4500
Nancy Outside in July XV:										
Nancy over the Trees	PE	SH/P	1981	EC/HC	41 X 34	R/BFK	15		2000	6000
Nancy Outside in July XVI:										
Japanese Bristro	PE	SH/P	1981	EC	31 X 27	R/BFK	19		1250	3500
Nancy Outside in July XVII:										
The Reddish One	AC	AC/AtC	1981	EC	30 X 22	R/BFK	26		1250	4500
Nancy Outside in July SVII	AC	AC/AtC	1981	EC/AC/PH/HC	24 X 20	R/BFK	15		1250	4000
A Heart on the Rue de Grenelle	PE	AC/AtC	1981	EC/HC	42 X 30	R/BFK	36	3	3500	35000
Nancy Outside in July XVIII:										
Full of Expression	PE	SH/P	1981	EC	36 X 25	R/BFK	15		2000	7500
Nancy XIX: The Fish in the Wind	AC	AC/AtC	1981	EB	30 X 23	AP/BL	25	1	1500	3500
Nancy XX: Among French Plants	AC	AC/AtC	1981	EB	36 X 25	R/BFK	26	1	1500	2500
Nancy XXI: The Red Frame	AC	AC/AtC	1981	EB/HC	36 X 25	R/BFK	22	Varies	1500	2500
Nancy XXII: Ten Layers of Grey	PE	SH/P	1981	EC	36 X 25	R/BFK	28		2000	7500
Tree										
A Female Robe for Karen McCready	PE	SH/P	1981	EC	44 X 35	AP/ROL	23		2500	6500
A Tree Covered with Rust	PE	SH/P	1981	EC	46 X 35	HMP	14		2500	5000
A Tree in Soot	PE	SH/P	1981	EB/MON	46 X 36	HMP	6		2500	5000
A Tree, Curvaceous and Blue	PE	SH/P	1981	EB/MON/HC	46 X 36	AP	6		2500	6500
A Tree Painted in South Florida	PE	SH/P	1981	EC	46 X 36	AP	15		2500	6500
Three Trees in the Shadow of Mt Zion (Trip)	PE	SH/P	1981	SP/EB	38 X 28 EA	AP	27		4500	12000
Two Hearts in a Forest	PE	JJ/ART	1981	LC/WC	36 X 60	AP	24	3	4500	20000
Shell from the Gulf of Acaba	PE	BG	1981	SP/EB	40 X 30	HMP	30	3	1500	2500
Two Tomatoes (Dipt)	PE	BG	1981	EB/AC/HC	42 X 59 TOT	R/BFK	25 EA		4500 SET	45000 SET
Etching Heart	PE	MF/ART	1981	EB	42 X 30	CD	42	1	1800	3500
Key West Print	PE	MF/ART	1981	EB/LC/PH/OFF	41 X 30	CD	40	4	1800	3000
Blue (Dipt)	PE	MF/ART	1981	EB/A/ENG	41 X 27 EA	CD	29 EA		3500	5000
White Ground, Night Tree	PE	SH	1981	EC	46 X 35	AP/ROL	15	3	1500	3500
Nancy XXIII: Squeezed out on Japanese Paper	PE	SH	1981	EC	36 X 25	HMP	25	1	1000	1500
Nancy XXIV: Brilliant Dutch Gloss	AC	AC/AtC	1981	EB	36 X 25	AP/ROL	18	1	2000	7500
Nancy XXV: Charcoal Cycle	PE	SH	1981	EC	36 X 25	AP/ROL	9		3000	8000
Rachel Cohen's Flags, State II (6 Sheets)	PE	BG	1981	EB/ENG/HC	22 X 138 TOT	R/BFK	14 EA		2000 SET	50000 SET
The Big Black and White Woodcut Tree	ULAE	ULAE	1981	WB	59 X 42	HMP	25	1	2000	3500
Nancy Outside in July XIII:										
Dissolving in Eden	AC	AC/AtC	1981	EC	42 X 25	R/BFK	30		2000	7500
The Bezalel Woodcut (with Rubber Stamp)	PE	BG	1981	WC/HC	40 X 30	R/BFK	6		2000	10000
Rancho Woodcut Heart	PE	RT	1982	WC	48 X 41	R/BFK	75	3	2500	18000
The Jerusalem Plant Series:										
The Jerusalem Plant #1	ULAE	ULAE	1982	WB	40 X 26	FAB	10		2000	7500
The Jerusalem Plant #2 (Dipt)	ULAE	ULAE	1982	WC	40 X 52 TOT	CP	11		2000	7500
The Jerusalem Plant #3	ULAE	ULAE	1982	WC	41 X 52	KOZO	11		2000	7500
The Jerusalem Plant #4	PE	AC/AtC	1982	LC	41 X 28	HMP	20		2000	4500
The Jerusalem Plant #5	PE	AC/AtC	1982	LC	39 X 30	HMP	9		2500	7500
The Jerusalem Plant #6	PE	AC/AtC	1982	LC	40 X 60	HMP	20		1500	4500
The Handpainted Bee	PE	AC/AtC	1982	EB/CAR/HC	27 X 23	HMP	40		1200	8500
The Handpainted Bee	PE	AC/AtC	1982	EC	27 X 23	HMP	40		2000	15000
The Jerusalem Woodcut Heart (with Rubber Stamp)	PE	JJ/ART	1982	WB	37 X 30	HMP	20	1	1500	10000
A Sunny Woodcut	PE	AC/AtC	1982	WC	32 X 31	HMP	42	4	1500	7500
A Night Woodcut	PE	AC/AtC	1982	WC	45 X 30	HMP	38		1200	5000
Eight Little Nudes (Set of 8)	PE	AC/AtC	1982	EC	22 X 17 EA	HMP	30 EA		8000 SET / 1000 EA	17500 SET / 2500 EA
Red and Blue Crommelynck Gates (Dipt)	PE	AC/AtC	1982	LC	72 X 36 EA	HMP	12 EA		3500 SET	7500 SET
Blue Crommelynck Gates (Dipt)	PE	AC/AtC	1982	LC	72 X 36 EA	HMP	15 EA		3000 SET	4000 SET
Blue Detail from the Crommelynck Gates	PE	AC/AtC	1982	EB/HC	40 X 26	R/BFK	30	Varies	2000	4500

JIM DINE CONTINUED

TITLE	PUBLISHER	PRINTER	DATE	MEDIUM	DIMENSION (PAPER SIZE) IN INCHES	TYPE OF PAPER	EDITION NUMBER	NO. OF COLORS	ORIGINAL OPENING PRICE	CURRENT RETAIL PRICE
SOLD OUT EDITIONS (RARE):										
Winter Windows on Chapel Street (4 Sheets)	PE	AC/AtC	1982	EB/CAR	51 X 44	R/BFK	40		2000	30000
The Hammer (with Watercolor Marks) (Dipt)	PE	AC/AtC	1982	LC/WA/HC	45 X 36 EA	HMP	46 EA		3000 SET	15000 SET
Winter Windows on Chapter Street	PE	AC/AtC	1982	EC	50 X 44	HMP	40	2	1500	2500
The Heart Called Paris Spring	AC	AC/AtC	1982	EC	36 X 25	HMP	90	3	2500	25000
The Jewish Heart (for United Jewish Appeal)	ART	PP	1982	EB/DPT	12 X 9	RdB	100	1	2000	6500
L A Eye Works	PE	GP	1982	EB/CAR	51 X 44	HMP	70	Varies	3500	25000
Fourteen Color Woodcut Bathrobe	PE	EP	1982	WC	78 X 42	HMP	75	14	5000	40000
Desire in Primary Colors	PE	EP	1982	AC	30 X 66	HMP	40		3000	20000
Five Hand-Painted Shells	PE	EP	1982	EB/HC	30 X 36	HMP	50	Varies	1500	4000
Fortress of the Heart, State II	PE	MS	1982	LC	36 X 61	HMP	22	4	4500	25000
Apocalypse (29 Woodblock Prints)	ArPr	MS	1982	IL/BK	15 X 11 EA	HMP	150		3000 SET	5000 SET
The Three Sydney Close Woodcuts (Trip)	PE	MS	1983	WC	46 X 32 EA	HMP	24 EA		2000 SET	6500 SET
The Robe Goes to Town	PE	MS	1983	COL/SP/A/SG	57 X 36	HMP	59		2000	5000
A Grey Version of the Heart	PE	AP	1983	LC	47 X 32	HMP	15		2000	8500
The Heart and the Wall (4 Sheets)	PE	MS	1983	EC/ENG	44 X 35	HMP	28		12500	25000
Swaying in the Florida Night	PE	MS	1983	EC/ENG	47 X 71	HMP	65		2500	6500
The Kindergarten Robes	PE	MS	1983	WC	60 X 75	HMP	75		4500	30000
The Black and White Nancy Woodcut, 1st Version	PE	MS	1983	WC	48 X 37	HMP	27		1800	4000
The Black and White Nancy Woodcut, 2nd Version	PE	MS	1983	WC	48 X 37	HMP	27		1800	4000
Two Robes with Watercolor	PE	MS	1983	LC/HC	38 X 59	HMP	9		5000	25000
Two Hand-Colored Colorado Robes (Dipt)	PE	MS	1983	LC/HC	38 X 30 EA	HMP	10		5000	30000
Cooper Street Robe	PE	MS	1983	WC/HC	36 X 25	HMP	13		5000	15000
The First Woodcut Gate (The Landscape)	PE	MS	1983	WC/HC	36 X 45	HMP	49		1800	4500
The Hand-Painted Nancy (Woodcut)	PE	ART	1983	WC/HC	51 X 39	MASA	12	Varies	2500	5000
A Double Feature (Woodcut)	PE	ART	1983	WC/HC	51 X 76	HMP	8		3500	7500
Two Very Strange Hearts (Dipt)	PE	ART	1983	WC	36 X 24 EA	HMP	18 EA		5000 SET	35000 SET
A Woodcut in the Snow	PE	ART	1983	WC/LC/CC	36 X 32	HMP	22		2500	20000
Handmade Double Venus	PE	ART	1983	WC/LC/HC	54 X 35	HMP	15		2000	6000
The Yellow Venus	PE	AP	1983	WC	60 X 37	OKP	20	4	2500	10000
The Sky (Venus Image)	PE	AP	1983	LC/WB	54 X 35	HMP	25		2000	6500
Double Venus in the Sky at Night	PE	AP	1983	LC/SP	42 X 30	SILK	50		2500	18000
Black Venus in the Wood	PE	AP	1983	WC	60 X 37	HMP	20		1500	4500
The Jerusalem Plant #7	PE		1983	LC/I	40 X 52	HMP	11		2500	8500
Black and White Nancy . . . (1st Version)	PE	AP	1983	WC	48 X 36	HMP	26		2500	4500
Black and White Nancy . . . (2nd Version)	PE	AP	1983	WC	48 X 36	HMP	27		2500	4500
Handmade Double Venus (Dipt)	PE	AP	1983	LC	54 X 35	HMP	15	2	2500	8500
Double Venus Woodcut Series:										
Double Venus Woodcut I	PE	AP	1983	WC	48 X 32	HMP	36		1200	5000
Double Venus Woodcut II	PE	AP	1983	WC	48 X 32	HMP	36		1200	5000
The Earth	PE	AP	1983	LC	46 X 32	AP/B	50		2500	15000
A Robe in Los Angeles	PE	AP	1983	LC	54 X 35	AP/B	50		2500	12000
A Grey Version of the Robe	PF	AP	1983	LC	54 X 35	HMP	12		2000	8500
A Grey Version of Los Angeles (Dipt)	PE	AP	1983	LC	54 X 35	HMP	15	2	2000	15000
The Heart and the Wall (4 Sheets) (F-145)	PE	MS	1983	EB/A	85 X 67	SOM	28		12500	50000
The Kindergarten Robes (F-146)	PE	MS	1983	WC	72 X 55	LEN	75	5	2500	30000
Two Hand-Colored Colorado Robes (Dipt) (F-151)	PE	ART	1980–83	LC/WA/HC	38 X 59	AC/B	10	3	5000	45000
Black Heart	PE	AP	1984	LB	51 X 35	HMP	20	1	1800	5000
The New French Tools Series:										
The New French Tools 1—Wise	PE	AP	1984	EB/A/HG/DPT	31 X 23	HMP	50		1200	1800
The New French Tools 2—Three Saws from the Rue Cler (F-172)	PE	AP	1984	EB/A/HG/DPT	36 X 25	HMP	50		1500	2800
The New French Tools 3—For Pep	PE	AP	1984	EB/A/HG/DPT	43 X 30	HMP	50		1500	3500
The New French Tools 4	PE	AP	1984	EB/A/HG/DPT	43 X 30	HMP	50		1800	3000
The New French Tools 5	PE	AP	1984	EB/A/HG/DPT	31 X 45	HMP	50		1800	4000

JIM DINE CONTINUED

TITLE	PUBLISHER	PRINTER	DATE	MEDIUM	DIMENSION (PAPER SIZE) IN INCHES	TYPE OF PAPER	EDITION NUMBER	NO. OF COLORS	ORIGINAL OPENING PRICE	CURRENT RETAIL PRICE
SOLD OUT EDITIONS (RARE):										
Boulevard Victor, Double Sky			1984	EB/A/HG/DPT	23 X 39	HMP	50		1500	5000
Temple of Flora Book (28 Prints)	ArPr	AP	1984	EB/A/PH/DPT/ENG	14 X 20 EA	HMP	150 EA		2000 SET	12500 SET
The Jerusalem Plant #8	ULAE	ULAE	1984	EB/A/PH/DPT	39 X 31	HMP	26	3	2500	3500
Tools and Dreams	PE	AP	1985	EB/A/DPT/HC	30 X 44	R/BFK	50	Varies	2500	8500
Lost Shells (Dipt)	PE	AP	1985	EB/SG/DPT/HC	30 X 21 EA	R/BFK	32 EA	Varies	2000 SET	3500 SET
Nine Views of Winter Series:										
Nine Views of Winter #1 (DO/F-197)	PE		1985	WC	53 X 37	AP/B	24		3000	12000
Nine Views of Winter #2 (DO/F-198)	PE		1985	WC	53 X 37	AP/B	24		3000	7500
Nine Views of Winter #3 (DO/F-199)	PE		1985	WC	53 X 37	AP/B	35		3000	12000
Nine Views of Winter #4 (DO/F-200)	PE		1985	WC	53 X 37	AP/B	24		3000	7500
Nine Views of Winter #5 (DO/F-201)	PE		1985	WC	53 X 37	AP/B	24		3000	8500
Nine Views of Winter #6 (DO/F-202)	PE		1985	WC	53 X 37	AP/B	24		3000	7500
Nine Views of Winter #7 (DO/F-203)	PE		1985	WC	53 X 37	AP/B	24		3000	15000
Nine Views of Winter #8 (DO/F-204)	PE		1985	WC	53 X 37	AP/B	24		3000	15000
Nine Views of Winter #9 (DO/F-205)	PE		1985	WC	53 X 37	AP/B	24		3000	7500
Rise Up, Solitude! (DO/F-206)	PE		1985	WC/EB/HC	52 X 58	R/BFK	34		3000	25000
Venus Series:										
Venus at Sea	PE		1985	EB/SG/HC	36 X 28	R/BFK	30		3000	12000
Venus on Chiri Paper	PE		1985	EB/SG	34 X 25	CHIRI	16	1	3000	8500
Venus on Beige Rives	PE		1985	EB/SG	45 X 30	RP	16	1	3000	6000
The French Watercolor Venus	PE		1985	EB/SH/HC	42 X 32	HMP	8		3000	35000
Night Venus and Sappho	PE		1985	EB/SG	39 X 30	R/BFK	15	1	2000	5000
Black and White Cubist Venus	PE		1985	AB/DPT	42 X 31	R/BFK	50	1	2000	7500
Wallpaper in Paris	PE		1985	EB/SG/A/DPT	34 X 44	DIEU	30		2000	4500
The Robe in France	PE		1985	EB/SG/LB	39 X 28	R/BFK	35	1	3000	20000
Two Hearts for the Moment	PE		1985	EB/SG/LB	28 X 41	R/BFK	36	1	3000	25000
The Double Pacific Gift (Dipt)	PE		1986	LC/LI	60 X 46 EA	R/BFK	6 EA		3500	7500
The Side View	PE		1986	EB/SG/DPT	46 X 43	R/BFK	20		3000	7500
Me in Denmark	PE		1986	DPT/SG/CC	37 X 30	R/BFK	12	1	2000	2500
Sovereign Nights	PE		1986	EB/CC	33 X 47	R/BFK	45	1	2000	5000
The Garrity Necklace	PE		1986	AB/DPT	53 X 41	R/BFK	30	1	3000	15000
The Channel	PE		1986	EB/A/DPT	42 X 31	R/BFK	20	1	2000	4500
The Channel/My Heart/A Hand	PE		1986	EB/A/DPT	29 X 47	R/BFK	20	1	2000	4500
12 rue Jacob	PE		1986	LB/A/DPT	43 X 31	R/BFK	20	1	2000	3000
The Channel, Two Side Views	PE		1986	WC	49 X 39	HMP	12	Varies	2000	4500
A Side View in Florida	PE		1986	EB/DPT/HC	52 X 40	R/BFK	15		3000	5000
Shellac on a Hand	PE		1986	EB/DPT/HC	58 X 40	R/BFK	30		2000	7500
Black and White Blossom	PE		1986	EB/DPT/A	62 X 39	R/BFK	60		2000	3800
Red Robe in France	PE		1986	EB/LB/HC	40 X 28	R/BFK	15		3000	30000
Robe in France (Sec)	PE		1986	EB/HC	40 X 28	R/BFK	20		3000	25000
My Nights in Santa Monica (Bistro Version)	PE/USF	PF/DS/GS/USF	1986	EB/DPT/SG	36 X 72	AP/B	20	5	2000	3000
Snow in France	PE		1986	EB/SG/DPT	30 X 23	AP/B	5		3000	10000
Atheism	PE		1986	LB/HC	69 X 48	AP	35		3000	30000
Yellow Robe	GAC/LACM		1986	LC	25 X 20	AP	50		2000	7500
Quartet	AC	AtC	1986	EB/A	36 X 28	AP	50		3000	5000
My Nights in Santa Monica	PE/USF	PF/DS/GS	1986	EC	35 X 72	AP/B	20	5	2500	6500
Hand Painting on the Mandala	PE	ART	1986	EC/HC	50 X 40	HMP	60	8	20000	35000
Two Florida Bathrobes (Dipt)	ART	GS/USF	1986	EB/LC	32 X 47	R/BFK	70	7	25000	18000
The Oil of Gladness	PE/WG	GS/USF	1987	EB/WC	79 X 38	AC	50		25000	30000
Red Dancer on the Western Shore	PE/WG	GS/USF	1987	EB/WC	79 X 48	AC	14	3	40000	25000
Youth and Maiden (Trip)	PE/WG	GS/USF	1987	EB/WC/HC	78 X 92 TOT	AC	16		65000	30000
The Mead of Poetry Series:										
The Mead of Poetry #1	PE/WG	GS/USF	1987	WC/CC	60 X 41	AC	16		6500	7500
The Mead of Poetry #2	PE/WG	GS/USF	1987	WC/CC	60 X 41	AC	15		6500	6000
The Mead of Poetry #3	PE/WG	GS/USF	1987	WC/CC	42 X 32	AC	15		6500	5000
Ravenna in November	PE/WG	GS/USF	1987	WC/EB/HC	79 X 52	AC	14		25000	35000
The Foreign Plowman	PE/WG	GS/USF	1987	WC/EB/HC	74 X 48	AC	10		20000	30000
Running Hammers in a Landscape	PE/WG	GS/USF	1987	WC/EB/HC	32 X 55	AC	18		6500	8500

JIM DINE CONTINUED

TITLE	PUBLISHER	PRINTER	DATE	MEDIUM	DIMENSION (PAPER SIZE) IN INCHES	TYPE OF PAPER	EDITION NUMBER	NO. OF COLORS	ORIGINAL OPENING PRICE	CURRENT RETAIL PRICE
CURRENT EDITIONS:										
Youth and the Maiden (Trip)	PE/WG	GS/USF	1987–88	WC/EB/HC	78 X 92	AC	16		65000	70000
Glyptotek Book (Book Containing 40 Clacies Transferes Intaglio Prints) (DO/F-193—DO/F-229)	PE/WG	GS/USF	1988	I	27 X 21 EA	AP	90 EA		10000 SET	10000 SET
Glyptotek Portfolio (Set of 14) (DO/F-193—DO/F-230)	PE/WG	GS/USF	1988	I/CC	27 X 21 EA	R/BFK	60 EA		25000 SET	60000 SET
Untitled Robe for the Korean Olympics	PE/WG	AP	1988	LC	34 X 26	R/BFK	300		5000	10000
Youth and the Maiden (Trip)	PE/WG	GS/USF	1988	WC	78 X 24	AC	16		25000	50000
Red Dancer on the Western Shore (Dipt)	PE/WG	GS/USF	1988	WC/EB		AC	14		12000	13500
Ten Hand-Colored Winter Tools II (Set of 10)	PE/WG	NBJ	1973–89	LC/HC	18 X 24 EA	HMP	18 EA	Varies	25000 SET	70000 SET
Hand-Colored Flowers II	PE/WG	NBJ	1977–89	EB/HC	28 X 39	AC	30	Varies	12000	15000
The Hand-Colored Viennese Hearts I-VII (Set of 7)	PE/WG	NBJ	1987–90	SP/EB/A/HC	47 X 36 EA	AC	40 EA		35000	40000 SET
Fo Dog in Hell	PE/WG	NBJ	1990	EB/HC	40 X 30	AC	30		12000	15000
The Foam	PE/WG	NBJ	1990	EB/A/HC	42 X 31	AC	30		18000	21000
Irish	PE/WG	NBJ	1990	EB	12 X 9	AC	12		2500	3500
Neptune and Venus (3 Sheets)	PE/WG	NBJ	1990	EB/A	48 X 50	AC	18		12000	18000
These Three Dogs are for Nina D (Trip)	PE/WG	NBJ	1990	EB/HC	37 X 80	AC	10		20000	35000
The World	PE/WG	NBJ	1990	DPT	14 X 10		250		350	500
Two Danish Red Robes (Dipt)	PE/WG	NBJ	1991	EB/A	30 X 45	ZER	14	2	7500	8500
Self in the Ocean	PE/WG	NBJ	1991	EB/A	60 X 40	ZER	30	Varies	7500	9500
Blue Wash (Four Robes)	PE/WG	NBJ	1991	EB/HC	66 X 51	AC	17	Varies	8500	9500
Two Dark Robes	PE/WG	NBJ	1991	EB/HC	28 X 39	AC	18	Varies	7500	7500
Calla Lilies Verona (Set of 3):										
Calla Lilies Verona #1	PE	LB/MB/SdA	1992	WB/EB/HC	32 X 27	HAHN	50	Varies	3500	3500
Calla Lilies Verona #2	PE	LB/MB/SdA	1992	WB/EB/HC	34 X 27	HAHN	50	Varies	3500	3500
Calla Lilies Verona #3	PE	LB/MB/SdA	1992	WB/EB/HC	32 X 25	HAHN	50	Varies	3500	3500

Jim Dine
14-Color Woodcut Bathrobe
Courtesy Pace Editions, Inc

Jim Dine
Picabia II (Forgot)
Courtesy Pace Editions, Inc

ROLANDO LOPEZ DIRUBE

BORN: Havana, Cuba; August 14, 1928; US Citizen
EDUCATION: San Alejandro Nat Sch of Fine Arts, Havana, Cuba; Univ of Havana, Cuba, 1947–48; Art Students League, NY 1948–49, with George Grosz & Kuniyoshi; S Fernando Sch of Fine Arts, Madrid, Spain
TEACHING: Prof, Design, Inter-Am, Univ of Puerto Rico, Sch of Arch, 1964–65; Lectr, Design, Sch of Arch, Univ of Puerto Rico, San Juan, PR, 1967; Prof, Painting, Art Students League, San Juan, PR, 1968 to present
AWARDS: First Prize, Gold Medal, Painting, Univ of Tampa, FL, 1951; First Prize, Sculpture, R J Reynolds Tobacco Co, VA, 1979

COLLECTIONS: Mus Nacional, Havana, Cuba; Mus Arte Contemp, Madrid, Spain; Metropolitan Mus, NY; Mus of Contemp Art, Caracas, Venezuela; Philadelphia Mus of Art, PA; Ponce Mus, PR
PRINTERS: Artist (ART)
PUBLISHERS: Balz Graphics, Catano, PR (BG); Editorial, Madrid, Spain (E)
GALLERIES: Estudio Actual, Apartado Caracas, Venezuela; Balz Graphics, Catano, PR; Galeria Botello I, San Juan, PR; Galeria Botello II, Hato Rey, PR
MAILING ADDRESS: 124 West Ocean Dr, Bay View, Catano, PR 00632

TITLE	PUBLISHER	PRINTER	DATE	MEDIUM	DIMENSION (PAPER SIZE) IN INCHES	TYPE OF PAPER	EDITION NUMBER	NO. OF COLORS	ORIGINAL OPENING PRICE	CURRENT RETAIL PRICE
SOLD OUT EDITIONS (RARE):										
Mujer En Rojo	BG	ART	1971	WC	25 X 13	AP	25	2	175	600
Estructuras Flotantes Series (I,II,III)	BG	ART	1971	WC	25 X 13 EA	AP	15 EA	4 EA	175 EA	600 EA
Estructuras Folgantes Series (I,II,III)	BG	ART	1971	WC	25 X 34 EA	AP	15 EA	7 EA	250 EA	1200 EA
Figura I	BG	ART	1974	WC	23 X 35	AP	30	4	300	900
CURRENT EDITIONS:										
El Piso Series (I,II,III)	BG	ART	1973	SP	25 X 12 EA	AP	30 EA	8 EA	175 EA	400 EA
El Pequeno Muro	BG	ART	1973	MM	25 X 12 EA	AP	30 EA	6 EA	175 EA	400 EA
Variaciones Series (I,II,III)	BG	ART	1973	SP	25 X 12 EA	AP	30 EA	5 EA	175 EA	400 EA
Cabezas Series (I–VI)	BG	ART	1973	SP	25 X 12 EA	AP	40 EA	5 EA	175 EA	400 EA
Cabezas Grandes Series (7–11)	BG	ART	1973	SP	18 X 25 EA	AP	65 EA	5 EA	200 EA	450 EA
Elmuro Series (I,II,III,IV)	BG	ART	1974	WC	24 X 34 EA	AP	30 EA	4 EA	250 EA	500 EA
Variaciones Modulares (1–100)	BG	ART	1981	W/EMB	28 X 40 EA	AP	70 EA	1 EA	500 EA	600 EA
Love Letters Series (1–10)	BG	ART	1981	MM	28 X 40 EA	AP	70 EA	1 EA	500 EA	600 EA

MARTIN DISLER

BORN: Seewen, Switzerland; 1949
PRINTERS: Atelier Crommelynck, Paris, France (AZ); Patricia Branstead, NY (PB); Aeropress, Inc, NY (A)
PUBLISHERS: Galerie Eric Franck, Geneva, Switzerland (GEF); Peter Blum Edition, NY (PBE); Multiples, NY (M)
GALLERIES: Galerie Eric Franck, Geneva, Switzerland; Peter Blum Edition, New York, NY; Marian Goodman Gallery, New York, NY; Signet Arts, St Louis, MO

Martin Disler
Totenwache
Courtesy Edition Schellmann

TITLE	PUBLISHER	PRINTER	DATE	MEDIUM	DIMENSION (PAPER SIZE) IN INCHES	TYPE OF PAPER	EDITION NUMBER	NO. OF COLORS	ORIGINAL OPENING PRICE	CURRENT RETAIL PRICE
SOLD OUT EDITIONS (RARE):										
Endless Licking of Crashing Globe by Black Doggie—Time Bomb (Contains Tape by the Artist and Text in English & German (Set of 8)	PBE	PB/A	1981	EB/A/SL/ DPT/PH	22 X 30 EA	VG/DE	49 EA	1 EA	3000 SET	12000 SET
Untitled	GEF	AC	1983	EB/A/DPT	15 X 20	R/BFK	50	1	400	2000
CURRENT EDITIONS:										
The Pains of Love (Silkscreen Book)	M	PB/A	1982	SP	18 X 22 EA	AP	30 EA		500	1200
Untitled	M	PB/A	1982	EC	35 X 23	R/BFK	50		500	900
Untitled	M	PB/A	1982	EC	43 X 30	R/BFK	50		500	1200
Untitled	M	PB/A	1982	EC	20 X 24	R/BFK	50		400	900
Untitled	M	PB/A	1982	EC	35 X 23	R/BFK	50		500	900
Untitled (Series of Linocuts & Monoprints)	M	PB/A	1983	LI/MON	40 X 26 EA	R/BFK	1 EA		600 EA	1200 EA
					26 X 40 EA	R/BFK	1 EA		600 EA	1200 EA
Untitled (Trip)	GEF	AC	1986	A/SL	42 X 70	ZER	7		5000	10000

JOHN MANFORD DIVOLA

BORN: Santa Monica, CA; June 6, 1949
EDUCATION: California State Univ, Northridge, CA, BA, 1971; Univ of California, Los Angeles, CA, MA, 1973, MFA, 1974
TEACHING: Instr, Photog, Loyola Marymount Univ, Los Angeles, CA, 1976–80; Instr, Photog, California Inst of Arts, Oakland, CA, 1978–88; Assoc Prof, Univ of California, Riverside, CA, 1988–89
AWARDS: Nat Endowment for the Arts, Photography Fel, 1973,76,79; Guggenheim Fel, NY, 1986; Jayne H Baum Gallery, NY, 1990
RECENT EXHIB: Mus of Mod Art, NY, 1989; Jayne H Baum Gallery, NY, 1990; Univ of California, Riverside, CA, 1992; Cincinnati Art Mus, OH, 1992

COLLECTIONS: Mus of Mod Art, San Francisco, CA; Mus of Mod Art, NY; Mus of Fine Arts, Houston, TX; Fogg Mus of Art, Cambridge, MA; Denver Art Mus, CO; Int Mus of Photography, George Eastman House, NY; New Orleans Art Mus, LA; Univ of California, Los Angeles, CA
PRINTERS: Artist (ART)
PUBLISHERS: Artist (ART)
GALLERIES: Susan Spiritus Gallery, Newport Beach, CA; Jeffrey Fuller Fine Arts, Phila, PA; Image Gallery, Seattle, WA; Visual Studies Workshop, New York, NY; Jan Kesner Gallery, Los Angeles, CA; Leonarda Di Mauro Gallery, New York, NY; Jayne H Baum Gallery, New York, NY
MAILING ADDRESS: 245 Ruth Ave, Venice, CA 90291

TITLE	PUBLISHER	PRINTER	DATE	MEDIUM	DIMENSION (PAPER SIZE) IN INCHES	TYPE OF PAPER	EDITION NUMBER	NO. OF COLORS	ORIGINAL OPENING PRICE	CURRENT RETAIL PRICE
SOLD OUT EDITIONS (RARE):										
Magnetism	ART	ART	1982	PH/DT	20 X 24	AP	20		500	1000
Zuma (Set of 10)	ART	ART	1982	PH/DT	16 X 20 EA	AP	30 EA		2500 SET	4500 SET

OTTO DIX

Karsch (K)

BORN: (1891–1969)
PRINTERS: Artist (ART)
PUBLISHERS: Artist (ART)
GALLERIES: Lafayette Parke Gallery, New York, NY

TITLE	PUBLISHER	PRINTER	DATE	MEDIUM	DIMENSION (PAPER SIZE) IN INCHES	TYPE OF PAPER	EDITION NUMBER	NO. OF COLORS	ORIGINAL OPENING PRICE	CURRENT RETAIL PRICE
SOLD OUT EDITIONS (RARE):										
Streichholzhändler (from Radierwerk II) (K-116)	ART	ART	1920	EB	14 X 12	WOVE	20	1	50	28000
Der Selbstmorder	ART	ART	1922	EB	14 X 11	WOVE	50	1	50	25000
Selbstporträt in Profile	ART	ART	1922	LB	8 X 6	CPP	100	1	25	6000
Dompteuse	ART	ART	1922	DPT	16 X 12	WOVE	50	1	35	15000
Kupplerin	ART	ART	1923	LC	19 X 15	LAID	65		60	22000
Frau Otto Mueller (Only Printed 15)	ART	ART	1923	LB	19 X 15	WOVE	50	1	50	7500
Dam mit Reiher	ART	ART	1923	LB	15 X 10	WOVE	120	1	50	15000
Nellie mit Spitzen Kragen	ART	ART	1924	LB	11 X 8	WOVE		1	50	300
Sterbender Soldat	ART	ART	1924	EB/A/DPT	8 X 6	WOVE	70		50	7500
Verschüttete	ART	ART	1924	EB	6 X 8	WOVE		1	35	4000
Die Katze (K-231-1)	ART	ART	1959	LC	15 X 20	HMP	63		100	15000

DMITRIENKO

PRINTERS: Maeght Editeur, Paris, France (ME); Galerie Maeght Lelong, Paris, France (ML)
PUBLISHERS: Maeght Editions, Paris, France (ME); Galerie Maeght Lelong, Paris, France (ML)
GALLERIES: Galerie Lelong, Paris, France & Zürich, Switzerland & New York, NY

TITLE	PUBLISHER	PRINTER	DATE	MEDIUM	DIMENSION (PAPER SIZE) IN INCHES	TYPE OF PAPER	EDITION NUMBER	NO. OF COLORS	ORIGINAL OPENING PRICE	CURRENT RETAIL PRICE
SOLD OUT EDITIONS (RARE):										
Tete a Croix	ME	ME	1978	EB	42 X 25	AP	75		1400 FF	2000 FF
Le Coeur de Marie	ME	ME	1978	EB	42 X 25	AP	75		1000 FF	1500 FF
L'Oeil u Vide	ME	ME	1978	EB	31 X 23	AP	75		750 FF	1200 FF
Les Victimes	ME	ME	1978	EB	41 X 30	AP	75		1000 FF	1500 FF
Sourire	ME	ME	1978	EB	20 X 15	AP	50		600 FF	1000 FF
Dernier Sommeil	ME	ME	1978	EB	42 X 30	AP	75		1200 FF	1500 FF

HOLLY DOWNING

BORN: San Francisco, CA; 1948
EDUCATION: Univ of California, Santa Cruz, CA, BFA, 1972; Royal Col of Art, London, England, 1974–75
PRINTERS: Artist (ART)
PUBLISHERS: Artist (ART)
GALLERIES: Mary Ryan Gallery, New York, NY; Curwen Gallery, London, England

TITLE	PUBLISHER	PRINTER	DATE	MEDIUM	DIMENSION (PAPER SIZE) IN INCHES	TYPE OF PAPER	EDITION NUMBER	NO. OF COLORS	ORIGINAL OPENING PRICE	CURRENT RETAIL PRICE
CURRENT EDITIONS:										
Untitled	ART	ART	1985	MEZ	11 X 15	R/BFK	30	1	125	300

The Printworld Directory is accepting new applications for the seventh edition. Approximately 300 new artists will be accepted. Please use the two forms provided in the back section of this directory to submit biographical data and documentation of prints. Edition number of each print must not exceed 500 and the retail price must be $100 or more.

JIRI GEORG DOKOUPIL

BORN: Bruntal, Czechoslovakia; 1954
EDUCATION: Studied in Cologne, Germany, Frankfurt, Germany; Cooper Union, New York, NY, 1976–78
TEACHING: Prof, Kunstakademie, Düsseldorf, Germany, 1983–84; Circulo de Ballas Artes, Madrid, Spain, 1989
RECENT EXHIB: Galerie Paul Maenz, Cologne, West Germany, 1987; Studio Marconi, Milan, Italy, 1987; Gallery Bruno Bischofberger, Zurich, Switzerland, 1987–88; Galleria Bonomo, Bari, Italy, 1988; Galerie Sonne, Berlin, West Germany, 1988; Galleria Massimo Minini, Brescia, Italy, 1989; Tony Shafrazi Gallery, NY, 1992; Galeria Leyendecker, Santa Cruz de Tenerife, 1990,91,92; Robert Miller Gallery, NY, 1989,90,92
COLLECTIONS: Nat Galerie, Berlin, Germany; Van Abbemuseum Eindhoven, Germany; Mus Folkwang, Essen, Germany; Boymans-van-Beuningen, Rotterdam, The Netherlands; Fundaco Caixa de Pensiones, Barcelona, Spain
PRINTERS: Bert Berens, Cologne, West Germany (BB), Seri-Grafic, Cologne, West Germany (SG); Larry B Wright Art Productions, NY (LBWAP); Kurt Zein, Vienna, Austria (KZ)
PUBLISHERS: Delano Greenridge Editions, NY (DGE); Edition Krinzinger, Vienna, Austria (EdKr)
GALLERIES: Castelli Graphics, New York, NY; Sonnabend Gallery, New York, NY; Gallery Bruno Bischofberger, Zürich, Switzerland; Robert Miller Gallery, New York, NY; Galleria Massimo Minini, Brescia, Italy; Galerie Sonne, Berlin, West Germany; Galerie Paul Maenz, Cologne, West Germany; Tony Shafrazi Gallery, New York, NY; Baumgartner Gallery, Wash, DC; Paul Kasmin Gallery, New York, NY; Edition Krinzinger, Vienna, Austria (EdKr)

TITLE	PUBLISHER	PRINTER	DATE	MEDIUM	DIMENSION (PAPER SIZE) IN INCHES	TYPE OF PAPER	EDITION NUMBER	NO. OF COLORS	ORIGINAL OPENING PRICE	CURRENT RETAIL PRICE
CURRENT EDITIONS:										
The Dokoupil Portfolio (Set of 9)	DGE	BB/SG/LBWAP	1986	SP/HC	22 X 22	R/BFK	33	2	3000 SET	4000 SET
Weichgrund (Set of 4)	EdKr	KZ	1991	I	31 X 47 EA	RP/300	16 EA	1 EA	SF1500 SET	SF1500 SET

LYDIA DONA

BORN: Rumania, 1955
EDUCATION: Bezalel Acad, Jerusalem, Israel, BFA, 1973–77; Sch of Visual Arts, NY, 1987–80; Hunter Col, NY, MFA, 1982–84
RECENT EXHIB: Gallerie Barbara Farber, Amsterdam, The Netherlands, 1987; Hillman Holland Fine Arts, Atlanta, GA, 1987
PRINTERS: Jon Cone, East Topsham, VT (JC); Cone Editions Press, East Topsham, VT (CEd)
PUBLISHERS: Cone Editions, East Topsham, VT (CEd)
GALLERIES: Salander-O'Reilly Galleries, New York, NY; Cone Editions, East Topsham, VT; Gallerie Barbara Farber, Amsterdam, The Netherlands; Carl Solway Gallery, Cincinnati, OH

TITLE	PUBLISHER	PRINTER	DATE	MEDIUM	DIMENSION (PAPER SIZE) IN INCHES	TYPE OF PAPER	EDITION NUMBER	NO. OF COLORS	ORIGINAL OPENING PRICE	CURRENT RETAIL PRICE
CURRENT EDITIONS:										
Untitled	CEd	JC/CEd	1986	SP	50 X 38	LEN/100	40	7	450	1800

DAVID MICHAEL DONNANGELO

BORN: Bethlehem, PA; September 3, 1957
EDUCATION: Moravian Col, Bethlehem, PA; Bucknell Univ, Lewisburg, PA; Temple Univ, Tyler Sch of Art, Phila, PA; Pennsylvania Governors Sch for the Art, Harrisburg, PA
COLLECTIONS: William Penn Mus, Harrisburg, PA; Pennsylvania State Univ, University Park, PA; The Vatican Coll, Rome, Italy
PRINTERS: D Wamsley Studio, NY (DWS); Avi Farin, NY (AF); Farin Design Studios, NY (FDS); Marvic Color, NY (MC); Artist (ART)
PUBLISHERS: Metropolitan Art Associates, Huntington, NY (MAA); Gallery Enterprises, Bethlehem, PA (GE); Brooks Gallery, Phila, PA; Studio A, Bethlehem, PA (StA)
GALLERIES: Emil Leonard Gallery, New York, NY; Howard Mann Art Center, Lambertville, NJ; Avanti Galleries, Lambertville, NJ; Brooks Gallery, Phila, PA; Metropolitan Art, Huntington, NY; Gallery Enterprises, Bethlehem, PA
MAILING ADDRESS: 1881 Abington Rd, Bethlehem, PA 18018

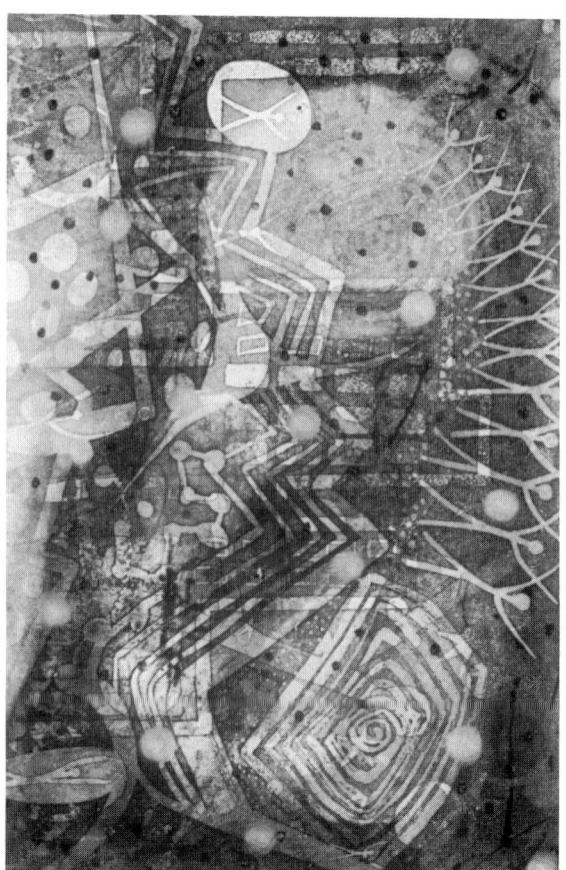

David Michael Donnangelo
In the Night
Courtesy the Artist

DAVID MICHAEL DONNANGELO CONTINUED

TITLE	PUBLISHER	PRINTER	DATE	MEDIUM	DIMENSION (PAPER SIZE) IN INCHES	TYPE OF PAPER	EDITION NUMBER	NO. OF COLORS	ORIGINAL OPENING PRICE	CURRENT RETAIL PRICE
CURRENT EDITIONS:										
In the Night	StA	ART	1982	EB/A	20 X 28	DE	75	7	250	600
Metaphysical Fantasy	FDS	AF/FDS	1984	LC/OFF	22 X 30	VEL/100	50	6	300	750
Blue Moon	BG	ART/SA	1988	EB/A	24 X 30	DE	50	4	300	600
The Goddess	BG	ART/SA	1988	EB/A	24 X 30	DE	50	4	300	600

PIERO DORAZIO

BORN: Rome, Italy; 1927
EDUCATION: Universitá degli Studi, Rome, Italy, 1945–51; Ecole des Beaux Art, Paris, France, 1947–48

COLLECTIONS: Albright-Knox Art Gallery, Buffalo, NY; Dartmouth Col, Hanover, NH
PUBLISHERS: Marlborough Gallery, London, England (MG)
GALLERIES: Marlborough Gallery, New York, NY; Nina Freudenheim Gallery, Buffalo, NY; Andre Emmerich Gallery, New York, NY; Achim Moeller Fine Art, New York, NY

TITLE	PUBLISHER	PRINTER	DATE	MEDIUM	DIMENSION (PAPER SIZE) IN INCHES	TYPE OF PAPER	EDITION NUMBER	NO. OF COLORS	ORIGINAL OPENING PRICE	CURRENT RETAIL PRICE
SOLD OUT EDITIONS (RARE):										
Fragments Frontales	MG		1966	LC	25 X 25	AP	90		75	1200
Coda di Paglia	MG		1966	LC	26 X 25	AP	90		75	1200
Untitled I	MG		1966	LC	25 X 19	AP	90		75	1000
Untitled II	MG		1966	LC	19 X 24	AP	90		75	1000
Accomplissments Libres	MG		1967	LC	31 X 22	AP	75		75	1500
Animation Interne	MG		1967	LC	20 X 26	AP	80		75	1000
Carrefour et Attraction	MG		1967	LC	26 X 18	AP	75		75	1000
Proposition	MG		1967	SP	26 X 26	AP	120		100	500
Watertower 1–5	MG		1973	SP	33 X 26 EA	AP	50 EA		150 EA	1000 EA

TONI DOVE

BORN: Flushing, NY; May 1, 1946
EDUCATION: Rhode Island Sch of Design, Providence, RI, BFA, 1968
TEACHING: Vis Critic & Lectr, Brown Univ, Providence, RI, 1974; Vis Lectr, Worcester Art Mus Sch, MA, 1974,79; Instr, Studio of Art, Pine Manor Jr. Col, 1975–79; Sch of Mus of Fine Arts, Boston, MA, 1978,81,82; Vis Lectr, Massachusetts Col of Art, Boston, MA, 1978,81,82,85; Boston Col, MA, 1979–86
AWARDS: Brown Univ, Providence, RI, 1974; Pine Manor Col, Brookline, MA, 1975–79; Boston Col, Newton, MA, 1979–80
RECENT EXHIB: Corcoran Armand Hammer Gallery, Wash, DC, 1989; Mesmer, Art in Anchorage, Brooklyn, NY, 1990

COLLECTIONS: Mus of Fine Arts, Boston, MA; Worcester Art Mus, MA; Hyatt Regency Hotel, Cambridge, MA; Achenbach Foundation for Graphic Arts, San Francisco, CA; San Francisco Mus of Mod Art, CA; Santa Cruz County Art Mus, CA
PRINTERS: Janet Kent, NY (JK); Sally Mara Sturman, NY (SMS); Patricia Branstead, NY (PB); Aeropress, NY (A)
PUBLISHERS: Diane Villani Editions, NY (DVE); Aeropress, NY (A); Corinthian Editions, NY (COR)
GALLERIES: Roger Ramsay, Chicago, IL; Diane Villani Editions, New York, NY; Robert Miller Gallery, New York, NY; Terry Dintenfass Gallery, New York, NY
MAILING ADDRESS: 115 West Broadway, New York, NY 10013

TITLE	PUBLISHER	PRINTER	DATE	MEDIUM	DIMENSION (PAPER SIZE) IN INCHES	TYPE OF PAPER	EDITION NUMBER	NO. OF COLORS	ORIGINAL OPENING PRICE	CURRENT RETAIL PRICE
SOLD OUT EDITIONS (RARE):										
Untitled, State I (Dipt) (Shell and Flower)	DVE/A	PB/A	1981	EMB/A/HC	17 X 60	AC/W	20	3	650	1500
Untitled, State II (Dipt) (Shell and Flower)	DVE/A	PB/A	1981	EMB/A/HC	17 X 60	AC/W	20	4	650	1500
Untitled (Orchid)	DVE/A	PB/A	1981	E/CO	30 X 40	MASA/GE	50		600	1200
Traces	DVE/A	PB/A	1981	A/HG/SB	30 X 42	MASA/GE	50	3	600	1200
Untitled (Series of 30)	COR	PB/A	1983	WB	50 X 30 EA	GE	1 EA	1 EA	500 EA	1000 EA
CURRENT EDITIONS:										
Untitled, State I (Flower)	JK/SMS	JK/SMS	1980	A/HC	17 X 30	RP	20		650	1200
Untitled, State II (Flower)	JK/SMS	JK/SMS	1980	A/HC	17 X 30	RP	20		650	1200

RACKSTRAW DOWNES

BORN: Kent, England; November 8, 1939; U S Citizen
EDUCATION: Cambridge Univ, England, BA, 1961; Yale Univ, New Haven, CT, BFA, 1963, MFA, 1964
TEACHING: Asst Prof, Fine Arts, Univ of Pennsylvania, Phila, PA 1967–79
AWARDS: Ind Grant, Ingram Merrill Found, 1975; Creative Artists Public Service Award, 1978; Nat Endowment for the Arts Grant, 1980

COLLECTIONS: Whitney Mus of Am Art, NY; Hirshhorn Mus, Wash, DC; Pennsylvania Acad of Fine Art, Phila, PA; Witherspoon Mus, Univ of North Carolina, NC; Metropolitan Mus of Art, NY
RECENT EXHIB: Kornbluth Gallery, Fair Lawn, NJ, 1990; Hirschl & Adler Modern, NY, 1992
PUBLISHERS: Crown Point Press, San Francisco, CA (CPP)
PRINTERS: Crown Point Press, San Francisco, CA (CPP)
GALLERIES: Hirschl & Adler Modern, New York, NY; Crown Point Press, New York, NY & San Francisco, CA; Claude Bernard Gallery, New York, NY; Kornbluth Gallery, Fair Lawn, NJ
MAILING ADDRESS: 16 Hudson St, New York, NY 10013

The retail prices of the 100,000 limited edition prints quoted in this directory are subject to change. Print publishers, artists and galleries were the direct sources for these quotations. Prices in the secondary market listed as "Sold Out Editions (Rare)" indicate that the publisher has a limited supply of that print or that the print is difficult to locate in the galleries.

RACKSTRAW DOWNES CONTINUED

TITLE	PUBLISHER	PRINTER	DATE	MEDIUM	DIMENSION (PAPER SIZE) IN INCHES	TYPE OF PAPER	EDITION NUMBER	NO. OF COLORS	ORIGINAL OPENING PRICE	CURRENT RETAIL PRICE
SOLD OUT EDITIONS: (RARE)										
Irving Trust, College of Insurance and a Flight into Newark	CPP	CPP	1986	EB/SG	19 X 24		25		1250	2000
CURRENT EDITIONS:										
Latham Square	CPP	CPP	1986	EB/SG	22 X 15		25		750	850

JOE DOYLE

BORN: New York, NY; February 27, 1941
EDUCATION: San Francisco State Univ, CA, BA, 1969, MFA, 1971
TEACHING: Instr, Painting, Laney Col, Oakland, CA, 1971–73; Co-Chmn, Fine Arts, Acad of Art, San Francisco, CA, 1975–76; Prof, Fine Art, Univ of San Francisco, CA 1975–76; Instr, Painting, Drawing, Figure Drawing, San Francisco Acad of Art, CA, 1978–79; Instr, California Col of Arts & Crafts, Oakland, CA, 1979–80
RECENT EXHIB: Merging One Gallery, Santa Monica, CA, 1987; Harcourts Contemp Gallery, San Francisco, CA, 1988; Davenport Art Center, IA, 1988
COLLECTIONS: Oakland Mus of Art, CA
PUBLISHERS: Editions Press, San Francisco, CA (EP); Merging One Gallery, Santa Monica, CA (MOG)
PRINTERS: Editions Press, San Francisco, CA (EP)
GALLERIES: Merging One Gallery, Santa Monica, CA; Walton-Gilbert Gallery, San Francisco, CA; Harcourts Contemporary Gallery, San Francisco, CA
MAILING ADDRESS: 4545 Toyon Place, Oakland, CA 94619

TITLE	PUBLISHER	PRINTER	DATE	MEDIUM	DIMENSION (PAPER SIZE) IN INCHES	TYPE OF PAPER	EDITION NUMBER	NO. OF COLORS	ORIGINAL OPENING PRICE	CURRENT RETAIL PRICE
SOLD OUT EDITIONS (RARE):										
Synesis Series	EP	EP	1985	SP/HC	30 X 35	R/BFK	20	21	900	2500
Synesis Series	EP	EP	1985	SP/HC	30 X 35	R/BFK	20	21	900	2500
Matta Series	EP	EP	1985	SP/HC	31 X 35	R/BFK	34	17	900	2500
Matta Series	EP	EP	1985	SP/HC	31 X 35	R/BFK	34	17	900	2500
Corium Series	EP	EP	1986	SP/HC	28 X 34	AP88	52	13	900	2500
Corium Series	EP	EP	1986	SP/HC	28 X 34	AP88	52	13	900	2500

JAMES DRAKE

BORN: Lubbock, TX; September 12, 1946
EDUCATION: Art Center, Col of Design, Los Angeles, CA, Fel, BFA, with Honors, 1969, MFA, 1970
TEACHING: Instr, Life Drawing, Art Center, Col of Design, Los Angeles, CA, 1969–70; Univ of Texas, El Paso, TX, 1971 to present
AWARDS: Nat Endowment for the Arts Awards, Visual Arts Fel, 1988, Artist Fel Grant, 1989–90, Int Exchange Fel, 1990
RECENT EXHIB: Adair Margo Gallery, El Paso, TX, 1987; Barbara Fendrick Gallery, Wash, DC, 1987,88; Univ of Texas, San Antonio, TX, 1988; Contemp Arts Mus, Houston, TX, 1988; Alternative Mus, NY, 1988; Palmer Art Mus, Pennsylvania State Univ, University Park, PA, 1988; La Jolla Mus of Contemp Art, CA, 1989; Arthur Roger Gallery, New Orleans, LA, 1989; Anderson Gallery, Virginia Commonwealth Univ, Richmond, VA, 1989,92
COLLECTIONS: El Paso Mus of Art, TX; Phoenix Art Mus, AZ; Univ of New Mexico, Albuquerque, NM; Univ of Texas, El Paso, TX; Mathews Art Center, Arizona State Univ, Tempe, AR; Pennsylvania State Univ, Palmer Mus of Art, University Park, PA; Contemp Arts Mus, Houston, TX; Virginia Commonwealth Univ, Richmond, VA
PRINTERS: Eric Katter, Albuquerque, NM (EK); Bill Lagattuta, Albuquerque, NM (BL); Anya K Szykitka, Albuquerque, NM (AKS); Tamarind Inst, Albuquerque, NM (TI); Lisa Sette, Tempe, AZ (LS); Sette Publishing Company, Tempe, AZ (SPC)
PUBLISHERS: Tamarind Inst, Albuquerque, NM (TI); Sette Publishing Company, Tempe, AZ (SPC)
GALLERIES: Tamarind Inst, Albuquerque, AZ; Arthur Roger Gallery, New York, NY & New Orleans, LA; Adair Margo Gallery, El Paso, TX; Barbara Fendrick Gallery, New York, NY; Sette Gallery, Scottsdale, AZ; Shea & Bornstein Gallery, Santa Monica, CA; David Lawrence Editions, Beverly Hills, CA; Richard Levy Gallery, Albuquerque, NM
MAILING ADDRESS: 5028 Love Rd, El Paso, TX 79922

James Drake
Tap
Courtesy Sette Publishing Company

The retail prices of the 100,000 limited edition prints quoted in this directory are subject to change. Print publishers, artists and galleries were the direct sources for these quotations. Prices in the secondary market listed as "Sold Out Editions (Rare)" indicate that the publisher has a limited supply of that print or that the print is difficult to locate in the galleries.

The Printworld Directory is accepting new applications for the seventh edition. Approximately 300 new artists will be accepted. Please use the two forms provided in the back section of this directory to submit biographical data and documentation of prints. Edition number of each print must not exceed 500 and the retail price must be $100 or more.

JAMES DRAKE CONTINUED

TITLE	PUBLISHER	PRINTER	DATE	MEDIUM	DIMENSION (PAPER SIZE) IN INCHES	TYPE OF PAPER	EDITION NUMBER	NO. OF COLORS	ORIGINAL OPENING PRICE	CURRENT RETAIL PRICE
CURRENT EDITIONS:										
Tap	SPC	LS/SPC	1986	LC	30 X 22	AC	25		300	500
Catnip I	SPC	LS/SPC	1986	WC	21 X 15	AC	20		300	500
Fiesta Food Chain	SPC	LS/SPC	1988	WC	22 X 17	AC	20		300	500
Hiding Your Words	SPC	LS/SPC	1988	WC	22 X 17	AC	20		300	500
Blue Gun	TI	EK/BL/TI	1989	LC	30 X 44	R/BFK	10		500	600
Third World Street Girls I	TI	EK/BL/TI	1989	LC	30 X 44	R/BFK	10		800	1000
Third World Street Girls II (Dipt)	TI	BL/TI	1989	LC	154 X 113 cm	R/BFK	10	3	800	1000
Green Knife	TI	AKS/BL/TI	1989	LC	77 X 113 cm	R/BFK	10	2	500	600
Let's Kiss Like We Were Really Lovers	TI	ART/EK/TI	1989	LC	44 X 61	R/BFK	12	3	800	1000

DAVID FRAISER DRIESBACH

BORN: Wausau, WI; October 7, 1922
EDUCATION: Univ of Illinois, Chicago, IL; Beloit Col; Univ of Wisconsin; Pennsylvania Acad of Fine Arts, Phila, PA; Iowa State Univ, MFA, 1951; Atelier 17, Paris, France, with S W Hayter, 1969
TEACHING: Hendrix Col, Conway, AR, 1952–53; Iowa State Teachers Col, Cedar Falls, IA, 1953–54; Milliken Univ, Decatur, IL, 1954–59; Ohio Univ, Athens, OH, 1959–64; Northern Illinois, Univ, De Kalb, IL 1964 to present
COLLECTIONS: Notre Dame Univ, South Bend, IN; Dayton Art Inst, OH; Purdue Univ, Hammond, IN; Carlton Col, Northfield, MN; Kalamazoo Art Center, MI; Ohio State Univ, Columbus, OH; Univ of Maryland, College Park, MD; Beloit Col, WI; Boston Mus of Fine Arts, MA; Seattle Mus of Art, WA; Columbus Gallery of Fine Arts, OH; Bibliotheque Nat, Paris, France
PRINTERS: AGB Graphics, Madison, WI (AGB); Nelson-Wagner Litho Workshop, Edwardsville, IL (NW); Tyminson (T); Gene Coon (GC); Mike Gulas (MG); Artist (ART)
PUBLISHERS: Pilot Rock Press, Normal, IL (PRP); Univ of Indiana, Evansville, IN (UI); Nelson-Wagner, Edwardsville, IL (N-W); Artist (ART)
GALLERIES: Merrill Chase Galleries, Chicago, IL; Associated American Artists, New York, NY; Joan Hodgell Gallery, Sarasota, FL; Clare Spitler Works of Art, Ann Arbor, MI; Joy Horwitch Gallery, Chicago, IL; Wenniger Graphics, Boston, MA; Chicago Center for the Print, Chicago, IL
MAILING ADDRESS: RR 810 Lawnwood Ave, De Kalb, IL 60115

TITLE	PUBLISHER	PRINTER	DATE	MEDIUM	DIMENSION (PAPER SIZE) IN INCHES	TYPE OF PAPER	EDITION NUMBER	NO. OF COLORS	ORIGINAL OPENING PRICE	CURRENT RETAIL PRICE
SOLD OUT EDITIONS (RARE):										
The Butterfly People	ART	ART	1968	EC	36 X 24	AP	30	4	250	600
All Children Must be Accompanied By Adults	ART	ART	1971–72	EC	24 X 36	AP	30	22	250	600
Lucky Mashed Patatoes	ART	ART	1972	EB/A	9 X 12	AP	250		100	300
Tuxedo 5-1234	ART	ART	1974	EC	20 X 24	AP	25	5	200	500
The Search (Triptych)	ART	ART	1963	EC	36 X 24 EA	AP	50	12	600	1300
Albert's Dog	ART	ART	1977	ENG	22 X 36	AP	60	1	150	400
The Everyday Occurrence	ART	ART	1973	ENG	24 X 36	AP	100	1	100	400
Roxy	ART	ART	1977	EC	23 X 24	AP	35	8	250	500
Trucker's Cafe	ART	ART	1977	EC	26 X 21	AP	50	5	250	350
Flaming Meatballs	N-W	T	1977	LC	24 X 16	AP	30	4	100	350
Art Ferrer and the Spectators	ART	GC	1980	EC	17 X 18	AP	50	6	200	350
Expensive Ties or Who in Hell is Ethel Lundberg	ART	MG	1981	E/ENG	20 X 16	AP	50	3	100	250
The Princess Walks in Her Sleep	ART	GC	1982	EC	10 X 16	AP	50	7	200	300
Uffda! My Dear	UI	ART	1982	EC	18 X 18	AP	30	8	400	500

SYDNEY MARIA DRUM

BORN: Calgary, Alta, Canada; November 20, 1952
EDUCATION: Univ of Calgary, Can, BFA, 1974; York Univ, Downsville, Can, MFA, 1976
TEACHING: Univ of Alberta, Edmonton, Can, 1976–78; Nova Scotia Col of Art & Design, Halifax, Can, 1978–83; Univ of Illinois, Chicago, IL, 1983 to present
AWARDS: Canadian Council of the Arts Grant, 1976–77; A-N-W Prof Prize, Print Club, Phila, PA, 1979; Artist Fel, Yaddo Found, 1980
RECENT EXHIB: Northwestern Univ, Evanston, IL, 1987; Bau-Xi Gallery, Toronto, ON, Canada, 1987,90,92
COLLECTIONS: Mus of Mod Art, NY; Philadelphia Mus of Art, PA; Nat Mus of Am Art, Wash, DC; Univ of Nebraska, Lincoln, NE; Univ of South Dakota, Vermillion, SD; Univ of Toronto, Can; Canadian Council Art Bank, Ottawa, Can; Southern Illinois Univ, Edwardsville, IL
PRINTERS: Orlando Condeso, NY (OC); Pat Kaufman (PK); Sue Kleinman (SK); Peter Almeida (PA); Brian Lynch (BL); Artist (ART)
PUBLISHERS: Condeso/Lawler Gallery, NY (C-L); Artist (ART)
GALLERIES: Condeso/Lawler Gallery, New York, NY; van Straaten Gallery, Chicago, IL; Jan Cicero Gallery, Chicago, IL; Gallery Pascal, Toronto, Canada; Klimpton Gallery, San Francisco, CA; Burns Fine Art, New York, NY; Bau-Xi Gallery, Toronto, ON, Canada
MAILING ADDRESS: 138 W 120th St, New York, NY 10027

TITLE	PUBLISHER	PRINTER	DATE	MEDIUM	DIMENSION (PAPER SIZE) IN INCHES	TYPE OF PAPER	EDITION NUMBER	NO. OF COLORS	ORIGINAL OPENING PRICE	CURRENT RETAIL PRICE
SOLD OUT EDITIONS (RARE):										
1st Large Mezzotint	ART	ART	1976	MEZ	18 X 24	R/BFK	15	1	200	400
1st Small Mezzotint	ART	ART	1976	MEZ	18 X 24	R/BFK	15	1	200	400
2nd Large Mezzotint	ART	ART	1976	MEZ	18 X 24	R/BFK	20	1	200	400
4th Large Mezzotint	ART	ART	1977	MEZ	18 X 24	R/BFK	20	1	200	400
5th Large Mezzotint	ART	ART	1977	MEZ	18 X 24	R/BFK	20	1	200	400

The print market has become very selective. For the first time since we published the first edition of The Printworld Directory in 1982, the prices of prints have been greatly reduced and greatly increased for the same artists by the most reputable and established print publishers. Check the fifth edition to understand the movement.

SYDNEY MARIA DRUM CONTINUED

TITLE	PUBLISHER	PRINTER	DATE	MEDIUM	DIMENSION (PAPER SIZE) IN INCHES	TYPE OF PAPER	EDITION NUMBER	NO. OF COLORS	ORIGINAL OPENING PRICE	CURRENT RETAIL PRICE
CURRENT EDITIONS:										
CURRENT EDITIONS:										
Untitled (G20)	C-L	OC	1981	EC	30 X 44	R/BFK	50	2	350	400
Untitled (G21)	C-L	OC	1981	EC	30 X 44	R/BFK	50	2	350	400
Untitled (G22)	ART	PK	1981	EC	20 X 30	R/BFK	25	2	275	350
Untitled (G23)	ART	SK	1981	EC	20 X 30	R/BFK	20	2	275	350
Untitled (G24)	ART	PA	1981	EC	20 X 30	R/BFK	25	2	275	350
Untitled (G26)	ART	ART	1982	EC	20 X 30	R/BFK	35	2	275	350
Untitled (G27)	ART	PA	1982	EC	20 X 30	R/BFK	50	2	275	350
Untitled (G28)	ART	PA	1982	EC	20 X 30	R/BFK	40	2	275	350
Untitled (G29)	ART	BL	1982	EC	20 X 30	R/BFK	50	3	275	350
Urbana	ART	PA	1982	EC	20 X 30	R/BFK	50	5	275	350
Untitled Urbana (G30)	ART	ART	1982	EC	20 X 30	R/BFK	45	2	275	350
Untitled (G31)	ART	ART	1982	EC	20 X 30	R/BFK	50	1	275	350

W DU NIKO

BORN: Piekary Slaskie, Poland; September 8, 1947
EDUCATION: Acad of Fine Arts, Krakow, Poland, 1974
PRINTERS: Artist (ART)
PUBLISHERS: Ed Hill Editions, El Paso, TX (EHE)
GALLERIES: Ed Hill Editions, El Paso, TX

TITLE	PUBLISHER	PRINTER	DATE	MEDIUM	DIMENSION (PAPER SIZE) IN INCHES	TYPE OF PAPER	EDITION NUMBER	NO. OF COLORS	ORIGINAL OPENING PRICE	CURRENT RETAIL PRICE
SOLD OUT EDITIONS (RARE):										
Visual Transposition Album XVIII	EHE	ART	1981	W/MT	29 X 35	HMP	35	2	350	650

VALENTINA DUBASKY

BORN: Washington, DC; March 1, 1951
EDUCATION: Washington Gallery of Mod Art Studios, Wash, DC, 1968; Corcoran Sch of Art, Wash, DC, 1969; Goddard Col, Plainfield, VT, MA, 1974; Goddard Col Grad Sch, NY, MFA, 1977
AWARDS: Artist's Grant, Ariana Found for the Arts; Independent Exhib Grant, Artists Space, NY; Pollock-Krasner Found Award, 1986
COLLECTIONS: Aldrich Mus of Contemp Art, Ridgefield, CT; Alternative Mus, NY; Newark Mus, NJ; Seattle Art Mus, WA; Jane Voorhees Zimmerli Art Mus, Rutgers Univ, New Brunswick, NJ
PRINTERS: Cheryl Pelavin Printmaker, NY (CP); Solo Press, NY (SP); Pamela Moore, NY (PM)
PUBLISHERS: Cheryl Pelavin Printmaker, NY (CP); Bristol Art Editions, NY (BA)
GALLERIES: Pelavin Editions, New York, NY; Robert Kidd Gallery, Birmingham, MI
MAILING ADDRESS: 253 E Tenth St, New York, NY 10009

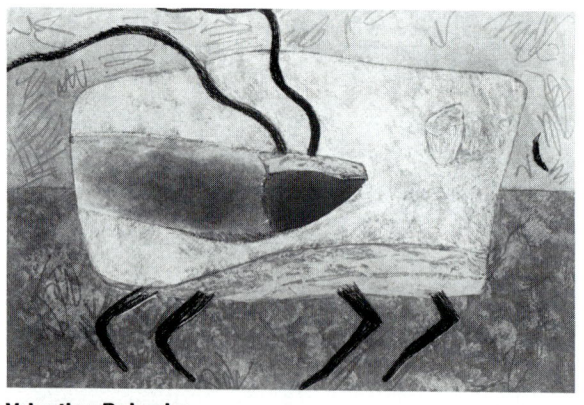

Valentina Dubasky
Leaping Bridled Stag
Courtesy Cheryl Pelavin Printmaker

TITLE	PUBLISHER	PRINTER	DATE	MEDIUM	DIMENSION (PAPER SIZE) IN INCHES	TYPE OF PAPER	EDITION NUMBER	NO. OF COLORS	ORIGINAL OPENING PRICE	CURRENT RETAIL PRICE
CURRENT EDITIONS:										
Dune Horse/Starry Night	BA	PM/SP	1983	LC	22 X 30	AP/B	40	6	450	1200
Leaping Brindled Stag	CP	CP	1984	EC/A/CC	27 X 37	SOM/GAMPS	50	8	625	1400
Plum Stag in Claret	CP	CP	1984	EC/A/CC	27 X 37	SOM/KIN	50	11	625	1400

JOHN EWING DUFF

BORN: Layfayette, IN; December 2, 1943
EDUCATION: San Francisco Art Inst, CA, BFA, 1967
AWARDS: Theodore Award, Guggenheim Mus, NY, 1977; Brandeis Award for Visual Arts, Waltham, MA, 1987
RECENT EXHIB: BlumHelman Gallery, Santa Monica, CA, 1987; Lorence • Monk Gallery, NY, 1987; BlumHelman Gallery, NY, 1988; Amy Lipton Gallery, NY, 1990; San Jose Mus of Art, CA, 1992
COLLECTIONS: Mus of Mod Art, NY; Solomon R Guggenheim Mus, NY; Whitney Mus of Am Art, NY; Kaiser Wilhelm Mus, Krefeld, West Germany; Metropolitan Art Mus, NY; Inst of Contemp Art, Chicago, IL
PRINTERS: William Katz, NY (WK); Artist (ART)
PUBLISHERS: William Katz, NY (WK); Artist (ART)
GALLERIES: Brooke Alexander, Inc, New York, NY; Margo Leavin Gallery, Los Angeles, CA; BlumHelman Gallery, New York, NY; Amy Lipton Gallery, New York, NY
MAILING ADDRESS: 7 Doyers St, New York, NY 10013

TITLE	PUBLISHER	PRINTER	DATE	MEDIUM	DIMENSION (PAPER SIZE) IN INCHES	TYPE OF PAPER	EDITION NUMBER	NO. OF COLORS	ORIGINAL OPENING PRICE	CURRENT RETAIL PRICE
SOLD OUT EDITIONS (RARE):										
Untitled	ART/WK	ART/WK	1974	SP	22 X 34	RB	20		200	750

JEAN DUBUFFET

BORN: Le Havre, France; (1901–1985)
EDUCATION: Academie Julian, Paris, France, 1918
RECENT EXHIB: Retrosp, Wildenstein Gallery, NY, 1987; Retrosp, Pace Gallery, NY, 1987; Galerie Michael Haas, Berlin, West Germany, 1987; Florida State Univ, Tallahassee, FL, 1992; Hirshhorn Mus, Wash, DC, 1992,93; Pace Gallery, NY, 1993
COLLECTIONS: Hirshhorn Mus, Wash, DC; Art Inst of Chicago, IL; Albright-Knox Art Gallery, Buffalo, NY
PRINTERS: M Broutelles, Paris, France (MB); Lacouriére & Frelaut, Paris, France (L/F)
PUBLISHERS: Editions Alecto, Ltd, London, England (EAL); Edition Galerie Beyeler, Basel, Switzerland (EGB); Pace Editions, Inc, NY (PE)
GALLERIES: Pace Prints, New York, NY; Editions Fata Morgana, Paris, France; Charles Foley Gallery, Columbus, OH; Donald Morris Gallery, Birmingham, MI; Barbara Krakow Gallery, Boston, MA; Solomon & Co Fine Art, New York, NY; Jane Kahan Gallery, New York, NY; Posner Gallery, Milwaukee, WI; Gallery Urban, New York, NY; Barbara Mathes Gallery, New York, NY; Scherer Gallery, Marlboro, NJ; Hokin Gallery, Bay Harbor Islands, FL; Galerie Michael Haas, Berlin, West Germany; Jonathan Novak, Los Angeles, CA; Connecticut Fine Arts, Westport, CT; Jupiter Fine Arts, Jupiter, FL; Richard Gray Gallery, Chicago, IL; Donald Morris Gallery, Birmingham, MI; Greenberg Gallery, St Louis, MO; Claude Bernard Gallery, New York, NY; Andre Emmerich Gallery, New York, NY; Sigrid Freundorfer Fine Art, New York, NY; Lillian Heidenberg Gallery, New York, NY; Alexander Kahan Fine Arts, New York, NY; Barbara Leibowits Graphics, New York, NY; Scharf Fine Art, New York, NY; Harcourts Modern & Contemporary, San Francisco, CA; Jupiter Fine Arts, FL; Yoshii Gallery, New York, NY; Posner Gallery, Milwaukee, WI; Sidney Janis Gallery, New York, NY; Enrico Navarra Gallery, New York, NY; Elkon Gallery, Inc, New York, NY; Foster Goldstrom, Inc, New York, NY; James Goodman Gallery, New York, NY; Stephen Haller Fine Art, New York, NY

Jean Dubuffet
Aborescences II
Courtesy Pace Editions

Loreau (L)—Webel/Lebon (W/L)

TITLE	PUBLISHER	PRINTER	DATE	MEDIUM	DIMENSION (PAPER SIZE) IN INCHES	TYPE OF PAPER	EDITION NUMBER	NO. OF COLORS	ORIGINAL OPENING PRICE	CURRENT RETAIL PRICE
SOLD OUT EDITIONS (RARE):										
Les Murs, Planache V: Danse au Mur (L-409)			1949	LB	15 X 11	R/100	195		20	6000
Corps de Dames (Set of 6)			1950	LB	12 X 10 EA	WOVE	3 EA	1 EA	500 SET	60000 SET
Les Montagnards (L-IX)			1953	LC	14 X 17	LANA	25	2	30	20000
Personnage au Costume Rouge			1961	LC	21 X 15	R/BFK	50		90	45000
Nez Carotte			1962	LC	23 X 15	R/BFK	50		90	45000
Sourire II (with 8 proofs)			1962	LC	21 X 15 EA	AP	3 EA			175000 SET
Banque de L'Hourloupe-Cartes a Jouer et a Tirer (Set of 52 Playing Cards)	EAL	EAL	1967	SP	10 X 7 EA		350		150	3500
Arborescence I (Vacuum-Formed Multiple) (Framed)	PE	MB	1972	SP/REL	13 X 10	AP	75		500	12000
Presences Fugaces (Set of 6):									3000 SET	90000 SET
Protestator (Green)	PE	MB	1973	SP	30 X 22	DE	100	4	500	20000
Exaltador (Blue)	PE	MB	1973	SP	30 X 22	DE	100	4	500	20000
Denegator (Buff)	PE	MB	1973	SP	30 X 22	DE	100	4	500	20000
Celebrator (Kraft)	PE	MB	1973	SP	30 X 22	DE	100	4	500	20000
Objectador (Rose)	PE	MB	1973	SP	30 X 22	DE	100	4	500	20000
Epiphanor (Black)	PE	MB	1973	SP	30 X 22	DE	100	4	500	20000
Quatre Personnages	EB	MB	1974	SP	25 X 36	ARJ	50		500	15000
Organisme	EB	MB	1974	SP	26 X 36	ARJ	50		600	15000
Territoire et Paysan	EB	MB	1975	SP	21 X 16	ARJ	50		600	15000
Recit	PE	MB	1975	SP	13 X 17	AP	50	3	500	9000
Marche en Compagne	PE	MB	1975	SP	31 X 28	AP	70		500	20000
Ontogenese	PE	MB	1975	SP	30 X 36	AP	50		500	20000
Solitude Illuminee	PE	MB	1975	SP	38 X 28	AP	50		500	20000
Site avec Trois Personages	PE	MB	1976	SP	27 X 40	AP	50		1500	20000
Fables (Set of 6):									4500 SET	95000 SET
Villa Duplex	PE	MB	1976	SP	35 X 28	AP	50	3	750	15000
Evocations	PE	MB	1976	SP	27 X 35	AP	50	2	750	15000
Lion Heraldique	PE	MB	1976	SP	27 X 35	AP	50	4	750	20000
Course Ta Galope	PE	MB	1976	SP	27 X 35	AP	50	4	750	15000
Immeuble	PE	MB	1976	SP	27 X 35	AP	50	4	750	15000
Le Visir	PE	MB	1976	SP	35 X 27	AP	50	4	750	15000
Le Fugitif (Enameled Steel & Aluminum, Magnetic)	PE	MB	1977	MULT	29 X 21	Steel/Alum	50	40	1500	25000

JEAN DUBUFFET CONTINUED

TITLE	PUBLISHER	PRINTER	DATE	MEDIUM	DIMENSION (PAPER SIZE) IN INCHES	TYPE OF PAPER	EDITION NUMBER	NO. OF COLORS	ORIGINAL OPENING PRICE	CURRENT RETAIL PRICE
SOLD OUT EDITIONS (RARE):										
Faits Memorables I, II, III (Set of 3)	PE	MB	1978	SP	30 X 39 EA	AP	70 EA	60 EA	4500 SET	65000 SET
									1800 EA	25000 EA
Ilya Book with Set of 13 Prints	PE	MB	1979	SP	14 X 10 EA	AP	80 EA	2 EA	10000 SET	80000 SET
Ilya Book with Limited Edition (Deluxe Edition)	PE	MB	1979	SP	14 X 10	AP	10 EA			POR
Ilya	PE	MB	1979	SP	14 X 10	AP	80		500	5000
Site de Memoire Series:										
Site de Memoire I	PE	AA	1979	SP	99 X 68	CAN	10	2	15000	80000
Site de Memoire II	PE	AA	1979	SP	84 X 58	CAN	10	2	10000	65000
Site de Memoire III	PE	AA	1979	SP	58 X 83	CAN	10	2	10000	65000
Parcours (Scroll on Rag Paper, Backed with Silk, Encased in Silkscreened Woodbox)	PE	AA	1981	SP	20 X 19	RAG/SILK	80	2	2000	20000
Les Passants	PE	AA	1982	LC	32 X 44	AP	50		2000	15000
Bonne Annee	PE	AA	1982	LC	15 X 17	AP	50		600	9000
Lieu Virtuel	PE	AA	1984	LC	32 X 43	AP	50		1000	15000
Personnage au Chapeau (L-XVI, 221)			1962	LC	22 X 15	LAID	50		90	20000
Vignettes Lorgnettes (Set of 24) (W/L-149-172)	EGB	L/F	1962	EB		R/BFK	20 EA	1 EA	2000 SET	30000 SET
Samedi Tantot (L-xxx,325)			1964	LC	22 X 16	AP	125		100	7500
Le Surintendant	PE	MB	1972	SP	20 X 12	AP	120		250	12000
Arborescence II	PE	MB	1972	SP/REL	13 X 10	AP	75		500	15000
Parade Nuptiale	PE	MB	1973	SP	15 X 13	AP	85		500	8500

MICHAEL DUFFY

RECENT EXHIB: Kyle Belding Gallery, Denver, CO, 1987
PRINTERS: Bud Shark, Boulder, CO (BS); Shark's, Inc, Boulder, CO (SI)
PUBLISHERS: Shark's, Inc, Boulder, CO (SI)
GALLERIES: Kyle Belding Gallery, Denver, CO; A Clean, Well-Lighted Place, New York, NY; C G Rein Galleries, St Paul, MN & Scottsdale, AZ & Santa Fe, NM & Houston, TX & Minneapolis, MN; Shark's Inc, Boulder, CO; Quartet Editions, New York, NY

TITLE	PUBLISHER	PRINTER	DATE	MEDIUM	DIMENSION (PAPER SIZE) IN INCHES	TYPE OF PAPER	EDITION NUMBER	NO. OF COLORS	ORIGINAL OPENING PRICE	CURRENT RETAIL PRICE
CURRENT EDITIONS:										
Burden	SI	BS/SLL	1986	WB	48 X 32	R/BFK	10	1	500	800
Cane Factory	SI	BS/SLL	1986	WB	48 X 32	R/BFK	10	1	500	800
Fields	SI	BS/SLL	1986	WB	48 X 32	R/BFK	10	1	500	800
Woman	SI	BS/SLL	1986	WB	48 X 32	R/BFK	10	1	500	800
Head 1,3	SI	BS/SLL	1987	MON	30 X 22 EA	AC	1 EA	Varies	500 EA	500 EA
Cross 1,2	SI	BS/SLL	1987	MON	30 X 22 EA	AC	1 EA	Varies	500 EA	500 EA
Byrnes 1,2	SI	BS/SLL	1987	MON	42 X 30 EA	AC	1 EA	Varies	500 EA	800 EA
Eve 1,2	SI	BS/SLL	1987	MON	30 X 42 EA	AC	1 EA	Varies	500 EA	800 EA
Henri 1,2	SI	BS/SLL	1987	MON	42 X 30 EA	AC	1 EA	Varies	500 EA	800 EA
Still Life	SI	BS/SLL	1988	WC	52 X 32	AC	10		600	800

FRANCOISE DUMONTIER

BORN: Lagny, France
PRINTERS: American Atelier, NY (AA)
PUBLISHERS: Circle Fine Art, NY (CFA)
GALLERIES: Circle Galleries, San Diego, CA & San Francisco, CA & Northbrook, IL & Pittsburgh, PA & Houston, TX & Soho, NY & Chicago, IL & Scottsdale, AZ & Beverly Hills, CA & Costa Mesa, CA & Sherman Oaks, CA & Palm Beach, FL & Honolulu, HI & New Orleans, LA & Las Vegas, NV & Seattle, WA

TITLE	PUBLISHER	PRINTER	DATE	MEDIUM	DIMENSION (PAPER SIZE) IN INCHES	TYPE OF PAPER	EDITION NUMBER	NO. OF COLORS	ORIGINAL OPENING PRICE	CURRENT RETAIL PRICE
SOLD OUT EDITIONS (RARE):										
Friponnerie	CFA	AA	1976	EC	13 X 16	AP	150		35	150
Pommier Deux	CFA	AA	1976	EC	10 X 10	AP	150		35	150
CURRENT EDITIONS:										
Noces de Dentelles	CFA	AA	1976	EC	13 X 14	AP	150		35	150

CARROLL DUNHAM

RECENT EXHIB: Editions Ilene Kurtz, NY, 1987; Sonnabend Gallery, NY, 1989
PRINTERS: Keith Brintzenhofe, NY (KB); Douglas Volle, NY (DV); John Lund, NY (JL); Hitoshi Kido, NY (HK); Craig Zammiello, NH (CZ); Universal Limited Art Editions, West Islip, NY (ULAE); Valter Rossi, Rome, Italy (VR); Atleier Vigna Antoniniana Stamperia d'Arte, Rome, Italy (AVAS); Leslie Miller, NY (LM); Grenfell Press, NY (GrPr)
PUBLISHERS: Universal Limited Art Editions, West Islip, NY (ULAE); Editions Ilene Kurtz, NY (EIK); Grenfell Press, NY (GrPr)

CARROLL DUNHAM CONTINUED

GALLERIES: Editions Ilene Kurtz, New York, NY; Daniel Weinberg Gallery, Santa Monica, CA; Thomas Smith Fine Art, Fort Wayne, IN; Barbara Krakow Gallery, Boston, MA; Flanders Contemporary Art, Minneapolis, MN; Carol M Penn Fine Art, Great Neck, NY; Elizabeth Paul Gallery, Cincinnati, OH; Simon Watson Gallery, New York, NY; Sonnabend Gallery, New York, NY; Editions Ilene Kurtz, New York, NY; David Nolan Gallery, New York, NY; Betsy Senior Contemporary Prints, New York, NY

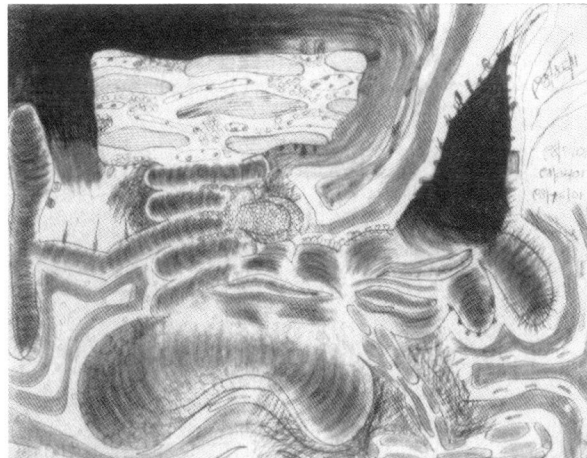

Carroll Dunham
Touching Two Sides
Courtesy Universal Limited Art Editions

Carroll Dunham
Full Spectrum
Courtesy Universal Limited Art Editions

TITLE	PUBLISHER	PRINTER	DATE	MEDIUM	DIMENSION (PAPER SIZE) IN INCHES	TYPE OF PAPER	EDITION NUMBER	NO. OF COLORS	ORIGINAL OPENING PRICE	CURRENT RETAIL PRICE
SOLD OUT EDITONS (RARE):										
Untitled	ULAE	KB/DV/ULAE	1984–85	LB	28 X 19	JWP/1951	42	1	500	1200
Untitled	ULAE	KB/DV/ULAE	1985	LC	25 X 18	HMP	31	2	500	1200
Accelerator	ULAE	KB/DV/ULAE	1985	LC	42 X 30	R/BFK	51	4	1200	2000
Full Spectrum	ULAE	KB/DV/ULAE	1985–87	LC/SP	42 X 28	JBG	68		2500	4500
Color Messages A,B,C (Set of 3)	ULAE	KB/DV/ULAE	1986–87	LC	13 X 9 EA	GAAP	52 EA	4 EA	1500 SET 600 EA	4200 SET 1400 EA
Three Etchings (Series of 3)	EIK	VR/AVAS	1987	EB/A/DPT	55 X 38 EA	FAB	50 EA		3500 EA	4200 EA
Red Shift (Set of 5)	ULAE	KB/DV/ULAE	1987–88	LC	30 X 22 EA	AP	49 EA		15000 SET	18000 SET
Untitled	ULAE	ULAE	1988	I	69 X 50	R/BFK	53	1	3000	4500
Wave	ULAE	ULAE	1988	EC	53 X 74	R/BFK	43		3000	4500
Touching Two Sides	ULAE	ULAE	1989	DPT	24 X 28	RdB	52	1	2000	3000
Floating Shape with...	ULAE	ULAE	1989	LC	23 X 29	R/BFK	47		1000	1800
Pumping Shape	ULAE	ULAE	1990	EB	18 X 23	R/BFK	38	1	850	1000
Place and Things (Boxed) (Set of 6)	EIK/GrPr	LM/GrPr	1992	LI	13 X 17	KOZO	36	20	4000 SET	4000 SET
Point of Origin	ULAE	JL/HK/CZ/ULAE	1988–92	I	49 X 69	TOR	30	2	3000	3000

DAVID A DUNLOP

PRINTERS: Artist (Art)
PUBLISHERS: Orion Editions, NY (OE)
GALLERIES: Mona Berman Fine Arts, New Haven, CT; Orion Editions, New York, NY

TITLE	PUBLISHER	PRINTER	DATE	MEDIUM	DIMENSION (PAPER SIZE) IN INCHES	TYPE OF PAPER	EDITION NUMBER	NO. OF COLORS	ORIGINAL OPENING PRICE	CURRENT RETAIL PRICE
CURRENT EDITIONS:										
Flood Plain	OE	ART	1988	SP	30 X 42	AP	150	32	550	675
Bourbeuse	OE	ART	1988	SP	30 X 42	AP	150	32	550	750
Water Turns	OE	ART	1989	SP	30 X 42	AP	175	32	700	750
Tanglewood	OE	ART	1989	EB	50 X 27	R/BFK	80	1	700	750

JORGE DURON

BORN: Mexico City, Mexico; 1930
EDUCATION: Architect; Univ of Americas, Mexico City, Mex, BFA, 1969; Univ of California, Berkeley, CA, MA in Sculpture
TEACHING: Prof, Art, Univ of the Americas, Mexico City, Mex, 1970–71; Dir, Dept of Visual Expression, Nat Univ of Mexico, 1970–71; Dir, Art Dept, Univ of the Americas, 1975
PUBLISHERS: Editions Press, San Francisco, CA (EP)
GALLERIES: Walton-Gilbert Galleries, San Francisco, CA

JORGE DURON CONTINUED

TITLE	PUBLISHER	PRINTER	DATE	MEDIUM	DIMENSION (PAPER SIZE) IN INCHES	TYPE OF PAPER	EDITION NUMBER	NO. OF COLORS	ORIGINAL OPENING PRICE	CURRENT RETAIL PRICE
CURRENT EDITIONS:										
Las Viejas	EP	EP	1979	LC	22 X 30	AC/B	60	6	400	650
Amalia	EP	EP	1979	LC	30 X 22	AC/W	100	5	400	650
La Pensativa	EP	EP	1979	LC	30 X 22	AC/W	100	4	400	650

NANCY DWYER

PRINTERS: Jack Lemon, Chicago, IL (JL); Landfall Press, Inc, Chicago, IL (LPI)

PUBLISHERS: Landfall Press, Inc, Chicago, IL (LPI)
GALLERIES: Rhona Hoffman Gallery, Chicago, IL; Josh Baer Gallery, New York, NY; Landfall Press, Inc, Chicago, IL

TITLE	PUBLISHER	PRINTER	DATE	MEDIUM	DIMENSION (PAPER SIZE) IN INCHES	TYPE OF PAPER	EDITION NUMBER	NO. OF COLORS	ORIGINAL OPENING PRICE	CURRENT RETAIL PRICE
CURRENT EDITIONS:										
Mayhem	LPI	JL/LPI	1990	LC	20 X 18	AC	25		650	650
Out of My Mind	LPI	JL/LPI	1990	LC	18 X 18	AC	25		650	650

EYVIND EARLE

BORN: New York, NY: 1916
RECENT EXHIB: Tamara Bane Gallery, Los Angeles, CA 1987,91; Conacher Galleries, San Francisco, CA, 1993
PRINTERS: Accent Studios (AC), Colton Graphics (CG), Atelier Giroudon, Paris, France (AG)

PUBLISHERS: Circle Fine Art Corp, Chicago, IL (CFA); Hammer Publishing Co, NY (HP); Robert Bane Publishing Inc, Los Angeles, CA (RBP)
GALLERIES: Tamara Bane Gallery, Los Angeles, CA; Conacher Galleries, San Francisco, CA; Nuance Galleries, Tampa, FL; Metropolitan Art Gallery, Los Angeles, CA

TITLE	PUBLISHER	PRINTER	DATE	MEDIUM	DIMENSION (PAPER SIZE) IN INCHES	TYPE OF PAPER	EDITION NUMBER	NO. OF COLORS	ORIGINAL OPENING PRICE	CURRENT RETAIL PRICE
SOLD OUT EDITIONS (RARE):										
California Coastline	HP	ART	1975	SP	10 X 8	COR	300	5 EA	200	1350
Santa Ynez Valley	HP	SS	1979	SP	20 X 40	MB	300	14	400	4500
Autumn	HP	ART/SS	1979	SP	28 X 22	AP	300	17	400	4500
La Viejas	HP	ART	1979	SP	20 X 40	MB	300	14	400	1200
Black Evergreen Forest	HP	ART	1979	SP	40 X 30	AP	300	20	550	5000
California Suite (Series of 4)									1000 SET	3500 SET
Carmel Valley	HP	ART	1979	SP	8 X 10	AP	100	11	250	1000
Santa Barbara Mountains	HP	ART	1979	SP	10 X 8	AP	100	12	250	1000
Seaside Pastures	HP	ART	1979	SP	10 X 8	AP	100	8	250	1000
Big Sur Calm	HP	ART	1979	SP	8 X 10	AP	100	10	250	1000
Enchanted Coast	HP	ART	1980	SP	40 X 20	AP	300		500	4500
Gothic Forest	HP	ART	1980	SP	24 X 26	AP	300	20	500	7500
Awakening	HP	ART	1981	SP	30 X 19	AP	260		350	2800
Girl with Raven Hair	HP	ART	1981	LC	30 X 20	AP	260		350	2800
Village	HP	ART	1981	SP	21 X 17	AP	300	24	400	2500
Winter	HP	ART	1981	SP	15 X 30	AP	300	20	400	4200
Spring	HP	ART	1981	SP	28 X 22	AP	280	20	450	3500
Summer	HP	ART	1981	SP	22 X 29	AP	300	37	500	4500
Eucalyptus	HP	ART	1982	SP	22 X 28	AP/260	85	10	600	2700
Winter Bonzai	HP	ART	1982	SP	28 X 22	STP	85	10	1000	3000
Winter Quiet	HP	ART	1982	SP	24 X 36	AP	300	19	400	4500
Seven White Horses	HP	ART	1982	SP	20 X 30	AP	40	11	600	1800
Carmel Highlands	HP	ART	1982	SP	20 X 16	STP	85	22	1000	3800
American Barns	HP	ART	1982	SP	12 X 30	AP	85		500	3200
Autumn Leaves	HP	ART	1982	SP	30 X 20	AP	75		400	1800
Big Sur and Branch	HP	ART	1982	SP	10 X 8	AP	300		250	1200
Black Oak	HP	ART	1982	SP	20 X 16	AP	40		400	2800
Valley	HP	ART	1982	SP	8 X 10	AP	300	9	250	1000
Blue Pine	HP	ART	1982	SP	28 X 20	AP	300		400	4500
Mountain Rise	HP	ART	1982	SP	40 X 20	AP	300		400	4200
Western Barns	HP	ART	1982	SP	10 X 8	AP/260	300	5	600	4000
Central Park	HP	ART	1983	SP	30 X 20	RG/100	85	7	600	2000
Winter Barn Suite (Set of 4)	HP	ART	1983	SP	20 X 16 EA	RG/100	100 EA	9 EA	1000 SET	6000 SET
Green Valley	HP	ART	1983	SP	20 X 30	MB	300	16	1000	2500
Land of the Midnight Sun	HP	ART	1983	SP	26 X 34	MB/100	85	10	800	4500
Gaviota Pass	HP	ART	1983	SP	20 X 30	MB	300	12	750	2800
Midnight Blue	HP	ART	1983	SP	30 X 20	MB	80	21	750	4000
Medieval Promenade	HP	ART	1983	SP	24 X 34	MB/STP	80	11	800	4200
Cattle Country	HP	ART	1983	SP	20 X 30	RG/100	150	7	650	2000

EYVIND EARLE CONTINUED

TITLE	PUBLISHER	PRINTER	DATE	MEDIUM	DIMENSION (PAPER SIZE) IN INCHES	TYPE OF PAPER	EDITION NUMBER	NO. OF COLORS	ORIGINAL OPENING PRICE	CURRENT RETAIL PRICE
SOLD OUT EDITIONS (RARE):										
Alamo Pintado	HP	ART	1984	SP	8 X 10	RG/100	300	10	300	1200
Sunlight	HP	ART	1984	SP	20 X 30	RG/100	300		800	2200
Reflections	HP	ART	1985	SP	30 X 20	RG/100	120		600	2500
Blue Fog	RBP	CG	1985	SP	30 X 42	STP	250		900	8500
Blue Fog (Deluxe)	RBP	CG	1985	SP	30 X 42	MB	100		1000	9000
Above the Sea	RBP	AS	1985	SP	30 X 38	STP	250		900	6000
Above the Sea (Deluxe)	RBP	AS	1985	SP	30 X 38	MB	100		1200	7000
Enchanted Forest	RBP	CG	1985	SP	29 X 41	STP	250		900	8500
Enchanted Forest (Deluxe)	RBP	CG	1985	SP	29 X 41	MB	100		1000	9000
The Great Red Barn	RBP	AS	1985	SP	24 X 44	STP	350		900	7500
Santa Ynez	RBP	CG	1985	SP	36 X 46	STP	350		900	7500
Beyond the Valley	RBP	AS	1986	SP	30 X 38	AP	300		1200	7500
Beyond the Valley (Deluxe)	RBP	AS	1986	SP	30 X 38	AP/BL	150		1500	8000
The Garden of Eden	RBP	AS	1986	SP	30 X 38	AP	350		1200	7500
The Garden of Eden (Deluxe)	RBP	AS	1986	SP	30 X 38	AP/BL	100		1500	8000
Factory	RBP	AG	1986	AC	24 X 33	HMP	195		1000	3000
Silent Thunder	RBP	AS	1986	SP	30 X 38	STP	310		1200	6500
Silent Thunder (Deluxe)	RBP	AS	1986	SP	30 X 38	AP/BL	150		1500	7000
Still Valley	RBP	ART	1986	SP	14 X 16	SP/100	265		400	2000
Eucalyptus Forest	RBP	ART	1986	SP	14 X 16	SP/100	267		400	2000
Cliffs of Darkness	RBP	ART	1986	LC	20 X 26	AP	95		500	1500
Winter Morning	RBP	ART	1986	SP	8 X 10	AP	126		600	2000
Snow Tree	RBP	ART	1986	SP	23 X 29	RP/100	100		1300	4500
Three Horses	RBP	AS	1986	SP	26 X 44	MB	300		1200	3500
Three Horses (Deluxe)	RBP	AS	1986	SP	26 X 44	AP/BL	100		1500	4000
Santa Ynez Oaks II	RBP	ART	1986	SP	15 X 40	MB	124		1200	2500
Purple Eucalyptus	RBP	ART	1987	SP	26 X 34	AP	100		800	7000
Mystical Coastline	RBP	ART	1987	SP	20 X 16	AP	125		500	5000
Seaside Pasture	RBP	AS	1987	SP	30 X 38	AP	320		1200	7500
Seaside Pasture (Deluxe)	RBP	AS	1987	SP	30 X 38	AP/BL	150		1500	8000
Purple Monument	RBP	ART	1987	SP	31 X 43	MB	120		1500	8000
Rainshower	RBP	ART	1987	SP	28 X 34	MB	80		1000	3000
Wildflowers	RBP	ART	1987	SP	23 X 29	SP/100	100		1000	2500
Towering Oak	RBP	ART	1987	SP	25 X 23	SP/100			1200	6500
Towering Oak (Deluxe)	RBP	ART	1987	SP	25 X 23	AP/BL			1500	7000
Inland from the Sea	RBP	ART	1987	SP	33 X 25	SP/100			1200	7000
Inland from the Sea (Deluxe)	RBP	ART	1987	SP	33 X 25	AP/BL			1500	7500
Coastal Fog	RBP	ART	1987	SP	15 X 17	SP/100	100		450	1800
California Tapestry	RBP	ART	1987	SP	17 X 40	MB	75		650	2500
Mauve, Red & Purple	RBP	AS	1987	SP	29 X 38	SP/100	495		1800	7000
Mauve, Red & Purple (Deluxe)	RBP	AS	1987	SP	29 X 38	AP/BL	495		2000	7500
Tall Trees	RBP	AS	1987	SP	32 X 24	SP/100	495		1800	5500
Tall Trees (Deluxe)	RBP	AS	1987	SP	32 X 24	AP/BL	495		2000	6000
Sea, Wind & Fog	RBP	AS	1988	SP	38 X 28	SP/100	495		1800	8500
Sea, Wind & Fog (Deluxe)	RBP	AS	1988	SP	38 X 28	AP/BL	495		2000	9000
Carmel Gold	RBP	AS	1988	SP	24 X 36	SP/100	495		1800	7000
Carmel Gold (Deluxe)	RBP	AS	1988	SP	24 X 36	AP/BL	495		2000	7500
Day's End	RBP	AS	1989	SP	33 X 26	SP/100	581		2000	8500
Day's End (Deluxe)	RBP	AS	1989	SP	33 X 26	AP/BL	581		2400	9000
Beyond Paradise	RBP	AS	1989	SP	25 X 38	SP/100	644		2000	5500
Beyond Paradise (Deluxe)	RBP	AS	1989	SP	25 X 38	AP/BL	644		2400	6000
Mystic Mountain	RBP	AS	1989	SP	26 X 34	SP/100	695		2000	5500
Mystic Mountain (Deluxe)	RBP	AS	1989	SP	26 X 34	AP/BL	695		2400	6000
Radiant Splendor	RBP	AS	1990	SP	34 X 26	SP/100	600		2000	7000
Radiant Splendor (Deluxe)	RBP	AS	1990	SP	34 X 26	AP/BL	600		2400	7500
Black Spruce	RBP	AS	1990	SP	21 X 41	SP/100	670		2200	6000
Black Spruce (Deluxe)	RBP	AS	1990	SP	21 X 41	AP/BL	670		2500	6500
Symphonic Fantasy	RBP	AS	1990	SP	26 X 33	SP/100	596		2200	7000
Symphonic Fantasy (Deluxe)	RBP	AS	1990	SP	26 X 33	AP/BL	596		2500	7500
Trees Draped in Autumn	RBP	AS	1990	SP	45 X 34	SP/100	616		2200	6000
Trees Draped in Autumn (Deluxe)	RBP	AS	1990	SP	45 X 34	AP/BL	616		2500	6500
Silent Meadow	RBP	AS	1990	SP	26 X 39	SP/100	579		2200	5500
Silent Meadow (Deluxe)	RBP	AS	1990	SP	26 X 39	AP/BL	579		2500	6000
Fog Light	RBP	AS	1990	SP	40 X 50	AP	630		2500	7500
Green Pastures	RBP	AS	1991	SP	30 X 40	AP	550		2200	7000
Gardener's Ranch (Special 75th Anniversary Series)	RBP	AS	1991	SP	30 X 40	AP			550	6500
Ocean Cliffs (Special 75th Anniversary Series)	RBP	AS	1991	SP	30 X 40	AP			550	6500
Ancient Tree (Special 75th Anniversary Series)	RBP	AS	1991	SP	30 X 40	AP			550	3600

EYVIND EARLE CONTINUED

TITLE	PUBLISHER	PRINTER	DATE	MEDIUM	DIMENSION (PAPER SIZE) IN INCHES	TYPE OF PAPER	EDITION NUMBER	NO. OF COLORS	ORIGINAL OPENING PRICE	CURRENT RETAIL PRICE
CURRENT EDITIONS:										
Garden of Dreams	RBP	AS	1990	SP	37 X 28	SP/100	623		2200	5500
Garden of Dreams (Deluxe)	RBP	AS	1990	SP	37 X 28	AP/BL	623		2500	6000
Autumn Fields	RBP	AS	1990	SP	24 X 36	AP	627		2200	3500
Winter Barnyard	RBP	AS	1991	SP	24 X 48	AP	610		2200	3600
Valley of Dreams	RBP	AS	1992	SP		AP			3600	3600
Homage to Planet Earth (Special Earth Day Suite) (Set of 6):									12000 SET	12000 SET
Blue Nocturne	RBP	AS	1992	SP		AP			2200	2200
Fog Enshrouded	RBP	AS	1992	SP		AP			2200	2200
Forest Symphony	RBP	AS	1992	SP		AP			2200	2200
Live Oak Country	RBP	AS	1992	SP		AP			2200	2200
Sea, Cliff & Redwood	RBP	AS	1992	SP		AP			2200	2200
Tocata & Fugue	RBP	AS	1992	SP		AP			2200	2200
Mist in the Dark Woods	RBP	AS	1992	SP		AP			3600	3600

ALEX ECHO

PRINTERS: Noblett Serigraphie, Inc, NY (NSI); Moross Studio Originals, Inc, Gardena, CA (MSO)
PUBLISHERS: Chalk & Vermilion Fine Arts, Greenwich, CT (CVFA)
MAILING ADDRESS: c/o Chalk & Vermilion Fine Arts, 200 Greenwich Ave, Greenwich, CT 06830

TITLE	PUBLISHER	PRINTER	DATE	MEDIUM	DIMENSION (PAPER SIZE) IN INCHES	TYPE OF PAPER	EDITION NUMBER	NO. OF COLORS	ORIGINAL OPENING PRICE	CURRENT RETAIL PRICE
CURRENT EDITIONS:										
Dream of Three Roses	CVFA	NSI	1992	SP/HS	30 X 23	AC/BL	250		425	425
Portrait of the Artist and His Wife	CVFA	NSI	1992	SP/HS	14 X 30	AC/BL	250		325	325
Waterlillies	CVFA	NSI	1992	SP/HS	14 X 30	COV	250		475	475
Sunflowers	CVFA	NSI	1992	SP/HS	32 X 25	COV	250		475	475
Seven Moons (Monday through Sunday) (Set of 7)	CVFA	MSO/NSI	1992	SP/FS	27 X 21 EA	AP-BL/AP-W	125 EA			

CHRISTIAN ECKART

BORN: Calgary, Alta, Canada; January 9, 1959
EDUCATION: Hunter Col, NY; City Univ of New York, NY, MFA, 1986
RECENT EXHIB: Galerie Tanit, Munich, Germany, 1987; Galerie Venster, Rotterdam, The Netherlands, 1988; Galerie Philippe Kriwin, Paris, France, 1989; Rhona Hoffman Gallery, Chicago, IL, 1987,89; Massimo Audiello Gallery, NY, 1988,89; Univ of Hartford, Joseloff Gallery, West Hartford, CT, 1992
PRINTERS: Watanabe Studios, Brooklyn, NY (WatSt); Brenda Zlamany, Brooklyn, NY (BZ); Erie-Lackawanna Editions, Brooklyn, NY (E-LE)
PUBLISHERS: Tomoko Liguori Gallery, NY (TLG); Edition Deger, Sag Harbor, NY (EdDeg)
GALLERIES: Tomoko Liguori Gallery, New York, NY; Rhona Hoffman Gallery, Chicago, IL; Galerie Philippe Kriwin, Paris, France; Galerie T Venster, Rotterdam, The Netherlands; Galerie Tanit, Munich, Germany; Steven Leiber Fine Art, New York, NY
MAILING ADDRESS: 438 Bedford Ave, Brooklyn, NY 11211

TITLE	PUBLISHER	PRINTER	DATE	MEDIUM	DIMENSION (PAPER SIZE) IN INCHES	TYPE OF PAPER	EDITION NUMBER	NO. OF COLORS	ORIGINAL OPENING PRICE	CURRENT RETAIL PRICE
CURRENT EDITIONS:										
Shadow Paintings Project Portfolio I (Set of 6)	TLG	WatSt	1992	SP	50 X 35 EA	SOM/S	25 EA		400 SET 800 EA	4000 SET 800 EA
The Power-Chord Cycle (Set of 6)	EdDeg	BZ/E-LE	1993	EB/A/SB	15 X 10 EA	R/BFK	25 EA	1 EA	2500 SET	2500 SET

RUTH ECKSTEIN

BORN: Nuremberg, West Germany; May 11, 1916; US Citizen
EDUCATION: New Sch for Social Research, NY, with Stuart Davis; Art Students League, NY; Pratt Graphics Center, NY
TEACHING: Pratt Graphics Center, NY
AWARDS: Purchase Prize, Hofstra Univ, 1956; Nassau Com Col, Garden City, NY, 1973; Art of Northeast USA, Silvermine, CT, 1983; Audubon Artists Award, 1977,78,85
RECENT EXHIB: Benton Gallery, Southampton, NY, 1988; Neuberger Mus, State Univ of New York, Purchase, NY, 1989; New York Inst of Tech, Old Westbury, NY, 1990; New Jersey State Mus, Trenton, NJ, 1992; Grants Pass Mus of Art, Eugene, OR, 1992
COLLECTIONS: Mus of Mod Art, NY; Metropolitan Mus of Art, NY; Guggenheim Mus, NY; Phila Mus of Art, PA; Brooklyn Mus, NY; Everson Mus, Syracuse, NY; Herbert F Johnson Mus, Cornell Univ, Ithaca, NY; Israel Mus, Jerusalem, Israel; Univ of Massachusetts, Amherst, MA
PRINTERS: Roni Henning (S A M Studios, NY) (RH); Print Editions, Ltd, Port Washington, NY (PEL); Artist (ART)
PUBLISHERS: Artist (ART)
GALLERIES: Anita Shapolsky Gallery, New York, NY; Suzuki Gallery, New York, NY; Sandra Soll Assoc, Phila, PA; EAC Gallery, Albertson, NY
MAILING ADDRESS: 5 Cricket Lane, Great Neck, NY 11024

The retail prices of the 100,000 limited edition prints quoted in this directory are subject to change. Print publishers, artists and galleries were the direct sources for these quotations. Prices in the secondary market listed as "Sold Out Editions (Rare)" indicate that the publisher has a limited supply of that print or that the print is difficult to locate in the galleries.

RUTH ECKSTEIN CONTINUED

TITLE	PUBLISHER	PRINTER	DATE	MEDIUM	DIMENSION (PAPER SIZE) IN INCHES	TYPE OF PAPER	EDITION NUMBER	NO. OF COLORS	ORIGINAL OPENING PRICE	CURRENT RETAIL PRICE
CURRENT EDITIONS:										
Clear Light of Winter	ART	RH	1973	SP	35 X 23	CC	40		90	350
Sense of Summer	ART	RH	1973	SP	35 X 23	CC	40		90	350
Kommos: King's Chamber	ART	ART	1977	MM	26 X 21	K/C	50	4	175	325
Kommos: Queen's Chamber	ART	ART	1977	MM	26 X 21	K/C	50	4	175	325
Kommos: Marble Wall	ART	ART	1977	MM	21 X 26	K/C	50	6	175	325
Maghreb I-VI (Set of 6)	ART	PEL	1979	MM	22 X 30 EA	K/C	60 EA	Varies	1150 SET / 225 EA	2500 SET / 500 EA
Maghreb VII	ART	PEL	1979	MM	30 X 44	K/C	60		400	650
Maghreb VIII	ART	PEL	1979	MM	22 X 59	K/C	60		400	650
Sites & Signs, I-VI	ART	PEL	1983	WC	22 X 30 EA	SOM	40 EA	4-6 EA	1500 SET / 300 EA	2500 SET / 500 EA
Alpha Suite I-V (Set of 5)	ART	ART	1992	WC/CO	27 X 21 EA	KOCHI	20 EA	3-6 EA	2500 SET	2500 SET

NANCY EDELL

BORN: Omaha, NE; November 12, 1942
EDUCATION: Univ of Omaha, NE, BFA, 1964; Filmmaking, Univ of Bristol, England, 1968–69
TEACHING: Workshops, Univ of Manitoba, Winnipeg Art Gallery, Manitoba Arts Council, Manitoba Theatre Workshop, Manitoba, Canada, 1976–79; Vis Art, Printmaking, St Michael's Printshop, St Johns, Newfoundland, 1987; Vis Fac, Visual Art, Banff Sch of Fine Arts, Banff, Alta, Can, 1988; Adj Prof, Drawing & Printmaking, Nova Scotia Col of Art & Design, Halifax, NS, Can, 1982–92
AWARDS: Manitoba Arts Council Grants, 1978, 79; Purchase Prize, Art Gallery of Brandt, Brantford, ON, Canada, 1979; Canada Council "B" Grants, 1974,80,84,87,88,90,92; Canada Council Grant, Paris Studio, 1990
RECENT EXHIB: Univ of Toronto, Scarborough, ON, Can, 1987; Articule Gallery, Montreal, Can, 1987; Winnipeg Art Gallery, Can, 1987–88; Art Gallery, Halifax, NS, Can, 1988; Univ of Nebraska, Omaha Art Gallery, NE, 1988; Univ of Moncton Art Gallery, NB, Can, 1989; Art Gallery of Nova Scotia, Halifax, NS, Canada, 1991–92
COLLECTIONS: Canada Council Bank, Ottawa, ON, Canada; Mount St Vincent Univ Art Gallery, Halifax, NS, Canada; Nova Scotia Art Bank, Canada; Winnipeg Art Gallery, Canada; Acadia Univ, Wolfville, NS, Canada; Dalhousie Univ Art Gallery, Halifax, NS, Canada; Art Gallery of Nova Scotia, Halifax, NS, Canada
PRINTERS: David Umholz, Winnipeg, Manitoba, Can (DU); Moosehead Press, Winnipeg, Canada (MP); Artist (ART); Judith Leidl (JL)
PUBLISHERS: Moosehead Press, Winnipeg, Manitoba, Canada (MP); Artist (ART)
GALLERIES: Studio 21, Halifax, NS, Canada
MAILING ADDRESS: 6051 Welsford St, Halifax, NS, Canada B3K 1G3

TITLE	PUBLISHER	PRINTER	DATE	MEDIUM	DIMENSION (PAPER SIZE) IN INCHES	TYPE OF PAPER	EDITION NUMBER	NO. OF COLORS	ORIGINAL OPENING PRICE	CURRENT RETAIL PRICE
CURRENT EDITIONS:										
Blomidon Bird Dance (Colored with Feather)	ART	DU/MP	1981	LC	26 X 20	AP	28	7	150	300
Boudoir-Egyptian	ART	ART	1982	LC	30 X 22	R/BFK	20	5	150	250
Madonna with Porcupine	ART	ART	1983	LC	29 X 22	KOZU	8	3	150	275
Home Entertainment	ART	DU/MP	1985	LC	20 X 26	AP	46	7	225	300
Boudoir-Lemur	ART	DU/MP	1985	LC	22 X 30	R/BFK	52	6	225	300
Fragile Structures	ART	JL	1989	LC/CC	30 X 42	R/BFK	14	2	450	450

STEPHEN EDLICH

BORN: New York, NY; 1944
EDUCATION: New York Univ, NY; Square Col, 1961–67
PUBLISHERS: Marlborough Gallery, NY (MG)
GALLERIES: Marlborough Gallery, New York, NY; Hokin Galleries, Palm Beach, FL & Bay Harbor Islands, FL; Alice Simsar Gallery, Ann Arbor, MI; Stephen Mazoh & Co, New York, NY; Alan Brown Gallery, Hartsdale, NY

TITLE	PUBLISHER	PRINTER	DATE	MEDIUM	DIMENSION (PAPER SIZE) IN INCHES	TYPE OF PAPER	EDITION NUMBER	NO. OF COLORS	ORIGINAL OPENING PRICE	CURRENT RETAIL PRICE
SOLD OUT EDITIONS (RARE):										
Seasons I, Summer V	MG		1980	EC	31 X 22	AP	45		500	1200
Untitled, View 66	MG		1980	EC	26 X 20	AP	39		500	1200

DORTHEA TANNING

BORN: Galesburg, IL; 1910
PRINTERS: Artist (ART)
PUBLISHERS: Artist (ART)
GALLERIES: Gimpel & Weitzenhoffer Gallery, New York, NY; Schlesinger Gallery, New York, NY; Enrico Navarra Gallery, New York, NY; Gallery of Surrealism & the Fantastic, New York, NY

TITLE	PUBLISHER	PRINTER	DATE	MEDIUM	DIMENSION (PAPER SIZE) IN INCHES	TYPE OF PAPER	EDITION NUMBER	NO. OF COLORS	ORIGINAL OPENING PRICE	CURRENT RETAIL PRICE
SOLD OUT EDITIONS (RARE):										
Premier Peril	ART	ART	1950	LC	14 X 11	AP	50		250	1800
Quatrieme Peril	ART	ART	1950	LC	14 X 11	AP	50		250	1800
Troisieme Peril	ART	ART	1950	LC	14 X 11	AP	50		250	1800

The print market has become very selective. For the first time since we published the first edition of The Printworld Directory in 1982, the prices of prints have been greatly reduced and greatly increased for the same artists by the most reputable and established print publishers. Check the fifth edition to understand the movement.

WILLIAM EGGLESTON

BORN: Memphis, TN; 1939
EDUCATION: Vanderbilt Univ, Nashville, TN; Delta State Col, Cleveland, OH, MS
RECENT EXHIB: Univ of Mississippi, University, MS, 1992; Nat Acad of Sciences, Wash, DC, 1992

PRINTERS: Dimension Color Labs, NY (DCL)
PUBLISHERS: Middendorf Gallery, Wash, DC (MG)
GALLERIES: Middendorf Gallery, Wash, DC; Fay Gold Gallery, Atlanta, GA; Turner/Krull Gallery, Los Angeles, CA; Jackson Fine Art, Atlanta, GA; Laurence Miller Gallery, New York, NY

TITLE	PUBLISHER	PRINTER	DATE	MEDIUM	DIMENSION (PAPER SIZE) IN INCHES	TYPE OF PAPER	EDITION NUMBER	NO. OF COLORS	ORIGINAL OPENING PRICE	CURRENT RETAIL PRICE
CURRENT EDITIONS:										
William Eggleston's Graceland (Set of 11)	MG	DCL	1983	DT	20 X 24 EA	AP	31 EA	Varies	20000 SET 2000 EA	25000 SET 2500 EA

SHEILA ELIAS

BORN: Chicago, IL
EDUCATION: Art Inst of Chicago, IL, 1960–68; Columbus Col of Art & Design, OH, BFA, 1974; California State Univ, Northridge, CA, MA, 1978
RECENT EXHIB: Univ of North Carolina, Chapel Hill, NC, 1989; Danville Mus of Fine Arts, VA, 1989; Paula Allen Gallery, New York, NY, 1989; Gallery 99, Bay Harbor Islands, FL, 1989

COLLECTIONS: Brooklyn Mus, NY; Los Angeles Inst of Contemp Art, CA; Univ of Michigan, Dearborn, MI; Kunsan Contemp Mus, Korea; Laguna Beach Art Mus, CA; Miami Dade Comm Col, Miami, FL
PRINTERS: Magnolia Press, Oakland, CA (MP); Pelavin Editions, NY (PeEd)
PUBLISHERS: Magnolia Press, Oakland, CA (MP); Artist (ART)
GALLERIES: Ratner Gallery, Chicago, IL; Paula Allen Gallery, New York, NY; Ann Jaffe Gallery, Bay Harbor Islands, FL; Vallerie Miller Gallery, Palm Springs, CA

TITLE	PUBLISHER	PRINTER	DATE	MEDIUM	DIMENSION (PAPER SIZE) IN INCHES	TYPE OF PAPER	EDITION NUMBER	NO. OF COLORS	ORIGINAL OPENING PRICE	CURRENT RETAIL PRICE
CURRENT EDITIONS:										
San Pedro Street Scenes	ART/MP	MP	1984	LC/HC	33 X 24	MYLAR	70	7	600	1200
Another Planet	ART	PeEd	1987	MON	31 X 43 EA	R/BFK	1 EA	Varies	2200 EA	2400 EA
Planetary I	ART	PeEd	1987	MON	32 X 38 EA	R/BFK	1 EA	Varies	2200 EA	2400 EA
Planetary II	ART	PeEd	1987	MON	32 X 43 EA	R/BFK	1 EA	Varies	2200 EA	2400 EA
Gregory I	ART	PeEd	1987	MON	22 X 30 EA	R/BFK	1 EA	Varies	1700 EA	1900 EA
Gregory II, IV	ART	PeEd	1987	MON	17 X 24 EA	R/BFK	1 EA	Varies	1700 EA	1900 EA
Gregory III	ART	PeEd	1987	MON	23 X 30 EA	R/BFK	1 EA	Varies	1700 EA	1900 EA
Palace I, II	ART	PeEd	1987	MON	22 X 30 EA	R/BFK	1 EA	Varies	1700 EA	1900 EA
The Tuna Club I	ART	PeEd	1987	MON	22 X 38 EA	R/BFK	1 EA	Varies	2000 EA	2200 EA
The Tuna Club II	ART	PeEd	1987	MON	36 X 40 EA	R/BFK	1 EA	Varies	2000 EA	2200 EA

SUSAN ELIAS

EDUCATION: Philadelphia Col of Art, PA, BFA, 1963; Columbia Univ, NY, 1964; New York Studio Sch, NY, 1965
AWARDS: First Prize, Sculpture, Philadelphia Col of Art, PA, 1963; Second Prize, Fine Arts Dept, Philadelphia Col of Art, PA, 1963; First Prize, Skowhegan Sch of Art, ME, 1963; Louis Comfort Tiffany Award, Sculpture, 1964; Cite des Arts Fel, Paris, France, 1972; Yaddo Fel, Saratoga Springs, NY, 1971,77; Creative Artists Public Service Award, 1978,79
PRINTERS: Artist (ART)
PUBLISHERS: Transworld Art, Inc, NY (TAI)
GALLERIES: Kirk DeGooyer Gallery, Los Angeles, CA

TITLE	PUBLISHER	PRINTER	DATE	MEDIUM	DIMENSION (PAPER SIZE) IN INCHES	TYPE OF PAPER	EDITION NUMBER	NO. OF COLORS	ORIGINAL OPENING PRICE	CURRENT RETAIL PRICE
SOLD OUT EDITIONS (RARE):										
Jungle Jazz, State I	TAI	ART	1980	LC	23 X 28	AP	125		250	400

PETER ELLENSHAW

BORN: London, England
EDUCATION: Royal Acad, London, England

PRINTERS: Atelier Royce, Paris, France (AR); Maccoy Studio (MS); Osiris Publications, NY (OP); Accent Studios (AS); Joseph Pelky (JP); Artist (ART)
PUBLISHERS: Hammer Publishing Co, NY (HP)
GALLERIES: Hammer Galleries, New York, NY; Conacher Galleries, San Francisco, CA

TITLE	PUBLISHER	PRINTER	DATE	MEDIUM	DIMENSION (PAPER SIZE) IN INCHES	TYPE OF PAPER	EDITION NUMBER	NO. OF COLORS	ORIGINAL OPENING PRICE	CURRENT RETAIL PRICE
SOLD OUT EDITIONS (RARE):										
Rivulet	HP	AR	1977	EC	24 X 36	AP	300	39	500	750
Clipper Ships	HP	AR	1977	EB	24 X 36	AP	100	1	250	550
Kerry Springtime	HP	MS	1978	SP	24 X 36	AP	300	65	400	750
Road to Coomcallee	HP	MS	1978	SP	24 X 36	AP	300	65	400	750
Tide Turning	HP	MS	1978	SP	24 X 36	AP	300	71	400	900
Afternoon Tide	HP	ART	1979	SP	24 X 20	AP	200	71	400	650
Hyde Park	HP	MS	1979	SP	24 X 20	AP	200	75	400	750
California Sands	HP	JP	1981	SP	20 X 20	EXV	200	24	400	750
Mayflowers	HP	AS	1981	SP	20 X 31	R/100	300	103	400	750
Bookhill Kerry	HP	OP	1981	SP	20 X 30	EVP	260	50	400	750
Crystal Stream	HP	OP	1981	SP	20 X 30	GPP	240	34	400	750

ROBERT M ELLIS

BORN: Cleveland, OH; 1922
EDUCATION: Western Reserve Univ, Sch of Architecture, OH, 1940–42; Cleveland Sch of Art, OH, 1946–48 (Grad); Mexico City Col, Mexico City, Mexico, BA, 1949; Univ of Southern California, Los Angeles, CA, MFA, 1952
TEACHING: Univ of New Mexico, Albuquerque, NM, Currently; Instr, Dept of Art, 1964–87, Prof Emeritus, Currently
RECENT EXHIB: Wildine Gallery, Albuquerque, NM, 1989
COLLECTIONS: Herbert Johnson Mus, Cornell Univ, Ithaca, NY; Utah Mus of Art, Salt Lake City, UT; Mus of Albuquerque, NM; Mus of Fine Arts, Santa Fe, NM
PRINTERS: Catherine Kuhn, Albuquerque, NM (CK); Lynne Allen, Albuquerque, NM (LA); Tamarind Inst, Albuquerque, NM (TI)
PUBLISHERS: Tamarind Inst, Albuquerque, NM (TI)
GALLERIES: Wildine Gallery, Albuquerque, NM; Tamarind Inst, Albuquerque, NM
MAILING ADDRESS: P O Box 1449, Taos, NM 87571

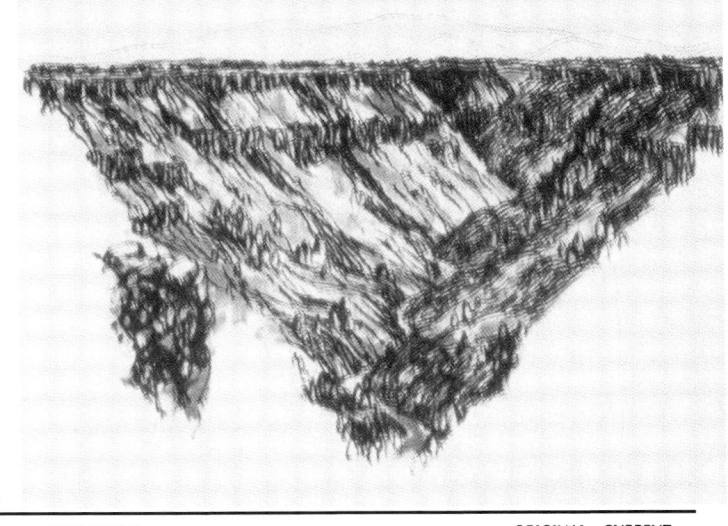

Robert M Ellis
Rio Grande Gorge #17
Courtesy Tamarind Institute

TITLE	PUBLISHER	PRINTER	DATE	MEDIUM	DIMENSION (PAPER SIZE) IN INCHES	TYPE OF PAPER	EDITION NUMBER	NO. OF COLORS	ORIGINAL OPENING PRICE	CURRENT RETAIL PRICE
CURRENT EDITIONS:										
Rio Grande Gorge #16	TI	CK/TI	1982	LC	22 X 30	R/BFK	40	3	150	375
Rio Grande Gorge #17	TI	LA/TI	1982	LC	31 X 41	GE	32	2	150	450

STEPHEN ELLIS

BORN: High Point, NC; 1951
EDUCATION: Boston Univ Art Prog, Tanglewood, Lenox, MA, 1969,73; Cornell Univ, Ithaca, NY BFA, 1973; New York Studio Sch, NY, 1973–74
RECENT EXHIB: Galerie Alfred Kren, Cologne, Germany, 1987; Galerie 86, Eurpaische Akademie Für Bildende Kunst, Trier, Germany, 1989; Koury Wingate Gallery, NY, 1989; Galerie Ascan Crone, Hamburg, Germany, 1990
PRINTERS: Kristine Suhr, Copenhagen, Denmark (KS); Niels Borch Jansen, Copenhagen, Denmark (NBJ); Mette Ulstrup, Copenhagen, Denmark (MU); Niels Borch Jensen, Copenhagen, Denmark (NBJ); Elizabeth Koury, NY (EK)
PUBLISHERS: Galerie Alfred Kren, Cologne, West Germany (GAK)
GALLERIES: Galerie Alfred Kren, Cologne, Germany; Galerie Ascan Crone, Hamburg, Germany; Baumgartner Galleries, Wash, DC; Elizabeth Koury Gallery, New York, NY

TITLE	PUBLISHER	PRINTER	DATE	MEDIUM	DIMENSION (PAPER SIZE) IN INCHES	TYPE OF PAPER	EDITION NUMBER	NO. OF COLORS	ORIGINAL OPENING PRICE	CURRENT RETAIL PRICE
CURRENT EDITIONS:										
Japanese Gothic (Set of 13)	GAK	KS/NBJ	1988	DPT/EB/AC	21 X 16 EA	HAHN	15 EA		4000 SET	6000 SET
Escorial (Set of 8)	EK	MU/NBJ	1991	I	30 X 21 EA	HAHN	15 EA		8500 SET	8500 SET

NISSAN ENGEL

BORN: Haifa, Israel; 1931
COLLECTIONS: Jewish Mus, NY; Muscarelle Mus, Williamsburg, VA; Weitzman Inst, Israel; Foundation Schlumberger, Paris, France
PRINTERS: Dutrou Atelier, Paris, France (DUT)
PUBLISHERS: Nahan Editions, Inc, NY (NE)
GALLERIES: Nahan Galleries, New York, NY & New Orleans, LA & Tokyo, Japan; Weil Gallery, Paris, France; Goldman Gallery, Haifa, Israel; Jaquester Gallery, Paris, France; Britt Olson Gallery, Stockholm, Sweden

Nissan Engel
Recital
Courtesy Nahan Editions

TITLE	PUBLISHER	PRINTER	DATE	MEDIUM	DIMENSION (PAPER SIZE) IN INCHES	TYPE OF PAPER	EDITION NUMBER	NO. OF COLORS	ORIGINAL OPENING PRICE	CURRENT RETAIL PRICE
SOLD OUT EDITIONS (RARE):										
Musica	NE	DUT	1989	AC/CAR	34 X 26	AP	150	8	1400	2200
Vision Lyrique	NE	DUT	1990	AC/CAR	48 X 40	HMP	150		1900	2500

NISSAN ENGEL CONTINUED

TITLE	PUBLISHER	PRINTER	DATE	MEDIUM	DIMENSION (PAPER SIZE) IN INCHES	TYPE OF PAPER	EDITION NUMBER	NO. OF COLORS	ORIGINAL OPENING PRICE	CURRENT RETAIL PRICE
CURRENT EDITIONS:										
Lieder	NE	DUT	1989	AC/CAR	28 X 36	AP	150	6	1400	2200
Recital	NE	DUT	1989	AC/CAR	28 X 36	AP	150	8	1400	1800
Opera	NE	DUT	1990	AC/CAR	31 X 23	HMP	150		1400	1800
Festival	NE	DUT	1990	AC/CAR	48 X 40	AP	150	8	2600	2600
Le Chant de la Terre	NE	DUT	1990	AC/CAR	48 X 40	AP	150	8	2600	2600
Vision Lyrique	NE	DUT	1990	AC/CAR	48 X 40	HMP	150		1900	2500
Allegorie	NE	DUT	1990	AC/CAR	29 X 44	HMP	150		1800	1800
Cristal (Set of 7)	NE	DUT	1990	AC/CAR	20 X 16 EA	AP	50 EA		2800 SET	2800 SET
Tempo	NE	DUT	1991	AC/CAR	38 X 29	HMP	150	12	1200	1400
Reve Bleu	NE	DUT	1991	AC/CAR	32 X 23	HMP	150	8	1800	2200
Quartet	NE	DUT	1992	AC/CAR	21 X 21	AP	150		1200	1200
Crepuscules	NE	DUT	1992	AC/CAR	20 X 23	HMP	150		1800	1800

E WAYNE ENSRUD

BORN: Albert Lea, MN
EDUCATION: Minneapolis Col of Art & Design, BFA, MN; Studied with Oskar Kokoschka, 1956–79
TEACHING: Instr, Film Animation, Pratt Inst, NY, 1967–72; Guest Prof, Figure Painting, Simon's Rock Early Cl, Great Barrington, CT, 1978; Instr, Painting & Drawing, Cumberland Sch, Great Neck, NY, 1967–79
AWARDS: Minneapolis Inst of Art, MN, 1957; Second Prize, Oil, Lever House, NY, 1966
RECENT EXHIB: Gryphin Gallery, Detroit, MI, 1988; Gallery Sho, Tokyo, Japan, 1988; Atrium, NY 1989; Klabal Gallery, Minneapolis, MN, 1989; Carmichael-Gallagher Gallery, Minneapolis, MN, 1989; Joden Gallery, Tokyo, Japan, 1989

COLLECTIONS: Bristol Art Mus, RI; Musee d'Art Moderne, Ceret, France; Collioure Musee, France
PRINTERS: American Atelier, NY (AE)
PUBLISHERS: Jackie Fine Arts, Inc, New York, NY (JFA); Marigold Enterprises, Ltd, New York, NY (ME)
GALLERIES: Pavillion Gallery, Portland, OR; Pioneer Square Gallery, Seattle, WA; Caroline Summers Gallery, New Orleans, LA; Circle Gallery, Chicago, IL & New York, NY; Cherry Creek Gallery, Denver, CO; Owl Gallery, San Francisco, CA; T R Gallery, New York, NY; Barney Weinger Gallery, New York, NY; Omni Gallery, Fort Lauderdale, FL; Central Gallery, New York, NY; Sherry-Lehman, New York, NY; Atrium Gallery, New York, NY; Klabal Gallery, Minneapolis, MN; Carmichael-Gallagher Gallery, Minneapolis, MN: Joden Gallery; Tokyo, Japan; Gallery Sho, Tokyo, Japan; Ro Gallery Image Makers, Inc, New York, NY
MAILING ADDRESS: 65 Central Park West, New York, NY 10023

TITLE	PUBLISHER	PRINTER	DATE	MEDIUM	DIMENSION (PAPER SIZE) IN INCHES	TYPE OF PAPER	EDITION NUMBER	NO. OF COLORS	ORIGINAL OPENING PRICE	CURRENT RETAIL PRICE
SOLD OUT EDITIONS (RARE):										
Manhattan II	JFA	AE	1980	LC	24 X 30	AP	300	11	300	1500
Mediterranean	JFA	AE	1980	LC	29 X 21	AP	300	12	300	1500
Maybe Manhattan-View from Governer's Island I	JFA	AE	1980	LC	30 X 22	AP	300	10	300	1500
	JFA	AE	1980	LC	23 X 31	AP	300	13	300	1500
Portofino	JFA	AE	1980	LC	20 X 25	AP	300	13	300	1500
Salzburg	JFA	AE	1980	LC	19 X 24	AP	300	13	300	1500
Flower Dance	JFA	AE	1980	LC	35 X 24	AP	300	13	300	1500
Leaving Port	JFA	AE	1980	LC	23 X 31	AP	300	12	300	1500
Bernkastel	JFA	AE	1980	LC	19 X 26	AP	300	11	300	1500
New York	JFA	AE	1980	LC	25 X 28	AP	300	11	300	1500
Afternoon Sails	JFA	AE	1981	LC	23 X 31	AP	300	9	300	1500
Bayside	JFA	AE	1981	LC	19 X 25	AP	300	9	300	1500
Blue Bouquet	JFA	AE	1981	LC	30 X 21	AP	300	5	300	1500
Blue Table	JFA	AE	1981	LC	35 X 26	AP	300	11	300	1500
Cheryl with Green Stockings	JFA	AE	1981	LC	35 X 25	AP	300	12	300	1500
Comogli, Italy	JFA	AE	1981	LC	20 X 28	AP	300	12	300	1500
Enchanted City	JFA	AE	1981	LC	21 X 29	AP	300	8	300	1500
Florence	JFA	AE	1981	LC	22 X 27	AP	300	10	300	1500
Homage to Degas II	JFA	AE	1981	LC	31 X 24	AP	300	8	300	1500
Lady with Cat	JFA	AE	1981	LC	27 X 21	AP	300	10	300	1500
Lorie	JFA	AE	1981	LC	34 X 25	AP	300	7	300	1500
Manhattan View from Brooklyn Bridge	JFA	AE	1981	LC	26 X 36	AP	300	11	300	1500
Ponte Vecchio	JFA	AE	1981	LC	27 X 36	AP	300	9	300	1500
Potter's Point	JFA	AE	1981	LC	21 X 30	AP	300	10	300	1500
Red Bouquet	JFA	AE	1981	LC	29 X 20	AP	300	10	300	1500
Rehearsal	JFA	AE	1981	LC	27 X 37	AP	300	10	300	1500
Santa Marherita	JFA	AE	1981	LC	20 X 27	AP	300	8	300	1500
Sigrid	JFA	AE	1981	LC	21 X 28	AP	300	11	300	1500
Upwind	JFA	AE	1981	LC	19 X 27	AP	300	9	300	1500
Venice Rialto	JFA	AE	1981	LC	25 X 19	AP	300	9	300	1500
Yellow Bouquet	JFA	AE	1981	LC	30 X 21	AP	300	5	300	1500
Flower Flight	JFA	AE	1982	LC	37 X 28	AP	300	10	300	1500
Homage to Degas III	JFA	AE	1982	LC	27 X 37	AP	300	10	300	1500
Piazza Navonna, Rome	JFA	AE	1982	LC	27 X 37	AP	300	10	300	1500
Sail Day	JFA	AE	1982	LC	27 X 31	AP	300	11	300	1500
Faces	ME	AE	1982	SP	18 X 14	AP	100	12	300	1500

YALE EPSTEIN

BORN: New Haven, CT; January 26, 1934
EDUCATION: Brooklyn Col, NY, BFA, 1955–58; MFA, 1958; Columbia Univ, NY, Art History; New York Univ, NY, Art Education; Brooklyn Mus Sch, NY, Painting & Drawing: Student's League, NY; Pratt Graphics Center, NY, Printmaking, 1972–75
TEACHING: Instr, Brooklyn Col, NY, 1976–83; Instr, Sch of Visual Arts, NY, 1982–90
AWARDS: First Prize, Graphics, Hudson River Mus, NY, 1984
RECENT EXHIB: Summa Gallery, NY, 1988; Woodstock Artists Assoc, NY, 1988; Somerhill Gallery, Chapel Hill, NC, 1990; Falkenstern Gallery, NY, 1990; Galerie Domberger, Stuttgart, West Germany, 1990
COLLECTIONS: Albright-Knox Art Gallery, Buffalo, NY; Brooklyn Mus, NY; Delaware Art Mus, Wilmington, DE; Yale Univ, New Haven, CT; City of Chicago, IL; Bibleotheque Nat, Paris, France; Library of Congress, Wash, DC; Univ of Wisconsin, Madison, WI
PRINTERS: Domberger KG, Stuttgart, West Germany (DOM); Cleveland Editions, NY (ClEd); Pelavin Editions, NY (Pel); Werner Graphics, NY (WG); Essig Editions, NY (EEd)
PUBLISHERS: Artist (ART)
GALLERIES: Galerie Domberger, Stuttgart, West Germany; Somerhill Gallery, Chapel Hill, NC; Summa Galleries, New York, NY & Brooklyn, NY; Orion Editions, New York, NY; Mona Berman Fine Arts, New Haven, CT; Chicago Center for the Print, Chicago, IL
MAILING ADDRESS: 135 Hudson St, New York, NY 10013; 9 Wiley Lane, Woodstock, NY 12498

TITLE	PUBLISHER	PRINTER	DATE	MEDIUM	DIMENSION (PAPER SIZE) IN INCHES	TYPE OF PAPER	EDITION NUMBER	NO. OF COLORS	ORIGINAL OPENING PRICE	CURRENT RETAIL PRICE
SOLD OUT EDITIONS (RARE):										
Mystikon I, II	ART	DOM	1982	SP	43 X 31 EA	RP	100 EA	8 EA	375 EA	900 EA
Samadhi	ART	WG	1983	EC	39 X 28	SOM	60	8	375	800
Summerfields	ART	WG	1983	EC	39 X 28	SOM	60	6	375	800
Autumnmist	ART	DOM	1984	SP	42 X 30	RP	94	8	500	900
CURRENT EDITIONS:										
Wintermist	ART	ClEd	1983	EC	40 X 30	RP	60	6	375	800
Binah	ART	ClEd	1983-84	EC	44 X 30	SOM	94	8	500	900
Makor	ART	ClEd	1983-84	EC	44 X 30	SOM	84	8	500	900
Mystikon III	ART	ClEd	1984	EC	45 X 30	SOM	90	6	500	800
Islandmist	ART	ClEd	1984	SP	42 X 31	RP	90	8	500	800
Innervision	ART	ClEd	1984	EC	45 X 30	RP	90	6	500	800
Ancient Echoes	ART	DOM	1985	SP	28 X 20	RP	80	6	300	350
Winter Window	ART	DOM	1985	SP	42 X 29	R/BFK	92	6	600	700
Meditation	ART	ClEd	1985	EC	40 X 30	RP	90	6	600	800
Island Rain	ART	ClEd	1986	EC	42 X 30	AP	90	6	650	800
Aurora	ART	DOM	1986	SP	31 X 41	RP	92	9	700	800
Western Cascade	ART	Pel/EEd	1988	EC	34 X 48	AP	80	8	900	950
Silent Sentry	ART	EEd	1988	EC	34 X 48	AP	90	8	900	900
Tomorrow's Memories	ART	DOM	1989	SP	43 X 30	RP	92	12	900	900
Mesa Valley	ART	EEd	1990	EC	48 X 30	AP	60	9	900	900

GARY L ERIKSEN

BORN: Jackson, MI; September 11, 1943
EDUCATION: Oberlin Col, OH, BA, 1966; Kent State Univ, OH, MA, 1968; Univ of Chicago, IL, 1971–73; Academia delle Belle Arti Di Roma, Italy, 1973–77; Scuola dell'Arte della Medaglia, Sch of italian Govt Mint, Rome, Italy, Diploma, 1977; Mechanic Inst, NY, 1979–81
AWARDS: New York State Council on the Arts, NY, 1982; First Prize, Meisner Foundry Award, Salmagundi Club, NY, 1982
COLLECTIONS: Sch of Italian Govt, Rome, Italy; Hungarian Nat Gallery, Budapest, Hungary; Nat Gallery of Art, Budapest, Hungary; Smithsonian Inst, Wash, DC; Cooper-Hewitt Mus, New York, NY
PRINTERS: Bulla Lithographing, Rome, Italy (BL)
PUBLISHERS: Artist (ART)
MAILING ADDRESS: P O Box 1668, New York, NY 10013

TITLE	PUBLISHER	PRINTER	DATE	MEDIUM	DIMENSION (PAPER SIZE) IN INCHES	TYPE OF PAPER	EDITION NUMBER	NO. OF COLORS	ORIGINAL OPENING PRICE	CURRENT RETAIL PRICE
CURRENT EDITIONS:										
In Arte Libertas	ART	BL	1977	LC	20 X 14	ITALIA	50	2	30	200
Thirst #2	ART	BL	1977	LC	20 X 14	ITALIA	50	3	30	200

ULF ERIKSSON

BORN: Helsingborg, Sweden; November 4, 1942
AWARDS: Swedish State Grand Bourse, 1974; Swedish State's Work Stipendary, 1979; City Bac Munster Am Steins Stipendary, 1979
COLLECTIONS: Nationalmuseum, Stockholm, Sweden; Nat Mus, Warsaw, Poland; Mus of Mod Art, San Francisco, CA; Metropolitan Mus of Art, NY; New York Public Library, NY; Guggenheim Mus, NY; Brooklyn Mus, NY; Library of Congress, Wash, DC
PRINTERS: CBS Grafik, Helsingborg, Sweden (CBS); Artist (ART)
PUBLISHERS: CBS Grafik, Helsingborg, Sweden (CBS); Bülow (BH); Artist (ART)
GALLERIES: Galerie Rolandshof, Rolandseck, Germany; Galerie 10/Jansem, Paris, France; Konstnarshusets Grafik Galleri, Stockholm, Sweden

TITLE	PUBLISHER	PRINTER	DATE	MEDIUM	DIMENSION (PAPER SIZE) IN INCHES	TYPE OF PAPER	EDITION NUMBER	NO. OF COLORS	ORIGINAL OPENING PRICE	CURRENT RETAIL PRICE
SOLD OUT EDITIONS (RARE):										
Regard the Fence	ART	ART	1969	EC	20 X 26	AP	5	5	100	1000
Seven Steps	ART	ART	1972	EC	36 X 29	AP	75	15	350	850
I Have a Dream	ART	ART	1973	I/EC	30 X 26	AP	30	3	250	650
SOS	ART	ART	1974	I/EC	6 X 12	AP	30	5	150	900
Sonate D'Automne	CBS	CBS	1980	LC	20 X 18	R/BFK	220	6	175	350

ULF ERIKSSON CONTINUED

TITLE	PUBLISHER	PRINTER	DATE	MEDIUM	DIMENSION (PAPER SIZE) IN INCHES	TYPE OF PAPER	EDITION NUMBER	NO. OF COLORS	ORIGINAL OPENING PRICE	CURRENT RETAIL PRICE
CURRENT EDITIONS:										
Sonate D'Automne II	ART	ART	1981	LC	20 X 18	R/BFK	275	6	200	250
I Remember (Set of 4)	BH	CBS	1980	EB	5 X 6 EA	R/BFK	30 EA	1 EA	300 SET	350 SET
Memories (Set of 8)	BH	CBS	1980	EB	5 X 6 EA	R/BFK	30 EA	1 EA	450 SET	500 SET
The Fence	ART	ART	1980	EC	36 X 29	R/BFK	75	8	300	450
Storm	ART	ART	1981	EC	14 X 12	R/BFK	75	8	150	250
Steps	ART	ART	1981	EC	36 X 29	R/BFK	75	5	300	450
My Window	ART	ART	1981	EC	36 X 29	R/BFK	75	12	300	350
Landscapes (Set of 4)	CBS	CBS	1982	E/HC	5 X 6 EA	R/BFK	30 EA	1 EA	400 SET	600 SET
Erotic Scenes (Set of 4)	CBS/BH	CBS	1982	E/HC	5 X 6 EA	R/BFK	30 EA	1 EA	450 SET	600 SET
Landscape	CBS	CBS	1982	E/HC	5 X 6	R/BFK	10	Multi	275	350

MARTHA MAYER ERLEBACHER

BORN: Jersey City, NJ; November 21, 1937
EDUCATION: Gettysburg Col, PA, 1955–56; Pratt Inst, NY, Bachelor of Industrial Design, 1960; MFA, 1963
TEACHING: Instr, Art League, NY, 1962–64; Instr, Pratt Inst, NY, 1964–65; Instr, Parsons Sch of Design, NY, 1965–66; Instr, Philadelphia Col of Art, PA, 1966–68; 1975–77
AWARDS: Pratt Inst, NY, Dean's Medal, 1960; Yaddo Fel, 1966; Bertha Shay Award, Cheltenham Art Center, Phila, PA, 1967; Netsky-Sernaker Mem Prize, Cheltenham Art Center, Phila, PA, 1973; Yaddo Fel, 1973; Vivian and Meyer P Potamkin Prize, Cheltenham Art Center, Phila, PA, 1974; Nat Endowment for the Arts, Sr Fel, 1982; Pennsylvania Council for the Arts Fel, Visual Art, 1988
RECENT EXHIB: Boise Gallery of Art, ID, 1987; Nat Acad of Design, NY, 1987–88; Arkansas Arts Center, Little Rock, AR, 1989–90
COLLECTIONS: Yale Univ, New Haven, CT; Cleveland Mus, OH; Fort Wayne Mus, TX; Ball State Univ, Muncie, IN; Univ of Notre Dame, South Bend, IN; Art Inst of Chicago, IL; Canton Art Inst, OH; Pennsylvania State Univ, University Park, PA; Flint Inst of Art, MI; Albrecht Art Mus, St Joseph, MO; Fogg Mus of Art, Harvard Univ, Boston, MA; Univ of Michigan, Ann Arbor, MI; Pennsylvania Acad of the Fine Arts, Phila, PA
PRINTERS: Artist (ART); Jack Lemon, Chicago, IL (JL); Mary McDonald, Chicago, IL (MM); Landfall Press Inc, Chicago, IL (LPI); Fred Gude, Chicago, IL (FG)
PUBLISHERS: Associated Am Artists, NY (AAA); Landfall Press Inc, Chicago, IL (LPI)
GALLERIES: Dart Gallery, Chicago, IL; Landfall Press Inc, Chicago, IL & New York, NY; Associated American Artists, New York, NY; Marian Looks Gallery, Phila, PA; Koplin Gallery, Santa Monica, CA; J Rosenthal Fine Arts, Ltd, Chicago, IL; Fischbach Gallery, New York, NY
MAILING ADDRESS: 7733 Mill Rd, Elkins Park, PA 19117

TITLE	PUBLISHER	PRINTER	DATE	MEDIUM	DIMENSION (PAPER SIZE) IN INCHES	TYPE OF PAPER	EDITION NUMBER	NO. OF COLORS	ORIGINAL OPENING PRICE	CURRENT RETAIL PRICE
SOLD OUT EDITIONS (RARE):										
Still Life I, II, III	AAA	ART	1974	LC	22 X 30 EA	AP	100 EA		200 EA	1000 EA
Still Life I	LPI	JL/LPI	1977	LC	25 X 33	AP/W	60	5	375	1000
Still Life I, State I	LPI	JL/LPI	1977	LC	25 X 33	AP/W	7	1	275	500
Still Life II	LPI	JL/FG/LPI	1977	LC	26 X 35	AP/S	60	5	375	800
Still Life II, State II	LPI	JL/LPI	1977	LC	25 X 33	AP/S	25	1	275	600
CURRENT EDITIONS:										
Torso I, II (Dipt)	LPI	JL/MM/LPI	1981	LC	22 X 25 EA	AP/S	25 EA	4 EA	600 SET	900 SET
Shawl	LPI	JL/LPI	1984	LC	22 X 20	AP/S	25	6	350	450
Brocade	LPI	JL/LPI	1985	LC	22 X 27	AP/S	25	2	350	450
Spanish Still Life	LPI	JL/LPI	1987	LC	24 X 36	AP/S	45	9	850	850
Spanish Still Life, State I	LPI	JL/LPI	1987	LB	24 X 36	AP/S	20		450	450

JIMMY ERNST

BORN: Cologne, Germany; (1920–1984)
EDUCATION: Lidenthal Real-Gymnasium Cologne, Germany; Altoona Arts & Crafts Sch, Germany
TEACHING: Brooklyn Col, NY, 1951–80
AWARDS: Award, Pasadena Art Mus, CA, 1946; Purchase Prize, Juliana Force Mem Award, Whitney Mus of Am Art, NY, 1951; Bronze Medal, Norman Wait Harris Prize, Art Inst, Chicago, IL, 1954; Purchase Prize Award, Hattie Brooks Stevens Mem, Pasadena Art Mus, CA, 1956; Brandeis Univ, Creative Arts Award, Waltham, MA, 1957; Simon R Guggenheim Found Fel, 1961
COLLECTIONS: Metropolitan Mus of Art, NY; Mus of Mod Art, NY; Whitney Mus of Am Art, NY; Solomon R Guggenheim Mus, NY; San Francisco Mus of Mod Art, CA; Nat Coll of Fine Art, Wash, DC; Pasadena Art Mus, CA; Brooklyn Mus, NY; Art Inst of Chicago, IL; Albright-Knox Art Gallery, Buffalo, NY; Brandeis Mus, Waltham, MA; Univ of Colorado, Boulder, CO; Univ of Connecticut, Storrs, CT; Corcoran Gallery of Art, Wash, DC; Detroit Inst of Art, MI; University of Michigan, Ann Arbor, MI; Michigan State Univ, East Lansing, MI; Mus of Fine Art, Houston, TX; Lehigh Univ, Bethlehem, PA; Wadsworth Atheneum, Hartford, CT; Cranbrook Acad, MI; Walker Art Center, Minneapolis, MN; Southern Illinois Univ, Carbondale, IL; Toledo Art Mus, OH; Virginia Mus of Fine Art, Richmond, VA; Norton Mus, West Palm Beach, FL; Toronto Art Mus, Canada; Wallraf-Richartz Mus, Cologne, Germany
PRINTERS: La Poligrafa, SA, Barcelona, Spain (LP); David Keister, Keister, Bloomington, IN (DK); Echo Press, Bloomington Press, IN (EPr)
PUBLISHERS: Ediciones Poligrafa, SA, Barcelona, Spain (EdP); Echo Press, Bloomington, IN (EPr)
GALLERIES: Michael Rosenfeld Gallery, New York, NY; Harmon-Meek Gallery, Naples, FL; Foster Harmon Galleries of Art, Sarasota, FL; Thornapple Corporate Art Associates, Wilmington, DE

TITLE	PUBLISHER	PRINTER	DATE	MEDIUM	DIMENSION (PAPER SIZE) IN INCHES	TYPE OF PAPER	EDITION NUMBER	NO. OF COLORS	ORIGINAL OPENING PRICE	CURRENT RETAIL PRICE
CURRENT EDITIONS:										
Terra Incognita Suite (Set of 15)	EdP	LP	1973	LC	22 X 28 EA	GP	75 EA	3-5 EA	3000 SET	4500 SET
									220 EA	350 EA
Terra Incognita (Color Variations) (Set of 15)	EdP	LP	1973	LC	22 X 28 EA	GP	XXV EA	3-5 EA	4000 SET	6000 SET
									280 EA	450 EA
Perede	EPr	DEK/EPr	1982	LC	24 X 30	AP/W	30	5	750	1000

MAX ERNST

BORN: Cologne, Germany; (1891–1976)
RECENT EXHIB: Newport Harbor Art Mus, Newport Beach, CA, 1992; Univ Art Mus, Berkeley, CA, 1992-93; Indianapolis Mus of Art, IN, 1993; Menil Coll, Houston, TX, 1993
Spies-Leppien (S-L); Spies (S)

PRINTERS: La Poligrafa, SA, Barcelona, Spain (LP)
PUBLISHERS: Ediciones Poligrafa, SA, Barcelona, Spain (EdP); Les Cahiers du Sud, Marseilles, France (LCS); Edition Georges Visat, Paris, France (EGV)
GALLERIES: Galeria Joan Prats, New York, NY & Barcelona, Spain

TITLE	PUBLISHER	PRINTER	DATE	MEDIUM	DIMENSION (PAPER SIZE) IN INCHES	TYPE OF PAPER	EDITION NUMBER	NO. OF COLORS	ORIGINAL OPENING PRICE	CURRENT RETAIL PRICE
SOLD OUT EDITIONS (RARE):										
Portrait de Paul et Gala Eluard (S-46) (Frontispiece for Les Dessous d'une vie ou la Pyramide Humaine)	LCS	ART	1926	EB	5 X 4	WOVE		1	25	5000
Danseuses (S-L 46 8/g)			1950	LB	20 X 13	LAID	100	1	95	3000
Masque	ART	ART	1950	EC	9 X 7	AP	100	2	80	2750
Ohne Titel	ART	ART	1950	EB	7 X 5	AP	100	1	65	5000
Ohne Titel	ART	ART	1950	EB/HC	7 X 5	AP	30	Varies	90	450
Hibou-Arlequin	ART	ART	1955	LC	18 X 13	AP	200		125	3000
Terre des Nebaleuses	ART	ART	1965	EC	8 X 6	AP	75	5	200	2750
Oiseaux en Péril by Dorothea Tanning (Set of 8)	EGV	ART	1975	AB/EB		LAID/JP	100 EA	1 EA	3000 SET	15000 SET

ERTÉ (ROMAIN DE TIRTOFF)

BORN: St Petersburg, Russia; (1892–1990)
EDUCATION: Acad Julian, Paris, France; Officer of Arts & Letters, French Govt, Paris, France, 1976; Legion of Honor Award, 1985
RECENT EXHIB: McAllen Inst Mus, TX, 1989
PRINTERS: Frank Rowland Workshop, Wheeling, IL (FRW); Superior Silkscreen, Chicago, IL (SS); Atelier Guillard, Gourdon & Cie, Paris, France (GGC); American Atelier, NY (AA); Chicago Serigraph Workshop, Chicago, IL (CSW); Mary Rowland Studios, Lake Zurich, IL (MRS); Atelier Arcay, Paris, France (ARCAY); Crystal Haze, San Francisco, CA (CH); Coriander Studios, London, England (CS); ChromaComp, Inc, NY (CC); Alexander Heinrici, NY (AH); Studio Heinrici, NY (SH)
PUBLISHERS: Circle Gallery, Ltd, Chicago, IL (CGL); Circle Fine Arts, Inc, Chicago, IL (CFA); Crystal Haze, San Francisco, CA (CH); Seven Arts, Ltd, London, England (SL); Chalk & Vermilion Fine Arts, Greenwich, CT (CVFA)
GALLERIES: Circle Galleries, San Diego, CA & San Francisco, CA & Northbrook, IL & Houston, TX & Soho, NY & Chicago, IL & Pittsburgh, PA; Jeffrey Ruesch Fine Art Ltd, New York, NY; TR's Gallery, New York, NY; Laura Paul Galleries, Cincinnati, OH & Columbus, OH; Emporium Enterprises, Inc, Dallas, TX; Swahn Fine Arts, San Diego, CA; Owl Gallery, San Francisco, CA; Horoshak Contemporary Art, Sunnyvale, CA; Petrini Art Gallery, Rocky Hill, CT; Georgetown Fine Art, Wash, DC; Davidson Gallery, Daytona Beach, FL; Graphic Art Collection, Hallandale, FL; P C Hart Gallery, Jupiter, FL; Park Shore Gallery, Naples, FL; Art Brokerage, Ketchum, ID; Merrill Chase Galleries, Chicago, IL; Walton Street Gallery, Chicago, IL; Fernette's Gallery of Art, Des Moines, IA; Downtown Gallery, New Orleans, LA; Allyson Louis Gallery, Bethesda, MD; Charles Barry International, Rockville, MD; J Todd Galleries, Wellesley, MA; Saper Gallery, East Lansing, MI; David Gallery, Ltd, Milbourn, NJ; Short Hills Art Gallery, Short Hills, NJ; Artists Showcase International, Hartsdale, NY; Art Spectrum, New York, NY; Dyansen Eclipse Gallery, New York, NY; Professional Fine Arts Services, Inc, New York, NY

Erté (Romain De Tirtoff)
The Portrait
Courtesy Circle Fine Art, Inc

TITLE	PUBLISHER	PRINTER	DATE	MEDIUM	DIMENSION (PAPER SIZE) IN INCHES	TYPE OF PAPER	EDITION NUMBER	NO. OF COLORS	ORIGINAL OPENING PRICE	CURRENT RETAIL PRICE
SOLD OUT EDITIONS (RARE):										
Splendeur	CFA	RW	1974	SP	34 X 26	SOM	260	4	225	10800
Winter Resort, Nice	CFA	RW	1974	SP	30 X 24	SOM	260	6	175	3300
Fashions	CFA	RW	1974	SP	30 X 24	SOM	260	5	175	3600
Furs	CFA	RW	1974	SP	30 X 24	SOM	260	5	175	9000
Compact Vanities	CFA	RW	1974	SP	30 X 24	SOM	260	5	175	4150
Winter Resorts	CFA	SS	1974	SP	30 X 24	SOM	260	6	175	5350
Three Faces	CFA	RW	1974	SP	30 X 24	SOM	260	6	175	3950
Brown Boot	CFA	SS	1974	SP	20 X 17	R/BFK	260	4	135	3800
Mystique	CFA	SS	1974	SP	40 X 26	SOM	260	5	225	8500
Black Rose	CFA	SS	1974	SP	25 X 20	R/BFK	260	3	185	7350
Top Hats	CFA	SS	1975	SP	24 X 19	R/BFK	260	3	225	11800
Tennis	CFA	RW	1974	SP	30 X 24	SOM	260	4	175	2950
Love	CFA	RW	1974	SP	30 X 24	SOM	260	3	175	3000
Printemps	CFA	RW	1975	SP	29 X 23	H	260	3	225	4000

ERTÉ (ROMAIN DE TIRTOFF)

TITLE	PUBLISHER	PRINTER	DATE	MEDIUM	DIMENSION (PAPER SIZE) IN INCHES	TYPE OF PAPER	EDITION NUMBER	NO. OF COLORS	ORIGINAL OPENING PRICE	CURRENT RETAIL PRICE
SOLD OUT EDITIONS (RARE):										
Renée	CFA	GGC	1975	LC	17 X 11	AP	260	3	65	3350
Nicole	CFA	GGC	1975	LC	17 X 11	AP	260	3	65	3700
Yvette	CFA	GGC	1975	LC	17 X 11	AP	260	5	65	3650
Simone	CFA	GGC	1975	LC	17 X 11	AP	260	3	65	3650
Zsa Zsa	CFA	AA	1975	LC	35 X 21	AP	260	3	200	6200
Premier	CFA	AA	1975	LC	16 X 12	AP	300	3	65	3000
The Four Seasons Folio (Set of 4):									450 SET	12800 SET
Winter	CFA	SS	1975	SP	20 X 14	AP	260	4	125	3150
Spring	CFA	SS	1975	SP	20 X 14	AP	260	4	125	3650
Summer	CFA	SS	1975	SP	20 X 14	AP	260	4	125	3250
Autumn	CFA	SS	1975	SP	20 X 14	AP	260	4	125	3350
Bon Soir	CFA	AA	1975	LC	16 X 12	AP	300	3	65	3350
Elegance	CFA	AA	1975	LC	16 X 12	AP	300	3	65	3350
Tres Chic	CFA	AA	1975	LC	16 X 12	AP	300	3	65	3000
The Kiss	CFA	AA	1975	LC/EMB	12 X 10	AP	300	2	60	9000
Summer and Winter	CFA	AA	1975	LC/EMB	11 X 12	AP	300	3	60	5600
The Veil	CFA	AA	1975	LC/EMB	12 X 9	AP	300	3	50	4900
Evening Creation	CFA	AA	1976	EC	15 X 11	AP	175	1	65	4050
Feathers	CFA	AA	1976	LC/EMB	12 X 9	AP	300	3	50	4950
Dancers	CFA	AA	1976	LC/EMB	6 X 13	AP	300	3	50	3350
La Belle	CFA	AG	1976	LC	15 X 11	AP	300	2	65	3350
Ficelle	CFA	AG	1976	LC	15 X 11	AP	300	3	65	3350
Muff	CFA	AG	1976	LC	15 X 11	AP	300	3	65	3350
Fantaisie	CFA	AG	1976	LC	15 X 11	AP	300	3	65	3350
Reflections	CFA	CSW	1976	SP	26 X 21	AP	300	10	175	6000 SET
The Alphabet Suite (Set of 26):										125000 SET
Letter A	CFA	CSW	1977	LC/SP	26 X 19	AP	350		175	5450
Letter B	CFA	CSW	1977	LC/SP	26 X 19	AP	350		175	5650
Letter C	CFA	CSW	1977	LC/SP	26 X 19	AP	350		175	3650
Letter D	CFA	CSW	1977	LC/SP	26 X 19	AP	350		175	5650
Letter E	CFA	CSW	1977	LC/SP	26 X 19	AP	350		175	5100
Letter F	CFA	CSW	1977	LC/SP	26 X 19	AP	350		175	6700
Letter G	CFA	CSW	1977	LC/SP	26 X 19	AP	350		175	5450
Letter H	CFA	CSW	1977	LC/SP	26 X 19	AP	350		175	5450
Letter I	CFA	CSW	1977	LC/SP	26 X 19	AP	350		175	3550
Letter J	CFA	CSW	1977	LC/SP	26 X 19	AP	350		175	5200
Letter K	CFA	CSW	1977	LC/SP	26 X 19	AP	350		175	6100
Letter L	CFA	CSW	1977	LC/SP	26 X 19	AP	350		175	11800
Letter M	CFA	CSW	1977	LC/SP	26 X 19	AP	350		175	9100
Letter N	CFA	CSW	1977	LC/SP	26 X 19	AP	350		175	3550
Letter O	CFA	CSW	1977	LC/SP	26 X 19	AP	350		175	3550
Letter P	CFA	CSW	1977	LC/SP	26 X 19	AP	350		175	7350
Letter Q	CFA	CSW	1977	LC/SP	26 X 19	AP	350		175	3650
Letter R	CFA	CSW	1977	LC/SP	26 X 19	AP	350		175	7350
Letter S	CFA	CSW	1977	LC/SP	26 X 19	AP	350		175	8000
Letter T	CFA	CSW	1977	LC/SP	26 X 19	AP	350		175	7350
Letter U	CFA	CSW	1977	LC/SP	26 X 19	AP	350		175	3550
The Curtain	CFA	CSW	1977	SP/FL	26 X 18	CSWS	300	4	160	6000
Broadway's in Fashion	CFA	CSW	1977	SP/EMB	14 X 18	CSWS	300	4	200	6950
Summer Breeze	CFA	CSW	1977	SP	31 X 23	R/100	300	4	450	7700
Flames of Love	CFA	CSW	1977	SP	27 X 21	R/100	300	4	300	8800
Twenties Remembered Folio (Set of 8):									1500 SET	50500 SET
The Bride	CFA	FRW	1977	SP	24 X 20	WC	300	4	175	6950
Amoureuse	CFA	FRW	1977	SP	24 X 20	WC	300	4	160	4400
Les Jolies Dames	CFA	FRW	1977	SP	24 X 20	WC	300	4	175	5200
Rainbow in Blossom	CFA	FRW	1977	SP	24 X 20	WC	300	4	175	5250
Beauty of the Beast	CFA	FRW	1977	SP	25 X 22	WC	300	16	250	14700
Autumn Song	CFA	FRW	1977	SP	25 X 22	WC	300	11	200	5450
Fish Bowl	CFA	FRW	1977	SP	25 X 22	WC	300	17	200	5250
Dream Voyage	CFA	FRW	1977	SP	25 X 22	WC	300	13	250	7850
Twenties Remembered Again Folio (Set of 8):									1500 SET	44000 SET
Spring Opening	CFA	CSW	1978	SP	24 X 19	R/100	4	185	1400	4950
Légerèté	CFA	CSW	1978	SP	24 X 19	R/100	300	3	200	5450
Selection of a Heart	CFA	CSW	1978	SP	24 X 19	R/100	300	3	250	5650
Tempest	CFA	CSW	1978	SP	24 X 19	R/100	300	3	250	9450
Russian Fairytale	CFA	CSW	1978	SP	24 X 19	R/100	300	3	250	5850
Earth's Dream	CFA	CSW	1978	SP	24 X 19	R/100	300	2	250	7300
Makeup	CFA	CSW	1978	SP	24 X 19	R/100	300	3	200	6000
First Dress	CFA	CSW	1978	SP	24 X 19	R/100	300	3	250	6350

ERTÉ (ROMAIN DE TIRTOFF)

TITLE	PUBLISHER	PRINTER	DATE	MEDIUM	DIMENSION (PAPER SIZE) IN INCHES	TYPE OF PAPER	EDITION NUMBER	NO. OF COLORS	ORIGINAL OPENING PRICE	CURRENT RETAIL PRICE
SOLD OUT EDITIONS (RARE):										
Turban Suite (Set of 3):									1500 SET	13750 SET
Rose Turban	CFA	AA	1979	LC	20 X 16	STP	300	3	525	4500
Yellow Turban	CFA	AA	1979	LC	20 X 16	STP	300	3	525	4500
The Mirror	CFA	AA	1979	LC	20 X 16	STP	300	3	525	5500
The Four Emotions Folio #1 (Set of 4):									2500 SET	15000 SET
L'Amour	CFA	CSW	1979	SP	23 X 18	R/100	300	4	625	4150
La Tristesse	CFA	CSW	1979	SP	23 X 18	R/100	300	4	625	4150
La Indifference	CFA	CSW	1979	SP	23 X 18	R/100	300	4	625	4150
La Jalouise	CFA	CSW	1979	SP	23 X 18	R/100	300	4	625	4150
The Four Emotions Folios #2 (Set of 4):									3000 SET	33200 SET
L'Amour	CFA	CSW	1979	SP/EMB	23 X 18	R/100	300	4	800	8500
La Tristesse	CFA	CSW	1979	SP/EMB	23 X 18	R/100	300	4	800	8500
La Indifference	CFA	CSW	1979	SP/EMB	23 X 18	R/100	300	4	800	8500
La Jalousie	CFA	CSW	1979	SP/EMB	23 X 18	R/100	300	4	800	8500
Riviera	CFA	CSW	1979	SP	24 X 19	R/100	300	14	300	5000
Les Poupées Russes	CFA	CSW	1979	SP	31 X 23	R/100	300	4	425	8000
Bagdad	CFA	AA	1979	LC	16 X 13	SOM	300	4	250	3250
Zobeide	CFA	AA	1979	LC	16 X 13	SOM	300	3	250	3250
Dinarzade	CFA	AA	1979	LC	16 X 13	SOM	300	5	250	3050
King's Favorite	CFA	AA	1979	LC	26 X 20	SOM	300	3	500	4550
Gaby Deslys	CFA	AA	1979	LC	26 X 20	SOM	300	3	600	5050
Manhattan Mary I	CFA	AA	1979	LC	22 X 18	SOM	300	4	225	4000
Manhattan Mary II	CFA	AA	1979	LC/SP	25 X 17	SOM	300	5	250	3350
Spring Fashions	CFA	CSW	1979	SP	31 X 23	R/100	300	3	275	4900
Blossom Umbrella	CFA	CSW	1979	SP	30 X 23	R/100	300	3	350	10000
The Golden Cloak	CFA	AA	1979	LC	25 X 17	SOM	300	4	325	5050
Lafayette	CFA	CSW	1979	SP	32 X 24	R/100	300	3	375	4800
After the Rain	CFA	CSW	1979	SP	31 X 23	R/100	300	4	475	3350
The Blue Dress	CFA	AA	1980	LC	25 X 19	SOM	300	3	350	2800
Fall	CFA	AA	1980	SP	31 X 24	R/100	300		1350	6100
Heat	CFA	MRS	1980	SP	25 X 19	R/100	300	26	450	11000
The Chaste Susanna	CFA	CSW	1980	SP	24 X 19	R/100	300	28	375	8000
Fireflies	CFA	CSW	1980	SP	32 X 24	R/100	300	23	650	11500
The French Rooster	CFA	CSW	1980	SP	31 X 22	R/100	300	24	950	11000
Vintage	CFA	CSW	1980	SP	31 X 23	R/100	300	30	1350	11500
The Bath of the Marquise	CFA	CSW	1980	SP	24 X 18	R/100	300	3	1350	5850
La Toilette	CFA	CSW	1980	SP	11 X 14	R/100	300	19	350	4550
The Wave	CFA	CSW	1980	SP	11 X 13	R/100	300	10	400	6500
The Riviera	CFA	CSW	1980	SP	10 X 15	R/100	300		350	3650
Noon	CFA	CSW	1980	SP	14 X 11	R/100	300	14	400	4900
Queen of Sheba	CFA	CSW	1980	SP	30 X 22	R/100	300	3	1150	9000
Michelle	CFA	CSW	1980	SP	30 X 22	R/100	300		1000	4950
Paresseuse	CFA	MRS	1980	SP	31 X 23	R/100	300	3	1350	8000
Rain	CFA	CSW	1980	SP/EMB	10 X 20	R/100	300	3	550	4600
La Merveilleuse	CFA	CSW	1980	SP	31 X 23	R/100	300		1150	5500
Woman and Satyr	CFA	AA	1980	SP	32 X 23	R/100	300		1350	11000
Mystére	CFA	AA	1980	SP	32 X 24	AP	300		1150	4200
Samson and Delilah	CFA	AA	1981	SP/EMB	19 X 24	R/BFK	300		1500	11000
Charleston Couple	CFA	AA	1981	SP	17 X 15	AP	300		750	4200
Twin Sisters	CFA	AA	1981	SP	40 X 55	AP	300		1800	14500
The Duel	CFA	AA	1981	SP	31 X 23	AP	300		1250	6700
Rendezvous	CFA	AA	1981	SP	30 X 23	AP	300		1250	6600
Applause	CFA	AA	1981	SP	29 X 23	AP	300		1250	8350
The Choice	CFA	AA	1981	SP	21 X 37	AP	300		1500	9000
Purity	CFA	AA	1981	SP/EMB	27 X 22	R/BFK	300		1250	11900
Ocean de Lumiere	CFA	AA	1981	SP/EMB	16 X 19	R/BFK	300		1150	11000
Pink Lady	CFA	AA	1981	SP	33 X 25	AP	300		1250	5800
The Bird Cage	CFA	AA	1981	SP	34 X 24	AP	300		1250	6100
Resting	CFA	AA	1981	SP/EMB	25 X 16	R/BFK	300		1000	5100
Salome	CFA	AA	1981	SP/EMB	21 X 27	R/BFK	300		1250	7450
Coquette	CFA	AA	1981	SP	24 X 19	AP	300		550	4000
Vamps Folio (Set of 6):									5000 SET	24000 SET
Circe	CFA	AA	1982	LC	21 X 15	AP	300		900	3650
Seductress	CFA	AA	1982	LC	21 X 15	AP	300		900	3500
Temptress	CFA	AA	1982	LC	21 X 15	AP	300		900	3700
Black Magic	CFA	AA	1982	LC	21 X 15	AP	300		900	3700
La Prétentieuse	CFA	AA	1982	LC	21 X 15	AP	300		900	5750
L'Empanachée	CFA	AA	1982	LC	21 X 15	AP	300		900	3700
Lovers and Idol	CFA	AA	1981	SP	23 X 17	AP	300		1250	6300
La Serenade	CFA	AA	1982	LC	20 X 16	SOM	300		550	6600

ERTÉ (ROMAIN DE TIRTOFF)

TITLE	PUBLISHER	PRINTER	DATE	MEDIUM	DIMENSION (PAPER SIZE) IN INCHES	TYPE OF PAPER	EDITION NUMBER	NO. OF COLORS	ORIGINAL OPENING PRICE	CURRENT RETAIL PRICE
SOLD OUT EDITIONS (RARE):										
Spider Web	CFA	AA	1982	SP	23 X 18	R/100	300		750	6400
Le Rideau de l'Hiver (The Curtain of Winter)	CFA	AA	1982	SP	23 X 18	R/100	300		750	3850
Summer Snow	CFA	AA	1982	SP	12 X 16	R/100	300		550	3250
Love's Screen	CFA	AA	1982	SP	12 X 14	R/100	300		550	4000
Lady with a Rose	CFA	AA	1982	SP/LC	22 X 16	R/100	300		550	3700
The Suitors	CFA	AA	1982	SP/EMB	16 X 18	R/100	300		750	3700
Ready for the Ball (Dipt)	CFA	AA	1982	SP	25 X 19	R/100	300		1500	10000
The Portrait	CFA	AA	1982	SP	30 X 23	R/100	300		1500	7000
The Coming of Spring	CFA	AA	1982	SP	30 X 23	R/100	300		1500	7800
The End of Romance	CFA	AA	1982	SP	30 X 23	R/100	300		1500	6700
The Arctic Sea	CFA	AA	1982	SP/ST	25 X 19	R/100	300		1250	12700
The Bubbles	CFA	AA	1982	SP	30 X 24	R/100	300		1500	6700
The Nile	CFA	AA	1982	SP	23 X 28	R/100	300		1500	10500
Set of Two Serigraphs (Set of 2):									3000 SET	12000 SET
Zeus	CFA	AA	1983	SP/EMB	28 X 24	R/100	300		1500	10500
Hera	CFA	AA	1982	SP/EMB	28 X 24	R/100	300		1500	10500
CURRENT EDITIONS:										
Adam & Eve	CVFA	AH/SH	1982	SP	37 X 21	AP	473		750	2000
The Coming of Spring	CVFA	AH/SH	1982	SP	30 X 24	AP	483		900	2500
Harlequin	CVFA	AH/SH	1982	SP	31 X 24	AP	488		950	2500
La Traviata	CVFA	AH/SH	1982	SP	32 X 24	AP	489		800	2000
Nature's Vanity	CVFA	AH/SH	1982	SP	32 X 24	AP	483		900	4000
Oriental Tale	CVFA	AH/SH	1982	SP	30 X 24	AP	480		850	3500
Love's Captive	CVFA	CCI	1982	SP	33 X 24	AP	492		950	2500
Stolen Kisses	CVFA	CCI	1982	SP	29 X 24	AP	480		825	2000
Fantasia	CVFA	AH/SH	1982	SP	33 X 25	AP	488		850	4500
Her Secret Admirers	CVFA	AH/SH	1982	SP	33 X 24	AP	481		900	4250
The Surprises of the Sea	CVFA	CCI	1982	SP	33 X 25	AP	486		950	2250
The Angel	CVFA	CCI	1983	SP	27 X 38	AP	510		1250	6250
The Slave	CVFA	CCI	1983	SP	35 X 27	AP	495		900	6250
Stranded	CVFA	CCI	1983	SP	33 X 27	AP	520		950	4500
The Phoenix Suite (Set of 2):									1975 SET	9000 SET
Phoenix Reborn	CVFA	CCI	1983	SP	28 X 40	AP	518		1150	5000
Phoenix Triumphant	CVFA	CCI	1983	SP	28 X 40	AP	515		1150	5000
L'Orientale	CVFA	CCI	1983	SP	30 X 22	AP	350		550	4000
Columbine	CVFA	CCI	1983	SP	33 X 25	AP	393		900	3000
Eyes of Love	CVFA	CCI	1983	SP	25 X 40	AP	514		1250	4000
Eyes of Jealousy	CVFA	CCI	1983	SP	25 X 40	AP	514		1250	4000
Swept Away	CVFA	CCI	1983	SP	33 X 24	AP	485		900	4500
Monte Carlo	CVFA	CCI	1983	SP	25 X 19	AP	402		450	2000
Sleeping Beauty	CVFA	CCI	1984	SP	27 X 33	AP	393		850	3000
Spring Shadows	CVFA	CCI	1984	SP	32 X 31	AP	474		675	2500
Rose Dancer	CVFA	CCI	1984	SP	20 X 27	AP	450		900	5750
Love and Passion Suite (Set of 2):									2375 SET	22500 SET
Kiss of Fire	CVFA	CCI	1984	SP	34 X 29	AP	550	12	1250	11250
Marriage Dance	CVFA	CCI	1984	SP	29 X 34	AP	535	13	1250	11250
Diva Suite (Set of 2)	CVFA	CCI	1984	SP	36 X 28 EA	AP	370 EA		1975 SET 1000 EA	20000 SET 10000 EA
Loge de Théâtre	CVFA	CCI	1984	SP	27 X 33	AP	490		975	7250
Sunrise/Moonlight Suite (Set of 2):									1175 SET	10000 SET
Sunrise	CVFA	CCI	1984	SP	27 X 33	AP	495		650	5000
Moonlight	CVFA	CCI	1984	SP	27 X 33	AP	495		650	5000
Three Graces	CVFA	CCI	1985	SP	33 X 25	AP	460	23	950	7750
Myths Suite (Set of 2):									2475 SET	16000 SET
Circe	CVFA	CCI	1985	SP	25 X 34	AP	525	17	1250	8500
Diana	CVFA	CCI	1985	SP	25 X 34	AP	525	12	1250	8500
Rigoletto	CVFA	CCI	1985	SP	31 X 38	AP	505	21	1250	13500
Pillow Swing	CVFA	CCI	1985	SP	30 X 22	AP	490	15	975	7500
Suite of Five:										
Copacabana	CVFA	CCI	1985	SP		AP	400		1250	3750
Deception	CVFA	CCI	1985	SP		AP	346		1250	2750
Debutante	CVFA	CCI	1985	SP		AP	358		1250	2750
Freedom & Captivity	CVFA	CCI	1985	SP		AP	495		1250	3000
Spring Showers	CVFA	CCI	1985	SP		AP	384		1250	3750
Winter's Arrival	CVFA	CCI	1985	SP	33 X 25	AP			950	5750
Enchanted Melody	CVFA	CCI	1985	SP	43 X 30	AP	515	23	1300	6250
Memories	CVFA	CCI	1985	SP	26 X 32	AP	460	14	900	3000
Opium/Mah Jongg Suite (Set of 2):									2275 SET	13500 SET
Opium	CVFA	CCI	1985	SP	30 X 27	AP	510	21	1200	6250
Mah-Jongg	CVFA	CCI	1985	SP	30 X 41	AP	510	13	1200	7250

ERTÉ (ROMAIN DE TIRTOFF)

TITLE	PUBLISHER	PRINTER	DATE	MEDIUM	DIMENSION (PAPER SIZE) IN INCHES	TYPE OF PAPER	EDITION NUMBER	NO. OF COLORS	ORIGINAL OPENING PRICE	CURRENT RETAIL PRICE
CURRENT EDITIONS:										
The Pursuit of Flore										
Morning, Day/Evening, Night	CVFA	CCI	1985	SP		AP	510		1200	3250
Suite (Set of 2):									2375 SET	20000 SET
Morning, Day	CVFA	CCI	1985	SP	44 X 32	AP	505	16	1250	10000
Evening, Night	CVFA	CCI	1985	SP	44 X 32	AP	505	25	1250	10000
Mystery of the Courtesan	CVFA	CCI	1986	SP/HS/EMB	26 X 31	COV/W	521		1500	4750
Perfume	CVFA	CCI	1986	SP	39 X 24	AP	520	31	1500	13500
Hearts & Zephyrs (Set of 4)	CVFA	CCI	1986	SP	12 X 12 EA	AP	510 EA	8 EA	2375 SET	7000 SET
At the Ball	CFA	AA	1986	SP	22 X 18	AP	300		1250	3700
Statue of Liberty Suite (Set of 2):									2675 SET	16000 SET
Statue of Liberty—Day	CVFA	CCI	1986	SP	36 X 27	AP	539	16	1450	8000
Statue of Liberty—Night	CVFA	CCI	1986	SP	36 X 27	AP	545	22	1450	9000
June Brides Suite (Set of 2):									2750 SET	26000 SET
Veil Gown	CVFA	CCI	1986	SP	39 X 30	AP	559		1450	13500
Fringe Gown	CVFA	CCI	1986	SP	39 X 30	AP	552		1450	13000
Metropolis Suite (Set of 2):									2750 SET	22500 SET
Opening Night	CVFA	CCI	1986	SP	30 X 25	AP	495	18	1450	13000
On the Avenue	CVFA	CCI	1986	SP	30 X 25	AP	482	20	1450	10000
Asian Princess Suite (Set of 3):									2975 SET	16000 SET
Bamboo	CVFA	CCI	1986	SP	29 X 21	AP	494	18	1100	6000
Willow Tree	CVFA	CCI	1986	SP	29 X 21	AP	496	16	1100	5250
Plum Blossom	CVFA	CCI	1986	SP	29 X 21	AP	488	16	1100	5250
Queen of the Night	CVFA	CCI	1986	SP	29 X 33	AP	541		1650	12000
Pearls & Diamonds	CVFA	CCI	1986	SP/HS/EMB	37 X 28	DOVE/BL	507		1500	4750
Plum Blossom	CVFA	CCI	1986	SP/HS/EMB	37 X 28	COV/W			1500	5250
The Flowered Cape	CFA	AA	1986	SP	27 X 21	AP	300		1500	7000
Feather Gown	CVFA	CCI	1987	SP	30 X 21	AP	516		1250	6750
Firebird	CVFA	CCI	1987	SP/HS/EMB	43 X 29	AP	596		1850	4000
Gala	CVFA	CCI	1987	SP/HS/EMB	40 X 29	AP	580		1850	4500
Helen of Troy	CVFA	CCI	1987	SP/HS/EMB	40 X 29	AP	480		1850	6750
Bacchante	CVFA	CCI	1987	SP/HS/EMB	41 X 29	COV/W	580	20	1850	7000
Haute Couture	CVFA	CCI	1987	SP/HS/EMB	38 X 28	COV/W	565		1850	7500
Devotion	CVFA	CCI	1987	SP/HS/EMB	42 X 31	COV/W	579		1850	7500
Hindu Princess	CVFA	CCI	1987	SP/HS/EMB	30 X 41	AP/BL	581		1850	5750
Ladies in Waiting	CVFA	CCI	1987	SP/HS/EMB	39 X 28	AP/BL	587		1850	5750
A Dream	CVFA	CCI	1987	SP/HS/EMB	40 X 30	COV/W	586		1850	3500
Moon Garden	CVFA	CCI	1987	SP/HS/EMB	39 X 29	AP/BL	575		1850	8000
Tuxedo	CVFA	CCI	1987	SP/HS/EMB	31 X 22	AP	472		1450	6750
The Celestial Virtues Suite										
(Set of 2):									3000 SET	18000 SET
Radiance	CVFA	CCI	1987	SP/HS/EMB	34 X 27	AP	560		1500	9000
Wisdom	CVFA	CCI	1987	SP/HS/EMB	34 X 27	AP	560		1500	9000
Roses and Carnations (Set of 2):									1500 SET	6500 SET
Roses	CVFA	CCI	1987	SP/HS/EMB	21 X 24	AP	325	21	800	3000
Carnations	CVFA	CCI	1987	SP/HS/EMB	21 X 24	AP	333	15	800	3500
The Love & Beauty Suite (Set of 2):									3375 SET	20000 SET
Aphrodite	CVFA	CCI	1987	SP/HS/EMB	40 X 31	AP88	550	15	1750	10000
Venus	CVFA	CCI	1987	SP/HS/EMB	40 X 29	AP88	500	21	1750	10000
Blue Asia	CVFA	CCI	1987	SP/HS/EMB	29 X 22	AP88	476	15	1175	4250
New York/Monaco Suite (Set of 2):									3500 SET	20000 SET
New York, New York	CVFA	CCI	1987	SP/HS/EMB	33 X 30	AP/BL	542	15	1850	10000
Monaco	CVFA	CCI	1987	SP/HS/EMB	39 X 32	COV	508	21	1850	10000
The Jeweled Gown Suite (Set of 2):									3950 SET	20000 SET
Byzantine	CVFA	CCI	1988	SP/HS/EMB	35 X 26	AP/BL	515	18	2000	10000
Pearls and Diamonds	CVFA	CCI	1988	SP/HS/EMB	37 X 28	AP/BL	507	17	2000	10000
Emerald Vase (Black & White)										
Black Vase	CVFA	CCI	1988	SP/HS/EMB	42 X 29	AP	294	20	1875	12000
White Vase	CVFA	CCI	1988	SP/HS/EMB	42 X 29	COV	297	20	1875	10000
Nocturne										
(with Gold & Silver Foil Stamping)	CVFA	CCI	1988	SP/HS/EMB	35 X 25	AP	479	18	1350	6250
Starfish	CVFA	CCI	1988	SP/HS/EMB	40 X 29	AP/BL	491	16	1975	8500
Legends Suite (Set of 2):									3500 SET	16000 SET
Sisters	CVFA	CCI	1988	SP/HS/EMB	23 X 29	COV/W	533	17	1975	8000
Athena	CVFA	CCI	1988	SP/HS/EMB	35 X 26	COV/W	507	22	1975	8000
Myth and Magic Suite (Set of 2):									3500 SET	13500 SET
Golden Fleece	CVFA	CCI	1988	SP/HS/EMB	36 X 30	COV	534	17	1975	6750
Enchantress	CVFA	CCI	1988	SP/HS/EMB	33 X 26	AP/BL	548	12	1975	6750
Harmony	CVFA	CCI	1988	SP/HS/EMB	33 X 28	COV	521	12	1975	9000
Spring Dress of Venus	CVFA	CCI	1988	SP/HS/EMB	32 X 24	R/BFK	335	18	1975	2500
The Swing	CVFA	CCI	1988	SP/HS/EMB	23 X 32	AP/W	385	24	1975	2500
Fox Fur	CVFA	CCI	1988	SP/HS/EMB	34 X 27	COV	500	20	1975	8000
Winter Flowers	CVFA	CCI	1988	SP/HS/EMB	33 X 29	R/BFK/W	377	21	1875	2750
Starstruck	CVFA	CCI	1989	SP/HS/EMB	33 X 24	AP/BL	521	15	1975	8000

ERTÉ (ROMAIN DE TIRTOFF)

TITLE	PUBLISHER	PRINTER	DATE	MEDIUM	DIMENSION (PAPER SIZE) IN INCHES	TYPE OF PAPER	EDITION NUMBER	NO. OF COLORS	ORIGINAL OPENING PRICE	CURRENT RETAIL PRICE
CURRENT EDITIONS:										
Masquerade Suite (Set of 2):										
Masquerade I (Black)	CVFA	CCI	1989	SP/HS/EMB	28 X 40	AP/BL	337		1975	4500
Masquerade II (White)	CVFA	CCI	1989	SP/HS/EMB	28 X 40	COV/W	340		1975	4000
Mary Garden	CVFA	CCI	1989	SP/HS/EMB	41 X 30	COV/W	585		1975	4000
Directoire	CVFA	CCI	1989	SP/HS/EMB	42 X 31	DOVE	517		1975	10000
Melisande and Golaud	CVFA	CCI	1989	SP/HS/EMB	32 X 25	AP/BL	448		2250	2950
The Necklace	CVFA	CCI	1989	SP/HS/EMB	31 X 40	COV/BL	590		2250	3500
Emerald Eyes	CVFA	CCI	1989	SP/HS/EMB	32 X 25	COV/W	537		1800	3500
The Mirror	CVFA	CCI	1989	SP/HS/EMB	29 X 25	AP/BL	463	25	2250	8000
The Storm/The Harvest Suite (Set of 2):									3950 SET	11000 SET
The Storm	CVFA	CCI	1989	SP/HS/EMB	26 X 38	COV/W	588	28	2250	5750
The Harvest	CVFA	CCI	1989	SP/HS/EMB	25 X 37	COV/W	578	21	2250	5250
The Contessa	CVFA	CCI	1989	SP/HS/EMB	29 X 23	AP/BL	525	14	2250	8000
American Millionairess Suite (Set of 2):									4500 SET	20000 SET
Tussel Gown	CVFA	CCI	1989	SP/HS/EMB	40 X 28	AP/BL	571		2500	10000
Fringe Cape	CVFA	CCI	1989	SP/HS/EMB	40 X 28	AP/BL	571		2500	10000
Twilight	CVFA	CCI	1990	SP/HS/EMB	37 X 27	AP/BL	601		2500	9500
Paris Days & Nights Suite (Set of 2):									4500 SET	20000 SET
Faubourg St Honore	CVFA	CCI	1990	SP/HS/EMB	43 X 29	AP/BL	580		2250	10000
Place de l'Opera	CVFA	CCI	1990	SP/HS/EMB	43 X 29	AP/BL	580		2250	10000
Tanegra (Blue)	CVFA	CCI	1990	SP/HS/EMB	41 X 31	COV/W	249		2500	3500

BARBARA ESS

BORN: Brooklyn, NY; 1948
EDUCATION: Univ of Michigan, Ann Arbor, MI, BA, 1969; London Sch of Film Technique, London, England, 1971
AWARDS: Mid-Atlantic Arts Found, Nat Endowment for the Arts Regional Fel, Photography, 1990–91
RECENT EXHIB: Honolulu Acad of Arts, HI, 1987; Interim Art, London, England, 1987; Johnen & Schottle Galerie, Cologne, Germany, 1987; Galerie Micheline Szwajcer, Antwerp, Belgium, 1988; Galerie Ghislaine Hussenot, Paris, France, 1989; Michael Kohn Gallery, Los Angeles, CA, 1987,91; Galerie La Maquina Espanola, Madrid, Spain, 1990,92; High Mus of Art, Atlanta, GA, 1992; Curt Marcus Gallery, NY, 1988,90,92; Queens Mus, Flushing, NY, 1993

COLLECTIONS: Art Gallery of Western Australia, Perth, Australia; Nat Mus of Am Art, Smithsonian Inst, Wash, DC; La Jolla Mus of Contemp Art, CA; Carnegie Mus of Art, Pittsburgh, PA; Princeton Univ Art Mus, NJ; Mus of Contemp Art, Los Angeles, CA; Mus of Fine Arts, Allan Chasanoff Photographic Coll, Houston, TX; Toledo Mus of Art, OH; Musee Nat de'Art Moderne, Centre Georges Pompidou, Paris, France; Tampa Mus of Art, FL; List Art Center, David Winton Bell Gallery, Brown Univ, Providence, RI; Musee de La Roche sur Yon, France; New Sch for Social Research, NY; FRAC, Loire, France; New Orleans Mus of Art, LA
PRINTERS: Deli Sacilotto, NY (DS); Iris Editions, NY (IrED)
PUBLISHERS: Kimberly Mock Editions, Oak View, CA (KME)
GALLERIES: Curt Marcus Gallery, New York, NY

TITLE	PUBLISHER	PRINTER	DATE	MEDIUM	DIMENSION (PAPER SIZE) IN INCHES	TYPE OF PAPER	EDITION NUMBER	NO. OF COLORS	ORIGINAL OPENING PRICE	CURRENT RETAIL PRICE
CURRENT EDITIONS:										
Things in the World (Set of 4)	KME	DS/IrEd	1992	PHG	17 X 20 EA	AP	40 EA		1100 SET	1100 SET

JOSEPH ESSIG

PUBLISHERS: Orion Editions, NY (OE)
GALLERIES: Orion Editions, New York, NY

TITLE	PUBLISHER	PRINTER	DATE	MEDIUM	DIMENSION (PAPER SIZE) IN INCHES	TYPE OF PAPER	EDITION NUMBER	NO. OF COLORS	ORIGINAL OPENING PRICE	CURRENT RETAIL PRICE
CURRENT EDITIONS:										
Hudson Echo	OE	ART/MP	1988	EC	36 X 53	SOM	75	3	800	950
Taconic View	OE	ART/MP	1988	EB	30 X 37	SOM	75	1	350	400
Vermont Weather	OE	ART/MP	1988	EB	30 X 37	SOM	75	1	350	400
East of Chatham	OE	ART/MP	1988	EB	30 X 37	SOM	75	1	350	400
Tilled Fields	OE	ART/MP	1989	EC	24 X 30	SOM	75	10	350	375
Western View I	OE	ART/MP	1989	EC	24 X 30	SOM	75	10	350	375
Western View II	OE	ART/MP	1989	EC	36 X 44	SOM	75	10	700	750

MAURITS CORNELIS ESCHER

BORN: The Netherlands; (1898–1972)
PRINTERS: Artist (ART)
PUBLISHERS: Artist (ART)

Bool/Kist/Locher/Wierda (B/K/L/W)

The retail prices of the 100,000 limited edition prints quoted in this directory are subject to change. Print publishers, artists and galleries were the direct sources for these quotations. Prices in the secondary market listed as "Sold Out Editions (Rare)" indicate that the publisher has a limited supply of that print or that the print is difficult to locate in the galleries.

MAURITS CORNELIS ESCHER CONTINUED

Maurits Cornelis Escher
Day and Night
Courtesy Avantgarde Art Associates

TITLE	PUBLISHER	PRINTER	DATE	MEDIUM	DIMENSION (PAPER SIZE) IN INCHES	TYPE OF PAPER	EDITION NUMBER	NO. OF COLORS	ORIGINAL OPENING PRICE	CURRENT RETAIL PRICE
SOLD OUT EDITIONS (RARE):										
The Sixth Day of Creation	ART	ART	1926	WB	15 X 11	WOVE		1	50	10000
Tower of Babel (B/K/L/W-118)	ART	ART	1928	WB	25 X 15	JP		1	50	8000
Barbarano, Cimino (B/K/L/W-129)	ART	ART	1929	LB	7 X 9	WOVE	24	1	35	3500
Hand with Reflecting Sphere (B/K/L/W- 268)	ART	ART	1935	LB	13 X 9	WOVE	30	1	100	30000
Day and Night (B/K/L/W-303)	ART	ART	1938	WC	17 X 27	JP		2	120	14000
Sky and Water I (B/K/L/W-306)	ART	ART	1938	WB	18 X 17	JP		1	90	9000
Three Spheres I (B/K/L/W-336)	ART	ART	1945	WE	11 X 7	JP		1	125	1500
Three Spheres II (B/K/L/W-339)	ART	ART	1946	LB	10 X 18	WOVE	40	1	125	30000
Horseman (B/K/L/W-342)	ART	ART	1946	WC	10 X 18	JP			150	6000
Other World (B/K/L/W-348)	ART	ART	1947	WE	13 X 10	JP			125	7000
Drawing Hands (B/K/L/W-355)	ART	ART	1948	LB	11 X 13	WOVE	43	1	150	25000
Puddle (B/K/L/W-378)	ART	ART	1952	WC	9 X 13	WOVE		3	200	6000
The Four Elements (Set of 4)	ART	ART	1953	WC	7 X 6	WOVE			600 SET	3000 SET
Plane Filling II (B/K/L/W-422)	ART	ART	1957	LB	13 X 15	HP/Cr	56	1	300	5000
Belvedere (B/K/L/W-426)	ART	ART	1958	LB	18 X 12	HP/Cr	56	1	350	6000

IVAN EYRE

BORN: Tullymet, Sask, Canada; April 15, 1935
EDUCATION: Univ of Saskatchewan, 1952; Univ of Manitoba, BFA, 1957; Univ of North Dakota, 1958
TEACHING: Univ of North Dakota, 1958–59; Univ of Manitoba, Can, 1960–65,67,72,75–78,79–80
AWARDS: Senior Arts Awards, Canadian Council, 1966, 78; Queen's Silver Jubilee Medal, Gov Gen of Canada, 1977; Univ of Manitoba Jubilee Award, 1982

RECENT EXHIB: Nat Gallery of Canada, Ottawa, Canada, 1988
COLLECTIONS: Nat Gallery of Canada, Ottawa, Canada; Art Gallery of Ontario, Toronto, Canada; Art Gallery of Vancouver, Canada; Art Gallery of Winnipeg, Canada; Glenbow Inst, Calgary, Canada
PUBLISHERS: Editions Trout, Toronto, Can (ET)
GALLERIES: Mira Godard Gallery, Toronto, Canada; Equinox Gallery, Vancouver, Canada
MAILING ADDRESS: 1098 Trappistes St, St Norbert, MB R3V 1B8, Canada

TITLE	PUBLISHER	PRINTER	DATE	MEDIUM	DIMENSION (PAPER SIZE) IN INCHES	TYPE OF PAPER	EDITION NUMBER	NO. OF COLORS	ORIGINAL OPENING PRICE	CURRENT RETAIL PRICE
CURRENT EDITIONS:										
Close-Cut	ET	ET	1979–80	I/E	15 X 18	AP	75	1	225	500
Watcher	ET	ET	1979–80	I/E	15 X 18	AP	75	1	225	500
Search	ET	ET	1979–80	I/E	15 X 18	AP	75	1	225	500
Horsemen	ET	ET	1979–80	I/E	15 X 18	AP	75	1	225	500

RICHARD ESTES

BORN: Evanston, IL; 1936
EDUCATION: Chicago Art Inst, IL, 1952–56
AWARDS: Nat Endowment for the Arts Fel, 1971
COLLECTIONS: Whitney Mus of Am Art, NY; Toledo Mus of Art, OH; Chicago Art Inst, IL; Rockhill Nelson Mus, Kansas City, MO; Des Moines Art Center, IA; Hirshhorn Mus, Wash, DC
PRINTERS: Michael Domberger, Stuttgart, West Germany, (MD)
PUBLISHERS: Parasol Press, Ltd, NY (PaP); V & R Fine Arts, Inc, Temple Terrace, FL (VR)
GALLERIES: Martina Hamilton Gallery, New York, NY; Graystone Gallery, San Francisco, CA; David Adamson Gallery, Wash, DC; Elizabeth Leach Gallery, Portland, OR; Stein Bartlow Gallery, Ltd, Chicago, IL; Allyson Louis Gallery, Bethesda, MD; Greenhut Galleries, Santa Fe, NM; Foster Goldstrom, Inc, New York, NY; Sorrentino/Mayer Fine Art, New York, NY & Great Neck, NY; Maine Coast Artists Gallery, Rockport, ME; Jonathan Novak Contemporary Art, Los Angeles, CA
MAILING ADDRESS: 300 Central Park, West, New York, NY 10028

Richard Estes
Eiffel Tower Restaurant
Courtesy Parasol Press

TITLE	PUBLISHER	PRINTER	DATE	MEDIUM	DIMENSION (PAPER SIZE) IN INCHES	TYPE OF PAPER	EDITION NUMBER	NO. OF COLORS	ORIGINAL OPENING PRICE	CURRENT RETAIL PRICE
SOLD OUT EDITIONS (RARE):										
Untitled	PaP	MD	1971	SP	31 X 47	FAB	100		500	12000
St Louis Arch	PaP	MD	1972	SP	20 X 28	FAB	75		400	5000
Urban	PaP	MD	1972	SP	20 X 28	FAB	75		400	5000
Qualicraft Shoes (The Chinese Lady)	PaP	MD	1974	SP	33 X 47	FAB	100		600	6000
Cash 40 Cents (From Urban Landscapes II)	PaP	MD	1979	SP	20 X 28	FAB	100		750	6000
(From Urban Landscapes II)	PaP	MD	1979	SP	20 X 28	FAB	100		750	6000
Escalator (from Urban Landscapes II)	Pap	MD	1979	SP	20 X 28	FAB	100		750	5000
NY Steampressing Venezia	PaP	MD	1979	SP	28 X 20	FAB	100		750	5000
Meat Department	PaP	MD	1979	SP	28 X 20	FAB	100		750	5000
Sherman Shoes	PaP	MD	1981	SP	14 X 20	FAB	250		500	3000
Urban Landscapes III (Set of 8):									18000 SET	38000 SET
Airport	PaP	MD	1981	SP	20 X 28	FAB	250	75	2500	5000
Subway Car	PaP	MD	1981	SP	20 X 28	FAB	250	75	2500	5000
42nd Street	PaP	MD	1981	SP	20 X 28	FAB	250	75	2500	5000
Bus	PaP	MD	1981	SP	20 X 28	FAB	250	75	2500	5000
Roma	PaP	MD	1981	SP	20 X 28	FAB	250	75	2500	5000
Eiffel Tower	PaP	MD	1981	SP	20 X 28	FAB	250	75	2500	5000
Shopping Center	PaP	MD	1981	SP	20 X 28	FAB	250	75	2500	5000
Manhattan	PaP	MD	1981	SP	20 X 28	FAB	250	75	2500	5000
Salzburg Cathedral	Pap/VR	MD	1982	SP	27 X 21	FAB	250	75	2500	5000
Holland Hotel	PaP	MD	1984	SP	48 X 72	WOVE	100	200	10000	15000
CURRENT EDITIONS:										
D Train	PaP	MD	1988	SP	36 X 72	WOVE	1		12000	15000

CONNOR EVERTS

BORN: Bellingham, WA; January 24, 1926
EDUCATION: Univ of London, London, England; Univ de Las Americas, Mexico City, Mexico; Univ of Washington, Seattle, WA; Chouinard Art Inst, Los Angeles, CA
TEACHING: Univ of Washington, Seattle, WA; Cranbrook Acad of Art, Bloomfield Hills, MI; Univ of California, Riverside, CA; Univ of Southern California, Los Angeles, CA; California Inst of the Arts, Valencia, CA
AWARDS: Los Angeles County Mus, Painting Prize, 1955
RECENT EXHIB: Whatcom Mus of History & Art, Bellingham, WA, 1987; Ruth Bachofner Gallery, Santa Monica, CA, 1987,89; California State Univ, Fine Arts Mus, Dominguez Hills, CA, 1989; Univ of Florida, Ginton Galleries, Gainesville, FL, 1989; Fresno City Gallery, Fresno, CA, 1989; City of Gainesville, Thomas Center Gallery, Gainesville, FL, 1989; Printworks, Chicago, IL, 1988,90; Joy Emery Gallery, Grosse Pointe, MI, 1990
COLLECTIONS: Inst of Chicago, IL; Brooklyn Mus, NY; California State Univ, Long Beach, CA; California State Univ, Los Angeles, CA; Des Moines Art Center, IA; Detroit Inst of Art, MI; Janco-Dad Mus, Israel; Los Angeles County Mus, CA; Mus of Mod Art, NY; Mus of Mod Art, San Francisco, CA; Mus of Mod Art, Tokyo, Japan; Milwaukee Mus of Art, WI; Nat Gallery of Art, Wash, DC; Pushkin Mus, Moscow, Russia; Rosenwald Print Coll, Phila, PA; San Diego Mus, CA; Whatcom Mus of History & Art, Bellingham, WA
PRINTERS: Norman Stewart, Bloomfield Hills, MI (NS); Stewart & Stewart, Bloomfield Hills, MI (S-S)
PUBLISHERS: Stewart & Stewart, Bloomfield Hills, MI (S-S); Harvey Littleton Studio, Spruce Pine, NC (HLS); Quiet Sun Press, Torrance, CA (QSP); Spartan Press, California State Univ, San Jose, CA (SparPr); Gator Press, Univ of Florida, Gainesville, FL (GaPr)
GALLERIES: Printworks, Chicago, IL; Joy Emery Gallery, Grosse Pointe, MI; Ruth Bachofner Gallery, Santa Monica, CA; Stewart & Stewart, Bloomfield Hills, MI
MAILING ADDRESS: 1521 Madrid Ave, Torrance, CA 90501

TITLE	PUBLISHER	PRINTER	DATE	MEDIUM	DIMENSION (PAPER SIZE) IN INCHES	TYPE OF PAPER	EDITION NUMBER	NO. OF COLORS	ORIGINAL OPENING PRICE	CURRENT RETAIL PRICE
CURRENT EDITIONS:										
Romabrite	S-S	NS/JK/S-S	1988	SP	30 X 22	R/BFK/W	65	21	400	750

LAWRENCE STEVEN FADEN

BORN: Brooklyn, NY; October 21, 1942
EDUCATION: Brooklyn Mus, NY; Sch of Visual Art, NY
TEACHING: Instr, Education Alliance Art Sch, 1982–84
RECENT EXHIB: Southern Alleghenies Mus of Art, Loretto, PA, 1990; G W Einstein Company, Inc, NY, 1991

PRINTERS: Steven Miller, NY (SM)
PUBLISHERS: G W Einstein & Co, NY (GWE)
GALLERIES: G W Einstein Company, Inc, New York, NY
MAILING ADDRESS: 184 E Seventh St, New York, NY 10003

TITLE	PUBLISHER	PRINTER	DATE	MEDIUM	DIMENSION (PAPER SIZE) IN INCHES	TYPE OF PAPER	EDITION NUMBER	NO. OF COLORS	ORIGINAL OPENING PRICE	CURRENT RETAIL PRICE
SOLD OUT EDITIONS (RARE):										
True Ghost Stories	GWE	SM	1981	HC/LB	16 X 20	R/BFK	25		300	500

CLAIRE FALKENSTEIN

BORN: Coos Bay, OR
EDUCATION: Univ of California, Berkeley, CA
RECENT EXHIB: Utah State Univ, Nora Eccles Harrison Mus of Art, Logan, UT, 1989; Coos Art Mus, Coos Bay, OR, 1989

COLLECTIONS: Addison Gallery of Am Art, Andover, MA; Baltimore Mus of Art, MD; Guggenheim Mus, NY; Los Angeles Mus of Art, CA
PRINTERS: Smith Andersen Gallery, Palo Alto, CA (3EP)
PUBLISHERS: Smith Andersen Gallery, Palo Alto, CA (3EP)
GALLERIES: Tortue Gallery, Santa Monica, CA; Jack Rutberg Fine Arts, Los Angeles, CA; Smith Andersen Gallery, Palo Alto, CA; Anita Shapolsky Gallery, New York, NY
MAILING ADDRESS: 719 Ocean Front Walk, Venice, CA 90291

TITLE	PUBLISHER	PRINTER	DATE	MEDIUM	DIMENSION (PAPER SIZE) IN INCHES	TYPE OF PAPER	EDITION NUMBER	NO. OF COLORS	ORIGINAL OPENING PRICE	CURRENT RETAIL PRICE
SOLD OUT EDITIONS (RARE):										
Fiori (Set of 3)			1968	LC	26 X 16 EA	AP	60 EA		500 SET	3000 SET
Lively Moment	3EP	3EP	1981	EB/A	25 X 30	AP	9		600	850
Allegory IV	3EP	3EP	1981	EB	30 X 23	AP	24	1	400	600
Allegory V	3EP	3EP	1981	EB	37 X 25	AP	16	1	500	750
Allegory VI	3EP	3EP	1982	EB	42 X 56	AP	6	1	2000	3000

DONALD FARNSWORTH

PRINTERS: Magnolia Editions, Oakland, CA (MaEd)
PUBLISHERS: Magnolia Editions, Oakland, CA (MaEd)
GALLERIES: Walter/White Fine Arts, Carmel, CA; Brendan Walter Gallery, Santa Monica, CA; Joanne Warfield Gallery, Los Angeles, CA

TITLE	PUBLISHER	PRINTER	DATE	MEDIUM	DIMENSION (PAPER SIZE) IN INCHES	TYPE OF PAPER	EDITION NUMBER	NO. OF COLORS	ORIGINAL OPENING PRICE	CURRENT RETAIL PRICE
CURRENT EDITIONS:										
Counterpoint/Baptistry I, II (Dipt)	MaEd	MaEd	1988	LC/HC	30 X 22 EA	Abaca	100 EA		1400 SET	1800 SET

MARY FAULCONER (FULLERTON)

BORN: Pittsburgh, PA
EDUCATION: Philadelphia Mus Sch of Art, PA
TEACHING: Instr, Philadelphia Mus Sch of Art, PA, 1936–40
AWARDS: Distinctive Merit Awards, 1954,57,61; Silver Medal Awards, 1958,59; Art Director's Club, Gold Medal, Am Rose Soc, 1978

PRINTERS: American Atelier, NY (AA)
PUBLISHERS: Circle Fine Art, Chicago, IL (CFA)
GALLERIES: ACA Galleries, New York, NY; Circle Galleries, San Diego, CA & San Francisco, CA & Northbrook, IL & Pittsburgh, PA & Houston, TX & Soho, NY & Chicago, IL & Scottsdale, AZ & Beverly Hills, CA & Costa Mesa, CA & Sherman Oaks, CA & Palm Beach, FL & Honolulu, HI & New Orleans, LA & Las Vegas, NV & Seattle, WA; Ro Gallery Image Makers, Inc, New York, NY

TITLE	PUBLISHER	PRINTER	DATE	MEDIUM	DIMENSION (PAPER SIZE) IN INCHES	TYPE OF PAPER	EDITION NUMBER	NO. OF COLORS	ORIGINAL OPENING PRICE	CURRENT RETAIL PRICE
CURRENT EDITIONS:										
Sag Harbor Antique Shop	CFA	AA	1982	LC	25 X 23	AP	250		250	275

FRANK FAULKNER

BORN: Sumter, NC; July 27, 1946
EDUCATION: Univ of North Carolina, Chapel Hill, NC, BFA, 1968, MFA, 1972
AWARDS: Nat Endowment for the Arts Grants, 1975,76; North Carolina Architects Award, 1976
COLLECTIONS: Hirshhorn Mus, Wash, DC; Nat Coll of Fine Arts, Wash, DC; Albright-Knox Art Gallery, Buffalo, NY; Smith Col, Northampton, MA

PRINTERS: Solo Press, NY (SP); Anthony Kirk, NY (AK); Eldindean Press, NY (Eld)
PUBLISHERS: Judith Solodkin, NY (JS); Tracey Register, NY (TR); Arnie Samet, NY (AS); Cinda Sparling, NY (CS); Solo Press, NY (SP); Associated American Artists, NY (AAA); Artist (ART)
GALLERIES: Monique Knowlton Gallery, New York, NY; Davis-McClain Galleries, Houston, TX; Roy Boyd Gallery, Chicago, IL; Jerald Melberg Gallery, Charlotte, NC; Associated American Artists, New York, NY; Hodges Taylor Gallery, Charlotte, NC; Marita Gilliam Gallery, Raleigh, NC
MAILING ADDRESS: 150 W 26th St, New York, NY 10001

TITLE	PUBLISHER	PRINTER	DATE	MEDIUM	DIMENSION (PAPER SIZE) IN INCHES	TYPE OF PAPER	EDITION NUMBER	NO. OF COLORS	ORIGINAL OPENING PRICE	CURRENT RETAIL PRICE
CURRENT EDITIONS:										
Mirror (Set of 46 Unique Proofs)	ART/SP	JS/TR/AS/CS	1983	EMB/PEN/WA	42 X 48	AP	1 EA	Varies	2500	3500
Matrix	AAA	AK/Eld	1987	EB/HC/CC	25 X 31	MOR/SOM	50		1000	1500

ROY FAIRCHILD-WOODARD

BORN: Surrey, England; 1953
RECENT EXHIB: Gallery Kisha, Osaka, Japan, 1993; Centre Gallery, Glasgow, Scotland, 1993; Gallery Grand Prix Art, Osaka, Japan; Wentworth Gallery, Palm Beach, FL, 1993
PRINTERS: London Contemporary Art, Inc, London, England (LCA)
PUBLISHERS: London Contemporary Art, Inc, Prospect Heights, IL & London, England (LCA)
GALLERIES: Gallery Kisha, Osaka, Japan; Centre Gallery, Glasgow, Scotland; Gallery Grand Prix Art, Osaka, Japan; Wentworth Gallery, Palm Beach, FL; Artists' Den, Valparaiso, IN
MAILING ADDRESS: c/o London Contemporary Art, Inc, 729 Pinecrest, Prospect Heights, IL 60070

Roy Fairchild-Woodard
Anna
Courtesy London Contemp Art, Inc

Roy Fairchild-Woodard
Bright Colours
Courtesy London Contemp Art, Inc

TITLE	PUBLISHER	PRINTER	DATE	MEDIUM	DIMENSION (PAPER SIZE) IN INCHES	TYPE OF PAPER	EDITION NUMBER	NO. OF COLORS	ORIGINAL OPENING PRICE	CURRENT RETAIL PRICE
SOLD OUT EDITIONS (RARE):										
Quiet Moment	LCA	LCA	1990	SP	22 X 31	AP	350		350	1200
Muse	LCA	LCA	1990	SP	26 X 18	AP	350		350	900
Backstage I, II	LCA	LCA	1990	SP	16 X 11 EA	AP	350 EA		275 EA	600 EA
Study in Green	LCA	LCA	1990	SP	35 X 24	AP	350		450	1400
Music Room	LCA	LCA	1990	SP	34 X 24	AP	350		450	1200
Blue Flowers	LCA	LCA	1990	SP	19 X 14	AP	350		275	700
White Lilies	LCA	LCA	1990	SP	19 X 14	AP	350		275	700
Reminiscence	LCA	LCA	1990	SP	35 X 24	AP	350		450	900
Red Dress	LCA	LCA	1990	SP	28 X 25	AP	350		450	1400
Dejeuner	LCA	LCA	1991	SP	35 X 24	AP	350		500	1400
Pink Roses	LCA	LCA	1991	SP	30 X 24	AP	350		500	1400
Peonies	LCA	LCA	1991	SP	19 X 14	AP	350		325	700
Fan & Flowers	LCA	LCA	1991	SP	19 X 14	AP	350		325	700
La Fenetre I, II	LCA	LCA	1991	SP	22 X 16 EA	AP	350 EA		350 EA	800 EA
Cafe Cresp	LCA	LCA	1991	SP	37 X 28	AP	350	51	600	1600
Red Flowers	LCA	LCA	1991	SP	26 X 35	AP	350	51	500	1500
Tristesse	LCA	LCA	1992	SP	38 X 30	AP	350		500	1600
Girl with Lilies	LCA	LCA	1992	SP	27 X 36	AP	350	45	500	1100
Nude with Gold	LCA	LCA	1992	AC	31 X 24	AP	350		500	1500
Golden Flowers	LCA	LCA	1992	SP	27 X 34	AP	350	46	700	1300
Fleur Rouges I	LCA	LCA	1992	SP	26 X 21	AP	350	42	500	900
Fleurs Rouges II	LCA	LCA	1992	SP	26 X 21	AP	350	38	500	900
Girl Undressing	LCA	LCA	1992	AC	31 X 24	AP	300	12	700	1500
Anna	LCA	LCA	1992	SP	28 X 22	AP	350	56	500	1200
Bright Colours	LCA	LCA	1992	SP	28 X 22	AP	350	56	500	1200
Jeunesse	LCA	LCA	1992	SP	41 X 29	AP	350		700	1600
Bal Masque	LCA	LCA	1992	SP	33 X 38	AP	350	62	900	2000
White Flowers	LCA	LCA	1992	SP	32 X 40	AP	350	52	800	1700

ROY FAIRCHILD-WOODARD CONTINUED

TITLE	PUBLISHER	PRINTER	DATE	MEDIUM	DIMENSION (PAPER SIZE) IN INCHES	TYPE OF PAPER	EDITION NUMBER	NO. OF COLORS	ORIGINAL OPENING PRICE	CURRENT RETAIL PRICE
SOLD OUT EDITIONS (RARE):										
Masquerade	LCA	LCA	1993	SP	35 X 52	AP	350	67	1500	3400
Gift of Keys	LCA	LCA	1993	SP	35 X 40	AP	350		1100	1500
CURRENT EDITIONS:										
Veronique	LCA	LCA	1991	SP	36 X 26	AP	350	48	500	900
Sitting Nude	LCA	LCA	1993	AC	30 X 24	AP	350	12	700	1200
Murano Memories I, II	LCA	LCA	1993	SP	22 X 30 EA	AP	350 EA		700 EA	900 EA
Writing on Walls	LCA	LCA	1993	SP	38 X 29	AP	350		900	900

Roy Fairchild-Woodard
White Flowers
Courtesy London Contemp Art, Inc

GEORGE GROSZ

BORN: Berlin, Germany; (1893–1959)
EDUCATION: Royal Saxon Acad of Fine Art, Dresden, Germany, 1909–11; Sch of Fine & Applied Arts, Berlin, Germany, 1911; Acad Colarassi, Paris, France, 1913
AWARDS: Guggenheim Found Fel, 1937; Carol H Beck Gold Medal Award, Pennsylvania Acad of Fine Arts, Phila, PA, 1940; Second Prize, Carnegie Inst, Pittsburgh, PA, 1945
RECENT EXHIB: Florida Gulf Coast Art Center, Belleair, FL, 1992; Hecksher Mus, Huntington, NY
COLLECTIONS: Whitney Mus of Am Art, NY; Mus of Mod Art, NY; Art Inst of Chicago, IL; Newark Mus, NJ; Cleveland Mus of Art, OH; Mus of Fine Arts, Boston, MA; Detroit Inst of Art, MI; Harvard Univ, Cambridge, MA; Huntington Mus, NY; Berlin Nat Gallery, Germany; Stuttgart Mus, Germany

PRINTERS: Artist (ART)
PUBLISHERS: Artist (ART); Associated American Artists, NY (AAA)
GALLERIES: Worthington Gallery, Chicago, IL; Alice Adam, Ltd, Chicago, IL; Sheldon Ross Gallery, Birmingham, MI; William R Davis Fine Arts, New York, NY; Rosenfeld Fine Arts, New York, NY; Simon/Newman Gallery, New York, NY; Soufer Gallery, New York, NY; Gallery 609, Lakewood, CO; Richard A Cohn, Ltd, New York, NY; Kimmel/Cohn Photography Arts, New York, NY; Lafayette Parke Gallery, New York, NY; La Boetie, Inc, New York, NY

TITLE	PUBLISHER	PRINTER	DATE	MEDIUM	DIMENSION (PAPER SIZE) IN INCHES	TYPE OF PAPER	EDITION NUMBER	NO. OF COLORS	ORIGINAL OPENING PRICE	CURRENT RETAIL PRICE
SOLD OUT EDITIONS (RARE):										
Das Ende	ART	ART	1917	LB	11 X 8	WOVE	100	1	25	700
Volkommene Menschen	ART	ART	1920	LB	11 X 9	WOVE	125	1	35	3000
Schaferstundchen	ART	ART	1921	LB	11 X 8	WOVE	77	1	40	900
Married Couple	ART	ART	1922	LB	17 X 14	WOVE	40	1	50	2200
Selbtbildnismit Hund Vor...	ART	ART	1925	LB	16 X 12	WOVE	40	1	60	1500
Self Portrait with Dog	ART	ART	1925	LB	16 X 12	WOVE	40	1	60	1500
Bagdad-on-the-Subway (Set of 6)	ART	ART	1933	LC	17 X 12 EA	WOVE	150 EA	1 EA	400 SET	10000 SET
The End of a Perfect Day	AAA	ART	1939	DPT	10 X 13	WOVE	250	1		700

CHARLES FAZZINO

BORN: Westchester County, NY; 1955
EDUCATION: Sch of Visual Arts, NY, BFA, 1955; Parsons Sch of Design, NY
PRINTERS: Fine Art Press, MA (FAP); Color, Inc, OH (CI)
PRINTERS: Andrea Ruoff Art Associates, Ltd, Fort Lee, NJ (ARAAL)
COLLECTIONS: United Nations Coll, NY; Rockefeller Center Col, NY; Mummers Mus, Phila, PA; Metropolitan Opera Guild & Lincoln Center, NY
GALLERIES: Legends of Art, Las Vegas, NV; Renjeau Galleries, Natick, MA; Collection Fine Art, Kailua-Kona, HI; Art Show, West Bloomfield, MI; O J Art, New York, NY; Leslie Fine Art, Scottsdale, AZ; Art Collection, Key West, FL

Charles Fazzino
A Night on Broadway
Courtesy Andrea Ruoff Art Associates, Ltd

TITLE	PUBLISHER	PRINTER	DATE	MEDIUM	DIMENSION (PAPER SIZE) IN INCHES	TYPE OF PAPER	EDITION NUMBER	NO. OF COLORS	ORIGINAL OPENING PRICE	CURRENT RETAIL PRICE
SOLD OUT EDITIONS (RARE):										
Washington Square Park	ARAAL	CI	1984	3-D/MM/LC	7 X 9 X ¼	COV/MB	200	Varies	75	500
New York City	ARAAL	CI	1986	3-D/MM/LC	7 X 9 X ¼	COV/MB	200	Varies	100	500
Greenwich Village	ARAAL	FAP	1986	3-D/SP	18 X 22 X ¼	COV/MB	150	Varies	300	1800
Broadway Nights	ARAAL	FAP	1986	3-D/MM/LC	9 X 7 X ¼	COV/MB	200	Varies	100	500
Broadway I	ARAAL	FAP	1986	3-D/SP	18 X 22 X ¼	COV/MB	150	Varies	300	1800
Broadway II	ARAAL	FAP	1987	3-D/SP	18 X 22 X ¼	COV/MB	200	Varies	390	1800
Lincoln Center	ARAAL	CI	1987	3-D/MM/LC	7 X 9 X ¼	COV/MB	200	Varies	100	500
Coney Island	ARAAL	CI	1987	3-D/MM/LC	7 X 9 X ¼	COV/MB	200	Varies	100	500
Baseball	ARAAL	CI	1987	3-D/MM/LC	7 X 9 X ¼	COV/MB	200	Varies	100	500
On Broadway	ARAAL	CI	1987	3-D/MM/LC	7 X 9 X ¼	COV/MB	400	Varies	100	500
Only in New York	ARAAL	CI	1987	3-D/MM/LC	7 X 9 X ¼	COV/MB	475	Varies	150	500
New York, New York	ARAAL	FAP	1987	3-D/SP	18 X 22 X ¼	COV/MB	200	Varies	390	1800
City Promenade	ARAAL	FAP	1987	3-D/SP	24 X 32 X ¼	COV/MB	200	Varies	500	2000
Sun and Fun	ARAAL	FAP	1988	3-D/SP	19 X 25 X ¼	COV/MB	200	Varies	425	500
Ski, Ski, Ski	ARAAL	FAP	1988	3-D/SP	29 X 33 X ¼	COV/MB	200	Varies	600	1800
San Francisco	ARAAL	CI	1988	3-D/MM/LC	13 X 19 X ¼	COV/MB	200	Varies	180	900
Village Parade	ARAAL	CI	1988	3-D/MM/LC	13 X 11 X ¼	COV/MB	350	Varies	180	280
Tennis	ARAAL	CI	1988	3-D/MM/LC	7 X 9 X ¼	COV/MB	200	Varies	150	500
Hollywood	ARAAL	CI	1988	3-D/MM/LC	7 X 9 X ¼	COV/MB	475	Varies	150	500
Godzilla, It's Kong!	ARAAL	CI	1988	3-D/MM/LC	7 X 9 X ¼	COV/MB	475	Varies	150	190
Golfing ?	ARAAL	CI	1988	3-D/MM/LC	7 X 9 X ¼	COV/MB	475	Varies	150	500
Rock and Roll	ARAAL	CI	1988	3-D/MM/LC	7 X 9 X ¼	COV/MB	475	Varies	150	500
Philly by Night	ARAAL	CI	1988	3-D/MM/LC	7 X 9 X ¼	COV/MB	200	Varies	150	500
Atlantic City	ARAAL	CI	1988	3-D/MM/LC	7 X 9 X ¼	COV/MB	200	Varies	150	500
Wall Street	ARAAL	FAP	1988	3-D/SP	25 X 30 X ¼	COV/MB	200	Varies	450	2800
Crossing Houston Street	ARAAL	FAP	1989	3-D/SP	23 X 34 X ¼	COV/MB	200	Varies	600	2800
Broadway I, Ser 2	ARAAL	FAP	1989	3-D/SP	13 X 11 X ¼	COV/MB	50	Varies	300	800
A Night on Broadway	ARAAL	CI	1989	3-D/SP	28 X 36 X ¼	COV/MB	250	Varies	600	3000
Evening at the Met	ARAAL	CI	1989	3-D/MM/LC	9 X 7 X ¼	COV/MB	475	Varies	160	500
Only in the Subway	ARAAL	FAP	1989	3-D/SP	14 X 34 X ¼	COV/MB	250	Varies	500	1800
Our Town, DC	ARAAL	CI	1989	3-D/MM/LC	13 X 11 X ¼	COV/MB	350	Varies	225	800
Just Boston	ARAAL	CI	1989	3-D/MM/LC	10 X 11 X ¼	COV/MB	475	Varies	230	900
Viva Las Vegas	ARAAL	FAP	1990	3-D/SP	24 X 30 X ¼	COV/MB	250	Varies	600	650
Dancing on Delancey	ARAAL	FAP	1990	3-D/SP	28 X 36 X ¼	COV/MB	350	Varies	600	2800
Regards from B-Way	ARAAL	FAP	1990	3-D/SP	36 X 28 X ¼	COV/MB	350	Varies	800	3000
I Luv LA	ARAAL	FAP	1990	3-D/SP	30 X 25 X ¼	COV/MB	200	Varies	600	1200
Stock Exchange	ARAAL	FAP	1990	3-D/MM/LC	10 X 12 X ¼	COV/MB	475	Varies	225	800
I'll Take Manhattan	ARAAL	FAP	1991	3-D/SP	36 X 28	COV/MB	350	Varies	850	2600
My Kind of Town	ARAAL	CI	1990	3-D/MM/LC	13 X 10 X ¼	COV/MB	475	Varies	230	300
Fireworks Over Baltimore	ARAAL	CI	1990	3-D/MM/LC	10 X 14 X ¼	COV/MB	475	Varies	230	280
Going Up Town	ARAAL	CI	1990	3-D/MM/LC	7 X 9 X ¼	COV/MB	475	Varies	160	500
Batters Up	ARAAL	CI	1990	3-D/MM/LC	7 X 9 X ¼	COV/MB	475	Varies	160	220
Hooray! New York	ARAAL	CI	1990	3-D/MM/LC	7 X 9 X ¼	COV/MB	475	Varies	160	500
Off Broadway	ARAAL	CI	1990	3-D/MM/LC	9 X 7 X ¼	COV/MB	475	Varies	160	500
Ooh-La-La, Paris	ARAAL	CI	1991	3-D/MM/LC	13 X 9 X ¼	COV/MB	475	Varies	240	800
Rockefeller Center	ARAAL	CI	1991	3-D/MM/LC	13 X 9 X ¼	COV/MB	475	Varies	240	280
On the Green	ARAAL	CI	1991	3-D/MM/LC	9 X 7 X ¼	COV/MB	475	Varies	170	190
Whats to Nosh	ARAAL	FAP	1991	3-D/SP	9 X 11 X ¼	COV/MB	475	Varies	280	900
The Great White Way	ARAAL	FAP	1991	3-D/SP	32 X 44 X ¼	COV/MB	50	Varies	600	1850
Broadway Bound	ARAAL	FAP	1991	3-D/SP	10 X 14 X ¼	COV/MB	475	Varies	280	800
Crazy about Broadway	ARAAL	FAP	1992	3-D/SP	14 X 10 X ¼	COV/MB	50	Varies	290	800
Remembering '60's TV	ARAAL	FAP	1992	3-D/SP	22 X 28 X ¼	COV/MB	400	Varies	800	2000
Bargains on Orchard Street	ARAAL	FAP	1992	3-D/SP	28 X 36 X ¼	COV/MB	50	Varies	1200	2200

CHARLES FAZZINO CONTINUED

TITLE	PUBLISHER	PRINTER	DATE	MEDIUM	DIMENSION (PAPER SIZE) IN INCHES	TYPE OF PAPER	EDITION NUMBER	NO. OF COLORS	ORIGINAL OPENING PRICE	CURRENT RETAIL PRICE
CURRENT EDITIONS:										
Philly by Day	ARAAL	CI	1989	3-D/MM/LC	9 X 7 X ¼	COV/MB	475	Varies	160	190
I Luv Football	ARAAL	CI	1989	3-D/MM/LC	7 X 9 X ¼	COV/MB	475	Varies	160	190
Little Chinatown	ARAAL	CI	1989	3-D/MM/LC	7 X 6 X ¼	COV/MB	475	Varies	160	190
Coney Baloney	ARAAL	CI	1989	3-D/MM/LC	9 X 7 X ¼	COV/MB	475	Varies	160	190
Out West	ARAAL	CI	1989	3-D/MM/LC	9 X 7 X ¼	COV/MB	475	Varies	160	190
City Silhouette	ARAAL	FAP	1990	3-D/SP	7 X 22 X ¼	COV/MB	200	Varies	250	350
Kangaroo Court	ARAAL	FAP	1990	3-D/SP	25 X 30 X ¼	COV/MB	350	Varies	600	700
City Marathon	ARAAL	FAP	1990	3-D/MM/LC	12 X 10 X ¼	COV/MB	475	Varies	225	350
Miami Heat	ARAAL	CI	1990	3-D/MM/LC	10 X 12 X ¼	COV/MB	475	Varies	230	260
Invasion of Ginza (Tokyo)	ARAAL	CI	1990	3-D/MM/LC	13 X 9 X ¼	COV/MB	475	Varies	230	260
Life's a Horse Race	ARAAL	CI	1990	3-D/MM/LC	8 X 9 X ¼	COV/MB	475	Varies	160	190
Fat Tuesday (Mardi Gras)	ARAAL	CI	1990	3-D/MM/LC	6 X 7 X ¼	COV/MB	475	Varies	160	190
Bumper to Bumper	ARAAL	CI	1990	3-D/MM/LC	9 X 7 X ¼	COV/MB	475	Varies	160	190
Clowns	ARAAL	CI	1990	3-D/MM/LC	9 X 7 X ¼	COV/MB	475	Varies	170	190
Barefoot in the Park	ARAAL	CI	1990	3-D/MM/LC	9 X 7 X ¼	COV/MB	475	Varies	160	190
Lady Liberty	ARAAL	CI	1991	3-D/MM/LC	9 X 7 X ¼	COV/MB	475	Varies	170	190
Using Grannys Sauna	ARAAL	FAP	1991	3-D/SP	9 X 25 X ¼	COV/MB	200	Varies	300	350
London	ARAAL	CI	1991	3-DM/LC	13 X 10 X ¼	COV/MB	475	Varies	220	260
Bean Town (Boston)	ARAAL	FAP	1991	3-D/SP	17 X 27 X ¼	COV/MB	400	Varies	440	500
Gateway to New York	ARAAL	FAP	1991	3-D/SP	28 X 36 X ¼	COV/MB	400	Varies	650	950
Under the Boardwalk (Atlantic City)	ARAAL	FAP	1991	3-D/SP	21 X 27 X ¼	COV/MB	400	Varies	440	500
Brunch at the Met	ARAAL	FAP	1992	3-D/SP	28 X 36 X ¼	COV/MB	400	Varies	650	950
Best of Boca Raton	ARAAL	FAP	1992	3-D/SP	22 X 31 X ¼	COV/MB	400	Varies	440	700
I Left My Heart . . . (San Francisco)	ARAAL	FAP	1992	3-D/SP	31 X 24 X ¼	COV/MB	400	Varies	440	700
Hester Street	ARAAL	FAP	1992	3-D/SP	10 X 14 X ¼	COV/MB	475	Varies	290	350
Winter at the Met	ARAAL	FAP	1992	3-D/SP	10 X 14 X ¼	COV/MB	475	Varies		350
Motor City (Detroit, Michigan)	ARAAL	CI	1992	3-DM/LC	14 X 10 X ¼	COV/MB	475	Varies	220	280
Nashville Nights	ARAAL	CI	1992	3-DM/LC	9 X 11 X ¼	COV/MB	475	Varies	220	280
Vadeling at Vale	ARAAL	CI	1992	3-DM/LC	13 X 10 X ¼	COV/MB	475	Varies	220	280
City of Love (Paris)	ARAAL	FAP	1993	3-D/SP	30 X 24 X ¼	COV/MB	400	Varies	850	850
Desert Green (Golf)	ARAAL	FAP	1993	3-D/SP	21 X 32 X ¼	COV/MB	450	Varies	650	700
Greetings from NY	ARAAL	FAP	1993	3-D/SP	35 X 28 X ¼	COV/MB	450	Varies	1200	1200
South Beach (Miami)	ARAAL	FAP	1993	3-D/SP	23 X 33 X ¼	COV/MB	450	Varies	650	700
Stepping Out on Broadway	ARAAL	FAP	1993	3-D/SP	32 X 42 X ¼	COV/MB	450	Varies	1700	1750
Wedding Nite-New York	ARAAL	FAP	1993	3-D/SP	28 X 36 X ¼	COV/MB	450	Varies	1200	1200
90210 to Melrose (LA)	ARAAL	FAP	1993	3-D/SP	9 X 13 X ¼	COV/MB	475	Varies	350	350
Jerusalem	ARAAL	FAP	1993	3-D/SP	10 X 14 X ¼	COV/MB	475	Varies	350	350
Manhattan Mania	ARAAL	FAP	1993	3-D/SP	13 X 9 X ¼	COV/MB	475	Varies	350	350

HELMUT FEDERLE

RECENT EXHIB: Barbara Gladstone Gallery, NY, 1990

PRINTERS: Druckatelier Kurt Zein, Vienna, Austria (DKZ)
PUBLISHERS: Peter Blum Edition, NY (PBE)
GALLERIES: Barbara Gladstone Gallery, New York, NY; Donald Young Gallery, Seattle, WA

TITLE	PUBLISHER	PRINTER	DATE	MEDIUM	DIMENSION (PAPER SIZE) IN INCHES	TYPE OF PAPER	EDITION NUMBER	NO. OF COLORS	ORIGINAL OPENING PRICE	CURRENT RETAIL PRICE
CURRENT EDITIONS:										
5 + 1 (Set of 6)	PBE	DKZ	1989	I/EB/A/SG	30 X 21	ZER	35		7000 SET	10000 SET

FRED FEHLAU

BORN: Long Beach, CA; 1958
EDUCATION: Art Center, Pasadena, CA, BFA, MFA
RECENT EXHIB: Newport Harbor Art Mus, Newport Beach, CA, 1989; Burnett Miller Gallery, Los Angeles, CA, 1988,90; Miller/Nordenhake Gallery, Cologne, Germany, 1991; Tony Shafrazi Gallery, New York, NY

PRINTERS: Cirrus Editions Workshop, Los Angeles, CA (CEW)
PUBLISHERS: Cirrus Editions, Lrd, Los Angeles, CA (CE)
GALLERIES: Cirrus Gallery, Los Angeles, CA; Burnett Miller Galleries, Los Angeles, CA; Hope Weiss Fine Art, Los Angeles, CA; Miller/Nordenhake Gallery, Cologne, Germany, Tony Shafrazi Gallery, New York, NY.

TITLE	PUBLISHER	PRINTER	DATE	MEDIUM	DIMENSION (PAPER SIZE) IN INCHES	TYPE OF PAPER	EDITION NUMBER	NO. OF COLORS	ORIGINAL OPENING PRICE	CURRENT RETAIL PRICE
CURRENT EDITIONS:										
Between a Rock and a Hard Place (Inside/Outside) (Dipt) (464c)	CE	CEW	1991	SP	15 X 15 EA	R/BFK	30 EA		900 SET	1200 SET
Between a Rock and a Hard Place (Me/You) (Dipt) (468c)	CE	CEW	1991	SP	15 X 15 EA	R/BFK	30 EA		900 SET	1200 SET
Between a Rock and a Hard Place (Center (492c)	CE	CEW	1991	SP	15 X 15	R/BFK	30		450	750

ELEN FEINBERG

BORN: New York, NY; 1955
EDUCATION: Art Student's League, NY, 1972; Tyler Sch of Art, Rome, Italy, 1974–75; Cornell Univ, Ithaca, NY, BFA, 1976; Indiana Univ, Bloomington, IN, MFA, 1978
TEACHING: Indiana Univ, Bloomington, IN, 1976–78; Univ of New Mexico, Albuquerque, NM, 1978 to present
AWARDS: Artist in Res, Roswell Mus & Art Center, NM, 1985–86; MacDowell Colony Fel, Petersborough, NH, 1987; Nat Endowment for the Arts Fel, Painting, 1987; Faculty Res Grant, Albuquerque, NM, 1988; Award, Painting, Ingram Merrill Found, NY, 1988
RECENT EXHIB: Roswell Mus, Albuquerque, NM, 1987; Van Straaten Gallery, Chicago, IL, 1987; G W Einstein Gallery, NY, 1987; B Z Wagman Gallery, St Louis, MO, 1987; Zimmerman/Saturn Gallery, Nashville, TX, 1988; Mekler Gallery, Los Angeles, CA, 1988,89; Watson Gallery, Houston, TX, 1989; Ruth Siegel Gallery, NY, 1989; Contemporary Realist Gallery, San Francisco, CA, 1989; Fresno Art Mus, CA, 1989; Bill Bace Galleries, NY, 1990
COLLECTIONS: Albuquerque Mus, NM; Israel Mus, Jerusalem, Israel; Milwaukee Mus of Art, WI; Arizona State Univ Art Mus, Tempe, AZ; Los Angeles County Mus of Art, CA; Roswell Mus & Art Center, NM; Univ of California, Santa Cruz, CA
PRINTERS: Bob Chew, Albuquerque, NM (BC); Tamarind Inst, Albuquerque, NM (TI)
PUBLISHERS: Tamarind Inst, Albuquerque, NM (TI)
GALLERIES: Mekler Gallery, Los Angeles, CA; Roger Ramsay Gallery, Chicago, IL; B Z Wagman Gallery, St Louis, MO; Zimmerman/Saturn Gallery, Nashville, TN; Watson Gallery, Houston, TX; Tamarind Inst, Albuquerque, NM; Bill Bace Galleries, New York, NY
MAILING ADDRESS: 613 Ridge Place, NE, Albuquerque, NM 87106

Elen Feinberg
Exegesis I
Courtesy Tamarind Institute

Elen Feinberg
Fortuna's Song
Courtesy Tamarind Institute

TITLE	PUBLISHER	PRINTER	DATE	MEDIUM	DIMENSION (PAPER SIZE) IN INCHES	TYPE OF PAPER	EDITION NUMBER	NO. OF COLORS	ORIGINAL OPENING PRICE	CURRENT RETAIL PRICE
CURRENT EDITIONS:										
Fortuna's Song	TI	BC/TI	1984	LC	19 X 25	SOM/CR	40	4	200	275
Exegesis I	TI	BC/TI	1984	LC	19 X 25	MBD/CP	40	4	200	275

JEAN FEINBERG

BORN: New Rochelle, NY; 1948
EDUCATION: Skidmore Col, Saratoga Springs, NY, BS, 1970; Hunter Col, NY, MA, 1977
AWARDS: McDowell Colony, 1977; Edward Albee Found, 1979; Nat Endowment for the Arts Fel, 1978,83,89
RECENT EXHIB: Victoria Munroe Gallery, NY, 1988,89
PRINTERS: John Nichols, NY (JN)
PUBLISHERS: John Nichols, NY (JN)
GALLERIES: Rosa Esman Gallery, New York, NY; John Davis Gallery, Akron, OH; Victoria Munroe Gallery, New York, NY
MAILING ADDRESS: c/o Victoria Munroe Gallery, 415 W Broadway, New York, NY 10012

TITLE	PUBLISHER	PRINTER	DATE	MEDIUM	DIMENSION (PAPER SIZE) IN INCHES	TYPE OF PAPER	EDITION NUMBER	NO. OF COLORS	ORIGINAL OPENING PRICE	CURRENT RETAIL PRICE
CURRENT EDITIONS:										
Untitled '84	JN	JN	1984	WB	23 X 18	MUL	35	1	400	650

ROCHELLE H FEINSTEIN

BORN: New York, NY; 1946
EDUCATION: Pratt Inst, NY; Columbia Univ, NY
TEACHING: Univ of Minnesota, Minneapolis, MN
COLLECTIONS: Pratt Inst, NY; Cornell Univ, Ithaca, NY
PRINTERS: Patricia Branstead, NY (PB); Aeropress, NY (A); Atelier Ettinger, NY (AE)
PUBLISHERS: Fred Dorfman Inc, NY (FDI); Diane Villani Editions, NY (DVE)
GALLERIES: Fred Dorfman Gallery, New York, NY; Diane Villani Editions, New York, NY; Sorkin Gallery, New York, NY

The retail prices of the 100,000 limited edition prints quoted in this directory are subject to change. Print publishers, artists and galleries were the direct sources for these quotations. Prices in the secondary market listed as "Sold Out Editions (Rare)" indicate that the publisher has a limited supply of that print or that the print is difficult to locate in the galleries.

ROCHELLE H FEINSTEIN CONTINUED

TITLE	PUBLISHER	PRINTER	DATE	MEDIUM	DIMENSION (PAPER SIZE) IN INCHES	TYPE OF PAPER	EDITION NUMBER	NO. OF COLORS	ORIGINAL OPENING PRICE	CURRENT RETAIL PRICE
CURRENT EDITIONS:										
Able Baker	FDI	AE	1980	LC	25 X 32	AP	100	6	300	500
Fortune Hunter	FDI	AE	1980	LC	25 X 32	AP	100	6	300	500
Strange Fruits	FDI	AE	1980	LC	25 X 32	AP	100	6	300	500
Columbus & Isabella	FDI	AE	1980	LC	25 X 32	AP	100	2	250	500
Pink & Blue	DVE	PB/A	1981	WC	22 X 30	KOZO	50		300	600
Spuyteydyuil	DVE	PB/A	1982	WC	34 X 26	KOZO	20		300	600

LUIS FEITO

BORN: Madrid, Spain; 1929
EDUCATION: Instr, Drawing, Escuela de Bellas Artes de San Fernando, Madrid, Spain
AWARDS: Carnegie Prize, Pittsburgh, PA, 1961
COLLECTIONS: Alexandria Mus, Egypt; Helsinki Atheneum, Finland; Guggenheim Mus, NY; Houston Mus, TX; Albright-Knox Art Gallery, Buffalo, NY; Rio de Janeiro Mus, Brazil; Lissone Mus, Italy; Goteborg Mus, Sweden
PRINTERS: La Poligrafa, SA, Barcelona, Spain (LP)
PUBLISHERS: Ediciones Poligrafa, SA, Barcelona, Spain (EdP)
GALLERIES: Galeria Joan Prats, Barcelona, Spain & New York, NY; Michael Delecea Fine Art, New York, NY

TITLE	PUBLISHER	PRINTER	DATE	MEDIUM	DIMENSION (PAPER SIZE) IN INCHES	TYPE OF PAPER	EDITION NUMBER	NO. OF COLORS	ORIGINAL OPENING PRICE	CURRENT RETAIL PRICE
SOLD OUT EDITIONS (RARE):										
5 Polychrome Lithographs (Set of 5)	EdP	LP	1973	LC/PO	30 X 22 EA	GP	75 EA		750 SET / 180 EA	4500 SET / 900 EA
Variants (Set of 5)	EdP	LP	1973	LC/PO	30 X 22 EA	GP	75 EA		930 SET / 210 EA	4800 SET / 1000 EA

ALINE FELDMAN

BORN: Kansas; May 11, 1928
EDUCATION: Indiana Univ, Bloomington, IN, BS
COLLECTIONS: Johns Hopkins Univ, Baltimore, MD; US Embassy, Paris, France; Ottawa Art & State Building Program, Canada; US State Dept Art Coll, Montgomery County, MD
PRINTERS: Artist (ART); Juliana Netschert, Columbia, MD (JN)
PUBLISHERS: Artist (ART)
GALLERIES: Associated American Artists, New York, NY; Marsha Mateyka Gallery, Wash, DC; Mary Ryan Gallery, New York, NY; Callen McJunkin Gallery, Charleston, WV

TITLE	PUBLISHER	PRINTER	DATE	MEDIUM	DIMENSION (PAPER SIZE) IN INCHES	TYPE OF PAPER	EDITION NUMBER	NO. OF COLORS	ORIGINAL OPENING PRICE	CURRENT RETAIL PRICE
SOLD OUT EDITIONS (RARE):										
Neighborhood in Early Evening	ART	ART	1979	WC	17 X 41	OKP	10	9	200	350
Neighborhood in the Afternoon	ART	ART	1979	WC	17 X 41	OKP	10	14	200	350
At the Edge of the Neighborhood	ART	ART	1980	WC	30 X 32	OKP	10	24	200	350
Harpers Ferry Rain	ART	ART	1980	WC	24 X 32	OKP	25	23	350	425
Changing Land Forms	ART	ART	1980	WC	30 X 32	OKP	10	25	250	325
Yellow Sky	ART	ART	1980	WC	24 X 32	OKP	25	17	200	325
Shadows (Setting on the Land)	ART	ART	1981	WC	30 X 32	OKP	25	10	250	375
Nearing St. Louis	ART	ART	1981	WC	30 X 32	OKP	25	12	350	425
Looking over Illinois	ART	ART	1982	WC	18 X 24	OKP	25	14	225	300
Calligraphies of Night	ART	ART	1982	WC	18 X 24	OKP	25	18	200	300
CURRENT EDITIONS:										
City Evening	ART	ART/JN	1990	WC	50 X 32	OKP	25	63	1200	1500

FRANKLIN FELDMAN

BORN: New York, NY; November 12, 1927
EDUCATION: New York Univ, NY, AB, 1948; Columbia Law Sch, NY, LLB, 1951; Art Students League, NY, Pratt Graphic Center, Brooklyn, NY; New Sch for Social Research, NY
TEACHING: Columbia Law Sch, NY, 1979 to present
AWARDS: Sharon Creative Arts Found, CT, 1970; Yaddo Fel, Saratoga Springs, NY, 1983
COLLECTIONS: Nat Portrait Gallery, Smithsonian Inst, Wash, DC
PRINTERS: Emiliano Sorini, NY (ES); Galeria Fort, Barcelona, Spain; Timothy Ross, Englewood, NJ (TR); Artist (ART)
PUBLISHERS: Artist (ART)
MAILING ADDRESS: 15 W 81st St, New York, NY 10024

TITLE	PUBLISHER	PRINTER	DATE	MEDIUM	DIMENSION (PAPER SIZE) IN INCHES	TYPE OF PAPER	EDITION NUMBER	NO. OF COLORS	ORIGINAL OPENING PRICE	CURRENT RETAIL PRICE
CURRENT EDITIONS:										
Metamorphosis	ART	ART	1982	EB/A	22 X 15	AP	50	1	200	250
Head in Gray	ART	ART	1983	EB/A	11 X 8	AP	50	1	150	200
Thrust	ART	ART	1983	EB/WA	11 X 8	AP	50	2	150	200
Friendly	ART	ART	1983	EB/WA	11 X 8	AP	50	3	150	200

The retail prices of the 100,000 limited edition prints quoted in this directory are subject to change. Print publishers, artists and galleries were the direct sources for these quotations. Prices in the secondary market listed as "Sold Out Editions (Rare)" indicate that the publisher has a limited supply of that print or that the print is difficult to locate in the galleries.

ALAN EVAN FELTUS

BORN: Washington, DC; May 1, 1943
EDUCATION: Temple Univ, Tyler Sch of Fine Arts, Phila, PA, 1961–62; Cooper Union, NY, BFA, 1966; Yale Univ Art Sch, New Haven, CT, MFA, 1968
TEACHING: Dayton Art Inst, OH, 1968–70; American Univ, Wash, DC, 1972 to present
AWARDS: Painting Fel, Am Acad in Rome, Italy, 1970–72; Tiffany Found Grant, 1980; Nat Endowment for the Arts Individual Grant, 1981
RECENT EXHIB: Louis Newman Galleries, Beverly Hills, CA, 1992
COLLECTIONS: Hirshhorn Mus, Wash, DC; Oklahoma Art Center, Oklahoma City, OK; Dayton Art Inst, OH; Corcoran Gallery of Art, Wash, DC; Univ of Virginia Art Mus, Charlottesville, VA; Nat Mus of Am Art, Wash, DC; New Jersey State Mus, Newark, NJ
PRINTERS: Editions Press, San Francisco, CA (EP)
PUBLISHERS: Editions Press, San Francisco, CA (EP)
GALLERIES: Walton-Gilbert Galleries, San Francisco, CA; Forum Gallery, New York, NY; Louis Newman Gallery, Beverly Hills, CA
MAILING ADDRESS: c/o Forum Gallery, 1018 Madison Ave, New York, NY 10021

TITLE	PUBLISHER	PRINTER	DATE	MEDIUM	DIMENSION (PAPER SIZE) IN INCHES	TYPE OF PAPER	EDITION NUMBER	NO. OF COLORS	ORIGINAL OPENING PRICE	CURRENT RETAIL PRICE
SOLD OUT EDITIONS (RARE):										
Reflection	EP	EP	1980	LC	21 X 29	AC/W	60	8	525	750
Moment	EP	EP	1980	LC	22 X 30	AC/W	60	7	525	750
The Letter, State I	EP	EP	1981	LC	30 X 22	AC/W	30	4	475	750
The Window	EP	EP	1981	EC	21 X 26	GE/W	60	5	525	900
The Letter, State II	EP	EP	1981	LC	30 X 22	AC/W	30	4	475	750

MAX FERGUSON

BORN: New York, NY
EDUCATION: Gerit Reitveld Acad, Amsterdam, The Netherlands; New York Univ, NY, BS, 1980
COLLECTIONS: City of New York Mus, NY; New York Historical Society, NY; City of Amsterdam, The Netherlands
PRINTERS: Sabina Klein Studio, NY (SKS)
PUBLISHERS: John Szoke Graphics, Inc, NY (JSG)
GALLERIES: John Szoke Graphics, Inc, New York, NY; Gallery Henoch, New York, NY; Littlejohn-Smith Gallery, New York, NY

TITLE	PUBLISHER	PRINTER	DATE	MEDIUM	DIMENSION (PAPER SIZE) IN INCHES	TYPE OF PAPER	EDITION NUMBER	NO. OF COLORS	ORIGINAL OPENING PRICE	CURRENT RETAIL PRICE
CURRENT EDITIONS:										
Coney Island—Self-Portrait (50 Hand-Colored)	JSG	SKS	1991	EB/A	15 X 19	R/BFK	100	Varies	1000	1000
Coney Island III (50 Hand-Colored)	JSG	SKS	1991	EB/A	15 X 19	R/BFK	100	Varies	1000	1000

Max Ferguson
Coney Island—Self-Portrait
Courtesy John Szoke Graphics

Max Ferguson
Coney Island III
Courtesy John Szoke Graphics

AGUSTIN FERNANDEZ

BORN: Cuba; 1928
AWARDS: Castro Govt, Cuba Fel, 1959; Cintas, 1978
COLLECTIONS: Mus of Mod Art, NY; Detroit Inst of Art, IL; Library of Congress, Wash, DC; New York Public Library; Yale Univ, New Haven, CT; Worcester Art Mus, MA; Victoria and Albert Mus, London, England; Circulo de Bellas Artes, Maracaibo, Venezuela; Mus de Bellas Arte, Havana, Cuba; Patrick Lennan Found, Palm Beach, FL; Mus of Ponce, Puerto Rico; Univ of Austin Mus, TX; Mus of Cali, Colombia; Newark Mus, NJ
PUBLISHERS: London Arts, Inc, Detroit, MI (LAI)
GALLERIES: London Arts Gallery, Detroit, MI

TITLE	PUBLISHER	PRINTER	DATE	MEDIUM	DIMENSION (PAPER SIZE) IN INCHES	TYPE OF PAPER	EDITION NUMBER	NO. OF COLORS	ORIGINAL OPENING PRICE	CURRENT RETAIL PRICE
SOLD OUT EDITIONS (RARE):										
Armour	LAI		1979	SP/CO	30 X 22	AP	300	4	300	350
Midnight Blue	LAI		1979	SP/CO	30 X 22	AP	300	3	300	350

AGUSTIN FERNANDEZ CONTINUED

TITLE	PUBLISHER	PRINTER	DATE	MEDIUM	DIMENSION (PAPER SIZE) IN INCHES	TYPE OF PAPER	EDITION NUMBER	NO. OF COLORS	ORIGINAL OPENING PRICE	CURRENT RETAIL PRICE
CURRENT EDITIONS:										
Construction	LAI		1979	SP/CO	30 X 22	AP	300	6	300	350

ROBERTO GONZALES FERNANDEZ

BORN: Monteforte de Lemos, Lugo, Spain; 1948
EDUCATION: La Escuela Superior de Bellas, Artes de Madrid, Spain
RECENT EXHIB: Galeria Esti-Arte, Madrid, Spain, 1984
COLLECTIONS: Mus de Bellas Artes de La Coruna, Spain; Hunterian Art Gallery, Glasgow, Scotland; Edinburgh Art Centre, Scotland; Galeria de Arte Mod de Lubiana, Yugoslavia; Forbes Coll, NY
PRINTERS: Taller Don Herbert, Madrid, Spain (TDH)
PUBLISHERS: Esti-Arte Ediciones, SA, Madrid, Spain (EAE)
GALLERIES: Galerie Esti-Arte, Madrid, Spain; Ruth Siegel Gallery, New York, NY

TITLE	PUBLISHER	PRINTER	DATE	MEDIUM	DIMENSION (PAPER SIZE) IN INCHES	TYPE OF PAPER	EDITION NUMBER	NO. OF COLORS	ORIGINAL OPENING PRICE	CURRENT RETAIL PRICE
CURRENT EDITIONS:										
O Seda Que Despliegan	EAE	TDH	1983	LB	31 X 23	R/BFK	50	1	300	400
Como Bloque de Vida	EAE	TDH	1983	LB	31 X 23	R/BFK	50	1	300	400
Por la Sombra Antares (Dipt)	EAE	TDH	1983	LB	31 X 45	R/BFK	50	1	600	700
La Verdad de si Mismo (Dipt)	EAE	TDH	1983	LB	45 X 31	R/BFK	50	1	600	700
Por el Aire el Deseo (Dipt)	EAE	TDH	1983	LB	45 X 31	R/BFK	50	1	600	700
Como la Piel (Trip)	EAE	TDH	1983	LB	67 X 31	R/BFK	50	1	900	1000
Otro Vacio Estrechan (4 part Lithograph	EAE	TDH	1983	LB	61 X 45	R/BFK	50	1	1200	1350
Ternura sin Servicio	EAE	TDH	1983	LB	31 X 23	R/BFK	50	1	300	400
Me Sentiras	EAE	TDH	1983	LB	31 X 23	R/BFK	50	1	300	400
Un Hombre Con Su Amor	EAE	TDH	1983	LB	31 X 23	R/BFK	50	1	300	400
Si Todo Fuera Dicho	EAE	TDH	1983	LB	31 X 23	R/BFK	50	1	300	400
Mira Tambien Hacia Lo Lejos	EAE	TDH	1983	LB	31 X 23	R/BFK	50	1	300	400
Sus Matorrales de Desea	EAE	TDH	1983	LB	25 X 20	R/BFK	50	1	300	400
El Invisible Muro	EAE	TDH	1983	LB	20 X 25	R/BFK	50	1	300	400

RUDY M FERNANDEZ, JR

BORN: Trinidad, CO; September 21, 1948
EDUCATION: Univ of Colorado, Boulder, CO, BFA, 1974; Washington State Univ, Pullman, WA, MFA, 1977
AWARDS: Arizona Comm on the Arts, Visual Arts Award, Painting, 1981; Commemorative Poster, Scottsdale Center for the Arts, 1982
COLLECTIONS: Smithsonian Inst, Wash, DC; Univ of Arizona, Tucson, AZ
PRINTERS: Ernest F De Soto, San Francisco, CA (EDS); Ernest De Soto Workshop, San Francisco, CA (EDSW)
PUBLISHERS: Ernest De Soto Workshop, San Francisco, CA (EDSW); Elaine Horwitch Galleries, Santa Fe, NM (EHG); Sette Publishing Co, Tempe, AZ (SPC)
GALLERIES: Sette Publishing Co, Tempe, AZ; Ernest De Soto Workshop, San Francisco, CA; Elaine Horwitch Galleries, Scottsdale, AZ & Sedona, AZ & Palm Springs, CA & Santa Fe, NM; Natoli-Ross Gallery, Los Angeles, CA; Mill Street Gallery, Aspen, CO
MAILING ADDRESS: c/o Ernest DeSoto Workshop, 319 11th St, San Francisco, CA 94103

TITLE	PUBLISHER	PRINTER	DATE	MEDIUM	DIMENSION (PAPER SIZE) IN INCHES	TYPE OF PAPER	EDITION NUMBER	NO. OF COLORS	ORIGINAL OPENING PRICE	CURRENT RETAIL PRICE
CURRENT EDITIONS:										
Sangre de Vida (with Glitter & Metallic Tape Hearts)	EDS	EDS/EDSW	1985	LC	31 X 24	HMP	75	14	650	800
No Vale la Peña (with Wood & Tacks)	EDS	EDS/EDSW	1985	MM	30 X 23 X 6	HMP	50	17+	1500	1800

CAROLE JEANE FEUERMAN

BORN: Hartford, CT; September 21, 1945
EDUCATION: Hofstra Univ, NY, 1963; Temple Univ, Phila, PA, 1964; Sch of Visual Arts, NY, BFA, 1967
AWARDS: Am Inst of Graphic Arts, Cert of Excellence, 1979; Charles D Murphy Sculpture Award, 1981; Amelia Peabody Sculpture Award, 1982; First Prize, U S Nat Fine Arts Competition, Tallahassee, FL, 1984
RECENT EXHIB: Laura Larkin Gallery, Del Mar, CA, 1990; Larkin Gallery, Santa Monica, CA, 1990; Arneson Gallery, Vail, CO, 1990; Sync Gallery, Northampton, MA 1990; Gallery Henoch, NY, 1991,92
PRINTERS: Artist (ART)
PUBLISHERS: Artist (ART)
GALLERIES: Gallery Henoch, New York, NY; Ann Jaffe Gallery, Bay Harbor Islands, FL; Jaffe Baker Gallery, Boca Raton, FL
MAILING ADDRESS: 371 Sagamore Ave, Mineola, NY 11501

TITLE	PUBLISHER	PRINTER	DATE	MEDIUM	DIMENSION (PAPER SIZE) IN INCHES	TYPE OF PAPER	EDITION NUMBER	NO. OF COLORS	ORIGINAL OPENING PRICE	CURRENT RETAIL PRICE
SOLD OUT EDITIONS (RARE):										
Joe's Belly	ART	ART	1981	CP	16 X 16 X 8	CP	20		2000	2500
Leg Iron	ART	ART	1981	CP	16 X 26 X 8	CP	20		2000	2500

RAFAEL FERRER

BORN: Santurce, PR; 1933
EDUCATION: Syracuse Univ, NY, 1951–52; Univ of Puerto Rico, Mavaquez, PR, 1952–54
TEACHING: Instr, Philadelphia Col of Art, PA, 1967–77; Vis Prof, San Francisco Art Inst, CA, 1975; Instr, Sch of Visual Art, NY, 1978–80; Vis Prof, Univ of Pennsylvania, Phila, PA, 1984
AWARDS: Solomon Guggenheim Award, NY, 1975; Nat Endowment for the Arts Fel, 1972,78
RECENT EXHIB: Mangel Gallery, Phila, PA, 1988; Tatistcheff Gallery, Santa Monica, CA, 1989; Philbrook Art Center, Tulsa, OK, 1987,89; Miami-Dade Com Col, South Campus Art Gallery, Miami, FL, 1992; Nancy Hoffman Gallery, NY, 1988,89,90,92
COLLECTIONS: Mocha Mus of Contemp Hispanic Art, NY; Beaver Col Art Gallery, Glendale, PA; Museo de Bellas Artes, Inst of Puerto Rican Culture, Old San Juan, PR; Mus of Mod Art, NY; Philadelphia Art Mus, PA; Mus de Ponce, PR; Ackland Art Mus, Chapel Hill, NC; Albright-Knox Art Gallery, Buffalo, NY; Metroplitan Mus of Art, NY; Whitney Mus of Am Art, NY; Acad of Fine Arts, Phila, PA; Denver Art Mus, CO; Mus of Fine Arts, Richmond, VA
PRINTERS: Betty Winkler, NY (BEW); X Press, NY (XP); Claude Pigot, NY (CP); Yama Prints, NY (YP); Bill Weege (BW); Andrew Rubin (AR); Tandem Press, Univ of Wisconsin, Madison, WI (TanPr); Artist (ART); Bud Shark, Boulder, CO (BS); Matthew Christie, Boulder, CO (MC); Shark's Inc, Boulder, CO (SI)
PUBLISHERS: Betty Winkler, NY (BEW); Artist (ART); Yama Prints, NY (YP); Tandem Press, Univ of Wisconsin, Madison, WI (TanPr); Shark's Inc, Boulder, CO (SI)
GALLERIES: Nancy Hoffman Gallery, New York, NY; Betsy Rosenfield Gallery, Chicago, IL; Tavelli Williams Gallery, Aspen, CO; Mangel Gallery, Phila, PA; Shark's, Inc, Boulder, CO; Quartet Editions, New York, NY
MAILING ADDRESS: c/o Nancy Hoffman Gallery, 429 West Broadway, New York, NY 10012

Rafael Ferrer
El Sol Asombra
Courtesy Shark's, Inc

Rafael Ferrer
Mercado
Courtesy Shark's, Inc

TITLE	PUBLISHER	PRINTER	DATE	MEDIUM	DIMENSION (PAPER SIZE) IN INCHES	TYPE OF PAPER	EDITION NUMBER	NO. OF COLORS	ORIGINAL OPENING PRICE	CURRENT RETAIL PRICE
CURRENT EDITIONS:										
Plenilunio	ART/BW	BW/XP	1986	COL/CAR	22 X 30	SOM	20		800	3000
Autoretrato (Self-Portrait)	TanPr	BW/AR/TanPr	1988	WC	20 X 13	Goya	20	2	750	750
Amanecer Sobre el Cabo	TanPr	BW/AR/TanPr	1988	WC	22 X 26	AC/B	36	9	1200	1500
Oriente Tropical	TanPr	BW/AR/TanPr	1988	WC	35 X 22	RP/HWT/B	36	18	1500	2000
Tempestad #1	ART/YP	BEW/CP/YP	1988	AC	11 X 18	R/BFK	20	4	1000	2500
Tempestad #2	ART/YP	BEW/CP/YP	1988	AC	22 X 30	DIEU/HMP	16	5	1200	3000
Playa Bonita	ART/SI	BS/MC/SLL	1989	MON	48 X 32 EA	R/BFK/W	1 EA	Varies	4500 EA	4500 EA
Marea Baja	ART/SI	BS/MC/SLL	1989	MON	48 X 32 EA	R/BFK/W	1 EA	Varies	5000 EA	5500 EA
Silencio	ART/SI	BS/MC/SLL	1989	MON	30 X 45 EA	R/BFK/W	1 EA	Varies	4500 EA	4500 EA
Rincon de las Galeras	ART/SI	BS/MC/SLL	1989	MON	32 X 48 EA	R/BFK/W	1 EA	Varies	5000 EA	5500 EA
Delicia	ART/SI	BS/MC/SLL	1989	MON	30 X 20 EA	R/BFK/W	1 EA	Varies	2500 EA	2500 EA
Pescador	ART/SI	BS/MC/SLL	1989	MON	20 X 30 EA	R/BFK/W	1 EA	Varies	2500 EA	2500 EA
? Y Tu ?	ART/SI	BS/MC/SLL	1989	MON	20 X 30 EA	R/BFK/W	1 EA	Varies	2500 EA	3000 EA
Remos	ART/SI	BS/MC/SLL	1989	MON	20 X 30 EA	R/BFK/W	1 EA	Varies	2500 EA	2500 EA
Ansiedad	ART/SI	BS/MC/SLL	1989	MON	20 X 30 EA	R/BFK/W	1 EA	Varies	2500 EA	3000 EA
Sombrero	ART/SI	BS/MC/SLL	1989	MON	20 X 30 EA	R/BFK/W	1 EA	Varies	2500 EA	2500 EA
Paseo (Dipt)	ART/SI	BS/MC/SLL	1989	MON	30 X 40 EA	R/BFK/W	1 EA	Varies	4500 EA	4500 EA
Recodo (Cove) (Hand-Drawn)	ART/SI	BS/MC/ART/SLL	1989	LC/DRAW	32 X 40	R/BFK/W	25	7	2500	3000
Mercado	ART/SI	BS/MC/SLL	1989	LC	30 X 45	R/BFK/W	30	9	2000	2000
El Sol Asombra	ART/SI	BS/MC/SI	1990	MON	35 X 42 EA	R/BFK/W	1 EA	Varies	5500 EA	5500 EA
El Sol Asombra	ART/SI	BS/MC/SI	1990	LC	35 X 42	R/BFK/W	30	9	2500	2500 EA
En la Hamaca	ART/SI	BS/MS/SI	1990	MON	18 X 48 EA	R/BFK/W	1 EA	Varies	3000 EA	3000 EA
Rio Balata	ART/SI	BS/MS/SI	1990	MON	48 X 32 EA	R/BFK/W	1 EA	Varies	5500 EA	5500 EA
Lavanderas	ART/SI	BS/MS/SI	1990	MON	32 X 43 EA	R/BFK/W	1 EA	Varies	4500 EA	4500 EA
Piña Parada	ART/SI	BS/MS/SI	1990	MON	32 X 22 EA	R/BFK/W	1 EA	Varies	3000 EA	3000 EA
Piña en la Sombra	ART/SI	BS/MS/SI	1990	MON	48 X 31 EA	R/BFK/W	1 EA	Varies	3500 EA	3500 EA
Atardecor	ART/SI	BS/MS/SI	1990	MON	48 X 32 EA	R/BFK/W	1 EA	Varies	5000 EA	5000 EA
Piña Acostada	ART/SI	BS/MS/SI	1990	MON	30 X 22 EA	R/BFK/W	1 EA	Varies	3000 EA	3000 EA
Tres Piñas	ART/SI	BS/MS/SI	1990	MON	20 X 48 EA	R/BFK/W	1 EA	Varies	2500 EA	2500 EA
Cayena Amarilla	ART/SI	BS/MS/SI	1990	MON	18 X 22 EA	R/BFK/W	1 EA	Varies	2000 EA	2000 EA

RAFAEL FERRER CONTINUED

TITLE	PUBLISHER	PRINTER	DATE	MEDIUM	DIMENSION (PAPER SIZE) IN INCHES	TYPE OF PAPER	EDITION NUMBER	NO. OF COLORS	ORIGINAL OPENING PRICE	CURRENT RETAIL PRICE
CURRENT EDITIONS:										
Cayena Roja	ART/SI	BS/MS/SI	1990	MON	18 X 22	R/BFK/W	1 EA	Varies	2000 EA	2000 EA
Nadadora que Viene	ART/SI	BS/MS/SI	1990	MON	20 X 48 EA	R/BFK/W	1 EA	Varies	3000 EA	3000 EA
Me Vine	ART/SI	BS/MS/SI	1990	MON	30 X 22 EA	R/BFK/W	1 EA	Varies	2000 EA	2000 EA
Verduras	TanPr	BW/AR/TanPr	1990	WC	22 X 19	RP/HWT/B		25	1800	1800
Sosua III	ART/SI	BS/MS/SI	1991	MON	30 X 22 EA	R/BFK/W	1 EA	Varies	2000 EA	2000 EA
Sombrero de Palma	ART/SI	BS/MS/SI	1991	MON	30 X 22 EA	R/BFK/W	1 EA	Varies	2000 EA	2000 EA
La Ola I, II	ART/SI	BS/MS/SI	1991	MON	30 X 22 EA	R/BFK/W	1 EA	Varies	2000 EA	2000 EA
La Gallina	ART/SI	BS/MS/SI	1991	MON	30 X 22 EA	R/BFK/W	1 EA	Varies	2000 EA	2000 EA

RAINER FETTING

BORN: Wilhelmshaven, West Germany; December 31, 1949
EDUCATION: Hochscule der Kunste, Berlin, Germany, 1977; Columbia Univ, NY, 1978–79
COLLECTIONS: Mus Gegenwartskunst, Basel, Switzerland; Portland Art Mus, OR; Mus of Contemp Art, Sydney, Australia; Mus des Beaux Arts, Toulon, France
PRINTERS: Frank Copello Print Shop, NY (FCPS)
PUBLISHERS: Marlborough Graphics, Inc, NY (MG); Raab Galerie, Berlin, Germany (RG)
GALLERIES: Dolly Fiterman, Gallery Gallery, Minneapolis, MN; Dorsky Gallery, New York, NY; Marlborough Galleries, New York, NY & London, England

TITLE	PUBLISHER	PRINTER	DATE	MEDIUM	DIMENSION (PAPER SIZE) IN INCHES	TYPE OF PAPER	EDITION NUMBER	NO. OF COLORS	ORIGINAL OPENING PRICE	CURRENT RETAIL PRICE
CURRENT EDITIONS:										
Black Wolf	MG		1984	EC	35 X 45	AP	10		900	1500
Dog	MG		1984	EC	35 X 45	AP	10		900	1500
Face	MG		1984	EC	49 X 40	AP	10		900	1500
White Wolf	MG		1984	EC	35 X 45	AP	10		900	1000
Indian Suite (Set of 4)										
Indian I (Blue)	RG	FCPS	1992	AC/SL	46 X 32	AP	100	1	950	950
Indian II (Blue & Brown)	RG	FCPS	1992	AC/SL	46 X 32	AP	100	2	950	950
Indian III (Blue, Brown & Red)	RG	FCPS	1992	AC/SL	46 X 32	AP	100	3	950	950
Indian IV (Blue, Brown & Red Variation)	RG	FCPS	1992	AC/SL	46 X 32	AP	100	3	950	950

ROBERT W FICHTER

BORN: Fort Meyers, FL; 1939
EDUCATION: Univ of Florida, Gainesville, FL, BFA, Printmaking & Painting, 1963; Indiana Univ Bloomington, IN, MFA, 1966
TEACHING: Prof, Art, Florida State Univ, Tallahassee, FL, 1972 to present
AWARDS: Nat Endowment for the Arts Fel, Photog, 1979–80; Florida Arts Fel, Developing Sch Award, Florida State Univ, Tallahassee, FL, 1981–82; Nat Endowment for the Arts Fel, Photog, 1984
RECENT EXHIB: Univ of Connecticut, Atrium Gallery, Storrs, CT, 1992; Stetson Univ, Duncan Gallery of Art, Deland, FL, 1992; Univ of Northern Iowa, Cedar Falls, IA, 1992
COLLECTIONS: Mus of Fine Arts, Boston, MA; Minneapolis Inst of Art, MN; Los Angeles County Mus, CA; Australian Nat Gallery, Canberra, Australia; Nat Gallery of Canada, Ottawa, ON, Canada; Mus of Fine Arts, St Petersburg, FL; Pasadena Art Mus, CA; Princeton Univ Mus, NJ; George Eastman House, Rochester, NY; Center for Creative Photography, Tucson, AZ
PRINTERS: Craig Cornwall, Albuquerque, NM (CC); Beth Lovendusky, Albuquerque, NM (BL); Tamarind Inst, Albuquerque, NM (TI)
PUBLISHERS: Tamarind Inst, Albuquerque, NM (TI)
GALLERIES: Tamarind Inst, Albuquerque, NM
MAILING ADDRESS: 612 W Eighth Ave, Tallahassee, FL 32303/Florida State University, Tallahassee, FL 32306

Robert Fichter
Only Bones Has Looked on Beauty Bare
Courtesy Tamarind Institute

TITLE	PUBLISHER	PRINTER	DATE	MEDIUM	DIMENSION (PAPER SIZE) IN INCHES	TYPE OF PAPER	EDITION NUMBER	NO. OF COLORS	ORIGINAL OPENING PRICE	CURRENT RETAIL PRICE
CURRENT EDITIONS:										
Only Bones Has Looked on Beauty Bare (Hand-Printed with Photographic Element)	TI	CC/TI	1987	LC/HC	32 X 45	ARJ		9	750	850
Bones Dancing in the Dark	TI	BL/TI	1987	LC	24 X 28	SOM/CR	25	3	350	450
Fish in Water #1	TI	BL/TI	1987	LC	16 X 24	CHIRI	30	2	250	350

The retail prices of the 100,000 limited edition prints quoted in this directory are subject to change. Print publishers, artists and galleries were the direct sources for these quotations. Prices in the secondary market listed as "Sold Out Editions (Rare)" indicate that the publisher has a limited supply of that print or that the print is difficult to locate in the galleries.

JUD FINE

BORN: Los Angeles, CA; November 20, 1944
EDUCATION: Univ of California, Santa Barbara, CA, BA, 1966; Cornell Univ, Ithaca, NY, MFA, 1970
TEACHING: Assoc Prof, Art, Univ of Southern California, Los Angeles, CA, 1979 to present
AWARDS: Contemp Art Council, New Talent Grant, Los Angeles County Art Mus, CA, 1972; Laura Slobe Mem Award, Art Inst of Chicago, IL, 1974; Nat Endowment for the Arts Grant, Individual Artist Fel, 1982; California State Arts Council, Sculpture Comm, Exposition Park, Los Angeles, CA, 1983
RECENT EXHIB: Univ of California, Irvine, CA, 1987; Laguna Beach Mus of Art, CA, 1988
COLLECTIONS: Yale Univ, New Haven, CT; Mus of Contemp Art, Los Angeles, CA; Los Angeles County Art Mus, CA; Guggenheim Mus of Art, NY; La Jolla Mus of Contemp Art, CA; Power Inst of Fine Arts, Sydney, Australia; Minneapolis Inst of Art, MN
PUBLISHERS: Ronald Feldman Fine Arts, NY (RFFA)
GALLERIES: Ronald Feldman Fine Arts, New York, NY
MAILING ADDRESS: 329 Wolly, Carpinteria, CA 93013

TITLE	PUBLISHER	PRINTER	DATE	MEDIUM	DIMENSION (PAPER SIZE) IN INCHES	TYPE OF PAPER	EDITION NUMBER	NO. OF COLORS	ORIGINAL OPENING PRICE	CURRENT RETAIL PRICE
CURRENT EDITIONS:										
3.3.3./2.2./1.	RFFA		1975	SP	22 X 29	AP	100		500	800
Untitled (Equal Sign)	RFFA		1977	LB	22 X 30	AP	100	1	500	800
Untitled (Curved Arrow)	RFFA		1977	LB	22 X 30	AP	100	1	500	800
Untitled (Straight Arrow)	RFFA		1977	LB	22 X 30	AP	95	1	500	800
Untitled (Waving Line)	RFFA		1977	LB	22 X 30	AP	95	1	500	800

LEONOR FINI

BORN: Buenos Aires, Argentina; August 31, 1908
RECENT EXHIB: CFM, NY, 1988,90,92
TEACHING: Univ of Trieste, France
COLLECTIONS: Mus d'Arte Moderna, Rome, Italy; Mus des Beaux Arts, Grenoble, France; Musees Royaux des Beaux Arts, Brussels, Belgium; Mus of Fine Art, Lodz, Poland; Peggy Guggenheim Mus, Venice, Italy; Mus Nat d'Art Moderne, Centre Georges Pompidou, Paris, France
PRINTERS: Serigraphie Michel Caza, Francoville, France (SMC); Atelier d'Art Michel Caza, Paris, France (AMC); Maitre-Imprimeur Marchand, Paris, France (M-IM); Dietz-Offizin, Lengmoos-Soyen, Germany (DO); Alain Satie Atelier, Paris, France (ASA); Atelier Manequin, Paris, France, (AM)
PUBLISHERS: Editions d'Art Agori, Zürich, Switzerland (EdAA); Société des Amis Des Livres, Paris, France (SdAdL); E Navarra, NY (EN); Circle Fine Art Corp, Chicago, IL (CFA); Contemporary Art Masters, NY (CAM); Joseph Foret, Paris, France (JF); Proscinium Gallerie, Paris, France (PG); Ariane Lancell, Paris, France (AL); Galerie Bosquet, Paris, France (GB); Editions Alain Satie Arts, Paris, France (EASA); Relais d'Art, Zürich, Switzerland (RDA); Claude Tchou, Paris, France (CT)
GALLERIES: CFM Gallery, New York, NY; Circle Galleries, San Diego, CA & San Francisco, CA & Northbrook, IL & Pittsburgh, PA & Houston, TX & Soho, NY & Chicago, IL & Scottsdale, AZ & Beverly Hills, CA & Costa Mesa, CA & Sherman Oaks, CA & Palm Beach, FL & Honolulu, HI & New Orleans, LA & Las Vegas, NV & Seattle, WA; Short Hills Art Gallery, Short Hills, NJ; Professional Fine Arts Services, Inc, New York, NY

TITLE	PUBLISHER	PRINTER	DATE	MEDIUM	DIMENSION (PAPER SIZE) IN INCHES	TYPE OF PAPER	EDITION NUMBER	NO. OF COLORS	ORIGINAL OPENING PRICE	CURRENT RETAIL PRICE
SOLD OUT EDITIONS (RARE):										
La Galere (Set of 6)			1947	LB	9 X 13 EA	AP	80 EA	1 EA	300 SET	15000 SET
Le Sabbat Ressuscite (Set of 35)	SdAdl			EB	15 X 11 EA	R/BFK	105 EA	1 EA	1800 SET	35000 SET
L' Apocalypse Suite (Set of 3):									125 SET	25000 SET
L'Apparition de la Femme	JF	AM	1963	LC	15 X 18	R/BFK	7	7	50	8500
Le Combat des Anges	JF	AM	1963	LC	15 X 18	R/BFK	7	7	50	8500
La Bete de la Mer	JF	AM	1963	LC	15 X 18	R/BFK	7	7	50	8500
Juliette (from Marquis de Sade Series)			1965	EB	11 X 9	R/BFK	99	1	60	900
Tete de Jeune Fille			1970	LC	26 X 19	AP			75	1500
Woman at Sewing Machine			1970	LC	21 X 30	AP	250		75	1700
Young Woman with Flowers in Her Hair			1970	COL	12 X 16	AP			75	700
Monsieur Vénus	EdAA		1972	ENG	17 X 13	R/BFK	275		100	2000
Tete de Variations des Apparences (Head from Variations of Appearances)	EASA	ASA	1973	EC	21 X 27	R/BFK	280	3	300	1000
Vibrissa (Cat's Whisker)	CT	M-IM	1973	DPT	20 X 26	AP	250	1	150	1350
Der Paravent (the Screen) (Set of 8 Panels)	RDA	DO	1973	SP	20 X 60 EA	AP	120 EA	130 EA	2000 SET	35000 SET
Heliodora	PG		1974	LC	22 X 30	R/BFK	275	Full	600	2650
Le Temps de la Mue (Set of 20)	GB		1974	ENG	11 X 15 EA	R/BFK	230 EA			6000 SET
Le Temps de la Mue (Set of 16)	GB		1975	ENG	11 X 15 EA	R/BFK	185 EA			5000 SET
The Witch on the Broom	CAM	AMC	1975	EC	20 X 26	AP	175		225	1000
The Entire Afternoon	CAM	AMC	1975	EC	20 X 27	AP	175		300	1200
Tristan und Isolde (Metropolitan Suite #1)	CFA	SMC	1977	SP	22 X 30	AP	250	12	500	2500
La Machine a' Coudre (Sewing Machine)	CFA	AMC	1979	SP	30 X 21	R/BFK	250	19	575	1100
La Machine a' Coudre (Sewing Machine) (DE)	CFA	AMC	1979	SP	30 X 21	JP	25	19	595	1050
Untitled			1980	EC	17 X 15	R/BFK	280		450	1000
Harmonika Zig (The Train)	CFA	AMC	1980	SP	20 X 30	R/BFK	250	19	550	800
Harmonika Zig (The Train) (DE)	CFA	AMC	1980	SP	20 X 29	JP	25	19	600	850
Rafaela	CFA	AMC	1981	SP	23 X 18	R/BFK	250	14	600	800
Rafaela (DE)	CFA	AMC	1981	SP	23 X 18	JP	250	14	650	850

LEONOR FINI CONTINUED

TITLE	PUBLISHER	PRINTER	DATE	MEDIUM	DIMENSION (PAPER SIZE) IN INCHES	TYPE OF PAPER	EDITION NUMBER	NO. OF COLORS	ORIGINAL OPENING PRICE	CURRENT RETAIL PRICE
SOLD OUT EDITIONS (RARE):										
La Tenebrosa (Shadowy Figure)	CFA	AMC	1982	SP	29 X 21	R/BFK	275	12	650	850
CURRENT EDITIONS:										
Dimanche Apres-Midi (Sunday Afternoon)	AL		1982	SP	21 X 29	AP	100	Full	400	5500
Visage d'Emanuelle (Face of Emanuelle)	GB		1985	LC	20 X 29	AP	275	4	550	1300
Le Chats de Madame Helvetius (Set of 16)	EN		1985	ENG	17 X 11 EA	R/BFK			3000 SET	10000 SET

AARON FINK

BORN: Boston, MA; March 10, 1955
EDUCATION: Maryland Inst Col of Art, Baltimore, MD, BFA; Yale Univ, New Haven, CT, MFA; Skohegan Sch of Art, ME
AWARDS: Massachusetts Council of the Arts & Humanities Fel, 1984; Nat Endowment for the Arts Fel, 1982,87
RECENT EXHIB: Portland Art Mus, ME, 1987; Jack Shainman Gallery, Wash, DC, 1988; David Beitzel Gallery, NY, 1988; Hartje Gallery, Frankfurt, Germany, 1989; Alpha Gallery, Boston, MA, 1989;
COLLECTIONS: Mus of Mod Art, NY; Philadelphia Mus of Art, PA; Metropolitan Mus of Art, NY; Mus of Fine Arts, Boston, MA; Art Inst of Chicago, IL; New York Public Library, NY

PRINTERS: Herbert A Fox, Merrimac, MA (HF); Fox Graphics, Merrimac, MA (FG); James Stroud, Glouster, MA (JS); Center Street Studio, Glouster, MA (CSS)
PUBLISHERS: Fox Graphics, Merrimac, MA (FG); Artist (ART)
GALLERIES: Alpha Gallery, Boston, MA; American Grafitti Gallery, Amsterdam, The Netherlands, Fox Graphics, Merrimac, MA; Lisa Sette Gallery, Scottsdale, AZ; Sette & Segura Publishing Company, Tempe, AZ; David Beitzel Gallery, New York, NY; Experimental Workshop, San Francisco, CA; Janet Levitt Fine Arts, San Francisco, CA; Albertson-Paterson Gallery, Winter Park, FL; Axis Twenty, Inc, Atlanta, GA; Roger Ramsay Gallery, Chicago, IL
MAILING ADDRESS: 63 Maverick Square, East Boston, MA 02128

TITLE	PUBLISHER	PRINTER	DATE	MEDIUM	DIMENSION (PAPER SIZE) IN INCHES	TYPE OF PAPER	EDITION NUMBER	NO. OF COLORS	ORIGINAL OPENING PRICE	CURRENT RETAIL PRICE
CURRENT EDITIONS:										
Four Color Cherry	ART/FG	HF/FG	1981	LC	30 X 22	AP/W	60	4	150	500
Smoker	ART	JS/CSS	1984	I	37 X 30	AP	35	1	225	500
Coffee Drinker	ART	JS/CSS	1984	I	37 X 30	AP	35	1	225	500
Untitled (Man/Bust)	ART	JS/CSS	1984	I	37 X 30	AP	35	1	225	500
Untitled (Man/Bust with Graphite)	ART	JS/CSS	1985	I	37 X 30	AP	35	1	225	500
Untitled (Man Drinking)	ART	JS/CSS	1985	I	37 X 30	AP	35	1	225	500
Untitled (Man/Hat)	ART	JS/CSS	1985	I	37 X 30	AP	35	4	225	500
Untitled	EW	EW	1989	MON	16 X 12 EA	AC	1 EA	Varies	600 EA	1000 EA
Untitled	EW	EW	1989	MON	48 X 36 EA	AC	1 EA	Varies	2500 EA	3500 EA
Untitled	EW	EW	1989	MON	36 X 60 EA	AC	1 EA	Varies	3000 EA	4000 EA
Steaming Cup	EW	EW	1990	WC	42 X 32	AC	40	22	1800	2000

LARRY FINK (LAURENCE B)

BORN: Brooklyn, NY; March 1, 1941
PRINTERS: Artist (ART)
PUBLISHERS: Prestige Art Ltd, Mamaroneck, NY (PA)

GALLERIES: Alan Brown Gallery, Hartsdale, NY; Light Gallery, New York, NY; Sander Gallery, New York, NY; Ledel Gallery, New York, NY; Jeffrey Fuller Fine Art, Phila, PA; Lieberman & Saul Gallery, New York, NY; Burden Gallery, Aperture, New York, NY
MAILING ADDRESS: PO Box 295, Martins Creek, PA 18063

TITLE	PUBLISHER	PRINTER	DATE	MEDIUM	DIMENSION (PAPER SIZE) IN INCHES	TYPE OF PAPER	EDITION NUMBER	NO. OF COLORS	ORIGINAL OPENING PRICE	CURRENT RETAIL PRICE
CURRENT EDITIONS:										
82 Photographs (Each Print Limited to 100 Examples)	PA	ART	1974–82	PH	16 X 20 EA	CFB	30		20000 SET 400 EA	30000 SET 600 EA

PINO FINOCCHIARO

BORN: Catania, Italy

EDUCATION: Inst of Art, Catania, Italy; Inst of Art, Urbino, Italy
AWARDS: Ambrogino Award, City of Milan, Italy
PRINTERS: Stamperia d'Arte, Urbino, Italy (SdA)
PUBLISHERS: John Szoke Graphics, NY (JSG)
GALLERIES: John Szoke Graphics, New York, NY

TITLE	PUBLISHER	PRINTER	DATE	MEDIUM	DIMENSION (PAPER SIZE) IN INCHES	TYPE OF PAPER	EDITION NUMBER	NO. OF COLORS	ORIGINAL OPENING PRICE	CURRENT RETAIL PRICE
CURRENT EDITIONS:										
Collina	JSG	SdA	1983	EC	30 X 22	R/BFK	100	8	175	300
Chiusa	JSG	SdA	1983	EC	30 X 22	R/BFK	150	8	175	300
Artimino	JSG	SdA	1985	EC	22 X 30	R/BFK	50	8	175	300
Houses & Cypresses	JSG	SdA	1986	EC	22 X 30	R/BFK	100	8	175	300
Coral Drive	JSG	SdA	1986	EC	22 X 30	R/BFK	100	8	190	325

ERIC FISCHL

BORN: New York, NY; March 9, 1948
EDUCATION: California Inst of the Arts, Valencia, CA, BFA, 1972
RECENT EXHIB: Mary Boone Gallery, NY, 1987; Inst of Contemp Art, London, England, 1987; Los Angeles County Art Mus, CA, 1987; Sara Hilden Art Mus, Tampere, Finland, 1988; Hood Mus of Art, Hanover, MA, 1991; Mary Boone/Michael Werner, NY, 1988; Portsmouth Mus, VA, 1989; Univ of Colorado, Colorado Springs, CO, 1992; Univ of Maine Mus, Orono, ME, 1989,92; Guild Hall Mus, East Hampton, NY, 1992; Sch of Mus of Fine Arts, Barbara & Steven Grossman Gallery, Boston, MA; Michael Kohn Gallery, Santa Monica, CA, 1992; Galeria Soledad Lorenzo, Madrid, Spain, 1993
COLLECTIONS: Metropolitan Mus of Art, NY
PRINTERS: Aeropress, NY (A); Patricia Branstead, NY (PB); John Shera, NY (JS); Lori Haselrick, NY (LH); Peter Kneubühler, Zürich, Switzerland (PK); Aldo Crommelynck, Paris, France (AC); Atelier Crommelynck, Paris, France (AtC); Tadashi Toda (TT); Shunzo Matsuda (SM); Crown Point Press, San Francisco, CA (CPP); Color By Pergament, NY (CBP); Jennifer Melby, NY (JM); Dan Welden, Sag Harbor, NY (DW); Hampton Editions, Sag Harbor, NY (HEd)
PUBLISHERS: Corinthian Editions (Aeropress, Getler/Pall & van Straaten), NY (COR); Peter Blum Edition, NY (PBE); Crown Point Press, San Francisco, CA (CPP); Parasol Press, Ltd, NY (PaP); Koury Wingate, NY (KW); Artist (ART)
GALLERIES: van Straaten Galleries, Chicago, IL; Peter Blum Gallery, New York, NY; Mary Boone Gallery, New York, NY; Edward Thorp Gallery, New York, NY; Marian Goodman Gallery, New York, NY; Thomas Smith Fine Art, Fort Wayne, IN; Rubenstein/Diacono Gallery, New York, NY; Barbara Gladstone Gallery, New York, NY; J J Brookings Gallery, San Jose, CA; Opus Art Studios, Miami, FL; Nancy Singer Gallery, St Louis, MO; Ruth Harf, Great Neck, NY; Sondra Mayer, Great Neck, NY; Karen Amiel Modern & Contemporary Art, New York, NY; Crown Point Galleries, New York, NY & San Francisco, CA; Martina Hamilton Gallery, New York, NY; Jim Kempner Fine Art, New York, NY; Mary Ryan Gallery, New York, NY; Tomoko Liguori Gallery, New York, NY; Michael Kohn Gallery, Santa Monica, CA; Signet Arts, St Louis, MO; Green Gallery Miami, FL; Magnuson Gallery, Boston, MA; Katie Block Fine Art, Boston, MA; Sorrentino/Mayer Fine Art, New York, NY & Great Neck, NY; Johnathan Novak Contemporary Art, Los Angeles, CA; Jan Anderson Gallery, New York, NY; Graystone Gallery, San Francisco, CA
MAILING ADDRESS: c/o Mary Boone Gallery, 417 West Broadway, New York, NY 10012

Eric Fischl
Beach
Courtesy Parasol Press, Ltd

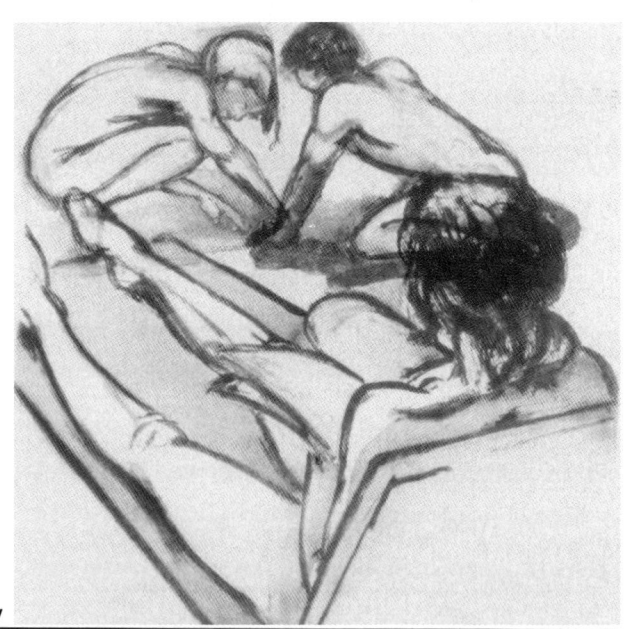

Eric Fischl
Digging Kids
Courtesy van Straaten Gallery

TITLE	PUBLISHER	PRINTER	DATE	MEDIUM	DIMENSION (PAPER SIZE) IN INCHES	TYPE OF PAPER	EDITION NUMBER	NO. OF COLORS	ORIGINAL OPENING PRICE	CURRENT RETAIL PRICE
SOLD OUT EDITIONS (RARE):										
Digging Kids	COR	PB/JS/LH	1982	EB/A/SG	54 X 39	THS	40	2	600	10500
Beach Balls	COR	PB/JS/LH	1982	EB/A	54 X 39	THS	40	2	600	10500
Year of the Drowned Dog (6 Parts)	PBE	PK	1983	EB/A/DPT	23 X 35	ZER	35		3000 SET	80000 SET
					22 X 17					
					18 X 17					
					23 X 11					
					13 X 10					
					23 X 19					
Untitled	PBE	PK	1984	A/SG	23 X 15	AP	50	1	430	3000
Puppet Tears	PBE	PK	1985	AC/DPT	7 X 10	ZER	50		600	2500
Floating Islands (Set of 5)	PBE	PK	1985	FR/A/SL/DPT	12 X 32 (4) 23 X 17 (1)	ZER	45 EA		5500 SET	25000 SET
Untitled 12.10.86	PBE	PK	1986	MON	11 X 16 EA	HMP	1 EA	Varies	3000 EA	12500 EA
Shower (with Burnishing)	PaP	AC/AtC	1987	EB/A/SG/BUR	22 X 25	HAHN	100		800	4000
CURRENT EDITIONS:										
Untitled	CPP	TT/SM/CPP	1988	WC	17 X 17	AC	200	9	2200	2200
Untitled (Set of 4)	PaP	JM	1989–90	AC	36 X 54 EA	SOM	100 EA		42000 SET	42000 SET
St Tropez 1981–1988 (Set of 16)	KW	CBP	1990	DT	16 X 20 EA	HMP	35 EA		35000 SET	35000 SET

ERIC FISCHL CONTINUED

TITLE	PUBLISHER	PRINTER	DATE	MEDIUM	DIMENSION (PAPER SIZE) IN INCHES	TYPE OF PAPER	EDITION NUMBER	NO. OF COLORS	ORIGINAL OPENING PRICE	CURRENT RETAIL PRICE
CURRENT EDITIONS:										
Untitled (Set of 4):									15000 SET	30000 SET
Beach	KW	CBP	1990	EB/A/SG/DPT	36 X 54	HMP	100		4000	5000
Dog	KW	CBP	1990	AC	36 X 54	HMP	100		4000	10000
Untitled (Set of 5)	ART	DW/HEd	1992	I	22 X 30 EA	AP	25 EA	1 EA	8000 SET	8000 SET
									1800 EA	1800 EA

Eric Fischl
Floating Islands
Courtesy Peter Blum Edition

JOEL A FISHER

BORN: Salem, OH; June 6, 1947
EDUCATION: Kenyon Col, OH, BA, 1969
TEACHING: Shiller Col, Berlin, Germany, 1973–74; Goldsmiths Col, (London Univ), England, 1979; Bath Acad of Art, England, 1980–82; Rhode Island Sch of Design, Providence, RI, 1985,90; Vermont Studio Sch, 1988-90; Tryler Sch of Art, Phila, PA, 1988; SVA, NY, 1988,90,91; Parsons Sch of Design, NY, 1990; Boston Mus Sch, MA, 1990; Guest Prof, Ecole des Beaux-Arts, Paris France, 1991
AWARDS: Kress Foundation Award, Art History, 1967, 68; Thomas J Watson Traveling Fellowship, 1971–72; Berliner Kunstler Program des DAAD, 1973–74; RTE Award, Limerick, Ireland, 1978; Nat Endowment Fel, Sculpture, 1984; Prize, George A & Eliza Gardner Howard Found, 1986–87
RECENT EXHIB: BlumHelman Gallery, NY, 1987; Albright-Knox Art Gallery, Buffalo, NY, 1987; Brooklyn Mus, NY, 1989; Butler Inst of Am Art, Youngstown, OH, 1989; Farideh Cadot Gallery, NY, 1990; Farideh Cadot Gallery, Paris, France, 1990,91; Art Affairs/Antoinette De Stigter, Amsterdam, Netherlands, 1991; Galerie Raymond Bollag, Zurich, Switzerland, 1991; Gallery Hubert Winter, Wien, Austria, 1991; Galeria Comicos/Luis Serpa, Lisbon, Portugal, 1991

COLLECTIONS: Butler Inst of Art, Youngstown, OH; Victoria and Albert Mus, London, England; Tehran Mus of Contemp Art, Iran; Coburn Gallery, Kenyon Col, Gambier, OH; Stedelijk Mus, Amsterdam, Holland; Muzeum Sztuki, Lodz, Poland; Mus of Mod Art, NY; Tate Gallery, London, England; Kunstmuseum Bern, Switzerland; Brooklyn Mus, NY; Kunstmuseum Luzern, Switzerland; Georgia Mus of Art, Athens, GA; Neues Mus Weserburg, Bremen, Germany; Center Georges Pompidou, Paris, France; Stadisches Mus, Monchengladbach, Germany; Wadsworth Atheneum, Hartford, CT; Malmo Mus, Sweden; Moderna Museet, Stockholm, Sweden; Mus of Fine Art, Richmond, VA; Mus of Contemp Art, Ghent, Belgium
PRINTERS: Lilah Toland (LT); Paul Singdahlsen (PS); Pamela Paulson (PP); Paul Mullowney (PM); Mari Andrews (MA); Crown Point Press, San Francisco, CA (CPP)
PUBLISHERS: Crown Point Press, San Francisco, CA (CPP)
GALLERIES: Crown Point Press, New York, NY & San Francisco, CA; Diane Brown Gallery, New York, NY; Costas Grimaldis Gallery, Baltimore, MD; Nigel Greenberg Gallery, London, England; Farideh Cadot Gallery, Paris, France; Shimada Gallery, Yamagauchi, Japan; Anders Tornberg, Lund, Sweden; Barbara Gross, Munich, Germany; Galery S-65, Aalst, Belgium; Antoinette De Stigter Gallery, Amsterdam, Netherlands
MAILING ADDRESS: 99 Commercial St, Brooklyn, NY 11222/ Box 348, River Rd, North Troy, VT 05859

TITLE	PUBLISHER	PRINTER	DATE	MEDIUM	DIMENSION (PAPER SIZE) IN INCHES	TYPE OF PAPER	EDITION NUMBER	NO. OF COLORS	ORIGINAL OPENING PRICE	CURRENT RETAIL PRICE
SOLD OUT EDITIONS (RARE):										
Softground II (4 States)	CPP	LT/PS	1980	EC	26 X 21 EA	AP/HMP/CC	10 EA	6 EA	1800	3500
Responsibility (Vertical)	CPP	LT/PS	1980	AB	48 X 36	AP88	15	1	500	2000
Drypoint (5 States)	CPP	LT/PS	1980	EC	26 X 21 EA	AP/HMP/CC	10 EA	6 EA	2250 EA	3500 EA
Hardground II (5 States)	CPP	LT/PS	1980	EC	26 X 21 EA	AP/HMP/CC	10 EA	6 EA	2250 EA	3500 EA
Softground (10 States)	CPP	LT/PS	1980	EC	26 X 21 EA	AP/HMP/CC	10 EA	6 EA	3150 EA	3500 EA
Sugarlift II (4 States)	CPP	LT/PS	1980	EC	26 X 21 EA	AP/HMP/CC	10 EA	6 EA	1800 EA	3500 EA
Tree	CPP	PP/PM/MA/CPP	1990	AC		SOM/T	7	7	1800	2800
CURRENT EDITIONS:										
Responsibility (Horizontal)	CPP	LT/PS	1980	AB/SL/CC	40 X 42	AP88	15	1	500	2000
First Etching (Diptych)	CPP	LT/PS	1980	EB	27 X 54	HMP	15	1	400	1500
Tree (Four Panels)	CPP	PP/PM/MA/CPP	1990	EB/A	86 X 65	SOM/W	10	7	1800	1800
Drypoint Drawings	CPP	PP/PM/MA/CPP	1990	DPT/CC	Varies	HMP	23 EA	Varies	650/1250 EA	950/1250 EA
Softground Drawings	CPP	PP/PM/MA/CPP	1990	EB/SG/CC	Varies	HMP	13 EA	Varies	650/950 EA	750/950 EA

JANET FISH

BORN: Boston, MA; May 18, 1938
EDUCATION: Smith Col, BA with Leonard Baskin; Yale Sch of Art & Arch with Alex Katz, Philip Pearlstein, BFA, 1962, MFA, 1963
AWARDS: MacDowell Fel, 1968,69,72; Harris Award 71st Chicago Biennale, 1974; Australian Council of Arts Grant, 1975
RECENT EXHIB: Jewish Mus, NY, 1988; Brevard Art Center & Mus, Melbourne, FL, 1989; Univ of Richmond, VA, 1989; Gerald Peters Gallery, Santa Fe, NM, 1991; Robert Miller Gallery, NY, 1987,88,89,91; Linda Cathcart Gallery, Santa Monica, CA, 1990,91; Univ of Colorado, Colorado Springs, CO, 1992; Fort Wayne Mus of Art, IN, 1992; Albrecht-Kemper Mus, St Joseph, MO, 1992; Univ of Wisconsin, Carlsten Art Gallery, Stevens Point, WI, 1992
COLLECTIONS: Whitney Mus of Am Art, NY; Dallas Mus of Art, TX; Minneapolis Mus of Art, MN; Cleveland Mus of Art, OH; Nat Gallery of Victoria, Melbourne, Australia; Graham Gund Coll, Mus of Fine Arts, Boston, MA; Metropolitan Mus of Art, NY; Albright-Knox Art Gallery, Buffalo, NY; Yale Univ, New Haven, CT; Art Inst of Chicago, IL; Colby Col, Waterville, ME; Newark Mus, NJ; Oberlin Col, OH; Rhode Island Sch of Design, Providence, RI; Acad of Fine Arts, Phila, PA
PRINTERS: Judith Solodkin, NY (JS); Solo Press, NY (SP); American Atelier, NY (AA); Tamarind Inst, Albuquerque, NM (TI); Lynne Allen (LA); Melissa Braggins-Katzman, NY (MB-K); William Haberman, NY, (WH); Resam Press, NY (RP); Deli Sacilloto, NY (DS); Burr Miller, NY (BM); Dana Sievertson, NY (DSN); Tony Kirk, NY (TK); John Hutcheson, MA (JH); Dwight Pogue, MA (DP); Chip Elwell, NY (CE); Andrew Bovel, NY (AB); Steven Rodriguez, NY (SR); Norman Stewart, Bloomfield Hills, MI (NS); Joe Keenan, Bloomfield Hills, MI (JK); Corey Stewart, Bloomfield Hills, MI (CS); Stewart & Stewart, Bloomfield Hills, MI (S-S); Jon Cone, East Topsham, VT (JC); Cone Editions, East Topsham, VT (CEd); Jennifer Melby Studio, NY (JMS); Bill Weege, Madison, WI (BW); Andrew Rubin, Madison, WI (AR); Tandem Press, Univ of Wisconsin, Madison, WI (TanPr)
PUBLISHERS: Brooke Alexander, Inc, NY (BAI); 724 Prints, NY (724P); Tamarind Inst, Albuquerque, NM (T); Vera List, Special Projects Inc (SPI); Oxbow Sch, Saugatuck, MI (OS); Jewish Mus, NY (JM); YMYWHA, Union, NJ (YMYWHA); Smith Col, Northampton, MA (SC); Stewart & Stewart, Bloomfield Hills, MI (S-S); Tandem Press, Univ of Wisconsin, Madison, WI (TanPr); John Szoke Graphics, NY (JSG)
GALLERIES: Brooke Alexander, Inc, New York, NY; Robert Miller Gallery, New York, NY; Betsy Rosenfield Gallery, Chicago, IL; Holoweski & Arnold Gallery, Royal Oak, MI; Linda Cathcart Gallery, Santa Monica, CA; Gerald Peters Gallery, Santa Fe, NM; Joy Tash Gallery, Scottsdale, AZ; Marianne Friedland Gallery, Naples, FL; Stewart & Stewart, Bloomfield Hills, MI; John Szoke Graphics, Inc, New York, NY; Meredith Long & Company, Houston, TX; Cone Editions, East Topsham, VT
MAILING ADDRESS: 101 Prince St, New York, NY 10012

Janet Fish
Leyden
Courtesy Stewart & Stewart

TITLE	PUBLISHER	PRINTER	DATE	MEDIUM	DIMENSION (PAPER SIZE) IN INCHES	TYPE OF PAPER	EDITION NUMBER	NO. OF COLORS	ORIGINAL OPENING PRICE	CURRENT RETAIL PRICE
SOLD OUT EDITIONS (RARE):										
Four Glasses	BAI	AA	1976	LCH	30 X 22	AP	150	6	250	2000
Cherries in Brandy	BAI	RP	1973	LC/HC	29 X 23	CAN	27		250	1500
Glasses for the Jewish Museum	VL	DS	1975	LC/HC	37 X 30	AP	144	6	200	1850
Preserved Peaches	SPI	BM	1975	LC	30 X 22	AP	75	5	300	1600
West Yellow Bowls	OS	DSN	1977	LC	15 X 11	AP	25	3	200	800
Green Bowls	724P	JS/SP	1978	LC	28 X 22	R/BFK	50	4	375	1500
Tulips and Teacups	TI	LA/TI	1981	LC	40 X 30	SS/W	43	6	600	2000
Yellow Bowl	TI	MB-K/TI	1981	LC	20 X 26	CD	43	4	500	1500
Wise Guy	TI	WH/TI	1982	LC	27 X 23	R/BFK	25	4	500	2000
Sandwich	YMYWHA	TK	1983	EB	15 X 18	R/BFK	150	1	300	750
Pears and Mitten	724P	CE/AB/SR	1985	WC	20 X 28	SEK/W	45	12	900	1200
CURRENT EDITIONS:										
Winsome Shells	SC	JH/DP	1985	LC/SP	20 X 30	AC	50	10	1200	1350
Pears and Autumn Leaves	ART	JM	1988	EB/A/DPT	39 X 30	R/BFK/W	60	12	1500	2500
Butterfly Wings	S-S	NS/JK/CS/S-S	1991	SP	22 X 30	R/BFK	61	12	1850	2400
Bananas	S-S	NS/JK/S-S	1991	SP	22 X 30	R/BFK	59	13	1850	1850
Leyden	S-S	NS/JK/S-S	1991	SP	29 X 41	R/BFK	44	12	2500	2500
Autumn Still Life	TanPr	BW/AR/TanPr	1991	LC	37 X 27	AC	40	12	1800	1800
Cerises	S-S	NS/JK/S-S	1992	SP	34 X 29	R/BFK/W	60	12	1800	1800
Rose Bowl	S-S	NS/JK/S-S	1992	SP	22 X 30	R/BFK/W	60	12	1500	1500
Tropical Fish	JSG	JC/CEd	1992	SP	41 X 46	AP88	75	3	2500	3000

ASTRID FITZGERALD

BORN: Wil, Switzerland; July 28, 1938; US Citizen
EDUCATION: St Agnes Col, Fribourg, Switzerland, 1955; Art Students League, NY, 1962; Pratt Inst, Brooklyn, NY, 1972
AWARDS: Michael M Engel Mem Award, Nat Arts Club, NY, 1973; Charles Levitt Award, Nat Acad Galleries, NY, 1978; Juror's Award, New York, Univ, NY, 1980
RECENT EXHIB: Danforth Mus of Art, Framingham, MA, 1988; Oklahoma Art Center, Oklahoma City, OK, 1988; Queens Mus, Flushing, NY, 1988; Pennsylvania Acad of Fine Arts, Phil, PA, 1989
COLLECTIONS: Marymount Col, Tarrytown, NY; Aldrich Mus of Contemp Art, Ridgefield, CT; Wellesley Col, MA
PRINTERS: Artist (ART)
PUBLISHERS: Artist (ART)
GALLERIES: Ellen Price Gallery, New York, NY; Art Sources, Orange Park, FL; Colmin Gallery, Toronto, ON, Canada
MAILING ADDRESS: 650 West End Ave, New York, NY 10025

The retail prices of the 100,000 limited edition prints quoted in this directory are subject to change. Print publishers, artists and galleries were the direct sources for these quotations. Prices in the secondary market listed as "Sold Out Editions (Rare)" indicate that the publisher has a limited supply of that print or that the print is difficult to locate in the galleries.

ASTRID FITZGERALD CONTINUED

TITLE	PUBLISHER	PRINTER	DATE	MEDIUM	DIMENSION (PAPER SIZE) IN INCHES	TYPE OF PAPER	EDITION NUMBER	NO. OF COLORS	ORIGINAL OPENING PRICE	CURRENT RETAIL PRICE
SOLD OUT EDITIONS (RARE):										
Break Away	ART	ART	1972	SP	32 X 26	AE	70	5	75	300
Clover Leaf	ART	ART	1972	SP	32 X 26	AE	65	5	75	300
Blue Core	ART	ART	1972	SP	32 X 26	AE	65	5	75	300
Cloud of Unknowing	ART	ART	1973	SP	22 X 30	AP	35	5	85	300
Dawning	ART	ART	1973	SP	22 X 30	AP	50	5	85	300
Winter Remembered	ART	ART	1973	SP	22 X 30	AP	45	5	85	300
Contemplation	ART	ART	1973	SP	22 X 30	AP	40	5	85	300
Moment in June	ART	ART	1973	SP	22 X 30	AP	30	5	85	300
CURRENT EDITIONS:										
Auspex I	ART	ART	1975	SP	22 X 30	AP	65	13	100	330
Auspex II	ART	ART	1975	SP	22 X 30	AP	55	7	100	330
Auspex III	ART	ART	1975	SP	22 X 30	AP	55	7	100	330
Acadia I	ART	ART	1978	SP	25 X 30	R/BFK	70	1	120	250
Acadia II	ART	ART	1978	SP	25 X 30	R/BFK	70	1	120	250
Acadia III	ART	ART	1978	SP	25 X 30	R/BFK	70	1	120	250
Acadia IV	ART	ART	1978	SP	25 X 30	R/BFK	70	1	120	250
Xenos I	ART	ART	1979	SP	25 X 35	AP	60	10	160	380
Xenos II	ART	ART	1979	SP	25 X 35	AP	55	9	160	380
Xenos III	ART	ART	1979	SP	25 X 35	AP	30	10	160	380
Xenos IV	ART	ART	1979	SP	25 X 35	AP	40	7	160	380
Xenos V	ART	ART	1979	SP	25 X 35	AP	15	9	160	380

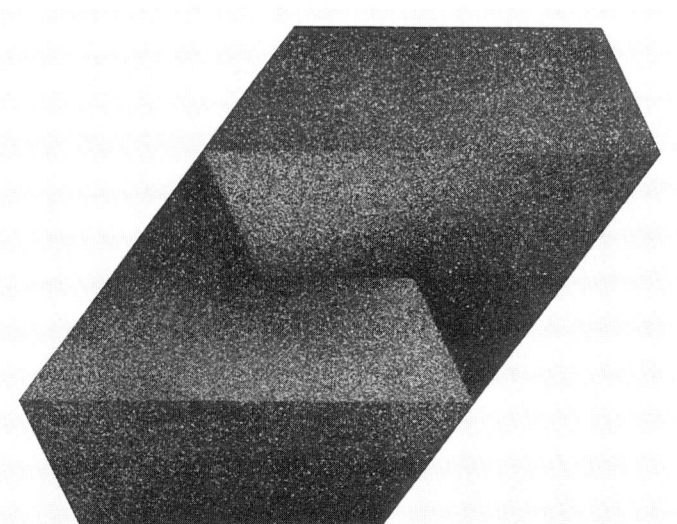

Astrid Fitzgerald
Xenos V
Courtesy the Artist

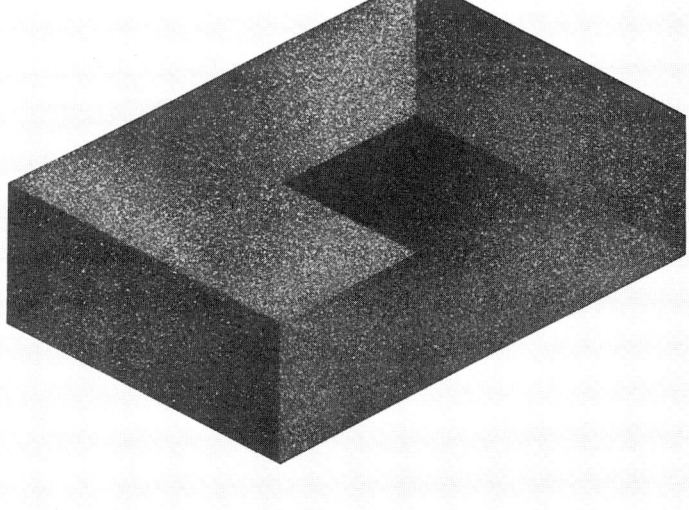

Astrid Fitzgerald
Xenos I
Courtesy the Artist

VERNON FISHER

BORN: Fort Worth, TX; 1943
EDUCATION: Hardin-Simmons Univ, Abilene, TX, BA, 1967; Univ of Illinois, Champaign-Urbana, IL, MFA, 1969
TEACHING: Assoc Prof, Art, Austin Col, Sherman, TX, 1969–78; Prof, Art, North Texas State Univ, TX, 1978 to present
AWARDS: Louis Comfort Tiffany Found Grant, 1980–81,84; Visual Art Award Grant, SECCA, 1981,88
RECENT EXHIB: Walker Art Center, Minneapolis, MN, 1987; Los Angeles County Mus of Art, CA, 1987; Inst of Contemp Arts, London, England, 1987; Lannan Mus, Lake Worth, FL, 1987; Barbara Gladstone Gallery, NY, 1987; Hiram Butler Gallery, Houston, TX, 1987; La Jolla Mus of Contemp Art, CA, 1989; Yellowstone Art Center, Billings, MT, 1992; Univ of North Texas, Cora Stafford Gallery, Denton, TX, 1992; Modernism, San Francisco, CA, 1993
COLLECTIONS: Mus of Mod Art, NY; Solomon R Guggenheim Mus, NY; Albright-Knox Art Gallery, Buffalo, NY; Corcoran Gallery of Art, Wash, DC; Hirshhorn Mus of Art, Wash, DC; Smithsonian Inst, Wash, DC
PRINTERS: Jack Lemon, Chicago, IL (JL); Landfall Press Inc, Chicago, IL (LPI); Barbara Spies, Chicago, IL (BS); Kenneth Hale (KH); Univ of Texas Printmaking Workshop, Austin, TX (UT); Artist (ART)
PUBLISHERS: Landfall Press Inc, Chicago, IL (LPI); Univ of Texas Art Dept, Austin, TX (UT)
GALLERIES: Landfall Press Inc, Chicago, IL; Betty Moody Gallery, Houston, TX; Barbara Gladstone Gallery, New York, NY; Hiram Butler Gallery, Houston, TX; Asher/Faure Gallery, Los Angeles, CA; John Weber Gallery, New York, NY; Fred Hoffman Gallery, Santa Monica, CA; Res Nova, New Orleans, LA; Barry Whistler Gallery, Dallas, TX; Works Gallery, Long Beach, CA; Park Granada Editions, Tarzana, CA; Jan Weiner Gallery, Kansas City, MO; Quartet Editions, New York, NY; Modernism, San Francisco, CA
MAILING ADDRESS: 1109 N Main, Fort Worth, TX 76106

The print market has become very selective. For the first time since we published the first edition of The Printworld Directory in 1982, the prices of prints have been greatly reduced and greatly increased for the same artists by the most reputable and established print publishers. Check the fifth edition to understand the movement.

VERNON FISHER CONTINUED

TITLE	PUBLISHER	PRINTER	DATE	MEDIUM	DIMENSION (PAPER SIZE) IN INCHES	TYPE OF PAPER	EDITION NUMBER	NO. OF COLORS	ORIGINAL OPENING PRICE	CURRENT RETAIL PRICE
CURRENT EDITIONS:										
Genetic Variations/Natural Selections (Set of 2)	LPI	JL/BS/LPI	1983	LC	32 X 42 EA	AC/W	35 EA	4 EA	900 SET	1600 SET
Dark Night Full of Stars	LPI	JL/LPI	1985	LC	30 X 33	AC/W	35	2	550	950
Composition in Red, White & Blue	LPI	JL/LPI	1985	LC	30 X 43	AC/W	20	6	750	750
Hanging Man	UT	ART/KH/UT	1985	LC/SP/PH	26 X 36	AC/W	40		600	750
Navigating by the Stars	LPI	JL/LPI	1989	LC	30 X 35	AC/W	50	4	1200	1200
Perdido en el Mar	LPI	JL/LPI	1989	LC	30 X 37	AC	50		2000	2000
Objects in a Field	LPI	JL/LPI	1990	LC	36 X 36	AC	35		1200	1200
Scenes from the American West	LPI	JL/LPI	1990	LB	36 X 40	AC	50	1	1800	1800
Aardvark	LPI	JL/LPI	1992	LC/SP	35 X 39	AC	50		1200	1200

TONY FITZPATRICK

PRINTERS: Jack Lemon, Chicago, IL (JL); Landfall Press, Inc, Chicago, IL (LPI); Steve Campbell, Chicago, IL (SC); Big Cat Press, Chicago, IL (BCP)

PUBLISHERS: Landfall Press, Inc, Chicago, IL (LPI); Artist (ART)
GALLERIES: Landfall Press, Inc, Chicago, IL; Carl Hammer Gallery, Chicago, IL; Janet Fleisher Gallery, Phila, PA; Quartet Editions, New York, NY; Bridgewater/Lustberg Gallery, New York, NY

TITLE	PUBLISHER	PRINTER	DATE	MEDIUM	DIMENSION (PAPER SIZE) IN INCHES	TYPE OF PAPER	EDITION NUMBER	NO. OF COLORS	ORIGINAL OPENING PRICE	CURRENT RETAIL PRICE
CURRENT EDITIONS:										
Songbird's Hurricane	LPI	JL/LPI	1991	EB/CC	24 X 23	GE	20	1	800	800
Circus Dog	LPI	JL/LPI	1991	EB/CC	24 X 23	GE	20	1	800	800
Black-Eyed Fight Dog	LPI	JL/LPI	1991	EB/CC	24 X 23	GE	20	1	800	800
Homage to a Big Cat	LPI	JL/LPI	1992	EB/CC	16 X 14	GE	25	1	300	300
Fly Man	LPI	JL/LPI	1992	EB/CC	16 X 14	GE	25	1	400	400
8 Count	LPI	JL/LPI	1992	EB/CC	20 X 15	GE	25	1	600	600
Hoodoo Bull	LPI	JL/LPI	1992	EB/CC	20 X 15	GE	25	1	600	600
Little Hot Diablo	LPI	JL/LPI	1992	EB/CC	16 X 14	GE	25	1	500	500
Shoeless Joe	LPI	JL/LPI	1992	EB/CC	16 X 14	GE	25	1	400	400
Saint of the Rain	LPI	JL/LPI	1992	EB/CC	15 X 14	GE	25	1	400	400
Smoke Dog	LPI	JL/LPI	1992	EB/CC	16 X 14	GE	25	1	400	400
Crow House	LPI	JL/LPI	1992	EB/CC	16 X 14	GE	25	1	500	500
Chez Rat	LPI	JL/LPI	1992	EB/CC	14 X 14	GE	25	1	400	400
Keyhole Kutie	LPI	JL/LPI	1992	EB/CC	16 X 14	GE	35	1	500	500
Atom Ant	LPI	JL/LPI	1992	EB/CC	12 X 12	GE	25	1	300	300
B-A-A-D Blind Dummy	LPI	JL/LPI	1992	EB/CC	12 X 12	GE	25	1	300	300
Cats Cradle	LPI	JL/LPI	1992	EB/CC	12 X 12	GE	25	1	300	300
Summer Etching	LPI	JL/LPI	1992	EB/CC	15 X 13	GE	25	1	300	300
Frank	LPI	JL/LPI	1992	EB/CC	14 X 13	GE	25	1	300	300
Cain	LPI	JL/LPI	1992	EB/CC	16 X 14	GE	25	1	400	400
Jail-Diary Page One	LPI	JL/LPI	1992	EB/CC	16 X 14	GE	25	1	400	400
The Coming of Locusts	LPI	JL/LPI	1992	EB/CC	16 X 14	GE	25	1	400	400
Rain Dog	LPI	JL/LPI	1992	EB/CC	15 X 15	GE	25	1	300	300
The Crow of the Plague	ART	SC/BCP	1992	EB/A	15 X 18	GE	25	2	800	800

AUDREY FLACK

BORN: New York, NY; May 30, 1931
EDUCATION: Cooper Univ, NY, 1951; Cranbrook Acad of Art, Bloomfield Hills, MI; Yale Univ, New Haven, CT, with Josef Albers
TEACHING: Instr, Drawing, Pratt Inst, Brooklyn, NY 1965–71; Instr, New York Univ, NY, 1968–71; Instr, Drawing, Sch of Visual Arts, NY, 1971–74; Mellon Prof, Anatomy, Cooper Union, NY, 1982
AWARDS: Second Prize, Nat Exhib of Paintings, Butler Inst of Am Art, Youngstown, OH, 1974; The Cooper Union Citation, NY, 1977; St Gaudens Medal, Cooper Union, NY, 1982
RECENT EXHIB: Gallery of Fine Arts, Daytona Beach Comm Col, FL, 1987; Ohio State Univ, Columbus, OH, 1987; Col of Wooster Art Mus, OH, 1987; Univ of California, Irvine, CA, 1988; Danforth Mus, Framington, MA, 1988; Oklahoma Art Center, Oklahoma City, OK, 1988; Queens Mus, Flushing, NY, 1988; Pennsylvania Acad of Fine Arts, Phila, PA, 1989; Univ of Florida, Samuel P Horn Mus, Gainesville, FL, 1992; Louis K Meisel Gallery, NY, 1992
COLLECTIONS: Mus of Mod Art, NY; Rose Art Mus, Brandeis Univ, Waltham, MA; Whitney Mus of Am Art, NY; Canberra Mus, Australia; St Louis Mus, MO; Smithsonian Inst, Wash, DC; Metropolitan Mus of Art, NY; Solomon R Guggenheim Mus, NY; San Francisco Mus of Mod Art, NY
PRINTERS: Shorewood Atelier, Inc, NY (SA); CVI Labs, NY (CVI); Vermillion Editions, Ltd, Minneapolis, MN (VEL)
PUBLISHERS: Prestige Art, Inc, Mamaroneck, NY; Vermillion Editions, Ltd, Minneapolis, MN (VEL)
GALLERIES: Louis K Meisel Gallery, NY; Morningstar Gallery, New York, NY; Alan Brown Gallery, Hartsdale, NY; Vermillion Editions, Ltd, Minneapolis, MN; Vered Gallery, East Hampton, NY
MAILING ADDRESS: c/o Louis K Meisel Gallery, 141 Prince St, New York, NY 10024

AUDREY FLACK CONTINUED

TITLE	PUBLISHER	PRINTER	DATE	MEDIUM	DIMENSION (PAPER SIZE) IN INCHES	TYPE OF PAPER	EDITION NUMBER	NO. OF COLORS	ORIGINAL OPENING PRICE	CURRENT RETAIL PRICE
CURRENT EDITIONS:										
Lady Madonna	PA	SA	1980	LC	24 X 34	AP	150	17	350	1000
12 Photographs	PA	CVI	1983	PH/DT	20 X 24 EA	AP	50 EA		7200 SET	8000 SET
									700 EA	800 EA
Self Portrait	VEL	VEL	1984	LC	20 X 26	AP	100		500	1200
Spirit Dancer	VEL	VEL	1984	LC	20 X 26	AP	100		500	1200
Banana Split	VEL	VEL	1986	LC/SP	20 X 26	AP	100		1000	1500

BARRY FLANAGAN

BORN: Flintshire, North Wales; 1941
EDUCATION: Birmingham Col of Arts & Crafts, Fine Arts Dept, MI, 1958; St Martin's Sch of Art, London, England, 1964–66
TEACHING: Central Sch of Art, London, England; St Martin's Sch of Art, London, England
COLLECTIONS: Mus of Mod Art, NY; Nat Gallery of Canada; Rijksmuseum Kroller-Muller, Holland; Nagoaka Mus, Tokyo, Japan; Kunsthaus, Zurich, Switzerland; Tate Gallery of Art, London, England; Arts Council of Great Britain, London, England; San Francisco Mus of Mod Art, CA; Art Inst of Chicago, IL
PRINTERS: Carol Docherty, London, England (CD); Colin Dyer, London, England (CD); Artist's Studio, London, England (AS)
PUBLISHERS: Waddington Graphics, London, England (WG)
GALLERIES: Waddington Graphics, London, England; Pace Editions, New York, NY; Nicola Jacobs Gallery, London, England; Art & Project, Amsterdam, The Netherlands; John Berggruen Gallery, San Francisco, CA
MAILING ADDRESS: 505 La Guardia Place, New York, NY 10012

Barry Flanagan
Valentine
Courtesy Waddington Graphics

TITLE	PUBLISHER	PRINTER	DATE	MEDIUM	DIMENSION (PAPER SIZE) IN INCHES	TYPE OF PAPER	EDITION NUMBER	NO. OF COLORS	ORIGINAL OPENING PRICE	CURRENT RETAIL PRICE
SOLD OUT EDITIONS (RARE):										
Killary Bay	WG	CD/AS	1980	LB	15 X 22	AP	30	1	180	1500
Killary Harbour I	WG	CD/AS	1980	LB	15 X 22	AP	30	1	180	1500
Killary Harbour II	WG	CD/AS	1980	LB	15 X 22	AP	30	1	180	1500
Valentine	WG	CD/AS	1981	LB	22 X 15	AP	30	1	220	1800
Pilgrim	WG	CD/AS	1981	LB	15 X 16	AP	30	1	180	1500
Atlantic Moon	WG	CD/AS	1983	LC	8 X 6	AP	45		180	1200
Cob Study	WG	CD/AS	1983	EB	9 X 6	AP	27	1	220	1000
Cup & Quill	WG	CD/AS	1983	EB	6 X 8	AP	40	1	220	1000
Field Day	WG	CD/AS	1983	EB	7 X 9	AP	75	1	220	1000
Jolly Dog	WG	CD/AS	1983	EB	10 X 8	AP	27	1	220	1500
Mule	WG	CD/AS	1983	EB	7 X 9	AP	41	1	180	1000
Stepney Green	WG	CD/AS	1983	EB	7 X 9	AP	46	1	180	1000
Truffle Hunt	WG	CD/AS	1983	EB	5 X 7	AP	50	1	180	1200
The Wren's Nest	WG	CD/AS	1983	EB	8 X 10	AP	77	1	180	1000
Ganymede	WG	CD/AS	1983	LB	22 X 15	AP	50	1	600	1350
Welsh Girl	WG	CD/AS	1983	LB	22 X 15	AP	32	1	375	1350
Welsh Cob	WG	CD/AS	1983	LB	22 X 15	AP	50	1	600	1350
Welsh Lights	WG	CD/AS	1983	LB	22 X 15	AP	30	1	600	1350
Yacht I,II	WG	CD/AS	1983	LB	15 X 23 EA	AP	48 EA	1 EA	375 EA	1200 EA
Atlantic Moon	WG	CD/AS	1983	LB	11 X 15	AP	45	1	300	1000
McBrayne's Ferry	WG	CD/AS	1983	LB	15 X 22	AP	35	1	525	1350
CURRENT EDITIONS:										
After Rembrandt	WG	CD/AS	1987	EB	7 X 5	AC	25	1	400	800
Baby Crawling (5 Proofs Only)	WG	CD/AS	1987	EB	7 X 5	AC	5 Pr	1	400	800
Baby Face Sketches (5 Proofs Only)	WG	CD/AS	1987	EB	7 X 5	AC	5 Pr	1	400	800
Camp Site (5 Proofs Only)	WG	CD/As	1987	EB	7 X 5	AC	5 Pr	1	400	800
Child Suckling I	WG	CD/AS	1987	EB	10 X 8	AC	10	1	400	800
Child Suckling II	WG	CS/AS	1987	EB	7 X 5	AC	10	1	400	800

BARRY FLANAGAN CONTINUED

TITLE	PUBLISHER	PRINTER	DATE	MEDIUM	DIMENSION (PAPER SIZE) IN INCHES	TYPE OF PAPER	EDITION NUMBER	NO. OF COLORS	ORIGINAL OPENING PRICE	CURRENT RETAIL PRICE
CURRENT EDITIONS:										
Hare, Tree and Figure (5 Proofs Only)	WG	CD/AS	1987	EB	7 X 5	AC	5 Pr	1	400	800
Harlequin	WG	CD/AS	1987	EB	8 X 6	AC	25	1	400	600
Insects	WG	CD/AS	1987	EB	5 X 6	AC	5	1	400	800
Leaves (5 Proofs Only)	WG	CD/AS	1987	EB	7 X 5	AC	5 Pr	1	400	800
Mother and Baby	WG	CD/AS	1987	EB	10 X 8	AC	25	1	400	800
Portrait of Kenneth Martin	WG	CD/AS	1987	EB	5 X 7	AC	25	1	400	800
Reclining Nude	WG	CD/AS	1987	EB	5 X 7	AC	25	1	400	800
Two Baby Heads (5 Proofs Only)	WG	CD/AS	1987	EB	7 X 5	AC	5 Pr	1	408	800

GAIL FLANERY

EDUCATION: Cooper Union, NY, BFA, 1972
PRINTERS: Roni Henning, NY (RH); Jennifer Melby, NY (JM); Kathleen Caraccio, NY (KC); Bruce Cleveland, NY (BC)
PUBLISHERS: Orion Editions, NY (OE)
GALLERIES: Orion Editions, New York, NY; Kimpton Gallery, San Francisco, CA; Cumberland Gallery, Nashville, TN
MAILING ADDRESS: 511 Eighth St, Brooklyn, NY 11215

TITLE	PUBLISHER	PRINTER	DATE	MEDIUM	DIMENSION (PAPER SIZE) IN INCHES	TYPE OF PAPER	EDITION NUMBER	NO. OF COLORS	ORIGINAL OPENING PRICE	CURRENT RETAIL PRICE
SOLD OUT EDITIONS (RARE):										
Northern River	OE	JM	1979	AC	22 X 30	AP	30	HC	225	500
CURRENT EDITIONS:										
Garnet Lake	OE	RH	1982	STEN	28 X 39	AP	65	21	425	500
Turner Bay	OE	RH	1983	STEN	26 X 38	AP	85	16	375	450
Rose Reflections	OE	KC	1984	AC	30 X 42	AP	100	18	425	450
Devil's Creek	OE	BC	1986	EC	30 X 41	AP	100	10	450	500
Below the Miter	OE	BC	1988	EC	24 X 41	AP	100	10	500	500
Near Shore	OE	BC	1988	EC	24 X 41	AP	100	10	500	500

DAN FLAVIN

BORN: New York, NY; April 1, 1933
EDUCATION: Univ of Maryland, Baltimore, MD; Republic of Korea; New Sch of Social Research, NY; Columbia Univ, NY
TEACHING: Univ of North Carolina, Greensboro, NC, Spring, 1967; Albert Dorne Vis Prof, Univ of Bridgeport, CT, 1973
AWARDS: William & Norma Copley Found Award, 1964; Nat Found of Arts & Humanities Award, 1966; Skowhegan Medal for Sculpture, ME, 1976
RECENT EXHIB: Galerie Thaddaeus Ropac, Salzburg, Austria, 1987; Donald Young Gallery, Chicago, IL, 1987; Karsten Schubert, Ltd, London, England, 1988; Pat Hearn Gallery, NY, 1988; Staatliche Kunsthalle, Baden, Germany, 1989; Langer Fine Arts, NY, 1989; Grob Gallery, London, England, 1989; Margo Leavin Gallery, Los Angeles, CA, 1989; Hirschl & Adler Modern, NY, 1989; Greenberg Gallery, St Louis, MO, 1989; Marisa del Re, NY, 1989; Leo Castelli Gallery, NY, 1989; Dia Art Found: the Dan Flavin Art Inst, Bridgehampton, NY, 1989; Columbia Univ, Wallach Art Gallery, New York, NY, 1989; Museé d'Art Contemporain, Lyon, France, 1989; Thomas Segal Gallery, Boston, MA, 1990; Hudson River Mus of Westchester, Yonkers, NY, 1992; Dia Center for the Arts, Bridgehampton, NY, 1992; Pace Gallery, NY, 1992
COLLECTIONS: Metropolitan Mus of Art, NY; Mus of Mod Art, NY; Whitney Mus of Am Art, NY; Guggenheim Mus, NY; Philadelphia Art Mus, PA; Kroller-Muller Mus, Einhoven, Holland; Hudson River Mus, Yonkers, NY
PRINTERS: Crown Point Press, San Francisco, CA (CPP); Patricia Branstead, NY (PB); Aeropress, Inc, NY (A); Daniel Weldin, NY (DW); Aldo Crommelynck, NY (AC); Atelier Crommelynck, Paris, France (AtC); Gemini GEL, Los Angeles, CA (GEM)
PUBLISHERS: Multiples, NY (M); Crown Point Press, San Francisco, CA (CPP); Castelli Graphics, NY (CG); Aldo Crommelynck, NY (AC); Editions Schellmann, Inc, NY (ES); Gemini GEL, Los Angeles, CA (GEM)
GALLERIES: Marian Goodman, New York, NY; Margo Leavin Gallery, Los Angeles, CA; Donald Young Gallery, Seattle, WA; Crown Point Press, San Francisco, CA & New York, NY; Dolly Fiterman Gallery, Minneapolis, MN; Gemini GEL, Los Angeles, CA; Pace Prints, New York, NY; Castelli Graphics, New York, NY; Thomas Segal Gallery, Boston, MA; Jonathan Novak Contemporary Art, Los Angeles, CA; John C Stoller & Company, Minneapolis, MN; Barbara Krakow Gallery, Boston, MA; 65 Thompson Street Gallery, New York, NY
MAILING ADDRESS: c/o Leo Castelli Gallery, 420 W Broadway, New York, NY 10012

TITLE	PUBLISHER	PRINTER	DATE	MEDIUM	DIMENSION (PAPER SIZE) IN INCHES	TYPE OF PAPER	EDITION NUMBER	NO. OF COLORS	ORIGINAL OPENING PRICE	CURRENT RETAIL PRICE
SOLD OUT EDITIONS (RARE):										
For Circular Florescent Light of One Wall (Set of 3)	M/CG	PB/A	1973	DPT	9 X 11 EA	AP	18 EA	1 EA	600 SET	3000 SET
Old Woman	M	PB/A	1974	EB/DPT	9 X 11	AP	9		250	750
Set of Fourteen Sailboat Pieces	M	PB/A	1974	EB/DPT	9 X 11 EA	AP	9 EA		3500 SET	7500 SET
Set of Two Colored Corner Pieces	M	PB/A	1974	EB/DPT	9 X 11 EA	AP	9 EA		500 SET	1500 SET
Set of Three Circular Light Pieces	M	PB/A	1974	EB/DPT	9 X 11 EA	AP	9 EA		900 SET	1800 SET
To Don Judd, Colorist, I-VII (Set of 7)	GEM	GEM	1987	LC	29 X 41 EA	AC	30 EA	1 EA	15000 SET	25000 SET
CURRENT EDITIONS:										
For One Walled Circular Florescent Light (Set of 5)	M	PB/A	1974	LB	22 X 30 EA	R/BFK	35 EA	1 EA	1200 SET / 250 EA	4500 SET / 900 EA
In March, in Oakland (Set of 9)	CPP	CPP	1978	EB	13 X 11 EA	R/BFK	25 EA	1 EA	1800 SET / 250 EA	1800 SET / 250 EA

DAN FLAVIN CONTINUED

TITLE	PUBLISHER	PRINTER	DATE	MEDIUM	DIMENSION (PAPER SIZE) IN INCHES	TYPE OF PAPER	EDITION NUMBER	NO. OF COLORS	ORIGINAL OPENING PRICE	CURRENT RETAIL PRICE
CURRENT EDITIONS:										
Second Sails (Set of 8)	CPP	CPP	1978	EB	11 X 15 EA	R/BFK	10 EA		1800 SET	1800 SET
									250 EA	250 EA
A Young Woman in a Raincoat	CPP	CPP	1978	DPT	15 X 11	R/BFK	10	1	250	250
Sixth Sails/1,2,3,4 (to Jim Fields) (Set of 4)	M	DW	1982	LC	15 X 14	R/BFK	25 EA	2	1500 SET	2400 SET
									400 EA	650 EA
Untitled (for Rento) (Set of 2)	ES		1986	SP	30 X 42 EA	AC	40 EA	3	2000 SET	3000 SET
Untitled (Set of 3):									1800 SET	2500 SET
Untitled A (Black on White Paper)	ES		1986	LB	22 X 30	AP/W	25	1	600	850
Untitled A (Black on GrayPaper)	ES		1986	LB	22 X 30	AP/W	25	1	600	850
Untitled A (White on Black Paper)	ES		1986	LB	22 X 30	AP/W	25	1	600	850
Untitled I (to Don Judd, Colorist)	ES		1986	LC	29 X 41	AP	30	2	1800	2200
Mia	AC	AC/AtC	1987	DPT	12 X 12	HAHN	30	1	400	1000
Sabina Looking into the Sun	AC	AC/AtC	1987	EB	14 X 11	HAHN	40	1	400	1000
For Jeanette O	AC	AC/AtC	1988	AC	23 X 30	HAHN	30	3	2500	4500
For K Malevich I	AC	AC/AtC	1988	AC	23 X 31	HAHN	18	2	2500	4500
For K Malevich II	AC	AC/AtC	1988	AC	23 X 31	HAHN	18	2	2500	4500

JAMES FLORA

BORN: Bellefontaine, OH; January 25, 1914
EDUCATION: Urbana Univ, OH, 1931–33; Art Acad of Cincinnati, OH, 1934–39; Studied with Stanley William Hayter at Atelier 17
AWARDS: Bronze Medal, Printing, Silvermine Guild, 1983
RECENT EXHIB: Galerie Bonheur, Greenwich, CT, 1987–88; Portland Place Galleries, South Norwalk, CT, 1989; Green Gallery, Guilford, CT, 1990
COLLECTIONS: Smithsonian Inst, Wash, DC
PRINTERS: Fine Art Press, MA (FAP)
PUBLISHERS: Andrea Ruoff Art Associates, Ltd, Fort Lee, NJ (ARAAL)
GALLERIES: Pearl Art/Art Vivant, Tokyo, Japan; Mystic Maritime Gallery, Mystic, CT; St James Place Gallery, Rowayton, CT; Portland Place Gallery, Norwalk, CT; Artworks Fine Art, Old Greenwich, CT

TITLE	PUBLISHER	PRINTER	DATE	MEDIUM	DIMENSION (PAPER SIZE) IN INCHES	TYPE OF PAPER	EDITION NUMBER	NO. OF COLORS	ORIGINAL OPENING PRICE	CURRENT RETAIL PRICE
CURRENT EDITIONS:										
United States Coming up the Hudson	ARAAL	FAP	1990	SP	12 X 36	COV/MB	250	40	400	500
Showtime on the Hudson	ARAAL	FAP	1990	SP	24 X 36	COV/MB	250	50	500	600
Venice & the Andrea Doria	ARAAL	FAP	1991	SP	18 X 36	COR/MB	250	40	500	500
Eiffel Tower & the Norway	ARAAL	FAP	1992	SP	18 X 36	COR/MB	250	40	500	500
Empire State Building & the Queen Mary	ARAAL	FAP	1993	SP	18 X 36	COR/MB	250	40	500	500

RICHARD A FLORSHEIM

BORN: Chicago, IL; (1916–1979)
EDUCATION: Univ of Chicago, IL; Studied in Paris and Rome
TEACHING: Layton Sch of Art, Milwaukee, WI; Contemp Art Workshop, Chicago, IL
COLLECTIONS: Mus of Mod Art, NY; Metropolitan Mus of Art, NY; Chicago Art Inst, IL; NY Public Library, NY; Smithsonian Inst, Wash, DC; Bibliotheque Nat, Paris, France; Victoria and Albert Mus, London, England; Nat de Belles Artes, Mexico City, Mex; Library of Congress, Wash, DC; Nat Gallery of Canada, Ottawa, Can; Philadelphia Mus of Arts, PA, Mills Col, Oakland, CA, Atlanta Mus of Art, GA, Art Mus of Tel Aviv, Israel
PRINTERS: Mourlot, Paris, France (M); Landfall Press Inc, Chicago, IL (LPI); David Panosh (DP); Chicago Serigraphic Workshop, Chicago, IL (CSW); Burr Miller, NY (BM)
PUBLISHERS: Associated American Artists, NY (AA); Landfall Inc, Chicago, IL (LPI); New York Graphic Society, CT (NYGS); Circle Fine Art, Chicago, IL (CFA)
GALLERIES: ACA Gallery, New York, NY; Lakeside Studio, Lakeside, MI; Benjamin-Beattie, Chicago, IL; Associated American Artists, New York, NY; Harmon-Meek Gallery, Naples, FL; Oehlschlaeger Galleries, Sarasota, FL; Circle Galleries, San Diego, CA & San Francisco, CA & Northbrook, IL & Pittsburgh, PA & Houston, TX & Soho, NY & Chicago, IL & Scottsdale, AZ & Beverly Hills, CA & Costa Mesa, CA & Sherman Oaks, CA & Palm Beach, FL & Honolulu, HI & New Orleans, LA & Las Vegas, NV & Seattle, WA

TITLE	PUBLISHER	PRINTER	DATE	MEDIUM	DIMENSION (PAPER SIZE) IN INCHES	TYPE OF PAPER	EDITION NUMBER	NO. OF COLORS	ORIGINAL OPENING PRICE	CURRENT RETAIL PRICE
SOLD OUT EDITIONS (RARE):										
Skyscrapers	AAA	M	1960	LC	11 X 30	R/100	250	3	150	600
Twilight	AAA	M	1963	LC	30 X 10	R/100	250	3	150	600
Shoreline	AAA	M	1964	LB	10 X 14	R/100	35	1	150	600
Oil Wells	AAA	M	1964	LC	21 X 15	R/100	50	4	150	600
Spars	AAA	M	1965	LC	30 X 10	R/100	250	4	175	600

The retail prices of the 100,000 limited edition prints quoted in this directory are subject to change. Print publishers, artists and galleries were the direct sources for these quotations. Prices in the secondary market listed as "Sold Out Editions (Rare)" indicate that the publisher has a limited supply of that print or that the print is difficult to locate in the galleries.

RICHARD A FLORSHEIM CONTINUED

TITLE	PUBLISHER	PRINTER	DATE	MEDIUM	DIMENSION (PAPER SIZE) IN INCHES	TYPE OF PAPER	EDITION NUMBER	NO. OF COLORS	ORIGINAL OPENING PRICE	CURRENT RETAIL PRICE
SOLD OUT EDITIONS (RARE):										
Nets	AAA	M	1968	LC	10 X 30	R/100	250		150	600
Glowing City	AAA	M	1968	LC	10 X 30	R/100	250		150	600
Night Storm	AAA	M	1968	LC	14 X 10	R/100	250		150	600
Urban Metaphor	LPI	DP/LPI	1973	LC	22 X 30	DE	30	4	200	750
Moonlight	NYGS	LPI	1978	LC	15 X 10	R/100	50	5	100	450
Fireworks	LS	LPI	1978	LC	21 X 16	R/100	30	5	200	450
Sand Flats	NYGS	LPI	1978	LC	21 X 16	R/100	50	4	75	450
Flags	LS	M	1978	LC	21 X 16	R/100	50	4	75	450
Silhouette I	AAA	LPI	1979	LC	20 X 8	R/100	100	5	180	450
Pennants	AAA	LPI	1979	LC	21 X 15	R/100	100	4	180	600
Low Tide	CFA	CSW	1979	SP/EMB	18 X 41	CSW/100R	300	11	225	600
Metropolis	CFA	CSW	1979	SP/EMB	35 X 45	CSW/100R	300	13	250	600

EDWARD C FLOOD

BORN: Chicago, IL; (1944–1985)
EDUCATION: Art Inst Sch, Chicago, IL, BFA, 1967, MFA, 1969
TEACHING: Lectr, Roosevelt Univ, Chicago, IL, 1969–72; Lectr, Univ of Texas, Austin, TX, 1984
AWARDS: Cassandra Found Grant, 1970; Nat Endowment for the Arts Fel, 1978; AVA/SECCA Grant, 1981; Pollock/Krasner Found Grant, 1985
COLLECTIONS: Art Inst of Chiago, IL; Metropolitan Mus of Art, NY; Nat Coll of Fine Arts, Koffler Coll, Wash, DC
PRINTERS: Mark Rottman, Chicago, IL (MR); Jerry Raidiger, Chicago, IL (JR); Landfall Press, Chicago, IL (LPI)
PUBLISHERS: Landfall Press, Inc, Chicago, IL (LPI)
GALLERIES: Klein Gallery, Chicago, IL
MAILING ADDRESS: Estate of Edward C Flood, c/o Cheryl C Flood, Box 64, Williamsburgh Station, Brooklyn, NY 11211

TITLE	PUBLISHER	PRINTER	DATE	MEDIUM	DIMENSION (PAPER SIZE) IN INCHES	TYPE OF PAPER	EDITION NUMBER	NO. OF COLORS	ORIGINAL OPENING PRICE	CURRENT RETAIL PRICE
SOLD OUT EDITIONS (RARE):										
Two Palms Menaced by a Wave	LPI	JR/MR/LPI	1971	LC	16 X 20	AP/W	30	5	100	800

JEAN MICHEL FOLON

BORN: Brussels, Belgium; March 1, 1934
PUBLISHERS: Alice Editions, Geneva, Switzerland (AEd); Blue Shadow, Paris, France (BS); André Sauret, Monte Carlo, Monaco (AS); Abrams Original Editions, NY (AOE); Transworld Art Inc, NY (TAI)
PRINTERS: Claude Manesse, France (CM); Philippe Lejeune, Burcy par Beaumont du Gatinais, France (PL); Tanguy Garric, Paris, France (CG); Blandine et Stéphane Lalou, Lucy, France (BL) & (SL)
GALLERIES: Galerie la Hune, Paris, France; Navin Kumar, New York, NY; Martin Lawrence Galleries, Los Angeles, CA & Newport Beach, CA & Sherman Oaks, CA & West Los Angeles, CA & Short Hills, CA & Phila, PA; Charles Whitchurch Fine Arts, Huntington Beach, CA; Newmark Gallery, New York, NY; Studio L'Atelier, Nashville, TN; Gala Art Gallery, Palm Beach, FL; Gallery 121 International, New York, NY; Langman Gallery, Willow Grove, PA; Ro Gallery Image Makers, Inc, New York, NY; Professional Fine Arts Services, Inc, New York, NY

TITLE	PUBLISHER	PRINTER	DATE	MEDIUM	DIMENSION (PAPER SIZE) IN INCHES	TYPE OF PAPER	EDITION NUMBER	NO. OF COLORS	ORIGINAL OPENING PRICE	CURRENT RETAIL PRICE
SOLD OUT EDITIONS (RARE):										
Les Ruines Circulaires (Set of 10):	AS	CM	1974	EB/A	26 X 20 EA	AP	95 EA		5000 SET	6000 SET
Qui	TAI	CG	1979	EB/A	20 X 26	AP	90		700	850
Le Guardian	TAI	CG	1979	EB/A	20 X 26	AP	90		700	850
Le Secret	TAI	CG	1979	EB/A	20 X 26	AP	90		700	850
L'Etranger	TAI	CG	1979	EB/A	20 X 26	AP	90		700	850
Theatre (Set of 4):									2000 SET	3000 SET
Road	AOE	PL	1979	EB/A	20 X 23	MG	100		500	750
Marionette	AOE	PL	1979	EB/A	20 X 23	MG	100		500	750
Arena	AOE	PL	1979	EB/A	20 X 23	MG	100		500	750
Scene	AOE	PL	1979	EB/A	20 X 23	MG	100		500	750
Jeux de Mains (Set of 4):									2000 SET	3000 SET
Hier	AEd	CG	1980	EB/A	20 X 26	AP	90		500	750
Aujourd'Hui	AEd	CG	1980	EB/A	20 X 26	AP	90		500	750
Demain	AEd	CG	1980	EB/A	20 X 26	AP	90		500	750
Dialogue	AEd	CG	1980	EB/A	20 X 26	AP	90		500	750
Over the Rainbow (Set of 7):									3500 SET	4500 SET
Lundi	AEd	CG	1981	EB/A	20 X 26	AP	90		500	650
Mardi	AEd	CG	1981	EB/A	20 X 26	AP	90		500	650
Mercredi	AEd	CG	1981	EB/A	20 X 26	AP	90		500	650
Jeudi	AEd	CG	1981	EB/A	20 X 26	AP	90		500	650
Vendredi	AEd	CG	1981	EB/A	20 X 26	AP	90		500	650
Samedi	AEd	CG	1981	EB/A	20 X 26	AP	90		500	650
Dimanche	AEd	CG	1981	EB/A	20 X 26	AP	90		500	650

The print market has become very selective. For the first time since we published the first edition of The Printworld Directory in 1982, the prices of prints have been greatly reduced and greatly increased for the same artists by the most reputable and established print publishers. Check the fifth edition to understand the movement.

JEAN MICHEL FOLON CONTINUED

TITLE	PUBLISHER	PRINTER	DATE	MEDIUM	DIMENSION (PAPER SIZE) IN INCHES	TYPE OF PAPER	EDITION NUMBER	NO. OF COLORS	ORIGINAL OPENING PRICE	CURRENT RETAIL PRICE
SOLD OUT EDITIONS (RARE):										
Cities (Set of 4):									2000 SET	2500 SET
Arrows	AOE	BL	1982	EB/A	22 X 23	R/BFK	100		500	650
Honeycomb Office	AOE	BL	1982	EB/A	22 X 23	R/BFK	100		500	650
Question Mark	AOE	BL	1982	EB/A	22 X 23	R/BFK	100		500	650
Numbers	AOE	BL	1982	EB/A	22 X 23	R/BFK	100		500	650

JAMES FORD

EDUCATION: Univ of California, Santa Barbara, CA, BA, 1965–69; California State Univ, Arcata, CA, MA, 1970; Univ of California, Santa Barbara, CA, MFA, 1971–72
AWARDS: Nat Endowment for the Arts, Ind Artist Grant, 1980; Art Matters Grants, Boulder, CO, 1985,87
RECENT EXHIB: Harcus Gallery, Boston, MA, 1987–88; 3 EP Ltd, Palo Alto, CA, 1988; Pence Gallery, Santa Monica, CA, 1987,89
COLLECTIONS: Brooklyn Mus of Art, NY; Los Angeles Municipal Art Gallery, CA; Univ of California, Santa Barbara, CA; Univ of California, Irvine, CA; Univ Art Mus, Berkeley, CA; Newport Harbor Art Mus, Newport Beach, CA; La Jolla Mus of Contemp Art, CA; Laguna Art Mus, Laguna Beach, CA; de Saisset Mus, Santa Clara, CA
PRINTERS: Artist (ART); Timothy Berry, Santa Monica, CA (TB); Teaberry Press, Santa Monica, CA (TP)
PUBLISHERS: 3 EP, Ltd, Palo Alto, CA (3EP)
GALLERIES: Pence Gallery, Los Angeles, CA; Harcus Gallery, Boston, MA; 3 EP, Ltd, Palo Alto, CA

TITLE	PUBLISHER	PRINTER	DATE	MEDIUM	DIMENSION (PAPER SIZE) IN INCHES	TYPE OF PAPER	EDITION NUMBER	NO. OF COLORS	ORIGINAL OPENING PRICE	CURRENT RETAIL PRICE
CURRENT EDITIONS:										
Basin, Beakers, Blades (Series of 21 Monotypes)	3EP	ART/TB/TP	1989	MON	Varies	AP	1 EA	Varies	1800–2500	1800–2500

GÜNTHER FÖRG

RECENT EXHIB: Newport Harbor Art Mus, Newport Beach, CA, 1992; Luhring/Augustine Gallery, NY, 1993
PRINTERS: Karl Imhoff, Munich, Germany (KI); Sander Photography GmbH, Cologne, Germany (SaPh); Hans Mayer, Munich, Germany (HM); Maurice Sanchez, NY (MS); Derriére L'Etoile Studio, NY (DES); Creative Color GmbH, Hamburg, Germany (CC); Niels Borch Jensen, Copenhagen, Denmark (NBJ)
PUBLISHERS: Galerie Bergman-Capitain, Cologne, Germany (GBC); Edition Julie Sylvester, NY (EJS); Editions Schellmann, Inc, NY (ES); Maximillian Verlag Sabine Knust, Munich, Germany (MV)
GALLERIES: David Nolan Gallery, New York, NY; Luhring & Augustine Gallery, New York, NY; Barbara Krakow Gallery, Boston, MA; Margarete Roeder Gallery/Editions, New York, NY; Goodman/Tinnon Fine Art, San Francisco, CA; Signet Arts, St Louis, MO; Edition Julie Sylvester, New York, NY; Montgomery Glasoe Fine Art, Minneapolis, MN; Jim Kemper Fine Art, Inc, New York, NY; Davis/McClain Gallery, Houston, TX; Editions Schellmann, Inc, New York, NY

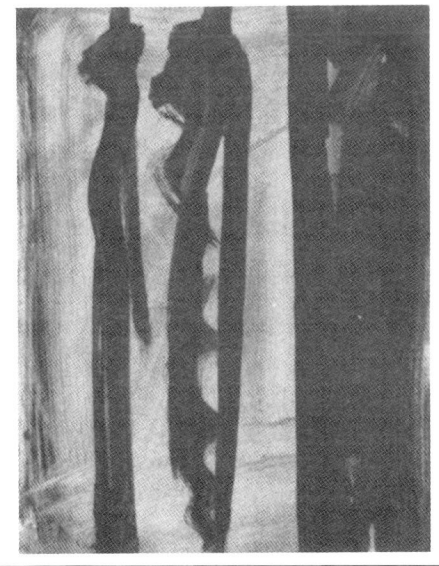

Günther Förg
Station of the Cross
Courtesy Edition Julie Sylvester

TITLE	PUBLISHER	PRINTER	DATE	MEDIUM	DIMENSION (PAPER SIZE) IN INCHES	TYPE OF PAPER	EDITION NUMBER	NO. OF COLORS	ORIGINAL OPENING PRICE	CURRENT RETAIL PRICE
CURRENT EDITIONS:										
Gardone (in Exotic Wood Box) (Set of 5)	GBC	SaPh	1986	PH	47 X 31 EA		9 EA		DM7500 SET	DM 10000 SET
Formen (Set of 5)	GBC	KI	1987	LC	27 X 23 EA	R/BFK	25 EA	2 EA	1500 SET	2000 SET
Häuser und Fenster (Set of 9)	GBC	CC	1987	DT	23 X 20 EA	R/BFK	15 EA		9000 EA	10000 SET
Krefeld Suite (Bronze Relief with 4 Lithographs)									8000 SET	9000 SET
	EJS	KI	1987	LC	27 X 21 EA	AC	12 EA	2 EA	XXX	XXX
	EJS	HM	1987	BR/REL	30 X 19 X 2	BRONZE	12		XXX	XXX
Raum (Set of 12)			1987	LC		AC	20 EA		5000 SET	7500 SET
Relief			1988	LC	25 X 18	AC	25		800	1000
Series of Monotypes on Dkawara (Set of 5)	EJS	MS/DES	1988	MON	19 X 15 EA	OKP	6 EA		3600 SET	3600 SET
Series of Monotypes on Rives (Set of 4)	EJS	MS/DES	1988	MON	25 X 19 EA	R/BFK	8 EA		3600 SET	3600 SET
Acht Holzschnitte (Set of 8)	ES		1990	WC	41 X 32 EA	AC	20 EA	2 EA	14000 SET	14000 SET
Ohne Titel (Set of 6)	ES		1990	SP	26 X 19 EA	AC	50 EA	2 EA	3000 SET	3000 SET
Bauhaus-Mappe (Set of 6)	MV	NBJ	1993	PH/G	15 X 12 EA	SOM/S	15 EA	2 EA	DM4500 SET	DM 4500 SET

PATRICIA TOBACCO FORRESTER

BORN: Northampton, MA; September 17, 1940
EDUCATION: Yale Summer Sch, Music & Art, New Haven, CT, 1961; Smith Col, Northampton, MA, BA, 1962; Yale Univ Art Sch, New Haven, CT, BFA, 1963, MFA, 1965
TEACHING: Asst Prof, Printmaking, California Col of Arts & Crafts, Oakland, CA, 1972–81; Guest Art, Painting, Kent State Univ, Canton, OH, 1981; Guest Art, Art Inst of Chicago, IL, 1982; Guest Art, Acad of Fine Arts, New Orleans, LA, 1984
AWARDS: Guggenheim Fel, Printmaking, 1967; MacDowell Colony Fel, 1980; Yaddo Fel, 1979,81
RECENT EXHIB: Reynolds/Minor Gallery, Richmond, VA, 1987; Fischbach Gallery, NY, 1987,88; Sierra Nevada Mus of Art, Reno, NV, 1988
COLLECTIONS: Brooklyn Mus, NY; San Antonio Mus of Art, TX; Oakland Mus, CA; Mem Art Gallery, Univ of Rochester, NY; Achenbach Found, Legion of Honor, CA
PRINTERS: Derriére L'Etoile Studio, NY (DES)
PUBLISHERS: John Szoke Graphics, NY (JSG)
GALLERIES: John Szoke Graphics, New York, NY; Fischbach Gallry, New York, NY; Braunstein/Quay Gallry, San Francisco, CA; Steven Scott Gallery, Baltimore, MD
MAILING ADDRESS: 2220 20th St, NW, Wash, DC 20009

Patricia Tobacco Forrester
Lily Triangle
Courtesy John Szoke Graphics, Inc

Patricia Tobacco Forrester
Royal Flush
Courtesy John Szoke Graphics, Inc

TITLE	PUBLISHER	PRINTER	DATE	MEDIUM	DIMENSION (PAPER SIZE) IN INCHES	TYPE OF PAPER	EDITION NUMBER	NO. OF COLORS	ORIGINAL OPENING PRICE	CURRENT RETAIL PRICE
CURRENT EDITIONS:										
Lily Triangle	JSG	DES	1987	LC	30 X 46	SOM	75	8	300	1000
Royal Flush	JSG	DES	1990	LC	30 X 46	SOM	75	6	1200	1600

CHUCK FORSMAN (CHARLES STANLEY)

BORN: Nampa, ID; May 5, 1944
EDUCATION: Univ of California, Davis, CA, BA, 1967, with Wayne Thiebaud & William Wiley, MFA, 1971, with Gabriel Laderman
TEACHING: Asst Prof, Painting & Sculpture, Univ of California, Davis, CA, 1970–71; Prof, Fine Arts, Univ of Colorado, Boulder, CO, 1971 to present
AWARDS: Purchase Award, Am Acad of Arts & Letters, NY, 1979; Nat Endowment for the Arts Grants, 1979,85; Faculty Fel, Univ of Colorado, Boulder, CO, 1979,88
RECENT EXHIB: Orlando Mus of Art, FL, 1987; Hudson River Mus, Yonkers, NY, 1988; Tibor de Nagy Gallery, NY, 1988; Virginia Mus of Fine Arts, Richmond, VA, 1990; Nat Acad of Sciences, Wash, DC, 1992
PRINTERS: Richard Finch, Normal, IL (RF); Xiaowen Chen, Normal, IL (XC); Richard Folse, Normal, IL (RFo); Sharon Merrill, Normal, IL (SM); Joe Sim, Normal, IL (JS); Normal Editions Workshop, Illinois State Univ, Normal, IL (NEW)
PUBLISHERS: Normal Editions Workshop, Illinois State Univ, Normal, IL (NEW)
GALLERIES: Tibor de Nagy Gallery, New York, NY; Robischon Gallery, Denver, CO; John Post Lee Gallery, New York, NY
MAILING ADDRESS: 511 Pleasant St, Boulder, CO 80302

TITLE	PUBLISHER	PRINTER	DATE	MEDIUM	DIMENSION (PAPER SIZE) IN INCHES	TYPE OF PAPER	EDITION NUMBER	NO. OF COLORS	ORIGINAL OPENING PRICE	CURRENT RETAIL PRICE
CURRENT EDITIONS:										
Untitled	NEW	RF/XC/RFo/ SM/JS/NEW	1989	LC	23 X 27	R/BFK/W	44	6	350	450

RICHARD F FOULGER

BORN: Kamloops, BC, Canada; April 30, 1949
EDUCATION: Alberta Col of Art, Calgary, Can, 1967–69; Vancouver Sch of Art, Can, 1970–72; Notre Dame Univ, Nelson, Can, 1974; Simon Fraser Univ, Burnaby, Can, BFA, 1974–75
COLLECTIONS: Alberta Col of Art, Calgary, Can; Soc of Canadian Painters, Etchers and Engravers, Toronto, Can; York Univ, Toronto, Can; Vancouver Art Gallery, BC, Can; The Print Club, Phila, PA
PRINTERS: Artist (ART)
PUBLISHERS: Artist (ART)
GALLERIES: Gallery 93, Ottawa, Toronto, Canada; Danish Art Gallery, Vancouver, BC, Canada;Bau-Xi Galleries, Vancouver, Canada & Toronto, Canada; Canadian Art Gallery, Canada; Downstairs Gallery, Edmonton, Canada; Fleet Galleries, Winnipeg, Canada; Nancy Poole's Gallery, London, Canada & Toronto, Canada
MAILING ADDRESS: Cobble Hill Loft Studio, RR 1, Winlaw, BC, Canada V0G 2J0

The retail prices of the 100,000 limited edition prints quoted in this directory are subject to change. Print publishers, artists and galleries were the direct sources for these quotations. Prices in the secondary market listed as "Sold Out Editions (Rare)" indicate that the publisher has a limited supply of that print or that the print is difficult to locate in the galleries.

RICHARD F FOULGER CONTINUED

TITLE	PUBLISHER	PRINTER	DATE	MEDIUM	DIMENSION (PAPER SIZE) IN INCHES	TYPE OF PAPER	EDITION NUMBER	NO. OF COLORS	ORIGINAL OPENING PRICE	CURRENT RETAIL PRICE
SOLD OUT EDITIONS (RARE):										
Landscape I	ART	ART	1971	SP	15 X 19	AP	25	1	75	200
Linear Tension	ART	ART	1971	SP	11 X 15	AP	7	4	75	200
Curvilinear Variation	ART	ART	1972	SP	16 X 16	AP	21	5	75	200
Image Four-Nancy's Drawing	ART	ART	1972	SP	16 X 17	AP	20	6	75	200
Legend of Blackloam	ART	ART	1972	SP	17 X 21	AP	29	8	75	200
Legend of Stone	ART	ART	1972	SP	15 X 17	AP	24	8	75	200
Rock Spirit	ART	ART	1972	SP	15 X 18	AP	20	8	75	200
Legend of Night	ART	ART	1973	SP	15 X 17	AP	20	8	75	200
Earth Spirit	ART	ART	1973	SP	18 X 22	AP	24	9	75	200
Mountain Spirit	ART	ART	1973	SP	17 X 20	AP	24	9	75	200
Mountain Mythology	ART	ART	1974	SP	17 X 17	AP	25	9	75	200
Landscape II	ART	ART	1981	SP	18 X 18	AP	30	1	125	200

TERRY FOX

BORN: Seattle, WA; May 10, 1943
EDUCATION: Self-Taught
RECENT EXHIB: Capp Street Project, San Francisco, CA, 1987; Gallery Paule Anglim, San Francisco, CA, 1992; Moore Col of Art & Design, Goldie Paley Gallery, Phila, PA, 1992
COLLECTIONS: Univ of California Art Mus, Berkeley, CA; Mus of Mod Art, NY; San Francisco Mus of Mod Art, CA; Kuntzmuseum, Luzern, Switzerland; Folkwang Mus, Essen, Germany; Mus of Contemp Art, Vienna, Austria
PRINTERS: Stephen Thomas (ST); Doris Simmelink (DS); Crown Point Press, San Francisco, CA (CPP)
PUBLISHERS: Crown Point Press, San Francisco, CA (CPP)
GALLERIES: Ronald Feldman Fine Arts, New York, NY; Crown Point Press, San Francisco, CA & New York, NY; Gallery Paule Anglim, San Francisco, CA
MAILING ADDRESS: Via Dell' Albero, 13 Firenze, Italy 50123

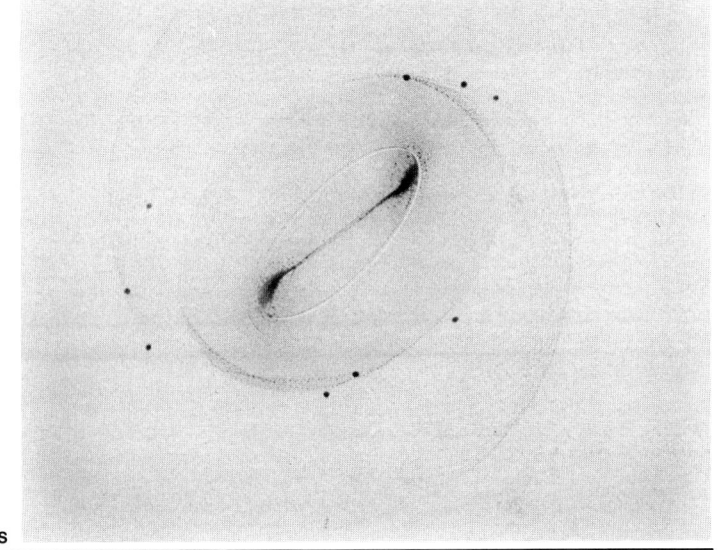

Terry Fox
Pendulum Spit Bite
Courtesy Crown Point Press

TITLE	PUBLISHER	PRINTER	DATE	MEDIUM	DIMENSION (PAPER SIZE) IN INCHES	TYPE OF PAPER	EDITION NUMBER	NO. OF COLORS	ORIGINAL OPENING PRICE	CURRENT RETAIL PRICE
CURRENT EDITIONS:										
Pendulum Spit Bite	CPP	ST/DS/CPP	1977	AB	40 X 49	R/BFK	25	1	550	1200

MARY FRANK

BORN: London, England; 1933
TEACHING: Instr, New Sch for Social Research, Drawing, NY, 1965–70; Instr, Queens Col, Grad Sch, Bronx, NY, Drawing & Sculpture, 1970–75; Vis Art, Skowhegan of Painting & Sculpture, 1976
AWARDS: Ingram Merrill Found Grant, 1961; Longview Found Grant, 1962,63,64; Nat Coun of the Arts, 1968; Am Acad of Arts & Letters, 1972; Creative Artists Public Service Grant, 1973, Brandeis Univ Creative Arts Award, 1977; Guggenheim Awards, 1973,83; Elected, Am Acad of Arts & Letters, 1984
RECENT EXHIB: Brooklyn Mus, NY, 1987; Roger Ramsay Gallery, Chicago, IL, 1987; DeCordova Mus, Lincoln, MA, 1988; Nielson Gallery, Boston, MA, 1988; Dalsheimer Gallery, Baltimore, MD, 1988; Dana Mus, Lincoln, MA, 1988; Everson Mus, Syracuse, NY, 1989; Pennsylvania Acad of Fine Arts, Phila, PA, 1989; Zabriskie Gallery, NY, 1989; Allene Lapides Gallery, Santa Fe, NM, 1992; Midtown Payson Gallery, NY, 1992,93
COLLECTIONS: Mus of Mod Art, NY; Metropolitan Mus of Art, NY; Whitney Mus of Am Art, NY; Brooklyn Mus, NY; Chicago Art Inst, IL; Des Moines Art Center, IA; Neuberger Mus, State Univ of New York, Purchase, NY; Kalamazoo Inst of Art, MI; Univ of Massachusetts, Northampton, MA; Worcester Art Mus, MA; Yale Univ, New Haven, CT; Univ of Brown Univ, Providence, RI; Mus of Fine Art, Boston, MA; Jewish Mus, NY; De Cordova Mus, Lincoln, MA; Akron Art Inst, OH; Hirshhorn Mus, Wash, DC; Southern Illinois Univ, Carbondale, IL; Virginia Mus of Art, Richmond, VA; Storm King Art Center, ME; Library of Congress, Wash, DC; Univ of Bridgeport, Michael C Arnot Art Mus, Elmira, NY; Univ of New Mexico, Albuquerque, NM; Connecticut Col Art Gallery
PRINTERS: Pondside Press, Rhinebeck, NY (PoPr); Judith Solodkin, NY (JS); Solo Press, NY (SP); Artist (ART)
PUBLISHERS: Solo Press, NY (SP); Artist (ART)
GALLERIES: Marsha Mateyka Gallery, Wash, DC; Associated American Artists, New York, NY; Zabriskie Gallery, New York, NY; Solo Gallery, New York, NY; Pondside Press, Rhinebeck, NY; Allene Lapides Gallery, Santa Fe, NM; Midtown Payson Gallery, New York, NY

TITLE	PUBLISHER	PRINTER	DATE	MEDIUM	DIMENSION (PAPER SIZE) IN INCHES	TYPE OF PAPER	EDITION NUMBER	NO. OF COLORS	ORIGINAL OPENING PRICE	CURRENT RETAIL PRICE
CURRENT EDITIONS:										
Constellation	ART	ART	1985	MON	36 X 28 EA	RICE	1 EA	Varies	2500 EA	4000 EA
Untitled	ART	ART	1985	MON	36 X 28 EA	RICE	1 EA	Varies	2500 EA	4000 EA
Untitled	ART	ART	1986–87	MON	37 X 24 EA	RICE	1 EA	Varies	2800 EA	4000 EA
Man in the Water, State II	SP	JS/SP	1987	LC	23 X 32	AC	30		600	800

SAM FRANCIS

BORN: San Mateo, CA; June 25, 1923
EDUCATION: Univ of California, Berkeley, CA, BA, 1941–43, MFA, 1948–50; Atelier Fernand Leger, Paris, France; Univ of California, Berkeley, CA, Hon DFA, 1969
AWARDS: First Prize, Int Biennial Exhib of Prints, Tokyo, Japan, 1962; Tate Mus, Dunn Int Prize, London, England, 1963; Tamarind Fel, Albuquerque, NM, 1963
RECENT EXHIB: Gallery de Seoul, Korea, 1988; Charles H MacNider Mus, Mason City, IA, 1989; Gallery Delaive, Amsterdam, The Netherlands, 1990; Heland Wetterling Gallery, Stockholm, Sweden, 1990; Ogawa Art Found, Tokyo, Japan, 1990; Ochi Gallery, Sun Valley, ID, 1990; Talbot Rice Gallery, Edinburgh, Scotland, 1990; Andre Emmerich Gallery, NY, 1990; Smith/Andersen Gallery, Palo Alto, CA, 1990; Retrosp, Galerie Kornfeld, Bern, Switzerland, 1991; Galerie Jean Fournier, Paris, France, 1991; James Corcoran Gallery, Los Angeles, CA 1991; Angeles Gallery, Los Angeles, CA, 1991; Gana Art Gallery, Seoul, Korea, 1991; Gagosian Gallery, NY, 1991; Centre Regional d'Art Contempora Midi-Pyrenees, Toulouse-Labege, France, 1991; Galerie Daniel Papierski, Paris, France, 1992; Mus van der Togt, Amsterdam, The Netherlands 1992; Kukje Gallery, Seoul, Korea, 1992; Galerie Wild, Frankfurt, Germany, 1992; Retrosp, Kunst-und Ausstellungshalle der Bundesrepublik Deutchland, Bon, Germany, 1993; Galerie Pudelko, Bonn, Germany, 1993; Bobbie Greenfield Fine Art, Venice, CA, 1993; M Cohen Gallery, NY, 1993; Ochi Galleries, Ketchum, ID, 1993; Manny Silverman Gallery, Los Angeles, CA, 1993; Associated American Artists, NY, 1989,90,91,93
COLLECTIONS: Guggenheim Mus, NY; Mus of Mod Art, NY; Whitney Mus of Am Art, NY; Tate Gallery, London, England; Stedelijk Mus, Amsterdam, Holland; Albright-Knox Art Gallery, Buffalo, NY; Art Inst, Dayton, OH; Univ of California, Los Angeles, CA; Nat Gallery of Art, Wash, DC; Nat Mus of Western Art, Tokyo, Japan; Ohara Art Mus, Basel, Switzerland; Pasadena Art Mus, CA; Seattle Mus of Art, WA; Washington Univ, St Louis, MO; Nat Mus of Art, Stockholm, Sweden; Toronto Art Mus, Canada; Albright Art Gallery, Kunsthaus, Zürich, Switzerland; Dayton Art Inst, OH
PRINTERS: The Litho Shop, Santa Monica, CA (LS); Tyler Graphics Ltd, Bedford Village, NY (TGL); Ikuru Kuwahara, Palo Alto, CA (IK); 3EP Workshop, Palo Alto, CA (3EP); Experimental Workshop, San Francisco, CA (EW); David Kelso, Palo Alto, CA (DK); Sienna Studios, NY (SS); Joe Petruzzelli, NY (JP); Garner Tullis Workshop, Santa Barbara, CA (GTW); Joe Zirkir, NY (JZ); Joseph Press, NY (JP); Irwin Hollander, NY (IH); Tamarind Inst Workshop, Albuquerque, NM (TI); Edicion de la Difference, Paris, France (EdLD); 2RC, Rome, Italy (2RC); Rossi, Rome, Italy (Ros); Jacob Samuel, Santa Monica, CA (JS); George Page, Santa Monica, CA (GP)
PUBLISHERS: The Litho Shop, Santa Monica, CA (LS); Brooke Alexander, Inc, NY (BAI); Gemini GEL, Los Angeles, CA (GEM); Tyler Graphics, Ltd, Bedford Village, NY (TGL); Abrams Original Editions, NY (AOE); 3EP, Palo Alto, CA (3EP); Experimental Workshop, San Francisco, CA (EW); Garner Tullis Workshop, Santa Barbara, CA (GTW); Pasadena Art Mus Art Alliance, CA (PMAA); Louisiana Mus, Denmark (LM); Tamarind Inst, Albuquerque, NM (TI); Kornfeld (KORN); Ediciones de la Difference (EdLD); Artist (ART); Edition Schellmann, Inc, NY (ES); 2 RC Editions, Rome, Italy (2RC); Gardner Litho (GL)
GALLERIES: Brooke Alexander, Inc, New York, NY; Smith Andersen Gallery, Palo Alto, CA; Minami Gallery, Tokyo, Japan; André Emmerich Gallery, New York, NY; Adler Gallery, Los Angeles, CA; Susan Gersh Gallery, Beverly Hills, CA; Herbert Palmer Gallery, Los Angeles, CA; Jack Rutberg Fine Art, Los Angeles, CA; Harcourts Contemp, San Francisco, CA; Graphics Gallery, San Francisco, CA; Marsha Mateyka Gallery, Wash, DC; Nancy Singer Gallery, New York, NY; Richard Gray Gallery, Chicago, IL; Lemberg Gallery, Birmingham, MI; Wirtz Gallery, San Francisco, CA; Pamela Auchincloss, Santa Barbara, CA; John Berggruen Gallery, San Francisco, CA; Graystone Gallery, San Francisco, CA; Irene Drori Graphics, Los Angeles, CA; Hokin Gallery, Bay Harbor Islands, FL & Palm Beach, FL; Alexander Kahan Fine Arts, New York, NY; Elizabeth Leach Gallery, Portland, OR; Michael H Lord Gallery, Milwaukee, WI; Martin Lawrence Galleries, Los Angeles, CA & Sherman Oaks, CA & West Los Angeles, CA & Short Hills, NJ & Phila, PA; Charles Whitchurch Gallery, Huntington Beach, CA; Art Source, Los Angeles, CA; Andrew Dierken Fine Art, Los Angeles, CA; Gemini GEL, Los Angeles, CA; R K Goldman Contemporary Gallery, Los Angeles, CA; Jonathan Novak, Los Angeles, CA; Manny Silverman Gallery, Los Angeles, CA; Joni Moisant Weyl Gallery, Los Angeles, CA; Smith Anderson Gallery, Palo Alto, CA; Shirley Cerf, Inc, San Francisco, CA; Michael Dunev Gallery, San Francisco, CA; Greenberg Gallery, St Louis, MO; Ronnie Meyerson, Inc, Bayville, NY; Carol M Penn Fine Art, Great Neck, NY; Margot Gallery, Inc, Larchmont, NY; Maxwell Davidson Gallery, New York, NY; Elkon Gallery, Inc, New York, NY; Gemini GEL at Joni Weyl, New York, NY; Foster Goldstrom, Inc, New York, NY; Jane Kahan Gallery, New York, NY; Magidson Fine Arts, New York, NY; Petersburg Press, New York, NY; Michelle Rosenfeld Fine Arts, New York, NY; Laura Paul Galleries, Cincinnati, OH & Columbus, OH; Argus Fine Arts, Eugene, OR; Posner Gallery, Milwaukee, WI; Ochi Galleries, Boise, ID & Sun Valley, ID; Kass/Meridian Gallery, Chicago, IL; R H Love Galleries, Chicago, IL; Corcoran Gallery, Santa Monica, CA; Thomas Segal Gallery, Boston, MA; Philip Samuels Fine Art, Clayton, MO; Angeles Gallery, Santa Monica, CA; Horoshak Contemporary Art, Sunnyvale, CA; Xiliary Twil Fine Arts, Santa Monica, CA & Venice, CA; Opus Art Studios, Miami, FL; Hibbard McGrath Gallery, Breckenridge, CO; Associated American Artists, New York, NY; Galerie Wild, Frankfurt, Germany; Edition Schellmann, Inc, New York, NY; Ro Gallery Image Makers, Inc, New York, NY
MAILING ADDRESS: c/o Sam Francis/The Litho Shop, 2058 Broadway, Santa Monica, CA 90404

Gemini GEL (G); Experimental Workshop (EXP); Sam Francis (SF); Sam Francis Etchings (SFE); 2 RC Editions (2RC)

Sam Francis
Untitled (SF-65)
Courtesy Art Alliance, Pasadena Museum

TITLE	PUBLISHER	PRINTER	DATE	MEDIUM	DIMENSION (PAPER SIZE) IN INCHES	TYPE OF PAPER	EDITION NUMBER	NO. OF COLORS	ORIGINAL OPENING PRICE	CURRENT RETAIL PRICE
SOLD OUT EDITIONS (RARE):										
Coldest Stone			1960	LC	25 X 35	AP	65		100	40000
First Stone			1960	LC	25 X 36	AP	65		100	40000
The White Line			1960	LC	36 X 25	AP	75		100	40000

SAM FRANCIS CONTINUED

TITLE	PUBLISHER	PRINTER	DATE	MEDIUM	DIMENSION (PAPER SIZE) IN INCHES	TYPE OF PAPER	EDITION NUMBER	NO. OF COLORS	ORIGINAL OPENING PRICE	CURRENT RETAIL PRICE
SOLD OUT EDITIONS (RARE):										
Untitled (K&K-12)			1963	LC	25 X 36	HMP	65		200	20000
Untitled (SF-65)	PMAA	JZ/JP	1963	LC	13 X 10	AP	100		200	6000
Yellow Speck (SF-24)	TI	IH/TI	1963	LC	22 X 30	AP	20		300	15000
Flying Love	TI	IH/TI	1963	LC	24 X 19	AP	10		300	5000
Untitled	TI	IH/TI	1963	LC	24 X 19	AP	20		300	5000
Lithograph Number 7 (from Paradise Box Suite)	TI	IH/TI	1963	LC	20 X 26	AP	40		300	7000
Heart Stone			1963	LB	24 X 35	AP	65		200	18000
Bright Jade Gold Ghost (SF-28)	KORN		1963	LC	25 X 36	R/BFK	125		200	16000
Untitled (SF-68)	PMAA	JZ/JP	1964	LC	11 X 15	R/BFK	100		200	5000
Voilá	ES		1964	LC	20 X 26	AP	300	4	200	7000
The Upper Red (SF-48)	ES		1963–65	LC	21 X 26	R/BFK	300	4	200	7000
Untitled (Up and Down)	ES		1966	LC	30 X 22	AP	25		300	2500
Untitled (SF-56) (G-18)	GEM	GEM	1966	LC	24 X 16	R/BFK	100		200	7000
Untitled (SF-62)	JP	JP	1966	LC	25 X 19	AP	15		300	6000
Untitled (SF-73)	AA/PM		1966	LC/CO	31 X 19	RICE/SILK	100		200	15000
Untitled (SF-94)	JP	JP	1967	LC	26 X 20	AP	7		300	7000
Damp (SF-90)	TI	TI	1969	LC	26 X 37	AP	20		300	4000
Sulfur Sails (SF-93)	TI	TI	1969	LC	38 X 26	AP	20		300	6000
The East is Red (SF-103)	LS	LS	1970	LC	25 X 35	R/BFK	15		250	15000
For Ebi			1970	LC	18 X 23	R/BFK	15		200	12000
Cut Throat (SF-116) (G-312)	GEM	GEM	1971	LC	45 X 31	ARJ	62		300	15000
White Bone	GEM	GEM	1971	LC	28 X 40	AP	69		300	10000
Yunan, State I (MOMA-315)	TGL	TGL	1971	LC	42 X 29	ARJ	15	5	300	15000
Yunan, State II (MOMA-317)	TGL	TGL	1971	LC	42 X 30	TOR	15	5	300	15000
Vegetable Series:										
Vegetable I (SF-112-I)	LS	LS	1971	LC	35 X 24	R/BFK	15		300	16000
Vegetable II (SF-112-II)	LS	LS	1971	LC	35 X 24	R/BFK	15		300	16000
Silver Line (SF-110)	LS	LS	1972	LC	15 X 11	R/BFK	57		300	5000
Of Vega (MOMA-409)	TGL	TGL	1972	SP	38 X 26	ARJ	80	4	400	8000
For James Kirsch (SF-121)	LS	LS	1972	LC	28 X 41	ARJ	32		500	12000
Freshet (SF-131)(G-412)	GEM	GEM	1972	SP	38 X 29	AP88	100		500	5000
Ting (SF-137) (G-407)	GEM	GEM	1972	SP	24 X 30	ARJ	75		400	8000
Salmon (SFE-4B)	2RC	2RC	1973	AC	16 X 18	AC	45		500	3000
Red Coral (SFE-3A)	2RC	2RC	1973	AC	18 X 20	AC	45		500	8000
Coral Marine	2RC	2RC	1973	LC	26 X 35	AC	23		500	8000
Untitled	AOE	LS	1974	LC	22 X 39	R/BFK	100		400	4000
Burnout	TGL	TGL	1974	SP	30 X 38	AP88	60	5	600	10000
Ariel's Ring (SF-197) (G-494)	GEM	GEM	1974	SP	41 X 51	ARJ	80	8	550	12500
Straight Line of the Sun	GEM	GEM	1976	LC	51 X 90	ARJ	32	15	2200	30000
Point	GEM	GEM	1976	LC	36 X 36	ARJ	26	5	700	10000
Deft and Sudden Gain	GEM	GEM	1976	LC	51 X 51	ARJ	38	6	950	12000
Untitled (SF-220)	LS	LS	1976	LC	30 X 22	R/BFK	20		750	9500
Concert Hall I, II, III (Set of 3) (SF 230, 231, 232)	LM		1977	LC	26 X 35 EA	R/BFK	75 EA		2000 SET	18000 SET
Untitled	GEM	GEM	1977	LC	51 X 51		25	10	950	10000
Pointing at the Future I (2 Panels)	GEM	GEM	1977	LC	44 X 72	AP	16		950	10000
Pointing at the Future II (2 Panels)	GEM	GEM	1977	LC	44 X 72	AP	16		950	10000
Living in Our Own Light (6 Panels)	GEM	GEM	1977	LC	88 X 108	AP	20		3000	36000
Untitled (SF-335) (G-820)	GEM	GEM	1978	LC	60 X 60	OKP	15		1200	25000
Untitled	GEM	GEM	1978	LC	51 X 51	OKP	25	5	950	20000
In, on, of Paper	GEM	GEM	1978	MON	30 X 25 EA	HMP	1 EA	Varies	2000 EA	20000 EA
Untitled (SF-255)	LS	LS	1978–79	LC	29 X 42	R/BFK	20		750	12000
Untitled (SF-256)	LS	LS	1979	LC	19 X 23	R/BFK	75		500	8000
Untitled (SF-260)	LS	LS	1981	LC	24 X 18	AP	150		750	4000
Falling Star (from Eight Lithographs to Benefit the Found for Contemp Performance Arts, Inc)	GEM	GEM	1981	LC	36 X 28	AP88	50		900	5000
Pivot	3EP	JK/3EP	1981	REL/M	38 X 31	AP88	16		900	8000
Untitled	EW	EW	1982	WC/MON	25 X 30	HMP	1 EA		750	20000 EA
Untitled (from Wood & Metal Plates) (EXP-57-03-82)	EW	EW	1982	MON	30 X 24 EA	HMP	1 EA		750 EA	35000 EA
Untitled (from Wood & Metal Plates) (EXP-SF-54-05-82)	EW	EW	1982	MON	43 X 79 EA	TOY	1 EA		2500	65000 EA
Untitled (from Wood & Metal Plates) (EXP-58-05-82)	EW	EW	1982	MON	25 X 32 EA	TOY	1 EA		2000	40000 EA
Untitled	AOE	LS	1982	EC	31 X 25	SOM		4	1000	3000
Self Portrait	3EP	IK/3EP	1982	AB/SL	15 X 11	FAB	20	1	800	2500
Untitled	3EP	KD/3EP	1982	AB/SL	22 X 25	R/BFK	20	1	1000	3000
Untitled (SF-268)	LS	LS	1982	LC	42 X 30	R/BFK	18		1500	12000
Generated (2 Panels)	GEM	GEM	1982	LC	41 X 61	AP88	40 EA	8 EA	2400 SET	15000 SET
Paradise of Ash (2 Panels)	GEM	GEM	1982	LC	46 X 65	AP88	43 EA	10 EA	2400 SET	15000 SET
Dark and Fast	GEM	GEM	1982	LC	38 X 30	AP88	20	5	1500	18000

SAM FRANCIS CONTINUED

TITLE	PUBLISHER	PRINTER	DATE	MEDIUM	DIMENSION (PAPER SIZE) IN INCHES	TYPE OF PAPER	EDITION NUMBER	NO. OF COLORS	ORIGINAL OPENING PRICE	CURRENT RETAIL PRICE
SOLD OUT EDITIONS (RARE):										
Vorstellung	GEM	GEM	1982	AC	37 X 30	AP88	40	1	900	10000
Untitled (SFE-001)	LS	LS	1982	EC	24 X 18	SOM	100		600	5000
Totem	GEM	GEM	1982	AB	38 X 20	AP88	29	1	750	10000
Second Mother	GEM	GEM	1982	AB	37 X 24	AP88	12	1	750	10000
First Subject	GEM	GEM	1982	AB/CC	45 X 36	AP88	20	1	1100	10000
Untitled (SF-269)	BAI	JP/SiS	1982	LC	48 X 35	AP88	250		1750	15000
Untitled			1982	EB	12 X 10	AP	8		1000	7500
Untitled			1982	EB	24 X 18	AP	20		600	3500
Untitled			1982	EB	17 X 5	AP	17		600	3500
Untitled (EXP-SF 61-01)	EW	EW	1983	WC/MON/OIL	24 X 32 EA	HMP	1 EA	Varies	15000	40000
Untitled (SFM 84–522)	ART	GTW	1984	MON	32 X 25 EA		1 EA	Varies	10000 EA	24000 EA
Green Buddha	GEM	GEM	1984	LC	59 X 50	HMP	20			
Mountain's Gate	GEM	GEM	1984	LC	60 X 100	AP88	15	6	4500	15000
Double Room	GEM	GEM	1984	LC	50 X 60	AP88	16	2	2400	15000
Not Deceived	GEM	GEM	1984	LC	50 X 60	AP88	20	2	2400	15000
Fragrant Breath	GEM	GEM	1984	LC	60 X 50	AP88	22	2	2400	15000
Deep Ground	GEM	GEM	1984	LC	60 X 50	AP88	15	5	2400	15000
Indigo Wood	GEM	GEM	1984	LC	60 X 50	AP88	22	6	2400	15000
Untitled (SFE-014)	LS	LS	1984	AC	26 X 11	AP	29	8	1200	12000
Untitled (Dipt) (SFE-028)	LS	LS	1985	EC	36 X 139 / 36 X 105	AP	23		4500	15000
Untitled (SFE-030)	LS	LS	1985	AC	10 X 8	AP	25		2000	6000
Untitled			1985	EB	46 X 33	AP	17		4500	15000
Untitled (SFE-031)	LS	LS	1985	EC	45 X 32	AP	23		4500	15000
Untitled (SFE-291) (G-1298)	GEM	GEM	1986	SP	84 X 60	EXP	56		6000	55000
Untitled (SFE-003)	LS	LS	1986	AC	24 X 18	AP	20		3000	12000
Poemesdans le Ciel (SF-316)	EdLD		1986	LC	30 X 22	AC	100		2500	7000
King Corpse (G-1296)	GEM	GEM	1986	SP	42 X 59	AC	65		3500	45000
Meteorite (G-1297)	GEM	GEM	1986	SP	72 X 42	AC	65		3000	35000
Beadelaire	GEM	GEM	1986	LC	43 X 59	AC	50	5	3500	15000
Senza Titolo I (SFE-064)	2RC	2RC	1987	EB/A	35 X 39	FAB	58		4500	20000
Senza Titolo II (SFE-065)	2RC	2RC	1987	AC	35 X 39	FAB	56		4500	20000
Senza Titolo III (SFE-066)	2RC	2RC	1987	AC	35 X 39	SOM	76		4500	20000
Untitled (SFE-059)	LS	LS	1988	AC	48 X 16	AP	22		5000	15000
Untitled Triptych (SFE-060)	LS	LS	1988	EB/A	36 X 27	AP	20		5000	25000
Untitled (for Chicago International Art Exposition 10th Anniversary) (SF-331)	LS	LS	1988	LC	45 X 29	AP	50		3000	5000
Untitled (SF-LP04)	LP	LP	1989	SP	28 X 38	AP	115		3500	6000
CURRENT EDITIONS:										
Untitled (SF-343)	LS	GP/LS	1990	LC	46 X 30	R/BFK/ROL	50		10000	10000
Untitled (SF-344)	LS	GP/LS	1990	LC	46 X 30	R/BFK/ROL	50		12500	12500
Untitled (SFE-073)	LS	JS/LS	1990	EC	35 X 28	R/BFK/ROL	21		12000	12000
Untitled (SFE-074)	LS	JS/LC	1990	EC	34 X 27	R/BFK/ROL	20		12000	12000
Untitled (SFE-075)	LS	JS/LC	1990	EC	33 X 27	R/BFK/ROL	22		10000	10000
Untitled (SFE-076)	LS	JS/LC	1990	EC	47 X 28	R/BFK/ROL	20		12000	12000
Trietto 1 (SFE-074RC)	2RC	Ros/2RC	1991	EC	53 X 66	R/BFK/ROL	66		12500	12500
Trietto 2 (SFE-075RC)	2RC	Ros/2RC	1991	EC	39 X 53	R/BFK/ROL	66		9500	9500
Trietto 3 (SFE-076RC)	2RC	Ros/2RC	1991	EC	39 X 53	R/BFK/ROL	66		9500	9500
Trietto 4 (SFE-077RC)	2RC	Ros/2RC	1991	EC	53 X 66	R/BFK/ROL	66		12500	12500
Trietto 5 (SFE-078RC)	2RC	Ros/2RC	1991	EC	53 X 66	R/BFK/ROL	66		12500	12500
Untitled (SFE-077)	LS	JS/LS	1991	EC	47 X 28	R/BFK/ROL	20		12000	12000
Leo Rising (SFE-078)	LS	JS/LS	1991	EC	47 X 28	R/BFK/ROL	20		12000	12000
Untitled (SFE-079)	LC	JS/LS	1991	EC	47 X 28	R/BFK/ROL	20		12000	12000
Untitled (SFE-080)	LC	JS/LS	1991	EC	47 X 28	R/BFK/ROL	19		12500	12500
Untitled (SFE-081)	LC	JS/LS	1991	EC	24 X 18	R/BFK/ROL	27		6000	6000
Untitled (SF-345)	LS	GP/LS	1991	LC	47 X 30	PTI/120	50		10000	10000
Untitled (SF-346)	LS	GP/LS	1991	LC	30 X 46	PTI/120	100		8500	8500
Untitled (SFE-082)	LC	JS/LS	1992	EC	26 X 23	R/BFK/ROL	21		7000	7000
Untitled (SFE-083)	LC	JS/LS	1992	EC	33 X 23	R/BFK/ROL	20		5000	5000
Untitled (SFE-084)	LC	JS/LS	1992	EC	45 X 31	R/BFK/ROL	20		8500	8500
Untitled (SFE-085)	LC	JS/LS	1992	EC	32 X 22	R/BFK/ROL	28		6500	6500
Untitled (SFE-086)	LC	JS/LS	1992	EC	16 X 13	R/BFK/ROL	36		1500	1500
Brutitied (Papierski Portfolio) (Set of 7) (SF-349-355)	GL		1992	LC	30 X 22 EA		50 EA		28800 SET	28800 SET
Untitled (SF-356)	LS	GP/LS	1992	LC	30 X 47	PTI/120	50	7	8000	8000
Untitled (SF-357)	LS	GP/LS	1992	LC	47 X 30	PTI/120	50		8000	8000
Untitled (SF-358)	LS	GP/LS	1993	LC	32 X 23	PTI/120	50	9	6500	6500
Untitled (SF-359)	LS	GP/LS	1993	LC	23 DIA	PTI/120	100		15000	15000
Untitled (SFE-087)	LS	JS/LS	1993	EC	16 X 13	R/BFK/ROL	12		1500	1500
Untitled (SFE-088)	LS	JS/LS	1993	EC	32 X 43	R/BFK/ROL	22	29	6500	6500
Untitled (SFE-089)	LS	JS/LS	1993	EC	32 X 43	R/BFK/ROL	21		6500	6500

SAM FRANCIS CONTINUED

Sam Francis
Untitled (SFE-088)
Courtesy The Litho Shop, Inc

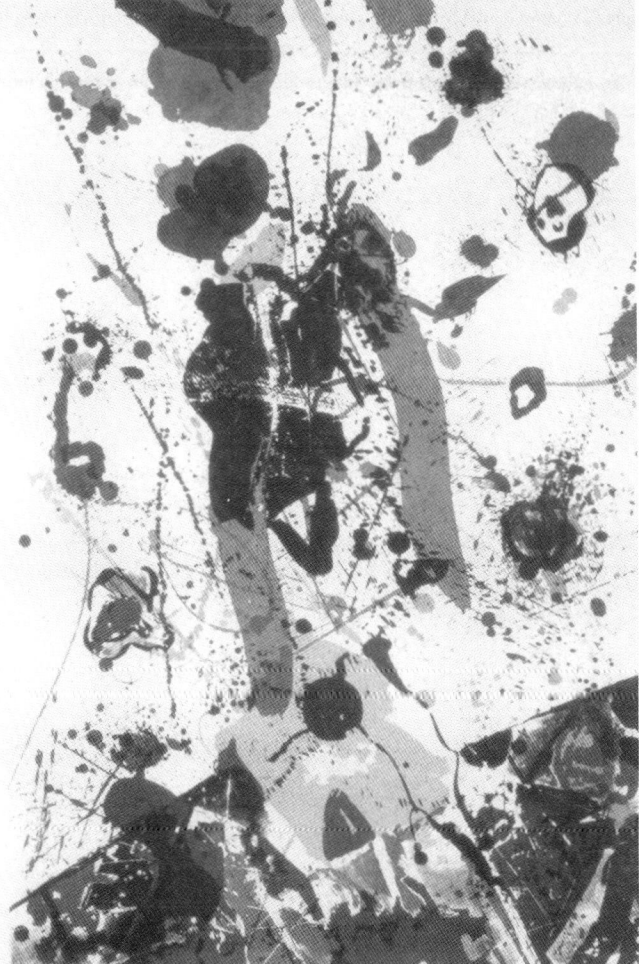

Sam Francis
Untitled (SFE-031)
Courtesy The Litho Shop, Inc

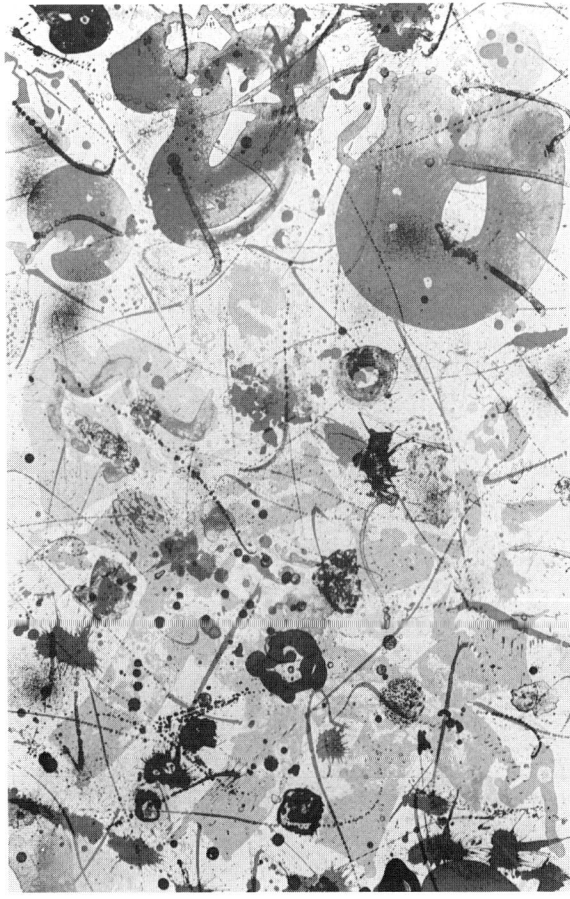

Sam Francis
Untitled (SF-358)
Courtesy The Litho Shop, Inc

The retail prices of the 100,000 limited edition prints quoted in this directory are subject to change. Print publishers, artists and galleries were the direct sources for these quotations. Prices in the secondary market listed as "Sold Out Editions (Rare)" indicate that the publisher has a limited supply of that print or that the print is difficult to locate in the galleries.

HELEN FRANKENTHALER

BORN: New York, NY; December 12, 1928
EDUCATION: Bennington Col, VT, BA, 1945–49
TEACHING: New York Univ, NY, 1958; Univ of Pennsylvania, Phila, PA, 1958; Yale Univ, New Haven, CT, 1967,70; Sch of Visual Arts, NY, 1967; Hunter Col, NY, 1970; Univ of Rochester, NY, 1971; Bennington Col, VT, 1972; Brooklyn Mus, NY, 1973; Swarthmore Col, PA, 1974; Drew Univ, Madison, NJ, 1975
AWARDS: Gold Medal, Pennsylvania Acad of Fine Arts, Phila, PA, Joseph E Temple Award, 1968; Spirit of Achievement Award, Albert Einstein Col, 1970; Chicago Inst of Art, IL, Ada S Garrett Prize, 1972; Gold Medal, Biennale della Grafica d'Arte, Florence, Italy, 1972; Creative Arts Award, American Jewish Congress, 1974; Nat Conf of Christian & Jews Award, 1978; Alumni Award, Bennington Col, VT, 1979; New York Mayor's Award of Hon for Arts & Culture, 1986
RECENT EXHIB: Tyler Graphics, Ltd, Mount Kisco, NY, 1987; John Berggruen Gallery, San Francisco, CA, 1987,88; Andre Emmerich Gallery, NY, 1988; Galeria Joan Prats, NY, 1988; Munson-Williams-Proctor Inst, Utica, NY, 1988; Am Print Renaissance, Stamford, CT, 1988; Buschlen Mowatt Gallery, Vancouver, BC, Canada, 1990; Occidental Col, Thorne Hall & Weigart Gallery, Los Angeles, CA, 1989; Merryman Coll, Stanford, CT, 1989; Nat Mus of Women in the Arts, Wash, DC, 1990; Buschlen Mowatt Gallery, Vancouver, Canada, 1990; Associated American Artists, NY, 1992; M Knoedler & Co, NY, 1992–93; Nat Gallery of Art, Wash, DC, 1993
COLLECTIONS: Metropolitan Mus of Art, NY; Mus of Mod Art, NY; Guggenheim Mus of Art, NY; Whitney Mus of Am Art, NY; Brooklyn Mus, NY; Cooper Hewitt Mus, NY; New York Univ; Art Inst of Chicago, IL; Cleveland Mus of Art, OH; Pasadena Art Mus, CA; Baltimore Mus of Art, MD; Albright-Knox Art Gallery, Buffalo, NY; Bennington Col, VT; Univ of California, Los Angeles, CA; Columbia Univ, NY; Wadsworth Atheneum, Hartford, CT; Detroit Inst of Art, MI; Victoria and Albert Mus, London, England; Smithsonian Mus, Wash, DC; Walker Art Center, Newark Mus, NJ; Honolulu Acad, Hawaii; San Francisco Mus of Art, CA; Univ of Sidney, Australia; Yale Univ, New Haven, CT; Univ of Wisconsin; Mus of Fine Arts, Houston, TX

PRINTERS: Universal Limited Art Editions, West Islip, LI, NY (ULAE); Lee Funderburg, NY (LF); John Hutcheson, NY (JH); Tyler Graphics Ltd, Mount Kisco, NY (TGL); 2 RC Editrice, Rome Italy (2RC); Tadashi Toda, Kyoto, Japan (TT); Shi-un-do Print Shop, Kyoto Japan (SPS); Rodney Konopaki (RK); Bob Cross (BC); John Hutcheson (JH); River Press, NY (RP); Crown Point Press, San Francisco, CA (CPP); Emanvele Cacciatore, NY (EC); Benjamin Gervis, NY (BG); Garner Tullis Workshop, NY (GTW); Ediciones Poligrafa, SA, Barcelona, Spain (EdP)
PUBLISHERS: Tyler Graphics, Ltd, Mount Kisco, NY (TGL); Abrams Original Editions, NY (AOE); Universal Limited Art Editions, West Islip, LI, NY (ULAE); 2 RC Editrice, Rome, Italy (2RC); Cleveland Orchestra, OH (CO); Crown Point Press, San Francisco, CA (CPP); Multiples, NY (M); Artist (ART); Garner Tullis Workshop, NY (GTW); La Poligrafa, SA, Barcelona, Spain (LP)
GALLERIES: Andre Emmerich Gallery, New York, NY; John Berggruen Gallery, San Francisco, CA; Crown Point Press, New York, NY & San Francisco, CA; Marvin Ross Friedman & Co, Miami, FL; Texann Ivy Fine Arts, Orlando, FL; Marian Goodman, New York, NY; Greenberg Gallery, St Louis, MO; Nancy Singer Gallery, St Louis, MO; Garner Tullis Workshop, Santa Barbara, CA; Irving Galleries, Palm Beach, FL; Barbara Krakow Gallery, Boston, MA; Flanders Contemporary Art, Minneapolis, MN; Meyerson Fine Art, New York, NY; Greg Kucera Gallery, Wash, DC; Mammen Gallery II, Scottsdale, AZ; Mixografia Gallery, Los Angeles, CA; Shirley Cerf, Inc, Los Angeles, CA; Graystone Gallery, San Francisco, CA; Mary Singer Gallery, Wash, DC; Opus Art Studios, Miami, FL; Heath Gallery, Atlanta, GA; Kass/Meridian Gallery, Chicago, IL; Sylvia Cordish Fine Art, Baltimore, MD; Gerald Peters Gallery, Santa Fe, NM; Tyler Graphics, Mount Kisco, NY; Douglas Drake Gallery, New York, NY; Galeria Joan Prats, New York, NY & Barcelona, Spain; Richard Green Gallery, New York, NY; Janie C Lee Galleries, New York, NY & Houston, TX; Jim Kemper Fine Art, New York, NY; Elizabeth Paul Gallery, Cincinnati, OH; Associated American Artists, New York, NY; Buschlen Mowatt Gallery, Vancouver, Canada; Rosa Esman Gallery, New York, NY; M Knoedler & Company, New York, NY
MAILING ADDRESS: 175 E 94th St, New York, NY 10021

Williams College (WC); Sparks (S); Tyler Graphics, Ltd (T); Helen Frankenthaler (HF)

TITLE	PUBLISHER	PRINTER	DATE	MEDIUM	DIMENSION (PAPER SIZE) IN INCHES	TYPE OF PAPER	EDITION NUMBER	NO. OF COLORS	ORIGINAL OPENING PRICE	CURRENT RETAIL PRICE
SOLD OUT EDITIONS (RARE):										
First Stone (WC-1)	ULAE	ULAE	1961	LC	23 X 30	AP/S	12	6	50	28000
Persian Garden (WC-8) (S-7)	ULAE	ULAE	1965–66	LC	26 X 20	AMP	24		100	6000
Sun Corner (WC-13)	ULAE	ULAE	1968	SP	36 X 36	ALUM	50		900	4000
Southwest Blues	ULAE	ULAE	1969	LC	24 X 19	AMP	19		150	4500
Sanguine Mood	ULAE	ULAE	1971	SP/PO	23 X 18	JBG	75	4	600	6000
What Red Lines Can Do (Set of 5) (WC-25-29)	M		1970	SP	39 X 26	HMP	75		400	6000
Savage Breeze	ULAE	ULAE		WC	30 X 25	HMP	31		650	25000
Connected by Joy	ULAE	ULAE	1969–73	EB/A	17 X 21	JBG	27	4	600	8000
Ponti	2RC	2RC	1973	AB/DPT	27 X 35	FAB	21	1	750	8000
East and Beyond (WC-44)	ULAE	ULAE	1973	WC	24 X 18	HMP	18	4	800	32000
Painted Book Cover (Each Handpainted by Artist)	AOE	ART	1973	HP	11 X 11	LIN	51		1000	7000
Message from Degas (WC-53) (S-31)	ULAE	ULAE	1972–74	EB/A	7 X 10	JWP	36	4	600	10000
Vineyard Storm	ULAE	ULAE	1974–76	WC	30 X 25	HMP	4			
Essence Mulberry	TGL	TGL	1977	WC	40 X 19	GP/HMP	46	7	2500	22000
Harvest	TGL	TGL	1977	LC	26 X 22	HMP	43	6	1250	4000
Dream Walk (WC-60) (T-178) (HF-2)	TGL	TGL	1977	LC	26 X 35	HMP	47	6	1000	4500
Barcelona (WC-61) (T-179) (HF-3)	TGL	TGL	1977	LC	41 X 32	HMP	30	9	3000	12000
Earth Slice	TGL	TGL	1978	AC/SL/SG	16 X 26	HMP	46		1000	3500
Attitudes	TGL	TGL	1978	LC	22 X 31	HMP	42		1000	5000
Bronze Smoke	TGL	TGL	1978	LC	31 X 22	HMP	42		1000	5000
Untitled (for Cleveland Orchestra)	CO	TGL	1978	SP	23 X 30	AC	150		300	2000
Ganymede	TGL	TGL	1978	AC/SL/SG	23 X 17	AC	49		1000	3500
Door	TGL	TGL	1976–79	LC	22 X 41	HMP	34		1000	8000
Sure Violet	TGL	TGL	1979	AC/SL/SG/DPT	31 X 43	TGL/HMP	50	12	3000	15000
Cameo	TGL	TGL	1980	WC	42 X 32	TGL/HMP	51	8	4000	12000
Monotype VI (with Pastel, Lithographic Ink & Paintstik)	TGL	TGL	1981	MON/HC	41 X 34 EA	SUK	1 EA		6000 EA	40000 EA
Monotype IX (Framed)	TGL	TGL	1981	MON	19 X 39 EA	GAM	1 EA	Varies	5000 EA	15000 EA
The Red Sea (T-200)	TGL	TGL	1978–82	LC	24 X 28	TGL/HMP	58	8	2000	8000
Deep Sun (T-20) (HF-33)	TGL	RK/BC/TGL	1983	I/EB/A/SB/MEZ	30 X 41	SAP	59	22	3600	12000
Divertimento	M	JH/RP	1983	LC	37 X 27	HMP	39	4	2400	7500

HELEN FRANKENTHALER CONTINUED

Helen Frankenthaler
In the Wings
Courtesy Tyler Graphics, Ltd

TITLE	PUBLISHER	PRINTER	DATE	MEDIUM	DIMENSION (PAPER SIZE) IN INCHES	TYPE OF PAPER	EDITION NUMBER	NO. OF COLORS	ORIGINAL OPENING PRICE	CURRENT RETAIL PRICE
SOLD OUT EDITIONS (RARE):										
Cedar Hill	CPP	TT/SPS/CPP	1983	WC	20 X 25	MM/HMP	75	10	2600	9000
Yellow Jack (with Hand-Coloring in Acrylic & Pastels)	TGL	TGL	1985–87	LC/HC	30 X 38	AC	54		3500	10000
Tribal Sign	TGL	TGL	1987	LC	24 X 19	TGL/HMP	47	11	3500	12000
Tiger's Eye	TGL	TGL	1987	EB/AC/LC/SP	19 X 22	TGL/HMP	56	9	3500	10000
Carot's Mark	TGL	TGL	1987	EB/AC/LC	27 X 31	R/BFK	52	5	3500	10000
Day One	TGL	TGL	1987	EB/AC/DPT	26 X 25	HMP	58	4	1800	6000
Blue Current	TGL	TGL	1987	EB/AC/LC	31 X 38	R/BFK	52		3500	10000
Walking Rain	TGL	TGL	1987	LC/SG/EB/A	30 X 22	THS	54		3500	12000
In the Wings	TGL	TGL	1987	LC/EB/A	14 X 21	TGL/HMP	50	11	2500	10000
Parets Series:										
Parets III	EdP	LP	1987	MON	50 X 38 EA	GP	1 EA		3000 EA	25000 EA
Broom Street at Night	ART/2RC	ART/2RC	1987	EC/AC/DPT	39 X 39	R/BFK	50		3000	10000
Ramblas	EdP	LP	1987	EB/LC	34 X 27	RP	75		2500	7500
Gateway (12 Unique Hand-Painted, Hand-Patinated Sculptural Bronze Screens with a 3-Panel Intaglio Print Framed in Cast Bronze Panels on One Side & a Unique Painting on Sand-Blasted Bronze Panels by the Artist on the Other Side (Weighs 630 lbs)	TGL	ART/TGL	1988	SCULP/I	7' X 9' EA	BRONZE	1 EA		200000 SET	250000 SET
Gateway (with Stenciled Borders) (Trip)	TGL	TGL	1988	EB/A/STEN	70 X 30	TGL/HMP	30	28	25000	40000
CURRENT EDITIONS:										
La Sardana	EdP	LP	1987	LC/EB	35 X 25	RP/300	60	5		
Un Poco Más	EdP	LP	1987	LC	27 X 37	AP/300	60	8		
Ramblas	EdP	LP	1987	LC/EB	34 X 27	RP/300	75	6		
Parets	EdP	LP	1987	EB/CAR	51 X 38	HMP	20	1		
Plaza Real	EdP	LP	1987–88	EC	29 X 35	RP/300	60	7		
Guadalupe	MIX	MIX	1989		69 X 45	HMP	74	5		
Alaska	MIX	MIX	1989		48 X 37	HMP	50	4		
Hermes	MIX	MIX	1989		44 X 92	HMP	50	5		
Sirocco	MIX	MIX	1989		37 X 35	HMP	52	5		
Tahiti	MIX	MIX	1989		32 X 54	HMP	45	5		
Bird of Paradise (Bas Relief-Microcast Copper)	MIX	MIX	1989		8' X 4' X 4"	COP	14	4		
Mirabelle	TGL	LF/JH/TGL	1990	LC	30 X 37	AC	56	24	10500	12000
The Clearing Grove	ART/GTW	EC/BG/GTW	1991	WC	24 X 32	RBT/HMP	28	4	4000	4000

ELIZABETH FRANZHEIM

BORN: Chicago, IL; 1923
EDUCATION: Shipley Sch, Bryn Mawr, PA, 1938–40; Yale Univ Sch of Fine Arts, New Haven, CT, 1940–42, MFA, 1947; Corcoran Sch of Art, Wash, DC, 1942

PRINTERS: Makor Press, NY (MaP)
PUBLISHERS: Post Oak Fine Art, Houston, TX (POFA)
GALLERIES: Galerie d'Art International, Paris, France

TITLE	PUBLISHER	PRINTER	DATE	MEDIUM	DIMENSION (PAPER SIZE) IN INCHES	TYPE OF PAPER	EDITION NUMBER	NO. OF COLORS	ORIGINAL OPENING PRICE	CURRENT RETAIL PRICE
CURRENT EDITIONS:										
Anchor Man	POFA	MaP	1982	LC	22 X 30	AP	200	6	500	600
From the Presidential Podium	POFA	MaP	1982	LC	22 X 30	AP	200	6	500	600
Guest Star	POFA	MaP	1982	LC	22 X 30	AP	200	6	500	600
Texas, 1950	POFA	MaP	1982	LC	22 X 30	AP	200	6	500	600
Maternity	POFA	MaP	1982	LC	22 X 30	AP	200	6	500	600
My Children the Acrobats	POFA	MaP	1982	LC	22 X 30	AP	200	6	500	600

SONDRA FRECKELTON

BORN: Dearborn, MI; 1936
EDUCATION: Art Inst of Chicago, IL
COLLECTIONS: Virginia Mus of Fine Arts, Richard, VA; Springfield Art Mus, MO; Nat Mus of Am Art, Wash, DC

PRINTERS: J Petruzzeli, NY (JP); Sienna Studio, NY (SS); Norman Stewart, Bloomfield Hills, MI (NS); Tobin Smith (TS); Wing Lake Studio, Bloomfield Hills, MI (WLS); Joe Keenan (JK); Cece Stack (CS); Stewart & Stewart, Bloomfield Hills, MI (S-S); Bill Weege, Madison, WI (BW); Andrew Rubin, Madison, WI (AR); Tandem Press, Univ of Wisconsin, Madison, WI (TanPr)
PUBLISHERS: Brooke Alexander, Inc, BY (BAI); Art Matters, Boulder, CO (AM); Stewart & Stewart, Bloomfield Hills, MI (S-S); Mount Holyoke Col, South Hadley, MA (MHC); Alice Simsar Gallery, Ann Arbor, MI (ASG); Gryphon Gallery (GG); Tandem Press, Univ of Wisconsin, Madison, WI (TanPr)
GALLERIES: Brooke Alexander, Inc, New York, NY; Signet Arts, St Louis, MO; Alice Simsar Gallery, Ann Arbor, MI; Stewart & Stewart Gallery, Bloomfield Hills, MI; Robert Schoelkopf Gallery, New York, NY
MAILING ADDRESS: 67 Vestry St, New York, NY 10013

Sondra Freckelton
Keeping Autumn
Courtesy Stewart & Stewart

Sondra Freckelton
Mirror Image
Courtesy Stewart & Stewart

TITLE	PUBLISHER	PRINTER	DATE	MEDIUM	DIMENSION (PAPER SIZE) IN INCHES	TYPE OF PAPER	EDITION NUMBER	NO. OF COLORS	ORIGINAL OPENING PRICE	CURRENT RETAIL PRICE
SOLD OUT EDITIONS (RARE):										
Self-Portrait with Begonia	BAI	JP/SS	1973	LB/HC/WA	14 X 22	R/BFK	29		150	2000
Begonia with Quilt	BAI	JP/SS	1979–80	LC	29 X 23	R/BFK	49		350	2000
Plums and Gloriosa Daisies	BAI	JP/SS	1980	LC	28 X 24	R/BFK	150		350	1500
Red Chair	S-S	MS/TS/WLS	1984	SP	29 X 21	R/BFK/W	50	20	600	4500
CURRENT EDITIONS:										
Begonia	BAI	JP/SS	1976	LC	22 X 18	R/BFK	75		150	500
Tulips	BAI	JP/SS	1977	LC	28 X 21	R/BFK	75		175	600
Still Life with Apples	BAI	JP/SS	1978	LC	19 X 24	R/BFK	68		200	1000
Still Life with Apples, Grey State	BAI	JP/SS	1978	LC	19 X 24	R/BFK	28		200	200

SONDRA FRECKELTON CONTINUED

TITLE	PUBLISHER	PRINTER	DATE	MEDIUM	DIMENSION (PAPER SIZE) IN INCHES	TYPE OF PAPER	EDITION NUMBER	NO. OF COLORS	ORIGINAL OPENING PRICE	CURRENT RETAIL PRICE
CURRENT EDITIONS:										
Poppies	BAI	JP/SS	1979–80	STEN	28 X 23	R/BFK	49		500	900
Sunflowers, State I	BAI/AM	JP/SS	1980	LC	36 X 28	R/BFK	80	7	500	500
Sunflowers, State II	BAI/AM	JP/SS	1980	LB/HC	36 X 28	R/BFK	30	4	600	600
Ladder Chair	BAI	JP/SS	1982	PO	34 X 25	R/BFK	49		750	900
Blue Chenille	S-S	NS/WLS	1985	SP	29 X 21	R/BFK/W	56	18	600	2100
Drawingroom Still Life	S-S	NS/WLS	1986	SP	29 X 21	R/BFK/W	59	20	585	1500
Openwork	MHC/ASG/GG/S-S	NS/JK/CS/WLS	1987	SP	21 X 28	R/BFK/W	67	17	650	1500
Souvenir	S-S	NS/JK/CS/WLS	1989	SP	22 X 30	R/BFK/W	61	18	950	1500
Red Poppies	S-S	NS/JK/CS/WLS	1990	SP	22 X 30	R/BFK/W	62	14	1350	1350
Keeping Autumn	S-S	NS/JK/S-S	1991	SP	41 X 29	R/BFK/W	42	19	1800	1800
Mirror Image	S-S	NS/JK/S-S	1992	SP	29 X 41	R/BFK/W	37	14	1750	1750
All over Red	TanPr	BW/AR/TanPr	1988	PO	33 X 25	AP/WA/140 lb	45	10	1500	1750
Pears	TanPr	BW/AR/TanPr	1988	PO	28 X 22	AP/WA/140 lb	30	14	1250	1500

DAVID FREED

BORN: Toledo, OH; May 23, 1936
EDUCATION: Miami Univ, OH, BFA, 1958; Univ of Iowa, Iowa City, IA, MFA, with honors, 1962; Royal Col of Art, London, England, 1964
TEACHING: Vis Lectr, Etching, Centeor Sch of Art, London, England, 1969; Prof, Printmaking, Virginia Commonwealth Univ, Richmond, VA, 1966 to present
AWARDS: Fulbright Fel, 1963–64; World Print Council Comp, San Francisco Mus, CA, 1976; Nattie Marie Jones Fel, 1983; Virginia Mus Fel, Richmond, VA, 1983–84
RECENT EXHIB: Reynolds Minor Gallery, Richmond, VA, 1987; Duck Blind Gallery, Kitty Hawk, NC, 1988; Cudahy's Gallery, Richmond, VA, 1989; Il Bisonte, Florence, Italy, 1989

COLLECTIONS: Mus of Mod Art, NY; Brooklyn Mus, NY; Chicago Inst of Art, IL; Corcoran Gallery of Art, Wash, DC; Nat Coll of Fine Art, Wash, DC; Victoria and Albert Mus, London, England; Mus Boymans Van Beuningen, Rotterdam, Holland
PRINTERS: Robert Frelout, Paris, France (RF); Lacouriere et Frelout, Paris France (LF); Artist (ART)
PUBLISHERS: Artist (ART)
GALLERIES: Laurel Press, Richmond, VA; Reynolds Minor Gallery, Richmond, VA; Duck Blind Gallery, Kitty Hawk, NC; Cudahy's Gallery, Richmond, VA; Il Bisonte, Florence, Italy
MAILING ADDRESS: 1825 W Grace St, Richmond, VA 23220

TITLE	PUBLISHER	PRINTER	DATE	MEDIUM	DIMENSION (PAPER SIZE) IN INCHES	TYPE OF PAPER	EDITION NUMBER	NO. OF COLORS	ORIGINAL OPENING PRICE	CURRENT RETAIL PRICE
CURRENT EDITIONS										
Whistler	ART	ART	1976	I	10 X 28	R/BFK	25	5	75	200
Hear Heart	ART	ART	1979	I	18 X 24	R/BFK	25	3	75	200
Afternoon	ART	ART	1980	I	18 X 24	STP	25	4	125	200
Cicada	ART	ART	1980	I	18 X 24	STP	25	4	125	200
Night on the Mountain	ART	ART	1981	I	22 X 30	STP	20	3	175	250
Autumn Voice I	ART	ART	1981	I	21 X 25	ROMA	15	4	175	200
Autumn Voice II	ART	ART	1981	I	21 X 25	ROMA	15	4	175	200
Spring Bones	ART	ART	1982	I/MON	10 X 44	STP	8	8	300	800
Appalachian Ariel	ART	ART	1982	I/MON	30 X 44	STP	5	8	400	800
And I Am the Arrow	ART	ART	1982	I/MON	30 X 44	STP	3	8	400	800
November Variations	ART	ART	1982-83	I/MON/CO	11 X 44	STP	8	8	400	600
Baudelaire Theme—La Beauté	ART	ART	1983	I/MON/CO	22 X 30	STP	6	8	400	600
Baudelaire Theme—Les Bijoux	ART	ART	1983	I/MON/CO	22 X 30	STP	6	8	400	600
Baudelaire Theme—Parfum	ART	ART	1983	I/MON	22 X 30	STP	8	8	400	600
Four Portraits of Baudelaire (Set of 4)	ART	RF/LF	1984	EC	8 X 11 11 X 21	R/BFK	15 EA	2 EA	400 SET 125 EA	400 SET 125 EA
A Paris	ART	RF/LF	1984	I	11 X 21	R/BFK	12	2	175	175
A Meryon	ART	RF/LF	1904	I	11 X 21	R/BFK	10	4	175	175
A Printemps	ART	RF/LF	1904	I	11 X 21	R/BFK	12	3	175	250
A Vincent	ART	RF/LF	1984	I	11 X 21	R/BFK	10	2	175	175
A Resistance	ART	RF/LF	1984	I	11 X 21	R/BFK	10	4	175	175
A Baudelaire	ART	RF/LF	1984	I	11 X 21	R/BFK	12	2	175	175
Yard Journal (Book with 6 Etchings with Poem by Charles Wright)	ART	ART	1985	I	10 X 22 EA	R/BFK	30 EA	18 EA	600 SET	750 SET
Genesis—7 Days (Set of 7)	ART	ART	1985	I	11 X 15 15 X 18	R/BFK	30 EA	15 EA	750 SET	1800 SET
Inimate Music: Arrow/Touch (Set of 2)	ART	ART	1986	I	18 X 24	R/BFK	10 EA	9 EA	300 SET 200 EA	500 SET 250 EA
Creation	ART	ART	1987	IC	20 X 45	R/BFK	30	9	600 SET	750 SET
Temptation	ART	ART	1987	IC	20 X 45	R/BFK	30	9	XXX	XXX
Expulsion	ART	ART	1987	IC	20 X 45	R/BFK	30	9	XXX	XXX
Genesis—Cain and Abel	ART	ART	1987	IC	15 X 22	R/BFK	30	3	200	200
Genesis—The Flood	ART	ART	1987	IC	15 X 22	R/BFK	30	2	200	200
Genesis—The Tower	ART	ART	1987	IC	15 X 22	R/BFK	30	3	200	200
Genesis—Cities of the Plain	ART	ART	1988	IC	15 X 22	R/BFK	30	2	200	200
Genesis—The Sacrifice	ART	ART	1988	IC	15 X 22	R/BFK	30	2	200	200

DAVID FREED CONTINUED

TITLE	PUBLISHER	PRINTER	DATE	MEDIUM	DIMENSION (PAPER SIZE) IN INCHES	TYPE OF PAPER	EDITION NUMBER	NO. OF COLORS	ORIGINAL OPENING PRICE	CURRENT RETAIL PRICE
CURRENT EDITIONS:										
Genesis—The Ladder	ART	ART	1988	IC	15 X 22	R/BFK	30	2	200	200
Genesis—Israel	ART	ART	1988	IC	15 X 22	R/BFK	30	2	200	200
Abraham and Sarah	ART	ART	1988	IC	22 X 15	CP	30	2	200	200
Ishmael	ART	ART	1988	IC	22 X 15	CP	30	2	200	200
Jacob and Esau	ART	ART	1988	IC	22 X 15	CP	30	2	200	200
Rebecca	ART	ART	1988	IC	22 X 15	CP	30	4	200	200
Joseph	ART	ART	1988	IC	22 X 15	CP	30	2	200	200
Aaron	ART	ART	1988	IC	22 X 15	CP	30	3	200	200
Moses	ART	ART	1988	IC	22 X 15	CP	30	3	200	200
I Am	ART	ART	1989	IC	22 X 45	CP	30	10	600 SET	750 SET
Remember	ART	ART	1989	IC	22 X 45	CP	30	10	XXX	XXX
The Law	ART	ART	1989	IC	22 X 45	CP	30	10	XXX	XXX
Orville and Wilber	ART	ART	1989	IC	22 X 28	LANA	50	3	200	200

HERMINE FREED

BORN: New York, NY; May 29, 1940
EDUCATION: Cornell Univ, Ithaca, NY, BA, 1961; New York Univ, NY, MA, 1967
TEACHING: Instr, New York Univ, NY, 1968–72; Assoc Prof, Univ of Illinois, Chicago, IL, 1976; Instr, Video & Photo Art Workshop, Sch of Visual Arts, NY, 1972 to present
AWARDS: Nat Endowment for the Arts Grant, NY, 1974; Creative Artists Public Service Grant, New York State Council on the Arts, 1978; Rockefeller Found Grant, NY, 1978
RECENT EXHIB: Southern Light Gallery, Amarillo Col, TX, 1987; Sherkat Gallery, NY, 1987; Elaine Benson Gallery, Bridgehampton, NY, 1990; Univ of Colorado, Boulder, CO, 1992; Douglass Col, North Brunswick, NY, 1992
COLLECTIONS: Chicago Art Inst, IL; California Inst of Arts, Valencia, CA; Hartwick Col, Oneonta, NY; Everson Mus, Syracuse, NY
PRINTERS: Peter X, NY (PX); X + (C), NY (X+C)
PUBLISHERS: Artist (ART)
GALLERIES: Castelli Graphics, New York, NY; Elaine Benson Gallery, Bridgehampton, NY
MAILING ADDRESS: 60 Gramercy Park, North, New York, NY 10010

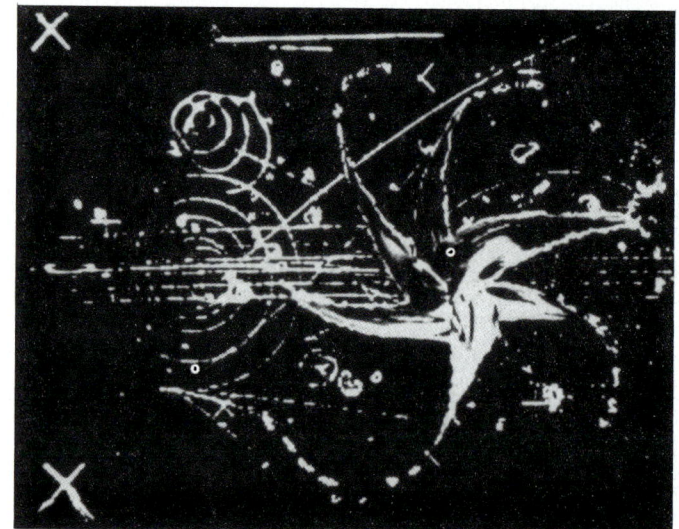

Hermine Freed
Alice Constellation
Courtesy the Artist

TITLE	PUBLISHER	PRINTER	DATE	MEDIUM	DIMENSION (PAPER SIZE) IN INCHES	TYPE OF PAPER	EDITION NUMBER	NO. OF COLORS	ORIGINAL OPENING PRICE	CURRENT RETAIL PRICE
CURRENT EDITIONS:										
Alice Constellation	ART	PX/X+C	1990–93	DIG	22 X 28	AP	10		500	500

PEDRO FRIEDEBERG

BORN: Florence, Italy; January 11, 1937
EDUCATION: Iberoamerican Univ, Mexico City, Mexico
AWARDS: Second Prize, Expos Solar, 1968; First Prize, Bienal de Grabado de San Juan, PR, 1979; Second Prize, Bienal Buenos Sires, Brazil, 1979
RECENT EXHIB: Carmen Llewellyn Gallery, New Orleans, LA, 1989
COLLECTIONS: Mus of Mod Art, NY; Rose Art Mus, Brandeis Mus, Waltham, MA; Mus of Mod Art, Paris, France; Israel Mus, Jerusalem, Israel
PRINTERS: Kyron Edicion Graficas Limitadas Limitadas, Mexico City, Mexico (KEG)
PUBLISHERS: Kyron Ediciones Graficas Limitadas, Mexico City, Mexico (KEG)
GALLERIES: Brooke Alexander Inc, New York, NY; Galeria Misrachi Genova, Mexico City, Mexico; Galeria of Circulo Hamburgo, Mexico City, Mexico; Phyllis Needlman Gallery, Chicago, IL; Carmen Llewellyn Gallery, New Orleans, LA
MAILING ADDRESS: c/o Phyllis Needlman Gallery, 1515 N Astor, Chicago, IL 60610

TITLE	PUBLISHER	PRINTER	DATE	MEDIUM	DIMENSION (PAPER SIZE) IN INCHES	TYPE OF PAPER	EDITION NUMBER	NO. OF COLORS	ORIGINAL OPENING PRICE	CURRENT RETAIL PRICE
SOLD OUT EDITIONS (RARE):										
Untitled	KEG	KEG	1973	SP	21 X 21	AP	100	Multi	150	600

The retail prices of the 100,000 limited edition prints quoted in this directory are subject to change. Print publishers, artists and galleries were the direct sources for these quotations. Prices in the secondary market listed as "Sold Out Editions (Rare)" indicate that the publisher has a limited supply of that print or that the print is difficult to locate in the galleries.

JANE FREILICHER

BORN: New York, NY; November 29, 1924
EDUCATION: Brooklyn Col, NY, BA; Columbia Univ, NY, MA; Hans Hofmann Sch, NY; Studied with Meyer Schapiro; Parsons Sch of Design, NY, MFA Program, 1989,90
TEACHING: Vis Critic & Lectr, Univ of Pennsylvania Grad Sch of Fine Arts, Phila, PA, 1968; Skowhegan Sch of Art, ME, 1968; Carnegie-Mellon Inst, Pittsburgh, PA, 1971; Sch of the Mus of Fine Arts, Boston, MA; Col of Creative Studies, NY; Univ of Santa Barbara, CA
AWARDS: Hallmark Int Art Award, 1960; Am Assn of Univ Women, 1974; Nat Endowment for the Arts, NY, 1976; Saltus Gold Medal, Nat Acad of Design, Annual Exhib, 1987
RECENT EXHIB: Retrosp, Currier Gallery, NH, 1986–87; Retrosp, Parrish Art Mus, Southampton, NY, 1986–87; Retrosp, Marian Koogler McNay Mus, San Antonio, TX, 1986–87; Lafayette Col Gallery, Easton, PA, 1989; Parrish Art Mus, Southhampton, NY, 1989; Artists Mus (Soho), NY, 1992; Fischbach Gallery, NY, 1992
COLLECTIONS: Brooklyn Mus, NY; Mus of Mod Art, NY; Metropolitan Mus, NY; Brandeis Art Mus, Waltham, MA; Univ of Utah, Salt Lake City, UT; Whitney Mus of Am Art, NY; Univ of North Carolina, Greensboro, NC; Rhode Island Sch of Design, Providence, RI
PRINTERS: Artist (ART); Condeso & Brokopp Studio, NY (CBS); Jennifer Melby Studio, NY (JMS); Orlando Condeso Studio, NY (OCS)
PUBLISHERS: Associated Am Artists, NY (AAA); Orion Editions, NY (OE); 724 Prints, NY (724P); John Szoke Graphics, NY (JSG)
GALLERIES: Orion Editions, New York, NY; Elaine Benson Gallery, Bridgehampton, NY; John Szoke Graphics, New York, NY; Associated American Artists, New York, NY; Fischbach Gallery, New York, NY; Morningstar Gallery, New York, NY
MAILING ADDRESS: 51 Fifth Ave, New York, NY 10003

Jane Freilicher
Peonies
Courtesy John Szoke Graphics, Inc

Jane Freilicher
Bouquet
Courtesy John Szoke Graphics, Inc

TITLE	PUBLISHER	PRINTER	DATE	MEDIUM	DIMENSION (PAPER SIZE) IN INCHES	TYPE OF PAPER	EDITION NUMBER	NO. OF COLORS	ORIGINAL OPENING PRICE	CURRENT RETAIL PRICE
SOLD OUT EDITIONS (RARE):										
Bouquet	AAA	ART	1978	LC	30 X 22	AP	60		350	1500
Flowering Cherry	OE	ART	1979	STEN	30 X 30	AP	68	20	500	1800
Poppies & Peonies	724P	CBS	1983	EB/A	37 X 37	R/BFK	50	8	800	1800
CURRENT EDITIONS:										
Peonies	JSG	OCS	1989–90	EB/A	30 X 22	R/BFK/W	65	6	1500	1800
Bouquet	JSG	JMS	1991	EB/A/DPT	25 X 24	R/BFK/W	75	8	1800	1800

BOB FREIMARK

BORN: Doster, MI; January 27, 1922
EDUCATION: Univ of Toledo, OH, B Ed; Cranbrook Acad of Art, MI, MFA
TEACHING: Instr, Drawing, Toledo Mus, OH, 1952–55; Instr, Painting, Ohio Univ, Athens, CA, 1956–59; Res Art, Des Moines Art Center, IA, 1959–63; Instr, Painting, Columbia Univ, NY, 1963; Prof, Painting, Harvard Univ, Cambridge, MA, 1972–73; Instr, Graphics, San Jose State Univ, CA, CA, 1964–72, 1973–86
AWARDS: New Talent in USA Award, Art in America, 1957; Ford Foundation Grant, WV, 1965; Western Interstate Comm for Higher Ed, 1967
RECENT EXHIB: Triton Mus of Art, Santa Clara, CA, 1989–90; Amerika Haus, Stuttgart, Germany, 1992; Guatemalteco, Guatemala City, Guatemala, 1992; Max Planck Inst, Munich, Germany, 1993; New England Fine Arts Inst, Boston, MA, 1993

BOB FREIMARK CONTINUED

COLLECTIONS: Bibliotheque Nat, Paris, France; British Mus, London, England; Boston Mus of Fine Arts, MA; Smithsonian Inst, Wash, DC; Nat Gallery, Prague, Czech; North Am Inst of Culture, Mexico City, Mex; Los Angeles County Mus, CA; Seattle Mus, WA; Cranbrook Mus, Bloomfield Hills, MI; Library of Congress, Wash, DC; Achenbach Found for Graphic Arts, San Francisco, CA; Fogg Mus, Cambridge, MA; Des Moines Art Center, IA; Nat Gallery, Wash, DC; Portland Art Mus, OR
PRINTERS: Harvard Press, Cambridge, MA (HP); Impressions Workshop, Boston, MA (IW) (OB); Grass Valley Studios, Morgan Hill, CA (GVS); Vaerksted fur Grafisk Kunst, Hjorring, Denmark (V); Lakeside Press, MI (LP); Cranbrook Press, Bloomfield Hills, MI (CP); Santa Reparata Graphic Workshop, Florence, Italy (SRGW); Peter Lewis (PL); Trillium Press, San Francisco, CA (TrPr); Littleton Studios, Spruce Pine, NC (LSt)
PUBLISHERS: Impressions Gallery, Boston, MA (IG) (OB); Grass Valley Studios, Morgan Hill, CA (GVS); Lakeside Press, Lakeside, MI (LP); Vaerksted fur Grafisk Kunst, Hjorring, Denmark (VGK); New York Graphic Society (NYGS); Littleton Studios, Spruce Pine, NC (LSt)
GALLERIES: Percival Galleries, Ltd, Des Moines, IA; Grass Valley Studios, Morgan Hill, CA; Aartvark Gallery, Phila, PA
MAILING ADDRESS: Route 2, Box 539A, Morgan Hill, CA 95037

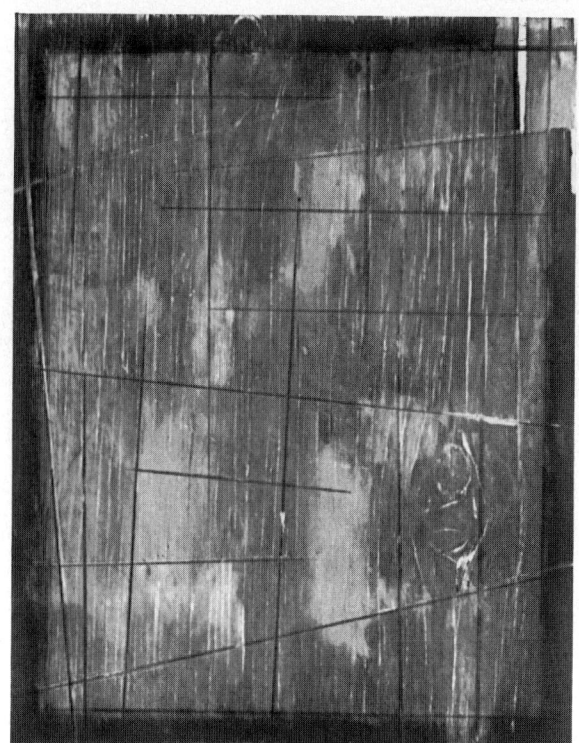

Bob Freimark
Vignette I
Courtesy the Artist

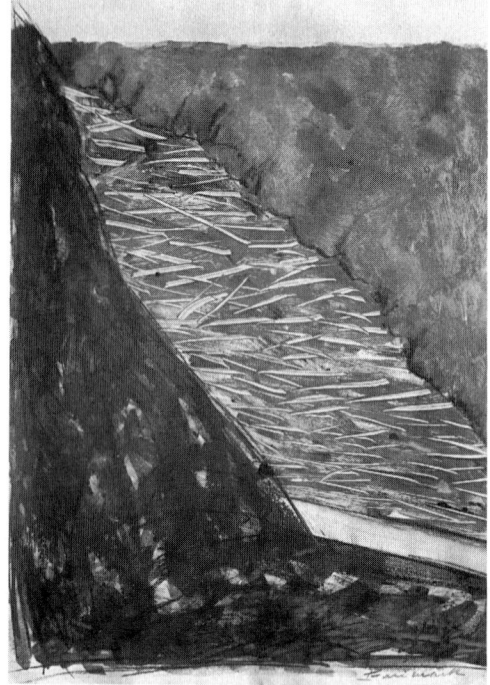

Bob Freimark
Clear Cut No 2
Courtesy the Artist

Bob Freimark
Free Kuwait
Courtesy the Artist

TITLE	PUBLISHER	PRINTER	DATE	MEDIUM	DIMENSION (PAPER SIZE) IN INCHES	TYPE OF PAPER	EDITION NUMBER	NO. OF COLORS	ORIGINAL OPENING PRICE	CURRENT RETAIL PRICE
SOLD OUT EDITIONS (RARE):										
The Four Horsemen	GVS	GVS	1959	WB	25 X 35	UT	20	1	150	600
Survivor	GVS	GVS	1959	SP	24 X 15	UT	21	8	125	500
South Dakota	GVS	GVS	1962	SP	16 X 22	UT	69	4	125	300
Michigan	GVS	GVS	1963	SP	16 X 23	UT	67	5	100	500
The Dissenter	GVS	GVS	1963	SP	16 X 23	UT	25	3	125	500
Nevada	GVS	GVS	1963	SP	15 X 22	UT	61	8	125	250
Vermont	GVS	GVS	1964	SP	17 X 23	UT	64	2	150	300
Maine	GVS	GVS	1964	SP	21 X 16	UT	61	6	125	300
Self-Portrait (Harvard)	GVS	HP	1973	LB	20 X 16	MUR	20	1	150	300
Enigmatic Woman	NYGS	HP	1973	SP	23 X 28	UT	100	4	125	250
Greek Island	NYGS	HP	1973	SP	23 X 30	UT	100	8	125	250
Greek Sea	LP	LP	1973	LC	22 X 30	AR	50	6	200	500
Czech Romance	IG	IW	1973	LC	30 X 21	R/FBK	100	8	175	500
Firenze (2 Editions)	GVS	SRGW	1974	LB	28 X 20 EA	IT	10 EA	1 EA	250 EA	350 EA
Blue Wave	IG	IW	1974	LC	30 X 18	R/BFK	60	4	200	500

BOB FREIMARK CONTINUED

Bob Freimark
Carolina Count-Down
Courtesy the Artist

TITLE	PUBLISHER	PRINTER	DATE	MEDIUM	DIMENSION (PAPER SIZE) IN INCHES	TYPE OF PAPER	EDITION NUMBER	NO. OF COLORS	ORIGINAL OPENING PRICE	CURRENT RETAIL PRICE
SOLD OUT EDITIONS (RARE):										
Elliptical Landscape	IG	IW	1974	LC	22 X 30	R/BFK	60	4	200	500
Blue Plate Special I,II	GVS	GVS	1975	LC	30 X 24 EA	CR	100 EA	6 EA	200 EA	400 EA
Obra	IG	IW	1976	LC	28 X 20	R/BFK	46	3	175	500
Myself at Cranbrook	CP	CP	1977	LC	22 X 30	R/BFK	20	4	250	400
CURRENT EDITIONS:										
Viking Ship	VGK	VGK	1971	LC	22 X 30	R/BFK	103	4	150	300
Seventeen	VGK	VGK	1971	LC	20 X 30	R/BFK	100	4	125	300
Meat and Potatoes	VGK	VGK	1971	LC	21 X 26	R/BFK	79	9	150	300
Homage to Whistler, Inc	GVS	HP	1973	SP	18 X 24	UT	100	4	125	200
Portal	GVS	IW	1976	LC	30 X 21	R/BFK	50	2	175	400
San Jose	KC	GVS	1976	LC	28 X 20	FAB	100	3	150	150
Polish Writer	GVS	GVS	1977	LC	27 X 20	R/BFK	50	3	175	500
Vineyard	GVS	IW	1977	LC	22 X 30	R/BFK	50	3	200	500
Two Women	GVS	GVS	1978	LC	30 X 22	R/BFK	22	2	150	250
Marshland	GVS	GVS	1978	LC	22 X 30	R/BFK	81	9	200	500
Fiesta in San Jose	GVS	GVS	1978	LC	22 X 29	AP	41	6	200	250
Krematorium (Auschwits Series) (Set of 4):										
der Wach Turm	GVS	GVS	1979	LC	27 X 30	FAB	25	4	300	600
Daniel Valdez	GVS	GVS	1979	LB	28 X 20	MUR	22	1	150	150
Paricutin	GVS	GVS	1979	LC	29 X 22	R/BFK	30	5	200	200
Mexican Love Suite (Set of 4):										
Mujer con Mantilla (with Lace)	GVS	GVS	1980	LB/CO	30 X 22	AP/B	48	2	300	500
Mujer Sentada	GVS	GVS	1980	LC	30 X 22	RPNP	50	3	300	500
Rosalia	GVS	GVS	1980	LC	30 X 22	R/BFK	40	2	300	500
Yo Te Amo	GVS	GVS	1980	LC	22 X 30	R/BFK	50	4	300	500
Awakening	GVS	GVS	1981	LC	22 X 30	LANA	44	2	250	500
Big Santa Teresa	GVS	GVS	1981	LC	22 X 30	LANA	47	2	200	400
Campesinos (Rom.)	GVS	GVS	1981	LC	22 X 30	LANA	50	4	250	500
Campesinos (Arab)	GVS	GVS	1981	LC	22 X 30	LANA	51	5	250	500
Young Sycamores	GVS	GVS	1981	LC	15 X 22	LANA	25	1	125	150
Arivederci Roma	GVS	GVS	1982	LC	15 X 22	LANA	50	5	200	350
Connemara (Celtic Series)	GVS	GVS	1982	LC	15 X 22	R/BFK	50	5	200	350
Fountain of Youth	GVS	GVS	1982	LC	22 X 15	LANA	48	4	175	350
Mantle (diptych)	GVS	GVS	1982	LC	45 X 30	AP/BL	50	5	450	600
Sugar Lips	GVS	GVS	1982	LC	15 X 22	R/BFK	11	2	150	200
Border Town	GVS	GVS	1982–83	LC	30 X 22	LANA	50	8	400	600
Corib (Celtic Series)	GVS	GVS	1983	LC	22 X 15	LANA	50	6	250	250
Cornwall	GVS	GVS	1983	LC	15 X 22	LANA	58	10	250	300
Curve of Developing Consciousness	GVS	GVS	1983	LC/SP	30 X 22	LANA	60	8	400	500
Modulation in All Things	GVS	GVS	1984	SP	30 X 42	AP	25	8	500	500

BOB FREIMARK CONTINUED

TITLE	PUBLISHER	PRINTER	DATE	MEDIUM	DIMENSION (PAPER SIZE) IN INCHES	TYPE OF PAPER	EDITION NUMBER	NO. OF COLORS	ORIGINAL OPENING PRICE	CURRENT RETAIL PRICE
CURRENT EDITIONS:										
Man and Wife I (Dipt)	GVS	GVS	1985	LB/CC	22 X 15 EA	RP/G	14 EA	1 EA	350 SET	350 SET
									200 EA	200 EA
Man and Wife II (Dipt)	GVS	GVS	1985	LB/CC	22 X 15 EA	RP/G	15 EA	1 EA	350 SET	350 SET
									200 EA	200 EA
C W Hayes	GVS	GVS	1985	LB	63 X 42 cm	R/BFK	22	1	200	300
California Fruit & Nuts Series:										
Quinces	GVS	GVS	1985	LC	35 X 45 cm	LANA	25	6	300	350
Granadas	GVS	GVS	1985	LC	35 X 45 cm	R/BFK	25	5	300	350
Kumquats	GVS	GVS	1986	LC	35 X 45 cm	R/BFK	25	5	300	350
Spring Willow	GVS	GVS	1986	EB	30 X 40 cm	Tumba	20	1	200	300
Live Oak	GVS	GVS	1986	LB	50 X 38 cm	R/BFK/G	40	1	150	150
Blue Cafe I,II (Series of 2)	GVS	GVS	1987	MON	30 X 22 EA	LANA	1 EA	Varies	1400 SET	1800 SET
									700 EA	900 EA
Red Dress I,II,III (Erotica) (Series of 3)	GVS		1987	MON	22 X 30 EA	LANA	1 EA	Varies	1500 SET	2000 SET
									500 EA	700 EA
Ristrade de Chilis I-VII (Series of 7) (California Fruits and Nuts Series)	GVS	GVS	1987	MON	30 X 22 EA	LANA	1 EA	Varies	700 EA	1000 EA
Tunas I-VI (Series)	GVS	GVS	1987	MON	30 X 22 EA	LANA	1 EA	Varies	3000 SET	5000 SET
									600 EA	1000 EA
Xian Series I-VI (Series of 6)	GVS	GVS	1988	MON/WA	22 X 30 EA	LANA	1 EA	Varies	1100 EA	1100 EA
Pacheco Pass I-V (Series of 5)	GVS	GVS	1988	MON	22 X 30 EA	LANA	1 EA	Varies	800 EA	1200 EA
Century Plant I-V (Series of 5)	GVS	GVS	1988	MON	26 X 20 EA	LANA	1 EA	Varies	4000 SET	4000 SET
									900 EA	900 EA
Dolores Huerta: The Pain I-VI (Series of 6)	GVS	GVS	1988	MON	26 X 20 EA	LANA	1 EA	Varies	5000 SET	6000 SET
									900 EA	1200 EA
Dusseldorf I,II (Series of 2)	GVS	GVS	1988	MON	26 X 20 EA	LANA	1 EA	Varies	1500 SET	1500 SET
									900 EA	900 EA
El Toro I-V (Series of 5)	GVS	GVS	1988	MON	22 X 30 EA	LANA	1 EA	Varies	4000 SET	4000 SET
									900 EA	900 EA
Fleur de Lis I,II,III (Erotica) (Series of 3)	GVS	GVS	1988	MON	26 X 20 EA	AP	1 EA	Varies	2100 SET	2100 SET
									800 EA	800 EA
Floral Landscape I,II (Series of 2)	GVS	GVS	1988	MON	7 X 12 EA	FAB	1 EA	Varies	200 EA	250 EA
Grand Canyon Suite I-XVII (Series of 17)	GVS	GVS	1988	MON	22 X 30 EA	AP/B	1 EA	Varies	1000 EA	1500 EA
Green Heron I,II,III (Series of 3)	GVS	GVS	1988	MON	20 X 26 EA	AP/W	1 EA	Varies	1500 SET	1500 SET
									700 EA	700 EA
Irreverant Flag I,II (Series of 2)	GVS	GVS	1988	MON	30 X 22 EA	AP/W	1 EA	Varies	2500 SET	2500 SET
									1500 EA	1500 EA
Moonlight and Roses I-IV (Series of 4)	GVS	GVS	1988	MON	22 X 30 EA	AP/B	1 EA	Varies	2200 SET	2200 SET
									600 EA	800 EA
Myself at the Easel Plus Myself as Francis Bacon I-V (Series of 5)	GVS	GVS	1988	MON	30 X 22 EA	AP	1 EA	Varies	2500 SET	2500 SET
									700 EA	700 EA
Lost and Found (Dipt)	GVS	PL/GVS	1988	LC	30 X 22 EA	R/BFK	10 EA	3 EA	900 SET	1800 SET
Fly Leaf (Dipt)	GVS	PL/GVS	1988	LC	30 X 22 EA	R/BFK	10 EA	4 EA	900 SET	1800 SET
Vanishing Rail	GVS	GVS	1989	MON	20 X 28 EA	INC	1 EA	Varies	1000	1000
Now that the Buffalo are Gone . . . (Trip) (Framed)	GVS	GVS	1989	MON	30 X 22 X 3	AP	1 EA	Varies	2500	2500
Hawaiian Icon	GVS		1991	LC	22 X 30	SOM	100	5	800	800
Ace of Hearts	GVS		1991	LC	20 X 26	R/BFK	100	3	545	545
Blind Instinct	LSt	LSt	1991	VIT	40 X 30	SOM	50	2	600	600
Carolina Count-Down	LSt	LSt	1991	VIT	31 X 50	SOM	40	3	800	1000
Carolina Red	LSt	LSt	1991	VIT	30 X 34	SOM	50	3	500	600
Catawba (Dipt)	LSt	LSt	1991	VIT	20 X 30	SOM	50	1	350	350
Cherokee	LSt	LSt	1991	VIT	20 X 30	SOM	50	1	350	350
Change-Up	LSt	LSt	1991	VIT	29 X 34	SOM	46	2	500	600
Roanoke	LSt	LSt	1991	VIT	23 X 20	SOM	50	4	300	350
Free Kuwait	GVS	TrPr	1993	LC	21 X 30	AP	50	5	600	800
Clear Out (Set of 2)	GVS	GVS	1993	MON	30 X 22 EA	R/BFK/G	1 EA	Varies	3000 SET	3000 SET
									1800 EA	1800 EA

The retail prices of the 100,000 limited edition prints quoted in this directory are subject to change. Print publishers, artists and galleries were the direct sources for these quotations. Prices in the secondary market listed as "Sold Out Editions (Rare)" indicate that the publisher has a limited supply of that print or that the print is difficult to locate in the galleries.

The Printworld Directory is accepting new applications for the seventh edition. Approximately 300 new artists will be accepted. Please use the two forms provided in the back section of this directory to submit biographical data and documentation of prints. Edition number of each print must not exceed 500 and the retail price must be $100 or more.

LUCIAN FREUD

BORN: Berlin, Germany; 1922
EDUCATION: Central Sch of Arts & Crafts, London, England, 1939; Goldsmith's Col, London, England, 1942
RECENT EXHIB: Hirshhorn Mus, Wash, DC, 1987; Hayward Gallery, London, England, 1988; Berlin Nat Galerie, West Germany, 1988; Brooke Alexander, Inc, NY, 1989; Thomas Gibson Fine Art, Ltd, London, England, 1991; Tate Gallery, London, England, 1992; Mary Ryan Gallery, NY, 1992
COLLECTIONS: Arts Council of Great Britain, London, England
PRINTERS: Palm Tree Editions, London, England (PTE); Mark Balakjian, London, England (MBS); Studio Prints, London, England (StPr)
PUBLISHERS: Brooke Alexander, Inc, New York, NY (BAI); James Kirkman, Ltd, London, England (JKL); Matthew Marks Gallery, NY (MMG)
GALLERIES: Brooke Alexander, Inc, New York, NY; Hayward Gallery, London, England; Joy Emery Gallery, Grosse Point Farms, MI; Mary Ryan Gallery, New York, NY; Matthew Marks Gallery, New York, NY; R K Goldman Contemporary, Los Angeles, CA; Stiebel Modern, New York, NY; Thomas Gibson Fine Art, Ltd, London, England; Marlborough Gallery, New York, NY

TITLE	PUBLISHER	PRINTER	DATE	MEDIUM	DIMENSION (PAPER SIZE) IN INCHES	TYPE OF PAPER	EDITION NUMBER	NO. OF COLORS	ORIGINAL OPENING PRICE	CURRENT RETAIL PRICE
SOLD OUT EDITIONS (RARE):										
Lawrence Growing	JKL		1982	EB	7 X 6	AP	25	1	800	7000
Head of a Girl II	JKL		1982	EB	6 X 5	AP	16	1	800	7000
Ib	BAI/JKL	PTE	1984	EB	22 X 21	AP	50	1	2000	7500
Blond Girl	BAI/JKL	PTE	1985	EC	35 X 28	AP	50		4000	17500
Girl Holding Her Foot	BAI/JKL	PTE	1985	EC	35 X 28	AP	50		4000	12500
Head of Bruce Bernard	BAI/JKL	PTE	1985	EC	20 X 19	AP	50		2400	7500
Man Posing	BAI/JKL	PTE	1985	EC	35 X 29	AP	50		4000	12500
Thistle	BAI/JKL	PTE	1985	EC	12 X 10	AP	30		1200	8000
Head of a Man	BAI/JKL	PTE	1987	EB	20 X 17	R/BFK	20	1	2500	8000
Lord Goodman	BAI/JKL	MBS	1987	EB/HC	19 X 22	R/BFK	50	Varies	5500	8000
Bella	BAI/JKL	PTE	1987	EB	27 X 22	R/BFK	50	1	3000	12000
Girl Sitting	BAI/JKL	PTE	1987	EC	27 X 32	R/BFK	50		5000	12500
Head of Ib	BAI/JKL	PTE	1988	EB	14 X 11	R/BFK	40	1	2500	7000
Man Resting	BAI/JKL	MB/StPr	1988	EB	20 X 21	SOM/S	30	1	4500	10000
Two Men in the Studio	BAI/JKL	MB/StPr	1989	EB	17 X 14	SOM/S	25	1	6000	7500
Naked Man on a Bed	BAI/JKL	MB/StPr	1990	EB	23 X 23	SOM/S	40	1	7000	7500
Esther	BAI/JKL	MB/StPr	1991	EB	17 X 15	SOM/S	25	1	6500	7500
Four Figures	BAI/JKL	MB/StPr	1991	EB	27 X 37	SOM/S	30	1	12500	13500
Head and Shoulders of a Girl	BAI/JKL	MB/StPr	1990	EB	20 X 19	SOM/S	50	1	12000	13500
CURRENT EDITIONS:										
Kai	JKL/MMG	MB/StPr	1991–92	EB	31 X 25	SOM/S	40	1	10000	10000

JOHNNY FRIEDLAENDER

BORN: Pless (Upper Silesia); (1912–1992)
EDUCATION: Breslau Acad of Fine Arts, 1928–30
PRINTERS: Atelier George Leblanc, Paris, France (AGL); Artist (ART)
PUBLISHERS: Contemporary Art Masters, NY (CAM); Horn Editions, NY (HE); Artist (ART); Galerie Schnake (SCH); Manus Presse (MPres)
GALLERIES: Galerie Select Ltd, New York, NY; Multiple Impressions, New York, NY; Robert Green Fine Arts, Mill Valley, CA; Laura Paul Gallery, Cincinnati, OH; Ro Gallery Image Makers, Inc, New York, NY Schmuckling (Sch); Peelings (P)

TITLE	PUBLISHER	PRINTER	DATE	MEDIUM	DIMENSION (PAPER SIZE) IN INCHES	TYPE OF PAPER	EDITION NUMBER	NO. OF COLORS	ORIGINAL OPENING PRICE	CURRENT RETAIL PRICE
SOLD OUT EDITIONS (RARE):										
Femme Debout	ART	ART	1948	EB		AP	5	1	35	3500
Stehender Frauenaki (Sch-41)	SCH	ART	1949	EB		AP	125	1	35	1500
Oiseau Blanc	ART	ART	1950	EB/A	14 X 10				40	2500
Couple (Sch-54)	SCH	ART	1950	EB	12 X 9		110	1	35	1500
Le Coq I	ART	ART	1951	EC	23 X 15	AP	200		40	2000
Nu Debout (Sch-103)	SCH	ART	1952	EB/A		AP	200		40	5000
Les Betes (Sch-119)	SCH	ART	1953	EB/A		AP	50		40	5000
Fleurs II (Sch-120)	SCH	ART	1953	EB/A	13 X 11	AP	200		50	2500
Collines I (Sch-147)	SCH	ART	1955	EC/A	17 X 32	AP			60	1500
Les Causses (Sch-167)	SCH	ART	1957	AC	21 X 16	AP	167		60	1500
Chevaux III (Sch-172)	SCH	ART	1958	EB/A		AP	40		65	4500
Oiseaux IV (Sch-184)	SCH	ART	1959	EB/A		AP	95		65	3750
Composition II (Sch-189)	SCH	ART	1960	EB/A	19 X 18	AP	80		65	3000
Verticales (Sch-213)	SCH	ART	1962	EB/A		AP	95		75	3500
Jaune sur Noir (Sch-215)	SCH	ART	1962	EB/A	22 X 17	AP	95		75	3500
Rouge-Bleu-Noir (Sch-216)	SCH	ART	1962	EB/A		AP	95		75	3750
Gris Ocre	ART	ART	1962–63	EB/A	23 X 18	AP	95		75	3500
Petit Bestiare	MPres	ART	1963	EB/A	20 X 13	AP	240		75	2000
L'Oiseau Bleu	MPres	ART	1963	EC/A	19 X 12	AP	20		75	3000
Titre (Sch-226)	SCH	ART	1963	EB	4 X 3	AP	240	1	50	800
Coq (Sch-231)	SCH	ART	1963	EB	4 X 3	AP	240	1	50	800
Beliers (Sch-233)	SCH	ART	1963	EB	4 X 3	AP	240	1	50	800
Bannieres (Sch-240)	SCH	ART	1964	EC/A	22 X 16	AP	95		75	2500
Composition sur fond Vert (Sch-252)			1965	EB/A	19 X 23	AP	95		80	3500
Three Couples (Set of 6)	MPres	ART	1965	EB/A	12 X 9 EA	AP	120 EA		400 SET	5000 SET
Galerie Schmückling Exhibition	GS	ART	1965	AB	12 X 9	AP	95	1	75	2000
Prisme (Sch-324)	SCH	ART	1968	EC/A	30 X 22	AP	95		80	3500
Montagne Verte (Sch-324)	SCH	ART	1968	EC/A	23 X 28	AP	95		80	3500
Gravure pour un Poeme	GS	ART	1969	EB/A	7 X 5	AP	155	1	90	1500
Mi-Octobre	GS	ART	1969	EC/A	27 X 18	AP	95		100	3500

JOHNNY FRIEDLAENDER CONTINUED

TITLE	PUBLISHER	PRINTER	DATE	MEDIUM	DIMENSION (PAPER SIZE) IN INCHES	TYPE OF PAPER	EDITION NUMBER	NO. OF COLORS	ORIGINAL OPENING PRICE	CURRENT RETAIL PRICE
SOLD OUT EDITIONS (RARE):										
La Nuit (Sch-348)	SCH	ART	1969	EC/A	30 X 22	AP	95		100	5000
Janvier (Sch-357)	SCH	ART	1969	EB/A	25 X 19	AP	95	1	100	2500
Les Deux Soleils (Sch-360)	SCH	ART	1970	EB/A		AP	99		125	4500
Abstrakte Komposition	SCH	ART	1970	LC	11 X 8	AP	200		70	800
Blason (Sch-375)	SCH	ART	1970	EC/A	30 X 22	AP	95		125	1500
La Presle	SCH	ART	1971	EC/A	30 X 23	AP	99		125	2500
Composition a la Guitare			1974	AC	19 X 15	AP	95			1500
Haalem	HE	AGL	1976	SP	22 X 30	AP	200		150	1500
Sao Paulo	HE	AGL	1976	LC	24 X 36	AP	275		250	2000
Sao Paulo	HE	AGL	1976	SP	24 X 36	AP	100		150	1500
Three Poems	HE	AGL	1976	LC	13 X 20	AP	225		150	1500
Fugue Around the Festival	CAM	AGL	1976	LC	22 X 30	AP	150		200	2000
Images in a Garden	HE	AGL	1976	AC	21 X 17	AP	135		400	2000
Images in Sur Fond Cris	HE	AGL	1976	AC	10 X 10	AP	175		250	1500
Mirage (Sch-575)	SCH	A	1977	EB/A		AUV	150		400	2750
Mirage (Sch-575)	SCH	A	1977	EB/A		AP	100		450	2750
Sur des Fleurs	SCH	A	1977	EB/A		AP	135		400	2500
Diaphonie	SCH	A	1978	EB/A	30 X 23	AP	95		450	3000
Fugue Miroir (Sch-618)	SCH	A	1978	AC	30 X 23	AP	95		450	3000
Two Forms in 3 Variations	HE	AGL	1978	AC	26 X 36	AP	95		800	2500
The Hours (Trip)	HE	AGL	1978	AC/ENG	30 X 23 EA	AP	95 EA		2250 SET	15000 SET
The Sao Paulo Lithograph	HE	AGL	1978	LC	30 X 19	AP	325		300	2500
Fleurs '79	HE	AGL	1979	EB/A	30 X 23	AP	95		850	3000
Two Forms in Three Variations (Set of 3)	HE	AGL	1979	AC/ENG	30 X 23 EA	AP	95 EA		2490 SET	12500 SET
Croissance	HE	AGL	1979	AC/ENG	30 X 23	AP	95		830	2500
Matinal (Sch-621)	HE	AGL	1979	EC/A	20 X 19	AP	95		400	3000
Etude	ART	ART	1980	AB/DPT	20 X 18	AP	95	1	400	1500
Eclosion	HE	AGL	1980	EB/A	30 X 23	AP	95	24	900	2500
Verticales	HE	AGL	1980	EB/A	30 X 23	AP	95	24	875	2500
Paysage Romantique	HE	AGL	1981	EB/A	21 X 30	AP	95	24	800	2000
Wildflower (Composition III) (Sch-719)	ART	ART	1981	EB/A		AP	95		400	725
Fleurs (Sch-722)	ART	ART	1982	EB/A		AP	95		400	2500
Avant L'Aube (Sch-723)	ART	ART	1982	EB/A		AP	95		400	4000
Lumen	HE	AGL	1982	EB/A	19 X 21	AP	95	24	700	2000
Scherzo	HE	AGL	1982	EB/A	30 X 23	AP	95	24	950	2500
Eclats (P-744)	ART	ART	1983	AC	30 X 22	AP	95		450	2500
Prelude III (Sch-741)	ART	ART	1983	EB/A		AP	95		450	2750
Lumier d'Automne (Sch-753)	ART	ART	1984	EB/A		AP	95		450	3500
Composition	ART	ART	1984	EC	10 X 8	AP	95		450	2500
Magie	ART	ART	1988	EB/A	21 X 17	AP	95		500	1500
Celesta	ART	ART	1990	EB/A		AP	95		500	1750

LEE FRIEDLANDER

BORN: Aberdeen, WA; 1934
EDUCATION: Art Center, Los Angeles, CA
RECENT EXHIB: California State Univ, Long Beach, CA, 1988; Corcoran Gallery of Art, Wash, DC, 1989
COLLECTIONS: California State Univ, Long Beach, CA
PRINTERS: Artist (ART)
PUBLISHERS: Double Elephant Press (DEP); Haywire Press (HP)
GALLERIES: Zabriskie Gallery, New York, NY; Texas Gallery, Houston, TX; Fraenkel Gallery, San Francisco, CA; Laurence Miller Gallery, New York, NY; A Gallery for Fine Art Photography, New Orleans, LA; Paul Kopeikin Gallery, Los Angeles, CA; Dean Jensen Gallery, Milwaukee, WI; Howard Yezerski Gallery, Boston, MA

TITLE	PUBLISHER	PRINTER	DATE	MEDIUM	DIMENSION (PAPER SIZE) IN INCHES	TYPE OF PAPER	EDITION NUMBER	NO. OF COLORS	ORIGINAL OPENING PRICE	CURRENT RETAIL PRICE
SOLD OUT EDITIONS (RARE):										
15 Photographs	DEP	ART	1973	PH	16 X 20 EA	DV	75		1500 SET	6000 SET
Shiloh (Set of 32)	HP	ART	1981	PH	7 X 11 EA	AP	20		19000 SET	25000 SET

JEAN FRELAUT

BORN: Paris, France; (1879–1954)
PRINTERS: Artists (ART)
PUBLISHERS: Artist (ART)

TITLE	PUBLISHER	PRINTER	DATE	MEDIUM	DIMENSION (PAPER SIZE) IN INCHES	TYPE OF PAPER	EDITION NUMBER	NO. OF COLORS	ORIGINAL OPENING PRICE	CURRENT RETAIL PRICE
SOLD OUT EDITIONS (RARE):										
Arbre dans la Lande	ART	ART	1907	EB	5 X 7	WOVE		1	20	250
Cote de Lurcasien	ART	ART	1913	EB	5 X 8	WOVE		1	20	150
Tete de Mendiante	ART	ART	1921	DPT	6 X 5	WOVE	25	1	25	200
Le Marché aux Chevaux	ART	ART	1923	EB	5 X 7	WOVE	50	1	25	250
Ferme	ART	ART	1923	EB	7 X 5	WOVE	50	1	25	150
Journée d'Hiver	ART	ART	1924	DPT	5 X 7	WOVE	40	1	25	350
Paysage	ART	ART	1943	EB	6 X 5	WOVE	50	1	75	300

DENNIS FRINGS

BORN: Streatore, IL; June 24, 1945
EDUCATION: Univ of Illinois, Urbana-Champaign, IL, BA, 1967; Univ of Texas, Austin, TX, 1970
TEACHING: Pearsal High Sch, Pearsal, TX, currently
AWARDS: Award of Excellence, Virginia Beach Mus, VA, 1986
COLLECTIONS: Royal Ontario Mus, Toronto, Can; Danforth Mus of Art, Framingham, MA; Brevard Art Center & Mus, Melbourne, FL; Nat Air & Space Mus, Wash, DC

PUBLISHERS: American Design, Ltd, Denver, CO (AD); Atlantic Arts, Annapolis, MD (AA); Spring Street Editions, NY (SSE); David Lawrence Editions, San Francisco, CA (DLE)
PRINTERS: O'Connell Graphics, NY (OG); Ed Bordett, Roanoke, VA (EB); Clay Huffman, Alexandria, VA (CH)
GALLERIES: Premier Gallery, Fredericksburg, VA; McMann Fine Arts, Roanoke, VA
MAILING ADDRESS: Studio 84, 105 North Union St, Alexandria, VA 22314

TITLE	PUBLISHER	PRINTER	DATE	MEDIUM	DIMENSION (PAPER SIZE) IN INCHES	TYPE OF PAPER	EDITION NUMBER	NO. OF COLORS	ORIGINAL OPENING PRICE	CURRENT RETAIL PRICE
SOLD OUT EDITIONS (RARE):										
Suite of Three:									750 SET	1500 SET
Action/Reaction	AD	OG	1980	SP	30 X 40	STP	195	9	250	500
Resumptive Patterns	AD	OG	1980	SP	30 X 40	STP	195	9	250	500
Nexus	AD	OG	1980	SP	30 X 40	STP	195	9	250	500
Suite of Three:									900 SET	1500 SET
Nigrosin Violet	AD	OG	1982	SP	30 X 40	STP	250	8	300	500
Double Slated	AD	OG	1982	SP	30 X 40	STP	250	8	300	500
Refracture	AD	OG	1982	SP	30 X 40	STP	250	8	300	500
Suite of Five:									1500 SET	1800 SET
Earth & Sky: A Dichotomy	AA	CH	1983	SP	22 X 30	STP	195	12	300	375
Whimsey and a Story Told	AA	CH	1983	SP	22 X 30	STP	195	12	300	375
Mouvement for Triangle in T2 Minor	AA	CH	1983	SP	22 X 30	STP	195	12	300	375
South Toward Emerald Seas	AA	CH	1983	SP	22 X 30	STP	195	12	300	375
Proportional Perception	AA	CH	1983	SP	22 X 30	STP	195	12	300	375
Suite of Eight:									2000 SET	3200 SET
Equinox	AA	CH	1984	SP	22 X 26	STP	150	13	300	400
Solstice	AA	CH	1984	SP	22 X 26	STP	150	13	300	400
Intrusion	AA	CH	1984	SP	22 X 26	STP	150	13	300	400
Irridescence	AA	CH	1984	SP	22 X 26	STP	150	13	300	400
Intergalatic	AA	CH	1984	SP	22 X 26	STP	150	13	300	400
Reverie	AA	CH	1984	SP	22 X 26	STP	150	13	300	400
Spaces	AA	CH	1984	SP	22 X 26	STP	150	13	300	400
Diffusion	AA	CH	1984	SP	22 X 26	STP	150	13	300	400
CURRENT EDITIONS:										
Aries I, II	AA	EB	1984	SP	29 X 40 EA	HEN	15 EA	14 EA	450 EA	500 EA
Kaleidoscope	SSE/DLE	OG	1985	SP	32 X 39	COV	91	8	450	500
Suite of Two:									750 SET	850 SET
Twilight	AA	EB	1986	SP	29 X 29	HEN	175	13	375	425
Eclipse	AA	EB	1986	SP	29 X 29	HEN	175	13	375	425

ELISABETH FRINK

BORN: Thurlow, England; November 14, 1930
EDUCATION: Guildford Art Sch, England, 1947–48; Chelsea Sch of Art, London, England, 1948–51
TEACHING: Chelsea Sch of Art, London, England; Royal Col of Art, London, England

COLLECTIONS: Mus of Mod Art, NY; Hirshhorn Mus, Wash, DC; Nat Gallery of Australia; Tate Gallery of Art, London, England
PRINTERS: Stanley Jones (SJ); Curwen Studios, London, England (CS); Cliff White (CW); White Ink, London, England (WI); Chris Prater (CP); Kelpra Studio, London, England (KS)
PUBLISHERS: Waddington Graphics, London, England (WG)
GALLERIES: Waddington Graphics, London, England; Terry Dintenfass, New York, NY; Nicola Jacobs Gallery, London, England; Margulies Taplin Gallery, Boca Raton, FL; Gala Art Gallery, Palm Beach, FL

TITLE	PUBLISHER	PRINTER	DATE	MEDIUM	DIMENSION (PAPER SIZE) IN INCHES	TYPE OF PAPER	EDITION NUMBER	NO. OF COLORS	ORIGINAL OPENING PRICE	CURRENT RETAIL PRICE
SOLD OUT EDITIONS (RARE):										
Wild Boar	WG	CW/WI	1967	LB	33 X 25	AP	25	1	60	1350
Bull	WG	CW/WI	1967	LB	33 X 25	AP	25	1	60	1350
Ducks	WG	CW/WI	1967	LB	33 X 25	AP	25	1	60	1350
Hare	WG	CW/WI	1967	LB	33 X 25	AP	25	1	60	1350
Horse	WG	CW/WI	1967	LB	33 X 25	AP	25	1	60	1350
Lioness	WG	CW/WI	1967	LB	33 X 25	AP	25	1	60	1350
Long Earred Owl	WG	CW/WI	1967	LB	33 X 25	AP	25	1	60	1350
Wild Goat	WG	CW/WI	1967	LB	33 X 25	AP	25	1	60	1350
Badger	WG	CW/WI	1970	LB	21 X 26	AP	70	1	75	1350
Bear	WG	CW/WI	1970	LB	21 X 26	AP	70	1	75	1350
Boar	WG	CW/WI	1970	LB	21 X 26	AP	70	1	75	1350
The Canterbury Tales I (Set of 5):										
The Reeve's Tale	WG	CW/WI	1970	EB	15 X 23	AP	70	1	75	650
The Miller's Tale I	WG	CW/WI	1970	EB	23 X 15	AP	70	1	75	650
The Miller's Tale II	WG	CW/WI	1970	EB	23 X 15	AP	70	1	75	650
Chanticleer and Pertelote	WG	CW/WI	1970	EB	15 X 23	AP	70	1	75	650
Chanticleer and the Fox	WG	CW/WI	1970	EB	15 X 23	AP	70	1	75	650
Hare	WG	CW/WI	1970	LB	21 X 26	AP	70	1	90	1350

ELISABETH FRINK CONTINUED

TITLE	PUBLISHER	PRINTER	DATE	MEDIUM	DIMENSION (PAPER SIZE) IN INCHES	TYPE OF PAPER	EDITION NUMBER	NO. OF COLORS	ORIGINAL OPENING PRICE	CURRENT RETAIL PRICE
SOLD OUT EDITIONS (RARE):										
Horse and Rider I-VI	WG	CW/WI	1970	LB	23 X 31 EA	AP	70 EA	1 EA	90 EA	1800 EA
Horse's Head	WG	CW/WI	1970	LB	16 X 23	AP	60	1	75	500
Lynx	WG	CW/WI	1970	LB	21 X 26	AP	70	1	90	1350
Mouflon	WG	CW/WI	1970	LB	21 X 26	AP	70	1	90	1350
Small Horse and Rider	WG	CW/WI	1970	LB	16 X 24	AP	60	1	75	950
Wolf	WG	CW/WI	1970	LB	21 X 26	AP	70	1	90	1350
Man & Horse, I-VI	WG	CW/WI	1971	LB	24 X 32 EA	AP	70 EA	1 EA	100 EA	1650 EA
CAS Horse & Rider	WG	CW/WI	1971	LB	24 X 32	AP	70	1	100	1650
Small Boar	WG	CW/WI	1971	LB	20 X 25	AP	70	1	75	950
The Canterbury Tales II (Set of 19):										
Chaucer's Sir Topaz	WG	CW/WI	1972	EB	32 X 24	AP	50	1	80	950
Clerk's Table	WG	CW/WI	1972	EB	32 X 24	AP	50	1	80	950
The Franklin's Tale	WG	CW/WI	1972	LB	32 X 24	AP	50	1	80	950
The Knights Tale	WG	CW/WI	1972	EB	32 X 24	AP	50	1	80	950
The Manciple's Tale	WG	CW/WI	1972	EB	32 X 24	AP	50	1	80	950
The Merchant's Tale	WG	CW/WI	1972	LB	32 X 24	AP	50	1	80	950
The Miller's Tale I	WG	CW/WI	1972	EB	32 X 24	AP	50	1	80	950
The Nun's Priest's	WG	CW/WI	1972	EB	32 X 24	AP	50	1	80	950
The Pardoner's Tale	WG	CW/WI	1972	EB	32 X 24	AP	50	1	80	950
The Physician's Tale	WG	CW/WI	1972	EB	32 X 24	AP	50	1	80	950
The Prioress's Tale	WG	CW/WI	1972	EB	32 X 24	AP	50	1	80	950
The Prologue	WG	CW/WI	1972	EB	32 X 24	AP	50	1	80	950
The Reeve's Tale	WG	CW/WI	1972	EB	32 X 24	AP	50	1	80	950
The Second Nun's Tale	WG	CW/WI	1972	EB	32 X 24	AP	50	1	80	950
The Shipman's Tale	WG	CW/WI	1972	EB	32 X 24	AP	50	1	80	950
The Squire's Tale	WG	CW/WI	1972	EB	32 X 24	AP	50	1	80	950
Summoner's Prologue Tale	WG	CW/WI	1972	EB	32 X 24	AP	50	1	80	950
The Wife of Bath's Tale	WG	CW/WI	1972	EB	32 X 24	AP	50	1	80	950
Arrival at Canterbury	WG	CW/WI	1972	EB	32 X 24	AP	50	1	80	950
Bullfight	WG	CW/WI	1973	EB	23 X 31	AP	72	1	100	800
Corida III	WG	CW/WI	1973	LB	18 X 31	AP	72	1	80	500
Goggled Head	WG	CW/WI	1973	EB	31 X 26	AP	52	1	100	1200
Rejoneadora I	WG	CW/WI	1973	EB	22 X 31	AP	72	1	100	900
The Odyssey:										
The Book of the Dead	WG	CW/WI	1974	LB	10 X 6	AP	30	1	80	350
Calypso	WG	CW/WI	1974	LB	10 X 6	AP	30	1	80	350
Circe	WG	CW/WI	1974	LB	10 X 6	AP	30	1	80	350
Cyclops	WG	CW/WI	1974	LB	10 X 6	AP	30	1	80	350
Debate in Ithaca	WG	CW/WI	1974	LB	10 X 6	AP	30	1	80	350
The Great Bow	WG	CW/WI	1974	LB	10 X 6	AP	30	1	80	350
In Eumaeus' Hut	WG	CW/WI	1974	LB	10 X 6	AP	30	1	80	350
Menelaus & Helen	WG	CW/WI	1974	LB	10 X 6	AP	30	1	80	350
Odysseus and Penelope	WG	CW/WI	1974	LB	10 X 6	AP	30	1	80	350
Odysseus Meets His Son	WG	CW/WI	1974	LB	10 X 6	AP	30	1	80	350
Telemachus with Nestor	WG	CW/WI	1974	LB	10 X 6	AP	30	1	80	350
Nausicas	WG	CW/WI	1974	LB	10 X 6	AP	30	1	80	350
Birds of Prey:										
Golden Eagle	WG	CW/WI	1974	EB	37 X 26	AP	50	1	135	1800
Goshawk	WG	CW/WI	1974	EB	37 X 26	AP	50	1	135	1800
Honey Buzzard	WG	CW/WI	1974	EB	37 X 26	AP	50	1	135	1800
Kestrel	WG	CW/WI	1974	EB	37 X 26	AP	50	1	135	1800
Lammergeier	WG	CW/WI	1974	EB	37 X 26	AP	50	1	135	1800
Long-Eared Owl	WG	CW/WI	1974	EB	37 X 26	AP	50	1	135	1800
Marsh Harrier	WG	CW/WI	1974	EB	37 X 26	AP	50	1	135	1800
Osprey	WG	CW/WI	1974	EB	37 X 26	AP	50	1	135	1800
Peregrine Falcon	WG	CW/WI	1974	EB	37 X 26	AP	50	1	135	1800
Sparrow Hawk	WG	CW/WI	1974	EB	37 X 26	AP	50	1	135	1800
Owl Series:										
Barn Owl	WG	CW/WI	1977	EB	21 X 18	AP	75	1	200	1800
Little Owl	WG	CW/WI	1977	EB	21 X 18	AP	75	1	200	1800
Long Erred Owl	WG	CW/WI	1977	EB	21 X 18	AP	75	1	200	1800
Snowy Owl	WG	CW/WI	1977	EB	21 X 18	AP	75	1	200	1800
Tawny Owl	WG	CW/WI	1977	EB	21 X 18	AP	75	1	200	1800
Young Barn Owl	WG	CW/WI	1977	EB	21 X 18	AP	75	1	200	1800
Rolling Over Horse	WG	CW/KS	1980	EB	27 X 36	AP	75	1	270	1800
Strawberry Roan	WG	CW/KS	1980	EB	27 X 36	AP	75	1	270	1800
Viszla (a)	WG	CW/KS	1980	EB	27 X 36	AP	75	1	270	1800
Viszla (b)	WG	CW/KS	1980	EB	27 X 36	AP	75	1	270	1800
Anthony and Cleopatra	WG	CW/KS	1982	EB	30 X 22	AP	200	1	250	600
Babboon	WG	CW/KS	1985	EB/A	9 X 9	R/BFK	40	1	250	750
The Bullring	WG	CW/KS	1985	EB	9 X 14	R/BFK	45	1	250	750
Panther	WG	CW/KS	1985	EB/A	9 X 9	R/BFK	40	1	250	750
Running Man	WG	CW/KS	1985	EB	8 X 8	R/BFK	30	1	250	600

ELISABETH FRINK CONTINUED

TITLE	PUBLISHER	PRINTER	DATE	MEDIUM	DIMENSION (PAPER SIZE) IN INCHES	TYPE OF PAPER	EDITION NUMBER	NO. OF COLORS	ORIGINAL OPENING PRICE	CURRENT RETAIL PRICE
SOLD OUT EDITIONS (RARE):										
Tiger	WG	CW/KS	1985	EB/A	9 X 9	R/BFK	40	1	250	750
CURRENT EDITIONS:										
Old Man of the Sea (Brown Ink)	WG	CW/KS	1988	EB	21 X 15	R/BFK	70	1	500	800
Herakles and the Bull (Brown Ink)	WG	CW/KS	1988	EB/A	21 X 15	R/BFK	70	1	500	800
The Dalgdonean Boar (Brown Ink)	WG	CW/KS	1988	EB/A	22 X 15	R/BFK	70	1	500	800

SHIRLEY FUERST

BORN: Brooklyn, NY; June 3, 1928
EDUCATION: Hunter Col, 1944–48, BA; Brooklyn Mus Art Sch, 1958–65; Pratt Graphics Center, Brooklyn, NY, 1965; Hunter Col, NY, MFA, 1967–71
AWARDS: Nat Assoc of Women Artists, Eric Schwartz Graphics Award, 1970
COLLECTIONS: James A Michener Found Coll, Univ of TX, Austin, TX; Allentown Art Mus, PA
PRINTERS: Artist (ART)
PUBLISHERS: Artist (ART)
GALLERIES: Atlantic Gallery, New York, NY
MAILING ADDRESS: 266 Marlborough Rd, Brooklyn, NY 11226

TITLE	PUBLISHER	PRINTER	DATE	MEDIUM	DIMENSION (PAPER SIZE) IN INCHES	TYPE OF PAPER	EDITION NUMBER	NO. OF COLORS	ORIGINAL OPENING PRICE	CURRENT RETAIL PRICE
SOLD OUT EDITIONS (RARE):										
Form from an Unknown Region	ART	ART	1968	EA	14 X 17	GE	40	3	150	400
Movable Metaphors I	ART	ART	1969	E/I	16 X 22	GE	20	2	175	500
Movable Metaphors II	ART	ART	1969	A/I	17 X 23	GE	20	1	175	500
Movable Metaphors III	ART	ART	1969	I	22 X 28	GE	40	5	250	700
CURRENT EDITIONS:										
Improbable Monument #1–#9	ART	ART	1976–77	HD/COL	13 X 14 X 2 EA		30 EA	4–8 EA	250 EA	600 EA
Little Big Box I (5 Parts)	ART	ART	1978	HD/COL	3 X 13 X 3		80	3	250	600
Little Big Box II (4 Parts)	ART	ART	1979	HD/COL	5 X 5 X 2		80	3	200	500
Deep Space I–VI	ART	ART	1980–81	HD/COL	12 X 12 X 1 EA		10 EA	6 EA	350 EA	500 EA
Cloud and Hexagon	ART	ART	1982	HD/COL	12 X 13 X 2		30	2	250	500
The Effect of Floating Eggs										
Upon a Balancing Heart	ART	ART	1982	HD/COL	17 X 12 X 2		30	6	400	600
Frieze I, II, III	ART	ART	1984	HD/COL	90 X 40 X 16 EA		10 EA	9 EA	1700 EA	2000 EA

HAMISH FULTON

BORN: London, England, 1946
EDUCATION: Hammersmith Col of Art; St Martins Sch of Art; Royal Col of Art, London, England
RECENT EXHIB: Tyler Sch of Art, Temple Univ, Phila, PA, 1988; Inst for Contemp Art, PS 1 Mus, NY, 1989; Retrosp, Albright-Knox Art Gallery, Buffalo, NY, 1990; John Weber Gallery, NY, 1987,92
COLLECTIONS: Mus of Mod Art, New York, NY; Nat Gallery, Ottawa, Canada; Stedelijk Mus, Amsterdam, Holland; Tate Gallery, London, England; British Council, London, England; Basel Kunstmuseum, Switzerland; Kroller Muller Mus, Otterlo, Holland
PRINTERS: Peter Pettengill (PP); Paul Singdahlsen (PS); Marcia Bartholme (MB); Crown Point Press, San Francisco, CA (CPP); Marc Hostettler, Neuchâtel, Switzerland (MH); Editions Média, Neuchâtel, Switzerland (EM); Tristam Kent, London, England (TK); Paragon Press, London, England (ParPr); Coriander Studio, London, England (CorSt)
PUBLISHERS: Crown Point Press, San Francisco, CA (CPP); Waddington Graphics, London, England (WG); Paragon Press, London, England (ParPr)
GALLERIES: Waddington Galleries, Ltd, London, England; Crown Point Press, New York, NY & San Francisco, CA; John Weber Gallery, New York, NY
MAILING ADDRESS: Orchard Cottage, Barne to Jane, Broad Oak, Canterbury, Kent, England 0227

TITLE	PUBLISHER	PRINTER	DATE	MEDIUM	DIMENSION (PAPER SIZE) IN INCHES	TYPE OF PAPER	EDITION NUMBER	NO. OF COLORS	ORIGINAL OPENING PRICE	CURRENT RETAIL PRICE
CURRENT EDITIONS:										
Porcupine	WG/CPP	PP	1982	EC	94 X 24	SOM/S	25		800	1500
Humming Heart (3 parts):	WG	ME/EM	1983	SP/COL	24 X 18 EA	SOM/S	60 EA		525 SET	2000 SET
Humming Heart										
Cloud/Rock										
Dust to Snow to Dust										
Fourteen Works, 1982–89										
(Wood Portfolio Case)	ParPr	TK/ParPr	1989	LC/OFF	Varies	HER	35 EA		10000 SET	12000 SET
Ten Toes Towards the Rainbow										
(Set of 9)	ParPr	CorSt	1993	SP	Varies	SOM/S	35 EA		9000 SET	9000 SET

The retail prices of the 100,000 limited edition prints quoted in this directory are subject to change. Print publishers, artists and galleries were the direct sources for these quotations. Prices in the secondary market listed as "Sold Out Editions (Rare)" indicate that the publisher has a limited supply of that print or that the print is difficult to locate in the galleries.

The Printworld Directory is accepting new applications for the seventh edition. Approximately 300 new artists will be accepted. Please use the two forms provided in the back section of this directory to submit biographical data and documentation of prints. Edition number of each print must not exceed 500 and the retail price must be $100 or more.

The print market has become very selective. For the first time since we published the first edition of The Printworld Directory in 1982, the prices of prints have been greatly reduced and greatly increased for the same artists by the most reputable and established print publishers. Check the fifth edition to understand the movement.

BARBARA FUMAGALLI

BORN: Kirkwood, MO; March 15, 1926
EDUCATION: Univ of Iowa, Iowa City, IA, BFA, 1948, MFA, 1950; Univ of New Mexico, Albuquerque, NM 1980–81
TEACHING: Instr, Univ of Wisconsin-Stout, Menomonie, WI, 1979,81
AWARDS: City Art Mus, St Louis, MO, 1947; Purchase Prize, Univ of Illinois, Urbana, IL 1954
RECENT EXHIB: Univ of Louisville, KY, 1993
COLLECTIONS: Mus of Mod Art, NY; Nelson Rockefeller Coll, NY; Univ of Illinois, Urbana, IL; Univ of Iowa, Iowa City, IA; Univ of Wisconsin-Stout, Menomonie, WI; Hamline Univ, St Paul, MN; St John's Univ, Collegeville, MN
PRINTERS: Artist (ART)
PUBLISHERS: Artist (ART)
GALLERIES: Galerie Kuhl, Hannover, West Germany
MAILING ADDRESS: Rt 4, Box 282A, Menomonie, WI 54751

Barbara Fumagalli
Night Visitor
Courtesy the Artist

TITLE	PUBLISHER	PRINTER	DATE	MEDIUM	DIMENSION (PAPER SIZE) IN INCHES	TYPE OF PAPER	EDITION NUMBER	NO. OF COLORS	ORIGINAL OPENING PRICE	CURRENT RETAIL PRICE
SOLD OUT EDITIONS (RARE):										
Study of Insects No 2	ART	ART	1947	ENG	9 X 12	JP	25	1	30	300
Study of Insects No 3	ART	ART	1947	ENG	12 X 14	JP	25	1	30	300
Self Portrait	ART	ART	1950	DPT	13 X 19	JP	25	1	35	400
Girl with Flowers	ART	ART	1953	DPT	19 X 26	JP	25	1	35	400
Nine Days Old	ART	ART	1956	DPT	13 X 19	JP	25	1	40	400
A Walk in the Night	ART	ART	1958	DPT	19 X 26	AP	25	1	40	300
CURRENT EDITIONS:										
Toto's Woods	ART	ART	1963	ENG	14 X 20	R/BFK	50	1	75	150
Louise	ART	ART	1963	ENG	22 X 29	R/BFK	50	1	100	200
Broken Fruit	ART	ART	1964	ENG	22 X 17	R/BFK	50	1	75	150
Helios	ART	ART	1964	ENG	21 X 28	R/BFK	50	1	100	200
Cat's Cradle	ART	ART	1965	ENG	20 X 40	R/BFK	50	1	125	250
Exotic Blooms	ART	ART	1965	ENG	20 X 29	R/BFK	50	1	100	200
Gretchen	ART	ART	1966	ENG	13 X 40	R/BFK	50	1	100	200
After Summer	ART	ART	1966	ENG	27 X 21	R/BFK	50	1	100	200
1735 Wallace Avenue	ART	ART	1967	ENG	21 X 24	R/BFK	50	1	100	200
Remember Robin	ART	ART	1967	ENG	20 X 24	R/BFK	50	1	100	200
Paisley	ART	ART	1968	ENG	16 X 40	R/BFK	50	1	100	200
Willow in the River	ART	ART	1968	ENG	22 X 29	R/BFK	50	1	100	200
Man with Pinks	ART	ART	1968	ENG	19 X 28	R/BFK	50	1	100	200
Yesterday	ART	ART	1969	ENG	16 X 40	R/BFK	50	1	100	200
Sunflower	ART	ART	1974	ENG	25 X 26	R/BFK	50	1	150	250
Passionflower	ART	ART	1978	ENG	26 X 26	R/BFK	50	1	150	250
Grasshoppers, 1st State	ART	ART	1980	LB	15 X 14	R/BFK	19	1	100	150
Corn, 2nd State	ART	ART	1980	LC	20 X 15	R/BFK	11	2	100	150
Black Cherries	ART	ART	1980	LB	16 X 15	AP/B	20		100	150
In the Pond	ART	ART	1980	SP	15 X 21	R/BFK	19	7	100	200
Under the Ferns	ART	ART	1980	SP	15 X 22	AP/B	14	6	100	200
In the Wind	ART	ART	1980	SP	14 X 22	R/BFK	24	8	100	200
English Breakfast	ART	ART	1980	LC	17 X 15	R/BFK	11	3	100	200
Salt Shaker	ART	ART	1981	LB/HC	15 X 18	R/BFK	20	3	100	250
Perennial Garden	ART	ART	1981	SP	21 X 15	AP	16	9	100	200
Floating Down Stream	ART	ART	1981	LC	19 X 15	R/BFK	21	3	100	200
Corsage	ART	ART	1981	LC	19 X 15	R/BFK	43	4	100	200
Nearly Wild	ART	ART	1983	SP/ENG	10 X 8	R/BFK/G	45	5	75	100
Ring from Childhood	ART	ART	1985	SP/ENG	5 X 6	MAG/IT	45	4	75	100
August Aviators	ART	ART	1985	SP/ENG	8 X 10	AP/W	55	8	75	100
Toad Life	ART	ART	1985	SP/ENG	8 X 11	HMP	88	7	75	100
Evening Visitor	ART	ART	1986	SP/ENG	8 X 10	R/BFK	88	11	75	100
Jewelweed	ART	ART	1988	SP/ENG	15 X 21	R/BFK	43	6	100	200

KATSURA FUNAKOSHI

BORN: Iwate, Japan; 1951
PRINTERS: Crown Point Press, San Francisco, CA (CPP)
PUBLISHERS: Crown Point Press, San Francisco, CA (CPP)
GALLERIES: Crown Point Press, San Francisco & New York, NY

TITLE	PUBLISHER	PRINTER	DATE	MEDIUM	DIMENSION (PAPER SIZE) IN INCHES	TYPE OF PAPER	EDITION NUMBER	NO. OF COLORS	ORIGINAL OPENING PRICE	CURRENT RETAIL PRICE
SOLD OUT EDITIONS (RARE):										
Dancer—Moon	CPP	CPP	1990	EB/DPT/SG	41 X 32		30	1	1500	1500
Dream of the Bird	CPP	CPP	1990	EB/DPT/SG	54 X 40		30	1	2000	2000
In the Room with High Ceiling	CPP	CPP	1990	EB/A/DPT/SB/SG	30 X 22		30	1	1100	1100
The Book Half Read	CPP	CPP	1990	EB/DPT/SG	27 X 21		30	1	1100	1100
Water Blue	CPP	CPP	1990	EB/A/DPT/SB	41 X 33		30	1	1500	1500
Quiet Summer	CPP	CPP	1990	EB/DPT/SG	41 X 32		30	1	1500	1800
CURRENT EDITIONS:										
After Mirror Reflecting Fingers	CPP	CPP	1990	EB/A/DPT/SL/SB	24 X 33		35	1	850	850
Study	CPP	CPP	1990	EB/DPT/HG	30 X 22		30	1	750	750

GEORGE JOSEPH GABIN

BORN: Brooklyn, NY; April 16, 1931
EDUCATION: Brooklyn Mus Art Sch, NY, 1949–52; Art Students League, NY, 1949–54; Studied printmaking with Harry Sternberg & Will Barnet
TEACHING: Instr, Drawing, New England Sch of Art, Boston, MA, 1964–70; Instr, Drawing & Painting, Montserrat Col of Art, Beverly, MA, 1970 to present
AWARDS: Lindley I Dean Mem Award, Rockport Art Assoc, MA, 1981; Stow Wengenroth Award for Lithography, Rockport Art Assoc, MA, 1982; Ralph Fabri Medal of Merit, Allied Artists of Am, NY, 1983; Grumbacher Gold Award, Holyoke Art Council, MA, 1981; Stow Wengenroth Award, Rockport Art Assn, ME, 1982; Ralph Fabi Medal of Merit, Allied Artists of America, 1983
COLLECTIONS: Davidson Col, NC; Echerd Col, St Petersburg, FL; Honolulu Acad of Arts, HI; Manhattan Col, Riverdale, NY; Skidmore Col, Sarasota Col, Sarasota, NY; Syracuse Univ, NY; Univ of California, Grunewald Center for the Graphic Arts, Los Angeles, CA; Univ of Virginia Bagly Mem Mus, Charlottesville, VA; Rutgers Univ, Jane Voorhees Zimmerli Art Mus, New Brunswick, NJ; St Lawrence Univ, Brush Art Gallery, Canton, NY; California State Univ, Chico, CA
PUBLISHERS: Fox Graphics, Merrimac, MA (FG); Impressions Workshop, Boston, MA (IW) (OB); Flat Rock Press, Boston, MA (FRP); Peter Benin, Wilton, CT (PB)
PRINTERS: Herbert A Fox, Merrimac, MA (HF); Fox Graphics, Merrimac, MA (FG); Impressions Workshop, Boston, MA (IW) (OB); Paul Maguire, Boston, MA (PM); Flat Rock Press, Boston, MA (FRP)
GALLERIES: Another Atmosphere, Newburyport, MA; Fox Graphics, Merrimac, MA; Carl Seimbab Gallery, Boston, MA
MAILING ADDRESS: 1 Fitchburg St, #B554, Somerville, MA 02143

TITLE	PUBLISHER	PRINTER	DATE	MEDIUM	DIMENSION (PAPER SIZE) IN INCHES	TYPE OF PAPER	EDITION NUMBER	NO. OF COLORS	ORIGINAL OPENING PRICE	CURRENT RETAIL PRICE
CURRENT EDITIONS:										
The Cyclist	IW/PB	PM/IW	1977	LB	32 X 23	AP/W	30	1	100	250
The Cyclist	IW/PB	PM/IW	1977	LB	32 X 23	AP/B	30	1	100	250
Penny Arcade	IW/PB	PM/IW	1978	LB	24 X 20	R/BFK/W	30	1	100	250
Penny Arcade	IW/PB	PM/IW	1978	LB	24 X 20	R/BFK/G	30	1	100	250
The Bed	FG/PB	HF/FG	1981	LB	22 X 30	R/BFK	60	1	150	400
Four Color Cherry	FG/ART	HF/FG	1981	LC	30 X 22	AP/W	60	4	150	450
The Last Train	FG/PB	HF/FG	1982	LB	24 X 32	R/BFK	60	1	150	400
The Conversation	FRP/PB	PM/FRP	1986	LB	24 X 22	R/BFK	100	1	125	200

WOLFGANG GÄFGEN

PRINTERS: Atelier Rigal, Fontenay-aux-Roses, France (AR)
PUBLISHERS: Boudoin Lebon, Paris, France (BL)
GALLERIES: Boudoin Lebon Gallery, Paris, France

TITLE	PUBLISHER	PRINTER	DATE	MEDIUM	DIMENSION (PAPER SIZE) IN INCHES	TYPE OF PAPER	EDITION NUMBER	NO. OF COLORS	ORIGINAL OPENING PRICE	CURRENT RETAIL PRICE
CURRENT EDITIONS:										
Nids (Nests) (Set of 6)	BL	AR	1983	AC	21 X 38 EA	AP	52 EA		1500 SET	2500 SET

CHARLES GAINES

RECENT EXHIB: John Weber Gallery, NY, 1989,91; Leo Castelli Gallery, NY, 1991
PRINTERS: Mary McDonald, Chicago, IL (MM); Landfall Press Inc, Chicago, IL (LPI)
PUBLISHERS: Landfall Press Inc, Chicago, IL (LPI)
GALLERIES: Margo Leavin Gallery, Los Angeles, CA; John Weber Gallery, New York, NY; Landfall Press Inc, Chicago, IL; Leo Castelli Gallery, New York, NY; Quartet Editions, New York, NY

TITLE	PUBLISHER	PRINTER	DATE	MEDIUM	DIMENSION (PAPER SIZE) IN INCHES	TYPE OF PAPER	EDITION NUMBER	NO. OF COLORS	ORIGINAL OPENING PRICE	CURRENT RETAIL PRICE
SOLD OUT EDITIONS (RARE):										
Color Regression I, II, III	LPI	MM/LPI	1980	LC	29 X 34 EA	R/BFK	30 EA	6 EA	900 SET	2000 SET

AMADEO GABINO

BORN: Valencia, Spain; 1922
EDUCATION: Escuela Superior de Bellas de Carlos, Valencia, Spain
AWARDS: Scholarship, Italian Government, 1949; Scholarship, French Government, Paris, France, 1952; Scholarship, Acad de Bellas Artes, Madrid, Spain, 1957; Ford Found Fel, NY, 1961
PRINTERS: La Poligrafa, SA, Barcelona, Spain (LP)
PUBLISHERS: Ediciones Poligrafa, SA, Barcelona, Spain (EdP)
GALLERIES: Galeria Joan Prats, New York, NY & Barcelona, Spain

TITLE	PUBLISHER	PRINTER	DATE	MEDIUM	DIMENSION (PAPER SIZE) IN INCHES	TYPE OF PAPER	EDITION NUMBER	NO. OF COLORS	ORIGINAL OPENING PRICE	CURRENT RETAIL PRICE
CURRENT EDITIONS:										
Barcelona Suite (Set of 13):									3000 SET	4500 SET
Barcelona #1-#12	EdP	LP	1977	EC	22 X 30	GP	75 EA	3 EA	250 EA	400 EA
Barcelona #13	EdP	LP	1977	EC	28 X 34	GP	75	3	350	500
Series of 13 Etchings (Set of 13):									3500 SET	5000 SET
Sombra del Viento	EdP	LP	1980	EC	22 X 30	GP	75	3	300	450
Espejo de la Noche	EdP	LP	1980	EC	22 X 30	GP	75	3	300	450
Yelmo del Sol	EdP	LP	1980	EC	22 X 30	GP	75	3	300	450
Polifemo	EdP	LP	1980	EC	22 X 30	GP	75	3	300	450
Polifemo II	EdP	LP	1980	EC	22 X 30	GP	75	3	300	450
Espejo de Venus	EdP	LP	1980	EC	22 X 30	GP	75	3	300	450
Rotura de la Nada	EdP	LP	1980	EC	22 X 30	GP	75	3	300	450
Mirada del Sol	EdP	LP	1980	EC	22 X 30	GP	75	3	300	450
Espejo de la Niebla	EdP	LP	1980	EC	22 X 30	GP	75	3	300	450
Sueño del Silencio	EdP	LP	1980	EC	22 X 30	GP	75	3	300	450
Bruma sin Limite	EdP	LP	1980	EC	22 X 30	GP	75	3	300	450
Homenaje a Rothko	EdP	LP	1980	EC	40 X 28	GP	75	3	400	550
Series of 4 Lithographs (Set of 4):									800 SET	1200 SET
Chicago	EdP	LP	1980	LC	30 X 22	GP	99	5	220	330
New York	EdP	LP	1980	LC	30 X 22	GP	99	5	220	330
Barcelona	EdP	LP	1980	LC	30 X 22	GP	99	6	220	330
Rotura de la Niebla	EdP	LP	1980	LC	30 X 22	GP	99	6	220	330
Photoscop	EdP	LP	1980	EC	8 X 8	GP	50	6	180	280

YANNIS GAITIS

BORN: Athens, Greece, 1923
COLLECTIONS: Tel Aviv Mus, Israel
PRINTERS: American Atelier, NY (AA)
PUBLISHERS: Circle Fine Art, Chicago, IL (CFA)
GALLERIES: Circle Galleries, San Diego, CA & San Francisco, CA & Northbrook, IL & Pittsburgh, PA & Houston, TX & Soho, NY & Chicago, IL & Scottsdale, AZ & Beverly Hills, CA & Costa Mesa, CA & Sherman Oaks, CA & Palm Beach, FL & Honolulu, HI & New Orleans, LA & Las Vegas, NV & Seattle, WA

TITLE	PUBLISHER	PRINTER	DATE	MEDIUM	DIMENSION (PAPER SIZE) IN INCHES	TYPE OF PAPER	EDITION NUMBER	NO. OF COLORS	ORIGINAL OPENING PRICE	CURRENT RETAIL PRICE
SOLD OUT EDITIONS (RARE):										
Red Bowler	CFA	AA	1979	LC	31 X 24	AP	250		50	300
Can	CFA	AA	1979	LC	31 X 24	AP	250		50	450
White Collars	CFA	AA	1979	LC	24 X 31	AP	250		50	300
Bowler	CFA	AA	1979	LC	24 X 31	AP	250		50	300
Dirty Dozen	CFA	AA	1979	LC	34 X 24	AP	250		50	300
Red Men	CFA	AA	1979	LC	24 X 31	AP	250		50	300
Car Pool	CFA	AA	1979	LC	32 X 24	AP	250		50	250
Opposition	CFA	AA	1980	LC/EMB	32 X 24	AP	250		75	250
CURRENT EDITIONS:										
Square Head	CFA	AA	1980	LC/EMB	32 X 24	AP	250		75	250
Profiles	CFA	AA	1980	LC/EMB	24 X 32	AP	250		75	250
Progression of Heads	CFA	AA	1980	LC/EMB	32 X 24	AP	250		75	250
Rejection	CFA	AA	1980	LC/EMB	24 X 32	AP	250		75	250

NORMAN GALINSKY

BORN: Charleston, W VA; January 28, 1942
EDUCATION: Univ of Cincinnati, OH, BS, ChE, 1959–64; Columbia Univ, NY, MFA, 1970–73, with Philip Guston, Theodorus Stamos, Malcolm Morley & Jack Tworkov; Art Students League, NY, Printmaking Workshop with Bob Blackburn; New York Univ, The New Sch, NY; Pratt Graphics Center, NY; Printmaking Workshop, NY; Sch for Visual Arts, NY
COLLECTIONS: Columbia Univ, NY; Emporia State Univ Coll, KS
PRINTERS: Kathleen Caraccio, NY (KC); Sylvia Roth, NY (SR); Hudson River Editions, NY (HRE)
PUBLISHERS: Orion Editions, NY (OE)
GALLERIES: Orion Editions, New York, NY; Katonah Gallery, Katonah, NY
MAILING ADDRESS: Lawrence Lane, Palisades, NY 10964

TITLE	PUBLISHER	PRINTER	DATE	MEDIUM	DIMENSION (PAPER SIZE) IN INCHES	TYPE OF PAPER	EDITION NUMBER	NO. OF COLORS	ORIGINAL OPENING PRICE	CURRENT RETAIL PRICE
SOLD OUT EDITIONS (RARE):										
Ildefonso Series (Series of 7)	OE	KC	1978	AC	23 X 30 EA	AP	40 EA	8–10 EA	250 EA	500 EA
Aquarian Series (Series of 50)	OE	SR/HRE	1982	MON	29 X 41 EA	AP	1 EA	1 EA	375 EA	750 EA
Aquarian Transformation	OE	SR/HRE	1983	EC	30 X 41	AP	15	7	350	750

CYNTHIA GALLAGHER

EDUCATION: Philadelphia Col of Art, PA, BFA, 1968–72; Queens Col, Flushing, NY, MFA, 1972–74
TEACHING: Vis Critic, New York Univ, NY, 1974–75; Philadelphia Col of Art, PA, 1976–77; Manhattan Com Col, City Univ of New York, NY, 1977–78; Yale Univ, Summer Sch of Music & Art, Norfolk, CT, 1980; Instr, New York Inst of Tech, Old Westbury, NY 1976–88; Instr, Fashion Inst of Tech, NY, 1988; Instr, Queens Col, City of New York, Bronx, NY, 1974–89
AWARDS: Creative Artists Public Service Prog, Grant, Graphics, 1981–82; Nat Endowment for the Arts Grant, Painting, 1983–84,89; New York Found of the Arts, 1989
RECENT EXHIB: Albright-Knox Art Gallery, Buffalo, NY, 1987; Luise Ross Gallery, NY, 1987; Alice Simsar Gallery, Ann Arbor, MI, 1988; Arkansas Art Center, Little Rock, AR, 1988; Edward Thorden Gallery, Goteborg, Sweden, 1989; Charles More Gallery, Phila, PA, 1990
COLLECTIONS: Metropolitan Mus of Art, NY
PRINTERS: New York Inst of Tech, Old Westbury, NY (NYIT); Ronni Henning, NY (RH); Judith Solodkin, NY (JS); Solo Press, NY (SP)
PUBLISHERS: Ronni Henning, NY (RH); Solo Press, NY (SP)
GALLERIES: Alice Simsar Gallery, Ann Arbor, MI; Luise Ross Gallery, New York, NY; Solo Gallery, New York, NY; Ellen Sragow Gallery, New York, NY; Holly Solomon Gallery, New York, NY; Charles More Gallery, Phila, PA; Edward Thorden Gallery, Goteborg, Sweden
MAILING ADDRESS: 178 Franklin St, New York, NY 10013

TITLE	PUBLISHER	PRINTER	DATE	MEDIUM	DIMENSION (PAPER SIZE) IN INCHES	TYPE OF PAPER	EDITION NUMBER	NO. OF COLORS	ORIGINAL OPENING PRICE	CURRENT RETAIL PRICE
CURRENT EDITIONS:										
Babycakes	RH	RH/NYIT	1982	SP	48 X 38	AP	50	16	450	950
Savannah's Pot	SP	JS/SP	1988	WC/LC	44 X 30	AP	45		850	950

MICHAEL R GALLAGHER

BORN: Los Angeles, CA; 1945
EDUCATION: Univ of Southern California, Los Angeles, CA, BFA, 1967; Yale Univ Sch of Art & Arch, New Haven, CT, MFA, 1970
AWARDS: Eli Harwood Schless Draughtsmanship Award, Yale Univ Art Gallery, New Haven, CT, 1970
COLLECTIONS: Univ of Southern California, Los Angeles, CA; Honolulu Acad of Art, HI; Guggenheim Mus, NY
PRINTERS: Artist (ART)
PUBLISHERS: Fred Dorfman, Inc, NY (FDI)
GALLERIES: Fred Dorfman Gallery, New York, NY; Louis K Meisel Gallery, New York, NY

TITLE	PUBLISHER	PRINTER	DATE	MEDIUM	DIMENSION (PAPER SIZE) IN INCHES	TYPE OF PAPER	EDITION NUMBER	NO. OF COLORS	ORIGINAL OPENING PRICE	CURRENT RETAIL PRICE
CURRENT EDITIONS:										
Barnabas' Voyage I–IV (Series of 4 States):									6000 SET	7500 SET
States I, II	FDI	ART	1985	SP	49 X 37 EA	LEN/100	20 EA	17–20 EA	1800 EA	2000 EA
States III, IV	FDI	ART	1985	SP	49 X 37 EA	LEN/100	35 EA	17–20 EA	1800 EA	2000 EA

MARGARET W GALLEGOS

BORN: Santa Monica, CA; August 7, 1938
EDUCATION: Univ of California, Los Angeles, CA, BA, 1960
AWARDS: Purchase Award, New Jersey Printmaking Council, Somerville, NJ, 1987
RECENT EXHIB: Hard Times Gallery, Bristol, England, 1987; Fort Hays State Univ, KS, 1987; Univ of North Dakota, Grand Forks, ND, 1987; Art Store Gallery, Pasadena, CA, 1987; Atkinson Gallery, Santa Barbara City Col, CA, 1987; Auburn Univ, AL, 1987; Corner Gallery, Salem, OR, 1987; Downey Mus of Art, CA, 1987; Zimmerli Mus, Rutgers Univ, Montclair, NJ, 1987
COLLECTIONS: New Jersey Printmaking Council, Somerville, NH
PRINTERS: Artist (ART)
PUBLISHERS: Artist (ART)

TITLE	PUBLISHER	PRINTER	DATE	MEDIUM	DIMENSION (PAPER SIZE) IN INCHES	TYPE OF PAPER	EDITION NUMBER	NO. OF COLORS	ORIGINAL OPENING PRICE	CURRENT RETAIL PRICE
CURRENT EDITIONS:										
??!!	ART	ART	1987	DPT	6 X 8	R/BFK	20	1	100	150

FRANK GALLO

BORN: Toledo, OH; Jan 13, 1933
EDUCATION: Toledo Mus Sch of Art, OH, BFA, 1954; Cranbrook Acad of Art, MI, 1955; Univ of Iowa, Iowa City, IA, 1959; Univ of Illinois, Urbana-Champaign, IL, Senior Scholar, 1985
TEACHING: Univ of Illinois, Champaign-Urbana, IL, 1960 to present
AWARDS: First Prize, Des Moines, 1958; Guggenheim Found Fel, 1966; Nat Acad of Arts & Letters Award of Excellence; First Prize, Sculpture, Cincinnati Art Mus, OH; Fel, Center for Advanced Studies, Univ of Illinois, Champaign-Urbana, IL
RECENT EXHIB: Whitney Mus of Am Art, Philip Morris Gallery, NY, 1988; Northern Arizona Univ, Flagstaff, AZ, 1987,92
COLLECTIONS: Whitney Mus of Am Art, NY; Mus of Mod Art, NY; Art Inst of Chicago, IL; Los Angeles County Mus of Art, CA; Baltimore Mus of Art, MD; Cleveland Mus of Art, OH; Nat Gallery of Victoria, Melbourne, Australia; Kalamazoo Inst of Arts. MI; Art Gallery of Toronto, Can; Museo de Bellas Artes, Caracas,Venezuela; Princeton Univ, NJ; Joseph Hirshhorn Found Coll, NY
PRINTERS: Atelier Desjobert, Paris, France(ADJ); Inst for Experimental Printmaking, San Francisco, CA (IEP); Univ of Illinois, Urbana, IL (UI); American Atelier, NY (AA); Artist (ART)
PUBLISHERS: Circle Gallery, Ltd, Chicago, IL (CGL); Circle Fine Art, Chicago, IL (CFA)
GALLERIES: Tower Park Gallery, Peoria Heights, IL; Laura Paul Galleries, Cincinnati, OH & Columbus, OH; Circle Galleries, San Diego, CA & San Francisco, CA & Northbrook, IL & Pittsburgh, PA & Houston TX & NY & Chicago, IL & Scottsdale, AZ & Beverly Hills, CA & Costa Mesa, CA & Sherman Oaks, CA & Palm Beach, FL & Honolulu, HI & New Orleans, LA & Las Vegas, NV & Seattle, WA; Gordon Upton, New York, NY; Fernette's Gallery, Des Moines, IA; Merrill Chase Galleries, Chicago, IL; Graphic Art Collection, Hallandale, FL; Gilman/Gruen Galleries, Chicago, IL; Campanile Galleries, Chicago, IL; Donna Rose Gallery, Ketchum, ID; Owl Gallery, San Francisco, CA; Russell Klatt Gallery, Birmingham, MI; Lysographics Fine Arts, St Louis, MO
MAILING ADDRESS: Dept of Art, Univ of Illinois, Urbana-Champaign, IL 61820

FRANK GALLO CONTINUED

TITLE	PUBLISHER	PRINTER	DATE	MEDIUM	DIMENSION (PAPER SIZE) IN INCHES	TYPE OF PAPER	EDITION NUMBER	NO. OF COLORS	ORIGINAL OPENING PRICE	CURRENT RETAIL PRICE
SOLD OUT EDITIONS (RARE):										
Carol	CGL	ART	1970	SP	41 X 29	R/BFK	300	3	190	3000
Girl Bending Down	CGL	ADJ	1970	LC	22 X 30	AP	250	4	150	1000
Flowing Hair	CGL	ADJ	1970	LC	23 X 30	AP	250	3	150	1000
Orange Hair	CGL	ADJ	1970	LC	23 X 30	AP	250	3	150	1000
Irene	CGL	UI	1971	SP	30 X 42	AP	200	5	175	1000
Sue	CGL	UI/IEP	1972	SP	22 X 30	R/BFK	285	4	150	600
The Bride	CGL	UI/IEP	1973	SP	25 X 38	WJP	250	4	175	800
The Dancer	CGL	UI/IEP	1978	CP	32 X 54 X 1	R/100	150	0	1000	9000
Legs	CFA	UI/IEP	1980	CP	31 X 51 X 3	R/100	150	0	1500	9000
Sleeping Girl with Respect to Klimt	CFA	UI/IEP	1980	CP	20 X 23 X 1	R/100	50	0	1050	3000
Concetta	CFA	UI/IEP	1980	CP	40 X 35 X 3	R/100	200	0	1900	9000
Secrets	CFA	UI/IEP	1980	CP	54 X 40 X 3	R/100	200	0	2700	9000
Verity	CFA	UI/IEP	1980	CP	24 X 17 X 2	HMP	200	0	1800	9500
Feathered Hat	CFA	UI/IEP	1981	CP	37 X 29 X 3	R/100	200	0	2700	10000
The Glance, The Gaze	CFA	ART	1981	CP	54 X 43 X 3	HMP	200	0	2100	6000
Secret Player	CFA	ART	1982	CP	37 X 46 X 2	HMP	200	0	2600	9500
Angela	CFA	ART	1982	CP	25 X 32	HMP	200	0	2450	10000
Untitled Profile	CFA	ART	1982	CP	18 X 20	HMP	200	0	1500	4000
Recent Memories	CFA	ART	1983	CP	38 X 28	HMP	200	0	2400	5000
The Letter	CFA	ART	1983	CP	31 X 22	HMP	200	0	2100	4500
Bronze Cygnus (with Stand)	CFA	ART	1983	MULT	28 X 24	BRONZE	10	0	4500	5000
The Actress	CFA	ART	1984	CP	49 X 37	HMP	250	0	3200	5500
Walking Figure	CFA	ART	1985	MULT	21 HT	BRONZE	200	0	3000	6200
Reclining Nude	CFA	ART	1986	CP	32 X 47	HMP	250	0	3000	7000
Paradiso	CFA	ART	1989	CP	42 X 31	HMP	100	0	2400	4000
CURRENT EDITIONS:										
Vegetable Lady	CFL	UI/IEP	1972	SP	29 X 41	R/BFK	300	7	150	550
There's a Strange Girl at my Table	CGL	AA	1976	LC/EMB	35 X 24	LEW/100	300	3	165	800
There's a Strange Girl in my Bath	CGL	AA	1976	LC/EMB	24 X 34	LEW/100	300	3	165	800
Bust of a Young Woman I	CFA	ART	1982	CP	36 X 20	HMP	200	0	2450	3850
Bust of a Young Woman II	CFA	ART	1982	CP	20 X 16	HMP	200	0	2450	3350
Cygnus	CFA	ART	1983	CP	28 X 24	HMP	200	0	3500	3600
Still Life	CFA	ART	1984	CP	25 X 34	HMP	200	0	2100	2500
Primavera (Spring)	CFA	ART	1984	CP	29 X 22	HMP	200	0	2000	2500
Sunbathers	CFA	ART	1984	CP	33 X 40	HMP	200	0	2000	2500
Pink Lips	CFA	ART	1989	CP	40 X 31	HMP	200	0	2800	2900
Sinfonia, State I	CFA	ART	1989	CP	38 X 26	HMP	100	0	2200	2600
Sinfonia, State II	CFA	ART	1989	CP	38 X 26	HMP	50	0	2500	2900
Girl with Green Hair	CFA	ART	1989	CP	25 X 38	HMP	100	0	2400	2500
Chapeau	CFA	ART	1989	CP	40 X 32	HMP	100	0	2400	2900
Persephone I	CFA	ART	1990	CP	39 X 31	HMP	100	0	2400	2500
Persephone II	CFA	ART	1990	CP	39 X 31	HMP	100	0	2400	2500

DIANA GONZALEZ GANDOLFI

EDUCATION: Tufts Univ, Boston, MA, BFA; Sch of Mus of Fine Arts, Boston, MA, MFA; Masters in Education & Arts Therapy
TEACHING: Sch of Mus of Fine Arts, Boston, MA, currently
AWARDS: Alumni Traveling Fel, Sch of Mus of Fine Arts, Boston, MA; Clarriss Bartlett Scholarship, Sch of Mus of Fine Arts, Boston, MA; James William Paige Traveling Fel, Sch of Mus of Fine Arts, Boston, MA; New Jersey State Council, Visual Arts Fel; Morris J Helman Mem Prize, Works on Paper, Nat Assoc of Women Artists, NY
COLLECTIONS: Mus of Fine Arts, Boston, MA
PUBLISHERS: John Szoke Graphics, NY (JSG)
PRINTERS: Sabina Klein Studios, NY (SKS)
GALLERIES: Randall Beck Gallery, Boston, MA; Bess Cutler Gallery, New York, NY; John Szoke Graphics, Inc, New York, NY

TITLE	PUBLISHER	PRINTER	DATE	MEDIUM	DIMENSION (PAPER SIZE) IN INCHES	TYPE OF PAPER	EDITION NUMBER	NO. OF COLORS	ORIGINAL OPENING PRICE	CURRENT RETAIL PRICE
CURRENT EDITIONS:										
Bridge in Merida (Dipt)	JSG	SKS	1986	EC	37 X 30 EA	R/BFK	50	11	1000 SET	1500 SET

ANN CUSHING GANTZ

BORN: Dallas, TX; August 27, 1935
EDUCATION: Memphis Acad of Arts, TN; Southwestern Univ, Memphis, TN; Newcomb Col, Tulane, LA, BFA, 1955
TEACHING: Instr, Printmaking & Painting, Dallas Mus of Fine Arts, TX, 1956–62; Cushing Galleries, Dallas, TX, 1967–79; Cushing Studio, Dallas, TX, 1979 to present
AWARDS: Felix Harris Award, Dallas Mus of Fine Arts, TX, 1956; Joseph Pennell Found, Smithsonian Inst, Wash, DC, 1960; Texas Fine Arts Award, Artist of the Year, 1979, Oak Award, 1981; McMurray Found Award, 1983; Delta Kappa Award, 1987; Alpha Omicron Pi Award, 1991; TVAA Award, 1992
RECENT EXHIB: Trammell Crow Pavilion, Dallas, TX, 1988; Tension House Gallery, Dallas, TX, 1989; Tension House Gallery, Dallas, TX 1991
COLLECTIONS: Dallas Mus of Fine Arts, TX; Denver Mus, CO; Norfolk Mus, VA; Smithsonian Inst, Wash, DC; Rhode Island Sch of Design, Providence, RI; S F Austin Col, Sherman, TX; McNay Mus, Austin, TX; Brooks Mem Col, Memphis, TN; Boston Mus of Fine Arts, MA; Los Angeles State Mus, CA; Univ of Texas, Arlington, TX; Smithsonian Inst, Wash, DC; Univ of Kentucky, Lexington, KY
PRINTERS: Artist (ART)
PUBLISHERS: Artist (ART)

ANN CUSHING GANTZ CONTINUED

GALLERIES: Stewart Gallery, Dallas, TX; Valerie Miller Gallery, Los Angeles, CA; Tension House Gallery, Dallas, TX
MAILING ADDRESS: 4654 Edmondson, Dallas, TX 75209

TITLE	PUBLISHER	PRINTER	DATE	MEDIUM	DIMENSION (PAPER SIZE) IN INCHES	TYPE OF PAPER	EDITION NUMBER	NO. OF COLORS	ORIGINAL OPENING PRICE	CURRENT RETAIL PRICE
SOLD OUT EDITIONS (RARE):										
The Game	ART	ART	1977	SP	9 X 8	AP	10	16	125	400
Last Doll	ART	ART	1978	WC	12 X 27	AP	24	10	225	375
Procession	ART	ART	1979	EC	10 X 17	AP	15	2	200	300
Spiral	ART	ART	1979	WC	14 X 30	AP	24	5	250	375
Escape	ART	ART	1979	A/E	16 X 22	AP	20	8	175	400
Consolation	ART	ART	1979	WC	11 X 22	AP	20	8	250	600
Fencer	ART	ART	1979	WC	9 X 18	AP	25	10	150	600
Feline	ART	ART	1979	EC	30 X 20	AP	10	2	500	1500
Recollection	ART	ART	1979	SP	30 X 30	AP	10	12	500	1500
Crystal	ART	ART	1979	SP	14 X 20	AP	20	6	250	500
Catenation	ART	ART	1981	WC	20 X 30	AP	15	8	350	400
CURRENT EDITIONS:										
Departure	ART	ART	1980	SP	17 X 24	AP	25	15	300	350
Evanescent	ART	ART	1980	WC	16 X 20	AP	25	10	250	300
Dale	ART	ART	1980	SP	16 X 28	AP	25	9	250	300
Red #4	ART	ART	1980	SP	20 X 20	AP	20	15	200	250
Crystal Vase by Day II	ART	ART	1980	SP	30 X 42	AP	10	32	525	600
Monarda: Series F	ART	ART	1981	SP	12 X 20	AP	8	20	250	300
Shasta: Series F	ART	ART	1981	SP	12 X 20	AP	8	20	250	300
The Bristol Fairy: Series F	ART	ART	1981	SP	12 X 20	AP	8	20	250	300
Landview: Series A	ART	ART	1981	SP	10 X 10	AP	10	20	250	300
Seaview: Series A	ART	ART	1981	SP	10 X 20	AP	10	20	250	300
Airview: Series A	ART	ART	1981	SP	10 X 20	AP	10	20	250	300
Laurel	ART	ART	1981	SP	15 X 29	AP	28	18	275	350
Not Church's Iceberg	ART	ART	1981	SP	14 X 18	AP	24	12	300	350
Palm	ART	ART	1981	SP	12 X 20	AP	15	9	300	350
Arboretum	ART	ART	1981	SP	20 X 20	AP	35	8	325	375
Retrospection	ART	ART	1981	WC	14 X 14	AP	35	14	300	350
Contemplation	ART	ART	1981	WC	16 X 32	AP	20	27	300	350
Tryptych	ART	ART	1981	LC	24 X 40	AP	20	25	400	450
Circle	ART	ART	1981	MM	28 X 30	AP	20	14	375	425

JEANNE ALICE GANTZ

BORN: Canton, OH; (1929–1987)
EDUCATION: Grad, Choate Sch, Boston, MA; Goucher Col, Baltimore, MD, 1949; Studied Etching with Kathan Brown, Crown Point Press, Oakland, CA, 1967–69
TEACHING: Instr, Intaglio Printing, Univ of California, Berkeley, CA, 1969–71
AWARDS: Purchase Award, Oakland Mus, CA, 1967; Purchase Award, Potsdam Nat Print Exhib, NY, 1967
PUBLISHERS: Made in California, Oakland, CA (MIC)
PRINTERS: David Kelso, Oakland, CA (DK); Chris Mehling, Oakland, CA (CM); Made in California, Oakland, CA (MIC)
GALLERIES: Made in California, Oakland, CA

TITLE	PUBLISHER	PRINTER	DATE	MEDIUM	DIMENSION (PAPER SIZE) IN INCHES	TYPE OF PAPER	EDITION NUMBER	NO. OF COLORS	ORIGINAL OPENING PRICE	CURRENT RETAIL PRICE
SOLD OUT EDITIONS (RARE):										
Fake Thiebaud	MIC	DK/CM/MIC	1978	EC/SG	12 X 11	R/BFK/W	30	6	125	500

ERNEST P GARTHWAITE

BORN: Saskatoon, Saskatchewan; 1940
EDUCATION: Loras Col, Dubuque, IA, BA, 1961; Univ of Notre Dame, South Bend, IN, MA, 1962; Univ of Wisconsin, Madison, WI, 1964–65; Art Student's League, Woodstock, NY 1966
TEACHING: Loras Col, Dubuque, IA, 1962–65; Col of New Rochelle, NY, 1965–68; City Univ of New York, NY, 1968 to present
PRINTERS: Bruce Cleveland, NY (BC)
PUBLISHERS: Orion Editions, NY (OE)
GALLERIES: Orion Editions, New York, NY; Sound Shore Gallery, Stamford, CT; Windmueller Fine Arts, Scarsdale, NY

TITLE	PUBLISHER	PRINTER	DATE	MEDIUM	DIMENSION (PAPER SIZE) IN INCHES	TYPE OF PAPER	EDITION NUMBER	NO. OF COLORS	ORIGINAL OPENING PRICE	CURRENT RETAIL PRICE
CURRENT EDITIONS:										
Series of Nine Etchings:										
Green Field Landing	OE	BC	1984	EC	32 X 45	AP	30	4–8	500	650
Gold Field Landing	OE	BC	1984	EC	32 X 45	AP	10	4–8	500	650
Dawn Gold Field Landing	OE	BC	1984	EC	32 X 45	AP	15	4–8	500	650
Noon Green Field Landing	OE	BC	1984	EC	32 X 45	AP	15	4–8	500	650
Dusk Green Field Landing	OE	BC	1984	EC	32 X 45	AP	15	4–8	500	650
Night Blue Field Landing	OE	BC	1984	EC	32 X 45	AP	15	4–8	500	650
Night Green Field Landing	OE	BC	1984	EC	32 X 45	AP	15	4–8	500	650
Dawn Green Field Landing I, II	OE	BC	1984	EC	32 X 45 EA	AP	15 EA	4–8 EA	500 EA	650 EA

CHARLES GARABEDIAN

BORN: Detroit, MI; 1923
EDUCATION: Univ of California, Los Angeles, CA, MFA, 1961
TEACHING: Univ of California, Los Angeles, CA, Santa Barbara, CA
AWARDS: Nordjyllands Kunstmuseum, Aalborg, Denmark, 1980, L A Louver Gallery, Venice, CA, 1980; La Jolla Mus of Contemp Art, 1981; Holly Solomon, NY, 1982
RECENT EXHIB: Hirschl & Adler Modern, NY, 1987; L A Louver Gallery, Venice, CA, 1989; Muhlenberg Col, Frank Martin Art Gallery, Allentown, PA, 1989
PRINTERS: Leslie Sutcliff, Los Angeles, CA (LS); Robert Aull, Los Angeles, CA (RA); Helen Abe Ichien, Los Angeles, CA (HI); Bud Shark, Boulder, CO (BS); Matthew Christie, Los Angeles, CA (MC); Ron Trujillo, Los Angeles, CA (RT); Cirrus Editions Workshop, Los Angeles, CA (CEW); Francesco Siqueiros, Los Angeles, CA (FS); Robert Dansby, Los Angeles, CA (RD); Bud Shark, Boulder, CO (BS); Matthew Christie, Boulder, CO (MC); Shark's, Inc, Boulder, CO (SI)
PUBLISHERS: L A Louver Publications, Venice, CA (LAL); Cirrus Editions Ltd, Los Angeles, CA (CEL); Shark's, Inc, Boulder, Inc (SI)
GALLERIES: Holly Solomon Editions, New York, NY; Cirrus Editions, Los Angeles, CA; Hirschl & Adler Modern, New York, NY; Gallery Paule Anglim, San Francisco, CA; Louver Galleries, Venice, CA & New York, NY; Betsy Senior Contemporary Prints, New York, NY; Hope Weiss Fine Art, Los Angeles, CA

TITLE	PUBLISHER	PRINTER	DATE	MEDIUM	DIMENSION (PAPER SIZE) IN INCHES	TYPE OF PAPER	EDITION NUMBER	NO. OF COLORS	ORIGINAL OPENING PRICE	CURRENT RETAIL PRICE
SOLD OUT EDITIONS (RARE):										
You Are Going on a Trip (9 Etchings and 2 Lithographs) (Set of 11):									4500 SET	7500 SET
China, Korea, Cambodia	LAL	HI/LS/RA	1974	EB	30 X 21	AC/W	50	1	400	750
The Vampire	LAL	HI/LS/RA	1975	LB	23 X 30	AC/W	37	1	350	750
Culver City Flood	LAL	BS/RT	1979	LC	20 X 22	AC/W	50	7	450	900
Graveyard	LAL	BS/MC	1979	LB	30 X 22	AC/W	50	1	400	750
Henry Inn #7	LAL	HI/LS/RA	1979	EB/A	21 X 30	R/BFK/W	50	1	400	750
You are Going on a Trip	LAL	HI/LS/RA	1961-80	EB	21 X 28	R/BFK/W	50	1	300	600
Crucifixion	LAL	HI/LS/RA	1961-80	EB/DPT	22 X 30	R/BFK/W	50	1	350	750
Artist and Model	LAL	HI/LS/RA	1980	EB/A	22 X 30	AC/W	50	1	450	750
Prehistoric Figures	LAL	HI/LS/RA	1980	EB/A	22 X 30	AC/W	50	3	650	1250
Night Parthenon	LAL	HI/LS/RA	1980	EB	16 X 20	AC/W	50	1	600	1250
Brick through the Window	LAl	HI/LS/RA	1980	EB/A	22 X 30	AC/W	50	1	450	750
Man Tearing His Heart Out	LAL	HI/LS/RA	1980	EC	22 X 30	R/BFK	50	4	650	1000
CURRENT EDITIONS:										
Untitled (188c)	CE	CEW	1975	LB	30 X 22	AC/W	37	1	350	1500
RIV (with Brian Murphy) (497c)	CE	FS/RD/CEW	1992	LB	12 X 42	R/BFK	40	1	850	850
RIV (with Brian Murphy) (498c)	CE	FS/RD/CEW	1992	LB	17 X 60	R/BFK	40	1	1200	1200
RIV (with Brian Murphy) (499c)	CE	FS/RD/CEW	1992	LB	18 X 53	R/BFK	40	1	1000	1000
Series of Monotypes	SI	BS/MC/SI	1992	MON	30 X 42 EA	SUZ	1 EA	Varies	2500 EA	2500 EA

CLAUDE GARACHE

BORN: Paris, France; 1930
PRINTERS: Maeght Editions, Paris, France (ME); Galerie Maeght Lelong, Paris, France (ML)
PUBLISHERS: Maeght Editions, Paris, France (ME); Galerie Maeght Lelong, Paris, France (ML)
GALLERIES: Galerie Lelong, New York, NY & Paris, France & Zürich, Switzerland; Spaightwood Galleries, Madison, WI

TITLE	PUBLISHER	PRINTER	DATE	MEDIUM	DIMENSION (PAPER SIZE) IN INCHES	TYPE OF PAPER	EDITION NUMBER	NO. OF COLORS	ORIGINAL OPENING PRICE	CURRENT RETAIL PRICE
SOLD OUT EDITIONS (RARE):										
Bresque Rogue	ME	ME	1978	EC	25 X 31	AP	50		500 FF	1200 FF
Sandre	ME	ME	1978	EC	25 X 30	AP	50		500 FF	1200 FF
Breville	ME	ME	1978	EC	25 X 30	AP	50		500 FF	1200 FF
Couzane	ME	ME	1978	EC	26 X 20	AP	50		500 FF	1200 FF
Dode I, II	ME	ME	1978	EC	29 X 23 EA	AP	50 EA		500 FF EA	1200 FF EA
Yvie	ME	ME	1979	EC	29 X 23	AP	50		500 FF	1200 FF
Meouge	ME	ME	1979	EC	25 X 20	AP	50		500 FF	1200 FF
Naisse	ME	ME	1979	EC	66 X 51 cm	AP	50		600 FF	1500 FF
Sauvechanne	ME	ME	1979	EC	51 X 67 cm	AP	50		600 FF	1500 FF
Auche II	ME	ME	1979	EC	51 X 67 cm	AP	50		600 FF	1500 FF
Tourette	ME	ME	1980	EC	65 X 51 cm	AP	50		700 FF	1500 FF
Stanton	ME	ME	1980	EC	67 X 52 cm	LAR	50		800 FF	1500 FF
Bloise	ME	ME	1980	EC	50 X 66 cm	INGRES	50		800 FF	1500 FF
Bleve	ME	ME	1980	EC	65 X 51 cm	INGRES	50		800 FF	1500 FF
Tourasse	ME	ME	1980	EC	66 X 50 cm	INGRES	50		800 FF	1500 FF
Suite Rouge sur Ingres Rose Fonce (Set of 7)	ME	ME	1980	LC	20 X 13	AP	50		3000 FF SET	10000 FF SET
Suite Vermillon sur Ingres Gris (Set of 8)	ME	ME	1980	LC	50 X 33 cm	AP	50		3000 FF SET	10000 FF SET
Derriere le Miroir I	ME	ME	1981	LC	48 X 65 cm	AP	80	2		2500 FF
Stanton II	ML	ML	1982	EC	65 X 50 cm	CAN	50	2		2500 FF
Dos de Méouge	ML	ML	1982	EC	65 X 50 cm	ING/C	50	2		2500 FF
Aouchet	ML	ML	1982	EC	65 X 50 cm	CAN	50	2		2500 FF
Stanton III	ML	ML	1982	EC	65 X 50 cm	VGZ	50	2		2500 FF
Matte	ML	ML	1982	EC	65 X 50 cm	MDL	50	1		2500 FF
Bleve II	ML	ML	1982	EC	45 X 54 cm	CB	50	2		2500 FF
Stanton IV	ML	ML	1982	EC	65 X 51 cm	CAN	50	1		2500 FF
Auche I	ML	ML	1982	EC	65 X 51 cm	CAN	50	2		2500 FF
2 Personnes I	ML	ML	1983	EC	50 X 67 cm	AP	50	2		2500 FF

CARME GARCES

BORN: Barcelona, Spain; 1928
EDUCATION: Ramon Togent Sch, Barcelona, Spain; Fine Art Conservatory of the Book, Barcelona, Spain
AWARDS: Scholarship, French Inst. Paris, France, 1956
PRINTERS: La Poligrafa, SA, Barcelona, Spain (LP)
PUBLISHERS: Ediciones Poligrafa, SA, Barcelona, Spain (EdP)
GALLERIES: Galeria Joan Prats, New York, NY & Barcelona, Spain

TITLE	PUBLISHER	PRINTER	DATE	MEDIUM	DIMENSION (PAPER SIZE) IN INCHES	TYPE OF PAPER	EDITION NUMBER	NO. OF COLORS	ORIGINAL OPENING PRICE	CURRENT RETAIL PRICE
CURRENT EDITIONS:										
Series of 5 Lithographs (Set of 5)	EdP	LP	1980	LC	22 X 30 EA	GP	99 EA	3 EA	500 SET	1000 SET
									180 EA	280 EA

JOAN A GARDNER

BORN: Joliet, IL; May 3, 1933
EDUCATION: Univ of Illinois, Champaign, IL, BFA, 1955; MFA, 1957
TEACHING: Instr of Art, Southern Connecticut State Col, 1965–78; Assoc Prof, Univ of New Haven, 1971–1982; Kent State Univ, Kent, OH 1982 to present
AWARDS: Kate Neal Kinley Mem Fellowship, 1955; Yale Univ Fellowship, 1956 with Rico Lebrun; Connecticut Acad of Fine Arts Award, New Britain Mus, 1969; Fulbright-Hays Award, 1974–75; Connecticut Comm on the Arts Grant, 1979–80
RECENT EXHIB: Univ of Akron, Emily H Davis Gallery, OH, 1992; 55 Mercer Street Gallery, NY, 1992
COLLECTIONS: Mus of Mod Art, NY; Univ of Illinois, Champaign-Urbana, IL; Chicago Art Inst, IL; Lyman Allyn Mus, New London, CT; Yale Univ, New Haven, CT; Illinois State Univ, Normal, IL; Tweed Mus, Duluth, MN; Southern Connecticut State Col, New Haven, CT; Univ of New Haven, West Haven, CT
PRINTERS: Artist (ART)
PUBLISHERS: White Elephant Press, East Haven, CT (WEP); CCM (CCM) Normal State Editions, Illinois State Teachers, Col, Normal, IL (NSE)
GALLERIES: 55 Mercer Street Gallery, New York, NY; John Davis Gallery, Akron, OH; Munson Galleries, New Haven, CT & Chatham, MA & Santa Fe, NM
MAILING ADDRESS: 547 S Lincoln, Kent, OH 44240

Joan A Gardner
Four O'Clock
Courtesy the Artist

TITLE	PUBLISHER	PRINTER	DATE	MEDIUM	DIMENSION (PAPER SIZE) IN INCHES	TYPE OF PAPER	EDITION NUMBER	NO. OF COLORS	ORIGINAL OPENING PRICE	CURRENT RETAIL PRICE
CURRENT EDITIONS:										
House Afire	WEP	ART	1980	I	24 X 33	AP	30	1	250	350
Escape Artists	WEP	ART	1980	I	24 X 33	RP	30	1	250	350
Listening In	WEP	ART	1980	I	24 X 32	RP	30	1	250	300
When all of a Sudden	WEP	ART	1981	I	24 X 32	RP	30	1	250	300
Battle of the Paintings	WEP	ART	1981	LB	22 X 17	RP	30	1	150	200
Masked Elephant	WEP	ART	1981	I	24 X 33	RP	30	1	250	300
Four O'Clock	NSE	ART	1981	LB	22 X 30	AP	30	1	250	300
Sunday 2 PM	NSE	ART	1981	LB	22 X 30	AP	30	1	250	300
Next Attraction	NSE	ART	1981	LB	22 X 30	AP	30	1	250	300
Late for Dinner	NSE	ART	1981	LB	22 X 30	AP	30	1	250	300
The Queen at Home	WEP	ART	1982	LB	17 X 22	AP	30	1	150	250
Midnight Carousel	WEP	ART	1982	LB	17 X 22	AP	30	1	150	250
Doll-House	WEP	ART	1982	LB	22 X 17	AP	30	1	150	250
Shopping	WEP	ART	1982	LB	17 X 22	AP	30	1	150	250
Next Attraction	NSE	NSE	1982	LB	22 X 30	AP	30	1	250	350
Late for Dinner	NSE	NSE	1982	LB	30 X 22	AP	30	1	250	350
Four O'Clock	NSE	NSE	1982	LB	22 X 30	AP	30	1	250	350
Sunday 2 PM	NSE	NSE	1982	LB	30 X 22	AP	30	1	250	350
Masked Elephant	WEP	ART	1982	I	24 X 33	AP	30	1	250	350
Battle of the Paintings	WEP	ART	1982	LB	17 X 22	AP	30	1	150	250
When all of a Sudden	WEP	ART	1982	I	24 X 32	AP	30	1	250	350
Listening In	WEP	ART	1982	I	24 X 32	AP	30	1	250	350

JEDD GARET

BORN: Los Angeles, CA; 1955
EDUCATION: Rhode Island Sch of Design, Providence, RI, 1973; Sch of Visual Arts, NY, 1975
RECENT EXHIB: Yares Gallery, Scottsdale, AZ, 1987; Gallery Lelong, NY, 1987; The Contemporary Mus, Honolulu, HI, 1989; Robert Miller Gallery, NY, 1989,91
PRINTERS: Cirrus Editions Workshop, Los Angeles, CA (CEW); Maurice Sanchez, NY (MS); Derrier L'Etoile Studios, NY (DES); Richard Hammond, Los Angeles, CA (RH); Francesco Siqueiros, Los Angeles, CA (FS); Robert Gingras, Los Angeles, CA (RG)
PUBLISHERS: Barbara Gladstone Editions, NY (BGE); Cirrus Editions, Los Angeles, CA (CE); Derrier L'Etoile Studios, NY (DES)

JEDD GARET CONTINUED

GALLERIES: Robert Miller Gallery, New York, NY; Texas Gallery, Houston, TX; Cirrus Editions, Ltd, Los Angeles, CA; Michael H Lord Gallery, Milwaukee, WI; Wirtz Gallery, San Francisco, CA; Betsy Rosenfield Gallery, Chicago, IL; Wolff Gallery, New York, NY; Riva Yares Gallery, Scottsdale, AZ; Galerie Lelong, New York, NY & Paris, France & Zurich, Switzerland; Reece Galleries, New York, NY; Schweitzer Gallery, New York, NY
MAILING ADDRESS: c/o Robert Miller Gallery, 41 E 57th St, New York, NY 10022

TITLE	PUBLISHER	PRINTER	DATE	MEDIUM	DIMENSION (PAPER SIZE) IN INCHES	TYPE OF PAPER	EDITION NUMBER	NO. OF COLORS	ORIGINAL OPENING PRICE	CURRENT RETAIL PRICE
CURRENT EDITIONS:										
Spheres	BGE	MS/DLE	1982	LC	58 X 36	AP	40		1200	2500
Column	BGE	MS/DLE	1982	LC	58 X 36	AP	40		1200	2500
Marble	BGE	MS/DLE	1982	LC	58 X 36	AP	40		1200	2500
Blood	CE	CEW	1982	LC	22 X 40	AC	45		650	950
Nice Sky	CE	CEW	1982	LC	22 X 40	AC	45		650	2500
Behind Your Back	CE	RG/CEW	1983	LC	40 X 30	AC	50	6	950	1000
Orange Rocks	CE	RG/CEW	1983	LC	40 X 30	AC	50	11	950	1000
Night Boy	CE	RG/CEW	1983	LC	40 X 30	AC	50	7	950	2000
Lush Life	CE	RG/CEW	1983	LB	40 X 30	AC/W	50	1	450	850
Center Structure	CE	RG/CEW	1983	LB	40 X 30	AC/W	50	1	450	850
Stump	CE	RG/CEW	1983	LB	40 X 30	AC/W	50	1	450	850
Spheres, Column, Marble, State II Gold (Set of 3):	DES	MS/DES	1984	LB/GP	59 X 38	CAN		1	3000 SET 1000 EA	3500 SET 1200 EA
Wonderous Orbs of Life (Dipt)	CE	RH/FS/CEW	1985	LC	36 X 90	AP88	50	12	2500	3800
Slide (Dipt)	CE	RH/FS/CEW	1986	LC	36 X 96	AP88	35	2	2800	3800

MARCO GASTINI

RECENT EXHIB: John Weber Gallery, NY, 1990
PRINTERS: Cirrus Editions Workshop, Los Angeles, CA (CEW); Parasol Press, NY (PaP)
PUBLISHERS: Cirrus Editions Ltd, Los Angeles, CA (CE)
GALLERIES: Cirrus Editions Ltd, Los Angeles, CA; Felicity Samuels, London, England; John Weber Gallery, New York, NY

TITLE	PUBLISHER	PRINTER	DATE	MEDIUM	DIMENSION (PAPER SIZE) IN INCHES	TYPE OF PAPER	EDITION NUMBER	NO. OF COLORS	ORIGINAL OPENING PRICE	CURRENT RETAIL PRICE
CURRENT EDITIONS:										
M/ABC/A, M/ABC/B, M/ABC/C (Triptych)	CE	CEW	1975	LC/SP	15 X 19	AP	25		375	1200

SONIA GECHTOFF

BORN: Philadelphia, PA; September 25, 1926
EDUCATION: Philadelphia Mus Sch of Art, PA, BFA, 1950
TEACHING: California Sch of Fine Art, 1956–57; New York Univ, NY, 1960–70; Queens Col, NY, 1970–74; Assoc Prof, Art, Univ of New Mexico, Albuquerque, NM, 1974–75; Art in Res, Skidmore Col, NY, 1988,89,90; Vis Artist, Chicago Art Inst, IL, 1989
AWARDS: Purchase Award, San Francisco Mus of Mod Art, CA, 1957; Ford Found Fel, Tamarind Lithography Inst, Los Angeles, CA, 1963; Drawing Prize, Four Corners States Bienale, Phoenix Art Mus, AR, 1975; First Prize, Painting, Santa Barbara Mus, CA, 1975; Gottlieb Found Grant, 1987; Mid-Atlantic Nat Endowment for the Arts Grant, 1988
RECENT EXHIB: Gruenebaum Gallery, NY, 1987; Kraushaar Galleries, NY, 1990,92
COLLECTIONS: Mus of Mod Art, NY; Baltimore Mus of Art, MD; San Francisco Mus of Art, CA; Oakland Mus of Art, CA; Metropolitan Mus, NY; Solomon R Guggenheim Mus, NY; Achenbach Found, California Palace of Legion of Honor, San Francisco, CA; Univ of Massachusetts, Amherst, MA; Arkansas Arts Center, Little Rock, AR
PRINTERS: Hudson River Editions, Garnerville, NY (HRE)
PUBLISHERS: Gruenebaum Graphics, Ltd, NY (GG)
GALLERIES: Kraushaar Galleries, New York, NY; Witkin Galleries, New York, NY
MAILING ADDRESS: 463 West St, #936, New York, NY 10014

TITLE	PUBLISHER	PRINTER	DATE	MEDIUM	DIMENSION (PAPER SIZE) IN INCHES	TYPE OF PAPER	EDITION NUMBER	NO. OF COLORS	ORIGINAL OPENING PRICE	CURRENT RETAIL PRICE
CURRENT EDITIONS:										
Brooklyn Bridge	GG	HRE	1984	EC	40 X 30	GE	50	4	650	2000
Tropics	GG	HRE	1984	EC	40 X 30	GE	50	4	650	2000

ARTHUR FREDERICK GEISERT

BORN: Dallas, TX; September 20, 1941
EDUCATION: Concordia Col, Seward, NE, BS, 1963; Univ of California, Davis, CA, MA, 1965; Chouinard Art Inst, Los Angeles, CA; Otis Art Inst, Los Angeles, CA; Art Inst of Chicago, IL
TEACHING: Concordia Col, River Forest, IL 1965–70; Concordia Col, Seward, NE, 1970–71; Clark Col, Dubuque, IA, 1973 to present
AWARDS: Purchase Award, Owensboro Mus of Fine Art, KY, 1980; Purchase Award, Univ of Wisconsin, Platteville, WI, 1980
COLLECTIONS: Clarke Col, Dubuque, IA; Valparasio Univ, IN; Univ of Illinois, Champaign-Urbana, IL; Western Illinois Univ, Macomb, IL; Eastern Illinois Univ, Charleston, IL; Univ of Wisconsin, Platteville, WI; Univ of Dallas, TX; Dulin Gallery of Art, Knoxville, TN; Owensboro Mus, KY; Freeport Art Mus, IL; Mus of Art, Lodz, Poland
PRINTERS: Artist (ART)
PUBLISHERS: Artist (ART)
GALLERIES: Associated American Artists, New York, NY; Wenniger Graphics, Boston, MA; Chicago Center for the Print, Chicago, IL
MAILING ADDRESS: P O Box 3, Galena, IL 61036

ARTHUR FREDERICK GEISERT CONTINUED

TITLE	PUBLISHER	PRINTER	DATE	MEDIUM	DIMENSION (PAPER SIZE) IN INCHES	TYPE OF PAPER	EDITION NUMBER	NO. OF COLORS	ORIGINAL OPENING PRICE	CURRENT RETAIL PRICE
CURRENT EDITIONS:										
Oink	ART	ART	1978	EB/HC	20 X 28	R/BFK	150	1	60	150
Pig ABC	ART	ART	1978	EB	24 X 36	R/BFK	150	1	100	150
Adam and Eve Naming the Animals	ART	ART	1978	EB	24 X 36	R/BFK	150	1	100	150
Ark V (4 panels)	ART	ART	1980	EB/HC	48 X 72	R/BFK	150	20	1000	1200
Over the North Pole	ART	ART	1981	EB/HC	24 X 36	R/BFK	150	15	150	200
Picnic	ART	ART	1981	EB/HC	24 X 36	R/BFK	150	15	150	200
Balloon Race	ART	ART	1981	EB/HC	24 X 36	R/BFK	150	15	150	200
Noah's Ark	ART	ART	1984	EB	24 X 36	R/BFK	150	15	150	200

SANDY GELLIS

BORN: New York, NY
EDUCATION: Sch of Visual Arts, NY; City Col of New York; New Sch for Social Research, NY
TEACHING: Instr, Fashion Inst of Tech, NY, 1980–83; Instr, Sch of Visual Arts, NY, 1979–89
AWARDS: MacDowell Colony Fel, 1979; New York Experimental Glass Workshop Grant, NY, 1984; Nat Endowment for the Arts Fel, 1979–82, 1987–88
RECENT EXHIB: Islip Art Mus, Long Island, NY, 1987; Mary Delahoyd Gallery, NY, 1988; Luise Ross Gallery, NY, 1989; Clocktown Gallery, NY, 1989; Storefront for Art & Arch, NY, 1989; Soc Art Crafts, Pittsburgh, PA, 1989; Sundered Ground, NY, 1989; Nat Print Biennial, Brooklyn, NY, 1989; Hillwood Art Mus, C W Post Univ, Greenvale, NY, 1990; Municipal Art Soc, NY, 1990
PRINTERS: Julie D'Amario, NY (JDA); Printmaking Workshop, NY (PW)
PUBLISHERS: Artist (ART)
GALLERIES: Luise Ross Gallery, New York, NY; Fulcrum Gallery, New York, NY; Mary Delahoyd Gallery, New York, NY; Actual Art Foundation, New York, NY; Gallery Three Zero, New York, NY
MAILING ADDRESS: 39 Bond St, New York, NY 10012

TITLE	PUBLISHER	PRINTER	DATE	MEDIUM	DIMENSION (PAPER SIZE) IN INCHES	TYPE OF PAPER	EDITION NUMBER	NO. OF COLORS	ORIGINAL OPENING PRICE	CURRENT RETAIL PRICE
CURRENT EDITIONS:										
Spring in the Northern Hemisphere (Set of 12)	ART	JDA/PW	1987	EC	12 X 12 EA	FAB	12 EA		1400 SET	1800 SET

GENERAL IDEA

Conceptual Group of Three Artists which was Formed in 1968:
A A BRONSON (ALIEAS MICHAEL TIMS)
BORN: Vancouver, BC, Canada; 1946
FELIX PARTZ (ALIAS RON GABE)
BORN: Winnipeg, Manitoba, Canada; 1945
JORGE ZONTAL (ALIAS JORGE SAIA)
BORN: Parma, Italy; 1944
RECENT EXHIB: New Mus of Contemp Art, NY, 1989; Koury Wingate Gallery, NY, 1990; Württembergischer Kunstverein, Stuttgart, Germany, 1993; Power Plant, Toronto, Canada, 1993; Wexner Center for the Arts, Ohio State Univ, Columbus, OH, 1993; Mus of Mod Art, San Francisco, CA, 1993
PRINTERS: Sheila Marbain, NY (SM); Maurel Studios, NY (MS)
PUBLISHERS: Peter Blum Edition, NY (PBE)
GALLERIES: Peter Blum Edition, New York, NY; Hillman Holland Gallery, Atlanta, GA

General Idea
The Honeymoon is Over
(From Fear Management Suite)
Courtesy Peter Blum Edition

TITLE	PUBLISHER	PRINTER	DATE	MEDIUM	DIMENSION (PAPER SIZE) IN INCHES	TYPE OF PAPER	EDITION NUMBER	NO. OF COLORS	ORIGINAL OPENING PRICE	CURRENT RETAIL PRICE
CURRENT EDITIONS:										
Fear Management (Set of 8)	PBE	SM/MS	1987	SP	33 X 22 EA	R/BFK	50 EA		3800 SET	5500 SET

JUAN GENOVES

BORN: Valencia, Spain; 1930
EDUCATION: Escuela Superior de Bellas Artes, Valencia, Spain
AWARDS: Gold Medal, Biennale d'Arte, Republica de San Marino, 1967; Marzotto Prize 1968
COLLECTIONS: Mus of Mod Art, NY; Guggenheim Mus, NY; Mus of Mod Art, Rio de Janeiro, Brazil; Worcester Art Mus, MA; Mus of Abstract Art, Cuenca, Spain; Mus of Contemp Art, Barcelon, Spain; Nat Gallery, Rome, Italy; Nat Gallery of South Africa, Cape Town, SA; Mus Boymans-van-Beuningen, Rotterdam, Holland; Chicago Inst of Art, IL; Nat Center of Contemp Art, Paris, France; Mus Royaux des Beaux Arts, Brussels, Belgium
PUBLISHERS: Marlborough Graphics, NY (MG)
GALLERIES: Marlborough Graphics, New York, NY

JUAN GENOVES CONTINUED

TITLE	PUBLISHER	PRINTER	DATE	MEDIUM	DIMENSION (PAPER SIZE) IN INCHES	TYPE OF PAPER	EDITION NUMBER	NO. OF COLORS	ORIGINAL OPENING PRICE	CURRENT RETAIL PRICE
SOLD OUT EDITIONS (RARE):										
Silencio, Silencio (Set of 10)	MG		1970	EC	20 X 26	AP	92			45000 SET 1000 EA
Untitled	MG		1971	SP	26 X 36	AP	170			1000
El Lugar y el Tiempo (Set of 10)	MG		1973	EC	20 X 26	AP	92			10000 SET 1000 EA

JEREMY GENTILLI

BORN: London, England, 1926
EDUCATION: Studied with Fernand Leger in Paris, France, 1951; Studied with Stanley W Hayter, Atelier 17, NY
COLLECTIONS: Arts Council of London, England; Victoria & Albert Mus, London, England; Stedelijk Mus, Amsterdam, The Netherlands; Bibliotheque Royale, Brussels, Belgium; Coll de la Ville de Paris, France

PRINTERS: Circle Fine Art, Chicago, IL (CFA)
PUBLISHERS: Circle Fine Art, Chicago, IL (CFA)
GALLERIES: Circle Galleries, San Diego, CA & San Francisco, CA & Northbrook, IL & Pittsburgh, PA & Houston, TX & Soho, NY & Chicago, IL & Scottsdale, AZ & Beverly Hills, CA & Costa Mesa, CA & Sherman Oaks, CA & Palm Beach, FL & Honolulu, HI & New Orleans, LA & Las Vegas, NV & Seattle, WA

TITLE	PUBLISHER	PRINTER	DATE	MEDIUM	DIMENSION (PAPER SIZE) IN INCHES	TYPE OF PAPER	EDITION NUMBER	NO. OF COLORS	ORIGINAL OPENING PRICE	CURRENT RETAIL PRICE
SOLD OUT EDITIONS (RARE):										
Red Nude	CFA	AA	1980	LC	16 X 20	AP	200		35	175
Visage	CFA	AA	1980	LC	13 X 14	AP	200		35	175
Clown	CFA	AA	1980	LC	12 X 13	AP	200		35	175

DARCY GERBARG

BORN: May 20, 1949
EDUCATION: Univ of Pennsylvania, Phila, PA, BA,1966–76; Univ of San Diego, CA, Design, 1971; Univ of California, San Diego, CA, Math, 1972; New York, Studio Sch of Drawing, Painting & Sculpture, NY, 1973–74; Bennington Col, VT, Papermaking, 1977
TEACHING: New York Univ, NY, Tisch Sch of the Arts, Interactive Telecommunications Prog & Inst of Film & TV, 1981–83; Lect, Tratt Inst, Computer Graphics Center, NY, 1984; Sch of Visual Arts, NY, 1984; Dir, MFA Prog, Computer Art, Sch of Visual Arts, NY, 1987–88; Art in Res, New York Univ, Courant Inst of Mathematical Sciences, Robotics & Manufacturing Laboratory, 1988 to present

RECENT EXHIB: Massachusetts Inst of Tech, Cambridge, MA, 1987; Everson Mus, Syracuse, NY, 1987; IBM Gallery of Science & Art, 1988; Fine Arts Mus of Long Island, NY, 1988; Wenniger Graphics, Boston, MA & Provincetown, MA, 1989; Arnolfini Gallery, Bristol, England, 1989; Smithsonian Inst, Wash, DC, 1990
PUBLISHERS: Digital Visuals, Inc, NY (DVI)
PRINTERS: Roni Henning, NY (RH); Henning Screen Print Workshop, NY (HSPW)
GALLERIES: Wenniger Graphics, Boston, MA; Joy Moos Gallery, Miami,FL
MAILING ADDRESS: P O Box 413, Old Chelsea Station, New York, NY, 10113

TITLE	PUBLISHER	PRINTER	DATE	MEDIUM	DIMENSION (PAPER SIZE) IN INCHES	TYPE OF PAPER	EDITION NUMBER	NO. OF COLORS	ORIGINAL OPENING PRICE	CURRENT RETAIL PRICE
CURRENT EDITIONS:										
May 1	DVI	RH/HCPW	1982	SP		R/BFK	90		400	500
Qspace	DVI	RH/HCPW	1983	SP		R/BFK	100		400	500
Veld 1	DVI	RH/HCPW	1988	SP		R/BFK	30		800	800
Veld 2	DVI	RH/HCPW	1988	SP		R/BFK	30		800	800
Garden	DVI	RH/HCPW	1988	SP	26 X 57	R/BFK	30	1	800	800

SARAH VALERIE GERSOVITZ, RCA

BORN: Montreal, Canada
EDUCATION: Concordia Univ, Canada, MA; Montreal Mus of Fine Arts, Canada
TEACHING: Bronfman Ctr, Montreal, Canada, 1972 to present
AWARDS: Anaconda Award, Canada Soc of Painters, Etchers, & Engravers, 1963, 67; Purchase Prize, Quebec Mus, Canada, 1966; Purchase Prize, Nat Gallery of South Australia, 1967; Purchase Prize, Dawson Col, 1974; First Prize, Univ of Sherbrooke, Canada, 1977; Thomas Moore Purchase Award, 1977; Purchase Prize, Sherbrooke Law Faculty, Canada, 1979; Travel Award, House of Humour & Satire, Gabrovo, Bulgaria, 1985; First Prize, Int Jury, Graphics, Gabrovo, Bulgaria, 1989; Travel Award, House of Humour & Satire, Gabrovo, Bulgaria, 1991
RECENT EXHIB: Bienal de Arte Valparaiso, Chili, 1987,89; Galerie Barbara Silverberg, Montreal, Canada, 1991
COLLECTIONS: Library of Congress, Wash, DC; New York Public Library, NY; Nat Gallery of South Australia; Am Embassy, Ottawa, Canada; Nat Gallery of Canada, Ottawa, Canada; Cultural Inst of Peru, Lima, Peru; McGill Univ, Montreal, Canada; Concordia Univ, Canada; Thomas More Inst, Canada; Israel Mus, Jerusalem, Israel; Mus d'Art Contemp, London, ON, Canada; Univ Kaiserslautern, Germany; Univ of Quebec, Canada; Univ of Sherbrooke, Canada; Mem Univ Art Gallery, St John's, Newfoundland; Univ of Alberta, Edmonton, Canada; Univ of Waterloo, Canada; Trent Univ, Canada; Mount Allison Univ, Canada; Thomas Inst, Canada; Dawson Col, Canada; House of Humour & Satire, Gabrovo, Bulgaria; Montreal Mus of Fine Arts, Canada; Art Gallery of Greater Victoria, Canada; Winnipeg Art Gallery, Canada; Art Gallery of Hamiliton, Canada; Art Gallery of Windsor, Canada; Kitchener-Waterloo Art Gallery, Canada; London Regional Art Gallery, Canada; Owens Art Gallery, Canada; Confederation Art Gallery, Canada; Cornerbrook Art Gallery, Newfoundland, Canada; Stewart Hall Art Gallery, Pointe Claire, Canada
PRINTERS: Artist (ART)
PUBLISHERS: Artist (ART)
GALLERIES: Galerie Lauze, Inc, Montreal, Canada; Fleet Galleries, East Winnipeg, Canada; Dresden Galleries, Halifax, NS, Canada, Le Centre d'Art, Montreal, Canada; West End Gallery, Edmonton, Alta, Canada; Galerie Daniel, Montreal, Canada; Dominion Galleries, Montreal, Canada; Galerie Barbara Silverberg, Montreal, Canada

SARAH VALERIE GERSOVITZ, RCA CONTINUED

TITLE	PUBLISHER	PRINTER	DATE	MEDIUM	DIMENSION (PAPER SIZE) IN INCHES	TYPE OF PAPER	EDITION NUMBER	NO. OF COLORS	ORIGINAL OPENING PRICE	CURRENT RETAIL PRICE
SOLD OUT EDITIONS (RARE):										
Inmate	ART	ART	1966	EC	20 X 15	R/BFK	25	4	60	400
Druid Dawn	ART	ART	1968	EC	15 X 20	R/BFK	20	4	85	400
Introspection	ART	ART	1972	SP	22 X 26	R/BFK	30	3	90	450
Tallit Kattan	ART	ART	1973	SP	30 X 22	AP	12	3	75	400
The Tour	ART	ART	1974	SP	15 X 17	AP	50	7	50	150
Observer Observed	ART	ART	1977	SP	22 X 30	AP	20	5	150	500
CURRENT EDITIONS:										
Chocolate Box for a Cannibal I	ART	ART	1971	SP	22 X 30	AP	35	3	150	500
Chocolate Box for a Cannibal II	ART	ART	1971	SP	22 X 30	AP	35	4	150	500
Pigscape	ART	ART	1972	SP	30 X 22	AP	20	5	150	400
Silk and Wood I	ART	ART	1972	SP	30 X 22	AP	25	4	300	300
Silk and Wood II	ART	ART	1972	SP	30 X 22	AP	30	4	300	350
Secret Windows	ART	ART	1973	AP	30 X 22	AP	20	7	100	350
Reception Committee	ART	ART	1974	SP	30 X 22	AP	10	7	200	400
Lancaster Tattoo	ART	ART	1975	SP	30 X 22	AP	20	6	150	400
Tear Along the Dotted Line	ART	ART	1975	SP	22 X 30	AP	15	6	150	450
Tattooed Sailor	ART	ART	1975	Sp	30 X 22	AP	19	5	150	450
It Won't Fit	ART	ART	1975	SP	22 X 30	AP	19	4	150	350
Tatooed Lady	ART	ART	1976	SP	30 X 22	AP	18	9	200	450
One Left	ART	ART	1977	SP	22 X 30	AP	19	7	250	500
Les Connaisseurs	ART	ART	1977	SP	30 X 22	AP	50	6	150	350
Bouquet	ART	ART	1977	SP	30 X 22	AP	40	5	150	400
Friends-Amis	ART	ART	1980	WC	21 X 29	AP	20	6	250	550
Spectator Sport	ART	ART	1980	WC	21 X 29	AP	20	6	250	550
Deserted House	ART	ART	1981	SP	22 X 30	AP	40	7	250	425
Oeuf-Oeuf	ART	ART	1982	SR	30 X 22	AP	25	4	250	300
More Eggs	ART	ART	1984	SP	22 X 30	AP	30	6	250	300
Self Portrait	ART	ART	1985	SP	22 X 30	AP	12	4	300	425
Distant Relatives	ART	ART	1985	SP	22 X 30	AP	20	5	350	425
Poet Carrying the World's Woes on His Non-Existent Shoulders	ART	ART	1989	WC	7 X 7	Rice	25	1	75	100
Imperious Presence	ART	ART	1989	WC	7 X 7	Rice	25	1	75	100
Pursuit	ART	ART	1990	WC	16 X 24	Rice	20	3	200	200
The Bath Houses of Thomas Mann	ART	ART	1991	WC	18 X 21	Rice	25	5	200	200

ILSE GETZ

BORN: Nurenberg, Germany; October 24, 1933
EDUCATION: Art Students League, NY, with Morris Kantor, George Grosz
TEACHING: Art Inst, Positano, Italy, Summers, 1956, 58
AWARDS: Yaddo Fellowship, 1959
COLLECTIONS: Phoenix Art Mus, AZ; Tel Aviv Mus, Israel; Dartmouth Col, Hanover, NH; Allentown Art Mus, PA; Kunsthalle, Nurenberg, Germany; Carnegie Inst, Pittsburgh, PA; New York Univ, NY; Neuberger Mus, Purchase, NY; Larry Aldrich Mus, Ridgefield, CT; Hirshhorn Mus, Wash, DC; Wadsworth Atheneum, Hartford, CT; Finch Col, NY
PRINTERS: Atelier Ettinger, NY (AE)
PUBLISHERS: Transworld Art, Inc, NY (TAI)
MAILING ADDRESS: 69 Litchfield Ponds, Litchfield, CT 06759

TITLE	PUBLISHER	PRINTER	DATE	MEDIUM	DIMENSION (PAPER SIZE) IN INCHES	TYPE OF PAPER	EDITION NUMBER	NO. OF COLORS	ORIGINAL OPENING PRICE	CURRENT RETAIL PRICE
CURRENT EDITIONS:										
Ninth Avenue Window	TAI	AE	1980	LC	20 X 17	AP	125		250	400
The Blue Door	TAI	AE	1980	LC	23 X 17	AP	125		250	400
Black Bird	TAI	AE	1980	LC	23 X 17	AP	125		250	400
Timeless Game	TAI	AE	1980	LC	23 X 17	AP	175		250	400

RALPH H GIBSON

BORN: January 16, 1939
EDUCATION: San Francisco Art Inst, CA, 1960–61
AWARDS: Creative Artists Public Service Award, 1977; Solomon R Guggenheim Found Fel, Photography, 1985; Nat Endowment for the Arts Grants, 1973,75,86; Officer de L'Ordre de Arts et Letters, France, 1986; Leica Medal of Excellence Award, 1988
RECENT EXHIB: International Center for Photography, NY, 1987; Photographer's Gallery, London, England, 1988; Bibliotheque Nat, Paris, France, 1988; Musee de L'Elysee, Lausaune, France, 1988; Minneapolis Inst of Art, MN, 1988; Phila Inst of Contemp Art, PA, 1988; Ringling Mus of Art, Sarasota, FL, 1988; Bucknell Univ, Lewisburg, PA, 1992
COLLECTIONS: Mus of Mod Art, NY; Metropolitan Mus of Art, NY; International Mus of Photography, George Eastman House, Rochester, NY; Center for Creative Photography, Univ of Arizona, Tucson, AZ; Fogg Art Mus, Cambridge, MA; Nat Gallery of Canada, Ottawa, Canada; Corcoran Gallery of Art, Wash, DC; Bibliotheque Nat, Paris, France
PRINTERS: John Nichols, NY (JN); Artist (ART)
PUBLISHERS: Hyperion Press, San Francisco, CA (HP); John Nichols, NY (JN)
GALLERIES: Light Impressions/Spectrum Gallery, Rochester, NY; G Ray Hawkins Gallery, Los Angeles, CA; Thomas V Meyer Fine Art, San Francisco, CA; Leo Castelli Gallery, New York, NY
MAILING ADDRESS: 331 W Broadway, New York, NY 10013

TITLE	PUBLISHER	PRINTER	DATE	MEDIUM	DIMENSION (PAPER SIZE) IN INCHES	TYPE OF PAPER	EDITION NUMBER	NO. OF COLORS	ORIGINAL OPENING PRICE	CURRENT RETAIL PRICE
CURRENT EDITIONS:										
Chiaroscuro (Set of 15)	HP	ART	1982	PH	11 X 14 EA		100 EA		9750 SET	15000 SET

FRANZ GERTSCH

BORN: Morigen, Switzerland; 1930
RECENT EXHIB: Turske & Turske Gallery, Zürich, Switzerland, 1987; Galerie Michael Haas, Berlin, Germany, 1988–89; Musee Rath, Geneva, Switzerland, 1989; Perimeter Gallery, Chicago, IL, 1989; San Jose Mus of Art, CA, 1992; Turske Hue-Williams Gallery, London, England, 1992; Twining Gallery, NY, 1992
COLLECTIONS: Kunstmuseum, Bern, Switzerland; Staatsgallerie, Stuttgart, Germany; Bayerische Staatsgemaldessammlung, Munich, Germany; Sprengel Mus, Hannover, Germany; Nat Gallerie, Berlin, Germany; Künsthaus, Zürich, Switzerland
PRINTERS: Nik Hausmann, Zürich, Switzerland (NH); Artist (ART)
PUBLISHERS: Turske & Turske, Zurich, Switzerland (TT); Artist (ART); Shorewood Atelier, NY (ShAt); Veith Turske, Zürich, Switzerland (VT)
GALLERIES: Perimeter Gallery, Chicago, IL; Turske & Turske Gallery, Zürich, Switzerland; Turske Hue-Williams Gallery, London, England; Twining Gallery, New York, NY; Perimeter Gallery, Chicago, IL; Louis K Meisel Gallery, New York, NY

Franz Gertsch
Schwarzwasser
Courtesy Turske & Turske

Franz Gertsch
Rueschegg
Courtesy Terske & Terske

TITLE	PUBLISHER	PRINTER	DATE	MEDIUM	DIMENSION (PAPER SIZE) IN INCHES	TYPE OF PAPER	EDITION NUMBER	NO. OF COLORS	ORIGINAL OPENING PRICE	CURRENT RETAIL PRICE
SOLD OUT EDITIONS (RARE):										
Jean-Frederic Schnyder (from Documenta: The Super Realists, NY)	ShAt	ShAt	1972	LC	63 X 90 cm	AP	300	2	500	8000
Tabea	VT/ART	NH	1981	LC	64 X 92 cm	AP	18	3	3000	16000
Christina	VT/ART	NH	1983	LC	64 X 91 cm	AP	12	6	4000	16000
Natascha I, II, III (Small)	ART/TT	NH/ART	1986	WC/ENG	114 X 94 cm EA	SHOIS/HANGA	33 EA	Varies	17000 EA	40000 EA
Natascha IV (Large)	ART/TT	NH/ART	1987-88	WC/ENG	276 X 217 cm	HEIZO	18	Varies	80000	160000
Dominique	FG/TT	NH/ART	1988	WC/ENG	276 X 217 cm	HEIZO	18	Varies	80000	160000
Rueschegg	FG/TT	NH/ART	1988-89	WC/ENG	276 X 217 cm	HEIZO	18	Varies	80000	160000
Doris	FG/TT	NH/ART	1989-90	WC/ENG	244 X 184 cm	HEIZO	18	Varies	80000	160000
CURRENT EDITIONS:										
Cima del Mar	FG/TT	NH/ART	1990-91	WC/ENG	71 X 64	HEIZO	30	Varies	55000	55000
Schwarzwasser	FG/TT	NH/ART	1990-91	WC	107 X 83	HEIZO	20	Varies	60000	60000

CRISTOS GIANAKOS

BORN: New York, NY; January 4, 1934
EDUCATION: Sch of Visual Arts, NY, 1952–56
TEACHING: Instr, Sch of Visual Arts, NY, 1965 to present
AWARDS: Creative Artists Public Service Grants, NY, Sculpture, 1976–77, 1979–80; Nat Endowment for the Arts Award, NY, Sculpture, 1980; Adolph & Esther Gottlieb Found, Ind Grant, 1989; Pollock-Krasner Found Grant, 1990
RECENT EXHIB: Siegeltuch Gallery, NY, 1988; Univ of Massachusetts, Amherst, MA, 1989; Brooklyn Mus, NY, 1989; Alpha Delta Gallery, Athens, Greece, 1992; Stark Gallery, NY, 1990, 92
COLLECTIONS: Mus of Mod Art, NY; Moderna Museet, Stockholm, Sweden; Nassau County Mus, Roslyn, NY; Malmo Mus, Sweden; Art Mus of Lund, Sweden; Malmo Konsthall, Malmo, Sweden; Nat Mus, Stockholm, Sweden; Brooklyn Mus, NY; Smithsonian Inst, Wash, DC
PRINTERS: Printmaking Workshop, NY (PW); Bill Hall, Ossining, NY (BH); Julie D'Amario, NY (JD); Lynn Rogan, NY (LR); Jennifer Lyncut, NY (JL); NYLE Press, Brooklyn, NY (NP); Spring Street Workshop, NY (SprSW)

CRISTOS GIANAKOS CONTINUED

PUBLISHERS: 724 Prints, NY (724P); Galerie Nordenhake, Stockholm, Sweden (GN); NYLE Press, Brooklyn, NY (NP); Artist (ART); Stark Gallery, NY (SG); Schwartz/Art, NY (S/A)

GALLERIES: Galerie Nordenhake, Stockholm, Sweden; Stark Gallery, New York, NY; Alpha Delta Gallery, Athens, Greece
MAILING ADDRESS: 93 Mercer St, New York, NY 10012

TITLE	PUBLISHER	PRINTER	DATE	MEDIUM	DIMENSION (PAPER SIZE) IN INCHES	TYPE OF PAPER	EDITION NUMBER	NO. OF COLORS	ORIGINAL OPENING PRICE	CURRENT RETAIL PRICE
CURRENT EDITIONS:										
Ramp 120	724P		1980	EC	22 X 30	R/BFK			200	300
Aurora (Set of 5)	GN	BH/PW	1985	I	29 X 41 EA	R/BFK/W	30 EA	2 EA	4500 SET	5000 SET
									900 EA	1000 EA
Post & Lintel	GN	BH/PW	1985	I	22 X 14	R/BFK	7	2	800	900
Bobo	GN	BH/PW	1985	I	18 X 12	R/BFK	7	2	800	900
Delta Series	GN	BH/PW	1985	I	14 X 22	R/BFK	7	2	800	900
Delta Series	GN	BH/JD/PW	1985	I	14 X 22	R/BFK	9	2	800	900
Doric	GN	BH/LR/PW	1985	I	22 X 14	R/BFK	7	2	800	900
Shield	GN	BH/JD/JL/PW	1985	I	22 X 30	R/BFK	5	2	800	900
Maia's Ladder	GN	BH/PW	1985	I	22 X 14	R/BFK	7	2	800	900
Red Site	GN	BH/PW	1985	I	14 X 11	R/BFK	7	2	750	800
Shakkei (Set of 7)	ART/NP	BH/PW/NP	1987	EC/REL	30 X 22 EA	R/BFK	15 EA		4500 SET	5000 SET
Alpha Series (Set of 13)	ART	ART	1991	PH/CO	26 X 20 EA	VEL	6 EA	2 EA	6500 SET	6500 SET
									900 EA	900 EA
Mirage (Set of 4)	SG	BH/SprSW	1991	EC	30 X 22 EA	R/BFK	20 EA	2 EA	4000 SET	4000 SET
									1200 EA	1200 EA
Mirage (Set of 3)	S/A	BH/SprSW	1992	EC/A	30 X 22 EA	R/BFK	20 EA	2 EA	2700 SET	2700 SET

STEVE GIANAKOS

BORN: New York, NY; 1938
EDUCATION: Pratt Inst, Brooklyn, NY
RECENT EXHIB: New York State Mus, Albany, NY, 1987; Asher-Faure Gallery, Los Angeles, CA, 1990; Barbara Toll Fine Arts, NY, 1988,92
PRINTERS: O'Connell Graphics, NY (OCG); Artist (ART); Clear Plasic Press, NY (CPPr)
PUBLISHERS: 724 Prints, NY (724P); Barbara Toll Fine Arts, NY (BTFA)
GALLERIES: Barbara Toll Fine Arts, New York, NY; Solo Gallery, New York, NY; Asher-Faure Gallery, Los Angeles, CA
MAILING ADDRESS: c/o Barbara Toll Fine Arts, 146 Greene St, New York, NY 10012

TITLE	PUBLISHER	PRINTER	DATE	MEDIUM	DIMENSION (PAPER SIZE) IN INCHES	TYPE OF PAPER	EDITION NUMBER	NO. OF COLORS	ORIGINAL OPENING PRICE	CURRENT RETAIL PRICE
SOLD OUT EDITIONS (RARE):										
Connect the Zits	SP	JS/SP	1979	LB	15 X 19	AP	20	1	250	400
Moving	SP	JS/SP	1984	LC	32 X 48	AP	60		450	800
CURRENT EDITIONS:										
Planter I,II,III	724P	ART	1978	LC	20 X 19 EA	AP	30 EA	3/3/4	225 EA	400 EA
Short, I Said, "You're Short"	BTFA	OCG	1985	SP	29 X 29	R/BFK	100	1	200	400
How Ya Doin'	BTFA	OCG	1986	SP	29 X 39	AC	50	3	250	400
Missing Children II (Set of 8)	SP	JS/SP	1986	LC	16 X 13 EA	AP	50 EA		1400 SET	1400 SET
Persons, Places & Things	CPPr	ART	1988	SP	37 X 31	SOM	50	1	500	750

JILL GIEGERICH

BORN: Chappaqua, NY; 1951
EDUCATION: San Francisco City Col, CA, 1970–71; Mount Angel Col, OR, 1971–72; California Inst of the Arts, Valencia, CA, BFA, 1975, MFA, 1977
AWARDS: John Simon Guggenheim Fel, 1992
RECENT EXHIB: Carnegie Mellon Univ, Pittsburgh, PA, 1987; Margo Leavin Gallery, Los Angeles, CA, 1987,89; Fred Hoffman Gallery, Santa Monica, CA, 1991; Phoenix Art Mus, AZ, 1992
COLLECTIONS: Carnegie Mellon Univ, Pittsburgh, PA
PRINTERS: Francesco Siqueiros, Los Angeles, CA (FS); Robert Dansby, Los Angeles, CA (RD); Alexia Montibon, Los Angeles, CA (AM); Cirrus Editions Workshop, Los Angeles, CA (CEW)
PUBLISHERS: Cirrus Editions, Ltd, Los Angeles, CA (CE)
GALLERIES: Cirrus Gallery, Los Angeles, CA; Margo Leavin Gallery, Los Angeles, CA; Fred Hoffman Gallery, Santa Monica, CA

TITLE	PUBLISHER	PRINTER	DATE	MEDIUM	DIMENSION (PAPER SIZE) IN INCHES	TYPE OF PAPER	EDITION NUMBER	NO. OF COLORS	ORIGINAL OPENING PRICE	CURRENT RETAIL PRICE
CURRENT EDITIONS:										
Soma I, State I (439c)	CE	CEW	1990	LC/CC	50 X 38	CORK/JP	45		1500	1500
Soma I, State II (439c)	CE	CEW	1990	LC	50 X 38	AC	18		1800	1800
Soma II, State I (447c)	CE	CEW	1990	LC/CC	50 X 38	CORK/JP	45		1500	1500
Soma II, State II (447ca)	CE	CEW	1990	LC	50 X 38	AC	18		1800	1800
Soma III, State I (448c)	CE	CEW	1990	LC/CC	50 X 38	CORK/JP	45		1500	1500
Soma III, State II (448ca)	CE	CEW	1990	LC	50 X 38	AC	18		1800	1800

The retail prices of the 100,000 limited edition prints quoted in this directory are subject to change. Print publishers, artists and galleries were the direct sources for these quotations. Prices in the secondary market listed as "Sold Out Editions (Rare)" indicate that the publisher has a limited supply of that print or that the print is difficult to locate in the galleries.

The Printworld Directory is accepting new applications for the seventh edition. Approximately 300 new artists will be accepted. Please use the two forms provided in the back section of this directory to submit biographical data and documentation of prints. Edition number of each print must not exceed 500 and the retail price must be $100 or more.

J NEBRASKA GIFFORD

BORN: Omaha, NE; November 25, 1939
EDUCATION: Bennington Col, VT, BA; Atelier 17, Paris, France, with S W Hayter
AWARDS: MacDowell Fel, 1976; CVA Grant, 1977; Pratt Inst Prize, NY, 1983
RECENT EXHIB: Noah's Art, NY, 1989; Drawing & Ceramics Gallery, Omaha, NE, 1990; Zodiac Gallery, Omaha, NE, 1990; Susan Teller Gallery, NY, 1990
COLLECTIONS: Univ of Nebraska, Omaha, NE; Pratt Inst, Brooklyn, NY; New York Univ, NY: Bennington Col Fine Arts Center, VT; Joslyn Art Mus, Omaha, NE; San Juan Col, NM; Sheldon Mus, Lincoln, NE
PRINTERS: John Nichols, NY (JN); Timothy Cramer, NY (TC); Artist (ART)
PUBLISHERS: John Nichols, NY (JN); Artist (ART)
GALLERIES: John Nichols Gallery, New York, NY; Louis K Meisel Gallery, New York, NY; Harm Bouckaert Gallery, New York, NY; Graham Gallery, Houston, TX; Associated American Artists, New York, NY; Mary Ryan Gallery, New York, NY; Zodiac Gallery, Omaha, NE; Susan Teller Gallery, New York, NY
MAILING ADDRESS: 4 Great Jones St, New York, NY 10012

TITLE	PUBLISHER	PRINTER	DATE	MEDIUM	DIMENSION (PAPER SIZE) IN INCHES	TYPE OF PAPER	EDITION NUMBER	NO. OF COLORS	ORIGINAL OPENING PRICE	CURRENT RETAIL PRICE
CURRENT EDITIONS:										
Bovinitron at the Seagram's Plaza	JN	JN	1984	LC/SP/NL	33 X 22	R/BFK	75	8	400	650
Red Sky	ART	ART/TC	1987	WC	22 X 27	MASA	20	14	500	650

DAVID JAMES GILHOOLY, III

BORN: Auburn, CA; April 15, 1943
EDUCATION: Univ of California, Davis, CA, BA, 1965, MA, 1967
TEACHING: San Jose State Col, CA, 1967–69; Univ of Saskatchewan, Can, 1969–71; York Univ, Toronto, Can, 1971–75, 76–77; Univ of California, Davis, CA, 1975–76
RECENT EXHIB: Oakland Mus, CA, 1988; Natsoulas Gallery, Davis, CA, 1988; Canton Art Inst, OH, 1989
COLLECTIONS: Australian Nat Gallery, Canberra, Australia; Oakland Mus of Art, CA; Bronfman Coll, Canadian Art Gallery; Nat Gallery, Ottawa, Can; Stedelijk Mus, Amsterdam, The Netherlands; San Antonio Mus of Art, TX; Whitney Mus of Am Art, NY; Long Beach Mus, CA; San Francisco Mus of Mod Art, CA; Philadelphia Mus, PA; Albright-Knox Art Gallery, Buffalo, NY; Utah Mus of Fine Arts, Salt Lake City, UT; Stanford Univ, Palo Alto, CA; San Jose Mus, CA; Nickle Art Mus, Univ of Calgary, Can; Univ of Washington, Seattle, WA; Univ of Arizona, Tempe, AZ; E B Crocker Art Mus, Sacramento, CA; Dartmouth Col, NH; Norman McKenzie Art Gallery, Regina, Can; Univ of Hawaii, Honolulu, HI; York Univ, Toronto, Can; Art Bank, Ottawa, Can; Vancouver Art Gallery, Can; Art Gallery of Greater Victoria, Can; Glenbow-Alberta Inst, Calgary, Can; Grossmont Col, San Diego, CA; Sir George Williams Art Gallery, Concordia Univ, Montreal, Can
PRINTERS: Ikuru Kuwahara, Palo Alto, CA (IK); 3 EP Ltd, Palo Alto, CA (3EP); Smith Andersen Editions, Palo Alto (SAE); Ann Hirsh, Oakland, CA (AH); Scott Greene, Oakland, CA (SG); Hirsh-Greene Press, Oakland, CA (HGP); Rick Dula (RD); Camille Gilhooly (CG); Donald Farnsworth (DF); Roxane Gilbert (RG); Magnolia Editions, Oakland, CA (MEd)
PUBLISHERS: 3 EP Ltd, Palo Alto, CA (3EP); Hirsh-Greene Press, Oakland, CA (HGP); Magnolia Editions, Oakland, CA (MEd)
GALLERIES: Smith Andersen Gallery, Palo Alto, CA; Joseph Chowning Gallery, San Francisco, CA; Asher/Faure Gallery, Los Angeles, CA; Harcourts Contemporary Gallery, San Francisco, CA; Delphine Gallery, Santa Barbara, CA; John Natsoulas Gallery, Davis, CA; Magnolia Editions, Oakland, CA; Sherry Frumkin Gallery, Santa Monica, CA; Lemberg Gallery, Birmingham, MI; Peter M David Gallery, Minneapolis, MN; Morgan Gallery, Kansas City, MO
MAILING ADDRESS: c/o Smith Anderson Gallery, 200 Homer St, Palo Alto, CA 94301

TITLE	PUBLISHER	PRINTER	DATE	MEDIUM	DIMENSION (PAPER SIZE) IN INCHES	TYPE OF PAPER	EDITION NUMBER	NO. OF COLORS	ORIGINAL OPENING PRICE	CURRENT RETAIL PRICE
CURRENT EDITIONS:										
Queen Victoria Presents the 20th Century Series	3EP	3EP	1983	MON	30 X 70	AP88	1 EA		1800	2000
My Daily Bread	3EP	3EP	1983	EB	24 X 43	AP88	12	1	600	800
My Daily Bread Series	3EP	3EP	1983	MON	24 X 43	AP88	1 EA		1800	2000
Food Descending the Staircase	3EP	3EP	1983	EB	36 X 37	AP88	12		900	1200
Food Descending the Staircase	3EP	3EP	1983	MON	36 X 37	AP88	1 EA		1800	2000
Selbstbildnis Mit Tod	3EP	3EP	1983	EB	23 X 30	R/BFK	12		500	700
Selbstbildnis Mit Tod	3EP	3EP	1983	MON	23 X 30	R/BFK	1 EA		700	900
First Morning Cup of Paula's Coffee	3EP	3EP	1983	EB	30 X 23	FAB	12		500	700
First Morning Cup of Paula's Coffee	3EP	3EP	1983	MON	30 X 23	FAB	1 EA		700	900
Self Portrait as Sandwich Fixing with a Punk Sardine Haircut (Series of 5)	3EP	3EP/SG	1983	MON/DPT	30 X 26 EA	AP88	1 EA		1800 EA	2000 EA
Fast Food Fallout over San Francisco	SAE	SG/HGP/SAE	1986	EC/A	23 X 31	TIEP	1 EA	8	1200 EA	1500 EA
San Francisco Devoured by Jello	HGP/ART	SG/AH/HGP	1986	EC/A	22 X 28	R/BFK	1 EA	7	1200 EA	1500 EA
Silver Leaf Dog	MEd	ART/RD/CG DF/RG/MEd	1988	LC	30 X 22	R/BFK	32	2	750	900

LUNDA HOYLE GILL

BORN: California
EDUCATION: Pomona Col, Claremont, CA, BA; Chouinard Art Inst, Los Angeles, CA; Art Students League, NY; Acad de Belli Arte, Florence, Italy
COLLECTIONS: Hermitage Mus, Lenningrad, Russia; Frye Mus, Seattle, WA; Oklahoma Art Mus, Oklahoma City, OK
PRINTERS: Vistec Graphics, Rochester, NY (VG); Artist (ART)
PUBLISHERS: Hammer Publishing Co, NY (HP)
GALLERIES: Hammer Galleries, New York, NY

The print market has become very selective. For the first time since we published the first edition of The Printworld Directory in 1982, the prices of prints have been greatly reduced and greatly increased for the same artists by the most reputable and established print publishers. Check the fifth edition to understand the movement.

LUNDA HOYLE GILL CONTINUED

TITLE	PUBLISHER	PRINTER	DATE	MEDIUM	DIMENSION (PAPER SIZE) IN INCHES	TYPE OF PAPER	EDITION NUMBER	NO. OF COLORS	ORIGINAL OPENING PRICE	CURRENT RETAIL PRICE
CURRENT EDITIONS:										
Natives of the North (Set of 3):									1200 SET	2000 SET
My Land	HP	ART/VG	1980	SP	21 X 28	AP88	300	26	450	750
Sewing My Mukluks	HP	ART/VG	1980	SP	20 X 24	AP88	300	26	400	650
Wise Kakanuk	HP	ART/VG	1980	SP	20 X 16	AP88	300	26	350	600

GREGORY JOSEPH GILLESPIE

BORN: Elizabeth, NJ; November 29, 1936
EDUCATION: Cooper Union for the Advancement of Science & Art, NY; San Francisco Art Inst, CA, BA, MFA, 1962
AWARDS: Am Acad in Rome Award, Italy, 1965–68; Fulbright Fel, 1967; Nat Inst of Arts & Letters Award, 1969
RECENT EXHIB: J Rosenthal Fine Arts, NY, 1988; Fitchburg Art Mus, MA, 1989; Forum Gallery, NY, 1989; Nielsen Gallery, Boston, MA, 1990; Harcourts Mod & Contemp Art, San Francisco, CA, 1992
COLLECTIONS: Hirshhorn Mus, Wash, DC; Whitney Mus of Am Art, NY; McNay Art Inst, San Antonio, TX; Mus of Mod Art, NY; Oklahoma Art Center, Oklahoma City, OK; Boston Mus of Fine Art, MA; San Francisco Mus of Mod Art, CA; Oakland Mus, CA
PRINTERS: Editions Press, San Francisco, CA (EP)
PUBLISHERS: Editions Press, San Francisco, CA (EP)
GALLERIES: Forum Gallery, New York, NY; John Berggruen Gallery, San Francisco, CA; J Rosenthal Fine Arts, Chicago, IL; R Michelson Galleries, Northampton, MA; Nielsen Gallery, Boston, MA; Harcourts Modern & Contemporary Art, San Francisco, CA
MAILING ADDRESS: c/o Forum Gallery, 1018 Madison Ave, New York, NY 10021

TITLE	PUBLISHER	PRINTER	DATE	MEDIUM	DIMENSION (PAPER SIZE) IN INCHES	TYPE OF PAPER	EDITION NUMBER	NO. OF COLORS	ORIGINAL OPENING PRICE	CURRENT RETAIL PRICE
CURRENT EDITIONS:										
Portfolio of Five Images	EP	EP	1984	LC/EC/I		Varies	Varies	45	6000 SET	8500 SET
Grandmother			1986	LC	24 X 20	AC		45	800	1000

MAX GIMBLETT (MAXWELL)

BORN: Auckland, New Zealand; December 5, 1935; US & NZ Citizen
EDUCATION: Ontario Col of Art, Toronto, Can, 1964; San Francisco Art Inst, CA, 1965
TEACHING: Vis Art, Printmaking, Indiana Univ, Bloomington, IN, 1979; Vis Lectr, Univ of Canterbury, Christchurch, NZ, 1981; Vis Assoc Prof, Int Honors Program in Japan, India, & Kenya; Vis Art, City Art Inst, Sydney, Australia, 1986; Vis Assoc Prof, Pratt Inst, Brooklyn, NY, 1979–89
AWARDS: Grant, Queen Elizabeth II Arts Council, New Zealand, 1980,86; Nat Endowment for the Arts Fel, Painting, 1989
RECENT EXHIB: White Columns Gallery, NY, 1988; Genovese Gallery, Boston, MA, 1987,89; Artis Gallery, Auckland, New Zealand, 1988,89,90
COLLECTIONS: Marion Koogler McNay Art Inst, San Antonio, TX; Laguna Gloria Art Mus, Austin, TX; San Francisco Mus of Mod Art, CA; Achenbach Found, San Francisco, CA; Pennsylvania Acad of Fine Arts, Phila, PA; Power Gallery of Contemp Art, Sydney, Australia; Art Gallery of New South Wales, Australia; Kunsthall Mälmo, Sweden
PRINTERS: Genovese Graphics, Boston, MA (GG)
PUBLISHERS: Genovese Graphics, Boston, MA (GG)
GALLERIES: Genovese Gallery, Boston, MA; Modernism, San Francisco, CA; R C Erpf Fine Art, New York, NY; Galerie Nordenhake, Mälmo, Sweden; Artis Gallery, Auckland, New Zealand; Jan Turner Gallery, Los Angeles, CA; Haines Gallery, San Francisco, CA
MAILING ADDRESS: 231 Bowery, New York, NY 10003

TITLE	PUBLISHER	PRINTER	DATE	MEDIUM	DIMENSION (PAPER SIZE) IN INCHES	TYPE OF PAPER	EDITION NUMBER	NO. OF COLORS	ORIGINAL OPENING PRICE	CURRENT RETAIL PRICE
CURRENT EDITIONS:										
Untitled (Set of 7)	GG	GG	1983	SP	30 X 20 EA	TOR	28 EA	1 EA	1800 SET	3000 SET
Silk Route (Set of 7)	GG	GG	1984	SP	30 X 20 EA	AP88	28 EA	1 EA	1800 SET	3000 SET
Jade	GG	GG	1986	SP	32 X 43	AP/CR	35	1	500	650
Onyx	GG	GG	1986	SP	32 X 43	AP/W	35	1	500	650

JOSEPH GIORDANO

EDUCATION: Maryland Inst Col of Art, Baltimore, MD, BFA, Painting; Univ of Pennsylvania, Grad Sch of Fine Arts, Phila, PA, MFA, Painting
AWARDS: Nat Endowment for the Arts, Visual Arts Fel Grant, Painting, 1986–86; New York State Council on the Arts Grant, 1988
RECENT EXHIB: Col of Notre Dame of Maryland, Baltimore, MD, 1991; Haupert Union Building Gallery, Moravian Col, Bethlehem, PA, 1991; Reading Public Mus, Reading, PA, 1992; Galerie Francoise, Baltimore, MD, 1992; Blue Mountain Gallery, NY, 1988,90,92
PRINTERS: Anthony Kirk, NY (AK); Eldindean Press, NY (ElP)
PUBLISHERS: Marcus Editions, NY (MarEd)
GALLERIES: Blue Mountain Gallery, New York, NY: Galerie Francois, Baltimore, MD
MAILING ADDRESS: 4613 Wilmslow Rd, Baltimore, MD 21210

TITLE	PUBLISHER	PRINTER	DATE	MEDIUM	DIMENSION (PAPER SIZE) IN INCHES	TYPE OF PAPER	EDITION NUMBER	NO. OF COLORS	ORIGINAL OPENING PRICE	CURRENT RETAIL PRICE
SOLD OUT EDITIONS (RARE):										
Umbrella	MarEd	AK/ElP	1983	A/HC	29 X 37	SOM	50	Multi	400	850
Umbrella	MarEd	AK/ElP	1983	AB	29 X 37	SOM	10	1	350	650
Madeleine	MarEd	AK/ElP	1984	AB	9 X 7	SOM	40	1	35	100
Biplane	MarEd	AK/ElP	1985	AB	9 X 8	SOM	100	1	35	200

The retail prices of the 100,000 limited edition prints quoted in this directory are subject to change. Print publishers, artists and galleries were the direct sources for these quotations. Prices in the secondary market listed as "Sold Out Editions (Rare)" indicate that the publisher has a limited supply of that print or that the print is difficult to locate in the galleries.

SAM GILLIAM

BORN: Tupelo, MS; 1933
EDUCATION: Univ of Louisville, KY, BA, 1955, MA, 1961
TEACHING: Instr Art, Public Sch System, Wash, DC, 1958–67; Instr, Painting, Corcoran Sch of Art, Wash, DC, 1964–76; Tenured Prof, Painting, Univ of Maryland, College Park, MD, 1982–85; Prof, Art, Carnegie-Mellon Univ, Pittsburgh, PA, 1985 to present
AWARDS: Norman Walt Harris Prize, Art Inst of Chicago, IL, 1970; Longview Found Purchase Award, 1970; Guggenheim Mem Fel 1971; Workshop Activities Grants, 1973–75; Nat Endowment for the Arts Grant, 1987; President's Award, Maryland Col of Art & Design, 1987; Order of Merit Award, Univ of Louisville, Alumni Assn, 1987; Ind Artist Endowment of the Arts Grant, 1989; Honorary Doctor of Arts & Letters, Northwestern Univ, Evanston, IL, 1990
RECENT EXHIB: Smithsonian Inst, Wash, DC, 1987; Robert Kidd Gallery, Birmington, MI, 1987; Carl Solway Gallery, Cincinnati, OH, 1987; Klein Gallery, Chicago, IL, 1987,88; Iannetti-Lanzone Gallery, San Francisco, CA, 1988; Owensboro Mus of Fine Art, KY, 1988; Birmingham Mus of Art, AL, 1988; Iannetti Lanzone Gallery, Inc, San Francisco, CA, 1988; Carnegie Mellon Univ Art Gallery, Pittsburgh, PA, 1989; Klein Art Works, Chicago, IL, 1990; Univ of Wisconsin, Crossman Gallery, Whitewater, WI, 1992
COLLECTIONS: Mus of Mod Art, NY; Art Inst of Chicago, IL; Corcoran Gallery of Art, Wash, DC; Hirshhorn Mus, Wash, DC; High Mus of Art, Atlanta, GA; Baltimore Mus, MD; Walker Art Center, Minneapolis, MN; Boymans-Von-Beunigen Mus, Rotterdam, Holland; Tate Gallery of Art, London, England; Howard Univ, DC; Phillips Coll, Wash, DC; Nat Coll for Fine Art, Wash, DC; Rutgers Univ, New Brunswick, NJ; Madison Art Center, WI; Carnegie Inst, Pittsburgh, PA; Princeton Univ, NJ; Baltimore Mus of Art, MD; Metropolitan Mus of Art, NY; Smithsonian Inst, Wash, DC; Musee d'Art Mod de la Ville de Paris, Paris, France
PRINTERS: Vermillion Editions Ltd, Minneapolis, MN (VEL); Jones Road Stable (JRS); William Weege (WW); David Keister, Bloomington, IN (DK); Echo Press, Bloomington, IN (EPr); Gary Denmark (GD); Tamela Martin (TM); Smith Andersen Editions, Palo Alto, CA (SAE); Andrew Rubin, Madison, WI (AR); Tandem Press, Univ of Wisconsin, Madison, WI (TanPr)
PUBLISHERS: Middendorf-Lane Gallery, Wash, DC (M–L); Vermillion Editions, Ltd, Minneapolis, MN (VEL); Fendrick Gallery, Wash, DC (FG); Jones Road Stable (JRS); Echo Press, Bloomington, IN (EPr); Smith Andersen Editions, Palo Alto, CA (SAE); Tandem Press, Univ of Wisconsin, Madison, WI (TanPr)
GALLERIES: Hamilton Gallery, New York, NY; Dart Gallery, Chicago, IL; Galerie Darthea Speyer, Paris, France; Carl Solway Gallery, Cincinnati, OH; Middendorf Gallery, Wash, DC; Robert Kidd, Birmingham, MI; Vermillion Editions, Minneapolis, MN; Nina Freudenheim Gallery, Buffalo, NY; McIntosh/Drysdale Gallery, Houston, TX; Davis/McClain Galleries, Houston, TX; Klein Art Works, Chicago, IL; Echo Press, Bloomington, IN; Barbara Fendrick Gallery, New York, NY & Wash, DC; Alice Simsar Gallery, Ann Arbor, MI; Brett Mitchell Collection, Cleveland, OH; Smith Andersen Gallery, Palo Alto, CA; Nancy Drysdale Gallery, Wash, DC; Peter M David Gallery, Minneapolis, MN; Carolyn Ruff Gallery, Minneapolis, MN; S Cara BB Galleries, Cleveland, OH
MAILING ADDRESS: 1752 Lamont St, NW, Wash, DC 20010

Sam Gilliam
Purple Antelope Space Squeeze
Courtesy Tandem Press

Sam Gilliam
Fast Track
Courtesy Tandem Press

TITLE	PUBLISHER	PRINTER	DATE	MEDIUM	DIMENSION (PAPER SIZE) IN INCHES	TYPE OF PAPER	EDITION NUMBER	NO. OF COLORS	ORIGINAL OPENING PRICE	CURRENT RETAIL PRICE
SOLD OUT EDITIONS (RARE):										
Pink Horseshoes	FG	JRS	1973	SP	18 X 25	AP	42	3	200	1000
Trail's End	JRS	WW	1980	I/CO	24 X 33	JWP	12	2	750	1200
Coffee Thyme	M–L	VEL	1981	LC/SP/I	31 X 41	HMP	65	10	850	1200
Coffee Thyme II	M–L	VEL	1981	LC/SP/I	31 X 41	HMP	39	11	1000	1600
Purple Antelope Space Squeeze	TanPr	AR/TanPr	1987	EB/A/REL/COL/HC/EMB	44 X 39	HMP	40	Varies		POR
CURRENT EDITIONS:										
Buoy Landscape I, II, III, IV, V	VEL	VEL	1982	DPT/EC	32 X 23 EA	HMP	25 EA	4 EA	400 EA	1200 EA
Last Coffee Thyme	VEL/M–L	VEL	1981	LC/SP/I	31 X 41	HMP	10	11	1200	2000

SAM GILLIAM CONTINUED

TITLE	PUBLISHER	PRINTER	DATE	MEDIUM	DIMENSION (PAPER SIZE) IN INCHES	TYPE OF PAPER	EDITION NUMBER	NO. OF COLORS	ORIGINAL OPENING PRICE	CURRENT RETAIL PRICE
CURRENT EDITIONS:										
Lattice I, II, III, IV	VEL	VEL	1982	LC/EC	32 X 44 EA	HMP	38 EA	12 EA	1000 EA	1600 EA
Pegram Medieval Larry (Unique Woodcut)	EPr	DK/EPr	1986	WC/HC	85 X 42 EA	AC&R/BFK&MIT	1 EA	Varies	5000 EA	8000 EA
Pittsburgh Sam (Unique Woodcut)	EPr	DK/EPr	1986	WC/HC	85 X 42 EA	AP/B&R/BFK&MIT	1 EA	Varies	5000 EA	8000 EA
Indiana Tom (Unique Woodcut)	EPr	DK/EPr	1986	WC/HC	79 X 49 EA	AP/B&R/BFK&MIT	1 EA	Varies	5000 EA	8000 EA
Going (Unique Woodcut)	EPr	DK/EPr	1986	WC/HC	61 X 48 EA	AP/B&R/BFK&MIT	1 EA	Varies	4500 EA	6000 EA
To Vancouver (Unique Woodcut)	EPr	DK/EPr	1986	WC/HC	49 X 49 EA	AP/B&R/BFK&MIT	1 EA	Varies	4000 EA	5000 EA
For Romare; 8	EPr	DK/EPr	1988	MON/MM	35 X 54 EA	HMP	1 EA	Varies	4500 EA	8000 EA
Chehaw	TanPr	AR/TanPr	1990	WC/EB	30 X 44	RP/BL	40	Varies	2000	2400
Aviation 4	SAE	GD/TM/SAE	1990	MON	30 X 23 EA	R/BFK	1 EA		2800 EA	3500 EA
Mother's March (Unique) (Round Plastic Frame)	EPr	DK/DC/EPr	1991	LB/COL/HC	48" Round	R/BFK&AC/W	1 EA	Varies	10000 EA	11000 EA
A January (Unique) (Round Plastic Frame)	EPr	DK/DC/EPr	1991	LB/COL/HC	48" Round	R/BFK&AC	1 EA	Varies	10000 EA	11000 EA
April (Unique) (Round Plastic Frame)	EPr	DK/DC/EPr	1991	LB/COL/HC	48" Round	R/BFK&AC	1 EA	Varies	10000 EA	11000 EA
June Moon (Unique) (Round Plastic Frame)	EPr	DK/DC/EPr	1991	LB/COL/HC	48" Round	R/BFK&AC	1 EA	Varies	10000 EA	11000 EA
July (Unique) (Round Plastic Frame)	EPr	DK/DC/EPr	1991	LB/COL/HC	48" Round	R/BFK&AC	1 EA	Varies	10000 EA	11000 EA
August (Unique) (Round Plastic Frame)	EPr	DK/DC/EPr	1991	LB/COL/HC	48" Round	R/BFK&AC	1 EA	Varies	10000 EA	11000 EA
September (Unique) (Round Plastic Frame)	EPr	DK/DC/EPr	1991	LB/COL/HC	48" Round	R/BFK&AC	1 EA	Varies	10000 EA	11000 EA
October (Unique) (Round Plastic Frame)	EPr	DK/DC/EPr	1991	LB/COL/HC	48" Round	R/BFK&AC	1 EA	Varies	10000 EA	11000 EA
Fast Track	TanPr	AR/TanPr	1992	EB/REL	25 X 25	HMP	49	11	1500	1500

LAWRENCE GIPE

BORN: Baltimore, MD; 1962
EDUCATION: Virginia Commonwealth Univ, Richmond, VA, BFA, 1984; Otis Art Inst/Parsons Sch of Design, Los Angeles, CA, MFA, 1986
AWARDS: Nat Endowment for the Arts Fel, 1989
RECENT EXHIB: Richard/Bennett Gallery, Los Angeles, CA, 1987; Claremont Col, CA, 1987; Laguna Art Mus, Laguna Beach, CA, 1988; Galerie Six Friedrich, Munich, Germany, 1989; Amerika Haus, Berlin, Germany, 1989; Hartje Gallery, Frankfurt, Germany, 1989; Barbara Fendrick Gallery, NY & Wash, DC, 1989; Shea & Beker Gallery, NY, 1990; Katonah Mus, NY, 1990; Federal Reserve Board Art Gallery, Wash, DC, 1992; Modernism, San Francisco, CA, 1993; Pelavin Editions, NY, 1992; BlumHelman Gallery, NY, 1993; Modernism, San Francisco, CA, 1993
PRINTERS: Cheryl Pelavin, NY (CP); Pelavin Editions, NY (PelEd)
PUBLISHERS: Pelavin Editions, NY (PelEd); Rutgers Archives, Zimmerli Art Mus, New Brunswick, NJ (RA/ZAM)
GALLERIES: Shea & Bornstein Gallery, Santa Monica, CA; BlumHelman Gallery, New York, NY; Pelavin Editions, New York, NY; Modernism, San Francisco, CA
MAILING ADDRESS: c/o Shea & Bornstein Gallery, 2114 Broadway, Santa Monica, CA 90404

Lawrence Gipe
Study 15
Courtesy Zimmerli Art Museum

TITLE	PUBLISHER	PRINTER	DATE	MEDIUM	DIMENSION (PAPER SIZE) IN INCHES	TYPE OF PAPER	EDITION NUMBER	NO. OF COLORS	ORIGINAL OPENING PRICE	CURRENT RETAIL PRICE
CURRENT EDITIONS:										
Themes for a Fin de Siécle (Series of 16)	CP	CP/PelEd	1991	MON	47 X 32 EA	AP	1 EA	Varies	2500 EA	2500 EA
Study A for Themes for a fin de Siécle	RA/ZAM	CP/PelEd	1992	AC	22 X 30	AC	71	2	1200	1200

YANKEL GINZBURG (JACOB)

BORN: Alma-Ata, Russia; March 23, 1945; US Citizen
EDUCATION: Inst of Fine Arts, Tel Aviv, Israel, Diploma, 1961
TEACHING: Inst of Fine Arts, Tel Aviv, Israel, 1965–67
AWARDS: Silver Medal, Biennal, Rome, 1962; First Prize, Bat-Yam Mus, Israel, 1965
COLLECTIONS: Cairo Mus, Egypt; Bat Yam Mus, Israel; Israel Mus, Jerusalem, Israel; Hirshhorn Mus, Wash, DC; Skirball Mus, Los Angeles, CA; Tel Aviv Mus, Israel
PUBLISHERS: Martin Lawrence Limited Editions, Van Nuys, CA (MLLE); Zimmerman Editions, Ltd, Baltimore, MD (ZE); Contemporary Editions, Sparta, NJ (ConEd)
PRINTERS: Accent Studios (AS); Zimmerman Editions, Ltd, Baltimore, MD (ZE); Artist (ART)
GALLERIES: Martin Lawrence Galleries, Sherman Oaks, CA & West Los Angeles, CA & Newport Beach, CA & Palm Springs, CA & Santa Clara, CA & Redondo Beach, CA & Thousand Oaks, CA & Escondido, CA & Los Angeles, CA & Phila, PA & Short Hills, NJ; Dyansen Eclipse Gallery, New York, NY
MAILING ADDRESS: 5710 Connecticut Ave, Chevy Chase, MD 20815

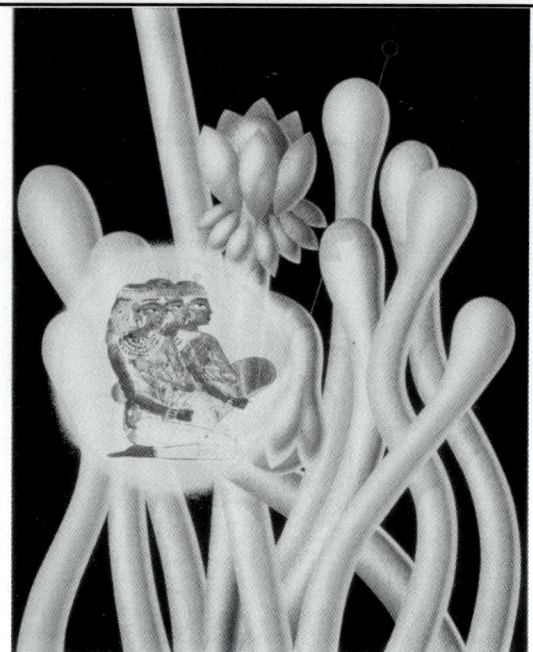

Yankel Ginzburg (Jacob)
Continuity
Courtesy Zimmerman Editions, Ltd

TITLE	PUBLISHER	PRINTER	DATE	MEDIUM	DIMENSION (PAPER SIZE) IN INCHES	TYPE OF PAPER	EDITION NUMBER	NO. OF COLORS	ORIGINAL OPENING PRICE	CURRENT RETAIL PRICE
SOLD OUT EDITIONS (RARE):										
Running Colors	MLLE	AH/SH	1982	SP	25 X 33	LEN	350	14	600	1500
Blackjack	MLLE	AS	1982	SP	36 X 30	AP	350	96	600	1800
Blackjack (Deluxe Edition)	MLLE	AS	1982	SP	36 X 30	JP	175	96	650	1800
Quilted	MLLE	AH/SH	1982	SP	29 X 37	AP	238	42	750	1500
Royalty	MLLE	AS	1983	SP	36 X 30	AP	350	98	600	1500
Royalty (Deluxe Edition)	MLLE	AS	1983	SP	36 X 30	JP	175	98	650	1500
Continuity	ZE	ZE	1983	SP	29 X 41	AP	362	31	600	1500
CURRENT EDITIONS:										
Treasures of the Sea (Set of 3):									1200 SET	2500 SET
Treasures of the Sea (Deluxe) (Set of 3):									1350 SET	2750 SET
Reflections	MLLE	ART	1978	SP	27 X 31	AP	350	36	350	1000
Reflections (Deluxe)	MLLE	ART	1978	SP	27 X 31	JP	175	36	375	1100
Inner Seascape	MLLE	ART	1978	SP	27 X 31	AP	350	36	350	1000
Inner Seascape (Deluxe)	MLLE	ART	1978	SP	27 X 31	JP	175	36	375	1100
Deep Waters	MLLE	ART	1978	SP	27 X 31	AP	350	36	350	1000
Deep Waters (Deluxe)	MLLE	ART	1978	SP	27 X 31	JP	175	36	375	1100
Ocelot in Fantastic Lands	MLLE	AS	1980	SP	30 X 40	AP	380	80	450	1500
Time Change	MLLE	AH/SH	1983	SP	29 X 34	AP	305	21	650	1500
King Lear	MLLE	AH/SH	1983	SP	38 X 50	AP	234	28	750	1500
Union	MLLE	AH/SH	1983	SP	41 X 47	AP	490	31	750	1500
Candy Store (Gray)	MLLE	AH/SH	1983	SP	31 X 37	AP	231	30	750	1500
Candy Store (Black)	MLLE	AH/SH	1983	SP	31 X 37	AP	231	30	750	1500
Space Odyssey	MLLE	AH/SH	1983	SP	33 X 29	AP	306	42	650	1500
Life in the Fast Lane	MLLE	AH/SH	1983	SP	29 X 41	AP	462	31	750	1500
City in Blue	ZE	ZE	1983	SP		AP	350		450	1200
Thru the Looking Glass	ZE	ZE	1983	SP/AC	12 X 16 X 19	AP	50		1000	9000
Sphere	ZE	ZE	1983	SP/AC		AP	70		900	5000
The Lovers	ZE	ZE	1983	SP		AP	350		700	1500
Spring	ZE	ZE	1983	SP		AP	350		600	1500
Self Portrait	ZE	ZE	1983	SP		AP	350		600	1500
Celebrating the Constitution (Set of 3):									1500 SET	3500 SET
Birth of a Nation	ConEd		1987	SP		AP	350		600	1350
Glorious Document	ConEd		1987	SP		AP	350		600	1350
Celebration	ConEd		1987	SP		AP	350		600	1350
Inner City	ConEd		1987	SP		AP	350		600	1350

The retail prices of the 100,000 limited edition prints quoted in this directory are subject to change. Print publishers, artists and galleries were the direct sources for these quotations. Prices in the secondary market listed as "Sold Out Editions (Rare)" indicate that the publisher has a limited supply of that print or that the print is difficult to locate in the galleries.

The Printworld Directory is accepting new applications for the seventh edition. Approximately 300 new artists will be accepted. Please use the two forms provided in the back section of this directory to submit biographical data and documentation of prints. Edition number of each print must not exceed 500 and the retail price must be $100 or more.

MARIA GIRONA

BORN: Barcelona, Spain
AWARDS: French Inst, Barcelona, Spain, Scholarship to study in Paris, France, 1950

PRINTERS: La Poligrafa, SA, Barcelona, Spain (LP)
PUBLISHERS: Ediciones Poligrafa, SA, Barcelona, Spain (EdP)
GALLERIES: Galeria Juan Prats, Barcelona, Spain & New York, NY

TITLE	PUBLISHER	PRINTER	DATE	MEDIUM	DIMENSION (PAPER SIZE) IN INCHES	TYPE OF PAPER	EDITION NUMBER	NO. OF COLORS	ORIGINAL OPENING PRICE	CURRENT RETAIL PRICE
CURRENT EDITIONS:										
Set of 10 Lithographs (Set of 10):									1500 SET	2500 SET
Vas i Flors	EdP	LP	1982	LC	30 X 22	GP	99	5	180	280
Mar i Flors	EdP	LP	1982	LC	30 X 22	GP	99	5	180	280
Gerro Rosat Glicina	EdP	LP	1982	LC	30 X 22	GP	99	5	180	280
Sindria	EdP	LP	1982	LC	30 X 22	GP	99	5	180	280
Els Lilás	EdP	LP	1982	LC	30 X 22	GP	99	5	180	280
Magranes i Ocells	EdP	LP	1982	LC	30 X 22	GP	99	5	180	280
Gerro i Finestra	EdP	LP	1982	LC	30 X 22	GP	99	5	180	280
Fruitera i Cieres	EdP	LP	1982	LC	30 X 22	GP	99	5	180	280
Bol i Lliris	EdP	LP	1982	LC	30 X 22	GP	99	5	180	280
Fruitera i Finestra	EdP	LP	1982	LC	30 X 22	GP	99	5	180	280

TINA GIROUARD

BORN: De Quincy, LA; May 26, 1946
EDUCATION: Univ of Southwestern Louisiana, Lafayette, LA, BFA, 1968
AWARDS: Creative Artists Public Service Award, 1973–74; Nat Endowment for the Arts Award, 1976; YAYA, Zagreb, Yugoslavia, Sponsored by ICA, Wash, DC
RECENT EXHIB: Univ of Southwestern Louisiana, Univ Art Mus, Lafayette, LA, 1989
PRINTERS: Larry B. Wright Art Productions, NY (LBW)
PUBLISHERS: Holly Solomon Editions, NY (HSE); Fabric Workshop, Phila, PA (FW)
GALLERIES: Holly Solomon Editions, Ltd, New York, NY; Mary Delahoyd Gallery, New York, NY

TITLE	PUBLISHER	PRINTER	DATE	MEDIUM	DIMENSION (PAPER SIZE) IN INCHES	TYPE OF PAPER	EDITION NUMBER	NO. OF COLORS	ORIGINAL OPENING PRICE	CURRENT RETAIL PRICE
CURRENT EDITIONS:										
Conflicting Evidence										
(50 Unique Pcs)	FW	FW	1980	SP/F	36 X 36		1		750	900
	FW	FW	1980	SP/F	36 X 72		1		1200	1350
	FW	FW	1980	SP/F	36 X 108		1		1800	2000
	FW	FW	1980	SP/F	72 X 72		1		2500	2750
	FW	FW	1980	SP/F	36 X 144		1		2500	2750
Stacked Signs (25 Unique Pcs)	HSE	LBW	1980	SP/EMB	31 X 31 EA	THS/W	25 EA	4 EA	750 EA	1000 EA
Hidden Meanings (Series of 25)	HSE	LBW	1980	SP/EMB	31 X 53 EA	THS/W	25 EA	4 EA	1200 EA	1350 EA

SAM GLANKOFF

BORN: New York, NY; (1894–1982)
EDUCATION: Self-Taught
RECENT EXHIB: Roger Ramsay Gallery, Chicago, IL, 1987; Tilden-Foley Gallery, New Orleans, LA, 1989
COLLECTIONS: Solomon R Guggenheim Mus, NY; Metropolitan Mus of Art, NY; Detroit Inst of Arts, MI; Brooklyn Mus, NY; Montclair Mus, NJ; Jewish Mus, NY; Jane Voorhees Zimmerli Mus, NJ; New York Public Library, NY; Davison Art Center, Wesleyan Univ, Middletown, CT
PRINTERS: Artist (ART)
PUBLISHERS: Artist (ART)
GALLERIES: Wendy Snyder Associates, New York, NY; Tilden-Foley Gallery, New Orleans, LA; Victoria Munroe Gallery, New York, NY
MAILING ADDRESS: c/o Wendy Snyder, 88 Lexington Ave, New York, NY 10016

TITLE	PUBLISHER	PRINTER	DATE	MEDIUM	DIMENSION (PAPER SIZE) IN INCHES	TYPE OF PAPER	EDITION NUMBER	NO. OF COLORS	ORIGINAL OPENING PRICE	CURRENT RETAIL PRICE
CURRENT EDITIONS:										
Untitled (Print-Painting 4003)	ART	ART	1972	INK	39 X 48 EA	HMP	1 EA	2 EA	3500 EA	13500 EA
Untitled (Print-Painting 4200)	ART	ART	1981	INK	49 X 39 EA	HMP	1 EA	4 EA	3800 EA	15000 EA

LLOYD GOFF

EDUCATION: Art Students League, NY; Univ of New Mexico, Albuquerque, NM; Académie Julian, Paris, France
TEACHING: Univ of New Mexico, Albuquerque, NM
AWARDS: Schnakenberg Scholarship, NY; Louis Comfort Tiffany Found Fel
COLLECTIONS: Whitney Mus of Am Art, NY; Dallas Mus, TX; Wadsworth Atheneum, Hartford, CT; Museo de Bellas Artes, Mexico City, Mexico
PRINTERS: American Atelier, NY (AA)
PUBLISHERS: Circle Fine Art, Chicago, IL (CFA)
GALLERIES: Circle Galleries, Chicago, IL & San Diego, CA & San Francisco, CA & Northbrook, IL & Pittsburgh, PA & Houston, TX & Soho, NY & Chicago, IL & Scottsdale, AZ & Beverly Hills, CA & Costa Mesa, CA & Sherman Oaks, CA & Palm Beach, FL & Honolulu, HI & New Orleans, LA & Las Vegas, NV & Seattle, WA

TITLE	PUBLISHER	PRINTER	DATE	MEDIUM	DIMENSION (PAPER SIZE) IN INCHES	TYPE OF PAPER	EDITION NUMBER	NO. OF COLORS	ORIGINAL OPENING PRICE	CURRENT RETAIL PRICE
SOLD OUT EDITIONS (RARE):										
Lincoln Center Fantasy	CFA	AA	1980	LC	23 X 29	AP	250		100	150

FRITZ GLARNER

BORN: Zürich, Switzerland; (1899–1972)
EDUCATION: Royal Inst of Fine Arts, Naples, Italy
COLLECTIONS: Mus of Mod Art, NY; Whitney Mus of Am Art, NY; Brooklyn Mus, NY; Albright-Knox Art Gallery, Buffalo, NY; Philadelphia Art Mus, PA; Yale Univ Art Mus, New Haven, CT; Brandeis Univ, Waltham, MA; Kunsthaus, Zürich, Switzerland; Mus of Winterthus, Switzerland; State Univ of New York, Purchase, NY
PRINTERS: Universal Limited Art Editions, West Islip, NY (ULAE)
PUBLISHERS: Universal Limited Art Editions, West Islip, NY (ULAE)
GALLERIES: Washburn Gallery, New York, NY; Graham Gallery, New York, NY

Sparks (S)

TITLE	PUBLISHER	PRINTER	DATE	MEDIUM	DIMENSION (PAPER SIZE) IN INCHES	TYPE OF PAPER	EDITION NUMBER	NO. OF COLORS	ORIGINAL OPENING PRICE	CURRENT RETAIL PRICE
SOLD OUT EDITIONS (RARE):										
Drawing for Tondo (Hors Commerce Only)			1962	LB	17 X 8	KOCHI	5	1	100	3500
Color Drawing for Relational Painting (S-9)	ULAE	ULAE	1963	LC	21 X 12	CHRIS	35		100	5000

JOHN P GLICK

BORN: Detroit, MI; July 1, 1938
EDUCATION: Wayne State Univ, Detroit, MI, 1960; Cranbrook Acad of Art, Bloomfield Hills, MI 1962
AWARDS: Louis Comfort Tiffany Grants, 1961,73; Nat Endowment for the Arts Fel Grants, 1977,88
RECENT EXHIB: Canton Art Inst, OH, 1987; Campbell Mus, Camden, NJ, 1987; Detroit Inst of Arts, MI, 1988; Univ of Wisconsin, Eau Claire, WI, 1988; Everson Mus of Art, Syracuse, NY, 1989; Detroit Artists Market, MI, 1989
COLLECTIONS: Detroit Inst of Arts, MI; Kansas City Art Inst, Kansas City, MO; Cranbrook Art Acad, Bloomfield Hills, MI; Everson Mus of Art, Syracuse, NY; Los Angeles County Mus, CA; Canton Inst of Art, OH; Renwick Gallery, Wash, DC; Nat Mus of Am Art, Wash, DC; Smithsonian Inst, Wash, DC; Auckland War Mem Mus, New Zealand; Dunedin City Mus, New Zealand; Christchurch City Art Gallery, New Zealand; Hawkes Bay Art Gallery, New Zealand; Wanganui Com Col, New Zealand; Otago Polytech, Dunedin, New Zealand; Manchester Polytechnic, New Zealand; Wayne State Univ, Detroit, MI; Arizona State Univ, Phoenix, AZ; Alfred Univ, NY; Lannan Found, Palm Beach, FL; South Bend Art Assn, Jackson, MS
PRINTERS: Norman Stewart, Birmingham, MI (NS); Joe Keenan, Birmingham, MI (JK); Stewart & Stewart, Birmingham, MI (S-S)
PUBLISHERS: Harvey Littleton Studio, Spruce Pine, NC (HLS); Stewart & Stewart, Birmingham, MI (S-S)
GALLERIES: Pro Art, St Louis, MO; Stewart & Stewart, Birmingham, MI; Schneider-Bluhm-Loeb Gallery, Inc, Chicago, IL
MAILING ADDRESS: 30435 West Ten Mile Rd, Farmington Hills, MI 48024

TITLE	PUBLISHER	PRINTER	DATE	MEDIUM	DIMENSION (PAPER SIZE) IN INCHES	TYPE OF PAPER	EDITION NUMBER	NO. OF COLORS	ORIGINAL OPENING PRICE	CURRENT RETAIL PRICE
CURRENT EDITIONS:										
Overflight	S-S	NS/JK/S-S	1989	SP	22 X 30	R/BFK/W	57	15	675	750

MIKE GLIER

BORN: Kentucky; 1953
EDUCATION: Rhode Island Sch of Design, Providence, RI, 1975; Williams Col, Williamstown, MA, BA, 1976; Hunter Col, NY, MA, 1979
AWARDS: Berkshire Mus Traveling Fel, Pittsfield, MA, 1976; Whitney Mus of Am Art, Independent Study Prog, NY, 1977; Nat Endowment for the Arts Fel, Drawing, 1981; Award, Visual Arts, New Orleans Mus, LA, 1990
RECENT EXHIB: Mus of Mod Art, NY, 1987; Williams Col Mus, Williamstown, MA, 1987; Hallwalls Contemp Art Center, Buffalo, NY, 1988; Mus of Mod Art, NY, 1988; Two First Union Center, Charlotte, NC, 1989; San Jose Mus of Art, CA, 1989; Wave Hill, Bronx, NY, 1989; Barbara Gladstone Gallery, NY, 1989
PUBLISHERS: Barbara Gladstone Editions, NY (BGE)
GALLERIES: Barbara Gladstone Gallery, New York, NY

TITLE	PUBLISHER	PRINTER	DATE	MEDIUM	DIMENSION (PAPER SIZE) IN INCHES	TYPE OF PAPER	EDITION NUMBER	NO. OF COLORS	ORIGINAL OPENING PRICE	CURRENT RETAIL PRICE
CURRENT EDITIONS:										
Lena Calling	BGE		1983	LC	30 X 23	AP	25		250	400
Barbara Calling	BGE		1983	LC	30 X 23	AP	25		250	400
Jenny Calling	BGE		1983	LC	30 X 23	AP	21		250	400
Men at Home: Necking	BGE		1985	EB/A/DPT	36 X 25	AP/W	60		350	500
Men at Home: Entertaining	BGE		1985	EB/A/DPT	36 X 25	AP/W	60		350	500
Men at Home: Grooming	BGE		1985	EB/A/DPT	36 X 25	AP/W	60		350	500
Men at Home: Mopping	BGE		1985	EB/A/DPT	36 X 25	AP/W	60		350	500
Men at Home: Sitting	BGE		1985	EB/A/DPT	36 X 25	AP/W	60		350	500

ABBY JANE GOELL

BORN: New York, NY
EDUCATION: Art Students League, NY; Syracuse Univ, NY, BA; Columbia Univ, NY, Painting, MFA, 1965, with Robert Motherwell; Pratt Graphic Arts Workshop, Brooklyn, NY, 1967
TEACHING: Instr, Art History, Hunter Col, NY, 1967; Lectr, Lab Inst Merchandising, 1967–70
AWARDS: Yaddo Fel, Saratoga Springs, NY, 1968; Virginia Center for Creative Arts Fel, Sweet Briar, VA, 1981
RECENT EXHIB: John Szoke Gallery, NY, 1988–89
COLLECTIONS: Mus of Mod Art, NY; Yale Univ, New Haven, CT; Syracuse Univ, NY; Stanford Mus, CT; Denver Mus, CO; NY Univ, NY

ABBY JANE GOELL CONTINUED

PRINTERS: Artist (ART)
PUBLISHERS: Pratt Graphic Center, Brooklyn, NY (PG); Joseph Kroll, Munich, Germany (JK); Stamperia Due Rossi, Rome, Italy (SDR); Artist (ART)
GALLERIES: Associated American Artists, New York, NY
MAILING ADDRESS: 37 Washington Sq, W, New York, NY 10011

TITLE	PUBLISHER	PRINTER	DATE	MEDIUM	DIMENSION (PAPER SIZE) IN INCHES	TYPE OF PAPER	EDITION NUMBER	NO. OF COLORS	ORIGINAL OPENING PRICE	CURRENT RETAIL PRICE
SOLD OUT EDITIONS (RARE):										
Come On Honey	PG	ART	1966	LC	24 X 36	R/100	20	3	35	300
Mid August	JK	ART	1972	SP	24 X 36	R/100	50	5	150	300
Old Game, New Rules	PG	ART	1975	LC	24 X 36	R/100	75	5	75	300
CURRENT EDITIONS:										
Variations on a Masque	ART	ART	1969	LC	19 X 27	R/100	100	3	90	200
Exits	ART	ART	1969	LC	19 X 27	R/100	100	3	90	200
Due Rossi	ART	ART	1969	LC	19 X 27	R/100	100	3	90	200
Munich Playground	JK	ART	1972	SP	24 X 36	R/100	50	4	150	250
Japanese Garden	ART	ART	1977	LC	19 X 25	R/100	75	3	95	200

E J GOLD

BORN: 1941
EDUCATION: Gutai Sch, Hokaido, Japan; Otis Art Inst, Los Angeles, CA
TEACHING: Otis Art Inst, Los Angeles, CA
RECENT EXHIB: Salon des Artistes/Galerie Matrix, NY, 1988; Mus of Ancient & Mod Art, Nevada City, CA, 1989; Connell Found for the Fine Arts, East Haven, CT, 1989; Hoho Gallery, Holyoke, MA, 1989
COLLECTIONS: Mus of Mod Art, NY; Univ of California, Los Angeles, CA; Houston Mus of Fine Arts, TX; Santa Barbara Mus, CA; Long Beach Mus, CA; Arizona State Univ, Tempe, AZ; Connoll Found for Fine Arts, East Haven, CT; Otis Art Inst, Los Angeles, CA; Mus of Ancient & Mod Art, Nevada City, CA; Univ of Southern California, Los Angeles, CA; Univ of California, Santa Barbara, CA; Crocker Mus, Sacramento, CA
PRINTERS: Robert Comara (RC); Bob Clarke (BC); Joe Green (JG); Karen Hellmich (KH); Artist (ART); Nancy Christie, CA (NC); Rose-Marie Jodouin, CA (RMJ)
PUBLISHERS: Robert Comara, Los Angeles, CA (RC); Heidelberg Editions International, Nevada City, CA (HEI); Mus of Ancient & Modern Art, Nevada City, CA (MAMA); Artist (ART)
GALLERIES: H Heather Edelman Gallery, New York, NY; Apocalypse Gallery, Vancouver, Canada; In-Between Gallery, Hollywood, CA; Nardin Fine Arts, Cross River, CT; State Street Gallery, New Haven, CT; Troov Gallery, Brooklyn, NY; Galleri Tonne, Oslo, Norway; Thunder Bear Gallery, Santa Fe, NM; Sergei Diaghilev Art Center, St Petersburg, Russia; Amherst Art Association, Amherst, MA
MAILING ADDRESS: c/o hei, P O Box 370, Nevada City, CA 95959

E J Gold
Odalisque IV
Courtesy Heidelberg Editions International

TITLE	PUBLISHER	PRINTER	DATE	MEDIUM	DIMENSION (PAPER SIZE) IN INCHES	TYPE OF PAPER	EDITION NUMBER	NO. OF COLORS	ORIGINAL OPENING PRICE	CURRENT RETAIL PRICE
SOLD OUT EDITIONS (RARE):										
May Rosenberg at the Cedar Bar	ART	ART	1959	MON	15 X 11 EA	AP	1 EA		200 EA	6200 EA
Artist at the Minetta Tavern	ART	ART	1959	WC	15 X 22	AP	10	1	150	1250
Portrait of Bill de Kooning at the Cedar Bar	ART	ART	1959	LB	15 X 11	AP	10	1	25	3000
Woman and Crutch	ART	ART	1963	LC	30 X 40	AP	10	3	100	3500
Study for the Crucifixion	ART	ART	1964	EC/SG	12 X 18	GE	16	2	100	2500
Prison Camp Floor	ART	ART	1964	EB/A	12 X 18	GE	10	2	100	4800
Jump God Jump	RC	ART	1965	WB	32 X 40	RICE	25	1	3500	9500
Mother with Child	ART	ART	1965	EB/A/DPT	15 X 17	CP	10	1	125	1500
Luciana	HEI	ART	1965	LB	11 X 15	AP	20	1	450	950
Black Crow with Sun	ART	ART	1966	EB/HC	12 X 14	AE	10	6	50	750
Nearly Naked Nun	ART	ART/JG	1966	I	12 X 14	GE	15	1	100	2500
Nearly Naked Nun	RC	ART	1966	LB	32 X 40	R/BFK	50	1	1200	7500
Sister Felicity	RC	ART/BC	1967	EB/DPT	12 X 14	GE	25	1	100	1500
Demiurge	HEI	ART	1967	LB	11 X 15	AP	20	1	600	1250
Long Neck Nude Madonna	HEI	ART	1967	LB	11 X 15	AP	50	1	600	800
Big Bird	HEI	ART	1986	SP	33 X 23	HC/RT	20	6	1000	3200

E J GOLD CONTINUED

E J Gold
Odalisque II
Courtesy Heidelberg Editions International

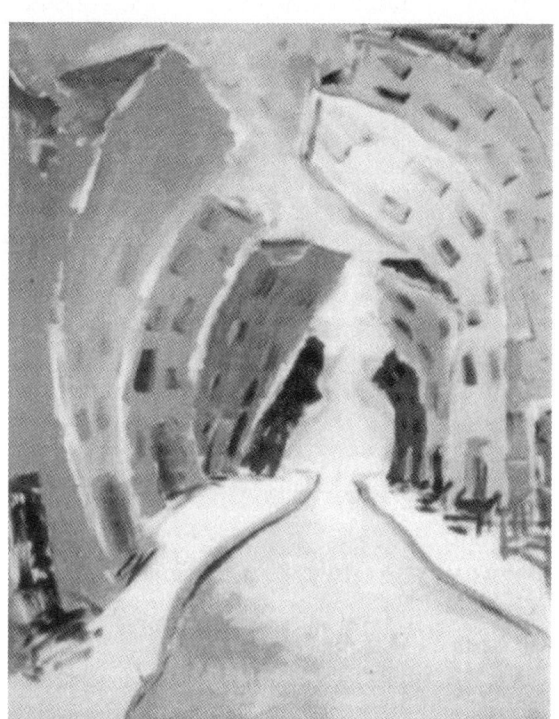

E J Gold
City in the Sky
Courtesy Heidelberg Editions International

TITLE	PUBLISHER	PRINTER	DATE	MEDIUM	DIMENSION (PAPER SIZE) IN INCHES	TYPE OF PAPER	EDITION NUMBER	NO. OF COLORS	ORIGINAL OPENING PRICE	CURRENT RETAIL PRICE
SOLD OUT EDITIONS (RARE):										
Disjointed Man	HEI	ART	1986	WB	38 X 50	LEN	10	1	1000	3500
The Bare Light Bulb	HEI	ART	1987	WB	15 X 22	R/BFK	75	1	2000	7500
Despair	HEI	ART	1987	WB	22 X 15	R/BFK	75	1	2000	5000
The White Folio (Set of 30)	MAMA	ART	1987	LB(20) SP(10)	11 X 15 EA	AP	50 EA		1500 SET	30000 SET
Es Regnet	HEI	ART	1987	WB	15 X 22	R/BFK	75	1	2000	4200
Checkered Table in Cafe	HEI	ART	1987	WB	15 X 22	AP	75	1	2000	4000
Checkered Table at Cafe	HEI	ART/KH	1987	SP	30 X 22	R/BFK	75	1	1200	2000
The Cellist	HEI	ART	1987	WB	22 X 15	R/BFK	75	1	2000	3000
The Edge of Thought	HEI	ART	1987	WB	15 X 22	R/BFK	75	1	2000	4800
The Coffee Cup	HEI	ART	1987	LI	15 X 22	R/BFK	75	1	2000	6500
A Bevy of Birdbrains	HEI	ART	1987	LB	11 X 15	AP	20	1	600	800
Circe La Femme	HEI	ART	1987	LB	11 X 15	AP	20	1	600	1400
The Matador's Woman	HEI	ART	1987	LB	11 X 15	AP	20	1	600	1400
The Matador's Ascension	HEI	ART	1987	LB	11 X 15	AP	15	1	600	1200
Young John Cage	HEI	ART	1987	LB	11 X 15	AP	10	1	500	900
Trying to Decide (Whether 6 + 6 is 12 or 6 + 6 are 12)	HEI	ART	1987	LB	11 X 15	AP	25	1	600	2100
Despair	HEI	ART/KH	1987	SP	22 X 30	R/BFK	75	1	500	500
The Bare Bulb	HEI	ART/KH	1987	SP	22 X 30	AP	75	1	800	1500
Odalisque I,II,III,IV	HEI	ART/KH	1987	SP	15 X 22 EA	R/BFK	75 EA	7/8/7/7	1200 EA	2000 EA
The Oak Room	HEI	ART/KH	1987	SP	15 X 22	R/BFK	45	10	1200	2200
The Cellist	HEI	ART/RH	1987	SP	22 X 30	AP	125	1	800	1200
The Cellist	HEI	ART	1987	LI	15 X 22	R/BFK	75	1	2000	3200
The Root is Taking Effect	HEI	ART	1986	SP	38 X 26	LEN	25	2	1000	2000
Nearly Naked Nun Standing	HEI	ART	1987	LB	11 X 15	AP	50	1	300	600
Mother Shapiro	HEI	ART	1987	LB	11 X 15	AP	50	1	300	700
Under the Penetrating Radiation	HEI	ART	1987	LB	11 X 15	AP	50	1	600	900
Oak Tree above the Road	HEI	ART	1987	LB	11 X 15	AP	10	1	500	600
Old Oak Tree	HEI	ART	1987	LB	11 X 15	AP	15	1	400	1800
Woodshed Behind the Artist's Studio	HEI	ART	1987	LB	11 X 15	AP	16	1	500	1800
Tahitian Long House	HEI	ART	1987	LB	11 X 15	AP	12	1	400	1500
Tree on the Bluff	HEI	ART	1987	LB	11 X 15	AP	8	1	300	500
Fisherman and Passing Boat	HEI	ART	1987	LB	11 X 15	AP	8	1	400	450
Larrabee Nude	HEI	ART	1987	LB	11 X 15	AP	50	1	300	800
Mayan Pterodactyl Rider	HEI	ART	1987	LB	11 X 15	AP	25	1	500	1800
Michaux Dancers	HEI	ART	1987	LB	11 X 15	AP	13	1	500	2500
Chapeau et Guitare I	HEI	ART	1987	LB	11 X 15	AP	16	1	700	1200

E J GOLD CONTINUED

TITLE	PUBLISHER	PRINTER	DATE	MEDIUM	DIMENSION (PAPER SIZE) IN INCHES	TYPE OF PAPER	EDITION NUMBER	NO. OF COLORS	ORIGINAL OPENING PRICE	CURRENT RETAIL PRICE
SOLD OUT EDITIONS (RARE):										
Chapeau et Guitare II	HEI	ART	1987	LB	11 X 15	AP	20	1	700	1200
Pleasant Conversation with Sombrero and Serape	HEI	ART	1987	LB	11 X 15	AP	15	1	700	700
Fresh Fruit	HEI	ART	1987	LB	11 X 15	AP	18	1	500	800
Street Corner Manhole	HEI	ART	1987	LB	11 X 15	AP	22	1	800	800
Backstage Curtain	HEI	ART	1987	LB	11 X 15	AP	20	1	700	900
Corner with Lamp Post and Fire Hydrant	HEI	ART	1987	LB	11 X 15	AP	20	1	700	900
A Very Narrow Alley	HEI	ART	1987	LB	11 X 15	AP	25	1	800	1200
Room with Window and Drape	HEI	ART	1987	LB	11 X 15	AP	15	1	600	1200
HMS Teapot	HEI	ART	1987	LB	11 X 15	AP	35	1	600	1500
Le Pompier Funebre	HEI	ART	1987	LB	11 X 15	AP	35	1	800	800
Cocktail Crocodile	HEI	ART	1987	LB	11 X 15	AP	50	1	600	900
Scarf and Jacket Series I	HEI	ART	1987	LB	11 X 15	AP	35	1	700	900
Nude in the Bijou Theatre	HEI	ART	1987	LB	11 X 15	AP	15	1	200	1400
Phantom Form	HEI	ART	1987	LB	11 X 15	AP	15	1	400	2100
Death Comes as a lover	HEI	ART	1987	LB	11 X 15	AP	25	1	500	2100
Inside Outside	HEI	ART	1987	LB	11 X 15	AP	25	1	600	2500
Tet Offensive '63	HEI	ART	1987	LB	11 X 15	AP	35	1	600	1800
Norton Street	HEI	ART	1987	LB	11 X 15	AP	20	1	500	1800
Overhead Perspective	HEI	ART	1987	LB	11 X 15	AP	10	1	600	1200
Room with No Door	HEI	ART	1987	LB	11 X 15	AP	25	1	600	2250
Dry Bones (in Mathematical Configuration #9)	HEI	ART	1987	LB	11 X 15	AP	10	1	200	650
Chamber with Stairs	HEI	ART	1987	LB	11 X 15	AP	10	1	600	800
In the Womb	HEI	ART	1987	SP	30 X 22	R/BFK	20	2	1200	1450
Whalemeat	HEI	ART	1987	SP	30 X 22	R/BFK	15	2	1800	2200
Io Plume	HEI	ART	1987	SP	20 X 13	R/BFK	15	3	1000	1250
Lady with Hairdo	HEI	ART	1987	SP	30 X 22	R/BFK	15	2	1800	2200
Matisse Monolith	HEI	ART	1987	SP	20 X 13	AP/TW	25	4	1200	1450
Musician	HEI	ART	1987	SP	20 X 13	AP/TW	25	4	1100	1350
Cactus Flower	HEI	ART	1987	SP	30 X 22	R/BFK	15	2	1200	1500
Simurgh	HEI	ART	1987	SP	20 X 13	AP/TW	25	4	600	900
Woman in Shower	HEI	ART/KH	1987	SP	30 X 22	R/BFK	75	1	800	2000
Woman Who Wasn't There in the Kitchen with Coffee Cup	HEI	ART/KH	1987	SP	30 X 22	R/BFK	75	1	800	2000
Odalisque I,III,IV	HEI	ART/KH	1987	SP	22 X 15 EA	R/BFK	75 EA	7 EA	1200 EA	1200 EA
Laundry Line, 10th Street	HEI	ART	1987	LB	11 X 15	AP	20	1	600	900
Javelin Thrower	HEI	ART	1987	LB	11 X 15	AP	25	1	500	600
Hypnotic Glance	HEI	ART	1987	LB	11 X 15	AP	10	1	600	2200
Exactitude is Not the Truth	HEI	ART	1987	LB	11 X 15	AP	10	1	500	2500
Danseuse Nue dans la Renombre	HEI	ART	1987	LB	11 X 15	AP	15	1	300	1350
Coffee Cup	HEI	ART/KH	1987	SP	30 X 22	R/BFK	75	1	1000	2000
Edge of Thought	HEI	ART/KH	1987	SP	30 X 22	R/BFK	75	1	800	2000
Es Regnet	HEI	ART/KH	1987	SP	30 X 22	R/BFK	75	1	800	2000
Relaxing Between Meals	HEI	ART	1987	LB	11 X 15	AP	50	1	400	1800
Pilgrim Monk	HEI	ART	1987	LB	11 X 15	AP	20	1	800	1800
Mad Woman	HEI	ART	1987	LB	11 X 15	AP	75	1	500	1500
Overhead Perspective, Cosmo St, 1970 (Brown Ink)	HEI	ART	1987	LC	11 X 15	AP	20	1	1200	1200
Macrodimensional Lovers (Brown Ink)	HEI	ART	1987	LC	11 X 15	AP	25	1	500	1800
Swept Away on the Wing (Brown Ink)	HEI	ART	1987	LC	11 X 15	AP	10	1	300	2000
Tet Offensive '63 (Sepia Ink)	HEI	ART	1987	LC	11 X 15	AP	35	1	700	1800
The Hermit (Sepia Ink)	HEI	ART	1987	LC	11 X 15	AP	25	1	700	1800
Guide (Sepia Ink)	HEI	ART	1987	LC	11 X 15	AP	10	1	300	1500
Odalisque II	HEI	ART/KH	1987	SP	22 X 15	R/BFK	75	8	1200	1200
Odalisque V, VI	HEI	ART/KH	1987	SP	22 X 15	R/BFK	75 EA	8 EA	1200 EA	2000 EA
Odalisque VII	HEI	ART/KH	1987	SP	22 X 15	R/BFK	75	9	1200	2000
Odalisque VIII	HEI	ART/KH	1987	SP	22 X 15	R/BFK	75	6	1200	2000
Looking Backwards (Brown Ink)	HEI	ART	1987	LC	11 X 15	AP	45	1	800	2000
Ne Plus Etre surson Terrain (Blue Ink)	HEI	ART	1987	LC	11 X 15	AP	12	1	400	900
Seated Death	HEI	ART	1987	LB	11 X 15	AP	15	1	500	1200
Snoman	HEI	ART	1987	LB	11 X 15	AP	10	1	250	1250
Very Thoughtful	HEI	ART	1987	LB	11 X 15	AP	50	1	400	1800
What Waits Outside	HEI	ART	1987	LB	11 X 15	AP	15	1	400	2100
Woodshed Behind the Artist's Studio	HEI	ART	1987	LB	11 X 15	AP	16	1	800	1800
Zen Circle Round Face	HEI	ART	1987	LB	11 X 15	AP	10	1	300	900
Despair	HEI	ART/KH	1987	SP	30 X 22	R/BFK	75	1	500	1800
Chess Player II	HEI	ART/KH	1987	SP	22 X 15	R/BFK	75	5	800	1200
Grinning Staircase (Brown Ink)	HEI	ART	1987	LC	11 X 15	AP	12	1	300	2500
Fat Monk (Sepia Ink)	HEI	ART	1987	LC	11 X 15	AP	10	1	500	2400
Dimensional Tweak (Green Ink)	HEI	ART	1987	LC	11 X 15	AP	II	1	500	800

E J GOLD CONTINUED

TITLE	PUBLISHER	PRINTER	DATE	MEDIUM	DIMENSION (PAPER SIZE) IN INCHES	TYPE OF PAPER	EDITION NUMBER	NO. OF COLORS	ORIGINAL OPENING PRICE	CURRENT RETAIL PRICE
SOLD OUT EDITIONS (RARE):										
Dreaming Monk, State I (Blue Ink)	HEI	ART	1987	LC	11 X 15	AP	20	1	400	1800
May Rosenberg	HEI	ART	1987	LB	11 X 15	AP	100	1	400	1400
An Amiable Disposition	HEI	ART	1987	LB	11 X 15	AP	6	1	450	1500
A Matter of Delicate Balance	HEI	ART	1988	LB	11 X 15	AP	35	1	300	2200
Persian Lamb	HEI	ART	1988	LB	11 X 15	AP	10	1	400	1200
Cactus Flower Buddha	HEI	ART	1988	LB	11 X 15	AP	15	1	300	2000
Curved Line Abstract	HEI	ART	1988	LB	11 X 15	AP	7	1	300	1000
He is So Delighted with His Nature	HEI	ART	1988	LB	11 X 15	AP	90	1	500	900
Inside Outside II	HEI	ART	1988	LB	11 X 15	AP	20	1	700	1000
Inside Outside III	HEI	ART	1988	LB	11 X 15	AP	50	1	700	1000
Kline's Trike	HEI	ART	1988	LB	11 X 15	AP	35	1	500	800
Kline's Bridge Trike	HEI	ART	1988	LB	11 X 15	AP	55	1	500	800
Corridor I,II,III	HEI	ART	1988	SP	30 X 22 EA	R/BFK	75 EA	5 EA	1200 EA	1500 EA
Horn Player at the Blue Note	HEI	ART/KH	1988	SP	22 X 15	R/BFK	75	4	900	1500
Michaux Dancers	HEI	ART/KH	1988	SP	25 X 19	HAM	75	1	1000	2000
Flying Boobs	HEI	ART/KH	1988	SP	22 X 15	R/BFK	75	3	800	1200
Riding the Broom	HEI	ART/KH	1988	SP	22 X 15	R/BFK	75	4	800	1200
Sanitarium Series Melting	HEI	ART/KH	1988	SP	30 X 22	R/BFK	75	12	1700	2200
Shrimpboat Boy	HEI	ART/KH	1988	SP	22 X 15	R/BFK	75	8	1100	1500
Morning Scene	HEI	ART	1989	SP	11 X 15	AP/W	25	10	100	1000
Red Sky in the Morning	HEI	ART	1989	SP	11 X 15	AP/W	25	22	100	1200
CURRENT EDITIONS:										
The Apprentice	HEI	ART	1988	SP	11 X 15	AP/W	25	6	100	450
Turquoise Table	HEI	ART	1988	SP	11 X 15	AP/W	25	5	100	650
Ladies in Blue	HEI	ART	1988	SP	11 X 15	AP/W	25	8	100	350
The Face in the Living Room Wall	HEI	ART	1988	SP	11 X 15	AP/W	25	7	100	350
The Deep Blue Window	HEI	ART	1988	SP	11 X 15	AP/W	25	10	100	650
The Flying Carousel	HEI	ART	1988	SP	11 X 15	AP/W	25	20	100	500
Weeping Madonna	HEI	ART	1988	SP	11 X 15	AP/W	25	4	100	400
10th Street	HEI	ART	1988	SP	11 X 15	AP/W	25	7	100	750
Landscape with Red Tile Roof	HEI	ART	1988	SP	11 X 15	AP/W	25	30	100	850
So Amused	HEI	ART	1988	SP	11 X 15	AP/W	25	6	100	400
Washington Bridge	HEI	ART	1988	SP	11 X 15	AP/W	25	20	100	600
And They Laughed with Joy	HEI	ART	1988	SP	11 X 15	AP/W	25	6	100	550
Dancing Cheek to Cheek	HEI	ART	1989	SP	11 X 15	AP/W	25	6	100	300
Spaced Invader	HEI	ART	1989	SP	11 X 15	AP/W	25	7	100	350
Lagash	HEI	ART	1989	SP	11 X 15	AP/W	25	8	100	300
The Lighthouse at Harrington Point	HEI	ART	1989	SP	11 X 15	AP/W	25	7	100	450
The Mirrored Carousel	HEI	ART	1989	SP	11 X 15	AP/W	25	11	100	500
Lady in Waiting	HEI	ART	1989	SP	11 X 15	AP/W	25	6	100	350
Under the Peak	HEI	ART	1989	SP	11 X 15	AP/W	25	11	100	450
Cote d'Azur	HEI	ART	1989	SP	11 X 15	AP/W	25	9	100	300
Countess Verushka	HEI	ART	1989	SP	11 X 15	AP/W	25	6	100	650
Bardo Station Bookstore	HEI	ART	1989	SP	11 X 15	AP/W	25	15	100	400
Brooding City	HEI	ART	1989	SP	11 X 15	AP/W	25	5	100	400
The Dog in the Moon is Now in Sight	HEI	ART	1989	SP	11 X 15	AP/W	25	4	100	350
The Hermit	HEI	ART	1989	SP	11 X 15	AP/W	25	5	100	750
The Small Pond	HEI	ART	1989	SP	11 X 15	AP/W	25	20	100	1000
Martha Graham	HEI	ART	1989	SP	11 X 15	AP/W	25	2	100	500
City in the Sky—Cobblestone	HEI	ART	1989	SP	11 X 15	AP/W	25	8	100	750
Which Way Did She Go?	HEI	ART	1989	SP	11 X 15	AP/W	25	6	100	300
Red Head Has the Blues	HEI	ART	1989	SP	11 X 15	AP/W	25	4	100	450
Harlequin	HEI	ART	1989	SP	11 X 15	AP/W	25	7	100	450
And Now for Dessert	HEI	ART	1989	SP	11 X 15	AP/W	25	4	100	450
Afternoon on the Lake	HEI	ART	1989	SP	11 X 15	AP/W	25	7	100	325
Village Square	HEI	ART	1989	SP	11 X 15	AP/W	25	20	100	1000
Monsoon Bay	HEI	ART	1989	SP	11 X 15	AP/W	25	8	100	450
Daisy in the Field	HEI	ART	1989	SP	11 X 15	AP/W	25	8	100	400
Posing	HEI	ART	1989	SP	11 X 15	AP/W	25	6	100	350
All Around Me—Sun, Sun, Sun	HEI	ART	1989	SP	11 X 15	AP/W	25	9	100	750
The Blue Nun	HEI	ART	1989	SP	11 X 15	AP/W	25	9	100	400
Mirror, Mirror on the Wall	HEI	ART	1989	SP	11 X 15	AP/W	25	7	100	350
Sitting at the Window	HEI	ART	1989	SP	11 X 15	AP/W	25	7	100	450
At the Opera	HEI	ART	1989	SP	11 X 15	AP/W	25	7	100	400
The Eternal Dilemma—Elevator or Stairs	HEI	ART	1989	SP	11 X 15	AP/W	25	8	100	600
Ecstatic Woman II	HEI	ART/NC	1990	SP	11 X 15	AP/W	25	15	100	300
She Who Sits by the Stove	HEI	ART/NC	1990	SP	11 X 15	AP/W	25	4	100	350
Landscape with Yellow Sun	HEI	ART/NC	1990	SP	11 X 15	AP/W	25	17	100	1000
Cubicula	HEI	ART	1990	SP	11 X 15	AP/W	25	6	100	400
Cosmo Turquoise with Green Vase	HEI	ART	1990	SP	11 X 15	AP/W	25	7	100	550
Star Eater	HEI	ART	1990	SP	11 X 15	AP/W	25	5	100	350

E J GOLD CONTINUED

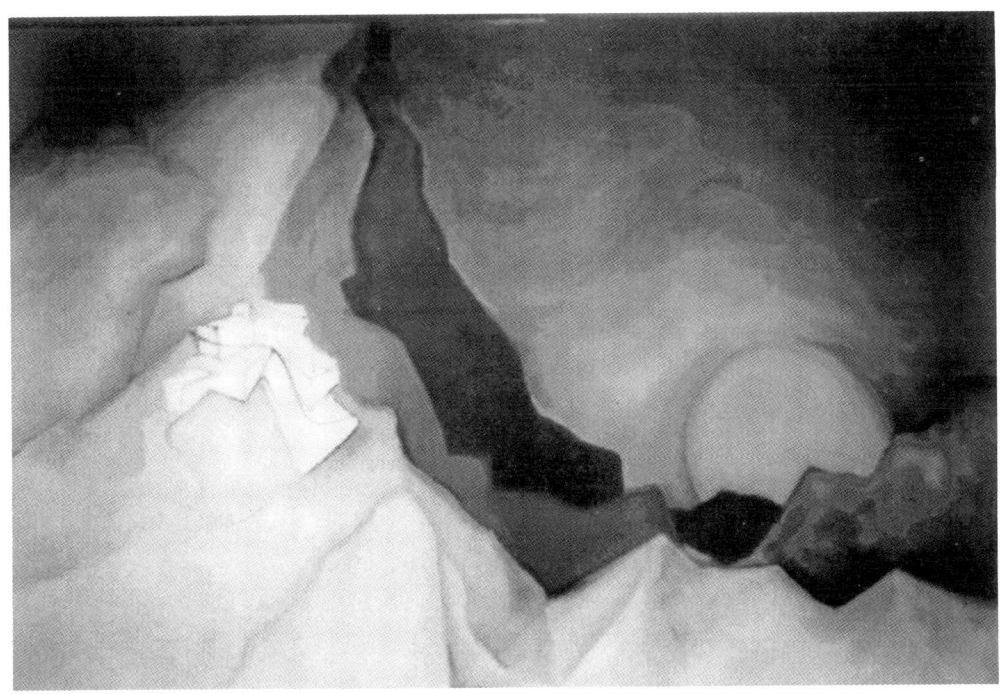

E J Gold
Landscape with Yellow Sun
Courtesy Heidelberg Editions International

TITLE	PUBLISHER	PRINTER	DATE	MEDIUM	DIMENSION (PAPER SIZE) IN INCHES	TYPE OF PAPER	EDITION NUMBER	NO. OF COLORS	ORIGINAL OPENING PRICE	CURRENT RETAIL PRICE
CURRENT EDITIONS:										
The Cat Walk	HEI	ART/NC	1990	SP	11 X 15	AP/W	25	7	100	300
The Quiet Gazebo	HEI	ART	1990	SP	11 X 15	AP/W	25	33	100	850
Natasha	HEI	ART	1990	SP	11 X 15	AP/W	25	7	100	500
L A Stetl	HEI	ART	1990	SP	11 X 15	AP/W	25	8	100	650
Valkyrie	HEI	ART	1990	SP	11 X 15	AP/W	25	4	100	400
Still Life with Red Table	HEI	ART	1990	SP	11 X 15	AP/W	25	13	100	750
Together Again	HEI	ART/NC	1990	SP	11 X 15	AP/W	25	6	100	350
Shangri-La	HEI	ART	1990	SP	11 X 15	AP/W	25	10	100	400
Duke of Earl	HEI	ART	1990	SP	11 X 15	AP/W	25	10	100	450
The Shadow Under the Door	HEI	ART	1990	SP	11 X 15	AP/W	25	7	100	300
My Public School	HEI	ART	1990	SP	11 X 15	AP/W	25	11	100	450
Macro Friends	HEI	ART	1990	SP	11 X 15	AP/W	25	4	100	450
The Wall is Covered with My Portrait	HEI	ART/NC	1990	SP	11 X 15	AP/W	25	4	100	350
Lake Placid	HEI	ART/NC	1990	SP	11 X 15	AP/W	25	8	100	450
Just a Little Sunday Stroll	HEI	ART/NC	1990	SP	11 X 15	AP/W	25	7	100	500
Young at Heart	HEI	ART/NC	1990	SP	11 X 15	AP/W	25	10	100	450
Le Pecheur	HEI	ART/NC	1991	SP	11 X 15	AP/W	25	9	100	500
Zaphod & Arthur at the Photomat	HEI	ART	1991	SP	11 X 15	AP/W	25	12	100	600
After School	HEI	ART/NC	1991	SP	11 X 15	AP/W	25	7	100	450
Yellow Haired Girl in a Green Wall	HEI	ART/NC	1991	SP	11 X 15	AP/W	25	6	100	350
Shamanic Voyage—Eagles										
Nest Sunday	HEI	ART/NC	1991	SP	11 X 15	AP/W	25	17	100	650
Through the Yellow	HEI	ART/NC	1991	SP	11 X 15	AP/W	25	9	100	300
Lady at Her Mirror	HEI	ART	1991	SP	11 X 15	AP/W	25	10	100	500
Class Clown	HEI	ART	1991	SP	11 X 15	AP/W	25	17	100	450
My Teal Blue Friends	HEI	ART/RMJ	1992	SP	9 X 15	AP/BL	25	8	100	500
Yellow Door	HEI	ART/RMJ	1992	SP	11 X 15	AP/BL	25	9	100	550
The Midway	HEI	ART/RMJ	1992	SP	9 X 15	AP/BL	25	15	100	450
In the Theatre	HEI	ART/RMJ	1992	SP	9 X 15	AP/BL	25	7	100	550
Empty Corridor	HEI	ART/RMJ	1992	SP	11 X 15	AP/BL	25	11	100	500
Angelic Warden	HEI	ART/RMJ	1992	SP	9 X 15	AP/BL	25	10	100	550
Land Beyond the Snow	HEI	ART/RMJ	1992	SP	9 X 15	AP/BL	25	6	100	500
House on the Side of the Road	HEI	ART/RMJ	1992	SP	9 X 15	AP/BL	25	8	100	500
Zen Gladness	HEI	ART	1993	SP	11 X 15	AP/W	25	6	100	300
Thirty Birds in a Full Moon for Late Night Tea	HEI	ART	1993	SP	11 X 15	AP/BL	25	12	100	500
A Narrow Escape	HEI	ART/RMJ	1993	SP	11 X 15	AP/W	25	8	100	400
One Moment Nearer My Eternity	HEI	ART/RMJ	1993	SP	9 X 11	AP/BL	25	11	100	400
She Waited at Home for the One	HEI	ART/RMJ	1993	SP	11 X 15	AP/BL	25	12	100	450
A Warm Welcome	HEI	ART/RMJ	1993	SP	9 X 11	AP/W	25	12	100	450
The Sun Knew the Valley from an Earlier Rise	HEI	ART	1993	SP	9 X 11	AP/W	25	7	100	350
Be It Ever So Humble	HEI	ART	1993	SP	9 X 11	AP/BL	25	10	100	450
The Blue Astronaut	HEI	ART/RMJ	1993	SP	9 X 11	AP/BL	25	9	100	400
Me and My Money	HEI	ART	1993	SP	11 X 15	AP/BL	25	15	100	500

GLENN GOLDBERG

BORN: Bronx, NY; August 31, 1953
EDUCATION: New York Studio Sch, NY; Queens Col, Flushing, NY, MFA
AWARDS: Edward Albee Found Grant, Montauk, NY, 1984; Guggenheim Fel, 1988–89
TEACHING: Lectr, New York Studio Sch, NY, 1988; Lectr, Montclair State Col, NJ, 1988; Lectr, Univ of Texas, Austin, TX, 1988
RECENT EXHIB: Willard Gallery, NY, 1987; Barbara Krakow Gallery, Boston, MA, 1988; Editions Ilene Kurtz, NY, 1988; Hoffman Borman Gallery, Santa Monica, CA, 1988; Albany Mus of Art, NY, 1989; Greenberg Gallery, St Louis, MO, 1988,90; Lincoln Center, Fine Arts Prints, Avery Fisher Hall, NY, 1992; J Rosenthal Fine Art, Chicago, IL, 1992; Wilkey Fine Art, Seattle, WA, 1992; M Knoedler Gallery, NY, 1988,92
COLLECTIONS: Metropolitan Mus of Art, NY; Nat Gallery of Art, Wash, DC; Brooklyn Mus, NY; High Mus, Atlanta, GA; Mus of Contemp Art, Los Angeles, CA
PRINTERS: Spring Street Workshop, NY (SSW); Karl Hecksher, NY (KH); K5, Brooklyn, NY (K5); Artist (ART)
PUBLISHERS: Editions Ilene Kurtz, NY (EIK); Spring Street Workshop, NY (SSW); K5, Brooklyn, NY (K5); Artist (ART)
GALLERIES: Fred Hoffman Gallery, Los Angeles, CA; Barbara Krakow Gallery, Boston, MA; Editions Ilene Kurtz, New York, NY; M Knoedler & Company, New York, NY; Pace Prints, New York, NY; Greenberg Gallery, St Louis, MO; J Rosenthal Fine Art, Chicago, IL; Wilkey Fine Art, Seattle, WA; Klein Art Works, Chicago, IL; Hill Gallery, Birmingham, MI
MAILING ADDRESS: c/o Editions Ilene Kurtz, Room 1004, 568 Broadway, New York, NY 10012

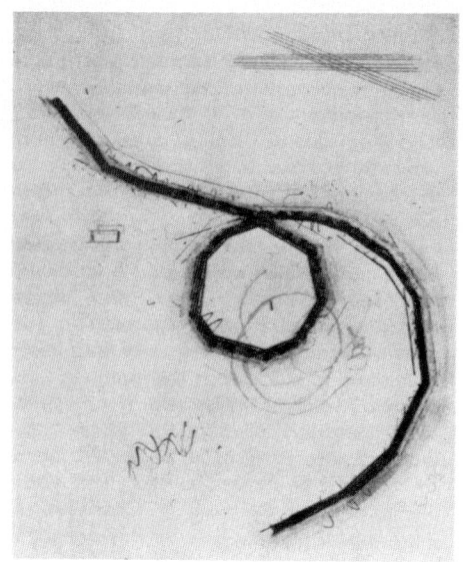
Glenn Goldberg
Coil Print
Courtesy Editions Ilene Kurtz

TITLE	PUBLISHER	PRINTER	DATE	MEDIUM	DIMENSION (PAPER SIZE) IN INCHES	TYPE OF PAPER	EDITION NUMBER	NO. OF COLORS	ORIGINAL OPENING PRICE	CURRENT RETAIL PRICE
CURRENT EDITIONS:										
Coil Print	EIK		1986	EC/DPT	30 X 22	AC	35		1200	1500
Paco & JJ	EIK		1987	EB/A	36 X 29	AC	25		1500	1700
Drifter Plus (Set of 3)	SSW	SSW	1989	REL	26 X 20 EA	AC	35 EA		2500 SET	2700 SET
Delta #1–#4 (Set of 4)	ART/KH	ART/KH/K5	1991	WC		KOZO	16 EA		2500 SET	2500 SET

MICHAEL GOLDBERG

BORN: New York, NY; December 24, 1924
EDUCATION: Arts Students League, NY, 1938–42; City Col of New York, NY, 1940–42; Han Hofmann Sch, 1941–42; 1948–50; Art Students League, NY, 1946
TEACHING: Univ of California, Berkeley, CA, 1961–62; Yale Univ, New Haven, CT, 1967; Univ of Minnesota, Saint Paul, MN 1968
RECENT EXHIB: Louver Gallery, Venice, CA, 1987; Bass Art Mus, Miami Beach, FL, 1987; Gallery Camino Real, Boca Raton, FL, 1987; Bette Stoller Gallery, NY, 1987; Claudia Nastuzzo, Salo, Italy, 1988; Stacke Gallery, Copenhagen, Denmark, 1988,89; Vanderwoude/Tananbaum Gallery, NY, 1987,90; Galerie Peccolo, Livorno, Italy, 1988,90; Galerie Weinberger, Copenhagen, Denmark, 1990; Plumira Gallery, Udine, Italy, 1990; Turchetto/Plumira Gallery, Milan, Italy, 1990; Lennon/Weinberg Gallery, NY, 1991; Lafayette Col Gallery, Easton, PA, 1989,92
COLLECTIONS: Mus of Mod Art, Israel; Art Inst of Chicago, IL; Dayton Art Inst, OH; Nat Gallery of Art, Wash, DC; Mus of Western Art, Tokyo, Japan
PRINTERS: X-Press, NY (XP)
PUBLISHERS: Orion Editions, NY (OE)
GALLERIES: Orion Editions, New York, NY; Vanderwoude/Tananbaum Gallery, New York, NY; Manny Silverman Gallery, Los Angeles, CA; Harris Samuel & Co, Inc, Miami Beach, FL; Edward Tyler Nahem Fine Art, New York, NY; Lennon/Weinberg Gallery, New York, NY; Stacke Gallery, Copenhagen, Denmark; Galerie Peccolo, Livorno, Italy; Bette Stoller Gallery, New York, NY; Turchetto/Plurima Gallery, Milan, Italy; Claudia Nastuzzo, Salo, Italy; CompassRose Gallery, Ltd, Chicago, IL
MAILING ADDRESS: 222 Bowery, New York, NY 10012

Michael Goldberg
Family V
Courtesy the Artist

The retail prices of the 100,000 limited edition prints quoted in this directory are subject to change. Print publishers, artists and galleries were the direct sources for these quotations. Prices in the secondary market listed as "Sold Out Editions (Rare)" indicate that the publisher has a limited supply of that print or that the print is difficult to locate in the galleries.

The Printworld Directory is accepting new applications for the seventh edition. Approximately 300 new artists will be accepted. Please use the two forms provided in the back section of this directory to submit biographical data and documentation of prints. Edition number of each print must not exceed 500 and the retail price must be $100 or more.

MICHAEL GOLDBERG CONTINUED

TITLE	PUBLISHER	PRINTER	DATE	MEDIUM	DIMENSION (PAPER SIZE) IN INCHES	TYPE OF PAPER	EDITION NUMBER	NO. OF COLORS	ORIGINAL OPENING PRICE	CURRENT RETAIL PRICE
CURRENT EDITIONS:										
Codex Coner Mesura di Ventura (with Bronze Powder)	OE	XP	1981	EC	42 X 32	GE	38	4	450	850
Codex Coner Braccio Fiorentino State I (with Bronze Powder)	OE	XP	1981	EC/PO/CO	31 X 44	GE	12	4	400	850
Codex Coner Braccio Fiorentino State II (with Bronze Powder)	OE	XP	1981	EC/PO/CO	31 X 33	GE	20	4	400	850
Codex Coner Braccio Fiorento (with Bronze Powder)	OE	XP	1981	EB	30 X 22	GE	20	2	200	200

LIBBY GOLDEN

BORN: New York, NY; November 18, 1913
EDUCATION: Cooper Union, NY, 1934; Art Students League, NY, Hunter Col, NY, 1934–38; Art Students League, NY, 1938–42; New York Univ, NY; Pratt Graphics Art Inst, NY, 1958–60
AWARDS: Print Prizes, Michigan State Fair, 1965–69; Grant, Nat Acad of Design, NY, 1969; Purchase Prize, Michigan Painters & Printmakers & Colorprint, USA, 1970
RECENT EXHIB: Preston Burke Gallery, Detroit, MI, 1988
COLLECTIONS: Philadelphia Mus of Art, PA; Detroit Inst of Art, MI; Grand Rapids Art Mus, MI; Art Mus of Richmond, VA; Arizona State Univ, Tempe, AZ; Scottsdale Center for the Arts, AZ; Flint Inst of Art, MI; Colby Col Art Mus, Waterville, ME
PRINTERS: Artist (ART)
PUBLISHERS: Artist (ART)
GALLERIES: Joy Tash Gallery, Scottsdale, AZ; Associated American Artists, New York, NY
MAILING ADDRESS: 7527 N Del Norte Dr, Scottsdale, AZ 85258

TITLE	PUBLISHER	PRINTER	DATE	MEDIUM	DIMENSION (PAPER SIZE) IN INCHES	TYPE OF PAPER	EDITION NUMBER	NO. OF COLORS	ORIGINAL OPENING PRICE	CURRENT RETAIL PRICE
SOLD OUT EDITIONS (RARE):										
Quintette	ART	ART	1966	SP	5 X 14	STR	12	22	60	300
Zealots	ART	ART	1966	SP	22 X 28	AP	15	35	75	650
Masada	ART	ART	1967	SP	20 X 28	STR	18	80	75	850
Mirrors	ART	ART	1968	SP	22 X 28	AP	15	50	75	750
Kabuki Dialogue	ART	ART	1971	SP	24 X 30	JP	15	40	125	800
CURRENT EDITIONS:										
Series of 25	ART	ART	1982	MON	18 X 24 EA	STR	1 EA	10 EA	750 EA	800 EA
Suite of 14	ART	ART	1982	SP	22 X 28 EA	STR	50 EA	30 EA	750 EA	800 EA

ROLLAND HARVE GOLDEN

BORN: New Orleans, LA; 1931
AWARDS: First Peace Award, Nat Arts Club, NY, 1979–90
RECENT EXHIB: Nat Arts Club, NY, 1987,88,90
COLLECTIONS: Paskin Mus, Moscow, Russia; Springfield Mus of Art, MO; New Orleans Mus, LA; Mississippi Mus of Art, Jackson, MS; Masur Mus, Monroe, LA; Wichita Falls Mus, KS; Zigler Mus, Jennings, LA; St John's Mus of Art, Wilmington, NC
PUBLISHERS: Nahan Editions, New Orleans, LA (NE)
MAILING ADDRESS: 78207 Woods Hole Lane, Folsom, LA 70437

TITLE	PUBLISHER	PRINTER	DATE	MEDIUM	DIMENSION (PAPER SIZE) IN INCHES	TYPE OF PAPER	EDITION NUMBER	NO. OF COLORS	ORIGINAL OPENING PRICE	CURRENT RETAIL PRICE
CURRENT EDITIONS:										
Autumn Tapestry I,II	NE		1988	LC	37 X 26 EA	AP	125 EA	6 EA	300 EA	300 EA
Woodland Symphony/Opus I–IV	NE		1988	LC/CO	35 X 25 EA	AP	65 EA	8 EA	550 EA	550 EA
Reverie	NE		1989	LC	34 X 24	AP	175		600	600
Parc Mysterieux	NE		1990	LC	33 X 24	AP	175	8	600	600

JANE E GOLDMAN

BORN: Dallas, TX; June 26, 1951
EDUCATION: Smith Col, Northampton, MA, Studio Art, BFA; Univ of Wisconsin, Madison, WI, Graphics Arts, MFA
TEACHING: Univ of California, Los Angeles, CA, Printmaking, 1981
AWARDS: Massachusetts Council on the Arts Fel, 1979; Yaddo Residency, 1981; MacDowell Colony Residency, 1982; Projection Completion Award, Massachusetts Council on the Arts, 1984
COLLECTIONS: Elvehjem Mus, Univ of Wisconsin, Madison, WI; Cleveland Mus, OH; Brooklyn Mus, NY; Detroit Inst of Art, MI; DeCordova Mus, Lincoln, MA; Smith Col Library, Northampton, MA; Univ of Texas, Austin, TX; Toledo Mus, OH; Wellesley Col, MA; Bibliotheque Nat, Paris, France; Grunewald Center, Univ of California, Los Angeles, CA
PRINTERS: Paul M Maguire, Boston, MA (PM); Flat Rock Press, Boston, MA (FRP); Norman Stewart, Bloomfield Hills, MI (NS); Wing Lake Studio, Bloomfield Hills, MI (WLS); Joe Keenan (JK); B Palmer (BP); Peter Juneau (PJ); Artist (ART)
PUBLISHERS: Stewart & Stewart, Bloomfield Hills, MI (S-S); Artist (ART)
GALLERIES: Clifford Gallery, Dallas, TX; Associated American Artists, New York, NY; van Straaten Gallery, Chicago, IL; Randall Beck Gallery, Boston, MA; Grace Chosy Gallery, Madison, WI
MAILING ADDRESS: 32 Clifton St, Somerville, MA 02144

The retail prices of the 100,000 limited edition prints quoted in this directory are subject to change. Print publishers, artists and galleries were the direct sources for these quotations. Prices in the secondary market listed as "Sold Out Editions (Rare)" indicate that the publisher has a limited supply of that print or that the print is difficult to locate in the galleries.

The Printworld Directory is accepting new applications for the seventh edition. Approximately 300 new artists will be accepted. Please use the two forms provided in the back section of this directory to submit biographical data and documentation of prints. Edition number of each print must not exceed 500 and the retail price must be $100 or more.

JANE E GOLDMAN CONTINUED

TITLE	PUBLISHER	PRINTER	DATE	MEDIUM	DIMENSION (PAPER SIZE) IN INCHES	TYPE OF PAPER	EDITION NUMBER	NO. OF COLORS	ORIGINAL OPENING PRICE	CURRENT RETAIL PRICE
SOLD OUT EDITIONS:										
Back Porch Reflections #3	ART	ART	1981	EC	17 X 32	R/BFK	100	8	300	1800
Back Porch Reflections #5	ART	PM/FRP	1982	LC	22 X 30	R/BFK	55	5	275	2100
Corner Reflections #2	ART	ART	1982	EC	22 X 30	R/BFK	100	9	250	2100
Dallas Reflections #15	S-S	NS/JK/WLS	1983	SP	22 X 30	R/BFK	47	29	350	1500
Green Street	ART	ART	1983	EC	23 X 41	R/BFK	100	12	325	2400
Grassmere Lane	S-S	NS/WLS	1983	SP	22 X 30	R/BFK	44	22	350	2400
Dallas Reflections #16	ART	ART	1984	EC	27 X 35	R/BFK	100	16	350	1500
Breezeway #7	S-S	NS/JK/WLS	1986	SP	29 X 21	R/BFK/W	67	24	325	2100
CURRENT EDITIONS:										
Summer Nights	S-S	NS/JK/WLS	1984	SP	22 X 30	R/BFK	60	30	350	900
Mid-Summer Light	S-S	NS/JK/WLS	1987	SP	22 X 30	R/BFK/W	66	28	450	1500
Sun Porch	S-S	NS/JK/BP/PJ/WLS	1988	SP	29 X 21	R/BFK/W	60	29	500	950
To the Garden	S-S	NS/JK/WLS	1989	SP	22 X 30	R/BFK/W	62	20	600	900
Ellen's Window	S-S	NS/JK/WLS	1990	SP	30 X 22	R/BFK/W	64	20	850	850

JACK GOLDSTEIN

BORN: Montreal, Canada; September 27, 1945
EDUCATION: Chouinard Art Inst, Los Angeles, CA, BFA, 1970; California Inst of the Arts, Valencia, CA, MFA, 1972
AWARDS: Canadian Council on the Arts Grant, 1973–74; Production Grant, New York State Council on the Arts, 1977; Nat Endowment for the Arts Fel, 1979–80
RECENT EXHIB: Dart Gallery, Chicago, IL, 1988; Mus of Contemp Arts, Los Angeles, CA, 1989; Scott Hanson Gallery, NY, 1989
COLLECTIONS: Mus of Mod Art, Geneva, Switzerland; Brooklyn Mus, NY

PRINTERS: Handworks, NY (H); Maurel Studio, NY; Sheila Marbain (SM); Frank Versaggi (FV); Editions Schellmann & Klüser, Munich, West Germany & NY (SK)
PUBLISHERS: Editions Schellmann & Klüser, Munich, West Germany (SK)
GALLERIES: Editions Schellmann, New York, NY; Dart Gallery, Chicago, IL; Vared Gallery, East Hampton, NY; Metro Pictures, New York, NY; Pace Prints, New York, NY; John Weber Gallery, New York, NY; Asher/Faure Gallery, Los Angeles, CA; Eve Mannes Gallery, Atlanta, GA; Carl Solway Gallery, Cincinnati, OH
MAILING ADDRESS: 138 Prince St, New York, NY 10012

TITLE	PUBLISHER	PRINTER	DATE	MEDIUM	DIMENSION (PAPER SIZE) IN INCHES	TYPE OF PAPER	EDITION NUMBER	NO. OF COLORS	ORIGINAL OPENING PRICE	CURRENT RETAIL PRICE
CURRENT EDITIONS:										
Untitled (Set of 2):										
Fireworks	SK	SM/FV/SK	1983	LC/SP	30 X 40	AP	55	Multi	500	1200
Lightning	SK	SM/FV/SK	1983	LC/SP	30 X 40	AP	55	Multi	500	1200

DANIEL JOSHUA GOLDSTEIN

BORN: Mount Vernon, NY; June 19, 1950
EDUCATION: Brandeis Univ, Waltham, MA; Univ of Santa Cruz, CA, BA; St Martins Col, London, England
AWARDS: Purchase Prize, Palo Alto Cultural Center, CA, 1973
COLLECTIONS: Brooklyn Mus, NY; Achenbach Found, San Francisco, CA; Rhode Island Sch of Design, Providence, RI; Chicago Art Inst, IL; Hunt Inst, Pittsburgh, PA; Carnegie Inst, Pittsburgh, PA

PRINTERS: James Phelan, San Francisco, CA (JP); Canyon Editions, San Francisco, CA (CanEd); Artist (ART)
PUBLISHERS: Canyon Editions, San Francisco, CA (CanEd); Artist (ART)
GALLERIES: Fischbach Gallery, New York, NY; Concept Gallery, Pittsburgh, PA; Nancy Singer Gallery, St Louis, MO; The Art Collector, San Diego, CA; Neville-Sargent Gallery, Chicago, IL; Robley Gallery, Roslyn, NY; Ed Hill Gallery, El Paso, TX; Young Gallery, Los Gatos, CA
MAILING ADDRESS: 224 Guerrero St, San Francisco, CA 94103

TITLE	PUBLISHER	PRINTER	DATE	MEDIUM	DIMENSION (PAPER SIZE) IN INCHES	TYPE OF PAPER	EDITION NUMBER	NO. OF COLORS	ORIGINAL OPENING PRICE	CURRENT RETAIL PRICE
SOLD OUT EDITIONS (RARE):										
Suite for Virginia Woolf: Daybreak, Afternoon, Evening, Night (Set of 4):	ART	ART	1975	WB	30 X 23 EA	HOSH	75 EA	7 EA	400 SET	3000 SET
Rocks I, the Lake	ART	ART	1976	WC	41 X 29	OKP	75	10	120	1000
Rocks II, the Cove	ART	ART	1976	WC	41 X 29	OKP	75	10	120	1000
Evening Iris	ART	ART	1976	WC	29 X 58	OKP	75	10	180	2000
Rocks III, Shumisen (Trip)	ART	ART	1977	WC	29 X 37	LEN/100	90	6	450	2000
Water Garden/Homage to Bachelard (Dipt)	ART	ART	1977	WC	41 X 29	LEN/100	125	10	350	1800
Islands	ART	ART	1978	WC	36 X 48	LEN/100	90	6	275	1000
Canyon/Passages Suite	ART	ART	1978	WC	24 X 19 EA	LANA	75 EA	1 EA	400 SET	2000 SET
Red Canyon	CanEd	JP/CanED	1978	WC	40 X 29	LEN/100	100	7	250	1000
Green Canyon	CanEd	JP/CanED	1978	WC	40 X 29	LEN/100	100	7	250	1000
Tulips and Window	ART	ART	1979	WC	48 X 30	LEN/100	100	16	375	1200
Iris Suite	CanEd	JP/CanED	1980	WC	29 X 29 EA	LANA	100	7	800 SET	2500 SET
CURRENT EDITIONS:										
Grey Canyon	CanEd	JP/CanED	1978	WC	40 X 29	LEN/100	100	7	250	1000

DANIEL JOSHUA GOLDSTEIN CONTINUED

TITLE	PUBLISHER	PRINTER	DATE	MEDIUM	DIMENSION (PAPER SIZE) IN INCHES	TYPE OF PAPER	EDITION NUMBER	NO. OF COLORS	ORIGINAL OPENING PRICE	CURRENT RETAIL PRICE
CURRENT EDITIONS:										
Nectarine Blossoms	ART	JP/CanED	1981	WC	24 X 39		100		250	500
Nocturne (Dipt)	ART	JP/CanED	1983	MM	38 X 27	LEN/AP	100	18	800	2000
The Purple Room	CanEd	JP/CanED	1983	WC/CO	36 X 27	LEN/AP	100	20	375	800
Offering Suite, IV, V, VI, VII, VIII	ART	JP/CanED	1984	MM	29 X 29 EA	LEN/OKP	100 EA	Varies	1600 EA	2000 EA

JOSEPH GOLDYNE

BORN: Chicago, IL; 1942
EDUCATION: Univ of California, Berkeley, CA, AB, 1964; Univ of California, San Francisco, CA, MD; 1968; Harvard Univ, Cambridge, MA, 1970
RECENT EXHIB: John Berggruen Gallery, San Francisco, CA, 1990
COLLECTIONS: Achenbach Found for the Graphic Arts, San Francisco Fine Arts Mus, CA; Crocker Mus, Sacramento, CA; Davidson Col, NC
PRINTERS: Smith Andersen Gallery, Palo Alto, CA (3EP); David Kelso, Oakland, CA (DK); Made in California, Oakland, CA (MIC); Magnolia Editions, Oakland, CA (MEd); Donald Farnsworth (DF); Stuart McKee (SM); Rick Dula (RD); Roxanne Gilbert (RG)
PUBLISHERS: Smith Andersen Gallery, Palo Alto, CA (3EP); Magnolia Editions, Oakland, CA (MEd); Made in California, Oakland, CA (MIC); Artist (ART)
GALLERIES: John Berggruen Gallery, San Francisco, CA; Klein Art Works, Chicago, IL; Victoria Munroe Gallery, New York, NY; Smith Andersen Gallery, Palo Alto, CA; Graystone Gallery, San Francisco, CA; Young Gallery, Los Gatos, CA; Made in California, Oakland, CA; Magnolia Editions, Oakland, CA; Roger Ramsay Gallery, Chicago, IL; Richard York Gallery, New York, NY

TITLE	PUBLISHER	PRINTER	DATE	MEDIUM	DIMENSION (PAPER SIZE) IN INCHES	TYPE OF PAPER	EDITION NUMBER	NO. OF COLORS	ORIGINAL OPENING PRICE	CURRENT RETAIL PRICE
SOLD OUT EDITIONS (RARE):										
Crystal Vase	3EP	3EP	1979	EB/A	16 X 13	HMP	20		200	900
Palm Promenade	3EP	3EP	1981	EB/HC	18 X 10	HMP	20	Varies	250	600
CURRENT EDITIONS:										
Dirty Dish	3EP	3EP	1979	EB/HC	16 X 22	HMP	20	Varies	200	900
Garbage Can	3EP	3EP	1979	EB/A	22 X 15	HMP	25		200	900
Sandstorm	3EP	3EP	1981	EB/A	14 X 10	HMP	25		250	750
Palm Promenade	3EP	3EP	1981	EB/HC	18 X 10	HMP	20	Varies	250	750
Tall & Thin	ART/MIC	DK/MIC	1981	EB/CC	14 X 10	KIT/R-BFK	26	1	225	600
Jewish Cemetery, Colma	ART/MIC	DK/MIC	1981	EB/DPT/A/HC/CC	14 X 10	HOSHO/AP-B	6	Varies	225	500
Fish Platter	ART/MIC	DK/MIC	1981	A/DPT/SB/SC/M	22 X 15	R/BFK/W	25		225	500
Three Green Peppers	ART	MIC	1981	A/DPT/SB	15 X 11	R/BFK	10		400	500
Three Peppers Red	ART	MIC	1981	A/DPT/SB	15 X 11	R/BFK	10		400	500
Three Tulips	MEd		1983	LC	40 X 19	AP/B	50		600	800
Three Pots	MEd		1983	LC	40 X 19	AP/B	50		600	800
Night Choir	ART	DK/MIC	1983	A/DPT	14 X 10	JWP	20	4	700	800
Opening	ART	DK/MIC	1983	A/DPT	14 X 10	JWP	20	4	700	800
Mum	ART	DK/MIC	1983	MON	9 X 6 EA	JWP	1 EA	Varies	800 EA	1000 EA
Sweater Closet at Dusk	ART/MEd	DF/SM/MEd	1984	LC	30 X 22	AP	70	25	650	800
Sweater Closet at Dusk	ART/MEd	DF/SM/MEd	1984	LC	30 X 22	HMP	70	25	650	800
Quartet	ART/MEd	DF/SM/MEd	1986	EB	7 X 5	HMP	130	1	800	900
High Spectacle (with Gold Leaf)	MEd	DF/RD/RG/MEd	1988	WC	30 X 21	FrP	39		1000	1200

FÉLIX GONZÁLEZ-TORRES

BORN: Cuba; 1957; US Citizen
EDUCATION: Pratt Inst, Brooklyn, NY, BFA, 1983; Whitney Mus Independent Study Program, NY, 1981,83; Int Center for Photography, New York Univ, NY, MFA, 1987
TEACHING: Adj Inst, Art, New York Univ, NY, 1989; Calarts, Los Angeles, CA, 1990; Prof, New York Univ, NY, 1992
AWARDS: Artist Fel, Art Matter, Inc, 1988,89; Cintas Found Fel, 1989; Pollock-Krasner Found Grant, 1989; Nat Endowment for the Arts Fel, 1989, Fordon Matta-Clark Found Award, 1991; Deutscher Akademischer Austauschdienst Fel, Artist in Residence Program, Berlin, Germany, 1992
RECENT EXHIB: New Mus of Contemp Art, NY, 1988; Intar Gallery, NY, 1988; Rastovski Gallery, NY, 1988; Brooklyn Mus, NY, 1989; Univ of British Columbia, Vancouver, Canada, 1990; Neue Gesellschaft fur Bildende Kunst, Berlin, Germany, 1990; Julia Sylvester Editions, NY, 1991; Mus Fridericianum, Kassel, Germany, 1991; Massimo de Carl, Milan, Italy, 1991; Luhring Augustine Hetzler, Los Angeles, CA, 1991; Galerie Peter Pakesch, Vienna, Austria, 1992; Teweles Gallery, Milwaukee Art Mus, WI, 1993; Andrea Rosen Gallery, NY, 1990,92,93
PRINTERS: Columbia Graphics, NY (CGr)
PUBLISHERS: Andrea Rosen Gallery, NY (ARG); Santa Monica Editions, CA (SME)
GALLERIES: Andrea Rosen Gallery, New York, NY; Galerie Peter Pakesch, Vienna, Austria
MAILING ADDRESS: c/o Andrea Rosen Gallery, 130 Prince St, New York, NY 10012

TITLE	PUBLISHER	PRINTER	DATE	MEDIUM	DIMENSION (PAPER SIZE) IN INCHES	TYPE OF PAPER	EDITION NUMBER	NO. OF COLORS	ORIGINAL OPENING PRICE	CURRENT RETAIL PRICE
SOLD OUT EDITIONS (RARE):										
Untitled (Boxed Paper Stack—1500 Sheets in Each Stack)	ARG/SME	CGr	1990-91	MULT	14 X 14 X 8	HamC/65	12 EA		3500	6000

LEON GOLUB

BORN: Chicago, IL; January 23, 1922
EDUCATION: Univ of Chicago, IL, BA, 1942; Chicago Art Inst Sch, IL, BFA, 1949, MFA, 1950; Indiana Univ, Bloomington, IN, 1957–59
TEACHING: Tyler Sch of Fine Arts, Temple Univ, Phila, PA, 1965–66; Sch of Visual Arts, NY, 1966–69; Rutgers Univ, Newark, NJ, 1970 to present
AWARDS: Florsheim Mem Prize, Art Inst of Chicago, IL, 1954; Ford Found Grant, 1960; Watson F Blair Prize, Art Inst of Chicago, IL, 1960; Cassandra Found Grant, 1967; Guggenheim Found Fel, 1968; Nat Inst of Arts & Letters, NY, 1973; Am Acad of Arts & Letters, NY, 1973; William H Bartels, Martin B Cahn & Walter M Campana Award, Art Inst of Chicago, IL, 1986; Skowhegan Medal for Painting, ME, 1988
RECENT EXHIB: Orchard Gallery, Derry, Northern Ireland, 1987; Kunstmuseum, Luzern, Switzerland, 1987; Saatchi Collection, London, England, 1988; Douglas Hyde Gallery, Dublin, Northern Ireland, 1988; Fawbush Gallery, NY, 1988; Barbara Gladstone Gallery, NY, 1988; Rhona Hoffman Gallery, Chicago, IL, 1989; Eli Broad Family Found, Los Angeles, CA, 1989; Whatcom Mus of History & Art, Bellingham, WA, 1989; Cleveland Center for Contemporary Art-The Galleria, OH, 1989; Galerie Darthea Speyer, Paris, France, 1987,90; Inst of Comtemp Art, Phila, PA, 1992; Spertus Mus of Judaica, Chicago, IL, 1992; Cleveland Inst of Art, Reinberger Galleries, OH, 1992; Palo Alto Cultural Center, CA, 1992
COLLECTIONS: Mus of Mod Art, NY; Art Inst of Chicago, IL; Amon Carter Mus of Western Art, Fort Worth, TX; Hirshhorn Mus, Wash, DC; Pasadena Art Mus, CA; Nat Coll of Fine Arts, Wash, DC; Saatchi Coll, London, England; Eli Broad Family Found, Los Angeles, CA
PRINTERS: Maurice Sanchez, NY (MS); Derriere L'Etoile Studios, NY (DES); Master Print Workshop, Mason Gross Sch of Visual Arts, Rutgers Univ, New Brunswick, NJ (MPW); John Hutcheson (JH); Tamarind Inst, Albuquerque, NM (TI); Judith Solodkin, NY (JS); Solo Press, NY (SP); Solo Impressions, NY (SoImp)
PUBLISHERS: Artists Call, NY (AC); Master Print Workshop, Mason Gross Sch of Visual Arts, Rutgers Univ, New Brunswick, NJ (MPW); Solo Press, NY (SP); Vinalhaven Press, NY (VP); Tamarind Inst, Albuquerque, NM (TI); Malmö Konsthall, Malmö, Sweden (MK)
GALLERIES: Galerie Neuendorf, Frankfort, West Germany; Fawbush Gallery, New York, NY; Burnett Miller Gallery, Los Angeles, CA; Rhona Hoffman Gallery, Chicago, IL; Printworks Gallery, Chicago, IL; Barbara Gladstone Gallery, New York, NY; Solo Gallery, New York, NY; Dean Jensen Gallery, Milwaukee, WI; Vinalhaven Press, Vinalhaven, ME; Josh Baer Gallery, New York, NY; Susan Caldwell & Company, New York, NY
MAILING ADDRESS: 530 La Guardia Place, New York, NY

TITLE	PUBLISHER	PRINTER	DATE	MEDIUM	DIMENSION (PAPER SIZE) IN INCHES	TYPE OF PAPER	EDITION NUMBER	NO. OF COLORS	ORIGINAL OPENING PRICE	CURRENT RETAIL PRICE
SOLD OUT EDITIONS (RARE):										
Transformation of the Lineament II	ART	ART	1949	LC	20 X 13	AP			50	2400
Sphinx and Victim I	ART	ART	1949	LC	19 X 25	AP			50	2400
Workers	ART	ART	1949	LC	13 X 11	AP			35	2000
Mother and Child I	ART	ART	1949	LC	25 X 22	AP			50	3600
The Mind—The Charnel House	ART	ART	1949	LC	28 X 22	AP			50	2400
PreColumbian	ART	ART	1949	LC	28 X 22	AP			50	3600
Fleeing Woman	TI	TI	1965	LC	29 X 41	AP	20		50	3000
Fleeing Men	TI	TI	1965	LC	22 X 30	AP	20		50	2000
Niobe	TI	TI	1965	LC	29 X 41	AP	20		50	3000
Struggle	TI	TI	1965	LC	29 X 41	AP	20		50	3000
Wounded Sphinx	TI	TI	1965	LC	29 X 41	AP	20		50	3000
Wounded Sphinx	TI	TI	1965	LC	22 X 30	AP	20		50	2000
Man and Woman	TI	TI	1965	LC	29 X 41	AP	20		50	3000
Niobid	TI	TI	1965	LC	29 X 41	AP	20		50	4000
Niobid II	TI	TI	1965	LC	22 X 30	AP	20		50	2000
Combat	TI	TI	1965	LC	29 X 41	AP	20		50	3000
Running Man III	TI	TI	1965	LC	22 X 30	AP	20		50	2000
Orator II	TI	TI	1965	LC	22 X 30	AP	20		50	2000
Orange Sphinx	TI	TI	1965	LC	22 X 30	AP	20		50	2000
The Fighter	TI	TI	1965	LC	22 X 30	AP	20		50	2000
Fallen Fighter	TI	TI	1965	LC	22 X 30	AP	20		50	2000
Seated Man	TI	TI	1965	LC	22 X 30	AP	20		50	2000
Agon (set of 7):									350 SET	2000 SET
Orator	TI	TI	1965	LC	22 X 30	AP	20		50	800
Fallen Warrior	TI	TI	1965	LC	22 X 30	AP	20		50	800
Running Man I	TI	TI	1965	LC	22 X 30	AP	20		50	800
Running Man II	TI	TI	1965	LC	22 X 30	AP	20		50	800
Wounded Warrior	TI	TI	1965	LC	22 X 30	AP	20		50	800
Running Blue Sphinx	TI	TI	1965	LC	22 X 30	AP	20		50	800
The Winged Sphinx	TI	TI	1965	LC	22 X 30	AP	20		50	800
CURRENT EDITIONS:										
The Burnt Man (Men are Not for Burning)	ART	ART	1970	SP/PH/C	38 X 50	AP	36		100	3000
Combat I	ART	ART	1970	SP/PH/C	50 X 35	AP	31		100	3000
Combat II	ART	ART	1970	SP/PH/C	50 X 35	AP	31		100	3000
Winged Sphinx	ART	ART	1972	SP/PH/C	50 X 38	AP	40		150	2500
Winged Sphinx I,II	ART	ART	1972	SP/PH/C	38 X 50 EA	AP	20 EA		150 EA	2500 EA
Winged Sphinx III,IV	ART	ART	1972	SP/PH/C	38 X 50 EA	AP	12 EA		150 EA	2500 EA
The Heretic's Fork	ART	ART	1975	LC	30 X 22	AP			200	1200
The Branks	ART	ART	1975	LC	30 X 22	AP			200	1200
Merc	AC	MS/DES	1985	LC	30 X 22	AC	58	2	600	1200
South Africa	AC	MS/DES	1985	LC	30 X 22	AC	90		600	1200
Encounter	MPW	JH/MPW	1986	LC	22 X 30	AP	70	4	900	1200
Riot I	MPW	JH/MPW	1986	LC	22 X 30	AP			900	1200
White Squad	MPW	JH/MPW	1986	LC	30 X 42	AC	60		1000	1800
The Reading of the Law	ART	ART	1949–87	EB	14 X 22	AP	15	1	900	1000
The Reading of the Law	ART	ART	1949–87	EC	14 X 22	AP	7		1000	1200
Foreboding	ART	ART	1949–87	EB	22 X 15	AP	15	1	900	1000
Foreboding II	ART	ART	1949–87	EC	22 X 15	AP	10		1000	1200
The Devil	ART	ART	1949–87	EB	22 X 15	AP	16	1	900	1000
The Devil II	ART	ART	1949–87	EC	22 X 15	AP	8		1000	1200
Aware	ART	ART	1949–87	EB	22 X 14	AP	15	1	900	1000

LEON GOLUB CONTINUED

TITLE	PUBLISHER	PRINTER	DATE	MEDIUM	DIMENSION (PAPER SIZE) IN INCHES	TYPE OF PAPER	EDITION NUMBER	NO. OF COLORS	ORIGINAL OPENING PRICE	CURRENT RETAIL PRICE
CURRENT EDITIONS:										
Aware I	ART	ART	1949–87	EC	22 X 14	AP	8		1000	1200
Head	ART	ART	1949–87	EB	22 X 15	AP	7	1	900	1000
Head II	ART	ART	1949–87	EC	22 X 15	AP	10		1000	1200
Myth	ART	ART	1949–87	EB	15 X 22	AP	20	1	900	1000
Myth II	ART	ART	1949–87	EC	15 X 22	AP	7		1000	1200
Alerted	ART	ART	1949–87	EB	22 X 15	AP	15	1	900	1000
Alerted II	ART	ART	1949–87	EC	22 X 15	AP	9		1000	1200
Gestures	ART	ART	1949–87	EC	22 X 27	AP	18		900	1000
Gestures II	ART	ART	1949–87	EC	22 X 27	AP	6		1000	1200
Three Heads	ART	ART	1949–87	EC	15 X 22	AP	11		1000	1200
The Caress (Versions I-IV)	ART	ART	1949–87	EC	30 X 22 EA	AP	10 EA		1000 EA	1500 EA
Facings: Black Women/Black Men (Dipt)	VP	VP	1988	LC	29 X 83	AC	30	8	2500	3000
Untitled	SP	JS/SP	1988	LC	30 X 41	AC	100		800	1000
Classic Head? Claw, Hand	MK	JS/Solmp	1989	LC	22 X 30	R/BFK	42		1800	1800
Facing	SP	JS/SP	1992	LC	30 X 22	AC	200		1500	1500
The Lovers	MK	JS/Solmp	1952–92	LC	30 X 22	R/BFK	90		1000	1000

ALI GOLKAR

BORN: Israel
PRINTERS: Har-El Printers, Tel Aviv, Israel (Har-El)
PUBLISHERS: London Contemporary Art, Inc, Prospect Heights, IL (LCA)

TITLE	PUBLISHER	PRINTER	DATE	MEDIUM	DIMENSION (PAPER SIZE) IN INCHES	TYPE OF PAPER	EDITION NUMBER	NO. OF COLORS	ORIGINAL OPENING PRICE	CURRENT RETAIL PRICE
CURRENT EDITIONS:										
Mirror of Dreams I, II	LCA	HarEl	1993	SP	25 X 19 EA	AP	350 EA		400 EA	400 EA
Blue Serenade I, II	LCA	HarEl	1993	SP	38 X 26 EA	AP	350 EA		500 EA	500 EA
Ode to Music	LCA	HarEl	1993	SP	31 X 44	AP	350		700	700

KEN GOODMAN (KENNETH HUNT)

BORN: New York, NY; October 22, 1950
EDUCATION: Rhode Island Sch of Design, Providence, RI, BFA, 1972
COLLECTIONS: Dannheisser Found, NY; Hunter Art Mus, Chattanooga, TN; Huntington Art Gallery, Austin, TX
PRINTERS: Editions Sheridan-Bardin, Brooklyn, NY (ES-B)
PUBLISHERS: Artist (ART)
GALLERIES: Brooke Alexander, Inc, New York, NY
MAILING ADDRESS: c/o Brooke Alexander, Inc, 59 Wooster St, New York, NY 10012

TITLE	PUBLISHER	PRINTER	DATE	MEDIUM	DIMENSION (PAPER SIZE) IN INCHES	TYPE OF PAPER	EDITION NUMBER	NO. OF COLORS	ORIGINAL OPENING PRICE	CURRENT RETAIL PRICE
CURRENT EDITIONS:										
Untitled I, State I	ART	ES-B	1985	SP	30 X 22	STP	30		350	400
Untitled I, State II	ART	ES-B	1985	SP	25 X 20	STP	30		350	400

SIDNEY GOODMAN

BORN: Philadelphia, PA; January 19, 1936
EDUCATION: Philadelphia Col of Art, PA, 1958
TEACHING: Instr, Tyler Sch of Art, Temple Univ, Phila, PA, 1977; Instr, Drawing & Painting, Philadelphia Col of Art, 1960–78; Distinguished Vis Prof, Univ of California, Davis, CA, 1987; Prof, Pennsylvania Acad of Fine Arts, Phila, PA, 1978 to present
AWARDS: Yale-Norfolk Fel, 1957; Purchase Award, Ford Found, 1962; Guggenheim Fel, 1964; Nat Acad of Design, 1971; Nat Endowment for the Arts Grant, 1974; First Prize, Butler Inst of Am Art, Youngstown, OH, 1975; AVA Awards, Visual Arts, 1985; Hazlett Award, Painting, Governor's Award, 1986;
RECENT EXHIB: J Rosenthal Fine Arts, Chicago, IL, 1989; Terry Dintenfass Gallery, NY, 1987,89,90,92
COLLECTIONS: Mus of Mod Art, NY; Whitney Mus of Am Art, NY; Brooklyn Mus, NY; Metropolitan Mus of Art, NY; Art Inst of Chicago, IL; Philadelphia Art Mus, PA; Pennsylvania Acad of Arts, Phila, PA; Weatherspoon Art Gallery, Univ of North Carolina, Greensboro, NC; Wake Forest Univ, NC; Univ of Wisconsin, Madison, WI; Wichita Mus of Art, KS; Univ of Maine, Orono, ME; Syracuse Univ, NY; Sheldon Mem Art Gallery, Univ of Nebraska, Lincoln, NE; Pennsylvania State Univ, University Park, PA; Sara Roby Found, NY; Nat Acad of Arts & Letters, NY; Brandeis Univ, Waltham, MA; Delaware Art Mus, Wilmington, DE; Hirshhorn Mus, Wash, DC; Kalamazoo Inst of Arts, MI; Minnesota Mus of Art, Minneapolis, MN; Miami-Dade Junior Col, FL; Arkansas Arts Center, Little Rock, AR; Library of Congress, Wash, DC; Moravian Col, Bethlehem, PA
PRINTERS: Richard Finch, Normal, IL (RF); Craig Martin, Normal, IL (CM); Normal Editions Workshop, Illinois State Univ, Normal, IL (NEW)
PUBLISHERS: Normal Editions Workshop, Illinois State Univ, Normal, IL (NEW)
GALLERIES: Terry Dintenfass Gallery, New York, NY; J Rosenthal Fine Arts, Chicago, IL; More Gallery, Phila, PA
MAILING ADDRESS: c/o Terry Dintenfass Gallery, 50 W 57th St, New York, NY 10019

TITLE	PUBLISHER	PRINTER	DATE	MEDIUM	DIMENSION (PAPER SIZE) IN INCHES	TYPE OF PAPER	EDITION NUMBER	NO. OF COLORS	ORIGINAL OPENING PRICE	CURRENT RETAIL PRICE
CURRENT EDITIONS:										
Boy with Raised Arm	NEW	RF/CM/NEW	1986	LB	29 X 22	R/BFK/W	55	1	600	600

JOE GOODE (JOSE BUENO)

BORN: Oklahoma City, OK; March 23, 1937
EDUCATION: Chouinard Art Inst, Los Angeles, CA, 1959–61
AWARDS: Cassandra Found Award; Am Fed of Arts Award
RECENT EXHIB: CompassRose Gallery, Chicago, IL, 1989; James Corcoran Gallery, Santa Monica, CA, 1989,90
COLLECTIONS: Mus of Mod Art, NY; Pasadena Art Mus, CA; Los Angeles County Mus of Art, CA; Victoria and Albert Mus, London, England; Fort Worth Art Mus, TX
PRINTERS: Cirrus Editions Workshop, Los Angeles, CA (CEW); Ed Hamilton (EH); David Ordaz (DO); William Law (WL); Chris Cordes (CC); Robert Gingras, Los Angeles, CA (RG); Richard Hammond, Los Angeles, CA (RH); Gemini GEL, Los Angeles, CA (GEM)

PUBLISHERS: Cirrus Editions, Los Angeles, CA (CE); Multiples, NY (M); Gemini GEL, Los Angeles, CA (GEM)
GALLERIES: Cirrus Editions, Ltd, Los Angeles, CA; Marian Goodman Gallery, New York, NY; Charles Cowles Gallery, New York, NY; Asher/Faure Gallery, Los Angeles, CA; Braunstein-Quay Gallery, San Francisco, CA; James Corcoran Gallery, Santa Monica, CA; CompassRose Gallery, Chicago, IL; Stein Bartlow Gallery, Ltd, Chicago, IL; Takada Fine Arts, San Francisco, CA
MAILING ADDRESS: c/o James Corcoran Gallery, 1327 Fifth St, Santa Monica, CA 90401

TITLE	PUBLISHER	PRINTER	DATE	MEDIUM	DIMENSION (PAPER SIZE) IN INCHES	TYPE OF PAPER	EDITION NUMBER	NO. OF COLORS	ORIGINAL OPENING PRICE	CURRENT RETAIL PRICE
SOLD OUT EDITIONS:										
Untitled (237c)	CE	CEW	1978	LC	28 X 40	AP	30	3	450	1200
Untitled (250c)	CE	WL/CEW	1978	LC	28 X 40	AP	30	3	250	1200
Untitled (317C Dipt) (with Gunshots)	CE	CEW	1982	LC/GS	14 X 21	TW/AMP	30	2	450	850
CURRENT EDITIONS:										
Untitled (28c)	CE	CEW	1971	LC/SP	18 X 29	AP	90	Multi	150	3500
Untitled (31c)	CE	CEW	1971	LC	9 X 10	AP	110	1	50	400
Untitled (32c)	CE	CEW	1971	LC	14 X 23	AP	50	Multi	125	2500
Untitled (33c)	CE	CEW	1971	LC	14 X 23	AP	50	Multi	125	2500
Untitled (85c) (Trip)	CE/M	CEW	1972	LC	24 X 126	RP	75	Multi	750 SET	8500 SET
Untitled (127c)	CE	CEW	1973	LC	18 X 24	AP	75		275	950
Untitled (167c) (Dipt with Tears)	CE	CC/CEW	1974	LC	30 X 42	RP	25	1–2	450	1200
Tissue Tear Series (Multi Layered, Torn Lithographs) (Set of 3):										
Untitled	GEM	GEM	1975	LC	20 X 26	AP	37		300	1200
Untitled	GEM	GEM	1975	LC	20 X 26	AP	26		300	1200
Untitled	GEM	GEM	1975	LC	28 X 38	AP	35		300	1200
Wash and Tear Series (Screen Prints on Fabric, Water Sprayed, Sewn and Torn) (Set of 3):										
Untitled	GEM	GEM	1975	SP	21 X 24	AP	24		350	1200
Untitled	GEM	GEM	1975	SP	29 X 39	AP	23		350	1200
Untitled	GEM	GEM	1975	SP	38 X 53	AP	25		350	1500
Untitled—Slick Watts, State 1 (226c)	CE	WL/CEW	1977	LC	15 X 20	AP	125		250	300
Untitled—Slick Watts, State 2 (226c)	CE	WL/CEW	1977	LC	15 X 20	AP	125		250	300
Untitled (238c) (with Razor Marks)	CE	WL/CEW	1978	LC	28 X 40	AP	30		450	1200
Untitled (245c) (with Razor Marks)	CE	WL/CEW	1978	LC	28 X 40	AP/BL	30	3	450	1200
Untitled (246c) (with Razor Marks)	CE	WL/CEW	1978	LC	28 X 40	AP	30	3	450	1200
Untitled (247c) (with Razor Marks)	CE	WL/CEW	1978	LC	18 X 15	AP/BL	30	4	250	850
Untitled (248c) (with Razor Marks)	CE	WL/CEW	1978	LC	18 X 15	AP/BL	30	3	250	850
Untitled (249c) (with Razor Marks)	CE	WL/CEW	1978	LC	18 X 15	TW/MP	25	4	250	850
Rainy Season '78 (Set of 6)	CE	WL/CEW	1978	LC	18 X 14 EA	AP	30		1500 SET 250 EA	5100 SET 850 EA
Untitled (301C) (Dipt) (with Gunshots)	CE	DO/CEW	1981	LC/GS	15 X 23	TW/HMP	30	4	450	1200
Untitled (305C) (Dipt) (with Gunshots)	CE	DO/CEW	1981	LC/GS	15 X 23	TW/HMP	30	4	450	1000
Untitled (306C) (Dipt) (with Gunshots)	CE	DO/CEW	1981	LC/GS	15 X 23	TW/HMP	30	3	450	1000
Untitled (307C) (Dipt) (with Gunshots)	CE	DO/CEW	1981	LC/GS	15 X 23	TW/HMP	30	4	450	1000
Untitled (308C) (Dipt) (with Gunshots)	CE	DO/CEW	1981	LC/GS	15 X 23	TW/HMP	30	4	450	1000
Untitled (309C) (Dipt) (with Gunshots)	CE	DO/CEW	1981	LC/GS	15 X 23	TW/HMP	30	2	450	1000
Untitled (310C) (Dipt) (with Gunshots)	CE	DO/CEW	1981	LC/GS	15 X 23	TW/HMP	30	2	450	1000
Untitled (311C) (with Gunshots)	CE	DO/CEW	1981	LC/GS	15 X 11	TW/HMP	30	2	350	850
Untitled (312C) (Dipt) (with Gunshots)	CE	EH/DO	1982	LC/GS	14 X 21	TW/HMP	30	2	300	1000
Untitled (313C) (Dipt) (with Gunshots)	CE	EH/DO	1982	LC/GS	14 X 21	TW/HMP	30	2	450	1000
Untitled (314C) (Dipt) (with Gunshots)	CE	EH/DO	1982	LC/GS	14 X 21	TW/HMP	30	4	450	1000
Untitled (315C) (Dipt) (with Gunshots)	CE	EH/DO	1982	LC/GS	14 X 21	TW/HMP	30	2	450	1000

JOE GOODE (JOSE BUENO) CONTINUED

TITLE	PUBLISHER	PRINTER	DATE	MEDIUM	DIMENSION (PAPER SIZE) IN INCHES	TYPE OF PAPER	EDITION NUMBER	NO. OF COLORS	ORIGINAL OPENING PRICE	CURRENT RETAIL PRICE
CURRENT EDITIONS:										
Untitled (316C) (Dipt) (with Gunshots)	CE	EH/DO	1982	LC/GS	14 X 21	TW/HMP	30	2	450	1000
Forest Fire Series:										
Untitled (337C	CE	RG/CEW	1983	LC	7 X 22	AP88	25	4	350	350
Untitled (339C	CE	RG/CEW	1983	LC	29 X 41	AP88	40		750	1200
Untitled (340C) (Trip)	CE	RG/CEW	1983	LC	41 X 74 EA	AP88	25 EA		1200	1200
Forest Fire (Set of 6)	CE	RH/CEW	1984	LC	14 X 26 EA	AP/BL	30 EA	4–5	2500 SET	3600 SET
									450 EA	750 EA
Forest Fire Aftermath	GEM	GEM	1984	LC	15 X 44	AP	75	1	275	275
Forest Fire (366c)	CE	RH/CEW	1984	LC	14 X 26 EA	AP/BL	15		450	750

RON GORCHOV

BORN: Chicago, Illinois; April 5, 1930
EDUCATION: Art Inst of Chicago Sch, IL, 1947–50; Univ of Illinois, 1950–51
TEACHING: Asst Prof, Art, Hunter Col, NY, presently
COLLECTIONS: Metropolitan Mus of Art, NY; Whitney Mus of Am Art, NY; Detroit Inst of Art, MI; Wadsworth Atheneum, Hartford, CT; Everson Mus of Art, Syracuse, NY
PRINTERS: Landfall Press, Inc, Chicago, IL (LPI); Jack Lemon, Chicago, IL (JL); Frank Gude, Chicago, IL (FG); Bummy Huss, NY (BH)
PUBLISHERS: Barbara Gladstone Editions, NY (BGE); Landfall Press, Inc, Chicago, IL (LPI); NAME Gallery, Chicago, IL (NG)
GALLERIES: Landfall Press, Inc, Chicago, IL; Marlborough Gallery, New York, NY; Susanne Hilberry Gallery, Birmingham, MI; Mangel Gallery, Phila, PA; Jack Tilton Gallery, New York, NY
MAILING ADDRESS: Canal St Sta, Box 337, New York, NY 10013

TITLE	PUBLISHER	PRINTER	DATE	MEDIUM	DIMENSION (PAPER SIZE) IN INCHES	TYPE OF PAPER	EDITION NUMBER	NO. OF COLORS	ORIGINAL OPENING PRICE	CURRENT RETAIL PRICE
SOLD OUT EDITIONS (RARE):										
Untitled	LPI/NG	JL/FG	1979	LC	22 X 30	AP/W	100	5	400	600
CURRENT EDITIONS:										
Untitled (30 Unique Hand-Cast Paper Multiples)	BGE	BH	1980	HC/MULT	28 X 23 X 7 EA	HMP	30		2500 EA	3000 EA

P S GORDON

BORN: Claremore, OK; 1953
EDUCATION: Univ of Oklahoma, Norman, OK, 1971–72; Univ of Tulsa, OK, BFA, 1972–74; Univ of Tulsa, OK, Grad Studies, Watercolor, 1974–75
AWARDS: Nat Endowment for the Arts Grant, 1979
RECENT EXHIB: Gallery at Lincoln Center, NY, 1992
PRINTERS: ChromaComp, Inc, NY (CCI)
PUBLISHERS: Chalk & Vermilion Fine Art, Greenwich, CT (CVFA)
GALLERIES: Fischbach Gallery, New York, NY; M A Doran Gallery, Tulsa, OK; Tower Park Gallery, Peoria Heights, IL

TITLE	PUBLISHER	PRINTER	DATE	MEDIUM	DIMENSION (PAPER SIZE) IN INCHES	TYPE OF PAPER	EDITION NUMBER	NO. OF COLORS	ORIGINAL OPENING PRICE	CURRENT RETAIL PRICE
CURRENT EDITIONS:										
To Catch a Mockingbird	CVFA	CCI	1986	SP	39 X 30	COV	392	40	500	650
4 No Trump, I'm Asking for Aces	CVFA	CCI	1986	SP	39 X 30	COV	392	40	500	650
Red Hot Mama	CVFA	CCI	1986	SP	39 X 29	COV	392	40	500	550
Basic Black with Pearls	CVFA	CCI	1986	SP	40 X 27	COV	392	40	500	850
A Well-Bred Painting	CVFA	CCI	1987	SP	39 X 31	COV	392	40	550	550
The Captain's All Vegged Out	CVFA	CCI	1987	SP	39 X 33	COV	392	40	550	550
Satsuma Vase	CVFA	CCI	1987	SP	31 X 38	COV	392	40	550	550
Flora, Flora, Where's the Fauna? (Sterling Under Glass)	CVFA	CCI	1987	SP	45 X 35	COV	392	40	600	800
Lady of Spain	CVFA	CCI	1987	SP	28 X 38	COV	392	40	550	550
Royal Doulton	CVFA	CCI	1987	SP	39 X 31	COV	392	40	550	550
Chinese Silk Kite	CVFA	CCI	1987	SP	39 X 31	COV	392	40	550	550
Narcissus	CVFA	CCI	1987	SP	39 X 31	COV	392	40	550	550
Tug of War	CVFA	CCI	1988	SP	32 X 21	COV	392	38	550	550
Mary's Marbles	CVFA	CCI	1989	SP	39 X 31	COV	392	38	650	650

RUSSELL TALBERT GORDON

BORN: Philadelphia, PA; June 3, 1936
EDUCATION: Temple Univ, Tyler Sch of Art, Phila, PA, BFA, 1962; Univ of Wisconsin, Madison, WI, MS, 1966, MFA, 1967
TEACHING: Assoc Prof, Art, Concordia Univ, Montreal, Canada; Asst Beginning Drawing, Univ of Wisconsin, Madison, WI, 1965–67; Asst Prof, Printmaking & Grad Seminars, Univ of Utah, Salt Lake City, UT, 1967–69. Asst Prof, Univ of California, Berkeley, CA, 1969, 72; Assoc Prof, Art, Concordia Univ, Montreal, Can, Currently
AWARDS: Facilty Res Grant Limited Ed Bk, Univ of Utah, Salt Lake City, UT, 1969; George Marshall Fel, Vikingsberg Kunst Mus, Am Scandinavian Found, 1972; Nat Endowment for the Arts Grant, Painting, 1981
RECENT EXHIB: Waddington & Gorce, Inc, Montreal, Canada, 1992

RUSSELL TALBERT GORDON CONTINUED

COLLECTIONS: Philadelphia Mus, PA; Oakland Mus, CA; New Jersey State Mus, Trenton, NJ; Univ of Utah, Salt Lake City, UT; Cincinnati Mus, OH; Walker Art Center, Minneapolis, MN; Univ of Wisconsin, Madison; Univ of New Hampshire, Durham, NH; Duke Univ, Durham, NC; Rosenwald Coll, Phila, PA; Mills Col, Oakland, CA; Philadelphia Print Club, PA; Oakland Mus, CA; Miami-Dade Public Library, FL; Canada Council Art Bank; Achenbach Found, Palace of the Legion of Honor, San Francisco, CA

PRINTERS: Artist (ART)
PUBLISHERS: Smith Andersen Gallery, Palo Alto, CA (SA)
GALLERIES: Braunstein-Quay Gallery, San Francisco, CA; Smith Andersen Gallery, Palo Alto, CA; Lakeside Studio Gallery, Lakeside, MI; Waddington & Gorce, Inc, Montreal, Canada
MAILING ADDRESS: c/o Dept of Art, Concordia University, G Williams Maisonneuve, Montreal, PQ, Canada H3G 1M8

TITLE	PUBLISHER	PRINTER	DATE	MEDIUM	DIMENSION (PAPER SIZE) IN INCHES	TYPE OF PAPER	EDITION NUMBER	NO. OF COLORS	ORIGINAL OPENING PRICE	CURRENT RETAIL PRICE
SOLD OUT EDITIONS (RARE):										
Untitled Monotype Series	SA	ART	1981	MON	25 X 20 EA	HMP	1 EA		400 EA	600 EA
Untitled Monotype Series	SA	ART	1981	MON	22 X 30 EA	HMP	1 EA		400 EA	800 EA
Untitled Monotype Series	SA	ART	1981	MON	23 X 19 EA	HMP	1 EA		400 EA	600 EA
Untitled, 1981	SA	ART	1981	EB/A	30 X 22	HMP	17		300	500

ROBERT GORDY

BORN: Jefferson Island, LA; (1933–1986)
EDUCATION: Yale-Norfolk Fel, 1954, with Hans Hofmann; Louisiana State Univ, Baton Rouge, LA, BA, 1955, MA, 1957; Iowa State Univ, Ames, IA, 1956
AWARDS: Yale-Norfolk Fel, 1954; Purchase Award, New Orleans Mus of Art, LA 1958,67,71,73; Tamarind Fel, Albuquerque, NM, 1970; Nat Endowment for the Arts Grants, 1967,78
RECENT EXHIB: Alexandria Mus of Art, LA, 1992

COLLECTIONS: New Orleans Mus of Art, LA; Whitney Mus of Am Art, NY; Wichita Art Mus, KS; Dallas Mus of Fine Arts, TX; Fort Worth Art Center, TX; Corcoran Gallery of Art, Wash, DC; Nat Gallery of Art, Wash, DC; Chicago Mus of Contemp Art, IL
PRINTERS: Liz Jordan (LJ); Julio Juristo (JJ); Artist (ART)
PUBLISHERS: Tamarind Inst, Albuquerque, NM (TI); Topaz Editions, Inc, Tampa, FL (TE); Bell Street Editions, New Orleans, LA (BSE); New Orleans Mus of Art, LA (NOM); Artist (ART)
GALLERIES: Phyllis Kind Gallery, Chicago, IL & New York, NY; Arthur Roger Gallery, New Orleans, LA; Peregrine Press Gallery, Dallas, TX; Graphics Gallery, San Francisco, CA; Topaz Editions, Inc, Tampa, FL

TITLE	PUBLISHER	PRINTER	DATE	MEDIUM	DIMENSION (PAPER SIZE) IN INCHES	TYPE OF PAPER	EDITION NUMBER	NO. OF COLORS	ORIGINAL OPENING PRICE	CURRENT RETAIL PRICE
SOLD OUT EDITIONS (RARE):										
Ramparts	TE	LJ	1981	LC/HC	22 X 30	AC/BL	40	10	350	800
Suspicious Head, First Version	ART	ART	1983	MONO/HC	24 X 18	STP	1	Multi	1200	1500
Female Head	TE	JJ	1984	LC	22 X 30	MAG	55	5	450	750

ARNOLD S GORE

BORN: Chicago, IL; August 21, 1935
EDUCATION: Univ of Iowa, BA, 1953
AWARDS: Art Directions II, Merit, 1978; Terrance Gallery, Palenville, NY, Nat Juried Art Show, Merit, 1981
RECENT EXHIB: Cudahy Gallery, Milwaukee Art Mus, WI, 1987

PRINTERS: Realistic Screen Process Studio, Milwaukee, WI (RSPS); Custom Screen, Milwaukee, WI (CS)
PUBLISHERS: Judith L. Posner & Assoc, Milwaukee, WI (JLP); Artist (ART)
GALLERIES: Judith L Posner & Assoc, Milwaukee, WI; Eve Mannes Gallery, Atlanta, GA; Cudahy Gallery, Milwaukee Art Mus, Milwaukee, WI

TITLE	PUBLISHER	PRINTER	DATE	MEDIUM	DIMENSION (PAPER SIZE) IN INCHES	TYPE OF PAPER	EDITION NUMBER	NO. OF COLORS	ORIGINAL OPENING PRICE	CURRENT RETAIL PRICE
SOLD OUT EDITIONS (RARE):										
Water Gateway	JLP	RSPS	1980	PH/SP	30 X 40	AC	30	7	200	300
Lakefront Festival	JLP	RSPS	1980	PH/SP	30 X 40	AC	30	6	200	300
P.A.C.	JLP	RSPS	1980	PH/SP	30 X 40	AC	30	7	200	300
Summerfest	JLP	RSPS	1980	PH/SP	30 X 40	AC	30	6	200	300
CURRENT EDITIONS:										
SMC '77 I–VI	ART	CS	1977	PH/SP	12 X 16 EA	AC	50 EA	2–5	130 EA	200 EA
Body Waves I–IV	ART	CS	1978	PH/SP	26 X 34 EA	AC	50 EA	5 EA	130 EA	200 EA
Doctor's Part	JLP	RSPS	1980	PH/SP	30 X 40	AC	30	5	200	250
Justice Varies	ART	RSPS	1981	PH/SP	30 X 30	AC	30	13	200	250
Outta Here!	JLP	RSPS	1982	PH/SP	30 X 40	AC	50	6	200	250
Excursion	JLP	RSPS	1982	PH/SP	30 X 40	AC	50	6	200	250
Beginnings	JLP	RSPS	1082	PH/SP	30 X 40	AC	50	5	200	250
Mosaic	JLP	RSPS	1982	PH/SP	30 X 40	AC	50	10	200	250
Power City	ART	RSPS	1982	PH/SP	30 X 40	AC	22	5	200	250
Birds	ART	RSPS	1982	PH/SP	30 X 40	AC	23	7	200	250

The retail prices of the 100,000 limited edition prints quoted in this directory are subject to change. Print publishers, artists and galleries were the direct sources for these quotations. Prices in the secondary market listed as "Sold Out Editions (Rare)" indicate that the publisher has a limited supply of that print or that the print is difficult to locate in the galleries.

The Printworld Directory is accepting new applications for the seventh edition. Approximately 300 new artists will be accepted. Please use the two forms provided in the back section of this directory to submit biographical data and documentation of prints. Edition number of each print must not exceed 500 and the retail price must be $100 or more.

JÜRGEN GÖRG

BORN: Dernbach, Germany; 1951
EDUCATION: Johannes-Gutenberg Univ, Mainz, West Germany
RECENT EXHIB: Kroos Gallery, Columbus, OH, 1987
PRINTERS: Weber Berlag, Mainz, West Germany (WB); Matthieu Atelier, Geneva, Switzerland (MA)
PUBLISHERS: John Szoke Graphics, Inc, NY (JSG)
GALLERIES: Brenda Kroos Gallery, Columbus, OH; John Szoke Graphics, Inc, New York, NY; Joy Tash Gallery, Scottsdale, AZ; Riggs Galleries, La Jolla, CA; Caldwell-Snyder Gallery, San Francisco, CA; CFM Gallery, New York, NY
MAILING ADDRESS: 373 Geary St, San Francisco, CA 94102

TITLE	PUBLISHER	PRINTER	DATE	MEDIUM	DIMENSION (PAPER SIZE) IN INCHES	TYPE OF PAPER	EDITION NUMBER	NO. OF COLORS	ORIGINAL OPENING PRICE	CURRENT RETAIL PRICE
CURRENT EDITIONS:										
Of Three Kinds	JSG	MA	1985	LC	39 X 28	R/BFK	180	4	350	400
Eva	JSG	MA	1985	LC	39 X 28	R/BFK	180	4	350	400

R C GORMAN

BORN: Chinle, Arizona: July 26, 1931
EDUCATION: Northern Arizona Univ, Flagstaff, AZ; Mexico City Col, Mexico
AWARDS: First Award, Heard Mus, Phoenix, AZ, 1968
RECENT EXHIB: Grycner Gallery, Lahaina, HI, 1989; Rio Grande Gallery, Santa Fe, NM, 1989,90; Galerie Capistrano, San Juan Capistrano, CA, 1989,90; Artistic Gallery, Scottsdale, AZ, 1991; Sunset Gallery, Maui, HI, 1991; American West, Chicago, IL, 1991; Adagio Gallery, Palm Springs, CA, 1989,91; Studio 53, NY, 1989,91; Navajo Gallery, Taos, NM, 1989,90,91
COLLECTIONS: Metropolitan Mus of Art, NY; Heard Mus, Phoenix, AZ; Santa Fe Mus of Fine Arts, NM; Philbrook Art Center, Tulsa, OK; Indianapolis Mus of Art, IN; El Paso Mus of Art, TX; Gonzaga Univ, Pacific Northwest Indian Center, Spokane, WA; Navajo Tribal Mus, Window Rock, AZ, Mus of Indian Arts, San Francisco, CA; Mus of the Am Indian, Heye Found, NY; U.S. Dept of the Interior, Wash, DC; Bureau of Indian Affairs, Wash, DC; Northern Arizona Univ, Flagstaff, AZ
PRINTERS: Greg Grycner, Taos, NM (GG); Grycner Editions, Taos, NM (GEd); Artist (ART); Tamarind Inst, Albuquerque, NM (TI); Windmill Press (WPr); Hand Graphics, Santa Fe, NM (HG); Ben Q Adams (BA); Bill Haberman (BH); Western Graphics, Albuquerque, NM (WGr); Richard Newlin (RN); Houston Fine Art Press, TX (HFAP); Peter C Holmes (PH); Origin Press, Tucson, AZ (OPr) (OB); George La Monte (GLM); Welles La Monte (WLM); Editions Press, San Francisco, CA (EP); Stephen Grace (SG); Krystine Graziano (KG); Brenda Hall (BH); Gary Feuge (GF); Consuelo Chavez (CC); Marcia Brown (MB); Peter Webb (PW); Lou Thompson (LT); Chris Fox (CF); Frances Thiel (FT); Kim Baker (KB); Kieron Walsh (KW); Robert Arber (RA); Richard Frush (RF); Molly Sauders (MS); Darrell Warnock (DW); Guy Kaiser (GK); Taos Editions, Ltd, NM (TEL); Craig Cornwall (CrC); Rodney Harmon (RH); Craig Keller (CK); Western Graphics, Albuquerque, NM (WGr)
PUBLISHERS: Artist (ART); Jose Sanches, Mexico City, Mexico (JS); Tamarind Inst, Albuquerque, NM (TI); Art Consultants (AC) (OB); Heritage West Gallery (HWG); Heye Foundation, NY (HF); Western Art Gallery, Albuquerque, NM (WAG); Albuquerque Opera Guild, NM (AOG); Phoenix Art League, AR (PAL); Albuquerque Mus, NM (AM); Windmill Press (WPr); Hand Graphics, Santa Fe, NM (HG); Pyramid Editions (PyrEd); Western Graphics, Albuquerque, NM (WGr); Serigraphics, Albuquerque, NM (SER); Sewey-Kofron Gallery (SKG); Ferre, Ltd (FL); Grycner Editions, Taos, NM (GEd); Editions Press, San Francisco, CA (FP); P & M Publications, Albuquerque, NM (PM); Origin Press, Tucson, AZ (OPr); Houston Art League, TX (HAL); Taos Editioin Editions, Ltd, NM (TEL); Papeles Press, Taos, NM (PaPr)
GALLERIES: Navajo Gallery, Taos, NM; Grycner Gallery, Taos, NM; Avanti Gallery, San Francisco, CA; MacLaren/Markowitz Gallery, Boulder, CO; Gallery One at Second Avenue, Denver, CO; Sunset Galleries, Maui, HI; Joan Cawley Gallery, Lenexa, KS; Chetkin Gallery, Red Bank, NJ; New Riverside Gallery, Red Bank, NJ; Studio 53, New York, NY; Renaissance Gallery, Pittsburgh, PA; Southwest Gallery, Dallas, TX; Kauffman Galleries, Houston, TX; Gallery Mack NW, Wash, DC; Adagio Gallery, Palm Springs, CA; Jamison Galleries, Santa Fe, NM; Mary Livingston Gallery II, Santa Ana, CA
MAILING ADDRESS: P O Box 1756, Taos, NM 87671

TITLE	PUBLISHER	PRINTER	DATE	MEDIUM	DIMENSION (PAPER SIZE) IN INCHES	TYPE OF PAPER	EDITION NUMBER	NO. OF COLORS	ORIGINAL OPENING PRICE	CURRENT RETAIL PRICE
CURRENT EDITIONS:										
Rainbow Jar	ART/HFAP	RN/HFAP	1982	LC	30 X 22	AP/W	200		500	5000
Hana	ART/HFAP	RN/HFAP	1982	LC	30 X 22	R/BFK/CR	250	3	500	2500
Chama	ART/HFAP	RN/HFAP	1982	LC	27 X 21	AP/B	200	5	450	2400
Pueblo	ART/HFAP	RN/HFAP	1982	LC	27 X 21	AP/W	150		450	3000
Chimayo/Day	ART/HFAP	RN/HFAP	1982	LC	30 X 22	AP/W	200	8	500	2000
Chimayo/Night	ART/HFAP	RN/HFAP	1982	LC	30 X 22	AP/W	200	6	500	2000
Salvanna (Barcelona)	ART/TEL	BA/RN/TEL	1982	LC	30 X 22	AP/W	250		500	1500
Barcelona Rose (Barcelona)	ART/TEL	BA/RN/TEL	1982	LC	30 X 22	AP/W	250		500	1500
Maya	ART/TEL	BA/RN/TEL	1982	WC	20 X 15	MUJ	250	10	500	1400
Monica	ART/TEL	BA/RN/TEL	1982	WC	15 X 20	MUJ	210	8	500	1800
Reunion	ART/OPr	PH/OPr	1982	LC	36 X 24	AP/W	200	12	600	4000
Lightening Blanket	ART/HFAP	RN/HFAP	1982	LC	23 X 30	AP/W	200	10	500	5500
Parasol	ART/OPr	PH/OPr	1982	LC	28 X 34	ARJ	200	15	600	2500
Rosalie	ART/WGr	BA/WGr	1982	LC	35 X 28	ARJ	200	5	550	2000
Navajo Rug	ART/WGr	BA/WGr	1982	LC	36 X 28	ARJ	200	8	550	2200
Chinle	ART/WGr	BA/WGr	1982	LC	36 X 27	ARJ	225	8	550	2500
Minna	ART/OPr	PH/OPr	1982	LC	28 X 22	AC/B	200	5	500	1800
Luana	ART/OPr	PH/OPr	1982	LC	23 X 31	AC/B	200	3	500	2200
Two Sisters	ART/OPr	PH/OPr	1982	LC	23 X 29	AC/B	200	8	500	1400
Nomad	ART/OPr	PH/OPr	1982	LC	34 X 23	AC/W	150	8	550	2000
Jeanette	ART/OPr	PH/OPr	1982	LC	22 X 30	AC/B	200	6	500	2000
Harvest	ART/OPr	PH/OPr	1982	LC	30 X 22	AC/B	200	6	500	2200
Winona, State I (Knee) (Red-Purple Line)	ART/EP	GLM/EP	1982	SP	27 X 32	AP88	150	13	575	2500
Winona, State II (Knee) (Blue-Purple Line)	ART/EP	GLM/EP	1982	SP	27 X 32	AP88	150	13	575	2500
Suzy, State I (Yellow Skirt)	ART/EP	GLM/EP	1982	SP	34 X 26	AP88	150	38	675	1800
Suzy, State II (Red Skirt)	ART/EP	GLM/EP	1982	SP	34 X 26	AP88	150	38	675	1800

R C GORMAN CONTINUED

TITLE	PUBLISHER	PRINTER	DATE	MEDIUM	DIMENSION (PAPER SIZE) IN INCHES	TYPE OF PAPER	EDITION NUMBER	NO. OF COLORS	ORIGINAL OPENING PRICE	CURRENT RETAIL PRICE
CURRENT EDITIONS:										
Painted Desert Women	ART/WGr	BA/BH/WGr	1983	LC	30 X 22	AC	200	8	600	3000
Hopi	ART/WGr	BA/BH/WGr	1983	LC	23 X 30	AC	200	6	600	2000
Acoma	ART/HFAP	RN/HFAP	1983	LC	38 X 30	AP/W	225	8	650	4000
Taos Shadows	ART/OPr	PH/OPr	1983	LC	31 X 25	ARJ	200	10	600	3000
Woman with Oranges	ART/HFAP	RN/HFAP	1983	LC	36 X 26	AC/B	200	8	650	4000
Virginia's Kitty	ART/HFAP	RN/HFAP	1983	LC	33 X 27	AP/B	200	6	600	2500
Thunderstorm	ART/HFAP	RN/HFAP	1983	LC	38 X 30	AP/W	175	15	600	6000
Ruins	ART/HFAP	RN/HFAP	1983	LC	28 X 21	AP/W	400	15	600	3200
Woman from Taos	ART/TEL	BA/RN/TEL	1983	LC	14 X 11	AP/B	350	6	450	2000
Daydreamer	ART/EP	GLM/EP	1983	SP	36 X 27	AP88	200	24	750	2400
Doreen, State I (Coral Skirt)	ART/EP	GLM/EP	1983	SP	33 X 26	AP88	150	10	750	1800
Doreen, State II (Lavander Skirt)	ART/EP	WLM/EP	1983	SP	33 X 26	AP88	150	10	750	1800
Woman from Maui, State I (Lavander-Pink Dress)	ART/EP	SG/EP	1983	SP	34 X 29	AP88	150		750	1600
Woman from Maui, State II (Blue Dress)	ART/EP	SG/EP	1983	SP	34 X 29	AP88	150		750	1600
Earring (Frances)	ART/HFAP	RN/HFAP	1983	LC	23 X 31	AP/B	200	10	600	2800
Indian Market	ART/WGr	BA/BH/KG/WGr	1983	LC	35 X 26	AP88	200	10	600	7500
Women from Chaco Canyon	ART/WGr	BA/WGr	1983	LC	32 X 24	AC/B	200	5	600	3200
Woman with Basket	ART/OPr	PH/OPr	1983	LC	37 X 28	AP/W	200	8	600	3000
Bosque Redondo	ART/WGr	BA/BH/WGr	1983	LC	36 X 26	AC/W	200	8	600	2500
Prickly Pear	ART/WGr	BA/BH/KG/WGr	1983	LC	36 X 28	AC/W	200	10	600	6000
La Rosa	ART/HFAP	RN/HFAP	1984	LC	23 X 30	AP/W	200	6	600	2500
Red Peppers	ART/HFAP	RN/CC/HFAP	1984	LC	34 X 25	AP/W	200	12	600	4000
Reina	ART/HFAP	RN/BH/GF/HFAP	1984	LC	36 X 28	R/BFK/CR	200	8	600	3000
Alma	ART/HFAP	RN/CC/HFAP	1984	LC	29 X 36	AC/W	200	10	600	2600
Anna	ART/GEd	GG/GEd	1984	CP	22 X 30	AC/W	60		500	2400
Bernadetta	ART/GEd	GG/GEd	1984	CP	22 X 30	AC/W	60		500	2400
Navajo Mother and Child	ART/GEd	GG/GEd	1984	CP	22 X 30	AC/W	90		500	3000
Ladle Maker	ART/WGr	BA/BH/KG/WGr	1984	LC	33 X 25	AC/W	200	6	600	4500
Lovilla	ART/OPr	PH/OPr	1984	LC	30 X 22	ARJ	200	6	650	2200
Chuska Woman	ART/OPr	PH/OPr	1984	LC	34 X 25	AP/W	200	10	650	1800
Canyon Harvest	ART/EP	WLM/EP	1984	SP	59 X 39	R/BFK	175	18	1200	5000
Janis, State I (Red)	ART/EP	WLM/EP	1984	SP	38 X 32	AP88	150	22	750	3000
Janis, State II (Lavender)	ART/EP	WLM/EP	1984	SP	38 X 32	AP88	150	22	750	3000
Carol's Blanket, State I (Brown)	ART/EP	WLM/EP	1984	SP	50 X 38	AC/W	150	22	900	3000
Carol's Blanket, State II (Blue)	ART/EP	WLM/EP	1984	SP	50 X 38	AC/W	150	22	900	3000
Tewa (Japan)	ART/TEL	BA/RN/TEL	1984	WC	20 X 15	MUL	250	10	750	1000
Mimbres	ART/TEL	BA/RN/TEL	1984	LC	32 X 28	AC/W	225	6	800	1800
Desert Twilight	ART/WGr	BA/RN/WGr	1984	LC	40 X 30	ARJ	225	13	750	5000
Khisani's Belt	ART/OPr	PH/OPr	1984	LC	27 X 36	AP/W	200	8	800	2400
Navajo Weaver	ART/WGr	BA/WGr	1984	LC	34 X 25	AC/W	200	8	800	4500
Bead Maker	ART/WGr	BA/BH/MB/PW	1984	LC	34 X 26	AC/W	250	6	800	3000
Tanya	ART/HFAP	RN/GF/HFAP	1984	LC	40 X 30	AC/W	200	10	800	2800
Kanolda	ART/OPr	KB/OPr	1985	LC	37 X 30	AP/W	200	6	750	3800
Cochiti	ART/WGr	BA/BH/MB/WGr	1985	LC	34 X 26	ARJ	200	14	750	3500
Blue Corn	ART/WGr	BA/BH/MB/WGr	1985	LC	37 X 26	AC/W	200	6	750	4000
Trading Woman	ART/WGr	BA/MB/KG/WGr	1985	LC	32 X 24	AC/W	200	14	750	2800
Red Blanket	ART/WGr	BA/BH/MB/KG/WGr	1985	LC	33 X 25	AC/W	200	10	750	2600
Mia	ART/OPr	PH/OPr	1985	LC	25 X 33	AP/W	200	6	750	2500
Maria, State I (Blue)	ART/EP	WLM/EP	1985	SP	38 X 32	AP/W	150	18	800	2000
Maria, State II (Red)	ART/EP	WLM/EP	1985	SP	38 X 32	AP/W	150	18	800	2500
Lucia	ART/HFAP	RN/GF/HFAP	1985	LC	39 X 29	AP/W	200	8	750	2400
Woman with Apples	ART/HFAP	RN/HFAP	1985	LC	38 X 29	AC/W	200	8	750	3000
Zia Jar	ART/HFAP	RN/CF/HFAP	1985	LC	38 X 29	AC/W	200	8	750	3500
Pomo	ART/HFAP	RN/FT/LT/HFAP	1985	LC	39 X 30	AC/W	200	8	750	3600
Tawzi	ART/GEd	GG/GEd	1985	CP		AC/W	90		600	2500
Noni	ART/GEd	GG/GEd	1985	CP		AC/W	90		600	2500
Angelina	ART/GEd	GG/GEd	1985	CP		AC/W	150		600	3500
Glenna	ART/GEd	GG/GEd	1985	CP		AC/W	150		600	2000
Winona I, II	ART/GEd	GG/GEd	1985	CP		AC/W	150 EA		600 EA	2500 EA
Chili Peppers	ART/TEL	BA/RN/RA/TEL	1985	LC	35 X 28	AC/W	250	10	700	6000
Lena	ART/WGr	BA/BH/MB/PW/WGr	1985	LC	32 X 25	AC/W	200	10	700	3500
Corn Woman	ART/WGr	BA/BH/PW/DW/WGr	1985	LC	36 X 26	AC/W	200	8	700	2800
Abiquiu Rainstorm	ART/HFAP	RN/HFAP	1985	LC	40 X 30	AC/W	250	8	700	4000
Valencia	ART/OPr	KB/RF/OPr	1985	LC	21 X 28	AP/CR	230	10	700	3000
Falling Star	ART/HFAP	RN/GF/HFAP	1985	LC	40 X 32	AP	200	8	700	6000
Anasazi Jar	ART/WGr	BA/BH/MB/HFAP	1985	LC	35 X 27	ARJ	200	6	700	3500
Paloma	ART/OPr	PH/OPr	1985	LC	27 X 34	AP/CR	200	5	700	3500
Marisa	ART/OPr	PH/KW/OPr	1985	LC	29 X 38	R/BFK	225	5	700	2500
Taos Night	ART/WGr	BA/BH/MB/PW	1985	LC	41 X 30	ARJ	200	8	700	3800

R C GORMAN CONTINUED

TITLE	PUBLISHER	PRINTER	DATE	MEDIUM	DIMENSION (PAPER SIZE) IN INCHES	TYPE OF PAPER	EDITION NUMBER	NO. OF COLORS	ORIGINAL OPENING PRICE	CURRENT RETAIL PRICE
CURRENT EDITIONS:										
Ristra	ART/HFAP	RN/GF/FT/HFAP	1985	LC	39 X 29	AC/W	200	10	700	4000
Carolina, State I (Orange)	ART/EP	WLM/EP	1986	SP	36 X 26	AP/W	150	28	900	2200
Carolina, State II (Blue)	ART/EP	WLM/EP	1986	SP	36 X 26	AP/W	150	28	900	2200
Tamara, State I (Blue)	ART/EP	WLM/EP	1986	SP	32 X 36	AP88	150	22	900	2200
Tamara, State II (Pink)	ART/EP	WLM/EP	1986	SP	32 X 36	AP88	150	22	900	2200
Trilogy, State I (Peach Paper)	ART/EP	WLM/EP	1986	SP	37 X 81	AP88	150	7	1400	3500
Trilogy, State II (Blue Paper)	ART/EP	WLM/EP	1986	SP	37 X 81	AP88	150	7	1400	3500
Monument Valley	ART/WGr	BA/BH/PW/DW/ WGr	1986	LC	36 X 29	R/BFK/T	200	10	800	4000
Concha	ART/WGr	BA/BH/PW/WGr	1986	LC	35 X 25	AC/W	200	12	800	3500
Pima	ART/WGr	BA/BH/PW/DW/ WGr	1986	LC	38 X 27	AC/W	200	8	800	5000
Florencita	ART/OPr	PH/KB/OPr	1986	LC	36 X 28	AP/W	200	6	800	3000
Wedding Basket	ART/OPr	KW/KB/OPr	1986	LC	33 X 25	AP/W	200	6	800	3800
Taos Woman	ART/WGr	BA/BH/PW/GK/ WGr	1986	LC	32 X 42	ARJ	200	6	800	2800
Desert Madonna	ART/WGr	BA/BH/PW/GK/ WGr	1986	LC	24 X 30	AC/W	225	6	800	2500
Ranchos Twilight	ART/WGr	BA/BH/PW/GK/ WGr	1986	LC	42 X 32	ARJ	225	12	800	4000
Pueblo Jar	ART/WGr	BA/BH/MB/PW/ WGr	1986	LC	36 X 39	ARJ	200	10	800	3000
Peshlakai's Concho	ART/WGr	BA/BH/PW/DW/ WGr	1986	LC	33 X 25	AC/W	200	8	800	3000
Woman from Third Mesa	ART/WGr	BA/BH/PW/GK/ WGr	1986	LC	36 X 27	AC/B	225	8	800	3000
Aletha	ART/HFAP	RN/CF/HFAP	1986	LC	36 X 26	AC/W	200	8	800	2800
Harvest Jar	ART/HFAP	RN/GF/HFAP	1986	LC	36 X 27	AC/W	200	8	800	3000
Nopales	ART/HFAP	RN/FT/HFAP	1986	LC	36 X 27	AC/W	200	8	800	4000
Night Blooming Cactus	ART/HFAP	RN/FT/HFAP	1986	LC	40 X 31	AC/W	200	15	800	6000
Julia	ART/GEd	GG/GEd	1986	CP		AC/W	150	0	750	2200
Carol	ART/GEd	GG/GEd	1986	CP		AC/W	150	0	750	2000
Elaine	ART/GEd	GG/GEd	1986	CP		AC/W	150	0	750	2000
Benally	ART/WGr	BA/PW/WGr	1987	LC	30 X 19	AC/W	225	8	850	3000
Grand Canyon	ART/WGr	BA/BH/PW/MS	1987	LC	38 X 30	AC/W	225	8	850	3000
Storage Jar	ART/WGr	BA/BH/PW/GK/ WGr	1987	LC	36 X 26	AC/W	225	8	900	2500
Lelani	ART/WGr	BA/PW/WGr	1987	LC	27 X 18	AC/W	225	8	850	3500
Masa	ART/OPr	PH/KW/OPr	1987	LC	36 X 29	R/BFK	200	6	900	2600
Secrets	ART/OPr	PH/KW/OPr	1987	LC	53 X 37	AC/W	225	6	1200	5500
Marissa	ART/OPr	PH/KW/OPr	1987	LC		AC/W	225		1200	2500
Ristra	ART/HFAP	RN/HFAP	1987	LC		AC/W	200		1200	4000
Crescent Moon	ART/HFAP	RN/HFAP	1987	LC		AC/W	225		1200	4500
Flower of Los Lunas	ART/HFAP	RN/HFAP	1987	LC		AC/W	200		1200	4000
Water Carrier	ART/HFAP	RN/HFAP	1987	LC		AC/W	225		750	4000
Thistle Jar	ART/HFAP	RN/HFAP	1987	LC		AC/W	200		750	3500
Naranja	ART/HFAP	RN/HFAP	1987	LC		AC/W	200		750	3500
Chili Picker	ART/TEL	TEL	1987	LC		AC/W	250		750	2500
Woman with Pottery	ART/GEd	GG/GEd	1987	CP		AC/W	150	0	700	2000
Two Women I, II	ART/GEd	GG/GEd	1987	CP		AC/W	150 EA	0	700 EA	2500 EA
Indian Woman in Desert	ART/GEd	GG/GEd	1987	SP	30 X 40	AC/W	266		750	3000
Indian Woman with Jar	ART/GEd	GG/GEd	1988	SP	27 X 36	AC/W	225		800	2500
Autumn Jar	ART/GEd	GG/GEd	1987	CP		AC/W	150	0	700	2000
Chaco Canyon	ART/GEd	GG/GEd	1987	CP		AC/W	150	0	700	2200
Snowflake Olla	ART/WGr	BA/BH/PW/MS	1987	LC	36 X 26	AC/W	225	8	750	2500
Canyon de Chelly Twilight	ART/WGr	BA/PW/CrC/ WGr	1988	LC	38 X 28	AC/W	224	81	850	3500
Escalera	ART/OPr	PH/OPr	1988	LC	30 X 41	R/BFK	225		850	3000
Breadmaker	ART/OPr	PH/OPr	1988	LC			225		850	3000
Estrella	ART/OPr	PH/KB/KW/RH	1988	LC	30 X 38	AP/W	225		850	3000
Dolly Nez	ART/OPr	PH/KB/KW/RH	1988	LC	27 X 37	R/BFK/W	225		850	3000
Evelyn	ART/PaPr		1988	SP			200		700	1200
Yossi-bah	ART/PaPr		1988	SP			200		700	1200
Jessica	ART/PaPr		1988	SP			200		700	1200
Bisbee	ART/HFAP	RN/HFAP	1988	LC			225		800	3200
Moonrise	ART/HFAP	RN/HFAP	1988	LC			225		800	3500
Silver Bracelet	ART/HFAP	RN/HFAP	1988	LC			225		850	3200
Woman with Lemons	ART/HFAP	RN/HFAP	1988	LC			225		850	3200
Carmen and Child	ART/HFAP	RN/HFAP	1988	LC	27 X 36	AC/W	225	73	850	3500
Sunset Woman	ART/HFAP	RN/HFAP	1988	LC			225		850	2000
Taos Poppies	ART/HFAP	RN/HFAP	1988	LC	27 X 36	AC/W	225	66	850	3500
Kiana	ART/GEd	GG/GEd	1988	CP			150	0	750	1200

R C GORMAN CONTINUED

TITLE	PUBLISHER	PRINTER	DATE	MEDIUM	DIMENSION (PAPER SIZE) IN INCHES	TYPE OF PAPER	EDITION NUMBER	NO. OF COLORS	ORIGINAL OPENING PRICE	CURRENT RETAIL PRICE
CURRENT EDITIONS:										
Flute Player	ART/GEd	GG/GEd	1988	CP			150	0	750	900
Yoko	ART/GEd	GG/GEd	1988	CP			200	0	750	900
Mother and Child	ART/GEd	GG/GEd	1988	CP			200	0	750	1000
Nellie Begay	ART/OPr	PH/KW/OPr	1988	LC	27 X 35	R/BFK/W	225	12	750	4000
Nizhoni	ART/WGr	BA/PW/CrC/RH	1989	LC	36 X 28	AC/W	224	57	900	1700
Mimbres Woman	ART/WGr	BA/PW/CrC/WGr	1989	LC	30 X 36	AC/B	224	46	900	1700
Salina	ART/WGr	BA/PW/CrC/RH	1989	LC	36 X 26	AC/W	224	61	900	1800
Taos Traders	ART/WGr	BA/PW/CrC/RH	1989	LC	36 X 26	AC/W	224	46	900	1800
Cactus Flowers	ART/WGr	BA/PW/CrC/RH	1989	LC	37 X 30	AC/B	224	67	900	1800
Enchanted Mesa	ART/WGr	BA/PW/CrC/RH	1989	LC	41 X 29	ARJ	224	57	900	1500
Catalina de Mora	ART/WGr	BA/PW/CrC/RH	1989	LC	37 X 30	AC/B	224	51	900	1800
Twilight in the Grand Canyon	ART/WGr	BA/PW/CrC/RH	1989	LC	42 X 30	ARJ	224	89	900	2000
Mesa Visit	ART/OPr	PH/OPr	1989	LC	30 X 38	AC/W	225		900	1800
Aurora	ART/OPr	KW/KB/PH/OPr	1989	LC	30 X 38	R/BFK	225		900	3500
Whispers	ART/OPr	PH/KB/OPr	1989	LC	38 X 37	AP/W	225		900	1800
First Choice	ART/OPr	PH/KB/OPr	1989	LC	30 X 38	R/BFK	225		900	1800
Kirsten	ART/PaPr		1989	SP	30 X 38	R/BFK	200		900	800
Blue Door	ART/HFAP	RN/HFAP	1989	LC	28 X 37	AC/W	225	62	900	2200
Desert Lily	ART/HFAP	RN/HFAP	1989	LC	30 X 39	AC/W	225	58	900	2800
Woman at the Lake	ART/HFAP	RN/HFAP	1989	LC	30 X 39	AC/W	225	58	900	2000
Eye Dazzler	ART/WGr		1989	LC	32 X 41	ARJ	224	58	900	1700
Waterfall	ART/HFAP	RN/HFAP	1989	LC	30 X 39	AC/W	225	84	1000	2000
Canyon Woman	ART/HFAP	RN/HFAP	1989	LC	30 X 39	AC/W	225	100	1000	2000
Tulips	ART/HFAP	RN/HFAP	1989	LC	26 X 37	AC/W	225	59	1000	1800
Red Concho (with Book)	ART/TEL	BA/TEL	1989	LC			300		850	900
Storyteller	ART/GEd	GG/GEd	1989	CP			200	0	1000	1800
Mystic Mesa	ART/HFAP	RN/HFAP	1990	LC	31 X 39	AC/W	225	71	1200	1800
Wild Flowers	ART/WGr	BA/PW/RH/CK	1990	LC	36 X 28	AC/W	224	58	1200	1800
Taos Flowers	ART/WGr	BA/PW/CrC/RH	1990	LC	45 X 33	AP/HWT	224	166	1500	3500
Saquaro	ART/WGr	BA/RH/CK/WGr	1990	LC	30 X 31	ARJ	224	83	1200	2000
Modesta	ART/OPr	PH/OPr	1990	LC	30 X 38	R/BFK	225		1200	1800
Sunrise	ART/OPr	PH/OPr	1990	LC	30 X 38	R/BFK	225		1200	1600
Maria Elena	ART/OPr	PH/OPr	1990	LC	30 X 38	R/BFK	225		1200	1800
Atole	ART/OPr	PH/OPr	1990	LC	30 X 36	R/BFK	225		1200	1800
Navajo Dancer	ART/OPr	PH/OPr	1990	LC	30 X 38	R/BFK	225		1200	1700
Dusk	ART/PaPr		1990	SP			200		700	800
Nicole	ART/PaPr		1990	SP			200		700	700
Ginny	ART/PaPr		1990	SP			200		700	800
Daughter of the Moon	ART/HFAP	RN/HFAP	1990	LC	32 X 39	SOM/W	225	69	1200	2000
Beauty Way	ART/HFAP	RN/HFAP	1990	LC	31 X 37	AC/W	225	62	1200	2000
La Chilera	ART/HFAP	RN/HFAP	1990	LC	30 X 39	AC/W	225	59	1200	2000
Star Gazer	ART/HFAP	RN/HFAP	1990	LC	31 X 36	AC/W	225	41	1200	2000
Gladia	ART/TEL	BA/TEL	1990	LC		AC/W	160		850	1800
Sacred Corn	ART/WGr	BA/WGr	1991	LC	32 X 42	ARJ	160	130	1500	2000
Panadera	ART/OPr	PH/OPr	1991	LC	31 X 38	R/BFK	225		1500	1800
Morning Star	ART/OPr	PH/OPr	1991	LC	36 X 29	R/BFK	225		1500	1600
Woman with Poppies	ART/HFAP	RN/HFAP	1991	LC	27 X 36	AC/W	225	55	1500	2000
Blanca	ART	ART	1991	CP			90	0	700	700
Consuelo	ART	ART	1991	CP			90	0	800	800

ANTONY GORMLEY

RECENT EXHIB: Mus of Contemp Art, San Diego, CA, 1992
PRINTERS: John Fitzgerald, CA (JF); Marc Morikawa, CA (MM); Hope Weiss, Los Angeles, CA (HW); La Paloma, Tujunga, CA (LaPal)
PUBLISHERS: Okeanos Editions, Los Angeles, CA (OkEd)
GALLERIES: Betsy Senior Contemporary Prints, New York, NY; Hope Weiss Fine Art, Los Angeles, CA; Salvatore Ala, New York, NY; Burnett Miller Gallery, Los Angeles, CA

TITLE	PUBLISHER	PRINTER	DATE	MEDIUM	DIMENSION (PAPER SIZE) IN INCHES	TYPE OF PAPER	EDITION NUMBER	NO. OF COLORS	ORIGINAL OPENING PRICE	CURRENT RETAIL PRICE
CURRENT EDITIONS:										
Bearing Light (Set of 12)	OkEd	JF/MM/HW/L	1990	WB	23 X 20 EA	R/BFK	30 EA	1 EA	7500 SET	7500 SET

The retail prices of the 100,000 limited edition prints quoted in this directory are subject to change. Print publishers, artists and galleries were the direct sources for these quotations. Prices in the secondary market listed as "Sold Out Editions (Rare)" indicate that the publisher has a limited supply of that print or that the print is difficult to locate in the galleries.

The Printworld Directory is accepting new applications for the seventh edition. Approximately 300 new artists will be accepted. Please use the two forms provided in the back section of this directory to submit biographical data and documentation of prints. Edition number of each print must not exceed 500 and the retail price must be $100 or more.

APRIL GORNIK

BORN: Cleveland, OH; April 20, 1953
EDUCATION: Cleveland Inst of Art, OH, 1971–75; Nova Scotia Col of Art & Design, Nova Scotia, Canada, BFA, 1976
RECENT EXHIB: California State Univ Art Mus, Long Beach, CA, 1988; Sable-Castelli Gallery, Toronto, ON, Canada, 1988; Whitney Mus of Am Art, NY, 1989; Art Gallery of Western Australia, Perth, Australia, 1990; Rhode Island Sch of Design, Providence, RI, 1990; Virginia Mus of Fine Arts, Richmond, VA, 1990; Guild Hall Mus, East Hampton, NY, 1992; William Paterson Col, Ben Shahn Galleries, Wayne, NJ, 1988,92; Edward Thorp Gallery, NY, 1987,92
COLLECTIONS: Metropolitan Mus of Art, NY; California State Univ Art Mus, Long Beach, CA; Nova Scotia Art Bank, Canada
PRINTERS: Maurice Sanchez, NY (MS); Derriére L'Etoile Studio, NY (DES); David Keister, Bloomington, IN (EPr); David Calkins, Bloomington, IN (DC); Echo Press, Bloomington, IN (EPr); Crown Point Press, San Francisco, CA (CPP); Tadashi Toda, Kyota, Japan (TT); Joe Wilfer (JW); Spring Street Workshop, NY (SprSW)
PUBLISHERS: Fred Dorfman, Inc, NY (FDI); Art Issue Editions, Inc, NY (AIE); Echo Press, Bloomington, IN (EPr); Crown Point Press, San Francisco, CA (CPP); Spring Street Workshop, NY (SprSW)
GALLERIES: Edward Thorp Gallery, New York, NY; Sable-Castelli Gallery, Toronto, Canada; Texas Gallery, Houston, TX; Michael Kohn Gallery, Los Angeles, CA; Elliot Smith Gallery, St Louis, MO; Mary Ryan Gallery, New York, NY; Luhring Augustine, New York, NY; Fred Dorfman Gallery, New York, NY; Jefferson Gallery, Effingham, IL; Crown Point Press, New York, NY & San Francisco, CA; Betsy Senior Contemporary Prints, New York, NY; Pace Prints, New York, NY; Sable-Castelli Gallery, Toronto, ON, Canada; Hudson River Editions, South Nyack, NY; Steven Scott Gallery, Baltimore, MD
MAILING ADDRESS: c/o Edward Thorp Gallery, 103 Prince St, New York, NY 10012

TITLE	PUBLISHER	PRINTER	DATE	MEDIUM	DIMENSION (PAPER SIZE) IN INCHES	TYPE OF PAPER	EDITION NUMBER	NO. OF COLORS	ORIGINAL OPENING PRICE	CURRENT RETAIL PRICE
CURRENT EDITIONS:										
Dust and Rain	FDI		1985	EB/A	31 X 43 EA	R/BFK	1 EA	Varies	1050 EA	1800 EA
Remember the Sabbath Day (from Ten Commandments Suite)	AIE	MS/DES	1987	LC	24 X 19	DIEU	84	3	500	1800
Light at the Source	EPr	DK/DC/EPr	1987	LC	38 X 28	R/BFK	35	5	900	1500
Light after the Flood	SprSW	JW/SprSW	1987	EB/SG	28 X 43	R/BFK	23	1	1800	4000
Light after the Flood, State II	SprSW	JW/SprSW	1988	EB/SG	24 X 41	R/BFK	40	1	2000	3500
Charente	CPP	TT/CPP	1988	WC	23 X 28	ECHIZEN/ MASHI	100	7	1200	2800
Rivers Meeting	CPP	TT/CPP	1989	LB	24 X 31	R/BFK	50	1	2500	3000
Equinox	SprSW	JW/SprSW	1990	EB/SG/SB	31 X 38	R/BFK	50	1	2000	2000
Sun & Storm	SprSW	JW/SprSW	1991	EB/SG/SB	29 X 23	R/BFK	35	1	1500	1500
Moon & Sea	SprSW	JW/SprSW	1991	EB/SG/SB	29 X 23	R/BFK	35	1	1500	1500

ANTHONY-PETR GÓRNY

BORN: Buffalo, NY; 1950
EDUCATION: State Univ of New York, Buffalo, NY, BFA, 1972 Yale Univ Sch of Art, New Haven, CT. MFA, 1974
AWARDS: Nat Arts Club, Best in Show Award, NY, 1973,74; Pennell Fund Purchase Prize, Library of Congress, Wash, DC, 1973,75; Eugene Feldman Mem Award, Print Club, Phila, PA, 1980; Board of Governor's Award, Print Club, Phila, PA, 1981; Pennsylvania Council on the Arts, Phila, PA, Ind Artist Fel, 1983; Second Prize, Philadelphia Art Alliance, PA, 1984,85; Philadelphia Mus of Art, Purchase Award, 1986; Friends of the Philadelphia Mus of Art, PA, Print Project Comm, 1987; Beaver Col Art Gallery Directors Award Prize, Glenside, PA, 1989; Nat Endowment for the Arts, Ind Visual Artist, Major Grant, 1989-90
TEACHING: Assoc Prof, Prints & Drawing, Tyler Sch of Art, Temple Univ, Phila, PA, 1974–81; Instr, Prints, Flesher Art Mem, Phila Art Mus, PA, 1986 to present; Assoc Prof, Photog & Performance Art, Univ of Arts, Phila, PA, 1989 to present
RECENT EXHIB: Inst of Contemp Art, Univ of Pennsylvania, Phila, PA, 1987; Lawrence Oliver Gallery, Phila, PA, 1988; Rosenwald Wolfe Gallery, Univ of the Arts, Phila, PA, 1989; Mednick Gallery, Univ of the Arts, Phila, PA, 1989
COLLECTIONS: Albright-Knox Art Gallery, Buffalo, NY; Ball Mus of Art, Ohio State Univ, Columbus, OH; Brooklyn Mus of Art, NY; Charles Burchfield Center, NY; State Univ of New York, Buffalo, NY; Charles Rand Penney Coll, Lockport, NY; Cleveland Mus of Art, OH; Kyoto Univ Coll of Fine Arts, Kyoto, Japan; Library of Congress, Wash, DC; Nat Mus of Am Art, Wash, DC; New Orleans Mus of Art, LA; Pennsyvania Acad of the Fine Arts, Phila, PA; Philadelphia Mus of Art, PA; Pratt Graphics Center Coll, NY; Solomon R Guggenheim Mus, NY; Vatican Coll, Rome, Italy; Victoria & Albert Mus, London, England; Yale Univ Art Gallery, New Haven, CT

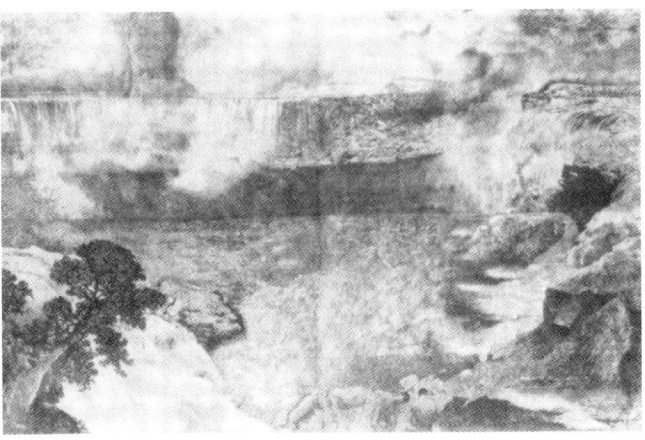

Anthony-Petr Górny
Centers of Power
Courtesy Echo Press

PRINTERS: Tim Sheesley, Phila, PA (TS); Corridor Press, Phila, PA (COR); David Keister, Bloomington, IN (DK); David Calkins, Bloomington, IN (DC); Echo Press, Bloomington, IN (EPr)
PUBLISHERS: Friends of the Philadelphia Mus, PA (FPM); Echo Press, Bloomington, IN (EPr)
GALLERIES: Nina Freudenheim Gallery, Buffalo, NY; Dolan/Maxwell Gallery, New York, NY & Phila, PA; Echo Press, Bloomington, IN
MAILING ADDRESS: 102 N Second St, Phila, PA 19106

TITLE	PUBLISHER	PRINTER	DATE	MEDIUM	DIMENSION (PAPER SIZE) IN INCHES	TYPE OF PAPER	EDITION NUMBER	NO. OF COLORS	ORIGINAL OPENING PRICE	CURRENT RETAIL PRICE
CURRENT EDITIONS:										
Magpie Caliper	EPr	DK/EPr	1980	LC	36 X 55	OKP	33	5	500	950
Centers of Power	EPr	DK/DC/EPr	1985-86	LB	36 X 55	OKP	35	3	1350	2500
Pitch Darkness (Dipt)	FPM	TS/COR	1987	LB/CC	34 X 24	GAMPI/FAB	100	1	900	2000

ADOLPH GOTTLIEB

BORN: New York, NY; (1903–1974)
EDUCATION: Art Students League, NY, with John Sloan, Robert Henri, 1919; Acad de la Grande Chaumiere, Paris, France, 1921; Parsons Sch of Design, NY 1923
TEACHING: Pratt Inst, NY, 1958; Univ of California, Los Angeles, CA, 1958
RECENT EXHIB: Florida Int Univ Art Mus, Miami, Fl, 1989; Heland Wetterling Gallery, Stockholm, Sweden, 1989; Manny Silverman Gallery, Los Angeles, CA, 1992; Univ of Oklahoma, Norman, OK, 1992; Muhlenberg Col, Frank Martin Art Gallery, Allentown, PA, 1989,92; Charles H MacNider Mus, Mason City, IA, 1989,92; Mills Col, Oakland, CA 1992; Florida Int Univ, Miami, FL, 1992
COLLECTIONS: Metropolitan Mus of Art, NY; Mus of Mod Art, NY; Whitney Mus of Am Art, NY; Jewish Mus, NY; Brooklyn Mus, NY; Brandeis Mus, Waltham, MA; Albright-Knox Mus, Buffalo, NY; Carnegie Inst, Pittsburgh, PA; Chicago Art Inst, IL; Corcoran Gallery of Art, Wash, DC; Cornell Univ, Ithaca, NY; Detroit Inst of Art, MI; Wadsworth Atheneum, Hartford, CT; Yale Univ, New Haven, CT; Walker Art Center, Minneapolis, MN; Smith Col, MA; Butler Inst of Am Art, Youngstown, OH; Newark Mus, NJ; Pasadena Art Mus, CA; Virginia Mus of Fine, Richmond, VA; Tel Aviv Univ, Israel; Mus of Fine Arts, Dallas, TX; Ball State Univ; Delgado Mus, New Orleans, LA; Univ of Illinois; Los Angeles County Mus of Art, CA; Soc of the Four Arts; Univ of Miami, Fl
PUBLISHERS: Marlborough Graphics, Inc, NY (MG); Brooke Alexander, Inc, NY (BAI); Artist (ART)
GALLERIES: Marlborough Graphics, Inc, New York, NY; Harcus Gallery, Boston, MA; Adler Gallery, Los Angeles, CA; Flanders Contemporary Arts, Minneapolis, MN; M Knoedler & Company, New York, NY; Benjamin-Beattie Gallery, Chicago, IL; Brooke Alexander, Inc, New York; Richard Green Gallery, New York, NY; Barry Rosen & Jaap Van Liere Modern & Contemporary Art, New York, NY; Jeffery Fuller Fine Art, Ltd, Phila, PA; Manny Silverman Gallery, Los Angeles, CA; Thomson Gallery, Minneapolis, MN; Solomon & Company Fine Art, Inc, New York, NY; Linda R Silverman Fine Art, Inc, New York, NY

Adolph Gottlieb
Green Foreground
Courtesy Marlborough Graphics

TITLE	PUBLISHER	PRINTER	DATE	MEDIUM	DIMENSION (PAPER SIZE) IN INCHES	TYPE OF PAPER	EDITION NUMBER	NO. OF COLORS	ORIGINAL OPENING PRICE	CURRENT RETAIL PRICE
SOLD OUT EDITIONS (RARE):										
Red Ground	MG		1966	SP	20 X 15	AP	50		200	3500
Pictograph	MG		1942	EC	8 X 10	AP	10		100	5000
Green Ground-Black Form	MG		1966	LC	30 X 22	AP	50		200	5000
Untitled	MG		1966	SP	32 X 30	AP	50		200	6000
Magenta Disc	MG		1966	SP	24 X 18	AP	50		200	6000
Maroon Disc	MG		1966	SP	24 X 18	AP	50		200	6000
Black Ground-Red Disc	MG		1966	SP	24 X 20	AP	50		200	5000
Chrome Yellow-Green Disc	MG		1966	LC	30 X 22	AP	50		200	5000
Green Halo	MG		1966	SP	24 X 18	AP	50		200	6000
Black and Grey	MG		1967	SP	24 X 18	AP	75		300	4500
Black Splash	MG		1967	SP	31 X 23	AP	75		300	4000
Arabesque	MG		1967	LC	30 X 22	AP	75		200	3000
Black on Silver	MG		1967	SP	23 X 17	AP	75		200	3000
Expanding	MG		1967	SP	24 X 18	AP	75		300	4000
Figure Eight	MG		1967	SP	18 X 24	AP	75		500	5000
Flotsam	MG		1967	SP	30 X 22	AP	75		500	6000
Flurry	MG		1967	SP	20 X 30	AP	75		500	5000
Flying Lines	MG		1967	SP	30 X 22	AP	75		500	5000
Jetsam	MG		1967	SP	24 X 18	AP	75		500	5000
Rosy Mood	MG		1967	SP	25 X 19	AP	75		500	5000
Signs	MG		1967	SP	24 X 18	AP	75		500	4000
Germination I	MG		1969	LC	22 X 30	AP	60		500	4000
Germination II	MG		1969	LC	22 X 30	AP	65		600	4000
Germination III	MG		1969	LC	30 X 22	AP	75		600	4000
Green Dream	MG		1969	SP	27 X 22	AP	95		500	3000
Pink High	MG		1969	SP	24 X 19	AP	95		500	5000
Two Bars	MG		1969	LC	30 X 21	AP	100		500	5000
Beacon	MG		1969	LC	29 X 21	AP	100		500	5000
Blue Night	MG		1970	SP	31 X 24	FAB	200		300	3000
Blues on Green	MG		1971	SP	33 X 26	AP	150		300	4500
Imaginary Landscape I	MG		1971	AC	26 X 33	AP	90		1000	8000
Imaginary Landscape II	MG		1971	AC	34 X 31	AP	55		1000	8000
Black Field	MG		1972	SP	36 X 28	AP	150		600	3000
Chrome Green	MG		1972	SP	36 X 28	AP	130		600	7000
Crimson Ground	MG		1972	SP	36 X 28	AP	150		600	4500
Green Foreground	MG		1972	SP	36 X 28	AP	150		600	3000
Orange Oval	MG		1972	SP	27 X 37	AP	150		600	6000
Pink Ground	MG		1972	SP	36 X 28	AP	150		600	5000
Untitled	BAI		1972	AC	32 X 24	AP	125		600	5000
Untitled	ART	ART	1972	EB/A	24 X 18		125		600	3500

ARI GRADUS

BORN: Israel; 1943
EDUCATION: New York Univ, NY
PRINTERS: Artist (ART)
PUBLISHERS: Jackie Fine Arts, NY (JFA); Original Collectors Guild, NY

GALLERIES: Circle Galleries, New York, NY & San Diego, CA & San Francisco, CA & Northbrook, IL & Pittsburgh, PA & Houston, TX & Chicago, IL & Scottsdale, AZ & Beverly Hills, CA & Costa Mesa, CA & Sherman Oaks, CA & Palm Beach, FL & Honolulu, HI & New Orleans, LA & Las Vegas, NV & Seattle, WA
MAILING ADDRESS: 423 6th St, Brooklyn, NY 11215

TITLE	PUBLISHER	PRINTER	DATE	MEDIUM	DIMENSION (PAPER SIZE) IN INCHES	TYPE OF PAPER	EDITION NUMBER	NO. OF COLORS	ORIGINAL OPENING PRICE	CURRENT RETAIL PRICE
SOLD OUT EDITIONS (RARE):										
Way Out West	JFA	ART	1979	LC	18 X 26	AP	300	13	200	300
Notre Quantier	JFA	ART	1979	LC	18 X 26	AP	300	14	200	300
The Puppet Show	JFA	ART	1979	LC	18 X 26	AP	300	13	200	300
On the Canal	JFA	ART	1979	LC	18 X 26	AP	300	13	200	300
Early Days Lower	JFA	ART	1979	LC	18 X 26	AP	300	12	200	300
Lower East Side	JFA	ART	1979	LC	18 X 26	AP	300	12	200	300
At the Fair	JFA	ART	1979	LC	18 X 25	AP	300	12	200	300
Jerusalem Market	JFA	ART	1979	LC	18 X 26	AP	300	12	200	300
Old New York	JFA	ART	1979	LC	18 X 26	AP	245	12	200	300
Afternoon Stroll	JFA	ART	1979	LC	18 X 26	AP	300	13	200	300
The Knife Sharpener	JFA	ART	1979	LC	18 X 25	AP	300	12	200	300
Jerusalem, Old City	JFA	ART	1979	LC	18 X 25	AP	300	13	200	300
Gypsy Fever	JFA	ART	1980	LC	18 X 26	AP	245	13	200	300
Jerusalem Bazar	JFA	ART	1980	LC	18 X 26	AP	245	12	200	300
Parisian Morning	JFA	ART	1980	LC	18 X 26	AP	300	12	200	300
Bringing in the Catch	JFA	ART	1980	LC	18 X 26	AP	245	12	200	300
Main Street USA	JFA	ART	1980	LC	19 X 26	AP	245	12	200	300
The Old Quarter	JFA	ART	1980	LC	18 X 26	AP	245	12	200	300
Winter's Play	JFA	ART	1980	LC	18 X 26	AP	245	12	200	300
The Bird Man	JFA	ART	1980	LC	18 X 26	AP	245	12	200	300
Winter Fantasy	JFA	ART	1980	LC	18 X 26	AP	245	12	200	300
Sidewalk Cafe	JFA	ART	1980	LC	18 X 26	AP	245	12	200	300
The Fountain Square	JFA	ART	1980	LC	18 X 26	AP	245	12	200	300
The Pidgeon Feeder	JFA	ART	1981	LC	19 X 26	AP	245	12	200	300
Main Street	OCG	ART	1982	LC	19 X 26	AP	250	16	225	300

ROBERT GRAHAM

BORN: Mexico City, Mexico; August 19, 1938; U S Citizen
EDUCATION: San Jose State Col, CA, 1961–63; San Francisco Art Inst, CA, MFA, 1963–64
RECENT EXHIB: Los Angeles Count Mus of Art, CA, 1988; Whitney Mus of Am Art, NY, 1988,89; Mus of Fine Arts, Houston, TX 1987–89; Contemp Mus, Honolulu, HI, 1989; Robert Miller Gallery, NY, 1990; Mixografia, Venice, CA & Los Angeles, CA, 1990; Contemp Arts Center, New Orleans, LA, 1990; Fine Arts Center for New River Valley, Pulaski, VA, 1992
COLLECTIONS: Whitney Mus of Am Art, NY; Mus of Mod Art, NY; Los Angeles County Mus, CA; Hirshhorn Mus, Wash, DC; Houston Mus of Fine Arts, TX; Dallas Mus of Fine Art, TX; Kunstmuseum, Cologne, Germany

PUBLISHERS: Gemini GEL, Los Angeles, CA (GEM); Mixografia, Santa Monica, CA (MIX)
PRINTERS: Gemini GEL, Los Angeles, CA (GEM); Mixografia, Santa Monica, CA (MIX)
GALLERIES: Art School Gallery, Carrboro, NC; Cynthia Drennon Fine Arts Resources, Los Angeles, CA; Gemini GEL, Los Angeles, CA; Joni Moisant Weyl Gallery, Los Angeles, CA; Dorothy Rosenthal Art Gallery, Chicago, IL; Robert Miller Gallery, New York, NY; Remba Gallery/Mixografia Workshop, Santa Monica, CA; John Berggruen Gallery, San Francisco, CA; Earl McGrath Gallery, Los Angeles, CA; Ginny Williams Gallery, Denver, CO
MAILING ADDRESS: 69 Windward Ave, Venice, CA 90291

TITLE	PUBLISHER	PRINTER	DATE	MEDIUM	DIMENSION (PAPER SIZE) IN INCHES	TYPE OF PAPER	EDITION NUMBER	NO. OF COLORS	ORIGINAL OPENING PRICE	CURRENT RETAIL PRICE
CURRENT EDITIONS:										
Figure/Table Series:										
Untitled	GEM	GEM	1975	SP	48 X 37	AP	33			1000
Untitled	GEM	GEM	1975	SP	37 X 45	AP	33			1000
Untitled	GEM	GEM	1975	SP	40 X 51	AP	35			1000
Untitled	GEM	GEM	1975	SP	35 X 45	AP	35			1000
Untitled	GEM	GEM	1975	SP	35 X 45	AP	35			1000
Untitled (Unglazed Porcelain Head-Light Purple)	GEM	GEM	1984	MULT	4 X 3 X 2 EA	Porcelain	1 EA	1 EA		3500 EA
Untitled (Unglazed Porcelain Head-Medium Purple)	GEM	GEM	1984	MULT	4 X 3 X 2 EA	Porcelain	1 EA	1 EA		3500 EA
Untitled (Unglazed Porcelain Head-Dark Purple)	GEM	GEM	1984	MULT	4 X 3 X 2 EA	Porcelain	1 EA	1 EA		3500 EA
Untitled (Unglazed Porcelain Head-Gray)	GEM	GEM	1984	MULT	4 X 3 X 2 EA	Porcelain	1 EA	1 EA		3500 EA
Untitled (Glazed Porcelain Bowl-White)	GEM	GEM	1984	MULT	8 X 9 DIA	Porcelain	1 EA	1 EA		4500 EA
Untitled (Glazed Porcelain Bowl-White)	GEM	GEM	1984	MULT	5 X 10 DIA	Porcelain	1 EA	1 EA		6000 EA
Untitled (Unglazed Porcelain Bowl)	GEM	GEM	1984	MULT	5 X 11 DIA	Porcelain	1 EA	1 EA		6000 EA

ROBERT GRAHAM CONTINUED

TITLE	PUBLISHER	PRINTER	DATE	MEDIUM	DIMENSION (PAPER SIZE) IN INCHES	TYPE OF PAPER	EDITION NUMBER	NO. OF COLORS	ORIGINAL OPENING PRICE	CURRENT RETAIL PRICE
CURRENT EDITIONS:										
Untitled (Glazed Porcelain Cube with Unglazed White Arm)	GEM	GEM	1984	MULT	10 X 9 X 9 EA	Porcelain	1 EA	1 EA		12000 EA
Untitled (Unglazed Porcelain Plaque)	GEM	GEM	1984	MULT	5 X 6 X 2	Porcelain	1 EA	1 EA		3000 EA
Untitled (Glazed Porcelain Plaque-White)	GEM	GEM	1984	MULT	5 X 6 X 2	Porcelain	1 EA	1 EA		3000 EA
Untitled (Glazed Porcelain Plaque-Black)	GEM	GEM	1984	MULT	5 X 6 X 2	Porcelain	1 EA	1 EA		3000 EA
Untitled (Glazed Porcelain Plaque-White)	GEM	GEM	1984	MULT	10 X 7 X 1	Porcelain	1 EA	1 EA		3500 EA
Untitled (Glazed Porcelain Plaque-Black)	GEM	GEM	1984	MULT	10 X 7 X 1 EA	Porcelain	1 EA	1 EA		3500 EA
Untitled (Unglazed Porcelain Cylinder with Glazed Head-White)	GEM	GEM	1984	MULT	12 X 9 DIA	Porcelain	1 EA	1 EA		12000 EA
Untitled (Glazed Porcelain Cylinder-White)	GEM	GEM	1984	MULT	12 X 9 DIA	Porcelain	1 EA	1 EA		12000 EA
Untitled (Glazed Porcelain Cylinder-with Unglazed Head-Black)	GEM	GEM	1984	MULT	12 X 9 DIA	Porcelain	1 EA	1 EA		12000 EA
Untitled (Unglazed Porcelain Head)	GEM	GEM	1984	MULT	4 X 3 X 2 EA	Porcelain	1 EA	1 EA		2000 EA
Untitled (Unglazed Porcelain Medallion)	GEM	GEM	1984	MULT	6 X 6 X 1 EA	Porcelain	1 EA	1 EA		1200 EA
Untitled No 35 (Freepoint)	MIX	MIX	1990	FP	33 X 27	HMP	10	1		

LILIANA GRAMBERG

BORN: Treviso, Italy; U S Citizen
EDUCATION: Univ of Rome, Italy, Laurea; California Col of Arts & Crafts, CA, MFA; Escuela Naacional Bellas Artes, Madrid, Spain; Atelier 17, Paris, France
AWARDS: Treadwell Prize, Graphics, Nat Assn of Women Artists, 1963; Silver Medal, Incisori d'Italia Assn, 1964
COLLECTIONS: British Mus, London, England; Galleria Nazionale Arte Moderna, Rome, Italy; Nat Gallery of Art, Wash, DC; Wesleyan Univ, Middletown, CT; Albertina Graphische Sammlung, Vienna, Austria; Ashmolean Mus, Oxford, England; Grunwald Center for the Graphic Arts, Los Angeles, CA; Bibliotheque Nat, Paris, France; Biblioteca Nacional, Madrid, Spain; E T H Graphische Sammlung, Zurich, Switzerland; Usher Art Gallery, Lincolnshire, England; Kestner Mus, Hannover, Germany; Mus of Mod Art, Buenos Aires; Nat Gallery of Mod Art, New Delhi, India; Staatliche Graphische Sammlung, Munich, Germany; Univ of Minnesota, Minneapolis, MN; Australian Nat Gallery, Canberra, Australia
PRINTERS: Artist (ART)
PUBLISHERS: Artist (ART)
GALLERIES: Munson William Proctor Rental Gallery, Utica, NY; Galleria Cartesius, Trieste, Italy
MAILING ADDRESS: 6322 32nd St, NW, Wash, DC 20015

TITLE	PUBLISHER	PRINTER	DATE	MEDIUM	DIMENSION (PAPER SIZE) IN INCHES	TYPE OF PAPER	EDITION NUMBER	NO. OF COLORS	ORIGINAL OPENING PRICE	CURRENT RETAIL PRICE
CURRENT EDITIONS:										
The Exhibition	ART	ART	1977	EB/A		AP	36	1	200	500

JUDITH ANN GRANITZ

PRINTERS: American Atelier, NY (AA)
PUBLISHERS: Circle Fine Art, Chicago, IL (CFA)
GALLERIES: Circle Galleries, San Diego, CA & San Francisco, CA & Northbrook, IL & Pittsburgh, PA & Houston, TX & Soho, NY & Chicago, IL & Scottsdale, AZ & Beverly Hills, CA & Costa Mesa, CA & Sherman Oaks, CA & Palm Beach, FL & Honolulu, HI & New Orleans, LA & Las Vegas, NV & Seattle, WA

TITLE	PUBLISHER	PRINTER	DATE	MEDIUM	DIMENSION (PAPER SIZE) IN INCHES	TYPE OF PAPER	EDITION NUMBER	NO. OF COLORS	ORIGINAL OPENING PRICE	CURRENT RETAIL PRICE
SOLD OUT EDITIONS (RARE):										
Vibrations	CFA	AA	1976	SP	20 X 24	AP	50		35	150
Equivalent I	CFA	AA	1976	SP	26 X 35	AP	60		50	200

REGINA GRANNE

EDUCATION: Cooper Union, NY, Cert, 1959; Hunter Col, NY, 1959–60; Yale Univ, BFA, 1961, MFA, 1963
TEACHING: Instr, Painting & Drawing, Ridgewood Sch of Art, NJ, 1967–73; Vis Prof, Art, Manhattanville Col, NY, 1973–74; Adj Lectr, Art, Queens Col, City Univ of New York, Flushing, NY, 1973–84; Vis Art, Milton Avery Grad Sch, Bard Col, NY, 1983 to present; Instr, Painting, Parsons Sch of Design, NY, 1970 to present
RECENT EXHIB: Genovese Gallery, Boston, MA, 1987; Tatistcheff Gallery, NY, 1989
PRINTERS: Camellia Sullivan, Boston, MA (CA); Genovese Graphics, Boston, MA (GG)
PUBLISHERS: Genovese Graphics, Boston, MA (GG)
GALLERIES: Genovese Gallery, Boston, MA; Tatistcheff Gallery, New York, NY

The print market has become very selective. For the first time since we published the first edition of The Printworld Directory in 1982, the prices of prints have been greatly reduced and greatly increased for the same artists by the most reputable and established print publishers. Check the fifth edition to understand the movement.

REGINA GRANNE CONTINUED

TITLE	PUBLISHER	PRINTER	DATE	MEDIUM	DIMENSION (PAPER SIZE) IN INCHES	TYPE OF PAPER	EDITION NUMBER	NO. OF COLORS	ORIGINAL OPENING PRICE	CURRENT RETAIL PRICE
CURRENT EDITIONS:										
Table and Chair and Plums #1	GG	CS/GG	1987	SP	30 X 39	AP88	50	26	800	900
Table and Chair and Plums #2	GG	CS/GG	1987	SP	30 X 39	AP88	30	13	500	550

GÜNTER GRASS

BORN: Danzig, Germany; October 16, 1927
COLLECTIONS: Davison Art Ctr, Wesleyan, Univ, Middletown, CT; Mus of Mod Art, NY; Cincinnati Art Mus, OH; San Francisco Mus, CA; Rose Art Mus, Brandeis Univ, Waltham, MA; Baltimore Mus of Art, MD; Musse D'Art Moderne, Paris, France; Mus Dahlem, Berlin, West Germany; Cleveland Mus of Art, OH
PRINTERS: Artist (ART)
PUBLISHERS: Artist (ART)
GALLERIES: Miller Gallery, Cincinnati, OH; Gallery 72, Omaha, NE; Mary Ryan Gallery, New York, NY

TITLE	PUBLISHER	PRINTER	DATE	MEDIUM	DIMENSION (PAPER SIZE) IN INCHES	TYPE OF PAPER	EDITION NUMBER	NO. OF COLORS	ORIGINAL OPENING PRICE	CURRENT RETAIL PRICE
SOLD OUT EDITIONS (RARE):										
Flounder over the Land	ART/GA	AD	1978	DB	20 X 26	KBR	100	1	450	750
CURRENT EDITIONS:										
Self Portrait I	ART/GA	AD	1972	EB	20 X 26	KBR	50	1	220	850
Self Portrait II	ART/GA	AD	1972	EB	20 X 26	KBR	50	1	220	850
Shark over the Land	ART/GA	AD	1973	EB	20 X 26	KBR	120	1	340	650
Sated (Self Portrait)	ART/GA	AD	1974	EB	20 X 26	KBR	100	1	300	650
Double Max (Frisch)	ART/GA	AD	1975	EB	20 X 26	KBR	60	1	220	500
All that Remains of the Flounder Are the Bones (Set of 7):									1250 SET	2500 SET
(1) Flounder on the Sand	ART/GA	AD	1977	EB	20 X 26	KBR	150	1	200	400
(2) Flounder	ART/GA	AD	1977	EB	20 X 26	KBR	150	1	200	400
(3) The Flounder	ART/GA	AD	1977	EB	20 X 26	KBR	150	1	200	400
(4) Flounder with Knife	ART/GA	AD	1977	EB	20 X 26	KBR	150	1	200	400
(5) All that Remains of the Flounder are the Bones	ART/GA	AD	1977	EB	20 X 26	KBR	150	1	200	400
(6) Head and Bones	ART/GA	AD	1977	EB	20 X 26	KBR	150	1	200	400
(7) The End of the Tale	ART/GA	AD	1977	EB	20 X 26	KBR	150	1	200	400
David as Oscar II (Tin Drum)	ART/GA	AD	1979	EB	20 X 26	KBR	150	1	450	600
The Writer's Hand	ART/GA	AD	1979	EB	20 X 26	KBR	100	1	390	500
Self Portrait with Fly	ART/GA	AD	1980	EB	20 X 26	KBR	150	1	250	450
Headbirth	ART/GA	AD	1981	EB	20 X 26	KBR	100	1	325	450
Self Portrait with Crawfish	ART/GA	AD	1981	EB	20 X 26	KBR	20	1	320	450
Self Portrait with Feather and Pen	ART/GA	AD	1981	EB	20 X 26	KBR	150	1	450	650
Testamonial to a Glove (7 Etchings Poem)	ART/GA	AD	1981	EB	20 X 26 EA	KBR	150 EA	1 EA	1200 SET	2000 SET
Among the Birds	ART	ART	1981	LB	25 X 32	KBR	60	1	400	600

PETER GRASS

PRINTERS: Alexander Heinrici, NY (AH); Studio Heinrici, Ltd, NY (SH)
PUBLISHERS: London Arts, Inc, Detroit, MI (LAI)
GALLERIES: Barbara Braathen, New York, NY; M-13 Gallery, New York, NY

TITLE	PUBLISHER	PRINTER	DATE	MEDIUM	DIMENSION (PAPER SIZE) IN INCHES	TYPE OF PAPER	EDITION NUMBER	NO. OF COLORS	ORIGINAL OPENING PRICE	CURRENT RETAIL PRICE
CURRENT EDITIONS:										
Beta Nova #1	LAI	AH/SH	1979	SP	31 X 26	AP	200	5	300	350
Arabian Nights #4	LAI	AH/SH	1979	SP	29 X 26	AP	200	5	300	350
Space Moor	LAI	AH/SH	1979	SP	31 X 26	AP	200	5	300	350

GRACE GRAUPE-PILLARD

BORN: New York, NY
EDUCATION: Music & Art High Sch, NY; City Col of New York, NY, Cum Laude, Phi Beta Kappa; City Univ of New York, NY, Grad Assistantship; Art Students League, NY
TEACHING: Instr, Painting & Drawing, Monmouth County Parks, NJ, 1976 to present
AWARDS: George Bridgman Mem Sch, Art Students League, NY, Philip Guston, Juror, 1968; New Jersey State Coun for the Arts, 1982–83; Nat Endowment for the Arts, 1985–86
RECENT EXHIB: Hallwalls, Buffalo, NY, 1987; Lyman Allyn Mus, CT, 1988; Hudson River Mus, NY, 1988; Hal Bromm, NY, 1987,89; Hillwood Gallery, Long Island Univ, NY, 1989–90; Sally Hawkins Gallery, NY, 1990; Aljira Center for Contemp Art, Newark, NJ, 1992
COLLECTIONS: New Jersey State Mus, Trenton, NJ
PRINTERS: Judith Solodkin, NY (JS); Solo Press, NY (SP)
PUBLISHERS: Solo Press, NY (SP)
GALLERIES: Solo Press, New York, NY; Hal Bromm Gallery, New York, NY; Sally Hawkins Gallery, New York, NY
MAILING ADDRESS: P.O. Box 1032, Freehold, NJ 07728

The Printworld Directory is accepting new applications for the seventh edition. Approximately 300 new artists will be accepted. Please use the two forms provided in the back section of this directory to submit biographical data and documentation of prints. Edition number of each print must not exceed 500 and the retail price must be $100 or more.

GRACE GRAUPE-PILLARD CONTINUED

TITLE	PUBLISHER	PRINTER	DATE	MEDIUM	DIMENSION (PAPER SIZE) IN INCHES	TYPE OF PAPER	EDITION NUMBER	NO. OF COLORS	ORIGINAL OPENING PRICE	CURRENT RETAIL PRICE
CURRENT EDITIONS:										
Self Portrait/Portrait (with Daze)	SP	JS/JP	1987	LC/PAS	31 X 47	AC	20		1200	1800

MICHAEL GRAVES

BORN: Indianapolis, IN; July 9, 1934
EDUCATION: Univ of Cincinnati, OH, BS, 1958; Harvard Univ, Cambridge, MA, MA, 1959
TEACHING: Vis Prof, Arch, Univ of Texas, Austin, TX, 1974; Vis Prof, Univ of California, Los Angeles, CA, 1977; Vis Prof, Univ of Houston, TX, 1978; Vis Prof, Univ of North Carolina, Charlotte, NC, 1979; Arch in Res, Am Acad in Rome, Italy, 1979; Lectr, Arch, Princeton Univ, NJ, 1962-67, Assoc Prof, 1968-72, Prof, 1972 to present
AWARDS: Design Award, Progressive Arch, 1970, 1975-80; Arnold W Brunner Mem Prize, 1980; Nat Honor Awards, Am Inst of Arch, 1975,79,82; Four Interiors Design Awards, Henry Hering Mem Medal & Am Sculpture Soc, 1986
RECENT EXHIB: Duke Univ, Durham, NC, 1988; Contemp Arts Center, Cincinnati, OH, 1989; Washington Design Center, DC, 1989; Kunstnernes Mus, Oslo, Norway, 1990; Fort Wayne Mus, IN, 1992; Contemp Arts Center, Cincinnati, OH, 1992
COLLECTIONS: Mus of Mod Art, NY; Cooper-Hewitt Mus, NY; Berlin Mus, Germany; Vassar Col Mus, Poughkeepsie, NY; Smith Col Mus, Northampton, MA
PRINTERS: Sally Sturman, NY (SS); Jane Kent, NY (JK); Toshiro Ito, Tokyo, Japan (TI)
PUBLISHERS: Soc of Fellows, American Acad, Rome, Italy (SFAA); RYU & Co, Tokyo, Japan (RYU)
GALLERIES: Max Protetch Gallery, New York, NY; Struve Gallery, Chicago, IL; Joy Moos Gallery, Miami, FL; John Nichols Gallery, New York, NY; Arion Press, San Francisco, CA
MAILING ADDRESS: 341 Nassau St, Princeton, NY 08540

TITLE	PUBLISHER	PRINTER	DATE	MEDIUM	DIMENSION (PAPER SIZE) IN INCHES	TYPE OF PAPER	EDITION NUMBER	NO. OF COLORS	ORIGINAL OPENING PRICE	CURRENT RETAIL PRICE
CURRENT EDITIONS:										
Composite Landscape	SFAA	JK/SS	1981	EC	21 X 16	JBG/MCC	125		300	650
Alternate Landscape	RYU	TI	1984	WC	16 X 20	EKH	150	24	750	900
Domestic Landscape	RYU	TI	1984	WC	16 X 12	EKH	150	32	750	900

NANCY STEVENSON GRAVES

BORN: Pittsfield, MA; 1940
EDUCATION: Vassar Col Poughkeepsie, NY, BA, 1961; Yale Univ, New Haven, CT, BFA, MFA, 1964
AWARDS: Fulbright-Hays Fel, Paris, France, 1964-68; Nat Endowment for the Arts Fel, 1972; Award, Am Art, Pennsylvania Acad of Fine Arts, Phila, PA 1987; Spirit Achievement Award, Albert Einstein Col Medal, 1988; Am Acad of Inst of Arts & Letters, NY, 1990
RECENT EXHIB: Albright-Knox Art Gallery, Buffalo, NY, 1987; Galleria d'Arte Moderna di Ca' Pesaro, Venice, Italy, 1987; Katonah Gallery, NY, 1987; Siebu Mus, Tokyo, Japan, 1988; Williams Col Art Mus, Williamstown, MA, 1988; Milwaukee Art Mus, WI, 1988; Thomas Fine Arts, Pasadena, CA, 1988; Heland Wetterling Gallery, Stockholm, Sweden, 1988; New Britain Mus of Am Art, CT, 1989; Scottsdale Center for the Arts, AZ, 1989; Nat Mus of Women in the Arts, Wash, DC, 1989; Univ of Maryland, Catonsville, MD, 1992; Berkshire Mus, Pittsfield, MA, 1992; Univ of South Forida, Graphicstudio, Tampa, FL, 1992; Lincoln Center, Fine Art Prints, Avery Fisher Hall, NY, 1992; M Knoedler & Co, NY, 1990,92,93
COLLECTIONS: Whitney Mus of Am Art, NY; Nat Gallery, Ottawa, Can; Wallraf-Richartz Mus, Koln, Germany; Chicago Art Inst, IL; Mus of Fine Arts, Houston, TX; Walker Art Center, Minneapolis, MN; Albright-Knox Art Gallery, Buffalo, NY; Corcoran Gallery of Art, Wash, DC
PRINTERS: Tyler Graphics Ltd, Mount Kisco, NY (TGL); Simca Print Artists, NY (SPA); Artist (ART)
PUBLISHERS: Tyler Graphics Ltd, Mount Kisco, NY (TGL); Simca Print Artists, NY (SPA); Artist (ART)
GALLERIES: M Knoedler & Co, New York, NY; Gloria Luria Gallery, Bay Harbor Island, FL; Irving Galleries, Palm Beach, FL; Richard Gray Gallery, Chicago, IL; Janie C Lee Gallery, Houston, TX; Michael H Lord Gallery, Milwaukee, WI; Mary Singer Gallery, Wash, DC; Ochi Galleries, Boise, ID & Sun Valley, ID; Nancy Singer Gallery, St Louis, MO; Flanders Graphics, Minneapolis, MN; Diane Villani, Inc, New York, NY; Thomas Fine Arts, Pasadena, CA; Linda Cathcart Gallery, Santa Monica, CA; Margulies Taplin Gallery Boca Raton, FL; Tyler Graphics, Ltd, Mount Kisco, NY; Betsy Senior Contemporary Prints, New York, NY; Garner Tullis, New York, NY; Locks Gallery, Phila, PA; Meredith Long & Company, Houston, TX; Heland Wetterling Gallery, Stockholm, Sweden
MAILING ADDRESS: 69 Wooster St, New York, NY 10012

TITLE	PUBLISHER	PRINTER	DATE	MEDIUM	DIMENSION (PAPER SIZE) IN INCHES	TYPE OF PAPER	EDITION NUMBER	NO. OF COLORS	ORIGINAL OPENING PRICE	CURRENT RETAIL PRICE
SOLD OUT EDITIONS (RARE):										
Muin	TGL	TGL	1977	EB/A/DPT	32 X 36	AC	32	18	450	5000
Ngetal	TGL	TGL	1977	EB/A/DPT	32 X 36	AC	33	20	450	5000
Toch	TGL	TGL	1977	EB/A/DPT	32 X 36	AC	28	13	450	5000
Onon (with Pastel)	TGL	TGL	1977	EB/A/DPT/ENG	32 X 36	AC	29	15	450	4500
Saille (with Pastel)	TGL	TGL	1977	EB/A	32 X 36	AC	27	14	450	4500
Ruis (with Solidified Oil Paint Stick)	TGL	TGL	1977	EB/A/ENG/HC	32 X 36	AC	33	9	450	4500
Approaches the Limit of—, I	TGL	TGL	1981	LC	46 X 32	AP/300	30	8	1000	4500
Approaches the Limit of—, II	TGL	TGL	1981	LC/ENG	48 X 32	AP/300	30	16	1200	5000
Calibrate	TGL	TGL	1981	EB/A/SG/ENG/LC	29 X 32	LANA	30	16	1000	4500
75 X 75	SPA/ART	ART	1984	SP	30 X 42	AP88	75	79	1400	4500
Six Frogs	SPA/ART	ART	1985	SP	30 X 41	AP88	66	90	1400	4500

ALAN GREEN

BORN: London, England; 1932
EDUCATION: Beckenham Sch of Art, London, England, 1949–53; Royal Col of Art, London, England, 1955–58
PRINTERS: Alecto, NY (AL)
PUBLISHERS: Annely Juda Fine Art, London, England (AJ)
GALLERIES: Annely Juda Fine Art, London, England; Gimpel Weitzenhoffer, New York, NY; Donald Morris Gallery, Birmingham, MI

TITLE	PUBLISHER	PRINTER	DATE	MEDIUM	DIMENSION (PAPER SIZE) IN INCHES	TYPE OF PAPER	EDITION NUMBER	NO. OF COLORS	ORIGINAL OPENING PRICE	CURRENT RETAIL PRICE
SOLD OUT EDITIONS (RARE):										
Five Out of Five (Set of 5)	AJ	AL	1973	EC	27 X 34 EA	AP	25 EA		200 EA	600 EA

DENISE G GREEN

BORN: Melbourne, Australia; April 7, 1946; U S Citizen
EDUCATION: Ecole Nat Superiere des Beaux Arts, Paris, France; Sorbonne Univ, Paris, France, BA, 1969; Hunter Col, NY, MFA, 1976
TEACHING: Roger Williams Col, Bristol, RI, 1972; Fairleigh Dickinson Univ, Rutherford, NJ, 1972–75; Pratt Inst, Brooklyn, NY, 1974; Art Inst of Chicago, IL, 1977; Virginia Commonwealth Univ, Richmond, VA, 1981
AWARDS: Ingram Merrill Found Grant, 1972,73; Visual Arts Board Grant, 1974,77
RECENT EXHIB: Solomon R Guggenheim Mus, NY, 1987; Gallery of Contemp Art, Ahmedabad, India, 1987; Althea Viafora Gallery, 1987, 88; Rosa Esman Gallery, NY, 1988; Univ Gallery, Melbourne Univ, Australia, 1988; Christine Abrahams Gallery, Melboune, Australia, 1988; Roslyn Oxley Gallery, Sydney, Australia, 1988
PRINTERS: Landfall Press Inc, Chicago, IL (LPI); Jack Lemon, Chicago, IL (JL); Mary McDonald (MM)
PUBLISHERS: Landfall Press Inc, Chicago, IL (LPI)
GALLERIES: Max Protetch Gallery, New York, NY; Landfall Press Inc, Chicago, IL & New York, NY; Althea Viafora, New York, NY; M–13, New York, NY; Rosa Esman Gallery, New York, NY; Roslyn Oxley Gallery, Sydney, Australia; Christine Abrahams Gallery, Melbourne, Australia
MAILING ADDRESS: 13 Laight St, New York, NY 10013

TITLE	PUBLISHER	PRINTER	DATE	MEDIUM	DIMENSION (PAPER SIZE) IN INCHES	TYPE OF PAPER	EDITION NUMBER	NO. OF COLORS	ORIGINAL OPENING PRICE	CURRENT RETAIL PRICE
SOLD OUT EDITIONS (RARE):										
Black and Pink	LPI	MM/LPI	1981	LC	26 X 20	AP/W	10	4	150	500
Circle Invaded by a Square	LPI	JL/LPI	1982	LC	36 X 36	AP/W	30	3	550	800
CURRENT EDITIONS:										
Delhi Morn	LPI	JL/LPI	1988	LC	24 X 32	AP/W	35	7	550	550
Love Song	LPI	JL/LPI	1988	LC	24 X 32	AP/W	35	10	550	550
Olive Park	LPI	JL/LPI	1988	LC	24 X 32	AP/W	35	8	550	550
Rocca Barbera	LPI	JL/LPI	1988	LC	24 X 32	AP/W	35	5	550	550

JASHA GREEN

BORN: Boston, MA; May 1, 1927
EDUCATION: Boston Mus Sch, MA, 1941,46–47; Studied with F Leger, Paris, France, 1948–50
COLLECTIONS: Guggenheim Mus, NY; Kansas City Art Mus, Kansas City, MO; Brooklyn Mus, NY; Philadelphia Mus of Art, PA; Denver Art Mus, CO
PRINTERS: Artist (ART)
PUBLISHERS: Fred Dorfman, Inc, NY (FDI)
GALLERIES: Fred Dorfman Gallery, New York, NY; Images Gallery, Toledo, OH
MAILING ADDRESS: 117 E 18th St, New York, NY 10003

TITLE	PUBLISHER	PRINTER	DATE	MEDIUM	DIMENSION (PAPER SIZE) IN INCHES	TYPE OF PAPER	EDITION NUMBER	NO. OF COLORS	ORIGINAL OPENING PRICE	CURRENT RETAIL PRICE
CURRENT EDITIONS:										
Hommage To Teddy Kollek, II	FDI	ART	1979	LC	32 X 25 EA	AP	250 EA	4 EA	250 EA	400 EA
Peace Prelude I–IV	FDI	ART	1979	LC	32 X 25 EA	AP	250 EA	4 EA	250 EA	400 EA

MARTIN LEONARD GREEN

BORN: Monterey Park, CA; October 4, 1936
EDUCATION: Brandt-Dike Sch of Painting, 1953–54; Pomona Col, CA, 1954–58; Mexico City Col, Mexico, 1957; Orange Coast Col, CA, 1975–76
COLLECTIONS: Los Angeles County Mus of Art, CA; Grunwald Center for Graphic Arts, Univ of California, Los Angeles, CA; Fogg Art Mus, Harvard Univ, Cambridge, MA
PRINTERS: Ernest F De Soto Workshop, San Francisco, CA (DSW); Spectrum Press, Orange, CA (SP); Richard Royce Atelier, Los Angeles, CA (RRA); Nancy E Bowen Studios, Anaheim, CA (NEBS); Artist (ART)
PUBLISHERS: Louis Newman Galleries, Beverly Hills, CA (LNG)
GALLERIES: Art Angles Gallery, Orange, CA; Nuance Galleries, Tampa, FL; Austin Galleries, Palatine, IL; Bergsma Gallery, Grand Rapids, MI; Riggs Galleries, La Jolla, CA
MAILING ADDRESS: 341 Chapman, Orange, CA 92669

TITLE	PUBLISHER	PRINTER	DATE	MEDIUM	DIMENSION (PAPER SIZE) IN INCHES	TYPE OF PAPER	EDITION NUMBER	NO. OF COLORS	ORIGINAL OPENING PRICE	CURRENT RETAIL PRICE
SOLD OUT EDITIONS (RARE):										
Waterfall	LNG	RRA	1975	I	70 X 35	GE	75	5	750	2200
Koi	LNG	DSW	1976	LC	28 X 39	GE	200	10	275	2500
Night Bridge	LNG	DSW	1977	LC	15 X 30	R/BFK	30	2	250	600
Moon Garden	LNG	DSW	1977	LC	25 X 36	AP	30	2	275	600

MARTIN LEONARD GREEN CONTINUED

TITLE	PUBLISHER	PRINTER	DATE	MEDIUM	DIMENSION (PAPER SIZE) IN INCHES	TYPE OF PAPER	EDITION NUMBER	NO. OF COLORS	ORIGINAL OPENING PRICE	CURRENT RETAIL PRICE
SOLD OUT EDITIONS (RARE):										
Eden I	LNG		1980	CV	38 X 23	CIBA	50		500	800
Moon Flowers	LNG	ART	1981	CV	19 X 23	CIBA	50		300	600
CURRENT EDITIONS:										
Passages	LNG	SP	1979	EC	30 X 22	AP	100	2	250	400
Bonsai	LNG	SP	1980	EC	28 X 42	AP	100		300	500
Idyllwild	LNG	ART	1980	CV	28 X 18	CIBA	50		300	550
Deep Blooming	LNG	ART	1980	CV	36 X 17	CIBA	50		350	650
Autumn Plumage	LNG	ART	1980	CV	38 X 23	CIBA	50		500	800
Rain Flowers	LNG	ART	1980	CV	38 X 23	CIBA	50		500	800
Mesa	LNG	ART	1980	CV	38 X 23	CIBA	50		500	800
First Bloom	LNG	ART	1980	CV	28 X 18	CIBA	50		300	550
Vernal Moon	LNG	ART	1982	CV	19 X 23	CIBA	50		300	550
Wood Spirit	LNG	ART	1982	CV	23 X 19	CIBA	50		300	550
Woodland Stream	LNG	ART	1982	CV	38 X 22	CIBA	50		500	800
Earth Spirit	LNG	ART	1982	CV	29 X 37	CIBA	50		825	1000
Bloom	LNG	ART	1982	CV	29 X 37	CIBA	50		825	1000
San Jacinto Peaks	LNG	ART	1983	CV	38 X 23	CIBA	50		600	800
Ni Koi	LNG	NEBS	1983	I	22 X 30	AP	50	18	275	400
Ichi Koi	LNG	NEBS	1983	I	22 X 30	AP	50	18	275	400

RICHARD GREENBERG

PRINTERS: American Atelier, NY (AA)
PUBLISHERS: Circle Fine Art, Chicago, IL (CFA)

GALLERIES: Circle Galleries, San Diego, CA & San Francisco, CA & Northbrook, IL & Pittsburgh, PA & Houston, TX & Soho, NY & Chicago, IL & Scottsdale, AZ & Beverly Hills, CA & Costa Mesa, CA & Sherman Oaks, CA & Palm Beach, FL & Honolulu, HI & New Orleans, LA & Las Vegas, NV & Seattle, WA

TITLE	PUBLISHER	PRINTER	DATE	MEDIUM	DIMENSION (PAPER SIZE) IN INCHES	TYPE OF PAPER	EDITION NUMBER	NO. OF COLORS	ORIGINAL OPENING PRICE	CURRENT RETAIL PRICE
SOLD OUT EDITIONS (RARE):										
Blue Nude	CFA	AA	1978	SP	26 X 35	AP	45		75	100

RODNEY ALAN GREENBLAT

RECENT EXHIB: Pennsylvania State Univ Mus, University Park, PA, 1987; William Paterson Col, Ben Shahn Galleries, Wayne, NY, 1987; Gracie Mansion Gallery, NY, 1987; Martin Lawrence Limited Editions Gallery, CA, 1989; Contemp Arts Mus, Houston, TX, 1989; John Berggruen Gallery, San Francisco, CA, 1989; Queens Mus of Art, NY, 1992
PRINTERS: Larry B Wright, NY (LBW); Larry B Wright Art Productions, NY (LBWAP)

PUBLISHERS: Bruce Spector, NY (BS); Larry B Wright Art Productions, NY (LBWAP); Martin Lawrence Limited Editions, Van Nuys, CA (MLLE)
GALLERIES: Karl Bornstein Gallery, Santa Monica, CA; Gracie Mansion Gallery, New York, NY; Delaware Art Mus, Sales Gallery, Wilmington, DE; Hokin Kaufman Gallery, Chicago, IL; Martin Lawrence Galleries, Escondido, CA & Newport Beach, CA & Palm Springs, CA & Redondo Beach, CA & Santa Monica, CA & Sherman Oaks, CA & Thousand Oaks, CA & West Los Angeles, CA & Short Hills, NJ & Soho, NY & Phila, PA; John Berggruen Gallery, San Francisco, CA; Fred Dorfman Gallery, New York, NY

TITLE	PUBLISHER	PRINTER	DATE	MEDIUM	DIMENSION (PAPER SIZE) IN INCHES	TYPE OF PAPER	EDITION NUMBER	NO. OF COLORS	ORIGINAL OPENING PRICE	CURRENT RETAIL PRICE
SOLD OUT EDITIONS (RARE):										
Mr. Whatever and the Watermellon Mandolin	BS/LBWAP	LBW/LBWAP	1986	SP	15 X 18	AC/W	90		400	1500
CURRENT EDITIONS:										
Set of 3:									1200 SET	5500 SET
Go-Go Golf	MLLE		1988	SP	32 X 43	AC/W	296		500	2050
Research Pays-Off	MLLE		1988	SP	33 X 43	AC/W	296		500	2050
Christina's World	MLLE		1988	SP	34 X 43	AC/W	296		500	2050
Bird Bath at Beak Pointe	MLLE		1989	SP	33 X 42	AC/W	297		600	1950

MILTON GREENE

PRINTERS: American Atelier, NY (AA)
PUBLISHERS: Circle Fine Art, Chicago, IL (CFA)

GALLERIES: Circle Galleries, San Diego, CA & San Francisco, CA & Northbrook, IL & Pittsburgh, PA & Houston, TX & Soho, NY & Chicago, IL & Scottsdale, AZ & Beverly Hills, CA & Costa Mesa, CA & Sherman Oaks, CA & Palm Beach, FL & Honolulu, HI & New Orleans, LA & Las Vegas, NV & Seattle, WA & Edward Weston Fine Arts, Northridge, CA

TITLE	PUBLISHER	PRINTER	DATE	MEDIUM	DIMENSION (PAPER SIZE) IN INCHES	TYPE OF PAPER	EDITION NUMBER	NO. OF COLORS	ORIGINAL OPENING PRICE	CURRENT RETAIL PRICE
SOLD OUT EDITIONS (RARE):										
Stockings	CFA	AA	1980	SP	35 X 46	SOM	300		150	850
Crossed Legs	CFA	AA	1980	SP	35 X 46	SOM	300		150	900

MILTON GREENE CONTINUED

TITLE	PUBLISHER	PRINTER	DATE	MEDIUM	DIMENSION (PAPER SIZE) IN INCHES	TYPE OF PAPER	EDITION NUMBER	NO. OF COLORS	ORIGINAL OPENING PRICE	CURRENT RETAIL PRICE
SOLD OUT EDITIONS (RARE):										
Little Drink	CFA	AA	1980	SP	35 X 46	SOM	300		150	800
Lying Down	CFA	AA	1980	SP	35 X 46	SOM	300		150	800
Reclining	CFA	AA	1980	SP	35 X 46	SOM	300		150	800
Face	CFA	AA	1980	SP	35 X 46	SOM	300		150	900

TIMOTHY GREENFIELD-SANDERS

BORN: Florida; February 16, 1952
EDUCATION: Columbia Univ, NY, BA, 1974; Am Firm Inst, NY, MFA, 1977
AWARDS: Fel, Am Film Inst, NY
RECENT EXHIB: Leo Castelli Gallery, NY, 1987; Zeit Foto Gallery, Tokyo, Japan, 1987; Mary Boone Gallery, NY, 1988
COLLECTIONS: Mus of Mod Art, NY; Australian Nat Gallery, Canberra, Australia; Whitney Mus of Am Art, NY; Metropolitan Mus of Art, NY; Nat Portrait Gallery, Wash, DC
PRINTERS: Artist (ART)
PUBLISHERS: Marcuse Pfeifer Gallery, NY (MPG)
GALLERIES: James Danziger Gallery, New York, NY; Zeit Foto Gallery, Tokyo, Japan
MAILING ADDRESS: 135 E Second St, New York, NY 10009

TITLE	PUBLISHER	PRINTER	DATE	MEDIUM	DIMENSION (PAPER SIZE) IN INCHES	TYPE OF PAPER	EDITION NUMBER	NO. OF COLORS	ORIGINAL OPENING PRICE	CURRENT RETAIL PRICE
CURRENT EDITIONS:										
Marcia Marcus (From Avant-Garde Portfolio—Artists of the Fifties)	MPG	ART	1980	PH	11 X 14		15		400	900

HAROLD GREGOR

BORN: Detroit, MI; September 10, 1929
EDUCATION: Wayne State Univ, NE, BS Ed, 1951; Michigan State Univ, East Lansing, MI, MS, Painting, 1953; Detroit Soc of Arts & Crafts, Oakland, CA, 1955–57; Ohio State Univ, Athens, OH, Painting, PhD, 1960
TEACHING: Head, Art Dept, Chapman Col, Los Angeles, CA; Prof, Art, Illinois State Univ, Normal, IL, 1970 to present
AWARDS: Purchase Award, Watercolor USA, 1984,85; Nat Endowment for the Arts Grants, 1973,86; Outstanding Teach & Researcher, Illinois State Univ, Norman, IL, 1985,86
COLLECTIONS: Rose Art Mus, Brandeis Univ, Waltham, MA; California Col of Arts & Crafts, Oakland, CA; Mus of Contemp Art, Chicago, IL; Illinois State Mus, Springfield, IL; Col of Guam; Fine Arts Gallery of San Diego, CA
RECENT EXHIB: Retrosp, Lakeview Mus of Arts & Science, Peoria, IL, 1987–88; Richard Gray Gallery, Chicago, IL, 1988; Tibor De Nagy Gallery, NY, 1987,88,89; Nat Acad of Design, NY, 1989; Bradley Univ, Heuser Art Center Gallery, Peoria, IL, 1992; Peoria Art Guild, IL, 1992
PRINTERS: Will Petersen, Evanston, IL (WP); Plucked Chicken Press, Evanston, IL (PCP); Artist (ART); Illinois State Univ, Normal, IL (ISU)
PUBLISHERS: Plucked Chicken Press, Evanston, IL (PCP); John Szoke Graphics, NY (JSG)
GALLERIES: Richard Gray Gallery, Chicago, IL; Tibor de Nagy Gallery, New York, NY; Harcourts Contemporary Gallery, San Francisco, CA; Marisa Del Re Gallery, New York, NY; Peoria Art Guild, Peoria, IL; John Szoke Graphics, New York, NY
MAILING ADDRESS: 107 W Market St, Bloomington, IL 61701

TITLE	PUBLISHER	PRINTER	DATE	MEDIUM	DIMENSION (PAPER SIZE) IN INCHES	TYPE OF PAPER	EDITION NUMBER	NO. OF COLORS	ORIGINAL OPENING PRICE	CURRENT RETAIL PRICE
CURRENT EDITIONS:										
Heartlands VI	PCP	ART/PCP	1985	LC	23 X 29	AC/W	30		375	600
Above the Farm, States I-V	JSG	ISU	1990	LI	30 X 46 EA	SOM	15 EA	1–3 EA	750 EA	750 EA

ELLNA KAY GREGORY-GOODRUM

BORN: Houston, TX; October 3, 1943
EDUCATION: Univ of Oklahoma, Norman, OK, BFA, 1965; North Texas State Univ, Denton, TX, MFA, 1979
TEACHING: Inst, Art Appreciation & Painting, Richland Col, Dallas, TX, 1980 to present
AWARDS: Best Abstract, Pastel Soc of Am, 1979; Texas Watercolor Soc, 1986; Nat Watercolor Award, Oklahoma City, OK, 1988; Southwestern Watercolor Soc, 1979,83,85,88
RECENT EXHIB: Springfield Mus, MO, 1988; Nat Watercolor Soc, NY, 1987,88; Transco Energy Center, Houston, TX, 1988; Foothill Art Center, 1988
COLLECTIONS: Renaissance Center, Detroit, MI; Rockwell International, Dallas, TX
PRINTERS: Artist (ART)
PUBLISHERS: Artist (ART)
GALLERIES: Edith Baker Gallery, Dallas, TX
MAILING ADDRESS: 7214 Lane Park Drive, Dallas, TX 75225

TITLE	PUBLISHER	PRINTER	DATE	MEDIUM	DIMENSION (PAPER SIZE) IN INCHES	TYPE OF PAPER	EDITION NUMBER	NO. OF COLORS	ORIGINAL OPENING PRICE	CURRENT RETAIL PRICE
SOLD OUT EDITIONS (RARE):										
Strata IV Series	ART	ART	1977	COL	30 X 22	AP/B	6	2	300	750
Strata Extensions	ART	ART	1977	COL	22 X 30	AP/B	6	2	300	750
Strata VII Series	ART	ART	1979	I	30 X 22	AP/B	6	3	300	750
Pendulum Series	ART	ART	1979	EMB	30 X 22	AP/B	4	10	400	900
Strata Line Series	ART	ART	1979	EMB	30 X 22	AP/W	4	4	400	900

MICHAEL GREGORY

PRINTERS: Marcia Bartholme, Seattle, WA (MB); Berit Bardarson, Seattle, WA (BB); Beta Press, Seattle, WA (BPr); Tamarind Inst, Albuquerque, NM (TI)
PUBLISHERS: Beta Press, Seattle, WA (BPr); Tamarind Inst, Albuquerque, NM (TI)
GALLERIES: Nancy Hoffman Gallery, New York, NY; John Berggruen Gallery, San Francisco, CA; Thomas Gallery, Minneapolis, MN; Tamarind Inst, Albuquerque, NM

TITLE	PUBLISHER	PRINTER	DATE	MEDIUM	DIMENSION (PAPER SIZE) IN INCHES	TYPE OF PAPER	EDITION NUMBER	NO. OF COLORS	ORIGINAL OPENING PRICE	CURRENT RETAIL PRICE
CURRENT EDITIONS:										
Green Arc	BPr	MB/BB/BPr	1992	DPt/SB	26 X 43	SOM	30	1	900	900
B/W Arc	BPr	MB/BB/BPr	1992	DPt/SB	26 X 43	SOM	30	1	900	900
Ochre Arc	BPr	MB/BB/BPr	1992	DPt/SB	26 X 43	SOM	30	1	900	900
Dark Spiral	BPr	MB/BB/BPr	1992	DPt/SB	26 X 43	SOM	15	1	900	900
On Gampi	BPr	MB/BB/BPr	1992	DPt/SB/CC	26 X 43	SOM/Gampi	35	1	900	900

GERRIT GREVE

BORN: Bandung (Java), Indonesia; 1948
EDUCATION: Elmhurst Col, IL
PRINTERS: Atelier Ettinger, NY (AE)
PUBLISHERS: Eleanor Ettinger Inc, NY (EEI)
GALLERIES: Miller Gallery, San Francisco, CA; Nuance Gallery, Tampa, FL

TITLE	PUBLISHER	PRINTER	DATE	MEDIUM	DIMENSION (PAPER SIZE) IN INCHES	TYPE OF PAPER	EDITION NUMBER	NO. OF COLORS	ORIGINAL OPENING PRICE	CURRENT RETAIL PRICE
SOLD OUT EDITIONS (RARE):										
La Boheme	EEI	AE	1981	LC	22 X 29	AP	350		275	400
La Boheme	EEI	AE	1981	LC	22 X 29	JP	50		300	400
Elektra	EEI	AE	1981	LC	22 X 29	AP	350		275	400
Elektra	EEI	AE	1981	LC	22 X 29	JP	50		300	400
Thoughts	EEI	AE	1981	LC	22 X 28	AP	350		275	400
Thoughts	EEI	AE	1981	LC	22 X 28	JP	50		300	400
Cat & Toad	EEI	AE	1981	LC	33 X 22	AP	400		275	400
Old Indian	EEI	AE	1981	LC	23 X 28	AP	350		275	400
Old Indian	EEI	AE	1981	LC	23 X 29	JP	50		300	400
Indigo Bunting	EEI	AE	1981	LC	23 X 29	AP	350		275	400
Indigo Bunting	EEI	AE	1981	LC	23 X 29	JP	50		300	400
Desert Dream	EEI	AE	1981	LC	23 X 29	AP	350		275	400
Desert Dream	EEI	AE	1981	LC	23 X 29	JP	50		300	400

ALEX V GREY

PRINTERS: Strother/Elwood Art Editions, Brooklyn, NY (SEAE)
PUBLISHERS: John Nichols, NY (JN)
GALLERIES: Stux Gallery, New York, NY; Du Bois International, Ltd, New York, NY; Thomas Erben Gallery, Inc, New York, NY

TITLE	PUBLISHER	PRINTER	DATE	MEDIUM	DIMENSION (PAPER SIZE) IN INCHES	TYPE OF PAPER	EDITION NUMBER	NO. OF COLORS	ORIGINAL OPENING PRICE	CURRENT RETAIL PRICE
Praying	SEAE	JN	1984	LC/SP	30 X 22	AC	30		400	650

JOHN GRILLO

BORN: Lawrence, MA; July 4, 1917
EDUCATION: Hartford Art Sch, CT, 1935–38; California Sch of Fine Arts, San Francisco, CA, 1946; Hans Hofmann Sch, NY, 1949–50
TEACHING: Southern Illinois Univ, 1960; Sch of Visual Arts, NY, 1961; Univ of California, Berkeley, CA, 1962–63; New Sch for Social Research, NY; 1964–66; Pratt Inst, NY, 1965–66; State Univ of Iowa, 1967 to present
AWARDS: Research Grant, Univ of Massachusetts, Amherst, MA; Albert M Bender Fel, 1947; Ford Found Fel, Butler Inst, Youngstown, OH, 1964; Ford Found Grant, Lithography, Tamarind Workshop, Los Angeles, CA 1964
RECENT EXHIB: Lane Comm Col, Art Gallery, Eugene, OR, 1989; Mus of Fine Arts, Springfield, MA, 1989
COLLECTIONS: Whitney Mus of Am Art, NY; Guggenheim Mus, NY; Brooklyn Mus, NY; Walker Art Center, Minneapolis, MN; Wadsworth Atheneum, Hartford, CT; Dartmouth Col, NH; Univ of Texas, Austin, TX; Newark Mus, NJ; Los Angeles County Mus, CA; Bennington Col, VT; Portland Mus, ME; Norfolk Mus, VA; Univ of California, Berkeley, CA; Butler Inst of Am Art, Youngstown, OH; Bundy Art Gallery, Waitsfield, VT; Univ of Massachusetts, Amherst, MA; Smith Col, MA
PRINTERS: Alexander Heinrici, NY (AH); Studio Heinrici, Ltd, NY (SH); American Atelier, NY (AA)
PUBLISHERS: London Arts, Inc, Detroit, MI (LAI); Circle Fine Art, Chicago, IL (CFA)
GALLERIES: Thronja Original Art, Springfield, MA; Jean Lumbard Fine Art, New York, NY; Aaron Gallery, Wash, DC; Cove Gallery, Wellfleet, MA; Circle Galleries, San Francisco, CA & San Diego, CA & Beverly Hills, CA & Costa Mesa, CA & Sherman Oaks, CA & Scottsdale, AZ & Palm Beach, FL & Honolulu, HI & New Orleans, LA & Las Vegas, NV & Seattle, WA & Chicago, IL & Northbrook, IL & Houston, TX & Pittsburgh, PA & Soho, NY

TITLE	PUBLISHER	PRINTER	DATE	MEDIUM	DIMENSION (PAPER SIZE) IN INCHES	TYPE OF PAPER	EDITION NUMBER	NO. OF COLORS	ORIGINAL OPENING PRICE	CURRENT RETAIL PRICE
CURRENT EDITIONS:										
Tantra Abstractions	LAI	AH/SH	1978	LC	34 X 25	SOM	200	6	175	175
Girl with Hat I-IV	CFA	AA	1980	SP	33 X 26 EA	AP	200 EA		175 EA	175 EA
Del Greco a' Goya	CFA	AA	1980	SP	33 X 26	AP	200		175	175
Portrait	CFA	AA	1981	SP	34 X 26	AP	200		175	175
Woman with Flowers	CFA	AA	1981	SP	26 X 34	AP	200		175	175

BURT GROEDEL

BORN: New York, NY, 1937
EDUCATION: Art Students League, NY; Pratt Inst, Brooklyn, NY
RECENT EXHIB: Polynero Gallery, Antwerp, Belgium, 1987; Chiaroscuro Gallery, Chicago, IL, 198–88; Lillian Heidenberg Gallery, NY, 1988
PRINTERS: Atelier Ettinger, NY (AE)
PUBLISHERS: Eleanor Ettinger Inc, NY (EEI)
GALLERIES: Jentra Art Gallery, Freehold, NY; Studio 53 Gallery, New York, NY; Polynero Gallery, Antwerp, Belgium; Chiaroscuro Gallery, Chicago, IL; Lillian Heidenberg Gallery, New York, NY; Straus Gallery, New York, NY
MAILING ADDRESS: 200 E 15th St, New York, NY 10003

TITLE	PUBLISHER	PRINTER	DATE	MEDIUM	DIMENSION (PAPER SIZE) IN INCHES	TYPE OF PAPER	EDITION NUMBER	NO. OF COLORS	ORIGINAL OPENING PRICE	CURRENT RETAIL PRICE
SOLD OUT EDITIONS (RARE):										
Her Serene Highness	EEI	AE	1980	LC	22 X 28	AP	300		225	300
Edifice Complex	EEI	AE	1980	LC	22 X 28	AP	300		225	325
Lady Go-Diva	EEI	AE	1980	LC	22 X 28	AP	300		200	300
Lady Worthington's Bird	EEI	AE	1980	LC	22 X 28	AP	300		200	375
Take Me to Your Leda	EEI	AE	1980	LC	22 X 28	AP	300		200	325
I've Grown Accustomed to Your Pace	EEI	AE	1980	LC	22 X 28	AP	300		200	425
Sea Fantasy	EEI	AE	1983	LC	23 X 24	AP	300	10	225	300
Still Life Fantasy	EEI	AE	1983	LC	22 X 33	AP	300	12	225	300

JAMES GROFF

BORN: Kankakee, IL; March 7, 1937
EDUCATION: Art Inst of Chicago, IL, 1953; Southern Illinois Univ, Carbondale, IL, BA, 1959; MFA, 1961
AWARDS: Am Soc of Printmakers, NY, 1959; Printmakers of Am, NY, 1960; Young Americans Painting Show, Andover, MA, 1961
COLLECTIONS: Southern Illinois Univ Mus, Carbondale, IL
PRINTERS: Artist (ART)
PUBLISHERS: Artist (ART)
GALLERIES: Clifford Gallery, Dallas, TX; Morgan Gallery, Kansas City, MO; Malton Gallery, Cincinnati, OH; Associated American Artists Gallery, New York, NY; Miriam Perlman Gallery, Chicago, IL; Heath Gallery, Atlanta, GA; Jack Rutberg Fine Arts, Los Angeles, CA; Harcourts Contemporary & Modern, San Francisco, CA; Galerie Simonne Stern, New Orleans, LA; Jan Weiner Gallery, Kansas City, MO; Dunlap-Freidenrich Fine Art, Newport Beach, CA; Charles Whitchurch, Huntington Beach, CA; Gremillion & Company Fine Art, Inc, Houston, TX; Trinity Gallery, Atlanta, GA; Virginia Miller Galleries, Miami, FL
MAILING ADDRESS: 7723 Brushwood Drive, Houston, TX 77088

TITLE	PUBLISHER	PRINTER	DATE	MEDIUM	DIMENSION (PAPER SIZE) IN INCHES	TYPE OF PAPER	EDITION NUMBER	NO. OF COLORS	ORIGINAL OPENING PRICE	CURRENT RETAIL PRICE
CURRENT EDITIONS:										
Sand Echo	ART	ART	1983	AC	30 X 22	R/BFK/CR	25	3	250	300
Blue Mist	ART	ART	1983	AC	30 X 22	R/BFK/CR	25	3	250	300
Yellow Fever	ART	ART	1983	AC	30 X 22	R/BFK/CR	25	3	250	300
Keyline	ART	ART	1983	AC	38 X 28 EA	R/BFK/CR	25 EA	3/3/4/3 EA	350 EA	400 EA
Red Velvet	ART	ART	1983	AC	30 X 22	R/BFK/CR	25	3	250	300
Et Alia #1	ART	ART	1983	AC	38 X 28	R/BFK/CR	25	3	350	400
Et Cetera #1–#4	ART	ART	1983	AC	20 X 22 EA	R/BFK/CR	25 EA	4/3 EA	250 EA	300 EA
Byline #1–#4	ART	ART	1983	AC	38 X 28	R/BFK/CR	25 EA	4 EA	350 EA	400 EA
Aging Sun #1–#4	ART	ART	1984	AC	38 X 28 EA	R/BFK/CR	25 EA	3 EA	350 EA	400 EA
Eclipse #1, #2	ART	ART	1984	AC	38 X 28 EA	R/BFK/CR	25 EA	3 EA	350 EA	400 EA
Earth Exit #1	ART	ART	1984	AC	30 X 22	R/BFK/CR	25	4	300	350

JAN GROOVER

BORN: Plainfield, NJ; 1943
EDUCATION: Pratt Inst, NY, BFA, 1965; State Univ of Ohio, Columbus, OH, MFA, 1970
TEACHING: Asst Prof, Art Sch, Univ of Hartford, CT, 1970–73; Prof, State Univ of New York, Purchase, NY, 1979 to present
AWARDS: Guggenheim Mem Found Grant, NY, 1979; Nat Endowment for the Arts Grant, 1978, 90
RECENT EXHIB: Retrosp, Mus of Mod Art, NY, 1987; California State Univ, Long Beach, CA, 1988; Berkshire Mus, Pittsfield, MA, 1989
COLLECTIONS: Metropolitan Mus of Art, NY; Mus of Mod Art, NY; Whitney Mus of Am Art, NY; Baltimore Mus of Art, MD; Mus of Fine Arts, Minneapolis, MN
PRINTERS: Artist (ART)
PUBLISHERS: Carol Goldberg, Inc, NY (CGI)
GALLERIES: BlumHelman Gallery, New York, NY; Robert Miller Gallery, New York, NY; Richard Green Gallery, Los Angeles, CA; Michael H Lord Gallery, Milwaukee, WI; Betsy Rosenfield Gallery, Chicago, IL
MAILING ADDRESS: 189 Bowery, New York, NY 10002

TITLE	PUBLISHER	PRINTER	DATE	MEDIUM	DIMENSION (PAPER SIZE) IN INCHES	TYPE OF PAPER	EDITION NUMBER	NO. OF COLORS	ORIGINAL OPENING PRICE	CURRENT RETAIL PRICE
SOLD OUT EDITIONS (RARE):										
Untitled, Washington Cars (Trip)	ART	ART	1974	PH	9 X 18	R/100			500	1200
Untitled, (Still Life)	ART	ART	1978	PH	15 X 19	R/100		3	600	1500
CURRENT EDITIONS:										
Plain Fields (Platinum Prints) (Set of 10)	CGI	ART	1981	PH	7 X 9 EA	R/100	20 EA		8000 SET	12000 SET
Untitled (Still Life of Bottles) (Mounted on Aluminum & Framed)	CGI	ART	1988	PH/C	28 X 36	SOM		5	3000	6000

The retail prices of the 100,000 limited edition prints quoted in this directory are subject to change. Print publishers, artists and galleries were the direct sources for these quotations. Prices in the secondary market listed as "Sold Out Editions (Rare)" indicate that the publisher has a limited supply of that print or that the print is difficult to locate in the galleries.

RED GROOMS

BORN: Nashville, TN; June 10, 1937
EDUCATION: Art Inst of Chicago, IL; Peabody Col, Nashville, TN; New Sch for Social Research, NY; Hans Hofmann sch, Provincetown, MA
TEACHING: Vis Art, Syracuse, NY, 1980; Vis Art, Southern Illinois, Carbondale, IL, 1980; Vis Art, Colorado State Univ, Boulder, CO, 1981; Albert Dorn Prof, Univ of Bridgeport, CT, 1982
AWARDS: Creative Artists Public Service Award, 1970; Lower Manhattan Cultural Council Award, 1982; President's Award, Rhode Island Sch of Design, Providence, RI, 1985; Gold Medal of Honor, Nat Arts Club, 1986; Mayor's Award of Honor for Art & Culture, NY, 1988
RECENT EXHIB: Retrosp, Whitney Mus of Am Art, NY, 1987; Retrosp, Pennsylvania Acad of Fine Arts, Phila, PA, 1987; Stanton Gallery, Denver, CO, 1987; Sims Fine Art, New Orleans, LA, 1987; Cleveland Center for Contemp Art, OH, 1988; North Dakota Mus of Art, Grand Forks, ND, 1989; Masur Mus of Art, Monroe, LA, 1989; Marlborough Gallery, NY, 1987,90; James Madison Univ, Sawhill Gallery, Harrisonburg, VA, 1992; Madison Art Center, WI, 1992; Hudson River Mus of Westchester, Yonkers, NY, 1992; Southeast Arkansas Arts & Sciences Center, Pine Bluff, AR, 1992; Redding Mus & Art Center, Ca, 1992; Univ of Colorado, Colorado Springs, CO, 1992; Pennsylvania Acad of Fine Arts, Phila, PA, 1992; Masur Mus of Art, Monroe, LA, 1992; Quartet Editions, NY, 1993
COLLECTIONS: Mint Mus of Art, Charlotte, NC; Art Inst of Chicago, IL; Mus of Mod Art, NY; North Carolina Mus of Art, Raleigh, NC; Chrysler Mus, Provincetown, MA; Brooklyn Mus, NY; Cheekwood Art Mus, Nashville, TN; Delaware Art Mus, Wilmington, DE; Denver Art Mus, CO; Everson Mus, Syracuse, NY; Fort Worth Art Center, TX; Hirshhorn Mus, Wash, DC; Hudson River Mus, Yonkers, NY; Museet Moderna, Stockholm, Sweden; Museo de Arts Contemporaneo, Caracas, Venezuela; New Jersey State Mus, Trenton, NJ; New Sch Art Center, NY; Northern Kentucky Univ, Highland Heights, KY; Southern Illinois Univ, Carbondale, IL
PRINTERS: Vermillion Editions, Ltd, Minneapolis, MN (VEL); A Kirk, NY (AK); J Melby, NY (JM); Chip Elwell, NY (CE); Wil Foo (WF); John Stemmer (JS); Experimental Workshop, San Francisco, CA (EW); John Campione (JC); Bud Shark, Boulder, CO (BS); Alexander Heinrici, NY (AH); Studio Heinrici, NY (SH); Matthew Christie, Boulder, CO (MC); Mark Villarreal, Boulder, CO (MV); Shark's, Inc, Boulder, CO (SI); Spring Street Workshop, NY (SpSW)
PUBLISHERS: Brooke Alexander, Inc, NY (BAI); Marlborough Graphics, NY (MG); Contemporary Artists (CA); Signet Arts, St Louis, MO (SA); Vermillion Editions, Ltd, Minneapolis, MN (VEL); Chicago Sculpture Society (CSS); Shark's Inc, Boulder, CO (SI); Experimental Workshop, San Francisco, CA (EW); Unicorn Gallery, Aspen, CO (UG); Anderson Ranch Arts Center, Aspen, CO (ARAC); Artist (ART); Spring Street Workshop, NY (SpSW); Bard Col, NY (BC)
GALLERIES: Brooke Alexander, Inc, New York, NY; Shark's, Inc, Boulder, CO; Signet Arts, St Louis, MO; Mangel Gallery, Phila, PA; Krakow Gallery, Boston, MA; Nicola Jacobs Gallery, London, England; Leila Taghinia-Milani, New York, NY; Nancy Hoffman Gallery, New York, NY; Horoshak Contemporary Art, Sunnyvale, CA; Opus Art Studios, Miami, FL; Marvin Ross Freedman & Co, Miami, FL; Morgan Gallery, Boston, MA; Vermillion Editions, Ltd, Minneapolis, MN; Marlborough Gallery, New York, NY & London, England; Quartet Editions, New York, NY; John Natsoulas Gallery, Davis, CA; Herbert Palmer Gallery, Los Angeles, CA; Daniel Saxon Gallery, Los Angeles, CA; John Berggruen Gallery, San Francisco, CA; Greenhut Gallery, Portland, ME; Joseph Petrone Fine Arts, New York, NY; Joseph Petrone Fine Arts, New York, NY; Pace Prints, New York, NY; Ro Gallery Image Makers, Inc, New York, NY
MAILING ADDRESS: c/o Shark's Inc, 2020 Ninth St, Boulder, CO 80302

Red Grooms
Gertrude
Courtesy Brooke Alexander Editions

Red Grooms
Dali Salad
Courtesy Brooke Alexander Editions

Alexander & Cowles (A&C)

TITLE	PUBLISHER	PRINTER	DATE	MEDIUM	DIMENSION (PAPER SIZE) IN INCHES	TYPE OF PAPER	EDITION NUMBER	NO. OF COLORS	ORIGINAL OPENING PRICE	CURRENT RETAIL PRICE
SOLD OUT EDITIONS (RARE):										
No Gas AARRRRRRHH (Cut-Out, Folded & Assembled in Plexiglas Box) (A&C 11A)	A&C		1971	LC/3D	29 X 10 X 24	AC	75		750	12000
Gangster and the Moll Dancing the Tango			1973	SP	39 X 29	AP	99		100	6000
The Daily Arf	CA	JC	1974	SP/EMB	20 X 15	GE	75	13	150	7500
Gertrude	MG		1975	LC/3-D	19 X 23 X 11	AC	46		750	15000
Gertrude Stein	BAI		1975	LC/PO	19 X 22 X 10	AC	46		750	15000
Picasso Goes To Heaven	BAI/MG		1976	E/PO	29 X 30	R/BFK	43		500	6000
Picasso Goes To Heaven	BAI/MG		1976	EB	29 X 30	R/BFK	20		300	6000
Cafe Manet	MG/BAI		1976	EB	13 X 15	R/BFK	40	1	150	3500

RED GROOMS CONTINUED

Red Grooms
Noa Noa
Courtesy Shark's, Inc

Red Grooms
South Sea Sonata
Courtesy Shark's, Inc

TITLE	PUBLISHER	PRINTER	DATE	MEDIUM	DIMENSION (PAPER SIZE) IN INCHES	TYPE OF PAPER	EDITION NUMBER	NO. OF COLORS	ORIGINAL OPENING PRICE	CURRENT RETAIL PRICE
SOLD OUT EDITIONS (RARE):										
Self Portrait with Liz	MG/BAI	AK	1982	LC	21 X 16	AP	44		800	3000
Manet/Romanco	MG/BAI	AK	1976	EB	34 X 26	R/BFK	40	1	350	3000
Matisse in his Studio	BAI/MG	AK	1976	LB	26 X 35	AP	75	1	175	3000
Nineteenth Century Artists (Set of 10):									1500 SET	20000 SET
Whistler	MG/BAI	AK	1976	EB	15 X 11	R/BFK	40	1	150	2000
Constintine Guys	MG/BAI	AK	1976	EB	15 X 11	R/BFK	40	1	150	2000
Courbet	MG/BAI	AK	1976	EB	15 X 11	R/BFK	40	1	150	2000
Degas	MG/BAI	AK	1976	DPT	15 X 11	R/BFK	40	1	150	2000
Rodin	MG	AK	1976	EB/A	15 X 11	R/BFK	40	1	150	2000
Cezanne	MG/BAI	AK	1976	EB/A	15 X 11	R/BFK	40	1	150	2000
Bazille	MG/BAI	AK	1976	EB/A	15 X 11	R/BFK	40	1	150	2000
Baudelaire	MG/BAI	AK	1976	EB	15 X 11	R/BFK	40	1	150	2000
Delacroix	MG/BAI	AK	1976	EB	15 X 11	R/BFK	40	1	150	2000
Naclar	MG/BAI	AK	1976	EB/A/DPT	15 X 11	R/BFK	40	1	150	2000
Coney Island	MG	AK	1976–78	AC	22 X 26	R/BFK	34		300	4500
Chuck Berry	MG	AK	1978	SP/DI	24 X 18	R/BFK	150		300	6000
A Body Like Mine	MG	AK	1978	SP	24 X 18	R/BFK	150		300	6000
Museum	BAI	AK	1978	LC	10 X 24	R/BFK	150		300	1000
Truck	BAI/MG	AK	1979	LB	24 X 62	AP	30	1	600	5000
Truck	BAI/MG	AK	1979	LC	24 X 62	AP	75		1250	15000
Peking Delight (Multi)	BAI	AK	1979	SP/WO	16 X 18 X 5	HMP	50		1500	15000
Frank Tarkenton (Multi)	BAI	AK	1979	PV/AL/PO	72 X 48 X 8	AP	8		3500	15000
Lorna Doone (2 Sheets)	BAI	AK	1979–80	LC/RS	49 X 32	AP	48		900	3600
Dallas 14, Jack 6	BAI	AK	1980	EB/A	18 X 14	R/BFK	25		200	3500
Jack Beal Watching the Superbowl	BAI	AK	1980	EB/A	18 X 15	R/BFK	15		175	3500
The Tatoo Artist	BAI	AK	1980	LC	38 X 25	AP	38		500	1200
Heads Up DH	BAI	AK	1980	EB/A	27 X 30	AP	26		300	7500
Dali Salad (Blue)	BAI/MG	AK	1980	LC/SP	27 X 20 X 13	AP/JP	10		2000	12000
Dali Salad (Multi) (AC-48)	BAI/MG	AK	1980–81	LC/SP	27 X 28 X 13	AP/JP	55		2000	15000
Mountaintime	SA	BS/SI	1981	LC	30 X 22	AP	65	6	900	6000
Mid-Rats	VEL	VEL	1981	LC	22 X 30	R/BFK	88	13	500	3000
Pancake Eater	BAI/MG/VEL	AK	1981	LC	42 X 30 X 3	HMP	31		2500	15000
Pierpont Morgan Library	BAI/MG	AK	1982	LC	15 X 38	AP	300		300	6000
Ruckus Taxi (A&C-57)	SI/ART	BS/SI	1982	LC	16 X 29 X 14	AC/W	75	5	1500	18000
Chicago Mile of Sculpture	VEL/CSS	VEL	1982	LC	36 X 23	AC/W	100	13	600	600
Chicago Mile of Sculpture	VEL/CSS	VEL	1982	LC/HC	32 X 23	AC/W	100	Varies	1000	2000
Downhiller	UG/ARAC	BS/SI	1983	LC	41 X 29	AC/W	75	6	1000	7500
Subway Riders	CFA	AA	1983	SP	30 X 36	AC/W	250		1000	7500
*Tonto/Condo (A&C-66)	SI/ART	BS/SI	1983	LC	23 X 31 X 7	R/BFK	75	7	1500	8000
*Wheeler Opera House	SI/ART	BS/SI	1984	LC	4 X 17 X 20	AP88	30	6	2000	15000
*London Bus	SI/ART	BS/SI	1984	LC	20 X 22 X 14	R/BFK	63	7	2000	15000
*Fats Domino	SI/ART	BS/SI	1984	LC	17 X 21 X 17	AP88	54		2000	15000
Giacometti	EW	WF/JS/EW	1984	WC	76 X 43	SAP/HMP	15	18	3000	12000
Charlie Chaplin	SI/ART	BS/SI	1985	LC	22 X 18 X 11	HMP	75		5000	15000
Cafe Tabu	MG		1985	EB/A	14 X 16	HMP	50		800	2000
Portrait of Giacometti	GT	GTW	1985	WC	71 X 43	R/BFK	15	5	2500	7500
Red's Roxy (in Plexiglas Box)	SI/ART	BS/SI	1985	LC	8 X 6 X 12	R/BFK-MYLAR	200		1400	6000

RED GROOMS CONTINUED

Red Grooms
Little Italy
Courtesy Shark's, Inc

TITLE	PUBLISHER	PRINTER	DATE	MEDIUM	DIMENSION (PAPER SIZE) IN INCHES	TYPE OF PAPER	EDITION NUMBER	NO. OF COLORS	ORIGINAL OPENING PRICE	CURRENT RETAIL PRICE
SOLD OUT EDITIONS (RARE):										
American Geisha	SI/ART	BS/SI	1985	LC/WC/LI	18 X 22	AC/W	25		1400	4000
CURRENT EDITIONS:										
Chaplin	SI/ART	BS/SI	1986	MON	72 X 36 EA	HMP	1 EA	Varies	6500 EA	12000 EA
Subway	SI/ART	BS/SI	1986	LC	15 X 41 X 7	HMP	75		4000	20000
De Kooning Breaks Through (Assembled by Hand & Mounted in Plexiglas Case) (3 Sheets)	SI/ART	BS/SI	1986/87	LC/3D	47 X 33 X 9	HMP	75	8	8000	15000
Elvis	SI	BS/SI	1987	LC	44 X 30	R/BFK	75		1800	5000
Elvis I, II, III, IV	SI	BS/SI	1987	MON	44 X 30 EA	HMP	1 EA	Varies	3500 EA	7500 EA
Center and Mott Street II	SI	BS/MC/SI	1987	MON	30 X 42 EA	HMP	1 EA	Varies	3500 EA	10000 EA
Old Business II	SI	BS/MC/SI	1987	MON	30 X 45 EA	HMP	1 EA	Varies	3500 EA	12000 EA
New Business II	SI	BS/MC/SI	1987	MON	30 X 45 EA	HMP	1 EA	Varies	3500 EA	12000 EA
Banderllias, Muerte, Capa, Muleta II (4 Panels)	SI	BS/MC/SI	1987	MON	73 X 18 EA	HMP	1 EA	Varies	20000 SET	45000 SET
Cafe Deux Magots	MG		1987	EB/A	29 X 33	HMP	90		1200	1500
Cedar Bar	MG		1987	LC	24 X 32	TRP	200		1000	1500
Van Gogh with Sunflowers	SI	BS/ART/SI	1988	LC	19 X 25	TRP	75	5	2500	4500
Little Italy	SI	BS/MC/SI	1988–89	LC/3D	27 X 39 X 17	R/BFK	90		7500	18000
Sunday Funnies	SI	BS/MC/SI	1989	LC	30 X 45	HMP	120		2500	6000
Los Aficionados	SI	BS/MC/SI	1989–90	LC/3D	25 X 35 X 24	HMP	90		2500	18000
Holy Hula (2 Sheets)	SI	BS/MC/SI	1990–91	LC/CO	29 X 37 X 2	R/BFK	90		8000	10000
Elaine de Kooning at the Cedar Bar	SpSW/BC	SpSW	1991	STR	30 X 22	SUZ	50		1000	1000
Noa Noa	SI	BS/MC/MV/SI	1992	WC	20 X 30	HMP	40		2500	2500
South Sea Sonata (2 Sheets)	SI	BS/MC/MV/SI	1992	LC/30	20 X 22 X 11	R/BFK	60		5000	6000
Marnalahoa Highway I, II	SI	BS/MC/MV/SI	1992	MON	24 X 34 EA	SUZ	1 EA	Varies	6000 EA	6000 EA
Peacock Grouper & Others I	SI	BS/MC/MV/SI	1992	MON	24 X 34 EA	SUZ	1 EA	Varies	6000 EA	6000 EA
Blue Goatfish & Others II	SI	BS/MC/MV/SI	1992	MON	24 X 34 EA	SUZ	1 EA	Varies	6000 EA	6000 EA
Bullethead Parrotfish & Others III	SI	BS/MC/MV/SI	1992	MON	24 X 34 EA	SUZ	1 EA	Varies	6000 EA	6000 EA
Blackspot Sergeant & Others IV	SI	BS/MC/MV/SI	1992	MON	24 X 34 EA	SUZ	1 EA	Varies	6000 EA	6000 EA
Gauguin and Van Gogh	SI	BS/MC/MV/SI	1992	MON	32 X 48 EA	SUZ	1 EA	Varies	10000 EA	10000 EA
Van Gogh with Sunflowers IV	SI	BS/MC/MV/SI	1992	MON	32 X 48 EA	SUZ	1 EA	Varies	10000 EA	10000 EA
Calf Roper I, II	SI	BS/MC/SI	1992	MON	22 X 30 EA	SUZ	1 EA	Varies	6000 EA	6000 EA
Bull Rider I, III, IV	SI	BS/MC/SI	1992	MON	30 X 22 EA	SUZ	1 EA	Varies	6000 EA	6000 EA
At the Beach I, II	SI	BS/MC/SI	1992	MON/WA	22 X 30 EA	SUZ	1 EA	Varies	6000 EA	6000 EA
Matisse in Nice	SI	BS/MC/SI	1993	LC	22 X 30	R/BFK	45	8	1800	2000
*Slam Dunk	SI	BS/MC/SI	1993	LC/3D	21 X 18 X 13	R/BFK	60	7	5000	5500

*Lithographed, Cut, Folded & Assembled into Plexiglas Case

LAURA GROSCH

BORN: Worcester, MA; April 1, 1945
EDUCATION: Wellesley Col, MA, BA, Art History; Univ of Pennsylvania, Phila, PA, BFA, Painting; Wellesley Col, MA, BA, Art History, 1963–67; Univ of Pennsylvania, Phila, PA, BFA, Painting, 1968; Studied with Sigmund Abeles & Neil Welliver
TEACHING: Falmouth Arts Guild, MA; Davidson Com Center, NC
AWARDS: Purchase Award, Boston Printmakers, First Nat Bank of Boston, MA, 1975; Purchase Award & Special Commendation, Greenville County Mus of Art, SC, 1976; Charlotte Printmakers Award, NC, 1978; Arts & Science Council of Artists Showcase, Charlotte, NC, 1979
RECENT EXHIB: Greenville County Art Mus, SC, 1987; Syracuse Univ, NY, 1987; Jerald Melberg Gallery, Charlotte, NC, 1987; Hodges Taylor Gallery, Charlotte, NC, 1989; Christa Faut Gallery, Davidson, NC, 1990
COLLECTIONS: Victoria & Albert Mus, London, England; Davidson Col, NC; Michigan State Univ, East Lansing, MI; Nasson Col, Springvale, ME; Smithsonian Inst, Wash, DC; Southern Illinois Univ, Edwardsville, IL; Univ of Nebraska, Lincoln, NE; Univ of Utah, Salt Lake City, UT; Kalamazoo Inst of Art, MI; Univ of Georgia, Athens, GA; Univ of West Virginia, Morgantown, WVA; Bowdoin Col, Brunswick, ME; Mesa Com Col, AZ; Washburn Univ, Topeka, KS; Northern Illinois Univ, Dekalb, IL; Ringling Mus, Sarasota, FL; Rockford Col, IL; Univ of Iowa, Iowa City, IA; Univ of Maine, Orono, ME; Beloit Col, WI; Florida State Univ, Tallahassee, FL; Mint Mus of Art, Charlotte, NC; Greenville County Mus, SC; Indiana State Univ, Evansville, IN; Dayton Art Inst, OH; Univ of North Carolina, Chapel Hill, NC; British Mus, London, England; Drury Col, Springfield, MO; Wittenburg Univ, Springfield, OH; Carnegie-Mellon Univ, Pittsburgh, PA; Boston Mus of Fine Arts, MA; Minneapolis Inst for the Arts, MN; Dickinson State Col, ND; Western Illinois Univ, Macomb, IL; Brooklyn Mus, NY; Univ of California, Riverside, CA; California Palace of the Legion of Honor, San Francisco, CA; Huntsville Mus of Art, AL; Eckerd Col, St Petersburg, FL; Honolulu Acad of Arts, HI; Lafayette Col, Skillman Library, Easton, PA; Madison Art Center, WI; Manhattan Col, Riverdale, NY; Northwood Inst, Dallas, TX; Skidmore Col, Sarasota Springs, NY; Syracuse Univ, NY; Tennessee Botanical Garden & Fine Arts Center, Cheekwood, Nashville, TN; Univ of California, Grunewald Center for the Graphic Arts, Los Angeles, CA; Univ of Virginia, Bagly Mem Mus, Charlotteville, VA; Westminister Col, New Wilmington, PA; California State Univ, Chico, CA; Rutgers Univ, Jane Voohees Zimmerli Art Mus, New Brunswick, NJ; St Lawrence Univ, Brush Art Gallery, Canton, NY
PRINTERS: Paul M Maquire, Boston, MA (PM); Lisa Mackie (LM), Tom Tracy (TT), John Clemmons (JC), Herbert Fox (HF), Fox Graphics Editions, Boston, MA; Flat Rock Press, Boston, MA (FRP); Jennifer Hilton, Boston, MA (JH); Catherine Kuhn (CK); Winstone Press, Mocksville, NC (WP)
PUBLISHERS: Impressions Workshop, Boston, MA (IW) (OB); Lakeside Studio, Lakeside, MI (LS) (OB); Artist (ART)
GALLERIES: Somerhill Gallery, Durham, NC; van Straaten Gallery, Chicago, IL; Suzanne Kohn Gallery, St Paul, MN; Marita Gilliam Gallery, Raleigh, NC; Jerald Melberg Gallery, Charlotte, NC; G W Einstein, Inc, New York, NY; Hodges Taylor Gallery, Charlotte, NC
MAILING ADDRESS: 497 S Main St, P O Box 10, Davidson, NC 28036

TITLE	PUBLISHER	PRINTER	DATE	MEDIUM	DIMENSION (PAPER SIZE) IN INCHES	TYPE OF PAPER	EDITION NUMBER	NO. OF COLORS	ORIGINAL OPENING PRICE	CURRENT RETAIL PRICE
SOLD OUT EDITIONS (RARE):										
Two Artichokes	LS	HF	1973	LC	22 X 30	AP	50	3	80	500
Dried Artichokes in a Basket	IW	LM	1974	LC	30 X 22	R/BFK	65	3	100	500
Gloxinia on an Oriental Rug	IW	LM	1974	LC	30 X 22	R/BFK	75	4	100	600
Daffodils	IW	LM	1975	LC	22 X 30	R/BFK	100	4	125	500
Dragon Flower	ART	TT	1976	LC	30 X 22	AP	50	4	200	500
CURRENT EDITIONS:										
Boston Lettuce	LS	JC	1972	LC	22 X 30	AP	50	3	50	250
Asparagus	IW	LM	1973	LC	30 X 22	AP/W	100	3	80	350
Borchelt Lettuce	IW	LM	1973	LC	22 X 30	R/BFK	100	3	380	350
Rose	IW	LM	1973	LC	22 X 30	R/BFK	100	4	100	350
Amaryllis on Adire Cloth	IW	LM	1973	LC	22 X 30	R/BFK	100	4	100	350
Rattan	IW	LM	1974	LC	21 X 30	AP	75	3	100	350
Iris on Bokhara	IW	PM	1975	LC	22 X 30	R/BFK	75	4	125	450
African Violet	ART	TT	1976	LC	20 X 25	R/BFK	50	6	200	450
Parrot Tulip	ART	PM/JH/FRP	1983	LC	22 X 30	R/BFK	50	5	400	450
Gladiolus	ART	CK	1984	LC	30 X 22	R/BFK	50	7	400	550
Blue Parrot Tulips and Nigerian Tie-Dy	ART	CK	1985	LC	15 X 11	R/BFK	25	4	150	200

CHAIM GROSS

BORN: Kolomea, Austria; (1904–1991)
EDUCATION: Beaux Arts Inst of Design, Art Students League, NY
TEACHING: Instr, Mus of Mod Art, NY, 1952–57; Instr, Sculpture, Ed Alliance Art Sch, 1927 to present; Instr, New Sch for Social Research, NY, 1948 to present
AWARDS: Award of Merit Medal, Nat Inst of Arts & Letters, 1963; Gold Medal, Nat Acad of Design, 1985
RECENT EXHIB: Cape Mus of Fine Arts, Dennis, MA, 1989,92; Hebrew Union Col, Skirball Mus, Cincinnati, OH, 1992; Provincetown Art Assoc, MA, 1992
COLLECTIONS: Metropolitan Mus of Art, NY; Mus of Mod Art, NY; Whitney Mus of Am Art, NY; Philadelphia Mus of Art, PA; Art Inst of Chicago, IL; Baltimore Mus of Art, MD; Brooklyn Mus of Art, NY; Jewish Mus of Art, NY; Tel Aviv Mus of Art, Israel; Pennsylvania Acad of Fine Art, PA; Newark Mus, NJ; Worcester Art Mus, MA
PRINTERS: Artist (ART)
PUBLISHERS: London Arts, Inc, Detroit, MI (LAI); Circle Fine Arts, Chicago, IL (CFA); Mourlot, Paris, France (M); Balkin Arts (BA)
GALLERIES: Forum Gallery, New York, NY; Glass Art Gallery, New York, NY; American Scene Gallery, Sarasota, FL; David Barnett Gallery, Milwaukee, WI; Farber Fine Arts, Secaucus, NJ; Rosenfeld Fine Arts, New York, NY; Michael Rosenfeld Gallery, New York, NY; Barry Rosen & Jaap Van Liere Modern & Contemporary, New York, NY & Beverly Hills, CA & Costa Mesa, CA & Sherman Oaks, CA & Scottsdale, AZ & Palm Beach, FL & Honolulu, HI & New Orleans, LA & Las Vegas, NV & Seattle, WA; Ro Gallery Image Makers, Inc, New York, NY
MAILING ADDRESS: c/o Estate of Chaim Gross, 526 La Guardia Place, New York, NY 10012

TITLE	PUBLISHER	PRINTER	DATE	MEDIUM	DIMENSION (PAPER SIZE) IN INCHES	TYPE OF PAPER	EDITION NUMBER	NO. OF COLORS	ORIGINAL OPENING PRICE	CURRENT RETAIL PRICE
SOLD OUT EDITIONS (RARE):										
Jewish Holidays (Set of 11):	ART	ART	1968–70	LC		JP		9–11		4000 SET

CHAIM GROSS CONTINUED

TITLE	PUBLISHER	PRINTER	DATE	MEDIUM	DIMENSION (PAPER SIZE) IN INCHES	TYPE OF PAPER	EDITION NUMBER	NO. OF COLORS	ORIGINAL OPENING PRICE	CURRENT RETAIL PRICE
CURRENT EDITIONS:										
Mother Playing	CFA	ART	1964	LB	19 X 26	AP	200	1	75	350
Rabbi	CFA	ART	1964	LB	19 X 26	AP	200	1	75	350
In Front of the Ark	P	ART	1970	LC	19 X 26	AP	20	6	400	750
Children's Game	BA	ART	1972	LC	15 X 21	AP	200	3	275	600
In the Synogogue	ART	ART	1974	LC	13 X 18	AP	110		200	700
Bar Mitzvah	ART	ART	1974	LC	14 X 18	AP	110		200	700
Mother and Children	M	ART	1975	LC	18 X 14	AP	125	4	200	400
Chasidic Fiddler	M	ART	1975	LC	16 X 22	AP	100	4	200	500
Homage to Sigmund Freud	ART	ART	1976	LC	14 X 18	AP	150		200	350
Song of Songs (Set of 9)	LE/BC	ART	1979	LC	22 X 18 EA	AP	15 EA	9 EA	2750 SET / 350 EA	4500 SET / 600 EA
Jacob's Dream	M	ART	1979	LC	23 X 19	AP	20	5	250	500
Three on a Unicycle	P	ART	1979	LC	24 X 14	AP	105	4	200	400
Side Street in New England	LAI	ART	1980	LC	29 X 17	AP	250	7	100	200

FREIDRICH GROSS

PRINTERS: John Nichols, NY (JN)
PUBLISHERS: John Nichols, NY (JN)

TITLE	PUBLISHER	PRINTER	DATE	MEDIUM	DIMENSION (PAPER SIZE) IN INCHES	TYPE OF PAPER	EDITION NUMBER	NO. OF COLORS	ORIGINAL OPENING PRICE	CURRENT RETAIL PRICE
CURRENT EDITIONS:										
La Guardia	JN	JN	1982	SP	20 X 40	R/BFK	200	35	300	600
Half & Half	JN	JN	1982	LC/SP	21 X 22	R/BFK	85	6	250	500

NANCY GROSSMAN

BORN: New York, NY; April 28, 1940
EDUCATION: Pratt Inst, Brooklyn, NY
TEACHING: Instr, Sculpture, Boston Fine Arts Sch, MA, 1985; Instr, Drawing, Cooper Union, NY, 1989
AWARDS: Ida C Haskell Found Fel, 1962; Guggenheim Mem Found Fel, 1965; Am Acad of Arts and Letters, 1974; Nat Inst of Arts and Letters, 1974; Nat Endowment for the Arts Fel, Sculpture, 1985
RECENT EXHIB: Long Island Univ, Hillwood Art Mus, Brookville, NY, 1992; Beacon Street Gallery, Chicago, IL 1992
COLLECTIONS: Whitney Mus of Am Art, NY; Princeton Univ, NJ; Univ of California, Berkeley, CA; Dallas Mus of Fine Art, TX; Israel Mus, Jerusalem, Israel; Phoenix Art Mus, AZ; Nat Mus of Am Art, Wash, DC; Virginia Mus of Fine Art, Richmond, VA; Metropolitan Mus of Art, NY
PRINTERS: Styria Studios, NY (SS)
PUBLISHERS: Transworld Art, Inc, NY (TAI)
GALLERIES: Cordier & Ekstrom, New York, NY; Barbara Gladstone Gallery, New York, NY; Terry Dintenfass, New York, NY; Heath Gallery, Atlanta, GA; Exit Art, New York, NY
MAILING ADDRESS: 105 Eldridge St, New York, NY 10002

TITLE	PUBLISHER	PRINTER	DATE	MEDIUM	DIMENSION (PAPER SIZE) IN INCHES	TYPE OF PAPER	EDITION NUMBER	NO. OF COLORS	ORIGINAL OPENING PRICE	CURRENT RETAIL PRICE
SOLD OUT EDITIONS (RARE):										
The Road to Life	TAI	SS	1976	LC	20 X 26	HMP	175	1	500	600

KATHY GROVE

PRINTERS: Julia D'Amario, NY (JDA); Bill Hall, NY (BH); Kathy Kuehn, NY (KK); Spring Street Workshop, NY (SprSW)
PUBLISHERS: Artist (ART)
GALLERIES: Genovese Graphics, Boston, MA; Golden Gallery, Boston, MA

TITLE	PUBLISHER	PRINTER	DATE	MEDIUM	DIMENSION (PAPER SIZE) IN INCHES	TYPE OF PAPER	EDITION NUMBER	NO. OF COLORS	ORIGINAL OPENING PRICE	CURRENT RETAIL PRICE
CURRENT EDITIONS:										
The Other Series: After Sloan	ART	JDA/BH/KK/SprSW	1992	PH/G	12 X 13	R/BFK	10	1	1000	1000
The Other Series: After Muybridge	ART	JDA/BH/KK/SprSW	1992	PH/G	12 X 13	R/BFK	5	1	2000	2000

RENE GRUAU

RECENT EXHIB: Jose Drudis-Biada Art Gallery, Jose Drudis, Mount St Mary's Col, Los Angeles, CA, 1988
PRINTERS: American Atelier, Chicago, IL (AA)
PUBLISHERS: Circle Fine Arts, Chicago, IL (CFA)
GALLERIES: Circle Galleries, San Francisco, CA & San Diego, CA & Houston, TX & Northbrook, IL & Pittsburgh, PA & Chicago, IL & Soho, NY & Scottsdale, AZ & Beverly Hills, CA & Costa Mesa, CA & Sherman Oaks, CA & New Orleans, LA & Honolulu, HI & Las Vegas, NV & Palm Beach, FL & Seattle, WA; Samuel Stein Fine Arts, Ltd, Chicago, IL

The retail prices of the 100,000 limited edition prints quoted in this directory are subject to change. Print publishers, artists and galleries were the direct sources for these quotations. Prices in the secondary market listed as "Sold Out Editions (Rare)" indicate that the publisher has a limited supply of that print or that the print is difficult to locate in the galleries.

RENE GRUAU CONTINUED

TITLE	PUBLISHER	PRINTER	DATE	MEDIUM	DIMENSION (PAPER SIZE) IN INCHES	TYPE OF PAPER	EDITION NUMBER	NO. OF COLORS	ORIGINAL OPENING PRICE	CURRENT RETAIL PRICE
SOLD OUT EDITIONS (RARE):										
Seba (Red Glove)	CFA	ART	1987	LC	25 X 33	AP	300		650	2200
Le Secret (The Secret)	CFA	ART	1987	LC	29 X 20	AP	300		650	2750
La Rose Rouge (The Red Rose)	CFA	ART	1987	LC	30 X 23	AP	300		650	2800
La Voilette (The Veil)	CFA	ART	1987	LC	27 X 22	AP	300		650	2200
La Chapeau Noir (The Black Hat)	CFA	ART	1987	LC	22 X 21	AP	300		650	1150
La Toque Rouge (The Red Hat)	CFA	ART	1987	LC	24 X 19	AP	300		650	3000
Les Girls Series (Set of 3):										9350 SET
Peut-Etre (Perhaps)	CFA	ART	1988	LC	51 X 29	AP	300		1200	3250
Plus Tard (Later)	CFA	ART	1988	LC	51 X 29	AP	300		1200	3250
Pourquoi Pas (Why Not?)	CFA	ART	1988	LC	51 X 29	AP	300		1200	3500
Les Perles (The Pearls)	CFA	ART	1988	LC	34 X 26	AP	300		1000	2300
Que la Fete Commence! (Let the Fun Begin!)	CFA	ART	1988	LC	34 X 26	AP	300		1000	2100
CURRENT EDITIONS:										
Rouge (Red)	CFA	ART	1989	LC	26 X 21	AP	300		750	1100
La Drape Rouge (Red Cloth)	CFA	ART	1989	LC	23 X 32	AP	300		650	1250
Esquisse de Brigitte (Sketch of Brigitte)	CFA	ART	1989	LC	18 X 16	AP	300		650	850
La Rose de Bagatelle (Sweetheart's Rose)	CFA	ART	1989	LC	35 X 46	AP	300		1000	2800
Le Parfum de Femme (Essence of Woman)	CFA	ART	1989	LC	27 X 20	AP	300		800	1200
Dolce Far Niente (Sweet Leisure)	CFA	ART	1989	LC	39 X 47	AP	300		1000	2850
Diane au Bain (Diane in the Bath)	CFA	ART	1989	LC	23 X 18	AP	300		500	750
Reverie (Dreaming)	CFA	ART	1989	LC	35 X 26	AP	300		900	1500
Paris en Vogue	CFA	ART	1989	LC	50 X 36	AP	300		1000	2700
L'Heure Bleue (Blue Hour)	CFA	ART	1990	LC	21 X 28	AP	300		850	1200
La Femme en laune	CFA	ART	1990	LC	48 X 35	AP	300		1000	2400
Night Life	CFA	ART	1990	LC		AP	300		800	800
Le Gant Noir (Black Glove)	CFA	ART	1990	LC	31 X 15	AP	300		875	1200
L'Hommes a Femmes	CFA	ART	1990	LC	25 X 23	AP	300		600	1200
Fifi	CFA	ART	1990	LC	23 X 32	AP	300		1250	1650
Springtime Shower	CFA	ART	1990	LC		AP	300		800	1000
Jacques	CFA	ART	1990	LC		AP	300		675	950
Bon Jour, Cheri	CFA	ART	1990	LC		AP	300		800	850
Rouge et Noir	CFA	ART	1990	LC	51 X 38	AP	300		1650	2700
Le Revue Balmáin	CFA	ART	1990	LC	39 X 54	AP	300		1750	2700
Clubfellow	CFA	ART	1990	LC		AP	300		800	900
Georges—Man with Hat	CFA	ART	1990	LC	23 X 18	AP	300		800	800
Il Pluie	CFA	ART	1990	LC		AP	300		800	900
Follies	CFA	ART	1990	LC	34 X 43	AP	300		850	1850
Le Parasol	CFA	ART	1990	LC	27 X 20	AP	300		1200	1000

DAVID GRUBB

BORN: Indiana; 1948
EDUCATION: Skowhegan Sch of Art, ME, 1968; Indiana Univ, Bloomington, IN, BFA, 1969; Queens Col, NY, MFA, 1972
COLLECTIONS: Skowhegan Sch of Art, ME; Virginia Center for the Creative Arts, Sweet Briar, VA
PRINTERS: Sheila Marbain, NY (SM); T E Black Studio, NY (TEB)
PUBLISHERS: Orion Editions, NY (OE)
GALLERIES: Orion Editions, New York, NY; Curt Marcus Gallery, New York, NY

TITLE	PUBLISHER	PRINTER	DATE	MEDIUM	DIMENSION (PAPER SIZE) IN INCHES	TYPE OF PAPER	EDITION NUMBER	NO. OF COLORS	ORIGINAL OPENING PRICE	CURRENT RETAIL PRICE
CURRENT EDITIONS:										
Dragon Rock (Series of 29)	OE	ART	1983	PO/HC	40 X 23 EA	R/BFK	1 EA	Varies 2	475 EA	550 EA
Shaded Stream (Series of 100)	OE	ART	1983	PO/HC	40 X 23 EA	R/BFK	1 EA	Varies 2	475 EA	550 EA
Lake Monroe	OE	SM	1983	SP	31 X 47	R/BFK	80	15	425	550
Hemlock Stream (Series of 100)	OE	ART	1983	PO/HC	36 X 35 EA	AP	1 EA	Varies 2	500 EA	650 EA
Harriman Park (Series of 100)	OE	ART	1983	PO/HC	36 X 35 EA	AP	1 EA	Varies 2	500 EA	650 EA
Wesley's Place (Series of 18)	OE	ART	1983	MON/PAS	22 X 30 EA	R/BFK	1 EA	1 EA	400 EA	450 EA
Salt Creek in Sunlight (Series of 100)	OE	ART	1984	PO/HC	36 X 35 EA	AP	1 EA	Varies 2	550 EA	950 EA
Salt Creek in Moonlight (Series of 100)	OE	ART	1984	PO/HC	36 X 35 EA	AP	1 EA	Varies 2	550 EA	950 EA
Owl Creek (Series of 100)	OE	ART	1984	PO/HC	35 X 37 EA	AP	1 EA	Varies 2	550 EA	850 EA
House in the Village (Series of 100)	OE	ART	1985	PO/HC	35 X 37 EA	AP	1 EA	Varies 2	550 EA	850 EA
Yellowwood Lake (Series of 100)	OE	ART	1985	PO/HC	26 X 32 EA	AP	1 EA	Varies 3	400 EA	450 EA
Down by the Branch (Series of 100)	OE	ART	1985	PO/HC	26 X 32 EA	AP	1 EA	Varies 3	400 EA	450 EA
Brummett's Meadow (Series of 100)	OE	ART	1985	PO/HC	26 X 32 EA	AP	1 EA	Varies 3	400 EA	450 EA
Brown County (Series of 100)	OE	ART	1985	PO/HC	26 X 36 EA	AP	1 EA	Varies	450 EA	450 EA
In the Woods (Series of 100)	OE	ART	1986	PO/HC	22 X 36 EA	AP	1 EA	Varies	400 EA	400 EA
City View I (Series of 75)	OE	ART	1986	PO/HC	19 X 30 EA	AP	1 EA	Varies	350 EA	350 EA

DAVID GRUBB CONTINUED

TITLE	PUBLISHER	PRINTER	DATE	MEDIUM	DIMENSION (PAPER SIZE) IN INCHES	TYPE OF PAPER	EDITION NUMBER	NO. OF COLORS	ORIGINAL OPENING PRICE	CURRENT RETAIL PRICE
CURRENT EDITIONS:										
Belmont Series:										
Belmont, Overcast	OE	TEB	1986	SP	26 X 50	STP	150	24	675	850
Belmont, Brightening Up	OE	TEB	1986	SP	26 X 50	STP	100	24	675	850
Fields Near Landenberg, Summer	OE	TEB	1986	PO/HC	26 X 32	AP	100	Varies	400	450
Fields Near Landenberg, Winter	OE	TEB	1986	PO/HC	26 X 32	AP	100	Varies	400	450
Potomac	OE	TEB	1986	PO/HC	26 X 32	AP	100	Varies	400	450
Diptych (Series of 100)	OE	TEB	1986	PO/HC	33 X 31	HMP	1 EA	Varies	500	550
Bright Water	OE	TEB	1988	EB	23 X 30	STP	75	1	350	350
MacIntosh Headwaters	OE	TEB	1988	EC	24 X 32	STP	80	10	500	500
Norfolk Gardens I, II	OE	TEB	1989	EC	38 X 29	STP	75	1	500 EA	500 EA

JOHN GRUEN

BORN: Enghien-lis-Bains, France; September 12, 1926; U S Citizen
EDUCATION: City Col of New York, NY; Univ of Iowa, Iowa City, IA, BA, MA
PRINTERS: Artist (ART)
PUBLISHERS: Symbax, Inc, NY (SI)
GALLERIES: Pierce Street Gallery, Birmingham, MI
MAILING ADDRESS: 317 W 83rd St, New York, NY 10024

TITLE	PUBLISHER	PRINTER	DATE	MEDIUM	DIMENSION (PAPER SIZE) IN INCHES	TYPE OF PAPER	EDITION NUMBER	NO. OF COLORS	ORIGINAL OPENING PRICE	CURRENT RETAIL PRICE
CURRENT EDITIONS:										
Still Lives (Set of 10):										
#21–#30	SI	ART	1981	PH	15 X 18 EA	KOD	60 EA		3000 SET	4000 SET
#31–#40	SI	ART	1981	PH	15 X 18 EA	KOD	60 EA		4000 SET	5000 SET
#51–#60	SI	ART	1981	PH	15 X 18 EA	KOD	60 EA		5000 SET	6000 SET

DENNIS GUASTELLA

EDUCATION: Macomb Com Col, Warren, MI, Assoc Degree, Technology, 1965–67; Ferris State Col, Big Rapids, MI, 1968–69; Wayne State Univ, Detroit, MI, BFA, Painting, 1969–72; Eastern Michigan Univ, Ypsilanti, MI, MFA, Painting, 1973–75
TEACHING: Asst Prof, Art, South Dakota State Univ, Brookings, SD, 1975–80; Washtenaw Com Col, Ann Arbor, MI, Chmn, Visual Arts Tech Dept, 1980 to present
AWARDS: Michigan Creative Artist Grant, 1982–83; Excellence in Performance for Teaching Award, Board of Trustees, Washtenaw Com Col, Ann Arbor, MI, 1985; Michigan Creative Artist Grant, 1986–87
RECENT EXHIB: Mott Com Col, Flint, MI, 1987; Battle Creek Art Center, MI, 1987
COLLECTIONS: Rutgers Univ, Camden, NJ; South Dakota Mem Art Center, Brookings, SD; Sioux City Art Center, IA; Univ of Nebraska, Sheldon Art Galleries, Lincoln, NE; Univ of North Dakota, Grand Forks, ND; South Dakota State Univ, Brookings, SD; Joslyn Art Mus, Omaha, NE; City of Livonia, City Hall, MI; Oakland Univ, Rochester, MI; Washtenaw Com Col, Ann Arbor, MI
PRINTERS: Norman Stewart, Bloomfield Hills, MI (NS); Stewart & Stewart, Bloomfield Hills, MI (S-S)
PUBLISHERS: Stewart & Stewart, Bloomfield Hills, MI (S-S)
GALLERIES: T'Marra Gallery, Ann Arbor, MI; Stewart & Stewart; Bloomfield Hills, MI
MAILING ADDRESS: 9025 McClumpha, Plymouth, MI 48170-7073

TITLE	PUBLISHER	PRINTER	DATE	MEDIUM	DIMENSION (PAPER SIZE) IN INCHES	TYPE OF PAPER	EDITION NUMBER	NO. OF COLORS	ORIGINAL OPENING PRICE	CURRENT RETAIL PRICE
CURRENT EDITIONS:										
Timepiece	S-S	NS/S-S	1982	SP	22 X 30	R/BFK/W	30	10	450	750
Patching	S-S	NS/S-S	1982	SP	22 X 30	R/BFK/W	30	15	450	750

BOB GUCCIONE

BORN: Brooklyn, NY
RECENT EXHIB: Ambassador Galleries, NY, 1992
COLLECTIONS: Fine Art Mus of Long Island, NY
PRINTERS: Chamelion Editions, Jersey City, NY (ChEd)
PUBLISHERS: Ambassador Publishing, Inc, NY (AmbP)
GALLERIES: Ambassador Galleries, New York, NY; Newbury Fine Art, Boston, MA; Squash Blossom Gallery, Rancho Mirage, CA; Art Insights, New York, NY; La Galeria du Arte, Newport Beach, CA; I Brewster Gallery, Phila, PA; Lublin Gallery, Greenwich, CT; Soho Collection, New York, NY
MAILING ADDRESS: c/o Ambassador Galleries, Inc, 137 Spring St, New York, NY 10012

TITLE	PUBLISHER	PRINTER	DATE	MEDIUM	DIMENSION (PAPER SIZE) IN INCHES	TYPE OF PAPER	EDITION NUMBER	NO. OF COLORS	ORIGINAL OPENING PRICE	CURRENT RETAIL PRICE
CURRENT EDITIONS:										
Bathers	AmbP	ChEd	1992	LC	34 X 28	AP	300	60	900	900
La Jeune Clown	AmbP	ChEd	1992	LC	29 X 36	AP	300	60	900	900
Still Life in Motion	AmbP	ChEd	1992	LC	28 X 35	AP	300	60	900	900
Three Women at a Round Table	AmbP	ChEd	1992	LC	29 X 35	AP	300	60	900	900

The retail prices of the 100,000 limited edition prints quoted in this directory are subject to change. Print publishers, artists and galleries were the direct sources for these quotations. Prices in the secondary market listed as "Sold Out Editions (Rare)" indicate that the publisher has a limited supply of that print or that the print is difficult to locate in the galleries.

RAUL GUERRERO

BORN: Brawley, CA; 1945
EDUCATION: Laguna Beach Art Assoc, Laguna Beach, CA; Southwestern Col, Nat City, CA; Inst of Nat Fine Arts, Mex: Chouinard Art Sch, Los Angeles, CA, BFA, 1966–69; Univ of California Dept of Arch, Los Angeles, CA, 1970–71
AWARDS: Photography Fel, Nat Endowment for the Arts, 1979
RECENT EXHIB: Phoenix Art Mus, AZ, 1987; Saxon-Lee Gallery, Los Angeles, CA, 1987,88; Linda Moore Gallery, San Diego, CA, 1993; Galeria Jorge Mara, Madrid, Spain, 1993
COLLECTIONS: Phoenix Art Mus, AZ; Long Beach Art Mus, CA; La Jolla Mus of Contemp Art, CA
PRINTERS: Jan Aman, CA (JA); Cirrus Editions Workshop, Los Angeles, CA (CEW)
PUBLISHERS: Cirrus Editions, Los Angeles, CA (CE)
GALLERIES: Cirrus Editions, Ltd, Los Angeles, CA; Barbara Braathen Gallery, New York, NY; Richard Kuhlenschmidt Simon, Gallery, Los Angeles, CA; Daniel Saxon Gallery, San Diego, CA; David Zapf Gallery, San Diego, CA; Schiller & Bodo, New York, NY; Linda Moore Gallery, San Diego, CA; Galeria Jorge Mara, Madrid, Spain
MAILING ADDRESS: c/o Daniel Saxon Gallery, 7525 Beverly Blvd, San Diego, CA 90036

TITLE	PUBLISHER	PRINTER	DATE	MEDIUM	DIMENSION (PAPER SIZE) IN INCHES	TYPE OF PAPER	EDITION NUMBER	NO. OF COLORS	ORIGINAL OPENING PRICE	CURRENT RETAIL PRICE
CURRENT EDITIONS:										
Untitled	CE	JA/CEW	1974	SP	22 X 26	AP	50	Multi	125	450

HELENE GUETARY

BORN: Paris, France, 1957
EDUCATION: Ecole des Beaux-Arts, Paris, France; Chicago Art Inst, IL; Sch of Visual Arts, NY
AWARDS: Caba Award, NY, 1981; Foundation de L'Archipel Grant, Paris, France, 1982
COLLECTIONS: Pace Univ, NY; Colby Sawyer Col, NH; Kennedy Mus, San Francisco, CA; Mus of Industrial Design, NY; Hamozi Coll, Tehran; Harkness Coll, NY
PRINTERS: Sienna Studios, NY (SS)
PUBLISHERS: Fred Dorfman, Inc, NY (FDI); Francis Fine Arts, Wenonah, NJ (FFA)
GALLERIES: Jentra Fine Art, Freehold, NY; Fred Dorman Gallery, New York, NY

TITLE	PUBLISHER	PRINTER	DATE	MEDIUM	DIMENSION (PAPER SIZE) IN INCHES	TYPE OF PAPER	EDITION NUMBER	NO. OF COLORS	ORIGINAL OPENING PRICE	CURRENT RETAIL PRICE
SOLD OUT EDITIONS (RARE):										
Move #1, #2	FFA	SS	1979	LC	36 X 25 EA	DE	250 EA	4 EA	200 EA	500 EA
Move #9	FDI	SS	1980	LC	36 X 25	DE	200	4	200	600
Pas de Deux #1	FDI	SS	1980	LC	36 X 25	DE	200	4	200	500
Arched Figure #1	FFA	SS	1980	LC	36 X 25	DE	250	4	200	500
Torticolli, #1, #2	FDI	SS	1984	LC	18 X 24 EA	AP	200 EA	6 EA	175 EA	400 EA
Torticolli	FDI	SS	1984	LC	38 X 26	AP	100	6	400	600
Allures	FDI	SS	1985	LC/CO/HC	25 X 22 EA	AP	30 EA	Varies	400 EA	600 EA

JOSÉP GUINOVART

BORN: Barcelona, Spain; 1927
RECENT EXHIB: Fine Arts Mus of Long Island, Hempstead, NY, 1987,92
PRINTERS: La Poligrafa, SA, Barcelona, Spain (LP)
PUBLISHERS: Ediciones Poligrafa, SA, Barcelona, Spain (EdP)
GALLERIES: Galeria Joan Prats, Barcelona, Spain & New York, NY; River Gallery, Westport CT; Spaightwood Galleries, Madison, WI; Brenda Kroos Gallery, Cleveland, OH

TITLE	PUBLISHER	PRINTER	DATE	MEDIUM	DIMENSION (PAPER SIZE) IN INCHES	TYPE OF PAPER	EDITION NUMBER	NO. OF COLORS	ORIGINAL OPENING PRICE	CURRENT RETAIL PRICE
SOLD OUT EDITIONS (RARE):										
Fang (Set of 4)	EdP	LP	1972	LC	30 X 22 EA	GP	75 EA		1000 SET	2500 SET
									250 EA	650 EA
Series of 38 Etchings:									7000 SET	22000SET
#1, #2	EdP	LP	1973	EB	28 X 35 EA	GP	50 EA	1 EA	360 EA	800 EA
#3–#7	EdP	LP	1973	EB	22 X 30 EA	GP	50 EA	1 EA	340 EA	800 EA
#8–#21	EdP	LP	1973	EB	20 X 15 EA	GP	50 EA	1 EA	320 EA	800 EA
#22–#38	EdP	LP	1973	EB	15 X 11 EA	GP	50 EA	1 EA	320 EA	600 EA
Polychrome Lithographs (Set of 7)	EdP	LP	1974	LC	30 X 22 EA	GP	75 EA		1100 SET	4000 SET
									180 EA	600 EA
Polychrome Lithographs (Set of 14)	EdP	LP	1976	LC	30 X 22 EA	GP	75		2200 SET	7500 SET
									180 EA	600 EA
Homenatge a Joan Prats (Set of 2)	EdP	LP	1975	LC	22 X 30 EA	GP	100 EA		400 SET	1100 SET
									200 EA	600 EA
12 Handcoloured Etchings (Set of 12)	EdP	LP	1976	EB/HC	28 X 33 EA	GP	50 EA	Varies	3400 SET	10000 SET
Series of 10 AL Lithographs (G) (Set of 10)	EdP	LP	1978–82	LC	30 X 22 EA	CP	99 EA		1600 SET	6000 SET
									180 EA	650 EA
Series of 10 Handcoloured Lithographs (P) (Set of 10)	EdP	LP	1982	LC	30 X 22 EA	GP	75 EA		2500 SET	5000 SET
									280 EA	550 EA
Series of 10 Handcoloured Lithographs (Set of 10)	EdP	LP	1982	LC	22 X 15 EA	GP	75 EA		2000 SET	3600 SET
									220 EA	400 EA
Series of 17 Hand Coloured Etchings— Mare Nostrum #1–#17 (Set of 17)	EdP	LP	1985	EB/HC	21 X 14 EA	GP	50 EA	2-5 EA	6500 SET	10000 SET
									400 EA	600 EA

JOSÉP GUINOVART

TITLE	PUBLISHER	PRINTER	DATE	MEDIUM	DIMENSION (PAPER SIZE) IN INCHES	TYPE OF PAPER	EDITION NUMBER	NO. OF COLORS	ORIGINAL OPENING PRICE	CURRENT RETAIL PRICE
CURRENT EDITIONS:										
Series of 7 Hand Coloured Etchings (Set of 7):									5500 SET	8000 SET
#1—Incis i Vermell	EdP	LP	1985	EB/HC	44 X 30	GP	50	5	850	1200
#2—Cargol	EdP	LP	1985	EB/HC	44 X 30	GP	50	3	850	1200
#3—Forma i Marge	EdP	LP	1985	EB/HC	44 X 30	GP	50	5	850	1200
#4—Com una Fletxa	EdP	LP	1985	EB/HC	44 X 30	GP	50	4	850	1200
#5—Com la Cara	EdP	LP	1985	EB/HC	44 X 30	GP	50	3	850	1200
#6—Figures Recolzades	EdP	LP	1985	EB/HC	44 X 30	GP	50	3	850	1200
#7—Plor Passat	EdP	LP	1985	EB/HC	44 X 30	GP	50	4	850	1200
L'Amor i L'Espina	EdP	LP	1986	EB		GP	50		1200	1300
Series of 13 Hand Coloured Etchings with Gouache (Set of 13):									6000 SET	8000 SET
#1—Con una Cuchara de Palo	EdP	LP	1987	EB/HC/GOU	19 X 19	GP	75	4	480	700
#2—Es Preciso Cruzar Puentes	EdP	LP	1987	EB/HC/GOU	19 X 19	GP	75	4	480	700
#3—Para que los Cocodrilos Duerman en Largas Filas Bajo Amianto de la Luna	EdP	LP	1987	EB/HC/GOU	19 X 19	GP	75	4	480	700
#4—A Tu Violencia Granate, Sordomudos en la Penumbra	EdP	LP	1987	EB/HC/GOU	19 X 19	GP	75	5	480	700
#5—Los Mulatos Estiraban Gomas de Liagar al Torso Blanco	EdP	LP	1987	EB/HC/GOU	19 X 19	GP	75	4	480	700
#6—La Sangre Notiene Puertas en Vuestra Noche Boca Arriba	EdP	LP	1987	EB/HC/GOU	19 X 19	GP	75	4	480	700
#7—Huir por las Esquinas y Encerrarse en los Altimos Pisos	EdP	LP	1987	EB/HC/GOU	19 X 19	GP	75	5	480	700
#8—Jamás Sierpe, Ni Cebra, Ni Mula Palidecieron al Morir	EdP	LP	1987	EB/HC/GOU	19 X 19	GP	75	4	480	700
#9—Asesinado por el Cielo, Entre las Formas que van Hacía la Sierpe y las Formas que Buscan el Cristal	EdP	LP	1987	EB/HC/GOU	19 X 19	GP	75	4	480	700
#10—Con la Ciencia del Tronco y el Rastro Llenan de Nervios Luminosos la Arcilla	EdP	LP	1987	EB/HC/GOU	19 X 19	GP	75	4	480	700
#11—A la Izquierda, a la Derecha, Porel sur y por el Norte se Levanta el Muro Impasible	EdP	LP	1987	EB/HC/GOU	19 X 19	GP	75	4	480	700
#12—Yo Estaba en la Terraza Luchando con la Luna	EdP	LP	1987	EB/HC/GOU	19 X 19	GP	75	5	480	700
#13—Enjambres de Ventanas Acribillaban an Muslo de la Noche	EdP	LP	1987	EB/HC/GOU	19 X 19	GP	75	5	480	700
Series of 2 Hand Coloured Etchings (Set of 2):									2000 SET	3500 SET
Me Llega Tu Rumor Atravesando Troncos y Ascensores	EdP	LP	1987	LC	51 X 39	GP	50	4	1100	1800
Un Viento Sur Lleva Colmillos, Girasoles y Alfabetos	EdP	LP	1987	LC	51 X 39	GP	50	6	1100	1800

KAREN GUNDERSON

BORN: Racine, WI; August 14, 1943
EDUCATION: Wisconsin State Univ, Whitewater, WI, BEd, 1966; Univ of Iowa, Owa City, IA, MA & MFA, 1968
TEACHING: Adj Asst Prof, New York Univ, Art Sch, NY, 1973–76; Vis Art, Painting, Chicago Art Inst, IL, 1977; Instr, Maryland Art Inst, Baltimore, MD, 1986

AWARDS: Distinguished Alumni Award, Univ of Wisconsin, Whitewater, WI, 1985
COLLECTIONS: Wustum Art Mus, Racine, WI; Milwaukee Art Center, WI
PRINTERS: Artist (ART)
PUBLISHERS: Artist (ART)
GALLERIES: Perimeter Gallery, Chicago, IL; Gremillion & Company, Houston, TX
MAILING ADDRESS: 26 Beaver St, New York, NY 10004

TITLE	PUBLISHER	PRINTER	DATE	MEDIUM	DIMENSION (PAPER SIZE) IN INCHES	TYPE OF PAPER	EDITION NUMBER	NO. OF COLORS	ORIGINAL OPENING PRICE	CURRENT RETAIL PRICE
SOLD OUT EDITIONS (RARE):										
Sky Passage	ART	ART	1984	WC	11 X 24	KOZO	16	2	325	400

The retail prices of the 100,000 limited edition prints quoted in this directory are subject to change. Print publishers, artists and galleries were the direct sources for these quotations. Prices in the secondary market listed as "Sold Out Editions (Rare)" indicate that the publisher has a limited supply of that print or that the print is difficult to locate in the galleries.

The Printworld Directory is accepting new applications for the seventh edition. Approximately 300 new artists will be accepted. Please use the two forms provided in the back section of this directory to submit biographical data and documentation of prints. Edition number of each print must not exceed 500 and the retail price must be $100 or more.

PHILIP GUSTON

BORN: Montreal, Canada; (1913–1980)
EDUCATION: Otis Art Inst, Los Angeles, CA, 1930
TEACHING: State Univ of Iowa, Ames, IA, 1941–45; Washington Univ, 1945–47; Univ of Minnesota, St Paul, MN; New York Univ, NY, 1951–59; Pratt Inst, NY, 1953–57; Yale Univ, New Haven, CT, 1963; Brandeis Univ, Waltham, MA, 1966; Columbia Univ, NY, 1966,70,74; New York Studio Sch, NY; Skidmore Col, Sarasota Springs, NY, 1968; Boston Univ, MA, 1973–80
AWARDS: First Prize, Carnegie Inst, Pittsburgh, PA, 1945; Prix de Rome, Italy, 1948; Am Acad of Arts & Letters Grant, NY, 1948; Ford Found Grant, NY, 1948,59; Guggenheim Found Fel, NY, 1947,68; Hon DFA, Boston Univ, MA, 1970; Distinguished Teaching of Art Award, College Art Assoc, 1975
RECENT EXHIB: Charles H MacNider Mus, Mason City, IA,1989,92; St Louis Art Mus, MO, 1992
COLLECTIONS: Allentown Mus, PA; Baltimore Mus, MD; Albright-Knox Art Gallery, Buffalo, NY; Chicago Inst, IL; Detroit Inst, MI; High Mus, Atlanta, GA; Hirshhorn Mus, Wash, DC; Univ of Illinois, Champaign, IL; State Univ of Iowa, Ames, IA; Los Angeles County Mus, CA; Mus of Mod Art, NY; Metropolitan Mus, NY; Minneapolis Inst of Art, MN; Nat Coll of Fine Arts, Wash, DC; Phillips Coll, Wash, DC; State Univ of New York, Purchase, NY; San Francisco Mus of Mod Art, CA; Guggenheim Mus, NY; St Louis Mus, MO; Tate Gallery, London, England; Whitney Mus of Am Art, NY; Washington Univ, St Louis, MO; Yale Univ, New Haven, CT; Worcester Mus, MA
PUBLISHERS: Gemini GEL, Los Angeles, CA (GEM); Skowhegan School of Art, ME (SSA); Artist (ART)
PRINTERS: Gemini GEL, Los Angeles, CA (GEM)
GALLERIES: John Berggruen Gallery, San Francisco, CA; David McKee Gallery, New York, NY; Gemini GEL at Joni Weyl, New York, NY; Gemini GEL, Los Angeles, CA; Janie C Lee Galleries, New York, NY & Houston, TX; Cava Gallery, Phila, PA; Andrew Dierken Fine Art, Los Angeles, CA; Anthony Meier Fine Arts, San Francisco, CA; Peter Wallach Gallery, St Louis, MO; Louis K Meisel Gallery, New York, NY; Edward Tyler Nahem Fine Art, New York; Sragow Gallery, New York, NY

Gemini GEL (G)

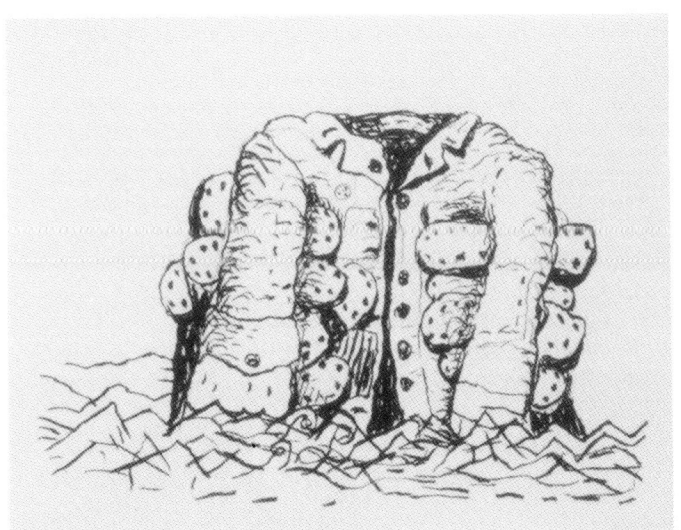

Philip Guston
Door
Courtesy Gemini GEL

Philip Guston
East Side
Courtesy Gemini GEL

TITLE	PUBLISHER	PRINTER	DATE	MEDIUM	DIMENSION (PAPER SIZE) IN INCHES	TYPE OF PAPER	EDITION NUMBER	NO. OF COLORS	ORIGINAL OPENING PRICE	CURRENT RETAIL PRICE
SOLD OUT EDITIONS (RARE):										
The Street	SSA		1970	LB	20 X 26	AP	120	1	100	10000
Studio Forms	GEM	GEM	1980	LB	32 X 43	AC	100	1	300	7500
Sea (G-869)	GEM	GEM	1980	LB	32 X 43	R/BFK	50	1	300	7500
Room (G-870)	GEM	GEM	1980	LC	33 X 43	R/BFK	50	1	300	7500
Coat (G-873)	GEM	GEM	1980	LC	32 X 43	R/BFK	50	1	300	7500
Car	GEM	GEM	1980	LC	20 X 30	R/BFK	50	1	300	7500
Elements	GEM	GEM	1980	LC	33 X 43	R/BFK	50	1	300	10000
East Side	GEM	GEM	1980	LC	33 X 43	R/BFK	50	1	300	7500
Remains	GEM	GEM	1980	LC	19 X 30	R/BFK	50	1	300	6500
Summer	GEM	GEM	1980	LC	20 X 30	R/BFK	50	1	300	6500
Rug (G-876)	GEM	GEM	1981	LC	20 X 29	R/BFK	50	1	350	6500
Group	GEM	GEM	1981	LC	30 X 20	R/BFK	50	1	350	6000
Curtain	GEM	GEM	1981	LC	31 X 41	R/BFK	50	1	350	6000
Agean	GEM	GEM	1981	LC	32 X 43	R/BFK	50	1	350	6000
Studio Corner	GEM	GEM	1981	LC	32 X 43	R/BFK	50	1	350	6000
Scene	GEM	GEM	1981	LC	20 X 30	R/BFK	50	1	350	6000
Shoes	GEM	GEM	1981	LC	20 X 30	R/BFK	50	1	350	9000
Door (G-931)	GEM	GEM	1981	LC	22 X 30	R/BFK	50	1	350	6000
Sea Group	GEM	GEM	1983	LC	32 X 43	R/BFK	50	1	400	6000
Gulf	GEM	GEM	1983	LC	32 X 43	R/BFK	50	1	400	10000
View	GEM	GEM	1983	LC	30 X 43	R/BFK	50	1	400	6000
Painter	GEM	GEM	1983	LC	32 X 43	R/BFK	50	1	400	6500
Sky	GEM	GEM	1983	LC	20 X 30	R/BFK	50	1	400	6000
Pile Up	GEM	GEM	1983	LC	20 X 30	R/BFK	50	1	400	6000
Easel	GEM	GEM	1983	LC	20 X 30	R/BFK	50	1	400	6000
Objects	GEM	GEM	1983	LC	20 X 30	R/BFK	50	1	400	6000

PETER GUTKIN

BORN: Brooklyn, NY; 1944
EDUCATION: Tyler Sch of Art, Temple Univ, Phila, PA, BFA, 1966; San Francisco Art Inst, CA, MFA, 1968
TEACHING: Instr, Aspen Sch of Contemp Art, CO, 1966; Univ of California, Berkeley, CA, 1972–74; San Francisco Art Inst, CA, 1978; California Col of Arts & Crafts, Oakland, CA 1982
AWARDS: Nat Endowment Humanities & Art Award, 1966; Purchase Prize, San Francisco Art Festival, CA, 1972; Nat Endowment for the Arts Fel, 1982,84; Prod Design Award, Resources Council, 1986
RECENT EXHIB: Laforet Mus, Tokyo, Japan, 1987; Modernism, San Francisco, CA, 1990
COLLECTIONS: Temple Univ, Phila, PA; Oakland Mus, CA; Portland Mus, OR; San Francisco Art Mus of Mod Art, CA
PUBLISHERS: Made in California, Oakland, CA (MIC)
PRINTERS: David Kelso, Oakland, CA (DK); Made in California, Oakland, CA (MIC)
GALLERIES: Modernism, San Francisco, CA
MAILING ADDRESS: 170 Capp, San Francisco, CA 94110

TITLE	PUBLISHER	PRINTER	DATE	MEDIUM	DIMENSION (PAPER SIZE) IN INCHES	TYPE OF PAPER	EDITION NUMBER	NO. OF COLORS	ORIGINAL OPENING PRICE	CURRENT RETAIL PRICE
CURRENT EDITIONS:										
Sonora Run	MIC	DK/MIC	1981	MEZ	30 X 22	R/BFK/W	50	1	300	500

KAREN GUZAK

BORN: Cambridge, MA; 1939
EDUCATION: Univ of Colorado, Boulder, CO, Boettcher Scholar, BS, 1961
TEACHING: Instr, Watermedia Painting, Factory of Visual Arts, Seattle, WA, 1976–81; Instr, Experimental Watercolor Workshop, Humbold Univ, Arcata, CA, 1982; Instr, Centrum Found, Port Townsend, WA, 1977,78,83; Instr, Watermedia Painting, Seattle Pacific Univ, WA, 1983; Instr, Color Lithography, Edmonds Com Col, WA, 1986; Instr, High Tech/Low Tech Workshop, Univ of Oregon, Eugene, OR, 1989
AWARDS: Juror's Award, Renton Show, WA, 1980
RECENT EXHIB: Musee Hyacinth Rigaud, Perpignan, France, 1988; Laura Russo Gallery, Portland, OR, 1989; Foster/White Gallery, Seattle, WA, 1989
COLLECTIONS: Musee de Carcassonne, Carcassonee, France; Portland Art Mus, OR; Brooklyn Mus, NY; New York City Library, NY; Whatcom Coun Art Mus, Bellingham, WA; Evergreen State Col, Olympia, WA; Emily Carr Col, Vancouver, BC, Canada; Seattle Pacific Univ, Seattle, WA; Baylor Col of Medicine, Houston, TX
PRINTERS: Debra Van Tuinen (DVT); Coburn Press (CP)
PUBLISHERS: Artist (ART)
GALLERIES: American Art, Tacoma, WA; Artists Circle, Potomac, MD; Bau XI, Vancouver, BC, Canada; Gergus Jean Gallery, Columbus, OH; Brentwood Gallery, St Louis, MO; Carson-Sapiro, Denver, CO; Davidson Gallery, Seattle, WA; Foster/White Gallery, Seattle, WA; Harris Gallery, Houston, TX; Hefner Gallery, Grand Rapids, MI; Miller Brown Gallery, San Francisco, CA; Northwest Print Council, Portland, OR; Laura Russo Gallery, Portland, OR; Shoshana Wayne Gallery, Santa Monica, CA; Ellen Sragow Gallery, New York, NY; Windsors Gallery, Dania, FL; Gallery 44, Boulder, CO; Brenda Forbig Gallery, Grand Rapids, MI; Chandler Gallery, Wellfleet, MA; La Boutique d'Art, Carcassonne, France; Buschlen/Mowatt Gallery, Vancouver, BC, Canada
MAILING ADDRESS: 707 S Snoqualmie, Seattle, WA 98108

TITLE	PUBLISHER	PRINTER	DATE	MEDIUM	DIMENSION (PAPER SIZE) IN INCHES	TYPE OF PAPER	EDITION NUMBER	NO. OF COLORS	ORIGINAL OPENING PRICE	CURRENT RETAIL PRICE
CURRENT EDITIONS:										
Duet I,II,III (Trip)	WP	DC/CM	1983	LC	35 X 84	LEN/100	36	60	950	950
A New Light	WP	DC/CM	1983	LC	44 X 32	LEN/100	300	60	380	450
Sunrise Dance	WP	DC/CM	1983	LC	44 X 32	LEN/100	24	35	380	450
Night Poem	ART	CoPr	1984	LC	31 X 42	AC/B	50	11	500	700
Blue Too (Dipt)	ART	DC/CM	1985	LC	30 X 44	MAG	50	35	800	800
Double X I,II (Dipt)	ART	DVT	1985	EC/WB	18 X 22	TR/WF	30	4	500 SET	500 SET
Phase Change	ART	DC/CM	1985	LC	22 X 30	HMP	50	13	450	450
Dream Dancer (Dipt)	ART	DC/CM	1985	LC	40 X 55	INCI/HC	50	11	950	950
Double Helix Warm and Cool (Dipt)	ART	DC/CM	1986	LC	30 X 42	R/BFK	42	11	650 SET	650 SET
Jewel Box	ART	IOP	1987	LC	22 X 29	LEN/100	125	25	400	400
Double Crisscross	ART	IOP	1987	LC	22 X 29	LEN/100	120	27	400	400
Quartz Quartet	ART	IOP	1987	LC	22 X 29	LEN/100	120	33	400	400
Crystal Code	ART	IOP	1987	LC	22 X 29	LEN/100	120	28	400	400
Making Time	ART	IOP	1987	LC	22 X 29	LEN/100	120	29	400	400
Silver Shimmy	ART	IOP	1987	LC	22 X 29	LEN/100	120	25	400	400
Moondancer (Dipt)	ART	CP	1987	LC	41 X 29	R/BFK/T	50	18	750	750
Range Finder	ART	IOP	1987	LC	22 X 29	LEN/100	120	26	400	400
Kaibob Trail	ART	IOP	1987	LC	22 X 29	LEN/100	120	28	400	400
Jewels for Taj	ART	IOP	1987	LC	22 X 29	LEN/100	120	28	400	400
Red Ridge	ART	IOP	1987	LC	22 X 29	LEN/100	120	26	400	400
Nevada Dazzler	ART	IOP	1987	LC	22 X 29	LEN/100	120	28	400	400
Quartz Dance	ART	IOP	1987	LC	22 X 29	LEN/100	120	25	400	400
Logos	ART	DC/CM	1987	LC	32 X 40	R/BFK/T	50	9	750	750
Centers of Seeing	ART	DC/CM	1987	LC	32 X 42	R/BFK	50	9	800	800
Double Dancer I,II	ART	DVT	1988	EC/WB	18 X 22	TR/WF	30	3+1	500 SET	500 SET
Fortification of the Center I,II (Dipt)	ART	DVT	1988	EC/WB	18 X 22	TR/WF	30	4	500 SET	500 SET

ROBERT GWATHMEY

BORN: Richmond, VA (1903–1988)
EDUCATION: North Carolina State Col, Raleigh, NC; Maryland Inst of Art, Baltimore, MD
COLLECTIONS: Whitney Mus of Am Art, NY; Brandeis Univ, Waltham, MA; Brooklyn Mus, NY; Springfield Mus of Art, MA; Virginia Mus of Fine Art, Richmond, VA; Pennsylvania Acad of Fine Arts, Phila, PA; Los Angeles County Art Mus, CA; Smithsonian Inst, Wash, DC; Butler Inst of Am Art, Youngstown, OH; Carnegie Inst, Pittsburgh, PA; Birmingham Mus, AL; San Diego Mus of Fine Art, CA; Mus of Mod Art, Sao Paulo, Brazil; Mus of Mod Art, NY; Univ of Nebraska, Lincoln, NE; Univ of Georgia, Athens, GA; Univ of Texas, Austin, TX; Oklahoma State Univ, Stillwater, OK; Randolph Macon Woman's Col, Lynchburg, VA

ROBERT GWATHMEY CONTINUED

PRINTERS: Artist (ART)
PUBLISHERS: Artist (ART)

GALLERIES: Terry Dintenfass, New York, NY; Michael Rosenfeld Gallery, New York, NY

TITLE	PUBLISHER	PRINTER	DATE	MEDIUM	DIMENSION (PAPER SIZE) IN INCHES	TYPE OF PAPER	EDITION NUMBER	NO. OF COLORS	ORIGINAL OPENING PRICE	CURRENT RETAIL PRICE
SOLD OUT EDITIONS (RARE):										
Topping Tobacco	ART	ART	1947	SP	13 X 9	AP			35	2500
Tin of Lard	ART	ART	1950	LC	18 X 13	AP	125		50	1500
Grandmother	ART	ART	1954	SP	17 X 13	AP	200		65	2500

HANS HAACKE

BORN: Cologne, Germany; August 12, 1936
EDUCATION: Staatliche Werkakademie, Kassel, West Germany, MFA; Atelier 17, Paris, France, with S W Hayter; Tyler Sch of Art, Temple Univ, Phila, PA
TEACHING: Prof, Art, Cooper Union Sch, NY, 1967 to present
AWARDS: Fulbright Fel, 1961; Guggenheim Fel, 1973; Nat Endowment for the Arts Fel, 1978
RECENT EXHIB: Mus of Mod Art, NY, 1988; Whitney Mus of Am Art, NY, 1989; Centre George Pompidou, Paris, France, 1987,90; Endleichkeit der Freiheit, Berlin, Germany, 1990; Renaissance Soc, Univ of Chicago, Il, 1989,92; John Weber Gallery, NY, 1988,90,92
COLLECTIONS: Philadelphia Mus of Art, PA; New Mus of Contemp Art, NY; Nat Gallery of Canada, Ottawa, Can; Nat Gallery of Australia, Canberra, Australia; Centre Georges Pompidou, Paris, France; Tate Gallery, London, England; Mod Museet, Stockholm, Sweden; Art Gallery of Ontario, Toronto, ON, Canada
PRINTERS: Crown Point Press, San Francisco, CA (CPP); Hidekatsu Takada, CA (HT); Nancy Anello, CA (NA); Stephen Thomas, CA (ST); Lilah Toland, CA (LT)
PUBLISHERS: Crown Point Press, San Francisco, CA (CPP)
GALLERIES: John Weber Gallery, New York, NY; Crown Point Press, New York, NY & San Francisco, CA
MAILING ADDRESS: 463 West St, New York, NY 10014

TITLE	PUBLISHER	PRINTER	DATE	MEDIUM	DIMENSION (PAPER SIZE) IN INCHES	TYPE OF PAPER	EDITION NUMBER	NO. OF COLORS	ORIGINAL OPENING PRICE	CURRENT RETAIL PRICE
SOLD OUT EDITIONS (RARE):										
Tiffany Cares	CPP	ST/LT	1978	PH/EB	29 X 41 TOT	HMP	35	1	500	4500
Upstair's at Mobil (Printed on 10 Sheets)	CPP	HT/NA	1982	PH/EC	36 X 21 EA 71 X 105 TOT	BHP	10	5	5000	12000

RICHARD JOHN HAAS

BORN: Spring Green, WI; August 29, 1936
EDUCATION: Univ of Wisconsin, Milwaukee, WI, BS, 1959; Univ of Minnesota, Saint Paul, MN, MFA, 1964; Michigan State Univ, East Lansing, MI, 1964–68; Olivet Col, MI, 1967; Bennington Col, VT, 1968–69
TEACHING: Instr, Art, Univ of Minnesota, Saint Paul, MN, 1963–64; Instr, Art, Walker Art Ctr, Minneapolis, MN, 1964; Asst Prof, Michigan State Univ, East Lansing, MI, 1964–68; Instr, Printmaking, Bennington Col, VT, 1968–80
AWARDS: Ford Foundation Purchase Prize, 1964; Creative Artists Service Grant, NY, 1972,75; Nat Endowment for the Arts Grant, Printmaking; Am Inst of Arch Medal, 1978; Annual Award, Municipal Arts Soc of NY, 1979; John Simon Guggenheim Found Mem Fel, NY, 1983; Doris C Freedman Award, NY, 1989
RECENT EXHIB: Williams Col Mus, Williamstown, MA, 1987; Nat Acad of Design, NY, 1987; Hudson River Mus, NY, 1988; Brooke Alexander, Inc, NY, 1989; Rona Hoffman Gallery, Chicago, IL, 1990
COLLECTIONS: Mus of Mod Art, NY; Metropolitan Mus Art, NY; Whitney Mus of Am Art, NY; Yale Univ Art Gallery, New Haven, CT; Fogg Mus, Cambridge, MA; Art Inst of Chicago, IL; Mus of Fine Arts, Boston, MA; Detroit Art Center, Ft Worth Art Art Mus, TX; High Mus of Art, Atlanta, GA; Houston Mus of Art, TX; Nat Coll of Fine Arts, Wash, DC; Library of Congress, Wash, DC; Newark Mus, NJ; Allentown Art Mus, PA; Minneapolis Mus of Art, MN; Free Library of Phila, PA; Lessing Rosenwald Coll, Phila, PA
PRINTERS: Landfall Press, Inc, Chicago, IL (LPI); Jack Lemon, Chicago, IL (JL); Tamarind Inst, Albuquerque, NM (TI); Hiromitsu Mirimoto, NY (HM); Paul Narkiewicz, NY (PN); Judy Solodkin, NY (JS); Solo Press, NY (SP); C Mousley, NY (CM); Patricia Branstead, NY (PB); Branstead Studio, NY (BS); Sienna Studio, NY (SS); Bruce Cleveland, Brooklyn, NY (BC); Bruce Cleveland Editions, Brooklyn, NY (BCE); Bruce Cleveland Editions, Brooklyn, NY (BCE); H Morimoto, NY (HM); Sheila Marbain, NY (SM); Maurel Studio, NY (MS); Maurice Sanchez, NY (MS); Jim Cooper, NY (JC); Derriére L'Etoile Studios, NY (DES); ChromaComp, Inc, NY (CCI); River House Editions, Chicago, IL (RHE)

Richard John Haas
Downtown LA—MOCA
Courtesy Riverhouse Editions

RICHARD JOHN HAAS CONTINUED

PUBLISHERS: Tamarind Inst, Albuquerque, NM (TI); Brooke Alexander, Inc, NY (BAI); Delahunty, Inc, NY (DI); Landfall Press, Inc, Chicago, IL (LPI); John Szoke Graphics, NY (JSG); Solo Press, NY (SP); River House Editions, Chicago, IL (RHE)

GALLERIES: Brooke Alexander, Inc, New York, NY; Landfall Press, Inc, Chicago, IL; Rhona Hoffman Gallery, Chicago, IL; Joy Moos Gallery, Miami, FL; Holly Solomon Gallery, New York, NY; Van Straaten Gallery, Chicago, IL; Quartet Editions, New York, NY
MAILING ADDRESS: 361 W 36th St, New York, NY 10018

Richard John Haas
Times Square Building Looking North
Courtesy Riverhouse Editions

Richard John Haas
Hong Kong View—Bank of China Tower
Courtesy Riverhouse Editions

TITLE	PUBLISHER	PRINTER	DATE	MEDIUM	DIMENSION (PAPER SIZE) IN INCHES	TYPE OF PAPER	EDITION NUMBER	NO. OF COLORS	ORIGINAL OPENING PRICE	CURRENT RETAIL PRICE
SOLD OUT EDITIONS (RARE):										
New Era Building I	BAI	PB/BS	1971	DPT	34 X 20	AP	20	1	200	1500
Dakota Courtyard	BAI	PB/BS	1971	EB	29 X 22	AP	50	1	200	1000
Bryn Mawr Hotel	BAI	PB/BS	1973	EB	29 X 20	AP	20	1	200	800
Greene Street	BAI	PB/BS	1973	EB	22 X 25	AP	27	1	200	1200
Alwyn Court	BAI	PB/BS	1973	EB	30 X 22	AP	50	1	200	1800
Corner of Broom & Broadway	BAI	PB/BS	1973	EB	37 X 19	AP	60	1	200	2000
Erie-Lackawanna Hoboken Terminal	BAI	PB/BS	1973	EB	21 X 37	AP	60	1	200	2000
Hoboken Terminal	BAI	PB/BS	1973	EB	23 X 41	AP	40	1	200	1000
Ansonia Entrance	BAI	PB/BS	1974	LC	19 X 16	AP	20		250	1000
Ansonia Entrance (State II)	BAI	PB/BS	1974	LB	19 X 16	AP	20	1	200	800
Corner of William & Maiden Lane	BAI	PB/BS	1974	LC	30 X 19	AP	40		225	1200
The Dorilton	BAI	PB/BS	1974	LC	20 X 23	AP	30		200	1000
Hugh O'Neill Building	BAI	PB/BS	1974	LC	24 X 23	AP	35		250	1000
Hugh O'Neill Building, State II	BAI	PB/BS	1974	LB	24 X 23	AP	20	1	250	750
Pennsylvania Academy	BAI	PB/BS	1974	LC	22 X 26	AP	40		250	1000
Olana	BAI	PB/BS	1974	LC	24 X 22	AP	20		250	1500
Olana, State II	BAI	PB/BS	1974	LC	24 X 23	AP	20		150	1000
The Potter Building, State II	BAI	PB/BS	1974	LB	22 X 26	AP	20		350	800
Rookery Courtyard	BAI	PB/BS	1974	EB/A	23 X 22	AP	50		150	800
Dakota Entrance	BAI/TI	TI	1974	LC	19 X 22	AP	50	Multi	175	1200
The Potter Building	BAI	PB/BS	1974	LC	22 X 26	AP	40		250	1000
Terrace, Washington Heights	BAI	PB/BS	1975	EB/A	22 X 27	AP	30		200	900
Office Facades, State II	BAI	PN	1976	LC	22 X 29	R/BFK	20		350	1000
Victorian Houses	BAI/DI	HM	1976	LC	22 X 29	R/BFK	40	5	250	1200

RICHARD JOHN HAAS CONTINUED

Richard John Haas
Chicago View, Morning
Courtesy Riverhouse Editions

TITLE	PUBLISHER	PRINTER	DATE	MEDIUM	DIMENSION (PAPER SIZE) IN INCHES	TYPE OF PAPER	EDITION NUMBER	NO. OF COLORS	ORIGINAL OPENING PRICE	CURRENT RETAIL PRICE
SOLD OUT EDITIONS (RARE):										
View of Chicago	BAI	HM	1976	LC	14 X 48	AP	150		200	800
Texas Architecture (Set of 6):									1200 SET	6000 SET
Victoria Houses	BAI/DI	HM	1976	LC	22 X 29	R/BFK/AC	40	5	300	1000
Storefronts	BAI/DI	HM	1976	LC	22 X 29	R/BFK/AC	40	5	300	1000
Courthouses	BAI/DI	JS/SP	1976	LC	22 X 29	R/BFK/AC	40	4	300	1000
Office Facades I	BAI/DI	PN	1976	LC	22 X 29	R/BFK/AC	40	4	300	1000
Office Facades II	BAI/DI	PN	1976	LC	22 X 29	R/BFK/AC	20	2	300	1000
Adolphus Hotel	BAI/DI	CM/PB	1976	EB/A	22 X 29	R/BFK/AC	40		300	1000
Driskill Motel	BAI/DI	CM/PB	1976	EB/A	22 X 29	R/BFK/AC	40		300	1000
Omaha Building	BAI	SiS	1977	EB	31 X 25	R/BFK	75		200	1200
View of 55th & Fifth Avenue	BAI	SiS	1977	LC	19 X 23	R/BFK	75	4	90	500
View of Munich	BAI	SiS	1978	LC	18 X 43	R/BFK	150		175	600
The Whitney	BAI	SiS	1979	WC	23 X 18	AP	60		250	400
Manhattan View, Battery Park (Day)	BAI	SiS	1979–80	EB/A	27 X 47	R/BFK	50	4	600	3500
Manhattan View, Battery Park (Night)	BAI	SiS	1980	EB/A	27 X 47	R/BFK	50		600	3000
Manhattan View, Battery Park (Black & White State)	BAI	SiS	1980	EB/A	26 X 47	AP	10		500	3500
State Capital Building, Albany	BAI	SiS	1981	LC	29 X 34	R/BFK	325		200	600
Centre Theatre Facade . . .	JSG	CCI	1981	SP	41 X 29	AC	100		400	1800
Villard Courtyard St Patrick's Cathedral	LPI	JL/LPI	1982	LC	29 X 42	R/BFK	50	4	500	1800
Railroad Terminal Cincinnati	LPI	JL/LPI	1985	LC	22 X 50	R/BFK	50	4	500	1200
Helmsley, Pan Am	JSG	BC/BCE	1985	EC	41 X 29	R/BFK	100	3	750	1800
Edison Brothers . . . (Trip)	JSG	BC/BCE	1985	SP	29 X 41	AC	100		750	3500
Ren Cen/City Country	JSG	BC/BCE	1985	LB	26 X 19	R/BFK	100		350	750
CURRENT EDITIONS:										
Garden Court	JSG	CCI	1979		96 X 72		200	8	450	3000
Architectural Facades, 1976–1986 (Set of 7):									6000 SET	6000 SET
Brotherhood Building, the Kroger Company, Cincinnati	BAI	MS/JC/DES	1989	SP	41 X 30	R/BFK	100		900	900
Center Theatre Facade, Milwaukee	BAI	MS/JC/DES	1989	SP	42 X 29	R/BFK	100		900	900
Chisholm Trail, Sundance Square, Fort Worth	BAI	MS/JC/DES	1989	SP	30 X 48	R/BFK	100		900	900
Edison Brothers Stores, Inc, St Louis (Trip)	BAI	MS/JC/DES	1989	SP	30 X 23	R/BFK	100 EA		1600 SET	1600 SET
				SP	30 X 42	R/BFK				
				SP	30 X 23	R/BFK				

RICHARD JOHN HAAS CONTINUED

TITLE	PUBLISHER	PRINTER	DATE	MEDIUM	DIMENSION (PAPER SIZE) IN INCHES	TYPE OF PAPER	EDITION NUMBER	NO. OF COLORS	ORIGINAL OPENING PRICE	CURRENT RETAIL PRICE
CURRENT EDITIONS:										
Fontainebleau Hilton Hotel, Miami Beach	BAI	MS/JC/DES	1989	SP	30 X 42	R/BFK	100		900	900
31 Milk Street, Boston	BAI	MS/JC/DES	1989	SP	41 X 30	R/BFK	100		900	900
West Facade, Boston Architectural Center	BAI	MS/JC/DES	1989	SP	30 X 45	R/BFK	100		900	900
Dallas Skyline	SP	JS/SP	1989	LC	29 X 32	R/BFK	50		1500	1500
Chicago Views:										
Chicago View, Day	RHE	PB/RHE	1989	EB	27 X 44	SOM	25	3	1500	1500
Chicago View, Evening	RHE	PB/RHE	1989	EB	27 X 44	SOM	50	3	1500	1500
Chicago View, Evening Fog	RHE	PB/RHE	1989	EB	27 X 44	R/BFK	50	1	1500	1500
Chicago View, Haze	RHE	PB/RHE	1989	EB	27 X 44	SOM	50	4	1500	1500
Chicago View, Morning	RHE	PB/RHE	1989	EB	27 X 44	R/BFK	25	1	1500	1500
Chicago View, Night Fog	RHE	PB/RHE	1989	EB	27 X 44	SOM	50	3	1500	1500
Down Town LA, MOCA	RHE	PB/RHE	1990	EB	30 X 22	AC	35	3	750	750
Hong Kong View, Bank of China Tower	RHE	PB/RHE	1990	EB	30 X 22	AC	35	4	750	750
New York Times Square Looking North	RHE	PB/RHE	1990	EB	30 X 22	AC	35	4	750	750
New York Lexington, Looking North—Central Synogogue	RHE	PB/RHE	1991	EB	30 X 22	AC	35	4	750	750

TERRY HAASS

BORN: Czechoslovakia; 1923
EDUCATION: Art Students League, NY; Atelier 17, with Stanley W Hayter, 1947; Ecole des Louvre, Architecture, MA, 1970
TEACHING: Brooklyn Col, NY; New York City Col, NY
AWARDS: Wooley Fel, 1951; Fulbright Travel Grant, Printmaking, 1951
COLLECTIONS: Brooklyn Mus, NY; Mus of Mod Art, NY; Victoria & Albert Mus, London, England; Guggenheim Mus, NY; Smithsonian Inst, Wash, DC; Israel Nat Mus, Jerusalem, Israel; Paula Modersohn Becker Mus, Bremen, Germany; Bibliotheque Nat, Paris, France
PRINTERS: American Atelier, NY (AA)
PUBLISHERS: Circle Fine Art, Chicago, IL (CFA); Associated American Artists, NY (AAA)
GALLERIES: Circle Galleries, San Francisco, CA & San Diego, CA & Northbrook, IL & Pittsburgh, PA & Houston, TX & Soho, NY & Chicago, IL & Scottsdale, AZ & Beverly Hills, CA & Costa Mesa, CA & Sherman Oaks, CA & Palm Beach, FL & Honolulu, HI & New Orleans, LA & Las Vegas, NV & Seattle WA

TITLE	PUBLISHER	PRINTER	DATE	MEDIUM	DIMENSION (PAPER SIZE) IN INCHES	TYPE OF PAPER	EDITION NUMBER	NO. OF COLORS	ORIGINAL OPENING PRICE	CURRENT RETAIL PRICE
SOLD OUT EDITIONS (RARE):										
Corsican Shore	AAA	AA	1967	EC	8 X 13	AP	100		35	150
Chasse Sauvage	AAA	AA	1967	EC	12 X 16	AP	35		40	150
Green Pie	CFA	AA	1968	EC	11 X 12	AP	100		35	125
Red and Blue	CFA	AA	1968	EC	11 X 12	AP	100		35	125
Green and Blue	CFA	AA	1968	EC	11 X 12	AP	100		35	125
Half Black/Half Red	CFA	AA	1968	EC	11 X 12	AP	100		35	125
Half Orange/Half Red	CFA	AA	1968	EC	11 X 12	AP	100		35	150
Two Purple Half Circles	CFA	AA	1968	EC	11 X 12	AP	100		35	150
Half Blue/Half Green	CFA	AA	1968	EC	11 X 12	AP	100		35	150
Blue Circle on Black	CFA	AA	1968	EC	11 X 12	AP	100		35	150
Nexus Portfolio, #1–#6	AAA	AA	1968	EC	11 DIA EA	AP	50 EA		35 EA	200 EA
Mouvement Lunaire	CFA	AA	1969	LC	26 X 35	AP	175		75	225
Diad Yellow, Green	CFA	AA	1969	EC	11 X 12	AP	100		35	125
Mouvement Solaire	CFA	AA	1969	LC	26 X 34	AP	175		75	225
Triad Red and Purple	CFA	AA	1969	EC	11 X 12	AP	100		35	150
Triad Yellow and Green	CFA	AA	1969	EC	11 X 12	AP	100		35	125
Biad Blue, Orange	CFA	AA	1969	EC	11 X 12	AP	100		35	125
Triad Blue, Orange	CFA	AA	1969	EC	11 X 12	AP	100		35	130
Triad Blue, Red	CFA	AA	1969	EC	11 X 12	AP	100		35	125
3 Triangles, Green	CFA	AA	1970	EC	11 X 12	AP	100		35	125
2 Triangles Red, Blue	CFA	AA	1970	EC	11 X 12	AP	100		35	125
4 Triangles Red, Orange	CFA	AA	1970	EC	11 X 12	AP	100		35	135
3 Triangles Orange	CFA	AA	1970	EC	11 X 12	AP	100		35	125
3 Triangles Green	CFA	AA	1970	EC	11 X 12	AP	100		35	125
2 Triangles Blue	CFA	AA	1970	EC	12 X 11	AP	100		35	100
No Infinity	CFA	AA	1971	LC	24 X 36	AP	250		75	200

VIDA HACKMAN

BORN: Bakersfield, CA; 1935
EDUCATION: Univ of California, Santa Barbara, CA, BA, 1956, MFA, 1967; California State Univ, Northridge, CA, MA, 1965
TEACHING: Asst Prof, Univ of California, Santa Barbara, CA, 1965–67; Los Angeles Com Col, CA, 1968–79; California State Univ, Northridge, CA, 1979–80
AWARDS: First Prize, Phelan Award
COLLECTIONS: Univ of California, Santa Barbara, CA; Lawrence Univ, Canton, OH, California State Univ, Long Beach, CA
PRINTERS: Artist (ART); A Goldman (AG); B Labadie (BL); W Weaver (WW); Black Dolphin Workshop, Los Angeles, CA (BDW)
PUBLISHERS: Artist (ART)
GALLERIES: Marilyn Pink Gallery, Los Angeles, CA; Orlando Gallery, Sherman Oaks, CA

VIDA HACKMAN CONTINUED

TITLE	PUBLISHER	PRINTER	DATE	MEDIUM	DIMENSION (PAPER SIZE) IN INCHES	TYPE OF PAPER	EDITION NUMBER	NO. OF COLORS	ORIGINAL OPENING PRICE	CURRENT RETAIL PRICE
SOLD OUT EDITIONS (RARE):										
San Simeon Collage IV	ART	ART	1980	MM	7 X 24	AP	1	5	350	550
San Simeon Collage V	ART	ART	1980	MM	7 X 24	AP	1	5	350	550
San Simeon Collage VII	ART	ART	1980	MM	7 X 17	AP	1	5	225	450
San Simeon Collage IX	ART	ART	1980	MM	7 X 20	AP	1	5	275	450
San Simeon Collage X	ART	ART	1980	MM	7 X 21	AP	1	5	350	550
San Simeon Collage XI	ART	ART	1980	MM	7 X 27	AP	2	5	350	550
Budge II	ART	ART	1981	EC	40 X 28	R/BFK	50	1	500	650
Double Red Phoenix	ART	ART	1981	EC	40 X 29	R/BFK	50	2	600	750
Pleiadis I	ART	ART	1981	EC	28 X 25	R/BFK	50	1	450	550
Black Warrier I	BDW	AG/BL/WW/BDW	1977	EB	29 X 40	GE/BL	10		200	600

VINCENT HADDELSEY

BORN: Lincolnshire, England; 1929
COLLECTIONS: Victoria & Albert Mus, London, England; Royal Coll, British Mus, London, England
PRINTERS: American Atelier, NY (AA)

PUBLISHERS: Circle Fine Art, Chicago, IL (CFA)
GALLERIES: Circle Galleries, San Diego, CA & San Francisco, CA & Northbrook, IL & Pittsburgh, PA & Houston, TX & Soho, NY & Chicago, IL & Scottsdale, AZ & Beverly Hills, CA & Costa Mesa, CA & Sherman Oaks, CA & Palm Beach, CA & Honolulu, HI & New Orleans, LA & Las Vegas, NV & Seattle, WA; David Findlay Gallery, New York, NY

TITLE	PUBLISHER	PRINTER	DATE	MEDIUM	DIMENSION (PAPER SIZE) IN INCHES	TYPE OF PAPER	EDITION NUMBER	NO. OF COLORS	ORIGINAL OPENING PRICE	CURRENT RETAIL PRICE
SOLD OUT EDITIONS (RARE):										
Hunting	CFA	AA	1972	EC	15 X 11	AP	130		50	500
Steeple Chase	CFA	AA	1972	EC	15 X 11	AP	130		50	500

MICHAEL HAFFTKA

BORN: 1954
AWARDS: Creative Artists Public Service Grant, Painting, 1983
RECENT EXHIB: Marc Richards Gallery, Los Angeles, CA, 1987; Mary Ryan Gallery, NY, 1987; Janet Steinberg Gallery, San Francisco, CA; DiLaurenti Gallery, NY, 1987; Gallery K Kawabata, Tokyo, Japan, 1988
COLLECTIONS: Mus of Mod Art, NY; Metropolitan Mus of Art, NY; Brooklyn Mus, NY; Carnegie Inst of Art, Pittsburgh, PA; New York Public Library, NY

PRINTERS: Artist (ART)
PUBLISHERS: Mary Ryan Gallery, NY (MRG)
GALLERIES: Mary Ryan Gallery, New York, NY; Marc Richards Gallery, Los Angeles, CA; Janet Steinberg Gallery, San Francisco, CA; DiLaurenti Gallery, New York, NY; Gallery K Kawabata, Tokyo, Japan; William Turner Gallery, Venice, CA
MAILNG ADDRESS: c/o Mary Ryan Gallery, 452 Columbus Ave, New York, NY 10024

TITLE	PUBLISHER	PRINTER	DATE	MEDIUM	DIMENSION (PAPER SIZE) IN INCHES	TYPE OF PAPER	EDITION NUMBER	NO. OF COLORS	ORIGINAL OPENING PRICE	CURRENT RETAIL PRICE
CURRENT EDITIONS:										
Neighbors (Set of 8)	MRG	ART	1986	DPT/MON	24 X 17 EA	FAB	VIII EA		2000 SET	3500 SET

FREDERICK HAGAN

BORN: Toronto, Canada; May 21, 1918
EDUCATION: Ontario Col of Art, Can, 1937–41; Art Students League, NY

TEACHING: Res Art, Pickering Col, Newmarket, Can, 1942–46; Instr, Drawing, Ontario Col of Art, Toronto, Can, 1946–83
COLLECTIONS: McMaster Univ, Hamilton, Can; Univ of Quelph, Can; Glenbow Coll, Calvary, Can; Nat Gallery, Ottawa, Can
GALLERIES: Gadatsy Gallery, Toronto, Canada
MAILING ADDRESS: 53 Lundy's Ave, Newmarket ON, Canada L3Y 3R9

TITLE	PUBLISHER	PRINTER	DATE	MEDIUM	DIMENSION (PAPER SIZE) IN INCHES	TYPE OF PAPER	EDITION NUMBER	NO. OF COLORS	ORIGINAL OPENING PRICE	CURRENT RETAIL PRICE
CURRENT EDITIONS:										
Surrounding Evidence	ART	ART	1971	LB	21 X 26		10	1	100	250
Spring Run Off	ART	ART	1974	LB	21 X 26		30	1	100	250
Open Door To Snow	ART	ART	1976	LB	16 X 21		24	1	100	250
Newfoundland (Set of 6)	ART	ART	1976	LB	16 X 20 EA		14 EA	1 EA	600 SET	900 SET
Woodcuts for Alice (Set of 7)	ART	ART	1980	WB	7 X 14 EA		10 EA	1 EA	350 SET	500 SET

NANCY HAGIN

BORN: Elizabeth, NJ; 1940
EDUCATION: Carnegie-Mellon Univ, Pittsburgh, PA, BFA, 1962; Yale Univ, New Haven, CT, MFA, 1964

TEACHING: Instr, Maryland Inst, Col of Art, Baltimore, MO, 1964–73; Instr, Rhode Island Sch of Design, Providence, RI, 1974; Instr, Fashion Inst of Tech, NY, 1974 to present; Cooper Union Sch of Art, NY, 1982 to present

NANCY HAGIN CONTINUED

AWARDS: Yale/Norfolk Award, New Haven, CT, 1961; Fulbright Grant, Rome, Italy, 1966–67; Municipal Art Soc of Baltimore Award, MO, 1969,70; Robert & Ann Merrick Found Award, 1970; Creative Artists Public Service Prog Grant, 1975; Art in Res, Palisades Interstate Park, NJ, 1975; Purchase Award, Fashion Inst of Tech, NY, 1976; Purchase Award, Butler Inst of Am Art, Youngstown, OH, 1977; Nat Endowment for the Arts Grant, 1982; MacDowell Colony Fel, 1974,79,82
RECENT EXHIB: Lafayette Col, Williams Center for the Arts, Easton, PA, 1987

COLLECTIONS: Mus of Fine Arts, Boston, MA; Butler Inst of Am Art, Youngstown, OH; Rose Art Mus, Brandeis Univ, Waltham, MA; Stern Col for Women, Yeshiva Univ, NY; Utah Mus of Fine Arts, Salt Lake City, UT; New Britain Mus of Am Art, CT; Fashion Inst of Tech, NY
PRINTERS: Orion Editions, NY (OE); Roni Henning, NY (RH); NYIT Screenprint Workshop, NY (NYIT); ChromaComp, Inc, NY (CCI)
PUBLISHERS: Orion Editions, NY (OE); Chalk & Vermilion Fine Arts, Greenwich, CT (CVFA)
GALLERIES: Orion Editions, New York, NY; Alpha Gallery, Boston, MA; Fischbach Gallery, New York, NY; Marcus Gordon Gallery, Pittsburgh, PA
MAILING ADDRESS: 55 W 28th St, New York, NY 10001

TITLE	PUBLISHER	PRINTER	DATE	MEDIUM	DIMENSION (PAPER SIZE) IN INCHES	TYPE OF PAPER	EDITION NUMBER	NO. OF COLORS	ORIGINAL OPENING PRICE	CURRENT RETAIL PRICE
CURRENT EDITIONS:										
North Window	OE	OE/NYIT	1981	SP	23 X 30	LEN	68	22	300	850
Morning Glory			1982	EB/A/SG/SG/DPT	42 X 28	R/BFK	40	1	600	1500
Lace Curtain	OE	RH/NYIT	1983	SP	35 X 41	LEN	125	20	575	750
Blue and White Agate	OE		1985	PO	35 X 41	LEN	125	22	650	750
Optimo	CVFA	CCI	1986	SP	28 X 28	COV	392	40	500	650
Country Lace	CVFA	CCI	1986	SP	40 X 29	COV	392	40	500	650
Pink Quilt	CVFA	CCI	1986	SP	31 X 36	COV	392	45	500	650
Blue Agate	CVFA	CCI	1986	SP	39 X 29	COV	392	40	500	650
Three Red Cloths	CVFA	CCI	1987	SP	29 X 38	COV	392		550	550
Tin Doll House	CVFA	CCI	1987	SP	30 X 38	COV	392		550	550
East of Suez	CVFA	CCI	1987	SP	39 X 31	COV	392		550	550
Milk Glass Bouquet	CVFA	CCI	1987	SP	38 X 34	COV	392		550	650
Red and White Quilt	CVFA	CCI	1987	SP	38 X 36	COV	392	50	550	550
Guest Room	CVFA	CCI	1987	SP	30 X 39	COV	392	34	550	625
Summer House	CVFA	CCI	1988	SP	30 X 38	COV	392	34	550	625
Checked Quilt	CVFA	CCI	1988	SP	38 X 34	COV	392	32	550	550

KATHERINE HAGSTRUM

BORN: Washington, DC; 1943
EDUCATION: Carlton Col, Northfield, MN; Northwestern Univ, Evanston, IL, MAT

PRINTERS: Artist (ART)
PUBLISHERS: John Szoke Graphics, NY (JSG)
GALLERIES: Vorpal Gallery, New York, NY & San Francisco, CA; Munson Gallery, Santa Fe, NM; Jane Lamond Gallery, London, England; C G Rein Galleries, Santa Fe, NM & Scottsdale, AZ & Houston, TX

TITLE	PUBLISHER	PRINTER	DATE	MEDIUM	DIMENSION (PAPER SIZE) IN INCHES	TYPE OF PAPER	EDITION NUMBER	NO. OF COLORS	ORIGINAL OPENING PRICE	CURRENT RETAIL PRICE
CURRENT EDITIONS:										
Lofty (Diptych)	JSG	ART	1983	EC	23 X 32	R/BFK	100	10	300	400
Aurora (Diptych)	JSG	ART	1984	EC	16 X 47	R/BFK	100	10	350	450

SAMIA ASAAD HALABY

BORN: Jerusalem, Palestine; December 12, 1936
EDUCATION: Univ of Cincinnati, OH, BS, 1954–59; Michigan State Univ, East Lansing, MI, MA, 1959–60; Indiana Univ, Bloomington, IN, MFA, 1961–63
TEACHING: Univ of Hawaii, Honolulu, HI, 1963–64; Kansas City Art Inst, MO, 1964–66; Univ of Michigan, Ann Arbor, MI, 1967–69; Indiana Univ, Bloomington, IN, 1962–63, 1969–72; Yale Univ, New Haven, CT, 1972–82; Univ of Hawaii, Honolulu, HI, 1985–86; Instr, Cooper Union, NY, 1989–90
AWARDS: Kansas City Council on the Arts, Traveling Grant, 1965; Tamarind Lithography Workshop, Artist in Residence, 1972; Creative Artists Public Service Grant, 1978–79
RECENT EXHIB: Jacksonville Art Mus, FL, 1992

COLLECTIONS: Guggenheim Mus, NY; Indianapolis Mus, IN; Detroit Inst of Art, MI; Cleveland Mus, OH; Yale Univ, New Haven, CT; Tamarind Inst Coll, Albuquerque, NM; Cooper Hewitt Mus, NY; Art Inst of Chicago, IL; Speed Art Mus, Louisville, KY; Fort Wayne Mus, IN; Michigan State Univ, East Lansing, MI; Indiana Univ Mus, Bloomington, IN; Nelson Rockhill Gallery of Art, Kansas City, MO; Honolulu Acad of Art, HI; Palm Springs Desert Mus, CA; Alternative Mus, NY
PRINTERS: Sheila Marbain, NY (SM); Maurel Studio, NY (MS)
PUBLISHERS: Impressions Workshop, Boston, MA (IW); Tamarind Lithography Workshop, Albuquerque, NM (TI); Sirroco Screen Prints, North Haven, CT (SSP); Maurel Studios, NY (MS); Cleveland Print Club, OH (CPC); Artist (ART)
GALLERIES: Ellen Sragow Ltd, New York, NY; Marian Locks Gallery, Phila, PA; van Straaten Gallery, Chicago, IL; New Gallery, Cleveland, OH; The Gallery, Bloomington, IN; Tossan-Tossan, New York, NY
MAILING ADDRESS: 103 Franklin St, New York, NY 10013

TITLE	PUBLISHER	PRINTER	DATE	MEDIUM	DIMENSION (PAPER SIZE) IN INCHES	TYPE OF PAPER	EDITION NUMBER	NO. OF COLORS	ORIGINAL OPENING PRICE	CURRENT RETAIL PRICE
CURRENT EDITIONS:										
Bright Crayon	TI	CC/TI	1972	LC	24 X 22	AP	14	3	325	600
Bruce's Blend	TI	BP/TI	1972	LC	23 X 23	AP	20	4	350	500
Triangles	TI	JS/TI	1972	LC	25 X 22	AP	14	4	375	600
Position Delay	SSP	WW/SSP	1981	SP	21 X 23	AP	75	6	125	350
Position Interplay: Noon	SSP	WW/SSP	1981	SP	21 X 27	AP	52	6	175	350
Position Interplay: Midnight	SSP	WW/SSP	1981	SP	21 X 27	AP	45	6	175	350

SAMIA ASAAD HALABY CONTINUED

TITLE	PUBLISHER	PRINTER	DATE	MEDIUM	DIMENSION (PAPER SIZE) IN INCHES	TYPE OF PAPER	EDITION NUMBER	NO. OF COLORS	ORIGINAL OPENING PRICE	CURRENT RETAIL PRICE
CURRENT EDITIONS:										
Pulsating	SSP	JT/SSP	1982	SP	22 X 30	AP	86	7	175	350
Seasoning Turning	ART	SM/MS	1983	SP	22 X 30	AP	40	5	210	400
City Turnings	ART	SM/MS	1983	SP	22 X 30	AP	39	5	210	400

ERNST HALBERSTADT

BORN: Budingen, Germany; August 26, 1920; U S Citizen
TEACHING: Mus Sch of Fine Arts, Boston, MA, 1950–53; Photography, Penlands, NC, 1973
COLLECTIONS: Metropolitan Mus of Art, NY; Mus of Mod Art, NY; Fogg Mus of Art, Harvard Univ, Cambridge, MA; DeCordova Mus, Lincoln, MA; Rose Art Mus, Brandeis Mus, Waltham, MA; Univ of Georgia Mus; Cleveland Mus of Art, OH; Brockton MA Art Mus; Addison Gallery of Am Art, Andover, MA
PRINTERS: Artist (ART)
PUBLISHERS: Artist (ART)
MAILING ADDRESS: 35 Staunton Road, Belmont, MA 02178

TITLE	PUBLISHER	PRINTER	DATE	MEDIUM	DIMENSION (PAPER SIZE) IN INCHES	TYPE OF PAPER	EDITION NUMBER	NO. OF COLORS	ORIGINAL OPENING PRICE	CURRENT RETAIL PRICE
SOLD OUT EDITIONS (RARE):										
Brothers Keeper	ART	ART	1938	LB	16 X 20	AP	25	1	25	350
Head, Young Girl	ART	ART	1938	LB	9 X 12	AP	25	1	25	550
CURRENT EDITIONS:										
Ogunquit Seacoast Series 1–7	ART	ART	1980–81	PH/C	36 X 36 EA	KOD	25 EA	FULL	400 EA	450 EA

EMANUEL HALLER

BORN: Newark, NJ; September 7, 1927
EDUCATION: Newark Sch of Fine & Industrial Art, NJ, Certificate 1949
TEACHING: Instr, Newark Mus, NJ; Printmaking Council of New Jersey, Somerville, NJ, currently
AWARDS: New Jersey State Mus, Trenton, NJ, 1965,69; Newark Mus, NJ, 1978; State of New Jersey Visual Arts Fel, 1985; New Jersey Center for Visual Arts Award, Summit, NJ, 1985
RECENT EXHIB: Johnson & Johnson World Headquarters, New Brunswick, NJ, 1990; Printmaking Council of New Jersey, Somerville, NJ, 1992
COLLECTIONS: New Jersey State Mus, Trenton, NJ; Newark Mus, NJ; Monmouth Col, West Long Branch, NJ; Rosenwald Coll, Jenkintown, PA; New Jersey State Mus, Trenton, NJ
PRINTERS: Artist (ART)
PUBISHERS: Artist (ART)
GALLERIES: Wenniger Graphics, Boston, MA; Swain Galleries, Plainfield, NJ; Printmaking Council of New Jersey, Somerville, NJ
MAILING ADDRESS: 121 Greenbrook Rd, North Plainfield, NJ 07060

TITLE	PUBLISHER	PRINTER	DATE	MEDIUM	DIMENSION (PAPER SIZE) IN INCHES	TYPE OF PAPER	EDITION NUMBER	NO. OF COLORS	ORIGINAL OPENING PRICE	CURRENT RETAIL PRICE
SOLD OUT EDITIONS (RARE):										
Eddie's Bunny	ART	ART	1970	EB	10 X 8	INDEX	100	1	50	250
Rembrandt's World	JBI	ART	1971	DPT	20 X 26	R/BFK	250	7	100	500
Bill's Buick	ART	ART	1973	EB/ENG	14 X 17	R/BFK	100	1	35	300
Toulouse-Lautrec	JBI	ART	1974	DPT	20 X 26	R/BFK	250	7	100	400
Jeans	ART	ART	1985	SP	22 X 30	INDEX	9	2	150	300
CURRENT EDITIONS:										
Eraser	ART	ART	1976	EC	18 X 14	R/BFK	100	2	100	275
Half Timbered	ART	ART	1981	EB	17 X 14	INDEX	150	1	125	250
Arlene's Socks	ART	ART	1982	EC/ENG	19 X 26	RP/HWT	50	4	275	400
Color Socks Series (Set of 3):									195 SET	350 SET
Red Socks	ART	ART	1984	ENG	13 X 19	RP/LTWT	50	4	70	150
Blue Socks	ART	ART	1984	ENG	13 X 19	RP/LTWT	50	4	70	150
Yellow Socks	ART	ART	1984	ENG	13 X 19	RP/LTWT	50	4	70	150
Tube	ART	ART	1984	DPT	17 X 14	INDEX	30	1	120	250
Doctor K	ART	ART	1986	LI	14 X 17	TAB	150	1	100	200
Basket Case	ART	ART	1987	DPT	10 X 15	RP	20	1	150	250
His Royal Highness	ART	ART	1988	EB/ENG	12 X 16	INDEX	100	1	150	250
Jacob Lawrence	ART	ART	1989	EB	11 X 14	INDEX	100	1	180	250
Mousey Tongue	ART	ART	1989	EB	14 X 18	INDEX	100	1	200	225
Tuscan Village	ART	ART	1991	DPT	11 X 14	DE	25	1	125	175
O'Neill	ART	ART	1991	WB	12 X 16	TAB	75	1	125	125
Beckett	ART	ART	1991	WB	16 X 20	TAB	75	1	250	250

STEVE HANKS

EDUCATION: Acad of Art, San Francisco, CA; California Col of Arts & Crafts, Oakland, CA
RECENT EXHIB: Leslie Levy Gallery, Scottsdale, AZ
PRINTERS: Eleanor Ettinger, Inc, NY (EEI); Messinger, Inc, NY (MI)
PUBLISHERS: Leslie Levy Gallery, Scottsdale, AZ (LLG)
GALLERIES: Leslie Levy Gallery, Scottsdale, AZ

TITLE	PUBLISHER	PRINTER	DATE	MEDIUM	DIMENSION (PAPER SIZE) IN INCHES	TYPE OF PAPER	EDITION NUMBER	NO. OF COLORS	ORIGINAL OPENING PRICE	CURRENT RETAIL PRICE
CURRENT EDITIONS:										
The Letter	LLG	EEI	1987	LC	41 X 23	AP	300	14	450	600

SUSAN HALL

BORN: Point Reyes Station, CA; March 19, 1943
EDUCATION: California Col of Arts & Crafts, Oakland, CA, BFA, 1962–65; Univ of California, Berkeley, CA, MA, 1965–67
TEACHING: Instr, Univ of California, Berkeley, CA, 1967–69; Sarah Lawrence Col, Bronxville, NY, 1972–75; Univ of Colorado, Boulder, CO; 1973,81; Art Inst of Chicago, IL, 1981; Sch of Visual Arts, NY, 1981 to present
AWARDS: Nat Endowment for the Arts Grant, 1979,88
RECENT EXHIB: Ovsey Gallery, Los Angeles, CA, 1987,89; Trabia-MacAfee Gallery, NY, 1987,88,89
COLLECTIONS: Whitney Mus of Am Art, NY; San Francisco Mus, CA; Storm King Art Center, Mountainville, NY; Brooklyn Mus, NY; Carnegie Inst, Pittsburgh, PA; Currier Mus of Art, Manchester, NH
PRINTERS: Aeropress, NY (A); Patricia Branstead, NY (PB); Movex, Ltd (ML); A Givati (AG); Bud Shark, Boulder, CO (BS); Ron Trujillo, Boulder, CO (RT); Shark's, Inc, Boulder, CO (SI); Maurice Sanchez, NY (MS); Jack Lemon, Chicago, IL (JL); Landfall Press, Inc, Chicago, IL (LPI); Artist (ART); Julio Juristo, Tampa, FL (JJ); Topaz Editions, Inc, Tampa, FL (TE)
PUBLISHERS: Barbara Gladstone Editions, NY (BGE); Brooke Alexander, Inc, NY (BAI); Diane Villani Editions, NY (DVE); Signet Arts, NY (SA); Pace Editions, NY (PE); Shark's, Inc, Boulder, CO (SI); Prestige Art Ltd, Mamaroneck, NY (PA); Art Matters, Boulder, CO (AM); Landfall Press, Inc, Chicago, IL (LPI); Artist (ART); Topaz Editions, Inc, Tampa, FL (TE)
GALLERIES: Barbara Gladstone Gallery, New York, NY; Brooke Alexander, Inc, New York, NY; Magnuson Gallery, Boston, MA; Roger Ramsay, Chicago, IL; Diane Villani Editions, New York, NY; Ovsey Gallery, Los Angeles, CA; Shark's, Inc, Boulder, CO; Alan Brown Gallery, Hartsdale, NY; Gallery Paule Anglim Gallery, San Francisco, CA; Nancy Hoffman Gallery, New York, NY; Landfall Press, Inc, Chicago, IL; Trabia-MacAfee Gallery, New York, NY; Pace Prints, New York, NY; Gump's Gallery, San Francisco, CA; Topaz Editions, Inc, Tampa, FL; Lise Hoshour Gallery, Albuquerque, NM; Quartet Editions, New York, NY
MAILING ADDRESS: 10 White St, New York, NY 10013

Susan Hall
Keone'ele, the Cove at City of Refuge
Courtesy Shark's, Inc

TITLE	PUBLISHER	PRINTER	DATE	MEDIUM	DIMENSION (PAPER SIZE) IN INCHES	TYPE OF PAPER	EDITION NUMBER	NO. OF COLORS	ORIGINAL OPENING PRICE	CURRENT RETAIL PRICE
SOLD OUT EDITIONS (RARE):										
New York Portrait #1,#2,#3	PE	AG/ML	1976	SP	36 X 28 EA	AC	8 EA	2 EA	200 EA	1000 EA
Morning Glory (Sanding, Scraping, Spit Bite, Soft Ground)	DVE/SA	PB/A	1982	A/DPT/CC	42 X 28		40	4	800	1400
CURRENT EDITIONS:										
Carrot Salad	BAI		1973	E/HC/WA	21 X 17		34		200	500
The Dinner	BAI		1973	E/HC/WA	18 X 23		34		200	500
Glove Display	BAI		1973	E/HC/WA	19 X 17		34		200	500
Summer Slices	BGE		1979	LC	29 X 22		50	4	400	500
Night Flight	BGE		1979	LC	29 X 22		50	5	400	500
Greetings from Afar	PA	MS	1980	SP/LC/HC	28 X 41	AP	100	7	600	750
Pages from the Diaries	PA	MS	1980	SP/LC/HC	28 X 41	AP	100	8	600	750
Landfall, States I,II	AM	JL/LPI	1981	LC	40 X 25 EA	AP	25 EA		600 EA	1000 EA
Shadow Moment	SI/ART	BS/SI	1983	LC	25 X 42	R/BFK/W	50	6	650	900
Maroon Bells I,II,III (Trip)	SI/ART	BS/SI	1984	MON	42 X 30 EA	AP	1 EA	Varies	3600 SET	4500 SET
Kitchen Clock I,II	SI/ART	BS/SI	1984	MON	42 X 30 EA	AP	1 EA	Varies	1200 EA	1500 EA
Shadow Moment II	SI/ART	BS/SI	1985	MON	25 X 42 EA	AP	1 EA	Varies	1000 EA	1400 EA
The Snorkler 1,2,3	SI/ART	BS/SI	1986	MON	40 X 30 EA	AP	1 EA	Varies	1000 EA	1600 EA
Sailing 1,2,3	SI/ART	BS/SI	1986	MON	28 X 40 EA	AP	1 EA	Varies	1000 EA	1600 EA
Shell Cove 2	SI/ART	BS/SI	1986	MON	28 X 40 EA	AP	1 EA	Varies	1000 EA	1600 EA
The Swimming Raft (I-V)	LPI	JL/LPI	1989	MON	33 X 42 EA	AC	1 EA	Varies	1800 EA	1800 EA
Jessie's Dream	LPI	JL/LPI	1989	MON	33 X 42 EA	AC	1 EA	Varies	1800 EA	1800 EA
Night Wading	LPI	JL/LPI	1989	MON	33 X 42 EA	AC	1 EA	Varies	1800 EA	1800 EA
Ruby's	LPI	JL/LPI	1989	MON	33 X 42 EA	AC	1 EA	Varies	1800 EA	1800 EA
Woman on a Diving Platform	SI	BS/RT/SI	1990	LC/HC	23 X 30	AC/B	25	Varies	1000	1000
Keene'ele, Cove at the City of Refuge	SI	BS/RT/SI	1992	WC	25 X 18	AC	15	6	1000	1000
Two Lights & the Moon II	SI	BS/SI	1992	MON/WA	22 X 30 EA	R/BFK	1 EA	Varies	1500 EA	1500 EA
Moonlight on the Lake	SI	BS/SI	1992	MON/WA	22 X 30 EA	R/BFK	1 EA	Varies	1500 EA	1500 EA

The retail prices of the 100,000 limited edition prints quoted in this directory are subject to change. Print publishers, artists and galleries were the direct sources for these quotations. Prices in the secondary market listed as "Sold Out Editions (Rare)" indicate that the publisher has a limited supply of that print or that the print is difficult to locate in the galleries.

The Printworld Directory is accepting new applications for the seventh edition. Approximately 300 new artists will be accepted. Please use the two forms provided in the back section of this directory to submit biographical data and documentation of prints. Edition number of each print must not exceed 500 and the retail price must be $100 or more.

PETER HALLEY

BORN: New York, NY; September 24, 1924
EDUCATION: Yale Univ, New Haven, CT, BA; Univ of New Orleans, LA, MFA
TEACHING: Instr, Painting & Sculpture, Sch of Visual Arts, NY 1989 to present
RECENT EXHIB: Whitney Mus of Am Art, NY, 1987; Guggenheim Mus, NY, 1988; Carnegie Mus, Pittsburgh, PA, 1988; Mus of Fine Arts, Boston, MA, 1988; Brooklyn Mus, NY 1989; Columbia Univ, Wallach Art Gallery, NY, 1989; Sonnabend Gallery, NY, 1990; Gagosian Gallery, NY, 1992; Edition Schellmann, NY, 1993
COLLECTIONS: Solomon Guggeheim Mus, NY; Albright-Knox Art Gallery, Buffalo, NY; Carnegie Mus of Art, Pittsburgh, PA; Wright State Univ, Dayton, OH; Addison Gallery of Am Art, Andover, MA
PRINTERS: Spring Street Workshop, NY (SprSW); MNM, Brooklyn, NY (MNM); Maurice Sanchez, NY (MS); Derriere L'Etoile Studios, NY (DES)
PUBLISHERS: Editions Ilene Kurtz, NY (EIK); Editions Schellmann, NY & Cologne, Germany (ES); Spring Street Workshop, NY (SprSW); Edition Julie Sylvester, NY (EJS)
GALLERIES: Pace Prints, New York, NY; Editions Ilene Kurtz, New York, NY; Rhona Hoffman Gallery, Chicago, IL; Thomas Smith Fine Art, Fort Wayne, IN; Gagosian Gallery, New York, NY; Sonnabend Gallery, New York, NY; Daniel Weinberg Gallery, Santa Monica, CA; Goodman/Tinnon Fine Art, San Francisco, CA; Michael Kohn Gallery, Santa Monica, CA; Margulies Taplin Gallery, Boca Raton, FL; Edition Julie Sylvester, New York, NY; Edition Schellmann, New York, NY
MAILING ADDRESS: 12 Harrison St, New York, NY 10013

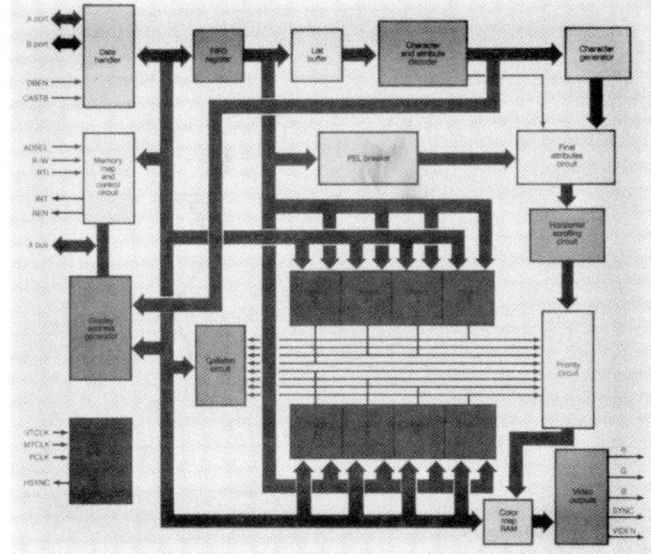

Peter Halley
Final Attributes
Courtesy Pace Editions, Inc & Edition Schellmann

TITLE	PUBLISHER	PRINTER	DATE	MEDIUM	DIMENSION (PAPER SIZE) IN INCHES	TYPE OF PAPER	EDITION NUMBER	NO. OF COLORS	ORIGINAL OPENING PRICE	CURRENT RETAIL PRICE
CURRENT EDITIONS:										
Prison (Framed) (Vacuum-Formed)	EIK	MNM	1988	REL	45 X 42	Plastic	18		8000	12000
A Tour of the Monuments of Passaic, New Jersey (Set of 5)	SprSW/ES	AH/SH/SprSW	1989	EB	16 X 20 EA	KIT	50 EA		6500 SET	9000 SET
Untitled (Set of 4):									7500 SET	6000 SET
Final Attributes	SprSW/ES	AH/SH/SprSW	1990	SP	31 X 39	MYLAR	50		2000	1800
Is It an Arrival or Departure?	SprSW/ES	AH/SH/SprSW	1990	SP	31 X 39	MYLAR	50		2000	1800
Limited Partners	SprSW/ES	AH/SH/SprSW	1990	SP	31 X 39	MYLAR	50		2000	1800
Station, Cell, Factory	SprSW/ES	AH/SH/SprSW	1990	SP	31 X 39	MYLAR	50		2000	1800
Untitled (Bam III)	EJS	MS/DES	1990	EB/REL	22 X 16	KIT	75	1	1800	2500
Untitled Number One (Cell with Conduit and Smoke Stack)	EJS	MS/DES	1991	LB	23 X 30	SOM	40	1	3000	3000
Untitled Number Two (Cell with Conduit and Smokestack)	EJS	MS/DES	1991	LB	23 X 30	SOM	75	1	3000	3000
Set of Three Screenprints:									4000 SET	4000 SET
Core	SpSW/ES	AH/SH/SH	1991	SP	26 X 38	AC	50		1500	2000
Fluke	SpSW/ES	AH/SH/SH	1991	SP	26 X 38	AC	50		1500	2000
Display	SpSW/ES	AH/SH/SH	1991	SP	26 X 38	AC	50		1500	1500
Nowhere (with Grid)	ES	AH/SH	1992	SP	40 X 55	AP88	50	16	3000	3000
Elsewhere (with Grid)	ES	AH/SH	1992	SP	40 X 55	AP88	50	16	3000	3000
Suite of 4 Related States:										
State I	ES	AH/SH	1992	SP	40 X 55	AP88	12	3	4000	4000
State II	ES	AH/SH	1992	SP	40 X 55	COV	12	9	4000	4000
State III (with Grid)	ES	AH/SH	1992	SP	40 X 55	AP88	12	12	4000	4000
State IV (with Grid)	ES	AH/SH	1992	SP	40 X 55	AP88	12	14	4000	4000

BRIAN ELLIOT HALSEY

BORN: Kendallville, IN; July 16, 1942
EDUCATION: Wheaton Col, IL, BA, 1960–64; Trinity Divinity Sch, IL, MA, 1964–67; Florida State Univ, Tallahassee, FL, PhD, 1969–72
TEACHING: Assoc Prof, Art & Art History, Spring Arbor Col, MI, 1967–76
AWARDS: U S Steel Fel, Humanities, 1969–71; Nat Acad of Design, NY, 1975
COLLECTIONS: Nat Mus of Mod Art, Kyoto, Japan; Los Angeles County Mus, CA; Metropolitan Mus of Art, NY; Brooklyn Mus, NY; Norton Gallery, West Palm Beach, FL; Achenbach Found for Graphic Arts, Fine Arts Mus of San Francisco, CA; Marion Koogler McNay Art Inst, San Antonio, TX; Albright-Knox Mus, Buffalo, NY; Denver Art Mus, CO; Baltimore Mus of Art, MD; Grunewald Center for Graphic Art, Los Angeles, CA; Minneapolis Inst of Arts, MN; Phoenix Art Mus, AZ; Detroit Art Inst, MI; Indianapolis Mus of Art, IN; Nat Gallery of Art, Wash, DC
PRINTERS: Larry Kotz, Ann Arbor, MI (LK); Vistec Graphics, Rochester, NY (VG) (OR); Artist (ART)
PUBLISHERS: Scaglione Editions, Southfield, MI (SE); Peterson Fine Arts, Dallas, TX (PFA); John Baughman Assoc, Grand Rapids, MI (JB); Robert Lount Assoc, Clawson, MI (RL); Artists Editions Ltd, Ann Arbor, MI (AE); Artist (ART)
GALLERIES: Bonfoey's Gallery, Cleveland, OH; Brenda Kroos Gallery, Columbus, OH; Editions Limited, Indianapolis, IN; Hefner Galleries Ltd, Grand Rapids, MI; Joan Hodgell Gallery, Sarasota, FL; Images Gallery, Toledo, OH; Merrill Chase Galleries, Chicago, IL; Partner's Gallery, Okemos, MI; Texann Ivy Fine Arts, Orlando, FL; Michael Gallery, Edina, MN; Larmers-Art Agentur, Dortmund, West Germany; DeGraaf Fine Art, Inc, Costa Mesa, CA
MAILING ADDRESS: 2288 Morrison Rd, Dexter, MI 48130

BRIAN ELLIOT HALSEY CONTINUED

TITLE	PUBLISHER	PRINTER	DATE	MEDIUM	DIMENSION (PAPER SIZE) IN INCHES	TYPE OF PAPER	EDITION NUMBER	NO. OF COLORS	ORIGINAL OPENING PRICE	CURRENT RETAIL PRICE
SOLD OUT EDITIONS (RARE):										
Suspension I	ART	ART	1973	SP	19 X 20	STP	125	9	100	300
Time-Space, States I, II	ART	ART	1973	SP	17 X 17 EA	STP	60 EA	9 EA	75 EA	300 EA
Suspension II	ART	ART	1974	SP	17 X 26	RP	90	9	125	350
Centroid I	ART	ART	1975	SP	19 X 19	RP	140	8	125	300
Alpha	ART	ART	1975	SP	6 X 7	RP	100	5	35	200
Micros	ART	ART	1975	RP	5 X 5	RP	100	5	35	200
Cosmos Suite (Set of 5):									750 SET	3000 SET
Suspension IV	SE	ART/LK	1976	SP	22 X 30	R/BFK	226	9	150	550
Alpha III	SE	ART/LK	1976	SP	22 X 30	R/BFK	226	11	150	650
Novem I	SE	ART/LK	1976	SP	22 X 30	R/BFK	226	9	150	800
Numinos II	SE	ART/LK	1976	SP	22 X 30	R/BFK	226	7	150	550
Nucleon I	SE	ART/LK	1976	SP	22 X 30	R/BFK	226	9	175	550
Nucleon II	SE	ART/LK	1976	SP	30 X 29	STP	200	9	175	350
Numinos, States I, II, III, IV	SE	ART/LK	1976	SP	35 X 35 EA	STP	95 EA	7 EA	175 EA	550 EA
Emanos, States I, II	SE	ART/LK	1977	SP	10 X 27 EA	R/BFK	55/28	8 EA	100 EA	350 EA
Entos, States I, II	SE	ART/LK	1977	SP	30 X 30 EA	R/BFK	70 EA	8 EA	150 EA	450 EA
Centron	SE	ART/LK	1977	SP	30 X 30	STP	195	9	150	550
Dynaton States:										
Dynaton, State I	SE	ART/LK	1977	SP	41 X 13	STP	72	8	135	450
Dynaton, State II	SE	ART/LK	1977	SP	41 X 13	STP	56	8	135	400
Dynaton, State III	SE	ART/LK	1977	SP	41 X 13	STP	20	8	135	400
Emanos States:										
Emanos II, State I	SE	ART/LK	1977	SP	15 X 40	STP	67	8	135	400
Emanos II, State II	SE	ART/LK	1977	SP	15 X 40	STP	56	8	135	400
Emanos II, State III	SE	ART/LK	1977	SP	15 X 40	STP	20	8	135	400
Luminos States: Luminos, State I	SE	ART/LK	1977	SP	29 X 50	LEN/100	130	7	250	550
Luminos, State II	SE	ART/LK	1977	SP	29 X 50	LEN/100	25	7	250	550
Novatron States:										
Novatron, State I	SE	ART/LK	1977	SP	30 X 30	STP	50	11	200	800
Novatron, State II	SE	ART/LK	1977	SP	30 X 30	STP	45	11	200	650
Novatron, State III	SE	ART/LK	1977	SP	30 X 30	STP	45	11	200	800
Novatron, State IV	SE	ART/LK	1977	SP	30 X 30	STP	50	11	200	600
Microcosms (Set of 6):									500 SET	1800 SET
Astron	SE/PFA	ART/LK	1978	SP	13 X 12	R/100	300	8	100	400
Centros	SE/PFA	ART/LK	1978	SP	13 X 12	R/100	300	7	100	350
Nuclead	SE/PFA	ART/LK	1978	SP	13 X 12	R/100	300	8	100	350
Theon	SE/PFA	ART/LK	1978	SP	13 X 12	R/100	300	7	100	350
Quatrad	SE/PFA	ART/LK	1978	SP	13 X 12	R/100	300	8	100	350
Isotron	SE/PFA	ART/LK	1978	SP	13 X 12	R/100	300	8	100	350
Triptych States:										
Triptych, State I	SE	ART/VG	1978	SP	22 X 27	STP	85	8	150	450
Triptych, State II	SE	ART/VG	1978	SP	21 X 27	STP	40	8	150	350
Triptych, State III	SE	ART/VG	1978	SP	21 X 27	STP	70	8	150	350
Triptych, State IV	SE	ART/VG	1978	SP	21 X 27	STP	35	8	150	350
Triptych, State V	SE	ART/VG	1978	SP	21 X 27	STP	90	8	150	450
Astron States:										
Astron, State I	SE	ART/VG	1978	SP	27 X 27	FAB	87	12	175	650
Astron, States II, III	SE	ART/VG	1978	SP	27 X 27 EA	FAB	82 EA	12 EA	175 EA	550 EA
Astron, State IV	SE	ART/VG	1978	SP	27 X 27	FAB	52	12	175	440
Septron States:										
Septron, State I	SE	ART/VG	1979	SP	27 X 27	FAB	94	11	175	800
Septron, State II	SE	ART/VG	1979	SP	27 X 27	FAB	88	11	175	550
Septron, State III	SE	ART/VG	1979	SP	27 X 27	FAB	108	11	175	800
Mandalas (Set of 6):									750 SET	2500 SET
Deltron	SE	ART/VG	1979	SP	22 X 21	SOM	300	11	125	450
Nuclead	SE	ART/VG	1979	SP	22 X 21	SOM	300	10	125	450
Trinovem	SE	ART/VG	1979	SP	22 X 21	SOM	300	9	125	450
Trion	SE	ART/VG	1979	SP	22 X 21	SOM	300	10	125	450
Novatron	SE	ART/VG	1979	SP	22 X 21	SOM	300	9	125	450
Triaxon	SE	ART/VG	1979	SP	22 X 21	SOM	300	11	125	450
Centrion States:										
Centrion, State I	JB	ART/VG	1980	SP	14 X 13	SOM	23	10	110	250
Centrion, State II	JB	ART/VG	1980	SP	14 X 13	SOM	33	10	110	250
Centrion, State II	JB	ART/VG	1980	SP	14 X 13	SOM	43	10	110	250
CURRENT EDITIONS:										
Continuum '80 (Set of 5):									550 SET	1000 SET
Monad	JB	ART/VG	1980	SP	15 X 13	SOM	295	10	110	200
Centrigon	JB	ART/VG	1980	SP	15 X 13	SOM	295	10	110	200
Vertigon	JB	ART/VG	1980	SP	16 X 13	SOM	295	10	110	200
Syntron	JB	ART/VG	1980	SP	14 X 17	SOM	295	10	110	200
Dodekon	JB	ART/VG	1980	SP	14 X 17	SOM	295	10	110	200
Architron, States I, II, III	JB	ART/VG	1980	SP	23 X 16 EA	SOM	99 EA	9 EA	160 EA	300 EA

BRIAN ELLIOT HALSEY CONTINUED

TITLE	PUBLISHER	PRINTER	DATE	MEDIUM	DIMENSION (PAPER SIZE) IN INCHES	TYPE OF PAPER	EDITION NUMBER	NO. OF COLORS	ORIGINAL OPENING PRICE	CURRENT RETAIL PRICE
CURRENT EDITIONS:										
Dynon States:										
Dynon I, States I, II, IV	JB	ART/VG	1980	SP	26 X 12 EA	SOM	74 EA	8 EA	125 EA	200 EA
Dynon I, States III, V	JB	ART/VG	1980	SP	26 X 12 EA	SOM	49 EA	8 EA	125 EA	250 EA
Dynon II, States I, III	JB	ART/VG	1980	SP	26 X 12 EA	SOM	74 EA	8 EA	125 EA	250 EA
Dynon II, State II	JB	ART/VG	1980	SP	26 X 12	SOM	49	8	125	200
Emanations States:										
Emanations, State I	JB	ART	1980	SP	29 X 40	R/BFK	65	8	300	525
Emanations, States II, III, IV	JB	ART	1980	SP	29 X 40 EA	R/BFK	65 EA	8 EA	300 EA	425 EA
Novem States:										
Novem II, State I	AE	ART	1981	SP	13 X 26	R/BFK	56	8	125	225
Novem II, State II	AE	ART	1981	SP	13 X 26	R/BFK	56	8	125	200
Novem III, States I, II, III	AE	ART	1982	SP	20 X 37 EA	R/BFK	71 EA	8 EA	250 EA	375 EA
Centrigon	AE	ART	1981	SP	28 X 28	R/BFK	150	8	200	525
Nucleon III, States I, II	AE	ART	1982	SP	26 X 26 EA	R/BFK	71 EA	11 EA	250 EA	375 EA
Macrocosms (Set of 7):							198 EA		1500 SET	3000 SET
Apotheosis, States I, II	AE	ART	1983	SP	20 X 26 EA	M/100	99 EA	11 EA	200 EA	350 EA
Matrix, States I, II	AE	ART	1983	SP	20 X 26 EA	M/100	99 EA	13 EA	200 EA	350 EA
Macron, States I, II	AE	ART	1983	SP	26 X 20 EA	M/100	99 EA	12 EA	200 EA	350 EA
Conundrum, States I, II	AE	ART	1983	SP	20 X 20 EA	M/100	99 EA	12 EA	175 EA	350 EA
Triune, States I, II	AE	ART	1983	SP	20 X 20 EA	M/100	99 EA	12 EA	175 EA	350 EA
Moleculon, States I, II	AE	ART	1983	SP	20 X 20 EA	M/100	99 EA	12 EA	175 EA	350 EA
Embryon, States I, II	AE	ART	1983	SP	20 X 20 EA	M/100	99 EA	12 EA	175 EA	350 EA
Microcosms II (Set of 6):							178		600 SET	1000 SET
Triune, States I, II	AE	ART	1983	SP	6 X 6 EA	M/100	89 EA	11 EA	100 EA	175 EA
Astron II, States I, II	AE	ART	1983	SP	6 X 6 EA	M/100	89 EA	11 EA	100 EA	175 EA
Archon, States I, II	AE	ART	1983	SP	6 X 8 EA	M/100	89 EA	11 EA	100 EA	175 EA
Archon, State II	AE	ART	1983	SP	6 X 8	M/100	74	11	100	175
Archon, State IV	AE	ART	1983	SP	6 X 8	M/100	54	11	100	175
Monad II, States I, II, IV	AE	ART	1983	SP	6 X 8 EA	M/100	89 EA	11 EA	100 EA	175 EA
Monad II, State III	AE	ART	1983	SP	6 X 8	M/100	74	11	100	175
Totem, States I, II, III, IV	AE	ART	1983	SP	7 X 6 EA	M/100	89 EA	11 EA	100 EA	175 EA
Alpha V, States I, II, III, IV	AE	ART	1983	SP	9 X 9 EA	M/100	89 EA	10 EA	100 EA	175 EA

YOZO HAMAGUCHI

BORN: Wakayama-ken, Japan; April 5, 1909
EDUCATION: Sch of Fine Arts, Tokyo, Japan, 1928–30; Independent Study, Painting & Engraving, Paris, France, 1930–39
AWARDS: First Prize, Sao Paulo Biennale, Brazil, 1957; Grand Prize, Ljublijana Int Print Biennale, 1961,72; Purchase Prize, Warsaw Nat Mus, Poland, 1966,72
RECENT EXHIB: Green Art Gallery & New England Sculpture Guild, Guilford, CT, 1989

COLLECTIONS: Mus of Mod Art, NY; Mus of Fine Arts, Boston, MA; Nat Gallery of Art, Wash, DC; Victoria & Albert Mus, London, England; Cleveland Mus, OH; Warsaw Mus, Poland; Mus of Mod Art, Wakayama, Japan; Library of Congress, Wash, DC; Bibliotheque Nationale, Paris, France; Nat Mus of Mod Art, Tokyo, Japan
PRINTERS: Atelier Leblanc, Paris, France, (AL)
PUBLISHERS: Artist (ART)
GALLERIES: John Szoke Graphics, Inc, New York, NY; Vorpal Galleries, New York, NY & San Francisco, CA
MAILING ADDRESS: c/o Vorpal Gallery, 411 W Broadway, New York, NY 10012

TITLE	PUBLISHER	PRINTER	DATE	MEDIUM	DIMENSION (PAPER SIZE) IN INCHES	TYPE OF PAPER	EDITION NUMBER	NO. OF COLORS	ORIGINAL OPENING PRICE	CURRENT RETAIL PRICE
SOLD OUT EDITIONS (RARE):										
Poplar			1962	MEZ/HC	8 X 11	R/BFK	50	Varies	500	15000
Two Cherries (MGall-96)	ART	AL	1964	MEZ	3 X 3	R/BFK	50	1	350	10000
Yarn (MGall-98)	ART	AL	1964	MEZ	3 X 3	R/BFK	50	1	350	10000
Nineteen Cherries and One	ART	AL	1965	MEZ	9 X 21	R/BFK	50	1	500	65000
Patrick's Cherry	ART	AL	1980	MEZ	20 X 30	WOVE/W	100		6000	30000
Pasteque	ART	AL	1981	MEZ	20 X 30	WOVE/W	150		5000	30000
Watermelon	ART	AL	1981	MEZ	9 X 22	WOVE/W	150		3000	30000
Bottle with One and One-Quarter Lemons (MGall-162)	ART	AL	1983	MEZ		WOVE/W	150	1		10500
Bottle with Yellow Lemons in Darkness	ART	AL	1981-89	MEZ	24 X 19	R/BFK	180		6000	50000

MARY HAMBLETON

BORN: Baltimore, MD; 1952
EDUCATION: Bennington Col, VT, 1971; Art Students League, NY, 1973; San Francisco Art Inst, CA, BFA, 1976
AWARDS: New York Found for the Arts Fel, 1989

RECENT EXHIB: Galerie Sigma, Bregenz, Austria & Vienna, Austria, 1989; Pamela Auchincloss Gallery, NY, 1988,89,93
PRINTERS: Garner Tullis Workshop, Santa Barbara, CA (GTW)
PUBLISHERS: Garner Tullis NY (GT); Artist (ART)
GALLERIES: Pamela Auchincloss Gallery, New York, NY; Galerie Sigma, Bregenz, Austria & Vienna, Austria

---

The retail prices of the 100,000 limited edition prints quoted in this directory are subject to change. Print publishers, artists and galleries were the direct sources for these quotations. Prices in the secondary market listed as "Sold Out Editions (Rare)" indicate that the publisher has a limited supply of that print or that the print is difficult to locate in the galleries.

MARY HAMBLETON CONTINUED

TITLE	PUBLISHER	PRINTER	DATE	MEDIUM	DIMENSION (PAPER SIZE) IN INCHES	TYPE OF PAPER	EDITION NUMBER	NO. OF COLORS	ORIGINAL OPENING PRICE	CURRENT RETAIL PRICE
CURRENT EDITIONS:										
#30 (Oil Monotype) (Series of 60)	ART/GTW	GTW	1986	MON/WB	30 X 23 EA	HMP	1 EA	1 EA	600 EA	600 EA
#30 (Oil Monotype) (Series of 60)	ART/GTW	GTW	1986	MON/WB	30 X 23 EA	HMP	1 EA	5 EA	800 EA	800 EA

RICHARD HAMILTON

BORN: London, England; February 24, 1922
EDUCATION: Royal Academy Sch, London, England, 1938–40, 1946–47; Slade Sch of Fine Art, London, England, 1948–51
TEACHING: King's Col, Univ of Durham, London, England, 1953–66; Royal Col of Art, London, England, 1957–61
AWARDS: William & Norma Copley Found Award, 1960
RECENT EXHIB: Anthony d'Offay Gallery, London, England, 1991
COLLECTIONS: Guggenheim Mus, NY; Tate Gallery of Art, London, England; Arts Council of Great Britain, London, England; Wallraf-Richartz Mus, Cologne, Germany
PRINTERS: Aldo Crommelynck, Paris, France (AC); Atelier Crommelynck, Paris, France (AtC); Frank Kicherer, Stuttgart, Germany (FK); E Schreiber, Stuttgart, Germany (ES); Schreiber Studio, Stuttgart, Germany; Manfred Heiting (MH); Peter Van Beveren (PVB); Ken Tyler, NY (KT); J Hutcheson, NY (JH); R Bigelow, NY (RB); Tyler Graphics, Ltd, Mount Kisco, NY (TGL); Petersburg Press, London, England (PP); Patricia Branstead, NY (PB); Aeropress, NY (A)
PUBLISHERS: Waddington Graphics, London, England (WG); Tyler Graphics, Ltd, Mount Kisco, NY (TGL); Petersburg Press, London, England (PP); Artist (ART); Propylaen Verlag, Berlin, Germany (PV); Editions Schellmann, Inc, NY (ES); Editions Alecto, London, England (EA)
GALLERIES: Waddington Graphics, London, England; Charles Cowles Gallery, New York, NY; Marian Goodman Gallery, New York, NY; David Adamson Gallery, Wash, DC; Robert Miller Gallery, New York, NY; Barbara Krakow Gallery, Boston, MA; Anthony d'Offay Gallery, London, England; Editions Schellmann, Inc, New York, NY

Richard Hamilton
My Marilyn
Courtesy the Artist

Waddington (W)

TITLE	PUBLISHER	PRINTER	DATE	MEDIUM	DIMENSION (PAPER SIZE) IN INCHES	TYPE OF PAPER	EDITION NUMBER	NO. OF COLORS	ORIGINAL OPENING PRICE	CURRENT RETAIL PRICE
SOLD OUT EDITIONS (RARE):										
Adonis in Y Fronts	PP	PP	1963	SP	27 X 33	AP	40		100	10000
Five Tyres Abandoned	PP	PP	1964	SP	27 X 36	AP	40		100	5000
My Marilyn (W-59)	EA		1965	SP	27 X 33	THS	75		150	10000
Self Portrait	PP	PP	1965–67	SP	21 X 16	SchP	75		150	5000
Toaster	PP	PP	1967	SP/LC/OFF/CO	35 X 25	AP	75		250	6000
I'm Dreaming of a White Christmas	ART	PP	1967	SP	30 X 41	AP	75		200	8500
Bathers (a)	PP	PP	1967	SP	27 X 37	AP	75		200	5000
People (with Gouache and Letterscreen)	PP	PP	1968	SP/PH/CO	25 X 33		26		100	10000
Swinging London '67 Poster (W-67)	WG	ED912	1968	LC/OFF	28 X 20	AP	1000		100	2500
Swinging London '67	WG	ED912	1968	EB/A/EMB/CO	22 X 29	AP	70		100	8500
La Scala Milano	PP	PP	1968	PH/E/SP	19 X 23	AP	65		100	5000
Bathers	PP	PP	1969	DT	19 X 25	AP	75		100	3500
Vignette	PP	PP	1969	DT	23 X 19	AP	50		100	3500
Fashion Plate (W-30)	PP	PP	1969–70	LC/SP/PO/CO/OFF	29 X 24	FAB	70		100	8000
Portrait of the Artists by Francis Bacon	PP	PP	1970–71	SP/COL	32 X 27	AP	140		150	6000
I'm Dreaming of a Black Christmas	PP	PP	1971	SP/COL/CO	29 X 39	AP	150		150	5500
Eine Kleine Schone Scheisse fur Dieter	PP	PP	1971	COL	17 X 14	AP	50		200	5000
Release	PP	PP	1972	SP/CO	27 X 37	AP	150		200	6000
Swinging London III	PP	PP	1972	SP/CO	27 X 37	AP	19		200	6000
By the Soft Blue Waters of Miers	PP	PP	1972	EB/A/DPT/HC	35 X 27	AP	12		350	8000
Esquisse	PP	PP	1972	EB/HC	14 X 17	AP	40		300	3000
Picasso's Meninas (with Stippling)	PV	PP	1972	EB/A/ENG	81 X 35	AP	135		500	25000
Five Tyres Remoulded (Set of 8)	PP	PP	1972	SP(7) COL(1)	23 X 33 EA	AP	150 EA		2000 SET	12000 SET
By the Waters of Miers	PP	PP	1972	EB/A/DPT	35 X 27	AP	75		300	3500

RICHARD HAMILTON CONTINUED

TITLE	PUBLISHER	PRINTER	DATE	MEDIUM	DIMENSION (PAPER SIZE) IN INCHES	TYPE OF PAPER	EDITION NUMBER	NO. OF COLORS	ORIGINAL OPENING PRICE	CURRENT RETAIL PRICE
SOLD OUT EDITIONS (RARE):										
Three Studies of Bloom	PP	PP	1973	EB	14 X 19	R/BFK	28	1	300	2500
Un des Effets des Eaux de Miers (with Stippling)	PP	PP	1973	EB/A	4 X 7	AP	100		200	2500
Flower-Piece Progressives (Set of 7):									2500 SET	25000 SET
Yellow	PP	PP	1974	EB/A	25 X 20	R/BFK	24		300	3500
Magenta	PP	PP	1974	EB/A	25 X 20	R/BFK	24		300	3500
Yellow and Magenta	PP	PP	1974	EB/A	25 X 20	R/BFK	24		300	3500
Cyan	PP	PP	1974	EB/A	25 X 20	R/BFK	24		300	3500
Yellow, Magenta, Cyan and Black	PP	PP	1974	EB/A	25 X 20	R/BFK	24		300	3500
Black	PP	PP	1974	EB/A	25 X 20	R/BFK	24		300	3500
Yellow, Magenta, Cyan and Black	PP	PP	1974	EB/A	25 X 20	R/BFK	24		300	3500
Trichromatic Flower-Piece	PP	PP	1974	EB/A	25 X 20	R/BFK	150		300	5000
Multi-Coloured Flower-Piece	PP	PP	1974	EC	19 X 16	R/BFK	100		300	3500
Mirror Image	M	PB/A	1975	COL	24 X 18	R/BFK	50		350	2000
Palindrome	M	PB/A	1975	COL/3D	24 X 18 EA	R/BFK	1 EA		350	4500
Flower-Piece B	TGL	TGL	1976	LC	26 X 20	AC	75	10	650	2000
Flower-Piece B (Crayon Study)	TGL	TGL	1976	LC	26 X 20	AC	34	4	500	2000
Flower-Piece B (Crayon Separation)	TGL	TGL	1976	LB	26 X 20	AC	23	1	350	1500
Sunset (f)	TGL	KT/TGL	1976	LB	17 X 21	HMP/AC	50	1	350	1500
Motel I	WG	AC/AtC	1979	EB/A	17 X 21	R/BFK	40		450	4000
Interior with Monochromes (W-106)	WG	FK/S	1979	COU/SP	16 X 28	IP	96		500	8500
Putting on de Stijl (W-107)	WG	FK/S	1979	COU/SP	20 X 24	AP	90	6	500	9000
Soft-Blue Landscape	WG	FK/S	1979	COL/SP	28 X 36	R/BFK	136	7	450	5000
Soft-Pink Landscape	WG	FK/S	1980	COL/SP	28 X 36	R/BFK	136	7	720	8000
Berlin Interior	WG	AC/AtC	1980	EB/A	22 X 30	R/BFK	100		540	7000
Motel II	WG	AC/AtC	1980	EB/A	17 X 21	R/BFK	40		540	4000
A Dedicated Follower of Fashion	WG	AC/AtC	1980	EB/A	30 X 22	R/BFK	100		540	7000
Instant Painting	WG	MH	1980	PH	24 X 20	R/BFK	17		800	5000
Archive I	WG	PVB	1981	LC	31 X 23	R/BFK	60		720	10000
Archive II	WG	PVB	1981	IB	31 X 23	R/BFK	15		800	8000
In Horne's House	WG	AC/AtC	1981–82	EB/A/ENG	30 X 22	R/BFK	120		1800	13500
Homage to Seghers	WG	AC/AtC	1982	EB/A	10 X 13	R/BFK	40		720	2500
Patricia Knight I	WG	AC/AtC	1982	EB/A	15 X 15	AP	50		900	6000
Patricia Knight II, III	WG	AC/AtC	1982	EB/A	15 X 15 EA	AP	50 EA	12 EA	900 EA	4000 EA
Collected Words (Nine Studies, 1957–65)	ES		1982	SP/COL	16 X 20 EA	AP	100 EA	4 EA	2000 SET 500 EA	3200 SET 1000 EA
Hers is a Lush Situation (1957)	WG	AC/AtC	1982	SP	9 X 15	AP	100		350	1500
How GatisekII as a Famous . . .	WG	AC/AtC	1982	SP	15 X 15	AP	100		500	1500
Pin-Up (1961)	WG	AC/AtC	1982	SP	14 X 10	AP	100		500	1200
Self-Portrait (1965)	WG	AC/AtC	1982	SP	11 X 8	AP	100		500	1200
She ($he) (1958)	WG	AC/AtC	1982	SP	10 X 7	AP	100		500	1500
Towards a Definitive . . . (b) (1962)	WG	AC/AtC	1982	SP	10 X 14	AP	100		500	1500
'AAH!' in Perspective (1963)	WG	AC/AtC	1983	SP	10 X 16	AP	100		350	1500
AAH! (1961)	WG	AC/AtC	1983	SP	9 X 15	AP	100		500	1500
Finn MacCool	WG	AC/AtC	1983	PH/A/ENG	30 X 22	AP	120		1350	7000
Leopold Bloom	WG	AC/AtC	1983	EB/A	30 X 22	AP	120		1350	4000
A Languid Floating Flower	WG	AC/AtC	1983	EB/A	18 X 19	AP	30		675	3500
Of the Tirbe of Finn	WG	AC/AtC	1983	EB/A	14 X 13	AP	30		675	3000
Lobby	WG	AC/AtC	1984	COL/SP	13 X 19	AP	88		900	5000
Self Portrait	WG	AC/AtC	1985	EB/A	15 X 11	AP	30		1000	5000
Self-Portrait in a Cracked . . .	WG	AC/AtC	1985	EB/A	12 X 9	AP	30		1000	5500
Transmogrifications of . . .	WC	AC/AtC	1985	EB/A/SG	30 X 22	AP	120		1350	8000
CURRENT EDITIONS:										
Bronze by Gold I, II	WG	AC/AtC	1987	EB/A/ENG	21 X 17 EA	R/BFK	120 EA		1500 EA	9000 EA
Buck Mulligan	WG	AC/AtC	1987	ENG/SG	9 X 8	R/BFK	24		900	3000
How a Great Daily Organ is . . .	WG	AC/AtC	1987	ENG	21 X 16	R/BFK	120		1000	5500
In What Posture?	WG	AC/AtC	1987	HEL/GRA	12 X 17	R/BFK	40		1200	3200
A Brief Libation	WG	AC/AtC	1988	EB/A	5 X 6	R/BFK	12		950	1500
Gentlemen of the Press	WC	AC/AtC	1988	EB/A	3 X 5	R/BFK	12		750	1200
Garryowen	WC	AC/AtC	1988	EB/A	2 X 3	R/BFK	12		750	1200
Gogarty (Stippled)	WC	AC/AtC	1988	EB/A/SG	5 X 4	R/BFK	12		950	1500
The House of Keyes	WC	AC/AtC	1988	EB/A/SG	4 X 3	R/BFK	12		750	1200
Molly	WC	AC/AtC	1988	EB/A	5 X 4	R/BFK	12		950	1500
Nora Barnacle	WC	AC/AtC	1988	EB/A	5 X 3	R/BFK	12		750	1200
O How the Waters	WC	AC/AtC	1988	EB/A/SB	5 X 4	R/BFK	12		950	1500
One Corned and Cabbage	WC	AC/AtC	1988	ENG	3 X 4	R/BFK	12	1	950	1500
Papli	WC	AC/AtC	1988	EB/SL	5 X 4	R/BFK	12	1	750	1200
Private Carr	WC	AC/AtC	1988	EB/A	7 X 3	R/BFK	12		750	1200
Sandycove	WC	AC/AtC	1988	EB/A	5 X 4	R/BFK	12		950	1500
Simon Dedalus	WC	AC/AtC	1988	MEZ	5 X 4	R/BFK	12	1	950	1500
Tame Essence of Wilde	WC	AC/AtC	1988	EB/SG	4 X 2	R/BFK	12	1	750	1500
With Unfeigned Regret	WC	AC/AtC	1988	DPT	3 X 5	R/BFK	12	1	750	1500

RICHARD HAMILTON CONTINUED

TITLE	PUBLISHER	PRINTER	DATE	MEDIUM	DIMENSION (PAPER SIZE) IN INCHES	TYPE OF PAPER	EDITION NUMBER	NO. OF COLORS	ORIGINAL OPENING PRICE	CURRENT RETAIL PRICE
CURRENT EDITIONS:										
Yes	WC	AC/AtC	1988	EB	3 X 4	R/BFK	12	1	750	1500
Ireland a Nation	AC	AC/AtC	1989	EB/ENG	5 X 4	R/BFK	12	1	750	1200
Madame Tweedy is in Her ...	AC	AC/AtC	1989	EB/A/GRA	2 X 4	R/BFK	12		950	1500
He Foresaw His Pale Body ...	AC	AC/AtC	1991	EB/A/HEL/GRA	20 X 15	R/BFK	120		2500	4000

PAT JO HAMMERMAN

EDUCATION: Queens Col, Flushing, NY, BA; Hunter Col, NY, MA
TEACHING: Prof, Printmaking & Papermaking, Queens/Borough Com Col, Bayside, NY
COLLECTIONS: Columbus Mus of Art, OH; Huntsville Mus, AL; Tucson Mus, AZ; Queens Mus, Flushing, NY; Kyoto Municipal Mus, Japan; Brooklyn Mus, NY; Grand Rapid Mus, MI; American Craft Mus, NY
PRINTERS: Artist (ART)
PUBLISHERS: John Szoke Graphics, NY (JSG)
GALLERIES: Texann Ivy Fine Arts, Orlando, FL; Jan Weiner Gallery, Topeka, KS; Andrea Marquit Fine Arts, New York, NY; Peter Rose Gallery, New York, NY
MAILING ADDRESS: 91–06 104th St, Richmond Hill, NY 11418

TITLE	PUBLISHER	PRINTER	DATE	MEDIUM	DIMENSION (PAPER SIZE) IN INCHES	TYPE OF PAPER	EDITION NUMBER	NO. OF COLORS	ORIGINAL OPENING PRICE	CURRENT RETAIL PRICE
SOLD OUT EDITIONS (RARE):										
Symbol 36	JSG	ART	1984	EC	30 X 40	HMP	25	8	650	750
CURRENT EDITIONS:										
Symbol 37	JSG	ART	1984	EC	30 X 40	HMP	25	8	650	750
Symbol 38	JSG	ART	1984	EC	30 X 40	HMP	25	8	650	750
Symbol 35	JSG	ART	1985	EC	30 X 40	HMP	25	8	650	750
Symbol 18	JSG	ART	1987	EC	22 X 28	HMP	50		375	450
Symbol 19	JSG	ART	1987	EC	22 X 28	HMP	50		375	450

FREDERICK HAMMERSLEY

BORN: Salt Lake City, UT; January 5, 1919
EDUCATION: Univ of Idaho, Southern Branch, Pacatello, ID, 1936–38; Chouinard Art Sch, Los Angeles, CA, 1940–42, 1946–47; Ecole des Beaux Arts, Paris, France, 1945; Jepson Art Inst, Los Angeles, CA, 1947–50
TEACHING: Instr, Jepson Art Sch, Los Angeles, CA, 1948–51; Lectr, Painting, Drawing & Design, Pomona Col, CA, 1953–62; Instr, Pasadena Art Mus, CA, 1956–61; Instr, Painting, Drawing & Design, Chouinard Art Inst, Los Angeles, CA, 1964–68; Assoc Vis Prof, Painting & Drawing, Univ of New Mexico, Albuquerque, NM, 1968–71
AWARDS: Purchase Award, Painting, Butler Inst of Am Art, Youngstown, OH, 1961; Los Angeles All City Annual, CA, 164–66; Guggenheim Awards, Painting, 1975,77
RECENT EXHIB: Modernism Gallery, San Francisco, CA, 1987,90
COLLECTIONS: San Francisco Mus of Mod Art, CA; Corcoran Gallery of Art, Wash, DC; Butler Inst of Am Art, Youngstown, OH; La Jolla Art Mus, CA; Los Angeles County Art Mus, CA; City of Claremont, CA; Univ of New Mexico, Albuquerque, NM; Univ of California, Santa Barbara, CA; Univ of Santa Barbara, CA
PRINTERS: Artist (ART)
PUBLISHERS: Artist (ART)
GALLERIES: Modernism, San Francisco, CA; Owings-Dewey Fine Art, Santa Fe, NM
MAILING ADDRESS: 608 Carlisle, SE, Albuquerque, NM 87106

TITLE	PUBLISHER	PRINTER	DATE	MEDIUM	DIMENSION (PAPER SIZE) IN INCHES	TYPE OF PAPER	EDITION NUMBER	NO. OF COLORS	ORIGINAL OPENING PRICE	CURRENT RETAIL PRICE
SOLD OUT EDITIONS (RARE):										
Light Switch	ART	ART	1988	LC	AP	AC			350	500

HARMONY HAMMOND

BORN: Chicago, IL; February 8, 1944
EDUCATION: Art Inst of Chicago, IL, Jr Sch, 1960–61; Milliken Univ, Decatur, IL, 1961–63; Univ of Minnesota, Minneapolis, MN, BFA, 1963–67
TEACHING: Nova Scotia Col of Art & Design, Canada, 1979; Notre Dame Univ, South Bend, IN, 1980; Univ of North Carolina, Chapel Hill, NC, 1981–82; Mason Gross Sch of Art, New Brunswick, NJ, 1982; Hunter Col, NY, 1983; Philadelphia Col of Art, PA, 1984; Univ of Arizona, Tucson, AZ, 1988 to present
AWARDS: Nat Endowment for the Arts Fel, Sculpture 1979; Yaddo Fel, 1980; MacDowell Fel, 1979,81; New York State Council of the Arts CAPS Grant, NY, Sculpture, 1982; Nat Endowment for the Arts Fel, Graphics, 1983; New York Council on the Arts Award, Painting, 1989; Pollock Krasner Fel, 1989–90
RECENT EXHIB: Miami-Dade Com Col, South, South Campus Art Gallery, Miami, FL, 1989; Dolan/Maxwell Gallery, NY, 1989; Fiction/Non-Fiction Gallery, NY, 1990; New Mexico State Univ, Las Cruces, NM, 1989; Cleveland State Univ, OH, 1990; Jose Freire Gallery, NY, 1993
COLLECTIONS: Everson Mus, Syracuse, NY; Walker Art Center, Minneapolis, MN; Inst of Fine Arts, Minneapolis, MN; Denver Art Mus, CO; Indianapolis, IN; Brooklyn Mus, NY
PRINTERS: Philip Barber, Minneapolis, MN (PB); Michael Reid, Minneapolis, MN (MR); Agnes Story, Minneapolis, MN (AS); Vermillion Editions Ltd, Minneapolis, MN (VEL); Steven Andersen, Minneapolis, MN (SA); Dana Stieverton, NY (DS); Oxbow Editions, NY (OxE); Printmaking Workshop, NY (PW); Bill Lagattuta (BL); Stephen Britko (SB); Tamarind Inst, Albuquerque, NM (TI); Jeffrey Ryan (JR); Tamarind Inst, Albuquerque, NM (TI); Shelly Sirmans, Baltimore, MD (SS); Maryland Inst, Baltimore, MD (MI); Artist (ART)
PUBLISHERS: Lerner-Heller Editions, NY (LHE); Oxbow Editions, NY (OxE); Tamarind Institute, Albuquerque, NM (TI); Vermillion Editions Ltd, Minneapolis, MN (VEL); Yellowstone Print Club, Billings, MT (YPC); Tamarind Institute, Albuquerque, NM (TI)
GALLERIES: Vermillion Editions Ltd, Minneapolis, MN; Bernice Steinbaum Gallery, New York, NY; Gerald Peters Gallery, Santa Fe, NM; Etherton-Stern Gallery, Tucson, AZ, Castelli Graphics, New York, NY
MAILING ADDRESS: c/o University of Arizona, Art Department, Speedway & Park Ave, Tucson, AZ 85721

HARMONY HAMMOND CONTINUED

TITLE	PUBLISHER	PRINTER	DATE	MEDIUM	DIMENSION (PAPER SIZE) IN INCHES	TYPE OF PAPER	EDITION NUMBER	NO. OF COLORS	ORIGINAL OPENING PRICE	CURRENT RETAIL PRICE
SOLD OUT EDITIONS (RARE):										
Shoe	OxE	DS/OxE	1978	I	8 X 5	RP	20	1	150	400
Spirit Personage	YPC	SA/VEL	1985	SP	30 X 22	AP	65	8	350	500
CURRENT EDITIONS:										
Crying Bead	OxE	DS/OxE	1978	I	8 X 5	RP	20	1	150	300
Oval Braid	OxE	DS/OxE	1978	I	8 X 5	RP	20	2	150	300
Spinster Braid	OxE	DS/OxE	1978	I	8 X 5	RP	20	1	150	300
Blue Spirit	TI	SB/BL/TI	1978	LC/CC	24 X 15	GE	20	5	300	500
Chicken Lady	VEL	VEL	1981	LC/SP	30 X 22	AP			300	500
Dance of the Ladder, I–IV (Set of 4)	VEL	SA/PB/MR/AS	1981	LC/SP	30 X 21 EA	TW/HMP	46	5/7/8/6	1000 SET	2000 SET
Fan Lady Meets Cactus Lady (with Chiné Colle)	VEL	SA/PB/MR/AS	1981	LC/SP/PO/I	30 X 41	AP/BL	48	17	550	800
Forms of Desire	LHE/PW	AN/RMN/PW	1982	EC	30 X 42	AP/B	65	4	300	400
Las Animas II	TI	JR/TI	1988	LC	30 X 45	R/BFK/CR	24	2	500	500
Untitled (Series of 100 Monoprints)		ART/SS/MI	1984–89	MON	28 X 32 EA		1 EA		1400 EA	1400 EA

JACK HANLEY

BORN: New York, NY; January 8, 1952
EDUCATION: State Univ of New York, NY, BFA, 1974; Univ of California, Berkeley, CA, MA, 1980, MFA, 1982
TEACHING: Vis Lectr, Fine Arts, Princeton Univ, NJ, 1984; Asst Prof, Fine Arts, Univ of Texas, Austin, TX, 1984 to present
AWARDS: Visual Artist Fel, Nat Endowment for the Arts Award, 1987
RECENT EXHIB: Contemp Art Mus, Houston, TX, 1988; Hal Bromm Gallery, NY, 1988

COLLECTIONS: Mus of Southern Texas, Corpus Christi, TX
PRINTERS: Katherine Brimberry, Austin, TX (KB); Gerald Manson, Austin, TX (GM); Flatbed Press, Austin, TX (FP)
PUBLISHERS: Flatbed Press, Austin, TX (FP)
GALLERIES: Barry Whistler Gallery, Dallas, TX; Trans Avant-Garde Gallery San Francisco, CA; James Gallery, Houston, TX
MAILING ADDRESS: c/o Barry Whistler Gallery, 2909-A Canton St, Dallas, TX 75226

TITLE	PUBLISHER	PRINTER	DATE	MEDIUM	DIMENSION (PAPER SIZE) IN INCHES	TYPE OF PAPER	EDITION NUMBER	NO. OF COLORS	ORIGINAL OPENING PRICE	CURRENT RETAIL PRICE
CURRENT EDITIONS:										
Ideologies Suite (Set of 3):										
Plaque Doctor	FP	KB/GM/FP	1990	I/C	42 X 30	R/BFK	20		600	600
Prince	FP	KB/GM/FP	1990	I/C	42 X 30	R/BFK	20		600	600
Shaman	FP	KB/GM/FP	1990	I/C	42 X 30	R/BFK	20		600	600

BOYD EVERETT HANNA

BORN: Irwin, PA; (1907–1987)
EDUCATION: Univ of Pittsburgh, PA, 1925–28; Carnegie-Mellon Univ, PA, 1928–30
AWARDS: Purchase Prize, Albany Print Club, NY, 1972, First Prize, 1974; Certificate of Merit, Soc of Illustrators, 1985

COLLECTIONS: Metropolitan Mus of Art, NY; Carnegie Inst of Art, Pittsburgh, PA; Pennell Coll, Library of Congress, Wash, DC; New York Public Library, NY; Boston Public Library, MA
PRINTERS: Artist (ART)
PUBLISHERS: Limited Editions Club, NY (LE); Peter Pauper Press, Mt Vernon, NY (PPP); John J Crawley & Co, Union City, NJ (JC); Sander Gallery, Porter, IN (SG); Print Club of Albany, NY (PCA); Hunt Inst, Pittsburgh, PA (HI); Artist (ART)
MAILING ADDRESS: 1475 S Jones Blvd, Apt G-16, Tucson, AZ 85713

TITLE	PUBLISHER	PRINTER	DATE	MEDIUM	DIMENSION (PAPER SIZE) IN INCHES	TYPE OF PAPER	EDITION NUMBER	NO. OF COLORS	ORIGINAL OPENING PRICE	CURRENT RETAIL PRICE
SOLD OUT EDITIONS (RARE):										
Partridge Berry	ART	ART	1941	WEC	5 X 6	J/VEL	14	5	25	600
Bobwhite	ART	ART	1942	WEC	6 X 8	J/VEL	5	5	10	600
Survival of the Fitter	ART	ART	1943	WEC	9 X 13	J/VEL	3	3	25	1200
Longfellow's Poems (20 Subjects)	LE	ART	1944	WEC	Varies	J/VEL	3 EA	3 EA	35	750 EA
The Compleat Angler (20 Subjects)	PPP	ART	1945	WEC	5 X 6 EA	BB	3 EA	2 EA	25 EA	350 EA
McKelvey's Barn	ART	ART	1946	WEB	7 X 6	J/VEL	50	1	15	600
Dreamthorp (8 Subjects)	PPP	ART	1947	WEB	5 X 6 EA	BB	2 EA	1 EA	65 EA	350 EA
The Prodigal Son	ART	ART	1951	WEB	5 X 4	RICE	25	1	10	200
Leaves of Grass (15 Subjects)	PPP	ART	1952	WEC	7 X 10 EA	RICE	3 EA	2 EA	65 EA	1200 EA
Professor Bishop Brown	ART	ART	1952	WEB	8 X 11	RICE	2	1	100	1200
The Road to Emmaus	ART	ART	1953	WEB	8 X 11	J/VEL	50	1	25	600
CURRENT EDITIONS:										
Bluet II	ART	ART	1971	WEC	6 X 7	J/VEL	20	5	25	200
Saguaro	HI	ART	1972	WEC	6 X 9	J/VEL	50	6	12	400
Totem Pole Formation	ART	ART	1973	WEC	8 X 10	J/VEL	25	4	50	300
Passion Series (6 Subjects)	JC	ART	1974	WEC	9 X 11 EA	J/VEL	20 EA	2 EA	25 EA	200 EA
Spring Beauty	ART	ART	1974	WEC	6 X 7	J/VEL	25	7	50	300
Peanut Cactus	PCA	ART	1975	WEC	9 X 11	J/VEL	80	7	10	600
Partridge Berry II	ART	ART	1976	WEC	7 X 8	J/INO	25	5	25	200
Timber Line	ART	ART	1977	WEC	8 X 10	J/INO	20	7	75	500
Birthplace	ART	ART	1977	WEC	6 X 6	J/VEL	80	1	25	200

BOYD EVERETT HANNA CONTINUED

TITLE	PUBLISHER	PRINTER	DATE	MEDIUM	DIMENSION (PAPER SIZE) IN INCHES	TYPE OF PAPER	EDITION NUMBER	NO. OF COLORS	ORIGINAL OPENING PRICE	CURRENT RETAIL PRICE
CURRENT EDITIONS:										
Tumacacori	ART	ART	1981	WEC	5 X 6	AP 88	94	2	50	300
Arbutus	ART	ART	1981	WEC	7 X 9	AP 88	13	7	50	400
Chief Kokush	ART	ART	1981	LINO	13 X 17	AP 88	11	6	100	300
Kris	ART	ART	1981	WEC	8 X 9	AP 88	10	7	100	300
Spindrift	SG	ART	1982	WEC	8 X 8	AP 88	50	9	100	200
The Unicorn	ART	ART	1982	WEB	7 X 6	AP/WA	100	1	25	200
Jim	ART	ART	1983	WEC	8 X 9	AP 88	12	8	100	200
Navajo Girl	ART	ART	1983	WEC	5 X 5	AP 88	14	7	50	200
Amaryllis	ART	ART	1985	LI	14 X 18	AP/WA	20	6	100	200

KEIKO HARA

BORN: Japan; October 1, 1942
EDUCATION: Mississippi Univ for Women, Columbus, MS, BFA, Painting, 1974; Univ of Wisconsin, Milwaukee, WI, MS, Printmaking, 1975; Cranbrook Acad of Art, Bloomfield Hills, MI, MFA, Printmaking, 1976;
TEACHING: Instr, Printmaking, Carthage Col, Kenosha, WI, 1979–80; Instr, Printmaking, Univ of Wisconsin, River Falls, WI, 1980–85; Asst Prof, Art, Whitman Col, Walla Walla, WA, 1985 to present
AWARDS: First Prize, Detroit Inst of Art, MI, 1976; Artist in Res, Art Park, NY, 1983; Select Award, Philadelphia Print Club, PA 1984
RECENT EXHIB: Whitman Col, Sheehan Gallery, Walla Walla, WA, 1992; Wise Coll, Bronxville, NY, 1992

COLLECTIONS: Detroit Inst of Art, MI; Art Inst of Chicago, IL; Milwaukee Art Mus, WI; Wustum Mus, Racine, WI; Muskegon Mus of Art, MI
PRINTERS: Bernie Swanson, Chicago, IL (BS); Jon Swanson, Chicago, IL (JS); Perimeter Press Inc, Chicago, IL (PER); Norman Stewart, Birmingham, MI (NS); Stewart & Stewart, Birmingham, MI (S-S); Yasushi Ishibashi, Tokyo, Japan, (YI); Litho Workshop May, Tokyo, Japan (LWM); Artist (ART)
PUBLISHERS: Perimeter Press Inc, Chicago, IL (PER); Stewart & Stewart, Birmingham, MI (S-S); Artist (ART)
GALLERIES: Perimeter Gallery, Chicago, IL; Bradley Galleries, Milwaukee, WI; Suzanne Kohn Gallery, St Paul, MN & Minneapolis, MN
MAILING ADDRESS: 336 N Division, Walla Walla, WA 99362

TITLE	PUBLISHER	PRINTER	DATE	MEDIUM	DIMENSION (PAPER SIZE) IN INCHES	TYPE OF PAPER	EDITION NUMBER	NO. OF COLORS	ORIGINAL OPENING PRICE	CURRENT RETAIL PRICE
SOLD OUT EDITIONS (RARE):										
Drawn in the Moon IV	S-S	NS/S-S	1980	LC/SP/CO	22 X 30	R/BFK/W	7	Multi	400	750
CURRENT EDITIONS:										
Topophila (Set of 24)	PER	BS/JS	1981	LC/CO	24 X 34 EA	HMP	20 EA	26 EA	4400 SET	6500 SET
Verse 2-8-2	ART	ART	1983	MON	68 X 64	HMP	1	3-7	3000	3500

MARVIN HARDEN

BORN: Austin, TX
EDUCATION: Univ of California, Los Angeles, CA, BFA, MFA, Los Angeles City Col, CA
TEACHING: Instr, Drawing, Univ of California, Los Angeles, CA, 1964–68; Instr, Drawing, Los Angeles Harbor Col, CA, 1965–68; Prof, California State Univ, Northridge, CA, 1968–84, Distinguished Prof, 1984 to present
AWARDS: Nat Endowment of the Arts Fel, 1972; Guggenheim Fel, 1983; Visual Arts Fel, 1983; Exceptional Merit Service Award, California State Univ, Northridge, CA, 1984

COLLECTIONS: Whitney Mus of Am Art, NY; Mus of Mod Art, NY; Univ of California, Berkeley, CA
PRINTERS: Ed Hamilton, CA (EH); David Ordaz, CA (DO); Cirrus Editions Workshop, Los Angeles, CA (CEW)
PUBLISHERS: Cirrus Editions Ltd, Los Angeles, CA (CE)
GALLERIES: Cirrus Editions, Ltd, Los Angeles, CA; James Corcoran Gallery, Santa Monica, CA
MAILING ADDRESS: c/o California State University, Painting Dept, 18111 Nordhoff St, Northridge, CA 91330

TITLE	PUBLISHER	PRINTER	DATE	MEDIUM	DIMENSION (PAPER SIZE) IN INCHES	TYPE OF PAPER	EDITION NUMBER	NO. OF COLORS	ORIGINAL OPENING PRICE	CURRENT RETAIL PRICE
SOLD OUT EDITIONS (RARE):										
The Thing Seen Suggest, This and Other Existences (156c)	CE	EH/CEW	1974	LC	20 X 14	AP	30	2	125	1000
CURRENT EDITIONS:										
A Line, Align in Mind, a Direct Indirection by Which We Find Directions Out; The Act, The Very Process-An Essential Transitoriness: A Line Align in Mind (286c, 304c, 306c) (Trip)	CE	DO/CEW	1981	LC	30 X 68	AP/B	15	1	1200	1500
A Line Align in Mind (286c)	CE	DO/CEW	1981-91	LC	30 X 22	AP/B	25	1	500	500
A Line Align in Mind (304c)	CE	DO/CEW	1981-91	LC	30 X 22	AP/B	25	1	500	500

The retail prices of the 100,000 limited edition prints quoted in this directory are subject to change. Print publishers, artists and galleries were the direct sources for these quotations. Prices in the secondary market listed as "Sold Out Editions (Rare)" indicate that the publisher has a limited supply of that print or that the print is difficult to locate in the galleries.

The Printworld Directory is accepting new applications for the seventh edition. Approximately 300 new artists will be accepted. Please use the two forms provided in the back section of this directory to submit biographical data and documentation of prints. Edition number of each print must not exceed 500 and the retail price must be $100 or more.

RICHARD C HARDEN

BORN: Canton, NY; 1956
EDUCATION: Col of Visual & Performing Arts, Syracuse Univ, NY, BFA, 1978
TEACHING: Nat Endowment for the Arts Sch Prog, Lectr, Harvard Univ, Cambridge, MA, 1984; Vis Art, Syracuse Univ, NY, 1984,85
AWARDS: Ford Found Grant, 1977; Award, Elizabeth T Greenshields Found, 1980; Award, Massachusetts Council on the Arts, Boston, MA, 1984; First Prize, Massachusetts Council on the Arts, 1986; Albert W Moore Awards, Boston Center for the Arts, MA, 1984,86
RECENT EXHIB: M S Gallery, Hartford, CT, 1988
COLLECTIONS: Metropolitan Mus of Art, NY; Cooper Hewitt Mus, NY; New Britain Mus of Am Art, CT; Syracuse Univ, NY; Vatican Mus, Rome, Italy
PRINTERS: Paul Maguire, Boston, MA (PM); Jennifer Hilton, Boston, MA (JH); Flat Rock Press, Boston, MA (FRP)
PUBLISHERS: Artist (ART)
GALLERIES: Mary Ryan Gallery, New York, NY; Wenniger Graphics, Boston, MA
MAILING ADDRESS: Star Route, New Hartford, CT 06057

TITLE	PUBLISHER	PRINTER	DATE	MEDIUM	DIMENSION (PAPER SIZE) IN INCHES	TYPE OF PAPER	EDITION NUMBER	NO. OF COLORS	ORIGINAL OPENING PRICE	CURRENT RETAIL PRICE
SOLD OUT EDITIONS (RARE):										
Poland (Set of 6):	ART	PM/JH/FRP	1983	LB	22 X 30	AP		1	1650 SET 350 EA	5000 SET 500 EA

DEWITT HARDY (CLARION)

BORN: St Louis, MO; June 25, 1940
EDUCATION: Syracuse Univ, NY, 1958-62
TEACHING: Kalamazoo Inst of Art, MI; St Lawrence Univ, Canton, NY; Mus of Art, Ogonquit, ME; Butler Inst of Am Art, Youngstown, OH
AWARDS: First Prize, Summit Art Center, NJ, 1965; Purchase Award, Butler Inst of Am Art, Youngstown, OH, 1969
COLLECTIONS: Bowdoin Col Mus, Brunswick, ME; Butler Inst of Am Art, Youngstown, OH; Mus of Art, Ogunquit, ME; Cleveland Mus, OH; British Mus, London, England; Hirshhorn Mus, Wash, DC; California Palace Legion of Honor, San Francisco, CA
PRINTERS: Herbert A Fox, Merrimac, MA (HF); Fox Graphics, Merrimac, MA (FG)
PUBLISHERS: Fox Graphics, Merrimac, MA (FG); Impressions Gallery, Boston, MA (IG) (OB); Lakeside Studio, Lakeside, MI (LS); Artist (ART)
GALLERIES: Fox Graphics, Merrimac, MA; Allport Gallery, San Francisco, CA; Robert Schoelkopf Gallery, New York, NY; Olga Dollar Gallery, San Francisco, CA; Frost Gully Gallery, Portland, ME
MAILING ADDRESS: Oak Woods Rd, North Berwick, ME 03906

TITLE	PUBLISHER	PRINTER	DATE	MEDIUM	DIMENSION (PAPER SIZE) IN INCHES	TYPE OF PAPER	EDITION NUMBER	NO. OF COLORS	ORIGINAL OPENING PRICE	CURRENT RETAIL PRICE
CURRENT EDITIONS:										
Untitled	ART/FG	HF/FG	1977	LC	14 X 16	R/BFK	60	5	90	300

DAVID HARE

BORN: New York, NY; (1917-1992)
EDUCATION: Degrees in Biology & Chemistry, 1923-39; Hon PhD, Maryland Inst of Art, Baltimore, MD, Hon PhD, 1969
RECENT EXHIB: Gruenbaum Gallery, NY, 1987; William Paterson Col, Ben Shahn Galleries, Wayne, NJ, 1989,92; Stamford Mus, Leonhardt Galleries, CT, 1992; Rutgers Barclay Gallery, Santa Fe, NM, 1992
COLLECTIONS: Metropolitan Mus of Art, NY; Whitney Mus of Am Art, NY; Brooklyn Mus, NY; San Francisco Mus of Mod Art, CA; Los Angeles County Mus of Art, CA; Akron Art Inst, OH; Delgado Mus of Art, New Orleans, LA; Carnegie Inst Art Mus, Pittsburgh, PA; Yale Univ Art Mus, New Haven, CT; Washington Univ Art Mus, St Louis, MO
PRINTERS: Rodney Hamon, Albuquerque, NM (RH); Lynne Allen, Albuquerque, NM (LA); Beth Lovendusky, Albuquerque, NM (BL); BQ Adam (BQA); L Baker (LB); Tamarind Inst, Albuquerque, NM (TI)
PUBLISHERS: Tamarind Inst, Albuquerque, NM (TI)
GALLERIES: Tamarind Inst, Albuquerque, NM; Shippee Gallery, New York, NY; G H Dalsheimer Gallery, Baltimore, MD; Rutgers Barclay Gallery, Santa Fe, NM
MAILING ADDRESS: c/o Rutgers Barclay Gallery, 325 W San Francisco St, Santa Fe, NM 87501

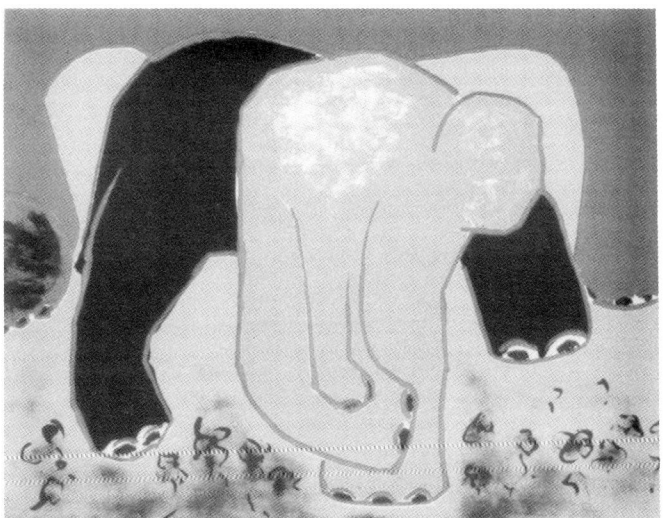

David Hare
Elephant in Violets
Courtesy Tamarind Institute

TITLE	PUBLISHER	PRINTER	DATE	MEDIUM	DIMENSION (PAPER SIZE) IN INCHES	TYPE OF PAPER	EDITION NUMBER	NO. OF COLORS	ORIGINAL OPENING PRICE	CURRENT RETAIL PRICE
SOLD OUT EDITIONS (RARE):										
Untitled	TI	BQA/LB/TI	1977	LC	56 X 72 cm	AC	70	5	375	800
CURRENT EDITIONS:										
Creeping Lion	TI	RH/TI	1987	LC	23 X 31	SOM/CR	20	5	600	800
Elephant in Violets	TI	LA/TI	1987	LC	23 X 30	ARJ	30	7	500	700
Two Figures	TI	LA/TI	1987	LC/CC	21 X 19	MUL-R/BFK	26	3	250	300
Venus Rising	TI	LA/TI	1987	LC/CC	18 X 22	MUL-R/BFK	30	5	250	300
Flying Head	TI	BL/TI	1987	LC	31 X 23	SOM/CR	20	5	600	800

KEITH HARING

BORN: Kutztown, PA; (1958–1990)
EDUCATION: Sch of Visual Arts, NY, 1978–70
RECENT EXHIB: Michael Kohn Gallery, Los Angeles, CA, 1988; Illinois State Univ, Art Gallery, Normal, IL, 1989; Art Inst of Boston, MA, 1989; Univ of Missouri, St Louis, MO, 1989; Huntington Library, San Marino, CA, 1989; Nassau County Mus of Fine Art, Roslyn Harbor, NY, 1989; Philip Samuels Fine Art, St Louis, MO, 1990; Studio 53 Art Gallery, NY, 1990; Queens Mus, NY, 1990; Illinois State Univ Mus, Normal, IL, 1991; Univ of Houston, Blaffer Gallery, Houston, TX, 1992; Univ of Colorado, Colorado Springs, CO, 1992; William Paterson Col, Ben Shahn Galleries, Wayne, NJ, 1989,92; Tony Shafrazi Gallery, NY, 1988–89,92
PRINTERS: Maurice Sanchez, NY (MS); Derriére L'Etoile Studio, NY (DES); Alexander Heinrici, NY (AH); Studio Heinrici, NY (SH); Matthieu Printers, Zürich, Switzerland (MP); Domberger KG, Stuttgart, Germany (DOM); Rupert Jason Smith, NY (RJS); Karl Mauer, Munich, West Germany (KM); Karl Imhof, Munich, West Germany (KI); Stuckzentrum Bender, Munich, West Germany (SB); L'Atelier Arts-Litho, Paris, France (AR); Durham Press, Durham, PA (DP)
PUBLISHERS: Barbara Gladstone Editions, NY (BGE); Tony Shafrazi, Gallery, NY (TSG); Fred Dorfman, Inc, NY (FDI); Editions Schellmann, NY (ES); George C Mulder, Amsterdam, The Netherlands & NY (GCM); House Bébert, Amsterdam, Netherlands (HB); Martin Lawrence Limited Editions, Van Nuys, CA (MLLE); Editions F B, Paris, France (EFB); Outreach Fund for Aids, NY (AOFFA); Paris Review, Paris, France (PR); Lococo-Mulder, Inc, St Louis, MO (L-M)
GALLERIES: Tony Shafrazi Gallery, New York, NY; Hal Bromm Gallery, New York, NY; Annina Nosei Gallery, New York, NY; Fay Gold Gallery, Atlanta, GA; Joy Moos Gallery, Miami, FL; Editions Schellmann, New York, NY; Michael Kohn Gallery, Los Angeles, CA; Martin Lawrence Galleries, New York, NY & Phila, PA; Stein Gladstone Gallery, New York, NY; Philip Samuels Fine Art, St Louis, MO; Fenton Fine Arts, Fort Worth, TX; G R N'Namdi Gallery, Detroit, MI; Metropolitan Art Gallery, Los Angeles, CA; Erika Meyerovich Gallery, San Francisco, CA; Robert Berman Gallery, Santa Monica, CA; Hokin Galleries, Bay Harbor Islands, FL & Palm Beach, FL; Alias Gallery, Atlanta, GA; Barbara Braathen Gallery, New York, NY; Gallery 121 International, New York, NY; Nan Miller Gallery, Rochester, NY; Mendelson Gallery, Pittsburgh, PA; Govinda Gallery, Wash, DC; TwoSixtyOne Art, New York, NY; Jaipaul Galleries, Phila, PA; Professional Fine Arts Services, Inc, New York, NY
MAILING ADDRESS: 325 Broome St, New York, NY 10014

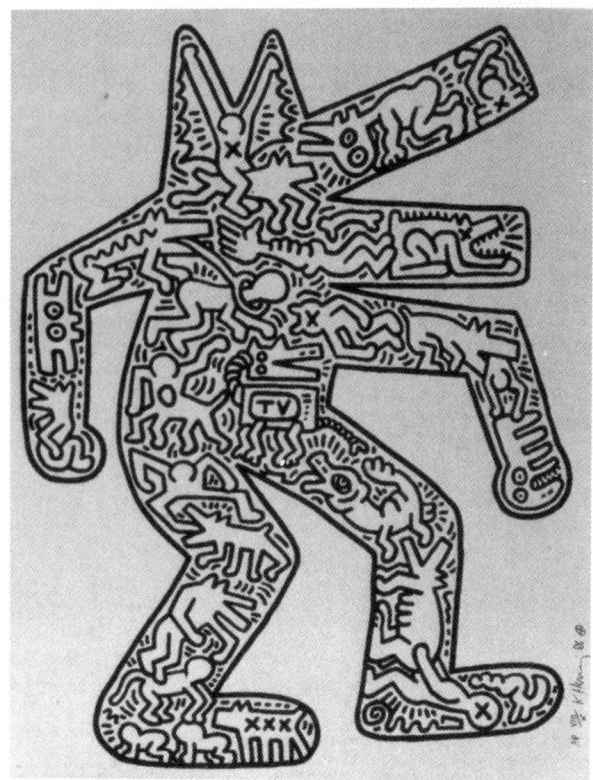

Keith Haring
Dog
Courtesy Edition Schellmann

TITLE	PUBLISHER	PRINTER	DATE	MEDIUM	DIMENSION (PAPER SIZE) IN INCHES	TYPE OF PAPER	EDITION NUMBER	NO. OF COLORS	ORIGINAL OPENING PRICE	CURRENT RETAIL PRICE
SOLD OUT EDITIONS (RARE):										
Untitled I-VI (Set of 6)	BGE	MS/DES	1982	LB	24 X 36 EA	AP88	40 EA	1 EA	1250 EA	60000 SET
Untitled (Set of 5)	TSG	AH/SH	1983	SP	42 X 50 EA	R/BFK	100 EA	6 EA	3500 SET	50000 SET
Untitled (Set of 3)	ES	MP	1985	LC	32 X 40 EA	R/BFK	60 EA	2 EA	1200 SET	20000 SET
Three Lithographs with Collotype (Set of 3)	ES	MP	1985	LC	32 X 40 EA	R/BFK	80 EA	2 EA	1200 SET	25000 SET
Ludo (Set of 5)	EFB		1985	LC	26 X 19 EA	AP	90 EA	2 EA	2500 SET	18000 SET
Fault Lines			1986	LC/OFF/COL	9 X 11	AP	200		350	800
Portrait of Joseph Beuys			1986	SP	32 X 24	CANVAS	90		1200	4000
Statue of Liberty			1986	SP	28 X 38	R/BFK	100		1200	6000
City Kids Speak on Liberty	FDI		1986	SP	38 X 28	R/BFK	100		1200	10000
Andy Mouse (with Andy Warhol) (Set of 4)	GCM	MP	1986	SP	38 X 38 EA	R/BFK	30 EA		3500 SET	30000 SET
Andy Mouse 2 (Homage to Andy Warhol) (Set of 4)	GCM	MP	1987	SP	38 X 38 EA	R/BFK	30 EA		4000 EA	25000 SET
Bad Boys (Set of 6)	HB		1986	SP	20 X 26 EA	AC	30 EA	1 EA	5000 SET	30000 SET
Double Man	ART		1986	LC	20 X 26	AC	85	2	800	9000
Dog (Painted Plywood with Screenprint)	ES	DOM	1986	SP	50 X 38 X 2	R/BFK	15		3000	8000
Dog	ES	MP	1986-87	SP	45 X 36	RP/300	40		1500	5000
Andy Mouse 2 (Keith Haring's Homage to Andy Warhol) (Set of 4)	GCM	MP	1986	SP	38 X 38 EA	LEN/MB	30 EA	7–8 EA	7500 SET	60000 SET
Growing Suite (Set of 5):									8000 SET	70000 SET
Growing Suite #1	MLLE	RJS	1988	SP	40 X 30	LEN/MB	100	4	1800	15000
Growing Suite #2	MLLE	RJS	1988	SP	30 X 40	LEN/MB	100	4	1800	14000
Growing Suite #3	MLLE	RJS	1988	SP	30 X 40	LEN/MB	100	3	1800	14000
Growing Suite #4	MLLE	RJS	1988	SP	30 X 40	LEN/MB	100	4	1800	14000
Growing Suite #5	MLLE	RJS	1988	SP	30 X 40	LEN/MB	100	5	1800	14000
Apocalypse Portfolio (Set of 21)	L-M	AR	1988	SP	38 X 38 EA	LEN/MB	90 EA	5–8 EA	15000 SET	25000 SET
Apocalypse (10 Screenprint Images by Keith Haring—with Screenprint Prose & Introduction by William S Burroughs) (Set of 21)	L-M	AR	1988	SP	38 X 38 EA	LEN/MB	90 EA	5–8 EA	15000 SET	25000 SET
Apocalypse I-X									3000 EA	3000 EA
Totem (Lacquered Carved Plywood)	ES	KM	1988	MULT	72 X 22 X 3	Wood	35			
Chocolate Budha (Set of 5)	EFB	AR	1989	LC	22 X 28 EA		90 EA		5000 SET	50000 SET
The Paris Review	PR		1989	SP	24 X 32		200		1200	5000
Untitled (Set of 4)	ART		1989	SP	17 X 14 EA		200 EA		4500 SET	35000 SET

KEITH HARING CONTINUED

TITLE	PUBLISHER	PRINTER	DATE	MEDIUM	DIMENSION (PAPER SIZE) IN INCHES	TYPE OF PAPER	EDITION NUMBER	NO. OF COLORS	ORIGINAL OPENING PRICE	CURRENT RETAIL PRICE
SOLD OUT EDITIONS (RARE):										
Totem (3-Part Woodcut—Top + Bottom Painted in Red)	ES	KI	1989	WC	76 X 35	JP	60		3500	8500
Totem (Wall Relief Cast in Concrete)	ES	SB	1989	MULT	72 X 22 X 3		25			
The Valley	GCM	AM	1989	EB	14 X 13 EA	HMP	80 EA		15000 SET	25000 SET
The Valley (16 Etchings by Keith Haring with 15 Etched Pages of Text by William S Burroughs—Cased in a Double Portfolio Box of Belgian Linen & Leather) (Set of 31)	GCM	AM	1989	EC	14 X 13 EA	HMP	80 EA	1–2 EA	15000 SET	25000 SET
Retrospect	MLLE		1989	SP	46 X 82					
Untitled (Set of 4)	ART		1989	SP	17 X 14 EA	LEN/MB	200 EA		4000 SET	22000 SET
Silence Equals Death	AOFFA	DP	1989	SP	39 X 39	LEN/MB	200	3	2000	10000
Totem (3 Parts)			1989	WC	75 X 35	JP	60		3000	8500
Best Buddies			1990	SP	26 X 32	LEN/MB	200		2000	5500
The Valley I-XVI	GCM	AM	1989	EC	14 X 13 EA	HMP	80 EA	1–2 EA	1500 SET	2000 EA

Keith Haring
Bad Boys
Courtesy House Bebert

Keith Haring
Ludo
Courtesy Editions FB

PAUL HARMON

BORN: Nashville, TN; January 23, 1939
EDUCATION: Univ of Tennessee, Knoxville, TN
AWARDS: Prix Int d'Art Contemporain de Monte-Carlo, 1990; Prix de la Ville de Monaco, 1990; Prix de la Societe EJA, 1990; Recipient of Commemorative Medal, City of Saint Martin de Tertre, 1990
RECENT EXHIB: Malton Gallery, Cincinnati, OH, 1987; Hoyle Gallery, Boston, MA, 1988; Galerie d'Art Public, Paris, France, 1989; South Wharf Gallery, Nantucket, MA, 1989; Zantman Art Galleries, Palm Desert, CA, 1989; Sande Webster Gallery, Phila, PA, 1990; Malton Gallery, Cincinnati, OH, 1990; Galerie Sabala, Paris, France, 1990; Bennett Galleries, Knoxville, TN, 1987,90; South Wharf Gallery, Nantucket, MA, 1990; Carl Van Vechten Gallery, Fisk Univ, Nashville, TN, 1991; Malton Gallery, Cincinnati OH, 1990,93; Galerie Art Expo, Paris, France, 1990,91,93
COLLECTIONS: Tampa Mus of Art, FL; Jacksonville Art Mus, FL; Tennessee State Mus, Nashville, TN; Cheekwood Fine Arts Center, TN; Vanderbilt Univ Fine Arts Center, Nashville, TN; Fisk Univ, Carl Van Vechten Gallery, Nashville, TN; Univ of South Florida, Tampa, FL; Belmont Col, Nashville, TN
PRINTERS: Philippe LeJeune Atelier, Burcy, France (PLJA); Topaz Editions, Inc, Tampa, FL (TE); Artist (ART); Petro III Graphics, Lexington, KY (PIII); Les Impressions d'Art, E & J Desjobert, Paris, France (LIA/EJD)
PUBLISHERS: GMB Galerie Internationale, Royal Oaks, MI (GMB); Cavaliero Fine Arts, NY (CAV); L'Atelier/The Studio, Brentwood, TN (LA); Biological Therapy Institute, Franklin, TN (BTI); Studio Meridian, Brentwood, TN (SM); Artist (ART); Art Multi, Paris, France (AM); International Fine Art Publishers, Bloomfield Hills, MI (IFAP)
GALLERIES: Sande Webster Gallery, Phila, PA; Malton Gallery, Cincinnati, OH; Bennett Galleries, Knoxville, TN; The Studio/L'Atelier, Nashville, TN; Fay Gold Gallery, Atlanta, GA; Michael Murphy Gallery, Tampa, FL; South Wharf Gallery, Nantucket, MA; Galerie Sabala, Paris, France; Galerie Art Expo, Paris, France; Galerie International, Bloomfield Hills, MI; Windsors Gallery, Dania, FL
MAILING ADDRESS: 1304 Wilson Pike, Brentwood, TN 37027; 1, Boulevard Saint Michel, Paris 75005, France

---

The retail prices of the 100,000 limited edition prints quoted in this directory are subject to change. Print publishers, artists and galleries were the direct sources for these quotations. Prices in the secondary market listed as "Sold Out Editions (Rare)" indicate that the publisher has a limited supply of that print or that the print is difficult to locate in the galleries.

PAUL HARMON CONTINUED

TITLE	PUBLISHER	PRINTER	DATE	MEDIUM	DIMENSION (PAPER SIZE) IN INCHES	TYPE OF PAPER	EDITION NUMBER	NO. OF COLORS	ORIGINAL OPENING PRICE	CURRENT RETAIL PRICE
SOLD OUT EDITIONS (RARE):										
The Pink Lady	LA	PLJA	1978	EC/A	10 X 13	AC	40	3	50	125
Dream	LA	PLJA	1978	EC/A	10 X 13	AC	50	2	50	125
The Cloud Lady	LA	PLJA	1978	EB/HC	10 X 13	AC	20	Varies	50	100
Chaplin	LA	PLJA	1978	EB	10 X 13	AC	25	1	50	140
The Collector	LA	PLJA	1978	EB	10 X 13	AC	25	1	50	100
Old Plate	LA	PLJA	1978	EB	10 X 13	AC	25	1	50	115
Le Voyage	AM	LIA/EJD	1989	LC	86 X 116 cm	AP	60	12	550	550
Jeanne Duval (with Acrylic & Enamel) (Series of 5 Variations)	AM	LIA/EJD	1989	MON/PO	116 X 86 cm EA	AP	1 EA	Varies	1500 EA	1500 EA
Steps on Earth (with Acrylic & Enamel) (Series of 5 Variations)	AM	LIA/EJD	1989	MON/PO	116 X 86 cm EA	AP	1 EA	Varies	1500 EA	1500 EA
Paysage du Midi (with Acrylic & Enamel) (Series of 5 Variations)	AM	LIA/EJD	1989	MON/PO	116 X 86 cm EA	AP	1 EA	Varies	1500 EA	1500 EA
CURRENT EDITIONS:										
A Time before Now (Set of 6)	GMB	TE	1980	LC	13 X 15 EA	AC	75 EA	3 EA	425 EA	550 SET
A Place before Here (Set of 6)	GMB	TE	1980	LC	13 X 15 EA	AC	75 EA	3 EA	425 EA	550 SET
Le Concorde	ART	TE	1980	LC	24 X 32	AC	90	7	220	400
Festival in Another Town	ART	TE	1980	LC	24 X 32	AC	90	7	220	400
Village Mirage	ART	TE	1981	LC	24 X 32	AC	90	9	220	400
Azimuth Series (Series of 41)	SM	TE	1983	LC/MON	21 X 29 EA	AC	1 EA	Varies	425 EA	600 EA
Interiors/Exteriors (Series of 4)	SM	TE	1983	LC/MON	21 X 29 EA	AC	1 EA	Varies	425 EA	600 EA
Collective Studies (Series of 50)	SM	TE	1984	LC/STEN/MON	21 X 31 EA	AC	1 EA	Varies	425 EA	600 EA
The Passage Series (Series of 54)	ART	ART	1985	STEN/MON	21 X 31	THS	1 EA	Varies	425 EA	600 EA
Voyageur Series (Series of 200)	ART	ART	1986	STEN/MON	21 X 31	THS	1 EA	Varies	425 EA	600 EA
Philosopher's Pupil Series (Series of 27)	ART	ART	1986	STEN/MON	21 X 31	THS	1 EA	Varies	425 EA	600 EA
The Kiss Series (Series of 200)	ART	ART	1987	STEN/MON	21 X 31	THS	1 EA	Varies	425 EA	600 EA
Colette Series (Series of 27)	ART	ART	1987	STEN/MON	21 X 31	THS	1 EA	Varies	425 EA	600 EA
The Earth Suite (Set of 4)	BTI	TE	1987	LC	25 X 32 EA	AC	90 EA	9–12	2400 SET	2400 SET
Mankind Suite (Set of 4)	BTI	TE	1987	LC	25 X 32 EA	AC	90 EA	9–12	2400 SET	2400 SET
Beyond Suite (Set of 4)	BTI	TE	1987	LC	25 X 32	AC	90 EA	9–12	2400 SET 600 EA	2400 SET 600 EA
The Boy	SM	PIII	1988	LC	30 X 22	THS	40	10	350	400
The Philosopher's Pupil	SM	PIII	1989	LC	30 X 22	THS	40	15	350	400
L'Amante de Baudelaire (Jeanne Duval)	AM	LIA/EJD	1989	LC	116 X 86 cm	AP	60	11	550	550
La Villa	AM	LIA/EJD	1989	LC	86 X 116 cm	AP	60	13	550	550
Invites Imaginairs (Set of 4)	AM	LIA/EJD	1992	LC	116 X 86 cm EA	AC	60 EA	2 EA	2000 SET	2600 SET
Sacred Planet	IFAP	LIA/EJD	1992	LC	86 X 116 cm	AC	75	5	600	650
The Kiss	IFAP	LIA/EJD	1992	LC	86 X 116 cm	AC	75	5	600	650
Sailing to Byzantium	IFAP	LIA/EJD	1992	LC	86 X 116 cm	AC	75	5	600	650
Music and the Medicis	IFAP	LIA/EJD	1992	LC	116 X 86 cm	AC	75	5	600	650

JAMES HARRILL

BORN: North Carolina; March 21, 1936
EDUCATION: New York Univ, NY; Parsons Sch of Design, NY; Ogunquit Sch of Sculpture & Painting, ME; Univ of Washington, Seattle, WA
AWARDS: Thalheimer Found Award, 1960; Purchase Award, Mus of New Mexico, 1971
RECENT EXHIB: Leslie Levy Gallery, Scottsdale, AZ, 1987
COLLECTIONS: Mus of New Mexico, Santa Fe, NM; Roswell Mus & Art Center, NM
PRINTERS: Wasserman Silkscreen Company, NY (WSC); Ultra Color, NY (UC); Messinger, Inc, NY (MI)
PUBLISHERS: Leslie Levy Gallery, Scottsdale, AZ (LLG)
GALLERIES: Leslie Levy Gallery, Scottsdale, AZ

TITLE	PUBLISHER	PRINTER	DATE	MEDIUM	DIMENSION (PAPER SIZE) IN INCHES	TYPE OF PAPER	EDITION NUMBER	NO. OF COLORS	ORIGINAL OPENING PRICE	CURRENT RETAIL PRICE
CURRENT EDITIONS:										
Greek Steps	LLG	WSC	1985	SP	32 X 28	WWP	200	20	400	1500
Desert Morning, Abiquin	LLG	WSC	1986	SP	15 X 48	WWP	275	18	450	850
Red Doors	LLG	WSC	1986	SP	32 X 28	WWP	275	12	400	700
Monastery Near Salonika	LLG	WSC	1986	SP	26 X 35	WWP	275	18	450	850
Steps to the Sky	LLG	WSC	1987	SP	28 X 58	WWP	150	40	1200	1800
Sunlit House, Canones	LLG	WSC	1988	LC	30 X 20	StP	100	11	700	800
Island Village	LLG	WSC	1988	SP	29 X 45	WWP	190	24	1000	1500
Delphi	LLG	WSC	1988	SP	32 X 42	WWP	190	32	1000	1500

HELEN MAYER HARRISON

BORN: New York, NY; 1927
EDUCATION: Queens Col, NY, BA; Cornell Univ, Ithaca, NY; New York Univ, NY, MA, 1953
TEACHING: Prof, Visual Arts, Univ of California, San Diego, CA, 1981 to present
AWARDS: Sea Grant, U S Dept of Commerce, 1974–76; DAAD Fel, Berlin, Germany, 1988

HELEN MAYER HARRISON CONTINUED

RECENT EXHIB: Los Angeles County Art Mus, CA, 1987; Grey Gallery, NY, 1987; Kunsterverein, Berlin, Germany, 1989; Moderna Galerja, Ljubljana, Czechoslavakia, 1990
COLLECTIONS: La Jolla Mus of Contemp Art, CA; Mus of Mod Art, NY; Brooklyn Mus, NY; Johnson Mus, Cornell Univ, Ithaca, NY; Powers Inst, Univ of Sydney, Australia; Tel Aviv Mus, Israel
PRINTERS: Artist (ART); Newton A Harrison, Del Mar, CA (NAH)
PUBLISHERS: Ronald Feldman Fine Arts, NY (RFFA)
GALLERIES: Ronald Feldman Fine Arts, New York, NY
MAILING ADDRESS: P O Box 466, Del Mar, CA 92014

TITLE	PUBLISHER	PRINTER	DATE	MEDIUM	DIMENSION (PAPER SIZE) IN INCHES	TYPE OF PAPER	EDITION NUMBER	NO. OF COLORS	ORIGINAL OPENING PRICE	CURRENT RETAIL PRICE
CURRENT EDITIONS:										
Book of the Seven Lagoons (Bound Portfolio of 45 Painted, Archivally-Processed, Sepia-Toned Photographs, One with Collage) (With Newton A Harrison) (Set of 45)	RFFA	ART/NEH	1987	PH	20 X 24 EA	AP	31 EA	1 EA	30000 SET	35000 SET

NEWTON A HARRISON

BORN: New York, NY; October 20, 1932
EDUCATION: Yale Univ, Sch of Art & Arch, New Haven, CT, BFA, MFA; Pennsylvania Acad of Fine Arts, Phila, PA, Certificate
TEACHING: Asst Prof, Art, Univ of New Mexico, Albuquerque, NM, 1965–67; Assoc Prof, Univ of California, San Diego, CA, 1967–77, Prof & Chmn, Art Dept, 1973–76, Prof, 1975 to present
AWARDS: Award for EAT: Projects Outside Art; Nat Endowment for the Arts Grant, 1975; Sea Grant, U S Dept of Commerce, 1974–76; DAAD Fel, Berlin, Germany, 1988
RECENT EXHIB: Los Angeles County Art Mus, CA, 1987; Grey Gallery, NY, 1987; Kinsterverein, Berlin, Germany, 1989; Moderna Galerja, Ljubljana, Czechoslavakia, 1990
COLLECTIONS: Mus of Mod Art, NY; Brooklyn Mus, NY; La Jolla Mus of Contemp Art, CA; Mus of Photographic Art, San Diego, CA; Powers Inst, Mus of Sydney, Australia; Los Angeles County Art Mus, CA; Tel Aviv Mus, Israel
PRINTERS: Artist (ART); Helen Mayer Harrison, Del Mar, CA (HMH)
PUBLISHERS: Ronald Feldman Fine Arts, NY (RFFA)
GALLERIES: Ronald Feldman Fine Arts, New York, NY
MAILING ADDRESS: P O Box 446, Del Mar, CA 92014

TITLE	PUBLISHER	PRINTER	DATE	MEDIUM	DIMENSION (PAPER SIZE) IN INCHES	TYPE OF PAPER	EDITION NUMBER	NO. OF COLORS	ORIGINAL OPENING PRICE	CURRENT RETAIL PRICE
CURRENT EDITIONS:										
Book of the Seven Lagoons (Bound Portfolio of 45 Painted, Archivally-Processed, Sepia-Toned Photographs, One with Collage) (with Helen Mayer Harrison) (Set of 45)	RFFA	ART/HMH	1987	PH	20 X 24 EA	AP	31 EA	1 EA	30000 SET	35000 SET

GORDON HART

BORN: Glasgow, Scotland; 1940
EDUCATION: Central Sch of Art, London, England, 1961–69
AWARDS: Arts Council of Great Britian Awards, 1964; Gulbenkian Scholarship, London, England, 1964; Max Beckman Scholarship, NY, 1964; Nat Endowment for the Arts Fel, 1975; Guggenheim Mem Fel, NY, 1977
COLLECTIONS: Albright-Knox Mus, Buffalo, NY; High Mus, Atlanta, GA; Neuberger Mus, Purchase, NY
PRINTERS: Osiris Publications, Ltd, NY (OP); Maurice Sanchez, NY (MS); Derriére L'Etoile Studio, NY (DES); John Nichols, NY (JN)
PUBLISHERS: Holly Solomon Editions, NY (HSE); Maurice Sanchez, NY (MS); Fred Dorfman, Inc, NY (FDI)
GALLERIES: Holly Solomon Gallery, New York, NY; Fred Dorfman Gallery, New York, NY; Acquavella Contemp Art, New York, NY; Stephen Rosenberg Gallery, New York, NY; Michael Leonard & Assoc, Inc, New York, NY
MAILING ADDRESS: 533 Canal St, New York, NY 10013

TITLE	PUBLISHER	PRINTER	DATE	MEDIUM	DIMENSION (PAPER SIZE) IN INCHES	TYPE OF PAPER	EDITION NUMBER	NO. OF COLORS	ORIGINAL OPENING PRICE	CURRENT RETAIL PRICE
SOLD OUT EDITIONS (RARE):										
Untitled (Purple)	MS	MS/DES	1980	LC/SP	41 X 30		10		450	600
Untitled (Red)	MS	MS/DES	1980	LC/SP	41 X 30		30		450	600
Untitled (Yellow)	MS	MS/DES	1980	LC/SP	41 X 30		29		450	600
Silverprint/White	HSE	JN	1981	MY/SL/SP	42 X 32	4MM	15		600	900
Silverprint/Magenta	HSE	JN	1981	MY/SL/SP	42 X 32	4MM	15		600	900
Silverprint/Yellow	HSE	JN	1981	MY/SL/SP	42 X 32	4MM	15		600	900
Yellow	HSE	OP	1981	SP	39 X 26	KRP/C	30	4	125	300
Violet	HSE	OP	1981	SP	39 X 26	KRP/C	30	4	125	300
One on One I–IV (Set of 4)	FDI	JN	1981	SP	30 X 25 EA	AE	25 EA	3–5 EA	1200 SET	1500 SET
									375 SET	500 SET
Two Screenprints with Aluminum/Copper Chine Collé (Set of 2)									1200 SET	1500 SET
Solar Print	FDI	JN	1981	SP	49 X 37	AE	25	3	600	850
Lunar Print	FDI	JN	1981	SP	49 X 36	AE	25	2	600	850

The retail prices of the 100,000 limited edition prints quoted in this directory are subject to change. Print publishers, artists and galleries were the direct sources for these quotations. Prices in the secondary market listed as "Sold Out Editions (Rare)" indicate that the publisher has a limited supply of that print or that the print is difficult to locate in the galleries.

GRACE HARTIGAN

BORN: Newark, NJ; March 28, 1922
TEACHING: Maryland Inst, Baltimore, MD, Artist in Res, 1967 to present
AWARDS: Moore Inst of Art & Science, Hon DFA, 1969; AAAL Childe Hassam Fund Purchase, 1975
RECENT EXHIB: Guild Hall Mus, East Hampton, NY, 1992; Lafayette Col, Easton, PA, 1992
COLLECTIONS: Mus of Mod Art, NY; Metropolitan Mus of Art, NY; Wadsworth Atheneum, Hartford, CT; Art Inst of Chicago, IL; Univ of Chicago, IL; Carnegie Inst, Pittsburgh, PA; Brooklyn Mus, NY; Brandeis Mus, Waltham, MA; Nelson Inst, Kansas City, KS; Walker Art Center, Minneapolis, MN; Whitney Mus of Am Art, NY; Flint Inst, MI; Vassar Col, Poughkeepsie, NY; Washington Univ, St Louis, MO; Rhode Island Inst of Design, Providence, RI; Princeton Univ, NJ; Philadelphia Mus of Art, PA; State Univ of New York, New Paltz, NY; North Carolina Mus of Art, Raleigh, NC; Washington Gallery Of Mod Art, Seattle, WA; Pennsylvania Acad of Fine Arts, Phila, PA; Minneapolis Inst of Art, MN; Nat Coll of Am Art, Wash, DC
PRINTERS: Universal Limited Art Editions, West Islip, NY (ULAE); Artist (ART); Sylvia Roth, Nyack, NY (SR); Sue Mallozzi, NY (SM); Hudson River Editions, Nyack, NY (HRE)
PUBLISHERS: Universal Limited Art Editions, West Islip, NY (ULAE); Artist (ART); Thomas Gruenbaum, NY (TG); Gruenbaum Graphics, NY (GG)
GALLERIES: ACA Galleries, New York, NY; Dolly Fiterman Fine Arts, Minneapolis, MN; C Grimaldis Gallery, Baltimore, MD
MAILING ADDRESS: 1710½ Eastern Ave, Baltimore, MD 21231

TITLE	PUBLISHER	PRINTER	DATE	MEDIUM	DIMENSION (PAPER SIZE) IN INCHES	TYPE OF PAPER	EDITION NUMBER	NO. OF COLORS	ORIGINAL OPENING PRICE	CURRENT RETAIL PRICE
SOLD OUT EDITIONS (RARE):										
Flowers in Goblet, No 1	ART	ART	1923	LC	18 X 11	WOVE	25		50	6000
Grapes	ART	ART	1923	LC	10 X 12	WOVE	25		50	4500
Pomegranate, Pear and...	ART	ART	1923	LC	10 X 15	WOVE	25		50	6000
Hero Leaves His Ship III	ULAE	ULAE	1960	LC	13 X 21	AC	26		350	4000
Elizabeth Etched	GG/TG	ART/SR/SM/HRE	1983	EB/A/SB	41 X 32	GE	50	10	900	1500

HANS HARTUNG

BORN: Leipzig, Germany; (1904–1989)
EDUCATION: Acad of Art, Leipzig, Germany, 1924–25; Acad of Art, Dresden, Germany, 1925–26; Acad of Art, Munich, Germany, 1928
PRINTERS: La Poligrafa, SA, Barcelona, Spain (LP); Erker Press, St Gallen, France (ErkPr); Artist (ART)
PUBLISHERS: Ediciones Poligrafa, SA, Barcelona, Spain (EdP); Erker Press, St Gallen, France (ErkPr); Marbach (Mar); Artist (ART)
GALLERIES: Galeria Joan Prats, New York, NY & Barcelona, Spain; River Gallery, Westport, CT

Schmücking (S)

TITLE	PUBLISHER	PRINTER	DATE	MEDIUM	DIMENSION (PAPER SIZE) IN INCHES	TYPE OF PAPER	EDITION NUMBER	NO. OF COLORS	ORIGINAL OPENING PRICE	CURRENT RETAIL PRICE
SOLD OUT EDITIONS: (RARE)										
Komposition 22 (S-22)	ART	ART	1953	EB	20 X 15	AP	100	1	50	1500
Komposition 3 (S-32)	ART	ART	1953	AB/DPT	4 X 11	AP	75	1	50	3500
Komposition 9 (S-38)	ART	ART	1953	EB/A	12 X 16	AP	75	1	50	3500
Komposition 14 (S-43)	ART	ART	1953	AB/DPT	15 X 21	AP	75	1	50	3500
Komposition 25 (S-54)	ART	ART	1953	EB	15 X 20	AP	75	1	50	1800
Composition	ART	ART	1953	EC	4 X 11	AP	75		65	900
Composition	ART	ART	1953	EC	20 X 31	AP	75		65	1200
Deux Compositions	ART	ART	1953	EC	15 X 21	AP	75		65	1500
Deux Compositions	ART	ART	1953	LB	41 X 30	AP	75	1	50	1500
5 Aquatint (S-34)	ART	ART	1953	AC	9 X 12	AP	100		65	2500
Composition: No 2	ART	ART	1953	EB/A	5 X 11	AP	100	4	65	1500
Composition: No 4	ART	ART	1953	EB/A	9 X 26	AP	100	5	65	6000
Composition: No 5	ART	ART	1953	EB/A	9 X 12	AP	100	2	65	5000
Composition: No 7	ART	ART	1953	EB/A	16 X 13	AP	75	4	65	5000
Composition: No 9	ART	ART	1953	EB/A	12 X 16	AP	75	3	65	5000
Gravure No 27	ART	ART	1957	EB/A	17 X 12	AP	100		65	1500
Lithograph L-112	ART	ART	1963	LC	21 X 28	AP	50		60	2500
Composition L-123			1964	LB	18 X 24	AP	75	1	60	3500
Untitled	ErkPr	ErkPr	1970	LB	16 X 22	AP		1	75	2200
Komposition	ErkPr	ErkPr	1970	LB	18 X 19	AP	75	1	75	900
Komposition	ErkPr	ErkPr	1970	LC	20 X 30	AP	75		100	2000
Farandole Portfolio (Set of 15)	EdP	LP	1971	LC	30 X 22 EA	GP	75 EA		8000 SET	28000 SET
Farandole Portfolio (Set of 5)	EdP	LP	1971	LC	30 X 22 EA	GP	75 EA		2500 SET	8000 SET
Aus: Hommage a Picasso			1973	LC	19 X 25	AP	90		150	1500
Composition LI	EckPr	EckPr	1973	LB	22 X 30	AP	75	1	125	800
Composition	EckPr	EckPr	1973	LC	22 X 30	AP	75		150	800
Komposition L-5	EckPr	EckPr	1973	LC	22 X 32	AP	75		150	800
Komposition L-6	EckPr	EckPr	1973	LC	22 X 18	AP	75		150	800
Komposition L-7	EckPr	EckPr	1973	LC	34 X 21	AP	75		150	800
Komposition L-12	EckPr	EckPr	1973	LC	32 X 24	AP	75		150	1000
Komposition L-15	EckPr	EckPr	1973	LC	25 X 35	AP	75		150	800
Komposition L-17	EckPr	EckPr	1973	LC	32 X 20	AP	75		150	800
Komposition L-19	EckPr	EckPr	1973	LC	23 X 28	AP	75		150	800
Komposition L-22	EckPr	EckPr	1973	LC	22 X 30	AP	75		150	800
Komposition L-24	EckPr	EckPr	1973	LC	25 X 35	AP	75		150	800
Set of 4 Lithographs	EdP	LP	1977	LC	30 X 22 EA	GP	75 EA		1800 SET / 470 EA	4000 SET / 1100 EA
Lithograph AL (Number 5)	EdP	LP	1977	LC	30 X 22 EA	GP	100 EA		450 EA	1100 EA

DONALD HARVEY

BORN: Walthamstow, England; June 14, 1930
EDUCATION: West Sussex Col of Art, England; Brighton Col of Art, England
TEACHING: Prof, Painting, Univ of Victoria, BC, Can, 1961 to present
AWARDS: Purchase Prize, Sadie & Samuel Bronfmann, Award, Montreal Mus, Can, 1963; First Prize Vancouver Art Gallery, Can, 1964; Art Gallery of Greater Victoria, Can, 1964–66, 69
RECENT EXHIB: Temple Univ, Tyler Sch of Art, Phila, PA, 1992
COLLECTIONS: Nat Gallery of Canada, Ottawa, Can; Albright-Knox Art Gallery, Buffalo, NY; Montreal Mus of Fine Arts, Can; Seattle Art Mus, WA
PRINTERS: Artist (ART)
PUBLISHERS: Artist (ART)
GALLERIES: Gallery Pascal, Toronto, Canada; Kyles Art Gallery, Victoria, Canada; Ken Heffle, Inc, Vancouver, Canada; Spaces, Cleveland, OH; Dart Gallery, Chicago, IL
MAILING ADDRESS: 1025 Joan Crescent, Victoria, BC, Canada V8S 3L3

TITLE	PUBLISHER	PRINTER	DATE	MEDIUM	DIMENSION (PAPER SIZE) IN INCHES	TYPE OF PAPER	EDITION NUMBER	NO. OF COLORS	ORIGINAL OPENING PRICE	CURRENT RETAIL PRICE
SOLD OUT EDITIONS (RARE):										
Mind Where You Tread	ART	ART	1966	SP	21 X 28	AP	20	5	80	300
Cortex	ART	ART	1966	SP	21 X 28	AP	20	5	80	300
Tumble	ART	ART	1967	SP	21 X 28	AP	20	5	80	300
Transistor FM	ART	ART	1967	SP	21 X 28	AP	20	6	80	300
CURRENT EDITIONS:										
Day Scape 1, 2, 3	ART	ART	1977	SP	22 X 28 EA	AP	21/17/19	5 EA	100 EA	200 EA
Nightscape 1, 2, 3	ART	ART	1977	SP	22 X 28 EA	AP	15/18/17	5 EA	100 EA	200 EA

BURT STANLY HASEN

BORN: New York, NY; December 19, 1921
EDUCATION: Art Students League, NY, 1940,42,44; Hans Hofmann Sch of Fine Arts, NY, 1947–48; Acad de la Grande-Chaumiere, Paris, France, 1948–50; Acad delle Belli Arti, Rome, Italy, 1959–60
TEACHING: Instr, Painting, Col of Art & Design, Minneapolis, MN, 1966; Instr, Painting & Drawing, Sch of Visual Arts, NY, 1953 to present
AWARDS: Emily Lowe Found, 1954; Fulbright Fel, Rome, Italy, 1959–66; New York Found for the Arts Grant, Painting, NY, 1990
RECENT EXHIB: Anita Shapolsky Gallery, NY, 1992
COLLECTIONS: Walker Art Center, Minneapolis, MN; Worcester Art Mus, MA; Hampton Inst, VA; Crestview Col, Allentown, PA; Bibliotheque Nat, Paris, France; New York Public Library, NY
PRINTERS: Artist (ART)
PUBLISHERS: Artist (ART)
GALLERIES: Martin Sumers Graphics, New York, NY; Galerie T'Pandje, Asselt, Belgium; Paarpsedemer Straat, Asselt, Belgium; Neo Persona Gallery, New York, NY; Anita Shapolsky Gallery, New York, NY
MAILING ADDRESS: 7 Dutch St, New York, NY 10038

TITLE	PUBLISHER	PRINTER	DATE	MEDIUM	DIMENSION (PAPER SIZE) IN INCHES	TYPE OF PAPER	EDITION NUMBER	NO. OF COLORS	ORIGINAL OPENING PRICE	CURRENT RETAIL PRICE
CURRENT EDITIONS:										
Faces Metamorphosis	ART	ART	1977	EB	18 X 24	AP	50	1	200	350
Souvenir From Pompei	ART	ART	1977	EB	18 X 24	AP	75	1	200	350
Les Bos Triumphant, No III	ART	ART	1977	E/A	16 X 20	AP	75	1	200	350
Between Light and Shadow	ART	ART	1977	E/A	18 X 24	AP	75	1	200	350
Poem-Image	ART	ART	1977	EC	18 X 24	AP	75	2	200	350
Homage to Mt Rushmore	ART	ART	1980	EC	16 X 20	AP	75	2	300	450
The Star Gazer	ART	ART	1980	E/A	9 X 12	AP	40	3	300	450

ZARINA HASHMI

EDUCATION: Studied woodcut printmaking, Bangkok, Thailand, 1958–61; Aligarh Univ, India, 1958; Hayter Atelier, Paris, France, 1963–67; St Martins Sch of Art, London, England, 1966; Studied papermaking, Bangkok, Thailand, 1968; Studied silkscreen printing, West Germany, 1971; Studied wood-block printing & papermaking, Japan, 1974
TEACHING: Bennington Col, VT, Spring, 1983; New York Feminist Art Inst, NY, 1979 to present
AWARDS: President's Award for Graphics, India, 1969; Japan Found Fel, 1974; Traveling Fel, New Delhi, India, 1982; New York Found for the Arts Grant, Painting, NY, 1990
COLLECTIONS: Mus of Mod Art, NY; Nat Gallery of Mod Art, New Delhi, India; Japan Found, Tokyo, Japan
PRINTERS: Printmaking Workshop, NY (PW); Artist (ART)
PUBLISHERS: Orion Editions, NY (OE); Artist (ART)
GALLERIES: Orion Editions, New York, NY; Objects Gallery, San Antonio, TX; Roberta English Gallery, San Francisco, CA
MAILING ADDRESS: 231 W 29th St, New York, NY 10001

TITLE	PUBLISHER	PRINTER	DATE	MEDIUM	DIMENSION (PAPER SIZE) IN INCHES	TYPE OF PAPER	EDITION NUMBER	NO. OF COLORS	ORIGINAL OPENING PRICE	CURRENT RETAIL PRICE
CURRENT EDITIONS:										
One Day the City was Golden (with Gold Powder)	ART/OE	ART/PW	1981	EB	28 X 25	ZAAN	35	1	275	500
Golden Route (with Gold Powder)	OE	ART/PW	1982	EB	30 X 22	HMP	35	1	275	500
Agni (Flame)	ART	ART/PW	1984	LB	33 X 25	HMP	18	1	400	500

MICHAEL HASTED

BORN: London, England; 1945
PRINTERS: Joseph Kleineman, NY (JK)
PUBLISHERS: London Arts, Inc, Detroit, MI (LAI); Post Oak Fine Art Distributors, Houston, TX (POFA)
GALLERIES: London Arts Gallery, Detroit, MI; Ro Gallery Image Makers, Inc, New York, NY

MICHAEL HASTED CONTINUED

TITLE	PUBLISHER	PRINTER	DATE	MEDIUM	DIMENSION (PAPER SIZE) IN INCHES	TYPE OF PAPER	EDITION NUMBER	NO. OF COLORS	ORIGINAL OPENING PRICE	CURRENT RETAIL PRICE
CURRENT EDITIONS:										
Light of Discovery	LAI	JK	1979	LC	24 X 19	SOM	250	9	250	600
A Point of Honour	POFA	JK	1979	LC	23 X 18	SOM	250	9	250	600
Public Outcry	POFA	JK	1979	LC	24 X 18	SOM	250	12	250	600
A Song of Praise	LAI	JK	1979	LC	24 X 18	SOM	250	10	250	600
Random Selection #2	LAI	JK	1980	CL	24 X 18	SOM	250	10	250	600
The Big Parade	LAI	JK	1980	LC	24 X 18	SOM	250	12	250	600
The Main Attraction	POFA	JK	1981	LC	16 X 12	SOM	250	11	250	600

JAMES HAVARD

BORN: Galveston, TX; 1937
EDUCATION: Sam Houston State Col, Huntsville, TX, BS, 1959; Atelier Chapman Kelley, Dallas, TX, 1960; Pennsylvania Acad of Fine Arts, Phila, PA, 1965
RECENT EXHIB: Elaine Horwitch Gallery, Santa Fe, NM, 1988; Marian Locks Gallery, Phila, PA, 1988; Allan Stone Gallery, New York, NY, 1989; Elaine Horwitch Gallery, Scottsdale, AZ, 1992
COLLECTIONS: Metropolitan Mus of Art, NY; Pennsylvania Acad of Fine Arts, Phila, PA; Philadelphia Art Mus, PA; Solomon R Guggenheim Mus, NY; Los Angeles County Mus, CA; Smithsonian Inst, Wash, DC
PRINTERS: Lynne Allen (LA); Marcia Brown (MB); Tamarind Inst, Albuquerque, NM
PUBLISHERS: Tamarind Inst, Albuquerque, NM (TI)
GALLERIES: Elaine Horwitch Galleries, Santa Fe, NM & Scottsdale, AZ; Locks Gallery, Phila, PA; Hokin Gallery, Palm Beach, FL; Allan Stone Gallery, New York, NY; Tavelli Williams Gallery, Aspen, CO; Jeremy Stone Gallery, San Francisco, CA; Somerville Manning Gallery, Greenville, DE; Naravisa Press, Santa Fe, NM; Roger La Pelle Gallery, Phila, PA
MAILING ADDRESS: P O Box 2945, Santa Fe, NM 87504

TITLE	PUBLISHER	PRINTER	DATE	MEDIUM	DIMENSION (PAPER SIZE) IN INCHES	TYPE OF PAPER	EDITION NUMBER	NO. OF COLORS	ORIGINAL OPENING PRICE	CURRENT RETAIL PRICE
SOLD OUT EDITIONS (RARE):										
Fallen Eagle	TI	LA/TI	1983	LC	42 X 30	R/BFK	40	9	600	1200
Peyote Meeting	TI	MB/TI	1983	LC	42 X 30	R/BFK	40	9	600	1200
Lakota	TI	LA/TI	1983	LC	36 X 24	AP/B	35	8	500	950

STANLEY WILLIAM HAYTER

BORN: London, England; (1901–1989)
EDUCATION: King's Col Univ, London, England
TEACHING: Dir, Atelier 17, Paris, France
AWARDS: Chevalie de la Legion d'Honneur France; Order of the British Empire
RECENT EXHIB: Associated American Artists, NY, 1992
COLLECTIONS: Mus of Mod Art, NY; Brooklyn Mus, NY; British Mus, London, England; Tate Gallery, London, England; Victoria and Albert Mus, London, England; Virginia Mus of Fine Art, Richmond, VA; San Francisco Mus of Mod Art, CA; Art Inst of Chicago, IL; Fogg Mus, Cambridge, MA; Albertina Mus, Vienna, Austria; City Art Mus, St Louis, MO; Grenoble Mus, France; Bibliotheque Nat, Paris, France; Bibliotheque Royale, Brussels, Belgium; Nat Gallery of Art, Wash, DC
PRINTERS: Artist (ART); Hecht, Paris, France (H); Hector Saunier, Paris, France (HS); Milen Poenau, Paris, France (MP); Atelier 17, Paris, France (A-17)
PUBLISHERS: Artist (ART); Guilde de la Gravure, Paris, France (GdG); L'Oeuve Gravee, Paris, France (LOGra); Editions Jeanne Bucher, Paris, France (EdJB)
GALLERIES: Don Soker Gallery, San Francisco, CA; Mary Ryan Gallery, New York, NY; Associated American Artists, New York, NY; Georgetown Gallery of Art, Wash, DC; Martha Tepper Contemp Fine Arts, West Newton, MA; Elaine Benson Gallery, Bridghampton, NY; Modernism Gallery, Coral Gables, FL; Virginia Lust Gallery, New York, NY
MAILING ADDRESS: 737 Washington St, New York, NY 10014

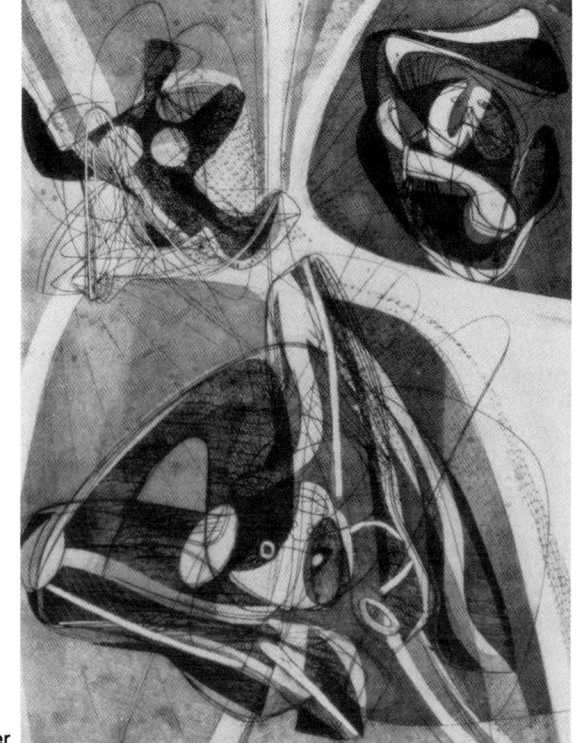

Stanley William Hayter
Day and Night
Courtesy Estate of S W Hayter

TITLE	PUBLISHER	PRINTER	DATE	MEDIUM	DIMENSION (PAPER SIZE) IN INCHES	TYPE OF PAPER	EDITION NUMBER	NO. OF COLORS	ORIGINAL OPENING PRICE	CURRENT RETAIL PRICE
SOLD OUT EDITIONS (RARE):										
Compositions Baigneuses	ART	ART	1927	LB	15 X 10	AP	10	1	30	5000
Place	ART	ART	1930	ENG/DPT	8 X 11	WOVE	50	1	35	4000
L'Apocalypse (Set of 6)	EdJB	ART	1932	ENG/DPT	21 X 16 EA	WOVE	60 EA	1 EA	150 SET	15000 SET
Horizon Bars	ART	ART	1932	ENG/REL	6 X 5	WOVE	100	1	30	1500
Croquis au Burin	ART	ART	1943	I	6 X 11	R/100	30	1	35	3000

STANLEY WILLIAM HAYTER CONTINUED

TITLE	PUBLISHER	PRINTER	DATE	MEDIUM	DIMENSION (PAPER SIZE) IN INCHES	TYPE OF PAPER	EDITION NUMBER	NO. OF COLORS	ORIGINAL OPENING PRICE	CURRENT RETAIL PRICE
SOLD OUT EDITIONS (RARE):										
Cronos	ART	ART	1944	EB/ENG/EMB	16 X 20	R/100	50	1	35	12500
Danse au Soleil	ART	ART	1945	EB/ENG/EMB	16 X 9	R/100	200	1	35	6000
Unstable Woman	ART	ART	1946	EB/ENG	15 X 20	R/100	50	1	50	7500
E	ART	ART/H	1946	I	6 X 7	R/100	50	1	50	2500
La Noyee	ART	ART/H	1946	I	14 X 17	R/100	50	1	75	5000
Sea Myth	ART	ART	1947	ENG/EMB	11 X 15	R/BFK	30	1	75	6000
Ceres	ART	ART	1948	ENG	28 X 21	R/BFK	2	1	85	8500
Death by Water	ART	ART	1948	I	14 X 24	AP	50	1	75	7000
Tropic of Cancer	ART	ART	1949	EB/ENG	22 X 27	R/BFK	50	1	75	6000
Night and Day	ART	ART	1951	EC/ENG	24 X 18	R/BFK	50	4	120	8500
Sun Dancer	ART	ART	1951	EC/ENG	16 X 9	R/BFK	200		75	3000
Composition	ART	ART	1951	EB/A	5 X 3	R/BFK	200		60	1800
Couple	CdG	ART	1952	EB/ENG/EMB	18 X 12	R/BFK	200	1	85	5500
Warriors	ART	ART	1953	EB/ENG	19 X 13	R/BFK	200		85	3000
Day and Night	ART	ART	1953	EB/ENG/EMB	23 X 18	AP	50	1	150	6000
Danäe	ART	ART	1954	EB/ENG	16 X 12	R/BFK	95	5	125	8500
La Noyee	LOGra	ART	1955	EB/ENG/S	14 X 19	R/BFK	175	1	135	4500
Ixion	LOGra	ART	1959	EB	19 X 20	R/BFK	50	17	125	5000
Noctiluca	LOGra	ART	1963	EC	12 X 15	R/BFK	50		125	3500
Floating Figure	LOGra	ART	1964	EB	20 X 25	R/BFK	50		125	3500
Nautilus	LOGra	ART	1969	EC	21 X 17	R/BFK			125	1500
Ripple	ART	ART	1970	EB/SG	18 X 23	R/BFK	100	1	150	2000
Gemini	ART	ART	1970	EC	19 X 23	R/BFK	100		150	1500
Mooring	ART	ART	1970	EC	23 X 18	R/BFK	100		150	1500
Symmetry	ART	ART	1970	EC	24 X 19	R/BFK	100		150	1500
Lake	ART	ART/HS/MP/A-17	1973	EB/A	18 X 22	R/BFK	100	2	150	1000
Nine Engravings (Set of 9)	ART	ART/HS/MP/A-17	1973	EB	16 X 12 EA	JBG	100 EA	1 EA	1000 SET	25000 SET
City	ART	ART/HS/MP/A-17	1974	EB/SG	19 X 24	R/BFK	75	1	150	2500
Drommond	ART	ART/HS/MP/A-17	1974	EB/SG	23 X 19	R/BFK	75	1	150	2500
Violet	ART	ART/HS/MP/A-17	1977	EC	25 X 19	R/BFK	50		200	3000
Death by Hektor	ART	ART/HS/MP/A-17	1979	ENG	12 X 19	R/BFK	35	1	200	3000

JAMES HAYWARD

BORN: San Francisco, CA; September 22, 1943
EDUCATION: San Diego State Univ, CA, BA; Univ of California, Los Angeles, CA; Univ of Washington, Seattle, WA, MFA
TEACHING: Instr, Painting, Univ of California, Berkeley, CA, 1983
AWARDS: New Talent, Los Angeles County Mus, CA, 1977; Japan-US Friendship Comm Fel, 1981–82; Guggenheim Fel, NY, 1983–84
RECENT EXHIB: Ace Gallery, Los Angeles, CA, 1991
COLLECTIONS: Los Angeles County Mus, CA; San Francisco Mus of Mod Art, CA
PRINTERS: Camilla Sullivan, Boston, MA (CS); Genovese Graphics, Boston, MA (GenG)
PUBLISHERS: Genovese Graphics, Boston, MA (GenG)
GALLERIES: Modernism, San Francisco, CA; Mizuno Gallery, Los Angeles, CA; M-13 Gallery, New York, NY; Genovese Gallery, Boston, MA; Ace Gallery, Los Angeles, CA
MAILING ADDRESS: 12241 Broadway Rd, Moorpark, CA 93021

TITLE	PUBLISHER	PRINTER	DATE	MEDIUM	DIMENSION (PAPER SIZE) IN INCHES	TYPE OF PAPER	EDITION NUMBER	NO. OF COLORS	ORIGINAL OPENING PRICE	CURRENT RETAIL PRICE
CURRENT EDITIONS:										
Red, Yellow, Blue (Series of 6)	GenG	CS/GenG	1986	SP	22 X 30 EA	HANGA	15 EA		4000 SET 800 EA	4250 SET 850 EA

PETER HEARD

BORN: London, England; December 3, 1939
RECENT EXHIB: Portal Gallery, London, England, 1989
PRINTERS: Chelsea Art Press, London, England (CAP); Pefiar Printing Workshop, Israel (PPW)
PUBLISHERS: Flanagan Graphics, Linwood, NJ (FG)
GALLERIES: Portal Gallery, London, England; Jerry Horn Gallery, Pittsburgh, PA; Central Square Fine Arts, Linewood, NJ; Wentworth Galleries, Nationwide; Renjeau Gallery, Natick, MA; Lake Falls Gallery, Baltimore, MD; Steve Stein Gallery, Sherman Oaks, CA

TITLE	PUBLISHER	PRINTER	DATE	MEDIUM	DIMENSION (PAPER SIZE) IN INCHES	TYPE OF PAPER	EDITION NUMBER	NO. OF COLORS	ORIGINAL OPENING PRICE	CURRENT RETAIL PRICE
CURRENT EDITIONS:										
Another Missed Tiddler	FG	CAP	1988	SP	34 X 29	AP	300	40	550	650
Mixed Doubles	FG	CAP	1989	SP	34 X 28	AP	300	40	550	650
Leander Blues?	FG	CAP	1989	SP	34 X 29	AP	300	35	550	650
Sea Breeze	FG	CAP	1989	SP	28 X 24	AP	300	35	450	550
The Kings Arms	FG	PPW	1990	SP	30 X 22	AP	300	35	450	550
Chucks Away	FG	CAP	1991	SP	28 X 24	AP	300	40	450	550

MILTON ELTING HEBALD

BORN: New York, NY; May 24, 1917
EDUCATION: Nat Acad, NY, 1931–32; Beaux Arts Inst, NY, 1932–35; Art Students League, NY, 1927–28
TEACHING: Brooklyn Mus Art Sch, NY, 1948–54; Cooper Union, NY, 1948–55
AWARDS: Prix de Rome, Italy, Sculpture, 1955–59
COLLECTIONS: Whitney Mus of Am Art, NY; Mus of Mod Art, NY; Philadelphia Mus, PA; Yale Univ, New Haven, CT; Acad of Arts & Letters, NY
PUBLISHERS: Alberto Caprini, Rome, Italy (AC); Touchtone Publishers, Ltd, NY (TPL); Il Torcoliere, Rome, Italy (TOR)
PRINTERS: Il Torcoliere, Rome, Italy (TOR); Alberto Caprini, Rome, Italy (AC)
GALLERIES: Harmon-Meek Gallery, Naples, FL; Heritage Gallery, Los Angeles, CA
MAILING ADDRESS: 840 20th St, Santa Monica, CA 90401; Via Santa Celso 22, Bracciano, Italy 00062

Milton Hebald
Oedipus
Courtesy the Artist

TITLE	PUBLISHER	PRINTER	DATE	MEDIUM	DIMENSION (PAPER SIZE) IN INCHES	TYPE OF PAPER	EDITION NUMBER	NO. OF COLORS	ORIGINAL OPENING PRICE	CURRENT RETAIL PRICE
SOLD OUT EDITIONS (RARE):										
An Alphabestiary (Set of 26) (with Poems by John Ciardi)	TPL	TOR	1963	LC	24 X 14 EA	AP	100 EA	1–2 EA	350 SET	1500 SET
Watchfull Lions I	TOR	TOR	1963	LC	22 X 20	AP	100	2	50	200
From the Ruins	AC	AC	1966	LB	20 X 27	AP	30	1	100	400
Poster Mickelson Gallery, Washington	TOR	TOR	1966	LC	22 X 20	AP	100	3	100	300
Dancing Family	AC	AC	1973	LB	28 X 20	AP	100	1	100	200
CURRENT EDITIONS:										
Watchful Lions II	TOR	TOR	1963	LC	28 X 20	AP	50	2	75	300
Susanna and the Elders	TOR	TOR	1963	LC	27 X 20	AP	30	2	200	600
Three Graces	TOR	TOR	1963	LC	28 X 20	AP	50	3	200	500
Spanish Dancers	TOR	TOR	1963	LB	27 X 20	AP	40	1	50	300
A Clodion	TOR	TOR	1963	LC	28 X 20	AP	25	2	75	400
Oedipus	TOR	TOR	1963	LC	20 X 27	AP	25	2	100	500
Frieze	TOR	TOR	1963	LC	27 X 20	AP	33	2	80	400
Siamese Family	TOR	TOR	1963	LC	19 X 18	AP	20	2	75	400
Rape of the Sabines	TOR	TOR	1963	LC	27 X 19	AP	20	2	100	400
Civic Justice	TOR	TOR	1963	LC	27 X 28	AP	60	2	150	400
Figures without Weight I	TOR	TOR	1966	LC	28 X 20	AP	30	2	150	400
Nature and the Child	TOR	TOR	1970	LB	16 X 14	AP	30	1	50	200
Figures without Weight II	AC	AC	1971	LC	28 X 20	AP	30	2	150	400
Ring Around the Roses	AC	AC	1975	LC	28 X 22	AP	250	3	25	200

WILLY HEEKS

BORN: Providence, RI; April, 28, 1951
EDUCATION: Univ of Rhode Island, Providence, RI, BFA, 1973; Whitney Mus of Am Art, Independent Study Prog, 1973
AWARDS: Yaddo Fel, Visual Arts, Saratoga Sprins, NY, 1980,84; Harriet & Esteban Vicente Fel, Painting, 1984; Louis Comfort Tiffany Award, 1985; Am Acad & Inst of Arts & Letters, NY, 1989; Nat Endowment for the Arts Fel, 1978,87,89
RECENT EXHIB: McNeil Gallery, Phila, PA, 1988; Gallerie Barbara Farber, Amsterdam, The Netherlands, 1987,89; Trans Avant Garde Gallery, Austin, TX, 1989; Boston Mus of Fine Arts, MA, 1990; David Beitzel Gallery, NY, 1987,88,90; Rena Bransten Gallery, San Francisco, CA, 1989,90; Nelson-Atkins Mus of Art, Kansas City, MO, 1990–91
COLLECTIONS: Middle Tennessee State Univ, Murfreesboro, TN; Univ of Rhode Island, Kingston, RI
PRINTERS: Artist (ART); Jon Cone, East Topsham, VT (JC); Cone Editions, East Topsham, VT (CEd); Judith Solodkin, NY (JS); Solo Press, NY (SP)
PUBLISHERS: Cone Editions, East Topsham, VT; Solo Press, NY (SP)
GALLERIES: David Beitzel Gallery, New York, NY; Gallerie Barbara Farber, Amsterdam, The Netherlands; Rena Bransten Gallery, San Francisco, CA; Cumberland Gallery, Nashville, TN; Cone Editions, East Topsham, VT; Solo Gallery, New York, NY; Experimental Workshop, San Francisco, Ca; Nielsen Gallery, Boston, MA

TITLE	PUBLISHER	PRINTER	DATE	MEDIUM	DIMENSION (PAPER SIZE) IN INCHES	TYPE OF PAPER	EDITION NUMBER	NO. OF COLORS	ORIGINAL OPENING PRICE	CURRENT RETAIL PRICE
CURRENT EDITIONS:										
Untitled	CEd	JC/CEd	1988	SP/DPT	30 X 22	R/BFK	35	9	1000	1200
Atlantic (One)	CEd	JC/CEd	1988	SP/EC	22 X 30	R/BFK	35		1000	1200
Affirming Flame	CEd	JC/CEd	1988	SP/EC	30 X 22	R/BFK	35		750	900
Blue Branch	SP	JS/SP	1992	MON	24 X 22 EA	HMP	1 EA	Varies	2500 EA	2500 EA

WILLY HEEKS CONTINUED

TITLE	PUBLISHER	PRINTER	DATE	MEDIUM	DIMENSION (PAPER SIZE) IN INCHES	TYPE OF PAPER	EDITION NUMBER	NO. OF COLORS	ORIGINAL OPENING PRICE	CURRENT RETAIL PRICE
CURRENT EDITIONS:										
China Door	SP	JS/SP	1992	MON	24 X 22 EA	HMP	1 EA	Varies	2500 EA	2500 EA
Inner Logic	SP	JS/SP	1992	MON	22 X 24 EA	HMP	1 EA	Varies	2500 EA	2500 EA
La Tern	SP	JS/SP	1992	MON	22 X 24 EA	HMP	1 EA	Varies	2500 EA	2500 EA
View	SP	JS/SP	1992	MON	22 X 24 EA	HMP	1 EA	Varies	2500 EA	2500 EA

MARY HEILMANN

BORN: San Francisco, CA; 1940
RECENT EXHIB: Gallery Mukai, Tokyo, Japan, 1988; Fuller Gross Gallery, San Francisco, CA, 1990; Inst of Contemp Art, Boston, MA, 1990; Robin Lockett Gallery, Chicago, IL, 1990; Galerie Isabella Kacprzak, Cologne, Germany, 1990; Green Gallery, Bay Harbor Islands, FL, 1991; Pat Hearn Gallery, NY, 1987,88,89,91

PRINTERS: Joe Wilfer, NY (JW); Ruth Lingen, NY (RL); Julie D'Amario, NY (JDA); Bill Hall, NY (BH); Kathy Kuehn, NY (KK); Spring Street Workshop, NY (SprSW)
PUBLISHERS: Spring Street Workshop, NY (SprSW)
GALLERIES: Pace Prints, New York, NY; Pat Hearn Gallery, New York, NY; Green Gallery, Bay Harbor Islands, FL; Robin Lockett Gallery, Chicago, IL

TITLE	PUBLISHER	PRINTER	DATE	MEDIUM	DIMENSION (PAPER SIZE) IN INCHES	TYPE OF PAPER	EDITION NUMBER	NO. OF COLORS	ORIGINAL OPENING PRICE	CURRENT RETAIL PRICE
CURRENT EDITIONS:										
Untitled (Set of 4):									2500 SET	2500 SET
Cut	SprSW	SW/RL/SprSW	1990	EB	16 X 12	HMP	30	1	750	750
Touch	SprSW	SW/RL/SprSW	1990	EB	16 X 12	HMP	30	1	750	750
Kiss	SprSW	SW/RL/SprSW	1990	EB	16 X 12	HMP	30	1	750	750
Valentine	SprSW	SW/RL/SprSW	1990	EB	16 X 12	HMP	30	1	750	750
Untitled (Set of 3):									2500 SET	2500 SET
Rincon	SprSW	SW/RL/SprSW	1990	EB	20 X 20	HMP	30	1	900	900
House	SprSW	SW/RL/SprSW	1990	EB	20 X 20	HMP	30	1	900	900
White Water	SprSW	SW/RL/SprSW	1990	EB	20 X 20	HMP	30	1	900	900
Crackle Suite (Set of 4):									3000 SET	3000 SET
Violet Crackle	SprSW	JW/RL/SprSW	1991	EB	18 X 18	HMP	30	1	900	900
Yellow Crackle	SprSW	JW/RL/SprSW	1991	EB	18 X 18	HMP	30	1	900	900
Blue Crackle	SprSW	JW/RL/SprSW	1991	EB	18 X 18	HMP	30	1	900	900
Double Red Crackle	SprSW	JW/RL/SprSW	1991	EB	18 X 18	HMP	30	1	900	900
All Night Movie	SprSW	JDA/BH/KK/SprSW	1991	EB	20 X 20	DCBP	30	1	900	900

MICHAEL HEINDORFF

BORN: Germany; 1949
EDUCATION: Univ of Braunschweig, Germany, 1970–74; Royal Col of Art, London, England, 1975–77
AWARDS: Schmidt-Rotluff Prize (German Prix de Rome), 1984
RECENT EXHIB: Bernard Jacobson Gallery, Los Angeles, CA, 1987

COLLECTIONS: Mus of Mod Art, NY; Victoria Albert Mus, London, England; Liverpool Univ, England; Arts Council of Great Britain; Herzog Anton Ulrich Mus, Braunschweig, Germany; Tate Gallery of Art, London, England
PRINTERS: Nick Tite (NT); Alan Cox (AC); Kevin Jackson (KJ); Richard Michel (RM); Silver Lake Press, London, England (SLP); Jack Shirreff, London, England (JS)
PUBLISHERS: Bernard Jacobson Ltd, London, England (BJL)
GALLERIES: Marsha Mateyka Gallery, Wash, DC; Dolly Fiterman Gallery, Minneapolis, MN

TITLE	PUBLISHER	PRINTER	DATE	MEDIUM	DIMENSION (PAPER SIZE) IN INCHES	TYPE OF PAPER	EDITION NUMBER	NO. OF COLORS	ORIGINAL OPENING PRICE	CURRENT RETAIL PRICE
SOLD OUT EDITIONS (RARE):										
Interior at Evelyn Gardens (Set of 5)	BJL	NT	1977	EB	15 X 12 EA	RKB	25 EA	1 EA	60 EA	900 EA
CURRENT EDITIONS:										
Interrogation (Set of 3)	BJL	AC	1978	LC	33 X 28 EA	R/BFK	30 EA	4 EA	200 EA	600 EA
Untitled (Set of 4)	BJL	KJ	1979	EB	19 X 23 EA	RKB	40 EA	1 EA	100 EA	400 EA
For SC (Set of 3)	BJL	KJ	1979	EB	19 X 23 EA	RKB	40 EA	1 EA	100 EA	400 EA
Affirmations (Set of 10)	BJL	RM	1980	EB	28 X 38 EA	RKB	30 EA	1 EA	1500 SET	6000 SET
Untitled (Set of 5)	BJL	AC	1981	LB/CC	23 X 30 EA	AP/JAP/T	20 EA	1 EA	200 EA	600 EA
Suitcases (Set of 3)	BJL	RM	1982	LB/CC	15 X 20 EA	AP/JAP/T	50 EA	1 EA	250 EA	400 EA
Huntington Library Gardens (Set of 6):										
Jungle I,II,III	BJL	SLP	1982	EB/HC	36 X 48 EA	AP	40 EA	1 EA	1500 EA	1800 EA
Elizabethan Garden	BJL	SLP	1982	EB/HC	36 X 48	AP	40	1	1500	1800
Coast Live Oak	BJL	SLP	1982	EB/HC	36 X 48	AP	40	1	2000	2250
Pan	BJL	SLP	1982	EB/HC	36 X 48	AP	40	1	1500	1800
Trout I	BJL	JS	1982	CAR	30 X 42	AP	50	8	750	1000
Lobster I	BJL	JS	1982	CAR	30 X 42	AP	50	16	750	1000
Rhine Etchings (Set of 4):										
Laacher Sea	BJL	JS	1982	CAR	36 X 48	AP	50	16	1200	2250
Katz	BJL	JS	1982	CAR	36 X 48	AP	50	16	1200	2250
Burresheim	BJL	JS	1982	CAR	36 X 48	AP	50	16	1200	2250
Linz	BJL	JS	1982	CAR	36 X 48	AP	50	16	1200	2250

MICHAEL HEINDORFF CONTINUED

TITLE	PUBLISHER	PRINTER	DATE	MEDIUM	DIMENSION (PAPER SIZE) IN INCHES	TYPE OF PAPER	EDITION NUMBER	NO. OF COLORS	ORIGINAL OPENING PRICE	CURRENT RETAIL PRICE
CURRENT EDITIONS:										
England Landscapes (Set of 4):										
Chiltern Hills	BJL	JS	1983	CAR	36 X 48	AP	35	16	1500	1800
Apollo	BJL	JS	1983	CAR	36 X 48	AP	35	16	1500	1800
Dashwood House	BJL	JS	1983	CAR	36 X 48	AP	35	16	1500	1800
Mausoleum	BJL	JS	1983	CAR	36 X 48	AP	35	16	1500	1800

MICHAEL HEIZER

BORN: Berkeley, CA; 1944
EDUCATION: San Francisco Art Inst, CA, 1963–64
RECENT EXHIB: M Knoedler & Co, NY, 1990; Art Center, Col of Design, Pasadena, CA, 1987,92; Univ of Nebraska, Sheldon Mem Art Gallery, Lincoln, NE, 1992
PRINTERS: Gemini GEL, Los Angeles, CA (GEM); Tyler Graphics, Mount Kisco, NY (TGL); B Fiske, NY (BF); R Konopaki (RK); Houston Fine Art Press, TX (HFAP); Achenbach Art Editions, Düsseldorf, Germany (AAE); Jean-Paul Russell, Durham, PA (JPR); Durham Press, Durham, PA (DurPr)
PUBLISHERS: Gemini GEL, Los Angeles, CA (GEM); Tyler Graphics, Mount Kisco, NY (TGL); Hines, Inc, San Francisco, CA (HI); Achenbach Art Edition, Düsseldorf, Germany (AAE); Durham Press, Durham, PA (DurPr)
GALLERIES: Richard Hines Gallery, Seattle, WA; Hill Gallery, Birmingham, MI; Barbara Krakow Gallery, Boston, MA; Tony Shafrazi Gallery, New York, NY; Gemini GEL, Los Angeles, CA; Fred Hoffman Gallery, Santa Monica, CA; Ochi Galleries, Boise, ID & Sun Valley ID; Tyler Graphics, Ltd, Mount Kisco, NY; Edward Tyler Nahem Fine Art, New York, NY; Pace Prints, New York, NY; M Knoedler & Company, New York, NY

Michael Heizer
Dragged Mass Diametric
Courtesy Edition Schellmann

TITLE	PUBLISHER	PRINTER	DATE	MEDIUM	DIMENSION (PAPER SIZE) IN INCHES	TYPE OF PAPER	EDITION NUMBER	NO. OF COLORS	ORIGINAL OPENING PRICE	CURRENT RETAIL PRICE
SOLD OUT EDITIONS (RARE):										
Circle III	TGL	TGL	1977	EB/A	41 X 31	HMP	14	1	500	2500
Scrap Metal Drypoint #1	GEM	GEM	1978	DPT	36 X 85	HMP	15	1	800	4000
Scrap Metal Drypoint #4	GEM	GEM	1978	DPT	36 X 85	HMP	14	1	800	4000
CURRENT EDITIONS:										
Circle Series (Set of 4):										
Circle I	TGL	TGL	1977	EB/A	41 X 31	HMP	6	1	400	2500
Circle II	TGL	TGL	1977	LC	41 X 31	HMP	21	1	450	2500
Circle IV	TGL	TGL	1977	LC	37 X 31	R/BFK	15	5	450	3000
Scrap Metal Drypoints:										
Scrap Metal Drypoint #2	GEM	GEM	1978	DPT	36 X 85	HMP	20	1	800	4000
Scrap Metal Drypoint #3	GEM	GEM	1978	DPT	36 X 85	HMP	20	1	800	4000
Scrap Metal Drypoint #5	GEM	GEM	1978	DPT	36 X 85	HMP	12	1	800	4000
Scrap Metal Drypoint #6	GEM	GEM	1978	DPT	36 X 85	HMP	20	1	800	4000
Untitled Collages (Series of 24)	TGL	TGL	1979	LC/SP/CO	30 X 30 EA	AC/R-BFK/R-100	1 EA	Varies	1000 EA	3000 EA
Monotypes (with Rubber Stamping, Drawing & Painting by the Artist)										
Single Sheets	TGL	TGL	1979	MON	24 X 32 to 29 X 37	TGL/HMP	1 EA		1800 EA	2500/ 4500 EA
Diptychs	TGL	TGL	1979	MON	26 X 47 EA	TGL/HMP	1 EA			5000 EA

MICHAEL HEIZER CONTINUED

TITLE	PUBLISHER	PRINTER	DATE	MEDIUM	DIMENSION (PAPER SIZE) IN INCHES	TYPE OF PAPER	EDITION NUMBER	NO. OF COLORS	ORIGINAL OPENING PRICE	CURRENT RETAIL PRICE
CURRENT EDITIONS:										
Levitated Mass	TGL	TGL	1983	LC/SP/EB	32 X 47	TGL/HMP	40	24	1200	2500
Dragged Mass	TGL	TGL	1983	LC/SP/EB	32 X 47	TGL/HMP	40	19	1200	2500
40°, 90°, 180° (with Rubber Stamping	TGL	TGL	1983	LC/SP/EB	32 X 47	TGL/HMP	40	16	1200	4500
Swiss Survey Series:										
Swiss Survey #1	GEM	GEM	1984	LC/SP/OFF	34 X 53	HMP	34	14	700	1500
Swiss Survey #2	GEM	GEM	1984	LC/SP/OFF	31 X 53	HMP	23	15	700	1500
Swiss Survey #3	GEM	GEM	1984	LC/SP/OFF	42 X 39	HMP	29	1	700	1500
Montana Survey Series:										
Montana Survey #1	GEM	GEM	1985	EC/PH/DPT	16 X 15	HMP	42	2	300	800
Montana Survey #2	GEM	GEM	1985	EC/PH/DPT	16 X 15	HMP	50	2	300	800
Montana Survey #3	GEM	GEM	1985	EC/PH/DPT	16 X 15	HMP	55	2	300	800
Vertical Displacement	GEM	GEM	1985	EC/DPT	29 X 35	HMP	45	1	400	900
Platform #1, #2, #3	GEM	GEM	1985	EC	50 X 65 EA	HMP	12 EA	1 EA	900 EA	1500 EA
Dragged Mass Geometric	AAE	AAE	1989	SP	140 X 257 CM	AP88	36	120	5000	6800
Offering I	DurPr	JPR/DurPr	1992	SP/EMB	108 X 36 X 4	WatPr	21	Varies	12000	12000

BRUCE HELANDER

BORN: Great Bend, KS; January 27, 1946
EDUCATION: Univ of Kansas, Col of Art, Lawrence, KS, 1964; Rhode Island Sch of Design, Providence, RI, BFA, 1969, MFA, 1972
TEACHING: Vis Art, Art Part, Lewiston, NY, 1975; Vis Art, North Miami Mus, FL, 1985; Vis Art, Vero Beach Mus, FL, 1986; Instr, Northwood Inst, West Palm Beach, FL, 1987; Vis Art, St Andrews Sch, Boca Raton, FL, 1988; Lectr, Painting, Inst of Am Indian Art, Santa Fe, NM, 1975 to present; Lectr, Design, Rhode Island Sch of Design, Providence, RI, 1971 to present
AWARDS: Purchase Prize, Providence Art Club, RI, 1971; Nat Endowment for the Arts Grant, 1974
RECENT EXHIB: O K Harris, South, Miami, FL, 1987; J P Natkin Gallery, NY, 1987; Littlejohn-Smith Gallery, NY, 1988; Shippee Gallery, NY, 1989; Virginia Lynch Gallery, Tiverton, RI, 1990; Carlo Lamagna Gallery, NY, 1990; Galerie Marine Namy-Caulier, Paris, France, 1993
COLLECTIONS: Hudson River Mus, Yonkers, NY; Danville Mus of Fine Arts, VA; Portland Art Mus, OR; Spencer Mus of Art, Lawrence, KS; Union Coun Col Mus, NJ; Mus of Art, Fort Lauderdale, FL; Albany Mus of Art, GA; Center for the Arts, Vero Beach, FL; Grand Rapids Art Mus, MI
PRINTERS: Brad Fain, London, England (BF); Coriander London, Ltd, London, England (COR)
PUBLISHERS: CM-2, Inc, New York, NY & Palm Beach, FL (CM2)
GALLERIES: Carlo Lamagna Gallery, New York, NY; Virginia Lynch Gallery, Tiverton, RI; Helander Gallery, Palm Beach, FL
MAILING ADDRESS: 151 Power St, Providence, RI 02906

TITLE	PUBLISHER	PRINTER	DATE	MEDIUM	DIMENSION (PAPER SIZE) IN INCHES	TYPE OF PAPER	EDITION NUMBER	NO. OF COLORS	ORIGINAL OPENING PRICE	CURRENT RETAIL PRICE
CURRENT EDITIONS:										
Storm Showers	CM2	BF/COR	1990	SP/CO	30 X 47	AP	250		950	1450
Rhode Island Red	CM2	BF/COR	1990	SP/CO	30 X 47	AP	250		950	1450

AL HELD

BORN: Brooklyn, NY; October 12, 1928
EDUCATION: Art Students League, NY; Acad de la Grande Chaumiere, Paris, France
TEACHING: Prof, Art, Yale Univ, New Haven, CT, 1962–78; Adj Prof, Painting, 1978 to present
AWARDS: Mr & Mrs Frank G Logan Medal, Art Inst of Chicago, IL, 1964; Guggenheim Found Fel, 1966; Jack I & Lillian L Posner Medal, Painting, Brandeis Univ Creative Arts Award, 1983
RECENT EXHIB: 650 Madison Avenue Gallery, NY, 1992; Andre Emmerich Gallery, NY, 1989,92; Allene Lapides Gallery, Santa Fe, NM, 1992
COLLECTIONS: Art Inst, Akron, OH; Brandeis Univ, Waltham, MA; Albright-Knox Art Gallery, Buffalo, NY; Art Inst, Dayton, OH; Mus of Mod Art, NY; San Francisco Mus of Mod Art, CA; Everson Mus, Syracuse, NY; Whitney Mus of Am Art, NY; Kunthalle, Basel, Switzerland; High Mus, Atlanta, GA; Hirshhorn Mus, Wash, DC; Metropolitan Mus of Art, NY; Kunsthaus, Zürich, Switzerland; Straatsgalerie, Stuttgart, Germany
PRINTERS: Mohammad Khalil, NY (MK); Crown Point Press, San Francisco, CA (CPP); Hidekatsu Takada (HT); Renée Bott (RB); Lawrence Hamlin (LH); Anita Heimbecker (AH); Mark Callen (MC); Nancy Anello, (NA); Deborah Feldman (DF); Brian Shure (BS); Daria Sywulak (DS); Sabina Klein, NY (SK); Tadashi Toda, Kyoto, Japan (TT)
PUBLISHERS: Pace Editions, NY (PE); Crown Point Press, San Francisco, CA (CPP)

Al Held
Pablo 7
Courtesy Crown Point Press

The print market has become very selective. For the first time since we published the first edition of The Printworld Directory in 1982, the prices of prints have been greatly reduced and greatly increased for the same artists by the most reputable and established print publishers. Check the fifth edition to understand the movement.

AL HELD CONTINUED

GALLERIES: André Emmerich Gallery, New York, NY; Pace Prints, New York, NY; Adler Gallery, Los Angeles, CA; Donald Morris Gallery, Birmingham, MI; Robert Miller Gallery, New York, NY; Crown Point Press, New York, & San Francisco, CA; Art Source, Los Angeles, CA; Manny Silverman Gallery, Los Angeles, CA; John Berggruen Gallery, San Francisco, CA; Ellen Erpf Miller, Newton, MA; Edward Tyler Nahem Fine Art, New York, NY; Allene Lapides Gallery, Santa Fe, NM
MAILING ADDRESS: 435 West Broadway, New York, NY 10012

TITLE	PUBLISHER	PRINTER	DATE	MEDIUM	DIMENSION (PAPER SIZE) IN INCHES	TYPE OF PAPER	EDITION NUMBER	NO. OF COLORS	ORIGINAL OPENING PRICE	CURRENT RETAIL PRICE
SOLD OUT EDITIONS (RARE):										
Untitled			1969	LC	35 X 30	AP	100		100	5000
Out and In	CPP	RB/LH/MC/CPP	1987	AC/SB/HG	41 X 53	SOM/S	50	45	3000	10000
Putu	CPP	RB/BS/MA/DS/DF/CPP	1989	EB/A	41 X 54	SOM/S	25	1	9500	10000
Almost There	CPP	RB/BS/NA/DS/CPP	1989	A/HG/DPT/ENG	37 X 29	SOM/S	60		4000	6500
CURRENT EDITIONS:										
Stone Ridge #1	PE	MK/SK	1983	EC	27 X 40	THS	65	17	1750	3000
Stone Ridge #2	PE	MK/SK	1983	EC	27 X 40	THS	65	17	1750	3000
Stone Ridge #3	PE	MK/SK	1983	EC	27 X 40	THS	65	17	1750	3000
Stone Ridge #4	PE	MK/SK	1983	EC	27 X 40	THS	65	17	1750	5000
Stone Ridge #5,#6,#7	PE	MK/SK	1984	EC	27 X 40 EA	THS	50 EA	17 EA	1800 EA	3000 EA
Stone Ridge #5,#6, States II	PE	MK/SK	1985	EB	27 X 40 EA	THS	20 EA	17 EA	2000 EA	4000 EA
Kyoto-Wa	CPP	RB/LH/CPP	1985	WC	27 X 40	THS	100	15	2200	4000
Oakland	CPP	RB/LH/CPP	1986	DPT	23 X 22	THS	25	1	900	1200
Pablo 7	CPP	HT/RB/NA/CPP	1986	EC	24 X 36	AP/WA	50	10	2200	3500
SF	CPP	RB/LH/CPP	1986	DPT	23 X 22	THS	25	1	900	1200
Straits of Magellan	CPP	RG/NA/LH/AH/CPP	1986	EB/HG	42 X 52	AP/WA	50	1	2800	5500
2 + 4	CPP	RL/LH/CPP	1987	EB	27 X 32	AP/WA	10	1	900	1000
Straits of Malacca	CPP	RB/LH/CPP	1987	EB	42 X 52	AP/WA	50	1	2800	5500
Straights of Malacca II	CPP	RB/BS/NA/CPP	1989	EB/HG	42 X 52	AP/WA	20	1	3500	6500
Russell's Way	CPP	RB/CPP	1989	AC	41 X 54	SOM/S	50		12000	10000
Pachinko	CPP	TT/CPP	1989–90	WC	26 X 34	KOZO	125	17	6500	6500
Indigo	CPP	CPP	1990	AC/SB	41 X 54	KOZO	50		8000	10000
Magenta	CPP	CPP	1990	AC/SB	41 X 54	KOZO	50		8000	10000
Straits of Pohai	CPP	CPP	1990	EB/HG	45 X 67	KOZO	50	1	6000	7000
Untitled (Black on White) (Set of 10)	PE		1973–90	SP	22 X 270 EA	HMP	10 EA	1 EA	20000 SET	20000 SET
Untitled (White on Black) (Set of 10)	PE		1973–90	SP	22 X 270 EA	HMP	10 EA	1 EA	20000 SET	20000 SET
Mark's Maze (Accordian Book)	SprSW	SprSW	1990	SP	7 X 90	AP	200		1000	1000
Scholes I, II	MMA	HN/WS	1991	SP	29 X 34 EA	AC	80 EA	38/58	3000 EA	3000 EA
The Space Between the Two	CPP	CPP	1992	AB/SB	50 X 41	AC	50	1	5500	5500
The Space Between the Two	CPP	CPP	1992	AB/SB	50 X 41	AC	50	1	5500	5500
Liv	CPP	CPP	1992	EB/A/HG	41 X 54	AC	50	1	6500	6500
Fly Away	CPP	CPP	1992	AB/SB	32 X 40	AC	50	1	2500	2500

JULES HELLER

BORN: New York, NY; November 16, 1919
EDUCATION: Arizona State Univ, Tempe, AZ, BA, 1939; Columbia Univ, NY, MA, 1940; Univ of Southern California, Los Angeles, CA, PhD, 1948
TEACHING: Prof, Printmaking, Univ of Southern California, Los Angeles, CA, 1946–61; Prof, Fine Arts, York Univ, Toronto, Can, 1972–76; Prof, Printmaking, Arizona State Univ, Tempe, AZ, 1976 to present
AWARDS: Canadian Council Grant, 1975; Doctor of Humane Letters, York Univ, Canada, 1985
COLLECTIONS: Allan R Hite Inst, Univ of Louisville, KY; Tamarind Inst, Univ of New Mexico, Albuquerque, NM; Toronto Dominion Centre, Can; Canadian Council Art Bank, York Univ, Can; York Univ, Can
PRINTERS: Smith Andersen Gallery, Palo Alto, CA (3EP); Sette Publishing Co, Tempe, AZ (SPC); Scorpio Press, Scottsdale, AZ (ScP)
PUBLISHERS: Smith Andersen Gallery, Palo Alto, CA
GALLERIES: Sette Gallery, Tempe, AZ; Smith Andersen Gallery, Palo Alto, CA
MAILING ADDRESS: 6838 E Cheney Rd, Scottsdale, AZ 85253

TITLE	PUBLISHER	PRINTER	DATE	MEDIUM	DIMENSION (PAPER SIZE) IN INCHES	TYPE OF PAPER	EDITION NUMBER	NO. OF COLORS	ORIGINAL OPENING PRICE	CURRENT RETAIL PRICE
CURRENT EDITIONS:										
Icarus Series	ScP	SPC	1983	MON	22 X 30 EA	AP88	1 EA	Varies	600 EA	1000 EA
Icarus Series	ScP	SPC	1983	MON	30 X 42 EA	AP88	1 EA	Varies	1000 EA	1400 EA
Dancers Series	ScP	SPC	1984	MON	22 X 30 EA	AP88	1 EA	Varies	600 EA	1000 EA
Dancers Series	ScP	SPC	1984	MON	30 X 42 EA	AP88	1 EA	Varies	1000 EA	1400 EA
Critter Series	ScP	SPC	1985	MON	22 X 30 EA	AP88	1 EA	Varies	600 EA	1000 EA
Critter Series	ScP	SPC	1985	MON	30 X 42 EA	AP88	1 EA	Varies	1000 EA	1400 EA

INARS HELMUTS

BORN: Riga, Latvia, USSR; 1934
EDUCATION: Latvian Acad of Art, Riga, Latvia, 1958–63
AWARDS: Int Graphic Biennale Award, Cracow, Poland, 1974; First Prize, Tallinn Triennalle, Russia, 1974
PRINTERS: Artist (ART)
PUBLISHERS: Russian International, Ltd, Sewickley, PA (RI)
GALLERIES: USSR Union of Artists, Moscow, Russia, USSR; Russian International Ltd, Sewickley, PA

INARS HELMUTS CONTINUED

TITLE	PUBLISHER	PRINTER	DATE	MEDIUM	DIMENSION (PAPER SIZE) IN INCHES	TYPE OF PAPER	EDITION NUMBER	NO. OF COLORS	ORIGINAL OPENING PRICE	CURRENT RETAIL PRICE
CURRENT EDITIONS:										
Start	RI	ART	1971	EC	20 X 25	LP	7	5	350	500
The Shift	RI	ART	1972	EC	25 X 30	LP	100	5	285	450
Still Life By the Sea	RI	ART	1972	LI/SP	20 X 24	LP	10	5	395	500
The Boats	RI	ART	1973	LI/SP	20 X 24	LP	25	5	285	400
Steel	RI	ART	1973	EC	24 X 31	LP	100	5	340	500
Flight (from Rhythm of Our Days)	RI	ART	1973	EC	19 X 25	LP	15	5	550	700
Old Riga	RI	ART	1974	EC	19 X 25	LP	15	3	480	600
Nuclear Reactor	RI	ART	1975	EC	20 X 25	LP	15	5	300	400
Circus	RI	ART	1975	EC	20 X 25	LP	15	5	350	450
Sea Wind	RI	ART	1975	LI/SP	20 X 26	LP	20	5	350	450
Acrobats (From Circus)	RI	ART	1975	EC	20 X 24	LP	20	5	385	450
Cosmonauts	RI	ART	1976	EC	20 X 25	LP	20	5	300	350
The Countdown	RI	ART	1976	EC	19 X 25	LP	20	4	350	400
Habitat	RI	ART	1978	EC	20 X 25	LP	25	5	450	500
Before the Start	RI	ART	1979	EC	20 X 25	LP	15	5	350	400
On the Wave	RI	ART	1979	LI/SP	20 X 25	LP	20	5	300	350
On the Beach	RI	ART	1979	LI/SP	14 X 27	LP	20	5	350	400
Limbazhi	RI	ART	1980	EC	18 X 24	LP	20	5	350	400

EDWARD HENDERSON

BORN: Connecticut; 1951
AWARDS: Guggenheim Mem Found Fel, NY, 1988; Nat Endowment for the Arts Grant, Wash, DC, 1989
RECENT EXHIB: Janie C Lee Gallery, Houston, TX, 1987; James Corcoran Gallery, Los Angeles, CA, 1987; Univ of Northern Iowa, Cedar Falls, IA, 1992
COLLECTIONS: Walker Art Center, Minneapolis, MN; Cleveland Center of Contemp Art, OH; Museo Tamayo, Mexico; Mus of Fine Arts, Boston, MA
PRINTERS: Aldo Crommelynck, NY (AC); Atelier Crommelynck, NY (AtC); Tamarind Inst, Albuquerque, NM (TI); Ko Muto, Kyoto, Japan (KM); Hiroyuki Taguchi, Kyoto, Japan (TK); Yamanaka Fine Arts Center, Kyoto, Japan (YFAC)
PUBLISHERS: Aldo Crommelynck, NY (AC); Tamarind Inst, Albuquerque, NM (TI); Yamanaka Fine Arts Center, Kyoto, Japan (YFAC)
GALLERIES: Pace Prints, New York, NY; Zolla/Lieberman Gallery, Chicago, IL; Tamarind Inst, Albuquerque, NM; Janie C Lee Gallery, Houston, TX; James Corcoran Gallery, Los Angeles, CA

TITLE	PUBLISHER	PRINTER	DATE	MEDIUM	DIMENSION (PAPER SIZE) IN INCHES	TYPE OF PAPER	EDITION NUMBER	NO. OF COLORS	ORIGINAL OPENING PRICE	CURRENT RETAIL PRICE
CURRENT EDITIONS:										
Untitled	AC	AC/AtC	1989	EB/A	16 X 18	R/BFK	55		850	850
Untitled	AC	AC/AtC	1991	EB/A	37 X 29	R/BFK	50		1000	1000
House Safe	YFAC	KM/HT/YFAC	1993	LC	15 X 19	R/BFK	68		400	400

CHAM HENDON

BORN: Birmingham, AL; 1936
EDUCATION: Sch of Art Inst of Chicago, IL, BFA, 1963; Univ of New Mexico, Albuquerque, NM, MA, 1965; Univ of Wisconsin, Madison, WI, MFA, 1977
TEACHING: Vis Artist, Mankato State Univ, MN, 1982; Vis Artist, Univ of Wisconsin, Madison, WI, 1984; Vis Artist, Virginia Commonwealth Univ, Richmond, VA, 1986
RECENT EXHIB: Univ of Alabama, Moody Gallery, Tuscaloosa, AL, 1992; Univ of North Iowa, Cedar Falls, IA, 1992; Phyllis Kind Gallery, NY, 1987,92
COLLECTIONS: Birmingham Mus of Art, AL; City Col of New York, NY; Madison Art Center, WI; Metropolitan Mus of Art, NY; New York State Univ, Neuberger Mus, Purchase, NY; Princeton Univ, NJ
PRINTERS: Artist (ART); Bill Weege, Madison, WI (BW); Andrew Rubin, Madison, WI (AR); Tandem Press, Univ of Wisconsin, Madison, WI (TanPr)
PUBLISHERS: Tandem Press, Univ of Wisconsin, Madison, WI (TanPr)
GALLERIES: Phyllis Kind Galleries, New York, NY & Chicago, IL; Monty Stabler Galleries, Birmingham, AL

TITLE	PUBLISHER	PRINTER	DATE	MEDIUM	DIMENSION (PAPER SIZE) IN INCHES	TYPE OF PAPER	EDITION NUMBER	NO. OF COLORS	ORIGINAL OPENING PRICE	CURRENT RETAIL PRICE
CURRENT EDITIONS:										
Musings (with Acrylic Wash) (Trip)	TanPr	ART/BW/ AR/TanPr	1987	WC/REL	44 X 30 EA	STP/W-AC/G	36	Varies	3000 SET 1200 EA	3000 SET 1200 EA

BARBARA HEPWORTH

BORN: Wakefield, Yorkshire, England; (1903-1975)
EDUCATION: Leeds Sch of Art, London, England; Royal Col of Art, London, England
RECENT EXHIB: Univ of California, Wight Art Mus Complex, Los Angeles, CA, 1988,92
COLLECTIONS: British Mus, London, England; Tate Gallery of Art, London, England; Victoria and Albert Mus, London, England; Detroit Inst of Art, MI
PUBLISHERS: Marlborough Graphics, Inc, NY (MG)
GALLERIES: Marlborough Graphics, Inc, New York, NY; Feingarten Galleries, Los Angeles, CA; Gimpel & Weitzenhoffer Gallery, New York, NY; Hirschl & Adler Modern, New York, NY; Sigrid Freundorfer Fine Art, New York, NY; Pasquale Iannetti Art Galleries, New York, NY

BARBARA HEPWORTH CONTINUED

TITLE	PUBLISHER	PRINTER	DATE	MEDIUM	DIMENSION (PAPER SIZE) IN INCHES	TYPE OF PAPER	EDITION NUMBER	NO. OF COLORS	ORIGINAL OPENING PRICE	CURRENT RETAIL PRICE
SOLD OUT EDITIONS (RARE):										
Assembly of Square Forms	MG		1970	SP	31 X 23	AP	60		250	1800
December Forms	MG		1970	SP	31 X 23	AP	60		250	1800
Forms in a Flurry	MG		1970	SP	31 X 23	AP	60		250	1800
High Tide	MG		1970	SP	23 X 31	AP	60		250	1800
November Green	MG		1970	SP	31 X 23	AP	60		250	1800
Orchid	MG		1970	SP	31 X 23	AP	60		250	1800
Rangatira I	MG		1970	SP	31 X 23	AP	60		250	2700
Rangatira II	MG		1970	SP	31 X 23	AP	60		250	1800
Three forms	MG		1970	SP	31 X 23	AP	60		250	1800
Two Ancestral Figures	MG		1970	SP	31 X 23	AP	60		250	1800
Opposing Forms (Set of 12)	MG		1970	SP	31 X 23 EA	AP	60 EA		2700 SET 250 EA	20000 SET 1800 EA

PHYLLIS HERFIELD

BORN: Staten Island, NY; December 6, 1947
EDUCATION: Art Students League, NY, 1964–65; Tyler Sch of Art, Rome, Italy, 1957–68; Temple Univ, Tyler Sch of Art, Phila, PA, BFA, 1969; Nat Acad of Fine Arts, NY, 1979–80
AWARDS: Edward Mooney Traveling Scholarship, Nat Acad Sch of Fine Arts, 1981; Prize, Julius Hallgarten Award, Nat Acad of Design, NY, 1981
RECENT EXHIB: Parkerson Gallery, Houston, TX, 1987; Hanson Gallery, Los Angeles, CA, 1988; Helander Galleries, NY, 1991; O K Harris Works of Art, NY, 1991; Helander Galleries, Palm Beach, FL, 1992
COLLECTIONS: Mus of Mod Art, NY; Metropolitan Mus of Art, NY; Hunter Col, NY; Brooklyn Acad of Music, NY
PRINTERS: Mohamed Khalil, NY (MK)
PUBLISHERS: Orion Editions NY (OE)
GALLERIES: Helander Galleries, New York, NY & Palm Beach, FL; O K Harris works of Art, New York, NY; Louis Stern Gallery, Beverly Hills, CA; Orion Editions, New York, NY; Salander-O'Reilly Galleries, New York, NY; Portraits, Inc, New York, NY
MAILING ADDRESS: P O Box 6366, 172 E 90th St, New York, NY 10128

TITLE	PUBLISHER	PRINTER	DATE	MEDIUM	DIMENSION (PAPER SIZE) IN INCHES	TYPE OF PAPER	EDITION NUMBER	NO. OF COLORS	ORIGINAL OPENING PRICE	CURRENT RETAIL PRICE
SOLD OUT EDITIONS (RARE):										
Frianium	OE	MK	1978	EC/HC	22 X 30	AP	65	AC	200	400

ALAN HERMAN

BORN: New York, NY; 1944
EDUCATION: Philadelphia Col of Art, Phila, PA, BFA, 1966; Tyler Sch of Art, Temple Univ, Phila, PA, MFA, 1968
PRINTERS: Patricia Branstead, NY (PB); Aeropress, NY (A)
PUBLISHERS: Diane Villani Editions, NY (DVE); Aeropress, NY (A)
GALLERIES: Betsy Magnuson Lee Gallery, Boston, MA; Roger Ramsay, Chicago, IL; Diane Villani Editions, New York, NY; Carl Solway Gallery, Cincinnati, OH

TITLE	PUBLISHER	PRINTER	DATE	MEDIUM	DIMENSION (PAPER SIZE) IN INCHES	TYPE OF PAPER	EDITION NUMBER	NO. OF COLORS	ORIGINAL OPENING PRICE	CURRENT RETAIL PRICE
CURRENT EDITIONS:										
Untitled (Pink Wall)	DVE/A	PB/A	1980	A/SB	22 X 30	AP	35	4	350	550
Untitled (Green Wall)	DVE/A	PB/A	1980	A/SB	22 X 30	AP	35	4	350	550

ROGER HERMAN

BORN: Saarbruchen, Saarland; November 21, 1947; German Citizen
EDUCATION: Kunstakademie Karlsruhe, MFA, 1979
TEACHING: Prof, Painting, Univ of California, LA, 1984 to present
AWARDS: New Talent Award, Los Angeles County Mus, CA, 1983
COLLECTIONS: Walker Art Center, Minneapolis, MN; Los Angeles County Mus of Art, Minneapolis, MN; San Francisco Mus of Art, CA; Newport Harbor Art Mus, Newport Beach, CA
PRINTERS: Artist (ART)
PUBLISHERS: Artist (ART)
GALLERIES: Gagosian Gallery, New York, NY; Hal Bromm Gallery, New York, NY
MAILING ADDRESS: 729 Academy Rd, Los Angeles, CA 90012

TITLE	PUBLISHER	PRINTER	DATE	MEDIUM	DIMENSION (PAPER SIZE) IN INCHES	TYPE OF PAPER	EDITION NUMBER	NO. OF COLORS	ORIGINAL OPENING PRICE	CURRENT RETAIL PRICE
SOLD OUT EDITIONS (RARE):										
Vincent Van Gogh (2 Sheets)	ART	ART	1983	WB	9 ft X 10 ft	BAR	3		3000	5000

MICHEL HERMEL

BORN: Paris, France, 1934
PRINTERS: American Atelier, NY (AA)
PUBLISHERS: Circle Fine Art, Chicago, IL (CFA)
GALLERIES: Circle Galleries, San Diego, CA & San Francisco, CA & Northbrook, IL & Pittsburgh, PA & Houston, TX & Soho, NY & Chicago, IL & Scottsdale, AZ & Beverly Hills, CA & Costa Mesa, CA & Sherman Oaks, CA & Palm Beach, FL & Honolulu, HI & New Orleans, LA & Las Vegas, NV & Seattle, WA

MICHEL HERMEL CONTINUED

TITLE	PUBLISHER	PRINTER	DATE	MEDIUM	DIMENSION (PAPER SIZE) IN INCHES	TYPE OF PAPER	EDITION NUMBER	NO. OF COLORS	ORIGINAL OPENING PRICE	CURRENT RETAIL PRICE
SOLD OUT EDITIONS (RARE):										
14th of July Ball	CFA	AA		LC	20 X 26	AP	200		125	325

LUIS HERNANDEZ-CRUZ

BORN: San Juan, Puerto Rico; October 17, 1936
EDUCATION: American Univ, Wash, DC, MA
TEACHING: Univ of Puerto Rico, PR, 1966 to present
PRINTERS: Artist (ART)
PUBLISHERS: Artist (ART)
GALLERIES: Galeria Botello I, San Juan, PR; Galeria Botello II, Hato Ray, PR; Meeting Point Art, Coral Gables, Miami, FL; Art Space/Virginia Miller Galleries, Coral Gables, FL; Galeria 2, Dorado, PR; Galeria San Juan, Old San Juan, PR; Galeria San Jeronimo, San Juan, PR; Galeria San Jeronimo, San Jeronimo, PR
MAILING ADDRESS: Patricia, 6, Susan Court, Guaynabo, PR 00657

TITLE	PUBLISHER	PRINTER	DATE	MEDIUM	DIMENSION (PAPER SIZE) IN INCHES	TYPE OF PAPER	EDITION NUMBER	NO. OF COLORS	ORIGINAL OPENING PRICE	CURRENT RETAIL PRICE
SOLD OUT EDITIONS (RARE):										
Momento de Huellas	ART	ART	1975	SP	29 X 23	AP	60	4	125	250
Puntal de Flechas	ART	ART	1975	SP	18 X 24	AP	60	5	100	250
CURRENT EDITIONS:										
Contra Campo Verde	ART	ART	1976	SP	18 X 24	AP	60	5	100	200
Contra Campa Mar-Fil	ART	ART	1976	SP	18 X 24	AP	60	5	100	200
Contra Campo Azul	ART	ART	1976	SP	18 X 24	AP	60	5	100	200
Planta e Insecto I,II,III	ART	ART	1979	SP	29 X 23 EA	AP	80 EA	6 EA	150 EA	300 EA
Sombra Anguelogia V	ART	ART	1979	SP	23 X 29	AP	80	7	150	300
Insectos	ART	ART	1980	SP	18 X 24	AP	80	6	125	300
Figura I,II	ART	ART	1980	SP	18 X 24 EA	AP	80 EA	6 EA	125 EA	200 EA
Compi con Dos Centros	ART	ART	1980	SP	26 X 18	AP	80	5	125	200
Compi en Amarillos	ART	ART	1980	SP	24 X 18	AP	80	6	125	200
Compi en Rojos	ART	ART	1980	SP	24 X 18	AP	80	6	125	300

PATRICK HERON

BORN: Leeds, London; January 30, 1920
EDUCATION: Slade Sch of Art, London, England
COLLECTIONS: Albright-Knox Art Gallery, Buffalo, NY; Toledo Mus of Art, Toledo, OH; Brooklyn Mus, NY; Toronto Art Gallery, Toronto, Can; Vancouver Art Gallery, Vancouver, Can; Power Coll, Sydney, Australia; Tate Gallery of Art, London, England; Arts Council of Great Britain, London, England
PRINTERS: Chris Prater, London, England (CP); Kelpra Studio, London, England (KS)
PUBLISHERS: Waddington Graphics, London, England (WG)
GALLERIES: Waddington Graphics, London, England

TITLE	PUBLISHER	PRINTER	DATE	MEDIUM	DIMENSION (PAPER SIZE) IN INCHES	TYPE OF PAPER	EDITION NUMBER	NO. OF COLORS	ORIGINAL OPENING PRICE	CURRENT RETAIL PRICE
SOLD OUT EDITIONS (RARE):										
Morning Reds-November 1979	WG	CP/KS	1980	EB/A	27 X 37	AP	50		270	1200
Blue Day Disc-December 1979	WG	CP/KS	1980	EB/A	27 X 37	AP	50		270	1200
Night Violet-January 1980	WG	CP/KS	1980	EB/A	27 X 37	AP	50		270	1200

NONA HERSHEY

BORN: New York, NY; October 31, 1946
EDUCATION: Tyler Sch of Art, Phila, PA, BFA, 1967; Tyler Sch of Art, Rome, Italy, MFA, 1969; Istituto Statale d'Arte di Urbino, Italy, 1979,80; Yoshida Hanga Acad, Tokyo, Japan, 1990
TEACHING: Asst Prof, Printmaking, Daemen Col, Buffalo, NY, 1972-73; Asst Prof, Printmaking, Temple Abroad, Rome, Italy, 1979-90; Assoc Prof, Drawing & Printmaking, Temple Univ Japan, Tokyo, Japan, 1990-91; Assoc Prof, Printmaking Wesleyan Univ, Middletown, CT, 1991-92
AWARDS: Purchase Awards, Davidson Nat Print & Drawing Comp, NC, 1973,75; Premio Lario, Como, Italy, 1981; Eastern US Print & Drawing Comp, NC, 1985; The MacDowell Colony, Peterborough, NH, 8-Week Residency, 1989; Ucross Found, Clearmont, WY, 6-Week Residency, 1990
RECENT EXHIB: Galleria Il Ponte, Rome, Italy, 1990
COLLECTIONS: Metropolitan Mus of Art, NY; Library of Congress, Wash, DC; Pennsylvania Acad of Fine Arts, Phila, PA; Civic Mus, Piacenza, Italy; Municipal Mus of Graphic Art, Caracas, Venezuela; Crakow Nat Mus, Poland; Yale Univ Art Gallery, New Haven, CT; Hunterdon Art Center, NJ; Graphic Inst, Latina, Italy; Barry Col, FL; Municipality of Cadorago, Italy; Municipal Library, Piacenza, Italy; Municipal Library, Como, Italy; Minnesota Mus, St Paul, MN; Davidson Col, NC; Skopje Mus of Contemp Art, Yugoslavia; Calcografia Nazionale, Rome, Italy; Utah State Univ, Logan, UT; Mint Mus, Charlotte, NC; Davison Art Center, Middletown, CT
PRINTERS: Stamperia 3K, Rome, Italy (S3K); Sannino, Rome, Italy (S); Bruno Bossetti, Rome, Italy (BB); Angelo Gabbanini, Rome, Italy (AG); Giancarlo Iacconucci, Rome, Italy (GI); Artist (ART)
PUBLISHERS: Il Ponte Editrice, Rome, Italy (IPE); Associated American Artists, New York, NY (AAA); Mary Ryan Gallery, NY (MRG); Artist (ART); Mezzanine Gallery, Metropolitan Mus of Art, NY (MMA)
GALLERIES: Associated American Artists, New York, NY; Galleria Il Ponte, Rome, Italy; Mary Ryan Gallery, New York, NY; Mezzanine Gallery, Metropolitan Mus of Art, New York, NY
MAILING ADDRESS: 301 Newport Road, Glen Gardner, NJ 08826

The retail prices of the 100,000 limited edition prints quoted in this directory are subject to change. Print publishers, artists and galleries were the direct sources for these quotations. Prices in the secondary market listed as "Sold Out Editions (Rare)" indicate that the publisher has a limited supply of that print or that the print is difficult to locate in the galleries.

NONA HERSHEY CONTINUED

TITLE	PUBLISHER	PRINTER	DATE	MEDIUM	DIMENSION (PAPER SIZE) IN INCHES	TYPE OF PAPER	EDITION NUMBER	NO. OF COLORS	ORIGINAL OPENING PRICE	CURRENT RETAIL PRICE
SOLD OUT EDITIONS (RARE):										
April	ART	ART	1980	I	14 X 17	PM	19	3	40	300
September 1980	ART	ART	1980	AB	24 X 31	PM	15	1	160	650
CURRENT EDITIONS:										
Finestre du Roma	IPE	S3K	1982	AC/SL	28 X 20	MAG	32	2	250	500
December 1982	ART	ART	1983	I	24 X 31	PM	20	1	175	500
July 1983-Shadows	ART	ART	1983	AC	24 X 31	PM	17	2	200	500
July 1983-Doorway I	ART	ART	1983	AC	24 X 31	PM	25	2	200	500
Suite	IPE	S3K	1985	I	27 X 78	MAG	30	1	650	1000
Quartet (4 Parts)	MRG	BB/AG/GI/S3K	1986	EB/A	24 X 77	MAG	20		1000	1100
Mirage I, II (Set of 2)	MRG	BB/AG/GI/S3K	1987	EB/A	56 X 27 EA	MAG	20 EA		1500 SET / 900 EA	1800 SET / 950 EA
Celebration	IPE/ART	AG/ART	1990	I	24 X 32	MAG	30	2	500	600

ANTON HEYBOER

PRINTERS: Artist, Den Ilp, The Netherlands (ART)
PUBLISHERS: Artist (ART)
GALLERIES: Kerr Gallery, New York, NY

TITLE	PUBLISHER	PRINTER	DATE	MEDIUM	DIMENSION (PAPER SIZE) IN INCHES	TYPE OF PAPER	EDITION NUMBER	NO. OF COLORS	ORIGINAL OPENING PRICE	CURRENT RETAIL PRICE
SOLD OUT EDITIONS (RARE):										
Mother and Daughter and Man 1-4 (Four Parts) (Unique)	ART	ART	1983	EB/HC/CO/DRAW	39 X 94	R/BFK	1	4+	6000	8000

LAWRENCE HEYMAN

BORN: Wash, DC; June 30, 1932
EDUCATION: Tyler Sch of Art, Phila, PA, BFA, 1954, BA, 1955; Atelier 17, Paris, France, S W Hayter, 1960–63, 1969–70; American Univ, Wash, DC, MFA, 1972
TEACHING: Instr, Printmaking, Rhode Island Sch of Design, Providence, RI, 1967–69; Lectr, Printmaking, Am Univ, Wash, DC, 1971–72; Asst Prof, Printmaking, Rhode Island Sch of Design, Providence, RI, 1972–79; Head, Printmaking, Rhode Island, Sch of Design, Providence, RI, 1976–79
AWARDS: Purchase Prize, Contemp Am Arts, DePaux Univ, Greencastle, IN, 1963; First Prize, Providence Art Club, RI 1974,76; Purchase Award, Bibliotheque Nat, Salon Le Trait, Paris, France, 1977; Nat Endowment for the Arts Award, 1987

RECENT EXHIB: Newport Art Mus, RI, 1988; Plum Gallery, Kensington, MD, 1989
COLLECTIONS: Bibliotheque Nat, Paris, France; St John's Univ, Collegeville, MN; Brooklyn Mus, NY; Univ of Maine, Portland, ME; Osaka Univ, Japan; Mankota State Univ, MN; Free Library, Phila, PA; Mus of the City of New York, NY; Brooks Mem Mus, Memphis, TN; Portland Art Mus, OR; American Mus, Wash, DC
PRINTERS: Artist (ART)
PUBLISHERS: Associated American Artists, NY (AAA); Judith Selkowitz Fine Arts, NY (JS); Antarés Éditions d'Art, Saint-Cloud, France (AE); Artist (ART)
GALLERIES: Wenniger Graphics, Boston, MA; Plum Gallery, Kensington, MD
MAILING ADDRESS: 182 Raleigh Ave, Pawtucket, RI 02860

TITLE	PUBLISHER	PRINTER	DATE	MEDIUM	DIMENSION (PAPER SIZE) IN INCHES	TYPE OF PAPER	EDITION NUMBER	NO. OF COLORS	ORIGINAL OPENING PRICE	CURRENT RETAIL PRICE
SOLD OUT EDITIONS (RARE):										
Seacoast	ART	ART	1961–62	IC	12 X 18	AP	95	6	90	350
Alpes-Maritimes	AAA	ART	1964	IC	16 X 20	AP	50	7	70	300
Summer Storm	AAA	ART	1968	IC	16 X 20	AP	100	6	60	300
Bridge	AAA	ART	1969	IC	16 X 20	AP	100	6	60	300
Raga du Soir	AE	ART	1970	IC	13 X 19	AP	135	6	90	350
Source	AE	ART	1971	IC	13 X 19	AP	135	6	90	250
Soleil	AE	ART	1971	IC	13 X 19	AP	135	5	90	250
Peacock	AE	ART	1972	IC	18 X 22	AP	60	6	90	400
CURRENT EDITIONS:										
Mother Cat	ART	ART	1962	IC	12 X 16	AP	45	5	45	250
Fog	ART	ART	1965	IC	10 X 11	AP	50	4	60	200
Running Boy	ART	ART	1967	IC	20 X 16	AP	35	6	50	250
Melting City	ART	ART	1971	IC	25 X 17	AP	25	5	70	250
Self-Taught	ART	ART	1975	IC	10 X 7	AP	20	4	40	150
Eye	ART	ART	1976	IC	24 X 18	AP	20	3	120	250
Sunset II	ART	ART	1976	IC	12 X 18	AP	50	6	120	250
Ephemera II	ART	ART	1976	IC	18 X 24	AP	50	5	130	300
Light Waves	ART	ART	1978–79	EC	18 X 24	AP	50	4	150	300
Canigou	ART	ART	1977–82	EC	24 X 33	AP	50	6	175	350

The retail prices of the 100,000 limited edition prints quoted in this directory are subject to change. Print publishers, artists and galleries were the direct sources for these quotations. Prices in the secondary market listed as "Sold Out Editions (Rare)" indicate that the publisher has a limited supply of that print or that the print is difficult to locate in the galleries.

The Printworld Directory is accepting new applications for the seventh edition. Approximately 300 new artists will be accepted. Please use the two forms provided in the back section of this directory to submit biographical data and documentation of prints. Edition number of each print must not exceed 500 and the retail price must be $100 or more.

J C HEYWOOD

BORN: Toronto, Canada; June 6, 1941
EDUCATION: Ontario Col of Art, Toronto, Can, 1959–63; Atelier 17, Paris, France, 1967–69
TEACHING: Instr, Sheridan Col, Can, 1969–71; Prof, Drawing & Painting, Univ of Guelph, Can, 1973–74; Prof, Printmaking & Painting, Queen's Univ, Kingston, Can, 1974 to present
AWARDS: Graphex Award, Art Gallery of Brantford, Can, 1975,78,79,81; Prize, Int Print Biennale, Krakow, Poland, 1980; World Print Ed Award, San Francisco, CA 1983
COLLECTIONS: Mus of Mod Art, Paris, France; Albertina Mus, Vienna, Austria; Royal Library, Brussels, Belgium; Victoria & Albert Mus, London, England; Art Inst of Chicago, IL; Nat Gallery, Can; Montreal Mus of Fine Arts, Can; Moderna Galerija, Ljubljana; Cleveland Mus, OH; Mus of Contemp Art, Montreal, Can; Bradford Art Gallery, England; Mus of Mod Art, Lodz, Poland
PRINTERS: Akagawa Print Workshop, Tokyo, Japan (AP); Mintmark Press Division, Toronto, Can (MP); Open Studio, Toronto, Can (OS); David Skuse, Can (BH); Chris Davy (CD); Artist (ART)
PUBLISHERS: Artist (ART)
GALLERIES: Mira Godard Gallery, Toronto, Can; Associated American Artists, New York, NY
MAILING ADDRESS: Department of Art, Queen's University, Kingston, ON, Canada K7L 3N6

TITLE	PUBLISHER	PRINTER	DATE	MEDIUM	DIMENSION (PAPER SIZE) IN INCHES	TYPE OF PAPER	EDITION NUMBER	NO. OF COLORS	ORIGINAL OPENING PRICE	CURRENT RETAIL PRICE
SOLD OUT EDITIONS (RARE):										
Door No 7	ART	ART	1975	SP	40 X 26	JP	20	9	125	1000
Beware the Past Version One	ART	ART	1975	SP	26 X 40		40	1	125	500
Enjoy	ART	ART	1975	SP	26 X 40	STP	20	12	125	700
Stasis Version One	ART	ART	1976	SP	26 X 40	STP	40	9	125	1300
Vanity Vanity Version One	ART	DS/MP	1977	LC/SP	30 X 40	NEWS	40	7	175	1000
Love	ART	ART/MP	1978	LC/SP	20 X 29	R/BFK	30	10	150	900
Story in Sunshine	ART	ART/MP	1979	LC/SP	30 X 40	STP	55	9	200	800
Me Modifying Matisse	ART	KD	1979	SP/HC	30 X 38	NEWS	30	34	200	800
Carpe Diem	ART	JC/MP	1979	LC/SP	24 X 20	R/BFK	80	13	200	800
CURRENT EDITIONS:										
Vanity Vanity Version Two	ART	ART/MP	1980	LC/SP	30 X 40	R/BFK	50	7	250	400
Triple Entendre	ART	BH/MP	1981	LC/SP/HC	28 X 38	R/BFK	40	8	250	450
My Wife	ART	ART/MP	1981	LC/SP/HC	29 X 41	R/BFK	30	20	250	450
Untitled Etching KV101	ART	OS	1981	EC	22 X 30	St AR	43	2	250	300
Untitled Etching KV102	ART	ART	1981	EC	22 X 30	St AR	43	2	250	350
Springtime	ART	ART	1981	LC/SP/HC	22 X 30	R/BFK	55	11	250	300
The Screen-Ness of Screen	ART	ART	1981	SPEC	29 X 41	R/BFK	27	14	250	300
Japan Flowers with Water	ART	AP	1982	EC	22 X 30	HAN	35	3	250	600
Japan Flower with Matsutani	ART	AP	1982	EC	20 X 26	HAN	40	2	250	350
Japan Flowers with Nick Wade	ART	AP	1982	EC/CO	20 X 26	HAN	40	2	250	400
Japan Flowers with Books	ART	AP	1982	EC	20 X 26	HAN	40	2	250	300
Japan Flowers with Cloth	ART	AP	1982	EC	20 X 26	HAN	40	3	250	300
Japan Paper with Ink	ART	ART/MP	1982	LC/SP/CO	32 X 41	THS	40	9	250	400
Blue Niche	ART	ART/CD	1983	I	22 X 30	SA	50	4	250	400
Red Niche	ART	CD	1983	I	30 X 42	AP88	75	4	300	300
Morning Coffee	ART	ART	1983	EC	22 X 30	SA	40	3	250	400
Three Part Invention	ART	ART	1983	I	30 X 42	AP88	40	6	300	350

EDNA HIBEL

BORN: Boston, MA; January 13, 1917
EDUCATION: Boston Mus of Fine Arts Sch, MA, 1935–39, Special Student, 1941–42
AWARDS: Int Year of the Child Award, LA, 1981; Artistic Achievement & Humanitarian Award, LA, 1981; Medal of Honor, Minister of Netherlands Culture, 1981; Medal of Honor & Citation, Pope John Paul II, Vatican, Rome, Italy, 1983; Fel, World Acad of Art & Science, 1984; Blue Ribbon Award, Art, Cordon Bleu Soc, 1984; United States Postal Stamp, 1986; Honorary Doctorates, Art & Literature, Univ for Peace & Mount Saint Mary's Col, 1988; Tributes in United States Congressional Records, 1979, 1989
RECENT EXHIB: China Nat Art Gallery, Beijing, China, 1986; Nat Mus of Costa Rica, 1988; Dubrovnik Mus, Yugoslavia, 1988; Nat Mus of Women in the Arts, Wash, DC, 1989; St Peter au der Sperr, Wiener Neustadt, Austria, 1989; Mus of Soviet Union, Acad of At, Leningrad, Russia, 1990; Northern Indiana Arts Assn, Munster, IN, 1990
COLLECTIONS: Boston Mus of Fine Arts, MA; Detroit Art Inst, MI; Phoenix Art Mus, AZ; Springfield Mus of Art, MA; Harvard Univ, Cambridge, MA; La Jolla Mus, CA; Boston Univ, MA; Univ of Miami, FL; Univ of New Hampshire, Durham, NH; Columbus Mus of Arts & Crafts, GA; Fleischman Coll, Cincinnati, OH; Palais des Nations Philatelic Mus, Geneva, Switzerland; United Nations Headquarters, NY; Hibel Mus of Art, Palm Beach, FL
PRINTERS: Edna Atelier, Zurich, Switzerland (EA); Wolfensberger AG, Zurich, Switzerland (WAG)
PUBLISHERS: JAR Publishers, Mangonia Park, FL (JAR); Edna Hibel Corp, Mangonia Park, FL (EHC)
GALLERIES: Graphic Art Collection, Hallandale, FL; Cobbs Gallery, St Petersburg, Fl; Prestige Gallery, Peabody, MA; Shropshire Shop, Shrewsbury, MA; Bilmar Galleries, Franklin Lakes, NJ; Dorothy Pollack, Jenkintown, PA; Terri Galleries, Atlanta, GA; American Business Concept, Centerline, MI; L Brandy's, Addison, IL; Art Tower Gallery, Cambria, CA; Edna Hibel Gallery, Palm Beach, FL; Professional Fine Arts Services, Inc, New York, NY; Artists' Den, Valparaiso, IN
MAILING ADDRESS: 1530 W 53rd Magnolia Park, FL 33407

TITLE	PUBLISHER	PRINTER	DATE	MEDIUM	DIMENSION (PAPER SIZE) IN INCHES	TYPE OF PAPER	EDITION NUMBER	NO. OF COLORS	ORIGINAL OPENING PRICE	CURRENT RETAIL PRICE
SOLD OUT EDITIONS (RARE):										
Sami the Artist	JAR	EA	1974	LC	14 X 18	R/BFK	148	4	125	1000
Lovers of Florence	JAR	EA	1975	LC	27 X 34	R/BFK	140	6	175	900
Sami No 9	JAR	EA	1976	LC	17 X 25	R/BFK	250	14	125	1000
March of Dimes Mother and Baby	JAR	EA	1976	LC	7 X 12	R/BFK	190	1	75	800
Ellie & Child	JAR	EA	1976	LC	12 X 18	R/BFK	295	14	150	900
Sophia & Children	JAR	EA	1976	LC	28 X 39	R/BFK	296	11	325	1600
Jennie	JAR	EA	1977	LC	9 X 12	JP	398	16	300	1300

EDNA HIBEL CONTINUED

TITLE	PUBLISHER	PRINTER	DATE	MEDIUM	DIMENSION (PAPER SIZE) IN INCHES	TYPE OF PAPER	EDITION NUMBER	NO. OF COLORS	ORIGINAL OPENING PRICE	CURRENT RETAIL PRICE
SOLD OUT EDITIONS (RARE):										
Felicia	JAR	EA	1978	LC	21 X 31	R/BFK	148	16	900	2600
Tina	EHC	EA	1980	LC	24 X 20	R/BFK	200	10	750	1200
Severine & Children	EHC	HA	1985	LC	26 X 38	RP	267	9/1 Gold	475	595
Papageno	EHC	HA	1986	LC	18 X 9	RP	196	2/1 Gold	195	275
Nancy with Megan	EHC	HA	1986	LC	31 X 21	JP	367	10/1 Gold	510	795
Flowers of Kashmir	EHC	HA	1987	LC	23 X 17	RP	297	11/2 Golds	295	450
Once Upon a Time	EHC	HA	1987	LC	19 X 28	JP	287	4/2 Golds	410	550
Aida	EHC	HA	1987	LC	26 X 36	RP	275	9/1 Gold	595	625
The New Hat	EHC	HA	1988	LC	19 X 15	JP	298	9/1 Gold	330	450
Amelia and Children	EHC	HA	1988	LC	40 X 28	JP	268	8/1 Gold	695	775
Xin-Xin of the High Mountain (with Platinum)	EHC	HA	1988	LC	14 X 10	PLAT	325	9/1 Gold		
John M	EHC	HA	1988	LC	13 X 8	RP	308	2	185	275
CURRENT EDITIONS:										
Zorina	EHC	EA	1982	LC	21 X 14	R/BFK	329	9	295	350
Zorina	EHC	EA	1982	LC	21 X 14	JP	329	9	325	375
Toni	EHC	EA	1982	LC	16 X 9	HMP	298	4	225	250
Toni	EHC	EA	1982	LC	16 X 9	R/BFK	298	1	185	250
January	EHC	EA	1982	LC	15 X 13	R/BFK	319	8	295	350
January	EHC	EA	1982	LC	15 X 14	JP	319	8	345	400
Portrait of a Family	EHC	EA	1982	LC	40 X 29	R/BFK	330	8	750	800
Little Rajah and the Unicorns	EHC	EA	1982	LC	41 X 29	R/BFK	319	8	1000	1100
Katrina & Children	EHC	EA	1982	LC	29 X 19	R/BFK	329	9	345	400
Katrina & Children	EHC	EA	1982	LC	29 X 19	JP	329	9	425	450
Rena & Rachel	EHC	EA	1982	LC	24 X 18	R/BFK	329	10	345	400
Rena & Rachel	EHC	EA	1982	LC	24 X 18	JP	329	10	395	450
Naro-San	EHC	EA	1982	LC	13 X 11	R/BFK	322	8	275	300
Naro-San	EHC	EA	1982	LC	13 X 11	JP	322	8	310	350
Thai Family	EHC	EA	1982	LC	16 X 12	HMP	383	16	225	250
Willa & Child	EHC	EA	1982	LC/HC	8 X 7	R/BFK	361	10	195	250
Willa & Child	EHC	EA	1982	LC/HC	8 X 7	HMP	361	10	350	400
Prima Ballarina	EHC	HA	1983	LC	17 X 10	JP	186	3	175	175
Japanese Rose	EHC	HA	1984	LC	24 X 10	SILK	295	6	325	375
Willie and the Two Quan Yins	EHC	HA	1984	LC	10 X 16	RP	289	12/2 Golds	365	365
Todd	EHC	HA	1986	LC	17 X 15	RP	298	10/1 Gold	310	325
Worcestershire Cat	EHC	HA	1986	LC	14 X 20	JP	280	7/1 Gold	295	295
Princess of the Imperial Palace	EHC	HA	1987	LC	40 X 28	JP	282	8/1 Gold	650	775
Lei Jeigiong & Her Baby in the Garden of Yun-Tai	EHC	HA	1987	LC	19 X 14	RP	273	1/1 Gold	250	275
Monica, Matteao & Vanessa	EHC	HA	1987	LC	24 X 18	JP	300	8/1 Gold	350	550
Robert with Mother and Sister	EHC	HA	1987	LC	23 X 15	RP	295	1	230	250
Leaving the Garden	EHC	HA	1987	LC	15 X 11	RP	299	10/2 Golds	345	345
Whistle of Grass	EHC	HA	1987	LC	12 X 10	RP	299	11/1 Gold	250	250
The Forest Friend	EHC	HA	1988	LC	18 X 16	RP	293	7/1 Gold	295	295
Vega Crossing the Bridge of Birds to Her Lover	EHC	HA	1988	LC	19 X 14	RP	279	7/1 Gold	350	350
Then and Now	EHC	HA	1988	LC	16 X 20	RP	278	8/1 Gold	350	350
Flowers of the Adriatic	EHC	HA	1988	LC	23 X 17	RP	286	8/1 Gold	300	300
Primavera	EHC	HA	1988	LC	10 X 18	JP	196	1	225	225
Festival Flower Girl	EHC	HA	1989	LC	14 X 18	RP	265	8/1 Gold	340	340
Papillon	EHC	HA	1989	LC	15 X 13	RP	295	4/1 Gold	295	295
Eva & Baby	EHC	HA	1989	LC	30 X 20	RP	285	9/1 Gold	535	535

JENE HIGHSTEIN

BORN: Baltimore, MD; 1942
EDUCATION: Univ of Maryland, Baltimore, MD, BA, 1963; Univ of Chicago, IL, 1963–65; New York Studio Sch, NY, 1966; Royal Acad Sch, London, England, Dipl, 1970
TEACHING: Instr, Sch of Visual Art, NY, 1973; Vis Art, Yale Univ, New Haven, CT, 1973; Artist-in-Residence, Sarah Lawrence Col, Bronxville, NY, 1976; Vis Art, C W Post Col, Old Westbury, NY, 1975,79; Vis Art, Emily Carr Col, Vancouver, BC, Canada, 1980; Vis Art, Rutgers Univ, Camden, NJ, 1982; Vis Art, Miami-Dade Com Col, FL, 1983
AWARDS: Sculpture Award, Creative Artists Public Service Program, 1979; Sculpture Award, Nat Endowment for the Arts, 1984; Sculpture Award, Guggenheim Fel, 1985
RECENT EXHIB: Art Mus of South Texas, Corpus Christi, TX, 1992; Governors State Univ, Nathan Manilow Sculpture Park, University Park, IL, 1992; Portland Art Mus, OR, 1993; Ace Contemporary Art, Los Angeles, CA, 1993
COLLECTIONS: Victoria & Albert Mus, London, England; Musee de la Ville de Paris, France; La Jolla Mus of Contemp Art, CA; Rose Art Mus, Brandeis Univ, Waltham, MA; Guggenheim, NY
PRINTERS: Mahaffey Fine Art, Portland, OR (MFA); Jacob Samuel, Santa Monica, CA (JS); Litho Shop, Santa Monica, CA (LS); Artist (ART)
PUBLISHERS: Mahaffey Fine Arts, Portland, OR (MFA); Artist (ART)
GALLERIES: G Grimaldis Gallery, Baltimore, MD; Michael Klein, Inc, New York, NY; Mattress Factory, Pittsburgh, PA; Mahaffey Fine Arts, Santa Monica, CA
MAILING ADDRESS: 145 Chambers St, New York, NY 10007

The print market has become very selective. For the first time since we published the first edition of The Printworld Directory in 1982, the prices of prints have been greatly reduced and greatly increased for the same artists by the most reputable and established print publishers. Check the fifth edition to understand the movement.

JENE HIGHSTEIN CONTINUED

TITLE	PUBLISHER	PRINTER	DATE	MEDIUM	DIMENSION (PAPER SIZE) IN INCHES	TYPE OF PAPER	EDITION NUMBER	NO. OF COLORS	ORIGINAL OPENING PRICE	CURRENT RETAIL PRICE
CURRENT EDITIONS:										
Swedish Black Granite	ART	ART	1988	MON	61 X 43 EA	AP	1 EA	Varies	1200 EA	2500 EA
Barge	MFA	MFA	1993	LB	31 X 47	AC	25	1	1400	1400
Diagonal Pipe Piece	MFA	MFA	1993	LB	31 X 47	AC	25	1	1400	1400
Diagonal Pipe in Eight Parts	ART	JS/LS	1993	EB	44 X 31	R/BFK/ROL	10	1	2000	2000

CHARLES CHRISTOPHER HILL

BORN: Greensburg, PA; March 4, 1948
EDUCATION: Univ of California, Irvine, CA, BA, 1970, MFA, 1973
TEACHING: Vis Instr, Art Center Col of Design, 1978–79; Instr, Univ of California, Los Angeles, CA, 1980–81
AWARDS: Young Talent Award, Los Angeles County Mus of Art, CA, 1976; Nat Endowment for the Arts, Wash, DC, 1976
RECENT EXHIB: Centre d'Action Culturelle de St-Brieuc, France, 1987; Cirrus Gallery, Los Angeles, CA, 1987–88
COLLECTIONS: Solomon R Guggenheim Mus, NY; Metropolitan Mus of Art, NY; Mus Nat d'Art Mod, Centre Georges Pompidou, Paris, France; Los Angeles County Mus, CA; Honolulu Acad of Art, HI; Mus of Mod Art, NY
PRINTERS: Cirrus Editions Workshop, Los Angeles, CA (CEW); Perry Tymeson, Los Angeles, CA (PT); William Law III, Los Angeles, CA (WL); James Allen, Los Angeles, CA (JA); Toby Michel, Los Angeles, CA (TM); Francesco Siqueiros, Los Angeles, CA (FS); Robert Dansby, Los Angeles, CA (RD)
PUBLISHERS: Cirrus Editions, Ltd, Los Angeles, CA (CE)
GALLERIES: Cirrus Editions Ltd, Los Angeles, CA
MAILING ADDRESS: 1158 Palms Blvd, Venice, CA 90201

TITLE	PUBLISHER	PRINTER	DATE	MEDIUM	DIMENSION (PAPER SIZE) IN INCHES	TYPE OF PAPER	EDITION NUMBER	NO. OF COLORS	ORIGINAL OPENING PRICE	CURRENT RETAIL PRICE
SOLD OUT EDITIONS (RARE):										
Quando Vayas a Cagar	CE	PT/CEW	1974	SP	24 X 29	NEWS	50	2	150	2500
CURRENT EDITIONS:										
Set of 4:										
Armstrong	CE	JA/CEW	1977	LC	28 X 39	R/BFK	50	5	250	2500
Atlatl	CE	JA/CEW	1977	LC	28 X 39	R/BFK	50	7	250	2500
Dibble	CE	WL/CEW	1977	LC	28 X 29	AP/B	50	3	250	2500
Lightning	CE	WL/CEW	1977	LC	28 X 39	AP/B	50	2	250	2500
Solomonic	CE	TM/CEW	1980	LC	31 X 24	AC/BL	75	4	300	750
Between Athens and Rome	CE	TM/CEW	1980	LC	31 X 24	R/BFK	50	5	300	750
Socony	CE	TM/CEW	1980	LC	31 X 23	R/BFK	19	4	350	750
Pringle	CE	TM/CEW	1980	LC	30 X 22	TW/HMP	30	4	350	750
Optimo	CE	TM/CEW	1980	LC/HP	30 X 22	TW/HMP	8	Multi	350	850
Apostolic (Trip)	CE	CEW	1980	LC	30 X 68	TW/HMP	10	Multi	1300	2000
Quinsey (Dipt)	CE	CEW	1980	LC/HP	30 X 45	TW/HMP	2	Multi	700	1500
Pyramis and Thisbe	CE	TM/CEW	1980	LC	30 X 45	TW/HMP	9	Multi	700	2000
Ecstatic	CE	TM/CEW	1980	LC	30 X 22	TW/HMP	30		350	750
Lothario	CE	CEW	1980	LC/HP	30 X 22	TW/HMP	16	2	350	850
John Beresford Tipton	CE	CEW	1980	LC/HP	30 X 90	TW/HMP	19		1500	2500
Monoprints (4 pcs)	CE	CEW	1980	MON	30 X 22	TW/HMP	1 EA		350 EA	500 EA
Monoprint Diptych	CE	CEW	1980	MON	30 X 45	TW/HMP	1 EA		700 EA	900 EA
Untitled, 1983 (Trip)	CE	CEW	1983	MON	30 X 61	TW/HMP	1 EA	1 EA	1800 EA	2500 EA
Roxanne	CE	FS/RD/CEW	1988	LC/WC	43 X 37	COV	40		950	1200
The Adventure	CE	FS/RD/CEW	1988	LC	43 X 37	COV	40		950	1200
Sovereign I,II,III (428c,429c,430c)	CE	FS/RD/CEW	1990	LC/WC/CC	42 X 34 EA	COV	35 EA		5400 SET / 1800 EA	5400 SET / 1800 EA

CLINTON J HILL

BORN: Payette, ID; March 8, 1922
EDUCATION: Univ of Oregon, Eugene, OR, BS, 1947; Brooklyn Mus Sch, NY, 1949–51; Academie de la Grande Chaumiere, Paris, France, 1951; Inst d'Arte Statale, Florence, Italy, 1951–52
TEACHING: Prof Emeritus, Queens Col, Flushing, NY, 1968–88
AWARDS: Fulbright Fel, India, 1956; Creative Artists Public Service Grant, 1975; Nat Endowment for the Arts, 1976–77, 1980–81; City Univ of New York, Faculty Research Awards, 1975,79,84
RECENT EXHIB: Centro Culturale, Villa Borzino, Italy, 1987; Marilyn Pearl Gallery, NY, 1988; Marilyn Pearl Gallery, NY, 1990; Worcester Mus, MA, 1992; Alice Simsar Gallery, Ann Arbor, MI, 1987,89,92; Marilyn Pearl Gallery, NY, 1990,92
COLLECTIONS: Mus of Mod Art, NY; Metropolitan Mus of Art, NY; Philadelphia Mus, PA; Phoenix Art Mus, AZ; Albright-Knox Art Gallery, Buffalo, NY; Corcoran Gallery of Art, Wash, DC; Hampton Inst, VA; Montclair Art Mus, NJ; Brooklyn Mus, NY; Worcester Mus, MA; Nat Gallery of Australia, Canberra, Australia
PRINTERS: Sergio Tosi Stampatore, Paris France (STS); Artist (ART); John Koller, Woodstock Vallery, CT (JK)
PUBLISHERS: Sergio Tosi Stampatore, Paris, France (STS)
GALLERIES: Marilyn Pearl Gallery, New York, NY; William Sawyer Gallery, San Francisco, CA; Alice Simsar Gallery, Ann Arbor, MI; Galerie Flora, Paris, France
MAILING ADDRESS: 178 Prince St, New York, NY 10012

TITLE	PUBLISHER	PRINTER	DATE	MEDIUM	DIMENSION (PAPER SIZE) IN INCHES	TYPE OF PAPER	EDITION NUMBER	NO. OF COLORS	ORIGINAL OPENING PRICE	CURRENT RETAIL PRICE
CURRENT EDITIONS:										
Vault	STS	ART	1980	DPT	24 X 35	HMP	6	1	400	500
Broad Jump (Fiberglass Relief)	STS	STS	1980	EC/REL	25 X 26	HMP	15	4	350	350
Broken Field Run	STS	STS	1980	EB/CO	30 X 41	HMP	12	1	350	350

CLINTON J HILL CONTINUED

TITLE	PUBLISHER	PRINTER	DATE	MEDIUM	DIMENSION (PAPER SIZE) IN INCHES	TYPE OF PAPER	EDITION NUMBER	NO. OF COLORS	ORIGINAL OPENING PRICE	CURRENT RETAIL PRICE
CURRENT EDITIONS:										
Black Track	STS	STS	1980	EB	25 X 36	HMP	10	1	350	350
Ansedonia	STS	STS	1980	EB/WM	17 X 22	HMP	16	1	350	350
Cosa	STS	STS	1980	EB/WM	17 X 22	HMP	16	1	350	350
Nite Ride (with Pigmented Pulp)	ART	ART	1986	CP	23 X 18	HMP	10	7	600	600
Reverse Track	ART	ART	1987	WC	24 X 18	HMP	5	4	925	925
Interference	ART	ART	1988	WC	37 X 25	HMP	5	6	1050	1050
Fast Track	ART	ART	1988	WC	30 X 17	HMP	5	5	925	925
Slide	ART	ART	1988	WC	30 X 17	HMP	5	6	925	925
Downhill	ART	ART	1988	WC	30 X 17	HMP	5	3	925	925
Run Around	ART	ART	1988	WC	30 X 24	HMP	6	6	925	925
Shuffle (with Pigmented Pulp)	ART	ART	1990	CP	23 X 18	HMP	5	11	600	600
Hot Hop (with Pigmented Pulp)	ART	ART	1990	CP	23 X 18	HMP	5	9	600	600
Hot Flash (with Pigmented Pulp)	ART	ART	1990	CP	23 X 18	HMP	5	8	600	600
Cool Passage (with Pigmented Pulp)	ART	ART	1990	CP	23 X 18	HMP	5	8	600	600

DARRELL HILL

EDUCATION: Arizona State Univ, Tempe, AZ, BA

PRINTERS: Land Mark Editions, Minneapolis, MN (LME)
PUBLISHERS: C G Rein Publishers, St Paul, MN (CGR)
GALLERIES: C G Rein Galleries, Scottsdale, AZ & Santa Fe, NM & Houston, TX & Minneapolis, MN

TITLE	PUBLISHER	PRINTER	DATE	MEDIUM	DIMENSION (PAPER SIZE) IN INCHES	TYPE OF PAPER	EDITION NUMBER	NO. OF COLORS	ORIGINAL OPENING PRICE	CURRENT RETAIL PRICE
CURRENT EDITIONS:										
Two Fords	CGR	LME	1982	LC	22 X 30	AP	100	6	250	350
Fancy Roadster	CGR	LME	1982	LC	22 X 29	AP	100	6	250	350
Hibiscus (Flower Arrangement)	CGR	LME	1982	LC	21 X 30	AP	100	6	250	350

JOHN HIMMELFARB

BORN: Chicago, IL; June 3, 1946
EDUCATION: Harvard Univ, Cambridge, MA, BA, 1968, MAT, 1968–70
AWARDS: First Prize, Western IL Univ, 1979; Yaddo Fel, 1979
RECENT EXHIB: Evanston Art Center, IL, 1987; Oregon Sch of Arts & Crafts, Portland, OR, 1987; Art Inst of Chicago, IL, 1988; Kalamazoo Inst of Art, MI, 1989
COLLECTIONS: Chicago Art Inst, IL; Fogg Art Mus, Cambridge, MA; Baltimore Mus of Art, MD; Nat Coll of Fine Arts, Wash, DC; Minneapolis Inst of Art, MN; Brooklyn Mus, NY; Cleveland Art Mus, OH; Univ of Iowa Art Mus, Iowa City, IA; Illinois State Mus, Springfield, IL; Minnesota Art Mus, St Paul, MN; Elvehjem Arts Center, Univ of Wisconsin, Madison, WI; Sheldon Mem Art Gallery, Univ of Nebraska, Lincoln, NE; Univ of Minnesota Art Gallery, Minneapolis, MN; Portland Art Mus, OR; Albrecht Art Mus, St Joseph, MO; Univ of Oregon Art Mus, Eugene, OR; Des Moines Art Center, IA; Smithsonian Inst, Wash, DC; Indianapolis Mus of Art, IN

PRINTERS: Will Peterson, Chicago, IL (WP); Plucked Chicken Press, Chicago, IL (PCP); John Nichols, Printmakers & Publishers, NY (JN); J Nebraska Gifford, NY (JNG); Jack Lemon, Chicago, IL (JL); Landfall Press, Chicago, IL (LPI); Norman Stewart, Bloomfield Hills, MI (NS); Joe Keenan, Blooomfield Hills, MI (JK); Stewart & Stewart, Bloomfield Hills, MI (S-S); Andrew Rubin, Madison, WI (AR); Tandem Press, Univ of Wisconsin, Madison, WI (TanPr)
PUBLISHERS: Balkin Editions, Chicago, IL (BE); John Nichols, Printmakers & Publishers, NY (JN); Landfall Press, Inc, Chicago, IL (LPI); Stewart & Stewart, Bloomfield Hills, MI (S-S); Tandem Press, Univ of Wisconsin, Madison, WI (TanPr)
GALLERIES: Terry Dintenfass Gallery, New York, NY; Brody's Gallery, Wash, DC; Landfall Press, Chicago, IL; Echo Press, Bloomington, IN; Gallery 72, Omaha, NE; Chicago Street Gallery, Lincoln, IL; Spaightwood Galleries, Madison, WI; Peltz Gallery, Milwaukee, WI
MAILING ADDRESS: 163 N Humphrey Ave, Oak Park, IL 60302

TITLE	PUBLISHER	PRINTER	DATE	MEDIUM	DIMENSION (PAPER SIZE) IN INCHES	TYPE OF PAPER	EDITION NUMBER	NO. OF COLORS	ORIGINAL OPENING PRICE	CURRENT RETAIL PRICE
SOLD OUT EDITIONS (RARE):										
Storyteller	BE	WP/PCP	1981	LC	30 X 40	AP/W	50	5	500	1000
Trio	BE	WP/PCP	1982	LC	25 X 33	MOR/G	25	1	200	800
Balance Sheet	BE	WP/PCP	1982	LC	28 X 33	R/BFK	25	1	200	800
Boatman	BE	WP/PCP	1982	LC	23 X 37	R/BFK	25	1	200	800
Bone	BE	WP/PCP	1982	LC	19 X 34	SHO	25	1	200	800
Bridge	BE	WP/PCP	1982	LC	25 X 32	MOR/G	25	1	200	800
Earth Dwellers/Line Dance	S-S	NS/JK/S-S	1991	SP	41 X 29	R/BFK/W	4	2	100	1800
CURRENT EDITIONS:										
Grand Street Meeting	JN	JN	1985	LC/SP	30 X 43	AP88	65	9	650	900
Lengthy Meeting	JN	JN/JNG	1986	WB	24 X 96	GOYA	10	1	600	850
Lumber Street Meeting	LPI	LPI	1988	WC	37 X 69	SOM	20		1500	2000
Serena Lane Meeting	EPr	DK/DC/EPr	1988	AC/SL/REL	42 X 49	AC	12	2	800	1200
Red and Black Face	TanPr	AR/TanPr	1989	MON	106 X 54 EA	HMP	1 EA	2 EA	6000 EA	6000 EA
Kandy Mountain	TanPr	AR/TanPr	1989	MON	52 X 107 EA	HMP	1 EA		6000 EA	6000 EA
Grown Woman in a Promised Land	TanPr	AR/TanPr	1989	MON	60 X 90 EA	SWP	1 EA		6000 EA	6000 EA
Ascending the Ladder (Dipt)	TanPr	AR/TanPr	1989	MON	43 X 51 EA	AP88	1 EA		2400 EA	2400 EA
Elevator	TanPr	AR/TanPr	1990	MON	54 X 106 EA	HMP	1 EA		6000 EA	6000 EA
Illustration without Words	TanPr	AR/TanPr	1990	LB	30 X 21	R/BFK/W	14	1	400	400
Catalan	TanPr	AR/TanPr	1990	LB/DRAW	21 X 30	R/BFK/W	34	1	800	800
Earth Dwellers/Mambo	S-S	NS/JK/S-S	1991	SP	41 X 29	R/BFK/W	37	8	1250	1250

JOHN HIMMELFARB CONTINUED

TITLE	PUBLISHER	PRINTER	DATE	MEDIUM	DIMENSION (PAPER SIZE) IN INCHES	TYPE OF PAPER	EDITION NUMBER	NO. OF COLORS	ORIGINAL OPENING PRICE	CURRENT RETAIL PRICE
CURRENT EDITIONS:										
Earth Dwellers/Fox Trot	S-S	NS/JK/S-S	1991	SP	41 X 29	R/BFK/W	34	8	1250	1250
Juggler	S-S	NS/JS/S-S	1992	SP	41 X 29	R/BFK/W	11	2	1000	1000
Juggler on Stage	S-S	NS/JS/S-S	1992	SP	41 X 29	R/BFK/W	24	5	1250	1250
Yellow Rose	S-S	NS/JS/S-S	1992	SP	41 X 29	R/BFK/W	25	4	1250	1250
Stolen Glance	S-S	NS/JS/S-S	1992	SP	41 X 29	R/BFK/W	10	2	1000	1000

John Himmelfarb
Juggler on Stage
Courtesy Stewart & Stewart

John Himmelfarb
Yellow Rose
Courtesy Stewart & Stewart

CHARLES B HINMAN

BORN: Syracuse, NY; December 29, 1932
EDUCATION: Syracuse Univ, NY, BFA, 1955; Art Students League, NY
AWARDS: First Prize, Mus Nagaoka, Japan, 1966; Nat Endowment for the Arts Grant, 1980
RECENT EXHIB: Virginia Lust Gallery, NY, 1989; Douglas Drake Gallery, NY, 1990,91
COLLECTIONS: Mus of Mod Art, NY; Larry Aldrich Mus of Contemp Art, Ridgefield, CT; Los Angeles County Mus, CA; Detroit Inst of Art, MI; Whitney Mus of Am Art, NY; Nat Gallery of Art, Wash,DC; Hirshhorn Mus, Wash, DC; Mus of Contemp Art, Nagoaka, Japan; Louisiana Mus, Humblebaek, Denmark; Mus des Beaux Arts de'l Ontario, Toronto, ON, Canada

PRINTERS: Bummy Huss, NY (BH); Dan Stack, NY (DS); Copperplate Editions, NY (CopEd); A Givat (AG); K Caraccio (KC); A Moskowitz (AM); Moxex, Ltd (ML); Tanglewood Press, NY (TP); Sillman & Ives, New Haven, CT (S/I); Domberger, Stuttgart, Germany (DOM); Arkay, Paris, France (A)
PUBLISHERS: Artist (ART); Pace Editions, NY (PE); Artist (ART); Pace Editions, NY (PE); Denise Rene, Paris, France (DR); Richard Feigen Graphics, NY (RFG)
GALLERIES: Virginia Lust Gallery, New York, NY; Pace Prints, New York, NY; Douglas Drake Gallery, New York, NY; Margaret Lipworth Gallery,Boca Raton, FL; Ann Jaffe Gallery, Miami, FL; Irving Galleries, Palm Beach, FL; Images Gallery, Toledo, OH; Sylvia Cordish Fine Arts, Baltimore, MD; Andrea Marquit Fine Art, Boston, MA
MAILING ADDRESS: 231 Bowery, New York, NY 10002

The retail prices of the 100,000 limited edition prints quoted in this directory are subject to change. Print publishers, artists and galleries were the direct sources for these quotations. Prices in the secondary market listed as "Sold Out Editions (Rare)" indicate that the publisher has a limited supply of that print or that the print is difficult to locate in the galleries.

The Printworld Directory is accepting new applications for the seventh edition. Approximately 300 new artists will be accepted. Please use the two forms provided in the back section of this directory to submit biographical data and documentation of prints. Edition number of each print must not exceed 500 and the retail price must be $100 or more.

CHARLES B HINMAN CONTINUED

TITLE	PUBLISHER	PRINTER	DATE	MEDIUM	DIMENSION (PAPER SIZE) IN INCHES	TYPE OF PAPER	EDITION NUMBER	NO. OF COLORS	ORIGINAL OPENING PRICE	CURRENT RETAIL PRICE
SOLD OUT EDITIONS (RARE):										
Untitled (Set of 4)	PE	AG/KS/AM/ML	1976	SP/EMB	38 X 42 EA	LEN/100	100 EA	3-4 EA	1200 SET	2500 SET
Domberger Suite, Plus 3 Singles (Untitled) (Set of 7)	DR	DOM		SP/MB	28 X 28 EA	GE	100 EA	3-6 EA	1500 SET 250 EA	2500 SET 400 EA
CURRENT EDITIONS:										
Nightrider	RFG	S/I	1968	SP	22 X 39	AC	100	4	100	2000
Color Wave	RFG	S/I	1968	SP	22 X 39	AC	100	4	100	2000
Color Door	RFG	S/I	1968	SP	22 X 39	AC	100	4	100	2000
Portfolio (Set of 8)	DR	A	1974	SP/EMB	26 X 34 EA		200 EA	2 EA	900 SET 125 EA	7500 SET 1000 EA
Untitled	ART	BH	1981	PC	22 X 28 X 2	HMP	50		2500	6000
Meteor Showers	ART	DS/CopEd	1987	EB/EMB/HC	30 X 41	AP	50		500	1000

THEO HIOS

BORN: Sparta, Greece; February 2, 1910; US Citizen
EDUCATION: Nat Univ of Athens, Greece; Art Students League, NY; Pratt Inst, Brooklyn, NY
TEACHING: Instr, Painting & Drawing, City Col of New York, NY, 1958-61; Instr, Painting & Drawing, Dalton Sch, 1962-73; Instr, Painting & Drawing, New Sch for Social Research, NY, 1962 to present
AWARDS: First Prize, New England Exhib, Silvermine Guild Artists, 1948; Purchase Award, Guild Hall Mus, NY, 1969; Purchase Award, Parish Art Mus, NY, 1970; Purchase Award, Adolph & Esther Gottlieb Found Grant, 1981
RECENT EXHIB: Pinakothiki Mus, Sparta, Greece, 1989; Long Island Univ, Southampton, NY, 1990; Hudson Guild Art Gallery, NY, 1992
COLLECTIONS: Guild Hall Mus, Easthampton, NY; Parrish Art Mus, Southampton, NY; New Sch of Social Research, NY; Carnegie Inst, Pittsburgh, PA; Nat Coll of Fine Arts, Wash, DC; Nat Pinakothike, Athens, Greece; Newark Mus, NJ; Smith Col, Northampton, MA; Brandeis Univ, Waltham, MA; Cornell Univ, Ithaca, NY; Wichita State Univ, KS
PRINTERS: Artist (ART)
PUBLISHERS: Artist (ART)
GALLERIES: Summit Gallery, New York, NY; Marian Goodman, New York, NY; Hudson Guild Art Gallery, New York, NY; Nancy Stein Gallery, New York, NY
MAILING ADDRESS: 136 W 95th St, New York, NY 10025

TITLE	PUBLISHER	PRINTER	DATE	MEDIUM	DIMENSION (PAPER SIZE) IN INCHES	TYPE OF PAPER	EDITION NUMBER	NO. OF COLORS	ORIGINAL OPENING PRICE	CURRENT RETAIL PRICE
SOLD OUT EDITIONS (RARE):										
Thunderbolt #1	ART	ART	1971	SP	23 X 19	AP	30	4	125	300
Untitled	ART	ART	1971	SP	18 X 22	AP	20	4	125	250
CURRENT EDITIONS:										
Involution #2	ART	ART	1974	SP	24 X 19	AP	14	4	140	250
Grand Canyon	ART	ART	1981	SP	18 X 24	AP	18	20	350	350
Vernal Fall-Yosemite Park	ART	ART	1981	SP	18 X 24	AP	20	27	350	350
Yosemite Valley	ART	ART	1982	SP	18 X 24	AP	45	18	400	400
Majestic Saquaros	ART	ART	1982	SP	24 X 18	AP	40	28	400	400
Sunset on Sifnos Island	ART	ART	1983	MON	11 X 16	AP	1	12	250	250
Pine Forest #1	ART	ART	1984	MON	15 X 20	AP	1	10	400	400
Pine Forest #2	ART	ART	1984	MON	15 X 20	AP	1	10	400	400
Sunset #1	ART	ART	1984	MON	15 X 20	AP	1	10	400	400
Sunset #2	ART	ART	1984	MON	15 X 20	AP	1	10	400	400
Old Olive Tree	ART	ART	1984	MON	19 X 13	AP	1	15	300	300
Old Olive Tree	ART	ART	1984	MON	18 X 12	AP	1	10	200	200
Two Olive Trees	ART	ART	1984	MON	18 X 12	AP	1	10	250	250
Nude-Ida	ART	ART	1947-85	MON	19 X 12	AP	1	10	250	250
Portrait of Alice	ART	ART	1946-85	MON	20 X 14	AP	1	12	200	200
Reclining Nude	ART	ART	1947-85	MON	12 X 19	AP	1	12	250	250
Peonies	ART	ART	1986	MON	16 X 22	AP	1	15	500	500
Grand Canyon	ART	ART	1986	MON	15 X 20	AP	1	15	450	450
Wild Cherry Trees	ART	ART	1986	MON	17 X 20	AP	1	15	450	450
Four Pine Studies #1	ART	ART	1986	MON	14 X 16	AP	1	12	400	400
Four Pine Studies #2	ART	ART	1986	MON	14 X 16	AP	1	12	400	400
Four Studies of Trees	ART	ART	1986	MON	14 X 17	AP	1	12	400	400
Four Studies of a Tree	ART	ART	1986	MON	14 X 17	AP	1	12	400	400
Four Tree Landscape	ART	ART	1986	MON	14 X 17	AP	1	12	400	400
Four Studies of Landscape	ART	ART	1986	MON	14 X 17	AP	1	12	400	400
Cocoanut Tree	ART	ART	1986	MON	17 X 12	AP	1	15	400	400
Flower Still Life	ART	ART	1986	MON	20 X 15	AP	1	15	400	400
Studio Corner with Flowers	ART	ART	1986	MON	23 X 17	AP	1	15	400	400

JOSEPH HIRSCH

BORN: Philadelphia, PA; (1910-1981)
EDUCATION: Philadelphia Col of Art, PA, 1927-31
TEACHING: Art Inst of Chicago; Nat Acad of Design, NY; Art Students League, NY, 1959-67; Dartmouth Col, 1966; Brigham Young Univ, 1971; Univ of UT, 1975
AWARDS: Fulbright Nat Acad of Design, Altman Prize, 1959,67,78; Metropolitan Mus of Art Prize; Butler Inst of Art Prize, 1964; Carnegie Prize, 1968; Oklahoma Art Center, Oklahoma City, OK, 1974
COLLECTIONS: Whitney Mus of Am Art, NY; Metropolitan Mus of Art, NY; Hirshhorn Mus of Art, Wash, DC; Mus of Fine Arts, Boston, MA
PRINTERS: George C Miller, NY (GCM); Artist (ART)
PUBLISHERS: Associated American Artists, NY (AAA); Kennedy Graphics, NY (KG); Artist (ART)

JOSEPH HIRSCH CONTINUED

GALLERIES: Kennedy Galleries, New York, NY; Forum Gallery, New York, NY; Associated American Artists, New York, NY; Fine Art Unlimited, St Petersburg Beach, FL; Sidney Rothman/The Gallery, Barnegat Light, NY

TITLE	PUBLISHER	PRINTER	DATE	MEDIUM	DIMENSION (PAPER SIZE) IN INCHES	TYPE OF PAPER	EDITION NUMBER	NO. OF COLORS	ORIGINAL OPENING PRICE	CURRENT RETAIL PRICE
SOLD OUT EDITIONS (RARE):										
Clowns and the News	AAA	ART	1942	LB	8 X 13	WOVE	250	1	35	800
The Hecklers	AAA	ART	1943	LB	11 X 17	WOVE	250	1	50	1200
The Confidence	AAA	ART	1944	LB	10 X 11	WOVE	250	1	50	1000
Father and Son	AAA	ART	1945	LB	10 X 12	WOVE	250	1	50	800
Private Enterprise	AAA	ART	1945	LB	8 X 12	WOVE	250	1	50	750
The Bánquet	AAA	ART	1946	LB	10 X 14	WOVE	250	1	50	1000
The Brief	AAA		1946	LB	13 X 9	WOVE	250	1	75	800
Man and Beast	AAA	GCM	1946	LB	14 X 7	WOVE	250	1	75	800
The Law	ART	ART	1948	LB	5 X 2	WOVE		1	50	350
Combat	ART	ART	1951	LB	12 X 20	WOVE	35	1	90	1500
Music	AAA	ART	1951	LB	10 X 8	WOVE	250	1	60	750
Man with Logs	AAA	GCM	1954	LB	9 X 12	WOVE	250	1	125	800
Soup	AAA	GCM	1963	LB	14 X 10	AP	250	1	150	650
Eyes	ART	ART	1963	LB	9 X 18	AP		1	150	650
Drink	ART	ART	1964	LB	9 X 12	AP		1	150	650
Duo	ART	ART	1964	LB	26 X 20	R/BFK	60	1	100	1500
Booth	AAA	CGM	1964	LB	28 X 21	R/BFK	60	1	100	1500
Sleeping Face	AAA	CGM	1966	SP	22 X 18	R/BFK	50		200	1500
September Mom	ART	ART	1966	LC	26 X 29	AP	90	6	200	1800
Shark	AAA	GCM	1967	LB	16 X 11	R/BFK	100	1	150	1500
Deposition	ART	ART	1967	LB	17 X 21	R/BFK	75	1	150	2000
Cellist	ART	ART	1969	LB	26 X 20	R/BFK	100	1	225	1500
Nereid and Poseidon	ART	GCM	1969	LB	17 X 22	R/BFK	160	1	135	1500
Hands at Rest	ART	CGM	1969	LB	17 X 22	R/BFK	160	1	135	1500
Man with Mask	ART	ART	1969	LB	22 X 18	R/BFK	100	1	150	1500
Triad	ART	ART	1970	LC	22 X 30	R/BFK	100	2	150	1500
Couples Portfolio (Set of 6)	AAA	CGM	1970	LC	15 X 11 EA	R/BFK	100 EA		1000 SET	5000 SET
Dreamers	ART	ART	1971	LB	17 X 20	AP	150	1	300	1800
Canal Fisherman	ART	ART	1974	LB	25 X 13	R/100	125	1	100	1200
Cup	ART	ART	1974	LB	26 X 20	R/BFK	90	1	200	2500
The Necklace	ART	ART	1974	LC	17 X 23	R/100	100	3	200	2000
Strictly from the Record	ART	ART	1974	LB	16 X 13	R/BFK	300	1	150	800
The Whole Truth	ART	ART	1974	LB	16 X 13	R/BFK	300	1	150	800
Woman Listening	KG	ART	1975	LB	27 X 19	R/100	125	1	300	1500
Windows	KG	ART	1977	LB	21 X 14	R/BFK	110	1	300	1500
Player	KG	ART	1977	LC	22 X 30	R/BFK	75	2	300	1500
Auctioneer	ART	ART	1979	LB	14 X 19	R/BFK	100	1	250	1200
Melancholy Baby	ART	ART	1979	LC	20 X 23	R/BFK	55	2	475	1500

SUE HIRTZEL

BORN: Buffalo, NY; February 8, 1945
EDUCATION: Daemen Col, Amherst, NY, BFA, 1962–69; State Univ of New York, Buffalo, Post Degree, 1969–70; Wayne State Univ, Detroit, MI, MA, MFA, 1970–73
TEACHING: Inst, Printmaking & Drawing, Wayne State Univ, Art Dept, Part-Time, 1973 to present
COLLECTIONS: Muskegon Mus, MI; Detroit Inst of Arts, MI; Univ of California, Chico, CA; Univ of Arizona, Tucson, AZ; Arizona State Univ, Tempe, AZ
PRINTERS: Wing Lake Studio, Bloomfield Hills, MI (S-S); Artist (ART)
PUBLISHERS: Stewart & Stewart, Bloomfield Hills, MI (S-S); Artist (ART)
GALLERIES: Stewart & Stewart, Bloomfield Hills, MI

TITLE	PUBLISHER	PRINTER	DATE	MEDIUM	DIMENSION (PAPER SIZE) IN INCHES	TYPE OF PAPER	EDITION NUMBER	NO. OF COLORS	ORIGINAL OPENING PRICE	CURRENT RETAIL PRICE
SOLD OUT EDITIONS (RARE):										
Paul's Window	ART	ART	1979	CV	18 X 22	AP/WA	6	3	200	1200
Trepass	ART	ART	1981	CV	22 X 30	AP/WA	6	2	250	1500
Infinity Dance	S-S	ART/WLS	1982	CV	22 X 30	AP/WA	22	4	250	1200
Grace	S-S	ART/WLS	1982	CV	22 X 30	AP/WA	16	3	250	1200

T HISACHIKA

PRINTERS: Untitled Press, Captiva, FL (UP); Artist (ART)
PUBLISHERS: Untitled Press, Captiva, FL (UP)
GALLERIES: Castelli Graphics, New York, NY; Sonnabend Gallery, New York, NY

TITLE	PUBLISHER	PRINTER	DATE	MEDIUM	DIMENSION (PAPER SIZE) IN INCHES	TYPE OF PAPER	EDITION NUMBER	NO. OF COLORS	ORIGINAL OPENING PRICE	CURRENT RETAIL PRICE
SOLD OUT EDITIONS (RARE):										
Bird and Shell and Orange	UP	ART/UP	1973	CO	11 X 31	MP	10	Multi	200	500

STEWART HITCH

BORN: Lincoln, NE; February 26, 1940
EDUCATION: Univ of Nebraska, Lincoln, NE, BFA, 1964, MFA, 1968
TEACHING: Art in Res, Florida Int Univ, Miami, FL, 1973; Vis Art, Syracuse Univ, NY, 1983–86; New York Univ, NY, 1987
RECENT EXHIB: Jack Shainman Gallery, NY, 1987; Ruth Siegel Contemp Art, NY, 1990
COLLECTIONS: Aldrich Mus of Contemp Art, Ridgefield, CT; Ewing Mus of Art, Normal, IL
PRINTERS: Jack Lemon, Chicago, IL (JL); Landfall Press, Inc, Chicago, IL (LPI)
PUBLISHERS: Landfall Press, Inc, Chicago, IL (LPI)
GALLERIES: Landfall Press, Inc, Chicago, IL; Edward Thorp Gallery, New York, NY; Jack Shainman Gallery, New York, NY; Trenkmann Gallery, New York, NY
MAILING ADDRESS: c/o Edward Thorp Gallery, 103 Prince St, New York, NY 10012

TITLE	PUBLISHER	PRINTER	DATE	MEDIUM	DIMENSION (PAPER SIZE) IN INCHES	TYPE OF PAPER	EDITION NUMBER	NO. OF COLORS	ORIGINAL OPENING PRICE	CURRENT RETAIL PRICE
SOLD OUT EDITIONS (RARE):										
Slum Goddess	LPI	JL/LPI	1985	LC	34 X 34	AP	35	7	750	800
Infidel	LPI	JL/LPI	1985	WC	19 X 19	AP	20	5	450	500

FRANZ HITZLER

BORN: Thalmassing bei Regensburg, Germany
EDUCATION: Kunstschule, Augsberg, West Germany, 1962–64; Akademie der Bilden den Kunste, Munich, West Germany, with Franz Nagels, 1967–72
COLLECTIONS: Stadtmuseum, Munich, West Germany
PRINTERS: Karl Imhof, Munich, West Germany (KI)
PUBLISHERS: Fred Jahn, Munich, West Germany (FJ)
GALLERIES: David Nolan Gallery, New York, NY

TITLE	PUBLISHER	PRINTER	DATE	MEDIUM	DIMENSION (PAPER SIZE) IN INCHES	TYPE OF PAPER	EDITION NUMBER	NO. OF COLORS	ORIGINAL OPENING PRICE	CURRENT RETAIL PRICE
CURRENT EDITIONS:										
Untitled (Set of 6)	FJ	KI	1986	LB	Varies	JP	35 EA	1 EA	950 SET	1800 SET

TYLER JAMES HOARE

BORN: Joplin, MO; June 5, 1940
EDUCATION: Sculpture, Univ of Colorado, Boulder, CO, 1959; Drawing & Painting, Univ of Kansas, Lawrence, KS, BFA, 1963; Sculpture Center, NY, 1960; Sculpture, California Col of Arts & Crafts, Oakland, CA, 1966; Univ Arti, Italy
TEACHING: Instr, Univ of California, Berkeley, CA, 1973,74; Vis Lectr, San Francisco Art Inst, CA, 1972; Instr, Univ of California, Berkeley, CA, 1973–74; Vis Art, Oakland Mus, CA, 1974; Vis Art, San Francisco State Univ, CA, 1972–75; Vis Art, Col of San Mateo, CA, 1975; Vis Art, California State Univ, Hayward, CA, 1974,79; Vis Art, Missouri Southern State Col, 1979; Vis Art, Univ of Wyoming, Laramie, WY, 1979; Colorado State Univ, Boulder, CO, 1979; Solano Comm Col, Suisun City, CA, 1983; California Col of Arts & Crafts, Oakland, CA, 1984
AWARDS: Diploma of Merit, Univ delle Arti, Italy; Focuserie Award, Nat Photography, Erie, PA, 1974
COLLECTIONS: California Col of Arts & Crafts, Oakland, CA; State Univ of New York, Albany, NY; Oakland Mus, CA; Mills Col, Oakland, CA; De Anza Col, Cupertino, CA; Harvard Univ, Cambridge, MA; Univ of Oklahoma, Norman, OK
PRINTERS: Artist (ART)
PUBLISHERS: Artist (ART)
MAILING ADDRESS: 30 Menlo Place, Berkeley, CA 94707

TITLE	PUBLISHER	PRINTER	DATE	MEDIUM	DIMENSION (PAPER SIZE) IN INCHES	TYPE OF PAPER	EDITION NUMBER	NO. OF COLORS	ORIGINAL OPENING PRICE	CURRENT RETAIL PRICE
CURRENT EDITIONS:										
Classic	ART	ART	1977	XER/C	11 X 17	PLAS	10	Multi	150	250
Xerox Car	ART	ART	1979	XER/C	11 X 16	PLAS	10	Multi	150	250
Car	ART	ART	1985	XER/C	9 X 11	PLAS	10	Multi	150	200
Tank	ART	ART	1985	XER/C	9 X 16	PLAS	10	Multi	150	200

ROBERT DEAN HOBBS

BORN: Merkel, TX; April 21, 1928
EDUCATION: Western Texas State Univ, Canyon, TX, BA; Northern Colorado State Univ, Greeley, CO; Pennsylvania State Univ, University Park, PA, DEd
TEACHING: Clarion State Col, PA, 1971 to present
COLLECTIONS: Northern Colorado State Univ, Greeley, CO; Western Texas State Univ, Canyon, TX; Pennsylvania State Univ, University Park, PA; Taxco Art Gallery, Mexico; Bloomsburg State Col, PA; Lockhaven State Col, PA; Clarion State Col, PA; Smithsonian Inst, Wash, DC
PRINTERS: Artist (ART)
PUBLISHERS: Artist (ART)
GALLERIES: West Broadway Gallery, New York, NY; Sanford Gallery, Clarion State Col, Clarion, PA; Upstairs-Downstairs, Arlington, TX; Amarillo Art Gallery, Amarillo, TX
MAILING ADDRESS: 1001 Tramway Blvd, NE, #113, Albuquerque, NM 87112

TITLE	PUBLISHER	PRINTER	DATE	MEDIUM	DIMENSION (PAPER SIZE) IN INCHES	TYPE OF PAPER	EDITION NUMBER	NO. OF COLORS	ORIGINAL OPENING PRICE	CURRENT RETAIL PRICE
CURRENT EDITIONS:										
Roaring Twenty's	ART	ART	1980	LC	15 X 20	CP	25	3	75	150
Texas	ART	ART	1980	LC	15 X 20	CP	25	3	75	150
The Law	ART	ART	1980	LB	15 X 20	CP	25	1	75	150
Madonna	ART	ART	1981	LB	15 X 20	CP	25	1	75	150
Anatomy Chart	ART	ART	1981	LB	15 X 20	CP	25	1	75	150
Birthplace of Justice	ART	ART	1981	SP	22 X 26	CP	6	4	125	175

ROBERT DEAN HOBBS CONTINUED

TITLE	PUBLISHER	PRINTER	DATE	MEDIUM	DIMENSION (PAPER SIZE) IN INCHES	TYPE OF PAPER	EDITION NUMBER	NO. OF COLORS	ORIGINAL OPENING PRICE	CURRENT RETAIL PRICE
CURRENT EDITIONS:										
Class of '51	ART	ART	1982	SP	22 X 31	CP	12	4	150	200
Airline Industry	ART	ART	1982	SP	21 X 31	CP	12	4	150	200
Lucky Lindy	ART	ART	1982	SP	15 X 20	CP	6	4	100	150
Epic of Flight	ART	ART	1982	SP	24 X 75	CP	6	4	200	275

DAVID HOCKNEY

BORN: Bradford, England; 1937
EDUCATION: Bradford Sch of Art, England, 1953–57; Royal Col of Art, London, England, 1959–62
TEACHING: Univ of Colorado, Boulder, CO, 1965; Univ of California, Los Angeles, CA, 1966; Univ of California, Berkeley, CA, 1967
RECENT EXHIB: Evelyn Aimis Fine Art, Toronto, Canada, 1987; L A Louver, Venice, CA, 1987; Retrosp, Los Angeles County Mus, CA, 1988; Metropolitan Mus, NY, 1988; Tate Gallery, London, England, 1988–89; DeCordova Mus, Lincoln, MA, 1988; Petersburg Press, Inc, NY, 1989; André Emmerich Gallery, NY, 1989; Los Angeles Municipal Art Gallery, Los Angeles, CA, 1990; Contemp Mus, Honolulu, HI, 1990; Lakeview Mus of Arts & Sciences, Peoria, IL, 1990; Wright State Univ, Dayton, OH, 1990; Berkeley Square Gallery, London, England, 1990; Albrecht-Kemper Mus, St Joseph, MO, 1992; Southern Alleghenies Mus of Art, Loretto, PA, 1992; Arlene Lapides Gallery, Santa Fe, NM, 1992; Richard Gray Gallery, Chicago, IL, 1992; Athena Fine Arts, NY, 1993; Andre Emmerich Fine Art, NY, 1993
PRINTERS: Gemini GEL, Los Angeles, CA (GEM); Tyler Graphics, Ltd, Mount Kisco, NY (TGL); Donna Rae Hirt, Los Angeles, CA (DRH); Serge Lozingot, Los Angeles, Ca (SL); Aldo Crommelynck, Paris, France (AC); Atelier Crommelynck, Paris, France (AtC); Maurice Payne, NY (MP); Petersburg Press, London, England, (PP); Office Copier (OC); Editions Alecto, London, England (EA); Letterio Calapai, Rome, Italy (LC); Artist (ART); Studio Bruckman, Munich, Germany (SB); Matthieu AG, Zürich, Switzerland (MAG)
PUBLISHERS: Gemini GEL, Los Angeles, CA (GEM); Petersburg Press, London, England (PP); Tyler Graphics, Ltd, Mount Kisco, NY (TGL); Sonnabend Editions, NY (SE); Editions Alecto, London, England (EA); Galerie Wolfgang Ketterer (GWK); Associated American Artists, NY (AAA); Kasmin Gallery, London, England (KG); Parasol Press, Ltd, NY (PaP); Metropolitan Mus of Art, NY (MMA); Bernard Jacobson, Ltd, London, England (BJL); Artist (ART); Brooke Alexander, Inc, NY (BAI); Observer, London, England (OB); Bruckman (Br); Matthieu, Zürich, Switzerland (Mat); Edition Olympia, Munich, Germany (EO)
GALLERIES: Associated American Artists, New York, NY; Richard Green Galleries, New York, NY & Los Angeles, CA; Andrew Dierken Fine Art, Los Angeles, CA; Gemini GEL, Los Angeles, CA; Irene Drori Fine Art, Los Angeles, CA; Jack Rutberg Fine Arts, Los Angeles, CA; R K Goldman Contemporary, Los Angeles, CA; Charles Whitchurch Gallery, Huntington Beach, CA; Galerie Michael, Beverly Hills, CA; Tokoro Gallery, Los Angeles, CA; Goodman/Tinnon Fine Art, San Francisco, CA; Erika Meyerovich Gallery, San Francisco, CA; Richard Gray Gallery, Chicago, IL; Kass/Meridian Gallery, Chicago, IL; Dorothy Rosenthal Art, Chicago, IL; Hokin Galleries, Palm Beach, FL & Bay Harbor Islands, FL; Morgan Gallery, Boston, MA; Golden Gallery, Boston, MA; Tyler Graphics, Mount Kisco, NY; André Emmerich Gallery, New York, NY; Novo Arts, New York, NY; Pace Prints, New York, NY; Charles Foley Gallery, Columbus, OH; Jeffrey Fuller Fine Art, Ltd, Phila, PA; Fenton Fine Arts, Fort Worth, TX; Greg Kucera Gallery, Seattle, WA; Michael H Lord Gallery, Milwaukee, WI; Posner Gallery, Milwaukee, WI; Berkeley Square Gallery, London, England; Arlene Lapides Gallery, Santa Fe, NM; Bowles-Sorokko Galleries, Beverly Hills, CA & San Francisco, CA & Soho, NY; Thomas Babeor Gallery, La Jolla, CA; Herbert Palmer Gallery, Los Angeles, CA; Calder-Snyder Gallery, San Francisco, CA; Park Granada Editions, Tarzana, CA; L A Louver, Inc, Venice, CA; William Turner Gallery, Venice, CA; River Gallery, Westport, CT; Foundry Gallery, Wash, DC; Mary Singer Gallery, Wash, DC; Nancy Singer Gallery, St Louis, MO; Margo Gallery, Inc, Palm Beach, FL; Zephyr Gallery, Louisville, KY; Joy Emery Gallery, Grosse Point Farms, MI; Jan Weiner Gallery, Kansas City, MO; DEL Fine Art Galleries, Taos, NM; Andre Emmerich Gallery, New York, NY; Professional Fine Arts Services, Inc, New York, NY

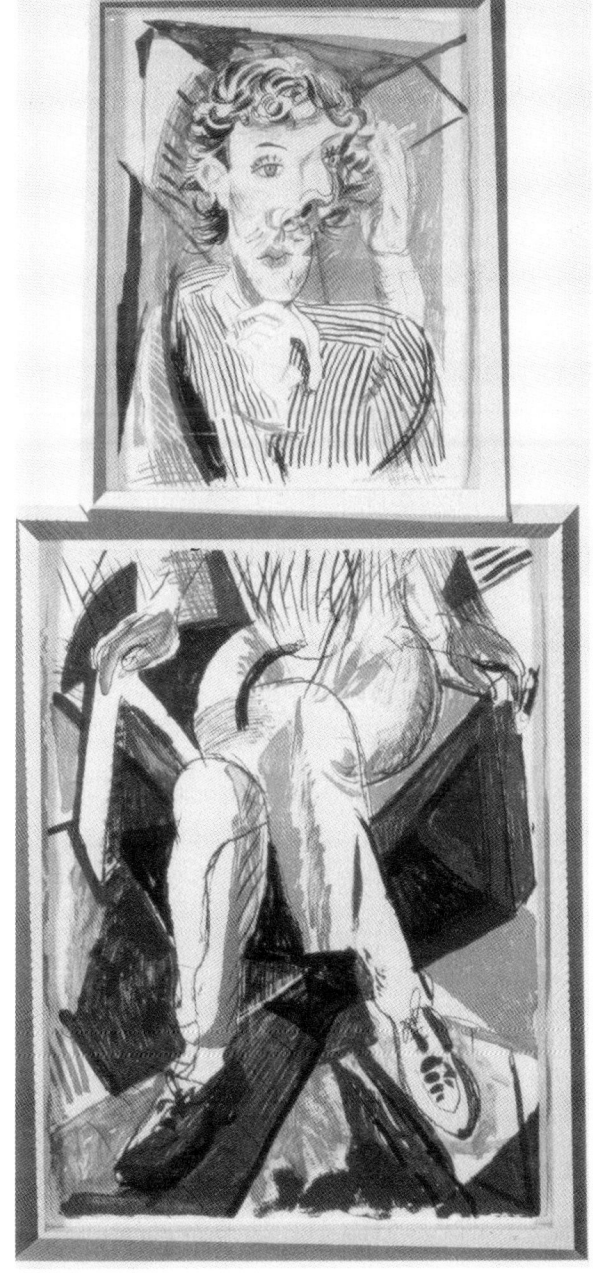

David Hockney
An Image of Gregory
Courtesy Tyler Graphics, Ltd

Scottish Arts Council (SAC)—Gemini GEL (G)—Tyler Graphics (T)—Emmerich (E)—David Hockney (DH)

The retail prices of the 100,000 limited edition prints quoted in this directory are subject to change. Print publishers, artists and galleries were the direct sources for these quotations. Prices in the secondary market listed as "Sold Out Editions (Rare)" indicate that the publisher has a limited supply of that print or that the print is difficult to locate in the galleries.

DAVID HOCKNEY CONTINUED

David Hockney
Hotel Acatlan: Second Day
Courtesy Tyler Graphics, Ltd

TITLE	PUBLISHER	PRINTER	DATE	MEDIUM	DIMENSION (PAPER SIZE) IN INCHES	TYPE OF PAPER	EDITION NUMBER	NO. OF COLORS	ORIGINAL OPENING PRICE	CURRENT RETAIL PRICE
SOLD OUT EDITIONS (RARE):										
Fires of Furious Desire	PP	MP	1961	EB	12 X 16	AP	75	1	100	6000
Alka Seltzer	PP	MP	1961	EB	16 X 11	AP	15	1	100	6000
Three Kings and a Queen	PP	MP	1961	EB/A	22 X 31	AP	50		250	9000
Kaisarion and all His Beauty	PP	MP	1961	EB/A	22 X 16	AP	50		250	18000
Gretchen and the Snurl	PP	MP	1961	EB/A	11 X 31	AP	75		250	9000
Mirror Mirror on the Wall (SAC-10)	PP	MP	1961	EB/A	22 X 31	HMP	50	2	250	18000
The Marriage (SAC-14)	PP	MP	1962	EB/A	13 X 16	JGP	75		150	9000
A Rake's Progress (Set of 16)	PP	MP	1963	EC	19 X 24 EA	AP	50 EA		5000 SET	90000 SET
Pacific Mutual Life	PP	MP	1964	LC	21 X 25	AP	20	1	500	8500
The Acrobat	PP	MP	1964	EB	23 X 31	AP	15	1	400	18000
Figure by a Curtain	PP	MP	1964	LC	19 X 26	AP	75		300	9000
Water Pouring into Swimming Pool, Santa Monica	PP	MP	1964	LC	20 X 26	AP	75		300	15000
Edward Lear	AAA	LC	1964	EB/A	20 X 16	AP	50		300	8500
Still Life	PP	MP	1965	LC	30 X 22	AP	50		300	15000
A Hollywood Collection (Set of 6) (SAC-41-46)	EdA	EdA	1965	LC	30 X 22 EA	R/BFK	85 EA		1500 SET	50000 SET
Picture of a Still Life . . .	EdA	EdA	1965	LC	31 X 23	R/BFK		7	300	18000
Illustrations for Thirteen Poems from CD Cavafy: Portrait of Cavafy in Alexandria	EdA	EdA	1966	EB/A	14 X 9	HMP	75		400	2000
Illustrations: The Shop Window of a Tobacco Store	EdA	EdA	1966	EB/A	14 X 9	HMP	75		400	2000
Illustrations: Portrait of Cavafy I	EdA	EdA	1966	EB/A	14 X 9	HMP	75		400	2000
Henry and Christopher	PP	MP	1967	LC/CO/HC	22 X 30	AP	75		600	20000
A Portrait of Rolf Nelson Six Fairy Tales from the Brothers Grim (Six Stories with 39 Etchings) Illustrations and Text Translated by Heiner Bastian. Each Edition is Bound in Blue Leather & Signed & Accompanied by a Sleeve in Six Loose Etchings & Numbered	PP	MP	1965–68	LC/HC	41 X 29	R/BFK	12	3	200	25000
Kasmin Twice	PP/KG	MP	1968	EB	22 X 31	R/BFK	10	1	400	20000
Ossie and Mo	PP	MP	1968	EB	19 X 20	LAID	75	1	300	3500
Vase & Flowers	PP	MP	1968	EB	36 X 28	AP	75	1	600	13000
Glass Table with Objects	PP	MP	1969	LC	9 X 15	AP	75	5	300	10000
Portrait of Felix Mann	GWK	MP	1969	LC	30 X 21	AP	65	1	300	6000
Still Life (SAC-111)	PP	MP	1969	EB/A	21 X 27	JGP	75		300	10000
Impressions Selected from the Book Six Fairy Tales from the Brothers Grim Portfolio (Boxed with Six Stories Bound Separately as a Concertina Fold & the 39 Etchings, Signed & Numbered)	PP	PP	1969	EB	25 X 19 EA		100 EA		500	60000
Edition A (Book with 39 Etchings & Text & Six Etchings, Loose & Signed, Nos 6, 12, 17, 20, 35, 37)	PP	PP	1969	EB	18 X 12 EA		100 EA		500	15000

DAVID HOCKNEY CONTINUED

TITLE	PUBLISHER	PRINTER	DATE	MEDIUM	DIMENSION (PAPER SIZE) IN INCHES	TYPE OF PAPER	EDITION NUMBER	NO. OF COLORS	ORIGINAL OPENING PRICE	CURRENT RETAIL PRICE
SOLD OUT EDITIONS (RARE):										
Edition B (Book with 39 Etchings & Text & Six Etchings, Loose & Signed, Nos 16, 27, 28, 30, 34, 39)	PP	PP	1969	EB	18 X 12 EA		100 EA		500	15000
Edition C (Book with 39 Etchings & Text & Six Etchings, Loose & Signed, Nos 11, 15, 18, 19, 22, 33)	PP	PP	1969	EB	18 X 12 EA		100 EA		500	15000
Edition D (Book with 39 Etchings & Text & Six Etchings, Loose & Signed, Nos 2, 14, 21, 23, 25, 29)	PP	PP	1969	EB	18 X 12 EA		100 EA		500	15000
Wayne Sleep	MP	MP	1969	EB	10 X 10	HMP	30		200	2000
Celia	PP	MP	1969	EB	28 X 22	JEP	75		300	30000
Olympische Spiele Munchen	EO	MAG	1970	LC	35 X 25	AP	200		200	5500
Flowers Made of Paper and Black Ink			1971	LC	39 X 39	AP	50		300	5000
Rue de Seine	PP	MP	1971	EB/A	21 X 17	JGB	150		275	32000
French Shop (SAC-122)	OB	MP	1971	EB/A	21 X 18	R/BFK	500	2	200	6000
Mo Asleep	PP	MP	1971	EB/A	35 X 28	R/BFK	75		300	5000
Mo with Five Leaves	PP	MP	1971	EC	35 X 28	R/BFK	75		300	6000
Portrait of Maurice Payne	PP	MP	1971	EB/A	35 X 28	R/BFK	75		350	5000
Portrait of Richard Hamilton	PP	MP	1971	EB/A	14 X 11	HMP	30		300	3500
The Restauranteur	PP	MP	1972	EB/A	17 X 14	AP	80		300	5000
Panama Hat (SAC-127)	PP/BAI	MP	1972	EB/A	17 X 13	HMP	125		300	20000
Slightly Damaged Chair, Malibu (G-453)	GEM	GEM	1973	LB	30 X 23	AP	60	1	125	5000
Study Lightning Medium (SAC-133) (G-455)	GEM	GEM	1973	LB	25 X 19	AP	60	1	125	6000
Two Peppers	PP	MP	1973	EB/A	15 X 19	R/BFK	100		300	6000
Marguerites (SAC-157)	PP	AtC	1973	EB/A	16 X 12	AP/HMP	100	4	450	18000
Tulips (SAC-158)	PP	MP	1973	EB/A	36 X 28	GMP	75		600	18000
Snow without Color	GEM	GEM	1973	LC	42 X 33	ARJ	38	9	450	40000
Celia 8365 Melrose Avenue Celia (SAC-148) (G-447)	GEM	GEM	1973	LB	43 X 29	HMP/B	52		400	48000
Celia Smoking (SAC-146) (G-449)	GEM	GEM	1973	LC	32 X 20	HMP	70		400	40000
Hollywood (G-448) (SAC-147)	GEM	SL/GEM	1973	LB	45 X 32	AP	46	1	275	30000
George Sand	PP	MP	1973	EB	31 X 23	R/BFK	25	1	300	7500
Gustave Flaubert	PP	MP	1973	EB	31 X 23	R/BFK	25	1	300	7500
Smaller Study of Lightning	TGL	TGL	1973	LC	20 X 16	AMG	75	3	125	3000

David Hockney
Number One Chair
Courtesy Tyler Graphics, Ltd

David Hockney
The Perspective Lesson
Courtesy Tyler Graphics, Ltd

DAVID HOCKNEY CONTINUED

David Hockney
Artist and Model
Courtesy Petersburg Press

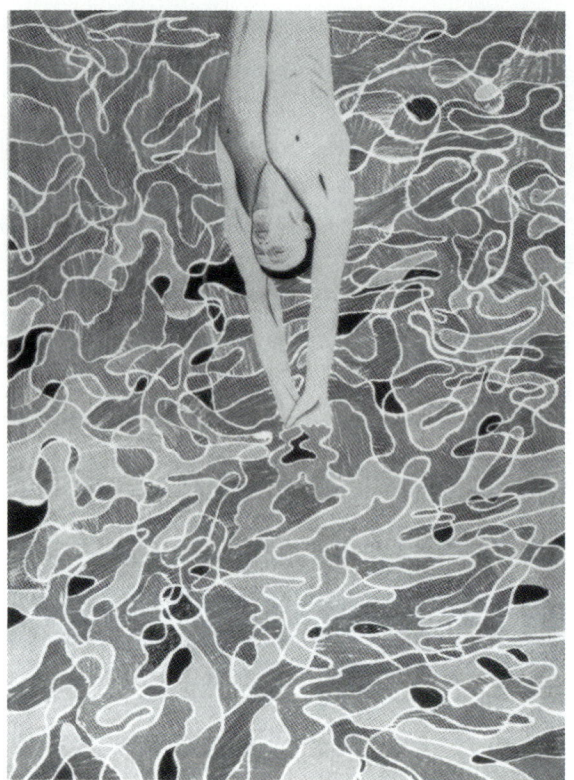

David Hockney
Olympische Spiele Munchen
Courtesy Edition Olympia

TITLE	PUBLISHER	PRINTER	DATE	MEDIUM	DIMENSION (PAPER SIZE) IN INCHES	TYPE OF PAPER	EDITION NUMBER	NO. OF COLORS	ORIGINAL OPENING PRICE	CURRENT RETAIL PRICE
SOLD OUT EDITIONS (RARE):										
My Mother at the Age of Twenty (from a Photograph) as a Study for Felicite in "A Simple Heart" of Gustave Flaubert	PP	PP	1973	EB	11 X 9	AMG	10	1	200	3000
Still Life with Book			1973	LC	27 X 22	AMG	88	1	150	2000
Study of Lightning Medium	PP	MP	1973	LC	30 X 22	AMG	60		150	2000
Chair-38, The Colony, Malibu	GEM	DRH/GEM	1973	LB	30 X 22	AMG	60	1	200	7500
Dark Mist	PP	MP	1973	LC	35 X 29	AMG	25	6	200	25000
Henry (G-450)	GEM	GEM	1973	LB	16 X 12	HMP	50	1	125	7500
The Master Printer of Los Angeles	PP	PP	1973	LC	48 X 32	AP	27		450	15000
The Student: Homage to Picasso	PP	PP	1973	EC	30 X 22	R/BFK	120		400	12000
Postcard of Richard Wagner with a Glass	PP	PP	1973	EB	8 X 6	R/BFK	75	1	350	15000
Godetia (SAC-155)	PP	AC/AtC	1973	EB/A	17 X 11	AP	100		400	22000
The Weather Series (Set of 6):									1500 SET	130000 SET
Mist (SAC-138) (G-442)	GEM	GEM	1973	LC	29 X 25	ARJ	98		350	25000
Lightning (SAC-139) (G-441)	GEM	GEM	1973	LC/SP	31 X 26	ARJ	98		350	15000
Wind (SAC-141) (G-440)	GEM	GEM	1973	LC/SP	31 X 24	ARJ	98		350	15000
Snow (SAC-140) (G-445)	GEM	GEM	1973	LC	34 X 28	ARJ	98		350	25000
Still Life with Book (SAC-144) (G-454)	GEM	GEM	1973	LC	27 X 22	ARJ	88		350	60000
Postcard of Richard Wagner with a Glass of Water (SAC-154)	BJL	AC/AtC	1973	EB/MON	7 X 5	HMP	100	3	350	5000
Artist and Model (SAC-160)	PP	AC/AtC	1973-74	EB/A	30 X 20	AMP	100		400	20000
The Desk	PP	AC/AtC	1974	PH/CO	48 X 46	KOD	20		500	22000
Yves Marie	PP	PP	1974	LB	30 X 23	R/BFK	75	1	250	3500
My Mother with Parrot (Two Etchings, One in Black, One in Color) (Set of 2)	PP	PP	1974	EB/A	26 X 20 EA	R/BFK	100 EA		500 SET	8000 SET
My Mother Today: As a Study for Felicite in "A Simple Heart" of Gustave Flaubert	PP	PP	1974	EB	15 X 12	R/BFK	12	1	300	3000
Geography Book (Felicite's Only View from Abroad): Illustration for "A Simple Heart" of Gustave Flaubert	PP	PP	1974	EC	15 X 16	R/BFK	100		300	4000
Gregory (SAC-169)	PP	PP	1974	EC	27 X 21	IP	75	3	300	9000

DAVID HOCKNEY CONTINUED

TITLE	PUBLISHER	PRINTER	DATE	MEDIUM	DIMENSION (PAPER SIZE) IN INCHES	TYPE OF PAPER	EDITION NUMBER	NO. OF COLORS	ORIGINAL OPENING PRICE	CURRENT RETAIL PRICE
SOLD OUT EDITIONS (RARE):										
Simplified Faces, State I, II (Set of 2)	PP	PP	1974	EC	22 X 20 EA	AP	30 EA		600 SET	20000 SET
Man Ray	PP	PP	1974	LC	26 X 20	AP	50		300	15000
Celia Seated on an Office Chair	PP	PP	1974	EB	35 X 29	R/BFK	20	1	400	18000
Celia Seated on an Office Chair	PP	PP	1974	EB/A	35 X 29	R/BFK	60		500	35000
Celia in a Wicker Chair	PP	PP	1974	EB	35 X 29	R/BFK	20	1	400	25000
Celia in a Wicker Chair	PP	PP	1974	EB/A	35 X 29	R/BFK	60		500	35000
Celia Observing	PP	PP	1974	EB	35 X 29	R/BFK	20	1	400	12000
Celia Observing	PP	PP	1974	EB/A	35 X 29	R/BFK	60		500	20000
Contrejour in the French Style (SAC-167)	PP	PP	1975	EB/A	29 X 29	IN	75		300	50000
Two Vases in the Louvre (SAC-168)	PP	PP	1974	EB/A	29 X 29	AP	75		400	55000
Homage to Michelangelo (SAC-173)	PP	PP	1975	EB/A	32 X 31	HMP	200	2	600	10000
Reclining Figure	PP	PP	1975	EB/A	18 X 20	HMP	75		500	5000
Henry Geldzahler	GEM	GEM	1976	LB	15 X 12	AP	96	1	600	13000
Henry Geldzahler with Hat (SAC-181) (G-711)	GEM	JW/BT/GEM	1976	LB	14 X 12	AP/B	96	1	1000	10000
Henry at the Table (SAC-188) (G-736)	GEM	JW/BT/GEM	1976	LB	30 X 41	HMP	96	1	600	15000
Henry Seated with Tulips (G-737)	GEM	JW/SL/MS/ AZ/EH/GEM	1976	LC	42 X 26	AC	90	5	1600	15000
Henry in His Office (G-766)	GEM	SL/MS/M5/EH/ AZ/JW/GEM	1976	LB	13 X 12	RNP	20	1	400	6000
Henry Reading the Newspaper	GEM	GEM	1976	LB	25 X 18	LBP	71	1	400	8000
For John Constable	PP	PP	1976	LB	15 X 17	HMP	100	1	400	4000
Celia Observing	GEM	GEM	1976	EB/A/SG	35 X 39	R/BFK	60		800	15000
Brooke Hopper	GEM	GEM	1976	LC	38 X 28	AP/B	92	2	1000	8000
Friends Series:										
Christopher Isherwood & Don Bachardy	GEM	GEM	1976	LB	29 X 37	AP/B	96	1	1400	12000
Joe McDonald	GEM	JW/SL/AZ/ EH/GEM	1976	LC	42 X 29	AP/B	99	2	1400	12000
Gregory Evans	GEM	GEM	1976	LB	42 X 30	AP/B	90	1	1400	10000
Nicholas Wilder	GEM	JW/RM/GEM	1976	LB	33 X 25	RP	95	1	1250	10000
Michael Crichton	GEM	JW/EH/GEM	1976	LC	42 X 11	AP/B	93	2	600	6500
Don Cribb	GEM	GEM	1976	LB	17 X 11	AC/W	59	1	600	6500
Peter Schlesinger (G-734)	GEM	JW/MS/GEM	1976–77	LB	16 X 12	AC/W	90	1	600	6500
Mo McDermott (G-735)	GEM	JW/MS/GEM	1976–77	LB	38 X 24	AP/B	100	1	1000	10000

David Hockney
Walking Past Two Chairs
Courtesy Tyler Graphics, Ltd

DAVID HOCKNEY CONTINUED

David Hockney
Ann Combing Her Hair
Courtesy Gemini GEL

David Hockney
Celia with Green Hat
Courtesy Tyler Graphics, Ltd

TITLE	PUBLISHER	PRINTER	DATE	MEDIUM	DIMENSION (PAPER SIZE) IN INCHES	TYPE OF PAPER	EDITION NUMBER	NO. OF COLORS	ORIGINAL OPENING PRICE	CURRENT RETAIL PRICE
SOLD OUT EDITIONS (RARE):										
Sidney in His Office (G-770)	GEM	JW/JS/AZ/GEM	1976–77	LC	20 X 21	HMP	60	2	750	3500
Homage to Michelangelo (SAC-173)	BR		1975	EB/AC	24 X 31	R/BFK	200	2	600	10000
Small Head of Gregory	GEM	JW/EH/GEM	1976–77	LB	11 X 10	AP/B	98	1	450	2000
Gregory Thinking of Henry	GEM	EH/JW/AZ/GEM	1977	LB	37 X 24	RNP	30	1	500	7500
Gregory Reclining	GEM	JW/EH/AZ/GEM	1977	LC	26 X 20	RNP	28	1	400	7500
Gregory with Gym Socks	GEM	JW/EH/AZ/GEM	1977	LC	28 X 19	HMP	14	1	450	7500
Henry with Cigar	GEM	EH/AZ/SL/ MS/GEM	1977	LC	11 X 11	RNP	25	1	500	8500
The Blue Guitar (Set of 20):									9000 SET	75000 SET
The Blue Guitar	PP	PP	1977	EB/A	18 X 21	HMP	200	2	450	2100
The Old Guitarist	PP	PP	1977	EB/A	18 X 21	HMP	200	3	450	4200
A Tune	PP	PP	1977	EB/A	18 X 21	HMP	200	5	450	3600
It Picks its Way	PP	PP	1977	EB/A	18 X 21	HMP	200	2	450	3000
Franco-American Mail	PP	PP	1977	EB/A	18 X 21	HMP	200	4	450	3000
Parade	PP	PP	1977	EB/A	18 X 21	HMP	200	3	450	3200
Discord Merely Magnifies	PP	PP	1977	EB/A	18 X 21	HMP	200	3	450	3200
The Buzzing of the Blue Guitar	PP	PP	1977	EB/A	18 X 21	HMP	200	3	450	3000
In a Chiarascuro	PP	PP	1977	EB/A	18 X 21	HMP	200	2	450	4200
Figures with Still Life	PP	PP	1977	EB/A	18 X 21	HMP	200	3	450	4200
Made in April	PP	PP	1977	EB/A	18 X 21	HMP	200	5	450	2500
A Picture of Ourselves	PP	PP	1977	EB/A	18 X 21	HMP	200	3	450	5000
The Poet	PP	PP	1977	EB/A	18 X 21	HMP	200	4	450	4200
Etching is the Subject	PP	PP	1977	EB/A	18 X 21	HMP	200	5	450	3200
Tick it, Tock it, Turn it	PP	PP	1977	EB/A	18 X 21	HMP	200	4	450	3500
I Say they Are	PP	PP	1977	EB/A	18 X 21	HMP	200	4	450	3000
On it May Stay His Eye	PP	PP	1977	EB/A	18 X 21	HMP	200	3	450	2100
A Moving Still Life	PP	PP	1977	EB/A	18 X 21	HMP	200	3	450	4200
Serenade	PP	PP	1977	EB/A	18 X 21	HMP	200	3	450	4200
What is a Picasso?	PP	PP	1977	EB/A	18 X 21	HMP	200	1	450	5000
Afternoon Swimming	GEM	GEM	1979	LC	32 X 40	HMP	55		1500	80000
Celia-Weary (G-833)	GEM	GEM	1979	LC	40 X 30	TOY/80	100	1	1250	10000
Ann Combing Her Hair	GEM	GEM	1979	LB	24 X 31	HMP	75	1	1800	10000
A Lot More of Ann Combing Her Hair (G-828)	GEM	GEM	1979	LB	49 X 37	TOY/50	67	1	2000	15000
Ann Putting on Lipstick (G-829)	GEM	GEM	1979	LB	47 X 19	OKP	75	1	1800	12000
Ann Seated in Director's Chair	TGL	TGL	1979	LB	30 X 44	R/BFK	5	1	2000	12000
Celia Inquiring	PP	PP	1979	LB	40 X 30	HMP	78	1	2000	18000
Celia Reclining	PP	PP	1979	LB	23 X 22	HMP	100	1	1800	8500
Celia Musing (G-832)	GEM	GEM	1979	LB	40 X 29	HMP	100	1	1250	8500
Celia Elegant (G-836)	GEM	GEM	1979	LB	40 X 30	HMP	100	1	1250	8500
Celia Amused	GEM	GEM	1979	LB	40 X 30	HMP	100	1	1250	8500
Celia Adjusting Her Eyelashes	PP	PP	1979	LB	23 X 31	HMP	100	1	1000	3000
Jerry Sohn	PP	PP	1979	LB	24 X 18	HMP	30	1	1250	4000
Joe with David Harte	TGL	TGL	1979	LC	47 X 32	AC	39	7	2000	8000

DAVID HOCKNEY CONTINUED

TITLE	PUBLISHER	PRINTER	DATE	MEDIUM	DIMENSION (PAPER SIZE) IN INCHES	TYPE OF PAPER	EDITION NUMBER	NO. OF COLORS	ORIGINAL OPENING PRICE	CURRENT RETAIL PRICE
SOLD OUT EDITIONS (RARE):										
Flowers and a Liriope Plant	GEM	GEM	1979	LC	42 X 59	AC	98		2500	15000
Two Vases of Cut Flowers and Liriope Plant	PP	PP	1979	LB	42 X 59	AC	98		2500	15000
Lithograph of Water Made of Thick and Thin Lines, a Green Wash, a Light Blue Wash and a Dark Blue Wash (Pool I) (T-245) (DH-32)	TGL	TGL	1980	LC	26 X 35	TGL/HMP	80	7	2100	28000
Lithograph of Water Made of Lines (Pool IA) (T-246) (T-247) (DH-33)	TGL	TGL	1980	LC	26 X 35	TGL/HMP	39	2	2100	18000
Lithograph of Water Made of Lines and a Green Wash (T-247)	TGL	KT/LF/RC/TGL	1978–80	LC	20 X 28	TGL/HMP	36		2100	10000
Lithograph of Water Made of Lines, a Green Wash and a Light Blue Wash (Pool IB)	TGL	TGL	1980	LC	26 X 35	TGL/HMP	36	3	2100	18000
Lithograph of Water Made of Lines, a Green Wash and a Light Blue Wash (Pool IC)	TGL	TGL	1980	LC	26 X 35	TGL/HMP	37	5	2100	20000
Lithograph of Water Made of Lines with Two Light Blue Washes (Pool ID)	TGL	TGL	1980	LC	26 X 35	TGL/HMP	35	5	2100	20000
Lithograph of Water Made of Thick and Thin Lines, and Two Light Blue Washes (Pool IE)	TGL	TGL	1980	LC	26 X 35	TGL/HMP	40	6	2100	18000
Lithograph of Water Made of Thick and Thin Lines, a Light Blue Wash and a Dark Blue Wash (Pool IF)	TGL	TGL	1980	LC	26 X 35	TGL/HMP	34	6	2100	20000
Lithographic Water Made of Lines, Crayon, and Two Blue Washes (Pool II)	TGL	TGL	1980	LC	30 X 34	TGL/HMP	85	7	2100	18000
Lithographic Water Made of Lines (Pool IIA) (T-253) (DH-40)	TGL	TGL	1980	LB	30 X 34	TGL/HMP	42	1	2100	10000
Lithographic Water Made of Lines and Crayon (Pool IIB)	TGL	TGL	1980	LC	29 X 34	TGL/HMP	42	2	2100	18000
Lithographic Water Made of Lines, Crayon and a Blue Wash (Pool IIC)	TGL	TGL	1980	LC	30 X 34	TGL/HMP	48	5	2100	26000
Lithograph of Water Made of Thick and Thin Lines and Two Blue Washes	TGL	TGL	1980	LC	26 X 34	TGL/HMP	40		2000	12000
Afternoon Swimming	TGL	TGL	1980	LC	32 X 40	AC	55	8	3600	70000
Johnny and Lindsay	TGL	TGL	1980	LC	30 X 44	R/BFK	54	2	1800	8500
Joe with Green Window (T-261)	TGL	TGL	1980	LC	44 X 30	R/BFK/CR	54	2	2000	12000
Study of Byron	TGL	TGL	1980	LB	20 X 16	AC	60	1	900	4000

David Hockney
Two Vases of Cut Flowers and a Liriope Plant
Courtesy Gemini GEL

DAVID HOCKNEY CONTINUED

David Hockney
Green Gray & Blue Plant,
July 1986
Courtesy the Artist

David Hockney
Black Plant on a Table
April 1986
Courtesy the Artist

TITLE	PUBLISHER	PRINTER	DATE	MEDIUM	DIMENSION (PAPER SIZE) IN INCHES	TYPE OF PAPER	EDITION NUMBER	NO. OF COLORS	ORIGINAL OPENING PRICE	CURRENT RETAIL PRICE
SOLD OUT EDITIONS (RARE):										
Afternoon Swimming (T-266) (DH-53)	TGL	TGL	1980	LC	32 X 40	AC/HMP	55	9	1200	90000
The Commissioner	TGL	TGL	1980	LC	16 X 30	AC	50		1000	4000
Potted Daffodils (T-249) (DH-46)	TGL	TGL	1980	LB	44 X 30	R/BFK	98	1	3000	22000
Green Bora Bora	TGL	TGL	1980	LC	35 X 42	R/BFK	50	2	1500	4000
Bora Bora	TGL	TGL	1980	LC	35 X 48	AP88	100	5	2000	10000
Black Tulip (T-258) (DH-45)	TGL	TGL	1980	LB	44 X 30	R/BFK	100	1	3000	22000
Celia in a Polka Dot Skirt	GEM	GEM	1980	LC	40 X 36	HMP	100		3500	20000
Celia in an Armchair (G-918)	GEM	GEM	1980	LC	44 X 48	AC	74	2	3000	30000
James	GEM	GEM	1981	LC	24 X 20	HMP	100	1	800	4500
William Burroughs	GEM	GEM	1981	LC	21 X 18	HMP	100	1	800	4500
Celia in the Director's Chair	GEM	GEM	1981	LB	42 X 38	HMP	98	1	3500	20000
Celia (La Bergere) (G-955)	GEM	GEM	1981	LC	24 X 35	AC	50		800	8000
Celia with Green Plant (G-919)	GEM	GEM	1981	LC	30 X 40	AC	90		1500	18000
John Hockney	GEM	GEM	1981	LC	16 X 15	HMP	100	1	700	4500
Two Vases of Cut Flowers and a Liriope Plant	GEM	GEM	1981	LB	42 X 59	TOY/80	98	1	8000	30000
The Brooklyn Bridge (G-915)	GEM	GEM	1982	PH/CO	108 X 58	KOD	20		5000	35000
Big Celia Print #1 (G-980)	GEM	GEM	1982	LB	48 X 57	AC	100	1	6000	20000
Big Celia Print #2 (G-981)	GEM	GEM	1982	LB	53 X 58	AC	100	1	7000	22000
The Steering Wheel	GEM	GEM	1982	PH/CO	20 X 25	KOD	5		2500	10000
Conversation in the Studio	TGL	TGL	1984	LC	24 X 29	TGL/HMP	45	7	5000	30000
The Marriage in Hawaii of David and Ann	GEM	GEM	1984	EC	43 X 30	HMP	60	1	1800	4500
House Doodle (G-1189)	GEM	GEM	1984	EC	31 X 42	R/BFK	60	1	2000	6000
Ann Looking at Her Picture (T-270)	TGL	TGL	1984	LB	44 X 30	R/BFK	50	1	2500	6000
Mexican Hotel Garden	GEM	GEM	1984	EC	32 X 47	HMP	65	1	2500	5000
Ann in the Studio	GEM	GEM	1984	EC	31 X 42	HMP	61	1	1800	4500
My Pool & Terrace			1984	EB	30 X 42	HMP	250	1	1500	12000
View of Hotel Well I (T-280) (DH-67)	TGL	TGL	1985	LC	32 X 41	TGL/HMP	75	16	6000	80000
View of Hotel Well II (T-281) (DH-68)	TGL	TGL	1985	LC	25 X 32	TGL/HMP	75	14	4500	80000
View of Hotel Well III (T-282) (DH-69)	TGL	TGL	1985	LC	49 X 38	TGL/HMP	80	24	12000	90000
Hotel Acatlan: First Day (Dipt) (T-282) (DH-69)	TGL	TGL	1985	LC	29 X 74	TGL/HMP	70		12000	120000
Hotel Acatlan: Second Day (Dipt) (T-203) (DH-70)	TGL	TGL	1985	LC	29 X 75	TGL/HMP	90	20	12000	100000
Hotel Acatlan: Two Weeks Later (T-286) (DH-73)	TGL	TGL	1985	LC	28 X 37 EA	TGL/HMP	98	20	14000	170000
Pembroke Studio with Blue Chairs and Lamp (T-275) (DH-62)	TGL	TGL	1985	LC	19 X 22	TGL/HMP	98	12	3500	15000
Pembroke Studio Interior (T-277) (DH-64)	TGL	TGL	1985	LC	46 X 55	TGL/HMP	70	10	5000	65000

DAVID HOCKNEY CONTINUED

TITLE	PUBLISHER	PRINTER	DATE	MEDIUM	DIMENSION (PAPER SIZE) IN INCHES	TYPE OF PAPER	EDITION NUMBER	NO. OF COLORS	ORIGINAL OPENING PRICE	CURRENT RETAIL PRICE
SOLD OUT EDITIONS (RARE):										
Two Pembroke Studio Chairs (T-276)	TGL	TGL	1985	LC	19 X 22	TGL/HMP/W	98	4	2500	15000
Tyler Dining Room (T-278) (DH-65)	TGL	TGL	1985	LC	32 X 40	TGL/HMP/W	98	14	7000	50000
Amaryllis in Vase (T-272) (DH-59)	TGL	TGL	1985	LC	50 X 36	TGL/HMP/W	80	10	12000	100000
The Perspective Lesson (T-284) (DHTGL-71)	TGL	TGL	1985	LC	30 X 22	TGL/HMP/G	50	4	3000	15000
An Image of Gregory (Top) (T-285)	TGL	TGL	1985	LC/CO	32 X 26	TGL/HMP/W	75	27	12000	30000
An Image of Gregory (Bottom) (T-285)	TGL	TGL	1985	LC/CO	46 X 35	TGL/HMP/W	75	12	12000	30000
Celia with Green Hat (T-274) (DH-61)	TGL	TGL	1985	LC	30 X 22	TGL/HMP/W	98	13	6000	60000
Red Celia (T-275) (DH-60)	TGL	TGL	1985	LC	31 X 22	TGL/HMP	82	4	12000	55000
An Image of Celia	TGL	TGL	1984–86	LC/OFF/SP/CO	60 X 41	TGL/CR&GE/Bl	40	35	20000	150000
An Image of Celia, State II	TGL	TGL	1986	LC/CO	66 X 49	TGL/HMP-GE	10		2000	160000
White Porcelain	TGL	TGL	1985–86	EB/LC/OFF	19 X 22	TGL/HMP/W	80		6000	20000
Number One Chair	TGL	TGL	1985–86	LC/EC	22 X 19	HMP	60		2500	10000
A Picture of Two Chairs	TGL	TGL	1986	EB/LC/OFF	19 X 21	TGL/HMP	60	5	6000	12000
Black Plant on a Table, April 1986 (6 Sheets) (E-2)	ART	ART/OC	1986	XER	29 X 33	AP	30		3000	9000
Green Gray & Blue Plant, July 1986 (Dipt) (E-33)	ART	ART/OC	1986	XER/HC	22 X 27	AP	60		3000	10000
The Drooping Plant	ART	ART/OC	1986	XER/HC	21 X 18	AP	46		3000	14000
Mulholland Drive	ART	ART/OC	1986	XER/HC	11 X 17	HMP	50	Varies	3000	10000
Red, Blue & Green Flowers	ART	ART/OC	1986	XER/HC	28 X 9	HMP	59	2	2500	8000
The Red Pot	ART	ART/OC	1986	XER/HC	14 X 9	HMP	60	Varies	3000	18000
Walking Past Two Chairs	TGL	TGL	1986	LC	22 X 40	HMP	38	21	5000	80000
Caribbean Tea Time (Double Sided Four Panel Folding Screen)	TGL	TGL	1987	LC/OFF/HC/CO	844 X 137	TGL/HMP	36	51	6000	350000
An Image of Ken	TGL	TGL	1987	LB	28 X 21	MdV	20	1	3000	8000
Portrait of Mother III	TGL	TGL	1987	LC	20 X 17	TGL/HMP	25		2500	3000
Apples, Grapes, Lemons on a Table (Dipt)	PaP	ART/OC	1988	XER/HC	17 X 22	AP	91		6000	22000
Red Flowers and Green Leaves, Separate, May 1988 (Dipt)	MMA	ART/OC	1988	XER/HC	14 X 17	AP	70		6000	20000
Still Life with Lemon	ART	ART/OC	1988	XER/HC	17 X 21	AP	91	Varies	3000	10000

David Hockney
Celia (La Bergere)
Courtesy Gemini GEL

The retail prices of the 100,000 limited edition prints quoted in this directory are subject to change. Print publishers, artists and galleries were the direct sources for these quotations. Prices in the secondary market listed as "Sold Out Editions (Rare)" indicate that the publisher has a limited supply of that print or that the print is difficult to locate in the galleries.

HOWARD HODGKIN

BORN: London, England; 1932
EDUCATION: Camberwell Sch of Art, 1949–50; Bath Acad of Art, England 1950–54
TEACHING: Charterhouse Sch, 1954–56; Bath Acad of Art, 1956–66; Chelsea Sch of Art, 1966; Art in Res, Brasenose Col, Oxford, 1976–77
AWARDS: Second Prize, John Moore Exhib, Liverpool, England, 1976; Commander of the British Empire Award, 1977
RECENT EXHIB: Bernard Jacobson Gallery, London, England, 1990; Greene Art Gallery & New England Sculptors Guild, Guilford, CT, 1989,92; Yale Univ, Yale Center for British Art, New Haven, CT, 1989,92; Whitney Mus of Am Art, Fairfield County Gallery, Stamford, CT, 1992; Lincoln Center, Fine Art Prints, Avery Fisher Hall, NY, 1992; Small Space Gallery, Arts Council of Greater New Haven, CT, 1992
COLLECTIONS: Mus of Mod Art, NY; Tate Gallery, London, England; Arts Council of Great Britain; Contemp Arts Soc, London, England; Peter Stuyvesant Foundation; Sao Paulo Mus, Brazil; Victoria and Albert Mus, London, England; British Mus, London, England; Walker Art Center, Minneapolis, MN
PRINTERS: Ian Lawson, London, England (IL); Alan Cox, London, England (AC); Kelpra Studio, London, England (KS); Solo Press, NY (SP); Norman Lassiter, NY (NL); M Payne (MP); D Levy (DL); B Porter (BP); J Welty (JW); K Farley (KF); Petersburg, London, England (PP); Perry Tymeson, NY (PT); Cinda Sparling, NY (CS); Judith Solodkin, NY (JS); Solo Press, NY (SP); Jack Shirreff, Wiltshire, England (JS); Stephen Doell, Wiltshire, England (SD); Samuel Lee, Wiltshire, England (SL); Andrew Smith, Wiltshire, England (AS); 107 Workshop, Wiltshire, England (107W)
PUBLISHERS: Bernard Jacobson, Ltd, London, England (BJL); Petersburg Press, London, England (PP); Waddington Graphics, London, England (WG)
GALLERIES: L A Louver, Venice, CA; M Knoedler & Company, New York, NY; André Emmerich Gallery, NY; Stein Gladstone Gallery, New York, NY; Bernard Jacobson Gallery, London, England; Marsha Mateyka Gallery, Wash, DC; Mary Ryan Gallery, New York, NY; Solo Gallery, New York, NY; Petersburg Press, Inc, New York, NY; Mary Singer Gallery, Wash, DC; Stephen Solovy Fine Art, Chicago, IL; Jan Weiner Gallery, Topeka, KS; Randall Beck Gallery, Boston, MA; Joy Emery Gallery, Grosse Pointe Farms, MI; Peter M David Gallery, Minneapolis, MN; Images Gallery, Toledo, OH; Locks Gallery, Phila, PA

Knowles (K)

Howard Hodgkin
Moonlight
Courtesy the Artist

TITLE	PUBLISHER	PRINTER	DATE	MEDIUM	DIMENSION (PAPER SIZE) IN INCHES	TYPE OF PAPER	EDITION NUMBER	NO. OF COLORS	ORIGINAL OPENING PRICE	CURRENT RETAIL PRICE
SOLD OUT EDITIONS (RARE):										
Untitled	EA	EA	1967	LC	20 X 25	AP	75		100	10000
Girl on a Sofa	EA	EA	1968	LC	20 X 26	AP	75		100	10000
Composition in Yellow . . .	EA	EA	1971	LC	21 X 29	AP	35		150	2000
More Indian Views (Set of 5)	BJL	IL	1976	LC	9 X 12 EA	SP	60 EA	3–5 EA	700 SET	15000 SET
For John Constable	BJL	IL	1976	LC	18 X 22	SP	100	2	200	5000
A Storm (K-5)	PP	BP/JW/KF	1977	LC/WA/HC	21 X 24	HMP	100		450	12000
Nick's Room	PP	BP/JW/KF	1977	LC/WA/HC	21 X 24	HMP	100	3	450	5000
A Furnished Room	PP	BP/JW/KF	1977	EB/A/HWA	21 X 27	HMP	100		450	2000
Jarid's Porch	PP	BP/JW/KF	1977	LC/HWA	22 X 25	HMP	100		450	5000
Nick	PP	MP/DL	1977	LC	23 X 23	SP	100		450	12000
Julian and Alexis	BJL	IL	1977	LC	28 X 40	SP	30	5	400	20000
Green Chateau (Set of 4)	BJL	AC	1978	LC/HC	10 X 15 EA	AP	12 EA		1000 SET	6000 SET
Bed and Breakfast (Set of 2)	PP	BP/JW/KF	1978	A/G	8 X 13 EA	AP	50 EA		1200 SET	5000 SET
Birthday Party	BJL	SP	1978	LC	16 X 20	AP	50	3	300	2500
Alexander Street	BJL	AC	1978	LC	14 X 24	AP	90	4	300	2500
You and Me	BJL	AC	1978	LC	9 X 16	AP	100	2	200	2500
For Bernard Jacobson (Dipt)	BJL	AC/AtC	1979	LC/HC	42 X 60	AP/CR	80	8	2000	35000
Cardo's Bar (Black)	PP		1979	LC/HC	6 X 5	SP	50		300	8000
Cardo's Bar (Red)	PP		1979	EB/HC	6 X 5	SP	50		300	15000
Here We Are in Croydon			1979	LC/HC	22 X 30		100		600	8000
Late Afternoon	PP		1979	EB	39 X 29		100		600	3500
Thinking Aloud (Black)	PP		1979	EB	47 X 30		100	1	600	6000
Early Evening	PP		1979	EB/HC	45 X 30		100		600	6000
All Alone in the Museum of . . .	PP		1979	EB/HC	47 X 30		100		600	3500
Those Plants			1980	EB/HC	33 X 41		100		600	3500
Artist and Model			1980	EB/A/SG/HC	33 X 42		100		600	3500
Artist and Model (In Green and Yellow)			1980	EB/A/SG/HC	33 X 41	JBG	100		750	5000
After Lunch			1980	EB/A/SG/HC	32 X 42	JBG	100		750	6000
Lotus (K-25)	BJL	KS	1980	SP	32 X 42	JBG	100	5	750	6500
Moonlight (Dipt)	BJL	JS/CS/SP	1980	LC/HC	47 X 56	R/BFK	100	6	2000	20000
Black Moonlight (Dipt)	BJL	JS/CS/SP	1980	LB	47 X 56	R/BFK	50	3	2000	10000
Still Life	BJL	KS	1981	SP	31 X 29	AP	100	5	750	6000
Tropic Fruit	BJL	KS	1981	SP	31 X 37	AP	100	23	700	6000
Souvenir	PP	NL	1981	SP	45 X 55	AP	100		1800	8000
Bleeding	BJL	JS/CS/SP	1982	LC/HC	36 X 60	AP	100		2000	9000
One Down	BJL	JS/CS/SP	1982	LC/HC	36 X 48	AP/B	100		1800	6500
Two to Go (K-39)	BJL	JS/CS/SP	1982	LC/HC	36 X 48	AP/B	100		1800	10000
Mourning	BJL	JS/CS/SP	1982	LC/HC	36 X 60	AP	50		2000	10000

HOWARD HODGKIN CONTINUED

TITLE	PUBLISHER	PRINTER	DATE	MEDIUM	DIMENSION (PAPER SIZE) IN INCHES	TYPE OF PAPER	EDITION NUMBER	NO. OF COLORS	ORIGINAL OPENING PRICE	CURRENT RETAIL PRICE
SOLD OUT EDITIONS (RARE):										
Redeye	BJL	JS/CS/SP	1982	LC/HC	10 X 12	AP	100	3	700	2500
Mourning	BJL	JS/CS/SP	1983	LC/HC	36 X 59	AP	50	Varies	2000	6000
Arrow (Red & Green)	BJL	JS/CS/SP	1983	LC	33 X 24	AP	150		800	1500
D H in Hollywood	PP	PT/CS/PP	1985	EB/SG		R/BFK	100	1	800	3000
Sand	PP	PT/CS/PP	1982–85	LC/HC	31 X 40	AP/B	50	Varies	1500	6000
Blood	PP	PT/CS/PP	1982–85	LC/HC	31 X 40	AC/B	50	Varies	1800	6000
David's Pool	PP	CS/AC/AtC	1979–85	EC/A/SG/HC	25 X 31	HAHN	100	Varies	1800	15000
David's Pool at Night	PP	CS/AC/AtC	1985	EC/A/SG/HC	25 X 31	HAHN	100	Varies	1200	10000
Red Listening Ear	BJL	JS/CS/SP	1986	EB/CAR/HC	19 X 26	HAHN	100	Varies	3000	10000
Blue Listening Ear	BJL	JS/CS/SP	1986	EB/CAR/HC	19 X 25	HAHN	100	Varies	3000	10000
Red Palm	WG	CS/SP	1986	LC/HC	43 X 53	AP/B	85	Varies	3000	10000
Red Palm, State I	WG	CS/SP	1987	LC/HC	43 X 53	AP/B	40	Varies	3000	8000
Black Palm	WG	CS/SP	1986	LC/HC	43 X 53	AP/B	85	Varies	2000	8000
Black Palm, State I	WG	CS/SP	1987	LC/HC	43 X 53	AP/B	40	Varies	2000	8000
Monsoon	WG	CS/SP	1987	LC/HC	43 X 53	AP/B	85	Varies	5000	22000
Black Monsoon	WG	CS/SP	1987	LC	42 X 53	AP/B	40		5000	8000
Moon	WG	CS/SP	1988	LC/HC	20 X 12	AP/B	35		1200	1500
Mango	WG	CS/SP	1990	EB/CAR/HC	30 X 44	AP/B	55		5000	8000
In an Empty Room	WG	CS/SP	1990	EB/CAR/HC	47 X 59	AP/B	55		8500	10000
Indian Tree	WG	CS/SP	1990	EB/CAR/HC	36 X 48	AP/B	55		8500	10000
Moroccan Door	WG	CS/SP	1990	EB/CAR/HC	30 X 44	AP/B	55		6000	7500
Night Palm	WG	CS/SP	1990	EB/CAR/HC	59 X 48	AP/B	55		8500	12000
Palm Window	WG	CS/SP	1990	EB/CAR/HC	59 X 48	AP/B	55		8500	15000
Street Palm	WG	JS/SD/107W	1990	EB/CAR/HC	58 X 47	AP/B	55		8500	15000
Flowering Palm	WG	CS/SP	1990	EB/CAR/HC	59 X 48	AP/B	55		8500	12000

JACK HOFFLANDER

EDUCATION: Chicago Acad of Fine Art, IL; Art Students League, NY
PRINTERS: American Atelier, NY (AA)
PUBLISHERS: Circle Fine Art, Chicago, IL (CFA)
GALLERIES: Circle Galleries, San Diego, CA & San Francisco, CA & Northbrook, IL & Pittsburgh, PA & Houston, TX & Soho, NY & Chicago, IL & Scottsdale, AZ & Beverly Hills, CA & Costa Mesa, CA & Sherman Oaks, CA & Palm Beach, FL & Honolulu, HI & New Orleans, LA & Las Vegas, NV & Seattle, WA

TITLE	PUBLISHER	PRINTER	DATE	MEDIUM	DIMENSION (PAPER SIZE) IN INCHES	TYPE OF PAPER	EDITION NUMBER	NO. OF COLORS	ORIGINAL OPENING PRICE	CURRENT RETAIL PRICE
SOLD OUT EDITIONS (RARE):										
Bennington Factory	CFA	AA	1980	SP	26 X 34	AP	250		100	250
Up, Up and Away	CFA	AA	1982	LC	22 X 28	AP	250		200	250

DOUGLAS WILLIAM HOFMANN

BORN: Baltimore, MD; February 13, 1945
EDUCATION: Maryland Inst, Col of Art, Baltimore, MD, BFA, Cum Laude, 1964-68
TEACHING: Instr, Painting, Maryland Inst, Baltimore, MD, 1974-75
AWARDS: Best in Show, Washington County Mus, 1972; Grant, Stacy Scholarship Fund, 1975
COLLECTIONS: Delaware Art Mus, Wilmington, DE; Joslyn Art Mus, Omaha, NE; Marquette Univ of Fine Art, Milwaukee, WI
PRINTERS: American Atelier, NY (AA)
PUBLISHERS: Circle Fine Art, Chicago, IL (CFA)
GALLERIES: Charles Barry International, Bethesda, MD; Owl Gallery, San Francisco, CA; Circle Galleries, San Diego, CA & San Francisco, CA & Northbrook, IL & Clayton, MO & Pittsburgh, PA & Houston, TX & Soho, NY & Chicago, IL & Scottsdale, AZ & Beverly Hills, CA & Costa Mesa, CA & Sherman Oaks, CA & Palm Beach, FL & Honolulu, HI & New Orleans, LA & Las Vegas, NV & Seattle, WA; Fernette's Gallery of Art, Des Moines, IA
MAILING ADDRESS: 114 Waren Ave, Baltimore, MD 21230

TITLE	PUBLISHER	PRINTER	DATE	MEDIUM	DIMENSION (PAPER SIZE) IN INCHES	TYPE OF PAPER	EDITION NUMBER	NO. OF COLORS	ORIGINAL OPENING PRICE	CURRENT RETAIL PRICE
SOLD OUT EDITIONS (RARE):										
Salon des Cent, State I	CFA	AA	1980	LC	27 X 21	AP	300		250	4000
Salon des Cent, State II	CFA	AA	1980	LC	27 X 21	SOM/W	100		275	4200
Bieres de la Meuse, State I	CFA	AA	1980	LC	31 X 25	AP	300		250	4000
Bieres de la Meuse, State II	CFA	AA	1980	LC	31 X 25	SOM/T	100		275	4200
La Femme en Bleu, State I	CFA	AA	1981	LC	26 X 25	AP	300		300	2000
La Femme en Bleu, State II	CFA	AA	1981	LC	26 X 25	SOM/T	100		300	2100
Moods of Light Folio (Set of 4)									1100 SET	5000 SET
China Closet	CFA	AA	1982	LC	19 X 23	AP	300		325	1400
Morning Light	CFA	AA	1982	LC	19 X 23	AP	300		325	1500
Robe de Satin	CFA	AA	1982	LC	19 X 23	AP	300		325	1400
Night Work	CFA	AA	1982	LC	19 X 23	AP	300		325	1500
Moods of Light Folio (Deluxe) (Set of 4)									1300 SET	6500 SET
China Closet	CFA	AA	1982	LC	23 X 19	SOM	100		350	2000
Morning Light	CFA	AA	1982	LC	23 X 19	SOM	100		350	2000
Robe de Satin	CFA	AA	1982	LC	19 X 23	SOM	100		350	2000
Night Work	CFA	AA	1982	LC	19 X 23	SOM	100		350	2000

DOUGLAS WILLIAM HOFMANN CONTINUED

TITLE	PUBLISHER	PRINTER	DATE	MEDIUM	DIMENSION (PAPER SIZE) IN INCHES	TYPE OF PAPER	EDITION NUMBER	NO. OF COLORS	ORIGINAL OPENING PRICE	CURRENT RETAIL PRICE
SOLD OUT EDITIONS (RARE):										
Jessica, State I	CFA	AA	1983	LC	35 X 43	AP	300		425	4600
Jessica, State II	CFA	AA	1983	LC	35 X 43	SOM/B	75		525	4650
Red Kimono	CFA	AA	1983	LC	31 X 25	AP	300		350	5750
Morning Rehearsal, State I	CFA	AA	1983	LC	31 X 25	AP	300		425	5000
Morning Rehearsal, State II (Deluxe)	CFA	AA	1984	LC	31 X 21	AP	130		475	5100
Lady of Shalot	CFA	AA	1984	LC	33 X 25	AP	300		350	5000
Dancing at Dusk, State I	CFA	AA	1984	LC	40 X 37	AP	275		600	6000
Dancing at Dusk, State II (Deluxe)	CFA	AA	1984	LC	39 X 36	AP	100		650	6200
Tapestry	CFA	AA	1988	LC	26 X 20	AP	300		750	3700
Oriental Bouquet	CFA	AA	1989	LC	23 X 20	AP	300		700	1000
Pink Flowers, State I	CFA	AA	1989	LC	22 X 20	AP	200		700	1500
Variation on Pink Flowers	CFA	AA	1989	LC	26 X 20	AP	100		625	900
Antheriums	CFA	AA	1989	LC	12 X 24	AP	300		600	900
Dance Suite Folio (Set of 4):									2600 SET	2600 SET
At the Barre I	CFA	AA	1990	LC	13 X 13	AP	300		775	775
At the Barre II	CFA	AA	1990	LC	13 X 13	AP	300		725	725
Tarlatans	CFA	AA	1990	LC	13 X 13	AP	300		750	750
Class	CFA	AA	1990	LC	13 X 13	AP	300		750	750
Rehearsal Suite (Set of 4):									2600 SET	3400 SET
Concentrate	CFA	AA	1990	LC	13 X 13	AP	300		750	850
Stretch	CFA	AA	1990	LC	13 X 13	AP	300		750	850
Fury	CFA	AA	1990	LC	13 X 13	AP	300		750	850
Relax	CFA	AA	1990	LC	13 X 13	AP	300		750	850
Before the Ballet, State I (Sepia)	CFA	AA	1990	LC	13 X 13	AP	300	1	1000	1000
Before the Ballet, State II (Green)	CFA	AA	1990	LC	13 X 13	AP	300	1	1000	1000
CURRENT EDITIONS:										
Developpe	CFA	AA	1991	LC	14 X 16	AC	300		900	900
Port de Bras	CFA	AA	1991	LC	14 X 16	AC	300		900	900
Reverence	CFA	AA	1991	LC	14 X 16	AC	300		900	900

CLAUS HOIE

BORN: Stavanger, Norway; November 3, 1911; US Citizen
EDUCATION: Pratt Inst, Brooklyn, NY; Art Students League, NY; Ecole des Beaux Arts, Paris, France
AWARDS: Gold Medal of Honor, Am Watercolor Soc, 1962; Award, Painting, Nat Inst of Arts & Letters, 197 ; Award of Merit, Nat Acad of Design, 1981; Obrig Prize, Nat Acad of Design, 1985
COLLECTIONS: Brooklyn Mus, NY; Norfolk Mus, VA; Butler Inst of Am Art, Youngstown, OH; Oklahoma Mus of Art; Guild Hall Mus, East Hampton, NY; Nat Acad of Design, NY; Univ of Minnesota, Minneapolis, MN; Norwegian-American Mus, Decora, IA; Brigham Young Univ, Salt Lake City, UT
PRINTERS: Artist (ART)
PUBLISHERS: Transworld Art, Inc, NY (TAI)
GALLERIES: Romano Gallery, Barnegat Light, NJ; Vered Gallery, East Hampton, NY
MAILING ADDRESS: 20 W 12th St, New York, NY 1011

TITLE	PUBLISHER	PRINTER	DATE	MEDIUM	DIMENSION (PAPER SIZE) IN INCHES	TYPE OF PAPER	EDITION NUMBER	NO. OF COLORS	ORIGINAL OPENING PRICE	CURRENT RETAIL PRICE
CURRENT EDITIONS:										
The Traveller	TAI	ART	1979	LC	22 X 29	AP	300		250	375
Pitcher and Grapefruit	TAI	ART	1979	LC	25 X 32	AP	300		250	350
Black Raven	TAI	ART	1979	LC	23 X 16	AP	300		250	350
Whirligig	TAI	ART	1979	LC	26 X 33	AP	300		250	350

BARRY HOLDEN

PRINTERS: Fred Gude, Chicago, IL (FG); Landfall Press Inc, Chicago, IL (LPI)
PUBLISHERS: Landfall Press Inc, Chicago, IL (LPI); NAME Gallery, Chicago, IL (NAME)
GALLERIES: Landfall Press Inc, Chicago, IL; Quartet Editions, New York, NY

TITLE	PUBLISHER	PRINTER	DATE	MEDIUM	DIMENSION (PAPER SIZE) IN INCHES	TYPE OF PAPER	EDITION NUMBER	NO. OF COLORS	ORIGINAL OPENING PRICE	CURRENT RETAIL PRICE
SOLD OUT EDITIONS (RARE):										
I Feel the Intruder	LPI/NAME	FG/LPI	1980	LC	22 X 30	AP/W	100	4	150	400

TOM HOLLAND

BORN: Seattle, WA; 1936
EDUCATION: Williamette Univ, George Putnam Univ Center, Salem, OR, 1954–56; Univ of California, Santa Barbara, CA, 1957–58; Univ of California, Berkeley, CA, 1958–59
TEACHING: Art Instr, San Francisco Art Inst, CA, 1961–68; 1972–80; Instr, Art, Univ of California, Los Angeles, CA 1968–69; Instr, Art, Berkeley, CA, 1978–79; Instr, Art, Cornish Inst, Seattle, WA, 1978
AWARDS: Fulbright Grant, Santiago, Chile, 1959–60; Nat Endowment for the Arts Grant, Sculpture, 1975–76; Guggenheim Fel, 1979

TOM HOLLAND CONTINUED

RECENT EXHIB: James Corcoran Gallery, Los Angeles, CA, 1987,88; Berggruen Gallery, San Francisco, CA, 1987,88,89; Charles Cowles Gallery, NY, 1988,89,90
COLLECTIONS: Whitney Mus of Am Art; St Louis City Mus, MO; San Francisco Mus of Art, CA; Mus of Mod Art, NY; Art Inst of Chicago, IL; Guggenheim Mus, NY; Hirshhorn Mus, Wash, DC; Walker Art Center, Minneapolis, MN; Aldrich Mus of Contemp Art, Ridgefield, CT
PRINTERS: Experimental Printmaking, San Francisco, CA (EP); Cirrus Editions Workshop, Los Angeles, CA (CEW); Jack Richard (JR); Nuristani Press (NP); 3EP Ltd, Palo Alto, CA (3EP); Crown Point Press, San Francisco, CA (CPP)

PUBLISHERS: Cirrus Editions, Los Angeles, CA (CE); Brooke Alexander, Inc, NY (BAI); Pace Editions, NY (PE); 3EP Ltd, Palo Alto, CA (3EP); Crown Point Press, San Francisco, CA (CPP)
GALLERIES: Cirrus Editions, Ltd, Los Angeles, CA; Pace Prints, New York, NY; Thomas Babeor Gallery, La Jolla, CA; Smith Andersen Gallery, Palo Alto, CA; John Berggruen Gallery, San Francisco, CA; Linda Farris Gallery, Seattle, WA; Peter M David Gallery, Minneapolis, MN; Nancy Singer Gallery, St Louis, MO; Crown Point Press, San Francisco, CA & New York, NY; James Corcoran Gallery, Santa Monica, CA; Kass/Meridian Gallery, Chicago, IL
MAILING ADDRESS: 28 Roble Rd, Berkeley, CA 94705

TITLE	PUBLISHER	PRINTER	DATE	MEDIUM	DIMENSION (PAPER SIZE) IN INCHES	TYPE OF PAPER	EDITION NUMBER	NO. OF COLORS	ORIGINAL OPENING PRICE	CURRENT RETAIL PRICE
SOLD OUT EDITIONS (RARE):										
Ryder	CE	CEW	1972	LC	30 X 42	CP	55	5	250	1500
Kuo	BAI	JR/NP	1973	LC	43 X 29	R/BFK	42	4	225	1000
Monotype Series	3EP	3EP	1979	MON	20 X 24 EA	SILK	1 EA	Varies	600 EA	1000 EA
Monotype Series	3EP	3EP	1979	MON	22 X 29 EA	SILK	1 EA	Varies	600 EA	900 EA
Monotype Series	3EP	3EP	1979	MON	22 X 30 EA	SILK	1 EA	Varies	600 EA	900 EA
Mariposa Series I–VI (Unique)	PE	EP	1982	HC/CP/3D	36 X 27 EA	CP	1 EA	Varies	2500 EA	4000 EA
Monterey Series, I–XIII (Unique)	PE	EP	1982	HC/CP/3D	36 X 27 EA	CP	1 EA	Varies	3000 EA	4000 EA
Santa Del Series	PE	EP	1983	MON/HC	24 X 36 EA	CP	1 EA	Varies	3000 EA	4000 EA
La Mell Series	PE	EP	1983	MON/HC	20 X 19 EA	CP	1 EA	Varies	2000 EA	3000 EA
Manca	CPP	CPP	1984	EC	22 X 46	HMP	35		1800	1800
Tetton	CPP	CPP	1984	EC	30 X 32	HMP	50		1500	1800
Rici	CPP	CPP	1984	EC	22 X 32	HMP	35		1200	1200
Pamino	CPP	CPP	1986	EC	31 X 47	HMP	40		1500	1800
CURRENT EDITIONS:										
Neiman	CE	CEW	1973	LC	30 X 42	CP	30	3	250	1000
Nichols	CE	CEW	1973	LC	30 X 42	CP	55	3	250	1000
Nelson	CE	CEW	1973	LC	30 X 42	CP	55	4	250	1000
Izio (Dark Head)	CPP	CPP	1984	EC	22 X 20	HMP	25		900	1000
Tali (Light Head)	CPP	CPP	1984	EC	22 X 20	HMP	25		900	1000
Pont	CPP	CPP	1986	EC	33 X 47	HMP	38		1500	1800
Tow	CPP	CPP	1986	EC	48 X 36	HMP	35		1500	1800

GINO HOLLANDER

BORN: New Jersey; 1924
EDUCATION: Rutgers Univ, Newark, NJ; Hobart & William Smith Col
COLLECTIONS: Museo de Bellas Artes, Spain; Greenville County Mus of Art, SC; Churchill Col, Cambridge, England; New York Univ, NY; DePaw Univ, Greencastle, IN

PRINTERS: American Atelier, NY (AA); Artist (ART)
PUBLISHERS: Circle Fine Art, Chicago, IL (CFA); Artist (ART)
GALLERIES: Circle Galleries, San Diego, CA & San Francisco, CA & Northbrook, IL & Pittsburgh, PA & Houston, TX & Soho, NY & Chicago, IL & Scottsdale, AZ & Beverly Hills, CA & Costa Mesa, CA & Sherman Oaks, CA & Palm Beach, FL & Honolulu, HI & New Orleans, LA & Las Vegas, NV & Seattle, WA

TITLE	PUBLISHER	PRINTER	DATE	MEDIUM	DIMENSION (PAPER SIZE) IN INCHES	TYPE OF PAPER	EDITION NUMBER	NO. OF COLORS	ORIGINAL OPENING PRICE	CURRENT RETAIL PRICE
SOLD OUT EDITIONS (RARE):										
Lise	CFA	AA	1979	LC	30 X 22	AP	300		75	450
Siri	CFA	AA	1979	LC	22 X 30	AP	300		100	400
Toro	CFA	AA	1979	LC	25 X 35	AP	300		100	400
Hermana	CFA	AA	1979	LC	30 X 22	AP	300		100	300
Groupo de Figures des Nudes	CFA	AA	1980	LC	21 X 29	AP	300		150	325
Las Dos Mujeres	CFA	AA	1980	LC	24 X 36	AP	300		150	350
Nina Sentada	CFA	AA	1980	LC	35 X 24	AP	300		150	350
Des Nuda con Manos	CFA	AA	1980	LC	29 X 21	AP	300		150	300
Cara de Blanca y Negra	CFA	AA	1980	LC	22 X 30	AP	300		150	325
Barco de Madrugasa	CFA	AA	1980	LC	36 X 24	AP	300		150	325
Sawyers Ridge Triptych	FDI	ART	1980	SP	28 X 28	K/80	275	11	360	500
Glass Corridor	ART	ART	1985	EB	23 X 32	R/BFK	77	1	250	350

CHUCK HOLZMAN

PRINTERS: Robert Townsend, Georgetown, MA (RT)
PUBLISHERS: Daniel Elias Editions, Lincoln, MA (DEEd)

TITLE	PUBLISHER	PRINTER	DATE	MEDIUM	DIMENSION (PAPER SIZE) IN INCHES	TYPE OF PAPER	EDITION NUMBER	NO. OF COLORS	ORIGINAL OPENING PRICE	CURRENT RETAIL PRICE
CURRENT EDITIONS:										
Untitled	DEEd	RT	1992	EB/A/HG/SL/DPT/CC	24 X 20	JP	35	1	300	300

MOHAMMAD HOURIAN

BORN: Iran; February 17, 1955
EDUCATION: Univ of Tehran, Iran, BA, 1973–77; Apprentice for 10 Years, with Haj Hosen-I-Esalrniyan, Iran (Age 12–22 Years)
TEACHING: Univ of Tehran, Iran, 1978; Berkeley Adult Ed, Berkeley, CA, 1987
AWARDS: Gold Medal, Int Tehran Exhib, 1975; First Prize, Tehran Painter's Exhibit, 1976
RECENT EXHIB: Hourian Fine Art Gallery, San Francisco, CA 1987,88; Columbia Univ, NY, 1989; Noori Gallery, San Francisco, CA, 1990; Swanson Fine Art Gallery, San Francisco, CA, 1992
COLLECTIONS: Fine Art Mus, Tehran, Iran; Mus of Fine Art, Brussels, Belgium; Mus of Mod Art, Tehran, Iran; Fine Art Mus, Tokyo, Japan; Tate Gallery, London, England; Columbia Univ, NY
PRINTERS: Lompa Print & Lithographing Company, Albany, CA (LPLC)
PUBLISHERS: Hourian Fine Art Publishing, San Francisco, CA (HFAP)
GALLERIES: Hourian Fine Art, San Francisco, CA; Swanson Fine Art Gallery, San Francisco, CA; Galerie Rivolta, Lausanne, Switzerland; Roma Gallery, Rome, Italy; Hilton Art Gallery, Tokyo, Japan; Sheraton Art Gallery, Munich, Germany; Noori Gallery, San Francisco, CA; Goethe Inst, Munich Germany & Berlin, Germany
MAILING ADDRESS: 1843 Union Street, San Francisco, CA 94123

Mohammad Hourian
Mother Earth Under the Sea
Courtesy the Artist

Mohammad Hourian
Dreams of Five Seasons
Courtesy the Artist

Mohammad Hourian
The G Clef with Two Lovers
Courtesy the Artist

The retail prices of the 100,000 limited edition prints quoted in this directory are subject to change. Print publishers, artists and galleries were the direct sources for these quotations. Prices in the secondary market listed as "Sold Out Editions (Rare)" indicate that the publisher has a limited supply of that print or that the print is difficult to locate in the galleries.

MOHAMMAD HOURIAN CONTINUED

Mohammad Hourian
Poet Watching a Polo Game
Courtesy the Artist

TITLE	PUBLISHER	PRINTER	DATE	MEDIUM	DIMENSION (PAPER SIZE) IN INCHES	TYPE OF PAPER	EDITION NUMBER	NO. OF COLORS	ORIGINAL OPENING PRICE	CURRENT RETAIL PRICE
SOLD OUT EDITIONS (RARE):										
Phoenix "Symorgh"	HFA	LPLC	1990	LC	20 X 30	QUIN	47	27	300	1600
CURRENT EDITIONS:										
Traditional Dancer with G Clef	HFA	LPLC	1988	LB	8 X 12	QUIN	47	1	150	450
Black and White G Clef	HFA	LPLC	1988	LC	22 X 27	QUIN	500	2	180	350
Dreams of Five Seasons	HFA	LPLC	1989	LC	23 X 35	QUIN	275	30	250	680
G Clef with Two Lovers	HFA	LPLC	1990	LC	9 X 14	QUIN	500	12	180	350
Lover with Arabesque	HFA	LPLC	1990	LC	9 X 14	QUIN	500	12	180	350
Polo Scene	HFA	LPLC	1990	LC	11 X 14	QUIN	500	25	180	350
Poet Watching a Polo Game	HFA	LPLC	1990	LC	16 X 24	QUIN	500	28	250	680

GORDON HOUSE

BORN: Wales; 1932
EDUCATION: St Albans Sch of Art
TEACHING: Hornsey Col of Art, London, England
COLLECTIONS: Mus of Mod Art, NY; Brooklyn Mus, NY; Tate Gallery of Art, London, England; British Council, London, England; Arts Council of Great Britain, London, England; Arco, Los Angeles, CA

PUBLISHERS: Artist (ART)
PRINTERS: Chris Prater, London, England (CP); Kelpra Studio, London, England (KS); Cliff White, London, England (CW); White Ink, London, England (WI); Atelier Wolfensberger, Zurich, Switzerland (AW); Harry Godfrey, London, England (HG)
GALLERIES: Waddington Graphics, London, England

TITLE	PUBLISHER	PRINTER	DATE	MEDIUM	DIMENSION (PAPER SIZE) IN INCHES	TYPE OF PAPER	EDITION NUMBER	NO. OF COLORS	ORIGINAL OPENING PRICE	CURRENT RETAIL PRICE
SOLD OUT EDITIONS (RARE):										
Crystal Red	ART	AW	1979	LC	43 X 31	AP	80		180	1200
Manx Red	ART	AW	1979	LC	43 X 31	AP	80		180	1200
Strand Green	ART	AW	1979	LC	43 X 31	AP	80		180	1200
Gothic Blue	ART	AW	1979	LC	43 X 31	AP	80		180	1200
Celt Green	ART	AW	1979	LC	43 X 31	AP	80		180	1200
Quarter Yellow	ART	AW	1979	LC	43 X 31	AP	80		180	1200
Directional Pink	ART	CP/KS	1979	EC	23 X 16	R/BFK	40		135	1000
Gothic Green	ART	CP/KS	1979	EC	23 X 17	R/BFK	40		135	1000
Manuscript Red	ART	CP/KS	1979	EC	23 X 17	R/BFK	40		135	1000
Crystal Earth	ART	CP/KS	1979	EC	23 X 17	R/BFK	40		135	1000
Manx Yellow	ART	CP/KS	1979	EC	23 X 17	R/BFK	40		135	1000
Still Life at Millbank	ART	CP/KS	1980	SP	24 X 30	AP	150		180	1000
5 + 2 First Phase with Green	ART	CP/KS	1981	LC	27 X 31	AP	70		180	800
5 + 2 First Phase with Red	ART	CP/KS	1981	LC	27 X 31	AP	70		180	800
London Bridge (Set of 8)	ART	CP/KS	1985	EB	12 X 8 EA	R/BFK	30 EA	1 EA	1500 SET	3000 SET

The print market has become very selective. For the first time since we published the first edition of The Printworld Directory in 1982, the prices of prints have been greatly reduced and greatly increased for the same artists by the most reputable and established print publishers. Check the fifth edition to understand the movement.

KAZUHISA HONDA

BORN: Japan; 1948
EDUCATION: Univ of Osaka, Japan; Atelier 17, Paris, France
TEACHING: Pratt Graphics Center, NY
PRINTERS: Artist (ART)

PUBLISHERS: John Szoke Graphics, NY (JSG)
GALLERIES: Wenniger Graphics, Boston, MA; Troy Art Gallery, Troy, NY; Summa Gallery, New York, NY & Brooklyn, NY; Newmark Gallery, New York, NY

TITLE	PUBLISHER	PRINTER	DATE	MEDIUM	DIMENSION (PAPER SIZE) IN INCHES	TYPE OF PAPER	EDITION NUMBER	NO. OF COLORS	ORIGINAL OPENING PRICE	CURRENT RETAIL PRICE
CURRENT EDITIONS:										
Piano and Violin	JSG	ART	1984	MEZ	9 X 7	R/BFK	85	4	150	250
Jumping Frog	JSG	ART	1984	MEZ/CC	12 X 10	R/BFK	50	4	175	275
Village	JSG	ART	1985	MEZ	20 X 25	R/BFK	75	4	250	350
Y's House	JSG	ART	1985	MEZ	20 X 25	R/BFK	60	4	250	350
Baby's Breath	JSG	ART	1986	MEZ	25 X 18	R/BFK	65	4	250	350

BUDD HOPKINS

BORN: Wheeling, WVA; June 15, 1931
EDUCATION: Oberlin Col, OH, BA, 1953; Columbia Univ, NY, 1953–54
TEACHING: Instr, Pratt Inst, Brooklyn, NY; Instr, Rhode Island Sch of Design, Providence, RI
AWARDS: Guggenheim Fel, 1975; Nat Endowment for the Arts Grant, 1979; Special Project Grant, New York State Council of the Arts, 1982
RECENT EXHIB: Marilyn Pearl Gallery, NY, 1988

COLLECTIONS: Guggenheim Mus, NY; Whitney Mus of Am Art, NY; Brooklyn Mus, NY; Corcoran Gallery of Art, Wash, DC; Hirshhorn Mus, Wash, DC; Allen Mem Art Mus; Delaware Art Mus, Wilmington, DE; Williams Col, Williamstown, MA
PRINTERS: Alexander Heinrici, NY (AH); Studio Heinrici, NY (SH); American Atelier, NY (AA)
PUBLISHERS: Jackie Fine Arts, NY (JFA); Worldwide Artistic Enterprises, DE (WAE); Frank Fedele Fine Arts, NY (FF); Artist (ART); Circle Fine Art, Chicago, IL (CFA)
GALLERIES: Long Point Gallery, Provincetown, MA; Kornbluth Gallery, Fair Lawn, NJ
MAILING ADDRESS: 246 W 16th St, New York, NY 10011

TITLE	PUBLISHER	PRINTER	DATE	MEDIUM	DIMENSION (PAPER SIZE) IN INCHES	TYPE OF PAPER	EDITION NUMBER	NO. OF COLORS	ORIGINAL OPENING PRICE	CURRENT RETAIL PRICE
SOLD OUT EDITIONS (RARE):										
Orange United	ART	AH/SH	1970	LB/SP	20 X 29	AP	250	5	400	500
Blue Hiram	ART	AH/SH	1973	SP	41 X 28	AP	150	5	250	600
Blue Assembled Image	ART	AH/SH	1975	SP	29 X 22	AP	200	4	150	400
CURRENT EDITIONS:										
Jutland	JFA	AH/SH	1979	SP	46 X 32	AP	250	5	400	500
Guardian I, II	JFA	AH/SH	1979	SP	40 X 27 EA	AP	250 EA	6 EA	400 EA	500 EA
Guardian III	WAE	AH/SH	1980	SP	40 X 27	AP	200	7	400	500
Guardian IV	WAE	AH/SH	1980	SP	40 X 27	AP	200	5	400	500
Guardian V, VI	ART	AH/SH	1980	SP	40 X 27 EA	AP	200 EA	10 EA	400 EA	500 EA
Guardian VII	WAE	AH/SH	1980	SP	40 X 27	AP	200	8	400	500
Guardian VIII, IX, X	CFA	AA	1980	SP	40 X 26 EA	AP	250 EA		200 EA	200 EA
Ixion IV, V	WAE	AH/SH	1980	SP	40 X 27 EA	AP	200 EA	9 EA	400 EA	500 EA
Gansevoort Street	WAE	AH/SH	1980	SP	40 X 27	AP	200	6	400	500

STEVE HORAN

BORN: Chicago, IL; April 1, 1940
EDUCATION: Univ of Chicago, IL, BA, 1961
AWARDS: Travel Fellowship to Europe, Univ of Chicago, Dept of Art History, Chicago, IL, 1964

COLLECTIONS: Univ of Wisconsin, La Crosse, WI
PRINTERS: Rupert Smith, NY (RS); Artist (ART)
PUBLISHERS: Fred Dorfman, Inc, NY (FDI); Artist (ART)
GALLERIES: Fred Dorfman, New York, NY; Roy Boyd Gallery, Chicago, IL; Neville-Sargent Gallery, Evanston, IL; Charlotte Brauer Fine Art, Munster, IN

TITLE	PUBLISHER	PRINTER	DATE	MEDIUM	DIMENSION (PAPER SIZE) IN INCHES	TYPE OF PAPER	EDITION NUMBER	NO. OF COLORS	ORIGINAL OPENING PRICE	CURRENT RETAIL PRICE
SOLD OUT EDITIONS (RARE):										
Town and Country	FDI	ART	1976	SP	30 X 40	K/80	150	8	225	500
Winter Haven	FDI	ART	1976	SP	30 X 40	K/80	150	8	225	500
City	FDI	ART	1976	SP	30 X 40	K/80	150	16	225	500
Stacy Triptych	FDI	ART	1978	SP	22 X 28 / 22 X 22 / 14 X 22	K/80	150	10	250	500
River Source Triptych	FDI	ART	1979	SP	28 X 28 / 22 X 28 / 14 X 28	K/80	150	6	275	500
Motoring	FDI	ART	1980	SP	30 X 40	K/80	150	19	300	400
Leaves	FDI	ART	1980	SP	30 X 40	K/80	150	9	200	400
Sawyers Ridge Triptych	FDI	ART	1980	SP	28 X 28 / 20 X 28 / 20 X 28	K/80 / K/80 / K/80	275	11	360	600
CURRENT EDITIONS:										
Holsteins	ART	ART	1976	SP	30 X 40	K/80	150	14	150	400
Golden Butte	FDI	ART	1979	SP	22 X 28	Q/100	175	7	125	250

STEVE HORAN CONTINUED

TITLE	PUBLISHER	PRINTER	DATE	MEDIUM	DIMENSION (PAPER SIZE) IN INCHES	TYPE OF PAPER	EDITION NUMBER	NO. OF COLORS	ORIGINAL OPENING PRICE	CURRENT RETAIL PRICE
CURRENT EDITIONS:										
Brian's Hill	FDI	ART	1979	SP	22 X 28	Q/100	150	8	125	250
Homewood	ART	ART	1980	SP	30 X 40	R/BFK	150	9	150	400
City Lights	FDI	ART	1982	SP	30 X 30	L/2P	150	11	150	300
White River	FDI	ART	1982	SP	30 X 30	L/2P	150	11	150	300
Portage	FDI	ART	1982	SP	30 X 30	L/2P	150	10	150	300
Strawberries	FDI	ART	1982	SP	30 X 30	L/2P	150	9	150	300
Kettle Moraine	FDI	RS	1982	SP	30 X 60	L/2P	100	7	500	600
Driving Home	FDI	RS	1982	SP	30 X 60	L/2P	100	11	500	600

IAN JOHN HORNAK

BORN: Philadelphia, PA; January 9, 1944
EDUCATION: Univ of Michigan, Ann Arbor, MI; Wayne State Univ, Detroit, MI, BFA, MFA
TEACHING: Instr, Drawing, Wayne State Univ, Detroit, MI, 1965–67; Henry Ford Col, Dearborn, MI, 1966 to present
RECENT EXHIB: Katharina Rich Perlow Gallery, NY, 1988
COLLECTIONS: Corcoran Gallery of Art, Wash, DC; Hecksher Mus, Huntington, NY; Albrecht Art Mus, St Joseph, MO; Oklahoma Art Center, OK; Indianapolis Mus of Art, IN; Canton Art Inst, OH
PRINTERS: John Nichols, NY (JN); Joseph Kleineman, NY (JK)
PUBLISHERS: Fred Dorfman, Inc, NY (FDI); London Arts, Inc, Detroit, MI (LAI)
GALLERIES: Fischbach Gallery, New York, NY; Robert L Kidd Associates, Birmingham, MI; Katharina Rich Perlow Gallery, New York, NY; Armstrong Gallery, New York, NY
MAILING ADDRESS: c/o Dept of Art, Henry Ford Col, Dearborn, MI 48128

TITLE	PUBLISHER	PRINTER	DATE	MEDIUM	DIMENSION (PAPER SIZE) IN INCHES	TYPE OF PAPER	EDITION NUMBER	NO. OF COLORS	ORIGINAL OPENING PRICE	CURRENT RETAIL PRICE
CURRENT EDITIONS:										
Angel's Concert	LAI	JK	1978	SP	22 X 29	JK	200	10	200	250
Transparent Barricades	FDI	JN	1981	SP	27 X 40	R/BFK	200	20	350	400
The Unexpected Frontier	FDI	JN	1981	SP	30 X 40	R/BFK	150	9	250	300

LARRY HOROWITZ

BORN: Plainview, NY; April 3, 1957
EDUCATION: Art Students League, NY, 1974; State Univ of New York, Purchase, NY, BFA, 1974–78
PRINTERS: Cone Editions, East Topsham, VT (CEd); Jon Cone, East Topsham, VT (JC)
PUBLISHERS: Cone Editions, East Topsham, VT (CEd)
GALLERIES: Condeso/Lawler, New York, NY; Windmueller Fine Arts, Scarsdale, NY; Artworks Fine Art, Old Greenwich, CT; Kornbluth Gallery, Inc, Fair Lawn, NJ; Gallery North, Setauket, NY; Images Gallery, Toledo, OH; Meredith Long & Company, Houston, TX

TITLE	PUBLISHER	PRINTER	DATE	MEDIUM	DIMENSION (PAPER SIZE) IN INCHES	TYPE OF PAPER	EDITION NUMBER	NO. OF COLORS	ORIGINAL OPENING PRICE	CURRENT RETAIL PRICE
CURRENT EDITIONS:										
Reflections	CEd	CEd/JC	1982	SP	8 X 10	AP	30	12	100	200
Notch	CEd	CEd/JC	1982	SP	17 X 25	AP	60	12	150	450

SHIRAZEH HOUSHIARY

PRINTERS: Peter Kosowicz, London, England (PK); Hope Sufferance Studios, London, England (HSS)
PUBLISHERS: Paragon Press, London, England (ParaPr)
GALLERIES: Paragon Press, London, England

TITLE	PUBLISHER	PRINTER	DATE	MEDIUM	DIMENSION (PAPER SIZE) IN INCHES	TYPE OF PAPER	EDITION NUMBER	NO. OF COLORS	ORIGINAL OPENING PRICE	CURRENT RETAIL PRICE
CURRENT EDITIONS:										
Round Dance (Set of 5)	ParaPr	PK/HSS	1992	EB	30 X 30 EA	ZER	20 EA	1 EA	£3000 SET	£3000 SET

DAVID HOWARD

BORN: Brooklyn, NY; January 25, 1948
EDUCATION: Ohio Univ, Athens, OH, 1969–71; San Francisco Art Inst, CA, MFA; San Francisco Center for Visual Studies, CA
TEACHING: Vis Instr, San Francisco City Col, CA, 1973; San Francisco Art Inst, CA; San Francisco Center for Visual Studies, CA, 1974 to present
AWARDS: Purchase Award, City of San Francisco, CA, 1973
RECENT EXHIB: San Francisco Public Library, CA, 1987; Hadley Martin Gallery, San Francisco, CA, 1987; Marc Richards Gallery, Los Angeles, CA, 1987; California State Univ, Northridge, CA, 1988; G Ray Hawkins Gallery, Santa Monica, CA, 1988; Hirshhorn Mus, Wash, DC, 1990; Smithsonian Mus, Wash, DC, 1990; Philadelphia Mus of Art, PA, 1990
COLLECTIONS: Mus of Mod Art, NY; San Francisco Mus of Mod Art, CA; Oakland Mus of Art, CA; de Saisset Art Gallery Mus, Santa Clara, CA; Hirshhorn Mus, Wash, DC; Smithsonian Inst, Wash, DC; San Francisco Art Inst, CA; Whitney Mus of Am Art, NY
PRINTERS: Artist (ART)
PUBLISHERS: San Francisco Center for Visual Studies, CA (SFC); Artist (ART)
GALLERIES: San Francisco Center for Visual Studies, San Francisco, CA; G Ray Hawkins Gallery, Santa Monica, CA; Marc Richards Gallery, Los Angeles, CA; Hadley Martin Gallery, San Francisco, CA
MAILING ADDRESS: 49 Rivoli St, San Francisco, CA 94117

DAVID HOWARD CONTINUED

TITLE	PUBLISHER	PRINTER	DATE	MEDIUM	DIMENSION (PAPER SIZE) IN INCHES	TYPE OF PAPER	EDITION NUMBER	NO. OF COLORS	ORIGINAL OPENING PRICE	CURRENT RETAIL PRICE
SOLD OUT EDITIONS (RARE):										
Conception	ART	ART	1970	PH	11 X 14	AP	50		35	850
Objective Reality	ART	ART	1973	PH	16 X 20	AP	100		75	1000
Realities I	SFVS	ART	1976	PH	20 X 24	AP	200		300	1500
Perspectives I	SFVS	ART	1978	PH	16 X 20	AP	100		450	1800
Perceptions I	SFVS	ART	1979	PH	8 X 10	AP	200		175	500
CURRENT EDITIONS:										
Mexico	SFVS	ART	1980	SP	20 X 24	AP	100	5	300	450
Mexico II	SFVS	ART	1980	PH/C	16 X 20	AP	50	FULL	250	400
Illusions	SFVS	ART	1981	PH/C	16 X 20	AP	50	FULL	250	300
Perceptions II	SFVS	ART	1981	PH/C	16 X 20	AP	50	FULL	250	300
Realities II	SFVS	ART	1981	PH/C	16 X 20	AP	50	FULL	250	300
Perspectives II	SFVS	ART	1981	PH/C	16 X 20	AP	50	FULL	250	300
Realism	SFVS	ART	1981	PH/C	16 X 20	AP	50	FULL	250	300
Abstraction	SFVS	ART	1981	PH/C	16 X 20	AP	50	FULL	250	300
Minimalism	SFVS	ART	1981	PH/C	16 X 20	AP	50	FULL	250	300
Nude Views	LW	ART	1981	SP	20 X 24	R/100	250	6	250	300
Life Lovers	LW	ART	1981	PH	16 X 20	R/100	150	1	185	250
Found Object #1	SFVS	ART	1981	PH/C	16 X 20	R/100	50	FULL	250	300
Altered Found Object #1	SFVS	ART	1981	PH	30 X 40	R/100	30	FULL	350	400
Altered Found Object #2	SFVS	ART	1982	PH	30 X 40	R/100	30	FULL	350	400
Found Object #2	SFVS	ART	1982	PH	30 X 40	R/100	30	1	200	250

LINDA HOWARD

BORN: Evanston, IL; October 22, 1934
EDUCATION: Univ of Colorado, Boulder, CO; Northwestern Univ, Chicago, IL; Chicago Art Inst, IL, 1953–55; Univ of Denver, CO, 1957; Hunter Col, NY, MA, 1971
TEACHING: Asst Prof, Sculpture, Hunter Col, NY, 1969–72; Lehman Col, NY, 1973–76; Assoc Prof, Hunter Col, NY, 1976–82
AWARDS: Creative Artists Public Service Grant, New York State, NY, 1975; Faculty Res Grant, City Univ of New York, NY 1975
RECENT EXHIB: Univ of Florida, Univ Gallery, Gainesville, FL, 1987
COLLECTIONS: Virlane Found, New Orleans, LA; City of Chicago, IL
PRINTERS: John Nichols, NY (JN)
PUBLISHERS: John Nichols, NY (JN)
GALLERIES: John Nichols Gallery, New York, NY; Barbara Gillman, Miami, FL; Joan Hodgell Gallery, Sarasota, FL; Heath Gallery, Atlanta, GA
MAILING ADDRESS: 527 72nd St, Holmes Beach, FL 33510–1508

TITLE	PUBLISHER	PRINTER	DATE	MEDIUM	DIMENSION (PAPER SIZE) IN INCHES	TYPE OF PAPER	EDITION NUMBER	NO. OF COLORS	ORIGINAL OPENING PRICE	CURRENT RETAIL PRICE
CURRENT EDITIONS:										
Imaginary Organic Structures	JN	JN	1984	LC/SP	30 X 40 EA	AP88	65 EA	25 EA	400 EA	500 EA
The I Ching Series	JN	JN	1984	SP/SL	30 X 22 EA	Mylar	40 EA	3 EA	500 EA	600 EA

FRANK HOWELL

BORN: Sioux City, IA; July 31, 1937
EDUCATION: Univ of Northern Iowa, Cedar Falls, IA; Univ of Iowa, Iowa City, IA; Chicago Art Inst, IL
RECENT EXHIB: John A Boler, Indian & Western Art, Minneapolis, MN, 1992
PRINTERS: Master Editions, Ltd, Englewood, CO (MEd)
PUBLISHERS: C G Rein Publishers, St Paul, MN (CGR)
GALLERIES: C G Rein Galleries, Scottsdale, AZ & Santa Fe, NM & Mount Lebanon, PA & Houston, TX & Minneapolis, MN; Lake Galleries, Inc, Tahoe City, CA; Gallery One at Second Avenue, Denver, CO; Renaissance Gallery, Mount Lebanon, PA & Pittsburgh, PA; Valhalla Gallery, Dallas, TX; Gomes Gallery, Inc, St Louis, MO

TITLE	PUBLISHER	PRINTER	DATE	MEDIUM	DIMENSION (PAPER SIZE) IN INCHES	TYPE OF PAPER	EDITION NUMBER	NO. OF COLORS	ORIGINAL OPENING PRICE	CURRENT RETAIL PRICE
SOLD OUT EDITIONS (RARE):										
The Crow Messengers	CGR	MEd	1984	LC	22 X 40	TSH/100	150		1000	1750
CURRENT EDITIONS:										
Dark Night	CGR	MEd	1983	LC	22 X 31	R/BFK/T	100		600	975
Ghost Dancer	CGR	MEd	1985	LC	29 X 16	STP	100	5	550	750
Sisters	CGR	MEd	1985	LC	45 X 30	STP	100		800	1200
Red Feathers	CGR	MEd	1985	LC	39 X 25	STP	200		800	1400

NICHOLAS HOWEY

BORN: Dubois, PA; 1948
EDUCATION: Univ of Pittsburgh, PA, BA; New York Univ, NY, MA
RECENT EXHIB: Greenberg Wilson Gallery, NY, 1991; Galleria in Arco, Turin, Italy, 1992; John Lee Gallery, NY, 1992
PRINTERS: Robert Blanton, NY (RB); Cinda Sparling, NY (CS); Joseph Stauber, NY (JS); Brand X Editions, NY (BX)
PUBLISHERS: Brand X Editions, NY (BX)
GALLERIES: John Post Lee Gallery, New York, NY

The retail prices of the 100,000 limited edition prints quoted in this directory are subject to change. Print publishers, artists and galleries were the direct sources for these quotations. Prices in the secondary market listed as "Sold Out Editions (Rare)" indicate that the publisher has a limited supply of that print or that the print is difficult to locate in the galleries.

NICHOLAS HOWEY CONTINUED

TITLE	PUBLISHER	PRINTER	DATE	MEDIUM	DIMENSION (PAPER SIZE) IN INCHES	TYPE OF PAPER	EDITION NUMBER	NO. OF COLORS	ORIGINAL OPENING PRICE	CURRENT RETAIL PRICE
CURRENT EDITIONS:										
Late Night (Set of 4)	BX	RB/CS/JS/BX	1992	SP	22 X 31 EA	SWP	40 EA		1800 SET	1800 SET

JOHN HOYLAND

BORN: Sheffield, England; 1934
EDUCATION: Sheffield Col of Art, England, 1951–56; Royal Acad Sch, London, England, 1956–60; Central Sch of Art, London, England
TEACHING: Chelsea Sch of Art, London, England
COLLECTIONS: Arts Council of Great Britain, London, England; British Council, London, England; Tate Gallery of Art, London, England; Power Coll, Sydney, Australia; Albright-Knox Art Gallery, Buffalo, NY; Toledo Mus of Art, OH; Phoenix Mus of Art, AZ

PRINTERS: Chris Prater, London, England (CP); Kelpra Studios, London, England (KS); James Collyer, London, England (JC); J C Editions, London, England (JCE); Chiron Press, NY (ChP); Advanced Graphics, London, England (AG); Roger Frélaut, Paris, France (RF); Atelier Lacouriere et Frélaut, Paris, France (ALF); Jack Shirreff, Wiltshire, England (JS); 107 Workshop, Wiltshire, England (107W)
PUBLISHERS: Waddington Graphics, London, England (WG)
GALLERIES: Waddington Graphics, London, England; Bernard Jacobson Ltd, London, England; Erika Meyerovich Gallery, San Francisco, CA; Eva Cahon Galleries, Ltd, Chicago, IL & Highland Park, IL; Fisher Island Gallery, Fisher Island, FL

TITLE	PUBLISHER	PRINTER	DATE	MEDIUM	DIMENSION (PAPER SIZE) IN INCHES	TYPE OF PAPER	EDITION NUMBER	NO. OF COLORS	ORIGINAL OPENING PRICE	CURRENT RETAIL PRICE
SOLD OUT EDITIONS (RARE):										
Small Green (Curwen)	WG		1968	LB	22 X 29	AP	75	1	75	1500
Small Grey (Swiss)	WG		1968	LB	18 X 27	AP	75	1	75	1500
Small Red	WG		1968	LB	18 X 27	AP	75	1	75	1800
Large Green (Swiss)	WG		1968	LB	20 X 31	AP	75	1	80	2200
Large Red, Documenta	WG		1968	LB	25 X 35	AP	100	1	80	2200
Blues/Red	WG	ChP	1969	SP	24 X 36	AP	75		100	3000
Red Blue	WG	ChP	1969	SP	24 X 36	AP	75		100	3000
Red/Greens	WG	ChP	1969	SP	22 X 36	AP	75		100	3000
Yellows	WG	ChP	1969	SP	21 X 36	AP	75		100	1800
Brown-Beige-Pink	WG	ChP	1970	LB	23 X 31	AP	100	1	120	1500
Ochre, Pink	WG		1971	EB	31 X 23	R/BFK	40	1	120	1500
Orange-Pink	WG	ChP	1971	SP	23 X 31	AP	75		120	1500
Orange-Pink-Green	WG	ChP	1971	SP	23 X 31	AP	75		120	1500
The New York Suite (Set of 9):										
Green, Orange, Pink	WG	ChP	1971	SP	41 X 28	AP	100		135	1800
Grey/Blue	WG	ChP	1971	SP	41 X 28	AP	100		135	1800
Yellow and Pink	WG	ChP	1971	SP	28 X 41	AP	100		135	1800
Pale Yellow, Pink and Brown	WG	ChP	1971	SP	28 X 41	AP	100		135	1800
Red Block on Grey	WG	ChP	1971	SP	41 X 28	AP	100		135	1800
Red Block on Pink	WG	ChP	1971	SP	41 X 28	AP	100		135	1800
Grey/Blue on Pink	WG	ChP	1971	SP	28 X 41	AP	100		135	1800
Brown Block on Pink	WG	ChP	1971	SP	41 X 28	AP	100		135	1800
Grey/Blue on Green	WG	ChP	1971	SP	41 X 28	AP	100		135	1800
Untitled I,II,III	WG		1974	LB	31 X 24 EA	AP	50 EA	1 EA	125 EA	1200 EA
Slade	WG		1978	LB	23 X 17	AP	50	1	150	800
Anking	WG	JC/JCE	1979	EB/A	27 X 21	R/BFK	50		200	2800
Splay	WG	JC/JCE	1979	EB/A	27 X 21	R/BFK	50		200	2500
Trace	WG	JC/JCE	1979	EB/A	27 X 21	R/BFK	50		200	2500
Trickster	WG	JC/JCE	1979	EB/A	27 X 21	R/BFK	50		200	2500
A–H King	WG	C/JC/JCE	1979	EB/A	36 X 27	R/BFK	50		225	3000
Dido	WG	JCE/JC	1979	EB/A	36 X 27	R/BFK	50		270	2200
View	WG	JCE/JC	1979	EB/A	36 X 27	R/BFK	50		270	2200
Rankin	WG	KS/CP	1979	EB/A	36 X 27	R/BFK	60		360	2200
Tembi	WG	KS/CP	1980	EB/A	27 X 36	R/BFK	60		360	2500
Memphis Blue	WG	KS/CP	1980	EB/A	36 X 27	R/BFK	60		360	2200
Vigil	WG	KS/CP	1980	EB/A	27 X 36	R/BFK	60		360	2500
Night Music	WG	KS/CP	1981	EB/A	27 X 36	R/BFK	60		450	2200
Realm	WG	KS/CP	1981	EB/A	27 X 36	R/BFK	60		450	2200
Fly Away	WG	KS/CP	1981	EB/A	27 X 36	R/BFK	60		450	1800
Xingu	WG	AG	1982	SP	58 X 45	R/BFK	65		720	3000
Betwixt and Between	WG	AG	1982	SP	56 X 41	R/BFK	60		720	3000
Little Dancer	WG	JS/107W	1982	MON	35 X 30 EA		1 EA	Varies	1000 EA	3500 EA
Tiger Mountain	WG	JS/107W	1982	MON	35 X 30 EA		1 EA	Varies	1000 EA	3500 EA
Tipasaw	WG	JS/107W	1982	MON	47 X 32 EA		1 EA	Varies	1200 EA	3500 EA
Bouquet	WG	JS/107W	1983	EC	48 X 36	R/BFK	60		675	1800
Reverie	WG	RF/ALF	1983	EC	36 X 25	R/BFK	50		450	1800
Broken Bride	WG	RF/ALF	1983	MON	39 X 31 EA	AC	1 EA	Varies	1000 EA	3000 EA
Dreamer	WG	RF/ALF	1983	MON	35 X 32 EA	AC	1 EA	Varies	1000 EA	3500 EA
Geron	WG	RF/ALF	1983	MON	28 X 25 EA	AC	1 EA	Varies	900 EA	2800 EA
Jamaica Series I-VI	WG	RF/ALF	1983	MON	33 X 30 EA	AC	1 EA	Varies	900 EA	2500 EA
Mizan	WG	RF/ALF	1983	MON	39 X 31 EA	AC	1 EA	Varies	1000 EA	3000 EA
Wheels in Motion	WG	RF/ALF	1983	MON	25 X 20 EA	AC	1 EA	Varies	900 EA	2000 EA
Mona Lisa	WG	RF/ALF	1984	MON	36 X 32	AC	1 EA	Varies	1200 EA	3500 EA
Angel Over	WG	RF/ALF	1985	MON	32 X 35 EA	AC	1 EA	Varies	1000 EA	2800 EA

JOHN HOYLAND CONTINUED

TITLE	PUBLISHER	PRINTER	DATE	MEDIUM	DIMENSION (PAPER SIZE) IN INCHES	TYPE OF PAPER	EDITION NUMBER	NO. OF COLORS	ORIGINAL OPENING PRICE	CURRENT RETAIL PRICE
SOLD OUT EDITIONS (RARE):										
The Ark	WG	RF/ALF	1985	MON	32 X 35 EA	AC	1 EA	Varies	1000 EA	2800 EA
Calabash View	WG	RF/ALF	1985	MON	36 X 35 EA	AC	1 EA	Varies	1000 EA	3000 EA
Dagon	WG	RF/ALF	1985	MON	32 X 35 EA	AC	1 EA	Varies	1000 EA	2800 EA
Sukotra	WG	RF/ALF	1985	MON	32 X 35 EA	AC	1 EA	Varies	1000 EA	2800 EA
Zada	WG	RF/ALF	1986	EB	24 X 22	R/BFK	34	1	950 EA	1800 EA
Ekel Suite (Set of 5):									2000 SET	5000 SET
Ekel	WG	RF/ALF	1986	EB	11 X 10	R/BFK	40	1	450	1200
Encircling Stone	WG	RF/ALF	1986	EB	11 X 10	R/BFK	40	1	450	1200
Kinor	WG	RF/ALF	1986	EB	11 X 10	R/BFK	40	1	450	1200
Mael	WG	RF/ALF	1986	EB	11 X 10	R/BFK	40	1	450	1200
Mahi	WG	RF/ALF	1986	EB	11 X 10	R/BFK	40	1	450	1200
Mirage	WG	RF/ALF	1986	EB	24 X 22	R/BFK	44	1	950	1800
Quas	WG	RF/ALF	1986	EB	24 X 22	R/BFK	40	1	950	1800
Ramal	WG	RF/ALF	1986	EB	24 X 22	R/BFK	42	1	950	2500
Wish	WG	RF/ALF	1986	EB	24 X 22	R/BFK	40	1	950	1800
CURRENT EDITIONS:										
Caracasa	WG		1988	MON	32 X 36 EA	AC	1 EA	Varies	1200 EA	3000 EA
Forest	WG		1988	MON	32 X 36 EA	AC	1 EA	Varies	1200 EA	3000 EA
Fourth Day	WG		1988	MON	32 X 36 EA	AC	1 EA	Varies	1200 EA	3000 EA
Jazar	WG		1988	MON	36 X 32 EA	AC	1 EA	Varies	1200 EA	3000 EA
Mador	WG		1988	MON	32 X 36 EA	AC	1 EA	Varies	1200 EA	3000 EA
Ring of Fire	WG		1988	MON	32 X 36 EA	AC	1 EA	Varies	1200 EA	3000 EA
When Morning Stars Sang	WG		1988	MON	36 X 32 EA	AC	1 EA	Varies	1200 EA	3000 EA
Banda Oriental	WG		1989	EB/A	25 X 19	R/BFK	65	1	950	1500
Captive Circle	WG		1989	EB/A	25 X 20	R/BFK	65	1	950	1500
Carib (2)	WG		1989	MON	46 X 32 EA	AC	1 EA	Varies	1200 EA	3000 EA
Jinel	WG		1989	EB/A	25 X 20	R/BFK	30		1250	1500
Jinel (2)	WG		1989	MON	46 X 32 EA	AC	1 EA	Varies	1200 EA	3000 EA
King	WG		1989	EB/A	25 X 19	R/BFK	50		1250	1500
La Manga	WG		1989	EB/A	25 X 20	R/BFK	30		1200	1500
Rivers of Surprise	WG		1989	EB/A	25 X 19	R/BFK	50		1200	1500
The Sorcerer	WG		1989	EB/A	25 X 19	R/BFK	65		1200	1500
Sun Animal	WG		1989	EB/A/CAR	25 X 19	R/BFK	45		1200	1500
Hating and Dreaming	WG		1990	WC/SP	45 X 41	AC	40		1500	1800

JOHN HUBBARD

BORN: Ridgefield, CT; February 26, 1931
EDUCATION: Harvard Univ, Cambridge, MA, BA, 1953; Art Students League, NY, 1956–58; Hans Hofmann Sch, Provincetown, MA
TEACHING: Vis Instr, Painting, Camberwell Sch of Art, London, England, 1963–65; Slade Sch of Fine Art, London, England 1975–77
RECENT EXHIB: Yale Univ, Center for British Art, New Haven, CT, 1989
COLLECTIONS: Scottish Gallery of Mod Art, Edinburgh, Scotland; Tate Gallery, London, England; Nat Gallery of Victoria, Melbourne, Can; Arts Council of Great Britain, London, England; Arts Council of Northern Ireland, Belfast, Ireland; Australian Nat Gallery, Melbourne, Australia
PRINTERS: Artist (ART)
PUBLISHERS: Contemp Art Soc (CAS); Artist (ART)
GALLERIES: Fischer Fine Art, Ltd, London, England
MAILING ADDRESS: c/o Yale University Center for British Art, 1080 Chapel St, P.O. Box 2120, New Haven, CT 06520

TITLE	PUBLISHER	PRINTER	DATE	MEDIUM	DIMENSION (PAPER SIZE) IN INCHES	TYPE OF PAPER	EDITION NUMBER	NO. OF COLORS	ORIGINAL OPENING PRICE	CURRENT RETAIL PRICE
SOLD OUT EDITIONS (RARE):										
4 Studies	CAS	ART	1971	LB	23 X 31	AP	20	1	100	200
Landscape	CAS	ART	1971	LB	24 X 31	AP	20	1	125	250
CURRENT EDITIONS:										
Chalk Landscape	ART	ART	1971	LC	24 X 30	AP	40	4	150	300
Marrakech	ART	ART	1972	LC	30 X 24	AP	50	7	175	300
Rothko Memorial Print	ART	ART	1972	LC	30 X 25	AP	75	6	175	350
Haytor Quarry	ART	ART	1981	EB	6 X 5	AP	20	1	150	200
Roussillon #1, #2	ART	ART	1981	EB	6 X 5 EA	AP	20 EA	1 EA	150 EA	200 EA
Double Quarry	ART	ART	1981	EB	6 X 8	AP	30	1	200	250
Fantastic Landscape	ART	ART	1981	EB	6 X 5	AP	30	1	175	250
Water Currents	ART	ART	1981	EB	6 X 5	AP	25	1	150	200

JULIUS HUBLER

BORN: Granite City, IL; December 11, 1919
EDUCATION: Southeast Missouri State Univ, Cape Girardeau, MO, BS, 1942; State Univ of Iowa, Iowa City, IA; Columbia Univ, NY, MA, EdD, 1951; Studied with Philip Guston
TEACHING: Instr, City Col of New York, NY, 1946–48; Prof, State Univ of New York, Buffalo, NY, 1948–82
AWARDS: Warren Mack Mem Award, Soc of Am Graphic Artists, NY, 1962; Samuel F B Morse Medal, Nat Acad of Design, NY, 1977,80; Leo Meissner Prize, Nat Acad of Design, NY, 1989
COLLECTIONS: Benton Spruance Coll, Philadelphia Mus, PA; Nat Acad of Design, NY; John Von Wicht Coll, Brooklyn Mus, NY; Everson Mus of Art, Syracuse, NY; New York Public Library, NY
PRINTERS: Artist (ART)
PUBLISHERS: Artist (ART)
MAILING ADDRESS: 94 Danbury Lane, Buffalo, NY 14217

JULIUS HUBLER CONTINUED

TITLE	PUBLISHER	PRINTER	DATE	MEDIUM	DIMENSION (PAPER SIZE) IN INCHES	TYPE OF PAPER	EDITION NUMBER	NO. OF COLORS	ORIGINAL OPENING PRICE	CURRENT RETAIL PRICE
CURRENT EDITIONS:										
Tyranny, Like Hell, is Not Easily Conquered. In Memory of Thomas Paine. The Crisis	ART	ART	1965	WE	22 X 32	BAS	12	1	100	1000
In Memory of a Great Man: The Will of Democritus	ART	ART	1985	REL/EMB	24 X 34	FAB	5	4	2500	2500

ROBERT H HUDSON

BORN: Salt Lake City, UT; September 8, 1938
EDUCATION: San Francisco Art Inst, CA, BFA, 1962; MFA, 1963
TEACHING: Instr, San Francisco Art Inst, CA, 1964–65; Chmn, Sculpture & Ceramic Dept, 1965–66; Asst Prof, Art, Univ of California, Berkeley, CA, 1966–73; Asst Prof, Art, San Francisco Art, Inst, CA, 1976 to present
AWARDS: Purchase Prize, San Francisco Mus, CA, 1963; Purchase Prize, San Jose State Col, CA, 1964; Neallie Sullivan Award, San Francisco Mus, CA, 1965; Guggenheim Found Fel, NY, 1976
RECENT EXHIB: Frumkin/Adams Gallery, NY, 1989; Redding Mus, CA, 1992; Florida Int Art Mus, Miami, FL, 1992; Dorothy Goldeen Gallery, Santa Monica, CA, 1992
COLLECTIONS: San Francisco Mus, CA; Los Angeles County Mus, CA; Oakland Mus, CA; Stedelijk Mus, Amsterdam, The Netherlands; San Jose State Col, CA; San Diego Mus, CA; San Francisco Art Inst, CA
PUBLISHERS: Shark's Lithography, Ltd, Boulder, CO (SLL); Crown Point Press, San Francisco, CA (CPP)
PRINTERS: Bud Shark, Boulder, CO (BS); Shark's Lithography, Ltd, Boulder, CO (SLL); Lawrence Hamlin, San Francisco, CA (FH); Nancy Anello, San Francisco, CA (NA); Crown Point Press, San Francisco, CA (CPP)
GALLERIES: Morgan Gallery, Kansas City, MO; Struve Gallery, Chicago, IL; Crown Point Press, San Francisco, CA & New York, NY; Dorothy Goldeen Gallery, Santa Monica, CA; Frumkin/Adams Gallery, New York, NY; John Berggruen Gallery, San Francisco, CA
MAILING ADDRESS: 392 Eucalyptus Ave, Cotati, CA 94928

TITLE	PUBLISHER	PRINTER	DATE	MEDIUM	DIMENSION (PAPER SIZE) IN INCHES	TYPE OF PAPER	EDITION NUMBER	NO. OF COLORS	ORIGINAL OPENING PRICE	CURRENT RETAIL PRICE
CURRENT EDITIONS:										
White of the Eye	SLL	BS/SLL	1985	LC	48 X 32	AP	40		1000	1200
Out of Orbit	CPP	LH/NA/CPP	1986	A/DPT/HG/SB	29 X 28	SOM	35		700	950
Untitled	CPP	LH/NA/CPP	1986	A/DPT/HG/SP	42 X 50	SOM	35		850	1200
River	CPP	LH/NA/CPP	1986	A/DPT/HG/SP	52 X 42	SOM	35		850	1200
Green and Red Rhyme	CPP	LH/NA/CPP	1986	A/DPT/HG/SP	26 X 40	SOM	40		500	850

VICTOR HUGGINS, JR

BORN: Chapel Hill, NC; July 23, 1936
EDUCATION: Univ of North Carolina, Chapel Hill, NC, BA, 1962; MACA, 1966; Post Grad Work, Teachers Col, Columbia Univ, NY, 1973–74
TEACHING: Univ of North Carolina, 1963–68; Asst Prof, Art, Vanderbilt Univ, Nashville, TN, 1968–69; Prof, Head of Art Dept, Virginia Tech, Blackburg, VA, 1969 to present
AWARDS: First Prize, Purchase Award, North Carolina Nat Bank, 1967; First Prize, Purchase Award, Spring Art Contest, Spring Mills, NC, 1967; First Prize, Purchase Award, Annual Southern Contemp Painting Exhib, 1968
RECENT EXHIB: Gaston County Mus, Dallas, TX, 1989
COLLECTIONS: Salem Col, Salem, NC; Weatherspoon Art Gallery, Univ of North Carolina, Greensboro, NC; Asheville Art Mus, Asheville, NC; Amherst Col, Amherst, MA; Vanderbilt Univ, Nashville, TN; Hunter Mus, Chattanooga, TN; Roanoke Mus of Fine Arts, Roanoke, VA; Ackland Art Center, Univ of North Carolina, Chapel Hill, NC; Brooks Mem Gallery, Memphis, TN; B Carroll Reece Mus, East Tennessee State Univ, Johnson City, TN
PRINTERS: David Adamson, Wash, DC (DA); Atlantic Editions, Richmond, VA (AE); Richmond Printmaking Workshop, Richmond, VA (RPW)
PUBLISHERS: Artist (ART)
GALLERIES: Somerhill Gallery, Chapel Hill, NC; Hodges/Taylor, Charlotte, NC
MAILING ADDRESS: c/o Dept of Art, Virginia Polytech Inst & State University, Blacksburg, VA 24060

TITLE	PUBLISHER	PRINTER	DATE	MEDIUM	DIMENSION (PAPER SIZE) IN INCHES	TYPE OF PAPER	EDITION NUMBER	NO. OF COLORS	ORIGINAL OPENING PRICE	CURRENT RETAIL PRICE
CURRENT EDITIONS:										
View Near Afton	ART	RPW	1979	LC	23 X 18	AP	25	5	150	250
Near Stuarts Draft	ART	RPW	1979	LC	16 X 21	AP	50	4	150	250
Fancy Gap	ART	RPW	1980	LC	16 X 21	AP	50	4	150	250
View Near Mountain Lake	ART	AE	1981	LC	15 X 15	AP	50	5	150	250
View Near Luray	ART	AE	1981	LC	22 X 17	AP	50	5	185	275
Wintergreen	ART	DA	1982	LC	22 X 17	AP	50	5	185	275

RICHARD HULL

RECENT EXHIB: Illinois State Mus, Springfield, IL, 1989
COLLECTIONS: Illinois State Mus, Springfield, IL
PRINTERS: Jack Lemon, Chicago, IL (JL); Landfall Press, Inc, Chicago, IL (LPI)
PUBLISHERS: Landfall Press, Inc, Chicago, IL (LPI); Phyllis Kind Gallery, Chicago, IL (PKG)
GALLERIES: Phyllis Kind Galleries, Chicago, IL & New York, NY; Landfall Press, Inc, Chicago, IL

The Printworld Directory is accepting new applications for the seventh edition. Approximately 300 new artists will be accepted. Please use the two forms provided in the back section of this directory to submit biographical data and documentation of prints. Edition number of each print must not exceed 500 and the retail price must be $100 or more.

RICHARD HULL CONTINUED

TITLE	PUBLISHER	PRINTER	DATE	MEDIUM	DIMENSION (PAPER SIZE) IN INCHES	TYPE OF PAPER	EDITION NUMBER	NO. OF COLORS	ORIGINAL OPENING PRICE	CURRENT RETAIL PRICE
CURRENT EDITIONS:										
Change	LPI/PKG	JL/LPI	1986	LC	30 X 40	AP	65	5	650	850
Return	LPI/PKG	JL/LPI	1986	LC	31 X 31	AP	65	4	450	650
Gate	LPI	JL/LPI	1989	MON	43 X 36 EA	AP	1 EA	Varies	1800 EA	1800 EA
Play	LPI	JL/LPI	1989	LC	22 X 30	AP	50		500	500
Now	LPI	JL/LPI	1990	EC	22 X 30	R/BFK	25		650	650
Veil	LPI	JL/LPI	1991	LB	31 X 36	AP	15	1	500	500
Net of Jewels Series (12 Color Monoprints)	LPI	JL/LPI	1992	MON	31 X 36 EA	AP	1 EA	Varies	1000 EA	1000 EA

JOHN HULTBERG

BORN: Berkeley, CA; February 8, 1922
EDUCATION: Fresno State Col, CA, BA, 1943; CA Sch of Fine Arts, 1947–49; Art Students League, NY, 1949–51
TEACHING: Instr, Painting, Art Students League, NY, Summer, 1960; Instr, Painting, San Francisco Art Inst, CA, 1963–64; Art in Res, Honolulu Art Acad, HI, 1966–67
AWARDS: First Prize, Corcoran Biennial, Wash, DC, 1955; Guggenheim Fel, 1956; Norman Harris Medal, Art Inst of Chicago, IL, 1962; Tamarind Fel, 1963; Am Fed of Arts, Ford Foundation Grant, 1964; Nat Education Assn Grant, 1981; Nat Endowment for the Arts Grant, 1981; Benjamin Altman Prize, Landscape, Nat Acad of Design, 1972,85; Pollock-Krasner Award, 1988
COLLECTIONS: Metropolitan Mus of Art, NY; Mus of Mod Art, NY; Guggenheim Mus, NY; Albright-Knox Art Gallery, Buffalo, NY; Stedelijk Mus, Eindhoven, Netherlands
PRINTERS: Alexander Heinrici, NY (AH); Studio Heinrici, NY (SH)
PUBLISHERS: London Arts, Inc. Detroit, MI (LAI)
GALLERIES: Barridoff Galleries, Portland, ME; Wyckoff Gallery, Wyckoff, NJ; Anderson Gallery, Brooklyn, NY; Anita Shapolsky Gallery, New York, NY
MAILING ADDRESS: c/o Anita Shapolsky Gallery, 99 Spring St, New York, NY 10012

John Hultberg
Sinking Ship
Courtesy London Arts, Inc

TITLE	PUBLISHER	PRINTER	DATE	MEDIUM	DIMENSION (PAPER SIZE) IN INCHES	TYPE OF PAPER	EDITION NUMBER	NO. OF COLORS	ORIGINAL OPENING PRICE	CURRENT RETAIL PRICE
CURRENT EDITIONS:										
Fragments of a Dream	LAI	AH/SH	1977	LC	26 X 35	SOM	200	8	300	350
Wide Window I,II	LAI	AH/SH	1978	SP	24 X 33 EA	SOM	200 EA	11 EA	150 EA	200 EA
Sketch	LAI	AH/SH	1978	SP	24 X 28	SOM	200	4	150	200
Barricade	LAI	AH/SH	1978	SP	24 X 28	SOM	200	9	150	200
Actors	LAI	AH/SH	1978	SP	24 X 36	SOM	200	11	150	200
Whitness	LAI	AH/SH	1978	SP	24 X 28	SOM	200	9	150	200
Sinking Ship	LAI	AH/SH	1978	SP	24 X 25	SOM	200	6	150	200
After the Party	LAI	AH/SH	1978	LC	26 X 34	SOM	200	10	150	200
Greenhouse	LAI	AH/SH	1978	LC	26 X 34	SOM	200	10	150	200

DAVID AIKEN HUMPHREY

BORN: Augsburg, Germany; August 30, 1955; US Citizen
EDUCATION: New York Studio Sch, 1976–77; Maryland Inst Col of Art, Baltimore, MD, BFA, 1973–77; New York Univ, NY, MA, 1980
TEACHING: Instr, Drawing, Cooper Union, NY, 1985
AWARDS: Creative Artist Public Service Grant, NY, 1979–80; New York State Council of the Arts Award, Painting, 1985; Nat Endowment for the Arts Grant, 1985
RECENT EXHIB: Rena Bransted Gallery, San Francisco, CA, 1987; David McKee Gallery, NY, 1988; Carnegie-Mellon Univ Art Gallery, Pittsburgh, PA, 1988; Krygier/Landau Gallery, Santa Monica, CA, 1989
COLLECTIONS: Seattle Mus of Art, WA; Carnegie Inst, Pittsburgh, PA; Metropolitan Mus, NY; Brooklyn Mus, NY; New York Public Library, NY

PRINTERS: Jon Cone, East Topsham, VT (JC); Cone Editions, East Topsham, Topsham, VT (CEd); Pelavin Editions, NY (PeEd)
PUBLISHERS: Cone Editions, East Topsham, VT (CEd); Pelavin Editions, NY (PeEd)
GALLERIES: McKee Gallery, New York, NY; Tibor de Nagy Gallery, New York, NY; Lawrence Mangel Gallery, Phila, PA; Hill Gallery, Birmingham, MI; Fred Hoffman Gallery, Santa Monica, CA; Alpha Gallery, Boston, MA; Pelavin Editions, New York, NY; Cone Editions, East Topsham, VT; Rena Bransten Gallery, San Francisco, CA; Krygier/Landau Gallery, Santa Monica, CA
MAILING ADDRESS: c/o McKee Gallery, 41 E 57th St, 5th Floor, New York, NY 10022

DAVID HUMPHREY CONTINUED

TITLE	PUBLISHER	PRINTER	DATE	MEDIUM	DIMENSION (PAPER SIZE) IN INCHES	TYPE OF PAPER	EDITION NUMBER	NO. OF COLORS	ORIGINAL OPENING PRICE	CURRENT RETAIL PRICE
CURRENT EDITIONS:										
Reading and Writing Suite (Set of 3):									750 SET	1500 SET
Calculations	CEd	JC/CEd	1986	SP	24 X 18	CARD	33		250	500
Silent Reading	CEd	JC/CEd	1986	SP	24 X 18	CARD	33		250	500
Writing on Water	CEd	JC/CEd	1986	SP	24 X 18	CARD	33		250	500
Harvest	PelEd	PelEd	1986	MON	22 X 30 EA	R/BFK	1 EA	Varies	800 EA	800 EA
Shovel	PelEd	PelEd	1986	MON	16 X 12 EA	R/BFK	1 EA	Varies	800 EA	800 EA
Garden II	PelEd	PelEd	1986	MON	20 X 32 EA	R/BFK	1 EA	Varies	1200 EA	1200 EA
Hello Simone	CEd	JC/CEd	1987	AC/SB	25 X 19	R/BFK	33	2	550	550
Survey	CEd	JC/CEd	1987	AC/SP/SB/DPT	25 X 19	R/BFK	33	2	550	550
Quarry	CEd	JC/CEd	1987	AC/SB	19 X 25	R/BFK	33	2	550	550
Migrant	CEd	JC/CEd	1987	AB	19 X 25	R/BFK	33	1	550	550
Shovel	CEd	JC/CEd	1987	AC/PH/HG	25 X 19	R/BFK	33	3	550	550
Plug	CEd	JC/CEd	1987	AC/EB/DPT	25 X 19	R/BFK	33	2	550	550
Lies	CEd	JC/CEd	1987	AC/SB/SP/DPT	25 X 19	R/BFK	33	2	550	550
Lies (Computer Generated Etching)	CEd	JC/CEd	1987	EB/COMP	15 X 10	R/BFK	35	1	300	300
Precipitate	CEd	JC/CEd	1987	EB/A/DPT	19 X 25	R/BFK	9	2	500	500
Along the Shining Path #1–#8 (Set of 8)	CEd	JC/CEd	1988	EB/A/DPT	16 X 15 EA	R/BFK	13 EA	1 EA	1400 SET / 200 EA	1800 SET / 250 EA

FRIEDENSREICH HUNDERTWASSER

BORN: Vienna, Austria; December 15, 1928; Artist's name was originally Friedrich Strowasser)

PRINTERS: Rotaprint Burodruckmashinen, Vienna, Austria (Rota); Artist (ART); Arta Lithographieranstalt, Zürich, Switzerland (ARTA); Matashiro Uchikawa Surishi, Tokyo, Japan (MUS); Renato Cardazzo, Venice, Italy (RC); Edizione del Cavallino, Venice, Italy (EC); Art School, Brunswick, Germany (AS); Fernand Mourlot, Paris, France (FM); Nakamura, Sr, Tokyo, Japan (NS); Nakamura Hanga Kobo, Tokyo, Japan (NHK); Nakamura, Jr, Tokyo, Japan (NJ); Michel Cassé, Paris, France (MC); Roger Lacouriére, Paris, France (RL); Jacques Davis, Paris, France (JD); Alberti Caprini, Rome, Italy (Cap); Galleria L'Elefante, Venice, Italy (GLE); Giorgio Verrati, Venice, Italy (GV); Studio Quattro, Venice, Italy (SQ); Gunter Dietz, Bavaria, Germany (GD); Dietz Offizin, Bavaria, Germany (DO); Multigraphic, Venice, Italy (MULT); T Matsuoka Surishi, Tokyo, Japan (TMS); Uchida Kogei Kobo, Kyoto, Japan (UKK); Robert Finger, Vienna, Autria (RF); Carl Laszlo, Basel, Switzerland (CL)

PUBLISHERS: Alfred Schmeller, Vienna, Austria (AS); Art Club, Vienna, Austria, Vienna (AC); Gustav K Beck, Salzburg, Austria (GKB); Slavi Soucek, Salzburg, Austria (SS); Galerie Kunst der Gegenwart, Salzburg, Austria (GKG); Arta Lithographieranstalt, Zurich, Switzerland (ARTA); Samuel Dubiner, Ramat-Gan, Israel (SD); Renato Cardazzo, Venice, Italy (RC); Edizione del Cavallino, Venice, Italy (EC); Wieland Schmied, Hanover, Germany (WS); Kestner-Gesellschaft, Hanover, Germany (KG); Documenta III, Kassel, Germany (D-III); Gruener Janura AG, Glarus, Switzerland (GJ); Claude Givaudan, SA, Geneva, Switzerland (CG); Jacques Lazar-Vernet, Paris, France (JLV); Galerie Krugier & Moos, Geneva, Switzerland (GK/M); Hanover Gallery, London, England (HG); Galleria La Medusa, Rome, Italy (GLM); Felix Landau, Los Angeles, CA (FL); University Art Mus, Berkeley, CA (UAM); Artist (ART); Schunemann Verlag, Bremen, Germany (SV); Ars Viva, Zurich, Switzerland (AV); Ugo Meneghini, Venice, Italy (UM)

Koschatzky-K

TITLE	PUBLISHER	PRINTER	DATE	MEDIUM	DIMENSION (PAPER SIZE) IN INCHES	TYPE OF PAPER	EDITION NUMBER	NO. OF COLORS	ORIGINAL OPENING PRICE	CURRENT RETAIL PRICE
SOLD OUT EDITIONS (RARE):										
Stadtteil von Oben) (City from Above) (K-2)	AS/AC	Rota	1951	LC	295 X 210 cm	AP	100	2	25	3000
Hochhaus mit Bäumen (Skyscraper with Trees) (K-3)	AS/AC	Rota	1951	LC	295 X 210 cm	AP	100	3	25	3000
Mädchen mit Augengläsern (Girl with Eyeglasses) (K-4)	AS/AC	Rota	1951	LC	295 X 210 cm	AP	100	3	25	3500
Gesicht (The Face) (K-6)	AS/AC	Rota	1951	LC	295 X 210 cm	AP	100	2	25	3000
Singende Dampfer (Singing Steamers) (K-9)	AS/AC	Rota	1951	LC	210 X 295 cm	AP	100	3	25	3500
Drei Hohe Häuser (Three High Houses) (K-12)	GKB/SS/GKG	ART	1953	LI	750 X 540 cm	AP	100	3	35	6500
Araberin (Arabian Woman) (K-13)	ARTA	ARTA	1955	LC	580 X 460 cm	AP	100	4	35	5000
Häuser im Bluttegen (Houses in Rain of Blood) (K-16)	SD	MUS	1961	WC	400 X 535 cm	JP	100	30	75	7500
Haus und Spirale im Regen (House and Spiral in the Rain) (K-19)	RC/EC	RC/EC	1962	LC	300 X 380 cm	AC	102	4	60	6000
Mädchenfund im Gras (Girl-Finding in the Grass) (K-20)	WS/KG	AS	1964	EC/OFF	420 X 530 cm	AP	300	3	75	8000
Automobil mit Roten Regentropfen (Automobil with Red Raindrops) (2 Sheets) (K-21)	D-III	FM	1964	LC	615 X 850 cm	AP	101	6	120	12000
Sonnenuntergang (Sunset) (K-22)	GJ	NS/NHK	1966	WC	255 X 330 cm	JP	200	20	150	8500
Die Augen von Machu Picchú (The Eyes of Machu Picchú) (K-23)	CG	MC	1966	LC	500 X 660 cm	AP	132	4	120	6000
Die Seereise I (The Journey I) (K-24)	JLV	RL/JD	1967	EC	395 X 290 cm	AP	107	4	100	6000
Seereise II-Reise zur See und mit der Bahn (Journey II & Travel by Rail) (K-25)	GK/M	MC	1967	LC	655 X 505 cm	RP	267	5	135	5000
Der Knabe mit den Grünen Haaren (The Boy with the Green Hair) (K-21)	GKF	FM	1967	LC	600 X 400 cm	AP	100	8	135	8000

FRIEDENSREICH HUNDERTWASSER CONTINUED

TITLE	PUBLISHER	PRINTER	DATE	MEDIUM	DIMENSION (PAPER SIZE) IN INCHES	TYPE OF PAPER	EDITION NUMBER	NO. OF COLORS	ORIGINAL OPENING PRICE	CURRENT RETAIL PRICE
SOLD OUT EDITIONS (RARE):										
Der Endlose Weg du Dir (The Endless Way to You) (K-27)	GKF	FM	1967	LC	520 X 620 cm	AP	100	10	135	18000
L'Expulsion (The Expulsion) (K-28)	GK/M	FM	1967	LC	715 X 900 cm	AP	154	14	175	8000
Das Falsche Augenlid (The False Eyelash) (K-29)	HG	FM	1967	LC	710 X 500 cm	AP	181	10	150	6000
Die Schatten der Sterne (Shadow of the Stars) (K-30)	GK/M	FM	1967	LC	520 X 610 cm	AP	150	15	150	6000
Abschied aus Afrika (2 Metal Imprints) (Good-bye from Africa) (K-31)	GLM	Cap	1967	LC	500 X 700 cm	AP	90	5	175	12000
Die Nachbarn I-Spiralsonne und Mondhaus (Spiral Sun and Moonhouse-The Neighbours) (K-32)	GJ	NJ/NHK	1967	WC	355 X 522 cm	JP	200	20	150	6000
Brillen im Kleinen Gesicht (Spectacles in the Small Face) (K-33)	GJ	NJ/NHK	1967	WC	350 X 430 cm	JP	200	20	150	5000
King Kong (with Gold & Silver) (K-34)	GLE	GLE/GV	1968	SP	645 X 490 cm	AP	115	19	200	7500
Konigreich der Toro (Kingdom of the Toro) (K-35)	GLE	GLE/GV	1968	SP	520 X 690 cm	AP	170	9	200	15000
La Barca-Regentag (Slow Travel Under the Sun) (K-40)	FL	SQ/GV	1969	SP	760 X 560 cm	AP	251	10	175	15000
Ein Regentag mit Walter Kampmann (5 Metal Colors) (A Rainy Day with Walter Kampmann) (K-36)	UM	SQ/GV	1969	SP	520 X 700 cm	AP	170	12/5	200	15000
Wartende (Waiting Houses) (K-37)	GJ	NJ/NHK	1969	WC	320 X 415 cm	JP	200	20	250	10000
Kleiner Palast der Krankheit (Little Palace of Illness) (K-38)	GJ	NJ/NHK	1970	WC	365 X 260 cm	JP	200	20	275	10000
Triste pas si Triste (Sad is not So Sad is Rainshine from Rainday on a Rainy Day) (K-39)	UAM/ART	GLE/SQ	1968/70	SP	740 X 560 cm	AP	250	10/15	200	12000
Testament in Gelb (Yellow Last Will) (K-43)	SV	GD/DO	1971	SP	525 X 745 cm	AP	475	22	300	16500
La Liaison d'Une Araigneé (Relations of a Spider) (K-55)	GJ	NJ/NHK	1971	WC	312 X 240 cm	JP	200	20	275	8000
Homage to Shröder-Sonnenstern (5 Metal Colors) (K-56)	AV	GD/DO	1972	SP	1000 X 700 cm	AP	416	8	250	7500
Pouvoir Vert (Green Power) (K-57)	GJ/UM	SQ/MULT	1972	SP	835 X 635 cm	AP	249	21	300	8500
Pluie de Sang Tombe dans le Jardin (Rain of Blood is Falling into the Garden) (K-59)	GJ	TMS/UKK	1972	WC	430 X 555 cm	JP	200	20	350	9500
Deux Nuages Pleuvant Sept Couleurs (Two Clouds Raining Seven Colors) (K-60)	GJ	MUS	1972	WC	430 X 570 cm	JP	200	25	350	9500
La Pluie Tombe Loin de Nous (The Rain Falls Far from Us) (K-61)	GJ	MUS	1972	WC	425 X 540 cm	JP	200	31	350	9500
Sommeil Inonde (Flooded Sleep) (K-62)	GJ	MUS	1973	WC	427 X 565 cm	JP	200	33	400	9000
Blutregenfieberhaus (Blood Garden House) (K-63)	GJ	TMS/UKK	1974	WC	540 X 430 cm	JP	200	20	450	9000
Les Larmes de L'Artiste (Tears of an Artist) (K-64)	GJ	MUS	1974	WC	570 X 430 cm	JP	200	25	450	12000
Wiesenmann (Meadowman) (K-65)	GJ	RF	1974	EC/A	655 X 500 cm	R/BFK	240	3	400	10000
Zwei Baüme auf dem Schiff Retentag (Two Trees on Board of Retentag) (K-58)	GJ	MUS	1975	WC	425 X 540 cm	JP	236	38	400	9500
Il Marinaio (One of Five Seamen) (K-66)	GJ	SQ/MULT	1975	SP	900 X 600 cm	AP	250	18	350	8000
Winter Lichterloh (Burning Winter) (K-67)	GJ	SQ	1976	SP	760 X 585 cm	AP	227	16	350	12000

The retail prices of the 100,000 limited edition prints quoted in this directory are subject to change. Print publishers, artists and galleries were the direct sources for these quotations. Prices in the secondary market listed as "Sold Out Editions (Rare)" indicate that the publisher has a limited supply of that print or that the print is difficult to locate in the galleries.

The Printworld Directory is accepting new applications for the seventh edition. Approximately 300 new artists will be accepted. Please use the two forms provided in the back section of this directory to submit biographical data and documentation of prints. Edition number of each print must not exceed 500 and the retail price must be $100 or more.

The print market has become very selective. For the first time since we published the first edition of The Printworld Directory in 1982, the prices of prints have been greatly reduced and greatly increased for the same artists by the most reputable and established print publishers. Check the fifth edition to understand the movement.

BRYAN HUNT

BORN: Terre Haute, IN; June 7, 1947
EDUCATION: Univ of South Florida, Tampa, FL, 1966–68; Otis Art Inst, Los Angeles, CA, BFA, 1969–72; Whitney Mus of Am Art, NY, 1972
AWARDS: Seoul Int Art Festival Grand Prize, Drawings, Korea, 1991
RECENT EXHIB: Barbara Mathes Gallery, NY, 1987; BlumHelman Gallery, NY, 1987; Retrosp, Herbert F Johnson Mus, Cornell Univ, Ithaca, NY, 1988; Crown Point Press, New York, NY & San Francisco, CA, 1989; Williams Col Mus of Art, Williamstown, MA, 1989; Wilhelm-Lehmbruck-Mus der Stadt Duisberg, West Germany, 1989; Herbert F Johnson Mus, Cornell Univ, Ithaca, NY, 1989; Indianapolis Center for Contemp Art, Herron Gallery, Indianapolis, IN, 1989; State Univ of New York, Neuberger Mus, Purchase, NY, 1989; Muhlenberg Col, Frank Martin Gallery, Allentown, PA, 1989,92; BlumHelman Gallery, NY, 1989,92
COLLECTIONS: Solomon R Guggenheim Mus, NY; Mus of Mod Art, NY; Whitney Mus of Am Art, NY; Yale Univ, New Haven, CT; Stedelijk Mus, Amsterdam, Netherlands; Metropolitan Mus of Art, NY; Mus of Contemp Art, Los Angeles, CA; Lehmbruck Mus, Duisburg, West Germany; Parc del Clot, Barcelona, Spain; San Francisco Mus of Mod Art, CA; Art Inst of Chicago, IL
PRINTERS: Tadashi Toda, Kyoto, Japan (TT); Shunzo Matsuda, Kyoto, Japan (SM); Lothar Osterburg, San Francisco, CA (LO); Lawrence Hamlin, San Francisco, CA (LH); Daria Sywulak, San Francisco, CA (DS); Crown Point Press, San Francisco, CA (CPP); Gemini GEL, Los Angeles, CA (GEM); Artist (ART)
PUBLISHERS: Crown Point Press, San Francisco, CA (CPP); Gemini GEL, Los Angeles, CA (GEM)
GALLERIES: Crown Point Press, San Francisco, CA & New York, NY; BlumHelman Gallery, New York, NY; Barbara Mathes Gallery, New York, NY; Ronnie Greenberg Gallery, St Louis, MO; Janet Steinberg Fine Arts, San Francisco, CA; Thomas Segal Gallery, Boston, MA; John C Stoller & Company, Minneapolis, MN; Gemini GEL, Los Angeles, CA
MAILING ADDRESS: 9 White St, New York, NY 10013

TITLE	PUBLISHER	PRINTER	DATE	MEDIUM	DIMENSION (PAPER SIZE) IN INCHES	TYPE OF PAPER	EDITION NUMBER	NO. OF COLORS	ORIGINAL OPENING PRICE	CURRENT RETAIL PRICE
SOLD OUT EDITIONS (RARE):										
Fall with Bend			1979	EB/A	88 X 18	SOM	31		1000	11000
Straight Fall			1979	EB/A	88 X 18	SOM	31		1000	11000
Waterfall with Bend			1979	EB/A	20 X 13	SOM	31		450	2000
Straits of Consequence	CPP	ART/RB/PP/DS/CPP	1988	MON/HC	55 X 36	SOM	1 EA	Varies	6500	8500
Navigator 1	CPP	RB/PP/DS/CPP	1988	EC	54 X 36	SOM	50		2250	5500
Navigator 3	CPP	RB/PP/DS/CPP	1988	A/DPT/SOG/BU	54 X 36	SOM	25		2000	5000
Quarry at Tuy	CPP	RB/PP/DS/CPP	1988	A/DPT/SG/SB/SOG/DRT	22 X 30	SOM	35		1000	2500
CURRENT EDITIONS:										
Duet: Wind and Thunder (Set of 2)	CPP	TT/ART/CPP	1986	WC	18 X 14 EA	SOM	25 EA	2 EA	500 SET	500 SET
Window	CPP	TT/SM/CPP	1986	WC	22 X 18	KOZO	200	7	650	950
Vector	CPP	RB/PP/DS/CPP	1988	A/DPT/SOG/DRT	30 X 22	SOM	25		650	950
Navigator 2	CPP	RB/PP/DS/CPP	1988	A/DPT/SOG/BU	54 X 36	SOM	25		2000	5000
Five Nights 1,2,3,4,5 (Set of 5)	CPP	RB/PP/DS/CPP	1988	A/DPT/SOG/DRT/BU	22 X 19 EA	SOM	15 EA		2000 SET 500 EA	5000 SET 1100 EA
Ovoid	CPP	RB/PP/DS/CPP	1988	A/DPT/SOG/DRT/BU	30 X 22	SOM	25	1	650	950
Phobos (with Encaustic)	CPP	ART/CPP	1988–90	EB/HC	44 X 30	SOM	6	Varies	3500	5000
Deimos (with Encaustic)	CPP	ART/CPP	1988–90	AB/HC	44 X 30	SOM	6	Varies	3500	5000
Sedona Precipice	CPP	LO/LH/DS/CPP	1992	EB/SG/SL/DPT	42 X 32	SOM/W/T	35	3	2000	2000
Wall	CPP	LO/LH/DS/CPP	1992	EB/A/SG/DPT	45 X 36	SOM/W/T	10	1	1800	1800
Temple Ruins (Portfolio of 5 etchings & 6 Photogravures)	CPP	LO/LH/DS/CPP	1992	EB/DPT (5) & PH/G (6)	16 X 17 EA	SOM/W/T	20 EA	1 EA	2000 SET	2000 SET
Island	CPP	LO/LH/DS/CPP	1992	EB/A/SG/SL	42 X 32	SOM/W/T	35	3	2000	2000
Memnon I,II,III	CPP	LO/LH/DS/CPP	1992	EB/A/SG DPT	23 X 19 EA	SOM/W/T	15 EA		1250 SET 500 EA	1250 SET 500 EA
Hoo Doo	CPP	LO/LH/DS/CPP	1992	EB/SG/HC	45 X 36	SOM	5	Varies	3000	3000

DIANE HUNT

BORN: Shanghai, China; 1948
EDUCATION: Univ of California, Los Angeles, CA, BFA, 1973; State Univ of New York, Albany, NY, MFA, Printmaking, 1976
PRINTERS: Frank Versaggi, NY (FV)
PUBLISHERS: Orion Editions, NY (OE)
GALLERIES: Orion Editions, New York, NY

TITLE	PUBLISHER	PRINTER	DATE	MEDIUM	DIMENSION (PAPER SIZE) IN INCHES	TYPE OF PAPER	EDITION NUMBER	NO. OF COLORS	ORIGINAL OPENING PRICE	CURRENT RETAIL PRICE
CURRENT EDITIONS:										
Study for Zora	OE	FV	1979	LC	34 X 40	AP	30	5	300	450

RICHARD HOWARD HUNT

BORN: Chicago, IL; September 12, 1935
EDUCATION: Art Inst of Chicago, IL, BA
TEACHING: Asst Prof, Sch of Art Inst, Chicago, IL, 1960–62; Univ of Illinois, Champaign, IL, 1961–63; Vis Art, Yale Univ, New Haven, CT, 1964; Northwestern Univ, Evanston, IL, 1968–69; Vis Art, Washington Univ, St Louis, MO, 1977–78; Art in Res, Eastern Michigan Univ, Ypsilanti, MI, 1988

RICHARD HOWARD HUNT CONTINUED

AWARDS: Guggenheim Fel, 1962–63; Tamarind Artist Fel, Ford Found, 1965; Cassandra Found Fel, 1970
RECENT EXHIB: Dorsky Gallery, NY, 1989; Daniel Templon Gallery, Paris, France, 1990; Lakeview Mus of Arts & Sciences, Peoria, IL, 1992; Fort Wayne Mus of Art, IN, 1992; New Jersey State Mus, Trenton, NY, 1992; Miami Univ Art Mus, Oxford, OH, 1992; Kalamazoo Inst of Art, MI, 1989,92; Governors State Univ, Nathan Manilow Sculpture Park, University Park, IL, 1989,92; Shidoni Contemp Art, Tesuque, NM, 1992
COLLECTIONS: Mus of Mod Art, NY; Cleveland Mus, OH; Art Inst of Chicago, IL; Nat Mus of Israel, Jerusalem, Israel; Mus of the 20th Century, Vienna, Austria Metropolitan Mus of Art, NY; Whitney Mus of Am Art, NY; Mus of Mod Art, NY; Hirshhorn Mus, Wash, DC; Portland Mus of Art, OR; Illinois State Mus, Springfield, IL; Cleveland Mus of Art, OH; Art Inst of Chicago, IL; Nat Mus of Israel, Jerusalem, Israel; Los Angeles County Art Mus, CA; Oakton Com Col, Des Plaines, IL; Mus of the 20th Century, Vienna, Austria
PRINTERS: Jerry Raidiger, Chicago, IL (JR); David Keister, Chicago, IL (DK); Landfall Press, Inc, Chicago, IL (LPI); Artist (ART); Cynthia Archer, Evanston, IL (CA); Will Petersen, Evanston, IL (WP); Plucked Chicken Press, Evanston, IL (PCP)
PUBLISHERS: Landfall Press, Inc, Chicago, IL (LPI); Plucked Chicken Press, Evanston, IL (PCP)
GALLERIES: B C Holland Gallery, Inc, Chicago, IL; Dorsky Gallery, New York, NY; Terry Dintenfass, New York, NY; Thomas Babeor Gallery, La Jolla, CA; De Graaf Fine Art, Inc, Chicago, IL; G H N'Namdi Gallery, Birmingham, MI; Daniel Templon Galleries, Paris, France & Tokyo, Japan; Shidoni Contemporary Art, Tesuque, NM; Gwenda Jay Gallery, Chicago, IL; Printworks Gallery, Chicago, IL
MAILING ADDRESS: 1017 W Lill Ave, Chicago, IL 60614

TITLE	PUBLISHER	PRINTER	DATE	MEDIUM	DIMENSION (PAPER SIZE) IN INCHES	TYPE OF PAPER	EDITION NUMBER	NO. OF COLORS	ORIGINAL OPENING PRICE	CURRENT RETAIL PRICE
SOLD OUT EDITIONS (RARE):										
Ravinia Print	LPI	JR/DK/LPI	1971	LC	30 X 21	GE	200	3	200	800
Not Fixed	PCP	CA/WP/PCP	1985	LC	40 X 30	SOM	40	6	325	800

MEL HUNTER

BORN: Oak Park, IL; July 27, 1927
EDUCATION: Northwestern Univ, Chicago, IL
PRINTERS: American Atelier, NY (AA)
PUBLISHERS: Circle Fine Art, Chicago, IL (CFA)
GALLERIES: Pegasus Fine Art, Grafton, VT; Circle Galleries, San Diego, CA & San Francisco, CA & Northbrook, IL & Clayton, MO & Pittsburgh, PA & Houston, TX & Soho, NY & Chicago, IL & Scottsdale, AZ & Beverly Hills, CA & Costa Mesa, CA & Sherman Oaks, CA & Palm Beach, FL & Honolulu, HI & New Orleans, LA & Las Vegas, NV & Seattle, WA; Jack Arnold Fine Arts, New York, NY
MAILING ADDRESS: Route 7, Ferrisburg, VT 05456

TITLE	PUBLISHER	PRINTER	DATE	MEDIUM	DIMENSION (PAPER SIZE) IN INCHES	TYPE OF PAPER	EDITION NUMBER	NO. OF COLORS	ORIGINAL OPENING PRICE	CURRENT RETAIL PRICE
SOLD OUT EDITIONS (RARE):										
Along Together	CFA	AA	1978	LC	22 X 19	AP	200		100	275
Alone Together (Deluxe Edition)	CFA	AA	1978	LC	22 X 19	R/BFK	35		100	325
Stag Hound in Full Gate	CFA	AA	1978	LC	22 X 25	AP	300		100	300
The Raven Ahead off Timor	CFA	AA	1978	LC	22 X 25	AP	300		100	300
Challenge off Chile	CFA	AA	1978	LC	26 X 19	AP	300		100	475
Dreadnaught	CFA	AA	1978	LC	24 X 31	AP	300		100	525
Snow Geese over Canadian Rockies	CFA	AA	1979	LC	20 X 30	AP	300		125	650
Night Winds	CFA	AA	1979	LC	19 X 29	AP	300		125	500
Snowies Nesting	CFA	AA	1979	LC/SP	22 X 32	AP	300		125	450
Light at Emerald Point	CFA	AA	1980	LC	22 X 36	AP	300		150	600
Dawn Meadow	CFA	AA	1981	LC	22 X 30	AP	300		150	500
Doll House	CFA	AA	1981	LC	22 X 30	AP	300		150	625
Horse Folio (Set of 10):									900 SET	1300 SET
Appaloosa	CFA	AA	1981	LC	26 X 32	AP	500		100	200
Standard Breed	CFA	AA	1981	LC	26 X 32	AP	500		100	200
Arabian	CFA	AA	1981	LC	26 X 32	AP	500		100	175
Hunter Jumper	CFA	AA	1981	LC	26 X 32	AP	500		100	175
Thoroughbred	CFA	AA	1981	LC	26 X 32	AP	500		100	200
Pinto	CFA	AA	1981	LC	26 X 32	AP	500		100	200
Tennessee Walker	CFA	AA	1981	LC	26 X 32	AP	500		100	175
Morgan	CFA	AA	1981	LC	26 X 32	AP	500		100	175
Saddlebred	CFA	AA	1981	LC	26 X 32	AP	500		100	175
Quarterhorse	CFA	AA	1981	LC	26 X 32	AP	500		100	175
CURRENT EDITIONS:										
Patriarch	CFA	AA	1981	LC	23 X 30	AP	300		150	500
Painted Lady	CFA	AA	1982	LC	28 X 19	AP	300		150	300

PETER HURD

BORN: Roswell, NM; February 22, 1904
EDUCATION: U S Military Acad, 1921–24; Haverford Col, PA, 1923–24; Pennsylvania Acad of Fine Arts, Phila, PA, 1924–26 with N C Wyeth; Texas Tech Univ, DFA, 1966; New Mexico State Univ, LLD, 1968
AWARDS: Wilmington Soc of Fine Arts, 1941, 45; Pennsylvania Acad of Fine Arts Medal, 1945; Isaac Maynard Prize, Nat Acad of Design, 1954
COLLECTIONS: Metropolitan Mus, NY; Art Inst of Chicago, IL; Delaware Art Mus, Wilmington, DE; Dallas Art Mus, TX; Roswell Mus, NW; Nat Gallery, Wash, DC; San Diego Art Mus, CA; Nat Gallery, Edinburgh, Scotland
RECENT EXHIB: Albuquerque Mus of Art History & Science Mus, NM, 1989; Roswell Mus & Art Center, NM, 1989
PRINTERS: American Atelier, NY (AA)
PUBLISHERS: Circle Fine Art, Chicago, IL (CFA)
GALLERIES: Jackson Gallery, Dallas, TX; Circle Galleries, San Diego, CA & San Francisco, CA & Northbrook, IL & Pittsburgh, PA & Houston, TX & Soho, NY & Chicago, IL & Scottsdale, AZ & Beverly Hills, CA & Costa Mesa, CA & Sherman Oaks, CA & Palm Beach, FL & Honolulu, HI & New Orleans, LA & Las Vegas, NV & Seattle, WA
MAILING ADDRESS: Sentinel Ranch, San Patricio, NM 88348

PETER HURD CONTINUED

TITLE	PUBLISHER	PRINTER	DATE	MEDIUM	DIMENSION (PAPER SIZE) IN INCHES	TYPE OF PAPER	EDITION NUMBER	NO. OF COLORS	ORIGINAL OPENING PRICE	CURRENT RETAIL PRICE
SOLD OUT EDITIONS (RARE):										
Apache Plume	CFA	AA	1972	SP	15 X 19	AP	250		100	1100
A Watering at Sundown	CFA	AA	1972	SP	26 X 30	AP	250		125	1850
A Practice Game	CFA	AA	1972	SP	32 X 44	AP	250		125	1350
A Race with the Rain	CFA	AA	1972	SP	32 X 45	AP	250		125	1350
Sunset through Dust	CFA	AA	1972	SP	24 X 36	AP	250		125	1350
Dusty Sun	CFA	AA	1972	LC	17 X 20	AP	250		100	1100
Dusty Sun (Japon)	CFA	AA	1972	LC	17 X 20	JP	25		125	1150
Fence Rider	CFA	AA	1972	LC	11 X 12	AP	250		75	1075
Fence Rider (Japon)	CFA	AA	1972	LC	11 X 12	AP	25		100	1175
A Far Away Place	CFA	AA	1972	LC	24 X 34	AP	260		125	1250
Night Visitor	CFA	AA	1973	LC	20 X 24	AP	260		125	1450
Night Visitor (Japon)	CFA	AA	1973	LC	24 X 20	JP	25		150	1550
A Ranch at Dawn	CFA	AA	1973	LC	15 X 15	AP	250		100	1050
A Ranch at Dawn (Japon)	CFA	AA	1973	LC	15 X 15	AP	25		125	1100
Day's End	CFA	AA	1973	SP	29 X 26	AP	260		150	1650
A Surging Cumulus (Japon)	CFA	AA	1974	LC	20 X 16	JP	25		175	1200
Dominiquez Well	CFA	AA	1974	LC	16 X 18	AP	260		150	1050
Dominiquez Well (Japon)	CFA	AA	1974	LC	16 X 18	JP	25		175	1200
Shower on the Prairie	CFA	AA	1975	LC	20 X 29	AP	260		200	1050
Shower on the Prairie (Japon)	CFA	AA	1975	LC	20 X 29	JP	25		225	1100
The Day it Rained	CFA	AA	1976	LC	22 X 29	AP	260		200	1000
CURRENT EDITIONS:										
Windmill Trouble	CFA	AA	1974	LC	19 X 24	AP	260		125	1050
Windmill Trouble (Japon)	CFA	AA	1974	LC	19 X 24	JP	25		150	1100
A Surging Cumulus	CFA	AA	1974	LC	20 X 16	AP	260		150	1050
The Day it Rained (Japon)	CFA	AA	1976	LC	22 X 29	JP	35		225	1100
Westward into Night	CFA	AA	1976	LC	22 X 34	AP	275		200	1050

MICHAEL HURSON

BORN: Youngstown, OH; 1941
EDUCATION: Oxbow Summer Sch, Saugatuck, MI, 1960,61; Yale Univ, Norfolk, CT, 1962; Art Inst of Chicago, IL, BFA, 1963
AWARDS: Nat Endowment for the Arts Grant, NY, 1974–75; Theodoron Award, Guggenheim Mus, NY, 1977; Vaklova Purchase Award, Mus of Contemp Art, Chicago, IL, 1980
RECENT EXHIB: Duke Univ Mus, Durham, NC, 1988; Paula Cooper Gallery, NY, 1987,88,89; Art Inst of Chicago, IL, 1990; BlumHelman Gallery, NY, 1990
COLLECTIONS: Art Inst of Chicago, IL; Guggenheim Mus, NY; Whitney Mus of Am Art, NY; Metropolitan Mus, NY; Nat Gallery of Australia, Camberra, Australia

PRINTERS: Jennifer Melby, NY (JM); Perry Tymeson, NY (PT); Petersburg Press, NY (PP); Leslie Miller, NY (LM); Grenfel Press, NY (GP)
PUBLISHERS: Fawbush Editions, NY (FE); Petersburg Press, NY (PP); Grenfel Press, NY (GP)
GALLERIES: Joe Fawbush Editions, New York, NY; Petersburg Press, New York, NY & London, England; Paula Cooper Gallery, New York, NY; DeGraaf Fine Art, Chicago, IL; Dart Gallery, Chicago, IL; Betsy Senior Contemporary Prints, New York, NY; BlumHelman Gallery, New York, NY; John Peet Gallery, New York, NY
MAILING ADDRESS: c/o Paula Cooper Gallery, 155 Wooster St, New York, NY 10012

TITLE	PUBLISHER	PRINTER	DATE	MEDIUM	DIMENSION (PAPER SIZE) IN INCHES	TYPE OF PAPER	EDITION NUMBER	NO. OF COLORS	ORIGINAL OPENING PRICE	CURRENT RETAIL PRICE
CURRENT EDITIONS:										
Deux Crayons dans un Chambre (with Scraping and Burnishing)	FE	JM	1987	EB/A/SB	18 X 26	R/BFK	35		1200	1500
Gravure de Crayon (with Scraping and Burnishing)	FE	JM	1987	EB/A/SB	20 X 17	R/BFK	35		900	1350
Papa Travaille (with Scraping and Burnishing)	FE	JM	1987	EB/A/SB	20 X 13	R/BFK	35		750	1000
Vladimir	PP	PT/PP	1987	LB/SP	24 X 10 X 3	AP/PLEX	35	4	1500	2500
Knife, Fork and Spoon (Diner Solitaire)	GP	LM/GP	1991	LC/LI	12 X 8	RdB	25		450	500

CLAUDIA JANE HUTCHINSON

BORN: New York, NY; September 22, 1949
EDUCATION: Sch of Visual Arts, NY, 1969–70; Art Students League, NY, 1967–75; Printmaking Workshop, NY, 1977–80
AWARDS: Art Students League Fel, NY, 1968; George Bridgeman Award, 1969; Art Students League, NY, 1971–75
COLLECTIONS: Museo Rayo, Rodanillo, Valle De Colombia, South America
PRINTERS: Artist (ART)
PUBLISHERS: Artist (ART)
MAILING ADDRESS: 158 Nassau Ave, Brooklyn, NY 11222

The retail prices of the 100,000 limited edition prints quoted in this directory are subject to change. Print publishers, artists and galleries were the direct sources for these quotations. Prices in the secondary market listed as "Sold Out Editions (Rare)" indicate that the publisher has a limited supply of that print or that the print is difficult to locate in the galleries.

CLAUDIA JANE HUTCHINSON CONTINUED

TITLE	PUBLISHER	PRINTER	DATE	MEDIUM	DIMENSION (PAPER SIZE) IN INCHES	TYPE OF PAPER	EDITION NUMBER	NO. OF COLORS	ORIGINAL OPENING PRICE	CURRENT RETAIL PRICE
CURRENT EDITIONS:										
Eleda Re Re	ART	ART	1982	EC	30 X 42	AP	25	4	150	200
The Sea	ART	ART	1982	EC	30 X 42	AP	20	3	200	250
Prototype	ART	ART	1982	EB	22 X 30	AP	20	1	125	200
The Offering	ART	ART	1982	EC	30 X 42	AP	20	3	175	250
If We Only Knew	ART	ART	1982	ENG	29 X 41	AP	20	1	150	200

PETER ARTHUR HUTCHINSON

BORN: London, England; March 4, 1930
EDUCATION: Univ of Illinois, Normal, IL, BFA, 1960
AWARDS: Nat Endowment for the Arts Fel, 1974; A & E Gottlieb Found Grant, 1987; Krasner-Pollock Grant, 1989
COLLECTIONS: Mus of Mod Art, NY; Monchengladbach Mus, Germany; Krefeld Mus, Germany; Chrysler Mus, Norfolk, VA; Musee Pompidou, Paris, France; Hoffmann Found, Basel, Switzerland
PRINTERS: Staeck Editions, Germany (SE); Yaki Kornblit, Amsterdam, Netherlands (YK); Atelier Laage, Paris, France (AL);
PUBLISHERS: Staeck Editions, Germany (SE); Yaki Kornblit, Amsterdam, Netherlands (YK); Atelier Laage, Paris, France (AL); Multiples, Inc, NY (M)
GALLERIES: Holly Solomon Editions, Ltd, New York, NY; John Gibson Gallery, New York, NY; Impulse, Provincetown, MA; Marian Goodman Gallery, New York, NY; Berta Walker Gallery, Provincetown, MA
MAILING ADDRESS: 10 Holway Ave, Provincetown, MA 02657

TITLE	PUBLISHER	PRINTER	DATE	MEDIUM	DIMENSION (PAPER SIZE) IN INCHES	TYPE OF PAPER	EDITION NUMBER	NO. OF COLORS	ORIGINAL OPENING PRICE	CURRENT RETAIL PRICE
CURRENT EDITIONS:										
Dissolving Clouds	YK	YK	1972	SP/PH/C	22 X 22	AP	75		200	600
Continental Divide	SE	SE	1973	SP/PH/CO	30 X 20	AP	75		300	750
Untitled	M		1974	SP/PH/C	30 X 22	AP	50		300	750
Beach Zebra	AL	AL	1975	SP/PH/C	15 X 22	AP	50		200	600
Raven	SK	SK	1975	PH/C	18 X 24	AP	48		200	600
Sketch Book, 1968–74	AL	AL	1975	SP/PH/CO	13 X 10	AP	50		1000	1500

PETER HUTTINGER

BORN: West Palm Beach, FL; 1953
PRINTERS: Prasada Press, Cleveland, OH (PrP)
PUBLISHERS: Prasada Press, Cleveland, OH (PrP)
GALLERIES: Feature Gallery, New York, NY; Patrick King Contemporary Art, Indianapolis, IN; Toni Birckhead Gallery, Cincinnati, OH

TITLE	PUBLISHER	PRINTER	DATE	MEDIUM	DIMENSION (PAPER SIZE) IN INCHES	TYPE OF PAPER	EDITION NUMBER	NO. OF COLORS	ORIGINAL OPENING PRICE	CURRENT RETAIL PRICE
CURRENT EDITIONS:										
Not Playing with a Full Deck (3 Part Litho Recto-Verso)	PrP	PrP	1981	LC	14 X 18 EA	AP/R/BFK	20		225	300

KYU-BAIK HWANG

BORN: Busan, Korea; 1932
EDUCATION: Ecole du Louvre, Paris, France; S W Hayter, Atelier 17, Paris, France
COLLECTIONS: Mus of Mod Art, NY; Musee d'Art Moderne, Paris, France; British Mus, London, England; Victoria & Albert Mus, London, England; Uffizi Gallery, Florence, Italy; Montreal Mus, Canada; Art Inst of Chicago, IL; Brooklyn Mus, NY; Philadelphia Mus, PA; Art Inst of Chicago, IL
PRINTERS: Artist (ART)
PUBLISHERS: John Szoke Graphics, NY (JSG)
GALLERIES: Fernette's Gallery of Art, Des Moines, IA; Newmark Gallery, New York, NY; Nladinska Kniica Gallery, Ljubljana, Yugoslavia; Wenniger Graphics, Boston, MA; Stephen Gill Gallery, New York, NY; ART Fine Art, Bellevue, WA

Kyu-Baik Hwang
Black Chair
Courtesy John Szoke Graphics

TITLE	PUBLISHER	PRINTER	DATE	MEDIUM	DIMENSION (PAPER SIZE) IN INCHES	TYPE OF PAPER	EDITION NUMBER	NO. OF COLORS	ORIGINAL OPENING PRICE	CURRENT RETAIL PRICE
CURRENT EDITIONS:										
Flower	JSG	ART	1982	MEZ	26 X 20	R/BFK	150	4	400	450
Umbrella	JSG	ART	1982	MEZ	26 X 20	R/BFK	150	5	450	500

KYU-BAIK HWANG CONTINUED

TITLE	PUBLISHER	PRINTER	DATE	MEDIUM	DIMENSION (PAPER SIZE) IN INCHES	TYPE OF PAPER	EDITION NUMBER	NO. OF COLORS	ORIGINAL OPENING PRICE	CURRENT RETAIL PRICE
CURRENT EDITIONS:										
Alarm Clock	JSG	ART	1983	MEZ	19 X 26	R/BFK	100	5	400	450
Basket	JSG	ART	1983	MEZ	19 X 26	R/BFK	100	5	400	450
Watch in Bowl	JSG	ART	1983	MEZ	20 X 26	R/BFK	100	5	400	450
Two Chains	JSG	ART	1983	MEZ	19 X 26	R/BFK	100	5	400	450
Geranium	JSG	ART	1984	MEZ	13 X 20	R/BFK	150	5	200	250
Poppy	JSG	ART	1984	MEZ	13 X 20	R/BFK	150	5	200	250
Black Chair	JSG	ART	1984	MEZ	19 X 26	R/BFK	100	7	425	500
Bird and Alarm Clock	JSG	ART	1984	MEZ	26 X 20	R/BFK	80	7	400	450
Evergreen	JSG	ART	1984	MEZ	30 X 23	R/BFK	90	6	550	600

DOROTHY IANNONE

BORN: Boston, MA; August 9, 1933
EDUCATION: Boston Univ, MA, BA, 1953–57; Brandeis Univ, Waltham, MA, Grad Studies, 1957–58
TEACHING: Acad of Art, West Berlin, Germany, 1977,79; Acad of Art, Maastricht, Holland, 1981,84; Royal Acad of Art, Amsterdam, Holland, 1981,84
AWARDS: Deutscher Akad Austauschienst, West Berlin, Germany, 1976; Senate for Science and Art, West Berlin, Germany, 1980; Art Found, Bonn, Germany, 1989
COLLECTIONS: Ludwig Mus Coll, Aachen, Germany; Senate for Science and Art, Berlin, Germany; Neue Berliner Kunstverein, Germany; Bibliotheque Nat, Paris, France; Basel Kunst Mus, Basel, Switzerland; Nat Women's Gallery, Wash, DC; Nat Galerie, Mus of Drawings & Prints, Berlin, Germany
PRINTERS: P Haas, Stuttgart, Germany (PH); K E Schultz, Braunschweig, Germany (KES); H Kaminsky, Düsseldorf, Germany (HK); W Simboeck, West Berlin, Germany (WS)
PUBLISHERS: Studio Galerie, Mike Steiner, Berlin, Germany (SGMS); Galerie Wilbrand, Cologne, Germany (GW)
GALLERIES: Galerie Mike Steiner, Berlin, Germany; Galerie Wilbrand, Cologne, Germany; Galerie Peterson, Berlin, Germany; Boekie Woekie Artists' Publications, Amsterdam, The Netherlands
MAILING ADDRESS: c/o DAAD Jaeger Strasse 23, D-1080 Berlin, Federal Republic of Germany

TITLE	PUBLISHER	PRINTER	DATE	MEDIUM	DIMENSION (PAPER SIZE) IN INCHES	TYPE OF PAPER	EDITION NUMBER	NO. OF COLORS	ORIGINAL OPENING PRICE	CURRENT RETAIL PRICE
SOLD OUT EDITIONS (RARE):										
At Home	GW	PH	1970	SP	29 X 35	BUE	100	7	85	300
CURRENT EDITIONS:										
Ten Scenes	GW	PH	1970	SP	28 X 38	BUE	100	7	85	300
Black Dick	GW	PH	1970	SP	26 X 33	BUE	100	7	85	300
Human Liberation	GW	HK	1971	SP	20 X 28	BUE	100	7	65	200
The Next Great Moment	GW	KES	1971	SP	29 X 41	BUE	100	7	85	300
The White Goddess	GW	KES	1971	SP	29 X 41	BUE	50	7	100	350
Lions	SGMS	KES	1971	EB	30 X 34	BUE	50	1	300	800
The Statue of Liberty	SGMS	WS	1977	SP	24 X 33	BUE	100	7	100	250

LOUIS ICART

BORN: Toulouse, France; (1888–1950)
AWARDS: Chevalier de French Légion d'Honneur, 1927
PRINTERS: Artist (ART)
PUBLISHERS: L'Estampe Moderne, Paris, France (LEM); Les Gravvures Modernes, Paris, France (LGM); Galerie George Petit, Paris, France (GGP); Artist (ART)
GALLERIES: I Brewster & Company Gallery, Inc, Phila, PA

TITLE	PUBLISHER	PRINTER	DATE	MEDIUM	DIMENSION (PAPER SIZE) IN INCHES	TYPE OF PAPER	EDITION NUMBER	NO. OF COLORS	ORIGINAL OPENING PRICE	CURRENT RETAIL PRICE
SOLD OUT EDITIONS (RARE):										
Coursing I	ART	ART	1914	EC	16 X 12	R/100	75		25	7500
Golf	ART	ART	1914	EC	11 X 17	R/100	75		25	9500
The Butterfly	ART	ART	1914	EC	11 X 19	R/100	75		25	4250
First Beautiful Days	ART	ART	1914	EC	10 X 15	R/100	75		25	4250
Springtime Vision	ART	ART	1914	EC	12 X 19	R/100	75		25	4250
Munitions Worker	ART	ART	1917	EC	7 X 10	R/100	250		25	2450
The Replacement	ART	ART	1917	EC	7 X 10	R/100	250		25	2450
Nurse	ART	ART	1917	EC	7 X 10	R/100	250		25	2450
Off to War	ART	ART	1917	EC	7 X 10	R/100	250		25	2450
Woman in Chains	ART	ART	1917	EC	7 X 10	R/100	250		25	2450
Flag Lady	ART	ART	1917	EC	7 X 10	R/100	250		25	2450
At the Grave	ART	ART	1917	EC	7 X 10	R/100	250		25	2450
Voice of the Cannon	ART	ART	1917	EC	23 X 16	R/100	100		25	5500
Winged Victory	ART	ART	1918	EC	15 X 22	R/100	100		25	4950
Marianne	ART	ART	1918	EC	12 X 20	R/100	75		25	3500
The Indiscreet Cockatoo	ART	ART	1921	EC	11 X 13	R/100	300		25	4900
The Blindfold	ART	ART	1922	EC	18 X 15	R/100	300		25	5500
The Open Cage	ART	ART	1922	EC	12 X 18	R/100	300		25	4500
The Broken Jug	ART	ART	1922	EC	12 X 19	R/100	300		25	4500
Behind the Fan	ART	ART	1922	EC	19 X 14	R/100	300		25	4000
The Lacquer Screen	ART	ART	1922	EC		R/100	300		25	4250

LOUIS ICART CONTINUED

TITLE	PUBLISHER	PRINTER	DATE	MEDIUM	DIMENSION (PAPER SIZE) IN INCHES	TYPE OF PAPER	EDITION NUMBER	NO. OF COLORS	ORIGINAL OPENING PRICE	CURRENT RETAIL PRICE
SOLD OUT EDITIONS (RARE):										
Laziness	ART	ART	1925	EC	19 X 15	R/100	350	35		4250
White Underwear	ART	ART	1925	EC	19 X 15	R/100	350	35		4000
In the Open	ART	ART	1925	EC	16 X 11	R/100	350	35		3950
On the Beach	ART	ART	1925	EC	16 X 11	R/100	350	35		3950
The Story Teller	ART	ART	1926	EC	17 X 14	R/100	350	35		3950
Impudence	ART	ART	1926	EC	14 X 18	R/100	350	35		3950
Autumn Leaves	ART	ART	1926	EC	16 X 20	R/100	350	35		3750
Love Letters	ART	ART	1926	EC	18 X 14	R/100	350	35		4000
The Masks	ART	ART	1926	EC	15 X 19	R/100	350	35		4000
Seagulls	ART	ART	1926	EC	16 X 20	R/100	350	35		4500
Spanish Night	ART	ART	1926	EC	13 X 21	R/100	350	35		4250
Venetian Night	ART	ART	1926	EC	13 X 21	R/100	350	35		4250
French Doll	ART	ART	1926	EC	18 X 14	R/100	350	35		4000
The Silk Robe	ART	ART	1926	EC	19 X 15	R/100	350	35		4500
Manon	ART	ART	1927	EC	13 X 20	R/100	500	35		4500
Scheherazade	ART	ART	1927	EC	20 X 13	R/100	500	35		4000
Thai's	ART	ART	1927	EC	20 X 16	R/100	500	35		6000
Sleeping Beauty	ART	ART	1927	EC	20 X 16	R/100	500	35		5000
SOLD OUT EDITIONS (RARE):										
Red Riding Hood	ART	ART	1927	EC	14 X 21	R/100	500	35		4000
Cinderella	ART	ART	1927	EC	18 X 15	R/100	500	35		4000
Autumn	ART	ART	1928	EC	7 X 9	R/100	500	35		4000
Cassanova	ART	ART	1928	EC	14 X 21	R/100	500	35		4000
Don Juan	ART	ART	1928	EC	14 X 21	R/100	500	35		3000
Zest	ART	ART	1928	EC	14 X 19	R/100	500	35		3500
Summer	ART	ART	1928	EC	7 X 9	R/100	500	35		6500
Faust	ART	ART	1928	EC	13 X 21	R/100	500	35		9000
Winter	ART	ART	1928	EC	7 X 9	R/100	500	35		3000
Green Screen	ART	ART	1928	EC	18 X 16	R/100	500	35		4000
Flower Vendor	ART	ART	1928	EC	14 X 19	R/100	500	35		4000
Chestnut Vendor	ART	ART	1928	EC	14 X 19	R/100	500	35		4000
Mignon	ART	ART	1928	EC	14 X 20	R/100	500	35		4000
Montmartre I	ART	ART	1928	EC	15 X 21	R/100	500	35		4000
Red Screen	ART	ART	1928	EC	18 X 16	R/100	100	35		4250
Fallen Nest	ART	ART	1928	EC	15 X 19	R/100	500	35		4000
Spilled Apples	ART	ART	1928	EC	13 X 20	R/100	500	35		4000
The Green Parakeet	ART	ART	1928	EC	9 X 11	R/100	500	35		4000
The Blue Parakeet	ART	ART	1928	EC	9 X 11	R/100	500	35		4000
Milkmaid	ART	ART	1928	EC	13 X 20	R/100	500	35		4000
The Parasol	ART	ART	1928	EC	14 X 18	R/100	500	35		4000
Spring	ART	ART	1928	EC	7 X 9	R/100	500	35		3750
Seville	ART	ART	1928	EC	13 X 20	R/100	500	35		3750
Tosca	ART	ART	1928	EC	13 X 21	R/100	500	35		4500
Werther	ART	ART	1928	EC	13 X 20	R/100	500	35		10000
Coursing II	ART	ART	1929	EC	25 X 16	R/100	350	35		10000
Youth	ART	ART	1930	EC	16 X 24	R/100			50	4500
Golden Vail	ART	ART	1930	EC	16 X 24	R/100			50	3500
Perfect Harmony	ART	ART	1932	EC	17 X 13	R/100			50	10000
Speed	ART	ART	1933	EC	25 X 16	R/100			50	10000
Repose	ART	ART	1933	EC	45 X 19	R/100			50	20000
Leda and the Swan	ART	ART	1934	EC	31 X 21	R/100			50	12500
Gay Trio	ART	ART	1936	EC	12 X 20	R/100			50	10000
Love's Blossom	ART	ART	1937	EC	25 X 17	R/100			50	10000
The Sofa	ART	ART	1937	EC	25 X 17	R/100			50	10500
Illusion	ART	ART	1940	EC	9 X 19	R/100			50	12500

YASUO IHARA

BORN: Japan; 1932
PRINTERS: American Atelier, NY (AA)
PUBLISHERS: Circle Fine Art, Chicago, IL (CFA)

GALLERIES: Circle Galleries, San Diego, CA & San Francisco, CA & Northbrook, IL & Pittsburgh, PA & Houston, TX & Soho, NY & Chicago, IL & Scottsdale, AZ & Beverly Hills, CA & Costa Mesa, CA & Sherman Oaks, CA & Palm Beach, FL & New Orleans, LA & Las Vegas, NV & Seattle, WA

TITLE	PUBLISHER	PRINTER	DATE	MEDIUM	DIMENSION (PAPER SIZE) IN INCHES	TYPE OF PAPER	EDITION NUMBER	NO. OF COLORS	ORIGINAL OPENING PRICE	CURRENT RETAIL PRICE
SOLD OUT EDITIONS (RARE):										
Reneé	CFA	AA	1976	SP	30 X 24	AP	200		50	150
Judith	CFA	AA	1976	SP	24 X 30	AP	200		50	150
Diana	CFA	AA	1976	SP	24 X 30	AP	200		50	150
Triad	CFA	AA	1976	SP	30 X 24	AP	200		50	150

SHOICHI IDA

BORN: Kyoto, Japan; September 13, 1941
EDUCATION: Kyoto Municipal Univ of Art, Japan, 1965
TEACHING: Kyoto Municipal Univ of Art, Japan, Sculpture, 1965–68, Printmaking, 1968
AWARDS: Scholarship, French Govt, 1968; Scholarship, Japan Society, NY, 1974
COLLECTIONS: Mus of Mod Art, NY; Mus of Mod Art, Paris, France; Victoria & Albert Mus, London, England; Stedelijk Mus, Amsterdam, The Netherlands; Nat Mus of Mod Art, Kyoto, Japan; Mus of Mod Art, Tokyo, Japan; Mus of Mod Art, San Francisco, CA; Walker Art Center, Minneapolis, MN; Portland Art Mus, OR; Univ of California Mus, Berkeley, CA; Mus of Mod Art, Rijeka, Yugoslavia; Mus of Mod Art, Krakow, Poland; Nat Mus of Mod Art, Ljubljana, Yugoslavia; Nat Mus of Warsaw, Poland; Santa Barbara Mus, CA; Cincinnati Mus, OH; Hunterian Art Gallery, Glasgow, Scotland; Ibiza Mus of Contemp Art, Spain; Univ of Alberta, Canada
PRINTERS: Prasada Press, Cleveland, OH (PrP); Hidekatsu Takada (HT); Marcia Bartholme (MB); Crown Point Press, San Francisco, CA (CPP); Tadashi Toda, Kyoto, Japan (TT); Hiroshi Taguchi, Japan (HTa); Nancy Anello, San Francisco, CA (NA); Lawrence Hamlin, San Francisco, CA (LH); Artist (ART); Mark Patsfall Graphics, Cincinnati, OH (MPG)
PUBLISHERS: Prasada Press, Cleveland, OH (PrP); Crown Point Press, San Francisco, CA (CPP); Gallery Ueda, Tokyo, Japan (GaUe); Irene Drori Graphics, Los Angeles, CA (IDG); Art Academy, Cincinnati, OH (AAcad)
GALLERIES: Don Soker Gallery, San Francisco, CA; Yoh Art Gallery, Osaka, Japan; Gallery Ueda, Tokyo, Japan; Crown Point Press, San Francisco, CA & New York, NY; Irene Drori Fine Art, Los Angeles, CA; Takada Fine Arts, San Francisco, CA; Perimeter Gallery, Chicago, IL; Wise Collection, Bronxville, NY; Perimeter Gallery, Chicago, IL; J J Brookings Gallery, San Jose, CA; Herbert Palmer Gallery, Los Angeles, CA
MAILING ADDRESS: 4-5-2 Kagamishhi Okitayama, Kita-ku, Kyoto, Japan 603

TITLE	PUBLISHER	PRINTER	DATE	MEDIUM	DIMENSION (PAPER SIZE) IN INCHES	TYPE OF PAPER	EDITION NUMBER	NO. OF COLORS	ORIGINAL OPENING PRICE	CURRENT RETAIL PRICE
SOLD OUT EDITIONS (RARE):										
Surface is the Between Series: Paper Between Raindrops and Waterstain	PrP	PrP	1981	LC	30 X 22	GE/CC/KOZO	22	2	180	2250
Surface is the Between Series: Between Vertical and Horizon, San Pablo Ave, No 1	CPP	HT/MB/CPP	1984	EB/A/CC	40 X 37	AP88	21	3	650	2250
Between Vertical and Horizon, San Pablo Ave, No 2	CPP	HT/MB/CPP	1984	AC/DPT/CC	36 X 55	AP88/KOZO	35	3	650	2250
Between Vertical and Horizon, San Pablo Ave, No 3	CPP	HT/MB/CPP	1984	EB/A/CC	37 X 55	AP88	35	3	650	2250
Between Vertical and Horizon, San Pablo Ave, No 4	CPP	HT/MB/CPP	1984	EB/A/CC	38 X 52	FAB	35	3	750	2250
Between Vertical and Horizon, San Pablo Ave, No 5	CPP	HT/MB/CPP	1984	EB/A	21 X 18	FAB	25	3	300	750
Between Vertical and Horizon, San Pablo, No 6	CPP	HT/MB/CPP	1984	EB/A/DPT/SB	20 X 18	AP88	25	1	300	750
Between Vertical and Horizon, San Pablo, No 7	CPP	HT/MB/CPP	1984	A/DPT/CC/SG	23 X 30	FAB	25	3	300	750
Between Vertical and Horizontal— Garden Project-Wood, Paper, Fire and Rain	CPP	TT/CPP	1985	WB/CC	29 X 21	KOZO-T/KOZO-U	100	8	250	1000
Between Vertical and Horizontal— Between Corrosion of Iron, Copper and Gold, No 1	GaUe	HTa	1986	EB/A/DPT/SB	22 X 30	THS	30	5	430	1000
Between Vertical and Horizontal— Field Horizon One, Two, Three I–IV (Set of 4)	GaUe	HTa	1986	EC/A/DPT/SB/CC	23 X 15	THS/KOZO	40 EA	2 EA	660 EA	1500 EA
Between Vertical and Horizon— Descended Triangle #1–#6	CPP	NA/LH/CPP	1987	EB/A/CC	26 X 22 EA	SOM	15 EA		4000 SET	6000 SET
Between Vertical and Horizon Descended Triangle	CPP	NA/LH/CPP	1987	AC	44 X 13	SOM	20		700	850
Between Vertical and Horizon— Descended Triangle (A)	CPP	NA/LH/CPP	1987	EC	20 X 25	SOM	40		700	850
Between Vertical and Horizon— Descended Triangle (B)	CPP	NA/LH/CPP	1987	AC	20 X 25	SOM	40		700	850
Between Vertical and Horizon— Descended Triangle (C)	CPP	NA/LH/CPP	1987	AC	26 X 17	SOM	20		700	850
Between Vertical and Horizon— Descended Triangle (D)	CPP	NA/LH/CPP	1987	AC	26 X 17	SOM	20		700	850
Between Vertical and Horizon— Descended Triangle (Square)	CPP	NA/LH/CPP	1987	EC	51 X 42	SOM	40		1800	2500
Descended Triangle (Well 1,2,3) (Set of 3)	CPP	NA/LH/CPP	1987	EC	20 X 13 EA	SOM	10 EA		1200 SET	1500 SET
Well from Karma Series:										
Well from Karma—Echo Blue	CPP	CPP	1989	AC	50 X 42	SOM	15		2500	3500
Well from Karma—Echo—Blue #1	CPP	CPP	1989	AC/CC	36 X 69	SOM	10		3000	4500
Well from Karma—Echo—Red	CPP	CPP	1989	AC	50 X 42	SOM	15		2500	3500
Well from Karma—Trap in Echo #1	CPP	CPP	1989	AC/CC	26 X 23	SOM	15		950	950
Between Air and Water, Nos 9,10,11,12	CPP	CPP	1992	SG/SB/DPT/CC	27 X 17 EA	GAMPI	5 EA		950 EA	950 EA
CURRENT EDITIONS:										
Between Vertical and Horizon Series: Paper Between a Snowed Stone and Water Stain (2 Sheets)	IDG		1981	LC/SP	22 X 31	AP88/KOZO	29		180	850

SHOICHI IDA CONTINUED

TITLE	PUBLISHER	PRINTER	DATE	MEDIUM	DIMENSION (PAPER SIZE) IN INCHES	TYPE OF PAPER	EDITION NUMBER	NO. OF COLORS	ORIGINAL OPENING PRICE	CURRENT RETAIL PRICE
CURRENT EDITIONS:										
Paper Between Four Stones and Water No 50 (2 Sheets)	IDG		1981	LC/SP	22 X 31	AP88/KOZO	34		180	850
Paper Between a Leaf and Water Stain (2 Sheets)	IDG		1981	LC/SP	22 X 31	AP88/KOZO	29		180	850
Paper Between a Twig and Water, No 22 (2 Sheets)	IDG		1981	LC/SP	22 X 15	AP88/KOZO	74		180	850
Paper Between Two Twigs and Stain (2 Sheets)	IDG		1981	LC/SP	22 X 16	AP88/KOZO	36		180	850
Paper Between a Snowed Stone and Road (2 Sheets)	IDG		1981	LC/SP	22 X 16	AP88/KOZO	30		180	850
Between Vertical and Horizon—Between Corrosion of Iron, Copper and Gold, No 1	GaUe	HTa	1986	EB/A/DPT/SB	22 X 30	THS	30	5	430	800
Between Vertical and Horizon—Field Horizon One, Two, Three, I–IV (Set of 4)	GaUe	HTa	1986	EC/A/DPT/SB/C	23 X 15 EA	THS/KOZO	40 EA	2 EA	660 EA	1500 EA
Between Vertical and Horizon—Between Scratching and Corrosion Nos 1,2,3,4	GaUe	HTa	1986	EC/A/DPT/SB	22 X 30 EA	AP99/THS	30 EA	2 EA	430 EA	1000 EA
Between Vertical and Horizon—Descended Triangle (E)	CPP	NA/LH/CPP	1987	EC	20 X 13	SOM	20		600	650
Between Vertical and Horizon—Descended Triangle (Triangle)	CPP	NA/LH/CPP	1987	EC	50 X 40	SOM	40		1800	2500
Between Vertical and Horizon—Descended Triangle (Circle)	CPP	NA/LH/CPP	1987	EC	51 X 42	SOM	40		2000	2500
Between Vertical and Horizon—Descended Triangle (Still Life)	CPP	NA/LH/CPP	1987	EC	31 X 44	SOM	25		1000	1800
Between Opening and Closing—Blue and Orange, Nos 1–4 (Printed on 2 Sheets) (Series of 4)	IDG	ART	1987	DPT/SB/SG/CO	14 X 10 EA	AP	20 EA		1800 SET / 500 EA	2800 SET / 750 EA
Between Vertical and Horizon—Descended Triangle—Triangle (Black)	CPP	CPP	1987	AC	51 X 41	SOM	12	1	1800	2250
Between Vertical and Horizon—Descended Triangle—Square (Black)	CPP	CPP	1987	AC	51 X 41	SOM	12	1	1800	2250
Between Vertical and Horizon—Descended Triangle—Circle (Black)	CPP	CPP	1987	AC	51 X 41	SOM	12	1	1800	2250
Well from Karma—Trap in Echo #1,#2,#3	CPP	CPP	1989	AC/CC	26 X 23 EA	SOM	15 EA		950 EA	950 EA
Well from Karma—Trap in Echo #4,#5	CPP	CPP	1989	AC/CC	31 X 24 EA	SOM	20 EA		1200 EA	1500 EA
Well from Karma—Trap in Echo #6–#13 (Set of 8)	CPP	CPP	1989	AC/CC	25 X 24 EA	SOM	10 EA		8500 SET / 1100 EA	10000 SET / 1250 EA
Four Seasons of Eden Park (Set of 4):									4000 SET	4000 SET
Spring	AAcad	ART	1991–92	EB/DPT/CC	30 X 22	AP	20		1200	1200
Summer	AAcad	MPG	1991–92	EB/DPT/CC	30 X 22	AP	20		1200	1200
Fall	AAcad	MPG	1991–92	EB/DPT/CC	30 X 22	AP	20		1200	1200
Winter	AAcad	MPG	1991–92	EB/DPT/CC	30 X 22	AP	20		1200	1200
Between Air and Water, No 1	CPP	CPP	1992	AC/SG/HG/DPT/CC	46 X 45	GAMPI	40		2500	2500
Between Air and Water, No 2	CPP	CPP	1992	AC/SG/HG/DPT/CC	46 X 45	GAMPI	33		2500	2500
Between Air and Water, No 3	CPP	CPP	1992	AC/DPT/CC	39 X 51	GAMPI	19		2500	2500
Between Air and Water, No 4	CPP	CPP	1992	SG/SB/DPT/CC	39 X 48	GAMPI	26		2500	2500
Between Air and Water, No 5	CPP	CPP	1992	SG/SB/DPT/CC	32 X 26	GAMPI	10		1500	1500
Between Air and Water, No 6	CPP	CPP	1992	SG/HG/SB/DPT/CC	22 X 20	GAMPI	10		700	700
Between Air and Water, No 7	CPP	CPP	1992	SG/SB/DPT/CC	41 X 45	GAMPI	30		2500	2500
Between Air and Water, No 8	CPP	CPP	1992	SG/SB/DPT/CC	43 X 67	GAMPI	10		3500	3500

The retail prices of the 100,000 limited edition prints quoted in this directory are subject to change. Print publishers, artists and galleries were the direct sources for these quotations. Prices in the secondary market listed as "Sold Out Editions (Rare)" indicate that the publisher has a limited supply of that print or that the print is difficult to locate in the galleries.

The print market has become very selective. For the first time since we published the first edition of The Printworld Directory in 1982, the prices of prints have been greatly reduced and greatly increased for the same artists by the most reputable and established print publishers. Check the fifth edition to understand the movement.

JÖRG IMMENDORFF

BORN: Bleckede, Germany; 1945
EDUCATION: Kunstakademie, Düsseldorf, West Germany
RECENT EXHIB: Michael Werner Gallery, NY, 1992
PRINTERS: Artist (ART); Till Verclas, Hamburg, Germany (TV)
PUBLISHERS: Maximilian Verlag, Sabine Knust, Munich, Germany (MV/SK)
GALLERIES: Sonnabend Gallery, New York, NY; Fay Gold Gallery, Atlanta, GA; Brody's Gallery, Wash, DC; Lawrence Oliver Gallery, Phila, PA; Mary Boone Gallery, New York, NY; Nicola Jacobs Gallery, London, England; Michael Werner Gallery, New York, NY

TITLE	PUBLISHER	PRINTER	DATE	MEDIUM	DIMENSION (PAPER SIZE) IN INCHES	TYPE OF PAPER	EDITION NUMBER	NO. OF COLORS	ORIGINAL OPENING PRICE	CURRENT RETAIL PRICE
CURRENT EDITIONS:										
Café Deutschland Gut (Set of 10)	MV/SK	ART	1983	LI/HC	70 X 90	AP/W	10 EA	10 EA	3000 EA	3500 EA
Babel (Series of 26)	MV/SK	ART	1987	LI		BUT	7 EA		20000 SET	25000 SET
									900 EA	1000 EA
Langer Marsch auf Adler (Set of 7)	MV/SK	TV	1991–92	LI	Varies	ANW	12 EA		9400 EA	9400 EA

GIANCARLO IMPIGLIA

BORN: Rome, Italy; March 9, 1940; US Citizen
EDUCATION: Fine Arts Lyceum, Rome, Italy; Acad of Fine Arts, Rome, Italy; Italian Center of Cinematography, Rome, Italy; Technical Sch of Photography, Rome, Italy
RECENT EXHIB: Metropolis Gallery, Boston, MA, 1987; Allyson-Louis Gallery, Bethesda, MD, 1987; Uptown Gallery, NY, 1990
COLLECTIONS: New York City Mus, NY; Mus Italo-Americano, San Francisco, CA; Jane Voorhees Zimmerli Art Mus, Rutgers Univ, New Brunswick, NJ; Snite Mus of Art, Notre Dame, IN; Kentucky Derby Mus, KY
PRINTERS: Grin Graphics, NY (GG); Screened Images, Port Washington, NY (SI); Chelsea Art Press, London, England (CAP); ChromComp, Inc, NY (CCI)
PUBLISHERS: Transworld Art Inc, NY (YAI); Marigold Enterprises, Ltd, NY (MEL); Giancarlo Impiglia Studio, Inc, NY (GIS); Chalk & Vermilion Fine Arts, Greenwich, CT (CVFA)
GALLERIES: Petrini Art Gallery, Rocky Hill, CT; Allyson Louis Gallery, Bethesda, MO; Mussavi Gallery, New York, NY; Newmark Gallery, New York, NY; Jeffrey Ruesch Fine Art, Ltd, New York, NY; Uptown Gallery, New York, NY; RVS Fine Art, Southampton, NY
MAILING ADDRESS: 182 Grand St, New York, NY 10013

TITLE	PUBLISHER	PRINTER	DATE	MEDIUM	DIMENSION (PAPER SIZE) IN INCHES	TYPE OF PAPER	EDITION NUMBER	NO. OF COLORS	ORIGINAL OPENING PRICE	CURRENT RETAIL PRICE
SOLD OUT EDITIONS (RARE):										
Intermission	GIS	GG	1980	SP	22 X 30	AP88	75	6	450	2000
Top of the City	GIS	GG	1981	SP	29 X 40	R/BFK	165	18	900	2500
The Party is Over	GIS	GG	1982	SP	28 X 36	R/BFK	165	21	900	1500
Brooklyn Bridge	CFA	AA	1983	SP	36 X 25	R/BFK	250		500	1000
The Kiss	GIS	SI	1983	SP	24 X 31	R/BFK	175	16	800	1200
Night Lights	GIS	SI	1983	SP	29 X 38	R/BFK	175	35	900	1500
Homage	GIS	SI	1984	SP	27 X 37	R/BFK	175	34	800	1350
CURRENT EDITIONS:										
An Evening to Remember	CVFA	CCI	1989	SP	39 X 37	COV	376	42	1250	1250
The Joy of Life	CVFA	CCI	1989	SP	28 X 38	COV	376	35	1250	1250
Crowd	CVFA	CCI	1989	SP	28 X 38	COV	376	35	1250	1250
Half Past Five	CVFA	CCI	1989	SP	28 X 38	COV	376	35	1250	1250

ROBERT INDIANA

BORN: New Castle, IN; September 13, 1928
EDUCATION: John Herron Art Inst, Indianapolis, IN, 1945–46; Munson-Williams-Proctor Inst, Utica, NY, 1947–48; Chicago Art Inst, IL, BFA, 1949–53; Skowhegan Sch, ME, 1953; Univ of Edinburgh, Scotland, 1953–54; Aspen Inst, CO, 1968
AWARDS: Chicago Inst of Art, IL, 1953; Franklin and Marshall Col, Lancaster, PA, Hon DFA, 1970; Indiana State Com on the Arts Award, 1973
RECENT EXHIB: Miami New Art Mus, Oxford, OH, 1989; Glabman Ring Gallery, Los Angeles, CA, 1990; Ramnarine Gallery, Long Island City, NY, 1992; Virginia Lust Gallery, NY, 1993
COLLECTIONS: Mus of Mod Art, NY; Whitney Mus of Am Art, NY; Stedelijk Mus, Schiedam, Netherlands; Carnegie Inst, Pittsburgh, PA; Detroit Inst of Art, MI; Allentown Mus of Art, PA; Baltimore Mus of Art, MD; Brandeis Mus, Waltham, MA; Albright-Knox Gallery of Art, Buffalo, NY; Delaware Art Mus, Wilmington, DE; Inst of Contemp Art, Univ of Pennsylvania, Phila, PA; Kaiser Wilhelm Mus, Krefeld, Germany; Los Angeles County Mus, CA; Metropolitan Mus of Art, NY; Aldrich Mus of Contemp Art, Ridgefield, CT; Walker Art Center, Minneapolis, MN; San Francisco Mus of Mod Art, CA
PRINTERS: Landfall Press, Inc, Chicago, IL (LPI); Jack Lemon, Chicago, IL (JL); Fred Gude, Chicago, IL (FG); Michael Domberger, Germany (MD); Simca Print Artists, Inc, NY (SPA); Patricia Branstead, NY (PB); Aeropress, NY (A)
PUBLISHERS: Multiples, NY (M); Transworld Art, Inc, NY (TAI); Abrams Original Editions, NY (AOE); South Bend Art Ctr, Inc (SBAC); Landfall Press, Inc, Chicago, IL (LPI); Prestige Art, Inc, Mamaroneck, NY (PA); Domberger Stuttgart-Schmela, Düsseldorf, Germany (DS-S)

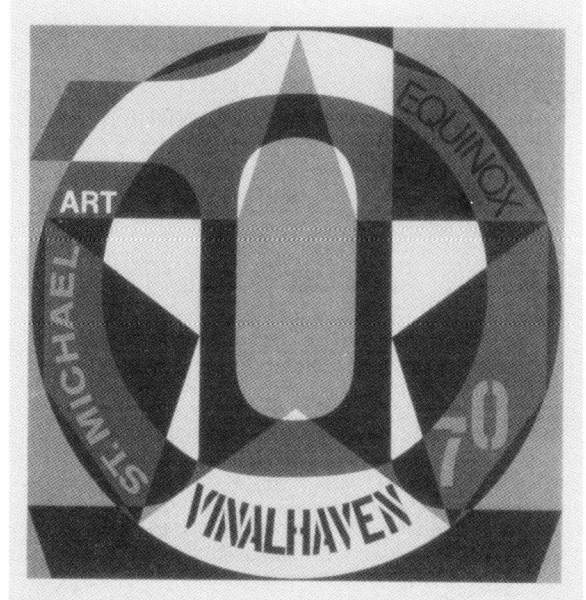

Robert Indiana
Decade: Autoportraits
Courtesy Multiples, Inc

ROBERT INDIANA CONTINUED

GALLERIES: Marian Goodman, New York, NY; Posner Gallery, Milwaukee, WI; Landfall Press, Inc, Chicago, IL; Graphics Gallery, San Francisco, CA; O'Farrell Gallery, Brunswick, ME; Ruth Siegel Gallery, New York, NY; Glabman Ring Gallery, Los Angeles, CA; Ramnarine Gallery, Long Island City, NY; Virginia Lust Gallery, New York, NY; Quartet Editions, New York, NY
MAILING ADDRESS: c/o Star of Hope, Vinalhaven, ME 94863

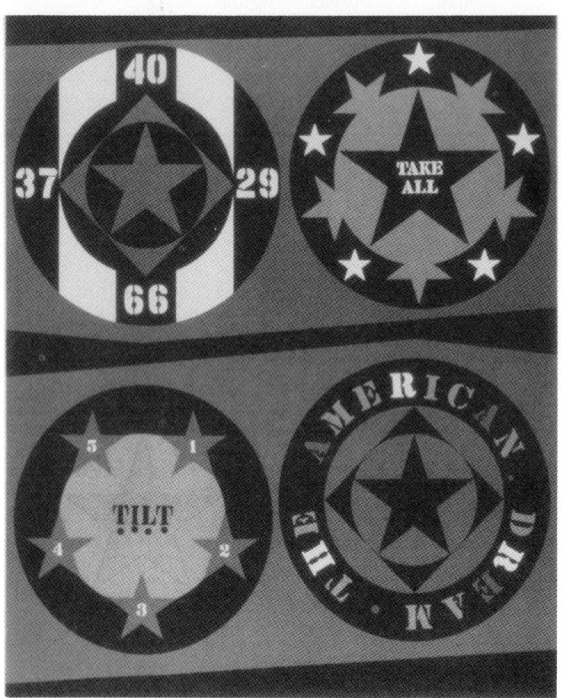

Robert Indiana
American Dream
Courtesy Multiples, Inc

Robert Indiana
Decade
Courtesy Multiples, Inc

TITLE	PUBLISHER	PRINTER	DATE	MEDIUM	DIMENSION (PAPER SIZE) IN INCHES	TYPE OF PAPER	EDITION NUMBER	NO. OF COLORS	ORIGINAL OPENING PRICE	CURRENT RETAIL PRICE
SOLD OUT EDITIONS (RARE):										
Numbers (Set of 10)	DS-S		1968	SP	26 X 20 EA	AP	275 EA		2500 SET	15000 SET
Decades (Set of 10)	M	PB/A	1971	SP	39 X 32 EA	SchPar	200 EA		2500 SET	20000 SET
Love			1971	SP	39 X 31	WOVE	200		300	3500
On the Mountains of the Prairie Gitche Manito the Mighty Called the Tribes of Men Together			1971	SP	32 X 30	AP			300	3000
The Golden Future of America	TAI	SPA	1976	SP	26 X 20	AP	175	5	500	2000
South Bend	SBAC/LPI	JL/FG	1978	LC	31 X 28	ARJ	150	7	500	2000
Decade: Autoportraits, 1980 (Set of 10)	M	PB/A	1980	SP	28 X 28 EA	ARJ	125 EA	9 EA	6000 SET 600 EA	18000 SET 2500 EA
Golden Five (Set of 5)	M	PB/A	1980	SP	27 X 27 EA	FAB	100 EA	9 EA	3750 SET	10000 SET
Demuth American Dream (Set of 5)	PA	MD	1980	SP	24 X 24 EA	FAB	100 EA	9 EA	3750 SET	10000 SET
An American Dream (Set of 4)	M	PB/A	1982	SP	27 X 27 EA	FAB	100 EA	9 EA	3000 SET	8000 SET
An American Dream #2 (Set of 4)	AOE	MD	1982	SP	27 X 27 EA	FAB	100 EA		3000 SET	8000 SET
A Garden of Love (Set of 6)	AOE	MD	1982	SP	27 X 27 EA	FAB	100 EA		4500 SET	8000 SET

MARK INNERST

BORN: York, PA; 1957
EDUCATION: Kutztown, PA, BFA, 1980
RECENT EXHIB: Galerie Montenay, Paris, France, 1987; Illinois State Univ, Normal, IL, 1988; Wright State Univ, Dayton, OH, 1988; Contemp Arts Mus, Houston, TX, 1988, Chicago Mus of Contemp Art, IL, 1988, Curt Marcus Gallery, NY, 1988; Folker Skulima Gallery, Berlin, West Germany, 1989; Nelson-Atkins Mus of Art, Kansas City, MO, 1989; Greenberg Gallery, St Louis, MO, 1990; Curt Marcus Gallery, NY, 1990
COLLECTIONS: Mus of Mod Art, NY; Albright-Knox Art Gallery, Buffalo, NY; Brooklyn Mus, NY; Solomon R Guggenheim Mus, NY; Indianapolis Mus of Art, IN; Los Angeles County Mus of Art, CA; Mus of Contemp Art, Barry Lowen Coll, Los Angeles, CA
PRINTERS: Richard Finch, Normal, IL (RF); Todd DeVriese, Normal, IL (TDV), Richard Fulse, Normal, IL (RFu), Eric Kuchn, Normal, IL (EK), Andrew Hatterman, Normal, IL (AH); Normal Editions Workshop, Illinois State Univ, Normal, IL (NEW)
PUBLISHERS: Normal Editions Workshop, Illinois State Univ, Normal, IL (NEW)
GALLERIES: Curt Marcus Gallery, New York, NY; Galerie Montenay, Paris, France; Michael Kohn Gallery, Los Angeles, CA; Greenberg Gallery, St Louis, MO

MARK INNERST CONTINUED

TITLE	PUBLISHER	PRINTER	DATE	MEDIUM	DIMENSION (PAPER SIZE) IN INCHES	TYPE OF PAPER	EDITION NUMBER	NO. OF COLORS	ORIGINAL OPENING PRICE	CURRENT RETAIL PRICE
SOLD OUT EDITIONS (RARE):										
Pocket Watch	NEW	RF/TDV/RFo/NEW	1989	LC	12 X 9	KIT/HMP	30	3	1500	2000
CURRENT EDITIONS:										
Lantern	NEW	RF/TDV/RFo/EK/AH/NEW	1989	LC	12 X 9	R/BFK-KIT	10	3	1800	2000

KYOHEI INUKAI

BORN: Chicago, IL; (1913–1985)
EDUCATION: Art Inst of Chicago, IL; Nat Acad of Design, NY; Arts Students League, NY
AWARDS: Louis Comfort Tiffany Found Fel
COLLECTIONS: Brandeis Univ, Waltham, MA; Portland Mus of Art, ME; Albright-Knox Art Gallery, Buffalo, NY; Philbrook Arts Center, Tulsa, OK; Wichita Univ, KS; Portland Mus of Fine Art, OR
PRINTERS: Editions Domberger, Stuttgart, West Germany (ED); Herb Fox, New Haven, CT (HF); Tom Black, College Point, NY (TB); Isaac Inbal, NY (II); Alexander Heinrici, NY (AH); Jim Shaikh, NY (JS); Moshin Graphics, NY (MG); Richard Mills, Mt Vernon, NY (RM); Artist (ART); American Atelier, NY (AA)

PUBLISHERS: Grippi Gallery, NY (GG); C & D Editions, NY (CDE); Dorsky Gallery, NY (DG); Richard Feigen Gallery, NY (RFG); Jackie Fine Arts, NY (JFA); London Arts, Inc, Detroit, MI (LAI); Editions Domberger, Stuttgart, West Germany (ED); Original Print Collectors, NY (OPC); Associated American Artist, NY (AAA); Graphic Society, Greenwich, CT (GS); Artist (ART); Circle Fine Art, NY (CFA)
GALLERIES: Associated American Artists, New York, NY; London Arts Gallery, Detroit, MI; Daruma Gallery, Cedarhurst, NY; Sylvan Cole Gallery, New York, NY; Circle Galleries, Chicago, Il & Soho, NY & Scottsdale, AZ & Beverly Hills, CA & Costa Mesa, CA & Sherman Oaks, CA & Palm Beach, FL & Honolulu, HI & New Orleans, LA & Las Vegas, NV & Seattle, WA & San Diego, CA & San Francisco, CA & Pittsburgh, PA & Houston, TX & Northbrook, IL

TITLE	PUBLISHER	PRINTER	DATE	MEDIUM	DIMENSION (PAPER SIZE) IN INCHES	TYPE OF PAPER	EDITION NUMBER	NO. OF COLORS	ORIGINAL OPENING PRICE	CURRENT RETAIL PRICE
SOLD OUT EDITIONS (RARE):										
Echo	RFG	ED	1968	SP	24 X 35	R/100	75	7	110	1800
Pulse	GG	ART	1969	SP	23 X 27		100	12	90	1800
Serpentine II	GG	ART	1970	SP	23 X 35		110	4	75	1000
Concentrum	GG	ART	1970	SP	27 X 27	AP	90	5	100	1800
Triangloform V	CDE	HF	1970	SP	26 X 22	WP80	100	17	90	1500
Triangloform VI, VII	DG	ART	1972	SP	38 X 38 EA	AE	80 EA	4 EA	150 EA	1800 EA
Flight Lines	JFA	AH	1979	SP	35 X 26	R/100	200	6	250	1000
Trinity	JFA	TB	1979	SP	23 X 30	AP88	200	4	225	1000
Life Forces	LAI	TB	1980	SP	23 X 30	AP88	200	4	150	1200
Zeno	JFA	TB	1980	SP	23 X 30	AP88	200	5	225	1200
Aquarius	JFA	TB	1981	SP	23 X 30	AP88	250	7	250	1200
Signal	JFA	II	1982	SP	23 X 30	AP88	250	8	250	1200
Cat Watching Pigeons	ART	ART	1982	WC	10 X 13	AP	45	2	75	500
Cat Drinking	ART	ART	1982	WB	9 X 11	MUL	50	1	50	400
Spring Riverside Park	ART	RM/ART	1983	SP	22 X 30	LEN	140	10	250	1000
Misty Morning Vermont	OPC	JS/MG	1983	LC	22 X 30	AP	245	20	190	650
Begonia	ART	RM/ART	1984	SP	15 X 22	LEN	135	10	200	1000
CURRENT EDITIONS:										
Flying High	CFA	AA	1984	SP	35 X 26	AP	200		125	225
Idea	CFA	AA	1984	SP	35 X 26	AP	200		125	225
Index	CFA	AA	1984	SP	22 X 30	AP	200		125	225
Shadow Lines	CFA	AA	1984	SP	26 X 34	AP	200		125	225

MICHIKO ITATANI

BORN: Osaka, Japan; May 8, 1948
EDUCATION: Art Inst of Chicago, IL, MFA, 1976
TEACHING: Vis Prof, Painting & Drawing Art Inst of Chicago, IL, 1979 to present
AWARDS: Illinois Arts Council Grants, Chicago, IL, 1979,81; Nat Endowment for the Arts Fel, 1980–81; Illinois Council Artist's Grant, 1984,85; John Simon Guggenheim Fel, 1990–91
RECENT EXHIB: Rockford Mus, IL, 1987; Musee de Quebec, Canada, 1988; Univ of Colorado, Boulder, CO, 1989; State of Illinois Art Gallery, Chicago, IL, 1989; Illinois State Mus, Springfield, IL, 1989; Alternative Mus, NY, 1989; Asashi Broadcasting Gallery, Japan, 1990

COLLECTIONS: Art Inst of Chicago, IL; Mus of Contemp Arts, Chicago, IL
PRINTERS: Mary McDonald, Chicago, IL (MM); Landfall Press, Inc, Chicago, IL (LPI)
PUBLISHERS: Landfall Press, Inc, Chicago, IL (LPI); NAME Gallery, Chicago, IL (NAME)
GALLERIES: Landfall Press, Inc, Chicago, IL; Deson-Saunders Gallery, Chicago, IL
MAILING ADDRESS: c/o Art Institute of Chicago, School of Art, Columbus Dr, Chicago, IL 60603

TITLE	PUBLISHER	PRINTER	DATE	MEDIUM	DIMENSION (PAPER SIZE) IN INCHES	TYPE OF PAPER	EDITION NUMBER	NO. OF COLORS	ORIGINAL OPENING PRICE	CURRENT RETAIL PRICE
SOLD OUT EDITIONS (RARE):										
Untitled	LPI/NAME	MM/LPI	1980	LC	22 X 30	AP/W	100	3	150	300

MARGARET ISRAEL

BORN: Havana, Cuba; (1929–1985)
EDUCATION: Syracuse Univ, NY; L'Ecole des Beaux Arts, Paris, France; Académie de la Grande Chaumiére; Atelier 17, NY, with Stanley Hayter
TEACHING: Parsons Sch of Design, NY
PRINTERS: American Atelier, NY (AA)
PUBLISHERS: Circle Fine Art, Chicago, IL (CFA)
GALLERIES: Circle Galleries, Chicago, IL & New York, NY & Scottsdale, AZ & Beverly Hills, CA & Sherman Oaks, CA & San Diego, CA & San Francisco, CA & Houston, TX & Costa Mesa, CA & Pittsburgh, PA & Seattle, WA & New Orleans, LA & Las Vegas, NV & Northbrook, IL & Palm Beach, FL & Honolulu, HI; Cordier & Ekstrom Gallery, New York, NY; Twining Gallery, New York, NY;

TITLE	PUBLISHER	PRINTER	DATE	MEDIUM	DIMENSION (PAPER SIZE) IN INCHES	TYPE OF PAPER	EDITION NUMBER	NO. OF COLORS	ORIGINAL OPENING PRICE	CURRENT RETAIL PRICE
SOLD OUT EDITIONS (RARE):										
Roosters	CFA	AA	1980	LC	23 X 28	AP	300		150	400
Chickens	CFA	AA	1980	LC	23 X 28	AP	300		150	400

CAROL JABLONSKY

BORN: Port Washington, NY; 1939
EDUCATION: Boston Univ, MA; Art Students League, NY; Institute Allende, Mexico City, Mexico
PRINTERS: American Atelier, NY (AA)
PUBLISHERS: Circle Fine Art, Chicago, IL (CFA)
GALLERIES: Circle Galleries, San Diego, CA & San Francisco, CA & Northbrook, IL & Houston, TX & Pittsburgh, PA & Soho, NY & Chicago, IL & Scottsdale, AZ & Beverly Hills, CA & Costa Mesa, CA & Sherman Oaks, CA & Palm Beach, FL & Honolulu, HI & New Orleans, LA & Las Vegas, NV & Seattle, WA; Walton Street Gallery, Chicago, IL

TITLE	PUBLISHER	PRINTER	DATE	MEDIUM	DIMENSION (PAPER SIZE) IN INCHES	TYPE OF PAPER	EDITION NUMBER	NO. OF COLORS	ORIGINAL OPENING PRICE	CURRENT RETAIL PRICE
SOLD OUT EDITIONS (RARE):										
Rocking Horse	CFA	AA	1972	LC	11 X 13	AP	300		35	575
Rocking Horse (Rives Journal)	CFA	AA	1972	LC	11 X 13	AP	15		50	600
Rocking Leopard	CFA	AA	1972	LC	11 X 13	AP	300		35	525
Rocking Leopard (Rives Journal)	CFA	AA	1972	LC	11 X 13	AP	15		50	550
Tulip	CFA	AA	1972	LC	15 X 21	AP	300		35	725
Rocking Unicorn	CFA	AA	1972	LC	11 X 13	AP	300		35	525
Rocking Unicorn (Rives Journal)	CFA	AA	1972	LC	11 X 13	AP	15		50	475
Rocking Dove	CFA	AA	1972	LC	11 X 13	AP	300		35	400
Rocking Dove (Rives Journal)	CFA	AA	1972	LC	11 X 13	AP	15		50	600
Eggs and Bird	CFA	AA	1973	EC	15 X 11	R/BFK	50		50	775
Juggler	CFA	AA	1973	EC	11 X 15	R/BFK	100		50	775
Clown	CFA	AA	1973	EC	11 X 15	R/BFK	100		50	800
Nestlings	CFA	AA	1973	EC	15 X 11	R/BFK	100		50	800
White Horse and Friends	CFA	AA	1973	LC	32 X 20	AP	300		75	850
Dancing Horse	CFA	AA	1973	LC	27 X 20	AP	300		75	825
Peaceable Kingdom	CFA	AA	1973	LC	22 X 27	AP	300		75	1025
Fable I	CFA	AA	1973	EC	11 X 15	R/BFK	100		50	825
A Fable II	CFA	AA	1973	EC	11 X 15	R/BFK	100		50	1100
Double Jester	CFA	AA	1973	EC	11 X 15	R/BFK	100		50	1100
Young Winged Lion	CFA	AA	1973	EC	11 X 15	R/BFK	100		50	850
Peter's Cat	CFA	AA	1973	EC	22 X 15	R/BFK	100		50	975
Mirror Image	CFA	AA	1973	EC	22 X 15	R/BFK	100		50	750
Leopard	CFA	AA	1973	EC	15 X 11	R/BFK	100		50	800
The Chair	CFA	AA	1973	EC	15 X 11	R/BFK	100		50	825
Leopard Dancing	CFA	AA	1973	LC	22 X 26	AP	300		50	1025
Spotted Cat	CFA	AA	1973	EC	15 X 18	R/BFK	100		50	900
Goodbye Michael	CFA	AA	1973	LC	23 X 24	AP	300		50	1475
Waiting for Pharoah's Daughter	CFA	AA	1973	EC	22 X 30	R/BFK	100		60	1000
Gus Mozart	CFA	AA	1973	EC	22 X 30	R/BFK	200		60	850
The Lotus	CFA	AA	1973	EC	18 X 15	R/BFK	100		50	600
The Turtle	CFA	AA	1973	DPT	15 X 11	R/BFK	100		50	600
The Butterfly	CFA	AA	1973	LC/I	15 X 11	R/BFK	100		50	700
Two Fish	CFA	AA	1973	DPT	11 X 7	R/BFK	100		50	700
Noctura	CFA	AA	1974	LC	18 X 19	AP	300		50	400
Kingdom with Minerva	CFA	AA	1974	LC	20 X 25	AP	300		60	825
Two Nests	CFA	AA	1974	LC	8 X 5	AP	300		50	750
Windows	CFA	AA	1975	LC	30 X 22	AP	300		75	525
Parrot Conversation	CFA	AA	1975	LC	12 X 17	AP	300		50	600
Talking Bird	CFA	AA	1975	EC	12 X 17	AP	300		50	700
Parrot and Friend	CFA	AA	1975	LC	12 X 17	AP	300		50	725
The Parrot	CFA	AA	1975	LC	12 X 17	AP	300		50	700
Tightrope Walker	CFA	AA	1975	LC/DPT	21 X 29	R/BFK	200		75	800
Bestiary	CFA	AA	1975	LC	29 X 30	AP	100		75	900
Linnaeus	CFA	AA	1975	LC	22 X 22	AP	10		75	950
Rose	CFA	AA	1975	LC	19 X 20	AP	300		75	750
Lyre and Cat Musician	CFA	AA	1975	LC	11 X 11	AP	300		50	400
The Acrobat	CFA	AA	1976	EC	15 X 11	R/BFK	50		75	675
The Lion	CFA	AA	1976	EC	15 X 11	R/BFK	50		75	675
The Unicorn	CFA	AA	1976	EC	15 X 11	R/BFK	50		75	675
The Owl	CFA	AA	1976	EC	15 X 11	R/BFK	50		75	675
The Jester	CFA	AA	1976	EC	15 X 11	R/BFK	50		75	675

CAROL JABLONSKY CONTINUED

TITLE	PUBLISHER	PRINTER	DATE	MEDIUM	DIMENSION (PAPER SIZE) IN INCHES	TYPE OF PAPER	EDITION NUMBER	NO. OF COLORS	ORIGINAL OPENING PRICE	CURRENT RETAIL PRICE
SOLD OUT EDITIONS (RARE):										
The Dove	CFA	AA	1976	EC	15 X 11	R/BFK	50		75	675
Equestrian Owls	CFA	AA	1976	LC	18 X 26	AP	300		80	875
Leopard Dreaming	CFA	AA	1976	LC	15 X 21	AP	300		80	775
Sunflower	CFA	AA	1976	LC	14 X 30	AP	300		75	775
Puppet Theatre	CFA	AA	1976	SP	36 X 36	AP	250		125	2600
Expectant Owls	CFA	AA	1976	LC	20 X 14	AP	300		75	750
Two Doves	CFA	AA	1976	LC	15 X 20	AP	275		75	700
Lion and Rider	CFA	AA	1976	EC	15 X 17	AP	100		50	750
Horse and Rider	CFA	AA	1976	EC	15 X 17	AP	100		50	825
Fish and Fowl	CFA	AA	1976	EC	11 X 15	AP	100		50	750
Pegasus	CFA	AA	1976	EC	11 X 10	AP	100		50	750
Dove and Dancer	CFA	AA	1976	EC	15 X 11	AP	100		50	825
Cat and Mouse	CFA	AA	1976	LC	22 X 23	AP	300		75	950
Kingdom and Ibis	CFA	AA	1977	LC	24 X 27	AP	300		80	925
Tiger	CFA	AA	1977	I	13 X 10	AP	100		50	775
Rose	CFA	AA	1977	I	12 X 10	AP	100		50	625
Helicopter	CFA	AA	1977	I	12 X 10	AP	100		50	575
Nightflower	CFA	AA	1977	I	12 X 10	AP	100		50	575
Winged Horse	CFA	AA	1977	I	13 X 15	AP	100		50	550
Bird in Hand I	CFA	AA	1977	I/HC	12 X 10	AP	100		50	950
Bird in Hand II	CFA	AA	1977	I/HC	13 X 10	R/BFK	100		50	1000
Fledermaus	CFA	AA	1977	I	12 X 10	R/BFK	100		50	575
Clown	CFA	AA	1977	I	12 X 10	R/BFK	100		50	300
Two Cats	CFA	AA	1977	LC	22 X 28	AP	300		80	1000
In the Garden	CFA	AA	1978	DPT	22 X 30	R/BFK	125		75	500
Chinese Dog	CFA	AA	1978	LC	21 X 27	AP	300		75	1200
House Cat	CFA	AA	1979	I/EMB	18 X 14	R/BFK	150		75	1050
Painted Horse	CFA	AA	1979	I	19 X 21	R/BFK	150		75	1050
Orpheus	CFA	AA	1980	LC	22 X 29	AP	300		150	650
In the Forest of the Night	CFA	AA	1980	LC	26 X 33	AP	300		75	1175
Red Poppy	CFA	AA	1980	LC	28 X 22	AP	300		75	750
Helianthus (Sunflower)	CFA	AA	1980	LC	37 X 27	AP	300		75	750
Birds of Paradise	CFA	AA	1981	LC	36 X 26	AP	300		75	1000
Bestiary Folio (Set of 10):									1000 SET	4200 SET
Bestiary	CFA	AA	1981	EC	15 X 13	R/BFK	100		125	600
Unicorn	CFA	AA	1981	EC	15 X 13	R/BFK	100		125	600
Sea Horse	CFA	AA	1981	EC	15 X 13	R/BFK	100		125	600
Taurus	CFA	AA	1981	EC	15 X 13	R/BFK	100		125	600
Sphinx	CFA	AA	1981	EC	15 X 13	R/BFK	100		125	600
Ursus	CFA	AA	1981	EC	15 X 13	R/BFK	100		125	600
Elephas Maximus	CFA	AA	1981	EC	15 X 13	R/BFK	100		125	600
Mus	CFA	AA	1981	EC	15 X 13	R/BFK	100		125	600
Cebus	CFA	AA	1981	EC	15 X 13	R/BFK	100		125	600
Centaur	CFA	AA	1981	EC	15 X 13	R/BFK	100		125	600
Eden Folio (Set of 10):									900 SET	2700 SET
Before Adam	CFA	AA	1981	LC	13 X 11	AP	300		100	375
Night	CFA	AA	1981	LC	13 X 11	AP	300		100	375
Eden Flower	CFA	AA	1981	LC	13 X 11	AP	300		100	275
Sleeping Adam	CFA	AA	1981	LC	13 X 11	AP	300		100	275
Forest	CFA	AA	1981	LC	13 X 11	AP	300		100	250
The Garden	CFA	AA	1981	LC	11 X 13	AP	300		100	500
Hummingbird	CFA	AA	1981	LC	13 X 11	AP	300		100	275
The Serpent	CFA	AA	1981	LC	13 X 11	AP	300		100	275
Adam & Eve	CFA	AA	1981	LC	11 X 13	AP	300		100	450
Forbidden Fruit	CFA	AA	1971	LC	13 X 11	AP	300		100	275
Authors Folio (Set of 8):									700 SET	2650 SET
Gertrude	CFA	AA	1981	EB/DPT/EMB	14 X 11	R/BFK	150		100	450
Falcon	CFA	AA	1981	EB/DPT/EMB	14 X 11	R/BFK	150		100	375
Poe	CFA	AA	1981	EB/DPT/EMB	14 X 11	R/BFK	150		100	425
Tyger	CFA	AA	1981	EB/DPT/EMB	14 X 11	R/BFK	150		100	425
Kafka	CFA	AA	1981	EB/DPT/EMB	14 X 11	R/BFK	150		100	375
Melville	CFA	AA	1981	EB/DPT/EMB	14 X 11	R/BFK	150		100	300
Isak Dinesen	CFA	AA	1981	EB/DPT/EMB	14 X 11	R/BFK	150		100	375
Pen and Ink	CFA	AA	1981	EB/DPT/EMB	14 X 11	R/BFK	150		100	400
Tulip	CFA	AA	1982	LC	15 X 21	AP	300		150	650
Ginger	CFA	AA	1982	LC	15 X 21	AP	300		150	725
Oriental Poppy	CFA	AA	1982	LC	29 X 22	AP	300		200	725
Sleeping Cat Game (Trip)	CFA	AA	1986	LC	33 X 65	AP	300		750	4800
Mermaids and a Peach	CFA	AA	1986	DPT/EMB	13 X 16	R/BFK	125		175	1475
Musical Menagerie	CFA	AA	1987	LC	28 X 21	R/BFK	300		450	700
Flora Puzzle	CFA	AA	1987	LC	19 X 37	R/BFK	30		950	2800

CAROL JABLONSKY CONTINUED

TITLE	PUBLISHER	PRINTER	DATE	MEDIUM	DIMENSION (PAPER SIZE) IN INCHES	TYPE OF PAPER	EDITION NUMBER	NO. OF COLORS	ORIGINAL OPENING PRICE	CURRENT RETAIL PRICE
CURRENT EDITIONS:										
Angel	CFA	AA	1972	EC	10 X 10	AP	150		50	660
Cat Disguise I, II (Set of 2)	CFA	AA	1972	LC	14 X 11 EA	AP	300 EA		100 SET	1325 SET
									50 EA	800 EA
Celeste	CFA	AA	1972	EC		AP	15		35	1500
Sea Change	CFA	AA	1972	EC	8 X 8	AP	150		35	675
Seabird	CFA	AA	1972	EC	8 X 8	AP	150		35	660
Seashell	CFA	AA	1972	EC	9 X 10	AP	150		50	660
Tempus Fugit Dog (Sirius)	CFA	AA	1972	LC	26 X 25	AP	300		50	725
Summer Table, White Cat	CFA	AA	1972	LC	36 X 22	AP	300		50	2250
Pegasus II	CFA	AA	1973	LC	17 X 13	AP	300		35	375
Minerva	CFA	AA	1973	LC	17 X 13	AP	300		35	350
The Owl Within	CFA	AA	1973	LC	21 X 25	AP	300		40	450
Duet	CFA	AA	1974	LC	19 X 11	AP	300		35	350
Portraits	CFA	AA	1975	LC	30 X 22	AP	300		40	450
Rana	CFA	AA	1975	LC	15 X 20	AP	300		35	300
Elphas and Others	CFA	AA	1975	LC/EC	30 X 21	R/BFK	300		40	400
Dovecote	CFA	AA	1975	LC	34 X 23	AP	300		40	450
Ram and Lute Musician	CFA	AA	1975	LC	11 X 11	AP	300		35	450
Horse and Horn Musician	CFA	AA	1975	LC	11 X 11	AP	300		35	350
Bird and Flute Musician	CFA	AA	1975	LC	11 X 11	AP	300		35	350
The Rabbits Motto	CFA	AA	1977	LC	24 X 30	AP	250		40	450
The Hat I	CFA	AA	1977	I	12 X 11	R/BFK	100		35	375
The Hat II	CFA	AA	1977	I	12 X 10	R/BFK	100		35	375
The Hat III	CFA	AA	1977	I	12 X 13	R/BFK	100		35	300
The Hat IV	CFA	AA	1977	I	12 X 13	R/BFK	100		35	300
Waltzing Mice	CFA	AA	1977	LC	21 X 20	AP	300		100	350
Ram	CFA	AA	1977	LC	7 X 20	AP	300		75	275
Winter Solstice	CFA	AA	1977	I	16 X 15	R/BFK	100		75	275
Moon	CFA	AA	1977	I	9 X 8	R/BFK	100		60	250
Flyer	CFA	AA	1977	I	9 X 8	R/BFK	100		60	250
Eden Windows	CFA	AA	1978	LC	34 X 25	AP	300		100	400
Paradisiaca	CFA	AA	1978	LC	22 X 26	AP	300		100	400
Abracadabra	CFA	AA	1978	EC	29 X 21	AP	300		100	400
Circus Entertainer	CFA	AA	1979	LC	24 X 32	AP	250		40	450
Horatio	CFA	AA	1979	I/EMB	16 X 14	R/BFK	150		75	350
Quintus	CFA	AA	1979	I/EMB	16 X 14	R/BFK	150		75	350
Cheetah	CFA	AA	1979	LC	21 X 26	AP	300		75	450
Red Pony (Minerva and Friend)	CFA	AA	1979	LC	22 X 30	AP	300		100	500
Fox Totem	CFA	AA	1980	LC	16 X 14	AP	300		50	275
Basket	CFA	AA	1980	LC	22 X 28	AP	300		150	500
Tyger and Rose	CFA	AA	1980	LC	20 X 25	AP	300		150	450
Frog Totem	CFA	AA	1980	LC	16 X 14	AP	300		50	300
Feather Totem	CFA	AA	1980	LC	16 X 14	AP	300		50	300
Monkey Totem	CFA	AA	1980	LC	16 X 14	AP	300		50	275
Owl and Mouse Game	CFA	AA	1982	LC	22 X 27	AP	300		175	400
Artists Folio I (Set of 8):									700 SET	1950 SET
Giotto and Weeping Angel	CFA	AA	1982	LC	14 X 11	AP	300		100	300
Vincent van Gogh and Sunflower	CFA	AA	1982	LC	14 X 11	AP	300		100	300
Rosa Bonheur and the Horse Fair	CFA	AA	1982	LC	14 X 11	AP	300		100	300
Claude Monet and Water Lily	CFA	AA	1982	LC	14 X 11	AP	300		100	300
Henri Rousseau and Gypsy Guitar	CFA	AA	1982	LC	14 X 11	AP	300		100	300
Georges Seurat and Grande Jatte Sailboat	CFA	AA	1982	LC	14 X 11	AP	300		100	300
Georgia O'Keeffe and White Hibiscus Flower	CFA	AA	1982	LC	14 X 11	AP	300		100	300
Joan Miro and Women, Bird and Moon	CFA	AA	1982	LC	14 X 11	AP	300		100	300
Artists Folio II (Set of 8):									700 SET	1950 SET
Sandro Botticelli & Venus Shell	CFA	AA	1983	LC	14 X 11	AP	300		100	300
Goya & Don Manuel Osorio's Cat	CFA	AA	1983	LC	14 X 11	AP	300		100	300
Henri Matisse Flower	CFA	AA	1983	LC	14 X 11	AP	300		100	399
Toulouse-Lautrec Moulin Rouge	CFA	AA	1983	LC	14 X 11	AP	300		100	300
Georges Rouault & Clown	CFA	AA	1983	LC	14 X 11	AP	300		100	300
Marc Chagall & The Red Goat	CFA	AA	1983	LC	14 X 11	AP	300		100	300
Paul Cezanne & Apple & Bowl	CFA	AA	1983	LC	14 X 11	AP	300		100	300
Pablo Picasso & the Blue Guitar	CFA	AA	1983	LC	14 X 11	AP	300		100	300
Proteus	CFA	AA	1983	LC	23 X 29	AP	300		150	575
Year of the Horse	CFA	AA	1986	LC	25 X 20	AP	300		325	700
Delphinus	CFA	AA	1987	LC	14 X 20	AP	300		200	350
Morning of a Jester	CFA	AA	1988	LC	31 X 25	AP	300		450	675
The Green World	CFA	AA	1988	LC	22 X 29	AP	300		450	675
The Chinese Bowl	CFA	AA	1989	LC	22 X 34	AP	300		500	725

BILL JACKLIN

BORN: Hampstead, London, England; 1945
EDUCATION: Walthamstow Sch of Art, London, England, Graphics 1960–61, Painting, 1962–64; Royal Col of Art, Painting, London, England, 1964–67
AWARDS: Arts Council Bursary, London, England, 1975
RECENT EXHIB: Marlborough Gallery, Inc, NY, 1987,90; Marlborough Fine Art, London, England, 1988,92; Mus of Mod Art, Oxford, England, 1992; Ministerio de Culture, Argentina, 1993; Santiago de Compostela, Spain, 1993
COLLECTIONS: British Mus, London, England; Tate Gallery, London, England; Victoria & Albert Mus, London, England; Mus of Mod Art, NY; Metropolitan Mus of Art, NY; Mus Boymans van Beuningen, Rotterdam, The Netherlands; Tampa Mus, FL; Hunterian Art Gallery, Glasgow, Scotland; Univ of Guelph, Ontario, Canada; Yale Center for British Art, New Haven, CT; Jane Voorhees Zimmerli Art Mus, Rutgers Univ, New Brunswick, NJ; Irish Art Council, Dublin, Ireland; Government Art Coll, London, England; Found Verannoman, Kruishoutem, Belgium; Contemp Art Society, London; England; City Art Gallery, Bradford, England; British Council of Art, London, England; Arts Council of Great Britain, London, England; Art Gallery of New South Wales, Sydney, Australia; Ashmolcan Mus, Oxford, England; Arkansas Arts Center, Little Rock, AR
PRINTERS: Angeles Press, Los Angeles, CA (APr); Pat Branstead, NY (PB); Branstead Studio, NY (BS)
PUBLISHERS: Marlborough Fine Art, London, England (MFA); Marlborough Graphics, NY (MG)
GALLERIES: Marlborough Galleries, New York, NY & London, England

TITLE	PUBLISHER	PRINTER	DATE	MEDIUM	DIMENSION (PAPER SIZE) IN INCHES	TYPE OF PAPER	EDITION NUMBER	NO. OF COLORS	ORIGINAL OPENING PRICE	CURRENT RETAIL PRICE
CURRENT EDITIONS:										
Anemones (Set of 7)	MG	APr	1977	EB/A	26 X 20 EA	FAB	40 EA			5500 SET
Woman in a Chair	MG	APr	1984	LC	14 X 10	AP	10			750
Chessplayers	MG	APr	1987	LC	37 X 49	AP	50			2000
The March—6th Avenue	MG	APr	1987	LC	50 X 36	AP	50			2000
Meatpackers—7 AM	MG	APr	1987	LC	50 X 36	AP	50			2000
Sandwich Eaters	MG	APr	1987	LC	37 X 49	AP	50			2000
Coney Island Monoprints	MG	PB/BS	1993	MON	Varies	AP	1 EA		1800/ 4500 EA	1800/ 4500 EA

HERB JACKSON

BORN: Raleigh, NC; August 16, 1945
EDUCATION: Davidson Col, NC, BA, 1963–67; Philips Univ, Marburg, West Germany, 1965–66; Univ of North Carolina, Greensboro, NC, MFA, 1969–70
TEACHING: Davidson Col, NC, 1969 to present
AWARDS: Purchase Award, Philadelphia Mus, PA, 1980; Purchase Award, Mint Mus, Charlotte, NC, 1981; Southeastern Center Contemp Art Grant, 1981; Nat Endowment for the Arts Grant, 1982; Secca Seven Fel, NY, 1982; North Carolina Visual Arts Fel, 1984
RECENT EXHIB: Nat Acad of Sciences, Wash, DC, 1989; Greenville Mus of Art, NC, 1989; Grace Coll of Popular Art in the Americas, Houston, TX, 1989; Lorenzelli Fine Art, Milan, Italy, 1989; Exhibition Hall of Moscow Artists, Russia, 1989; Samuel P Horn Mus, Gainesville, FL, 1990
COLLECTIONS: Whitney Mus of Am Art, NY; Brooklyn Mus, NY; British Mus, London, England; Mus of Fine Arts, Boston, MA; Philadelphia Mus of Art, PA; Library of Congress, Wash, DC; Baltimore Mus of Art, MO
PRINTERS: Paul Maguire, Boston, MA (PM); Robert Townsend, Boston, MA (RT); Katherine Kuhn, Tamarind Institute, Albuquerque, NM (KK); M Oshima, Boston, MA (MO); Impressions Workshop, Boston, MA (IW); June Lambla, Spruce Pine, NC (JL); Littleton Studio, Spruce Pine, NC (LitS); Herb Fox, Boston, MA (HF); Lynne Allen, Tamarind Inst, Albuquerque, NM (TI)
PUBLISHERS: Impressions Workshop, Boston, MA (IW); Robert Townsend Editions, Boston, MA (RTE); Lakeside Studio, MI (LS); Littleton Studio, Spruce Pine, NC (LitS); Artist (ART)
GALLERIES: van Straaten Gallery, Chicago, IL; Jerald Melberg Gallery, Charlotte, NC; Oxford Gallery, Oxford, England; Marita Gilliam Gallery, Raleigh, NC; Princeton Gallery of Fine Art, Princeton, NJ; Judy Youens Gallery, Houston, TX; Phyllis Weil & Company, New York, NY; Brenda Kroos Gallery, Columbus, OH

Herb Jackson
Turning East
Courtesy the Artist

MAILING ADDRESS: PO Box 2495, Davidson, NC 28036

TITLE	PUBLISHER	PRINTER	DATE	MEDIUM	DIMENSION (PAPER SIZE) IN INCHES	TYPE OF PAPER	EDITION NUMBER	NO. OF COLORS	ORIGINAL OPENING PRICE	CURRENT RETAIL PRICE
SOLD OUT EDITIONS (RARE):										
Warm Beam	IW	PM	1972	LC	22 X 30	R/BFK	50	3	80	750
Element Suite (Set of 4)	IW	PM	1973	LC	22 X 30 EA	R/BFK	100 EA	14 EA	500 SET	2500 SET
Cumulus	IW	PM	1973	LC	38 X 50	AE	50	1	150	1200
Oriental	IW	HF	1973	LC	22 X 30	R/BFK	50	3	100	750
Summit	IW	RT/IW	1976	EB/A	30 X 22	R/BFK	70	3	125	750
Magellan	IW	PM	1976	LC	41 X 30	R/BFK	70	4	200	800
CURRENT EDITIONS:										
Gold Coast	ART	RT	1976	EB/A	28 X 24	R/BFK	50	3	300	650
Golden Fleece	ART	PM	1977	LC	30 X 22	R/BFK	25	3	200	450
Lotus	ART	RT	1977	EB/A	32 X 48	R/BFK	50	3	500	850
Mojo	ART	PM	1977	LC	37 X 28	AP	35	2	200	450
Rising	ART	RT	1979	EB/A	28 X 24	R/BFK	50	3	300	550

HERB JACKSON CONTINUED

TITLE	PUBLISHER	PRINTER	DATE	MEDIUM	DIMENSION (PAPER SIZE) IN INCHES	TYPE OF PAPER	EDITION NUMBER	NO. OF COLORS	ORIGINAL OPENING PRICE	CURRENT RETAIL PRICE
CURRENT EDITIONS:										
Zamathu	ART	RT	1979	EB/A	28 X 24	R/BFK	50	3	300	550
Tanker	RTE	RT	1981	DPT	48 X 36	R/BFK	40	1	200	650
Sappho	ART	PM	1981	LC	30 X 22	R/BFK	60	4	300	450
Tenth Muse	ART	KK	1981	LC	41 X 29	R/BFK	50	4	450	550
Night Heat	ART	LA	1982	LC	30 X 22	R/BFK	37	3	300	450
French Angel	ART	KK	1982	LC	30 X 22	R/BFK	50	3	300	450
Opening	LitS	JL/LitS	1985	EB/A	16 X 16	AP	40	3	350	400
Ridge Secret	LitS	JL/LitS	1985	EB/A	35 X 25	AP	30	3	600	800
Turning East	LitS	JL/LitS	1985	EB/A	16 X 16	AP	40	4	400	450

JETT JACKSON

BORN: Laguna Beach, CA; February 17, 1958
EDUCATION: California Inst of Arts, Valencia, CA
RECENT EXHIB: LACE, Los Angeles, CA, 1987; Downey Mus of Art, CA, 1988; American Gallery, Los Angeles, CA, 1989; Rico Gallery, Los Angeles, CA, 1990
PRINTERS: Clearwater Publishing, Santa Ana, CA (ClPub); Multiples, Los Angeles, CA (MULT)
PUBLISHERS: Brana Publishing, Santa Monica, CA (BrP)
GALLERIES: Brana Gallery, Santa Monica, CA; Lemuria Gallery, Phila, PA; Rico Gallery, Los Angeles, CA
MAILING ADDRESS: 2525 Main St, Santa Monica, CA 90405

TITLE	PUBLISHER	PRINTER	DATE	MEDIUM	DIMENSION (PAPER SIZE) IN INCHES	TYPE OF PAPER	EDITION NUMBER	NO. OF COLORS	ORIGINAL OPENING PRICE	CURRENT RETAIL PRICE
CURRENT EDITIONS:										
Don't Worry—Everything Will be Okay	BrP	ClPub	1990	SP	37 X 38	AP	400	75	650	950
Not Picasso	BrP	MULT	1990	SP	36 X 40	AP	400	42	650	850
Circus Girl	BrP	MULT	1990	SP	36 X 40	AP	400	42	650	750

OLIVER LEE JACKSON

BORN: St Louis, MO; June 23, 1935
EDUCATION: Wesleyan University, Bloomington, IL, BFA, 1958; Univ of Iowa, Iowa City, IA, MFA, 1963
TEACHING: St Louis Com Col, MO, 1964–67; Washington Univ, St Louis, MO, 1967–69; Instr, Southern Illinois Univ, East St Louis, IL, 1967–69; Oberlin Col, OH, 1969–70; Prof, Art, California State Univ, Sacramento, CA, 1971 to present
AWARDS: Nat Endowment for the Arts, Award in Painting, 1980–81; Nettie Marie Jones Fel, Lake Placid Center for the Arts, NY, 1984
RECENT EXHIB: Palm Springs Desert Mus, CA, 1987; Albright-Knox Art Gallery, Buffalo, NY, 1989; Univ of Illinois, Champaign, IL, 1988; Univ of California, Berkeley, CA, 1989
COLLECTIONS: San Francisco Mus of Mod Art, CA; Seattle Art Mus, WA; Oakland Mus, CA; Mus of Nat Center of Afro Am Art, Boston, MA; New Orleans Mus of Art, LA; Crocker Art Mus, Sacramento, CA
PRINTERS: Timothy Berry, San Francisco, CA (TB); Teaberry Press, San Francisco, CA (TP)
PUBLISHERS: Artist (ART)
GALLERIES: Rena Bransten Gallery, San Francisco, CA; Arthur Roger Gallery, New Orleans, LA; Iannetti-Lanzone Gallery, San Francisco, CA; Eve Mannes Gallery, Atlanta, GA; Liz Harris Gallery, Boston, MA
MAILING ADDRESS: 251 Post St, #540, San Francisco, CA 94108

Oliver L Jackson
Intaglio Drypoint I
Courtesy the Artist

TITLE	PUBLISHER	PRINTER	DATE	MEDIUM	DIMENSION (PAPER SIZE) IN INCHES	TYPE OF PAPER	EDITION NUMBER	NO. OF COLORS	ORIGINAL OPENING PRICE	CURRENT RETAIL PRICE
CURRENT EDITIONS:										
Intaglio Drypoint I	ART	TB/TP	1985	DPT	36 X 48	AC/W	23	1	1000	1200
Intaglio Drypoint II	ART	TB/TP	1985	DPT/ENG/HB	36 X 24	AP/W	35	1	750	900
Intaglio Drypoint III	ART	TB/TP	1985	DPT/HB	36 X 48	AP/W	32	1	1000	1200

JIM JACOBS

BORN: New York, NY; May 26, 1945
EDUCATION: Boston Univ, MA, BA; Bryn Mawr Col, PA; Harvard Univ, Cambridge, MA; Mus of Fine Arts, Boston, MA
TEACHING: Instr, Boston Univ, MA, 1965; Instr, Harvard Univ, Cambridge, MA, 1966,67; Instr, Bryn Mawr Col, PA, 1967; Lectr, Mus of Fine Arts, Mus Sch, Boston, MA, 1967
AWARDS: Creative Artists Public Service Program Grant, 1981–82
COLLECTIONS: Rose Art Mus, Brandeis Univ, Waltham, MA; Smith Col Mus, Northampton, MA

JIM JACOBS CONTINUED

PRINTERS: American Atelier, NY (AA)
PUBLISHERS: Circle Fine Art, Chicago, IL (CFA)
GALLERIES: Swanston Fine Arts, Atlanta, GA; Andrea Marquit Fine Art, New York, NY; Edward Tyler Nahem Fine Art, New York, NY; Circle Galleries, San Diego, CA & San Francisco, CA & Northbrook, IL & Pittsburgh, PA & Houston, TX & Soho, NY & Chicago, IL & Scottsdale, AZ & Beverly Hills, CA & Costa Mesa, CA & Sherman Oaks, CA & Palm Beach, FL & Honolulu, HI & New Orleans, LA & Las Vegas, NV & Seattle, WA
MAILING ADDRESS: 26 W 20th St, New York, NY 10011

TITLE	PUBLISHER	PRINTER	DATE	MEDIUM	DIMENSION (PAPER SIZE) IN INCHES	TYPE OF PAPER	EDITION NUMBER	NO. OF COLORS	ORIGINAL OPENING PRICE	CURRENT RETAIL PRICE
CURRENT EDITIONS:										
Folded Flag	CFA	AA	1982	SP	30 X 22	R/BFK	200		150	250

KEITH JACOBSHAGEN

BORN: Wichita, KS; September 8, 1941
EDUCATION: Kansas City Art Inst, MO, BFA; Art Ctr, Col of Design, Los Angeles, CA; Univ of Kansas, Lawrence, KS, MFA
AWARDS: Owen H Kenan Award, Painting, 1972; Frank Woods Fel, Univ of Nebraska, Lincoln, NE, 1975
RECENT EXHIB: Sheldon Mem Art Gallery, Univ of Nebraska, Lincoln, NE, 1989; Sioux City Art Center, IA, 1989,92
COLLECTIONS: Sheldon Mem Gallery, Univ of Nebraska, Lincoln, NE; Univ of Kansas Mus of Art, Lawrence, KS; Oklahoma Univ Mus, Norman, OK; Oakland Mus, CA; Pasadena Art Mus, CA
PRINTERS: Richard Finch, Normal, IL (RF); Todd DeVriese, Normal IL (TDV); Eric Kuehn, Normal, IL (EK); Andrew Hatterman, Normal, IL (AH); Richard Folse, Normal, IL (RFo); Tom Hyde, Normal, IL (TH); Sharon Merrill, Normal, IL (SM); Normal Editions Workshop, Illinois State Univ, Normal, IL (NEW); Jack Lemon, Chicago, IL (JL); Landfall Press, Inc, Chicago, IL (LPI)
PUBLISHERS: Normal Editions Workshop, Illinois State Univ, Normal, IL (NEW); Landfall Press, Inc, Chicago, IL (LPI)
GALLERIES: Dorry Gates Gallery, Kansas City, MO; Charles Campbell Gallery, San Francisco, CA; Jan Turner Gallery, Los Angeles, CA; Roger Ramsay Gallery, Chicago, IL; Landfall Press, Inc, Chicago, IL
MAILING ADDRESS: 2030 "C" St, Lincoln, NE 68502

TITLE	PUBLISHER	PRINTER	DATE	MEDIUM	DIMENSION (PAPER SIZE) IN INCHES	TYPE OF PAPER	EDITION NUMBER	NO. OF COLORS	ORIGINAL OPENING PRICE	CURRENT RETAIL PRICE
CURRENT EDITIONS:										
North	NEW	RF/TDV/EK/ AH/RFo/TH/ SM/NEW	1989	LC	30 X 22	R/BFK/W	15	7	450	600
Near Hollow Eve	LPI	JL/LPI	1990	MON	22 X 30 EA	AC	1 EA	Varies	1300 EA	1300 EA
August	LPI	JL/LPI	1990	EC	16 X 34	R/BFK	20		800	800
Cut Brush	LPI	JL/LPI	1990	MON	42 X 33	AC	1 EA	Varies	1800 EA	1800 EA

LEE JAFFE

BORN: New York, NY; 1950
EDUCATION: Pennsylvania State Univ, University Park, PA, 1965–69
RECENT EXHIB: L A Louver Gallery, Venice, CA, 1987; L A Louver Gallery, Los Angeles, CA, 1988; Anders Tornberg Gallery, Lund, Sweden, 1987; Edvard Thorden Gallery, Goteberg, Sweden, 1988; Univ of Missouri Art Gallery, Kansas City, MO, 1989; Georges Lavrov Galerie, Paris, France, 1989; Galerie Grafiart, Turku, Finland, 1989; Kaj Forsblom Gallery, Helsinki, Finland, 1989; Marc Jancou Galerie, Zürich, Switzerland, 1990; Moderna Museet, Stockholm, Sweden, 1991
COLLECTIONS: Metropolitan Mus of Art, NY; Saatchi Col, London, England; Univ of Missouri, Kansas City, MO; Tate Gallery, London, England; Detroit Inst of Art, MI; Eli Brood Found, Los Angeles, CA
PRINTERS: Artist (ART); Lynn Forgach, NY (LF); Exeter Press, NY (ExPr); Jeff Wasserman, Santa Monica, CA (JW); Wasserman Silkscreen, Santa Monica, CA (WS); Robert Aull, Los Angeles, CA (RA); Robert Hollister, Los Angeles, CA (RH)
PUBLISHERS: Artist (ART); David Lawrence Editions, Beverly Hills, CA (DLE)
GALLERIES: L A Louver, Los Angeles, CA & New York, NY; Vanessa Devereux Gallery, London, England; Marc Jancou Galerie, Zürich, Switzerland; Georges Lavrov Galerie, Paris, France; Future Perfect Gallery, Los Angeles, CA; Anders Tornberg Gallery, Lund, Sweden; Kaj Forsblom Gallery, Helsinki, Finland

TITLE	PUBLISHER	PRINTER	DATE	MEDIUM	DIMENSION (PAPER SIZE) IN INCHES	TYPE OF PAPER	EDITION NUMBER	NO. OF COLORS	ORIGINAL OPENING PRICE	CURRENT RETAIL PRICE
CURRENT EDITIONS:										
The Strömholm Painting (with Silver Metalic Powders)	ART	ART/LF/ExPr	1987	XER/HC	10 X 11 FT TOT 60 X 44 (1) 30 X 22 (20)	HMP	1 EA	Varies	21000 SET 3000 EA	25000 SET 3200 EA
The Life and Times of Primo Carnera: The Sucker Punches (Series of 5):										
The Sucker Punch #1	DLE	RA/RH	1990	EB/LC	38 X 25	RICE/HMP	9	8	2400	2400
The Sucker Punch #2	DLE	RA/RH	1990	EB/LC	38 X 25	RICE/HMP	11	8	2400	2400
The Sucker Punch #3	DLE	RA/RH	1990	EB/LC	38 X 25	RICE/HMP	10	8	2400	2400
The Sucker Punch #4	DLE	RA/RH	1990	EB/LC	38 X 25	RICE/HMP	10	8	2400	2400
The Sucker Punch #5	DLE	RA/RH	1990	EB/LC	38 X 25	RICE/HMP	10	8	2400	2400
Cordially Yours, Blind Arthur Brake*	DLE	JW/WS	1990	MM	25 X 19	RICE/HMP	19	1	1950	1950
Cordially Yours, Blind Lemon Jefferson*	DLE	JW/WS	1990	MM	25 X 19	RICE/HMP	13	1	1950	1950
Cordially Yours, Blind Boy Fuller*	DLE	JW/WS	1990	MM	25 X 19	RICE/HMP	13	1	1950	1950
Cordially Yours, Blind Willie Johnson*	DLE	JW/WS	1990	MM	25 X 19	RICE/HMP	13	1	1950	1950
Cordially Yours, Blind McTell*	DLE	JW/WS	1990	MM	25 X 19	RICE/HMP	13	1	1950	1950

*Medium—Steel, Wax Encaustic, Hand-Writing, Painting & Drilling on Handmade Rice Paper on Wood & Canvas

ARTHUR JACOBSON

BORN: Chicago, IL; January 10, 1924
EDUCATION: Univ of Wisconsin, Madison, WI, BA, 1948, MA, 1950
TEACHING: Prof Emeritus, Arizona State Univ, Tempe, AZ
AWARDS: Pennsylvania Acad of Fine Arts, Phila, PA, 1965; Dallas Mus, TX, 1965; Phoenix Art Mus, AZ, 1971
COLLECTIONS: Pennsylvania Acad of Fine Arts, Phila, PA; Dallas Mus, TX; Mus of New Mexico, Santa Fe, NM; Hastings Col, NE; Phoenix Art Mus, AZ; Arizona State Univ, Tempe, AZ
PRINTERS: Artist (ART)
PUBLISHERS: Artist (ART)
GALLERIES: Print Consortium, Kansas City, MO
MAILING ADDRESS: 7209 E McDonald Drive, #47, Scottsdale, AZ 85250

TITLE	PUBLISHER	PRINTER	DATE	MEDIUM	DIMENSION (PAPER SIZE) IN INCHES	TYPE OF PAPER	EDITION NUMBER	NO. OF COLORS	ORIGINAL OPENING PRICE	CURRENT RETAIL PRICE
SOLD OUT EDITIONS (RARE):										
Quartet	ART	ART	1965	I	12 X 18	AP	50	3	200	600
Orange Flower	ART	ART	1970	EMB/REL	22 X 30	AP	25	1	250	600
Concept Blue	ART	ART	1972	EMB/REL	22 X 30	AP	25	1	250	600
CURRENT EDITIONS:										
London Series-Trafalgar	ART	ART	1975	LC	22 X 30	AP	25	4	350	400
Astro Series II, III, IV, VIII	ART	ART	1975	LC	22 X 30 EA	AP	25 EA	4–5 EA	350 EA	400 EA
Pandoras Puzzle I	ART	ART	1976	LC	22 X 30	AP	30	3	350	400
Pandoras Puzzle II	ART	ART	1976	LC	22 X 30	AP	35	3	350	400
Quantum I	ART	ART	1977	LC	22 X 30	AP	30	4	350	400
Quantum II	ART	ART	1977	LC	23 X 34	AP	25	5	400	450
London Series Picadilly	ART	ART	1978	LC	22 X 30	AP	25	4	350	400
London Series Soho	ART	ART	1979	LB	22 X 30	AP	25	1	350	400
Cello Player	ART	ART	1981	WC	16 X 24	AP	100	3	350	400
The Musician	ART	ART	1981	WC	24 X 33	MUL	50	3	600	800
Horn Player	ART	ART	1982	WC	24 X 33	MUL	50	3	600	800
Violinist	ART	ART	1983	WC	24 X 33	MUL	50	3	600	800
Bassoonist	ART	ART	1983	WC	24 X 33	MUL	50	3	600	800
Clarinetist	ART	ART	1984	WC	24 X 33	MUL	50	3	600	800
Flutist	ART	ART	1984	WC	24 X 33	MUL	50	3	600	800
Trumpeter	ART	ART	1984	WC	24 X 33	MUL	50	3	600	800
Trombonist	ART	ART	1984	WC	24 X 33	MUL	50	3	600	800
Pianist	ART	ART	1984	WC	24 X 33	MUL	50	3	600	800
The Symphony	ART	ART	1984	WC	36 X 72	SUZ	50	5	1200	1500
Oboe Player	ART	ART	1985	WC	24 X 33	MUL	50	3	600	800
Conductor	ART	ART	1985	WC	24 X 33	MUL	50	3	600	800

YVONNE JACQUETTE

BORN: Pittsburgh, PA; December 15, 1934
EDUCATION: Rhode Island Sch of Design, Providence, RI 1952–56
TEACHING: Instr, Moore Col of Art, Phila, PA, 1972; Vis Art & Instr, Painting, Univ of Pennsylvania, 1972–76, 1979–82; Vis Art, Nova Scotia Col of Art, Can, 1974; Instr, Parsons Sch of Design, NY, 1975–78; Instr, Grad Sch of Fine Arts, Univ of Pennsylvania, Phila, PA, 1979–84
AWARDS: Ingram Merrill Grant, 1974; Creative Artists Public Service Program Grant, Painting, NY, 1979; Painting, New York State Council on the Arts Fel, 1985; Am Acad of Inst of Arts & Letters, NY, 1990
RECENT EXHIB: O'Farrell Gallery, Brunswick, ME, 1990; Berggruen Gallery, San Francisco, CA, 1991; Univ of Maine, Jewett Hall Gallery, Augusta, ME, 1992; Univ of Maine, Orono, ME, 1989,92; Brooke Alexander, Inc, NY, 1988,89,90,92
COLLECTIONS: Weatherspoon Gallery, Univ of North Carolina, Greensboro, NC; Whitney Mus of Am Art, Ny; Metropolitan Mus of Art, NY; Colby Col Mus, Waterville, ME; Mus of Mod Art, NY; Staatliche Mus, Berlin, Germany; Carnegie Inst Art Mus, Pittsburgh, PA; Am Acad Inst of Arts & Letters, NY
PRINTERS: Sienna Studios, NY (SS); Paul Narkiewicz, NY (PM); Aeropress Inc, NY (A); Patricia Branstead, NY (PB); Dan Leary, NY (DL); Chris Erickson, NY (ChE); Anthony Kirk, NY (AK); Eldindean Press, NY (EldP); Doris Simmelink, San Francisco, CA (DS); Marcia Bartholme, San Francisco, CA (MB); Crown Point Press, San Francisco, CA (CPP); Bud Shark, Boulder, CO (BS); Shark's Lithography, Ltd, Boulder, CO (SLL); John Stemmer, San Francisco, CA (JS); David Crook, San Francisco, CA (DC); Experimental Workshop, San Francisco, CA (EW); Maurice Sanchez, NY (MS); Jim Cooper, NY (JC); Derriére L' Etoile Studios, NY (DES); Norman Stewart, Bloomfield Hills, MI (NS); Joe Keenan, Bloomfield Hills, MI (JK); Stewart & Stewart, Bloomfield Hills, MI (S-S)
PUBLISHERS: Brooke Alexander, Inc, NY (BAI); Eldindean Press, NY (EldP); Crown Point Press, San Francisco, CA (CPP); Shark's Lithography, Ltd, Boulder, CO (SLL); Experimental Workshop, San Francisco, CA (EW); Artist (ART); Stewart & Stewart, Bloomfield Hills, MI (S-S)
GALLERIES: Brooke Alexander, Inc, New York, NY; Crown Point Press, San Francisco, CA & New York, NY; Experimental Workshop, San Francisco, CA; Sharks, Inc, Boulder, CO; Betsy Senior Contemporary Prints, New York, NY; O'Farrell Gallery, Brusnwick, ME; Vinalhaven Press, Vinalhaven, ME
MAILING ADDRESS: 50 W 29th St, New York, NY 10001

TITLE	PUBLISHER	PRINTER	DATE	MEDIUM	DIMENSION (PAPER SIZE) IN INCHES	TYPE OF PAPER	EDITION NUMBER	NO. OF COLORS	ORIGINAL OPENING PRICE	CURRENT RETAIL PRICE
SOLD OUT EDITIONS (RARE):										
22nd Street (36 Examples)	BAI		1974	LC/HS/PAS	19 X 24 EA	RP	1 EA		150 EA	2500 EA
Aerial View of 33rd Street	BAI	PB/A	1981	LC	50 X 31	MUL	60		900	2500
Northwest View from the Empire State Building	BAI	ChE	1982	LB	50 X 35	TRANS	60	1	900	2500
Two Ferries Passing (Set of 10)	BAI	PB/DL/A	1982–83	AC	30 X 22 EA	FAB	8 EA	3 EA	5000 SET	12000 SET
Two Ferries Passing (Printed in Black)	BAI	PB/DL/A	1982–83	AB	30 X 22	FAB	20	1	450	1200
A Glimpse of Lower Manhattan (Day)	SLL	BS/SLL	1984	LC/3D	21 X 15 X 4	SOM	60		1600	2000
A Glimpse of Lower Manhattan (Night)	SLL	BS/SLL	1984	LC/3D	21 X 15 X 4	SOM	60		1600	2000
A Glimpse of Lower Manhattan (Dawn)	SLL	BS/SLL	1984	LC/HC	21 X 15 X 4	SOM	10		2000	2500

YVONNE JACQUETTE CONTINUED

TITLE	PUBLISHER	PRINTER	DATE	MEDIUM	DIMENSION (PAPER SIZE) IN INCHES	TYPE OF PAPER	EDITION NUMBER	NO. OF COLORS	ORIGINAL OPENING PRICE	CURRENT RETAIL PRICE
SOLD OUT EDITIONS (RARE):										
High Beams	ART/EldP	AK/EldP	1985	EB	8 X 7	MAG	60	1	90	500
Peoples Express	ART/EldP	AK/EldP	1985	EB	8 X 7	MAG	30	1	90	500
Full Beams	ART/EldP	AK/EldP	1985–86	EB	8 X 7	MAG	60	1	90	500
Mississippi Night Lights (Minneapolis)	BAI	MS/DES	1985–86	LC/SP	58 X 36	AP/ROL	60	13	2500	5000
NY4	SLL	BS/SLL	1986	MON/3D	21 X 15 X 4 EA	AC	1 EA		2500 EA	3600 EA
NY2	SLL	BS/SLL	1986	MON/3D	21 X 15 X 4 EA	AC	1 EA		2500 EA	3600 EA
CA2	SLL	BS/SLL	1986	MON/3D	21 X 15 X 4 EA	AC	1 EA		2500 EA	3600 EA
CA3	SLL	BS/SLL	1986	MON/3D	21 X 15 X 4 EA	AC	1 EA		2500 EA	3600 EA
CO2	SLL	BS/SLL	1986	MON/3D	21 X 15 X 4 EA	AC	1 EA		2500 EA	3600 EA
CL2	SLL	BS/SLL	1986	MON/3D	21 X 15 X 4 EA	AC	1 EA		2500 EA	3600 EA
CURRENT EDITIONS:										
East 15th Street	BAI	SS	1974	LC	18 X 22	RP	125		200	750
Fog River IV	BAI	SS	1976	LC	16 X 18	RP	79	3	100	400
Green Light, Grey Day	BAI	PN	1976	LC	20 X 24	MUL	38	3	250	750
Clouds Obscuring San Diego	CPP	DS/MB/CPP	1987	AC/SG/HC	25 X 21	SOM	60	14	1500	1500
Showhegan I	CPP	DS/MB/CPP	1987	EC	30 X 22	SOM			1000	1500
Showhegan II	CPP	DS/MB/CPP	1987	EB	30 X 22	SOM	35	1	800	950
NVI	SLL	BS/SLL	1987	MON	30 X 22 EA	SOM	1 EA		2500 EA	3200 EA
Speeding Jet View	SLL	BS/SLL	1987	MON	30 X 22 EA	SOM	1 EA		3000 EA	4500 EA
Speeding Tilted Night	SLL	BS/SLL	1987	MON	30 X 22 EA	SOM	1 EA		3000 EA	4500 EA
Speeding Tilted Dusk	SLL	BS/SLL	1987	MON	30 X 22 EA	SOM	1 EA		3000 EA	4500 EA
Tip of Manhattan	EW	JS/DC/EW	1987	WC	30 X 56	OKP	30	2	2400 EA	3000 EA
Motion Picture (Times Square)	BAI	MS/JC/DES	1989–90	LC	49 X 36	AC	60		3000	3000
Winging It	BAI	MS/JC/DES	1990	EC	25 X 26	R/BFK	40		1200	1200
Winging It	BAI	MS/JC/DES	1990	EC	25 X 26	R/BFK	20		1200	1200
Winging It	BAI	MS/JC/DES	1990	EB/CC	25 X 26	R/BFK	20	1	900	900
Winging It	BAI	MS/JC/DES	1990	EB	25 X 26	R/BFK	20	1	900	900
Winging It	BAI	MS/JC/DES	1990	EC	25 X 26	R/BFK	20	2	900	900
Night View Wing I	S-S	NS/JK/WLS	1992	SP	30 X 22	R/BFK/W	48	15	1500	1500
Night View Wing II	S-S	NS/JK/WLS	1992	SP	30 X 22	R/BFK/W	23	5	1250	1250

JUDITH C JAIDINGER

BORN: Chicago, IL; April 10, 1941
EDUCATION: Art Inst of Chicago, IL, BFA, 1970
TEACHING: Instr, Northeastern Illinois Univ, Chicago, IL, 1980 to present
AWARDS: Graphic Award, 1st Prize, New Mexico Art League, Albuquerque, NM, 1974; Graphic Award, Oklahoma Art Guild, Oklahoma City, OK, 1974; Oklahoma Mus of Art, Oklahoma City, OK, 1975; Purchase Awards, Minot State Col, ND, 1970,77

COLLECTIONS: Minot State Col, ND; Illinois State Mus, Springfield, IL; Washington & Jefferson Col, Wash, PA; Prairie State Col, Chicago Heights, IL; New Mexico Art League, Albuquerque, NM; Hunterdon Art Center, Clinton, NJ; Eastern Illinois Univ, Charleston, IL; Brand Library, Glendale, CA; Columbia-Greene Community Col, Palenville, NY; J P Speed Art Mus, Louisville, KY; Art Inst of Chicago, IL
PRINTERS: Artist (ART)
PUBLISHERS: Artist (ART)
GALLERIES: Chicago Center for the Print Ltd, Chicago, IL
MAILING ADDRESS: 6110 N Newburg Ave, Chicago, IL 60631

TITLE	PUBLISHER	PRINTER	DATE	MEDIUM	DIMENSION (PAPER SIZE) IN INCHES	TYPE OF PAPER	EDITION NUMBER	NO. OF COLORS	ORIGINAL OPENING PRICE	CURRENT RETAIL PRICE
CURRENT EDITIONS:										
The Pollination of Martha	ART	ART	1972	WE	10 X 12	BHP	50	2	80	400
Puppet Masters	ART	ART	1973	WE	8 X 20	BHP	22	1	50	175
From Day to Day	ART	ART	1974	WE	9 X 10	BHP	40	1	80	175
Flesh of My Flesh	ART	ART	1975	WE	8 X 16	BHP	32	1	100	400
In My Mother's House	ART	ART	1976	WE	9 X 10	BHP	25	1	100	350
Had We but World Enough and Time	ART	ART	1977	WE	8 X 10	BHP	40	4	100	400
A Matter of Time	ART	ART	1978	WE	8 X 11	BHP	30	1	125	350
Giving Up the Ghost	ART	ART	1979	WE	9 X 8	BHP	46	1	125	350
Guilty Pleasures	ART	ART	1980	WE	8 X 11	BHP	41	1	125	350
The Heart has Many Doors	ART	ART	1981	WE	9 X 9	BHP	45	1	125	350
It's Just a Turn and Freedom	ART	ART	1982	WE	9 X 10	BHP	50	1	125	350
Tis' in My Memory Locked	ART	ART	1983	WE	9 X 12	BHP	50	1	300	350
I Shall Know Why, When Time is Over	ART	ART	1984	WE	10 X 12		25	1	300	350
Let Us Prey	ART	ART	1985	WE	11 X 9		100	1	300	350
In My End is My Beginning	ART	ART	1985	WE	8 X 6		100	1	150	200
The Deserts Lived Beneath the Floorboards	ART	ART	1986	WE	7 X 8		100	1	150	200

The retail prices of the 100,000 limited edition prints quoted in this directory are subject to change. Print publishers, artists and galleries were the direct sources for these quotations. Prices in the secondary market listed as "Sold Out Editions (Rare)" indicate that the publisher has a limited supply of that print or that the print is difficult to locate in the galleries.

PIERRE JACQUOT

BORN: Nancy, France, 1929
EDUCATION: L'Ecole Nationale des Beaux Arts, Paris, France
TEACHING: Prof, L'Ecole Nationale des Beaux Arts, Paris, France
AWARDS: Chevalier de L'Ordre des Arts et Letters, French Govt, 1968
COLLECTIONS: Musee de Nancy, France; Bydogoszcz Mus; L'Ecole Nationale de Geologie, Paris, France
PRINTERS: American Atelier, NY (AA)
PUBLISHERS: Circle Fine Art, Chicago, IL (CFA)
GALLERIES: Circle Galleries, San Diego, CA & San Francisco, CA & Northbrook, IL & Pittsburgh, PA & Houston, TX & Soho, NY & Chicago, IL & Scottsdale, AZ & Beverly Hills, CA & Costa Mesa, CA & Sherman Oaks, CA & Palm Beach, FL & Honolulu, HI & New Orleans, LA & Las Vegas, NV & Seattle, WA

TITLE	PUBLISHER	PRINTER	DATE	MEDIUM	DIMENSION (PAPER SIZE) IN INCHES	TYPE OF PAPER	EDITION NUMBER	NO. OF COLORS	ORIGINAL OPENING PRICE	CURRENT RETAIL PRICE
SOLD OUT EDITIONS (RARE):										
Le Pélerin (Pilgrim)	CFA	AA	1979	LC	30 X 22	AP	150		75	250
Janus	CFA	AA	1979	LC	26 X 20	AP	150		75	200
Eloe	CFA	AA	1979	LC	26 X 20	AP	150		75	200
UFO	CFA	AA	1979	LC	20 X 26	AP	150		75	275
Arlequin Comédien	CFA	AA	1979	LC	30 X 22	AP	200		75	200

CHRISTOPHER P JAMES

BORN: Boston, MA; May 8, 1947
EDUCATION: Cummington Col for the Arts, 1968; Massachusetts Col of Art, Boston, MA, BFA, 1969; Sch of Design, Boston, MA, MAT, 1971
TEACHING: Asst Prof, Photography & Design, Greenfield Com Col, MA, 1971–78; Art in Res, Keene State Col, NH, 1977–78; Lectr, Massachusetts Inst of Tech, Cambridge, MA; Lectr, Philadelphia Col of Art, PA; Lectr, Univ of Oregon, Eugene, OR; Lectr, Parsons Sch of Design, NY; Lectr, Rhode Island Sch of Design, Providence, RI; Instr, Chulalongkorn Univ, Bangkok, Thailand; Recontres Int de La Photographics, Arles, France; Prof, Harvard Univ, Cambridge, MA, 1978
AWARDS: Nat Endowment for the Arts Fel, 1977–78; Massachusetts Arts Found Fel, 1978
RECENT EXHIB: Witkin Gallery, NY, 1987,90; Lizardi/Harp Gallery, Pasadena, CA, 1987,88,90; Weston Gallery, Carmel, CA, 1989,91
COLLECTIONS: Mus of Mod Art, NY; International Mus of Photography, George Eastman House, Rochester, NY; Boston Mus of Fine Arts, MA; Minneapolis Inst of the Arts, MN; Bibliotheque Nat, Paris, France
PRINTERS: Artist (ART)
PUBLISHERS: Symbax Inc, NY (SI); Artist (ART)
GALLERIES: Witkin Gallery, New York, NY; Maine Photographic Workshops, Rockport, ME; Halsted Gallery, Birmingham, MI; Lizard/Harp Gallery, Pasadena, CA
MAILING ADDRESS: P O Box 399, Dublin, NH 03444

TITLE	PUBLISHER	PRINTER	DATE	MEDIUM	DIMENSION (PAPER SIZE) IN INCHES	TYPE OF PAPER	EDITION NUMBER	NO. OF COLORS	ORIGINAL OPENING PRICE	CURRENT RETAIL PRICE
CURRENT EDITIONS:										
Union Boat Club	ART	ART	1980	PH/HC	6 X 9	Agfa	25	Varies	325	450
Portfolio	SI	ART	1982	PH/HC	8 X 8 EA	Agfa	25 EA		3500 SET	4000 SET

GEOFFREY JAMES

BORN: St Asaph, Wales; January 9, 1942
EDUCATION: Wadham Col, Oxford, England, BA, MA
PRINTERS: Artist (ART)
PUBLISHERS: Vajima Galerie, Montreal, Canada (YG); Artist (ART)
GALLERIES: Twining Gallery, New York, NY

TITLE	PUBLISHER	PRINTER	DATE	MEDIUM	DIMENSION (PAPER SIZE) IN INCHES	TYPE OF PAPER	EDITION NUMBER	NO. OF COLORS	ORIGINAL OPENING PRICE	CURRENT RETAIL PRICE
CURRENT EDITIONS:										
French Gardens (Set of 10)	ART/YG	ART	1981	PH	16 X 20 EA	KOD	20 EA		1500 SET	2000 SET

TONY JANNETTI

BORN: Yonkers, NY; May 27, 1947
EDUCATION: Carnegie-Mellon Inst, Pittsburgh, PA, Summer, 1968; Pratt Inst, NY, BFA, 1965–69
TEACHING: Fordham Univ, NY, 1983,84
RECENT EXHIB: 55 Mercer Street Gallery, NY, 1987; Jane Voorhees Zimmerli Mus, Rutgers Univ, New Brunswick, NJ, 1988; Mary Ryan Gallery, NY, 1988; Marcus Gordon Gallery, Pittsburgh, PA, 1989
COLLECTIONS: Yale Univ, New Haven, CT; Mus of Mod Art, NY; Jane Voorhees Zimmerli Mus, Rutgers Univ, New Brunswick, NJ
PRINTERS: Chip Elwell, NY (CE); Ted Warner, NY (TW); Marina Epstein, NY (ME); Chip Elwell Studio, NY (CES); Artist (ART)
PUBLISHERS: Orion Editions, NY (OE); Chip Elwell, NY (CE); Artist (ART)
GALLERIES: Gallery 101, Stamford, CT; Ann Goodman Fine Art, Marina Del Rey, CA; Judith Selkowitz Fine Art, New York, NY; Jayne Baum Gallery, New York, NY; 55 Mercer Street Gallery, New York, NY; Marcus Gordon Gallery, Pittsburgh, PA; Gallery 500, Elkins Park, PA
MAILING ADDRESS: 261 Bowery, New York, NY 10002

TITLE	PUBLISHER	PRINTER	DATE	MEDIUM	DIMENSION (PAPER SIZE) IN INCHES	TYPE OF PAPER	EDITION NUMBER	NO. OF COLORS	ORIGINAL OPENING PRICE	CURRENT RETAIL PRICE
SOLD OUT EDITIONS (RARE):										
Untitled	CE/ART	CE	1977	PO	30 X 35	R/BFK	50	17	150	5000
Monk	OE	CE	1978	PO	28 X 41	R/BFK	20	7	225	2000
Hoopoe	OE	CE	1978	PO	28 X 41	R/BFK	40	14	250	3000
Fourth Valley	OE/ART	CE	1978	PO	28 X 41	ACW	60	14	250	3000
Voice	OE/ART	CE	1979	PO	29 X 41	R/BFK	60	15	300	2000
Zia	ART	ART	1981	PO	31 X 21	BOD	30	13	275	600
Man	CE/ART	CE/CES	1981	PO	32 X 46	HMP	42	16	500	1500
Pine Hill Series	ART	ART	1986–87	WC	29 X 41	SOM	9	20	700	2000

TONY JANNETTI CONTINUED

TITLE	PUBLISHER	PRINTER	DATE	MEDIUM	DIMENSION (PAPER SIZE) IN INCHES	TYPE OF PAPER	EDITION NUMBER	NO. OF COLORS	ORIGINAL OPENING PRICE	CURRENT RETAIL PRICE
CURRENT EDITIONS:										
Red Shoes	OE	CE	1978	PO	29 X 41	GE/BL	10	15	175	500
Oriole	OE	CE	1979	PO	29 X 41	GE/BL	10	7	200	500
Simurgh	ART	CE	1979	PO	29 X 41	R/BFK	60	15	300	1000
Fifth Valley	OE/ART	CE	1979	PO	29 X 41	ACW	60	15	250	1500
The Baker Makes Good His Escape (2 Sheets)	ART	CE/CES	1980	LI	39 X 47	MUL	60	12	450	2000
Robert Le Ver Seeks Entrance to the Great Lady's Nation	ART	TW/CES	1982	REL	17 X 33	NAT	64	14	325	500
The Governor's Hunt for His Wife's Presence (2 Sheets)	CE/ART	CE/TW/CES	1983	WC/LI	37 X 45	MIN	35	16	650	850
Fast Foxtrot for Maty and Magenta (3 Monoprints)	ART	KC/ART	1987	MON	37 X 58	KOZU	1 EA	10	950	2200

VASILIOS JANOPOULOS

BORN: Greece, November 12, 1951

PRINTERS: Atelier Unlimited, NY (AU)
PUBLISHERS: Jackie Fine Arts, Inc, NY (JFA); Stefanotti Gallery, NY (SG); Marigold Enterprises, NY (ME)
MAILING ADDRESS: 155 E 34th St, New York, NY 10016

TITLE	PUBLISHER	PRINTER	DATE	MEDIUM	DIMENSION (PAPER SIZE) IN INCHES	TYPE OF PAPER	EDITION NUMBER	NO. OF COLORS	ORIGINAL OPENING PRICE	CURRENT RETAIL PRICE
CURRENT EDITIONS:										
Marcella-La Cabana	JFA	AU	1981	SP	22 X 29	AP	300		150	250
Beach Family	JFA	AU	1980	SP	29 X 23	AP	500		125	200
Iris Terrace	JFA	AU	1980	SP	21 X 26	AP	500		125	200
Nurit	JFA	AU	1980	SP	21 X 27	AP	500		125	200
Circus Twins	JFA	AU	1980	SP	29 X 23	AP	500		125	200
Raggae Woman	JFA	AU	1980	SP	30 X 21	AP	500		125	200

JOEL JANOWITZ

BORN: Newark, NJ; November 29, 1945
EDUCATION: Brandeis Univ, Waltham, MA, BA, 1967; Univ of California, Santa Barbara, CA, BFA, 1969
TEACHING: Instr, Univ of California, Santa Barbara, CA, 1968–69; Instr, DeCordova Mus, Lincoln, MA, 1972–73; Asst Prof, Painting & Drawing, Brown Univ, Providence, RI, 1973–75,77; Instr, Boston Col, Newton, MA, 1979; Inst, Painting, Harvard Univ, Summer Sch, Cambridge, MA, 1980,81; Instr, Painting, Mus of Fine Arts Sch, Boston, MA, 1985
AWARDS: Artist Fel, Massachusetts State Grants, 1975,79; Nat Endowment for the Arts Awards, 1976,82; Purchase Award, Hassam & Speicher Fund, 1980,87; Am Acad & Inst of Arts & Letters, NY, 1980,87; Artist's Fel, New York Found for the Arts, 1988
RECENT EXHIB: Victoria Munroe Gallery, NY, 1988
COLLECTIONS: Whitney Mus of Am Art, NY; Wellesley Col Mus, MA; Brandeis Univ, Waltham, MA; Mus of Fine Arts, Boston, MA; Brown Univ, Providence, RI; Colby Col, Waterville, ME; Univ of California, Santa Barbara, CA; Wheaton Col, Norton, MA; Massachusetts Inst of Tech, Cambridge, MA; Metropolitan Mus of Art, NY; Brooklyn Mus, NY
PRINTERS: Artist (ART)
PUBLISHERS: Harcus Krakow Gallery, Boston, MA (HK)
GALLERIES: Barbara Krakow Gallery, Boston, MA; Victoria Munroe Gallery, New York, NY

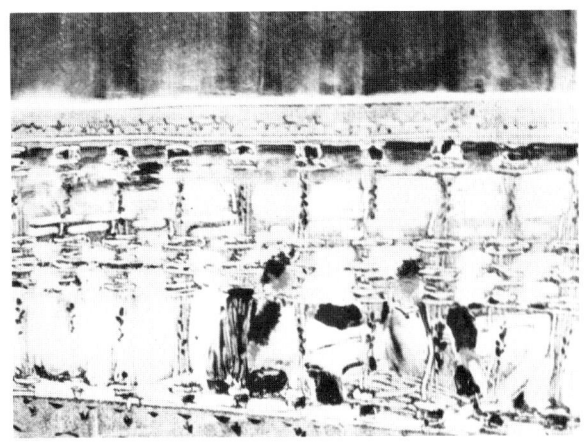

Joel Janowitz
Balustrade/Glance
Courtesy the Artist

MAILING ADDRESS: 183 E Broadway, New York, NY 10002

TITLE	PUBLISHER	PRINTER	DATE	MEDIUM	DIMENSION (PAPER SIZE) IN INCHES	TYPE OF PAPER	EDITION NUMBER	NO. OF COLORS	ORIGINAL OPENING PRICE	CURRENT RETAIL PRICE
CURRENT EDITIONS:										
Balustrade/Tree	HK	ART	1981	C/MON	16 X 20	AP	1		550	650
Balustrade/Conversation	HK	ART	1981	C/MON	16 X 20	AP	1		550	650
Balustrade/Breaking Light	HK	ART	1981	C/MON/PAS	16 X 20	AP	1		575	650
Balustrade/Boats	HK	ART	1981	C/MON	10 X 20	AP	1		450	600
Balustrade/Glance	HK	ART	1981	C/MON	16 X 20	AP	1		550	650
Balustrade/Landscape	HK	ART	1981	C/MON/PAS	11 X 20	AP	1		475	600

The retail prices of the 100,000 limited edition prints quoted in this directory are subject to change. Print publishers, artists and galleries were the direct sources for these quotations. Prices in the secondary market listed as "Sold Out Editions (Rare)" indicate that the publisher has a limited supply of that print or that the print is difficult to locate in the galleries.

ANGELA BING JANSEN

BORN: New York, NY; August 17, 1929
EDUCATION: Brooklyn Col, NY, BA; New York Univ, NY, MA; Atelier 17, NY, with S W Hayter; Brooklyn Mus Sch, NY
AWARDS: Associated American Artists Gallery Award, NY, 1971; George Roth Prize, Philadelphia Print Club, PA, 1971,74; Nat Endowment for the Arts, 1974–75

COLLECTIONS: Metropolitan Mus, NY; Mus of Mod Art, NY; Philadelphia Mus of Art, PA; Art Inst of Chicago, IL; Tate Gallery of Art, London, England; Worcester Mus, MA
PRINTERS: Artist (ART)
PUBLISHERS: Orion Editions, NY (OE)
GALLERIES: Gimpel & Weitzenhoffer Gallery, New York, NY; Orion Editions, New York, NY; Witkin Gallery, New York, NY
MAILING ADDRESS: 1646 First Ave, New York, NY 10028

TITLE	PUBLISHER	PRINTER	DATE	MEDIUM	DIMENSION (PAPER SIZE) IN INCHES	TYPE OF PAPER	EDITION NUMBER	NO. OF COLORS	ORIGINAL OPENING PRICE	CURRENT RETAIL PRICE
CURRENT EDITIONS:										
Concerning Time	OE	ART	1974–79	PH/E/A	22 X 30	AP	25		200	400
Uffizi	OE	ART	1979	PH/E/A	22 X 15	AP	25		150	250

ROBERT JANZ

BORN: Belfast, Ireland; 1932
EDUCATION: Glasgow Sch of Art, Glasgow, Scotland; St Martin's Sch of Art, London, England
TEACHING: Instr, Wimbledon Sch of Art, London, England, 1968–80; Instr, Middlesex Polytechnic, London, England, 1976–80; North London Polytechnic, London, England, 1976–80
AWARDS: Fulbright Scholarship, 1964; DAAD Fellowship, Berlin, West Germany, 1980,81
RECENT EXHIB: L A Louver Gallery, Venice, CA, 1987; Art at Work, NY, 1988; Oliver Dowling Gallery, Dublin, Ireland, 1989
PRINTERS: Leslie Sutcliff, Los Angeles, CA (LS); Robert Aull, Los Angeles, CA (RA); Helen Abe Ichien, Los Angeles, CA (HI); Bill Weege, Madison, WI (BW); Andrew Rubin, Madison, WI (AR); Tandem Press, Univ of Wisconsin, Madison, WI (TanPr)
PUBLISHERS: L A Louver Publications, Venice, CA (LAL); Tandem Press, Univ of Wisconsin, Madison, WI (TanPr)
GALLERIES: L A Louver Gallery, Venice, CA; Nina Freudenheim Gallery, Buffalo, NY; Oliver Dowling Gallery, Dublin, Ireland

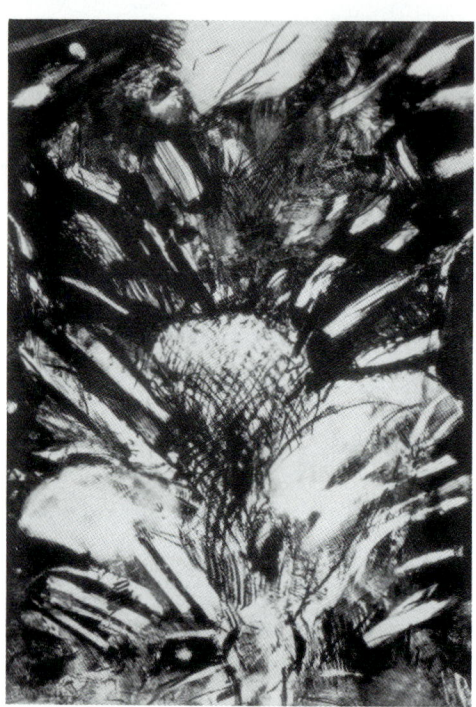

Robert Janz
Passover Rose, State IV
Courtesy Tandem Press

TITLE	PUBLISHER	PRINTER	DATE	MEDIUM	DIMENSION (PAPER SIZE) IN INCHES	TYPE OF PAPER	EDITION NUMBER	NO. OF COLORS	ORIGINAL OPENING PRICE	CURRENT RETAIL PRICE
SOLD OUT EDITIONS (RARE):										
Passover Rose, State I	TanPr	BW/AR/TanPr	1988	LB	35 X 25	R/BFK/W	4	1	750	900
Passover Rose, State II	TanPr	BW/AR/TanPr	1988	LB	35 X 25	R/BFK/W	5	1	750	900
Passover Rose, State III	TanPr	BW/AR/TanPr	1988	LB	35 X 25	R/BFK/W	4	1	750	900
CURRENT EDITIONS:										
Changing Lines (Set of 6):									2500 SET	4500 SET
Expanding Circle	LAL	HI/LS/RA	1980	EB/PH	30 X 22	R/BFK/W	50	1	450	750
Three Lines	LAL	LS/RA	1980	EB/PH	30 X 22	R/BFK/W	50	1	450	750
Expanding Square	LAL	HI/LS/RA	1980	EB/PH	30 X 22	R/BFK/W	50	1	450	750
Waves Triangle	LAL	HI/LS/RA	1980	EB/PH	30 X 22	R/BFK/W	50	1	450	750
Parking Lot Glyph	LAL	HI/LS/RA	1980	EB/PH	30 X 22	R/BFK/W	50	1	450	750
Pedagogic Line	LAL	HI/LS/RA	1980	EB/PH	30 X 22	R/BFK/W	50	1	450	750
Passover Rose, State IV	TanPr	BW/AR/TanPr	1988	LB	35 X 25	R/BFK/W	15	1	750	750
Passover Rose, State V	TanPr	BW/AR/TanPr	1988	LB	35 X 25	R/BFK/W	23	1	750	750

VALERIE JAUDON

BORN: Greenville, MS; August 6, 1945
EDUCATION: Mississippi State Col; Memphis Acad of Art, TN; Univ of the Americas, Mexico City, Mex; St Martins Sch of Art, London, England
TEACHING: Instr, Sch of Visual Arts, NY, 1983–84; Hunter Col, NY, 1986 to present
AWARDS: Creative Artists Public Service Grant, 1980; Mississippi Inst of Arts & Letters, 1981; Award, City of New York, NY, 1987; Nat Endowment for the Arts Fel, 1988; Art Award, Excellence in Design, Art Commission, NY, 1988
RECENT EXHIB: Sidney Janis Gallery, NY, 1988,90
COLLECTIONS: Hirshhorn Mus, Wash, DC; Aldrich Mus of Contemp Art, Ridgefield, CT; Louisiana Mus, Humlebaek, Denmark; Mus of Mod Arts, NY; Fogg Mus, Cambridge, MA; Sammlung-Ludwig Mus, Aachen, West Germany
PRINTERS: Morris Payne, NY (MP); Paul Marcus, NY (PM); Felix Harlan, NY (FH)
PUBLISHERS: Barbara Gladstone Editions, NY (BGE); Corinthian Editions, NY (COR); Aeropress Publishing, Inc, NY (A); Getler/Pall Gallery, NY (G–P); van Straaten, Chicago, IL (VS)
GALLERIES: Holly Solomon Editions, New York, NY; van Straaten Gallery, Chicago, IL; Dart Gallery, Chicago, IL; Sidney Janis Gallery, New York, NY; Fay Gold Gallery, Atlanta, GA
MAILING ADDRESS: 139 Bowery Ave, New York, NY 10002

VALERIE JAUDON CONTINUED

TITLE	PUBLISHER	PRINTER	DATE	MEDIUM	DIMENSION (PAPER SIZE) IN INCHES	TYPE OF PAPER	EDITION NUMBER	NO. OF COLORS	ORIGINAL OPENING PRICE	CURRENT RETAIL PRICE
CURRENT EDITIONS:										
Untitled	BGE	MP	1980	EB	31 X 30	R/BFK	45	1	550	800
Red & Black	COR	PM/FH	1982	SUG/DB/A	33 X 30	ACW	30	2	750	850
Blue & Black	COR	PM/FH	1982	SUB/DB/A	33 X 30	ACW	30	2	750	850
White & Blue-Gray	COR	PM/FH	1982	SUG/DB/A	33 X 30	ACW	15	1	1200	1350
Gold Leaf, Red & Black	COR	PM/FH	1982	SUG/DB/A	33 X 30	ACW	12	2	1200	1350

DANSK JAWORSKA

PRINTERS: Artist (ART)
PUBLISHERS: Fred Dorfman, Inc, NY (FDI)
GALLERIES: Fred Dorfman, Inc, New York, NY

TITLE	PUBLISHER	PRINTER	DATE	MEDIUM	DIMENSION (PAPER SIZE) IN INCHES	TYPE OF PAPER	EDITION NUMBER	NO. OF COLORS	ORIGINAL OPENING PRICE	CURRENT RETAIL PRICE
CURRENT EDITIONS:										
Water Colour (Trip)	FDI	ART	1985	SP	22 X 41 EA	AC	50 EA		350 EA	450 EA
Poolside	FDI	ART	1985	SP	26 X 36	AC	100		350	450
Yellow Pool	FDI	ART	1985	SP	36 X 26	AC	100		350	450
Whirlpool	FDI	ART	1985	SP	36 X 26	AC	100		350	450

VINCE JEFFERDS

BORN: Jersey City, NJ; 1916
EDUCATION: Rutgers Univ, New Brunswick, NJ
PRINTERS: American Atelier, NY (AA)
PUBLISHERS: Circle Fine Art, Chicago, IL (CFA)
GALLERIES: Manus Gallery, Stuttgart, Germany; Circle Galleries, San Diego, CA & San Francisco, CA & Northbrook, IL & Pittsburgh, PA & Houston, TX & Soho, NY & Chicago, IL & Scottsdale, AZ & Beverly Hills, CA & Costa Mesa, CA & Sherman Oaks, CA & Palm Beach, FL & Honolulu, HI & New orleans, LA & Las Vegas, NV & Seattle, WA

TITLE	PUBLISHER	PRINTER	DATE	MEDIUM	DIMENSION (PAPER SIZE) IN INCHES	TYPE OF PAPER	EDITION NUMBER	NO. OF COLORS	ORIGINAL OPENING PRICE	CURRENT RETAIL PRICE
CURRENT EDITIONS:										
Narcissism	CFA	AA	1978	SP	32 X 32		175		75	200

JACK JEFFERSON

BORN: Lead, SD; 1921
EDUCATION: Univ of Iowa, Iowa City, IA, 1940–42; California Sch of Fine Arts, San Francisco, CA, 1946–50
TEACHING: San Francisco Art Inst, 1959–79
AWARDS: Abraham Rosenberg Traveling Fel, Addison Gallery of Am Art, Andover, MA, 1953; Am Fed of Arts Traveling Fel, 1954; Madelaine Diamond Found Award, San Francisco, CA, 1991
RECENT EXHIB: Gallery Paule Anglim, San Francisco, CA, 1991
COLLECTIONS: M H de Young Mem Mus, San Francisco, CA; Smithsonian Inst, Wash, DC; Oakland Mus, CA
PRINTERS: David Kelso, Oakland, CA (DK); Made in California, Oakland, CA (MIC)
PUBLISHERS: Made in California, Oakland, CA (MIC)
GALLERIES: Gallery Paule Anglim, San Francisco, CA; Made in California, Oakland, CA; Betsy Senior Contemporary Prints, New York, NY
MAILING ADDRESS: c/o Made in California, 3246 Ettie St, #16, Oakland, CA 94608

TITLE	PUBLISHER	PRINTER	DATE	MEDIUM	DIMENSION (PAPER SIZE) IN INCHES	TYPE OF PAPER	EDITION NUMBER	NO. OF COLORS	ORIGINAL OPENING PRICE	CURRENT RETAIL PRICE
CURRENT EDITIONS:										
#1	MIC	DK/MIC	1984	A/DPT/SG	30 X 23	R/BFK/W	42	1	275	525
#2 (with Burnishing)	MIC	DK/MIC	1984	A/DPT	30 X 23	R/BFK/W	42	1	275	525
#3	MIC	DK/MIC	1984	EB/HG	15 X 23	R/BFK/W	32	1	150	300
#4	MIC	DK/MIC	1985	EB/DPT/HG	15 X 23	R/BFK/W	28	1	150	300
#5	MIC	DK/MIC	1985	AC/DPT	23 X 30	R/BFK/W	40	4	500	800
#6	MIC	DK/MIC	1988	AC	23 X 30	RdL	40	3	600	800
#7	MIC	DK/MIC	1989	EB/A/HG	23 X 15	R/BFK/W	20	1	275	425
#8	MIC	DK/MIC	1990	EB/A/HG	23 X 15	R/BFK/W	20	1	300	425
#9	MIC	DK/MIC	1992	EB/A/HG	23 X 15	R/BFK/W	20	1	350	475

HANS JELINEK

BORN: Vienna, Austria; August 21, 1910
EDUCATION: Grad Acad of Applied Arts, Vienna, Austria; Univ of Vienna, Austria
TEACHING: Instr, Graphic Art, New Sch of Social Res, NY 1945–50; Prof, Art, City Col of New York, NY, 1948–79; Nat Acad of Sch of Fine Arts, NY, 1973 to present; Prof Emeritus, City Col of New York, NY, 1979 to present
AWARDS: First Prize, Woodcut, Artists for Victory, Nat Graphics Art Exhib, 1943; Pennell Prize, Library of Congress, Wash, DC, 1945; Tiffany Award for Graphic Art, 1947; Paul Sachs Award, Boston, MA, 1962; Audubon Artists Medal and Award for Creative Graphics; People's Prize, Art Assoc of Newport; Samuel Finley Breese Morse Medal, Nat Acad, NY
COLLECTIONS: Metropolitan Mus, NY; Victoria and Albert Mus, London, England; Philadelphia Mus, PA; Cooper Mus, NY; Virginia Mus of Fine Arts, Richmond, VA; Swarthmore Col, PA; Williams Col, Williamstown, MA; Dartmouth Col, Hanover, NH; Mus of Fine Arts, Boston, MA

HANS JELINEK CONTINUED

PRINTERS: Joseph Blumenthal, NY (JB); The Spiral Press, NY (TSP) (OB); Artist (ART)
PUBLISHERS: International Graphic Art Society, NY (IGAS); Society of American Graphic Artists, NY (SAGA); Artist (ART)
GALLERIES: Associated American Artists, New York, NY
MAILING ADDRESS: 675 West End Ave, New York, NY 10025

TITLE	PUBLISHER	PRINTER	DATE	MEDIUM	DIMENSION (PAPER SIZE) IN INCHES	TYPE OF PAPER	EDITION NUMBER	NO. OF COLORS	ORIGINAL OPENING PRICE	CURRENT RETAIL PRICE
SOLD OUT EDITIONS (RARE):										
Culture	ART	ART	1947	WC	23 X 18	TROYA	OP	1	25	600
Three Mourning Women	ART	ART	1947	WC	18 X 12	TROYA/SEK	OP	1	25	600
The Final Victors	ART	ART	1949	WC	18 X 24	TROYA	OP	1	25	600
The Politician	ART	ART	1954	WC	13 X 20	SEK	OP	3	50	500
Three Thistles	ART	ART	1962	WC	34 X 18	SEK	OP	3	75	1000
Wildflowers	ART	ART	1965	WC	18 X 25	SEK	OP	3	100	600
The Trial	ART	ART	1966	WC	12 X 18	SEK/MOR	OP	3	100	700
CURRENT EDITIONS:										
Oblivion	ART	JB/TSP	1968	WC	22 X 14	JAP	250	1	100	500
Wheat	ART	JB/TSP	1970	WC	11 X 26	JAP	250	1	125	450
Lutenist	ART	JB/TSP	1971	WC	14 X 20	JAP	250	1	125	450
Metamorphosis	ART	ART	1974	WC	20 X 12	BAS	OP	1	150	600

PAUL JENKINS

BORN: Kansas City, MO; July 12, 1923
EDUCATION: Kansas City Art Inst & Sch of Design, KS, 1938–41; Art Students League, NY, 1948–52; DH, 1973
AWARDS: Golden Eagle Award, 1967; Officier des Arts & Letters Award, France, 1980; Art Directors Club Medal, 1984
RECENT EXHIB: Charles B Goddard Center for Visual & Performing Arts, Ardmore, OK, 1989; Samuel Stein Fine Arts, Ltd, Chicago, IL, 1989; Associated American Artists, NY, 1992,93
COLLECTIONS: Mus of Mod Art, NY; Solomon R Guggenheim Mus, NY; Whitney Mus of Am Art, NY; Brooklyn Mus, NY; Baltimore Mus, MD; Albright-Knox Mus, Buffalo, NY; Harvard Univ, Cambridge, MA; Detroit Inst of Art, MI; Walker Art Center, Minneapolis, MN; Chrysler Mus, Norfolk, VA; Philadelphia Mus of Art, PA; Nat Coll of Fine Arts, Wash, DC; Corcoran Gallery of Art, Wash, DC; Hirshhorn Mus, Wash, DC; Tate Gallery, London, England; Victoria and Albert Mus, London, England; Stedelijk Mus, Amsterdam, Holland; Mus of Mod Art, Paris, France; Art Gallery of Ontario, Toronto, Can; Centre Georges Pompidou, Paris, France; Mus of Western Art, Tokyo, Japan
PRINTERS: F Mourlot, Paris, France (FM); Imprimerie Mourlot, Paris, France (IM); Artist (ART)
PUBLISHERS: Transworld Art, Inc, NY (TAI); Tyler Graphics, Ltd, Bedford Village, NY (TGL); Abrams Original Editions, NY (AOE)
GALLERIES: Karl Flinker Gallery, Paris, France; Fingerhut Gallery, Minneapolis, MN; Carone Gallery, Fort Lauderdale, FL; Samuel Stein Fine Arts, Chicago, IL; Gimpel Fils Gallery, London, England; Gimpel & Weitzenhoffer Gallery, New York, NY; Evelyn Aimis Fine Art, Toronto, Canada; Argus Fine Arts, Eugene, OR; Eva Cohon Gallery, Ltd, Chicago, IL & Highland Park, IL; Fernette's Gallery of Art, Des Moines, IA; David Anderson Gallery, Buffalo, NY; MCL Fine Arts, Roslyn Heights, NY; Samuel Stein Fine Arts, Chicago, IL; Associated American Artists, New York, NY
MAILING ADDRESS: 831 Broadway, New York, NY 10003

TITLE	PUBLISHER	PRINTER	DATE	MEDIUM	DIMENSION (PAPER SIZE) IN INCHES	TYPE OF PAPER	EDITION NUMBER	NO. OF COLORS	ORIGINAL OPENING PRICE	CURRENT RETAIL PRICE
SOLD OUT EDITIONS (RARE):										
Phenomena Franklin's Kite	TAI	FM/IM	1976	LC	28 X 20	AP	175	5	500	1000
Katherine Wheel	TGL	TGL	1979	LC/MON	29 X 43	HMP	50		800	2500
Cardinal Rain Palace	TAI	FM/IM	1980	SP	60 X 40	AP	100		2000	2500
Emissary	TGL	TGL	1980	EB/AC	26 X 16	HMP	20	4	600	750
Himalayan Hourglass	TGL	TGL	1980	EB/AC	30 X 22	HMP	20	6	600	1000
Over the Cusp	TGL	TGL	1980	EB/DPT/MEZ	16 X 26	HMP	20	4	600	1000
Four Winds I	TGL	TGL	1980	EB/WA	48 X 33	HMP	58	Varies	2000	3500
East Winds II	TGL	TGL	1980	EB/WA	51 X 37	TW/HMP	18	Varies	2000	3500
West Winds III	TGL	TGL	1980	EB/WA	51 X 37	HMP	53	Varies	2200	3500
Portrait New York, New York	AOE	ART	1981	SP/AC	46 X 34	ST/R/100	125	40	2500	3500
Continental Divide	TAI	ART	1982	LC	38 X 29	SOM	150		1500	2000
Cardinal Prism	TAI	ART	1982	LC	38 X 29	SOM	94		1500	2000
Sheffield Blue	TAI	ART	1982	LC	38 X 29	SOM	150		1500	2000
Sinclair Red	TAI	ART	1982	LC	38 X 29	SOM	150		1500	2000

STEVAN JENNIS

BORN: Newark, NJ; 1945
EDUCATION: San Fernando Valley Col, CA, BFA, 1967; Univ of California, Los Angeles, CA, MA, 1970; Univ of Massachusetts, Boston, MA, MFA, 1973
TEACHING: Mount Holyoke Col, South Hadley, MA, 1973; Univ of Massachusetts, Amherst, MA, 1973–74
RECENT EXHIB: Helander Gallery, NY, 1992
COLLECTIONS: Neuberger Mus, Purchase, NY; Newark Mus, NJ; Univ of Massachusetts, Boston, MA; Washington and Jefferson Col, Washington, PA; Weatherspoon Art Gallery, Univ of North Carolina, Greensboro, NC
PRINTERS: XPress, NY (XP); Alan Koslin, NY (AK)
PUBLISHERS: Diane Villani Editions, NY (DVE); Barbara Toll Fine Art, NY (BTFA)
GALLERIES: Magnuson Gallery, Boston, MA; Roger Ramsay, Chicago, IL; CA; Diane Villani Editions, New York, NY; Barbara Toll Fine Arts, New York, NY; Helander Gallery, New York, NY

The retail prices of the 100,000 limited edition prints quoted in this directory are subject to change. Print publishers, artists and galleries were the direct sources for these quotations. Prices in the secondary market listed as "Sold Out Editions (Rare)" indicate that the publisher has a limited supply of that print or that the print is difficult to locate in the galleries.

STEVAN JENNIS CONTINUED

TITLE	PUBLISHER	PRINTER	DATE	MEDIUM	DIMENSION (PAPER SIZE) IN INCHES	TYPE OF PAPER	EDITION NUMBER	NO. OF COLORS	ORIGINAL OPENING PRICE	CURRENT RETAIL PRICE
CURRENT EDITIONS:										
Black House	DVE/BTFA	AK/XP	1981	E/HC	39 X 30	AP	60	10	600	600

ALFRED JENSEN

BORN: Guatemala City, Guatemala; 1903
EDUCATION: San Diego Fine Arts, Sch, CA, 1925; Hans Hofmann Sch, Munich, Germany, 1927-28; Ecole Scandinavien, Paris, France, 1929-34
RECENT EXHIB: Pace Downtown, NY, 1991
PRINTERS: Sheila Marbain, NY (SM); Carl Lindgren, NY (CL); Maurel Studio, NY (MS)
PUBLISHERS: Pace Editions, NY (PE)
GALLERIES: Pace Prints, New York, NY; Wenger Gallery, San Diego, CA; Vanderwoude Tananbaum Gallery, New York, NY; Rothschild Fine Arts, New York, NY; Pace Downtown, New York, NY

TITLE	PUBLISHER	PRINTER	DATE	MEDIUM	DIMENSION (PAPER SIZE) IN INCHES	TYPE OF PAPER	EDITION NUMBER	NO. OF COLORS	ORIGINAL OPENING PRICE	CURRENT RETAIL PRICE
CURRENT EDITIONS:										
Untitled (Set of 4)	PE	SM/CL/MS	1973	SP	35 X 35 EA	TUS	150 EA	10 EA	500 SET / 150 EA	1500 SET / 400 EA

BILL JENSEN

BORN: Minneapolis, MN; November 26, 1945
EDUCATION: Univ of Minnesota, Minneapolis, MN, BFA, 1968, MFA, 1970
TEACHING: Inst, Univ of Minnesota, Minneapolis, MN, 1965-70; Instr, Brooklyn Mus of Art, NY, 1971-75; Instr, York Col, Queens, NY, 1972-73
AWARDS: Creative Artists Public Service Program Grant, 1979; Artist's Fel, Nat Endowment for the Arts, 1985-86
RECENT EXHIB: Phillips Coll, Wash, DC, 1987; Lannan Mus, Lake Worth, FL, 1988
COLLECTIONS: Whitney Mus of Am Art, NY; Metropolitan Mus of Art, NY; Worcester Mus, MA; Lannan Mus, Lake Worth, FL; Phillips Coll, Wash, DC; Mus of Mod Art, NY; Fogg Mus, Cambridge, MA; Los Angeles County Mus of Art, CA; Columbia Green Col, Hudson, NY; Carnegie Inst Art Mus, Pittsburgh, PA
PRINTERS: John Lund, NY (JL); Hitoshi Kido (HK); Universal Limited Editions, West Islip, NY (ULAE); Shi Ji-hong, West Islip, NY (SJH)
PUBLISHERS: Universal Limited Art Editions, West Islip, NY (ULAE)
GALLERIES: Washburn Gallery, New York, NY; Thomas Smith Fine Art, Fort Wayne, IN; Barbara Krakow Gallery, Boston, MA; Elizabeth Paul Gallery, Cincinnati, OH; Greg Kucera Gallery, Seattle, WA; Graystone, San Francisco, CA
MAILING ADDRESS: c/o Washburn Gallery, 41 E 57th St, 8th Fl, New York, NY 10022

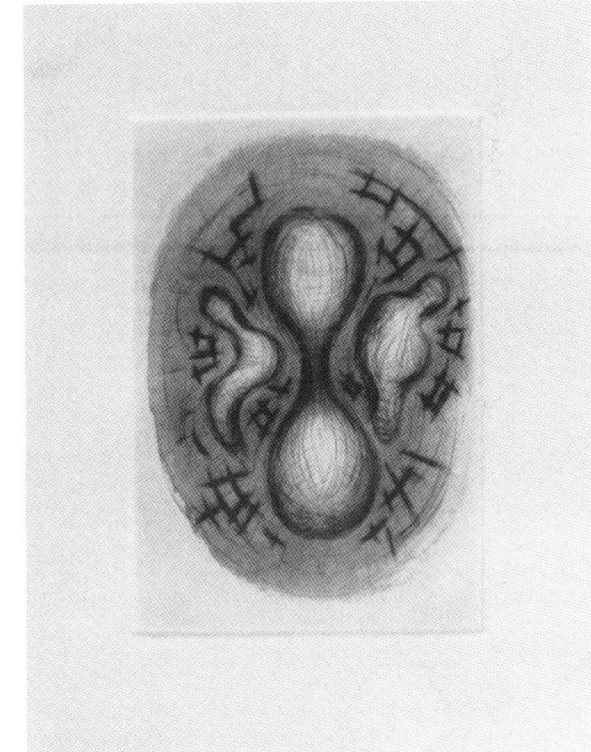

Bill Jensen
From Endless Suite
Courtesy Universal Limited Art Editions

TITLE	PUBLISHER	PRINTER	DATE	MEDIUM	DIMENSION (PAPER SIZE) IN INCHES	TYPE OF PAPER	EDITION NUMBER	NO. OF COLORS	ORIGINAL OPENING PRICE	CURRENT RETAIL PRICE
CURRENT EDITIONS:										
Endless (Set of 11) (Boxed)	ULAE	ULAE	1983-85	I	20 X 15 EA	HMP	38 EA		7500 SET	10000 SET
Ancestors	ULAE	JL/HK/ULAE	1984-87	I	20 X 15	HMP	45	5	1500	2500
For Alice Too	ULAE	JL/SJH/ULAE	1990	EC	21 X 21	AP/TCP	51	7	2500	3000

MICHAEL FLORIAN JILG

BORN: Great Bend, KS; June 28, 1947
EDUCATION: Fort Hays Kansas State Univ, Hays, KS, BA, 1969, MA, 1970; Blossom-Kent Art Prog, Kent State Univ, OH, 1972; Wichita State Univ, KS, MFA, 1972; Pratt Graphics, Studio Camnitzer, Valdottavo, Italy, 1984; Santa Reparata Graphics Inst, Florence, Italy, 1985
TEACHING: Asst Prof, Painting, Fort Hays State Univ, Hays, KS, 1981 to present
AWARDS: Purchase Prize, Kansas Arts Com, Topeka, KS, 1980,81
COLLECTIONS: Wichita Art Mus, KS; Joslyn Art Mus, Omaha, NE; Kansas Arts Com, Topeka, KS; Kent State Univ, OH; Purdue Univ, Hammond, IN; Bucks County Col, PA; Fort Hays State Univ, Hays, KS; Wichita State Univ, KS
PRINTERS: Arrow Printers, Salina, KA; Artist (ART)
PUBLISHERS: Krantz Publishers, Chicago, IL (KP); Artist (ART)
MAILING ADDRESS: 317 W 20th, Hays, KS 67601

MICHAEL FLORIAN JILG CONTINUED

TITLE	PUBLISHER	PRINTER	DATE	MEDIUM	DIMENSION (PAPER SIZE) IN INCHES	TYPE OF PAPER	EDITION NUMBER	NO. OF COLORS	ORIGINAL OPENING PRICE	CURRENT RETAIL PRICE
CURRENT EDITIONS:										
Sculpture Critics	ART	ART	1985	EB	12 X 10	FAB	75	1	75	125
Swimsuit	ART	ART	1985	EB	16 X 16	R/BFK	75	1	75	125
The Bishop's Nephew	ART	ART	1986	EB	16 X 16	FAB	75	1	75	125
The Bishop's Neice	ART	ART	1986	EB	16 X 16	FAB	75	1	75	125

JIANG (TIE-FENG)

BORN: Ningbo, China; October 3, 1939
EDUCATION: Studied with Huang Yong-Yu, 1959–63; Central Art Inst, Beijing, China, BA, 1964
TEACHING: Instr, Yunnan Art Acad, Kumming, China, 1978–83
AWARDS: Mural, Great Hall of the People, Beijing, China, 1979; Second Place, United Nations Int Children's Picture Grant, 1980
RECENT EXHIB: Dyansen Gallery, Boston, MA, 1987; Patricia Judith Gallery, Boca Raton, FL, 1987; American Design, Aspen, CO, 1987,88; Dyansen Gallery, Soho, NY, 1987,88; Benjamin's Gallery, Buffalo, NY, 1988; Kenneth Behm Gallery, Bellevue, WA, 1988; Tower Gallery, Sacramento, CA, 1988; Jean Stephen Gallery, Minneapolis, MN, 1988; Dyansen Gallery, San Diego, CA, 1988,89; Bishop's Gallery, Georgetown, Wash, DC, 1987,89; Reid Gallery, Carmel, CA, 1989; Saper Gallery, East Lansing, MI, 1989; Fine Art Collectors, Sausalito, CA, 1989,90; Merrill Chase Galleries, Chicago, IL & Wash, DC, 1990; Lawrence Gallery, Santa Rosa, CA, 1988,90; Livingston Gallery, Honolulu, HI; 1989,90; Bishop's Gallery, Scottsdale, AZ, 1988,90,91
COLLECTIONS: Norfolk Mus, VA; Great Hall of the People, Beijing, China
PRINTERS: ChromComp, Inc, NY (CCI); Colton Graphics, Mondeleine, IL (CGr)
PUBLISHERS: Fingerhut Group Publishers, Inc, Minneapolis, MN (FGP)
GALLERIES: Bishop's Gallery, Scottsdale, AZ; Livingston Gallery, Honolulu, HI; Lawrence Gallery, Santa Rosa, CA; Merrill Chase Galleries, Chicago, IL & Wash, DC; Renaissance Gallery, Pittsburgh, PA; Park Shore Gallery, Naples, FL; Saper Gallery, East Lansing, MI

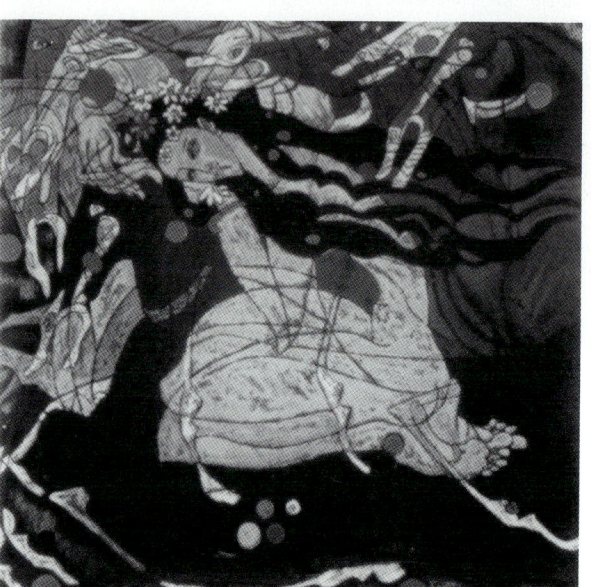
Jiang (Tie-Feng)
Emerald Lady
Courtesy Fingerhut Group Publishers

TITLE	PUBLISHER	PRINTER	DATE	MEDIUM	DIMENSION (PAPER SIZE) IN INCHES	TYPE OF PAPER	EDITION NUMBER	NO. OF COLORS	ORIGINAL OPENING PRICE	CURRENT RETAIL PRICE
SOLD OUT EDITIONS (RARE):										
Emerald Lady	FGP	CCI	1985	SP	40 X 40	AP	300	34	490	8000
Mother & Child	FGP	CCI	1985	SP	40 X 40	AP	300	24	490	5500
Girl of T'ang Dynasty	FGP	CCI	1985	SP	40 X 40	AP	300	29	490	4500
Moonlight Dance	FGP	CCI	1986	SP	40 X 40	AP	300		490	5500
Four Seasons	FGP	CCI	1986	SP	40 X 40	AP	260	29	490	7000
Horse Series (Set of 2):										
Red Horse	FGP	CCI	1986	SP	24 X 24		260	25	375	2500
Green Horse	FGP	CCI	1986	SP	24 X 24	AP	260	20	375	2500
Speed	FGP	CCI	1986	SP	20 X 40	AP	260	25	490	9000
Flight	FGP	CCI	1986	SP	30 X 30	AP	260	25	490	5000
Springtime	FGP	CCI	1987	SP	33 X 33	AP	293	28	825	5000
Calla Lilies	FGP	CGr	1987	SP	32 X 32	AP	293	27	830	5500
Flower Suite (Set of 2):										
White	FGP	CGr	1988	SP	25 X 25	AP	293	27	660	3500
Radiant Violet	FGP	CGr	1988	SP	25 X 25	AP	293	30	660	4000
Black Horse	FGP	CGr	1988	SP	40 X 40	AP	293	27	1200	9000
Whisper	FGP	CGr	1989	SP	32 X 32	AP	293	45	1100	5000
Running Horses	FGP	CGr	1989	SP	44 X 30	AP	293	34	1250	9000
Mysterious & Ancient	FGP	CGr	1989	SP	40 X 42	AP	293	38	1750	5500
Line Symphony	FGP	CGr	1989	SP	40 X 40	AP	350	32	1750	5500
Blue Lady	FGP	CGr	1990	SP		AP	350		2250	12000
Zebras	FGP	CGr	1990	SP	36 X 36	AP	300	27	1500	4000
Purple Dream	FGP	CGr	1990	SP	36 X 36	AP	300	36	1500	3500
Stone Forest	FGP	CGr	1991	SP	40 X 40	AP	300		2250	5000
Nature Suite (Set of 4)	FGP	CGr	1993	SP		AP	300 EA		3500 SET	3500 SET
Lovers' Trees	FGP	CGr	1993	SP		AP	300		3000	3000
CURRENT EDITIONS:										
Mermaid	FGP	CGr	1987	SP	35 X 35	AP	293	28	830	4500
Love Suite (Set of 2):										
Love	FGP	CGr	1987	SP	20 X 20	AP	293	19	520	3000
Girls	FGP	CGr	1987	SP	20 X 20	AP	293	19	520	3000
Blossoming Flowers	FGP	CGr	1987	SP	38 X 38	AP	293	45	1210	5500

JIANG (TIE-FENG) CONTINUED

TITLE	PUBLISHER	PRINTER	DATE	MEDIUM	DIMENSION (PAPER SIZE) IN INCHES	TYPE OF PAPER	EDITION NUMBER	NO. OF COLORS	ORIGINAL OPENING PRICE	CURRENT RETAIL PRICE
CURRENT EDITIONS:										
Girl of Suzhou	FGP	CGr	1987	SP	32 X 33	AP	293	30	960	4500
Playing Water	FGP	CGr	1988	SP	32 X 32	AP	293	33	960	5000
A Mountain Ghost	FGP	CGr	1988	SP	32 X 32	AP	293	30	760	5000
White Mermaid	FGP	CGr	1988	SP	32 X 32	AP	293	34	994	4500
To Soar	FGP	CGr	1988	SP	29 X 42	AP	293	43	1060	5000
Spring	FGP	CGr	1989	SP	33 X 33	AP	293	37	1450	5000
Little Horses Suite (Set of 2)										
Horse I	FGP	CGr	1989	SP	25 X 25	AP	293	39	670	3000
Horse II	FGP	CGr	1989	SP	25 X 25	AP	293	35	670	3000
Morning Flowers	FGP	CGr	1990	SP	36 X 36	AP	350		1500	4500
Huntress	FGP	CGr	1990	SP	34 X 34	AP	350	47	1500	4500
Pipa Melody	FGP	CGr	1990	SP	36 X 36	AP	300	43	1500	4500
Large Bouquet	FGP	CGr	1990	SP	40 X 40	AP	300	31	1750	5000
Emerald Forest	FGP	CGr	1990	SP	36 X 36	AP	300	41	1500	4500
Freedom Suite	FGP	CGr	1991	SP		AP	300		2200 SET	2750 SET
The Empress	FGP	CGr	1991	SP		AP	300		1500	2200
Spirit of Fire	FGP	CGr	1992	SP		AP	300		1500	2500
Imperial Zebras	FGP	CGr	1992	SP		AP	300		1500	2800
Rhythm	FGP	CGr	1992	SP		AP	300		1500	2500
Panda Suite (Set of 2)	FGP	CGr	1993	SP		AP	300		1500 SET	1500 SET
Elephant Family	FGP	CGr	1993	SP		AP	300		1500	1500

LUIS ALFONSO JIMENEZ, JR

BORN: El Paso, TX; July 30, 1940
EDUCATION: Univ of Mexico City, Mexico, BFA, 1964
AWARDS: Nat Endowment for the Arts, 1977
RECENT EXHIB: Redding Mus & Art Center, CA, 1989; Lakeview Mus of Arts & Sciences, Peoria, IL, 1989; Utah State Univ, Nora Eccles Harrison Mus, Logan, UT, 1989; Lew Allen/Butler Fine Art, Santa Fe, NM, 1990; Univ of Colorado, Colorado Springs, CO, 1992; Univ of Nevada, Donna Beam Fine Art Gallery, Las Vegas, NV, 1992; Roswell Mus, NM, 1989,92; Alternative Mus, NY, 1989,92
COLLECTIONS: Long Beach Mus, CA; New Orleans Mus, LA; Roswell Mus, NM; Plains Mus, Fargo, ND; Nat Coll of Fine Arts, Wash, DC
PRINTERS: Landfall Press Inc, Chicago, IL (LPI); Jack Lemon, Chicago, IL (JL); Mary McDonald, Chicago, IL (MM); Ernest F DeSoto, San Francisco, CA (EDS); Ernest DeSoto Workshop, San Francisco, CA (EDSW); Sette Workshop, Tempe, AZ (SeW)
PUBLISHERS: Landfall Press Inc, Chicago, IL (LPI); Ernest DeSoto Workshop, San Francisco, CA (EDSW); Sette Publishing Company, Tempe, AZ (SPC)
GALLERIES: Elaine Horwitch Galleries, Scottsdale, AZ & Santa Fe, NM; Phyllis Kind Gallery, Chicago, IL & New York, NY; Robischon Gallery, Denver, CO; Landfall Press, Inc, Chicago, IL; Ernest DeSoto Workshop, San Francisco, CA; Adair Margo Gallery, El Paso, TX; Moody Gallery, Houston, TX; Lisa Sette Gallery, Scottsdale, AZ; Etherton/Stern Gallery, Tucson, AZ; Lew Allen Gallery, Santa Fe, NM; Naravisa Press, Santa Fe, NM
MAILING ADDRESS: P O Box 175, Hondo, NM 88336

TITLE	PUBLISHER	PRINTER	DATE	MEDIUM	DIMENSION (PAPER SIZE) IN INCHES	TYPE OF PAPER	EDITION NUMBER	NO. OF COLORS	ORIGINAL OPENING PRICE	CURRENT RETAIL PRICE
SOLD OUT EDITIONS (RARE):										
Vaquero	LPI	JL/LPI	1981	LC	46 X 34	ARP	50	6	750	1200
Honky Tonk	LPI	JL/LPI	1981	LC	35 X 50	AP/W	50	7	1000	1500
Coyote	LPI	JL/LPI	1986	LC	34 X 28	AP/W	50	6	650	950
Bronco (Horse)	LPI	JL/LPI	1978	LC	40 X 28	AP/W	35	5	300	800
Bronco (Cowboy)	LPI	JL/LPI	1978	LC	40 X 28	AP/W	35	5	300	800
Rodeo Queen	LPI	JL/LPI	1981	LC	42 X 29	AP/W	50	5	600	950
Sodbuster	LPI	JL/LPI	1982	LC	32 X 45	AP/W	50	6	750	950
Steve Jordan	LPI	JL/LPI	1984	LC	30 X 23	AP/W	40	5	500	650
Dancing Couple	LPI	JL/LPI	1984	LC	48 X 34	AP/W	50	5	800	800
Texas Waltz	LPI	JL/LPI	1984	LC	48 X 35	AP/W	50	5	800	950
Fiesta (Dipt)	EDSW	EDS/EDSW	1985	LC	64 X 48	AP/W	76	5	1000	1500
CURRENT EDITIONS:										
Dead Coyote	LPI	JL/LPI	1985	LC	34 X 28	AP/W	50		800	800

THOMAS ALIX JOHNSTON

BORN: Oklahoma City, OK; June 4, 1941
EDUCATION: San Diego State Univ, CA, BA, 1965; Univ of California, Santa Barbara, CA, MFA, 1967; Atelier 17, Paris, France, 1980
TEACHING: Prof, Art, Western Washington Univ, Bellingham, WA, currently
AWARDS: Purchase Award, Henry Art Gallery, Univ of Washington, Seattle, WA, 1967; First Place, Graphics, California State Univ, Chico, CA, 1970; Purchase Award, Seattle Art Mus, WA, 1972; Purchase Award, Western New Mexico, Univ, Silver City, NM; Univ of North Dakota, Grand Forks, ND; Univ of Texas, El Paso, TX
RECENT EXHIB: Francine Seders Gallery, Seattle, WA, 1987
COLLECTIONS: Portland Art Mus, OR; Cheney Cowles Mus, Spokane, WA; Henry Art Gallery, Univ of Washington, Seattle, WA; Univ of Texas, El Paso, TX; Western New Mexico Univ, Silver City, NM; Univ of North Dakota, Grand Forks, ND; Seattle Art Mus, WA; California State Univ, Chico, CA; Mod Art Mus, Kobe, Japan; Whatcom Mus, Bellingham, WA
PRINTERS: Lacouriere et Frelaut, Paris, France (L/F); Artist (ART)
PUBLISHERS: Artist (ART)
GALLERIES: Francine Seders Gallery, Seattle, WA; Figura, Inc, New York, NY
MAILING ADDRESS: c/o Art Dept, Western Washington Univ, Bellingham, WA 98225

THOMAS ALIX JOHNSTON CONTINUED

TITLE	PUBLISHER	PRINTER	DATE	MEDIUM	DIMENSION (PAPER SIZE) IN INCHES	TYPE OF PAPER	EDITION NUMBER	NO. OF COLORS	ORIGINAL OPENING PRICE	CURRENT RETAIL PRICE
CURRENT EDITIONS:										
Metro	ART	L/F	1981	AB	24 X 30	R/BFK	30	1	100	250
Primary X	ART	L/F	1982	AC	30 X 22	R/BFK	50	3	100	375
Vertigo	ART	ART	1984	I/VIS	28 X 28	AP	10	3	200	675
Untitled	ART	ART	1984	LB	26 X 39	VGZ	5	1	350	1000

LESTER JOHNSON

BORN: Minneapolis, MN; January 27, 1919
EDUCATION: Art Inst of Chicago, IL
TEACHING: Art in Res, Univ of Wisconsin, Milwaukee, WI, 1964; Director, Studies, Grad Sch, Painting Sch of Art & Arch, Yale Univ, New Haven, CT, 1969–74; Adj Prof Painting, Yale Univ, New Haven, CT, 1964 to present
AWARDS: Guggenheim Fel, 1972, Painting, 1973; Creative Arts Award, Painting, Brandeis Univ, Waltham, MA, 1978
RECENT EXHIB: Brandeis Univ, Rose Art Mus, Waltham, MA, 1987; Westmoreland Mus of Art, Greenburg, PA, 1987; Gallery Moos, NY, 1987,88; Retrosp, David Barnett Gallery, Milwaukee, WI, 1989; Gimpel/Weitzenhoffer Gallery, NY, 1990; Passaic Count Com Col, LRC Gallery, Paterson, NJ, 1992
COLLECTIONS: Phoenix Art Mus, AZ; Univ of Arizona Mus, Tucson, AZ; Connecticut Wadsworth Atheneum, Hartford, CT; Yale Univ Art Gallery, New Haven, CT; Detroit Art Inst, MI; Kalamazoo Inst of Arts, MI; Univ of Michigan, Ann Arbor, MI; Minneapolis Inst of Arts, MN; Walker Art Center, Minneapolis, MN; Univ of Nebraska, Lincoln, NE; Albright-Knox Art Gallery, Buffalo, NY; Solomon R Guggenheim Mus, NY; Guild Hall, East Hampton, NY; Mus of Mod Art, NY; Neuberger Mus, State Univ of New York, Purchase, NY; New Sch for Social Research, NY; Dayton Art Inst, OH; Ohio State Univ, Columbus, OH; Fort Worth Art Mus, TX; Chrysler Mus, Norfolk, VA; Hirshhorn Mus, Wash, DC; Nat Mus of Am Art, Wash, DC; Univ of Wisconsin, Milwaukee, WI
PRINTERS: Jon Cone, Port Chester, NY (JC); Cone Editions, Port Chester, NY (CEd); Judith Solodkin, NY (JS); Solo Press, NY (SP)
PUBLISHERS: London Arts Inc, Detroit, MI (LAI); Cone Editions, NY (CEd); Solo Press, NY (SP)
GALLERIES: Zabriskie Gallery, New York, NY; Donald Morris Gallery, Birmingham, MI; Munson Gallery, New Haven, CT; Connecticut Fine Arts, Westport, CT; Gimpel/Weitzenhoffer Gallery, New York, NY; Anderson Gallery, Buffalo, NY; Peter M David Gallery, Minneapolis, MN; David Barnett Gallery, Milwaukee, WI; Gallery Moos, New York, NY; Gallery Gemini, Palm Beach, FL; Cantor/Lemberg Gallery, Birmingham, MI; Cone Editions, East Topsham, VT; Solo Gallery, New York, NY; Branchville Soho Gallery, Ridgefield, CT; Margaret Lipworth Fine Art, Boca Raton, FL
MAILING ADDRESS: c/o Sch of Art, Yale Univ, New Haven, CT 06520

Lester Johnson
Close Up
Courtesy London Arts, Inc

Lester Johnson
City Graces
Courtesy London Arts, Inc

TITLE	PUBLISHER	PRINTER	DATE	MEDIUM	DIMENSION (PAPER SIZE) IN INCHES	TYPE OF PAPER	EDITION NUMBER	NO. OF COLORS	ORIGINAL OPENING PRICE	CURRENT RETAIL PRICE
SOLD OUT EDITIONS (RARE):										
City Graces	LAI		1980	LC	29 X 22	SOM	175	10	450	1500
Close Up	LAI		1980	LC	29 X 21	SOM	175	10	450	1500
Group	POFA		1980	LC	29 X 21	SOM	175	10	450	1500
City Venus	LAI		1980	LC	30 X 22	SOM	175	10	450	1500
Untitled	CEd	JC/CEd	1983	SP	30 X 42	AP88	60	21	600	3500
Gold Series 3	SUNY	JC/CEd	1984	SP	34 X 42	G-100	100	3	750	2500
Untitled (Gold Series)	HAD	JC/CEd	1985	SP	20 X 25	R/BFK	200	6	150	1000
Single Girl	CEd	JC/CEd	1986	EB/SG	14 X 12	LANA	9	1	600	1000
Girl's Head	CEd	JC/CEd	1986	DPT	14 X 12	LANA	8	1	600	1000
Spring Scene, State II	CEd	JC/CEd	1986	AB/SB	20 X 17	LANA	21	1	600	1200
Noon	CEd	JC/CEd	1987	SP	49 X 36	R/BFK	35	3	1200	3500

LESTER JOHNSON CONTINUED

TITLE	PUBLISHER	PRINTER	DATE	MEDIUM	DIMENSION (PAPER SIZE) IN INCHES	TYPE OF PAPER	EDITION NUMBER	NO. OF COLORS	ORIGINAL OPENING PRICE	CURRENT RETAIL PRICE
SOLD OUT EDITIONS (RARE):										
New York Trip	LAI		1980	LC	29 X 22	SOM	175	10	450	1500
Three Women	LAI		1980	LC	29 X 22	SOM	175	10	450	1500
Street Scene: Men & Women	LAI		1980	LC	28 X 21	SOM	175	19	450	1500
New York Scene	LAI		1980	LC	29 X 22	SOM	175	12	450	1500
Passine Crowd #1	LAI		1980	LC	28 X 21	SOM	175	10	450	1500
Group Passing	CEd	JC/CEd	1984	SP	42 X 30	AP88	66	2	750	1500
Gold Series 4, State 1	CEd	JC/CEd	1984	SP	22 X 30	AP88	50	4	600	1000
Gold Series 4, State 2	CEd	JC/CEd	1984	SP	22 X 30	AP88	50	8	750	1500
Arabesque	CEd	JC/CEd	1985	SP	20 X 25	R/BFK	66	7	600	1000
Three Girls	CEd	JC/CEd	1986	SP	30 X 42	AP88	60	3	750	1500
Man in Woodcut, 1953–1986 (Set of 6)	CEd	JC/CEd	1986	WB	22 X 16 EA	KIT	30 EA	1 EA	1800 SET	6000 SET
City Trio	CEd	JC/CEd	1986	EB/SK/SB/DPT	14 X 12	LANA	80	1	400	800
City Couple	CEd	JC/CEd	1986	EB/SL	14 X 12	LANA	30	1	500	900
City Group, State 1	CEd	JC/CEd	1986	AB	20 X 17	LANA	26	1	500	1000
City Group, State 2 (with Burnishing)	CEd	JC/CEd	1986	AB/SG/SL	20 X 17	LANA	26	1	600	1000
Girls Walking, State 1	CEd	JC/CEd	1986	AB	20 X 17	LANA	26	1	500	1000
Girls Walking, State 3	CEd	JC/CEd	1986	AB/DPT	20 X 17	LANA	26	1	600	1000
Spring Scene, State 1	CEd	JC/CEd	1986	AB	20 X 17	LANA	21	1	500	1000
Three Girls Close Up	CEd	JC/CEd	1986	EB/SB/SL	13 X 15	LANA	80	1	400	800
Three Heads	CEd	JC/CEd	1986	AB/SB/DPT	19 X 25	LANA	28	1	600	1000
Gold Series 2	CEd	JC/CEd	1986	SP	38 X 50	LEN/100	40		750	1500
CURRENT EDITIONS:										
St Marks	CEd	JC/CEd	1987	EB/DPT	20 X 26	LANA	36	1	600	1000
Spring	CEd	JC/CEd	1987	EB/SL	18 X 13	LANA	14	1	500	900
Passing Scene	SP	JS/SP	1992	LC	63 X 46	AC	40		3500	3500

ALLEN JONES

BORN: London, England; 1937
EDUCATION: Hornsey Col of Art, London, England; Royal Col of Art, London, England
TEACHING: Croydon Col of Art, London, England
AWARDS: Tamarind Lithography Fellowship, Albuquerque, NM, 1966
COLLECTIONS: Mus of Mod Art, NY; Chicago Art Inst, Chicago, IL; Fogg Art Mus, Cambridge, MA; Pasadena Art Mus, Pasadena, CA; Stedelijk Mus, Amsterdam, Netherlands; Moderna Museet, Stockholm, Sweden; Mus of the 20th Century, Vienna, Austria; Tate Gallery of Art, London, England

PRINTERS: Petersburg Press, London, England (PP); Jack Lemon, Chicago, IL (JL); Landfall Press, Inc, Chicago, IL (LPI); Judy Solodkin, NY (JS); Solo Press, NY (SP); Ian Lawson, Wales (IL); Houston Univ, Houston, TX (HU); Ian Brice, London, England (IB); Richard Mitchell, London, England (RM); The Printworkshop, London, England (TP); Advanced Graphics, London, England (AG)
PUBLISHERS: Petersburg Press, London, England (PP); Waddington Graphics, London, England (WG)
GALLERIES: Waddington Graphics, London, England; Petersburg Press, London, England & New York, NY; James Corcoran Gallery, Santa Monica, CA; Zack/Shuster Gallery, Boca Raton, FL

TITLE	PUBLISHER	PRINTER	DATE	MEDIUM	DIMENSION (PAPER SIZE) IN INCHES	TYPE OF PAPER	EDITION NUMBER	NO. OF COLORS	ORIGINAL OPENING PRICE	CURRENT RETAIL PRICE
SOLD OUT EDITIONS (RARE):										
A Fleet of Buses (Set of 5)	PP	PP	1966	LC	25 X 23 EA	HMP	20 EA		1000 SET	2500 SET
Shoe Box									1200 SET	5000 SET
(One Silkscreen, Seven	PP	PP	1968	SP(1)	15 X 12 EA	AP	200 EA		XXX	XXX
Lithographs, One Aluminum				LC(7)	16 X 13 EA	AP	200 EA		XXX	XXX
Multiple)				MULT(1)	10 X 6 X 7 EA	ALUM	200 EA		XXX	XXX
Magician Suite I–VI	WG	JL/LPI	1976	LC	33 X 23 EA	HMP	60 EA	5/6 EA	270 EA	1800 EA
Black Feat	WG	JL/LPI	1976	LB	41 X 29	HMP	60		270	1800
Red Feat	WG	JL/LPI	1976	LC	41 X 29	HMP	60		270	1800
Beach Scene	WG	JS/SP	1979	LC	26 X 38	HMP	55		270	2000
Totem (Diptych)	WG	JS/SP	1979	LC	26 X 19	HMP	15		180	1500
Box (4-part Lithograph)	WG	IL	1980	LC	41 X 60	HMP	70		720	2000
Prompt	WG	HU	1981	LC	10 X 12	HMP	35		180	1000
Question	WG	HU	1981	LC	30 X 23	HMP	35		540	1500
Impromptu (4-Part Lithographs)	WG	IL	1981	LC	48 X 80	HMP	80		900	2000
Cue	WG	JL/LPI	1981	LC	42 X 28	HMP	75		540	1500
Magic Moment	WG	JL/LPI	1981	LC	31 X 22	HMP	75		450	1500
Stage Set (4-Part Lithograph)	WG	JL/LPI	1982	LC	45 X 61	HMP	75		900	1800
Take it from the Top	WG	JS/SP	1982	LB	29 X 37	HMP	80		450	1500
Paso Double	WG	AG	1983	SP	39 X 29	HMP	65		450	1500
Chalice Portfolio (Set of 4):									1200 SET	2500 SET
Chalice I (Sold Only with Portfolio)	WG	IB/TP	1983	LC	12 X 12	HMP	20		XXX	XXX
Chalice II, III, IV	WG	IB/TP	1983	LC	12 X 12 EA	HMP	40 EA		300 EA	600 EA

The retail prices of the 100,000 limited edition prints quoted in this directory are subject to change. Print publishers, artists and galleries were the direct sources for these quotations. Prices in the secondary market listed as "Sold Out Editions (Rare)" indicate that the publisher has a limited supply of that print or that the print is difficult to locate in the galleries.

JASPER JOHNS

BORN: Augusta, GA; May 15, 1930
EDUCATION: Univ of South Carolina, Columbia, SC
AWARDS: First Prize, Mus of Mod Art, Ljubljana, Yugoslavia, 1967; Carnegie Inst, Pittsburgh Prize; Am Acad & Inst of Arts & Letters, NY, Gold Medal, Graphic Art, 1986,89
RECENT EXHIB: Leo Castelli Gallery, NY, 1988; Margo Leavin Gallery, Los Angeles, CA, 1988; High Mus, Atlanta, GA, 1988; Gagosian Gallery, NY, 1989; Heland Wetterling Gallery, Stockholm, Sweden, 1989; Univ of California, Wight Art Mus, Los Angeles, CA, 1990; Univ of Maine, Orono Mus of Art, ME, 1990; Columbia Univ, Wallach Art Gallery, NY, 1990; State Univ of New York, Neuberger Mus, Purchase, NY, 1990; St Louis Art Mus, MO, 1991; Gagosian Gallery, NY, 1990,92
COLLECTIONS: Victoria and Albert Mus, London, England; Mus of Mod Art, NY; Whitney Mus of Am Art, NY; Albright-Knox Gallery of Art, Buffalo, NY; Wadsworth Atheneum, Hartford, CT; Mus of Mod Art, Paris, France; Tate Gallery, London, England; Nat Mus of Stockholm, Sweden; San Francisco Mus of Mod Art, CA; Stedelijk Mus, Amsterdam, The Netherlands; Hirshhorn Mus, Wash, DC; Moderna Museet, Stockholm, Sweden; Kunst Mus, Basel, Switzerland
PRINTERS: Tyler Graphics, Ltd, Mount Kisco, NY (TGL); Petersburg Press, London, England (PP); Keith Brintzenhofe, NY (KB); Shi Ji-Hong, NY (SJH); Hitoshi Kido, NY (HK); John Lund, NY (JL); Craig Zammiello, NY (CZ); Aetna Printing Co, NY (APC); Alexander Heinrici, NY (AH); Aetna Screen Products, NY (ACP); Aldo Crommelynck, NY (AC); Atelier Crommelynck, NY (AtC); Universal Limited Editions, West Islip, NY (ULAE); Gemini GEL, Los Angeles, CA (GEM); Simca Print Artists, Tokyo, Japan (SPA); Keith Brintzenhofe, NY (KB); Bill Goldston, NY (BG)
PUBLISHERS: Tyler Graphics, Ltd, Mount Kisco, NY (TGL); Petersburg Press, London, England (PP); Universal Limited Art Editions, West Islip, NY (ULAE); Gemini GEL, Los Angeles, CA (GEM); Simca Print Artists, Tokyo, Japan (SPA); Aetna Printing Co, NY (APC); Committee to Endow a Chair in Honor of Meyer Schapiro at Columbia University (CECHMSCU); Brooke Alexander, Inc, NY (BAI)
GALLERIES: Thomas Segal Gallery, Boston, MA; L A Louver, Venice, CA; Castelli Graphics, New York, NY; Marian Goodman, New York, NY; Solomon & Co, New York, NY; Paula Cooper Gallery, New York, NY; James Goodman Gallery, New York, NY; Thomas Babeor Gallery, La Jolla, CA; Gemini GEL, Los Angeles, CA; Donald Young Gallery, Seattle, WA; Magnuson Gallery, Boston, MA; Nancy Singer Gallery, St Louis, MO; Del Fine Art, Taos, NM; BlumHelman Gallery, New York, NY; Janie C Lee Gallery, Houston, TX & New York, NY; Michael H Lord Gallery, Milwaukee, WI; Texann Ivy Fine Art, Orlando, FL; Barbara Krakow Gallery, Boston, MA; Michael Campbell Fine Art, Scottsdale, AZ; Andrew Dierken Fine Art, Los Angeles, CA; Cynthia Drennon Fine Arts, Los Angeles, CA; R K Goldman & Company, Los Angeles, CA; Margo Leavin Gallery, Los Angeles, CA; Tokoro Gallery, Los Angeles, CA; Goodman/Tinnon Fine Art, San Francisco, CA; Graphics Gallery, San Francisco, CA; Graystone Gallery, San Francisco, CA; Harcourts Contemporary, San Francisco, CA; Jupiter Fine Arts, Jupiter, FL; R S Johnson Fine Art, Chicago, IL; Thomas Smith Fine Art, Fort Wayne, IN; Morgan Gallery, Boston, MA; Golden Gallery, Chestnut Hill, MA; John C Stoller & Company, Minneapolis, MN; Leo Castelli Gallery, New York, NY; Gagosian Gallery, New York, NY; Pace Prints, New York, NY; Petersburg Press, New York, NY; Owl 57 Galleries, Woodmere, NY; Elizabeth Paul Gallery, Cincinnati, OH; Jeffrey Fuller Fine Art, Ltd, Phila, PA; Fenton Fine Arts, Fort Worth, TX; Heland Wetterling Gallery, Stockholm, Sweden; Brooke Alexander Gallery, New York, NY
MAILING ADDRESS: 340 Riverside Dr, New York, NY 10025

Field (F)—Gemini (G)—Segal (S)—Sparks (Sp)

Jasper Johns
Savarin
Courtesy Universal Limited Art Editions

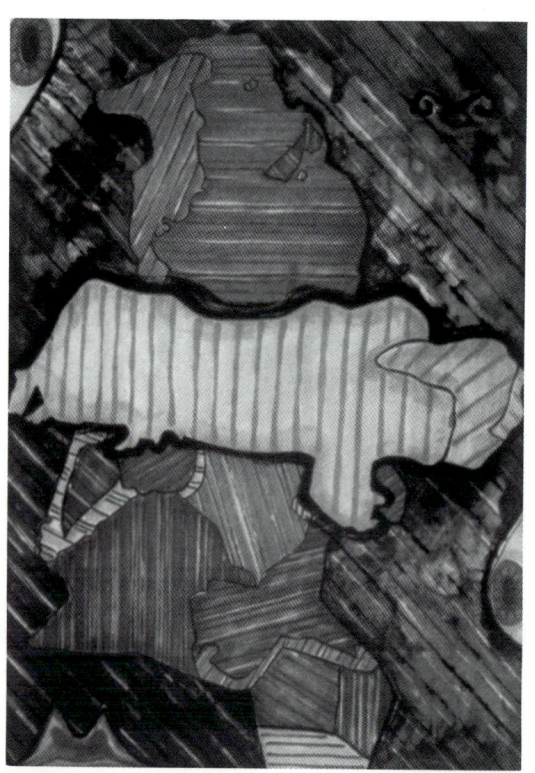

Jasper Johns
Green Angel
Courtesy Universal Limited Art Editions

TITLE	PUBLISHER	PRINTER	DATE	MEDIUM	DIMENSION (PAPER SIZE) IN INCHES	TYPE OF PAPER	EDITION NUMBER	NO. OF COLORS	ORIGINAL OPENING PRICE	CURRENT RETAIL PRICE
SOLD OUT EDITIONS (RARE):										
0 through 9 (F-4) (Sp-4)	ULAE	ULAE	1960	LC	25 X 19	AP	35		300	150000
0 through 9	ULAE	ULAE	1960	LC	30 X 22	JP	35		300	130000
False Start (F-10)	ULAE	ULAE	1962	LC	30 X 22	HMP	35	2	500	175000
False Start II (F-11)	ULAE	ULAE	1962	LC	18 X 14	HMP	30		500	190000
Coat Hanger I (F-2)	ULAE	ULAE	1962	LC	26 X 21	GCP	35		500	80000
Painting with Two Balls I (F-8)	ULAE	ULAE	1962	LC	21 X 17	JP	39		500	80000

JASPER JOHNS CONTINUED

TITLE	PUBLISHER	PRINTER	DATE	MEDIUM	DIMENSION (PAPER SIZE) IN INCHES	TYPE OF PAPER	EDITION NUMBER	NO. OF COLORS	ORIGINAL OPENING PRICE	CURRENT RETAIL PRICE
SOLD OUT EDITIONS (RARE):										
Red, Yellow, Blue	ULAE	ULAE	1962–63	LC	18 X 13	AP	25			
0 through 9 (Presented in a Natural Wood Box) (Set of 10)	ULAE	ULAE	1960–63	LC	20 X 16 EA	JP	10 EA		7500 SET	290000 SET
Skin with O'Hara Poem (with Frank O'Hara) (F-48)	ULAE	ULAE	1963–65	LB	22 X 34	SFP	30		600	35000
Pinion (F-49)	ULAE	ULAE	1963–66	LC	40 X 28	HMP	35		650	30000
Recent Still Life (F-50)	ULAE	ULAE	1965–66	LC	35 X 20	HMP	100		600	10000
Voice (F-59)	ULAE	ULAE	1966–67	LB	49 X 32	HMP	30	2	700	30000
0 through 9 (F-62)	ULAE	ULAE	1967	LC	22 X 20	JP/BL	50	4	500	75000
Target (F-63)	ULAE	ULAE	1967	LC	22 X 20	HMP	28		600	35000
Ten from Leo Castelli: The Critic Sees (Embossed Paper) (F-68)	TP	TP	1967	SP/EMB	24 X 20 EA	RP/I	200 EA		5000 SET	75000 SET
Targets (F-69)	ULAE	ULAE	1967–68	LC	34 X 26	HMP	42		600	60000
Flags (F-70)	ULAE	ULAE	1967–68	LC	35 X 26	HMP	43		600	75000
First Etchings (Set of 6) (F-71–F-77)	ULAE	ULAE	1967	EB/PH/ENG	28 X 23 EA	ALM	26 EA		4500 SET	60000 SET
First Etchings State II (Set of 7) (F-78–F-90):									5000 SET	95000 SET
Painted Bronze	ULAE	ULAE	1967	EB/PH/ENG	26 X 20	ALM	40		500	10000
Ale Cans (F-80)	ULAE	ULAE	1967–69	EB/A	26 X 20	ALM	40		800	20000
Paint Brushes (F-81)	ULAE	ULAE	1967–69	EB/A	26 X 20	ALM	40		800	15000
White Target (F-91)	ULAE	ULAE	1967–68	LC/CO	30 X 22	JP/BR	34	1	600	70000
Untitled (Ruler)	APC	APC	1968	SP	36 X 25	AP	110		800	6000
Figure 8 (G-95)	GEM	GEM	1968	LC	28 X 22	AP	70		600	15000
Black and White Numerals:										
Black and White Numerals: Figure 0 (F-94) (G-87)	GEM	GEM	1968	LB	28 X 22	GCD	70	2	600	20000
Black and White Numerals: Figure 1 (F-95) (G-88)	GEM	GEM	1968	LB	27 X 22	GCD	70	2	600	30000
Black and White Numerals: Figure 3 (F-97) (G-90)	GEM	GEM	1968	LB	27 X 21	GCD	70	2	600	25000
Black and White Numerals: Figure 4 (F-) (G-9)	GEM	GEM	1968	LB	28 X 21	GCD	70	2	600	20000
Black and White Numerals: Figure 6 (F-100) (G-93)	GEM	GEM	1968	LB	28 X 22	GCD	70	2	600	60000
Black and White Numerals: Figure 7 (F-101) (G-94)	GEM	GEM	1968	LB	28 X 22	GCD	70	2	600	50000
Black and White Numerals: Figure 9 (F-103) (G-96)	GEM	GEM	1968	LB	28 X 22	GCD	70	2	600	60000
Target with Four Faces (F-92)	APC	APC	1968	SP	36 X 26	RP	100	7	800	45000
Untitled (Ruler)	APC	APC	1968	SP	36 X 25	AP	110		800	6000
Figure 8 (G-95)	GEM	GEM	1968	LC	28 X 22	AP	70		600	15000
0 through 9: Figures from 0–9 (Set of 10)	GEM	GEM	1968–69	LC	38 X 31 EA	ARJ	40 EA	1 EA	5000 SET	800000 SET
Color Numerals (Set of 10):									9000 SET	800000 SET
Color Numerals: Figure 5 (F-109) (G-121)	GEM	GEM	1968–69	LC	27 X 23	ARJ	40		1000	45000
Color Numerals: Figure 7 (F-111) (G-123)	GEM	GEM	1968–69	LC	38 X 31	ARJ	40		1000	90000
Gray Alphabets (F-114) (G-97)	GEM	GEM	1968	LC	51 X 34	RP	59	3	1000	60000
0 through 9	ULAE	ULAE	1967–69	EC/PH/ENG	26 X 19	RdB	40		800	10000
Flightlight I	ULAE	ULAE	1967–69	EC	26 X 19	AP	40		800	10000
Alphabet (F-115) (G-126)	GEM	GEM	1968–69	LB	31 X 37	GCD	70	2	1000	16000
Embossed Alphabet (F-116) (G-127)	GEM	GEM	1968–69	EMB	30 X 37	GCD	70	0	1000	10000
No (F-117) (G-128)	GEM	GEM	1968–69	LC/EMB	46 X 28	GCD	80	2	1000	20000
Lead Reliefs:										
High School Days	GEM	GEM	1960–69	REL/LD/EMB	23 X 17	AP	60	2	1500	30000
Flag (F-120) (G-131)	GEM	GEM	1960–69	REL/LD/EMB	23 X 43	AP	60	2	1500	60000
The Critic Smiles	GEM	GEM	1960–69	REL/LD/EMB	23 X 17	AP	60	2	1500	30000
Bread (Hand Painted in Oil) (F-122) (G-133)	GEM	GEM	1969	REL/LD/EMB	23 X 17	AP	60	3	1500	35000
Light Bulb (F-128)	ULAE	ULAE	1970	LC	19 X 12	HMP	40	2	1500	15000
Painting with Two Balls (F-132)	ART	AH/ASP	1971	SP	30 X 25	GE	59	2	2000	35000
Painting with Two Balls (Gray) (F-133)	ULAE	ULAE	1971	SP	30 X 25	JBG	66	2	2000	20000
Decoy (F-134)	ULAE	ULAE	1971	LC	42 X 30	R/BFK	55		2500	150000
Fragments—According to What Series:										
Fragments—According to What: Bent Blue, State II (F-138) (G-286)	GEM	GEM	1971	LC	26 X 29	GE	66	3	2000	25000
Fragments—According to What: Hinged Canvas (F-139) (G-288)	GEM	GEM	1971	LC	36 X 30	AP	69	7	2000	8500

JASPER JOHNS CONTINUED

Jasper Johns
0 Through 9 (F-206)
Courtesy Petersburg Press

TITLE	PUBLISHER	PRINTER	DATE	MEDIUM	DIMENSION (PAPER SIZE) IN INCHES	TYPE OF PAPER	EDITION NUMBER	NO. OF COLORS	ORIGINAL OPENING PRICE	CURRENT RETAIL PRICE
SOLD OUT EDITIONS (RARE):										
Fragments—According to What: Bent Stencil (F-141) (G-289)	GEM	GEM	1971	LC	30 X 20	AP	79		2000	7000
Fragments—According to What: Coathanger and Spoon (F-142) (G-290)	GEM	GEM	1971	LC	34 X 25	AP	76		2000	8000
Fragments—According to What: Leg and Chair	GEM	GEM	1971	LC	35 X 30	AP	68	7	2000	10000
Bent U	GEM	GEM	1971	LC	25 X 20	AP	69		1000	8000
Untitled	GEM	GEM	1971	LC	39 X 30	AP	66		1200	10000
Souvenir I (F-156) (G-342)	GEM	GEM	1972	LC	34 X 30	AMG	63		1200	15000
Souvenir (Black State)	GEM	GEM	1972	LB	34 X 27	AMG	16		1200	12000
Screen Piece (F-146)	ART/SPA	SPA	1972	SP	31 X 20	R/BFK	67	8	1200	20000
Zone (F-150) (G-354)	GEM	GEM	1972	LC	44 X 29	ARJ	65		1000	10000
Zone—Black State (F-151) (G-355)	GEM	GEM	1972	LB	44 X 29	ARJ	16	2	1200	12000
Fool's House (F-154) (G-348)	GEM	GEM	1971–72	LC	41 X 20	ALM	67	3	1200	40000
M (F-158) (G-344)	GEM	GEM	1971–72	LC	27 X 19	ALM	67		1000	18000
Evion (F-160) (G-346)	GEM	GEM	1971–72	LC	44 X 29	ALM	64		1200	15000
Device	GEM	GEM	1972	LC	39 X 30	ALM	62		1200	15000
Good Time Charlie (G-349)	GEM	GEM	1972	LC	44 X 29	ALM	69		1200	15000
Viola	GEM	GEM	1972	LC	29 X 43	ALM	70	8	1200	15000
Viola (Black State)	GEM	GEM	1972	LC	32 X 44	ALM	18		1200	15000
Two Flags (Gray) (F-164)	ULAE	ULAE	1970–72	LB	22 X 27	JP	36	1	1500	40000
Cup II Picasso (F-168)	ULAE	ULAE	1973	LC	19 X 12	GPap	11		1200	8000
Decoy (F-169)	ULAE	BG/ULAE	1971–73	LC	42 X 30	R/BFK	31		2000	12500
Decoy II (F-170)	ULAE	BG/ULAE	1971–73	LC	42 X 30	R/BFK	31		2000	12500
For Meyer Schapiro: Target (F-171)	CECHMSCU		1973	SP	12 X 12	HMP	100		1000	15000
Painting with a Ball	ULAE	BG/ULAE	1971–73	LC	41 X 29	R/BFK	31		2000	10000
Flags I (F-173)	ART/SPA	SPA	1973	SP	28 X 35	JBG	65	5	1500	150000
Flags II (F-174)	ART/SPA	SPA	1973	SP	28 X 35	JBG	60		1200	50000
Target	ART/SPA	SPA	1974	SP	35 X 27	JBG	70		1200	150000
Four Panels from Untitled 1972 (F-194–F-197) (G-557)	GEM	GEM	1973–74	LC/EMB	40 X 28 EA	HMP	45 EA		4500 SET	190000 SET
Sketch From Untitled I	GEM	GEM	1974	LC	43 X 29	AMG	50	11	900	10000
Sketch From Untitled II	GEM	GEM	1974	LC	37 X 26	WASHI	50	3	900	10000
Handfootsockfloor	GEM	GEM	1974	LC	31 X 23		48		750	12000
Casts from Untitled—Black States										
Torso	TGL	TGL	1974	LC	16 X 19	WASHI	14	3	750	8000
Casts from Untitled:										
Torso	GEM	GEM	1974	LC	31 X 23	LNP	50	3	750	8000
Face	GEM	GEM	1974	LC	31 X 23	LNP	49	3	750	8000
Buttocks	GEM	GEM	1974	LC	31 X 23	LNP	49	3	750	8000
Leg	GEM	GEM	1974	LC	31 X 23	LNP	50	3	750	8000
Knee	GEM	GEM	1974	LC	31 X 23	LNP	47	3	750	8000

JASPER JOHNS CONTINUED

TITLE	PUBLISHER	PRINTER	DATE	MEDIUM	DIMENSION (PAPER SIZE) IN INCHES	TYPE OF PAPER	EDITION NUMBER	NO. OF COLORS	ORIGINAL OPENING PRICE	CURRENT RETAIL PRICE
SOLD OUT EDITIONS (RARE):										
Four Panels from Untitled 1972 (Grays and Black) (F-198–201) (G-615)	GEM	GEM	1973–75	LB	41 X 32	HMP/G	20 EA	2	2500 SET	200000 SET
Ale Cans (I) (F-202) (G-611)	GEM	GEM	1975	LC	23 X 32	HMP	41	2	750	10000
Ale Cans (II) (F-203) (G-612)	GEM	GEM	1975	LC	19 X 15	HMP	14	2	750	10000
Ale Cans (IV) (F-205) (G-614)	GEM	GEM	1975	LB	13 X 19	HMP	22	1	750	16000
0–9 (F-206)	PP	AC/AtC	1975	EB/A	17 X 14	JBG	100		750	32000
0–9 (Set of 10)	PP	AC/AtC	1975	EB	9 X 7 EA	HMP	100 EA		5000 SET	75000 SET
0 through 9: Figures (Set of 10):										
0–9: Figure 5 (F-207)	PP	AC/AtC	1975	EB/A/SG/OB	16 X 13	JBG	100		750	9000
0–9: Figure 6 (F-207)	PP	AC/AtC	1975	EB/A/SG/OB	16 X 13	JBG	100		750	10000
0–9: Figure 7 (F-207)	PP	AC/AtC	1975	EB/A/SG/OB	16 X 13	JBG	100		750	12000
0–9: Figure 9 (F-207)	PP	AC/AtC	1975	EB/A/SG/OB	16 X 13	JBG	100		750	9000
Fizzles/Foirades (Set of 33) (F-215–F-248)	PP	AC/AtC	1975–76	EB (31) EC (2)	13 X 10 EA	RdB	250 EA		5000 SET	60000 SET
Scent	ULAE	ULAE	1975–76	LC (1) LB/OFF	45 X 35	TRP/HMP	42	4	2400	30000
Corpse and Mirror (F-209)	PP	AC/AtC	1975–76	AC/DPT	11 X 14	GE/BL	50		750	35000
Corpse and Mirror (F-210)	ULAE	ULAE	1976	LC/OFF	31 X 40	GE/BL	58	2	900	80000
Corpse and Mirror (Screenprint) (F-211)	ART/SPA	SPA	1976	SP	42 X 53	MIT/KOZO	65	4	1800	90000
Untitled I (Hatching) (F-213)	PP	AC/AtC	1976	EB/AC	13 X 19	RdB	55		1000	30000
Untitled II (Flagstones) (F-214)	PP	AC/AtC	1976	AC	13 X 20	RdB	55		900	15000
Light Bulb	GEM	GEM	1976	LC	17 X 14	HMP	48		1000	35000
6 Lithographs (after Untitled 1975):										
#1 (F-249) (G-740)	GEM	GEM	1976	LC	30 X 30	RNP	60	11	1800	18000
#2 (F-250) (G-741)	GEM	GEM	1976	LC	30 X 30	RNP	60	12	1200	15000
#3 (F-251) (G-742)	GEM	GEM	1976	LC	30 X 30	RNP	60	11	1200	15000
#4 (F-252) (G-743)	GEM	GEM	1976	LC	30 X 30	RNP	60	12	900	12000
#5 (F-253) (G-744)	GEM	GEM	1976	LC	30 X 30	RNP	60	11	900	12000
#6 (F-254) (G-745)	GEM	GEM	1976	LC	30 X 30	RNP	60	16	2400	30000
Untitled (F-258)	ULAE	ULAE	1977	LC	28 X 40	JBG	53		2000	75000
Savarin (F-259)(Grey)	ULAE	ULAE	1977	LB/OFF	45 X 34	TRP	50	1	900	270000
Dutch Wives (S-1)	SPA	SPA	1977	SP	43 X 56	JP	70		2400	34000
Dutch Wives (S-2)	SPA	SPA	1977	SP	43 X 56	HMP	53		2400	30000
Untitled	SPA	SPA	1977	LC	11 X 8	HMP	60		1500	10000
0 through 9 (G-781)	GEM	GEM	1977–78	LC	6 X 5	HMP	60		1500	45000
Set of 6 Savarins:										
Savarin 2 (Wash and Line) (S-6)	ULAE	ULAE	1978	LB	26 X 20	RdB	42	2	2000	20000
Savarin 3 (Red) (S-7)	ULAE	ULAE	1978	LC	26 X 20	RdB	42	2	2000	40000
Savarin 4 (Oval) (S-8)	ULAE	ULAE	1978	LB	26 X 20	RdB	42	2	2000	32000
Savarin 6 (Blue) (S-1)	ULAE	ULAE	1979	LC	26 X 20	RdB	42	3	2000	40000
Land's End	PP	AC/AtC	1978	LC	42 X 30	HMP	56	9	3600	50000
Land's End (S-13) (G-831)	GEM	GEM	1979	LB	52 X 36	KUR	70	1	4500	50000
Land's End II (Black)	GEM	GEM	1979	EB/A	52 X 36	R/BFK	60		3000	20000
Land's End II	PP	AC/AtC	1979	EB/A	52 X 36	R/BFK	60		3000	20000
Target with Four Faces	PP	AC/AtC	1979	EC	30 X 22	HMP	88	5	4500	50000
Periscope I (G-840)	GEM	GEM	1979	LC	50 X 36	KUR	65		4500	45000
Periscope II (G-841)	GEM	GEM	1979	LC	56 X 41	HMP	28		4800	50000
Usuyuki	PP	AC/AtC	1979	LC	35 X 51	R/BFK	57		5000	70000
Usuyuki (S-25)	SPA	SPA	1980	SP	52 X 20	JP	90		5000	85000
Usuyuki (S-26)	ULAE	ULAE	1980	LC	46 X 15	R/BFK	57		5000	80000
Target with Plaster Casts (S-22)	PP	AC/AtC	1978–80	EB/A	30 X 23	RP/HMP	88		3600	50000
Untitled (S-20) (G-853)	GEM	GEM	1977–80	LC	34 X 31	KUR	60	12	3600	90000
Two Flags (Whitney Anniversary) (S-21) (G-854)	GEM	GEM	1980	LC	50 X 34	AP88	51	7	5000	35000
Two Flags	GEM	GEM	1980	LC	48 X 36	HMP	56	4	4800	40000
Two Flags	GEM	GEM	1981	LC	48 X 36	HMP	45	1	5000	40000
Cicada (S-29–S-34) (Set of 6)	SPA	SPA	1979–81	SP	22 X 18 EA	KUR			18000 SET	200000 SET
Cicada (S-27) (G-923)	GEM	GEM	1979–81	LC	27 X 20	AP88	58		4000	25000
Cicada II (S-28)	ART/SPA	SPA	1979–81	SP	18 X 13	KUR	50		3500	45000
Cicada (G-956)	GEM	GEM	1979–81	LC	26 X 21	DUCH	50		3500	42000
Usuyuki (S-35)	SPA	SPA	1979–81	SP	28 X 45	JP	85		5000	150000
Savarin	ULAE	ULAE	1977–81	LC	40 X 30	HMP	60	4	5000	90000
Untitled	PP	AC/AtC	1981	EB/A	16 X 13	HMP	78		1800	9000
Untitled (3 Black States)	PP	AC/AtC	1981	EB	8 X 6 EA	HMP	25 EA	1 EA	1500 EA	10000 EA
Periscope	PP	AC/AtC	1981	EB/A	34 X 24	RP/B	88		5000	30000
Untitled	PP	AC/AtC	1981	EC	16 X 13	HMP	78		1800	10000
Voice 2 (Trip)	ULAE	ULAE	1982	LC	36 X 24	HANGA	54		10000	160000

The print market has become very selective. For the first time since we published the first edition of The Printworld Directory in 1982, the prices of prints have been greatly reduced and greatly increased for the same artists by the most reputable and established print publishers. Check the fifth edition to understand the movement.

JASPER JOHNS CONTINUED

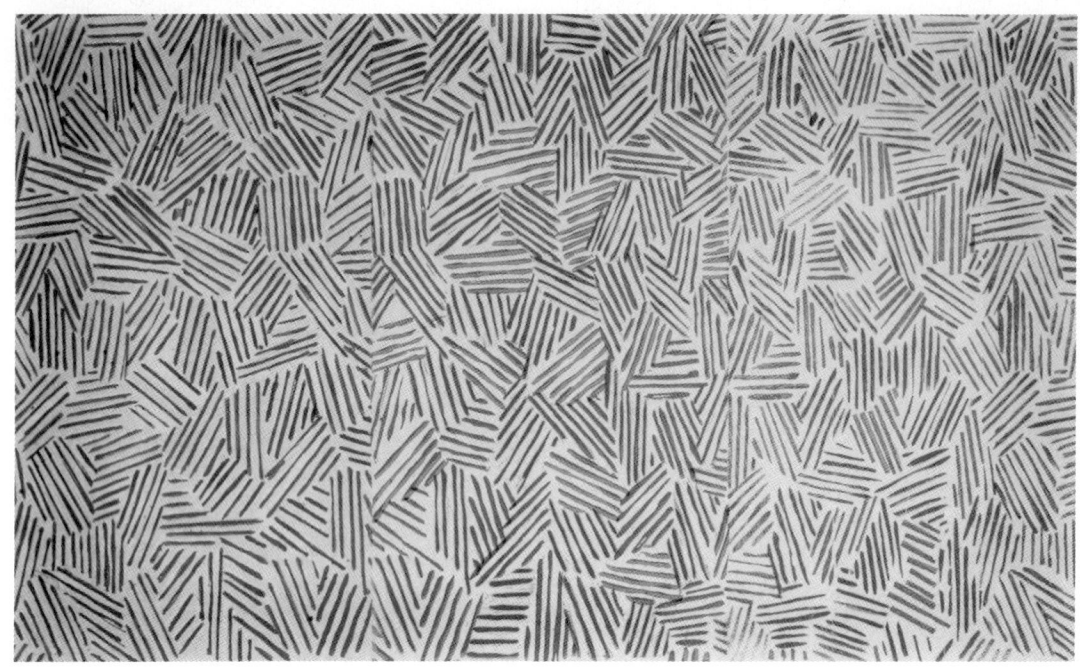

Jasper Johns
Scent
Courtesy Universal Limited Art Editions

TITLE	PUBLISHER	PRINTER	DATE	MEDIUM	DIMENSION (PAPER SIZE) IN INCHES	TYPE OF PAPER	EDITION NUMBER	NO. OF COLORS	ORIGINAL OPENING PRICE	CURRENT RETAIL PRICE
SOLD OUT EDITIONS (RARE):										
Three Colour Etchings:									10000 SET	60000 SET
Untitled (Red)	PP	AC/AtC	1982	EC	42 X 30	HMP	77		3500	20000
Untitled (Yellow)	PP	AC/AtC	1982	EC	42 X 30	HMP	77		3500	20000
Untitled (Blue)	PP	AC/AtC	1982	EC	42 X 30	HMP	77		3500	20000
Poems (Book of Poems by Wallace Stevens with One Etching and Aquatint)	AP		1985		12 X 8		320		3500	12500
Ventriloquist	ULAE	KB/ULAE	1985	LC	42 X 28	JBG	67	8	7500	20000
Ventriloquist	ULAE	KB/BG/ULAE	1986	LC	42 X 21	HMP	69	11	8500	20000
Winter	ULAE	KB/BG/ULAE	1986	EC	16 X 12	HMP	34		3800	20000
The Seasons (Set of 4)	ULAE	HK/JL/CZ/ULAE	1987	I	26 X 19 EA	SOM	73 EA	1	40000 SET	160000 SET
The Seasons (Set of 4)	ULAE	JL/SJH/CZ/ULAE	1989	EB	47 X 33	AP/MUL	59	1	40000 SET	160000 SET
Between the Clock and Bed	ULAE	JL/SJH/CZ/ULAE	1989	LB	26 X 40		50	1		
Untitled	ULAE	JL/SJH/CZ/ULAE	1990	LB	9 X 8		250	1	2000	2500
The Seasons	ULAE	KB/SJH/HK/JL/ CZ/ULAE	1990	I	50 X 45	AP	50	1	50000	60000
Summer	BAI		1985–91	LC	16 X 14		225		2000	2000
Green Angel	ULAE	JL/SJH/CZ/ULAE	1991	EC	32 X 22	JBG/BOX	46	8	20000	25000

TOM JOHNSON

BORN: New Orleans, LA; 1944
EDUCATION: Vancouver Sch of Art, BC, Canada; Univ of Colorado, Boulder, CO; San Francisco Art Inst, CA; Art Students League, NY; Newcomb Art Sch, New Orleans, LA
TEACHING: Vancouver Sch of Art, BC, Canada; Univ of Colorado, Boulder, CO
AWARDS: Vancouver Sch of Art, Fel, BC, Canada; Art Students League Scolarship, NY
RECENT EXHIB: Djurovich Gallery, Sacramento, CA, 1987

COLLECTIONS: Santa Barbara Mus, CA; Crocker Mus of Art, Sacramento, CA; Vancouver Art Gallery, BC, Canada; Mus of Ancient & Mod Art, Nevada City, CA
PRINTERS: Greg Ludlum, Grass Valley, CA (GL); Karen Hellmich, Rough and Ready, CA (KH); Artist (ART)
PUBLISHERS: Artist (ART)
GALLERIES: Knight-Gomez Fine Art, Baltimore, MD; Joyce Kenyon & Associates, Nevada City, CA; Schossig Gallery, Berlin, West Germany; Per Heiberg-Sorgenfri, Oslo, Norway; Connell Found for the Fine Arts, East Haven, CT; Bachtold Collection, San Francisco, CA
MAILING ADDRESS: c/o Heidelberg Editions International, P O Box 370, Nevada City, CA 95959

TITLE	PUBLISHER	PRINTER	DATE	MEDIUM	DIMENSION (PAPER SIZE) IN INCHES	TYPE OF PAPER	EDITION NUMBER	NO. OF COLORS	ORIGINAL OPENING PRICE	CURRENT RETAIL PRICE
CURRENT EDITIONS:										
Joan on Violin	ART	GL	1985	SP	15 X 11	AC	85	1	100	350
The Red Hat	ART	ART	1987	LB	30 X 22	AP/B	60	15	750	2800

TOM JOHNSON CONTINUED

TITLE	PUBLISHER	PRINTER	DATE	MEDIUM	DIMENSION (PAPER SIZE) IN INCHES	TYPE OF PAPER	EDITION NUMBER	NO. OF COLORS	ORIGINAL OPENING PRICE	CURRENT RETAIL PRICE
CURRENT EDITIONS:										
The Guitar Player	ART	ART	1987	LB	30 X 22	AP	60	3	750	2800
The Lady and the Duke	ART	ART	1987	LB	30 X 22	AC/BL	60	1	350	1800
The Acrobat	ART	KH	1987	SP	30 X 22	AC/BL	60	1	200	950
The Smoker	ART	ART	1987	AC	15 X 11	AC	20	8	750	1850
The Striped Cat	ART	ART	1987	AC	11 X 15	AC	20	7	500	1800
Red Poppies	ART	ART	1987	AC	15 X 20	AC	20	7	500	1850
The Prince	ART	GL	1987	SP	25 X 19	AP	60	8	450	1400
The Flute Player	ART	GL	1987	SP	30 X 22	AC/BL	60	1	350	1650
The Red Scarf	ART	GL	1987	SP	30 X 22	AP/WA	60	5	350	2200
Night in Madrid	ART	GL	1987	SP	30 X 22	AP/WA	60	5	300	2400
Head in Hands	ART	GL	1987	SP	11 X 15	AC	85	1	125	250
Woman on Her Elbow	ART	GL	1988	SP	15 X 22	AC	85	1	150	350
Sleeping Youth	ART	GL	1988	SP	15 X 22	AC	85	1	150	450
Sleeping Youth	ART	GL	1988	SP	15 X 22	AC	85	1	150	450
Seated Girl	ART	GL	1988	SP	22 X 15	AC	85	1	200	450
Leaning on an Elbow	ART	GL	1988	SP	15 X 22	AC	85	1	150	350
Leaning Back	ART	GL	1988	SP	15 X 22	AC	85	1	150	300
Young Girl	ART	GL	1988	SP	15 X 11	AC	85	1	125	225
Mardi Gras Mambo	ART	GL	1988	SP	22 X 15	AC	85	1	200	500
Antman	ART	GL	1988	SP	22 X 15	AC	85	1	200	450
Lady with Curls	ART	GL	1988	SP	15 X 11	AC	85	1	125	250
Standing Youth	ART	GL	1988	SP	22 X 15	AC	85	1	200	450
Head of a Man	ART	GL	1988	SP	15 X 11	AC	85	1	125	250
The Striped Cat	ART	GL	1988	SP	15 X 11	AC	85	1	125	350
Man with a Nose	ART	GL	1988	SP	22 X 15	AC	85	1	200	450
Man with a Hat	ART	GL	1988	SP	30 X 22	AC	85	1	450	1850
Man with a Hat	ART	GL	1989	SP	15 X 11	AC	95	1	100	200
Lady with a Polka Dot Necklace	ART	GL	1989	SP	30 X 22	AC	95	1	450	750
Still Life with Room Service	ART	GL	1988	SP	15 X 20	AC/BL	95	1	250	850
The Fish Plate	ART	GL	1988	MM	11 X 15	AP/WA	95	9	200	1250
L'Homme a la Pipe	ART	GL	1988	MM	36 X 24	AP/WA	95	9	1200	3200
Leaning on Her Elbows	ART	GL	1988	SP	15 X 15	AC	95	1	150	250
Man with a Pipe (Study)	ART	GL	1988	SP	15 X 11	AC	95	1	100	200
Woman's Back	ART	GL	1989	SP	22 X 15	AC	95	1	200	450
Leaning on Her Hand	ART	GL	1989	SP	15 X 11	AC	95	1	125	250
Lady with Dots	ART	GL	1989	SP	15 X 11	AC	95	1	125	250
Three Musicians	ART	GL	1989	SP	15 X 22	AC	95	1	200	400
Still Life with Guitar	ART	GL	1989	SP	15 X 20	AC/BL	95	1	450	850
Still Life with Guitar	ART	GL	1989	MM	15 X 20	AP/WA	95	9	1800	2800
Man in the Mirror	ART	GL	1989	SP	22 X 15	AC/BL	95	1	200	450
Lady with a Hat	ART	GL	1989	SP	36 X 24	AP/WA	95	9	1200	1859
Self-Portrait	ART	GL	1989	SP	24 X 18	AP/WA	95	9	950	2200

JOAN JONAS

BORN: New York, NY; July 13, 1936
EDUCATION: Mount Holyoke Col, MA; Boston Mus Sch, MA; Columbia Univ, NY, MFA, 1965
AWARDS: Creative Artists Public Service Program Award, 1972,73,75; Nat Endowment for the Arts Grants, 1973,75; Maya Dern Award, Video, Am Film Inst, NY, 1988; Rockefeller Award, NY, 1990
COLLECTIONS: Mus of Mod Art, NY
RECENT EXHIB: Performing Garage, NY, 1987; Whitney Mus of Am Art, NY; Mus of Mod Art, NY, 1987; Walker Art Center, Milwaukee, WI; Carnegie Inst, Pittsburgh, PA, 1988
PRINTERS: Lilah Toland (LT); Nancy Anello (NA); Peter Pettengill (PP); Crown Point Press, San Francisco, CA (CPP)
PUBLISHERS: Crown Point Press, San Francisco, CA (CPP)
GALLERIES: Crown Point Press, New York, NY & San Francisco, CA; Elizabeth Leach Gallery, Portland, OR; Performing Garage, New York, NY; Leo Castelli Gallery, New York, NY; Electronic Arts Intermix, New York, NY
MAILING ADDRESS: 112 Mercer St, New York, NY 10012

TITLE	PUBLISHER	PRINTER	DATE	MEDIUM	DIMENSION (PAPER SIZE) IN INCHES	TYPE OF PAPER	EDITION NUMBER	NO. OF COLORS	ORIGINAL OPENING PRICE	CURRENT RETAIL PRICE
CURRENT EDITIONS:										
Hurricane Series (Set of 5)	CPP	LT/NA/CPP	1979	EB	23 X 35 EA	R/BFK	25 EA	1 EA	750 SET / 250 EA	3500 SET / 750 EA
Magic Circle	CPP	LT/NA/CPP	1979	EB	26 X 19	R/HW/B	10	1	125	550
Spring Mountain	CPP	LT/NA/CPP	1979	EB	42 X 51	RO/BFK	15	1	400	850
Rose	CPP	PP/CPP	1982	EB	11 X 11	SOM/S	18	1	150	350
Desert Guardian	CPP	PP/CPP	1982	EB	40 X 30	SOM/S	25	1	400	850
Double Wheel	CPP	PP/CPP	1982	EB	24 X 36	SOM/S	20	1	300	850
Double Dogs	CPP	PP/CPP	1982	EB	39 X 44	SOM/S	10	1	300	850
Double Lunar Dogs	CPP	PP/CPP	1982	EB	24 X 36	SOM/S	10	1	300	850

The retail prices of the 100,000 limited edition prints quoted in this directory are subject to change. Print publishers, artists and galleries were the direct sources for these quotations. Prices in the secondary market listed as "Sold Out Editions (Rare)" indicate that the publisher has a limited supply of that print or that the print is difficult to locate in the galleries.

RONALD WARREN JONES

BORN: Ft. Belvoir, VA; July 8, 1952
EDUCATION: Huntington Col, Montgomery, AL, BA, 1974; Univ of South Carolina, Columbia, SC, MFA, 1976; Ohio Univ, Athens, OH, PhD, Art History, 1981
TEACHING: Instr, Rhode Island Sch of Design, Providence, RI, 1988–90; Sch of Visual Arts, NY, 1989–90; Prof, Yale Univ, New Haven, CT, 1989 to present
AWARDS: Mellon Found Stipend, Pittsburgh, PA, 1983; Univ Resident Grant, Univ of the South, TN, 1983; Nat Endowment for the Arts, Fel, Visual Arts, 1984; Southeastern Col of Art Conference, Individual Artist Grant, 1985
RECENT EXHIB: Whitney Mus of Am Art, NY, 1990; Seibu Mus, Tokyo, Japan, 1990; Isabella Kacprzak Gallery, Cologne, Germany, 1988,90; Metro Pictures, NY, 1987,88,89,90
COLLECTIONS: Moderna Museet, Stockholm, Sweden; Baltimore Mus of Art, MD
PRINTERS: Jack Lemon, Chicago, IL (JL); Landfall Press, Inc, Chicago, IL (LPI); Sylvia Karger, Berlin, Germany (SK); Andreas Muhs, Berlin, Germany (AM); Julie Sylvester, Berlin, Germany (JS); PPS Photo Fachlabor, Berlin, Germany (PPS); Lisa Mackie, NY (LM); Deli Sacilotto, NY (DS); Iris Editions, NY (IEd)
PUBLISHERS: Landfall Press, Inc, Chicago, IL (LPI); Edition Julie Sylvester, NY (EJS); Serena & Warren, NY (S&W)
GALLERIES: Metro Gallery, New York, NY; Lawrence Mangel Fine Art, Phila, PA; Landfall Press, Chicago, IL; Quartet Editions, New York, NY; Brooke Alexander Editions, New York, NY
MAILING ADDRESS: 90-96 Stanton St, #3-B, New York, NY 10002

TITLE	PUBLISHER	PRINTER	DATE	MEDIUM	DIMENSION (PAPER SIZE) IN INCHES	TYPE OF PAPER	EDITION NUMBER	NO. OF COLORS	ORIGINAL OPENING PRICE	CURRENT RETAIL PRICE
CURRENT EDITIONS:										
Untitled	LPI	JL/LPI	1990	WC	81 X 26	AC	10		1500	1500
Untitled	LPI	JL/LPI	1990	WC	64 X 26	AC	10		1500	1500
16 Isarstrasse (Unique Photograms)	EJS	SK/AM/JS/PPS		PHG	46 X 34 EA	UN/BN	111	1 EA		5500 EA
Three Color Photogravure Prints (Set of 3)									4000 SET	4000 SET
Jesus Built My Hot Rod . . .	S&W	LM/DS/IEd	1992	PHC/G	20 X 40	STP	50		1500	1500
Rapunzel's Syndrome . . .	S&W	LM/DS/IEd	1992	PHC/G	20 X 40	STP	50		1500	1500
The Fool in His Mirror . . .	S&W	LM/DS/IEd	1992	PHC/G	20 X 40	STP	50		1500	1500

JIM JONSON

BORN: St Louis, MO; 1928
EDUCATION: St Louis Art Mus, MO; Washington Univ, St Louis, MO; Chouinard Sch of Art, Los Angeles, CA
RECENT EXHIB: Burchfield Art Center, Buffalo, NY, 1992
PRINTERS: American Atelier NY (AA); Bud Shark, Boulder, CO (BS); Shark's, Inc, Boulder, CO (SI)
PUBLISHERS: Circle Fine Art, Chicago, IL (CFA); Shark's Inc, Boulder, CO (SI)
GALLERIES: Shark's, Inc, Boulder, CO; Circle Galleries, Pittsburgh, PA & Chicago, IL & Northbrook, IL & Houston, TX & San Diego, CA & San Francisco, CA & Soho, NY & Scottsdale, AZ & Beverly Hills, CA & Costa Mesa, CA & Sherman Oaks, CA & Palm Beach, FL & Honolulu, HI & New Orleans, LA & Las Vegas, NV & Seattle, WA; Ann Jacob Gallery, Atlanta, GA

TITLE	PUBLISHER	PRINTER	DATE	MEDIUM	DIMENSION (PAPER SIZE) IN INCHES	TYPE OF PAPER	EDITION NUMBER	NO. OF COLORS	ORIGINAL OPENING PRICE	CURRENT RETAIL PRICE
SOLD OUT EDITIONS (RARE):										
The Serve	CFA	AA	1980	LC	28 X 21	AP	300		100	250
Tee Shot	CFA	AA	1980	LC	28 X 22	AP	300		100	275
CURRENT EDITIONS:										
The Dance Suite (Set of 6):									400 SET	600 SET
On Pointe	CFA	AA	1978	LC	17 X 14	AP	300		75	150
Cabriole	CFA	AA	1978	LC	17 X 14	AP	300		75	175
Adagio	CFA	AA	1978	LC	17 X 14	AP	300		75	175
Free Spirit	CFA	AA	1978	LC	17 X 14	AP	300		75	150
Arabesque	CFA	AA	1978	LC	17 X 14	AP	300		75	150
Rehearsal	CFA	AA	1978	LC	17 X 14	AP	300		75	175
Grid Iron	CFA	AA	1978	SP	25 X 21	R/BFK	300		100	200
Soccer	CFA	AA	1979	LC	22 X 28	AP	300		125	250
Reclining Half-Nude	CFA	AA	1979	LC	24 X 32	AP	300		125	250
Jumper	CFA	AA	1979	LC	23 X 26	AP	300		125	250
Giant Slalom	CFA	AA	1979	LC	24 X 36	AP	300		125	300
Hockey II	CFA	AA	1980	LC	22 X 27	AP	300		150	275
Secret Love	SI	BS/SI	1986	LC	30 X 22	AP	30		225	450
Mondrian Shadowed	SI	BS/SI	1986	LC	25 X 22	AP	30		225	450

ROBERTO JUAREZ

BORN: Chicago, IL; 1952
EDUCATION: San Francisco Art Inst, CA, BFA, 1977; Univ of California, Los Angeles, CA, 1978–79
TEACHING: Art in Res, Gulf & Western Co, Altos de Chavon, Dominican Republic, 1984
AWARDS: Altos de Chavon, Dominican Republic, 1984
RECENT EXHIB: Texas Gallery, Houston, TX, 1987; Stephen Wirtz Gallery, San Francisco, CA, 1988; Gloria Luria Gallery, Bay Harbor Islands, FL, 1988; Sette Gallery, Scottsdale, AZ, 1989; Betsy Rosenfeld Gallery, Chicago, IL, 1989; Robert Miller Gallery, NY, 1987,89,90
COLLECTIONS: The Newark Mus, NJ; Rutgers Univ, New Brunswick, NJ; Metropolitan Mus of Art, NY
PRINTERS: Chip Elwell, NY (CE); Andrew Bovell, NY (AB); Earl Bovell, NY (EB); Martin Willgohs, Tempe, AZ (MW); Sette Publishing Co, Tempe, AZ (SPC); Bill Lagattuta, Albuquerque, NM (BL); Tamarind Inst Workshop, Albuquerque, NM (TI)
PUBLISHERS: Diane Villani Editions, NY (DVE); Rutgers Archives for Printmaking Studios, Zimmerli Art Mus, Rutgers State Univ, NJ (RAPS); Chip Elwell, NY (CE); School Graphics, Miami, FL (SG); Sette Publishing Co, Tempe, AZ (SPC); Artist (ART); Tamarind Inst, Albuquerque, NM (TI)

ROBERTO JUAREZ CONTINUED

GALLERIES: Robert Miller Gallery, New York, NY; Betsy Rosenfield Gallery, Chicago, IL; Signet Arts, St Louis, MO; Roger Ramsay Gallery, Chicago, IL; Diane Villani Editions, New York, NY; Lisa Sette Gallery, Scottsdale, AZ; Tavelli Williams Gallery, Aspen, CO; Stephen Wirtz Gallery, San Francisco, CA; Gloria Luria Gallery, Bay Harbor Islands, FL; Richard Green Gallery, Santa Monica, CA; Richard Levy Gallery, Albuquerque, NM; Tamarind Inst, Albuquerque, NM; Betsy Senior Contempory Prints, New York, NY; Meredith Long & Company, Houston, TX
MAILING ADDRESS: 303 E 8th St, New York, NY 10009

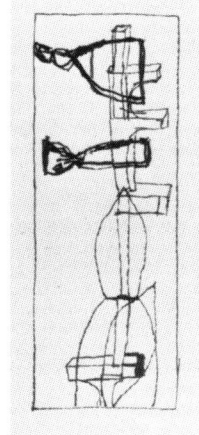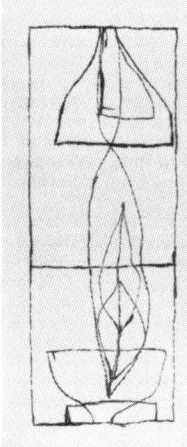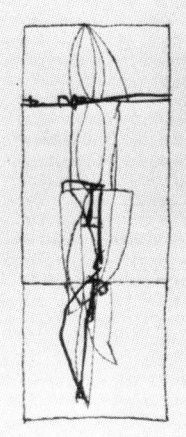

Roberto Juarez
Diving Platform, Tea Bowl and Nail Section
Courtesy Sette Publishing Company

TITLE	PUBLISHER	PRINTER	DATE	MEDIUM	DIMENSION (PAPER SIZE) IN INCHES	TYPE OF PAPER	EDITION NUMBER	NO. OF COLORS	ORIGINAL OPENING PRICE	CURRENT RETAIL PRICE
SOLD OUT EDITIONS (RARE):										
Father & Son (Yellow)	DVE/CE	CE	1983	WC	32 X 25	KOZO	15	2	350	800
Boy with Bird (Black)	ART/CE	CE	1983	WC	30 X 21	KOZO	20		350	800
Father & Son	DVE/CE	CE	1983	WB	30 X 21	KOZO	15	1	350	800
Two Sons	DVE/CE	CE	1983	WB	20 X 25	TOR	15	1	350	800
Boy with Bird (Turquoise)	DVE/CE	CE	1983	WB	30 X 23	KOZO	20	1	350	800
Boy with Bird (Yellow)	CVE/CE	CE	1983	WB	30 X 23	KOZO	20	1	350	800
Juncos	DVE/CE	CE	1983	WC	19 X 13	UDA	18	2	250	600
Sweet Sweat	DVE/CE	CE	1983	WC	36 X 36	SUZ	25	9	600	1500
Southwest Pieta	SPC	MW/SPC	1983	LC	30 X 44	SUZ	50		800	2000
Bellhop	RAPS	CE	1984	PO/HC	32 X 47	AC	40	17	700	1800
Arrowroot	ART/CE/SG	CE/AB/EB	1985	WC	47 X 36	KOZO	40	11	1500	2500
CURRENT EDITIONS:										
Pine Palm	DVE	CE	1986–87	WC	72 X 36	OKP	15		1800	3500
Driving Platform, Tea Bowl and Nail Section	SPC	MW/SPC	1987	LC/CC	44 X 21 EA	OKP-R/BFK	34 EA		1200 SET	2000 SET
Raindrops	SPC	MW/SPC	1987		38 X 25	OKP	34		500	800
Spira Swirl	SPC	MW/SPC	1988		33 X 26	OKP	30		500	600
Cut Flowers (Dipt)	TI	ART/BL/TI	1989	LC	42 X 48	OKP	15	2	2000	3000
The First Thirty Beans	TI	ART/BL/TI	1989	LC	26 X 20	JEP	18	1	450	500

PETER JULIAN

BORN: Buffalo, NY; 1952
EDUCATION: Southern Methodist Univ, Dallas, TX, 1975
PRINTERS: Landfall Press, Inc, Chicago, IL (LPI); Jack Lemon, Chicago, IL (JL); Peregrine Press, Dallas, TX (PeP); Thomas Piper, Wales, Ireland (TP)
PUBLISHERS: Landfall Press, Inc, Chicago, IL (LPI); Peregrine Press, Dallas, TX (PeP); Artist (ART)
GALLERIES: Hal Bromm Gallery, New York, NY; Peregrine Press Gallery, Dallas, TX

Peter Julian
Untitled
Courtesy Landfall Press, Inc

TITLE	PUBLISHER	PRINTER	DATE	MEDIUM	DIMENSION (PAPER SIZE) IN INCHES	TYPE OF PAPER	EDITION NUMBER	NO. OF COLORS	ORIGINAL OPENING PRICE	CURRENT RETAIL PRICE
SOLD OUT EDITIONS (RARE):										
Untitled-Diptych	LPI	JL/LPI	1982	LC	26 X 38	AP/W	30	7 EA	450	800
Broad Axe	PeP	T/PeP	1983	LC	36 X 30	R/BFK	50	2	325	800
CURRENT EDITIONS:										
Untitled (January 1, 1985)	ART	PeP	1985	MON	45 X 32 EA	AP	1 EA	Varies	1200 EA	1800 EA

The retail prices of the 100,000 limited edition prints quoted in this directory are subject to change. Print publishers, artists and galleries were the direct sources for these quotations. Prices in the secondary market listed as "Sold Out Editions (Rare)" indicate that the publisher has a limited supply of that print or that the print is difficult to locate in the galleries.

DONALD CLARENCE JUDD

BORN: Excelsior Springs, MO; June 3, 1928
EDUCATION: Art Student's League, NY, 1947-53; Columbia Univ, NY, BS, Philosophy, 1953, Grad Study, 1958-61
AWARDS: Guggenheim Found Fel, 1968; US Govt Grants, 1967,76; Skowhegan Medal, Sculpture, 1987; Brandeis Univ Medal, Sculpture, 1987
RECENT EXHIB: Paula Cooper Gallery, NY, 1988; Whitney Mus of Am Art, NY, 1988; Galerie Arnowitsch, Stockholm, Sweden, 1988; Whitney Mus of Am Art, NY, 1988; Dallas Mus of Contemp Art, TX, 1989; Arkansas State Univ Fine Arts Gallery, State University, AR, 1989; Chinati Found, Marfa, TX, 1989; Western Washington Univ, Bellingham, WA, 1992; Pasadena Col of Design Art Center, CA, 1989,92; Laumeier Sculpture Park, St Louis, MO, 1992; Edition Schellmann, NY, 1992; Pace Gallery, NY, 1992,93
COLLECTIONS: Mus of Mod Art, NY; Whitney Mus of Am Art, NY; Walker Art Ctr, Minneapolis, MN; Los Angeles County Mus, CA; Albright-Knox Art Gallery, Buffalo, NY
PRINTERS: Styria Studio, NY (SS); Patricia Branstead, NY (PB); Aeropress, Inc, NY (A); Gemini GEL, Los Angeles, CA (GEM); Editions Schellmann & Klüser, Munich, Germany (SK); XPress, NY (XP); Styria Studio, NY (SS); Maurice Sanchez, NY (MS); Jim Cooper, NY (JC); James Miller, NY (JM); Derriére L'Etoile Studios, NY (DES)
PUBLISHERS: Gemini GEL, Los Angeles, CA (GEM); Multiples, NY (M); Editions Schellmann & Klüsser, Munich, Germany (SK); Styria Studio, NY (SS); Prestige Art Ltd, Mamaroneck, NY (PA); Brooke Alexander, Inc, NY (BAI); Artist (ART); Editions Schellmann, NY (ES)
GALLERIES: Marian Goodman Gallery, New York, NY; Rhona Hoffman Gallery, Chicago, IL; Donald Young Gallery, Seattle, WA; BlumHelman Gallery, New York, NY; Peder Bonnier Gallery, New York, NY; Edition Schellmann, New York, NY; Alan Brown Gallery, Hartsdale, NY; Jayne H Baum Gallery, New York, NY; Marlborough Gallery, New York, NY; Margo Leavin Gallery, Los Angeles, CA; Angles Gallery, Santa Monica, CA; Brooke Alexander, Inc, New York, NY; Paula Cooper Gallery, New York, NY; Galerie Aronowitsch, Stockholm, Sweden; Gagosian Gallery, New York, NY; Barbara Krakow Gallery, Boston, MA; Aneri Art Ltd, New York, NY; Simon/Neuman Gallery, New York, NY; Studio 53, New York, NY & Locust Valley, NY; Lawrence Mangel Gallery, Phila, PA; Adair Margo Gallery, El Paso, TX; Charles Whitchurch Gallery, Huntington Beach, CA; Jan Weiner Gallery, Topeka, KS; Scherer Gallery, Marlboro, NJ; Stephen Solovy Fine Art, Chicago, IL; C & L Fine Arts, Inc, Bohemia, NY; Carol Evans Fine Art, Brooklyn, NY; Castelli Gallery, New York, NY; Galerie Lelong, New York, NY; Susan Sheehan Gallery, Inc, New York, NY; Styria Studio, New York, NY; Davis/McClain Gallery, Houston, TX; Rubenstein/Diacono Gallery, New York, NY; Alsuko Murayama Fine Art, New York, NY; Pace Gallery, New York, NY; Ro Gallery Image Makers, Inc, New York, NY
MAILING ADDRESS: 101 Spring St, New York, NY 10013

Donald Judd
Woodcut Etchings, 1974
Courtesy Styria Studio

TITLE	PUBLISHER	PRINTER	DATE	MEDIUM	DIMENSION (PAPER SIZE) IN INCHES	TYPE OF PAPER	EDITION NUMBER	NO. OF COLORS	ORIGINAL OPENING PRICE	CURRENT RETAIL PRICE
SOLD OUT EDITIONS (RARE):										
Untitled (Variant of Woodcut 3-L)			1963	WC	30 X 22	AP	31		200	7500
Untitled			1961–69	WC	21 X 17	AP	10		250	7500
Orange Grid Design Series (Set of 7)				WC	31 X 22 EA	WOVE/W	10 EA		800 SET	8500 SET
Untitled (Box)	SK		1970	SP	22 X 29		100		100	3000
Untitled (Room)	SK		1970	SP	22 X 29		100		100	3000
Untitled	GEM	GEM	1971	SS/AC	23 X 27 X 4		50		600	5000
Untitled (Set of 6)	M/CG	PB/A	1974	EB	30 X 42 EA		35 EA	1 EA	3000 SET 500 EA	20000 SET 2200 EA
Woodcut Etchings (Set of 3):									1200 SET	20000 SET
Woodcut Etchings (DJ0177)	SS	SS	1974	WB	42 X 30	GE	70	1	450	8000
Woodcut Etchings (DJ0178)	SS	SS	1974	WB	42 X 30	GE	70	1	450	8000
Woodcut Etchings (DJ0179)	SS	SS	1974	WB	42 X 30	GE	70	1	450	8000
Untitled	SS	SS	1979	WB/EB	35 X 25	GE	100	1	900	3000
Untitled	SS	SS	1980	EB/A	25 X 29	GE	150		800	2000
Untitled	SS	SS	1980	EB/A	30 X 36	GE	150		800	2000
Folded Meter (Set of 3) (Cold Rolled Steel, Stainless Steel, Galvanized Iron)	SK		1983	MULT	39 X 39 EA	Metal	3 EA		5000 EA	7500 EA
Untitled (Set of 27)	ART	XP/SS	1983	EB	41 X 29 EA	AC	15 EA	1 EA	1500 EA	3000 SET
Untitled (for Benefit of New Museum of Contemporary Art, NY)	BAI		1986	MULT	28 X 28 X 3	AC	40		5000	20000
Untitled Suite (Set of 16)	PA	SS	1987–88	EB	30 X 35	GE	75 EA	1 EA	6400 SET	8500 SET
Untitled (Red Edition) (Set of 10)	BAI	MS/JC/DES	1988	WB	23 X 31 EA	OKP	25 EA	1 EA	12000 SET	15000 SET
Untitled (Black Edition) (Set of 10)	BAI	MS/JC/DES	1988	WB	23 X 31 EA	OKP	25 EA	1 EA	12000 SET	15000 SET
Untitled (Blue Edition) (Set of 10)	BAI	MS/JC/DES	1988	WB	23 X 31 EA	OKP	25 EA	1 EA	12000 SET	15000 SET
CURRENT EDITIONS:										
Untitled #1 (Cadmium Yellow with Black)	BAI	MS/JC/DES	1990	WC/STEN	24 X 32	HANGA	25	2	3000	3000

DONALD CLARENCE JUDD CONTINUED

TITLE	PUBLISHER	PRINTER	DATE	MEDIUM	DIMENSION (PAPER SIZE) IN INCHES	TYPE OF PAPER	EDITION NUMBER	NO. OF COLORS	ORIGINAL OPENING PRICE	CURRENT RETAIL PRICE
CURRENT EDITIONS:										
Untitled #2 (Cadmium Yellow with Red)	BAI	MS/JC/DES	1990	WC/STEN	24 X 32	HANGA	25	2	3000	3000
Untitled #3 (Cadmium Yellow with Blue & Black)	BAI	MS/JC/DES	1990	WC/STEN	24 X 32	HANGA	25	3	3000	3000
Untitled #4 (Cadmium Yellow with Black & Red)	BAI	MS/JC/DES	1990	WC/STEN	24 X 32	HANGA	25	3	3000	3000
Untitled #5 (Cadmium Red with Black)	BAI	MS/JC/DES	1990	WC/STEN	24 X 32	HANGA	25	2	3000	3000
Untitled #6 (Cadmium Black with Green & Red)	BAI	MS/JC/DES	1990	WC/STEN	24 X 32	HANGA	25	3	3000	3000
Untitled #7 (Cadmium Red with Black)	BAI	MS/JC/DES	1990	WC/STEN	24 X 32	HANGA	25	2	3000	3000
Untitled (Horizontal) (Green) (Set of 4)	BAI	MS/JC/DES	1991	WC	27 X 39 EA	OKP	25 EA	1 EA	9000 SET	9000 SET
Untitled (Vertical) (Green) (Set of 4)	BAI	MS/JC/DES	1991	WC	27 X 39 EA	OKP	25 EA	1 EA	9000 SET	9000 SET
Untitled (Vertical) (Red) (Set of 4)	BAI	MS/JC/DES	1991	WC	27 X 39 EA	OKP	25 EA	1 EA	9000 SET	9000 SET
Untitled (Anodized Aluminum in 12 Colors)	ES		1991	MULT	6 X 41 X 6	ALUM	144 EA	1 EA	12000 EA	12000 EA
Untitled (Chinati 1,2) (Dipt)	BAI	JM/MS/DES	1992	WC/SP	24 X 31 EA	TOSA	25 EA	2 EA	4500 SET	4500 SET

JAMES JOSEPH JUSZCZYK

BORN: Chicago, IL; January 30, 1943
EDUCATION: Univ of Illinois, Champaign, IL, 1960–62; Cleveland Art Inst, OH, BFA, 1966; Univ of Pennsylvania, Phila, PA, MFA, 1969
TEACHING: Case Western Reserve Univ, Cleveland, OH, 1966–67; Illinois State Univ, Bloomington, IL, 1979; Ohio State Univ, Columbus, OH, 1989; Lectr, "Understanding Acrylic", sponsored by Binney & Smith (Liquitex)
AWARDS: Ford Found Grant, 1966; Univ of Pennsylvania Fel, Phila, PA, 1968

RECENT EXHIB: Jan Cicero Gallery, Chicago, IL, 1987; Found Constructive & Concrete Art, Zurich, Switzerland, 1991; Galerie Bruno Bucher, Poitiers, France, 1992; ACP Viviane Ehrli Gallerie, Zurich, Switzerland, 1993
PRINTERS: Landfall Press, Inc, Chicago, IL (LPI); Jack Lemon, Chicago; Daniel Burgin, Basel, Switzerland (DB); Flora Pongan, Basel, Switzerland (FP); Editions Fanal, Basel, Switzerland (EdF)
PUBLISHERS: Landfall Press, Inc, Chicago, IL (LPI); Editions Fanal, Basel, Switzerland (EdF)
GALLERIES: Jan Cicero Gallery, Chicago, IL; ACP Viviane Ehrli Galerie, Zurich, Switzerland
MAILING ADDRESS: 74 Grand St, 4th Fl, New York, NY 10013-2253

TITLE	PUBLISHER	PRINTER	DATE	MEDIUM	DIMENSION (PAPER SIZE) IN INCHES	TYPE OF PAPER	EDITION NUMBER	NO. OF COLORS	ORIGINAL OPENING PRICE	CURRENT RETAIL PRICE
SOLD OUT EDITIONS (RARE):										
Juszczyk Suite (Set of 3):									900 SET	1800 SET
Reach	LPI	JL/MM	1980	LC	20 X 34	R/BFK	35	7	300	600
Press	LPI	MM/LPI	1980	LC	20 X 34	R/BFK	35	7	300	600
Gate	LPI	MM/LPI	1980	LC	20 X 34	R/BFK	35	7	300	600
Deep Diamond Suite (Set of 5)	EdF	DB/FP/EdF	1992	SP	60 X 50 cm EA	R/BFK	35 EA	8 EA	1500 SET	1500 SET
									320 EA	320 EA

ILYA KABAKOV

BORN: Russia; 1933

RECENT EXHIB: Marsha Mateyka Gallery, Wash, DC, 1993
PUBLISHERS: Ronald Feldman Fine Arts, NY (RFFA)
GALLERIES: Ronald Feldman Fine Arts, New York, NY; Sloane Gallery of Art, Denver, CO; Michael Kizhner Fine Art, Los Angeles, CA; Marsha Mateyka Gallery, Wash, DC

TITLE	PUBLISHER	PRINTER	DATE	MEDIUM	DIMENSION (PAPER SIZE) IN INCHES	TYPE OF PAPER	EDITION NUMBER	NO. OF COLORS	ORIGINAL OPENING PRICE	CURRENT RETAIL PRICE
CURRENT EDITIONS:										
The Beautiful Sixties (with Michael Grobman (3) (Set of 6)	RFFA		1989	LB	24 X 32 EA	SOM	150 EA	1 EA	4000 SET	4500 SET
Untitled (from the Departure from Moscow Portfolio) (20 Artists)	RFFA		1990	LB	24 X 30	R/BFK	100	1	1800	2000

JOHN C KACERE

BORN: Walker, IA; June 23, 1920
EDUCATION: Mizen Acad of Art, Chicago, IL, 1938–42; State Univ of Iowa, Ames, IA, BFA, 1949, MFA, 1951
TEACHING: Asst Instr, State Univ of Iowa, Ames, IA, 1949–50; Instr, Univ of Manitoba, Can, 1950–53; Univ of Florida, Gainesville, FL, 1953–65; Instr, Cooper Union, NY, 1958; Instr, Parsons Sch of Design, NY, 1964; Instr, Univ of New Mexico, Albuquerque, NM, 1964–72; New York Univ, NY, 1973–77; Sch of Visual Arts, NY, 1977
RECENT EXHIB: Brenda Kroos Gallery, Columbus, Oh, 1988; La Vignes-Bastille, Paris, France, 1989; O K Harris Gallery, NY, 1987,89
COLLECTIONS: Wadsworth Atheneum, Hartford, CT; Brandeis Univ, Waltham, MA; Stedelijk Mus, Amsterdam, The Netherlands; Yale Univ, New Haven, CT; Mt Holyoke Col, MA; Portland Art Mus, OR; J B Speed Mus, Louisville, KY

JOHN C KACERE CONTINUED

PRINTERS: American Atelier, NY (AA)
PUBLISHERS: Circle Fine Art, Chicago, IL (CFA)
GALLERIES: Circle Galleries, San Diego, CA & San Francisco, CA & Northbrook, IL & Pittsburgh, PA & Houston, TX & Soho, NY & Chicago, IL & Scottsdale, AZ & Beverly Hills, CA & Costa Mesa, CA & Sherman Oaks, CA & Palm Beach, CA & Honolulu, HI & New Orleans, LA & Las Vegas, NV & Seattle, WA; O K Harris Gallery, New York, NY
MAILING ADDRESS: 43 Great Jones St, New York, NY 10012

TITLE	PUBLISHER	PRINTER	DATE	MEDIUM	DIMENSION (PAPER SIZE) IN INCHES	TYPE OF PAPER	EDITION NUMBER	NO. OF COLORS	ORIGINAL OPENING PRICE	CURRENT RETAIL PRICE
SOLD OUT EDITIONS (RARE):										
Maija I	CFA	AA	1978	LC/OFF	27 X 22	AP	200		150	375
Diane	CFA	AA	1978	LC/OFF	27 X 22	AP	200		150	350
CURRENT EDITIONS:										
Linda	CFA	AA	1978	LC/OFF	27 X 22	AP	200		150	350
Maija II	CFA	AA	1978	LC/OFF	27 X 22	AP	200		150	350
Judi 79	CFA	AA	1979	SP	29 X 21	AP	300		150	350
Loretta II	CFA	AA	1979	LC/OFF	21 X 25	AP	200		150	325

MENASHE KADISHMAN

BORN: Israel; 1932
EDUCATION: St Martin's Sch of Art, London, England
COLLECTIONS: Tate Gallery, London, England; Hirshhorn Mus, Wash, DC; Israel Mus, Jerusalem, Israel
PRINTERS: Styria Studio, NY (SS)
PUBLISHERS: Prestige Art Ltd, Mamaroneck, NY (PA)
GALLERIES: Jayne H Baum Gallery, New York, NY; Judith Posner, Milwaukee, WI; Nohra Haime Gallery, New York, NY; Ann Jaffe Gallery, Bay Harbor Islands, NY

TITLE	PUBLISHER	PRINTER	DATE	MEDIUM	DIMENSION (PAPER SIZE) IN INCHES	TYPE OF PAPER	EDITION NUMBER	NO. OF COLORS	ORIGINAL OPENING PRICE	CURRENT RETAIL PRICE
CURRENT EDITIONS:										
Cracked Earth	PA	SS	1980	SP	26 X 35	AP	99	6	300	400

ERIKA KAHN

BORN: Berlin, Germany
EDUCATION: Art Students League, NY; Pratt Inst, NY; California State Univ, Los Angeles, CA, BA; Univ of California, Long Beach, CA, MA
TEACHING: Prof, Printmaking & Papermaking, Los Angeles County Mus, CA
COLLECTIONS: Los Angeles County Mus, CA; Denver Mus, CO
PRINTERS: Artist (ART)
PUBLISHERS: John Szoke Graphics, NY (JSG)
GALLERIES: Art Angles Gallery, Orange, CA; Stones Gallery, Lihue, Kauai, HI

TITLE	PUBLISHER	PRINTER	DATE	MEDIUM	DIMENSION (PAPER SIZE) IN INCHES	TYPE OF PAPER	EDITION NUMBER	NO. OF COLORS	ORIGINAL OPENING PRICE	CURRENT RETAIL PRICE
CURRENT EDITIONS:										
Santa Lucia (Diptych)	JSG	ART	1981	EC/EMB/HC	30 X 36	R/BFK	150	6	500	600
Willows (Diptych)	JSG	ART	1984	EC/EMB/HC	22 X 60	R/BFK	175	6	500	750

WOLF KAHN

BORN: Stuttgart, Germany; October 4, 1927
EDUCATION: New Sch for Social Research, NY, with Stuart Davis; Hans Hofmann Sch, 1947–49; Univ of Chicago, IL, BA, 1950–51
TEACHINGS: Adj Assoc Prof, Painting, Cooper Union Art Sch, NY, 1960–77; Hunter Col, NY; Vis Assoc Prof, Painting, Univ of California, Berkeley, CA, 1960–61; Art in Res, Dartmouth Col, Hanover, NH, 1984
AWARDS: Fulbright Scholarship to Italy, 1963–65; Guggenheim Fel, 1961; Am Acad Art Award, Inst of Arts & Letters, NY, 1979; Purchase Award, Hassam Found, NY, 1979
RECENT EXHIB: Grace Borgenicht Gallery, NY, 1989; Kornbluth Gallery, Fairlawn, NJ, 1990; Associated American Artists, NY, 1991; Thomas Segal Gallery, Boston, MA, 1992; Gerald Peters Gallery, Santa Fe, NM, 1990,92
COLLECTIONS: Mus of Mod Art, NY; Brooklyn Mus, NY; Metropolitan Mus of Art, NY; Whitney Mus of Am Art, NY; Los Angeles County Mus, CA; Houston Mus of Fine Art, TX
PRINTERS: Solo Press, NY (SP); Tiber Press, NY (TP); Tamarind Inst Workshop, Albuquerque, NM (TI); Lynne Allen, Albuquerque, NM (LA); Garner Tullis Workshop, New York, NY (GTW); Judith Solodkin, NY (JS); Solo Press, NY (SP); Jon Cone, East Topsham, VT (JC); Cone Editions, East Topsham, VT (CEd); Tony Kirk, NY (TK); Eldindean Press, NY (EldP); Artist (ART)
PUBLISHERS: Solo Press, NY (SP); Hadassah, Westfield, NJ (HAD); Garner Tullis Workshop, Santa Barbara, CA (GTW); Cone Editions, East Topsham, VT (CEd); Artist (ART); Eldindean Press, NY (EldP)
GALLERIES: Grace Borgenicht Gallery, New York, NY; Thomas Segal Gallery, Boston, MA; Carone Gallery, Fort Lauderdale, FL; Stremmel Galleries, Reno, NV; Kornbluth Gallery, Fair Lawn, NJ; Dumont-Landis Fine Art, New Brunswick, NJ; Jerald Melberg Gallery, Charlotte, NC; Associated American Artists, New York, NY; Rothschild Fine Arts, New York, NY; Cone Editions, East Topsham, VT; Arlene McDaniel Galleries/Ellsworth & Wiley Galleries, Simsbury, CT; Gerald Peters Gallery, Santa Fe, NM; M Friedland Gallery, Toronto, Canada & Naples, FL; Virginia Lynch Gallery, Tiverton, RI; Gallery 30, Burlingame, CA; Gallery 3, Roanoke, VA; Nan Miller Gallery, Rochester, NY; Reynolds/Minor Gallery, Richmond, VA; Metropolitan Museum Mezzanine Gallery, New York, NY
MAILING ADDRESS: 32 W 20th St, New York, NY 10011

The retail prices of the 100,000 limited edition prints quoted in this directory are subject to change. Print publishers, artists and galleries were the direct sources for these quotations. Prices in the secondary market listed as "Sold Out Editions (Rare)" indicate that the publisher has a limited supply of that print or that the print is difficult to locate in the galleries.

The Printworld Directory is accepting new applications for the seventh edition. Approximately 300 new artists will be accepted. Please use the two forms provided in the back section of this directory to submit biographical data and documentation of prints. Edition number of each print must not exceed 500 and the retail price must be $100 or more.

WOLF KAHN CONTINUED

TITLE	PUBLISHER	PRINTER	DATE	MEDIUM	DIMENSION (PAPER SIZE) IN INCHES	TYPE OF PAPER	EDITION NUMBER	NO. OF COLORS	ORIGINAL OPENING PRICE	CURRENT RETAIL PRICE
SOLD OUT EDITIONS (RARE):										
100-Mile Barn	ART	JS/SP	1978	LC	15 X 23	AP	135	4	135	850
New Barn Doors	HAD	SC/CEd	1983	SP	22 X 30	AP88	200	6	100	1100
CURRENT EDITIONS:										
Gray Barn	ART	TP	1970	LB	26 X 32	AP	30	1	150	1100
White Barn	ART/SP	JS/SP	1978	LC	20 X 25	AP	50	3	150	1100
River Bend	ART	JS/SP	1979	EB	26 X 26	AP	40	1	300	1100
Near Saxton's River	ART	JS/SP	1979	EB	16 X 22	AP	40	1	300	850
Corral	ART	JS/SP	1980	LC	18 X 26	AP	50	5	300	1200
Twin Barns	ART	JS/SP	1980	LC	18 X 26	AP	50	5	300	1200
Tobacco Sheds	ART	JS/SP	1980	LC	18 X 26	AP	50	5	300	1200
Martha's Vineyard	ART	JS/SP	1980	LC	18 X 26	AP	50	5	300	1200
New Growth	ART	JC/CEd	1982	SP	22 X 30	AP	80	6	400	1000
Trailer	ART	JS/SP	1982	LC	22 X 30	AP	50	5	400	1000
Barn Head-On	ART	JS/SP	1982	LC	22 X 30	AP	50	5	400	1000
Kentucky Barn I	ART	JC/CEd	1983	SP	22 X 30	AP88	60	5	400	1000
Kentucky Barn II	ART	JC/CEd	1983	SP	22 X 30	AP/WA	40	7	400	1100
Kentucky Barn, States (Each Unique)	ART	JC/CEd	1983	SP	22 X 30	AP88	22	3–10	400	1300
Open Door	ART	JS/SP	1983	LC	22 X 30	AP88	50	6	400	1000
Barn and Cart	ART	JS/SP	1983	LC	22 X 30	AP88	50	7	450	1000
Greens and Greys of Summer	CEd	JC/CEd	1984	SP	22 X 30	AP88	60	10	600	1000
House with a Painted Roof I	CEd	JC/CEd	1984	SP	22 X 30	AP88	30	7	600	1000
House with a Painted Roof II	CEd	JC/CEd	1984	SP	22 X 30	AP88	60	5	600	1000
Barn in the Woods	ART	LA/TI	1985	LC	30 X 40	LANA	60	5	700	1400
Flood Plain Farm	EldP	TK/EldP	1987	DPT	13 X 20	LANA	35	3	400	1500
Winter River	ART	TK/EldP	1987	DPT	13 X 20	LANA	40	1	400	900
1000 Points	ART	ART	1991	MON	12 X 24 EA	LANA	1 EA	Varies	2000 EA	2500 EA
Purple and Yellow Cove	ART	ART	1991	MON	12 X 15 EA	LANA	1 EA	Varies	1500 EA	1800 EA

RAFFI KAISER

BORN: Jerusalem, Israel; 1931
EDUCATION: L'Ecole Nationale Sperieure des Beaux Arts, Paris, France; Arts Academy, Florence, Italy, 1955
AWARDS: First Prize, Painting, Adolphe Neuman Award, Israel, 1967
PRINTERS: American Atelier, NY (AA)
PUBLISHERS: Circle Fine Art, Chicago, IL (CFA)
GALLERIES: Gallery 44, Brussels, Belgium; Gordon Gallery, Tel Aviv, Israel; Aberbach Fine Art, New York, NY & London, England; Circle Galleries, San Diego, CA & San Francisco, CA & Northbrook, IL & Pittsburgh, PA & Houston, TX & Soho, NY & Chicago, IL & Scottsdale, AZ & Beverly Hills, CA & Costa Mesa, CA & Sherman Oaks, CA & Palm Beach, FL & Honolulu, HI & New Orleans, LA & Las Vegas, NV & Seattle, WA

TITLE	PUBLISHER	PRINTER	DATE	MEDIUM	DIMENSION (PAPER SIZE) IN INCHES	TYPE OF PAPER	EDITION NUMBER	NO. OF COLORS	ORIGINAL OPENING PRICE	CURRENT RETAIL PRICE
CURRENT EDITIONS:										
Floating Female	CFA	AA	1978	LC	26 X 19	AP	200		50	225
Nu au Divan	CFA	AA	1978	LC	22 X 30	AP	200		50	225

S BURKETT KAISER

BORN: San Francisco, CA; 1946
EDUCATION: San Diego State Univ, CA, BA; Brandes Sch of Art, California Art Inst, CA; Sergei Bongart Sch of Art, CA
PUBLISHERS: Marco Fine Arts, Gardena, CA (MFA)
GALLERIES: Marco Fine Arts, Beverly Hills, CA & Santa Monica, CA
MAILING ADDRESS: c/o Marco Fine Arts, 1633 West 135th St, Gardena, CA 90249

S Burkett Kaiser
Malibu Breeze
Courtesy Marco Fine Arts

S BURKETT KAISER CONTINUED

TITLE	PUBLISHER	PRINTER	DATE	MEDIUM	DIMENSION (PAPER SIZE) IN INCHES	TYPE OF PAPER	EDITION NUMBER	NO. OF COLORS	ORIGINAL OPENING PRICE	CURRENT RETAIL PRICE
CURRENT EDITIONS:										
Malibu Breeze	MFA		1992	SP	26 X 26		195	125	750	750
Sunflowers	MFA		1992	SP	26 X 26		195	125	750	750
Morning Roses	MFA		1992	SP	26 X 26		195	125	750	750

RICHARD KALINA

BORN: New York, NY; May 21, 1946
EDUCATION: Univ. of Pennsylvania, Phila, PA, 1966
TEACHING: Bennington Col, VT; Fordham Univ, NY
RECENT EXHIB: Piezo Electric Gallery, NY, 1987; Elizabeth McDonald Gallery, NY, 1988–89; John Good Gallery, New York, NY; John Davis Gallery, NY, 1989; J B Speed Art Mus, Louisville, KY, 1989; Gallerie Rohmel, Cologne, Germany, 1989; Shea & Beker Gallery, NY, 1989–90; Scott Hanson Gallery, NY, 1990
COLLECTIONS: Indianapolis Mus, IN; Norton Gallery of Art, Palm Beach, FL; New York Univ, NY
PRINTERS: Sue Evans, NY (SE); Evans Editions, NY (EE)
PUBLISHERS: Dumbarton Press, NY (DPr)
GALLERIES: Diane Brown Gallery, New York, NY; Dumbarton Press, New York, NY
MAILING ADDRESS: 139 Bowery, New York, NY 10002

TITLE	PUBLISHER	PRINTER	DATE	MEDIUM	DIMENSION (PAPER SIZE) IN INCHES	TYPE OF PAPER	EDITION NUMBER	NO. OF COLORS	ORIGINAL OPENING PRICE	CURRENT RETAIL PRICE
CURRENT EDITIONS:										
Untitled	DPr	SE/EE	1992	EB	18 X 17	SOM/S	24	1	500	500

JACK ALLAN KAMINSKY

BORN: New Brunswick, NJ; September 8, 1949
EDUCATION: Brooklyn Col, NY, BS, 1972, MFA, 1975
TEACHING: Head, Graphics & Photography Dept, Brooklyn Mus Art Sch, NY, 1973–85; Instr, Photography, Pratt Inst, Continuing Ed, Brooklyn Botanic Gardens, NY, 1985; Long Island Univ, NY, Continuing Ed, Brooklyn, NY, 1985 to present; Ed Alliance, NY, 1985 to present
AWARDS: Brooklyn Col Fel, NY, 1974–75
RECENT EXHIB: Wiesner Gallery, Brooklyn, NY, 1987; Soho Photography Gallery, NY, 1988; Lever House, NY, 1988; Stuhr Mus, Grand Island, NE, 1990; Governor's Mansion, Lincoln, NE, 1990
COLLECTIONS: Smithsonian Inst, Wash, DC; La Grange Col, GA
PRINTERS: Artist (ART)
PUBLISHERS: Artist (ART)
GALLERIES: Ann Kendall Richards, New York, NY; Wiesner Gallery, Brooklyn, NY
MAILING ADDRESS: 1760 Marine Parkway, Brooklyn, NY 11234

TITLE	PUBLISHER	PRINTER	DATE	MEDIUM	DIMENSION (PAPER SIZE) IN INCHES	TYPE OF PAPER	EDITION NUMBER	NO. OF COLORS	ORIGINAL OPENING PRICE	CURRENT RETAIL PRICE
CURRENT EDITIONS:										
The Path	ART	ART	1982	SP	20 X 13	LEN	15	1	100	150
The Mosaic	ART	ART	1982	SP	20 X 13	LEN	15	1	100	150
The Palms	ART	ART	1982	SP	20 X 13	LEN	15	1	100	150
The Trellis	ART	ART	1982	SP	20 X 13	LEN	15	1	100	150
Electra	ART	ART	1982	SP	20 X 13	LEN	15	3	125	175
Phoenix	ART	ART	1982	SP	20 X 13	LEN	15	3	125	175
Pegasus	ART	ART	1982	SP	20 X 13	LEN	15	3	125	175
Apollo	ART	ART	1982	SP	20 X 13	LEN	15	3	125	175
Icarus	ART	ART	1983	SP	13 X 20	LEN	15	3	125	175
Babylon	ART	ART	1983	SP	13 X 20	LEN	15	3	125	175
The Great Hall	ART	ART	1983	XC	9 X 11	LEN	50	Multi	200	275
Roll Those Bones	ART	ART	1983	XC	9 X 11	LEN	50	Multi	200	275
The Guggenheim II	ART	ART	1983	XC	9 X 11	LEN	50	Multi	300	375

BOB KANE

BORN: 1921
COLLECTIONS: Mus of Mod Art, NY; Whitney Mus of Am Art, NY; St John's Univ, Jamaica, NY
PRINTERS: American Atelier, NY (AA)
PUBLISHERS: Circle Fine Art, Chicago, IL (CFA)
GALLERIES: Roy Boyd Gallery, Santa Monica, CA; Circle Gallery of Animation Art, NY; Harmon-Meek Gallery II, Naples, FL

TITLE	PUBLISHER	PRINTER	DATE	MEDIUM	DIMENSION (PAPER SIZE) IN INCHES	TYPE OF PAPER	EDITION NUMBER	NO. OF COLORS	ORIGINAL OPENING PRICE	CURRENT RETAIL PRICE
SOLD OUT EDITIONS (RARE):										
Batman and Robin in the Spotlight	CFA	AA	1977	LC	32 X 25	SOM	300	4	100	1500
Batman Suite (Set of 4)									350 SET	5750 SET
Batman and Castle	CFA	AA	1978	LC	33 X 24	AP	300	5	100	1500
Batman and Robin Running	CFA	AA	1978	LC	32 X 24	AP	300	3	100	1500
Over Gotham	CFA	AA	1978	LC	33 X 24	AP	300	11	100	1500
The Joker	CFA	AA	1978	LC	34 X 24	AP	300	3	100	1500

The print market has become very selective. For the first time since we published the first edition of The Printworld Directory in 1982, the prices of prints have been greatly reduced and greatly increased for the same artists by the most reputable and established print publishers. Check the fifth edition to understand the movement.

BOB PAUL KANE

BORN: Cleveland, OH; July 11, 1937
EDUCATION: Cleveland Inst of Art, OH; Cornell Univ, Ithaca, NY, Pratt Inst, Brooklyn, NY; Art Students League, NY
TEACHING: Instr, Painting & Art History, Montclair State Col, NJ, 1960-70

COLLECTIONS: Cincinnati Mus, OH; Mus Municipal, St Paul de Vence, France; Hirshhorn Mus, Wash, DC; Palm Springs Desert Mus, CA; Pennsylvania Acad of Fine Arts, Phila, PA
PUBLISHERS: Fred Dorfman, Inc, NY (FDI)
GALLERIES: Mangel Gallery, Phila, PA
MAILING ADDRESS: 125 Riverside Dr, New York, NY 10024

TITLE	PUBLISHER	PRINTER	DATE	MEDIUM	DIMENSION (PAPER SIZE) IN INCHES	TYPE OF PAPER	EDITION NUMBER	NO. OF COLORS	ORIGINAL OPENING PRICE	CURRENT RETAIL PRICE
CURRENT EDITIONS:										
Fleurs Nicoises	FDI	ART	1979	LC	27 X 38	AP	225	5	200	350
St Tropez	FDI	ART	1979	LC	27 X 37	AP	225	5	200	350

HOWARD KANOVITZ

BORN: Fall River, MA; February 9, 1929
EDUCATION: Providence Col, RI, BS, 1949; Rhode Island Sch of Design, 1949-51; Art Students League, NY, 1951; New Sch for Social Research, NY, 1949-52; Studied with Franz Kline, NY, 1951-52; Univ of Southern California, Los Angeles, CA, 1958; Inst of Fine Arts, New York Univ, NY, 1959-61
TEACHING: Instr, Painting & Design, Brooklyn Col, NY, 1961-64; Instr, 2-D Design, Pratt Inst, NY, 1964-66; Prof, Painting, Southampton Col, NY, 1977-78; Sch of Visual Arts, NY, 1980-85

AWARDS: Berlin Deutscher Akademischer Austauschdienst Fel, 1979-80
RECENT EXHIB: Parrish Art Mus, Southampton, NY, 1988; Florida International Univ Mus, Miami, FL, 1989; Marlborough Gallery, NY, 1990
COLLECTIONS: Whitney Mus of Am Art, NY; Wallraf-Richartz Mus, Cologne, Germany; Neue Galerie Stadt Aachen, Germany; Mus of Contemp Art, Utrecht, Holland; Goteborgs Konstmuseum, Sweden; Boymans-Van Beuningen, Rotterdam, The Netherlands; Ludwig Mus, Cologne, West Germany; Metropolitan Mus of Art, NY
PUBLISHERS: Transworld Art, Inc, NY (TAI)
GALLERIES: Galerie Inge Baecker, Cologne, Germany; Marlborough Gallery, New York, NY; Hokin/Kaufman Gallery, Chicago, IL; Vered Gallery, East Hampton, NY
MAILING ADDRESS: 463 Broome St, New York, NY 10013

TITLE	PUBLISHER	PRINTER	DATE	MEDIUM	DIMENSION (PAPER SIZE) IN INCHES	TYPE OF PAPER	EDITION NUMBER	NO. OF COLORS	ORIGINAL OPENING PRICE	CURRENT RETAIL PRICE
CURRENT EDITIONS:										
Visible Difference	TAI		1980	LC	33 X 24	AP	125		400	1200
Windmill Antilles	TAI		1980	LC	33 X 24	AP	175		400	1200
The Ground Above Us	TAI		1980	LC	33 X 24	AP	125		400	1200
East End Trilogy	TAI		1980	LC	33 X 24	AP	125		400	1200

SANDRA KAPLAN

BORN: Cincinnati, OH
EDUCATION: Art Acad of Cincinnati, OH, 1960-61; with Julian Stanczak; Pratt Inst, Brooklyn, NY, BFA, with honors, 1965; City Univ of New York, 1968-70, with Richard Lindner, Stephen Greene & Jacob Landau
TEACHING: Instr, Painting & Design, Araphoe Comm Col, 1974-75; Instr, Oil Painting, Emily Griffith Opportunity Sch, 1974-76; Art Instr, Metro State Col, 1977-78; Guest Art, Instr, Denver Univ, CO, 1978-79
AWARDS: Dean's Medal, Graphic Arts, Pratt Inst, NY, 1975; Best of Show, Jefferson Unitarian Church, Golden, CO, 1975; Rocky Mountain Nat Watermedia Award, Golden, CO, 1979; First Place, Rocky Mountain Regional Print Show, Golden, CO, 1982; Ludwig Vogelstein Found Grant, 1986; Phillip Morris Fel, 1986; Yaddo Artists Colony Grant, 1986

RECENT EXHIB: Eva Cohon Galleries, Ltd, Chicago, IL & Highland Park, IL, 1989; Dubins Gallery, Los Angeles, CA, 1988,90; Olson Larsen Gallery, Des Moines, IA, 1990
PRINTERS: Bud Shark, Boulder, CO (BS); Matthew Christie, Boulder, CO (MC); Shark's Inc, Boulder, CO (SI)
PUBLISHERS: Art Group Partners, Denver, CO (AG); Nathaniel Jessup, Denver, CO (NJ); Shark's, Inc, Boulder, CO (SI); Artist (ART)
GALLERIES: Inkfish Gallery, Denver, CO; Ventana Fine Art, Santa Fe, NM; Dubins Gallery, Los Angeles, CA; Janus Gallery, Santa Fe, NM; Parker Blake, Inc, Denver, CO; Shark's, Inc, Boulder, CO; Eva Cohon Galleries, Ltd, Chicago, IL & Highland Park, IL; Olson Larsen Gallery, Des Moines, IA; Quartet Editions, New York, NY
MAILING ADDRESS: 828 S Pennsylvania, Denver, CO 80209

TITLE	PUBLISHER	PRINTER	DATE	MEDIUM	DIMENSION (PAPER SIZE) IN INCHES	TYPE OF PAPER	EDITION NUMBER	NO. OF COLORS	ORIGINAL OPENING PRICE	CURRENT RETAIL PRICE
CURRENT EDITIONS:										
Clivia (SK Dragul)	ART	BS/SI	1981	LC	30 X 45	R/BFK/W	75	6	400	1000
Prickly Pear I, State I	ART	BS/MC/SI	1983	LC	30 X 44	R/BFK/W	50	6	400	1000
Prickly Pear I, State II	ART	BS/MC/SI	1983	LC	30 X 44	R/BFK/W	50	6	500	1200
Prickly Pear II, State I	ART	BS/MC/SI	1983	LC	30 X 44	R/BFK/W	50	6	400	1000
Prickly Pear II, State II	ART	BS/MC/SI	1983	LC	30 X 44	R/BFK/W	50	6	500	1200
Bromeliad I, State I	ART/AG/NJ	BS/SI	1984	LC	30 X 45	R/BFK/W	50	6	500	1000
Bromeliad II, State I	ART/AG/NJ	BS/SI	1984	LC	30 X 45	R/BFK/W	50	6	500	1200
The Gazebo	SI	BS/SI	1985	MON	30 X 45 EA	SOM	1 EA	Varies	1000 EA	1200 EA
The Desert at 4	SI	BS/SI	1985	MON	30 X 45 EA	SOM	1 EA	Varies	1000 EA	1200 EA
Anne's Roses	SI	BS/SI	1985	MON	30 X 45 EA	SOM	1 EA	Varies	1000 EA	1200 EA
Pool	SI	BS/SI	1986	MON	35 X 36 EA	SOM	1 EA	Varies	1200 EA	1400 EA
Bench	SI	BS/SI	1986	MON	35 X 36 EA	SOM	1 EA	Varies	1200 EA	1400 EA
Path	SI	BS/SI	1986	MON	35 X 36 EA	SOM	1 EA	Varies	1200 EA	1400 EA
Canna	SI	BS/SI	1986	MON	35 X 36 EA	SOM	1 EA	Varies	1200 EA	1400 EA
Ginger Shadows	SI	BS/SI	1986	MON	35 X 45 EA	SOM	1 EA	Varies	1200 EA	1200 EA
Barbara's Tulips	SI	BS/SI	1987	MON	32 X 48 EA	SOM	1 EA	Varies	1400 EA	1600 EA
Day/Night	SI	BS/SI	1992	MON	43 X 22 EA	SOM	1 EA	Varies	1200 EA	1200 EA

ANISH KAPOOR

BORN: Bombay, India
EDUCATION: Hornsey Col of Art, London, England, 1973–77; Chelsea Sch of Art, London, England, 1977–78
TEACHING: Art in Res, Walker Art Gallery, Liverpool, England, 1979; Instr, Wolverhampton Polytechnic, Liverpool, England, 1979
AWARDS: Turner Prize, $20,000, Tate Gallery, London, England, 1991
RECENT EXHIB: Ray Hughes Gallery, Sydney, Australia, 1987; Crown Point Press, NY, 1989; Barbara Gladstone Gallery, NY, 1989,90; Mus of Contemp Art, La Jolla, CA, 1992; Univ of Massachusetts, Amherst, MA, 1992; Lisson Gallery, London, England, 1988,93
COLLECTIONS: Tate Gallery, London, England; Mus of Mod Art, NY; San Francisco Mus of Mod Art, CA
PRINTERS: Lawrence Hamlin, San Francisco, CA (LH); Nancy Anello, San Francisco, CA (NA); Daria Sywulak, San Francisco, CA (DS); Crown Point Press, San Francisco, CA (CPP); Tadashi Toda (TT); Shunzo Matsuda, Kyoto, Japan (SM)
PUBLISHERS: Crown Point Press, San Francisco, CA (CPP)
GALLERIES: Crown Point Press, San Francisco, CA & New York, NY; Barbara Gladstone Gallery, New York, NY; Lisson Gallery, London, England; Stuart Regen Gallery, Los Angeles, CA; Marsha Mateyka Gallery, Wash, DC; Adobe Gallery, Albuquerque, NM; David Beitzel Gallery, New York, NY

TITLE	PUBLISHER	PRINTER	DATE	MEDIUM	DIMENSION (PAPER SIZE) IN INCHES	TYPE OF PAPER	EDITION NUMBER	NO. OF COLORS	ORIGINAL OPENING PRICE	CURRENT RETAIL PRICE
SOLD OUT EDITIONS (RARE):										
Untitled #8	CPP	LH/NA/DS/CPP	1988	AC/SB	27 X 20	AC	20		1500	1700
Untitled I	CPP	LH/NA/DS/CPP	1988	EB/A/SB	53 X 42	AC	20		3000	4500
CURRENT EDITIONS:										
Untitled II	CPP	LH/NA/DS/CPP	1988	EB/A/SB	53 X 42	AC	20		3000	3500
Untitled III	CPP	LH/NA/DS/CPP	1988	EB/A/SB	53 X 42	AC	20		3000	3500
Untitled #1	CPP	LH/NA/DS/CPP	1988	AC	27 X 21	RdB	20		1500	1500
Untitled #2	CPP	LH/NA/DS/CPP	1988	AC	23 X 18	RdB	20		1500	1500
Untitled #3	CPP	LH/NA/DS/CPP	1988	AC	27 X 20	AC	20		1500	1500
Untitled #4	CPP	LH/NA/DS/CPP	1988	AC/SB	23 X 18	AC	20		1500	1500
Untitled #5	CPP	LH/NA/DS/CPP	1988	AC/SB	27 X 20	RdB	20		1500	1500
Untitled #6	CPP	LH/NA/DS/CPP	1988	AC/SB	27 X 20	RdB	20		1500	1500
Untitled #7	CPP	LH/NA/DS/CPP	1988	AC/SB	27 X 20	RdB	20		1500	1500
Untitled #9	CPP	LH/NA/DS/CPP	1988	AC/SB	27 X 20	RdB	20		1500	1500
Untitled (Woodblock Prints) (Set of 2):									1500 SET	1650 SET
Untitled #10	CPP	LH/NA/DS/CPP	1990	WC	28 X 24	AC	75	3	850	950
Untitled #11	CPP	LH/NA/DS/CPP	1990	WC	28 X 24	AC	75	3	850	950
Untitled A	CPP	LH/NA/DS/CPP	1991	AB/PIG	54 X 41	AC	5		4500	4500
Untitled B	CPP	LH/NA/DS/CPP	1991	AB/PIG	54 X 41	AC	5		5000	5000
Untitled C	CPP	LH/NA/DS/CPP	1991	AB/PIG	54 X 41	AC	5		3500	3500
Untitled D	CPP	LH/NA/DS/CPP	1991	AB/PIG	44 X 30	AC	5		4000	4000
Untitled 12	CPP	LH/NA/DS/CPP	1991	EB/A/SB	40 X 34	AC	15	1	1500	1500
Racine	CPP	LH/NA/DS/CPP	1991	EB/A/SB	36 X 31	AC	20	1	1500	1500
Mother as a Void	CPP	LH/NA/DS/CPP	1991	AB/PIG	54 X 41	AC	5		5500	5500
Mother of Light	CPP	LH/NA/DS/CPP	1991	EB/A/SB	53 X 43	AC	15	1	1800	1800
Magnetic Field	CPP	LH/NA/DS/CPP	1991	DPT	47 X 38	AC	15	1	1800	1800
Door	CPP	LH/NA/DS/CPP	1991	EB/A/SB	36 X 31	AC	20	1	1500	1500

SUSAN KAPROV

BORN: New York, NY; August 11, 194
EDUCATION: City Col of New York, NY; BA, 1967; Dartmouth Col, Hanover, NH, MA, 1968
TEACHING: Bard Col, NY; George Washington Univ, Wash, DC; City Col of New York, NY
AWARDS: MacDowell Colony Fel, 1971,73; Ossabow Island Project Fel, 1973; Creative Arts Public Service Program Fel, New York State Council on the Arts, 1979–80
RECENT EXHIB: Fay Gold Gallery, Atlanta, GA, 1990
COLLECTIONS: Mus of Mod Art, NY; Metropolitan Mus of Art, NY; Corcoran Gallery of Art, Wash, DC; Mus Boymans-van-Beuningen, Rotterdam, Holland; Nat Mus of Am Art, Wash, DC; Brooklyn Mus, NY; Nat Coll of Fine Arts, Wash, DC; Nat Mus of Am Art, Wash, DC
PRINTERS: Artist (ART)
PUBLISHERS: Artist (ART)
GALLERIES: Laurence Miller Gallery, New York, NY
MAILING ADDRESS: 149 Willow St, Brooklyn Heights, NY 11201

TITLE	PUBLISHER	PRINTER	DATE	MEDIUM	DIMENSION (PAPER SIZE) IN INCHES	TYPE OF PAPER	EDITION NUMBER	NO. OF COLORS	ORIGINAL OPENING PRICE	CURRENT RETAIL PRICE
SOLD OUT EDITIONS (RARE):										
Self Portraits	ART	ART	1975	MON	9 X 14	R/100	30	4	250	800
Remembrance of Things Present	ART	ART	1978	MON	23 X 30	R/100	15	4	225	800
CURRENT EDITIONS:										
Compositions for Night	ART	ART	1982	MON/AC	30 X 44	R/100	15	6	1500	1800

BARBARA KASSEL

PRINTERS: Mike Costello, Santa Fe, NM (MC); Hand Graphics, Santa Fe, NM (HG)
PUBLISHERS: Markel/Tremaine Press, NY (M/TP)
GALLERIES: Markel/Sears Fine Arts, New York, NY

TITLE	PUBLISHER	PRINTER	DATE	MEDIUM	DIMENSION (PAPER SIZE) IN INCHES	TYPE OF PAPER	EDITION NUMBER	NO. OF COLORS	ORIGINAL OPENING PRICE	CURRENT RETAIL PRICE
CURRENT EDITIONS:										
The Tent	M/TP	MC/HG	1990	MON/HC	15 X 22 EA	R/BFK	1 EA	Varies	900	900

The retail prices of the 100,000 limited edition prints quoted in this directory are subject to change. Print publishers, artists and galleries were the direct sources for these quotations. Prices in the secondary market listed as "Sold Out Editions (Rare)" indicate that the publisher has a limited supply of that print or that the print is difficult to locate in the galleries.

DAVID KAPP

BORN: New York, NY; 1953
EDUCATION: Windham Col, Putney, VT, BFA, 1974; Queens Col, NY, MFA, 1977
AWARDS: Hassam Purchase Prize, 1979; Creative Artists Public Service Fel, Painting, 1982; Rosenthal Found Award, 1985
RECENT EXHIB: Anne Plumb Gallery, NY, 1987; Alpha Gallery, Boston, MA, 1988; Feigenson/Preston Gallery, Birmingham, MI, 1988; David Beitzel Gallery, NY, 1989,91,92
PRINTERS: Jon Cone, East Topsham, VT (JC); Cone Editions Press, East Topsham, VT (CEd); Judith Solodkin, NY (JS); Solo Press, NY (SP)
PUBLISHERS: Cone Editions, East Topsham, VT (CEd); Solo Press, NY (SP)
GALLERIES: David Beitzel Gallery, New York, NY; Alpha Gallery, Boston, MA; Feigenson/Preston Gallery, Birmingham, MI; Watson Gallery, Houston, TX; Cone Editions, East Topsham, VT; Solo Gallery, New York, NY
MAILING ADDRESS: 305 Canal Ave, New York, NY 10013

TITLE	PUBLISHER	PRINTER	DATE	MEDIUM	DIMENSION (PAPER SIZE) IN INCHES	TYPE OF PAPER	EDITION NUMBER	NO. OF COLORS	ORIGINAL OPENING PRICE	CURRENT RETAIL PRICE
CURRENT EDITIONS:										
Oncoming (26 Variations)	CEd	JC/CEd	1985	MON/SP	24 X 35	AC	1 EA	Varies	500	600
Oncoming Car	CEd	JC/CEd	1985	SP	16 X 22	HMP	50	1	400	400
Oncoming Cars	CEd	JC/CEd	1987	DPT	16 X 12	R/BFK	35	1	400	400
Vertical Oncoming	CEd	JC/CEd	1987	AB/EB	20 X 18	R/BFK	40	1	500	500
Rear View	CEd	JC/CEd	1987	AB/EB	20 X 18	R/BFK	40	1	500	500
Grid and Sign	SP	JS/SP	1991	MON	29 X 29 EA	AC	1 EA	Varies	1500 EA	1500 EA
The Hill & Merge Portfolio (Set of 2)									1800 SET	1800 SET
The Hill	SP	JS/SP	1992	LC	25 X 36	AC	40	2	950	950
Merge	SP	JS/SP	1992	LC	25 X 36	AC	40	2	950	950

DENNIS KARDON

PRINTERS: Solo Press, NY (SP); Victoria Sclatani, NY (VS); David Keister, Bloomington, IN (DK); David Calkins, Bloomington, IN (DC); Echo Press, Bloomington, IN (EPr); Orlando Condeso, Vinalhaven, ME (OC); Susan Volker, Vinalhaven, ME (SV); Vinalhaven Press, Vinalhaven, ME (VP)
PUBLISHERS: Perma Press, NY (PPr); Echo Press, Bloomington, IN (EPr); Vinalhaven Press, ME (VP)
GALLERIES: Barbara Toll Fine Arts, New York, NY; Vinalhaven Press Gallery, New York, NY; Echo Press, Bloomington, IN; Drawing Center, New York, NY; Simon Watson Gallery, New York, NY

TITLE	PUBLISHER	PRINTER	DATE	MEDIUM	DIMENSION (PAPER SIZE) IN INCHES	TYPE OF PAPER	EDITION NUMBER	NO. OF COLORS	ORIGINAL OPENING PRICE	CURRENT RETAIL PRICE
CURRENT EDITIONS:										
Conspiracy	PPr	SP	1981	WC	26 X 28	KCJP	47	1	350	1000
Death of Marat	PPr	VS/SP	1981	WC	26 X 28	KCJP	47	1	350	1000
Charlotte's Gaze	EPr	DK/DC/EPr	1985	LC/WC	24 X 27	GAS	38	11	550	850
Charlotte's Gaze, State II	EPr	DK/DC/EPr	1986	LC/WC	25 X 27	KOZO	10	1	450	650
Pleasure and Power	EPr	DK/DC/EPr	1986	LC	24 X 31	KUR	38	3	650	850
Pleasure and Power, State II	EPr	DK/DC/EPr	1987	LB	24 X 31	KOZO	16	1	400	650
Critical Mass	VP	OC/SV/VP	1987	AC/SB	24 X 29	HMP	20		800	1000
And Julia's Legs	EPr	DK/DC/EPr	1988–89	LC	25 X 25	KOZO	34	5	850	850
Born Again	EPr	DK/DC/EPr	1989	PH/LB	18 X 23	MOR/BL	10	1	500	500

DONALD C KARWELIS

BORN: Rockford, IL; September 18, 1934
EDUCATION: Univ of California, Irvine, CA, BFA, 1969; MFA, 1971
TEACHING: Lectr, Drawing & Painting, Riverside City Col, NY, 1971–72; Lectr, Sculpture, Univ of California, Irvine, CA, 1969–71, 1986–87
AWARDS: Nat Defense Education Research Grant, US Govt, 1970; Nat Endowment for the Arts Grant, 1976–77
RECENT EXHIB: L J Gallery, Newport Beach, CA, 1989; Irvine Fine Arts, CT, 1990; Lithuanian Art Mus, Lemont, IL, 1990; Works Gallery, Long Beach, CA, 1991; Antoinette A Sullivan Gallery, Irvine, CA, 1992
COLLECTIONS: Long Beach Art Mus, CA; Orange Coast Col, Costa Mesa, CA; Brand Art Center, Los Angeles, CA; Riverside City Col, CA; Los Angeles County Mus, CA; Newport Harbor Art Mus, CA; Laguna Art Mus, CA
PRINTERS: Ocean Works, Medical Lake, WA (OW); Conrad Schwable, Medical Lake, WA (CS)
PUBLISHERS: Ocean Works Limited Editions, Medical Lake, WA (OW)
GALLERIES: Ruth Bachofner Gallery, Los Angeles, CA; Hunsaker/Schlessinger Gallery, Los Angeles, CA; Marilyn Pink/Master Prints & Drawings, Los Angeles, CA; Works Gallery, Long Beach, CA; Antoinette A Sullivan Gallery, Irvine, CA
MAILING ADDRESS: 202-K E Stevens, Santa Ana, CA 92707

TITLE	PUBLISHER	PRINTER	DATE	MEDIUM	DIMENSION (PAPER SIZE) IN INCHES	TYPE OF PAPER	EDITION NUMBER	NO. OF COLORS	ORIGINAL OPENING PRICE	CURRENT RETAIL PRICE
SOLD OUT EDITIONS (RARE):										
Shikan	OW	CS/OW	1982	LB	23 X 30	R/BFK	20	1	250	750
CURRENT EDITIONS:										
Head	ART	ART	1965	WC	18 X 12	RICE	20	3	35	750
Figure	ART	ART	1967	WE	24 X 18	RICE	10	3	50	750
Untitled	ART	ART	1967	SP	24 X 18	STP	50	2	35	600
Figure	ART	ART	1967	SP	19 X 24	STP	5	Multi	150	950
Artichoke	ART	ART	1968	SP	24 X 19	STP	49	2	35	650
Judy	ART	ART	1968	SP	24 X 19	STP	15	2	50	900
Head of Girl	ART	ART	1968	WB	24 X 18	STP	47	1	35	900
Cicada	OW	CS/OW	1982	LC	23 X 30	R/BFK	20	3	275	650
Momoyama Razzmataz (Trip)	OW	CS/OW	1982	LC	41 X 89	R/BFK	20	3	1200	3000
Edo Boogie-Woogie	ART	ART	1986	E	12 X 16	MASA/RICE	20	7	275	575

RICHARD C KARWOSKI

BORN: Brooklyn, NY; October 3, 1938
EDUCATION: Pratt Inst, Brooklyn, NY, BA, 1961, Studied with Richard Lindner & Jacob Landau; Columbia Univ, NY, MA, 1963
TEACHING: Prof, Art, Painting & Design, New York City Tech Col, City Univ of New York, Brooklyn, NY, 1969 to present
AWARDS: Purchase Prize, Prints USA, 1982; President's Award, Oklahoma Watercolor Soc, NY, 1984; Saltzman Award, Nat Arts Club, 1985; Purchase Award, Kutztown Univ, PA 1985; New York City Tech Col, Outstanding Scholar Award, 1989
RECENT EXHIB: Wagner Col, Staten Island, NY, 1987; Retrosp, Ashwagh Hall, Springs, East Hampton, NY, 1988; Gallery East, East Hampton, NY, 1988; New York City Tech Col, Brooklyn, NY, 1988; Guild Hall Mus, Leidy Gallery, East Hampton, NY, 1988; Nat Arts Club, NY, 1988; Montauk Chamber of Commerce, NY, 1989; Elaine Benson Gallery, Bridgehampton, NY, 1989
COLLECTIONS: Newark Mus, NJ; Wichita Mus, KS; Everson Mus, Syracuse, NY; Heckscher Mus, Huntington, NY; Univ of Pennsylvania, Phila, PA; Detroit Art Inst, MI; Butler Inst of Am Art, Youngstown, OH; Guild Hall Mus, East Hampton, NY; Everhart Mus, Scranton, PA; Kosciuszko Found, NY; Helen Foresman Spencer Mus of Art, Lawrence, KS; Tennessee Fine Art Center, Nashville, TN; Arkansas Fine Art Center, Little Rock, AR; Oklahoma Art Center, Oklahoma City, OK; Portland Mus, ME; Asheville Art Mus, NC; Tyler Art Gallery, State Univ of New York, Oswego, NY; Pratt Inst, NY; New York City Tech Col, Brooklyn, NY; Univ of Pennsylvania, Phila, PA; Kutztown Univ, PA; Salmagundi Club, NY; Library of Congress, Wash, DC; Tyler Art Gallery, State Univ of New York, Oswego, NY; Bryant Library, Roslyn, NY
PRINTERS: American Atelier, NY (AA)
PUBLISHERS: Circle Fine Art, Chicago, IL (CFA); Art Prints, NY (AP); Artist (ART)
GALLERIES: Gallery East, East Hampton, NY; Elaine Benson Gallery, Bridgehampton, NY; Nancy Stein Art Consultant, New York, NY; Reece Gallery, New York, NY; Images Gallery, Toledo, OH; The Art Collector, San Diego, CA; The Frame Shop, East Hampton, NY; Circle Galleries, Chicago, IL & New York, NY & San Diego, CA & San Francisco, CA & Scottsdale, AZ & Costa Mesa, CA & Beverly Hills, CA & Sherman Oaks, CA & Palm Beach, FL & Honolulu, HI & Northbrook, IL & New Orleans, LA & Las Vegas, NV & Pittsburgh, PA & Houston, TX & Seattle, WA
MAILING ADDRESS: 28 E 4th St, New York, NY 10003

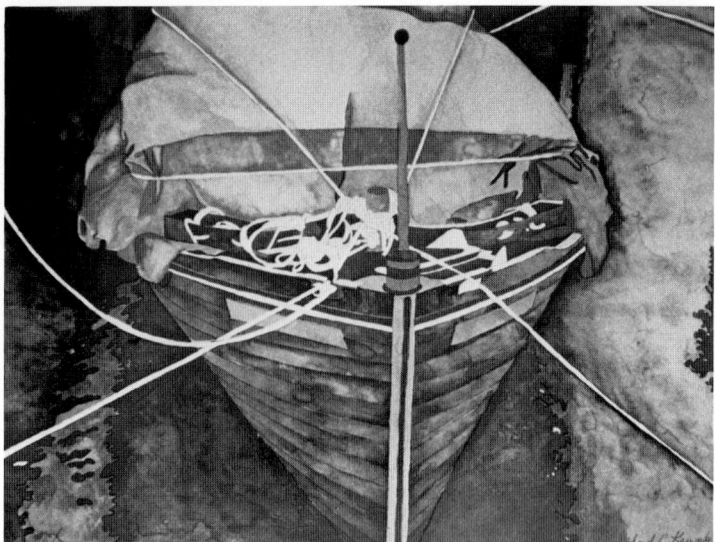

Richard C Karwoski
At the Marina
Courtesy the Artist

TITLE	PUBLISHER	PRINTER	DATE	MEDIUM	DIMENSION (PAPER SIZE) IN INCHES	TYPE OF PAPER	EDITION NUMBER	NO. OF COLORS	ORIGINAL OPENING PRICE	CURRENT RETAIL PRICE
SOLD OUT EDITIONS (RARE):										
Trees in Washington Square	CFA	AA	1980	LC	22 X 30	SOM	300	6	200	400
Another October	CFA	AA	1980	LC	22 X 30	R/BFK	300	10	200	400
All Apples	CFA	AA	1980	LC	22 X 30	SOM	300	10	200	400
Sunflower #1	CFA	AA	1980	LC	22 X 30	SOM	300	9	200	400
A Dream Pang	CFA	AA	1981	LC	22 X 30	SOM	300	10	200	400
CURRENT EDITIONS:										
Marigold Garden	AP	AA	1983	LC	22 X 30	SOM	250	12	300	350
At the Marina	AP	AA	1983	LC	22 X 30	SOM	250	12	300	350
All Boats	ART	AA	1983	LC	22 X 30	SOM	250	12	300	400

DEBORAH KASS

BORN: San Antonio, TX; 1952
EDUCATION: Art Students League, NY, 1968–70; Whitney Mus, Independent Study Program, NY, 1972; Carnegie-Mellon Univ, Pittsburgh, PA, MFA, 1974
TEACHING: Distinguished Vis Artist, Rhode Island Sch of Design, Providence, RI, 1990
AWARDS: Nat Endowment for the Arts Fel, Painting, 1987
RECENT EXHIB: Joy Moos Gallery, Miami, FL, 1987; Scott Hanson Gallery, NY, 1988; Simon Watson Gallery, NY, 1989–90
COLLECTIONS: Guggenheim Mus, NY; Cincinnati Mus, OH; La Jolla Mus, CA
PRINTERS: David Keister, Bloomington, IN (DK); David Calkins, Bloomington, IN (DC); Echo Press, Bloomington, IN (EPr)
PUBLISHERS: Echo Press, Bloomington, IN (EPr)
GALLERIES: Joy Moos Gallery, Miami, FL; Echo Press, Bloomington, IN; Simon Watson Gallery, New York, NY

TITLE	PUBLISHER	PRINTER	DATE	MEDIUM	DIMENSION (PAPER SIZE) IN INCHES	TYPE OF PAPER	EDITION NUMBER	NO. OF COLORS	ORIGINAL OPENING PRICE	CURRENT RETAIL PRICE
CURRENT EDITIONS:										
Sense and Sensibility (2 Sheets)	EPr	DK/DC/EPr	1987	LC/WC	18 X 23	AP88	26	11	500	650
Untitled	EPr	DK/DC/EPr	1987	LC/WC	17 X 44	R/BFK/W	22	8	500	550

BERNARD KASSOY

BORN: New York, NY; (1914–1990)
EDUCATION: City Col of NY, BS, 1935, MS, 1936; Cooper Union Art Sch, 1937, with Isaac Soyer
TEACHING: Instr, Fine Arts, High Sch of Music & Art, NY, 1939–72; Instr, Lithography, City Col of New York, NY, 1966–67; Instr, Lithography, Nat Acad of Design, NY, 1968, Instr, Painting, Harriet Febland, Advanced Painters Workshop, New Rochelle, NY, 1974 to present
AWARDS: Merit Award, Art Directors Club, NY, 1979; Award of Merit Award, Pastel, Am Soc of Contemp Artists, 1981; Award, Painting, Am Soc of Contemp Artists, 1984; Florian Kramer Mem Award, Painting, City Col of Art, Alumni Exhib, 1985; Artist's Fel, Virginia Center for the Creative Arts, Richmond, VA, 1986,88

BERNARD KASSOY CONTINUED

COLLECTIONS: Butler Inst of Am Art, Youngstown, OH; Slater Mem Mus, Norwich, CT; Univ of Georgia Mus of Art, Athens, GA
PRINTERS: Il Bisonte, Florence, Italy (IB); Graphic Workshop, Piestrasanta, Italy (GW); Artist (ART)
PUBLISHERS: Artist (ART)
GALLERIES: Ward-Nasse Gallery, New York, NY; Pioneer Gallery, Cooperstown, NY
MAILING ADDRESS: c/o Estate of Bernard Kassoy, Route 1, Box 74, Burlington, NY 13315

TITLE	PUBLISHER	PRINTER	DATE	MEDIUM	DIMENSION (PAPER SIZE) IN INCHES	TYPE OF PAPER	EDITION NUMBER	NO. OF COLORS	ORIGINAL OPENING PRICE	CURRENT RETAIL PRICE
CURRENT EDITIONS:										
Monte Altissimmo	ART	JB	1970	LB/ZINC	12 X 15	AP	20	1	125	200
Portrait of the Artist	ART	ART	1975	WB	11 X 12	AP	20	1	150	250
Mountains, Red Sun	ART	ART	1975	WC	7 X 7	AP	20	4	150	250
Visions, I	ART	ART	1975	WB	12 X 18	AP	10	1	150	250
Visions, II	ART	ART	1975	WB	14 X 16	AP	10	1	150	250
Black Sun	ART	ART	1975	WB	6 X 12	AP	10	1	150	250
Flute Player (Version 1)	ART	ART	1976	WB	13 X 15	AP	20	1	150	250
Flute Player (Version 2)	ART	ART	1976	WC	13 X 15	AP	20	3	150	250
Untitled Abstract	ART	ART	1976	AC	10 X 14	AP	20	4	175	250
Mountainscape	ART	GW	1976	EB/A/ZINC	4 X 14	MAG/RAG	20	1	125	200
Abstract I, '76	ART	GW	1976	A/ZINC	10 X 14	MAG/RAG	20	1	125	200
Visions, III	ART	ART	1977	WB	14 X 16	AP	10	1	150	250
Visions, IV	ART	ART	1977	WB	13 X 15	AP	10	1	150	250
Woman	ART	ART	1983	WB	9 X 23	SEK/RICE	20	1	175	250
Decoration I	ART	ART	1983	I/ZINC	10 X 14	RR	20	4	125	200
Decoration II	ART	ART	1983	I/ZINC	7 X 14	RR	20	4	125	200
Pond	ART	ART	1983	EB/ZINC	8 X 10	SEK/RICE	20	1	125	200
Trees	ART	ART	1983	DPT/ZINC	5 X 6	SEK/RICE	20	1	125	200
Triptych	ART	ART	1984	EB/A/ZINC	8 X 14	SEK/RICE	20	2	125	200
Helicopter	ART	ART	1984	EB/A/ZINC	9 X 12	SEK/RICE	20	1	125	200

KARL ALBERT KASTEN

BORN: San Francisco, CA; March 5, 1916
EDUCATION: Marin Col, CA; Univ of California, Berkeley, CA, AB, MA; Univ of Iowa, Iowa City, IA; Hans Hofmann Sch of Art, NY
TEACHING: Instr, Painting & Drawing, Univ of Michigan, Ann Arbor, MI, 1946–47; Asst Prof, Painting & Drawing, San Francisco State Col, CA, 1947–50; Prof, Painting & Graphics, Univ of California, Berkeley, CA, 1950–82, Prof Emeritus, Art, 1983 to present
AWARDS: Purchase Prize, Oakland Art Mus, Women's Bd, Western Painters Exhib, 1954; Tamarind Lithography Fel, 1968; Creative Arts Inst Fel, 1964,71; Humanities Research Fel, 1971
COLLECTIONS: Mus of Mod Art, NY; Los Angeles County Art Mus, CA; Victoria & Albert Mus, London, England; Pasadena Art Mus, CA; San Francisco Mus of Mod Art, CA; Oakland Mus, CA; Musee des Beaux Arts, Rennes, France; Auckland City Mus, New Zealand; New York Public Library, NY; Mills Col, Oakland, CA; Univ of Oklahoma, Oklahoma City, OK
PRINTERS: Giorgio Upiglio, Milan, Italy (GU); Giorgio Upiglio Press, Milan, Italy (GUP); Artist (ART)
PUBLISHERS: Grafica Uno Press, Milan, Italy (GUP); Giorgio Upiglio Press, Milan, Italy (GUP); Artist (ART)
GALLERIES: Gallerita, Milan, Italy; Galerie G Linder Basle, Switzerland; Wenniger Graphics, Boston, MA; Gallerita, Milan, Italy; Holloway Howard Gallery, San Francisco, CA
MAILING ADDRESS: 1884 San Lorenzo Ave, Berkeley, CA 94707

TITLE	PUBLISHER	PRINTER	DATE	MEDIUM	DIMENSION (PAPER SIZE) IN INCHES	TYPE OF PAPER	EDITION NUMBER	NO. OF COLORS	ORIGINAL OPENING PRICE	CURRENT RETAIL PRICE
CURRENT EDITIONS:										
High Tor II	GUP	GU	1979	DPT	22 X 30	R/BFK	30	1	250	350
St George V	GUP	GU	1979	COL	20 X 20	IT	30	3	200	250
Sky-Lab	GUP	GU	1979	COL	20 X 20	IT	30	2	200	250
Demeter	GUP	GU	1979	COL	7 DIA	IT	30	2	150	200
Campanile Summer	ART	ART	1980	DPT/HC	6 X 7	R/BFK	20	Multi	100	150
Byzantium II	ART	ART	1981	COL	16 X 24	R/BFK	1	2	400	450
The City	ART	ART	1982	DPT	18 X 24	AP	30	2	200	250
Verdi	ART	ART	1982	COL	16 X 20	AP	30	3	225	250
Kachina-B	ART	ART	1982	COL	18 X 11	AP	30	2	200	250
Kachina-C	ART	ART	1982	COL	17 X 11	AP	30	2	200	250
Lac	ART	ART	1982	COL	9 X 11	AP	30	3	100	150
Campanile Blue	ART	ART	1983	COL	16 X 20	AP	30	2	100	150
San Francisco Skyline	ART	ART	1988	COL	20 X 24	R/BFK	5	3	300	300
Trastevere	GUP	GU	1988	DPT	11 X 13	ITALIA	30	1	200	200
Pisa	GUP	GU	1988	COL	18 X 18	ITALIA	30	1	300	300
Torre di Giotto	GUP	GU	1988	COL	18 X 18	ITALIA	30	1	300	300
St George Unhorsed	GUP	GU	1989	DPT	8 X 8	ITALIA	15	2	100	100
Bay Bridge	GUP	GU	1989	DPT	9 X 12	ITALIA	30	1	200	200
St George & Horse	ART	ART	1990	COL	16 X 20	R/BFK	20	4	350	350
Sara	ART	ART	1991	COL	20 X 18	R/BFK	20	2	250	250
Celia	ART	ART	1991	COL	18 X 20	R/BFK	30	1	200	200
Jan	ART	ART	1991	DPT	15 X 20	R/BFK	10	3	150	175
Lu	GUP	GU	1991	COL	15 X 20	ITALIA	20	3	250	250
Bix	GUP	GU	1992	COL	12 X 13	ITALIA	20	1	175	175

The retail prices of the 100,000 limited edition prints quoted in this directory are subject to change. Print publishers, artists and galleries were the direct sources for these quotations. Prices in the secondary market listed as "Sold Out Editions (Rare)" indicate that the publisher has a limited supply of that print or that the print is difficult to locate in the galleries.

ALEX KATZ

BORN: New York, NY; July 24, 1927
EDUCATION: Cooper Union Art Sch, NY, 1946–49; Skowhegan Sch of Painting & Sculpture, ME, 1949–50; Colby Col, ME, Hon PhD, 1985
TEACHING: Adj Prof, Yale Univ, New Haven, CT, 1962–63; Prof, New York Univ, NY, 1983–84
AWARDS: Guggenheim Fel, 1972; Saint Gaudens Medal, 1980; Cooper Union Skowhegan Award, ME, 1980
RECENT EXHIB: New York State Mus Cultural Education Center, Albany, NY, 1987; Rahr-West Art Mus, Manitowoc, WI, 1987; Brooklyn Mus, NY, 1988; North Dakota Mus of Art, Grand Forks, ND, 1989; Masur Mus of Art, Monroe, LA, 1989; Munson-Williams-Proctor Inst, Sch of Art, Utica, NY, 1989; Arkansas Arts Center, Little Rock, AR, 1992; Southeast Arkansas Arts & Sciences Center, Pine Bluff, AR, 1992; Univ of Colorado, Colorado Springs, CO, 1992; Sioux City Art Center, IA, 1989,92; Masur Mus of Art, Monroe, LA, 1989,92; Colby Col, Waterville, ME, 1987,92; Marlborough Gallery, NY, 1987,88,89,90,92; Rubenstein/Diacono Gallery, NY, 1993; Allene Lapides Gallery, Santa Fe, NM, 1993
COLLECTIONS: Metropolitan Mus of Art, NY; Mus of Mod Art, NY; Whitney Mus of Am Art, NY; NY Univ, NY; Boston Mus of Fine Arts, MA; Fogg Art Mus, Harvard Univ, MA; Art Inst of Chicago, IL; Cincinnati Mus of Art, OH; Hirshhorn Mus of Art, Wash, DC; Dartmouth Col of Mus, Hanover, NH; Wadsworth Atheneum, Hartford, CT; Allentown Art Mus, PA; Brandeis Univ, Waltham, MA; New Jersey State Mus, Trenton, NJ; Worcester Mus, MA; Tate Gallery, London, England; Butler Inst of Am Art, Youngstown, OH
PRINTERS: Mourlot, Paris, France (M); Chiron Press, NY (CP); Paul Narkiewicz (PN); H Nakazato (HN); P Laucheron (PL); Styria Studios, NY (SS); Simca Print Artists, Tokyo, Japan (SPA); Chris Erikson, NY (CE); Chip Elwell, NY (CE); Patricia Branstead, NY (PB); Aeropress, NY (A); Nancy Brokopp, NY (NB); Sienna Studio, NY (SiS); Brand X, NY (BX); Jeryl Parker Editions, NY (JPE); American Atelier, NY (AA); Crown Point Press, San Francisco, CA (CPP); John Erickson, NY (JE); Aldo Crommelynck, NY (AC); Atelier Crommelynck, NY (AtC); Bernard Manhertz, NY (BM); Styria Studio, NY (SS); Doris Simmelink, Marina del Rey, CA (DS); Derrick Isono, Marina del Rey, CA (DI); Chris Sukimoto, Marina del Rey, CA (CK); Simmelink/Sukimoto Editions, Marina del Rey, CA (SSE); Matthew Christie, Boulder, CO (MC); Garner Tullis Workshop, Santa Barbara, CA (GTW)
PUBLISHERS: Fischbach Gallery, NY (FG); Bo Alveryd, Sweden (BA); Brooke Alexander Editions, NY (BAI); Kennedy Graphics, NY (KG); Marlborough Graphics, NY (MG); Tamarind Institute, Albuquerque, NM (TI); Jackie Fine Arts, NY (JFA); Abrams Original Editions, NY (AOE); Prowat Laucharoen (PL); Transworld Art, Inc (TAI); Styria Studios, NY (SS); John Christian Erikson, NY (JCE); Circle Fine Art, Chicago, IL (CFA); Crown Point Press, San Francisco, CA (CPP); Peter Blum Edition, NY (PBE); Aldo Crommelynck, NY (AC); International Images, Inc, NY (InIm); Gaultney-Kleineman Art, NY (GKA); Artist (ART); Simca Print Artists, Tokyo, Japan (SPA); Simmelink/Sukimoto Editions, Marina del Rey, CA (SSE); Garner Tullis, Santa Barbara, CA (GT); Chalk & Vermilion Fine Arts, NY (CVFA)
GALLERIES: Marlborough Graphics, New York, NY; Brooke Alexander, Inc, New York, NY; Kennedy Graphics, New York, NY; Texas Gallery, Houston, TX; David Adamson Gallery, Wash, DC; Hokin/Kaufman Gallery, Chicago, IL; Susanne Hilberry Gallery, Birmingham, MI; Harcus Gallery, Boston, MA; Nancy Singer Gallery, St Louis, MO; Robert Miller Gallery, New York, NY; Benjamin Mangel Gallery, Phila, PA; Michael H Lord Gallery, Milwaukee, WI; Crown Point Press, San Francisco, CA & New York, NY; Erika Meyerovich Gallery, San Francisco, CA; O'Farrell Gallery, Brunswick, ME; Robley Gallery, Roslyn, NY; Images Gallery, Toledo, OH; Charles Foley Gallery, Columbus, OH; Argus Fine Arts, Eugene, OR; International Images, New York, NY; Riva Yares Gallery, Scottsdale, AZ & Santa Fe, NM; Opus Art Studios, Miami, FL; Golden Gallery, Chestnut Hill, MA; Thomson Gallery, Minneapolis, MN; Fred Dorfman, Inc, New York, NY; Joanne Lyon Gallery, Aspen, CO; Hokin Gallery, Bay Harbor Islands, FL & Palm Beach, FL; Mira Goddard Gallery, Toronto, Canada; Mangel Gallery, Phila, PA; Mary Ryan Gallery, New York, NY; Shaw Satakay Gallery, Tokyo, Japan; Styria Studios, New York, NY; Pace Prints, New York, NY; Circle Galleries, San Francisco, CA & San Diego, CA & Northbrook, IL & Pittsburgh, PA & Houston, TX & Chicago, IL & Soho, NY & Scottsdale, AZ & Beverly Hills, CA & Costa Mesa, CA & Sherman Oaks, CA & Palm Beach, FL & Honolulu, HI & New Orleans, LA & Las Vegas, NV & Seattle, WA; Betsy Senior Contemporary Prints, New York, NY; Greenhut Galleries, Albany, NY; Nan Miller Gallery, Rochester, NY; Dean Jensen Gallery, Milwaukee, WI; Michael Kohn Gallery, Santa Monica, CA; Tavelli Williams Gallery, Aspen, CO; Signet Arts, St Louis, MO; Maine Coast Artists Gallery, Rockport, ME; Bobbie Greenfield Fine Arts, Inc, Venice, CA; Allene Lapides Gallery, Santa Fe, NM; Rubenstein/Diacono Gallery, New York, NY; Ro Gallery Image Makers, Inc, New York, NY
MAILING ADDRESS: 435 West Broadway, New York, NY 10012

Alex Katz
Ada with Flowers
Courtesy Simca Print Artists, Inc

Alex Katz
Anne
Courtesy Brooke Alexander, Inc & Marlborough Graphics, Inc

Brooklyn Museum (B)—Maravell (M)—Walker (W)

ALEX KATZ CONTINUED

TITLE	PUBLISHER	PRINTER	DATE	MEDIUM	DIMENSION (PAPER SIZE) IN INCHES	TYPE OF PAPER	EDITION NUMBER	NO. OF COLORS	ORIGINAL OPENING PRICE	CURRENT RETAIL PRICE
SOLD OUT EDITIONS (RARE):										
Gray Interior (M-17)	FG		1968	SP	17 X 22	Becket	50		200	3000
White Petuna	BAI	M	1969	LC	30 X 22	AP	100		225	4500
Alex	KG	M	1970	LC	30 X 22	AP	100	9	200	4500
Swamp Maple	BAI	M	1970	LC	41 X 27	AP	84	7	350	4000
Swamp Maple II	BAI	M	1970	LC	41 X 28	AP	90	7	250	3500
Late July II	BAI	M	1970	LC	22 X 29	AP	120		200	2000
Portrait of a Poet: Kenneth Koch	BAI	M	1970	LC	28 X 22	AP	200		150	9000
Head of Vincent	BAI	M	1972	LB	14 X 21	AP	120		200	9000
June Ekman's Class (Set of 12): June, Harmony, Judy, Naomi, Nancy, Yvonne, Timmie, Kasha, Fran, Mary, Roxanne, Thalia	BAI	M	1972	EB/AC	11 X 15 EA	AP	50 EA	5 EA	1200 SET 100 EA	5000 SET 5000 EA
Lake Wesserunset, I, II	MG	CP	1972	SP	36 X 30 EA	AP	60 EA	5 EA	325 EA	3000 EA
Lake Wesserunset III	MG	CP	1972	SP	36 X 30	AP	30	5	325	3500
Lake Wesserunset IV	MG	CP	1972	SP	30 X 36	AP	60	5	350	3000
Superb Lilies	MG	PN	1972	LC	19 X 20	AP	90	7	300	4500
Homage to Frank O'Hara: William Dunas	BAI	M	1972	LC	33 X 26	AP	90		400	5000
Large Head of Ada	MG	HN	1973	EB/AC	15 X 40	AP	44	1	350	7500
Anne	MG	PN	1973	LC	27 X 36	AP	83	9	350	8500
Luna Park II	MG	CP	1973	SP	30 x 40	AP	60	6	300	3000
Provincetown, Late Afternoon I, II	BAI	M	1973	SP	18 X 24 EA	AP	60 EA		300 EA	1000 EA
Red Sails	BAI	M	1973	SP	23 X 29	AP	60		300	3500
Still Life	BAI	PL	1974	DPT/AC	22 X 31	AP/GE	62		250	2500
Sunny	BAI	PL	1974	DPT/AC	15 X 22	AP	52		250	1800
Vincent with Open Mouth	BAI	PL	1974	DPT	23 X 15	AP	58		250	1200
Profile of Vincent	BAI	M	1974	DPT	15 X 22	AP	62		200	500
The Swimmer	KG	M	1974	SP	40 X 25	AP	200	5	400	6000
The Swimmer	MG	M	1974	AC	40 X 25	AP	84		350	7500
Good Morning	MG	CP	1975	SP	38 X 29	AP	91	9	350	6000
Rowboat I, II	MG	SS	1975	LC/SP	36 X 28 EA	AP	80 EA	12 EA	450 EA	6000 EA
Boy with Branch I (M-77)	MG/BA	PL	1975	AC	41 X 25	AP	90	7	550	3000
Boy with Branch II (M-78)	MG/BA	PL	1975	AC	41 X 25	AP	60	7	550	5000
Good Afternoon I (M-68)	MG/BAI	SS	1975	LC	36 X 28	AP	100	13	400	4000
Good Afternoon II (M-69)	MG/BAI	SS	1975	LC/SP	28 X 36	AC	80	12	400	5000
Dog at Duck Trap	MG	SS	1975–76	LC	29 X 43	AC/W	90	10	400	3000
Black and White Sunny	BAI/MG	SS	1976	LC	25 X 23	R/100	40	3	250	1500
Al Held	BAI	SS	1976	PO	16 X 16	FAB	24	29	500	3500
Susan (M-89)	TAI	CP	1976	SP	26 X 20	JP	50		500	3500
Susan (M-90)	TAI	CP	1976	SP	26 X 20	R/100	175	11	450	3500
Ann Lauterbach (M-91)	BAI/MG	PL	1977	AC	15 X 22	AC	40	6	500	3500
Caroline	BAI	PL	1977	LC	27 X 21	AC	60		250	1000
Blue Pamela	BAI/MG	SS	1977	LC/SP/PO	29 X 22	CD	30	2	300	1500
Grey Pamela	BAI/MG	SS	1977	LC/SP/PO	29 X 22	CD	30	2	300	1500
Five Women	AOE		1977	SP	18 X 47	JP	100		500	6000
Face of the Poet (Set of 14)	BAI/MG	SS	1978	AC	15 X 19 EA	AP	25 EA		3500 SET	20000 SET
Self-Portrait	MG	PL	1978	AC	36 X 30	AP	32		300	5000
The Dog	MG	PL	1978	AC	10 X 13	AP	90		150	1500
Twilight I	MG	SPA	1978	SP	42 X 33	AP	50	7	500	1800
Twilight II	MG	SPA	1978	SP	42 X 33	AP	65	7	500	1800
Twilight III	MG	SPA	1978	SP	42 X 33	AP	55	3	500	1500
Ada in the Rain	BAI	PL	1978–79	LB	22 X 30	AP	120		500	3500
Blue Umbrella I, II	BAI	PL	1978–79	LC	22 X 30 EA	AP	120 EA		450 EA	5000 EA
The Orange Band	ART/SPA	SPA	1979	SP	40 X 28	AC	80	25	1200	9500
Polka Dot Blouse I–IV (Series of 4)	MG	SS	1979	SP	30 X 22	AP	120	10	2400 SET 600 EA	10000 SET 4000 EA
The Red Band	SPA/ART	SPA	1979	SP	55 X 37	AC	60		1800	6000
Song (M-126)	BAI	SS	1980–81	LC/SP	33 X 44	AP	99		1800	4000
Ada in the Woods	SPA	SPA	1981	SP	48 X 36	GRAM	65		3200	15000
Ada with Flowers	SPA	SPA	1981	SP	48 X 36	GRAM	65		3200	15000
Plaid Shirt	SPA/ART	SPA	1981	SP	47 X 31	AC	71	16	1500	8000
Striped Jacket	ART	CE	1981	LC	30 X 37	AC	58	6	2000	8000
Large Head of Vincent	BAI	PB/A	1982	AC	60 X 36	AP	50		1800	3500
Julia and Alexandria	SS	SS	1983	SP	37 X 74	AP/RR	75	47	2000	8000
Edwin Denby	MG	SS	1983	LC	30 X 40	AP	50		1200	2200
Night: William Duncas Dancers #1–#4 (Set of 4)	JFA		1983	LC	25 X 31 EA	AP	100 EA		4500 SET	8000 SET
Bicycling in Central Park	CFA	AA	1983	LC	22 X 30	AP	250		1200	5000
Red Coat	SPA/ART	SPA	1983	SP	58 X 29	STP	73	34	1800	30000
The Moose	ART	NB	1983	AC	23 X 41	R/BFK	50	5	1600	1800
Ada and Alex	SS	SS	1984	SP	30 X 36	AP	75	37	1500	6000

ALEX KATZ CONTINUED

Alex Katz
Julia and Alexandria
Courtesy Styria Studio

TITLE	PUBLISHER	PRINTER	DATE	MEDIUM	DIMENSION (PAPER SIZE) IN INCHES	TYPE OF PAPER	EDITION NUMBER	NO. OF COLORS	ORIGINAL OPENING PRICE	CURRENT RETAIL PRICE
SOLD OUT EDITIONS (RARE):										
Sunset	JCE	SiS/BX	1984	LC/SP/OFF	70 X 5	AP88	41	3	2000	7500
Give Me Tomorrow (Set of 13)	JCE	SiS/BX	1983–85	EC/A	18 X 13 EA				5000 SET	6500 SET
The Green Cap	CPP	CPP	1985	WC	17 X 24	AP	200	13	1400	3500
Joan	CPP	DS/JPE	1986	AC	31 X 39	SOM	65		3000	9500
Tremor in the Morning (Set of 10):									4800 SET	50000 SET
Eric & Anni	PBE	CE	1986	WC	21 X 20	R/BFK	45	1	500	5000
Jennifer & Eric	PBE	CE	1986	WC	21 X 20	R/BFK	45	1	500	5000
Julian & Jessica	PBE	CE	1986	WC	21 X 20	R/BFK	45	1	500	5000
Kriti & Vincent	PBE	CE	1986	WC	21 X 20	R/BFK	45	1	500	5000
Ada & Alex	PBE	CE	1986	WC	21 X 20	R/BFK	45	1	500	5000
Rackstraw & Peggy	PBE	CE	1986	WC	21 X 20	R/BFK	45	1	500	5000
Danny & Laura	PBE	CE	1986	WC	21 X 20	R/BFK	45	1	500	5000
Carter & Phyllis	PBE	CE	1986	WC	21 X 20	R/BFK	45	1	500	5000
Ando & Dino	PBE	CE	1986	WC	21 X 20	R/BFK	45	1	500	5000
Peter & Linda	PBE	CE	1986	WC	21 X 20	R/BFK	45	1	500	5000
Samantha	ART/SPA	CPP	1987	SP	66 X 29	AC	80	32	3000	10000
Reclining Figure	CPP	DS/CS/CPP	1987	AC	36 X 43	AC	60		2500	12000
CURRENT EDITIONS:										
John Ashbery	CPP	DS/JPE	1986	AB	57 X 22	SOM	25	1	1800	7500
Ada (on Cat Aluminum)	SS	BM/SS	1987	SP	65" HT ALUM		75		5000	25000
Beach Sandals	CPP	DS/CS/CPP	1987	AC	25 X 29	AC	60		1200	3000
Black Shoes	CPP	DS/CS/CPP	1988	EB/A/SG	23 X 29	SOM	60		1500	3500
3 PM, 1988	PBE	JE	1988	WB	37 X 72	ADG	50	1	4000	6000
Ada	SS/ART	BM/SS	1988	SP/ALUM	65 X 10 X ¼	ALUM	75	65	8000	10000
Red Cap	CPP	DS/DI/CS/SSE	1989–90	EB/A	21 X 70	SOM/S	50		10000	12000
Light as Air (Illustrated Book) (12 Etchings & Aquatints, Text by Ron Padgett)	AC	AtC	1989	EB/A	18 X 30 EA	AP	30 EA		7500 SET	7500 SET
Light as Air (Illustrated Book) (12 Etchings & Aquatints, Text by Ron Padgett) (Deluxe Edition)	AC	AtC	1989	EB/A	18 X 15 EA	AP	10 EA		12000 SET	15000 SET
Alex and Ada Suite (The 1960's to the 1980's) (Set of 8):									24000 SET	24000 SET
Ada in Hat (1961)	GFA	SS	1990	SP	27 X 36	AP/ROL	150	14	XXXX	XXXX
Alex with Hat, a Self Portrait (1963)	GFA	SS	1990	SP	32 X 36	AP/ROL	150	19	XXXX	XXXX
Ada with Sun Glasses (1969)	GFA	SS	1990	SP	36 X 24	AP/ROL	150	29	XXXX	XXXX
Ada in White Hat (1978)	GFA	SS	1990	SP	36 X 26	AP/ROL	150	30	XXXX	XXXX
Alex Sweat Shirt II (1986)	GFA	SS	1990	SP	36 X 29	AP/ROL	150	26	XXXX	XXXX
Triple Ada with Gray Ribbon (1987)	GFA	SS	1990	SP	28 X 36	AP/ROL	150	21	XXXX	XXXX
Ada with Orange Hat (1988)	GFA	SS	1990	SP	18 X 36	AP/ROL	150	24	XXXX	XXXX
Alex in Green Jacket (1989)	GFA	SS	1990	SP	36 X 24	AP/ROL	150	33	XXXX	XXXX
Black Brook	CPP	DS/DI/CS/SSE	1990	EB/AC	40 X 29	AP88	50		4000	5000
Swimmer	MG	CPP	1990	WC	24 X 28	AP88	100		2000	2000
Tree	MG	CPP	1990	WC	18 x 17	AP88	30		1200	1200
Ursula	MG	CPP	1990	WC	12 X 30	AP88	100		2000	2000
Corine	Inlm	JCE	1992				50	4		
Grey Day	CVFA	SS	1992	SP	22 X 72	AP	75	28	6500	6500
Forest	SSE	DS/DI/CS/SSE	1992	AC	29 X 66	SOM	40	5	6000	6000

ROBERT CRAIG KAUFFMAN

BORN: Los Angeles, CA; March 31, 1932
EDUCATION: Univ of California, Los Angeles, CA, MFA, 1956
TEACHING: Assoc Prof, Painting & Sculpture, Univ of California, Irvine, CA, 1967–72; Instr, Painting & Sculpture, Univ of California, Berkeley, CA, 1969; Instr, Painting & Sculpture, Sch of Visual Arts, NY, 1970–71
AWARDS: U S Govt Fel for the Arts, 1967; First Prize, Art Inst of Chicago, IL, 1970
COLLECTIONS: Whitney Mus of Am Art, NY; Tate Gallery of Art, London, England; Art Inst of Chicago, IL; Los Angeles County Mus of Art, CA; Pasadena Art Mus, CA
PRINTERS: Cirrus Editions Workshop, Los Angeles, CA (CEW); David Ordaz, Los Angeles, CA (DO); Ed Hamilton, Los Angeles, CA (EH); Jane Aman, Los Angeles, CA (JA); Tamarind Inst, Albuquerque, NM (TI); Lynne D Allen (LA); Barbara Telleen (BT); Robert Gingras, Los Angeles, CA (RG)
PUBLISHERS: Cirrus Editions, Los Angeles, CA (CE); Tamarind Inst, Albuquerque, NM (TI)
GALLERIES: Cirrus Editions, Ltd, Los Angeles, CA; Pace Gallery, New York, NY; Asher/Faure Gallery, Los Angeles, CA; BlumHelman Gallery, New York, NY; Works Gallery, Long Beach, CA
MAILING ADDRESS: Dept of Art, Univ of California, Irvine, CA 92717

Robert Craig Kauffman
Yellow Chair #1
Courtesy Tamarind Institute

TITLE	PUBLISHER	PRINTER	DATE	MEDIUM	DIMENSION (PAPER SIZE) IN INCHES	TYPE OF PAPER	EDITION NUMBER	NO. OF COLORS	ORIGINAL OPENING PRICE	CURRENT RETAIL PRICE
CURRENT EDITIONS:										
Untitled (Set of 4) (#39c, #40c, #41c, #42c)	CE	CEW	1971	LC	22 X 27	RP/ROL	80	2	600 SET 150 EA	1400 SET 350 EA
Untitled (#73cs)	CE	JA/CEW	1973	SP	40 X 26	VTP	50	Multi	300	1200
Untitled (#285c)	CE	DO/CEW	1980	LC/SP	33 X 24	CD	50	6	400	750
Untitled (#290c)	CE	DO/CEW	1980	LC/SP	33 X 24	CD	50	5	400	750
Untitled (#298c) State I	CE	DO/CEW	1980	LC/SP	33 X 24	CD	25	5	475	800
Untitled (#298c) State II	CE	DO/CEW	1980	LC/SP	33 X 24	CD	25	6	475	800
Untitled (#299c) State I	CE	DO/CEW	1980	LC/SP	43 X 30	CD	25	5	650	1000
Untitled (#299c) State II	CE	DO/CEW	1980	LC/SP	43 X 30	CD	25	6	650	1000
Untitled (#299c) State III	CE	DO/CEW	1980	LC/SP	43 X 30	CD	15	7	750	1200
Untitled (#317c)	CE	EH/CEW	1981	LC/SP	15 X 20	TWP	45	8	400	550
Untitled (#318c)	CE	EH/CEW	1981	LC/SP	8 X 49	R/BFK	45	8	650	850
Untitled (#327c)	CE	CEW	1982	LC	41 X 23	AP/W	45		650	850
Untitled (#328c)	CE	CEW	1982	LC	29 X 34	AP/W	60		650	850
Pink Chair #2	TI	LA/BT/TI	1983	LC	31 X 20	AP/W	50	8	500	850
Yellow Chair #1	TI	BT/TI	1983	LC	41 X 28	AP/W	40	9	650	850
Untitled (336c)	CE	CEW	1983	LC	19 X 14	AP/W	300		200	250
Untitled (#35c)	CE	RG/CEW	1984	LC	30 X 40	AP/W	50	4	650	750

PETER KEEFER

BORN: New York, NY; 1933
EDUCATION: California Col of Arts & Crafts, Los Angeles, CA, BFA, 1958; California State Univ, Northridge, CA, MA, 1970
PRINTERS: Spectrum Press, Orange, CA (SP); Larry Taylor, CA (LT); Daysprings Press, Albuquerque, NM (DP); Mike Vogel, Albuquerque, NM (MV); Edgewater Works, Denver, CO (EW); Paula Crane, Denver, CO (PC); Chameleon Press, El Paso, TX (CP); R J Barry, El Paso, TX (RJB)
PUBLISHERS: London Arts Inc, Detroit, MI (LAI); American Design, Denver, CO (AD); Bowles/Hopkins, San Francisco, CA (BH); Post Oak Fine Art Distributors, Houston, TX (POFA)
GALLERIES: London Arts Gallery, Detroit, MI; Wenniger Gallery, Boston, MA; Ro Gallery Image Makers, Inc, New York, NY
MAILING ADDRESS: 4637 Livingston Dr, Long Beach, CA 90803

TITLE	PUBLISHER	PRINTER	DATE	MEDIUM	DIMENSION (PAPER SIZE) IN INCHES	TYPE OF PAPER	EDITION NUMBER	NO. OF COLORS	ORIGINAL OPENING PRICE	CURRENT RETAIL PRICE
SOLD OUT EDITIONS (RARE):										
Taos Blue Lake	POFA	SP	1981	COLG	22 X 30	R/100	250	6	160	250
CURRENT EDITIONS:										
Mesa Petaca	LAI	RJB/CP	1981	COLG	22 X 30	STP	250	4	160	180
Castle Rock	LAI	LT/SP	1981	COLG	22 X 30	STP	250	4	160	180
Taos Dusk	LAI	LT/SP	1981	COLG	22 X 30	STP	250	5	160	180

MILDRED ELAINE KAYE

BORN: New York, NY; September 24, 1929
EDUCATION: High Sch of Mus & Art, NY; Indiana Univ, PA, BA, 1951; Montclair State Col, Upper Montclair, NJ, MA, 1977
TEACHING: Instr, Graphics Arts, Bergen County Vocational Technical High School, NJ, 1972 to present
AWARDS: Best in Show, Cork Gallery, Lincoln Center, NY, 1981; Judges Choice, Leona Library Assn, 1981; Judges Choice, Lever House, NY, 1983; Second Prize, Salute Small Works, 1990; Second Prize, Pavilion Gallery, 1991; First Prizes, Mari Invitational, Mamaroneck, NY 1989,92
RECENT EXHIB: Mari Gallery, Mamaroneck, NY, 1989; Jacob Javits Fed Bldg, NY, 1989; Nat Assoc of Women Artists Indian Cult Exchange Tour, 1990; Paterson Mus, 1991; Intermission Gallery, 1992
COLLECTIONS: Indiana Univ, Bloomington, IN; Montclair State Col, Upper Montclair, NJ; John Herron Inst, Indianapolis, IN; Am Cultural Center, Taipei, China; The Print Consortium, NY
PRINTERS: Artist (ART)
PUBLISHERS: Artist (ART)
GALLERIES: Nathan's Gallery, West Paterson, NJ; Mari Gallery, Mamaroneck, NY; Margaret D'Ayala, Upper Saddle River, NJ; White Gallery, Franklin Lakes, NJ
MAILING ADDRESS: 87 Kern Place, Saddle Brook, NJ 07662

Mildred Elaine Kaye
Fantasy on a Persian Rug
Courtesy the Artist

TITLE	PUBLISHER	PRINTER	DATE	MEDIUM	DIMENSION (PAPER SIZE) IN INCHES	TYPE OF PAPER	EDITION NUMBER	NO. OF COLORS	ORIGINAL OPENING PRICE	CURRENT RETAIL PRICE
SOLD OUT EDITIONS (RARE):										
Hey! Diddle Diddle	ART	ART		SP/COL	26 X 32	AC	25	14	125	300
The Juggler	ART	ART	1978	SP/COL	20 X 26	AC	25	10	95	200
Birth of Pegassus	ART	ART	1977	SP	19 X 26	R/100	25	10	95	150
Rosecone	ART	ART	1979	SP/COL	18 X 26	AC	25	20	100	150
CURRENT EDITIONS:										
Sardines	ART	ART	1976	SP	15 X 22	AC	25	12	100	125
Upon the Earth's Sweet Flowing Breast	ART	ART	1980	SP/COL	19 X 28	AC	25	4	100	200
This Little Piggy	ART	ART	1981	CP	20 X 16	HMP	50		85	150
Blessed Be You in Your Coming, Blessed Be You in Your Going Forth	ART	ART	1981	CP	16 X 20	HMP	50		100	200
The Cat and . . .	ART	ART	1981	SP/COL	16 X 25	AC	25	6	100	150
Persistance of Vision	ART	ART	1981	SP	22 X 29	AC	25	20	100	200
Summer of Many Realities	ART	ART	1982	SP	28 X 32	AC	25	18	150	200
Hyper Eclectia	ART	ART	1982	SP/COL	20 X 27	AC	25	15	100	200
For Spacious Skies	ART	ART	1983	SP/COL	28 X 32	AC	25	15	100	200
Still She Haunts Me, Phantomwise, Alice Moving Under Skies, Never Seen by Waking Eyes	ART	ART	1985	SP/COL	28 X 32	AC	25	25	150	200
Bride of Silence	ART	ART	1985	SP/CP	25 X 27	HMP	50	7	400	450
The Judgment of Paris	ART	ART	1985	SP	20 X 27	AC	25	14	110	125
My Father's Tallis	ART	ART	1986	SP/COL	28 X 32	AC	35	18	145	300
And the Dish . . .	ART	ART	1986	SP/COL	27 X 32	AC	50	18	175	250
The Juggler II	ART	ART	1986	SP/COL	20 X 26	AC	50	13	150	250
Ode to the Muse	ART	ART	1987	SP/COL	20 X 27	AC	25	8	100	175
A Tallis in Time	ART	ART	1986	SP	25 X 32	AC	25	23	200	225
Mythscape	ART	ART	1987	SP/COL	28 X 32	AC	20	21	250	300
The Trophy	ART	ART	1987	SP	25 X 34	AC	20	25	200	250
Thou Yet Unravished Bride	ART	ART	1988	SP	25 X 28	AC	20	21	250	300
On Lydig Avenue	ART	ART	1988	SP	25 X 40	AC	25	26	250	325
Fantasy on a Persian Rug	ART	ART	1989	SP	20 X 28	AC	20	30	275	300
Folio Fantasia	ART	ART	1989	SP/COL	28 X 32	AC	25	30	125	200
And the Cat Jumped over the Moon	ART	ART	1990	SP/COL	26 X 32	AC	25	14	300	300
Class Roots	ART	ART	1991	SP	22 X 27	AC	20	4	200	200
And All Our Yesterdays	ART	ART	1991	SP	15 X 23	CAN	15	18	175	175
Tea for Two	ART	ART	1991	SP	12 X 16	CAN	15	10	200	200
Rose of Brighton Beach	ART	ART	1992	SP	27 X 32	AC	15	33	350	350
Sacred and Profane Love	ART	ART	1992	SP	20 X 27	AC	20	26	300	300
Succubi and Furies	ART	ART	1992	SP	12 X 12	AC	2	12	100	125

MILDRED ELAINE KAYE CONTINUED

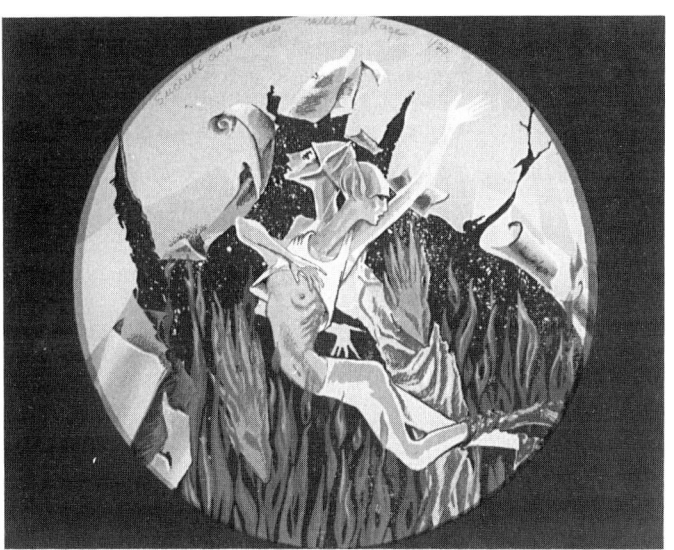

Mildred Elaine Kaye
Succubi and Furies
Courtesy the Artist

Mildred Elaine Kaye
Sacred and Profane Love
Courtesy the Artist

Mildred Elaine Kaye
Thou Yet Unravished Bride
Courtesy the Artist

Mildred Elaine Kaye
The Juggler
Courtesy the Artist

JERRY KEARNS

BORN: Petersburg, VA; 1943
EDUCATION: Univ of California, Santa Barbara, CA, 1968
TEACHING: Univ of California, Los Angeles, CA, 1970–71; Univ of California, Amherst, MA, 1971 to present
AWARDS: Prix de Rome, Am Acad, Rome, Italy, 1968–70; Nat Endowment for the Arts Grant, 1974; New York State Council for the Arts Proj Grant, NY, Painting, 1987; Comm, Public Art Fund, Inc, NY, 1988; Comm, ZONE Art Gallery, Springfield, MA, 1988,89
RECENT EXHIB: Univ of Connecticut, Atrium Gallery, Storrs, CT, 1987; Meyers/Bloom Gallery, 1988; ZONE Art Gallery, Springfield, MA, 1988; Galeria Temple, Valencia, Spain, 1989; Cleveland State Univ Art Gallery, OH, 1989; Kent Fine Art, NY, 1988,89; Lehman Col Art Gallery, NY, 1992
COLLECTIONS: Mus of Mod Art, NY; Hofstra Univ, Hempstead, NY; Art Gallery of Western Australia, Perth, Australia; Centro Wilfredo Lam, Havana, Cuba; Western Washington Univ, Bellingham, WA; Frederick R Weisman Coll, Los Angeles, CA
PRINTERS: Alix Heyeler, Amherst, MA (AH); Univ of Massachusetts Printmaking Studios, Amherst, MA (UMPS); Maxwell Nova Fine Arts, New Rochelle, NY (MNFA); Artist (ART)
PUBLISHERS: Associated American Artists, NY (AAA); Artist (ART); Kent Fine Art, NY (KFA)
GALLERIES: Kent Fine Art, New York, NY

TITLE	PUBLISHER	PRINTER	DATE	MEDIUM	DIMENSION (PAPER SIZE) IN INCHES	TYPE OF PAPER	EDITION NUMBER	NO. OF COLORS	ORIGINAL OPENING PRICE	CURRENT RETAIL PRICE
SOLD OUT EDITIONS (RARE):										
Musing	AAA	ART	1972	LC	13 X 10	AP	250		35	500
CURRENT EDITIONS:										
White Lies	ART	AH/UMPS	1985	LB	20 X 30	RP/HWT	5	1	700	1000
Dentente	KFA	MNFA	1989	SP	33 X 37	COV	75	6	900	1200
Hard Rock	KFA	MNFA	1989	SP	33 X 37	COV	75	3	900	1200

STEVE KEISTER

BORN: Lancaster, PA; 1949
EDUCATION: Tyler Sch of Art, Temple Univ, Phila, PA, BFA, 1970, MFA, 1972
TEACHING: Instr, Sch of Visual Arts, NY
AWARDS: Pollock-Krasner Found Scholar, 1987; Nat Endowment for the Arts Fel, 1988
COLLECTIONS: Mus of Contemp Art, Chicago, IL; Temple Univ, Phila, PA; Whitney Mus of Am Art, NY; Milwaukee Art Mus, WI; High Mus, Atlanta, GA; Dallas Mus of Fine Arts, TX; Mus of Contemp Art, Los Angeles, CA; Lannan Found, West Palm Beach, FL
PRINTERS: Judith Solodkin, NY (JS); Solo Press, NY (SP)
PUBLISHERS: Solo Press, NY (SP)
GALLERIES: Solo Press, New York, NY; BlumHelman Gallery, New York, NY
MAILING ADDRESS: 46 Laight St, New York, NY 10013

TITLE	PUBLISHER	PRINTER	DATE	MEDIUM	DIMENSION (PAPER SIZE) IN INCHES	TYPE OF PAPER	EDITION NUMBER	NO. OF COLORS	ORIGINAL OPENING PRICE	CURRENT RETAIL PRICE
CURRENT EDITIONS:										
Cat Scan	SP	JS/SP	1989	SP/XER	34 X 45	MASA	25	2	850	850
Reverse Angle Replay	SP	JS/SP	1989	WC/SP/CC	24 X 56	MASA/CHIRI	45	3	1200	1500
Super Conductor	SP	JS/SP	1989	LC/SP/PH	34 X 72	MASA	45	3	1600	1600
Tango (with Safety Fencing, Foam Rubber, Chiffon Paper & Artist's Tapes)	SP	JS/SP	1989	SP/CO/MULT	36 X 108	CAN		6	4500	4500

MIKE KELLEY

BORN: Detroit, MI; 1954
EDUCATION: Univ of Michigan, Ann Arbor, MI, BFA, 1976; California Inst of Art, Valencia, CA, MFA, 1978
RECENT EXHIB: Los Angeles County Mus, CA, 1987; Whitney Mus of Am Art, NY; Jablonka Galerie, Cologne, Germany, 1989; Galerie Peter Pakesch, Vienna, Austria, 1989; Mus of Fine Art, Boston, MA, 1990; Seibu Contemp Art Gallery, Tokyo, Japan, 1990; Ghislaine Hussenot Gallery, Paris, France, 1990; Lannan Found, Los Angeles, CA, 1991
PRINTERS: Fabric Workshop, Phila, PA (FW)
PUBLISHERS: Edition Julie Sylvester, NY (EJS)
GALLERIES: Rosamund Felsen Gallery, Los Angeles, CA; Metro Pictures, New York, NY; Galerie Peter Pakesch, Vienna, Austria; Jablonka Galerie, Cologne, Germany
MAILING ADDRESS: c/o Metro Pictures, 150 Greene St, New York, NY 10012

TITLE	PUBLISHER	PRINTER	DATE	MEDIUM	DIMENSION (PAPER SIZE) IN INCHES	TYPE OF PAPER	EDITION NUMBER	NO. OF COLORS	ORIGINAL OPENING PRICE	CURRENT RETAIL PRICE
SOLD OUT EDITIONS (RARE):										
Pansy Metal/Clovered Hoof (Series of 10 Oversized Screen Printed Scarves) (Set of 10):									6500 SET	7500 SET
Blood & Soil (Potato Print)	EJS	FW	1989	SP	53 X 58	SILK	40		750	850
Country Cousin	EJS	FW	1989	SP	53 X 58	SILK	40		750	850
Emerald Eyehole	EJS	FW	1989	SP	53 X 58	SILK	40		750	850
Hangin' Heavy	EJS	FW	1989	SP	53 X 58	SILK	40		750	850
Hairy—Horney	EJS	FW	1989	SP	53 X 58	SILK	40		750	850
Master Dik	EJS	FW	1989	SP	53 X 58	SILK	40		750	850
The Orange & Green	EJS	FW	1989	SP	53 X 58	SILK	40		750	850
Peat Shade	EJS	FW	1989	SP	53 X 58	SILK	40		750	850
Satan's Nostrils	EJS	FW	1989	SP	53 X 58	SILK	40		750	850
Twisted Shamrock	EJS	FW	1989	SP	53 X 58	SILK	40		750	850
Unlucky Clover	EJS	FW	1989	SP	53 X 58	SILK	40		750	850

DANIEL KELLY

PRINTERS: Segoshi Yoshimitsu, Tokyo, Japan (SY); Edition Works, Tokyo, Japan (EdW)

PUBLISHERS: Artist (ART)
GALLERIES: Joe Fawbush Editions, New York, NY; Mary Ryan Gallery, New York, NY; Brody's Gallery, Wash, DC; Carter Arcand Gallery, Portland, OR; Spark Gallery, Denver, CO

TITLE	PUBLISHER	PRINTER	DATE	MEDIUM	DIMENSION (PAPER SIZE) IN INCHES	TYPE OF PAPER	EDITION NUMBER	NO. OF COLORS	ORIGINAL OPENING PRICE	CURRENT RETAIL PRICE
CURRENT EDITIONS:										
Blaine	ART	SY/EdW	1985	LC	31 X 19	WASHI	50	3	450	900
Fumiko	ART	SY/EdW	1985	LC/HC/CC	14 X 31	JAP	15	Varies	600	900
Michael	ART	SY/EdW	1986	LC	39 X 27	KOZO	25	3	600	1000
Shiga's Overcoat	ART	SY/EdW	1989	WC/LC/CO	38 X 25	PCP	48		1000	1000

ELLSWORTH KELLY

BORN: Newburgh, NY; May 31, 1923
EDUCATION: Pratt Inst, NY, 1941–42; Boston Mus Sch, MA, 1946–48; Acad des Beaux-Arts, Paris, France, 1948–49
AWARDS: Carnegie Inst Prizes, 1962,64; Brandeis Univ, MA, Creative Arts Award, 1962; Tokyo Int Educational Ministry Award, 1963; Chicago Art Inst, IL, Flora Mayer Witkowsky Prize, 1964; Chicago Art Inst, IL, 1974
RECENT EXHIB: Print Retrosp, Detroit Inst of Art, MI, 1987; Mus of Art, Huntsville, AL, 1987–88; Des Moines Art Center, IA, 1988; Neuberger Mus, Purchase, NY, 1988; Long Beach Univ Art Mus, CA, 1988; Los Angeles County Mus, CA, 1988; Print Retrosp, Long Beach Univ Art Mus, CA, 1988; Nelson-Atkins Mus of Art, Kansas City, MO, 1988; San Francisco Mus of Mod Art, CA, 1988; Mus of Mod Art, NY, 1988; BMW Gallery NY, 1988; BlumHelman Gallery, NY, 1988; Milwaukee Art Mus, WI, 1988; Laguna Gloria Art Mus, Austin, TX, 1989; Print Retrosp, Berkshire Mus, Pittsfield, MA, 1989; Massachusetts Inst of Tech, List Visual Arts Center, Cambridge, MA, 1989; BlumHelman Gallery, NY, 1988,89; Hood Mus, Hanover, NH, 1989–90; Susan Sheehan Gallery, NY, 1990; Galerie Max, Turnberry, North Miami Beach, FL, 1990; Gallery Kashahara, Osaka, Japan, 1990; State Univ of New York, Plattsburgh Art Mus, NY, 1990; Gagosian Gallery, NY, 1991; Dallas Mus of Art, TX, 1989,92; Lannan Found, Los Angeles, CA, 1992; Berkshire Mus, Pittsfield, MA, 1992; Anthony d'Offay Gallery, London, England, 1992; Leo Castelli Graphics, NY, 1988, 92; Benedicte Saxe Gallery, Beverly Hills, CA, 1992; Laura Carpenter Fine Art, Santa Fe, NM, 1992
COLLECTIONS: Metropolitan Mus of Art, NY; Mus of Mod Art, NY; Guggenheim Mus, NY; Whitney Mus of Am Art, NY; Stedelijk Mus, Schiedam, Netherlands; Brandeis Univ, Waltham, MA; Albright-Knox Gallery of Art, Buffalo, NY; Carnegie-Mellon Mus, Pittsburgh, PA; Chicago Art Inst, IL; Cincinnati Mus of Art, OH; Cleveland Mus of Art, OH; Dartmouth Col, MA; Found Maeght, Paris, France; Harvard Univ, Cambridge, MA; Los Angeles County Mus, CA; San Francisco Mus of Art, CA; Yale Univ, New Haven, CT; Mus of Art, Pasadena, CA; Tate Gallery, London, England; Walker Art Center, Minneapolis, MN; Toronto Mus of Art, Can; Corcoran Gallery of Art, Wash, DC; Seattle Mus of Art, WA
PRINTERS: Gemini GEL, Los Angeles, CA (GEM); Tyler Graphics Workshop, Mount Kisco, NY (TGL); Maeght Editeur, Paris, France (ME); Galerie Maeght Lelong, Paris, France (ML); James Reid, Los Angeles, CA (JR); Diana Kingsley, Los Angeles, CA (DK), Maggie Pari, Los Angeles, CA (MP); Claudio Stickmar, Los Angeles, CA (CS); Andrew Rubin, Los Angeles, CA (AR)
PUBLISHERS: Gemini GEL, Los Angeles, CA (GEM); Tyler Graphics, Ltd, Mount Kisco, NY (TGL); Maeght Editions, Paris, France (ME); Brooke Alexander, Inc, NY (BAI); Galerie Maeght Lelong, Paris, France (ML)
GALLERIES: Castelli Graphics, New York, NY; Tyler Graphics, Ltd, Mount Kisco, NY; BlumHelman Galleries, New York, NY; R K Goldman Contemporary, Los Angeles, CA; Travelli Williams Gallery, Aspen, CO; John C Stoller & Company, Minneapolis, MN; Greenberg Gallery, St Louis, MO; Jan Weiner Gallery, Kansas City, MO; Susan Sheehan Gallery, Inc, New York, NY; DEL Fine Art Galleries, Taos, NM; Reynolds Gallery, Richmond, VA; Elizabeth Paul Gallery, Cincinnati, OH; Janie C Lee Gallery, Houston, TX & New York, NY; Gagosian Gallery, New York, NY; BenedictesSaxe Gallery, Beverly Hills, CA; Laura Carpenter Fine Art, Santa Fe, NM; 65 Thompson Street, New York, NY; Matthew Marks Gallery, New York, NY; Stux Modern, New York, NY; John Berggruen Gallery, San Francisco, CA; Thomas Babeor Gallery, La Jolla, CA; Irene Drori Fine Art, Los Angeles, CA; TwoSixtyOne Art, New York, NY

Ellsworth Kelly
Grand Case
Courtesy Gemini GEL

Ellsworth Kelly
Orient Beach
Courtesy Gemini GEL

ELLSWORTH KELLY CONTINUED

TITLE	PUBLISHER	PRINTER	DATE	MEDIUM	DIMENSION (PAPER SIZE) IN INCHES	TYPE OF PAPER	EDITION NUMBER	NO. OF COLORS	ORIGINAL OPENING PRICE	CURRENT RETAIL PRICE
SOLD OUT EDITIONS (RARE):										
Red-Orange	ME	ME	1964	LC	35 X 24	R/BFK	75		100	5000
Black	ME	ME	1964	LC	35 X 24	R/BFK	75		100	5000
Yellow	ME	ME	1964	LC	35 X 24	R/BFK	75		100	5000
Green	ME	ME	1964	LC	35 X 24	R/BFK	75		100	5000
Orange with Blue	ME	ME	1964	LC	35 X 24	R/BFK	75		100	5000
Light Blue with Orange	ME	ME	1964	LC	35 X 24	R/BFK	75		100	5000
Green with Red	ME	ME	1964	LC	35 X 24	R/BFK	75		100	5000
Orange with Green	ME	ME	1964	LC	35 X 24	R/BFK	75		100	5000
Yellow with Dark Blue	ME	ME	1964	LC	35 X 24	R/BFK	75		100	5000
Dark Blue with Red	ME	ME	1964	LC	35 X 24	R/BFK	75		100	5000
Black with White	ME	ME	1964	LC	35 X 24	R/BFK	75		100	5000
Blue with Orange and Green	ME	ME	1964	LC	35 X 24	R/BFK	75		100	5000
Blue and Yellow and Red-Orange	ME	ME	1964	LC	35 X 24	R/BFK	75		100	5000
Blue and Orange	ME	ME	1964	LC	35 X 24	R/BFK	75		100	5000
Orange and Blue over Yellow	ME	ME	1964	LC	24 X 35	R/BFK	75		100	5000
Blue and Green over Orange	ME	ME	1964	LC	24 X 35	R/BFK	75		100	5000
Red over Yellow	ME	ME	1964	LC	35 X 24	R/BFK	75		100	5000
Yellow over Dark Blue	ME	ME	1964	LC	35 X 24	R/BFK	75		100	5000
Yellow over Black	ME	ME	1964	LC	35 X 24	R/BFK	75		100	5000
Red Orange over Blue	ME	ME	1964	LC	35 X 20	R/BFK	75		100	5000
Yellow over Yellow	ME	ME	1964	LC	35 X 24	R/BFK	75		100	5000
Orange and Green	ME	ME	1964	LC	35 X 24	R/BFK	75		100	5000
Black over Yellow	ME	ME	1964	LC	35 X 24	R/BFK	75		100	5000
Blue over Orange	ME	ME	1964	LC	35 X 24	R/BFK	75		100	5000
Blue over Green	ME	ME	1964	LC	35 X 24	R/BFK	75		100	5000
Orange over Blue	ME	ME	1964	LC	35 X 24	R/BFK	75		100	5000
Dark Blue with Red	ME	ME	1964	LC	24 X 35	R/BFK	75		100	5000
Derrier Le Mirror	ME	ME	1964	LC		R/BFK	150		100	5000
Cyclamen Series, I–V	ME	ME	1964–66	LC	35 X 24 EA	R/BFK	75 EA		150 EA	5000 EA
Grapefruit	ME	ME	1964–66	LC	35 X 24	R/BFK	75		150	5000
Leaves	ME	ME	1964–66	LC	35 X 24	R/BFK	75		150	5000
Camellia Series, I–II, III	ME	ME	1964–66	LC	35 X 24 EA	R/BFK	75 EA		150 EA	5000 EA
Tangerine	ME	ME	1964–66	LC	35 X 24	R/BFK	75		150	5000
Lemon	ME	ME	1964–66	LC	35 X 24	R/BFK	75		150	5000
Seaweed	ME	ME	1964–66	LC	35 X 24	R/BFK	75		150	5000
Locust	ME	ME	1964–66	LC	35 X 24	R/BFK	75		150	5000
Catalpa Leaf	ME	ME	1964–66	LC	35 X 24	R/BFK	75		150	5000
Pear Series I, II, III	ME	ME	1964–66	LC	35 X 24 EA	R/BFK	75 EA		150 EA	5000 EA
String Bean Leaves Series I, II, III	ME	ME	1964–66	LC	35 X 24 EA	R/BFK	75 EA		150 EA	5000 EA
Melon Leaf	ME	ME	1964–66	LC	35 X 24	R/BFK	75		150	5000
Fig Branch	ME	ME	1964–66	LC	35 X 24	R/BFK	75		150	2500
Ilanthus Leaves I	ME	ME	1964–66	LC	24 X 35	R/BFK	75		150	6000
Ilanthus Leaves II	ME	ME	1964–66	LC	35 X 24	R/BFK	75		150	6000
Lemon Branch	ME	ME	1964–66	LC	35 X 24	R/BFK	75		150	5000
Magnolia	ME	ME	1964–66	LC	24 X 35	R/BFK	75		150	2500
Oranges	ME	ME	1964–66	LC	24 X 35	R/BFK	75		150	5000
David	ME	ME	1964–66	LC	35 X 24	R/BFK	75		150	5000
Red Orange over Black	GEM	ME	1970	SP	25 X 30	AP	250	2	200	4500
Yellow/Orange	GEM	GEM	1970	LC	35 X 41	ARJ	75	2	300	6500
Black/White/Black	GEM	GEM	1970	LC	42 X 30	ARJ	75	3	300	6000
Blue/Black	GEM	GEM	1970	LC	36 X 34	ARJ	75	2	300	5500
Yellow/Black	GEM	GEM	1970	LC	42 X 36	ARJ	75	2	300	8000
Blue/Red Orange/Green	GEM	GEM	1971	LC	42 X 30	ARJ	64	4	300	6500
Blue/Green/Black/Red	M	M	1971	LC	30 X 28	ARJ	100	3	300	6500
Blue/White/Red (G-265)	GEM	GEM	1971	LC	43 X 30	ARJ	54	3	300	8000
Green/Black	GEM	GEM	1972	LC	40 X 30	ARJ	50	2	400	8000
Black Curve	GEM	GEM	1972	LI/C	29 X 29	ARJ	75	1	350	4500
Black/Yellow	GEM	GEM	1972	LC	40 X 34	ARJ	55	2	400	5300
Black/Green II	GEM	GEM	1972	LC	28 X 24	ARJ	50	2	400	5300
Green/White	GEM	GEM	1972	LC	27 X 44	ARJ	60	2	400	5300
Untitled	BAI	GEM	1972	LC	36 X 27	ARJ	125	1	150	1800
White Curve I	GEM	GEM	1973	LB	34 X 34	AP	49	1	400	4500
White Bar with Black	GEM	GEM	1973	LC/PL	29 X 42	ARJ	50	1	400	4500
Spectrum	GEM	GEM	1973	SP	34 X 83	ARJ	34	14	500	34000
Two Whites and Black	GEM	GEM	1973	SP/EMB	23 X 47	ARJ	75	1	400	5000
Two Blacks and White	GEM	GEM	1973	SP/EMB	23 X 47	ARJ	75	1	400	3500
White and Black	GEM	GEM	1973	SP	23 X 35	ARJ	75	1	350	4000
Black and White Pyramid	GEM	GEM	1973	SP/EMB	32 X 46	ARJ	50	1	600	3000
Black Curve I	GEM	GEM	1973	LC/PL	34 X 34	ARJ	50	1	500	4500
Peach Branch	GEM	GEM	1974	LC	47 X 32	AP	50	1	500	5500
Blue with Black I	GEM	GEM	1974	LC	42 X 37	ARJ	50	2	500	3500
Large Black Curve	GEM	GEM	1974	SP	24 X 84	ARJ	30	1	1000	16000
Grape Leaves I	GEM	GEM	1974	LC	31 X 47	AP	50	1	500	5500
Grape Leaves II, III	GEM	GEM	1974	LC	47 X 31 EA	AP	50 EA	1 EA	500 EA	5500 EA

ELLSWORTH KELLY CONTINUED

TITLE	PUBLISHER	PRINTER	DATE	MEDIUM	DIMENSION (PAPER SIZE) IN INCHES	TYPE OF PAPER	EDITION NUMBER	NO. OF COLORS	ORIGINAL OPENING PRICE	CURRENT RETAIL PRICE
SOLD OUT EDITIONS (RARE):										
Blue with Black II	GEM	GEM	1974	SP	31 X 28	ARJ	50	2	400	4000
Yellow	GEM	GEM	1975	LC	38 X 38	ARJ	48	1	400	4500
Two Yellows	GEM	GEM	1975	LC	36 X 33	ARJ	44	1	400	4500
Variation Series:										
Black Variation 2	GEM	GEM	1975	LC	38 X 38	HMP	24	1	400	3500
Black Variation 3	GEM	GEM	1975	LC/I/DEB	40 X 39	HMP	25	1	400	3500
Black Variation 4	GEM	GEM	1975	SP	46 X 35	HMP	25	1	400	3000
Black Variation 5	GEM	GEM	1975	LC/I/DEB	39 X 38	HMP	21	1	400	4000
Black Variation 6	GEM	GEM	1975	LC	39 X 38	HMP	25	1	400	3000
Gray Variation	GEM	GEM	1975	I/DEB	39 X 38	HMP	27	1	400	3000
Blue I	GEM	GEM	1975	LC/EMB	40 X 39	HMP	23	1	400	3000
Blue II	GEM	GEM	1975	LC/EMB	40 X 39	HMP	24	1	400	3000
Thoronet			1976	LC	34 X 41	HMP	16	1	400	4000
Poitiers	GEM	GEM	1976	LC/EMB	41 X 34	RRP	16	1	400	4000
Third Curve Series (Series of 16):										
Corneilla	GEM	GEM	1976	LC/EMB	35 X 41	RP/ROL	16	1	400	3000
Moissac	GEM	GEM	1976	LC	34 X 41	RP/ROL	16	1	400	3000
Talmont	GEM	GEM	1976	LC/EMB	34 X 41	RP/ROL	16	1	400	3000
Chauvigny	GEM	GEM	1976	LC/EMB	34 X 41	RP/ROL	16	1	400	3000
Caen	GEM	GEM	1976	LC/DEB	41 X 34	RP/ROL	16	1	400	4000
Fontenay	GEM	GEM	1976	LC/DEB	34 X 41	RP/ROL	16	1	400	3000
Angers	GEM	GEM	1976	LC/DEB	34 X 41	RP/ROL	16	1	400	4000
Tournus	GEM	GEM	1976	LC/DEB	34 X 41	RP/ROL	16	1	400	3000
Canigou	GEM	GEM	1976	LC/DEB	34 X 41	RP/ROL	16	1	400	3000
St Savin	GEM	GEM	1976	LC/I/DEB	34 X 41	RP/ROL	16	1	400	4000
Montmorillon (G-691)	GEM	GEM	1976	I/EMB/DEB	34 X 41	RP/ROL	16	1	400	3000
Vic	GEM	GEM	1976	I/EMB/DEB	34 X 41	RP/ROL	16	1	400	3000
Fontevrault	GEM	GEM	1976	I/EMB/DEB	34 X 41	RP/ROL	16	1	400	3000
Souillac	GEM	GEM	1976	I/EMB/DEB	34 X 41	RP/ROL	16	1	400	3000
Colors on a Grid	TGL	TGL	1976	LC/SP	48 X 48	AP88	46	15	4000	25000
Colored Paper Images:										
Untitled I	TGL	TGL	1976	CP/HMP	46 X 32	HMP	20	1	400	20000
Untitled II	TGL	TGL	1976	CP/HMP	46 X 32	HMP	17	1	400	20000
Untitled II, State I	TGL	TGL	1976	CP/HMP	46 X 32	HMP	9	1	400	20000
Untitled III	TGL	TGL	1976	CP/HMP	46 X 32	HMP	21	1	400	20000
Untitled IV	TGL	TGL	1976	CP/HMP	46 X 32	HMP	20	1	400	20000
Untitled V	TGL	TGL	1976	CP/HMP	46 X 32	HMP	19	1	400	20000
Untitled VI	TGL	TGL	1976	CP/HMP	46 X 32	HMP	23	1	400	20000
Untitled VII	TGL	TGL	1976	CP/HMP	46 X 32	HMP	20	1	400	20000
Untitled VIII	TGL	TGL	1976	CP/HMP	46 X 32	HMP	20	1	400	20000
Untitled IX	TGL	TGL	1976	CP/HMP	46 X 32	HMP	18	1	400	20000
Untitled IX, State I	TGL	TGL	1976	CP/HMP	46 X 32	HMP	10	1	400	20000
Untitled X	TGL	TGL	1976	CP/HMP	46 X 32	HMP	20	1	400	20000
Untitled XI	TGL	TGL	1976	CP/HMP	46 X 32	HMP	18	1	400	20000
Untitled XII	TGL	TGL	1976	CP/HMP	46 X 32	HMP	20	1	400	20000
Untitled XIII	TGL	TGL	1976	CP/HMP	33 X 32	HMP	23	1	400	18000
Untitled XIV	TGL	TGL	1976	CP/HMP	33 X 32	HMP	24	1	400	18000
Untitled XV	TGL	TGL	1976	CP/HMP	33 X 32	HMP	23	1	400	18000
Untitled XVI	TGL	TGL	1976	CP/HMP	33 X 32	HMP	24	1	400	18000
Untitled XVII	TGL	TGL	1976	CP/HMP	33 X 32	HMP	24	1	400	18000
Untitled XVIII	TGL	TGL	1976	CP/HMP	33 X 32	HMP	22	1	400	18000
Untitled XIX	TGL	TGL	1976	CP/HMP	33 X 32	HMP	17	1	400	18000
Untitled XX	TGL	TGL	1976	CP/HMP	33 X 32	HMP	22	1	400	18000
Untitled XXI	TGL	TGL	1976	CP/HMP	33 X 32	HMP	10	1	400	18000
Nine Colors	TGL	TGL	1977	CP/HMP	30 X 30	HMP	10	9	2000	18000
Nine Squares	TGL	TGL	1977	LC/SP	40 X 40	R/BFK	44	10	1500	10000
Blue/Green/Yellow/Orange/Red	TGL	TGL	1977	CP/HMP	13 X 46	HMP	14	5	2000	10000
Leaves	GEM	GEM	1978	LC	30 X 42	AP88	30	1	600	7500
Leaf Series II, III, IV, X	GEM	GEM	1978	LC	30 X 42 EA	AP88	20 EA	1 EA	600 EA	7500 EA
Leaf Series V-XI	GEM	GEM	1978	LC	30 X 42 EA	AP88	20 EA	1 EA	600 EA	7500 EA
Dark Gray and White	TGL	TGL	1978	SP	30 X 42	RP/NEW	41	1	1000	10000
Saint Martin Landscape	TGL	TGL	1979	LC/SP/CO	27 X 33	AP88/W	39	14	800	4500
Dark Gray and White	TGL	TGL	1979	SP/CO	30 X 42	RNP/G	41	1	2000	10000
Wall	TGL	TGL	1979	EB/A	31 X 28	AC	50	1	2250	18000
Woodland Plant	TGL	TGL	1979	LB	31 X 47	AC	100	1	500	10000
Wild Grape Leaf	TGL	TGL	1980	LC	27 X 25	AC/300	50	1	500	4000
Mulberry Leaf	TGL	TGL	1980	LC	36 X 26	AC/300	50	1	500	4000
Sarsaparilla	TGL	TGL	1980	LC	32 X 48	AC/300	50	1	500	6000
Daffodil	TGL	TGL	1980	LC	40 X 28	AC/300	50	1	500	6000
Jacmel	GEM	GEM	1980	LC	35 X 30	AC	25	2	1000	4500
Jacmel, State I	GEM	GEM	1980	LC	35 X 30	AC	10	1	500	2500
Grand Case	GEM	GEM	1980	LC	30 X 35	AC	25	2	1000	6500
Grand Case, State I	GEM	GEM	1980	LC	30 X 35	AC	10	1	500	1000

ELLSWORTH KELLY CONTINUED

TITLE	PUBLISHER	PRINTER	DATE	MEDIUM	DIMENSION (PAPER SIZE) IN INCHES	TYPE OF PAPER	EDITION NUMBER	NO. OF COLORS	ORIGINAL OPENING PRICE	CURRENT RETAIL PRICE
SOLD OUT EDITIONS (RARE):										
Marigot	GEM	GEM	1980	LC	30 X 35	AC	25	2	1000	5500
Marigot, State I	GEM	GEM	1980	LC	30 X 35	AC	10	1	500	1000
Amden	GEM	GEM	1980	LC	29 X 32	AC	25	2	1000	4500
Amden, State I	GEM	GEM	1980	LC	29 X 32	AC	10	1	500	1500
Braunwald	GEM	GEM	1980	LC	30 X 35	AC	25	2	1000	4500
Braunwald, State I	GEM	GEM	1980	LC	30 X 35	AC	10	1	500	1000
Bordrouant	GEM	GEM	1980	LC	30 X 35	AC	25	2	1000	5500
Bordrouant, State I	GEM	GEM	1980	LC	30 X 35	AC	10	1	500	1000
Bandol	GEM	GEM	1980	LC	35 X 31	AC	25	2	1000	5500
Bandol, State I	GEM	GEM	1980	LC	35 X 31	AC	10	1	500	1000
18 Colors (Cincinnati)	GEM	GEM	1982	LC	16 X 91	HMP	57	18	4000	10000
The Concorde Series:										
Square with Black	GEM	GEM	1982	AB	30 X 28	HMP	18	1	800	2200
Square with Black, State I	GEM	GEM	1982	AB	30 X 28	HMP	18	1	800	3800
Diagonal with Black	GEM	GEM	1982	AB	34 X 29	HMP	18	1	1000	2200
Diagonal with Black, State I	GEM	GEM	1982	AB	34 X 29	HMP	18	1	1000	3800
Concorde I	GEM	GEM	1982	AB	42 X 30	HMP	18	1	1200	5000
Concorde I, State I	GEM	GEM	1982	AB	42 X 30	HMP	18	1	1200	6200
Concorde II	GEM	GEM	1982	AB	33 X 25	HMP	18	1	1000	3800
Concorde II, State I	GEM	GEM	1982	AB	33 X 25	HMP	18	1	1000	5000
Concorde III	GEM	GEM	1982	AB	42 X 30	HMP	18	1	1200	4000
Concorde III, State I	GEM	GEM	1982	AB	42 X 30	HMP	18	1	1200	6200
Concorde IV	GEM	GEM	1982	AB	35 X 26	HMP	18	1	1000	3800
Concorde IV, State I	GEM	GEM	1982	AB	35 X 26	HMP	18	1	1000	3800
Concorde V	GEM	GEM	1982	AB	27 X 21	HMP	18	1	750	3500
Concorde V, State I	GEM	GEM	1982	AB	27 X 21	HMP	18	1	750	5000
Cupecoy	GEM	GEM	1984	LB	58 X 50	AP88	25	1	1500	4500
Cul de Sac	GEM	GEM	1984	LB	43 X 57	AP88	25	1	1200	6000
Baie Rouge	GEM	GEM	1984	LB	51 X 52	AP88	25	1	1400	5000
Orient Beach	GEM	GEM	1984	LB	48 X 50	AP88	16	1	1200	2500
Orient Beach, State I	GEM	GEM	1984	LB/CO	48 X 50	AP88	10	1	1500	3000
St Martin Triptych	GEM	GEM	1984	LC	(L) 58 X 52 (M) 56 X 52 (R) 56 X 52	HMP	6		10000	15000
Philodendron Series:										
Philodendron I	GEM	GEM	1985	LC	25 X 36	HMP	30	1	800	6500
Philodendron II	GEM	GEM	1985	LC	25 X 36	HMP	30	1	800	7500
Calla Lily Series:										
Calla Lily I	GEM	GEM	1985	LC	30 X 39	HMP	30	1	900	5500
Calla Lily II	GEM	GEM	1985	LC	36 X 25	HMP	30	1	800	5500
Calla Lily III	GEM	GEM	1985	LC	36 X 25	HMP	30	1	800	5500
Dracena I	GEM	GEM	1985	LC	43 X 32	HMP	30	1	1000	4500
Dracena II	GEM	GEM	1985	LC	43 X 32	HMP	30	1	1000	4500
CURRENT EDITIONS:										
Red Curve	GEM	GEM	1986	LC		AP88			5000	15000
Red Curve, State I	GEM	GEM	1986	LC		AP88			5000	15000
Red Curve, State II	GEM	GEM	1986	LC		AP88			5000	15000
Blue Curve	GEM	GEM	1986	LC		AP88			5000	15000
Blue Curve, State I	GEM	GEM	1986	LC		AP88			5000	15000
Blue Curve, State II	GEM	GEM	1986	LC		AP88			5000	15000
Green Curve	GEM	GEM	1986	LC	38 X 84	AP88	15	1	5000	12000
Green Curve, State I	GEM	GEM	1986	LC	38 X 84	AP88			5000	15000
Green Curve, State II	GEM	GEM	1986	LC	38 X 84	AP88			5000	15000
Black Curve	GEM	GEM	1986	LC	38 X 84	AP88	25	1	5000	12000
Dark Gray Curve	GEM	GEM	1986	LC	26 X 84	AP88	25	1	5000	12000
Dark Gray Curve, State I	GEM	GEM	1986	LC		AP88			5000	9000
Gray Curve	GEM	GEM	1986	LC		AP88			5000	15000
Untitled (Red)	GEM	GEM	1987	LC		AP88			5000	15000
Untitled (Red), State I	GEM	GEM	1987	LC		AP88			5000	15000
Untitled (Purple)	GEM	GEM	1987	LC		AP88			5000	15000
Untitled (Purple), State I	GEM	GEM	1987	LC		AP88	18	1	5000	9000
Untitled (Orange)	GEM	GEM	1987	LC	51 X 46	AP88			5000	15000
Untitled (Orange), State I	GEM	GEM	1987	LC	47 X 46	AP88			5000	8000
Untitled (Gray)	GEM	GEM	1987	LC	47 X 46	AP88	18	1	5000	15000
Untitled (Gray), State I	GEM	GEM	1987	LC	42 X 46	AP88			5000	15000
Blue Curve, State III	GEM	GEM	1987	LC	42 X 46	AP88	18	1	5000	8000
Yellow Curve	GEM	GEM	1987	LC		AP88			5000	15000
Purple/Red/Gray/Orange	GEM	JR/DK/MP/CS/ AR/GEM	1987–88	LC	52 X 222	AP88	18	4	35000	120000
Gray Curve	GEM	GEM	1988	LC	26 X 84	AP88	15		12000	15000
Green Curve	GEM	GEM	1988	LC	37 X 84	AP88	25		12000	15000
Green Curve, State I	GEM	GEM	1988	LC	38 X 84	AP88	15		12000	15000

ELLSWORTH KELLY CONTINUED

Ellsworth Kelly
Blue Curve, State I
Courtesy Gemini GEL

TITLE	PUBLISHER	PRINTER	DATE	MEDIUM	DIMENSION (PAPER SIZE) IN INCHES	TYPE OF PAPER	EDITION NUMBER	NO. OF COLORS	ORIGINAL OPENING PRICE	CURRENT RETAIL PRICE
CURRENT EDITIONS:										
Untitled (Red,Purple,Orange) (Set of 4)	GEM	GEM	1988	LC	46 X 46 EA	AP88	18 EA		25000 SET	30000 SET
Untitled (Red, Purple, Orange, Gray) (Set of 4)	GEM	GEM	1988	LC	46 X 46 EA	AP88	18 EA		35000 SET	40000 SET
Oak Series										
Oak I (Benefit J Carter Brown Fund/ American Federation of Arts)	GEM	GEM	1992	LB	30 X 36	R/BFK	35	1	3500	3500
Oak II-VI	GEM	GEM	1992	LB	30 X 36 EA	R/BFK	30 EA	1 EA	3500 EA	3500 EA
Oak VII	GEM	GEM	1992	LB	24 X 32	HMP/T	30	1	3500	3500
Set of Four 1 Color Lithographs (Set of 4):									12000 SET	12000 SET
EK	GEM	GEM	1989	LC	47 X 38	AP88	50	1	3500	3500
Jack I	GEM	GEM	1989	LC	47 X 37	AP88	35	1	3500	3500
Jack II	GEM	GEM	1989	LC	47 X 38	AP88	35	1	3500	3500
Jack III	GEM	GEM	1989	LC	47 X 39	AP88	35	1	3500	3500
Set of Four 2 Color Lithographs (Set of 4):										
EK/Green	GEM	GEM	1989	LC	47 X 36	AP88	50	2	6500	6500
Jack/Blue	GEM	GEM	1989	LC	47 X 36	AP88	35	2	6500	6500
Jack/Gray	GEM	GEM	1989	LC	47 X 38	AP88	35	2	6500	6500
Jack/Red	GEM	GEM	1989	LC	47 X 37	AP88	35	2	6500	6500
Set of Four 6 Color Lithographs (Set of 4):										
EK/Spectrum II	GEM	GEM	1990	LC	25 X 94	AP88	50	6	12000	15000
EK/Spectrum I	GEM	GEM	1990	LC	25 X 94	AP88	50	6	20000	25000
Jack/Spectrum	GEM	GEM	1990	LC	25 X 9	AP88	35	6	12500	15000
EK/Spcetrum III	GEM	GEM	1990	LC	14 X 40	AP88	50	6	9000	10000

DOUGLAS KENT

BORN: Leicester, MA; November 2, 1944
EDUCATION: Worcester Art Mus Sch, MA
AWARDS: Ford Foundation Grant
PRINTERS: John Nichols, NY (JN)
PUBLISHERS: Fred Dorfman, Inc, NY (FDI)
GALLERIES: Martina Hamilton, New York, NY; Fred Dorfman, New York, NY

TITLE	PUBLISHER	PRINTER	DATE	MEDIUM	DIMENSION (PAPER SIZE) IN INCHES	TYPE OF PAPER	EDITION NUMBER	NO. OF COLORS	ORIGINAL OPENING PRICE	CURRENT RETAIL PRICE
CURRENT EDITIONS:										
Cowboys & Indians	FDI	JN	1981	SP	40 X 40	AE/R	75	14	250	450
Indians & Rabbits	FDI	JN	1981	SP	40 X 40	AE/R	75	10	250	450

The retail prices of the 100,000 limited edition prints quoted in this directory are subject to change. Print publishers, artists and galleries were the direct sources for these quotations. Prices in the secondary market listed as "Sold Out Editions (Rare)" indicate that the publisher has a limited supply of that print or that the print is difficult to locate in the galleries.

DAVID WILLIAM KELSO

BORN: Van Nuys, CA; January 29, 1948
EDUCATION: Univ of California, Riverside, CA, English Literature, Phi Beta Kappa, 1965–69; Studied with James Strombotne, Art, Univ of California, Riverside, CA, 1968–69-Grad Study, Victorian English, Univ of California, Berkeley, CA, 1969–70; Studied Etching with Kathan Brown, Univ of California Ext, CA, 1971; Apprenticeship, Intaglio Printmaking, with Jeanne Gantz, El Dorado Press, CA, 1972–73
TEACHING: Printmaking Workshop with Frank Lobdell, Yale Univ, New Haven, CT, 1992
AWARDS: Purchase Awards, Northwest Int Small Format Print Exhib, Art Services, 1978; Jurors Award, Berkeley Art Center, CA, 1991
RECENT EXHIB: Zimmerli Mus, Rutgers Univ, NJ, 1990; Olga Dollar Gallery, San Francisco, CA, 1991; Silvermine Guild Prints, New Canaan, CT, 1992
COLLECTIONS: Rutgers Archives, Zimmerli Mus, New Brunswick, NJ; Fine Arts Mus, Achenbach Found, San Francisco, CA
PRINTERS: Artist (ART)
PUBLISHERS: Made in California, Oakland, CA (MIC)
GALLERIES: Betsy Senior Contemporary Prints, New York, NY; Olga Dollar Gallery, San Francisco, CA
MAILING ADDRESS: 3246 Ettie Street, #16, Oakland, CA 94608

TITLE	PUBLISHER	PRINTER	DATE	MEDIUM	DIMENSION (PAPER SIZE) IN INCHES	TYPE OF PAPER	EDITION NUMBER	NO. OF COLORS	ORIGINAL OPENING PRICE	CURRENT RETAIL PRICE
SOLD OUT EDITIONS (RARE):										
Chrome Yellow Light	MIC	ART/MIC	1981	A/SB/HG/SG	30 X 22	R/BFK/W	15	6	250	950
CURRENT EDITIONS:										
Influence	MIC	ART/MIC	1983	A/SB/HG/SG	30 X 23	R/BFK/W	30	5	300	575
Snare	MIC	ART/MIC	1985	A/SB/HG/SG	30 X 23	R/BFK/W	40	4	375	500
Closing	MIC	ART/MIC	1989	A/SB/HG/SG	30 X 23	R/BFK/W	30	5	400	525
Echo	MIC	ART/MIC	1990	A/HG/SG	30 X 23	R/BFK/W	30	6	475	600
Bubble Boy	MIC	ART/MIC	1990	EB/A/HG/SH	23 X 30	R/BFK/W	15	1	325	375
Game Boy	MIC	ART/MIC	1992	EB/A/SG/ENG	30 X 23	R/BFK/W	20	1	375	375

MEL KENDRICK

BORN: Boston, MA; 1949
EDUCATION: Trinity Col, Hartford, CT, BA, 1971; Hunter Col, NY, 1973
AWARDS: Creative Artists Public Service Prog Grant, 1974,78; Nat Endowment for the Arts Grants, 1978,81
RECENT EXHIB: Galeria 57, Madrid, Spain, 1987; St Louis Art Mus, MO, 1987; New Britain Mus of Am Art, CT, 1987; Metropolitan Mus of Art, NY, 1988; John Weber Gallery, NY, 1987,89; Brooklyn Mus, NY, 1990; Margo Leavin Gallery, Los Angeles, CA, 1988,90; C Grimaldi Gallery, Baltimore, MD, 1990; Univ of Massachusetts, Amherst, MA, 1992
COLLECTIONS: Metropolitan Mus of Art, NY; Brooklyn Mus, NY; Storm King Art Center, Mountainville, NY; Centro Cultural Art Contemporeo, Mexico City, Mexico; Walker Art Center, Minneapolis, MN; High Mus, Atlanta, GA; Whitney Mus of Am Art, NY; Addison Gallery of Am Art, Andover, MA
PRINTERS: Leslie Miller, NY (LM); Grenfell Press, NY (GP)
PUBLISHERS: Editions Ilene Kurtz, NY (EIK)
GALLERIES: BlumHelman Gallery, New York, NY; John Weber Gallery, New York, NY; Margo Leavin Gallery, Los Angeles, CA; Editions Ilene Kurtz, New York, NY
MAILING ADDRESS: 134 Duane St, New York, NY 10007

Mel Kendrick
Untitled
Courtesy Editions Ilene Kurtz

TITLE	PUBLISHER	PRINTER	DATE	MEDIUM	DIMENSION (PAPER SIZE) IN INCHES	TYPE OF PAPER	EDITION NUMBER	NO. OF COLORS	ORIGINAL OPENING PRICE	CURRENT RETAIL PRICE
CURRENT EDITIONS:										
Untitled (Set of 6)	EIK	LM/GP	1990		25 X 19	SEK	25		5000 SET	5000 SET

WILLIAM KENTRIDGE

BORN: Johannesburg, South Africa; 1955
EDUCATION: Univ of Witwatersrand, Johannesburg, South Africa, BA, Politics & African Studies, 1973–76; Johannesburg Art Found, South Africa, Studied with Bill Ainslie, 1976; Studied Mime and Theatre, Ecole Jacques Lecoq, Paris, France, 1981-82
TEACHING: Instr, Johannesburg Art Found, South Africa, Etching, 1978–80
RECENT EXHIB: Cassirer Fine Art, Johannesburg, South Africa, 1988,90; Gallery on the Market, Johannesburg, South Africa, 1990; Gallery International, Cape Town, South Africa, 1990; Goodman Gallery, Johannesburg, South Africa, 1992; Vanessa Deverau Gallery, London, England, 1987,89,92
PRINTERS: Jack Shireff, Shaw, Wiltshire, England (JS); Workshop 107, Shaw, Wiltshire, England (W107)
PUBLISHERS: David Krut Fine Art, London, England (DKFA)
GALLERIES: Deborah Ripley Fine Arts, New York, NY; David Krut Fine Art, London, England

TITLE	PUBLISHER	PRINTER	DATE	MEDIUM	DIMENSION (PAPER SIZE) IN INCHES	TYPE OF PAPER	EDITION NUMBER	NO. OF COLORS	ORIGINAL OPENING PRICE	CURRENT RETAIL PRICE
CURRENT EDITIONS										
Iris	DKFA	JS/W107	1992	I/HC	47 X 36	SOM	30		£600	£600

JANE KENT

PRINTERS: David Keister, Bloomington, IN (DK); David Calkins, Bloomington, IN (DC); Echo Press, Bloomington, IN (EPr); Cindy Ettinger, NY (CE)
PUBLISHERS: Echo Press, Bloomington, IN (EPr); Dolan/Maxwell, Phila, PA (D/M)
GALLERIES: Betsy Senior Contemporary Prints, New York, NY; Dumbarton Press, New York, NY; Echo Press, Bloomington, IN

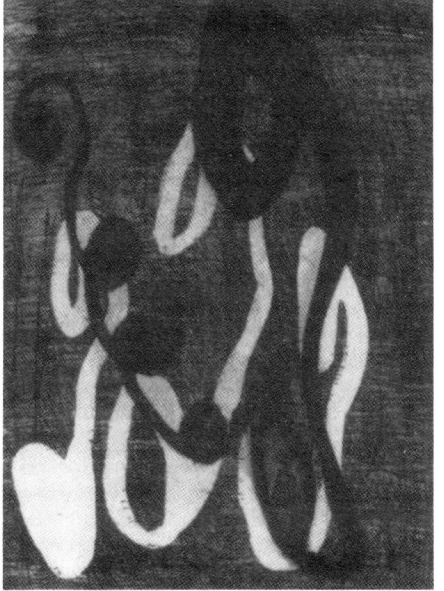

Jane Kent
Untitled, 1989–90
Courtesy the Artist

TITLE	PUBLISHER	PRINTER	DATE	MEDIUM	DIMENSION (PAPER SIZE) IN INCHES	TYPE OF PAPER	EDITION NUMBER	NO. OF COLORS	ORIGINAL OPENING PRICE	CURRENT RETAIL PRICE
CURRENT EDITIONS:										
Untitled	ART	ART	1989–90	MON	32 X 26 EA	R/BFK	5 EA	Varies	900/2100 EA	900/2100 EA
Untitled #1 (Orange)	D/M	CE	1990	I	26 X 22	R/BFK	20	1	700	700
Untitled #2 (Maroon & Blue)	D/M		1990	I	26 X 22	R/BFK	20	2	700	700
Untitled #3 (White & Black)	D/M	CE	1990	I	26 X 22	R/BFK	20	1	700	700
O-Me (with Handstamping)	EPr	DK/DC/EPr	1991	LC	18 X 12	R/BFK/LANA	5	5	600	600
O-My	EPr	DK/DC/EPr	1991	LC	18 X 12	TRP	4	6	600	600
U-B	EPr	DK/DC/EPr	1991	LC/LI	18 X 12	R/BFK/W	5	3	600	600
Y-Y	EPr	DK/DC/EPr	1991	LC	18 X 12	R/BFK/W	5	2	600	600
O-O-O	EPr	DK/DC/EPr	1991	LC/DPT/LI	29 X 20	LANA/HOSHO	8	5	1200	1200
O-Y	EPr	DK/DC/EPr	1991	LC	29 X 20	LANA	8	4	1200	1200
Portrait	EPr	DK/DC/EPr	1991	LC	29 X 20	LANA	8	3	1200	1200

ZOE KERAMEA

PRINTERS: Artist (ART); Printmaking Workshop, NY (PW)
PUBLISHERS: Museum Tower Editions, NY (MTE)
GALLERIES: Museum Tower Editions, New York, NY

TITLE	PUBLISHER	PRINTER	DATE	MEDIUM	DIMENSION (PAPER SIZE) IN INCHES	TYPE OF PAPER	EDITION NUMBER	NO. OF COLORS	ORIGINAL OPENING PRICE	CURRENT RETAIL PRICE
CURRENT EDITIONS:										
Black & White on Black and White I	ART	ART/PW	1990	ZOE	16 X 42 EA	HAHN	18	1	3600	4000
Black & White on Black and White II	ART	ART/PW	1990	ZOE	16 X 42 EA	HAHN	18	1	4000	4500
Eclipse (White on Black) (Set of 4)	MTE	ART/PW	1992	ZOE	8 X 8 EA	HAHN	18 EA	1 EA	1500 SET	1500 SET

HAIM KERN

BORN: Leipzig, Germany; 1930
EDUCATION: L'Ecole Nationale des Beaux Arts, Paris, France; L'Académie de la Grane Chaumiére, Paris, France; L'Académie Julian, Paris, France

PRINTERS: American Atelier, NY (AA)
PUBLISHERS: Circle Fine Art, Chicago, IL (CFA)
GALLERIES: Circle Galleries, San Diego, CA & San Francisco, CA & Northbrook, IL & Pittsburgh, PA & Houston, TX & Soho, NY & Chicago, IL & Scottsdale, AZ & Beverly Hills, CA & Costa Mesa, CA & Sherman Oaks, CA & Palm Beach, FL & Honolulu, HI & New Orleans, LA & Las Vegas, NV & Seattle, WA

TITLE	PUBLISHER	PRINTER	DATE	MEDIUM	DIMENSION (PAPER SIZE) IN INCHES	TYPE OF PAPER	EDITION NUMBER	NO. OF COLORS	ORIGINAL OPENING PRICE	CURRENT RETAIL PRICE
SOLD OUT EDITIONS (RARE):										
So Did I	CFA	AA	1979	LC	22 X 30	AP	200		75	175
CURRENT EDITIONS:										
Une Ha, Attaque de Coeur	CFA	AA	1978	LC	22 X 30	AP	200		75	150
Bonne Huit, Mme Ingres	CFA	AA	1980	LC	30 X 21	AP	200		75	150
Lithography Drives Me Mad	CFA	AA	1980	LC	30 X 22	AP	200		75	150

The retail prices of the 100,000 limited edition prints quoted in this directory are subject to change. Print publishers, artists and galleries were the direct sources for these quotations. Prices in the secondary market listed as "Sold Out Editions (Rare)" indicate that the publisher has a limited supply of that print or that the print is difficult to locate in the galleries.

HUGH KEPETS

BORN: Cleveland, OH; February 6, 1946
EDUCATION: Carnegie-Mellon Univ, Pittsburgh, PA, BFA, 1968; Ohio Univ, Athens, OH, MFA, 1972
AWARDS: Purchase Award, Cleveland Mus, OH, 1974; Philadelphia Print Club, PA, 1975; Davidson Nat Comp, 1976; Nat Endowment for the Arts Fel, 1976; Cleveland Arts Prize, 1979; Creative Artists Public Service Grants, 1975,80
RECENT EXHIB: Roger Ramsay Gallery, Chicago, IL, 1988; Ingrid Cusson Gallery, NY, 1989; Lyman Allyn Mus, New London, CT, 1992; David Adamson Gallery, Wash, DC, 1992
COLLECTIONS: Metropolitan Mus, NY; Philadelphia Mus, PA; Yale Univ, New Haven, CT; Cleveland Mus, OH; Art Inst of Chicago, IL; Delaware Art Mus, Wilmington, DE; Indianapolis Mus, IN; Fogg Mus, Harvard Univ, Boston, MA; Worcester Art Mus, MA; Currier Art Mus, Manchester, NH; Westmoreland County Art Mus, Greensburg, PA; Notre Dame Univ, South Bend, IN; Grey Art Gallery, New York, Univ, NY; Ablion Col, MI; Ackland Art Center, Univ of North Carolina, Chapel Hill, NC; Kresge Art Gallery, Michigan State Univ, East Lansing, MI; Utah State Univ, Logan, UT; Brandeis Univ, Waltham, MA; Mills Col, Oakland, CA; Middlebury Col, VT; Weatherspoon Art Gallery, Univ of North Carolina, Greensboro, NC; Yale Univ, New Haven, CT
PRINTERS: K Caraccio, NY (KC); Burr Miller, NY (BM); Maurel Studio, NY (MS); Sheila Marbain, NY (SM); Mohammad Khalil, NY (MK); Frank Versaggi, NY (FV); John Campione, NY (JC); Norman Stewart, Bloomfield Hills, MI (NS); Joe Keenan (JK); Wing Lake Studio, Bloomfield Hills, MI (WLS); Julie Fein, NY (JF); Roni Henning, NY (RH); Steve Maiorano, NY (SMa); Screened Images, Port Washington, NY (SI); Michael Reck, NY (MR)
PUBLISHERS: Orion Editions, NY (OE); G W Einstein & Co, NY (GWE); Print Club of Cleveland, OH (PCC); 724 Prints, NY (724P); Stewart & Stewart, Bloomfield Hills, MI (S-S); Artist (ART)
GALLERIES: David Adamson Gallery, Wash, DC; Roger Ramsay Gallery, Chicago, IL; Randall Beck Gallery, Boston, MA; Stewart & Stewart, Bloomfield Hills, MI; Brenda Kroos Gallery, Columbus, OH; Orion Editions, New York, NY; Concept Art Gallery, Pittsburgh, PA
MAILING ADDRESS: 134 E 16th St, New York, NY 10003

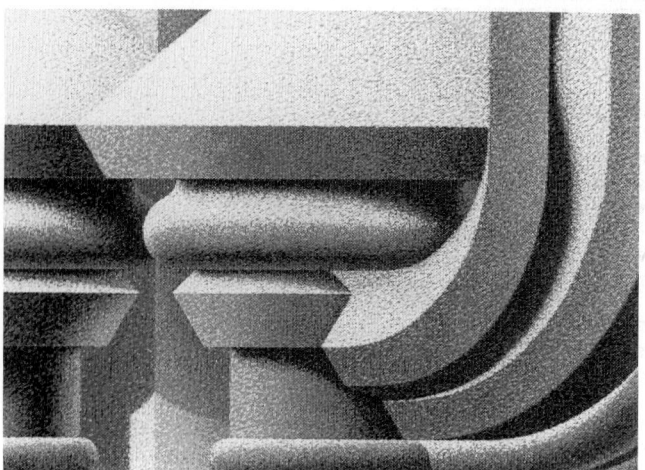

Hugh Kepets
Astor
Courtesy Stewart & Stewart

TITLE	PUBLISHER	PRINTER	DATE	MEDIUM	DIMENSION (PAPER SIZE) IN INCHES	TYPE OF PAPER	EDITION NUMBER	NO. OF COLORS	ORIGINAL OPENING PRICE	CURRENT RETAIL PRICE
SOLD OUT EDITIONS (RARE):										
Beverley Road	ART	JC/BM	1974	LC/SP	27 X 21	R/BFK	40	5	200	800
Cortelyu Road	ART	JC/BM	1974	LC/SP	27 X 21	R/BFK	40	4	200	800
Brooklyn Botanical Garden I	GWE	SM/BM	1975	LC/SP	21 X 27	R/BFK	80	5	200	800
Brooklyn Botanical Garden II	GWE	SM/BM	1975	LC/SP	21 X 27	R/BFK	80	5	200	800
Sixth Avenue	GWE	SM/MS	1976	SP	41 X 35	STAR	85	11	250	1200
Seventh Avenue	GWE	SM/MS	1976	SP	41 X 35	STAR	85	11	250	1200
Eighth Avenue	GWE	SM/MS	1976	SP	41 X 35	STAR	85	11	250	1200
West 74th Street	GWE	SM/MS	1976	SP	41 X 35	STAR	100	13	250	1200
Lower Broadway I,II,III	GEW	SM/BM	1977	LC/SP	27 X 21 EA	STAR	85 EA	4 EA	250 EA	1200 EA
Hudson Street I,II	GWE	MK	1977	I	22 X 30 EA	STAR	65 EA	2 EA	200 EA	700 EA
Demitasse	OE	SM/FV	1977	LC/SP	22 X 30	R/BFK	85	6	250	650
West 71st Street	OE	SM/MS	1979	SP	35 X 49	R/BFK	85	15	350	1850
18th Street	OE	SM/MS	1979	SP	35 X 49	R/BFK	85	16	350	1850
West 79th Street I	OE	SM/FV	1979	SP	35 X 49	R/BFK	85	15	350	1250
Allegheny I (Blue)	OE	SM/MS	1980	SP	31 X 35	R/BFK	50	15	435	750
Allegheny II (Gray)	OE	SM/MS	1980	SP	31 X 35	R/BFK	38	15	435	1000
Allegheny III (Red)	OE	SM/MS	1980	SP	31 X 35	R/BFK	50	15	435	750
Smithfield Street Bridge I	PA	SM/MS	1980	SP	30 X 35	R/BFK/G	100	15	425	750
West 11th Street I, Red Rail	OE	KC	1983	I	29 X 40	AP	65	4	475	1200
West 11th Street I, Blue Rail	OE	KC	1983	I	29 X 40	AP	65	4	475	850
Met Gates II	PCC	KC	1984	I	15 X 12	AP	250	2	200	350
CURRENT EDITIONS:										
Iroquois	OE	SM/FV	1979	LC/SP	22 X 30	R/BFK	85	6	250	500
10 Spoons (1–15, Gray/16–50, Blue/ 51–85, Green)	OE	KC	1980	AC	29 X 21		85	3	185	300
Tama (1–42, Gray/43–85, Red)	OE	KC	1980	LC/SP	22 X 41		85	3	375	600
41 CPW	OE	SM/FV	1980	LC/SP	30 X 22		85	5	300	600
Allegheny IV (Gray)	OE	SM/MS	1981	SP	31 X 35		100	15	425	750
E 9th & Euclid	OE	SM/MS	1981	SP	31 X 35		95	15	425	650
39 GPN	OE	KC	1981	AC	30 X 41	RP/T-RP/G	85	54	375	600
GW Bridge	OE	SM/MS	1981	SP	44 X 30		100	15	475	1500
Cuyahoga	OE	SM/MS	1982	SP	44 X 30		95	16	500	850
Grant Avenue I,II	OE	KC	1982	I	24 X 30 EA		50 EA	4 EA	275 EA	325 EA
Syracuse	OE	SM/FV	1982	LC/SP	25 X 24		100	5	275	325
West 11th Street II, Green Rail	OE	KC	1982	AC	30 X 40	R/BFK	60	4	550	850
West 11th Street III, Green Rail	OE	KC	1982	AC	40 X 30	R/BFK	60	5	550	850
West 11th Street II, Brass Rail	OE	KC	1983	AC	30 X 40	R/BFK	60	4	550	850
West 11th Street III, Brass Rail	OE	KC	1983	AC	39 X 29	R/BFK	60	5	550	850
1889 YDR II	OE	SM/FV	1983	LC/SP	23 X 30	R/BFK	60	6	300	350
Met Gates III	ART	JF/KC	1984	I	22 X 30	AC	45	2	300	550
Westside I	724P	SM/MS	1984	SP	25 X 35	R/BFK	90	14	400	1200
Westside II	724P	SM/MS	1984	SP	25 X 35	R/BFK	90	14	400	900
Westside III	724P	SM/MS	1985	SP	25 X 35	R/BFK	90	14	400	800

HUGH KEPETS CONTINUED

TITLE	PUBLISHER	PRINTER	DATE	MEDIUM	DIMENSION (PAPER SIZE) IN INCHES	TYPE OF PAPER	EDITION NUMBER	NO. OF COLORS	ORIGINAL OPENING PRICE	CURRENT RETAIL PRICE
CURRENT EDITIONS:										
St Luke's Place #1,#2,#3	ART	JF/KC	1985	I	22 X 30 EA	AC	40 EA	2 EA	300 EA	550 EA
St Luke's Place #4 (Red/Grey)	ART	KC	1986	I	40 X 52	AC	15	2	950	1600
St Luke's Place #4 (Blue/Grey)	ART	KC	1986	I	40 X 52	AC	15	2	950	1600
9th Avenue I (Gray)	ART/OE	SMa/SI	1986	SP	46 X 35	COV	98	16	800	1200
9th Avenue II (Red)	ART/OE	SMa/SI	1986	SP	46 X 35	COV	98	16	800	1200
10th Avenue I (Gray)	ART/OE	SMa/SI	1986	SP	46 X 36	COV	98	15	800	1200
10th Avenue II (Red)	ART/OE	SMa/SI	1986	SP	46 X 36	COV	98	15	800	1200
Astor	S-S	NS/WLS	1986	SP	21 X 29	R/BFK/W	67	32	475	1000
Lenox	S-S	NS/WLS	1986	SP	21 X 29	R/BFK/W	68	31	425	850
St Luke's Place #5,#6	OE	RH	1986	SP	42 X 66 EA	AC/W	40 EA	25 EA	1000 EA	1850 EA
St Luke's Place #7,#8	OE	RH	1987	SP	48 X 36 EA	AC/W	40 EA	26 EA	1000 EA	1800 EA
Tilden	S-S	NS/WLS	1987	SP	21 X 29	R/BFK/W	68	26	450	850
Lincoln	ART/OE	SM/MS	1988	SP	41 X 31	COV	95	14	700	1000
Madison	ART/OE	SM/MS	1988	SP	41 X 31	COV	95	14	700	1000
Williamsberg	ART/OE	SM/MS	1988	SP	41 X 31	COV	95	14	700	1000
Park Avenue South I,II	ART/OE	SMa/SI	1989	SP	46 X 36 EA	COV	98 EA	15 EA	900 EA	900 EA
Huron	ART/OE	RH	1989	SP	30 X 22	AC/W	90	17	750	850
Akron	ART/OE	RH	1989	SP	30 X 22	AC/W	90	17	750	850
Columbus I,II	ART/OE	RH	1990	SP	48 X 36 EA	AC/W	50 EA	14 EA	1400 EA	1400 EA
Morningside Drive, #1,#2,#3	ART	MR/KC	1992	I	22 X 30 EA	AC/W	15 EA	4 EA	1200 SET / 450 EA	1200 SET / 450 EA
Riverside Drive, #1,#2,#3	ART	MR/KC	1992	I	22 X 30 EA	AC/W	15 EA	4 EA	1200 SET / 450 EA	1200 SET / 450 EA

CATHERINE KERNAN

BORN: Cooperstown, NY; June 9, 1948
EDUCATION: Cooper Union, NY, BFA; Univ of Wisconsin, Madison, WI, MFA
AWARDS: First Prize, Midwestern Print & Drawing Comp, 1979
COLLECTIONS: Detroit Inst of Art, MI; Elvehjem Mus of Art, Madison, WI; Madison Art Center, WI
PRINTERS: Norman Stewart, Bloomfield Hills, MI (NS); Stewart & Stewart, Bloomfield Hills, MI (S–S); Stephen Calwalader, Boston, MA (SC); Artist (ART); Joe Keenan (JK)
PUBLISHERS: Ronbie Editions Inc, Bensalem, PA (RE); Wing Lake Studio, Bloomfield Hills, MI (WLS); Artist (ART)
GALLERIES: Associated American Artists, New York, NY; Clifford Gallery, Dallas, TX; Stone Press Gallery, Seattle, WA; Bess Cutler Gallery, New York, NY; Stewart & Stewart, Bloomfield Hills, MI;
MAILING ADDRESS: 32 Clifton St, Somerville, MA 02144

TITLE	PUBLISHER	PRINTER	DATE	MEDIUM	DIMENSION (PAPER SIZE) IN INCHES	TYPE OF PAPER	EDITION NUMBER	NO. OF COLORS	ORIGINAL OPENING PRICE	CURRENT RETAIL PRICE
CURRENT EDITIONS:										
Cutaway I, II, III	RE	ART	1982	I	34 X 27	AC/W	100	21	300	900
Cutaway II	RE	ART	1982	I	34 X 27	AC/W	100	16	300	900
Cutaway III	RE	ART	1982	I	34 X 27	AC/W	100	21	300	900
Cutaway IV	ART	ART	1983	I	34 X 27	AC/W	100	19	300	900
Cutaway V	ART	ART	1983	I	34 X 27	AC/W	100	16	300	900
Traversal I	S-S	NS/WLS	1983	SP	21 X 29	R/BFK/W	41	32	350	750
Traversal II	S-S	NS/WLS	1983	SP	21 X 29	R/BFK/W	44	24	350	750
Syra I	ART	ART/SC	1984	I	26 X 22	AC/W	50	17	225	650
Syra II	ART	ART/SC	1984	I	22 X 25	AC/W	70	14	225	650
Cascade Series #3 (Dipt)	ART	ART	1986	MON	42 X 60 EA	AP	1 EA		1200 EA	1500 EA
Sticks I	S-S	NS/JK/WLS	1988	SP	29 X 21	R/BFK/W	55	21	400	750
Sticks II	S-S	NS/JK/WLS	1988	SP	29 X 21	R/BFK/W	61	18	400	750

BARBARA DAVIS KERNE

BORN: Bronx, NY; January 1, 1938
EDUCATION: Brooklyn Col, NY, BA, 1960; Univ of Maryland, College Park, MD, MA, 1961
TEACHING: Prof, Art, Montgomery Col, Rockville, MD, 1972 to present
AWARDS: Best in Show, Maryland Federation of Arts, Annapolis, MD, 1984; Purchase Award, Owensboro Mus, KY, 1986; Fel, Frans Masereel Center, Kasterlee, Belgium, 1987
RECENT EXHIB: Philadelphia Print Club, PA, 1987; Acad Arts Coll, Easton, MD, 1987; Wenniger Graphics, Provincetown, MA, 1988; Franz Bader Gallery, Wash, DC, 1988; Mills Col Art Gallery, Oakland, CA, 1988; Rowe Art Gallery, Univ of North Carolina, Charlotte, NC, 1989; Society of Am Graphic Artists, Nat Print Exhib, NY, 1989; Selby Gallery, Ringling Sch of Art, Sarasota, FL, 1990
COLLECTIONS: Corcoran Gallery Art, Wash, DC; Norton Gallery of Art, Palm Beach, FL; Acad of Arts, Easton, MD; Montgomery County Contemp Art Coll, Rockville, MD; Owensboro Mus, KY; Franz Masereel Centre Graphic Arts, Kasterlee, Belgium
PRINTERS: C Caraccio, NY (CC); Tom Ranses, Wash, DC (TR); Artist (ART)
PUBLISHERS: Artist (ART)
GALLERIES: Franz Bader Gallery, Wash, DC; Print Club, Phila, PA; Miriam Perlman, Inc, Chicago, IL; Swanston Fine Arts, Inc, Atlanta, GA; Ed Hill Editions, El Paso, TX
MAILING ADDRESS: 10409 Lloyd Rd, Potomac, MD 20854

The retail prices of the 100,000 limited edition prints quoted in this directory are subject to change. Print publishers, artists and galleries were the direct sources for these quotations. Prices in the secondary market listed as "Sold Out Editions (Rare)" indicate that the publisher has a limited supply of that print or that the print is difficult to locate in the galleries.

BARBARA DAVIS KERNE CONTINUED

TITLE	PUBLISHER	PRINTER	DATE	MEDIUM	DIMENSION (PAPER SIZE) IN INCHES	TYPE OF PAPER	EDITION NUMBER	NO. OF COLORS	ORIGINAL OPENING PRICE	CURRENT RETAIL PRICE
SOLD OUT EDITIONS (RARE):										
Transition	ART	ART	1982	EB	22 X 18	AP	30	1	100	250
Looking for Tomorrow	ART	ART	1982	EB	18 X 12	AP	30	1	100	250
CURRENT EDITIONS:										
The Striped Stair	ART	ART	1981	EB	18 X 15	AP	30	1	60	125
Threshold	ART	ART	1981	EB	18 X 15	AP	30	1	60	125
From the Arbor	ART	ART	1982	EB	22 X 18	AP	30	1	100	175
Rest and Be Thankful	ART	ART	1982	EB	22 X 18	AP	30	1	100	175
Palmetto Dunes	ART	ART	1983	EB	22 X 30	AP	25	1	200	250
Under the Green Umbrella	ART	ART	1983	EB	30 X 22	AP	30	1	200	250
Cinzano	ART	ART	1983	EB	30 X 22	AP	30	1	200	250
Late Afternoon	ART	ART	1983	EB	22 X 30	AP	25	1	200	250
Solitude	ART	ART	1984	EB	22 X 18	AP	50	1	200	250
Brazilian Court	ART	ART	1984	EB/A	22 X 18	R/BFK	30	4	125	250
Late Afternoon II	ART	CC	1984	EB/A	22 X 30	R/BFK	50	4	250	375
Palmetto Dunes II	ART	CC	1984	EB/A	22 X 30	R/BFK	50	4	250	375
Transition II	ART	ART	1985	EB/A	22 X 18	R/BFK	30	4	150	275
Gateway	ART	ART	1985	EB/A	22 X 30	R/BFK	50	3	300	375
Beyond the Fountain	ART	ART	1985	EB/A	22 X 30	R/BFK	50	3	300	375
Garden of Silence	ART	ART	1985	EB/DPT	22 X 30	AP	30	1	200	275
Ecco la Primavera	ART	ART	1985	EB/DPT	22 X 30	AP	30	1	200	275
Arbor	ART	TR	1986	EB/A/DPT/HC	30 X 22	R/BFK	40	3	350	375
Dreaming of Spring	ART	TR	1986	EB/A/DPT/HC	30 X 35	R/BFK	50	3	400	450
Private Space	ART	TR	1986	EB/DPT	22 X 30	AP	35	1	250	275
Monoprints, EV 4–6	ART	ART	1986	MON	18 X 24 EA	R/BFK	1 EA		400 EA	450 EA
Monoprints, EV 4–6	ART	ART	1986	MON	24 X 30 EA	R/BFK	1 EA		450 EA	500 EA

MAURIE KERRIGAN

BORN: Jersey City, NJ; April 28, 1951
EDUCATION: Moore Col of Art, Phila, PA, BFA, 1973; Art Inst of Chicago, IL, MFA, 1977; Whitney Mus of Am Art, NY, 1977
AWARDS: Visual Arts, Nat Endowment for the Arts Fel, 1981; Artists Fel, Pennsylvania Council for the Arts, Phila, PA, 1982; Penn's Landing Sculpture Award, Phila, PA, 1983; MacDowell Colony Fel, 1986,87; Penny McCall Found Award, 1987
RECENT EXHIB: Philadelphia Mus of Art, PA, 1987; Pennsylvania Acad of Fine Arts, Phila, PA, 1989
COLLECTIONS: Philadelphia Mus of Art, PA; Lannon Found, Palm Beach, FL; Phillips Coll, Wash, DC; Smithsonian Inst, Wash, DC; Nat Women's Mus, Wash, DC
PUBLISHERS: Landfall Press, Inc, Chicago, IL (LPI)
PRINTERS: Jack Lemon, Chicago, IL (JL); Landfall Press, Inc, Chicago, IL (LPI)
GALLERIES: Max Hutchinson Gallery, New York, NY; Jeffrey Fuller Fine Art Gallery, Phila, PA; Landfall Press, Inc, Chicago, IL
MAILING ADDRESS: 2426 Lombard St, Phila, PA 19146

TITLE	PUBLISHER	PRINTER	DATE	MEDIUM	DIMENSION (PAPER SIZE) IN INCHES	TYPE OF PAPER	EDITION NUMBER	NO. OF COLORS	ORIGINAL OPENING PRICE	CURRENT RETAIL PRICE
CURRENT EDITIONS:										
Oxidation	LPI	JL/LPI	1985	WC	23 X 22	AP	30	4	350	350

ROBERT GLENN KETCHUM

BORN: Los Angeles, CA; December 1, 1947
EDUCATION: Univ of California, Los Angeles, CA, BA, 1970; California Inst of the Arts, Valencia, CA, MFA, Photography, 1974
TEACHING: Founder & Teacher, Photography Workshop, Sun Valley Ctr for the Arts & Humanities, CA, 1970–73; Instr, Photography, California Inst of the Arts, Valencia, CA, 1974–75; Tahoe Photographic Workshop, NV, 1981; Instr, Adv Bd, Appalachian Arts Center, Highlands, NC, 1982 to present
AWARDS: Int Artist of the Year, 1974; MAT Research Award, Ciba-Geigy, 1979; Nat Park Found, 1978,79; Pentax Corp, 1983; New York State Council of the Arts Grant, 1985
COLLECTIONS: Mus of Mod Art, NY; Corcoran Gallery of Art, Wash, DC; Los Angeles County Mus of Art, CA; George Eastman House, NY; Univ of California, Los Angeles, CA; Fogg Art Mus, Harvard Univ, MA; Univ of New Mexico, Albuquerque, NM; Metropolitan Mus of Art, NY; Nat Mus of Art, Wash, DC; Metropolitan Mus of Art, NY; Nat Mus of Am Art, Wash, DC
PRINTERS: Michael Wilder, Venice, CA (MW)
PUBLISHERS: Artist (ART)
GALLERIES: Afterimage Gallery, Dallas, TX; Photography Gallery, La Jolla, CA; G Ray Hawkins Gallery, Los Angeles, CA; Silver Image Gallery, Seattle, WA; Photographer's Gallery, Palo Alto, CA; J J Brookings Gallery, San Jose, CA; Photographic Image Gallery, Portland, OR
MAILING ADDRESS: 696 Stone Canyon Rd, Los Angeles, CA 90077

TITLE	PUBLISHER	PRINTER	DATE	MEDIUM	DIMENSION (PAPER SIZE) IN INCHES	TYPE OF PAPER	EDITION NUMBER	NO. OF COLORS	ORIGINAL OPENING PRICE	CURRENT RETAIL PRICE
SOLD OUT EDITIONS (RARE):										
Cottonwood Thicket	ART	MW	1972	PH/C	20 X 24	CIBA	10		200	2800
Madrugada	ART	MW	1974	PH/C	24 X 30	CIBA	10		300	3300
Winter Sun	ART	MW	1974	PH/C	24 X 30	CIBA	9		300	3300
Targhee Fall	ART	MW	1976	PH/C	20 X 24	CIBA	13		200	2000
Monument Valley	ART	MW	1977	PH/C	24 X 30	CIBA	12		1500	1800
First Light	ART	MW	1978	PH/C	20 X 24	CIBA	15		400	1000
Cottonwood Thicket	ART	MW	1980	PH/C	30 X 40	CIBA	14		3000	5500
From the Point at Jons	ART	MW	1981	PH/C	24 X 30	CIBA	12		1500	1800

ROBERT GLENN KETCHUM CONTINUED

TITLE	PUBLISHER	PRINTER	DATE	MEDIUM	DIMENSION (PAPER SIZE) IN INCHES	TYPE OF PAPER	EDITION NUMBER	NO. OF COLORS	ORIGINAL OPENING PRICE	CURRENT RETAIL PRICE
SOLD OUT EDITIONS (RARE):										
Window in the Forest	ART	MW	1982	PH/C	30 X 40	CIBA	15		3000	3300
Trail Creek Beaver Ponds	ART	MW	1982	PH/C	30 X 40	CIBA	12		3000	3300
Window in the Forest	ART	MW	1983	PH/C	30 X 40	CIBA	15		1000	3300
CURRENT EDITIONS:										
Willows	ART	MW	1972	PH/C	20 X 24	CIBA	15		400	1800
Limekiln	ART	MW	1977	PH/C	20 X 24	CIBA	15		400	1800
Gambel Oak, Mesa Verde	ART	MW	1977	PH/C	20 X 24	CIBA	15		400	1000
Morning Fog, Big Sur	ART	MW	1978	PH/C	20 X 24	CIBA	15		400	1800
Good Dog Constellation	ART	MW	1983	PH/C	30 X 40	CIBA	20		750	1650
Autumnal Warp	ART	MW	1983	PH/C	30 X 40	CIBA	20		750	1650
Altar/Apparition in Blue	ART	MW	1983	PH/C	30 X 40	CIBA	20		750	1650
The Dark Wood of Error	ART	MW	1983	PH/C	30 X 40	CIBA	20		750	1650
La Couleur de Mon Amour	ART	MW	1983	PH/C	30 X 40	CIBA	20		750	1650
Brewster Boogie Woogie 27	ART	MW	1983	PH/C	30 X 40	CIBA	20		750	1650
Brewster Boogie Woogie 11	ART	MW	1983	PH/C	30 X 40	CIBA	20		750	1650
Dielectric for the Eye/Homage to Jackie Priestman	ART	MW	1983	PH/C	30 X 40	CIBA	20		750	1650

HARVEY KIDDER

BORN: Cambridge, MA
EDUCATION: Child-Walker Sch of Design, Boston, MA
COLLECTIONS: Mendenhall Mus, PA; Millicent Rogers Mus, Taos, NM

PRINTERS: David Wander, NY (DW); Bruce Cleveland, Brooklyn, NY (BC); Cleveland Editions Brooklyn, NY (ClEd); Werner Graphics, NY (WG)
PUBLISHERS: John Szoke Graphics, NY (JSG)
GALLERIES: John Szoke Graphics, New York, NY; Images Art Gallery, Briarcliff, NY; River Gallery, Irvington-On-Hudson, NY

TITLE	PUBLISHER	PRINTER	DATE	MEDIUM	DIMENSION (PAPER SIZE) IN INCHES	TYPE OF PAPER	EDITION NUMBER	NO. OF COLORS	ORIGINAL OPENING PRICE	CURRENT RETAIL PRICE
CURRENT EDITIONS:										
Salt March	JSG	WG	1984	EC	25 X 32	AC	150	6	190	250
Beach Road	JSG	WG	1984	EC	25 X 32	AC	150	6	190	250
Red Rocks	JSG	WG	1984	EC	25 X 36	AC	175	6	250	300
Canyon Steam	JSG	WG	1984	EC	25 X 33	AC	176	6	250	300
Park Suite (Set of 3):									475 SET	600 SET
Autumn Haze	JSG	DW	1984	EC	30 X 22	AC	150	6	175	250
Cityscape	JSG	DW	1984	EC	30 X 22	AC	150	6	175	250
Park Walk	JSG	DW	1984	EC	30 X 22	AC	150	6	175	250
Coastal Rocks	JSG	BC/ClEd	1984	EC	29 X 34	AC	150	6	275	350
Springtime (Blue Bonnet)	JSG	BC/ClEd	1984	EC	30 X 42	AC	150	6	250	300
Panorama	JSG	BC/ClEd	1985	EC	30 X 42	AC	60	6	300	350
The Path	JSG	BC/ClEd	1986	EC	30 X 42	AC	125	6	275	350

HUBERT KIECOL

BORN: Cologne, Germany

PRINTERS: Artist (ART)
PUBLISHERS: Galerie Gisela Capitain, Cologne, Germany (GGC)
GALLERIES: Bruno Brunnet Fine Arts, Berlin, Germany; David Nolan Gallery, New York, NY

TITLE	PUBLISHER	PRINTER	DATE	MEDIUM	DIMENSION (PAPER SIZE) IN INCHES	TYPE OF PAPER	EDITION NUMBER	NO. OF COLORS	ORIGINAL OPENING PRICE	CURRENT RETAIL PRICE
CURRENT EDITIONS:										
Fünf Treppen (Set of 5)	GGC	DTV	1988	AB		RP	20 EA	1 EA	1900 SET	3000 SET
Astronomie (Set of 5)	GGC	ART	1992	WC	29 X 21 EA	BU	12 EA	2 EA	DM 5400 SET	DM 5400 SET

CHRIS KILLIP

BORN: England; 1946

PRINTERS: Artist (ART)
PUBLISHERS: Witkin Berley, Ltd, NY (WBL)
GALLERIES: Witkin Gallery, New York, NY

TITLE	PUBLISHER	PRINTER	DATE	MEDIUM	DIMENSION (PAPER SIZE) IN INCHES	TYPE OF PAPER	EDITION NUMBER	NO. OF COLORS	ORIGINAL OPENING PRICE	CURRENT RETAIL PRICE
SOLD OUT EDITIONS (RARE):										
Isle of Man (Set of 12)	WBL	ART	1973	PH	11 X 14 EA		25 EA		350 SET	2500 SET

The print market has become very selective. For the first time since we published the first edition of The Printworld Directory in 1982, the prices of prints have been greatly reduced and greatly increased for the same artists by the most reputable and established print publishers. Check the fifth edition to understand the movement.

LANCE KILAND

BORN: Fargo, ND; November 27, 1947
EDUCATION: Moorhead State Univ, MN, BA; Southern Illinois Univ, Carbondale, IL, MFA
TEACHING: North Hennepin Comm Col, Minneapolis, MN, 1972 to present
AWARDS: Bush Found Fel, 1984; McKnight Found Fel, 1985; Nat Endowment for the Arts Fel, 1985; Minnesota State Arts Grant, 1988
RECENT EXHIB: Thomson Gallery, Minneapolis, MN, 1987,89; Art Inst of Chicago, IL, 1991; North Dakota Mus of Art, Grand Forks, ND, 1991
COLLECTIONS: Walker Art Center, Minneapolis, MN; Art Inst of Chicago, IL
PRINTERS: Jack Lemon, Chicago, IL (JL); Landfall Press, Inc, Chicago, IL (LPI)
PUBLISHERS: Landfall Press, Inc, Chicago, IL (LPI)
GALLERIES: Thimmesch Gallery, Minneapolis, MN; Landfall Press, Inc, Chicago, IL; Quartet Editions, New York, NY
MAILING ADDRESS: 3153 Bloomington Ave, South, Minneapolis, MN 55407

TITLE	PUBLISHER	PRINTER	DATE	MEDIUM	DIMENSION (PAPER SIZE) IN INCHES	TYPE OF PAPER	EDITION NUMBER	NO. OF COLORS	ORIGINAL OPENING PRICE	CURRENT RETAIL PRICE
CURRENT EDITIONS:										
Pilot Stone	LPI	JL/LPI	1988	WC	40 X 36	AC/W	35	4	600	600
Hole in the Day	LPI	JL/LPI	1988	WC/LC	40 X 36	AC/W	35	6	600	600
Beehive	LPI	JL/LPI	1988	LC/WC	17 X 20	AC/W	35	4	250	250
A Sharp Eye	LPI	JL/LPI	1988	LC/WC	17 X 20	AC/W	35	4	250	250
Red River	LPI	JL/LPI	1988	LC/WC	17 X 20	AC/W	35	4	250	250
Take Note	LPI	JL/LPI	1988	LC/WC	17 X 20	AC/W	35	4	250	250

STEPHEN KILAR

BORN: Hungary; 1935
EDUCATION: L'Ecole Nationale des Beaux Arts, Paris, France
COLLECTIONS: Musée d'Art Moderne de la Ville, Paris, France
PRINTERS: American Atelier, NY (AA)
PUBLISHERS: Circle Fine Art, Chicago, IL (CFA)
GALLERIES: Circle Galleries, San Diego, CA & San Francisco, CA & Northbrook, IL & Pittsburgh, PA & Houston, TX & Soho, NY & Chicago, IL & Scottsdale, AZ & Beverly Hills, CA & Costa Mesa, CA & Sherman Oaks, CA & Palm Beach, FL & Honolulu, HI & New Orleans, LA & Las Vegas, NV & Seattle, WA

TITLE	PUBLISHER	PRINTER	DATE	MEDIUM	DIMENSION (PAPER SIZE) IN INCHES	TYPE OF PAPER	EDITION NUMBER	NO. OF COLORS	ORIGINAL OPENING PRICE	CURRENT RETAIL PRICE
SOLD OUT EDITIONS (RARE):										
Poles Magnétiques	CFA	AA	1980	EC	13 X 20	R/BFK	50		35	150
Fin des Plantes	CFA	AA	1980	EC	13 X 18	R/BFK	50		35	150

MARK KING

PRINTERS: American Atelier, NY (AA); Alexander Heinrici, NY (AH); Studio Heinrici, NY (SH)
PUBLISHERS: Martin Lawrence Limited Editions, Van Nuys, CA (MLLE); Alliance Art Publishing, Hayward, WI (AAP)
GALLERIES: Martin Lawrence Galleries, Sherman Oaks, CA & Los Angeles, CA & Newport Beach, CA & Short Hills, NJ & Phila, PA & Palm Springs, CA & Redondo Beach, CA & Escondido, CA & Thousand Oaks, CA & West Los Angeles, CA & Santa Clara, CA; Renaissance Galleries, Pittsburgh, PA & Mt Lebanon, PA; Post Gallery, Houston, TX; Art Brokerage, Ketchum, ID; Professional Fine Arts Services, Inc, New York, NY

Mark King
Lone Tusker
Martin Lawrence Limited Editions

The retail prices of the 100,000 limited edition prints quoted in this directory are subject to change. Print publishers, artists and galleries were the direct sources for these quotations. Prices in the secondary market listed as "Sold Out Editions (Rare)" indicate that the publisher has a limited supply of that print or that the print is difficult to locate in the galleries.

MARK KING CONTINUED

Mark King
Augusta Glory
Courtesy Martin Lawrence Limited Editions

Mark King
Cherry Blossom Corner
Courtesy Martin Lawrence Limited Editions

TITLE	PUBLISHER	PRINTER	DATE	MEDIUM	DIMENSION (PAPER SIZE) IN INCHES	TYPE OF PAPER	EDITION NUMBER	NO. OF COLORS	ORIGINAL OPENING PRICE	CURRENT RETAIL PRICE
SOLD OUT EDITIONS (RARE):										
Parasol	MLLE	AH/SH	1986	SP	33 X 40	SOM	550		750	3500
Orchestra	MLLE	AH/SH	1986	SP	38 X 42	SOM	550		750	4000
Picking up the Scent	MLLE	IL	1987	SP	35 X 44	SOM	550		750	4500
Amen Corner	MLLE	IL	1987	SP	36 X 43	SOM	550		750	4500
Spyglass Hill	MLLE	IL	1987	SP	43 X 36	SOM	550		750	4000
Cypress Point #15	MLLE	IL	1988	SP	37 X 42	SOM	550		850	4500
Pink Umbrella	MLLE	IL	1988	SP	34 X 42	SOM	550		850	4500
Desoto Springs Pond	MLLE	IL	1988	SP	37 X 46	SOM	550		850	4500
Augusta #11	MLLE	IL	1989	SP	37 X 46	SOM	550		1200	4500
Golf Series:										
Seaside Green	MLLE	IL	1989	SP	20 X 24	SOM	595		850	1400
Sawgrass #17	MLLE	IL	1989	SP	20 X 24	SOM	595		850	1400
Riviera #5	MLLE	IL	1989	SP	20 X 24	SOM	595		850	1400
Augusta Landscape	MLLE	IL	1989	SP	20 X 24	SOM	550		850	1400
Morning Splendor	MLLE	IL	1990	SP	52 X 73	SOM	325		1800	5000
CURRENT EDITIONS:										
Bengal Family	AAP		1976	SP	40 X 40	AP			250	3000
Zebras	AAP		1976	SP	45 X 35	AP			250	3000
Foxhunt	AAP		1977	SP	41 X 33	AP			350	3000
Pulse of the City	AAP		1977	SP	42 X 54	AP			400	5500
Spinnakers	AAP		1977	SP	45 X 36	AP			350	3500
Polo	AAP		1979	SP	30 X 46	AP			350	2800
Champions Both (Hockey)	AAP		1979	SP	42 X 32	AP			250	1400
Concerto	AAP		1980	SP	38 X 32	AP			400	2800
Genuine Risk	AAP		1981	SP	38 X 31	AP			400	1500
Powder Skier	AAP		1982	SP	44 X 34	AP			450	2800
Asea	AAP		1983	SP	34 X 28	AP			200	1000
Huntsman	AAP		1983	SP	20 X 25	AP			250	800
Jour et Nuit	AAP		1983	SP	35 X 36	AP			500	2800
La Terrasse	AAP		1983	SP	45 X 36	AP			500	2800
Lioness and Cubs	AAP		1983	SP	40 X 32	AP			450	1800
Pacer	AAP		1984	SP	25 X 32	AP			250	1000
Café de Flore	MLLE	AH/SH	1986	SP	33 X 40	SOM	550		750	3500
Leopard	AAP		1987	SP	45 X 36	AP			400	2800
St Tropez	MLLE	AH/SH	1987	SP	37 X 42	SOM	550		750	2400
Foyer des Artistes	MLLE	IL	1987	SP	44 X 34	SOM	550		750	3000
St Michel	MLLE	IL	1987	SP	37 X 46	SOM	550		750	2800
Flower Market	MLLE	IL	1988	SP	34 X 42	SOM	550		850	2250
High Powder	MLLE	IL	1988	SP	38 X 46	SOM	550		850	3000
Ponts des Arts	MLLE	IL	1988	SP	34 X 42	SOM	550		850	2000
Morning Light	MLLE	IL	1989	SP	37 X 46	SOM	550		1200	2400
Tennis Landscape	MLLE	IL	1989	SP	38 X 46	SOM	550		1200	2525
Lake Course at Olympic #8	MLLE	IL	1989	SP	37 X 46	SOM	550		1200	3500
Hunt Suite (Set of 2):									2000 SET	4500 SET
Hunt Crossing	MLLE	IL	1989	SP	34 X 44	SOM	550		1200	2600
Morning Hunt	MLLE	IL	1989	SP	35 X 43	SOM	550		1200	2200

MARK KING CONTINUED

Mark King
Reflections of Imperial Gardens
Courtesy Martin Lawrence Limited Editions

Mark King
Hook Shot
Courtesy Martin Lawrence Limited Editions

TITLE	PUBLISHER	PRINTER	DATE	MEDIUM	DIMENSION (PAPER SIZE) IN INCHES	TYPE OF PAPER	EDITION NUMBER	NO. OF COLORS	ORIGINAL OPENING PRICE	CURRENT RETAIL PRICE
CURRENT EDITIONS:										
The Equestrian Suite:									2500 SET	3500 SET
Morning Workout	MLLE	IL	1990	SP	25 X 19	SOM	550		800	1000
Polo	MLLE	IL	1990	SP	25 X 19	SOM	550		800	1000
Setting Out	MLLE	IL	1990	SP	25 X 19	SOM	550		800	1000
Into the Stretch	MLLE	IL	1990	SP	20 X 24	SOM	550		800	1000
Concerto for Harpischord	MLLE	IL	1990	SP	35 X 42	SOM	550		1200	2250
Two Piece Suite:									2000 SET	4500 SET
Golf Landscape	MLLE	IL	1990	SP	35 X 42	SOM	550		1200	2425
Wimbledon Afternoon	MLLE	IL	1990	SP	37 X 46	SOM	550		1200	2425
Two Piece Suite:									2000 SET	4500 SET
Summer Rose Garden	MLLE	IL	1990	SP	34 X 42	SOM	550		1200	2250
The Tryst	MLLE	IL	1990	SP	37 X 46	SOM	550		1200	2450
Golf Series II:									3000 SET	4500 SET
Morning Putt	MLLE	IL	1990	SP	21 X 25	SOM	595		900	1200
Approach Shot	MLLE	IL	1990	SP	21 X 25	SOM	595		900	1200
Doughnut Hole	MLLE	IL	1990	SP	21 X 25	SOM	595		900	1200
Putting Green, Rancho Bernardo	MLLE	IL	1990	SP	21 X 25	SOM	595		900	1200
Sierra Glow	MLLE	IL	1991	SP	35 X 43	SOM	550		1200	1800
Reflections Suite (with Book):									2400 SET	3500 SET
By the Sea	MLLE	IL	1991	SP	21 X 24	SOM	1200		675	900
Montmartre	MLLE	IL	1991	SP	21 X 24	SOM	1200		675	800
Rainy Day	MLLE	IL	1991	SP	21 X 24	SOM	1200		675	1200
Spring Magnolia Blossoms	MLLE	IL	1991	SP	21 X 24	SOM	1200		675	1000
Two Piece Suite:									2750 SET	3500 SET
Harbour Town	MLLE	IL	1991	SP	29 X 37	SOM	595		1350	1850
Hills of Lakeway	MLLE	IL	1991	SP	29 X 37	SOM	595		1350	1850
Reflections of Imperial Gardens	MLLE	IL	1991	SP	34 X 41	SOM	595		1350	2250
Kentucky Derby	MLLE	IL	1990	SP	37 X 46	SOM	550		1200	2425
Morning Splendor	MLLE	IL	1990	SP	52 X 73	SOM	325		1800	5000
An English Water Garden	MLLE	IL	1991	SP	35 X 43	SOM	550		1200	2100
Lone Tusker	MLLE	IL	1991	SP	47 X 38	SOM	595		1200	2125
Giverny, Wisteria and Agapanthes										
Bridge	MLLE	IL	1992	SP	35 X 40	SOM	595		1000	1700
Hook Shot	MLLE	IL	1992	SP	31 X 42	SOM	595		1000	1650
The White House	MLLE	IL	1992	SP	34 X 42	SOM	595		1250	1800
Concerto II	MLLE	IL	1992	SP	35 X 41	SOM	595		1000	1675
Golf Series III (Set of 4):									2400 SET	2400 SET
Pinehurst	MLLE	IL	1993	SP	21 X 24	SOM	595		800	800
Myrtle Beach Dunes Golf	MLLE	IL	1993	SP	21 X 24	SOM	595		800	800
Augusta #12 in Fall	MLLE	IL	1993	SP	21 X 24	SOM	595		800	800
Bel-Air #6	MLLE	IL	1993	SP	21 X 24	SOM	595		800	800
Augusta Glory	MLLE	IL	1993	SP	31 X 38	SOM	595		900	1400
Cherry Blossom Corner	MLLE	IL	1993	SP	24 X 42	SOM	595		1200	1500

The retail prices of the 100,000 limited edition prints quoted in this directory are subject to change. Print publishers, artists and galleries were the direct sources for these quotations. Prices in the secondary market listed as "Sold Out Editions (Rare)" indicate that the publisher has a limited supply of that print or that the print is difficult to locate in the galleries.

TONY KING

BORN: Concord, MA; 1944
PRINTERS: John Nichols, NY (JN)
PUBLISHERS: Prestige Art Ltd, Mamaroneck, NY (PA); Artist (ART)

GALLERIES: O K Harris Works of Art, New York, NY; Alan Brown Gallery, Hartsdale, NY; John Nichols Gallery, New York, NY; Mincher/Wilcox Gallery, San Francisco, CA

TITLE	PUBLISHER	PRINTER	DATE	MEDIUM	DIMENSION (PAPER SIZE) IN INCHES	TYPE OF PAPER	EDITION NUMBER	NO. OF COLORS	ORIGINAL OPENING PRICE	CURRENT RETAIL PRICE
CURRENT EDITIONS:										
Twenty Dollars	PA	JN	1983	SP	20 X 35	R/BFK	100	15	450	600
Franklin 100	ART	JN	1983	SP	24 X 46	R/BFK	100	15	675	800

DONG M KINGMAN

BORN: Oakland, CA; 1911
TEACHING: Instr, Hunter Col, NY, Watercolor & Chinese Art History, 1948-53; Instr, Columbus Univ, NY, 1946-54; Famous Artists Sch, Westport, CT, 1954 to present
AWARDS: Guggenheim Fel, NY (2); Purchase Prize, San Francisco Art Association, CA; Walter Bigg Mem Award; Nat Acad of Design, NY; Barse Mem Award; Am Watercolor Soc; Award for Advancement of Watercolor Art, Philadelphia Watercolor Club, PA

COLLECTIONS: Metropolitan Mus, NY; Whitney Mus of Am Art, NY; Mus of Mod Art, NY; San Francisco Mus of Mod Art, CA; M H De Young Mem Mus, San Francisco, CA; Art Inst of Chicago, IL; Wadsworth Atheneum, Hartford, CT; Mus of Fine Arts, Boston, MA; Hirshhorn Mus, Wash, DC
PRINTERS: American Atelier, NY (AA)
PUBLISHERS: Circle Fine Art, Chicago, IL (CFA)
GALLERIES: Circle Galleries, San Diego, CA & San Francisco, CA & Northbrook, IL & Pittsburgh, PA & Houston, TX & Soho, NY & Chicago, IL; Conacher Galleries, San Francisco, CA
MAILING ADDRESS: 21 W 58th St, New York, NY 10019

TITLE	PUBLISHER	PRINTER	DATE	MEDIUM	DIMENSION (PAPER SIZE) IN INCHES	TYPE OF PAPER	EDITION NUMBER	NO. OF COLORS	ORIGINAL OPENING PRICE	CURRENT RETAIL PRICE
SOLD OUT EDITIONS (RARE):										
Golden Gate	CFA	AA	1976	LC	21 X 32	AP	300		100	400
Spirit of July 4, 1976	CFA	AA	1976	LC	35 X 24	AP	500		100	400

SANDY KINNEE (FLOYD)

BORN: Port Huron, MI; March 30, 1947
EDUCATION: Univ of Michigan, Ann Arbor, MI, BFA, Printmaking, 1969, Grad Study, 1970; Wayne State Univ, Detroit, MI, MFA, Printmaking, 1976; Atelier 17, Paris, France, 1979
TEACHING: Instr, Printmaking, Colorado Fine Arts Center, CO, 1977-78, 78-80,86
AWARDS: Purchase Award, Mus of New Mexico, Santa Fe, NM, 1978; Printmakers Fel, Western State Arts Found, 1979; Pollack-Krasner Found Grant, 1987
RECENT EXHIB: Marcus Gordon Gallery, Pittsburgh, PA, 1987; Joslyn Art Mus, Omaha, NE, 1987; Gallery Two Nine One, Atlanta, GA, 1987; Colorado Col, Coburn Gallery, Colorado Springs, CO, 1989; William Campbell Contemp Art, Fort Worth, TX, 1989; Virginia Miller Galleries, Coral Gables, FL, 1989; Peter M David Gallery, Minneapolis, MN, 1990
COLLECTIONS: Metropolitan Mus of Art, NY; Allen Art Mus, Oberlin, OH; Portland Art Mus, OR; New Mexico Mus, Santa Fe, NM; Madison Art Center, WI; Evergreen State Col, CO
PRINTERS: Artists (ART)
PUBLISHERS: Orion Editions, NY (OE); Artist (ART)
GALLERIES: Peter M. David, Minneapolis, MN; Orion Editions, New York, NY; Gallery 500, Phila, PA; Texann Ivy Fine Arts, Orlando, FL; Marcus Gordon Fine Arts, Pittsburgh, PA; William Campbell Contemporary Art, Fort Worth, TX; Gallery Two Nine One, Atlanta, GA
MAILING ADDRESS: 847 E Cache la Poudre, Colorado Springs, CO 80903

TITLE	PUBLISHER	PRINTER	DATE	MEDIUM	DIMENSION (PAPER SIZE) IN INCHES	TYPE OF PAPER	EDITION NUMBER	NO. OF COLORS	ORIGINAL OPENING PRICE	CURRENT RETAIL PRICE
SOLD OUT EDITIONS: (RARE)										
Empress of China	ART	ART	1976	SP	25 X 23	HMP	22	29	150	450
Green Fan	ART	ART	1976	EB	24 X 13	HMP	15	1	100	350
Monet's Bridge Fan	ART	ART	1977	EC/HC	24 X 20	HMP	28	Varies	175	800
Bridge Fan/From a Screen	ART	ART	1977	EB	31 X 14	HMP	19	1	100	350
Baseball Fan	ART	ART	1977	SP	23 X 24	HMP	16	13	130	450
Big Indians	ART	ART	1979	EC/HC	16 X 20	HMP	50	Varies	200	450
A Non-Geometric Kimono	ART	ART	1979	EC/HC	24 X 26	HMP	100	Varies	350	800
Traditional Stylized Clouds	ART	ART	1981	EC/HC	28 X 23	HMP	30	Varies	500	550
Hybird	ART	ART	1981	EC/HC	22 X 28	HMP	50	Varies	500	650
Geometric Kimono Suite (G/Dark Headed)	ART	ART	1981	EC/HC	22 X 26	HMP	150	Varies	500	750
Geometric Kimono Suite (A/Morning Glory)	ART	ART	1981	EC/HC	22 X 28	HMP	150	Varies	500	750
Guide	ART	ART	1981	EC/HC	30 X 41	HMP	33	Varies	700	750
Matisse Tablita	ART	ART	1982	STEN	22 X 21	HMP	9	1	350	450
Gillnet Tablita	ART	ART	1982	SP/HC	22 X 21	HMP	12	Varies	350	450
Fishscale Tablita	ART	ART	1982	SP	22 X 21	HMP	12	8	350	400
Pictish Tablita	ART	ART	1982	SP	22 X 21	HMP	13	7	350	450
Red RiverTablita	ART	ART	1982	STEN	21 X 21	HMP	11	2	350	450
Distorting	ART	ART	1983	SP	34 X 21	HMP	24	22	350	400
Falling	ART	ART	1983	SP	34 X 21	HMP	36	28	350	400
Rising	ART	ART	1983	SP	34 X 21	HMP	24	24	350	400
Embassy Split	ART	ART	1983	SP	34 X 21	HMP	39	25	350	400
Slippery Ladder	ART	ART	1983	SP	36 X 24	HMP	35	31	350	400
Traditional Stylized Clouds, Step #2	OE	ART	1984	EC/HC	29 X 24	HMP	48	Varies	500	550

ROBERT KIPNISS

BORN: New York, NY; February 1, 1931
EDUCATION: Art Students League, NY; Wittenberg Univ, Springfield, OH; Univ of Iowa, Iowa City, IA, BA, Literature, 1952; MFA, 1954
AWARDS: Honorary Doctorate, Wittenberg Univ, Springfield, OH, 1979; Lithography Prize, Soc of Am Graphic Artists, 1979; Purchase Award, Charlotte Printmakers, NC, 1979; Charles M Lea Prize, Print Club, Phila, PA; Ralph Fabbri Prize, Nat Acad of Design, NY, 1976,80,81; Medal of Honor, Audubon Artists, 1983
COLLECTIONS: Whitney Mus of Am Art, NY; Yale Univ, New Haven, CT; Univ of Fine Arts, San Francisco, CA; Chicago Art Inst, IL; Albright-Knox Mus, Buffalo, NY; Cleveland Mus, OH; Detroit Inst of Art, MI; Los Angeles County Mus, CA; Nat Coll of Fine Arts, Smithsonian Inst, Wash, DC; Metropolitan Mus, NY; Philadelphia Mus, PA; Cleveland Mus, OH
RECENT EXHIB: Concept Art Gallery, Pittsburgh, PA, 1987
PRINTERS: George C Miller & Sons, NY (GCM)
PUBLISHERS: John Szoke Graphics, NY (JSG); Associated American Artists, NY (AAA); Artist (ART)
GALLERIES: Summa Gallery, Brooklyn, NY; & New York, NY; Merrill Chase Gallery, Chicago, IL; Gerhard Wurzer Gallery, Houston, TX; Alan Brown Gallery, Hartsdale, NY; Strecker Gallery, Manhattan, KS; J Todd Galleries, Wellesley, MA; Saper Galleries, East Lansing, MI; Galerie Select, Ltd, New York, NY; River Gallery, Irvington-On-Hudson, NY; Jean Lumbard Fine Art, New York, NY
MAILING ADDRESS: Hudson House, P O Box 7099, Ardley-On-Hudson, NY 10503

TITLE	PUBLISHER	PRINTER	DATE	MEDIUM	DIMENSION (PAPER SIZE) IN INCHES	TYPE OF PAPER	EDITION NUMBER	NO. OF COLORS	ORIGINAL OPENING PRICE	CURRENT RETAIL PRICE
SOLD OUT EDITIONS (RARE):										
Four Seasons Suite (Deluxe) (Set of 8)	AAA	GCM	1977	LB(4) LC(4)	17 X 13 EA	AP	100 EA		2500 SET	4000 SET
Green Roofs	ART	GCM	1978	LC	19 X 17	AP	90	5	500	1500
A Private Porch	ART	GCM	1984	LC	21 X 20	AP	120	7	550	1000
CURRENT EDITIONS:										
Morning	JSG	GCM	1982	LC	18 X 14	AP	175	5	150	200
Studio Flower	JSG	GCM	1982	LC	29 X 22	AP	120	5	800	850
Fences and Steps	JSG	GCM	1983	LC	17 X 20	AP	130	5	400	450
Through Bedroom Curtains	JSG	GCM	1983	LC	24 X 22	AP	120	7	750	800
Window Pots	JSG	GCM	1983	LC	21 X 18	AP	130	5	400	450
Upstate	ART	GCM	1984	LC	21 X 20	AP	120	6	550	600
The Entrance	ART	GCM	1984	LC	26 X 23	AP	120	7	800	850
The Upper Garden	ART	GCM	1985	LC	10 X 9	AP	175	7	100	150
An Evening Look	ART	GCM	1985	LC	10 X 9	AP	175	5	100	150

KENT BRUCE KIRBY

BORN: Fargo, ND; December 31, 1934
EDUCATION: Carleton Col, Northfield, MN, BA, 1956; Univ of North Dakota, Grand Forks, ND, MA, 1959; Univ of Michigan, Ann Arbor, MI, MFA, 1970
TEACHING: Muskingum Col, New Concord, OH, 1959–61; Wilkes Col, Wilkes-Barre, PA, 1961–62; Alma Col, MI, 1962–90; Dana Col, Blair, NE, 1976–90
AWARDS: Newberry Library Research Fel, 1974; Nat Endowment for the Arts Grant, 1976; Michigan Council for the Arts Grant, 1975,79,81
RECENT EXHIB: Nat Mus of Am History, 1988–89
COLLECTIONS: Metropolitan Mus of Art, NY; Walker Art Center, Minneapolis, MN; Guggenheim Mus, NY; Detroit Inst of Art, Detroit, MI; Art Inst of Chicago, IL; Philadelphia Mus of Art, PA
PRINTERS: Artist (ART)
PUBLISHERS: Light-Print Press (LPP)
GALLERIES: Miriam Perlman, Inc, Chicago, IL; Chicago Center for the Print, Chicago, IL
MAILING ADDRESS: 614 W Superior St, Alma, MT 48801

TITLE	PUBLISHER	PRINTER	DATE	MEDIUM	DIMENSION (PAPER SIZE) IN INCHES	TYPE OF PAPER	EDITION NUMBER	NO. OF COLORS	ORIGINAL OPENING PRICE	CURRENT RETAIL PRICE
SOLD OUT EDITIONS (RARE):										
Bouquet	LPP	ART	1978	COL	10 X 13	AP88	5	1	100	400
Italian Red Apples	LPP	ART	1978	COL	10 X 13	AP88	5	1	100	400
Red Villa Doors	LPP	ART	1978	COL	7 X 9	AP88	10	6	100	300
Cannon	LPP	ART	1979	COL	8 X 9	AP88	10	3	100	300
Atlanta Manikins	LPP	ART	1980	COL	6 X 9	AP88	10	5	100	300
CURRENT EDITIONS:										
Grand River Suite	LPP	ART	1975	COL	10 X 13	AP88	250	3	300 SET	1200 SET
Michigan Portfolio I (Set of 10)	LPP	ART	1978	COL	15 X 19 EA	AP88	20 EA	1 EA	300 SET	1200 SET
Mask	LPP	ART	1979	COL	11 X 13	AP88	8	3	100	250
Michigan Portfolio II (Set of 5)	LPP	ART	1980	COL	15 X 19 EA	AP88	15 EA	1–5 EA	500 SET	1800 SET
Girl in the Corn	LPP	ART	1980	COL	7 X 9	AP88	6	4	150	250
Two Models	LPP	ART	1980	COL	7 X 10	AP88	12	5	150	250
Old Coats	LPP	ART	1980	COL	7 X 9	AP88	7	3	150	250
Italian Red Apples II	LPP	ART	1981	COL	12 X 15	RP/COV	5	3	175	250
Garden (Brown)	LPP	ART	1981	COL	10 X 12	RP/COV	10	2	175	250
Fish/Dancer	LPP	ART	1982	COL	12 X 15	DOVE	15	3	175	250

ERNST LUDWIG KIRCHNER

BORN: Germany; (1880-1938)
PRINTERS: Artist (ART)
PUBLISHERS: Artist (ART)
GALLERIES: David Tunick, Inc, New York, NY; Lafayette Parke Gallery, New York, NY; Carus Gallery, New York, NY; Worthington Gallery, Chicago, IL; Marilyn Pink Fine Arts, Los Angeles, CA; Theodore B Donson, Ltd, New York, NY; Alice Adam, Ltd, Chicago, IL

Sohn (S); Schiefler (Sch); Dube (D)

ERNST LUDWIG KIRCHNER CONTINUED

TITLE	PUBLISHER	PRINTER	DATE	MEDIUM	DIMENSION (PAPER SIZE) IN INCHES	TYPE OF PAPER	EDITION NUMBER	NO. OF COLORS	ORIGINAL OPENING PRICE	CURRENT RETAIL PRICE
SOLD OUT EDITIONS (RARE):										
Schlussvignette (Sch-68)	ART	ART	1905	WB	5 X 5	WOVE		1	20	1800
Schreibendes Mädchen (D-4)	ART	ART	1906	DPT	4 X 3	WOVE	70	1	25	5000
Das Grüne Haus (D-50)	ART	ART	1908	LC	17 X 21	WOVE		4	35	60000
Rappenhengst, Reiterin, und Clown (D-128)	ART	ART	1909	LC	21 X 25	WOVE		5	35	300000
Funfte Jahresmappe der Kunstlergruppe Brücke (Set of 4 Prints) (S-215)	ART	ART	1909-10	WB(2) WC(1) DPT(1)		WOVE			50	200000 SET
Fränzikopf mit Puppe (D-150)	ART	ART	1910	LB		WOVE		1	50	25000
Blond Pippa in Weissem Tanzkostüm mit Schirm (Sch-130)	ART	ART	1911	DPT	10 X 7	WOVE		1	50	8500
Liebespaar VI (D-190)	ART	ART	1911	LB	7 X 8	WOVE		1	50	9500
Nackte Frau am Fenster (D-147)	ART	ART	1912	EB	6 X 5	WOVE	50	1	40	1000
Berliner Vorstadtlandschaft (D-228)	ART	ART	1912	LB	17 X 13	WOVE		1	50	10500
Drei Badende am Strandel (D-234)	ART	ART	1913	LB	12 X 17	WOVE		1	60	22500
Fünf Kokotten auf der Strasse (D-240)	ART	ART	1913-14	WB					75	275000
Frauen am Potsdamerplatz (D-239b)	ART	ART	1914	WC/MON	21 X 15	WOVE			75	45000
Der Tennisspieler	ART	ART	1915	EB/A	8 X 9	WOVE			80	1000
Stefelalp (D-301)	ART	ART	1917	WB	18 X 23	WOVE		1	100	60000
Portrait Frau Dr Robert (Marie-Luise) Binswager (D-315/II)	ART	ART	1917-18	WB	22 X 9	WOVE		1	80	32000
Kuh und Baer Vor Almhütten	ART	ART	1918	WB	5 X 8	WOVE		1	75	2500
Träumendes Mädchen (D-341/III)	ART	ART	1918	WB	15 X 12	WOVE		1	80	15000
Kopf Ludwig Schames, Kirchners Freund un Kunsthandler in Frankfurt (D-330/II)	ART	ART	1918	WB	22 X 10	WOVE		1	80	93000
Bertannen im Nebel	ART	ART	1919	WB		WOVE		1	90	30000
Der Kranke (Sch-346/II)	ART	ART	1919	WB	6 X 35	WOVE		1	80	3500
Berghäuser (Blue)	ART	ART	1919	EB	11 X 10	WOVE		1	85	15000
Hirt, Bauer, Mädchen (D-400/I)	ART	ART	1919	WB		WOVE		1	85	16000
Mädchen mit Kleinkind auf dem Arm, das Eine Katze im Schoss Hält)	ART	ART	1919	WB	17 X 14	WOVE		1	85	32000
Der Tanz Zwischen den Frauen (D-289/V)	ART	ART	1919	EB/A	6 X 3	WOVE	70	1	80	2000
Vignette Staffel Apl	ART	ART	1920	WB	5 X 7	WOVE		1	90	3000
Alter Mann (Sch-327)	ART	ART	1920	EB	10 X 8	WOVE		1	90	8500
Zimmerleute (Sch-382)	ART	ART	1920	WB	7 X 7	WOVE		1	90	3000
Baumgrenze I,II (Sch-403)	ART	ART	1920	LB	20 X 23	Yellow		1	100	25000
Bavernliebespaar (Sch-427)	ART	ART	1920	WB	8 X 8	WOVE		1	90	5000
Alte und Junge Frau (D-436B)	ART	ART	1921	LB	13 X 9	WOVE		1	90	3000
Melancholisches Mädchen (D-480 II/II)	ART	ART	1922	WB	31 X 18	JP		1	100	55000
Melancholisches Mädchen (D-480/b)	ART	ART	1922	WC	28 X 16	JP			100	110000
Sertig Dörfli (D-507/B/III)	ART	ART	1924	DPT	12 X 14	WOVE		1	100	20000
Gerichtsszene aus Shaw's Heiliger Johann (D-533 III)	ART	ART	1925	WC	17 X 13		50		100	6500
Kopf Albert Muller (D-543/b)	ART	ART	1925	WC	21 X 12				90	60000
Strasse (S-436) (D-430/II)	ART	ART	1926	LB	13 X 11	WOVE		1	90	12000
Selbstbildnis (D-550/II)	ART	ART	1926	WB	7 X 4	WOVE		1	90	1800
Sertigweg im Winter (II/II) (Sch-546)	ART	ART	1927	WB	15 X 17	WOVE		1	100	10000
Der Geiger-Häusermann (D-H-590)	ART	ART	1927	WB	16 X 11	WOVE		1	100	10000

GLORIA KISCH

BORN: New York, NY; November 14, 1941
EDUCATION: Sarah Lawrence Col, NY, BA, 1963; Boston Mus Sch, MA, 1964–65; Otis Art Inst, Los Angeles, CA, BFA, MFA, 1969
RECENT EXHIB: Robert Miles Plaza, Lincoln Center, NY, 1987; Art et Industre, NY, 1989

COLLECTIONS: Mildura Art Mus, Victoria, Australia; Palm Springs Desert Mus, CA; Newport Harbor Art Mus, CA; Denver Art Mus, CO
PRINTERS: Cirrus Editions Workshop, Los Angeles, CA (CEW)
PUBLISHERS: Cirrus Editions, Los Angeles, CA (CE)
GALLERIES: Cirrus Editions, Ltd, Los Angeles, CA; Touchstone Gallery, New York, NY; Eva J Pape Fine Art, New York, NY
MAILING ADDRESS: 620 Broadway, New York, NY 10012

TITLE	PUBLISHER	PRINTER	DATE	MEDIUM	DIMENSION (PAPER SIZE) IN INCHES	TYPE OF PAPER	EDITION NUMBER	NO. OF COLORS	ORIGINAL OPENING PRICE	CURRENT RETAIL PRICE
CURRENT EDITIONS:										
The Right Place, States I–IV (Set of 4)	CE	CEW	1977	LC/PO	26 X 20	HMP	50	1–2	400 SET / 100 EA	1000 SET / 250 EA

R B KITAJ

BORN: Chagrin Falls, Ohio; 1932
EDUCATION: Cooper Union, NY, 1950–51; Acad of Fine Arts, Vienna, Austria, 1951–52; Ruskin Sch of Drawing, Oxford, England, 1960; Royal Col of Art, London, England, 1959–61; Ealing & Camberwell Schools of Art, London, England, 1961–62; Univ of London, England, Hon PhD, 1982
TEACHING: Slade Sch, Univ of London; Univ of California, Berkeley, CA; Univ of California, Los Angeles, CA
AWARDS: Cooper Union Citation, NY, 1982; Skowhegan Medal for Drawing, 1985
RECENT EXHIB: Penson Gallery, NY, 1988
COLLECTIONS: Mus of Mod Art, NY; Tate Gallery, London, England; Stedelijk Mus, Amsterdam, Holland; High Mus, Atlanta, GA; Albright-Knox Art Gallery, Buffalo, NY; Cincinnati Mus, OH; Gemeentmuseum, The Hague, The Netherlands; Art Council, London, England; Stuyvesant Found, London, England; Baltimore Mus of Art, MD; Art Inst of Chicago, IL; Univ of Glasgow, Scotland; Victoria and Albert Mus, London, England; Mus of Mod Art, Oxford, England; St Lawrence Univ, NY; Sao Paulo Mus of Mod Art; Wallraf-Richartz Mus, Cologne, Germany; Boymans Mus, Rotterdam, The Netherlands; Walker Art Gallery, Liverpool, England; Arts Council of Northern Ireland; Kunsthalle, Basel, Switzerland; Art Gallery of Southern Australia
PRINTERS: Petersburg Press, London, England (PP)
PUBLISHERS: Marlborough Graphics, NY (MG); E Donagh, London, England (ED); Petersburg Press, Ltd, London, England (PP)
GALLERIES: Marlborough Graphics, New York, NY; Petersburg Press, London, England & New York, NY; Penson Gallery, New York, NY; Graphics Gallery, San Francisco, CA
MAILING ADDRESS: c/o Marlborough Fine Arts, Ltd, 6 Albermarle St, London W1X 4BY, England

R B Kitaj
Addled Art
Courtesy Marlborough Graphics

TITLE	PUBLISHER	PRINTER	DATE	MEDIUM	DIMENSION (PAPER SIZE) IN INCHES	TYPE OF PAPER	EDITION NUMBER	NO. OF COLORS	ORIGINAL OPENING PRICE	CURRENT RETAIL PRICE
SOLD OUT EDITIONS (RARE):										
Atcheson Go Home	MG		1963	SP	29 X 21	AP	40		50	1500
The Flood of Laymen	MG		1964	SP	30 X 20	AP	70		50	1500
Errata	MG		1964	SP	29 X 20	AP	40		50	1500
Old and New Tables	MG		1964	SP	24 X 17	AP	45		50	1200
Photograph and Philosophy	MG		1964	SP	20 X 31	AP	40		50	1500
What is Comparison?	MG		1964	SP	30 X 20	AP	70		50	1500
The Cultural Valve of Fear, Distrust, and Hypochondria	MG		1965	SP	21 X 31	AP	70		60	1500
The Desire for Lunch is a Bourgeois Obsessional Neurosis	MG		1965	SP	30 X 20	AP	70		60	1500
The Gay Science	MG		1965	SP	30 X 20	AP	70		60	1600
Hellebore for Georg Trakl	MG		1965	SP	30 X 22	AP	70		60	1600
The Republican of the Southern Cross	MG		1965	SP	30 X 20	AP	70		60	1600
Some Poets: for Love (Robert Creely)	MG		1966	SP	26 X 18	AP	70		60	800
Go and Get Killed	MG		1966	SP	32 X 22	AP	70		75	1600
Heart	MG		1966	SP	24 X 32	AP	70		75	1500
His Everypoor, Defeated Losers, Hopeless Move, Loser, Buried	MG		1966	SP	30 X 20	AP	70		75	1200
Let Us Call It Arden and Live in It	MG		1966	SP	33 X 23	AP	70		75	2000
Mort	MG		1966	SP	40 X 28	AP	70		75	1200
Truman in the White House	MG		1966	SP	40 X 27	AP	70		75	2000
Vernissage Cocktail	MG		1966	SP	41 X 28	AP	70		75	2000
Barrio	MG		1967	SP	34 X 24	AP	70		75	2000
Civic Virtue	MG		1967	SP	21 X 26	AP	100		75	1500
Some Poets: Ed Dorn	MG		1967	SP	26 X 26	AP	70		75	1200
For Fear	MG		1967	SP	20 X 30	AP	70		75	1200
Glue Words	MG		1967	SP	33 X 23	AP	70		75	1600
Home Truths	MG		1967	SP	22 X 36	AP	70		75	1200
In His Forthcoming Book	MG		1967	SP	33 X 20	AP	70		75	1400
I've Balled Every Waitress in this Club	MG		1967	SP	23 X 33	AP	70		75	1400
Nerves Massage Defeat Heart	MG		1967	SP	33 X 23	AP	70		75	1200
Some Poets: Revolt on the Clyde (Hugh MacDairmid)	MG		1967	SP	26 X 21	AP	70		75	1200
Some Poets: Star Betelguese (Robert Duncan)	MG		1968	SP	31 X 22	AP	70		80	1200
Critic News Topi	MG		1968	SP	27 X 40	AP	70		80	2000
Plays for Total Stakes	MG		1968	SP	26 X 26	AP	70		80	1200
Bacon I	MG		1969	SP	40 X 19	AP	70		80	1500
Bacon II	MG		1969	SP	40 X 15	AP	70		80	1500

R B KITAJ CONTINUED

TITLE	PUBLISHER	PRINTER	DATE	MEDIUM	DIMENSION (PAPER SIZE) IN INCHES	TYPE OF PAPER	EDITION NUMBER	NO. OF COLORS	ORIGINAL OPENING PRICE	CURRENT RETAIL PRICE
SOLD OUT EDITIONS (RARE):										
Hail Thee Who Play (Michael McClure)	MG		1969	SP	33 X 18	AP	70		80	1200
									1000 SET	10000 SET
In Our Time (Set of 50)	MG		1970	SP	31 X 23 EA	AP	150 EA		100 EA	800 EA
Nancy and Jim Dine	MG		1970	SP	34 X 23	AP	70		100	1000
Bedroom	MG		1971	SP	38 X 26	AP	70		100	1200
Kenneth Koch	MG		1971	SP	37 X 25	AP	70		100	800
Modern Painters	MG		1971	SP	23 X 16	AP	70		100	800
Robert Duncan	MG		1971	EB	21 X 16	AP	150		100	1000
The Adding Machine	MG		1972	SP	22 X 30	AP	70		100	600
Cutie	MG		1974	SP	25 X 20	AP	70		250	1000
Ezra Pound II	MG		1974	SP	36 X 30	AP	70		360	1200
French Subjects	MG		1974	SP/CO	40 X 26	AP	70		360	2000
Waiting for Lefty	MG		1974	SP	37 X 25	AP	70		360	1500
Addled Art	MG		1975	SP	41 X 28	AP	70		500	2000
Nude Sculpture	PP	ED/PP	1975	LC	22 X 16	AP	30		400	1000
Cap'n A B Dick (A)	MG		1975	LB	18 X 22	AP	30		500	1000
Cap'n A B Dick (B)	MG		1975	LB	18 X 22	AP	20		500	1000
A Life (A)	PP	ED/PP	1975	LC	30 X 21	AUV/CR	75	3	600	1200
A Life (B)	PP	ED/PP	1975	LC	30 X 21	AUV/CR	50	3	600	1200
Orgasm	PP	ED/PP	1975	LB	18 X 22	WH/MP	30		500	1000
The Rash Act (A)	PP	ED/PP	1975	LB	30 X 21	WH/MP	30		500	1400
The Rash Act (B1)	PP	ED/PP	1975	LC	30 X 21	WH/MP	75		500	1400
The Rash Act (B2)	PP	ED/PP	1975	LC	30 X 21	WH/MP	25		500	1400
The Red Dancer from Moscow	MG		1975	SP	40 X 30	AP	70		500	1300
Some Do Not . . . (A)	MG		1975	LB	21 X 29	AP	50		500	1200
Some Do Not . . . (B)	MG		1975	LB	21 X 29	AP	75		500	1200
Sleeping Fires	MG		1975	LB	20 X 15	AP	75		500	2500
Lives of the Saints Suite	MG		1975	SP	41 X 28 EA	AP	70 EA		500 EA	1200 EA
Melancholie after Vincent	MG		1976	EB	6 X 6	AP	50		500	800
Actress	MG		1977	LB	26 X 20	AP	50		500	1000
Dominie in Catalonia	MG		1977	EB	11 X 11	AP	50		450	800
Man with Matisse Tattoo	MG		1978	SP	20 X 22	AP	50		500	1200
CURRENT EDITIONS:										
Self Portrait (After Matteo)	MG		1983	EB	26 X 20	AP	50	1	1000	2000
Self Portrait (Hand on Chin)	MG		1983	EB	18 X 13	AP	30	1	800	1500
Self Portrait (Papillon)	MG		1983	EB/SG	19 X 15	AP	30	1	1000	2000

CHARLES S KLABUNDE

BORN: Omah, NE; October 1, 1935
EDUCATION: Univ of Nebraska, Omaha, NE, BFA, 1958; Univ of Iowa, Iowa City, IA, MFA, 1962; Studied with Maruicio Lasansky
TEACHING: Asst Prof, Printmaking, Cooper Union Art Sch, NY 1969–75
AWARDS: Guggenheim Fel, 1971–72; Purchase Award, Davidson Nat Print & Drawing Competition, 1973; Purchase Award, The Print Club, Phila, PA, 1975; Nat Acad of Design Award, 1979
COLLECTIONS: Metropolitan Mus, NY; Mus of Mod Art, NY; Philadelphia Mus, PA; Whitney Mus of Am Art, NY; Art Inst of Chicago, IL; Bibliotheque Nat, Paris, France; Nat Gallery of Art, Wash, DC; Pierpont Morgan Library, NY; New York Public Library, NY; Brooklyn Mus, NY; Minneapolis Inst of Art, MN; Minnesota Mus, Minneapolis, MN; Indianapolis Mus, IN; Museo La Tertulia, Cali, Columbia; Sheldon Mem Art Gallery, Lincoln, NE; Mem Art Gallery, Rochester, NY; Kemper Art Coll, Chicago, IL; Arkansas Art Center, Little Rock, AR; Harvard Univ, Cambridge, MA; Columbia Univ, NY; Williams Col, Williamstown, MA; Arizona State Univ, Tempe, AZ; Ohio State Univ, Columbus, OH; Newberry Library, Chicago, IL; Brooklyn Col, NY; Southern Illinois Univ, Carbondale, IL; Davidson Col, NC; Univ of Nebraska, Omaha, NE; Univ of Iowa, Iowa City, IA
PRINTERS: Artist (ART)
PUBLISHERS: Artist (ART)
GALLERIES: Sylvan Cole Gallery, New York, NY; Franz Bader Gallery, Wash, DC; CFM Gallery, New York, NY
MAILING ADDRESS: 25 Fifth St, Frenchtown, NJ 08825

TITLE	PUBLISHER	PRINTER	DATE	MEDIUM	DIMENSION (PAPER SIZE) IN INCHES	TYPE OF PAPER	EDITION NUMBER	NO. OF COLORS	ORIGINAL OPENING PRICE	CURRENT RETAIL PRICE
SOLD OUT EDITIONS (RARE):										
Cycle of Sangsaric (Set of 6)	ART	ART	1968	I/ENG	18 X 24	R/BFK	40	1	450 SET	6000 SET
San Andreas Annunzio	ART	ART	1970	I/ENG	18 X 33	R/BFK	100	2	125	3500
The Seven Deadly Sins (Set of 7) (Anger, Greed, Lust, Vanity, Gluttony, Envy, Sloth)	ART	ART	1971	I/ENG	17 X 21 EA	R/BFK	60 EA	2 EA	350 SET	7500 SET
									80 EA	1800 EA
Linn County Fair	ART	ART	1973	I/ENG	12 X 18	R/BFK	80	4	90	2800
Stone City	ART	ART	1973	I/ENG	18 X 24	R/BFK	80	4	125	3200
Happy Birthday PT Barnum	ART	ART	1974	I/ENG	18 X 24	R/BFK	100	4	125	3200
The Promise	ART	ART	1975	I/ENG	12 X 18	R/BFK	150	4	150	1000
La Grande Execution du Robespierre	ART	ART	1975	I/ENG	18 X 24	R/BFK	120	1	150	1800
The Aberration of St Paul	ART	ART	1975	I/ENG	24 X 36	R/BFK	150	1	250	1500
Moon Basin Project	ART	ART	1976	I/ENG	18 X 31	R/BFK	136	4	200	2200
Jedediah's Maypole	ART	ART	1976	I/ENG	18 X 24	R/BFK	118	4	175	1200
The Unicorn	ART	ART	1977	I/ENG	12 X 24	R/BFK	140	4	150	1800
The Automaton	ART	ART	1978	I/ENG	12 X 18	R/BFK	150	4	150	1000

CHARLES S KLABUNDE CONTINUED

TITLE	PUBLISHER	PRINTER	DATE	MEDIUM	DIMENSION (PAPER SIZE) IN INCHES	TYPE OF PAPER	EDITION NUMBER	NO. OF COLORS	ORIGINAL OPENING PRICE	CURRENT RETAIL PRICE
SOLD OUT EDITIONS (RARE):										
The Night Carousel	ART	ART	1978	I/ENG	17 X 24	R/BFK	131	4	175	1200
The Puppeteer	ART	ART	1979	I/ENG	17 X 24	R/BFK	150	4	200	1500
Paradise Aerial Tram	ART	ART	1980	I/ENG	22 X 26	R/BFK	125	4	350	2200
Memories of Brucemore	ART	ART	1980	I/ENG	18 X 24	R/BFK	110	4	250	1500
CURRENT EDITIONS:										
The Wedding	ART	ART	1975	I/ENG	17 X 24	R/BFK	125	4	250	1000
Studies of Levitation (Set of 6)	ART	ART	1977	I/ENG	6 X 9	R/BFK	150	4	360 SET / 90 EA	1800 SET / 500 EA
The Magicians	ART	ART	1979	I/ENG	19 X 24	R/BFK	150	4	200	1000
Aerial Duet	ART	ART	1979	I/ENG	9 X 12	R/BFK	150	4	100	600
David and Goliath	ART	ART	1979	I/ENG	5 X 8	R/BFK	100	4	75	500
Apotheosis USA	ART	ART	1980	I/ENG	9 X 24	R/BFK	150	4	225	750
Winged Equus	ART	ART	1981	I/ENG	18 X 23	R/BFK	150	5	250	1000
Nemesis Riding Pegasus	ART	ART	1981	I/ENG	22 X 22	R/BFK	150	4	400	1800
The Illusionist	ART	ART	1982	I/ENG	18 X 24	R/BFK	150	4	300	1000
Paradise Lost	ART	ART	1982	I/ENG	22 X 27	R/BFK	150	4	400	1500
The Lost Ones	ART	ART	1985	I/ENG	12 X 18 EA	R/BFK	350 EA	1 EA	2000 EA	2200 EA
The Superstitions of Mad Whales	ART	ART	1986	I/ENG	24 X 36	R/BFK	80	2	800	1000
Descent of Man	ART	ART	1986	I/ENG	22 X 27	R/BFK	80	2	800	1000
Studies of the Revolutionary Mind (Set of 6)	ART	ART	1986/87	I/ENG	16 X 22 EA	R/BFK	80 EA	2 EA	2000 SET / 600 EA	2500 SET / 800 EA

KONRAD KLAPHECK

BORN: Dusseldorf, Germany; 1935
EDUCATION: Acad of Fine Arts, Dusseldorf, Germany, 1954–58
PRINTERS: Maeght Editeur, Paris, France (ME); Galerie Maeght Lelong, Paris, France (ML)
PUBLISHERS: Maeght Editions, Paris, France (ME); Galerie Maeght Lelong, Paris, France (ML)
GALLERIES: Galerie Lelong, Paris, France & Zürich, Switzerland & New York, NY

TITLE	PUBLISHER	PRINTER	DATE	MEDIUM	DIMENSION (PAPER SIZE) IN INCHES	TYPE OF PAPER	EDITION NUMBER	NO. OF COLORS	ORIGINAL OPENING PRICE	CURRENT RETAIL PRICE
CURRENT EDITIONS:										
Richesse	ME	ME	1980	EB	22 X 15	AP	80	1	950 FF	3000 FF
Destin	ME	ME	1980	EB	29 X 21	AP	80	1	1200 FF	3000 FF
Vanite de la Gloire (Fond Bleu Aquarelle)	ME	ME	1980	EC	31 X 21	AP	20		1500 FF	3500 FF
Vanite de la Gloire	ME	ME	1980	EB	31 X 21	AP	80	1	1200 FF	3000 FF
Aux Aguets (Black)	ME	ME	1980	AC	26 X 34 cm	AP	60		850 FF	3000 FF
Patience	ME	ME	1980	EC	27 X 20 cm	AP	120		380 FF	2000 FF
L'élu	ME	ME	1981	LC	54 X 41 cm	AP	75		1200 FF	3000 FF
Le Pacha	ME	ME	1981	EC	39 X 27 cm	PN	30		1200 FF	3000 FF

MATI KLARWEIN

BORN: Hamburg, Germany; 1932
EDUCATION: Studied with Fernand Leger, Paris, France, 1949–51
PUBLISHERS: London Arts Inc, Detroit, MI (LAI)
GALLERIES: London Arts Gallery, Detroit, MI

TITLE	PUBLISHER	PRINTER	DATE	MEDIUM	DIMENSION (PAPER SIZE) IN INCHES	TYPE OF PAPER	EDITION NUMBER	NO. OF COLORS	ORIGINAL OPENING PRICE	CURRENT RETAIL PRICE
SOLD OUT EDITIONS (RARE):										
Parcellation	LAI		1979	SP	24 X 24	AP	300	5	250	400
CURRENT EDITIONS:										
The Good Life	LAI		1978	SP	25 X 25	AP	300	6	300	350
As Yourself	LAI		1979	SP	25 X 25	AP	300	5	250	300
Beautiful Beast	LAI		1979	SP	23 X 23	AP	300	6	300	350
Developments	LAI		1979	SP	24 X 24	AP	300	4	300	350

RON KLEEMANN

BORN: Bay City, MI; July 1937
EDUCATION: Univ of Michigan, Ann Arbor, MI, BS, 1961
RECENT EXHIB: Richard Perlow Gallery, NY, 1987; R H Love Galleries, Chicago, IL 1987
COLLECTIONS: Smithsonian Inst, Wash, DC; Univ of Virginia Mus of Art, Charlottesville, VA; Mus of Mod Art, NY; Guggenheim Mus, New York, NY; Indianapolis Mus of Art, IN; Hirshhorn Mus, Wash, DC; Boston Mus of Contemp Art, MA

The Printworld Directory is accepting new applications for the seventh edition. Approximately 300 new artists will be accepted. Please use the two forms provided in the back section of this directory to submit biographical data and documentation of prints. Edition number of each print must not exceed 500 and the retail price must be $100 or more.

RON KLEEMANN CONTINUED

PRINTERS: Editions Lassiter-Meisel, NY, (ELM); Shorewood Workshop (SW); Artist (ART)
PUBLISHERS: Post Oak Fine Art Distributors, Houston, TX (POFA); London Arts Inc, Detroit, MI (LAI); Artist (ART); Glenn Interests (GI)
GALLERIES: Louis K Meisel Gallery, New York, NY; Adams/Middleton Gallery, Dallas, TX; Katharina Rich Perlow Gallery, New York, NY; R H Love Galleries, Chicago, IL; Circle Galleries, San Diego, CA & San Francisco, CA & Northbrook, IL & Pittsburgh, PA & Houston, TX & Soho, NY & Chicago, IL & Scottsdale, AZ & Beverly Hills, CA & Costa Mesa, CA & Serman Oaks, CA & Palm Beach, FL & Honolulu, HI & New Orleans, LA & Las Vegas, NV & Seattle, WA
MAILING ADDRESS: c/o Louis K Meisel Gallery, 141 Prince St, New York, NY 10012

TITLE	PUBLISHER	PRINTER	DATE	MEDIUM	DIMENSION (PAPER SIZE) IN INCHES	TYPE OF PAPER	EDITION NUMBER	NO. OF COLORS	ORIGINAL OPENING PRICE	CURRENT RETAIL PRICE
SOLD OUT EDITIONS (RARE):										
R C Porsche	LAI	SW	1974	LC	22 X 32	AP	150	8	150	1600
Cartwheel Spinoffs Folio (Set of 4):									1400 SET	1550 SET
Tom Sneva	CFA	AA	1978	LC	24 X 30	AP	195	4	350	425
AJ and the Borg Warner Times 4	CFA	AA	1978	LC	24 X 30	AP	195	4	350	425
Rutherford	CFA	AA	1978	LC	24 X 30	AP	195	3	350	425
Johncock	CFA	AA	1978	LC	24 X 30	AP	195	4	350	425
CURRENT EDITIONS:										
Health Tex	LAI	NL/ELM	1980	SP	22 X 30	SOM	250	25	550	1000
Texas Tug	LAI	NL/ELM	1980	SP	22 X 30	SOM	250	20	550	1000
Straight Shot	LAI	NL/ELM	1980	SP	22 X 30	SOM	250	20	550	1000
White Knights	LAI	NL/ELM	1980	SP	22 X 30	SOM	250	20	550	1000
Old Indy	GI	ELM	1981	SP	22 X 30	SOM	250	20	550	1000
Fire Engine	POFA	ELM	1981	SP	22 X 30	SOM	250	20	550	1000

FRITZ KLEIN

BORN: Java; 1898
RECENT EXHIB: Bucknell Univ, Lewisburg, PA, 1992; Provincetown Art Mus, MA, 1992
COLLECTIONS: Mus of Amsterdam, The Netherlands; Central Mus, Utrecht, Belgium; Local Mus, Arnhem, The Netherlands; Musée Belfort, France
PRINTERS: American Atelier, NY (AA)
PUBLISHERS: Circle Fine Art, Chicago, IL (CFA)
GALLERIES: Circle Galleries, San Diego, CA & San Francisco, CA & Northbrook, IL & Pittsburgh, PA & Houston, TX & Soho, NY & Chicago, IL & Scottsdale, AZ & Beverly Hills, CA & Costa Mesa, CA & Sherman Oaks, CA & Palm Beach, FL & Honolulu, HI & New Orleans, LA & Las Vegas, NV & Seattle, WA; Greenberg Gallery, St Louis, MO; Reger Galleries, Tinton Falls, NJ; Sidney Janis Gallery, New York, NY; Stux Modern, New York, NY; Pat Kerny Fine Arts, New York, NY

TITLE	PUBLISHER	PRINTER	DATE	MEDIUM	DIMENSION (PAPER SIZE) IN INCHES	TYPE OF PAPER	EDITION NUMBER	NO. OF COLORS	ORIGINAL OPENING PRICE	CURRENT RETAIL PRICE
SOLD OUT EDITIONS (RARE):										
On the Beach (Japon)	CFA	AA	1980	LC	20 X 26	JP	25		100	175
CURRENT EDITIONS:										
On the Beach	CFA	AA	1980	LC	20 X 26	AP	200		75	150

LYNN KLEIN (ELLEN)

BORN: San Francisco, CA; April 14, 1951
EDUCATION: Univ of Minneapolis, MN, BA, 1974, MA, 1976
TEACHING: Instr, Design, Univ of Minnesota, Minneapolis, MN, 1974–84
AWARDS: Minnesota State Arts Grant, 1978; Photog Fel, Film in the Cities Gallery, 1983; James P Phelan Art Award, World Print Council, 1983; Rockefeller Found Fel, 1984–86
RECENT EXHIB: Grand Palais, Paris, France, 1987; Minneapolis Inst of Arts, MN, 1988; Foster White Gallery, Seattle, WA, 1989
COLLECTIONS: Minneapolis Inst of Arts, MN; Philadelphia Mus of Art, PA; Bibliotheque Nat, Paris, France; Dayton Mus, OH
PRINTERS: Vermillion Editions, Ltd, Minneapolis, MN (VEL)
PUBLISHERS: Vermillion Editions, Ltd, Minneapolis, MN (VEL)
GALLERIES: Allrich Gallery, San Francisco, CA; Vermillion Editions, Ltd, Minneapolis, MN
MAILING ADDRESS: 240 Beach Drive, Marrowstone Island, Norland, WA 98358

TITLE	PUBLISHER	PRINTER	DATE	MEDIUM	DIMENSION (PAPER SIZE) IN INCHES	TYPE OF PAPER	EDITION NUMBER	NO. OF COLORS	ORIGINAL OPENING PRICE	CURRENT RETAIL PRICE
CURRENT EDITIONS:										
Double/Absent	VEL	VEL	1983	LC/CL	30 X 44				400	600

ART KLEINMAN

BORN: Columbia, SC; 1949
EDUCATION: Univ of Kansas, BFA, 1967–71
COLLECTIONS: Wright State Univ, OH
PRINTERS: Will Petersen, Evanston, IL (WP); Plucked Chicken Press, Evanston, IL (PCP)
PUBLISHERS: Balkin Editions, Chicago, IL (BE)
GALLERIES: Atrium Gallery, St Louis, MO

TITLE	PUBLISHER	PRINTER	DATE	MEDIUM	DIMENSION (PAPER SIZE) IN INCHES	TYPE OF PAPER	EDITION NUMBER	NO. OF COLORS	ORIGINAL OPENING PRICE	CURRENT RETAIL PRICE
CURRENT EDITIONS:										
Litho I	BE	WP/PCP	1982	LC	26 X 39	AC/W	50	6	400	600

SYBIL KLEINROCK

BORN: New York, NY
EDUCATION: State Univ of New York, Purchase, NY; Univ of California, Berkeley, CA
TEACHING: State Univ of New York, Purchase, NY; Univ of California, Berkeley, CA
PRINTERS: Atelier Ettinger, NY (AE); Moshin Graphics, NY (MG); J K Fine Arts, NY (JK); Sienna Studio, NY (SiS)
PUBLISHERS: Fred Dorfman, Inc, NY (FDI)
GALLERIES: Touchstone Gallery, New York, NY; Fred Dorfman Gallery, New York, NY

TITLE	PUBLISHER	PRINTER	DATE	MEDIUM	DIMENSION (PAPER SIZE) IN INCHES	TYPE OF PAPER	EDITION NUMBER	NO. OF COLORS	ORIGINAL OPENING PRICE	CURRENT RETAIL PRICE
CURRENT EDITIONS:										
Landscape	FDI	AE	1981	LC	28 X 36	AP	200	6	250	400
Dream Markings I & II	FDI	AE	1981	LC	28 X 36 EA	AP	200 EA	6 EA	250 EA	400 EA
Notations I & II	FDI	JK	1981	LC	29 X 21 EA	AP	150 EA	6 EA	200 EA	350 EA
Dream Fields I & II	FDI	JK	1981	LC	29 X 21 EA	AP	150 EA	7 EA	200 EA	350 EA
Skymarking II	FDI	MG	1981	LC	23 X 26	RP	125	11	175	300
Skymarking III	FDI	MG	1981	LC	23 X 29	RP	125	12	175	300
Midway Series (Set of 3):									1200 SET	1500 SET
Midway I	FDI	SiS	1984	LC/HC	26 X 30	EXP	20	2	500	600
Midway II	FDI	SiS	1984	LC/HC	26 X 30	EXP	20	6	500	600
Midway III	FDI	SiS	1984	LC/HC	26 X 30	EXP	20	8	500	600

MICHAEL JAY KNIGIN

BORN: Brooklyn, NY; December 9, 1942
EDUCATION: Tyler Sch of Art, Phila, PA, BFA, 1966
TEACHING: Assoc Prof, Pratt Inst, Brooklyn, NY, Currently
AWARDS: Ford Found Grant, Tamarind Lithography Workshop, 1964; Mod Language Assn, Am Library Assn, Lithographic Tech Inst Award, 1969; John B. Turner Mem Award, Soc of Am Graphic Artists, 1979; NASA Art Team, 1989–90
RECENT EXHIB: Guild Hall Mus, East Hampton, NY, 1990; Elaine Benson Gallery, Bridgehampton, NY, 1993
COLLECTIONS: Whitney Mus of Am Art, NY; Mus of Mod Art, NY; Israel Mus, Jerusalem, Israel; Nat Coll of Fine Arts, Wash, DC; New York Univ, NY; Albright-Knox Art Gallery, Buffalo, NY; Portland Mus of Fine Arts, OR; Cooper Hewitt Mus, NY
PRINTERS: American Atelier, NY (AA); Atelier Ettinger, NY (AE); Mauro Giuffreda, NY (MG); Triton Press, NY (TP)
PUBLISHERS: Fred Dorfman, Inc, NY (FDI); Jackie Fine Arts, Inc, NY (JFA); Rachelle Ann Manning, NY (RAM); Circle Fine Art Corp, Chicago, IL (CFA); Beckman, Kaufman, Lapin, Rus (BKLR); Douglas P Dahl (DPD); H Walter Smith (HWS); Kenneth Gores (KG); John H Mittenthal (JHM); Joseph A Intile (JAI); Gordon Schramm (GS); George Cottingham (GC); Al C Giusti (ACF); M Lerman (ML); Kenneth T Haley (KTH); W M Ballard (WMB); Krido Fine Arts (KFA); American Graphic Partners (AGP); Graphic Art Partners (GAP); Carol C Halvorson (CCH); Paul Sloane (PS); Dana Art Management (DAM); International Partners (IAP); Bernard S Costello, Jr (BSC); Overhill Editions, NY (OHE)
GALLERIES: Uptown Gallery, New York, NY; Jack Gallery, New York, NY; Patricia Judith Art Gallery, Boca Raton, FL; Fred Dorfman Gallery, New York, NY; Associated American Artists, New York, NY; Circle Galleries, San Diego, CA & San Francisco, CA & Northbrook, IL & Pittsburgh, PA & Houston, TX & Soho, NY & Chicago, IL & Scottsdale, AZ & Beverly Hills, CA & Costa Mesa, CA & Sherman Oaks, CA & Palm Beach, FL & Honolulu, HI & New Orleans, LA & Las Vegas, NV & Seattle, WA
MAILING ADDRESS: c/o Department of Visual Art, Pratt Inst, Brooklyn, NY 11205; PO Box 95, Wainscott, NY 11975

TITLE	PUBLISHER	PRINTER	DATE	MEDIUM	DIMENSION (PAPER SIZE) IN INCHES	TYPE OF PAPER	EDITION NUMBER	NO. OF COLORS	ORIGINAL OPENING PRICE	CURRENT RETAIL PRICE
SOLD OUT EDITIONS (RARE):										
Ensaburo after Kunisige	CFA	AA	1977	LC	32 X 24	AP	300		150	450
Sambaso after Hirosada	CFA	AA	1977	LC	23 X 31	AP	300		150	400
Gathering Lotus Flowers	CFA	AA	1977	LC	25 X 24	AP	0		150	400
Sudden Shower after Hiroshige	PGC/CFA	MG/AA	1978	LC	19 X 24	RP	175	11	175	500
Japanese Series T:										
In the Hollow of the Deep Sea Wave, after Hokusai	BFLR	MG/AA	1978	LC/HC	29 X 21	R/BFK	100	4	250	400
The Love Letter after Kunimasa	BFLR	MG/AA	1978	LC/HC	19 X 32	R/BFK	200	6	250	400
Lovers, after Harunbu	BFLR	MG/AA	1978	LC/HC	33 X 9	R/BFK	200	4	250	400
53 Stations of Tokaido, after Hiroshiae	BFLR	MG/AA	1978	LC/HC	23 X 26	R/BFK	200	5	250	350
Miraculous Misfits (Set of 3)	FDI	AE	1978	LC	39 X 27 EA	AP	275 EA	9–12 EA	600 SET	1500 SET
CURRENT EDITIONS:									250 EA	450 EA
Silent Witness	FDI	AE	1978	LC	22 X 34	AP	275	7	250	350
East River Dance	FDI	AE	1978	LC	22 X 34	AP	275	11	250	350
Thunder and Shower Series:										
Thunder and Shower I after Yoshitaki	DPD	MG/AA	1978	LC	32 X 24	SOM	300	4	325	400
Thunder and Shower II, after Yoshitaki	HWS	MG/AA	1979	LC	32 X 24	SOM	300	23	325	400
Thunder and Shower III, after Yoshitaki	HWS	MG/AA	1979	LC	32 X 24	SOM	300	16	325	400
Osaka Series Ensahuro, after Kunishia	GS	MG/AA	1979	LC	32 X 24	SOM	300	19	325	400
Lion Dancer, after Hirosada	JAI	MG/AA	1979	LC	31 X 21	SOM	300	18	325	400
Somsoba, after Hirosada	JHM	MG/AA	1979	LC/SP	23 X 21	SOM	300	27	325	400
Rikaku, after Kunishige	KG	MC/AA	1979	LC	31 X 24	SOM	300	14	325	400
Actor, after Kunishige	HWS	MG/AA	1979	LC	31 X 23	SOM	300	13	325	400
Gathering Lotus Flowers, after Harunohu	CFA	MG/AA	1979	LC	25 X 24	SOM	250	20	325	400

MICHAEL JAY KNIGIN CONTINUED

TITLE	PUBLISHER	PRINTER	DATE	MEDIUM	DIMENSION (PAPER SIZE) IN INCHES	TYPE OF PAPER	EDITION NUMBER	NO. OF COLORS	ORIGINAL OPENING PRICE	CURRENT RETAIL PRICE
CURRENT EDITIONS:										
Sonja, after Hirosada	CCH	MG/AA	1980	LC	31 X 22	SOM	300	18	325	400
Day Command	PS	MG/AA	1980	LC	27 X 31	SOM	225	15	350	400
Boldest Flyer	PS	MG/AA	1980	LC	27 X 31	SOM	225	15	350	400
Preferred Position	FDI	AE	1982	LC	21 X 30	SOM	300		350	400
In the Clear	FDI	AE	1982	LC	21 X 30	SOM	300		350	400
Fair Passer	FDI	AE	1982	LC	19 X 36	SOM	300		350	400
Casual Encounter	FDI	AE	1982	LC	19 X 36	SOM	300		350	400
Our Golden Times (Set of 10)	OHE	TP	1984	COL/HC	10 X 16 EA	SOM	150 EA	Varies	1050 SET 150 EA	2000 SET 250 EA
Native Rival	CFA	AA	1979	LC	16 X 26	AP	300		250	400
Advance Notice	CFA	AA	1979	LC	27 X 17	AP	300		250	400
Finest Hope	CFA	AA	1979	LC	27 X 20	AP	300		250	400
Loyal to Me	CFA	AA	1979	LC	19 X 27	AP	300		250	400
Woman with Umbrella	CFA	AA	1979	LC	12 X 28	AP	300		250	400
Stations of Tokaido	CFA	AA	1979	LC	20 X 23	AP	300		250	400
Invading Night	CFA	AA	1979	LC	33 X 21	AP	300		250	350
Placid Way	CFA	AA	1979	LC	31 X 22	AP	300		250	350
Romantic Lead	CFA	AA	1979	LC	25 X 10	AP	300		250	325
Take the Point	CFA	AA	1979	LC	16 X 25	AP	300		250	400
Brave Venture	CFA	AA	1979	LC	17 X 25	AP	300		250	400
Royal Applause	CFA	AA	1979	LC	26 X 24	AP	300		250	400
Not Me Boy	CFA	AA	1979	LC	16 X 26	AP	300		250	400
Classic Heiress	CFA	AA	1979	LC	28 X 34	AP	300		250	400
Woman Playing a Poppon A/Uta	CFA	AA	1979	LC	29 X 21	AP	300		250	350
The 26 Station of Kiskaido	CFA	AA	1980	LC	17 X 27	AP	250		250	375
Fabled Ambassador	CFA	AA	1980	LC	24 X 18	AP	300		250	400
The Reflection fo Sugamati	CFA	AA	1980	LC	13 X 8	AP	250		175	250
Ohisa after Utamaro	CFA	AA	1980	LC	13 X 8	AP	250		175	250
Profound Love after Utamaro	CFA	AA	1980	LC	13 X 8	AP	250		175	250
Regal Chief	CFA	AA	1980	LC	17 X 15	AP	300		250	400
The Dreamer after Utamaro	CFA	AA	1980	LC	13 X 8	AP	250		175	250
New Evidence	CFA	AA	1980	LC	29 X 22	AP	300		250	375
Boldest Native	CFA	AA	1980	LC	22 X 22	AP	300		250	375
Real Form	CFA	AA	1980	LC	28 X 22	AP	300		250	375

IMI KNOEBEL

RECENT EXHIB: Simon/Neuman Gallery, NY 1987; Gallery Bruno Bischofberger, Zürich, Switzerland, 1987; Fred Hoffman Gallery, Santa Monica, CA, 1989
PRINTERS: Michel, Dusseldorf, Germany (Mi); Artist (ART); Carmen Knoebel, Düsseldorf, Germany (CK); Domberger Atelier, Stuttgart, Germany (DOM)

PUBLISHERS: Maximilian Verlag Sabine Knust, Munich, Germany (MVSK); Margarete Roeder Gallery Editions, NY (MRE); Achenbach Art Edition, Düsseldorf, Germany (AAE)
GALLERIES: Editions Ilene Kurtz, New York, NY; Simon/Neuman Gallery, New York, NY; Fred Hoffman Gallery, Santa Monica, CA; Gallery Bruno Bischofberger, Zürich, Switzerland; Barbara Gladstone Gallery, New York, NY; Margarete Roeder Gallery, New York, NY; Burnett Miller Gallery, Los Angeles, CA; Laura Carpenter Fine Art, Santa Fe, NM

TITLE	PUBLISHER	PRINTER	DATE	MEDIUM	DIMENSION (PAPER SIZE) IN INCHES	TYPE OF PAPER	EDITION NUMBER	NO. OF COLORS	ORIGINAL OPENING PRICE	CURRENT RETAIL PRICE
CURRENT EDITIONS:										
Untitled (Set of 6)	MVSK	Mi	1975–85	SP	40 X 29 EA	WP	20 EA		4000 SET 850 EA	8000 SET 1250 EA
The Russian Room (Set of 8)	MVSK	ART/CK	1988	SP	40 X 28 EA	S-H	20 EA		7000 SET	8500 SET
Grace Kelly	MVSK	ART/CK	1990	SP	28 X 39	WP	90		2500	2500
Series of Nine Screenprints (Portraits) (Set of 9):									25200 SET	25200 SET
Circe	AAE	DOM	1992	SP	79 X 55	FAB	25		3100	3100
Daphne	AAE	DOM	1992	SP	79 X 55	FAB	25		3100	3100
Diana	AAE	DOM	1992	SP	79 X 55	FAB	25		3100	3100
Dorothy	AAE	DOM	1992	SP	79 X 55	FAB	25		3100	3100
Jeanne	AAE	DOM	1992	SP	79 X 55	FAB	25		3100	3100
Lucretia	AAE	DOM	1992	SP	79 X 55	FAB	25		3100	3100
Penelope	AAE	DOM	1992	SP	79 X 55	FAB	25		3100	3100
Sophie	AAE	DOM	1992	SP	79 X 55	FAB	25		3100	3100
Victoria	AAE	DOM	1992	SP	79 X 55	FAB	25		3100	3100

ANDERS KNUTSSON

RECENT EXHIB: Orono Mus, Univ of Maine, ME, 1992

PUBLISHERS: Artist (ART)
PRINTERS: Ingbar Landberg, Stockholm, Sweden (IL)
GALLERIES: Ellen Price Gallery, New York, NY; Graystone Gallery, San Francisco, CA

ANDERS KNUTSSON CONTINUED

TITLE	PUBLISHER	PRINTER	DATE	MEDIUM	DIMENSION (PAPER SIZE) IN INCHES	TYPE OF PAPER	EDITION NUMBER	NO. OF COLORS	ORIGINAL OPENING PRICE	CURRENT RETAIL PRICE
CURRENT EDITIONS:										
Dancers in Delight	ART	IL	1986	SP	30 X 41	AP	95	16	675	850

HENRY KOEHLER

BORN: Louisville, KY; February 2, 1927
EDUCATION: Yale Univ, New Haven, CT, BA, 1950
RECENT EXHIB: Galerie La Cymoise, Paris, France, 1987; Spink and Son Gallery, London, England, 1990
COLLECTIONS: California Palace of Legion of Honor, San Francisco, CA; J B Speed Art Mus, Louisville, KY; Parrish Art Mus, Southampton, NY; Thomasville Cultural Center, GA
PRINTERS: American Atelier, NY (AA)
PUBLISHERS: Circle Fine Art, Chicago, IL (CFA)
GALLERIES: Circle Galleries, San Diego, CA & San Francisco, CA & Northbrook, IL & Pittsburgh, PA & Houston, TX & Soho, NY & Chicago, IL; Carol Swearington Art, Louisville, KY; Galerie La Cymoise, Paris, France; Arthur Ackermann & Son, New York, NY; Spink & Son Gallery, London, England
MAILING ADDRESS: 80 N Main St, Southampton, NY 11968

TITLE	PUBLISHER	PRINTER	DATE	MEDIUM	DIMENSION (PAPER SIZE) IN INCHES	TYPE OF PAPER	EDITION NUMBER	NO. OF COLORS	ORIGINAL OPENING PRICE	CURRENT RETAIL PRICE
SOLD OUT EDITIONS (RARE):										
Red Jockey Below	CFA	AA	1980	LC	31 X 23	AP	300		125	400
Constellation Below	CFA	AA	1980	LC	35 X 24	AP	300		125	400
Five English Jockeys	CFA	AA	1980	LC	23 X 31	AP	300		125	400

DEBORAH RAY KOGAN

BORN: Philadelphia, PA; August 31, 1940
EDUCATION: Philadelphia Col of Art; Pennsylvania Acad of Fine Arts, Phila, PA 1958-62; Univ of Pennsylvania; Phila, PA; Albert C Barnes Foundation, Merion, PA, 1962-64
TEACHING: Lectr, William and Mary Col; Lectr, Moore Col of Art, Phila, PA; Lectr, Univ of the Arts, Phila, PA, currently
AWARDS: Louis Comfort Tiffany Foundation Grant, 1968; Junior League Award, Earth Arts, 1973; Philadelphia Mus, and Civic Center Award, 1973; Am Inst of Graphic Arts Award, 1976; Moore Col of Art, Phila, PA, 1977; Purchase Award, Millersville State Col, PA; Carolyn W Field Award for Children's Literature, 1988
COLLECTIONS: Carnegie Mellon Univ, Pittsburgh, PA; Library of Congress, Wash, DC; Drexel Univ, Phila, PA; Univ of Minnesota, MN; Montgomery County Col, Center Square, PA; Free Library, Phila, PA
PRINTERS: Atelier Ettinger, NY (AE); Sienna Studio, NY (SS)
PUBLISHERS: Fred Dorfman, Inc, NY (FDI)
GALLERIES: Rosenfeld Gallery, Phila, PA

Deborah Ray Kogan
Teton I
Courtesy the Artist

TITLE	PUBLISHER	PRINTER	DATE	MEDIUM	DIMENSION (PAPER SIZE) IN INCHES	TYPE OF PAPER	EDITION NUMBER	NO. OF COLORS	ORIGINAL OPENING PRICE	CURRENT RETAIL PRICE
CURRENT EDITIONS:										
Canto I-IV	FDI	AE	1979	LC	21 X 29 EA	AP	125 EA	6 EA	125 EA	300 EA
Canadian Cycles I-IV	FDI	AE	1981	LC	21 X 29 EA	AP	125 EA	7 EA	250 EA	300 EA
Logan Pass I, II	FDI	SS	1981	LC	17 X 37 EA	AP	150 EA	6 EA	200 EA	350 EA
Teton I, II, III	FDI	SS	1981	LC	18 X 13 EA	AP	30 EA	5 EA	90 EA	250 EA
Springsong	FDI	SS	1981	LC	38 X 48	AP	150	5	375	600

KIKI KOGELNIK

BORN: Bleiburg, Austria
EDUCATION: Akademie of Fine Arts, Vienna, Austria
RECENT EXHIB: Galerie Uluv, Prague, Czeckoslavakia, 1992
PRINTERS: American Atelier, NY (AA)
PUBLISHERS: London Arts Inc, Detroit, MI (LAI); Circle Fine Art, Chicago, IL (CFA)
GALLERIES: London Arts Gallery, Detroit, MI

TITLE	PUBLISHER	PRINTER	DATE	MEDIUM	DIMENSION (PAPER SIZE) IN INCHES	TYPE OF PAPER	EDITION NUMBER	NO. OF COLORS	ORIGINAL OPENING PRICE	CURRENT RETAIL PRICE
SOLD OUT EDITIONS (RARE):										
Rally	CFA	AA	1970	LC	21 X 30	AP	200		150	275
Beach Ball	LAI		1978	SP	36 X 26	AP	200	13	200	225
Crazy Bird	LAI		1978	SP	34 X 26	AP	200	14	200	225
Triangle	CFA	AA	1979	SP	36 X 26	AP	200		200	225

The retail prices of the 100,000 limited edition prints quoted in this directory are subject to change. Print publishers, artists and galleries were the direct sources for these quotations. Prices in the secondary market listed as "Sold Out Editions (Rare)" indicate that the publisher has a limited supply of that print or that the print is difficult to locate in the galleries.

PETER KOGLER

PRINTERS: Kurt Zein, Vienna, Austria (KZ); Edition Artelier, Vienna, Austria (EdA)

PUBLISHERS: Edition Keinzinger, Vienna, Austria (EdK); Edition Artelier, Vienna, Austria (EdA)
GALLERIES: Galerie Krinzinger, Vienna, Austria; Edition Artelier, Vienna Austria

TITLE	PUBLISHER	PRINTER	DATE	MEDIUM	DIMENSION (PAPER SIZE) IN INCHES	TYPE OF PAPER	EDITION NUMBER	NO. OF COLORS	ORIGINAL OPENING PRICE	CURRENT RETAIL PRICE
CURRENT EDITIONS:										
Ameise (Set of 3)	EdK	KZ	1992	PH/EB	25 X 20 EA	AP	25 EA	1 EA	SF 1925 SET	SF 1925 SET
Untitled (Set of 4)	EdA	EdA	1992	SP	39 X 27 EA	FAB	15 EA	4 EA	DM 2860 SET	DM 2860 SET

BARBARA KOHL

BORN: Milwaukee, WI; February 10, 1940
EDUCATION: Univ of Wisconsin, Madison, WI, BS, Art History, 1963; Univ of Wisconsin, Milwaukee, WI
COLLECTIONS: Milwaukee Art Center, WI
PRINTERS: Custom Screen, Milwaukee, WI (CS); Brand X, NY (BX)
PUBLISHERS: Transworld Art, Inc, NY (TAI); Prestige Art Ltd, Mamaroneck, NY (PA)
GALLERIES: Barbara Gilman, Miami, FL; Posner Art Gallery, Milwaukee, WI; Carol Getz Gallery, Miami, FL; David Barnett Gallery, Milwaukee, WI

Barbara Kohl
Hallelujah
Courtesy the Artist

TITLE	PUBLISHER	PRINTER	DATE	MEDIUM	DIMENSION (PAPER SIZE) IN INCHES	TYPE OF PAPER	EDITION NUMBER	NO. OF COLORS	ORIGINAL OPENING PRICE	CURRENT RETAIL PRICE
SOLD OUT EDITIONS (RARE):										
Broken Dishes	TAI	CS	1979	SP	23 X 20	AP	250		250	300
Kaleidoscope	TAI	CS	1979	SP	23 X 21	AP	250		250	300
Fannie's Fan	TAI	CS	1979	SP	23 X 21	AP	250		250	300
Star of Jacob	TAI	CS	1979	SP	23 X 21	AP	250		250	300
Zahor-Remember	PA	BX	1980	SP	22 X 30	AP	100	8	300	325
Pinwheel & Pride	PA	BX	1980	SP	22 X 30	AP	100	8	300	325
Mensch	PA	BX	1980	SP	22 X 30	AP	100	8	300	325
Sweet Soul	PA	BX	1980	SP	22 X 30	AP	100	8	300	325
Hallelujah	PA	BX	1980	SP	22 X 30	AP	100	8	300	325

IDA KOHLMEYER

BORN: New Orleans, LA; November 3, 1912
EDUCATION: Newcomb Col, New Orleans, LA, BA, 1933, MFA, 1956; Studied with Hans Hofmann, 1956
TEACHING: Instr, Painting & Drawing, Newcomb Art Sch, New Orleans, LA, 1956-65; Assoc Prof, Painting, Univ of New Orleans, LA, 1973-75
AWARDS: Ford Found Purchase Award, Corcoran Gallery of Art, Wash, DC, 1963; Mus Purchase Awards, High Mus, Atlanta, GA, 1963,66; Artists of the Southeast, New Orleans Mus, LA, 1975; Outstanding Achievement in Visual Arts Awards, Nat Women's Caucus for the Arts, 1981
RECENT EXHIB: Univ of the South Mus, Sewanee, TN, 1989; Masur Mus, Monroe, LA, 1992; Allene Lapides Gallery, Santa Fe, NM, 1992; Mary Ryan Gallery, NY, 1993
COLLECTIONS: Metropolitan Mus of Art, NY; New Orleans Mus, LA; Brooklyn Mus, NY; San Francisco Mus of Mod Art, CA; High Mus, Atlanta, GA; Mus of Fine Arts, Houston, TX; Corcoran Gallery of Art, Wash, DC; Nat Coll, Smithsonian Inst, Wash, DC; Jewish Mus, NY
PRINTERS: Weldon Workshop (WW) (OB)
PUBLISHERS: Artist (ART)
GALLERIES: Arthur Roger Gallery, New Orleans, LA; Gimpel Weitzenhoffer Gallery, New York, NY; Moody Gallery, Houston, TX; Heath Gallery, Atlanta, GA; Robert L Kidd, Birmingham, MI; William Sawyer Gallery, San Francisco; CA; Gloria Luria Gallery, Bay Harbor Islands, FL; Hokin/Kaufman Gallery, Chicago, IL; Cumberland Gallery, Nashville, TN; Hokin Gallery, Palm Beach, FL; Van Straaten Gallery, Chicago, IL; Allene Lapides Gallery, Santa Fe, NM; Mary Ryan Gallery, New York, NY

The retail prices of the 100,000 limited edition prints quoted in this directory are subject to change. Print publishers, artists and galleries were the direct sources for these quotations. Prices in the secondary market listed as "Sold Out Editions (Rare)" indicate that the publisher has a limited supply of that print or that the print is difficult to locate in the galleries.

The Printworld Directory is accepting new applications for the seventh edition. Approximately 300 new artists will be accepted. Please use the two forms provided in the back section of this directory to submit biographical data and documentation of prints. Edition number of each print must not exceed 500 and the retail price must be $100 or more.

IDA KOHLMEYER CONTINUED

TITLE	PUBLISHER	PRINTER	DATE	MEDIUM	DIMENSION (PAPER SIZE) IN INCHES	TYPE OF PAPER	EDITION NUMBER	NO. OF COLORS	ORIGINAL OPENING PRICE	CURRENT RETAIL PRICE
CURRENT EDITIONS:										
Tokens of Identity	ART	WW	1981	SP	30 X 42	AP	135	21	350	500
Shape-Scape	ART	WW	1981	SP	39 X 52	AP	67	12	500	600
Quartered	ART	WW	1981	SP	38 X 35	GAL	135	10	400	500
Semiosis	ART	WW	1984	SP	37 X 38	COV	100	22	450	650
Mythic Print	ART	WW	1985	SP	48 X 36	AP	100	22	450	550
Mythic Print, States I, II	ART	WW	1985	SP	48 X 36 EA	AP	35 EA	22 EA	550 EA	650 EA

JIRÍ KOLÁR

BORN: Protivin, Czechoslavakia, 1914
PRINTERS: Maeght Editeur, Paris, France (ME); Galerie Maeght Lelong, Paris, France (ML)
PUBLISHERS: Maeght Editions, Paris, France (ME); Galerie Maeght Lelong, Paris, France (ML)
GALLERIES: Galerie Lelong, Paris France & Zürich, Switzerland & New York, NY; Hokin/Kaufman Gallery, Chicago, IL; Hokin Galleries, Palm Beach, FL & Bay Harbor Islands, FL; R K Goldman Contemporary, Chicago, IL

TITLE	PUBLISHER	PRINTER	DATE	MEDIUM	DIMENSION (PAPER SIZE) IN INCHES	TYPE OF PAPER	EDITION NUMBER	NO. OF COLORS	ORIGINAL OPENING PRICE	CURRENT RETAIL PRICE
CURRENT EDITIONS:										
Hommage á Mademoiselle Rivière	ME	ME	1981	EC	30 X 20 cm	AP	150		900 FF	1500 FF
Portrait de Mademoiselle Rivière	ME	ME	1981	EC	80 X 56 cm	AP	250		600 FF	1200 FF
Dans Ton Regard Abordent et sur Tes lèvres S' Endorment des Petites Barques	ME	ME	1981	EC	37 X 56 cm	AP	250		500 FF	1000 FF

KOMAR & MELAMID

BORN: Moscow, USSR; Komar, September 11, 1943, Melamid, July 14, 1945
EDUCATION: Stroganov Inst of Art & Design, Moscow, USSR, 1967
TEACHING: Instr, Visual Art, Moskov Regional Art Schole, USSR, 1968–76
AWARDS: Nat Endowment for the Arts Grant, 1982
RECENT EXHIB: Anderson Gallery, Virginia Commonwealth Univ, Richmond, VA, 1987; Beaver Col Art Gallery, Glenside, PA, 1987; Contemp Russian Art Center of America, NY, 1987; Neuen Gesellschaft fur Gildende Kunst, Berlin, Germany, 1988; Florida State Univ Gallery & Mus, Tallahassee, FL, 1989; Univ of North Texas Univ Art Gallery, Denton, TX, 1989; Ronald Feldman Fine Art, NY, 1989,91; Univ of Florida, Gainesville, FL, 1992; Miami-Dade Com Col, FL, 1992; Florida State Univ, Tallahassee, FL, 1992; Bucknell Univ, Lewisburg, PA, 1992; Sloane Gallery, Denver, CO, 1992
COLLECTIONS: Tel Aviv Mus, Israel; Solomon R Guggenheim Mus, NY; Mus of Mod Art, NY; Metropolitan Mus of Art, NY
PRINTERS: John Nichols, Printmakers & Publishers, NY (JN); Julio Juristo (JL); Barbara Balfour (BB); Randy Hemminghaus (RH); Vinalhaven Press, Vinalhaven, ME (VP); Judith Solodkin, NY (JS); Solo Press, NY (SP); Patricia Branstead, NY (PB); Branstead Studio, NY (BS); Stauber & Vendetti, NY (SV)
PUBLISHERS: St/Elwood Art Editions, Brooklyn, NY (SEAE); Vinalhaven Press, Vinalhaven, ME (VP); Solo Press, NY (SP); State Editions, NY (StEd); Riverhouse Editions, Clark, CO (REd); Artists (ART)
GALLERIES: Ronald Feldman Fine Arts, New York, NY; van Straaten Gallery, Chicago, IL; Temple Gallery, Phila, PA; Sloane Gallery of Art, Denver, CO; Gallery Paule Anglim, San Francisco, CA; Topaz Editions, Tampa, FL; L Bartman Fine Arts, Chicago, IL; Vinalhaven Press, Vinalhaven, ME; Artes Magnus, New York, NY; Holly Solomon Gallery, New York, NY; FUEL Gallery, Seattle, WA
MAILING ADDRESS: 164 E 33rd St, #3-D, New York, NY 10016

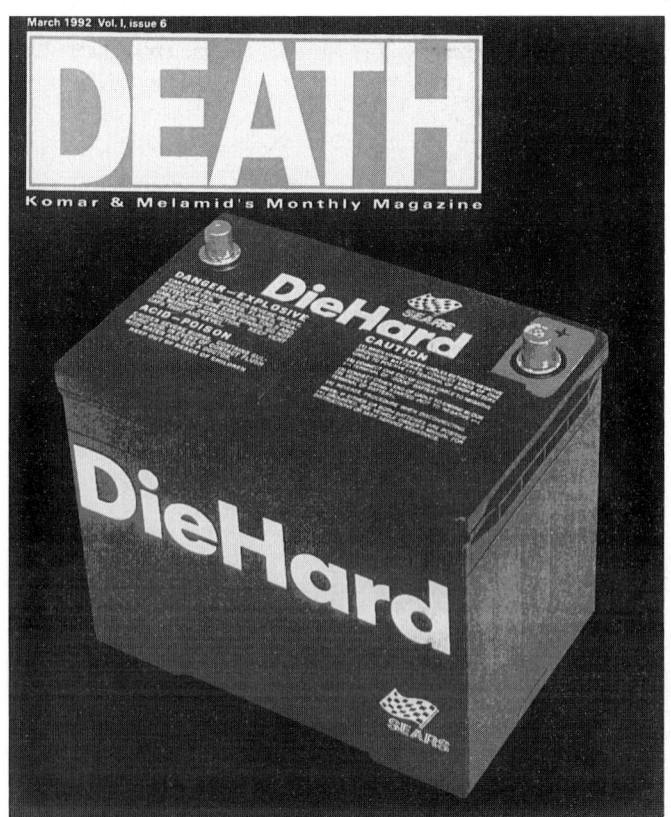

Komar & Melamid
Death Magazine, March
Volume 1, issue 6
Courtesy the Artists

TITLE	PUBLISHER	PRINTER	DATE	MEDIUM	DIMENSION (PAPER SIZE) IN INCHES	TYPE OF PAPER	EDITION NUMBER	NO. OF COLORS	ORIGINAL OPENING PRICE	CURRENT RETAIL PRICE
CURRENT EDITIONS:										
Tea with Lemon	SEAE	JN	1985	SP/CO/HC	14 X 30	SOM/NP	15		750	3000
Peace I (Set of 4 Diptychs)	VP	JJ/BB/RH/VP	1986	LC/PH/CC	36 X 24 EA	R/BFK	12 EA		3200 SET	6000 SET
Sunrise at Bayonne (with Copper)	REd	PB/REd	1988	EB/A	32 X 73	R/BFK	40	7	2500	5000

KOMAR & MELAMID CONTINUED

Komar & Melamid
Our Flag
(First Project)
Courtesy Riverhouse Editions

TITLE	PUBLISHER	PRINTER	DATE	MEDIUM	DIMENSION (PAPER SIZE) IN INCHES	TYPE OF PAPER	EDITION NUMBER	NO. OF COLORS	ORIGINAL OPENING PRICE	CURRENT RETAIL PRICE
CURRENT EDITIONS:										
Head of Worker (4 Parts) (Bergen Point Brass Foundry) (Woodcut on Brass Leaf Lithograph & Brass Stamping on Leather)	SP/StEd	JS/SP	1989	MM	24 X 88 EA	JP(1) AP(2) Leather(1)	40 EA		4500 SET	6000 SET
Heads of Workers (Xerox, Lithograph, Acrylic & Crayon)	SP	JS/SP	1989	MM	31 X 90	AC			7500	10000
Church, New Jersey	SP	JS/SP	1990	MON	30 X 53 EA	AC	20 EA		3000 EA	3500 EA
Our Flag (First Project)	REd	PB/BS	1990	PH/SG	40 X 59	R/BFK	75	2	1500	1500
Our Flag (Second Project)	REd	PB/BS	1990	PH/SG	59 X 39	R/BFK	75	2	1500	1500
God Bless America (Flag) (Woodcut on Fabric Front & Verso)	SP	JS/SP	1990	WC	60 X 44	FABRIC	6		2000	2000
God Bayonne New Jersey	REd	PB/REd	1990	MM	30 X 94	R/BFK	60		3000	3000
Death Magazine (Covers Dated Monthly from October 1991 to September 1992—to be Considered One Artwork)	ART	SV	1992	SP	10 X 12 EA	AP	250 EA	5–6 EA	3000 SET	3500 SET

EVA AND PAUL KOLOSVARY

BORN: Hungary (Both); Eva: May 14, 1937; Paul: May 23, 1921
EDUCATION: Eva: Sch of Fine Arts, Budapest, Hungary; California State Univ, Long Beach, CA, BA, MA & MFA, 1980
Paul: Atelier Art Inst, Budapest, Hungary; Acad of Fine Arts, Budapest, Hungary
AWARDS: Purchase Award, Col of the Siskiyous, Weed, CA, 1976; Award, Riverside, CA, 1977; Purchase Award, California State Univ, Northridge, CA, 1979; Purchase Award, Santa Monica Col, CA, 1981; Purchase Awards, Texas Tech Univ, Lubbock, TX, 1980, 83; Award, Dakota Western Univ, Minot, ND, 1984; Gold Medal in Printmaking, Int Art Comp, Los Angeles, CA, 1984; First Prize, Printmaking, California State Fair, Sacramento, CA, 1984; Purchase Prize, Univ of Texas, El Paso, TX, 1984; Purchase Award, New York State Univ, Potsdam, NY, 1984; Award, Southern Oregon State Col, Ashland, OR, 1984; First Prize, Graphics, Owensboro Mus of Fine Art, KY, 1986; First Prize, Printmaking, Boston/Los Angeles Nat Competition, 1987
RECENT EXHIB: Thinking Eye Gallery, Los Angeles, CA, 1987; Art Inst of Boston, MA, 1987; Carroll Reece Mus, Johnson City, TN, 1987; California State Univ, Northridge, CA, 1987
COLLECTIONS: Mus of Fine Arts, Budapest, Hungary; Downy Mus of Art, CA; Cheney Cowles Mem Mus, Spokane, WA; Huntsville Mus, AL; Texas Tech Univ, Lubbock, TX; State of New York Univ, Potsdam, NY; Univ of Texas, El Paso, TX; Norton Simon Coll, Fullerton, CA; Col of the Siskiyous, Weed, CA; Brand Library Art Center, Glendale, CA; Rockford Col, IL; Santa Monica Col, CA
PRINTERS: Artist (ART)
PUBLISHERS: Artist (ART)
GALLERIES: Thinking Eye Gallery, Los Angeles, CA; Wenniger Graphics, Boston, MA; Louis Congdon Art Publisher, Seattle, WA; Rubiner Gallery, West Bloomfield, MI
MAILING ADDRESS: 30211 Via Rivera, Rancho Palos Verdes, CA 90274

The Printworld Directory is accepting new applications for the seventh edition. Approximately 300 new artists will be accepted. Please use the two forms provided in the back section of this directory to submit biographical data and documentation of prints. Edition number of each print must not exceed 500 and the retail price must be $100 or more.

EVA AND PAUL KOLOSVARY

TITLE	PUBLISHER	PRINTER	DATE	MEDIUM	DIMENSION (PAPER SIZE) IN INCHES	TYPE OF PAPER	EDITION NUMBER	NO. OF COLORS	ORIGINAL OPENING PRICE	CURRENT RETAIL PRICE
SOLD OUT EDITIONS (RARE):										
The Cube Series:										
The Cube #1—Reality	ART	ART	1976	EC	30 X 22	AP	50		200	600
The Cube #2—Couple	ART	ART	1976	EC	30 X 22	AP	50		200	600
The Cube #3—Meditation	ART	ART	1976	EC	30 X 22	AP	50		200	600
The Cube #4	ART	ART	1978	EC	24 X 18	AP	50		150	500
The Cube #5—Seated Woman	ART	ART	1976	EC	30 X 22	AP	50		200	600
The Cube #6—Reclining Woman	ART	ART	1977	EC	22 X 30	AP	50		200	600
Volume in Space Series:										
#1—Stitches of Gravity	ART	ART	1978	EC	22 X 30	AP	50		200	500
#2—An Illusion	ART	ART	1978	EC	22 X 30	AP	50		300	600
#3—Journey	ART	ART	1978	EC	30 X 22	AP	50		300	600
#4—Window	ART	ART	1978	EC	22 X 30	AP	50		300	600
#5—Phenomenon	ART	ART	1978–80	EC	30 X 22	AP	50		300	600
#6—Passage	ART	ART	1978–80	EC	29 X 41	AP	50		600	1200
#7—Creation	ART	ART	1980	EC	22 X 30	AP	50		300	600
#8—Danae	ART	ART	1980	EC	22 X 30	AP	50		400	1000
#9—Cube	ART	ART	1981	EC	30 X 22	AP	25		400	600
#10—Cadillac	ART	ART	1981	EC	30 X 22	AP	25		400	600
CURRENT EDITIONS:										
Joshua Tree Monument:										
#1	ART	ART	1981	EC	29 X 28	AP	30	6	500	550
#2	ART	ART	1981	EC	31 X 29	AP	30	8	500	550
#3	ART	ART	1981	EC	36 X 29	AP	30	6	600	650
#4	ART	ART	1983	EC	36 X 29	AP	20	7	500	550
#5	ART	ART	1983	EC	31 X 30	AP	25	14	500	550
#6	ART	ART	1983	EC	29 X 41	AP	20	8	500	550
#7	ART	ART	1983	EC	39 X 28	AP	30	11	600	650
#8	ART	ART	1984	EC	41 X 29	AP	35	12	700	750
#10	ART	ART	1985	EC	29 X 41	AP	25	11	700	750
Papa, Papa, Where Are You Now?	ART	ART	1984	EC	41 X 29	AP	25	24	700	750
Self-Portrait-Paul	ART	ART	1984	EC	29 X 22	AP	30	13	400	450
Black Fish	ART	ART	1985	EC	29 X 41	AP	25	22	700	750
Debbie	ART	ART	1985	EC	29 X 22	AP	25	30	450	650
Ramona	ART	BW	1985	SP	22 X 25	AP	25	1	200	300
Ramona's Country-Fantasy	ART	ART	1986	EC	29 X 41	AP	25	11	700	750
Joshua Tree Monument (Dipt)	ART	ART	1986	EC	29 X 78	AP	25	22	1200	1300
Dying Tulips	ART	ART	1986	EC	30 X 22	AP	30	14	300	500

BILL KOMOSKI

PRINTERS: Judith Solodkin, NY (JS); Solo Press, NY (SP)

PUBLISHERS: Solo Press, NY (SP)
GALLERIES: Roy Boyd Gallery, Santa Monica, CA; Carol Getz Gallery, Coconut Grove, FL; Solo Impressions, New York, NY

TITLE	PUBLISHER	PRINTER	DATE	MEDIUM	DIMENSION (PAPER SIZE) IN INCHES	TYPE OF PAPER	EDITION NUMBER	NO. OF COLORS	ORIGINAL OPENING PRICE	CURRENT RETAIL PRICE
CURRENT EDITIONS:										
Untitled	SP	JS/SP	1989	MON	26 X 21 EA	AC	1 EA	Varies	1000 EA	1200 EA

JEFF KOONS

BORN: York, PA; 1955
EDUCATION: Maryland Inst Col of Art, Baltimore, MD, 1972–75; Sch of Art Inst of Chicago, IL, 1975–76; Maryland Inst Col of Art, Baltimore, MD, BFA, 1976

RECENT EXHIB: Whitney Mus of Am Art, NY, 1987,89
PRINTERS: Joe Petruzzelli, NY (JP); Maurice Sanchez, NY (MS); Derriére L'Etoile Studios, NY (DES)
PUBLISHERS: Editions Ilene Kurtz, NY (EIK)
GALLERIES: Daniel Weinberg Gallery, Santa Monica, CA; Donald Young Gallery, Seattle, WA; Sonnabend Gallery, New York, NY; Editions Ilene Kurtz, New York, NY; G W Einstein, New York, NY

TITLE	PUBLISHER	PRINTER	DATE	MEDIUM	DIMENSION (PAPER SIZE) IN INCHES	TYPE OF PAPER	EDITION NUMBER	NO. OF COLORS	ORIGINAL OPENING PRICE	CURRENT RETAIL PRICE
CURRENT EDITIONS:										
Luxury and Degradation (Set of 3):									1500 SET	5000 SET
Fisherman/Golfer	EIK	JP/MS/DES	1986	PH/LC	32 X 24	RCP	60		500	1700
Jim Beam J B Turner Engine	EIK	JP/MS/DES	1986	PH/LC	32 X 24	RCP	60		500	1700
Baccarat Crystal Set	EIK	JP/MS/DES	1986	PH/LC	32 X 24	RCP	60		500	1700

The retail prices of the 100,000 limited edition prints quoted in this directory are subject to change. Print publishers, artists and galleries were the direct sources for these quotations. Prices in the secondary market listed as "Sold Out Editions (Rare)" indicate that the publisher has a limited supply of that print or that the print is difficult to locate in the galleries.

CHAIM KOPPELMAN

BORN: Brooklyn, NY; November 17, 1920
EDUCATION: Am Artists' Sch, NY; Art Col of Western England, Bristol, England; Amadee Ozenfant, Sch of Fine Arts, with Eli Siegal, Founder of Aesthetic Realism
TEACHING: New York Univ, NY, 1947–55; Brooklyn Col, NY, 1950–60; State Univ of New York, New Paltz, NY, 1952–58; Sch of Visual Arts, NY, 1959 to present
AWARDS: Louis Comfort Tiffany Grants, 1956, 59; Soc of Am Graphics Artists Prize, 1966; Creative Artists Public Service Grant, NY, 1976; Cannon Prize, Nat Acad, 1986; Small Works Annual Exhib Award, 1986; Purchase Award, Philadelphia Mus & Print Club, Phila, PA, 1987; Cannon Prize, Nat Acad of Design, NY, 1986,89
RECENT EXHIB: Print Club, Phila, PA, 1988; Alternative Mus, NY, 1988
COLLECTIONS: Mus of Mod Art, NY; Metropolitan Mus of Art, NY; Whitney Mus of Am Art, NY; Victoria and Albert Mus, London, England; Mus of Fine Art, Caracas, Venezuela; Library of Congress, Wash, DC; Los Angeles County Mus, CA
PRINTERS: Artist (ART)
PUBLISHERS: Associated American Artists, NY (AAA); Artist (ART)
GALLERIES: Associated American Artists Gallery, New York, NY
MAILING ADDRESS: 498 Broome St, New York, NY 10012

TITLE	PUBLISHER	PRINTER	DATE	MEDIUM	DIMENSION (PAPER SIZE) IN INCHES	TYPE OF PAPER	EDITION NUMBER	NO. OF COLORS	ORIGINAL OPENING PRICE	CURRENT RETAIL PRICE
SOLD OUT EDITIONS (RARE):										
Hopeful Landscape	AAA	ART	1960	EB	7 X 14	R/BFK	220	1	35	150
Wings of the Dove	AAA	ART	1960	EB/A	18 X 15	R/BFK	220		50	300
Not There	ART	ART	1977	LC	22 X 22	AP	30	2	125	200
Doggie, Git Out of There	ART	ART	1977	LC	22 X 26	AP	30	3	125	200
Over Brooklyn	ART	ART	1977	LC	24 X 18	AP	30	5	125	200
Critical Still Life	ART	ART	1977	LC	19 X 26	AP	30	5	125	200
Once We were Two Smoothies	ART	ART	1977	LC	24 X 18	AP	30	4	125	200
Still Life with Touch of Class	ART	ART	1981	I	25 X 19	R/BFK	30	2	150	200
Still Life with Bottles	ART	ART	1981	EB	12 X 18	R/BFK	30	1	100	150

EDWARD B KOREN

BORN: New York, NY; December 13, 1935
EDUCATION: Columbia Univ, NY, BA, 1957; Atelier 17, Paris, France, with S W Hayter, 1958–62; Pratt Inst, NY, MFA, 1964; Union Col, NY, LHD, 1984
AWARDS: John Simon Guggenheim Fel, NY, 1970–71
COLLECTIONS: Fogg Mus, Cambridge, MA; Princeton Univ, NJ; Rhode Island Sch of Design, Providence, RI; U S Information Agency, Wash, DC; Library of Congress, Wash, DC
PRINTERS: Judith Solodkin, NY (JS); Solo Press, NY (SP)
PUBLISHERS: Solo Press, NY (SP)
GALLERIES: Solo Gallery, New York, NY
MAILING ADDRESS: c/o The New Yorker, 25 W 43rd St, New York, NY 10036

TITLE	PUBLISHER	PRINTER	DATE	MEDIUM	DIMENSION (PAPER SIZE) IN INCHES	TYPE OF PAPER	EDITION NUMBER	NO. OF COLORS	ORIGINAL OPENING PRICE	CURRENT RETAIL PRICE
CURRENT EDITIONS										
Beasties	SP	JS/SP	1987	MON/HC	16 X 19 EA	GE	1 EA	Varies	850 EA	950 EA
Beasties	SP	JS/SP	1987	MON/HC	24 X 30 EA	GE	1 EA	Varies	1000 EA	1200 EA
Microbes (set of 6)	SP	JS/SP	1991	EC	27 X 24 EA	R/BFK	15 EA		1800 SET	1800 SET
									350 EA	350 EA
So Quickly, So Slowly (Set of 5):									1200 SET	1200 SET
So Quickly, So Slowly I	SP	JS/SP	1991	EC	18 X 21	R/BFK	15		225	225
So Quickly, So Slowly II	SP	JS/SP	1991	EC	18 X 21	R/BFK	15		225	225
So Quickly, So Slowly III	SP	JS/SP	1991	EC	18 X 21	R/BFK	15		275	275
So Quickly, So Slowly IV	SP	JS/SP	1991	EC	21 X 18	R/BFK	15		225	225
So Quickly, So Slowly V	SP	JS/SP	1991	EC	18 X 21	R/BFK	15		350	350
This Suddenly Speeded Up Time (Set of 4)										
This Suddenly Speeded Up Time I	SP	JS/SP	1991	EC	18 X 21	AC	15		225	225
This Suddenly Speeded Up Time II	SP	JS/SP	1991	EC	21 X 18	AC	15		275	275
This Suddenly Speeded Up Time III	SP	JS/SP	1991	EC	21 X 18	AC	15		275	275
This Suddenly Speeded Up Time IV	SP	JS/SP	1991	EC	18 X 21	AC	15		225	225

LEONARD J KOSCIANSKI

BORN: Cleveland, OH; April 20, 1952
EDUCATION: Cleveland Inst of Art, OH, BFA, 1977; Univ of California, Davis, CA MFA, 1979
TEACHING: Asst Prof, Art, Univ of Tennessee, Knoxville, TN, 1980–84; Univ of Maryland, College Park, MO, 1984–87
AWARDS: Visual Arts Fel, 1983; Southeastern Center for Contemp Arts, Fel, 1983; Nat Endowment for the Arts Grants, 1983,85,89; Rockefeller Found Fel, Bellagio, Italy, 1990
RECENT EXHIB: Karl Bornstein Gallery, Santa Monica, CA, 1987; Florida State Univ Mus, Tallahassee, FL, 1988; Phyllis Kind Gallery, New York, NY & Chicago, IL, 1987,88,89,90
COLLECTIONS: Metropolitan Mus of Art, NY; Philadelphia Mus of Art, PA; Newport Harbor Mus, Newport Beach, CA; Phoenix Mus of Art, AZ
PRINTERS: Jack Lemon, Chicago, IL (JL); Landfall Press, Inc, Chicago, IL (LPI)
PUBLISHERS: Landfall Press, Inc, Chicago, IL (LPI)
GALLERIES: Karl Bornstein Gallery, Santa Monica, CA; Brody's Gallery, Wash, DC; Phyllis Kind Galleries, New York, NY & Chicago, IL; Landfall Press, Inc, Chicago, IL; Federal Reserve Board Art Gallery, Wash, DC
MAILING ADDRESS: 1712 S Harbor Lane, Annapolis, MD 21401

TITLE	PUBLISHER	PRINTER	DATE	MEDIUM	DIMENSION (PAPER SIZE) IN INCHES	TYPE OF PAPER	EDITION NUMBER	NO. OF COLORS	ORIGINAL OPENING PRICE	CURRENT RETAIL PRICE
CURRENT EDITIONS:										
Pleiades	LPI	JL/LPI	1989	LC	24 X 32	AP	35	6	900	900
Pleiades, State I	LPI	JL/LPI	1989	LC	24 X 32	AP	35	1	500	500
Red Boar	LPI	JL/LPI	1989	MON	33 X 42 EA	FAB	1 EA		4500 EA	4500 EA

LEONARD KOSCIANSKI CONTINUED

TITLE	PUBLISHER	PRINTER	DATE	MEDIUM	DIMENSION (PAPER SIZE) IN INCHES	TYPE OF PAPER	EDITION NUMBER	NO. OF COLORS	ORIGINAL OPENING PRICE	CURRENT RETAIL PRICE
CURRENT EDITIONS:										
Mad Dog	LPI	JL/LPI	1991	MON	27 X 35 EA	FAB	1 EA	Varies	1200 EA	1200 EA
Fire-Eaters	LPI	JL/LPI	1991	LC	30 X 24	AC	35		900	900
Fire-Eaters, State I	LPI	JL/LPI	1991	LB	30 X 24	AC	24	1	500	500
Wild Dog	LPI	JL/LPI	1991	MON	27 X 35 EA	FAB	1 EA	Varies	1200 EA	1200 EA
Medusa	LPI	JL/LPI	1991	MON	33 X 42 EA	FAB	1 EA	Varies	1200 EA	1200 EA

LEON KOSSOFF

BORN: London, England; 1926
EDUCATION: St Martin's Sch of Art, London, England, 1949–53; Royal Col of Art, London, England, 1953–56
TEACHING: Chelsea Sch of Art, London, England, 1966–69
RECENT EXHIB: Runkel-Hue-Williams Ltd, London, England, 1989
COLLECTIONS: British Mus, London, England; Tate Gallery of Art, London, England; Art Council of Great Britain, London, England; Australian Nat Gallery, Canberra, Australia; City Mus of Leicester, England
PRINTERS: American Atelier, NY (AA); Studio Prints, London, England (SP); Mark Balakjian, London, England (MB)
PUBLISHERS: Associated American Artists, NY (AAA); Bernard Jacobson Ltd, London, England (BJL)
GALLERIES: Bernard Jacobson Ltd, London, England; L A Louver, Venice, CA; Hirsch & Adler Modern, New York, NY; Runkel-Hue-Williams, Ltd, London, England; Robert Miller Gallery, New York, NY; Associated American Artists, New York, NY

TITLE	PUBLISHER	PRINTER	DATE	MEDIUM	DIMENSION (PAPER SIZE) IN INCHES	TYPE OF PAPER	EDITION NUMBER	NO. OF COLORS	ORIGINAL OPENING PRICE	CURRENT RETAIL PRICE
SOLD OUT EDITIONS (RARE):										
Wings of the Dove	AAA	AA	1960	EB/A	18 X 15	RP	220		50	1000
Set of Six Etchings:										
The Booking Hall	BJL	SP	1982	EB	16 X 14	THS	100	1	200	600
The Letter	BJL	SP	1982	EB	15 X 16	THS	100	1	200	600
Outside Kilburn Underground	BJL	SP	1982	EB	23 X 26	THS	40	1	500	1000
Mother	BJL	SP	1982	EB	24 X 20	THS	60	1	300	800
Father Asleep	BJL	SP	1982	EB	20 X 24	THS	60	1	300	800
Resting	BJL	SP	1982	EB	20 X 23	THS	60	1	300	800
Fidelma I, II, III, IV (Set of 4):	BJL	MB/SP	1984	EB	16 X 11 EA	SOM	60 EA	1 EA	900 SET	2000 SET
									250 EA	600 EA
The Window	BJL	MB/SP	1984	EB	13 X 12	SOM	100	1	350	750
Going Home	BJL	MB/SP	1984	EB	23 X 26	SOM/CR	100	1	800	1200

MARK KOSTABI

BORN: Los Angeles, CA; November 27, 1960
EDUCATION: Fullerton Comm Col, CA, 1978; California State Univ, Fullerton, CA, 1979–81
RECENT EXHIB: Albright Col, Freedman Gallery, Reading, PA, 1987; Beaver Col, Glenside, PA, 1987; Trova Found, Clayton, MO, 1989; Peterson Mus, Paterson, NJ, 1992; Retrosp, Seibu Mus, Japan, 1992; Retrosp, Mitsukoshi Mus, Japan, 1992; Martin Lawrence Galleries, Los Angeles, CA & New York, NY & Phila, PA & Wash, DC, 1993
COLLECTIONS: Mus of Mod Art, NY; Seibu Mus, Tokyo, Japan; Memphis Brooks Mus of Art, TN; Metropolitan Mus of Art, NY; Guggenheim Mus, NY; Groninger Mus, The Netherlands
PRINTERS: Editions Sheridan Bardin, Brooklyn, NY (ESB)
PUBLISHERS: Ronald Feldman Fine Arts, NY (RFFA); Artist (ART); Martin Lawrence Limited Editions, Van Nuys, CA (MLLE)
GALLERIES: Ronald Feldman Fine Arts, New York, NY; Roy Boyd Gallery, Santa Monica, CA; Peter Miller Gallery, Chicago, IL; Hokin Galleries, Bay Harbor Islands, FL & Palm Beach, FL; Morgan Gallery, Boston, MA; Fred Dorfman Gallery, New York, NY; Alan Brown Gallery, Hartdale, NY; Hanson Galleries, Beverly Hills, CA & San Francisco, CA & New Orleans, LA & La Jolla, CA & Maui, HI; Charlotte Brawer Fine Art, Munster, IL; C & L Fine Arts, Inc, Bohemia, NY; Martin Lawrence Galleries, Nationwide, USA
MAILING ADDRESS: c/o Ronald Feldman Fine Arts, 31 Mercer St, New York, NY 10013

TITLE	PUBLISHER	PRINTER	DATE	MEDIUM	DIMENSION (PAPER SIZE) IN INCHES	TYPE OF PAPER	EDITION NUMBER	NO. OF COLORS	ORIGINAL OPENING PRICE	CURRENT RETAIL PRICE
CURRENT EDITIONS:										
Kostabi's Factory	RFFA	ESB	1985	LB	22 X 30	R/BFK	100	1	350	1500
Climbing	ART	ESB	1985	SP/PH	30 X 22	STP	100		175	1200
Climbing	ART	ESB	1985	SP/PH/HC	30 X 22	STP	100	Varies	250	2000
Close Call	RFFA	ESB	1986	SP	42 X 30	AP88	40	15	750	1500
Close Call Portfolio (Set of 8)	RFFA	ESB	1986	SP	40 X 28 EA	AP88	10 EA		6000 SET	9000 SET
Enasaurs	RFFA	ESB	1986	SP	43 X 30	AP88	60		1800	2500
Two Cultures (Set of 2)	RFFA	ESB	1987	SP	42 X 30 EA	AP88	52 EA		1800 EA	2200 EA
Upwardly Mobile (Set of 3)	RFFA	ESB	1989	SP	40 X 30 EA	AP88	52 EA		5000 SET	5000 SET
The Art of the Deal II	RFFA	ESB	1989	SP	28 X 40	AP88	56		3000	3000
Art of the Deal (Iron Fist)	MLLE		1993	SP	26 X 39	AP88	353	10	900	1150
The Early Nerd Gets the Worm	MLLE		1993	SP	31 X 31	AP88	353	8	900	1150

The print market has become very selective. For the first time since we published the first edition of The Printworld Directory in 1982, the prices of prints have been greatly reduced and greatly increased for the same artists by the most reputable and established print publishers. Check the fifth edition to understand the movement.

The Printworld Directory is accepting new applications for the seventh edition. Approximately 300 new artists will be accepted. Please use the two forms provided in the back section of this directory to submit biographical data and documentation of prints. Edition number of each print must not exceed 500 and the retail price must be $100 or more.

MARK KOSTABI CONTINUED

Mark Kostabi
Art of the Deal (Iron Fist)
Courtesy Martin Lawrence Limited Editions

Mark Kostabi
The Early Nerd Gets the Worm
Courtesy Martin Lawrence Limited Editions

JOSEPH KOSUTH

BORN: Toledo, OH; January 31, 1945
EDUCATION: Toledo Mus Sch of Design, OH, 1955–62; Cleveland Art Inst, OH, 1963–64; Sch of Visual Arts, NY, 1966–67; New Sch for Social Research Grad Center, NY, 1970–73
TEACHING: Lectr, Univ of Santiago, Chile, 1971; Prof, Sch of Visual Arts, NY, 1968 to present
RECENT EXHIB: Wright State Univ, Dayton, OH, 1987; Knoll Galleria, Budapest, Hungary, 1988; Galerie Le Gall Peyroulet, Paris, France, 1989; Santa Barbara Contemp Art Forum, CA, 1989; Leo Castelli Gallery, NY, 1989; Brooklyn Mus, NY, 1990; Galeria Juana de Arizpuro, Madrid, Spain, 1990; Galeria Comicos, Lisbon, Portugal, 1990; Margo Leavin Gallery, Los Angeles, CA, 1990; Hirshhorn Mus, Wash, DC, 1992; Renaissance Soc, Univ of Chicago, IL, 1989,92; Leo Castelli Gallery, NY, 1993
COLLECTIONS: Mus of Mod Art, NY; Tate Gallery, London, England; Solomon Guggenheim Mus, NY; Whitney Mus of Am Art, NY; Nat Gallery of Canada, Ottawa, Canada
PRINTERS: Artist (ART); Dikko Faust, NY (DF); Purgatory Pie Press, NY (PPP)
PUBLISHERS: Wright State univ, Dayton, OH (WSU); Ruth Benzacar Editions, Buenos Aires, Argentina (RBE)
GALLERIES: Castelli Graphics, New York, NY; Margo Leavin Gallery, Los Angeles, CA; Wright State Univ, Dayton, OH; Sally Baker Gallery, Hudson, NY
MAILING ADDRESS: 591 Broadway, New York, NY 10012

TITLE	PUBLISHER	PRINTER	DATE	MEDIUM	DIMENSION (PAPER SIZE) IN INCHES	TYPE OF PAPER	EDITION NUMBER	NO. OF COLORS	ORIGINAL OPENING PRICE	CURRENT RETAIL PRICE
CURRENT EDITIONS:										
Text/Context (Conventional)	WSU	ART	1978	SP	30 X 40	AP	40		750	15000
Ten Unnumbered Corrections (7 Nights) (Set of 10)	DF/PPP		1991	EB/LP	10 X 10 EA	JOH	25 EA		7000 SET	7000 SET

HARRY KOURSAROS

BORN: Reading, PA; February 14, 1928
EDUCATION: Albright Col, Reading, PA, BA, 1950; George Washington Law Sch, Wash, DC, 1950 53; Am Univ, Wash, DC, MFA, 1956
TEACHING: Assoc Prof/Chairman, Art Dept, Albright Col, Reading, PA, 1964 to present
AWARDS: Soc of Washington Artists, Max Weber, Juror, 1955; Am Univ Writer Award, 1956; Fulbright Grants, 1956,57
COLLECTIONS: Birmingham Mus, Birmingham, AL; Reading Mus, Reading, PA; Neuberger Mus, Purchase, NY; Newark Mus, Newark, NJ
PRINTERS: Atelier Ettinger, NY (AE)
PUBLISHERS: Transworld Art, Inc, NY (TAI)
GALLERIES: Barry Rosen & Jaap van Liere Modern & Contemporary Art, New York, NY
MAILING ADDRESS: 362 W Broadway, New York, NY 10013

TITLE	PUBLISHER	PRINTER	DATE	MEDIUM	DIMENSION (PAPER SIZE) IN INCHES	TYPE OF PAPER	EDITION NUMBER	NO. OF COLORS	ORIGINAL OPENING PRICE	CURRENT RETAIL PRICE
SOLD OUT EDITIONS (RARE):										
Kition	TAI	AE	1980	LC	40 X 28	AP	175		200	350
Paphos	TAI	AE	1980	LC	29 X 35	AP	175		200	350
Minoan Ladder	TAI	AE	1980	LC	35 X 24	AP	175		200	350

The retail prices of the 100,000 limited edition prints quoted in this directory are subject to change. Print publishers, artists and galleries were the direct sources for these quotations. Prices in the secondary market listed as "Sold Out Editions (Rare)" indicate that the publisher has a limited supply of that print or that the print is difficult to locate in the galleries.

The Printworld Directory is accepting new applications for the seventh edition. Approximately 300 new artists will be accepted. Please use the two forms provided in the back section of this directory to submit biographical data and documentation of prints. Edition number of each print must not exceed 500 and the retail price must be $100 or more.

JANNIS KOUNELLIS

BORN: Pireasus, Greece; March 21, 1936
RECENT EXHIB: Galleria Sprovieri, Rome, Italy, 1987; Simon/Neuman Gallery, NY, 1987; Thomas Segal Gallery, Boston, MA, 1988; Galerie Lelong, Paris, France, 1993
PRINTERS: Crown Point Press, San Francisco, CA (CPP); Max Dunkes, Munich, West Germany (MD); Atelier Franck Bordas, Paris, France (AFB)
PUBLISHERS: Crown Point Press, San Francisco, CA (CPP); Editions Schellmann & Klüser, Munich, Germany & New (SK); Galerie Lelong, Paris, France (GL)

GALLERIES: Sonnabend Gallery, New York, NY; Crown Point Press, New York, NY & San Francisco, CA; Editions Schellmann, New York, NY; Whitechapel Art Gallery, London, England; Paul Cava Gallery, Phila, PA; Marian Goodman Gallery, New York, NY; Rhona Hoffman Gallery, Chicago, IL; Luhring & Augustine Gallery, New York, NY; Karsten Greve Galerie, Cologne, Germany; Galleria Sprovieri, Rome, Italy; Simon/Neuman Gallery, New York, NY; Thomas Segal Gallery, Boston, MA; Margo Leavin Gallery, Los Angeles, CA; Donald Young Gallery, Seattle, WA; Judi Rotenberg Gallery, Boston, MA; Galerie Lelong, New York, NY & Paris, France

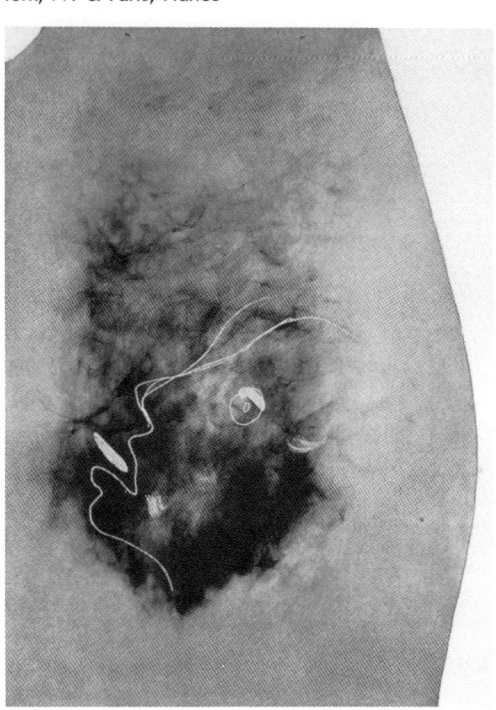

Jannis Kounellis
Frammenti di Danza
Courtesy Edition Schellmann

Jannis Kounellis
Untitled (Finestra)
Courtesy Edition Schellmann

TITLE	PUBLISHER	PRINTER	DATE	MEDIUM	DIMENSION (PAPER SIZE) IN INCHES	TYPE OF PAPER	EDITION NUMBER	NO. OF COLORS	ORIGINAL OPENING PRICE	CURRENT RETAIL PRICE
SOLD OUT EDITIONS (RARE):										
Untitled	CPP	CPP	1979	PH/EB/A	45 X 36	AP	21		1500	5000
CURRENT EDITIONS:										
Manifesto per un Teatro Utopistico (Manifesto for a Utopian Theatre)	CPP	CPP	1979	PH/EB	35 X 26	AP	35	600	1200	3500
Frammenti di Danza (Fragments of Dance) (Set of 7)	SK	MD	1982	EB/DPT	37 X 30 EA	R/BFK	75 EA	1 EA	4500 SET 750 EA	15000 SET 2500 EA
Fumo di Pietra I–X (Set of 10)	GL	AFB	1992	LB	24 X 22 EA to 41 X 68 EA	AP	21 EA	1 EA	2300 – 3400 EA	2300 – 3400 EA

JOYCE KOZLOFF

BORN: Somerville, NJ; December 14, 1942
EDUCATION: Carnegie Inst, BFA, 1964; Columbia Univ, MFA, 1967; Rutgers Univ, Univ of Florence Art Students League, Italy
TEACHING: Instr, Ace Program, Queens Col, Flushing, NY, 1972; Instr, Sch for Visual Arts, NY, 1973–74; Instr, Chicago Inst of Art, IL, 1975; Syracuse Univ, NY; Instr, Cooper Union, NY, 1990

AWARDS: Creative Artists Public Service Grants, NY, 1975; Am Assoc of Univ Women Grant, 1975; Nat Endowment for the Arts Grant, 1977; Yaddo Fel, Saratoga Springs, NY, 1981; Am Acad of Arts & Letters, NY, 1987,90
COLLECTIONS: Mus of Modern Art, NY
RECENT EXHIB: Lorence-Monk Gallery, NY, 1990; Nina Freudenheim Gallery, Buffalo, NY, 1990

The retail prices of the 100,000 limited edition prints quoted in this directory are subject to change. Print publishers, artists and galleries were the direct sources for these quotations. Prices in the secondary market listed as "Sold Out Editions (Rare)" indicate that the publisher has a limited supply of that print or that the print is difficult to locate in the galleries.

JOYCE KOZLOFF CONTINUED

PRINTERS: Lilah Toland (LT); Peter Pettengill (PP); June Lambla (JL); Paul Singahlsen (PS); Bartholme (MB); Crown Point Press, San Francisco, CA (CPP); Dan Stack, NY (DS); David Belzycki, NY (DB); Brian Finley, NY (BF); Solo Press, NY (SP); Artist (ART)
PUBLISHERS: Crown Point Press, San Francisco, CA (CPP); Barbara Gladstone Editions, NY (BGE); Solo Press, NY (SP)
GALLERIES: Tibor de Nagy Gallery, New York, NY; Barbara Gladstone Gallery, New York, NY; Crown Point Press, San Francisco, CA & New York, NY; Nancy Drysdale Gallery, Wash, DC
MAILING ADDRESS: 152 Wooster St, New York, NY 10012

TITLE	PUBLISHER	PRINTER	DATE	MEDIUM	DIMENSION (PAPER SIZE) IN INCHES	TYPE OF PAPER	EDITION NUMBER	NO. OF COLORS	ORIGINAL OPENING PRICE	CURRENT RETAIL PRICE
CURRENT EDITIONS:										
Is It Still High Art? (State 1A)	BGE	SP	1979	LC	17 X 31	CS	15	7	450	1200
Is It Still High Art? (State 1B)	BGE	SP	1979	LC	17 X 31	CS	30	7	350	1200
Is It Still High Art? (State 2)	BGE	SP	1979	LC	23 X 13	CS	15	7	450	1200
Is It Still High Art? (State 3)	BGE	SP	1979	LC	30 X 17	CS	45	7	450	1200
Tile Multiples (Two States)	BGE	ART	1980	MM	24 X 24 EA	CP	15 EA	5	1500 EA	2800 EA
Homage to Robert Adam, States I,II (Installation of 3 cast paper modules containing 19 color etchings to be installed singly or in a group)	CPP	LT/PP/JL	1981	EB/A	32 X 32 EA	R/BFK	25 EA	25 EA	2500 EA	1800 EA
San Francisco Victorian (Handpainted, Artist-designed frame is $350 additional)	CPP	PS/MB	1981	EB/A/EMB	23 X 32 EA	SOM	25 EA	43 EA	1200 EA	1800 EA
Harvard Litho	BGE	DS/DB/BF/SP	1984–86	LC/HC	86 X 11	AP/ROL	30	37	3500	3500

KOZO

EDUCATION: Keio Univ, Japan, 1956–60
AWARDS: Grand Prix de Serigraphie, Paris, France; Grand Prix du Contemp Art, Tokyo, Japan
COLLECTIONS: Musee de'Art Moderne, Paris, France; Bibliotheque Royale de Belgium, Brussels, Belgium; Musee d'Art Moderne de Calcutta, India; Osaka City Mus, Japan
PRINTERS: Artist (ART)
PUBLISHERS: John Szoke Graphics, NY (JSG)
GALLERIES: John Szoke Graphics, Inc, New York, NY; Greenhut Galleries, Albany, NY; Multiple Impressions, New York, NY; JRS Fine Art, Providence, RI

TITLE	PUBLISHER	PRINTER	DATE	MEDIUM	DIMENSION (PAPER SIZE) IN INCHES	TYPE OF PAPER	EDITION NUMBER	NO. OF COLORS	ORIGINAL OPENING PRICE	CURRENT RETAIL PRICE
CURRENT EDITIONS:										
Fleur Rouge	JSG	ART	1990	SP	17 X 25	AC	110	3	600	600
Camelia Blanc	JSG	ART	1990	SP	33 X 23	AC	120	3	850	850
Fruit Rouge	JSG	ART	1990	SP	33 X 23	AC	120	3	850	850

MIREILLE KRAMER

BORN: Cairo, Egypt; 1932
EDUCATION: Jerusalem Univ, Israel; Univ of Milan, Italy; L'Ecole du Louvre, Paris, France; L'Académie Jullian, Paris, France; Pratt Inst, NY
AWARDS: Millerman Prize, Young Artists of Israel Exhib, Israel, 1957
PRINTERS: American Atelier, NY (AA)
PUBLISHERS: Circle Fine Art, Chicago, IL (CFA)
GALLERIES: Circle Galleries, San Diego, CA & San Francisco, CA & Northbrook, IL & Pittsburgh, PA & Houston, TX & Soho, NY & Chicago, IL & Scottsdale, AZ & Beverly Hills, CA & Costa Mesa, CA & Sherman Oaks, CA & Palm Beach, FL & Honolulu, HI & New Orleans, LA & Las Vegas, NV & Seattle, WA

TITLE	PUBLISHER	PRINTER	DATE	MEDIUM	DIMENSION (PAPER SIZE) IN INCHES	TYPE OF PAPER	EDITION NUMBER	NO. OF COLORS	ORIGINAL OPENING PRICE	CURRENT RETAIL PRICE
SOLD OUT EDITIONS (RARE):										
After Love	CFA	AA	1978	EC	10 X 14	R/BFK	125		25	150
Free Love	CFA	AA	1978	EC	17 X 22	R/BFK	125		35	150
Family	CFA	AA	1978	EC	20 X 29	R/BFK	125		35	150
Les Fiances	CFA	AA	1978	EC	20 X 29	R/BFK	125		35	150
Swinging Lady	CFA	AA	1978	EC	20 X 29	R/BFK	125		35	150
CURRENT EDITIONS:										
Women's Liberation	CFA	AA	1979	EC	20 X 29	R/BFK	125		35	150
My First Tango	CFA	AA	1979	EC	16 X 21	R/BFK	125		35	150
1925	CFA	AA	1979	EC	15 X 20	R/BFK	125		35	150
Lovers in the Sky	CFA	AA	1979	EC	15 X 20	R/BFK	125		35	150

STEVE KRAMER

PRINTERS: Vermillion Editions, Ltd, Minneapolis, MN (VEL)
PUBLISHERS: Vermillion Editions, Ltd, Minneapolis, MN (VEL)
GALLERIES: Vermillion Editions, Ltd, Minneapolis, MN

TITLE	PUBLISHER	PRINTER	DATE	MEDIUM	DIMENSION (PAPER SIZE) IN INCHES	TYPE OF PAPER	EDITION NUMBER	NO. OF COLORS	ORIGINAL OPENING PRICE	CURRENT RETAIL PRICE
CURRENT EDITIONS:										
Totally Nude	VEL	VEL	1984	LC	35 X 25				200	250
Untitled	VEL	VEL	1985	MON	30 X 40 EA		1 EA		400	550
Monotype SK #1–#16	VEL	VEL	1985	MON	22 X 30 EA		1 EA		300	450

KATE KRASIN

BORN: Tucumcari, NM; 1943
EDUCATION: Univ of Texas, Arlington, TX, 1961; Kansas State Univ, Manhattan, KS, 1966
TEACHING: Kansas State Univ, Manhattan, KS, 1967–68
PUBLISHERS: Elaine Horwitch Gallery, Santa Fe, NM (EH); Ed Hill Editions, El Paso, TX (EHE)
GALLERIES: Ed Hill Galleries, El Paso, TX

TITLE	PUBLISHER	PRINTER	DATE	MEDIUM	DIMENSION (PAPER SIZE) IN INCHES	TYPE OF PAPER	EDITION NUMBER	NO. OF COLORS	ORIGINAL OPENING PRICE	CURRENT RETAIL PRICE
CURRENT EDITIONS:										
Winter Chamisa	EHE	ART	1981	SP	25 X 30	STP/W	55	16	225	500

LEE KRASNER

BORN: Brooklyn, New York; (1911–1984)
EDUCATION: Cooper Union Sch, NY, 1926–29; Nat Acad of Design, NY
AWARDS: Cooper Union, Saint-Gaudens Medal, 1974
RECENT EXHIB: State Univ of New York, Staller Center Art Gallery, Stony Brook, NY, 1989; Univ of Alabama, Moody Gallery of Art, Tuscaloosa, AL, 1992; Miami-Dade Com Col, Miami, FL, 1992; Robert Miller Gallery, NY, 1992
COLLECTIONS: Whitney Mus of Am Art, NY; Philadelphia Mus of Art, PA
PRINTERS: Chiron Press, NY (CP); Pratt Graphic Art Center, NY (PGAC)
PUBLISHERS: Marlborough Graphics, NY (MG); Transworld Art, Inc, NY (TAI); Artist (ART)
GALLERIES: Robert Miller Gallery, New York, NY; Meredith Long & Company, Houston, TX

Lee Krasner
Free Space
Courtesy Transworld Art, Inc

TITLE	PUBLISHER	PRINTER	DATE	MEDIUM	DIMENSION (PAPER SIZE) IN INCHES	TYPE OF PAPER	EDITION NUMBER	NO. OF COLORS	ORIGINAL OPENING PRICE	CURRENT RETAIL PRICE
SOLD OUT EDITIONS (RARE):										
Obsidian	ART	PGAC	1962	LB	15 X 19	AP	85	1	50	6000
Refractions	ART	PGAC	1962	LB	17 X 23	AP	70	1	50	6000
Primary Series:										
Primary Series: Blue Stone	MG		1969	LC	23 X 29	AP	100	1	100	5000
Primary Series: Gold Stone	MG		1969	LC	23 X 29	AP	100	1	100	5000
Primary Series: Rose Stone	MG		1969	LC	23 X 29	AP	100	1	100	5000
Free Space	TAI	CP	1976	SP	20 X 26	LEN	175		300	3000
Free Space (Deluxe)	TAI	CP	1976	PA/SP/CO	20 X 26	LEN	125		400	3500

MIKULAS KRAVJANSKY

BORN: Rudney, Czechoslovakia; May 3, 1928
EDUCATION: Acad of Fine Art, Bratislava, Czechoslovakia, PSV, 1957
TEACHING: Lectr, Scenography, Acad of Arts, Bratislava, Czechoslovakia, 1957–58; Asst Prof, Design, Acad Muzas Art, Bratislava, Czechoslovakia, 1965; Master, Art-Design, Humber Col, Toronto, Can, 1969–75
COLLECTIONS: Nat Mus of Slovakia, Bratislava, Czechoslovakia; Inst of Scenography, Int Mus, Prague, Czechoslovakia; Royal Ontario Mus, Toronto, ON, Can
PRINTERS: Artist (ART)
PUBLISHERS: Metropolitan Art Associates, Huntington, NY (MAA); Rose Art Ltd, Fort Lauderdale, FL (RAL); DIstinctive Graphics, Inc, Toronto, ON, Canada (DCI); Beaux Art Galleries, Toronto, ON, Canada (BAG); Collectors Group, FL (CGR); Artist (ART); L & D Editions, NY (LDE); Gemi Publishing, FL (GP); Dyansen Editions, NY (DYA); M K Publishing, Napa, CA (MKP); Lawrence Ross, Beverly Hills, CA (LR); International Fine Art, NY (IFA); Alliance Art Publishing, Hayward, WI (AAP)
GALLERIES: Hammer Galleries, New York, NY; Martin Lawrence Galleries, Los Angeles, CA & Sherman Oaks, CA & Newport Beach, CA & Phila, PA; Peterson Fine Art, Minneapolis, MN; Dyansen Eclipse Gallery, New York, NY; P C Hart Gallery, Jupiter, FL
MAILING ADDRESS: 23 South Newport Dr, Napa, CA 94559

TITLE	PUBLISHER	PRINTER	DATE	MEDIUM	DIMENSION (PAPER SIZE) IN INCHES	TYPE OF PAPER	EDITION NUMBER	NO. OF COLORS	ORIGINAL OPENING PRICE	CURRENT RETAIL PRICE
SOLD OUT EDITIONS (RARE):										
The Aztec's Time (Trip)	MAA	ART	1979	COL	22 X 30	AP	100		500	4000
The Mayan Legend (Trip)	MAA	ART	1980	COL	22 X 30 EA	AP	100		500 SET	3800 SET
Opera Suite:										
Aida	MAA	ART	1980	COL	20 X 30	AP	100		250	1000
Fidello	MAA	ART	1980	COL	22 X 30	AP	100		250	1000
Madama Butterfly	MAA	ART	1981	COL	22 X 30	AP	100		300	1000
Carmen	MAA	ART	1981	COL	22 X 30	AP	100		300	1000
Magic Flute	MAA	ART	1981	COL	22 X 30	AP	100		300	1000
Flying Dutchmen	MAA	ART	1981	COL	22 X 30	AP	100		300	1000
Shangri-La, Blue (Trip)	MAA	ART	1981	COL	22 X 30	TIEM	100		750	3500
Shangri-La, Brown (Trip)	MAA	ART	1981	COL	22 X 30	TIEM	100		750	3500

MIKULAS KRAVJANSKY CONTINUED

TITLE	PUBLISHER	PRINTER	DATE	MEDIUM	DIMENSION (PAPER SIZE) IN INCHES	TYPE OF PAPER	EDITION NUMBER	NO. OF COLORS	ORIGINAL OPENING PRICE	CURRENT RETAIL PRICE
SOLD OUT EDITIONS (RARE):										
Flags of the Earth I, II, III	MAA	ART	1982	I/MM	22 X 30 EA	AP	195 EA		350 EA	1000 EA
XVIII Dynasty (Trip)	MAA	ART	1982	COL	22 X 30	AP	190		1100	4500
Le Fleur de Passion I, II, III	MAA	ART	1983	I/MM	22 X 30 EA	AP	75 EA		750 EA	1800 EA
City Sights	MAA	ART	1983	I/MM	30 X 41	AP	75		750	2000
City Lights	MAA	ART	1983	I/MM	30 X 41	AP	75		750	2000
Mikado (Trip)	MAA	ART	1983	I/MM	30 X 40 (1) 12 X 30 (2)	COL	100		900	4500
Olympic Flame	LR	ART	1984	I/MM	30 X 42	HMP	50		850	1800
Olympic Gold	LR	ART	1984	I/MM	30 X 40	HMP	50		850	1800
Sumo Wrestlers	MK	ART	1984	I/MM	30 X 44	AP	25		750	1200
Toronto	MAA	ART	1984	I/MM	30 X 40	HMP	75		750	2500
Kabuki (Trip)	MAA	ART	1984	I/MM	30 X 40 (1) 12 X 30 (2)	COL	150 EA		1750 SET	4500 SET
Rodeo Drive LA: Day/Night	LR	ART	1984	I/MM	30 X 40	HMP	100		2400 SET	6000 SET
Princess (Trip)	MAA	ART	1984	I/MM	22 X 30 (1) 12 X 30 (2)	HMP	100 EA		600 SET	2500 SET
Tea Party	MAA	ART	1985	I/MM	30 X 40	COL	50		950	2500
The Tea Party (Trip)	MAA	ART	1985	I/MM	30 X 40 12 X 30 (2)	COL	50		1750 SET	4500 SET
Parasols (Dipt)	MAA	ART	1985	I/MM	22 X 30 (3)	COL	100 EA		1250 SET	2500 SET
Garden of the Mountain (Set of 6)	MAA	ART	1985	I/MM	12 X 30 (6)	JAP	100 EA		1800 SET	4800 SET
The Dream (Trip)	IFA	ART	1985	I/MM	22 X 30 EA	COL	75 EA		1500 SET	3500 SET
Ikebana	CGR	ART	1986	I/MM	30 X 40 EA	COL	75 EA		900 SET	2500 SET
The Holy City (Trip)	GP	ART	1986	I/MM	22 X 30 (3)	HMP	50 EA		2400 SET	4500 SET
Madama Butterfly (Ladies of the Opera)	DYA	ART	1986	I/MM	30 X 40	COL	95		1500	3000
Cherry Blossom (Trip)	DYA	ART	1987	I/MM	22 X 30 (3)	HMP	95		2100	2500
The Tea House (Trip)	DYA	ART	1987	I/MM	22 X 30 (3)	HMP	95 EA		2100 SET	3000 SET
Water Lillies (from Romantic Suite)	DYA	ART	1987	I/MM	22 X 30	HMP	120		700 EA	1800 EA
School of Ikebana (Trip)	MKP	ART	1987	I/MM	22 X 30 (3)	COL	150 EA		1800 SET	4000 SET
Past Revisited	DYA	ART	1988	I/MM	30 X 40	HMP	150		1000	1500
CURRENT EDITIONS:										
Hanashi (Trip)	MKP	ART	1985	I/MM	22 X 30 (3)	COL	100		1800	2500
Garden of the Classics (Horizontal)	MKP	ART	1986	I/MM	40 X 30	COL	50		750	1500
Garden of the Classics (Vertical)	MKP	ART	1986	I/MM	30 X 40	COL	50		750	1300
Acropolis (Trip)	GP	ART	1986	I/MM	22 X 30 (3)	HMP	50		2400	3500
The Eight Immortals (Set of 8)	GP	ART	1986	I/MM	19 X 28 (8)	HMP	100		4000 SET	7200 SET
Carmen (Ladies of the Opera)	DYA	ART	1986	I/MM	30 X 42	COL	95		900	2500
Midsummer Night's Dream (Trip)	DYA	ART	1987	I/MM	22 X 30 (3)	HMP	95 EA		1900 SET	2500 SET
Romeo and Juliet (Trip)	DYA	ART	1987	I/MM	22 X 30 (3)	HMP	95		1900 SET	2500 SET
Elements Suite:										
Water	LDE	ART	1987	I/MM	22 X 30	HMP	50		500	1400
Fire	LDE	ART	1987	I/MM	22 X 30	HMP	50		900	1400
Earth	LDE	ART	1987	I/MM	22 X 30	HMP	50		900	1400
Air	LDE	ART	1987	I/MM	22 X 30	HMP	50		900	1400
Romantic Suite:										
Jungle Romance	DYA	ART	1987	I/MM	22 X 30	HMP	120		650	1500
Bird in the Garden	DYA	ART	1987	I/MM	22 X 30	HMP	120		650	1500
Mardi Gras (Trip)	DYA	ART	1988	I/MM	22 X 30 (3)	HMP	120		2500	2300
Light on the Stairs	DYA	ART	1988	I/MM	30 X 40	HMP	150		1500	1200
In the Park	DYA	ART	1988	I/MM	30 X 40	HMP	150		1500	1200
Symbols from the Beginning	MKP	ART	1988	I/MM	30 X 40	HMP	50		1000	1200
Mayan Memories	MKP	ART	1988	I/MM	30 X 40	HMP	50		1000	1200
Morning, Day, Evening (Trip)	MAA	ART	1989	I/MM	22 X 30 (3)	HMP	100		1950	3500
Friends (Trip)	DYA	ART	1989	I/MM	22 X 30 (3)	HMP	120		1900	2500
Apples and Flowers	MAA	ART	1989	I/MM	19 X 29	WCP	50		500	700
Flowers in the Glass	MAA	ART	1989	I/MM	19 X 29	WCP	50		500	700
Pears with Vase	MAA	ART	1989	I/MM	19 X 29	WCP	50		500	700
The Painted Bridge	DYA	ART	1989	I/MM	22 X 30	HMP	120		675	800
The Hidden Gate	DYA	ART	1989	I/MM	22 X 30	HMP	120		675	800
The Decorated Wall	DYA	ART	1989	I/MM	22 X 30	HMP	120		675	800
Placid Flowers	DYA	ART	1989	I/MM	19 X 29	WCP	120		450	600
Life Passage	DYA	ART	1989	I/MM	19 X 29	WCP	120		450	600
Suspended Twilight	DYA	ART	1989	I/MM	19 X 29	WCP	120		450	600
Morning Song	DYA	ART	1989	I/MM	19 X 29	WCP	120		450	600
The Peach Experience	AAP	ART	1990	I/MM	22 X 30 (6)	WCP	50 EA		2250 SET	3500 SET
The Blue Spring Song	AAP	ART	1990	I/MM	22 X 30 (3)	WCP	50 EA		2250 SET	3500 SET
Mountain Symphony (Set of 6)	MAA	ART	1990	I/MM	11 X 30 (6)	WCP	50/50		2250 SET	3500 SET
The Love Letters	DYA	ART	1990	I/MM	30 X 40	WCP	120		1600	2200
Pentian Royal (Set of 3)	AAP	ART	1990	I/MM	22 X 30	WCP	100 EA		2250 SET	3500 SET
Nordic Skiing (Set of 3)	AAP	ART	1991	I/MM	22 X 30 EA	WCP	150 EA		2400 SET	2400 SET

LYNWOOD KRENECK

BORN: Kenedy, TX; June 11, 1936
EDUCATION: Univ of Texas, Austin, TX, BFA, 1958, MFA, 1965
TEACHING: Texas Tech Univ, Lubbock, TX, 1965–86
AWARDS: Purchase Prize, Auburn Univ, AL, 1986; Purchase Prize, Purdue Univ, Lafayette, IN, 1986; Purchase Prizes, Univ of North Dakota, Grand Forks, ND, 1983,86
COLLECTIONS: Philadelphia Mus, PA; Fine Arts Gallery of San Diego, CA; High Mus, Atlanta, GA; Springfield Art Mus, MO; Oklahoma Art Center, Oklahoma City, OK; Silvermine Guild, New Canaan, CT; Wichita Art Mus, KS
PRINTERS: Peregrine Press, Inc, Dallas, TX (PerP); Univ of Oklahoma, Sch of Art, Norman, OK (UO); Artist (ART)
PUBLISHERS: Peregrine Press, Inc, Dallas, TX (PerP); Univ of Oklahoma, Sch of Art, Norman, OK (UO); Artist (ART)
GALLERIES: Patrick Graphics Gallery, Austin, TX; Peregrine Gallery, Dallas, TX
MAILING ADDRESS: 5224 14th St, Lubbock TX 79416

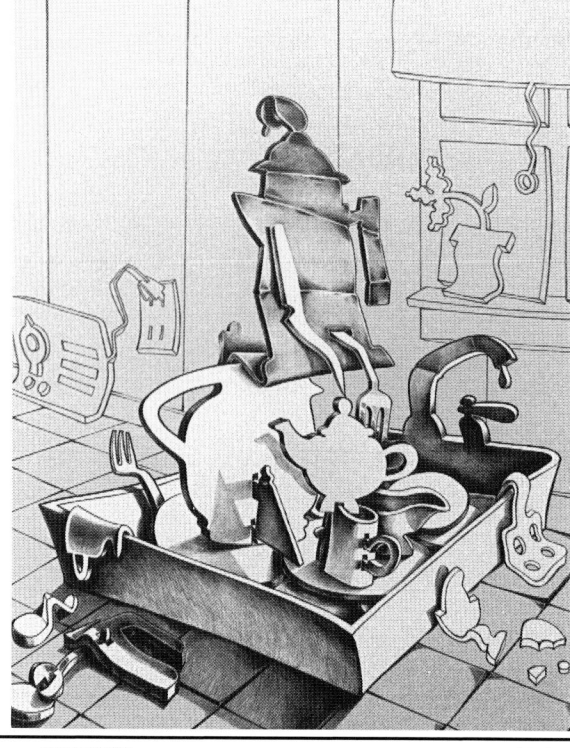

Lynwood Kreneck
Hot Day at Cardboard Cottage
Courtesy the Artist

TITLE	PUBLISHER	PRINTER	DATE	MEDIUM	DIMENSION (PAPER SIZE) IN INCHES	TYPE OF PAPER	EDITION NUMBER	NO. OF COLORS	ORIGINAL OPENING PRICE	CURRENT RETAIL PRICE
SOLD OUT EDITIONS (RARE):										
Every Artist Has an Attic	ART	ART	1984	SP/AS	25 X 23	AP88	14	60	300	450
CURRENT EDITIONS:										
Earth's Mysteries Solved/Flying Dutchman	PerP	PerP	1982	LC/SP/AS	22 X 30	AP88	51	22	300	350
Great Moments in Food Law/Shower Pie	ART	ART	1984	SP/AS	20 X 24	AP88	14	40	300	350
Hot Day at Cardboard Cottage	PerP	PerP	1985	LC/AS	19 X 22	AP88	20	4	200	250
Just Good Clean Fun	ART	ART	1985	SP/AS	23 X 11	AP88	32	24	300	350
The Artist's Attic	UO	UO	1986	SP/AS	36 X 24	AP88	24	95	500	550

BARBARA KRUGER

BORN: Newark, NY; January 26, 1945
EDUCATION: Syracuse Univ, NY; Parsons Sch of Design, NY; Sch of Visual Arts, NY
TEACHING: Vis Artist, California Inst of Art, Valencia, CA; Vis Artist, Art Inst of Chicago, IL; Vis Art, Univ of California, Berkeley, CA
AWARDS: Creative Artists Service Prog Grant, 1976–77; Nat Endowment for the Arts Grant, 1983–84
RECENT EXHIB: Crousel/Hussenot Gallery, Paris, France, 1987; Nat Art Gallery, Wellington, New Zealand, 1988; Univ of Nevada, Inst for Fine Art, Donna Beam Fine Art Gallery, Las Vegas, NV, 1989; William Peterson Col, Ben Shahn Galleries, Wayne, NJ, 1989; Mary Boone Gallery, NY, 1987,89; Whitney Mus of Am Art, NY, 1987,89; Galerie Bebert, Rotterdam, The Netherlands, 1989; Fred Hoffman Gallery, Santa Monica, CA, 1989; Monika Spruth Gallery, Cologne, Germany, 1987,90; San Jose Mus, CA, 1992; Cleveland Inst of Art, Reinberger Galleries, OH, 1992
PRINTERS: Maurice Sanchez, NY (MS); Derriere L'Etoile Studios, NY (DES)
PUBLISHERS: Peter Blum Edition, NY (PBE)
GALLERIES: Fred Hoffman Gallery, Santa Monica, CA; Rhona Hoffman Gallery, Chicago, IL; Mary Boone Gallery, New York, NY
MAILING ADDRESS: c/o Rhona Hoffman Gallery, 215 W Superior St, Chicago, IL 60610

TITLE	PUBLISHER	PRINTER	DATE	MEDIUM	DIMENSION (PAPER SIZE) IN INCHES	TYPE OF PAPER	EDITION NUMBER	NO. OF COLORS	ORIGINAL OPENING PRICE	CURRENT RETAIL PRICE
SOLD OUT EDITIONS (RARE):										
Untitled (We Will No Longer Be Seen and Not Heard) (Painted Frame)	ART	ART		PH	49 X 51	MB				30000
My Pretty Pony	ART	ART	1988	LB	21 X 15	AP	250	1	2000	2500

NICHOLAS KRUSHENICK

BORN: New York, NY; May 31, 1929
EDUCATION: Arts Student League, NY, 1948–50; Hans Hofmann Sch, NY, 1950–51
TEACHING: Univ of Wisconsin, Vis Art, 1969; Art in Res, Dartmouth Col, NH, 1969; Cornell Univ, Ithaca, NY, 1970; Yale Univ, New Haven, CT, Art Critic, 1969–70
AWARDS: Tamarind Lithography Award, 1965; Guggenheim Foundation Fellowship, 1967

NICHOLAS KRUSHENICK CONTINUED

COLLECTIONS: Metropolitan Mus of Art, NY; Mus of Mod Art, NY; Whitney Mus of Am Art, NY; Albright-Knox Art Gallery, Buffalo, NY; Smithsonian Inst, Wash, DC; Hirshhorn Mus, Wash, DC; Walker Art Center, Minneapolis, MN; Dallas Mus of Fine Arts, TX; Chrysler Art Mus, Provincetown, MA; Los Angeles County Mus of Art, CA; Kalamazoo Art Inst, MI; Finch Col Mus, NY; Stedelijk Mus, Amsterdam, Holland; Folkwang Mus, Essen, West Germany; Aldrich Mus of Contemp Art, CT; Norfolk Mus, VA; Galerie de Stadt, Stuttgart, Germany

PRINTERS: Chiron Press, NY (CP); Alexander Heinrici, NY (AH); Studio Heinrici, NY (SH)
PUBLISHERS: London Arts, Inc, Detroit, MI (LAI); Transworld Art, Inc, NY (TAI); Prestige Art, Ltd, Mamaroneck, NY (PA)
GALLERIES: River Gallery, Westport, CT; Daniel Newburg Gallery, New York, NY

TITLE	PUBLISHER	PRINTER	DATE	MEDIUM	DIMENSION (PAPER SIZE) IN INCHES	TYPE OF PAPER	EDITION NUMBER	NO. OF COLORS	ORIGINAL OPENING PRICE	CURRENT RETAIL PRICE
CURRENT EDITIONS:										
Boston Tea Party	TAI	CP	1975	SP	20 X 26	AP	175	5	200	500
Silver Liner	LAI	AH/SH	1977	SP	26 X 22	SOM	200	6	250	250
Over the Top	LAI	AH/SH	1978	SP	29 X 24	SOM	200	5	250	250
Tailgate	LAI	AH/SH	1978	SP	29 X 24	SOM	200	6	250	250
Over the Rainbow	LAI	AH/SH	1978	SP	28 X 38	SOM	200	5	250	250
Mount Cadillac	PA	JN	1980	SP	30 X 41	SOM	100	5	300	300
Big Moose Lake	PA	JN	1980	SP	30 X 41	SOM	100	4	300	300
Blue Hill	PA	JN	1980	Sp	33 X 40	SOM	100	5	300	300
Kennebunkport	PA	JN	1980	SP	33 X 40	SOM	100	4	300	300

JANET KRUSKAMP

BORN: Grants Pass, OR; December 10, 1934
EDUCATION: Chouinard Art Inst, Los Angeles, CA
COLLECTIONS: Rosicrucian Egyptian Mus, San Jose, CA; Triton Mus of Art, Santa Clara, CA; Springville Mus of Art, UT; Alexandria Mus of Art, LA; La Grange Col, GA
PRINTERS: American Atelier, NY (AA)
PUBLISHERS: Circle Fine Art, Chicago, IL (CFA)
GALLERIES: Circle Galleries, Chicago, IL & New York, NY; Circle Galleries, San Diego, CA & San Francisco, CA & Northbrook, IL & Pittsburgh, PA & Houston, TX & Soho, NY & Chicago, IL & Scottsdale, AZ & Beverly Hills, CA & Costa Mesa, CA & Sherman Oaks, CA & Palm Beach FL & Honolulu, HI & New Orleans, LA & Las Vegas, NV & Seattle, WA; Marjorie Cahn Gallery, Los Gatos, CA
MAILING ADDRESS: 1627 Hyde Drive, Los Gatos, CA 95030

TITLE	PUBLISHER	PRINTER	DATE	MEDIUM	DIMENSION (PAPER SIZE) IN INCHES	TYPE OF PAPER	EDITION NUMBER	NO. OF COLORS	ORIGINAL OPENING PRICE	CURRENT RETAIL PRICE
SOLD OUT EDITIONS (RARE):										
Discards	CFA	AA	1980	LC	23 X 24	AP	300		100	175

ANSEL JONATHAN KRUT

BORN: Capetown, South Africa; 1959
EDUCATION: Univ of Witwatersrand, South Africa, BFA, 1970–82, RCA, 1983–85
PRINTERS: 107 Workshop, Wiltshire, England (107W)
PUBLISHERS: Artist (ART)
GALLERIES: David Krut Fine Art, London, England
MAILING ADDRESS: 3-A Aylestone Ave, London NW6, England

TITLE	PUBLISHER	PRINTER	DATE	MEDIUM	DIMENSION (PAPER SIZE) IN INCHES	TYPE OF PAPER	EDITION NUMBER	NO. OF COLORS	ORIGINAL OPENING PRICE	CURRENT RETAIL PRICE
CURRENT EDITIONS:										
Untitled (Series of 11)	ART	107W	1986	MON	48 X 36 EA	AP	1 EA	Varies	500 EA	600 EA

OTTO AUGUST KUHLER

BORN: Germany; (1894–1977)
PRINTERS: Artist (ART)
PUBLISHERS: Artist (ART)

TITLE	PUBLISHER	PRINTER	DATE	MEDIUM	DIMENSION (PAPER SIZE) IN INCHES	TYPE OF PAPER	EDITION NUMBER	NO. OF COLORS	ORIGINAL OPENING PRICE	CURRENT RETAIL PRICE
SOLD OUT EDITIONS (RARE):										
Grand Central Station	ART	ART	1927	EB	15 X 9	WOVE	50	1	50	600
Mighty Metropolis, NY	ART	ART	1927	EB	9 X 13	WOVE	50	1	50	650
The Cables that Hold it All	ART	ART	1928	EB	13 X 9	AP	50	1	50	1200
Giants on Call	ART	ART	1928	EB/DPT	13 X 11	WOVE	50	1	50	1200
Hudson Bridge	ART	ART	1928	EB	11 X 9	WOVE	50	1	50	1200
Luminous Liberty	ART	ART	1928	EB	13 X 10	WOVE	50	1	50	1000
The Monster Grows	ART	ART	1928	EB	11 X 9	WOVE	50	1	50	1250
Fifth Avenue at 42nd Street	ART	ART	1929	EB	8 X 6	WOVE	50	1	50	600
Man-Made Canyon	ART	ART	1929	EB	12 X 8	WOVE	28	1	75	1000
New York Public Library	ART	ART	1929	EB	8 X 6	WOVE	25	1	50	400
The Valley of Work	ART	ART	1929	EB	12 X 16	WOVE	25	1	75	1000
Graf Zeppelin	ART	ART	1930	EB	9 X 11	WOVE	50	1	85	600
Cargo Carriers	ART	ART	1932	EB	11 X 14	WOVE	10	1	100	1500

MURAMASA KUDO

BORN: Tokyo, Japan; 1948
PRINTERS: Kato Art Studios, Gardenia, CA (KAS); ChromaComp, Inc, NY (CCI)
PUBLISHERS: Chalk & Vermilion Fine Arts, Greenwich, CT (CVFA)
GALLERIES: Hanson Galleries, Maui, HI

TITLE	PUBLISHER	PRINTER	DATE	MEDIUM	DIMENSION (PAPER SIZE) IN INCHES	TYPE OF PAPER	EDITION NUMBER	NO. OF COLORS	ORIGINAL OPENING PRICE	CURRENT RETAIL PRICE
SOLD OUT EDITIONS (RARE):										
Black Chiffon (with Hot Stamping)	CVFA	KAS/CCI	1988	SP/HS	29 X 40	WEST	416	130	750	2500
Twilight Reflections	CVFA	KAS/CCI	1988	SP/HS/EMB	27 X 47	WEST	416	135	750	1750
Fireflies	CVFA	KAS/CCI	1988	SP/HS/EMB	33 X 42	WEST	416	50	750	1500
Morning Irises	CVFA	KAS/CCI	1989	SP/HS/EMB	33 X 42	COV	416	43	750	2500
Sunflowers	CVFA	KAS/CCI	1989	SP/HS	43 X 32	WEST	416	52	750	1750
Ocean Breeze	CVFA	CCI	1989	SP/HS/EMB	34 X 45	COV	416	44	750	2000
Lilies in Stream	CVFA	KAS/CCI	1989	SP/HS	29 X 40	WEST	416	130	750	2000
Candlelight	CVFA	KAS/CCI	1990	SP/HS		COV	416		600	800
Debut	CVFA	KAS/CCI	1990	SP/HS		COV	416		875	1000
Deco Vase	CVFA	KAS/CCI	1990	SP/HS		COV	416		875	1000
Reclining with Roses	CVFA	KAS/CCI	1991	SP/HS		COV	416			
Surf	CVFA	KAS/CCI	1991	SP/HS		COV	416		1000	1200
Wicker Basket	CVFA	KAS/CCI	1991	SP/HS		COV	416		875	1000
Treasure & the Gatherer (Set of 2)	CVFA	KAS/CCI	1992	SP/HS		COV	416		1750	2000

KAREN KUNC

BORN: Omaha, NE; December 15, 1952
EDUCATION: Univ of Nebraska, Lincoln, NE, BFA, 1975; Ohio State Univ, Athens, OH, MFA, 1977
TEACHING: Vis Asst Prof, Printmaking, Univ. of California, Berkeley, CA, 1987; Vis Art, Instr, Carleton Col, Northfield, MN, 1989; Assoc Prof, Printmaking, Univ of Nebraska, Lincoln, NE, 1983 to present
AWARDS: Nat Endowment for the Arts Fel, 1984; First Prize, Graphica Atlantica, Reykjavik, Iceland, 1987; Purchase Award, Univ of Delaware, Wilmington, DE, 1988
RECENT EXHIB: Zimmerli Art Mus, Rutgers Univ, New Brunswick, NJ, 1988; Greenville County Art Mus, SC, 1988; California Palace Legion of Honor, San Francisco, CA, 1989; Univ of Alabama, Moody Gallery of Art, Tuscaloosa, AL, 1992; Sioux City Art Center, IA, 1992
COLLECTIONS: Nat Mus of Am Art, Smithsonian Inst, Wash, DC; Univ of Nebraska, Mem Art Gallery, Lincoln, NE; Victoria & Albert Mus, London, England; Nat Art Library, London, England; Philadelphia Mus of Art, PA; Art Mus of Reykjavik, Iceland; Elvehjem Mus of Art, Univ of Wisconsin, Madison, WI; New York Public Library
PRINTERS: David Keister, Bloomington, IN (DK); David Calkins, Bloomington, IN (DC); Echo Press, Bloomington, IN (EPr); Andrew Rubin, Madison, WI (AR); Tandem Press, Univ of Wisconsin, Madison, WI (TanPr)
PUBLISHERS: Echo Press, Bloomington, IN (EPr); Tandem Press, Univ of Wisconsin, Madison, WI (TanPr)
GALLERIES: Mary Ryan Gallery, New York, NY; Jane Haslem Gallery, Wash, DC; Jan Cicero Gallery, Chicago, IL; Atrium Gallery, St. Louis, MO
MAILING ADDRESS: RR #1, Avola, NE 68307

Karen Kunc
A Jaded Nature
Courtesy Tandem Press

TITLE	PUBLISHER	PRINTER	DATE	MEDIUM	DIMENSION (PAPER SIZE) IN INCHES	TYPE OF PAPER	EDITION NUMBER	NO. OF COLORS	ORIGINAL OPENING PRICE	CURRENT RETAIL PRICE
CURRENT EDITIONS:										
Submersive	EPr	DK/DC/EPr	1989	MON/WC	26 X 39 EA	KOZO	1 EA	Varies	800 EA	1000 EA
Garden	EPr	DK/DC/EPr	1989	MON/WC	26 X 39 EA	KOZO	1 EA	Varies	800 EA	1000 EA
Encored	EPr	DK/DC/EPr	1991	MON/WC	25 X 37 EA	KOZO	1 EA	Varies	1000 EA	1000 EA
Farplace	EPr	DK/DC/EPr	1991	MON/I/WC	25 X 37 EA	KOZO	1 EA	Varies	1000 EA	1000 EA
Fiction	EPr	DK/DC/EPr	1991	MON/I/WC	25 X 37 EA	KOZO	1 EA	Varies	1000 EA	1000 EA
Heartwood	EPr	DK/DC/EPr	1991	MON/I/WC	25 X 37 EA	KOZO	1 EA	Varies	1000 EA	1000 EA
Natural Origin	EPr	DK/DC/EPr	1991	MON/I/WC	25 X 37 EA	KOZO	1 EA	Varies	1000 EA	1000 EA
Walk on Water	EPr	DK/DC/EPr	1991	MON/I/WC	25 X 37 EA	KOZO	1 EA	Varies	1000 EA	1000 EA
A Jaded Nature	TanPr	AR/TanPr	1992	WC	45 X 30	SUZ	41	49	850	850

AUDREY GRENDAHL KUHN

BORN: Chicago, IL; May 3, 1929
EDUCATION: Univ Sch of Art, Ann Arbor, MI, BA, 1952; Russell Sage Col, Troy, NY, Cert; Skidmore Col, Saratoga Springs, NY, Cert, Art
AWARDS: First Prize, Albany Artists Show, NY, 1976
RECENT EXHIB: F Kendrick Gallery, Delmar, NY, 1990; Gallery at 211, Ossining, NY, 1990; Schweinfurth Mus, Auburn, NY, 1992; Print Club of Albany Biennial, Schenectady Mus, NY, 1992
COLLECTIONS: Mus of Mod Art, Haifa, Israel; Hudson Valley Com Col, Troy, NY; Russell Sage Col, Troy, NY
PRINTERS: Artist (ART)
PUBLISHERS: Artist (ART)
GALLERIES: Cove Gallery, Wellfleet, MA; Wenniger Graphics, Boston, MA; Dan Greenblat Gallery, New York, NY; Schoolhouse Gallery, Sanibel, FL; Somerhill Gallery, Chapel Hill, NC; Towne Gallery, Lenox, MA; F Kendrick Gallery, Delmar, NY; Gallery at 211, Ossinging, NY
MAILING ADDRESS: 10 Valdepenas Lane, Clifton Park, NY 12065

TITLE	PUBLISHER	PRINTER	DATE	MEDIUM	DIMENSION (PAPER SIZE) IN INCHES	TYPE OF PAPER	EDITION NUMBER	NO. OF COLORS	ORIGINAL OPENING PRICE	CURRENT RETAIL PRICE
SOLD OUT EDITIONS (RARE):										
Cartouche	ART	ART	1983	SP/I/EMB	29 X 40	R/BFK	125	12	250	400
Transparencies I–V	ART	ART	1983	SP/I/EMB	22 X 30 EA	R/BFK	100 EA	24 EA	200 EA	350 EA
Jewels I–IV	ART	ART	1986	SP/I/EMB	22 X 30 EA	R/BFK	150 EA	12 EA	200 EA	200 EA
Prism I–II	ART	ART	1987	SP/I/EMB	29 X 40 EA	R/BFK	125 EA	12 EA	250 EA	250 EA
Prism III, IV	ART	ART	1987	SP/I/EMB	29 X 40 EA	R/BFK	75 EA	12 EA	250 EA	250 EA
Silver Crossing Scarlet I, II	ART	ART	1990	SP/MM	27 X 40 EA	FAB	25 EA	11 EA	350 EA	350 EA

MORTON KUNSTLER

BORN: Brooklyn, NY; August 28, 1931
EDUCATION: Brooklyn Col, NY; Univ of California, Los Angeles, CA; Pratt Inst, NY, 1950
RECENT EXHIB: Mus of Westward Expansion, St Louis, MO, 1989; Hammer Galleries, NY, 1989
COLLECTIONS: Nassau County Mus, Roslyn, NY; Mus of Arts & Sciences, Daytona Beach, FL; San Mateo County Historical Mus, CA; Lowie Mus of Anthropology, Berkeley, CA; Hermitage, Nashville, TN; Favell Mus, Klameth Falls, OR; U S Navy Mem Mus, Wash, DC
PRINTERS: Lassiter Studio, NY (LS); Vistec Graphics, NY (VG); Visteck Graphics, Rochester, NY (VG); American Atelier, NY (AA); Dietz Offizin, Lengmoos, Soyen, West Germany (DO)
PUBLISHERS: Hammer Publishing, NY (HP); Circle Gallery, Ltd, Chicago, IL (CG); Dietz Art Limited, NY (DAL)
GALLERIES: Hammer Galleries, New York, NY; Conacher Galleries, San Francisco, CA
MAILING ADDRESS: Cove Neck, Oyster Bay, NY 11771

TITLE	PUBLISHER	PRINTER	DATE	MEDIUM	DIMENSION (PAPER SIZE) IN INCHES	TYPE OF PAPER	EDITION NUMBER	NO. OF COLORS	ORIGINAL OPENING PRICE	CURRENT RETAIL PRICE
SOLD OUT EDITIONS (RARE):										
The Kansan	CGL	AA	1976	LC	24 X 29	AP	300	9	110	325
Early Snow	CGL	AA	1977	LC	21 X 28	AP	300	10	165	275
Runnin' Late	HP	LS	1978	SP	23 X 30	SOM	300	45	400	700
CURRENT EDITIONS:										
Going after Big Bull	HP	VG	1980	SP	24 X 30	SOM	300	20	400	550
His New Blue Coat	HP	VG	1980	SP	25 X 20	SOM	300	22	400	500
Storm Clouds	HP	VG	1980	SP	32 X 23	R/100	300	19	400	550
Liberty/Ellis Island Suite (Set of 3):									9900 SET	9900 SET
Arrival of Immigrants in New York Harbor	DAL	DO	1986	SP	33 X 44	CAN	200	180	3600	3600
Ellis Island Main Hall	DAL	DO	1986	SP	33 X 44	CAN	200	180	3600	3600
Freedom	DAL	DO	1986	SP	33 X 44	CAN	200	180	3600	3600

CLINTON KUOPUS

BORN: Detroit, MI; December 8, 1942
EDUCATION: US Navy Photography Intelligence Sch, 1963; Eastern Michigan Univ, Ypsilanti, MI; Michigan State Univ, Lansing, MI; Wayne State Univ, NE
TEACHING: Instr, Visual Art, Bloomfield Hills Schs, MI, 1970–75; Instr, Youngstown State Univ, OH, 1980–82; Univ of Akron, OH, 1981–82; Asst Prof, Art, Lake Erie Col, Plainesville, OH, 1975–80, 82–83; Parsons Sch of Design, NY, 1983 to present
RECENT EXHIB: Detroit Inst of Art, MI, 1991; Kansas City Art Mus, MO, 1991–92
COLLECTIONS: Lake Erie Col, Plainesville, OH
PRINTERS: Norman Stewart, Bloomfield Hills, MI (NS); Joe Keenan, Bloomfield Hills, MI (JK); Corey Stewart, Bloomfield Hills, MI (CS); Stewart & Stewart, Bloomfield Hills, MI (S-S)
PUBLISHERS: Stewart & Stewart, Bloomfield Hills, MI (S-S)
GALLERIES: Stewart & Stewart, Bloomfield Hills, MI
MAILING ADDRESS: P O Box 6475, Yorkville Station, New York, NY 10128

TITLE	PUBLISHER	PRINTER	DATE	MEDIUM	DIMENSION (PAPER SIZE) IN INCHES	TYPE OF PAPER	EDITION NUMBER	NO. OF COLORS	ORIGINAL OPENING PRICE	CURRENT RETAIL PRICE
CURRENT EDITIONS:										
Downwind	S-S	NS/JK/CS/S-S	1990	SP	30 X 22	R/BFK/G	37	12	750	750
Mustard Fields	S-S	NS/JK/CS/S-S	1990	SP	22 X 30	R/BFK/G	37	9	750	750

HONEY W KURLANDER

BORN: Brooklyn, NY
EDUCATION: Parsons Sch of Design, NY; New York Univ, NY; Pratt Inst, Brooklyn, NY
COLLECTIONS: C W Post Col, Greenvale, NY; Long Island Univ, Brooklyn, NY; Nassau Comm Col, Garden City, NY
PRINTERS: Dietz Offizin, Lengmoos, Soyen, West Germany (DO)
PUBLISHERS: Dietz Art Limited, NY (DAL)
GALLERIES: Garden City Gallery, Ltd, New York, NY; Dietz Art Limited, New York, NY; Isis Gallery, Ltd, Searingtown, NY
MAILING ADDRESS: 6 Kings Dr, Old Westbury, NY 11568

HONEY W KURLANDER CONTINUED

TITLE	PUBLISHER	PRINTER	DATE	MEDIUM	DIMENSION (PAPER SIZE) IN INCHES	TYPE OF PAPER	EDITION NUMBER	NO. OF COLORS	ORIGINAL OPENING PRICE	CURRENT RETAIL PRICE
CURRENT EDITIONS:										
Spring Time Medley	DAL	DO	1986	SP	23 X 35	CANVAS	165	175	650	700
Planting Fields	DAL	DO	1986	SP	34 X 46	CANVAS	165	210	720	800

ROBERT ELLIS KUSHNER

BORN: Pasadena, CA; August 19, 1949
EDUCATION: Univ of California San Diego, CA, BA
RECENT EXHIB: Philadelphia Inst of Contemp Art, PA, 1987; State Univ of New York, Staller Center Art Gallery, Stony Brook, NY, 1989; Holly Solomon Gallery, NY, 1992; Rockefeller Center, NY, 1992; Midtown Payson Galleries, NY, 1992; Crown Point Press, San Francisco, CA & NY, 1990-91,92; Univ of California, Berkeley, CA, 1993; John Berggruen Gallery, San Francisco, CA, 1993
COLLECTIONS: Brooklyn Mus, NY; Denver Art Mus, CO; Mus Moderner Kunst, Palaia Leichtenstein, Vienna; Tate Gallery, London, England; Whitney Mus of Am Art, NY; Mus of Mod Art, NY; Australian Nat Gallery, Canberra, Australia; J Paul Getty Mus, Los Angeles, CA; Library of Congress, Wash, DC; Mus of Mod Art, San Francisco, CA; Oakland Mus, CA
PRINTERS: Judith Solodkin, NY (JS); Solo Press, NY (SP); Stephen Thomas (ST); Nancy Anello (NA); Peter Pettengill (PP); Crown Point Press, San Francisco, CA (CPP); Jeryl Parker, NY (JP); Marcia Bartholme (MB); Mark Callen (MC); Zhuo Guanyling (ZG); Fong Jin Da (FJD); Ku Jie-Juen (KJJ); Cai Yan (CY); Reizo Monjyu (RM); Shunzo Matsuda (SM); Bud Shark, Boulder, CO (BS); Matthew Christie, Boulder, CO (MC); Shark's, Inc, Boulder, CO (SI)
PUBLISHERS: Barbara Gladstone Editions, NY (BGE); Crown Point Press, San Francisco, CA (CPP); Holly Solomon Editions, NY (HSE); Solo Press, NY (SP); Art Issue Editions, Inc, NY (AIE); Art Matters, Boulder, CO (AMI); Artist (ART); Shark's Inc, Boulder, CO (SI)
GALLERIES: Holly Solomon Editions, New York, NY; Asher/Faure, Los Angeles, CA; Dart Gallery, Chicago, IL; Crown Point Press, New York, NY & San Francisco, CA; Nancy Singer Gallery, St Louis, MO; Harcourts Contemporary, San Francisco, CA; Fawbush Editions, New York, NY; Fay Gold Gallery, Atlanta, GA; Mary Singer Gallery, Wash, DC; Solo Gallery, New York, NY; Michael H Lord Gallery, Milwaukee, WI; Shark's, Inc, Boulder, CO; Quartet Editions, New York, NY; John Berggruen Gallery, San Francisco, CA
MAILING ADDRESS: c/o Crown Point Press, 568 Broadway, New York, NY 10012

Robert Ellis Kushner
Alpine Sunflower I
Courtesy Shark's, Inc

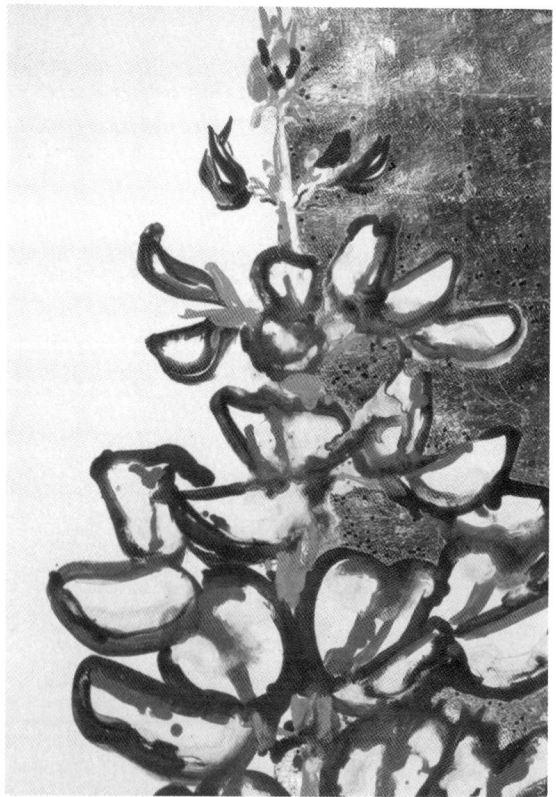

Robert Ellis Kushner
Lupine II
Courtesy Shark's, Inc

TITLE	PUBLISHER	PRINTER	DATE	MEDIUM	DIMENSION (PAPER SIZE) IN INCHES	TYPE OF PAPER	EDITION NUMBER	NO. OF COLORS	ORIGINAL OPENING PRICE	CURRENT RETAIL PRICE
SOLD OUT EDITIONS (RARE):										
Inez (Trip)	BGE	SP	1979	LC	30 X 33 EA	AP	35 EA		1200 SET	5000 SET
Paulette and Karla (Trip)	CPP	ST/NA/CPP	1980	AC	24 X 108 TOT	R/BFK	14 EA	6 EA	2500 SET	5000 SET
Blanche	CPP	ST/NA/CPP	1980	AC	24 X 36	R/BFK	5	1	700	1200
Blanchette	CPP	ST/NA/CPP	1980	AC	24 X 36	R/BFK	5	1	700	1200
Blanchine	CPP	ST/NA/CPP	1980	AC	24 X 36	R/BFK	5	1	700	1200

ROBERT ELLIS KUSHNER CONTINUED

TITLE	PUBLISHER	PRINTER	DATE	MEDIUM	DIMENSION (PAPER SIZE) IN INCHES	TYPE OF PAPER	EDITION NUMBER	NO. OF COLORS	ORIGINAL OPENING PRICE	CURRENT RETAIL PRICE
SOLD OUT EDITIONS (RARE):										
The Joy of Ornament (Set of 20)	CPP	ST/NA/CPP	1980	EC	12 X 6 EA	AP/HS	35 EA	1 EA	3000 SET 200 EA	5000 SET 350 EA
Flowered Nat for Joy of Ornament	CPP	PP/CPP	1980	EC	19 X 31	SOM/S	40		350	1200
Les Oiseaux Parisiens (Dipt)	CPP	PP/CPP	1982	EB/A	30 X 21 EA	SOM	25 EA		1200 SET	3500 SET
Cupid & Psyche (Fabric Collage)	CPP	JP/CPP	1985	MON/CO	42 X 60	HMP	23		2000 EA	7500 EA
At the Shore (Fabric Collage)	CPP	JP/CPP	1985	MON/CO	42 X 60	HMP	23		2000 EA	7500 EA
Resting (Fabric Collage)	CPP	JP/CPP	1985	MON/CO	42 X 60	HMP	23		2000 EA	8500 EA
Flora	CPP	MB/MC/CPP	1987	AB/DPT/CC	31 X 45	SOM/S	25		1500	3000
Hangzhou Tulip (Chinese Watercolor Woodblock Printed on Silk)	CPP	CY/CPP	1989	WB/WA	24 X 37	SILK/SOM-S-W	36		1500	1800
CURRENT EDITIONS:										
Angelique (with Sequins & Fabric)	BGE	SP	1980	LC	49 X 35	AP	35	2	2000	3500
The Question	BGE	SP	1981	LC	61 X 31	AP	20	6	2200	3500
The Answer	BGE	SP	1981	SP	61 X 31	AP	20	6	2200	3000
Another Question	BGE	SP	1981	SP	61 X 31	AP	20	6	2200	3000
Trellis (Two Hinged Sheets)	BGE	SP	1981	SP	28 X 20 EA	AP	16	3	850	1500
Desk Work	HSE	SP	1981	LC	30 X 23	AP/W/CC	35	3	800	1500
Cupids Making Borscht	HSE	SP	1981	LC	22 X 60	AP/W	30	6	1800	5000
More Borscht	HSE	SP	1981	LB	22 X 60	AP/BL/CC	15	1	1200	1800
More and More Borscht	HSE	SP	1981	LC	22 X 60	GE/BL	15	4	1600	2000
Cupids and Fans	HSE	SP	1981	LC	22 X 90	HMP	15	4	2200	4000
Gardening	HSE	SP	1981	LC	90 X 22	AP/W/CC	20	2	1800	2500
Music (Hand-Applied Feathers & Sequins)	HSE	SP	1981	LC	22 X 30	HMP	25	2	500	1800
Fandango (Horizontal)	HSE	SP	1981	LC	22 X 90	AP/W	10	4	2200	3500
Fandango (Vertical)	HSE	SP	1981	LC	67 X 30	AP/W	1	4	2200	4000
National Treasure	HSE	SP	1981	LC	67 X 30	AP/W/CC	25	4	2200	3500
New Baby	HSE	SP	1981	LC	22 X 29	R/BFK/W	35	3	900	3000
Nursery (Horizontal)	HSE	SP	1981	LC	15 X 88	R/BFK/W	4	1	500	3500
Nursery (Vertical)	HSE	SP	1981	LC	60 X 22	R/BFK/W	16	1	500	3000
Flowered Mat for the Joy of Ornament	CPP	PP/CPP	1982	EC	18 X 30	SOM	40		250	1200
Nubiana (Diptych)	CPP	PP/CPP	1982	EB/A	36 X 25 EA	KAS	25 EA		900 SET	3000 SET
Ballade Triste	SP	JS/SP	1982	PW	31 X 23	TRP/HMP	15	7	600	1500
Ina	SP	SP	1982	PW/LC	31 X 23	TRP	7		1200	2000
Violet	SP	SP	1982	LC/HC	37 X 25	RAK	20	5	800	1200
Chanson Egyptien (8 Variants)	AM		1982	LC	38 X 30 EA	SOM	40 EA		800 EA	1500 EA
Seraphina I	SP	SP	1983	LC/HC	25 X 38	JAP	30		1200	2500
Seraphina II	SP	SP	1983	LC/HC	25 X 38	JAP	20		1200	2500
Fruit Plate	SP/ART	SP	1983	LC/HC/CO	29 X 42	GE/BL	30	3	1200	3500
Daphne I	CPP	JP/CPP	1985	WC	32 X 25	AP	150	22	1500	1800
Daphne II	CPP	JP/CPP	1985	WC	32 X 25	AP	150	18	1500	1800
Bibelot	CPP	JP/CPP	1985	EC	61 X 40	SOM/S	10		4500	10000
Pineapple (Series of 12 Unique Lithographs)	SP	JS/SP	1986	LC/HC	31 X 25 EA	HMP	1 EA		2000 EA	4000 EA
Maple (Series of 15 Unique Lithographs)	SP	JS/SP	1986	LC/HC	23 X 30 EA	HMP	1 EA		2000 EA	4000 EA
Hiroko	SP	JS/SP	1986	LC	23 X 19	SOM	170		800	1200
Honor thy Father and thy Mother (from Ten Commandments Suite)	AIE	JS/SP	1987	LC	24 X 18	DIEU	84	5	500	1800
Summer	CPP	CPP	1987	AC	41 X 50	AP	35		2200	3000
Tondo	CPP	MB/MC/CPP	1987	AC/CO	41 X 41	FABRIC	50		3000	3500
Earring (Wax Drypoint Cast in Bronze)	CPP	MB/MC/CPP	1987	DPT	23 X 22	JBG/HMP	20		750	750
Vase	CPP	MB/MC/CPP	1987	DPT	23 X 22	JBG/HMP	20		750	750
Series of Three Unique Prints:										
Spring	CPP	MB/MC/CPP	1987	EB/A	24 X 19 EA	HMP	28	1 EA	1500 EA	1800 EA
Conch	CPP	MB/MC/CPP	1987	EB/A	24 X 19 EA	HMP	28	1 EA	1500 EA	1800 EA
Angel	CPP	MB/MC/CPP	1987	EB/A	24 X 19 EA	HMP	27	1 EA	1500 EA	1800 EA
Series of Four Unique Prints:										
Torchier	CPP	MB/MC/CPP	1987	AC/SB/SL	12 X 16 EA	HMP	36	1 EA	1000 EA	1200 EA
Reclining Man	CPP	MB/MC/CPP	1987	AC/SB/SL	12 X 16 EA	HMP	35	1 EA	1000 EA	1200 EA
Reclining Woman	CPP	MB/MC/CPP	1987	AC/SB/SL	12 X 16 EA	HMP	36	1 EA	1000 EA	1200 EA
Water Bearer	CPP	MB/MC/CPP	1987	AC/SB/SL	12 X 16 EA	HMP	38	1 EA	1000 EA	1200 EA
Nocturne	SP	JS/SP	1988	LC	25 X 37	UNRYU	30		900	1200
Red Anemone	CPP	ZG/CPP	1989	WB/SILK	41 X 17	SILK/AC	75		1500	1500
White Anemone, State I	CPP	FJD/KJJ/CPP	1989	WB/SILK	21 X 23	SILK/AC	26		950	950
White Anemone, State II	CPP	FJD/KJJ/CPP	1989	WB/SILK	21 X 23	SILK/AC	21		950	950
Black Jade	CPP	CY/CPP	1989	WB/SILK	21 X 38	SILK/SOM-S	35		1250	1500
Pelleás et Mélisande (Set of 7)	CPP	BS/MC/CPP	1990	DPT	24 X 18 EA	KOZO	20 EA	1 EA	5000 SET 900 EA	5000 SET 900 EA
Phlox I,II	SP	JS/SP	1990	LB	10 X 6 EA	AC	15 EA		500 EA	500 EA

ROBERT ELLIS KUSHNER CONTINUED

TITLE	PUBLISHER	PRINTER	DATE	MEDIUM	DIMENSION (PAPER SIZE) IN INCHES	TYPE OF PAPER	EDITION NUMBER	NO. OF COLORS	ORIGINAL OPENING PRICE	CURRENT RETAIL PRICE
CURRENT EDITIONS:										
Hand Painted Summer	CPP	MB/MC/CPP	1987–91	EC/HC	41 X 51	SOM	5	4+	4000	4000
Hand Painted Daphne I	CPP	TT/RM/CPP	1991	WB/HC	32 X 25	KOZO	7	22+	2500	2800
Hand Painted Daphne II	CPP	TT/RM/CPP	1991	WB/HC	32 X 25	KOZO	2	18+	2500	2800
Hand Painted Daphne (Series 2)	CPP	TT/RM/CPP	1985–91	WB/HC	32 X 26	KOZO	16	22+	3000	3000
Delpinium (Series of 36)	CPP	TT/SM/CPP	1991	WB	37 X 13 EA	Varies	1 EA	Varies	1500	1500
Peony (Series of 41)	CPP	TT/SM/CPP	1991	WB	18 X 18 EA	Varies	1 EA	Varies	1250	1250
Wildflower Series (with Metallic Leaf)	SI	BS/MC/SI	1992	MON	42 X 30 EA	SUZ	1 EA	Varies	5000 EA	5000 EA
Wildflower Series (with Metallic Leaf)	SI	BS/MC/SI	1992	MON	42 X 15 EA / 30 X 22 EA	SUZ	1 EA	Varies	3800 EA	3800 EA
Wildflower Series (with Metallic Leaf)	SI	BS/MC/SI	1992	MON	19 X 13 EA / 30 X 11 EA	SUZ	1 EA	Varies	2000 EA	2000 EA

TERENCE LA NOUE

BORN: Hammond, IN; December 4, 1941
EDUCATION: Ohio Wesleyan Univ, Delaware, OH, BFA, 1964; Hochscule für Bildenende Künste, West Berlin, Germany; Cornell Univ, Ithaca, NY, MFA, 1967
TEACHING: Instr, La Guardian Col, NY, 1972
AWARDS: Fulbright Fel, 1964–65; Guggenheim Fel, 1982; Nat Endowment for the Arts Grants, 1972–73, 1983
RECENT EXHIB: Heland Wetterling Gallery, Stockholm, Sweden, 1989; André Emmerich Gallery, NY, 1987,88–89; Siegel Contemp Art, NY, 1987,88,90; LewAllen Gallery, Santa Fe, NM, 1992
COLLECTIONS: Roy Neuberger Mus, State Univ of New York, Purchase, NY; Corcoran Gallery of Art, Wash, DC; Indianapolis Mus of Art, IN; Carnegie Inst, Pittsburgh, PA; Whitney Mus of Am Art, NY; Solomon R Guggenheim Mus, NY; Brooklyn Mus, NY; Albright-Knox Art Gallery, Buffalo, NY
PRINTERS: Alan Koslin, NY (AK); X Press, NY (XP); Tyler Graphics, Ltd, Mount Kisco, NY (TGL); Experimental Workshop, San Francisco, CA (EW)
PUBLISHERS: Orion Editions, NY (OE); 724 Prints, NY (724P); Tyler Graphics, Ltd, Mount Kisco, NY (TGL); Experimental Workshop, San Francisco, CA (EW); Artist (ART)
GALLERIES: Nancy Hoffman Gallery, New York, NY; Galerie Farideh Cadot, Paris France; Orion Editions, New York, NY; Eve Mannes Gallery, Atlanta, GA; Davis/McClain Galleries, Houston, TX; Ruth Siegel, Ltd, New York, NY; Experimental Workshop, San Francisco, CA; André Emmerich Gallery, New York, NY; Habatat Gallery, Bay Harbor Islands, FL; Zolla/Lieberman Gallery, Chicago, IL; Dorothy Goldeen Gallery, Santa Monica, CA; Hokin Galleries, Bay Harbor Islands, FL & Palm Beach, FL; Albertson-Peterson Gallery, Winter Park, FL; Betsy Senior Contemporary Prints, New York, NY; Heland Wetterling Gallery, Stockholm, Sweden; Siegel Contemporary Art, New York, NY; LewAllen Gallery, Santa Fe, NM
MAILING ADDRESS: 29-AS Portland Ave, Brooklyn, NY 11217

TITLE	PUBLISHER	PRINTER	DATE	MEDIUM	DIMENSION (PAPER SIZE) IN INCHES	TYPE OF PAPER	EDITION NUMBER	NO. OF COLORS	ORIGINAL OPENING PRICE	CURRENT RETAIL PRICE
CURRENT EDITIONS:										
Cochin	OE	AK/XP	1981	EB/A	38 X 31	HMP	65	12	650	1500
Atitlan	724P	AK/XP	1981	CP	28 X 49	HMP	15	9	1200	2500
Bangalore	724P	AK/XP	1981	CP	32 X 43	HMP	15	11	1500	2500
The Ritual Series:										
Papuan Gulf	TGL	TGL	1987	EC/A/LC/WC/ENG/DPT	36 X 40	KOZO/MdV	42	13	2000	4000
Papuan Gulf, State I	TGL	TGL	1987	EC/A/ENG	30 X 22	HMP	10	1	500	750
The Water Spirits	TGL	TGL	1987	EC/A/LC/WC/ENG/DPT	36 X 40	KOZO/MdV	42	23	2000	4000
The Water Spirits, State I	TGL	TGL	1987	EC/A/ENG	30 X 22	HMP	10	1	500	750
Palace of Quetzalcoati	TGL	TGL	1987	EC/A/LC/WC/ENG/DPT	36 X 40	KOZO/MdV	42	21	2000	4000
Palace of Quetzalcoati	TGL	TGL	1987	EC/A/ENG	30 X 22	HMP	10	1	500	750
The Talking Drums	TGL	TGL	1987	EC/A/DPT/WC	36 X 40	KOZO/MdV	42	12	1500	2000
The Talking Drums, State I	TGL	TGL	1987	EC/A/ENG	30 X 22	HMP	10	1	500	750
The Fossil Garden	TGL	TGL	1987	EC/A/LC/WC/ENG/DPT	36 X 40	KOZO/MdV	42	26	1500	2000
The Fossil Garden, State I	TGL	TGL	1987	EC/A/ENG	30 X 22	HMP	10	1	500	750
The Dream of Gods	TGL	TGL	1987	LC/WC	44 X 49	TGL/HMP/KOZO	50	21	3500	5000
Hand-Colored Monoprint II (Includes Frame)	TGL/ART	TGL	1987	MON/HC	36 X 24	KOZO	1 EA	Varies	4000 EA	5600 EA
Tarantella Series (Series of Unique Works in Colored & Pressed Paper Pulp, Hand-Colored by the Artist) (Includes Frame)	TGL/ART	TGL	1988	MULT/HC	48 X 77 to 59 X 85	HMP	1 EA	Varies	15000 EA	18500 EA

MIMI LA PLANT

BORN: San Francisco, CA; January 7, 1943
EDUCATION: Col of Marin, CA, 1968; Santa Rosa Junior Col, CA, AA, 1972; Univ of California, Berkeley, CA, BA, 1974; Humboldt State Univ, Arcata, CA, MA, 1982
TEACHING: Instr, Col of Redwoods, Eureka, CA; Mendocino Art Center, Mendo, CA; Humboldt State Univ, Eureka, CA
COLLECTIONS: Humboldt Cultural Center, Eureka, CA
PRINTERS: Artist (ART)
PUBLISHERS: Artist (ART)
GALLERIES: Hank Baum Gallery, San Francisco, CA; San Francisco Museum of Modern Art Rental Gallery, CA; Miriam Perlman, Inc, Chicago, IL
MAILING ADDRESS: P O Box 14383, Santa Barbara, CA 93107

MIMI LA PLANT CONTINUED

TITLE	PUBLISHER	PRINTER	DATE	MEDIUM	DIMENSION (PAPER SIZE) IN INCHES	TYPE OF PAPER	EDITION NUMBER	NO. OF COLORS	ORIGINAL OPENING PRICE	CURRENT RETAIL PRICE
CURRENT EDITIONS:										
Snow Country	ART	ART	1981	MON	20 X 30 EA	R/BFK	1 EA	3 EA	100 EA	250 EA
Tea Garden	ART	ART	1981	MON	30 X 22 EA	R/BFK	1 EA	3 EA	100 EA	250 EA
Miasma	ART	ART	1981	MON	30 X 22 EA	R/BFK	1 EA	1 EA	100 EA	200 EA
Counter Attack	ART	ART	1981	MON	30 X 22 EA	R/BFK	1 EA	2 EA	100 EA	250 EA
Kocina	ART	ART	1981	MON	30 X 22 EA	R/BFK	1 EA	1 EA	100 EA	250 EA
He's a Funny Guy	ART	ART	1982	MON	30 X 22 EA	R/BFK	1 EA	2 EA	100 EA	250 EA
Zen	ART	ART	1982	MON	30 X 22 EA	R/BFK	1 EA	2 EA	100 EA	250 EA
The Toy Soldier II	ART	ART	1982	MON	30 X 22 EA	R/BFK	1 EA	1 EA	100 EA	250 EA
The Red Mark	ART	ART	1982	MON	30 X 22 EA	R/BFK	1 EA	3 EA	100 EA	250 EA
Kandinsky	ART	ART	1982	MON	30 X 22 EA	R/BFK	1 EA	3 EA	100 EA	250 EA
Wave	ART	ART	1984	MON	22 X 30 EA	MAG	3 EA	3 EA	250 EA	450 EA
Sir Prince	ART	ART	1985	MON	22 X 30 EA	MAG	3 EA	4 EA	150 EA	300 EA
East View	ART	ART	1985	MON	22 X 30 EA	MAG	3 EA	3 EA	200 EA	300 EA
For Hank	ART	ART	1986	MON	22 X 30 EA	MAG	4 EA	4 EA	200 EA	300 EA
Circus	ART	ART	1986	MON	22 X 30 EA	MAG	4 EA	5 EA	300 EA	350 EA
Venice	ART	ART	1986	MON	22 X 30 EA	MAG	4 EA	4 EA	200 EA	300 EA

JOCHEN LABRIOLA

PRINTERS: American Atelier, NY (AA)
PUBLISHERS: Circle Fine Art, Chicago, IL (CFA)
GALLERIES: Circle Galleries, San Diego, CA & San Francisco, CA & Northbrook, IL & Pittsburgh, PA & Houston, TX & Soho, NY & Chicago, IL & Scottsdale, AZ & Beverly Hills, CA & Costa Mesa, CA & Sherman Oaks, CA & Palm Beach, FL & Honolulu, HI & New Orleans, LA & Las Vegas, NV & Seattle, WA

TITLE	PUBLISHER	PRINTER	DATE	MEDIUM	DIMENSION (PAPER SIZE) IN INCHES	TYPE OF PAPER	EDITION NUMBER	NO. OF COLORS	ORIGINAL OPENING PRICE	CURRENT RETAIL PRICE
SOLD OUT EDITIONS (RARE):										
Three Calla Lillies	CFA	AA	1981	LC	29 X 21	AP	300		250	1550
Five Calla Lillies on Grey	CFA	AA	1982	LC	25 X 34	AP	300		250	1800
Red Tulips on Blue	CFA	AA	1982	LC	29 X 21	AP	300		250	950
Calla Lillies (Dipt)	CFA	AA	1983	LC	35 X 24	AP	300		500	2800
Red Anthuriums	CFA	AA	1985	LC	35 X 25	AP	300		350	1050
Calla Lily with Shadow	CFA	AA	1985	LC	24 X 30	AP	300		300	950
Three Calla Lillies with Sunbeam	CFA	AA	1985	LC	25 X 24	AP	300		300	975

SYL LABROT

BORN: New Orleans, LA; 1929
TEACHING: State Univ of New York, Rochester, NY
PRINTERS: American Atelier, NY (AA)
PUBLISHERS: Circle Fine Art, Chicago, IL (CFA)
GALLERIES: Circle Galleries, San Diego, CA & San Francisco, CA & Northbrook, IL & Pittsburgh, PA & Houston, TX & Soho, NY & Chicago, IL & Scottsdale, AZ & Beverly Hills, CA & Costa Mesa, CA & Sherman Oaks, CA & Palm Beach, FL & Honolulu, HI & New Orleans, LA & Las Vegas, NV & Seattle, WA

TITLE	PUBLISHER	PRINTER	DATE	MEDIUM	DIMENSION (PAPER SIZE) IN INCHES	TYPE OF PAPER	EDITION NUMBER	NO. OF COLORS	ORIGINAL OPENING PRICE	CURRENT RETAIL PRICE
SOLD OUT EDITIONS (RARE):										
Square Root #1, Plum	CFA	AA	1980	SP	20 X 20	SOM	90		35	125
Square Root #2, Green	CFA	AA	1980	SP	20 X 20	SOM	95		35	125
Square Root #3, Turquoise	CFA	AA	1980	SP	20 X 20	SOM	80		35	125
Square Root #4, Purple	CFA	AA	1980	SP	20 X 20	SOM	92		35	125
Square Root #5, Light Blue	CFA	AA	1980	SP	20 X 20	SOM	88		35	125

STEPHEN LACK

BORN: August 27, 1946
EDUCATION: Columbia Univ, NY, with Tony Padovano, 1966; McGill Univ, Montreal, Canada, BA, 1967; Inst Allende, San Miguel, Mexico, MFA, 1968
TEACHING: Artist in Res, Banff Inst, Alta, Canada, 1987; Long Island Univ, Studio Workshop, Brooklyn, NY, 1988
AWARDS: Nat Endowment for the Arts Fel, 1987
RECENT EXHIB: Gracie Mansion Fine Art, NY, 1992
COLLECTIONS: Australian Art Gallery, Canberra, Australia
PRINTERS: Anthony Kirk, NY (AK); Eldindean Press, NY (EldP); Sylvia Roth, South Nyack, NY (SR); Mary Seibert, South Nyack, NY (MS); Hudson River Editions, South Nyack, NY (HRE)
PUBLISHERS: Eldindean Press, NY (EldP); Hudson River Editions, South Nyack, NY (HRE)
GALLERIES: Gracie Mansion Gallery, New York, NY
MAILING ADDRESS: 9 Willow Ave, Rockleigh, NJ 07647

TITLE	PUBLISHER	PRINTER	DATE	MEDIUM	DIMENSION (PAPER SIZE) IN INCHES	TYPE OF PAPER	EDITION NUMBER	NO. OF COLORS	ORIGINAL OPENING PRICE	CURRENT RETAIL PRICE
CURRENT EDITIONS:										
Just Get Me Out of Here (Set of 19)	EldP	AK/EldP	1987	EB/A	9 X 8 EA	AC/SOM	45 EA		900 SET	2000 SET
Danish Jews (Series of 3)	HRE	SR/MS/HRE	1992	MON	29 X 35 EA	GE	1 EA	Varies	1200 EA	1200 EA

CHERYL LAEMMLE

BORN: Minneapolis, MN; August 11, 1947
EDUCATION: Humboldt State Univ, Arcata, CA, BA, 1974; Washington State Univ, Pullman, WA, MFA, 1978
AWARDS: Creative Artists Public Service Program Fel, 1980; Vera G List Award, 1984; Nat Endowment for the Arts Fel, Painting, 1985–86, 1986–87
RECENT EXHIB: Hokin/Kaufman Gallery, Chicago, IL, 1988; Greg Kucera Gallery, Seattle, WA, 1988; Rena Bransten Gallery, San Francisco, CA, 1990
COLLECTIONS: Metropolitan Mus of Art, NY; Tamayo Mus, Mexico City, Mexico
PRINTERS: Aeropress, NY (A); Patricia Branstead, NY (PB)
PUBLISHERS: Deborah Sharpe Editions, NY (DSE)
GALLERIES: Barbara Toll Fine Arts, New York, NY; Hokin/Kaufman Gallery, Chicago, IL; Greg Kucera Gallery, Seattle, WA; Rena Bransten Gallery, San Francisco, CA; Fay Gold Gallry, Atlanta, GA; Morning Star Gallery, Santa Fe, NM; Terry Dintenfass, New York, NY
MAILING ADDRESS: 735 E 9th St, New York, NY 10009

TITLE	PUBLISHER	PRINTER	DATE	MEDIUM	DIMENSION (PAPER SIZE) IN INCHES	TYPE OF PAPER	EDITION NUMBER	NO. OF COLORS	ORIGINAL OPENING PRICE	CURRENT RETAIL PRICE
CURRENT EDITIONS:										
Monkey with Angel (Hardground, Aquatint, and Open Bite Etching)	DSE	PB/A	1982	EB/A	23 X 30	R/BFK	35	1	450	600

IRENE R LAGORIO

BORN: Oakland, CA; May 2, 1921
EDUCATION: California Col of Arts & Crafts, Oakland, CA, 1938–39; Univ of California, Berkeley, CA, AB & MA, 1942; Columbia Univ, NY, 1945
TEACHING: Special Lectr, Univ of California, Extension Courses, 1960 to present
AWARDS: Chapelbrook Found Grant, Graphics, Boston, MA, 1969; Best in Show, Monterey Peninsula Mus of Art, CA, 1971
COLLECTIONS: San Francisco Mus of Mod Art, CA; Monterey Peninsula Mus of Art, CA; Richmond Mus of Art, VA; Monterey Art Com Coll, CA; Museo Italo-Americano Coll, San Francisco, CA; Achenbach Coll, California Palace of Legion of Honor Mus, San Francisco, CA
PRINTERS: Artist (ART)
PUBLISHERS: Artist (ART)
GALLERIES: Valley Art Center, Walnut Creek, CA
MAILING ADDRESS: First & Mission Sts, P O Box 153, Carmel, CA 93921

TITLE	PUBLISHER	PRINTER	DATE	MEDIUM	DIMENSION (PAPER SIZE) IN INCHES	TYPE OF PAPER	EDITION NUMBER	NO. OF COLORS	ORIGINAL OPENING PRICE	CURRENT RETAIL PRICE
SOLD OUT EDITIONS (RARE):										
Man-O-War	ART	ART	1969	SP	22 X 26	JP	30	5	100	300
Griffins	ART	ART	1969	SP	22 X 26	JP	30	4	100	300
Horse	ART	ART	1969	SP	22 X 26	JP	30	4	100	300
Snake of the Apocalypse	ART	ART	1969	SP	22 X 26	JP	30	6	100	300
Blue Whale	ART	ART	1969	SP	22 X 26	JP	30	4	100	300
Yare Hawk	ART	ART	1971	SP	22 X 26	JP	30	5	75	200
Resplendent Declarations	ART	ART	1971	SP	30 X 40	JP	25	8	150	400
The Sign	ART	ART	1971	SP	30 X 40	JP	25	8	150	400
Unicorn in the Garden	ART	ART	1979	SP	22 X 26	JP	30	12	75	300
Varied Thrush on the Edge of Evening	ART	ART	1980	SP	22 X 26	JP	30	10	100	250
CURRENT EDITIONS:										
Resplendent Declarations	ART	ART	1971	SP	30 X 40	JP	25	8	150	400
Gull at Dusk	ART	ART	1979	SP	22 X 16	JP	30	5	100	250

BARBARA LAINERE

EDUCATION: Art Students League, NY
PRINTERS: American Atelier, NY (AA)
PUBLISHERS: Circle Fine Art, Chicago, IL (CFA)
GALLERIES: Circle Galleries, San Diego, CA & San Francisco, CA & Northbrook, IL & Pittsburgh, PA & Houston, TX & Soho, NY & Chicago, IL & Scottsdale, AZ & Beverly Hills, CA & Costa Mesa, CA & Sherman Oaks, CA & Palm Beach, FL & Honolulu, HI & New Orleans, LA & Las Vegas, NV & Seattle, WA

TITLE	PUBLISHER	PRINTER	DATE	MEDIUM	DIMENSION (PAPER SIZE) IN INCHES	TYPE OF PAPER	EDITION NUMBER	NO. OF COLORS	ORIGINAL OPENING PRICE	CURRENT RETAIL PRICE
SOLD OUT EDITIONS (RARE):										
Still Life	CFA	AA	1980	LC	31 X 25	AP	300		75	350

JACQUES LALANDE

BORN: France; 1921
EDUCATION: Sch of Fine Arts, Montpellier, France; Nat Sch of Fine Arts, Paris, France
PRINTERS: American Atelier, NY (AA); Arts Litho, Paris, France (AL)
PUBLISHERS: Circle Fine Art, Chicago, IL (CFA); Lublin Graphics, Greenwich, CT (LG)
GALLERIES: Circle Galleries, San Diego, CA & San Francisco, CA & Northbrook, IL & Pittsburgh, PA & Houston, TX & Soho, NY & Chicago, IL & Scottsdale, AZ & Beverly Hills, CA & Costa Mesa, CA & Sherman Oaks, CA & Palm Beach, FL & Honolulu, HI & New Orleans, LA & Las Vegas, NV & Seattle, WA; Professional Fine Arts Services, Inc, New York, NY

The retail prices of the 100,000 limited edition prints quoted in this directory are subject to change. Print publishers, artists and galleries were the direct sources for these quotations. Prices in the secondary market listed as "Sold Out Editions (Rare)" indicate that the publisher has a limited supply of that print or that the print is difficult to locate in the galleries.

JACQUES LALANDE CONTINUED

TITLE	PUBLISHER	PRINTER	DATE	MEDIUM	DIMENSION (PAPER SIZE) IN INCHES	TYPE OF PAPER	EDITION NUMBER	NO. OF COLORS	ORIGINAL OPENING PRICE	CURRENT RETAIL PRICE
SOLD OUT EDITIONS (RARE):										
Violin	CFA	AA	1976	LC	20 X 26	AP	200		100	400
Black Stockings	CFA	AA	1976	LC	20 X 26	AP	200		100	400
Sunshade	CFA	AA	1976	LC	20 X 26	AP	200		100	400
Floral Arrangement	CFA	AA	1976	LC	20 X 26	AP	200		100	400
3 Girls and Violin	CFA	AA	1977	LC	20 X 26	AP	200		125	400
Bikes	CFA	AA	1977	LC	20 X 26	AP	200		125	400
Red Shaw	CFA	AA	1977	LC	20 X 26	AP	200		125	400
Musicians in Venice	CFA	AA	1978	LC	20 X 26	AP	200		125	400
Musical Duo	LG	AL	1978	LC	19 X 25	AP	250		80	120
Musical Trio	LG	AL	1978	LC	19 X 25	AP	250		80	120
Le Balcon	LG	AL	1978	LC	19 X 25	AP	250		80	120
Maree Basse	LG	AL	1979	LC	19 X 25	AP	250		80	120
Concerto a la Chaise Blanche	LG	AL	1979	LC	19 X 25	AP	250		80	120
Ombrelle Bleue	LG	AL	1980	LC	19 X 25	AP	250		100	120
The Musicians	CFA	AA	1979	LC	20 X 26	AP	200		125	400
Tea Party	CFA	AA	1979	LC	20 X 26	AP	200		125	400
Musical Trio	CFA	AA	1979	LC	20 X 26	AP	200		125	400
Les Chevaux	CFA	AA	1980	LC	32 X 34	AP	200		150	400
Panier des Fleurs	CFA	AA	1980	LC	28 X 30	AP	200		150	400
Jetee a Deauville	LG	AL	1980	LC	19 X 25	AP	250		100	120
Deauville	LG	AL	1982	LC	19 X 25	AP	250		100	120
Le Pecheur au Phare	LG	AL	1982	LC	19 X 25	AP	250		100	120
Solo du Flutiste	LG	AL	1982	LC	19 X 25	AP	250		100	120
Trying on Hats	LG	AL	1982	LC	19 X 25	AP	250		100	120
La Halte	LG	AL	1982	LC	19 X 25	AP	250		100	120

NORMAN LALIBERTÉ

BORN: Montreal, Canada; 1925
EDUCATION: Illinois Inst of Tech, Chicago, IL, BS; Cranbrook Acad of Art, MI, 1952
TEACHING: Kansas City Art Inst, KS; Rhode Island Sch of Design, Providence, RI
AWARDS: Cranbrook Acad of Art Fel, MI, 1952
RECENT EXHIB: Clark Gallery, Lincoln, NE, 1989
COLLECTIONS: Albright-Knox Art Gallery, Buffalo, NY; Montreal Mus of Fine Arts, Canada; Univ of Chicago, IL; Nat Art Center, Ottawa, Canada; Spaeth Found, NY
PRINTERS: American Atelier, NY (AA)
PUBLISHERS: Circle Fine Art, Chicago, IL (CFA)
GALLERIES: Circle Galleries, San Diego, CA & San Francisco, CA & Houston, TX & Northbrook, IL & Pittsburgh, PA & Soho, NY & Chicago, IL & Scottsdale, AZ & Beverly Hills, CA & Costa Mesa, CA & Sherman Oaks, CA & Palm Beach, FL & Honolulu, HI & New Orleans, LA & Las Vegas, NV & Seattle, WA; Langman Gallery, Willow Grove, PA; Chase Gallery, Boston, MA; Beverly Gordon Gallery, Dallas, TX

TITLE	PUBLISHER	PRINTER	DATE	MEDIUM	DIMENSION (PAPER SIZE) IN INCHES	TYPE OF PAPER	EDITION NUMBER	NO. OF COLORS	ORIGINAL OPENING PRICE	CURRENT RETAIL PRICE
SOLD OUT EDITIONS (RARE):										
Clown	CFA	AA	1976	LC	22 X 30	AP	250		50	225
Major Arcana	CFA	AA	1977	LC	24 X 34	AP	250		60	250
SOLD OUT EDITIONS (RARE):										
Le Cirque Folio (Set of 7):									500 SET	1325 SET
Acrobats	CFA	AA	1978	LC	24 X 33	AP	250		75	250
Lion Tamers	CFA	AA	1978	LC	23 X 31	AP	250		75	250
Strong Man	CFA	AA	1978	LC	23 X 31	AP	250		75	250
Twins	CFA	AA	1978	LC	21 X 30	AP	250		75	250
Elephant with Pyramid	CFA	AA	1978	LC	22 X 30	AP	250		75	250
Cannon	CFA	AA	1978	LC	22 X 30	AP	250		75	250
Equestrian	CFA	AA	1978	LC	22 X 30	AP	250		75	250
Tarot Cards Folio (Set of 20):									900 SET	2525 SET
Title Page	CFA	AA	1980	LC	12 X 16	AP	250		50	200
The Page	CFA	AA	1980	LC	12 X 16	AP	250		50	200
I, The Magician	CFA	AA	1980	LC	12 X 16	AP	250		50	200
II, High Priestess	CFA	AA	1980	LC	12 X 16	AP	250		50	200
III, The Empress	CFA	AA	1980	LC	12 X 16	AP	250		50	200
IV, The Emperor	CFA	AA	1980	LC	12 X 16	AP	250		50	200
V, The Pope	CFA	AA	1980	LC	12 X 16	AP	250		50	200
VI, The Lovers	CFA	AA	1980	LC	12 X 16	AP	250		50	200
VII, The Chariot	CFA	AA	1980	LC	12 X 16	AP	250		50	200
VIII, Justice	CFA	AA	1980	LC	12 X 16	AP	250		50	200
IX, The Hermit	CFA	AA	1980	LC	12 X 16	AP	250		50	200
X, The Wheel of Fortune	CFA	AA	1980	LC	12 X 16	AP	250		50	200
XI, Strength	CFA	AA	1980	LC	12 X 16	AP	250		50	200
XII, through XV	CFA	AA	1980	LC	12 X 16 EA	AP	250 EA		50 EA	200 EA
XVI, Lightning Struck Tower	CFA	AA	1980	LC	12 X 16	AP	250		50	200
XVII, The Star	CFA	AA	1980	LC	12 X 16	AP	250		50	200
XVIII, The Moon	CFA	AA	1980	LC	12 X 16	AP	250		50	200
XIX, The Sun	CFA	AA	1980	LC	12 X 16	AP	250		50	200
XX, Judgment	CFA	AA	1980	LC	12 X 16	AP	250		50	200
XXI, The World	CFA	AA	1980	LC	12 X 16	AP	250		50	200

WILFREDO LAM

BORN: Sagua la Grande, Cuba; (1902–1982)
RECENT EXHIB: Hirshhorn Mus, Wash, DC, 1992; Arsenal de la Marina, San Juan, PR, 1992; Inst of Puertorrican Culture, San Juan, PR, 1992; Galerie Lelong, Paris, France, 1992
COLLECTIONS: Mus of Mod Art, NY; Guggenheim Mus, NY; Chicago Inst of Art, IL; Yale Univ Art Gallery, New Haven, CT; Tate Gallery, London, England; Stedelijk van Abbe Mus, Eindhoven, The Netherlands; Inst d'Arte, Lima, Peru; Musee Nat d'Art Moderne, Paris, France; Musees Royaux des Beaux Arts, Brussels, Belgium; Nationalgalerie Staatliche Museen, Berlin, Germany
PRINTERS: Giorgio Upiglio, Milan, Italy (GU); Grafica Uno, Milan, Italy (GrU); La Poligrafa, SA, Barcelona, Spain (LP); Artist (ART)
PUBLISHERS: Giorgio Upiglio, Milan, Italy (GU); Grafica Uno, Milan, Italy (GrU); Ediciones Poligrafa, SA, Barcelona, Spain (EdP); Artist (ART)
GALLERIES: Graphica Uno Studio, Milan, Italy; Gallerita, Milan, Italy; Galeria Joan Prats, New York, NY & Barcelona, Spain; George Belcher Gallery, San Francisco, CA; Carone Gallery, Fort Lauderdale, FL; Marta Gutierrez Fine Arts, Key Biscayne, FL; Arnold Herstand & Company, New York, NY; Mary-Anne Martin Fine Art, New York, NY; Galerie Cujas, San Diego, CA; Richard Arregui Fine Art, Coral Gables, FL; Modernism Gallery, Coral Gables, FL; Sande Garcia Fine Arts, Miami, FL; Galerie Lelong, New York, NY; Nohra Haime Gallery, New York, NY; Constance Kamens Fine Art, New York, NY; Sindin Gallery, New York, NY; TwoSixtyOne Art, New York, NY

TITLE	PUBLISHER	PRINTER	DATE	MEDIUM	DIMENSION (PAPER SIZE) IN INCHES	TYPE OF PAPER	EDITION NUMBER	NO. OF COLORS	ORIGINAL OPENING PRICE	CURRENT RETAIL PRICE
SOLD OUT EDITIONS (RARE):										
Quetxal			1947	LC	17 X 13	AP	70		75	2000
Oiseaux			1953	LC	15 X 21	AP	100		100	2000
El Ultimo Viaje del Buque Fantasma (Set of 12)	EdP	LP	1976	LC	22 X 30 EA	GP	99 EA		4000 SET / 350 EA	10000 SET / 900 EA
El Ultimo Viaje del Buque Fantasma (Set of 2)	EdP	LP	1976	LC	30 X 22 EA	GP	99 EA		600 SET	4000 SET
Annonciation (Set of 7)	GU/GrU	GU/GrU	1969–82	EC/A	24 X 31 EA	AP	125 EA	6	7000 SET	15000 SET

JACOB LANDAU

BORN: Philadelphia, PA; December 17, 1917
EDUCATION: Philadelphia Col of Art, PA, 1935–38; New Sch of Social Research, NY, 1948–49, 1952–53; Acad de la Grande Chaumiere, Paris, France, 1950–52
TEACHING: Philadelphia Col of Art, PA, 1954–57; Sch of Visual Arts, NY, 1954–56; From Instr to Assoc Prof, Pratt Inst, Brooklyn, NY 1957–68, Prof, Graphic Art, 1968–83; Found, University Without Walls Project, Prof Emeritus, 1983 to present
AWARDS: Nat Arts Council Endowment Grant, 1966; Guggenheim Fel, 1968; Childe Hassam Purchase Prize, Am Acad of Arts and Letters Award, 1973,74; Ford Found Travel-Study Grant, 1975; New Jersey State Council on the Arts Fel, 1987
RECENT EXHIB: Retrosp, Ryder Col, Laurenceville, NJ, 1988
COLLECTIONS: Metropolitan Mus of Art, NY; Mus of Modern Art, NY; Whitney Mus of Am Art, NY; Philadelphia Mus of Art, PA; Hirshhorn Mus, Wash, DC; Library of Congress, Wash, DC
PRINTERS: Deli Sacilotto Atelier, NY (DSA); Robert Franklin, NY (RF); Artist (ART)
PUBLISHERS: Associated American Artists, NY (AAA); Tamarind Inst, Albuquerque, NM (TI); Ferdinand Roten (FR); Brandywine Workshop, Phila, PA (BW); Georgetown Graphics Print Club Editions (GGPC); Artist (ART)
GALLERIES: Jentra Fine Art Gallery, Freehold, NJ; Neuheisel Gallery, Saarbrucken, West Germany; Martin Sumers Graphics, New York, NY; Brandywine Workshop, Phila, PA; Wenniger Graphics, Boston, MA; International Print Society, New Hope, PA; Drawing Room Gallery, Rahway, NJ; Tobey C Moss Gallery, Los Angeles, CA
MAILING ADDRESS: 2 Pine Drive, Roosevelt, NJ 08555

TITLE	PUBLISHER	PRINTER	DATE	MEDIUM	DIMENSION (PAPER SIZE) IN INCHES	TYPE OF PAPER	EDITION NUMBER	NO. OF COLORS	ORIGINAL OPENING PRICE	CURRENT RETAIL PRICE
SOLD OUT EDITIONS (RARE):										
Horses	AAA		1961	WB			100	1	75	450
Charades Suite (Set of 10)	TI		1965	LB	14 X 11 EA		20 EA	1 EA	400 SET	1000 SET
Horses and Men	AAA		1967	W	15 X 24		100	1	130	250
*Holocaust Suite (Set of 6)	AAA		1968	LB	15 X 20 EA		40 EA	1 EA	600 SET	3000 SET
I, John Brown	AAA		1968	W/PO	33 X 41		50	4	150	250
Attica	AAA		1973	LC	15 X 24		18	1	100	750
The Sucking Infant	AAA		1979	LC	26 X 19		210	4	200	350
Einstein	GGPB	DSA	1982	I	19 X 26	AP	100	1	100	300
CURRENT EDITIONS:										
Kingdom of Dreams (Set of 26)	AAA		1969	LB(6)	10 X 7 EA		100 EA		600 SET	2000 SET
But If the Cause . . .	FR		1972	LC(20)	27 X 18		175	2	140	200
If All Problems . . .			1975	SP	24 X 18		75	6	100	150
**Dante Cycle (Set of 7)										
The Violent against Art	ART	ART	1975	LC	24 X 20		36	1	120	300
The Violent against Themselves	ART	ART	1975	LC	23 X 17		35	1	120	300
The City of Dis	ART	ART	1975	LC	24 X 17		50	1	120	300
The Ninth Circle	ART	ART	1975	LC	22 X 19		50	1	120	300
The Noble Thieves	ART	ART	1976	LC	23 X 17		55	1	120	300
Paolo and Francesca	ART	ART	1976	LC	23 X 17		55	1	120	300
The Virtuous Pagans	ART	ART	1976	LC	24 X 16		120	1	120	300
Meditation on Love and Death	ART	ART	1976	LC	18 X 25		60	1	140	300
Isaiah	ART	ART	1976	PO	30 X 6		75	25	150	350
Malachi	ART	ART	1976	LC/PO	30 X 6		75	25	150	350
Mediation on Love I—Dantane and Beatrice	ART	ART	1981	LC	26 X 19		175	5	300	300
Mediation on Love II—Gaia	ART	ART	1981	LC	26 X 18		175	5	300	300
Third Vision	ART/BW	RF	1987	LC/OFF	22 X 30	AC	100		300	300
Thirty-Fourth Psalm	ART/BW	RF	1988	LC/OFF	22 X 30	AC	100		300	300

* Published by the artist under a Guggenheim Grant
** Published by the artist under a Ford Foundation Grant

EDWARD AUGUST LANDON

BORN: Hartford, CT; (1911–1984)
EDUCATION: Hartford Art Sch, CT; Art Students League, NY; Univ of Fine Arts, Mexico
AWARDS: Guggenheim Fel, 1939–41; Fulbright Fel, 1950–51
COLLECTIONS: Bibliotheque Nat, Paris, France; Metropolitan Mus, NY; Mus of Mod Art, NY; Nat Gallery of Fine Arts, Wash, DC; Nat Gallery, Stockholm, Sweden; Tel Aviv Mus, Israel; Turku Mus, Finland; Victoria and Albert Mus, London, England
PRINTERS: Artist (ART)
PUBLISHERS: Artist (ART)
GALLERIES: Bethesda Gallery, Bethesda, MD; Wenniger Graphics, Boston, MA; Gallery 2, Woodstock, VT; Gallery North Star, Grafton, VT

TITLE	PUBLISHER	PRINTER	DATE	MEDIUM	DIMENSION (PAPER SIZE) IN INCHES	TYPE OF PAPER	EDITION NUMBER	NO. OF COLORS	ORIGINAL OPENING PRICE	CURRENT RETAIL PRICE
SOLD OUT EDITIONS (RARE):										
French Farm	ART	ART	1942	SP	12 X 18	R/BFK	50	9	25	650
Counterpoint	ART	ART	1942	SP	13 X 14	R/BFK	25	5	25	650
Abstract	ART	ART	1943	SP	8 X 12	R/BFK	25		25	650
Salient in February	ART	ART	1945	SP	13 X 15	R/BFK	25	1	35	1800
Salient in February	ART	ART	1945	SP	13 X 15	R/BFK	40		35	2000
Wine and Fruit	ART	ART	1947	SP	10 X 12	R/BFK	50	5	35	650
Buffoon	ART	ART	1948	SP	12 X 15	R/BFK	30	4	30	650
Hall of Fame	ART	ART	1951	SP	11 X 14	R/BFK	30		30	600
Nothing Begins, Nothing Ends	ART	ART	1951	SP	11 X 14	R/BFK	30		300	600
Ferry Boat	ART	ART	1952	SP	12 X 18	R/BFK	25	8	50	600
Roots of Memory	ART	ART	1961	SP	8 X 18	AP	15	4	50	550
Roots of Memory	ART	ART	1961	SP	8 X 15	AP	17	4	35	550
Untitled	ART	ART	1963	SP	18 X 12	AP	24	5	75	550
At Home	ART	ART	1967	SP	7 X 4	AP	40	4	30	350
Shall We Dance	ART	ART	1969	SP	8 X 11	AP	30	3	50	350
January Day	ART	ART	1980	SP	14 X 10	AP	20	4	125	200
Prefiguration	ART	ART	1980	SP	10 X 13	CH	15	3	150	225
Cross Purpose	ART	ART	1980	SP	12 X 9	CH	20	3	125	175
Land's End	ART	ART	1981	SP	10 X 18	R/BFK	20	5	100	175
Lost	ART	ART	1981	SP	12 X 9	CH	25	3	100	175
Taos Revisited	ART	ART	1981	SP	11 X 9	MASA	20	3	125	175
At the Gallery	ART	ART	1981	SP	16 X 7	AP	30	6	100	150
A Lull in the Day's Conversation	ART	ART	1982	SP	10 X 10	MASA	25	3	125	175
Flying off at a Tangent	ART	ART	1982	SP	10 X 16	CH	25	6	150	225
Inscape	ART	ART	1982	SP	10 X 14	AP	25	7	150	225

THOMAS LANIGAN-SCHMIDT

BORN: Elizabeth, NJ; 1948
EDUCATION: Pratt Inst, Brooklyn, NY, 1965–66; Sch of Visual Arts, NY, 1967
RECENT EXHIB: Holly Solomon Gallery, NY, 1988
PUBLISHERS: Holly Solomon Editions, NY (HSE)
GALLERIES: Holly Solomon Gallery, New York, NY

TITLE	PUBLISHER	PRINTER	DATE	MEDIUM	DIMENSION (PAPER SIZE) IN INCHES	TYPE OF PAPER	EDITION NUMBER	NO. OF COLORS	ORIGINAL OPENING PRICE	CURRENT RETAIL PRICE
SOLD OUT EDITIONS (RARE):										
Ten Rats in Search of.... (Rats Made of Gold, Foil, Rhinestones, Straight Pins, Magic Marker & Hot Glue)	HSE	SP	1980	MF/RH/STP	4 X 9 X 3	HMP	10		300 EA	400 EA

FAY LANSNER

BORN: Philadelphia, PA
EDUCATION: Tyler Sch of Fine Arts, Temple Univ, Phila, PA, 1945–47; Art Students League, NY, 1947–48; Hans Hofmann Sch, NY, 1948–50; Studied with Leger & Lhote Pris, France, 1950–51
COLLECTIONS: Weatherspoon Art Mus, Univ of North Carolina, Greensboro, NC; Metropolitan Mus of Art, NY; State Univ of New York, Neuberger Mus, Purchase, NY; Guild Hall, Easthampton, NY; Philadelphia Mus, PA; Corcoran Gallery of Art, Wash, DC; Hood Col, Frederick, MD; Lehigh Univ, Bethlehem, PA; Univ of Newark, NJ; New York Univ, NY; Albright-Knox Art Gallery, Buffalo, NY
PRINTERS: Imprimerie Maeght, Paris, France (IM); Fernand Mourlot, Paris, France (FM); Atelier Mourlot, Paris, France (AM); Gino Diamuto, Paris, France (GD); Arte Atelier, Paris, France (ARTE); Guy Veliot, Paris, France (GV)
PUBLISHERS: Marlborough Graphics, NY (MG); Artist (ART)
GALLERIES: Marlborough Gallery, New York, NY; Ingber Gallery, New York, NY; Elaine Benson Gallery, Southampton, NY; Arras Gallery, New York, NY
MAILING ADDRESS: 317 W 80th St, New York, NY 10024

TITLE	PUBLISHER	PRINTER	DATE	MEDIUM	DIMENSION (PAPER SIZE) IN INCHES	TYPE OF PAPER	EDITION NUMBER	NO. OF COLORS	ORIGINAL OPENING PRICE	CURRENT RETAIL PRICE
CURRENT EDITIONS:										
Red and Blue	MG	FM/AM	1968	LC	22 X 27	AP	35	2	75	250
Silver and Blue	MG	FM/AM	1968	LC	25 X 19	AP	35	2	75	250
Untitled I/7-Color	ART	GD/FM/AM	1971	LC	27 X 43	AP	150	7	175	450
Untitled II/10-Color	ART	GV/ARTE	1973	LC	36 X 23	AP	75	10	150	400

The retail prices of the 100,000 limited edition prints quoted in this directory are subject to change. Print publishers, artists and galleries were the direct sources for these quotations. Prices in the secondary market listed as "Sold Out Editions (Rare)" indicate that the publisher has a limited supply of that print or that the print is difficult to locate in the galleries.

LOIS LANE

BORN: Philadelphia, PA; January 6, 1948
EDUCATION: Philadelphia Col of Art, PA, BFA, 1969; Yale Univ Summer Sch of Music & Art, New Haven, CT, 1968; Yale Univ, Sch of Art & Arch, MFA, 1971
AWARDS: Creative Artist Public Service Grant, Painting, New York State Council on the Arts, 1977; Nat Endowment for the Arts Grant, Painting, 1978
RECENT EXHIB: Willard Gallery, NY, 1987, John Berggruen Gallery, San Francisco, CA, 1987–88; Barbara Krakow Gallery, Boston, MA, 1989; Barbara Mathes Gallery, NY, 1988,89; Print Club, Phila, PA, 1992; Barbara Toll Fine Art, New York, NY, 1992
COLLECTIONS: Mus of Mod Art, NY; Whitney Mus of Am Art, NY; Art Mus of South Texas, Corpus Christi, TX; Des Moines Art Center, IA; Mus of Fine Arts, Houston, TX; Akron Art Mus, OH; Albright-Knox Art Gallery, Buffalo, NY; Nat Gallery of Art, Wash, DC
PRINTERS: Patricia Branstead, NY (PB); Aeropress, NY (A); Maurice Sanchez, NY (MS); James Miller, NY (JM); Derriére L'Etoile Studios, NY (DES); Joe Wilfer, NY (JW); Ruth Lingen, NY (RL); Spring Street Workshop, NY (SprSW)
PUBLISHERS: Parasol Press, Ltd, NY (PaP); Derrière L'Etoile Studios, NY (DES); Spring Street Workshop, NY (SprSW)
GALLERIES: Barbara Krakow Gallery, Boston, MA; Willard Gallery, New York, NY; Greenberg Gallery, St Louis, MO; Felicity Samuels Gallery, London, England; Barbara Toll Fine Arts, New York, NY; Pace Prints, New York, NY; Willard Gallery, New York, NY

Lois Lane
Untitled (3 Linocuts)
Courtesy Derrière L'Etoile Studios

TITLE	PUBLISHER	PRINTER	DATE	MEDIUM	DIMENSION (PAPER SIZE) IN INCHES	TYPE OF PAPER	EDITION NUMBER	NO. OF COLORS	ORIGINAL OPENING PRICE	CURRENT RETAIL PRICE
SOLD OUT EDITIONS (RARE):										
Six Aquatints: Untitled	PaP	PB/A	1979	AC	24 X 18 EA	R/BFK	75 EA	2 EA	1800 SET	4000 SET
Untitled	PaP	PB/A	1979	AC	30 X 24	R/BFK	45	2	350	850
CURRENT EDITIONS:										
Untitled I–VII (Set of 7)	DES	JM/MS/DES	1989	LI	21 X 17 EA	KIT	25		4200 SET	5000 SET
Untitled	SprSW	JW/RL/SprSW	1990	WC/SP	41 X 30	OKP	15		1500	1500
Untitled	SprSW	JW/RL/SprSW	1990	WC/SP/LI	41 X 30	OKP	15		1500	1500
Untitled	SprSW	JW/RL/SprSW	1990	REL/SP	41 X 30	OKP	15		1500	1500
Untitled	SprSW	JW/RL/SprSW	1990	REL/SP	41 X 30	OKP	15		1500	1500
Untitled	SprSW	JW/RL/SprSW	1990	MON	41 X 31 EA	OKP	1 EA		2500 EA	2500 EA

ROSEMARY LOUISE LANE

BORN: San Francisco, CA; Dec 6, 1944
EDUCATION: California Col of Arts and Crafts, 1962–66, BFA; California State Univ, Hayward, CA, 1970; Univ of California, Berkeley, CA, 1969–70; Univ of Oregon, MFA, 1971–73
TEACHING: Univ of Oregon, Eugene, OR, 1972–73; Univ of Delaware, Newark, DE, 1974 to present; Vis Instr, Printmaking, Univ of Oregon, Eugene, OR, 1973–74; From Instr to Asst Prof, Printmaking, Drawing & Papermaking, Univ of Delaware, Newark, DE, 1974–82, Assoc Prof, 1982–87
AWARDS: Purchase Award, Delaware Art Mus, Wilmington, DE, 1978; Research Stipend Award, Univ of Delaware, Prix du Centennaire de Raymond Duncan, Acad of Raymond Duncan, Medal of Bronze, Paris, France, 1981; Delaware Center for Contemp Art, 1982; Purchase Award, Univ of North Dakota, Grand Forks, ND, 1985; Purchase Award, Nat Print & Drawing Exhib, Minot State Col, ND, 1985
COLLECTIONS: Delaware Art Mus, Wilmington, DE; Portland Center of the Visual Arts, OR; Minot State Col, ND; Int Coll of Women's Art, Denmark; Univ of Oregon, Eugene, OR
PRINTERS: Artist (ART)
PUBLISHERS: Artist (ART)
GALLERIES: Associated American Artists, New York, NY
MAILING ADDRESS: 50 Cummings Court, Bear, DE 19701

TITLE	PUBLISHER	PRINTER	DATE	MEDIUM	DIMENSION (PAPER SIZE) IN INCHES	TYPE OF PAPER	EDITION NUMBER	NO. OF COLORS	ORIGINAL OPENING PRICE	CURRENT RETAIL PRICE
CURRENT EDITIONS:										
Entrapment	ART	ART	1973	LB	9 X 12	R/BFK	15	1	60	200
Medicalaid	ART	ART	1974	MON	24 X 30	R/BFK	1	2	250	600

ROSEMARY LOUISE LANE CONTINUED

TITLE	PUBLISHER	PRINTER	DATE	MEDIUM	DIMENSION (PAPER SIZE) IN INCHES	TYPE OF PAPER	EDITION NUMBER	NO. OF COLORS	ORIGINAL OPENING PRICE	CURRENT RETAIL PRICE
CURRENT EDITIONS:										
Revelation	ART	ART	1974	EB	12 X 18	R/BFK	60	1	60	200
Dryad Manifest	ART	ART	1974	EB	18 X 24	R/BFK	60	1	75	300
The Catch	ART	ART	1974	EB	18 X 24	R/BFK	60	1	75	300
Emergence	ART	ART	1974	EB	18 X 24	R/BFK	60	1	75	300
Prey	ART	ART	1974	EC	18 X 24	R/BFK	60	2	75	300
Blind Alternative	ART	ART	1974	EB	12 X 18	R/BFK	60	1	60	300
Symbiosis	ART	ART	1976	EC	18 X 24	R/BFK	60	2	75	300
Moon Cradle (Bichromate on Vinyl)	ART	ART	1979	BI/CHR	15 X 23	VINYL	20	10	250	500
Sawyer's Surprise	ART	ART	1979	BI/CHR	15 X 23	VINYL	20	18	250	500
Disclosure	ART	ART	1979	BI/CHR	12 X 15	VINYL	20	20	250	500
Dorothy's Slippers	ART	ART	1979	BI/CHR	15 X 23	VINYL	20	26	250	500
The Carpet Ride	ART	ART	1979	BI/CHR	15 X 23	VINYL	20	18	250	500
Apex Conceived	ART	ART	1980	BI/CHR	15 X 23	VINYL	20	23	250	500
Point of View	ART	ART	1981	BI/CHR	16 X 20	VINYL	20	8	250	400
A Matter of Principle	ART	ART	1981	BI/CHR	16 X 20	VINYL	20	28	325	500
Heart of the Matter	ART	ART	1981	HCP	15 X 16 X 4	HMP	5	8	295	550
Heritage	ART	ART	1981	HCP	15 X 23 X 3	HMP	5	6	295	750
Sacred Ground Coverings	ART	ART	1983	HCP	26 X 22 X 5	HMP	6	6	295	750
Ode to Maria	ART	ART	1983	HCP	22 X 30 X 5	HMP	5	8	495	750
Vestige: The Above	ART	ART	1983	HCP	24 X 36 X 12	HMP	5	8	495	750
Vestige I: Reliquary	ART	ART	1983	BI/CHR	17 X 18	VINYL	20	30	325	500
Vestige II: Sanctuary	ART	ART	1983	BI/CHR	18 X 22	VINYL	20	30	325	500
Vestige III: The Gift	ART	ART	1983	BI/CHR	18 X 22	VINYL	20	30	325	500
Vestige IV: Flight of Spirit	ART	ART	1984	BI/CHR	18 X 22	VINYL	20	30	325	500
Vestige: The Sound	ART	ART	1984	HCP	28 X 34 X 6	HMP	5	8	495	750

RICHARD LANDRY

BORN: Cecilia, LA; November 16, 1938
EDUCATION: Univ of Southwestern Louisiana, Lafayette, LA, BME
AWARDS: Creative Artists Public Service Program Award, Mixed Media, 1974; Nat Endowment for the Arts Fel, Video, 1975
PUBLISHERS: Larry B Wright, NY (LBW)
GALLERIES: Holly Solomon Editions, Ltd, New York, NY; Leo Castelli Gallery, New York, NY
MAILING ADDRESS: PO Box 64, Cecilia, LA 70521

TITLE	PUBLISHER	PRINTER	DATE	MEDIUM	DIMENSION (PAPER SIZE) IN INCHES	TYPE OF PAPER	EDITION NUMBER	NO. OF COLORS	ORIGINAL OPENING PRICE	CURRENT RETAIL PRICE
CURRENT EDITIONS:										
Untitled #1	LBW	LBW	1980	PH/SP	30 X 40	LEN	30		550	600

DANIEL S LANG

BORN: Tulsa, OK; March 17, 1935
EDUCATION: Northwestern Univ, Evanston, IL; Univ of Tulsa, OK, BFA; Univ of Iowa, Iowa City, IA, MFA, 1959 with Mauricio Lassansky
TEACHING: Asst Prof, Painting, Art Inst of Chicago, IL, 1962–64; Asst Prof, Painting, Washington Univ, St Louis, MO, 1964–65; Vis Art, Ohio State Univ, Columbus, OH, 1968–69; Univ of South Florida, Tampa, FL, Fall, 1972; Adj Prof, Univ of Utah, Salt Lake City, UT 1984–88
RECENT EXHIB: Moravian Col, Payne Gallery, Bethlehem, PA, 1989,92
COLLECTIONS: Mus of Mod Art, NY; Art Inst of Chicago, IL; California Palace Legion of Honor, San Francisco, CA; Quincy Found, IL; Nelson-Atkins Mus of Fine Arts, Kansas City, MO; Victoria & Albert Mus, London, England
PRINTERS: Herbert A. Fox, Merrimac, MA (HF); Fox Graphics, Merrimac, MA (FG); Roni Henning, NY (RH)
PUBLISHERS: Fox Graphics, Merrimac, MA (FG); Orion Editions, NY (OE); Artist (ART)
GALLERIES: Fischbach Gallery, New York, NY; Gimpel/Weizenhoffer Gallery, New York, NY; Tibor de Nagy Gallery, New York, NY; Arthur Tooth & Sons Gallery, London, England; Fox Graphics, Merrimac, MA; Orion Editions, New York, NY; Sherry French Gallery, New York, NY; Meredith Long Gallery, Houston, TX; Gallery Henoch, New York, NY; Hokin Gallery, Palm Beach, FL; Taylors' Contemporanea Fine Arts, Hot Springs National Park, AR
MAILING ADDRESS: 38 W 56th St, #5, New York, NY 10019

TITLE	PUBLISHER	PRINTER	DATE	MEDIUM	DIMENSION (PAPER SIZE) IN INCHES	TYPE OF PAPER	EDITION NUMBER	NO. OF COLORS	ORIGINAL OPENING PRICE	CURRENT RETAIL PRICE
CURRENT EDITIONS:										
Pomaia Tree	ART/FG	HF/FG	1978	LC	22 X 30	AP	60	4	250	500
Tuscan Landscape	OE	RH	1981	PO/OTL	28 X 36	AP	50	18	300	500

DORIS LANIER

EDUCATION: City Col of New York, NY, 1950; Brooklyn Mus Art Sch, NY, 1953–54; Phoenix Art Sch, AZ, 1956–60; New Sch of Art, NY, 1960–62; Pratt Graphic Center, NY, 1963–67
AWARDS: Purchase Prize, Mus of Mod Art, Rijeka, Yugoslavia, 1982; Creative Artists Public Service Grant, Multimedia, Film, 1984
RECENT EXHIB: June Kelly Gallery, NY, 1989
COLLECTIONS: Mus of Mod Art, Rijeka, Yugoslavia, City Col of New York, NY; Silvermine Guild Gallery, New Canaan, CT
PRINTERS: American Atelier, NY (AA)
PUBLISHERS: Orion Editions, NY (OE); Artist (ART)

DORIS LANIER CONTINUED

GALLERIES: Orion Editions, New York, NY; June Kelly Gallery, New York, NY; Circle Galleries, San Diego, CA & San Francisco, CA & Northbrook, IL & Pittsburgh, PA & Houston, TX & Soho, NY & Chicago, IL & Scottsdale, AZ & Beverly Hills, CA & Costa Mesa, CA & Sherman Oaks, CA & Palm Beach, FL & Honolulu, HI & New Orleans, LA & Las Vegas, NV & Seattle, WA
MAILING ADDRESS: 41 Union Square, New York, NY 10003

TITLE	PUBLISHER	PRINTER	DATE	MEDIUM	DIMENSION (PAPER SIZE) IN INCHES	TYPE OF PAPER	EDITION NUMBER	NO. OF COLORS	ORIGINAL OPENING PRICE	CURRENT RETAIL PRICE
CURRENT EDITIONS:										
Timea Sails III	OE		1978	LC/CO	29 X 42	AP	25		375	400
No Heads	ART	CP	1983	LC/HC/OFF	23 X 30	R/BFK	20	Multi	300	350

ELLEN LANYON

BORN: Chicago, IL; December 21, 1926
EDUCATION: Art Inst of Chicago, IL, BFA, 1948; Iowa State Univ, Iowa City, IA, MFA, with Mauricio Lasansky, 1950; Courtauld Inst, Univ of London, England
TEACHING: Vis Art, Lectr, Standford Univ, CA, 1973; Vis Art, Fel, Inst of Arts & Humanistic Studies, Pennsylvania State Univ, University Park PA, 1974; Vis Art, State Univ of Iowa, Salt Lake City, IA, Ames, IA, 1975; Vis Art, Lectr, Univ of California, Davis, CA, 1973,80; Vis Art, Instr, Parsons Sch of Design, NY, 1979–80; Vis Art, Instr, Sch of Visual Arts, NY, 1980–83; Instr, Painting & Director, Oxbow Sch of Painting, Saugatuck, MI, 1960 to present; Instr, Painting, State Univ of New York, Purchase, NY, 1978 to present; Instr, Painting, Cooper Union, NY, 1979–82, Assoc Prof, 1983 to present
AWARDS: Fulbright Fel, 1950; Cassandra Found Award, 1971; Yaddo Fel, 1974–75, 76; Hereward Lester Cooke Found, 1981; Nat Endowment for the Arts Grants, 1974,87
COLLECTIONS: Art Inst of Chicago, IL; Brooklyn Mus, NY; Nat Coll of Art, Wash, DC; Metropolitan Mus, NY; McNay Art Inst, San Antonio, TX; Denver Art Mus, CO; Illinois Wesleyan, Bloomington, IL; Krannert Mus, Univ of Illinois, Champaign, IL; Univ of Massachusetts, Amherst, MA; Finch Col, NY; New Jersey State Mus, Trenton, NJ; Illinois State Mus, Springfield, IL; Galleria Comunale d'Arte Contemporanea, Arezzo, Italy; Koffler Found, Chicago, IL; Albion Col, MI; Kansas State Univ, Manhattan, KS; Univ of Dallas, TX; Cornell Univ, Ithaca, NY; Mus of Contemp Art, Chicago, IL
RECENT EXHIB: Retrosp, Krannert Mus, Univ of Illinois, Champaign, IL, 1987–88
PRINTERS: Landfall Press, Inc, Chicago, IL (LPI); Jack Lemon, Chicago, IL (JL); Judith Solodkin, NY (JS); Solo Press, NY (SP); Melissa Braggins, Rhinebeck, NY (MB); Pondside Press, Rhineback, NY (PonPr)
PUBLISHERS: Landfall Press, Inc, Chicago, IL (LPI); Solo Press, NY (SP); Pondside Press, Rhinebeck, NY (PonPr)
GALLERIES: Richard Gray Gallery, Chicago, IL; Susan Caldwell Gallery, New York, NY; Landfall Press, Inc, Chicago, IL & New York, NY; Struve Gallery, Chicago, IL; Pondside Press, Rhinebeck, NY; Printworks Gallery, Chicago, IL; Chicago Street Gallery, Lincoln, IL; Berland Hall Gallery, New York, NY; Peltz Gallery, Milwaukee, WI
MAILING ADDRESS: 138 Prince St, New York, NY 10012

TITLE	PUBLISHER	PRINTER	DATE	MEDIUM	DIMENSION (PAPER SIZE) IN INCHES	TYPE OF PAPER	EDITION NUMBER	NO. OF COLORS	ORIGINAL OPENING PRICE	CURRENT RETAIL PRICE
SOLD OUT EDITIONS (RARE):										
Six Episodes-Monarch 600	LPI	JL/LPI	1979	LC	22 X 25	GE/BL	35	5	500	800
Strange Games A-Oxbow	LPI	JL/LPI	1980	LC/HC	48 X 34	TWP	9	1	1200	2000
Strange Games B-Talmadge	LPI	JL/LPI	1980	LC/HC	48 X 34	TWP	9	1	1200	2000
Strange Games C-Everglades	LPI	JL/LPI	1980	LC/HC	48 X 34	TWP	9	1	1200	2000
Strange Games D-Lincoln Park	LPI	JL/LPI	1980	LC/HC	48 X 34	TWP	9	1	1200	2000
Black Egret	LPI	JL/LPI	1984	LC	45 X 30	R/BFK/G	25	3	600	800
Eagle Beak	LPI	JL/LPI	1984	LC	45 X 30	R/BFK/G	25	3	600	800
CURRENT EDITIONS:										
Cloisonne	SP	JS/SP	1988	LC	30 X 40	AC	50		750	850
Niagara	SP	JS/SP	1989	LC	29 X 49	AC	50	8	950	950
The Elements (Set of 4):									4300 SET	4300 SET
Air	PonPr	MB/PonPr	1991-92	LC/HC	44 X 30	R/BFK	14	Varies	1200	1200
Water	PonPr	MB/PonPr	1991-92	LC/HC	44 X 30	R/BFK	14	Varies	1200	1200
Land	PonPr	MB/PonPr	1991-92	LC/HC	44 X 30	R/BFK	14	Varies	1200	1200
Fire (Trip)	PonPr	MB/PonPr	1991-92	LC/HC	15 X 90	R/BFK	14	Varies	1200	1200

TADEUSZ LAPINSKI

BORN: Rawo Mazowiecka, Poland; June 20, 1928; US Citizen
EDUCATION: Acad of Fine Arts, Warsaw, Poland, MFA, 1955
TEACHING: Assoc Prof, Lithography, Univ of Maryland, College Park, MD, 1972–82, Prof, 1983 to present
AWARDS: Cincinnati Mus Prize, OH; Medal of Honor, Printers and Sculptors Soc, NJ; UNESCO Prize, Paris, France; Silver Medal, Audubon Art Soc, NY; World Prize, Calvatore, Italy, 1985; First Prize, Int Print Festival, Vienna, Austria, 1981,86
RECENT EXHIB: Central Inst of Art, Beijing, Peoples Republic of China, 1988
COLLECTIONS: Mus of Mod Art, NY; Jewish Mus, NY; Mus of Fine Arts, Boston, MA; San Francisco Mus of Mod Art, CA; Nat Gallery of Art, Wash, DC; Nat Coll of Fine Arts, Wash, DC; Philadelphia Mus of Art, PA; Mus of Contemp Art, Sao Paolo, Brazil; Mus of Fine Art, Mexico City, Mexico; Albertina Graphics Coll, Vienna, Austria; Mus of Belgrade; Mus of Mod Art, Tokyo, Japan
PRINTERS: American Atelier, NY (AA)
PUBLISHERS: Circle Fine Art, Chicago, IL (CFA)
GALLERIES: Franz Bader Gallery, Wash, DC; Gordon Gallery, Los Angeles, CA; Circle Galleries, San Diego, CA & San Francisco, CA & Northbrook, IL & Pittsburgh, PA & Houston, TX & Soho, NY & Chicago, IL & Scottsdale, AZ & Beverly Hills, CA & Costa Mesa, CA & Sherman Oaks, CA & Palm Beach, FL & Honolulu, HI & New Orleans, LA & Las Vegas, NV & Seattle, WA
MAILING ADDRESS: 10413 Eastwood Ave, Silver Spring, MD 20901

TITLE	PUBLISHER	PRINTER	DATE	MEDIUM	DIMENSION (PAPER SIZE) IN INCHES	TYPE OF PAPER	EDITION NUMBER	NO. OF COLORS	ORIGINAL OPENING PRICE	CURRENT RETAIL PRICE
SOLD OUT EDITIONS (RARE):										
Italia 70	CFA	AA	1970	EC	22 X 30	R/BFK	50		35	250

The retail prices of the 100,000 limited edition prints quoted in this directory are subject to change. Print publishers, artists and galleries were the direct sources for these quotations. Prices in the secondary market listed as "Sold Out Editions (Rare)" indicate that the publisher has a limited supply of that print or that the print is difficult to locate in the galleries.

TADEUEZ LAPINSKI CONTINUED

TITLE	PUBLISHER	PRINTER	DATE	MEDIUM	DIMENSION (PAPER SIZE) IN INCHES	TYPE OF PAPER	EDITION NUMBER	NO. OF COLORS	ORIGINAL OPENING PRICE	CURRENT RETAIL PRICE
CURRENT EDITIONS:										
Targets	CFA	AA	1970	EC	22 X 30	R/BFK	50		35	250
Astrology	CFA	AA	1970	EC	22 X 30	R/BFK	50		35	250
Birth of a Dinosaur	CFA	AA	1970	EC	22 X 30	R/BFK	50		35	250

FRANK LAPOINTE

BORN: Port Rexton, Newfoundland, Can; November 5, 1942
EDUCATION: Ontario Col or Art, Can, 1962–66
TEACHING: Instr, Painting & Printmaking, Dundas Valley, Sch of Art, Dundas, ON, Can, 1969–70
AWARDS: Silver Medal, 1967; Bronze Medal, 1968; Newfoundland Arts & Letters Govt Grant, 1970; Canadian Council Grant, 1977
RECENT EXHIB: Mem Univ Gallery, St John's, Newfoundland, 1988,90
COLLECTIONS: Art Gallery of Ontario, Toronto, Can; Simon Fraser Univ, Burnaby, BC, Can; Univ of Lethoridege, Alberta, Can; Nat Gallery of Can, Ottawa, Can; Univ of New Brunswick; Univ of Oregon, Corvallis, OR
PRINTERS: Artist (ART)
PUBLISHERS: Artist (ART)
GALLERIES: Mira Godard Gallery, Toronto, Ontario, Canada; Southwest, Calgary, Canada; Bau-Xi Gallery, Vancouver, Canada
MAILING ADDRESS: Tors Cove, Southern Shore, NF, Canada A0A 4A0

TITLE	PUBLISHER	PRINTER	DATE	MEDIUM	DIMENSION (PAPER SIZE) IN INCHES	TYPE OF PAPER	EDITION NUMBER	NO. OF COLORS	ORIGINAL OPENING PRICE	CURRENT RETAIL PRICE
CURRENT EDITIONS:										
Heartiest Greetings	ART	ART	1977	LC	30 X 22	AP	28	6	160	225
Lamanche	ART	ART	1977	LC	30 X 22	AP	28	6	160	225
Peter's Last Hunt	ART	ART	1978	LC	30 X 22	AP	28	7	160	225
Oh, Happy Sight	ART	ART	1978	LC	13 X 19	AP	22	4	160	225
Razorbill	ART	ART	1981	LC	21 X 30	AP	35	7	200	225

KEVIN LARMEE

BORN: Ridgefield Park, NJ; June 15, 1946
EDUCATION: San Francisco Art Inst, CA, 1967–68; Shimer Col, Mt Carroll, IL, 1965–67, 1969–70; Columbia Col, Chicago, IL, 1974
AWARDS: Krasner-Pollack Grant, 1986
COLLECTIONS: Brooklyn Mus, NY; Fashion Inst of Tech, NY
PRINTERS: Printmaking Workshop, NY (PW); Holly Sears, NY (HS); Michael Richards, NY (MR)
PUBLISHERS: Martin Hason, NY (MH); Avenue B Gallery, NY (ABG)
GALLERIES: Vorpal Galleries, New York, NY & San Francisco, CA; Zolla/Lieberman Gallery, Chicago, IL
MAILING ADDRESS: 25 Mercer St, New York, NY 10013

TITLE	PUBLISHER	PRINTER	DATE	MEDIUM	DIMENSION (PAPER SIZE) IN INCHES	TYPE OF PAPER	EDITION NUMBER	NO. OF COLORS	ORIGINAL OPENING PRICE	CURRENT RETAIL PRICE
CURRENT EDITIONS:										
Cigarette	ABG	HS/MR/PW	1985	LC	48 X 32	R/BFK/W	75	5	350	600

EDWARD LARSON

RECENT EXHIB: Evanston Art Center, IL, 1987
PRINTERS: Jack Lemon, Chicago, IL (JL); Barbara Spies, Chicago, IL (BS); Landfall Press Inc, Chicago, IL (LPI)
PUBLISHERS: Landfall Press Inc, Chicago, IL (LPI)
GALLERIES: Zolla/Lieberman Gallery, Chicago, IL; Jan Baum Gallery, Los Angeles, CA; Landfall Press, Inc, Chicago, IL; Helander Galleries, Palm Beach, FL & Bay Harbor Islands, FL & New York, NY; Brigitte Schluger Gallery, Denver, CO; Hibberd McGrath Gallery, Breckenridge, CO; Artists on the Corner, Clayton, MO; Folliard Gallery, Milwaukee, WI

TITLE	PUBLISHER	PRINTER	DATE	MEDIUM	DIMENSION (PAPER SIZE) IN INCHES	TYPE OF PAPER	EDITION NUMBER	NO. OF COLORS	ORIGINAL OPENING PRICE	CURRENT RETAIL PRICE
SOLD OUT EDITIONS (RARE):										
The Big Parade	LPI	LPI	1982	WC	33 X 25	KUM	20	4	250	250
Parts	LPI	BS/LPI	1983	WC	38 X 24	KUM	20	4	350	350
Suite of 9 Woodcuts:									1000 SET	1800 SET
Self-Portrait	LPI	JL/LPI	1984	WC	24 X 18	NG	20	3	125	200
Norman Maier	LPI	JL/LPI	1984	WC	24 X 18	NG	20	4	125	200
Somewhere Else #3	LPI	JL/LPI	1984	WC	24 X 18	KUM	20	5	125	200
Commonwealth #4	LPI	JL/LPI	1984	WC	24 X 18	NG	20	5	125	200
Away from all That	LPI	JL/LPI	1984	WC	24 X 18	KUM	20	3	125	200
Twin Ladies	LPI	JL/LPI	1984	WC	24 X 18	KUM	20	6	125	200
Sleeping Beauty	LPI	JL/LPI	1984	WC	24 X 18	NG	20	4	125	200
Heaven	LPI	JL/LPI	1984	WC	24 X 18	KUM	20	4	125	200
Ronald Radiation	LPI	JL/LPI	1984	WC	24 X 18	NG	20	4	125	200

The print market has become very selective. For the first time since we published the first edition of The Printworld Directory in 1982, the prices of prints have been greatly reduced and greatly increased for the same artists by the most reputable and established print publishers. Check the fifth edition to understand the movement.

The Printworld Directory is accepting new applications for the seventh edition. Approximately 300 new artists will be accepted. Please use the two forms provided in the back section of this directory to submit biographical data and documentation of prints. Edition number of each print must not exceed 500 and the retail price must be $100 or more.

PHILIP SEELY LARSON

BORN: Ventura, CA; July 21, 1944
EDUCATION: Univ of Minnesota, MN, BA; 1966; Columbia Univ, NY, PhD, 1971
TEACHING: Prof, Minneapolis Col of Art & Design, MN, 1975 to present
AWARDS: Nat Endowment for the Arts Fel, 1979,81
COLLECTIONS: Walker Art Center Minneapolis, MN; Minneapolis Inst of Arts, MN; Solomon R Guggenheim Mus, NY

PRINTERS: Angus Davis, (AD); Vermillion Editions, Ltd, Minneapolis, MN (VEL); Minneapolis Col of Art & Design, MN (MCAD); Artist (ART)
PUBLISHERS: Bird Island Press, Minneapolis, MN (BIP) (OB); Artist (ART)
GALLERIES: Thomson Gallery, Minneapolis, MN
MAILING ADDRESS: c/o Minneapolis College of Art & Design, 133 E 25th St, Minneapolis, MN 55404

TITLE	PUBLISHER	PRINTER	DATE	MEDIUM	DIMENSION (PAPER SIZE) IN INCHES	TYPE OF PAPER	EDITION NUMBER	NO. OF COLORS	ORIGINAL OPENING PRICE	CURRENT RETAIL PRICE
SOLD OUT EDITIONS (RARE):										
The First Stencil (Richardson & White)	BIP	VEL	1978	EB/DPT	32 X 24	AP	25	1	150	850
The Second Stencil (Sullivan & Wright)	BIP	VEL	1978	EB/DPT	32 X 24	AP	25	1	150	850
The Third Stencil (Greene & Greene)	BIP	VEL	1978	EB/DPT	32 X 24	AP	25	1	150	850
The Fourth Stencil (Purcell & Elmslie)	BIP	VEL	1978	EB/DPT	32 X 24	AP	25	1	150	850
The First Grate (Knossos)	ART	VEL	1978	ENG/DPT	24 X 36	AP	15	1	200	900
The Second Grate (Ravenna)	ART	VEL	1978	ENG/DPT	24 X 36	AP	15	1	200	900
The Third Grate (Uxmal)	ART	VEL	1978	ENG/DPT	24 X 36	AP	15	1	200	900
The Fourth Grate (Giza)	ART	VEL	1978	ENG/DPT	24 X 36	AP	15	1	200	900
The First Hinge (BA)	ART	AD	1979	SP/GL	24 X 36	AL/BL	25	2	250	900
The Second Hinge	ART	AD	1979	SP/GL	24 X 36	AL/BL	25	2	250	900
The First Drain (Chicago-Rome)	ART	AD	1980	SP/STEN	24 X 36	KOZO	15	4	225	850
The Second Drain (Chicago-Rome)	ART	AD	1980	SP/STEN	24 X 36	KOZO	15	4	225	850
Cast Iron Fragments I	ART	AD	1981	SP	24 X 32	AL/WH	10	1	150	500
Cast Iron Fragments II	ART	AD	1981	SP	24 X 32	JP	10	1	150	500
The First Foundation (Minneapolis-Ravenna)	ART	AD	1980–82	SP/STEN	40 X 26	KOZO	20	3	225	600
The Second Foundation (Minneapolis-Ravenna)	ART	AD	1980–82	SP/STEN	40 X 26	KOZO	20	3	225	600
The Tile Floor (Geese in Flight)	ART	ART	1983	BP/STEN/GL	22 X 30	FAB	15	4	350	600
The First Snare (Dial & Drum)	ART	AD	1984	SP/GL	22 X 15	FAB	15	4	300	500
The Second Snare (Regulator & Rack)	ART	AD	1984	SP/GL	22 X 15	FAB	15	4	300	500
The Third Snare (Cylinder & Float)	ART	AD	1984	SP/GL	22 X 15	FAB	15	4	300	500
The Four Elements (The Four Times of Day) (Set of 4):									1600 SET	2500 SET
Morning Fire	ART	ART/MCAD	1984	EB/ENG/SB	30 X 22	AP/CR	12		400	650
Midday Earth	ART	ART/MCAD	1984	EB/ENG/SB	30 X 22	AP/CR	12		400	650
Evening Water	ART	ART/MCAD	1984	EB/ENG/SB	30 X 22	AP/CR	12		400	650
Night Air	ART	ART/MCAD	1984	EB/ENG/SB	30 X 22	AP/CR	12		400	650
CURRENT EDITIONS:										
Rock and Ladder (Jacob's Dream)	ART	ART	1986	PO	48 X 36	GE	4		1000	1500
Roman Weights and Measures	ART	ART	1986	PO	48 X 36	GE	4		1000	1500
Tippy-Toe Triangles	ART	ART	1986	PO	48 X 36	GE	4		1000	1500
Windows and Shutters (Dipt) (22-Karat Gold Leaf on Marbelized Paper)	ART	AD	1988–89	SP	44 X 30 EA	PaP			2600	2600

MAURICIO L LASANSKY

BORN: Buenos Aires, Argentina; October 12, 1914
EDUCATION: Superior Sch of Fine Arts, Buenos Aires, Argentina
TEACHING: Director, Free Fine Arts Sch, Villa Maria, Cordoba, Argentina, 1936; Taller Manualidades, Cordoba, Argentina, 1939; Vis Lectr, Univ of Iowa, Iowa City, IA, 1945, Asst Prof, 1946, Assoc Prof, 1947; Lucas Lectr, Carleton Col, Northfield, MN, 1965; Res Prof, 1965–67, Virgil M Hancher Distinguished Prof, 1967–71, Res Prof, 1971–72, Prof, 1948–88; Prof, Printmaking, Hamline Univ, St Paul, MN, 1988 to present
AWARDS: Ford Found Fel, 1962; Guggenheim Fel, 1943,44,63,64; Nat Acad of Arts & Design, NY, 1990

RECENT EXHIB: Museo del Grabado Latinoamericano Inst of Puerto Rican Culture, Old San Juan, PR, 1989; Sioux City Art Center, IA, 1989,92; Fairleigh Dickinson Univ, Phyllis Rothman Gallery, Madison, NJ, 1989,92
COLLECTIONS: Art Inst of Chicago, IL; Seattle Mus, WA; Uffizi Gallery, Florence, Italy; Mus Arte Contemp, Madrid, Spain; Brooklyn Mus, NY; Detroit Inst, MI; Philadelphia Mus, PA; Pennsylvania Acad of Fine Arts, Phila, PA; Portland Mus, OR; Yale Univ, New Haven, CT
PRINTERS: Artist (ART)
PUBLISHERS: Artist (ART)
GALLERIES: Jane Haslem Gallery, Wash, DC; Percival Galleries, Des Moines, IA
MAILING ADDRESS: c/o Hamline University, Snelling & Hewitt Ave, St Paul, MN 55104

TITLE	PUBLISHER	PRINTER	DATE	MEDIUM	DIMENSION (PAPER SIZE) IN INCHES	TYPE OF PAPER	EDITION NUMBER	NO. OF COLORS	ORIGINAL OPENING PRICE	CURRENT RETAIL PRICE
SOLD OUT EDITIONS (RARE):										
Dachau	ART	ART	1946	EB/A	16 X 24	AP	55	1	25	2000
For an Eye for an Eye	ART	ART	1946	I	27 X 21	AP	50	1	25	5000
My Wife	ART	ART	1947	EB/A/ENG		AP	50	1	50	2000
Near East (Pieta)	ART	ART	1948	I		AP	35	1	50	2000

MARUICIO L LASANSKY CONTINUED

TITLE	PUBLISHER	PRINTER	DATE	MEDIUM	DIMENSION (PAPER SIZE) IN INCHES	TYPE OF PAPER	EDITION NUMBER	NO. OF COLORS	ORIGINAL OPENING PRICE	CURRENT RETAIL PRICE
SOLD OUT EDITIONS (RARE):										
Self-Portrait	ART	ART	1948	EB/A		AP	50	1	50	2000
Sagittarius	ART	ART	1955	EB/A	21 X 35	AP	50	1	100	1800
Kaddish I	ART	ART	1975	EC/ENG	44 X 25	AP	70		100	1800
Kaddish II	ART	ART	1976	EC/ENG	41 X 25	AP	70		100	1800
Kaddish III	ART	ART	1976	EC/ENG	39 X 25	AP	70		100	1800
Kaddish IV	ART	ART	1977	EC/ENG	47 X 26	AP	70		200	1800
Kaddish V	ART	ART	1977	EC/ENG	42 X 24	AP	70		200	1800
Kaddish VI	ART	ART	1977	EC/ENG	40 X 24	AP	70		200	1800
Kaddish VII	ART	ART	1977	EC/ENG	45 X 24	AP	70		200	1800
Kaddish VIII	ART	ART	1977	EC/ENG	46 X 24	AP	70		200	1800
Old Man	ART	ART	1978	EC/ENG	29 X 21	AP	75		200	1500
Lady with Derby	ART	ART	1978	EC/ENG	24 X 18	AP	70		200	1500
Indian Chief Wounded Feather	ART	ART	1978	EC/ENG	28 X 24	AP	70		250	1500
Cosmoscape #2	ART	ART	1979	EC/ENG	24 X 28	AP	70		250	1500
Emilia at 10 with Black Cat	ART	ART	1979–80	EC/ENG	62 X 32	AP	70		1000	3500

PAT LASCH

BORN: New York, NY; November 20, 1944
EDUCATION: Queens Col, City Univ of New York, NY, BA; Mus of Mod Art, NY
TEACHING: Soho Center for Visual Arts, NY; Parsons Sch of Design, NY
AWARDS: Yaddo Fel, 1978,80; Creative Artists Public Service Award, 1980,81; Rome Prize, 1982–83; New York State Council on the Arts Grant, Special Project, NY, 1984–85
RECENT EXHIB: DeCordova Mus, Lincoln, MA, 1987; Queens Mus, NY, 1987;Parsons Sch of Design Exhib Center, NY, 1989; Marilyn Pearl Gallery, NY, 1988,90
COLLECTIONS: Mus of Mod Art, NY; Queens Col, City Univ, of New York, NY; Oberlin Mus, OH; Rutgers Univ, Rutherford, NJ
PRINTERS: Kathy Carraccio, NY (KC); Bristol Art Editions, NY (BA)
PUBLISHERS: Bristol Art Editions, NY (BA)
GALLERIES: Marilyn Pearl Gallery, New York, NY; Bernice Steinman Gallery, New York, NY; Thomas Segal Gallery, Boston, MA; Kathryn Markel Gallery, New York, NY
MAILING ADDRESS: 463 West St., #228–G, New York, NY 10014

TITLE	PUBLISHER	PRINTER	DATE	MEDIUM	DIMENSION (PAPER SIZE) IN INCHES	TYPE OF PAPER	EDITION NUMBER	NO. OF COLORS	ORIGINAL OPENING PRICE	CURRENT RETAIL PRICE
CURRENT EDITIONS:										
Royal Ring	BA	KC/BA	1981	DC/EMB	28 X 28 RD	JK/HMP	50	4	400	700

PAUL LASTER

BORN: Flint, MI; 1951
AWARDS: Award, New York Dept of Cultural Affairs, 1983; Nat Endowment for the Arts, Visual Arts Fel, Drawings, 1985; Grants, Art Matter, Inc, 1988,89; Nat Endowment for the Arts, Visual Arts Fel, New Genres, 1989
RECENT EXHIB: Galerie Arch, Amsterdam, The Netherlands, 1988; Pence Gallery, Santa Monica, CA, 1989,90; Hirschl & Adler Mod, NY,1990; Runel-Hue-Williams Gallery, London, England, 1991; Barbara Krakow Gallery, Boston, MA, 1991; Greenberg Gallery, St Louis, MO, 1992; Hamilton Gallery, London, England, 1992; Galerie Baudoin Lebon, Paris, France, 1992; Richard Levy Gallery, Albuquerque, NM, 1992
COLLECTIONS: Metropolitan Mus of Art, NY; Brooklyn Mus, NY; Aldrich Mus of Contemp Art, Ridgefield, CT; Mary & Leigh Block Gallery, Northwestern Univ, Evanston, IL
PRINTERS: Jean-Yves Noblet, NY (JYN); Noblet Serigraphie, NY (NSer)
PUBLISHERS: Caren Golden Fine Arts, NY (CGFA)
GALLERIES: Hirschl & Modern, New York, NY; Barbara Krakow Gallery, Boston, MA; Betsy Rosenfield Gallery, Chicago, IL; Caren Golden Fine Arts, New York, NY

TITLE	PUBLISHER	PRINTER	DATE	MEDIUM	DIMENSION (PAPER SIZE) IN INCHES	TYPE OF PAPER	EDITION NUMBER	NO. OF COLORS	ORIGINAL OPENING PRICE	CURRENT RETAIL PRICE
CURRENT EDITIONS:										
Endless Voyage (Set of 3):									1800 SET	1800 SET
Woman	CGFA	JYN/NSer	1992	SP	20 X 26	R/BFK	35		650	650
Pagoda	CGFA	JYN/NSer	1992	SP	20 X 26	R/BFK	35		650	650
Man	CGFA	JYN/NSer	1992	SP	20 X 26	R/BFK	35		650	650

MICHAEL LASUCHIN

BORN: Kramatorsk, USSR; July 24, 1923; U S Citizen
EDUCATION: Rostow Col of Art, USSR, 1940–41; Philadelphia Col of Art, PA, BFA; Tyler Sch of Art, Temple Univ, Phila, PA, MFA
TEACHING: Tyler Sch of Art, Phila, PA, 1979–71; Philadelphia Col of Art, PA, 1972 to present
AWARDS: Lessing Rosenwald Prize, Phila Print Club, PA, 1973; Medal of Honor, Painters & Sculptors Soc of New Jersey, Jersey City, NJ, 1975; Venture Fund Award, Mellon Found, 1977; Philip & Esther Klein Award, Am Color Print Soc, Phila, PA, 1979; Griffe's Tel Award, Nat Watercolor Soc, Los Angeles, CA, 1979; Medal of Honor, Audubon Artists, NY, 1980; John Taylor Award, Audubon Artist, NY, 1981; Purchase Award, Honolulu Acad of Fine Art, HI 1985
PRINTERS: Artist (ART)
PUBLISHERS: Print Club, Phila, PA (PC); Pratt Graphic Arts Ctr, NY (PG) Artist (ART)
GALLERIES: Venable-Neslage Gallery, Wash, DC; Rosenfeld Fine Art, Phila, PA; Signatures Gallery, Far Hills, NJ; Wenniger Graphics, Boston, MA; Plum Gallery, Paoli, PA
MAILING ADDRESS: 120 E Cliveden St, Phila, PA 19119

MICHAEL LASUCHIN CONTINUED

TITLE	PUBLISHER	PRINTER	DATE	MEDIUM	DIMENSION (PAPER SIZE) IN INCHES	TYPE OF PAPER	EDITION NUMBER	NO. OF COLORS	ORIGINAL OPENING PRICE	CURRENT RETAIL PRICE
SOLD OUT EDITIONS (RARE):										
Isogonic Inferential	ART	ART	1972	SP	54 X 40	STAR	25	13	180	650
Equation	ART	ART	1972	SP	42 X 30	STAR	50	5	80	400
Confluence	ART	ART	1973	MEZ	17 X 11	R/BFK	15	1	50	350
Tangram	ART	ART	1973	SP	53 X 40	STAR	30	9	170	550
Ariel's Conation	ART	ART	1973	SP	30 X 30	STAR	45	10	80	325
Epitaph	ART	ART	1975	SP	20 X 18	STAR	20	5	50	300
Visitation	ART	ART	1975	SP	21 X 17	STAR	30	8	60	350
Legend	ART	ART	1976	SP	37 X 30	STAR	12	13	150	400
Trans	ART	ART	1976	SP	21 X 15	AP	50	11	60	350
Triad	ART	ART	1976	SP	21 X 15	AP	50	14	60	300
CURRENT EDITIONS:										
Aldebaran	ART	ART	1976	SP	43 X 67	STAR	35	1	200	600
Atarax	ART	ART	1977	SP	32 X 30	STAR	50	3	90	300
Polaris	ART	ART	1977	SP	32 X 30	STAR	30	5	150	400
Manifestation	ART	ART	1978	SP	45 X 32	STAR	50	12	150	400
Orapronobis	ART	ART	1979	SP	32 X 23	STAR	50	5	140	400
Departure	ART	ART	1980	SP	18 X 28	STAR	100	10	130	300
Silvercloud	ART	ART	1980	SP	21 X 30	AP	125	6	130	300
Tribute	ART	ART	1982	SP	18 X 13	STAR	35	6	120	300
Apparition	ART	ART	1982	SP	37 X 29	R/BFK	50	8	200	350
Threnody	ART	ART	1982	SP	40 X 30	STAR	40	3	220	350

REX LAU

BORN: Trenton, NJ; February 26, 1947
EDUCATION: Sch of Visual Arts, NY
RECENT EXHIB: Ruth Siegel, Ltd, NY, 1987
COLLECTIONS: Metropolitan Mus of Art, NY; Guggenheim Mus of Am Art, NY; Albright-Knox Art Gallery, Buffalo, NY; Mus of Contemp Art, New Orleans, LA: Walker Art Center, Minneapolis, MN; Lannan Foundation, Palm Beach, FL
PRINTERS: Wil Foo, San Francisco, CA (WF); John Stemmer, San Francisco, CA (JS); Experimental Workshop, San Francisco, CA (EX)
PUBLISHERS: Experimental Workshop, San Francisco, CA (EX)
GALLERIES: Ruth Siegel, Ltd, New York, NY; John Berggruen Gallery, San Francisco, CA; Nina Freudenheim Gallery, Buffalo, NY

TITLE	PUBLISHER	PRINTER	DATE	MEDIUM	DIMENSION (PAPER SIZE) IN INCHES	TYPE OF PAPER	EDITION NUMBER	NO. OF COLORS	ORIGINAL OPENING PRICE	CURRENT RETAIL PRICE
CURRENT EDITIONS:										
The Wind Demons	EW	WF/JS/EW	1984	WC	31 X 25	HMP	30	7	650	800
Red Shadows	EW	WF/JS/EW	1984	WC	31 X 25	HMP	30	3	550	700
December Nights	EW	WF/JS/EW	1985	WC	31 X 25	HMP	20	1	500	650
Black Rock	EW	WF/JS/EW	1986	WC	60 X 28	OKP	30	1	750	900
Lion Head Point	EW	WF/JS/EW	1986	WC	31 X 25	HMP	30	5	650	800

SUSAN LAUFER

BORN: Tuckahoe, NY; 1950
EDUCATION: Boston Univ, MA, BFA, 1972; New York Univ, NY, MA, 1975
TEACHING: Vis Lectr, Boston Mus Sch, MA; Vis Lectr, Brown Univ, Providence, RI; Parsons Sch of Design, NY; Rhode Island Sch of Design, Providence, RI
AWARDS: Nat Endowment for the Arts Fel, 1984; Ariana Found Grant, NY, 1985
RECENT EXHIB: Barbara Krakow Gallery, Boston, MA, 1988; John C Stoller Gallery, Minneapolis, MN, 1988; Stephen Wirtz Gallery, San Francisco, CA, 1989; Germans van Eck Gallery, NY, 1987,89; Michael Lord Gallery, Milwaukee, WI, 1989; Univ of Connecticut, Atrium Gallery, Storrs, CT, 1992
COLLECTIONS: Albright-Knox Art Gallery, Buffalo, NY; Brooklyn Mus of Art, NY; Denver Art Mus, CO; Greenville County Art Mus, SC; Metropolitan Mus of Art, NY; Northern Illinois Univ, De Kalb, IL
PRINTERS: Experimental Workshop, San Francisco, CA (EW); Joe Wilfer, NY (JW); Spring Street Workshop, NY (SprSW)
PUBLISHERS: Experimental Workshop, San Francisco, CA (EW); Spring Street Workshop, NY (SprSW)
GALLERIES: Pace Prints, New York, NY; Experimental Workshop, San Francisco, CA; Betsy Senior Contemporary Prints, New York, NY; Germans van Eck Gallery, New York, NY; Michael Lord Gallery, Milwaukee, WI; Stephen Wirtz Gallery, San Francisco, CA; BlumHelman Gallery, New York, NY; Calvin-Morris Gallery, New York, NY; Davis/McClain Gallery, Houston, TX; Fraenkel Gallery, San Francisco, CA; CCA Gallery, Chicago, IL; Hill Gallery, Birmingham, MI; Lemberg Gallery, Birmingham, MI

TITLE	PUBLISHER	PRINTER	DATE	MEDIUM	DIMENSION (PAPER SIZE) IN INCHES	TYPE OF PAPER	EDITION NUMBER	NO. OF COLORS	ORIGINAL OPENING PRICE	CURRENT RETAIL PRICE
CURRENT EDITIONS:										
Strata I	EW	EW	1988	COL/HC	72 X 41	R/BFK	10	Varies	5000	5000
Strata II	EW	EW	1988	COL/HC	50 X 19	R/BFK	36	Varies	3000	3000
Transformation Series I (Set of 6)	SprSW	JW/SprSW	1989	REL/LI/HC	26 X 20 EA	R/BFK	35 EA	Varies	6500 SET 1200 EA	6500 SET 1200 EA

The retail prices of the 100,000 limited edition prints quoted in this directory are subject to change. Print publishers, artists and galleries were the direct sources for these quotations. Prices in the secondary market listed as "Sold Out Editions (Rare)" indicate that the publisher has a limited supply of that print or that the print is difficult to locate in the galleries.

HANNE H7L LAURIDSEN

BORN: Edbjerg, Denmark; U S Citizen
EDUCATION: Univ of California, Berkeley, CA, Double BA in Art & History of Art, 1980; Univ of California, La Jolla, CA, MFA, 1982
TEACHING: Univ of California, Berkeley, CA, 1980; Univ of California, San Diego, CA, 1982; Parrish Art Mus, Southampton, NY, Fall, 1986; Guild Hall Mus, East Hampton, NY, 1983–86
AWARDS: Ford Found Fel, 1981–82; Louis B Mayer Found Fel, 1982; Third Prize, All California Arts Competition, 1982; New York City Artist Housing Project Award, 1984
RECENT EXHIB: Ismael Gallery, NY, 1988; Germans Van Eck Gallery, NY, 1990; Rockefeller Town House Gallery, NY, 1992
PRINTERS: Artist (ART)
PUBLISHERS: Artist (ART)
GALLERIES: Ismael Gallery, New York, NY; PDG Gallery, New York, NY; E M Donahue Gallery, New York, NY
MAILING ADDRESS: 517 E 11th St, 2nd Fl, New York, NY 10009

TITLE	PUBLISHER	PRINTER	DATE	MEDIUM	DIMENSION (PAPER SIZE) IN INCHES	TYPE OF PAPER	EDITION NUMBER	NO. OF COLORS	ORIGINAL OPENING PRICE	CURRENT RETAIL PRICE
CURRENT EDITIONS:										
Ecology (with Tempora Paint and Oil Pastel)	ART	ART	1981	LC	20 X 26	AP	10	5	400	1000
—So Ugly—	ART	ART	1991	EB	10 X 13	AP	10	1	300	500
The Ugly Duckling Dream	ART	ART	1991	MON	20 X 26 EA	AP	1 EA	5 EA	500 EA	1000 EA
Onions or Appels	ART	ART	1992	LC	20 X 26	AP	10	2	300	500

BERTRAND LAVIER

BORN: Chatillon-sur-Seine, France; 1949
RECENT EXHIB: Ecole des Beaux-Arts, Macon, France, 1987; Mus de Peinture et de Sculpture, Grenoble, France, 1987; Locus-Solus, Genoa, Italy, 1987; Myers Bloom Gallery, Santa Monica, CA, 1988; Liliane and Michael Durand-Dessert, Paris, France, 1989; Galerie Hans Mayer, Dusseldorf, Germany, 1989; John Gibson Gallery, NY, 1987,89
PRINTERS: Mark Callen, San Francisco, CA (MC); Renée Bott, San Francisco, CA (RB); Crown Point Press, San Francisco, CA (CPP)
PUBLISHERS: Crown Point Press, San Francisco, CA (CPP)
GALLERIES: Crown Point Press, New York, NY & San Francisco, CA; Galerie Han Mayer, Dusseldorf, Germany; Myers Bloom Gallery, Santa Monica, CA; John Gibson Gallery, New York, NY; Dart Gallery, Chicago, IL

TITLE	PUBLISHER	PRINTER	DATE	MEDIUM	DIMENSION (PAPER SIZE) IN INCHES	TYPE OF PAPER	EDITION NUMBER	NO. OF COLORS	ORIGINAL OPENING PRICE	CURRENT RETAIL PRICE
SOLD OUT EDITIONS (RARE):										
Untitled Modern Painting No 1	CPP	MC/RB/CPP	1987	AC	45 X 40	SOM	25		1000	1800
CURRENT EDITIONS:										
Untitled Modern Painting No 2	CPP	MC/RB/CPP	1987	AC	20 X 50	SOM	25		1000	1800
Untitled Modern Painting No 3	CPP	MC/RB/CPP	1987	AC	52 X 40	SOM	25		1000	1800

JACOB LAWRENCE

BORN: Atlantic City, NJ; September 7, 1917
EDUCATION: Harlem Workshop, NY, 1934-39; Am Artists Sch, 1938; Denison Univ, OH, Honorary Degree, DFA, 1972
TEACHING: Instr, Summer, Black Mountain Col, Painting, 1947; Instr, Pratt Inst, NY, 1956-71; Art-in-Res, Brandeis Univ, 1965; Inst, New Sch for Social Research, 1966; Instr, Art Students League, NY, 1967; Coordinator of the Arts, Asst to Dean, Sch of Art, Pratt Inst, 1970-71; Prof of Art, Univ of Washington, Seattle, WA, 1972 to present
AWARDS: Rosenwald Fel, 1940,41,42,; Guggenheim Fel,NY, 1946; Atlanta Univ, GA, Pruchase Prize, 1948; Norman Wait Harris Medal, Art Inst of Chicago, IL, 1948; Nat Inst of Arts and Letters Grant, 1953; Chapelbrook Found Grant, 1955; Ford Found Award, 1960; Elected Member, Nat Inst of Arts and Letters, 1965; Spingarn Medal (NAACP), 1970; Nat Endowment for the Arts, 1977; Presidents for Art Award, President Bush, 1990
RECENT EXHIB: Dallas Mus of Art, Dallas, TX, 1987; Brooklyn Mus, NY, 1987; Univ of Missouri, Kansas City Gallery of Art, KS, 1989; Francine Seders Gallery, Ltd, Seattle, WA, 1990; Southeast Arkansas Arts Center, Pine Bluff, AR, 1992; Phillips Coll, Wash, DC, 1987,92; High Mus, Atlanta, GA, 1989,92; Phillips Acad, Addison Gallery of Am Art, Andover, MA, 1992; Montclair Art Mus, NJ, 1992; East Carolina Univ, Wellington B Gray Gallery, Greenville, NC, 1992; South Carolina State Col, I P Stanback Mus, Orangeburg, SC, 1992; Whatcom Mus of History & Art, Bellingham, WA, 1992; Clark Col, Vancouver, WA, 1992
COLLECTIONS: Metropolitan Mus of Art, NY; Whitney Mus of Am Art, NY; Phillips Col, Wash, DC; Portland Mus, OR; Worcester Mus, MA; Baltimore Mus, MD; Wichita Mus of Art, KS; Albright-Knox Art Gallery, Buffalo, NY; Am Acad of Arts and Letters, NY; Mus of Mod Art, Sao Paulo, Brazil; Brooklyn Mus, NY; Hirshhorn Mus, Wash, DC; Mus of Fine Art, Boston, MA; Nat Coll of Fine Art, Wash, DC; Smithsonian Inst, Wash, DC; Philadelphia Mus of Art, PA; Harlem Mus, NY; Mus of Mod Art, NY
PRINTERS: Ives Sillman, Hampden, CT (IS)
PUBLISHERS: Transworld Arts Ind, NY (TAI); Associated American Artists, NY (AAA)
GALLERIES: Terry Dintenfass Gallery, New York, NY; Francine Seders Gallery, Seattle, WA; Luise Ross Gallery, New York, NY; Sid Deutsch Gallery, New York, NY; McIntosh Gallery, Atlanta, GA; Alitash Kebede Fine Arts, Los Angeles, CA; G R N'Namdi Gallery, Birmingham, MI
MAILING ADDRESS: 4316 37th Ave, NE, Seattle, WA 98105

TITLE	PUBLISHER	PRINTER	DATE	MEDIUM	DIMENSION (PAPER SIZE) IN INCHES	TYPE OF PAPER	EDITION NUMBER	NO. OF COLORS	ORIGINAL OPENING PRICE	CURRENT RETAIL PRICE
SOLD OUT EDITIONS (RARE):										
Workshop	AAA	IS	1972	OC	22 X 18	AP	100		300	5000
Builders No 3	TAI	IS	1974	SP	32 X 32	AE	150		300	7000
Confrontation at the Bridge	TAI	IS	1975	SP	20 X 26	SP	175		300	7000
Morning Still Life	TAI	IS	1980	SP	20 X 26	AP	175		500	6000

The print market has become very selective. For the first time since we published the first edition of The Printworld Directory in 1982, the prices of prints have been greatly reduced and greatly increased for the same artists by the most reputable and established print publishers. Check the fifth edition to understand the movement.

SANDRA LAWRENCE

PRINTERS: American Atelier, NY (AA)
PUBLISHERS: Circle Fine Art, Chicago, IL (CFA)
GALLERIES: Circle Galleries, San Diego, CA & San Francisco, CA & Northbrook, IL & Houston, TX & Pittsburgh, PA & Soho, NY & Chicago, IL & Scottsdale, AZ & Beverly Hills, CA & Costa Mesa, CA & Sherman Oaks, CA & Palm Beach, FL & Honolulu, HI & New Orleans, LA & Las Vegas, NV & Seattle, WA

TITLE	PUBLISHER	PRINTER	DATE	MEDIUM	DIMENSION (PAPER SIZE) IN INCHES	TYPE OF PAPER	EDITION NUMBER	NO. OF COLORS	ORIGINAL OPENING PRICE	CURRENT RETAIL PRICE
CURRENT EDITIONS:										
Plant, Lettuce, Tomatoes	CFA	AA	1980	LC	21 X 29	AP	250		200	250
Poinsettia and Apples	CFA	AA	1980	LC	30 X 22	AP	250		200	250
Patio	CFA	AA	1980	LC	22 X 30	AP	250		200	250

ELEANORE BERMAN LAZAROF

BORN: New York, NY; September 2, 1928
EDUCATION: Univ of California, Los Angeles, CA, BA, 1950; Black Mountain Col, Studied with Josef Albers & Lyonel Feininger; Atelier Fernand Leger, Paris, France; New Sch for Social Research, NY, Studied with Adya Yunkers
AWARDS: Purchase Award, Allmanson Award, All City Art Show, Los Angeles, CA; Purchase Award, Brand Library
RECENT EXHIB: Downey Mus of Art, CA, 1988; Lisa Kurts Gallery, Memphis, TN, 1989; Fridholm Fine Arts, Asheville, NC, 1989
COLLECTIONS: Los Angeles County Mus of Art, CA; Milwaukee Art Center, WI; Brooklyn Mus, NY; Grunwald Center for Graphic Art, Univ of California, Los Angeles, CA; Achenbach Found, Palace of the Legion of Honor, San Francisco, CA
PRINTERS: Richard Royce, Stone Ridge, NY (RR); Atelier Royce, Stone Ridge, NY (AR); Robert Aull, Santa Monica, CA (RA)
PUBLISHERS: Artist (ART)
GALLERIES: Lisa Kurts Gallery, Memphis, TN; Shoshana Wayne Gallery, Santa Monica, CA
MAILING ADDRESS: 718 N Maple Dr, Beverly Hills, CA 90210

TITLE	PUBLISHER	PRINTER	DATE	MEDIUM	DIMENSION (PAPER SIZE) IN INCHES	TYPE OF PAPER	EDITION NUMBER	NO. OF COLORS	ORIGINAL OPENING PRICE	CURRENT RETAIL PRICE
SOLD OUT EDITIONS (RARE):										
Canto II	ART	AR	1975	EC	40 X 30	AP	75	2	300	500
Falling Forms, State I, II, III, IV (Set of 4)	ART	AR	1977	EC/AC	17 X 23 EA	AP	48 EA	2	800 SET 200 SET	1000 SET 275 EA
Dos Lados de la Manana	ART	RA	1979	EC/AC	30 X 41	AP	30	1	350	500
Due Volte	ART	RA	1978	EB	54 X 32	R/BFK	20	1	400	500
CURRENT EDITIONS:										
Canto Variation	ART	AR	1975	COL/AC	40 X 30	AP	75	2	300	450
Stones	ART	AR	1975	EB	30 X 40	AP	75	1	250	400
Interlude	ART	AR	1975	EC	40 X 30	AP	75	2	325	400
Lodestar	ART	AR	1977	EC	40 X 30	GE	40	2	300	400
Rifatto	ART	RA	1978	EC/A	45 X 20	R/BFK	42	2	400	450
Jericho I	ART	RA	1979	EB	54 X 32	R/BFK	25	1	400	500
Jericho II	ART	RA	1979	EB	54 X 32	R/BFK	20	1	400	500
Annunciation, State I	ART	AR	1980	EB	23 X 18	HMP	15	1	400	450
Annunciation, State II	ART	AR	1980	EB/EMB	23 X 18	HMP	35	1	400	450
Duo I (with Sugarlift)	ART	RA	1983	EB/A	39 X 26	R/BFK	15	1	450	450
Duo II, III (with Sugarlift)	ART	RA	1983	EC	40 X 30 EA	R/BFK	15 EA	2 EA	400 EA	450 EA

HAROLD M LE ROY

BORN: New York, NY; (1905–1992)
EDUCATION: Columbia Univ, NY, MFA; Brooklyn Mus Art Sch, NY; Art Students League, NY Hans Hofmann Sch, NY
TEACHING: Instr, Brooklyn Col, NY 1984,85,86
AWARDS: Heydenryk Award for Graphic Art, 1977; Am Veterans Soc of Artists Award, 1979; Binney & Smith Award, 1981; Am Soc of Contemp Artists Award, Painting, 1984
COLLECTIONS: Butler Inst of Am Art, Youngstown, OH; Mint Mus, Charlotte, NC; Mus of Mod Art, London, Ont, Can; Safad Mus, Israel; Skirball Mus of Art, Los Angeles, CA; Georgia Mus of Art, Athens, GA; Smithsonian Inst, Wash, DC; Chrysler Mus, Norfolk, CT; Slater Mem Mus, Norwich, CT; Lydia Drake Library Coll, Pembroke, MA; Fine Arts Mus of Long Island, NY; Brooklyn Mus, NY
PRINTERS: Artist (ART)
PUBLISHERS: Bestin Art, Brooklyn, NY (BA)
GALLERIES: Belanthi Gallery, Brooklyn, NY; Simon Fitoussi, Paris, France

TITLE	PUBLISHER	PRINTER	DATE	MEDIUM	DIMENSION (PAPER SIZE) IN INCHES	TYPE OF PAPER	EDITION NUMBER	NO. OF COLORS	ORIGINAL OPENING PRICE	CURRENT RETAIL PRICE
SOLD OUT EDITIONS (RARE):										
Cluster	BA	ART	1979	SP	16 X 14	AP	92	5	60	400
Floral Melody	BA	ART	1979	SP	20 X 24	AP	100	8	60	300
Conservatoire	BA	ART	1980	SP	22 X 28	AP	110	10	60	500
Shades of Tiffany	BA	ART	1980	SP	20 X 26	AP	125	10	60	500
Mod Cirque	BA	ART	1980	SP	20 X 26	AP	100	7	60	500
At the Spanish Steps	BA	ART	1980	SP	12 X 18	AP	100	7	50	300
Caladium	BA	ART	1982	SP	28 X 22	AP	125	6	200	500

The retail prices of the 100,000 limited edition prints quoted in this directory are subject to change. Print publishers, artists and galleries were the direct sources for these quotations. Prices in the secondary market listed as "Sold Out Editions (Rare)" indicate that the publisher has a limited supply of that print or that the print is difficult to locate in the galleries.

ROBERT LAZUKA

BORN: Chicago, IL; 1948
EDUCATION: Sch of Art Inst of Chicago, IL, Painting, 1968–69; Arizona State Univ, Tempe, AZ, BFA, 1981, MFA, 1984
TEACHING: Grad Teaching Asst, Sch of Art, Arizona State Univ, Tempe, AZ, 1982–83; Instr, Ohio Univ, Athens, OH, Sch of Art, Printmaking, 1984–85, Asst Prof, 1987 to present
COLLECTIONS: Clemson Univ, SC; Board of Regents, State of Arizona, Tempe, AZ
PRINTERS: Bill Weege, Madison, WI (BW); Andrew Rubin, Madison, WI (AR); Tandem Press, Univ of Wisconsin, Madison, WI (TanPr)
PUBLISHERS: Tandem Press, Univ of Wisconsin, Madison, WI (TanPr)
MAILING ADDRESS: c/o Ohio University, School of Art, Athens, OH 54701

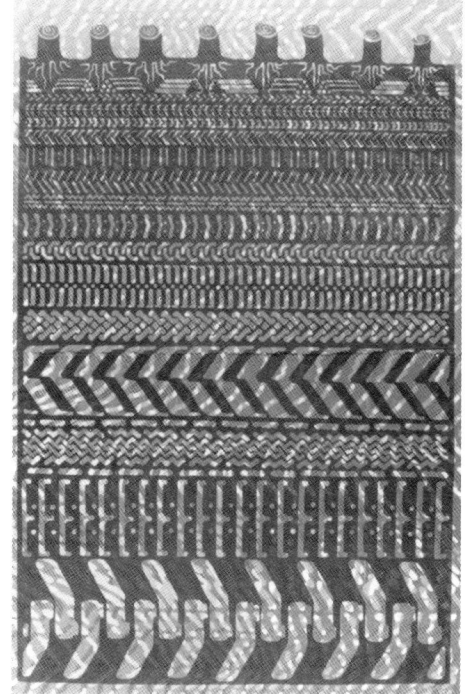

Robert Lazuka
National Forest: Clear Cut Decision
Courtesy Tandem Press

TITLE	PUBLISHER	PRINTER	DATE	MEDIUM	DIMENSION (PAPER SIZE) IN INCHES	TYPE OF PAPER	EDITION NUMBER	NO. OF COLORS	ORIGINAL OPENING PRICE	CURRENT RETAIL PRICE
SOLD OUT EDITIONS (RARE):										
National Forest: Clear Cut Decision (Series of 4) (Dipt)	TanPr	BW/AR/TanPr	1989	WC/MON	77 X 52 EA	HMP	1 EA	14 EA	2000 EA	2200 EA

BARRY LE VA

BORN: Long Beach, CA; 1941
EDUCATION: California State Univ, Long Beach, CA, 1960–63; Los Angeles Col of Art & Design, CA, 1963; Otis Art Inst, Los Angeles, CA, BFA, 1964, MFA 1967
TEACHING: Instr, Minneapolis Col of Art & Design, MN, 1968–70; Instr, Sculpture, Princeton Univ, NJ, 1973–74; Instr, Grad Dept, Sculpture, Yale Univ, New Haven, CT, 1976
AWARDS: Young Talent Grant, Los Angeles County Mus, CA, 1968; Guggenheim Found Fel, Sculpture, 1974; Nat Endowment for Arts Fel, 1976
RECENT EXHIB: Inst of Contemp Art, Univ of Pennsylvania, Phila, PA, 1987; Holly Solomon Gallery, NY, 1987; Laurie Rubin Gallery, NY, 1987; Barbara Gladstone Gallery, NY, 1987; Carnegie-Mellon Art Gallery, Pittsburgh, PA, 1987,88; Rijksmuseum Kröller-Müller, Otterloo, The Netherlands, 1988; Fred Jahn, Munich, Germany, 1988; High Mus, Atlanta, GA, 1989; Carnegie Mellon Univ, Pittsburgh, PA, 1989; Daniel Weinberg Gallery, Los Angeles, CA, 1989; Texas Gallery, Houston, TX, 1989; David Nolan Gallery, NY, 1987,89,90; New York Univ, NY, 1992
COLLECTIONS: Whitney Mus of Am Art, NY; Mus of Mod Art, NY; Chicago Art Inst, IL; Philadelphia Art Mus, PA; Rijksmueum Kröller-Müller, Otterloo, The Netherlands
PRINTERS: Karl Imhof, Munich, Germany (KI);
PUBLISHERS: Galerie Fred Jahn, Munich, Germany (GFJ)
GALLERIES: David Nolan Gallery, New York, NY; Daniel Weinberg, Santa Monica, CA; Texas Gallery, Houston, TX; Galerie Fred Jahn, Munich, Germany
MAILING ADDRESS: 160 W 24th St, #5-C, New York, NY 10011

TITLE	PUBLISHER	PRINTER	DATE	MEDIUM	DIMENSION (PAPER SIZE) IN INCHES	TYPE OF PAPER	EDITION NUMBER	NO. OF COLORS	ORIGINAL OPENING PRICE	CURRENT RETAIL PRICE
CURRENT EDITIONS:										
Sculptured Activities I–V (Set of 5)	GFJ	KI	1907–09	WC	40 X 31 EA	R/BFK	16 EA		8000 SET 2000 EA	8000 SET 2000 EA
NTZ (Dipt)	GFJ	KI	1990	LB	35 X 43	AP/CR	35	1	1500	1500
Saturation Horizontal—02	GFJ	KI	1990	LB	35 X 43	AP/CR	35	1	1500	1500

JUNE LEAF

BORN: Chicago, IL; 1929
EDUCATION: Inst of Design, Chicago, IL; Univ of Illinois, Champaign, IL; Roosevelt Univ, Chicago, IL
TEACHING: Instr, Painting & Drawing, Art Inst of Chicago, IL, 1954–58; Parsons Sch of Design, NY, 1966–68
AWARDS: Fulbright Grant, Paris, France, 1958; Canadian Council of the Arts Awards, 1978,82; Nat Endowment for the Arts Grant, 1989
RECENT EXHIB: Phyllis Kind Gallery, Chicago, Il, 1987; Pratt Inst, Brooklyn, NY, 1988; Edward Thorp Gallery, NY, 1987,88,90; Washington Project for the Arts, Wash, DC, 1992
COLLECTIONS: Mus of Mod Art, NY; Art Inst of Chicago, IL; Mus of Contemp Art, Chicago, IL; Smithsonian Inst, Wash, DC; Madison Art Center, WI; Col of Cape Breton, Sydney, NS, Canada
PRINTERS: Jack Lemon, Chicago, IL (JL); Landfall Press Inc, Chicago, IL (LPI)
PUBLISHERS: Landfall Press Inc, Chicago, IL (LPI)
GALLERIES: Rhona Hoffman Gallery, Chicago, IL; Landfall Press, Inc, Chicago, IL; Edward Thorp Gallery, New York, NY; Printworks Gallery, Chicago, IL
MAILING ADDRESS: c/o Edward Thorp Gallery, 103 Prince St, New York, NY 10012

JUNE LEAF CONTINUED

TITLE	PUBLISHER	PRINTER	DATE	MEDIUM	DIMENSION (PAPER SIZE) IN INCHES	TYPE OF PAPER	EDITION NUMBER	NO. OF COLORS	ORIGINAL OPENING PRICE	CURRENT RETAIL PRICE
SOLD OUT EDITIONS (RARE):										
Untitled	LPI	JL/LPI	1981	LC	36 X 25	AP/W	30	4	300	600
Untitled, State I	LPI	JL/LPI	1981	LC	36 X 25	AP/W	20	1	300	600
Untitled			1990	MON/HC	47 X 35 EA	AP/W	1 EA	Varies	4000 EA	4500 EA
Untitled			1990	MON/HC	47 X 41 EA	AP/W	1 EA		4500 EA	5000 EA

LEBADANG

BORN: Vietnam; 1922
EDUCATION: Ecole des Beaux Art, Toulouse, France, 1939–40
COLLECTIONS: Univ Art Gallery, Lund, Sweden; Loo Coll, Tokyo, Japan; Phoenix Art Mus, AZ
PRINTERS: Société Arts-Litho, Paris, France (SAL); Jean Claude Perrin, Paris, France (JCP); Chicago Serigraphic Workshop, IL (CSW); Artist (ART)

PUBLISHERS: Circle Fine Art Corp, Chicago, IL (CFA)
GALLERIES: I-Michael Galleries, Edina, MN; Circle Galleries, San Diego, CA & San Francisco, CA & Northbrook, IL & Pittsburgh, PA & Houston, TX & Soho, NY & Chicago, IL; Davidson Gallery, Daytona Beach, FL; Owl Gallery, San Francisco, CA; Walton Street Gallery, Chicago, IL; Park West Gallery, Southfield, MI; Laura Paul Galleries, Cincinnati, OH & Columbus, OH; Fernette's Gallery of Art, Des Moines, IA

TITLE	PUBLISHER	PRINTER	DATE	MEDIUM	DIMENSION (PAPER SIZE) IN INCHES	TYPE OF PAPER	EDITION NUMBER	NO. OF COLORS	ORIGINAL OPENING PRICE	CURRENT RETAIL PRICE
SOLD OUT EDITIONS (RARE):										
Lebadangraphy Series:										
Le Soleil Bleu	CFA	AA	1967	SP	22 X 30	AP	275		75	1000
La Montagne Fleurie	CFA	AA	1967	SP	22 X 30	AP	275		75	950
Le Cheval Noir	CFA	AA	1967	SP	22 X 30	AP	275		75	950
Le Chevalier Solitare	CFA	AA	1967	SP	22 X 30	AP	275		75	950
Les Voiliers	CFA	AA	1967	SP	22 X 30	AP	275		75	950
La Branche Seche	CFA	AA	1967	SP	31 X 47	AP	275		100	1150
Les Montagne Dorees	CFA	AA	1968	SP	31 X 47	AP	275		100	1150
Cheval D'Antan	CFA	AA	1968	SP	31 X 47	AP	275		100	1150
La Cavaliere Solitaire	CFA	AA	1968	SP	22 X 30	AP	275		100	1100
Le Rocher, La Mere et L'Enfant	CFA	AA	1968	SP	22 X 30	AP	275		100	1000
La Montagne de la Mere et L'Enfant	CFA	AA	1968	SP	22 X 30	AP	275		100	1000
Le Rocher de la Grande Dame	CFA	AA	1968	SP	22 X 30	AP	275		100	1000
La Montagne Ensoleillee	CFA	AA	1968	SP	31 X 31	AP	275		100	875
Le Rocher de la Grande Dame	CFA	AA	1968	SP	22 X 30	AP	275		100	1000
La Montagne Ensoleilee	CFA	AA	1968	SP	31 X 31	AP	275		100	875
Le Printemps	CFA	AA	1969	SP	21 X 47	AP	275		125	1000
Fleurs	CFA	AA	1969	SP	48 X 60	AP	300		125	1500
Pleasures	CFA	AA	1969	SP	11 X 11	AP	275		75	750
Dreams	CFA	AA	1969	SP	11 X 11	AP	275		75	750
Mysterieux	CFA	AA	1969	SP	11 X 11	AP	275		75	750
Imagination	CFA	AA	1969	SP	11 X 11	AP	275		75	750
Joyeux	CFA	AA	1969	SP	31 X 16	AP	275		75	900
Lollipop Tree	CFA	AA	1970	LC	20 X 26	AP	120		150	750
Orange Junks	CFA	AA	1972	LC	20 X 26	AP	120		150	750
Afrique	CFA	AA	1972	LC	19 X 26	AP	180		150	725
Les Chevaux Oranges	CFA	AA	1973	LC	19 X 26	AP	180		150	750
Reve	CFA	AA	1973	LC	19 X 26	AP	180		150	700
Jungle	CFA	AA	1973	LC	19 X 26	AP	180		150	725
Paysage aux Barques	CFA	AA	1974	LC	21 X 29	AP	250		150	750
La Lune Rouge	CFA	AA	1974	LC	21 X 29	AP	250		150	750
Le Lac	CFA	AA	1974	LC	21 X 29	AP	250		150	750
Le Cheval	CFA	AA	1974	LC	21 X 29	AP	250		150	750
Stallions	CFA	AA	1975	EC	11 X 15	AP	275		100	700
Arbre Jaune	CFA	AA	1975	EC	11 X 15	AP	275		100	700
Figure de la Lune	CFA	AA	1975	EC	11 X 15	AP	275		100	700
Femme Native	CFA	AA	1975	EC	11 X 15	AP	275		100	700
Travaille du Matin	CFA	AA	1975	EC	11 X 15	AP	275		100	700
Foret	CFA	AA	1975	EC	11 X 15	AP	275		100	700
Nue	CFA	AA	1975	EC	11 X 15	AP	275		100	700
Le Cheval Cavalier	CFA	AA	1975	EC	11 X 15	AP	275		100	700
Muthuswamy	CFA	AA	1975	EC	11 X 15	AP	275		100	700
Golden Orb	CFA	AA	1976	LC	26 X 38	AP	275		300	1550
Tempest	CFA	AA	1976	LC	27 X 38	AP	275		300	750
Moonshadow	CFA	AA	1976	LC	21 X 30	AP	275		250	750
Imaginative Landscape	CFA	AA	1976	LC	24 X 34	AP	275		250	750
Procession (4 Panels)	CFA	AA	1978	SP	73 X 24 EA / 73 X 96 TOT	Wood	150			1100
Le Monument	CFA	ART/JSP	1981	LC/EMB	24 X 30	AP	300	3	350	900
La Petite Cabane du Pecheur	CFA	ART/JCP	1981	LC/EMB	30 X 22	AP	300	3	375	900
L'Autre Monde	CFA	ART/JCP	1981	LC/EMB	34 X 25	AP	300	3	375	900
Le Papillon	CFA	ART/JCP	1981	LC/EMB	25 X 17	AP	300	3	325	1000
La Barque Solitaire I	CFA	ART/JCP	1981	LC/EMB	25 X 17	AP	300	3	250	700

LEBADANG CONTINUED

TITLE	PUBLISHER	PRINTER	DATE	MEDIUM	DIMENSION (PAPER SIZE) IN INCHES	TYPE OF PAPER	EDITION NUMBER	NO. OF COLORS	ORIGINAL OPENING PRICE	CURRENT RETAIL PRICE
SOLD OUT EDITIONS (RARE):										
La Barque et la Lune	CFA	ART/JCP	1981	LC/EMB	25 X 17	AP	300	3	325	1000
L'Aberration	CFA	ART/JCP	1981	LC/EMB	25 X 17	AP	300	3	250	750
La Comedie Humaine #5	CFA	ART/JCP	1981	LC/EMB	30 X 22	AP	300	3	375	750
La Lune Blanc	CFA	ART/JCP	1981	LC/EMB	30 X 23	AP	300		475	1150
Le Bout du Passage	CFA	ART/JCP	1981	LC/EMB	30 X 22	AP	300	3	350	700
La Demie Lune	CFA	ART/JCP	1981	LC/EMB	34 X 25	AP	300	3	350	750
La Barque Solitaire II	CFA	ART/CP	1981	LC/EMB	30 X 2	AP	300	3	325	750
La Lune Rouge et L'Hiver	CFA	ART/JCP	1981	LC/EMB	24 X 17	AP	300	3	275	700
Le Paysage Melancolique	CFA	ART/JCP	1981	LC/EMB	24 X 17	AP	300	3	275	800
La Comedie Humaine Series:										
La Comedie Humaine #1	CFA	ART/JCP	1981	LC/EMB	23 X 23	AP	300	3	275	700
La Comedie Humaine #2	CFA	ART/JCP	1981	LC/EMB	24 X 24	AP	300	3	350	700
La Comedie Humaine #3	CFA	ART/JCP	1981	LC/EMB	34 X 12	AP	300	3	275	575
La Comedie Humaine #4	CFA	ART/JCP	1981	LC/EMB	34 X 12	AP	300	3	275	575
La Comedie Humaine #5	CFA	ART/JCP	1981	LC/EMB	30 X 22	AP	300	3	275	750
Ce N'Est pas Encore L'Hiver	CFA	P/FR	1982	EC/EMB	14 X 10	AP	250		175	1000
Une Petite Chanson dans L'Espace (A Short Song Floating through Time)	CFA	P/FR	1982	EC/EMB	14 X 10	AP	250		175	900
Une Petite Chanson (A Short Song)	CFA	P/FR	1982	EC/EMB	14 X 10	AP	250		175	800
Tranquilité (Tranquility)	CFA	P/FR	1982	EC/EMB	14 X 10	AP	250		175	1000
Calme et Dignité (Calm and Dignity)	CFA	P/FR	1982	EC/EMB	31 X 10	AP	250		300	1100
La Vie et le Bonheur (Life and Happiness)	CFA	P/FR	1982	EC/EMB	32 X 10	AP	250		300	850
Calme et Beauté (Calm and Beauty)	CFA	P/FR	1982	EC/EMB	26 X 20	AP	250		375	1200
Mysterieux Rendezvous	CFA	CSW	1982	SP/CO	30 X 46	AP	275		550	1800
Espace Tranquilite	CFA	JCP	1985	SPC/EC/CO	19 X 20	AP	250		800	2000
Espace Calme	CFA	JCP	1985	SPC/EC/CO	19 X 20	AP	250		800	1550
Espace Amour	CFA	JCP	1985	SPC/EC/CO	36 X 18	AP	250		900	1675
Espace Beaute	CFA	JCP	1985	SPC/EC/CO	36 X 20	AP	250		900	1850
Memoire d'un Lieu Sacre (To Memory of a Spiritual Place)	CFA	JCP	1986	SPC/EC	26 X 40	HMP	250		1600	2500
Paysage Mentale (Landscape of the Mind)	CFA	JCP	1986	SPC/EC	26 X 20	HMP	250		1100	2400
Nadir	CFA	JCP	1986	SPC/EC	21 X 13	HMP	250		675	1400
La Femme Reposee	CFA	AA	1986	RL	15 X 22	AP	200		450	975
Petite Nature avec Verre	CFA	AA	1986	RL	15 X 22	AP	200		450	975
Les Fleurs de Minuit	CFA	AA	1986	RL	15 X 22	AP	200		450	1000
La Colombe	CFA	AA	1986	RL	15 X 22	AP	200		450	1000
La Branche Morte	CFA	AA	1986	RL	25 X 41	AP	200		600	1100
Fantasie du Soir	CFA	AA	1986	RL	26 X 39	AP	200		600	1150
Ten Horse Folio (Set of 10):									5000 SET	10000 SET
Plate #1	CFA	AA	1986	LC/EMB	21 X 30	AP	275		500	1000
Plate #2	CFA	AA	1986	LC/EMB	21 X 30	AP	275		500	1000
Plate #3	CFA	AA	1986	LC/EMB	21 X 30	AP	275		500	975
Plate #4	CFA	AA	1986	LC/EMB	21 X 30	AP	275		500	1000
Plate #5	CFA	AA	1986	LC/EMB	21 X 30	AP	275		500	1100
Plate #6	CFA	AA	1986	LC/EMB	21 X 30	AP	275		500	1000
Plate #7	CFA	AA	1986	LC/EMB	21 X 30	AP	275		500	1000
Plate #8	CFA	AA	1986	LC/EMB	21 X 30	AP	275		500	1000
Plate #9	CFA	AA	1986	LC/EMB	21 X 30	AP	275		500	1000
Plate #10	CFA	AA	1986	LC/EMB	21 X 30	AP	275		500	1100
Ten Horse Folio (Set of 10):									6000 SET	11500 SET
Plate #1	CFA	AA	1986	LC/EMB	21 X 30	JP	50		600	1100
Plate #2	CFA	AA	1986	LC/EMB	21 X 30	JP	50		600	1100
Plate #3	CFA	AA	1986	LC/EMB	21 X 30	JP	50		600	1100
Plate #4	CFA	AA	1986	LC/EMB	21 X 30	JP	50		600	1075
Plate #5	CFA	AA	1986	LC/EMB	21 X 30	JP	50		600	1100
Plate #6	CFA	AA	1986	LC/EMB	21 X 30	JP	50		600	1050
Plate #7	CFA	AA	1986	LC/EMB	21 X 30	JP	50		600	1200
Plate #8	CFA	AA	1986	LC/EMB	21 X 30	JP	50		600	1050
Plate #9	CFA	AA	1986	LC/EMB	21 X 30	JP	50		600	1250
Plate #10	CFA	AA	1986	LC/EMB	21 X 30	JP	50		600	1350
CURRENT EDITIONS:										
La Nature Prie sans Parole (Nature Prays without Words)	CFA	P/FR	1982	EC/EMB	26 X 20	AP	250		375	850
Les Volubiles (Twining Branches)	CFA	CSW	1982	SP	60 X 46	AP	275		1000	1400
Reminiscences Suite (Set of 10)										
Fleurs d'Amitie (Flowers of Friendship)	CFA	JCP	1983	LC	37 X 18	AP	250		250	500
Fleurs d'Amitie (With Gold and Silver)	CFA	JCP	1983	LC/ST	37 X 18	AP	100		350	600

LEBADANG CONTINUED

TITLE	PUBLISHER	PRINTER	DATE	MEDIUM	DIMENSION (PAPER SIZE) IN INCHES	TYPE OF PAPER	EDITION NUMBER	NO. OF COLORS	ORIGINAL OPENING PRICE	CURRENT RETAIL PRICE
CURRENT EDITIONS:										
Les Arbres en Hiver (Trees in Winter)	CFA	JCP	1983	LC	24 X 17	AP	250		250	500
Les Arbres en Hiver (With Gold and Silver)	CFA	JCP	1983	LC/ST	24 X 17	AP	100		350	600
La Barque Solitaire (Solitary Boat)	CFA	JCP	1983	LC	12 X 34	AP	250		250	500
La Barque Solitaire (With Gold and Silver)	CFA	JCP	1983	LC/ST	12 X 34	AP	100		350	600
Les Arbres Freres (Brother Trees)	CFA	JCP	1983	LC	34 X 12	AP	250		250	500
Les Arbres Freres (With Gold and Silver)	CFA	JCP	1983	LC/ST	34 X 12	AP	100		350	600
Fleurs d'Espoir (Flowers of Hope)	CFA	JCP	1983	LC	24 X 17	AP	250		250	600
Fleurs d'Espoir (With Gold and Silver)	CFA	JCP	1983	LC/ST	24 X 17	AP	100		350	700
Les Barques Soeurs (Sister Boats)	CFA	JCP	1983	LC	24 X 35	AP	250		250	700
Les Barques Soeurs (With Gold and Silver)	CFA	JCP	1983	LC/ST	24 X 35	AP	100		350	800
La Vallee Silencieuse (The Silent Valley)	CFA	JCP	1983	LC	35 X 24	AP	250		250	800
La Vallee Silencieuse (With Gold and Silver)	CFA	JCP	1983	LC/ST	35 X 24	AP	100		350	850
Barques au Rendezvous (Boats at Rendezvous)	CFA	JCP	1983	LC	37 X 18	AP	250		250	600
Barques au Rendezvous (With Gold and Silver)	CFA	JCP	1983	LC/ST	37 X 18	AP	100		350	800
Fleurs d'Amour (Flowers of Love)	CFA	JCP	1983	LC	50 X 35	AP	250		350	850
Fleurs d'Amour (With Gold and Silver)	CFA	JCP	1983	LC/ST	50 X 35	AP	100		450	950
La Tranquilite sur le Lac (Tranquility on the Water)	CFA	JCP	1983	LC	35 X 50	AP	250		350	850
La Tranquilite sur le Lac (With Gold and Silver)	CFA	JCP	1983	LC/ST	35 X 50	AP	100		450	950
Espace Dignite	CFA	JCP	1985	SPC/EC/CO	38 X 58	HMP	250		2000	2400
Espace Mysterieux	CFA	JCP	1986	SPC/EC	41 X 20	HMP	250		1200	1500
Espace Joyeux	CFA	JCP	1986	SPC/EC	20 X 20	HMP	250		850	1150
Espace Plaisir	CFA	JCP	1986	SPC/EC	20 X 20	HMP	250		850	1100
Espace Famille (Blue)	CFA	JCP	1986	SPC/EC	20 X 40	HMP	250		1200	1550
Quassar	CFA	JCP	1986	SPC/EC	25 X 15	HMP	250		1150	1440
Orion	CFA	JCP	1986	SPC/EC	25 X 24	HMP	250		1300	1500
Blue Solitude	CFA	JCP	1986	SPC/EC	26 X 10	HMP	250		750	1300
Le Miroir de la Nuit	CFA	JCP	1987	SPC/EC	30 X 22	HMP	250		1,800	2100
L'Espace de l'Amit	CFA	JCP	1987	SPC/EC/CO	25 X 15	HMP	250		1250	1700
L'Espace sans Dualisme	CFA	JCP	1987	SPC/EC/CO	21 X 21	HMP	250		1000	1350
L'Espace en Paix	CFA	JCP	1987	SPC/EC/CO	15 X 22	HMP	250		1500	1800
Suite of Six Horses (Set of 6):									8800 SET	8800 SET
Espaces Horse #1	CFA	JCP	1989	SPC/LC/CO	27 X 20	HMP	200		1800	1800
Espaces Horse #2	CFA	JCP	1989	SPC/LC/CO	27 X 20	HMP	200		1800	1800
Espaces Horse #3	CFA	JCP	1989	SPC/LC/CO	27 X 20	HMP	200		1800	1800
Espaces Horse #4	CPA	JCP	1989	SPC/LC/CO	27 X 20	HMP	200		1800	1800
Espaces Horse #5	CPA	JCP	1989	SPC/LC/CO	27 X 20	HMP	200		1800	1800
Espaces Horse #6	CPA	JCP	1989	SPC/LC/CO	27 X 20	HMP	200		1800	1800

FANCH LEDAN

BORN: Brittany, France; September 8, 1949
EDUCATION: Ecole Superieure des Sciences Commerciales, Paris, France, Master of Bus Administration, 1972; California State Univ, Sacramento, CA, 1973
RECENT EXHIB: Emporium Enterprises, Inc, Dallas, TX, 1989; Metropolis Gallery, Boston, MA, 1990

PRINTERS: American Atelier, NY (AA); Kato Art Studio, Torrance, CA (KAS); American Serigraph, Los Angeles, CA (AmS); Grapholith, Paris, France (Graph); Atelier Desjobert, Paris, France (AD); Impressions, Ltd, Los Angeles, CA (IL); Coriander Studio, London, England (COR)
PUBLISHERS: Studio 53 Editions, NY (S53); Circle Fine Art, Chicago, IL (CFA); Parkwest Galleries, Southfield, MI (PG); Impress Graphics, Stamford, CT (IG); Christie's Contemp, London, England (CC); Blinder Fine Arts, Inc, Santa Monica, CA (BA)

The retail prices of the 100,000 limited edition prints quoted in this directory are subject to change. Print publishers, artists and galleries were the direct sources for these quotations. Prices in the secondary market listed as "Sold Out Editions (Rare)" indicate that the publisher has a limited supply of that print or that the print is difficult to locate in the galleries.

The Printworld Directory is accepting new applications for the seventh edition. Approximately 300 new artists will be accepted. Please use the two forms provided in the back section of this directory to submit biographical data and documentation of prints. Edition number of each print must not exceed 500 and the retail price must be $100 or more.

FANCH LEDAN CONTINUED

GALLERIES: Art Moods, Atlanta, GA; Art City, Los Angeles, CA; Art Dimensions, Century City, CA; Art Forum, Honolulu, HI; Billy Hork Galleries, Chicago, IL; Bromberg Fine Art, Long Island, NY; Carol Lawrence Galleries, Beverly Hills, CA; Columbia Fine Art, Columbia, MD; Court Gallery, Cincinnati, OH; Donna Marie Gallery, Santa Ana, CA; Emporium Enterprises, Dallas, TX; Elayne Galleries, Minneapolis, MN; Gallery at Palmer Square, Princeton, NJ; Galerie des Champs Elysees, Paris, France; Galerie Maxis, Canyon Country, CA; Grossman Galerie, Franklin, MI; Hoffman-Porges Gallery, Tampa, FL; Hoitts Gallery, San Francisco, CA; JEM Alexander Gallery, Westchester, IL; JEM Fine Art, Newport Beach, CA; JMS Fine Arts, Redondo Beach, CA; Laurence Galleries, Santa Rosa, CA; Limited Editions, Portland, OR; Lori's Art Gallery, Woodland Hills, CA; MRL Fine Arts, Long Beach, CA; Marson Galleries, Baltimore, MD; Mary Roberts Gallery, Honolulu, HI; Metropolis Gallery, Boston, MA; Nan Miller Gallery, Rochester, NY; Ocean Avenue Galleries, Santa Monica, CA; Park Place Gallery, St Louis, MO; Portland Place Gallery, Norwalk, CT; Promenade Gallery, Santa Monica, CA; Rejeau Galleries, Natick, MA; Revann Galleries, Atlantic City, NJ; Rittenhouse Fine Arts, Jenkintown, PA; Scarsdale Gallery, Scarsdale, NY; Sherman Gallery, Manhattan Beach, CA; Silver K Gallery, Melbourne, Australia; Studio 53, New York, NY; Triangle Galleries, Newport Beach CA & Beverly Hills, CA; Uptown Gallery, Fresno, CA; Warwick Gallery, Warwick, RI; Westbelt Gallery, Wayne, NJ; Swahn Fine Arts, San Diego, CA; Fox International, Gardnerville, NE; Circle Galleries, San Diego, CA & San Francisco, CA & Northbrook, IL & Chicago, IL & Soho, NY & Houston, TX & Pittsburgh, PA; Fox International, Lake Tahoe, NV; Carteret Contemporary Art, Morehead City, NC

TITLE	PUBLISHER	PRINTER	DATE	MEDIUM	DIMENSION (PAPER SIZE) IN INCHES	TYPE OF PAPER	EDITION NUMBER	NO. OF COLORS	ORIGINAL OPENING PRICE	CURRENT RETAIL PRICE
SOLD OUT EDITIONS (RARE):										
Le Linge au Vent de Matin	CFA	AA	1978	LC	17 X 21	AP	300		100	500
Le Place de Dinard	CFA	AA	1978	LC	16 X 26	AP	300		125	600
Le Grand Boulevard	S53	GRA	1981	LC	24 X 32	AP	375	19	225	750
Le Grand Boulevard	S53	GRA	1981	LC	24 X 32	JP	375	19	250	750
Les Planches de Deauville	S53	GRA	1981	LC	24 X 32	AP	375	18	225	750
Les Planches de Deauville	S53	GRA	1981	LC	24 X 32	JP	375	18	250	750
Place du Marche	S53	GRA	1981	LC	24 X 32	AP	375	17	225	750
Place du Marche	S53	GRA	1981	LC	24 X 32	JP	375	17	250	750
Spring Show	S53	GRA	1981	LC	24 X 32	AP	375	16	225	750
Spring Show	S53	GRA	1981	LC	24 X 32	JP	375	16	250	750
Le Paradis	S53	GRA	1981	LC	24 X 32	AP	375	16	225	750
Le Paradis	S53	GRA	1981	LC	24 X 32	JP	375	16	250	750
Pont Neuf	S53	GRA	1981	LC	24 X 32	AP	325	19	250	750
Pont Neuf	S53	GRA	1981	LC	24 X 32	JP	50	19	250	750
Le Grand Escalier Rouge	IG	CS	1985	SP	31 X 30	AP/240	364	20	350	600
Interior with Miro	IG	CS	1986	SP	29 X 35	AP/260	414	25	350	600
Opening of the Bay	ChCON	GRA	1987	LC			230		350	450
Le Sofa de Julie	PWG	AD	1987	LC	31 X 23	AP/260	415	24	350	550
Balloons Place de la Concorde	PWG	AD	1988	LC	31 X 23	AP/260	415	26	350	550
The Villa	BFA	KAS	1989	SP	32 X 38	COV	370	65	550	750
Above Cannes	BFA	AD	1989	LC/SP	31 X 37	AP/300	300	22	550	700
CURRENT EDITIONS:										
Interior with Picasso	BFA	AS	1988	SP	29 X 41	COV	495	43	550	750
Antigua	BFA	IL	1988	SP	31 X 38	WWP	495	46	550	700
Interior with Guitar	BFA	AS	1989	SP	38 X 30	COV	495	86	650	800
Quiet Harber: St Tropez	BFA	AS	1989	LC/SP	31 X 38	AP/400	345	27	550	700
Piano Balcony	BFA	KAS	1990	SP	35 X 34	COV	360	60	650	750

CATHERINE LEE

BORN: Pampa, TX; April 11, 1950
EDUCATION: San Jose State Univ, CA, BA, 1975
TEACHING: Art in Res, Minneapolis Col of Art & Design, Minnesota Inst of Art, MN, 1982; Vis Asst Prof, Painting, Univ of Texas, San Antonio, TX, 1983; Adj Asst Prof, Columbia Univ, NY, 1986–87
AWARDS: Creative Artist Public Service Prog Fel, Painting, 1978
RECENT EXHIB: Galerie Weinberger, Copenhagen, Denmark, 1992; Stadtische Galerie im Lenbachhaus, Munich, Germany, 1992
COLLECTIONS: State Univ of New York, Dowd Gallery, Courtland, NY; Mus Fur Kultur, Hamburg, Germany
PRINTERS: Limestone Press, San Francisco, CA (LP)
PUBLISHERS: Diani Villani Editions, NY (DVE); Hine Editions, San Francisco, CA (HE); Limestone Press, San Francisco, CA (LP)
GALLERIES: John Davis Gallery, New York, NY; Marilyn Butler Gallery, Santa Monica, CA; Thomas Segal Gallery, Boston, MA; Garner Tullis Fine Art, New York, NY; Diane Villani Editions, New York, NY; Galerie Weinberger, Copenhagen, Denmark; Stephen Wirtz Gallery, San Francisco, CA
MAILING ADDRESS: 106 Spring St, New York, NY 10012

TITLE	PUBLISHER	PRINTER	DATE	MEDIUM	DIMENSION (PAPER SIZE) IN INCHES	TYPE OF PAPER	EDITION NUMBER	NO. OF COLORS	ORIGINAL OPENING PRICE	CURRENT RETAIL PRICE
CURRENT EDITIONS:										
Suite of Four Color Woodcut Prints (Set of 4):									5000 SET	6000 SET
Coast	DVE		1988	WC	39 X 27	KOZO	25		1300	1700
Borderline	DVE		1988	WC	39 X 27	KOZO	25		1300	1700
Savannah	DVE		1988	WC	27 X 39	KOZO	25		1300	1700
North Umberland	DVE		1988	WC	27 X 39	KOZO	25		1300	1700
Tehama I-VI (Set of 6)	HE/LP	LP	1992	EB	30 X 44 EA	SOM	20 EA	1 EA	3000 SET	3000 SET
Antrim, Armagh, Derry, Donegal, Down, Fermenagh, Tyrone, Ulster (Set of 8)	HE/LP	LP	1992	EB/A/DPT	19 X 19 EA	RP/HWT	10 EA	1 EA	600 EA	600 EA

The print market has become very selective. For the first time since we published the first edition of The Printworld Directory in 1982, the prices of prints have been greatly reduced and greatly increased for the same artists by the most reputable and established print publishers. Check the fifth edition to understand the movement.

LI LIN LEE

BORN: Jakarta, Indonesia; October 11, 1955
EDUCATION: Univ of Pittsburgh, PA, B S, Biochemistry, 1974–78
RECENT EXHIB: Lasorda-Iri Gallery, Los Angeles, CA, 1988; Reicher Gallery, Barat Col, Lake Forest, IL, 1989; Tilden Foley Gallery, New Orleans, LA, 1989,90; Richard Iri Gallery, Los Angeles, CA, 1990; Betsy Rosenfield Gallery, Chicago, IL, 1990; E M Donahue Gallery, NY, 1989,90,91

PRINTERS: Crown Point Press, San Francisco, CA (CPP)
PUBLISHERS: Crown Point Press, San Francisco, CA (CPP)
GALLERIES: Betsy Rosenfield Gallery, Chicago, IL; E M Donahue Gallery, New York, NY; Tilden Foley Gallery, New Orleans, LA; Richard Iri Gallery, Los Angeles, CA; Crown Point Press, San Francisco, CA & New York, NY; Payton Rule Gallery, Denver, CO

TITLE	PUBLISHER	PRINTER	DATE	MEDIUM	DIMENSION (PAPER SIZE) IN INCHES	TYPE OF PAPER	EDITION NUMBER	NO. OF COLORS	ORIGINAL OPENING PRICE	CURRENT RETAIL PRICE
CURRENT EDITIONS:										
A Hidden Place	CPP	CPP	1989	WC	23 X 22	RAG/SILK	25		750	750
In the Rainy Season	CPP	CPP	1989	WC	23 X 22	RAG/SILK	25		750	750
Mirror Image	CPP	CPP	1989	WC	23 X 22	RAG/SILK	25		750	750
Sacrament and Sorrow	CPP	CPP	1989	WC	23 X 22	RAG/SILK	25		750	750

TOM LEESON

BORN: Chicago, IL; March 16, 1945
EDUCATION: Ball State Univ, Muncie, IN, BS, 1968; Univ of California, Los Angeles, CA, MA, 1971
TEACHING: Vis Lectr, Drawing & Sculpture, Univ of California, Santa Barbara, CA, 1982; Vis Lectr, Drawing, Univ of California, Los Angeles, CA, 1977–79, Lectr, 1983 to present

COLLECTIONS: Los Angeles County Mus of Art, CA; Santa Monica City Col of Art Gallery, CA
PUBLISHERS: Landfall Press, Inc, Chicago, IL (LPI)
PRINTERS: Jack Lemon, Chicago, IL (JL); Landfall Press, Inc, Chicago, IL (LPI)
GALLERIES: Landfall Press, Inc, Chicago, IL; Ovsey Gallery, Los Angeles, CA
MAILING ADDRESS: 4748 W Washington Blvd, Los Angeles, CA 90016

TITLE	PUBLISHER	PRINTER	DATE	MEDIUM	DIMENSION (PAPER SIZE) IN INCHES	TYPE OF PAPER	EDITION NUMBER	NO. OF COLORS	ORIGINAL OPENING PRICE	CURRENT RETAIL PRICE
SOLD OUT EDITIONS (RARE):										
Erasure	LPI	JL/LPI	1976	LC	23 X 30	AP/W	60	5	150	600

LEONARD LEHRER

BORN: Philadelphia, PA; March 23, 1935
EDUCATION: Philadelphia Col of Art, PA, BFA, 1956; Univ of Pennsylvania, Phila, PA, MFA, 1960
TEACHING: Philadelphia Col of Art, PA, 1956–70; Tyler Art Sch, Temple Univ, Phila, PA, 1970; Univ of New Mexico, Albuquerque, NM, 1970–74; Univ of Texas, San Antonio, TX, 1974–77; Arizona State Univ, AZ, 1977 to present

COLLECTIONS: Philadelphia Mus, PA; Sprengel Mus of Mod Art, W Germany; Cleveland Mus, OH; Mus of Mod Art, NY; Yale Univ, New Haven, CT; Univ of Hartford, CT; Baylor Univ, Waco, TX; Univ of Texas, San Antonio, TX; Univ of Utah, Salt Lake City, UT; Univ of California, Los Angeles, CA; Nat Gallery of Art, Wash, DC
PRINTERS: Wayne Kimball, Mesa, AZ (WK); Stephen Britko (SB)
PUBLISHERS: Ed Hill Editions, El Paso, TX (EHE); Artist (ART)
GALLERIES: Marian Locks Gallery, Phila, PA; Davidson Gallery, Seattle WA; Ed Hill Editions, El Paso, TX: Sette Gallery, Scottsdale, AZ; Winstone Press, Winston-Salem, NC

TITLE	PUBLISHER	PRINTER	DATE	MEDIUM	DIMENSION (PAPER SIZE) IN INCHES	TYPE OF PAPER	EDITION NUMBER	NO. OF COLORS	ORIGINAL OPENING PRICE	CURRENT RETAIL PRICE
CURRENT EDITIONS:										
View of Puerto Vallarta	EHE	WK	1978	LB	22 X 31	GE	100	1	150	700
Puerto Vallarta II	ART	WK	1978	LC	9 X 13	R/BFK	100	4	150	500
La Granja de Sanil Defonso	EHE	WK	1978	LB	26 X 36	R/BFK	100	1	200	750
View of St Petersburg	EHE	SB	1978	LB	30 X 44	ARJ/AP	100	1	200	1000
Hampton Court	ART	WK	1981	LC	22 X 30	AP	100	4	325	800
Garden Diptych	ART	WK	1981	LB	22 X 30	AP	100	1	225	700
Veduta	ART	WK	1981	LB	22 X 30	AP	100	1	225	700

DANIEL LEIGHTON

BORN: Weston, England; October 10, 1967
EDUCATION: Leighton-Jones Studios, Plantation, FL; Cranbrook Art Sch, London, England; Dover Col, England

PUBLISHERS: Collectors Art Plus, Lauderhill, FL (CAP)
PRINTERS: American Screen Printing, Deerfield Beach, FL (ASP)
GALLERIES: B J Seger Fine Art, Deerfield Beach, FL
MAILING ADDRESS: 7 Cliffe House, Radnor Cliff, Sandgate Kent, England KT2 P2TY

TITLE	PUBLISHER	PRINTER	DATE	MEDIUM	DIMENSION (PAPER SIZE) IN INCHES	TYPE OF PAPER	EDITION NUMBER	NO. OF COLORS	ORIGINAL OPENING PRICE	CURRENT RETAIL PRICE
SOLD OUT EDITIONS (RARE):										
Sheri	CAP	ASP	1986	SP	30 X 40	LEN	300	2	300	500
Cindy	CAP	ASP	1986	SP	30 X 40	LEN	300	1	300	500

The Printworld Directory is accepting new applications for the seventh edition. Approximately 300 new artists will be accepted. Please use the two forms provided in the back section of this directory to submit biographical data and documentation of prints. Edition number of each print must not exceed 500 and the retail price must be $100 or more.

BARRY LEIGHTON-JONES

BORN: London, England; October 17, 1932
EDUCATION: Royal Col of Art, Brighton, England
TEACHING: Sidlup Art Sch, London, England
COLLECTIONS: Ringling Mus, Sarasota, FL
PRINTERS: American Screen Printing, Deerfield Beach, FL (ASP); Dynaprint, Inc, Hollywood, FL (Dyn)
PUBLISHERS: Collectors Art Plus, Lauderhill, FL (CAP)
GALLERIES: B J Seger Fine Art, Deerfield Beach, FL; Galerie Martin, Boca Raton, FL

TITLE	PUBLISHER	PRINTER	DATE	MEDIUM	DIMENSION (PAPER SIZE) IN INCHES	TYPE OF PAPER	EDITION NUMBER	NO. OF COLORS	ORIGINAL OPENING PRICE	CURRENT RETAIL PRICE
SOLD OUT EDITIONS (RARE):										
Andrea at the Hamptons	CAP	ASP	1986	SP	38 X 50	LEN	300	16	900	1200
Andrea at the Plaza	CAP	Dyn	1987	SP	38 X 50	LEN	275	32	750	900

KOSTAS LEKAKIS

PRINTERS: Richard/Bennett Press, Santa Barbara, CA (RBP); Artist (ART)
PUBLISHERS: Richard/Bennett Press, Santa Barbara, CA (RBP)

TITLE	PUBLISHER	PRINTER	DATE	MEDIUM	DIMENSION (PAPER SIZE) IN INCHES	TYPE OF PAPER	EDITION NUMBER	NO. OF COLORS	ORIGINAL OPENING PRICE	CURRENT RETAIL PRICE
CURRENT EDITIONS:										
I, Crooked Smile	RBP	ART/RBP	1985	WC	19 X 15	RP	4	8	800	900

ANNETTE ROSE LEMIEUX

BORN: Norfolk, VA; October 11, 1957
EDUCATION: Northwestern Connecticut Com Col, Winsted, CT, AA, 1977; Hartford Art Sch, Univ of Hartford, CT, BFA, 1981
AWARDS: Anna Ball Pierce Award, Hartford Art Sch, Univ of Hartford, CT, 1981; Pollock/Krasner Found, 1986; Nat Endowment for the Arts Awards, 1983,84,85,86,87,89; Mies van der Rohe Stipend, Kaiser-Wilhelm Mus, Krefeld, Germany, 1992
RECENT EXHIB: Inst of Contemp Art, Boston, MA, 1987; Lia Ruma Galerie, Naples, Italy, 1987; Wadsworth Atheneum, Hartford, CT, 1988; Whitney Mus of Am Art, NY, 1989; Ringling Mus, Sarasota, FL, 1989; New Mus, NY, 1989; Albright-Knox Art Gallery, Buffalo, NY, 1989; Corcoran Gallery of Art, Wash, DC, 1990; Newport Harbor Art Mus, Newport Beach, CA, 1990; Nat Mus of Am Art, Wash, DC, 1990; Galerie Monika Spru, Cologne, Germany; Rhona Hoffman Gallery, Chicago, IL, 1990; Oklahoma City Art Mus, OK, 1991; Maryland Inst, Col of Art, Decker & Meyerhoff Gallery, Baltimore, MD, 1992; Cleveland Center for Contemp Art, OH, 1992; Mus of Mod Art, NY, 1992; Josh Baer Gallery, NY, 1992
COLLECTIONS: Mus of Mod Art, NY; Rooseum, Malmo, Sweden; Eli Brode Found, Los Angeles, CA; Elaine Danheiser Found, NY; Oklahoma Art Mus, Oklahoma City, OK; Israel Mus, Jerusalem, Israel
PRINTERS: Trestle Editions, NY (TE); Kelton Labs, NY (KL)
PUBLISHERS: I C Editions, NY (ICE); Brooke Alexander, Inc, NY (BAI)
GALLERIES: Josh Baer Gallery, New York, NY; Rhona Hoffman Gallery, Chicago, IL; Galerie Monika Spru, Cologne, Germany; Lia Ruma Galerie, Naples, Italy; Brooke Alexander, Inc, New York, NY
MAILING ADDRESS: 153 W 27th St, #1005, New York, NY 10001-6203

TITLE	PUBLISHER	PRINTER	DATE	MEDIUM	DIMENSION (PAPER SIZE) IN INCHES	TYPE OF PAPER	EDITION NUMBER	NO. OF COLORS	ORIGINAL OPENING PRICE	CURRENT RETAIL PRICE
CURRENT EDITIONS:										
Stolen Faces (Trip)	ICE	TE	1991	LB	30 X 22 30 X 44 30 X 22	AP88	26	1	6000	6000
Scarehead	BAI	KL	1992-93	PH	20 X 16	Oriental	50		900	900

LEONE & MACDONALD

RECENT EXHIB: Fawbush Gallery, NY, 1992
PRINTERS: Artist (ART)
PUBLISHERS: Artist (ART); Fawbush Gallery, NY (FG)
GALLERIES: Fawbush Gallery, New York, NY

TITLE	PUBLISHER	PRINTER	DATE	MEDIUM	DIMENSION (PAPER SIZE) IN INCHES	TYPE OF PAPER	EDITION NUMBER	NO. OF COLORS	ORIGINAL OPENING PRICE	CURRENT RETAIL PRICE
CURRENT EDITIONS:										
Private Parts (Sites and Secretions) (Series of 4)	ART/FG	ART	1992	Brand	17 X 20 EA	DIEU	12 EA	1 EA	5000 SET 500 EA	5000 SET 500 EA

DENNIS LEON

BORN: London, England; 1933
EDUCATION: Temple Univ, Phila, PA, BS, BFA, MFA
TEACHING: Prof, Sculpture & Art History, Philadelphia Col of Art, Phila, PA, 1959-72; Prof & Chmn, Sculpture Dept, California Col of Arts & Crafts, Oakland, CA, 1972 to present
AWARDS: Nat Inst of Arts & letters Grant, 1967; John Simon Guggenheim Fel, 1967; San Francisco Mus of Mod Art, Golden Gate Nat Recreation Area, 1978; Nat Endowment for the Arts Fel, 1979; MacDowell Fel, 1981
COLLECTIONS: Philadelphia Mus of Art, PA; Storm King Art Center, NY; Philadelphia Col of Art, Phila, PA; Univ of North Carolina, Greensboro, NC: Oakland Mus, CA
PRINTERS: David Kelso, Oakland, CA (DK); Made in California, Oakland, CA (MIC)
PUBLISHERS: Made in California, Oakland, CA (MIC)
GALLERIES: J Noblett Gallery, Boyes Hot Springs, CA; Dorothy Goldeen Gallery, Santa Monica, CA; Haines Gallery, San Francisco, CA; Butters Gallery, Ltd, Portland, OR
MAILING ADDRESS: c/o Dept of Fine Arts, California College of Arts & Crafts, Oakland, CA 94618

DENNIS LEON CONTINUED

TITLE	PUBLISHER	PRINTER	DATE	MEDIUM	DIMENSION (PAPER SIZE) IN INCHES	TYPE OF PAPER	EDITION NUMBER	NO. OF COLORS	ORIGINAL OPENING PRICE	CURRENT RETAIL PRICE
CURRENT EDITIONS:										
Submerged Figure	MIC	DK/MIC	1984	A/DPT/HG	40 X 26	R/BFK/CR	30	1	300	600
Diving Figure	MIC	DK/MIC	1984	DPT/HG	15 X 11	R/BFK/W	30	1	100	300
Vertical Landscape	MIC	DK/MIC	1984	AB/HG	15 X 11	R/BFK/W	30	1	100	300

JAMES CHAN LEONG

BORN: San Francisco, CA; November 27, 1929
EDUCATION: California Col of Arts & Crafts, BFA, 1951; MFA, 1954; San Francisco State Col, CA, MA, 1955; Univ of Oslo, Norway 1956–58
TEACHING: Univ of Georgia, Athens, GA, 1971; Univ of Georgia, Cortona, Italy, 1970–86
AWARDS: John Hay Whitney Fel, 1953–54; Fulbright Grant for Norway, 1956–57; Guggenheim Found Grant, Rome, Italy, 1958–59
COLLECTIONS: Princeton Mus, NJ; Harvard Univ, Cambridge, MA; New York Univ Mus, NY; Univ of Texas, Austin, TX; Rochester Mus, NY; Dallas Mus of Fine Arts, TX; Indianapolis Mus of Art, IN; Georgia Art Mus, Athens, GA; Middle Tennessee State Univ, Murfreesboro, TN; Neuberger Mus, Purchase, NY; Weatherspoon Art Gallery, Univ of North Carolina, Greensboro, NC
PRINTERS: Artist (ART)
PUBLISHERS: Artist (ART)
GALLERIES: Gloria Luria Gallery, Bay Harbor Island, Miami, FL; Galleria IL Ponte, Rome, Italy
MAILING ADDRESS: Piazza del Biscione 95, Interno 4, Rome, 00186, Italy

TITLE	PUBLISHER	PRINTER	DATE	MEDIUM	DIMENSION (PAPER SIZE) IN INCHES	TYPE OF PAPER	EDITION NUMBER	NO. OF COLORS	ORIGINAL OPENING PRICE	CURRENT RETAIL PRICE
SOLD OUT EDITIONS (RARE):										
Leong at Cerberus	ART	ART	1969	LC	32 X 24	AP	150	5	25	200
Reflects	ART	ART	1970	LC	24 X 32	AP	150	4	50	150
Cracked Sky	ART	ART	1974	LC	15 X 11	AP	40	4	·65	300
CURRENT EDITIONS:										
Ripple Tank	ART	ART	1969	SP/PLEX	16 X 20 X 1	AP	50	2	75	300
Channel	ART	ART	1972	LC	14 X 17	AP	55	3	65	150

MARK LERE

BORN: La Moure, ND; May 13, 1950
EDUCATION: Metropolitan State Col, Denver, CO, BFA, 1973; Univ of California, Irvine, CA, MFA, 1976
AWARDS: Nat Endowment for the Arts Fel, Visual Arts, 1984; Nat Endowment for the Arts Fel, Sculpture, 1988
RECENT EXHIB: Los Angeles County Mus of Art, CA, 1987; Margo Leavin Gallery, Los Angeles, CA; Santa Barbara Mus of Art, CA, 1988; North Dakota Mus of Art, Grand Forks, ND, 1989–90; Art Center Col of Design, Pasadena, CA, 1992; John Berggruen Gallery, San Francisco, CA, 1992
COLLECTIONS: Mus of Mod Art, NY; Los Angeles County Mus, CA; Mus of Contemp Art, Los Angeles, CA
PRINTERS: Cirrus Editions Workshop, Los Angeles, CA (CEW); Francesco Siqueiros, Los Angeles, CA (FS); Robert Dansby, Los Angeles, CA (RD)
PUBLISHERS: Cirrus Editions Ltd, Los Angeles, CA (CE)
GALLERIES: Cirrus Gallery, Los Angeles, CA; Margo Leavin Gallery, Los Angeles, CA; Mary Ryan Gallery, New York, NY; John Berggruen Gallery, San Francisco, CA
MAILING ADDRESS: 2447 N Claremont Ave, Los Angeles, CA 90027

TITLE	PUBLISHER	PRINTER	DATE	MEDIUM	DIMENSION (PAPER SIZE) IN INCHES	TYPE OF PAPER	EDITION NUMBER	NO. OF COLORS	ORIGINAL OPENING PRICE	CURRENT RETAIL PRICE
CURRENT EDITIONS:										
Dowzey Fountain	CE	CEW	1980	LC/HC	23 X 30	AP	30	Varies	300	500
Cowl	CE	CEW	1986	LC	43 X 36	AP88	30	4	950	1200
Gullet	CE	CEW	1986	LC	43 X 36	AP88	30	4	950	1200
Spindle	CE	CEW	1986	LC	43 X 36	AP88	30	4	950	1200
Mylar Edition	CE	CEW	1986	LC	43 X 36	AP88	10	4	950	1400
Rope (Trial Proofs)	CE	CEW	1986	LC	43 X 36 EA	AP88	1 EA		1200 EA	1500 EA
Shadow #1,#2,#3, (Set of 3)	CE	FS/RD/CEW	1989	LC	60 X 40 EA	AP88	35 EA	8 EA	2700 SET	5400 SET
									900 EA	1800 EA

LESLIE LERNER

PRINTERS: Jill Livermore, San Francisco, CA (JL); Limestone Press, San Francisco, CA (LPr)
PUBLISHERS: Limestone Press, San Francisco, CA (LPr); Janet Steinberg Gallery, San Francisco, CA (JSG)
GALLERIES: Janet Steinberg Gallery, San Francisco, CA; Rena Bransten Gallery, San Francisco, CA; Roger Ramsay Gallery, Chicago, IL

TITLE	PUBLISHER	PRINTER	DATE	MEDIUM	DIMENSION (PAPER SIZE) IN INCHES	TYPE OF PAPER	EDITION NUMBER	NO. OF COLORS	ORIGINAL OPENING PRICE	CURRENT RETAIL PRICE
CURRENT EDITIONS:										
My Life in France: The Theater (Set of 5)	LPr/JSG	JL/LPr	1987	EB/A/HG/SG	14 X 9 EA	GE	25 EA		600 SET	1000 SET

The print market has become very selective. For the first time since we published the first edition of The Printworld Directory in 1982, the prices of prints have been greatly reduced and greatly increased for the same artists by the most reputable and established print publishers. Check the fifth edition to understand the movement.

ALFRED LESLIE

BORN: New York, NY; 1927
EDUCATION: New York Univ, NY, 1956–57
RECENT EXHIB: Vanderwoude Tananbaum Gallery, NY, 1987; Flynn Gallery, NY, 1991; Univ of Hartford, Joseloff Gallery, West Harford, CT, 1992
PRINTERS: Landfall Press, Inc, Chicago, IL (LPI); David Kiester, Chicago, IL (DK); Jack Lemon, Chicago, IL (JL); Patrick Foy, Tampa, FL (PF); Graphicstudio, Univ of South Florida, Tampa, FL (GS); Kathy Kuehn, NY (KK); Joe Wilfer, NY (JW); Ruth Lingen, NY (RL); Spring Street Workshop, NY (SprSW)

PUBLISHERS: Landfall Press, Inc, Chicago, IL (LPI); Graphicstudio, Univ of South Florida, Tampa, FL (GS); Artist (ART); Spring Street Workshop, NY (SprSW)
GALLERIES: Oil & Steel, Long Island City, NY; Adler Gallery, Los Angeles, CA; Hill Gallery, Birmingham, MI; Claude Bernard Gallery, New York, NY; Vanderwoude/Tananbaum Gallery, New York, NY; Manny Silverman Gallery, Los Angeles, CA; Edward Tyler Nahem Fine Art, New York, NY; Sharon Truax Fine Art, Venice, CA; Lemberg Gallery, Birmingham, MI; Flynn Gallery, New York, Ny; Stiebel Modern, New York, NY; Landfall Press, Inc, Chicago, IL; Pace Prints, New York, NY

TITLE	PUBLISHER	PRINTER	DATE	MEDIUM	DIMENSION (PAPER SIZE) IN INCHES	TYPE OF PAPER	EDITION NUMBER	NO. OF COLORS	ORIGINAL OPENING PRICE	CURRENT RETAIL PRICE
SOLD OUT EDITIONS (RARE):										
Alfred Leslie	LPI	DK/LPI	1974	LC	40 X 30	AP/W	50	1	600	2500
Connie Suite (Set of 5):									3000 SET	12500 SET
Connie with Milk	LPI	JL/LPI	1976	LC	40 X 30	AP/W	20	1	600	2500
Connie with Baby	LPI	JL/LPI	1976	LC	40 X 30	AP/W	20	1	600	2500
Connie with Baby Nursing	LPI	JL/LPI	1976	LC	40 X 30	AP/W	20	1	600	2500
Connie with Nursing Bra	LPI	JL/LPI	1976	LC	40 X 30	AP/W	30	1	600	2500
Connie with Book	LPI	JL/LPI	1976	LC	40 X 30	AP/W	20	1	600	2500
CURRENT EDITIONS:										
Richard Bellamy	LPI	DK/LPI	1974	LC	40 X 30	AP/W	50	2	600	2500
Frank Fata	LPI	DK/LPI	1974	LC	40 X 30	AP/W	50	1	600	2500
Folded Constance Pregnant	ART/GS	PF/GS	1985–86	EB/SG	97 X 74	THS	30	1	14000	18000
Montauk (Set of 3)	SprSW	KK/SprSW	1991	EB/A	17 X 17 EA	OKP	50 EA		2200 SET	2200 SET
Near David's Fields (Set of 2)	SprSW	KK/SprSW	1991	EB/A	17 X 17 EA	OKP	50 EA		1500 SET / 800 EA	1500 SET / 800 EA
Outside Blue Water, Again (Set of 3)	SprSW	JW/RL/SprSW	1991	EB/A	21 X 25 EA	OKP	50 EA		3000 SET / 1200 EA	3000 SET / 1200 EA
Hugh	SprSW	JW/RL/SprSW	1992	EB	70 X 46	OKP	20	1	4500	4500
Malena	SprSW	JW/RL/SprSW	1992	EB	70 X 46	OKP	20	1	4500	4500
Malena (Hand Colored)	SprSW	JW/RL/SprSW	1992	EB/A/SG/HC	50 X 39	OKP	20		5000	5000
Self Portrait	SprSW	JW/RL/SprSW	1992	EB/A/SG	50 X 39	OKP	20		3500	3500
Rainbow over Hadley, MA (Set of 2)	SprSW	JW/RL/SprSW	1992	EB/A	25 X 31 EA	OKP	20 EA		2500 SET / 1500 EA	2500 SET / 1500 EA

JULIAN LETHBRIDGE

PRINTERS: Lorena Salcedo-Watson, West Islip, NY (LSW); Douglas Volle, West Islip, NY (DV); Universal Limited Art Editions, West Islip, NY (ULAE)

PUBLISHERS: Universal Limited Art Editions, West Islip, NY (ULAE)
GALLERIES: Paula Cooper Gallery, New York, NY; Thomas Smith Fine Art, Fort Wayne, IN; Stuart Regen Gallery, Los Angeles, CA

TITLE	PUBLISHER	PRINTER	DATE	MEDIUM	DIMENSION (PAPER SIZE) IN INCHES	TYPE OF PAPER	EDITION NUMBER	NO. OF COLORS	ORIGINAL OPENING PRICE	CURRENT RETAIL PRICE
CURRENT EDITIONS:										
Access	ULAE	LSW/DV/ULAE	1992	LC/SP	26 X 19	TOR	50	4	1000	1000

JOSEPH LETITIA

BORN: New Britain, CT; 1960
EDUCATION: Mus of Fine Arts, Tufts Univ, Boston, MA, BS Ed, 1984; Nova Scotia Col of Art & Design, Can, 1985; Mus of Fine Arts, Boston, MA, 1986; Yale Univ, New Haven, CT, MFA, 1986
AWARDS: Boston Sch of Mus of Fine Arts, MA, 1981,83,85,86; Travelling Fel, Boston Sch of Mus of Fine Arts, MA, 1986; Yale Univ, New Haven, CT, Scholarship, 1986

RECENT EXHIB: Judi Rotenburg Gallery, Boston, MA, 1987; WET Gallery, Boston, MA, 1987
PRINTERS: Herbert A Fox, Merrimac, MA (HF) Fox Graphics, Merrimac, MA (FG)
PUBLISHERS: Fox Graphics, Merrimac, MA (FG); Merrimac Editions, Merrimac, MA (MerEd); Artist (ART)
GALLERIES: Fox Graphics, Merrimac, MA

TITLE	PUBLISHER	PRINTER	DATE	MEDIUM	DIMENSION (PAPER SIZE) IN INCHES	TYPE OF PAPER	EDITION NUMBER	NO. OF COLORS	ORIGINAL OPENING PRICE	CURRENT RETAIL PRICE
CURRENT EDITIONS:										
No Love Lost	ART/FG	HF/FG	1987	LB	60 X 42	AC	6	1	700	750
Bambino Delle Rose	ART/FG	HF/FG	1987	WB/LC	40 X 30	R/BFK	60	2	350	400

The retail prices of the 100,000 limited edition prints quoted in this directory are subject to change. Print publishers, artists and galleries were the direct sources for these quotations. Prices in the secondary market listed as "Sold Out Editions (Rare)" indicate that the publisher has a limited supply of that print or that the print is difficult to locate in the galleries.

The Printworld Directory is accepting new applications for the seventh edition. Approximately 300 new artists will be accepted. Please use the two forms provided in the back section of this directory to submit biographical data and documentation of prints. Edition number of each print must not exceed 500 and the retail price must be $100 or more.

JOSEF LEVI

BORN: New York, NY; February 17, 1938
EDUCATION: Univ of Connecticut, Storrs, CT, BA, 1959; Columbia Univ, NY, 1960
TEACHING: Art in Res, Appalachian State Univ, Boone, NC, 1969; Art in Res, Pennsylvania State Univ, University Park, PA, 1976
AWARDS: Purchase Award, Univ of Illinois, Urbana, IL, 1966; Selection, New Talent, USA, Art in America, NY, 1966
RECENT EXHIB: Oklahoma Art Center, Oklahoma City, OK, 1988; O K Harris Gallery, NY, 1987,90,92
COLLECTIONS: Mus of Mod Art, NY; Albright-Knox Mus, Buffalo, NY; Aldrich Mus of Contemp Art, Ridgefield, CT; Des Moines Art Center, IA; Krannert Art Mus, Univ of Illinois, Urbana, IL; J B Speed Art Mus, Louisville, KY; Corcoran Gallery of Art, Wash, DC; Virginia Mus of Fine Arts, Richmond, VA; Dartmouth Col, Hanover, NH
PRINTERS: La Salle (LS); John Nichols, Inc, NY (JN)
PUBLISHERS: Sienna Press, Inc, NY (SP); John Nichols, NY (JN); Master Editions, NY (ME); Eleanor Ettinger, NY (EE)
GALLERIES: John Nichols, New York, NY; O K Harris Gallery, New York, NY; Adams Middleton Gallery, Dallas, TX
MAILING ADDRESS: 171 West 71st St, New York, NY 10023

TITLE	PUBLISHER	PRINTER	DATE	MEDIUM	DIMENSION (PAPER SIZE) IN INCHES	TYPE OF PAPER	EDITION NUMBER	NO. OF COLORS	ORIGINAL OPENING PRICE	CURRENT RETAIL PRICE
SOLD OUT EDITIONS (RARE):										
Still Life with the Artist Francesco d'Este	JN	JN	1978	SP	24 X 29	AP	140	4	300	400
Still Life with Matisse (Red Studio)	JN	JN	1978	SP	29 X 29	AP	75	4	300	400
Still Life with Matisse (White Studio)	JN	JN	1978	SP	29 X 29	AP	75	4	300	400
Still Life with Ghirlandaio, Giovanna, Gail	LAI	LS	1978	SP	38 X 38	AP	300	5	200	400
Still Life with the Artist as a Bronzino	LAI	LS	1978	SP	32 X 40	AP	300	6	200	400
Still Life with Titian and Paladino	LAI	LS	1979	LB/MM/MEZ	21 X 24	AP	175	4	700	1200
Still Life with Cezanne and Caravaggio	LAI	LS	1979	LB/MM/MEZ	22 X 24	AP	175	4	700	1200
Still Life with Pisanello	LAI	LS	1979	SP/SB/MM	21 X 25	AP	175	9	700	1200
Still Life with Zurbaran	LAI	LS	1979	LB/MM/MEZ	21 X 22	AP	175	4	700	1200
Still Life with Hans Maler	LAI	LS	1979	SP/SB/MM	22 X 22	AP	175	8	700	900
Still Life with German Master	LAI	LS	1979	SP/SB/MM	22 X 26	AP	175	8	700	900
Still Life with Utamaro	LAI	LS	1979	SP/SB/MM	22 X 30	AP	175	7	700	1200
Still Life with Rae as a Cranach Venus	LAI	LS	1980	LC	20 X 30	AP	250	4	200	400
Still Life with Gail as Queen Elizabeth I	LAI	LS	1980	LC	21 X 24	AP	250	4	200	400

ERIK LEVINE

BORN: Los Angeles, CA; October 31, 1960
EDUCATION: California State Univ, Northridge, CA, 1980,81; Univ of California, Los Angeles, CA, 1982
RECENT EXHIB: Louisiana Mus of Mod Art, Humlelbaek, Denmark, 1989; Fundacio Joan Miro, Barcelona, Spain, 1989; Halle Sud, Geneva, Switzerland, 1989; Brandts Klaedelfabrik, Odense, Denmark, 1989; Meyers/Bloom Gallery, Santa Monica, CA, 1990; Diane Brown Gallery, NY, 1988,89,90
COLLECTIONS: Albright-Knox Art Gallery, Buffalo, NY; New Mus of Contemp Art, Geneva, Switzerland; High Mus of Art, Atlanta, GA; Louisiana Mus of Mod Art, Humlelbaek, Denmark; Walker Art Center, Minneapolis, MN
PRINTERS: Joe Wilfer, NY (JW); Ruth Lingen, NY (RL); Spring Street Workshop, NY (SprSW)
PUBLISHERS: Spring Street Workshop, NY (SprSW)
GALLERIES: Pace Prints, New York, NY; Diane Brown Gallery, New York, NY; Meyers/Bloom Gallery, Santa Monica, CA

TITLE	PUBLISHER	PRINTER	DATE	MEDIUM	DIMENSION (PAPER SIZE) IN INCHES	TYPE OF PAPER	EDITION NUMBER	NO. OF COLORS	ORIGINAL OPENING PRICE	CURRENT RETAIL PRICE
CURRENT EDITIONS:										
Fullerene A, B, C (Set of 3)	SprSW	JW/RL/SprSW	1991	EB	40 X 25 EA	OKP	25 EA	1 EA	1200 SET / 500 EA	1200 SET / 500

LES LEVINE

BORN: Dublin, Ireland; October 6, 1935; US Citizen
TEACHING: Art In Res, Aspen Inst, CO, 1967–69; Assoc Prof, New York Univ, NY, 1972; William Patterson Col, Wayne, NJ, 1974–75
AWARDS: Nat Endowment for the Arts Fel, 1974,80; New York State Council for the Arts, Video Award, 1980
RECENT EXHIB: Jewish Mus, NY, 1987; Mus of Mod Art, NY, 1988; Mai 36 Gallery, Luzern, Switzerland, 1988; New York Found for the Arts, NY, 1989; Everson Mus, Syracuse, NY, 1990
COLLECTIONS: Nat Gallery of Canada, Ottawa, Canada; Metropolitan Mus, NY; Whitney Mus of Am Art, NY; Mus of Mod Art, NY; Philadelphia Mus of Art, PA
PRINTERS: Outdoor Posters, Ltd, Knoxville, TN (OPL); GEM Screen Printing, NY (GSP); Herbert Okoskin, NY (HO)
PUBLISHERS: Ted Greenwald Gallery, NY (TG); Elizabeth Galasso Editions, Ossining, NY (EGE)
GALLERIES: Isaacs Gallery, Toronto, Canada; Michael Lowe Gallery, Cincinnati, OH; Carl Solway Gallery, Cincinnati, OH
MAILING ADDRESS: 20 E 20th St, New York, NY 10003

TITLE	PUBLISHER	PRINTER	DATE	MEDIUM	DIMENSION (PAPER SIZE) IN INCHES	TYPE OF PAPER	EDITION NUMBER	NO. OF COLORS	ORIGINAL OPENING PRICE	CURRENT RETAIL PRICE
CURRENT EDITIONS:										
Home Billboards (Set of 10): Appeal, Convey, Go, Model, Plant, Pull, Relax, Shed, Steer, Win	TG	OPL	1984	SP	59 X 51 EA	WPBB	13 EA		6000 SET / 700 EA	8500 SET / 850 EA
Crazy Wisdoms B (Relax, Plant, Watch & Set) (Set of 4)	EGE	HO/GSP	1986	SP/COMP	19 X 40 EA	RAG II	49 EA	11 EA	3000 SET / 750 EA	3200 SET / 800 EA

LES LEVINE CONTINUED

TITLE	PUBLISHER	PRINTER	DATE	MEDIUM	DIMENSION (PAPER SIZE) IN INCHES	TYPE OF PAPER	EDITION NUMBER	NO. OF COLORS	ORIGINAL OPENING PRICE	CURRENT RETAIL PRICE
CURRENT EDITIONS:										
Crazy Wisdoms Z (Form, Reflect & Light) (Set of 3)	EGE	HO/GSP	1986	SP/COMP	19 X 40 EA	RAG II	49 EA	11 EA	2250 SET 750 EA	2400 SET 800 EA

JACK LEVINE

BORN: Boston, MA; January 3, 1915
EDUCATION: Harvard Univ, 1929–31; Harvard Univ, Cambridge, MA, with Dr Denman W Ross, 1929–31; Studied with Harold Zimmerman; Colby Col, Waterville, ME, Hon DFA, 1946
TEACHING: Lectr, Cleveland Mus Art Sch, OH, 1950; Lectr, Skowhegan Sch of Painting & Sculpture, ME, 1956; Lectr, Pennsylvania Acad of Fine Arts, Phila, PA, 1966–69; Lectr, Univ of Illinois, Urbana, IL; Lectr, Art Inst of Chicago, IL
AWARDS: Guggenheim Fel, 1945,46; Pennsylvania Acad of Fine Arts Award, 1948; Corcoran Gallery of Art Award, 1959; Altman Prize, Nat Acad of Design, NY, 1975
RECENT EXHIB: Charles H MacNider Mus, Mason City, IA, 1989; Mus of Art, Ogunquit, ME, 1989; Jewish Mus, NY, 1990; Midtown Gallery, NY 1990; Illinois State Univ, Normal, IL, 1992
COLLECTIONS: Metropolitan Mus of Art, NY; Mus of Mod Art, NY; Whitney Mus of Am Art, NY; Boston Mus of Fine Arts, Boston, MA; Walker Art Center, Minneapolis, MN; Art Inst of Chicago, IL
PRINTERS: Herbert A Fox, Merrimac, MA (HF); Merrimac Editions, Merrimac, MA (MaEd); Artist (ART)
PUBLISHERS: Kennedy Graphics, Inc, NY (KG); Horn Editions, NY (HE); Artist (ART)
GALLERIES: Kennedy Graphics, New York, NY; Foster Harmon Galleries of American Art, Sarasota, FL; Midtown-Payson Galleries, New York, NY; Michael Rosenfield Gallery, New York, NY; American Scene Gallery, Sarasota, FL; Stein Bartlow Gallery, Ltd, Chicago, IL; Zolla/Lieberman Gallery, Chicago, IL
MAILING ADDRESS: 68 Morton St, New York, NY 10014

Jack Levine
Thought
Courtesy Kennedy Graphics, Inc

TITLE	PUBLISHER	PRINTER	DATE	MEDIUM	DIMENSION (PAPER SIZE) IN INCHES	TYPE OF PAPER	EDITION NUMBER	NO. OF COLORS	ORIGINAL OPENING PRICE	CURRENT RETAIL PRICE
SOLD OUT EDITIONS (RARE):										
The Spanish General	KG	ART	1962	EB/A	20 X 24	R/BFK	100	1	250	2000
Ashkenazi II	KG	ART	1964	EB/DPT	21 X 15	R/BFK	100	1	250	1000
Love, Careless Love	KG	ART	1965	EB/A	22 X 30	R/BFK	100	1	250	1800
El Greco	KG	ART	1966	EB/DPT	20 X 13	IT	100	1	250	1000
Prussian General	KG	ART	1966	EB/DPT	22 X 15	R/BFK	100	1	250	500
Double Eagle	ART	ART	1966	LB	10 X 8	R/BFK	120	1	250	400
Maimonides	KG	ART	1967	LB	27 X 21	AP	100	1	200	1000
The Art Lover	KG	ART	1968	LC	26 X 19	AP	100	1	250	900
Blue Angel	KG	ART	1968	LC	21 X 27	AP	120	5	250	1200
Gangsters Funeral	KG	ART	1968	ENG	25 X 35	R/BFK	120	1	200	2000
At the Ball	ART	ART	1968	EB	5 X 7	R/BFK	100	1	200	500
Warsaw Ghetto	ART	ART	1969	LB	19 X 25	AP	120	1	200	400
Cain and Abel	KG	ART	1969	LB	30 X 23	R/BFK	125	1	200	900
Texas Delegate	KG	ART	1970	LB	22 X 28	AP	120	1	200	900
The Feast of Pure Reason	KG	ART	1971	EB	26 X 32	R/BFK	120	1	300	2800
Thought	KG	ART	1972	LB	39 X 26	AP	100	1	300	2800
Hong Kong Tailor	KG	ART	1972	EB/DPT	13 X 11	R/BFK	100	1	300	800
Sacrifice of Isaac	KG	ART	1974	EB	22 X 15	R/BFK	100	1	350	1200
Shammai	KG	ART	1975	EB/DPT	28 X 23	R/BFK	100	1	400	1000
Head of David	KG	ART	1977	LB	22 X 15	AP	100	1	450	600
Silent Eulogy	HE	ART	1978	LC	54 X 25	AP	150	1	500	800
Requiem	KG		1979	LB	41 X 29	AP	150	1	500	1200
Sweet Bye and Bye	KG	ART	1980	EB/DPT/MEZ	15 X 21	R/BFK	100	1	500	1000
Lion of Praque	KG	ART	1982	EB/A	21 X 15	R/BFK	100	1	600	1200
Kronos	KG	ART	1983	LB		AP	50	1	450	800
Rabbi in White	KG	ART	1983	LB		AP	50	1	650	900
Solomon and David	ART	HF/MeEd	1987	LB	36 X 25	AC	40	1	850	1200

MARION LERNER LEVINE

BORN: London, England
EDUCATION: Sch of the Art Inst of Chicago, IL, BFA
TEACHING: Instr, Watercolor, Brooklyn Col, NY, 1976–80; Instr, Drawing & Painting, Col of Staten Island, NY, 1981–82
AWARDS: Award, Am Acad & Inst of Arts & Letters, NY, 1980; Adolph & Esther Gottlieb Found Grant, Painting, 1981; Creative Artists Public Service Fel, Painting, New York State Council on the Arts, 1983; Nat Endowment for the Arts Fel, Painting, 1986
RECENT EXHIB: Katharina Rich Perlow Gallery, NY, 1986–87; Butler Inst of Am Art, Youngstown, OH 1987; Prince Street Gallery, NY, 1992
COLLECTIONS: Brooklyn Mus, NY; McNay Art Inst, San Antonio TX; US State Dept, Wash, DC
PRINTERS: Bruce Cleveland, Brooklyn, NY (BC), Cleveland Editions, Brooklyn, NY (ClEd); Joe Essig, Brooklyn, NY (JE); March Press, Brooklyn, NY (MP); Artist (ART)
PUBLISHERS: Orion Editions, NY (OE); Artist (ART)
GALLERIES: Orion Editions, New York, NY; Judith Litvich Gallery, San Francisco, CA; Prince Street Gallery, New York, NY
MAILING ADDRESS: 359 Sixth Ave, Brooklyn, NY 11215

Marion Lerner Levine
Zinnia Reflections
Courtesy the Artist

Marion Lerner Levine
From a Place of Delight
Courtesy the Artist

TITLE	PUBLISHER	PRINTER	DATE	MEDIUM	DIMENSION (PAPER SIZE) IN INCHES	TYPE OF PAPER	EDITION NUMBER	NO. OF COLORS	ORIGINAL OPENING PRICE	CURRENT RETAIL PRICE
CURRENT EDITIONS:										
Garden Flowers in Color	OE	BC/ClEd	1985–86	EC/A/SG/HC	29 X 41	AC	60	2	550	850
Garden Flowers in Color II	OE	BC/ClEd	1985–86	EC	29 X 41	AC	6	1	350	450
A Rose Annual	OE	BC/ClEd	1985–86	EC/A/HC	29 X 41	AC	60	2	600	850
A Rose Annual II	OE	BC/ClEd	1985–86	EC	29 X 41	AC	6	1	350	450
White Ribbon	ART	BC/ClEd	1986	EC/A	14 X 20	AC	25	3	175	250
White Ribbon II	ART	BC/ClEd	1986	EC/A	14 X 20	R/BFK	25	3	175	250
Rose Willow	OE	JE/MP	1988	EC/A/HC	36 X 48	AC	75	10	750	850
Blue Willow Journey	OE	JE/MP	1988	SP	36 X 48	EC/A/HC	75	10	750	850
Zinnia Reflections	OE	JE/MP	1989	EB/HC	32 X 38	AC	60	6	750	750
Suite of Two (Set of 2):									750 SET	750 SET
Cherries and Blue Ribbons	ART	ART	1991	EC/A	22 X 26	AC	20	3	400	400
Daffadils	ART	ART	1991	EC/A	22 X 26	AC	20	3	400	400
From a Place of Delight	OE	JE/MP	1992	EC/A/HC	29 X 41	AC	60	4	750	750

TOM LEVINE

BORN: New York, NY; March 24, 1945
EDUCATION: City Col of New York, NY, BA, 1966; Brooklyn Col, NY, MFA, 1974
AWARDS: Yaddo Fel, 1984; Virginia City for Creative Arts, 1985; Cummington Com Arts, 1991
RECENT EXHIB: Deutsch-Amerikanisches Inst, Municipal Gallery, Regensburg, Germany, 1988–89
PRINTERS: Maurice Payne, NY (MP)
PUBLISHERS: Parasol Press, NY (PaP)
MAILING ADDRESS: 191 Claremont Ave, #43, New York, NY 10027

TITLE	PUBLISHER	PRINTER	DATE	MEDIUM	DIMENSION (PAPER SIZE) IN INCHES	TYPE OF PAPER	EDITION NUMBER	NO. OF COLORS	ORIGINAL OPENING PRICE	CURRENT RETAIL PRICE
CURRENT EDITIONS:										
More Sardines (Set of 22)	PaP	MP	1991	EB/DPT/SG/CC	14 X 14 EA	SOM	12 EA	1 EA	4500 SET	4500 SET

The retail prices of the 100,000 limited edition prints quoted in this directory are subject to change. Print publishers, artists and galleries were the direct sources for these quotations. Prices in the secondary market listed as "Sold Out Editions (Rare)" indicate that the publisher has a limited supply of that print or that the print is difficult to locate in the galleries.

SHERRIE LEVINE

BORN: 1947
EDUCATION: Univ of Wisconsin, Madison, WI, BA, 1969, MFA 1973
RECENT EXHIB: Whitney Mus of Am Art, NY, 1989; Mary Boone Gallery, NY, 1987,91; Univ of Oklahoma Mus, Norman, OK, 1992
COLLECTIONS: Northwestern Univ, Evanston, IL; De Saisset Art Mus, Santa Clara, CA
PRINTERS: Maurice Sanchez, NY (MS); James Miller, NY (JM); Derriére L'Etoile Studios, NY (DES); Crown Point Press, San Francisco, CA (CPP)
PUBLISHERS: Editions Ilene Kurtz, Inc, NY (ELK); Peter Blum Edition, NY (PBE); Crown Point Press, San Francisco, CA (CPP)
GALLERIES: Editions Ilene Kurtz, Inc, New York, NY; Daniel Weinberg Gallery, Santa Monica, CA; Barbara Krakow Gallery, Boston, MA; Mary Boone Gallery, New York, NY; Donald Young Gallery, Seattle, WA; Simon Watson Gallery, New York, NY; Richard Kuhlenschmidt Gallery, Los Angeles, CA; Crown Point Press, San Francisco, CA & New York, NY

 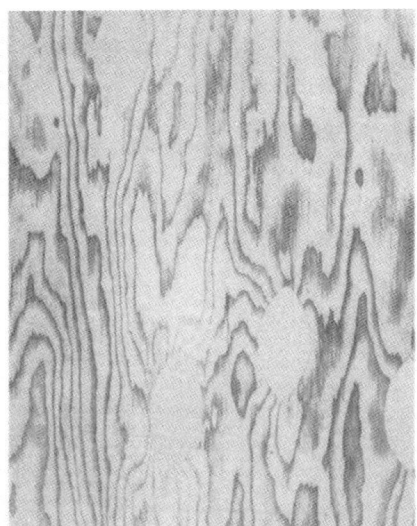 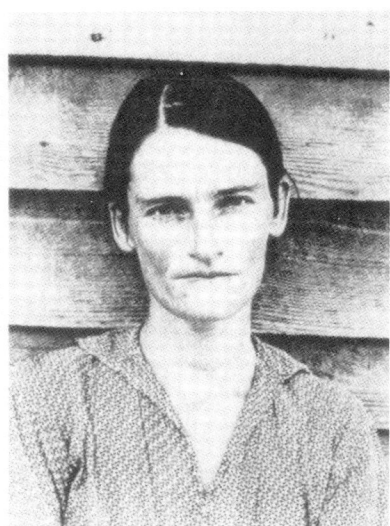

Sherrie Levine
From Barcham Green Portfolio
Courtesy Crown Point Press

TITLE	PUBLISHER	PRINTER	DATE	MEDIUM	DIMENSION (PAPER SIZE) IN INCHES	TYPE OF PAPER	EDITION NUMBER	NO. OF COLORS	ORIGINAL OPENING PRICE	CURRENT RETAIL PRICE
SOLD OUT EDITIONS (RARE):										
Barcham Green Portfolio, #4, #5	CPP	CPP	1986	PH/EB/A	31 X 23 EA	JBG	25 EA	1 EA	500 EA	1600 EA
CURRENT EDITIONS:										
Barcham Green Portfolio, #1, #2, #3	CPP	CPP	1986	EB/A	31 X 23 EA	JBG	25 EA	1 EA	500 EA	1600 EA
After Edgar Degas (Set of 5)	EIK	MS/JM/DES	1987	PH/LC	26 X 21 EA	RKP/HWT	35 EA		2500 SET	6000 SET
Meltdown (Set of 4)	PBE	MS/JM/DES	1989	WC	36 X 25 EA	KOZO	35 EA		6500 SET	8000 SET

MON LEVINSON

BORN: New York, NY; January 6, 1926
TEACHING: Long Island Univ, C W Post Col, Greenvale, NY, 1970–72, 1976–77
AWARDS: Cassandra Found Award, 1972; Creative Artists Public Service Program Award, New York State Council of Arts, NY, 1974; Nat Endowment for the Arts Fel, 1976
RECENT EXHIB: Andre Zarre Gallery, NY, 1989
COLLECTIONS: Whitney Mus of Am Art, NY; Joseph H Hirshhorn Mus, Wash, DC; New York Univ Art Coll; Rose Art Gallery, Brandeis Univ, Waltham, MA; Brooklyn Mus, NY; Albright-Knox Gallery, Buffalo, NY
PRINTERS: Bill Hall, NY (BH); Printmaking Workshop, NY (PW)
PUBLISHERS: Artist (ART)
GALLERIES: Lorence Monk Gallery, New York, NY; Andre Zarre Gallery, New York, NY; Fridholm Fine Arts Gallery, Asheville, NC
MAILING ADDRESS: 309 W Broadway, New York, NY 10013

TITLE	PUBLISHER	PRINTER	DATE	MEDIUM	DIMENSION (PAPER SIZE) IN INCHES	TYPE OF PAPER	EDITION NUMBER	NO. OF COLORS	ORIGINAL OPENING PRICE	CURRENT RETAIL PRICE
CURRENT EDITIONS:										
Doorway	ART	BH/PW	1986	REL	22 X 26	R/BFK	5	1	700	750
Doorway-Black Version	ART	BH/PW	1986	REL	22 X 26	AP	5	1	700	750

BENJAMIN LEVY

PRINTERS: American Atelier, NY (AA)
PUBLISHERS: Circle Fine Art, Chicago, IL (CFA)
GALLERIES: Circle Galleries, San Diego, CA & San Francisco, CA & Northbrook, IL & Pittsburgh, PA & Houston, TX & Soho, NY & Chicago, IL & Scottsdale, AZ & Beverly Hills, CA & Costa Mesa, CA & Sherman Oaks, CA & Honolulu, HI & Palm Beach, FL & New Orleans, LA & Las Vegas, NV & Seattle, WA

TITLE	PUBLISHER	PRINTER	DATE	MEDIUM	DIMENSION (PAPER SIZE) IN INCHES	TYPE OF PAPER	EDITION NUMBER	NO. OF COLORS	ORIGINAL OPENING PRICE	CURRENT RETAIL PRICE
SOLD OUT EDITIONS (RARE):										
Couple with Fox	CFA	AA	1982	LC	24 X 22	AP	250		125	250
Silhouette	CFA	AA	1982	SP	22 X 27	AP	250		125	250

BENJAMIN LEVY CONTINUED

TITLE	PUBLISHER	PRINTER	DATE	MEDIUM	DIMENSION (PAPER SIZE) IN INCHES	TYPE OF PAPER	EDITION NUMBER	NO. OF COLORS	ORIGINAL OPENING PRICE	CURRENT RETAIL PRICE
CURRENT EDITIONS:										
The Hunter	CFA	AA	1982	LC	22 X 29	AP	250		125	250
Man with Bird	CFA	AA	1982	SP	24 X 29	AP	300		125	250

DOUGLAS LEW

BORN: Shanghai, China; 1933
EDUCATION: Bradley Univ, Peoria, IL, BFA, MA
AWARDS: Merit Award, Southwest Artists, 1973; North Star's Award of Excellence, 1978; First Place, Watercolor, North Star Watercolor Soc, 1982
PRINTERS: Land Mark Editions, Minneapolis, MN (LME)
PUBLISHERS: C G Rein Publishers, St Paul, MN (CGR)
GALLERIES: C G Rein Galleries, Scottsdale, AZ & Santa Fe, NM & Houston, TX & Minneapolis, MN

TITLE	PUBLISHER	PRINTER	DATE	MEDIUM	DIMENSION (PAPER SIZE) IN INCHES	TYPE OF PAPER	EDITION NUMBER	NO. OF COLORS	ORIGINAL OPENING PRICE	CURRENT RETAIL PRICE
CURRENT EDITIONS:										
A Breeze at Last	CGR	LME	1984	LC	28 X 20	RP/HWT	100	13	350	400
The Drive	CGR	LME	1984	LC	21 X 29	RP/HWT	100	12	350	400
The Back Hand	CGR	LME	1984	LC	22 X 29	RP/HWT	100	13	350	400

JEFFEREY LEW

BORN: New York, 1946
EDUCATION: Nat Acad of Design, NY, 1965; Boston Mus Sch, Tuft Univ, MA, 1966–68
AWARDS: Rockefeller Travel Fel, 1972; Nat Endowment for the Arts Fel, 1972, 76
PRINTERS: Patricia Branstead, NY (PB); Aeropress, Inc, NY (A)
PUBLISHERS: Multiples Inc, NY (M)
GALLERIES: Marian Goodman Gallery, New York, NY

TITLE	PUBLISHER	PRINTER	DATE	MEDIUM	DIMENSION (PAPER SIZE) IN INCHES	TYPE OF PAPER	EDITION NUMBER	NO. OF COLORS	ORIGINAL OPENING PRICE	CURRENT RETAIL PRICE
SOLD OUT EDITIONS (RARE):										
Eight	M	PB/A	1979	LC	27 X 35	HMP	275		275	600
Four Books of Articulation	M	PB/A	1979	LC	36 X 28	HMP	275		275	600
Lying Books	M	PB/A	1979	LC	28 X 39	HMP	275		275	600
Read Color	M	PB/A	1979	LC	28 X 40	HMP	275		275	600
CURRENT EDITIONS:										
Open Book	M	PB/A	1980	AC/SG	31 X 42	HMP	50		750	900

WEYMAN LEW

BORN: San Francisco, CA; February 17, 1935
EDUCATION: Univ of California, Berkeley, CA, BS, 1957; San Francisco Art Inst, CA, 1965–66
TEACHING: Guest Lectr, Painting, Drawing & Serigraphy, M H de Young Mem Mus, San Francisco, CA, 1970–71
AWARDS: Merit Award, San Francisco Art Festival, CA, 1980; Distinguished Award for Culture, The Chinese Culture Found, San Francisco, CA, 1991
RECENT EXHIB: International Arts Exhib Hall, Beijing, China, 1991; Chinese Culture Center, San Francisco, CA, 1991
COLLECTIONS: Brooklyn Mus, NY; Oakland Mus, CA; MH de Young Mem Mus, San Francisco, CA; Univ of California, Berkeley, CA; Achenbach Found, San Francisco, CA; San Francisco Mus of Mod Art, CA; Santa Barbara Mus, CA; Inst Arte Contemporaneo, Lima, Peru
PRINTERS: Artist (ART)
PUBLISHERS: ADI, San Francisco, CA (ADI); Artist (ART)
GALLERIES: Robin Gibson Gallery, Paddington, Australia; Sande Webster Gallery, Phila, PA; Robin Gibson Gallery, Sydney, Australia; BMG Fine Art, Adelaide, Australia; Tahir Fine Arts, New Orleans, LA; Young Gallery, Los Gatos, CA; Collectors Gallery, Oakland Museum, Oakland, CA; Valley Art Center, Walnut Creek, CA; Windsors Gallery, Dania, FL; C et D, Paris, France; Anne Goodman Fine Art, Santa Monica, CA; Hank Baum Gallery, San Francisco, CA
MAILING ADDRESS: 2810 Pacific Ave, San Francisco, CA 94115

TITLE	PUBLISHER	PRINTER	DATE	MEDIUM	DIMENSION (PAPER SIZE) IN INCHES	TYPE OF PAPER	EDITION NUMBER	NO. OF COLORS	ORIGINAL OPENING PRICE	CURRENT RETAIL PRICE
SOLD OUT EDITIONS (RARE):										
Mates	ART	ART	1977	EB/HC	15 X 16	AP	75	Multi	60	300
CURRENT EDITIONS:										
Plum Moon	ADI	ADI	1977	SP	26 X 40	BECK	125	7	125	225
Secrets	ADI	ADI	1977	SP	26 X 40	BECK	125	7	125	225
At Long Last	ART	ART	1977	EB/HC	28 X 22	AP	75	3	175	250
Sitting Pretty	ART	ART	1977	EB/HC	22 X 30	AP	75	7	150	225
Wraparound	ART	ART	1977	EB/HC	22 X 30	AP	75	7	150	225
In Touch	ART	ART	1977	EB/HC	22 X 30	AP	75	3	150	225
Daybreak	ART	ART	1977	EB/HC	22 X 30	AP	75	3	150	225
A Lazy Day	ART	ART	1977	EB/HC	18 X 12	AP	75	3	100	175
Taking a Gander	ADI	ADI	1978	SP	40 X 26	BECK	125	7	125	225
Laze	ART	ART	1980	AC/HC	15 X 16	AP	80	3	100	200
Salone	ART	ART	1983	EB/HC	30 X 22	AP	50	6	225	250
Leda	ART	ART	1983	EB/HC	30 X 22	AP	50	9	275	300
She's a Big Girl Now	ART	ART	1988	EB/HC	30 X 22	AP	50	Multi	175	350

MARTIN LEWIS

BORN: American; (1888-1962)
PRINTERS: Artist (ART)
PUBLISHERS: Artist (ART); Chicago Society of Etchers, IL (SE); Society of American Etchers (SAE)

McCarron (Mc)

GALLERIES: Paul McCarron Fine Prints & Drawings, New York, NY; Newmark Gallery, New York, NY; Sragow Gallery, New York, NY; Old Print Shop/Kenneth M Newman, New York, NY; Bethesda Art Gallery, Glen Echo, MD; Sande Garcia Fine Art, Miami, FL

TITLE	PUBLISHER	PRINTER	DATE	MEDIUM	DIMENSION (PAPER SIZE) IN INCHES	TYPE OF PAPER	EDITION NUMBER	NO. OF COLORS	ORIGINAL OPENING PRICE	CURRENT RETAIL PRICE
SOLD OUT EDITIONS (RARE):										
The Old Timer's Battleship (Mc-12)	ART	ART	1916	EB	10 X 13	WOVE	50	1	20	2500
Rooftops	ART	ART	1918	EB	7 X 10	WOVE		1	25	8000
Skyline, New York (Mc-32)	ART	ART	1919	EB	9 X 10	WOVE	50	1	25	5500
The Great Shadow (Mc-33)	ART	ART	1925	DPT	10 X 7	WOVE		1	35	3500
Butter and Egg Man's Holiday (Mc-44)	ART	ART	1926	DPT	7 X 10	WOVE	25	1	35	1500
Charleston Practice (Mc-49)	ART	ART	1926	DPT	8 X 10	WOVE	25	1	35	4000
Tabloid Readers (Mc-56)	ART	ART	1927	DPT	7 X 10	WOVE	50	1	40	5000
Derricks (Mc-58)	ART	ART	1927	DPT	8 X 12	WOVE	100	1	40	9000
The Boyfriends (Mc-63)	ART	ART	1927	EB	8 X 8	WOVE	50	1	40	2500
Relics (Mc-65)	ART	ART	1928	DPT	12 X 10	WOVE	100	1	40	20000
Rain on Murray Hill (Mc-66)	ART	ART	1928	DPT	8 X 12	WOVE	100	1	40	15000
East Side Night—Williamsburgh Bridge (Mc-67)	ART	ART	1928	EB	10 X 12	WOVE	85	1	40	6500
Under the Street Lamp (Mc-68)	ART	ART	1928	DPT	15 X 10	WOVE	100	1	40	3500
Ice Cream Cones (Mc-70)	ART	ART	1928	DPT	9 X 15	WOVE	75	1	40	2500
Boss of the Block (Mc-74)	ART	ART	1928	EB/A/DPT	11 X 7	WOVE	200		35	2500
Shadows—Garage at Night (with Sandpaper-Ground) (Mc-75)	ART	ART	1928	DPT	10 X 12	WOVE	75	1	40	3300
Fifth Avenue Bridge (Mc-76)	ART	ART	1928	DPT	10 X 12	WOVE	85	1	35	8500
The Little Penthouse	ART	ART	1929	DPT	10 X 7	WOVE	100	1	40	10000
Building a Babylon	ART	ART	1929	DPT	13 X 8	WOVE	100	1	40	4500
Down to the Sea at Night (Mc-81)	ART	ART	1929	DPT	8 X 13	WOVE	75	1	40	4500
Bay Windows (Mc-86)	ART	ART	1929	DPT	12 X 8	WOVE	100	1	40	12000
Oncoming Rain	ART	ART	1929	DPT	8 X 10	WOVE	50	1	40	2000
Quarter of Nine—Saturday's Children (Mc-88)	ART	ART	1929	DPT	10 X 13	WOVE	100	1	40	12000
Snow on the El (Mc-89)	ART	ART	1929	DPT	14 X 9	WOVE	50	1	40	25000
Glow of the City (Mc-87)	ART	ART	1929	DPT	11 X 14	WOVE	100	1	40	20000
Corner Shadows (Mc-90)	ART	ART	1929	DPT	9 X 9	WOVE	100	1	40	8000
The Tree, Manhattan (Mc-92)	ART	ART	1930	DPT	13 X 10	WOVE	100	1	50	7500
Arch, Midnight (Mc-94)	ART	ART	1930	DPT	8 X 12	WOVE	100	1	50	9000
Stoops in Snow (Mc-95)	ART	ART	1930	DPT	10 X 15	WOVE	100	1	50	18000
Subway Steps (Mc-96)	ART	ART	1930	DPT	14 X 9	WOVE	100	1	50	13500
Shadow Dance (Mc-97)	ART	ART	1930	DPT	9 X 11	WOVE	100	1	50	18000
Break in the Thunderstorm (Mc-98)	ART	ART	1930	DPT	12 X 10	WOVE	85		50	12000
Manhattan Lights (Mc-102)	ART	ART	1931	DPT	16 X 10	WOVE	100	1	50	4500
2 AM (Mc-103)	ART	ART	1932	DPT/SP	9 X 15	WOVE	50	1	60	11000
Night in New York, 1926 (Mc-42)	CSE	ART	1932	EB	8 X 9	WOVE	135	1	60	7000
White Monday (Mc-105)	ART	ART	1932	DPT/AB	10 X 9	WOVE	100	1	60	3000
Cronies (Mc-107)	CSE	ART	1932	AB	10 X 11	WOVE	100	1	60	3000
Circus Night (Mc-109)	ART	ART				WOVE	100	1	65	10000
RFD (Mc-110)	ART	ART	1933	DPT/AB	10 X 12	WOVE	100	1	60	3000
Lost Railroad (Mc-112)	ART	ART	1933	DPT/AB	10 X 17	WOVE		1	60	5000
Grandpa Takes a Walk (Mc-114)	ART	ART	1933	EB	9 X 11	WOVE	100	1	60	3500
Trumbull Street (Mc-118)	ART	ART	1935	DPT	11 X 13	WOVE	100	1	65	6500
Sun Bath (Mc-119)	ART	ART	1935	LB	10 X 14	WOVE	50	1	65	5000
Politics (Mc-125)	ART	ART	1936	DPT	10 X 11	WOVE		1	65	3500
On the Roof (Mc-132)	ART	ART	1937	EB/A/REL	13 X 10	WOVE	10		70	1800
Passing Freight (Mc-133)	ART	ART	1940	DPT	10 X 7	AP	100	1	75	5000
Strength and Beauty (Mc-135)	ART	ART	1940	DPT	11 X 13	AP	50	1	75	3000
Shadow Magic (Mc-136)	ART	ART	1940	DPT	13 X 9	WOVE	100	1	75	4500
Chance Meeting (Mc-138)	SAE	ART	1941	DPT	10 X 7	LAID	100	1	75	6500
At the Wall	ART	ART	1949	EB/A/SG	15 X 12	AP	50		100	3500

STANLEY LEWIS

BORN: Montreal, Canada; March 28, 1930
EDUCATION: Montreal Mus of Fine Arts Sch of Arts & Design, Canada, 1948–51; Lithography, Instituto Allende, San Miguel, Mexico, 1953–55
TEACHING: Instr, Sculpture, McGill Univ, Montreal, Canada, 1952; Instr, Graphics, Saidye Bronfman Centre, Montreal, Canada, 1970; Head of Dept, Sculpute, Saidye Bronfman Centre, Montreal, Canada, 1973 to present
AWARDS: Concours Artistiques, Quebec City, Canada, Cash Prize, 1959; Prize, Stone-Cut Print, Quebec Mus, Canada, 1962
COLLECTIONS: Montreal Mus of Fine Arts, Canada; Nat Gallery of Canada, Ottawa, Canada
PRINTERS: Corinne Spiegel, Toronto, Canada (CP); La Magie de LÁrt, Toronto, Canada (LMA)
PUBLISHERS: Atelier J Lukacs, Montreal, Canada (AJL)
GALLERIES: Atelier J Lukacs, Montreal, Canada; La Magie de LÁrt, Toronto, Canada; Bowery Gallery, New York, NY
MAILING ADDRESS: 4131 Côte des Neiges, #4 Montreal, Quebec, Canada H3H 1X1

STANLEY LEWIS CONTINUED

TITLE	PUBLISHER	PRINTER	DATE	MEDIUM	DIMENSION (PAPER SIZE) IN INCHES	TYPE OF PAPER	EDITION NUMBER	NO. OF COLORS	ORIGINAL OPENING PRICE	CURRENT RETAIL PRICE
CURRENT EDITIONS:										
Set of Three Stone-Cut Prints:									1000 SET	1200 SET
The Discovery of Flight	LMA	LMA	1982	LC	36 X 24	RICE	35	3	350	400
Moment of Becoming	LMA	LMA	1982	LC	36 X 24	RICE	35	3	350	400
Meditation	LMA	LMA	1982	LC	36 X 24	RICE	35	3	350	400

SOL LEWITT

BORN: Hartford, CT; 1928
EDUCATION: Syracuse Univ, BFA, 1949
TEACHING: Inst, Mus Mod Art Sch, NY, 1964–67; Inst, Cooper Union, NY, 1967
RECENT EXHIB: Musee de'Art Moderne de la Ville de Paris, France, 1987; Westfälisher Kunstverein Munster, Germany, 1987; Kestner Gesellschraft, Hannover, Germany, 1988; Kunsthalle, Bern, Switzerland, 1989; Tokyo Mus, Japan, 1990; Daniel Weinberg Gallery, Los Angeles, CA, 1991; Lisson Gallery, London, England, 1991; Galeria 57, Madrid, Spain, 1991; Wesleyan Univ, Ezra & Cecile Zilkha Gallery, Middletown, CT, 1992; Daniel Weinberg Gallery, Santa Monica, CA, 1992,93; John Weber Gallery, NY, 1988,90,91,92,93
COLLECTIONS: Mus of Mod Art, NY; Whitney Mus of Am Art, NY; Art Inst of Chicago, IL; Detroit Inst of Art, MI; Stedelijk Mus, Amsterdam, Holland; Albright-Knox Art Gallery, Buffalo, NY; Art Gallery of Toronto, Can; Los Angeles County Art Mus, Los Angeles, CA
PRINTERS: Shorewood-Bank Street Atelier, NY (S-BSA); Michael Berden, Boston, MA (MB); Jennifer Melby, NY (JM); Jeryl Parker Editions, NY (JPE); Patricia Branstead, NY (PB); Branstead Studios, NY (BS); Aeropress, NY (A); John Campione, NY (JC); Peter Pettengill (PP); June Lambla (JL); Hidekatsu Takada (HT); Anthony O'Hare, Brooklyn, NY (AOH); Susan Hover, Brooklyn, NY (SH); Kevin Oster, Brooklyn, NY (KO); Jack Lemon, Chicago, IL (JL); Landfall Press, Inc, Chicago, IL (LPI); Jo Wantanabe, NY (JW); Joseph Montague, Brooklyn, NY (JM); Lawrence Hamlin (LH); Lothar Osterburg (LO); Paul Mullowney (PM); Pamela Paulson (PP); Crown Point Press, San Francisco, CA (CPP); Watanabe Studio, Brooklyn, NY (WS); Artist (ART); Kazuko Miyamoto, NY (KM); Riverhouse Editions Press, Clark, CO (REd); Takuji Hamanaka, Brooklyn, NY (TH)
PUBLISHERS: John Weber Gallery, NY (JWG); Multiples, NY (M); Crown Point Press, San Francisco, CA (CPP); Transworld Art, Inc, NY (TAI); Center for Constitutional Rights (CCR); Parasol Press, Ltd, NY (PaP); Artists Call, NY (AC); Matsumura Editions, NY (MEd); Achenbach Art Edition, Düsseldorf, Germany (AAE); Edition Schellmann, NY & Cologne, Germany (ES); Artist (ART); Galerie Lelong, NY & Paris, France (GL); Riverhouse Editions, Chicago, IL (REd); Watanabe Studio, Brooklyn, NY (WS)
GALLERIES: Marian Goodman, New York, NY; John Weber Gallery, New York, NY; Crown Point Press, New York, NY & San Francisco, CA; Marvin Ross Friedman & Co, Miami, FL; Rhona Hoffman Gallery, Chicago, IL; Tomoko Liguori Gallery, New York, NY; Daniel Weinberg Gallery, Santa Monica, CA; B R Kornblatt Gallery, Wash, DC; Thomas Segal Gallery, Boston, MA; Edition Schellmann, New York, NY; Landfall Press, Inc, Chicago, IL; Galeria 57, Madrid, Spain; Jonathan Novak Contemporary Art, Los Angeles, CA; Goodman/Tinnon Fine Arts, San Francisco, CA; Axis Twenty, Inc, Atlanta, GA; Van Straaten Gallery, Chicago, IL; Brenda Edelson Fine Art, Baltimore, MD; Barbara Krakow Gallery, Boston, MA; John C. Stoller & Company, Minneapolis, MN; James Francis Trezza Fine Art, Boston, MA & Palm Beach, FL; Nancy Singer Gallery, St Louis, MO; Laura Carpenter Fine Art, Santa Fe, NM; Carol Evans Fine Arts, Brooklyn, NY; Rico/Maresca Gallery, New York,NY; TwoSixtyOne Art, New York, NY; Donald Young Gallery, Seattle, WA; Lawrence Mangel Fine Art, Phila, PA

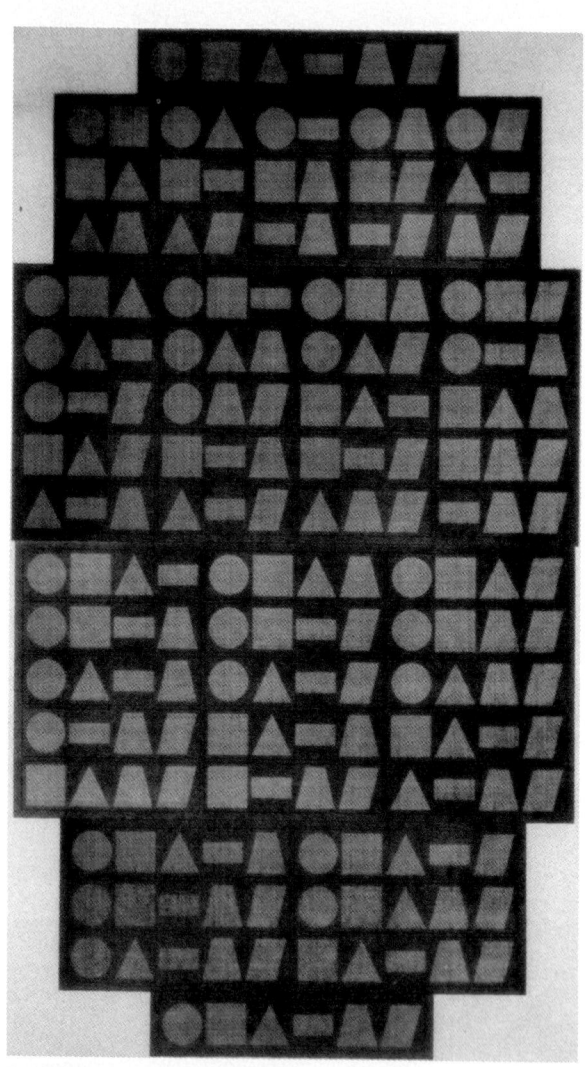

Sol LeWitt
All One, Two, Three, Four, Five & Six Part Combinations of Six Geometric Figures
Courtesy the Artist

MAILING ADDRESS: 117 Hester St, New York, NY 10022

Tate Gallery (TG)

TITLE	PUBLISHER	PRINTER	DATE	MEDIUM	DIMENSION (PAPER SIZE) IN INCHES	TYPE OF PAPER	EDITION NUMBER	NO. OF COLORS	ORIGINAL OPENING PRICE	CURRENT RETAIL PRICE
SOLD OUT EDITIONS (RARE):										
Horizontal Composite (TG-S-?)	IWC	ART	1970	SP	18 X 40	WOVE	150		150	6000
Composite Series (Yellow) (Set of 5)	ART	ART	1971	SP	20 X 20 EA	STP	35 EA	1 EA	600 SET	9000 SET
Suite of 16 (Color Lithographs)	LPI	JL/LPI	1971	LC	23 X 23 EA	AP	50 EA	4 EA	3500 SET	10000 SET
Suite of 16 (Black & White Lithographs)	LPI	JL/LPI	1971	LB	23 X 23 EA	AP	50 EA	1 EA	1500 SET	6000 SET
Vertical Lines Not Touching (Black)	CCR	S-BSA	1971	LB	7 X 23	AP	150	1	150	2500

SOL LEWITT CONTINUED

TITLE	PUBLISHER	PRINTER	DATE	MEDIUM	DIMENSION (PAPER SIZE) IN INCHES	TYPE OF PAPER	EDITION NUMBER	NO. OF COLORS	ORIGINAL OPENING PRICE	CURRENT RETAIL PRICE
SOLD OUT EDITIONS (RARE):										
Arcs from Corners and Sides... Lines of One Inch in Four Directions and all Combinations (Set of 16) (TG-L6)	ART	ART	1972	SP	28 X 28	STP	50		200	2000
						MAG	50 EA		2000 SET	20000 SET
The Location of Lines (Set of 5)	PaP	CPP	1975	EB	18 X 18 EA	R/BFK	25 EA	1 EA	600 SET	1500 SET
Straight, Wavy and Broken Lines (Set of 7)	PaP	CPP	1873	EB	27 X 21 EA	AP	25 EA	1 EA	2500 SET	20000 SET
All One Two Three and Four Part Combinations of Lines in Four Directions	M	JC	1976	SP	26 X 23 EA	AP	20	1	600	1800
All Combinations of Red Yellow Blue Straight and Broken Lines on Red, Yellow and Blue	M	JW	1976	SP	30 X 30	AP	50	4	450	1200
All One Two Three and Four Part Combinations of Lines in Four Directions and in Four Colors (Composite)	M	JC	1976	SP	30 X 42	AP	55	4	500	1500
Lines and Color Straight, Not Straight and Broken, Lines Using all Combinations of Black, Yellow and Blue for Lines and Intervals	M	JW	1977	SP	30 X 30	AP88	50		450	1200
Serial System Using Lines (Set of 6)	M	PB/A	1977	SP	15 X 19 EA	AP88	45 EA		1000 EA	2000 EA
Bands of Line in Four Directions in Black and White	M	PB/A	1977	SP	15 X 19	AP88	70	1	200	1000
Serial System Using Lines and Color (Set of 6)	M	PB/A	1977	SP	19 X 15 EA	AP88	45 EA		1000 SET	4000 SET
All Double Combinations of 6 Geometric Figures	PaP	CPP	1977	EB/A	6 X 6 EA	R/BFK	25 EA	1 EA	1500 SET	8000 SET
Lines from Sides, Corners, Center	PaP	CPP	1977	EB/A	35 X 35	R/BFK	25		750	4500
Points on a Grid (Set of 7)	M	PB/A	1978	SP	30 X 30 EA	R/BFK	25 EA		2100 SET	8000 SET
Lines in Color on Color to Points on a Grid (Set of 10)	M	PB/A	1978	SP	30 X 30 EA	AP88	25 EA		3000 SET	9000 SET
Six Geometric Figures in Three Colors on Three colors and all Their Combinations	M	PB/A	1978	SP	30 X 30	AP88	60		400	1200
Color Grids: all Vertical and Horizontal Combinations of Black, Yellow, Red and Blue Straight, Not Straight and Broken Lines	M	PB/A	1977–80	SP	30 X 30	AP	65		450	1000
All One-Two-Three-Four-Five & Six Part Combinations of Six Geometric Figures	ART		1980	SP	66 X 39	R/BFK	33		1500	3000
Four Part Combination of 6 Geometric Figures in Four Colors, I, II, III (Set of 3)	M	PB/A	1980	WC	8 X 17 EA	AP88	40 EA		950 SET	4000 SET
Different Sets of Color Woodcuts—4 Prints in Each Set (Set of 12)	M	PB/A	1980	WC	8 X 18 EA	AP88	40 EA		2500 SET	8000 SET
Windows	M	PB/A	1980	PH/C	34 X 30	AP88	20		1400	5000
Crown Point (Book of Photo Etchings) (40)	CPP	CPP	1980	PH/E	11 X 11	Book	25		2500 SET	3500 SET
Six Geometric Figures and all Their Combinations (Set of 63)	M	PB/A	1980	SP	11 X 11 (6) 11 X 19 (15) 11 X 26 (20) 11 X 34 (15) 11 X 41 (6) 11 X 49 (1)	AP	10 EA	1 EA	7500 SET	13500 SET
Untitled (Set of 10)	M	MB	1981	SP	20 X 20 EA	AP	25 EA		2500 SET	7500 SET
Set of 75	M	PB/A	1981	SP	22 X 22 EA	R/BFK	25 EA		10000 SET	20000 SET
Untitled (Set of 6)	M	MB	1982	WB	30 X 30 EA	AP	40 EA	1 EA	3000 SET	8000 SET
Untitled Composite (Set of 8)	M	MB	1982	SP	22 X 38 EA	AP	40 EA		5000 SET	12000 SET
									650 EA	2000 EA
Untitled	M	MB	1982	WB	30 X 30	KIZ	40		750	1800
Forms Derived from a Cube (Set of 24) (TG-E-28)	M	JM/JPE	1982	AC	21 X 21 EA	SOM	25 EA		5400 SET	25000 SET
Forms Derived from a Cube (Set of 8) (TG-E-28)	M	JM/JPE	1982	AC	21 X 21 EA	SOM	25 EA		3200 SET	10000 SET
Forms Derived from a Cube (Individual)	M	JM/JPE	1982	AC	21 X 21	SOM	25		400 EA	1800 EA

SOL LEWITT CONTINUED

TITLE	PUBLISHER	PRINTER	DATE	MEDIUM	DIMENSION (PAPER SIZE) IN INCHES	TYPE OF PAPER	EDITION NUMBER	NO. OF COLORS	ORIGINAL OPENING PRICE	CURRENT RETAIL PRICE
SOLD OUT EDITIONS (RARE):										
Doubles in Color (Set of 10):	M	JM/JPE	1982	AC	21 X 38 EA	AP88	10 EA		750 EA	1500 EA
Stars (Set of 28)									12000 SET	20000 SET
Stars (Set of 4 Stars):									2200 SET	6000 SET
Single Stars:									750 EA	1500 EA
Stars—Dark Center (Set of 7):	CPP	HT/PP/JL/CPP	1983	A/HG	21 X 21 EA	AP88	10 SETS		3600 SET	7000 SET
Stars—Light Center (Set of 7):	CPP	HT/PP/JL/CPP	1983	A/HG	21 X 21 EA	AP88	10 SETS		3600 SET	7000 SET
Double Stars (Set of 7):	CPP	HT/PP/JL/CPP	1983	A/HG	15 X 27 EA	AP88	25 SETS	4 EA	3600 SET	7000 SET
Stars—Blue Center (Set of 7):	CPP	HT/PP/JL/CPP	1983	A/HG	21 X 21 EA	AP88	10 EA	4 EA	3600 SET	7000 SET
Stars—Red Center (Set of 7):	CPP	HT/PP/JL/CPP	1983	A/HG	21 X 21 EA	AP88	10 EA	4 EA	3600 SET	7000 SET
Isometric Form with Lines in Four Directions and Four Colors	M	JW	1983	SP	42 X 42	AP88	20	4	900	2800
Isometric Cube with Lines in Four Directions and Four Colors	M	JW	1983	SP	42 X 42	AP88	20	4	900	2800
Forms Derived from a Cube— Twelve Images, Simple and Superimposed in Black and White and Color (Set of 48)	M	JW	1984	SP	8 X 8 EA	AP88	40 EA	1–3 EA	3000 SET	8000 SET
Untitled (Set of 6)	M	JW	1984	SP	20 X 52 EA	AC	20 EA		5000 SET	10000 SET
Ficciones (Book-J L Borges)			1984	SP	9 X 9	AP	1500			1000
Set of Two Color Silkscreens (Set of 2):									900 EA	2800 EA
Seven Part Three Color Composite	M	JW	1985	SP	30 X 28	AC	35	3	750	1500
Fifteen Part Four Color Composite	M	JW	1985	SP	38 X 36	AC	35	4	900	2800
Doubles in Black and Grey: (Set of 10)	M	JM	1984	AC	21 X 38 EA	AP88	10 EA	2 EA	6000 SET	8000 SET
									750 EA	1200 EA
Bands of Lines One Inch Wide in Four Directions & Four Colours (TG-S-49)	M	PB/A	1985	SP	29 X 96	AC	20	4	2500	5000
Bands of Lines One Inch Wide in Four Directions in Black & Grey (TG-S-50)	M	PB/A	1985	SP	29 X 96	AC	20	2	2500	5000
Two Pyramids—Four Colors (Set of 4)	M	JW	1986	SP	38 X 62 EA	AC	20 EA	4 EA	8000 SET	20000 SET
									2500 EA	6000 EA
CURRENT EDITIONS:										
Arcs from Four Corners	CPP	CPP	1986	WC	21 X 32	SOM	200	5	750	2000
Pyramids (Set of 6) (TG-E-35)	PaP		1987	AC	21 X 33	SOM/S	19		3000	10000
Centered Cube within a Yellow . . .			1987	SP	22 X 30	AC	30	20	800	1350
Centered Cube within a Red . . .			1987	SP	22 X 30	AC	30	20	800	1350
Two Cubes with Colors Superimposed: Untitled	ES/AGr	JW/WS	1988	SP	30 X 95	AC	30	25	3500	5000
Two Cubes with Colors Superimposed—Blue	ES/AGr	JW/WS	1988	SP	30 X 95	AC	30	25	3500	5000
Two Cubes with Colors Superimposed—Dark Red	ES/AGr	JW/WS	1988	SP	30 X 95	AC	30	25	3500	5000
Flat Top Pyramid with Colours Superimposed—(Rust)	ES/AGr	JW/WS	1988	SP	30 X 95	AC	30	20	3500	5000
Flat Top Pyramid with Colours Superimposed—(Red)	ES/AGr	JW/WS	1988	SP	30 X 95	AC	30	23	3500	5000
Wall Piece (16 Modules High) (Painted Pinewood Construction)	ES	KM	1988	MULT	76 X 5 X 5	WOOD	20		10000	12000
A Circle Divided into Eight Equal Parts, with Colours Superimposed in Each Part (Set of 4)	ES	JW/WS	1989	SP	30 X 30 EA	AC	40 EA	32–42 EA	7500 SET	8000 SET
									1800 EA	2000 EA
Complex Forms (Set of 5)	MaEd	JM/WS	1989	EC	24 X 18 EA	AP88	39 EA	5 EA	3500 SET	12000 SET
Red, Yellow, Blue and Gray Squares, Bordered by a Black Band (Set of 4)	ES	JW/WS	1989	AC	18 X 18 EA	MAG	25		4500	5000
Complex Form, Color Super . . . (Set of 5)			1989	EB	30 X 20 EA	AP88	39 EA	1 EA	12000 SET	13500 SET
Untitled			1989	EB/A	20 X 25	MAG	3		3000	5000
Circle . . . . (Set of 4)	AAE	WS	1989	SP	76 X 76 CM EA	SOM/T	40 EA	4	15000 SET	18000 SET
Art Bands in Colors			1990	EB/A	19 X 21	MAG	30		1200	1500
Complex Forms			1990	EB/A	36 X 36	MAG	27		6000	7500
Square with Colors Super . . . (Set of 6)			1991	EB/A	29 X 29 EA	MAG	25 EA		7500 SET	7500 SET
Black & Gray (Set of 4)	CPP	LH/LO/PM/ PP/CPP	1991	EB/A/HG/SB	12 X 12 EA	SOM/W/T	10 EA	1 EA	1950 SET	1950 SET
									650 EA	650 EA
Black & Gray (Set of 4)	CPP	LH/LO/PM/ PP/CPP	1991	EB/A/HG/SB	25 X 24 EA	SOM/W/T	10 EA	1 EA	4500 SET	4500 SET
									1500 EA	1500 EA

SOL LEWITT CONTINUED

Sol LeWitt
Flat Top Pyramid with Colors Superimposed
Courtesy Edition Schellmann

TITLE	PUBLISHER	PRINTER	DATE	MEDIUM	DIMENSION (PAPER SIZE) IN INCHES	TYPE OF PAPER	EDITION NUMBER	NO. OF COLORS	ORIGINAL OPENING PRICE	CURRENT RETAIL PRICE
CURRENT EDITIONS:										
Black & Gray (Set of 4)	CPP	LH/LO/PM/PP/CPP	1991	EB/A/HG/SB	30 X 17 EA	SOM/W/T	10 EA	1 EA	3000 SET 1000 EA	3000 SET 1000 EA
Black & Gray (Set of 4)	CPP	LH/LO/PM/PP/CPP	1991	EB/A/HG/SB	30 X 20 EA	SOM/W/T	10 EA	1 EA	3600 SET 1200 EA	3600 SET 1200 EA
Color & Black (Set of 4)	CPP	LH/LO/PM/PP/CPP	1991	EB/A/HG/SB	13 X 12 EA	SOM/W/T	25 EA	1 EA	1950 SET 650 EA	1950 SET 650 EA
Color & Black (Set of 4)	CPP	LH/LO/PM/PP/CPP	1991	EB/A/HG/SB	25 X 24 EA	SOM/W/T	25 EA	1 EA	4500 SET 1500 EA	4500 SET 1500 EA
Color & Black (Set of 4)	CPP	LH/LO/PM/PP/CPP	1991	EB/A/HG/SB	30 X 17 EA	SOM/W/T	10 EA	1 EA	3000 SET 1000 EA	3000 SET 1000 EA
Color & Black (Set of 4)	CPP	LH/LO/PM/PP/CPP	1991	EB/A/HG/SB	30 X 20 EA	SOM/W/T	10 EA	1 EA	3600 SET 1200 EA	3600 SET 1200 EA
Color & Black (Set of 4)	CPP	LH/LO/PM/PP/CPP	1991	EB/A/HG/SB	41 X 40 EA	SOM/W/T	15 EA	1 EA	5400 SET 1800 EA	5400 SET 1800 EA
All Combinations of Four Colors (Set of 15)	M	AOH/WS	1991	AC	14 X 14 EA	SOM/W/T	10 EA		7500 SET	7500 SET
Vertical Not Straight Lines—Not Touching on Color (Series of 6)	REd	PB/BS	1991	EB	47 X 33 EA	R/BFK	30 EA	2 EA	4000 SET 800 EA	8000 SET 1500 EA
Forms Derived from a Cube (Color) (Set of 12)	AAE	WS	1991	SP	32 X 32 EA	SOM/T	35 EA	4 EA	34000 SET 4000 EA	34000 SET 4000 EA
Bands of Lines in Four Directions (Horizontal & Square) (Set of 2)	WS	TH/WS	1993	WB	11 X 29 (Hor) 17 X 17 (Sq)	KOZO	125 EA	1 EA	2000 SET 1200 EA	2000 SET 1200 EA

PETER LIASHKOV

BORN: Rouen, France; 1939
EDUCATION: Otis Art Inst, Parsons Sch of Design, Los Angeles, CA, MFA, 1968
TEACHING: Otis Art Inst, Parsons Sch of Design, Los Angeles, CA, 1975; Art Center Col of Design, Pasadena, CA, 1974 to present

COLLECTIONS: Springfield Art Mus, MO; Pennsylvania Acad of Fine Arts, Phila, PA; Frye Art Mus, Seattle, WA
PRINTERS: Stephen Thomas, San Francisco, CA (ST); Katherine Lincoln Press, San Francisco, CA (KLP)
PUBLISHERS: Katherine Lincoln Press, San Francisco, CA (KLP); Artist (ART)
GALLERIES: Jan Baum Gallery, Los Angeles, CA
MAILING ADDRESS: 1909 5th Ave, Los Angeles, CA 90018

TITLE	PUBLISHER	PRINTER	DATE	MEDIUM	DIMENSION (PAPER SIZE) IN INCHES	TYPE OF PAPER	EDITION NUMBER	NO. OF COLORS	ORIGINAL OPENING PRICE	CURRENT RETAIL PRICE
CURRENT EDITIONS:										
Open Torso Series (Series of 40)	ART/KLP	ST/KLP	1984	MON/KC	23 X 31 EA	GE	1 EA	Multi	1000 EA	1200 EA

MANES LICHTENBERG

BORN: New York, NY; 1920
EDUCATION: Art Students League, NY; Acad de la Grand, Chaumiere, Paris, France; Studied with Fernand Leger, Paris, France

AWARDS: Prix Othon Friesz, Paris, France, 1961; Gold Medal of Honor, Allied Artists Am, NY, 1964; Prix Maurice Utrillo, Paris, France, 1964
PRINTERS: Atelier Ettinger Inc, NY (AE)
PUBLISHERS: Eleanor Ettinger Inc, NY (EEI)
GALLERIES: Phillips Gallery, Dallas, TX; Savage Galleries, Scottsdale, AZ; Loring Art Gallery, Cedarhurst, NY; Jones Gallery, La Jolla, CA
MAILING ADDRESS: 835 Mix Ave, Hamden, CT 06514

MANES LICHTENBERG CONTINUED

TITLE	PUBLISHER	PRINTER	DATE	MEDIUM	DIMENSION (PAPER SIZE) IN INCHES	TYPE OF PAPER	EDITION NUMBER	NO. OF COLORS	ORIGINAL OPENING PRICE	CURRENT RETAIL PRICE
SOLD OUT EDITIONS(RARE):										
Connecticut Shore	EEI	AE	1980	LC	23 X 28	AP	300		250	400
CURRENT EDITIONS:										
Dove Cote	EEI	AE	1980	LC	25 X 20	AP	300		250	300
Marché aux Fleurs, Paris	EEI	AE	1980	LC	23 X 28	AP	300		250	300

GARY LICHTENSTEIN

BORN: Waterbury, CT; October 23, 1953
EDUCATION: Syracuse Univ, NY; San Francisco Art Inst, CA; Antioch Col, Yellow Springs, OH, BFA, 1973, MFA, 1975
TEACHING: Vis Lectr, San Francisco Art Inst, CA, 1979; Printmaking Workshop, San Francisco Mus of Mod Art, CA, 1980; Instr, Printmaking, Univ of California, Berkeley, CA, 1981–86
COLLECTIONS: Univ of Connecticut, Torrington, CT; San Francisco Mus of Mod Art, CA; de Sassait Art Mus, Santa Clara; Light of Sweden Found, Goteborg, Sweden
PRINTERS: Soma Fine Art Press, San Francisco, CA (SFA)
PUBLISHERS: Franklin Henderson Fine Art, San Francisco, CA (FHFA)
GALLERIES: Soma Fine Art, San Francisco, CA; Franklin Henderson Fine Art, San Francisco, CA
MAILING ADDRESS: c/o Soma Fine Art Press, 665 Third St, #225, San Francisco, CA 94107

TITLE	PUBLISHER	PRINTER	DATE	MEDIUM	DIMENSION (PAPER SIZE) IN INCHES	TYPE OF PAPER	EDITION NUMBER	NO. OF COLORS	ORIGINAL OPENING PRICE	CURRENT RETAIL PRICE
SOLD OUT EDITIONS (RARE):										
Blend (Violet to Grey)	FHFA	SFA	1980	SP	30 X 40	AP	40	Blend	425	800
Blend (Ochre to Violet)	FHFA	SFA	1980	SP	30 X 40	AP	30	Blend	425	800
Blend (Purple to Green)	FHFA	SFA	1980	SP	30 X 40	AP	30	Blend	425	800
Blend-Seems Like Manhattan	FHFA	SFA	1980	SP	30 X 40	AP	50	Blend	425	950
Warm Wishes of Color	FHFA	SFA	1980	SP	30 X 40	AP	50	Blend	400	1250
A Italia	FHFA	SFA	1981	SP	26 X 38	AP	40	Blend	300	650
Silver Lining	FHFA	SFA	1982	SP	22 X 30	AP	15	Blend	285	650
Blend-Ocean Blue to Green	FHFA	SFA	1982	SP	30 X 40	AP	25	Blend	425	675
Blend-Horizontal Horizon	FHFA	SFA	1982	SP	30 X 40	AP	25	Blend	425	850
Vistazo West	FHFA	SFA	1983	SP	22 X 30	AP	20	Blend	275	650
After the Rains	FHFA	SFA	1983	SP	22 X 30	AP	30	Blend	285	650
CURRENT EDITIONS:										
Realm of the Senses, #1	FHFA	SFA	1980	SP	30 X 40	AP	25	9+	325	650
Realm of the Senses, #2	FHFA	SFA	1980	SP	30 X 40	AP	50	9+	325	650
Realm of the Senses, #3	FHFA	SFA	1980	SP	30 X 40	AP	75		300	575
Transparent Shadows	FHFA	SFA	1980	SP	30 X 40	AP	8	20	285	600
Crystal Blue	FHFA	SFA	1980	SP	30 X 40	AP	7	18	350	675
Mirrored Depths	FHFA	SFA	1980	SP	26 X 36	AP	15	18	280	525
Shelter from the Storm	FHFA	SFA	1980	SP	30 X 40	AP	60	24	320	650
Submergence	FHFA	SFA	1981	SP	22 X 30	AP	30	14	175	500
Blend-Autumn's Color	FHFA	SFA	1982	SP	30 X 40	AP	25	Blend	425	675
Silver Synchronism	FHFA	SFA	1982	SP	22 X 30	AP	60	8	175	350
Fathomed Depths, #1	FHFA	SFA	1982	SP	26 X 38	AP	40	12+	250	400
Fathomed Depths, #2	FHFA	SFA	1982	SP	26 X 38	AP	15	12+	250	550
Traverse Blends	FHFA	SFA	1983	MON	22 X 30	AP	15	Blend	280	550
Transverse Blend I,II,III	FHFA	SFA	1984	SP	22 X 30 EA	AP	25 EA	Blend	425 EA	650 EA
Lumiere	FHFA	SFA	1985	SP	22 X 30	AP	75	22	425	575
Often Times Unseen	FHFA	SFA	1985	SP	22 X 30	AP	50	18	425	575

LOUIS LIEBERMAN (KARL)

BORN: Brooklyn, NY; May 7, 1944
EDUCATION: Brooklyn Mus Sch, NY, 1961–64; Brooklyn Col, NY, BA, 1982; Rhode Island Sch of Design, Providence, RI, BFA, 1969
TEACHING: Adj Lectr, Sculpture & Design, Lehman Col, Bronx, NY, 1972–75; Adj Lectr, Drawing, Brooklyn Col, NY, 1971–78; Vis Art, Sculpture, Illinois State Univ, Normal, IL, 1979; Vis Art, Hamilton Col, Clinton, NY, 1982
AWARDS: Nat Endowment for the Arts, Visual Arts Fel, 1979–80; New York Council on the Arts, Creative Artist Prog Service Grants, 1970–71, 1980–81; New York Found for the Arts, NY, 1984–85; Pollock-Krasner Found Award, 1987; Adolph & Esther Gottlieb Found Award, 1989–90
RECENT EXHIB: Wilson Art Center, Rochester, NY, 1987; Stephen Rosenberg Gallery, NY, 1987–88; Philadelphia Mus, PA, 1988; Erie Art Mus, PA, 1988–89; Mus of Fine Art, Santa Cruz, CA, 1988–89; Hunter Mus, Chattanooga, TN, 1988–89; Henry Feiwel Gallery, NY, 1989; Philadelphia Art Alliance, PA, 1990; Conlon Gallery, Santa Fe, NM, 1990
COLLECTIONS: Metropolitan Mus of Art, NY; Staten Island Mus, Richmond, NY; Georgetown Col, KY; Philadelphia Mus, PA; Aldrich Mus of Contemp Art, Ridgefield, CT; Hamilton Col, Clinton, NY; Kenan Center, Lockport, NY; Stamford Mus of Art, CA; Weatherspoon Guild, Univ of North Carolina, Greensboro, NC
PRINTERS: Artist (ART)
PUBLISHERS: Artist (ART)
GALLERIES: Ellen Price Gallery, New York, NY; Nina Freudenheim Gallery, Buffalo, NY; Conlon Gallery, Santa Fe, NM
MAILING ADDRESS: 16 Greene St, New York, NY 10013

TITLE	PUBLISHER	PRINTER	DATE	MEDIUM	DIMENSION (PAPER SIZE) IN INCHES	TYPE OF PAPER	EDITION NUMBER	NO. OF COLORS	ORIGINAL OPENING PRICE	CURRENT RETAIL PRICE
SOLD OUT EDITIONS (RARE):										
Untitled	ART	ART	1976	CP	14 X 18 X 1	CD	8	0	200	1750
Untitled	ART	ART	1977	CP	19 X 29 X 1	R/100	3	0	650	2000
Untitled	ART	ART	1982	CP	43 X 36 X 3	R/100	12	0	1000	4000

ROY LICHTENSTEIN

BORN: New York, NY; October 27, 1923
EDUCATION: Art Students League, NY, 1939; Ohio State Univ, Columbus, OH, BFA, 1946, MFA, 1949
TEACHING: Instr, Ohio State Univ, Columbus, OH, 1946–51; Instr, State Univ of Oswego, 1957–60; Instr, Douglass Col, Rutgers Univ, New Brunswick, NJ, 1960–63
RECENT EXHIB: Castelli Uptown Gallery, NY, 1987; Corcoran Gallery of Art, Wash, DC, 1988; Martina Hamilton Gallery, NY, 1988; Ivory/Kimpton Gallery, San Francisco, CA, 1988; Florida State Univ Mus, Tallahassee, FL, 1989; Merryman Coll, Stanford, CA, 1989; State Univ of New York, Plattsburgh, NY, 1989; Heland Wetterling Gallery, Stockholm, Sweden, 1989; Erika Meyerovich Gallery, San Francisco, CA, 1990–91; Galerie Beyeler, Basil, Switzerland, 1991; Galerie Daniel Templon, Paris, France, 1992; Galerie Ulysses, Vienna, Austria, 1992; Gagosian Gallery, NY, 1992; Leo Castelli Gallery, NY, 1988,92; Mayor Gallery, London, England, 1988,92; Richard Gray Gallery, Chicago, IL, 1992; Galerie Kaj Forsblom, Zurich, Switzerland, 1992–93; Guggenheim Mus, NY, 1993; Musée des Beaux Arts, Montreal, Canada, 1993; Laura Carpenter Fine Art, Santa Fe, NM, 1993
COLLECTIONS: Mus of Mod Art, NY; in Solomon R Guggenheim Mus, NY; Whitney Mus of Am Art, NY; Tate Gallery, London, England; Stedelijk Mus, Schiedam, The Netherlands; Pasadena Mus of Art, CA; Metropolitan Mus of Art, NY
PRINTERS: Mourlot, Paris, France (M); Styria Studio, NY (SS); Gemini GEL, Los Angeles, CA (GEM); Tyler Graphics Ltd, Mount Kisco, NY (TGL); Gabriele Mazzotta Editore (GME); La Paloma, Los Angeles, CA (LP); Ron McPherson, Los Angeles, CA (RM); Shigemitsy Tsykaguchi, Phila, PA (ST); Michael Berdan, Cambridge, MA (MB); Burston Graphics Center, Jerusalem, Israel (BGC); Tanglewood Press (TP); Maeght Editeur, Paris, France (ME); La Paloma, Graphicstudio, Univ of South Florida, Tampa, FL (GS/USF); Waddington Graphics, London, England (WG)
PUBLISHERS: Multiples, NY (M); Tyler Graphics, Ltd, Mount Kisco, NY (TGL); Gemini GEL, Los Angeles, CA (GEM); Castelli Graphics, NY (CG); Leo Castelli, NY (LC); Feigen Gallery, NY (FG); Mourlot Paris, France (M); Gabriele Mazzotta Editore (GME); Arts, Letters, and Politics, NY (ALP); Petersburg Press, London, England (PP); List Art Posters, NY (LAP); Posters Original, Ltd, NY (POL); Editore Gabriele Mazzota, Milan, Italy (EGM); Galerie Maeght, Paris, France (GM); Tanglewood Press (TP); Leo Castelli Gallery, NY (LCG); Original Editions, NY (OEd); Jerusalem Mus, Jerusalem, Israel (JM); Inst of Contemp Art, Univ of Pennsylvania, Phila, PA (ICA/UP); APC Editions, Division Chermayeff & Geismar Assoc, Inc, NY (APC/DCGA); Committee to Endow a Chair in Honor of Meyer Schapiro at Columbia University, NY (CECHMSCU); Stedelijk Mus, Amsterdam, The Netherlands (SM); Pasadena Art Mus, CA (PAM); Metropolitan Mus of Art, NY (MMA)
GALLERIES: Gemini GEL, Los Angeles, CA; R K Goldman Contemporary, Los Angeles, CA; Andrew Dierken Fine Art, Los Angeles, CA; Irene Drori Fine Arts, Los Angeles, CA; Jack Rutberg Fine Arts, Los Angeles, CA; Richard Greene Gallery, Los Angeles, CA & New York, NY; Greystone Gallery, San Francisco, CA; Xiliary Twil Fine Arts, Santa Monica, CA; Mary Singer Gallery, Wash, DC; Hokin Galleries, Palm Beach, FL & Bay Harbor Islands, Miami, FL; Jupiter Fine Arts, Jupiter, FL; Opus Art Studios, Miami, FL; Marvin Ross Friedman & Co, Miami, FL; Barbara Gillman Gallery, Miami, FL; Ochi Galleries, Boise, ID & Sun Valley, ID; Richard Gray Gallery, Chicago, IL; Kass/Meridian Gallery, Chicago, IL; Magnuson Gallery, Boston, MA; Morgan Gallery, Boston, MA; Golden Gallery, Boston, MA; Nancy Singer Gallery, St Louis, MO; Greenberg Gallery, St Louis, MO; Tyler Graphics, Ltd, Mount Kisco, NY; Leo Castelli Gallery, New York, NY; Gagosian Gallery, New York, NY; James Goodman Gallery, New York, NY; Martina Hamilton Gallery, New York, NY; Jane Kahan Gallery, New York, NY; Petersburg Press, New York, NY & London, England; Reinhold-Brown Gallery, New York, NY; Fenton Fine Arts, Fort Worth, TX; Mayor Gallery, London, England; Heland Wetterling Gallery, Stockholm, Sweden; Galerie Kaj Forsblom, Zurich, Switzerland; Laura Carpenter Fine Art, Santa Fe, NM; Professional Fine Arts Services, Inc, New York, NY
MAILING ADDRESS: PO Box 1369, Southampton, NY 11968
Bianchini (B) Gemini GEL (G)

TITLE	PUBLISHER	PRINTER	DATE	MEDIUM	DIMENSION (PAPER SIZE) IN INCHES	TYPE OF PAPER	EDITION NUMBER	NO. OF COLORS	ORIGINAL OPENING PRICE	CURRENT RETAIL PRICE
SOLD OUT EDITIONS (RARE):										
Foot and Hand (B-2)	LCG		1962	LC/OFF	17 X 21	AP	300		75	3500
Crying Girl (Unlimited Edition) (B-4)	LCG		1963	LC/OFF	18 X 24	AP			50	8000
Foot Medication	LCG		1963	LC/OFF	23 X 17	AP	100		50	2500
Crak! (B-5)	LCG		1964	LC/OFF	19 X 27	AP	300		100	25000
As I Opened Fire . . . (Set of 3)	SM		1964	LC/OFF	25 X 21 EA	AP	3000 EA		300 SET	12000 SET
The Temple	LCG		1964	LC/OFF	24 X 18	AP	300		75	3000
Turkey Shopping Bag	LCG		1964	SP	23 X 17	AP	200		100	3500
Moonscape (Printed on Metallic Rowlex) (from 11 Pop Artists) (B-9)	OEd		1965	SP	20 X 24	M/ROW	200		100	4500
The Melody Haunts My Reverie (from 11 Pop Artists II) (B-10)	OEd		1965	SP	27 X 23	AP	200		100	25000
Sweet Dreams Baby! (from 11 Pop Artists III) (B-11)	OEd		1965	SP	38 X 28	WOVE/W	200		150	75000
Shipboard Girl (Unlimited Edition) (B-12)	LCG		1965	LC/OFF	26 X 19	AP			100	20000
Brushstroke (B-14)	LCG		1965	SP	22 X 28	AP	280		150	5000
Sunrise (Unlimited Edition) (B-15)	LCG		1965	LC/OFF	18 X 23	AP			100	4000
Lincoln Center Poster (on Silver Paper) (B-18)	LAP		1965	SP	46 X 30	SP	100		100	4500
Brushstrokes (B-20)	PAM		1967	SP	22 X 30	AP	300		150	6000
Modern Art Poster (B-21)	LCG		1967	SP	8 X 11	AP	300		100	5500
Fish and Sky (from Ten from Castelli) (B-25)	TP	TP	1967	SP/PH	11 X 14	PLAS	200	1	150	4000
Ten Landscapes (Set of 10) (B-26 a-j)	OEd/LCG		1967	SP/PH	12 X 17	ARJ	100		1000 SET	40000 SET
Salute to Aviation	FG		1968	SP	45 X 25	ARJ	135		200	3000
Pyramid (Mounted on Composition Board) (B-31)	LCG		1968	SP	20 X 20 X 20	BD	300	2	200	5000
Red Barn	EGM	LP/CPA/W	1969	SP	14 X 17	FAB	250		100	8500
Industry and Melody	GME	GME	1969	SP	17 X 14	FAB	100		100	7000
Industry and the Arts	GME	GME	1969	LC/SP	26 X 19	ARJ	250		125	5000
Modern Triptych	M	M	1969	LC	41 X 17	ARJ	100		200	5000
Haystack	M	M	1969	SP	19 X 26	ARJ	250		200	4000
Landscape (Red Barn)	M	M	1969	SP	20 X 26	ARJ	250		200	4000
Salute to Air Mail	ICS		1968	MULT	115 X 5	BRONZE	50		500	3000
Red Barn	EGM		1969	SP	14 X 17	FAB	250		200	4500
Pyramids (Yellow & Black)	M		1969	LC	12 X 35		101		200	5500

ROY LICHTENSTEIN CONTINUED

TITLE	PUBLISHER	PRINTER	DATE	MEDIUM	DIMENSION (PAPER SIZE) IN INCHES	TYPE OF PAPER	EDITION NUMBER	NO. OF COLORS	ORIGINAL OPENING PRICE	CURRENT RETAIL PRICE
SOLD OUT EDITIONS (RARE):										
Roven Cathedral (Yellow)	GEM	GEM	1969	SP	49 X 33	ARJ	75		200	4000
Cathedral #6	TGL	TGL	1969	LC	49 X 31	ARJ	75	2	200	4000
Haystack Series:										
Haystack #1	GEM	GEM	1969	LC/SP	21 X 31	R/BFK	100	2	200	3500
Haystack #2	GEM	GEM	1969	LC/SP	21 X 31	R/BFK	100	3	200	3500
Haystack #3	GEM	GEM	1969	LC/SP	21 X 31	R/BFK	100	3	200	3500
Haystack #4	GEM	GEM	1969	LC/SP	21 X 31	R/BFK	100	3	200	3500
Haystack #5	GEM	GEM	1969	LC/SP	21 X 31	R/BFK	100	3	200	3500
Haystack #6	GEM	GEM	1969	LC	21 X 31	R/BFK	100	2	200	3500
Haystack #6, State I	GEM	GEM	1969	LC	21 X 31	R/BFK	13	2	200	4000
Haystack #6, State III	GEM	GEM	1969	LC	21 X 31	R/BFK	13	2	200	3500
Haystack #7	GEM	GEM	1969	EMB	21 X 31	R/BFK	100	1	200	3500
Solomon R Guggenhaim Museum Poster (B-35)	LCG/POL		1969	LC	29 X 29	ARJ	250		100	7000
Peace through Chemistry II	GEM	GEM	1970	LC/SP	37 X 63	R/BFK	43		500	15000
Peace through Chemistry III	GEM	GEM	1970	LB	30 X 57	R/BFK	16	1	300	10000
Peace through Chemistry Bronze	GEM	GEM	1970	BR/REL	27 X 46 X 1	BRONZE	38		3000	50000
Litho/Litho (G-223)	GEM	GEM	1970	LC	35 X 48	ARJ	54	4	300	2000
Banner (with Felt)	M		1970	MULT	96 X 96	VINYL	30		500	15000
Twin Mirror	GEM	GEM	1970	SP	39 X 26	AP	250		200	5000
Modern Head Series:										
Modern Head #1 (G-242)	GEM	GEM	1970	WC	20 X 13	HOSHI	100		300	6000
Modern Head #2 (G-243)	GEM	GEM	1970	LC/LI/EMB	25 X 19	HOSHI	100	1	300	6000
Modern Head #3 (G-244)	GEM	GEM	1970	LC/LI/EMB	25 X 18	HOSHI	100	1	300	6000
Modern Head #5 (G-246)	GEM	GEM	1970	EMB/PT	28 X 20	HOSHI	100	1	300	6000
Modern Head Relief	GEM	GEM	1970	REI	24 X 18 X 1		100		300	15000
Modern Print (G-277)	GEM	GEM	1971	LC/SP	24 X 24	ARJ	200		300	3500
Mirror Series (Set of 8):										
Mirror #1 (G-382)	GEM	GEM	1972	LI/SP	28 X 28	ARJ	80		400	6000
Mirror #2 (G-383)	GEM	GEM	1972	LI/SP/EMB	28 X 28	ARJ	80	6	400	6000
Mirror #3 (G-384)	GEM	GEM	1972	LI/SP/EMB	28 X 28	ARJ	80		400	6000
Mirror #4 (G-385)	GEM	GEM	1972	LI/SP/EMB	28 X 28	ARJ	80		400	6000
Mirror #5 (G-386)	GEM	GEM	1972	LC/SP	34 X 24	ARJ	80	5	400	6000
Mirror #6 (G-387)	GEM	GEM	1972	LC/SP	40 X 30	ARJ	80	5	400	6000
Mirror #7 (G-388)	GEM	GEM	1972	LC/SP	38 X 26	ARJ	80	5	400	6000
Mirror #8 (G-389)	GEM	GEM	1972	LC/SP	41 X 53	ARJ	80	5	400	6000
Mirror	SS	SS	1972	SP	33 X 33	ARJ	75		400	7000
For Meyer Schapiro: Still Life	CECHMSCU		1973	LC/SP	25 X 24	ARJ	100		300	4500
Homage to Picasso: Still Life with Picasso (G-564)	GEM	GEM	1973	SP	30 X 22	AP88	90		400	32000
Bull Profile Series I–VI (Set of 6) (G-466–G-471)	GEM	GEM	1973	LC/SP/LI	27 X 35 EA	ARJ	100 EA		1500 SET	50000 SET
Bull Head Series (Set of 6):										
Bull Head I (G-488)	GEM	GEM	1973	LI/LB	27 X 35	ARJ	100	1	450	25000
Bull Head II (G-489)	GEM	GEM	1973	LI/LC	27 X 35	ARJ	100	2	450	25000
Bull Head III (G-490)	GEM	GEM	1973	LI/LC/SP	25 X 33	ARJ	100	5	450	25000
Bull Head IV (G-491)	GEM	GEM	1973	LI/LC/SP	27 X 35	ARJ	100	5	450	25000
Still Life with Cheese	GEM	GEM	1974	LC/SP	35 X 45	ARJ	100		850	9000
Six Still Lifes (Set of 6):										4800 SET	125000 SET
Still Life with Pitcher & Flowers	M/CG	SS	1974	LC	37 X 52	R/BFK	100		850	25000
Still Life with Portrait	M/CG	SS	1974	LC	38 X 48	R/BFK	100		900	12000
Still Life with Windmill	M/CG	SS	1974	LC	36 X 45	R/BFK	100		850	15000
Yellow Still Life	M/CG	SS	1974	LC	33 X 44	R/BFK	100		800	15000
Still Life with Figurine	M/CG	SS	1974	LC/SP	38 X 47	R/BFK	100		850	9000
Still Life with Lobster	M/CG	SS	1974	LC/SP	38 X 39	R/BFK	100		850	20000
Still Life with Crystal Bowl	M/CG	SS	1975	LC/SP	38 X 50	RF/ROL	45	8	900	30000
Homage to Max Ernst (T-333) (RL-1)	TGL	TGL	1975	SP	26 X 20	AP88	100	6	500	10000
Mirrors of the Mind:										
Before the Mirror	M/CG	SS	1975	LC/SP	44 X 32	ARJ	100		600	15000
Huh?	M/CG	BGC	1976	SP	42 X 30	AP	100	3	800	20000
Entablature Series:										
Entablature I (T-335) (RL-4)	TGL	TGL	1976	SP/CO/EMB	29 X 45	R/BFK	16	5	1800	4000
Entablature II (T-336) (RL-5)	TGL	TGL	1976	SP/CO/LC	29 X 45	R/BFK	30	4	1500	3000
Entablature III (T-337) (RL-6)	TGL	TGL	1976	SP/LC/CO	29 X 45	R/BFK	16	4	1800	3500
Entablature IV (T-338) (RL-7)	TGL	TGL	1976	SP/CO/EMB	29 X 45	R/BFK	30	5	1500	3000
Entablature V (T-339) (RL-8)	TGL	TGL	1976	SP/LC/CO	29 X 45	R/BFK	30	4	1500	3500
Entablature VI (T-340) (RL-9)	TGL	TGL	1976	SP/CO/EMB	29 X 45	R/BFK	30	5	1500	3000
Entablature VII (T-341) (RL-10)	TGL	TGL	1976	SP/CO/EMB	29 X 45	R/BFK	30	2	1500	3000
Entablature VIII (T-342) (RL-11)	TGL	TGL	1976	SP/CO/EMB	29 X 45	R/BFK	30	6	1500	3500
Entablature IX (T-343) (RL-12)	TGL	TGL	1976	SP/LC/CO	29 X 45	R/BFK	30	4	1500	4000
Entablature X (T-344) (RL-13)	TGL	TGL	1976	SP/LC/CO	29 X 45	R/BFK	18	3	1500	4000
Entablature XII (T-346) (RL-15)	TGL	TGL	1976	SP/LC/CO	29 X 45	R/BFK	18	3	1800	4000

ROY LICHENSTEIN CONTINUED

TITLE	PUBLISHER	PRINTER	DATE	MEDIUM	DIMENSION (PAPER SIZE) IN INCHES	TYPE OF PAPER	EDITION NUMBER	NO. OF COLORS	ORIGINAL OPENING PRICE	CURRENT RETAIL PRICE
SOLD OUT EDITIONS (RARE):										
America: The Third Century:										
Bicentennial Print	APC/DCGA		1976	LC/SP	25 X 18	AP88	200		500	7000
Inaugural Print	TGL	TGL	1977	SP	20 X 30	AP88	100	5	500	2500
Figures with Pope	GEM	GEM	1978	LC	22 X 30	ARJ	38		900	5000
Figures	GEM	GEM	1978	LC	22 X 24	ARJ	38		900	5000
At the Beach	GEM	GEM	1978	LC	26 X 43	ARJ	38		1200	8000
American Indian Theme (Set of 6):										
American Indian Theme I (T-346) (RL-14)	TGL	TGL	1980	WC/LC	33 X 32	SUZ/HMP	50	4	1800	4500
American Indian Theme II (T-347) (RL-15)	TGL	TGL	1980	WC/LC	33 X 38	SUZ/HMP	50	7	2400	4500
American Indian Theme III (T-348) (RL-16)	TGL	TGL	1980	WC/LC	35 X 27	SUZ/HMP	50	5	2500	5000
American Indian Theme IV (T-349) (RL-17)	TGL	TGL	1980	WC/LC	37 X 36	SUZ/HMP	50	5	2300	4500
American Indian Theme V (T-350) (RL-18)	TGL	TGL	1980	WC/LC	32 X 41	SUZ/HMP	50	6	2400	5000
American Indian Theme VI (T-351) (RL-19)	TGL	TGL	1980	WC/LC	38 X 50	SUZ/HMP	50	5	3500	6000
Head with Feathers and Braid (T-352) (RL-20)	TGL	TGL	1980	EB/A	24 X 20	LANA	32	4	950	3000
Figure with Teepee (T-353) (RL-21)	TGL	TGL	1980	EB/EMB	24 X 21	LANA	32	3	950	3000
Head with Braid	TGL	TGL	1980	AC/ENG	24 X 20	LANA	32	5	1250	3500
Expressionist Woodcuts (Set of 7)	GEM	GEM	1980	WC/EMB	40 X 34 EA	OKP	50 EA		8500 SET	70000 SET
Morton A Mort	GEM	GEM	1980	WC	30 X 39	OKP	50		1500	20000
Reclining Nude (G-880)	GEM	GEM	1980	WC	28 X 34	AC	50		1500	7500
Dr Waldmann (G-881)	GEM	GEM	1980	WC/EMB	40 X 34	AC	50		1500	7500
Head	GEM	GEM	1980	WC	40 X 34	OKP	50		1500	20000
Nude in the Woods	GEM	GEM	1980	WC	40 X 16	OKP	50		1500	22000
The Student (G-884)	GEM	GEM	1980	WC	38 X 34	AC	50		1500	22000
The Couple	GEM	GEM	1980	WC	40 X 36	OKP	50		1500	20000
Two Figures with Teepee (T-355)	TGL	TGL	1980	AC/ENG	24 X 21	LANA	32	5	1250	10000
Dancing Figures (RL-23)	TGL	TGL	1980	AC/ENG	25 X 22	LANA	32	5	1500	10000
Night Scene	TGL	TGL	1980	EB/A	21 X 21	LANA	32	7	1350	20000
Untitled I	TGL	TGL	1981	EC	23 X 21	LANA	8	4	2000	20000
Untitled II	TGL	TGL	1981	EC	23 X 21	LANA	8	4	2000	20000
Lamp (T-360) (RL-28)	TGL	TGL	1981	WC	25 X 18	OKP	30	4	1200	8000
Goldfish Bowl (T-362) (RL-30)	TGL	TGL	1981	WC	25 X 18	OKP	30	6	1500	8000
Study of Hands	CG		1981	LC/SP	32 X 33	R/BFK	100		1250	10000
Picture and Pitcher	TGL	TGL	1981	WC	25 X 18	OKP	30	3	1200	8000
I Love Liberty	LP	RM/LP	1982	SP	38 X 27	AP88	250	4	1200	22000
Seven Apple Woodcuts:										
Apple with Gray Background	PP	MB	1982	WC	30 X 33	HMP	60	9	3000	20000
Red and Yellow Apples	PP	MB	1982	WC	29 X 38	HMP	60	6	3000	20000
Two Apples	PP	MB	1982	WC	30 X 78	HMP	60	6	3000	20000
Red Apple	PP	MB	1982	WC	31 X 37	HMP	60	5	3000	20000
Apple and Lemon	PP	ST	1982	WC	32 X 42	HMP	60	5	3000	20000
Red Apple and Yellow Apple	PP	ST	1982	WC	28 X 38	HMP	60	4	3000	20000
Vertical Apple	PP	ST	1982	WC	38 X 33	HMP	60	6	3000	20000
Against Apartheid	GM	ME	1983	LC/SP	34 X 24	AP	110		2000	20000
Two Paintings Series:										
Two Paintings: Green Lamp (G-1140)	GEM	GEM	1984	WC/LC/SP/CO	36 X 50	AP88	60		3500	18000
Two Paintings: Sleeping Muse (G-1142)	GEM	GEM	1984	WC	38 X 49	AP88	60	15	3500	18000
Two Paintings: Beach Ball (G-1143)	GEM	GEM	1984	WC/LC/SP	37 X 36	AP88	60	4	3500	15000
Two Paintings (G-1144)	GEM	GEM	1984	WC/LC/SP/CO	43 X 36	AP88	60	8	3500	50000
Two Paintings: Painting in a Gold Frame (G-1145)	GEM	GEM	1984	WC/LC/SP/CO	44 X 33	AP	60	7	3500	22000
Painting on Canvas	GEM	GEM	1984	WC/LC/SP/CO	34 X 39	AP88	60	7	3500	22000
Forms in Space	ICA/UP		1985	SP	36 X 52	WOVE	125		5000	10000
Landscape Series:										
Landscapes: Road Before the Forest (G-1255)	GEM	GEM	1985	LC/WC/SP	37 X 52	AP88	60	8	5000	35000
Landscapes: Sunshine Through the Clouds (G-1258)	GEM	GEM	1985	LC/WC/SP	56 X 40	AP88	60	10	5000	35000
View from the Window	GEM	GEM	1985	WC/LC/SP	80 X 34	AP88	60	40	5000	45000
Yellow Brushstroke (G-1250)	GEM	GEM	1985	PH/EC	24 X 13	AP88	40		1500	6000

ROY LICHENSTEIN CONTINUED

TITLE	PUBLISHER	PRINTER	DATE	MEDIUM	DIMENSION (PAPER SIZE) IN INCHES	TYPE OF PAPER	EDITION NUMBER	NO. OF COLORS	ORIGINAL OPENING PRICE	CURRENT RETAIL PRICE
SOLD OUT EDITIONS (RARE):										
Brushstroke VI (Hand-Tooled from Cherry Wood & Painted with Epoxy, Acrylic, Resin & Enamel)	GEM	GEM	1986	REL/AC	60 X 58 X 10	WOOD	10	10	50000	55000
Untitled (From Brooklyn Academy of Music Portfolio)	PaP		1987	WC/SP	54 X 26	AP88	75	7	10000	10000
Two Paintings: Dagwood (G-1146)	GEM	GEM	1984	WC/LC	51 X 36	AP88	60		3500	18000
Landscapes: Moonscape (G-1254)	GEM	GEM	1985	WC/LC/SP	34 X 52	AP88	60		5000	18000
Imperfect Diptych (G-1360)	GEM	GEM	1988	WC/SP/CO	46 X 91	AP	45	21	20000	30000
Imperfect (G-1361)	GEM	GEM	1988	WC/SP/CO	45 X 103	RAG/4-Ply	45	25	25000	50000
Imperfect (G-1362)	GEM	GEM	1988	WC/SP/CO	67 X 86	MS	45	15	25000	40000
Imperfect	GEM	GEM	1988	WC/SP/CO	68 X 92	MS	45	21	35000	50000
Imperfect	GEM	GEM	1988	WC/SP/CO	63 X 89	MS	45	23	35000	50000
Imperfect (G-1364)	GEM	GEM	1988	WC/SP/CO	58 X 93	RAG/4-Ply	45	36	20000	40000
Brushstroke Figures (with Wax Encaustic) (Series of 7):									160000 SET	290000 SET
Blonde	WG	GS/USF	1988–89	LC/WC/SP/ENC	46 X 32	SWP	60		25000	42000
Blue Face	WG	GS/USF	1988–89	LC/WC/SP/ENC	46 X 32	SWP	60		25000	42000
Green Face	WG	GS/USF	1988–89	LC/WC/SP/ENC	46 X 32	SWP	60		25000	42000
Grandpa	WG	GS/USF	1988–89	LC/WC/SP/ENC	57 X 37	SWP	60	10	25000	42000
The Mask	WG	GS/USF	1988–89	LC/WC/SP/ENC	46 X 31	SWP	60		25000	25000
Nude	WG	GS/USF	1988–89	LC/WC/SP/ENC	57 X 37	SWP	60		25000	42000
Portrait	WG	GS/USF	1988–89	LC/WC/SP/ENC	53 X 30	SWP	60	8	25000	42000
Brushstroke on Canvas	MMA	TGL	1989	LC	34 X 32	R/BFK	40	7	10000	18000
Brushstroke Contest	TGL	TGL	1989	LC	48 X 38	R/BFK	36	10	10000	15000
Roads Collar	GS/USF	GS/USF	1989	LC/LC/SP	52 X 29	SWP	30		15000	20000
CURRENT EDITIONS:										
Interior Series:										
Bedroom	GEM	GEM	1991	WB/SP	57 X 79	AC	60	10	25000	25000
La Sortie	GEM	GEM	1991	WB	59 X 81	AC	60	6	35000	35000
The Den	GEM	GEM	1991	WB/SP	57 X 72	AC	60	7	25000	25000
The Living Room	GEM	GEM	1991	WB/SP	58 X 72	AC	60	11	25000	25000
Red Lamps	GEM	GEM	1991	WB/SP/LC	57 X 79	AC	60	11	25000	25000
Modern Room	GEM	GEM	1991	WB/SP/LC	56 X 81	AC	60	12	25000	25000
Yellow Vase	GEM	GEM	1991	WB/SP/LC	55 X 85	AC	60	11	25000	25000
Blue Floor	GEM	GEM	1991	WB/SP/LC	58 X 84	AC	60	12	30000	30000

DAVID LIGARE

BORN: Oak Park, IL; 1945
EDUCATION: Chouinard Art Inst, Los Angeles, Ca, 1961; Art Center Col of Design, Los Angeles, CA, 1964
RECENT EXHIB: Koplin Gallery, Los Angeles, CA, 1987
COLLECTIONS: Mus of Mod Art, NY; Weatherspoon Art Gallery, Univ of North Carolina, Greensboro, NC
PRINTERS: Landfall Press, Inc, Chicago, IL (LPI); Jerry Raidinger, Chicago, IL (JR)
PUBLISHERS: Landfall Press, Inc, Chicago, IL (LPI)
GALLERIES: Hall Galleries, Dallas, TX; Koplin Gallery, Santa Monica, CA; Stiebel Modern, New York, NY; Ron Hall Gallery, Dallas, TX

TITLE	PUBLISHER	PRINTER	DATE	MEDIUM	DIMENSION (PAPER SIZE) IN INCHES	TYPE OF PAPER	EDITION NUMBER	NO. OF COLORS	ORIGINAL OPENING PRICE	CURRENT RETAIL PRICE
SOLD OUT EDITIONS (RARE):										
Sand Drawing, #21,#22,#23,#24	LPI	JR/LPI	1973	LC	30 X 25 EA	JBG	75 EA	2 EA	125 EA	700 EA

GLENN LIGON

PRINTERS: Gregory Burnet, NY (GB); Burnet Editions, NY (BE)
PUBLISHERS: Max Protetch Gallery, NY (MPG)
GALLERIES: Max Protetch Gallery, New York, NY; White Columns, New York, NY

TITLE	PUBLISHER	PRINTER	DATE	MEDIUM	DIMENSION (PAPER SIZE) IN INCHES	TYPE OF PAPER	EDITION NUMBER	NO. OF COLORS	ORIGINAL OPENING PRICE	CURRENT RETAIL PRICE
CURRENT EDITIONS:										
Untitled (Two White/Two Black) (Set of 4)	MPG	GB/BE	1992	EB	25 X 17 EA	FAB/R-BFK	45 EA	1 EA	3000 SET	3000 SET

JOHN LIM

BORN: Singapore, China, 1937
EDUCATION: Univ of Pennsylvania, Wharton Sch, Phila, PA, 1959
AWARDS: Art Directors Merit Award, NY, 1978
PRINTERS: Steuber Silkscreen Studio, Downingtown, PA (SSS); Robert Benoit Pronovost, Toronto, Canada (RBP)
PUBLISHERS: Flanagan Graphics, Inc, Linwood, NJ (FG); NJ Fine Art Publications, Toronto, Canada (NJFA)
GALLERIES: Neville Gallery, Toronto, Canada
MAILING ADDRESS: 404 Palmerston Blvd, Toronto, ON, Canada M6G 2N8

TITLE	PUBLISHER	PRINTER	DATE	MEDIUM	DIMENSION (PAPER SIZE) IN INCHES	TYPE OF PAPER	EDITION NUMBER	NO. OF COLORS	ORIGINAL OPENING PRICE	CURRENT RETAIL PRICE
CURRENT EDITIONS:										
Count Your Stitches	FG	SSS	1980	SP	24 X 20	AP88	275	30	175	350
Kites Flying	FG	SSS	1980	SP	24 X 20	AP88	275	24	175	350
Mint Juleps	FG	SSS	1980	SP	20 X 24	AP88	275	30	200	350
Flower Shop	FG	SSS	1980	SP	20 X 24	AP88	275	28	200	350
Hot Chocolate	FG	SSS	1980	SP	20 X 24	AP88	275	31	200	350
Lovers	FG	SSS	1981	SP	20 X 24	AP88	275	29	200	350
Come Dance with Me	FG	SSS	1981	SP	24 X 36	AP88	275	27	300	550
Moonlight Serenade	NJFA	RBP	1984	SP	20 X 24	RPG	275		275	350
Honky Tonk Baby	NJFA	RBP	1984	SP	20 X 24	RPG	275		275	350
A Happy Family	NJFA	RBP	1985	SP	20 X 24	RPG	275		275	350
A Windy Day	NJFA	RBP	1985	SP	20 X 24	RPG	275		275	350

NAOMI LIMONT

BORN: Pottstown, PA; September 13, 1929
EDUCATION: Pennsylvania Acad of Fine Arts, Phila, PA, BFA; Pratt Graphics Center, NY, with Michael Ponce de Leon; Barnes Found, Merion, PA; Univ of Pennsylvania, Phila, PA, BFA; Tyler Sch of Art, Temple Univ, Phila, PA, with Romas Viesulas & Jerome Kaplan, MFA
TEACHING: Art in Res, Lock Haven State Col, PA, 1981; Instr, Graphics, Abington Art Center, PA, 1984 to present
AWARDS: Sun Oil Award, Earth Art Exhib, PA, 1975; Stella Drabkin Award & Bronze Medal, Am Color Print Soc, 1976; Grumbacher Award, 1981
COLLECTIONS: Philadelphia Mus of Art, PA; Yale Univ, New Haven, CT; Harvard Univ, Cambridge, MA; Rutgers Univ, New Brunswick, NJ; Pennsylvania Acad of Fine Arts, Phila, PA; Univ of Southern California, Los Angeles, CA
PRINTERS: Carl Pappendick, Phila, PA (CP); Barrett Pope, Horsham, PA (BP); Artist (ART)
PUBLISHERS: Primrose Press, New Hope, PA (PP); Philadelphia Print Club, PA (PPC); Artist (ART)
GALLERIES: Rosenfeld Gallery, Phila, PA; Hahn Gallery, Phila, PA; Langman Gallery, Jenkintown, PA
MAILING ADDRESS: RD 2, P O Box 180, Barto, PA 19504

TITLE	PUBLISHER	PRINTER	DATE	MEDIUM	DIMENSION (PAPER SIZE) IN INCHES	TYPE OF PAPER	EDITION NUMBER	NO. OF COLORS	ORIGINAL OPENING PRICE	CURRENT RETAIL PRICE
SOLD OUT EDITIONS (RARE):										
The Creation Folio	PPC	ART	1967	EC	6 X 8	AP	50	10	50	1000
Palindrome	ART	ART	1971	EC	16 X 19	AP	50	7	50	400
The Peaceable Kingdom	ART	ART	1974	EC	15 X 19	AP	50	3	50	400
The Seventh Day	ART	ART	1974	EC	18 X 18	AP	50	2	60	300
Penn's Treaty with the Indians	ART	ART	1976	EC	13 X 16	AP	50	10	90	300
CURRENT EDITIONS:										
Yosemite Falls	ART	ART	1973	COL	22 X 28	R/BFK	50	7	75	300
National Park	ART	BP	1973	COL	26 X 108	R/BFK	50	15	1000	3000
Arches National Park	ART	BP	1975	COL	26 X 132	R/BFK	50	25	1000	3500
Arctic Moonrise	ART	ART	1977	COL	26 X 20	R/BFK	50	5	70	200
The Little Lamb	ART	ART	1978	EC	13 X 17	R/BFK	100	7	100	200
Aesop's Fable	ART	ART	1978	EC	2 X 12	R/BFK	200	5	60	150
The Unruffled Grouse	ART	CP	1978	LC/HC	22 X 19	R/BFK	75	5	75	150
Watch the Birdie	ART	ART	1978	EC	15 X 19	R/BFK	100	3	80	150
In the Garden	ART	ART	1979	EC/VIS	14 X 17	R/BFK	50	6	80	150
The Waters Flow 'Round the Place of its Planting	ART	ART	1979	EC	18 X 24	R/BFK	300	6	150	250
North Cascade National Park	ART	BP	1979	COL	26 X 62	R/BFK	50	8	1000	1800
The Susquehanna	ART	ART	1981	COL	16 X 20	R/BFK	50	6	125	250
Blue Hills	ART	ART	1981	COL	10 X 15	R/BFK	80	8	80	150
Peace in Pennsylvania	ART	ART	1982	EC	17 X 11	R/BFK	200	7	200	250
Columbus Day	ART	ART	1982	COL	13 X 15	R/BFK	50	4	100	150
Mountain Landscape	ART	ART	1983	COL	18 X 19	R/BFK	25	3	100	150

DAVID LOCKHART

BORN: New York, NY; 1928
EDUCATION: Art Students League, NY
PRINTERS: American Atelier, NY (AA)
PUBLISHERS: Circle Fine Art, Chicago, IL (CFA)
GALLERIES: Circle Galleries, San Diego, CA & San Francisco, CA & Northbrook, IL & Pittsburgh, PA & Houston, TX & Soho, NY & Chicago, IL & Scottsdale, AZ & Beverly Hills, CA & Costa Mesa, Ca & Sherman Oaks, CA & Palm Beach, FL & Honolulu, HI & New Orleans, LA & Las Vegas, NV & Seattle, WA

TITLE	PUBLISHER	PRINTER	DATE	MEDIUM	DIMENSION (PAPER SIZE) IN INCHES	TYPE OF PAPER	EDITION NUMBER	NO. OF COLORS	ORIGINAL OPENING PRICE	CURRENT RETAIL PRICE
CURRENT EDITIONS:										
Constellation	CFA	AA	1977	LC	24 X 33	AP	300		75	250

RICHARD LINDNER

BORN: Hamburg, Germany; (1901–1978)
EDUCATION: Sch of Fine & Applied Arts, Nuremberg, Germany; Acad of Fine Arts, Munich, Germany, 1924, Berlin, 1927–28
TEACHING: Pratt inst, Brooklyn, NY, 1951-63; Yale Univ, New Haven, CT, 1963
AWARDS: William & Norma Copely Found Grant, 1957
COLLECTIONS: Mus of Mod Art, NY; Tate Gallery, London, England; Whitney Mus of Am Art, NY; Chicago Inst of Art, IL; Cleveland Mus of Art, OH
PRINTERS: Mourlot, Paris, France (M); Maeght Lelong, Paris, France (ML); The American Atelier, NY (AA); Shorewood Atelier, Inc, NY (SAI)
PUBLISHERS: Maeght Lelong, Paris, France (ML); Transworld Art, Inc, NY (TAI); Circle Gallery, Ltd, Chicago, IL (CGL); Multiples, NY (M); Marlborough Graphics, NY (MG); A C Mazo, Paris, France (ACM); Shorewood Publishers, Inc, NY (SPI) (OB)
GALLERIES: Galerie Lelong, New York, NY & Paris, France & Zürich, Switzerland; Marian Goodman, New York, NY; Morningstar Gallery, New York, NY; Marlborough Gallery, New York, NY; Harcourts Gallery, San Francisco, CA; Connecticut Fine Art, Westport, CT; Scherer Gallery, Marlboro, NJ; Short Hills Art Gallery, NJ; Kouros Gallery, New York, NY; Circle Galleries, San Diego, CA & San Francisco, CA & Northbrook, IL & Houston, TX & Pittsburgh, PA & Soho, NY & Chicago, IL & Scottsdale, AZ & Beverly Hills, CA & Costa Mesa, CA & Sherman Oaks, CA & Palm Beach, FL & Honolulu, HI & New Orleans, LA & Las Vegas, NV & Seattle, WA; Don Soker Gallery, San Francisco, CA; Richard Levy Gallery, Albuquerque, NM; Claude Bernard Gallery, New York, NY; Thomas Erben Gallery, Inc, New York, NY; Achim Moeller Fine Art, New York, NY

**Richard Lindner
Afternoon**
Courtesy Sherwood Atelier

TITLE	PUBLISHER	PRINTER	DATE	MEDIUM	DIMENSION (PAPER SIZE) IN INCHES	TYPE OF PAPER	EDITION NUMBER	NO. OF COLORS	ORIGINAL OPENING PRICE	CURRENT RETAIL PRICE
SOLD OUT EDITIONS (RARE):										
Banner #1	M		1965	F/S	84 X 48	AP	20		1500	7500
Banner #2	M		1966	F	84 X 48	AP	20		1500	6500
Banner #4	M	SPI	1971	LEA/CO	75 X 53	AP	18		1500	8500
Afternoon	SPI	SAI	1969	LC	28 X 22	JP	250		250	5000
Thank You	SPI	SAI	1969	SP/CO	28 X 18	AP	10		350	2500
Woman with a Parrot	SPI	SAI	1969	LC	22 X 14	AP	75		250	2000
Girl with Hoop	MG		1971	LC	24 X 20	AP	75		300	1500
Washington Holiday	TAI		1975	LC	26 X 20	AP	175		300	1250
Une Lettre de New York	ME	ME	1975	LC	28 X 21	AP	125		1000 FF	8000 FF
Femme Sur Fond Jaune	ME	ME	1975	LC	28 X 21	AP	125		1000 FF	8000 FF
Sans Titre	ME	ME	1975	LC	28 X 21	AP	125		1000 FF	8000 FF
As	ME	ME	1975	LC	28 X 21	AP	125		1000 FF	8000 FF
Femme Avec un Sac Jaune	ME	ME	1975	LC	28 X 21	AP	125		1000 FF	8000 FF
Nuages	ME	ME	1975	LC	28 X 21	AP	125		1000 FF	8000 FF
Face et Profil	ME	ME	1975	LC	28 X 21	AP	125		1000 FF	8000 FF
Amazone	ME	ME	1975	LC	28 X 21	AP	125		1000 FF	8000 FF
Blonde	ME	ME	1976	LC	28 X 21	AP	125		1000 FF	8000 FF
Arizona	ME	ME	1976	LC	28 X 21	AP	125		1000 FF	8000 FF
Heart	ME	ME	1976	LC	28 X 22	AP	250		1000 FF	8000 FF
Circle and Pillow	ME	ME	1976	LC	28 X 22	AP	250		1000 FF	8000 FF
Portrait No	ME	ME	1976	LC	28 X 22	AP	250		400 EA	3000 EA
How It All Began	ME	ME	1976	LC	28 X 22	AP	250		400	3000
Untitled 1975 (Set of 10)	ACM	M	1976	LC	28 X 21 EA	AP	125 EA		3500 SET	10000 SET
Afternoon (Set of 8)	SPI		1976	LC/COL	28 X 22 EA	AP	250 EA		2500 SET	6000 SET
Der Rosenkavalier	CGL	AA	1978	LC	22 X 30	AP/W	250	22	700	3000

EVAN LINDQUIST

BORN: Salina, KS; May 23, 1936
EDUCATION: Emporia State Univ, KS, BSE, 1958; Univ of Iowa, Iowa City, IA, MFA, 1963
TEACHING: Prof, Art, Arkansas State Univ, Jonesboro, AR, 1963 to present
AWARDS: Boston Printmakers, Silvermine Guild, MA, 1971–74; Potsdam Prints, New York State Univ Award, Potsdam, NY, 1972; New York State Univ Award, Potsdam, NY, 1972; Award, San Diego State Univ, CA, 1973; Awards, Boston Printmakers, MA, 1971,72,73; Int Graphic Arts Found Award, John Szoke Gallery, NY, 1989

RECENT EXHIB: Arkansas Arts Center, Little Rock, AR, 1987; Arkansas State Univ, Fine Arts Gallery, State University, AR, 1989; Memphis Col of Art, TN, 1990; NW Missouri State Univ, Maryville, MO, 1991; Society of Am Graphic Artists, NY, 1992; Prints Int, Silvermine Guild, New Canaan, CT, 1992
COLLECTIONS: Art Inst of Chicago, IL; Boston Mus of Fine Arts, MA; Whitney Mus of Am Art, NY; Museo Espanol de Arte Contemporeaneo Madrid, Spain; Nelson-Atkins Mus, Kansas City, MO; Galleria degli Uffizi, Florence, Italy; Brooks Mem Art Gallery, Memphis, TN; Arkansas Art Center, Little Rock, AR; Albertina, Vienna, Austria
PRINTERS: Artist (ART)
PUBLISHERS: Artist (ART)
GALLERIES: Gallery V, Kansas City, MO
MAILING ADDRESS: P O Box 2782, State University, AR 72467

EVAN LINDQUIST CONTINUED

TITLE	PUBLISHER	PRINTER	DATE	MEDIUM	DIMENSION (PAPER SIZE) IN INCHES	TYPE OF PAPER	EDITION NUMBER	NO. OF COLORS	ORIGINAL OPENING PRICE	CURRENT RETAIL PRICE
SOLD OUT EDITIONS (RARE):										
Emu	ART	ART	1961	ENG	22 X 22	INDEX	25	1	20	460
Rabbit	ART	ART	1962	ENG	13 X 16	R/BFK	25	1	20	210
Jackrabbit	ART	ART	1962	ENG	18 X 21	R/BFK	25	1	20	310
New World Landscape	ART	ART	1963	EB	13 X 17	R/BFK	50	1	20	240
View at the Entrance	ART	ART	1963	EB	16 X 20	R/BFK	50	1	20	130
Flight	ART	ART	1963	I	24 X 30	INDEX	25	1	40	800
Demon Woods	ART	ART	1964	ENG	22 X 28	R/BFK	25	1	25	650
Deep Summer	ART	ART	1965	EB	28 X 40	R/BFK	20	1	25	1500
Sweet Music	ART	ART	1965	EB	22 X 17	R/BFK	25	1	25	240
Changing Winds	ART	ART	1966	IC	19 X 15	R/BFK	15	2	50	220
Eric	ART	ART	1967	IC	40 X 26	R/BFK	30	8	50	350
The PHD's	ART	ART	1967	IC	22 X 22	R/BFK	15	2	50	250
Trees	ART	ART	1967	ENG	28 X 22	R/BFK	25	1	35	545
Ork	ART	ART	1967	IC	16 X 20	R/BFK	15	5	50	950
Fantasy	ART	ART	1968	ENG	24 X 28	R/BFK	40	1	75	2000
Adam & Eve	ART	ART	1968	EB	28 X 19	R/BFK	30	1	25	360
Gravity	ART	ART	1970	ENG	16 X 16	LAV	50	1	50	330
Creation	ART	ART	1970	ENG	14 X 14	LAV	50	1	50	300
Superego	ART	ART	1970	ENG	23 X 23	LAV	100	1	75	300
Thought	ART	ART	1970	ENG	16 X 16	LAV	100	1	75	375
Cosmos	ART	ART	1971	ENG	22 X 20	LAV	100	1	60	420
Collection of Cancelled Postage Stamps	ART	ART	1971	ENG(CO)	18 X 14	R/BFK	15		100	1100
Lute I	ART	ART	1974	ENG	17 X 24	LAV		1	60	470
Lute II	ART	ART	1974	ENG	18 X 24	LAV	25	1	125	650
Violin	ART	ART	1974	ENG	14 X 25	LAV	25	1	125	650
Lamp	ART	ART	1975	WE	7 X 5	JAP	300	1	25	150
Document	ART	ART	1975	ENG	19 X 28	LAV	25	1	75	240
Document: Man	ART	ART	1976	ENG	22 X 17	LAV	15	1	50	350
Document: Schema	ART	ART	1978	ENG	13 X 25	LAV	25	1	75	200
Lightning III	ART	ART	1978	ENG	16 X 21	LAV	25	1	75	210
Bird Cage	ART	ART	1979	ENG	19 X 16	LAV	25	1	75	175
Engraving Tools	ART	ART	1980	ENG/MEZ	14 X 20	ITALIA	25		50	300
Engraving Tools & Chessboard	ART	ART	1980	ENG/MEZ	14 X 20	ITALIA	25		50	195
Men & Beasts Stamps	ART	ART	1980	EB	12 X 15	R/BFK	20	1	75	200
Heroes & Monster Stamps	ART	ART	1980	EB	12 X 15	R/BFK	20	1	75	200
In Arkansas	ART	ART	1981	ENG	16 X 21	LAV	100	1	100	250
Landscape I	ART	ART	1981	ENG	20 X 29	LAV	5	6	300	680
Document: Bridge	ART	ART	1981	IC	23 X 35	LAV	10	4	200	445
Lily	ART	ART	1983	WC	29 X 21	ESSEX	25	4	200	380
Grapes	ART	ART	1983	WC	29 X 21	ESSEX	25	4	200	380
Hyacinth	ART	ART	1983	WC	29 X 21	ESSEX	25	4	200	380
Crown Imperial	ART	ART	1983	WC	29 X 21	ESSEX	25	4	200	400
Indian Quamash	ART	ART	1983	WC	29 X 21	ESSEX	25	4	200	380
CURRENT EDITIONS:										
Graven Image	ART	ART	1980	ENG	20 X 17	LAV	30	1	100	250
Concho (Set of 12)	ART	ART	1980	EB	14 X 12 EA	R/BFK	45 EA	1 EA	100 SET	250 SET
Second Monster Portrait	ART	ART	1981	ENG	13 X 16	LAV	25	1	75	200
First Monster Portrait	ART	ART	1981	ENG	13 X 16	LAV	25	1	75	200
Document: Torn Gravity Map	ART	ART	1981	ENG	8 X 8	AC	60	1	35	150
Ridge (Set of 3)	ART	ART	1982	ENG	24 X 23	R/BFK	30		250	350
Four Views of the Ridge	ART	ART	1982	ENG	27 X 27	LAV	20	1	275	355
Memory	ART	ART	1984	ENG/WC	16 X 16	LAV	30	3	165	205
Homage to Ukiyo-e: Celebrated Place	ART	ART	1984	ENG/WC	16 X 22	SOM	30	4	165	250
Homage to Ukiyo-e: Actor	ART	ART	1984	ENG/WC	15 X 17	SOM	25	2	165	205
Homge to Ukiyo-e: Dancer	ART	ART	1984	ENG/WC	17 X 22	SOM	25	2	165	205
Homage to Ukiyo-e: Foreignors Enter Edo	ART	ART	1984	ENG/WC	16 X 22	SOM	30	2	165	250
Homage to Ukiyo-e: Sumo Wrestlers	ART	ART	1984	ENG/WC	16 X 18	SOM	25	2	165	205
History Lesson: Borgia	ART	ART	1984	ENG/WC	25 X 16	SOM	30	7	165	250
History Lesson: Machiabelli	ART	ART	1984	ENG/WC	28 X 22	SOM	25	7	165	250
The River	ART	ART	1985	ENG	17 X 31	SOM	25	1	200	300
History Lesson: Napoleon	ART	ART	1985	ENG/WC	30 X 19	SOM	40	7	185	230
History Lesson: Tamerlane	ART	ART	1986	ENG/WC	28 X 22	SOM	40	7	195	230
History Lesson: Cleopatra	ART	ART	1986	ENG/WC	25 X 16	SOM	40	7	185	230
Gravity Flowering	ART	ART	1987	ENG	20 X 14	LAV	35	1	125	165
Gravity Expanding	ART	ART	1987	ENG	20 X 20	LAV	100	1	150	255
Thought V	ART	ART	1988	ENG	22 X 22	LAV	25	1	125	180
Idea	ART	ART	1989	ENG	19 X 13	LAV	25	1	125	165
Labyrinth VI	ART	ART	1989	ENG	13 X 13	LAV	25	1	150	165
Conscience	ART	ART	1991	ENG	28 X 22	LAV	100	1	600	600
Thought VI	ART	ART	1992	ENG	22 X 22	LAV	55	1	325	400

LINDA HAMMER LINDROTH

BORN: Miami, FL; September 4, 1946
EDUCATION: Douglass Col, New Brunswick, NJ, BA, 1968; Rutgers Univ, New Brunswick, NJ, MFA, 1979
TEACHING: Instr, Photog, Douglass Col, Rutgers Univ, New Brunswick, NJ, 1977–79
AWARDS: Documentary Photography Award, New Jersey Photography, 1974; New Jersey State Council on the Arts Fel, 1974, 83–84; New Jersey State Council of the Arts Fel, Mixed Media, 1984
RECENT EXHIB: Art Contemporain, Hull, Quebec, Can, 1987; Aetna Inst Gallery, Hartford, CT, 1987; Real Art Ways, Hartford, CT, 1988
PRINTERS: Artist (ART)
PUBLISHERS: W E Nordt, MD, New Haven, CT (WEN); Artist (ART)
GALLERIES: Simon Gallery, Montclair, NJ
MAILING ADDRESS: 219 Livingston St, New Haven, CT 06511

TITLE	PUBLISHER	PRINTER	DATE	MEDIUM	DIMENSION (PAPER SIZE) IN INCHES	TYPE OF PAPER	EDITION NUMBER	NO. OF COLORS	ORIGINAL OPENING PRICE	CURRENT RETAIL PRICE
SOLD OUT EDITIONS (RARE):										
Mixed Media Artist's Book	ART	ART	1975	MM	12 X 12	AP	100	Multi	35	300
CURRENT EDITIONS:										
Avalon Canyon Rd, Catalina Is, CA	ART	ART	1980	PH	16 X 20	AP	25	1	250	500
Avalon Canyon Rd, Catalina Is, CA	ART	ART	1981	PH	16 X 20	AP	25	1	250	500
The Jersey Meadows (A Series of Photos)	ART	ART	1981–82	PH	16 X 20	AP	25	1	250	500
Five triptyches (Polaroid Color Prints with b/w images enlarged onto photolinen	ART	ART	1983	PH	43 X 57 EA	Linen	5 EA		10000 EA	12000 EA
Triptych I, II, III (Set of 3)	WEN	GJ/HS	1984	PHC	20 X 24 EA	LF	5 EA	FULL	5000 SET	6000 SET

JACQUES LIPSCHITZ

BORN: Paris, France; (1891–1973)
EDUCATION: Ecole des Beaux-Arts, Paris, France; Acad Julian, Paris, France
AWARDS: Gold Medal, Am Acad, 1966; Award, Nat Inst of Arts & Letters, 1966
RECENT EXHIB: Marlborough Gallery, NY, 1987; St John's Col, Elizabeth Meyers Mitchell Art Gallery, Annapolis, MD, 1989; Dia Art Found, NY 1989; State Univ of New York, Neuberger Mus, Purchase, NY, 1989; Nelson-Atkins Mus of Art, Kansas City, MO 1989; Univ of Arizona Mus, Tucson, AZ, 1992; St John's Col, Elizabeth Myers Mitchell Art Gallery, Annapolis, MS, 1992; State Univ of New York, Neuberger Mus, Purchase, NY, 1992
COLLECTIONS: Mus of Mod Art, NY; Metropolitan Mus of Art, NY; Whitney Mus of Am Art, NY; Hirshhorn Mus, Wash, DC; Albright-Knox Art Gallery, Buffalo, NY; Philadelphia Art Mus, PA; Mus of Mod Art, Paris, France; Musée de Grenoble, France
PUBLISHERS: Marlborough Graphics, NY (MG)
GALLERIES: Marlborough Gallery, New York, NY; Fay Gold Gallery, Atlanta, GA; Herbert Palmer Gallery, Los Angeles, CA; Prakapas Gallery, La Jolla, CA; Harcourts Modern & Contemporary, San Francisco, CA; Galleria Durini, Ltd, New York, NY

TITLE	PUBLISHER	PRINTER	DATE	MEDIUM	DIMENSION (PAPER SIZE) IN INCHES	TYPE OF PAPER	EDITION NUMBER	NO. OF COLORS	ORIGINAL OPENING PRICE	CURRENT RETAIL PRICE
SOLD OUT EDITIONS (RARE):										
Biblical Subject	MB		1968	LC	28 X 22	AP	60		200	2800

SEYMOUR LIPTON

BORN: New York, NY; November 6, 1903
EDUCATION: City Col of New York, 1922–23; Columbia Univ, NY, 1923–27
TEACHING: Cooper Union, NY, 1943–44; Newark State Teachers Col, NJ, 1944–45; Yale Univ, New Haven, CT, 1957–59; New Sch for Social Research, NY, 1940–64
AWARDS: Art Inst of Chicago, IL, 1957; Nat Inst of Arts & Letters, NY, 1958; Guggenheim Found Fel, NY, 1960; New Sch for Social Research Grant, NY, 1960; Ford Found Grant, NY, 1961; George D Widener Mem Gold Medal, Pennsylvania Acad of Fine Arts, Phila, PA
RECENT EXHIB: Long Island Univ, Hillwood Art Mus, Brookville, NY, 1992
COLLECTIONS: Mus of Mod Art, NY; Metropolitan Mus of Art, NY; Whitney Mus of Am Art, NY; Philadelphia Mus, PA; Brooklyn Mus, NY; Yale Univ, New Haven, CT; Baltimore Mus, MD; Albright-Knox Art Gallery, Buffalo, NY; Phillips Mus, Wash, DC; Tel Aviv Mus, Israel; Cornell Univ, Ithaca, NY; Detroit Inst of Fine Arts, MI; Hirshhorn Mus, Wash, DC; Univ of Michigan, Ann Arbor, MI
PUBLISHERS: Marlborough Graphics, NY (MG)
GALLERIES: Marlborough Gallery, New York, NY; Weintraub Gallery, New York, NY; Jerald Melberg Gallery, Charlotte, NC; Babcock Galleries, New York, NY

TITLE	PUBLISHER	PRINTER	DATE	MEDIUM	DIMENSION (PAPER SIZE) IN INCHES	TYPE OF PAPER	EDITION NUMBER	NO. OF COLORS	ORIGINAL OPENING PRICE	CURRENT RETAIL PRICE
SOLD OUT EDITIONS (RARE):										
Study for Sculpture No 1	MG		1969	LC	27 X 19	AP	100		75	1200
Study for Sculpture No 2	MG		1969	LC	26 X 20	AP	100		75	1200

LAZAR EL LISSITSKY

Gmurzynska—G

BORN: (1890–1941)
PRINTERS: Artist (ART)
PUBLISHERS: Artist (ART); Kestner (Kes)

The Printworld Directory is accepting new applications for the seventh edition. Approximately 300 new artists will be accepted. Please use the two forms provided in the back section of this directory to submit biographical data and documentation of prints. Edition number of each print must not exceed 500 and the retail price must be $100 or more.

LAZAR EL LISSITSKY CONTINUED

TITLE	PUBLISHER	PRINTER	DATE	MEDIUM	DIMENSION (PAPER SIZE) IN INCHES	TYPE OF PAPER	EDITION NUMBER	NO. OF COLORS	ORIGINAL OPENING PRICE	CURRENT RETAIL PRICE
SOLD OUT EDITIONS (RARE):										
Chad Gadya (Tale of the Unk)	ART	ART	1919	LB	12 X 11 EA	WOVE		1	300 SET	75000 SET
Beat the Whites . . .	ART	ART	1919	LC	18 X 22	WOVE			25	85000
Proun I	ART	ART	1919	LB/CO	25 X 19	WOVE	50	1	1	35
Wendingen IV, #2 (Magazine Cover)	ART	ART	1921	LB	13 X 13	WOVE		1	25	5500
Ansager (from Sieg über die Sonne Portfolio) (G-56)	Kes	ART	1923	LC	14 X 10	WOVE	75		35	25000

FRANK LOBDELL

BORN: Kansas City, MO; 1921
EDUCATION: St Paul Sch of Fine Arts, St Paul, MN, 1938–39; California Sch of Fine Arts, San Francisco, CA, 1947–50; Acad Grande Chaumiere, Paris, France, 1950–51
TEACHING: Instr, California Sch of Fine Arts (now San Francisco Art Inst), San Francisco, CA, 1957–65; Prof, Art, Stanford Univ, Stanford, CA, 1966–91
AWARDS: San Francisco Mus of Art, Ca, Artists Council Prize, 1948; Purchase Prize, 1950, Nealie Sullivan Award, 1960; Tamarind Fel, Albuquerque, NM, 1966; A Knight of Mark Twain, 1971; Nat Acad & Inst of Arts & Letters Award of Merit, NY, 1988
RECENT EXHIB: Palo Alto Cultural Center, CA, 1989; Campbell-Thiebaud Gallery, San Francisco, CA, 1990; Smith Andersen Gallery, Palo Alto, CA, 1992

COLLECTIONS: Pasadena Art Mus, CA, Los Angeles County Mus, CA; Stanford Mus, CA; San Francisco Mus of Mod Art, CA; Oakland Mus of Art, CA; New York Public Library, NY; U S State Dept, Wash, DC; Zimmerli Mus, Rutgers Univ, NJ
PUBLISHERS: 3 EP Ltd, Palo Alto, CA (3EP); Smith Andersen Gallery, Palo Alto, CA (SA); Made in California, Oakland, CA (MIC); Artist (ART)
PRINTERS: Ikuru Kuwahara, Palo Alto, CA (IK); 3 EP Ltd, Palo Alto, CA (3EP); David Kelso, Oakland, CA (DK); Made in California, Oakland, CA (MIC)
GALLERIES: Smith Andersen Gallery, Palo Alto, CA; Campbell-Thiebaud Gallery, San Francisco, CA; Betsy Senior Contemporary Prints, New York, NY
MAILING ADDRESS: c/o Made in California, 3246 Etter St, #16, Oakland, CA 94608

TITLE	PUBLISHER	PRINTER	DATE	MEDIUM	DIMENSION (PAPER SIZE) IN INCHES	TYPE OF PAPER	EDITION NUMBER	NO. OF COLORS	ORIGINAL OPENING PRICE	CURRENT RETAIL PRICE
SOLD OUT EDITIONS (RARE):										
10.29.81	3EP	IK/3EP	1981	EB	25 X 19	R/BFK	5	1	400	600
10.31.81	3EP	IK/3EP	1981	EB	19 X 15	R/BFK	14	1	300	500
11.1.81	3EP	IK/3EP	1981	EB/A	19 X 15	R/BFK	15	1	400	600
11.2.81	3EP	IK/3EP	1981	EB/A	19 X 15	R/BFK	12	1	400	600
11.7.81	3EP	IK/3EP	1981	EB/A	23 X 15	R/BFK	15	1	400	600
11.13.81	3EP	IK/3EP	1981	EB	15 X 19	R/BFK	15	1	400	600
11.14.81	3EP	IK/3EP	1981	EB	15 X 19	R/BFK	13	1	400	600
11.20.81	3EP	IK/3EP	1981	EB	15 X 19	R/BFK	18	1	400	600
11.21.81	3EP	IK/3EP	1981	EB	15 X 19	R/BFK	14	1	400	600
12.5.81, State I	3EP	IK/3EP	1981	EB/A	28 X 22	R/BFK	7		800	1000
12.9.81	3EP	IK/3EP	1981	EB/A	23 X 15	R/BFK	15	1	400	600
2.25.83	SA/MIC	DK/MIC	1983	EC/A/HG	22 X 30	R/BFK	33	4	950	1100
CURRENT EDITIONS:										
2.25.83 (C, Yellow)	SA/MIC	DK/MIC	1983	EC/A/HG	23 X 30	R/BFK	33	4	850	1350
3.6.83 (A, Red)	SA/MIC	DK/MIC	1983	EC/A	23 X 30	R/BFK/W	33	4	850	1350
3.7.83 (B, Gray)	SA/MIC	DK/MIC	1983	EC/A/HG	23 X 30	R/BFK/W	39	2	800	1350
10.30.86A	MIC/ART	DK/MIC	1987	EB/A/HG	13 X 17	R/BFK/W	15	1	350	450
10.21.86B	MIC/ART	DK/MIC	1987	EB/A/HG/SG	23 X 30	R/BFK/W	35	1	450	550
10.22.86C	MIC/ART	DK/MIC	1987	EB/A/HG/SG	23 X 30	R/BFK/W	35	1	450	550
10.30.86D	MIC/ART	DK/MIC	1987	EB/A/HG/SG	19 X 23	R/BFK/W	35	1	400	500
11.3.86E	MIC/ART	DK/MIC	1987	EB/A/HG	13 X 17	R/BFK/W	15	1	350	450
10.29.86F	MIC/ART	DK/MIC	1987	EC/A/HG/SG	23 X 30	R/BFK/W	15	1	400	500
12.23.86G	MIC/ART	DK/MIC	1987	EC/A/HG	23 X 30	R/BFK/W	35	3	600	850
1.15.87H	MIC/ART	DK/MIC	1987	EC/A/HG/SG	19 X 23	R/BFK/W	35	3	500	650
1.12.87I	MIC/ART	DK/MIC	1987	EC/A/HG	13 X 17	R/BFK/W	35	3	475	600
5.23.87	MIC/ART	DK/MIC	1987	EC/A/HG/SG	23 X 19	R/BFK/W	35		475	700
Seven Etching Suite	MIC	DK/MIC	1988	EB/A/HG	10 X 9 EA	RdB	35 EA	1 EA	1575 SET	2000 SET
3.28.89	MIC	DK/MIC	1990	EB/A/HG	11 X 15	R/BFK/W	15	1	350	350
4.11.89	MIC	DK/MIC	1990	EB/A/HG	15 X 23	R/BFK/W	15	1	400	400
6.27.89	MIC	DK/MIC	1990	EB/A/HG/SG	15 X 23	R/BFK/W	15	1	425	425
6.28.89	MIC	DK/MIC	1990	EB/A/HG	15 X 23	R/BFK/W	15	1	425	425
7.6.89	MIC	DK/MIC	1989	EB/A/HG/SG	15 X 23	R/BFK/W	20	1	400	425
7.11.89 (State I)	MIC	DK/MIC	1989	EB/HG	30 X 23	R/BFK/W	10	1	550	600
8.4.89	MIC	DK/MIC	1990	EB/A/HG	30 X 23	R/BFK/W	38	1	550	675
9.21.89	MIC	DK/MIC	1989	EC/A/HG/SG	30 X 23	R/BFK/W	40	4	650	875
4.18.90	MIC	DK/MIC	1991	EB/A/HG	13 X 12	R/BFK/W	20	1	350	350
4.23.90	MIC	DK/MIC	1990	EC/A/SG	30 X 23	R/BFK/W	40	4	650	1200
5.25.90	MIC	DK/MIC	1991	EB/HG	13 X 12	RdL	20	1	350	350
6.12.91	MIC	DK/MIC	1991	EB/SG	13 X 12	RdL	20	1	350	350
6.25.91	MIC	DK/MIC	1991	EB/A/HG	13 X 12	RdL	20	1	350	350
7.20.91	MIC	DK/MIC	1991	EC/A/HG/SG	23 X 30	R/BFK/W	50	4	800	800

ROBERT LOBE

BORN: Detroit, MI; 1945
EDUCATION: Oberlin Col, Oh, BA, 1963–67; Hunter Col, NY, 1967–68
AWARDS: Creative Artists Public Service Award, 1981–82; Nat Endowment for the Arts Fel, 1979,83–84; Guggenheim Sculptor in Res, Chesterwood, 1985; Pollack-Krasner Found Grant, NY, 1992
RECENT EXHIB: Anderson Gallery, Virginia Commonwealth Univ, Richmond, VA, 1987; BlumHelman Gallery, Los Angeles, CA, 1989; Cleveland Mus of Art, OH, 1990; Beth Urdang Fine Art, Boston, MA, 1991; City Gallery of Contemp Art, Raleigh, NC; Art Center Col of Design, Pasadena, CA, 1992; Allene Lapidis Gallery, Santa Fe, NM, 1992; BlumHelman Warehouse, NY, 1989,91,92; BlumHelman Gallery, NY, 1989,92–93

COLLECTIONS: Albright-Knox Art Gallery, Buffalo, NY; Brooklyn Mus, NY; Cleveland Mus, OH; Contemp Mus, Honolulu, HI; Detroit Inst of Arts, MI; Indianapolis Mus of Art, IN; J Patrick Lannan Found, Los Angeles, CA; Mihanna-cho Int Outdoor Sculpture Garden, Mihama-cho, Japan; Milwaukee Art Mus, WI; Nat Gallery of Art, Washington, DC; Solomon R Guggenheim Mus, NY; Storm King Art Center, Mountainville, NY; Walker Art Center, Minneapolis, MN; Whitney Mus of Am Art, NY
PRINTERS: Judith Solodkin, NY (JS); Solo Press, NY (SP)
PUBLISHERS: Solo Press, NY (SP)
GALLERIES: BlumHelman Gallery, New York, NY; Solo Gallery, New York, NY; Allene Lapidis Gallery, Santa Fe, NM; Beth Urdang Fine Art, Boston, MA

TITLE	PUBLISHER	PRINTER	DATE	MEDIUM	DIMENSION (PAPER SIZE) IN INCHES	TYPE OF PAPER	EDITION NUMBER	NO. OF COLORS	ORIGINAL OPENING PRICE	CURRENT RETAIL PRICE
CURRENT EDITIONS:										
Woods Walk/Trees Talk (Set of 2):									1600 SET	1600 SET
Woods Walk	SP	JS/SP	1992	LC	33 X 33	SOM	30		850	850
Trees Talk	SP	JS/SP	1992	LC	33 X 33	SOM	30		850	850

PETER LOBELLO

BORN: New Orleans, LA; November 18, 1935
EDUCATION: Tulane Univ, Sch of Architecture, New Orleans, LA, 1953–55; Newcomb Sch of Art, 1954–55; Independent Study: Sicily, Tunisia, Libya, Egypt, Iran; Art in Residence, Rome, Italy, 1967–68

COLLECTIONS: Aldrich Mus of Contemp Art, Ridgefield, CT; New Orleans Mus, LA; Plains Art Mus, Moorhead, MN; Geneva Mus of Art, Switzerland; Phoenix Art Mus, AZ; Univ of Minnesota, Minneapolis, MN
PRINTERS: John Nichols, NY (JN)
PUBLISHERS: John Nichols, NY (JN)
GALLERIES: Jean Lumbard Fine Arts, New York, NY; John Nichols Gallery, New York, NY
MAILING ADDRESS: 71 Grand St, New York, NY 10013

TITLE	PUBLISHER	PRINTER	DATE	MEDIUM	DIMENSION (PAPER SIZE) IN INCHES	TYPE OF PAPER	EDITION NUMBER	NO. OF COLORS	ORIGINAL OPENING PRICE	CURRENT RETAIL PRICE
CURRENT EDITIONS:										
Spill	JN	JN	1981	LC	45 X 30	R/BFK	20	3	450	600

RAYMOND LOEWY

BORN: Paris, France, 1893
PRINTERS: American Atelier, NY (AA)

PUBLISHERS: Circle Fine Art, Chicago, IL (CFA)
GALLERIES: Circle Galleries, San Diego, CA & San Francisco, CA & Northbrook, IL & Pittsburgh, PA & Houston, TX & Soho, NY & Chicago, IL & Scottsdale, AZ & Beverly Hills, CA & Costa Mesa, CA & Sherman Oaks, CA & Palm Beach, FL & Honolulu, HI & New Orleans, LA & Las Vegas, NV, & Seattle, WA

TITLE	PUBLISHER	PRINTER	DATE	MEDIUM	DIMENSION (PAPER SIZE) IN INCHES	TYPE OF PAPER	EDITION NUMBER	NO. OF COLORS	ORIGINAL OPENING PRICE	CURRENT RETAIL PRICE
SOLD OUT EDITIONS (RARE):										
Folio (Mixed Media Graphics) (Set of 8):									1500 SET	3700 SET
Air Force One	CFA	AA	1979	LC/MM	21 X 28	AP	300		200	700
Avanti	CFA	AA	1979	LC	21 X 28	AP	300		200	850
Avanti II	CFA	AA	1979	LC/ST	28 X 22	AP	300		250	900
Moonlanding	CFA	AA	1979	SP/MM	21 X 28	AP	300		200	600
EVA (Extra Vehicular 400)	CFA	AA	1979	LC	21 X 28	AP	300		200	600
Space Maintenance Taxi	CFA	AA	1979	LC	21 X 28	AP	300		200	600
T–1 Locomotive	CFA	AA	1979	LC	21 X 28	AP	300		200	700
Hydrofoil	CFA	AA	1979	LC	21 X 28	AP	300		200	600
Skylab	CFA	AA	1979	LC	21 X 28	AP	300		200	600
CURRENT EDITIONS:										
S–1 Locomotive	CFA	AA	1978	LC	18 X 29	AP	300		150	600
Space Race Folio (Set of 8):									1800 SET	3200 SET
Rocket	CFA	AA	1985	LC	28 X 22	AP	300		250	600
Race Car with Flag	CFA	AA	1985	LC	28 X 22	AP	300		250	600
Race Car in Sun	CFA	AA	1985	LC	28 X 22	AP	300		250	600
Car with Headlights	CFA	AA	1985	LC	28 X 22	AP	300		250	600
Car with French Curve	CFA	AA	1985	LC/ST	28 X 22	AP	300		250	600
Formula Car in Mountains	CFA	AA	1985	LC	28 X 22	AP	300		250	600
Day and Night	CFA	AA	1985	LC	28 X 22	AP	300		250	600

GINA LOMBARDI

EDUCATION: Lehman Col, NY; Parson Sch of Design, NY
COLLECTIONS: Arizona State Univ, Tempe, AZ; Oklahoma State Univ, Stillwater, OK; Philadelphia Col of Art, PA

PRINTERS: The American Atelier, NY (AA)
PUBLISHERS: Georgina Graphics, Ltd (GG); Jackie Fine Arts, NY (JFA)
GALLERIES: Ro Gallery Image Makers, Inc, New York, NY

GINA LOMBARDI CONTINUED

Gina Lombardi
A Day in the Country
Courtesy the Artist

Gina Lombardi
Afternoon Rest
Courtesy the Artist

Gina Lombardi
Michelle
Courtesy the Artist

TITLE	PUBLISHER	PRINTER	DATE	MEDIUM	DIMENSION (PAPER SIZE) IN INCHES	TYPE OF PAPER	EDITION NUMBER	NO. OF COLORS	ORIGINAL OPENING PRICE	CURRENT RETAIL PRICE
SOLD OUT EDITIONS (RARE):										
The Offering	GC	AA	1975	VP	36 X 36	MUS	100	14	1200	1350
Vanity	GC	AA	1976	VP	24 X 30	MASA	50	12	250	350
Springtime II	GC	AA	1977	VP	20 X 40	SILK	50	10	300	350
Springtime I	GC	AA	1977	VP	20 X 40	SILK	50	10	300	350
Night Owl	GC	AA	1978	CH	30 X 40	AP			300	350
Bird of Paradise	GC	AA	1978	CH	30 X 40	AP			300	350
Arcari	GC	AA	1978	CH	30 X 40	AP			300	350
Landscape I	GG	AA	1979	VP	16 X 17	MASA	100	12	150	300
CURRENT EDITIONS:										
Tribal Warrior	JFA	AA	1979	LC	22 X 30	R/BFK	300	11	150	300
The Dancers	JFA	AA	1979	LC	22 X 30	R/BFK	300	12	150	300
Geisha	JFA	AA	1979	LC	22 X 30	R/BFK	300	12	125	200
Nubian Madian	JFA	AA	1979	LC	22 X 30	R/BFK	300	9	150	300
Two Women	JFA	AA	1979	LC	18 X 28	R/BFK	300	10	150	300
Summer Afternoon By the Pond	JFA	AA	1979	LC	22 X 30	R/BFK	300	16	150	200
Washing Clothes	JFA	AA	1979	LC	22 X 30	R/BFK	300	12	125	200
The Catch	JFA	AA	1980	LC	22 X 30	SOM	250	17	150	300
Returning Home	JFA	AA	1980	LC	22 X 30	SOM	250	14	150	300
Girl from Borneo	JFA	AA	1980	LC	20 X 28	SOM	250	14	150	300
Autumn	JFA	AA	1980	LC	22 X 30	SOM	250	15	150	300
Island Girl	JFA	AA	1980	LC	22 X 30	R/BFK	300	15	150	250
Solitary Dance	JFA	AA	1980	LC	22 X 30	SOM	250	14	150	300
Anne	JFA	AA	1980	LC	22 X 30	R/BFK	250	10	150	300
Afternoon Rest	JFA	AA	1980	LC	22 X 30	SOM	250	16	150	300
April	JFA	AA	1980	LC	22 X 30	R/BFK	250	21	150	300
Autumn Walk	JFA	AA	1980	LC	22 X 30	SOM	250	19	150	300
Spring Walk	JFA	AA	1980	LC	22 X 30	SOM	250	17	150	300
Summer Breeze	JFA	AA	1980	LC	22 X 30	SOM	250	18	150	300
Summer Day	JFA	AA	1981	LC	22 X 30	SOM	250	13	200	300
Michelle	JFA	AA	1981	LC	22 X 30	SOM	250	12	150	300
Friendly Interruptions	JFA	AA	1981	LC	22 X 30	SOM	250	12	200	300
A Day in the Country	JFA	AA	1981	LC	22 X 30	SOM	250	13	200	300
Preparing For the Dance	JFA	AA	1981	LC	22 X 30	SOM	250	11	200	300
Mountain Serenade	JFA	AA	1981	LC	22 X 30	SOM	250	12	200	300
Marisa	JFA	AA	1981	LC	22 X 30	SOM	250	12	200	300
Sharing Life	JFA	AA	1981	LC	22 X 30	SOM	250	12	200	300
Afternoon in the Park	JFA	AA	1981	LC	22 X 30	SOM	250	12	200	300

The retail prices of the 100,000 limited edition prints quoted in this directory are subject to change. Print publishers, artists and galleries were the direct sources for these quotations. Prices in the secondary market listed as "Sold Out Editions (Rare)" indicate that the publisher has a limited supply of that print or that the print is difficult to locate in the galleries.

ROBERT LONGO

BORN: Brooklyn, NY; 1953
EDUCATION: North Texas State Univ, Denton, TX; Nassau Com Col, NY; State Univ of New York, Buffalo, NY, BFA, 1975
RECENT EXHIB: Los Angeles County Mus, CA, 1989; North Miami Center of Contemp Art, FL, 1989; Mus d'Art Moderne, Saint-Etienne, France, 1989; Mus of Contemp Art, Chicago, IL, 1990; Wadsworth Atheneum, Hartford, CT, 1990; Metro Pictures, NY, 1990; North Miami Center of Contemp Art, FL, 1992; Galerie Hans Mayer, Düsseldorf, Germany, 1993
COLLECTIONS: Albright-Knox Art Gallery, Buffalo, NY; Walker Art Center, Minneapolis, MN; Mus of Mod Art, NY; Tate Gallery, London, England; High Mus, Atlanta, GA; Weatherspoon Art Gallery, Univ of North Carolina, Greensboro, NC

PRINTERS: Maurice Sanchez, NY (MS); Donna Schulman, NY (DS); James Miller, NY (JM); Derriere L'Etoile Studios, NY (DES); Karl Maurer, Munich, Germany (KM); Joe Joseph, NY (JJ); Brand X, NY (BX)
PUBLISHERS: Editions Schellmann & Klüser, Munich, Germany & NY (ESK); Edition Schellmann, NY & Munich, Germany (ES); Brooke Alexander, Inc, NY (BAI); Park Granada Editions, Tarzana, CA (PGE)
GALLERIES: Metro Pictures, New York, NY; Texas Gallery, Houston, TX; Brooke Alexander Inc, New York, NY; Pace Prints, New York, NY; Schlesinger Gallery, New York, NY; Editions Schellmann, New York, NY & Munich, Germany; J J Brookings Gallery, San Jose, CA; Linda Cathcart Gallery, Santa Monica, CA; Stephen Solovy Fine Art, Chicago, IL; Fred Dorfman Gallery, New York, NY; Galerie Hans Mayer, Düsseldorf, Germany
MAILING ADDRESS: 85 South St, New York, NY 10038

Robert Longo
Black Palms
Courtesy Edition Schellmann

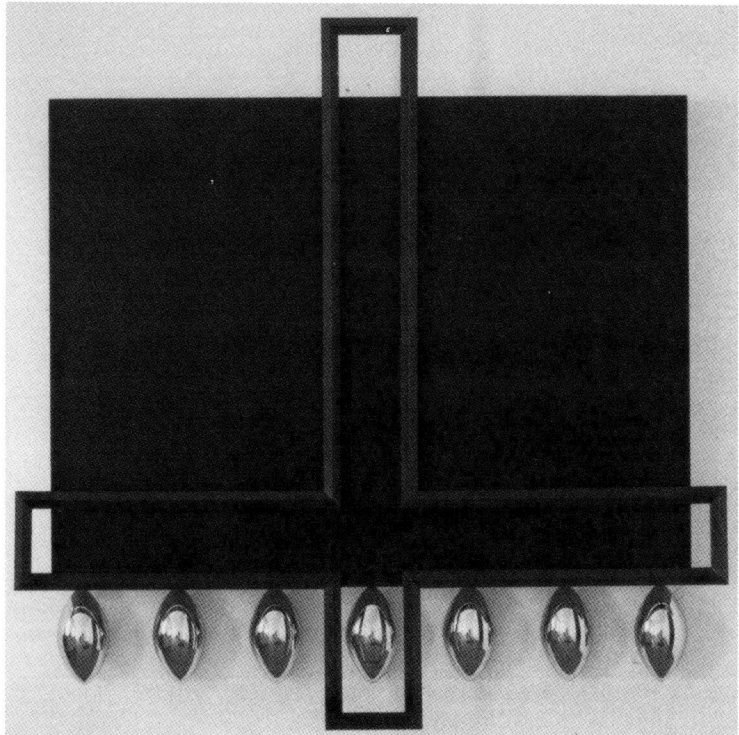

Robert Longo
End of the Season
Courtesy Edition Schellmann

TITLE	PUBLISHER	PRINTER	DATE	MEDIUM	DIMENSION (PAPER SIZE) IN INCHES	TYPE OF PAPER	EDITION NUMBER	NO. OF COLORS	ORIGINAL OPENING PRICE	CURRENT RETAIL PRICE
SOLD OUT EDITIONS (RARE):										
Jules/Gretchen/Mark, State II	BAI	MS/DES	1982–83	LC/EMB	37 X 68	AP	30	3	2500	15000
Government (Dipt)	ESK	KM/JJ/BX	1983	SP/PLEX/PL	72 X 28	AP88	15		5000	18000
Men in the Cities Series:										
Joanna and Larry	ESK	MS/DES	1983	LC	72 X 36	AP/350	48	3	1800	20000
Cindy	BAI	MS/DES	1984	LB	68 X 39	AP/350	38	1	2500	15000
Gretchen and Eric	BAI	MS/DES	1985	LC	68 X 39	AP/350	48	3	2500	20000
Anne and Edmund (Set of 2)	BAI	DS/JM/MS/DES	1985	LB	68 X 39	AP/ROL	38 EA	2 EA	5000 SET	35000 SET
CURRENT EDITIONS:										
Men in the Cities Series:										
Gretchen	BAI	MS/DES	1982–83	LC/EMB	37 X 21	AP	45	3	900	4500
Mark	BAI	MS/DES	1982–83	LC/EMB	37 X 21	AP	45	3	900	4500
Jules	BAI	MS/DES	1982–83	LC/EMB	37 X 21	AP	45	3	600	4500
Arena Brains	BAI	MS/DES	1986	LC	45 X 29	AP	75		2500	3000
Meryl and Jonathan	ESK	MS/DES	1988	LC	72 X 36	AP/350	18	3	1800	20000
Black Palms	ES	MS/DES	1989	LC	67 X 50	AP/350	35		3000	5000
End of the Season (Wall Object with Plywood, Linoleum, Lacquered Aluminum & Chromed Copper)	ES		1989	MULT	47 X 39 X 6		11		9000	12000
Solid Vision	BAI	MS/DES	1989	LC/WC	53 X 38	AP	42		3000	4500
Frank and Glen	BAI	MS/DES	1990	LC	38 X 55	AP	38		4000	4000
Strong in Love	BAI	MS/DES	1989–91	PH/EB/A	29 X 44	AP	15		1500	1500
Strong in Love (Yellow)	BAI	MS/DES	1989–91	PH/EB/A	29 X 44	AP	15		1500	1800

NINO LONGOBARDI

BORN: Italy
RECENT EXHIB: Germans van Eck, NY, 1990
PRINTERS: 3K Workshop, Rome, Italy (3KW); Il Ponte Editrice D'Art, Rome, Italy (IPE); Bruno Bassetti, Rome, Italy (BB); Angelo Gabbanini, Rome, Italy (AG); Giancarlo Iaccomucci, Rome, Italy (GI)
PUBLISHERS: Il Ponte Editrice D'Art, Rome, Italy (IPF); Metropolitan Mus of Art, Mezzanine Gallery, NY (MMA)
GALLERIES: Cowles Gallery, New York, NY; Paul Cava Gallery, Phila, PA; Germans van Eck Gallery, New York, NY

TITLE	PUBLISHER	PRINTER	DATE	MEDIUM	DIMENSION (PAPER SIZE) IN INCHES	TYPE OF PAPER	EDITION NUMBER	NO. OF COLORS	ORIGINAL OPENING PRICE	CURRENT RETAIL PRICE
CURRENT EDITIONS:										
Untitled I (Bull)	IPE	3KW	1982	LB	20 X 28	AP	60	1	275	750
Untitled II (Scull)	IPE	3KW	1982	LB	20 X 28	AP	60	1	275	750
Untitled 1982	IPE	3KW	1982	LC/SP	20 X 28	AP	70	2	300	850
Chair and Swimmer (with Watercolor)	IPE	3KW	1982	LC/WA	20 X 28	AP	70		500	900
Il Bestiaro (Set of 10):	IPE	BB/AG/3KW	1984	I	20 X 16 EA	SIC	60 EA	1 EA	1500 SET	5500 SET
The Runner	MMA	GI/3KW	1984	WC	16 X 20	AC	20	3	275	750
Green Vase (Black)	MMA	AG	1990	WC	31 X 23	MAG	50	2	3000	3000
Green Vase (Red)	MMA	AG	1990	WC	31 X 23	MAG	50	2	3000	3000

ANDREW LORD

RECENT EXHIB: Gallery Bruno Bischofberger, Zurich, Switzerland, 1992
PRINTERS: John Hutcheson, Jersey City, NJ (JH); Palisades Press, Jersey City, NJ (PalPr)
PUBLISHERS: Raymond Foye Editions, NY (RFE)
GALLERIES: Margo Leavin Gallery, Los Angeles, CA; Gallery Bruno Bischofberger, Zurich, Switzerland

TITLE	PUBLISHER	PRINTER	DATE	MEDIUM	DIMENSION (PAPER SIZE) IN INCHES	TYPE OF PAPER	EDITION NUMBER	NO. OF COLORS	ORIGINAL OPENING PRICE	CURRENT RETAIL PRICE
CURRENT EDITION:										
Series I (Set of 5)	RFE	JH/PalPr	1987	LC	42 X 30 EA	GE/BL	20 EA		3500 SET 900 EA	5000 SET 1000 EA
Series II (Set of 8)	RFE	JH/PalPr	1987	LC	39 X 26 EA	KAS	25 EA		4500 SET 750 EA	6500 SET 850 EA
Series III (Set of 3)	RFE	JH/PalPr	1987	LC	52 X 36 EA	KOZO	30 EA		2500 SET 900 EA	3000 SET 1000 EA
Series IV (Dipt)	RFA	JH/PalPr	1987	LC	45 X 30	R/BFK	25		1500	1800

LEE LORENZ

PRINTERS: Judith Solodkin, NY (JS); Solo Press, NY (SP)
PUBLISHERS: Solo Press, NY (SP)
GALLERIES: Solo Impressions, New York, NY

TITLE	PUBLISHER	PRINTER	DATE	MEDIUM	DIMENSION (PAPER SIZE) IN INCHES	TYPE OF PAPER	EDITION NUMBER	NO. OF COLORS	ORIGINAL OPENING PRICE	CURRENT RETAIL PRICE
CURRENT EDITIONS:										
Temptation of St. Anthony	SP	JS/SP	1981	LB	22 X 30	AP	50	1	150	250
Ecco Femina	SP	JS/SP	1982	LC	20 X 24	AP	80		250	350

YONA LOTAN

BORN: Israel
COLLECTIONS: Mus of Mod Art, Paris, France; Mus Boymans-Van-Beuningen, Rotterdam, The Netherlands; Mus Petit Palais, Geneva, Switzerland; Nat Gallery, Berlin, Germany
PRINTERS: ChromaComp, NY (CCI)
PUBLISHERS: Metropolitan Art Associates, NY (MAA); ChromaComp, NY (CCI)

TITLE	PUBLISHER	PRINTER	DATE	MEDIUM	DIMENSION (PAPER SIZE) IN INCHES	TYPE OF PAPER	EDITION NUMBER	NO. OF COLORS	ORIGINAL OPENING PRICE	CURRENT RETAIL PRICE
CURRENT EDITIONS:										
Moments In Our Life	CCI	CCI	1978	SP	20 X 27	AP	300		250	400
Together	CCI	CCI	1978	SP	27 X 35	AP	275	32	250	400
Yearning For Peace	CCI	CCI	1978	SP	25 X 17	AP	200		200	350
The Dance	MAA	CCI	1979	SP	16 X 21	AP	200		200	400
Intimate II	MAA	CCI	1979	SP	16 X 21	AP	200		200	400
Lost Paradise	MAA	CCI	1979	SP	16 X 21	AP	200		200	400

The retail prices of the 100,000 limited edition prints quoted in this directory are subject to change. Print publishers, artists and galleries were the direct sources for these quotations. Prices in the secondary market listed as "Sold Out Editions (Rare)" indicate that the publisher has a limited supply of that print or that the print is difficult to locate in the galleries.

STEPHEN NEIL LORBER

BORN: New York, NY; August 30, 1943
EDUCATION: Pratt Inst, NY, BFA, 1966; Yale Univ, New Haven, CT, Summer, 1964; Brooklyn Col, NY, MFA, 1969
AWARDS: Yale Univ Fel, New Haven, CT, 1964; Art in Res Grant, Roswell Mus & Art Center, NM; Yaddo Fel, 1971–75; Nat Endowment for the Arts Fel, 1976-77
RECENT EXHIB: Charles B Goddard Center for Visual & Performing Arts, Ardmore, OK, 1989
COLLECTIONS: Oklahoma Art Center, Oklahoma City, OK; Western New Mexico Univ, Silver City, NM; Roswell Mus, NM; Chicago Art Inst, IL
PRINTERS: Maurel Studio, NY (MS); Lynne Aikman, NY (LA); Mary Wood, NY (MW); K Carraccio, NY (KC); Blue Heron Press, Greenwich, NY (BHP)
PUBLISHERS: Barbara Gladstone Editions, NY (BGE); Diana Villani Editions, NY (DVE); Elaine Horwitch Graphics, Scottsdale, AZ (EHG); Blue Heron Press, Greenwich, NY (BHP); Artist (ART)
GALLERIES: Alexander F Milliken, Inc, New York, NY; Pace Prints, New York, NY
MAILING ADDRESS: RD 3, P O Box 198, Greenwich, NY 12834

Stephen Neil Lorber
Still Life with Street Musicians
Courtesy the Artist

TITLE	PUBLISHER	PRINTER	DATE	MEDIUM	DIMENSION (PAPER SIZE) IN INCHES	TYPE OF PAPER	EDITION NUMBER	NO. OF COLORS	ORIGINAL OPENING PRICE	CURRENT RETAIL PRICE
SOLD OUT EDITIONS (RARE):										
Sill Life with Quiver	ART	LA	1978	EC/A/ENG	22 X 30	AP	40	11	450	700
Camaroon Backpack	ART	KC	1978	EC/A/ENG	22 X 30	AP	50	9	450	1000
Sardinian Baskets	BGE/DVE	M	1979	SP	30 X 40	AP	80	22	450	850
Still Life with Jug	ART	KC	1980	EC/A/ENG	27 X 32	AP	65	14	450	1000
*Three Small Baskets	ART	KC	1980	EC/A/ENG	22 X 26	AP/CR	80	9	450	600
*Navajo Cermonial	ART	KC	1981	EC/A/ENG	22 X 26	AP/CR	80	12	450	1000
CURRENT EDITIONS:										
Still Life with Reeds and Quiver	BGE	MS	1978	SP	40 X 25	AP	80	22	450	850
Italian Veduta (Set of 4)										
Temple of the Dioscouri Agrigento	ART	KC	1978	EB/A/ENG	12 X 13	AP	50	1	150	300
Terme Caracalla, Rome	ART	KC	1978	EB/A/ENG	12 X 13	AP	50	1	150	300
Temple of Juno, Agrigento	ART	KC	1978	EB/A/ENG	12 X 13	AP	50	1	150	300
The Forum, Rome	ART	KC	1978	EB/A/ENG	12 X 13	AP	50	1	150	300
Still Life with Quiver, State II	ART	KC	1978	EB/A/ENG	22 X 30	AP	30	1	250	500
Red Paper	ART	KC	1979	EB/A/ENG	27 X 33	AP/CR	65	14	450	650
Camaroon Backpack, State II	ART	KC	1979	EB/A/ENG	22 X 30	RP/NP	25	2	300	500
Still Life with Twigs	ART	KC	1980	EB/A/ENG	27 X 33	AP	65	14	450	650
Still Life with Twigs	BGE	MS	1980	SP	30 X 40	AP	95	27	500	850
Still Life with Broom	BGE	MS	1980	SP	28 X 36	AP	90	25	550	750
*Painti Water Bottle	ART	KC	1980	EB/A/ENG	22 X 26	AP/CR	80	9	450	550
*Mission Basket	ART	KC	1981	EB/A/ENG	22 X 26	AP/CR	80	9	450	550
*Three from the North Coast	ART	KC	1981	EB/A/ENG	22 X 26	AP/CR	80	13	450	550
Large Yellow Basket	BGE	MS	1981	SP	39 X 31	AP	95	25	750	750
Still Life with Star Quilt	BGE	MS	1981	SP	39 X 31	AP	95	33	750	750
Still Life with Double Wedding Band Quilt	BGE/EHG	MS	1982	SP	39 X 31	AP	80		750	750
Large Shaker Basket	BHP	MW/BHP	1982	EB/A/ENG	27 X 30	AP	80	9	450	500
Original Red Paint	BHP	MW/BHP	1982	EB/A/ENG	30 X 40	AP	80	9	650	650
Still Life with Polka Dot Quilt	BHP	MW/BHP	1982	EB/A/ENG	30 X 40	AP	70	14	650	650
Two Shaker Baskets	BHP	MW/BHP	1983	EB/A/ENG	22 X 26	AP	80	10	450	450
Indian Feather Basket	BHP	MW/BHP	1983	EB/A/ENG	22 X 30	AP	80	9	450	450
Blue Bowl	BHP	BHP	1985	SP	23 X 32	AP88	50	25	750	750
Limes	BHP	BHP	1985	SP	19 X 27	AP	60	20	650	650
Orion's Nebula	BHP	BHP	1985	SP	26 X 38	AP	60	40	750	750
Oranges	BHP	BHP	1986	SP	19 X 26	AP	90	30	650	650
Sweet Peppers	BHP	BHP	1986	SP	20 X 33	AP	70	36	750	750
Lemons	BHP	BHP	1988	SP	18 X 28	AC	80	35	650	650
Still Life with Street Musicians	BHP	BHP	1988	Sp	18 X 27	AC	80	92	750	750
Democleides the Sailor	BHP	BHP	1990	SP	22 X 30	AC	60	40	750	750

*From the Native American Baskets of the Southwest and Northwest

---

The retail prices of the 100,000 limited edition prints quoted in this directory are subject to change. Print publishers, artists and galleries were the direct sources for these quotations. Prices in the secondary market listed as "Sold Out Editions (Rare)" indicate that the publisher has a limited supply of that print or that the print is difficult to locate in the galleries.

The Printworld Directory is accepting new applications for the seventh edition. Approximately 300 new artists will be accepted. Please use the two forms provided in the back section of this directory to submit biographical data and documentation of prints. Edition number of each print must not exceed 500 and the retail price must be $100 or more.

JOHN LORING

BORN: Chicago, IL; November 23, 1939
EDUCATION: Yale Univ, New Haven, CT, BA, 1960; Ecole des Beaux-Arts, Paris, France, 1961–64
TEACHING: Univ of California, Davis, CA, 1977
COLLECTIONS: Mus of Mod Art, NY; Art Inst of Chicago, IL; Whitney Mus of Am Art, NY; Boston Mus of Fine Art, MA; Metropolitan Mus of Art, NY; Princeton Univ, NJ; Vassar Col, Poughkeepsie, NY; Yale Univ, New Haven, CT
PRINTERS: Artist (ART)
PUBLISHERS: Pace Editions, NY (PE); Abrams Original Editions, NY (AOE); Judith Selkowitz Fine Art, NY (JSFA)
GALLERIES: Pace Prints, New York, NY; Judith Selkowitz Fine Art, New York, NY
MAILING ADDRESS: 860 Fifth Ave, New York, NY 10021

TITLE	PUBLISHER	PRINTER	DATE	MEDIUM	DIMENSION (PAPER SIZE) IN INCHES	TYPE OF PAPER	EDITION NUMBER	NO. OF COLORS	ORIGINAL OPENING PRICE	CURRENT RETAIL PRICE
SOLD OUT EDITIONS (RARE):										
Subway Scenes (Set of 4)	PE	ART	1972	SP	26 X 37 EA	STAR	50 EA		350 SET	3000 SET
Dollar Bill	JSFA	MS	1973	SP	26 X 40	STAR/W	50	6	125	1800
Ice Cream Chromes (Set of 3)	PE	ART	1973	SP	35 X 35 EA	STAR	50 EA		300 SET	2000 SET
Pull	PE	ART	1973	SP	39 X 35	STAR	30	10	200	1000
Pipelines #1, #2 (Set of 2)	PE	ART	1976	SP	35 X 50 EA	STAR	40 EA	6 EA	250 SET	2000 SET
Mortar Boards #1 Science (Set of 3)	PE	ART	1977	SP/PH/WB	23 X 27 EA	STAR	40 EA	3 EA	250 SET	2000 SET
Mortar Boards #2 Medicine (Set of 3)	PE	ART	1977	SP/WB	27 X 41 EA	STAR	40 EA	3 EA	250 SET	2000 SET
Mortar Boards #3 Law (Set of 3)	PE	ART	1977	SP/WB	25 X 43 EA	STAR	40 EA	3 EA	250 SET	2000 SET
TV Heroes (Set of 4):									700 SET	2500 SET
Antinous (Fire Sacred Flames of Art #1)	PE	ART	1977	SP	32 X 41	STAR	50	5	350	800
Cleopatra (Love Letters in the Sand)	PE	ART	1977	SP	32 X 41	STAR	50	5	200	600
Wittengenstein (Hot Ziggety)	PE	ART	1977	SP	32 X 41	STAR	50	5	200	600
Theresa of Avila	PE	ART	1977	SP	32 X 41	STAR	50	5	200	600
Pools	PE	ART	1978	LC/SP	30 X 43	STAR	40	8	350	800

ROBERT LOSTUTTER

RECENT EXHIB: Illinois State Mus, Springfield, IL, 1989
PRINTERS: Jack Lemon, Chicago, IL (JL); Landfall Press, Inc, Chicago, IL (LPI)
PUBLISHERS: Landfall Press, Inc, Chicago, IL (LPI)
GALLERIES: Dart Gallery, Chicago, IL; Landfall Press, Inc, Chicago, IL; LedisFlam Gallery, New York, NY; Quartet Editions, New York, NY

TITLE	PUBLISHER	PRINTER	DATE	MEDIUM	DIMENSION (PAPER SIZE) IN INCHES	TYPE OF PAPER	EDITION NUMBER	NO. OF COLORS	ORIGINAL OPENING PRICE	CURRENT RETAIL PRICE
CURRENT EDITIONS:										
Ross's Turaco Looking Back	LPI	JL/LPI	1988	EB/HC	9 X 10	SOM	20	Varies	1200	1200
Untitled	LPI	JL/LPI	1989	EB	14 X 11	SOM	10	1	600	600
American Flamingo	LPI	JL/LPI	1989	EB/HC	14 X 11	SOM	10	Varies	1000	1000
Ground Cuckoo	LPI	JL/LPI	1989	EB/HC	14 X 11	SOM	10	Varies	1000	1000
Crimson Rumped Toucanet	LPI	JL/LPI	1989	EB/HC	14 X 11	SOM	10	Varies	1000	1000
Violet Cuckoo	LPI	JL/LPI	1989	EB/HC	14 X 11	SOM	10	Varies	1000	1000
Green Orapandola	LPI	JL/LPI	1989	EB/HC	14 X 11	SOM	10	Varies	1000	1000

MARGOT LOVEJOY

BORN: Campbellton, NB, Canada; October 21, 1930
EDUCATION: Mount Allison Univ, Can, 1947–49; L'Academie Julian, Paris, France, 1949; St Martin's Sch of Art, London, England, 1950; Pratt Graphics Center, NY, 1966–71; Parson Sch, NY, 1979; New York Univ, NY, 1982
TEACHING: Instr, Herbert H Lehman Col, State Univ of New York, NY, 1974–75; Instr, Pratt Sch of Design, NY, 1972–78; Instr, Phoenix Sch of Design, NY, 1972–78; Instr, Pratt Graphic Center, NY, 1972–79; Instr, Parsons Sch of Design, NY, 1975–77; Asst Prof, Fine Art, State Univ of New York, Purchase, NY, 1978 to present
AWARDS: Pratt Graphics Center, Dr Paul Bradlow Award, NY, 1969; Nat Assn of Women Artists, Alice Bueli Mem Award, 1976; Bea Camhi Award for Graphics, YAA, 1976; Soc of Am Graphic Artists, Purchase Award, 1978; Nat Assn of Women Artists, Gayner Award, 1979; Purchase Award, Nat Copier Exhib, 1984; New York State Council on the Arts, Ind Artist Support Grant, 1986; John Simon Guggenheim Fel, 1987–88; Special Project Grant, Art Matters, Inc, 1989
RECENT EXHIB: Mus of Contemp Hispanic Art, NY, 1987; Massachusetts Inst of Technology, Cambridge, MA, 1987; Cloud Stage V, Inst of Art & Urban Resources, PSI, NY, 1987; PPOW Gallery, NY, 1987; Twining Gallery, NY, 1987; Everson Mus, Syracuse, NY, 1987–88; East End Arts, Long Island, NY, 1988; Mus of Mod Art, NY, 1988; Fine Arts Mus, Long Island, Hempstead, NY, 1989; Philadelpia Print Club, PA, 1989; Arvada Center, CO, 1989; Bowman & Megahan Gallery, Allegheny Col, PA, 1990; Alternative Mus, NY, 1990,92
COLLECTIONS: New Brunswick Mus, NB, Can; Hudson River Mus, NY; New York Univ Print Coll, NY; Bibliotheque Nat, Paris, France; Dresden Mus, Germany; Hunsterian Art Gallery, Glasgow, Scotland; Mus of Mod Art Library Coll, NY
PRINTERS: Cone Editions, Port Chester, NY (CEd); Jon Cone, Port Chester, NY (JC); Sheila Marbain, NY (SM)
PUBLISHERS: Artist (ART)
GALLERIES: Orion Editions, New York, NY; Pascal Gallery, Toronto, Canada; Wells Gallery, Ottawa, Canada
MAILING ADDRESS: 166-04 81st Ave, Jamaica, NY 11432

TITLE	PUBLISHER	PRINTER	DATE	MEDIUM	DIMENSION (PAPER SIZE) IN INCHES	TYPE OF PAPER	EDITION NUMBER	NO. OF COLORS	ORIGINAL OPENING PRICE	CURRENT RETAIL PRICE
CURRENT EDITIONS:										
Cosmic Code	ART	CEd/JC	1982	SP	30 X 42	AP	40	19	350	750
Azimuth I (Dipt)	ART	SM	1983	SP/CO	33 X 42	AP	33	20	425	750

MARVIN LOWE

BORN: Brooklyn, NY; May 19, 1927
EDUCATION: Julliard Sch of Music, NY, BA, 1950–52; Brooklyn Col, NY, BA, 19854; Univ of Iowa, Iowa City, IA, MFA, 1960
TEACHING: Prof. Fine Arts, Bucknell Univ, Lewisburg, PA, 1963–68; Bottegadarte Grafica, Florence, Italy, 1967; Prof. Fine Arts, Indiana Univ, Bloomington, IN, 1968 to present
AWARDS: Paul J Sachs Purchase Award, Boston, MA, 1965; Lessing J Rosenwald Purchase Award, Philadelphia Print Club, PA, 1966; Nat Endowment for the Arts Fel, 1975; Ford Found Fel, 1979; Indiana Arts Comm, Artist's Fel, 1987
RECENT EXHIB: Printworks, Ltd, Chicago, IL, 1987; Purdue Univ, IN, 1988; Kunstzentrum, Glende/Reinbek, Fed Republic, Germany, 1988; Privatgalerie Plenisast, Hamburg, Fed Republic, Germany, 1988
COLLECTIONS: British Mus, London, England; Brooklyn Mus, NY; Philadelphia Mus of Art, PA; Indianapolis Mus, IN; Columbia Univ, NY; American Embassy, London, England; Nat Coll of Fine Arts, Wash, DC; Japan Print Soc, Tokyo, Japan; Ringling Mus, Sarasota, FL; California Palace of Legion of Honor, San Francisco, CA; Honolulu Acad of Art, HI; Silvermine Sch of Art, New Canaan, CT; Springfield Mus, MO; Des Moines Art Center, IA; State Univ of New York; Potsdam, NY; Indianapolis Mus, IN; Univ of North Carolina, Chapel Hill, NC; Dayton Art Inst, OH; Mus of Fine Arts, Springfield, MA; Univ of Iowa, Iowa City, IA; Univ of Georgia, Athens, GA; Michigan State Univ, East Lansing, MI; Indiana Univ, Bloomington, IN; Univ of Maine, Orono, ME; Kalamazoo Inst of Art, MI; Wilson Library, NY; Southern Illinois Univ, Edwardsville, IL; Florida State Univ, Tallahassee, FL; Fort Wayne Mus, IN; Sheldon Mem Gallery of Art, Lincoln, NE; Smithsonian Inst, Wash, DC; New York Public Library, NY
PRINTERS: David Keister, Bloomington, IN (DK); Echo Press, Bloomington, IN (EP); Artist (ART)
PUBLISHERS: Lakeside Studio, MI (LS); Echo Press, Bloomington, IN (EP); Artist (ART)
GALLERIES: Printworks Gallery, Chicago, IL
MAILING ADDRESS: c/o School of Fine Arts, Indiana University, Bloomington, IN 47405

TITLE	PUBLISHER	PRINTER	DATE	MEDIUM	DIMENSION (PAPER SIZE) IN INCHES	TYPE OF PAPER	EDITION NUMBER	NO. OF COLORS	ORIGINAL OPENING PRICE	CURRENT RETAIL PRICE
SOLD OUT EDITIONS (RARE):										
Tybault and Mercutio	LS	LS	1970	EC	27 X 24	AP	30	8	150	650
Nautical Number	LS	LS	1972	SP	54 X 42	AP	25	25	250	1350
Who's Afraid of Relationships?	LS	LS	1972	SP	54 X 38	AP	25	36	300	1800
Malabar	LS	LS	1972	SP	51 X 36	AP	21	20	225	1200
Behind the Screen (Dawn)	ART	ART	1973	IC/REL	27 X 34	AC	20	5	125	600
Fourteen Hundred Little Circles	ART	ART	1974	IC/REL	14 X 36	R/BFK	20	5	150	600
Old Dress for the Galactic Ball	ART	ART	1974	IC/REL	16 X 36	AC	20	6	135	600
Shell Flowers	ART	ART	1974	IC/REL	14 X 36	AC	20	6	150	500
Last Night	LS	LS	1974	EC	24 X 30	AP	20	6	175	750
CURRENT EDITIONS:										
Voodoo of the Western World	LS	LS	1972	IC/SP	24 X 24	AC	50	8	100	350
Andromeda	LS	LS	1972	IC	24 X 24	AC	50	6	100	350
Green Up Front	ART	ART	1973	EC	36 X 24	AC	50	6	150	450
Behind the Screen: Dusk	ART	ART	1973	IC/REL	27 X 24	AC	19	5	125	500
Eight-and-One-Half Little Flowers	ART	ART	1974	IC/REL	27 X 24	AC	20	5	150	450
Cloud Mask (2 Panels)	ART	ART	1981	REL/MET	50 X 48	AC	10	1	450	550
Visitor (2 Panels)	ART	ART	1981	REL/MET	48 X 38	AC	10	1	300	400
Steam (2 Panels)	EP	DK	1981	LC/SP/EMB	42 X 42	AP/BL/G	16	3	350	450
Tracks (4 Panels)	ART	ART	1981	REL/MET	57 X 57	AC	10	1	750	900
Old Visitors	ART	ART	1981	REL/MET	33 X 24	AC	8	1	250	400
Old Eyes (2 Panels)	ART	ART	1981	EC/REL	61 X 41	AC	11	6	800	900
Jelly Fish (3 Panels)	LS	LS	1982	EC/ENG/R	35 X 51	AC	10	9	950	1000
Red Caterpillar	ART	ART	1982	EC/ENG/R	45 X 40	AC	10	7	700	800
Heat (2 Panels)	ART	ART	1982	EC/ENG/R	46 X 26	AC	10	8	700	800
Medusa (Triptych)	ART	ART	1982	IC/ENG/REL	48 X 92	AC	10	9	950	1000
Sodium (4 Panels)	ART	ART	1983	IC/REL	48 X 64	AC	10	8	950	1000
Sulphur	ART	ART	1983	IC/REL	58 X 28	AC	10	8	700	800
Orion Arm Series (20 Variations)	ART	ART	1983	IC/REL	40 X 28 EA	AC	1 EA	10 EA	650 EA	800 EA
Brownian Movement Series (Series of 24)	ART	ART	1984	IC/REL	40 X 28 EA	AC	1 EA	8 EA	650 EA	800 EA
Nebula Series (Series of 20)	ART	ART	1984	IC/REL	40 X 28 EA	AC	1 EA	8 EA	700 EA	800 EA
Diamond Anvil	ART	ART	1984	IC	75 x 31	AC	10	10	1250	1350
Water Series (Series of 25)	ART	ART	1984	REL/MET	40 X 28 EA	AC	1 EA	9 EA	650 EA	800 EA
Ejecta I	ART	ART	1984	IC/REL/HC	56 X 39	AC	1	6	950	1350
Weather Report	ART	ART	1984	IC/REL	95 X 37	AC	10	9	1400	1500
Light Bulb Series (Series of 24)	ART	ART	1984–85	IC/REL/HC	39 X 28 EA	AC	1 EA	8 EA	700 EA	800 EA
Iapetus	ART	ART	1985	IC/REL/HC	57 X 41	AC	10	7	1250	1350
Panthalassa	ART	ART	1985	IC/REL/HC	57 X 41	AC	10	8	1250	1350
10 GEV	ART	ART	1985	IC/REL/HC	52 X 40	AC	10	8	1250	1350
Tidal Series (Series of 20)	ART	ART	1985–86	IC/REL/HC	40 X 28 EA	AC	1 EA	6 EA	700 EA	800 EA
Water	EP	DK/EP	1986	LC/REL/HC	25 X 35	MOR	40	9	350	500

BRUCE STARK LOWNEY

BORN: Los Angeles, CA; October 16, 1937
EDUCATION: North Texas State Univ, Denton, TX, BA, 1959; San Francisco State Univ, CA, MA, 1966, Univ of New Mexico, Albuquerque, NM, Asst to Garo Antreasian; Tamarind Lithography Workshop, Albuquerque, NM
TEACHING: Instr, Univ of New Mexico, Albuquerque, NM; Instr, Minneapolis Col of Art & Design, MN; Inst, Fort Lewis Col, Univ of New Mexico, Albuquerque, NM; Univ of Texas, Austin, TX
AWARDS: Louis Comfort Tiffany Found Award, 1969; Nat Endowment for the Arts Award, 1974; Artist in Res Grant, Roswell Mus & Art Center, Roswell, NM, 1974; Western States Arts Found Award, 1979
COLLECTIONS: Art Inst of Chicago, IL; Minneapolis Inst of Art, Minneapolis, MN; Mus of Fine Arts, Santa Fe, NM; Yale Univ, New Haven, CT; Univ of New Mexico, Albuquerque, NM; North Dakota State Univ, Fargo, ND
PRINTERS: Steve Britko, Santa Fe, NM (SB); Lynne Allen, Albuquerque, NM (LA)
PUBLISHERS: Tamarind Inst, Albuquerque, NM (TI); Laura Richards Fine Arts, Inc, Albuquerque, NM (LRFA)
GALLERIES: Rettig & Martinez Gallery, Santa Fe, NM; Robischon Gallery, Denver, CO; Gump's Art Gallery, San Francisco, CA
MAILING ADDRESS: 800 Oso Ridge Route, Grants, NM 87020

BRUCE STARK LOWNEY CONTINUED

TITLE	PUBLISHER	PRINTER	DATE	MEDIUM	DIMENSION (PAPER SIZE) IN INCHES	TYPE OF PAPER	EDITION NUMBER	NO. OF COLORS	ORIGINAL OPENING PRICE	CURRENT RETAIL PRICE
CURRENT EDITIONS:										
The Triumphant Arch	LRFA	LA/TI	1986	LC	22 X 29	AP/B	38	4	500	600

LOUIS LOZOWICK

BORN: Russia; (1892–1973)
EDUCATION: Ohio State Univ, Columbus, OH, BA; Nat Acad of Design, NY
AWARDS: Art Inst of Chicago, 1929; Philadelphia Art Alliance, PA, 1930; Cleveland Mus of Art, OH, 1930; Oakland Art Gallery, CA, 1946; Rochester Print Club, NY, 1948; Brooklyn Mus, NY, 1950; Soc of Am Graphic Artists, NY, 1951,57,62; Dallas Mus of Fine Art, TX, 1953; Creative Graphics, NY, 1958; Newark Mus, 1959; Montclair Art Mus, NJ, 1959; Hunterdon Art Center, NJ, 1959; Purchase Award, New Jersey State Mus, Trenton, NJ, 1960; Jersey City Mus, NJ, 1960
COLLECTIONS: Whitney Mus of Am Art, NY; Mus of Mod Art, NY; Metropolitan Mus of Art, NY; Los Angeles County Mus, CA; Cleveland Mus of Art, OH; New York Public Library, NY; Honolulu Acad of Art, HI; Mus of Fine Arts, Houston, TX; Yale Univ, New Haven, CT; Mus of Western Art, Moscow, Russia; Syracuse Univ, NY; Montclair Art Mus, NJ; Rochester Mem Art Gallery, NY; Newark Mus, NJ; Victoria & Albert Mus, London, England; Carnegie Inst of Art, Pittsburgh, PA
PRINTERS: George C Miller, NY (GCM)
PUBLISHERS: Artist (ART); Cleveland Print Club, OH (CPC); American Artists Group, NY (AAG); Associated American Artists, NY (AAA)
GALLERIES: Herbert Palmer Gallery, Los Angeles, CA; Bethesda Art Gallery, Glen Echo, MD; Kornbluth Gallery, Inc, Fair Lawn, NJ; Sid Deutsch Gallery, New York, NY; Harbor Gallery, New York, NY; Sragow Gallery, New York, NY; Vanderwoude/Tananbaum Gallery, New York, NY

Flint (F)

TITLE	PUBLISHER	PRINTER	DATE	MEDIUM	DIMENSION (PAPER SIZE) IN INCHES	TYPE OF PAPER	EDITION NUMBER	NO. OF COLORS	ORIGINAL OPENING PRICE	CURRENT RETAIL PRICE
SOLD OUT EDITIONS (RARE):										
Chicago	ART	GCM	1923	LB	11 X 8	WOVE	5	1	25	10000
Tanks #1	ART	GCM	1925	LB	14 X 8	WOVE	50	1	25	5000
Minneapolis	ART	GCM	1925	LB	12 X 9	WOVE	20	1	25	30000
New York	ART	GCM	1925	LB	12 X 9	WOVE	20	1	25	30000
Coney Island (Luna Park)	ART	GCM	1926	LB	13 X 9	WOVE	20	1	25	23000
Checkerboard (Under the Elevated) (F-8)	ART	GCM	1927–28	LB	12 X 9	WOVE	20	1	25	11000
Still Life #2 (F-36)	ART	GCM	1929	LB	13 X 16	WOVE	50	1	30	14000
57th Street (Rubber Center)	ART	GCM	1929	LB	20 X 14	WOVE	40	1	35	14000
Allen Street (Under the El)	ART	GCM	1929	LB	8 X 11	WOVE	20	1	35	12000
Corner of a Steel Plant	ART	GCM	1929	LB	11 X 8	WOVE	25	1	35	3500
Hanover Square	ART	GCM	1929	LB	15 X 9	WOVE	25	1	35	16000
In the Park, No Job	ART	GCM	1929	LB	14 X 9	WOVE	50	1	35	1500
Tanks (Steel Plant)	ART	GCM	1929	LB	15 X 9	WOVE	50	1	35	6500
Bridge in Shadow	ART	GCM	1930	LB	12 X 9	WOVE	47	1	50	4000
Brooklyn Bridge	ART	GCM	1930	LB	14 X 9	WOVE	100	1	50	20000
Construction (Excavation)	ART	GCM	1930	LB	14 X 8	WOVE	25	1	50	6000
Queensboro Bridge	ART	GCM	1930	LB	14 X 8	WOVE	50	1	50	3500
Traffic	ART	GCM	1930	LB	9 X 16	WOVE	20	1	50	16000
City on a Rock	CPC	GCM	1931	LB	8 X 13	WOVE	242	1	50	1000
Kurgan Tube (Soviet)	ART	GCM	1931	LB	8 X 6	WOVE	15	1	50	1000
Mid-Air	ART	GCM	1931	LB	12 X 7	WOVE	50	1	50	4000
Quite Harbor (Swimming)	AAA	GCM	1932	LB	9 X 13	WOVE	250	1	50	800
Red Tea House (Tajikistan)	ART	GCM	1932	LB	10 X 11	WOVE	50	1	50	800
Border Guards (Red Army)	ART	GCM	1932	LB	13 X 8	WOVE	50	1	50	800
Tear Gas	ART	GCM	1932	LB	13 X 8	WOVE	10	1	50	4500
Storm over Manhattan	AAA	GCM	1935	LB	10 X 14	WOVE	189	1	60	3000
Angry Skies	ART	GCM	1935	LB	10 X 14	WOVE	20	1	60	2000
Abandoned Quarry, Rockport	ART	GCM	1936	LB	14 X 11	WOVE	20	1	60	750
Oil Country	AAG	GCM	1936	LB	13 X 7	WOVE	200	1	60	1000
Ship Building	ART	GCM	1936	LB	11 X 14	WOVE	20	1	60	1800
Spanning the Hudson	ART	GCM	1936	LB	9 X 13	WOVE	15	1	60	1800
Distant Manhattan	AAA	GCM	1937	LB	7 X 13	AP	250	1	60	800
Skater's Island	AAA	GCM	1937	LB	9 X 13	AP	250	1	60	800
Winter Fun	AAA	GCM	1940	LB	9 X 13	AP	250	1	60	1500
Steel Valley	AAA	GCM	1942	LB	9 X 13	AP	250	1	60	1800
Black Butterfly	ART	GCM	1948	LB	15 X 11	AP	15	1	100	1500
Angry Skies (Andante Cantabile) (1935) (F-123)	AAA	GCM	1948	LB	10 X 14	AP	250	1	100	1200
Conversation in Haiti	ART	GCM	1955	LB	14 X 8	AP	20	1	75	500
Where Gladiators Fought	ART	GCM	1972	LB	11 X 15	AP	20	1	75	500
Thanksgiving Dinner (1938) (F-157)	ART	GCM	1972	LB	13 X 8	WOVE	10	1	100	2200
Castle of Montezuma (Signed by Artist's Wife)	ART	GCM	1973	LB	9 X 13	AP	50	1	200	1500
Above the City (Printed in 1932)			1982	LB	17 X 8	AP	200	1	200	800

The print market has become very selective. For the first time since we published the first edition of The Printworld Directory in 1982, the prices of prints have been greatly reduced and greatly increased for the same artists by the most reputable and established print publishers. Check the fifth edition to understand the movement.

CHARLES LUCE

BORN: Phoenix, AZ; June 15, 1947
EDUCATION: Amherst Col, MA, AB, 1969; Univ of Washington, Seattle, WA, MAT, 1971
RECENT EXHIB: Saxon-Lee Gallery, Los Angeles, CA, 1988; Schrieber/Cutler Gallery, NY, 1988,89
COLLECTIONS: Albright-Knox Art Gallery, Buffalo, NY; Seattle Art Mus, WA; City of Seattle, WA; Library of Congress, Wash, DC
PRINTERS: John Nichols, NY (JN)
PUBLISHERS: Elise Meyer Gallery, NY (EMG); John Nichols, NY (JN)
GALLERIES: Luise Ross Gallery, New York, NY; John Nichols Gallery, New York, NY; Gracie Mansion Gallery, New York, NY; MIA Gallery, Seattle, WA
MAILING ADDRESS: 142 Henry St, #8W, New York, NY 10002

TITLE	PUBLISHER	PRINTER	DATE	MEDIUM	DIMENSION (PAPER SIZE) IN INCHES	TYPE OF PAPER	EDITION NUMBER	NO. OF COLORS	ORIGINAL OPENING PRICE	CURRENT RETAIL PRICE
CURRENT EDITIONS:										
Aim at the (L) Edge	EM/JN	JN	1984	LC/SP	18 X 43	AP88	50	14	450	800
Suit Spirit Trap #3	EM/JN	JN	1984	SP	38 X 26	MUL	50	42	650	1000

MICHAEL LUCERO (LEWIS)

BORN: Tracy, CA; April 1, 1953
EDUCATION: Humbolt State Univ, Arcata, CA, BA, 1975; Univ of California, Davis, CA, 1977; Univ of Washington, Seattle, WA, MFA, 1978
TEACHING: Vis Lectr, Rhode Island Sch of Design, Providence, RI, 1979; Wake Forest Univ, Winston-Salem, NC, 1980; Instr, New York Univ, NY, 1979–80; Instr, Parsons Sch of Design, NY, 1981–82
AWARDS: Ford Found Scholarship, Univ of Washington, Seattle, WA, 1977,78; Young Am Award, Mus of Contemp Crafts of Am Craft Council, NY, 1979; Creative Artists Public Service Program Fel, 1980–81; Nettie Marie Jones Fel, Center for Music, Drama & Art, Lake Placid, NY, 1983; Nat Endowment for the Arts Fel, 1979,82,84
RECENT EXHIB: Linda Ferris Gallery, Seattle, WA, 1987; ACA Contemp Art, NY, 1988; Philbrook Mus, Tulsa, OK, 1988; Whitney Mus of Am Art, NY, 1988; Contemp Arts Center, Cincinnati, OH, 1990; Stanford Mus, CT, 1990; Louisiana State Univ, Baton Rouge, LA, 1990; Fay Gold Gallery, Atlanta, GA, 1990,91; Univ of Connecticut, Atrium Gallery, Storrs, CT, 1992; Allene Lapides Gallery, Santa Fe, NM, 1992
COLLECTIONS: Metropolitan Art Mus, NY; Seattle Art Mus, WA; Museo Tamayo, Mexico City, Mexico; San Francisco Mus of Mod Art, CA; New Mus of Contemp Art, NY; Everson Mus, Syracuse, NY
PRINTERS: Aeropress, NY (A); Patricia Branstead, NY (PB)
PUBLISHERS: Deborah Sharpe Editions, NY (DSE)
GALLERIES: Charles Cowles Gallery, New York, NY; Linda Farris Gallery, Seattle, WA; Hokin/Kaufman Gallery, Chicago, IL; Sharpe Gallery, New York, NY; ACA Contemporary Galleries, New York, NY; Dorothy Weiss Gallery, San Francisco, CA; Allene Lapides Gallery, Santa Fe, NM
MAILING ADDRESS: 735 E Ninth St, New York, NY 10069

TITLE	PUBLISHER	PRINTER	DATE	MEDIUM	DIMENSION (PAPER SIZE) IN INCHES	TYPE OF PAPER	EDITION NUMBER	NO. OF COLORS	ORIGINAL OPENING PRICE	CURRENT RETAIL PRICE
CURRENT EDITIONS:										
Self-Portrait with Figure (Hardground Etching)	DSE	PB/A	1982	EB	23 X 30	R/BFK	29	1	450	750

LUIGI LUCIONI

BORN: Malnate, Italy; (1900–1988)
EDUCATION: Cooper Union Art Sch, NY; Nat Acad of Design, NY
AWARDS: Tiffany Medal, 1929; Carnegie Inst Prize, Pittsburgh, PA, 1939; Corcoran Gallery of Art, Wash, DC Awards, 1939,41,49; Purchase Award, Nat Acad of Design, NY, 1959
RECENT EXHIB: Print Club of Albany, NY, 1992
COLLECTIONS: Mus of Mod Art, NY; Whitney Mus of Am Art, NY; Metropolitan Mus of Art, NY; Pennsylvania Acad of Fine Arts, Phila, PA; Carnegie Inst of Art, Pittsburgh, PA; Toledo Mus, OH; Brooklyn Mus, NY; Seattle Art Mus, WA; Victoria & Albert Mus, London, England; Library of Congress, Wash, DC
PRINTERS: Artist (ART)
PUBLISHERS: Associated American Artists, NY (AAA); Prairie Print Makers (PPM); Print Club of Albany, NY (PCA)
GALLERIES: Shoshana Wayne Gallery, Santa Monica, CA; American Scene Gallery, Sarasota, FL; Richard York Gallery, New York, NY

TITLE	PUBLISHER	PRINTER	DATE	MEDIUM	DIMENSION (PAPER SIZE) IN INCHES	TYPE OF PAPER	EDITION NUMBER	NO. OF COLORS	ORIGINAL OPENING PRICE	CURRENT RETAIL PRICE
SOLD OUT EDITIONS (RARE):										
Landscape with Trees	ART	ART	1928	EB	7 X 9	WOVE	30	1	25	300
Nantucket	ART	ART	1928	EB	5 X 7	WOVE	30	1	25	500
My Birthplate	AAA	ART	1939	EB	8 X 11	WOVE	250	1	35	200
Promfret Church	AAA	ART	1939	EB	8 X 11	WOVE	250	1	35	300
Vermont Pastoral	AAA	ART	1939	EB	7 X 13	WOVE	203	1	50	300
Vermont Landscape	AAA	ART	1939	EB	9 X 11	WOVE	250	1	50	200
New England Landscape	AAA	ART	1939	EB	9 X 11	WOVE	250	1	50	250
Restful Ruins	AAA	ART	1941	EB	7 X 11	WOVE	200	1	50	250
Two Silos	AAA	ART	1942	EB	7 X 12	WOVE	200	1	50	250
Shadows and Substance	AAA	ART	1943	EB	8 X 11	WOVE	200	1	50	200
Stony Pastures	AAA	ART	1943	EB	8 X 11	WOVE	200	1	50	250
Sunlight Through the Clouds	AAA	ART	1943	EB	8 X 11	WOVE	200	1	50	200
Late Shadows	AAA	ART	1944	EB		WOVE	250	1	50	300
Pattern of Trees	AAA	ART	1944	EB	8 X 12	WOVE	250	1	50	300
Tree Tapestry	AAA	ART	1945	EB	9 X 11	WOVE	250	1	50	250
Route 7 (Sepia)	AAA	ART	1946	EB	9 X 12	WOVE	250	1	50	300
The Big Willow	AAA	ART	1946	EB	9 X 11	WOVE	250	1	50	200
Summer Shadows	AAA	ART	1946	EB	6 X 12	WOVE	250	1	50	250
Between Birches	AAA	ART	1947	EB	9 X 11	WOVE	250	1	50	200
The Big Haystack	AAA	ART	1947	EB	8 X 11	WOVE	250	1	50	250
Elm on the Hill	AAA	ART	1948	EB	8 X 11	WOVE	250	1	50	200
Weathered Barns	AAA	ART	1948	EB	8 X 12	WOVE	250	1	50	400

LUIGI LUCIONI CONTINUED

TITLE	PUBLISHER	PRINTER	DATE	MEDIUM	DIMENSION (PAPER SIZE) IN INCHES	TYPE OF PAPER	EDITION NUMBER	NO. OF COLORS	ORIGINAL OPENING PRICE	CURRENT RETAIL PRICE
SOLD OUT EDITIONS (RARE):										
The Nestled Barns	AAA	ART	1949	EB	9 X 11	WOVE	250	1	50	200
Leaning Silo	AAA	ART	1949	EB	7 X 11	WOVE	250	1	50	300
Moving Shadows	AAA	ART	1951	EB	7 X 12	WOVE	250	1	60	200
The Big Shadow	AAA	ART	1951	EB	9 X 11	WOVE	250	1	60	200
Birch Processional	AAA	ART	1951	EB	9 X 14	WOVE	250	1	60	250
The Edge of the Birches	AAA	ART	1951	EB	10 X 12	WOVE	250	1	60	250
White Arabesque	AAA	ART	1952	EB	11 X 10	WOVE	250	1	60	300
Elms by the Lake	AAA	ART	1952	EB	8 X 11	WOVE	250	1	60	200
Hovering Trees	AAA	ART	1952	EB	8 X 11	WOVE	250	1	60	350
On the Road	AAA	ART	1952	EB	9 X 11	WOVE	250	1	60	200
Stone and Shadows	AAA	ART	1952	EB	11 X 8	WOVE	250	1	60	200
Hilltop Elms	PPM	ART	1954	EB	11 X 10	WOVE	250	1	75	250
Theme in White	PPM	ART	1955	EB	9 X 11	WOVE	250	1	75	500
Enveloping Shadows	PCA	ART	1965	EB	11 X 8	AP	250	1	75	200
Barn in the Hills	PCA	ART	1966–67	EB	9 X 10	AP	250	1	75	250
White Sentinels	AAA	ART	1977	EB	11 X 8	R/BFK	250	1	100	200
Shadows in Lombardy		ART	1978	EB	9 X 6	R/BFK	100	1	100	300

MARKUS LÜPERTZ

BORN: Liberec, Germany; 1941
EDUCATION: Werkkunstschule, Krefeld, West Germany
COLLECTIONS: Staatliche Kunstakademie, Düsseldorf, West Germany; Neue Galerie-Sammlung Ludwig, Aachen, West Germany
RECENT EXHIB: Solomon R. Guggenheim Mus, NY, 1989; Kunsthalle Kiel, West Germany, 1989; Mus of Mod Art, NY, 1989; Los Angeles County Mus of Art, CA 1989; Galerie Lelong, Zürich, Switzerland, 1989; Rena Bransten Gallery, San Francisco, CA, 1989; Mary Boone Gallery, NY, 1990; Baltimore Mus of Art, MD, 1992; Michael Werner Gallery, NY, 1991,92
PRINTERS: Mark Callen, San Francisco, CA (MC); Brian Shure, San Francisco, CA (BS); Nancy Anello, San Francisco, CA (NA); Crown Point Press, San Francisco, CA (CPP); Artist (ART)
PUBLISHERS: Maximilian Verlag/Sabine Knust, Munich, Germany (MV/SK); Crown Point Press, San Francisco, CA (CPP)
GALLERIES: Editions Ilene Kurtz, New York, NY; Nicola Jacobs Gallery, London, England; Galerie Thaddaeus Ropoc, Saltzburg, Austria; Mary Boone Gallery, New York, NY; Travelli Gallery, Aspen, CO; David Nolan Gallery, New York, NY; Fay Gold Gallery, Atlanta, GA; Steven Lieber Gallery, New York, NY; Marian Goodman, New York, NY; Crown Point Press, San Francisco, CA & New York, NY; Galerie Lelong, Zürich, Switzerland; Rena Bransten Gallery, San Francisco, CA; Mary Boone Gallery, New York, NY; Michael Werner Gallery, New York, NY; Hine Editions/Limestone Press, San Francisco, CA

TITLE	PUBLISHER	PRINTER	DATE	MEDIUM	DIMENSION (PAPER SIZE) IN INCHES	TYPE OF PAPER	EDITION NUMBER	NO. OF COLORS	ORIGINAL OPENING PRICE	CURRENT RETAIL PRICE
CURRENT EDITIONS:										
Evening	MV/SK	ART	1985	WC/HC	55 X 41	R/100	8	Varies	4000	7500
Ganymede	MV/SK	ART	1986	WC/MON	82 X 38	Varies	20	Varies	7500	10000
Gedachtes und Gemachtes	CPP	MC/BS/NA/CPP	1988	EC	42 X 51	SS	25		1250	2500
Kopf	CPP	MC/BS/NA/CPP	1988	EB	25 X 21	SS	25		550	650
Monkey	CPP	MC/BS/NA/CPP	1988	EB	23 X 25	SS	25		600	1200
Pferd	CPP	MC/BS/NA/CPP	1988	EC	42 X 50	SOM/T	25		1250	2800
Pilzesammler	CPP	MC/BS/NA/CPP	1988	EC	23 X 25	SS	25		750	1200
Der Zwerg Erklärt dem Riesen die Schönheit der Blume	CPP	MC/BS/NA/CPP	1988	EC	23 X 25	SS	25		750	1200
Steel Points and Poems (Book)			1989	DPF	15 X 11	SS	60	1	1800	2000

JAMES LUTES (JIM)

BORN: Ft Louis, WA; December 5, 1995
EDUCATION: Washington State Univ, Pullman, WA, BA, 1978; Art Inst of Chicago, IL, BFA, 1982
TEACHING: Vis Artist, Art Inst of Chicago, IL, 1983 to present
AWARDS: Anna Louis Raymond Traveiing Fel, 1982, Visual Arts Awards, 1988
RECENT EXHIB: Los Angeles County Mus, CA, 1988; Dart Gallery, Chicago, IL, 1988; Mus of Contemp Art, Chicago, IL, 1989; Michael Kohn Gallery, Los Angeles, CA, 1989; Univ of Missouri, St Louis, MO, 1990; Illinois State Mus, Springfield, IL, 1992; State of Illinois Art Gallery, Chicago, IL, 1992
COLLECTIONS: Mus of Contemp Art, Chicago, IL
PRINTERS: Jack Lemon, Chicago, IL; Landfall Press, Inc, Chicago, IL (LPI)
PUBLISHERS: Landfall Press, Inc, Chicago, IL (LPI)
GALLERIES: Dart Gallery, Chicago, IL; S Bitter-Larkin Gallery, New York, NY; LedisFlam Gallery, New York, NY
MAILING ADDRESS: 1360 N Milwaukee Ave/Columbus Dr & Jackson, Chicago, IL 60622

TITLE	PUBLISHER	PRINTER	DATE	MEDIUM	DIMENSION (PAPER SIZE) IN INCHES	TYPE OF PAPER	EDITION NUMBER	NO. OF COLORS	ORIGINAL OPENING PRICE	CURRENT RETAIL PRICE
CURRENT EDITIONS:										
Assessor of Doubt	LPI	JL/LPI	1992	LC	22 X 30	AC	45		500	500

The retail prices of the 100,000 limited edition prints quoted in this directory are subject to change. Print publishers, artists and galleries were the direct sources for these quotations. Prices in the secondary market listed as "Sold Out Editions (Rare)" indicate that the publisher has a limited supply of that print or that the print is difficult to locate in the galleries.

ALDO LUONGO

BORN: Buenos Aires, Argentina; January 31, 1940
EDUCATION: Buenos Aires, Acad of Fine Art, Argentina
PRINTERS: Atelier Ettinger, NY (AE); Accent Studio, NY (AS); Accent Design, NY (AD); American Atelier, NY (AA)
PUBLISHERS: Martin Lawrence Limited Editions, Van Nuys, CA (MLLE); Circle Gallery, Ltd, Chicago, IL (CGL); Robert Bane Editions, Inc, Los Angeles, CA
GALLERIES: Martin Lawrence Galleries, Sherman Oaks, CA & West Los Angeles, CA & Newport Beach, CA & Palm Springs, CA & Santa Clara, CA & Redondo Beach, CA & Thousand Oaks, CA & Escondido, CA & Short Hills, NJ & Los Angeles, CA; Paideia Gallery, Los Angeles, CA; Petrini Art Gallery, Rocky Hill, CT; Georgetown Fine Art, Wash, DC; Emporium Enterprises, Inc, Dallas, TX; Professional Fine Arts Services, Inc, New York, NY

Aldo Luongo
Strawberries for Lunch
Courtesy Robert Bane Editions

TITLE	PUBLISHER	PRINTER	DATE	MEDIUM	DIMENSION (PAPER SIZE) IN INCHES	TYPE OF PAPER	EDITION NUMBER	NO. OF COLORS	ORIGINAL OPENING PRICE	CURRENT RETAIL PRICE
SOLD OUT EDITIONS (RARE):										
The Hawk	CGL	AA	1974	LC	23 X 34	AP	275	3	150	3000
Mathematics	CGL	AA	1974	LC	24 X 34	AP	275	3	125	1100
Lovers	CGL	AA	1974	LC	24 X 33	AP	275	3	125	2000
On the Beach	MLLE	AE	1977	LC		AP	300		200	2500
Romance	MLLE	AE	1977	LC		AP	300		200	2200
Bjorn Borg	MLLE	AE	1977	LC	23 X 32	AP	395	26	200	2000
The Bomb	MLLE	AE	1977	LC	26 X 28	AP	395	24	200	3000
Evening Lovers	MLLE	AE	1979	LC	29 X 25	AP	395	20	275	2500
Conversation	MLLE	AE	1979	LC	29 X 25	AP	395	30	275	2500
Hawk & Mug	MLLE	AS	1979	LC	29 X 25	STP	395	22	350	6500
Windy Day	MLLE	AS	1979	SP	29 X 25	STP	395	46	350	7500
First Day of School	MLLE	AS	1980	SP	26 X 32	STP	395	38	600	4000
Gray Sweater	MLLE	AD	1980	SP	24 X 29	STP	395	60	350	3000
Young	MLLE	AD	1981	SP	30 X 39	STP	395	52	400	600
Afternoon Beer	MLLE	AD	1981	SP	30 X 38	STP	395	58	500	5000
Cafe Tortoni	MLLE	AD	1981	SP	38 X 39	STP	395	64	600	6500
Alicia	MLLE	AD	1981	SP	30 X 40	STP	395	62	600	4500
Red Beach	MLLE	AD	1981	SP	43 X 35	STP	395	63	600	4500
Love Scene II	MLLE	AD	1981	SP	31 X 38	STP	395	54	600	2500
Dixieland	MLLE	AD	1982	SP	30 X 40	STP	395	46	600	2000
Tiernamente (Blue Dress)	MLLE	AD	1982	SP		STP	395		600	3000
Embrace	MLLE	AD	1982	SP		STP	395		600	2500
Morning Umbrellas	RBE	AD	1983	SP		STP	395		600	6500
Lovers in Reds & Purples	RBE	AD	1983	SP		STP	395		600	6000
Beyond Seiges	RBE	AD	1984	SP		STP	395		750	3000
Bar Union	RBE	AD	1984	SP		STP	395		750	5500
Fall Sun	RBE	AD	1984	SP		STP	395		750	4500
Dawn	RBE	AD	1984	SP		STP	395		900	4000
California	RBE	AD	1984	SP		STP	395		900	2400
The Hawk & His Brothers	RBE	AD	1984	SP		STP	395		1200	7000
My Favorite Redhead	RBE	AD	1984	SP		STP	395		900	4500
My Favorite Redhead (Deluxe)	RBE	AD	1984	SP		MB	100		1200	5000
Profile (Black & White)	RBE	AD	1985	LB		AP	395	1	750	1500
Friendly Walks	RBE	AD	1985	SP		STP	395		900	3500
Last Days of '44	RBE	AD	1985	SP		STP	395		1000	7000
Last Days of '44 (Deluxe)	RBE	AD	1985	SP		MB	100		1200	7500
Last Days of '44 (with Remarque)	RBE	AD	1985	SP		MB	100		1500	8000
La Recoletta	RBE	AD	1985	SP		STP	395		900	4500
La Recoletta (Deluxe)	RBE	AD	1985	SP		MB	100		1200	5000
Warmth	RBE	AD	1985	SP		STP	395		1200	4500
Profile (Deluxe) (Grey/Black)	RBE	AD	1985	LC		AP	100		850	1500
Profile (Deluxe) (Green/Grey)	RBE	AD	1985	LC		AP	100		850	1500
Profile (Deluxe) (Sepia)	RBE	AD	1985	LC		AP	100		850	1500
Cafe Select	RBE	AD	1986	SP		AP	395		1250	2200
Cafe Select (Deluxe) (Black Paper)	RBE	AD	1986	SP		AP/BL	100		1250	2400
Peaches & Purples	RBE	AD	1986	SP		STP	395		1000	7500
A Brew at Gardel's	RBE	AD	1986	SP		STP	395		1000	4500
A Brew at Gardel's (Deluxe)	RBE	AD	1986	SP		AC	100		1200	5000
Summer Fishing	RBE	AD	1986	SP		AP	395		900	4000
Fishing Harbor	RBE	AD	1986	SP		AP	395		1000	6000
Warmth in Purple (Lovers)	RBE	AD	1986	SP		AP	395		1400	4500

ALDO LUONGO CONTINUED

TITLE	PUBLISHER	PRINTER	DATE	MEDIUM	DIMENSION (PAPER SIZE) IN INCHES	TYPE OF PAPER	EDITION NUMBER	NO. OF COLORS	ORIGINAL OPENING PRICE	CURRENT RETAIL PRICE
SOLD OUT EDITIONS (RARE):										
Blue Coast	RBE	AD	1986	SP		AC	395		1200	8000
Blue Coast (Deluxe)	RBE	AD	1986	SP		AC	100		1400	8500
Homage to Monet (Luongo's California)	RBE	AD	1986	SP		AC	395		1200	8000
Windy Beach	RBE	AD	1987	SP		AC	395		1200	7000
Young Lovers	RBE	AD	1987	SP		AC	300		1400	3000
Country Bike Ride	RBE	AD	1987	SP		AC	300		1500	6000
Casa de Campo	RBE	AD	1987	SP		AC	300		1500	6000
Ballerina	RBE	AD	1988	SP		AC	300		1200	7000
Ballerina Suite (Set of 3):									1500 SET	2800 SET
Reverence	RBE	AE	1988	LC	21 X 29	AP	300	1	600	1000
Passé	RBE	AE	1988	LC	21 X 29	AP	300	1	600	1000
Kim	RBE	AE	1988	LC	21 X 29	AP	300	1	600	1000
Ballerina Suite (Deluxe) (Set of 3):									1600 SET	3200 SET
Reverence	RBE	AE	1988	LC	21 X 29	JP	60	1	650	1150
Passé	RBE	AE	1988	LC	21 X 29	JP	60	1	650	1150
Kim	RBE	AE	1988	LC	21 X 29	JP	60	1	650	1150
A Jump to Victory	RBE	AD	1988	SP		AP	300		1200	2000
La Bella Durmiente	RBE	AD	1989	SP		AP	300		1400	4000
Road in Cordoba	RBE	AD	1989	SP		AP	300		1400	4500
Bridge at Giverny	RBE	AE	1989	SP		AP	395		1600	5000
Bridge at Giverny (Deluxe) (with Remarque)	RBE	AE	1989	SP		AP	100		1800	5500
Bridge at Giverny (Black Paper)	RBE	AE	1989	SP		AP/BL	100		2000	5500
Springtime in Venice	RBE	AD	1990	SP		AP	300		1400	3500
Springtime in Venice (Deluxe) (Black Paper)	RBE	AD	1990	SP		AP/BL	100		1800	3200
Summer Smile	RBE	AE	1990	SP		AP	395		1800	4000
Summer Smile (Deluxe) (Black Paper)	RBE	AE	1990	SP		AP/BL	100		2000	4500
Sunny Ride through Palermo	RBE	AE	1990	SP		AP	395		1800	4000
Sunny Ride through Palermo (Deluxe) (Black Paper)	RBE	AE	1990	SP		AP/BL	100		2000	4500
Mediterranean Sunset	RBE	AE	1990	SP		AP	395		1800	4000
Mediterranean Sunset (Deluxe) (Black Paper)	RBE	AE	1990	SP		AP/BL	100		2000	4500
Three Cypress	RBE	AE	1991	SP		AP	395		1800	3000
CURRENT EDITIONS:										
Strawberries for Lunch	RBE	AD	1983	SP		STP	395		600	2400
Billiards at Cafe Palermo	RBE	AD	1984	LC		STP	395		1000	2500
Destiny	RBE	AD	1985	SP		STP	395		900	2000
Destiny (Deluxe) (with Remarque)	RBE	AD	1985	SP		MB	100		1200	2500
Destiny (Special Portfolio)	RBE	AD	1985	SP		MB	100		1400	3000
A Tango at the Glass Palace	RBE	AD	1985	SP		STP	395		900	2000
A Tango at the Glass Palace (Deluxe) (with Remarque)	RBE	AD	1985	SP		MB	100		1200	2500
A Tango at the Glass Palace (Special Portfolio)	RBE	AD	1985	SP		MB	100		1400	3000
High Flyer (Summer Olympics)	RBE	AD	1988	SP		AC	300		1200	2500
High Flyer (Summer Olympics) (Deluxe) (with Remarque)	RBE	AD	1988	SP		AC	300		1400	3000
Pacific Morning	RBE	AD	1991	SP		AP	300		2000	2500
Windy Beach II	RBE	AD	1991	SP		AP	300		1500	2000
Water Reflections	RBE	AD	1991	SP		AP	300		1500	2000
Amigo	RBE	AD	1991	SP		AP	300		1500	2000
Fishing Day	RBE	AD	1992	SP		AP	300		2400	2400
Homage to the Hawk Portfolio (Set of 3):									3000 SET	3000 SET
By the Corner	RBE	AD	1992	SP		AP	300		1200	1200
Redhead	RBE	AD	1992	SP		AP	300		1200	1200
White Cap	RBE	AD	1992	SP		AP	300		1200	1200
Romance Suite (Set of 3):									3000 SET	3000 SET
Study of Casa de Campo	RBE	AD	1992	SP		AP	300		1200	1200
Study of Girl with Bicycle	RBE	AD	1992	SP		AP	300		1200	1200
Sunbeams at Midday	RBE	AD	1992	SP		AP	300		1200	1200

The retail prices of the 100,000 limited edition prints quoted in this directory are subject to change. Print publishers, artists and galleries were the direct sources for these quotations. Prices in the secondary market listed as "Sold Out Editions (Rare)" indicate that the publisher has a limited supply of that print or that the print is difficult to locate in the galleries.

The Printworld Directory is accepting new applications for the seventh edition. Approximately 300 new artists will be accepted. Please use the two forms provided in the back section of this directory to submit biographical data and documentation of prints. Edition number of each print must not exceed 500 and the retail price must be $100 or more.

MARK LUYTEN

BORN: Belgium
PUBLISHERS: Echo Press, Bloomington, IN (EPr)
PRINTERS: David Calkins, Bloomington, IN (DC); David Keister, Bloomington, IN (DK); Echo Press, Bloomington, IN (EPr)
GALLERIES: Echo Press, Bloomington, IN; Barbara Krakow Gallery, Boston, MA; Betsy Senior Contemporary Prints, New York, NY

Mark Luyten
Quatorzieme Lettre
Courtesy Echo Press

TITLE	PUBLISHER	PRINTER	DATE	MEDIUM	DIMENSION (PAPER SIZE) IN INCHES	TYPE OF PAPER	EDITION NUMBER	NO. OF COLORS	ORIGINAL OPENING PRICE	CURRENT RETAIL PRICE
SOLD OUT EDITIONS (RARE):										
Intermezzo IX	EPr	DK/DC/EPr	1988	MON	42 X 30 EA	AC	1 EA	Varies	1800 EA	2500 EA
CURRENT EDITIONS:										
Intermezzo Series:										
La Memoire	EPr	DK/DC/EPr	1989	MON/CO	42 X 29 EA	AC/W	1 EA	Varies	1800 EA	2400 EA
Les Sons	EPr	DK/DC/EPr	1989	MON/CO	42 X 29 EA	AC/W	1 EA	Varies	1800 EA	2400 EA
L'Odeur	EPr	DK/DC/EPr	1989	MON/CO	42 X 29 EA	AC/W	1 EA	Varies	1800 EA	2400 EA
Varie Vedute Series:										
Le Labyrinthe	EPr	DK/DC/EPr	1989	PH/LC/CO/RS/EMB	42 X 29	AC	20	2	1000	1200
Le Miroir	EPr	DK/DC/EPr	1989	PH/LC/COL	42 X 29	AC	20	3	1000	1200
Divertimento III-V	EPr	DK/DC/EPr	1990	MON/CO	36 X 44 EA	AC/W	1 EA	Varies	2000 EA	2400 EA
Serre Series:										
Serre I	EPr	DK/DC/EPr	1991	PH/LC/CO	47 X 69	JP/AP/W	20	2	1400	1400
Serre II	EPr	DK/DC/EPr	1991	PH/LC/CO/RS	48 X 34	AC/W	20	2	1200	1200
Serre III	EPr	DK/DC/EPr	1991	PH/REL/CO/RS	36 X 40	AC/W	20	2	1200	1200
Lettre Series:										
Septiéme Lettre	EPr	DK/DC/EPr	1991	LC/CO	33 X 41	AC/W	4	2	1600	1600
Huitiéme Lettre	EPr	DK/DC/EPr	1991	MON/CO	33 X 48 EA	AC/W	1 EA	Varies	2200 EA	2200 EA
Dixiéme Lettre	EPr	DK/DC/EPr	1991	MON/CO	29 X 42 EA	LANA	1 EA	Varies	2200 EA	2200 EA
Onziéme Lettre	EPr	DK/DC/EPr	1991	MON/CO	29 X 42 EA	LANA	1 EA	Varies	2200 EA	2200 EA
Quatorziéme Lettre	EPr	DK/DC/EPr	1991	MON/CO	33 X 63 EA	AC/W	1 EA	Varies	2400 EA	2400 EA
Seiziéme Lettre	EPr	DK/DC/EPr	1991	MON/CO	33 X 63 EA	AC/W	1 EA	Varies	2400 EA	2400 EA
Dix-Septiéme Lettre	EPr	DK/DC/EPr	1991	PH/LC/CO	42 X 29	LANA/W	5	2	1600	1600
Dix-Neuviéme Lettre	EPr	DK/DC/EPr	1991	PH/LC/CO	33 X 48	AC/W	8	4	1200	1200
Vingtiéme Lettre	EPr	DK/DC/EPr	1991	MON/CO	33 X 39 EA	AC/W	1 EA	Varies	2200 EA	2200 EA

LAWRENCE MACARAY

BORN: Elsinore, CA; May 8, 1921
EDUCATION: Whittier Col, CA, BA, 1951; California State Univ, Long Beach, CA, MA, 1955
TEACHING: Prof, Drawing & Painting, El Camino Col, Torrance, CA 1962–87
AWARDS: Purchase Prize, Downey Mus of Art, CA, 1974; Purchase Prize, Southern California Artists, Del Mar, CA, 1974
COLLECTIONS: Bertrand Russell Peace Found, Nottingham, England; Bowers Mus, Santa Ana, CA; San Bernardino County Mus, Redland, CA
PRINTERS: Larry Taylor, Orange, CA (LT); Spectrum Press, Orange, CA (SP); Barbara Johnson, Torrance, CA (BJ); John Johnson, Torrance, CA (JJ); Prism Press, Torrance, CA (PP); Artist (ART)
PUBLISHERS: Prism Press, Torrance, CA (PP); Spectrum Press, Orange CA (SP); El Camino Col, Torrance, CA (EC)
GALLERIES: Ruskin Fine Art, Los Angeles, CA
MAILING ADDRESS: 1431 E La Palma Ave, Anaheim, CA 92805

TITLE	PUBLISHER	PRINTER	DATE	MEDIUM	DIMENSION (PAPER SIZE) IN INCHES	TYPE OF PAPER	EDITION NUMBER	NO. OF COLORS	ORIGINAL OPENING PRICE	CURRENT RETAIL PRICE
CURRENT EDITIONS:										
Death of a Friend	SP	LT/SP	1974	SP	24 X 36	STR/IM	100	5	75	300
The Grand Tour	EC	ART	1975	LB	26 X 20	R/BFK	25	1	65	250
Enigmatic Glime	SP	LT/SP	1976	LC	30 X 22	AP	25	1	75	300

LAWRENCE MACARAY CONTINUED

TITLE	PUBLISHER	PRINTER	DATE	MEDIUM	DIMENSION (PAPER SIZE) IN INCHES	TYPE OF PAPER	EDITION NUMBER	NO. OF COLORS	ORIGINAL OPENING PRICE	CURRENT RETAIL PRICE
CURRENT EDITIONS:										
Perspicious Intent	SP	LT/SP	1976	LC	30 X 22	AP	25	1	75	300
Thatched Cottage, Connemara	EC	ART	1976	LB	15 X 22	AP	20	1	65	250
January Floral	EC	ART	1977	SP	30 X 22	AP	15	11	75	300
Starry Shirt	EC	ART	1977	EB	15 X 11	AP	10	1	65	250
Sonny's Dream	EC	ART	1980	EB	15 X 11	AP	10	1	65	250
The Blue Rider	PP	BJ/JJ/PP	1984	SP	22 X 30	AP	50	21	175	350
Pagan Shrouds	PP	BJ/JJ/PP	1985	SP	22 X 30	AP	50	6	175	350

DAVID MACAULAY

BORN: Burton-on-Trent, England; December 2, 1946
EDUCATION: Rhode Island Sch of Design, BA, Arch, 1969
TEACHING: Instr, Rhode Island Sch of Design, Providence, RI, 1974–76, Adj Prof, 1976–85; Yale Univ, New Haven, CT, Vis Lectr, Yale Univ, New Haven, CT, 1978–79
TEACHING: Vis Lectr, Yale Univ, New Haven, Ct, 1978–79; Instr, Rhode Island Sch of Design, Providence, RI, 1974–76, Adj Prof, 1976–85; Vis Prof, Brown Univ, Providence, RI, 1982 to present; Wellesley Col, MA, 1985 to present

AWARDS: Deutscher Jungenbuchpreis, Germany, 1975; Caldescott Hon Medal, Am Library Assn, 1974,78
COLLECTIONS: Cooper Hewitt Mus, NY; Toledo Mus of Art, OH; Rhode Island Sch of Design, Providence, RI
PRINTERS: Judith Solodkin, NY (JS); Solo Press, NY (SP)
PUBLISHERS: Solo Press, NY (SP)
GALLERIES: Solo Gallery, New York, NY
MAILING ADDRESS: c/o Space Gallery of Architecture, 39 W 67th St, New York, NY 10023

TITLE	PUBLISHER	PRINTER	DATE	MEDIUM	DIMENSION (PAPER SIZE) IN INCHES	TYPE OF PAPER	EDITION NUMBER	NO. OF COLORS	ORIGINAL OPENING PRICE	CURRENT RETAIL PRICE
CURRENT EDITIONS:										
Time Off	SP	JS/SP	1982	LB	12 X 16	AP	50	1	150	300
Veduta della Stazione Grand Central	SP	JS/SP	1982	LB	32 X 41	AP	80		400	600

TURI SPEAR MACCOMBIE

BORN: Troy, NY; 1947
EDUCATION: Syracuse Univ Sch of Art, NY; Pomona Col, Claremont, CA
AWARDS: Mina Walker Smith Prize, Watercolor, New Haven Paint & Clay Club, John Slade Ely House, CT, 1975; Nat Prize, Letraset, Inc, Creativity Comp, 1976; Prize, Soundview Exhib, Lyman Allyn Mus, Outstanding Painting, 1979; Second Prize, Soundview Exhib, 1980; New Haven Paint & Clay Club Prize, Anna Held Audette, Juror, CT, 1980
PRINTERS: Artist (ART)
PUBLISHERS: Orion Editions, NY (OE)
GALLERIES: Orion Editions, New York, NY

TITLE	PUBLISHER	PRINTER	DATE	MEDIUM	DIMENSION (PAPER SIZE) IN INCHES	TYPE OF PAPER	EDITION NUMBER	NO. OF COLORS	ORIGINAL OPENING PRICE	CURRENT RETAIL PRICE
CURRENT EDITIONS:										
White Tulips	OE	ART	1989	PO		AC	75		1000	1000

KIM MACCONNEL

BORN: Oklahoma City, OK; 1946
EDUCATION: Univ of California, San Diego, CA, BA, 1969; MFA, 1972
AWARDS: California State Scholar, 1970
RECENT EXHIB: Holly Solomon Gallery, NY, 1992; Gian Enzo Sperone, Rome, Italy, 1992

PRINTERS: Rex Heftmann, San Diego, CA (RH); Fabric Workshop, NY & Phila, PA (FW)
PUBLISHERS: Holly Solomon Editions, NY (HSE); Brooke Alexander, Inc, NY (BAI)
GALLERIES: Holly Solomon Gallery, New York, NY; James Corcoran Gallery, Los Angeles, CA; Dart Gallery, Chicago, IL; Texas Gallery, Houston, TX; Gian Enzo Sperone, Rome, Italy

TITLE	PUBLISHER	PRINTER	DATE	MEDIUM	DIMENSION (PAPER SIZE) IN INCHES	TYPE OF PAPER	EDITION NUMBER	NO. OF COLORS	ORIGINAL OPENING PRICE	CURRENT RETAIL PRICE
SOLD OUT EDITIONS (RARE):										
Poetry Project Poster	BAI		1990	SP	30 X 30	AP	125		125	125
Poetry Project Print	BAI		1990	SP	27 X 30	AP	75		350	350
CURRENT EDITIONS:										
Bamboo Curtain	FW	FW	1980	SP/CS/BAM	108 X 54	COT	8	1	1200	3500
The Sliding Series (Set of 3):									3000 SET	3500 SET
Green	HSE	RH	1980	SP/DI	24 X 19 X 1	GM/W	40	2	1100	1300
Magenta	HSE	RH	1980	SP/DI	17 X 24 X 1	GM/W	40	2	1100	1300
Orange	HSE	RH	1980	SP/DI	23 X 20 X 1	GM/W	40	2	1100	1300

The print market has become very selective. For the first time since we published the first edition of The Printworld Directory in 1982, the prices of prints have been greatly reduced and greatly increased for the same artists by the most reputable and established print publishers. Check the fifth edition to understand the movement.

ISAAC MAIMON

BORN: Beersheba, Israel; December 15, 1951
EDUCATION: Avni Inst, Tel Aviv, Israel, Teaching, BA, 1978
TEACHING: Center for the Visual Arts, Beersheva, Israel Ben-Gurion Univ of the Negev, Israel
RECENT EXHIB: Tower Gallery, Sacramento, CA, 1991; Tower Gallery, Los Angeles, CA, 1992; Atlas Galleries, Chicago, IL, 1992,93; Fine Art Collections, Sausalito, CA, 1991,92,93; Network Gallery, La Jolla, CA, 1993; Sher Gallery, Miami, FL, 1991,93; Sundook Gallery, Boca Raton, FL, 1992,93; Minitaur Gallery, Las Vegas, NV, 1993
PRINTERS: Geo-Print, Tel Aviv-Jaffa, Israel (GP)
PUBLISHERS: B & R International Art, Ltd, Bonsall, CA
MAILING ADDRESS: c/o B & R International Art, Ltd, 5641 Circle View Dr, Bonsall, CA 92003

Isaac Maimon
Reception
Courtesy B & R International Art, Ltd

TITLE	PUBLISHER	PRINTER	DATE	MEDIUM	DIMENSION (PAPER SIZE) IN INCHES	TYPE OF PAPER	EDITION NUMBER	NO. OF COLORS	ORIGINAL OPENING PRICE	CURRENT RETAIL PRICE
SOLD OUT EDITIONS (RARE):										
Cafe Select	TW	GPA	1989	SP	35 X 26	AP	250		250	900
Two Women	TW	GPA	1989	SP	30 X 41	AP	250		250	900
Happy Hour/Seated Woman (Set of 2)	TW	GPA	1989	SP	13 X 18 EA	AP	250 EA		250	1200
Cafe Caze I, II	BR	GPA	1990	SP	17 X 13 EA	AP	275 EA		600 SET	1200 SET
Girl Talk	BR	GPA	1990	SP	26 X 34	AP	275		600	1200
Monique										
Cafe Napolitan	BR	GPA	1990	SP	26 X 35	AP	275		600	1200
At the Ball	BR	GPA	1991	SP	34 X 45	COV	275		900	2000
CURRENT EDITIONS:										
Champaigne Girl	BR	GPA	1990	SP	26 X 37	WWP	275		600	1000
Courtesan	BR	GPA	1991	SP	36 X 26	COV	275		600	700
Paris Nights (Set of 4):									1450 SET	1550 SET
Bonne Soirée	BR	GPA	1991	SP	19 X 15	WWP	275		xxx	xxx
C'Est la Vogue	BR	GPA	1991	SP	19 X 15	WWP	275		xxx	xxx
L'Affectation	BR	GPA	1991	SP	19 X 15	WWP	275		xxx	xxx
Le Rendez-vous	BR	GPA	1991	SP	19 X 15	WWP	275		xxx	xxx
Gazebo	BR	GPA	1991	SP	25 X 36	COV	275		900	1000
The Reception	BR	GPA	1991	SP	39 X 26	COV	275		600	700
Table for One	BR	GPA	1991	SP	25 X 36	COV	275		600	700
Cafe de Lion	BR	GPA	1992	SP	32 X 46	COV	275		900	1000
The Corner Cafe	BR	GPA	1992	SP	28 X 38	COV	275		600	900
High Society (Set of 2):									600 SET	600 SET
La Vie Francaise	BR	GPA	1992	SP	21 X 15	WWP	275		xxx	xxx
Le Beau Monde	BR	GPA	1992	SP	21 X 15	WWP	275		xxx	xxx
Once in a While	BR	GPA	1992	SP	28 X 40	WWP	275		600	600
City Cafes	BR	GPA	1993	SP		COV	275		1500	1500
Westbank Cafe	BR	GPA	1993	SP		COV	275		900	900

The retail prices of the 100,000 limited edition prints quoted in this directory are subject to change. Print publishers, artists and galleries were the direct sources for these quotations. Prices in the secondary market listed as "Sold Out Editions (Rare)" indicate that the publisher has a limited supply of that print or that the print is difficult to locate in the galleries.

The Printworld Directory is accepting new applications for the seventh edition. Approximately 300 new artists will be accepted. Please use the two forms provided in the back section of this directory to submit biographical data and documentation of prints. Edition number of each print must not exceed 500 and the retail price must be $100 or more.

ISAAC MAIMON CONTINUED

Isaac Maimon
Two Women
Courtesy B & R International Art, Ltd

Isaac Maimon
Monique
Courtesy B & R International Art, Ltd

Isaac Maimon
At the Ball
Courtesy B & R International Art, Ltd

GUY MACCOY

BORN: Kansas; (1904–1981)
EDUCATION: Kansas City Art Inst, KS; Art Students League, NY; Columbia Univ, NY, BA, 1940
TEACHING: Jepson Art Inst, Los Angeles, CA; Otis Art Inst, Los Angeles, CA
PRINTERS: Artist (ART); American Atelier, NY (AA)
PUBLISHERS: Artist (ART); Circle Fine Art, Chicago, IL (CFA)
GALLERIES: Circle Galleries, San Diego, CA & San Francisco, CA & Northbrook, IL & Pittsburgh, PA & Houston, TX & Soho, NY & Chicago, IL & Scottsdale, AZ & Beverly Hills, CA & Costa Mesa, CA & Sherman Oaks, CA & Palm Beach, FL & Honolulu, HI & New Orleans, LA & Las Vegas, NV & Seattle, WA

TITLE	PUBLISHER	PRINTER	DATE	MEDIUM	DIMENSION (PAPER SIZE) IN INCHES	TYPE OF PAPER	EDITION NUMBER	NO. OF COLORS	ORIGINAL OPENING PRICE	CURRENT RETAIL PRICE
SOLD OUT EDITIONS (RARE):										
Haunts of the Heron	ART	ART	1943	SP	11 X 14	AP	50			500
Two Men and Moon	ART	ART	1943	SP	11 X 14	AP	50			500
Vermont Grazing	ART	ART	1944	SP	11 X 14	AP	50			500
It is Evening	ART	ART	1944	SP	11 X 14	AP	50			600
Purple Still Life	ART	ART	1944	SP	11 X 14	AP	50			500
Wild Canary	ART	ART	1948	SP	11 X 14	AP	50			300
Open Door	ART	ART	1950	SP	11 X 14	AP	50			400
Billboard Birds	ART	ART	1951	SP	12 X 14	AP	30			350
Flight	ART	ART	1951	SP	11 X 14	AP	50			500
CURRENT EDITIONS:										
Golden Warriors	CFA	AA	1980	LC	30 X 41	AP	200	50		150

ANNE MACDOUGALL

EDUCATION: Randolph-Macon Woman's Col, Lynchburg, VA; Syracuse Univ, NY
AWARDS: Artists' Found Grant, Boston, MA; Virginia Center, Sweet Briar, VA; MacDowell Colony, Petersborough, NH
COLLECTIONS: Mus of Fine Arts, Boston, MA; Fogg Mus, Cambridge, MA; Boston Univ, MA; DeCordova Mus, Lincoln, MA; Cleveland Mus, OH; Virginia Mus of Fine Arts, Richmond, VA
PRINTERS: Sabina Klein Studio, NY (SKS)
PUBLISHERS: John Szoke Graphics, Inc, NY (JSG)
GALLERIES: John Szoke Graphics, Inc, New York, NY
MAILING ADDRESS: 98 Riverside Dr, New York, NY 10024

TITLE	PUBLISHER	PRINTER	DATE	MEDIUM	DIMENSION (PAPER SIZE) IN INCHES	TYPE OF PAPER	EDITION NUMBER	NO. OF COLORS	ORIGINAL OPENING PRICE	CURRENT RETAIL PRICE
CURRENT EDITIONS:										
Badlands II (Dipt)	JSG	SKS	1986	EC/HC	24 X 67	R/BFK	80	4	1000	1250

YAN MACS

BORN: Riga, Lativia; December 1933
EDUCATION: North Texas State Univ, Denton, TX, MA
TEACHING: Fort Worth Art Center, TX
AWARDS: Southwest Print & Drawing Award, 1963; Dallas Mus Awards, TX; Texas Wesleyan Col, Fort Worth, TX, Purchase Award
COLLECTIONS: Texas Wesleyan Col, Fort Worth, TX; Oklahoma Mus of Art, Oklahoma City, OK
PRINTERS: Herbert A Fox, Merrimac, MA (HF); Fox Graphics, Merrimac, MA (FG)
PUBLISHERS: Fox Graphics, Merrimac, MA (FG); Michael Strem, Newburyport, MA (MS)
GALLERIES: Fox Graphics, Merrimac, MA

TITLE	PUBLISHER	PRINTER	DATE	MEDIUM	DIMENSION (PAPER SIZE) IN INCHES	TYPE OF PAPER	EDITION NUMBER	NO. OF COLORS	ORIGINAL OPENING PRICE	CURRENT RETAIL PRICE
CURRENT EDITIONS:										
Sunday Afternoon	FG	HF/FG	1977	LC	28 X 28	AP	185	23	500	900
Strolling	FG	HF/FG	1977	LC	28 X 28	AP	185	28	500	900

CHRISTOPHER MAKOS

BORN: Lowell, MA; January 4, 1948
PUBLISHERS: Ronald Feldman Fine Arts, NY (RFFA)
GALLERIES: Ronald Feldman Fine Arts, New York, NY; Govinda Gallery, Wash, DC
MAILING ADDRESS: c/o Ronald Feldman Fine Arts, 31 Mercer St, New York, NY 10013

TITLE	PUBLISHER	PRINTER	DATE	MEDIUM	DIMENSION (PAPER SIZE) IN INCHES	TYPE OF PAPER	EDITION NUMBER	NO. OF COLORS	ORIGINAL OPENING PRICE	CURRENT RETAIL PRICE
CURRENT EDITIONS:										
Altered Image (Photographs of Andy Warhol in Drag) (Signed by Andy Warhol & Artist) (Set of 5)	RFFA		1982	PH	28 X 22 EA	KOD	25 EA	1 EA	5000 SET	20000 SET
Altered Image (Silkscreens of Andy Warhol in Drag) (Set of 5)	RFFA		1989	SP	40 X 32 EA	SOM	35 EA		2000 EA	2500 EA
Ten Images (Photographs taken 1978–1987 During Travel with Andy Warhol) (Set of 30)	RFFA		1989	PH	14 X 18 EA or 18 X 14 EA	KOD	30 EA	1 EA	7000 EA	7500 SET

SHEILA MAKI

BORN: Sudbury, Canada, August 31, 1932
EDUCATION: Camden Arts Centre, London, England, 1967–68; Univ of British Columbia, BC, Can; Centennial Col, Toronto, Can, 1973–79; George Brown Col, Toronto, Can, 1973–79
AWARDS: Palme d'or des Beaux Arts, Monte Carlo, 1973; Hon Mention, Burnaby Print Exhib, Burnaby Art Gallery, ON, Can, 1975; Ontario Arts Council Grants, 1979,80,91
RECENT EXHIB: Glenhyrst Art Gallery, Brantford, Can, ON, 1988; Peel Mus of Art, Brampton, Can, ON, 1988; Arts Centre, North Bay, ON, Can, 1989; Visual Arts Centre of Newcastle, ON, Can, 1990; Gloucester County Col, Sewell, NJ, 1990; Wilfred Laurier Univ, Waterloo, Can, 1991; Woodstock Public Art Gallery, Can, 1991; Int Print Society, New Hope, PA, 1991

COLLECTIONS: Burnaby Art Gallery, Can; Oregon State Univ, Corvallis, OR; Cornell Univ, Ithaca, NY; Univ of Waterloo, Can; Univ of Toronto, Can; Metropolitan Toronto Sch, Toronto, Can; Metropolitan Mus & Art Center, Miami, FL; Nat Mus of Manitoba, Ottawa, Can; Art Gallery of Ontario, Can; Art Gallery of Hamilton, Can; Kirchener-Waterloo Art Gallery, Can; Centennial Gallery, Canada; Wilfred Laurier Univ, Waterloo, Can
PRINTERS: Artist (ART)
PUBLISHERS: Merritt Fine Art Co, Toronto, Canada (MFA); Fidelity Arts of California, Los Angeles, CA (FAC); Artist (ART)
GALLERIES: CFAS Gallery, Toronto, ON, Canada; Steiner CAC, Willowdale, ON, Canada; Gallery 211, Ossining, NY; Corporate Art Association, St Louis, MO; Artsource, Greenwood Lake, NY
MAILING ADDRESS: c/o Venturgraph, Int, #19–400 Esna Park Dr, Markham, ON, Canada L3R 3K2

TITLE	PUBLISHER	PRINTER	DATE	MEDIUM	DIMENSION (PAPER SIZE) IN INCHES	TYPE OF PAPER	EDITION NUMBER	NO. OF COLORS	ORIGINAL OPENING PRICE	CURRENT RETAIL PRICE
SOLD OUT EDITIONS (RARE):										
Flying Up	ART	ART	1972	EC	16 X 20	AP	15	4	100	650
Fugue with Orange	ART	ART	1972	EC	16 X 20	AP	15	3	100	650
Northern Symphony	ART	ART	1972	EC	30 X 22	AP		2	100	650
Awareness of Life	ART	ART	1973	EC	30 X 22	AP	10	3	100	650
Bird of Fire	ART	ART	1973	EC	30 X 22	AP	10	3	100	650
Unspoiled Splendor	ART	ART	1973	EC	30 X 22	AP	25	2	100	500
Lighter Moments	ART	ART	1973	EC	24 X 20	AP	25	2	100	650
Softness of Dawn	ART	ART	1973	EC	10 X 12	AP	12	2	60	425
Forgotten Drama	ART	ART	1974	EC	22 X 30	AP	25	2	100	650
Forgotten Intrigues	ART	ART	1974	EC	16 X 20	AP	15	3	90	600
Procrastination	ART	ART	1974	EC	30 X 22	AP	30	2	100	650
Promise of Youth	ART	ART	1975	EC/COL	20 X 26	AP	45	2	100	500
Salutation	ART	ART	1975	EB/COL	30 X 22	AP	25	1	100	675
Sound Waves	ART	ART	1975	COL	34 X 25	AP	50	6	125	900
Atmospheric Rythm	ART	ART	1975	EC/COL	27 X 35	AP	50	5	125	900
Interlacing Rhythm	ART	ART	1976	EC/COL	22 X 30	AP	50	5	100	600
Living Legacy	ART	ART	1976	EC/COL	23 X 27	AP	45	4	100	625
Duo in Harmony	ART	ART	1976	SP	25 X 20	MAY	38	7	80	500
Currents of Energy	ART	ART	1976	EC/COL	30 X 26	AP	45	4	145	750
Memory of a Dream	FAC	ART	1977	EC/COL	34 X 28	AP	50	5	100	900
Interlocking Triads	ART	ART	1977	SP	20 X 25	MAY	38	9	80	525
Dynamics in Contrast	ART	ART	1977	SP	20 X 25	MAY	40	8	80	500
Orange is Beautiful	ART	ART	1977	SP	20 X 25	MAY	37	9	80	500
Airwave Adventure	ART	ART	1977	SP	20 X 25	MAY	39	5	80	500
Dramatic Advance	ART	ART	1977	SP	20 X 25	MAY	41	6	80	500
Illuminated Landmark	FAC	ART	1978	EC	22 X 30	AP	50	5	100	650
Beginning Spaces	ART	ART	1978	EC	18 X 24	AP	60	4	60	400
A New Entrance	ART	ART	1978	EC/COL	28 X 26	AP	50	7	145	850
Aerial Suspension	ART	ART	1978	EC/COL	30 X 22	AP	50	3	100	625
Grand Opening	FAC	ART	1978	EC/COL	22 X 30	AP	50	3	100	650
Northern Legend	FAC	ART	1978	EC/COL	30 X 22	AP	50	5	100	700
On the Sunny Side	FAC	ART	1978	EC/COL	22 X 30	AP	50	4	60	550
Journey's End	FAC	ART	1978	EC/COL	22 X 30	AP	50	4	100	700
Difference	FAC	ART	1979	EC/COL	29 DIA	AP	60	4	125	700
Somewhere I Have Never Travelled	FAC	ART	1979	EC/COL	33 X 28	AP	50	5	125	875
Trio One	FAC	ART	1979	EC/COL	29 DIA	AP	60	5	125	650
Jazz Interlude	FAC	ART	1980	EC/COL	30 X 40	AP	75	10	125	875
Future Rhythms	FAC	ART	1980	EC/SP	30 X 40	AP	75	8	125	900
Circling Around (Set of 4)	MFA	ART	1980	SP	22 X 30 EA	AP	55 EA	11 EA	900 SET	2800 SET
Reality of It All	ART	ART	1983	EC/SP/COL	26 X 30	AP	39	9	325	675
Magicial Medley	ART	ART	1983	SP	22 X 30	AP	32		300	625
The Celestial Wedge	ART	ART	1984	SP	22 X 30	AP	43	15	300	525
Bounds of Freedom	ART	ART	1984	SP	30 X 42	AP	29	16	475	775
About to Change	ART	ART	1986	SP	22 X 30	AP	9	13	375	900
CURRENT EDITIONS:										
Suspended Animation	ART	ART	1976	EC	22 X 30	AP	45	4	100	575
Pole of the North	ART	ART	1978	EC/COL/SP	30 X 42	AP	45	7	400	750
Wind of Chance	ART	ART	1979	EC/SP	30 X 42	AP	65	13	300	750
In Place of the Other	ART	ART	1979	EC/COL	22 X 29	AP	60	6	150	500
Lost and Gone Forever	ART	ART	1979	EC/SP/COL	23 X 30	AP	60	6	150	525
Beyond the Barrier	ART	ART	1980	SP	22 X 30	AP	60	11	200	475
Resulting Experience	ART	ART	1980	EC/SP/COL	28 DIA	AP	45	7	275	475
Soft into the New Realm	ART	ART	1980	SP	22 X 30	AP	60	11	200	600
With a Look of its Own	ART	ART	1980	SP	22 X 30	AP	60	9	200	475
The Depths of Calm	ART	ART	1981	SP	22 DIA	AP	30	6	200	450
The Roots of Life	ART	ART	1982	SP	30 X 42	AP	75	13	400	700
Encompassing of the North	ART	ART	1982	SP	22 X 30	AP	50	12	270	475
Fall Highlights	ART	ART	1982	SP/PENC	22 X 30	AP	29	5	250	475
More Discoveries	ART	ART	1983	SP	22 X 30	AP	45	13	300	475
The Endless Horizon	ART	ART	1984	SP	22 X 30	AP	20	12	300	475

SHEILA MAKI CONTINUED

TITLE	PUBLISHER	PRINTER	DATE	MEDIUM	DIMENSION (PAPER SIZE) IN INCHES	TYPE OF PAPER	EDITION NUMBER	NO. OF COLORS	ORIGINAL OPENING PRICE	CURRENT RETAIL PRICE
CURRENT EDITIONS:										
Around the Pole	ART	ART	1985	SP	22 X 30	SOM	64		325	500
Heavens are Rich	ART	ART	1985	SP	22 X 30	SOM	56		325	475
The Positive Flow	ART	ART	1985	SP	22 X 30	SOM	58		350	475
Perpetual Motion (Dipt)	ART	ART	1985	SP	44 X 60	SOM	35	39	1500	1900
Nine Metres Tall	ART	ART	1986	SP	29 X 43	SOM	25		480	725
Thoughts on the Matter (Tript)	ART	ART	1986	SP	30 X 66	AP	37		1500	1750
An Open Book	ART	ART	1986	SP	22 X 30	AP	35	7	375	500
Laser Option	ART	ART	1987	SP	22 X 30	SOM	33	10	400	475
A Star is Powerful	ART	ART	1987	SP	30 X 44	SOM	55	14	600	750
Contact with Mystery	ART	ART	1987	SP	22 X 30	SOM	31	9	400	475
Dreampath	ART	ART	1987	SP	28 X 30	SOM	25	14	450	550
On the Surface	ART	ART	1987	SP	22 X 30	SOM	55	11	375	475
Natures of the Land	ART	ART	1988	SP	22 X 30	AP	55	11	400	475
Drifting Stillness	ART	ART	1989	SP	30 X 44	SOM	44	8	600	700
Clear of the Surface	ART	ART	1989	SP	30 X 44	SOM	43	8	600	700
Climb into the Wind	ART	ART	1989	SP	30 X 44	SOM	45	9	650	700
Something Special	ART	ART	1989	SP	30 X 44	SOM	43	9	650	700
Shadows of the Drift	ART	ART	1989	SP	30 X 44	SOM	33	8	650	700
Egypt Revisited	ART	ART	1989	SP	30 X 22	SOM	45		425	475
Balloons over Miami	ART	ART	1989	SP	27 X 37	SOM	40		550	650
Low to the Sea	ART	ART	1989	SP	22 X 30	SOM	44	9	450	475
Something Special	ART	ART	1989	SP	30 X 44	SOM	43	9	650	700
Coming and Going	ART	ART	1990	SP	30 X 22	SOM	48		425	475
Living Elements	ART	ART	1990	SP	17 X 22	SOM	35		250	325
Five Shades of Blue	ART	ART	1990	SP	12 X 11	SOM	35	5	135	175
Through the Arch	ART	ART	1991	SP/COL	22 X 27	SOM	35	3	375	400
Arch of Ime	ART	ART	1991	SP/COL	18 X 21	SOM	33	5	350	375
From the Open Sea	ART	ART	1991	SP	22 X 30	SOM	30	9	425	475
Lost Heritage Portfolio (Set of 5)	ART	ART	1991	SP	12 X 10 EA	RP	50 EA	1 EA	450 SET	500 SET
Just for a Change	ART	ART	1992	SP	30 X 44	SOM	33		700	750
Except for the Wind	ART	ART	1992	SP	22 X 30	SOM	32		475	475

STANLEY MALTZMAN

BORN: New York, NY; July 4, 1921
EDUCATION: New York Phoenix Sch of Design, NY, 1948
TEACHING: Instr, Drawing, Hudson Valley Workshops, NY, 1987,88,89,90
AWARDS: Am Acad of Arts & Letters, NY; Connecticut Acad of Fine Arts, First Prize, CT, 1976; Ball State Univ Award, Muncie, IN, 1981; Berkshire Mus, Pittsfield, MA, 1981; Curatorship Grant, 1983; William Zahn Mem Award, Knickerbocker Artists, NY, 1983
RECENT EXHIB: Pastel Soc of Am Artists, NY, 1989; Nat Acad of Design, NY, 1990
COLLECTIONS: Mus of Fine Arts, Springfield, MA; Carnegie-Mellon Inst, Pittsburgh, PA; Hudson River Mus, Yonkers, NY; Schenectady Mus, NY; Eisenhower Col, Salem, NY
PRINTERS: George C Miller & Sons, NY (GCM)
PUBLISHERS: Artist (ART)
GALLERIES: Associated American Artist, New York, NY; Capricorn Gallery, Bethesda, MD
MAILING ADDRESS: Rte 1, PO Box 158, Freehold, NY 12431

TITLE	PUBLISHER	PRINTER	DATE	MEDIUM	DIMENSION (PAPER SIZE) IN INCHES	TYPE OF PAPER	EDITION NUMBER	NO. OF COLORS	ORIGINAL OPENING PRICE	CURRENT RETAIL PRICE
SOLD OUT EDITIONS (RARE):										
Bald Eagle	ART	GCM	1969	LB	30 X 22	AP	50	1	50	400
CURRENT EDITIONS:										
Wintercats	ART	GCM	1970	LB	30 X 22	AP	100	1	50	300
Woodcock I	ART	GCM	1970	LB	21 X 16	AP	100	1	50	275
Woodcock II	ART	GCM	1971	LB	19 X 17	AP	90	1	40	250
The Gladiator	ART	GCM	1971	LB	30 X 22	AP	100	1	50	300
Ruffed Grouse	ART	GCM	1974	LB	19 X 17	AP	90	1	50	250
Woodland Tennant	ART	GCM	1977	LB	16 X 20	AP	90	1	50	225
Ring Necked Pheasant	ART	GCM	1979	LB	21 X 17	AP	90	1	50	250
A Pleasant Surprise	ART	GCM	1979	LB	20 X 17	AP	45	1	50	225
A Genuine Antique	ART	GCM	1980	LC/HC	19 X 22	AP	90	2	125	275
Winter Leaves	ART	GCM	1981	LB	19 X 22	AP	50	1	125	250
Japanese Lace	ART	GCM	1984	LC	25 X 19	R/BFK	90	3	150	250

MATTHIAS MANSEN

PRINTERS: Artist (ART)
PUBLISHERS: Wolfgang Wittrock, Düsseldorf, Germany (WW)

TITLE	PUBLISHER	PRINTER	DATE	MEDIUM	DIMENSION (PAPER SIZE) IN INCHES	TYPE OF PAPER	EDITION NUMBER	NO. OF COLORS	ORIGINAL OPENING PRICE	CURRENT RETAIL PRICE
CURRENT EDITIONS:										
Küche (Kitchen) (Set of 5)	WW	ART	1990–91	WB	40 X 54 EA	SOM	5 EA	1 EA	14000 SET	14000 SET

MAN RAY (EMMANUEL RADINSKI)

BORN: Philadelphia, PA; (1890–1976)
EDUCATION: Acad of Design, NY, 1908; Art Students League, NY; Ferrer Ctr, NY
RECENT EXHIB: Zabriskie Gallery, NY, 1988–89; Kent Gallery, NY, 1989; Smithsonian Inst, Wash, DC, 1989; Philadelphia Mus of Art, PA, 1989; Int Center of Photography, Midtown, NY, 1990; Robert Miller Gallery, NY, 1991; Univ of California, Riverside, NY, 1992; Gallery Piazza Arts & Culture, Sausalito, CA, 1992; Kent Gallery, NY, 1992
COLLECTIONS: Mus of Modern Art, NY
PRINTERS: Atelier Mourlot, Paris, France (AM); Gemini GEL, Los Angeles, CA (GEM); Artist (ART)
PUBLISHERS: Transworld Art, Inc, NY (TAI); Gemini GEL, Los Angeles, CA (GEM); Artist (ART)

GALLERIES: Edwynn Houk Gallery, Chicago, IL; Kimmel/Cohn Photography, New York, NY; Prakapas Gallery, New York, NY; Robert Miller Gallery, New York, NY; Staley-Wise Gallery, New York, NY; Zabriskie Gallery, New York, NY; Kent Gallery, New York, NY; G Ray Hawkins Gallery, Los Angeles, CA; Robert Koch Gallery, San Francisco, CA; Middendorf Gallery, Wash, DC; Ehler Caudill Gallery, Chicago, IL; Beth Urdang Fine Art, Boston, MA; Karen Amiel Modern & Contemporary Art, New York, NY; G Ray Hawkins Gallery, Modernism Gallery, Coral Gables, FL; Gala Art Gallery, Palm Beach, FL; Gerald Peters Gallery, Santa Fe, NM; Virginia Lust Gallery, New York, NY; Magneststone Contemp Art, Paoli, PA; Jeffrey Fuller Fine Arts, Ltd, Phila, PA

Gemini—(G)

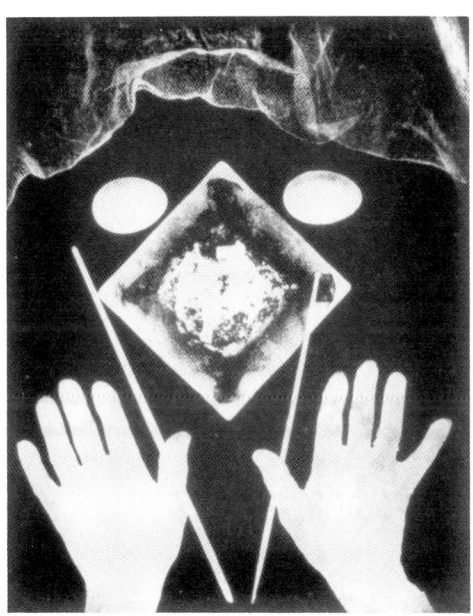

Man Ray
Untitled (G-20)
Courtesy Gemini GEL

Man Ray
Revolving Doors
Courtesy Gemini GEL

TITLE	PUBLISHER	PRINTER	DATE	MEDIUM	DIMENSION (PAPER SIZE) IN INCHES	TYPE OF PAPER	EDITION NUMBER	NO. OF COLORS	ORIGINAL OPENING PRICE	CURRENT RETAIL PRICE
SOLD OUT EDITIONS (RARE):										
Rayograph (Double-Brush)	ART	ART	1920	PH	9 X 7	AP			50	125000
Lila	ART	ART	1920	PH	5 X 9	AP			50	30000
Study of Legs in Stockings and Heels	ART	ART	1920	PH	6 X 5	AP	20		50	6000
Kiki Silhouette	ART	ART	1922	PH	11 X 8	AP			50	60000
The Primacy of Matter Over Thought	ART	ART	1929	PH	11 X 9	AP			50	110000
Nusch Ehuard and Ady	ART	ART	1930	PH	9 X 7	AP			100	36000
Self-Portrait with View Camera	ART	ART	1932	PH	9 X 8	AP			100	55000
Lee Miller in a Bathing Costume	ART	ART	1932	PH	7 X 4	AP			100	20000
Untitled (Buttons)	ART	ART	1945	PH	14 X 11	AP			150	32000
Letter Box (with Ceramic Letters)	GEM	GEM	1966	MULT	5 X 11 X 3	AP	25		300	7500
Untitled (G-20)	GEM	GEM	1966	LC	26 X 22	R/BFK	125	1	200	3000
Hands	GEM	GEM	1966	SP	27 X 21	PLEX	40	2	400	1800
One Hand	GEM	GEM	1966	SP	27 X 21	PLEX	40	2	400	2000
Personage	TAI	AM	1975	LC	26 X 30	AB	175	2	400	850
Les Grands Trans-Parents (from Mirrors of the Mind Suite)	M	ART	1975	LC/SP/EMB/CO	26 X 20	AB	100		400	2500

The retail prices of the 100,000 limited edition prints quoted in this directory are subject to change. Print publishers, artists and galleries were the direct sources for these quotations. Prices in the secondary market listed as "Sold Out Editions (Rare)" indicate that the publisher has a limited supply of that print or that the print is difficult to locate in the galleries.

ALFRED MANESSIER

BORN: Saint-Ouen, France; December 5, 1911
EDUCATION: Lyceum & Fine Arts Sch of Amiens, France
TEACHING: Salon de Mai, Paris, France
COLLECTIONS: Tate Gallery, London, England; Solomon R Guggenheim Mus, NY; National Galerie, Berlin, Germany; Museo de Arte Moderna, Rio de Janeiro, Brazil; Mus Boymans Van Beuningen, Rotterdam, The Netherlands; Mus Royaux des Beaux-Arts, Brussels, Belgium; Mod Museet, Stockholm, Sweden; Nationalgalleriet, Oslo, Norway; Nat Gallery, Canada; Mus d'Art Mod, Paris, France
PRINTERS: La Poligrafa, SA, Barcelona, Spain (LP)
PUBLISHERS: Ediciones Polifraca, SA, Barcelona, Spain (EdP)
GALLERIES: Galeria Joan Prats, Barcelona, Spain & New York, NY

TITLE	PUBLISHER	PRINTER	DATE	MEDIUM	DIMENSION (PAPER SIZE) IN INCHES	TYPE OF PAPER	EDITION NUMBER	NO. OF COLORS	ORIGINAL OPENING PRICE	CURRENT RETAIL PRICE
SOLD OUT EDITIONS (RARE):										
PrinTemps Hollandais			1958	LC/HC	17 X 23	AP	50	5	50	1000
CURRENT EDITIONS:										
Man Series–I–XV (Set of 15)	EdP	LP	1979	LC	30 X 22 EA	GP	99 EA		4100 SET	7000 SET
									300 EA	500 EA

ROBERT PETER MANGOLD

BORN: North Tonawanda, New York; October 12, 1937
EDUCATION: Cleveland Inst of Arts, OH, 1956–59; Yale Univ, New Haven, CT, 1959, BFA, 1960–62, MFA, 1963
TEACHING: Instr, Hunter Col, NY, 1964–65; Instr, Skohegan Summer Art Sch, ME, 1968; Instr, Yale-Norfolk Summer Art Sch, Norfolk, CT, 1969; Instr, Cornell Univ, Ithaca, NY, 1970; Instr, Art, Sch of Visual Arts, NY, 1963 to present
AWARDS: Nat Council on Arts Award, 1966; John Simon Guggenheim Mem Grant, 1969; Skowhegan Sch of Painting & Sculpture, ME, Painting, 1993
RECENT EXHIB: Paula Cooper Gallery, NY, 1987; Hallen für Neue Kunst, Schaffhausen, Switzerland, 1987; South Dakota Stat Univ, Art Mus, Brookings, SD, 1989; Galerie Lelong, NY, 1989; Lisson Gallery, London, England, 1987,90; Pace Gallery, NY, 1992; Pace Prints, NY, 1993
COLLECTIONS: Guggenheim Mus, NY; Mus of Mod Art, NY; Whitney Mus of Am Art, NY; New York Univ; Mus of Fine Arts, Houston, TX; La Jolla Mus of Contemp Art, CA; Tate Gallery, London, England; Stedelijk Mus, Amsterdam, The Netherlands; Los Angeles County Mus, CA; Rhode Island Sch of Design, Providence, RI; Oberlin Col, OH; Aldrich Mus of Contemp Art, Ridgefield, CT
PRINTERS: Workshop Inc (WI); Crown Point Press, San Francisco, CA (CPP); Hidekatsu Takada, CA (HT); David Kelso, CA (CK); Jeryl Parker, NY (JP); Doris Simmelink, Simmelink-Sukimoto Editions, Marina Del Rey, CA (SSE); Patrick Foy, San Francisco, CA (PF); Leslie Miller, NY (LM); Grenfell Press, NY (GrenPr)
PUBLISHERS: Max Protech, Inc, NY (MP); Parasol Press, NY (PaP); Crown Point Press, San Francisco, CA (CPP); Brooke Alexander, Inc, NY (BAI); Simmelink-Sukimoto Editions, Marina Del Rey, CA (SSE); Grenfell Press, NY (GrenPr)
GALLERIES: John Weber Gallery, New York, NY; Crown Point Press, New York, NY & San Francisco, CA; Rhona Hoffman Gallery, Chicago, IL; Donald Young Gallery, Seattle, WA; Sidney Janis Gallery, New York, NY; Texas Gallery, Houston, TX; Paula Cooper Gallery, New York, NY; Martina Hamilton Gallery, New York, NY; Lisson Gallery, London, England; Betsy Senior Contemporary Prints, New York, NY; Daniel Weinberg Gallery, Santa Monica, CA; Artyard, Denver, CO; Galerie Lelong, New York, NY; Pence Fine Art, Inc, Los Angeles, CA; Hope Weiss Fine Art, Los Angeles, CA; Janet Steinberg Fine Arts, San Francisco, CA; Takada Fine Arts, San Francisco, CA; Susan Sheehan Gallery, New York, NY; Stux Modern, New York, NY; Pace Gallery, New York, NY
MAILING ADDRESS: c/o Paula Cooper Gallery, 155 Wooster St, New York, NY 10012

TITLE	PUBLISHER	PRINTER	DATE	MEDIUM	DIMENSION (PAPER SIZE) IN INCHES	TYPE OF PAPER	EDITION NUMBER	NO. OF COLORS	ORIGINAL OPENING PRICE	CURRENT RETAIL PRICE
SOLD OUT EDITIONS (RARE):										
Distorted Square within a Circle (Set of 3):									525 SET	6000 SET
Distorted Square within a Circle 1	MP		1973	SP	27 X 27	MUR	75		175	2000
Distorted Square within a Circle 2	MP	WI	1973	SP	27 X 27	MUR	75		175	2000
Distorted Square within a Circle 3	MP	WI	1973	SP	27 X 27	MUR	75		175	2000
Seven Aquatints	PaP	CPP	1973	AC	27 X 22 EA	R/BFK	50 EA		1200 SET	24000 SET
Five Aquatints (Set of 5)	PaP	PF/CPP	1975	AC	9 X 9 EA	AP/S	50 EA	3 EA	1200 SET	18000 SET
Untitled Aquatint	CPP	HT/DK	1978	AC	22 X 21	R/BFK	20	2	500	3500
Orange	PaP	PF/CPP	1979	AC	41 X 41	R/BFK	50		1200	5000
Three Aquatints	PaP	PF/CPP	1979	AC	26 X 58	R/BFK	50		1200	5500
Two Aquatints (Set of 2):									3600 SET	10000 SET
Aquatint #1	PaP	JP/DS/JPE	1985	AC	53 X 37	SOM	20		2200	5000
Aquatint #2	PaP	JP/DS/JPE	1985	AC	55 X 37	SOM	20		2200	5000
CURRENT EDITIONS:										
Five Color Frame	CPP	CPP	1985	WC	25 X 21	SOM	200	10	1000	2500
Untitled (Set of 4)	BAI		1989	WC	15 X 27 EA	SOM	40		9000 SET	9000 SET
Pages (Set of 12)	SSE	SSE	1989	EB	14 X 14 EA	Varies	40 EA		8000 SET	16000 SET
Untitled	BAI		1989–90	WB	17 X 19	SOM	35		900	900
Untitled	BAI		1989–90	WB	16 X 19	SOM	35		900	900
The Nonconformist's Memorial (with Susan Howe, Poetry) (60-Page Bound Book with 6 Woodcuts):										
Paper	GrenPr	LM/GrenPr	1992		14 X 9		65		1500	1500
Vellum	GrenPr	LM/GrenPr	1992		14 X 9		18		2500	2500

The retail prices of the 100,000 limited edition prints quoted in this directory are subject to change. Print publishers, artists and galleries were the direct sources for these quotations. Prices in the secondary market listed as "Sold Out Editions (Rare)" indicate that the publisher has a limited supply of that print or that the print is difficult to locate in the galleries.

SYLVIA PLIMACK MANGOLD

BORN: New York, NY; September 18, 1938
EDUCATION: Cleveland Art Inst, OH, 1956–59; Cooper Union, NY, 1959; Yale Univ Art Sch, New Haven, CT, BFA, 1961
TEACHING: Sch for the Visual Arts, 1970–71, 1974–82
RECENT EXHIB: Lehman Col of Art Gallery, City Univ of New York, Bronx, NY, 1986–87; Aldrich Mus of Contemp Art, Ridgefield, CT, 1986–87; Brooke Alexander, Inc, NY, 1987; Fuller Goldeen Gallery, San Francisco, CA, 1987; Texas Gallery, Houston, TX, 1987; Flander's Contemp Art, Minneapolis, MN, 1987; Anne Marie Verna Galerie, Zürich, Switzerland, 1988
COLLECTIONS: Mus of Mod Art, NY; Brooklyn Mus, NY; Whitney Mus of Am Art, NY; Albright-Knox Art Gallery, Buffalo, NY; Yale Univ, New Haven, CT; Weatherspoon Art Gallery, Univ of North Carolina, Greensboro, NC; Walker Art Center, Minneapolis, MN; Utah Mus, Salt Lake City, UT
PRINTERS: Paul Narkiewicz, NY (PN); Styria Studio, NY (SS); Sarah Todd, Los Angeles, CA (ST); Tadashi Toda, Kyoto, Japan (TT); Shunzo Matsuda, Kyoto, Japan (SM); Crown Point Press, San Francisco, CA (CPP); Doris Simmelink, Marina Del Rey, CA (DS); Chris Sukimoto, Marina Del Rey, CA (CK); Simmelink/Sukimoto Editions, Marina Del Rey, CA (S/SE); Betty Winkler (BW); Riverhouse Editions, Clark, CO (REd)
PUBLISHERS: 724 Prints, NY (724P); Brooke Alexander, Inc, NY (BAI); Parasol Press, NY (PaP); Styria Studio, NY (SS); Crown Point Press, San Francisco, CA (CPP); Jeryl Parker, NY (JP); Doris Simmelink, NY (DS); Riverhouse Editions, Clark, CO (REd)
GALLERIES: Brooke Alexander, Inc, New York, NY; Donald Young Gallery, Seattle, WA; Rhona Hoffman Gallery, Chicago, IL; Styria Studio, New York, NY; Crown Point Press, New York, NY & San Francisco, CA; Texas Gallery, Houston, TX; Flander's Contemporary Art, Minneapolis, MN; Anne Marie Verna Galerie, Zürich, Switzerland; Betsy Senior Contemporary Prints, New York, NY; Takada Fine Arts, San Francisco, CA; Hope Weiss Fine Art, Los Angeles, CA; Van Straaten Gallery, Chicago, IL
MAILING ADDRESS: 1 Bull Rd, Washingtonville, NY 10992

Sylvia Plimack Mangold
Lodgepolo Pine
Courtesy Van Straaten Gallery

TITLE	PUBLISHER	PRINTER	DATE	MEDIUM	DIMENSION (PAPER SIZE) IN INCHES	TYPE OF PAPER	EDITION NUMBER	NO. OF COLORS	ORIGINAL OPENING PRICE	CURRENT RETAIL PRICE
SOLD OUT EDITIONS (RARE):										
Flexible and Stainless	BAI	PN	1972	LC	21 X 29	R/BFK	50		100	750
Floor	BAI	PN	1973	L/HC/AC	29 X 37	R/BFK	29		150	1500
Floor II	BAI	PN	1974	L/HC/AC	29 X 37	R/BFK	38		150	900
Aquatint, Sugarlift and Golden Changes (Set of 3)	PaP	CPP	1977	EB/A	11 X 14 EA	R/BFK	50 EA	1 EA	600 SET	1800 SET
Aquatint, Sugarlift and Golden Changes (As Above with Two Additional (Etchings)	PaP	CPP	1977	EB/A	11 X 14	R/BFK	10	1	400	2000
Paper Under Tape/Paint over Paper	PaP	CPP	1977	EB/A	22 X 30	R/BFK	50		250	1000
View of Schumnemunk Mt	724P		1980	LC	32 X 21	R/BFK	50	11	900	1500
Cropped Sunset with Plum Tree	SS	SS	1982	LC/SP	30 X 42	AC/W	60	8	1000	1500
Nut Trees Series:										
Nut Trees (Red)	JP/DS	DS/ST	1985	AC	25 X 20	KOCHI	25	1	750	1000
Nut Trees (Yellow)	JP/DS	DS/ST	1985	AC	25 X 20	KOCHI	25	1	750	1000
Nut Trees (Blue)	JP/DS	DS/ST	1985	AC	25 X 20	KOCHI	25	1	750	1000
The Nut Trees	CPP	TT/SM/CPP	1985	WC	16 X 23	KOZO	100	8	950	1000
The Pin Oak at the Pond	BAI	DS/CS/SSE	1985–86	A/DPT/SB	26 X 29	SOM	50	5	1250	2000
CURRENT EDITIONS:										
The Locust Trees	S/SE	DS/CS/SSE	1988	DPT/A	24 X 31	SOM	30	2	900	1000
The Locust Trees, State I	S/SE	DS/CS/SSE	1988	DPT	24 X 31	SOM	10	1	750	900
Elk River	REd	BW/REd	1992	MON	32 X 23 EA to 36 X 24 EA	HMP	1 EA	Varies	2000 EA	2000 EA
Mountain View	REd	BW/REd	1992	MON	16 X 22 EA to 17 X 22 EA	HMP	1 EA	Varies	1500 EA	1500 EA
Small Tree Monoprint	REd	BW/REd	1992	MON	22 X 17 EA to 25 X 20 EA	HMP	1 EA	Varies	1500 EA	1500 EA
Lodgepole Pine	REd	BW/REd	1992	EB/A/DPT/SB	31 X 21 EA	HAHN		2	1500	1500
Tall Trees	REd	BW/REd	1992	MON	25 X 20 EA to 30 X 23 EA	HMP	1 EA	Varies	2000 EA	2000 EA
Mountain View	REd	BW/REd	1992	EC	30 X 23 EA	IYO	10	Varies	750	750

ELSIE MANVILLE

BORN: Philadelphia, PA; May 11, 1922
EDUCATION: Tyler Sch of Fine Arts, Temple Univ, Phila, PA, BFA, BS, Ed, 1939–43
TEACHING: Adj Instr, Fashion Inst of Tech, NY, presently
AWARDS: Nat Acad of Design, NY, 1976; Purchase Award, Butler Inst of Am Art, Youngstown, OH, 1978; Nat Endowment of the Arts, Visual Arts Fel, 1981; Best Work on Paper, Guild Hall Mus, East Hampton, NY, 1982; Purchase Award, Guild Hall Mus, East Hampton, NY, 1984; Nat Endowment for the Arts, Artist Fel Grant, Painting, 1985; New York Found for the Arts Award, Painting, NY, 1990
COLLECTIONS: Temple Univ, Phila, PA; Butler Inst of Am Art, Youngstown, OH; Univ of Iowa Mus of Art, Iowa City, IA
PRINTERS: Roni Henning, NY (RH)
PUBLISHERS: Orion Editions, New York, NY (OE)
GALLERIES: Orion Editions, New York, NY; Kraushaar Galleries, New York, NY
MAILING ADDRESS: c/o Kraushaar Galleries, 724 Fifth Ave, New York, NY 10019

TITLE	PUBLISHER	PRINTER	DATE	MEDIUM	DIMENSION (PAPER SIZE) IN INCHES	TYPE OF PAPER	EDITION NUMBER	NO. OF COLORS	ORIGINAL OPENING PRICE	CURRENT RETAIL PRICE
CURRENT EDITIONS:										
Think of Me	OE	RH	1984	SP	32 X 38	AC	125	31	500	750
Bristol Blue	OE	RH	1986	SP	32 X 38	AC	125	39	600	750
Tea and Lemon	OE	RH	1989	SP	32 X 38	AC	125	39	600	750

MICHAEL MANZAVRAKOS

BORN: Minneapolis, MN; 1951
EDUCATION: Univ of Minnesota, Minneapolis, MN, 1969–74; Studio Arts Program
TEACHING: Instr, Photography, Studio Arts, Teaching Asst, Univ of Minnesota, Minneapolis, MN, 1974; Instr, Photography Workshop, Rochester Art Center, MN, 1978; Instr, Monotype Workshop, North Hennepin Com Col, Minneapolis, MN, 1986; Instr, Monotype Workshop, Univ of Minnesota, Minneapolis, MN, 1987
AWARDS: Minnesota State Arts Board Project Grants, Minneapolis MN, 1977,80; Minneapolis Independent Choreographers Alliance, MN, 1985
RECENT EXHIB: Thomson Gallery, Minneapolis, MN, 1987; Dolan/Maxwell Gallery, Phila, PA, 1988; Piper, Jaffray, Hopwood, Inc, Minneapolis, MN, 1990; Steensland Gallery, St Olaf Col, Northfield, MN, 1991; Carolyn Ruff Gallery, Minneapolis, MN, 1991
COLLECTIONS: Univ of Indiana, Bloomington, IN; Univ of Minnesota, Minneapolis, MN; Walker Art Center, Minneapolis, MN; Minneapolis Inst of Art, MN
PRINTERS: Steven Sorman's Studio, St. Croix, MN (SSS); David Keister, Bloomington, IN (OK); David Calkins, Bloomington, IN (DC); James Cheskaty, Bloomington, IN (JC); Echo Press, Bloomington, IN (EPr); Artist (ART); Smith Andersen Editions, Palo Alto, CA (SAE)
PUBLISHERS: Echo Press, Bloomington, IN (EPr); Artist (ART); Smith Andersen Editions, Palo Alto, CA (SAE)
GALLERIES: Thomson Gallery, Minneapolis, MN; Echo Press, Bloomington, IN; Carolyn Ruff Gallery, Minneapolis, MN; Smith Andersen Editions, Palo Alto, CA
MAILING ADDRESS: 2921 E 24th St, Minneapolis, MN 55406; Studio, 2418 University Avenue, Southeast, Minneapolis, MN 55414

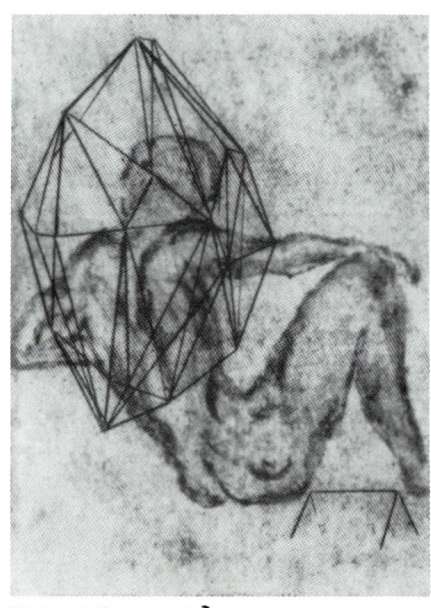

Michael Manzavrakos
Second Watcher
Courtesy Smith Andersen

TITLE	PUBLISHER	PRINTER	DATE	MEDIUM	DIMENSION (PAPER SIZE) IN INCHES	TYPE OF PAPER	EDITION NUMBER	NO. OF COLORS	ORIGINAL OPENING PRICE	CURRENT RETAIL PRICE
SOLD OUT EDITIONS (RARE):										
I Can't Hear You, I, II	ART	ART/SSS	1984	MON	42 X 28 EA	AP	1 EA	1 EA	900 EA	2500 EA
Dwelling Place (Set of 5)	ART	ART	1985	DPT	29 X 24 EA	GOYU	5 EA	2 EA	1500 SET	4500 SET
CURRENT EDITIONS:										
Along the Nile	EPr	DK/DC/EPr	1985	MON	22 X 16 EA	KOCHI	1 EA	Varies	450 EA	750 EA
Memory of the Paleologue I (2 Panels)	EPr	DK/DC/EPr	1986	MON	61 X 23 EA	IVP	1 EA	Varies	800 EA	1100 EA
Memory of the Paleologue II (3 Panels)	EPr	DK/DC/EPr	1986	MON	68 X 31 EA	IVP	1 EA	Varies	950 EA	1600 EA
The Keeper (2 Panels)	EPr	DK/DC/EPr	1986	MON	61 X 23 EA	IVP	1 EA	varies	800 EA	1100 EA
Small Room at Pylos I	EPr	DK/DC/EPr	1986	MON	31 X 23 EA	IVP	1 EA	Varies	350 EA	600 EA
Night Window I–IV	EPr	DK/DC/EPr	1987	MON	60 X 23 EA	ISP	1 EA	2 EA	1000 EA	1400 EA
Moving About I	EPr	DK/DC/DPr	1987	I/MON	61 X 45 EA	ISP	4 EA	3 EA	1500 EA	2200 EA
Night Shade	EPr	DK/DC/EPr	1987	MON/HC	60 X 23 EA	ISP	4 EA	3 EA	1200 EA	1550 EA
Cloister	EPr	DK/DC/EPr	1987	MON/HC	60 X 23 EA	ISP	1 EA	2 EA	1200 EA	1400 EA
Niobe	EPr	DK/DC/EPr	1988–89	COL	42 X 30 EA	TAK/AC	8	4	1200	1400
Naken I–VIII (Set of 8)	EPr	JC/EPr	1989	COL	26 X 22 EA	AC/W	8 EA	4 EA	800 EA	950 EA
First-Fourth Witness	EPr	DK/DC/EPr	1991	LC	30 X 22 EA	MIT & AC/B	15 EA	6 EA	850 EA	850 EA
Forgotten Witness	EPr	DK/DC/EPr	1991	MON	25 X 20 EA	AC	1 EA	Varies	950 EA	950 EA
First-Fifth Guardian	EPr	DK/DC/EPr	1991	MON	25 X 20 EA	CGP	1 EA	Varies	950 EA	950 EA
Undone Protector I,II	EPr	DK/DC/EPr	1991	MON	13 X 10 EA	IVP	1 EA	Varies	850 EA	850 EA
Becoming Protector I	EPr	DK/DC/EPr	1991	MON	19 X 15 EA	IVP/LANA	1 EA	Varies	850 EA	850 EA

MICHAEL MANZAVRAKOS CONTINUED

TITLE	PUBLISHER	PRINTER	DATE	MEDIUM	DIMENSION (PAPER SIZE) IN INCHES	TYPE OF PAPER	EDITION NUMBER	NO. OF COLORS	ORIGINAL OPENING PRICE	CURRENT RETAIL PRICE
CURRENT EDITIONS:										
Becoming Protector II	EPr	DK/DC/EPr	1991	MON	13 X 10 EA	IVP	1 EA	Varies	850 EA	850 EA
First Protector	EPr	DK/DC/EPr	1991	MON	19 X 14 EA	LANA	1 EA	Varies	850 EA	850 EA
Second-Sixth Protector	EPr	DK/DC/EPr	1991	MON	19 X 14 EA	LANA	1 EA	Varies	850 EA	850 EA
Monotypes (Series of 31)	SAE	SAE	1991	MON	30 X 22 EA	LANA	1 EA	Varies	1500 EA	1500 EA
Monotypes (Series of 6)	SAE	SAE	1991	MON	59 X 22 EA	LANA	1 EA	Varies	1900 EA	1900 EA

USHANNA MARALDO

BORN: Osnabruck, Lower Saxony, West Germany; US Citizen
EDUCATION: Michigan State Univ, East Lansing, MI, BFA with Honors; Univ of Mexico, Mexico City, Mexico; Univ of Osnabruck, Germany, MA, Psychology; Col of Arts & Crafts, Oakland, CA; San Francisco Art Inst, CA
TEACHING: Instr, Fine Art, Buser Inst, Switzerland, 1970; Produce & Director, New Visions & New Music, San Francisco, CA, 1975
AWARDS: First Prize, Mus of Mod Art, San Francisco, CA, Nat Drawing Comp, 1970; First Prize, Southern California Artists, Century City Chamber of Commerce, CA, 1979; Award of Excellence, Int Artists, IAC, NY, 1988

COLLECTIONS: Mus of Mod Art, San Francisco, CA; Santa Barbara Mus of Art, CA; Oakland Art Mus, CA; Goeth Inst, San Francisco, CA; Laguna Beach Mus, CA; Univ of California, Berkeley, CA; Ball State Univ Mus, Muncie, IN; Scripps Research Found, La Jolla, CA
PRINTERS: Richard Royce Studios, Santa, NY (RRS); Pentagraphics, Studio City, CA (Pen); Artist (ART)
PUBLISHERS: Lawrence Unlimited, Northridge, CA (LU); Luma Arts, Tarzana, CA (LA); Fidelity Arts of California, Inc, Los Angeles, CA (FAC)
GALLERIES: Ruth Bachofner Gallery, Los Angeles, CA; Art Collector, San Diego, CA
MAILING ADDRESS: 535 Barker Pass Rd, Santa Barbara, CA 93108

TITLE	PUBLISHER	PRINTER	DATE	MEDIUM	DIMENSION (PAPER SIZE) IN INCHES	TYPE OF PAPER	EDITION NUMBER	NO. OF COLORS	ORIGINAL OPENING PRICE	CURRENT RETAIL PRICE
SOLD OUT EDITIONS (RARE):										
Celestial Musician	LA	RRS	1976	AC/E/EMB/HC	29 X 34	GE	21	51	450	1500
Precision II	LU	ART	1983	SP/EMB/STEN	42 X 30	GE	15	9	400	600
Spring Grace	LA	ART	1984	SP/3-D/HC	48 X 15	AC	25	12	600	800
Summer Glow	LA	ART	1984	SP/3-D/HC	48 X 15	AC	75	12	600	800
Autumn Fire	LA	ART	1985	SP/3-D/HC	48 X 15	AC	35	12	600	800
Migration	LA	ART	1985	MM/HC	44 X 26	STP	20	9	595	800
Dunes	LA	ART	1985	MM/HC	44 X 26	STP	25	9	595	800
Spectrum (Woven Paper)	LA	ART	1986	SP/HC	36 X 36	STP	20	10	700	900
CURRENT EDITIONS:										
Tapestry	LU	ART	1982	SP/STEN	42 X 30	AC	22	8	400	500
Precision I	LU	ART	1983	SP/STEN/EMB	42 X 30	GE	15	9	400	500
Window to the Rose Garden I, II	LU	ART	1983	SP/STEN/EMB	42 X 30 EA	GE	25 EA	9 EA	400 EA	500 EA
Vast Horizon	LU	ART	1983	EC/HC	42 X 30	GE	20	12	500	600
Expanding View	LU	ART	1984	SP/HC	30 X 44	SOM	30	9	550	600
Winter Rest	LA	ART	1985	SP/3-D/HC	48 X 15	AC	25	12	600	700
Tigerlily	LA	ART	1985	SC/HC	44 X 30	STP	36	16	550	600
Genesis I	FAC	ART	1986	MM/EMB/HC	30 X 42	AC	200	9	395	500
Sky Journey	FAC	ART	1986	MM/EMB/HC	42 X 30	AC	200	9	395	500
Reflective River	LA	ART	1986	PSC/SP	23 X 43	STP/100	20	18	600	700
Wings on the Breeze	LA	ART	1986	PSC/SP	23 X 43	STP/100	20	15	600	700
Transparent Land	LA	ART	1987	MM/HC	30 X 40	STP	75	15	650	700
Desert Monuments	LA	ART	1987	MM/HC	30 X 44	STH	99	21	750	800
Natural Currents (Dipt)	LA	ART	1987	MM/EMB/HC	39 X 60	AC	75	21	1000	1200

LEO MARANZ

BORN: Chicago, IL; 1900
PRINTERS: American Atelier, NY (AA)
PUBLISHERS: Circle Fine Art, NY (CFA)
GALLERIES: Circle Galleries, San Diego, CA & San Francisco, CA & Northbrook, IL & Pittsburgh, PA & Houston, TX & Soho, NY & Chicago, IL & Scottsdale, AZ & Beverly Hills, CA & Costa Mesa, CA & Sherman Oaks, CA & Palm Beach, FL & Honolulu, HI & New Orleans, LA & Las Vegas, NV & Seattle, WA

TITLE	PUBLISHER	PRINTER	DATE	MEDIUM	DIMENSION (PAPER SIZE) IN INCHES	TYPE OF PAPER	EDITION NUMBER	NO. OF COLORS	ORIGINAL OPENING PRICE	CURRENT RETAIL PRICE
CURRENT EDITIONS:										
Balloons	CFA	AA	1978	SP	42 X 34	AP	250		200	500
Sextette Folio (Set of 6)									1000 SET	2050 SET
#1-Overture	CFA	AA	1979	SP	30 X 30	AP	300		175	450
#2-Allegro	CFA	AA	1979	SP	30 X 30	AP	300		175	450
#3-Stacatto	CFA	AA	1979	SP	30 X 30	AP	300		175	450
#4-Adagio	CFA	AA	1979	SP	30 X 30	AP	300		175	450
#5-Counter Point	CFA	AA	1979	SP	30 X 30	AP	300		175	450
#6-Crescendo	CFA	AA	1979	SP	30 X 30	AP	300		175	450

ROBERT MAPPLETHORPE

BORN: New York, NY; (1946–1989)
EDUCATION: Pratt Inst, NY, 1963–70
AWARDS: Creative Artists Public Service Program Award
COLLECTIONS: Metropolitan Mus of Art, NY; Mus of Mod Art, NY; Victoria & Albert Mus, London, England; Int Center of Photog, NY; George Eastman House, Rochester, NY; Mus of Fine Arts, Boston, MA; Corcoran Gallery of Art, Wash, DC; San Francisco Mus of Mod Art, CA; Georges Pompidou Mus, Paris, France
RECENT EXHIB: Whitney Mus of Am Art, NY, 1988; Betsy Rosenfield Gallery, Chicago, IL, 1988–89; Robert Miller Gallery, NY, 1988; Inst of Contemp Art, Chicago, IL, 1988–89; Corcoran Gallery, Wash, DC, 1989; Columbus Mus, GA, 1992; Tampa Mus of Art, FL, 1992; Univ of South Florida, Tampa, FL, 1992
PRINTERS: Deli Sacilotto, NY (DS); Artist (ART); Vermillion Editions, Ltd, Minneapolis, MN (VEL); Graphicstudio, Tampa, FL (GS); University of South Florida, Tampa, FL (USF)
PUBLISHERS: Lunn Gallery, New York, NY (LG); Robert Miller Gallery, New York, NY (RMG); Barbara Gladstone Gallery, NY (BGE); Deli Sacilotto, NY (DS); Edition Schellmann, NY (ES); Vermillion Editions, Ltd, Minneapolis, MN (VEL); Galerie Bernd Klüser, NY & Munich, Germany (GBK); Grahicstudio, Tampa, FL (GS); University of South Florida, Tampa, FL (USF)
GALLERIES: Fraenkel Gallery, San Francisco, CA; Texas Gallery, Houston, TX; Robert Miller Gallery, New York, NY; Gagosian Gallery, New York, NY; Michael H Lord Gallery, Milwaukee, WI; Barbara Gladstone Gallery, New York, NY; Betsy Rosenfield, Chicago, IL; Editions Schellmann, New York, NY; Richard Green Gallery, Santa Monica, CA; The Collector Art Gallery, Wash, DC; Middendorf Gallery, Wash, DC; Barbara Gillman Gallery, Miami, FL; Flanders Contemp Art, Minneapolis, MN; Vermillion Editions, Ltd, Minneapolis, MN; Karen Amiel Modern and Contemporary Art, New York, NY; Fahey/Klein Gallery, Los Angeles, CA; G Ray Hawkins Gallery, Santa Monica, CA; Tavelli Williams Gallery, Aspen, CO; Ginny Williams Gallery, Denver, CO; Fay Gold Gallery, Atlanta, GA; Weston Gallery, Carmel, CA; Thomson Gallery, Minneapolis, MN; BlumHelman Gallery, New York, NY; Bonnier Gallery, New York, NY; Martina Hamilton & Associates, Inc, New York, NY; Edition

Robert Mapplethorpe
From America Suite
Courtesy Edition Schellmann

Schellmann, New York, NY
MAILING ADDRESS: c/o Robert Miller Gallery, 41 E 57th St, New York, NY 10022

TITLE	PUBLISHER	PRINTER	DATE	MEDIUM	DIMENSION (PAPER SIZE) IN INCHES	TYPE OF PAPER	EDITION NUMBER	NO. OF COLORS	ORIGINAL OPENING PRICE	CURRENT RETAIL PRICE
SOLD OUT EDITIONS (RARE):										
Dan S	ART	ART	1980	PH	40 X 30	WOVE			800	20000
Z (Set of 13)	LG/RMG	ART	1981	PH	7 X 7 EA	R/100	25 EA		2500 SET	15000 SET
Floral Still (Set of 3)	ART	ART	1982	PH	33 X 32 EA	WOVE	30 EA		3000 SET	3500 SET
Flowers (Set of 10)	BGE/DS	DS	1983	PH/CC	31 X 25 EA	AP	40 EA		6500 SET	36000 SET
Mirror Image	ES	ART	1983	PH	19 X 15	AP			600	9000
America	ES	ART	1983	PH	19 X 15	AP			600	10000
Andy Warhol	ART	ART	1983	PH	19 X 15	HMP	10		600	32500
Self Portrait with Gun and Star	ART	ART	1983	PH	15 X 15	HMP	10		600	35000
Grace Jones Painted by Keith Haring (Trip)	ART	ART	1984	PH	15 X 15 EA				1500 SET	10000 SET
Untitled #1–#5 (Set of 5):									3000 SET	20000 SET
Untitled #1	BGE	DS	1985	PH/SP	30 X 25		60	3	600	4000
Untitled #2	BGE	DS	1985	PH/SP	30 X 25		60	1	600	4000
Untitled #3, #4 (with Watercolor)	BGE	DS	1985	PH/WA	30 X 25 EA		60 EA	1 EA	600 EA	4000 EA
Untitled #5 (with Flocking)	BGE	DS	1985	PH/FL	30 X 25		60	1	600	4000
Cross	VEL	VEL	1986	LB	32 X 24	AC	90	1	600	3000
Tampa Orchid	GS/USF	GS/USF	1986	SP/PH/G	22 X 36	AC	60		1500	12000
Untitled (from Suite: For Joseph Beuys)	ES/GBK		1986	LC/OFF	32 X 24	WOVE	90		400	3000
Floral Still Lifes (Set of 3):									3000 SET	55000 SET
Orchid	GS/USF	GS/USF	1987	PH/G	33 X 33	HMP	30		1200	20000
Hyacinth	GS/USF	GS/USF	1987	PH/G	33 X 33	HMP	30		1200	20000
Vase of Flowers	GS/USF	GS/USF	1987	PH/G	33 X 33	HMP	30		1200	20000
Poppy	ART	ART	1988	PH/G	19 X 19	HMP	7		2000	32500
Flowers	ART	ART	1988	PH/G	36 X 25	HMP	25		2500	7500
Cala Lily (Dipt)	VEL	VEL	1988	LC	26 X 26	AP	24		2500	27500
Untitled (Calla Lilies) (Set of 2)	VEL	VEL	1988	LC/OFF	26 X 26 EA	AP	24 EA	2 EA	4000 SET	20000 SET
Calla Lily (Dye Transfer)	VEL	VEL	1988	PH/DT	19 X 19	AP	24	7	2500	30000
America (Set of 3)	ES	ES	1988	LC	30 X 25 EA	AP	40 EA		2000 SET	18000 SET

The print market has become very selective. For the first time since we published the first edition of The Printworld Directory in 1982, the prices of prints have been greatly reduced and greatly increased for the same artists by the most reputable and established print publishers. Check the fifth edition to understand the movement.

ROBERT MAPPLETHORPE CONTINUED

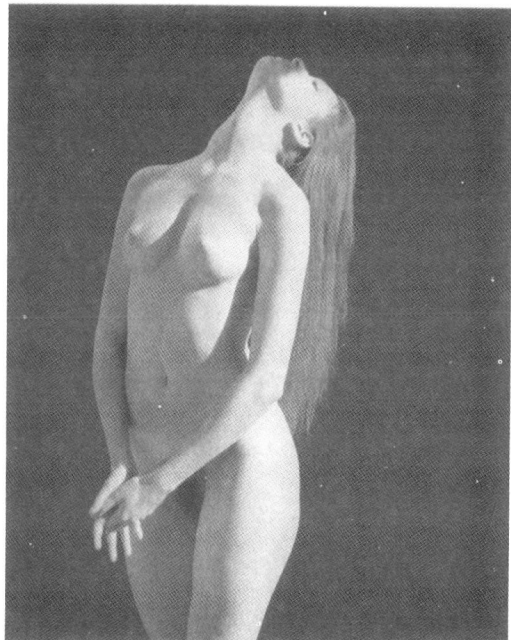

Robert Mapplethorpe
From America Suite
Courtesy Edition Schellmann

Robert Mapplethorpe
From America Suite
Courtesy Edition Schellmann

CONRAD MARCA-RELLI

BORN: Boston, MA; June 5, 1913
EDUCATION: Cooper Union, NY
TEACHING: Yale Univ, New Haven, CT, 1954–55, 59–60; Univ of California, Berkeley, CA, 1958; New Col, Sarasota, FL, 1966
AWARDS: Chicago Art Inst IL, Logan Medal & Purchase Prize, 1954; Ford Found Fel Grant, 1959; Detroit Inst of Art, 1960; Chicago Art Inst IL, M V Kohnstamm Prize, 1963
RECENT EXHIB: Marisa del Re, NY, 1992
COLLECTIONS: Metropolitan Mus of Art, NY; Mus of Mod Art, NY; Whitney Mus of Am Art, NY; Guggenheim Mus, NY; Art Inst of Chicago, IL; Brandeis Univ, Waltham, MA; Carnegie Inst, Pittsburgh, PA; Detroit Inst of Art, MI; Fogg Mus, Harvard Univ, Cambridge, MA; Albright-Knox Art Gallery, Buffalo, NY; High Mus, Atlanta, GA; Pennsylvania Acad of Fine Arts, PA; Seattle Art Mus, WA; Univ of Alabama, Tuscaloosa, AL; Yale Univ, New Haven, CT; Washington Univ, St Louis, MO; Wadsworth Atheneum, Hartford, CT; Walker Art Ctr, Minneapolis, MN; Univ of Michigan, Ann Arbor, MI; Allentown Mus of Art, PA; Cleveland Mus, OH; Colby Col, Waterville, ME; Herron Mus, Indianapolis, IN; Nat Gallery of Fine Arts, Wash, DC; Mus of Fine Arts, Houston, TX; San Francisco Mus of Mod Art, CA; Mus of Contemp Art, Los Angeles, CA; Mus of Contemp Art, Madrid, Spain
PRINTERS: American Atelier, NY (AA); Joseph Kleinman (JK); La Poligrafa, Barcelona, Spain (LP); Barcelona, Spain (EdP)
PUBLISHERS: Marlborough Graphics, NY (MG); Transworld Art Inc, NY (TAI); Post Oak Fine Art Distributors, Houston, TX (POFA); Ediciones Poligrafa S/A, Barcelona, Spain (EdP)
GALLERIES: Marlborough Graphics, New York, NY; Galeria Joan Prats, New York, NY; River Gallery, Westport CT; Hokin Gallery, Palm Beach, FL; & Bay Harbor Islands, FL; Hokin/Kaufman Gallery, Chicago, IL; Ianuzzi Gallery, Phoenix, AZ; Marisa del Re Gallery, New York, NY; R H Love Contemporary Galleries, Chicago, IL; Ianuzzi Gallery, Scottsdale, AZ; Rives Yares Galleries, Scottsdale, AZ & Santa Fe, NM
MAILING ADDRESS: 7337 Point of Rocks Rd, Sarasota, FL 33581

TITLE	PUBLISHER	PRINTER	DATE	MEDIUM	DIMENSION (PAPER SIZE) IN INCHES	TYPE OF PAPER	EDITION NUMBER	NO. OF COLORS	ORIGINAL OPENING PRICE	CURRENT RETAIL PRICE
SOLD OUT EDITIONS (RARE):										
Untitled 2	MG		1966	CO	24 X 19	AP	30		150	1000
Untitled 3	MG		1966	CO	30 X 21	AP	30		150	1000
Untitled 5	MG		1968	CO	22 X 30	AP	40		150	1000
Untitled 6	MG		1968	CO	22 X 30	AP	40		150	1000
Untitled 7	MG		1969	CO	20 X 26	AP	100		150	1000
Ibiza II	MG		1968	CO/P	21 X 26	AP	35		150	1000
Multiple A, B, C, D	MG		1969	MM	18 X 18 EA	AP	50 EA		250 EA	1000 EA
Summer Suite A, B, C, D, F	MG		1970	LC/CO	20 X 26 EA	AP/Burlap	50 EA		200 EA	1000 EA
Untitled A, B, C, D, E, F, G, H, I, J	MG		1971	CO/CAN	24 X 19 EA	AP	12 EA		225 EA	1000 EA
Autumn Suite A, B, C, D, E, F	MG		1974	LC/CO	32 X 25 EA	AP/Burlap	50 EA		150 EA	10000 EA
Set of 15 Etchings (MR1-15)	EdP	LP	1975	EB	22 X 30 EA	GP	75 EA	1 EA	8500 SET	9000 SET
									600 EA	650 EA
AL Joan Prats	EdP	LP	1975	FA	22 X 30	GP	99	1	500	550
Woman in Shower	TAI	AA	1982	LC	26 X 31	SOM	150	11	650	650
The Meeting Place	TAI	AA	1982	LC	26 X 31	SOM	150	11	650	650
Villa Neuve	POFA	JK	1982	LC	22 X 27	SOM	250	14	600	1000

The Printworld Directory is accepting new applications for the seventh edition. Approximately 300 new artists will be accepted. Please use the two forms provided in the back section of this directory to submit biographical data and documentation of prints. Edition number of each print must not exceed 500 and the retail price must be $100 or more.

MARCEL

BORN: Seattle, WA; September 2, 1946
EDUCATION: Cornish Sch of Allied Arts, Seattle, WA; New York Arts Student League, NY, Coranado Sch of Fine Arts, CA
AWARDS: Hallmark Fel, Art Students League, NY
COLLECTIONS: Charleston West Virginia Mus, W VA
PRINTERS: Artist (ART)
PUBLISHERS: Flanagan Graphics, Haverford, PA (FG)
GALLERIES: Newman Gallery, Phila, PA; Black Prints Gallery, Blacksburg, VA; Miller & Main Galleries, Blacksburg, VA; Short Hills Art Gallery, Short Hills, NJ; Capital Gallery of Contemporary Art, Frankfort, KY

TITLE	PUBLISHER	PRINTER	DATE	MEDIUM	DIMENSION (PAPER SIZE) IN INCHES	TYPE OF PAPER	EDITION NUMBER	NO. OF COLORS	ORIGINAL OPENING PRICE	CURRENT RETAIL PRICE
SOLD OUT EDITIONS (RARE):										
Night Comes Quietly	FG	ART	1981	SP	24 X 34	MUR	135	30	250	350
As Clouds Drift, Hushed	FG	ART	1981	SP	18 X 24	ST	130	37	175	250
Toward a Flower Form	FG	ART	1981	SP	18 X 24	AP88	136	47	175	250
On Pools of Quivering Shadows	FG	ART	1981	SP	24 X 36	MUR	139	38	250	350
Peter's Voyage	FG	ART	1982	SP	24 X 34	MUR	137	45	265	350
Puce, Peter, Sadie and Jasmine	FG	ART	1982	SP	18 X 24	LEN/100	140	43	180	250

CHRISTIAN MARCLAY

RECENT EXHIB: Indianapolis Center for Contemp Art, Herron Gallery, IN, 1992; Real Art Ways, Hartford, CT, 1992
PRINTERS: Judith Solodkin, NY (JS); Solo Press, NY (SP)
PUBLISHERS: Solo Press, NY (SP)
GALLERIES: Solo Gallery, New York, NY

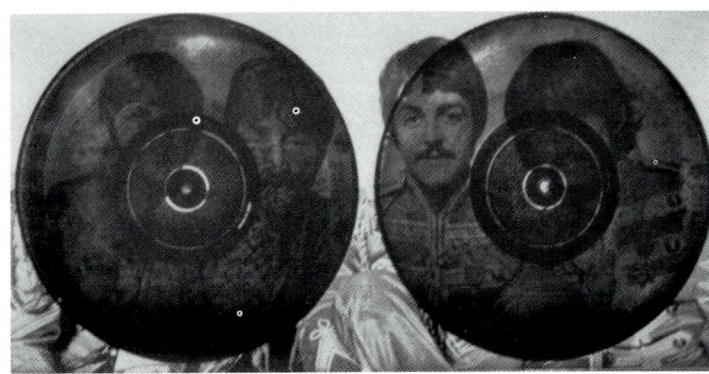

Christian Marclay
Sargent Pepper
Courtesy Solo Press

TITLE	PUBLISHER	PRINTER	DATE	MEDIUM	DIMENSION (PAPER SIZE) IN INCHES	TYPE OF PAPER	EDITION NUMBER	NO. OF COLORS	ORIGINAL OPENING PRICE	CURRENT RETAIL PRICE
CURRENT EDITIONS:										
Monotype (Surface)	SP	JS/SP	1990	MON	45 X 45 EA	AC	4 EA		3500 EA	4000 EA
Sargent Pepper (Surface Print on Album Jacket)	SP	JS/SP	1990	MON	12 X 25 EA	AC	20 EA		1800 EA	2000 EA
Untitled (Colored Surface Print)	SP	JS/SP	1990	MON	39 X 39 EA	AC	8 EA		3500 EA	4000 EA
White Album	SP	JS/SP	1990	MON	13 X 25 EA	AC	17 EA	Varies	2500 EA	3000 EA
Untitled (Victor)	SP	JS/SP	1991	MON	29 X 22 EA	AC	1 EA	Varies	1200 EA	1200 EA

MARCIA MARCUS

BORN: New York, NY; January 11, 1928
EDUCATION: New York Univ, BA, 1947; Cooper Union, NY, 1950–52; Art Students League, NY, 1954
TEACHING: New York Univ, NY; New Sch for Social Research, NY; Notre Dame, South Bend, IN; Adj Intr, Painting, Cooper Union Sch of Art, NY, 1970–71; Assoc Prof, Painting & Drawing, Louisiana State Univ, Baton Rouge, LA, Spring, 1972; Instr, Vassar Col, Poughkeepsie, NY, 1973–74; Vis Art, Cornell Univ, Ithaca, NY, Spring, 1975; Vis Art, Syracuse Univ, NY, 1976; Vis Art, Purdue Univ, IN, 1977–78; Asst Prof, Rhode Island Sch of Design, Providence, RI, 1978–79; Assoc Prof, Univ of Iowa, Champaign, IA, 1979–80; Adj Assoc Prof, Queens Col, NY, 1981; Ohio State Univ, Columbus, OH, Winter, 1983; Vis Art, Colorado State Univ, 1984; Vis Art, Univ of Wyoming, Laramie, WY, 1985; Vis Art, Northern Arizona Univ, Flagstaff, AZ, 1986; Vis Art, Univ of Maetland,1988; Vis Art, University of California, Davis, CA, 1989; Vis Art, Chautauqua Art Sch, NY, 1990; Vis Art, Col of Staten Island, NY, 1991
AWARDS: Walter K Gutman Award, 1961; Fulbright Fel, Paris, France, 1962–63; Rosenthal Award, 1964; Ford Found Grant, Art in Res, Rhode Island Sch of Design, Providence, RI, 1966; Childe Hassam Purchase Award, 1964,71; Ingram Merrill Award, 1964,77; Nat Endowment of the Arts, Painting, 1991-92
COLLECTIONS: Whitney Mus of Am Art, NY; Newark Mus, NJ; Rhode Island Sch of Design, Providence, RI; Phoenix Art Mus, AZ; Clark Univ, MA; Everson Univ, Syracuse, NY; Hirshhorn Mus, Wash, DC; Neuberger Mus, Purchase, NY; Randolph-Macon Women's Col, Lynchburg, VA; Purdue Univ, Lafayette, IN; Bowdoin Col, Brunswick, ME; Philadelphia Art Mus, PA; Univ of Wyoming, Laramie, WY; The Women's Museum, Wash, DC; Univ of Colorado, Boulder, CO; Canton Art Inst, OH; Guild Hall, Easthampton, NY
PRINTERS: Maurel Studio, NY (MS); Steve Poleski, NY (SP)
PUBLISHERS: Associated American Artists, NY (AAA); Kennedy Graphics, Inc, NY (KG); Pratt Inst, NY (PI); Artist (ART)
GALLERIES: Associated American Artist, New York, NY;
MAILING ADDRESS: 80 N Moore St, #32-B, New York, NY 10013

TITLE	PUBLISHER	PRINTER	DATE	MEDIUM	DIMENSION (PAPER SIZE) IN INCHES	TYPE OF PAPER	EDITION NUMBER	NO. OF COLORS	ORIGINAL OPENING PRICE	CURRENT RETAIL PRICE
SOLD OUT EDITIONS (RARE):										
Dunes	AAA	SP	1970	SP	20 X 26	R/BFK	100	3	150	500
Dunes II	ART	SP	1971	SP	7 X 44	AP	100	3	175	500
Olympic Print	KG	MS	1974	SP/PH	25 X 40	R/BFK	200	11	375	600
CURRENT EDITIONS:										
Shadow Self-Portrait	ART	MS	1981	SP	36 X 20	R/BFK	100	5	500	600

BRICE MARDEN

BORN: Bronxville, NY; October 15, 1938
EDUCATION: Boston Univ, MA, BFA, 1958–61; Yale-Norfolk Summer Sch for Music & Art, CT; Sch of Art & Arch, Yale Univ, New Haven, CT, MFA, 1961–63, with Esteban Vicente & Alex Katz
RECENT EXHIB: Anthony d'Offay Gallery, London, England, 1988; van Straaten Gallery, Chicago, IL, 1988; Karsten Greve Gallery, Cologne, Germany, 1992
COLLECTIONS: Mus of Mod Art, NY; Whitney Mus of Am Art, NY; Walker Art Center, Minneapolis, MN; Fort Worth Art Center, TX; Stedelijk Mus, Amsterdam, Holland; Mus of Art, San Francisco, CA; Fogg Art Mus, Harvard Univ, Cambridge, MA; Albright-Knox Art Gallery, Buffalo, NY
PRINTERS: United Press, Inc, Captiva Island, FL (UP); Richard Wilke, FL (RW); Steve Hartman, FL (SH); Simca Print Artists, NY (SPA); Jennifer Melby, NY (JM); Crown Point Press, San Francisco, CA (CPP); Artist (ART); Chiron Press, NY (ChPr); Patricia Branstead, NY (PB); Branstead Studio, NY (BS)
PUBLISHERS: United Press, Inc, Captiva Island, FL (UP); Brooke Alexander, Inc, NY (BAI); Parasol Press, Ltd, NY (PaP); Simca Print Artists, NY (SPA); Peter Blum Edition, NY (PBE); Artist (ART); Chiron Press, NY (ChPr)
GALLERIES: Brooke Alexander, Inc, New York, NY; Crown Point Press, New York, NY & San Francisco, CA; Pace Prints, New York, NY; Charles Cowles Gallery, New York, NY; Mary Boone Gallery, New York, NY; Anthony d'Offay Gallery, London, England; van Straaten Gallery, Chicago, IL; Karsten Greve Gallery, Cologne, Germany; Matthew Marks Gallery, New York, NY; Thomas Babeor Gallery, La Jolla, CA; Kim Light Gallery, Los Angeles, CA; Goodman/Tinnon Fine Art, San Francisco, CA; Anthony Meier Fine Arts, San Francisco, CA; L Bartman Fine Arts, Chicago, IL; Stephen Solovy Fine Art, Chicago, IL; Barbara Krakow Gallery, Boston, MA; Montgomery Glasoe Fine Art, Minneapolis, MN; Laura Carpenter Fine Art, Santa Fe, NM; Carol Evans Fine Art, Brooklyn, NY; A Clean, Well-Lighted Place, New York, NY; Karen Amiel Modern & Contemporary, New York, NY; Dranoff Fine Art, New York, NY; Gagosian Gallery, New York, NY; Hirschl & Adler Modern, New York, NY; Susan Sheehan Gallery, Inc, New York, NY; Linda R Silverman Fine Art, Inc, New York, NY; Matthew Marks Gallery, New York, NY
MAILING ADDRESS: 276 Bowery, New York, NY 10012

Brice Marden
Five Threes
Courtesy Parasol Press, Ltd

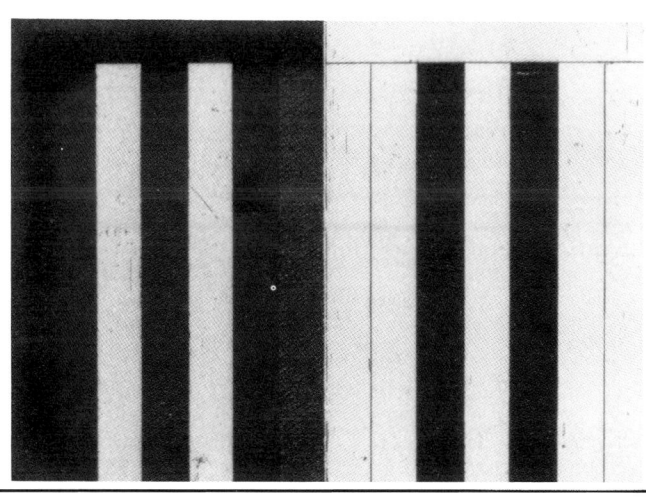

Brice Marden
12 Views for Caroline
Courtesy Parasol Press

TITLE	PUBLISHER	PRINTER	DATE	MEDIUM	DIMENSION (PAPER SIZE) IN INCHES	TYPE OF PAPER	EDITION NUMBER	NO. OF COLORS	ORIGINAL OPENING PRICE	CURRENT RETAIL PRICE
SOLD OUT EDITIONS (RARE):										
Gulf	ChPr	ChPr	1969	LB	14 X 20	R/BFK	100	2	100	7500
Untitled (Black & White)	ChPr	ChPr	1971	LB	15 X 23	R/BFK	50	1	100	6000
BM 72 (Set of 6):									1000 SET	42000 SET
BM 72 #1	UP	RW/SH	1972	LC	26 X 19	IT/W	42	2	200	8000
BM 72 #2	UP	RW/SH	1972	LC	19 X 26	IT/W	48	3	200	8000
BM 72 #3	UP	RW/SH	1972	LC	26 X 19	R/BFK	40	3	200	8000
BM 72 #4	UP	RW/SH	1972	LC	26 X 19	IT/W	46	3	200	8000
BM 72 #5	UP	RW/SH	1972	LC	26 X 19	IT/W	44	1	200	8000
BM 72 #6	UP	RW/SH	1972	LC	26 X 19	IT/W	46	1	200	8000
Five Plates (Set of 5)	PaP	CPP	1973	EB/A	41 X 31 EA	R/BFK	50 EA	1 EA	2000 SET	35000 SET
Adriatics (Set of 7):	PaP	CPP	1974	EB/A (5)	24 X 14 EA	R/BFK	40 EA		3000 SET	35000 SET
				EB/A (2)	24 X 28 EA		0		450 EA	4500 EA
									450 EA	7500 EA
Five Threes (Set of 5)	PaP	CPP	1977	AC	33 X 40 EA	R/BFK	25 EA		2500 SET	35000 SET
For Caroline (Set of 12)	PaP	CPP	1978	EB	27 X 21 EA	HMP	50 EA	1 EA	2500 SET	20000 SET
Tiles #1–#4 (Set of 4)	PaP	CPP	1979	EB/A/SL	22 X 30 EA	R/BFK	30 EA	1 EA	2000 SET	15000 SET
Untitled (Skowhegan)	PaP	CPP	1979	EB	6 X 5	R/BFK	40	1	350	4500
Focus I–V (Set of 5)	BAI		1979–80	EB/A	15 X 11 EA	R/BFK	75 EA	2 EA	1250 SET	15000 SET
Untitled	SPA/ART	SPA	1983	SP	38 X 50	KOZO	15	3	600	9000
1,2,3,4 (Set of 4)	SPA/ART	SPA	1983	SP	38 X 29 EA	KOZO	32 EA		1500 SET	10000 SET
CURRENT EDITIONS:										
Etchings to Rexroth (with Scraping & Burnishing) (Set of 25)	PBE	JM	1986	EB/A/DPT/SL	20 X 16 EA	R/BFK	45 EA	1 EA	12000 SET	45000 SET
Tu Fu (Book)			1987	EB	10 X 7	AP	140			1500
Cold Mountain Series Zen Studies I–VI (Set of 6)	ART	JM	1991	EB/A/SL/SB	28 X 35 EA	JWP	35 EA	1 EA	30000 SET	30000 SET
After Boticelli #1–#5 (Set of 5)	ART	PB/BS	1992–93	EB/A	27 X 21 EA	HMP	45 EA	1 EA	120000 SET	12000 SET
Han Shan Exit #1–#6 (Set of 6)	ART	PB/BS	1992–93	EB/A	15 X 11 EA	HMP	45 EA	1 EA	10000 SET	10000 SET

MARINO MARINI

BORN: Pistoia, Italy; (1901–1980)
EDUCATION: Academia di Belle Arti, Florence, Italy
RECENT EXHIB: Dominican Gallery, Montreal, Canada, 1991; Kent Gallery, NY, 1992; Harcourts Mod & Contemp, San Francisco, CA, 1992–93
COLLECTIONS: Mus of Mod Art, NY; Albright-Knox Art Gallery, Buffalo, NY; Art Inst of Chicago, IL; Tate Gallery, London, England; Musee du Jeu de Paume, Paris, France; Galleria d'Arte Moderna, Milan, Italy; Galleria Nazionale d'Arte Moderna, Rome, Italy
PRINTERS: American Atelier, NY (AA); Stamperia Salvioni, Rome, Italy (StSal); Atelier Mourlot, Paris, France (AM); Lacouriére et Fréulant, Paris, France (L/F); Aldo Crommelynck, Paris, France (AC); Atelier Crommelynck, Paris, France (AtC)
PUBLISHERS: Circle Fine Art, Chicago, IL (CFA); Edi Albra, Rome, Italy (EA); Curt Valentin Gallery, Paris, France (CVG); Berggruen & Company, San Francisco, CA (BC); Atelier Mourlot, Paris, France (AM); Toninelli, Rome, Italy (TON); XXe Siécle (XS); L de Tullio, Rome, Italy (LdT); L'Oeuvre Gravée, Paris, France (LOG); Aldo Crommelynck, Paris, France (AC); Transworld Art, Inc, NY (TAI)
GALLERIES: Tasende Gallery, La Jolla, CA; Fingerhut Gallery, Minneapolis, MN; Alexander Kahan Fine Arts, New York, NY; Jane Kahan Gallery, New York, NY; Pierre Matisse Gallery, New York, NY; Meridian Galleries, New York, NY & Chicago, IL; Circle Galleries, San Diego, CA & San Francisco, CA & Northbrook, IL & Pittsburgh, PA & Houston, TX & Soho, NY & Chicago, IL & Scottsdale, AZ & Beverly Hills, CA & Costa Mesa, CA & Sherman Oaks, CA & Palm Beach, FL & Honolulu, HI & New Orleans, LA & Las Vegas, NV & Seattle, WA; Dominican Gallery, Montreal, Canada; Kent Gallery, New York, NY; Stein Bartlow Gallery, Ltd, Chicago, IL; Galerie Mourlot, Boston, MA; Rolly-Michaux Gallery, Ltd, Boston, MA; Galerie Internationale, Bloomfield Hills, MI; Avanti Galleries, Inc, New York, NY; Galleria Durini, Ltd, New York, NY; Lillian Heidenberg Gallery, New York, NY; Weintraub Gallery, New York, NY; Miller Gallery, Cincinnati, OH; Harcourts Modern & Contemporary, San Francisco, CA

Marino Marini
Spartaco
Courtesy Alex Rosenberg

Bruckmann (B) — Guastalla (G)

TITLE	PUBLISHER	PRINTER	DATE	MEDIUM	DIMENSION (PAPER SIZE) IN INCHES	TYPE OF PAPER	EDITION NUMBER	NO. OF COLORS	ORIGINAL OPENING PRICE	CURRENT RETAIL PRICE
SOLD OUT EDITIONS (RARE):										
Nell' Appartamento		StSal	1943	LB	20 X 15	AP	10	1		1800
Lo Scudo		StSal	1943	LB	20 X 15	AP	10	1		1800
Gaukler			1951	EC	29 X 22	R/BFK				3500
Gaukler-Giocoliere (G-75)			1951	LC	23 X 15	AP	200			2000
Cavaliers et Chevraux, Bordure Verte (G-34)	CVG	AM	1951	LB	25 X 19	AP		1		1800
Giocolieri (B-L32)	GdG		1951	LC	19 X 13	AP	200			2500
Jugglers (SL-36)			1951	LC	19 X 13	AP	200			1200
Cavalier et Cheval Orange et Jaune (G-L39)			1952	LC	21 X 12	AP	50			2000
Juggler and Horses (G-L40)			1952	LC	24 X 18	AP	65			
Figure and Two Horses			1953	LC	24 X 16	AP				1000
Jongleur et Deux Chevaux, Bleu, Jeune et Noir (G-L45)	AIC	AM	1953	LC	24 X 16	AP				2000
Cavallo			1953	LC	22 X 15	AP	200			1800
Cavallo (G-L62)			1955	LC	13 X 23	AP	50			2200
Giocolieri (G-102)	AM	AM	1955	LC	26 X 20	AP	50			2800
Giocolieri (G-L48)			1955	LC		AP	50			2200
Man on Horseback			1955	LC	20 X 20	AP				1200
Reiter auf Violttem Grund, mit Roter Bordüre (G-50)			1955	LC		AP	65			5000
Reiter vor Rotem Grund			1955	EC	28 X 20	R/BFK	75			1200
Reiter vor Violettem Grund			1955	EC	28 X 20	R/BFK	75			1000
Reiter			1955	SP	32 X 26	AP	50			1800
Cavalier et Cheval Bordure Orange (G-L57)			1955	LC	24 X 18	AP	50			2500
Ceramica I (B-60)	BC		1955	LC	26 X 20	AP	50			2500
Ceramica II (G-L61)	AM	AM	1955–56	LC						
Cheval Rouge sur Fond Vert (G-105)			1955	LC	20 X 14	AP	175			1200
Composizione (L-58)			1955	LC	24 X 16	AP	50			2000
Due Pomone (B-52)	XS	L/F	1956	EB		R/BFK		1		1000
Giochi (G-L66)			1956	LC	26 X 20	AP	50			1500
Reiter auf Schwarzen Grund (T-67)			1956	LB	14 X 20	AP	50	1		1600
L'Idea del Cavaliere			1958	EB	14 X 12	R/BFK	50	1		800
Man and Two Horses			1960	LB	19 X 12	AP		1		2000
La Cavalier Noir (B-76)	LOG		1960	LC	23 X 19	AP	60			2000
Impressionabilita (G-53)	TON		1960	SP	26 X 27	AP				1500
Le Cavalier Noir (G-L81)			1962	LC	16 X 13	AP	50			1600
Guerriero (G-174)			1963	EB	23 X 18	R/BFK	50	1		1200
Idea e Spazio (Set of 12)		AC/AtC	1963	AC	21 X 16 EA	R/BFK	100 EA			3800 SET
Pferd			1964	LC	38 X 25	AP				500

MARINO MARINI CONTINUED

TITLE	PUBLISHER	PRINTER	DATE	MEDIUM	DIMENSION (PAPER SIZE) IN INCHES	TYPE OF PAPER	EDITION NUMBER	NO. OF COLORS	ORIGINAL OPENING PRICE	CURRENT RETAIL PRICE
SOLD OUT EDITIONS (RARE):										
L'Idea del Cavaliere (G-L90)			1968	LB	21 X 15	AP		1		1000
L'Album No 1 (Set of 12)	XS		1968	EB	20 X 15 EA	R/BFK	50 EA	1 EA		10000 SET
Apparazione			1968	DPT	27 X 20	R/BFK	60	1	100	1000
Gioco Felice (G-93)	LdT		1969	EB	28 X 20	R/BFK	60			1800
Tamburlano			1969	AB	28 X 20	R/BFK	60			2000
Trio Felice (B-R116)			1970	DPT	27 X 20	R/BFK		1		1000
Acrobat			1970	EB	25 X 19	R/BFK		1		1500
Miracolo			1970	EB/DPT	14 X 12	R/BFK	65	1		1250
Grand Teatro			1971	EB/A	20 X 25	R/BFK	75			2200
Miraculo (B-132)	XS	L/F	1971	EB		R/BFK		1		1000
Chevaux et Cavalier II (G-266)			1972	LC	19 X 25	AP	50			2000
Chevaux et Cavalier III (M-107)			1972	LC	15 X 20	AP	50			1500
Chevaux et Cavalier VI (M-109)			1972	LC	15 X 20	AP	50			1500
Danza Minima II (G-306)			1973	EB/A	39 X 28	R/BFK	25			1250
Il Profondo II (G-298)			1973	EB/A/DPT	28 X 39	R/BFK	25			1250
Il Teatro de Ma			1973	AB	19 X 25	R/BFK				1250
Il Teatro della Maschere: Giocolieri (B-R156)	Albra		1973	EB	28 X 39	R/BFK	75	1		2200
Gioco I (G-301)			1973	DPT	39 X 28					1000
Gioco II (G-302)			1973	EB/A	39 X 28					1200
Luci di Danza (from Il Teatro delle Maschere)			1973	EC/A	23 X 19	R/BFK	75			1800
Presentazione II (G-296)			1973	EB	28 X 39	R/BFK	25	1		1200
Personnages de Sacré Printemps (G-312)			1974	LC	26 X 20	AP	75			4000
Bizarria (G-326)			1975	EC	15 X 20	R/BFK	175			2200
Drei Grazien (G-A181)			1975	AC	21 X 17	R/BFK	75			1800
Furie de Danse			1975	EB/A/ENG	21 X 17	R/BFK	75			1800
Trois Graces			1975	EB/A/ENG	21 X 17	R/BFK	75			1800
Spartaco (from An American Portrait)	TAI	AC/AtC	1975	EC	20 X 26	R/BFK	175	6	250	2500
Untitled			1977	EB/A	19 X 15	R/BFK	75		800	6000
Grand Cavalier (G-220)			1978	EB/A	39 X 26	R/BFK	20			6000
La Traviata (Metropolitan Opera #1)	CFA	AA	1978	LC	30 X 22	AP	250		350	2400
Immaginazione di Colore (G-L132)			1979	LC	24 X 17	AP				4500
Marino from Goethe (G-A227)			1979	EB/A	19 X 25	R/BFK				4500
Studio di Cavaliere			1979	LC	23 X 18	AP				2800
Giaco Colorato	EA		1979	EC/A	13 X 10	R/BFK	150		900	2500
Red Horse	EA		1980	EC/A	22 X 15	R/BFK	150		900	2500
Grand Cavalier	EA		1980	EC/A	48 X 31	R/BFK	125		3000	7500

SUZANNE McCLELLAND

PRINTERS: Hitoshi Kido, West Islip, NY (HK); Lorena Salcedo-Watson, West Islip, NY (LSW); Douglas Volle, West Islip, NY (DV); Bruce Wankel, West Islip, NY (BW); Universal Limited Art Editions, West Islip, NY (ULAE)

PUBLISHERS: Universal Limited Art Editions, West Islip, NY (ULAE)
GALLERIES: Brooke Alexander Editions, New York, NY; Thomas Smith Fine Art, Fort Wayne, IN; Mark Masuoka Gallery, Las Vegas, NV

TITLE	PUBLISHER	PRINTER	DATE	MEDIUM	DIMENSION (PAPER SIZE) IN INCHES	TYPE OF PAPER	EDITION NUMBER	NO. OF COLORS	ORIGINAL OPENING PRICE	CURRENT RETAIL PRICE
CURRENT EDITIONS:										
Then	ULAE	HK/LSW/DV/ BW/ULAE	1993	LC/SP	22 X 30	AC	55	7	650	650

MELISSA MEYER

PRINTERS: Antony O'Hara, Brooklyn, NY (AOH); Watanabe Studio, Brooklyn, NY (WS); Dumbarton Press, NY (DPr)

PUBLISHERS: Artist (ART); Watanabe Studio, Brooklyn, NY (WS); Dumbarton Press, Brooklyn, NY (DPr)
GALLERIES: Holly Solomon Gallery, New York, NY; Miller/Block Gallery, Boston, MA; Dumbarton Press, New York, NY

TITLE	PUBLISHER	PRINTER	DATE	MEDIUM	DIMENSION (PAPER SIZE) IN INCHES	TYPE OF PAPER	EDITION NUMBER	NO. OF COLORS	ORIGINAL OPENING PRICE	CURRENT RETAIL PRICE
CURRENT EDITIONS:										
Survey Suite I (Set of 5)	ART/WS	AOH/WS	1992	I	18 X 15 EA	SOM	50 EA	1 EA	2250 SET	2250 SET
Survey Suite II (Set of 6)	ART/WS	AOH/WS	1992	I	18 X 15 EA	SOM	50 EA	1 EA	2700 SET	2700 SET

The retail prices of the 100,000 limited edition prints quoted in this directory are subject to change. Print publishers, artists and galleries were the direct sources for these quotations. Prices in the secondary market listed as "Sold Out Editions (Rare)" indicate that the publisher has a limited supply of that print or that the print is difficult to locate in the galleries.

ALLAN MARDON

BORN: Welland, ON, Canada, 1931
EDUCATION: Ontario Col of Art, Toronto, ON, Canada; Edinburgh Sch of Art, Scotland; Slade Sch of Fine Art, Univ of London, England
PRINTERS: American Atelier, NY (AA)
PUBLISHERS: Circle Fine Art, Chicago, IL (CFA)
GALLERIES: Circle Galleries, San Diego, CA & San Francisco, CA & Northbrook, IL & Pittsburgh, PA & Houston, TX & Soho, NY & Chicago, IL & Scottsdale, AZ & Beverly Hills, CA & Costa Mesa, CA & Sherman Oaks, CA & Palm Beach, FL & Honolulu, HI & New Orleans, LA & Las Vegas, NV & Seattle, WA

TITLE	PUBLISHER	PRINTER	DATE	MEDIUM	DIMENSION (PAPER SIZE) IN INCHES	TYPE OF PAPER	EDITION NUMBER	NO. OF COLORS	ORIGINAL OPENING PRICE	CURRENT RETAIL PRICE
CURRENT EDITIONS:										
Falcon	CFA	AA	1978	EB/LC	27 X 33	R/BFK	300		75	200
Football	CFA	AA	1978	LC	23 X 29	AP	300		75	200
Baseball	CFA	AA	1978	LC	23 X 29	AP	300		75	250
Fishing	CFA	AA	1978	LC	24 X 33	AP	300		75	200
Pheasant Hunting	CFA	AA	1978	LC	17 X 23	AP	300		50	175
Pheasants	CFA	AA	1978	LC	17 X 23	AP	300		50	175

JACQUES MARGERIN

BORN: Paris, France; 1930
EDUCATION: L'Ecole d'Arts et de Publicité, Paris, France
PRINTERS: American Atelier, NY (AA)
PUBLISHERS: Circle Fine Art, Chicago, IL (CFA)
GALLERIES: Circle Galleries, San Diego, CA & San Francisco, CA & Northbrook, IL & Pittsburgh, PA & Houston, TX & Soho, NY & Chicago, IL & Scottsdale, AZ & Beverly Hills, CA & Costa Mesa, CA & Sherman Oaks, CA & Palm Beach, CA & Honolulu, HI & New Orleans, LA & Las Vegas, NV & Seattle, WA

TITLE	PUBLISHER	PRINTER	DATE	MEDIUM	DIMENSION (PAPER SIZE) IN INCHES	TYPE OF PAPER	EDITION NUMBER	NO. OF COLORS	ORIGINAL OPENING PRICE	CURRENT RETAIL PRICE
SOLD OUT EDITIONS (RARE):										
Fiddler	CFA	AA	1980	LC	20 X 26	AP	200		50	250
Girl with Cat	CFA	AA	1980	LC	20 X 26	AP	200		50	250

DENISE MILAN

PRINTERS: Artist (ART)
PUBLISHERS: Artist (ART)
GALLERIES: Galeria Nara Roesler, São Paulo, Brazil

TITLE	PUBLISHER	PRINTER	DATE	MEDIUM	DIMENSION (PAPER SIZE) IN INCHES	TYPE OF PAPER	EDITION NUMBER	NO. OF COLORS	ORIGINAL OPENING PRICE	CURRENT RETAIL PRICE
CURRENT EDITIONS:										
Monoprint	ART	ART	1993	MON	17 X 20 EA	GE	1 EA	Varies	500/1000 EA	500/1000 EA

CHRISTIAN PHILIPP MÜELLER

RECENT EXHIB: Kunstverein München, Munich, Germany, 1992
PRINTERS: Edition Artelier, Graz, Germany (EdART)
PUBLISHERS: Edition Artelier, Graz, Germany (EdART)
GALLERIES: American Fine Arts, New York, NY; Nexus Foundation for Today's Art, Phila, PA

TITLE	PUBLISHER	PRINTER	DATE	MEDIUM	DIMENSION (PAPER SIZE) IN INCHES	TYPE OF PAPER	EDITION NUMBER	NO. OF COLORS	ORIGINAL OPENING PRICE	CURRENT RETAIL PRICE
CURRENT EDITIONS:										
Vergessene Zukunft, Forgotten Future (Set of 8)	EdART	EdART	1992	PH	13 X 18 EA		10 EA	1 EA	DM2000 SET	DM2000 SET

The retail prices of the 100,000 limited edition prints quoted in this directory are subject to change. Print publishers, artists and galleries were the direct sources for these quotations. Prices in the secondary market listed as "Sold Out Editions (Rare)" indicate that the publisher has a limited supply of that print or that the print is difficult to locate in the galleries.

The Printworld Directory is accepting new applications for the seventh edition. Approximately 300 new artists will be accepted. Please use the two forms provided in the back section of this directory to submit biographical data and documentation of prints. Edition number of each print must not exceed 500 and the retail price must be $100 or more.

The print market has become very selective. For the first time since we published the first edition of The Printworld Directory in 1982, the prices of prints have been greatly reduced and greatly increased for the same artists by the most reputable and established print publishers. Check the fifth edition to understand the movement.

TOM MARIONI

BORN: Cincinnati, OH; May 21, 1937
EDUCATION: Cincinnati Art Acad, OH, 1955–59
TEACHING: Instr, Univ of California, Berkeley, CA, 1979; Instr, Univ of California, Los Angeles, CA, 1986
AWARDS: John Simon Guggenheim Grant, 1980; Nat Endowment for the Arts Awards, 1979,80,84; Travel Grant, Asian Cultural Council, 1986
RECENT EXHIB: Gallery Paule Anglim, San Francisco, CA, 1993
COLLECTIONS: Oakland Mus of Art, CA; Richmond Art Center, Oakland, CA; Student Cultural Center, Belgrade, Yugoslavia; City of San Francisco; Santa Barbara Art Mus, CA
PRINTERS: Xu Yin She, Hangzhou, China (XYS); Rong Bao Zhai, Beijing, China (RBZ); Brian Shure, San Francisco, CA (BS); Julie Goldman, San Francisco, CA (JG); Lawrence J Hamlin, San Francisco, CA (LJH); Marcia Bartholme, San Francisco, CA (MB); Stephen Thomas, San Francisco, CA (ST); Doris Simmelink, San Francisco, CA (DS); Lilah Toland, San Francisco, CA (LT); Nancy Anello, San Francisco, CA (NA); Paul Mullowney, San Francisco, CA (PM); Crown Point Press, San Francisco, CA (CPP); Cai Yan (CY); Linda Geary (LG)
PUBLISHERS: Crown Point Press, San Francisco, CA (CPP)
GALLERIES: L A Louver, Venice, CA; Kendall Art Gallery, Wellfleet, MA; Crown Point Press, New York, NY & San Francisco, CA; Gallery Paule Anglim, San Francisco, CA; John Pence Gallery, San Francisco, CA; Margarete Roeder Gallery, New York, NY; Bill Bace Gallery, New York, NY
MAILING ADDRESS: 22 Howard St, San Francisco, CA 94105

TITLE	PUBLISHER	PRINTER	DATE	MEDIUM	DIMENSION (PAPER SIZE) IN INCHES	TYPE OF PAPER	EDITION NUMBER	NO. OF COLORS	ORIGINAL OPENING PRICE	CURRENT RETAIL PRICE
SOLD OUT EDITIONS (RARE):										
Cafe Society Beer (Bottle of Anchor Steam Beer with an Etching for a Label)	CPP	LT/NA/CPP	1979	HENG/E		AP/HS	100	3	100	250
Drawing a Line as Far as I Can Reach (Triptych)	CPP	CPP	1984	EB	75 X 30	R/BFK	5	1	650	2000
Finger Line	CPP	DS/LG/CPP	1991	SG/HG/DPT/CC	41 X 27	SOM/W	10		850	850
CURRENT EDITIONS:										
Religious Picture	CPP	DS/ST/CPP	1977	EC/SG	22 X 35	RP/H/W	25	1	175	650
Landing (Set of 7)	CPP	DS/ST/CPP	1977	MEZ	(6)10 X 12 (1)20 X 19	RP/H/B	25	1	250 SET	1500 SET
Spirit in the Dark	CPP	PS/NA/CPP	1980	AC	52 X 42	R/BFK	15	2	500	1000
Bending Light	CPP	CPP	1980	EB	22 X 28	R/BFK	10	1	300	300
Train Windows (Diptych)	CPP	CPP	1981	AC	30 X 44 EA 30 X 88 TOTAL	R/BFK	25	1	600	1200
Cross	CPP	CPP	1982	EB	19 X 20		15	1	400	650
Feather Circle	CPP	CPP	1986	AC	44 X 30	R/BFK	20	1	500	1200
Feather Line	CPP	LJH/NA/MB/CPP	1988	AC	44 X 30	SOM	20	1	650	1000
Pi	CPP	XYS/BS/JG/CPP	1989	WC	22 X 23	SILK	35	2	550	1000
Peking	CPP	RBZ/BS/JG/CPP	1989	WC	27 X 20	SILK	35	2	550	850
Flying Yen	CPP	CY/BS/CPP	1990	WB/WA/CC	23 X 20	SILK/XZP/AC	25		850	850
Finger Print	CPP	DS/LG/CPP	1991	SG/SL/DPT/CC	34 X 24	SM/W	10	3	700	700
Tree	CPP	DS/LG/CPP	1991	HG/WV/CC	22 X 14	SOM/W	10		300	300
Process Landscapes (Series of 47 Monotypes)	CPP	LH/PM/CPP	1992	MON	11 X 7 EA to 49 X 40 EA	AP88 or ColP	1 EA	Varies	850/2000	850/2000
Tree at Night (Blue)	CPP	LH/PM/CPP	1992	PH/ENG/MEZ	34 X 34	SOM	5	1	850	850
Tree at Night (Black)	CPP	LH/PM/CPP	1992	PH/ENG/MEZ	34 X 34	SOM	5	1	850	850

MARISOL ESCOBAR

BORN: Paris, France; 1930
EDUCATION: Ecole Beaux Arts, Paris, France, 1949; Art Students League, NY, 1950; New Sch for Social Research, NY, 1951–54; Hans Hofmann Sch, NY; Moore Col of Art, Phila, PA, Hon Dr, 1970
AWARDS: Acad of Achievement, San Diego, CA
RECENT EXHIB: Heckscher Mus, Huntington, NY, 1987; Nat Portrait Gallery, Wash, DC, 1987; Sidney Janis Gallery, NY, 1989; Arkansas State Univ Fine Arts Gallery, State Univ, AZ, 1989; Rose Art Mus, Brandeis Univ, Waltham, MA, 1990; Miami Univ Art Mus, Oxford, OH, 1989,92
COLLECTIONS: Mus of Mod Art, NY; Whitney Mus of Am Art, NY; Albright-Knox Art Gallery, Buffalo, NY; Mus Bellas Artes, Caracas, Venezuela; Nat Portrait Gallery, Wash, DC
PRINTERS: Styria Studio, NY (SS); Alexander Heinrici, NY (AH); Studio Heinrici, NY (SH); American Atelier, NY (AA)
PUBLISHERS: Multiples, NY (M); Universal Limited Art Editions, West Islip, NY (ULI); Transworld Art, Inc, NY (TAI); Atelier Royce, NY (AR); Sidney Janis Gallery Editions, NY (SJG); Styria Studio, NY (SS); Prestige Art Ltd, Mamaroneck, NY (PA); Circle Fine Art, NY (CFA)
GALLERIES: Sidney Janis Gallery, New York, NY; Marian Goodman, New York, NY; Styria Studio, New York, NY; Alan Brown Gallery, Hartsdale, NY; Posner Gallery, Milwaukee, WI; Circle Galleries, Scottsdale, AZ & Beverly Hills, CA & Costa Mesa, CA & San Diego, CA & San Francisco, CA & Sherman Oaks, CA & Palm Beach, FL & Honolulu, HI & Chicago, IL & New York, NY & Northbrook, IL & New Orleans, La & Las Vegas, NV & Pittsburgh, PA & Houston, TX & Seattle, WA
MAILING ADDRESS: c/o Sidney Janis Gallery, 6 W 57th St, New York, NY 10019

TITLE	PUBLISHER	PRINTER	DATE	MEDIUM	DIMENSION (PAPER SIZE) IN INCHES	TYPE OF PAPER	EDITION NUMBER	NO. OF COLORS	ORIGINAL OPENING PRICE	CURRENT RETAIL PRICE
CURRENT EDITIONS:										
Banner	M		1972	SP	88 X 50	SILK	20		900	2500
Pocohontas	TAI		1975	LC	26 X 20	AP	175		500	2000
Untitled Suite A–F (Set of 6)	PA	AH/SH	1979	LC	38 X 52 EA	R/BFK	100 EA	4 EA	1000 EA	2000 EA
Meeting of the Universe	CFA	AA	1979	LC	31 X 23	AP	150		125	350
Chief Joseph	SS	SS	1980	LC/HC	42 X 30	TWP	75	20	850	1500
Chief Joseph Special	SS	SS	1980	LC	42 X 30	TWP	20	1	750	1500
Sun Mask	SJG		1980	BRON	13 X 11	HMP	6		4500	6500

MARISOL ESCOBAR CONTINUED

TITLE	PUBLISHER	PRINTER	DATE	MEDIUM	DIMENSION (PAPER SIZE) IN INCHES	TYPE OF PAPER	EDITION NUMBER	NO. OF COLORS	ORIGINAL OPENING PRICE	CURRENT RETAIL PRICE
CURRENT EDITIONS:										
Leaf Woman	SJG		1980	BRON	23 X 7	HMP	6		8500	12000
Veil of Veronica	SJG		1980	BRON	36 X 16	HMP	6		8500	12000
The Sun	SJG		1981	CP	21 X 17	HMP	30		2100	4000
Colt 45	SJG		1981	CP	40 X 7	HMP	30		4500	6500
Self-Portrait with Hair	SJG		1981	CP	28 X 15	HMP	30		3600	5000

ROBERT MARKLE

BORN: Hamilton, Ontario, Canada; 1936
EDUCATION: New Sch of Art, Toronto, Can, 1966–72; Ontario Col of Art, Toronto, Can, 1970–71
COLLECTIONS: Nat Gallery of Canada, Ottawa, Can; McMaster Univ, Hamilton, Can; Philadelphia Mus of Art, PA; Art Gallery of Ontario, Toronto, Can; Montreal Mus of Fine Art, Can; Univ of Western Ontario, London, Can; Univ of Waterloo, Norman Mackenzie Art Gallery, Regina, Can; Canada Council Art Bank; Art Gallery of Hamilton, Can
PRINTERS: Sword Street Press, Toronto, Can (SSP)
PUBLISHERS: Sword Street Press Limited, Toronto, Can (SSP)
GALLERIES: The Isaacs Gallery, Toronto, Can

TITLE	PUBLISHER	PRINTER	DATE	MEDIUM	DIMENSION (PAPER SIZE) IN INCHES	TYPE OF PAPER	EDITION NUMBER	NO. OF COLORS	ORIGINAL OPENING PRICE	CURRENT RETAIL PRICE
CURRENT EDITIONS:										
Untitled	SSP	SSP	1979	LC	48 X 31	HMP	25	9	500	750
Untitled	SSP	SSP	1979	LC	23 X 32	HMP	16	3	250	500

RONALD MARKMAN

BORN: Bronx, NY; May 29, 1931
EDUCATION: Yale Univ, New Haven, CT, BFA, 1957, MFA, 1959
TEACHING: Instr, Univ of Florida, Gainesville, FL, 1959; Instr Art Inst of Chicago, IL, 1960–64; Instr, Indiana Univ, Bloomington, IN, 1964 to present
AWARDS: Fulbright Fel, 1962–63; Lily Open Faculty Fel, 1989; Am Inst of Arts & Letters, NY, 1989
COLLECTIONS: Brooklyn Mus, NY; Art Inst of Chicago, IL; Hirshhorn Mus, Wash, DC; Metropolitan Mus of Art, NY; Mus of Mod Art, NY; Smithsonian Inst, Wash, DC
PRINTERS: David Keister, Bloomington, IN (DK); David Calkins, Bloomington, IN (DC); Echo Press, Bloomington, IN (EPr)
PUBLISHERS: Echo Press, Bloomington, IN (EPr)
GALLERIES: Terry Dintenfass Gallery, New York, NY; Patrick King Contemp Art, Indianapolis, IN; Echo Press, Bloomington, IN
MAILING ADDRESS: 719 S Jordan, Bloomington, IN 47401

TITLE	PUBLISHER	PRINTER	DATE	MEDIUM	DIMENSION (PAPER SIZE) IN INCHES	TYPE OF PAPER	EDITION NUMBER	NO. OF COLORS	ORIGINAL OPENING PRICE	CURRENT RETAIL PRICE
CURRENT EDITIONS:										
Cityscape	EPr	DK/DC/EPr	1980	LC/REL/CO/WA	22 X 30 X ¼	AC/W	28	25	350	750

AGNES BERNICE MARTIN

BORN: Maklin, Sask, Canada; March 22, 1912; U S Citizen
EDUCATION: Columbia Univ, NY; Univ of New Mexico, Albuquerque, NM
AWARDS: Oskar Kokoschka Prize, Painting, 1992
RECENT EXHIB: Center for the Fine Arts, Miami, FL, 1992,93; Whitney Mus of Am Art, NY, 1992–93; Milwaukee Art Center, WI, 1993; Houston Contemp Arts Mus, TX, 1993; Reina Sofia Nat Mus, Madrid, Spain, 1993–94
COLLECTIONS: Mus of Mod Art, NY; Whitney Mus of Am Art, NY; Guggenheim Mus of Art, NY; Tate Gallery, London, England; Stedelijk Mus, Amsterdam, The Netherlands, Kunstraum, Munich, Germany; Mus of Fine Arts, Canberra, Australia; Art Mus of Ontario, Canada
PRINTERS: Editions Domberger, Stuttgart, Germany (DOM)
PUBLISHERS: Parasol Press, Ltd, NY (PaP)
GALLERIES: Pace Prints, New York, NY; Barbara Krakow Gallery, Boston, MA; Elkon Gallery, New York, NY; John C Stoller & Company, Minneapolis, MN; Laura Carpenter Fine Art, Santa Fe, NM
MAILING ADDRESS: Lamy, NM 87540

TITLE	PUBLISHER	PRINTER	DATE	MEDIUM	DIMENSION (PAPER SIZE) IN INCHES	TYPE OF PAPER	EDITION NUMBER	NO. OF COLORS	ORIGINAL OPENING PRICE	CURRENT RETAIL PRICE
SOLD OUT EDITIONS (RARE):										
On a Clear Day (Set of 30)	PaP	DOM	1973	SP	15 X 15 EA	JP	50 EA	1 EA	7500 SET	75000 SET

FRED THOMAS MARTIN

BORN: San Francisco, CA; June 13, 1927
EDUCATION: Univ of California, Berkeley, CA, BA, 1949; MA, 1952; San Francisco Art Inst, CA, with David Park, Clifford Still & Mark Rothko
TEACHING: Instr, Art History, San Francisco Art Inst, CA, 1979 to present
AWARDS: Nat Found, Artist Grant, 1970–71
COLLECTIONS: Mus of Mod Art, NY; Whitney Mus of Am Art, NY; San Francisco Mus of Art, CA; Oakland Art Mus, Fogg Art Mus, Cambridge, MA
PRINTERS: 3EP Ltd, Palo Alto, CA (3EP)
PUBLISHERS: 3EP Ltd, Palo Alto, CA (3EP)
GALLERIES: Rena Bransten, San Francisco, CA; John Natsoulas Gallery, Davis, CA
MAILING ADDRESS: 232 Monte Vista, Oakland, CA 94611

FRED THOMAS MARTIN CONTINUED

TITLE	PUBLISHER	PRINTER	DATE	MEDIUM	DIMENSION (PAPER SIZE) IN INCHES	TYPE OF PAPER	EDITION NUMBER	NO. OF COLORS	ORIGINAL OPENING PRICE	CURRENT RETAIL PRICE
CURRENT EDITIONS:										
Tarot of California (Set of 6)	3EP	3EP	1980	EC	23 X 27 EA	AP	20 EA		2200 SET	3000 SET
7 Scenes from the Birth of Venus	3EP	3EP	1981	MON	39 X 31 EA	AP	1 EA		1000 EA	1200 EA
Sunset Flowers	3EP	3EP	1981	MON	40 X 30 EA	AP	1 EA		1000 EA	1200 EA
Rabatment	3EP	3EP	1981	MON	54 X 39 EA	AP	1 EA		1500 EA	1800 EA

KENNETH MARTIN

BORN: Sheffield, England; 1905
EDUCATION: Sheffield Sch of Art, England, 1921–23; 27–29; Royal Col of Art, London, England, 1929–32
TEACHING: Goldsmiths Col, London, England
AWARDS: OBE (1971), Hon Doctorate, Royal Col of Art, London, England
COLLECTIONS: Mus of Mod Art, NY; Fogg Art Mus, Cambridge, MA; Rijksmuseum Kroler-Muller, Holland; Wilhelm Lehmbruck-Mus, Duisburg, Germany; Tate Gallery, London, England; British Mus, London, England; Arts Council of Great Britain, London, England
PRINTERS: Mark Hofstadtler, Neuchatel, Switzerland (MH); Editions Media, Neuchatel, Switzerland (EM); Chris Prater, London, England (CP); Kelpra Press, London, England (KP)
PUBLISHERS: Waddington Graphics, London, England (WG)
GALLERIES: Waddington Graphics, London, England

TITLE	PUBLISHER	PRINTER	DATE	MEDIUM	DIMENSION (PAPER SIZE) IN INCHES	TYPE OF PAPER	EDITION NUMBER	NO. OF COLORS	ORIGINAL OPENING PRICE	CURRENT RETAIL PRICE
SOLD OUT EDITIONS (RARE):										
Chance & Order, I, II, III, IV, V	WG	CP/KP	1971	SP	27 X 27 EA	AC	70 EA		70 EA	1500 EA
Chance & Order VI	WG	CP/KP	1976	SP	28 X 28	AC	51		100	1500
Key Drawing	WG	CP/KP	1977	SP	30 X 30	AC	61		120	1000
Pier and Ocean/Venice (Set of 2)	WG	MH/EM	1981	SP	24 X 35 EA	SOM	70 EA		270 SET	2500 SET
Chance, Order, Change . . .	WG	MH/EM	1981	SP	37 X 37	SOM	80		270	1500
14 Million Park B History Pictures (Set of 4)	WG	MH/EM	1982	SP	33 X 24 EA	SOM	90 EA		1100 SET	3000 SET

KNOX MARTIN

BORN: Barranquilla, Columbia; February 12, 1923; US Citizen
EDUCATION: Art Students League, NY (Four Years)
TEACHING: Asst Prof, Drawing & Painting, Yale Univ, New Haven, CT, 1965–70; Instr, Art Students League, NY, 1974–82; Instr, Univ of Minnesota, Minneapolis, MN; Instr, New York Univ, NY
AWARDS: Nat Endowment for the Arts, NY, 1972; Creative Artists Public Service Award, NY, 1978
RECENT EXHIB: Artists Mus of Soho, NY, 1992
COLLECTIONS: Corcoran Gallery of Art, Wash, DC; Mus of Mod Art, NY; Whitney Mus of Am Art, NY; Mus of Art, Austin, TX; Univ of California, Berkeley, CA; Baltimore Mus of Art, MD; Art Inst of Chicago, IL; Dallas Mus of Art, TX
PRINTERS: American Atelier, NY (AA)
PUBLISHERS: Circle Fine Art, Chicago, IL (CFA)
GALLERIES: Circle Galleries, San Diego, CA & San Francisco, CA & Northbrook, IL & Pittsburgh, PA & Houston, TX & Soho, NY & Chicago, IL & Scottsdale, AZ & Beverly Hills, CA & Costa Mesa, CA & Sherman Oaks, CA & Palm Beach, FL & Honolulu, HI & New Orleans, LA & Las Vegas, NV & Seattle, WA; Thomsen Gallery, Tappan, NY; Gremillion & Company Fine Art, Inc, Houston, TX
MAILING ADDRESS: 128 Fort Washington Ave, New York, NY 10032

TITLE	PUBLISHER	PRINTER	DATE	MEDIUM	DIMENSION (PAPER SIZE) IN INCHES	TYPE OF PAPER	EDITION NUMBER	NO. OF COLORS	ORIGINAL OPENING PRICE	CURRENT RETAIL PRICE
CURRENT EDITIONS:										
Woman with Bicycle	CFA	AA	1979	LC	28 X 35	AP	300		175	450
Flowers III	CFA	AA	1980	SP	30 X 22	R/BFK	300		200	450
Flowers IX	CFA	AA	1981	LC	30 X 22	AP	300		225	450
Palette of Flowers	CFA	AA	1982	SP	36 X 22	R/BFK	300		250	450

MICHAEL MARTIN

BORN: St Louis, MO; 1931
EDUCATION: Carnegie Art Inst, Pittsburgh, PA; Art Inst of Chicago, IL, 1953
PRINTERS: American Atelier, NY (AA)
PUBLISHERS: Circle Fine Art, Chicago, IL (CFA)
GALLERIES: Circle Galleries, San Francisco, CA & San Diego, CA & Northbrook, IL & Houston, TX & Pittsburgh, PA & Soho, NY & Chicago, IL & Scottsdale, AZ & Beverly Hills, CA & Costa Mesa, CA & Sherman Oaks, CA & Palm Beach, FL & Honolulu, HI & New Orleans, LA & Las Vegas, NV & Seattle, WA; Joyce Petter Galleries, Saugatuck, MI

TITLE	PUBLISHER	PRINTER	DATE	MEDIUM	DIMENSION (PAPER SIZE) IN INCHES	TYPE OF PAPER	EDITION NUMBER	NO. OF COLORS	ORIGINAL OPENING PRICE	CURRENT RETAIL PRICE
SOLD OUT EDITIONS (RARE):										
Girl with Balloon	CFA	AA	1978	LC	30 X 15	AP	300		50	250
CURRENT EDITIONS:										
Boy with Kite	CFA	AA	1978	LC	30 X 15	AP	300		50	225

The print market has become very selective. For the first time since we published the first edition of The Printworld Directory in 1982, the prices of prints have been greatly reduced and greatly increased for the same artists by the most reputable and established print publishers. Check the fifth edition to understand the movement.

STEFAN MARTIN

BORN: Elgin, IL; January 10, 1936
EDUCATION: Art Inst of Chicago, IL 1958
TEACHING: Beaver Col, Jenkintown, PA; Mercer County Col, NJ; Instr, Engraving, Printmaking Council of New Jersey, 1979 to present
AWARDS: Art Students League, Chicago, IL, 1958; Am Acad of Arts & Letters, NY, 1959; Philadelphia Print Club, PA, 1960; Metropolitan Mus, NY 1960; Tiffany Fel Grants, 1961–62, 1963–64; Int Graphic Soc, 1964,65,68; New Jersey State Mus, Trenton, NJ, 1966, 68; Art Directors Club of New Jersey, 1980
COLLECTIONS: Philadelphia Art Mus, PA; Charleton Col, Northfield, MN; Art Inst of Chicago, IL; Mus of Mod Art, NY; Metropolitan Art Mus, NY; Virginia Mus of Fine Arts, Richmond, VA; Columbia Univ, NY; Jersey City Mus, NJ; Smithsonian Inst, Wash, DC; New Jersey State Mus, Trenton, NJ
PUBLISHERS: Kennedy Graphics, KY (KG); Artist (ART)
PRINTERS: Artist (ART)
GALLERIES: Associated American Artists, New York, NY; Kornbluth Gallery, Fair Lawn NJ; Kennedy Graphics, New York, NY; Winkler Gallery Int, Salzburg, Austria; Gallery 500, Elkins Park, PA
MAILING ADDRESS: PO Box 304, Roosevelt, NJ 08555

TITLE	PUBLISHER	PRINTER	DATE	MEDIUM	DIMENSION (PAPER SIZE) IN INCHES	TYPE OF PAPER	EDITION NUMBER	NO. OF COLORS	ORIGINAL OPENING PRICE	CURRENT RETAIL PRICE
SOLD OUT EDITIONS (RARE):										
Rooster	ART	ART	1962	ENG	20 X 16	OP	20	1	40	150
Emergence	KG	ART	1965	ENG	15 X 18	OP	50	1	125	175
Group Unit	KG	ART	1967	ENG	14 X 19	OP	40	1	125	175
Animal Kingdom	KG	ART	1969	ENG	10 X 9	OP	100	1	50	125
Eclesiastes Series	KG	ART	1970	ENG	13 X 10	OP	100	2	300	475
Dove	KG	ART	1970	WC	9 X 8	OP	50	3	80	125
Summit	KG	ART	1970	ENG	25 X 16	OP	60	1	125	200
Ben Shahn Portrait	KG	ART	1971	ENG	13 X 10	OP	100	1	50	225
Mike Seeger's Thing	KG	ART	1972	ENG	13 X 10	OP	60	1	50	125
Holocaust	ART	ART	1980	ENG	13 X 10	OP	100	1	40	250
CURRENT EDITIONS:										
Field of Horns	KG	ART	1980	ENG	12 X 10	OP	100	1	100	150
Skowhegan	KG	ART	1980	ENG	8 X 7	OP	100	1	75	125
Aged Tree	KG	ART	1981	ENG	20 X 13	OP	50	1	125	175
Doodle Block	KG	ART	1982	ENG	13 X 25	OP	100	1	100	225
Oil Spill	KG	ART	1982	WB	12 X 13	OP	50	1	100	125
A Struggle	KG	ART	1982	ENG	11 X 13	OP	50	1	75	125

MARCIA MARX

BORN: Newark, NY; 1930
EDUCATION: Columbia Univ, NY; New Sch for Social Research, NY; Yale Univ, New Haven, CT
PRINTERS: American Atelier, NY (AA)
PUBLISHERS: Circle Fine Art, Chicago, IL (CFA)
GALLERIES: Circle Galleries, San Diego, CA & San Francisco, CA & Northbrook, IL & Pittsburgh, PA & Houston, TX & Soho, NY & Chicago, IL & Scottsdale, AZ & Beverly Hills, CA & Costa Mesa, CA & Sherman Oaks, CA & Palm Beach, FL & Honolulu, HI & New Orleans, LA & Las Vegas, NV Seattle, WA

TITLE	PUBLISHER	PRINTER	DATE	MEDIUM	DIMENSION (PAPER SIZE) IN INCHES	TYPE OF PAPER	EDITION NUMBER	NO. OF COLORS	ORIGINAL OPENING PRICE	CURRENT RETAIL PRICE
SOLD OUT EDITIONS (RARE):										
Tickle My Vanity	CFA	AA	1978	LC	21 X 17	AP	50		50	125
CURRENT EDITIONS:										
Balloons	CFA	AA	1978	LC	20 X 26	AP	200		50	125
Groom's Side	CFA	AA	1978	LC	20 X 25	AP	200		50	125

OLIVIERO MASI

BORN: Busto Arisizio, Italy; 1949
RECENT EXHIB: Robertson Gallery, Beverly Hills, CA, 1987
COLLECTIONS: Museo Nazionale d'Arte, La Paz, Bolivia
PRINTERS: Artist (ART)
PUBLISHERS: John Szoke Graphics, NY (JSG)
GALLERIES: John Szoke Graphics, New York, NY

TITLE	PUBLISHER	PRINTER	DATE	MEDIUM	DIMENSION (PAPER SIZE) IN INCHES	TYPE OF PAPER	EDITION NUMBER	NO. OF COLORS	ORIGINAL OPENING PRICE	CURRENT RETAIL PRICE
SOLD OUT EDITIONS (RARE):										
Papaveri	JSG	ART	1984	EC	15 X 12	R/BFK	150	10	175	250
Afternoon	JSG	ART	1984	EC	15 X 12	R/BFK	150	15	200	250
CURRENT EDITIONS:										
Summer Suite:										
SummerShadows	JSG	ART	1983	EC	15 X 23	R/BFK	150	15	225	275
Summer Time	JSG	ART	1983	EC	15 X 23	R/BFK	150	15	225	275
Fall Suite:										
Backyard	JSG	ART	1983–84	EC	19 X 15	R/BFK	99	20	250	300
Field	JSG	ART	1983–84	EC	19 X 15	R/BFK	99	20	225	275
Maple	JSG	ART	1983–84	EC	19 X 15	R/BFK	99	20	250	300
Lane	JSG	ART	1983–84	EC	19 X 15	R/BFK	99	20	200	250
Field of Poppies (Trip)	JSG	ART	1985	EC	27 X 20 EA	R/BFK	150		550	700
Oak (Trip)	JSG	ART	1985	EC	27 X 20 EA	R/BFK	150		550	700
Country Poppies (Trip)	JSG	ART	1986	EC	27 X 20 EA	R/BFK	150		650	700

LORNA MASSIE

BORN: Milwaukee, WI; December 27, 1938
EDUCATION: Layton Sch of Art, Milwaukee, WI; Smith Col, Northampton, MA; Univ of California, Berkeley, CA, BA, 1961; Woodstock Sch of Art, MA, 1974–76; Albert Handell Sch, 1977; Art Students League, NY, 1978; Women's Studio Workshop, Rosendale, NY
AWARDS: Hudson Valley Art Assoc Award, NY, 1981; Barrett House Graphics Award, Poughkeepsie, NY, 1986; Helen Apen Oehler Award, Graphics, Allied Artists of America, 1989; Philip Isenberg Award, Graphics & Drawing, Knickerbocker Artists, NY, 1990
RECENT EXHIB: Mark Gruber Gallery, New Paltz, NY, 1990
COLLECTIONS: Univ of Wisconsin Hospital, Madison, WI
PRINTERS: Artist (ART)
PUBLISHERS: Original Print Collectors Group, Ltd, NY (OPCG); Christie's Contemporary Art, London England (CCA); Artist (ART)
GALLERIES: Rogers Gallery, Mattapoisett, MA; Valperine Gallery, Madison, WI; Mark Gruber Gallery, New Paltz, NY; Gallery 4, Alexandria, VA; River Gallery, Irvington-on-Hudson, NY Ann Leonard Gallery, Woodstock, NY; Gallery 2, Morristown, NJ; J-Michael Gallery, Edina, MN; Petrucci Gallery, Saugerties, NY; Nancy Stein Gallery, New York, NY; Burd House Gallery, Nyack, NY; Wenniger Graphics, Boston, MA; Nan Miller Gallery, Rochester, NY; Arnould Gallery, Marblehead, MA; Bayview Gallery, Camden, ME; Uptown Art, Minneapolis, MN; Company Hill Gallery, Kingston, NY; White House Gallery, Stone Ridge, NY; Millbrook Gallery, Millbrook, NY; Sweetwater & Salt Tide Art Galleries, Cortland Manor, NY
MAILING ADDRESS: 452 Whitfield Rd, Accord, NY 12404

TITLE	PUBLISHER	PRINTER	DATE	MEDIUM	DIMENSION (PAPER SIZE) IN INCHES	TYPE OF PAPER	EDITION NUMBER	NO. OF COLORS	ORIGINAL OPENING PRICE	CURRENT RETAIL PRICE
SOLD OUT EDITIONS (RARE):										
Smith's Meadow	ART	ART	1978	SP	17 X 14	Bristol	32	5	50	125
Summer Duet	ART	ART	1979	SP	20 X 14	Italia	250	7	70	125
Winter Night	ART	ART	1979	SP	21 X 20	Italia	250	6	100	150
Jake's Pasture	ART	ART	1979	SP	20 X 24	Italia	250	6	125	300
Buzzard's Bay	ART	ART	1979	SP	22 X 30	SOM/S	160	7	140	350
Dry Wind	ART	ART	1979	SP	20 X 28	Italia	250	6	105	375
December Thaw	ART	ART	1979	SP	20 X 28	Italia	250	7	105	275
Tidal Waters	ART	ART	1979	SP	20 X 28	Italia	250	7	100	175
Lake Children	ART	ART	1979	SP	14 X 20	Italia	250	6	70	125
Amy's Resolve	ART	ART	1979	SP	14 X 20	Italia	250	6	70	125
Peconic View	CCA	ART	1981	SP	23 X 29	G/100	200	5	125	500
Summer Towel	CCA	ART	1981	SP	15 X 22	SOM/S	175	7	70	300
Mohonk Pasture	OPCG	ART	1981	SP	23 X 29	G/100	225	10	140	400
Harbor Morning	OPCG	ART	1981	SP	23 X 29	G/100	195	8	140	400
Kitchen Sonata	CCA	ART	1982	SP	22 X 30	SOM	175	7	150	400
Harbor Lilies	CCA	ART	1982	SP	23 X 29	G/100	225	6	150	400
October Garden	CCA	ART	1983	SP	22 X 27	SOM	150	7	150	275
Orchard Fox	ART	ART	1983	SP	22 X 27	SOM	85	6	140	350
Winter Story	CCA	ART	1983	SP	22 X 30	SOM	225	6	150	375
Thimble Island Rocks	CCA	ART	1984	SP	22 X 30	SOM	75	6	150	375
Moon Garden	CCA	ART	1985	SP	22 X 27	SOM	175	7	150	350
Mohonk Cloudbreak	ART	ART	1985	SP	14 X 19	Italia	101	6	115	175
Thimble Islands	CCA	ART	1985	SP	22 X 30	SOM	175	6	150	375
Winter Warm	ART	ART	1986	SP	23 X 29	G/100	75	8	150	300
Early Snow	ART	ART	1986	SP	23 X 30	COV	90	13	150	250
Watch Hill Window	ART	ART	1986	SP	23 X 29	G/100	75	6	150	375
Julie's Porch	CCA	ART	1987	SP	22 X 30	SOM/S	175	8	200	350
Best Cat	OPCG	ART	1990	SP	22 X 30	SOM	80	5	200	350
CURRENT EDITIONS:										
Shore Wind	ART	ART	1980	SP	22 X 30	SOM	150	6	135	225
Cloud Mountain	ART	ART	1980	SP	22 X 30	SOM/S	125	7	125	200
Before Sundown	ART	ART	1985	SP	18 X 22	G/100	120	9	125	150
Kripplebush Fields	ART	ART	1988	SP	22 X 30	SOM	150	8	200	250
Ocean Monarch	ART	ART	1988	SP	23 X 28	COV	175	9	175	200
Mohonk Red-Wing	ART	ART	1989	SP	23 X 30	COV	85	11	200	225
Watch Hill Swans	ART	ART	1989	SP	23 X 22	COV	80	7	200	250
St Thomas Pasture	ART	ART	1989	SP	20 X 30	COV	85	8	200	250
Ned's Point Bench	ART	ART	1990	SP	23 X 30	COV	120	9	250	250
Spring Pasture	ART	ART	1991	SP	21 X 30	COV	85	8	250	250

MAXINE MASTERFIELD

BORN: Los Angeles, CA; July 21, 1933
EDUCATION: Cleveland Inst of Art, OH, 1955
AWARDS: Purchase Award, Nat Watercolor Soc, 1978; High Winds Medal, Am Watercolor Soc, 1981; Grand Buckeye Leaf Award, Ohio Watercolor Soc, 1982
COLLECTIONS: Laguna Beach Mus of Art, CA
PRINTERS: Land Mark Editions, Minneapolis, MN (LME)
PUBLISHERS: C G Rein Publishers, St Paul, MN (CGR)
GALLERIES: C G Rein Galleries, Scottsdale, AZ & Santa Fe, NM & Houston, TX & Minneapolis, MN; Alan Gallery, Berea, OH; Nuance Galleries, Tampa, FL
MAILING ADDRESS: Glenoaks Villa, 3968 Lakeside Rd, Sarasota, FL 33582

TITLE	PUBLISHER	PRINTER	DATE	MEDIUM	DIMENSION (PAPER SIZE) IN INCHES	TYPE OF PAPER	EDITION NUMBER	NO. OF COLORS	ORIGINAL OPENING PRICE	CURRENT RETAIL PRICE
CURRENT EDITIONS:										
Craggy Canyons	CGR	LME	1982	LC	29 X 40	AP	100	4	300	350
Within the Sea	CGR	LME	1983	LC	29 X 40	AP	100	4	300	350

ANDRÉ MASSON

BORN: Balagny, France; January 4, 1896
RECENT EXHIB: Cranbrook Acad of Art Mus, Bloomfield, MI, 1992; Zabriski, NY, 1992; Cavaliero Fine Arts, NY, 1993
PRINTERS: Atelier Mourlot, Paris, France (AM); La Poligrafa, Barcelona, Spain, (LP); Barcelona, Spain (EdP)
PUBLISHERS: Transworld Art, Inc, NY (TAI); Ediciones Poligrafa, SA, Barcelona, Spain (EdP); Circle Gallery, Ltd, Chicago, IL (CGL)
GALLERIES: Joan Prats Gallery, New York, NY & Barcelona, Spain; Jack Rutberg Fine Arts, Los Angeles, CA; Gallerie Louise, York, PA; Saidenberg Gallery, New York, NY; Leila Taglhinia-Milani, New York, NY; Arnold Herstand & Co., New York, NY; Multiple Impressions, New York, NY; Galerie Lahumiere, Paris, France; Circle Galleries, San Diego, CA & San Francisco, CA & Northbrook, IL & Clayton, MO & Pittsburgh, PA & Houston, TX & Soho, NY & Chicago, IL & Scottsdale, AZ & Beverly Hills, CA & Costa Mesa, CA & Sherman Oaks, CA & Palm Beach, FL & Honolulu, HI & New Orleans, LA & Las Vegas, NV & Seattle, WA; Bond Street Gallery, Oakland, CA; Gala Art Gallery, Palm Beach, FL; Galerie Select, Ltd, New York, NY; Gallery of Surrealism & the Fantastic, New York, NY; Zabriskie Gallery, New York, NY
MAILING ADDRESS: 26 Rue de Sevigne, Paris, 4e, France

TITLE	PUBLISHER	PRINTER	DATE	MEDIUM	DIMENSION (PAPER SIZE) IN INCHES	TYPE OF PAPER	EDITION NUMBER	NO. OF COLORS	ORIGINAL OPENING PRICE	CURRENT RETAIL PRICE
SOLD OUT EDITIONS (RARE):										
Solidarité-L'Epagne...			1938	EB	3 X 4	WOVE	150	1	25	2500
Don Giovanni	CGL	AM	1977	LC	30 X 22	AP/W	250	9	200	2300
CURRENT EDITIONS:										
Wave of the Future	TAI	AM	1974	LC	20 X 26	AP	175	7	400	750
Quatre Dames 1900	EdP	LP	1978	LC	26 X 20	AP	99		300	500
Le Feu d'Herbes	EdP	LP	1978	LC	20 X 26	R/BFK	99		350	500

JULIA MATEU

BORN: Barcelona, Spain; 1941
EDUCATION: Art Acad Casa de Campo, Madrid, Spain
TEACHING: Art Sch Riba de Freser, Spain
COLLECTIONS: Mus Dorsten, West Germany; Catalan Mus, Barcelona, Spain
PRINTERS: Domberger KG, Dilderstadt, West Germany (DOM)
PUBLISHERS: Dietz Art Limited NY (DAL)
GALLERIES: Dietz Art Limited, New York, NY; Estol Galeria, Barcelona, Spain
MAILING ADDRESS: Sant Marti d'Empuries, L'Escala-Gerona, Spain

TITLE	PUBLISHER	PRINTER	DATE	MEDIUM	DIMENSION (PAPER SIZE) IN INCHES	TYPE OF PAPER	EDITION NUMBER	NO. OF COLORS	ORIGINAL OPENING PRICE	CURRENT RETAIL PRICE
CURRENT EDITIONS:										
E Divi Dali-Homage to Dali	DAL	DOM	1985	COL/SP	23 X 35	FAB/BUT	280	31	400	900

ROBERTO SEBASTIAN MATTA

BORN: Santiago, Chile; November 11, 1911
EDUCATION: Col of Sacred Heart, Santiago, Chile; Catholic Univ, Santiago, Chile; Studied with Le Corbursier, Paris, France, 1935–37
RECENT EXHIB: Arnold Herstand & Co, NY, 1989; Hirshhorn Mus, Wash, DC, 1992
COLLECTIONS: Mus of Mod Art, NY; Wadsworth Atheneum, Hartford, CT; St Louis Mus, MO
PRINTERS: Visat, Paris, France (V); Mourlot, Paris, France (M); La Poligrafa, Barcelona, Spain (LP); Alexander Heinrici, NY (AH); Studio Heinrici, NY (SH)
PUBLISHERS: Transworld Art Inc, NY (TAI); Contemporary Art Masters, NY (CAM); Ediciones Poligrafa, Barcelona, Spain (EdP); Studio Heinrici, NY (SH)
GALLERIES: Maxwell Davidson Gallery, New York, NY; Meridian Gallery, Chicago, IL, & New York, NY; Jack Rutberg Fine Arts, Los Angeles, CA; Carimor Galleries, New York, NY; Tasende Gallery, La Jolla, CA; Hilde Gerst Gallery, New York, NY; Alexander Kahan Fine Arts, New York, NY; Yares Gallery, Scottsdale, AZ; Leila Taghinia-Milani, New York, NY; Marta Gutierrez Fine Arts, Key Biscayne, FL; Galeria Joan Prats, Barcelona, Spain & New York, NY; Carone Gallery, Fort Lauderdale, FL; Sande Garcia Fine Arts, Miami, FL; Galerie Thomas R Monahan, Chicago, Il; Phyllis Needlman Gallery, Chicago, IL; Arnold Herstand & Company, New York, NY; Mary-Anne Martin Fine Art, New York, NY; Bond Street Gallery, Oakland, CA; George Belcher Gallery, San Francisco, CA; Gary Nader Fine Arts, Coconut Grove, FL; Richard Arregui Fine Art, Coral Gables, FL; Nohra Haime Gallery, New York, NY; Constance Kamens Fine Art, New York, NY; Sindin Galleries, New York, NY; TwoSixtyOne Art, New York, NY; Jane Kahan Gallery, New York, NY

Roberto Sebastian Matta
L'Ame est une Couronne
Courtesy Ediciones Poligrafa

MAILING ADDRESS: Boissy Sans Avoir, Seine-et-Oise, France

TITLE	PUBLISHER	PRINTER	DATE	MEDIUM	DIMENSION (PAPER SIZE) IN INCHES	TYPE OF PAPER	EDITION NUMBER	NO. OF COLORS	ORIGINAL OPENING PRICE	CURRENT RETAIL PRICE
SOLD OUT EDITIONS (RARE):										
New York Suite (Set of 10)			1944	EB		AP	70 EA	1 EA	1000 SET	20000 SET
Surreal Figure			1949	EB	6 X 4	AP	60	1	100	2000

ROBERTO SEBASTIAN MATTA CONTINUED

TITLE	PUBLISHER	PRINTER	DATE	MEDIUM	DIMENSION (PAPER SIZE) IN INCHES	TYPE OF PAPER	EDITION NUMBER	NO. OF COLORS	ORIGINAL OPENING PRICE	CURRENT RETAIL PRICE
SOLD OUT EDITIONS (RARE):										
Or Dur or Aison	TAI	V	1971	EB	20 X 26	AP	100	7	300	800
Pourquoi	TAI	M	1971	LC	20 X 26	AP	150		300	800
Set of 5 Lithographs	EdP	LP	1971	LC	30 X 21 EA	GP	100 EA		2000 SET	2500 SET
									400 EA	550 EA
Homer	SH	AH/SH	1971	EB/A		AP	100		350	1100
Explosions, I,II,III	SH	AH/SH	1971	LC	22 X 28 EA	AP	125 EA		350 EA	1100 EA
Oh! Les Tomobiles			1972	EB/A/SG	16 X 22	AP	100	1	300	850
Populated Surrelistic Landscape, Plate I,II	SH	AH/SH	1975	LC		AP	125 EA		185 EA	850 EA
CURRENT EDITIONS:										
Une Saison en Enfer (Set of 10):									6000 SET	8000 SET
Je Fixe des Vertiges	EdP	LP	1978	EB/A	26 X 20	AP	100		650	800
Plusieurs Autres Vies	EdP	LP	1978	EB/A	26 X 20	AP	100		650	800
Attire le Gai Venin	EdP	LP	1978	EB/A	26 X 20	AP	100		650	800
Nous ne Sommes Pas au Monde	EdP	LP	1978	EB/A	26 X 20	AP	100		650	800
Damnépar l'Are-en Ciel	EdP	LP	1978	EB/A	26 X 20	AP	100		650	800
Des Secrets pour Changer La Vie	EdP	LP	1978	EB/A	26 X 20	AP	100		650	800
L'explosion qui Eclair mon Abime	EdP	LP	1978	EB/A	26 X 20	AP	100		650	800
L'âme set une Couronne	EdP	LP	1978	EB/A	26 X 20	AP	100		650	800
Feu, Feu sur Moi	EdP	LP	1978	EB/A	26 X 20	AP	100		650	800
Je Suis Intact	EdP	LP	1978	EB/A	26 X 20	AP	100		650	800
Une Saison en Enfer (Set of 10)	EdP	LP	1978	EB/A	26 X 20	JP	100 EA		6500 SET	8500 SET
									700 EA	850 EA
Ouvre L'Instant	EdP	LP	1978	LC	26 X 20	AP	100		650	800
Series of 5, SM1–SM5	EdP	LP	1978	LC	30 X 21	AP	100 EA		2000 SET	2500 SET
									400 EA	550 EA
Antologia (Set of 5):									2000 SET	2500 SET
Sois Bastion et Cristobal	EdP	LP	1979	LC	30 X 21	AP	100	5	400	550
Cristifixion	EdP	LP	1979	LC	30 X 21	AP	100	5	400	550
D' Yeaux	EdP	LP	1979	LC	30 X 21	AP	100	5	400	550
Nue Bu	EdP	LP	1979	LC	30 X 21	AP	100	5	400	550
Le Coq	EdP	LP	1979	LC	30 X 21	AP	100	5	400	550
New School (Set of 10)			1980	EB	15 X 11 EA	AP	70 EA	1 EA	3000 SET	7000 SET

WANDA MILLER MATTHEWS

BORN: Barry, IL; September 15, 1930
EDUCATION: Bradley Univ, Peoria, IL, BFA, 1952; Univ of Iowa, Iowa City, IA, MFA, 1957, with Maurice Lasansky
AWARDS: Louis C Tiffany Found Grant, Graphic Arts, 1957,58; Purchase Awards, Nat print Exhib; Boston Printmakers, MA, 1959,70; State Univ Col, Potsdam, NY, 1962,70; Benton Spruance Prize, Phila Print Club, PA, 1971; Southwest Texas Univ, San Marcos, TX 1979; Purchase Award, Soc of Am Graphic Artists, Nat Print Exhib, New York, NY, 1979; Purchase Award, Dulin Nat Print Comp, Knoxville, Tn, 1968,81; S Drabkin Mem Award, Am Color Print Soc Nat Exhib, Phila, PA, 1981; Purchase Prize, Honolulu Acad of Art, HI, 1983; First Place, Color Prints, YBOR Nat Print Comp, Ybor City, FL 1985; Leila Sawyer Mem Award, Nat Assn of Women Artists, NY, 1986
RECENT EXHIB: Jane Haslem Gallery, Wash, DC, 1990; Brandts Klaedefabrik Mus, Odense, Denmark, 1989
COLLECTIONS: Philadelphia Mus of Art, PA; Los Angeles County Mus of Art, CA; Portland Art Mus, OR; DeCordova Mus, Lincoln, MA; Joslyn Art Mus, Omaha, NE; Bytow Nat Mus, Poland; Honolulu Acad of Art, HI; Boston Public Library, MA; Library of Congress, Wash, DC, Col Board Coll, NY
PRINTERS: Artist (ART)
PUBLISHERS: Artist (ART)
GALLERIES: Jane Haslem Gallery, Wash, DC; van Straaten Gallery, Chicago, IL; Brena Gallery, Denver, CO; Oxford Gallery, England; John Szoke Gallery, New York, NY; Print Club Gallery, Phila, PA; Wenniger Graphics, Boston, MA; Dubins Gallery, Los Angeles, CA; Gallery 500, Elkins Park, PA; Merida-Rapp Graphics, Louisville, KY; Robischon Gallery, Denver, CO; Riggs Gallery, La Jolla, CA; Artisan Interiors, Traverse City, MI
MAILING ADDRESS: 2865 Jay Rd, Boulder, CO 80301

TITLE	PUBLISHER	PRINTER	DATE	MEDIUM	DIMENSION (PAPER SIZE) IN INCHES	TYPE OF PAPER	EDITION NUMBER	NO. OF COLORS	ORIGINAL OPENING PRICE	CURRENT RETAIL PRICE
SOLD OUT EDITIONS (RARE):										
Self Portrait	ART	ART	1957	IB	28 X 16	HAM	35	1	35	350
Daughter of Harry Miller	ART	ART	1959	ENG	19 X 16	FAB	45	1	45	300
Inside	ART	ART	1970	IC	26 X 37	ALEX	40	Multi	150	700
One Morning	ART	ART	1975	I/EC	36 X 26	R/BFK	45	Multi	190	500
Turning	ART	ART	1976	IC	23 X 31	R/BFK	50	Multi	180	450
With Trees	ART	ART	1976	IC	26 X 29	R/BFK	30	Multi	165	500
Backyard	ART	ART	1978	IC	25 X 35	R/BFK	40	Multi	190	750
Window	ART	ART	1979	IC	26 X 22	R/BFK	80	Multi	250	1000
Mountain-Town II	ART	ART	1981	IC	33 X 22	R/BFK	60	Multi	375	900
Back Door	ART	ART	1981	IC	26 X 21	R/BFK	35	Multi	250	700
CURRENT EDITIONS:										
The Mulberry Tree	ART	ART	1980	IC	29 X 28	R/BFK	85	Multi	200	350
Chimneys	ART	ART	1980	IC	25 X 27	R/BFK	50	Multi	150	450
East Light	ART	ART	1981	IC	26 X 22	R/BFK	50	Multi	300	450
Mountain-Town I	ART	ART	1981	IC	29 X 24	R/BFK	7	Multi	325	500
Mountain-Town III	ART	ART	1982	IC	26 X 22	R/BFK	50	Multi	300	450
Mountian-Town IV	ART	ART	1982	IC	26 X 22	R/BFK	50	Multi	300	375

WANDA MILLER MATTHEWS CONTINUED

TITLE	PUBLISHER	PRINTER	DATE	MEDIUM	DIMENSION (PAPER SIZE) IN INCHES	TYPE OF PAPER	EDITION NUMBER	NO. OF COLORS	ORIGINAL OPENING PRICE	CURRENT RETAIL PRICE
CURRENT EDITIONS:										
Going	ART	ART	1982	IC	26 X 22	R/BFK	50	Multi	300	450
Stone Wall	ART	ART	1983	IC	26 X 22	R/BFK	50	Multi	300	450
Snow Light	ART	ART	1983	IC	24 X 23	R/BFK	50	Multi	240	450
China Tour: Were We Really There?	ART	ART	1984	IC	29 X 27	R/BFK	60	Multi	400	400
China Album	ART	ART	1984	IC	29 X 27	R/BFK	7	Multi	375	375
Foothills	ART	ART	1985	IC	29 X 25	R/BFK	50	Multi	350	400
Danny's Room	ART	ART	1985	IC	26 X 22	R/BFK	60	Multi	400	450
Mid-day	ART	ART	1985	IC	29 X 25	R/BFK	50	Multi	400	400
Between	ART	ART	1986	IC	36 X 26	R/BFK	60	Multi	500	500
A Light Inside	ART	ART	1987	IC	27 X 26	R/BFK	35	Multi	450	600
North Light	ART	ART	1987	IC	27 X 23	R/BFK	35	Multi	375	450
The Window Set (Set of 10):	ART	ART	1980–88	IC	82 X 72	R/BFK	5	Multi	5000 SET	5000 SET
Home, with Mountains	ART	ART	1988	IC	26 X 22	R/BFK	40	Multi	400	450
Inner Light	ART	ART	1988	IC	27 X 23	R/BFK	40	Multi	400	450

PETER MAX

BORN: Berlin, Germany; October 19, 1937; US Citizen
EDUCATION: Art Students League, NY; Pratt Inst, Brooklyn, NY; Sch of Visual Arts, NY
RECENT EXHIB: Hermitage Mus, Central Exhib Hall, St Petersberg, Russia, 1991; Moscow Acad of Fine Arts, Moscow, 1991; Hartmann Gallery, Munich, Germany, 1992; Lincoln Gallery, Dallas, TX, 1992; Daniel Peleg Gallery, Detroit, MI, 1992
COLLECTIONS: Mus of Mod Art, NY; El Paso Mus of Art, TX; Brooks Mem Art Gallery, Memphis, TN; Univ of Alabama, Birmingham, AL; Phoenix Mus of Art, AZ; Wichita Art Mus, KS; Newport Harbor Art Mus, Balboa, CA; Corcoran Gallery of Art, Wash, DC; Denver Art Mus, Munich, Germany; Stedelijk Mus, Amsterdam, The Netherlands; Kunstlerhaus, Vienna, Austria; Musee de L'Affiche, Paris, France
PRINTERS: Jorge Dumas, NY (JD); Atelier Dumas NY (AD); Peter Baum, NY (PB); Ismo Productions, NY (JP); Belline (BEL); Alexander Heinrici, NY (AH); Heinrici Studio, NY (HS); Izmo Productions, NY (IZMO); American Atelier, NY (AA); Sausalito Studio, CA (SAUS); Joseph Kleineman, NY (JK); A Nussbaum, NY (AN); Karl & Gail, NY (K/G); Miguel Herrara, NY (MH); Hoshida Print Studio, Japan (HPS); Kyoto Workshop, Japan (KW); Arabesque Studio, Boston, MA (AraSt); Max Studio, NY (MAX)
PUBLISHERS: London Arts, Inc, Detroit, MI (LAI); Martin Lawrence Limited Editions, Van Nuys, CA (MLLE); AMX Art Ltd, NY (AMX); Zero Megalopolis, NY (ZM); C G Rein Publishers, St Paul, MN (CGR); Frankel Art, NY (FA); Lawrence Ross Publishing, Beverly Hills, CA (LRP); Circle Fine Art, Chicago, IL (CFA); Tsumura Art Association, Tokyo, Japan (TAA); Hanson Art Galleries, San Francisco, CA (HAN)
GALLERIES: Martin Lawrence Galleries, Newport Beach, CA & Los Angeles, CA & Phila, PA & Sherman Oaks, CA & West Los Angeles, CA & Short Hills, NJ; Lake Gallery, Incline Village, NV; C G Rein Galleries, Scottsdale, AZ & Santa Fe, NM & Scottsdale, AZ & Houston, TX & Minneapolis, MN; Hanson Galleries, Beverly Hills, CA & Carmel, CA & Las La Jolla, CA & Sausalito, CA & San Francisco, CA & New Orleans, LA & Maui, HI; Stephen Gill Gallery, New York, NY; Merrill Chase Gallery, Chicago, IL; Access Gallery, New York, NY; Hartmann Gallery, Dallas, TX; Ro Gallery Image Makers, Inc, New York, NY; Professional Fine Arts Services, Inc, New York, NY
MAILING ADDRESS: 37 W 65th St, New York, NY 10023

Peter Max
Palm Beach Lady
Courtesy AMX Art, Ltd

TITLE	PUBLISHER	PRINTER	DATE	MEDIUM	DIMENSION (PAPER SIZE) IN INCHES	TYPE OF PAPER	EDITION NUMBER	NO. OF COLORS	ORIGINAL OPENING PRICE	CURRENT RETAIL PRICE
SOLD OUT EDITIONS (RARE):										
An Astral Question	LAI	PB	1970	SP	22 X 30	AP	100		100	8000
Astro Guide	LAI	PB	1970	SP	22 X 30	AP	100		100	8000
Astral Thinker	LAI	PB	1970	SP	18 X 12	AP	300		75	6000
Astral World Watcher	LAI	PB	1970	SP	22 X 30	AP	100		100	12000
At the Feet of My Master	LAI	PB	1970	SP	22 X 30	AP	100		100	14000
Coming into Red	LAI	PB	1970	SP	16 X 19	AP	300		75	6000
Going East	LAI	PB	1970	SP	22 X 30	AP	100		100	8000
Cosmic Confrontation	LAI	PB	1970	SP	22 X 30	AP	100		100	9000
Enigma 22	LAI	PB	1970	SP	22 X 30	AP	100		100	8000
Eternal Flow	LAI	PB	1970	SP	22 X 30	AP	100		100	8000

PETER MAX CONTINUED

TITLE	PUBLISHER	PRINTER	DATE	MEDIUM	DIMENSION (PAPER SIZE) IN INCHES	TYPE OF PAPER	EDITION NUMBER	NO. OF COLORS	ORIGINAL OPENING PRICE	CURRENT RETAIL PRICE
SOLD OUT EDITIONS (RARE):										
Eternal Guide	LAI	PB	1970	SP	22 X 30	AP	100		100	8000
Forever There	LAI	PB	1970	SP	22 X 30	AP	100		100	8000
Glimpse into Akashic Records	LAI	PB	1970	SP	22 X 30	AP	100		100	10000
Going East	LAI	PB	1970	SP	22 X 30	AP	100		100	8000
Good Loving	LAI	PB	1970	SP	19 X 16	AP	300		75	6000
Great Wave of Atlantis	LAI	PB	1970	SP	22 X 30	AP	100		100	8000
Hieroglyphic I	LAI	PB	1970	SP	22 X 30	THS	100		100	8000
Infinity Watchers	LAI	PB	1970	SP	19 X 16	AP	300		75	6000
Innocence	LAI	PB	1970	SP	22 X 30	AP	100		100	8000
Mexico	LAI	PB	1970	SP	22 X 30	AP	100		100	8000
Past Incarnations	LAI	PB	1970	SP	22 X 30	AP	100		100	8000
Remembering It	LAI	PB	1970	SP	22 X 30	AP	100		100	8000
Remembering the Flight	LAI	PB	1970	SP	19 X 16	THS	300		75	6000
Right Now	LAI	PB	1970	SP	22 X 30	AP	100		100	8000
Satchidanada	LAI	PB	1970	SP	19 X 15	THS	300		75	12000
Translucent Vision	LAI	PB	1970	SP	22 X 30	AP	100		100	8000
Universal Runner	LAI	PB	1970	SP	22 X 30	AP	100		100	8000
Winter Sunshine	LAI	PB	1970	SP	19 X 16	THS	300		75	6000
Witnessing from Above	LAI	PB	1970	SP	19 X 16	THS	300		75	6000
Atlanta 2000	LAI	PB	1971	SP	15 X 14	AP	300		75	6000
Being One with the Sun	LAI	PB	1971	SP	22 X 30	AP	100		120	8000
Bowing to the Beginning	LAI	PB	1971	SP	22 X 30	AP	100		120	8000
Christ	LAI	PB	1971	SP	22 X 30	AP	100		120	9000
Closer to God	LAI	PB	1971	SP	22 X 30	AP	100		120	8000
Colassus II	LAI	PB	1971	SP	22 X 30	AP	300		75	6000
Crab Nebular Man	LAI	PB	1971	SP	22 X 30	AP	100		120	12000
Desert Vision	LAI	PB	1971	SP	22 X 30	AP	100		120	8000
Eternal Bubble Dance	LAI	PB	1971	SP	22 X 30	AP	100		120	8000
Experiencing Nothing	LAI	PB	1971	SP	22 X 30	AP	100		120	8000
Gazing	LAI	PB	1971	SP	22 X 30	AP	100		120	8000
Going Home	LAI	PB	1971	SP	22 X 30	AP	100		120	8000
Great Sage Stepping Down	LAI	PB	1971	SP	22 X 30	AP	100		120	8000
Hidden Profile	LAI	PB	1971	SP	22 X 30	AP	100		120	8000
Hieroglyphic II	LAI	PB	1971	SP	22 X 30	AP	100		120	8000
Horizon Enigma	LAI	PB	1971	SP	22 X 30	AP	100		120	8000
House in the Clouds	LAI	PB	1971	SP	22 X 30	AP	100		120	8000
House on the Hill	LAI	PB	1971	SP	22 X 30	AP	100		120	9000
Illusion of Self	LAI	PB	1971	SP	22 X 30	AP	100		120	8000
Joy	LAI	PB	1971	SP	22 X 30	AP	100		120	8000
Knowledge Bliss Absolute	LAI	PB	1971	SP	22 X 30	AP	100		120	9000
Leaving It Behind	LAI	PB	1971	SP	22 X 30	AP	100		120	8000
Magical Moment	LAI	PB	1971	SP	22 X 30	AP	100		120	8000
Man on the Hill	LAI	PB	1971	SP	22 X 30	AP	100		120	8000
Mexican Welcoming Committee	LAI	PB	1971	SP	22 X 30	AP	100		120	8000
Moving Ahead	LAI	PB	1971	SP	22 X 30	AP	100		120	8000
Night of Magic	LAI	PB	1971	SP	22 X 30	AP	100		120	8000
Once There was Me	LAI	PB	1971	SP	22 X 30	AP	100		120	9000
Planetary Vision	LAI	PB	1971	SP	22 X 30	AP	100		120	8000
Pointing to Infinity	LAI	PB	1971	SP	22 X 30	AP	100		120	8000
Polka Dots	LAI	PB	1971	SP	22 X 30	AP	100		120	8000
Prostrations	LAI	PB	1971	SP	22 X 30	AP	100		120	8000
Rama	LAI	PB	1971	SP	22 X 30	AP	100		120	12000
Remembering How	LAI	PB	1971	SP	22 X 30	AP	100		120	8000
Rocks and Sun	LAI	PB	1971	SP	22 X 30	AP	100		120	8000
Running with Image of His Mother	LAI	PB	1971	SP	22 X 30	AP	100		120	8000
Rhythmic Man	LAI	PB	1971	SP	22 X 30	AP	100		120	12000
Splitting	LAI	PB	1971	SP	22 X 30	AP	100		120	8000
St Paul	LAI	PB	1971	SP	22 X 30	AP	100		120	8000
Stepping Down	LAI	PB	1971	SP	22 X 30	AP	100		120	8000
Sunshine Peace (Green)	LAI	PB	1971	SP	22 X 30	AP	100		120	8000
Sunshine Peace (Pink)	LAI	PB	1971	SP	22 X 30	AP	100		120	8000
The Thought of God	LAI	PB	1971	SP	22 X 30	AP	100		120	8000
Traveling in the Light	LAI	PB	1971	SP	22 X 30	AP	100		120	9000
Atlantic Runner	LAI	PB	1972	SP	15 X 14	AP	300		100	6000
Ball of Fire	LAI	PB	1972	SP	22 X 30	AP	150		135	10000
Baloo Baba	LAI	PB	1972	SP	16 X 18	AP	300		100	6000
Becoming of the Wave	LAI	PB	1972	SP	22 X 30	AP	100		135	7000
Being with Moort: (Top of America)	LAI	PB	1972	SP	22 X 30	AP	100		135	9000
Candidate for Peace	LAI	PB	1972	SP	22 X 30	AP	300		100	6000
Entering a New State	LAI	PB	1972	SP	22 X 30	AP	100		135	7000
Floating in Peace	LAI	PB	1972	SP	19 X 16	AP	300		135	7000
Galaxy Lady	LAI	PB	1972	SP	19 X 16	AP	300		100	6000
Getting There Quickly	LAI	PB	1972	SP	22 X 30	AP	100		135	7000

PETER MAX CONTINUED

TITLE	PUBLISHER	PRINTER	DATE	MEDIUM	DIMENSION (PAPER SIZE) IN INCHES	TYPE OF PAPER	EDITION NUMBER	NO. OF COLORS	ORIGINAL OPENING PRICE	CURRENT RETAIL PRICE
SOLD OUT EDITIONS (RARE):										
Giving the Light	LAI	PB	1972	SP	22 X 30	AP	100		135	7000
Golden Time	LAI	PB	1972	SP	22 X 30	AP	100		135	7000
The Guru	LAI	PB	1972	SP	22 X 30	AP	100		135	7000
Hendrix	LAI	PB	1972	SP	22 X 30	AP	100		135	9000
Magic Carpet Ride	LAI	PB	1972	SP	22 X 30	AP	100		135	7000
Magical Mystery	LAI	PB	1972	SP	22 X 30	AP	100		135	7000
Moving into New Spheres	LAI	PB	1972	SP	22 X 30	AP	100		135	7000
Moving with Father	LAI	PB	1972	SP	22 X 30	AP	100		135	7000
Mystic Sailing	LAI	PB	1972	SP	22 X 30	AP	100		135	7000
Peaceful Place	LAI	PB	1972	SP	22 X 30	AP	100		135	7000
Planetarian Traveler	LAI	PB	1972	SP	22 X 30	AP	100		135	7000
Playful Pair	LAI	PB	1972	SP	22 X 30	AP	100		135	7000
Playful Prince	LAI	PB	1972	SP	22 X 30	AP	100		135	7000
Praying to the Wind	LAI	PB	1972	SP	22 X 30	AP	100		135	7000
Rainbow Runner	LAI	PB	1972	SP	22 X 30	AP	100		135	7000
Sat Guru, Teacher of Light	LAI	PB	1972	SP	19 X 16	THS	300		100	6000
Atlantis Suite (Set of 4):									400 SET	24000 SET
Atlantis 2000	LAI	PB	1972	SP	14 X 15	AP	300		125	6500
Flowers of Atlantis	LAI	PB	1972	SP	14 X 15	AP	300		125	6500
Lords of Atlantis	LAI	PB	1972	SP	14 X 15	AP	300		125	6500
Atlantis Runner	LAI	PB	1972	SP	14 X 15	AP	300		125	6500
Wave of Ecstacy	LAI	PB	1972	SP	22 X 30	AP	100		135	7000
Within and Without	LAI	PB	1972	SP	22 X 30	AP	100		135	7000
Somewhere in Space	LAI	PB	1972	SP	22 X 30	AP	100		135	7000
Superbly Free	LAI	PB	1972	SP	22 X 30	AP	100		135	7000
Tip Toe Floating	LAI	PB	1972	SP	22 X 30	AP	100		150	7000
Cosmic Jumper (Palm Beach)	FA	GH	1973	SP	26 X 36	AP	75		400	14000
Cosmic Runner with Zooples	LAI	PB	1973	SP	22 X 14	AP	150		135	7000
Rainbow Jumper (Cosmic Jumper II)	AMX	PB	1973	SP	30 X 23	AP	150		400	4500
Aztec Man	FA	GH	1973	LC	24 X 30	AP	300		225	6000
Being Content	CFA	AA	1973	LC	7 X 7	AP	300		100	1800
Being God	CFA	AA	1973	LC	7 X 7	AP	300		100	1800
Being without Need	CFA	AA	1973	LC	7 X 7	AP	300		100	2000
Breakthrough	CFA	AA	1973	LC	3 X 9	AP	250		100	1600
Brown Lady	FA	GH	1973	LC	28 X 22	AP	300		225	15000
Cosmic Jumper II	FA	PB	1973	SP	22 X 30	AP	150		225	8000
Dawn	AMX	PB	1973	LC	7 X 7	AP	300		100	1800
Descending Flyer	AMX	AMX	1973	SP	22 X 30	AP	100		150	6000
Elegant Lady	CFA	AA	1973	SP	22 X 30	AP	100		150	9000
Entering Yellow	FA	GH	1973	LC	7 X 7	AP	300		100	1500
Facing Waves (Gemini)	CFA	AA	1973	LC	26 X 20	AP	300		225	6000
Five and One's Master	CFA	AA	1973	LC	3 X 9	AP	300		100	1600
Flower Lady	CFA	AA	1973	LC	7 X 7	AP	300		100	1500
Flute Dancer	CFA	AA	1973	LC	7 X 7	AP	300		100	1500
Geometric Man	CFA	AA	1973	LC	7 X 7	AP	300		100	2000
Giving of One's Self	CFA	AA	1973	LC	5 X 5	AP	250		100	1500
Going Within	CFA	AA	1973	LC	7 X 7	AP	300		100	1800
Heart (Orange)	FA	GH	1973	LC	26 X 20	AP	300		225	4000
Infinity Balancer	CFA	AA	1973	LC	7 X 7	AP	300		100	1700
La Femme	CFA	BEL	1973	LC	20 X 24	AP	250		150	4500
Lady on Couch #1	CFA	AA	1973	LC	24 X 30	AP	300		150	5000
Lady on Couch–Blue	FA	GH	1973	LC	26 X 20	AP	300		225	7000
Lady on Couch–Yellow	FA	GH	1973	LC	26 X 20	AP	300		225	7000
Lady on Yellow Couch	CFA	AA	1973	LC	24 X 30	AP	300		150	4500
Lav/Red/Blue Plant on Yellow	AMX	PB	1973	SP	30 X 22	AP	150		200	4000
Monk with Bird	AMX	PB	1973	LC	21 X 26	AP	200		225	7000
Music Team	CFA	AA	1973	LC	7 X 7	AP	300		100	1500
Peach Lady	FA	GH	1973	LC	24 X 30	AP	300		225	5000
Pink & Lavendar Flowers	AMX	PB	1973	SP	29 X 22	AP	150		200	4000
Playing in the Clouds	CFA	AA	1973	LC	7 X 7	AP	300		100	1600
Prince of Blue	AMX	AMX	1973	SP	22 X 30	AP	100		150	10000
Purple Sage	AMX	AMX	1973	SP	15 X 22	AP	150		150	3000
Quadrillage	CFA	BEL	1973	LC	14 X 20	AP	250		150	4500
Sage by Mount Fuji	CFA	AA	1973	LC	7 X 7	AP	300		100	1700
Sage by Mountain	CFA	AA	1973	LC	7 X 7	AP	300		100	1700
Seeing Everything	CFA	AA	1973	LC	7 X 7	AP	300		100	1600
Sitting on Top	CFA	AA	1973	LC	7 X 7	AP	300		100	1600
Sleeping in the Third Eye	CFA	AA	1973	LC	7 X 7	AP	300		100	2000
The Great Man	CFA	AA	1973	LC	7 X 7	AP	300		100	1600
The Great Wave	CFA	AA	1973	LC	7 X 7	AP	300		100	2000
Three Lords and Runner	FA	GH	1973	LC	15 X 21	AP	300		225	7000
Time and Space	CFA	AA	1973	LC	9 X 13	AP	250		100	2500
Traveling Along	CFA	AA	1973	LC	10 X 14	AP	250		100	2500

PETER MAX CONTINUED

TITLE	PUBLISHER	PRINTER	DATE	MEDIUM	DIMENSION (PAPER SIZE) IN INCHES	TYPE OF PAPER	EDITION NUMBER	NO. OF COLORS	ORIGINAL OPENING PRICE	CURRENT RETAIL PRICE
SOLD OUT EDITIONS (RARE):										
Waking Up	CFA	AA	1973	LC	7 X 7	AP	300		100	1500
Watching the Master	CFA	AA	1973	LC	7 X 7	AP	300		100	2000
Zapping the Light	CFA	AA	1973	LC	7 X 7	AP	300		100	2000
Zero Horizontal (Zero I)	FA	GH	1973	LC	20 X 26	AP	300		225	10000
Zero Vertical (Zero II)	FA	GH	1973	LC	20 X 26	AP	300		225	10000
Bluebeard	AMX	PB	1974	SP	10 X 14	AP	150		150	2750
Flowers in the Wind	FA	PB	1974	LC/SP	24 X 30	AP	150		350	8000
Man in Chair	FA	PB	1974	LC/SP	24 X 30	AP	150		350	12000
Monk in Garden	FA	GH	1974	LC/SP	26 X 31	AP	150		350	15000
Jagger	AMX	AH/HS	1974	SP	30 X 40	AP	300		275	6000
Jamaica (Palm Beach)	FA	PB	1974	LC/SP	25 X 31	AP	150		350	11000
Lady in Blue with Vase	FA	PB	1974	LC/SP	27 X 37	AP	150		350	7000
Little Sailboat	AMX	PB	1974	SP	13 X 10	AP	150		150	2500
Man in Chair	FA	PB	1974	SP	24 X 30	AP	150		350	12000
Monk in Garden	FA	GH	1974	LC/SP	26 X 31	AP	150		350	15000
Montana Sun	AMX	PB	1974	SP	13 X 10	AP	150		150	2500
Nude Descending	FA	PB	1974	LC/SP	29 X 20	AP	150		350	12000
Sage on Cliff	AMX	PB	1974	SP	10 X 11	AP	150		150	2500
Toulouse Lautrec	CFA	AA	1974	SP	30 X 42	AP	125		250	3500
76 Jumper	FA	PB	1975	SP	26 X 36	AP	75		500	14000
Cosmic Window	FA	PB	1975	SP	26 X 36	AP	75		500	14000
Peach Cinema	FA	PB	1975	SP	26 X 36	AP	75		500	14000
Sunday Afternoon	FA	PB	1975	SP	26 X 36	AP	75		500	14000
Angel into Box	CFA	AA	1976	LC	10 X 12	AP	300		150	2000
Angel Out of Box	CFA	AA	1976	LC	10 X 12	AP	300		150	2000
Bird in Hand	CFA	AA	1976	SP	23 X 28	AP	200		150	8000
Boat on a Wave	CFA	AA	1976	LC/SP	11 X 13	AP	300		150	2000
Circus Performer	CFA	AA	1976	LC	16 X 17	AP	300		450	3000
Circus Performer with Bird	CFA	AA	1976	LC	17 X 13	AP	300		150	3000
Cliff Dweller	CFA	AA	1976	LC	11 X 10	AP	300		150	2500
During Atlantis	CFA	AA	1976	LC	11 X 12	AP	300		175	3000
Facing East	CFA	AA	1976	LC	4 X 7	AP	300		100	2000
Facing Left	CFA	AA	1976	LC	4 X 7	AP	300		100	2000
Flower Angel I,II	CFA	AA	1976	LC	7 X 8 EA	AP	300 EA		150 EA	2000 EA
Flowers	CFA	AA	1976	LC	16 X 21	AP	300		450	2500
Flowers in Red	CFA	AA	1976	LC	7 X 6	AP	300		150	2500
Geometric #2	CFA	AA	1976	LC	5 X 5	AP	300		100	2000
Geometric #3	CFA	AA	1976	LC	5 X 5	AP	300		100	2000
House in the Sun	CFA	AA	1976	LC	6 X 7	AP	300		150	2750
Lady on Pattern	CFA	AA	1976	LC	9 X 10	AP	300		100	2000
Little Boat II	CFA	AA	1976	LC/SP	11 X 13	AP	300		100	2000
Prince Caspian of Narnia	CFA	AA	1976	LC	11 X 14	AP	300		150	2500
Reclining Woman	CFA	AA	1976	LC	22 X 26	AP	300		150	2000
Sage with Bird	CFA	AA	1976	LC	5 X 4	AP	300		100	2000
Sailing New Worlds	CFA	AA	1976	LC	13 X 12	AP	300		150	5000
Sun Sailing	CFA	AA	1976	LC	7 X 7	AP	300		100	2000
Sunrise	CFA	AA	1976	LC	8 X 9	AP	300		100	2000
The Great Genie	CFA	AA	1976	LC	8 X 11	AP	300		150	2500
Little Boat	CFA	AA	1976	LC	5 X 5	AP	300		100	2000
The Poet	CFA	AA	1976	LC	5 X 5	AP	300		100	4000
The Young Prince	CFA	AA	1976	LC	9 X 11	AP	300		150	2000
Winter Dream	CFA	AA	1976	LC	6 X 9	AP	300		150	2250
Man with Umbrella	CFA	AA	1977	LC	20 X 25	AP	300		200	4000
Visage	AMX	JD	1977	LC	17 X 24	AP	300		400	2200
A Long Time Ago	AMX	PB	1978	SP	30 X 22	FAB	250		400	4000
Angel	AMX	PB	1978	SP	30 X 22	FAB	250		400	3750
Before the Eclipse	AMX	PB	1978	SP	30 X 23	AP	175		450	3250
By the Window	AMX	PB	1978	LC	21 X 27	AP	300		450	3250
Close to the Sun	AMX	PB	1978	SP	19 X 23	SOM	150		400	3250
Early Morning I	AMX	PB	1978	SP	18 X 25	SOM	150		400	2750
Early Morning II	AMX	PB	1978	SP	30 X 23	AP	150		400	2900
Encounter	AMX	PB	1978	SP	30 X 23	AP	175		400	4000
Floating with Flowers	AMX	PB	1978	LC	29 X 21	AP	175		450	2750
Flower Jumper	AMX	PB	1978	SP	33 X 27	AP	200		400	2750
Flowers II	AMX	PB	1978	SP	30 X 23	AP	150		400	2750
Flowers in Brown	AMX	PB	1978	LC	27 X 21	AP	300		400	2750
His Own Eclipse	AMX	PB	1978	SP	30 X 22	FAB	250		400	2750
Lady in Brown	AMX	PB	1978	LC	20 X 17	AP	300			
Lady in Flowers	CFA	AA	1978	LC	21 X 16	AP	300		200	3500
Lady in Grey	CFA	AA	1978	LC	15 X 20	AP	300		200	3000
Lady with Picture	AMX	PB	1978	SP	30 X 23	AP	250		450	4000
Land of Sunshine	AMX	PB	1978	SP	30 X 19	SOM	200		450	4000
Light Planet	AMX	PB	1978	SP	9 X 13	SOM	75		175	2000

PETER MAX CONTINUED

TITLE	PUBLISHER	PRINTER	DATE	MEDIUM	DIMENSION (PAPER SIZE) IN INCHES	TYPE OF PAPER	EDITION NUMBER	NO. OF COLORS	ORIGINAL OPENING PRICE	CURRENT RETAIL PRICE
SOLD OUT EDITIONS (RARE):										
Lunar 2000	AMX	PB	1978	SP	9 X 13	SOM	75		175	2000
Monk in Beige	AMX	PB	1978	SP	36 X 26	AP	200		450	3250
Moon Flowers I	AMX	PB	1978	SP	22 X 30	AP	150		400	2750
Moon Flowers II	AMX	PB	1978	SP	19 X 27	AP	150		400	2750
Moon People	AMX	PB	1978	SP	23 X 30	AP	150		400	3000
Moonscape I,II	AMX	PB	1978	SP	19 X 24 EA	SOM	150 EA		400 EA	3000 EA
Morning Arrival	AMX	PB	1978	SP	30 X 23	AP	250		400	2750
Cosmic Runner III	FA	PB	1978	SP	26 X 36	AP	39		300	18000
Full Moon	CFA	AA	1978	LC	7 X 7	AP	300		100	2000
Movement East	AMX	PB	1978	SP	27 X 19	AP	250		400	3250
Moving Along	AMX	PB	1978	SP		AP	200		400	3500
Night Flowers	AMX	PB	1978	LC	28 X 22	AP	150		400	2750
Outer Spectrum	AMX	PB	1978	SP	9 X 13	SOM	75		175	2750
Red Sun	AMX	PB	1978	LC	21 X 27	AP	200		400	2250
Sam's Sphere	AMX	PB	1978	SP	29 X 22	AP	150		400	3500
Seasons	AMX	IZMO	1978	SP	29 X 38	AP	200		400	2750
Solar Flowers	AMX	PB	1978	SP	9 X 13	SOM	75		175	2000
Space Flowers I	AMX	PB	1978	SP	28 X 22	AP	165		400	3250
Space Flowers II	AMX	PB	1978	SP	19 X 25	AP	150		400	3250
Space Landscape I	AMX	PB	1978	SP	19 X 27	AP			400	3250
Space Landscape II	AMX	PB	1978	SP	22 X 30	AP	150		400	3250
Space Rainbow	AMX	PB	1978	SP	30 X 22	AP	150		400	3250
Spring Day	AMX	PB	1978	SP	19 X 27	AP	250		400	4200
Sun Moon Landscape	AMX	PB	1978	SP	19 X 24	SOM	150		400	3000
Sunrise Flowers	AMX	PB	1978	LC	30 X 22	FAB	250		400	4000
The Poet II	AMX	IZMO	1978	SP	26 X 36	AP	200		400	3500
Two with Umbrellas	AMX	PB	1978	SP	30 X 22	AP	200		400	4000
Winged Flyer II	AMX	IZMO	1978	SP	30 X 25	AP	250		400	3000
Woman in Derby	AMX	IZMO	1978	SP	25 X 19	AP	200		400	3000
Zero and Flowers	AMX	IZMO	1978	LC	16 X 21	AP	300		400	3000
Angel and Master	AMX	IZMO	1979	SP	30 X 23	AP	100		400	3500
Earth Flowers	AMX	JK	1979	LC	28 X 22	AP	165		400	3500
Flower at Sea	AMX	IZMO	1979	SP	30 X 23	AP	100		400	3250
Flower Pot	AMX	IZMO	1979	SP	30 X 23	AP	175		400	3500
Flower Set I	AMX	IZMO	1979	SP	30 X 23	AP	100		400	3000
Flowers in Circle	AMX	IZMO	1979	SP	30 X 23	AP	130		400	3200
Flying	AMX	IZMO	1979	SP	30 X 23	AP	100		400	3000
Flying Freely	AMX	IZMO	1979	SP	30 X 23	AP	100		400	3200
In Trance	AMX	IZMO	1979	SP	16 X 22	AP	100		400	2500
King Tut's Nanny	AMX	IZMO	1979	SP	30 X 23	AP	165		400	2500
Kite Flyer	AMX	IZMO	1979	SP	30 X 23	AP	100		400	4200
Lady against Clouds	AMX	IZMO	1979	SP	30 X 23	AP	250		300	3000
Lady in Weeds	AMX	IZMO	1979	SP	30 X 23	AP	100		400	4000
Lady on Couch with Vase	AMX	IZMO	1979	SP	30 X 23	AP	100		400	4000
Landscape through Window	AMX	IZMO	1979	SP	30 X 23	AP	100		400	3250
Life on Yellow Planet	AMX	IZMO	1979	SP	30 X 23	AP	175		400	2500
Lovers	AMX	IZMO	1979	SP	30 X 23	AP	100		400	3500
Marilyn's Flowers I	AMX	IZMO	1979	SP	30 X 23	AP	175		400	3500
Marilyn's Flowers II	AMX	IZMO	1979	SP	26 X 22	AP	165		400	3000
Mercury Dime III	AMX	IZMO	1979	SP	30 X 23	AP	100		400	2750
Monk with Hat	AMX	IZMO	1979	SP	30 X 23	AP	100		400	2250
Mountain Girl	AMX	IZMO	1979	SP	30 X 23	AP	250		300	4000
On a Distant Planet	AMX	JK	1979	LC	27 X 21	AP	165		400	2750
Pablo Casal	AMX	IZMO	1979	SP	25 X 23	AP	175		400	2250
Performer with Hat	AMX	IZMO	1979	SP	30 X 23	AP	100		400	2250
Pink Sailboat	AMX	IZMO	1979	SP	30 X 23	AP	175		400	3500
Pique Dame Series:										
Pique Dame: Electric Future Man	AMX	JD	1979	LC	10 X 13	AP	280		225	2250
Pique Dame: Pique Dame	AMX	JD	1979	LC	10 X 13	AP	280		225	2250
Pique Dame: Soft Chair & Wall	AMX	JD	1979	LC	10 X 13	AP	280		225	2250
Pique Dame: The Room	AMX	JD	1979	LC	10 X 13	AP	280		225	2250
Portrait of a Cat	AMX	IZMO	1979	SP	30 X 23	AP	100		400	2250
Reclining	AMX	IZMO	1979	SP	30 X 23	AP	130		400	4000
Reflections in Vase	AMX	IZMO	1979	SP	30 X 23	AP	130		400	4000
Royal Gardens	AMX	IZMO	1979	SP	26 X 22	AP	175		400	4500
Runner on Brown	AMX	PB	1979	SP	23 X 23	AP	175		450	2250
Saturn Messenger	AMX	PB	1979	SP	30 X 23	AP	175		400	3500
Seated Lady	AMX	IZMO	1979	SP	30 X 23	AP	175		400	3500
Sky Jumper	AMX	IZMO	1979	SP	30 X 23	AP	175		400	3500
Summer Season I	AMX	IZMO	1979	SP	23 X 30	AP	175		400	3500
Summer Season II	AMX	IZMO	1979	SP	23 X 30	AP	175		400	3000
Summer Season Voyage	AMX	JK	1979	SP	23 X 30	AP	175		400	3000
Tales from Beyond	AMX	IZMO	1979	SP	30 X 23	AP	175		400	3250

PETER MAX CONTINUED

TITLE	PUBLISHER	PRINTER	DATE	MEDIUM	DIMENSION (PAPER SIZE) IN INCHES	TYPE OF PAPER	EDITION NUMBER	NO. OF COLORS	ORIGINAL OPENING PRICE	CURRENT RETAIL PRICE
SOLD OUT EDITIONS (RARE):										
Talking to Karen	AMX	IZMO	1979	LC	28 X 22	AP	165		400	3000
The Dialogue	AMX	IZMO	1979	SP	30 X 23	AP	175		400	3500
The Room	AMX	JD	1979	LC	10 X 13	AP	280		225	2250
Three Faces	AMX	JD	1979	SP	30 X 23	AP	100		400	4200
Tibetan Scene	AMX	JD	1979	LC	28 X 21	SOM	150		400	4200
Tropical Flowers	AMX	JD	1979	SP	30 X 23	AP	175		400	3250
Untitled Abstract	AMX	IZMO	1979	SP	30 X 23	AP	100		400	2500
Walking in the Garden	AMX	PB	1979	SP	30 X 23	AP	100		400	3000
Woman's Face (Purple)	AMX	JK	1979	LC	25 X 34	AP	200		400	2500
At the Lake	AMX	JK	1980	SP	30 X 23	AP	100		400	3250
Vase in Room II	AMX	JK	1980	LC	22 X 26	AP	165		400	2750
American Woman	AMX	JK	1980	LC	28 X 21	SOM	200		450	3000
Beyond Horizon	AMX	IZMO	1980	SP	25 X 22	AP	165		420	3000
Boat Flyer	AMX	JK	1980	LC	23 X 18	AP	165		420	2750
Composition Red	AMX	JK	1980	LC	27 X 21	AP	165		420	3000
Composition Red and Green	AMX	JK	1980	LC	26 X 22	AP	165		420	3000
Daydreaming	AMX	JK	1980	LC	27 X 22	AP	165		420	3000
Flowers Abstract	AMX	JK	1980	LC	27 X 22	AP	165		420	3000
Freedom	AMX	JK	1980	LC	28 X 22	SOM	200		420	3000
From Another Planet	AMX	JK	1980	LC	28 X 22	SOM	165		420	3000
Himalayan Valley	AMX	JK	1980	LC	25 X 22	AP	165		450	3000
In His Garden	AMX	JK	1980	LC	26 X 22	AP	165		450	2750
Lady in Green	AMX	JK	1980	LC	17 X 22	AP	165		400	3000
Lady of Fashion	AMX	JK	1980	LC	24 X 19	AP	165		400	3000
Lady with Feathers	AMX	JD	1980	LC	24 X 21	AP	165		400	2750
Monk and Vase	AMX	IZMO	1980	SP	27 X 22	AP	165		400	3500
Monk at Red Sea	AMX	JK	1980	LC	28 X 22	AP	165		400	3500
New World Landscape	AMX	IZMO	1980	SP	25 X 22	AP	165		400	4200
Robed Man and Vase	AMX	JK	1980	LC	26 X 22	AP	165		400	4000
Sage at Window	AMX	JK	1980	LC	26 X 22	AP	165		400	3500
Sailboats	AMX	JK	1980	LC	26 X 22	AP	165		400	3000
Semi Nude with Flower Zoople	AMX	JK	1980	LC	27 X 22	AP	165		400	3000
Space Teacher	AMX	IZMO	1980	SP	22 X 25	AP	165		400	3500
Sunrise II	AMX	JK	1980	LC	27 X 22	AP	165		400	4500
The Garden	AMX	JK	1980	LC	25 X 22	AP	165		400	3500
Two Floating	AMX	JK	1980	LC	28 X 22	AP	165		400	3000
Two Flowers	AMX	JK	1980	LC	28 X 20	AP	165		400	3500
Vase in Room I	AMX	JK	1980	LC	27 X 21	AP	165		400	3000
Vase in Room II	AMX	JK	1980	LC	22 X 26	AP	165		400	2750
Zero's Friend	AMX	JK	1980	LC	27 X 22	AP	165		400	3200
At the Picture	AMX	JK	1981	LC	24 X 19	AP	165		400	2750
Ballet Story	AMX	JK	1981	LC	30 X 22	AP	165		400	3000
Barcelona	AMX	SAUS	1981	EC	16 X 14	AP	100		300	3000
Brown Lady with Vase	CGR	JD	1981	LC	19 X 23	AP	200		600	4500
Flower with Vase	CGR	JD	1981	LC	21 X 27	AP	200		600	4500
General Data	AMX	JD	1981	SP	30 X 22	AP	200		600	8000
Girl from Ibiza	AMX	JD	1981	LC	30 X 22	AP	165		400	4500
Girl with Flower	AMX	JD	1981	EC	14 X 16	AP	100		300	3750
Giving of the Flower	AMX	JD	1981	LC	30 X 21	AP	165		400	3500
Going West: Balancing Purple	AMX	JD	1981	LC	10 X 14	AP	250		250	2250
Going West: Going West	AMX	JD	1981	LC	10 X 14	AP	250		250	2250
Going West: Holding the Sun	AMX	JD	1981	LC	10 X 14	AP	250		250	2250
Going West: Peach Surprise	AMX	JD	1981	LC	10 X 14	AP	250		250	2250
Grey Flowers and Vase II	AMX	JD	1981	LC	27 x 21	AP	200		250	2500
Heart II	AMX	JD	1981	LC	30 X 22	AP	165		250	2500
If Series: Flower Garden	MLLE	IZMO	1981	SP	14 X 10	AP	200		300	2500
If Series: If	MLLE	IZMO	1981	SP	14 X 10	AP	200		300	2500
If Series: Runner	MLLE	IZMO	1981	SP	14 X 10	AP	200		300	2500
If Series: Space Place	MLLE	IZMO	1981	SP	14 X 10	AP	200		300	2500
In Dream State	AMX	JD	1981	LC	22 X 30	AP	165		400	2750
Lady On Green	AMX	JK	1981	LC	28 X 22	AP	165		400	2750
Large Christus	AMX	SAUS	1981	EC	7 X 9	AP	50		350	4000
Music Player	AMX	JD	1981	LC	26 X 21	AP	250		250	2750
Palm Court	AMX	SAUS	1981	EC	16 X 14	AP	100		300	2750
Pink Sky Flyer	AMX	IZMO	1981	SP	30 X 22	AP	165		300	2750
Rainbow and Clouds	AMX	JK	1981	LC	22 X 30	AP	165		450	3000
Reclining Nude	AMX	SAUS	1981	EC	16 X 14	AP	100		300	2750
Red Sail	AMX	JK	1981	LC	27 X 21	AP	165		400	3000
Reflections II	AMX	JK	1981	LC	19 x 25	AP	165		400	3000
Seated Man	CGR	JD	1981	LC/SP	30 X 40	AP	200		600	4000
Seated with Circle	AMX	JK	1981	LC	29 X 22	AP	165		400	3500
Solar View	AMX	JK	1981	LC	25 X 17	AP	165		400	2250
Spring Girl	AMX	JD	1981	LC	19 X 25	AP	165		400	2250

PETER MAX CONTINUED

TITLE	PUBLISHER	PRINTER	DATE	MEDIUM	DIMENSION (PAPER SIZE) IN INCHES	TYPE OF PAPER	EDITION NUMBER	NO. OF COLORS	ORIGINAL OPENING PRICE	CURRENT RETAIL PRICE
SOLD OUT EDITIONS (RARE):										
Suzin	AMX	JK	1981	LC	29 X 21	AP	100		400	6000
The Jockey	AMX	JK	1981	LC	29 X 22	AP	165		400	2750
Visage III	AMX	JK	1981	LC	29 X 21	AP	165		400	3000
With Feathers	AMX	JK	1981	LC	30 X 22	AP	165		400	2500
Yellow Bird	AMX	IZMO	1981	SP	30 X 22	AP	165		400	2250
Across the Room	AMX	AN	1982	LC	21 X 30	AP	200		400	2500
Bluegrass Pegasus	AMX	AN	1982	LC	38 X 27	AP	300		400	4000
Cosmic Holiday	MLLE	JD/AD	1982	LC	7 X 7	AP	280		150	2500
Day Dream	MLLE	JD/AD	1982	LC	7 X 7	AP	280		150	2500
Descending Angel	AMX	AN	1982	LC	21 X 30	AP	200		400	2500
Dressed Up	MLLE	JD/AD	1982	LC	7 X 7	AP	280		150	2500
From the Beginning	AMX	AN	1982	LC	21 X 30	AP	200		400	2500
Galactic Man	MLLE	JD/AD	1982	LC	7 X 7	AP	280		150	2500
In Horizon	AMX	AN	1982	LC	21 X 30	AP	200		400	2500
Ladies Man	MLLE	JD/AD	1982	LC	7 X 7	AP	280		150	2000
Melting Pot	MLLE	JD/AD	1982	LC	7 X 7	AP	280		150	2000
New Chair	MLLE	JD/AD	1982	LC	7 X 4	AP	280		150	2000
Old Chair	MLLE	JD/AD	1982	LC	7 X 4	AP	280		150	2000
Palm Beach Lady	AMX	AN	1982	LC/SP	36 X 27	AP	300		850	4000
Red Vase	AMX	AN	1982	LC	21 X 30	AP	200		400	3000
Runner and Flying Sage	AMX		1982	LC	27 X 22	AP	165		400	3000
Space Reunion	MLLE	JD/AD	1982	LC	7 X 7	AP	250		150	2000
Spring Day	MLLE	JD/AD	1982	LC	7 X 7	AP	250		150	2000
The Dancer	AMX	AN	1982	LC	30 X 21	AP	200		400	2000
The Dream	AMX	AN	1982	LC	21 X 30	AP	200		400	2000
The Dreamer	AMX	AN	1982	LC	21 X 30	AP	200		400	2000
Umbrella Man I	AMX	AN	1982	LC	30 X 21	AP	200		400	2000
Umbrella Man II	AMX	AN	1982	LC	21 X 30	AP	200		400	2000
Deco Lady	LR	AN	1983	LC	30 X 40	AP	75		1200	15000
Lady by Window	LR	AN	1983	LC	40 X 30	AP	75		1200	10000
Lady with Degas	LR	AN	1983	LC	40 X 30	AP	75		1200	10000
Lady with Flowers	LR	AN	1983	LC	40 X 30	AP	75		1200	8000
Nude and Vase	LR	AN	1983	LC	30 X 40	AP	75		1200	8000
Zero Amarillo	LR	AN	1984	SP	22 X 30	AP	300		900	5000
Statue of Liberty, Versions I–VI	AMX	IB	1985	MEZ	36 X 25 EA	AP	300 EA		950 EA	3500 EA
Blue Profile	CG	AA	1986	LC	31 X 25	AP	300		900	4000
Northern Dancer	AMX	AMX	1986	LC	25 X 35	AP	300		900	3500
Crimson Lady	CG	AA	1987	LC	36 X 26	AP	300		900	4000
Deco Lady	CG	AA	1987	LC	37 X 26	AP	300		900	6000
CURRENT EDITIONS:										
Blushing Beauty	HAN	SOMA	1988	SP	38 X 30	COV	300		1450	15000
Flag with Heart	HAN	K/G	1988	SP	33 X 40	COV	495		1800	7500
Les Mondrian Ladies	HAN	SOMA	1988	SP	30 X 40	COV	300		1250	9500
Mercury Dime	AMX	K/G	1988	LC	27 X 40	COV	300			POR
Midnight Profile	HAN	K/G	1988	SP	30 X 40	COV	300		1800	7500
Nude Fan Dancer	HAN	SOMA	1988	SP	30 X 40	COV	300		1250	7500
Reclining in Red	HAN	SOMA	1988	SP	40 X 32	COV	300		1450	7500
Lady on Red with Floating Vase	HAN	K/G	1988	SP	28 X 38	AP	300		1800	7500
Andy with Mustache	HAN	K/G	1989	SP	37 X 38	COV	300		1800	11000
Asia	HAN	MH	1989	SP	30 X 40	COV	300		1900	9500
Better World	HAN	MH	1989	SP/LC	40 X 32	COV	495		1800	9500
Blue Lady Planet	HAN	IZMO	1989	SP	37 X 38	COV	300			POR
Flower Lady	TAA	IZMO	1989	SP	30 X 40	AP	150		1800	4700
Grammy	HAN	K/G	1989	SP	32 X 40	COV	300		1900	15000
JFK—Four Kennedy's	HAN	K/G	1989	SP	32 X 40	COV	495		1900	3500
Mondrian Ladies (on Black)	TAA	HPS	1989	SP	30 X 36		150			
Neo Man	HAN	K/G	1989	SP	30 X 40	COV	300		1900	7500
Zero Megalopolis	TAA	KW	1989	SP	27 X 36		150			
Angel Suite (Set of 6):									3000 SET	7000 SET
Angel and Vase	HAN	MH	1989	EC	15 X 19	AP	100		XXXX	XXXX
Angel of Light	HAN	MH	1989	EC	15 X 19	AP	100		XXXX	XXXX
Angel and Pyramids	HAN	MH	1989	EC	15 X 19	AP	100		XXXX	XXXX
Angel in Thought	HAN	MH	1989	EC	15 X 19	AP	100		XXXX	XXXX
Angel Meeting	HAN	MH	1989	EC	15 X 19	AP	100		XXXX	XXXX
Three Angels	HAN	MH	1989	EC	15 X 19	AP	100		XXXX	XXXX
Angel with Heart	HAN	JK	1990	LC	36 X 27	AP	300		2350	7500
Balboa Park	TAA	JK	1990	LC	27 X 34	AP	150		2350	7500
French Zero's Girlfriend	TAA	JK	1990	LC	27 X 36	AP	150		4700	5500
Ioae Suite: (Set of 5)									8250 SET	25000 SET
Dega & Woman	HAN	K/G	1990	SP	28 X 38	AP	300		XXXX	XXXX
Profiles	HAN	K/G	1990	SP	28 X 38	AP	300		XXXX	XXXX
Sage	HAN	K/G	1990	SP	26 X 36	AP	300		XXXX	XXXX
Umbrella Man	HAN	K/G	1990	SP	26 X 36	AP	300		XXXX	XXXX

PETER MAX CONTINUED

TITLE	PUBLISHER	PRINTER	DATE	MEDIUM	DIMENSION (PAPER SIZE) IN INCHES	TYPE OF PAPER	EDITION NUMBER	NO. OF COLORS	ORIGINAL OPENING PRICE	CURRENT RETAIL PRICE
CURRENT EDITIONS:										
Zero	HAN	K/G	1990	SP	26 X 36	AP	300		XXXX	XXXX
Liberty	HAN	K/G	1990	SP	40 X 32	COV	300		2000	11000
Mona Lisa	HAN	K/G	1990	SP	40 X 32	COV	300		2000	7500
New Moon	TAA	JK	1990	SP	27 X 36	AP	150		4700	5600
Time Line Dega Man	TAA	JK	1990	SP	27 X 36	AP	150		4700	5600
Umbrella Man with Rainbow Sky	TAA	AraSt	1990	SP	27 X 36	AP	150		4700	4700
Zero in Love	HAN	IZMO	1990	SP	30 X 40	COV	300		1800	7500
Beauty and Fauve Suite (Set of 2):									3900 SET	10500 SET
Beauty	HAN	SOMA	1991	SP	40 X 30	AP	300		2350	9500
Fauve	HAN	SOMA	1991	SP	40 X 30	AP	300		2350	9500
Brown Lady	TAA	JK	1991	LC	27 X 36	AP	100		4700	4700
Flower Blossom III	TAA	SOMA	1991	SP	30 X 37	AP	100		4700	4700
Grammy '91	HAN	SOMA	1991	SP	30 X 40	COV	300		2450	5500
Homage to Picasso, Vol I, #1-#4	HAN	MAX	1991	EC	23 X 20 EA	AP	99 EA		4700 SET	4750 SET
Homage to Picasso, Vol II, #5-#8	HAN	MAX	1991	EC	23 X 20 EA	AP	99 EA		2750 SET	2750 SET
Homage to Picasso, Vol III, #9-#12	HAN	MAX	1991	EC	23 X 20 EA	AP	99 EA		2500 SET	2500 SET
Homage to Picasso, Vol IV,#13-#16	HAN	MAX	1991	EC	23 X 20 EA	AP	99 EA		2250 SET	2250 SET
I Love the World	HAN	SOMA	1991	SP	30 X 40	AP	320		2350	4500
Roseville Suite (Set of 2):									4500 SET	5500 SET
Roseville Bouquet	HAN	SOMA	1991	SP	40 X 30	AP	300		2250	2350
Roseville Profile	HAN	SOMA	1991	SP	40 X 30	AP	300		2250	2350
Three Faces	TAA	JK	1991	LC	27 X 36	AP	100		2800	2800
Walking in Reeds	TAA	AraSt	1991	SP	30 X 40	COV	100		3100	3100
Without Borders	HAN	SOMA	1991	SP	40 X 32	AP	300		2350	9500
Heart Suite (Set of 2):									2350 SET	7500 SET
Heart I,II	HAN	SOMA	1992	SP	16 X 32 EA	AP	300 EA		1250 EA	1250 EA
Discovery	HAN	SOMA	1992	SP	27 X 48	AP	300		2350	2350
Homage to Picasso, Vol V, #17-#20	HAN	MAX	1992	EC	23 X 20	AP	99		2250	2250
Walking in Reeds II	HAN	SOMA	1992	SP	30 X 40	AP	300		2350	2350
Stormy Sail	HAN	SOMA	1993	SP	26 X 40	AP	300		2350	2350
Mona Lisa Portraits	HAN	SOM	1993	SP	30 X 40 EA	AP	200 EA		2350 EA	2350 EA

PAUL MAXWELL

BORN: Frost Prairie, AR; 1925
EDUCATION: Principia Col, BFA, 1950; Claremont Grad Sch, CA; Univ of Houston, TX
TEACHING: Prof of Art, Univ of Houston, TX
COLLECTIONS: Smith Col Mus, Northhampton, MA; Wichita Art Mus, KS; Los Angeles Mus of Art, CA; Dallas Mus of Fine Arts, TX; Denver Art Mus, CO; Mus of Fine Arts, Houston, TX; Oklahoma Art Center, Oklahoma City, OK; DeCordova Mus, Lincoln, MA; Fort Worth Art Center, TX; Springfield Mus of Fine Art, MO; Univ of Texas Mus, Austin, TX

PRINTERS: Artist (ART)
PUBLISHERS: Fred Dorfman, Inc, NY (FDI); Multiples, Inc, Dallas, TX (MI)
GALLERIES: Fred Dorfman, New York, NY; C G Rein Galleries, Scottsdale, AZ & Houston, TX & Minneapolis, MN; Gallery 22, Bloomfield Hills, MI; Graphic Art Collection, Hallandale, FL; The Hang-Up, Sarasota, FL; Nuance Galleries, Tampa, FL; Owl 57 Galleries, Woodmere, NY; Laura Paul Galleries, Cincinnati, OH & Columbus, OH; Aaron Aubrey Contemporary Fine Art, Santa Monica, CA

TITLE	PUBLISHER	PRINTER	DATE	MEDIUM	DIMENSION (PAPER SIZE) IN INCHES	TYPE OF PAPER	EDITION NUMBER	NO. OF COLORS	ORIGINAL OPENING PRICE	CURRENT RETAIL PRICE
SOLD OUT EDITIONS (RARE):										
Rocker	FDI	ART	1980	A/CP	30 X 30	AP	100	5	270	450
Moondrops	FDI	ART	1980	A/CP	30 X 22	AP	150	7	360	500
Module I	FDI	ART	1980	A/CP	40 X 40	AP	150	8	450	650
CURRENT EDITIONS:										
Gemstones	FDI	M	1980	HP/CP/A	20 X 23	AP	100	8	275	400
Thermal	FDI	M	1981	HP/CP/A	60 X 40	AP	150	7	750	850
Proteus	FDI	M	1981	HP/CP/A	40 X 60	AP	100	6	750	850
Classic I	FDI	M	1981	WCA	40 X 60	AP	150	1	500	650
Classic II	FDI	M	1981	HP/CP/A	40 X 60	AP	150	9	750	900
Klimer	FDI	M	1981	HP/CP/A	40 X 48	AP	100	7	575	750
Sectoral	FDI	M	1981	HP/CP/A	40 X 48	AP	100	7	600	750
Lands End I–VIII	FDI	M	1981	SP	30 X 40	AP88	100	6	200	300
Lands End I–VIII	FDI	M	1981	PO	30 X 40	AP88	10	7	500	600

The retail prices of the 100,000 limited edition prints quoted in this directory are subject to change. Print publishers, artists and galleries were the direct sources for these quotations. Prices in the secondary market listed as "Sold Out Editions (Rare)" indicate that the publisher has a limited supply of that print or that the print is difficult to locate in the galleries.

The Printworld Directory is accepting new applications for the seventh edition. Approximately 300 new artists will be accepted. Please use the two forms provided in the back section of this directory to submit biographical data and documentation of prints. Edition number of each print must not exceed 500 and the retail price must be $100 or more.

WILLIAM C MAXWELL

BORN: Yonkers, NY; September 3, 1941
EDUCATION: Wagner Col, Staten Island, NY, BA, 1970; Columbia Univ, NY, MA, 1971, EdM, 1972, EdD, 1976
TEACHING: Chairman & Prof, Painting & Printmaking, Col of New Rochelle, NY, 1975 to present
AWARDS: President's Award, Nat Arts Club, NY, 1975; Shields Award, NY, 1975; Purchase Award, Univ of Dallas, Irving, TX, 1980; CAPS Finalist, 1981
RECENT EXHIB: Capp Street Project, San Francisco, CA, 1989; Gallery Stendahl, NY, 1991
COLLECTIONS: Mus of Mod Art, NY; Hudson River Mus, Yonkers, NY; Brooklyn Mus, NY; Univ of Massachusetts, Amherst, MA; Columbia Univ, NY; Univ of Dallas, Irving, TX

PRINTERS: Suzanne Williams, Brooklyn, NY (SW); Frank J Martinez, Brooklyn, NY (FM); Water Street Press, Ltd, Brooklyn, NY (WSP); Sienna Studios, NY (SS); Joe Petrocelli, NY (JP); Artist (ART); Maxwell-Nova Fine Arts, Inc, New Rochelle, NY (MNFA)
PUBLISHERS: Water Street Press, Ltd, Brooklyn, NY (WSP), Beaux Arts Editions, Ltd (BAEL); New Masters, Inc (NM); Artist (ART); Maxwell-Nova Fine Arts, Inc, New Rochelle, NY (MNFA)
GALLERIES: Windmueller Fine Arts, Scarsdale, NY; Gallery Stendahl, New York, NY; Art Placement International, New York, NY & Greenwich, CT
MAILING ADDRESS: 307 Canal St, New York, NY 10013; 170 Orchard St, Orient, NY 11958

William C Maxwell
The Etiology of Gravity and Dance
Courtesy the Artist

TITLE	PUBLISHER	PRINTER	DATE	MEDIUM	DIMENSION (PAPER SIZE) IN INCHES	TYPE OF PAPER	EDITION NUMBER	NO. OF COLORS	ORIGINAL OPENING PRICE	CURRENT RETAIL PRICE
SOLD OUT EDITIONS (RARE):										
Process: Twelve	ART	ART	1974	LC	21 X 27	R/BFK	50	8	250	450
Process: One Plus 280 (States I–V)	ART	ART	1976	LC	17 X 23	AP	50	8	250	450
Process: Ramose X 475 X One (States I–V)	ART	ART	1978	LC	21 X 23	AP	50	7–13	250	350
Process: Linear Intrusion (States I–V)	ART	ART	1979	LC	17 X 23	AP	50	7–16	250	350
Butterfly Trees	NM	SS	1980	LC/SP	22 X 30	R/BFK	300	9	200	350
CURRENT EDITIONS:										
To Further Wonder If There Is a Line at All	WSP	SW/FM/WSP	1982	LC/EC/SP	22 X 30	AP	200	37	250	450
Gambling with the Past	MNFA	MNFA	1992	SP	29 X 41	AP88	50	16	500	500
Etiology of Gravity and Dance	MNFA	MNFA	1992	SP	29 X 41	AP88	50	16	500	500
Deference of Toadspace	MNFA	MNFA	1992	SP	29 X 41	AP88	50	16	500	500

STEVEN LEE MAYES

BORN: Los Angeles, CA; November 7, 1939
EDUCATION: Wichita State Univ, KS, BFA & BAE, 1963, MFA, 1965
TEACHING: Southern State Col, Springfield, SD, 1966–71; South Dakota State Univ, Brookings, SD, 1971–77; West Texas State Univ, Canyon, TX, 1977 to present

COLLECTIONS: Univ of New Mexico, Albuquerque, NM; Sioux City Art Center, IA; Univ of North Dakota, Grand Forks, ND; Paul Edwards Coll, Wichita Art Mus, KS; South Dakota Mem Art Center, Brookings, SD; Wichita State Univ, KS; Southern Graphics Council, States Boro, GA
GALLERIES: Miriam Pearlman Gallery, Chicago, IL; Clifford Gallery, Dallas, TX; William Campbell Contemporary Art, Fort Worth, TX
MAILING ADDRESS: 1104 Creekmere, Canyon, TX 79015

TITLE	PUBLISHER	PRINTER	DATE	MEDIUM	DIMENSION (PAPER SIZE) IN INCHES	TYPE OF PAPER	EDITION NUMBER	NO. OF COLORS	ORIGINAL OPENING PRICE	CURRENT RETAIL PRICE
CURRENT EDITIONS:										
Binary Splash	ART	ART	1984	MON	18 X 20 EA	AC	1 EA	5 EA	250 EA	300 EA
Compu Series #1	ART	ART	1984	MON	20 X 18 EA	AC	1 EA	5 EA	250 EA	300 EA
Green Pyramid	ART	ART	1985	MON	22 X 30 EA	AC	1 EA	5 EA	350 EA	400 EA

STEVEN LEE MAYES CONTINUED

TITLE	PUBLISHER	PRINTER	DATE	MEDIUM	DIMENSION (PAPER SIZE) IN INCHES	TYPE OF PAPER	EDITION NUMBER	NO. OF COLORS	ORIGINAL OPENING PRICE	CURRENT RETAIL PRICE
CURRENT EDITIONS:										
Azure Pyramid	ART	ART	1985	MON	22 X 30 EA	AC	1 EA	5 EA	350 EA	400 EA
Spotty Message	ART	ART	1985	MON	22 X 30 EA	AC	1 EA	5 EA	350 EA	400 EA
Message for Tut	ART	ART	1985	MON	22 X 30 EA	AC	1 EA	5 EA	350 EA	400 EA
Arabesque (Violet)	ART	ART	1985	MON	22 X 30 EA	AC	1 EA	5 EA	350 EA	400 EA
Nebkheperura	ART	ART	1985	MON	22 X 30 EA	AC	1 EA	5 EA	350 EA	400 EA
Subtle Message	ART	ART	1985	MON	22 X 30 EA	AC	1 EA	5 EA	350 EA	400 EA
Ruby Texas	ART	ART	1985	MON	20 X 26 EA	AC	1 EA	5 EA	350 EA	400 EA
Sealed Message	ART	ART	1985	MON	22 X 30 EA	AC	1 EA	5 EA	350 EA	400 EA
Black Flame Pyramid	ART	ART	1985	MON	22 X 30 EA	AC	1 EA	5 EA	350 EA	400 EA
Arabesque in Black & Tan	ART	ART	1985	MON	22 X 30 EA	AC	1 EA	5 EA	350 EA	400 EA
Spotted Incisor	ART	ART	1985	MON	22 X 30 EA	AC	1 EA	5 EA	350 EA	400 EA
Blue Grey Incisor	ART	ART	1985	MON	22 X 30 EA	AC	1 EA	5 EA	350 EA	400 EA
Tectonic Shift	ART	ART	1986	MON	22 X 30 EA	AC	1 EA	5 EA	350 EA	400 EA
Aquarian Edge	ART	ART	1986	MON	22 X 30 EA	AC	1 EA	5 EA	350 EA	400 EA

DOUGLAS MAZONOWICZ

BORN: Wiltshire, England
EDUCATION: Swindon Col of Art, London, England
TEACHING: Instr, Graphics, Farnham Col of Art, England, until 1960; Research Assoc, Carnegie Mus of Nat Hist, Pittsburgh, PA, 1968 to present
COLLECTIONS: British Mus, London, England; Cleveland Mus of Nat Hist, OH; Everson Mus of Art, Syracuse, NY; Ohio State Univ, OH; Field Mus of Nat Hist, Chicago, IL
PRINTERS: Artist (ART)
PUBLISHERS: Transworld Art, Inc, NY (TAI); Hammer Publishing, NY (HP)
GALLERIES: Hammer Galleries, New York, NY

TITLE	PUBLISHER	PRINTER	DATE	MEDIUM	DIMENSION (PAPER SIZE) IN INCHES	TYPE OF PAPER	EDITION NUMBER	NO. OF COLORS	ORIGINAL OPENING PRICE	CURRENT RETAIL PRICE
SOLD OUT EDITIONS (RARE):										
The Ant Eater	TAI	ART	1979	SP	23 X 29	GPP	275	6	300	350
The Contemplative Unicorn	TAI	ART	1979	SP	23 X 29	GPP	275	6	300	350
Dark Warrior	TAI	ART	1979	SP	29 X 23	GPP	275	6	300	350
Friendly Totems	TAI	ART	1979	SP	29 X 23	GPP	275	6	300	350
The Hand of Man (Set of 10):									2500 SET	3000 SET
Crouching Bison	HP	ART	1981	SP	18 X 24	R/100	300	8	250	300
Bowman & Deer	HP	ART	1981	SP	24 X 18	R/100	300	8	250	300
Prancing Horse	HP	ART	1981	SP	18 X 24	R/100	300	8	250	300
Giraffe, Timenzouzine	HP	ART	1981	SP	24 X 18	R/100	300	8	250	300
Hunter & Ibex	HP	ART	1981	SP	18 X 24	R/100	300	8	250	300
Head of a Horse, Tito	HP	ART	1981	SP	24 X 18	R/100	300	8	250	300
Group of Antelopes	HP	ART	1981	SP	18 X 24	R/100	300	8	250	300
Helmeted Warrior	HP	ART	1981	SP	24 X 18	R/100	300	8	250	300
Engraved Frieze	HP	ART	1981	SP	18 X 24	R/100	300	8	250	300
Two Figures in Finery	HP	ART	1981	SP	24 X 18	R/100	300	8	250	300

MICHAEL MAZUR

BORN: New York, NY; November 2, 1935
EDUCATION: Horace Mann Sch, NY; Amherst Col, MA, BA, 1958; Yale Univ Sch of Art, New Haven, CT BFA, 1959, MFA, 1961
TEACHING: Rhode Island Sch of Design, Providence, RI, 1961–64; Yale Univ, New Haven, CT, 1971; Brandeis Univ, Waltham, MA, 1965–76; Harvard Univ, Cambridge, MA, 1976–78
AWARDS: Louis Comfort Tiffany Grant, 1962; Nat Inst of Arts & Letters, NY, 1964; Guggenheim Found Fel, NY, 1965; Tamarind Lithography Grant, Albuquerque, NM, 1968
RECENT EXHIB: Rutgers Univ, Jane Zimmerli Art Mus, New Brunswick, NJ, 1987; Mus of Fine Arts, Boston, MA, 1987; Univ Art Gallery, Sonoma State Univ, Northridge, CA, 1987; Hooks-Epstein Gallery, Houston, TX, 1987; Macalester Col, St Paul, MN, 1988; Southern Alleghenies Mus of Art, Loretto, PA, 1988; Ian Turner Gallery, Los Angeles, CA, 1988; Barbara Krakow Gallery, Boston, MA 1987,88; Fawbush Gallery, NY, 1987,88; Fawbush Editions Gallery, NY, 1990; Mus of Fine Arts, Boston, MA, 1990

COLLECTIONS: Mus of Mod Art, NY; Whitney Mus of Am Art, NY; Fogg Mus, Harvard Univ, Cambridge, MA; Yale Univ, New Haven, CT; Philadelphia Mus, PA; Art Inst of Chicago, IL; Brooklyn Mus, NY; Nat Coll of Fine Arts, Wash, DC; Los Angeles County Mus, CA; Smith Col, Northamptom, MA; Library of Congress, Wash, DC
PRINTERS: Robert Townsend, Inc, Georgetown, MA (RT); Solo Press, NY (SP); Experimental Workshop, San Francisco, CA (EW); Artist (ART)
PUBLISHERS: Harcus Krakow Gallery, Boston, MA (HK); Pace Editions, NY (PE); Joe Fawbush Editions, NY (JFE); Solo Press, NY (SP); Associated American Artists, NY (AAA); Experimental Workshop, San Francisco, CA (EW); Mary Ryan Gallery, NY (MRG)
GALLERIES: Robert Miller Gallery, New York, NY; Pace Prints, New York, NY; Barbara Krakow Gallery, Boston, MA; Jane Haslem Gallery, Wash, DC; Barbara Mathes Gallery, New York, NY; John C Stroller & Co, Minneapolis, MN; Charles Foley Gallery, Columbus, OH; Jan Turner Gallery, Los Angeles, CA; Fawbush Editions, New York, NY; Solo Gallery, New York, NY; Experimental Workshop, San Francisco, CA; Martha Tepper Contemporary Fine Arts, West Newton, MA; Mary Ryan Gallery, New York, NY

The retail prices of the 100,000 limited edition prints quoted in this directory are subject to change. Print publishers, artists and galleries were the direct sources for these quotations. Prices in the secondary market listed as "Sold Out Editions (Rare)" indicate that the publisher has a limited supply of that print or that the print is difficult to locate in the galleries.

MICHAEL MAZUR CONTINUED

TITLE	PUBLISHER	PRINTER	DATE	MEDIUM	DIMENSION (PAPER SIZE) IN INCHES	TYPE OF PAPER	EDITION NUMBER	NO. OF COLORS	ORIGINAL OPENING PRICE	CURRENT RETAIL PRICE
SOLD OUT EDITIONS (RARE):										
The Confrontation	AAA	ART	1951	EC		AP	50		50	2000
Confrontation across Easel	AAA	ART	1951	EC		AP	50		50	2000
Composition with Floor	AAA	ART	1951	EC		AP	50		50	2000
Artist/Model/Container	AAA	ART	1951	EC		AP	50		50	2000
The Artist & the Model (Set of 12)	AAA	ART	1968	EB	23 X 24	AP	50		2000 SET	8000 SET
Amaryllis/Calla Lilly I,II,III	PE/HK	RT/ART	1982	E/HC	44 X 32 EA	AP	10 EA		750 EA	2000 EA
Cyclamen I,II,III	PE/HK	RT/ART	1982	E/HC	44 X 32 EA	AP	20 EA		675 EA	2000 EA
Simple Calla Lily (Black)	PE/HK	RT/ART	1982	E/HC	44 X 32	AP	20		675	2500
Simple Calla Lily (Gray)	PE/HK	RT/ART	1982	E/HC	44 X 32	AP	20		675	2500
Red Roller	PE/HK	RT/ART	1982	E/HC	44 X 32	AP	20		675	2500
Wakeby Night (3 Sheets)	JFE/SP	JS/SP	1984	LC/WC/CC/MON	30 X 20 EA	AP	25 EA	Multi	2000	6000 SET
CURRENT EDITIONS:										
Wakeby Island I,II	FE	JS/SP	1985	WC	25 X 20 EA	AP	15 EA		600 EA	850 EA
Wakeby Island (20 Examples)	FE	JS/SP	1986	LC/PAS	21 X 27 EA	AP	1 EA		1000 EA	1600 EA
Wakeby Rain	FE	JS/SP	1986	WC	31 X 51	AP	10		1000	1600
Wakeby Day (3 Sheets)	FE	JS/SP	1986	LC/WC/CC/MON	31 X 15 EA	AP	50 EA		2500 SET	5600 SET
Wakeby Sunflower	FE	JS/SP	1986	MON/PAS	35 X 40	AP	1 EA		2500	3500
Two Ideas about a Garden	MRG	RT	1990	EB/A/WC/CC	27 X 62	AP-ROL/KOZO	50	1	2200	2500

JAY DAVID McCAFFERTY

BORN: San Pedro, CA; February 21, 1948
EDUCATION: Los Angeles State Col, BA; Univ of California, Irvine CA, MFA
TEACHING: Vis Art, Lectr, World Campus Afloat, Chapman Col, Orange, CA, 1974; Claremont Col, Grad Sch of Art, CA, 1978; Vis Art, Lectr, Univ of California, Irvine, CA, 1980; Instr, Los Angeles Harbor Col, Wilmington, CA, 1976 to present
AWARDS: New Talent Award, Los Angeles County Mus of Art, CA, 1974; Nat Endowment for the Arts, Fel, 1976
RECENT EXHIB: Cirrus Editions Gallery, Los Angeles, CA, 1990
COLLECTIONS: Los Angeles County Mus of Art, CA; Long Beach Mus of Art, CA
PRINTERS: James Allen, Los Angeles, CA (JA); David Ordaz, Los Angeles, CA (DO); Cirrus Editions Workshop, Los Angeles, CA (CEW)
PUBLISHERS: Cirrus Editions, Los Angeles, CA (CE)
GALLERIES: Cirrus Editions Gallery, Ltd, Los Angeles, CA; Galerie Krebs, Bern, Switzerland; The Works Gallery, Long Beach, CA
MAILING ADDRESS: 1017 Beacon St, San Pedro, CA 90731

TITLE	PUBLISHER	PRINTER	DATE	MEDIUM	DIMENSION (PAPER SIZE) IN INCHES	TYPE OF PAPER	EDITION NUMBER	NO. OF COLORS	ORIGINAL OPENING PRICE	CURRENT RETAIL PRICE
CURRENT EDITIONS:										
Arm	CE	JA/CEW	1977	LC	23 X 30	AC	50	1	175	450
Rock	CE	JA/CEW	1977	LC	23 X 30	AC	50	1	175	450
#1 Alive	CE	JA/CEW	1977	WB/SP	11 X 11	AC	25	2	100	500
#2 Incidence	CE	JA/CEW	1977	WB/SP	11 X 11	AC	25	2	100	500
#3 Instinct	CE	JA/CEW	1977	WB/SP	11 X 11	AC	25	2	100	500
#4 Thusfar	CE	JA/CEW	1977	WB/SP	11 X 11	AC	25	2	100	500
Emerge I–V (Set of 5)	CE	DO/CEW	1980	WB/SP	27 X 27	AC	50	2	1000 SET	3250 SET
									250 EA	650 EA
Untitled (402c)	CE	CEW	1987	LC	30 X 40	AC	35		400	850

JAMES McCAIN

BORN: Omaha, NE; 1944
EDUCATION: Univ of Montana, Missoula, MT; San Francisco Art Inst, CA
PUBLISHERS: C G Rein Publishers, St Paul, MN (CGR)
GALLERIES: C G Rein Galleries, Scottsdale, AZ & Santa Fe, NM & Houston, TX & Minneapolis, MN; Jones Gallery, La Jolla, CA

TITLE	PUBLISHER	PRINTER	DATE	MEDIUM	DIMENSION (PAPER SIZE) IN INCHES	TYPE OF PAPER	EDITION NUMBER	NO. OF COLORS	ORIGINAL OPENING PRICE	CURRENT RETAIL PRICE
CURRENT EDITIONS:										
Hunter	CGR		1987	MULT	12 X 6 X 6	BRONZE	250		950	1000

ANN McCALL

BORN: Toronto, Canada; December 12, 1941
EDUCATION: McGill Univ, Montreal, Can, BA, 1964; Univ of Pittsburgh, PA, 1971–74; Concordia Univ, Montral, Can, BFA, 1978
TEACHING: Makerere Univ, Uganda, 1965
AWARDS: Purchase Award, Dawson Col, Montreal, Can, 1981; Merit Awards, Boston Printmakers, MA, 1977,83
COLLECTIONS: Winnipeg Mus, Can; Vancouver Mus, Can; Canada Council Art Bank, Ottawa, Can; Univ of McGill, Montreal, Can; Mus of Lodz, Poland; DeCordova Mus, Lincoln, MA
PUBLISHERS: Waddington & Schiell Galleries, Toronto, Can (WS)
PRINTERS: Les Ateliers de Serigraphie Remi Bildeau, La Prairie, Quebec, Can (LAS)
GALLERIES: Waddington & Schiell Gallery, Toronto, Canada; Galerie Waddington & Gorce, Montreal, Canada
MAILING ADDRESS: 509 Argyle Ave, Montreal, PQ, Canada H3Y 3B6

ANN McCALL CONTINUED

TITLE	PUBLISHER	PRINTER	DATE	MEDIUM	DIMENSION (PAPER SIZE) IN INCHES	TYPE OF PAPER	EDITION NUMBER	NO. OF COLORS	ORIGINAL OPENING PRICE	CURRENT RETAIL PRICE
CURRENT EDITIONS:										
Farm Landscape Series (Set of 5):									1000 SET	2000 SET
Farm Landscape I	WS	LAS	1986	SP	22 X 30	AP88	35	13	230	400
Farm Landscape II	WS	LAS	1986	SP	22 X 30	AP88	35	16	230	400
Farm Landscape III	WS	LAS	1986	SP	22 X 30	AP88	35	24	230	400
Farm Landscape IV	WS	LAS	1986	SP	22 X 30	AP88	35	13	230	400
Farm Landscape V	WS	LAS	1986	SP	22 X 30	AP88	35	20	230	400

RICK McCARTHY

BORN: Montreal, Quebec; September 20, 1941
EDUCATION: Ontario Col of Art, Toronto, Can, 1967–69
TEACHING: Ontario Col of Art, Toronto, Can
COLLECTIONS: Canada Council Bank, Ottawa, Can
PUBLISHERS: Sword Street Press, Limited (SSP)
GALLERIES: Bau-Xi Gallery, Toronto, Canada

TITLE	PUBLISHER	PRINTER	DATE	MEDIUM	DIMENSION (PAPER SIZE) IN INCHES	TYPE OF PAPER	EDITION NUMBER	NO. OF COLORS	ORIGINAL OPENING PRICE	CURRENT RETAIL PRICE
CURRENT EDITIONS:										
Becoming One with the Time/Space										
Continuum	SSP	SSP	1980	LC	38 X 29	HMP	38	9	375	650
Purgatorio	SSP	SSP	1980	LC	38 X 29	HMP	14	14	375	650
Inferno	SSP	SSP	1980	LC	38 X 29	HMP	14	14	375	650

ALLAN McCOLLUM

BORN: Los Angeles, CA; August 4, 1944
AWARDS: Nat Endowment for the Arts Fel, 1987,88,89,90
RECENT EXHIB: Whitney Mus of Am Art, NY, 1989; John Weber Gallery, NY, 1988,89; Studio Trisorio, Naples, Italy, 1989; Galerie Fahnemann, Berlin, Germany, 1990; Julian Preto Gallery, NY, 1987,88,89,90; Galerie Yvon Lambert, Paris, France, 1988,90
COLLECTIONS: Long Beach Mus of Art, CA
PRINTERS: Jane Aman, Los Angeles, CA (JA); Cirrus Editions Workshop, Los Angeles, CA (CEW)
PUBLISHERS: Cirrus Editions, Los Angeles, CA (CE)
GALLERIES: Cirrus Editions, Ltd, Los Angeles, CA; Douglas Drake Gallery, Kansas City, KS; Marian Goodman Gallery, New York, NY; Heath Gallery, Atlanta, GA; John Weber Gallery, New York, NY; Richard Kuhlenschmidt Gallery, Santa Monica, CA; Rhona Hoffman Gallery, Chicago, IL; Brooke Alexander, Inc, New York, NY
MAILING ADDRESS: c/o John Weber Gallery, 142 Greene St, New York, NY 10012

TITLE	PUBLISHER	PRINTER	DATE	MEDIUM	DIMENSION (PAPER SIZE) IN INCHES	TYPE OF PAPER	EDITION NUMBER	NO. OF COLORS	ORIGINAL OPENING PRICE	CURRENT RETAIL PRICE
CURRENT EDITIONS:										
Untitled (77c)	CE	JA/CEW	1974	SP	6 X 34	AP	50	15	100	500

BRUCE McCOMBS

BORN: Cleveland, OH; August 18, 1943
EDUCATION: Cleveland Inst of Art, BFA, Printmaking, 1966; Tulane Univ, New Orleans, LA, MFA, Printmaking, 1968
TEACHING: Instr, Drawing & Printmaking, Muskingum Col, New Concord, OH, 1968–69; Art In Res, North Arizona Univ, Flagstaff, AR, 1976; Art in Res, Arizona State Univ, Tempe, AR, 1976; Assoc Prof, Printmaking, Hope Col, Holland, MI, 1969 to present
AWARDS: Purchase, New Jersey State Mus, Trenton, NY, 1967; Purchase, Soc of Am Graphic Artists, NY, 1968; Am Acad of Arts & Letters, NY, 1970; Purchasee, Nat Print Exhib, Silvermine Guild, CT, 1975; Purchase, Nat Print Exhib, Dickinson State Col, ND, 1975
COLLECTIONS: Whitney Mus of Am Art, NY; Ohio State Univ, Columbus, OH; Philadelphia Mus of Art, PA; Fort Wayne Mus of Art, IN; Dartmouth Col, Hanover, NH; Mount Holyoke Col, South Hadley, MA; Madison Art Center, WI; Silvermine Guild, New Canaan, CT; DeCordova Mus, Lincoln, MA; Nat Coll, Wash, DC; Library of Congress, Wash, DC; Norfolk Mus of Arts & Sciences, VA; Minnesota Mus, Minneapolis, MN; Kalamazoo Art Inst, MI; Springfield Mus of Art, MO; Hackley Art Mus, Muskegon, MT; Illinois State Mus, Normal, IL; Hope Col, Holland, MI; Univ of Dallas, TX; Univ of Louisville, KY; Bridgewater State Col, MA; Erie Art Center, PA; City of Grand Rapids, MI; Joshua B Speed Mus, Louisville, KY; Bucknell Univ, PA; Muskingum Col, New Concord, OH; Univ of Minnesota, Minneapolis, MN; Ithaca Col Mus, NY; New York State Univ, Potsdam, NY; St Lawrence Univ, NY; Muncie Art Assoc, IN; Auburn Univ, AL; Calvin Col, Grand Rapids, MI; Trenton State Univ, NJ; Arkansas Arts Center, Little Rock, AR; Arbrecht Art Mus, MO; Miami Art Center, FL; Grand Rapids Art Mus, MI; St Paul Art Center, MN; Massillion Mus, OH; New Jersey State Mus, Trenton, NJ; Masur Mus of Art, Monroe, LA; Bradley Univ, Peoria, IL; Univ of Georgia, Athens, GA; Wheaton Col. IL; Univ of Tennessee, Chattanooga, TN; Dulin Gallery of Art, TN; Anderson Art Center, IN; East Carolina Univ, Greenville, NC; Bowdoin Col, Brunswick, ME; Baldwin-Wallace Col, Berea, OH; Mercyhurst Col, Erie, PA; Purdue Univ, Hammond, IN; Univ of North Dakota, Grand Forks, ND; Western Illinois Univ, Macomb, IL; St John's Univ, Collegeville, MN; Silvermine Guild of Artists, CT; Peoria Art Guild, IL
PRINTERS: Artist (ART)
PUBLISHERS: Flanagan Graphics, Linwood, NJ (FG)
GALLERIES: Associated American Artists, New York, NY; Newman Galleries, Phila, PA & Bryn Mawr, PA; JRS Gallery, Providence, RI; Langman Gallery, Willow Grove, PA; Bergsma Gallery, Grand Rapids, MI; Xochipilli Art Gallery, Birmingham, MI; Central Square Gallery, Linwood, NJ

The print market has become very selective. For the first time since we published the first edition of The Printworld Directory in 1982, the prices of prints have been greatly reduced and greatly increased for the same artists by the most reputable and established print publishers. Check the fifth edition to understand the movement.

BRUCE McCOMBS CONTINUED

TITLE	PUBLISHER	PRINTER	DATE	MEDIUM	DIMENSION (PAPER SIZE) IN INCHES	TYPE OF PAPER	EDITION NUMBER	NO. OF COLORS	ORIGINAL OPENING PRICE	CURRENT RETAIL PRICE
SOLD OUT EDITIONS (RARE):										
Street Corner	FG	ART	1975	EB	27 X 39	R/BFK	200	1	125	1500
Five after Four	FG	ART	1976	EB	27 X 39	R/BFK	200	1	125	1500
Galveston Flyer	FG	ART	1977	EB	27 X 39	R/BFK	200	1	125	1500
New Concord Volunteers, 1896	FG	ART	1977	EB	25 X 31	R/BFK	200	1	150	1000
Gulliver's Packard	FG	ART	1978	EB	27 X 39	R/BFK	200	1	175	1500
Winslow and Emporia	FG	ART	1978	EB	27 X 39	R/BFK	200	1	200	750
Audubon Place	FG	ART	1978	EB	25 X 31	R/BFK	200	1	175	500
Coast to Coast	FG	ART	1979	EB	21 X 27	R/BFK	200	1	125	1000
Good Vibrations	FG	ART	1979	EB	27 X 39	R/BFK	200	1	200	1000
Airline Diner	FG	ART	1979	EB	25 X 31	R/BFK	200	1	175	1000
20th Century Limited	FG	ART	1982	EB	25 X 31	R/BFK	200	1	200	1200
CURRENT EDITIONS:										
Hollywood	FG	ART	1977	EB	2 X 3	R/BFK	200	1	200	750
Pause that Refreshes	FG	ART	1977	EB	21 X 27	R/BFK	200	1	125	375
August 18th, 1909	FG	ART	1977	EB	25 X 31	R/BFK	200	1	175	350
1907–1977	FG	ART	1977	EB	39 X 27	R/BFK	200	1	175	325
Rice's Drugs	FG	ART	1977	EB	27 X 39	R/BFK	200	1	200	450
White Tower Time	FG	ART	1977	EB	25 X 31	R/BFK	200	1	175	400
BM's Flying Circus	FG	ART	1978	EB	27 X 21	R/BFK	200	1	125	325
Billboard	FG	ART	1978	EB	31 X 25	R/BFK	200	1	175	375
Endurance	FG	ART	1978	EB	21 X 27	R/BFK	200	1	125	300
Lilliput Lunch	FG	ART	1979	EB	25 X 31	R/BFK	200	1	200	375
Paradise	FG	ART	1979	EB	25 X 31	R/BFK	200	1	225	375
Great Disaster Game	FG	ART	1980	EB	27 X 39	R/BFK	200	1	250	400
Skyscraper	FG	ART	1980	EB	31 X 25	R/BFK	200	1	200	375
Stainless Steel	FG	ART	1980	EB	17 X 25	R/BFK	200	1	150	250
White Tower II	FG	ART	1981	EB	25 X 31	R/BFK	200	1	200	400
Dryer Home	FG	ART	1981	EB	25 X 31	R/BFK	200	1	225	375
Metropolis	FG	ART	1981	EB	21 DIA	R/BFK	200	1	200	375
Night Flight	FG	ART	1981	EB	31 X 25	R/BFK	200	1	225	375
Night Tower	FG	ART	1981	EB	25 X 31	R/BFK	200	1	225	375
Real Steel	FG	ART	1981	EB	25 X 31	R/BFK	200	1	225	375
Skytrain	FG	ART	1981	EB	25 X 31	R/BFK	200	1	200	375
Marathon	FG	ART	1981	EB	25 X 31	R/BFK	200	1	200	375
Barnstorming	FG	ART	1981	EB	21 X 31	R/BFK	200	1	250	300
Bob's Happy Landing	FG	ART	1981	EB	26 X 31	R/BFK	200	1	200	375
Unfinished City	FG	ART	1981	EB	25 X 31	R/BFK	200	1	225	375
Last American Pinballs	FG	ART	1982	EB	25 X 31	R/BFK	200	1	200	400
Neon Time	FG	ART	1982	EB	25 X 31	R/BFK	200	1	225	375
Uptown	FG	ART	1982	EB	25 X 31	R/BFK	200	1	225	375
Art Deco Showroom	FG	ART	1982	EB	25 X 31	R/BFK	200	1	250	375
Brownstone	FG	ART	1982	EB	25 X 31	R/BFK	200	1	250	375
Airplane Works	FG	ART	1983	EB	25 X 31	R/BFK	200	1	250	375
Airstreams	FG	ART	1983	EB	25 X 31	R/BFK	200	1	250	375
Big Sleep	FG	ART	1983	EB	31 X 25	R/BFK	200	1	250	375
Lorain, Carnegie Bridge	FG	ART	1983	EB	25 X 31	R/BFK	200	1	225	375
Arcade	FG	ART	1984	EB	25 X 31	R/BFK	200	1	250	375
Joan Crawford's Bedroom	FG	ART	1984	EB	25 X 31	R/BFK	200	1	225	375
Movie Palace	FG	ART	1984	EB	25 X 31	R/BFK	200	1	225	375
Parade	FG	ART	1984	EB	31 X 25	R/BFK	200	1	225	375
Penthouse Showroom	FG	ART	1984	EB	25 X 31	R/BFK	200	1	225	375
Big Bucks	FG	ART	1985	EC	20 X 39	R/BFK	200	3	325	400
Ghost Car	FG	ART	1985	EB	25 X 31	R/BFK	200	1	275	375
Newsstand	FG	ART	1985	EB	25 X 31	R/BFK	200	1	225	400
Reflections	FG	ART	1985	EB	31 X 25	R/BFK	200	1	250	375
Sunbather	FG	ART	1985	EB	25 X 31	R/BFK	200	1	375	375
Gulliver's Lincoln	FG	ART	1986	EB	25 X 31	R/BFK	200	1	375	375
Bullitt	FG	ART	1986	EB	31 X 25	R/BFK	200	1	375	375
Intersection	FG	ART	1986	EB	15 X 39	R/BFK	200	1	325	325
American Icon	FG	ART	1986	EB	31 X 25	R/BFK	200	1	375	375
American Streamline	FG	ART	1986	EB	25 X 31	R/BFK	200	1	375	375
Anatomical Car	FG	ART	1986	EB	25 X 31	R/BFK	200	1	375	375
Arched Bridge	FG	ART	1986	EB	25 X 31	R/BFK	200	1	375	375
Beaux Arts Tower	FG	ART	1986	EB	25 X 31	R/BFK	200	1	375	375
Cadillac	FG	ART	1986	EB	25 X 31	R/BFK	200	1	375	375
Campus Drive-In	FG	ART	1986	EB	25 X 31	R/BFK	200	1	375	375
Club Car	FG	ART	1986	EB	25 X 31	R/BFK	200	1	375	375
Dashboard Clocks	FG	ART	1986	EB	25 X 31	R/BFK	200	1	375	375
Diner	FG	ART	1986	EB	25 X 31	R/BFK	200	1	375	375
Dream Room	FG	ART	1986	EB	25 X 31	R/BFK	200	1	375	375
Fossils	FG	ART	1986	EB	25 X 31	R/BFK	200	1	375	375
Greetings from Motor City	FG	ART	1986	EB	25 X 31	R/BFK	200	1	350	350

BRUCE McCOMBS CONTINUED

TITLE	PUBLISHER	PRINTER	DATE	MEDIUM	DIMENSION (PAPER SIZE) IN INCHES	TYPE OF PAPER	EDITION NUMBER	NO. OF COLORS	ORIGINAL OPENING PRICE	CURRENT RETAIL PRICE
CURRENT EDITIONS:										
Making of King Kong	FG	ART	1986	EB	25 X 31	R/BFK	200	1	375	375
Open City	FG	ART	1986	EB	31 X 25	R/BFK	200	1	375	375
Parkway	FG	ART	1986	EB	27 X 39	R/BFK	200	1	375	400
Self Portrait	FG	ART	1986	EB	25 X 31	R/BFK	200	1	375	375
Thriller	FG	ART	1986	EB	25 X 31	R/BFK	200	1	375	375
Hollywood Mirror	FG	ART	1988	EB	25 X 31	R/BFK	200	1	375	375
Parkway	FG	ART	1988	EB	27 X 39	R/BFK	200	1	400	400
Arch Bridge	FG	ART	1989	EB	25 X 31	R/BFK	200	1	375	375
Car Museum	FG	ART	1990	EB	25 X 31	R/BFK	200	1	375	375
Cathedral	FG	ART	1990	EB	27 X 39	R/BFK	200	1	400	400
Choo Choo Grill	FG	ART	1990	EB	25 X 31	R/BFK	200	1	375	375
Deep Space Traffic	FG	ART	1990	EB	25 X 31	R/BFK	200	1	375	375
Reo	FG	ART	1990	EB	25 X 31	R/BFK	200	1	375	375
Ocean Express	FG	ART	1991	EB	25 X 31	R/BFK	200	1	375	375
Wing Walker	FG	ART	1991	EB	25 X 31	R/BFK	200	1	375	375

HARRY McCORMICK

BORN: New Jersey, June 12, 1942
EDUCATION: Pratt Inst, Brooklyn, NY
COLLECTIONS: Brooklyn Mus, NY; Newark Mus, NJ; Vatican Coll, Rome, Italy; Univ of Southern Illinois, Carbondale, IL; Canton Art Inst, OH; Univ of Wyoming, Laramie, WY; St Lawrence Univ, Canton, NY
PRINTERS: Chromacomp Inc, NY (CI); Artist (ART)
PUBLISHERS: Brewster Editions, NY (BE); Circle Fine Art, Chicago, IL (CFA)
GALLERIES: Brewster Gallery, New York, NY; Merrill Chase Galleries, Chicago, IL; JRS Fine Art, Providence, RI; Loring Art Gallery, Cedarhurst, NY; Circle Galleries, San Diego, CA & San Francisco, CA & Northbrook, IL & Pittsburgh, PA & Houston, TX & Soho, NY & Chicago, IL & Scottsdale, AZ & Beverly Hills, CA & Costa Mesa, CA & Sherman Oaks, CA & Palm Beach, FL & Honolulu, HI & New Orleans, LA & Las Vegas, NV & Seattle, WA

TITLE	PUBLISHER	PRINTER	DATE	MEDIUM	DIMENSION (PAPER SIZE) IN INCHES	TYPE OF PAPER	EDITION NUMBER	NO. OF COLORS	ORIGINAL OPENING PRICE	CURRENT RETAIL PRICE
CURRENT EDITIONS:										
Flower Market	BE	CI	1979	SP	23 X 36	L/100	200	32	300	650
Empire Diner	BE	ART	1980	SP	24 X 32	ST	250	30	200	650
Nirvana	BE	ART	1980	SP	24 X 32	ST	250	32	200	650
Russian Tea Room	BE	ART	1980	SP	24 X 36	ST	250	35	200	750
Harvey's Chelsea Restaurant	BE	ART	1980	SP	24 X 32	ST	250	32	200	750
McSorely's Ale House	BE	ART	1981	SP	24 X 38	L/100	250	36	250	750
Paloma	BE	ART	1981	SP	24 X 38	L/100	250	35	300	750
Irish Mist	BE	ART	1981	SP	35 X 24	L/100	250	35	200	650
La Cabana	BE	ART	1982	SP	24 X 31	L/100	250	34	300	650
The Chinese Screen	BE	ART	1982	SP	24 X 26	L/100	250	32	300	650
Landmark Tavern	CFA	ART	1988	LC	26 X 31	AP	300		500	650

ANN McCOY

BORN: Boulder, Colorado; July 8, 1946
EDUCATION: Univ of Colorado, Boulder, CO, BFA, 1969; Univ of California, Los Angeles, CA, 1972
AWARDS: Contemp Arts Council, New Talent Award, Los Angeles County Mus, CA, 1972; Norman Wait Harris Award, Art Inst of Chicago, IL, 1974; Berliner Kunstlerprogramm, 1977; Prix de Rome, Italy, 1989–90; AVA Award, 1989–90
RECENT EXHIB: Arnold Herstand & Company, NY, 1990
COLLECTIONS: Mus of Mod Art, NY; Whitney Mus of Am Art, NY; Art Inst of Chicago, IL; Los Angeles County Art Mus, CA; Mus of Fine Arts, Houston, TX; Nat Gallery of Australia, Canberra, Australia; Allen Mem Art Mus, Oberlin, OH; Sara Roby Foundation, NY; Powis Art Gallery, Australia
PRINTERS: Bud Shark, Boulder, CO (BS); Shark's Lithography Ltd, Boulder, CO (SLL)
PUBLISHERS: Brooke Alexander, Inc, NY (BAI); Prestige Art, Ltd, Mamaroneck, NY (PA)
GALLERIES: Brooke Alexander, Inc, New York, NY; Margo Leavin Gallery, Los Angeles, CA; Jayne H Baum Gallery, New York, NY; Ruth Bachofner Gallery, Los Angles, CA; Sherry French Gallery, New York, NY; ACA Contemporary Gallery, New York, NY; Arnold Herstand & Company, New York, NY; Eugene Binder Gallery, Dallas, TX; Somerville Manning Gallery, Greenville, DE
MAILING ADDRESS: P O Box 1491, Stuyvesant Station, New York, NY 10009

TITLE	PUBLISHER	PRINTER	DATE	MEDIUM	DIMENSION (PAPER SIZE) IN INCHES	TYPE OF PAPER	EDITION NUMBER	NO. OF COLORS	ORIGINAL OPENING PRICE	CURRENT RETAIL PRICE
SOLD OUT EDITIONS (RARE):										
Cuttlefish: De Secretis Naturae	BAI	BS/SLL	1978	LC	42 X 30	AP	15		1800	2500
Cuttlefish: De Secretis Naturae	BAI	BS/SLL	1978	LC/HC	42 X 30	AP	35		2400	3500
The Night Sea (Dipt)	BAI	BS/SLL	1978	LC	65 X 35	AP	20	1		2500
The Night Sea (Dipt)	BAI	BS/SLL	1978	LC/HC	65 X 34	AP	30	1	1500	3500
Sea Serpents: Tractulus Aristolis (Trip)	BAI	BS/SLL	1978	LC	30 X 35	AP	20	1	1500	1800
Sea Serpents: Tractulus Artistolis (Trip)	BAI	BS/SLL	1978	LC/HC	30 X 42	AP	30	1	1800	2500

ANN McCOY CONTINUED

TITLE	PUBLISHER	PRINTER	DATE	MEDIUM	DIMENSION (PAPER SIZE) IN INCHES	TYPE OF PAPER	EDITION NUMBER	NO. OF COLORS	ORIGINAL OPENING PRICE	CURRENT RETAIL PRICE
SOLD OUT EDITIONS (RARE):										
Jelly Fish	BAI	BS/SLL	1978	LC/HC	42 X 30	AP	15		600	1500
Spotted Ray I	BAI	BS/SLL	1978	LC/HC	42 X 30	AP	25		600	1800
Spotted Ray II	BAI	BS/SLL	1979	LC/HC	42 X 29	AP	25		750	1500
Night Iguanas	BAI	BS/SLL	1979	LC/HC	29 X 42	AP	25		750	900
Sea Jellies	BAI	BS/SLL	1979	LC/HC	27 X 37	AP	15		750	900
Sharks	BAI	BS/SLL	1979	LC/HC	42 X 29	AP	25		750	1500
CURRENT EDITIONS:										
Meduse	BAI	BS/SLL	1978	LC/HC	30 X 22	AP	30		600	1200
Seven Planets for Michael Maier (7 Shades of Blue):										
State II	BAI	BS/SLL	1978	LC/HC	35 X 47	AC	7		600	900
State III	BAI	BS/SLL	1978	LC/HC	35 X 47	AC	7		600	900
State IV	BAI	BS/SLL	1978	LC/HC	35 X 47	AC	10		600	900
State V	BAI	BS/SLL	1978	LC/HC	35 X 47	AC	7		600	900
State VI	BAI	BS/SLL	1978	LC/HC	35 X 47	AC	6		600	900
State VII	BAI	BS/SLL	1978	LC/HC	35 X 47	AC	4		600	900
State VIII	BAI	BS/SLL	1978	LC/HC	35 X 47	AC	1		600	900
Untitled	BAI	BS/SLL	1978	LC/OFF	23 X 31	AC	75		125	200
Serpens II	BAI	BS/SLL	1979	LC/OFF	21 X 28	AC	90		125	200
Serpens III	BAI	BS/SLL	1979	LC/HC	21 X 29	AC	20		300	300
The Underworld, State I (Dipt)	PA	BS/SLL	1980	LC/HC	42 X 30	AC	100		900	1200
The Underworld, State II (Dipt)	PA	BS/SLL	1980	LC/HC	41 X 30	AC	100		900	1200

MARK MCDOWELL

BORN: PA; 1954
EDUCATION: Pennsylvania State Univ, University Park, BFA, 1976; Arizona State Univ, Tempe, AZ

PRINTERS: Melissa Katzman Braggins, Albuquerque, NM (MKB); William Haberman, Albuquerque, NM (WH); Tamarind Inst, Albuquerque, NM
PUBLISHERS: Tamarind Inst, Albuquerque, NM (TI)
GALLERIES: Udinotti Gallery, San Francisco, CA; Santa Fe East Gallery, NM; Tamarind Institute, Albuquerque, NM; Elaine Horwitch Galleries, Scottsdale, AZ

TITLE	PUBLISHER	PRINTER	DATE	MEDIUM	DIMENSION (PAPER SIZE) IN INCHES	TYPE OF PAPER	EDITION NUMBER	NO. OF COLORS	ORIGINAL OPENING PRICE	CURRENT RETAIL PRICE
CURRENT EDITIONS:										
Political Speech Yakkitty-Yak-Yakkitty-Yak	TI	MKB/TI	1982	LC	24 X 18	CD	30	6	200	450
Stereo Pyramids in the Land of Enchantment	TI	WH/TI	1982	LC/CO	18 X 24	GE	10	8	250	600

JAMES McGARRELL

BORN: Indianapolis, IN; February 22, 1930
EDUCATION: Indiana Univ, Bloomington, IN, BA, 1953; Skowhegan Sch of Painting, ME, 1953; Univ of California, Los Angeles, CA, MA, 1955; Fulbright Fel, Stuttgart Acad of Fine Arts, Germany, 1956
TEACHING: Reed Col, Portland, OR, 1956–59; Indiana Univ, Bloomington, IN, 1959–80; Washington Univ, St Louise, MO, 1981 to present
AWARDS: Fulbright Fel, 1956; Nat Inst of Arts & Letters Grant, 1963; Guggenheim Found Fel, NY, 1964; Nat Endowment for the Arts Fels, 1966,85
RECENT EXHIB: Miami-Dade Com Col, Wolfson Campus, Frances Wolfson Art Gallery, Miami, Fl, 1989; Eastern Illinois Univ, Tarble Arts Center, Charleston, IL, 1992
COLLECTIONS: Whitney Mus of Am Art, NY; Mus of Mod Art, NY; Mus of Mod Art, Paris, France; Mus Hambourg, Germany; Hirshhorn Mus, Wash, DC; Univ of Bridgeport, CT; Centre Georges Pompidou, Paris, France

PRINTERS: Landfall Press Inc, Chicago, IL (LP); Jack Lemon, Chicago, IL (JL); Washington Univ Printmaking Workshop, St Louis, MO (WUPW); Peregrine Press, Dallas, TX (PerP); David Calkins, Bloomington, IN (DC); David Keister, Bloomington, IN (DK); Echo Press, Bloomington, IN (EPr); S Britko, Albuquerque, NM (SB); Tamarind Inst, Albuquerque, NM (TI)
PUBLISHERS: Quincy Arts Club, IL (QAC); Washington Univ Printmaking Workshop, St Louis MO (WUPW); Peregrine Press, Dallas, TX (PerP); Artist (ART); Echo Press, Bloomington, IN (EPr); Tamarind Inst, Albuquerque, NM (TI)
GALLERIES: Frumkin/Adams, Gallery, New York, NY; Galerie Claude Bernard, Paris, France; Yares Gallery, Scottsdale AZ; Signet Arts, St Louis, MO; Graphics Gallery, San Francisco, CA; Struve Gallery, Chicago, IL; Peregrine Press, Dallas, TX; Galerie Simonne Stern, New Orleans, LA & Atlanta, GA; Jane Haslem Gallery, Wash, DC; Gagosian Gallery, New York, NY; More Gallery, Phila, PA; Printworks Gallery, Chicago, IL; William Shearburn Fine Art, St Louis, MO
MAILING ADDRESS: c/o School of Fine Arts, P O Box 1031, Washington Univ, St Louis, MO 63130

TITLE	PUBLISHER	PRINTER	DATE	MEDIUM	DIMENSION (PAPER SIZE) IN INCHES	TYPE OF PAPER	EDITION NUMBER	NO. OF COLORS	ORIGINAL OPENING PRICE	CURRENT RETAIL PRICE
SOLD OUT EDITIONS (RARE):										
Quincy Inventions, I–VI (Set of 6)	QAC	JL/LPI	1970	LC	22 X 30 EA	AP/WK	40 EA	4 EA	200 EA	1000 EA
Quotation with Twister	TI	SB/TI	1977	LC	76 X 56 cm	AP/B		4	300	800
Bianca & Blacky (Four Panels)	EPr	DK/DC/EPr	1980	LB	30 X 74	R/BFK/G	30	1	800	1500
Spring Pull	ART/WUPW	DG/WUPW	1983	AB	22 X 30	AC	35	1	200	800
CURRENT EDITIONS:										
Mixed Media	EPr	DK/DC/EPr	1988	MM	30 X 40 EA	R/BFK	1 EA		3000 EA	4000 EA
Coffee	EPr	DK/DC/EPr	1988	MM	30 X 40 EA	R/BFK	1 EA		3000 EA	4000 EA

JAMES McGARRELL CONTINUED

TITLE	PUBLISHER	PRINTER	DATE	MEDIUM	DIMENSION (PAPER SIZE) IN INCHES	TYPE OF PAPER	EDITION NUMBER	NO. OF COLORS	ORIGINAL OPENING PRICE	CURRENT RETAIL PRICE
CURRENT EDITIONS:										
Carver Mountain	EPr	DK/DC/EPr	1987	MON/HC	31 X 41 EA	JK/HMP	1 EA	4 EA	3000 EA	4000 EA
Oxen Flood	EPr	DK/DC/EPr	1987	MON/HC	31 X 41 EA	JK/HMP	1 EA	4 EA	3000 EA	4000 EA
Pergola	EPr	DK/DC/EPr	1987	MON/HC	31 X 41 EA	JK/HMP	1 EA	4 EA	3000 EA	4000 EA
Devil Dancing	EPr	DK/DC/EPr	1990	MON/HC	31 X 41 EA	JK/HMP	1 EA	4 EA	3500 EA	4000 EA
Dunes, Waves & Dark Rider	EPr	DK/DC/EPr	1990	MON/HC	31 X 41 EA	JK/HMP	1 EA	4 EA	3500 EA	4000 EA
Slow Drag	EPr	DK/DC/EPr	1990	MON/HC	31 X 41 EA	JK/HMP	1 EA	4 EA	3500 EA	4000 EA
Waves	EPr	DK/DC/EPr	1990	MON/HC	31 X 41 EA	JK/HMP	1 EA	4 EA	3500 EA	4000 EA
Red Diver	EPr	DK/DC/EPr	1990	MON/HC	29 X 42 EA	LANA/W	1 EA	4 EA	3500 EA	4000 EA
Band Shell	EPr	DK/DC/EPr	1990	MON/HC	29 X 42 EA	LANA/W	1 EA	4 EA	3500 EA	4000 EA
Women at Poolside	EPr	DK/DC/EPr	1992	MON/HC	29 X 42 EA	LANA/W	1 EA	4 EA	4000 EA	4000 EA
Women at Poolside Shadow	EPr	DK/DC/EPr	1992	MON/HC	29 X 42 EA	LANA/W	1 EA	4 EA	4000 EA	4000 EA
Pondlight	EPr	DK/DC/EPr	1992	MON/HC	29 X 42 EA	LANA/W	1 EA	4 EA	4000 EA	4000 EA
Pondlight Shadow	EPr	DK/DC/EPr	1992	MON/HC	29 X 42 EA	LANA/W	1 EA	4 EA	4000 EA	4000 EA
Redboat Diver	EPr	DK/DC/EPr	1992	MON/HC	29 X 42 EA	LANA/W	1 EA	4 EA	4000 EA	4000 EA
Redboat Diver Shadow	EPr	DK/DC/EPr	1992	MON/HC	29 X 42 EA	LANA/W	1 EA	4 EA	4000 EA	4000 EA

DELOSS MCGRAW

BORN: Okewah, OK; 1945
EDUCATION: California State Univ, Long Beach, CA, BA, 1969; Cranbrook Acad of Art, MI, MFA, 1972
RECENT EXHIB: Santa Clara Univ, De Saisset Mus, CA, 1992; Linda Moore Gallery, San Diego, CA, 1992
COLLECTIONS: Wichita State Univ, KS; Honolulu Acad of Art, HI; Cranbrook Acad of Art, MI
PRINTERS: Russell Craig, Albuquerque, NM (RC); Brian Haberman, Albuquerque, NM (BH); Tom Pruitt, Albuquerque, NM (TP); Tamarind Inst, Albuquerque, NM (TI)
PUBLISHERS: Tamarind Inst, Albuquerque, NM (TI)
GALLERIES Lizardi/Harp Gallery, Pasadena, CA; Harcourts Contemporary, San Francisco, CA; Alias Studio Gallery, Atlanta, GA; Robert Kidd Gallery, Birmingham, MI; Giannetta Gallery, Wynnewood, PA; Tamarind Institute, Albuquerque, NM; Bentley-Tomlinson Gallery, Scottsdale, AZ; Annex Gallery, Linda Moore Galllery, San Diego, CA; DeSoto Workshop, San Francisco, CA; Haines Gallery, San Francisco, CA

Deloss McGraw
The Poet Detects the
Nothingness of Mr. Evil
Courtesy Tamarind Institute

TITLE	PUBLISHER	PRINTER	DATE	MEDIUM	DIMENSION (PAPER SIZE) IN INCHES	TYPE OF PAPER	EDITION NUMBER	NO. OF COLORS	ORIGINAL OPENING PRICE	CURRENT RETAIL PRICE
CURRENT EDITIONS:										
W D Snodgrass Winged in Color Reflects on the Village	TI	RC/TI	1985	LC/HC	30 X 22	AP/BL	30	7	300	400
The Poet Wears a Hat of Color	TI	BH/TI	1985	LC/HC	30 X 22	AP/BL	30	4	300	400
The Poet Detects the Nothingness of Mr Evil	TI	TP/TI	1985	LC/HC	22 X 30	AP/B	30	6	300	400

WILLIAM WIND McKIM

BORN: Independence, MO; May 13, 1916
EDUCATION: Kansas City Art Inst, MO, with Thomas Hart Benton
TEACHING: Instr, Drawing, Kansas City Art Inst, MO, 1945– 48, Instr, Lithography, 1948–58, Prof, Lithography, 1958–86
AWARDS: D M Lighton Award, Midwestern Annual, Kansas City, MO, 1940

COLLECTIONS: William Rockhill Nelson Gallery, Kansas City Art Inst, MO
PRINTERS: Landfall Press, Inc, Chicago, IL (LPI); Jerry Raidiger, Chicago, IL (JR)
PUBLISHERS: Landfall Press, Inc, Chicago, IL (LPI)
GALLERIES: Landfall Press, Inc, Chicago, IL
MAILING ADDRESS: 8704 E 32nd St, Kansas City, MO 64129

TITLE	PUBLISHER	PRINTER	DATE	MEDIUM	DIMENSION (PAPER SIZE) IN INCHES	TYPE OF PAPER	EDITION NUMBER	NO. OF COLORS	ORIGINAL OPENING PRICE	CURRENT RETAIL PRICE
SOLD OUT EDITIONS (RARE):										
Danae	LPI	JR/LPI	1972	LC	22 X 28	ARJ	35	5	100	500

THOMAS MCKNIGHT

BORN: Lawrence, KS; 1941
EDUCATION: Wesleyan Univ, Middleton, CT, BA; Columbia Univ, NY, Art History
COLLECTIONS: Metropolitan Mus of Art, NY
PRINTERS: ChromaComp, Inc, NY (CCI); Willco Fine Art, Ltd, Brooklyn, NY (WFA); HMK Fine Arts, Ltd, NY (HMK)
PUBLISHERS: Chalk & Vermilion Fine Arts, Greenwich, CT (CVFA)
GALLERIES: Hanson Galleries, Beverly Hills, CA & Carmel, CA & San Francisco, CA & New Orleans, LA; Swahn Fine Arts, San Diego, CA; Greene Art Gallery, Guilford, CT; Petrini Art Gallery, Rocky Hill, CT; Georgetown Fine Art, Wash, DC; Art Collectors Gallery, Gainesville, FL; P C Hart Gallery, Jupiter, FL; Nuance Gallery, Tampa, FL; Greggie Fine Art, Atlanta, GA; Highland Gallery, Inc, Atlanta, GA; Art Brokerage, Ketchum, ID; Fernette's Gallery of Art, Des Moines, IA; Rolly-Micheau Galleries, Boston, MA; J Todd Galleries, Wellesley, MA; Short Hills Art Gallery, Short Hills, NJ; Artists Showcase International, Hartsdale, NY; Art Gallery, Studio 53, New York, NY; Jeffrey Ruesch Fine Art, Ltd, New York, NY; Landing Gallery of Woodbury, Inc, Woodbury, NY; Emporium Enterprises, Inc, Dallas, TX; American Art, Tacoma, WA; Fisher Island Gallery, Fisher Island, FL; Atlas Galleries, Inc, Chicago, IL; Allyson Louis Gallery, Bethesda, MD; Print Gallery, Southfield, MI; Central Galleries/JB Fine Arts, Inc, Lawrence, NY; Gallery 121 International, New York, NY; Post Gallery, Houston, TX; Professional Fine Arts Services, Inc, New York, NY

Thomas McKnight
Solitair
Courtesy Chalk & Vermilion Fine Arts

TITLE	PUBLISHER	PRINTER	DATE	MEDIUM	DIMENSION (PAPER SIZE) IN INCHES	TYPE OF PAPER	EDITION NUMBER	NO. OF COLORS	ORIGINAL OPENING PRICE	CURRENT RETAIL PRICE
CURRENT EDITIONS:										
Central Park I	CVFA	HMK	1980	SP	30 X 32	AP/W	352	29	275	1400
Central Park II	CVFA	HMK	1980	SP	30 X 35	AP/W	352	29	275	1000
Hunters	CVFA	HMK	1980	SP	29 X 35	AP/W	402		275	1400
Brooklyn Bridge I	CVFA	HMK	1980	SP	39 X 29	AP/W	352	28	275	1000
Schlossremseck	CVFA	HMK	1980	SP	29 X 38	AP/W	354		275	1000
Hour of the Wolf	CVFA	HMK	1980	SP	29 X 31	AP/W	354		275	1000
Citadel	CVFA	HMK	1980	SP	29 X 31	AP/W	354		275	1000
Breakfast Room	CVFA	HMK	1980	SP	29 X 31	AP/W	354		275	1750
Manhattan Interior	CVFA	HMK	1980	SP	29 X 33	AP/W	354		275	1400
Barbados Suite (Set of 2):										2250 SET
Montego Bay	CVFA	HMK	1980	SP	29 X 31	AP/W	354		275	1400
Irish Castle	CVFA	HMK	1981	SP	29 X 31	AP/W	354		275	1400
Bennington Room	CVFA	HMK	1981	SP	29 X 31	AP/B	354		425	5250
Brooklyn Bridge II	CVFA	HMK	1981	SP	29 X 32	AP/W	354		275	1600
The Seine	CVFA	HMK	1981	SP	29 X 34	AP/W	354		275	1000
Hammersmith Farms	CVFA	HMK	1981	SP	29 X 34	AP/W	354		275	1200
Manhattan Ballet	CVFA	HMK	1981	SP	29 X 29	AP/W	354		375	1400
Red Room (Beekman Place)	CVFA	HMK	1981	SP	29 X 31	AP/W	354		375	2750
Pans Oak	CVFA	HMK	1981	SP	29 X 31	AP/W	354		375	1000
Nantucket	CVFA	HMK	1981	SP	29 X 29	AP/W	354		375	5250
Delphi	CVFA	HMK	1981	SP	29 X 30	AP/W	328		375	1600
Conservatory	CVFA	HMK	1981	SP	28 X 30	AP/W	353		375	3750
Aegean Doorway	CVFA	HMK	1981	SP	29 X 31	AP/W	353		375	1000
Flowered Couch	CVFA	HMK	1982	SP	29 X 29	AP/W	354		425	6500
Music Room	CVFA	HMK	1982	SP	29 X 30	AP/B	354		425	4500
Picasso in Venice	CVFA	HMK	1982	SP	29 X 29	AP/B	354		425	2000
Moon Temple	CVFA	HMK	1982	SP	35 X 28	AP/W	354		425	2500
Apollo & Daphne	CVFA	HMK	1982	SP	29 X 29	AP/W	354		425	1000
Matisse Gallery	CVFA	HMK	1982	SP	29 X 31	AP/W	354		425	1600
Hanging Carpet	CVFA	HMK	1982	SP	29 X 30	AP/W	354		425	1600
Gothic Revival	CVFA	HMK	1982	SP	29 X 30	AP/W	364		425	1600
Harlequin	CVFA	HMK	1982	SP	29 X 32	AP/W	364		425	4500
Riviera Villa	CVFA	HMK	1982	SP	29 X 30	AP/W	364		425	4500
Different Places Suite (Set of 6):									1650 SET	6000 SET
Hobe Sound	CVFA	CCI	1983	SP	19 X 21	DOVE/CR	351	28	300	1200
Central Park West	CVFA	CCI	1983	SP	19 X 21	DOVE/CR	351	30	300	800
Monte Carlo	CVFA	CCI	1983	SP	19 X 21	DOVE/CR	351	28	300	600
Monterey	CVFA	CCI	1983	SP	19 X 21	DOVE/CR	351	29	300	800
Shelter Island	CVFA	CCI	1983	SP	19 X 21	DOVE/CR	351	27	300	2000
Strawberry Hill	CVFA	CCI	1983	SP	19 X 21	DOVE/CR	351	26	300	1500
Fifth Avenue	CVFA	HMK	1983	SP	29 X 30	AP/W	364		475	4000
Music in Manhattan	CVFA	HMK	1983	SP	29 X 31	AP/W	364		425	4500
Princeton	CVFA	HMK	1983	SP	29 X 29	AP/B	364		475	2600
Eros & Saturn/Neptune's Court (Set of 2):									425 SET	1800 SET
Eros & Saturn	CVFA	HMK	1983	SP	20 X 22	AP/B	364		275	1000
Neptune's Court	CVFA	HMK	1983	SP	22 X 19	AP/B	364		275	1000

THOMAS MCKNIGHT CONTINUED

TITLE	PUBLISHER	PRINTER	DATE	MEDIUM	DIMENSION (PAPER SIZE) IN INCHES	TYPE OF PAPER	EDITION NUMBER	NO. OF COLORS	ORIGINAL OPENING PRICE	CURRENT RETAIL PRICE
CURRENT EDITIONS:										
Newport Sailing	CVFA	HMK	1983	SP	29 X 30	AP	364		475	5000
The Red Clock	CVFA	HMK	1983	SP	29 X 30	AP	364		475	1750
Winter Breakfast Room	CVFA	HMK	1983	SP	29 X 31	AP/W	364		475	5250
Valencia	CVFA	HMK	1983	SP	29 X 30	AP/W	364		475	2750
Tarrytown	CVFA	CCI	1983	SP	29 X 32	AP/W	364		475	3000
Rialto	CVFA	CCI	1983	SP	29 X 30	AP/W	364		475	2500
Manhattan Suite (Set of 8):									2500 SET	8000 SET
57th Street Gallery	CVFA	WFA	1984	SP	19 X 21	DOVE/1000	351		350	2000
Park Avenue Christmas	CVFA	WFA	1984	SP	19 X 21	DOVE/1000	351		350	900
Washington Square Bedroom	CVFA	WFA	1984	SP	19 X 21	DOVE/1000	351		350	750
Fifth Avenue Teatime	CVFA	WFA	1984	SP	19 X 21	DOVE/1000	351		350	900
Central Park West Dining Room	CVFA	WFA	1984	SP	19 X 21	DOVE/1000	351		350	800
Gramerey Park Living Room	CVFA	WFA	1984	SP	19 X 21	DOVE/1000	351		350	1000
Beekman Place	CVFA	WFA	1984	SP	19 X 21	DOVE/1000	351		350	2000
Wall Street Office	CVFA	WFA	1984	SP	19 X 21	DOVE/1000	351		350	1500
Leger Room	CVFA	HMK	1984	SP	29 X 30	AP/W	364		475	1500
Cold Spring Harbor	CVFA	CCI	1984	SP	33 X 34	DOVE/W	351	40	475	3500
Lake George	CVFA	HMK	1984	SP	29 X 30	AP/W	364		475	3250
Antibes	CVFA	CCI	1984	SP	32 X 35	DOVE/W	351	40	475	1000
Mykonos	CVFA	HMK	1984	SP	29 X 30	AP/W	364		475	2750
Narcissus	CVFA	CCI	1984	SP	31 X 32	DOVE/W	351		475	1500
Marblehead	CVFA	CCI	1984	SP	41 X 45	DOVE/W	351	33	750	7500
Venice Suite (Set of 6):									1750 SET	6750 SET
Piazza San Marco	CVFA	CCI	1984	SP	19 X 21	DOVE/W	351	31	325	2000
Cafe Quadri	CVFA	CCI	1984	SP	19 X 21	DOVE/W	351	31	325	700
Palazzo with Garden	CVFA	CCI	1984	SP	19 X 21	DOVE/W	351	38	325	800
Morning at the Gritti	CVFA	CCI	1984	SP	19 X 21	DOVE/W	351	33	325	900
Rialto by Gondola	CVFA	CCI	1984	SP	19 X 21	DOVE/W	351	35	325	2000
Evening on the Grand Canal	CVFA	CCI	1984	SP	19 X 21	DOVE/W	351	30	325	2000
Montauk	CVFA	CCI	1984	SP	19 X 21	DOVE/W	351		300	1750
San Remo	CVFA	CCI	1984	SP	19 X 21	DOVE/W	351		300	1650
Solitaire	CVFA	CCI	1984	SP	35 X 36	DOVE/W	351	40	550	2500
Litchfield	CVFA	CCI	1984	SP	40 X 44	DOVE/W	351		750	6500
The Red Retreat	CVFA	WFA	1984	SP	11 X 10	DOVE/W			300	6500
Open Window	CVFA	WFA	1984	SP	35 X 36	DOVE/W	350		550	1250
Yellow Cradle	CVFA	CCI	1985	SP	32 X 35	DOVE/W	351	37	475	1000
North Shore	CVFA	CCI	1985	SP	32 X 35	DOVE/W	351	43	575	5000
Statue of Liberty	CVFA	CCI	1985	SP	28 X 22	DOVE/W	268	37	475	2000
Australia Garden	CVFA	CCI	1985	SP	35 X 36	DOVE/W	351	40	550	2250
Mykonos Suite (Set of 6):									1875 SET	8500 SET
Harbor	CVFA	WFA	1985	SP	21 X 23	SOM/W	351	42	325	1500
Street	CVFA	WFA	1985	SP	21 X 23	SOM/W	351	42	325	1250
Chapel	CVFA	WFA	1985	SP	21 X 23	SOM/W	351	42	325	1250
Taverna	CVFA	WFA	1985	SP	21 X 23	SOM/W	351	42	325	1750
Courtyard	CVFA	WFA	1985	SP	21 X 23	SOM/W	351	42	325	1500
Windmills	CVFA	WFA	1985	SP	21 X 23	SOM/W	351	42	325	2000
Log Cabin	CVFA	CCI	1985	SP	32 X 34	DOVE/W	351	45	575	1150
Blue Couch	CVFA	CCI	1985	SP	42 X 46	DOVE/W	386	55	825	7500
Newport Suite (Set of 7):									2275 SET	9000 SET
Swimming Pool	CVFA	WFA	1985	SP	21 X 23	SOM/W	386	41	350	2250
Regatta	CVFA	WFA	1985	SP	21 X 23	SOM/W	386	36	350	1500
Afternoon Nap	CVFA	WFA	1985	SP	21 X 23	SOM/W	386	42	350	1500
Cliff Walk	CVFA	WFA	1985	SP	21 X 23	SOM/W	386	46	350	1250
Red Matisse	CVFA	WFA	1985	SP	21 X 23	SOM/W	386	45	350	1250
Garden Room	CVFA	WFA	1985	SP	21 X 23	SOM/W	386	36	350	1250
Chinese Gazebo	CVFA	WFA	1985	SP	21 X 23	SOM/W	386	41	350	1250
Christmas in Connecticut	CVFA	WFA	1985	SP	33 X 34	COV	386	53	575	1600
Coconut Grove	CVFA	WFA	1986	SP	33 X 34	COV	386	54	650	7500
North Woods	CVFA	WFA	1986	SP	31 X 32	COV	386	51	575	1200
Hudson River Valley	CVFA	CCI	1986	SP	31 X 33	COV	386	40	575	2750
Lighthouse	CVFA	CCI	1986	SP	36 X 32	COV	386	43	575	4000
England Suite (Set of 7):									2275 SET	7250 SET
Stourhead Gardens	CVFA	WFA	1986	SP	19 X 21	SOM	386	45	350	900
Pilgrim Cottage	CVFA	WFA	1986	SP	19 X 21	SOM	386	45	350	1500
Cotswold Inn	CVFA	WFA	1986	SP	19 X 21	SOM	386	45	350	1000
Salisbury	CVFA	WFA	1986	SP	19 X 21	SOM	386	48	350	1750
Castle Combe	CVFA	WFA	1986	SP	19 X 21	SOM	386	44	350	1000
Elgin Place	CVFA	WFA	1986	SP	19 X 21	SOM	386	45	350	800
Wilton House	CVFA	WFA	1986	SP	19 X 21	SOM	386	44	350	1000
Seven Statues	CVFA	WFA	1986	SP	27 X 39	SOM	386	48	650	2000
Coctails in Greenwich	CVFA	CCI	1986	SP	41 X 44	DOVE/W	386	45	825	6500
Montparnasse	CVFA	CCI	1986	SP	21 X 19	DOVE/W	351	30	375	800
Eastern Shore	CVFA	CCI	1986	SP	40 X 44	COV	386	45	950	7000

THOMAS MCKNIGHT CONTINUED

TITLE	PUBLISHER	PRINTER	DATE	MEDIUM	DIMENSION (PAPER SIZE) IN INCHES	TYPE OF PAPER	EDITION NUMBER	NO. OF COLORS	ORIGINAL OPENING PRICE	CURRENT RETAIL PRICE
CURRENT EDITIONS:										
Mykonos II Suite (Set of 10):									3750 SET	13000 SET
Kastro	CVFA	WFA	1986	SP	23 X 21	SOM	386	40	400	1100
Agrari Beach	CVFA	WFA	1986	SP	23 X 21	SOM	386	36	400	1100
Vengera	CVFA	WFA	1986	SP	23 X 21	SOM	386	40	400	1100
Pan's Cove	CVFA	WFA	1986	SP	23 X 21	SOM	386	45	400	1300
Caprice	CVFA	WFA	1986	SP	23 X 21	SOM	386	45	400	2250
Lotus	CVFA	WFA	1986	SP	23 X 21	SOM	386	42	400	1750
Le Mer	CVFA	WFA	1986	SP	23 X 21	SOM	386	45	400	1600
Pierrot's	CVFA	WFA	1986	SP	23 X 21	SOM	386	40	400	1200
Remezzo	CVFA	WFA	1986	SP	23 X 21	SOM	386	45	400	1400
City Bar	CVFA	WFA	1986	SP	23 X 21	SOM	386	40	400	1500
Left Bank	CVFA	WFA	1986	SP	29 X 35	SOM	386		650	2750
Natchez	CVFA	CCI	1987	SP	42 X 43	COV	409	47	975	7000
Oyster Bay	CVFA	CCI	1987	SP	32 X 35	DOVE/W	415	47	650	2750
Red Room with Guitar	CVFA	WFA	1987	SP	29 X 32	AP/B	400		650	1750
Atlantis	CVFA	CCI	1987	SP	33 X 36	AP	415		650	3750
The Hampton's Suite (Set of 12):									4500 SET	13500 SET
Westhampton	CVFA	WFA	1987	SP	21 X 23	SOM/W	415	40	400	1500
Sagaponack	CVFA	WFA	1987	SP	21 X 23	SOM/W	415	40	400	1200
Georgica	CVFA	WFA	1987	SP	21 X 23	SOM/W	415	40	400	2250
Bridgehampton	CVFA	WFA	1987	SP	21 X 23	SOM/W	415	40	400	1500
Maidstone	CVFA	WFA	1987	SP	21 X 23	SOM/W	415	40	400	1000
Wainscott	CVFA	WFA	1987	SP	21 X 23	SOM/W	415	40	400	850
Mecox Bay	CVFA	WFA	1987	SP	21 X 23	SOM/W	415	40	400	1250
Amagansett	CVFA	WFA	1987	SP	21 X 23	SOM/W	415	40	400	1100
Sag Harbor	CVFA	WFA	1987	SP	21 X 23	SOM/W	415	40	400	1350
Southampton	CVFA	WFA	1987	SP	21 X 23	SOM/W	415	40	400	1500
Water Mill	CVFA	WFA	1987	SP	21 X 23	SOM/W	415	40	400	1750
East Hampton	CVFA	WFA	1987	SP	21 X 23	SOM/W	415	40	400	1000
Mykonos Rooftops	CVFA	CCI	1987	SP	43 X 45	COV	415		1150	6250
Belvedere	CVFA	HSW	1987	SP	33 X 34	COV	415	40	650	1900
La Jolla	CVFA	CCI	1987	SP	33 X 35	COV	435		650	1500
Southern Italy Suite (Set of 12):									4500 SET	13500 SET
Villa Rufolo	CVFA	WFA	1987	SP	21 X 23	SOM	415	41	400	1200
Villa Cimbrone	CVFA	WFA	1987	SP	21 X 23	SOM	415	41	400	950
Positano Terrace	CVFA	WFA	1987	SP	21 X 23	SOM	415	41	400	1750
Hotel Le Sirenuse	CVFA	WFA	1987	SP	21 X 23	SOM	415	41	400	1750
Positano Restaurant	CVFA	WFA	1987	SP	21 X 23	SOM	415	41	400	1100
Positano Streets	CVFA	WFA	1987	SP	21 X 23	SOM/W	415	41	400	1350
View of Vesuvius	CVFA	WFA	1987	SP	21 X 23	SOM/W	415	41	400	1000
Sorrento	CVFA	WFA	1987	SP	21 X 23	SOM/W	415	41	400	1200
Ravello Garden	CVFA	WFA	1987	SP	21 X 23	SOM/W	415	41	400	900
Capri	CVFA	WFA	1987	SP	21 X 23	SOM/W	415	41	400	1400
Amalfi Cloister	CVFA	WFA	1987	SP	21 X 23	SOM/W	415	41	400	1200
Amalfi Villa	CVFA	WFA	1987	SP	21 X 23	SOM/W	415	41	400	1000
Ports of Call	CVFA	WFA	1987	SP	41 X 44	COV	415	50	1150	4750
The Four Seasons Suite (Winter/Spring/Summer/Fall) with "A Vision of Earthly Happiness" Book	CVFA	WFA	1987	SP	10 X 12	COV			1175 SET	1850 SET
Christmas Eve	CVFA	CCI	1987	SP	37 X 34	COV	386	38	875	1750
Constitution	CVFA	CCI	1988	SP	39 X 42	COV	550	42	1150	2500
Cap Martin	CVFA	CCI	1988	SP	33 X 35	COV	415	47	650	1750
Bay of Naples	CVFA	CCI	1988	SP	40 X 44	COV	415	40	1150	4500
Art Deco Room	CVFA	CCI	1988	SP	40 X 43	COV	480	40	1150	4500
In the Tropics Suite (Set of 12):									4500 SET	14500 SET
St Barts	CVFA	WFA	1988	SP	21 X 23	COV	490	50	400	1300
Guadeloupe	CVFA	WFA	1988	SP	21 X 23	COV	490	50	400	1200
Dominica	CVFA	WFA	1988	SP	21 X 23	COV	490	50	400	1700
Antigua	CVFA	WFA	1988	SP	21 X 23	COV	490	50	400	1200
Puerto Vallerta	CVFA	WFA	1988	SP	21 X 23	COV	490	50	400	2250
Nassau	CVFA	WFA	1988	SP	21 X 23	COV	490	50	400	1000
La Samanna	CVFA	WFA	1988	SP	21 X 23	COV	490	50	400	1300
Tortola	CVFA	WFA	1988	SP	21 X 23	COV	490	50	400	1100
Martinique	CVFA	WFA	1988	SP	21 X 23	COV	490	50	400	1200
Anquilla	CVFA	WFA	1988	SP	21 X 23	COV	490	50	400	1000
Barbados	CVFA	WFA	1988	SP	21 X 23	COV	490	50	400	2250
Montego Bay	CVFA	WFA	1988	SP	21 X 23	COV	490	50	400	1400
Hyannisport	CVFA	CCI	1988	SP	37 X 66	COV	490	40	1500	7500
Manhattan Penthouses (Set of 5):									3875 SET	7500 SET
Murray Hill	CVFA	WFA	1988	SP	32 X 34	COV	490	40	800	2000
Madison Square	CVFA	WFA	1988	SP	32 X 34	COV	490	40	800	2250
Turtle Bay	CVFA	WFA	1988	SP	32 X 34	COV	490	40	800	1750
Rockefeller Center	CVFA	WFA	1988	SP	32 X 34	COV	490	40	800	1750
Midtown	CVFA	WFA	1988	SP	32 X 34	COV	490	40	800	2500

THOMAS MCKNIGHT CONTINUED

TITLE	PUBLISHER	PRINTER	DATE	MEDIUM	DIMENSION (PAPER SIZE) IN INCHES	TYPE OF PAPER	EDITION NUMBER	NO. OF COLORS	ORIGINAL OPENING PRICE	CURRENT RETAIL PRICE
CURRENT EDITIONS:										
Crescent Bay	CVFA	CCI	1988	SP	37 X 66	COV	490	47	1875	7500
Venetian Tale/Carnival in Venice (with Hot-Stamping) (Set of 2)	CVFA	CCI	1988	SP	40 X 43 EA	COV	500 EA	52 EA	2850 SET 1950 EA	4250 SET 2150 EA
Mustique	CVFA	CCI	1989	SP	33 X 36	COV	490	38	925	5000
Centre Island	CVFA	CCI	1989	SP	33 X 36	COV	490	41	925	3000
Palm Beach	CVFA	CCI	1989	SP	40 X 45	DOVE/W	449	35	1450	4500
Manhattan Fantasy	CVFA	CCI	1989	SP	37 X 66	COV	490	59	1975	3750
Palm Beach Suite (Set of 8):									9000 SET	9000 SET
Breakers	CVFA	WFA	1989	SP	21 X 23	COV	510		1000	1000
Grace Tail	CVFA	WFA	1989	SP	21 X 23	COV	510		1000	1000
Lagomar	CVFA	WFA	1989	SP	21 X 23	COV	510		1500	1500
Lake Worth	CVFA	WFA	1989	SP	21 X 23	COV	510		2000	2000
North Lake Way	CVFA	WFA	1989	SP	21 X 23	COV	510		1450	1450
North Ocean Boulevard	CVFA	WFA	1989	SP	21 X 23	COV	510		1500	1500
South Ocean Boulevard	CVFA	WFA	1989	SP	21 X 23	COV	510		2000	2000
Villa Rosa	CVFA	WFA	1989	SP	21 X 23	COV	510		900	900
St Martin	CVFA	CCI	1989	SP	34 X 36	COV	490		2250	2250
Century	CVFA	CCI	1989	SP	34 X 38	COV	490		1500	1500
Red Cauch	CVFA	CCI	1989	SP	33 X 36	COV	490		2250	2250
Bienestar Courtyard	CVFA	CCI	1989	SP	37 X 66	COV	510		2750	4000
Boca Raton	CVFA	WFA	1989	SP	39 X 43	COV	510		2250	2750
La Cote d'Azur Suite (Set of 8):									9000 SET	9000 SET
Antibes	CVFA	WFA	1989	SP	21 X 23	COV	490	49	1400	1400
Cannes	CVFA	WFA	1989	SP	21 X 23	COV	490	49	1750	1750
Cap-Ferrat	CVFA	WFA	1989	SP	21 X 23	COV	490	49	1400	1400
Eze	CVFA	WFA	1989	SP	21 X 23	COV	490	49	1800	1800
La Voila d'Or	CVFA	WFA	1989	SP	21 X 23	COV	490	49	1200	1200
Menton	CVFA	WFA	1989	SP	21 X 23	COV	490	49	2000	2000
Nice	CVFA	WFA	1989	SP	21 X 23	COV	490	49	2000	2000
St-Paul-de-Vence	CVFA	WFA	1989	SP	21 X 23	COV	490	49	900	900
Mykonos Panoramas (Set of 2):									6000 SET	7000 SET
Mykonos Harbor	CVFA	WFA	1989	SP	28 X 50	COV	510		3350	3850
Mykonos Windmills	CVFA	WFA	1989	SP	28 X 50	COV	510		3350	3850
El Dorado	CVFA	CCI	1989	SP	35 X 38	COV	490		1050	1275
Catalina	CVFA	CCI	1989	SP	36 X 33	COV	510		1250	1750
Return to Mykonos Suite (Set of 8):									7500 SET	9000 SET
Alefkandra	CVFA	WFA	1990	SP	21 X 23	COV	510		1000	1250
Kalafati	CVFA	WFA	1990	SP	21 X 23	COV	510		1000	1400
Kaminaki	CVFA	WFA	1990	SP	21 X 23	COV	510		1000	1400
Korfos	CVFA	WFA	1990	SP	21 X 23	COV	510		1000	1250
Livadi	CVFA	WFA	1990	SP	21 X 23	COV	510		1000	1250
Paralia	CVFA	WFA	1990	SP	21 X 23	COV	510		1000	1250
Paraportiani	CVFA	WFA	1990	SP	21 X 23	COV	510		1000	1250
Venetia	CVFA	WFA	1990	SP	21 X 23	COV	510		1000	1250
Bel Air	CVFA	WFA	1990	SP	39 X 43	COV	510		2250	2750
Venice Revisited (Set of 8):									7000 SET	8000 SET
Ca d'Oro	CVFA	WFA	1990	SP	21 X 23	COV	510		1450	1600
Campo Manin	CVFA	WFA	1990	SP	21 X 23	COV	510		600	750
Grand Canal	CVFA	WFA	1990	SP	21 X 23	COV	510		1450	1600
Ponte di Rialto	CVFA	WFA	1990	SP	21 X 23	COV	510		1050	1200
Rio San Toma	CVFA	WFA	1990	SP	21 X 23	COV	510		1050	1200
Rio Van Axel	CVFA	WFA	1990	SP	21 X 23	COV	510		850	1000
Santa Maria del Giglio	CVFA	WFA	1990	SP	21 X 23	COV	510		1200	1350
Saturnia	CVFA	WFA	1990	SP	21 X 23	COV	510		600	750
Palm Island	CVFA	WFA	1990	SP	25 X 50	COV	510		3000	3500
Gulfstream	CVFA	WFA	1990	SP	28 X 50	COV	510		2250	2750
Golf Course	CVFA	WFA	1990	SP	28 X 50	COV	510		3350	3850
Aegean Bar	CVFA	CCI	1990	SP	33 X 35	COV	490		1250	1400
Aegean Suite (Set of 2):									3250 SET	3750 SET
Aegean Chapel	CVFA	WFA	1990	SP	32 X 35	COV	510		1750	2250
Aegean Lane	CVFA	WFA	1990	SP	32 X 35	COV	510		1750	1750
Four Corners of America (Plus Book—Windows on Paradise) (Set of 4):									2550 SET	2750 SET
Golden Gate	CVFA	WFA	1990	SP	17 X 19	COV	1260		650	750
Desert Patio	CVFA	WFA	1990	SP	17 X 19	COV	1260		650	750
Plantation	CVFA	WFA	1990	SP	17 X 19	COV	1260		650	750
Northern Summer	CVFA	WFA	1990	SP	17 X 19	COV	1260		650	750
Four Seas Suite (Set of 4):									4250 SET	4500 SET
Pacific Pool	CVFA	WFA	1990	SP	21 X 23	COV	510		900	950
Gulf Pool	CVFA	WFA	1990	SP	21 X 23	COV	510		900	950
Atlantic Pool	CVFA	WFA	1990	SP	21 X 23	COV	510		900	950
Caribbean Pool	CVFA	WFA	1990	SP	21 X 23	COV	510		900	950

THOMAS MCKNIGHT CONTINUED

TITLE	PUBLISHER	PRINTER	DATE	MEDIUM	DIMENSION (PAPER SIZE) IN INCHES	TYPE OF PAPER	EDITION NUMBER	NO. OF COLORS	ORIGINAL OPENING PRICE	CURRENT RETAIL PRICE
CURRENT EDITIONS:										
Daydreams Suite (Set of 4):									2250 SET	2450 SET
California Salon	CVFA	WFA	1991	SP	18 X 20	COV	1260		500	550
Andalusian Pool	CVFA	WFA	1991	SP	18 X 20	COV	1260		650	750
Massachusetts Sun Porch	CVFA	WFA	1991	SP	18 X 20	COV	1260		650	850
Riviera Conservatory	CVFA	WFA	1991	SP	18 X 20	COV	1260		650	750
Nantucket Suite (Set of 4):									4550 SET	4750 SET
Harbor View	CVFA	WFA	1991	SP	21 X 23	COV	510		1400	1750
Madaket	CVFA	WFA	1991	SP	21 X 23	COV	510		1400	1400
Orange Street	CVFA	WFA	1991	SP	21 X 23	COV	510		1400	1400
Sconset	CVFA	WFA	1991	SP	21 X 23	COV	510		1400	1400
Nantucket Lighthouse	CVFA	WFA	1991	SP	50 X 28	COV	510		2550	2750
Antigua Beach	CVFA	WFA	1991	SP	32 X 35	COV	510		1225	1375
Pool Pavillion	CVFA	WFA	1991	SP	21 X 23	COV	510			
Mar-a-Lago	CVFA	WFA	1991	SP	21 X 23	COV	510			
Clarke Avenue	CVFA	WFA	1991	SP	21 X 23	COV	510			
Manalapan	CVFA	WFA	1991	SP	21 X 23	COV	510			
Villa Del Mar	CVFA	WFA	1991	SP	21 X 23	COV	510			
Villa Apollo	CVFA	WFA	1991	SP	21 X 23	COV	510			
Villa Diana	CVFA	WFA	1991	SP	21 X 23	COV	510			
Villa Laguna	CVFA	WFA	1991	SP	21 X 23	COV	510			
America's Cup Suite:										
Newport	CVFA	WFA	1992	SP	28 X 50	COV	510			2000
San Diego	CVFA	WFA	1992	SP	28 X 50	COV	510			2000

RICHARD McLEAN

BORN: Hoquiam, WA; April 12, 1934
EDUCATION: California Col of Arts & Crafts, Oakland, CA, BFA, 1958; Mills Col, Oakland, CA, MFA, 1962
TEACHING: California State Univ, San Francisco, CA, 1963; California Col of Arts & Crafts, Oakland, CA, 1963–65
COLLECTIONS: Solomon R Guggenheim Mus, NY; Whitney Mus of Am Art, NY; Virginia Mus of Fine Arts, Richmond, VA; Utrecht Mus of Contemp Art, Amsterdam, Netherlands; San Francisco Mus of Mod Art, CA; Mus Boymans-van Beuingen, Rotterdam, Netherlands; Oakland Mus of Art, CA
PRINTERS: Don Farnsworth Press, San Francisco, CA (DFP); Editions Lassiter-Meisel, NY (ELM); Archer Press, Oakland, CA (AP)
PUBLISHERS: London Arts Inc, Detroit, MI (LAI); Master Editions Inc, NY (MEI); Post Oak Fine Art, Houston, TX (POFA)
GALLERIES: London Arts Gallery, Detroit, MI; Ro Gallery Image Makers, Inc, New York, NY
MAILING ADDRESS: 5840 Heron Dr, Oakland, CA 94618

TITLE	PUBLISHER	PRINTER	DATE	MEDIUM	DIMENSION (PAPER SIZE) IN INCHES	TYPE OF PAPER	EDITION NUMBER	NO. OF COLORS	ORIGINAL OPENING PRICE	CURRENT RETAIL PRICE
SOLD OUT EDITIONS (RARE):										
Buzz Ballou	MEI	AP	1980	LC	22 X 28	R/BFK	250	4	425	1000
Banana Beau	LAI	DFP	1980	LC	22 X 30	SOM	250	5	425	1000
Jack Magill's Bourbon Jet	LAI	DFP	1980	LC	22 X 30	SOM	250	5	425	1000
Fillies with Two-Tone Trailer	POFA	DFP	1980	LC	22 X 30	SOM	250	5	400	1000

GEORGE McNEIL

BORN: New York, NY: February 22, 1908
EDUCATION: Pratt Inst, NY, 1927–29; Art Students League, NY, 1930–31,32,33; Hans Hofmann Sch of Fine Arts, NY, 1933–36; Columbia Univ, NY, MA, 1943, EdD, 1952; Pratt Inst, NY, Hon DFA, 1945; Maryland Inst, Col of Art, Baltimore, MD, 1988
TEACHING: Prof Emeritus, Pratt Inst, NY
AWARDS: John Simon Guggenheim Fel, 1969; Am Acad of Arts & Letters Award, 1982
RECENT EXHIB: Gruenebaum Gallery, NY, 1987; Rena Bransten Gallery, San Francisco, CA, 1987; Lannan Mus, Lake Worth, FL, 1987; Mus of Ancient & Mod Art, Nevada City, CA, 1989; Univ of Hartford, Joseloff Gallery, CT, 1992; Artists Mus of Soho, NY, 1992; Washington & Lee Univ, du Pont Gallery, Lexington, VA, 1992; Julian Weissman Fine Art, NY, 1993
COLLECTIONS: Mus of Mod Art, NY; Whitney Mus of Am Art, NY; Brooklyn Mus, NY; Walker Art Center; Minneapolis, MN; Univ of Michigan Art Mus, Ann Arbor, MI; Mus of Art, Fort Lauderdale, FL; Univ of New Mexico Mus, Albuquerque, NM
PRINTERS: Sylvia Roth, South Nyack, NY (SR); Sue Mallozzi, NY (SM); Steve Szczepanek, NY (SS); Hudson River Editions, South Nyack, NY (HRE); Hudson River Editions, Garnerville, NY (HRE); Artist (ART); Marcia Brown, Albuquerque, NM (MB); Lynne Allen, Albuquerque, NM (LA); Tamarind Inst, Albuquerque, NM (TI)
PUBLISHERS: Tom Gruenbaum, NY (TG); Gruenbaum Graphics, NY (CG); Gruenebaum Graphics, NY (GG); Tamarind Inst, Albuquerque, NM (TI)
GALLERIES: Dumont-Landis Fine Arts, Newark, NY; Rena Bransten Gallery, San Francisco, CA; M Knoedler & Company, New York, NY; Tamarind Institute, Albuquerque, NM; Dunlap-Freidenrich Fine Art, Newport Beach, CA; Galleria Maray, Allendale, NJ; Julian Weissman Fine Art, New York, NY
MAILING ADDRESS: 195 Waverly Ave, Brooklyn, NY 11205

The retail prices of the 100,000 limited edition prints quoted in this directory are subject to change. Print publishers, artists and galleries were the direct sources for these quotations. Prices in the secondary market listed as "Sold Out Editions (Rare)" indicate that the publisher has a limited supply of that print or that the print is difficult to locate in the galleries.

GEORGE McNEIL CONTINUED

TITLE	PUBLISHER	PRINTER	DATE	MEDIUM	DIMENSION (PAPER SIZE) IN INCHES	TYPE OF PAPER	EDITION NUMBER	NO. OF COLORS	ORIGINAL OPENING PRICE	CURRENT RETAIL PRICE
SOLD OUT EDITIONS (RARE):										
Delusion Disco	TG/GG	SR/SM/SS/HRE	1984	LC	23 X 28	R/BFK	11	3	900	1500
Philadelphia Woman	TI	TI	1977	LC	76 X 56 cm	CD	70	4	225	1000
CURRENT EDITIONS:										
Things Unknown	TI	MB/TI	1984	LC	22 X 28	GE	40	3	600	800
High Life	TI	LA/TI	1984	LC	22 X 28	GE	40	4	600	800
Rock Trio	TI	LA/TI	1984	LB	27 X 38	CD	35	1	600	600
Dionysus Agonistes	TI	MB/TI	1984	LC	44 X 32	AP/ROL	50	3	800	950
Dartmouth Disco	TI	LA/TI	1987	LC	28 X 22	SOM/S	30	4	600	800
Diana Dallies	TI	LA/TI	1987	LC	28 X 23	R/BFK	30	4	600	800

J JAY McVICKER

BORN: Vici, OK; October 18, 1911
EDUCATION: Oklahoma State Univ, Stillwater, OK, BA, MA, 1941
TEACHING: Prof, Chmn, Dept of Art, Oklahoma State Univ, Stillwater, OK, 1941–77
AWARDS: Purchase Award, Oklahoma Art Center, Oklahoma City, OK, 1967; Purchase Award, Dallas Mus of Fine Arts, TX, 1969; John Taylor Arms Graphic Award, Audubon Artists, NY, 1990
COLLECTIONS: Metropolitan Mus of Art, NY; Dallas Mus of Fine Arts, TX; US Nat Mus of Am Art, Wash, DC; Georgetown Univ, Wash, DC; Joslyn Art Mus, Omaha, NE; Oklahoma Art Center, Oklahoma City, OK
GALLERIES: Bethesda Art Gallery, Bethesda, MD
MAILING ADDRESS: 4212 N Washington, Stillwater, OK 74075

J Jay McVicker
Primordial Tensions
Courtesy the Artist

TITLE	PUBLISHER	PRINTER	DATE	MEDIUM	DIMENSION (PAPER SIZE) IN INCHES	TYPE OF PAPER	EDITION NUMBER	NO. OF COLORS	ORIGINAL OPENING PRICE	CURRENT RETAIL PRICE
SOLD OUT EDITIONS (RARE):										
Solitude	ART	ART	1940	AB	10 X 12	R/BFK	25	1	25	200
Three Figures	ART	ART	1952	SP	10 X 17	R/BFK	8	6	40	400
Two Figures	ART	ART	1953	SP	16 X 12	R/BFK	15	9	40	350
Astral-Geometric	ART	ART	1958	SP	16 X 12	R/BFK	24	6	50	350
CURRENT EDITIONS:										
September Symphony	ART	ART	1940	AB	11 X 15	RP/HWT	25	1	25	275
Abandoned	ART	ART	1940	AB	10 X 15	R/BFK	25	1	25	400
Oklahoma Twilight	ART	ART	1940	AB	10 X 16	R/BFK	25	1	25	300
Nocturne	ART	ART	1941	AB	10 X 15	RP/HWT	25	1	25	300
Nocturnal Sequence	ART	ART	1942	AB	11 X 16	R/BFK	25	1	25	350
The Wind	ART	ART	1942	AB	11 X 15	R/BFK	25	1	25	300
Spring Madness	ART	ART	1942	AB	11 X 16	AP	25	1	25	300
Moonlight and Mystery	ART	ART	1942	AB	10 X 15	R/BFK	25	1	25	350
January	ART	ART	1942	AB	10 X 16	R/BFK	25	1	25	350
Driftwood	ART	ART	1943	AB	8 X 17	R/BFK	50	1	25	275
The Cloud	ART	ART	1943	AB	11 X 16	R/BFK	25	1	25	350
Arc Welder	ART	ART	1943	AB	11 X 16	UMB	50	1	25	350
Night Shift	ART	ART	1943	AB	10 X 16	R/BFK	30	1	25	350
Afternoon Shadows	ART	ART	1943	AB	10 X 13	R/BFK	50	1	25	250
Night and the River	ART	ART	1943	AB	11 X 16	R/BFK	25	1	40	200
Spirit of the Night	ART	ART	1946	AB	10 X 14	R/BFK	50	1	40	200
Cottonwoods	ART	ART	1946	AB	10 X 7	R/BFK	50	1	40	200
The Pinto Colt	ART	ART	1947	AB	10 X 16	R/BFK	50	1	40	200
Pintos by the River	ART	ART	1947	AB	10 X 16	R/BFK	50	1	40	250
Nostalgic Moment	ART	ART	1947	AB	10 X 16	R/BFK	50	1	40	200
River Tapestry	ART	ART	1947	AB	11 X 9	R/BFK	50	1	40	200
The Road	ART	ART	1947	AB	11 X 16	R/BFK	50	1	40	350
Along the Cimarron	ART	ART	1947	AB	10 X 16	R/BFK	50	1	40	300
Prairie Elements	ART	ART	1947	AB	12 X 16	R/BFK	50	1	40	200
Sunscape	ART	ART	1948	AB	11 X 16	R/BFK	50	1	50	300
Embryonic Forms	ART	ART	1948	AB	16 X 10	R/BFK	50	1	50	250
Nude Contemplating a River	ART	ART	1949	A/E/SG	16 X 10	R/BFK	50	1	50	300
Small Town Elements	ART	ART	1949	AB	9 X 17	R/BFK	50	1	50	350

J JAY McVICKER CONTINUED

TITLE	PUBLISHER	PRINTER	DATE	MEDIUM	DIMENSION (PAPER SIZE) IN INCHES	TYPE OF PAPER	EDITION NUMBER	NO. OF COLORS	ORIGINAL OPENING PRICE	CURRENT RETAIL PRICE
CURRENT EDITIONS:										
Penitence and the Angel	ART	ART	1949	A/E/SG/EMB	15 X 11	R/BFK	75	1	50	300
Primordial Tensions	ART	ART	1950	A/E/SG/EMB	12 X 14	R/BFK	30	4	50	300
Centaur	ART	ART	1953	SP	17 X 10	R/BFK	30	10	50	350
Ideagraphic Elements #4	ART	ART	1953	SP	22 X 15	R/BFK	15	10	50	300
Dark Figure	ART	ART	1954	SP	18 X 12	R/BFK	20	5	50	350
Origins	ART	ART	1955	A/E/SG/EMB	17 X 12	AC	30	4	50	400
Cycle	ART	ART	1956	SP	11 X 19	AC	30	8	50	300
Replendent Forest	ART	ART	1956	SP	22 X 16	AC	20	4	50	300
Blue Ceramic	ART	ART	1956	SP	22 X 16	AC	40	6	50	400
Three Horsemen	ART	ART	1957	SP	16 X 12	AC	38	6	60	350
The Red Bottle	ART	ART	1957	SP	12 X 22	AC	47	7	60	350
Structural Elements	ART	ART	1958	AC	11 X 17	RP/HWT/B	40	6	60	350
Black Image	ART	ART	1958	AC	15 X 12	RP/HWT/W	25	4	60	300
Red Accent	ART	ART	1962	R/BFK	16 X 13	R/BFK	40	4	75	300
Blue Ambiance (State II)	ART	ART	1965	A/E/SG	12 X 16	RP/HWT/W	30	6	75	350
Two Yellow Squares	ART	ART	1968	EMB	18 X 14	AC	40	2	75	300
Scape #2	ART	ART	1975	A/E/SG	14 X 12	R/BFK	30	5	100	300
Black Sun over Pharaol's Garden II	ART	ART	1978	SP	12 X 16	R/BFK	12	14	100	300
Red Circle	ART	ART	1981	A/E/SG	12 X 16	R/BFK	25	5	100	300
Scape #3	ART	ART	1981	A/E/SG	12 X 12	R/BFK	40	5	100	300
Orange Accent (State II)	ART	ART	1981	A/E/SG	11 X 16	R/BFK	25	4	100	300
Lateral Passage	ART	ART	1982	AC	10 X 17	R/BFK	40	6	150	250
Red Rooster (State II)	ART	ART	1982	A/E/SG	16 X 11	R/BFK	40	4	150	400
Circumvention (State II)	ART	ART	1982	A/E/SG/EMB	12 X 18	R/BFK	25	5	150	350
Dark Structure (State II)	ART	ART	1983	AC	15 X 10	R/BFK	40	9	150	250
Ceramic Imagery (State II)	ART	ART	1985	A/E/SG/EMB	14 X 12	R/BFK	40	5	175	300
Specter in Green	ART	ART	1985	AC	14 X 12	R/BFK	50	1	175	250
Red Triangle	ART	ART	1986	A/E/LI/EMB	12 X 18	R/BFK	40	7	200	350

JONATHAN MEADER

BORN: Orange, NJ; August 29, 1943
EDUCATION: Wurlitzer Found Grant, 1967; Stern Family Grant, 1970; Corcoran Workshop Grant, 1970–72; Nat Endowment for the Arts Fel, 1974; Washington Print Club Com, 1975; Nat Inst of Health Com, 1978
AWARDS: Stern Family Grant, NY, 1970; Printmakers Grant, Nat Endowment for the Arts, 1974

COLLECTIONS: Baltimore Mus, MD; Corcoran Gallery, Wash, DC; Detroit Inst of Art, MI; Hirshhorn Mus, Wash, DC; Metropolitan Mus of Art, NY; Whitney Mus of Am Art, NY; Philadelphia Mus of Art, PA; Phillips Coll, Wash, DC; Nat Coll of Fine Arts, Wash, DC
PRINTERS: Artist (ART)
PUBLISHERS: Artist (ART)
GALLERIES: Zenith Gallery, Wash, DC; Arnold Klein Gallery, Royal Oak, MI
MAILING ADDRESS: 758 Marin Drive, Mill Valley, CA 94941

TITLE	PUBLISHER	PRINTER	DATE	MEDIUM	DIMENSION (PAPER SIZE) IN INCHES	TYPE OF PAPER	EDITION NUMBER	NO. OF COLORS	ORIGINAL OPENING PRICE	CURRENT RETAIL PRICE
SOLD OUT EDITIONS (RARE):										
Unicorn I	ART	ART	1972	SP	23 X 23	AP	81	31	50	2000
Pyramid Portfolio (Set of 4)	ART	ART	1974	SP	20 X 22 EA	AP	100 EA	11–15 EA	300 SET	1500 SET
Bear	ART	ART	1975	SP	20 X 23	AP	60	11	100	500
Accumulus	ART	ART	1976	SP	23 X 23	AP	140	16	120	500
Unicorn II	ART	ART	1977	SP	22 X 26	AP	100	47	250	1800
CURRENT EDITIONS:										
Psyche	ART	ART	1975	SP	23 X 23	AP	140	19	150	500
Passage (Set of 3)	ART	ART	1975	SP	20 X 20 EA	AP	150 EA	12–18 EA	400 SET	500 SET
Astral Self Portrait	ART	ART	1977	SP	20 X 23	AP	140	31	150	250
Reflections	ART	ART	1978	SP	26 X 21	AP	150	26	150	450
Stargazer	ART	ART	1978	SP	22 X 27	AP	160	10	175	200
Stonehenge	ART	ART	1979	SP	23 X 22	AP	162	16	200	250
Dejamour	ART	ART	1979	SP	22 X 26	AP	150	50	360	950
Nancy and the Bear	ART	ART	1980	SP	19 X 22	AP	150	33	200	250
Dream Cove	ART	ART	1981	SP	22 X 30	AP	120	14	200	250
Enchanted Spring	ART	ART	1981	SP	19 X 18	AP	200	31	400	450

SUSAN PEAR MEISEL

BORN: New York, NY; April 16, 1947
EDUCATION: Art Students League, NY; Sch of Visual Arts, NY; Parsons Sch of Design, NY; New Sch for Social Research, NY; Mus of Mod Art, NY; Univ of Florence, Italy
COLLECTIONS: Gerlach Coll, Vienna, Austria; Lovelace Coll, London, England; Olaffsson Coll, Omea, Sweden; Library of Congress, Wash, DC; Alfred Santos Gallery & Coll, Mexico City, Mexico

PRINTERS: Lassiter-Meisel, NY (LM)
PUBLISHERS: Transworld Art, Inc, NY (TAI); Edward Weston Graphics, NY (EWG); Circle Fine Art, Chicago, IL (CFA)
GALLERIES: Edward Weston Gallery, New York, NY; Louis K Meisel Gallery, New York, NY; Circle Galleries, San Diego, CA & San Francisco, CA & Northbrook, IL & Pittsburgh, PA & Houston, TX & Soho, NY & Chicago, IL & Scottsdale, AZ & Beverly Hills, CA & Costa Mesa, CA & Sherman Oaks, CA & Palm Beach, FL & Honolulu, HI & New Orleans, LA & Las Vegas, NV & Seattle, WA

SUSAN PEAR MEISEL CONTINUED

TITLE	PUBLISHER	PRINTER	DATE	MEDIUM	DIMENSION (PAPER SIZE) IN INCHES	TYPE OF PAPER	EDITION NUMBER	NO. OF COLORS	ORIGINAL OPENING PRICE	CURRENT RETAIL PRICE
SOLD OUT EDITIONS (RARE):										
Pantalone Rosa	CFA	AA	1975	LC	30 X 24	AP	275	4	35	425
Victorian House	CFA	AA	1976	LC	29 X 31	AP	275	4	35	400
Seven Drawers	CFA	AA	1976	LC	6 X 12	AP	275	4	35	150
Flowers	CFA	AA	1976	LC	7 X 11	AP	275	4	35	150
My Little Chest	CFA	AA	1976	LC	6 X 10	AP	275	4	35	125
Love Seat	CFA	AA	1976	LC	7 X 11	AP	275	4	35	125
Tick-Tock	CFA	AA	1976	LC	6 X 11	AP	275	4	35	125
Armoire	CFA	AA	1976	LC	11 X 16	AP	275	4	35	150
Splish-Splash	CFA	AA	1976	LC	7 X 11	AP	275	4	35	125
Bethesda Fountain	CFA	AA	1977	LC	24 X 29	AP	275	4	35	425
Wall Street (Set of 4):									1000 SET	1500 SET
Delmonico	TAI	LM	1977	SP	47 X 35	LEN	300		275	400
Old Customs House	TAI	LM	1977	SP	35 X 47	LEN	300		275	400
The Stock Exchange	TAI	LM	1977	SP	47 X 35	LEN	300		275	400
Sub Treasury Building	TAI	LM	1977	SP	35 X 47	LEN	300		275	400
New York (Series of 4):									1000 SET	1500 SET
Times Square	TAI	JM	1977	SP	24 X 29	LEN	300		275	450
Washington Square	TAI	LM	1977	SP	24 X 29	LEN	300		275	450
Grand Central	TAI	LM	1977	SP	24 X 29	LEN	300		275	450
Statue of Liberty	TAI	LM	1977	SP	24 X 29	LEN	300		275	450
Country Store	CFA	AA	1977	LC	24 X 29	AP	275	12	100	400
L'Oiseau Bleu	CFA	AA	1977	LC	18 X 21	AP	275	4	100	350
SOLD OUT EDITIONS (RARE):										
Public Library	EWG		1977	SP	23 X 28	LEN	175		275	450
My House	EWG		1977	SP	20 X 24	R/100	275		200	350
Happy Days	EWG		1977	SP	20 X 26	R/100	275		200	350
Moulin Rouge	EWG		1977	SP	22 X 29	R/100	275		200	350

HAIM MENDELSON

BORN: Semiatich, Builsk, Poland; October 15, 1923, US Citizen
EDUCATION: WPA Art Sch, NY, 1935–36; Am Artists Sch, NY, 1936–40; Saul Baizerman Art Sch, NY, 1940–43; Educational Alliance Art Sch, NY, 1946
TEACHING: Educational Alliance Art Sch, NY, 1956–61; City Col of New York, NY, 1961–64; Columbia Grammar Sch, NY, 1963–64; City & County Sch, NY, 1964–91
AWARDS: First Prize, Graphics Award, Village Art Center, NY, 1962; Knickerbocker Artists Graphics Award, 1964; Purchase Award, St Paul Art Center, MN, 1966; Knickerbocker Artists Presidents Award for Graphics, 1984; Painters & Sculptors Soc Awards for Graphics, 1968,74,85; Maury Leibovitz Special Merit Award, 1987
RECENT EXHIB: Missouri Western State Col, Saint Joseph, MO, 1988; Addrain Col, MI, 1988; Arts Council Galery, Winston-Salem, NC, 1988; Nat Acad of Design, NY, 1990; Hunterdon Art Center, Clinton, NJ, 1991; Nat Arts Club, NY, 1992; Hudson Guild Art Gallery, NY, 1992
COLLECTIONS: St Paul Art Center, MN; Edwin A Ulrich Mus, Wichita, KS; Manhattan Col, Riverdale, NY; Griffiths Art Center, Canton, NY; St Vincent Col, Latrobe, PA; New York Public Library, NY; Wichita State Univ, KS; Minnesota Mus of Art, St Paul, MN; Flint Inst of Fine Arts, MI
PRINTERS: Artist (ART)
PUBLISHERS: New York Graphic Society, Ltd, Greenwich, CT, (NYGS); Artist (ART)
GALLERIES: Yellow Poui Art Gallery, Grenada, West Indies; Hudson Guild Art Gallery, New York, NY
MAILING ADDRESS: 234 W 21st St, #63, New York, NY 10011

TITLE	PUBLISHER	PRINTER	DATE	MEDIUM	DIMENSION (PAPER SIZE) IN INCHES	TYPE OF PAPER	EDITION NUMBER	NO. OF COLORS	ORIGINAL OPENING PRICE	CURRENT RETAIL PRICE
SOLD OUT EDITIONS (RARE):										
Grass 1963 (Set of 11)	ART	ART	1963	ENG	19 X 12	RP/AV	20	1	250 SET	350 SET
Chess Players	ART	ART	1963	MEZ	18 X 12	CRIS	30	1	100	150
Growth	ART	ART	1963	AB	23 X 13	CRIS	60	1	100	125
Nuns in the Rain	ART	ART	1964	MEZ	23 X 13	CRIS	60	1	100	125
Bending Figure	ART	ART	1965	MEZ	13 X 23	RP	60	1	100	125
The Mary Anthony Dance Studio	ART	ART	1966	MEZ	13 X 24	RP	60	1	100	125
Vermont Rabbit	ART	ART	1967	AB	12 X 16	JBG	60	1	100	100
Summer	NYGS	ART	1970	ENG	20 X 13	RP/AV	200	1	75	150
Rain Arched	NYGS	ART	1971	ENG	13 X 20	RP/AV	200	1	75	150
Wild Wheat	NYGS	ART	1971	ENG	20 X 13	AP/T	200	1	75	150
Dune's Edge	NYGS	ART	1971	ENG	20 X 13	RP/AV	200	1	75	150
Moody Hill Grass	NYGS	ART	1971	ENG	20 X 13	UMB	200	1	75	150

ANA MENDIETA

PRINTERS: Ultimate Image, NY (UI)
PUBLISHERS: Galerie Lelong, NY (GL)
GALLERIES: Galerie Lelong, New York, NY & Paris, France; Laura Carpenter Fine Art, Santa Fe, NM; Virginia Miller Galleries, Miami, FL

TITLE	PUBLISHER	PRINTER	DATE	MEDIUM	DIMENSION (PAPER SIZE) IN INCHES	TYPE OF PAPER	EDITION NUMBER	NO. OF COLORS	ORIGINAL OPENING PRICE	CURRENT RETAIL PRICE
CURRENT EDITIONS:										
Silueta Works in Mexico, 1973–77 (Boxed Photographs)	GL	UI	1991	PH	16 X 20 EA	KOD	20 EA		6500 SET	6500 SET

ANA MENDIETA CONTINUED

TITLE	PUBLISHER	PRINTER	DATE	MEDIUM	DIMENSION (PAPER SIZE) IN INCHES	TYPE OF PAPER	EDITION NUMBER	NO. OF COLORS	ORIGINAL OPENING PRICE	CURRENT RETAIL PRICE
CURRENT EDITIONS:										
Silueta Works in Iowa, 1976–78 (Boxed Photographs)	GL	UI	1991	PH	16 X 20 EA	KOD	20 EA		6500 SET	6500 SET

RICHARD MARSHALL MERKIN

BORN: Brooklyn, NY; 1938
EDUCATION: Syracuse Univ, NY, BFA; Rhode Island Sch of Design, Providence, RI, MFA
AWARDS: Louis Comfort Tiffany Found Fel, 1962–63; Richard & Hinda Found Award, Nat Inst of Arts & Letters, NY, 1975
RECENT EXHIB: Foster-White Gallery, Seattle, WA, 1987; JRS Fine Art, Providence, RI, 1988; Helander Gallery, Palm Beach, FL, 1987,89
COLLECTIONS: Mus of Mod Art, NY; Rhode Island Sch of Design, Providence, RI; Finch Col, NY; Rose Art Mus, Brandeis Univ, Waltham, MA; Massachusetts Inst of Technology, MA; Am Fed of Arts, NY; Chrysler Mus of Art, Norfolk, VA; Fisk Univ, Nashville, TN; Miami-Dade Junior Col, FL; Michigan State Univ, East Lansing, MI; Minnesota Mus of Art, MN; McClurg Mus, Univ of Tennessee Knoxville, TN; Pennsylvania Acad of the Arts, Phila, PA; Sara Robey Found, NY; Smithsonian Inst, Wash, DC; State Univ of Brockport, NY; Whitney Mus of Am Art, NY
PRINTERS: Brand X, NY (BX); Artist (ART)
PUBLISHERS: Hammer Publishing, NY (HP)
GALLERIES: Terry Dintenfass Gallery, New York, NY; Hammer Galleries, New York, NY; Helander Gallery, Palm Beach, FL; C S Sculte Galleries, South Orange, NJ; JRS Fine Art, Providence, RI; Foster-White Gallery, Seattle, WA
MAILING ADDRESS: 500 West End Ave, #12–D, New York, NY 10024

TITLE	PUBLISHER	PRINTER	DATE	MEDIUM	DIMENSION (PAPER SIZE) IN INCHES	TYPE OF PAPER	EDITION NUMBER	NO. OF COLORS	ORIGINAL OPENING PRICE	CURRENT RETAIL PRICE
SOLD OUT EDITIONS (RARE):										
Byron and Shelly	HP	BX	1980	SP	21 X 31	AP88	260	26	260	800
Oedipus in Luxor	HP	BX	1980	SP	24 X 32	AP88	260	26	260	800
Fitz in Hollywood	HP	ART	1981	SP	29 X 28	AC/B	260	31	400	800
In Havana, 1941	HP	BX	1981	SP	18 X 24	R/BFK	260	26	260	700
Nagaski	HP	BX	1981	SP	25 X 36	AP88	260	28	260	700

MARIO MERZ

BORN: Milan, Italy; 1925
RECENT EXHIB: Retrosp, Soloman Guggenheim Mus, NY, 1989; Murray & Isabella Rayburn Found, NY, 1992; Sperone Westwater Gallery, NY, 1992
PRINTERS: Peter Kneubühler, Zürich, Switzerland (PK)
PUBLISHERS: Maximilian Verlag Sabine Knust, Munich, Germany (MV/SK)
GALLERIES: Margo Leavin Gallery, Los Angeles, CA; Margarete Roeder Gallery, New York, NY; Sperone Westwater Gallery, New York, NY; Whitechapel Art Gallery, London, England; Hayward Gallery, London, England; Carl Solway Gallery, Cincinnati, OH; SteinGladstone Gallery, New York, NY; Salvatore Ala, New York, NY

TITLE	PUBLISHER	PRINTER	DATE	MEDIUM	DIMENSION (PAPER SIZE) IN INCHES	TYPE OF PAPER	EDITION NUMBER	NO. OF COLORS	ORIGINAL OPENING PRICE	CURRENT RETAIL PRICE
CURRENT EDITIONS:										
Untitled (Set of 3):										
Untitled #1	MV/SK	PK	1988	AB	26 X 20	R/BFK	30		1100	2000
Untitled #2	MV/SK	PK	1988	AB	26 X 20	R/BFK	30		1300	2000
Untitled #3	MV/SK	PK	1988	AB	32 X 24	R/BFK	30		1600	2000
Untitled	MV/SK	PK	1993	AB/DPT	32 X 43	ZER	20	1	DM 3600	DM 3600

ARNOLD MESCHES

BORN: New York, NY; August 11, 1923
EDUCATION: Art Center Sch, Chouinard Art Inst, Los Angeles, CA
TEACHING: Instr, Painting & Drawing, Univ of Southern California, Summer, 1950; Instr, & Dir, New Sch of Art, Los Angeles, CA, 1954–57; Instr, Otis Art Inst, Los Angeles, CA, 1963–67, 1977–78; Univ of California, Ext, Los Angeles, CA, 1972–78; Otis/Parsons Award, San Francisco Mus of Art, CA, 1969; Nat Endowment for the Arts Grant, NY, 1982
AWARDS: Purchase Award, San Francisco Mus of Art, CA, 1969; Nat Endowment for the Arts Grant, NY, 1982
RECENT EXHIB: Centro di Cultura Ausoni, Rome, Italy, 1989; Seibu Art Forum, Tokyo, Japan, 1989; Kuznetsky Most Exhib Hall, Moscow, Russia, 1989; Carlo Lamagna Gallery, NY, 1989; Burchfield Art Center, Buffalo, NY, 1992
COLLECTIONS: Philadelphia Mus, PA; San Francisco Mus of Art, CA; Brooklyn Mus, NY; Palm Springs Mus, CA
PRINTERS: American Atelier, NY (AA)
PUBLISHERS: Circle Fine Art, Chicago, IL (CFA)
GALLERIES: Circle Galleries, San Diego, CA & San Francisco, CA & Northbrook, IL & Houston, TX & Pittsburgh, PA & Soho, NY & Chicago, IL & Scottsdale, AZ & Beverly Hills, CA & Costa Mesa, CA & Sherman Oaks, CA & Palm Beach, FL & Honolulu, HI & New Orleans, LA & Las Vegas, NV & Seattle, WA; Haines Gallery San Francisco, CA; Brody's Gallery, Washington, DC; Donahue Gallery, New York, NY
MAILING ADDRESS: 254 E 7th St, #15–16, New York, NY 10009

TITLE	PUBLISHER	PRINTER	DATE	MEDIUM	DIMENSION (PAPER SIZE) IN INCHES	TYPE OF PAPER	EDITION NUMBER	NO. OF COLORS	ORIGINAL OPENING PRICE	CURRENT RETAIL PRICE
SOLD OUT EDITIONS (RARE):										
The Chair II	CFA	AA	1978	SP	30 X 40	AP	100	50		250
The Chair in Black II	CFA	AA	1979	SP	31 X 42	AP	100	50		300
Chair in Brown	CFA	AA	1979	SP	31 X 42	AP	150	50		225
The Line II	CFA	AA	1979	SP	20 X 24	AP	100	50		125

The retail prices of the 100,000 limited edition prints quoted in this directory are subject to change. Print publishers, artists and galleries were the direct sources for these quotations. Prices in the secondary market listed as "Sold Out Editions (Rare)" indicate that the publisher has a limited supply of that print or that the print is difficult to locate in the galleries.

ARNOLD MESCHES CONTINUED

TITLE	PUBLISHER	PRINTER	DATE	MEDIUM	DIMENSION (PAPER SIZE) IN INCHES	TYPE OF PAPER	EDITION NUMBER	NO. OF COLORS	ORIGINAL OPENING PRICE	CURRENT RETAIL PRICE
SOLD OUT EDITIONS (RARE):										
Ode to a Tower	CFA	AA	1980	SP	20 X 30	AP	150		50	150
Telephone Poles/ Yellow	CFA	AA	1982	SP	24 X 24	AP	150		100	125
CURRENT EDITIONS:										
Bell Shapes II	CFA	AA	1982	SP	11 X 19	AP	150		75	125
Vertical Wires in Red	CFA	AA	1982	SP	30 X 22	AP	150		100	125

RAY K METZKER

BORN: Milwaukee, WI; September 10, 1931
EDUCATION: Beloit Col, WI, BA, 1953; Illinois Inst of Technology, MS, 1959
TEACHING: Prof, Photog, Philadelphia Col of Art, PA, 1962–81; Assoc Prof, Photog, Univ of New Mexico, Albuquerque, NM, 1970–72; Adj Prof, Photog, Rhode Island Sch of Design, Providence, RI, 1977; Columbia Col, Chicago, IL, 1980–83; Smith Distinguished Vis Art, George Washington Univ, Wash, DC, 1987–88

AWARDS: John Simon Guggenheim Fel, 1966–79; Nat Endowment for the Arts Fel, 1974,88
RECENT EXHIB: State of Illinois Art Gallery, Chicago, IL, 1989; Laurence Miller Gallery, NY, 1990
COLLECTIONS: Philadelphia Mus of Art, PA; Mus of Mod Art, NY; Art Inst of Chicago, IL; Mus of Fine Arts, Houston, TX
PRINTERS: Artist (ART)
PUBLISHERS: Apertune, NY (A); Sand Creatures, Millerton, NY (SC); Artist (ART); Vinalhaven Press, Vinalhaven, ME (VP)
GALLERIES: Laurence Miller Gallery, New York, NY
MAILING ADDRESS: 733 S Sixth St, Phila, PA 19147

TITLE	PUBLISHER	PRINTER	DATE	MEDIUM	DIMENSION (PAPER SIZE) IN INCHES	TYPE OF PAPER	EDITION NUMBER	NO. OF COLORS	ORIGINAL OPENING PRICE	CURRENT RETAIL PRICE
SOLD OUT EDITIONS (RARE):										
Untitled (Unique Composite of 11 Photographs	ART	ART	1966	PH	41 X 41 EA	Mason	1 EA		800 SET	50000 SET
Pictus Interruptus	ART	ART	1978	PH	11 X 14		20–30		250	800
Spring Tingle	ART	ART	1980	PH	16 X 20		20–30		450	800
CURRENT EDITIONS:										
New Mexico Suite	ART	ART	1970	PH	11 X 14		20–25		75	800
Sand Creatures	ART	ART	1976	PH	8 X 10		15–25		250	600
Pictus Interruptus	ART	ART	1978	PH	16 X 20		20–30		325	800
City Whispers	ART	ART	1983	PH	11 X 14		20–30		450	800
Earthly Delights (Silver Prints) (Series of 50)	VP	ART	1986–88	PH	20 X 16 EA		25 EA		2800 SET	3500 SET

JOEL MEYEROWITZ

BORN: New York, NY; March 6, 1938
EDUCATION: Ohio State Univ, Columbus, OH
TEACHING: Adj Prof, Cooper Union, NY, 1971–78; Lectr, Art, Princeton Univ, NJ, 1978
AWARDS: Nat Endowment for the Arts Fel, 1978; John Simon Guggenheim Fel, 1971,79; St Louis & Arch, MO, 1980, Wild Flowers, 1983; New York Graphic Soc, NY, 1985

RECENT EXHIB: New York State Mus, Albany, NY, 1988
COLLECTIONS: Mus of Mod Art, NY; Art Inst of Chicago, IL; Philadelphia Mus, PA; Mus of Fine Arts, Boston, MA; St Louis Art Mus, MO; New York State Mus, Albany, NY
PRINTERS: Grapestake Gallery, San Francisco, CA (GG)
GALLERIES: Witkin Gallery, New York, NY; Harcus Gallery, Boston, MA; Halsted Gallery, Birmingham, MI; Michael H Lord Gallery Milwaukee, WI; Nancy Hoffman Gallery, New York, NY
MAILING ADDRESS: 817 West End St, New York, 10025

TITLE	PUBLISHER	PRINTER	DATE	MEDIUM	DIMENSION (PAPER SIZE) IN INCHES	TYPE OF PAPER	EDITION NUMBER	NO. OF COLORS	ORIGINAL OPENING PRICE	CURRENT RETAIL PRICE
CURRENT EDITIONS:										
The French Portfolio (Set of 12)	GG	DCL	1980	PH/DT	16 X 20 EA		96 EA		3000 SET	7500 SET

JOHN MILLEI

RECENT EXHIB: Claremont Col, Montgomery Gallery & Lang Gallery, CA, 1992

PRINTERS: Cirrus Editions Workshop, Los Angeles, CA (CEW)
PUBLISHERS: Cirrus Editions, Ltd, Los Angeles, CA (CE)
GALLERIES: Cirrus Editions Gallery, Los Angeles, CA; Marc Richards Gallery, Los Angeles, CA; Marc Jancou Gallery, Zürich, Switzerland

TITLE	PUBLISHER	PRINTER	DATE	MEDIUM	DIMENSION (PAPER SIZE) IN INCHES	TYPE OF PAPER	EDITION NUMBER	NO. OF COLORS	ORIGINAL OPENING PRICE	CURRENT RETAIL PRICE
CURRENT EDITIONS:										
Couple Suite (Set of 2)									2730 SET	2730 SET
Couple 1	CE	CEW	1992	LC	44 X 34	R/BFK	40	3	1200	1200
Couple 2	CE	CEW	1992	LC	44 X 34	R/BFK	40	3	1200	1200
Untitled Series (Set of 16)	CE	CEW	1992	LC	24 X 20 EA	R/BFK	60 EA	4-6 EA	1680 SET	1680 SET
									650 EA	650 EA

The print market has become very selective. For the first time since we published the first edition of The Printworld Directory in 1982, the prices of prints have been greatly reduced and greatly increased for the same artists by the most reputable and established print publishers. Check the fifth edition to understand the movement.

DUANE MICHALS

BORN: McKeesport, PA; February 18, 1932
EDUCATION: Univ of Denver, CO, BA
RECENT EXHIB: Butler Inst of Am Art, Youngstown, OH, 1989; Southern Alleghenies Mus, Loretto, PA, 1989; Fay Gold Gallery, Atlanta, GA, 1990; San Francisco Mus of Mod Art, CA, 1991; Mus of Photographic Arts, San Diego, CA, 1992; Miami-Dade Com Col, Miami, FL, 1992; Southern Alleghenies Mus of Art, Loretto, PA, 1992; Sidney Janis Gallery, NY, 1987,92

COLLECTIONS: Mus of Mod Art, NY; Chicago Art Inst, IL; Mus Folkwang, Essen, Germany; George Eastman House, Rochester, NY
PRINTERS: Artist (ART)
PUBLISHERS: Galerie Wilde (GW); Artist (ART)
GALLERIES: Sidney Janis Gallery, New York, NY; Douglas Drake Gallery, Kansas City, KS; Witkin Gallery, New York, NY; Light Impressions Spectrum Gallery, Rochester, NY; Impulse Gallery, Providence, MA; Fay Gold Gallery, Atlanta, GA
MAILING ADDRESS: 109 E 19th St, New York, NY 10003

TITLE	PUBLISHER	PRINTER	DATE	MEDIUM	DIMENSION (PAPER SIZE) IN INCHES	TYPE OF PAPER	EDITION NUMBER	NO. OF COLORS	ORIGINAL OPENING PRICE	CURRENT RETAIL PRICE
SOLD OUT EDITIONS (RARE):										
Things are Queer (Series of 9 Photographs)	ART	ART	1971	PH	3 X 5 EA	AP	25 EA		500 SET	15000 SET
The Blue Sequence (Set of 7):	ART	ART	1973–74	PH	3 X 5 EA	AP	25 EA		500 SET	12000 SET
10 Fotografen (Set of 10)	GW	ART	1975	PH	17 X 13 EA	AP	30 EA		1800 SET	15000 SET

TOM MIELKO

BORN: Boston, MA; October 25, 1945
EDUCATION: Art Inst of Boston, MA; Boston Mus of Fine Arts Sch, MA
AWARDS: First Prize, George Walling Show, Nantucket, MA
RECENT EXHIB: Dyansen Gallery, NY, 1990; Arlington Gallery, Santa Barbara, CA 1990

COLLECTIONS: Smithsonian Inst, Wash, DC
PRINTERS: Hampson Printing, CT (HamPr); Kingswood Group, Ardmore, PA (KiPr)
PUBLISHERS: Artist (ART)
GALLERIES: Thalhainers Gallery, Naples, FL; Mielko Gallery, Nantucket, MA
MAILING ADDRESS: P O Box 4489, Santa Barbara, CA 93103

TITLE	PUBLISHER	PRINTER	DATE	MEDIUM	DIMENSION (PAPER SIZE) IN INCHES	TYPE OF PAPER	EDITION NUMBER	NO. OF COLORS	ORIGINAL OPENING PRICE	CURRENT RETAIL PRICE
SOLD OUT EDITIONS (RARE):										
A Quiet Place	ART	HamPr	1982	LC/OFF	17 X 23	80 lb Cov	100	4	50	200
Queen Ann's Lace	ART	HamPr	1982	LC/OFF	17 X 23	80 lb Cov	100	4	50	200
Sunday Afternoon	ART	HamPr	1982	LC/OFF	17 X 23	80 lb Cov	150	4	50	175
The Sentry	ART	HamPr	1984	LC/OFF	17 X 23	80 lb Cov	150	4	50	250
Lady on a Chestnut Mare	ART	HamPr	1984	LC/OFF	20 X 29	80 lb Cov	150	4	50	150
Summer Breeze	ART	HamPr	1984	LC/OFF	20 X 29	80 lb Cov	250	4	50	150
Afternoon Nap	ART	KiPr	1984	LC/OFF	20 X 29	90 lb Cov	250	4	50	150
CURRENT EDITIONS:										
Carousel	ART	HamPr	1984	LC/OFF	20 X 29	80 lb Cov	280	4	50	100
Crooked House	ART	HamPr	1984	LC/OFF	20 X 29	80 lb Cov	250	4	50	100
Afternoon Nap	ART	KiPr	1985	LC/OFF	17 X 23	80 lb Cov	500	4	50	100
The Outing	ART	KiPr	1985	LC/OFF	17 X 23	80 lb Cov	500	4	50	100
Summer Wishes	ART	KiPr	1985	LC/OFF	17 X 23	80 lb Cov	500	4	50	100
Water's Edge	ART	ART	1985	SP	18 X 24	90 lb Cov	280	15	75	200
Diana's Fantasy	ART	KiPr	1986	LC/OFF	17 X 23	80 lb Cov	500	4	50	100
A Summer Place	ART		1989	LC/OFF	17 X 23	90 lb Cov	500	4	60	100

JAY MILDER

BORN: Omaha, Nebraska; May 12, 1934
EDUCATION: The Sorbonne, Paris, France; William Hayter Graphics, NY; Chicago Art Inst, IL
TEACHING: New York City Col, NY, 1977 to present
AWARDS: Walter Gutman Award, 1960; First Prize, All Ohio Artists, 1964; First Prize, Figurative Artists, Bayonne, NY, 1977; Nat Endowment for the Arts Fel, 1989–90

COLLECTIONS: Tel Aviv Mus, Israel; Baltimore Mus, MD; Chrysler Mus, Norfolk, VA; Robert Schoelkopf Gallery, NY; Skidmore Col, NY
PRINTERS: Artist (ART)
PUBLISHERS: Fred Dorfman, Inc, NY (FDI)
GALLERIES: Shahin Requicha Gallery, Manhattan Beach, CA; Gallery Jupiter, Little Silver, NJ; Fred Dorfman Gallery, New York, NY
MAILING ADDRESS: 108 Wooster St, New York, NY 10012

TITLE	PUBLISHER	PRINTER	DATE	MEDIUM	DIMENSION (PAPER SIZE) IN INCHES	TYPE OF PAPER	EDITION NUMBER	NO. OF COLORS	ORIGINAL OPENING PRICE	CURRENT RETAIL PRICE
CURRENT EDITIONS:										
Homage to Robert Jones	FDI	ART	1979	LC	39 X 28	AP	275	4	200	275
Space Space	FDI	ART	1979	LC	40 X 28	AP	275	4	200	275
Spacelock	FDI	ART	1979	LC	28 X 36	AP	275	4	200	275

FRANCES ST CLAIR MILLER

BORN: England
EDUCATION: Slade Sch of Art, Univ Col, London, England
TEACHING: Prof, Printmaking, Sir John Cass Col, London, England; Master Printer, Octopus Press, London, England; Master Printer, Studio Prints, London, England
PRINTERS: Artist (ART)
PUBLISHERS: John Szoke Graphics, Inc, NY (JSG)
GALLERIES: John Szoke Graphics, Inc, New York, NY

FRANCES ST CLAIR MILLER CONTINUED

TITLE	PUBLISHER	PRINTER	DATE	MEDIUM	DIMENSION (PAPER SIZE) IN INCHES	TYPE OF PAPER	EDITION NUMBER	NO. OF COLORS	ORIGINAL OPENING PRICE	CURRENT RETAIL PRICE
CURRENT EDITIONS:										
Luxembourg Gardens	JSG	ART	1984	EC	23 X 30	TS	150	4	250	300
Westbury Court Garden	JSG	ART	1985	EC	22 X 30	TS	150	4	250	300
Autumn Garden	JSG	ART	1986	EC	26 X 21	TS	150	4	200	250
Evening Garden	JSG	ART	1986	EC	21 X 26	TS	150	4	200	250
Cherry Path	JSG	ART	1990	EC	15 X 21	TS	150	4	225	225
Late Autumn at Bredwardine	JSG	ART	1990	EC	17 X 23	TS	150	4	250	250

KATHRYN MILLER

BORN: Philadelphia, PA; June 21, 1935
EDUCATION: Univ of North Carolina, Chapell Hill, NC, 1957; Georgia Southern Col, Statesboro, GA, 1969; Savannah Col of Art & Design, GA, 1979–80
TEACHING: Instr, Armstrong State Col, Savannah, GA, 1987–88; Trenholm Artists Guild Workshop, GA, 1988
AWARDS: Award of Distinction, Drayton Hall, South Carolina Crafts Assn, 1985; Second Place, Manarin Art Assn, 1986: Award of Distinction, Tarpon Springs, 1989

COLLECTIONS: Savannah Col of Art & Design, GA; Marion County Mus, Marion, SC; Waycross Junior Col, Waycross, GA
PRINTERS: McGrew Color Graphics, Kansas City, MO (Mc); Artist (ART)
PUBLISHERS: Artist (ART)
GALLERIES: Friedman's Art Gallery, Savannah, GA; Tatler Gallery, Hilton Head Island, SC; Left Bank Art Gallery, St Simons, GA; Gallery House, Marietta, GA; Lyman Gallery, St Simons Island, GA
MAILING ADDRESS: 2 Stillwood Court, South, Savannah, GA 31419

TITLE	PUBLISHER	PRINTER	DATE	MEDIUM	DIMENSION (PAPER SIZE) IN INCHES	TYPE OF PAPER	EDITION NUMBER	NO. OF COLORS	ORIGINAL OPENING PRICE	CURRENT RETAIL PRICE
CURRENT EDITIONS:										
Georgia Backwater	ART	ART	1980	EB	14 X 18	AP/B	50	1	100	150
Shell Medley	ART	ART	1980	EB	14 X 18	AP/B	200	1	100	150
Preening Heron	ART	ART	1981	EB	14 X 18	R/BFK	200	1	100	150
White Heron	ART	ART	1981	WC	14 X 11	R/100	50	5	100	150
Toucan	ART	ART	1981	WC	14 X 11	R/100	10	8	200	250
Anhinga	ART	ART	1981	LC	16 X 20	R/100	50	4	60	150
Macaw State I,II	ART	ART	1981	LC	12 X 16 EA	R/100	50 EA	4 EA	60 EA	150 EA
Under Sea World	ART	ART	1982	EC	12 X 16	R/100	200	3	60	150
The Canadians	ART	ART	1982	EC	14 X 18	AP/B	200	2	100	150
The Egrets	ART	ART	1982	EB/EMB	14 X 18	R/BFK	200	1	100	150
Up and Away	ART	ART	1982	EC	12 X 18	AP/B	200	7	100	150
High Society	ART	ART	1982	EC	12 X 18	AP/B	200	2	60	150
Sundown	ART	ART	1982	EC	14 X 18	AP/B	200	3	100	150
Unicorn	ART	ART	1983	EB	14 X 18	R/BFK	200	1	100	150
Dragon	ART	ART	1985	EC/A/EMB	16 X 30	AP/B	200	6	140	200
Cats!	ART	ART	1985	EC/A/EMB	15 X 13	AP/B	200	3	100	150
The Great Blue	ART	ART	1985	EC/A/HC	17 X 15	R/BFK	200	3	100	150
Ducks and Daisies	ART	ART	1985	EC/A/HC	12 X 22	AP/B	200	4	100	150
Pelican Flight	ART	ART	1985	EC/A/EMB	20 X 16	AP/B	200	1	100	150
Pelican Bay	ART	ART	1985	EC/A/EMB	20 X 16	AP/B	200	4	100	150
The Hen Party	ART	ART	1985	EC/A/EMB	11 X 22	AP/B	200	3	100	150

ROBERT (BUCK) MILLER

BORN: Freeport, IL; November 19, 1937
TEACHING: Southern Illinois Univ, Carbondale, IL, 1975; Milwaukee Artists Teachers Col, WI, 1977–78
AWARDS: Special Merit Award, Photographer of the Year, 1975; United Nations Environmental Award, 1975

RECENT EXHIB: Clark Col, Vancouver, WA, 1989
COLLECTIONS: Milwaukee Art Center, WI, 1982; Posner Gallery, Milwaukee, WI, 1982
PRINTERS: Kolor-Krome, Milwaukee, WI (K-K)
PUBLISHERS: Univ of Kansas, Lawrence, KS (UK); Continental Heritage Press, Tulsa, OK (CHP); Judith Posner Associates, Milwaukee, WI (JPA)
GALLERIES: Posner Gallery, Milwaukee, WI; Gallery 72, Omaha, NE
MAILING ADDRESS: PO Box 33, Milwaukee, WI 53201

TITLE	PUBLISHER	PRINTER	DATE	MEDIUM	DIMENSION (PAPER SIZE) IN INCHES	TYPE OF PAPER	EDITION NUMBER	NO. OF COLORS	ORIGINAL OPENING PRICE	CURRENT RETAIL PRICE
CURRENT EDITIONS:										
Lake Michigan	JPA	K-K	1979	PH	16 X 20	CIBA	300		300	350
Hot Air Balloons	JPA	K-K	1980	PH	16 X 20	CIBA	300		300	350
Wolf River	JPA	K-K	1981	PH	16 X 20	CIBA	300		300	350
Lovers	JPA	K-K	1982	PH	16 X 20	CIBA	300		300	350
Lacrosse	JPA	K-K	1982	PH	16 X 20	CIBA	300		300	350

The retail prices of the 100,000 limited edition prints quoted in this directory are subject to change. Print publishers, artists and galleries were the direct sources for these quotations. Prices in the secondary market listed as "Sold Out Editions (Rare)" indicate that the publisher has a limited supply of that print or that the print is difficult to locate in the galleries.

HENRY MILLER

BORN: New York, NY; (1891–1980)
EDUCATION: Self-Taught
RECENT EXHIB: Matsuya Ginza, Tokyo, Japan, 1991; Coast Gallery, Big Sur, CA, 1991; Galerie Springer, Berlin, Germany, 1992
COLLECTIONS: Harvard Univ, Cambridge, MA; Yale Univ, New Haven, CT; San Francisco Mus of Mod Art, Univ of California, Los Angeles, CA
PRINTERS: Ed Holt, Carmel, CA (EH); Larissa Holt, Carmel, CA (LH); Coast Publishing Studio, Carmel, CA (CPS)
PUBLISHERS: Coast Publishing, Carmel, CA (CP)
GALLERIES: Coast Galleries, Big Sur, CA & Pebble Beach, CA & Wailea, Maui, HI & Hana, Maui, HI & Lahaina, Maui, HI
MAILING ADDRESS: c/o Coast Publishing, P O Box 223519, Carmel, CA 93922

Henry Miller
Antoine the Clown
Courtesy Coast Publishing

Henry Miller
Chagall's Horse
Courtesy Coast Publishing

TITLE	PUBLISHER	PRINTER	DATE	MEDIUM	DIMENSION (PAPER SIZE) IN INCHES	TYPE OF PAPER	EDITION NUMBER	NO. OF COLORS	ORIGINAL OPENING PRICE	CURRENT RETAIL PRICE
SOLD OUT EDITIONS (RARE):										
L'Amour Toujours	CP	EH/LH/CPS	1975	LC		AP	200		475	6000
Clown A	CP		1975	LC		AP	200		450	8000
Clown B	CP		1975	LC		AP	200		275	4500
Clownesque	CP		1975	LC		AP	200		200	3500
Childish Dream	CP		1975	LC		AP	200		225	3500
Open Labyrinth	CP		1975	LC		AP	200		225	3300
Dream of Spring	CP		1975	LC		AP	200		250	3500
Fantasy	CP		1975	LC		AP	200		225	3900
Maison de Fous	CP		1975	LC		AP	200		400	4000
After the Quake	CP		1975	LC		AP	200		200	3800
North Africa	CP		1975	LC		AP	200		350	6000
The Procession	CP		1975	LC		AP	200		425	4200
Gremlins	CP		1975	LC		AP	200		375	4400
Glow Worm	CP		1975	LC		AP	200		375	4000
Face to Face	CP		1975	LC		AP	200		300	2250
D'Apres Schatz	CP		1975	LC		AP	200		300	3000
Linear Fantasy	CP		1975	LC		AP	200		300	2500
Happy Days	CP		1975	LC		AP	200		300	2700
Hero (Head)	CP		1975	EC		R/BFK	120		225	3500
Jeune Fille	CP		1975	EC		R/BFK	120		200	2500
Creative World	CP		1975	EC		R/BFK	120		175	2300
Early Music	CP		1975	EC		R/BFK	120		175	2500
Broken Dreams	CP		1975	EC		R/BFK	120		200	2400
The Question	CP		1975	EC		R/BFK	120		200	2400
Initiations	CP		1975	EC		R/BFK	120		200	2500
Facing East	CP		1975	EC		R/BFK	120		175	2750

HENRY MILLER CONTINUED

TITLE	PUBLISHER	PRINTER	DATE	MEDIUM	DIMENSION (PAPER SIZE) IN INCHES	TYPE OF PAPER	EDITION NUMBER	NO. OF COLORS	ORIGINAL OPENING PRICE	CURRENT RETAIL PRICE
SOLD OUT EDITIONS (RARE):										
Good News	CP		1975	EC		R/BFK	120		175	3000
Just a Brooklyn Boy	CP		1983	LC		AP	200		675	6000
Smile at the Foot of the Ladder	CP		1983	LC		AP	200		675	5500
Sarasota	CP		1983	LC		AP	200		675	3000
Remembrance	CP		1983	LC		AP	200		550	4900
Enlarged Dream	CP		1983	LC		AP	200		675	3200
Siamese Night	CP		1983	LC		AP	200		650	3300
Looking East to the Sun	CP		1983	LC		AP	200		650	3300
CURRENT EDITIONS:										
Hawaiian Serenade	CP		1990	LC		AP	200		1200	3500
Going South to Mexico	CP		1990	LC		AP	200		1200	3800
Chagall's Horse	CP	EH/LH/CPS	1991	SP	12 X 14	AP	200	16	750	1250
Jerusalem	CP	EH/LH/CPS	1991	SP	12 X 13	AP	200	22	800	1250
The Blue Pitcher	CP	EH/LH/CPS	1991	SP	13 X 15	AP	200	26	800	1250
Antoine the Clown	CP	EH/LH/CPS	1991	SP	10 X 14	AP	200	17	850	1250
Bubu	CP	EH/LH/CPS	1992	SP	17 X 20	AP	200	11	1300	1300
Sunday Afternoon	CP	EH/LH/CPS	1992	SP	14 X 12	AP	200	17	1250	1250
Really the Blues	CP	EH/LH/CPS	1992	SP	16 X 10	AP	200	17	1250	1250
A la Durrell	CP	EH/LH/CPS	1992	SP	15 X 15	AP	200	20	1300	1300

Henry Miller
Jerusalem
Courtesy Coast Publishing

Henry Miller
Blue Pitcher
Courtesy Coast Publishing

RICHARD KIDWELL MILLER

BORN: Fairmont, West Virginia; March 15, 1930
EDUCATION: Pennsylvania Acad of Fine Arts, Phila, PA; American Univ, Wash, DC, BA, 1953; Columbia Univ, NY, MFA, 1956
TEACHING: Asst Prof, Painting, Kansas City Art Inst, MO, 1968–69; Adj Prof, Painting & Drawing, Westchester Comm Col, NY, 1980–83
AWARDS: Washington Times-Herald Scholar, 1947; Fulbright Fel, 1953; Gertrude Vanderbilt Whitney Scholar, Nat Inst of Arts & Letters, NY, 1948–53, 1955–56

COLLECTIONS: Hirshhorn Mus, Wash, DC; Phillips Coll, Wash, DC; Rochester Mus, NY; Albrecht Gallery of Art, St Louis, MO; Univ of Arizona, Tucson, AZ
PRINTERS: Artist (ART)
PUBLISHERS: Artist (ART)
GALLERIES: Peter Rose Gallery, New York, NY; Bell Gallery, Greenwich, CT
MAILING ADDRESS: 222 W 83rd St, Apt 8C, New York, NY 10024

TITLE	PUBLISHER	PRINTER	DATE	MEDIUM	DIMENSION (PAPER SIZE) IN INCHES	TYPE OF PAPER	EDITION NUMBER	NO. OF COLORS	ORIGINAL OPENING PRICE	CURRENT RETAIL PRICE
SOLD OUT EDITIONS (RARE):										
Coq	ART	ART	1960	EB/A	12 X 18	R/100	50	2	100	200

RICHARD KIDWELL MILLER CONTINUED

TITLE	PUBLISHER	PRINTER	DATE	MEDIUM	DIMENSION (PAPER SIZE) IN INCHES	TYPE OF PAPER	EDITION NUMBER	NO. OF COLORS	ORIGINAL OPENING PRICE	CURRENT RETAIL PRICE
CURRENT EDITIONS:										
Portent II	ART	ART	1978	SP	26 X 26	R/100	100	4	400	400
Tension Black	ART	ART	1978	SP	26 X 26	R/100	100	3	400	400
Side Winder	ART	ART	1978	SP	17 X 26	R/100	100	4	350	350
Flight Blue	ART	ART	1978	SP	16 X 22	R/100	50	3	250	250
Fire Wind	ART	ART	1978	SP	16 X 22	R/100	100	3	250	250
The Room	ART	ART	1978	SP	14 X 14	R/100	75	3	250	250
Signal I	ART	ART	1978	SP	12 X 12	R/100	75	3	250	250
Signal II	ART	ART	1978	SP	12 X 18	R/100	75	3	300	300
Haddonfield	ART	ART	1978	SP	14 X 14	R/100	75	3	300	300
Flight I	ART	ART	1979	EB/A	7 X 12	R/100	75	2	250	250
Flight Red	ART	ART	1979	EB/A	12 X 12	R/100	75	3	300	300

STEVE MILLER

BORN: Buffalo, NY; October 12, 1951
EDUCATION: Univ of Vermont, Burlington, VT, 1970; Middlebury Col, VT, BA, 1973; Skohegan Sch of Art & Sculpture, ME, 1973
AWARDS: Hans Hofmann Fel, Fine Arts Work Center, Providencetown, MA, 1973–74; Nat Endowment for the Arts Fel, 1987
RECENT EXHIB: Mint Mus, Charlotte, NC, 1987; Bronx Mus of Art, NY, 1987; Everson Mus of Art, Syracuse, NY, 1987; Josh Baer Gallery, NY, 1988; Fiction/Non-Fiction Gallery, NY, 1989; Carol Getz Gallery, Miami, FL, 1989; Galerie du Genie, Paris, France, 1988, 90; S-Bitter Larkin Gallery, NY, 1990

COLLECTIONS: Albright-Knox Art Gallery, Buffalo, NY; Burchfield Art Center, Buffalo, NY
PRINTERS: Donald Sheridan Fine Arts, Brooklyn, NY (DSFA)
PUBLISHERS: Artist (ART)
GALLERIES: Castelli Graphics, New York, NY; Josh Baer Gallery, New York, NY; Galerie du Genie, Paris, France; Editions Ilene Kurtz, New York, NY; Nina Freudenheim Gallery, Buffalo, NY; S-Bitter Larkin Gallery, New York, NY; Carol Getz Gallery, Miami, FL
MAILING ADDRESS: 48 Gold St, New York, NY 10038

TITLE	PUBLISHER	PRINTER	DATE	MEDIUM	DIMENSION (PAPER SIZE) IN INCHES	TYPE OF PAPER	EDITION NUMBER	NO. OF COLORS	ORIGINAL OPENING PRICE	CURRENT RETAIL PRICE
CURRENT EDITIONS:										
Untitled (Series of 29)	ART	DSFA	1986	MON	21 X 31 EA	LEN/MB	1 EA	Varies	1000 EA	1000 EA
Untitled (Series of 17)	ART	DSFA	1987	MON	24 X 31 EA	LEN/MB	1 EA	Varies	1000 EA	1000 EA
Untitled (Series of 20)	ART	DSFA	1989	MON	32 X 41 EA	LEN/MB	1 EA	Varies	1000 EA	1000 EA

RICHARD K MILLS

BORN: New York, NY; December 10, 1947
EDUCATION: Aspen Sch of Contemp Art, CO, 1965; City Col of New York, NY, BA, 1970, MFA, 1974; Pratt Graphics Center, NY, 1977–79
TEACHING: Instr, Screenprinting, Nat Acad Sch of Fine Arts, NY, 1984; Instr, Printmaking, Pratt Graphics Center, NY, 1982–85; Instr, Printmaking, C W Post, Long Island Univ, Greenvale, NY, 1985 to present

AWARDS: Best Print, City without Walls, Newark, NY, 1985
COLLECTIONS: American Mus, Bath, England; Haifa Mus of Mod Art, Israel
PRINTERS: Artist (ART)
PUBLISHERS: Orion Editions, NY (OE); International Graphic Arts Found, NY (CA); Pratt Graphics Center, NY (PGC); Artist (ART)
GALLERIES: Orion Editions, New York, NY; Images Art Gallery, Briarcliff, NY; Gross McCleaf Gallery, Phila, PA

TITLE	PUBLISHER	PRINTER	DATE	MEDIUM	DIMENSION (PAPER SIZE) IN INCHES	TYPE OF PAPER	EDITION NUMBER	NO. OF COLORS	ORIGINAL OPENING PRICE	CURRENT RETAIL PRICE
SOLD OUT EDITIONS (RARE):										
Madison Avenue Park	ART	ART	1977	SP	15 X 20	STP	20	13	100	200
Lexington Avenue (Wine & Liquors)	ART	ART	1978	SP	26 X 20	LEN	15	10	150	250
Cooper Square	ART	ART	1978	SP	20 X 26	LEN	20	15	175	300
Madison Square/Flat Iron Building	ART	ART	1982	SP	30 X 27	AP	50	8	250	650
PAS	ART	ART	1982	SP	30 X 38	RP/G	35	10	250	450
Porter's House II	ART	ART	1983	SP	26 X 29	LEN	20	6	250	350
Porter's House III	ART	ART	1983	SP	26 X 29	LEN	22	8	250	350
CURRENT EDITIONS:										
Third Avenue	PGC	ART	1978	SP	11 X 15	STP	70	8	100	200
Flatiron I	ART	ART	1979	SP	15 X 22	STP	60	3	100	200
Early Spring: Broadway	ART	ART	1979	SP	20 X 26	AP	25	6	150	200
Empire State (Gray Steps)	ART	ART	1979	SP	28 X 30	AP	47	7	150	200
Fifth Avenue	ART/OE	ART	1980	SP	39 X 30	GE	50	8	200	350
Children's Corner	ART	ART	1982	SP	36 X 28	GE	35	8	200	450
From 461	ART	ART	1982	SP	36 X 28	GE	35	8	250	450
Porter's House I	ART	ART	1983	SP	23 X 26	AP88	22	6	250	350
Ello	ART	ART	1983	SP	26 X 36	AP	22	10	275	400
Schwarzenbach Facade	ART	ART	1983	SP/LC	31 X 24	SOM	18	8	250	350
Schwarzenbach Facade/31st Street	ART	ART	1983	SP/LC	31 X 24	SOM	18	8	250	350
Toward Wellfleet Harbor	ART	ART	1983	PO	22 X 27	AP	14	18	250	350
Maine/Rain	ART	ART	1983	SP	26 X 25	AP/B	26	10	150	250

RICHARD K MILLS CONTINUED

TITLE	PUBLISHER	PRINTER	DATE	MEDIUM	DIMENSION (PAPER SIZE) IN INCHES	TYPE OF PAPER	EDITION NUMBER	NO. OF COLORS	ORIGINAL OPENING PRICE	CURRENT RETAIL PRICE
CURRENT EDITIONS:										
Autumn Haze I, II	ART	ART	1983	PO	28 X 36 EA	AP/WA	50 EA	15 EA	300 EA	350 EA
Eastern Standard #9	ART	ART	1984	SP	21 X 21	AP88	15	8	200	250
Ebb Tide, Wellfleet	ART	ART	1984	SP	23 X 33	AP	49	14	275	350
Madison Fragment	ART/IGA	ART	1984	SP	18 X 20	R/BFK	100	18	200	250
Buxton's Cove	ART	ART	1985	SP	23 X 30	AP	50	12	300	350
Lowe's House/Halls Mills	ART	ART	1985	SP	23 X 30	AP	50	15	250	300
Martin's Truck	ART	ART	1985	SP	23 X 30	AP	50	6	250	300
Lewis Gardiner's House	ART	ART	1985	SP	23 X 30	AP	50	6	250	300
Eagle Island Mailboat	ART	ART	1985	SP	23 X 30	AP	50	12	300	350
Porter House/Great Spruce Head Island	ART	ART	1985	SP	23 X 30	R/BFK	50	7	275	350
Quoddy I	ART	ART	1985	SP	23 X 30	AP	50	6	300	350
Quoddy II	ART	ART	1985	SP	23 X 30	AP	20	6	375	350
Pines	ART	ART	1985	SP	23 X 30	AP	50	8	300	350
Storefront, Stonington	ART	ART	1985	SP	23 X 30	AP	25	8	300	350
Self Portrait (from Self Portraits To Go Suite)	PGC	ART	1985	SP	15 X 15	R/BFK	40	4	100	150
Saggitarius in New York (from Cityscapes Suite)	PGC	ART	1985	SP	14 X 17	AP	21	4	100	150
Porter's House IV	ART	ART	1986	SP	25 X 29	Italia	35	5	300	350
Erotica (from Erotica Suite)	PGC	ART	1986	SP	14 X 17	CD	21	4	100	150
Black City Series I, II, III	OE	ART	1989	SP	35 X 41 EA	CD	80 EA		950 EA	950 EA

MARILYN MINTER

BORN: Shreveport, LA; July 19, 1948
EDUCATION: Univ of Florida, Gainesville, FL, BFA, 1970; Syracuse Univ, NY, MFA, Painting, 1972
TEACHING: Instr, Painting, Sch of Visual Arts, NY, 1987 to present
AWARDS: New York State Council of the Arts, 1988; Nat Endowment for the Arts Award, 1989
RECENT EXHIB: White Columns Gallery, NY, 1988; Nicola Jacobs Gallery, London, England, 1989; Max Protetch Gallery, NY, 1990; Simon Watson Gallery, NY, 1990; Meyers/Bloom Gallery, Santa Monica, CA, 1991; Max Protetch Gallery, NY, 1992
COLLECTIONS: Mus of Mod Art, NY; Denver Art Mus, CO; Everson Mus, Syracuse, NY
PRINTERS: Jack Lemon, Chicago, IL (JL); Landfall Press, Inc, Chicago, IL (LPI); Bob Blanton, NY (BB); Tom Little, NY (TL); New York Art Lab, NY (NYAL)
PUBLISHERS: Landfall Press, Inc, Chicago, IL (LPI); New York Art Lab, NY (NYAL)
GALLERIES: Greenberg Gallery, St Louis, MO; Myers/Bloom Gallery, Santa Monica, CA; Max Protetch Gallery, New York, NY; Simon Watson Gallery, New York, NY; Fred Dorfman Gallery, New York, NY; Nicola Jacobs Gallery, London, England; Landfall Press, Inc, Chicago, IL; Carol Getz Gallery, Coconut Grove, FL; Quartet Editions, New York, NY
MAILING ADDRESS: c/o Max Protetch Gallery, 560 Broadway, New York, NY 10012

TITLE	PUBLISHER	PRINTER	DATE	MEDIUM	DIMENSION (PAPER SIZE) IN INCHES	TYPE OF PAPER	EDITION NUMBER	NO. OF COLORS	ORIGINAL OPENING PRICE	CURRENT RETAIL PRICE
CURRENT EDITIONS:										
Hands Dumping	LPI	JL/LPI	1989	SP	24 X 30	ALUM	35		1500	1500
Hands Folding	LPI	JL/LPI	1989	SP	24 X 30	ALUM	35		1500	1500
Hands Washing	LPI	JL/LPI	1989	SP	24 X 30	ALUM	35		1500	1500
Fingered	NYAL	BB/TL/NYAL	1992	SP	28 X 21	ALUM	9	1	1500	1500
Funhouse Mirror, Series One	NYAL	BB/TL/NYAL	1992	SP	68 X 34	ALUM	5	2	3750	3750
Funhouse Mirror, Series Two	NYAL	BB/TL/NYAL	1992	SP	68 X 34	ALUM	5	3	3750	3750
Sleep, States I, II, III	NYAL	BB/TL/NYAL	1992	SP	96 X 32 EA	ALUM	1 EA	1 EA	5250 EA	5250 EA

HARRY MINTZ

BORN: September 27, 1909; US Citizen
TEACHING: Prof Emeritus, Art Inst of Chicago, IL
AWARDS: Art Inst of Chicago, IL, 1953; Jules F Bower Prize, 1952,54; Silver Prize, Art Inst of Chicago, IL, 1962
COLLECTIONS: Corcoran Gallery of Art, Wash, DC; Art Inst of Chicago, IL; New Evansville Mus, IN; Whitney Mus of Am Art, NY; Tel Aviv Mus of Mod Art, Israel; Rio de Janeiro Mus of Art, Brazil; Univ of Notre Dame, South Bend, IN; Northwestern Univ, Evanston, IL; Warsaw Acad of Fine Art, Warsaw, Poland
PRINTERS: Jean Barrau, NY (JP)
PUBLISHERS: Stanley Moss, NY (SM)
GALLERIES: Silver Cloud Fine Arts, Chicago, IL; Gilman/Gruen Gallery, Chicago, IL
MAILING ADDRESS: 429 W Briar Pl, Chicago, IL 60657

TITLE	PUBLISHER	PRINTER	DATE	MEDIUM	DIMENSION (PAPER SIZE) IN INCHES	TYPE OF PAPER	EDITION NUMBER	NO. OF COLORS	ORIGINAL OPENING PRICE	CURRENT RETAIL PRICE
CURRENT EDITIONS:										
In Flight	SM	JB	1982	SP	42 X 30	AP88	150	6	450	750

The Printworld Directory is accepting new applications for the seventh edition. Approximately 300 new artists will be accepted. Please use the two forms provided in the back section of this directory to submit biographical data and documentation of prints. Edition number of each print must not exceed 500 and the retail price must be $100 or more.

PETER WINSLOW MILTON

BORN: Lower Merion, PA; April 2, 1930
EDUCATION: Yale Univ, New Haven, CT, BFA, 1954, MFA, 1961, with Joseph Albers
TEACHING: Instr, Drawing & Basic Design, Maryland Inst, Col of Art, Baltimore, MD, 1961–68; Instr, Printmaking, Yale Univ Summer Sch of Music & Art, 1970
AWARDS: Yale-Norfolk Residency, 1953; Yale Traveling Fel, 1954; Louis Comfort Tiffany Found Grant, 1963; First Prize, Festival de Artes Graficas, Cali, Colombia, 1969; Grand Prize, Second Festival of Art, Seoul, Korea, 1972; Residency, Rockefeller Found, Bellagio, Italy, 1990; Medal of Honor, Int'l Print Exhib, USSR, 1990; Award, Int'l Triennial of Graphic Arts, Cracow, Poland, 1991
RECENT EXHIB: Allport-Caldwell Gallery, San Francisco, CA, 1987; More Gallery, Phila, PA, 1990; Francis Kyle Gallery, London, England, 1991; Davidson Gallery, Seattle, WA, 1991; Franz Bader Gallery, Wash, DC, 1991; Louis Newman Galleries, Beverly Hills, CA, 1992; Edith Caldwell Gallery, San Francisco, CA, 1992; John Szoke Gallery, NY, 1987,91,92
COLLECTIONS: Mus of Mod Art, NY; Metropolitan Mus, NY; Philadelphia Mus, PA; Tate Gallery, London, England; Library of Congress, Wash, DC; Brooklyn Mus, NY; Detroit Inst of Art, MI; Baltimore Mus, MD; Bibliotheque Nat, Paris, France; British Mus, London, England; Carnegie Mus, Pittsburgh, PA; Cincinnati Art Mus, OH; Cleveland Art Mus, OH; Corcoran Gallery, Wash, DC; CA; Mus of Mod Art, San Francisco, CA; Hirshhorn Mus, Wash, DC; Hood Mus, Hanover, NH; Mus of Fine Arts, Houston, TX; Los Angeles County Mus, CA; Minneapolis Inst of Arts, MN; Museo de Arte Moderno, Bogata, Colombia; Museo de Arte Moderno, Cali Colombia; Mus of Fine Arts, Boston, MA; Nat Coll of Fine Arts, Wash, DC; Nat Gallery of Art, Wash, DC; Phillips Coll, Wash, DC; Portland Art Mus, OR; Seattle Art Mus, WA; Yale Univ Art Gallery, New Haven, CT
PRINTERS: Robert Townsend, Boston, MA (RT); Impressions Workshop, Boston, MA (IW); Artist (ART)
PUBLISHERS: Artist (ART)
GALLERIES: Associated American Artists, New York, NY; Franz Bader Gallery, Wash, DC; Alpha Gallery, Boston, MA; Graystone Gallery, San Francisco, CA; Allport Gallery, San Francisco, CA; First Impressions/Barbara Linhard Gallery, Carmel, CA; Summa Gallery, New York, NY & Brooklyn, NY; Uptown Gallery, New York, NY; More Gallery, Phila, PA; Francis Kyle Gallery, London, England; John Szoke Gallery, New York, NY; Louis Newman Galleries, Beverly Hills, CA; Susan Cummins Gallery, Mill Valley, CA; Edith Caldwell Gallery, San Francisco, CA; Rubiner Gallery, West Bloomfield, MI; Ed Hill Gallery, El Paso, TX; David Galleries, Seattle, WA
MAILING ADDRESS: PO Box 237, Francestown, NH 03043

Peter Winslow Milton
American Interior: Family Reunion
Courtesy the Artist

TITLE	PUBLISHER	PRINTER	DATE	MEDIUM	DIMENSION (PAPER SIZE) IN INCHES	TYPE OF PAPER	EDITION NUMBER	NO. OF COLORS	ORIGINAL OPENING PRICE	CURRENT RETAIL PRICE
SOLD OUT EDITIONS (RARE):										
Julia Passing I, II	ART	ART	1967	EB/ENG	18 X 24 EA	MUR	100 EA	1 EA	80 EA	5000 EA
Victoria's Children	ART	ART	1967	EB/ENG	18 X 24	MUR	100	1	80	5000
Passage III	ART	RT	1972	EB/ENG	25 X 37	R/BFK	140	1	250	4000
Passage IV	ART	RT	1973	EB/ENG	19 X 36	R/BFK	140	1	350	4000
The First Gate	ART	RT/IW	1974	EB/ENG	27 X 39	MUR	140	1	500	3000
Second Opinion	ART	RT/IW	1974	EB/ENG	27 X 33	MUR	140	1	375	750
Daylillies	ART	RT/IW	1975	EB/ENG	26 X 28	RWW/B	160	1	600	14000
A Sky Blue Life	ART	RT/IW	1976	EB/ENG	26 X 40	GE/CO	160	1	850	3600
The Rehearsal	ART	RT/IW	1977	EB/ENG	31 X 42	RHW/B	160	1	900	3600
Before the Hunt	ART	RT/IW	1978	EB/ENG	22 X 39	R/BFK	160	1	850	4000
Sanctuary's Edge (Lift Ground)	ART	RT/IW	1981	EB	58 X 40	AC/B	171	1	1000	1500

The retail prices of the 100,000 limited edition prints quoted in this directory are subject to change. Print publishers, artists and galleries were the direct sources for these quotations. Prices in the secondary market listed as "Sold Out Editions (Rare)" indicate that the publisher has a limited supply of that print or that the print is difficult to locate in the galleries.

PETER WINSLOW MILTON CONTINUED

TITLE	PUBLISHER	PRINTER	DATE	MEDIUM	DIMENSION (PAPER SIZE) IN INCHES	TYPE OF PAPER	EDITION NUMBER	NO. OF COLORS	ORIGINAL OPENING PRICE	CURRENT RETAIL PRICE
SOLD OUT EDITIONS (RARE):										
Erotic Suite (Set of 4):									1200 SET	1200 SET
Butterfly	ART	RT	1982	EB/ENG	17 X 18	R/BFK	125	1	350	350
Europe	ART	RT	1982	EB/ENG	17 X 18	R/BFK	125	1	350	350
Friday's Children	ART	RT	1982	EB/ENG	17 X 18	R/BFK	125	1	350	350
Cotillion	ART	RT	1982	EB/ENG	17 X 18	R/BFK	125	1	350	350
CURRENT EDITIONS:										
Interior Series:										
Interior I: Family Reunion	ART	RT	1984	EB/ENG	27 X 42	R/BFK	175	1	900	7500
Interiors II: Stolen Moments	ART	RT	1986	EB/ENG	38 X 30	R/BFK	175	1	1500	2100
Interiors III: Time with Celia	ART	RT	1986	EB/ENG	38 X 30	R/BFK	175	1	1500	2100
Interior IV: Hotel Paradise Cafe	ART	RT	1987	EB/ENG	30 X 42	R/BFK	175	1	1800	13000
Interior V: Water Music	ART	RT	1988	EB/ENG	38 X 30	SOM	175	1	1500	2400
Interior VI: Soundings	ART	RT	1989	EB/ENG	38 X 30	SOM	175	1	1800	2600
Interior VII: The Train from Munich	ART	RT	1991	EB/ENG	28 X 42	R/BFK	175	1	2200	5200

MIRÁ PARIS

BORN: Near Russian Border; 1934
EDUCATION: Building & Arch Col, Nuremburg, Germany; T K Col, Malmö, Sweden, Lund Univ, Sweden
COLLECTIONS: Las Vegas Art Mus, NV; Safiro Castle, Stockholm, Sweden; Univ of California, Davis, CA; Richard Nixon Library, Yorbia Linda, CA; George Bush Library, Texas A & M Univ, College Station, TX; Jimmy Carter Library, GA; Bill Clinton Library, AR; Henry Kissinger Library, NY; Ronald Reagan Library; Gerald Ford Library; Las Vegas Art Mus, NV; Nat Wildlife Federation, Wash, DC
PRINTERS: Bowman & Son Printing, Las Vegas, NV (B/S); Lodge Graphics, Las Vegas, NV (LodGr)
PUBLISHERS: Royal Collection, Paris, France (RC); Art West Collections, Beverly Hills, CA (AWC); Art Affair, Las Vegas, NV (AA); Art Affair, Las Vegas, NV (AF)
GALLERIES: Scottsdale Auction House, Scottsdale, AZ; International Auction Associates, Las Vegas, NV; Art Affair, Las Vegas, NV

TITLE	PUBLISHER	PRINTER	DATE	MEDIUM	DIMENSION (PAPER SIZE) IN INCHES	TYPE OF PAPER	EDITION NUMBER	NO. OF COLORS	ORIGINAL OPENING PRICE	CURRENT RETAIL PRICE
SOLD OUT EDITONS (RARE):										
Midnight Moon	RC	B/S	1959	MM	20 X 24	AP	150	7	75	450
Interlude	RC	B/S	1959	MM	20 X 24	AP	250	5	125	700
Fantasy Sun	RC	B/S	1960	MM	20 X 24	AP	100	11	150	750
Evening Star	RC	B/S	1961	HI	22 X 28	AP	175	6	200	700
Moonrise	RC	B/S	1963	WC	22 X 28	AP	175	6	200	1100
Sunset Moons	RC	B/S	1965	OIL	20 X 24	AP/WA	100	4	220	1000
Oriental Jade	RC	B/S	1967	WC	24 X 36	AP	250	3	200	600
Nocturnal Star	RC	B/S	1969	MM	22 X 28	AP/WA	350	9	100	500
Revolution	RC	B/S	1969	MM	20 X 24	AP	110	112	225	400
Spectrum Sky	RC	B/S	1970	MM	30 X 40	AP	175	6	200	500
Jasmine Spring	RC	B/S	1971	ACRYLIC	30 X 40	AP	175	6	200	550
Creation Spark	RC	B/S	1974	ACRYLIC	24 X 36	AP	300	4	100	300
Evolution Eruption	RC	B/S	1975	WA	24 X 36	AP	300	6	140	600
Universal Fire	RC	B/S	1976	MM	30 X 40	AP/WA	200	7	150	550
China Seas	RC	B/S	1978	MM	20 X 24	AP	25	7	250	1800
Bamboo in Black	RC	B/S	1978	MM	30 X 40	AP	20	7	300	1600
Moonlite Sonata	RC	B/S	1980	MM	22 X 28	AP	350	6	275	1850
Sunburst	RC	B/S	1981	MM	22 X 38	AP	375	6	140	360
Black Sapphire	RC	B/S	1981	MM	30 X 40	AP	175	6	300	900
Storm Burst	RC	B/S	1982	WC	20 X 24	AP/WA	250	9	100	220
Amethyst Aura	RC	B/S	1982	MM	20 X 24	AP	150	6	190	250
Topaz Tempest	RC	B/S	1985	MM	24 X 36	AP	200	9	400	1180
Royal Flight	RC	B/S	1986	WC	20 X 24	AP/WA	100	7	200	900
Sapphire Sky	RC	B/S	1986	WC	22 X 20	AP/WA	175	12	100	1500
Series of 7 Pavillions for 7 Princesses:									1855 SET	6000 SET
#1-Gold Pavillion	AWC	B/S	1987	MM	24 X 36	CAM/D	350	6	275	1950
#2-Silver Pavillion	AWC	B/S	1987	MM	24 X 36	CAM/D	350	6	275	1800
#3-Green (Emerald) Pavillion	AWC	B/S	1987	MM	24 X 36	CAM/D	350	6	275	1750
#4-Bronze Pavillion	AWC	B/S	1987	MM	24 X 36	CAM/D	350	6	275	1750
#5-Black Pavillion	AWC	B/S	1987	MM	24 X 36	CAM/D	350	6	275	1700
#6-White Pavillion	AWC	B/S	1987	MM	24 X 36	CAM/D	350	6	275	1850
#7-Turquoise Pavillion	AWC	B/S	1987	MM	24 X 36	CAM/D	350	6	275	1750
Evolution Jewel	AWC	B/S	1988	MM	24 X 36	CAM/D	150	6	200	600
Birth of the Continents	AWC	B/S	1988	MM	24 X 36	CAM/D	375	6	225	550
Life Cycle	AWC	B/S	1988	MM	24 X 36	CAM/D	375	6	225	400
Sunburst Love	RC	B/S	1988	MM	20 X 24	AP	300	6	150	350
Rainbow Light	RC	B/S	1989	MM	20 X 24	AP	375	9	350	600
Sunset Embers	RC	B/S	1989	MM	20 X 24	AP	200	6	200	300
Sunrise of Life	RC	B/S	1989	MM	24 X 36	AP	200	6	200	300
Weeping Willow	AWC	B/S	1989	MM	24 X 36	CAM/D	375	6	275	400
Eruption	AWC	B/S	1989	MM	24 X 36	CAM/D	375	6	275	600
Love Story	AWC	B/S	1989	MM	24 X 36	CAM/D	375	6	295	485

MIRÁ PARIS CONTINUED

TITLE	PUBLISHER	PRINTER	DATE	MEDIUM	DIMENSION (PAPER SIZE) IN INCHES	TYPE OF PAPER	EDITION NUMBER	NO. OF COLORS	ORIGINAL OPENING PRICE	CURRENT RETAIL PRICE
SOLD OUT EDITIONS (RARE):										
Tree of Life	AWC	B/S	1989	MM	24 X 36	CAM/D	375	6	275	500
Four Seasons	AWC	B/S	1990	MM	24 X 36	CAM/D	375	6	275	500
ABC Alphabet	AWC	B/S	1990	MM	24 X 36	CAM/D	500	6	190	650
Majestic Sunset	AWC	B/S	1990	MM	24 X 36	CAM/D	350	6	290	400
Rainbow Willow	AWC	B/S	1990	MM	24 X 36	CAM/D	350	6	275	350
Golden Willows in the Sun	AWC	B/S	1990	MM	24 X 36	CAM/D	350	6	275	350
Oriental Cypress	AWC	B/S	1990	MM	24 X 36	CAM/D	350	6	275	300
Universal Power	AWC	B/S	1990	MM	24 X 36	CAM/D	350	6	325	610
Gem Explosion	AWC	B/S	1990	MM	24 X 36	CAM/D	350	6	275	485
Future Love	AWC	B/S	1990	MM	24 X 36	CAM/D	350	6	275	590
Modern Love	AWC	B/S	1990	MM	24 X 36	CAM/D	350	6	275	700
Lava Eruption	AWC	B/S	1990	MM	24 X 36	CAM/D	350	6	275	750
Cypress and Willow	AWC	B/S	1990	MM	24 X 36	CAM/D	350	6	275	300
Emerald Seas	AWC	B/S	1990	MM	24 X 36	CAM/D	350	6	295	480
Couden Willow	AWC	B/S	1990	MM	24 X 36	CAM/D	350	6	275	490
Evolution Ovum	AWC	B/S	1990	MM	24 X 36	CAM/D	350	6	285	400
Wild Stallion	AWC	B/S	1990	MM	24 X 36	CAM/D	350	6	290	780
Silvery Sunset	AWC	B/S	1990	MM	24 X 36	CAM/D	350	6	275	900
Rising Sun	AWC	B/S	1990	MM	24 X 36	CAM/D	350	6	275	380
Mount Fuji	AWC	B/S	1990	MM	24 X 36	CAM/D	350	6	275	350
Triumph	AWC	B/S	1990	MM	24 X 36	CAM/D	350	6	490	690
Parisian Fantasy	AWC	B/S	1990	MM	24 X 36	CAM/D	350	6	395	500
Venus	AWC	B/S	1990	MM	24 X 36	CAM/D	350	6	950	2100
Cosmos	FI	FI	1990	MM	22 X 30	CAM/D	1000	4	100	250
Phoenitia	FI	FI	1990	MM	22 X 30	CAM/D	1000	4	100	250
Midnight Blue	FI	FI	1990	MM	22 X 30	CAM/D	1000	4	100	175
Mars	FI	FI	1990	MM	22 X 30	CAM/D	1000	4	100	175
Pyramid Panarama	FI	FI	1990	MM	22 X 30	CAM/D	1000	4	100	175
Cosmic Comets	FI	FI	1990	MM	22 X 30	CAM/D	1000	4	100	270
Vermillion Pyramid	FI	FI	1990	MM	22 X 30	CAM	75	6	200	465
Heights of Heaven	FI	FI	1990	MM	22 X 30	CAM	75	6	200	350
Nile Nights	FI	FI	1990	MM	22 X 30	CAM	75	6	200	350
Heavenly Princess	FI	FI	1990	MM	22 X 30	CAM	75	6	200	910
Contemplation of Origin	FI	FI	1990	MM	22 X 30	CAM	75	6	200	1180
Solar Evolution	FI	FI	1990	MM	22 X 30	CAM	75	6	200	450
Mystery of Life	FI	FI	1990	MM	22 X 30	CAM	175	6	150	325
View of History	FI	FI	1990	MM	22 X 30	CAM	175	6	150	325
Planitary Mirá	FI	FI	1990	MM	22 X 30	CAM	1	10	200	3200
Triumph	FI	FI	1990	MM	22 X 30	CAM/D	500	4	75	250
Gem Explosion Future	FI	FI	1990	MM	22 X 30	CAM/D	500	6	125	420
Love Explosion	FI	FI	1990	MM	22 X 30	CAM/D	500	6	125	910
Modern Love	FI	FI	1990	MM	22 X 30	CAM/D	500	6	175	800
Purple Mountain	FI	FI	1990	MM	22 X 30	CAM/D	1	6	2500	9100
Golden Apollo	FI	FI	1990	MM	22 X 30	CAM/D	50	6	1000	3400
Fire and Ice Nude	FI	FI	1990	MM	22 X 30	CAM/D	50	6	1000	5400
Lava Eruption	FI	FI	1990	MM	22 X 30	CAM/D	AP	12	750	2700
Rainbow Sky	FI	FI	1990	MM	22 X 30	CAM/D	AP	6	350	1900
Evolution Ovum	FI	FI	1990	MM	22 X 30	CAM/D	AP	4	500	1640
Jewel Eruption	FI	FI	1990	MM	22 X 30	CAM/D	350	6	300	1600
Palette of Art	FI	FI	1990	MM	22 X 30	CAM/D	350	6	275	1400
Fiesta Willow	FI	FI	1990	MM	22 X 30	CAM/D	500	4	200	800
Black Pavillion	FI	FI	1990	MM	22 X 30	CAM/D	AP	12	1100	4600
Mount Fuji	FI	FI	1990	MM	22 X 30	CAM/D	AP	10	700	2900
Silver Pavillion	FI	FI	1990	MM	22 X 30	CAM/D	AP	10	700	3800
Tree of Life	FI	FI	1990	MM	22 X 30	CAM/D	AP	10	800	4300
Cypress and Willow	FI	FI	1990	MM	22 X 30	CAM/D	AP	10	300	710
Emerald Seas	FI	FI	1990	MM	22 X 30	CAM/D	175	12	1000	6200
Majestic Sunrise	FI	FI	1990	MM	22 X 30	CAM/D	75	14	1000	9100
Mirá does Dali	FI	FI	1990	MM	22 X 30	CAM/D	1	40	2500	4300
Beginning Life	FI	FI	1990	MM	22 X 30	CAM/D	500	6	300	350
Moon Beams	FI	FI	1990	MM	22 X 30	CAM/D	500	6	300	350
All Seeing Power	FI	FI	1990	MM	22 X 30	CAM/D	500	6	300	350
Horizontal Sunflower	FI	FI	1990	MM	22 X 30	CAM/D	500	6	300	350
Egrets	FI	FI	1990	MM	22 X 30	CAM/D	10	14	400	850
Euphora	FI	FI	1990	MM	22 X 30	CAM/D	10	14	400	800
Bahamian Beauty	FI	FI	1990	MM	22 X 30	CAM/D	10	14	400	760
Southwest Meditation	FI	FI	1990	MM	22 X 30	CAM/D	10	14	400	890
Watching Over All	FI	FI	1990	MM	22 X 30	CAM/D	5	10	1900	2200
Bali Bay	FI	FI	1990	MM	22 X 30	CAM/D	5	12	1450	1780
Palm Shadows	FI	FI	1990	MM	22 X 30	CAM/D	2	14	2200	2900
Palm Pair	FI	FI	1990	MM	22 X 30	CAM/D	2	8	1100	1700
Birth of Earth	FI	FI	1990	MM	22 X 30	CAM/D	75	6	500	700
Cosmic Boom	FI	FI	1990	MM	22 X 30	CAM/D	75	6	500	900

MIRÁ PARIS CONTINUED

Mirá Paris
Cosmic Princess of Ariana
Courtesy Royal Collections

Mirá Paris
Behind Every Man is a Beautiful Woman
Courtesy Royal Collections

TITLE	PUBLISHER	PRINTER	DATE	MEDIUM	DIMENSION (PAPER SIZE) IN INCHES	TYPE OF PAPER	EDITION NUMBER	NO. OF COLORS	ORIGINAL OPENING PRICE	CURRENT RETAIL PRICE
SOLD OUT EDITIONS (RARE):										
Ebony Reflection	FI	FI	1990	MM	22 X 30	CAM/D	75	6	400	1150
Sunset Sea	FI	FI	1990	MM	22 X 30	CAM/D	1	10	1000	4750
Gloval Vista Winters	FI	FI	1990	MM	22 X 30	CAM/D	500	4	150	210
Nocturnal Warden	FI	FI	1990	MM	22 X 30	CAM/D	1	10	2000	4400
Autumnal Bay	FI	FI	1990	MM	22 X 30	CAM/D	1	10	2500	8300
Peaceful Heaven and Fiery Earth	FI	FI	1990	MM	22 X 30	CAM/D	1	10	3600	7100
Smoky Flame	FI	FI	1990	MM	22 X 30	CAM/D	1	16	4000	24000
Fantasy Hillside	FI	FI	1990	MM	22 X 30	CAM/D	1	18	4000	35000
King & Queen of Nile	FI	FI	1990	MM	22 X 30	CAM/D	1	18	2500	2900
Golden View	FI	FI	1990	MM	22 X 30	CAM/D	1	12	2000	6500
Tree Fantasy	FI	FI	1990	MM	22 X 30	CAM/D	1	12	2000	3400
Mirá Self Portrait	FI	FI	1990	MM	22 X 30	CAM/D	1	12	1500	2100
Torso of Venus	FI	FI	1990	MM	22 X 30	CAM/D	1	12	1500	8600
Wild Stallion	FI	FI	1990	MM	22 X 30	CAM/D	500	10	200	950
Heat of Sunset	FI	FI	1990	MM	22 X 30	CAM/D	500	10	200	1100
Saphire Mountain	FI	FI	1990	MM	22 X 30	CAM/D	500	10	200	650
Aphrodite	FI	FI	1990	MM	22 X 30	CAM/D	500	10	200	780
World Seasons Universe	IMA	FI	1990	MM	22 X 30	CAM/D	500	4	100	350
Coral Sunset Bay	IMA	FI	1990	MM	22 X 30	CAM/D	500	4	100	300
Infinity	IMA	FI	1990	MM	22 X 30	CAM/D	500	4	100	300
Hillside of Eden	IMA	FI	1990	MM	22 X 30	CAM/D	500	4	100	150
River of Rainbows	IMA	FI	1990	MM	22 X 30	CAM/D	500	4	100	400
Eye of Power	IMA	FI	1990	MM	22 X 30	CAM/D	75	10	600	1450
Tangerine Scape	IMA	FI	1990	MM	22 X 30	CAM/D	75	10	600	1600
Reflection	IMA	FI	1990	MM	22 X 30	CAM/D	75	10	600	1400
Four Seasons: Winter	IMA	FI	1990	MM	22 X 30	CAM/D	75	10	600	1400
Four Seasons: Fall	IMA	FI	1990	MM	22 X 30	CAM/D	100	10	500	1100
Mt Fuji Fantasy	FI	FI	1990	MM	22 X 30	CAM/D	1	10	1000	6500
Primavera Floral	FI	FI	1990	MM	22 X 30	CAM/D	5	10	500	2100
Southern Sky	FI	FI	1990	MM	22 X 30	CAM/D	5	10	500	900
Tropical View	FI	FI	1990	MM	22 X 30	CAM/D	5	10	500	1650
Hidden Oak	FI	FI	1990	MM	22 X 30	CAM/D	75	6	200	680
Tropical Fuji	FI	FI	1990	MM	22 X 30	CAM/D	75	6	200	680
Golden Sky	FI	FI	1990	MM	22 X 30	CAM/D	100	8	300	750

MIRÁ PARIS CONTINUED

Mirá Paris
Trilogy
Courtesy Royal Collections

Mirá Paris
Cosmic Princess Melody
Courtesy Royal Collections

TITLE	PUBLISHER	PRINTER	DATE	MEDIUM	DIMENSION (PAPER SIZE) IN INCHES	TYPE OF PAPER	EDITION NUMBER	NO. OF COLORS	ORIGINAL OPENING PRICE	CURRENT RETAIL PRICE
SOLD OUT EDITIONS (RARE):										
Silvered Nude	FI	FI	1990	MM	22 X 30	CAM/D	100	8	300	750
Silvered Reflection	FI	FI	1990	MM	22 X 30	CAM/D	100	8	300	750
Enchanted Lake	FI	FI	1990	MM	22 X 30	CAM/D	350	12	450	1100
Tropical Storm	FI	FI	1990	MM	22 X 30	CAM/D	350	12	450	1100
Iced Vista	FI	FI	1990	MM	22 X 30	CAM/D	350	12	450	1100
Shades of the Seasons	FI	FI	1990	MM	22 X 30	CAM/D	350	12	450	1100
Fantasy Land	FI	FI	1990	MM	22 X 30	CAM/D	500	10	200	465
Southern Sunset	FI	FI	1990	MM	22 X 30	CAM/D	500	10	200	480
Delightful Day	FI	FI	1990	MM	22 X 30	CAM/D	500	10	200	580
Four Seasons: Spring	IMA	FI	1990	MM	22 X 30	CAM/D	AP	8	2000	3500
Four Seasons: Summer	IMA	FI	1990	MM	22 X 30	CAM/D	AP	10	2000	3000
Mt Fugi Explosion	IMA	FI	1990	MM	22 X 30	CAM/D	AP	12	1000	4900
Southwest Arch	IMA	FI	1990	MM	22 X 30	CAM/D	AP	18	1000	4600
Southwest Sunburst	IMA	FI	1990	MM	22 X 30	CAM/D	AP	10	1000	4600
Sunburst Mountain	FI	FI	1990	MM	22 X 30	CAM/D	AP	14	1500	8600
Ruby Explosion	FI	FI	1990	MM	22 X 30	CAM/D	AP	14	1500	9100
Eye of Life	FI	FI	1990	MM	22 X 30	CAM/D	AP	14	1000	2200
Natures Love Story	FI	FI	1990	MM	22 X 30	CAM/D	AP	14	1000	2800
Beginning Sunrise	FI	FI	1990	MM	22 X 30	CAM/D	AP	10	500	3250
Cats Psyche	FI	FI	1990	MM	22 X 30	CAM/D	AP	10	500	3100
Burst of Love	FI	FI	1990	MM	22 X 30	CAM/D	AP	12	600	900
Atlantis	FI	FI	1990	MM	22 X 30	CAM/D	50	4	500	3650
Maple Leaf	FI	FI	1990	MM	22 X 30	CAM/D	50	4	550	2150
Geometric Mirá	FI	FI	1990	MM	22 X 30	CAM/D	350	14	1500	8600
Autumn Leaves	FI	FI	1990	MM	22 X 30	CAM/D	350	6	300	1100
Reclyning Nude	FI	FI	1990	MM	22 X 30	CAM/D	350	6	300	910
Burst of Evolution	FI	FI	1990	MM	22 X 30	CAM/D	350	4	300	1800
Nude Statuesque	FI	FI	1990	MM	22 X 30	CAM/NTS	200	6	500	1400
Plum Tree by the Bay	FI	FI	1990	MM	22 X 30	CAM/D	200	6	500	1670
Isis	FI	FI	1990	MM	22 X 30	CAM/D	100	6	500	2100
Rainbow Coruption	FI	FI	1990	MM	22 X 30	CAM/D	100	8	500	3300
Plum Tree	FI	FI	1990	MM	22 X 30	CAM/D	100	10	500	3400
Yellow Sails in the Sunset	FI	FI	1990	MM	22 X 30	CAM/D	100	12	500	750

MIRÁ PARIS CONTINUED

TITLE	PUBLISHER	PRINTER	DATE	MEDIUM	DIMENSION (PAPER SIZE) IN INCHES	TYPE OF PAPER	EDITION NUMBER	NO. OF COLORS	ORIGINAL OPENING PRICE	CURRENT RETAIL PRICE
SOLD OUT EDITIONS (RARE):										
Black and White Pavilion	FI	FI	1990	MM	22 X 30	CAM/D	100	12	500	550
Eagle Protecting the Flaming Earth, #1	FI	FI	1990	MM	22 X 30	CAM/D	AP	12	1500	6500
Eagle Protecting the Flaming Earth, #2	FI	FI	1990	MM	22 X 30	CAM/D	500	4	500	1900
Moonlight Behind Great Wall	FI	FI	1990	MM	22 X 30	CAM/D	AP	10	1000	2500
Still Life of Spring	FI	FI	1990	MM	22 X 30	CAM/D	5	14	2000	6200
Generation of Life	FI	FI	1990	MM	22 X 30	CAM/D	10	10	1500	2900
Sunrise Magnolia	FI	FI	1990	MM	22 X 30	CAM/D	50	10	1000	3300
Contemplation	FI	FI	1990	MM	22 X 30	CAM/D	1	12	2000	6900
Shadowed Nude	FI	FI	1990	MM	22 X 30	CAM/D	5	12	1000	5400
Eye of Seasons	FI	FI	1990	MM	22 X 30	CAM/D	10	10	700	8500
Power of Heaven	FI	FI	1990	MM	22 X 30	CAM/D	10	6	600	1300
Window Sill	FI	FI	1990	MM	22 X 30	CAM/D	10	6	600	1900
Sunburst	FI	FI	1990	MM	22 X 30	CAM/D	50	6	500	3800
Revolutionary Era	FI	FI	1990	MM	22 X 30	CAM/D	50	6	500	4300
Birth of the Earth	FI	FI	1990	MM	22 X 30	CAM/D	350	6	300	4100
Saphire Landscape	FI	FI	1990	MM	22 X 30	CAM/D	350	6	300	3200
Plum Willow	FI	FI	1990	MM	22 X 30	CAM/D	500	6	350	2100
Geometric Mirá	FI	FI	1990	MM	22 X 30	CAM/D	100		100	220
Cosmic Sunset	FI	FI	1990	MM	22 X 30	CAM/D	500		50	175
Cosmic Burst	FI	FI	1990	MM	22 X 30	CAM/D	550		50	220
Fashion Lady	FI	FI	1990	MM	22 X 30	CAM/D	500		50	365
Aurora Bora Bora	FI	FI	1990	MM	22 X 30	CAM/D	500		50	350
Egyptian Moon	FI	FI	1990	MM	22 X 30	CAM/D	10/AP		500	950
Aura Bay	FI	FI	1990	MM	22 X 30	CAM/D	10/AP		500	1100
Cosmo Tropical	FI	FI	1990	MM	22 X 30	CAM/D	10/AP		500	900
Eclipse	FI	FI	1990	MM	22 X 30	CAM/D	10/AP		500	700
Storm Sky	FI	FI	1990	MM	22 X 30	CAM/D	10/AP		500	500
Cosmic Night	FI	FI	1990	MM	22 X 30	CAM/D	10/AP		500	500
Our Home Earth	FI	FI	1990	MM	22 X 30	CAM/D	10/AP		500	750
Primeval Power	FI	FI	1990	MM	22 X 30	CAM/D	1		1000	3800
Stone Henge	FI	FI	1990	MM	22 X 30	CAM/D	500	6	750	1900
Arabian Sunrise	FI	FI	1990	MM	22 X 30	CAM/D	350	6	750	750
Northwest Sailing	FI	FI	1990	MM	22 X 30	CAM/D	250	6	750	1100
Delightful Day	FI	FI	1990	MM	22 X 30	CAM/D	500	10	200	580
Bahama Eve	FI	FI	1990	MM	22 X 30	CAM/D	500	10	200	625
Paradise Setting	FI	FI	1990	MM	22 X 30	CAM/D	500	10	200	1150
Glacial Landscape	FI	FI	1990	MM	22 X 30	CAM/D	1	10	2000	4500
Row of Nature	FI	FI	1990	MM	22 X 30	CAM/D	1	10	2000	4500
Cosmic Earth	FI	FI	1990	MM	22 X 30	CAM/D	7/AP		1000	2200
Lake Vista	FI	FI	1990	MM	22 X 30	CAM/D	7/AP		1000	2100
Rainbow Waters	FI	FI	1990	MM	22 X 30	CAM/D	10/AP		1000	1550
Fantasy Scape	FI	FI	1990	MM	22 X 30	CAM/D	10/AP		1000	1500
Trinidad	FI	FI	1990	MM	22 X 30	CAM/D	10/AP		1000	2700
Hills & Valleys	FI	FI	1990	MM	22 X 30	CAM/D	35		300	350
Enchanted Couple	FI	FI	1990	MM	22 X 30	CAM/D	35		300	350
Luxury Lady	FI	FI	1990	MM	22 X 30	CAM/D	35		300	450
Peacefull Valley	FI	FI	1990	MM	22 X 30	CAM/D	100		100	175
Cosmic Paradise	FI	FI	1990	MM	22 X 30	CAM/D	100		100	175
Heatwave	FI	FI	1990	MM	22 X 30	CAM/D	50	6	400	1250
Platinum Planet	FI	FI	1990	MM	22 X 30	CAM/D	50	6	400	1150
Egyptian Eclipse	FI	FI	1990	MM	22 X 30	CAM/D	50	6	400	900
Unearthly Spire	FI	FI	1990	MM	22 X 30	CAM/D	50	6	400	1680
Utopia	FI	FI	1990	MM	22 X 30	CAM/D	50	6	400	550
Heavenly Pyramid	FI	FI	1990	MM	22 X 30	CAM/D	50	6	400	500
Broken Promise	FI	FI	1990	MM	22 X 30	CAM/D	100	4	200	350
Golden Pyramid	FI	FI	1990	MM	22 X 30	CAM/D	100	4	200	350
Majestic Journey	FI	FI	1990	MM	22 X 30	CAM/D	100	4	200	350
Misty Entity	FI	FI	1990	MM	22 X 30	CAM/D	350	10	150	750
Platinum Moon	FI	FI	1990	MM	22 X 30	CAM/D	300	10	100	685
Midnight	FI	FI	1990	MM	22 X 30	CAM/D	25	6	150	1190
Marble Space	FI	FI	1990	MM	22 X 30	CAM/D	1	10	2000	2910
Beautiful Vision	FI	FI	1990	MM	22 X 30	CAM/D	1	10	2000	3600
Focus of Power	FI	FI	1990	MM	22 X 30	CAM/D	1	10	2000	3600
Golden Topaz Sun	FI	FI	1990	MM	22 X 30	CAM/D	1	10	1000	3600
Bonsai	FI	FI	1990	MM	22 X 30	CAM/D				
Deco Mirá	FI	FI	1990	MM	22 X 30	CAM/D	1	12	1000	1450
Gentlemen Mirá	FI	FI	1990	MM	22 X 30	CAM/D	1	14	2000	16200
Samoan Sunset	FI	FI	1990	MM	22 X 30	CAM/D	1	18	2000	21000
Mountainside	FI	FI	1990	MM	22 X 30	CAM/D	1	18	2000	8100
Double Tree	FI	FI	1990	MM	22 X 30	CAM/D	1	18	2000	9300
Island Dream	FI	FI	1990	MM	22 X 30	CAM/D	1	18	2000	4300

MIRÁ PARIS CONTINUED

TITLE	PUBLISHER	PRINTER	DATE	MEDIUM	DIMENSION (PAPER SIZE) IN INCHES	TYPE OF PAPER	EDITION NUMBER	NO. OF COLORS	ORIGINAL OPENING PRICE	CURRENT RETAIL PRICE
SOLD OUT EDITIONS (RARE):										
Sensual Nude	FI	FI	1990	MM	22 X 30	CAM/D	1	10	1500	3100
Serenity Sunset	FI	FI	1990	MM	22 X 30	CAM/D	1	10	1500	3200
Hawaiian Vista	FI	FI	1990	MM	22 X 30	CAM/D	1	10	1500	6900
Rainbow Light	FI	FI	1990	MM	22 X 30	CAM/D	1	10	1500	2100
Bayou Sunrise	FI	FI	1990	MM	22 X 30	CAM/D	175	6	750	2200
Willows Dancing Reflection	FI	FI	1990	MM	22 X 30	CAM/D	200	10	800	2100
Sunflower Corner	FI	FI	1990	MM	22 X 30	CAM/D	750	10	350	600
Path of Winter	FI	FI	1990	MM	22 X 30	CAM/D	750	10	350	750
Mountain Lake	FI	FI	1990	MM	22 X 30	CAM/D	350	10	400	890
Black Willow	FI	FI	1990	MM	22 X 30	CAM/D	600	10	220	420
Oriental Cyprus	IMA	FI	1990	MM	30 X 40	CAM/D	75	14	600	1900
Mountain Peaks	IMA	FI	1990	MM	30 X 40	CAM/D	75	14	600	1550
Triple Range	IMA	FI	1990	MM	30 X 40	CAM/D	75	14	600	2400
Exotic Land	IMA	FI	1990	MM	30 X 40	CAM/D	75	14	600	2400
Molten Sea	IMA	FI	1990	MM	30 X 40	CAM/D	75	14	600	750
Heavenly Reflection	IMA	FI	1990	MM	30 X 40	CAM/D	75	14	600	600
Golden Sky	IMA	FI	1990	MM	30 X 40	CAM/D	75	14	600	4400
Tropical Waters	IMA	FI	1990	MM	30 X 40	CAM/D	75	14	600	4100
Evolution of Strength	IMA	FI	1990	MM	22 X 30	CAM/D	75	14	600	3600
Golden Tropics	IMA	FI	1990	MM	22 X 30	CAM/D	5	18	900	7500
Starflowers	IMA	FI	1990	MM	22 X 30	CAM/D	5	18	900	7700
Shadowed Bay	IMA	FI	1990	MM	22 X 30	CAM/D	5	18	900	7800
Venus II	IMA	FI	1990	MM	22 X 30	CAM/D	5	18	900	1100
Natural Interlude	IMA	FI	1990	MM	22 X 30	CAM/D	5	18	900	1450
Night Saphire	IMA	FI	1990	MM	22 X 30	CAM/D	5	18	900	11200
Perfect Sailing	IMA	FI	1990	MM	22 X 30	CAM/D	15	18	500	2200
Tree of Ages	IMA	FI	1990	MM	22 X 30	CAM/D	15	18	500	4500
Nocturnal Light	RC	B/S	1991	MM	30 X 40	CAM/D	5	12	2100	8000
Beauty of Life	RC	B/S	1991	MM	30 X 40	CAM/D	5	12	1900	4200
Vision of Heaven	RC	B/S	1991	MM	30 X 40	CAM/D	5	12	1900	3600
Tempest Storm	RC	B/S	1991	MM	30 X 40	CAM/D	10	12	1900	2200
Light Eternal	RC	B/S	1991	MM	30 X 40	CAM/D	25	10	1200	1500
Brilliant Bay	RC	B/S	1991	MM	30 X 40	CAM/D	25	10	1200	1750
Paramount Ray	RC	B/S	1991	MM	30 X 40	CAM/D	25	10	1200	1750
Eternal Star	RC	B/S	1991	MM	30 X 40	CAM/D	25	10	1000	3200
Princess Aura	RC	B/S	1991	MM	30 X 40	CAM/D	1	12	4000	8500
Willow of the Wild	RC	B/S	1991	MM	30 X 40	CAM/D	1	10	3500	4100
Border of Earth	RC	B/S	1991	MM	30 X 40	CAM/D	1	10	3000	3900
Princess Emerald	RC	B/S	1991	MM	30 X 40	CAM/D	1	10	3000	4900
Cosmic Vision	RC	B/S	1992	MM	22 X 30	CAM/D	1	12	3000	11800
Princess Victoria	RC	B/S	1992	MM	22 X 30	CAM/D	1	18	3500	22000
Azure Infinity	RC	B/S	1992	MM	22 X 30	CAM/D	1	18	3000	16000
Secret Watch	RC	B/S	1992	MM	22 X 30	CAM/D	125	4	500	900
Cosmic Hope	RC	B/S	1992	MM	10 X 20	CAM/D	150	6	400	1100
Princess Serina	RC	B/S	1992	MM	16 X 22	CAM/D	150	6	400	810
Vision of Tomorrow	RC	B/S	1992	MM	16 X 22	CAM/D	1000	6	350	1500
Life Utopia	RC	B/S	1992	MM	16 X 22	CAM/D	1000	6	350	1500
Beauty of Being	RC	B/S	1992	MM	16 X 22	CAM/D	1000	6	300	475
CURRENT EDITIONS										
Eagle Protecting Flaming Earth	AWL	LodGr	1991	MM	22 X 30	CAM/D	350		550	800
Origin of Life	AWL	LodGr	1991	MM	22 X 30	CAM/D	350		500	550
Origin of Life	AWL	LodGr	1991	MM	16 X 22	CAM/D	500		100	125
Mountain Majesty	AWL	LodGr	1991	MM	23 X 30	CAM/D	350		500	1500
Mountain Majesty	AWL	LodGr	1991	MM	16 X 22	CAM/D	500		200	450
Galaxia Cosmic Princess	AWL	LodGr	1991	MM	22 X 30	CAM/D	350		500	1000
Self Portrait-Gilded Mask	AWL	LodGr	1991	MM	22 X 30	CAM/D	350		500	0
Self Portrait-Gilded Mask	AWL	L	1991	MM	16 X 22	CAM/D	500		150	550
Gentlemen Mirá	AWL	L	1991	MM	22 X 30	CAM/D	350		500	775
Gentlemen Mirá	AWL	L	1991	MM	16 X 22	CAM/D	500		400	975
Ascension	AWL	L	1991	MM	22 X 30	CAM/D	350		400	840
Ascension	AWL	L	1992	MM	16 X 22	CAM/D	500		150	380
Behind Every Man is a Beautiful Woman	AWL	LodGr	1992	MM	22 X 30	CAM/D	350		600	900
Behind Every Man is a Beautiful Woman	AWL	LodGr	1992	MM	16 X 22	CAM/D	500		200	225
Checkmate Cosmic Princess	AWL	LodGr	1992	MD	22 X 30	CAM/D	350		500	600
Checkmate Cosmic Princess	AWL	LodGr	1992	MM	16 X 22	CAM/D	500		220	250
Eagle Protecting Flaming Earth	AWL	LodGr	1992	MM	16 X 22	CAM/D	500		150	175

The retail prices of the 100,000 limited edition prints quoted in this directory are subject to change. Print publishers, artists and galleries were the direct sources for these quotations. Prices in the secondary market listed as "Sold Out Editions (Rare)" indicate that the publisher has a limited supply of that print or that the print is difficult to locate in the galleries.

JOAN MIRÓ

BORN: Barcelona, Spain; (1938–1983)
AWARDS: First Prize, Guggenheim Found Int, 1954; Carnegie Prize for Painting, 1967
RECENT EXHIB: Wichita State Univ, Edwin A Ulrich Mus, KS, 1987; St Lawrence Univ, Richard F Brush Art Gallery, Canton, OH, 1987; Heckscher Mus, Huntington, NY, 1987; Philadelphia Mus, PA, 1987; Fort Worth Mus, TX, 1987–88; San Francisco Mus of Mod Art, CA, 1988; Thomas Ammann Fine Art, Zurich, Switzerland, 1992
PRINTERS: Atelier Lacouriére, Paris, France (AtLAC); Marcoussis Studio, Paris, France (MS); Atelier 17, Paris, France (At17); Atelier Mourlot, Paris, France (AtM); Crommelynck et Dutrou, Paris, France (C/D); J J Torralba, Barcelona, Spain (JJT); Joan Barbará, Barcelona, Spain (JB); Maeght Editeur, Paris, France (ME); Galerie Maeght Lelong, Paris, France (ML); Atelier Arte, Paris, France (ARTE); La Poligrafa, Barcelona, Spain (LP); Damia Caus, Barcelona, Spain (DC); Morsang Studio, Paris, France (MOR)
PUBLISHERS: Group Aldan, Barcelona, Spain (GA); Pierre Matisse, Paris, France (PM); Pierre Loeb, Paris, France (PL); Guy Levis Mano, Paris, France (GLM); Curt Valentin, NY (CV); Atelier Mourlot, Paris, France (AtM); Tériade, Paris, France (TER); Mus of Mod Art, NY (MMA); Sala Gaspar, Barcelona, Spain (SG); Omnium Cultural, Barcelona, Spain (OC); Futbal Club, Barcelona, Spain (FC); Maeght Editions, Paris, France (ME); Transworld Art, Inc, NY (TAI); Contemporary Art Masters, NY (CAM); Nathan Silberberg, NY (NS); Martin Lawrence Limited Editions, Van Nuys, CA (MLLE); Galerie Maeght Lelong, Paris, France (ML); Ediciones Poligrafa, Barcelona, Spain (EdP); Louis Broder, Paris, France (LB)
GALLERIES: Charles Whitchurch Fine Arts, Huntington Beach, CA; Galleries Touché, Laguna Beach, CA; Annette Couch Fine Arts, Los Angeles, CA; Wenger Gallery, Los Angeles, CA; Harcourts Gallery, San Francisco, CA; Horoshak Contemporary Art, San Francisco, CA; Erika Meyerovich Gallery, San Francisco, CA; Solomon Fima Fine Art, Sherman Oaks, CA; Lake Gallery, Tahoe City, CA; Connecticut Fine Art, Westport, CT; River Gallery, Westport, CT; Galerie Martin, Boca Raton, FL; Opus Art Studios, Coral Gables, FL; Centurion Galleries, Chicago, IL; Kass/Meridian Gallery, Chicago, IL; Masters Portfolio, Chicago, IL; Samuel Stein Fine Arts, Chicago, IL; Fernette's Gallery of Art, Des Moines, IA; Hanson Art Galleries, Carmel, CA & Sausalito, CA & New Orleans, LA; Randall Beck Gallery, Boston, MA; Rolly-Michaux Galleries, Boston, MA; Donald Morris Gallery, Birmingham, MI; Saper Galleries, East Lansing, MI; Peterson Fine Art, Minneapolis, MN; Delta Editions, St Louis, MO; Gallery of the Masters, St Louis, MO; Galeria Maray, Englewood, NJ; Print Loft, Englewood, NJ; Scherer Gallery, Marlboro, NJ; David Gary, Millburn, NJ; Short Hills Art Gallery, Short Hills, NJ; Arras Gallery, New York, NY; William Beadleston Fine Art, New York, NY; Claude Bernard Gallery, New York, NY; Brewster Gallery, New York, NY; CCA Galleries, New York, NY; Theodore B Donson, New York, NY; Dorsky Galleries, Ltd, New York, NY; Galerie Lelong, New York, NY & Paris, France & Zurich, Switzerland; Hilde Gerst Gallery, New York, NY; Judith Goldberg Gallery, New York, NY; James Goodman Gallery, New York, NY; Lillian Heidenberg Gallery, New York, NY; Alexander Kahan Fine Arts, New York, NY; Jane Kahan Gallery, New York, NY; Jan Krugier Gallery, New York, NY; Pace Master Prints, New York, NY; Nathan Silberberg Fine Arts, New York, NY; Simon/Neuman Gallery, New York, NY; Studio 53; New York, NY; Weintraub Gallery, New York, NY; Abanté Fine Art Gallery, Portland, OR; Spaightwood Gallery, Madison, WI; Posner Gallery, Milwaukee, WI; Galerie Marwan Hoss, Paris, France; Meridian Gallery, New York, NY; I Irving Galleries, West Bloomfield, MI; Nahan Galleries, New Orleans, LA & New York, NY & Tokyo, Japan; Arnold Herstand Gallery, New York, NY; Thomas Ammann Fine Art, Zurich, Switzerland; Professional Fine Arts Services, Inc, New York, NY

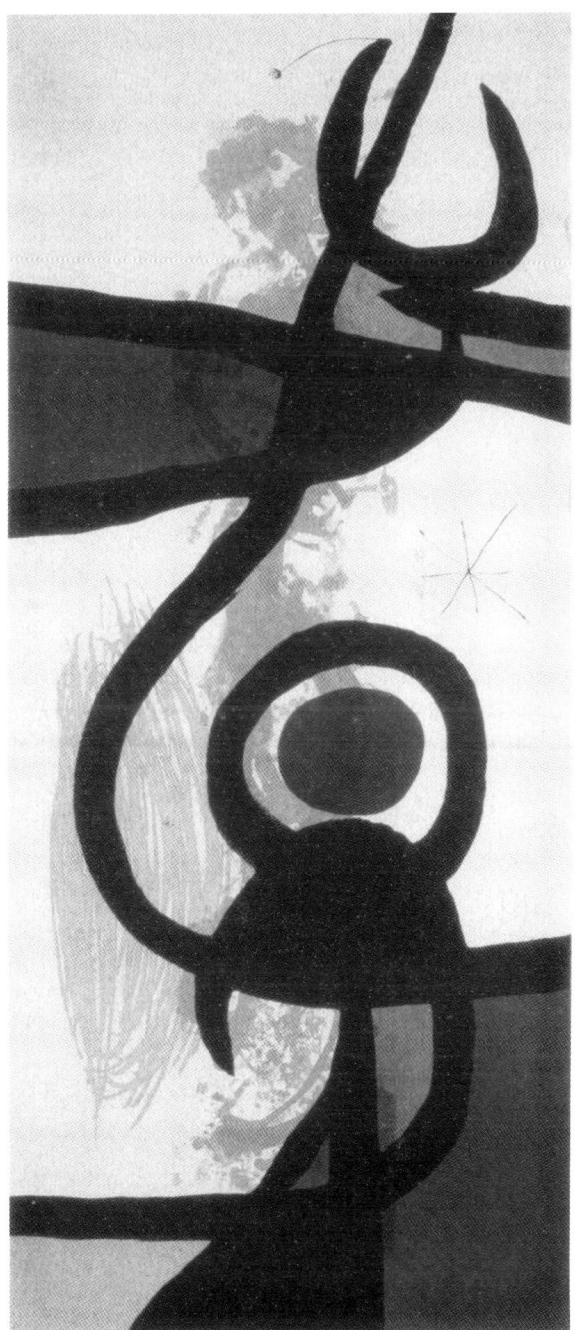

Joan Miró
Les Grandes Manoeuvres
Courtesy Editions Maeght

Wember (W); Benhoura (B); Dupain (D); Mourlot (M); Cramer (C); Benhoura/Gaillard (B/G)

TITLE	PUBLISHER	PRINTER	DATE	MEDIUM	DIMENSION (PAPER SIZE) IN INCHES	TYPE OF PAPER	EDITION NUMBER	NO. OF COLORS	ORIGINAL OPENING PRICE	CURRENT RETAIL PRICE
SOLD OUT EDITIONS (RARE):										
Erste Radierung (W-2)			1933	EB	10 X 13	HMP	100	1	25	40000
Femme et Chien DeVant la Lune (D-18)		GA	1935	PO	26 X 20	HMP	60	5	50	65000
L'Aigle et la Femme la Nuit (with Colored Drawings in the Margins (D-22) (B-2)	PL/PM	AtLAC/MS	1938	EB/DPT/HC	13 X 16	PARCH	4	8	50	35000

JOAN MIRÓ CONTINUED

TITLE	PUBLISHER	PRINTER	DATE	MEDIUM	DIMENSION (PAPER SIZE) IN INCHES	TYPE OF PAPER	EDITION NUMBER	NO. OF COLORS	ORIGINAL OPENING PRICE	CURRENT RETAIL PRICE
SOLD OUT EDITIONS (RARE):										
L'Aigle et la Femme la Nuit (D-22)	PL/PM	AtLAC/MS	1938	EB/DPT	13 X 16	AP	30	3	50	20000
L'Aigle et la Femme la Nuit (D-22)	PL/PM	AtLAC/MS	1938	EB/A	9 X 12	AP	30	1	50	9000
La Geante (D-27)	PL/PM	AtLAC/MS	1938	EB/DPT	14 X 9	AP	30	1	75	25000
Serie Noir et Rouge (D-34) (B-13)	PL/PM/AtLAC/MS		1938	DPT	7 X 10	AP/WOVE	30	2	35	6000
Solidarité: Composition (D-42) (B-401)	GLM	At17	1938	EB/A	4 X 3	MLP	165	1	35	15000
Solidarité	GLM	At17	1938	EC		LAID	150		50	18000
Bijou et Cadre (D-24) (B-5)	PL/PM	MS	1939	EB	5 X 4	AP/WOVE	2	1	75	20000
Barcelona Series:										
Barcelona Series: Plate VI (M-11)			1944	LB	28 X 21	AP	5	1	75	18000
Barcelona Series: Plate XVII (M-22)			1944	LB	25 X 17	AP	5	1	75	12000
The Prints of Joan Miró (Book) (D-4, D-48)	CV	At17	1947	LC	5 X 6 EA		1400 EA		100	25000 SET
La Main	ME	AtLAC	1947	EB/SG	14 X 19	R/BFK			100	42000
Composition	ME	At17/AtLAC	1947	EC	15 X 18	R/BFK	13		100	15000
L'Antitete (D-53)	BOR	At17	1947	EB	9 X 7	WOVE/HW	200	1	50	8000
L'Antitete (D-64)	BOR	At17	1947–48	EB/HC	6 X 5	VGP			100	8000
Parler Seul (Book) (M-102-M-106) (C-17)	ME	AtM	1948	LC	15 X 11 EA	R/100	250 EA		500 SET	25000 SET
Acrobats In the Night Garden (M-58)	ME	AtM	1948	LC	22 X 15	WOVE	75		125	3000
Figure and Bird (M-68)			1948	LC	23 X 17	RP/WOVE	75	6	100	40000
Album 13 (M-73-M-85)	ME		1948	LC			75 EA		100	4000 EA
Figure with a Red Sun II (M-94) (W-101)	ME		1950	LC	25 X 20	AP/WOVE	40	6	100	15000
Young Girl in the Moonlight (M-180)	AtM	AtM	1951	LC	21 X 29	AP	75	6	125	12500
Dog Barking at the Moon (M-189)	ME	AtM	1952	LC	14 X 22	AP	80	6	125	18000
Serie II (Set of 5)	ME	AtM	1952–53	AC		LAID	13 EA		900 SET	60000 SET
Serie III (D-91) (B-16)	ME	AtM	1952–53	EB/HC	20 X 28	AP	50	Varies	150	45000
La Main (D-100) (B-20)	ME	AtLAC	1953	EB/A	20 X 26	AP	75		100	45000
Lithographie pour le Centennaire de L'Imprimerie Mourlot (M-190) (B-247)	AtM	AtM	1953	LC	20 X 26	AP	75	12	100	85000
Untitled (M-122)	AtM	AtM	1953	LC		AP	5	10	125	60000
Night (Published in Derriére le Miroir) (M-200)			1953	LB	15 X 11	R/100	100	1	125	15000
Figure (M-212)	ME	AtM	1955	LC	30 X 22	AP	50		175	30000
L'Indifférent (M-143)	ME	AtM	1955	LC	20 X 25	AP	50		175	5500
Moon Star (M-214)	ME	AtM	1955	LC	28 X 17	WOVE	50		300	5000
Femme au Mirror (M-242)	ME	AtM	1956	LC	15 X 22	R/BFK	150	8	100	110000
Zephyr Bird (Published in Derriére le Miroir) (#87, #88, #89) (M-227)	ME		1956	LC	14 X 21	R/100	100		100	5000
La Baque d'Aurore Series:										
La Baque d'Aurore (D-126) (B-425)	LB	C/D	1957	EB/A	5 X 6	JP	87		125	8500
La Baque d'Aurore (D-137) (B-425)	LB	C/D	1957	EB/A/DPT/ENG	16 X 5	JP	87		125	15000
La Baque d'Aurore (D-139) (B-425)	LB	C/D	1957	EB/A/DPT/ENG		JP	87		125	15000
La Creole (D-147) (B-23)	ME	C/D	1958	AC/SG	12 X 5	AP	75	1	100	5500
Le Prophete (D-157) (B-33)	ME	C/D	1958	EB/A	6 X 5	AP	75		100	12000
Les Forestiers-Grîs (D-149)	ME	C/D	1958	EB/A	20 X 13	R/BFK	75		175	20000
Fusées (Set of 15) (B-438) (D-247–262)	LB	C/D	1959	AC/STEN	11 X 15 EA	R/BFK	50 EA	3 EA	10000 SET 1800 SET	250000 SET 75000 SET
Ciel Rouge (B-264)			1960	LC	15 X 22	AP	100		100	9500
The Cascade	ME	ME	1964	LC	36 X 24	AP	75		180	25000
Ubu Roi Series										
Ubu Roi: Plate III (M-468)	TER	AtM	1966	LC	16 X 25	AP	75		300	15000
Ubu Roi: Plate VI (M-477)	TER	AtM	1966	LC	16 X 25	AP	75		300	15000
Ubu Roi: Plate VIII (M-483)	TER	AtM	1966	LC	16 X 25	AP	75		300	15000
Ubu Roi: Plate XI (M-192)	TER	AtM	1966	LC	16 X 25	AP	75		300	15000
Ubu Roi: Plate XIII (M-498)	TER	AtM	1966	LC	16 X 25	AP	75		300	15000
Couple D'Oiseaux Series:										
Couple D'Oiseaux I	ME	ME	1966	EC	23 X 36	AP	50		300	15000
Couple D'Oiseaux III	ME	ME	1966	EC	23 X 36	AP	50		300	15000
L'Astre du Labyrinthe (D-425) (B-87)	ME	ME	1967	EB/A/CAR	28 X 41	AP	75		500	12000
L'Astre du Marecage (D-426) (B-88)	ME	ME	1967	EB/A/CAR	41 X 29	AP	75		500	22000
Equinoxe (D428) (B-91)	ME	ME	1967	EB/A/CAR	41 X 29	AP	75	8	500	16000
Petito Barriére (D-436) (B-99)	ME	ME	1967	AC/DPT	11 X 4	AP	75		300	13500
La Rebelle (D-439) (B-101)	ME	ME	1967	EB/A/CAR	37 X 25	AP	75		400	38000
Trace Sur la Paroi Series:										
Trace Sur la Paroi: III (D-442) (B-109)	ME	ME	1967	EB/A/CAR	23 X 37	AP	75		400	42000
Trace Sur la Paroi: VI (D-445) (B-111)	ME	ME	1967	EB/A/CAR	23 X 37	AP	75		400	35000
La Femme aux Bijoux (D-452) (B-115)	ME	ME	1968	EB/A/CAR	19 X 14	AP	75		60	35000

JOAN MIRÓ CONTINUED

Joan Miró
Grande Triptyque Noir
Courtesy Galerie Lelong

Joan Miró
Ruisselante Solaire
Courtesy Galerie Lelong

TITLE	PUBLISHER	PRINTER	DATE	MEDIUM	DIMENSION (PAPER SIZE) IN INCHES	TYPE OF PAPER	EDITION NUMBER	NO. OF COLORS	ORIGINAL OPENING PRICE	CURRENT RETAIL PRICE
SOLD OUT EDITIONS (RARE):										
Le Samourai (D-438)	ME	ME	1968	EB/CAR	31 X 23	AP	75		950	18000
Sumo (D-459) (B-123)	ME	ME	1968	AC/CAR	19 X 15	AP	75		600	2000
Les Esséncies de la Terra	EdP	LP	1968	LC	50 X 36 cm	JP	100		600	20000
L'Aieule Devant la Mer (D-484) (B-127)	ME	AtM	1969	EB/A/CAR	46 X 28	AP	75		800	25000
Le Caissier (D-487) (B-130)	ME	ME	1969	EB/A/CAR	36 X 27	AP	75		650	25000
Dancy (D-492) (B-135)	ME	ME	1969	EB/A/CAR	17 X 17	AP	75		400	22000
Les Deux Amis (D-493) (B-137)	ME	ME	1969	EB/A/CAR	28 X 42	AP	75	7	500	40000
La Femme Angora (D-499) (B-143)	ME	ME	1969	EB/A/CAR	42 X 27	AP	75		800	30000
La Fronde (D-501) (B-145)	ME	MOR	1969	EB/A/CAR	41 X 27	AP	75		600	18000
Le Grande Carnassier (D-502) (B-146)	ME	ME	1969	EB/A/CAR	41 X 27	AP	75		600	18000
L'Invitee du Dimanche (D-480) (B-152)	ME	ME	1969	EB/A	24 X 39	AP	75		500	30000
Oiseau Mongol (D-513) (B-159)	ME	MOR	1969	EB/A/CAR	41 X 27	AP/WOVE	75	7	600	25000
Prise a L'Hamecon (D-515) (B-161)	ME	MOR	1969	EB/A/CAR	39 X 24	AP	75		600	10000
La Ralentie	ME	ME	1969	EB/A/CAR	29 X 22	AP	75	12	600	2500
Soleil Ebouillante (D-518) (B-164)	ME	ME	1969	EB/A/CAR	39 X 24	AP	75		600	18500
Manniquin Parade Series:										
Manniquin Parade in Bahia (M-628)	ME	ME	1969	LC	47 X 32	AP	75		600	18000
Manniquin Parade in Ireland (M-630)	ME	ME	1969	LC	47 X 32	AP	75		600	18000
Manniquin Parade	ME	ME	1969	LC	47 X 32	AP	75		600	18000
Le Penseur Puissant	ME	ME	1969	EB/A/CAR		AP	75	7	600	18000
The Rebel	ME	ARTE	1969	EB/A/CAR		AP	75	7	600	18000
La Harpie	ME	ARTE	1969	EB/A/CAR		AP	75	7	600	18000
Old Irish Woman	ME	ARTE	1969	EB/A/CAR			75	7	600	18000
Sleep on the Moon	ME	ARTE	1969	EB/A/CAR			75	7	600	18000
Drawn on the Wall #2	ME	ARTE	1969	EB/A/CAR			75	7	600	22000
L' Adorateur du Soleil (D-483)	ME	MOR	1969	EB/A/CAR	42 X 27	AP	75		1000	10000
La Calabasse (D-488)	ME	MOR	1969	EB/A/CAR	40 X 28	AP	75		1000	12000
Dor mir Sous la Lune (D-495)	ME	MOR	1969	EB/A/DPT/CAR	29 X 41	AP	75		1200	12000
Poemes a la Main	EdP	AtM	1970	LC/HC	22 X 31	AP	25		1000	6000
Archipel Sauvage IV (D-530) (B-172)	ME	ME	1970	EB/A	23 X 36	AP	35		800	12000

JOAN MIRÓ CONTINUED

Joan Miró
Dormir sous la Lune
Courtesy Galerie Lelong

TITLE	PUBLISHER	PRINTER	DATE	MEDIUM	DIMENSION (PAPER SIZE) IN INCHES	TYPE OF PAPER	EDITION NUMBER	NO. OF COLORS	ORIGINAL OPENING PRICE	CURRENT RETAIL PRICE
SOLD OUT EDITIONS (RARE):										
Joan Miró I Catalunya	EdP	LP	1970	LC	50 X 66 cm	AP	160		800	18000
Ma' de Proverbs	EdP	LP	1970	LC	57 X 77 cm	AP	75		800	18000
Osaka	EdP	LP	1970	LC	55 X 77 cm	AP	75		800	18000
Homenaje a Joan Prats	EdP	LP	1971	LC	65 X 86 cm	GP	75		850	20000
Ubu aux Baleares Series (Set of 14) (M-720– 784)	TER	AtM	1971	LC	20 X 26 EA	AP	120 EA			5000 EA
Newspaper	ME		1972	LC	26 X 20	AP	50			10000
Miró Lithographs, Volume II			1972	LC	18 X 15 EA	AP	80			3000 EA
Ocellaire	EdP	LP	1972	EC	56 X 76 cm	AP	75		900	18000
Nocturn Catalá	EdP	LP	1972	EC	56 X 76 cm	AP	75		900	18000
Miró Litógrafo I	EdP	LP	1972	LC	33 X 26 cm	RP	150		700	15000
Homenaje a Josep-Lluis Sert (Set of 5)	EdP	LP	1972	LC	75 X 58 cm EA	GP	150 EA		800 SET	25000 SET
Barcelona 1972–1973: Plate XIII9 (D-604)	SG	JJT	1973	EB/A/CAR	67 X 27	AP	50		1200	20000
Le Sarrasin a L'Etoile Bleu (D-578) (B-207)	ME	MOR	1973	EB/A/CAR	55 X 24	AP	50		1000	20000
Mont-Roig III (B-386)	EdP	LP	1973	LC	30 X 23	AP	30		800	1800
Oda a Joan Miró (from Suite of 9) (B-506)	EdP	LP	1973	LC	35 X 24	AP	100		800	18000
Hommage to Miró (B-589)	MMA	ME	1973	LC	36 X 24	AP	150		800	20000
La Femme des Sables			1973	AC	41 X 27	R/BFK	75		1000	30000
Les Agulles del Pastor	EdP	LP	1973	LC	59 X 83 cm	GP	75		1000	20000
Claca	EdP	LP	1973	LC	59 X 83 cm	GP	75		1000	20000
Godalla	EdP	LP	1973	LC	83 X 59 cm	GP	75		1000	20000
El Fogainer	EdP	LP	1973	LC	83 X 59 cm	GP	75		1000	20000
El Marxant de Galls	EdP	LP	1973	LC	59 X 83 cm	GP	75		1000	15000
Ode a Joan Miró	EdP	LP	1973	LC	34 X 25 cm	GP	75		1000	18000
Les Grandes Manouevres (D-575)	ME	MOR	1973	EB/A/CAR	55 X 24	AP	50		1000	18000
Espiru-Miró (Set of 8) (B/G-608)	SG	JJT	1974	EB/A	28 X 34 EA	AP	50 EA		5500 SET	40000 SET

JOAN MIRÓ CONTINUED

TITLE	PUBLISHER	PRINTER	DATE	MEDIUM	DIMENSION (PAPER SIZE) IN INCHES	TYPE OF PAPER	EDITION NUMBER	NO. OF COLORS	ORIGINAL OPENING PRICE	CURRENT RETAIL PRICE
SOLD OUT EDITIONS (RARE):										
La Femme Aborescente	ME	MOR	1974	EB/A/CAR	44 X 29	AP	50	16	1000	15000
Somnambule (B-127) (D-127)	ME	MOR	1974	EB/A/CAR	45 X 30	AP	50	16	1000	100000
Gravures pour une Exposition (One of 4 Variants) (B-211)	PM	MOR	1974	EB/A	25 X 36	AP	75		1000	85000
Femme Toupie (B-214)	ME	MOR	1974	EB/A/CAR	46 X 29	AP	50	16	1000	50000
Permissionaire (B-215)	ME	MOR	1974	EB/A/CAR	45 X 29	AP	50		1000	50000
Le Cracheur de Flammes (B/G-221)	ME	MOR	1974	EB/A/CAR	44 X 29	AP	75	12	1000	20000
Ja Ajudeu la Cultura Catalana?	OC	LP	1974	LC	73 X 54 cm	GP	75		1000	20000
Futbol Club Barcelona	FC	LP	1974	LC	99 X 69 cm	GP	50		1000	25000
Mont-Roig (Set of 4)	EdP	LP	1974	LC	76 X 56 cm EA	GP	30 EA		2500 SET	38000 SET
Miró Ecultor (Set of 7)	EdP	LP	1974–75	LC	35 X 52 cm EA	GP	100 EA		2800 SET	50000 SET
L'Halterophile	ME	ME	1975	LC	89 X 42	AP	30		2000	12000
La Guerriérre de Cent Ans	ME		1975	LC	89 X 42	AP	30		2000	12000
L'Enfance d'Ubu			1975	LC	13 X 20	AP	100		1000	9500
Hommage a Helion			1975	LC	23 X 18	AP	99		1000	9500
Journal d'Un Graveur (Set of 48) (B/G-616)	ME	MOR	1964–75	EB/A/DPT	23 X 18 EA	R/BFK	85 EA	1–6 EA	8500 SET	40000 SET
Souris Rouge a la Mantille	ME	ME	1975	EB/A	45 X 29	R/BFK	50		1200	15000
Miró Litógrafo II (Set of 13)	ME	AtM	1975	LC	33 X 26 cm EA	RP	150 EA		1800 SET	45000 SET
Maravillas con Variaciones Acrosticas en el Jardín de Miró (Set of 20)	EdP	LP	1975	LC	33 X 26 cm EA	RP	150 EA		2500 SET	75000 SET
Acrosticas en el Jardín de Miró (Set of 20)	EdP	LP	1975	LC	50 X 36 cm EA	RP	200 EA		2500 SET	75000 SET
Déballage I, II	ME	ME	1975	EC	29 X 45 EA	AP	30 EA		1000 EA	10000 EA
Human Rights	CAM		1975	LC	24 X 31	AP	75		1000	12000
Homenatge a Joan Prats #1– #15	EdP	LP	1975	LC	22 X 30 EA	GP	100 EA		1000 EA	12000 EA
Rupestre 44	CAM		1975	LC	22 X 30	AP	50		1000	12000
Oiseau de Feu	ME	ME	1975	EC	30 X 41	AP	75		1200	35000
Eustache	ME	ME	1975	LC	36 X 25	AP	50		1000	25000
La Manucure Evaporee	ME	ME	1975	EC	38 X 54	AP	50		2000 FF	90000 FF
La Taupe Hilare	ME	ME	1975	EC	38 X 55	AP	50		2000 FF	90000 FF
L'Encerclement	ME	ME	1975	EC	38 X 54	AP	50		2000 FF	90000 FF
Souris Noire a la Manfille	ME	ME	1975	EC	54 X 38	AP	50		2000 FF	90000 FF
Pic de la Mirandole	ME	ME	1975	EC	42 X 29	AP	50		1500 FF	80000 FF
Souris Rouge à la Mantille	ME	ME	1975	EC	45 X 29	AP	50		1500 FF	80000 FF
Grand Triptyque Noir	ME	ME	1975	EC	160 X 120 cm	AP	50		2500 FF	120000 FF
Suécia (Set of 2)	EdP	LP	1975–76	LC	76 X 56 cm	AP	100 EA		2000 SET	30000
Ruisselante Lunaire	ME	ME	1976	LC	62 X 47	AP	30		2500	20000
Miró Litógrafo III (Set of 8)	ME/EdP	AM/LP	1977	LC	33 X 26 cm EA	RP	150 EA		1800 SET	35000 SET
Le Chat de la Voisine	ME	ME	1977	LC	21 X 30	AP	30		1500	10000
Ruisselante Solaire	ME	ME	1977	LC	62 X 47	AP	30		3500	25000
La Meneuse de Lune	ME	ME	1977	LC	91 X 48	AP	30		5000	35000
Creole Dancer	ME	ME	1977	EB/A/CAR	45 X 29	R/BFK	50		2500	20000
Le Grande Ecaillere	ME	ME	1977	LC	91 X 48	AP	30		5000	35000
Personnage a la Fleche Noire	ME	ME	1977	EC	32 X 24	AP	50		2000	15000
L'Invitee du Dimanche, Fond Moir I	ME	ME	1978	EC	32 X 48	AP	75		1800	12000
Grave sur Legivre I	ME	ME	1978	EC	36 X 25	AP	50		1500	10000
Le Rossignol Effronte	ME	ME	1978	EC	23 X 15	AP	50		1000	8000
Le Puisatier	ME	ME	1978	EC	42 X 27	AP	75		1800	12000
La Greve Noir	ME	ME	1978	EC	24 X 54	AP	50		2000	15000
Le Chef d'Orchestre	ME	ME	1978	EC	54 X 38	AP	50		2000	15000
La Rat des Sables	ME	ME	1978	EC	38 X 54	AP	50		2000	15000
Emballage	ME	ME	1978	EC	39 X 45	AP	30		1800	12000
Le Troubadour	ME	ME	1978	EC	21 X 28	AP	50		1000	8000
Le Chef des Equipages	MF	MF	1978	EC	55 X 24	AP	50		2000	15000
Mambo	ME	ME	1978	EC	55 X 38	AP	50		2000	15000
La Fugitive	ME	ME	1978	EC	53 X 38	AP	50		2000	15000
Tres Joans	EdP	LP	1978	LC	75 X 121 cm	AP	99		2000	25000
Album 21 (Set of 21)	ME	AtM	1978		20 X 26	AP	75		2000 SET	40000 SET
Le Mulot	ME	ME	1978	EC	51 X 67 cm	AP	30		1200	9000
Le Frelon	ME	ME	1978	EC	51 X 67 cm	AP	30		1200	9000
Le Termite	ME	ME	1978	EC	51 X 67 cm	AP	30		1200	9000
La Libellule	ME	ME	1978	EC	51 X 67 cm	AP	30		1200	9000
La Musaraigne	ME	ME	1978	EC	51 X 67 cm	AP	30		1200	9000
Le Cri-Cri	ME	ME	1978	EC	51 X 67 cm	AP	30		1200	9000
Le Souriceau	ME	ME	1978	EC	64 X 46 cm	AP	30		1200	9000
Le Scorpion Joufflu	ME	ME	1978	EC	64 X 46 cm	AP	30		1200	9000
Le Hanneton	ME	ME	1978	EC	51 X 67 cm	AP	30		1200	9000
La Fourmi Rose	ME	ME	1978	EC	51 X 67 cm	AP	30		1200	9000
Les Scarabées	ME	ME	1978	EC	46 X 64 cm	AP	30		1200	9000
L'Oustachi	ME	ME	1978	EC	107 X 75 cm	AP	50		1500	12000
La Fine Mouche	ME	ME	1978	EC	64 X 46 cm	AP	30		1200	9000
Les Troglodytes-Noir	ME	ME	1978	EC	49 X 141 cm	AP	30	1	1000	6000

JOAN MIRÓ CONTINUED

Joan Miró
Ruisselante Lunaire
Courtesy Galerie Lelong

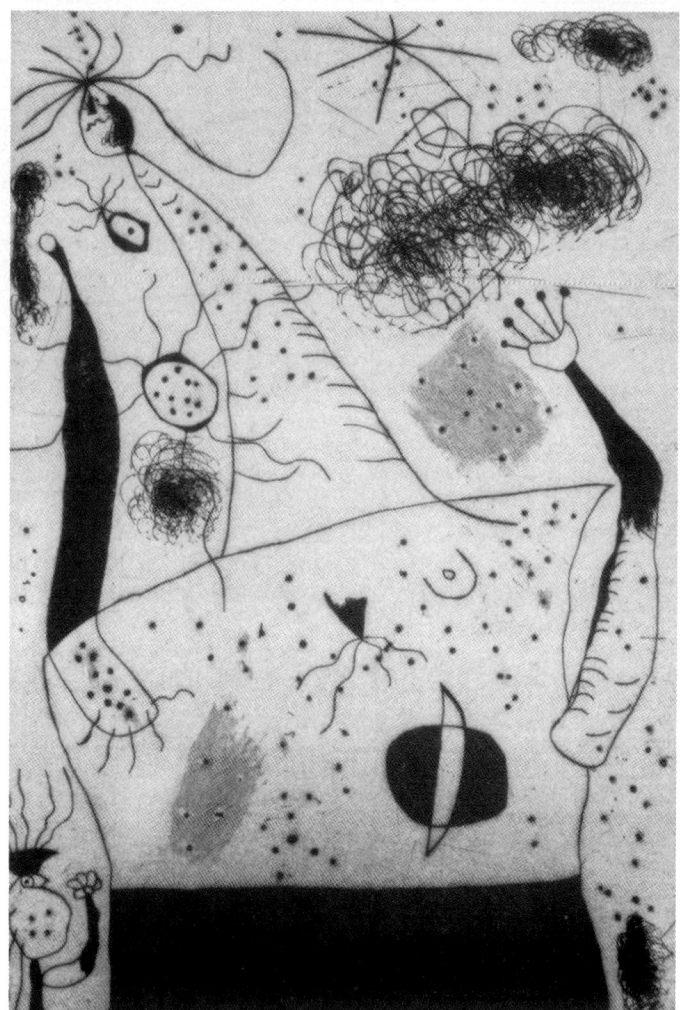

Joan Miró
La Geante
Courtesy Atelier Lacouriére

TITLE	PUBLISHER	PRINTER	DATE	MEDIUM	DIMENSION (PAPER SIZE) IN INCHES	TYPE OF PAPER	EDITION NUMBER	NO. OF COLORS	ORIGINAL OPENING PRICE	CURRENT RETAIL PRICE
SOLD OUT EDITIONS (RARE):										
La Rainette	ME	ME	1978	EB/A	25 X 18	R/BFK	30		1500	4000
Ocella	ME	DC	1978	LC	18 X 26	AP	75		1800	4500
Grans Rupestres (Set of 8) (B-248)	ME	JB	1979	AC	35 X 27 EA	R/BFK	30 EA		2000 EA	8000 EA
Grans Rupestres #24	TAI	ME	1979	EB/WO	36 X 27	AP	30		5500	15000
Els Gossos (B/G-257)	ME	JB	1979	EB/A	29 X 46	R/BFK	30		2500	8000
Personatge I Estels	ME	JB	1979	EB/A/WC	36 X 25	R/BFK	50		2500	6000
L'Otaire Savante	ME	JB	1979	EC	107 X 75 cm	AP	50		2000	12000
Arlequin Jongleur	ME	ME	1979	LC	36 X 24	AP	50		10000 FF	60000 FF
Arlequin Tourneur	ME	ME	1979	LC	36 X 24	AP	50		10000 FF	60000 FF
Arlequin Enturbanne	ME	ME	1979	LC	36 X 24	AP	50		10000 FF	60000 FF
Arlequin Artificier	ME	ME	1979	LC	36 X 24	AP	50		10000 FF	60000 FF
La Chasse aux Papillons	MLLE	ME	1979	AC	29 X 26	AP	50	8	4000	25000
L'Elagede la Main	MLLE	ME	1979	AC	20 X 26	AP	50	4	4000	25000
L'Evadé	ME	ME	1979	EC	64 X 46 cm	AP	50		2000 FF	10000 FF
La Metamorphose	ME	ME	1979	EC	139 X 97 cm	AP	50		2000 FF	10000 FF
La Brahmane	ME	ME	1979	EC	138 X 97 cm	AP	50		30000 FF	150000 FF
Le Roi des Lapins	ME	ME	1979	EC	96 X 71 cm	AP	50		30000 FF	150000 FF
Fête Galante	ME	ME	1979	EC	64 X 45 cm	AP	50		20000 FF	75000 FF
L'aveugle Parmiles Oiseaux	ME	ME	1979	EC	135 X 97 cm	AP	50		10000 FF	40000 FF
Reverie aux Piments Doux	ME	ME	1979	EC	67 X 51 cm	AP	50		10000 FF	35000 FF
L'Oiseleur etsa Compagne	ME	ME	1979	EC	81 X 63 cm	AP	50		6000	50000
Columbine Effarouchée	ME	ME	1980	LC	36 X 24	AP	50		1500	12000
Columbine au Miroir	ME	ME	1980	LC	36 X 24	AP	50		1500	12000
Columbine au Saut du Lit	ME	ME	1980	LC	36 X 24	AP	50		1500	12000
Columbine a la Fenetre	ME	ME	1980	LC	36 X 24	AP	50		1500	12000
Columbine aux Idées Noires	ME	ME	1980	LC	36 X 24	AP	50		1500	12000
Serie Gaudi 40	ME	ME	1980	EB/A/CO	17 X 14	AP/WOVE	50		1000	6500
Serie Gaudi 45	ME	ME	1980	EB/A/CAR	45 X 30	AP/WOVE	50		1500	25000
Serie Gaudi 46	ME	ME	1980	EB/A/CO	37 X 31	AP/WOVE	50		1200	25000
Serie Enrajolats No 53	ME	ME	1980	EB/A	16 X 21	AP/WOVE	30		1000	7000
Colpir Sense Nafrar	EdP	LP	1980	LC	96 X 7 cm	GP	50		2000	18000

RICHARD LAURENCE MISRACH

BORN: Los Angeles, CA; July 11, 1949
EDUCATION: Univ of California, Berkeley, CA, BA, 1971
TEACHING: Univ of California, Berkeley, CA, 1971–77,82
AWARDS: Friends of Photography, Ferguson Grant, 1976; Nat Endowment for the Arts Fel, 1973,77; Guggenheim Fel, NY, 1978,80
RECENT EXHIB: Santa Barbara Mus of Art, CA, 1988; Univ of Nevada, Sonna Beam Gallery, Las Vegas, NV, 1992; Univ of Nevada, Sheppard Fine Arts Gallery, Reno, NV, 1992
COLLECTIONS: Mus of Mod Art, NY; San Francisco Mus of Mod Art, CA; Smithsonian Inst, Wash, DC; Mus of Fine Arts, Houston, TX; Arco Ctr for the Visual Arts, Los Angeles, CA; Oakland Mus, CA; Mus of Mod Art, Georges Pompidou Ctr, Paris, France; Center for Creative Photography, Tucson, AZ; Fogg Art Mus, Harvard Univ, Cambridge, MA; Metropolitan Mus, NY; Santa Barbara Mus of Art, CA
PRINTERS: Myron's Dye Transfer Printing, San Francisco, CA (MDT); Artist (ART)
PUBLISHERS: Grapestake Gallery, San Francisco, CA (GG); Artist (ART)
GALLERIES: Light Gallery, New York, NY; Fraenkel Gallery, San Francisco, CA; Elizabeth Leach Gallery, Portland, OR; Etherton/Stern Gallery, Tucson, AZ; Jan Kesner Gallery, Los Angeles, CA; Thomas V Meyer Fine Art, San Francisco, CA; Middendorf Gallery, Wash, DC; Scott Alan Fine Arts, New York, NY; Gibson Gallery, Seattle, WA
MAILING ADDRESS: 1420 45th St, Emeryville, CA 94608

TITLE	PUBLISHER	PRINTER	DATE	MEDIUM	DIMENSION (PAPER SIZE) IN INCHES	TYPE OF PAPER	EDITION NUMBER	NO. OF COLORS	ORIGINAL OPENING PRICE	CURRENT RETAIL PRICE
SOLD OUT EDITIONS (RARE):										
Hawaii Portfolio (Set of 12):	GG	MDT	1980	PH/DT	16 X 20 EA		50 EA		1500 SET	5000 SET
Stonehenge #1,#2,#3,#4	ART	ART	1976–81	PH	16 X 20 EA				500 EA	2500 EA
Desert Photographs	ART	ART	1975–81	PH	16 X 20 EA				500 EA	2500 EA
CURRENT EDITIONS:										
Greece, Louisiana, Hawaii	GG	ART	1979–81	PH	40 X 30 EA		10 EA		750 EA	2000 EA
Graecism Portfolio (Set of 10):	GG	MDT	1982	PH/DT	16 X 20 EA		25 EA		4500 SET	7500 SET
Louisiana Series	GG	ART	1982	PH	20 X 16 EA				250 EA	400 EA
Greece Series	GG	ART	1982	PH	24 X 20 EA				400 EA	600 EA

JESSICA MITCHELL

BORN: Pittsburgh, PA; 1946
EDUCATION: Carnegie Mellon Univ, Pittsburgh, PA; Silvermine Col of Art, New Canaan, CT; Art Students League, NY
AWARDS: Bernard Klonis Mem Merit Scholarship, Art Students League, NY
PRINTERS: American Atelier, NY (AA)
PUBLISHERS: Circle Fine Art, Chicago, IL (CFA)
GALLERIES: Circle Galleries, San Diego, CA & San Francisco, CA & Northbrook, IL & Pittsburgh, PA & Houston, TX & Soho, NY & Chicago, IL & Scottsdale, AZ & Beverly Hills, CA & Costa Mesa, CA & Sherman Oaks, CA & Palm Beach, FL & Honolulu, HI & New Orleans, LA & Las Vegas, NV & Seattle, WA

TITLE	PUBLISHER	PRINTER	DATE	MEDIUM	DIMENSION (PAPER SIZE) IN INCHES	TYPE OF PAPER	EDITION NUMBER	NO. OF COLORS	ORIGINAL OPENING PRICE	CURRENT RETAIL PRICE
SOLD OUT EDITIONS (RARE):										
Peach and Flowers	CFA	AA	1978	EB	15 X 16	R/BFK	165		50	150
Still Life with Basket	CFA	AA	1978	EB	12 X 14	R/BFK	165		50	150
Small Still Life	CFA	AA	1978	EB	9 X 9	R/BFK	165	1	50	125
Still Life with Apple	CFA	AA	1978	EB	9 X 11	R/BFK	165	1	50	125
CURRENT EDITIONS:										
Faces	CFA	AA	1978	EB	16 X 12	R/BFK	110	1	50	100
Transformation	CFA	AA	1978	EB	20 X 12	R/BFK	110	1	50	100

JOAN MITCHELL

BORN: Chicago, IL; (1926–1992)
EDUCATION: Smith Col, Northampton, MA, 1942–44; Art Inst of Chicago, IL, BFA, 1944–47; Columbia Univ, NY, MFA, 1950
AWARDS: Distinguished Artist Award for Lifetime Achievement, College Art Assn, 1988; Award for Painting, French Ministry of Culture, Paris, France, 1989
RECENT EXHIB: Allentown Art Mus, PA, 1987; Niagra Univ, Buscaglia-Castellani Art Gallery, Niagra Falls, NY, 1987; San Francisco Mus of Mod Art, CA, 1988; Cornell Univ, Johnson Mus, Ithaca, NY, 1988; Corcoran Gallery, Wash, DC, 1988; La Jolla Mus of Contemp Art, CA, 1988–89; Manny Silverman Gallery, Los Angeles, CA, 1988–89; La Jolla Mus of Contemp Art, CA, 1988–89; Herbert F Johnson Mus of Art, Cornell Univ, Ithaca, NY, 1989; Jean Foumier Gallery, Paris, France, 1990; Albright-Knox Art Gallery, Buffalo, NY, 1988,92; Galerie Jean Fournier, Paris, France, 1992; Laura Carpenter Fine Art, Santa Fe, NM, 1992; Susan Sheehan Gallery, NY, 1993; Robert Miller Gallery, NY, 1993
COLLECTIONS: Mus of Mod Art, NY; Basel Mus, Switzerland; Hirshhorn Mus, Wash, DC; Albright-Knox Art Gallery, Buffalo, NY; Norman Mackenzie Art Gallery, Regina, Sask, Canada; Phillips Coll, Wash, DC; Art Inst of Chicago, IL; Pennsylvania Acad of Fine Art, Phila, PA; Jean Foumier Gallery, Paris, France
PRINTERS: Tyler Graphics Workshop, Mount Kisco, NY (TGL)
PUBLISHERS: Tyler Graphics Ltd, Mount Kisco, NY (TGL)
GALLERIES: Gloria Luria Gallery, Bay Harbor Islands, FL; David Anderson Gallery, Buffalo, NY; Harcus Gallery, Boston, MA; Spaightwood Galleries, Madison, WI; Manny Silverman Gallery, Los Angeles, CA; R K Goldman Contemporary, Los Angeles, CA; Marvin Ross Friedman & Co, Miami, FL; Robert Miller Gallery, New York, NY; Edward Tyler Nahem Fine Art, New York, NY; Jean Foumier Gallery, Paris, France; BenedicteSaxe Gallery, Beverly Hills, CA; Hine Editions/Limestone Press, San Francisco, CA; River Gallery, Westport, CT; John C Stoller & Company, Minneapolis, MN; Laura Carpenter Fine Art, Santa Fe, NM; Tyler Graphics, Ltd, Mount Kisco, NY; Lennon Weinberg Gallery, New York, NY; Carol M Penn Fine Art, New York, NY; Gianna M Carotenuro Fine Art, Yountville, CA; Ameringer & Avard Fine Art, Inc, New York, NY; Susan Sheehan Gallery, New York, NY
MAILING ADDRESS: c/o Robert Miller Gallery, 41 E 57th St, New York, NY 10022

The retail prices of the 100,000 limited edition prints quoted in this directory are subject to change. Print publishers, artists and galleries were the direct sources for these quotations. Prices in the secondary market listed as "Sold Out Editions (Rare)" indicate that the publisher has a limited supply of that print or that the print is difficult to locate in the galleries.

JOAN MITCHELL CONTINUED

TITLE	PUBLISHER	PRINTER	DATE	MEDIUM	DIMENSION (PAPER SIZE) IN INCHES	TYPE OF PAPER	EDITION NUMBER	NO. OF COLORS	ORIGINAL OPENING PRICE	CURRENT RETAIL PRICE
CURRENT EDITIONS:										
Bedford Series:										
Bedford I	TGL	TGL	1981	LC	43 X 33	AP88	70	10	1800	5000
Bedford II	TGL	TGL	1981	LC	43 X 33	AP88	70	8	1800	3500
Bedford III	TGL	TGL	1981	LC	43 X 33	AP88	70	7	1800	3500
Sides of a River Series:										
Sides of a River I	TGL	TGL	1981	LC	43 X 33	AP88	70	6	1800	3500
Sides of a River II	TGL	TGL	1981	LC	43 X 33	AP88	70	7	1800	3500
Sides of a River III	TGL	TGL	1981	LC	43 X 33	AP88	70	2	1200	2500
Flower Series:										
Flower I	TGL	TGL	1981	LC	43 X 33	AP88	70	8	1800	3500
Flower II	TGL	TGL	1981	LC	43 X 33	AP88	70	2	1200	2500
Flower III	TGL	TGL	1981	LC	43 X 33	AP88	70	4	1800	3500
Brush Series:										
Brush	TGL	TGL	1981	LC	43 X 33	AP88	70	4	1500	3500
Brush, State I	TGL	TGL	1981	LC	43 X 33	AP88	35	4	1500	2500
Sunflowers I-IV	TGL	TGL	1992	LC	57 X 82 EA	R/BFK	34 EA		4500 EA	4500 EA
Sunflowers V	TGL	TGL	1992	LC	57 X 41	R/BFK	34		2500	2500

MARGARETTA K MITCHELL

BORN: Brooklyn, NY; May 27, 1935
EDUCATION: Smith Col, Northampton, MA, BA, 1957; Boston Mus Sch, MA 1958–59; Escuela de Bellas Artes, Madrid, Spain, 1959–60; Univ of California, Berkeley, CA, MA, 1985
AWARDS: Nat Endowment for the Arts Mus Grant, 1978–79; Levi Strauss Found, 1979; California Council for the Arts Grant, Berkeley Art Center, CA, 1981–82; Mortimer Fleichhacker Found, 1985; L J & Mary C Skaggs Found Grant, 1981,85; California Council for the Humanities, 1980,85
TEACHING: City Col, San Francisco, CA, 1980; Rhode Island Sch of Design, Providence, RI, Summer, 1983; Civic Arts, Walnut Creek, CA, 1980–84; Univ of California Ext, San Francisco, CA, 1976–78,1985; Univ of California Ext, Berkeley, CA, 1986; California Col of Arts & Crafts, Oakland, CA, 1984,86

RECENT EXHIB: Carlton Col, Northfield, MN, 1988
COLLECTIONS: International Center of Photography, NY; Oakland Mus, CA; Royal Print Coll, Windsor, England; Smith Col, Northampton, MA; Bancroft Library, Univ of California, Berkeley, CA
PRINTERS: Katherine Lincoln Press, San Francisco, CA (KLP); Hirsh-Greene Press, Oakland, CA (HGP); Ann Hirsh, Oakland, CA (AH); Scott Greene, Oakland, CA (SG)
PUBLISHERS: Ed Hill Editions, El Paso, TX (EHE); Elysian Editions, Berkeley, CA (EE)
GALLERIES: Marcuse Pfeifer Gallery, New York, NY; Ed Hill Gallery, El Paso, TX
MAILING ADDRESS: 280 Hillcrest Rd, Berkeley, CA 94704

TITLE	PUBLISHER	PRINTER	DATE	MEDIUM	DIMENSION (PAPER SIZE) IN INCHES	TYPE OF PAPER	EDITION NUMBER	NO. OF COLORS	ORIGINAL OPENING PRICE	CURRENT RETAIL PRICE
SOLD OUT EDITIONS (RARE):										
Cyclamen	EHE	KLP	1982	PHG	30 X 22	R/BFK	60	7	275	700
CURRENT EDITIONS:										
Orchid	EHE	KLP	1982	PHG	30 X 22	R/BFK	60	7	275	550
Chinese Tree Peony	EHE	KLP	1982	PHG	30 X 22	R/BFK	60	13	275	600
Peony Blossom	EHE	KLP	1982	PHG	20 X 17	R/BFK	60	5	175	450
Nasturtium Leaves with Buds	EHE	KLP	1983	PH/GRA	30 X 22	R/BFK	60	3	275	450
Portfolio (Set of 13):									3750 SET	4000 SET
Come Dance with Me	EE	HG	1986	PH/GRA	19 X 15	AC	50	1	300	350
Dance for Life	EE	HG	1986	PH/GRA	15 X 19	AC	50	1	300	350
Benediction	EE	HG	1986	PH/GRA	19 X 15	AC	50	1	300	350
Thanksgiving	EE	HG	1986	PH/GRA	19 X 15	AC	50	1	300	350
Caryatid	EE	HG	1986	PH/GRA	19 X 15	AC	50	1	300	350
Sisters	EE	HG	1986	PH/GRA	19 X 15	AC	50	1	300	350
Flinging the Veil	EE	HG	1986	PH/GRA	19 X 15	AC	50	1	300	350
Victory	EE	HG	1986	PH/GRA	19 X 15	AC	50	1	300	350
Blessed Spirits	EE	HG	1986	PH/GRA	19 X 15	AC	50	1	300	350
Procession	EE	HG	1986	PH/GRA	19 X 15	AC	50	1	300	350
Weaving Garlands	EE	HG	1986	PH/GRA	19 X 15	AC	50	1	300	350
Sülgwynn Quitzow, Spring Festival	EE	HG	1986	PH/GRA	19 X 15	AC	50	1	300	350
Finale: Southern Roses	EE	HG	1986	PH/GRA	19 X 15	AC	50	1	300	350

WAYNE AKIRA MIYAMOTO

BORN: Honolulu, HI; September 6, 1947
EDUCATION: Rensslaer Polytech Inst, Troy, NY, 1965–68; Univ of Hawaii, Honolulu, HI, BA, BFA, 1970, MFA, 1974
TEACHING: Asst Prof, Florida Tech Univ, Orlando, FL, 1976–78; Vis Art, San Jose State Univ, CA, 1978; Vis Art, Sch of Art Inst, Chicago, IL, 1978; Vis Art, Univ of Hawaii, Hilo, HI, 1976, Asst Prof, 1981–86, Assoc Prof, 1986 to present, Dept Chmn, 1983 to present

AWARDS: State Found for Culture and the Arts Grants, Hawaii, 1972,74,75; Purchase Awards, Pacific States Regional Print & Drawing Exhib, 1984,85; Juror's Award, Print Club of Philadelphia, 1988
COLLECTIONS: Fine Arts Mus, Univ of Alaska, Fairbanks, AK; Florida Tech Univ, Orlando, FL; Univ of Hawaii, Honolulu, HI; Leeward Community Col, Pearl City, HI; Ft Hays State Univ, Hays, KS; C N Gorman Mus, Univ of California, Davis, CA; Univ of Central Florida, Orlando, FL

WAYNE AKIRA MIYAMOTO CONTINUED

PRINTERS: Artist (ART)
PUBLISHERS: CH-14 Print Studio, Dept of Art, Univ of Hawaii, Hilo, HI (CH-14); CSUS Print Studio, Dept of Art, California State Univ, Sacramento, CA (CSUS); UCF Print Studio, Dept of Art, Univ of Central Florida, Orlando, FL (UCF); Artist (ART)
GALLERIES: Texann Ivy Fine Arts, Orlando, FL; Gallery EAS, Honolulu, FL
MAILING ADDRESS: PO Box 1176, Hilo, HI 96720

TITLE	PUBLISHER	PRINTER	DATE	MEDIUM	DIMENSION (PAPER SIZE) IN INCHES	TYPE OF PAPER	EDITION NUMBER	NO. OF COLORS	ORIGINAL OPENING PRICE	CURRENT RETAIL PRICE
SOLD OUT EDITIONS (RARE):										
Torso XXV	ART	ART	1974	I	36 X 24	R/BFK	10	1	250	350
Bone Figure	CSUS	DK	1981	LB	30 X 22	R/BFK	9	1	200	350
O-SA-KA-NA	CH-14	ART	1982	I	18 X 24	MUR	10	1	200	350
CURRENT EDITIONS:										
Shimanagashi Map of the World	UCF	ART	1976	I	18 X 24	R/BFK	10	1	150	275
Aquarium	UCF	ART	1977	I	18 X 24	R/BFK	10	1	150	275
Trapeze Syndrome	UCF	ART	1977	I	18 X 24	R/HW	10	1	150	275
Robeson's Pillow	UCF	ART	1978	I	24 X 18	R/BFK	10	1	175	275
Kami Figure	CH-14	ART	1982	I	12 X 9	AP/B	7	1	75	150
Kami Figure, No. 2	CH-14	ART	1982	I	12 X 9	AP/B	7	1	75	150
Kami Figure No. 3	CH-14	ART	1982	I	12 X 9	AP/B	7	1	75	150
Two Figures	CH-14	ART	1983–84	I	24 X 18	R/BFK	8	2	300	350
KA-NE	CH-14	ART	1984	I	24 X 18	R/BFK	8	1	200	250
Figures-Three-Earth	CH-14	ART	1984	I	24 X 17	AP/CW	8	2	300	350
Figure (Wahine)	CH-14	ART	1984	I	24 X 18	TIEP	5	1	200	250
Haniwa	CH-14	ART	1985	I	24 X 18	R/BFK	8	2	300	350
Kami Figure-Ox	CH-14	ART	1985	I	24 X 18	R/BFK	8	2	300	350
Ancestor Figure	CH-14	ART	1985	I	24 X 18	AP/CW	8	2	300	350
Kappa Venus	CH-14	ART	1985	I	24 X 18	R/BFK/G	8	1	200	250

GEORGE JOJI MIYASAKI

BORN: Kalopa, Hawaii; March 24, 1935
EDUCATION: California College of Arts & Crafts, Oakland, CA, MFA, BA Ed 1958–64
TEACHING: Univ of California, Berkeley, CA, 1964 to present
AWARDS: Guggenheim Fel, 1963, Purchase Prize, Brooklyn Mus, 1968; Nat Endowment for the Arts Fel, 1980, 85
RECENT EXHIB: 311 Site Gallery, Pacific Grove, CA, 1987; Palo Alto Cultural Center, CA, 1989
COLLECTIONS: Brooklyn Mus, NY; Mus of Mod Art, NY; Madison Art Center, Madison, WI; Nat Gallery of Art, Wash, DC; San Francisco Mus of Mod Art, CA; Art Inst of Chicago, IL; Univ of Texas, Austin, TX; Auchenbach Found of Graphic Arts, San Francisco, CA; Pasadena Art Mus, CA; Oakland Art Mus, CA; Philadelphia Mus of Art, PA; Walker Art Center, Minneapolis, MN
PRINTERS: Tamarind Inst, Albuquerque, NM (TI); Lynne Allen (LA); Don Farnsworth (DF); Barbara Tolleen (BA); Wayne Kline (WK); Craig Cornwall (CC)
PUBLISHERS: Tamarind Inst, Albuquerque, NM (TI); Magnolia Fine Arts Press, Oakland, CA (MFAP)
GALLERIES: Stephen Wirtz Gallery, San Francisco, CA; Klein Gallery, Chicago, IL; Tamarind Institute, Albuquerque, NM; 311 Site Gallery, Pacific Grove, CA; Magnolia Editions, Oakland, CA
MAILING ADDRESS: 2844 Forest Ave, Berkeley, CA 94705

TITLE	PUBLISHER	PRINTER	DATE	MEDIUM	DIMENSION (PAPER SIZE) IN INCHES	TYPE OF PAPER	EDITION NUMBER	NO. OF COLORS	ORIGINAL OPENING PRICE	CURRENT RETAIL PRICE
SOLD OUT EDITIONS (RARE):										
Gallop	TI	LA/TI	1982	LC/CC	40 X 30	GE	50	4	800	1200
Trampas Mesa	TI	WK/TI	1982	LC	27 X 21	CD	50	5	500	1000
Tormenta de Truenos (Sandia Mt)	TI	BT/TI	1982	LC	25 X 21	ARJ	50	4	500	1000
Blue Ridge	MFAP	DF/MFAP	1985	LC	36 X 27	R/BFK	40	7	600	900
Signal Hill USA	MFAP	DF/MFAP	1985	LC	38 X 28	R/BFK	60	7	800	1100
CURRENT EDITIONS:										
White Signal	TI	LA/TI	1987	LC	30 X 23	GE	30	7	500	600
Mescalero	TI	CC/TI	1987	LC/CC	40 X 28	SOM/MUL	30	6	700	800

PAUL MOGENSEN

BORN: Los Angeles, CA; December 3, 1941
EDUCATION: Univ of Southern California, CA, BFA, 1963
AWARDS: Guggenheim Found Grant, 1976; Nat Endowment for the Arts Grant, 1980; Pollock-Krasner Found Grant, NY, 1988
RECENT EXHIB: Edward Thorp Gallery, NY, 1987
COLLECTIONS: Houston Mus of Fine Arts, Houston, TX; Mus of Mod Art, NY; High Mus of Art, Atlanta, GA; Wadsworth Atheneum, Hartford, CT
GALLERIES: Texas Gallery, Houston, TX; Brooke Alexander Inc, New York, NY; Edward Thorp Gallery, New York, NY; Hope-Weiss Fine Art, Los Angeles, CA
MAILING ADDRESS: 159 Mercer St, New York, NY 10012

TITLE	PUBLISHER	PRINTER	DATE	MEDIUM	DIMENSION (PAPER SIZE) IN INCHES	TYPE OF PAPER	EDITION NUMBER	NO. OF COLORS	ORIGINAL OPENING PRICE	CURRENT RETAIL PRICE
SOLD OUT EDITIONS (RARE):										
No Title (Double Spiral on Carmine)	ART	ART	1976	W/WAC	22 X 29	RICE	15	9	350	650
No Title (Prussian Blue Dot-Dash	ART	ART	1976	W/WAC	22 X 29	RICE	50	1	100	450
Set of Prints:										
Part I (Set of 14)	ART	ART	1981	W/WAC	10 X 15 EA	JP	30 EA	22 EA	4000 SET	5000 SET
Part II (Set of 14)	ART	ART	1981	W/WAC	10 X 15 EA	JP	30 EA	22 EA	4000 SET	5000 SET

RICHARD BASIL MOCK

BORN: Long Beach, CA; August 2, 1944
EDUCATION: Univ of Michigan, Ann Arbor, MI, BA; San Francisco Art Inst, CA; Skowhegan Sch of Painting & Sculpture, ME; New York Studio Sch, NY
TEACHING: Univ Oklahoma, Norman, OK
AWARDS: Nat Endowment for the Arts Grant; New York Studio Sch Alumni Grant; Fel, Painting, Roswell Mus, NM
RECENT EXHIB: Augen Gallery, Portland, OR, 1987; Howard Yezerski Gallery, Boston, MA, 1992
COLLECTIONS: Metropolitan Mus of Art, NY; Brooklyn Mus, NY; Victoria & Albert Mus, London, England; Walker Art Center, Minneapolis, MN; Worcester Art Mus, MA; American Embassy, London, England; Australia Nat Art Mus, Canberra, Australia; Culture Center, Monterrey, Mexico; Fort Worth Art Mus, TX; Museo de Monterrey, Mexico; Mus of Fine Arts, Boston, MA; Nat Army Mus, London, England; Nat Mus of Am Art, Wash, DC; New York Public Library, NY; Pentagon, Wash, DC
PRINTERS: Ted Warner, NY (TW); Chip Elwell, NY (CE); Bruce Porter, NY (BP); Trestle Editions, NY (TrE); Andrea Russell, Brooklyn, NY (AR); Grin Graphics, Brooklyn, NY (GG); Frank Martinez, Brooklyn, NY (FM); Chris Murray, Brooklyn, NY (CM); Water Street Press, Brooklyn, NY (WSP); Dan Stack, NY (DS); Copperplate Editions, NY (CPEd); Rinconada Press, Monterrey, Mexico (RinPr); Everglades Press, Brooklyn, NY (EvPr); Mark Dixon, Glasgow, Scotland (MD); Stuart Duffin, Glasgow, Scotland (SD); Glasgow Print Shop, Glasgow, Scotland (GPS); Arte Dos Graffico, Bogota, Colombia (ADG)
PUBLISHERS: Perma Press, NY (PeP); Chip Elwell, NY (CE); Fawbush Editions, NY (FE); Bruce Porter, NY (BP); John Szoke Graphics, NY (JSG); Waterstreet Press, Brooklyn, NY (WSP); Scott Siegler, Los Angeles, CA (ScS); Carla Singer, Los Angeles, CA (CS); Bruce Vinokour, Los Angeles, CA (BV); Copperplate Editions, NY (CPEd); Artist (ART); Kentler International Drawing Center, Brooklyn, NY (KIDC); Copper Plate Editions, Aripeka, FL (CPE); Glasgow Print Shop, Glasgow, Scotland (GPS); Miguel Garza Salinas, Bogota, Colombia (MGS); Maria Cocchiarelli, Bogota, Colombia (MC); Luis Angel Parra, Bogota, Colombia (LAP)
GALLERIES: Brooke Alexander, Inc, New York, NY; Diane Villani Editions, New York, NY; Hokin/Kaufman Gallery, Chicago, IL; Fawbush Editions, New York, NY; Asher/Faure Gallery, Los Angeles, CA; John Szoke Graphics, New York, NY; Rosa Esman Gallery, New York, NY; Evelyn Siegel Gallery, Fort Worth, TX; Gallery 72, Omaha, NE; Brody's Gallery, Wash, DC; Galeria Sextante, Bogota, Colombia; Howard Yezerski Gallery, Boston, MA
MAILING ADDRESS: 112 Sackett St, Brooklyn, NY 11231

Richard Basil Mock
I'm Bushed
Courtesy the Artist

TITLE	PUBLISHER	PRINTER	DATE	MEDIUM	DIMENSION (PAPER SIZE) IN INCHES	TYPE OF PAPER	EDITION NUMBER	NO. OF COLORS	ORIGINAL OPENING PRICE	CURRENT RETAIL PRICE
SOLD OUT EDITIONS (RARE):										
Mock of the Times (Editorial, Lincuts for the New York Times) (Set of 60)	ART/WSP	CE/FM/CM/WSP	1980–86	LI	20 X 26 EA	R/BFK	40 EA	1 EA	7000 SET	30000 SET
Urban Arms	KIDC	EvPr	1988	LI	22 X 30	R/BFK/W	35	1	800	1000
Arms Merchant	ART	EvPr	1988	LI	22 X 30	R/BFK/W	20	1	450	1000
Arc Angel San Miguel	MGS	RinPr	1990	LI	22 X 30	R/BFK/W	20	1	600	1000
CURRENT EDITIONS:										
Hawaiian Visions (Set of 4)	PeP	CE	1983	LI/HC	20 X 26 EA	R/BFK	30 EA	Varied	1500 SET	2500 SET
Printer's Devil	ART/CE	CE	1984	WC	37 X 29	SUZ	25	4	600	1200
Axis Crossing	FE		1985	LB	36 X 24		20		400	500
Totum Walker	FE		1985	LB	36 X 24		20		400	500
Crystal Gazer	FE		1986	LI/WA/HC	26 X 30		25		750	900
Insights	FE		1986	LC	33 X 38		40		900	1000
Sun, Moon, Soup (Set of 6)	ART/BP	BP/TrE	1986	LB	44 X 34 EA	THS	40 EA	1 EA	4000 SET	6000 SET
Hawaiian Series (Set of 4):									1000 SET	1500 SET
Kavai	JSG	CE	1986	LI		KOZO	33	2	350	400
Bird of Paradise	JSG	CE	1986	LI		KOZO	33	2	350	400
Original Surfer	JSG	CE	1986	LI		KOZO	33	2	350	400
Island Maker	JSG	CE	1986	LI		KOZO	33	2	350	400
Life Timer	JSG	CE	1986	WC	45 X 38	KOZO	34	12	1000	1250
Voids and Tangents (Set of 4)	ScS/CS/BV	AR/GG	1986	SP	22 X 22 EA	R/BFK/CR	40 EA	2 EA	2000 SET	2250 SET
Deception	CPEd	DS/CPEd	1988	EC/CO/HC	28 X 30	R/BFK	30	2	1500	1800
Deception	CPE	DS	1988	EB/A	28 X 36	BAS	35	4	1200	1500
Urban Warfare, Ten Act of Violence (Set of 10)	MGS	EvPr	1990	LI	22 X 30 EA	R/BFK	70 EA	1 EA	3500 SET	10000 SET
Gulf War (Confrontation Zone, Oil Spill Kill, Vapor Raper, Victim) (Set of 4)	GPS	SD/GPS	1991	LI/SP	20 X 27 EA	AP	50 EA	2 EA	4000 SET 1200 EA	4000 SET 1200 EA

The retail prices of the 100,000 limited edition prints quoted in this directory are subject to change. Print publishers, artists and galleries were the direct sources for these quotations. Prices in the secondary market listed as "Sold Out Editions (Rare)" indicate that the publisher has a limited supply of that print or that the print is difficult to locate in the galleries.

RICHARD BASIL MOCK CONTINUED

TITLE	PUBLISHER	PRINTER	DATE	MEDIUM	DIMENSION (PAPER SIZE) IN INCHES	TYPE OF PAPER	EDITION NUMBER	NO. OF COLORS	ORIGINAL OPENING PRICE	CURRENT RETAIL PRICE
CURRENT EDITIONS:										
Four Horses of the Apocalypse (Set of 4)	MGS	RinPr	1991	LI	22 X 30 EA	R/BFK/W	20 EA	1 EA	2400 SET / 600 EA	4000 SET / 1000 EA
World Environment (for United Newspaper-Development Forum) (Set of 10)	MC	EvPr	1992	LI	22 X 30 EA	R/BFK	70 EA	1 EA	3500 SET	3900 SET
Hurricane Andrew	LAP	ADG	1992	LI	50 X 70 cm	MAG/650	20	1	350	1000
Danza Cosmica No 2	LAP	ADG	1992	CAR	50 X 70 cm	MAG/650	25	5	500	500
El Hombre Electrico	LAP	ADG	1992	LI	50 X 70 cm	MAG/650	25	1	350	350
Libetad e Ilusiones	LAP	ADG	1992	LI	50 X 70 cm	MAG/650	25	1	350	350
La Responsabilidad de la Prensa	LAP	ADG	1992	LI	50 X 70 cm	MAG/650	25	1	350	350
Dos Conejos Impresos	LAP	ADG	1992	LI	50 X 70 cm	MAG/650	25	2	500	500
Danza Cosmica No 3	LAP	ADG	1992	LI	50 X 70 cm	MAG/650	25	6	500	500
I'm Bushed (Set of 3)	HYG	EvPr	1992	LI	22 X 30	R/BFK	70	1	1000 SET	1000 SET
Television	LAP	ADG	1992	LI	50 X 70 cm	MAG/650	25	1	350	350
Electricidad Primaria	LAP	ADG	1992	LI	50 X 70 cm	MAG/650	25	1	350	350

MARY K MODEEN-WATKINSON

BORN: Madison, WI; July 14, 1953
EDUCATION: Northeast Missouri State Univ, Kirksville, MO, MA; Louisiana State Univ, Baton Rouge, LA, MFA
TEACHING: Louisiana State Univ, Baton Rouge, LA; Northeast Missouri State Univ, Kirksville, MO; Asst Prof, Dartmouth Col, Hanover, NH, currently
PRINTERS: Artist (ART)
PUBLISHERS: Artist (ART)
GALLERIES: Mary Bell Galleries, Chicago, IL; Woodstock Gallery & Design Center, Woodstock, VT

TITLE	PUBLISHER	PRINTER	DATE	MEDIUM	DIMENSION (PAPER SIZE) IN INCHES	TYPE OF PAPER	EDITION NUMBER	NO. OF COLORS	ORIGINAL OPENING PRICE	CURRENT RETAIL PRICE
CURRENT EDITIONS:										
From Inside Out	ART	ART	1981	LC	16 X 20	R/BFK	9	6	100	125
Strata	ART	ART	1981	LC	16 X 20	STP/G	9	6	125	150
Rain	ART	ART	1981	LC	16 X 20	STP/G	8	5	125	150
Hills at Dusk	ART	ART	1982	LC	16 X 20	STP/G	9	8	150	175
Sky	ART	ART	1982	LC	18 X 24	RP/HNT	9	7	125	150
Deceptive Clouds	ART	ART	1982	LC	16 X 20	AP/C	7	7	150	175
Under the Overpass	ART	ART	1982	LC	16 X 20	AC/BL	6	5	125	150
Dusk & Dawn: Comparisons (Set of 2)	ART	ART	1982	LC	8 X 10 EA	STP/G	11/12 EA	7 EA	1 SET	175 SET
Dusk & Dawn: Comparisons (Set of 2)	ART	ART	1982	LC	8 X 10 EA	STP	14/13 EA	6 EA	150 SET	175 SET
Approaching Storm	ART	ART	1982	LC	18 X 22	STP/G	7	6	200	225
Convergence of Place	ART	ART	1983	LB	14 X 19	SOM/C	5	1	100	175
Daybreak/Nightfall (Set of 4)	ART	ART	1985	LC	20 X 25 EA	R/BFK	18 EA	6 EA	750 SET / 200 EA	850 SET / 250 EA

PHILIPPE MOHITZ

BORN: Bordeaux, France; 1941
EDUCATION: Atelier Jean Delpech, Paris, France
PRINTERS: Artist (ART); Bruno Kiefi, Paris, France (BK)
PUBLISHERS: Artist (ART)
GALLERIES: Fitch-Febvrel Gallery, New York, NY; John Szoke Graphics, New York, NY

TITLE	PUBLISHER	PRINTER	DATE	MEDIUM	DIMENSION (PAPER SIZE) IN INCHES	TYPE OF PAPER	EDITION NUMBER	NO. OF COLORS	ORIGINAL OPENING PRICE	CURRENT RETAIL PRICE
SOLD OUT EDITIONS (RARE):										
Planche Onje Me Suis Perdu	ART	ART	1972	ENG/DPT	11 X 14	JP	60	1	150	800
L' Eglise	ART	BK	1975	ENG	9 X 8	R/BFK	100	1	300	800
Eldorado	ART	ART	1977	ENG	13 X 16	R/BFK	100	1	440	800
La Tour	ART	ART	1978	ENG	18 X 15	R/BFK	100	1	600	800
Les Temps Modernes	ART	ART	1979	ENG	15 X 11	R/BFK	100	1	700	750
Icarus	ART	ART	1980	ENG	15 X 13	R/BFK	100	1	750	800
Escalade	ART	ART	1980	ENG	13 X 10	R/BFK	100	1	350	400
La Vierge	ART	ART	1980	ENG	12 X 9	R/BFK	100	1	300	350
Le Printemps	ART	ART	1980	ENG	11 X 15	R/BFK	100	1	350	400
Desertion	ART	ART	1981	ENG	15 X 18	R/BFK	100	1	750	800

SANTIAGO MOIX

BORN: Barcelona, Spain; 1960
RECENT EXHIB: Marovnochi Gallery, Tokyo, Japan, 1987; Pace Gallery, NY, 1987,88
PRINTERS: Joe Wilfer, NY (JW); Spring Street Workshop, NY (SprSW)
PUBLISHERS: Spring Street Workshop, NY (SprSW)
GALLERIES: Pace Prints, New York, NY; Renee Metras Gallery, Barcelona, Spain

SANTIAGO MOIX CONTINUED

TITLE	PUBLISHER	PRINTER	DATE	MEDIUM	DIMENSION (PAPER SIZE) IN INCHES	TYPE OF PAPER	EDITION NUMBER	NO. OF COLORS	ORIGINAL OPENING PRICE	CURRENT RETAIL PRICE
CURRENT EDITIONS:										
Untitled (Dipt)	SprSW	JW/SprSW	1987	WC	62 X 34	AP/W	10		800	1200
Untitled (Small Vase)	SprSW	JW/SprSW	1987	WC	15 X 15	AP/W	12		400	500
Untitled (Flower Pots)	SprSW	JW/SprSW	1987	WC	42 X 37	AP/W	10		600	800

JOHN MOMINEE

EDUCATION: Univ of Evansville, IN, BA, 1961–65; Southern Illinois Univ, Carbondale, IL, MFA, 1965–67; Salt Glaze Pottery Workshop, New Harmony, IN, 1967; Kalamazoo Art Inst, MI, Lithography Workshop, 1972
TEACHING: Teaching Asst, Southern Illinois Univ, Carbondale, IL, 1965–67; Instr, Art, Univ of Evansville, IN, 1967–70; Asst Prof, Art, Austin Peay State Univ, Clarksville, TN, 1971–77; Artist in Res, Univ of Wisconsin, Platteville, WI, 1980–82; Dir, Harry Nohr Art Gallery, Univ of Wisconsin, Platteville, WI, 1980 to present; Dir, Center for Arts, Univ of Wisconsin, Platteville, WI, 1982 to present
RECENT EXHIB: Chosy Gallery, Madison, WI, 1988; Madison Art Center, WI, 1989; Cudahy Gallery, Milwaukee Art Mus, WI, 1989
PRINTERS: Bill Weege, Madison, WI (BW); Andrew Rubin, Madison, WI (AR); Tandem Press, Univ of Wisconsin, Madison, WI (TanPr)
PUBLISHERS: Tandem Press, Univ of Wisconsin, Madison, WI (TanPr)
GALLERIES: Suzanne Kohn Gallery, Minneapolis, MN; Grace Chosy Gallery, Madison, WI; Katie Gingrass Gallery, Milwaukee, WI
MAILING ADDRESS: c/o University of Wisconsin, Director, Center for the Arts, Platteville, WI 53818

TITLE	PUBLISHER	PRINTER	DATE	MEDIUM	DIMENSION (PAPER SIZE) IN INCHES	TYPE OF PAPER	EDITION NUMBER	NO. OF COLORS	ORIGINAL OPENING PRICE	CURRENT RETAIL PRICE
SOLD OUT EDITIONS (RARE):										
Untitled, #1–#6 (Set of 6)	TanPr	BW/AR/TanPr	1989	MON	72 X 87 EA	HMP	1 EA	Varies	5000 EA	9500 EA

ALDO MONDINO

PRINTERS: American Atelier, NY (AA)
PUBLISHERS: Circle Fine Art, Chicago, IL (CFA)
GALLERIES: Circle Galleries, San Diego, CA & San Francisco, CA & Houston, TX & Northbrook, IL & Soho, NY & Chicago; IL & Scottsdale, AZ & Beverly Hills, CA & Costa Mesa, CA & Sherman Oaks, CA & Palm Beach, FL & Honolulu, HI & New Orleans, LA & Las Vegas, NV & Seattle, WA; Sperone Westwater, New York, NY

TITLE	PUBLISHER	PRINTER	DATE	MEDIUM	DIMENSION (PAPER SIZE) IN INCHES	TYPE OF PAPER	EDITION NUMBER	NO. OF COLORS	ORIGINAL OPENING PRICE	CURRENT RETAIL PRICE
CURRENT EDITIONS:										
Combinations I	CFA	AA	1981	SP	36 X 36	AP	200		150	300

JACQUES MONORY

BORN: Paris, France; 1934
PRINTERS: Maeght Editeur, Paris, France (ME); Galerie Maeght Lelong, Paris, France (ML)
PUBLISHERS: Maeght Editions, Paris, France (ME); Galerie Maeght Lelong, Paris, France (ML)
GALLERIES: Galerie Lelong, Paris, France & New York, NY

TITLE	PUBLISHER	PRINTER	DATE	MEDIUM	DIMENSION (PAPER SIZE) IN INCHES	TYPE OF PAPER	EDITION NUMBER	NO. OF COLORS	ORIGINAL OPENING PRICE	CURRENT RETAIL PRICE
CURRENT EDITIONS:										
Fuite, 1,2,3,4,5,6,7	ME	ME	1981	LC	73 X 10 cm	AP	75		1500 FF SET	5000 FF SET
Adieu Ma Jolie	ME	ME	1981	LC	56 X 76 cm	AP	75		900 FF	2000 FF
Fouillis Mathematique pour un Univers en Enroulement Torsadé	ME	ME	1981	LC	64 X 91 cm	AP	75	3	700 FF	2000 FF

VICKY MONTESINOS

PRINTERS: American Atelier, NY (AA)
PUBLISHERS: Circle Fine Art, Chicago, IL (CFA)
GALLERIES: Circle Galleries, San Diego, CA & San Francisco, CA & Northbrook, IL & Pittsburgh, PA & Houston, TX & Soho, NY & Chicago, IL & Scottsdale, AZ & Beverly Hills, CA & Costa Mesa, CA & Sherman Oaks, CA & Palm Beach, FL & Honolulu, HI & New Orleans, LA & Las Vegas, NV & Seattle, WA; Benedetti Gallery, New York, NY; Owl Gallery, San Francisco, CA

TITLE	PUBLISHER	PRINTER	DATE	MEDIUM	DIMENSION (PAPER SIZE) IN INCHES	TYPE OF PAPER	EDITION NUMBER	NO. OF COLORS	ORIGINAL OPENING PRICE	CURRENT RETAIL PRICE
SOLD OUT EDITIONS (RARE):										
Madame X	CFA	AA	1984	LC	34 X 25	AP	300		350	1200
Dama Misteriosa	CFA	AA	1984	LC	34 X 25	AP	300		350	1350
Amoureuse	CFA	AA	1984	LC	35 X 22	AP	300		350	1450
Imagenes de la Imaginacion (Trip)	CFA	AA	1985	LC	37 X 53	AP	300		500	2600
Mirage	CFA	AA	1985	LC	35 X 26	AP	300		500	2900
Dreams and Lace	CFA	AA	1985	LC	26 X 35	AP	300		500	1000
The Artist	CFA	AA	1986	MM/HC	55 X 27	AP	300		800	2800

VICKY MONTESINOS CONTINUED

TITLE	PUBLISHER	PRINTER	DATE	MEDIUM	DIMENSION (PAPER SIZE) IN INCHES	TYPE OF PAPER	EDITION NUMBER	NO. OF COLORS	ORIGINAL OPENING PRICE	CURRENT RETAIL PRICE
SOLD OUT EDITIONS (RARE):										
Las Damas de Otono (Trip)	CFA	AA	1986	LC	36 X 80	AP	300		800	2000
Those Silent Dreams	CFA	AA	1986	LC	25 X 35	AP	300		800	1300
Visage from the Past	CFA	AA	1987	MM	35 X 25	AP	300		800	1600
Fleurs d'Amour	CFA	AA	1987	MM	36 X 25	AP	300		800	1200
A Woman Remembered (with 24K Gold)	CFA	AA	1987	MM	36 X 26	AP	300		800	1700
Out of My Dreams (Trip)	CFA	AA	1987	MM	37 X 60	AP	300		800	1550
White over White (with Hand Painting)	CFA	AA	1987	MM	49 X 37	AP	300		800	2650
The Rose	CFA	AA	1988	MM	36 X 25	AP	300		800	1100
Portrait in Black (with 24K Gold)	CFA	AA	1988	MM	29 X 21	AP	300		800	1650
En Hiver	CFA	AA	1989	MM	22 X 30	AP	300		500	850
Two Dreams	CFA	AA	1989	MM	52 X 32	AP	300		800	1350
Elegance in White	CFA	AA	1989	LC	49 X 36	AP	300		600	1600
CURRENT EDITIONS:										
The Venetian (with Hand Painting)	CFA	AA	1988	MM	51 X 26	AP	300		800	1000
Mirage de L'Or (with 24K Gold)	CFA	AA	1988	MM	49 X 36	AP	300		800	2250
Isadora (with Gold & Silver Embellishments)	CFA	AA	1989	MM	51 X 26	AP	300		1000	1750
Black Lace (with Handmade Silver Leaf Paper)	CFA	AA	1989	MM	22 X 29	AP	300		800	950
Imaginary Portrait of George Sand	CFA	AA	1989	LC	36 X 26	AP	300		800	1100
The Mirror	CFA	AA	1989	LC	37 X 36	AP	300		1000	1600
Deco Personality	CFA	AA	1990	LC	35 X 24	AP	300		900	950

MICK MOON

BORN: Edinburgh, Scotland; 1937
EDUCATION: Chelsea Sch of Art, London, England, 1958-62; Royal Col of Art, London, England, 1962-63
TEACHING: Chelsea Sch of Art, London, England, 1963-73; Slade Sch of Fine Art, London, England, 1973 to present

PRINTERS: Artist (ART); Alan Cox, London, England (AC); David Costello, London, England (DC); Cameron Lindo, London, England (CL); John Pengally, London, England (JP); Robert Saich, London, England (RS); David Wood, London, England (DW); Advanced Graphics, London, England (AG)
PUBLISHERS: Artist (ART); Waddington Graphics, London, England (WG)
GALLERIES: Waddington Gallery, London, England

TITLE	PUBLISHER	PRINTER	DATE	MEDIUM	DIMENSION (PAPER SIZE) IN INCHES	TYPE OF PAPER	EDITION NUMBER	NO. OF COLORS	ORIGINAL OPENING PRICE	CURRENT RETAIL PRICE
CURRENT EDITIONS:										
Tiffany	ART	ART/AC	1985	MON	60 X 46 EA	CAN	1 EA	Varies	2500 EA	3500 EA
Hybrids (Set of 6)										
Blue Bend	WG	DC/CL/JP/RS/DW/AG	1990–91	SP/WC	54 X 43	AP	45		1285	1500
Green Spice	WG	DC/CL/JP/RS/DW/AG	1990–91	SP/WC	54 X 43	AP	45		1285	1500
Hybrids	WG	DC/CL/JP/RS/DW/AG	1990–91	SP/WC	54 X 43	AP	45		1285	1500
Marriage	WG	DC/CL/JP/RS/DW/AG	1990–91	SP/WC	54 X 43	AP	45		1285	1500
Melting Pot	WG	DC/CL/JP/RS/DW/AG	1990–91	SP/WC	54 X 43	AP	45		1285	1500
Mixed Spice	WG	DC/CL/JP/RS/DW/AG	1990–91	SP/WC	54 X 43	AP	45		1285	1500

BARBARA BROOKS MORGAN

BORN: Buffalo, Kansas; July 8, 1900
EDUCATION: Instr, Art, Univ of California, Los Angeles, CA, 1919–23; Marquette Univ, Milwaukee, WI, Hon DFA, 1978
TEACHING: Univ of California, Los Angeles, CA, 1925–30

AWARDS: Philadelphia Mus of Art Fel, 1970; Nat Endowment for the Arts, 1975; Nat Conf, Soc for Photographic Education, Fort Worth, TX, 1979
COLLECTIONS: Nat Gallery of Canada, Ottawa, Can; Marquette Univ, Milwaukee, WI; Fotografiska Museet, Stockholm, Sweden; Univ of California Library, Los Angeles, CA; Mus of Fine Arts, St Petersburg, FL
GALLERIES: Daniel Wolf Gallery, New York, NY; Jeffrey Fuller Fine Art, Phila, PA; Alan Brown Gallery, Hartsdale, NY
MAILING ADDRESS: 120 High Point Rd, Scarsdale, NY 10583

TITLE	PUBLISHER	PRINTER	DATE	MEDIUM	DIMENSION (PAPER SIZE) IN INCHES	TYPE OF PAPER	EDITION NUMBER	NO. OF COLORS	ORIGINAL OPENING PRICE	CURRENT RETAIL PRICE
SOLD OUT EDITIONS (RARE):										
Amaryllis I	ART	ART	1943	PH	18 X 7	AP			50	7500
Dance Portfolio (Set of 10)	ART	ART	1977	PH	14 X 11	AP	50		1800 SET	12000 SET
					20 X 16	AP	50		1800 SET	12000 SET

HENRY MOORE

BORN: Castleford, Yorkshire, England; (1898–1986)
EDUCATION: Leeds Sch of Art, London, England, 1919–21; Royal Col of Art, London, England, 1921–24
TEACHING: Royal Col of Art, London, England, 1925–32; Chelsea Sch of Art, London, England, 1932–39
RECENT EXHIB: Retrosp, Marlborough Fine Art, Ltd, London, England, 1987; Univ of Rochester Mem Art Gallery, NY, 1989; Palm Springs Desert Mus, CA, 1989; Albright-Knox Art Gallery, Buffalo, NY, 1989; King Storm Art Center, Mountainville, NY, 1989; Manhattan Psychiatric Center's Sculpture Garden, NY, 1989; Weintraub Gallery, NY, 1989; Maeght Editeur, Paris, France, 1990; Grob Gallery, London, England, 1990
COLLECTIONS: Mus of Mod Art, NY; Hirshhorn Philadelphia Mus of Art, PA; Art Gallery of Ontario, Toronto, Can; Lincoln Center, NY; Victoria and Albert Mus, London, England; Tate Gallery, London, England
PRINTERS: Curwen Press, London, England (CP); Atelier Lacouriére et Frélaut, Paris, France (ALF); Michael Rand, London, England (MR); Maeght Editeur, Paris, France (ME); Galerie Maeght Lelong, Paris, France (ML); J C Editions, London, England (JCEd); Mixografia Workshop, Los Angeles, CA (MW); Zika Ascher, London, England (ZA); Wolfensberger, Zürich, Switzerland (WOLF); Fequet et Baudier, Paris, France (F/B); Roy Crosset, London, England (RC)
PUBLISHERS: Transworld Art, Inc, NY (TAI); Raymond Spencer Co, Ltd, London, England (RSC); 2 RC Editrice, Rome Italy (2RCE); Henry Moore Foundation, London, England (HMF); Maeght Editions, Paris, France (ME); Galerie Maeght Lelong, Paris, France (ML); Gérard Cramer, Geneva, Switzerland (GC); Mixografia Workshop, Los Angeles, CA (MW); Orde Levinson, London, England (OL); Zika Ascher, London, England (ZA); Raymond Spencer Co, Ltd, London, England (RSC); Ganymed, London, England (GANY); George Rainbird, London, England (GR); New York Graphic Society, Greenwich, CT (NYGS)
GALLERIES: L A Louver, Venice, CA; Galerie Lelong, Paris, France & Zürich, Switzerland & New York, NY; Tasende Gallery, La Jolla, CA; Herbert Palmer Gallery, Los Angeles, CA; Harcourts Gallery, San Francisco, CA; Annette Couch Fine Arts, Los Angeles, CA; Marvin Ross Friedman & Co, Miami, FL; Galeria Joan Prats, New York, NY & Barcelona, Spain; James Goodman Gallery, New York, NY; Lillian Heidenberg Gallery, New York, NY; Jane Kahan Gallery, New York, NY; Feingarten Galleries, Los Angeles, CA; Mixografia Gallery, Los Angeles, CA; John Berggruen Gallery, San Francisco, CA; Harcourts Gallery, San Francisco, CA; Horoshak Contemporary Art, Sunnyvale, CA; Robert Brown Contemporary Art, Wash, DC; Hokin Galleries, Bay Harbor Islands, FL & Palm Beach, FL; Rolly-Michaux Galleries, Boston, MA;

Henry Moore
Two Standing Figures
Courtesy Avantgarde Art Associates

Beth Urdang Fine Arts, Brookline, MA; Dolly Fiterman Gallery, Minneapolis, MN; Greenberg Gallery, St Louis, MO; Nathan Silberberg Fine Arts, New York, NY; Charles Foley Gallery, Columbus, OH; Evelyn Aimis Fine Art, Toronto, Canada; Maxwell Davidson Gallery, New York, NY; Sigrid Freudorfer Fine Art, New York, NY; Phyllis Hattis Fine Arts, Inc, New York, NY; Marlborough Gallery, New York, NY; Posner Gallery, Milwaukee, WI; Grob Gallery, London, England

Cramer (C)

TITLE	PUBLISHER	PRINTER	DATE	MEDIUM	DIMENSION (PAPER SIZE) IN INCHES	TYPE OF PAPER	EDITION NUMBER	NO. OF COLORS	ORIGINAL OPENING PRICE	CURRENT RETAIL PRICE
SOLD OUT EDITIONS (RARE):										
Figures Sculptures (C-1)	GC	F/B	1931	WB	5 X 8	AP	50	1	50	20000
Reclining Nude	ZA	ZA	1949	SP	70 X 102	Linen	30		80	30000
Two Standing Figures	ZA	ZA	1949	SP	103 X 72	Linen	30		80	30000
Figures in Settings (C-5)	GANY		1951	COL	23 X 16	AP	75		50	16000
Woman Holding Cat (C-10)	GANY		1951	COL	14 X 21	AP	75		35	12000
Thirteen Standing Figures (C-41)	GR/NYGS	CP	1958	LC	18 X 12	AP	150		75	3000
Reclining Figure (C-55)	GC		1951–66		3 X 6	RP/WOVE	50		100	5000
Two Upright Motives	GC		1966	LB	6 X 6	AP	50	1	50	1800
Ideas for Sculpture	GC		1969	EB	26 X 20	AP	100	1	100	2850
Ideas for Sculpture in Landscape	GC		1969	EB	26 X 20	AP	100	1	100	2850
Project for Hill Sculpture	GC		1969	EB	26 X 20	AP	100	1	100	3150
Elephant Skull Album (Set of 28)	GC		1969–70	EB	20 X 14EA	AP	80 EA	1 EA	800 SET	22000 SET
Storm at Sea	GC		1970	EB/DPT	11 X 15	AP	50	1	50	1400
Wreck	GC		1970	EB/DPT	11 X 15	AP	50	1	50	1400
Tunnel, Arch and Window	GC		1971	EB/A/DPT	17 X 12	AP	50	1	125	1950
Three Reclining Figures	GC		1971	LC	21 X 16	AP	95		200	3675
Glenkiln Cross I,II	HMF	CP	1973	EB/A/DPT	12 X 10EA	AP	100 EA	1 EA	250 EA	1400 EA
Lullaby	HMF	CP	1973	LC	16 X 14	AP	25		250	2000
Lullaby Sleeping Head	HMF	CP	1973	LC	16 X 14	AP	25		250	2000
Shipwreck I,II	HMF	CP	1973	LB	10 X 14EA	AP	50 EA		250 EA	1400 EA
Man and Woman	HMF	CP	1973	LC	14 X 10	AP	25		250	2650
Six Stone Figures	HMF	CP	1973	LC	26 X 20	AP	75		250	2650
Reclining Figure with Red Stripes	HMF	CP	1973	LC	9 X 9	AP	250		250	2500
Three Reclining Figures	HMF	CP	1973	LC	26 X 20	AP	75		400	2800
Two Women Bathing Child I	HMF	CP	1973	LC	20 X 26	RP	175		400	7500
Reclining Figures (Set of 6) (C-236–241)			1973	LC	26 X 20EA	AP	50 EA		2000 SET	10000 SET

HENRY MOORE CONTINUED

TITLE	PUBLISHER	PRINTER	DATE	MEDIUM	DIMENSION (PAPER SIZE) IN INCHES	TYPE OF PAPER	EDITION NUMBER	NO. OF COLORS	ORIGINAL OPENING PRICE	CURRENT RETAIL PRICE
SOLD OUT EDITIONS (RARE):										
Auden/Moore Lithographs (Ed A and C)			1974	LC	16 X 13 EA	RP	150 EA		5000 SET	25000 SET
Auden/Moore Lithographs (Ed A—Bound, Red Linen) (11 Lithographs with 4 Loose Lithographs)			1974	LC	16 X 13 EA	RP	150 EA		5000 SET	25000 SET
Sheep Album (Set of 12)			1972-74	EB		RP	80 EA	1 EA	5000 SET	36000 SET
Three Grazing Sheep	HMF	CP	1974	LC	15 X 21	RP	30		600	2375
Sheep in Field	HMF	CP	1974	LC	18 X 23	RP	50		800	3000
Sheep in Landscape	HMF	CP	1974	LC	18 X 20	RP	50		800	3000
Two Fat Lambs	HMF	CP	1974	LC	23 X 28	RP	30		600	2375
Sheep Climbing	HMF	CP	1974	LC	7 X 8	RP	30		600	2350
Woman Seated on Fireside Stool	HMF	CP	1974	LC	26 X 20	RP	175		600	2650
Woman Seated at Desk I	HMF	CP	1974	LC	26 X 20	RP	75		600	2500
Group of Figures (C-341)	HMF	CP	1974	LB	9 X 13	RP	65	1	500	1800
Girl Seated at Desk I–IV	HMF	CP	1974	LC	17 X 14 EA	RP	50 EA		500 EA	1850 EA
Girl Seated at Desk V–VIII	HMF	CP	1974	LC	21 X 14 EA	RP	50 EA		500 EA	1850 EA
Black Reclining Figure I–IV	HMF	CP	1974	LC	11 X 15 EA	RP	20 EA		500 EA	1575 EA
Girl I	HMF	CP	1974	LC	15 X 13	RP	50		600	2000
Girl II	HMF	CP	1974	LC	15 X 13	RP	50		600	2150
Seated Figures	HMF	CP	1974	LC	15 X 12	RP	50		600	1900
Reclining Figure	HMF	CP	1974	LC	15 X 13	RP	50		600	1850
Reclining Figure Back	HMF	CP	1974	LC	15 X 13	RP	50		600	1850
Seated Girl	HMF	CP	1974	LC	15 X 13	RP	50		600	1850
Seated Girl in Bed	HMF	CP	1974	LC	15 X 13	RP	50		600	1850
Reclining Girl in Bed	HMF	CP	1974	LC	15 X 13	RP	50		600	1850
Seated Figure Back	HMF	CP	1974	LC	15 X 13	RP	50		600	1850
Resting Girl	HMF	CP	1974	LC	15 X 13	RP	50		600	1850
Seated Figure I, Line Drawing	HMF	CP	1974	LC	20 X 17	RP	50		800	1725
Seated Figure III, Dark Room	HMF	CP	1974	LC	20 X 17	RP	50		800	1825
Reclining Figures, Man & Woman I,II	HMF	CP	1975	EB/A	12 X 9 EA	RP	100 EA		600 EA	3150 EA
Seated Mother & Child	HMF	CP	1975	LC	12 X 9	RP	100		600	3150
Two Women Bathing Child II	TAI	CP	1975	LC	20 X 26	SP	175	4	800	7500
Draped Reclining Figure	HMF	CP	1975	LC	23 X 31	AP	50		800	7500
Friday Night Camden Town	HMF	CP	1975	LC	22 X 22	SP	50	7	800	2650
Group in Industrial Landscape	HMF	CP	1975	LC	20 X 16	AP	75		800	2650
Eightieth Anniversary Portfolio (Set of 9) (C-442–450)	OL	RC/CP	1975–76	LB	24 X 18 EA	RP	100 EA	1 EA	2500 SET	20000 SET
Reclining Figure	HMF	CP	1976	EB		AP	100	1	650	2500
Figure Against Architectural Background I	HMF	CP	1976	LC	22 X 25	SP	50	9	800	3000
Figure in a Room	HMF	CP	1977	LC	17 X 20	SP	50		650	1950
Three Reclining Personages	HMF	CP	1977	EB		AP	100	1	650	2500
Reclining Woman	HMF	CP	1977	EB		AP	100	1	650	2500
Dante Stones (Set of 5)	HMF	CP	1977	EB/A	21 X 16 EA	RP	50 EA		2000 SET	12000 SET
									450 EA	2500 EA
Stone I–IV	HMF	CP	1977	EB/A	21 X 16 EA	RP	50 EA		800 EA	2500 EA
Reclining Figure Portfolio (Set of 9)	HMF	CP	1977–78	LC	21 X 18 EA	AP	50 EA		6000 SET	20000 SET
Man Figure in Landscape	HMF	CP	1977–78	LC	21 X 24	SP	50 EA		800 EA	2550 EA
Man and Woman, ¾ View	HMF	CP	1978	LC	19 X 23	SP	50		800	2900
Reclining Figure	HMF	CP	1979	EB	7 X 9	AP	25	1	800	2500
Reclining Figure Cave	HMF	MR	1979	LC	21 X 25	AP	50		800	2900
Reclining Figure Arch Leg	HMF	MR	1979	LC	18 X 23	AP	50		800	2900
Opening Form I	HMF	MR	1979	LC	20 X 23	AP	50		800	2650
Man and Woman	HMF	MR	1979	LC	18 X 22	AP	50		800	2350
Feet on Holiday I,II	HMF	MR	1979	LC	18 X 21 EA	AP	50 EA		700 EA	2100 EA
Elephants	RSC	MR	1979	EB	15 X 19	R/BFK	50		750	2100
Reclining Mother & Child I,II	HMF	MR	1979	EB/DPT	17 X 19 EA	AP	50 EA	1 EA	500 EA	2300 EA
Profile	HMF	MR	1979	EB/DPT	18 X 19	AP	50	1	500	2300
Female Torso & Sculptural Ideas I,II	HMF	MR	1979	LB	20 X 29 EA	AP	50 EA	1 EA	500 EA	2800 EA
The Artist's Hand Portfolio (2 Etchings & 3 Lithographs) (Set of 5)	HMF	MR	1979	EB/LC	20 X 15 EA	AP	50 EA		3000 SET	12500 SET
Curved Reclining Figure in Landscape	HMF	MR	1979	EB/DPT	15 X 19	AP	50	1	1000	2500
Head of Girl and Reclining Figure	HMF	MR	1979	EB/DPT	18 X 21	AP	50	1	800	2525
Reclining Figure	HMF	MR	1979	EB/DPT	13 X 16	AP	50	1	800	2500
Reclining Figure Distorted	HMF	MR	1979	EB	17 X 19	AP	50	1	800	2000
Seated Nude	HMF	MR	1979	EB/DPT	19 X 15	AP	50	1	800	2100
Sisters with Children	HMF	MR	1979	LC	22 X 29	AP	50		900	2900
Six Sculptural Ideas	HMF	MR	1979	LC	21 X 26	AP	50		800	2900
Reclining Figure Pisello Baccello	HMF	MR	1979	EB/A/DPT/ ENG	26 X 37	AP	20		1200	7500

HENRY MOORE CONTINUED

Henry Moore
Woman Holding Cat
Courtesy Ganymed

TITLE	PUBLISHER	PRINTER	DATE	MEDIUM	DIMENSION (PAPER SIZE) IN INCHES	TYPE OF PAPER	EDITION NUMBER	NO. OF COLORS	ORIGINAL OPENING PRICE	CURRENT RETAIL PRICE
SOLD OUT EDITIONS (RARE):										
Seated Figure			1979	EB/DPT	19 X 15	R/BFK	50		800	2300
Seated Mother and Child	HMF	MR	1979	EB	12 X 9	R/BFK	100		800	2650
Mother and Child	HMF	MR	1979	EB/DPT	21 X 18	R/BFK	50		800	2525
Child Study	HMF	MR	1979	EB/DPT	19 X 15	R/BFK	50		800	2200
Two Reclining Mother and Child Studies	HMF	MR	1979	LC	12 X 9	AP	100		800	3150
Woman Putting on Stocking I	HMF	MR	1979	EB	19 X 16	R/BFK	50		800	2100
Trees Album (Set of 5):									2500 SET	12000 SET
Trees I—Bole and Creeper	HMF	MR	1979	EB/A	9 X 10	R/BFK			500	2400
Trees II-Upright Branches	HMF	MR	1979	EB/A	9 X 10	R/BFK			500	2000
Trees III—Knuckled Trunk	HMF	MR	1979	EB/A	9 X 10	R/BFK			500	2000
Trees IV—Tortured Roots	HMF	MR	1979	EB/A	9 X 10	R/BFK			500	2250
Trees V—Dead Ash	HMF	MR	1979	EB/A	9 X 10	R/BFK			500	2000
The Artist's Hand Portfolio	HMF	MR	1979	LC	20 X 15	AP	50		3000 SET	12500 SET
Five Sculptural Ideas	HMF	MR	1979–80	EB/A/DPT	38 X 38	AP	10		1200	8500
Reclining Figure Terra Cotta	HMF	MR	1979–80	EB/A/DPT	35 X 57	AP	10		1500	27500
Stone Reclining Figure	HMF	MR	1979–80	EB/A/DPT	48 X 92	AP	10		2500	37500
Female Figures with Grey Background	HMF	MR	1980	LC	18 X 22	AP	50		800	2650
Six Reclining Figures with Blue Background	HMF	MR	1980	LC	18 X 19	AP	50		800	2650
Seated Woman	ME	ME	1980	EB	16 X 13	RP	50	1	10000 FF	50000 FF
Seated Figure	HMF	MR	1980	EB/A	55 X 36	RP	10		3000	8500
Ideas for Relief Sculpture	HMF	MR	1980	EB	9 X 7	AP	25		1000	2000
Reclining Nude	HMF	MR	1980	EB	8 X 12	AP	75		1000	2400
The West Wind Relief Sketchbook, 1928, Ed A (Includes Two Etchings)	HMF		1980	Book	8 X 12				2500	7500
The West Wind Relief Sketchbook, 1928, Ed B (Includes One Etching)	HMF		1980	Book	8 X 12				1500	4500
The West Wind Relief Sketchbook, 1928, Ed C (Without Etching)	HMF		1980	Book	8 X 12				300	1500
Adam	HMF	MR	1980	LC	21 X 25	AP	50		900	2400
Eve	HMF	MR	1980	LC	21 X 25	AP	50		900	2400
Eve	HMF	MR	1981	LB	21 X 25	AP	50		900	2000
Reclining Woman Series:										
Reclining Woman I (C-591)	RSC	CP	1980–81	LC	25 X 29	AP	50		1000	6500
Reclining Woman II (C-592)	RSC	CP	1980–81	LC	25 X 29	AP	50		1000	6500
Reclining Woman III (C-593)	RSC	CP	1980–81	LC	25 X 36	AP	50		1000	6500
Reclining Woman IV (C-594)	RSC	CP	1980–81	LC	25 X 29	AP	50		1000	6500
Reclining Woman on Beach	HMF	MR	1980–81	LC	22 X 30	AP	50		1000	6000

HENRY MOORE CONTINUED

TITLE	PUBLISHER	PRINTER	DATE	MEDIUM	DIMENSION (PAPER SIZE) IN INCHES	TYPE OF PAPER	EDITION NUMBER	NO. OF COLORS	ORIGINAL OPENING PRICE	CURRENT RETAIL PRICE
SOLD OUT EDITIONS (RARE):										
Reclining Woman on Seashore	HMF	MR	1980–81	LC	25 X 34	AP	50		1000	6000
Seated Mother and Child	HMF	MR	1980–81	EB/A	27 X 23	AP	50		1000	2800
Seven Sculptural Ideas II	HMF	MR	1980–81	EB/A	27 X 23	AP	50		1000	2800
Three Sisters	HMF	MR	1981	LC	22 X 18	AP	50		1000	2800
Head of a Girl	HMF	MR	1981	LB	23 X 21	AP	10	1	1200	2000
Ideas for Metal Sculpture (Set of 6):										
Ideas for Metal Sculpture I	HMF	MR	1981	LC	18 X 17	AP	50		1000	1850
Ideas for Metal Sculpture II	HMF	MR	1981	LC	9 X 10	AP	50		1000	1850
Ideas for Metal Sculpture III	HMF	MR	1981	LC	18 X 17	AP	50		1000	1850
Ideas for Metal Sculpture IV	HMF	MR	1981	LC	17 X 18	AP	50		1000	1850
Ideas for Metal Sculpture V	HMF	MR	1981	LC	9 X 10	AP	50		1000	1850
Ideas for Metal Sculpture VI	HMF	MR	1981	LC	17 X 18	AP	50		1000	1850
Six Reclining Figures	HMF	MR	1981	LC	18 X 19	AP	50		1000	2350
Three Sculptural Ideas	HMF	MR	1981	LC	22 X 18	AP	50		1200	2000
Six Reclining Figures against Red Background	HMF	MR	1981	LC	17 X 18	AP	50		1000	2200
Figures with Sky Background I	HMF	MR	1981	LC	18 X 18	AP	50		1000	2500
Figures with Sky Background II	HMF	MR	1981	LC	20 X 24	AP	50		1200	2500
Three Seated Figures	HMF	MR	1981	LC	22 X 18	AP	50		1000	2000
Mary and Martha	HMF	MR	1981	LC	16 X 18	AP	50		1000	2200
Nativity	HMF	MR	1981	LC	9 X 10	AP	50		1000	1600
Rock Head	HMF	MR	1981	LC	10 X 9	AP	50		1000	1600
The Attendants	HMF	MR	1981	LC	9 X 10	AP	50		1000	1600
The Observers	HMF	MR	1981	LC	9 X 10	AP	50		1000	1600
The Three Marys	HMF	MR	1981	LC	9 X 10	AP	50		1000	1600
Visitation	HMF	MR	1981	LC	10 X 9	AP	50		1000	1600
Woman's Head	HMF	MR	1981	LC	10 X 9	AP	50		1000	1600
Five Sculptural Ideas	HMF	MR	1981	LC	22 X 17	AP	50		1500	2800
Five Ideas for Sculpture (C-610)	RSC	WOLF	1981	LC	14 X 10	AP	50		800	5000
Reclining Figure: Pisello Bocello II	ML	CP	1982	EC	26 X 39	AP	6	2	15000 FF	60000 FF
Reclining Figure Bone	ML	CP	1982	EC	26 X 39	R/BFK	50	8	15000 FF	60000 FF
Six Heads Olympians	HMF	MR	1982	LC	34 X 23	AP	50		1800	4000
Reclining Mother & Child with Blue Background	HMF	MR	1982	LC	22 X 29	AP	50		1800	7500
Reclining Figure Idea for Metal Sculpture	HMF	MR	1982	LC	18 X 22	AP	50		1600	3250
Reclining Mother & Child with Grey Background	HMF	MR	1982	LC	22 X 29	AP	50		1800	7500
Reclining Figure Bone	HMF	MR	1982	LC	18 X 22	AP	50		1600	3000
Reclining Woman with Yellow Background	HMF	MR	1982	LC	21 X 25	AP	50		1800	5500
Animals in the Zoo (Set of 10):									10000 SET	12500 SET
Rhinocerous	HMF	JCEd	1982	EB	18 X 21	R/BFK	65	1	1000	1300
Dromedary	HMF	JCEd	1982	EB	18 X 21	R/BFK	65	1	1000	1300
Vultures	HMF	JCEd	1982	EB	18 X 21	R/BFK	65	1	1000	1300
Baby Elephant	HMF	JCEd	1982	EB	18 X 21	R/BFK	65	1	1000	1300
Leopard in Tree	HMF	JCEd	1982	EB	18 X 21	R/BFK	65	1	1000	1300
Zebra	HMF	JCEd	1982	EB	18 X 21	R/BFK	65	1	1000	1300
Bison	HMF	JCEd	1982	EB	18 X 21	R/BFK	65	1	1000	1300
Jaguar Lying Down	HMF	JCEd	1982	EB	18 X 21	R/BFK	65	1	1000	1300
Antelope	HMF	JCEd	1982	EB	18 X 21	R/BFK	65	1	1000	1300
Tiger	HMF	JCEd	1982	EB	18 X 21	R/BFK	65	1	1000	1300
Elephant's Head I,II	HMF	JCEd	1982	EB	22 X 18EA	R/BFK	50 EA	1 EA	1000 EA	2350 EA
Four Ideas for Sculpture	HMF	CP	1982	LC	18 X 22	AP	50		1000	3250
Henry Moore 1980 Sketchbook (Ed A—Includes Two Color Etchings—Mother & Child, 1983 & Two Reclining Figures, 1983)	HMF	MR	1985	EC/DPT	15 X 12EA	AP	25 EA		3500 SET	7250 SET
Henry Moore Sketchbook (Ed B—Includes 1 Etching/Aquatint—Reclining Nude, 1983)	HMF	MR	1985	EB/A	15 X 12	AP	25		1800	4250
Henry Moore 1980 Sketchbook	HMF	MR	1985		15 X 12	R/100	350		500	1250
Mother and Child Album (with Etching)	HMF	MR	1985		15 X 13	AP	50		2500	12500

WAYLAND D MOORE

BORN: Belton, SC; September 8, 1935
EDUCATION: Ringling Sch of Art, Sarasota, FL
TEACHING: Special Adj Lectr, Emory Univ, Atlanta, GA 1983 to present
COLLECTIONS: Univ of Georgia, Athens, GA; Headley Mus, Lexington, KY; Clemson Univ, SC
PRINTERS: ChromaComp, Inc, NY (CC)
PUBLISHERS: Felicie Editions, NY (FE); Art Dimensions, NY (AD)
GALLERIES: Shirley Fox Galleries, Atlanta, GA; Studio 53, New York, NY; Only Originals, Watchung, NJ
MAILING ADDRESS: 2124 Azalea Circle, Atlanta, GA 30324

WAYLAND D MOORE CONTINUED

TITLE	PUBLISHER	PRINTER	DATE	MEDIUM	DIMENSION (PAPER SIZE) IN INCHES	TYPE OF PAPER	EDITION NUMBER	NO. OF COLORS	ORIGINAL OPENING PRICE	CURRENT RETAIL PRICE
SOLD OUT EDITIONS (RARE):										
Eighth Furlong	FE	CC	1976	SP	29 X 41	AP	300	27	200	2000
Balloon	FE	CC	1976	SP	40 X 32	AP	300	26	250	2500
Rough Seas	FE	CC	1976	SP	30 X 43	AP	300	28	200	2500
American's Champion	FE	CC	1977	SP	43 X 30	AP	300	27	250	1800
Giraffe	FE	CC	1977	SP	45 X 23	AP	300	22	300	1800
Lion	FE	CC	1977	SP	2 X 3	AP	300	26	300	2500
Golf	FE	CC	1977	SP	29 X 36	AP	300	24	325	1800
Undefeated	FE	CC	1977	SP	28 X 34	AP	300	22	300	2000
Sea Breeze	FE	CC	1978	SP	29 X 31	AP	300	25	300	1800
Stormy Weather	FE	CC	1979	SP	43 X 30	AP	300	27	375	2000
Churchill Downs	FE	CC	1979	SP	32 X 40	AP	300	24	350	1800
Marathon	FE	CC	1979	SP	26 X 36	AP	300	22	375	2000
Spinnakers	FE	CC	1979	SP	41 X 30	AP	300	28	350	1800
Lift Off	FE	CC	1980	SP	37 X 26	AP	300	28	375	1500
We're Number One	FE	CC	1980	SP	29 X 23	AP	300	24	350	1800
Go For It	FE	CC	1982	SP	23 X 28	AP	300	27	400	1200

ARMANDO MORALES

BORN: Granada, Nicaragua; January 15, 1927
EDUCATION: Sch of Fine Arts, Manague, Nicaragua; Pratt Graphic Art Center, NY; Art Inst of Detroit, MI; Philadelphia Mus Sch of Art, PA
TEACHING: Instr, Pratt Graphic Center, NY, 1960–61; Cooper Union, NY, 1972–73
AWARDS: Purchase Award, Mus of Fine Arts, Houston, TX, 1956; Travel Grant, Am Council of Education, Wash, DC, 1957; Guggenheim Fel, NY; NEA Travel Fel, Wash, DC, 1962–64; Award, Arte de America y Espana, Madrid, Spain, 1963; Award, Carnegie Int, Pittsburgh, PA, 1964; Medal Ruben Dario, Arts Award, Bestowed by the Government of Nicaragua, 1982
RECENT EXHIB: Galerie Claude Bernard, Paris, France, 1987; Ravel Fine Art Associates, Austin, TX, 1993
COLLECTIONS: Mus of Mod Art, NY; Solomon R Guggenheim Mus, NY; Inst of Contemp Art, Boston, MA; Museo de Arte Moderna, Sao Paulo, Brazil; Museo de Bellos Artes, Caracas, Venezuela; Detroit Art Inst, MI; Museo de Arte Contemporaneo, Bogata, Colombia; Mus of Fine Art, Houston, TX; Mus of Latin Am Art, Wash, DC; Princeton Mus of Art, NJ; Rhode Island Sch of Design, Providence, RI; Philbrook Art Center, Tulsa, OK; Texas Univ Art Mus, Austin, TX; Cincinnati Mus, OH; Museo Tamayo, Mexico City, Mexico
PRINTERS: Ediciones Graficas, Coyoacan, Mexico (EG); Andrew Vlady, Coyoacan, Mexico (AV); Kyron Ediciones Graficas Limitades, SA, Mexico City, Mexico (KEG); Herb Fox, Boston, MA (HF); Fox Graphics, Boston, MA (FG); Kenneth Hale, Austin, TX (KH); Univ of Texas, Austin, TX (UT)
PUBLISHERS: G-R Art Publishers, Austin, TX (G-R)
GALLERIES: Ravel Fine Art Associates, Austin, TX; CA Harris Gallery, Houston, TX; CDS, New York, NY; Southwest Gallery, Dallas, TX; Marta Gutierrez Fine Arts, Key Biscayne, FL; Galerie Claude Bernard, Paris, France & New York, NY; Daniel Saxon Gallery, Los Angeles, CA; Gary Nader Fine Art, Coconut Grove, FL; Martha Tepper Fine Arts, West Newton, MA; Nohra Haime Gallery, New York, NY; TwoSixtyOne Art, New York, NY
MAILING ADDRESS: 26 rue des Plantes, Paris, 14, France; c/o Claude Bernard Gallery, 33 E 74th St, New York, NY 10021

TITLE	PUBLISHER	PRINTER	DATE	MEDIUM	DIMENSION (PAPER SIZE) IN INCHES	TYPE OF PAPER	EDITION NUMBER	NO. OF COLORS	ORIGINAL OPENING PRICE	CURRENT RETAIL PRICE
SOLD OUT EDITIONS (RARE):										
Pescaderas	G-R	KEG	1979	LC	22 X 34	AP	75	5	500	1500
Desnudo Sentado	G-R	KEG	1979	LC	32 X 24	AP	75	5	500	1200
CURRENT EDITIONS:										
Tres Banistas	G-R	KEG	1979	LC	24 X 32	AP	75	6	500	900
Mujer Dormida	G-R	KEG	1979	LC	22 X 34	AP	75	5	500	900
Dos Banistas	G-R	HF/FG	1980	LC	22 X 30	AP	75	7	500	900
Despedida	G-R	HF/FG	1980	LC	22 X 30	AP	75	6	500	800
Bodegon	G-R	HF/FG	1980	LC	20 X 30	AP	75	6	500	800
Desnudo en Frente de Espejo Concaavo	G-R	HF/FG	1980	LC	22 X 30	AP	75	8	500	800
Dos Ciclistas	G-R	KH/UOT	1981	LC	23 X 28	AP	75	2	400	600

MAHER N MORCOS

BORN: Cairo, Egypt; February 23, 1946; U S Citizen
EDUCATION: Cairo Univ, Egypt, BA, Arch, 1969; Leonardo de Vinci, Italy, 1970
AWARDS: Gold Medal, Death Valley Show, CA, 1980; Best of Show, Western Heritage Show, Arapahoe County Assn, 1981; Best of Show, Western Artists of America, Reno, NV, 1981
PRINTERS: American Atelier, NY (AA)
PUBLISHERS: Circle Fine Art, Chicago, IL (CFA)
GALLERIES: Circle Galleries, San Francisco, CA & San Diego, CA & Northbrook, IL & Houston, TX & Pittsburgh, PA & Soho, NY & Chicago, IL; Scottsdale, AZ & Beverly Hills, CA & Costa Mesa, CA & Sherman Oaks, CA & Palm Beach, FL & Las Vegas, NV & Honolulu, HI & New Orleans, LA & Seattle, WA
MAILING ADDRESS: P O Box 22659, San Diego, CA 92122

TITLE	PUBLISHER	PRINTER	DATE	MEDIUM	DIMENSION (PAPER SIZE) IN INCHES	TYPE OF PAPER	EDITION NUMBER	NO. OF COLORS	ORIGINAL OPENING PRICE	CURRENT RETAIL PRICE
SOLD OUT EDITIONS (RARE):										
Indian	CFA	AA	1972	LC	18 X 26	AP	200		50	200
Brave Past	CFA	AA	1974	LC	18 X 26	AP	250		50	200
Indian II	CFA	AA	1974	LC	19 X 26	AP	200		50	200
Nude I	CFA	AA	1978	LC	18 X 25	AP	200		75	200
Nude II	CFA	AA	1978	LC	17 X 28	AP	200		75	225

FRANCOIS MORELLET

BORN: Chalet, France; 1926
EDUCATION: Self-Taught
RECENT EXHIB: International Inst for Mod Structural Art, Kansas City, MO, 1992
COLLECTIONS: Mus of Mod Art, NY
PRINTERS: Spiegel Studio, Saarbrucken, Germany (SpS)
PUBLISHERS: Galerie Dorothea van der Koelen, Munich, Germany (GDK)
GALLERIES: Galerie Hermanns, Munich, Germany; Hayward Gallery, London, England

TITLE	PUBLISHER	PRINTER	DATE	MEDIUM	DIMENSION (PAPER SIZE) IN INCHES	TYPE OF PAPER	EDITION NUMBER	NO. OF COLORS	ORIGINAL OPENING PRICE	CURRENT RETAIL PRICE
CURRENT EDITIONS:										
Straktur	GDK			SP	20 X 20	HMP	115		250	500
Twice (Set of 3)	GDK	SpS	1992	ENG	13 X 18 EA	HMP	60 EA	1 EA	1350 SET	1350 SET

HIROKI MORINOUE

BORN: Kealakekua, HI; September 28, 1947
EDUCATION: California Col of Arts & Crafts, Oakland, CA, BFA, 1973; Sumi (Japanese Brush Painting), Koh Ito Sensei, 1976; Moku-Hanga (Japanese Woodblock Painting), Takashi Okubu Sensei, 1982
AWARDS: First Prize, 13th Annual Exhib, 1974; Purchase Prize, Best of Show, Hilo, HI, 1974; Purchase Award, Best of Show, Honolulu City, HI, 1975; Kanagawa Prefectural Governor's Award, 1977; Best Painting Award, 7th Annual Easter Art Festival, Hilo, HI, 1979; First Prize Award, Kanagawa Suisai Renmei Ten, Yokohama, Japan, 1983; Purchase Award, Best of Show, Wailoa Center Exhib, Hilo, HI, 1986; State Found, Culture & the Arts Purchase Award, Hilo, HI, 1986,89,90; Second Prize, First Annual Japanese Chamber of Commerce & Industry, Hilo, HI, 1990; First Place Award, Second Annual Japanese Chamber of Commerce & Industry, Hilo, HI, 1991
RECENT EXHIB: Gallery EAS, Honolulu, HI, 1987, Volcano Art Center/Studio 7 Gallery, Volcano, HI, 1987,88; Editions Limited, San Francisco, CA, 1988; Contemporary Mus, Honolulu, HI, 1989; Gallery of the Pacific, Mauna Lani, HI, 1990; Mark Masuoka Gallery, Las Vegas, NV, 1990; Kala Institute Gallery, Berkeley, CA, 1990; Joanne Chappell Gallery, San Francisco, CA, 1991; Stones Gallery, Kauri, HI, 1988,90,92; Studio 7 Gallery, Holualoa, HI, 1992
COLLECTIONS: State Found on Culture & the Arts, HI; Honolulu Acad of Arts, HI; Contemp Mus of Art, HI; Nat Parks Coll, Baltimore, MD; Ueno No Mori Mus, Tokyo, Japan; City of Fujisawa, Kanagawa, Japan
PRINTERS: Bud Shark, Boulder, CO (BS); Shark's, Inc, Boulder, CO (SI)
PUBLISHERS: Shark's Inc, Boulder, CO (SI)
GALLERIES: Stones Gallery, Kauri, HI; Gallery EAS, Honolulu, HI; Joanne Chappell Gallery, San Francisco, CA; Mark Masuoka Gallery, Las Vegas, NV; Studio 7 Gallery, Holualoa, HI

TITLE	PUBLISHER	PRINTER	DATE	MEDIUM	DIMENSION (PAPER SIZE) IN INCHES	TYPE OF PAPER	EDITION NUMBER	NO. OF COLORS	ORIGINAL OPENING PRICE	CURRENT RETAIL PRICE
CURRENT EDITIONS:										
Land Space XXI-92	SI	BS/SI	1992	WC	45 X 30	R/BFK	10		1400	1400

MALCOLM MORLEY

BORN: London, England; 1931
EDUCATION: Royal Col of Art, London, England, 1954–57
TEACHING: Royal Col of Art, London, England, 1956; Ohio State Univ, Columbus, OH, 1965,66; Sch of Visual Arts, NY, 1967–69; State Univ of New York, Stoneybrook, NY, 1972
AWARDS: First Annual Turner Prize, Tate Gallery, London, England, 1984
RECENT EXHIB: Temperance Hall Gallery, Bellport, NY, 1988; Anthony d'Offay Gallery, London, England, 1990; Pace Gallery, NY, 1987,88–89,91; Mary Boone Gallery, NY, 1993
COLLECTIONS: Metropolitan Mus of Art, NY; Whitney Mus of Am Art, NY; Mus of Mod Art, NY; Detroit Inst of Arts, MI; Fordham Univ, NY; Hirshhorn Mus, Wash, DC; Louisiana Mus, Humblebaek, Denmark; Mus of Contemp Art, Chicago, IL; Musee d'Art Moderne, Paris, France; Victoria & Albert Mus, London, England; Wadsworth Atheneum, Hartford, CT; Neue Galerie, Cologne, West Germany
PRINTERS: Tyler Graphics, Ltd, Mount Kisco, NY (TGL); Gemini GEL, Los Angeles, CA (GEM); Vermillion Editions, Ltd, Minneapolis, MN (VEL); Novak Graphics, NY (NG); Felix Harlan, NY (FH); X-Press, NY (XP)
PUBLISHERS: Tyler Graphics, Ltd, Mount Kisco, NY (TGL); Brooke Alexander, Inc, NY (BAI); Vermillion Editions, Ltd, Minneapolis, MN (VEL); Gemini GEL, Los Angeles, CA (GEM); Novak Graphics, NY (NG); Artist (ART); X-Press, NY (XP); Abrams Original Editions, NY (AOE)
GALLERIES: Pace Prints, New York, NY; Pace Gallery, New York, NY; Gemini GEL, Los Angeles, CA; Tyler Graphics, Ltd, Mount Kisco, NY; Janet Steinberg Fine Arts, San Francisco, CA; Vermillion Editions, Ltd, Minneapolis, MN; Nohra Haime Gallery, New York, NY; Nicola Jacobs Gallery, London, England; Mary Boone Gallery, New York, NY; Sorrentino/Mayer Fine Art, New York, NY; Ro Gallery Image Makers, Inc, New York, NY
MAILING ADDRESS: 2 Spring St, New York, NY 10012

TITLE	PUBLISHER	PRINTER	DATE	MEDIUM	DIMENSION (PAPER SIZE) IN INCHES	TYPE OF PAPER	EDITION NUMBER	NO. OF COLORS	ORIGINAL OPENING PRICE	CURRENT RETAIL PRICE
SOLD OUT EDITIONS (RARE):										
Beach Scene (with Varnish Overprint)	BAI		1969	SP	30 X 22	AP	100		100	5000
Ship	AOE		1972	SP	23 X 34	AP	125		125	2500
Beach Scene	TGL	TGL	1982	LC	38 X 52	AP88	58	19	1600	16000
Parrots	TGL	TGL	1982	LC	43 X 40	AP88	55	11	1200	8500
Devonshire Cows	TGL	TGL	1982	LC	46 X 34	RP/300	65	12	950	4500
Devonshire Bullocks	TGL	TGL	1982	LC	48 X 35	RP/300	58	25	1200	4500
Horses	TGL	TGL	1982	LC	39 X 29	TGL/HMP	35	1	600	2000
Goats in Shed	TGL	TGL	1982	LC	29 X 40	NIM/HMP	30	1	600	2000
Goat	TGL	TGL	1982	LC	32 X 41	HMP	30	2	600	2000
Fish	TGL	TGL	1982	LC	26 X 39	HMP	30	1	500	2000
Carmel	ART/XP	FH/XP	1983	EB/SG	17 X 14	SWHP	38	1	500	2000
Our Tramp Steamer Hugging the Horizon off Coconut Island II	GEM	GEM	1987	LC	34 X 54	AP88	44	20	2000	4500
Kite on Gibson Beach	GEM	GEM	1987	LC	41 X 46	AP88	56	14	2000	4500
Rite of Passage	GEM	GEM	1988	EC	46 X 32	HMP	52	19	4500	10000

MALCOLM MORLEY CONTINUED

TITLE	PUBLISHER	PRINTER	DATE	MEDIUM	DIMENSION (PAPER SIZE) IN INCHES	TYPE OF PAPER	EDITION NUMBER	NO. OF COLORS	ORIGINAL OPENING PRICE	CURRENT RETAIL PRICE
CURRENT EDITIONS:										
Sailboat (Dark)	VEL	VEL	1985	LC	30 X 40	AP	30	13	2400	5000
Sailboat (Light)	VEL	VEL	1985	LC	30 X 40	AP	60	13	2400	5000
Fallacies of Enoch Suie (Set of 6):									12000 SET	18000 SET
French Legionaire Being										
Eaten by Lions	NG	NG	1986	EB/A	21 X 33	FAB	75		2500	3500
The Lone Ranger	NG	NG	1986	EB/A	21 X 33	FAB	75		2500	3500
Lonliness of a Warrior	NG	NG	1986	EB/A	21 X 33	FAB	75		2500	3500
Cradles of Civilization	NG	NG	1986	EB/A	21 X 33	FAB	75		2500	3500
Return of Ulysses	NG	NG	1986	EB/A	21 X 33	FAB	75		2500	3500
Aegean Fantasies	NG	NG	1986	EB/A	21 X 33	FAB	75		2500	3500
Odesseys of Enoch Suite:										10000 SET
Beach Scene	NG	NG	1986	EB/A	24 X 36	AP	69		2000	4000
Leopards	NG	NG	1986	EB/A	24 X 36	AP	69		2000	3500
Trojan Caluacade	NG	NG	1986	EB/A	24 X 36	AP	69		2000	3500
Kachina and Masai Ritual	NG	NG	1986	EB/A	24 X 36	AP	69		2000	3500
Aegean Crime	NG	NG	1986	EB/A	24 X 36	AP	69		2000	3500
Cathedral	NG	NG	1986	EB/A	24 X 36	AP	23		1400	1800
Lucy Pussy	NG	NG	1986	EB/A		AP	30		3000	3000
Devon Landscape	NG	NG	1986	EB/A	57 X 76	FAB	63		1400	1400
Our Tramp Steamer Hugging the Horizon off Coconut Island I	GEM	GEM	1987	LC	52 X 77	AP88	39	22	4000	8500
Devon Mare with Foal with Lake Tahoe above	GEM	GEM	1987	I	51 X 36	AP	60	9	3500	4500
Coconut Grove	GEM	GEM	1987	LC	35 X 28	AP88	47	9	1200	1500
Wind Surfers	GEM	GEM	1987	LC	26 X 35	AP88	56	11	1200	1500
Eve Born of Adam	GEM	GEM	1987	I	22 X 27	R/BFK	35	8	900	1200
Eve Born of Adam, State II	GEM	GEM	1987	I	22 X 26	JBG	19	1	700	1200
Jazz	GEM	GEM	1987	I	32 X 38	R/BFK	47	2	1200	1500
Black Rainbow over Oedipus at Thebes I	GEM	GEM	1988	LC/SP	47 X 58	AC/W	32	16	3000	3000
Black Rainbow over Oedipus at Thebes II	GEM	GEM	1988	LC/SP	47 X 58	AC/W	32	16	3000	3000
Black Rainbow over Oedipus at Thebes III	GEM	GEM	1988	LC	47 X 58	AC/W	32	5	2000	2000

DANIEL MORPER

PRINTERS: Artist (ART); Hand Graphics, NY (HG)
PUBLISHERS: John Szoke Graphics, NY (JSG)
GALLERIES: John Szoke Graphics, New York, NY

TITLE	PUBLISHER	PRINTER	DATE	MEDIUM	DIMENSION (PAPER SIZE) IN INCHES	TYPE OF PAPER	EDITION NUMBER	NO. OF COLORS	ORIGINAL OPENING PRICE	CURRENT RETAIL PRICE
CURRENT EDITIONS:										
Prow	JSG	ART	1987	EB/HC	24 X 30	R/BFK	75	Varies	500	900
Metropolis	JSG	HG	1989	EC	27 X 35	R/BFK	100		600	750

ROBERT MORRIS

BORN: Kansas City, MO; February 9, 1931
EDUCATION: Univ of Kansas City, MO & Kansas City Art Inst, MO, 1948–50; California Sch of Fine Arts, Valencia, CA, 1951; Reed Col, Portland, OR, 1953–55; Hunter Col, NY, 1961–62
TEACHING: Instr, Art, Hunter Col, NY, 1967 to present
AWARDS: Purchase Prize, Guggenheim Mus, NY, 1967; Guggenheim Found Fel, 1969; Sculpture Award, Soc of Four Arts, 1975; Skowhegan Medal for Progress & Environment, ME, 1978
RECENT EXHIB: 65 Thompson Street Gallery, NY, 1991; Univ of Maryland, Baltimore County Fine Arts Gallery, Catonsville, MD, 1992; Western Washington Univ, Bellingham, WA, 1992; Sonnabend Gallery, NY, 1991,92; Leo Castelli Gallery, NY, 1993
COLLECTIONS: Sterling & Francine Clark Art Inst, Williamstown, MA; Whitney Mus of Am Art, NY; Tate Gallery of Art, London, England; Dallas Mus of Fine Art, TX; Mod Museet, Stockholm, Sweden; Nat Gallery of Victoria, Melbourne, Australia
PRINTERS: John Nichols, NY (JN); Editions Schellmann & Klüser, Munich, Germany (SK); Artist (ART); Condeso, Vinalhaven, ME (OC); Susan Volker, Vinalhaven, ME (SV); Vinalhaven Press, Vinalhaven, ME (VP)
PUBLISHERS: John Nichols, NY (JN); Castelli Graphics, NY (CG); Hollander, NY (HOL); Editions Schellmann & Klüser, Munich, Germany (SK); Artist (ART); Vinalhaven Press, Vinalhaven, ME (VP); Friends of Modern Art, Detroit, MI (FMA); Detroit Inst of Arts, MI (DIA)
GALLERIES: John Nichols Gallery, New York, NY; Soufer Gallery, New York, NY; Washburn Gallery, New York, NY; Editions Schellmann, New York, NY; Sonnabend Gallery, New York, NY; Paul Cava Gallery, Phila, PA; Margo Leavin Gallery, Los Angeles, CA; 65 Thompson Street Gallery, New York, NY; Leo Castelli Gallery, New York, NY
MAILING ADDRESS: 186 Grand St, New York, NY 10013

TITLE	PUBLISHER	PRINTER	DATE	MEDIUM	DIMENSION (PAPER SIZE) IN INCHES	TYPE OF PAPER	EDITION NUMBER	NO. OF COLORS	ORIGINAL OPENING PRICE	CURRENT RETAIL PRICE
SOLD OUT EDITIONS (RARE):										
Earth Projects (Set of 10)	FMA/DIA		1969	LC	22 X 30 EA	R/BFK	125 EA		1000 SET	6000 SET
In the Realm of the Carceral	JN	JN	1979	EB/A	37 X 48	AE	150	1	500	1500

ROBERT MORRIS CONTINUED

TITLE	PUBLISHER	PRINTER	DATE	MEDIUM	DIMENSION (PAPER SIZE) IN INCHES	TYPE OF PAPER	EDITION NUMBER	NO. OF COLORS	ORIGINAL OPENING PRICE	CURRENT RETAIL PRICE
SOLD OUT EDITIONS (RARE):										
Five War Memorials (Set of 5):									1200 SET	6000 SET
Scattered Atomic Waste	CG/HOL		1970	LC	24 X 43	AP	40		300	1500
Smoking Center	CG/HOL		1970	LC	24 X 43	AP	40		300	1500
½ Mile Concrete Star with Names	CG/HOL		1970	LC	24 X 43	AP	40		300	1500
Infantry Archive	CG/HOL		1970	LC	24 X 43	AP	40		300	1500
Trench with Clorine Gas	CG/HOL		1970	LC	24 X 43	AP	40		300	1500
Untitled (L's)	CG		1972	CA	3 X 3 X 12	R/BFK	17		500	2000
Untitled (Wedges)	CG		1972	CA	5 X 5	R/BFK	25		300	1500
Location	ART	ART	1973	MM	15 X 15	AP	17		600	2000
Photo Cabinet	ART	ART	1975	PH/Wood	11 X 15 EA	AP	17		600	2000
Memory Drawings (Lead Intaglio Plaques) (Set of 5)	ART	SK	1975	MM	21 X 14 EA	R/BFK	20 EA		1000	7500
Golden Memories	ART	ART	1976	MM	6 X 30 X 6	R/BFK	17		600	2000
Cenotaph Series	SK	SK	1980	SP	26 X 14 X 2	AP	180 EA		400 EA	700 EA
Poppies			1986	WC			180		375	450
High Desert			1989	WC			150		375	375
Wild Phlox			1990	LC			150		225	225
CURRENT EDITIONS:										
Continuities (Set of 5)	VP	OC/SV/VP	1988	EB/A	20 X 15 EA	R/BFK	20 EA		2800 SET	3500 SET
Conundrums	VP	OC/SV/V		EB/A	15 X 20	R/BFK	20 EA	1 EA	3500 SET	4000 SET

ROBIN MORRIS

BORN: Yonkers, NY; August 30, 1953
EDUCATION: Syracuse Univ, NY, 1971–72; C W Post Col, Long Island, NY, 1973–75
RECENT EXHIB: Central Galleries, Larence, NY, 1989; Gallery at Turnberry, North Miami, FL 1989
COLLECTIONS: Mus of Arts & Sciences, Dayton, FL
PRINTERS: J K Fine Art Editions, NY (JKFA); Public Image Prints, Stephentown, NY (PIP); Color Technology (CT)
PUBLISHERS: New Deco, Boca Raton, FL (ND)
GALLERIES: Central Galleries, Lawrence, NY; New Art Gallery, Deerfield Beach, FL
MAILING ADDRESS: c/o New Deco, 10018 Spanish Isles Blvd, #A–11, Boca Raton, FL 33498

TITLE	PUBLISHER	PRINTER	DATE	MEDIUM	DIMENSION (PAPER SIZE) IN INCHES	TYPE OF PAPER	EDITION NUMBER	NO. OF COLORS	ORIGINAL OPENING PRICE	CURRENT RETAIL PRICE
SOLD OUT EDITIONS (RARE):										
The Couple	NDI	JKFAE	1982	LC	22 X 30	AP	250	12	150	3600
Bon Voyage	NDI	JKFAE	1983	LC	22 X 29	AP	300	12	200	2200
Waiting for the Boys	NDI	JKFAE	1983	LC	21 X 29	AP	350	13	250	2800
Rivals	NDI	JKFAE	1984	LC	22 X 29	AP	350	13	300	2800
The Gangsters	NDI	JKFAE	1984	LC	21 X 29	AP	350	14	300	2800
The Expedition	NDI	JKFAE	1984	LC/SP	22 X 29	AP	350	13	300	2800
Jazz Trio	NDI	JKFAE	1985	LC	21 X 29	AP	350	13	450	2400
At the Cat Club	NDI	JKFAE	1985	LC	21 X 29	AP	350	14	450	2000
At the Ocean Club	NDI	JKFAE	1986	LC	21 X 28	AP	350	15	500	1800
Excalibur	NDI	JKFAE	1987	LC	18 X 38	AP	350	12	600	2500
City Lights	NDI	JKFAE	1987	LC	27 X 39	AP	350	15	600	2500
Alone in a Crowd	NDI	JKFAE	1988	LC	27 X 39	AP	350	12	600	1800
Jazz Still Life	NDI	PIP	1989	SP	38 X 42	AP	150	16	700	1400
Cast Party	NDI	JKFAE	1987	LC	27 X 39	AP	350	14	600	1500
Slave to Fashion	NDI	JKFAE	1989	LC	26 X 39	AP	350	8	600	1300
CURRENT EDITIONS:										
Dress Rehearsal	NDI	JKFAE	1982	LC	23 X 30	AP	300	13	150	850
New Deco	NDI	JKFAE	1985	LC	20 X 27	AP	350	6	450	1000
The Dance	NDI	JKFAE	1985	LC	20 X 29	AP	350	13	450	800
Her New Blue Coat	NDI	JKFAE	1985	LC	21 X 29	AP	350	13	450	800
Paris Rage	NDI	JKFAE	1986	LC	20 X 29	AP	350	14	450	800
Francois and a Few Friends	NDI	JKFAE	1986	LC	21 X 29	AP	350	14	450	1100
Max the Sax	NDI	JKFAE	1986	LC	20 X 29	AP	350	14	500	850
Jumpin' Jive	NDI	JKFAE	1986	LC	21 X 29	AP	350	13	500	800
Commodore	NDI	JKFAE	1987	LC/SP	27 X 28	AP	350	14	600	800
Rhythm & Blues (Set of 4)									750 SET	1200 SET
Tres Amigos	NDI	JKFAE	1988	LC	13 X 17	AP	350	14	200	425
Urban Serenade	NDI	JKFAE	1988	LC	13 X 17	AP	350	14	200	475
Calypso	NDI	JKFAE	1988	LC	13 X 17	AP	350	14	200	350
Spotlight	NDI	JKFAE	1988	LC	13 X 17	AP	350	14	200	375
The First to Arrive	NDI	JKFAE	1988	LC	27 X 38	AP	350	14	600	850
Cigars, Cigarettes	NDI	JKFAE	1989	LC	26 X 37	AP	350	14	600	950
The Sunbathers	NDI	JKFAE	1989	LC	27 X 38	AP	350	15	700	850
Vicky	NDI	PIP	1989	SP	33 X 42	COV	150	16	700	900
Red Hot Suite	NDI	JKFAE	1989	LC	20 X 27 EA	COV	350 EA		800 SET	1000 SET
Cool Blue Suite	NDI	JKFAE	1989	LC	20 X 27 EA	COV	350 EA		800 SET	1000 SET
Steppin' Out	NDI	CT	1990	SP	32 X 47	COV	150	18	750	1500
The Ritz	NDI	PIP	1990	SP	35 X 47	COV	300	27	750	900

ROBIN MORRIS CONTINUED

TITLE	PUBLISHER	PRINTER	DATE	MEDIUM	DIMENSION (PAPER SIZE) IN INCHES	TYPE OF PAPER	EDITION NUMBER	NO. OF COLORS	ORIGINAL OPENING PRICE	CURRENT RETAIL PRICE
CURRENT EDITIONS:										
Trio	NDI	PIP	1990	SP	32 X 42	COV	250	23	750	800
Working Mom	NDI	JKFAE	1990	LC	14 X 17	COV	350		350	350
Sultry	NDI	JKFAE	1990	LC	13 X 18	COV	350		350	350
At Your Service	NDI	JKFAE	1991	LC	13 X 17	COV	350		350	350
Mary and Eddie	NDI	JKFAE	1991	LC	13 X 18	COV	350		350	350
Land of the Pharoahs	NDI	JKFAE	1991	LC	21 X 27	COV	350		600	600
Room Service	NDI	JKFAE	1991	LC	18 X 26	COV	350		600	600
Travesty of Justice	NDI	PIP	1991	SP	34 X 46	STP	200		700	800
The Conductor	NDI	PIP	1992	SP	31 X 41	STP	100		700	800

GORDON MORTENSEN

BORN: Arnegard, ND; April 27, 1938
EDUCATION: Minneapolis Col of Art & Design, MN, BFA; Univ of Minnesota, St Paul, MN
RECENT EXHIB: Concept Art Gallery, Pittsburgh, PA, 1987,89
COLLECTIONS: Brooklyn Mus, NY; Philadelphia Mus of Art, PA; Mus of Am Art, Wash, DC; Minnesota Mus, St Paul, MN; Chicago Art Inst, IL; Walker Art Center, Minneapolis, MN; Carnegie Inst, Pittsburgh, PA; Dulin Gallery of Art, Knoxville, TN; Achenbach Found of the Graphic Arts

PRINTERS: Artist (ART)
PUBLISHERS: Associated American Artists, NY (AAA); C G Rein Publishers, St Paul, MN (CGR); Steve Foster, San Francisco, CA (SF); Artist (ART)
GALLERIES: C G Rein Galleries, Santa Fe, NM & Houston, TX & Scottsdale, AZ & Minneapolis, MN; J Todd Gallery, Wellesley, MA; OR; Randell Beck Gallery, Boston, MA; Concept Gallery, Pittsburgh, PA; Images Gallery, Toledo, OH; Kauffman Galleries, Houston, TX; Malton Gallery, Cincinnati, OH; First Impressions/Barbara Linhard Gallery, Carmel, CA; Summa Gallery, New York, NY & Brooklyn, NY

TITLE	PUBLISHER	PRINTER	DATE	MEDIUM	DIMENSION (PAPER SIZE) IN INCHES	TYPE OF PAPER	EDITION NUMBER	NO. OF COLORS	ORIGINAL OPENING PRICE	CURRENT RETAIL PRICE
SOLD OUT EDITIONS (RARE):										
Marshes in Springtime	ART	ART	1971	WC	15 X 20	GOYA	30	7	30	1500
Late Afternoon	AAA	ART	1974	WC	20 X 27	GOYA	100	18	60	1500
Late January	AAA	ART	1975	WC	20 X 27	GOYA	100	23	60	1000
Late Summer	AAA	ART	1975	WC	20 X 27	GOYA	100	20	60	1000
Summer Bend	ART	ART	1976	WC	24 X 32	TOR	100	23	85	1200
September	ART	ART	1976	WC	24 X 32	HOS	115	41	125	1200
Lagoon and Highlands	ART	ART	1977	WC	21 X 28	HOS	125	23	100	1000
West Baker Park	ART	ART	1977	WC	21 X 28	HOS	125	27	100	1200
Shades of Winter	ART	ART	1978	WC	21 X 28	HOS	125	20	120	1000
Shades of Summer	ART	ART	1978	WC	20 X 27	HOS	132	22	125	900
Minnesota Winter	CGR	ART	1978	WC	11 X 12	TOR	125	25	90	900
The Big Sur River	ART	ART	1978	WC	24 X 32	HOS	130	21	175	1500
South Dakota Badlands	ART	ART	1979	WC	21 X 15	HOS	14	28	80	900
Wildflowers	ART	ART	1979	WC	15 X 21	HOS	300	32	80	900
Cachagua	ART	ART	1979	WC	15 X 21	HOS	140	26	80	1000
Cachagua II	SF	ART	1979	WC	15 X 21	OS	200	18	80	1000
Loch Raven	ART	ART	1980	WC	21 X 28	TOR	130	27	250	1000
Autumn Birch	ART	ART	1980	WC	26 X 34	TOR	125	28	250	1500
Autumn Pond	ART	ART	1981	WC	22 X 27	TOR	120	28	160	1200
California Wildflowers	ART	ART	1982	WC	21 X 28	TOR	130	31	200	1200
Apache Trail	CGR	ART	1982	WC	24 X 32	TOR	130	28	250	575
Evergreens	ART	ART	1982	WC	11 X 13	TOR	160	27	60	800
North Dakota Prairies	ART	ART	1982	WC	24 X 38	TOR	130	35	300	1200
Winter in Baker Park	ART	ART	1982	WC	24 X 32	TOR	130	31	250	1200
Laureles in Spring	ART	ART	1982	WC	21 X 28	TOR	130	27	200	1000
Cattle Country	ART	ART	1982	WC	24 X 34	TOR	130	30	250	1200
Northwest Iowa	ART	ART	1982	WC	21 X 28	TOR	130	28	200	1200
Waterlilies	ART	ART	1982	WC	13 X 11	TOR	160	19	60	800
Lower Oak Creek Canyon	CGR	ART	1983	WC	24 X 30	TOR	130	25	250	650
Neat Tortilla Flat	CGR	ART	1983	WC	24 X 32	TOR	130	34	250	575
River Beach	ART	ART	1983	WC	28 X 34	TOR	130	41	325	900
October	ART	ART	1983	WC	31 X 32	TOR	130	36	500	1000
Autumn Colour	ART	ART	1983	WC	24 X 34	TOR	130	29	290	800
Near Loch Raven	ART	ART	1983	WC	21 X 28	TOR	130	33	230	800
California Poppies	ART	ART	1983	WC	34 X 28	TOR	115	43	375	1500
River Birch	CGR	ART	1984	WC	26 X 40	TOR	130	35	400	1200
Cattails	CGR	ART	1984	WC	26 X 40	TOR	130	27	450	650
Southwest Desert	ART	ART	1984	WC	26 X 40	TOR	130	42	380	1000
Oak Creek	ART	ART	1984	WC	26 X 40	TOR	130	38	380	1000
September in Roosevelt Park	ART	ART	1984	WC	23 X 24	TOR	130	33	320	800
Rocks in Spanish Bay	ART	ART	1984	WC	21 X 26	TOR	130	26	250	800
October in Roosevelt Park	ART	ART	1985	WC	22 X 24	TOR	130	40	320	800
Early June	ART	ART	1985	WC	17 X 22	TOR	150	30	150	700
Spring Pond	CGR	ART	1985	WC	26 X 40	TOR	130	33	450	900

GORDON MORTENSEN CONTINUED

TITLE	PUBLISHER	PRINTER	DATE	MEDIUM	DIMENSION (PAPER SIZE) IN INCHES	TYPE OF PAPER	EDITION NUMBER	NO. OF COLORS	ORIGINAL OPENING PRICE	CURRENT RETAIL PRICE
SOLD OUT EDITIONS (RARE):										
Lily Pond	CGR	ART	1985	WC	40 X 26	TOR	130	26	450	1200
April in Tahoe	CGR	ART	1985	WC	26 X 40	TOR	130	37	450	1200
Near Carmel	ART	ART	1985	WC	38 X 24	TOR	130	29	380	600
Pinnacles	ART	ART	1985	WC	22 X 17	TOR	150	24	150	500
Green Mountain Lake	ART	ART	1985	WC	21 X 28	TOR	130	33	250	600
River Flowers	CGR	ART	1985	WC	26 X 40	TOR	130	31	450	900
The Superstitions	CGR	ART	1985	WC	26 X 40	TOR	130	41	500	575
Near Sedona	CGR	ART	1986	WC	26 X 40	TOR	130	25	500	900
Tahoe	CGR	ART	1986	WC	28 X 34	TOR	130	23	450	450
Autumn Currents	CGR	ART	1986	WC	66 X 40	TOR	130	23	500	850
Arizona Wildflowers	CGR	ART	1986	WC	22 X 36	TOR	130	33	450	600
Carmel Wildflowers	CGR	ART	1986	WC	26 X 40	TOR	130	32	450	1700
Desert Flowers	CGR	ART	1987	WC	42 X 32	TOR	130	44	500	1000
Carmel River Beach	CGR	ART	1987	WC	24 X 38	TOR	130	42	500	900
Desert Aloe	CGR	ART	1988	WC	28 X 34	TOR	130	31	500	800
Whispering Ridge	CGR	ART	1988	WC	17 X 24	TOR	130	28	500	350
Big Sur-Afternoon	CGR	ART	1989	WC	28 X 34	TOR	130	31	500	900
Seaside Daisies	CGR	ART	1989	WC	26 X 40	TOR	130	42	550	900
CURRENT EDITIONS										
The Little Sioux	CGR	ART	1984	WC	26 X 40	TOR	130	41	450	550
Arizona	CGR	ART	1986	WC	37 X 37	TOR	130	33	325	425
September in the Park	CGR	ART	1986	WC	26 X 40	TOR	130	30	325	550
Evening in Tahoe	CGR	ART	1987	WC	26 X 40	TOR	130	35	325	500
Red Rocks	CGR	ART	1987	WC	26 X 40	TOR	130	33	325	475
Seattle	CGR	ART	1987	WC	32 X 42	TOR	130	31	450	700
Verde River	CGR	ART	1987	WC	34 X 38	TOR	130	29	325	500
Meadows Beach	CGR	ART	1988	WC	26 X 40	TOR	130	34	450	550
Meadows Ridge	CGR	ART	1988	WC	42 X 32	TOR	130	37	450	750
Painted Caynon	CGR	ART	1988	WC	32 X 42	TOR	130	41	450	700
Sedona Gold	CGR	ART	1988	WC	10 X 12	TOR	180	27	80	100
Tonto Creek	CGR	ART	1988	WC	34 X 28	TOR	130	33	325	475
Wellesley Woods	CGR	ART	1989	WC	32 X 42	TOR	130	30	450	700
Carmel Bay	CGR	ART	1989	WC	34 X 28	TOR	130	54	325	450
Evening Pond	CGR	ART	1989	WC	40 X 26	TOR	130	34	450	550
Natick	CGR	ART	1990	WC	42 X 32	TOR	130	23	500	650
The Garden	CGR	ART	1990	WC	32 X 42	TOR	130	24	500	650
Coastal River	CGR	ART	1990	WC	32 X 42	TOR	130	26	500	650
Bullhead Lily	CGR	ART	1990	WC	40 X 26	TOR	130	26	325	475
Beach Flowers	CGR	ART	1990	WC	42 X 32	TOR	130	41	500	650
Natick Audubon	CGR	ART	1990	WC	26 X 40	TOR	130	25	500	900
Tea Rose	CGR	ART	1990	WC	26 X 40	TOR	130	29	425	475
September, Big Sur	CGR	ART	1991	WC	29 X 40	TOR	130	27	650	650

ED MOSES

BORN: Long Beach, CA; April 9, 1926
EDUCATION: Univ of California, Los Angeles, CA, BA, 1955; MA, 1958
TEACHING: Art Inst, Univ of California, Irvine, CA, 1968–71; Instr, Art, Univ of California, Los Angeles, CA, 1968–72, 1975–76; Instr, Art, Skowhegan Sch of Painting & Sculpture, ME, 1983; Instr, Art, California State Col, Long Beach, CA, 1985–86
AWARDS: Tamarind Lithography Grant; Nat Endowment for the Arts Grant, 1976; John Simon Guggenheim Fel, 1980
RECENT EXHIB: Iannetti Lanzone Gallery, San Francisco, CA, 1988; Univ of California, Los Angeles, CA, 1988; Galeria Joan Prats, NY, 1989; L A Louver Gallery, Venice, CA, 1987,88,89
COLLECTIONS: Chicago Inst of Art, IL; Corcoran Gallery of Art, Wash, DC; Pasadena Mus, CA; Walker Art Center, Minneapolis, MN; San Francisco Mus of Art, CA; Whitney Mus of Am Art, NY; Albright-Knox Art Gallery, Buffalo, NY; Philadelphia Art Mus, PA; Smithsonian Inst, Wash, DC; Mus of Contemp Art, Los Angeles, CA
PRINTERS: Ed Hamilton (EH); Jan Aman (JA); Cirrus Editions Workshop, Los Angeles, CA (CEW); Ikuru Kuwahara, Palo Alto, CA (IK); 3 EP Ltd, Palo Alto, CA; La Poligrafa, SA, Barcelona, Spain (LP)
PUBLISHERS: Cirrus Editions, Los Angeles, CA (CE); 3EP, Palo Alto, CA (3EP); Ediciones Poligrafa, SA, Barcelona, Spain (EdP)
GALLERIES: Cirrus Editions, Ltd, Los Angeles, CA; Emmerich Gallery, New York, NY; Smith-Andersen Gallery, Palo Alto, CA; Dorothy Rosenthal Art, Chicago, IL; Angles Gallery, Santa Monica, CA; L A Louver Gallery, Venice, CA; Galeria Joan Prats, New York, NY & Barcelona, Spain
MAILING ADDRESS: 1233 Palms Blvd, Venice, CA 90291

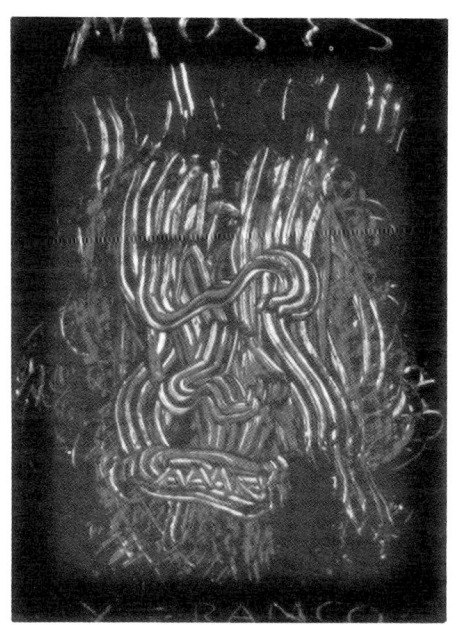

Ed Moses
Moses y Branco
Courtesy Ediciones Poligrafa

ED MOSES CONTINUED

TITLE	PUBLISHER	PRINTER	DATE	MEDIUM	DIMENSION (PAPER SIZE) IN INCHES	TYPE OF PAPER	EDITION NUMBER	NO. OF COLORS	ORIGINAL OPENING PRICE	CURRENT RETAIL PRICE
SOLD OUT EDITIONS (RARE):										
Broken Wedge Series 1–7	CE	EH/JA/CEW	1973	LC	24 X 18	AP	50	Multi	1450 SET 250 EA	12600 SET 1800 EA
Untitled	3EP	3EP	1980	MON	22 X 38 EA	AP	1 EA	Varies	500 EA	3500 EA
Untitled	3EP	3EP	1980	MON	14 X 37 EA	AP	1 EA	Varies	500 EA	3000 EA
Untitled (EM-G5B)	3EP	3EP	1980	DPT	31 X 22	AP	16		400	2200
Culp Wall	3EP	3EP	1982	PH/E/DPT	40 X 29	AP88	16	1	1500	2000
Ikuru	3EP	3EP	1982	DPT/EB	26 X 19	AP88	10		400	800
Bite Head I	3EP	3EP	1982	DPT/REL	30 X 22	AP88	16		600	1000
Bite Head II	3EP	3EP	1982	DPT/REL	32 X 22	AP88	16		600	1000
Portrait	3EP	3EP	1982	DPT	20 X 16	AP88	20		350	750
Nohbu Wall A	3EP	IK/3EP	1982	PH/E	40 X 29	AP88	12	4	1500	2000
Nohbu Wall B	3EP	IK/3EP	1982	PH/E	40 X 28	AP88	12	4	1500	2000
Nohbu Wall C	3EP	IK/3EP	1982	PH/E	40 X 29	AP88	12	1	1500	2000
Shard Series	3EP	3EP	1982	MON	42 X 30 EA	AP	1 EA	Varies	1500 EA	3500 EA
ACH	3EP	3EP	1982	MON	26 X 40 EA	AP	1 EA	Varies	1500 EA	3500 EA
Untitled (EM-L-7)	3EP	IK/3EP	1983	LC/CC	40 X 26	RP/BUT	40	3	800	1500
Untitled (EM-L-9)	3EP	IK/3EP	1983	LC	40 X 26	RP/B	40	3	800	1500
Untitled (EM-L-11)	3EP	IK/3EP	1983	LC/CC	40 X 26	RP/DB	40	2	800	1500
Untitled (EM-1-12)	3EP	IK/3EP	1983	LC	40 X 26	RP/G	40	3	800	1500
Krak Wall I	3EP	IK/3EP	1983	EB/DPT	23 X 31	GE	12	1	750	1000
Krak Wall II	3EP	IK/3EP	1983	EB	31 X 23	GE	12	1	750	1000
Krak Wall III	3EP	IK/3EP	1983	EB/DPT	30 X 23	GE	10	1	750	1000
CURRENT EDITIONS:										
Shago (Set of 6)	EdP	LP	1988-89	LC	30 X 22 EA	GP	25 EA	2-3 EA	950 EA	1100 EA
Untitled #1-#5	EdP	LP	1988-89	LC	33 X 25 EA	GP	25 EA	2-3 EA	100 EA	1100 EA
Cap de Patata	EdP	LP	1988-89	LC	32 X 24	GP	50	2	1100	1200
Moses y Branco	EdP	LP	1988-89	LC	32 X 24	GP	50	2	1100	1200
Eloi-Ricco II	EdP	LP	1988-89	LC	32 X 24	GP	50	2	1000	1200
Ricco-Trac	EdP	LP	1988-89	EC	32 X 24	GP	50	2	950	1100
Double-Trac I	EdP	LP	1988-89	EC	32 X 24	GP	50	2	1000	1100
Double-Trac II	EdP	LP	1988-89	EC	32 X 24	GP	50	2	1000	1100
Cargot-Trac	EdP	LP	1988-89	EC	32 X 24	GP	50	2	1000	1100
Eloi-Vador I	EdP	LP	1988-89	EC	32 X 24	GP	50	2	1200	1300
Eloi-Vador III	EdP	LP	1988-89	EC	32 X 24	GP	50	2	1200	1300
Afif I	EdP	LP	1988-89	EC	32 X 24	GP	50	2	1000	1100
Afif II	EdP	LP	1988-89	EC	32 X 24	GP	50	2	1000	1100

IRA MOSKOWITZ

BORN: Turla, Poland; March 15, 1912; U S Citizen
EDUCATION: Art Students League, NY, 1930–33
AWARDS: Guggenheim Fel, Creative Art, 1943; Am Art War Prize, Lithograph, 1944; Library of Congress Award, Pennell Show, 1945
COLLECTIONS: Metropolitan Mus of Art, NY; Whitney Mus of Am Art, NY; Nat Gallery of Art, Wash, DC; Bibliotheque Nat, Paris, France; Mus of New Mexico, Albuquerque, NM; Mus of Mod Art, NY; Brooklyn Mus, NY; Mus of Fine Arts, Houston, TX; Carnegie Inst, Pittsburgh, PA; Mus of Navajo Ceremonial Art, Santa Fe, NM; New York Public Library, NY; Library of Congress, Wash, DC; Albany Inst of History & Art, NY; Philbrook Art Center, MI; Mus of Nat History, Cincinnati, OH; Mus of Natural History, NY
GALLERIES: Brewster Gallery, New York, NY; Professional Fine Arts Services, Inc, New York, NY
MAILING ADDRESS: 390 West End Ave, New York, NY 10024

TITLE	PUBLISHER	PRINTER	DATE	MEDIUM	DIMENSION (PAPER SIZE) IN INCHES	TYPE OF PAPER	EDITION NUMBER	NO. OF COLORS	ORIGINAL OPENING PRICE	CURRENT RETAIL PRICE
SOLD OUT EDITIONS (RARE):										
Silver Smelter in Zimapan	ART	ART	1941	LB	11 X 15	AP			50	600
Arrival of the Shaliko-Zuni	ART	ART	1946	LB	12 X 13	AP			75	600

ROBERT S MOSKOWITZ

BORN: New York, NY; June 20, 1935
EDUCATION: Self-Taught
RECENT EXHIB: Hirshhorn Mus, Wash, DC, 1989; La Jolla Mus of Contemp Art, CA, 1989–1990; Mus of Mod Art, NY, 1990; Asheville Art us, Ashville, NC, 1992; BlumHelman Gallery, NY, 1992
COLLECTIONS: Mus of Mod Art, NY; Whitney Mus of Am Art, NY; Albright-Knox Art Gallery, Buffalo, NY; Rose Art Mus, Bradeis Mus, Waltham, MA; Wadsworth Atheneum, Hartford, CT; Joslyn Art Mus, NE; Kitakyushu Municipal Mus, Japan; Philadelphia Mus of Art, PA; La Jolla Mus of Contemp Art, CA; BlumHelman Galleries, New York, NY & Los Angeles, CA
PRINTERS: Simca Print Artists, NY (SPA); Crown Point Press, San Francisco, CA (CPP); Artist (ART)
PUBLISHERS: Simca Print Artists, NY (SPA); Crown Point Press, San Francisco, CA (CPP); Artist (ART)
GALLERIES: Crown Point Press, San Francisco, CA & New York, NY; BlumHelman Galleries, New York, NY & Los Angeles, CA; Terry Dintenfass Gallery, New York, NY
MAILING ADDRESS: 81 Leonard St, New York, NY 10013

TITLE	PUBLISHER	PRINTER	DATE	MEDIUM	DIMENSION (PAPER SIZE) IN INCHES	TYPE OF PAPER	EDITION NUMBER	NO. OF COLORS	ORIGINAL OPENING PRICE	CURRENT RETAIL PRICE
SOLD OUT EDITIONS (RARE):										
Eddystone	ART/SPA	SPA	1983	SP	77 X 34	HMP	23	10	2300	6000

ROBERT S MOSKOWITZ CONTINUED

TITLE	PUBLISHER	PRINTER	DATE	MEDIUM	DIMENSION (PAPER SIZE) IN INCHES	TYPE OF PAPER	EDITION NUMBER	NO. OF COLORS	ORIGINAL OPENING PRICE	CURRENT RETAIL PRICE
CURRENT EDITIONS										
Moon Dog	CPP	T/SM/CPP	1988	WC	19 X 12	KOZO	75	4	1000	2000
The Red and the Black	CPP	TT/SM/CPP	1988	WC	14 X 24	KOZO	75	5	1500	2800

JOE MOSS (FRANCIS)

BORN: Kincheloe, WVA; January 26, 1933
EDUCATION: West Virginia Univ, BA, 1951, MA, 1960
TEACHING: West Virginia Univ, 1960–1970; Univ of Delaware, 1970 to present
AWARDS: Cays Fel, MIT, Cambridge, MA, 1973; Nat Endowment for the Arts Fel, 1980
COLLECTIONS: St Louis Art Mus, St Louis, MO; Johnson Mus, Ithaca, NY; Delaware Art Mus, Wilmington, DE
PRINTERS: Artist (ART)
PUBLISHERS: Washington Univ, St Louis, MO (WU); Artist (ART)
GALLERIES: Max Hutchinson Gallery, New York, NY; Locks Gallery, Phila, PA; Barbara Gillman Gallery, Miami, FL; Somerville Manning Gallery, Greenville, MD

TITLE	PUBLISHER	PRINTER	DATE	MEDIUM	DIMENSION (PAPER SIZE) IN INCHES	TYPE OF PAPER	EDITION NUMBER	NO. OF COLORS	ORIGINAL OPENING PRICE	CURRENT RETAIL PRICE
CURRENT EDITIONS:										
Chant	ART	ART	1980	LC/I	29 X 36	AP	50	1	275	400

P BUCKLEY MOSS

BORN: Staten Island, NY; May 20, 1933
EDUCATION: Cooper Union, NY
COLLECTIONS: Fine Arts Mus, Roanoke, VA
PRINTERS: Lou Stovell Workshop, Inc, Wash, DC (LSW); Le Studio, Montreal, Can (LS)
GALLERIES: P Buckley Moss Gallery, Wash, DC
MAILING ADDRESS: 2878 Hartland Rd, Falls Church, VA 22043

TITLE	PUBLISHER	PRINTER	DATE	MEDIUM	DIMENSION (PAPER SIZE) IN INCHES	TYPE OF PAPER	EDITION NUMBER	NO. OF COLORS	ORIGINAL OPENING PRICE	CURRENT RETAIL PRICE
SOLD OUT EDITIONS (RARE):										
Winter's Joy	ART	LSW	1982	SP	25 X 25	R/180	99	34	500	1200
Together on Sunday	ART	LSW	1983	SP	36 X 29	Ris/2-Ply	99	49	600	2400
Imperial Majesty	ART	LSW	1984	SP	38 X 28	B-2-Ply	99	40	600	1500
Winter Geese	ART	LSPM	1985	EC	23 X 20	AP	99		400	1000
CURRENT EDITIONS:										
Canada Geese	ART	LSPM	1986	EC	23 X 23	SOM	99		600	800
Geese in Blue	ART	LSPM	1986	EC	12 X 25	AP	99		1000	1200
The Homesteaders	ART	LSPM	1986	EC	30 X 22	SOM	99		1200	1500
Stone House	ART	LSPM	1986	EC	23 X 20	SOM	99		600	800
Wedding Couple	ART	LSPM	1986	EC	33 X 19	AP	99		800	1000
Harmony	ART	LSW	1986	SP	37 X 30	B-2-Ply	99		1200	1500

MALDA MUIZULE

BORN: Latvia; 1937
EDUCATION: Latvian Acad of Art, Graphics Dept, 1963
AWARDS: First Prize, Latvian Triennale, 1980
COLLECTIONS: Cremona Found, Wash, DC
PRINTERS: Artist (ART)
PUBLISHERS: Artist (ART)
GALLERIES: International Images, Ltd, Sewickley, PA; USSR Union of Artists, Moscow, Russia, USSR

TITLE	PUBLISHER	PRINTER	DATE	MEDIUM	DIMENSION (PAPER SIZE) IN INCHES	TYPE OF PAPER	EDITION NUMBER	NO. OF COLORS	ORIGINAL OPENING PRICE	CURRENT RETAIL PRICE
CURRENT EDITIONS:										
Sea Image	ART	ART	1973	EC	19 X 25	LP	10	6	380	500
Evening	ART	ART	1977	EC	19 X 25	LP	10	7	350	500
Aurora	ART	ART	1977	EC	19 X 25	LP	7	6	380	500
Autumn Games	ART	ART	1977	EC	19 X 25	LP	12	8	380	500
Autumn Games I	ART	ART	1977	EC	19 X 25	LP	12	8	380	500
Landscape with Butterflies	ART	ART	1978	EC	19 X 25	LP	20	5	350	450
In the Old City	ART	ART	1978	EC	19 X 25	LP	15	6	350	450
The Youth	ART	ART	1978	EC	19 X 25	LP	20	6	350	450
Olympic Motive	ART	ART	1979	EC	20 X 25	LP	20	8	350	450
Tristan and Izolda	ART	ART	1979	EC	19 X 25	LP	20	6	350	450
New Species	ART	ART	1979	EC	19 X 25	LP	10	5	350	450
Fantastic Figure	ART	ART	1979	EC	14 X 19	LP	20	5	175	300
Female Portrait	ART	ART	1979	EC	14 X 19	LP	20	5	175	300
Reporting	ART	ART	1979	EC	19 X 25	LP	10	6	350	450
Ballade about the Sea	ART	ART	1980	EC	19 X 25	LP	20	5	350	450
Motive with a Cock	ART	ART	1980	EC	19 X 25	LP	20	8	350	450

ROBERT MOTHERWELL

BORN: Aberdeen, WA; (1915–1991)
EDUCATION: Stanford Univ, CA, BA, 1932–36; California Sch of Fine Arts, 1935; Harvard Univ Grad Sch, Cambridge, MA, 1937; Columbia Univ, NY, 1940–41
TEACHING: Instr, Painting, Black Mountain Col, 1945,51; Prof, Painting, Hunter Col, NY, 1950–58, Distinguished Prof, 1971–72; Columbia Univ, NY, 1964–65
AWARDS: Guggenheim Fel, 1964; Belgian Art Critics Prize, Brussels, Belgium, 1966; La Grande Medaille de Vermeil de la Villa de Paris, France, 1977; Gold Medal, Pennsylvania Acad of Fine Art, Phila, PA, 1979; Edward MacDowell Medal, Peterborough, NH, 1985; Guggenheim Mus Prize, 1985
RECENT EXHIB: M Knoedler & Co, NY, 1987,88; Marian Locks Gallery, Phila, PA, 1989; Heland Wetterling Gallery, Stockholm, Sweden, 1989; Harcourts Modern & Contemp Art, San Francisco, CA, 1989; Masur Mus of Art, Monroe, LA, 1992; Albrecht-Kemper Mus of Art, St Joseph, MO, 1992; Monclair Art Mus, NJ, 1992; North Miami Center of Contemp Art, FL, 1992; Arkansas Arts Center, Little Rock, AR; Associated Am Artists, NY, 1988,90,92,93
COLLECTIONS: Mus of Mod Art, NY; Metropolitan Mus of Art, NY; Whitney Mus of Art, NY; Brooklyn Mus of Art, NY; Fogg Mus, Harvard Univ, Cambridge, MA; Yale Univ, New Haven, CT; Albright-Knox Gallery of Art, Buffalo, NY; Addison Art Gallery, Andover, MA; Art Inst of Chicago, IL; Baltimore Mus of Art, MD; Bennington Col, VT; Brown Univ, Providence, RI; Cleveland Mus of Art, OH; Chrysler Art Mus, Provincetown, MA; Dallas Mus of Fine Art, TX; Dayton Art Inst, OH; Peggy Guggenheim Found, Venice, Italy; Houston Fine Arts Mus, TX; Los Angeles County Mus, CA; Mus of Mod Art, Rio de Janeiro, Brazil; New York Univ; North Carolina Mus, Raleigh, NC; Pasadena Art Mus, CA; San Francisco Art Mus, CA; Smithsonian Inst, Wash, DC; Stedelijk Mus, Amsterdam, Netherlands; Tel Aviv Art Mus, Israel; Art Gallery of Toronto, Can; Univ of Nebraska, Lincoln, NE; Univ of Washington, Seattle, WA; Walker Art Inst, Minneapolis, MN; Washington Univ, St Louis, MO; Worcester Art Mus, MA
PRINTERS: Irwin Hollander, NY (IH); Irwin Hollander Workshop, NY (IHW); Donn Steward, NY (DS); Artist (ART); Tyler Graphics, Mount Kisco, NY (TGL); Catherine Mousley, NY (CM); Toddy Belknap, NY (TB); Gemini GEL, Los Angeles, CA (GEM); Robert Bigelow (RB)
PUBLISHERS: American Federation of Arts, NY (AFA); Abrams Original Editions, NY (AOE); Marlborough Graphics, NY (MG); Tyler Graphics, Ltd, Mount Kisco, NY (TGL); Brooke Alexander Editions, NY (BAI); Petersburg Press, NY (PP); Berggruen & Cie, Paris, France (B/C); Robert Motherwell Editions, Greenwich, CT (RME); Waddington Graphics, London, England (WG)
GALLERIES: Marlborough Graphics, New York, NY; Brooke Alexander, Inc, New York, NY; L A Louver Gallery, Venice, CA; John Berggruen Gallery, San Francisco, CA; M Knoedler & Company, New York, NY; Harcourts Contemporary Gallery, San Francisco, CA; David Adamson Gallery, Wash, DC; Hokin Galleries, Bay Harbor Islands, FL & Palm Beach, FL; Thomas Smith Fine Art, Fort Wayne, IN; Douglas Drake Gallery, Kansas City, KS; Harcus Gallery, Boston, MA; Long Point Gallery, Provincetown, MA; Flanders Contemporary Art, Minneapolis, MN; Greenberg Gallery, St Louis, MO; Nancy Singer Gallery, St Louis, MO; Images Gallery, Toledo, OH; Paul Cava Gallery, Phila, PA; Michael H Lord Gallery, Milwaukee, WI; Associated American Artists, New York, NY; Pace Editions, New York, NY; Morgan Gallery, Boston, MA; Thomas Babeor Gallery, La Jolla, CA; Irene Drori Graphics, Los Angeles, CA; Graystone, San Francisco, CA; Fendrick Gallery, Wash, DC; Mary Ryan Gallery, New York, NY; Nan Miller Gallery, Rochester, NY; Contemporary Gallery, Dallas, TX; Spaightwood Galleries, Madison, WI; Greg Kucera Gallery, Seattle, WA; Marian Locks Gallery, Phila, PA; Heland Wetterling Gallery, Stockholm, Sweden; Dunlop-Freidenrich Fine Art, Newport Beach, CA; Arion Press, San Francisco, CA; Bowles-Sorokko Gallery, Beverly Hills, CA & San Francisco, CA & Soho, NY; Joanne Chappell Gallery, San Francisco, CA; Manny Silverman

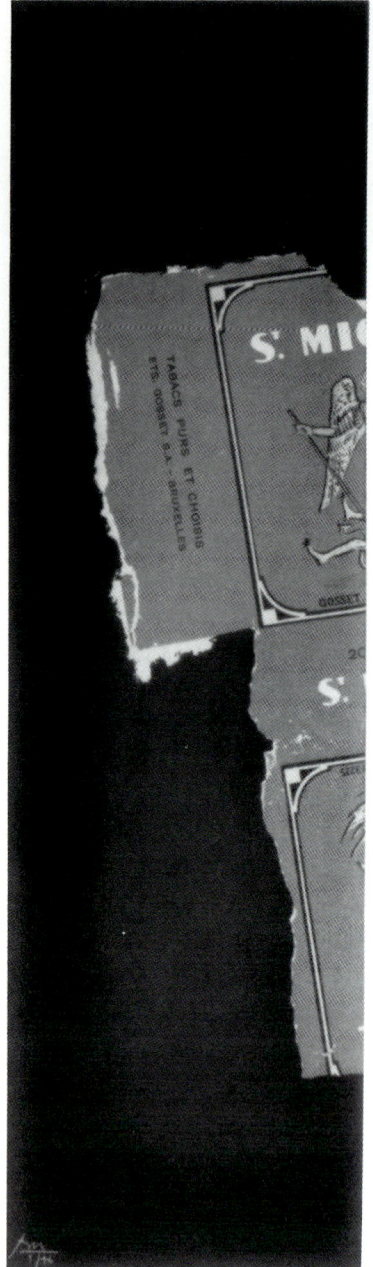

Robert Motherwell
St Michael II
Courtesy Tyler Graphics, Ltd

Gallery, Los Angeles, CA; Kass/Meridian Gallery, Chicago, IL; J Rosenthal Fine Arts, Chicago, IL; Levinison Kane Gallery, Boston, MA; Galerie Internationale, Bloomfield Hills, MI; Gottheiner Fine Arts, Ltd, St Louis, MO; Thomson Gallery, Minneapolis, MN; Moira Singer Gallery, Green Valley, NV; J J Brookings Gallery, San Jose, CA; William Turner Gallery, Venice, CA; River Gallery, Westport, CT; Marsha Mateyka Gallery, Wash, DC; Mary Singer Gallery, Wash, DC

Belknap (B); Tyler (T); Robert Motherwell (RM)

TITLE	PUBLISHER	PRINTER	DATE	MEDIUM	DIMENSION (PAPER SIZE) IN INCHES	TYPE OF PAPER	EDITION NUMBER	NO. OF COLORS	ORIGINAL OPENING PRICE	CURRENT RETAIL PRICE
SOLD OUT EDITIONS (RARE):										
Leonardo's Wall	IHW	IH/IHW	1965–66	LC	30 X 42	R/BFK	20		125	5000
Untitled	TGL	TGL	1965–66	EC	22 X 30	R/BFK	12	1	125	
Automatism A (Signed in Brown Crayon) (B-6)	IHW	IH/IHW	1965–66	LB	28 X 21	R/BFK	100	1	100	15000
Automatism B (B-7)	IHW	IH/IHW	1965–66	LB	30 X 21	R/BFK	100	1	100	15000
Calligraphy	IHW	IH/IHW	1965–66	LC	19 X 26	R/BFK	80	1	100	5000
Madrid Suite (Set of 10)	IHW	IH/IHW	1965–66	LC	22 X 30 EA	AC	100 EA	1 EA	900 SET	20000 SET
Untitled	TGL	TGL	1965–66	EB	24 X 18	R/BFK	25	1	125	6000

ROBERT MOTHERWELL CONTINUED

TITLE	PUBLISHER	PRINTER	DATE	MEDIUM	DIMENSION (PAPER SIZE) IN INCHES	TYPE OF PAPER	EDITION NUMBER	NO. OF COLORS	ORIGINAL OPENING PRICE	CURRENT RETAIL PRICE
SOLD OUT EDITIONS (RARE):										
Untitled (B-19)	TGL	TGL	1965–66	EB/OB	30 X 22	R/BFK	25	1	125	4500
Untitled (B-20)	TGL	TGL	1965–66	EB/OB	18 X 24	R/BFK	12	1	125	4500
Untitled (B-24A)	TGL	TGL	1965–66	LB	25 X 20	R/BFK	25	1	125	4500
Summertime in Italy (B-21)	IHW	IH/IHW	1965–66	LC	22 X 17	R/BFK	50	1	125	6000
Summertime in Italy (with Lines) (B-22)	IHW	IH/IHW	1965–66	LB	22 X 17	R/BFK	100	3	100	5000
Summertime in Italy (with Blue) (B-24)	IHW	IH/IHW	1965–66	LB	30 X 22	AC	100	1	125	5000
Summertime in Italy (with Crayon) (B-23)	IHW	IH/IHW	1965–66	LB	30 X 22	AC	100	1	125	5000
Untitled	TGL	TGL	1966	LC	22 X 17	R/BFK	30	1	100	5000
Untitled (B-26)	TGL	TGL	1966	LC	30 X 22	AC	45	2	125	5000
Untitled (B-27)	TGL	TGL	1966	LC	23 X 17	AC	100	1	100	5000
To Arp (B-30)	TGL	TGL	1966	LB	9 X 7	AC	100	1	100	3500
Pour Arp	TGL	TGL	1966	LC	10 X 22	AC			100	3500
Untitled	TGL	TGL	1965–66	EB	24 X 18	R/BFK	25	1	125	6000
Untitled (B-19)	TGL	TGL	1965–66	EB/OB	30 X 22	R/BFK	25	1	125	4500
Untitled (B-20)	TGL	TGL	1965–66	EB/OB	18 X 24	R/BFK	12	1	125	4500
Untitled (B-24A)	TGL	TGL	1965–66	LB	25 X 20	R/BFK	25	1	125	4500
Summertime in Italy (B-21)	IHW	IH/IHW	1965–66	LC	22 X 17	R/BFK	50	1	125	6000
Summertime in Italy (with Lines) (B-22)	IHW	IH/IHW	1965–66	LB	22 X 17	R/BFK	100	3	100	5000
Summertime in Italy (with Blue) (B-24)	IHW	IH/IHW	1965–66	LB	30 X 22	AC	100	1	125	5000
Summertime in Italy (with Crayon) (B-23)	IHW	IH/IHW	1965–66	LB	30 X 22	AC	100	1	125	5000
Untitled	TGL	TGL	1966	LC	22 X 17	R/BFK	30	1	100	5000
Untitled (B-26)	TGL	TGL	1966	LC	30 X 22	AC	45	2	125	5000
Untitled (B-27)	TGL	TGL	1966	LC	23 X 17	AC	100	1	100	5000
To Arp (B-30)	TGL	TGL	1966	LB	9 X 7	AC	100	1	100	3500
Pour Arp	TGL	TGL	1966	LC	10 X 22	AC			100	3500
Untitled (B-31)	TGL	TGL	1966	EC	10 X 7	AC	200	1	100	4000
Untitled	TGL	TGL	1967	EB	14 X 10	AC	200	1	100	3500
Gauloises Bleues (B-33)	ULAE	ULAE	1968	AC/CO	11 X 6	AC	75	1	200	4000
Gauloises Bleues (White)	ULAE	ULAE	1970	EB/A/LI	23 X 16	AC	40		250	4000
Africa Suite (Set of 10) (B-40-9)	MG		1970	SP	31 X 39 EA	AP	150 EA	1 EA	225 EA	9000 EA
Open on Two Whites	ULAE	ULAE	1971	LC	48 X 32	AP	30	2	250	6500
Basque Series: #3, #4, #7, #8, #11, #12 A, B, C, D	MG		1972	SP	40 X 29 EA	AP	150 EA	2 EA	175 EA	7000 EA
A La Pintura (24 Pages with 21 Aquatints) (B-82–B-102)	ULAE	DS	1968–72		26 X 38 EA	JBG	40 EA	2 EA	2000 SET	75000 SET
Five Circles	TGL	TGL	1971–72	LC	41 X 30	AC	80	1	125	3500
Chair	TGL	TGL	1971–72	LC	39 X 28	R/BFK	300	4	100	5000
Open Series, #1, #2, #9, #10, #13, #14, #15, #16	MG	TGL	1972	SP	31 X 39 EA	AP	150		175 EA	6000 EA
Summer Light Series:										
Summer Light Series: Pauillac #1 (B-119) (G-472)	GEM	GEM	1972	LC/EMB/CO	32 X 18	ARJ	92		200	6000
Summer Light Series: Pauillac #2 (B-120)	GEM	GEM	1973	LC/SP/PO/CO	30 X 12	ARJ	55		200	5500
Summer Light Series: Harvest, with Leaf (B-123)	GEM	GEM	1973	LC/CO	20 X 12	ARJ	54		200	5000
Summer Light Series: Harvest, in Scotland (B-129)	GEM	GEM	1973	LC/CO	36 X 18	ARJ	69		200	6000
Summer Light Series: Harvest, with Blue Bottom (G-477)	GEM	GEM	1973	LC	30 X 12	HMP	55		200	5000
Atascadero Suite (Set of 3):										
Atascadero I	GEM	GEM	1973	LC	36 X 19	HMP	21		250	5000
Atascadero II	GEM	GEM	1973	LC	36 X 19	HMP	25		250	5000
Atascadero III	GEM	GEM	1973	LC	36 X 19	HMP	24		250	5000
Untitled	TGL	TGL	1973	EB/A	42 X 30	AC	50	1	200	2500
Untitled	TGL	TGL	1973	EB/A	42 X 30	AC	50	2	200	6500
Untitled	TGL	TGL	1973	EB/A	42 X 24	AC	46	2	200	6500
Bird I	TGL	TGL	1973	EC	30 X 22	AC/B	21	1	200	5000
Bird II	TGL	TGL	1973	EC	30 X 22	AC/B	21	1	200	5000

The retail prices of the 100,000 limited edition prints quoted in this directory are subject to change. Print publishers, artists and galleries were the direct sources for these quotations. Prices in the secondary market listed as "Sold Out Editions (Rare)" indicate that the publisher has a limited supply of that print or that the print is difficult to locate in the galleries.

The Printworld Directory is accepting new applications for the seventh edition. Approximately 300 new artists will be accepted. Please use the two forms provided in the back section of this directory to submit biographical data and documentation of prints. Edition number of each print must not exceed 500 and the retail price must be $100 or more.

ROBERT MOTHERWELL CONTINUED

TITLE	PUBLISHER	PRINTER	DATE	MEDIUM	DIMENSION (PAPER SIZE) IN INCHES	TYPE OF PAPER	EDITION NUMBER	NO. OF COLORS	ORIGINAL OPENING PRICE	CURRENT RETAIL PRICE
SOLD OUT EDITIONS (RARE):										
Untitled	TGL	TGL	1973	EB/A	42 X 30	AC	50	2	200	5500
Soot Black Stone Series (Set of 6):									1100 SET	20000 SET
Soot Black Stone #1	TGL	TGL	1973	EB	36 X 18	LAR/HMP	50	1	200	4500
Soot Black Stone #2	TGL	TGL	1973	EB	36 X 24	LAR/HMP	47	1	200	4500
Soot Black Stone #3	TGL	TGL	1973	EB	36 X 24	LAR/HMP	52	1	200	4500
Soot Black Stone #4	TGL	TGL	1973	EB	36 X 24	LAR/HMP	50	1	200	4500
Soot Black Stone #5	TGL	TGL	1973	EB	36 X 24	LAR/HMP	53	1	200	4500
Soot Black Stone #6	TGL	TGL	1973	EB	36 X 18	LAR/HMP	50	1	200	4500
Untitled	TGL	TGL	1974	EB/A	29 X 22	GE	32		600	3500
Roth-Handle (B-137)	ART	ART	1974	AB/CO	20 X 16	ALM	53	1	500	7500
The Stoneness of Stone	TGL	TGL	1974	LB	41 X 30	TWP	75	1	300	7500
Dutch Linen Suite (Set of 4):										
Dutch Linen Suite, I			1974	EB/A	29 X 25	R/BFK	26		250	7500
Dutch Linen Suite, II			1974	EB/A	29 X 25	R/BFK	29		250	7500
Dutch Linen Suite, III			1974	EB/A	29 X 25	R/BFK	31		250	7500
Dutch Linen Suite, IV			1974	EB/A	29 X 25	R/BFK	25		250	7500
Untitled	TGL	TGL	1974	EB/A	29 X 22	GE	32	2	250	8000
Untitled	TGL	TGL	1975	EB/A	26 X 20	R/BFK	69	4	250	8000
Untitled	RME/BAI	ART/CM	1975	AC	30 X 22	AC/B	96	3	300	8000
Hermitage (B-149) (T-394) (RM-13)	MKC	TGL	1975	LC/SP	47 X 32	AC	200	6	800	18000
Slate Gray Pintura (B-152)	TGL	TGL	1975	EB/A/COL	32 X 27	JBG	59	3	250	7500
Roth-Handle II (B-153)	B/C	ART	1975	EB/A/HC	25 X 21	HMP	6	Varies	400	8000
Spanish Elegy Series:										
Spanish Elegy I	TGL	TGL	1975	LB	18 X 31	HMP/BR	38	1	500	10000
Spanish Elegy II	TGL	TGL	1975	LC	23 X 33	HMP/BR	38	2	550	10000
Mediterranean	TGL	TGL	1975	LC/SP	47 X 32	AC	26	8	600	6000
Mediterranean (State I, White)	TGL	TGL	1975	LC/SP	47 X 32	AC	26	8	600	6000
Mediterranean (State II, Yellow)	TGL	TGL	1975	LC/SP	47 X 32	AC	26	9	600	6000
Monster	TGL	TGL	1975	LB	41 X 31	HMP/G	26	1	600	15000
Bastos (T-383) (RM-2)	TGL	TGL	1975	LC	62 X 40	ARJ	49	6	1200	40000
Tobacco Roth-Handle (T-385) (RM-4)	TGL	TGL	1975	LC/SP	41 X 31	HMP/CR	45	4	1000	20000
Djarum (2 Sheets, Laminated) (B-145) (T-390) (RM-9)	TGL	TGL	1975	LC/SP	48 X 32	HMP/AC	18	4	1000	15000
Poe's Abyss	TGL	TGL	1975	LC	46 X 42	ARJ	16	2	600	10000
Le Coq	TGL	TGL	1975	LC/SP	38 X 25	AC	40	3	600	10000
Untitled (B-150)	BAI	CM	1975	EB/A	9 X 12	AC	69		700	10000
Untitled (Beige, Blue and Black)	BAI	CM	1976	EB/A	30 X 22	HMP	96	3	750	12000
Atascadero Series:										
Atascadero I	TGL	TGL	1973–76	LC	36 X 19	HMP	21	2	600	5000
Atascadero II	TGL	TGL	1973–76	LC	36 X 19	HMP	21	2	600	5000
Atascadero II	TGL	TGL	1973–76	LC	36 X 19	HMP	21	2	600	5000
Palo Alto	PP	PP	1973–76	LC	36 X 24	HMP	40		400	6000
Untitled	PP	PP	1976	LC	30 X 35	AC	70	1	300	2500
Red Sea I (B-158)	AOE	ART/CM	1976	EB/A	24 X 20	AC	100	2	750	7500
Calligraphic Study Series:										
Calligraphic Study I	BAI	CM	1976	EB/A	23 X 18	HMP	30	1	600	10000
Calligraphic Study II	BAI	CM	1976	EB/A	23 X 18	HMP	30	1	600	10000
Calligraphic Study III	BAI	CM	1976	EB/A	23 X 18	HMP	30	1	600	10000
Calligraphic Study IV	BAI	CM	1976–77	EB/A	23 X 18	HMP	30	1	600	10000
Untitled	PP	PP	1976	LC/CC	12 X 16	KIT	27	1	750	5000
Untitled			1976	MON	10 X 8 EA	R/BFK	1 EA		350 EA	6000 EA
Untitled (#7)			1976	MON	9 X 12 EA	R/BFK	1 EA		350 EA	6000 EA
Gesture Series:										
Gesture I (State I) (B-167)	BAI/RME	CM	1976–77	EB/A	35 X 26	JBG	75	2	900	15000
Gesture II (State II)	BAI/RME	CM	1976–77	EB/A	35 X 26	JBG	75	2	900	15000
Gesture III (B-171)	BAI/RME	CM	1976–77	EB/A	35 X 26	JBG	75	2	900	15000
Gesture IV (State I) (B-172)	BAI/RME	CM	1976–77	EB/A	35 X 26	JBG	100	2	900	20000
Untitled (State I)	TGL	TGL	1977	LC/CC	18 X 23	HMP	20	2	750	3500
Untitled (State II)	TGL	TGL	1977	LC/CC	18 X 23	AC/KIT	10	2	750	3500
Untitled (State III)	TGL	TGL	1977	LC/CC	18 X 23	AC/KIT	20	2	750	3500
Untitled	TGL	TGL	1977	LC/CC	22 X 30	AC	40	2	900	12000
Untitled	TGL	TGL	1977	LC	9 X 12	AC/B	100	1	350	6000
Untitled	TGL	TGL	1977	LC	13 X 18	KIT	40		500	3500
Untitled (State I)	TGL	TGL	1977	EB/A	15 X 17	HMP-G	30	1	350	6000
Untitled (State II)	TGL	TGL	1977	EB/A	15 X 17	HMP-G	10	1	350	6000
Untitled (State I)	TGL	TGL	1977	EB/A/HC	13 X 13	HMP-BK	30	1	800	10000
House of Atreus	TGL	TGL	1977	EB/A	12 X 10	RdL	40	2	350	5000
Espana Series:										
Espana I	TGL	TGL	1977	EB/A	12 X 10	RdL	40	2	350	5000
Espana II	TGL	TGL	1977	EB/A	12 X 10	RdL	40	2	350	5000
The 40's	TGL	TGL	1977	EB/A	14 X 16	RdL	80	2	350	3500
Phoeician Etching	TGL	TGL	1977	EB/A	14 X 16	RdL	40	2	350	4000
Abyss	TGL	TGL	1978	MON/CO	24 X 30	FAB/B	25	2	1500	20000

ROBERT MOTHERWELL CONTINUED

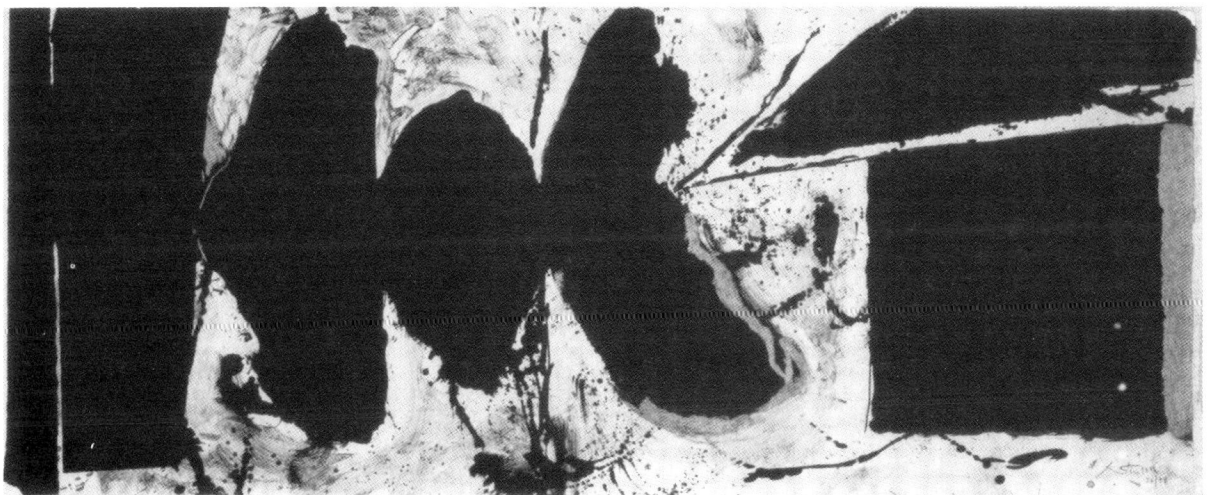

Robert Motherwell
Elegy Black Black
Courtesy Tyler Graphics, Ltd

TITLE	PUBLISHER	PRINTER	DATE	MEDIUM	DIMENSION (PAPER SIZE) IN INCHES	TYPE OF PAPER	EDITION NUMBER	NO. OF COLORS	ORIGINAL OPENING PRICE	CURRENT RETAIL PRICE
SOLD OUT EDITIONS (RARE):										
Black on Black	TGL	TGL	1978	LC/CC	28 X 22	AP/BL	58	1	400	10000
Untitled	TGL	TGL	1978	LC/CC	29 X 26	AC	24		400	10000
Untitled	TGL	TGL	1978	LC	28 X 24		46		400	15000
Oy/Yo	TGL	TGL	1978	EB/A/CC	27 X 22	R/BFK/B	78	3	500	7500
The Wave (B-198)	BAI/RME	ART	1974–78	EB/A/CC	31 X 26	R/BFK/RICE	60	1	5000	6000
Untitled	BAI/RME	RB	1978	LC/CC	22 X 16	KIT	19	1	500	5000
					30 X 22	AC				
Untitled	BAI/RME	RB	1978	LC/CC/HC	18 X 14	KIT/HMP	29	2	500	7500
					26 X 20					
Untitled	BAI/RME	RB	1978	LC/CC	20 X 20	KIT	24	1	500	5000
Dance Series:					29 X 2	AC				
Dance I (B-199)			1978	EB/A	20 X 31	JBG	30	1	1200	7500
Dance II (B-200)			1978	EB/A	26 X 41	JBG	30	1	1200	7500
Dance III (B-201)			1978	EB/A	28 X 31	JBG	30	1	1200	6000
Dance III (Red) (B-202)			1978	EB/A	28 X 31	JBG	50	1	1200	6500
Elegy Study (B-209)	PP	PP	1978–79	LB	26 X 37	TW/HMP	98	1	1200	12500
Red Open with White Stripe	TGL	CM/TGL	1979	EB/A	18 X 36	HMP	58	2	1200	15000
Red Open with White Line	BAI/RME	RB	1979	EB/A	18 X 36	HMP	56		1200	15000
Black Sea	BAI/RME		1979	EB/A	32 X 26	STP	40	1	1000	12000
Red Sea II (B-211)	AOE	CM/TB	1979	EB/A	32 X 29	GE/W	100	2	1000	20000
St Michael Series:										
St Michael I (State I)	TGL	TGL	1979	LC/SP	63 X 25	AC	14	6	4000	18000
St Michael I (State II) (B-204)										
(RM-15) (T-396)	TGL	TGL	1979	LC/SP/MON	63 X 25	AC	34	7	3000	15000
St Michael II (B-205) (T-397)	TGL	TGL	1979	LC/SP	60 X 18	AC	46	8	2000	15000
St Michael III (B-206) (RM16)	TGL	TGL	1979	LC/SP	42 X 32	HMP	99	6	1500	22000
The Dalton Print	TGL	ART	1979	LC	26 X 20	R/BFK	150	1	250	3500
Altamira Elegy	TGL	TGL	1979–80	LC	9 X 12	AC/B	75	2	350	6000
Springtime Dissonance (B-224)	TGL	TGL	1979–80	FR/A	21 X 28	DE	30	2	750	8500
The Berggruen Series (Set of 4):										
(B-225–B-228)									1600 SET	15000 SET
PS #1 Green/Blue Spring	BG/B/C	BAI	1979–80	LC	16 X 17	AC	100	3	400	4000
PS #2 Yellow/Gray Summer	BG/B/C	BAI	1979–80	LC	16 X 17	AC	100	3	400	4000
PS #3 Sienna/Blue Fall	BG/B/C	BAI	1979–80	LC	16 X 17	AC	100	3	400	4000
PS #4 Gray/Blue Winter	BG/B/C	BAI	1979–80	LC	16 X 17	AC	100	3	400	4000
St Marks	BAI		1979–80	LC	19 X 21	AC	50		400	8500
Automatism Elegy (State I—White)										
(B-238)	TGL	TGL	1979–80	LC	18 X 22	AC/W	40	1	400	5000
Automatism Elegy (State II—Buff)										
(B-239)	TGL	TGL	1979–80	LC	16 X 20	AC/B	50	1	400	5000
Los Angeles Sun	PP	PP	1979–80	EB/A	33 X 28	GE	25	2	1000	7500
Los Angeles Sun, State II	PP	PP	1979–80	EB/A	33 X 27	JBG	20	1	500	7500
Put out all Flags (B-230)	AFA	ART	1979–80	EB/A	12 X 20		50	2	400	10000
Paris Suite (Set of 4):									1200 SET	18000 SET
Paris I (Spring) (B-231)	RME	RB	1980	LC	16 X 16	JBG/HMP	75	3	350	5000
Paris II (Summer) (B-232)	RME	RB	1980	LC	16 X 16	JBG/HMP	75	3	350	5000
Paris III (Autumn) (B-233)	RME	RB	1980	LC	16 X 16	JBG/HMP	75	3	350	5000
Paris IV (Winter) (B-234)	RME	RB	1980	LC	16 X 16	JBG/HMP	75	3	350	5000

ROBERT MOTHERWELL CONTINUED

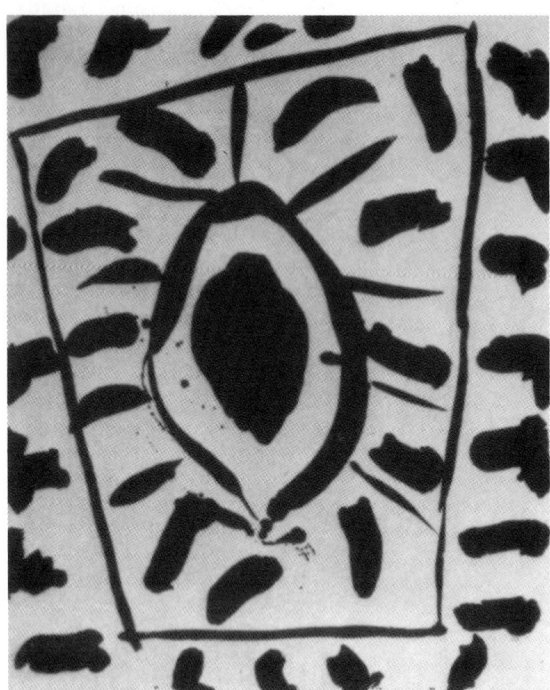

Robert Motherwell
Los Angeles Sun
Courtesy Brooke Alexander, Inc

Robert Motherwell
Mexican Night II
Courtesy the Artist

TITLE	PUBLISHER	PRINTER	DATE	MEDIUM	DIMENSION (PAPER SIZE) IN INCHES	TYPE OF PAPER	EDITION NUMBER	NO. OF COLORS	ORIGINAL OPENING PRICE	CURRENT RETAIL PRICE
SOLD OUT EDITIONS (RARE):										
Easter Day 1979	TGL	TGL	1980	LB	39 X 30	LANA	75	1	900	6500
Samurai II	TGL	TGL	1980	LB/CC	57 X 25	SEK	49	1	1500	8500
El General	TGL	TGL	1980	LC	41 X 28	KHD	49	2	950	12000
Rite of Passage Series:										
Rite Passage I	TGL	TGL	1980	LC	26 X 29	TGL/HMP	50	1	750	10000
Rite of Passage II	TGL	TGL	1980	LC	31 X 39	TGL/HMP	51	1	1000	10000
Rite of Passage III	TGL	TGL	1980	LC/CC	25 X 34	TGL/HMP	98	1	950	12000
Brushstroke	TGL	TGL	1980	LB	32 X 16	AC	49	1	350	12000
La Guerra Series:										
La Guerra I	TGL	TGL	1980	LC	37 X 49	SUZ	50	1	1000	8500
La Guerra II	TGL	TGL	1980	LC	32 X 45	AC	48	3	1000	7500
Primal Sign Series:										
Primal Sign I (B-223)	TGL	TGL	1979–80	EB/A	29 X 22	JWP	60	2	1000	8000
Primal Sign II	TGL	TGL	1979–80	EB/A	30 X 21	GE	45	2	1000	8000
Primal Sign III	TGL	TGL	1980	EB/A	29 X 21	AP	35	2	1000	8000
Primal Sign IV	TGL	TGL	1980	EB/A	30 X 21	GE	62	2	1000	8000
Primal Sign V (Copper)	TGL	TGL	1981	EB/A	33 X 26	AP	28	2	1000	8000
Primal Sign (Moss) (B-248)	TGL	TGL	1981	EB/A	33 X 26	AP	32	2	1000	8000
Black Gesture on Copper Ground (B-243)	PP	PP	1980–81	EB/A	39 X 21	GE	52	2	1800	9000
Beige Open			1981	EB/SG	22 X 28		80		1000	7500
Grey Open with White Paint	PP	PP	1981	EB/SG/PO	20 X 27	AMP	79	2	1000	7500
Yellow Chord (B-244)	TGL	TGL	1980–81	EB/A	39 X 22	GE	50	2	1500	9000
The Black Wall	TGL	TGL	1981	EB/A	18 X 36	HMP	36	1	3000	15000
Signs on White (B-251A)	PP	PP	1981	EB/A	27 X 32	GE	53	3	1000	8000
Signs on Copper	PP	PP	1981	EB/A	28 X 34	GE	59	1	1000	8000
Chicago Art Print	TGL	TGL	1981	LC	34 X 25	AC	150	4	1000	5000
Delta (B-255)	PP	PP	1981–82	EB/A	27 X 32	AP	48	2	1000	6500
Bloomsday	PP	PP	1982	EB/A	30 X 35	GE	31	2	1000	6000
Stephen's Iron Crown Etched (B-257)	PP	PP	1981–82	EB/A	25 X 28	GE	66	2	1000	6500
Lament for Lorca (B-254) (T-413) (RM-32)	TGL	TGL	1982	LC	44 X 61	TGL/HMP/W	52	4	4500	25000
Alberti Elegy	TGL	TGL	1982	LB/CC	14 X 15	TGL/HMP	100	1	750	6500
L'Amour (B-259)	TGL	TGL	1982	LB	12 X 12	GE	18	1	450	3000
Running Elegy	TGL	TGL	1983	EB/A/SL	19 X 36	LAR/HMP	31	1	1000	10000
Black Flag (B-262)	TGL	TGL	1982–83	EB	18 X 22	LAR/HMP	42	2	650	4000
Naples Yellow Open	TGL	TGL	1983	EB/A	12 X 18	LAR/HMP	62		650	4500
Mulligan's Tower	TGL	TGL	1983	EB	17 X 13	GE	32	1	500	3000
Wind	TGL	TGL	1983	EB/A/SL	20 X 18	RdB	27	1	500	3000

ROBERT MOTHERWELL CONTINUED

TITLE	PUBLISHER	PRINTER	DATE	MEDIUM	DIMENSION (PAPER SIZE) IN INCHES	TYPE OF PAPER	EDITION NUMBER	NO. OF COLORS	ORIGINAL OPENING PRICE	CURRENT RETAIL PRICE
SOLD OUT EDITIONS (RARE):										
Black Mountain, State I (B-266)	TGL	TGL	1980–83	EB/A/SL	24 X 31	LAR/HMP	21	1	750	10000
Black Mountain, State II (Red) (B-267)	TGL	TGL	1983	EB/A/SL	25 X 31	LAR/HMP	32	2	1000	12000
Gypsy Curse (B-286)	TGL	TGL	1983	LB/CC	9 X 6	MOR	98	1	500	5000
Athena	TGL	TGL	1983	EB/A/SL	20 X 18	RdB	19	1	450	4000
Red Sea III (B-292)	TGL	TGL	1982–83	EB/A	28 X 12	TGL/HMP	70	2	1000	20000
Running Elegy II, Blue State (B-295)	TGL	TGL	1983	EB/A/SG	12 X 29	TGL/HMP	10	2	900	10000
Airless Black (B-279)	TGL	TGL	1983	LC	15 X 26	TGL/HMP	98	2	600	3500
Black Concentrated	TGL	TGL	1983	LC	15 X 26	TGL/HMP	98	1	750	4000
Black Wall of Spain	TGL	TGL	1983	LC	15 X 26	TGL/HMP	98	3	900	3500
Through Black Emerge Purified	TGL	TGL	1983	LC	15 X 26	TGL/HMP	98	3	900	3500
Elegy Black Black (B-274) (T-423) (RM42)	TGL	TGL	1982–83	LC	15 X 38	TGL/HMP	98	3	2500	30000
Black with No Way Out (B-285)	TGL	TGL	1983	LC	15 X 38	TGL/HMP	98	2	2500	20000
Black Sounds	TGL	TGL	1983–84	LC/CO/LET	39 X 25	SOM/HMP	60	2	2000	15000
Black Rumble (B-308)	TGL	TGL	1983–84	LC	38 X 29	AC	65	3	900	5000
Burning Sun (B-310) (T-461) (RM-80)	TGL	TGL	1983–84	LC	43 X 29	AC	25	2	900	10000
At the Edge (B-315)	ART	ART	1983–84	AC	23 X 25	HMP	34	3	900	25000
Glass Garden	TGL	TGL	1984	EB/A/CC	18 X 31	LAR/HMP	59	2	900	3500
Australia	TGL	TGL	1984	EB/A	25 X 30	GE	25	2	900	3500
America—La France Variations Series: (B-297–B-305) (T-443–T-451) (RM-62–RM-70)										
America—La France Variations I	TGL	TGL	1984	LC/CO	47 X 32	TGL/HMP	70	12	1500	8000
America—La France Variations II	TGL	TGL	1984	LC/CO	46 X 29	TGL/HMP	70	11	1500	8000
America—La France Variations III	TGL	TGL	1984	LC/CO	48 X 31	TGL/HMP	70	10	1500	8000
America—La France Variations IV	TGL	TGL	1984	LC/CO	47 X 32	TGL/HMP	68	10	1500	8000
America—La France Variations V	TGL	TGL	1984	LC/CO	46 X 32	TGL/HMP	60	7	1500	8000
America—La France Variations VI	TGL	TGL	1984	LC/CO	46 X 32	TGL/HMP	60	11	1500	8000
America—La France Variations VII	TGL	TGL	1984	LC/CO	53 X 36	TGL/HMP	68	8	1500	9000
America—La France Variations VIII	TGL	TGL	1984	LC/CO	50 X 22	TGL/HMP	69	4	1500	8000
America—La France Variations IX	TGL	TGL	1984	LC/CO	29 X 22	TGL/HMP	60	5	1500	6000
Water's Edge	TGL	TGL	1984	LC	33 X 27	TGL/HMP	62	4	1000	9000
On the Wing (B-309) (T-454) (RM-73)	TGL	TGL	1984	LC/CO/EMB	47 X 31	AC	70	6	2000	15000
Naples Yellow Open	TGL	TGL	1984	EB/A	19 X 25	GE	62	3	900	9000
Blackened Sun	TGL	TGL	1984	EB/A	41 X 29	GE	30	1	900	10000
The Australian Stone (B-314)	TGL	TGL	1984	EB/A/CC	24 X 30	LAR/HMP	52	3	900	15000
Bistre Signs	TGL	TGL	1984	EB/A/CC	28 X 33	JWP	24	1	900	5500
Mexican Night II (B-318)	ART	ART	1984	EB/A	25 X 24	JWP	70	2	900	30000
La Casa de la Mancha	TGL	TGL	1984	EB/A	24 X 31	JWP	70	2	900	10000
The Persian II	TGL	TGL	1984	EB/A	26 X 22	JWP	70	3	900	15000
Ulysses Suite (Set of 22)	TGL	TGL	1985	EB	13 X 10 EA	HMP	40 EA	1 EA	15000 SET	30000 SET
Flesh Automatism (B-326)	TGL	TGL	1985	AC	24 X 30	HMP	15	2	2000	15000
The Redness of Red (T-458) (RM-77)	TGL	TGL	1985	LC/SP/CO	24 X 16	R/BFK-MOR	100	9	900	20000
Black Open	TGL	TGL	1986	EB/A	16 X 17	JWP-W	29	1	900	4500
Elegy Fragment I (B-327)	TGL	TGL	1986	EB/A/SL	34 X 24	LAR/HMP	18	1	900	8000
Elegy Fragment II (B-328)	TGL	TGL	1986	AC	34 X 24	LAR/HMP	52	2	900	10000
The Razor's Edge	TGL	TGL	1986	AC	24 X 27	GE/W	36	2	900	6000
Wanderers	WG	ART	1986	AC	24 X 27	JWP-W	35	2	900	6000
The Green Studio	TGL	TGL	1986	EB/A	12 X 18	GE/W	50	2	950	5000
Hollow Men Suite #1–#7 (Set of 7)			1985–86	EB/A/CC	4 X 5 to 4 X 7	HMP	49	1	5000 SET	25000 SET
Perpetual Summer	TGL	TGL	1986	EB/A/CO	33 X 25	JWP	26	4	6000	15000
In White with Green Stripe	TGL	TGL	1987	LC/LI/CO	34 X 24	JWP	75	9	5000	8000
Irish Suite (Set of 7)	TGL	TGL	1987	EB	4 X 6 EA	R/BFK	15 EA	1 EA	8000 SET	10000 SET
Blue Elegy (Pressed Paper Pulp)	TGL	TGL	1987	LC/REL	42 X 58	TGL/HMP	30	6	6000	75000
The Alphabet Series (26 Variations)	TGL	TGL	1987	AC/CO	37 X 28 EA	HMP	1 EA	3 EA	6000 EA	40000 EA
Riverrun	TGL	TGL	1988	EB/A/SL	11 X 20	HMP	37		7500	10000
CURRENT EDITIONS:										
Game of Chance	TGL	TGL	1987	LC/AC/HC/CO	23 X 16	TGL/HMP	100	Varies	1200	13000
The French Revolution Bicentennial Series:										
The French Revolution Bicentennial #1	TGL	TGL	1987	EB/A/CO	10 X 14	HMP	35		3500	9000
The French Revolution Bicentennial #2	TGL	TGL	1987	EB/A/CO	10 X 14	HMP	35		3500	9000
The French Revolution Bicentennial #3	TGL	TGL	1987	EB/A/CO	10 X 14	HMP	35		3500	9000

ROBERT MOTHERWELL CONTINUED

TITLE	PUBLISHER	PRINTER	DATE	MEDIUM	DIMENSION (PAPER SIZE) IN INCHES	TYPE OF PAPER	EDITION NUMBER	NO. OF COLORS	ORIGINAL OPENING PRICE	CURRENT RETAIL PRICE
CURRENT EDITIONS:										
The French Revolution Bicentennial #4	TGL	TGL	1988	EB/A/CO	10 X 14	HMP	35		3500	9000
The French Revolution Bicentennial #5	TGL	TGL	1988	EB/A/CO	10 X 14	HMP	35		3500	9000
Sirens Series:										
Sirens I	TGL	TGL	1988	EB/A	15 X 19	HMP	69		3500	9000
Sirens II	TGL	TGL	1988	EB/A	15 X 19	HMP	69		3500	9000
Flags (RM-88)	TGL	TGL	1989	LC/EMB	36 X 30	MOR	68		7500	16000
Beau Geste Suite, #1–#6 (Set of 6)	TGL	TGL	1989	LC	22 X 15 EA	HMP	100 EA		2200 EA	2500 EA
Beau Geste Series, I–VI	TGL	TGL	1989	LC	22 X 15 EA	HMP	XXV EA	2 EA	3000 EA	3500 EA
Beau Geste VII	TGL	TGL	1989	LC	22 X 15	HMP	35		3000	3500
Beau Geste VIII	TGL	TGL	1989	LC	22 X 15	HMP	35		3000	3500
Calligraphy I	TGL	TGL	1989	LC	54 X 40	HMP	50	3	12000	15000
The Cavern	TGL	TGL	1989	EB/A/CAR	18 X 24	R/BFK	23		4000	5000
Elegy Study I (B-425)	TGL	TGL	1989	LC	39 X 61	HMP	50	4	18000	35000
Long Point Music	TGL	TGL	1989	LC/CC	14 X 10	HMP	30		3500	4000
Mask (for Ingmar Bergman)	TGL	TGL	1989	LC	53 x 42	HMP	62	15	30000	50000
Mirror I	TGL	TGL	1989	LB	22 X 15	HMP	25	1	3500	4000
Mirror, State I	TGL	TGL	1989	LB	22 X 15	OP	25	1	2500	3000
Mirror, State II	TGL	TGL	1989	LB	22 X 15	AP	25	1	2500	3000
Orange Lyric	TGL	TGL	1989	EB/A/CAR	27 X 32	R/BFK	30		9000	10000
The Poet's Eye	TGL	TGL	1989	EB/A/CAR	18 X 24	R/BFK	35		8500	9000
The Red Queen	TGL	TGL	1989	EB/A/CO	24 X 18	R/BFK	40		12000	20000
Three Figures	TGL	TGL	1989	LC	55 X 40	AC	80	4	18000	20000
Three Forms	TGL	TGL	1989	EB/A/CAR	18 X 22	R/BFK	30		3000	3500
The Wave	TGL	TGL	1989	LC	41 X 57	AC	92	4	20000	30000
Burning Elegy	TGL	TGL	1990	LC/HC	53 X 63	HMP	36	Varies	25000	35000
España	TGL	TGL	1990	EB/A/CAR	16 X 24	HMP	40		5000	6000
Irish Suite (Set of 8)	TGL	TGL	1990	EB	17 X 15 EA	HMP	15 EA		12000 SET	15000 SET
May Linen Suite (Set of 8)	TGL	TGL	1990	EB	11 X 14 EA to 10 X 15 EA	HMP	15 EA		12000 SET	15000 SET
Seaside Studio	TGL	TGL	1990	EB/A	24 X 20	HMP	32	2	5000	7000
Summer Sign	TGL	TGL	1990	EB/CAR	17 X 34	R/BFK	38	1	7500	9000
Summer Sign	TGL	TGL	1990	EB/CAR	25 X 31	R/BFK	35	1	7500	8000
Window	TGL	TGL	1990	EB/A/CAR	12 X 16	R/BFK	30		3000	5000
Burning Elegy	TGL	TGL	1991	LC	43 X 53	TGL/HMP	36		15000	30000
Black for Mozart	TGL	TGL	1991	LC	64 X 41	TGL/HMP	40		10000	20000

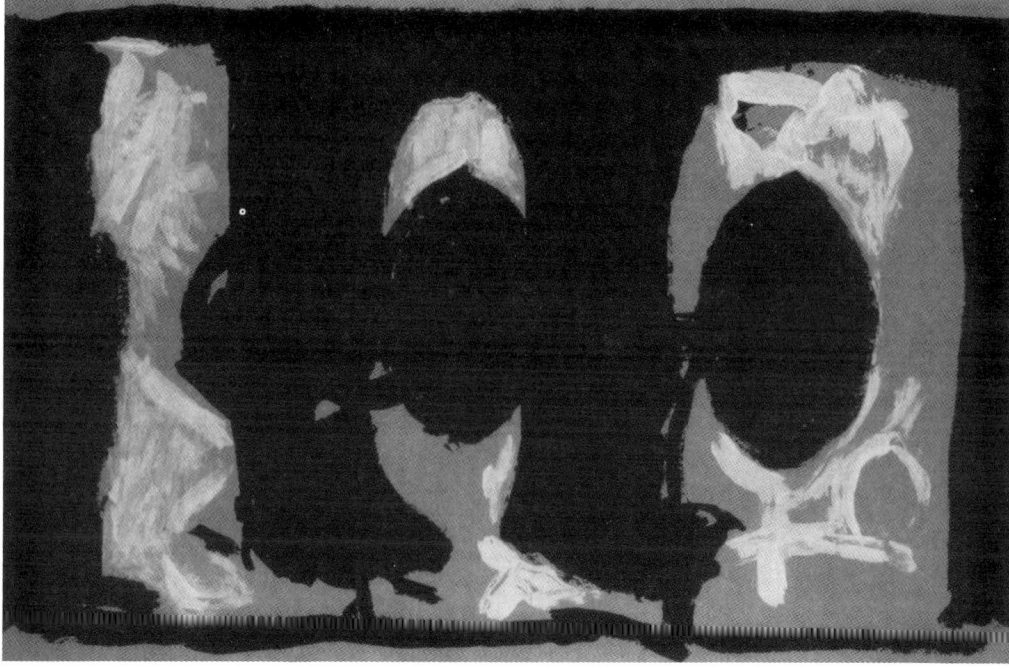

Robert Motherwell
Elegy Study I
Courtesy Tyler Graphics, Ltd

The print market has become very selective. For the first time since we published the first edition of The Printworld Directory in 1982, the prices of prints have been greatly reduced and greatly increased for the same artists by the most reputable and established print publishers. Check the fifth edition to understand the movement.

KAIKO MOTI

BORN: Bombay, India; (1921–1989)
EDUCATION: Bombay Sch of Fine Arts, India; Atelier Hayter, Paris, France
TEACHING: Univ of Wisconsin, Madison, WI
COLLECTIONS: Victoria and Albert Mus, London, England; Mus of Mod Art, Paris, France; Bibliotheque Nationale, Paris, France
PRINTERS: Atelier Capelle, Paris (AC); Atelier Robbe, Paris, France (AR); Atelier IAB, Paris, France (IAB); Arts Litho, Paris, France (AL); Atelier Colbert, Paris, France (ACol)
PUBLISHERS: Lublin Graphics, Greenwich, CT
GALLERIES: Brewster Gallery, New York, NY; Summa Gallery, Brooklyn, NY; Hammer Galleries, New York, NY; Gillary Gallery, Jericho, NY; Morningstar Gallery, New York, NY; J Todd Galleries, Wellesley, MA; Daruma Galleries, Cedarhurst, NY; JRS Fine Art, Providence, RI; Centurion Gallery, Chicago, IL

TITLE	PUBLISHER	PRINTER	DATE	MEDIUM	DIMENSION (PAPER SIZE) IN INCHES	TYPE OF PAPER	EDITION NUMBER	NO. OF COLORS	ORIGINAL OPENING PRICE	CURRENT RETAIL PRICE
CURRENT EDITIONS:										
Roses Jaunes	LG	AR	1972	EC	26 X 20	AP/JP	120/75		170	3200
Serenity	LG	AR	1972	EC	26 X 20	AP/JP	120/75		150	3200
Bison	LG	AR	1972	EC	26 X 20	AP/JP	120/75		150	3200
Cheval Blanc	LG	AR	1972	EC	26 X 20	AP/JP	120/75		200	3200
Owl	LG	AR	1972	EC	26 X 20	AP/JP	120/75		170	2000
Impatience	LG	AR	1972	EC	26 X 20	AP/JP	120/75		200	3000
Fleurs de Campagne	LG	AR	1972	EC	25 X 32 cm	AP/JP	120/75		180	4000
Le Chat	LG	AR	1972	EC	26 X 20	AP/JP	120/75		200	2000
Seascape	LG	AR	1973	EC	26 X 20	AP/JP	120/75		250	2000
Cheval Jaune	LG	AR	1973	EC	26 X 20	AP/JP	120/75		250	3200
Fleur Aquarelle	LG	AR	1973	EC	26 X 20	AP/JP	120/75	13	300	3200
Horse with Tether	LG	AR	1973	EC	26 X 20	AP/JP	120/75		250	2750
Horse with Orange Bit	LG	AR	1973	EC	26 X 20	AP/JP	120/75		300	2750
Young Tiger	LG	AR	1974	EC	26 X 20	AP	120		300	3200
Paysage	LG	AR	1974	EC	26 X 20	AP/JP	120/75		300	2000
Automne	LG	AR	1974	EC	26 X 20	AP/JP	120/75		300	2000
Oiseaux	LG	AR	1974	EC	26 X 20	AP/JP	120/75		300	3000
Marine Soleil	LG	AR	1974	EC	25 X 32 cm	AP	40		300	2600
Cheval Debout	LG	AR	1974	EC	25 X 32 cm	AP/JP	120/75		400	3000
Birch Trees	LG	AR	1974	EC	26 X 20	AP	145		300	2800
La Theiere	LG	AR	1974	EC	26 X 20	AP	100		300	2000
Fleur Rouge	LG	AR	1974	EC	25 X 32 cm	AP/JP	120/75		300	2500
Chateau d'If	LG	AR	1974	EC	26 X 20	AP/JP	120		300	4750
Aigle	LG	AR	1975	EC	26 X 20	AP/JP	120/75		300	2200
Coucher de Soleil	LG	AR	1975	EC	26 X 20	AP/JP	120/75		300	3000
Poisson	LG	AR	1975	EC	26 X 20	AP	120/75		300	1900
Paysage au Soleil	LG	AR	1975	EC	26 X 20	AP/JP	120/75		300	4750
Owl I	LG	AR	1975	EC	26 X 20	AP/JP	120/75	14	300	1800
La Chouette	LG	AR	1976	EC	26 X 20	AP/JP	120/75		300	1800
Crepuscule	LG	AR	1976	EC	26 X 20	AP/JP	120/75		300	3000
Rocher II	LG	AR	1976	EC	25 X 32 cm	AP/JP	120/75		300	4750
Colette	LG	AR	1976	EC	26 X 20	AP/JP	120/75		300	2500
Portrait de Jeune Fille	LG	AR	1976	EC	25 X 32 cm	AP/JP	120/75		350	4750
Falcon	LG	AR	1976	LC	26 X 20	AP/JP	120/75		300	2200
Cheval	LG	AC	1976	LC		AP/JP	250/250		200	1000
Pommegranates	LG	AR	1977	EC	25 X 32 cm	AP/JP	120/75	14	350	2800
Mustang	LG	AR	1977	EC	26 X 20	AP/JP	120/75		300	3500
Brume de Matin	LG	AC	1977	EC	26 X 20	AP/JP	120/75		300	3500
Cheval	LG	AC	1977	LC	12 X 14	AP	300	12	75	1000
Chat	LG	AC	1977	LC	12 X 14	AP	300		75	1000
Grand Arbre	LG	AC	1977	EC	25 X 32 cm	AP/JP	120/75		400	5000
Owl II	LG	AC	1977	EC	26 X 20	AP/JP	120/75		300	1800
Titou et Tao	LG	AC	1977	EC	22 X 32	AP/JP	120/75		300	4200
Night Watch	LG	AC	1977	EC	26 X 20	AP/JP	120/75	15	300	2200
Horizon	LG	AC	1977	EC	22 X 32	AP/JP	120/75		350	2800
Summer Afternoon	LG	AC	1977	EC	22 X 32	AP/JP	120/75		350	2900
Grand Arbre, State I	LG	AC	1977	EB	25 X 32 cm	AP	100	1	300	1800
Point du Jour	LG	AC	1977	EC	26 X 20	AP/JP	120/75		300	4000
Petite Marine	LG	AC	1978	EC	26 X 20	AP/JP	120/75		300	2500
Voir en Songe	LG	AC	1978	LC	26 X 20	AP/JP	200/100	14	250	1800
Sunrise	LG	AC	1978	EC	22 X 32	AP/JP	120/75		450	5000
Rose Glass & Bottle	LG	AC	1978	EC	26 X 20	AP/JP	120/75		380	3200
Crystal Vase & Flowers	LG	AR	1979	EC	26 X 20	AP/JP	120/75	13	380	2500
San Antonio	LG	ACol	1979	EC	26 X 20	AP/JP	120/75	16	380	2400
San Carlos	LG	ACol	1979	EC	25 X 32 cm	AP/JP	120/75		450	2400
Linden tree	LG	ACol	1979	EC	22 X 32	AP/JP	120/75		450	3000
Champs de Lavande	LG	AC	1979	EC	25 X 32 cm	AP/JP	120/75		600	5000
Homage to Turner	LG	AC	1979	EC	26 X 20	AP	140		200	2500
Aqua Blanca	LG	AC	1980	EC	25 X 32 cm	AP/JP	225/40	16	600	5000
Forest	LG	IAB	1980	EC	25 X 32 cm	AP/JP	225/40	12	650	5000
Clamart	LG	AC	1980	EC	25 X 32 cm	AP/JP	120/75		600	2500
Les Tulipes	LG	AC	1980	EC	25 X 32 cm	AP/JP	160/40	15	650	2500
Les Roses	LG	AC	1980	EC	25 X 32 cm	AP/JP	160/40	16	650	2500
Les Jonquilles	LG	AC	1980	EC	25 X 32 cm	AP/JP	120/75	14	650	2500
Chrysanthemums	LG	AC	1980	EC	25 X 32 cm	AP/JP	160/40	15	650	2800

KAIKO MOTI CONTINUED

TITLE	PUBLISHER	PRINTER	DATE	MEDIUM	DIMENSION (PAPER SIZE) IN INCHES	TYPE OF PAPER	EDITION NUMBER	NO. OF COLORS	ORIGINAL OPENING PRICE	CURRENT RETAIL PRICE
SOLD OUT EDITIONS (RARE):										
Morning Glow	LG	AC	1981	EC	25 X 32 cm	AP/JP	120/75	13	650	3000
Eventide	LG	AC	1981	EC	25 X 32 cm	AP/JP	160/40	12	600	2300
Lioness	LG	AC	1981	EC	26 X 20	AP/JP	120/75	14	600	2100
Petite Marine	LG	AC	1981	EC	26 X 20	AP/JP	160/40		600	2500
Autumn Mist	LG	AC	1981	EC	25 X 32 cm	AP/JP	120/75		700	3000
Grand Marine	LG	AC	1981	EC	25 X 32 cm	AP/JP	120/75		650	3000
La Mer	LG	AC	1981	EC	25 X 32 cm	AP/JP	120/75		650	3000
Petit Paysage	LG	AC	1982	EC		AP	195		350	2200
En Plein Vol	LG	AC	1982	EC	25 X 32 cm	AP/JP	120/75	15	650	1800
L'Abre	LG	AC	1982	EC	26 X 20	AP	120/75		350	1500
Force de Voile	LG	AC	1982	EC	26 X 20	AP	250	14	350	2500
L'Eau Qui Dort	LG	AR	1982	EC	26 X 20	AP	250		350	1800
Sur ma Table	LG	AC	1982	EC	26 X 20	AP	250		350	2500
Jeanot	LG	AC	1982	EC	26 X 20	AP/JP	120/75		400	1200
Still Life	LG	AC	1983	EC	25 X 32 cm	AP/JP	120/75		650	2800
Retour du Jour	LG	AC	1983	EC	26 X 20	AP	250		350	2500
Early Evening	LG	AC	1983	EC	25 X 32 cm	AP/JP	120/75		700	3000
Gita	LG	AC	1984	EC	26 X 20	AP/JP	120/75		600	1800
The Steed	LG	AC	1984	EC	26 X 20	AP/JP	120/75		600	1800
Summer Solstice	LG	AC	1984	EC	26 X 20	AP/JP	120/75		600	2500
Sentinel	LG	AC	1984	EC	26 X 20	AP	250		380	800
Promontory	LG	AR	1984	EC	26 X 20	AP	250		380	2000
Under Sail	LG	AC	1985	EC	26 X 20	AP	250		380	1800
Owl Light	LG	AC	1985	EC	26 X 20	AP/JP	120/75		800	1800
Golden Evening	LG	AC	1986	EC	26 X 20	AP	250		380	1500
Evening Glow	LG	AC	1986	EC	26 X 20	AP	250		380	1500
Les Oliviers	LG	AC	1986	EC	26 X 20	AP/JP	120/75		750	2250
Morning Passage	LG	AC	1986	EC	26 X 20	AP/JP	120/75		750	3000
Hidden Cove	LG	AC	1986	EC		AP	500		150	400
Study for a Still Life	LG	AC	1986	EC	26 X 20	AP/JP	220/75		450	1000
Cheval Dresse	LG	AC	1986	EC	27 X 22	AP/JP	220/75		750	1000
Cheval de Face	LG	AC	1987	EC	27 X 22	AP/JP	150/75		800	1000
Cheval Tranquille	LG	AC	1987	EC	27 X 22	AP/JP	150/75		800	1000
En Liberte	LG	AC	1987	EC	27 X 22	AP/JP	150/75		800	1000
Evening Passage	LG	AC	1987	EC	27 X 22	AP/JP	150/75		800	2800
Entre Ciel et Terre	LG	AC	1987	EC	19 X 26	AP/JP	150/75		800	2050
Abre Enchante	LG	AC	1987	EC	23 X 30	AP/JP	150/75		900	2050
The Road Not Taken	LG	AC	1987	EC	18 X 23	AP/JP	150/75		800	2200
A Fleur d'Eau	LG	AC	1988	EC	18 X 23	AP	500		1200	1500
Rose Fleuri	LG	AC	1988	EC	18 X 23	AP/JP	200/100		500	950
Anemones	LG	AC	1988	EC	13 X 18	AP/JP	200/100		600	1200
Still Life with Book	LG	AC	1988	EC	18 X 23	AP/JP	200/100		850	1500
Les Belles Roses	LG	AC	1988	EC	18 X 23	AP/JP	200/100		1000	2000
Siamese Cats II	LG	AC	1988	EC	18 X 23	AP/JP	200/100		1000	1600
Bois Caché	LG	AC	1989	EC	18 X 23	AP/JP	200/100		1000	1600
Two Horses	LG	AC	1989	EC	18 X 23	AP/JP	200/100		1000	1200
Deluxe Book with 3 Etchings										1500

OI MOTOI

BORN: Osaka, Japan; November 4, 1910; U S Citizen
EDUCATION: Pac Fine Art Col, Tokyo, Japan, 1928
TEACHING: Instr, Painting, Queens Col, City Univ of New York, Bronx, NY, 1960-72; Instr, Painting, Brooklyn Inst of Art & Science, NY, 1967-78
AWARDS: Rising Sun Emperor Award, Japan, 1981
COLLECTIONS: Metropolitan Mus, NY; Nat Gallery of Art, Wash, DC; Philadelphia Mus, PA; Cincinnati Mus, OH; Nagaoka Mus of Mod Art, Japan

PRINTERS: American Atelier, NY (AA)
PUBLISHERS: Associated American Artists, NY (AAA); Circle Fine Art, Chicago, IL (CFA)
GALLERIES: Circle Galleries, San Diego, CA & San Francisco, CA & Northbrook, IL & Pittsburgh, PA & Houston, TX & Soho, NY & Chicago, IL & Scottsdale, AZ & Beverly Hills, CA & Costa Mesa, CA & Sherman Oaks, CA & Palm Beach, FL & Honolulu, HI & New Orleans, LA & Las Vegas, NV & Seattle, WA
MAILING ADDRESS: 24-50 95th St, East Elmhurst, NY 11369

TITLE	PUBLISHER	PRINTER	DATE	MEDIUM	DIMENSION (PAPER SIZE) IN INCHES	TYPE OF PAPER	EDITION NUMBER	NO. OF COLORS	ORIGINAL OPENING PRICE	CURRENT RETAIL PRICE
SOLD OUT EDITIONS (RARE):										
Purple Hair Clown	AAA	AA	1968	REL	11 X 9	R/BFK	100		35	200
Family Head	CFA	AA	1970	EC	23 X 15	R/BFK	50		50	150

The retail prices of the 100,000 limited edition prints quoted in this directory are subject to change. Print publishers, artists and galleries were the direct sources for these quotations. Prices in the secondary market listed as "Sold Out Editions (Rare)" indicate that the publisher has a limited supply of that print or that the print is difficult to locate in the galleries.

MARCEL MOULY

BORN: Paris, France; 1918
AWARDS: Knight of the Order of Arts and Letters, Paris, France; First Prize, Lithography, Mérite Culturel Artistique, Paris, France, 1973
COLLECTIONS: Musée Nat de'Art Moderne, Paris, France; Princeton Univ, NJ; Mus of Art & History, Geneva, Switzerland
PRINTERS: American Atelier, NY (AA)

PUBLISHERS: Circle Fine Art, Chicago, IL (CFA)
GALLERIES: Circle Galleries, San Diego, CA & San Francisco, CA & Northbrook, IL & Pittsburgh, PA & Houston, TX & Soho, NY & Chicago, IL & Scottsdale, AZ & Beverly Hills, CA & Costa Mesa, CA & Sherman Oaks, CA & Palm Beach, FL & Honolulu, HI & New Orleans, LA & Las Vegas, NV & Seattle, WA

TITLE	PUBLISHER	PRINTER	DATE	MEDIUM	DIMENSION (PAPER SIZE) IN INCHES	TYPE OF PAPER	EDITION NUMBER	NO. OF COLORS	ORIGINAL OPENING PRICE	CURRENT RETAIL PRICE
SOLD OUT EDITIONS (RARE):										
La Fenetre Ouverte	CFA	AA	1970	LC	11 X 15	AP	220		50	200
Les Bateaux en Bleu	CFA	AA	1970	LC	14 X 16	AP	220		50	250
La Nuit Tombe	CFA	AA	1970	LC	13 X 18	AP	220		50	250
Femme Pensif	CFA	AA	1970	LC	18 X 13	AP	220		50	250
Studio de l'Artist	CFA	AA	1970	LC	26 X 35	AP	220		75	400
Bowl of Fruit	CFA	AA	1974	LC	17 X 12	AP	175		75	300
Checkmate	CFA	AA	1974	LC	17 X 14	AP	175		75	300
Chess	CFA	AA	1974	LC	16 X 12	AP	175		75	300
Woman with Red Chair	CFA	AA	1974	LC	17 X 14	AP	175		75	350
Two Women	CFA	AA	1974	LC	27 X 34	AP	175		125	550
Meditation	CFA	AA	1976	LC	35 X 28	AP	250		125	550
Still Life with Pitcher	CFA	AA	1978	LC	12 X 12	AP	200		50	300
Blue Chair	CFA	AA	1978	LC	13 X 15	AP	200		50	300
The Sailboats	CFA	AA	1978	LC	14 X 16	AP	200		50	275
Woman with Blue Scarf	CFA	AA	1978	LC	16 X 12	AP	200		50	350
Nude with Red Tablecloth	CFA	AA	1978	LC	24 X 31	AP	200		75	525
Composition in Blue	CFA	AA	1979	LC	11 X 17	AP	200		50	275
Femme Noire	CFA	AA	1979	LC	16 X 13	AP	200		50	275
Les Bouteilles	CFA	AA	1979	LC	17 X 15	AP	200		50	300
Orange Sailboats	CFA	AA	1979	LC	13 X 16	AP	200		50	300
Femme avec le Vase Rouge	CFA	AA	1979	LC	34 X 26	AP	200		75	400
Le Petite Dejeuner	CFA	AA	1980	LC	27 X 35	AP	250		125	550
CURRENT EDITIONS:										
Sailboat Suite (Set of 6):									300 SET	1600 SET
Sails under the Orange Moon	CFA	AA	1974	LC	21 X 30	AP	220		75	325
Green Sun in the Sails	CFA	AA	1974	LC	21 X 30	AP	220		75	325
Sailors at Port	CFA	AA	1974	LC	21 X 30	AP	220		75	325
Sail in the Blue Night	CFA	AA	1974	LC	30 X 21	AP	220		75	325
Boatmen with Orange Sail	CFA	AA	1974	LC	21 X 30	AP	220		75	325
Sailing in the Night	CFA	AA	1974	LC	30 X 21	AP	220		75	325

DONNA MOYLAN

PRINTERS: Sue Evans, NY (SE); Evans Editions, NY (EEd)
PUBLISHERS: Edition Julie Sylvester, NY (EJS)

TITLE	PUBLISHER	PRINTER	DATE	MEDIUM	DIMENSION (PAPER SIZE) IN INCHES	TYPE OF PAPER	EDITION NUMBER	NO. OF COLORS	ORIGINAL OPENING PRICE	CURRENT RETAIL PRICE
CURRENT EDITIONS:										
Bridges	EJS	SE/EEd	1992	DPT	18 X 19	AP	25		500	500

OTTO MÜELLER

Karsch (K); Dube (D)

BORN: German; (1874-1930)
PUBLISHERS: Galerie Ferinand Möller (GFM); A Beyer (AB); Kunstlerbund (KUN)
GALLERIES: Lafayette Parke Gallery, New York, NY

TITLE	PUBLISHER	PRINTER	DATE	MEDIUM	DIMENSION (PAPER SIZE) IN INCHES	TYPE OF PAPER	EDITION NUMBER	NO. OF COLORS	ORIGINAL OPENING PRICE	CURRENT RETAIL PRICE
SOLD OUT EDITIONS (RARE):										
Waldsee Mit Drei Badenden und Einem Sitzenden Madchen (K-112/B)			1918	LB	13 X 11	WOVE	100	1	25	13500
Waldlandschaft mit Kleinen Figuren (K-74)			1919	LB		WOVE	60	1	25	13500
Kniendes, Sitzendes un Zwei Liegende Mädchen im Gras (K-100)			1920	LB	10 X 7	WOVE	30	1	30	15000
Mutter und Kind II (K-107/II)			1920	LB	10 X 7	WOVE	30	1	30	12000
Ein Sitzendes und ein Kniendes Mädchen unter Blättern (K-110-C)			1920	LB	7 X 9	WOVE	30	1	30	2500
Die Affindung Mose (K-150/a)			1920	LC	10 X 7	WOVE	30		30	18000
Weisses Haus in Wiesen (D-H-418/III)			1920	WB	15 X 23	WOVE			30	35000

OTTO MÜELLER CONTINUED

TITLE	PUBLISHER	PRINTER	DATE	MEDIUM	DIMENSION (PAPER SIZE) IN INCHES	TYPE OF PAPER	EDITION NUMBER	NO. OF COLORS	ORIGINAL OPENING PRICE	CURRENT RETAIL PRICE
SOLD OUT EDITIONS (RARE):										
Zirkuspaar (K-113-C)			1920-21	LB	10 X 8	WOVE	100	1	35	13500
Zwei Figuren am Waldbach (K-145a/b)			1921	LB	12 X 16	WOVE	20	1	35	16500
Drei Mädchen im Profile (K-111-C) AB			1921	LB	11 X 15	WOVE	100	1	35	13500
Zwei Badende im Bach (K-151/A)			1922	LC	10 X 7	WOVE	60		35	25000
Sitzendes und Seitlich Aufgestützes			1922	LB		WOVE	22		35	18000
Adam and Eva (K-122/II)			1920-23	LB	17 X 13	WOVE		1	40	12500
Ein in Dünen Sitzendes und ein Liegendes Mädchen (K-154/b)			1920-24	LC		WOVE	30		40	60000
Olympia (Hand-Colored with Watercolor and Crayon) (K-137-A/B)			1924	LB/HC		WOVE	22		40	60000
Madchen am Wasser (K-127) Ummauerter Hofmit Baum und Düchern (K-135)			1920-25	LB		WOVE		1	40	5000
Paar am Tisch (Self Portrait with Maschka) (K-155/III)			1922-25	LC		WOVE	60		40	30000
Am Ufer Sitzendes Mädchen (K-116/I)			1922-26	LC/HC	15 X 10	WOVE	25	Varies	50	90000
Sitzendes und Zwei Liegende Mädchen im Gras (K-126/II)	KUN		1922-26	LB	12 X 17	WOVE	70	1	40	12000
Stehende Zigeunesin mit Einem Kind auf dem Arm (K-164/I)			1926-27	LC	27 X 20	WOVE			50	70000
Zigeunerkind im Dorf (K-159/II)			1925-27	LC		WOVE	8	5	40	60000
Waldlandschaft mit Bach (K-169/I)			1927	LB/HC		WOVE		Varies	40	15000
Knabe Zwischen Blattpflanzen, 1912 (K-2IIA)			1945-52	WB	11 X 15	AP	400			1800
Mädchen Zwischen Blattpfanzen, 1912 (K-3/IIA)			1945-52	WB	11 X 15	AP	500			6000

PHILIP EDWARD MULLEN

BORN: Akron, OH; October 10, 1942
EDUCATION: Univ of Minnesota, Minneapolis, MN, BA, 1964; Univ of North Dakota, Fargo, ND, MA, 1966; Ohio Univ, Athens, OH, PhD, 1970
TEACHING: Univ of South Carolina, Columbia, SC
AWARDS: Russel Award for Research in the Humanities, 1976
RECENT EXHIB: Schmidt-Bingham Gallery, NY, 1987
COLLECTIONS: Guggenheim Mus, NY; Brooklyn Mus, NY; Denver Mus, CO; Hunter Mus, Chattanooga, TN
PRINTERS: Steven Nevitt (SN); Larry Rosing (LR); Susan Heath (SH)
PUBLISHERS: Artist (ART)
GALLERIES: David Findlay, Jr, Inc, New York, NY; Dubins Gallery, Los Angeles, CA; Jan Weiner Gallery, Topeka, KS; Gillete-Frutchey Gallery, Atalnta, GA; Schmidt-Bingham Gallery, New York, NY; Malton Gallery, Cincinnati, OH; Eva Cohon Gallery, Highland, IL
MAILING ADDRESS: 1611 Hollywood Dr, Columbia, SC 29205

TITLE	PUBLISHER	PRINTER	DATE	MEDIUM	DIMENSION (PAPER SIZE) IN INCHES	TYPE OF PAPER	EDITION NUMBER	NO. OF COLORS	ORIGINAL OPENING PRICE	CURRENT RETAIL PRICE
SOLD OUT EDITIONS (RARE):										
Kathmandu Tapestry	ART	SN	1977	SP	30 X 21	KATH	34	16	150	500
A.D.I. Blue	ART	SH	1977	SP	28 X 18	DF/HMP	28	19	150	550
Striped Olive	ART	LR	1977	SP	24 X 17	MEX	32	12	150	450
Kathmandu Eccentric	ART	SN	1977	SP	30 X 21	KATH	34	17	150	450
Bahamian Dollar	ART	SN	1979	SP	36 X 26	DF/HMP	15	25	375	500
Nevitt Bahama	ART	SN	1979	SP	26 X 36	DF/HMP	20	24	375	500
Kinwashi Bahama	ART	SN	1979	SP	24 X 72	IND	10	15	450	600
Bahama Short	ART	SN	1979	SP	36 X 26	DF/HMP	18	17	375	500
CURRENT EDITIONS:										
Tutti Fruiti	ART	LR	1977	SP	28 X 19	DF/HMP	9	11	150	350
Olive Airplane	ART	LR	1977	SP	17 X 20	MEX	14	13	150	450
Roadside Rug	ART	SH	1977	SP	26 X 22	ENG	30	14	150	350
Nevitt Brown	ART	SH	1978	SP	17 X 24	DF/HMP	33	17	150	350
English Gold	ART	SH	1978	SP	23 X 31	ENG	31	26	150	400
Duel Runner	ART	SN	1981	SP	31 X 76	ARM	21	23	950	1000
Runner	ART	SN	1981	SP	31 X 42	ARM	22	25	575	650
Runner II	ART	SN	1981	SP	31 X 42	ARM	23	19	575	650
Mirror	ART	SN	1981	SP	24 X 17	DF/HMP	12	21	400	450
Mirror II	ART	SN	1981	SP	24 X 17	DF/HMP	12	21	400	450
Jog	ART	SN	1981	SP	24 X 18	DF/HMP	12	25	400	450
Jog II	ART	SN	1981	SP	24 X 18	DF/HMP	12	22	400	450

The print market has become very selective. For the first time since we published the first edition of The Printworld Directory in 1982, the prices of prints have been greatly reduced and greatly increased for the same artists by the most reputable and established print publishers. Check the fifth edition to understand the movement.

MATT MULLICAN

BORN: Santa Monica, CA; 1951
EDUCATION: California Inst of the Arts, Valencia, CA, BFA, 1974
RECENT EXHIB: Moore Col of Art, Phila, PA, 1987; Fuller Goldeen Gallery, San Francisco, CA, 1987; Dallas Mus of Art, TX, 1987; Kuhlenschmidt/Simon Gallery, Los Angeles, CA, 1987; Michael Klein, Inc, NY, 1987,88; Mai 36 Galerie, Luzerne, Switzerland, 1988; Carl Solway Gallery, Cincinnati, OH, 1988; Riverside Studios, London, England, 1988; Winnepeg Art Gallery, Canada, 1987–88; Brooklyn Mus, NY, 1988; San Diego State Univ, CA, 1988; Lawrence Oliver Gallery, Phila, PA, 1988; Hirshhorn Mus, Wash, DC, 1989; Fuller-Gross Gallery, San Francisco, CA, 1989; Mus of Mod Art, NY, 1989; Oregon Art Inst, Portland, OR, 1989; Western Washington Univ, Bellingham, WA, 1989; Galerie Bruges La Morte, Bruges, Belgium, 1989; Galerie Albert Baronian, Brussels, Belgium, 1989; Mario Diacono Gallery, Boston, MA, 1989; Portikus, Frankfurt, Germany, 1990; Magasin, Grenoble, France, 1990; List Art Center, Massachusetts Inst of Tech, Boston, MA, 1990; Weatherspoon Art Gallery, Univ of North Carolina, Greensboro, NC, 1991; Rijksmuseum Kroeller-Meuller, Otterlo, The Netherlands, 1991; De Appel, Amsterdam, The Netherlands, 1991; Galerie Fahnemann, Berlin, Ghislaine Hussenot, Paris, France, 1989,92; Fondation pour L'Artchitecture, Brussels, Belgium, 1992; Texas Gallery, Houston, TX, 1992; Richard Kuhlenschmidt Gallery, Los Angeles, CA, 1989,92; Architecktur Forum, Zurich, Switzerland, 1992; Brooke Alexander Editions, NY, 1991,92; Barbara Gladstone Gallery, NY, 1992; Univ of South Florida Contemp Art Mus, Tampa, FL, 1993
PRINTERS: Robert Blanton, NY (RB); Brand X Editions, NY (BX); Mark Patsfall Graphics, Cincinnati, OH (MPG)
PUBLISHERS: Carl Solway Gallery, Cincinnati, OH (CSG); Edition Julie Sylvester, NY (EJS)
GALLERIES: Richard Kuhlenschmidt Gallery, Santa Monica, CA; Brooke Alexander Editions, New York, NY; Michael Klein, Inc, New York, NY; Carl Solway Gallery, Cincinnati, OH; Lawrence Mangel Fine Art, Phila, PA

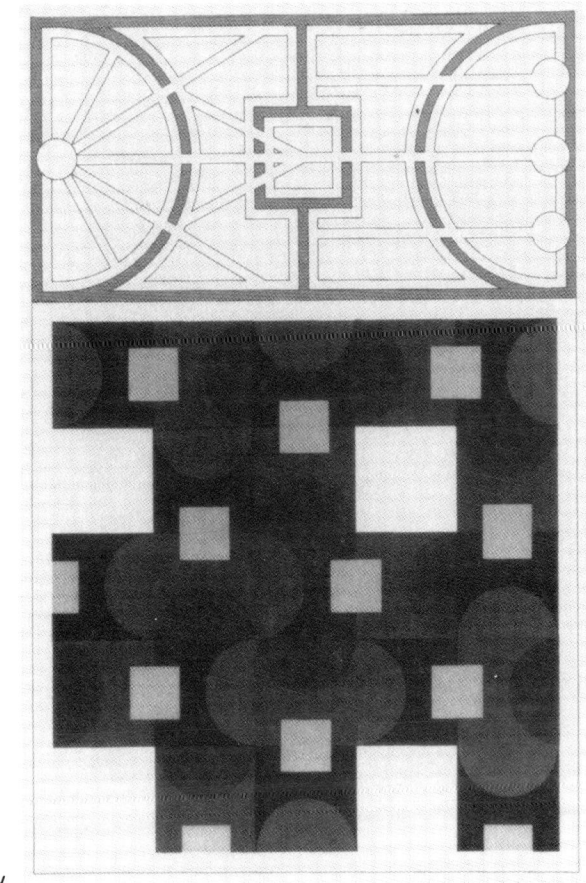

Matt Mullican
Untitled
Courtesy Carl Solway Gallery

TITLE	PUBLISHER	PRINTER	DATE	MEDIUM	DIMENSION (PAPER SIZE) IN INCHES	TYPE OF PAPER	EDITION NUMBER	NO. OF COLORS	ORIGINAL OPENING PRICE	CURRENT RETAIL PRICE
CURRENT EDITIONS:										
Untitled (Set of 16)	CSG		1988	EB/AC	22 X 15 EA	MAG	64 EA		7500 SET	10000 SET
Suite of Five Screenprints (Set of 5):									10000 SET	10000 SET
Subject	EJS	RB/BX	1992	SP	37 X 27	R/BFK	15		2200	2200
Sign	EJS	RB/BX	1992	SP	37 X 27	R/BFK	15		2200	2200
Frame	EJS	RB/BX	1992	SP	37 X 27	R/BFK	15		2200	2200
World	EJS	RB/BX	1992	SP	37 X 27	R/BFK	15		2200	2200
Elements	EJS	RB/BX	1992	SP	37 X 27	R/BFK	15		2200	2200
Untitled (Set of 10 Color Screenprints & 64 Black & White Etchings)	CSG	MPG	1993	SP/EB	30 X 22 EA (SP) 15 X 11 EA (EB)	MAG	32 EA		12000 SET	12000 SET

DAPHNE MUMFORD

EDUCATION: Bridgeport, CT; 1934
PRINTERS: Anthony Pratley, NY (AP); American Atelier, NY (AA)
PUBLISHERS: London Arts, Inc, Detroit, MI (LAI); Circle Fine Art, Chicago, IL (CFA)
GALLERIES: London Arts Gallery, Detroit, MI; Circle Galleries, Chicago, IL & New York, NY & Scottsdale, AZ & Beverly Hills, CA & Costa Mesa, CA & Sherman Oaks, CA & Palm Beach, FL & Honolulu, HI & Las Vegas, NV & New Orleans, LA & Pittsburgh, PA & Houston, TX & Seattle, WA & Northbrook, IL & San Diego, CA & San Francisco, CA

TITLE	PUBLISHER	PRINTER	DATE	MEDIUM	DIMENSION (PAPER SIZE) IN INCHES	TYPE OF PAPER	EDITION NUMBER	NO. OF COLORS	ORIGINAL OPENING PRICE	CURRENT RETAIL PRICE
CURRENT EDITIONS:										
Moonrise	LAI	AP	1978	SP	21 X 29	AP	200	6	150	200
Reflections and Penetrations	CFA	AA	1979	LC	26 X 25	AP	200		150	200

HIDEO MURANAKA

BORN: Tokyo, Japan; February 4, 1946
EDUCATION: Tokyo Nat Univ of Fine Arts & Music, Japan, BFA, 1970, MFA, 1972
TEACHING: Acad Muranaka, San Francisco, CA, 1976–79; Acad of Art Col, San Francisco, CA, 1974–75,84; San Francisco State Univ, CA, 1984,88,91 to present
AWARDS: Purchase Prizes, Wesleyan Int Exhib, Prints & Drawings, 1980; Mid-Am Biennial, Owensboro Mus of Fine Art, 1982; Second Prize, Museo Hosio, Capranica-Viterbo, Italy, 1984; Hon Mention, San Bernardino County Mus, Redland, CA, 1985; First Prize, Museo Hosio, Italy, 1988
RECENT EXHIB: San Diego Art Inst, CA, 1987; Knoxville Mus of Art, TN, 1988; Muscarelle Mus of Art, VA, 1988; Haggin Mus, Stockton, CA, 1988; Palazzo Castel Sant'Elia, Viterbo, Italy, 1988; Holter Mus of Art, MT, 1989; Chapelle de la Sorbone, Paris, France, 1990; Mus de la Commanderie, Bordeaux, France, 1990; Mus Int d'Art,, Montreal, Canada, 1991

HIDEO MURANAKA CONTINUED

COLLECTIONS: Brooklyn Mus, NY; Achenbach Found, San Francisco, CA; Palace of the Legion of Honor, San Francisco, CA; Mus Int d'Art, Montreal, Canada
PRINTERS: Artist (ART)
PUBLISHERS: Artist (ART)
GALLERIES: Collectors Gallery, Oakland Museum, Oakland, CA
MAILING ADDRESS: 179 Oak St, #W, San Francisco, CA 94102

TITLE	PUBLISHER	PRINTER	DATE	MEDIUM	DIMENSION (PAPER SIZE) IN INCHES	TYPE OF PAPER	EDITION NUMBER	NO. OF COLORS	ORIGINAL OPENING PRICE	CURRENT RETAIL PRICE
SOLD OUT EDITIONS (RARE):										
Flowing	ART	ART	1978	WC	17 X 17	HOS	20	3	200	400
CURRENT EDITIONS:										
Evening	ART	ART	1983	WC	34 X 24	KOZO	15	5	500	650
Stream	ART	ART	1984	WC	34 X 24	KOZO	15	4	500	650

HIROSHI MURATA

BORN: Tokyo, Japan; January 18, 1941
EDUCATION: Rhode Island Sch of Design, Providence, RI, BFA, 1964; Yale Univ Sch of Art, New Haven, CT, MFA, 1966
TEACHING: Asst Prof, Art, Western Michigan Univ, Kalamazoo, MI, 1966–70; From Asst Prof to Assoc Prof, Art, Trenton State Col, NJ, 1972 to present
AWARDS: Creative Artists Public Service Prog Grant, New York State Council on the Arts, NY, 1972–73; Nat Endowment for the Arts Grant, 1975–76
COLLECTIONS: Larry Aldrich Mus of Contemp Art, Ridgefield, CT; Tokyo Univ, Col of Art, Tokyo, Japan
PRINTERS: Oxbow Press, Amherst, MA (OP)
PUBLISHERS: Artist (ART)
GALLERIES: Sragow Gallery, New York, NY; Rabbet Gallery, New Brunswick, NJ
MAILING ADDRESS: c/o Dept of Art, Trenton State Col, Hillwood Lakes, Trenton, NJ 08625

TITLE	PUBLISHER	PRINTER	DATE	MEDIUM	DIMENSION (PAPER SIZE) IN INCHES	TYPE OF PAPER	EDITION NUMBER	NO. OF COLORS	ORIGINAL OPENING PRICE	CURRENT RETAIL PRICE
CURRENT EDITIONS:										
Aka Niwa	ART	OP	1980	LC	27 X 39	AP	30		300	600

ELIZABETH MURRAY

BORN: Chicago, IL; 1940
EDUCATION: Art Inst of Chicago, IL, BFA, 1962; Mills Col, Oakland, CA, MFA, 1964
TEACHING: Instr, Painting, Bard Col, Annadale on Hudson, NY, 1974–75, 76–77; Instr, Painting, Wayne State Univ, Detroit, MI, 1975; Vis Prof, Painting, California Inst of Arts, Valencia, CA, 1975–76; Vis Prof, Painting, Chicago Art Inst, IL, 1975–76; Yale Univ, New Haven, CT, 1977–78; Instr, Sch of Visual Arts, NY, 1978–80
AWARDS: Walter M Campana Award, Art Inst of Chicago, IL, 1982; Skowhegan, ME, Purchase Prize, Painting, 1986
RECENT EXHIB: Mus of Contemp Art, Los Angeles, CA, 1987; Massachusetts Inst of Technology, List Visual Arts Center, Cambridge, MA, 1987; Univ of Oklahoma, Norman, OK, 1987; Carnegie-Mellon Univ Art Gallery, Pittsburgh, PA, 1987; Paula Cooper Gallery, NY, 1987, 88; Trans Avant-Garde Gallery, Austin, TX, 1988; Inst of Contemp Art, London, England, 1988; Whitney Mus of Am Art, NY, 1988; Mus of Mod Art, NY, 1990; Graphische Sammlung Albertina, Vienna, Austria, 1990; David Winton Bell Gallery, Providence, RI, 1991; Wexner Center for the Arts, Ohio State Univ, Columbus, OH, 1991–92; Paula Cooper Gallery, NY, 1992; Locks Gallery, Phila, PA, 1993
COLLECTIONS: Detroit Inst of Arts, MI; Guggenheim Mus, NY; Hirshhorn Mus, Wash, DC; High Mus of Art, Atlanta, GA; Baltimore Mus of Art, MD; Mus of Fine Arts, Boston, MA; Art Inst of Chicago, Il; Mus of Contemp Art, Los Angeles, CA; Mus of Mod Art, NY; Metropolitan Mus of Art, NY; Philadelphia Mus of Art, PA
PRINTERS: Simca Print Artists, NY (SPA); Maurice Sanchez, NY (MS); Derriére L'Etoile Studios, NY (DES); James Miller, NY (JM); John Volny, NY (JV); Keith Brintzenhofe, NY (KB); Douglas Volle, NY (DV); John Lund, NY (JL); Hitoshi Kido, NY (HK); Nancy Mesenbourg, NY (NM); Jihon Shi, NY (JS); Bruce Wankel, NY (BW); Lorena Salcedo-Watson, NY (LSW); Universal Limited Art Editions, West Islip, NY (ULAE); Richard Dawson, NY (RD); Fine Creations, Inc, NY (FCI)
PUBLISHERS: Brooke Alexander, Inc, NY (BAI); Paula Cooper Editions, NY (PCE); Simca Print Artists, NY (SPA); Universal Limited Art Editions, West Islip, NY (ULAE); Lincoln Center, NY (LC); Gemini GEL, Los Angeles, CA (GEM)
GALLERIES: Paula Cooper Gallery, New York, NY; Locks Gallery, Phila, PA; Brooke Alexander Editions, New York, NY

Krakow (K)

Elizabeth Murray
Up Dog
Courtesy Universal Limited Art Editions

MAILING ADDRESS: c/o Paula Cooper Gallery, 155 Wooster St, New York, NY 10012

ELIZABETH MURRAY CONTINUED

TITLE	PUBLISHER	PRINTER	DATE	MEDIUM	DIMENSION (PAPER SIZE) IN INCHES	TYPE OF PAPER	EDITION NUMBER	NO. OF COLORS	ORIGINAL OPENING PRICE	CURRENT RETAIL PRICE
SOLD OUT EDITIONS (RARE):										
Mostly Mozart Festival	LC	FCI	1979	SP	30 X 30	AP	144		200	2500
SOLD OUT EDITIONS (RARE):										
Untitled States (I–IV) (Set of 5) States I, II, III-Black States IV, V-Black & Red	PCE/BAI	SPA	1980	LC	29 X 18 EA	AP	35 EA	1–2	1600 SET	12000 SET
Untitled, State Edition	PCE/BAI	SPA	1980–81	LC	28 X 22	AP	15		450	4000
Untitled	PCE/BAI	SPA	1981	LC	38 X 26	AP	35		450	3500
Untitled	SPA/ART	SPA	1982	SP	50 X 33	KOZO	50	15	1500	8000
Hand on Head	PCE/BAI	JM/JV/MS/DES	1983–84	LC	30 X 22	AP	40		750	3500
Snake Cup	PCE/BAI	JM/JV/MS/DES	1983 84	LC	32 X 25	AP	40	4	800	4000
Sniff	PCE/BAI	MS/DES	1984	LC	28 X 41	AP	31		900	4000
Untitled (Black Cup)	PCE/BAI	MS/DES	1984	LC/HC	59 X 36	AP	10		2000	8000
Inside Story	PCE/BAI	MS/DES	1984	LC/HC	59 X 36	AP/ROL	14		1800	8000
Blue Body	ULAE	KB/DV/ULAE	1986–87	LC	48 X 32	AP	70	11	2800	7500
Up Dog (K-18)	ULAE	KB/RD/DV/ULAE	1987–88	LC	53 X 36	AP	62		4000	9000
Down Dog (K-17)	ULAE	KB/RD/DV/ULAE	1988	LC	41 X 51	AP	65		3000	10000
Her Story (Book-13 Etchings & 13 Poems)		KB/JL/HK/NM JS/BW/ULAE	1988–90		12 X 18	TOR	74 EA		8500 SET	8500 SET
CURRENT EDITIONS:										
Quartet (Set of 4) (Bird, Chair, ?, Shoes)	ULAE	KB/JL/LS/	1989–90	EC	18 X 14 EA	AP/FAB	59 EA		10000 SET	12000 SET
Undoing	ULAE	HK/JL/DV/ULAE	1989–90	LC	29 X 23	SOM	60	9	3000	3000
Hat	ULAE	kB/JL/ULAE	1991	EB/MON	14 X 10	JBG	23	1	2500	2500
Birds	ULAE	kB/JL/ULAE	1991	EB/MON	14 X 10	JBG	21	1	2500	2500
Wiggle Manhattan	ULAE	KB/HK/LSW/DV/ULAE	1992	LC	59 X 29	TOR	47	15	3500	3500
Collaged Constructions (Series of 30)	GEM	GEM	1993	LC/SP/HC	30 X 23 X EA	COL/MB	1 EA	23 EA	7500 EA	7500 EA
Bulb	ULAE	JL/HK/CZ/ULAE	1993	MEZ	17 X 10	LANA	40	1	800	800

FRANCES MYERS

BORN: Racine, WI; April 16, 1936
EDUCATION: Univ of Wisconsin, Madison, WI, BA, 1959; MA, 1960; MFA, 1965; San Francisco Art Inst, CA
TEACHING: Lectr, Printmaking, St Martin's Sch of Art, London, England, 1966–67; Lectr, Printmaking, Col of Art & Design, Birmingham, England, 1966; Distinguished Prof, Art, Mills Col, Oakland, CA 1979; Vis Lectr, Art, Univ of California, Berkeley, CA, 1982; Lectr, Art, Univ of Wisconsin, Madison, WI, 1975,76,80,82,1986–88, Asst Prof, 1988–90; Assoc Prof, 1990 to present
AWARDS: H Lester Cooke Found Fel, 1977; Wisconsin Arts Council Grants, 1973,77; Nat Endowment for the Arts, Graphic Fels, 1974–75,1985–86; Print Club, Phila, PA, 1984,86,88; Purchase Award, Bradley Univ, Peoria, IL, 1989
RECENT EXHIB: Jane Haslem Gallery, Wash, DC, 1988; Univ of North Corolina, Charlotte Art Gallery, NC, 1988; Northwestern Univ, Dittman Gallery, Evanston, IL, 1989; Natasha Nicholson Works of Art, Madison, WI, 1989; Perimeter Gallery, Chicago, IL, 1988,90,92
COLLECTIONS: Metropolitan Mus of Art, NY; Chicago Art Inst, IL; Victoria & Albert Mus, London, England; Philadelphia Mus of Art, PA; Mus of Contemp Art, Chicago, IL; Brooklyn Mus, NY; Nat Coll of Fine Arts, Wash, DC; Mus of Fine Arts, Boston, MA; Nat Mus of Am Art, Smithsonian Inst, Wash, DC; Musee des Arts Decoratif, Paris, France; British Print Council, London, England
PRINTERS: Artist (ART); Gary Denmark, Palo Alto, CA (GD); Smith/Andersen Editions, Palo Alto, CA (SAE); Bill Weege, Madison, WI (BW); Andrew Rubin, Madison, WI (AR); Tandem Press, Univ of Wisconsin, Madison, WI (TanPr)
PUBLISHERS: Perimeter Press, Chicago, IL (PER); Artist (ART); Smith/Andersen Editions, Palo Alto, CA (SAE); Tandem Press, Univ of Wisconsin, Madison, WI (TanPr)
GALLERIES: Fanny Garver Gallery, Madison, WI; Gallery of Graphic Arts, New York, NY; Jane Haslem Gallery, Wash, DC; Perimeter Gallery, Chicago, IL; Paper Press Gallery & Studio, Chicago, IL; Smith/Andersen Editions, Palo Alto, CA; Natasha Nicholson Works of Art, Madison, WI

Frances Myers
Leaping Dog
Courtesy Tandem Press

MAILING ADDRESS: Rt 1, Hollandale, WI 53544

FRANCES MYERS CONTINUED

TITLE	PUBLISHER	PRINTER	DATE	MEDIUM	DIMENSION (PAPER SIZE) IN INCHES	TYPE OF PAPER	EDITION NUMBER	NO. OF COLORS	ORIGINAL OPENING PRICE	CURRENT RETAIL PRICE
CURRENT EDITIONS:										
The Frank Lloyd Wright Portfolio (Set of 6):									2100 SET	3500 SET
Johnson's Wax	PER	ART	1977	AC	22 X 30	AC	50		350	600
The Guggenheim	PER	ART	1978	AC	17 X 25	AC	50		350	600
Wingspread	PER	ART	1978	AB	22 X 30	AC	50	1	350	600
Taliesin West	PER	ART	1979	EC	20 X 24	AP/BL	50		350	600
Marin County Civic Center	PER	ART	1980	EC	18 X 28	RP/TAN	50		350	600
Unity Temple	PER	ART	1980	AC	20 X 26	RP/GREY	50		350	600
Hollyhock House	ART	ART	1980	EC	14 X 20	RP/TAN	50		200	400
Imperial Hotel	ART	ART	1980	EC	15 X 19	RP/TAN	50		200	400
Ennis House	ART	ART	1980	EC	24 X 32	AC	50		325	550
Falling Water	ART	ART	1981	AB	21 X 27	AC	50	1	300	500
Swans Down	SAE	GD/SAE	1989	MON	39 X 53 EA	AC	1 EA	Varies	1600 EA	2200 EA
Reprise	TanPr	BW/AR/TanPr	1990	EC/SG/REL/MON	38 X 52 EA	AC/W	1 EA	11 EA	1500 EA	1800 EA
Leaping Dog	TanPr	BW/AR/TanPr	1990	EC/SG/REL	74 X 48	SWP	6	5	2200	2200
Tete a Tete	TanPr	BW/AR/TanPr	1990	EC/SG/REL	67 X 48	AC/W	6	8	2500	2800
Curtain Call	TanPr	BW/AR/TanPr	1990	EC/SG/REL	38 X 52	AC/W	20	11	1350	1350
Tending Jan's Garden	TanPr	BW/AR/TanPr	1990	EC/SG/REL	40 X 62	AC/W	20	7	1750	1750
Out for Lunch	TanPr	BW/AR/TanPr	1990	EC/SG/REL	22 X 30	AC/W	40	7	450	450
Dragon Brew	TanPr	BW/AR/TanPr	1990	EC/SG/REL	41 X 29	AC/W	12	13	750	750

JOYCE STILLMAN MYERS

COLLECTIONS: Aldrich Mus, Ridgefield, CT
PRINTERS: Alexander Heinrici, NY (AH); Studio Heinrici, NY (SH)
PUBLISHERS: London Arts, Inc, Detroit, MI (LAI)
GALLERIES: Louis K Meisel, New York, NY; London Arts, Inc, Detroit, MI

TITLE	PUBLISHER	PRINTER	DATE	MEDIUM	DIMENSION (PAPER SIZE) IN INCHES	TYPE OF PAPER	EDITION NUMBER	NO. OF COLORS	ORIGINAL OPENING PRICE	CURRENT RETAIL PRICE
CURRENT EDITIONS:										
Eirodian Fantasy	LAI	AH/SH	1980	SP	22 X 29	SOM	250	28	500	500

JON NAAR

BORN: London, England
EDUCATION: Univ of Paris, France; Univ of London, England; Columbia Univ, NY
PRINTERS: American Atelier, NY (AA)
PUBLISHERS: Circle Fine Art, Chicago, IL (CFA)
GALLERIES: Circle Galleries, Chicago, IL & New York, NY & Scottsdale, AZ & Beverly Hills, CA & Costa Mesa, CA & San Diego, CA & San Francisco, CA & Sherman Oaks, CA & Palm Beach, FL & Honolulu, HI & Northbrook, IL & New Orleans, LA & Las Vegas, NV & Pittsburgh, PA & Houston, TX & Seattle, WA

TITLE	PUBLISHER	PRINTER	DATE	MEDIUM	DIMENSION (PAPER SIZE) IN INCHES	TYPE OF PAPER	EDITION NUMBER	NO. OF COLORS	ORIGINAL OPENING PRICE	CURRENT RETAIL PRICE
SOLD OUT EDITIONS (RARE):										
Kool	CFA	AA	1978	SP	22 X 28	AP	300		50	200
Hex	CFA	AA	1978	SP	26 X 42	AP	300		75	200
Franny	CFA	AA	1978	SP	26 X 42	AP	300		75	250
Red Door	CFA	AA	1978	SP	42 X 26	AP	300		75	250
CURRENT EDITIONS:										
Rube	CFA	AA	1978	SP	21 X 28	AP	300		50	200
Tree	CFA	AA	1978	SP	20 X 28	AP	300		50	200
155th Street	CFA	AA	1978	SP	20 X 28	AP	300		50	200
Eddie 135	CFA	AA	1978	SP	26 X 42	AP	300		75	250

PETER NAGY

BORN: Bridgeport, CT; 1959
EDUCATION: Parsons Sch of Design, NY, BFA, 1981
TEACHING: Vis Lectr, Grad Art Dept, Florida State Univ, Tallahassee, FL, 1984; Vis Lectr, Hartford Art Sch, CT, 1984; Vis Art, California Inst of the Arts, Valencia, CA, 1984; Vis Art, Brown Univ, Providence, RI, 1985; Lectr, International Center of Photography, NY, 1985; Grad Art Dept, Mason Gross Sch of the Arts, Rutgers Univ, New Brunswick, NJ, 1984,86
PRINTERS: Mark Patsfall, Cincinnati, OH (MP); Big Apple Sign Company, NY (BASC)
PUBLISHERS: Carl Solway Gallery, Cincinnati, OH (CSG); Baron/Boisanté Editions, NY (B/BE)
GALLERIES: Carl Solway Gallery, Cincinnati, OH; Margo Leavin Gallery, Los Angeles, CA; Jay Gorney Modern Art, New York, NY; Baron/Boisante Gallery, New York, NY

TITLE	PUBLISHER	PRINTER	DATE	MEDIUM	DIMENSION (PAPER SIZE) IN INCHES	TYPE OF PAPER	EDITION NUMBER	NO. OF COLORS	ORIGINAL OPENING PRICE	CURRENT RETAIL PRICE
CURRENT EDITIONS:										
Cancer Logos	CSG	MP	1988	WB	44 X 44	AP88	30		1500	1800
Lost (Framed)	B/BE	BASC	1990	SP	61 X 61	CANVAS	10	1	6500	6500

THOMAS VINCENT NAKASHIMA

BORN: Iowa; 1941
EDUCATION: Loras Col, Dubuque, IA, 1966; Univ of Notre Dame, South Bend, IN, MA, MFA, 1968
TEACHING: Notre Dame Univ, South Bend, IN, 1966–68; Columbus Col of Art & Design, Columbus, OH, 1968–73; West Virginia Univ, Morgantown, WVA, 1973–81
COLLECTIONS: Notre Dame Univ, South Bend, IN; Columbus Gallery of Fine Arts, OH; West Virginia Univ Art Gallery, Morgantown, WVA; Davidson Col, Davidson, NC; Univ of Tennessee, Knoxville, TN; Michigan State Univ, East Lansing, MI; Nasson Col, Springvale, ME; Emory Univ, Atlanta, GA; Southern Illinois Univ, Edwardsville, IL; Univ of Utah, Salt Lake City, UT; Univ of Nevada, Reno, NV; Kalamazoo Inst, Kalamazoo, MI; Univ of Georgia, Athens, GA; Univ of Nebraska, Lincoln, NE; Univ of Missouri, Columbia, MO; Ringling Mus of Art, Sarasota, FL; Univ of Oklahoma, Norman OK; Indianapolis Mus of Art, IN; Springfield Art Mus, MO; Madison Art Center, WI; Drake Univ, Des Moines, IA
PRINTERS: Will Petersen, Chicago, IL (WP); Plucked Chicken Press, Evanston, IL (PCP)
PUBLISHERS: Balkin Editions, Chicago, IL (BE)
GALLERIES: Henri Gallery, Wash, DC; Anton Gallery, Wash, DC; Bernice Steinbaum Gallery, New York, NY

TITLE	PUBLISHER	PRINTER	DATE	MEDIUM	DIMENSION (PAPER SIZE) IN INCHES	TYPE OF PAPER	EDITION NUMBER	NO. OF COLORS	ORIGINAL OPENING PRICE	CURRENT RETAIL PRICE
CURRENT EDITIONS:										
Kimono I	BE	WP/PCP	1981	LC	23 X 23	BBG	25	6	250	400
Komono II	BE	WP/PCP	1981	LC	22 X 23	AC/B	25	4	250	400
Blossom (With Yardstick and Ruler Affixed)	BE	WP/PCP	1982	LC	30 X 40	R/BFK	25	4	400	600

HITOSHI NAKAZATO

BORN: Tokyo, Japan; March 15, 1936
EDUCATION: Tama Col of Arts, Tokyo, Japan, BFA, Painting, 1960; Univ of Wisconsin, Milwaukee, WI, MS, Art, Printmaking, 1964; Univ of Wisconsin, Madison, WI, 1964; Univ of Pennsylvania, Phila, PA, MFA, Painting, with Piero Dorazio, 1966
TEACHING: Tama Col of Art, Tokyo, Japan, 1968–71; Univ of Pennsylvania, Phila, PA, 1971–73, 1973–79, 1979 to present
AWARDS: John D. Rockefeller Fel, 1966–67; Creative Artists Public Service Prog Grant, NY, 1974–75; Pennsylvania Acad of Fine Arts, Phila, PA
COLLECTIONS: Mus of Mod Art, NY; Philadelphia Mus of Art, PA; Nat Mus of Mod Art, Kyoto, Japan; Brooklyn Mus, NY; Nat Gallery of Art, Wash, DC; Moore Col of Art, Phila, PA
PRINTERS: Artist (ART)
PUBLISHERS: Artist (ART)
GALLERIES: Tokyo Gallery, Tokyo, Japan
MAILING ADDRESS: 361 W 36th St, New York, NY 10018

TITLE	PUBLISHER	PRINTER	DATE	MEDIUM	DIMENSION (PAPER SIZE) IN INCHES	TYPE OF PAPER	EDITION NUMBER	NO. OF COLORS	ORIGINAL OPENING PRICE	CURRENT RETAIL PRICE
CURRENT EDITIONS:										
Kerr #1, #2, #3	ART	ART	1981	AB	30 X 44 EA	R/BFK	50 EA	1 EA	800 EA	1500 EA
Cey #1, #2, #3	ART	ART	1981	AB	30 X 44 EA	R/BFK	50 EA	1 EA	800 EA	1500 EA
Ferro #1, #2, #3, #4	ART	ART	1982	AB	30 X 44 EA	R/BFK	50 EA	1 EA	800 EA	1500 EA

ANTHONY NAPONIC (GEORGE)

BORN: Adamsburg, PA; January 16, 1954
EDUCATION: Univ of Pittsburgh, PA, 1971–73; Kansas City Art Inst, Kansas City, MO, BFA, 1973–74
TEACHING: Instr, Printmaking, Kansas City Art Inst, MO, 1975–76,87
AWARDS: Mid-Am Art Alliance Grant, 1982–83; Emerging Artist Award, Nat Endowment for the Arts Grant, 1983
RECENT EXHIB: Douglas Drake Gallery, NY, 1988; Mus of Mod Art, NY, 1988
COLLECTIONS: Kansas City Art Inst, Kansas City, MO; Univ of Pittsburgh, PA; Madison Art Center, WI; Lake Forest Col Mus, IL
PRINTERS: Jack Lemon, Chicago, IL (JL); Landfall Press, Inc, Chicago, IL (LPI)
PUBLISHERS: Landfall Press, Inc, Chicago, IL (LPI)
GALLERIES: Zolla/Lieberman Gallery, Chicago, IL; Douglas Drake Gallery, New York, NY; Landfall Press, Inc, Chicago, IL; Concept Art Gallery, Pittsburgh, PA; Quartet Editions, New York, NY
MAILING ADDRESS: 106 Suffolk St, #5-A, New York, NY 10002

TITLE	PUBLISHER	PRINTER	DATE	MEDIUM	DIMENSION (PAPER SIZE) IN INCHES	TYPE OF PAPER	EDITION NUMBER	NO. OF COLORS	ORIGINAL OPENING PRICE	CURRENT RETAIL PRICE
CURRENT EDITIONS:										
Behind the Lines	LPI	JL/LPI	1982	LC	21 X 27	AP/W	35	6	250	400
Back Up Lady	LPI	JL/LPI	1982	LC	21 X 27	AP/W	35	5	250	400
Never Enough Water	LPI	JL/LPI	1982	LC	21 X 27	AP/W	35	5	250	400

PAUL NARKIEWICZ

BORN: USA; September 10, 1937
EDUCATION: Philadelphia Col of Art, PA
TEACHING: Moore Col of Art, Phila, PA; Cooper Union, NY; Rutgers Univ, Camden, NJ; Philadelphia Col of Art, PA
PRINTERS: Chip Elwell, NY (CE); Roni Henning, NY (RH); Artist (ART)
PUBLISHERS: 724 Prints, NY (724P); Orion Editions, NY (OE); Narkiewicz/Pavise/Monte, NY (NPM)
GALLERIES: Orion Editions, New York, NY

TITLE	PUBLISHER	PRINTER	DATE	MEDIUM	DIMENSION (PAPER SIZE) IN INCHES	TYPE OF PAPER	EDITION NUMBER	NO. OF COLORS	ORIGINAL OPENING PRICE	CURRENT RETAIL PRICE
SOLD OUT EDITIONS (RARE):										
Cypresses	OE	ART	1978	LC	20 X 25	AP	27	7	75	500
Pines	OE	ART	1978	PO	27 X 35	AP	74	18	200	1000
Meadow	OE	ART	1978	LC	15 X 21	AC/W	21	4	75	350
Road In	OE	CE	1978	LIN	16 X 23	AC/W	15	1	75	350
Shadows	OE	ART	1979	PO	24 X 33	AC/W	78	19	125	500

PAUL NARKIEWICZ CONTINUED

TITLE	PUBLISHER	PRINTER	DATE	MEDIUM	DIMENSION (PAPER SIZE) IN INCHES	TYPE OF PAPER	EDITION NUMBER	NO. OF COLORS	ORIGINAL OPENING PRICE	CURRENT RETAIL PRICE
SOLD OUT EDITIONS (RARE):										
Open Field	OE	ART	1979	LC	16 X 22	AC/W	97	9	75	350
Via Aprile	OE	RH	1979	PO	13 X 15	AC/W	25	7	75	250
Arles	OE	RH	1979	PO	22 X 30	AC/W	62	17	125	350
Untitled (Profile)	724P	ART	1981	LC	17 X 20	AP	23	8	300	400
Untitled (Smoker)	724P	ART	1981	LC	35 X 29	AC/W	44	8	400	500
Vase	724P	ART	1982	LC	37 X 29	AC/W	33	7	500	600
Cinnamon Hill I	OE	RH	1982	PO	26 X 33	AC/W	72	20	350	500
Goldfish	NPM	ART	1983	LC	26 X 20	RdB	14	2	250	400

JAMES NARES

RECENT EXHIB: Michael Klein Gallery, NY, 1989; Paul Kasmin Gallery, NY, 1993

PRINTERS: Maurice Payne, NY (MP); Leslie Miller, NY (LM); Grenfel Press, NY (GrP)
PUBLISHERS: Fawbush Editions, NY; Grenfel Press, NY (GrP)
GALLERIES: Fawbush Gallery, New York, NY; Paul Kasmin Gallery, New York, NY

TITLE	PUBLISHER	PRINTER	DATE	MEDIUM	DIMENSION (PAPER SIZE) IN INCHES	TYPE OF PAPER	EDITION NUMBER	NO. OF COLORS	ORIGINAL OPENING PRICE	CURRENT RETAIL PRICE
CURRENT EDITIONS:										
Panther Trumpets	FE	MP	1986	MON	39 X 29 EA	JP	1 EA	Varies	1200 EA	1500 EA
The Golden Ladder (Series of 12)	GrP	LM/GrP	1988	WC	30 X 15	KOZO	26		2400 SET 400 EA	3000 SET 425 EA

NORMAN NAROTZKY

BORN: Brooklyn, NY; March 14, 1928
EDUCATION: Brooklyn Col, NY, BA, 1949; Art Students League, NY, 1949–52; Cooper Union Art Sch, Certificate, 1952; BFA 1979; Atelier 17, Paris, France, 1954–56; Acad of Fine Arts, Munich, Germany, 1956–57; New York Univ Grad Sch of Arts and Science, 1957–58
TEACHING: Artist's Studio, Cadaques, Spain, 1959–69; Northern Michigan Univ, Marquette, MI, Summer, 1979; Artist's Studio, Barcelona, Spain, 1976 to present
AWARDS: Wooley Found Fel, Paris, France, 1954–55; French Govt Fel, Paris, France, 1955–56; Purchase Prize, Philadelphia Mus of Art, PA, 1956; Fulbright Fel, Munich, West Germany, 1956–57; Miniprint International Cadagues Award, 1982; Painting Grant, Generalitat de Catalunya, Barcelona, Spain, 1983; Honorable Mention, Premi de Dibuix Joan Miro, Barcelona, Spain, 1990; Grand Prize, Bienal, Barcelona, Spain, 1987
RECENT EXHIB: Rombach Scheuer Gallery, Staufen, West Germany, 1989; Manhattan East Gallery, NY, 1990; Centre Cultural Gallery, Barcelona, Spain, 1990; Centre d'Art, Barcelona, Spain, 1990; Galeria d'Art Port Lligat, Cadaques, Spain, 1989,91

COLLECTIONS: Philadelphia Mus of Art; Univ of Texas Art Gallery, Austin, TX (James A Michener Coll); Mill Col Art Gallery, Oakland, CA; Mus Popular de Arte Contemp de Villafames, Spain; Mus de Arte Contemp, Madrid, Spain; Mus de Arte Contemp, de Villaneauva y Geltru, Spain; Mus de Arte Contemp, FC, Barcelona, Spain
PRINTERS: Pons (PONS); Tomas Pi (TP); Barbara (BAR); Tobella (TOB); Zerkowitz (ZER); Torrents (TOR); Taller Galeria Fort, Barcelona, Spain (TGF); Joan Barbara, Barcelona, Spain (JB); Artist (ART); Masafumi Yamamoto, Barcelona, Spain (MY)
PUBLISHERS: Collectors Guild, Ltd, NY (CG); Fine Arts 260, NY (FA260); Taller-Galeria Fort, Barcelona, Spain (TGF); Galeria Eude, Barcelona, Spain (GE); Intra-Realist Group, Florence, Italy (IRG); Miquel Plana, Girona, Spain (MP)
GALLERIES: Intra-Realist Group, Florence, Italy; Fine Arts 260, NY; Taller Galeria Fort, Barcelona, Spain; Taller de Pintura, Barcelona, Spain; Galeria Eude, Barcelona, Spain; Arbitrage Gallery, New York, NY; Anita Shapolsky Gallery, New York, NY; Mahattan East Gallery, New York, NY
MAILING ADDRESS: Corcega 198-6, 08036, Barcelona, Spain

TITLE	PUBLISHER	PRINTER	DATE	MEDIUM	DIMENSION (PAPER SIZE) IN INCHES	TYPE OF PAPER	EDITION NUMBER	NO. OF COLORS	ORIGINAL OPENING PRICE	CURRENT RETAIL PRICE
SOLD OUT EDITIONS (RARE):										
Red Moon	ART	ART	1955	EC/ENG	20 X 26	AP	50	3	35	650
Vol d'Insectes	ART	PONS	1956	LC	15 X 22	VGZ	25	3	25	400
Los Ojos de Los Muertos	IRG	TOB	1968	M/REL	15 X 10	FAB	100	2	25	250
A Game, a Rose and Time	CG	TOR	1969	LC	27 X 20	GP	275	8	35	550
Death Flower	ART	TOR	1969	LC	20 X 22	AP	12	1	85	300
Renacimiente de Venus	FA260	ZER	1972	LC	27 X 21	GP	260	8	46	650
Woman	ART	TOB	1977	SP	26 X 20	GP	55	1	50	250
Living Landscape	TGF	TGF	1982	EC	8 X 8	AP	100	2	50	175
Llum de Ponent (Included in Book "Cadaques" by Josep Pla Together with Etchings by 19 Other Artists)	MP	MP	1989	EC	17 X 13	GP	125	5	1200 SET	POR
CURRENT EDITIONS:										
Pauture	ART	ART	1964	PO	26 X 20	GP	25	5	50	550
Odalisque	ART	ART	1964	PO	21 X 26	GP	25	8	50	550
Torso	ART	ART	1964	PO	26 X 20	GP	25	8	50	550
He Robbed the Glendale Train	ART	TOR	1965	LC	36 X 21	GP	45	3	50	550
Red Venus	ART	ZER	1973	LC	26 X 22	GP	140	8	75	475
Black Venus	TGF	TGF	1973	EB	20 X 28	GP	40	1	165	400
Birth of Venus I, II	TGF	TGF	1973	EC	20 X 28 EA	GP	40 EA	2 EA	165 EA	400 EA
Death of Venus I, II	TGF	TGF	1973	EC	20 X 28 EA	GP	40 EA	2 EA	165 EA	400 EA
La Flor de Tu Vientre	ART	TP	1977	LC	36 X 25	AP	125	9	150	500

NORMAN NAROTZKY CONTINUED

TITLE	PUBLISHER	PRINTER	DATE	MEDIUM	DIMENSION (PAPER SIZE) IN INCHES	TYPE OF PAPER	EDITION NUMBER	NO. OF COLORS	ORIGINAL OPENING PRICE	CURRENT RETAIL PRICE
CURRENT EDITIONS:										
Woman	ART	TOB	1977	SP	26 X 20	GP	55	1	50	200
Mountain El Pani	TGF	LA	1978	LC	21 X 31	GP	200	9	80	200
La Montaña	CE99	BAR	1982	EC	20 X 26	AP	99	1	POR	POR
Rocky Coast, Blue Sea	ART	ART	1983	PO	18 X 21	GP	10	18	200	400
Landscape: Green and Pink	ART	ART	1983	PO	18 X 21	GP	5	7	200	400
Landscape: Pink and Brown	ART	ART	1983	PO	18 X 21	GP	10	11	200	400
Landscape: Pink and Purple	ART	ART	1983	PO	18 X 21	GP	10	11	200	400
Black Sky	ART	ART	1983	PO	18 X 21	GP	10	16	200	400
Green Hills	ART	ART	1983	PO	18 X 21	GP	10	8	200	400
Muntanya Cremada	ART	ART	1987	COL	7 X 8	GP	29	2	100	175
Night Moutain	ART	ART	1991	PO	7 X 9	GP	25	3	160	175
The Raven Suite (Set of 9)	ART	MY	1992	EC	19 X 15 EA	AP	45 EA	2–4 EA	2000 SET / 400 EA	2000 SET / 400 EA

ROBERT NATKIN

BORN: Chicago, IL; November 7, 1930
EDUCATION: Art Inst of Chicago, IL, BA, 1952
TEACHING: Ford Found, Art in Res, Kalamazoo Inst of Arts, MI
RECENT EXHIB: Gimpel & Weitzenhoffer Gallery, NY, 1987,89; Hockaday Center for the Arts, Kalispell, MT, 1989; Bradley Univ, Heuser Art Center Gallery & Hartmann Center Gallery, Peoria, IL, 1992
COLLECTIONS: Solomon R Guggenheim Mus, NY; Whitney Mus of Am Art, NY; Los Angeles County Mus of Art; Mus of Fine Art, Houston, TX; Carnegie Inst, Pittsburgh, PA; Wadsworth Atheneum, Hartford, CT; Akron Art Inst, OH; Albright-Knox Art Gallery, Buffalo, NY; Art Inst of Chicago, Il; Brooklyn Mus, NY; Centre Pompidou, Paris, France; Columbus Mus, OH; Duke Univ, Durham, NC; Fine Arts Gallery of San Diego, CA; Hirshhorn Mus, Wash, DC; Krannert Art Mus, Univ of Illinois, Champaign-Urbana, IL; Metropolitan Mus, NY; Milwaukee Art Center, WI; Mint Mus, Charlotte, NC; Pennsylvania State Univ, University Park, PA; Rhode Island Sch of Design, Providence, RI; Univ of Oklahoma, Norman, OK; Mus of Fine Arts, Houston, TX; Mus of Mod Art, NY; Oklahoma Art Center, Oklahoma City, OK; San Francisco Mus, CA; Worcester Art Mus, MA
PRINTERS: Styria Studio, NY (SS)
PUBLISHERS: Styria Studio, NY (SS)
GALLERIES: Tortue Gallery, Santa Monica, CA; Gloria Luria Gallery, Bay Harbor Islands, FL; Gimpel & Weitzenhoffer Gallery, New York, NY; Meridian Gallery, New York, NY & Chicago, IL; Miller Gallery, Cincinnati, OH; Jeffrey Fuller Fine Art, Phila, PA; Graphics Gallery, San Francisco, CA; Baum Gallery, San Francisco, CA; Gimpel Fils Gallery, London, England; Klonarides Gallery, Toronto, Canada; André Emmerich Gallery, New York, NY; Helander Gallery, Palm Beach, CA; John Szoke Graphics, New York, NY; Brenda Kroos Gallery, Columbus, OH; Watson Gallery, Houston, TX; Stein Bartlow Gallery, Ltd, Chicago, IL; Douglas Drake Gallery, New York, NY; Galerie Internationale, Bloomfield Hills, MI
MAILING ADDRESS: 24 Mark Twain Lane, West Redding, CT 06896

TITLE	PUBLISHER	PRINTER	DATE	MEDIUM	DIMENSION (PAPER SIZE) IN INCHES	TYPE OF PAPER	EDITION NUMBER	NO. OF COLORS	ORIGINAL OPENING PRICE	CURRENT RETAIL PRICE
SOLD OUT EDITIONS (RARE):										
Large Colored Etching	SS	SS	1979	EC	50 X 38	AE	75		1300	2500
Black Etching	SS	SS	1979	EB	35 X 42	AE	75		1000	2000
Small Colored Etching	SS	SS	1979	EC	29 X 25	AC/W	50		900	1800
Small Colored Etching	SS	SS	1979	EC	25 X 29	AC/W	75		900	1800
Apollo Series	SS	SS	1980	LC	38 X 60	AP/WA	75		1500	3500
Bern Series	SS	SS	1980	LC	42 X 30	AP/B	31		1100	3000
Red Bern Series	SS	SS	1980	LC	44 X 34	R/BFK	75		1100	3000
Apollo	SS	SS	1980	LC	38 X 60	AWP	75	56	1500	3500
Face Series	SS	SS	1980	LC	43 X 42	AP/ROL	75	15	1300	2500
Face Series	SS	SS	1980	LC/CO	37 X 44	AP/ROL	75	10	1200	3000
Homage to Louis Sullivan and Frank Lloyd Wright Series	SS	SS	1980	LC/CO	42 X 30	AC/W	75		1000	2000
Color Bath Series Oval	SS	SS	1980	LC	48 X 30	AP/B	75		1000	2000
Bern Series (Blue X)	SS	SS	1981	LC	44 X 34	AC/W	35		1100	3000
Blue Bern Series	SS	SS	1981	LC	42 X 30	R/BFK	30	21	1100	3000
Yellow Bern Series	SS	SS	1981	LC	44 X 34	RP/ROL	50		1100	3000
Bern Series	SS	SS	1981	LC	30 X 45	RNP/G	50		1100	3000
Bern Series	SS	SS	1981	LC/CO	44 X 34	R/BFK	25		1000	3000
Face Series	SS	SS	1981	LC/CO	34 X 34	RP/ROL	35		1000	3000
Little Apollo Series	SS	SS	1982	LC/HC	42 X 30	AP/WA	75		1000	2000
Intimate Lighting Series	SS	SS	1983	LC	30 X 45	R/BFK	70		1000	2000
Bern Series	SS	SS	1983	LC/SP	42 X 78	AP/ROL	75	17	2000	4000

JOE NEILL

BORN: New Eagle, PA; August 29, 1944
EDUCATION: Westminster Col, New Wilmington, PA, BA, 1966; Bowling Green Univ, OH, MFA, 1968
COLLECTIONS: Mem Art Gallery, Rochester, NY; Tyler Mus of Art, TX
PRINTERS: Aeropress, NY (A); Patricia Branstead, NY (PB)
PUBLISHERS: Diane Villani Editions, NY (DVE); Robert Freidus Gallery, NY (RF)
GALLERIES: Robert Freidus Gallery, New York, NY; Magnuson Gallery, Boston, MA; Roger Ramsay Gallery, Chicago, IL; Diane Villani Editions, New York, NY; Vanderwoude/Tananbaum Gallery, New York, NY
MAILING ADDRESS: 392 Broadway, New York, NY 10013

TITLE	PUBLISHER	PRINTER	DATE	MEDIUM	DIMENSION (PAPER SIZE) IN INCHES	TYPE OF PAPER	EDITION NUMBER	NO. OF COLORS	ORIGINAL OPENING PRICE	CURRENT RETAIL PRICE
CURRENT EDITIONS:										
Earth Structure with Red Shift	DVE/RF	PB/A	1981	EB/A/EMB	24 X 24	R/BFK	50	2	400	850

BRUCE NAUMAN

BORN: Wayne, IN; December 6, 1941
EDUCATION: Univ of Wisconsin, Madison, WI, BS, 1960–64; Univ of California, Davis, CA, MFA, 1965–66, with William Wiley & Robert Arneson
TEACHING: Instr, San Francisco Inst, CA, 1966–68; Instr, Sculpture, Univ of California, Irvine, CA, 1970
AWARDS: Nat Endowment for the Arts Grant, 1968; Aspen Inst for Humanistic Studies Grant, CO, 1970
RECENT EXHIB: New Museum, NY, 1987; Houston Mus of Contemp Art, TX, 1987–88; Los Angeles Mus of Contemp Art, CA, 1988; Univ of California Art Mus, CA, 1988; Mus of Mod Art, NY, 1987,88; Whitney Mus of Am Art, 1987,88; Art Center Col of Design, Pasadena, CA, 1989; Mus d'Art Moderne, Saint-Etienne, France, 1989; Leo Castelli Gallery, NY, 1990; Mus of Holography, NY, 1989,92; Art Center, Col of Design, Pasadena, CA, 1992; Governors State Univ, Nathan Manilow Sculpture Park, University Park, IL, 1989,92; Sperone Westwater Gallery, NY, 1988,90,92
COLLECTIONS: Whitney Mus of Am Art, NY; Wallraf-Richartz Mus, Cologne, Germany; Kunstverein, Aachen, Germany; St Louis Mus, MO; Los Angeles County Mus, CA; Australian Nat Gallery, Canberra, Australia; Fogg Mus of Art, Cambridge, MA
PRINTERS: Cirrus Editions Workshop, Los Angeles, CA (CEW); Gemini GEL, Los Angeles, CA (GEM); Ed Hamilton, Los Angeles, CA (EG); Chris Cordes, Los Angeles, CA (CC); Ron Mills, Los Angeles, CA (RM); Arber & Son Editions, Alameda, NM (ASE)
PUBLISHERS: Cirrus Editions, Los Angeles, CA (CE); Gemini GEL, Los Angeles, CA (GEM); Aetna (A); Castelli Graphics, NY (CG); Nicholas Wilder Gallery, Los Angeles, CA (NWG); Brooke Alexander, Inc, NY (BAI)
GALLERIES: Cirrus Editions, Los Angeles, CA; Texas Gallery, Houston, TX; Richard Hines Gallery, Seattle, WA; Donald Young Gallery, Seattle, WA; Sperone Westwater Gallery, New York, NY; Leo Castelli Gallery, New York, NY; Brooke Alexander, Inc, New York, NY; Reinhold-Brown Gallery, New York, NY; Gemini GEL, Los Angeles, CA; Cynthia Drennon Fine Arts Resources, Los Angeles, CA; Daniel Weinberg Gallery, Santa Monica, CA; Pence Fine Art, Inc, Los Angeles, CA; Anthony Meier Fine Arts, San Francisco, CA; Laura Carpenter Fine Art, Santa Fe, NM; 65 Thompson Street, New York, NY
MAILING ADDRESS: c/o Castelli Gallery, 420 W Broadway, New York, NY 10012

Bruce Nauman
Pearl Masque
Courtesy Gemini GEL

Bruce Nauman
Double Face
Courtesy Gemini GEL

TITLE	PUBLISHER	PRINTER	DATE	MEDIUM	DIMENSION (PAPER SIZE) IN INCHES	TYPE OF PAPER	EDITION NUMBER	NO. OF COLORS	ORIGINAL OPENING PRICE	CURRENT RETAIL PRICE
SOLD OUT EDITIONS (RARE):										
Studies for Holograms (Set of 5)	A/CG	CEW	1970	SP	26 X 26 EA	AP/W	150 EA		700 SET	22000 SET
Untitled (Gray) (#43c)	CE/CG/NW	EH/CEW	1971	LC	30 X 42	AP/W	75	3	250	15000
Untitled (Green)	CG/NWG	EH/CEW	1971	LC	22 X 28	AP/W	100	3	250	15000
Untitled (Salmon Pink)	CG/NWG	EH/CEW	1971	LC	22 X 28	AP/W	100		250	15000
Raw War	CG/NWG	EH/CEW	1971	LC	22 X 28	AP/W	100	3	250	15000
Untitled (#2cl)	CE	EH/CEW	1972	EB	27 X 36	R/BFK	15	1	500	18000
Untitled (#1cl)	CE	EH/CEW	1972	DPT	27 X 36	R/BFK	25	1	500	18000
Untitled (#3cl)	CE	EH/CEW	1973	EB/A	36 X 27	R/BFK	25	1	350	18000
Doe Fawn	CE	CC/CEW	1973	LC	32 X 45	R/RO	50	2	250	15000
Perfect Door	CE	RM/CEW	1973	LC	32 X 26	R/RO	50	1	150	12000
Perfect Odor	CE	RM/CEW	1973	LC	32 X 26	R/RO	50	1	150	12000
Perfect Rodo	CE	RM/CEW	1973	LC	32 X 26	R/RO	50	1	150	12000
Eat Death	GEM	GEM	1973	LC	43 X 31	ARJ	68	3	250	15000
Sugar/Ragus	GEM	GEM	1973	LC/SP	28 X 36	ARJ	57	3	250	15000
Suck Cuts	GEM	GEM	1973	LC	39 X 31	ARJ	34	3	150	12000
Pay Attention	GEM	GEM	1973	LC	38 X 28	ARJ	50	1	500	18000
Vision	GEM	GEM	1973	LC	25 X 33	AP88	40		150	18000
Clear Vision	GEM	GEM	1973	LC/SP	36 X 49	ARJ	50	3	500	18000
Suposter	GEM	GEM	1973	LC/SP	36 X 30	AP88	72		150	18000
M Ampere	CE	EH/CEW	1973	LC	31 X 45	R/RO	50	2	250	18000
Normal Desires	CE	EH/CEW	1973	LC	24 X 35	CP	50	1	250	18000
Untitled (Black)	CE	CEW	1975	AC	36 X 27	AC	25	1	250	18000
Oiled Dead	GEM	GEM	1975	LC/SP	46 X 50	AC	10		350	20000
Oiled Dead, State I	GEM	GEM	1975	LC/SP	46 X 50	AC	14		350	20000
Proof of the Pudding	GEM	GEM	1975	LC	36 X 43	AC	18		350	18000
Sundry Obras Nuevas (Set of 5):										
Help Me, Hurt Me	GEM	GEM	1975	LC	36 X 51	AC	20	1	500	15000
Dead	GEM	GEM	1975	LC	34 X 49	AC	15	1	500	12000
Ah Ha	GEM	GEM	1975	SP	29 X 41	AC	44	1	500	12000
No Sweat	GEM	GEM	1975	SP	40 X 32	AC	25	1	400	5500
Silver Grotto/Yellow Grotto	GEM	GEM	1975	SP	30 X 83	AC	20		800	12000

BRUCE NAUMAN CONTINUED

TITLE	PUBLISHER	PRINTER	DATE	MEDIUM	DIMENSION (PAPER SIZE) IN INCHES	TYPE OF PAPER	EDITION NUMBER	NO. OF COLORS	ORIGINAL OPENING PRICE	CURRENT RETAIL PRICE
SOLD OUT EDITIONS (RARE):										
False Passage	GEM	GEM	1975	AC	26 X 35	AC	20	1	375	10000
Double Face	GEM	GEM	1981	LB	25 X 34	AC	50	1	375	6000
Life Mask (G-941)	GEM	GEM	1981	LB	28 X 38	AC	50	1	375	6000
Pearl Masque (G-942)	GEM	GEM	1981	LB	29 X 38	AC	50	1	375	6000
No-State	GEM	GEM	1981	LC	30 X 43	AC	25	2	500	12000
Underground Passage	GEM	GEM	1981	DPT	26 X 35	R/BFK	20	1	375	5000
Underground Passage	GEM	GEM	1981	DPT	26 X 35	R/BFK	20	1	375	5000
No	GEM	GEM	1981	LC	30 X 43	AC	21		500	15000
Floor Drain	GEM	GEM	1985	AC/DPT	39 X 28	R/BFK	32	1	600	11000
Shit and Die	GEM	GEM	1985	DPT	16 X 23	R/BFK	38	1	400	9500
TV Clown	BAI	ASE	1987–88	LB	30 X 44	TRANS	35	1	1500	9000
Clown Taking a Shit	BAI	ASE	1988	LC	42 X 30	AC	35		8000	12000
Small Carousel	BAI		1988	DPT	16 X 18	R/BFK	35		5000	6000
Large Carousel, State I	BAI		1988	DPT	34 X 40	R/BFK	12		8000	10000
Use Me	BAI		1988	EB	16 X 18	R/BFK	35	1	5000	6000
CURRENT EDITIONS:										
Violins/Violence	GEM	GEM	1985	DPT	28 X 39	R/BFK	23	1	700	4000
Suspended Chair	GEM	GEM	1985	DPT	39 X 28	R/BFK	31	1	600	4000
House Divided	GEM	GEM	1985	EC/DPT	28 X 39	R/BFK	23	1	700	4000
Untitled (Cast Iron Ring)	GEM	GEM	1985	MULT	23 X 23 X 3	IRON	25		2500	9000
I Learned Helplessness from Rats	BAI		1988	EB/DPT	16 X 18	R/BFK	35	1	3500	4500
Learned Helplessness from Rats	BAI		1988	EB	16 X 18	R/BFK	35	1	3500	4500
Untitled (#62)	BAI		1989–90	EB/HG	17 X 20	R/BFK	45	1	3000	3500
Untitled (#63)	BAI		1989–90	EB/HG	20 X 17	R/BFK	45	1	3000	3500
Untitled (#64)	BAI		1989–90	EB/HG	17 X 20	R/BFK	45	1	3000	3500
Untitled (#65)	BAI		1989–90	EB/HG	17 X 20	R/BFK	45	1	3000	3500
Untitled (#66)	BAI		1989–90	DPT	17 X 20	R/BFK	34	1	3000	3500
Untitled (#67)	BAI		1989–90	DPT	17 X 20	R/BFK	40	1	3000	3500
Untitled (#68-State)	BAI		1990–91	DPT/AB	17 X 20	R/BFK	38	1	3500	3500
Untitled (#69)	BAI		1989–90	DPT	17 X 20	R/BFK	45	1	3500	4000
Untitled (Hands)	BAI		1990–91	DPT/AB	17 X 20	R/BFK	38	1	2500	2500

JIM NAWARA

BORN: Chicago, IL; January 25, 1945
EDUCATION: Art Inst of Chicago, IL, BFA; Univ of Illinois, Champaign, IL, MFA; Inst of Chicago Art Sch, IL, BFA, 1967; Univ of Illinois, Champaign, IL, MFA, 1969
TEACHING: Prof, Dept of Art, Wayne State Univ, Detroit, MI, 1969 to present
AWARDS: Grants, Ball State Univ, Muncie, IN, 1971,74,75; Michigan Found for the Arts, 1981,83; Research Awards, Wayne State Univ, Detroit, MI, 1977,81,84; Purchase Award, Butler Inst of Am Art, Youngstown, OH, 1972; Ball State Univ Grants, Muncie, IN, 1971,74,75; Purchase Award, Michigan Printmakers, Detroit Inst of Arts, MI, 1977; Michigan Found for the Arts, 1981,83; Creative Artists Grants, Michigan Council for the Arts, 1982,85,88,89; Res Awards, Wayne State Univ, Detroit, MI, 1978,81,84,88,90
RECENT EXHIB: Nawara Gallery, Walled Lake, MI 1989; Wayne State Univ, MI, 1992
COLLECTIONS: Cleveland Mus, OH; Detroit Inst of Arts, MI; Boston Mus of Fine Arts, MA; Butler Inst of Am Art, Youngstown, OH; Bradford City Art Gallery, Bradford, England; Auckland City Art Gallery, New Zealand; Nat Mus of Warsaw, Poland; Jagiellonian Univ, Karkow, Poland; Auburn Univ, AL; Northern Illinois Univ, DeKalb, IL; Dulin Gallery, Knoxville, TN; Univ of Western Ontario, London, ON, Canada; Minot State Col, ND; Western Michigan Univ, Kalamazoo, MI; Georgia State Univ, Atlanta, GA; South Dakota State Univ, Brooklings, SD; Appalachian State Univ, Boone, NC; Alma Col, MI; Wesleyan Col, Macon, GA; Univ of California, Chico, CA; Nat Air and Space Mus, Wash, DC; Toledo Mus of Art, OH
PRINTERS: Norman Stewart, Bloomfield Hills, MI (NS); Stewart & Stewart, Bloomfield Hills, MI (S-S); Douglas Semivan, Royal Oak, MI (DS); Paul Martyka, Rock Hill, SC (PM); Typocraft Company, Detroit, MI (TC)
PUBLISHERS: Stewart & Stewart, Bloomfield Hills, MI (S-S); Michigan Workshop of Fine Prints, Detroit, MI (MWFP)
GALLERIES: Stewart & Stewart, Bloomfield Hills, MI
MAILING ADDRESS: 13343 Kingston Ave, Huntington Woods, MI 48070-1018

TITLE	PUBLISHER	PRINTER	DATE	MEDIUM	DIMENSION (PAPER SIZE) IN INCHES	TYPE OF PAPER	EDITION NUMBER	NO. OF COLORS	ORIGINAL OPENING PRICE	CURRENT RETAIL PRICE
SOLD OUT EDITIONS (RARE):										
Quebrada	S-S	NS/S-S	1980	SP	22 X 30	AP88	30	20	300	1000
CURRENT EDITIONS:										
Horseshoe Mound	ART	ART	1972	CV	16 X 20	AgP/R118	20	1	150	400
Moraine	ART	ART	1972	CV	16 X 20	AgP/R118	30	1	150	300
Bedrock	ART	TC	1974	LB/OFF	21 X 24	R/BFK	30	1	100	250
Deadwood	ART	DS	1975	LB	25 X 30	AP	25	1	250	400
Mosaic	MWFP	PM	1975	EB	27 X 21	R/BFK	50	1	150	300
Ebon	ART	PM	1978	MEZ	27 X 33	AP	50	1	300	500
Dartmoor	S-S	NS/S-S	1981	SP	22 X 30	R/BFK	60	28	375	750
Onyx	ART	DS	1982	MEZ/DPT	24 X 26	ITALIA	25	1	400	500
Triassic	ART	DS	1982	DPT	33 X 24	ITALIA	10	1	300	400
Tuff	ART	DS	1982	MEZ/DPT	18 X 21	ITALIA	10	1	300	400
Monhegan	ART	DS	1982	MEZ/DPT	25 X 30	ITALIA	25	1	400	500

The retail prices of the 100,000 limited edition prints quoted in this directory are subject to change. Print publishers, artists and galleries were the direct sources for these quotations. Prices in the secondary market listed as "Sold Out Editions (Rare)" indicate that the publisher has a limited supply of that print or that the print is difficult to locate in the galleries.

LUCILLE PROCTER NAWARA

BORN: Oklahoma City, OK; June 26, 1941
EDUCATION: Smith Col, Northampton, MA, 1962; Boston Univ, MA, BFA (Equiv), 1967; Univ of Illinois, Champaign, IL, MFA, 1969
TEACHING: Asst Prof, Wayne State Univ, Detroit, MI, 1969–76; Instr, Center for Creative Studies, Detroit, MI, 1982–84
AWARDS: Purchase Award, Bank of Commerce, Hamtramck, MI, 1983; Michigan Council for the Arts, Individual Artist Grants, 1981,83; Cash Award, Michigan Watercolor Soc, Univ of Michigan, Ann Arbor, MI, 1989
RECENT EXHIB: Northern Michigan Univ, Art Gallery, Marquette, MI, 1989; Joy Emery Gallery, Grosse Pointe Farms, MI, 1989

COLLECTIONS: Detroit Inst of Arts, MI; Grand Rapids Art Mus, MI; Kalamazoo Art Inst, MI; Flint Art Inst, MI; Univ of Michigan Art Mus, Ann Arbor, MI
PRINTERS: Norman Stewart, Bloomfield Hills, MI (NS); Joe Keenan, Bloomfield Hills, MI (JK); Wing Lake Studio, Bloomfield Hills, MI (WLS)
PUBLISHERS: Stewart & Stewart, Bloomfield Hills, MI (S-S)
GALLERIES: Joy Emery Gallery, Grosse Pointe Farms, MI; Stewart & Stewart, Bloomfield Hills, MI
MAILING ADDRESS: 13343 Kingston Ave, Huntington Woods, MI 48070-1018

TITLE	PUBLISHER	PRINTER	DATE	MEDIUM	DIMENSION (PAPER SIZE) IN INCHES	TYPE OF PAPER	EDITION NUMBER	NO. OF COLORS	ORIGINAL OPENING PRICE	CURRENT RETAIL PRICE
CURRENT EDITIONS:										
Bash Bish Falls	S-S	NS/JK/S-S	1989	SP	22 X 30	R/BFK/W	71	21	600	750

DENNIS NECHVATAL

BORN: Dodgeville, WI; 1948
EDUCATION: Lorcas Col, Dubuque, IA, 1966–67; Univ of Wisconsin, Stout-Menomonie, WI, BS, BA, 1971; Indiana Univ, Bloomington, IN, BFA, 1974
AWARDS: Wisconsin Arts Board Grant, 1985; Arts Midwest Fel, 1988

COLLECTIONS: Art Inst of Chicago, IL; Milwaukee Art Mus, WI; Madison Art Center, WI
PRINTERS: Bill Weege, Madison, WI (BW); Andrew Rubin, Madison, WI (AR); Tandem Press, Univ of Wisconsin, Madison, WI (TanPr)
PUBLISHERS: Tandem Press, Univ of Wisconsin, Madison, WI (TanPr)
GALLERIES: Tory Folliard Gallery, Milwaukee, WI

Dennis Nechvatal
Landscape Drama
Courtesy Tandem Press

Dennis Nechvatal
Birth
Courtesy Tandem Press

TITLE	PUBLISHER	PRINTER	DATE	MEDIUM	DIMENSION (PAPER SIZE) IN INCHES	TYPE OF PAPER	EDITION NUMBER	NO. OF COLORS	ORIGINAL OPENING PRICE	CURRENT RETAIL PRICE
CURRENT EDITIONS:										
Paradise	TanPr	BW/AR/TanPr	1990	WB	18 X 13	SUK	30	1	250	250
Landscape Drama	TanPr	BW/AR/TanPr	1990	WB	77 X 52	AC/W	20	1	1800	1800
Birth	TanPr	BW/AR/TanPr	1990	WB	77 X 52	AC/W	20	1	1800	1800
Hero	TanPr	BW/AR/TanPr	1990	WB	20 X 17	R/BFK/W	20	1	300	300
Lovers	TanPr	BW/AR/TanPr	1990	WB	53 X 52	AC	20	1	1500	1500

The print market has become very selective. For the first time since we published the first edition of The Printworld Directory in 1982, the prices of prints have been greatly reduced and greatly increased for the same artists by the most reputable and established print publishers. Check the fifth edition to understand the movement.

JOSEPH NECHVATAL

BORN: Chicago, IL; January 15, 1951
EDUCATION: Southern Illinois Univ, Carbondale, IL, BFA, 1975; Cornell Univ, Ithaca, NY, 1976; Columbia Univ, NY, 1977
AWARDS: Opera Award, Painting, 1985; Inter Arts Awards, 1986; Nat Endowment for the Arts Fel, 1988; Painting Award, New York State Council on the Arts, NY, 1988
RECENT EXHIB: Illinois State Univ, Normal, IL, 1989; Brooke Alexander, Inc, NY, 1987,90
PRINTERS: Alexander Heinrici, NY; Studio Heinrici, NY (SH); Vermillion Editions, Ltd, Minneapolis, MN (VEL); Maurice Sanchez, NY (MS); Derriére L'Estoile Studio, NY (DES); Maurice Payne, NY (MP)
PUBLISHERS: Studio Heinrici, NY (SH); Vermillion Editions, Ltd, Minneapolis, MN (VEL); Art Issue Editions, Inc, NY (AIE)
GALLERIES: Brooke Alexander, Inc. New York, NY; Jack Tilton Gallery, New York, NY; Fabric Workshop, New York, NY & Phila, PA; Asher/Faure Gallery, Los Angeles, CA; Rhona Hoffman Gallery, Chicago, IL; Shoshana Wayne Gallery, Santa Monica, CA
MAILING ADDRESS: c/o Brooke Alexander, Inc, 59 Wooster St, New York, NY 10012

Joseph Nechvatal
Diabolos Incarnatus
Courtesy Art Issue Editions, Inc

TITLE	PUBLISHER	PRINTER	DATE	MEDIUM	DIMENSION (PAPER SIZE) IN INCHES	TYPE OF PAPER	EDITION NUMBER	NO. OF COLORS	ORIGINAL OPENING PRICE	CURRENT RETAIL PRICE
CURRENT EDITIONS:										
Scab of Time	SH	AH/SH	1984	SP	38 X 44	GE	66	8	400	900
Diabolos Incarnatus	SH	AH/SH	1984	SP	20 X 18	Varies	55	5	150	600
Quartet (Set of 4)	VEL	VFI	1985	LC/HC	9 X 11 EA	HMP	8 EA		900 SET	2500 SET
Thou Shalt Not Make Graven Images (from Ten Commandments Suite)	AIE	MS/DES	1987	LC	24 X 19	DIEU	84	5	500	1500
The Flagellation of Real Passion	AIE	MP	1987	EC	26 X 36	MOR/Y	49	2	500	1000

ALICE NEEL

BORN: Merion Square, PA; (1900–1984)
EDUCATION: Philadelphia Sch of Design, PA, 1921–24
TEACHING: Univ of Pennsylvania Grad Sch, Phila, PA, 1971–72; Skowhegan Sch of Painting & Sculpture, ME, 1972
AWARDS: Acad of Arts & Letters Award, 1969; Benjamin Altman Figure Price, Nat Acad of Design, NY, 1971; Childe Hassam Fund Prize
RECENT EXHIB: Gallery Paule Anglim, San Francisco, CA, 1988; Nat Acad of Sciences, Wash, DC, 1989; Tufts Univ Art Gallery, Aidekman Arts Center, Medford, MA, 1992; Univ of Wisconsin, Carlsten Art Gallery, Stevens Point, WI, 1992
COLLECTIONS: Mus of Mod Art, NY; Whitney Mus of Am Art, NY; Metropolitan Mus, NY; American Mus, Moscow, USSR; Hirshhorn Mus, Wash, DC; Yale Univ, New Haven, CT; Princeton Univ, NJ; Baltimore Mus, MD; Dartmouth Col, Hanover, NH; Dillard Inst, New Orleans, LA; Oberlin Col, OH
PRINTERS: Atelier Ettinger Inc, NY (AE); Maurel Studio, NY (MS)
PUBLISHERS: Kennedy Graphics, NY (KG); 724 Prints, NY (724P); Eleanor Ettinger Inc, NY (EEI)
GALLERIES: Hahn Gallery, Phila, PA; Sandy Carson Gallery, Denver, CO; Graham Modern, New York, NY; Kennedy Graphics, New York, NY; C Grimaldis Gallery, Baltimore, MD; Susanne Hilberry Gallery, Birmingham, MI; Harcus Gallery, Boston, MA; Uptown Gallery, New York, NY; Gallery Paule Anglim, San Francisco, CA; Eleanor Ettinger, Inc, New York, NY; Robert Miller Gallery, New York, NY; Rothschild Fine Arts, New York, NY; Linda Cathcart Gallery, Santa Monica, CA; Bingham Kurts Gallery, Memphis,TN; Sragow Gallery, New York, NY

TITLE	PUBLISHER	PRINTER	DATE	MEDIUM	DIMENSION (PAPER SIZE) IN INCHES	TYPE OF PAPER	EDITION NUMBER	NO. OF COLORS	ORIGINAL OPENING PRICE	CURRENT RETAIL PRICE
SOLD OUT EDITIONS (RARE):										
Olympic Print	KG		1974	SP	40 X 25	AP	200		375	1000
Portrait of Benny Andrews	724P		1970	LC	35 X 24	AP	30	1	250	1200
Victoria and Cat		MS	1981	SP/LC/PO	40 X 26	AP	100		400	1500
Mother & Child	EEI	AE	1982	LC	28 X 31	AP	200		600	1500
The Bather	EEI	AE	1982	LC	27 X 44	AP	200		600	1800
Jar from Samarkand	EEI	AE	1982	LC	28 X 28	AP	200		600	1800
The Family	EEI	AE	1982	LC	27 X 32	AP	200		600	1800
Youth	EEI	AE	1983	LC	25 X 38	AP	200	22	800	1800
Light	EEI	AE	1983	LC	27 X 38	AP	200	22	800	1800

VICTOR NEWSOME

BORN: Leeds, England; 1935
EDUCATION: Leeds Col of Art, England, 1953–55, 1957–60
PRINTERS: Print Workshop, London, England (PW)
PUBLISHERS: Anne Berthaud Gallery, London, England (AB)
GALLERIES: Hester Van Royen Gallery, London, England; Anne Berthaud Gallery, London, England; Marlborough Gallery, New York, NY

TITLE	PUBLISHER	PRINTER	DATE	MEDIUM	DIMENSION (PAPER SIZE) IN INCHES	TYPE OF PAPER	EDITION NUMBER	NO. OF COLORS	ORIGINAL OPENING PRICE	CURRENT RETAIL PRICE
CURRENT EDITIONS:										
Head I	AB	PW	1981	LB	22 X 1	AP/W	35	1	150	400

LEROY NEIMAN

BORN: St Paul, MN; June 8, 1926
EDUCATION: Art Inst of Chicago, IL; Univ of Chicago, IL; Univ of Illinois, Chicago, IL
TEACHING: Atlanta Poverty Art Prog, GA, 1967–68; Univ of Kentucky, 1977–78; Instr, Figure Drawing, Art Inst of Chicago, IL, 1950–60; Instr, Painting, Winston-Salem Art Center, NC, 1964
AWARDS: Hamilton-Graham Award, Ball State Col, Muncie, IN, 1958; Municipal Prize, Chicago Exhib, IL, 1958; Gold Medal, Salon d'Art Mod. Paris, France, 1961; AAU Award of Merit, 1976; Honorary Doctor of Arts, St John's Univ, NY, 1980; Artist of the Century, Beaux Arts Soc, NY, 1981
RECENT EXHIB: New State Tretyakov Mus, 1988
COLLECTIONS: Illinois State Mus, Normal, IL; Joslyn Art Mus, Omaha, NE; Wodham Col, Oxford, England; Mus of Sport in Art, NY; Hermitage Lenningrad, USSR; Mus de Bellas Artes, Caracas, Venezuela; Art Inst of Chicago, IL; Indianapolis Mus, IN; Minnesota Mus, Minneapolis, MN; Art Inst of Chicago, IL
PRINTERS: Styria Studio, NY (SS); Seymour Hayden, NY (SA); American Atelier, NY (AA); Robert Blanton, NY (RB); Thomas Little, NY (TL); Isaiah Singleton, NY (IS); Joseph Stauber, NY (JS); Brand-X Editions, NY (BX)

PUBLISHERS: Knoedler Publishing Co, NY (KP); Circle Fine Art, Chicago, IL (CFA)
GALLERIES: Hammer Graphics, New York, NY; Foster Harmon Galleries of American Art, Sarasota, FL; Merrill Chase Galleries, Chicago, IL & Northbrook, IL; Circle Galleries, San Diego, CA & San Francisco, CA & Northbrook, IL & Scottsdale, AZ & Beverly Hills, CA & Costa Mesa, CA & Sherman Oaks, CA & Palm Beach, FL & Honolulu, HI & New Orleans, LA & Las Vegas, NV & Seattle, WA & Pittsburgh, PA & Houston, TX & Soho, NY & Chicago, IL; Gallery One at Second Avenue, Denver, CO; Graphic Art Collection, Hallandale, FL; The Hang-Up, Sarasota, FL; Shirley Fox Gallery, Atlanta, GA; Art Brokerage, Ketchum, ID; Allyson Louis Gallery, Bethesda, MD; Charles Barry International, Rockville MD; J Todd Galleries, Wellesley, MA; Short Hills Art Gallery, Short Hills, NJ; Artists Showcase International, Hartsdale, NY; Emporium Enterprises, Inc, Dallas, TX; Hanson Galleries, Beverly Hills, CA & San Francisco, CA & New Orleans, LA; Metropolitan Art Gallery, Los Angeles, CA; Edward Weston Fine Art, Northridge, CA; Bowles-Sorokko Galleries, San Francisco, CA; John Denton Gallery, Hiawassee, FL; Benedetti Gallery, New York, NY; Gallery 121 International, New York, NY; Professional Fine Arts Services, Inc, New York, NY

TITLE	PUBLISHER	PRINTER	DATE	MEDIUM	DIMENSION (PAPER SIZE) IN INCHES	TYPE OF PAPER	EDITION NUMBER	NO. OF COLORS	ORIGINAL OPENING PRICE	CURRENT RETAIL PRICE
SOLD OUT EDITIONS (RARE):										
Deuce	CFA	AA	1968	SP	32 X 26	AP	275		60	2250
Sailing	CFA	AA	1968	SP	20 X 24	AP	275		60	2250
Chipping on	CFA	AA	1968	SP	26 X 32	AP	275		60	1500
Match Point	CFA	AA	1968	SP	48 X 36	AP	300		75	3900
Tiger	CFA	AA	1968	SP	48 X 36	AP	300		75	5100
Tennis Players	CFA	AA	1968	SP	18 X 18	AP	300		50	1500
Pool Room	CFA	AA	1968	SP	23 X 26	AP	350		75	1800
The Race	CFA	AA	1969	SP	17 X 25	AP	300		75	1300
In the Stretch	CFA	AA	1969	SP	26 X 34	AP	250		75	1400
Stock Market	CFA	AA	1969	SP	30 X 42	AP	300		75	7900
Jockey	CFA	AA	1969	SP	26 X 22	AP	300		75	1600
Casino	CFA	AA	1969	SP	26 X 32	AP	300		75	2100
Paddock	CFA	AA	1969	SP	30 X 30	AP	300		75	1600
Punchinello	CFA	AA	1969	LC	30 X 21	AP	250		75	1400
Pierrot	CFA	AA	1969	LC	26 X 20	AP	250		75	1150
Pierrat the Juggler	CFA	AA	1969	LC	21 X 30	AP	200		125	1150
Sliding Home	CFA	AA	1970	SP	36 X 24	AP	300		125	1900
Skier	CFA	AA	1970	SP	27 X 18	AP	300		125	1500
Four Aces	CFA	AA	1970	SP	36 X 26	AP	300		125	1500
Slalom	CFA	AA	1970	SP	32 X 26	AP	300		125	1500
Leopard	CFA	AA	1970	SP	38 X 50	AP	300		225	8200
Al Capone	CFA	AA	1970	SP	40 X 30	AP	300		200	1400
Harlequin	CFA	AA	1970	LC	30 X 18	AP	200		125	1150
Harlequin with Sword	CFA	AA	1970	LC	30 X 19	AP	250		125	1150
Hockey Player	CFA	AA	1970	SP	30 X 40	AP	300		200	2800
Punchinello with Text	CFA	AA	1970	LC	30 X 24	AP	200		125	1600
Harlequin with Text	CFA	AA	1971	LC	30 X 24	AP	200		125	1150
Tee Shot	CFA	AA	1971	SP	30 X 24	AP	300		100	5000
End Around	CFA	AA	1971	SP	30 X 24	AP	300		100	1700
Lion's Pride	CFA	AA	1971	SP	36 X 48	AP	300		100	7000
Marathon	CFA	AA	1971	SP	35 X 27	AP	300		100	1800
Scramble	CFA	AA	1971	SP	28 X 38	AP	300		100	1800
Downhill Skier	CFA	AA	1971	SP	32 X 17	AP	300		100	1800
Innsbruck	CFA	AA	1971	SP	22 X 16	AP	300		100	1800
Doubles	CFA	AA	1971	SP	36 X 48	AP	300		100	3150
Trotters	CFA	AA	1971	SP	36 X 48	AP	300		100	1850
Goal	CFA	AA	1971	SP	24 X 30	AP	300		100	1500
Roulette	CFA	AA	1972	SP	48 X 50	AP	40		350	4500
Back Hand	CFA	AA	1972	SP	31 X 24	AP	300		200	1450
Slapshot	CFA	AA	1972	SP	36 X 30	AP	300		200	1600
Fox Hunt	CFA	AA	1972	SP	30 X 36	AP	300		200	1500
Smash	CFA	AA	1972	SP	26 X 26	AP	300		200	1750
Outlet	CFA	AA	1972	SP	30 X 39	AP	250		200	2000
Sudden Death	CFA	AA	1972	SP	31 X 39	AP	250		200	2350
Hommage to Boucher	CFA	AA	1972	SP	26 X 40	AP	250		200	1700
Twelve Meter Yacht Race	CFA	AA	1972	SP	30 X 19	AP	250		200	1800
Baseball Player Folio (Set of 10):									800 SET	7500 SET
Batting Practice	CFA	AA	1972	EC	16 X 15	AP	150		100	800
Wind Up	CFA	AA	1972	EC	16 X 15	AP	150		100	800
Awaiting the Decision	CFA	AA	1972	EC	16 X 15	AP	150		100	800
Warm Up Swings	CFA	AA	1972	EC	16 X 15	AP	150		100	800

LEROY NEIMAN CONTINUED

TITLE	PUBLISHER	PRINTER	DATE	MEDIUM	DIMENSION (PAPER SIZE) IN INCHES	TYPE OF PAPER	EDITION NUMBER	NO. OF COLORS	ORIGINAL OPENING PRICE	CURRENT RETAIL PRICE
SOLD OUT EDITIONS (RARE):										
Next at Bat	CFA	AA	1972	EC	16 X 15	AP	150		100	800
The Pitcher	CFA	AA	1972	EC	16 X 15	AP	150		100	800
The Argument	CFA	AA	1972	EC	16 X 15	AP	150		100	800
The Umps	CFA	AA	1972	EC	16 X 15	AP	150		100	800
Sliding Home	CFA	AA	1972	EC	16 X 15	AP	150		100	800
The Hit	CFA	AA	1972	EC	16 X 15	AP	150		100	800
Skiing Folio (Set of 10):									800 SET	7500 SET
Single Skier	CFA	AA	1973	EC	16 X 15	AP	150		100	800
Between Trees	CFA	AA	1973	EC	16 X 15	AP	150		100	800
Top of the Crest	CFA	AA	1973	EC	16 X 15	AP	150		100	800
Two Racers	CFA	AA	1973	EC	16 X 15	AP	150		100	800
Break	CFA	AA	1973	EC	16 X 15	AP	150		100	800
Jump	CFA	AA	1973	EC	16 X 15	AP	150		100	800
Village in the Valley	CFA	AA	1973	EC	16 X 15	AP	150		100	800
House on the Slope	CFA	AA	1973	EC	16 X 15	AP	150		100	800
Pine Trail	CFA	AA	1973	EC	16 X 15	AP	150		100	800
Three Skiers	CFA	AA	1973	EC	15 X 16	AP	150		100	800
Hockey Folio (Set of 10):									800 SET	7500 SET
Face off No 20	CFA	AA	1973	EC	15 X 16	AP	150		100	800
Score No 22	CFA	AA	1973	EC	16 X 15	AP	150		100	800
Fight	CFA	AA	1973	EC	15 X 16	AP	150		100	800
Fight with Policeman	CFA	AA	1973	EC	15 X 16	AP	150		100	800
Study of No 4	CFA	AA	1973	EC	16 X 15	AP	150		100	800
1 against 1 (Straight Shot)	CFA	AA	1973	EC	16 X 15	AP	150		100	800
1 against 1 (Goalie on Ice)	CFA	AA	1973	EC	15 X 16	AP	150		100	800
Goalie Down	CFA	AA	1973	EC	15 X 16	AP	150		100	800
Goal No 5	CFA	AA	1973	EC	15 X 16	AP	150		100	800
High Stick	CFA	AA	1973	EC	15 X 16	AP	150		100	800
Ali-Frazier Folio (Set of 15):									1200 SET	11000 SET
Study of Ali	CFA	AA	1974	EC	15 X 20	AP	150		100	800
Ali Down	CFA	AA	1974	EC	15 X 20	AP	150		100	800
The Introduction	CFA	AA	1974	EC	15 X 20	AP	150		100	800
Frazier's Corner	CFA	AA	1974	EC	15 X 20	AP	150		100	800
Ali's Corner	CFA	AA	1974	EC	15 X 20	AP	150		100	800
The Winner	CFA	AA	1974	EC	15 X 20	AP	150		100	800
After the Fight	CFA	AA	1974	EC	15 X 20	AP	150		100	800
Study of Frazier and Ali	CFA	AA	1974	EC	20 X 15	AP	150		100	800
Rounds Series:										
Rounds 1, 2	CFA	AA	1974	EC	20 X 15 EA	AP	150 EA		100 EA	800 EA
Rounds 3, 4	CFA	AA	1974	EC	20 X 15 EA	AP	150 EA		100 EA	800 EA
Rounds 7–9	CFA	AA	1974	EC	20 X 15 EA	AP	150 EA		100 EA	800 EA
Rounds 10, 11	CFA	AA	1974	EC	20 X 15 EA	AP	150 EA		100 EA	800 EA
Rounds 12–14	CFA	AA	1974	EC	20 X 15 EA	AP	150 EA		100 EA	800 EA
Round 15	CFA	AA	1974	EC	15 X 20	AP	150		100	800
Le Grand Escalier de L'Opera	KP	RB/BX	1975	SP	32 X 25	AP	300		500	12500
Toots Shor Bar	KP	RB/BX	1975	SP	31 X 25	AP	300		500	13500
Clubhouse Turn	KP	RB/BX	1975	SP	39 X 36	AP	300		500	10500
Black Panther	KP	RB/BX	1975	SP	29 X 39	AP	300		500	12000
Golf Landscape	KP	RB/BX	1976	SP	36 X 28	AP	300		600	14500
High Seas Sailing	KP	RB/BX	1976	SP	25 X 33	AP	300		600	11500
Vegas Blackjack	KP	RB/BX	1976	SP	22 X 32	AP	300		600	13500
Satchmo	KP	RB/BX	1976	SP	25 X 38	AP	300		600	12500
Elephant Stampede	KP	RB/BX	1976	SP	30 X 40	AP	300		800	27000
Sun Serve	KP	RB/BX	1976	SP	36 X 18	AP	300		600	8000
Grand Prix de Monaco	KP	RB/BX	1976	SP	36 X 24	AP	300		600	12500
Cafe Deux Magots	KP	RB/BX	1976	SP	23 X 34	AP	300		600	12500
Serengeti Leopard	KP	RB/BX	1976	SP	33 X 42	AP	300		600	13500
Willie Stargell	KP	RB/BX	1976	SP	18 X 36	AP	300		600	5500
Olympic Swimmer	KP	RB/BX	1976	SP	18 X 36	AP	300		600	4500
Olympic Gymnast	KP	RB/BX	1976	SP	18 X 36	AP	300		600	4500
Racquetball	KP	RB/BX	1976	SP	39 X 36	AP	500		600	5000
Olympic Basketball	KP	RB/BX	1976	SP	26 X 26	AP	300		600	6000
Olympic Track	KP	RB/BX	1976	SP	20 X 40	AP	300		600	6500
Borg/Connors	KP	RB/BX	1977	EB/HC	14 X 22	AP	125		800	3500
French Connection	KP	RB/BX	1977	SP	23 X 31	AP	300		800	8600
Harlem Streets	KP	RB/BX	1977	SP	40 X 26	AP	100		800	6500
La Nuit de Paris	KP	RB/BX	1977	SP	40 X 26	AP	100		800	5500
Neiman Montreal 76	KP	RB/BX	1977	SP	31 X 48	AP	600		800	15000
Basketball Superstars	KP	RB/BX	1977	SP	32 X 28	AP	300		800	10500
High Altitude Skiing	KP	RB/BX	1977	SP	25 X 34	AP	300		800	9500
Marlin Fishing	KP	RB/BX	1977	SP	26 X 34	AP	300		800	8500
Black Labrador	KP	RB/BX	1977	SP	27 X 36	AP	300		800	11500
Giraffe Family	KP	RB/BX	1977	SP	38 X 29	AP	300		800	13500
Ocean Sailing	KP	RB/BX	1977	SP	26 X 35	AP	300		800	10500

LEROY NEIMAN CONTINUED

TITLE	PUBLISHER	PRINTER	DATE	MEDIUM	DIMENSION (PAPER SIZE) IN INCHES	TYPE OF PAPER	EDITION NUMBER	NO. OF COLORS	ORIGINAL OPENING PRICE	CURRENT RETAIL PRICE
SOLD OUT EDITIONS (RARE):										
Red Square	KP	RB/BX	1977	SP	26 X 33	AP	300		800	10500
Bucking Bronc	KP	RB/BX	1977	SP	31 X 31	AP	300		800	8500
Delacroix's Tiger	KP	RB/BX	1977	SP	29 X 38	AP	300		800	7500
Introduction of the Champions at Madison Square Garden	KP	RB/BX	1977	SP	29 X 37	AP	300		800	13500
Red Sky	KP	RB/BX	1977	SP	19 X 31	AP	300		800	5500
Moby Dick Assaulting the Pequod	KP	RB/BX	1977	SP	19 X 31	AP	300		800	4500
Bjorn Borg	KP	RB/BX	1977	SP	24 X 17	AP	300		800	5000
French Connection	KP	RB/BX	1977	SP	23 X 31	AP	300		800	8500
Kentucky Wildcats	KP	RB/BX	1978	SP	36 X 27	AP	300		1000	6500
Blue Whale	KP	RB/BX	1978	SP	19 X 31	AP	300		1000	5000
Ahab at the Night Watch	KP	RB/BX	1978	SP	19 X 31	AP	300		1000	6000
Metropolitan Opera	KP	RB/BX	1978	SP	26 X 33	AP	300		1000	11500
Zebra Family	KP	RB/BX	1978	SP	28 X 38	AP	300		1000	13500
Regatta of the Gondoliers	KP	RB/BX	1978	SP	26 X 38		300		1000	7500
Spectators Fleet-America's Cup	KP	RB/BX	1978	SP	24 X 35	AP	300		1000	6500
Young Tiger	KP	RB/BX	1978	SP	12 X 27	AP	300		1000	9200
Willie Mays	KP	RB/BX	1978	SP	32 X 28	AP	300		1000	9200
PJ Clarke's	KP	RB/BX	1978	SP	26 X 39	AP	300		1000	25000
Golf Threesome	KP	RB/BX	1978	SP	24 X 36	AP	300		1000	17000
Polar Bears	KP	RB/BX	1979	SP	38 X 28	AP	300		1200	8000
The Beach at Cannes	KP	RB/BX	1979	SP	37 X 24	AP	300		1200	8000
American Bald Eagle	KP	RB/BX	1979	SP	29 X 38	AP	300		1200	16000
Aegean Sailing	KP	RB/BX	1979	SP	23 X 38	AP	300		1200	8500
Irish-American Bar	KP	RB/BX	1979	SP	26 X 39	AP	300		1200	16500
Stretch Stampede	KP	RB/BX	1979	SP	30 X 45	AP	300		1200	12500
Chateau Hunt	KP	RB/BX	1979	SP	26 X 39	AP	300		1200	12500
Kentucky Derby	KP	RB/BX	1979	SP	21 X 42	AP	300		1200	11000
Winter Olympic Skating Lake Placid 1980	KP	RB/BX	1980	SP	42 X 21	AP	300		1500	6500
Winter Olympic Skiing Lake Placid 1980	KP	RB/BX	1980	SP	42 X 21	AP	300		2000	8000
Olympic Boxing-Moscow 1980	KP	RB/BX	1980	SP	42 X 21	AP	300		1200	4800
Chicago Board of Trade	KP	RB/BX	1980	SP	25 X 38	AP	300		3000	15000
New York Marathon	KP	RB/BX	1980	SP	21 X 38	AP	300		2000	9500
Gorilla Family	KP	RB/BX	1980	SP	29 X 38	AP	300		2000	6500
Nantucket Sailing	KP	RB/BX	1980	SP	20 X 29	AP	300		2000	11000
Race of the Year	KP	RB/BX	1980	SP	22 X 32	AP	300		2000	8500
Neiman Lake Placid 1980	KP	RB/BX	1980	SP	32 X 48	AP	300		3000	10500
FX McCroy's Whiskey Bar	KP	RB/BX	1980	SP	23 X 45	AP	300		3000	16000
Jaguar Family	KP	RB/BX	1980	SP	17 X 23	AP	300		2000	7000
Shikar	KP	RB/BX	1980	SP	38 X 29	AP	300		4000	13500
Normandy Sailing	KP	RB/BX	1980	SP	9 X 12	AP	300		600	5800
Cafe de la Paix	KP	RB/BX	1980	SP	9 X 12	AP	300		600	10500
Blood Tennis	KP	RB/BX	1980	SP	29 X 23	AP	300		1500	5800
Stud Poker	KP	RB/BX	1980	SP	36 X 18	AP	300		2500	8500
Eaux Fortes 80 (Etching Portfolio)	KP	RB/BX	1980	EC	19 X 17	AP	300		2500	20000
Rodeo	KP	RB/BX	1980	EB/HC	19 X 17	AP	250		1500	5800
Stud Poker	KP	RB/BX	1980	EC	20 X 25	AP	250		800	3500
Dalmation	KP	RB/BX	1980	EC	25 X 20	AP	250		800	3200
Into the Open	KP	RB/BX	1980	EC	14 X 18	AP	250		800	3500
Six Nudes	KP	RB/BX	1980	EC	26 X 18	AP	250		800	3000
Soccer	KP	RB/BX	1980	EC	12 X 18	AP	250		800	2500
Daily Double	KP	RB/BX	1980	EC	12 X 18	AP	250		800	2500
Bovine Family	KP	RB/BX	1980	EC	9 X 15	AP	250		600	1500
Midnight Cheetah	KP	RB/BX	1980	EC	5 X 13	AP	250		600	1500
Game of Life	KP	RB/BX	1981	EC	20 X 25	AP	250		800	3200
Stenmark	KP	RB/BX	1981	SP	38 X 24	AP	300		1500	11500
Tour de France	KP	RB/BX	1981		33 X 24	AP	300		1500	13500
Lion Couple	KP	RB/BX	1981	SP	33 X 24	AP	300		1500	7500
Before the Race	KP	RB/BX	1981	SP	30 X 36	AP	300		1500	7500
Stadium Tennis	KP	RB/BX	1981	SP	30 X 36	AP	300		1500	6800
Paris Bourse	KP	RB/BX	1981	SP	30 X 38	AP	300		1500	9500
Vince Lombardi (Memorial Lithograph)	KP	RB/BX	1981	LC	14 X 17	AP	300		1200	6500
Sweet Serve	KP	RB/BX	1981	SP	36 X 18	AP	300		1200	5500
Olympic Pole Vaulting-Moscow 1980	KP	RB/BX	1981	SP	42 X 21	AP	300		1200	4200
Equestrienne	KP	RB/BX	1981	SP	24 X 12	AP	300		1200	5000
Power Serve	KP	RB/BX	1981	SP	25 X 33	AP	300		1200	5500
North Seas Sailing	KP	RB/BX	1981	SP	20 X 28	AP	300		1500	6500
Carnival Suite (Set of 2):									2000 SET	6500 SET
Panteras	KP	RB/BX	1981	SP	24 X 36	AP	300		1000	4000
Passistas	KP	RB/BX	1981	SP	30 X 38	AP	300		800	2700

LEROY NEIMAN CONTINUED

TITLE	PUBLISHER	PRINTER	DATE	MEDIUM	DIMENSION (PAPER SIZE) IN INCHES	TYPE OF PAPER	EDITION NUMBER	NO. OF COLORS	ORIGINAL OPENING PRICE	CURRENT RETAIL PRICE
SOLD OUT EDITIONS (RARE):										
Place du Casino, Monte Carlo	KP	RB/BX	1982	SP	38 X 27	AP	300		1500	10500
Silverdome-Superbowl	KP	RB/BX	1982	SP	38 X 27	AP	300		1500	9500
Vegas Craps	KP	RB/BX	1982	SP		AP	300		1500	10500
Cafe de la Flore la Nuit	KP	RB/BX	1982	SP	25 X 38	AP	300		1500	8500
Grand Prix, Caesar's Palace	KP	RB/BX	1982	SP	30 X 30	AP	300		1500	6000
Elephant Family	KP	RB/BX	1983	SP	29 X 38	AP	300		2000	13500
Stock Exchange, London	KP	RB/BX	1983	SP	29 X 38	AP	300		2000	8000
Hawaiian Sailing	KP	RB/BX	1983	SP	27 X 38	AP	300		2000	8200
My Fair Lady	KP	RB/BX	1983	SP	26 X 34	AP	300		1800	7500
Mixologist Bar	KP	RB/BX	1983	SP	27 X 39	AP	300		2000	8000
Skiing Twins	KP	RB/BX	1983	KP	36 X 30	AP	300		2000	9000
American Gold	KP	RB/BX	1984	SP	28 X 42	AP	600	41	2000	8000
Elephant Nocturne	KP	RB/BX	1984	SP	29 X 38	AP	500	31	2000	12000
Golf Winners	KP	RB/BX	1984	SP	24 X 40	AP	500	45	2000	8000
Regents Park	KP	RB/BX	1984	SP	28 X 35	AP	300	38	2250	8000
Wind Surfing	KP	RB/BX	1984	SP	28 X 29	AP	300	34	2250	6000
Rush Street Bar	KP	RB/BX	1984	SP	26 X 38	AP	300	36	1800	7500
18th at Pebble Beach	KP	RB/BX	1984	SP	24 X 42	AP	400	35	1800	16500
Classic Marathon Finish	KP	RB/BX	1985	SP	24 X 30	AP	350	33	2250	7500
Golden Girl (Mary Lou)	KP	RB/BX	1985	SP	24 X 30	AP	500	28	2150	4200
Harry's Wall Street Bar	KP	RB/BX	1985	SP	25 X 38	AP	600	38	2000	9500
Ice Castle (St Paul Winter Castle)	KP	RB/BX	1985	SP	29 X 38	AP	300	40	2250	4000
International Foursome	KP	RB/BX	1985	SP	38 X 31	AP	600	35	2000	8000
Khemosabi	KP	RB/BX	1985	SP	36 X 24	AP	300	29	2250	7000
Lady Skiier	KP	RB/BX	1985	SP	38 X 28	AP	300	26	2250	6000
The Plaza Square	KP	RB/BX	1985	SP	26 X 36	AP	300	32	2250	5000
Post-Season Football Classic	KP	RB/BX	1985	SP	27 X 38	AP	600	34	2000	7000
Texas Longhorns	KP	RB/BX	1985	SP	27 X 38	AP	500	36	2150	4500
The American Stock Exchange	KP	RB/BX	1986	SP	31 X 38	AP	375	38	2050	6000
Buena Vista Bar	KP	RB/BX	1986	SP	28 X 37	AP	375	36	2350	11000
Caspian Tiger	KP	RB/BX	1986	SP	26 X 33	AP	375	25	2350	7500
Rendez-vous a la Corvette	KP	RB/BX	1986	SP	24 X 36	AP	100	42	2800	15000
The Cove at Vintage	KP	RB/BX	1986	SP	32 X 36	AP	375	33	2350	11000
Kilimanjaro Cheetah	KP	RB/BX	1986	SP	20 X 27	AP	300	35	2350	8000
Lady Liberty	KP	RB/BX	1986	SP	38 X 31	AP	600	58	2500	13500
La Plage a Deauville	KP	RB/BX	1986	SP	29 X 36	AP	375	35	2350	5500
Nob Hill	KP	RB/BX	1986	SP	31 X 38	AP	300	40	2350	10000
CURRENT EDITIONS:										
Baden-Baden	KP	RB/BX	1987	SP	36 X 42	AP	375	60	2450	7500
Clubhouse at Old St Andrews	KP	RB/BX	1987	SP	27 X 36	AP	375	32	2450	8500
Great Dane	KP	RB/BX	1987	SP	36 X 27	AP	375	37	2450	5500
Bistro Garden-Bar	KP	RB/BX	1987	SP	24 X 36	AP	374	33	2450	7500
Left Bank Cafe	KP	RB/BX	1987	SP	26 X 38	AP	375	40	2450	5500
Red Square Panorama	KP	RB/BX	1987	SP	28 X 38	AP	375	46	2450	9500
Twenty-Four Hours of Le Mans	KP	RB/BX	1987	SP	28 X 38	AP	375	35	2450	5500
Borzoi/Changing Moscow Tape	KP	RB/BX	1988	SP	24 X 28	AP	375	26	2500	4500
Diamond Head-Hawaii	KP	RB/BX	1988	SP	28 X 38	AP	375	64	2500	4500
Magic Johnson	KP	RB/BX	1988	SP	38 X 25	AP	375	40	2500	7500
Monte Carlo Suite (with Book) (Set of 2):										
Harbor at Monaco	KP	RB/BX	1988	SP	38 X 29	AP	375	80	2300	3500
Salle Privee-Monte Carlo	KP	RB/BX	1988	SP	8 X 11	AP	700	37	2300	3500
In the Pocket	KP	RB/BX	1988	SP	28 X 38	AP	375	30	2500	5000
Napoleon at Waterloo	KP	RB/BX	1988	SP	31 X 38	AP	375	38	2500	5200
Piazza del Popolo-Rome	KP	RB/BX	1988	SP	28 X 37	AP	375	50	2500	5200
Chicago Key Club Bar	KP	RB/BX	1989	SP	29 X 36	AP	475	45	2500	4800
Johnny Bench, the Catcher	KP	RB/BX	1989	SP	38 X 19	AP	350	38	2350	5200
La Traviata	KP	RB/BX	1989	SP	20 X 36	AP	250	31	2500	5500
Bethesda Fountain-Central Park	KP	RB/BX	1989	SP	31 X 38	AP	500	45	2500	5500
Polo Lounge	KP	RB/BX	1989	SP	25 X 75	AP	700	55	2500	17500
The President's Birthday Party	KP	RB/BX	1989	SP	36 X 32	AP	600	45	2800	6200
Super Play	KP	RB/BX	1989	SP	21 X 38	AP	525	30	2800	4500
April at Augusta	KP	RB/BX	1990	SP	29 X 38	AP	550		2800	8500
Bay Area Baseball	KP	RB/BX	1990	SP	28 X 36	AP	450	41	2800	5500
Chicago Options	KP	RB/BX	1990	SP	29 X 39	AP	450		2800	15000
Dodger's Centennial	KP	RB/BX	1990	SP	32 X 40	AP	125		2500	9000
Orlando Magic	KP	RB/BX	1990	SP	35 X 26	AP	250	41	3000	7500
Quarterback of the Eighties	KP	RB/BX	1990	SP	27 X 15	AP	250	30	2800	6800
Secretariat II	KP	RB/BX	1990	SP	24 X 12	AP	250	19	2800	5200
The Slugger (Mike Schmidt)	KP	RB/BX	1990	SP	32 X 22	AP	300		3000	10000
The "21" Club	KP	RB/BX	1990	SP	26 X 36	AP	500		3000	6000
Homage to Ali	KP	RB/BX	1991	SP	28 X 38	AP	270		3000	7500

JOAN NELSON

BORN: Torrence, CA; 1958
EDUCATION: Washington Univ, St Louis, MO, 1981; Brooklyn Mus Sch, NY, Max Beckman Mem Sch, 1981–82
RECENT EXHIB: Fawbush Gallery, NY, 1987; Michael Kohn Gallery, Los Angeles, CA, 1987; Contemp Arts Mus, Houston, TX, 1988; St Louis Arts Mus, MO, 1989; Robert Miller Gallery, New York, NY, 1989,90
COLLECTIONS: Contemp Arts Mus, Houston, TX; St Louis Arts Mus, MO; Mus of Mod Art, NY; Solomon R Guggenheim Mus, NY; Toledo Mus of Art, OH

PRINTERS: Judith Solodkin, NY (JS); Solo Press, NY (SP); Artist (ART); Cirrus Editions Workshop, Los Angeles, CA (CEW)
PUBLISHERS: Fawbush Editions, NY (FE); Solo Press, NY (SP); Cirrus Editions Ltd, Los Angeles, CA (CE)
GALLERIES: Garth Clark Gallery, Los Angeles, CA; PPOW Gallery, New York, NY; Fawbush, New York, NY; Michael Kohn Gallery, Santa Monica, CA; Robert Miller Gallery, New York, NY; Solo Gallery, New York, NY; Cirrus Gallery, Los Angeles, CA

TITLE	PUBLISHER	PRINTER	DATE	MEDIUM	DIMENSION (PAPER SIZE) IN INCHES	TYPE OF PAPER	EDITION NUMBER	NO. OF COLORS	ORIGINAL OPENING PRICE	CURRENT RETAIL PRICE
CURRENT EDITIONS:										
Untitled (Set of 2) (with Acrylic Varnish)	FE/SP	JS/ART/SP	1986	LC	13 X 13 EA	AP	45		750 SET	7000 SET
Set of Five Lithographs (Set of 5)	CE	CEW	1990	LC	16 X 16 EA	R/BFK	45 EA		4500 SET	4500 SET

ROGER LAUX NELSON

BORN: Willmar, MN, 1945

PRINTERS: Catherine Mosely, NY (CM); Frank Versaggi, NY (FV); Roni Henning, NY (RH)
PUBLISHERS: Orion Editions, NY (OE)
GALLERIES: Orion Editions, New York, NY; B R Kornblatt Gallery, Wash, DC; Peter M David, Minneapolis, MN; van Straaten Gallery, Chicago, IL

TITLE	PUBLISHER	PRINTER	DATE	MEDIUM	DIMENSION (PAPER SIZE) IN INCHES	TYPE OF PAPER	EDITION NUMBER	NO. OF COLORS	ORIGINAL OPENING PRICE	CURRENT RETAIL PRICE
SOLD OUT EDITIONS (RARE):										
Six Landscapes (Set of 6)	OE	CM	1976	EC/HC	12 X 15 EA	AP	15 EA	6 EA	100 EA	200 EA
Shadows	OE	CM	1978	EC/HC	20 X 26	AP	15	HC	250	350
It's Picking Up	OE	CM	1978	EC/HC	20 X 26	AP	15	HC	250	350
Grove	OE	CM	1978	EC/HC	20 X 26	AP	15	HC	250	350
Lost Valley	OE	FV	1978	LC/HC	30 X 37	AP	34	HC	325	450
Boundaries	OE	CM/RH	1979	EB/PO	27 X 36	AP	48	9	325	450
Wind Rows	OE	CM/RH	1979	EB/PO	27 X 36	AP	48	6	325	450

NANCY NEMEC

BORN: Pinehurst, NC; November 30, 1923
EDUCATION: Colby-Sawyer Col, New London, NH, 1941; Vesper George Sch of Art, Boston, MA, 1944; Columbia Univ Sch, NY, General Studies, 1948
TEACHING: Instr, Hudson River Mus, Yonkers, NY, 1959–66; Instr, Westchester Art Workshop, White Plains, NY, 1966–71
AWARDS: Knickerbocker Artists Awards, NY, 1960,65,71,80,85; Acad of Artists Assoc Awards, 1965–67, 1973–74, 1976–78, 1980; Best in Graphic Art, Miniature Painters & Gravers Soc, Wash, DC, 1985; Purchase Award, New Hampshire Art Assoc, League of New Hampshire Craftsmen, 1985
COLLECTIONS: New Britain Mus of Am Art, CT; New York Public Library, NY; Hudson River Mus, NY; Library of Congress, Wash, DC; Free Library of Philadelphia, PA; Georgia Mus of Art, Athens, GA
PRINTERS: Artist (ART)
PUBLISHERS: Artist (ART)
GALLERIES: Alliance Museum Shop, Indianapolis, IN; Upper Echelon, Sausalito, CA; Ruth Green's Little Art Gallery, Raleigh, NC; 927 Gallery, New Orleans, LA; Schoolhouse Gallery, Sanibel, FL
MAILING ADDRESS: c/o Kearsarge Studio, Kearsarge Mountain Rd, RFD 2, P O Box 55, Warner, NH 03278

TITLE	PUBLISHER	PRINTER	DATE	MEDIUM	DIMENSION (PAPER SIZE) IN INCHES	TYPE OF PAPER	EDITION NUMBER	NO. OF COLORS	ORIGINAL OPENING PRICE	CURRENT RETAIL PRICE
CURRENT EDITIONS:										
To Sleep in Snow	ART	ART	1986	SP	23 X 30	BP	15	4	175	350

ILSE BUCHERT NESBITT

BORN: Frankfort, Germany; September 6, 1932
EDUCATION: Art Acad, Berlin, Germany, 1956–57; Art Acad, Hamburg, Germany, 1954–56, 1957–59
TEACHING: Instr, Typography & Book Design, Rhode Island Sch of Design, Providence, RI, 1960–65
AWARDS: First Prize, Prints, Newport Harbor Art Mus, RI, 1983
RECENT EXHIB: Univ Library, Hamburg, Germany, 1988; State Library, Hamburg, Germany, 1988; De Blois Gallery, Newport, RI, 1989; Gallerie Eva Wolf-Butow, Frankfort-Oberursel, Germany, 1991
COLLECTIONS: Brown Univ, Providence, RI; State Univ, Hamburg, Germany; Klingspor Mus, Offenbach, Germany
PRINTERS: Artist (ART)
PUBLISHERS: Third & Elm Press, Newport, RI (TEP)
GALLERIES: Gallerie Eva Wolf-Butow, Frankfort-Oberursel, Germany
MAILING ADDRESS: 29 Elm St, Newport, RI 02840

TITLE	PUBLISHER	PRINTER	DATE	MEDIUM	DIMENSION (PAPER SIZE) IN INCHES	TYPE OF PAPER	EDITION NUMBER	NO. OF COLORS	ORIGINAL OPENING PRICE	CURRENT RETAIL PRICE
SOLD OUT EDITIONS (RARE):										
As the Sunflower Turns	TEP	ART	1988	WC	21 X 15	MUL	5	Multi	200	350
CURRENT EDITIONS:										
Newport Winter	TEP	ART	1973	WC	16 X 12	OKP	20	1	100	100

ILSE BUCHERT NESBITT CONTINUED

TITLE	PUBLISHER	PRINTER	DATE	MEDIUM	DIMENSION (PAPER SIZE) IN INCHES	TYPE OF PAPER	EDITION NUMBER	NO. OF COLORS	ORIGINAL OPENING PRICE	CURRENT RETAIL PRICE
CURRENT EDITIONS										
The Best Tailor in the World (Set of 9)	TEP	ART	1983	WC	15 X 20 EA	MUL/RP	25 EA	1 EA	700 SET	700 SET
Wherefore the Rose	TEP	ART	1983	WC	22 X 15	MUL	25	Multi	200	200
Purple Spring	TEP	ART	1984	WC	23 X 14	MUL	15	Multi	250	250
Newport Harborside	TEP	ART	1984	WC	13 X 26	MUL	25	1	170	170
Garden with Cat	TEP	ART	1984	WC	13 X 20	MUL	25	1	150	150
Lilacs	TEP	ART	1986	WC	18 X 23	MUL	25	Multi	200	200
Fig Tree	TEP	ART	1989	WC	20 X 14	MUL	25	Multi	200	200
Summer Figs	TEP	ART	1989	WC	19 X 14	MUL	15	Multi	200	200
Autumn	TEP	ART	1990	WC	20 X 26	JP	15	Multi	500	500
Abundance	TEP	ART	1992	WC	16 X 20	JP	10	Multi	350	350

LOWELL NESBITT (BLAIR)

BORN: Baltimore, MD; (1933–1993)
EDUCATION: Tyler Sch of Fine Arts, Temple Univ, Phila, PA, BFA; Royal Col of Art, London, England; Sch of Visual Arts, NY, 1970–71
TEACHING: Instr, Printmaking, Towson State Col, MD, 1966–67; Instr, Printmaking, Baltimore Art Mus, MD, 1967–68; Hon Lectr, Univ of Miami, Coral Gables, FL, 1968,69,71; Hon Lectr, Univ of Richmond, VA, 1968,69,71; Hon Lectr, Baltimore Art Mus, MD, 1968,69,71; Instr, Painting, Sch of Visual Arts, NY, 1970–71
AWARDS: Purchase Award, Baltimore Art Mus, MD, 1956; Purchase Award, Nat Coll of Fine Arts, Wash, DC, 1969; Purchase Award, Baker Brush Company, Drawing, 1971
RECENT EXHIB: R H Love Modern, Chicago, IL, 1987; Joy Tash Gallery, Scottsdale, AZ, 1987; Larsen Dulman Gallery, New Hope, PA, 1988
COLLECTIONS: Mus of Mod Art, NY; Yale Univ, New Haven, CT; Corcoran Gallery of Art, Wash, DC; Detroit Inst of Art, MI; Chicago Inst of Art, IL; Baltimore Mus of Art, MD; Philadelphia Mus of Art, PA; La Jolla Mus, CA; Phillips Coll, Wash, DC; Carnegie-Mellon Univ, Pittsburgh, PA; Nat Coll of Fine Arts, Wash, DC; Library of Congress, Wash, DC; Nat Gallery of Fine Art, Wash, DC; Temple Univ, Phila, PA; Nat Art Gallery, Wellington, New Zealand; Bibliotheque Nat, Paris, France
PRINTERS: Mohammad Khalil, NY (MK); Orlando Condeso, NY (OC); Norman Lassiter, NY (NL); Editions Lassiter-Meisel, NY (ELM); Alexander Heinrici, NY (AH); Stuidio Heinrici, NY (SH); John Nichols, NY (JN); Fine Creations, NY (FC); American Atelier, NY (AA)

PUBLISHERS: Gimpel & Weitzenhoffer, NY (GW); Alecto International, NY (AI); London Arts, Inc, Detroit, MI (LAI); Metropolitan Art Associates, Huntington, NY (MAA); Marlborough Graphics, Inc, NY (MG); Pace Editions, NY (PE); Brooke Alexander, Inc, NY (BAI); Martin Lawrence Limited Editions, Van Nuys, CA (MLLE); John Nichols, NY (JN); Daytop Village (DV); Prestige Art Ltd, Mamaroneck, NY (PA); Circle Fine Art, Chicago, IL (CFA)
GALLERIES: Marlborough Graphics Gallery, New York, NY; Pace Prints, New York, NY; Brooke Alexander, Inc, New York, NY; Harmon Gallery, Naples, FL; Images Gallery, Toledo, OH; Hokin/Kaufman Gallery, Chicago, IL; Southwest Gallery, Dallas, TX; Alan Brown Gallery, Hartsdale, NY; G Sander Fine Art, Daytona Beach, FL; Foster Harmon Galleries of American Art, Sarasota, FL; Wenniger Graphics, Boston, MA; Now & Then Gallery, East Meadow, NY; Southwest Gallery, Dallas, TX; Martin Lawrence Galleries, Sherman Oaks, CA & Los Angeles, CA & West Los Angeles, CA & Newport Beach, CA & Palm Springs, CA & Santa Clara, CA & Redondo Beach, CA & Thousand Oaks, CA & Escondido, CA & Phila, PA & Short Hills, NJ & Soho, NY; R H Love Modern, Chicago, IL; Joy Tash Gallery, Scottsdale, AZ; Circle Galleries, Scottsdale, AZ & Beverly Hills, CA & Costa Mesa, CA & San Diego, CA & San Francisco, CA & Sherman Oaks, CA & Palm Beach, FL & Honolulu, HI & Chicago, IL & Northbrook, IL & New Orleans, LA & Las Vegas, NV & New York, NY & Pittsburgh, PA & Houston, TX & Seattle, WA
MAILING ADDRESS: 69 Wooster St, New York, NY 10012

TITLE	PUBLISHER	PRINTER	DATE	MEDIUM	DIMENSION (PAPER SIZE) IN INCHES	TYPE OF PAPER	EDITION NUMBER	NO. OF COLORS	ORIGINAL OPENING PRICE	CURRENT RETAIL PRICE
SOLD OUT EDITIONS (RARE):										
Parrot Tulip	BAI	OC	1973	EC	22 X 30	GE/HMP	8		200	900
Iris, '73	BAI/GW/AI	MK	1973	AC	30 X 44	AP	100	5	300	900
Three White Tulips on Black	CFA	AA	1976	SP	35 X 26	AP	200		500	950
Three White Lilies on Black	CFA	AA	1976	SP	44 X 3	AP	200		500	950
Two Dutch Iris on Black	CFA	AA	1976	SP	44 X 3	AP	200		500	950
Japanese Iris	MAA		1979	SP	36 X 37	AP	250		500	850
Pink Tulip	LAI	NL/ELM	1979	SP	26 X 22	SOM	175	6	500	850
Iris I '80	CFA	AA	1980	LC	25 X 36	AP	200		350	650
CURRENT EDITIONS:										
July '64	MAA		1964	SP	32 X 32	AP	200		450	850
Fruit	CFA	AA	1973	LC	24 X 32	AP	175		300	600
Narcissus and Daffodil on Black	CFA	AA	1974	SP	45 X 37	AP	200		500	800
Shoes, States I-XII	BAI		1974	DPT	27 X 36 EA	AP		14 EA	250 EA	450 EA
Andy Warhol's Studio '74	MG	MK	1974	AC	30 X 42	AP	50		350	650
Boots '74	MG	MK	1974	AC	30 X 42	AP	50		350	650
Brooklyn Bridge '74	MG	MK	1974	AC	30 X 39	AP	50		350	650
Iris '74	MG	MK	1974	AC	42 X 30	AP	50		350	650
Rose '75	LAI		1975	SP	24 X 24	SOM	175	6	500	500
Hats (Set of 6)	PE		1975	SP	35 X 35 EA	STAR	150 EA		900 SET	2800 SET
Yellow Rose	CFA	AA	1976	SP	30 X 28	AP	175		300	550
Standstone Tulip	BAI		1976	LC	39 X 31	AP	100		450	650
Yellow Spotted Lily	MAA		1976	SP	24 X 26	AP	175		450	500
Grapes	LAI		1977	LC	19 X 31	AP	175	5	400	400
Yellow Orchid	MAA	NL/ELM	1978	SP	29 X 30	AP	175		450	500
Three Morning	MAA	NL/ELM	1978	SP	36 X 45	AP	175		450	650
Rust Iris	LAI	NL/ELM	1979	SP	24 X 24	SOM	175	7	500	500
Iris and Rose on Gold	LAI	NL/ELM	1979	SP	25 X 38	SOM	175	8	500	500

LOWELL NESBITT (BLAIR) CONTINUED

TITLE	PUBLISHER	PRINTER	DATE	MEDIUM	DIMENSION (PAPER SIZE) IN INCHES	TYPE OF PAPER	EDITION NUMBER	NO. OF COLORS	ORIGINAL OPENING PRICE	CURRENT RETAIL PRICE
SOLD OUT EDITIONS (RARE):										
Ten Lemons	LAI	NL/ELM	1979	SP	24 X 27	SOM	175	8	500	500
Hybiscus	MAA	NL/ELM	1979	SP	36 X 37	AP	250		500	750
Oriental Iris I, II, III	MAA	NL/ELM	1979	SP	38 X 41 EA	AP	250 EA		1600 SET	2200 SET
CURRENT EDITIONS:										
White Lily On White	MAA	NL/ELM	1979	SP	32 X 32	AP	200		450	650
White and Violet Iris	MAA	NL/ELM	1979	SP	36 X 36	AP	200		450	650
White Emperor	MAA	NL/ELM	1979	SP	24 X 33	AP	200		450	550
Four Anemonies	MAA	NL/ELM	1979	SP	31 X 31	AP	200		450	550
Orchid Diamond	PA	FC	1979	SP	24 DIA	RG	175	8	350	400
Three White Tulips on Black	CFA	AA	1980	SP	35 X 26	AP	200		400	900
Black Parrot Tulip II	CFA	AA	1980	SP	36 X 46	AP	200		400	950
Viola Adorata	MAA	NL/ELM	1980	SP	41 X 36	AP	250		500	700
Violet Monochrome Flower	MAA	NL/ELM	1980	SP	31 X 31	AP	175		450	650
Water Lily II	MLLE	AH/SH	1981	SP	24 X 42	AP	200	23	550	650
Wild Life Suite (Set of 3):									1500 SET	1800 SET
Tiger Lily	MLLE	AH/SH	1982	SP	32 X 44	AP	200	10	650	850
Blue Bird	MLLE	AH/SH	1982	SP	33 X 42	AP	200	10	650	750
Flamingo	MLLE	AH/SH	1982	SP	34 X 42	AP	200	10	650	750
Iris	DV	JN	1984	LC/SP	19 DIA	TRP	50	5	350	500
Rose	JN	JN	1984	LC/SP	19 DIA	TRP	50	5	350	500
Lily	JN	JN	1984	LC/SP	19 DIA	TRP	50	5	350	500

BARBARA NESSIM

BORN: New York, NY; March 30, 1939
EDUCATION: Pratt Inst, NY, BFA, 1956–60; Pratt Graphic Art Center, NY, 1960
TEACHING: Pratt Inst, NY, 1977–84; Sch of Visual Arts, NY, 1967 to present; Fashion Inst of Tech, NY, 1976 to present
AWARDS: Artist in Res, Associated Council of the Arts, NY, 1969
COLLECTIONS: World Trade Center, NY
RECENT EXHIB: Community Col, Spokane, WA, 1987; Fine Arts Gallery, Spokane Falls, WA, 1987; Kansas City Art Inst, Charlotte Crosby Kemper Gallery, Kansas City, MO, 1989; Fine Arts Mus of Long Island, Hempstead, NY, 1989
PRINTERS: Matthieu Litho, Zurich, Switzerland (ML); Digix, Los Angeles, CA (DX)
PUBLISHERS: Artist (ART)
GALLERIES: Ginza Gallery, Tokyo, Japan; Fine Arts Gallery, Spokane, WA; Rempire Fine Art Gallery, New York, NY
MAILING ADDRESS: 63 Greene St, New York, NY 10012

TITLE	PUBLISHER	PRINTER	DATE	MEDIUM	DIMENSION (PAPER SIZE) IN INCHES	TYPE OF PAPER	EDITION NUMBER	NO. OF COLORS	ORIGINAL OPENING PRICE	CURRENT RETAIL PRICE
CURRENT EDITIONS:										
Woman Girl	ART	ML	1981	LC	30 X 22	R/BFK	90	12	600	900
Woman thinking about Night Dream	ART	ML	1981	LC	13 X 17	AP	30	2	200	500
Sea Form	ART	ML	1981	LC	29 X 22	R/BFK	90	12	600	900
Night Dream	ART	ML	1981	LC	32 X 22	R/BFK	100	12	600	900
The Information is the Picture (9 Prints with One Hand-Colored Pastel) (Set of 10)	ART	XM	1984	XER	9 X 11 EA	JP/A-MBM	10 EA	6 EA	1100 SET	2500 SET
Hand Memory	ART	DX	1986	COM/JET	30 X 24	Ph5	5	14	400	1350
Flowers in the Wind	ART	DX	1986	COM/JET	30 X 24	Ph5	5	14	400	1350
The Gift	ART	DX	1986	COM/JET	30 X 24	Ph5	5	14	400	1350
Without Hands	ART	DX	1986	COM/JET	30 X 24	Ph5	5	14	400	1350

ERVIN NEUHAUS

BORN: Yugoslavia; 1928
EDUCATION: Sch of Beaux Arts, Israel; L'Académie Supérieure des Beaux Arts, Paris, France
PRINTERS: American Atelier, NY (AA)
PUBLISHERS: Circle Fine Art, Chicago, IL (CFA)
GALLERIES: Circle Galleries, San Diego, CA & San Francisco, CA & Northbrook, IL & Pittsburgh, PA & Houston, TX & Soho, NY & Chicago, IL & Scottsdale, AZ & Beverly Hills, CA & Costa Mesa, CA & Sherman Oaks, CA & Palm Beach, FL & Honolulu, HI & New Orleans, LA & Las Vegas, NV & Seattle, WA

TITLE	PUBLISHER	PRINTER	DATE	MEDIUM	DIMENSION (PAPER SIZE) IN INCHES	TYPE OF PAPER	EDITION NUMBER	NO. OF COLORS	ORIGINAL OPENING PRICE	CURRENT RETAIL PRICE
SOLD OUT EDITIONS (RARE):										
Study in Blue	CFA	AA	1976	LC	20 X 26	AP	75		50	200
Study in Brown	CFA	AA	1976	LC	20 X 26	AP	75		50	250
Le Mage	CFA	AA	1976	LC	20 X 26	AP	75		50	250
Planet	CFA	AA	1977	EC	20 X 26	R/BFK	65		60	200
Les Etres Heureux	CFA	AA	1979	LC	20 X 26	AP	65		75	200
Le Petit Etre Blanc	CFA	AA	1980	LC	20 X 26	AP	65		80	200

The retail prices of the 100,000 limited edition prints quoted in this directory are subject to change. Print publishers, artists and galleries were the direct sources for these quotations. Prices in the secondary market listed as "Sold Out Editions (Rare)" indicate that the publisher has a limited supply of that print or that the print is difficult to locate in the galleries.

LOUISE NEVELSON

BORN: Kiev, Russia; (1900–1986)
EDUCATION: Art Students League, NY, 1929–30; Hofmann Sch, Munich, Germany, 1931
AWARDS: Chicago Art Inst, Frank G Logan Award, 1960; Tamarind Fel, 1963; MacDowell Colony Medal, 1969; Brandeis Univ, Creative Arts Award, 1971; Smith Col, MA, Hon DFA, 1973; New York State Governor's Award, 1987
COLLECTIONS: Mus of Mod Art, NY; Whitney Mus of Am Art, NY; Tate Gallery of Art, London, England; Walker Art Center, Minneapolis, MN; Hirshhorn Mus, Wash, DC; Brandeis Univ, Waltham, MA; Chicago Inst of Art, IL; Albright-Knox Gallery of Art, Buffalo, NY; Brooklyn Mus of Art, NY; Carnegie Inst, Pittsburgh, PA; Mus of Fine Art, Houston, TX; Indiana Univ; Nat Mus ot Art, Jerusalem, Israel; Jewish Mus, NY; Princeton Univ, NJ; Sara Robey Foundation; Julliard Sch of Music, NY; Arts Club of Chicago, IL; Univ of Alabama, Birmingham, AL; Hospital Corp of America; Queens Col, NY; Newark Mus, NJ; Pasadena Art Mus, CA
RECENT EXHIB: Krakow Gallery, Boston, MA, 1987; Reading Public Mus, PA, 1989; Nat Mus of Women in the Arts, Wash, DC, 1990,92; Nassau County Mus of Fine Art, Roslyn Harbor, NY, 1992; Muhlenberg Col, Frank Martin Art Gallery, Allentown, PA, 1989,92; Miami Univ Art Mus, Oxford, OH, 1989,92; Univ of Wisconsin, Carlsten Art Gallery, Stevens Point, WI, 1992; Wichita Art Mus, KS, 1989,92; William A Farnsworth Library & Art Mus, Rockland, ME, 1989,92; Storm King Art Center, Mountainville, NY, 1989,92; New York State Mus, Trenton, NJ, 1992; Univ of Florida, Samuel P Harn Mus, Gainesville, FL, 1992; Delaware Art Mus, Wilmington, DE, 1992; Stamford Mus & Nature Center, Leonhardt Galleries, CT, 1992; Pace Gallery, NY, 1989,92,93
PRINTERS: Emiliano Sorini, NY (ES); Irwin Hollander, NY (IH); Hollander Graphic Workshop, NY (HGW); Tamarind Inst Workshop, Albuquerque, NM (TI); Atelier 17 (A17); Chiron Press, NY (CP); Kathy Caraccio, NY (KC); Experimental Printmaking, NY (EXP); Sergio Tosi, Milan, Italy (ST)
PUBLISHERS: Hollander Graphic Workshop, NY (HGW); Tamarind Inst, Albuquerque, NM (TI); Pace Editions, NY (PE); Abrams Original Editions, NY (AOE)
GALLERIES: Pace Prints, New York, NY; Graphics Gallery, San Francisco, CA; Hokin Gallery, Palm Beach, FL & Bay Harbor Islands, FL; Foster Goldstrum Gallery, Dallas, TX; Richard Gray Gallery, Chicago, IL; Charles Foley Gallery, Columbus, OH; Barbara Krakow Gallery, Boston, MA; David Anderson Gallery, Buffalo, NY; Sigrid Freundorfer Fine Art, New York, NY; Elaine Horwitch Galleries, Scottsdale, AZ; Irving Galleries, Palm Beach, FL; Kass/Meridian Gallery, Chicago, IL; O'Farrell Gallery, Brunswick, ME; Laura Paul Galleries, Cincinnati, OH & Columbus, OH; Park Granada Editions, Tarzana, CA; Margulies Taplin Galleries, Boca Raton, FL; Faber Fine Arts, Secaucus, NJ; Bellas Artes, Santa Fe, NM; Vanderwoude/Tananbaum Gallery, New York, NY; Collector's Gallery, Nashville, TN; Locks Gallery, Phila, PA
MAILING ADDRESS: 21 Spring St, New York, NY 10012

Baro (B)

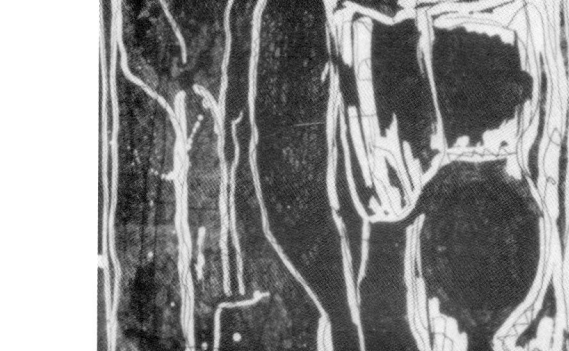

Louise Nevelson
Sky Garden
Courtesy Pace Editions, Inc.

Louise Nevelson
Flower Queen
Courtesy Pace Editions, Inc

TITLE	PUBLISHER	PRINTER	DATE	MEDIUM	DIMENSION (PAPER SIZE) IN INCHES	TYPE OF PAPER	EDITION NUMBER	NO. OF COLORS	ORIGINAL OPENING PRICE	CURRENT RETAIL PRICE
SOLD OUT EDITIONS (RARE):										
The Magic Garden		A17	1953–55	EB/HC	6 X 9	WOVE	20	4	200	5000
The Magic Garden in a Sea-Land A	HGW	ES/IH/HGW	1953–55	EB	15 X 17	R/BFK	20	1	200	3000
Flower Queen	HGW	ES/IH/HGW	1953–55	EB	20 X 16	R/BFK	20	1	200	3000
Ancient City	HGW	ES/IH/HGW	1953–55	EB/A/DPT	14 X 21	R/BFK	20		200	5000
Goddess One	HGW	ES/IH/HGW	1965–66	EB/A/DPT	17 X	R/BFK	20		500	3000
The West Queen	HGW	ES/IH/HGW	1965–66	EB/A/DPT	21 X 14	R/BFK	20		500	3000
Facades (Set of 12)	AOE	CP	1966	SP/PH/AC	23 X 17 EA	AP	125 EA		1250 SET	50000 SET
Double Imagery Series:										
Double Imagery	PE	ST	1967	LC	39 X 27	R/100	20		800	7500
Double Imagery	PE	ST	1967	LC	39 X 27	R/100	10		800	3500
Double Imagery	PE	ST	1967	LC	37 X 52	R/100	20		800	4500
Double Imagery (A)	PE	ST	1967	LC	34 X 57	R/100	20		800	4500
Double Imagery (B)	PE	ST	1967	LC	34 X 57	R/100	20		800	3500

LOUISE NEVELSON CONTINUED

TITLE	PUBLISHER	PRINTER	DATE	MEDIUM	DIMENSION (PAPER SIZE) IN INCHES	TYPE OF PAPER	EDITION NUMBER	NO. OF COLORS	ORIGINAL OPENING PRICE	CURRENT RETAIL PRICE
SOLD OUT EDITIONS (RARE):										
Double Imagery, State II	PE	ST	1967	LC	34 X 23	R/100	10		1000	4500
Double Imagery, State III	PE	ST	1967	LC	23 X 34	R/100	AP		1000	4500
Double Imagery	PE	ST	1967	LC	42 X 58	R/100	20		800	4500
Double Imagery	PE	ST	1967	LC	22 X 42	R/100	20		800	3500
Double Imagery	PE	ST	1967	LC	36 X 72	R/100	20		800	4500
Double Imagery	PE	ST	1967	LC	39 X 43	R/100	20		800	4500
Double Imagery (A)	PE	ST	1967	LC	39 X 43	R/100	20		800	4500
Double Imagery B	PE	ST	1967	LC	39 X 43	R/100	20		800	4500
Double Imagery	PE	ST	1967	LC	36 X 57	R/100	20		800	4500
Double Imagery	PE	ST	1967	LC	36 X 48	R/100	20		800	4500
Double Imagery (B)	PE	ST	1967	LC	36 X 48	R/100	20		800	4500
Double Imagery, State II	PE	ST	1967	LC	36 X 24	R/100	10		1000	4500
Double Imagery: Untitled I, II (Set of 2) (B-86)	TI	TI	1967	LC	43 X 39 EA	R/BFK	20 EA		1500 SET	7500 SET
Night Leaf (Wood Frame)	PE	ST	1969	AC/PLAS	13 X 13 X 2	CP	150		1000	10000
The Great Wall	PE	ST	1970	I/LEAD	30 X 25	RAG	150		1000	6500
Night Sound	PE	ST	1971	I/LEAD	30 X 25	RAG	150		1000	6500
Tropical Leaves	PE	ST	1972	I/LEAD	30 X 25	FAB	150		650	6500
Sky Garden	PE	ST	1972	I	30 X 25	R/BFK	150	1	750	6500
Sky Shadow	PE	ST	1973	REL/CO	30 X 25	FAB	150		550	6500
Untitled (Aquatints) (Set of 6)	PE	2RC	1973	AC/CO	37 X 26 EA	FAB	90 EA		3300 SET / 600 EA	25000 SET / 5000 EA
Night Tree	PE	ST	1974	I	30 X 26	R/BFK	150	1	750	6500
Symphony Three (Mult)	PE	ST	1974	MULT	18 X 1 X 2	CP	125	1	2000	10000
Dark Ellipse	PE	ST	1974	MULT	18 X 7	CP	125	1	1500	15000
Nightscape (Black)	PE	ST	1975	CP/MULT	27 X 31 X 6	CP	75	1	1500	8500
Dawnscape	PE	ST	1975	CP/MULT	27 X 31	CP	75	1	1500	8500
Dawn's Presence	PE	KC	1976	REL	32 X 22	CP	75	1	1750	8500
Moon Garden	PE	KC	1976	CP/REL	21 X 32	CP	75	1	1500	8500
Essences (Set of 17)	PE	KC	1977	SG/EC	42 X 28 EA	CP	30 EA		850 EA	5000 EA
Dawn's Clouds	PE	KC	1977	CP/REL	28 X 39	CP	75	1	2000	8500
Morning Haze (Dipt)	PE	KC	1978	CP/REL	33 X 46	CP/W	125	1	2500	10000
Celebration (Set of 6)	PE	KC	1979	A/E/CO	44 X 32 EA	AC	50 EA	4 EA	6500 SET	20000 SET / 4000 EA
Full Moon (Mult)	PE	KC	1980	MULT	19 X 19		125	1	2000	7500
Six-Pointed Star	PE	EXP	1980	REL/CO	41 X 35	CP	90	1	2500	8500
Night Star	PE	EXP	1981	REL/CO	32 X 36	CP	90	1	2500	8500
Sun-Set (Mult)	PE	EXP	1981	SG/E	12 X 17	CP	125	1	3500	6500
Tonalities (Set of 3):										
Tonality I (Red)	PE	EXP	1981	EB/A	48 X 32	AC	20	1	1200	5000
Tonality II (Orange)	PE	EXP	1981	EB/A	48 X 32	AC	20	1	1200	5000
Tonality III (Beige)	PE	EXP	1981	EB/A	48 X 32	AC	20	1	1200	5000
Sky Gate Series:										
Sky Gate I	PE	EXP	1982	CAST	34 X 20	CP/G	90	1	2000	6500
Sky Gate II (Dipt)	PE	EXP	1982	CAST	34 X 40 EA	CP/G	90	1	3000	8000
Reflections Series #I–#V	PE	EXP	1983	EC/A	46 X 35 EA	CP/G	50 EA		1750 EA	3500 EA

BARNETT NEWMAN

BORN: New York, NY; (1905–1970)
EDUCATION: City Col of New York, BA; Cornell Univ, Ithaca, NY, ASL with John Sloan
RECENT EXHIB: Gagosian Gallery, NY, 1992
COLLECTIONS: Mus of Mod Art, NY; Whitney Mus of Am Art, NY; Wadsworth Atheneum, Hartford, CT; Tate Gallery, London, England; Kunsthalle Mus, Basel, Switzerland; Moderna Museet, Stockholm, Sweden; Stedelijk Mus, Amsterdam, The Netherlands
PRINTERS: Artist (ART); Universal Limited Art Editions, West Islip, NY (ULAE)
PUBLISHERS: Artist (ART); Universal Limited Art Editions, West Islip, NY (ULAE)
GALLERIES: Gagosian Gallery, New York, NY; Linda R Silverman Fine Art, Inc, New York, NY; Janie C Lee Galleries, New York, NY & Houston, TX

TITLE	PUBLISHER	PRINTER	DATE	MEDIUM	DIMENSION (PAPER SIZE) IN INCHES	TYPE OF PAPER	EDITION NUMBER	NO. OF COLORS	ORIGINAL OPENING PRICE	CURRENT RETAIL PRICE
SOLD OUT EDITIONS (RARE):										
Untitled	ART	ART	1961	LB	30 X 22	AP	30	1	100	50000
18 Cantos (Set of 18)	ULAE	ULAE	1963–64	LC	28 X 22	JP	18 EA		2000 SET	375000 SET

DONALD NEWMAN

BORN: Point Pleasant, NJ
EDUCATION: California Inst of Art, Valencia, CA, 1976–77; Whitney Mus Ind Study Program, NY, 1977–78
PRINTERS: Chip Elwell, NY (CE); Orlando Condeso, NY (OC)
PUBLISHERS: Diane Villani Editions, NY (DVE)
GALLERIES: Magnuson Gallery, Boston, MA; Roger Ramsay, Chicago, IL; Diane Villani Editions, New York, NY

DONALD NEWMAN CONTINUED

TITLE	PUBLISHER	PRINTER	DATE	MEDIUM	DIMENSION (PAPER SIZE) IN INCHES	TYPE OF PAPER	EDITION NUMBER	NO. OF COLORS	ORIGINAL OPENING PRICE	CURRENT RETAIL PRICE
CURRENT EDITIONS:										
Temptation	DVE	OC	1982	EB/A/PH	38 X 30	R/BFK	25		450	750
Expulsion	DVE	OC	1982	EB/A/PH	38 X 30	R/BFK	25		450	750

LIBBY NEWMAN

BORN: Rockland, DE; November 17, 1925
EDUCATION: Tyler Sch of Fine Art, Phila, PA, 1954; Philadelphia Col of Art, PA, BFA, 1962; Univ of Pennsylvania, Phila, PA
AWARDS: Best Picture of the Year Award, Philadelphia Art Alliance, PA, 1965; Nat Print Award, Cheltenham Art Center, PA, 1970; Carl Zigrosser Nat Mem Award, Am Color Print Soc, 1981
RECENT EXHIB: Mangel Gallery, Phila, PA, 1987,88,92
COLLECTIONS: Philadelphia Mus, PA; Mus of Mod Art, Buenos Aires, Argentina; Nat Mus of Belgrade, Yugoslavia; Glassboro State Col, NJ; Univ of Pennsylvania, Law Sch, Phila, PA; St Charles Borromeo Seminary, Overbrook, PA
PUBLISHERS: Circle Fine Art, Chicago, IL (CFA); Artist (ART)
PRINTERS: Brandywine Graphics (BG); American Atelier, NY (AA)
GALLERIES: Mangel Gallery, Phila, PA; Circle Galleries, San Diego, CA & San Francisco, CA & Northbrook, IL & Pittsburgh, PA & Houston, TX & Soho, NY & Chicago, IL & Scottsdale, AZ & Beverly Hills, CA & Costa Mesa, CA & Sherman Oaks, CA & Palm Beach, FL & Honolulu, HI & New Orleans, LA & Las Vegas, NV & Seattle, WA
MAILING ADDRESS: 327 Meeting House Lane, Merion, PA 19066

TITLE	PUBLISHER	PRINTER	DATE	MEDIUM	DIMENSION (PAPER SIZE) IN INCHES	TYPE OF PAPER	EDITION NUMBER	NO. OF COLORS	ORIGINAL OPENING PRICE	CURRENT RETAIL PRICE
CURRENT EDITIONS:										
Aquarius Awakening	CFA	AA	1979	WC	24 X 19	AP	100		50	200
Pursuit	CFA	AA	1980	WC	19 X 28	AP	50		50	200
Ode to Jerusalem	CFA	AA	1980	WC	29 X 21	AP	50		100	250
Inside/Outside Series	ART	BG	1984	SP	21 X 30 EA	AP	30 EA	10 EA	250 EA	300 EA

JOHN NEWMAN

BORN: New York, NY; 1952
EDUCATION: Whitney Mus, Independent Study Prog, NY, 1972; Oberlin Col, OH, BA, 1973; Yale Sch of Art, New Haven, CT, MFA, 1975
AWARDS: New York Found for the Arts Award, Sculpture, 1990; John Simon Guggenheim Fel, 1992
COLLECTIONS: Reed Col, Portland, OR; Bennington Col, VT; Massachusetts Inst of Technology, Cambridge, MA
RECENT EXHIB: John Berggruen Gallery, San Francisco, CA, 1991; David Nolan Gallery, NY, 1991; Gerald Peters Gallery, Dallas, TX, 1993
PRINTERS: Jennifer Melby, NY (JM); 2RC, Rome, Italy (2RC); Keiji Shinohara, Boston, MA (KS); Tyler Graphics, Ltd, Mount Kisco, NY (TGL)
PUBLISHERS: Editions Ilene Kurtz, NY (EIK); Tyler Graphics, Ltd, Mount Kisco, NY (TGL)
GALLERIES: Madison Gallery, Toronto, Canada; Masters Gallery, Calgary, Canada; Flanders Contemporary Art, Minneapolis, MN; Vermillion Editions, Ltd, Minneapolis, NM; Editions Ilene Kurtz, New York, NY; John Berggruen Gallery, San Francisco, CA; John C Stoller & Company, Minneapolis, MN; David Nolan Gallery, New York, NY; Gerald Peters Gallery, Dallas, TX; Tyler Graphics, Ltd, Mount Kisco, NY; Thomas Smith Fine Art, Fort Wayne, IN; Katie Block Fine Art, Boston, MA

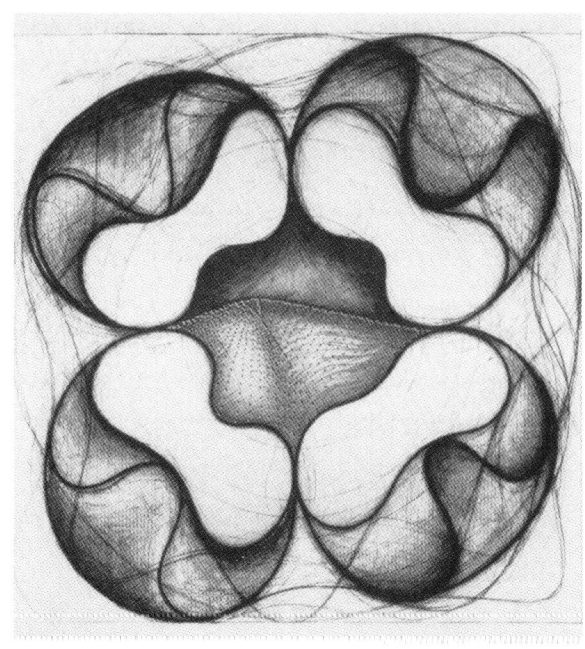

John Newman
Auto-Da-Fe
Courtesy Tyler Graphics, Ltd

TITLE	PUBLISHER	PRINTER	DATE	MEDIUM	DIMENSION (PAPER SIZE) IN INCHES	TYPE OF PAPER	EDITION NUMBER	NO. OF COLORS	ORIGINAL OPENING PRICE	CURRENT RETAIL PRICE
CURRENT EDITIONS:										
Two Pulls	EIK	JM	1986	EB/A/SG/HG/DPT	45 X 25	THS	39	2	1500	3000
Piccolo Romano Rosso	EIK	2RC	1988	EB/A/DPT/SG/CC	20 X 27	FAB	58		1500	2000
Medio Romano Giallo	EIK	2RC	1988	EB/A/DPT/SG	31 X 57	FAB	58		2500	3500
Grande Romano Blu	EIK	2RC	1988	EB/A/DPT/SG	61 X 29	FAB	58		2800	4000
Auto-Da-Fe	TGL	TGL	1990	LB/EB/A	58 X 57	THS	42		1500	2000
Sotto Voce	TGL	TGL	1990	LC	57 X 57	THS	42		1500	1500
Spin Cloud	TGL	TGL	1990	EB/A	22 X 19	R/BFK	35		900	1000
Untitled (Set of 3)	EIK	KS	1991	WB	30 X 21 EA	HOSHO	40 EA	1 EA	3500 SET / 1500 EA	3500 SET / 1500 EA

DON NICE

BORN: Visalia, CA; June 26, 1932
EDUCATION: Univ of Southern California, Los Angeles, CA, BFA, 1950–54; Yale Univ, New Haven, CT, MFA, 1962–64
TEACHING: Instr, Minneapolis Sch of Art, MN, 1960–62; Art in Res, Dartmouth Col, Hanover, NH, 1982–83; Instr, Sch of Visual Arts, NY, Dean, 1964–66, 1963 to present
AWARDS: Ford Found Purchase Award, 1963
RECENT EXHIB: Lake Placid Center for the Arts, NY, 1987; Elaine Horwitch Gallery, Palm Springs, CA, 1987; Fenrick Gallery, Wash, DC, 1989; Sun Valley Center for the Arts & Humanities, ID, 1988,90; Hofstra Univ Mus, Emily Lowe Gallery, Hempstead, NY, 1992; Lincoln Center, Avery Fisher Hall, NY, 1992; John Berggruen Gallery, San Francisco, CA, 1987, 89,92
COLLECTIONS: Mus of Mod Art, NY; Minneapolis Inst of Art, MN; Delaware Art Mus, Wilmington, DE; Whitney Mus of Am Art, NY; Walker Art Center, Minneapolis, MN; Arnhems Mus, The Netherlands; Art Gallery of Ontario, Canada; Nat Mus of Art, Canberra, Australia; Pennsylvania Acad of Fine Arts, Phila, PA
PRINTERS: Landfall Press Inc, Chicago, IL (LPI); Jack Lemon, Chicago, IL (JL); David Keister, Chicago, IL (DK); Timothy Berry, Chicago, IL (TB); Ian Lawson (IL); Crown Point Press, San Francisco, CA (CPP); Norman Stewart, Bloomfield Hills, MI (NS); Wing Lake Studio, Bloomfield Hills, MI (WLS); Bill Weege, Madison, WI (BW); Andrew Rubin, Madison, WI (AR); Tandem Press, Univ of Wisconsin, Madison, WI (TanPr)
PUBLISHERS: Pace Editions, NY (PE); Nancy Hoffman Gallery, NY (NHG); Parasol Press, NY (PaP); Landfall Press Inc, Chicago, IL (LPI); Univ of Michigan, Ann Arbor, MI (UM); Tandem Press, Univ of Wisconsin, Madison, WI (TanPr)
GALLERIES: Pace Prints, New York, NY; Nancy Hoffman Gallery, New York, NY; Images Gallery, Toledo, OH; Stewart & Stewart, Bloomfield Hills, MI; Martha Tepper Contemporary Fine Arts, West Newton, MA; Rutgers Barclay Gallery, Santa Fe, NM; Berggruen Gallery, San Francisco, CA
MAILING ADDRESS: c/o School of Visual Arts, Fine Arts Dept, 209 E 23rd St, New York, NY 10010

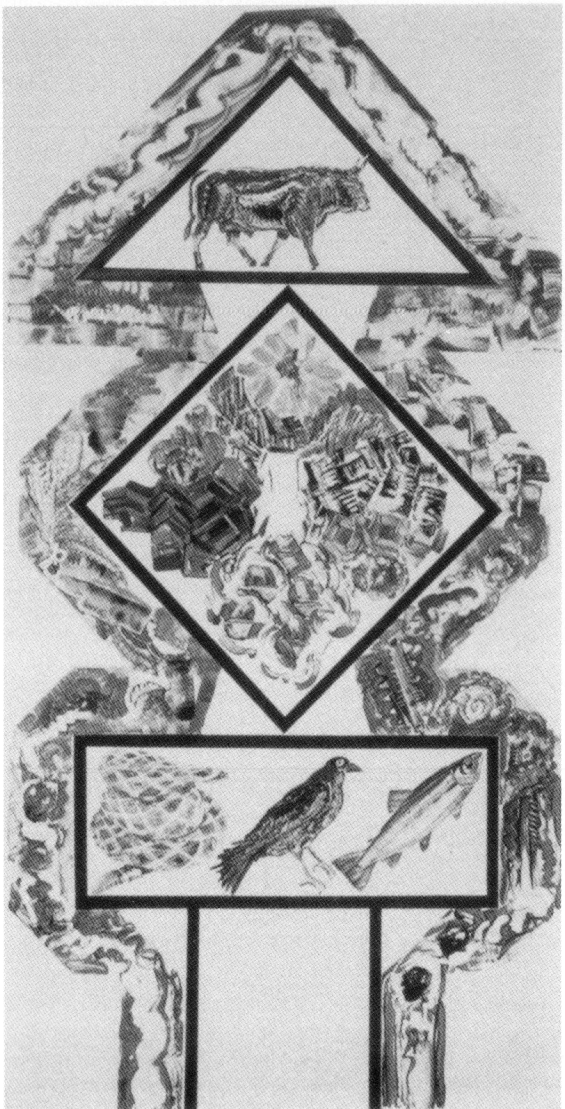

Don Nice
Gaia M II
Courtesy Tandem Press

TITLE	PUBLISHER	PRINTER	DATE	MEDIUM	DIMENSION (PAPER SIZE) IN INCHES	TYPE OF PAPER	EDITION NUMBER	NO. OF COLORS	ORIGINAL OPENING PRICE	CURRENT RETAIL PRICE
SOLD OUT EDITIONS (RARE):										
Radishes	PaP	IL	1973	LC	38 X 27	AP	50	8	350	2500
Owl	ART	C	1974	AC	37 X 30	AP	30	6	500	2200
Double Sneaker	LPI	DK/LPI	1975	LC	34 X 48	TRP	50	10	500	2500
Buffalo	NHG	JL/LPI	1976	LB	42 X 38	AP/W	50	11	450	2200
Bull Durham	NHG	TB/LPI	1976	AB	18 X 18	AP/W	25	1	175	1200
Raccoon	NHG	TB/LPI	1976	SP	22 X 30	AP/W	75		350	1500
Minnesota Predella	NHG	IL	1977	SP	16 X 63	AP/W	150		450	2200
Tootsie Pops	NHG	IL	1977	LB	28 X 40	AP/W	50		350	1200
Lion	NHG	IL	1977	SP	39 X 41	AP	144		450	1800
Hudson River Parrot (Triptych)	PE	JB/LPI	1980	LC/SP	10 X 29	AP	12		750	1800
American Still Life (Set of 3):									1100 SET	3500 SET
American Still Life #1	PE	JB/LPI	1980	LC	30 X 22	AC	50	5	450	1500
American Still Life #2	PE	JB/LPI	1980	LC	30 X 22	AC	50	5	450	1500
American Still Life #3	PE	JB/LPI	1980	LC	30 X 22	AC	50	5	450	1800
Two Pair	PE	JB/LPI	1981	AC/SUG	30 X 40	AP	50		750	1800
Heartland	UM	NS/WLS	1984	SP	15 X 29	R/BFK	50	9	500	1500
Fredericks Straits	LPI	JL/LPI	1985	LC	14 X 30	AC	30	8	450	1200
Ernest Sound	LPI	JL/LPI	1985	LC	14 X 30	AC	30	8	450	1200
Indian Brook	TanPr	BW/AR/TanPr	1990	MON	19 X 14 EA	AC	1 EA	Varies	750 EA	750 EA
Trout X	TanPr	BW/AR/TanPr	1990	MON	42 X 30 EA	AC	1 EA	Varies	1000 EA	1000 EA
Trout XIII	TanPr	BW/AR/TanPr	1990	MON	42 X 30 EA	AC	1 EA	Varies	2000 EA	2000 EA
Gaia MV II	TanPr	BW/AR/TanPr	1990	MON	72 X 39 EA	AC	1 EA	Varies	4000 EA	4000 EA
Gaia MV VI	TanPr	BW/AR/TanPr	1990	MON	71 X 40 EA	AC	1 EA	Varies	4000 EA	4000 EA
Trout	TanPr	BW/AR/TanPr	1991	LC	41 X 30	AC/W	40	9	1200	1200

The retail prices of the 100,000 limited edition prints quoted in this directory are subject to change. Print publishers, artists and galleries were the direct sources for these quotations. Prices in the secondary market listed as "Sold Out Editions (Rare)" indicate that the publisher has a limited supply of that print or that the print is difficult to locate in the galleries.

LEONARDO M NIERMAN

BORN: Mexico City, Mexico; November 1, 1932
EDUCATION: Nat Univ of Mexico, Mexico City, Mex, BA
AWARDS: First Prize, Art Inst of Mex, 1964; Palm D'Or Beaux Arts, Monaco, 1969; Gold Medal & Silver Medal, Tomasso Campanell Found, Italy, 1970,72
RECENT EXHIB: Museo de Arte Costarricense, San Jose, Costa Rica, 1987; Retrosp, Merrill Chase Gallery, Woodfield, IL, 1990; Merrill Chase Gallery, Chicago, IL, 1990; Merrill Chase Gallery, Oakbrooke, IL, 1990
COLLECTIONS: Mus of Fine Arts, Boston, MA; Ft Worth Art Mus, TX; Mus of Mod Art, Mexico City, Mex; Detroit Inst of Arts, MI; Acad of Fine Arts, Honolulu, Hawaii; Mus of Mod Art, Haifa, Israel; Mus of Contemp Arts, Madrid, Spain; Israel Mus, Jerusalem, Israel
PRINTERS: Arts Litho, Paris, France (AL); La Poligrafa, SA, Barcelona, Spain (LP)
PUBLISHERS: Lublin Graphics, Greenwich, CT (LG); Ediciones Poligrafa, SA, Barcelona, Spain (EdP)
GALLERIES: Nahan Galleries, New Orleans, LA; J Richards Gallery, Englewood, NJ; Jentra Fine Art Gallery, Freehold, NJ; B Lewin Galleries, Palm Beach, CA; Galeria Joan Prats, New York, NY & Barcelona, Spain; Hang-Up Gallery, Sarasota, FL; Centurion Galleries, Chicago, IL; Bryant Galleries, Jackson, MS & New Orleans, LA & Birmingham, AL; Lublin Graphics, Greenwich, CT & New York, NY; Merrill Chase Galleries, Chicago, IL & Northbrook, IL; de Ligney Art Galleries, Fort Lauderdale, FL; Galerie Martin, Boca Raton, FL
MAILING ADDRESS: Amsterdam 43 PH, Mexico 11 DF Mexico 06100

TITLE	PUBLISHER	PRINTER	DATE	MEDIUM	DIMENSION (PAPER SIZE) IN INCHES	TYPE OF PAPER	EDITION NUMBER	NO. OF COLORS	ORIGINAL OPENING PRICE	CURRENT RETAIL PRICE
SOLD OUT EDITIONS (RARE):										
Vent Eternal	LG	AL	1974	LC	18 X 24	AP	300	16	250	600
Chateau	LG	AL	1974	LC	18 X 24	JP	300	16	250	600
Brume de la Mer	LG	AL	1974	LC	18 X 24	AP/JP	300	16	250	600
La Vague	LG	AL	1974	LC	18 X 24	AP/JP	300	16	250	600
Oiseau de Feu	LG	AL	1974	LC	18 X 24	AP/JP	300	16	250	600
Forms in Space	LG	AL	1974	LC	18 X 24	AP/JP	275	13	200	500
Prismatic City	LG	AL	1977	LC	18 X 24	AP/JP	275	15	300	500
CURRENT EDITIONS:										
Stravinsky	LG	AL	1976	LC	18 X 24	AP/JP	270	14	300	400
Capriccio	LG	AL	1980	LC	18 X 24	AP/JP	350	15	400	400
Sonata	LG	AL	1980	LC	18 X 24	AP/JP	350	16	400	400
Moonlight	LG	AL	1980	LC	18 X 24	AP/JP	350	15	400	400
Musical Nocturne	LG	AL	1980	LC	18 X 24	AP/JP	350	16	400	400
Jerusalem	LG	AL	1980	LC	18 X 24	AP/JP	350	14	400	400
Set of Five Mixed Media Graphics:									2800 SET	3500 SET
Eclipse	EdP	LP	1983	MM	30 X 22	GP	99		600	750
Sũena	EdP	LP	1983	MM	30 X 22	GP	99		600	750
Vuelo	EdP	LP	1983	MM	22 X 30	GP	99		600	750
Espejismo	EdP	LP	1983	MM	30 X 22	GP	99		600	750
Primavera	EdP	LP	1983	MM	30 X 22	GP	99		600	750
Flight Sensation	LG	AL	1985	LC	23 X 17	AP/JP	350		400	400
Space Dynamics	LG	AL	1985	LC	23 X 17	AP/JP	350		400	400
Moment of Ignition	LG	AL	1985	LC	24 X 17	AP/JP	350		400	400
Autumn Wind	LG	AL	1985	LC	23 X 17	AP/JP	350		400	400
Form in Suspension	LG	AL	1985	LC	24 X 17	AP/JP	350		400	400

JEAN NIND

BORN: Miri, Sarawak, Borneo; June 17, 1930; Canadian Citizen
EDUCATION: Chelsea Art Sch, London, England, Univ of Saskatchewan, Saskatoon, Saskatchewan
TEACHING: Instr, Mendel Art Gallery, Saskatawan, Sask, Can, 1965–66; Instr, Painting, Sir Sandford Fleming Col, Peterborough, ON, Can, 1970–77; Instr, Painting, Trent Univ & Peterborough Art Gallery, Peterborough, ON, Can, 1970–77
AWARDS: Purchase Award, Saskatchewan Arts Council, Can, 1965; Purchase Award, Sir Sandford Fleming Col, Peterborough, ON, Can, 1975; Merit Award, Ontario Arts Council, Can, 1975,89,90
RECENT EXHIB: Williamson House Gallery, Peterborough, ON, Can, 1988; Art Space, Toronto, ON, Can, 1988; Art Gallery of Lindsay, Can, 1988; Art Gallery of Peterborough, Can, 1989; Magic Image, Ajax, ON, Canada, 1992
COLLECTIONS: Trent Univ, Peterborough, Can; Sir Sandford Fleming Col, Peterborough, Can; Art Gallery of Peterborough, Can
PRINTERS: Artist (ART)
PUBLISHERS: Artist (ART)
GALLERIES: Bau-Xi Galleries, Toronto, Canada & Vancouver, Canada; Sisler Gallery, Toronto, Canada; Sobot Gallery, Toronto, Canada; Williamson House Gallery, Peterborough, ON, Canada; Art Gallery of Peterborough, ON, Canada
MAILING ADDRESS: 29 Merino Rd, Peterborough, ON, Canada K9J 6M8

TITLE	PUBLISHER	PRINTER	DATE	MEDIUM	DIMENSION (PAPER SIZE) IN INCHES	TYPE OF PAPER	EDITION NUMBER	NO. OF COLORS	ORIGINAL OPENING PRICE	CURRENT RETAIL PRICE
SOLD OUT EDITIONS (RARE):										
Prairie Trees	ART	ART	1966	SP	17 X 24	AP	8	5	100	500
Eclypse	ART	ART	1968	SP	17 X 24	AP	6	7	100	500
Winter Grass	ART	ART	1976	SP	17 X 24	AP	9	5	200	350
Winter Tree	ART	ART	1976	SP	17 X 24	AP	10	5	200	350
Tree Variations #2	ART	ART	1976	SP	17 X 24	AP	8	6	200	500
Day Lilies, #1,#2	ART	ART	1989	SP	17 X 24 EA	AP	5 EA	4 EA	600 SET / 300 EA	600 SET / 300 EA
Jonathan and His Friends, #1, #2, #3	ART	ART	1990	SP	17 X 24 EA	AP	2 EA	4 EA	1000 SET / 350 EA	1000 SET / 350 EA
CURRENT EDITIONS:										
Elm Tree, #1, #2	ART	ART	1976	SP	17 X 24 EA	AP	8 EA	5 EA	400 SET / 200 EA	600 SET / 300 EA
Winter Birch #2	ART	ART	1976	SP	17 X 24	AP	12	5	250	250
Solitude	ART	ART	1977	SP	17 X 24	AP	5	5	250	250
Dying Elm #0, #1	ART	ART	1977	SP	17 X 24 EA	AP	8 EA	5 EA	250 EA	250 EA

JEAN NIND CONTINUED

TITLE	PUBLISHER	PRINTER	DATE	MEDIUM	DIMENSION (PAPER SIZE) IN INCHES	TYPE OF PAPER	EDITION NUMBER	NO. OF COLORS	ORIGINAL OPENING PRICE	CURRENT RETAIL PRICE
CURRENT EDITIONS:										
Carnival Trinidad #1, #2, #3	ART	ART	1978	SP	17 X 24 EA	AP	8 EA	6 EA	200 EA	200 EA
Algarve Orchard #1–#5 (Set of 5)	ART	ART	1982	SP	17 X 24 EA	AP	1 EA	5 EA	1250 SET	1250 SET
Algarve Variations #0	ART	ART	1983	SP	17 X 24	AP	12	4	250	250
Algarve Variations #1	ART	ART	1983	SP	17 X 24	AP	5	5	250	250
Algarve Variations #2	ART	ART	1983	SP	17 X 24	AP	5	6	250	250
Geranium Stock	ART	ART	1983	SP	17 X 24	AP	12	5	250	250
Algarve Winter Variations #1–#4 (Set of 4)	ART	ART	1984	SP	17 X 24 EA	AP	1 EA	7 EA	1000 SET	1000 SET
Swamp Grass Suite (Set of 8):									2250 SET	2250 SET
Swamp Grass, #1,#2,#3	ART	ART	1986	SP	17 X 24 EA	AP	4 EA	4 EA	300 EA	300 EA
Swamp Grass, #4,#5,#6,#7	ART	ART	1989	SP	17 X 24 EA	AP	4 EA	4 EA	300 EA	300 EA
Winter Morning Suite, #1,#2,#3 (Set of 3)	ART	ART	1989	SP	17 X 24 EA	AP	1 EA	4 EA	900 SET	900 SET
									300 EA	300 EA
Wild Lilies Suite, #1,#2,#3 (Set of 3)	ART	ART	1989	SP	17 X 24 EA	AP	3 EA	4 EA	900 SET	900 SET
									300 EA	300 EA

ANNE E NIPPER

BORN: Raleigh, NC; 1955
EDUCATION: Univ of North Carolina, Chapel Hill, NC, BFA, 1976
COLLECTIONS: Duke Univ, Durham, NC; Eastern Illinois Univ, Charleston, IL
PRINTERS: Tom Jones Graphics, Greensboro, NC (TJG) (OB)
PUBLISHERS: Tom Jones Graphics, Greensboro, NC (TJG) (OB); London Arts Inc, Detroit, MI (LAI)
GALLERIES: London Arts Gallery, Detroit, MI

TITLE	PUBLISHER	PRINTER	DATE	MEDIUM	DIMENSION (PAPER SIZE) IN INCHES	TYPE OF PAPER	EDITION NUMBER	NO. OF COLORS	ORIGINAL OPENING PRICE	CURRENT RETAIL PRICE
CURRENT EDITIONS:										
Three Tropical Robins	LAI	TJG	1980	SP	38 X 30	STP	250	5	175	200
Tree Top Treatise	LAI	TJG	1980	SP	30 X 22	STP	250	5	150	175

BRIAN NISSEN

PRINTERS: La Poligrafa, Barcelona, Spain (LP)
PUBLISHERS: Ediciones Poligrafa, Barcelona, Spain (EdP)
GALLERIES: Galeria Joan Prats, Barcelona, Spain & New York, NY; Galeria Venezuela, New York, NY

TITLE	PUBLISHER	PRINTER	DATE	MEDIUM	DIMENSION (PAPER SIZE) IN INCHES	TYPE OF PAPER	EDITION NUMBER	NO. OF COLORS	ORIGINAL OPENING PRICE	CURRENT RETAIL PRICE
SOLD OUT EDITIONS (RARE):										
Mariposa Obsidiana #1–#10 (Set of 10)	EdP	LP	1981	EC	28 X 21 EA	GP	75 EA		3000 SET	4000 SET
									350 EA	450 EA

HERMANN NITSCH

RECENT EXHIB: David Nolan Gallery, NY, 1988
PRINTERS: D P Druck & Publication, Munich, West Germany (DPD)
PUBLISHERS: Verlag Fred Jahn, Munich, West Germany (VFJ); David Nolan Gallery, NY (DNG)
GALLERIES: David Nolan Gallery, New York, NY; Karl Imhof, Munich, West Germany (KI); Modernism Gallery, San Francisco, CA

TITLE	PUBLISHER	PRINTER	DATE	MEDIUM	DIMENSION (PAPER SIZE) IN INCHES	TYPE OF PAPER	EDITION NUMBER	NO. OF COLORS	ORIGINAL OPENING PRICE	CURRENT RETAIL PRICE
CURRENT EDITIONS:										
The Architecture of the Orgies— Mysteries Theatre (Set of 36)	VFJ	DPD	1984-87	LC(28)	40 X 30 EA	R/BFK	35 EA	Varies	15000 SET	18000 SET
Die Achitektur des Mysterien Theatres Mappe (Set of 18)	FJ/DNG	KI	1984-89	LC/EB/HC	28 X 22 EA	R/BFK	35 EA	Varies	18000 DM	18000 DM

IRVING NORMAN

BORN: Poland; 1910
EDUCATION: California Sch of Fine Arts, 1945; Studied with Reginald Marsh and R B Hale
AWARDS: Albert M Bender Mem Fund, 1945–46; Purchase Awards, San Francisco Art Assn, 1945
PRINTERS: Editions Press, San Francisco, CA (EP)
PUBLISHERS: Editions Press, San Francisco, CA (EP)
GALLERIES: Simon Lowinsky Gallery, San Francisco, CA

TITLE	PUBLISHER	PRINTER	DATE	MEDIUM	DIMENSION (PAPER SIZE) IN INCHES	TYPE OF PAPER	EDITION NUMBER	NO. OF COLORS	ORIGINAL OPENING PRICE	CURRENT RETAIL PRICE
CURRENT EDITIONS:										
From Work	EP	EP	1979	LB	22 X 28	STP/C	90	1	400	600

KENNETH NOLAND

BORN: Asheville, NC; April 10, 1924
EDUCATION: Black Mountain Col, Beria, NC, 1946–48, with Ilya Bolotowsky; Zadkine Sch of Sculpture, Paris, France, 1948–49
TEACHING: Instr, Inst of Contemp Art, Wash, DC, 1949–51; Catholic Univ, Wash, DC, 1951–60; Washington Workshop Center for the Arts, Wash, DC, 1952–56; Milton Avery Prof, Arts, Bard Col, Annandale-on-Hudson, NY, 1985; Artist in Res, Computer Video Arts, Pratt Inst, NY, 1986–87
AWARDS: Corcoran Award, Wash, DC, 1967
RECENT EXHIB: Gallery One, Toronto, Canada, 1988; Hokin Gallery, Bay Harbor Islands, FL, 1989; Heath Gallery, Atlanta, GA, 1989; Salander-O'Reilly Gallery, Inc, NY, 1989; Helander Gallery, Palm Beach, FL, 1990; Salander-O'Reilly Gallery, Inc, Beverly Hills, CA, 1990; Edmonton Art Gallery, Alberta, Canada, 1990–91; Asheville Art Mus, NC, 1992
COLLECTIONS: Albright-Knox Art Gallery, Buffalo, NY; Detroit Inst of Fine Arts, MI; Baltimore Mus, MD; Stedelijk Mus, Schniedam, Netherlands; Worcester Art Mus, MA; Art Inst of Chicago, IL; Corcoran Gallery of Art, Wash, DC; Solomon R Guggenheim Mus, NY; Los Angeles County Mus, CA; Metropolitan Mus of Art, NY; Mus of Mod Art, NY; Nat Gallery of Art, Wash, DC; Walker Art Center, Minneapolis, MN; Whitney Mus of Am Art, NY
PRINTERS: Chiron Press, NY (CP); Sarah Lawrence Art Press, NY (SLAP); Artist (ART); Tyler Graphics Workshop, Mount Kisco, NY (TGL); Experimental Workshop, San Francisco, CA (ExW); Bob Franklin, Phila, PA (BF); Brandywine Graphic Workshop, Phila, PA (BGW)
PUBLISHERS: Tyler Graphics, Ltd, Mount Kisco, NY (TGL); Experimental Workshop, San Francisco, CA (ExW); Artist (ART); Artist (ART); Brandywine Graphic Workshop, Phila, PA (BGW)
GALLERIES: Nancy Singer Gallery, St Louis, MO; André Emmerich Gallery, New York, NY; Galeria Joan Prats, New York, NY & Barcelona, Spain; Flanders Modern, Minneapolis, MN; Experimental Workshop, San Francisco, CA; Constance Kamens Fine Art, Inc, New York, NY; Douglas Drake Gallery, New York, NY; Hokin Galleries, Bay Harbor Islands, FL & Palm Beach, FL; Eva Cohon Galleries, Ltd, Chicago, IL & Highland Park, IL; R H Love Galleries, Chicago, IL; Rembla Gallery, Mixografia Workshop, Santa Monica, CA; Helander Gallery, Palm Beach, FL; Stremmel Gallery, Reno, NV; Gallery Urban, New York, NY;

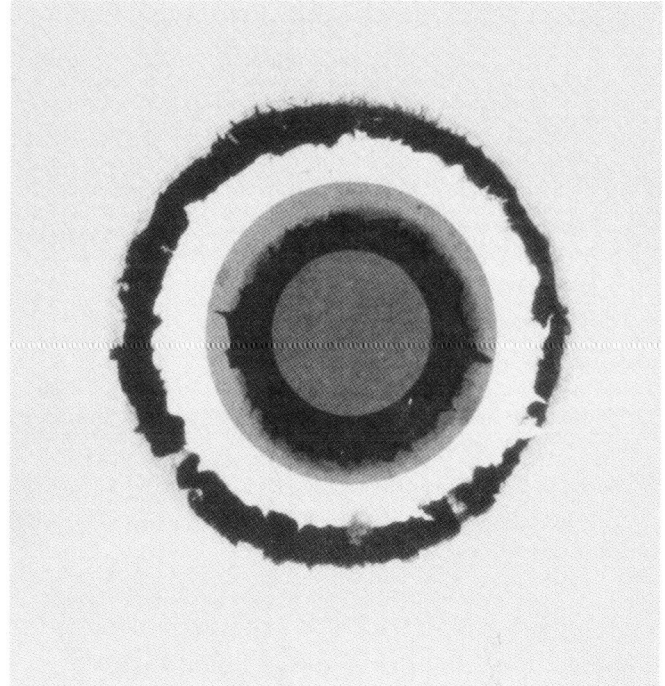

Kenneth Noland
Handmade Paper Project: Circle II
Courtesy Tyler Graphics, Ltd

Salander-O-Reilly Galleries, New York, NY; Gerald Peters Gallery, Dallas, TX; Meredith Long & Company, Houston, TX
MAILING ADDRESS: 125-A Kitchawan Rd, South Salem, NY 10590

Tyler Graphics, Ltd (T)

TITLE	PUBLISHER	PRINTER	DATE	MEDIUM	DIMENSION (PAPER SIZE) IN INCHES	TYPE OF PAPER	EDITION NUMBER	NO. OF COLORS	ORIGINAL OPENING PRICE	CURRENT RETAIL PRICE
SOLD OUT EDITIONS (RARE):										
Twin Planes		CP/SLAP	1969	SP	6 X 59	CAN	200		200	5500
Echo (Printed for 50th Anniversary of Sarah Lawrence College) (T-463) (KN-2)	TGL	TGL	1978	AC/EMB	20 X 24	AC	50	6	1000	6000
Blush (Printed for Inst of Contemp Art)	TGL	TGL	1978	LC	36 X 30	R/BFK	50	13	1200	6000
Untitled (PK-0393)	ART	ART	1981	MON	25 X 30 EA	HMP	1 EA	Varies	3000 EA	12000 EA
Winds	TGL	TGL	1982	MON/HC	86 X 32 EA	R/BFK	1 EA		2000 EA	15000 EA
CURRENT EDITIONS:										
Circle I Series (T-464) (3 Layers of Colored Pulp)	TGL	TGL	1978	LC/MON	20 X 16	HMP	110	Varies	2000	6500 EA
Circle II Series (5 Layers of Colored Pulp)	TGL	TGL	1978	LC/MON	32 X 21	HMP	110	Varies	3000	7500 EA
Horizontal Stripes Series (2–6 Layers of Colored Pulp):										
Horizontal Stripes I	TGL	TGL	1978	SP/MON	51 X 32 EA	HMP	1 EA	Varies	8000 EA	14000 EA
Horizontal Stripes II	TGL	TGL	1978	SP/MON	51 X 32 EA	HMP	1 EA	Varies	8000 EA	14000 EA
Horizontal Stripes III	TGL	TGL	1978	SP/MON	51 X 32 EA	HMP	1 EA	Varies	8000 EA	14000 EA
Horizontal Stripes IV	TGL	TGL	1978	SP/MON	51 X 32 EA	HMP	1 EA	Varies	8000 EA	14000 EA
Horizontal Stripes V	TGL	TGL	1978	SP/MON	51 X 32 EA	HMP	1 EA	Varies	8000 EA	14000 EA
Diagonal Stripes Series (8 Layers of Colored Pulp) Pairs (unique colored & Pressed Paper Pulp—Each with Two (16" Squares)	TGL	TGL	1982	MON	23 X 41 EA	HMP	1 EA	Varies	3000 EA	5500 EA
Montes Coloreados	TGL	TGL	1985	MON/HC	38 X 60 EA	HMP	1 EA	Varies	4500 EA	10000 EA
Brandywine	ART/BGW	BF/BGW	1991	LC/OFF/SP	22 X 30	AC/BL	19		2500	3500

GUSTAVO NOVOA

BORN: Santiago, Chile; March 1, 1941
EDUCATION: Acad of Fine Arts, Santiago, Chile

PRINTERS: Atelier Ettinger, NY (AE); Edmund et Jacques Desjobert, Paris, France (E-JD)
PUBLISHERS: Studio 53 Editions, NY (S53E)
GALLERIES: Art Gallery, Studio 53, New York, NY; Wally Findlay Galleries, Paris, France & Palm Beach, FL & New York, NY & Beverly Hills, CA & Chicago, IL; Fernette's Gallery of Art, Des Moines, IA; Steiner Galleries, Miami, FL; Jack Arnold Fine Arts, New York, NY

GUSTAVO NOVOA CONTINUED

TITLE	PUBLISHER	PRINTER	DATE	MEDIUM	DIMENSION (PAPER SIZE) IN INCHES	TYPE OF PAPER	EDITION NUMBER	NO. OF COLORS	ORIGINAL OPENING PRICE	CURRENT RETAIL PRICE
CURRENT EDITIONS:										
Company	S53E	E-JD	1980	LC	25 X 31	AP	350	14	400	500
Company	S53E	E-JD	1980	LC	25 X 31	JP	350	14	425	500
Drifters	S53E	E-JD	1980	LC	25 X 31	AP	350	17	325	450
Drifters	S53E	E-JD	1980	LC	25 X 31	JP	350	17	350	500
Audience	S53E	E-JD	1980	LC	25 X 32	AP	350	13	400	500
Audience	S53E	E-JD	1980	LC	25 X 32	JP	350	13	425	500
Plum River	S53E	E-JD	1980	LC	25 X 32	AP	350	11	400	500
Plum River	S53E	E-JD	1980	LC	25 X 32	JP	350	11	425	500
Novoa's Ark	S53E	E-JD	1981	LC	25 X 31	AP	350	14	325	450
Novoa's Ark	S53E	E-JD	1981	LC	25 X 31	JP	350	14	350	450
Lioness	S53E	E-JD	1981	LC	15 X 20	AP	350	16	175	300
Lioness	S53E	E-JD	1981	LC	15 X 20	JP	350	16	200	300
Lion	S53E	E-JD	1981	LC	15 X 20	AP	350	16	175	300
Lion	S53E	E-JD	1981	LC	15 X 20	JP	350	16	200	300
Compassion	S53E	E-JD	1981	LC	25 X 31	AP	350	15	325	450
Compassion	S53E	E-JD	1981	LC	25 X 31	JP	350	15	350	450
Central Park	S53E	E-JD	1981	LC	25 X 31	AP	350	17	325	450
Central Park	S53E	E-JD	1981	LC	25 X 31	JP	350	17	350	450
Ensemble	S53E	E-JD	1982	LC	25 X 31	AP	350	15	325	450
Ensemble	S53E	E-JD	1982	LC	25 X 31	JP	350	15	350	450

DENIS PAUL NOYER

BORN: Lyon, France; March 16, 1940
EDUCATION: Ecole des Beaux-Arts de Troyes, Paris, France; Studied with Philippe Noyer (Father)
RECENT EXHIB: Galerie Deo, Cannes, France, 1989; Manoir du Mod Gallery, Metz, France, 1990,91
COLLECTIONS: Sausalito Mus, CA
PRINTERS: Arts Litho, Paris, France (AL); Atelier Desjobert, Paris, France (AD)

PUBLISHERS: Editions des Maîtres Contemporains, Saint Raphaël, France (EMC); Rosenstiels Fine Art, London, England (RFA); Original Print Collector's Group, NY (OPCG); Gregory Editions, Woodland Hills, CA (GregEd)
GALLERIES: Florence Art Gallery, Dallas, TX; Railings Gallery, London, England; Gregory Editions, Woodland Hills, CA; Galerie Deo 70, Cannes, France; Galerie Anne Apesteguy, Deauville, France; Galerie Pierre Hautot, Paris, France
MAILING ADDRESS: 119 rue de la Tour, 75016 Paris, France

TITLE	PUBLISHER	PRINTER	DATE	MEDIUM	DIMENSION (PAPER SIZE) IN INCHES	TYPE OF PAPER	EDITION NUMBER	NO. OF COLORS	ORIGINAL OPENING PRICE	CURRENT RETAIL PRICE
CURRENT EDITIONS:										
Mercedes Suite (Set of 12):									5000 SET	7500 SET
Hotel Carlton (Cannes)	EMC	AD	1985–86	LC	105 X 75 cm	AP	300	16	500	700
Hotel de Paris (Monte Carlo)	EMC	AD	1985–86	LC	105 X 75 cm	AP	300	16	500	700
Hotel Ritz (Paris)	EMC	AD	1985–86	LC	105 X 75 cm	AP	300	16	500	700
Le Casino de Monte Carlo	EMC	AD	1985–86	LC	105 X 75 cm	AP	300	16	500	700
Le Grand Hotel de Cabourg	EMC	AD	1985–86	LC	105 X 75 cm	AP	300	16	500	700
Palais de la Mediterrannée (Nice)	EMC	AD	1985–86	LC	105 X 75 cm	AP	300	16	500	700
Le Casino de Deauville	EMC	AD	1985–86	LC	105 X 75 cm	AP	300	16	500	700
Hotel Crillon (Paris)	EMC	AD	1985–86	LC	105 X 75 cm	AP	300	16	500	700
Hotel Plaza Athenee (Paris)	EMC	AD	1985–86	LC	105 X 75 cm	AP	300	16	500	700
Hotel George V (Paris)	EMC	AD	1985–86	LC	105 X 75 cm	AP	300	16	500	700
Hotel Negresco (Nice)	EMC	AD	1985–86	LC	105 X 75 cm	AP	300	16	500	700
Hotel Gonnet (Cannes)	EMC	AD	1985–86	LC	105 X 75 cm	AP	300	16	500	700
Springtime Dream (Set of 4):										
Lady in Blue	GregEd	AD	1991	LC	15 X 20	AP	375	12	800	800
On the Deck	GregEd	AD	1991	LC	15 X 20	AP	375	12	800	800
Party	GregEd	AD	1991	LC	15 X 20	AP	375	12	800	800
The Park	GregEd	AD	1991	LC	15 X 20	AP	375	12	800	800

PHILIPPE NOYER

BORN: Lyon, France; June 28, 1917
EDUCATION: Ecole des Roches, Lyon, France; Beaux Arts Sch of Lyon, France
COLLECTIONS: Univ of Cincinnati, OH; Seattle Mus, WA; Mus of Mod Art, Paris, France; Mus of Fine Art, Phoenix, AZ; Mus of Mod Art, Omaha, NE; Mus of Mod Art, Boston, MA; Baltimore Mus, MD

PRINTERS: Arts Litho, Paris, France (AL); Atelier Desjobert, Paris France (AD)
PUBLISHERS: Edward Weston Graphics Inc, Northridge, CA (EWG); Metropolitan Art Associates, Huntington, NY (MAA); Amiel Publishing, Secaucus, NJ (AP); Michael Zabrin Publishing (MZP)
GALLERIES: Edward Weston Graphics Galleries, New York, NY & Paris, France & Los Angeles, CA & Milan, Italy; La Galeria, Kansas City, MO
MAILING ADDRESS: 9 Bis Rue Lalo, 75116 Paris, France

The print market has become very selective. For the first time since we published the first edition of The Printworld Directory in 1982, the prices of prints have been greatly reduced and greatly increased for the same artists by the most reputable and established print publishers. Check the fifth edition to understand the movement.

PHILIPPE NOYER CONTINUED

TITLE	PUBLISHER	PRINTER	DATE	MEDIUM	DIMENSION (PAPER SIZE) IN INCHES	TYPE OF PAPER	EDITION NUMBER	NO. OF COLORS	ORIGINAL OPENING PRICE	CURRENT RETAIL PRICE
SOLD OUT EDITIONS (RARE):										
Femme et Papillons	EWG			LC	24 X 31	R/100	325	12	200	1000
Ladies in Red	EWG			LC	32 X 25	R/100	220		200	800
Lady and the Peke	EWG			LC	21 X 27	R/100	275		200	1200
Villa Medici	EWG			LC	31 X 25	R/100	200		200	1200
From Ladies and Leopards Suite (Set of 5):										
Maude	EWG			LC	30 X 24	R/100	250		350	1800
Miss Otis	EWG			LC	30 X 30	R/100	250		350	1200
Daphne	EWG			LC	29 X 23	R/100	250		350	1800
Heidi	EWG			LC	30 X 16	R/100	250		350	1200
Lady from Macao	EWG			LC	31 X 44	R/100	250		350	1200
CURRENT EDITIONS:										
La Blanc Yacht	EWG		1979	LC	30 X 47	R/100	325		400	3000
Princess Elodie and the Ice Cream	EWG		1979	LC	25 X 33	R/100	325		400	750
L'Autrauche et Femme	EWG		1979	LC	46 X 29	R/100	325		400	800
Symphony to a Geranium	EWG		1980	SP	34 X 44	R/100	325		450	800
Les Petites Filles au Piano	EWG		1980	LC	38 X 25	R/100	325		450	750
White Rolls Royce (Reg)	EWG		1980	SP	34 X 46	R/100	325		450	2000
White Rolls Royce (Del)	EWG		1980	SP	33 X 46	R/100	150			1800
Femme Chez Maxim	EWG		1981	LC	34 X 23	R/100	325	15	500	750
Femme Aux Chevre	EWG		1981	LC	30 X 23	R/100	325		500	600
Moulin Rouge	EWG		1981	LC	32 X 32	R/100	325		750	900
La Tortue	EWG		1981	LC	30 X 23	PAP/FAB	180/60		600/700	800/900
Love	EWG		1981	LC	30 X 23	PAP/FAB	180/60		600/700	800/900
La Femme a Oiseau (Parrot)	EWG		1981	LC	30 X 23	PAP/FAB	180/60		600/700	800/900
La Rosier Rose	EWG		1981	LC	30 X 23	PAP/FAB	180/60		600/700	800/900
Frog and Ice Cream Cone	EWG		1981	LC	30 X 23	PAP/FAB	180/60		600/700	800/900
Le Dousett (Fish Bowl)	EWG		1981	LC	30 X 23	PAP/FAB	180/60		600/700	800/900
Chinese Garden	MAA	AL	1984	LC	30 X 41	AP	250	20	750	1000
Gold Eclipse	MAA	AL	1984	LC	30 X 41	AP	250		750	1000
Lady Libellula	MZP	AL	1984	LC	30 X 41	AP	250	20	800	1000
Dona Camilla	MAA	AL/AD	1984–85	LC	30 X 41	AP	250	20	750	900
Oderint Dum Metuant (The Red Eclipse)	AP	AD	1985	LC	30 X 41	AP	250	25	1000	1200
The Dictator	AP	AD	1985	LC	30 X 40	AP	250	20	800	1000
Blind Man's Buff at the Russian Imperial Court	AP	AD	1985	LC	30 X 41	AP	250	20	800	1000
Hollywood	AP	AD	1985	LC	30 X 41	AP	250	20	800	1000

BOB L NUGENT

BORN: Santa Monica, CA; August 15, 1947
EDUCATION: Col of Creative Studies, Univ of California, Santa Barbara, CA, BFA, 1969; MFA, 1971
TEACHING: Univ of Hawaii, Samoan Islands, 1971–72; Pepperdine Univ, Malibu, CA, 1972–73; Col of the Siskiyous, Weed, CA, 1973–81; Sonoma State Univ, Rohnert Park, CA, 1981 to present
AWARDS: Univ of California Regents Grant, 1967–71; Tyrus Wong Award for Painting, 1972; Louis Comfort Tiffany Found Fel, 1977; Nat Endowment for the Arts Fel, 1979
COLLECTIONS: Indianapolis Mus of Art, IN; Arizona State Univ, Tempe, AZ; Brooklyn Mus of Art, NY
PRINTERS: Katherine Lincoln Press, San Francisco, CA (KLP); Christopher Laehy, Bloomington, IN (CL); David Keister, Bloomington, IN (DK); Pegram Harrison, Bloomington, IN (PH); David Calkins, Bloomington, IN (DC); Echo Press, Bloomington, IN (EPr); Presstime Studio, Tucson, AZ (PS); Magnolia Editions, Oakland, CA (MEP)
PUBLISHERS: Bristol Art Editions, Ltd, NY (BA); Katherine Lincoln Press, San Francisco, CA (KLP); Echo Press, Bloomington, IN (EPr); Artist (ART)
GALLERIES: Cavallino, Venice, Italy; Gallerie Cammille, Brussels, Belgium; Robert L Kidd Galleries, Birmingham, MI; Futura, Stockholm, Sweden; Mary Ryan Gallery, New York, NY; Echo Press, Bloomington, IN; Thomson Gallery, Minneapolis, MN; Gallery 72, Omaha, NE; Roy Boyd Galleries, Chicago, IL & Santa Monica, CA; Cumberland Gallery, Nashville, TN; Magnolia Editions, Oakland, CA; I Wolk Gallery, St Helena, CA; Fay Gold Gallery, Atlanta, GA
MAILING ADDRESS: c/o Department of Art, Sonoma State University, 1801 E Cotati Ave, Rohner Park, CA 94928

TITLE	PUBLISHER	PRINTER	DATE	MEDIUM	DIMENSION (PAPER SIZE) IN INCHES	TYPE OF PAPER	EDITION NUMBER	NO. OF COLORS	ORIGINAL OPENING PRICE	CURRENT RETAIL PRICE
SOLD OUT EDITIONS (RARE):										
Kept Letter	BA	DK/CL/PH	1980	LC/CO	26 X 19	HMP	30	3	400	500
Canal Series I, II	BA	DK/CL/EPr	1980	LC	23 X 30 EA	AP/W	30 EA	4 EA	400 EA	500 EA
Valley Structure, I, II	ART/KLP	KLP	1980	PH/GRA	22 X 30 EA	R/BFK	16 EA	12 EA	400 EA	500 EA
T-Structure	ART/KLP	KLP	1980	PH/GRA	22 X 30	R/BFK	16	15	400	500
Untitled 1980 Monotypes (Series of 20)	ART/KLP	KLP	1980	MON	22 X 30 EA	AP88	1 EA	Multi	400 EA	500 EA
Untitled 1981 Monotypes	ART/KLP	KLP	1981	MON	22 X 30 EA	AP88	1 EA	Multi	400 EA	500 EA
Nanny's Note	BA	DK/CL/EPr	1982	LC/CO	26 X 19	HMP	30	11	400	500
Folio	BA	DK/CL/EPr	1982	LC/CO	18 X 12 X 1	HMP/CHIRI	30	7	400	500
Belen Poles XIII	EPr	DK/DC/EPr	1987	MM	24 X 55 EA	HMP	1 EA	Varies		
CURRENT EDITIONS:										
Obara I, II (Dipt)	ART	MEP	1983	LC/CO	18 X 15 EA	MASA/MUL	120 EA	5 EA	500 EA	600 EA
Obara Variations (Set of 4):										
Obara Variations I	EPr	DK/OC/EPr	1984	LC/CO/GL	11 X 14	CHP/SHIB	24	7	500	600
Obara Variations II, III, IV	EPr	DK/OC/EPr	1984	LC/CO/GL	11 X 14 EA	CHP/SHIB	24 EA	7/7/6	400 EA	500 EA

BOB L NUGENT CONTINUED

TITLE	PUBLISHER	PRINTER	DATE	MEDIUM	DIMENSION (PAPER SIZE) IN INCHES	TYPE OF PAPER	EDITION NUMBER	NO. OF COLORS	ORIGINAL OPENING PRICE	CURRENT RETAIL PRICE
CURRENT EDITIONS:										
Obara Aichi (with Gold Leaf) I-VI (Set of 6)	EPr	DK/DC/EPr	1985	LC	21 X 18 EA	KIT	26 EA	8-11 EA	600 EA	850 EA
Amazona I	EPr	DK/DC/EPr	1987	LC	45 X 31	JK/HMP	30	8	750	900
Amazona Study #1	EPr	DK/DC/EPr	1988	MON	24 X 28 EA	HMP	1 EA		1000 EA	1500 EA
Amazona Study #2	EPr	DK/DC/EPr	1988	MON	36 X 24 EA	HMP	1 EA		1200 EA	1800 EA
Batão (Unique)	EPr	DK/DC/EPr	1990	EB/HC/WA	20 X 15	TR/HMP/BL	1 EA	Varies	800 EA	800 EA
Archive I	EPr	DK/DC/EPr	1991	LC/DPT/HC	35 X 28	OD/AC	19	9	1200	1200
Archive II	EPr	DK/DC/EPr	1991	LC/DPT/HC	35 X 28	OD/AC	16	9	1200	1200
Chapada #1, #2	EPr	DK/DC/EPr	1990-92	LC/DPT/ENG/HC	20 X 28	AC/W	21 EA	Varies	1000 EA	1000 EA

EDWARD E O'CONNELL

BORN: New York, NY; July 9, 1936
EDUCATION: Hofstra Univ, Hempstead, NY, BS, 1954–58; Pratt Inst, NY, MFA, 1965–66
TEACHING: Asst Prof, Photography & Graphics, Montclair State Col, Upper Montclair, NJ, 1967–70; Sch of Visual Arts, NY, 1969–80; Asst Prof, Photography & Printmaking, Fordham Univ, NY, 1970–80
AWARDS: Harcourt Found Fel, 1965; Pratt Fel, NY, 1966; Printmaking Grant, Louis Comfort Tiffany Found, 1966; Award, Associated American Artists, Miniature Print Prize, NY, 1967; Purchase Award, Brooklyn Mus, NY, 1970

COLLECTIONS: Metropolitan Mus of Art, NY; Brooklyn Mus, NY; George Eastman House, Rochester, NY; Minneapolis Art Inst, MN; Univ of Massachusetts, Amherst, MA; Univ of Tennessee, Knoxville, TN; Univ of Wisconsin, Platteville, WI; Univ of Minnesota, Duluth, MN; Univ of Guam; Philadelphia Free Library, PA
PUBLISHERS: Spring Street Editions, NY (SSE); Migneco-Smith, Florence, Italy (MS)
PRINTERS: Gerald Johnson, NY (GJ); Michael Kirsky, NY (MK); O'Connell Graphics, NY (OCG); Artist (ART)
GALLERIES: John Szoke Gallery, New York, NY; Associated American Artists, New York, NY

TITLE	PUBLISHER	PRINTER	DATE	MEDIUM	DIMENSION (PAPER SIZE) IN INCHES	TYPE OF PAPER	EDITION NUMBER	NO. OF COLORS	ORIGINAL OPENING PRICE	CURRENT RETAIL PRICE
SOLD OUT EDITIONS (RARE):										
Totem	SSE	ART/OG	1965	SP	35 X 46	MO/S	20	1	150	450
American Still Life	SSE	ART/OG	1966	SP	5 X 7	NB	25	4	125	300
Suburbia in Four Installments	SSE	ART/OG	1967	SP	22 X 30	AP	5	6	125	500
Sky Mural (20 Panels)	SSE	ART/OG	1968	SP	144 X 180	MO/S	22	10	1500	3500
Flower Study	SSE	ART/OG	1970	SP	35 X 46	MO/S	8	1	125	400
CURRENT EDITIONS:										
Downtown	SSE	ART/OG	1968	SP	23 X 29	NB	25	4	100	350
Downtown Variations	SSE	ART/OG	1968	SP	23 X 29	NB	21	5	100	350
New York Reflections II	SSE	ART/OG	1968	SP	23 X 29	NB	15 AP	6	100	250
Rainbow's End	SSE	ART/OG	1969	SP	23 X 29	NB	50	4	100	300
Sentinel	SSE	ART/OG	1969	SP	38 X 50	MO/S	25	1	150	350
Silvery Trip	SSE	ART/OG	1969	SP	23 X 29	NB	50	5	125	350
Winter Creek	SSE	ART/OG	1969	SP	23 X 29	NB	40	2	75	250
Pigs Emerging	SSE	ART/OG	1970	SP	35 X 46	MO/S	35	1	125	350
Approaching Madrid	SSE	ART/OG	1970	SP	35 X 42	MO/S	35	2	100	250
The Swimmers	SSE	ART/OG	1970	SP	18 X 23	NB	55	6	100	350
Portrait of the Artist as a Young Man	SSE	ART/OG	1970	SP	18 X 23	NB	45	6	100	250
East River	SSE	GJ/OG	1980	SP	26 X 31	LEN	215	5	150	250
Hudson (Dipt)	SSE	GJ/OG	1983	SP	29 X 42	STP	225	8	600	650
Harborside	SSE/MS	MK/OG	1985	SP	30 X 50	LEN	57	9	400	450
Forms Emerging	SSE	ART	1987	MON	26 X 40 EA	STP	1 EA	14 EA	500 EA	550 EA
Beacon Series Dipt	SSE	ART	1987	MON	52 X 40 EA	STP	1 EA	14 EA	1500 EA	1800 EA

HUGH O'DONNELL

BORN: England
EDUCATION: Chamberwell Col of Art, London, England, 1968–69; Falmouth Col of Art, Cornwall, England, BA, with Honors, 1969–72; Birmingham Col of Art, H Dip Ad, 1972–73; Fel, Gloucestershire Col of Art, England, 1973–74; Fel, Kyoto Univ of Arts, Japan, (Japanese Govt Scholarship), 1974–75; Royal Col of Art, London, England, 1976–79
AWARDS: First Prize, Sir Whitworth Wallace Trust, Birmingham, England, 1973; Arts Council Awards, Purchase Prizes, 1978, 80
RECENT EXHIB: Marlborough Gallery, NY, 1987; Eva Cohon Gallery, Chicago, IL, 1988; Hokin Gallery, Palm Beach, FL; Univ of South Florida, Graphicstudio, Tampa, FL, 1992

COLLECTIONS: Metropolitan Art Mus, NY; Albright-Knox Art Gallery, Buffalo, NY; Solomon R Guggenheim Mus, NY; Walker Arts Center, Minneapolis, MN; Victoria and Albert Mus, London, England; Arts Council of Great Britain, London, England; Contemp Arts Center of Great Britain, London, England; Sidney & Frances Lewis Found, Richmond, VA
PRINTERS: Bud Shark, Boulder, CO; Matthew Christie, Boulder, CO (MC); Shark's, Inc, Boulder, CO (SI)
PUBLISHERS: Marlborough Gallery, Inc., NY (MG); Shark's, Inc, Boulder, CO (SI)
GALLERIES: Marlborough Gallery, New York, NY; Hokin Galleries, Bay Harbor Islands, FL & Palm Beach, FL; Eva Cohon Galleries, Ltd, Chicago, IL & Highland Park, IL; Shark's, Inc, Boulder, CO; Quartet Editions, New York, NY

The Printworld Directory is accepting new applications for the seventh edition. Approximately 300 new artists will be accepted. Please use the two forms provided in the back section of this directory to submit biographical data and documentation of prints. Edition number of each print must not exceed 500 and the retail price must be $100 or more.

HUGH O'DONNELL CONTINUED

TITLE	PUBLISHER	PRINTER	DATE	MEDIUM	DIMENSION (PAPER SIZE) IN INCHES	TYPE OF PAPER	EDITION NUMBER	NO. OF COLORS	ORIGINAL OPENING PRICE	CURRENT RETAIL PRICE
CURRENT EDITIONS:										
San Giovanni Series/Moving Target:										
Moving Target #1	MG		1985	EC	15 X 22	R/BFK/W	40		600	1000
Moving Target #2	MG		1985	EC	15 X 22	R/BFK/W	40		600	1000
Moving Target #3	MG		1985	EC	15 X 22	R/BFK/W	40		600	1000
San Giovanni Series/Untitled:										
Untitled #1	MG		1985	EC	32 X 24	R/BFK/W	40		600	1000
Untitled #2	MG		1985	EC	32 X 24	R/BFK/W	45		600	1000
Untitled #3	MG		1985	EC	32 X 24	R/BFK/W	60		600	1000
Boulder Series #1–#14	SI	BS/MC/SI	1988	MON	36 X 42 EA	HMP	1 EA	Varies	4000 EA	5000 EA

NILS OBEL

BORN: Copenhagen, Denmark; July 1, 1937
EDUCATION: M Anderson Sch, Copenhagen, Denmark, 1954–59; Ecole de la Grande Chaumiere, Paris, France, 1959–65
AWARDS: Prix de la Dome, Mus: d'Art Mod, Paris, France; Prix Charlottenborg, Denmark, 1971; Grand Prix Humanitaire de France, 1979; Prix Peter Paul Rubens, Antwerp, Belgium, 1979; Le Palme d'Or, Paris, France, 1980
RECENT EXHIB: Stoneley-Burnham Gallery, Greenfield, MA, 1987; Simms Fine Art, New Orleans, LA, 1988
COLLECTIONS: Royal Mus of Fine Arts, Copenhagen, Denmark; Art Inst of Chicago, IL; Int Cultural Ctr, Antwerp, Belgium; Royal Library, Copenhagen, Denmark; Univ of Copenhagen, Denmark; Mus of Fine Arts, Ghent, Belgium
PRINTERS: J & B Printers, Rockland, ME (J/B)
PUBLISHERS: Post Oak Fine Art Distributors, Houston, TX (POFA); Simms Fine Art, New Orleans, LA (SFA); Artist (ART)
GALLERIES: Gallery Alexandra Monett, Brussels, Belgium; Simms Fine Art, New Orleans, LA

TITLE	PUBLISHER	PRINTER	DATE	MEDIUM	DIMENSION (PAPER SIZE) IN INCHES	TYPE OF PAPER	EDITION NUMBER	NO. OF COLORS	ORIGINAL OPENING PRICE	CURRENT RETAIL PRICE
CURRENT EDITIONS:										
Sailing in the Mist	POFA	J/B	1981	SP	22 X 30	AP	200	16	250	350
Sailfish, Barbu	SFA		1988	LC	26 X 41	100/RAG	75	6	500	500

GERI OBLER

BORN: New York, NY; May 1, 1942
EDUCATION: Pratt Inst, NY, BFA, 1963, with Richard Lindner; Hunter Col, NY, MA, 1966, with Ron Gorchov; Columbia Univ, NY, EdD, 1974
TEACHING: Queens Mus, NY
COLLECTIONS: Berkshire Mus, Pittsfield, MA; Univ of Wyoming, Laramie, WY
PRINTERS: Artist (ART)
PUBLISHERS: Burns Fine Art, NY (BFA)
GALLERIES: Burns Fine Art, New York, NY; Gallery, 169, Great Neck, NY; Ars Graphics, Port Washington, NY; Henry Howells Gallery, New York, NY
MAILING ADDRESS: 26 Brokaw Lane, Great Neck, NY 11023

TITLE	PUBLISHER	PRINTER	DATE	MEDIUM	DIMENSION (PAPER SIZE) IN INCHES	TYPE OF PAPER	EDITION NUMBER	NO. OF COLORS	ORIGINAL OPENING PRICE	CURRENT RETAIL PRICE
CURRENT EDITIONS:										
Julie's Farewell I, II, III	BFA	ART	1985	REL	31 X 21 EA	HMP	95 EA	8 EA	1000 SET / 370 EA	1200 SET / 400 EA

LOUIS OCEPEK (DAVID)

BORN: Detroit, MI; August 27, 1942
EDUCATION: Wayne State Univ, Detroit, MI, BFA, 1964; Univ of Iowa, Iowa City, IA, MA, 1967
TEACHING: Prof, Design & Printmaking, Portland State Univ, OR, 1971–83; Prof, Design, Montana State Univ, Bozeman, MT, 1983–85; Prof, Art, New Mexico State Univ, Las Cruces, NM, 1985 to present
AWARDS: Purchase Award, State Univ of New York, 1968; San Diego State Print Exhib, CA, 1969; Western Michigan Univ, Kalamazoo, MI, 1970; Comm, Washington State Arts Comm, 1982; Research & Creativity Grant, Montana State Univ, Bozeman, MT, 1983; Research Grant, New Mexico State Univ, Las Cruces, NM, 1985
COLLECTIONS: Portland Art Mus, OR; City of Portland, OR; Montana State Univ, Bozeman, MT; Portland State Univ, OR; San Diego State Univ, Ca; Albion Col, MI; State Univ of New York, Oswego, NY; Western Michigan Univ, Kalamazoo, MI
PRINTERS: Artist (ART)
PUBLISHERS: Errollgraphics, Inc, Portland, OR (EI); Artist (ART)
GALLERIES: Cynthia Vonsuhr Gallery, Bellvue, WA; Miriam Perlman, Inc, Chicago, IL; Fountain Gallery, Portland, OR; Adair Margo Gallery, El Paso, TX
MAILING ADDRESS: 1935 Thomas Dr, Las Cruces, NM 88001

TITLE	PUBLISHER	PRINTER	DATE	MEDIUM	DIMENSION (PAPER SIZE) IN INCHES	TYPE OF PAPER	EDITION NUMBER	NO. OF COLORS	ORIGINAL OPENING PRICE	CURRENT RETAIL PRICE
SOLD OUT EDITIONS (RARE):										
Ships at Sea	ART	ART	1974	SP	19 X 24	AE	6	5	125	400
Possible Fracture	ART	ART	1975	SP	30 X 23	R/BFK	7	11	125	400
Halloween	ART	ART	1975	SP	32 X 21	JAP	5	10	125	350
While Waiting in the Garden	ART	ART	1975	SP	28 X 20	R/BFK	6	8	125	350
CURRENT EDITIONS:										
Delphi	ART	ART	1980	SP	28 X 20	AP88	13	10	150	300
Ocean Song	ART	ART	1982	SP	22 X 31	STP/100	11	18	225	300
Essence	ART	ART	1982	SP	28 X 20	ITAL	15	12	225	300
The Oracle	ART	ART	1982	SP	28 X 20	ITAL	10	14	225	300

LOUIS OCEPEK (DAVID) CONTINUED

TITLE	PUBLISHER	PRINTER	DATE	MEDIUM	DIMENSION (PAPER SIZE) IN INCHES	TYPE OF PAPER	EDITION NUMBER	NO. OF COLORS	ORIGINAL OPENING PRICE	CURRENT RETAIL PRICE
CURRENT EDITIONS:										
Kachina Suite: I–IV	ART	ART	1983	SP	28 X 20 EA	R/BFK	15 EA	10–20	850 SET / 225 EA	1000 SET / 300 EA
Bop	ART	ART	1985	SP	15 X 35	R/BFK	10	16	250	350
Jazz Variations	ART	ART	1985	SP	26 X 16	ITAL	9	11	250	300

ALBERT OEHLEN

RECENT EXHIB: Galerie Bleich Rossi, Burgergasse, Germany, 1989
PRINTERS: Till Verclas, Hamburg, Germany (TV)
PUBLISHERS: Editions Julie Sylvester, NY (EJS)
GALLERIES: Edition Julie Sylvester, New York, NY; Galerie Bleich Rossi, Burgergasse, Germany; Luhring Augustine Gallery, New York, NY

TITLE	PUBLISHER	PRINTER	DATE	MEDIUM	DIMENSION (PAPER SIZE) IN INCHES	TYPE OF PAPER	EDITION NUMBER	NO. OF COLORS	ORIGINAL OPENING PRICE	CURRENT RETAIL PRICE
CURRENT EDITIONS:										
Estrechiamento de Mente (Set of 4)									7000 SET	9000 SET
Trip	EJS	TV	1988	EB/DPT	84 X 50 EA	AP	10	1	2000	2500
Pot	EJS	TV	1988	EB/DPT	84 X 50 EA	AP	10	1	2000	2500
Downers	EJS	TV	1988	EB/DPT	84 X 50 EA	AP	10	1	2000	2500
The End	EJS	TV	1988	EB/DPT	84 X 50 EA	AP	10	1	2000	2500

ALEC OGLOFF

BORN: Wayne, Alta, Canada; November 12, 1946
EDUCATION: Self-Taught
RECENT EXHIB: Brackendale Art Gallery, Brackendale, BC, Canada, 1989; Kelowna Art Gallery, Kelowna, BC, Canada, 1991
PRINTERS: Midsummer Music Company, Inc, Vancouver, BC, Canada (MMC); Central Graphics, Inc, Clearbrooke, BC, Canada (CGI); Mitchell Press, Ltd, Vancouver, BC, Canada (MPL); H MacDonald Printing Company, Ltd, Vancouver, BC, Canada (HMPC)
PUBLISHERS: A Ogloff Graphics, Ltd, West Vancouver, BC, Canada (AOG)
GALLERIES: Brackendale Art Gallery, Brackendale, BC, Canada; Lloyd Gallery, Penticton, BC, Canada; A Ogloff Graphics, Ltd, West Vancouver, BC, Canada
MAILING ADDRESS: 1084 Highland Drive, West Vancouver, BC, Canada V7S 2X9

TITLE	PUBLISHER	PRINTER	DATE	MEDIUM	DIMENSION (PAPER SIZE) IN INCHES	TYPE OF PAPER	EDITION NUMBER	NO. OF COLORS	ORIGINAL OPENING PRICE	CURRENT RETAIL PRICE
CURRENT EDITIONS:										
Psalm 23	AOG	HMPC	1983	LC/OFF/SP	19 X 26	G/100	275	7/2	275	500
Alluring Bait	AOG	MPL	1989	LC/OFF	24 X 27	KC/80	275	4	300	300
Textures	AOG	CGI	1989	LC/OFF	19 X 24	MP	275	7	300	300

HELEN OJI

BORN: Sacramento, CA; August 27, 1950
EDUCATION: Yuba Col, Marysville, CA, AA, 1970; California State Univ, Sacramento, CA, BA, 1972; MA, 1975
AWARDS: Creative Artists Public Service Program, Graphics Fel, 1982–83; Ariana Found Arts, Inc, Mixed Media Grant, 1984; Jane Voorhees Zimmerli Art Mus, NJ, 1985
RECENT EXHIB: Mus of Mod Art, NY, 1988; Solena Gallery, Brooklyn, NY, 1988; Long Island Univ, Brooklyn, NY, 1988
COLLECTIONS: Jacksonville Art Mus, FL
PRINTERS: Cheryl Pelavin Printmaker, NY (CP)
PUBLISHERS: Cheryl Pelavin Printmaker, NY (CP)
GALLERIES: Monique Knowlton Gallery, New York, NY; van Straaten Gallery, Chicago, IL; Pelavin Editions, New York, NY
MAILING ADDRESS: 284 Lafayette St, #5D, New York, NY 10012

TITLE	PUBLISHER	PRINTER	DATE	MEDIUM	DIMENSION (PAPER SIZE) IN INCHES	TYPE OF PAPER	EDITION NUMBER	NO. OF COLORS	ORIGINAL OPENING PRICE	CURRENT RETAIL PRICE
CURRENT EDITIONS:										
Mt Vesuvius	CP	CP	1984	EB/HC	32 X 47	R/BFK	50	1	625	750

KENZO OKADA

BORN: Yokohama, Japan; (1902–1982)
EDUCATION: Tokyo Fine Arts Univ, Japan
AWARDS: Carnegie Int, 1955; Am Acad of Arts and Letters, 1955; Ford Found Grand, 1960; Mianichi Art Award, 1966; New York Council of the Arts, 1969
RECENT EXHIB: Fabian Carlsson Gallery, London, England, 1989
COLLECTIONS: Metropolitan Mus of Art, NY; Mus of Mod Art, NY; Guggenheim Mus, NY; Whitney Mus of Am Art, NY; Art Inst of Chicago, IL; Yale Univ, New Haven, CT; San Francisco Mus of Mod Art, CA; Boston Mus of Fine Arts, MA; Santa Barbara Mus, CA
PRINTERS: Artist (ART)
PUBLISHERS: Pace Editions, NY (PE)
GALLERIES: Pace Prints, New York, NY; Marisa del Re Gallery, New York, NY; Jack Tilton Gallery, NY; Fabian Carlsson Gallery, London, England

---

The retail prices of the 100,000 limited edition prints quoted in this directory are subject to change. Print publishers, artists and galleries were the direct sources for these quotations. Prices in the secondary market listed as "Sold Out Editions (Rare)" indicate that the publisher has a limited supply of that print or that the print is difficult to locate in the galleries.

KENZO OKADA CONTINUED

TITLE	PUBLISHER	PRINTER	DATE	MEDIUM	DIMENSION (PAPER SIZE) IN INCHES	TYPE OF PAPER	EDITION NUMBER	NO. OF COLORS	ORIGINAL OPENING PRICE	CURRENT RETAIL PRICE
CURRENT EDITIONS:										
Iris	PE	ART	1975	SP	30 X 33	STR	175	8	200	1000
Morning Glory	PE	ART	1975	SP	30 X 33	STR	175	7	200	1000
Bamboo	PE	ART	1977	SP	39 X 32	STR	150	8	250	900
Boat	PE	ART	1977	SP	32 X 38	STR	150	8	250	900

OKU (SHIGEO OKUMURA)

BORN: Tientsin, China; January 12, 1937
EDUCATION: Asagaya Univ, Tokyo, Japan
AWARDS: Symbols and Images, 1978

COLLECTIONS: Cincinnati Art Mus, OH
PRINTERS: Steuber Silkscreen Studio, Downingtown, PA (SSS); George C Miller and Son, NY (GCM); Galapagos, Phila, PA (GAL)
PUBLISHERS: Flanagan Graphics, Inc, Haverford, PA (FG)
GALLERIES: Newman Gallery, Phila, PA Langman Gallery, Phila, PA; Newman Galleries, Phila, PA & Bryn Mawr, PA;

TITLE	PUBLISHER	PRINTER	DATE	MEDIUM	DIMENSION (PAPER SIZE) IN INCHES	TYPE OF PAPER	EDITION NUMBER	NO. OF COLORS	ORIGINAL OPENING PRICE	CURRENT RETAIL PRICE
SOLD OUT EDITIONS (RARE):										
Cross Eyed Cat	FG	GCM	1977	LC	10 X 14	R/BFK	180	1	100	500
Tennis Match	FG	GCM	1977	LC	17 X 20	R/BFK	180	9	100	750
Jungle	FG	GCM	1977	LC	25 X 19	R/BFK	190	10	150	750
Oval Nude	FG	GCM	1977	LC	21 X 15	R/BFK	180	7	125	450
What a Day	FG	GCM	1977	LC	19 X 25	R/BFK	180	8	125	450
Snow Women	FG	GCM	1977	LC	23 X 19	R/BFK	180	9	125	450
Late Spring	FG	SSS	1978	SP	20 X 20	R/BFK	190	36	300	750
The Circus	FG	SSS	1978	SP	18 X 21	R/BFK	190	36	300	750
Family Cruise	FG	SSS	1978	SP	18 X 26	R/BFK	190	24	175	750
My Life Guard	FG	SSS	1978	SP	17 X 24	R/BFK	190	15	175	750
The Poets	FG	SSS	1979	SP	18 X 24	R/BFK	250	23	200	600
A Clear Day	FG	SSS	1979	SP	18 X 26	R/BFK	250	25	200	800
Three Cats	FG	SSS	1979	SP	18 X 24	R/BFK	200	20	175	1000
The Door is Open	FG	SSS	1979	LC/SP	16 X 22	R/BFK	140	11	150	450
How to Train A Lion	FG	SSS	1979	SP	20 X 18	R/BFK	250	15	150	450
Jimmy's Closet	FG	SSS	1979	SP	20 X 20	R/BFK	250	26	175	450
Sitting	FG	SSS	1979	SP	17 X 26	AP	250	25	200	500
After Practice	FG	SSS	1979	SP	20 X 20	AP	250	27	200	350
Sunday Afternoon	FG	SSS	1980	SP	26 X 31	AP	275	30	250	500
My Garden	FG	SSS	1980	SP	28 X 3	AP	275	37	280	1000
Friends	FG	SSS	1980	SP	18 X 24	AP	275	28	200	500
Sidney's Mother	FG	SSS	1981	SP	27 X 23	AP	150	29	200	450
Vacation	FG	SSS	1981	SP	30 X 23	AP	275	30	200	450
Boating	FG	SSS	1981	SP	20 X 25	AP	275	31	250	450
Duck Dinner	FG	SSS	1982	SP	20 X 24	AP	275	26	250	450
Pucci	FG	SSS	1982	SP	20 X 16	AP	275	11	150	450
Five Sisters	FG	JS	1983	SP	20 X 27	AP	275	25	300	450
Lunchbreak	FG	GAL	1984	SP	20 X 25	AP	275	23	300	450
A New Leaf	FG	SSS	1985	SP	20 X 20	AP	275	29	300	450
Lady with Cats	FG	SSS	1986	LC	17 X 14	AP	275		100	300
Lady with Roses	FG	SSS	1986	LC	17 X 14	AP	275		100	300
The Letter	FG	SSS	1986	LC	13 X 10	AP	275		100	300

JOSE ORTEGA

BORN: Castile, Spain; 1921
EDUCATION: Studied in Spain
AWARDS: Medal for Graphics, Nat Exhib Madrid, 1953; Gold Medal, International Festival of Youth, Warsaw, Poland, 1955

PRINTERS: Michel Casse, Paris, France (MIC); Georges Fressart, Sannois, France (GF); Artist (ART)
PUBLISHERS: Transworld Arts, Inc, NY (TAI)
GALLERIES: Helio Galleries, New York, NY

TITLE	PUBLISHER	PRINTER	DATE	MEDIUM	DIMENSION (PAPER SIZE) IN INCHES	TYPE OF PAPER	EDITION NUMBER	NO. OF COLORS	ORIGINAL OPENING PRICE	CURRENT RETAIL PRICE
SOLD OUT EDITIONS (RARE):										
Segadores (Set of 20)	TAI	MC-GF	1970	LC/I/HC	23 X 25 EA	AP	120 EA		11000 SET	20000 SET
Composition	TAI	ART	1972	LC/I/HC	23 X 25	AP	120		625	900
Eyes	TAI	ART	1972	LC/I/HC	25 X 22	AP	130		450	800
Reclining Nude	TAI	ART	1972	LC/I/HC	14 X 15	AP	150		180	500
Le Joueur de Flute	TAI	GF	1980	CAR/A/E	27 X 27	AP	130	18	750	900
Le Bain Turc	TAI	GF	1980	CAR/A/E	27 X 27	AP	130	19	850	900
Le Quatre Graces	TAI	GF	1980	CAR/A/E	28 X 27	AP	130	17	850	900

The print market has become very selective. For the first time since we published the first edition of The Printworld Directory in 1982, the prices of prints have been greatly reduced and greatly increased for the same artists by the most reputable and established print publishers. Check the fifth edition to understand the movement.

CLAES OLDENBURG

BORN: Stockholm, Sweden; January 28, 1929
EDUCATION: Yale Univ, New Haven, CT, BA, 1950-52; Art Inst of Chicago, IL, 1952-54
AWARDS: Skowhegan Award, 1972; Sao Paulo Award, 1977; Medal, Am Inst of Arch, 1977; Creative Artists for Public Service Prog, Graphic Grant, 1978; Japan Found Fel, 1979
RECENT EXHIB: Mus of Mod Art, NY, 1987,88; Inst of Contemp Art, London, England, 1987-88; Whitney Mus of Am Art, NY, 1988; Penson Gallery, NY, 1988; Contemp Mus, Honolulu, HI, 1989; Susan Sheehan Gallery, NY, 1990; Retrosp, Brooke Alexander Editions, NY, 1990; Univ of Wisconsin, Carlsten Art Gallery, Stevens Point, WI, 1992; Cleveland Center of Contemp Art, OH, 1992; Springfield Art Mus, MO, 1992; Pace Gallery, NY, 1992
COLLECTIONS: Albright-Knox Art Gallery, Buffalo, NY; Yale Univ, New Haven, CT; Mus of Mod Art, NY; Whitney Mus of Am Art, NY; Art Inst of Chicago, IL; Art Gallery of Ontario, Toronto, Can; Sidney Lewis, Richmond, VA
PRINTERS: Landfall Press, Inc, Chicago, IL (LPI); Jack Lemon, Chicago, IL (JL); Thomas Minkler, Chicago, IL (TM); David Keister, Chicago, IL (DK); Patricia Branstead, NY (PB); Aeropress, NY (A); Davison (DAV); Universal Limited Art Editions, West Islip, NY (ULAE); Maurice Sanchez, NY (MS); Linda Gray, NY (LG); James Miller, NY (JM); Joe Petruzelli, NY (JP); Derriére L'Etoile Studios, NY (DES); Aldo Crommelynck, NY (AC); Atelier Crommelynck, NY (AtC); Claudio Stickar, Los Angeles, CA (CS); Gemini GEL, Los Angeles, CA (GEM)

PUBLISHERS: Paul Bianchini, NY (PBi); Multiples, NY (M); Des Moines Art Ctr, IA (DMAC); New Gallery, Cleveland, OH (NG); Landfall Press, Chicago, IL (LPI); Petersburg Press, London, England (PP); Gemini GEL, Los Angeles, CA (GEM); Artists Call, NY (AC); Artist (ART); Editions Alecto, London, England (EA); Universal Limited Art Editions, West Islip, NY (ULAE); Brooke Alexander, Inc, NY (BAI); Pace Editions, Inc NY (PE); Aldo Crommelynck, NY (AC)
GALLERIES: Gemini GEL, Los Angeles, CA; R K Goldman Contemporary, Los Angeles, CA; Marvin Ross Friedman & Company, Miami, FL; O'Farrell Gallery, Brunswick, ME; Leo Castelli Gallery, New York, NY; Janie C Lee Galleries, New York, NY & Houston, TX; Contemporary Gallery, Dallas, TX; John Berggruen Gallery, San Francisco, CA; Margo Leavin Gallery, Los Angeles, CA; Susan Sheehan Gallery, New York, NY; Brooke Alexander, Inc, New York, NY; Marian Goodman Gallery, New York, NY; Mary Boone Gallery, New York, NY; Reinhold-Brown Gallery, New York, NY; Michael Lowe Gallery, Cincinnati, OH; Owl 57 Gallery, Woodmere, NY; Charles Whitchurch Gallery, Huntington Beach, CA; Dunlap-Freidenrich Fine Art, Newport Beach, CA; Park Granada Editions, Tarzana, CA; Randall Beck Gallery, Boston, MA; Golden Gallery, Boston, MA; J Rosenthal Fine Arts, Chicago, IL; Herbert Palmer Gallery, Los Angeles, CA; Andrew Dierken Fine Art, Los Angeles, CA; Rick Jones Modern & Contemporary Art, St Louis, MO; Carol Evans Fine Arts, Brooklyn, NY; Fenton Fine Arts, Fort Worth, TX; Atsuko Murayama, New York, NY; Pat Kery Fine Arts, New York, NY; Janet Levitt Fine Art, San Francisco, CA; Sorrentino/Mayer Fine Art, New York, NY; Pace Prints, New York, NY

Sparks (S)—Gemini GEL (G)

TITLE	PUBLISHER	PRINTER	DATE	MEDIUM	DIMENSION (PAPER SIZE) IN INCHES	TYPE OF PAPER	EDITION NUMBER	NO. OF COLORS	ORIGINAL OPENING PRICE	CURRENT RETAIL PRICE
SOLD OUT EDITIONS (RARE):										
The Store Poster	ART		1961	LC/OFF	28 X 22	CARD		3	50	3500
London Knees (Plastic Objects with Lithograph and Documentation in a Suitcase)			1966	LC	39cm HT Mult		120		500	15000
Tea Bag (Silkscreen, Collage & Vacuum Formed Plexiglas with Cloth)	M		1966	MM	39 X 28	PLEX	125		500	7500
Notes (Set of 12):										
Punching Bag	GEM	GEM	1968	LC	23 X 16	R/BFK	100	8	200	5000
Gym Shoes	GEM	GEM	1968	LC	23 X 16	R/BFK	100	6	200	5000
Skate Monument	GEM	GEM	1968	LC/EMB	23 X 16	R/BFK	100	6	200	5000
Kassel	GEM	GEM	1968	LC/EMB	23 X 16	R/BFK	100	12	200	5000
Pop	GEM	GEM	1968	LC/EMB	23 X 16	R/BFK	100	13	200	5000
Ice Cream Cones	GEM	GEM	1968	LC/EMB	23 X 16	R/BFK	100	11	200	5000
Flash Light	GEM	GEM	1968	LC	23 X 16	R/BFK	100	9	200	5000
Mickey Mouse	GEM	GEM	1968	LC	23 X 16	R/BFK	100	9	200	5000
Tar Pits	GEM	GEM	1968	LC	23 X 16	R/BFK	100	6	200	5000
City as Alphabet	GEM	GEM	1968	LC	23 X 16	R/BFK	100	6	200	5000
Body Buildings	GEM	GEM	1968	LC	23 X 16	R/BFK	100	9	200	5000
New Pasadena Museum	GEM	GEM	1968	LC	23 X 16	R/BFK	100	7	200	5000
Soft Drum Set (Soft Sculpture & Silkscreen on Canvas)	M		1969	MULT/SP	10 X 19 X 14	CAN	200		500	12000
Profile Airflow (Molded Polyurethane Relief over Two Color Lithograph on Wooden Stretcher Bars)	GEM	GEM	1969	MULT/LC	33 X 65	WOOD	75		600	35000
Double-Nose/Purse/Punching Bag/Ashtray	GEM	GEM	1970	LE/BR/WP	11 X 21 X 8	AC	75		500	8500
Double-Nose/Purse/Punching Bag/Ashtray	GEM	GEM	1970	LB	21 X 19	R/BFK	50	1	200	1800
Alphabet in the Form of a Good Humor Bar	PBi		1970	LC/OFF	29 X 20	R/BFK	250		200	3000
Typewriter Eraser	PBi		1970	LC/OFF	29 X 20	R/BFK	250		200	3000
Geometric Mouse—Scale C (G-281)	GEM	GEM	1971	LB/AL	25 X 20	ALUM	120		3000	12000
Baked Potato Studies:										
Colossal Baked Potato in a Landscape	PP	PP	1972	LC	26 X 33	HMP	100		200	6000
Baked Potato with Butter	PP	PP	1972	LC	31 X 40	HMP	100		300	7500
Soft Fireplug, Inverted	PP	PP	1972	LC	40 X 31		100		300	7500
Tea Bag	PP	PP	1972	LC	31 X 22		100		300	7500
Notes in Hand (Set of 50, Boxed)	PP	PP	1972	PH/OFF	10 X 8 EA		100 EA	4 EA	5000 SET	20000 SET
Soft Toilet #1	GEM	GEM	1972	LC	21 X 16	AMG	75	2	300	4000
Soft Toilet #2	GEM	GEM	1972	LB	20 X 15	AMG	75	1	300	4000
Soft Toilet #3—On Chalk Board	GEM	GEM	1972	SP	30 X 22	ARJ	70	3	350	4000
The Letter Q as Beach House, with Sailboat	GEM	GEM	1972	LC	39 X 30	ARJ	100	15	350	10000

CLAES OLDENBURG CONTINUED

TITLE	PUBLISHER	PRINTER	DATE	MEDIUM	DIMENSION (PAPER SIZE) IN INCHES	TYPE OF PAPER	EDITION NUMBER	NO. OF COLORS	ORIGINAL OPENING PRICE	CURRENT RETAIL PRICE
SOLD OUT EDITIONS (RARE):										
Soft Drum Set	GEM	GEM	1972	LC	29 X 40	AMG	68	1	350	10000
Lipstick on Caterpillar Tracks	M	PB/A	1972	LC	32 X 23	AP	100		300	2000
Typewriter Eraser as Tornado	M	PB/A	1972	LC/OFF	29 X 20	AP	200		200	1500
Hats Vesuvius	LPI	TM/LPI	1973	LC	20 X 26	JBG	25	7	300	6000
Store Window: Bow, Hats, Heart, Shirt, 29¢	LPI	DK/LPI	1973	LC	23 X 27	JBG	75	10	300	6000
Coffee Cup	DMAC	JL/LPI	1973	LC	18 X 23	TWP	50	4	300	5000
Mitt	ART/NG	DK/LPI	1973	LC	20 X 22	TWP	75	4	300	5000
Soft Picasso Cufflink	PP	PP	1973	LC	36 X 27		120		400	6000
Picasso Cufflink	PP	DK/DP	1974	LC	36 X 27	AP/W	185	13	400	6500
Study for a Monument in the Heroic/Erotic/Academic/Comic Style	PP	PP	1974–75	EC	37 X 42	AP/W	60	6	500	5000
Mermaid	PP	PP	1974–75	EC	25 X 20	AP/W	60	6	500	3000
Two Figures	PP	PP	1974–75	EC	25 X 20	AP/W	60	6	500	3000
Figure in Skirt with Phallus	PP	PP	1974–75	EC	28 X 36	AP/W	60	6	500	3500
Figure in Skirt with Phallus II	PP	PP	1974–75	EC	25 X 20	AP/W	60	6	500	3000
Medusa	PP	PP	1974–75	EC	26 X 20	AP/W	60	6	500	3000
Seated Figure	PP	PP	1974–75	EC	25 X 20	AP/W	60	6	500	3000
Figure and Phallus I	PP	PP	1974–75	EC	36 X 28	AP/W	60	6	500	4500
Two Profiles	PP	PP	1974–75	EC	36 X 28	AP/W	60	6	500	4500
Bust	PP	PP	1974–75	EC	35 X 28	AP/W	60	6	500	4500
Study for a Sculpture in the Form of A Inversted Q: Above and Below Ground	PP	PP	1975	EB/SG/LC	14 X 11	AP	100		300	3500
Landscape with Noses	M	PB/A	1975	EB/A	26 X 20	AP	35		500	3000
Bat Spinning at the Spead of Light Series:										
Bat Spinning at the Speed of Light, State I	LPI	JL/LPI	1975	LC	37 X 25	AP/W	14	4	750	3500
Bat Spinning at the Speed of Light, State II	LPI	JL/LPI	1975	LC	37 X 25	AP/W	35	6	750	3500
Bat Spinning at the Speed of Light, State III	LPI	JL/LPI	1975	LC	37 X 25	AP/W	60	3	700	3500
Bat Spinning at the Speed of Light, State IV	LPI	JL/LPI	1975	LC	37 X 25	AP/W	10	4	500	3500
Teapot (S-1)	ULAE	ULAE	1975	LB	18 X 26	MOR	34	1	400	17000
Spoon Pier	LPI	TB/LPI	1975	A/SUG	28 X 22	TWP	50	4	500	6000
Pile of Erasers	LPI	JL/LPI	1975	LC	23 X 29	HMP	75	7	500	6000
Smoke and Reflections	CG/M	PB/A	1975	EC	27 X 20	R/BFK	35		600	6000
Strawberry Skull Bike Seat	CG/M	PB/A	1975	EC	24 X 18	R/BFK	35		600	6000
Sketch of Three-Way Plug	CG/M	PB/A	1975	LC/OFF/AirBr	32 X 24	AP	100		300	3200
Ice Cream Desserts Series:										
Ice Cream Desserts (A)	PP	PP	1975–76	EB/A	22 X 30	AP/W	50	6	750	5000
Ice Cream Desserts (B)	PP	PP	1975–76	EB/A	22 X 31	AP/W	50	5	750	5000
Ice Cream Desserts (C)	PP	PP	1975–76	EB/A	22 X 32	AP/W	50	5	600	4000
Standing Mitt with Ball	M	PB/A	1976	LC	38 X 25	AP	50		300	1500
Tongue Cloud Over London with Thames Ball	PP	PP	1976	EC	41 X 31	AP	60	5	2400	12000
Ice Cream Desserts—Praline	PP	PP	1976	EC	18 X 15	AP	60		600	3500
Woman Hanging in Imitation of the Soft Fan	PP	PP	1976	EB	41 X 31	AP	50	1	1200	4500
Woman Entwined in Giant Electric Cord, Ed A (Blue/Black)	PP	PP	1976	EB	41 X 31	AP	50	1	1200	4500
Woman Entwined in Giant Electric Cord, Ed B (Serpia)	PP	PP	1976	EB	41 X 31	AP	50	1	1200	4500
Four Figures and Head on Giant Phallus	PP	PP	1976	EC	31 X 38	AP	60	2	900	4500
Hats, Bones, Q's, Etc	PP	PP	1976	EC	18 X 15	AP	60	1	600	3500
Figure Looking Through Legs	PP	PP	1976	EC	20 X 17	AP	60	2	600	3500
Study for Tongue Cloud	PP	PP	1976	EC	18 X 15	AP	60	5	600	3500
Soft Screw Series:										
Soft Screws, Tumbling #1	GEM	GEM	1976	LC	68 X 45	AP	35	1	900	15000
Soft Screws, Tumbling #2	GEM	GEM	1976	LC	68 X 41	AP	35	1	900	15000
Arch in the Form of a Screw for Times Square NYC	GEM	GEM	1976	LC	68 X 41	AP	35	1	900	15000
Soft Screw in Waterfall (G-702)	GEM	GEM	1976	LC	68 X 45	AP	35	1	900	15000
Colossal Screw in Landscape—Type 2	GEM	GEM	1976	LC	68 X 41	AP	35	1	900	15000
Sailboat and Hat	M	PB/A	1976	EC/A	24 X 17	AP	35	2	550	1200
Butter Pat in Berkeley Hills	M	PB/A	1976	EC	26 X 20	AP	35		350	1500
Landscape with Noses	M	PB/A	1976	EC	21 X 16	AP	35	1	350	900
Study for Steel and Lead Ashtray	M	PB/A	1976	EC/A	35 X 3	AP	50	4	1000	6000
Fag End Boot	M	PB/A	1976	EB/A	26 X 20	AP	25	5	600	4000

CLAES OLDENBURG CONTINUED

TITLE	PUBLISHER	PRINTER	DATE	MEDIUM	DIMENSION (PAPER SIZE) IN INCHES	TYPE OF PAPER	EDITION NUMBER	NO. OF COLORS	ORIGINAL OPENING PRICE	CURRENT RETAIL PRICE
SOLD OUT EDITIONS (RARE):										
Fag Ends Carved Rock	M	PB/A	1976	LC/OFF	38 X 25	AP	50		300	1500
Arched Soft Screw as Building	GEM	GEM	1976	LC	68 X 41	AP	35		800	4500
Geometric Mouse Pyramid Doubled	LPI/M	JL/LPI	1976	LC	35 X 26	AP/W	50	3	500	5000
Chicago Stuffed with Numbers	GEM	GEM	1977	LC	28 X 32	AC	85	9	500	12000
Soft Alphabet (Set of 41 pp)	M	PB/A	1978	SP	23 X 29 X 3	AC	16		6000	25000
The Alternate Proposal for the Allen Memorial Museum	M	PB/A	1979	EB/WA/PEN	32 X 39	AP			4000	12000
Postcard of the Spoon on the Isle St Louis with Needles	M	PB/A	1979	AC/CC	27 X 22	AP	50		650	2500
Crusoe's Umbrella	M	PB/A	1979	A/CO	21 X 24	AP	50		1200	5000
Braque's Nail	M	PB/A	1980	LB	25 X 19	AP	60		350	1000
Screw Arch Bridge Series:										
Screw Arch Bridge, State I	M	PB/A	1980	EB/LIN	32 X 58	AP	15		2400	20000
Screw Arch Bridge, State II	M	PB/A	1980	EB/A	32 X 58	AP	35		4000	28000
Screw Arch Bridge, State III	M	PB/A	1980	EB/A	32 X 58	AP	25		5000	32000
Broken Button (P-19)	M		1981	CP/REL	16 X 14 6	CP/HMP	100		2500	6000
Double Screw Arch Bridge, State II	M	PB/A	1980-81	EB/A	31 X 58	AC	35		5000	50000
Double Screw Arch Bridge, State III	M	PB/A	1981	AC/MON	22 X 51	AC	25		5000	65000
Colossal Flashlight in Place of Hoover Dam	M	DAV	1982	PH/LC/OFF	33 X 24	AP	100	Multi	350	1200
Pick-Axe Superimposed on a Drawing by Ludwig Grimm	M	PB/A	1982	EC	27 X 20	AP	100	Multi	450	1800
Proposal for a Monument to the University of El Salvador	M	PB/A	1984	EC	23 X 30	AP	35	Multi	750	3000
Proposal for a Monument to the Survival of the University of El Salvador: Blasted Pencil (Which Still Writes)	AC	PB/A	1984	A/SG/SB	23 X 30	THS	35		750	3000
Knife Ship Superimposed on the Guggenheim Museum	M	PB/A	1986	SP	31 X 37	THS	75		2800	4000
CURRENT EDITIONS:										
Apple Core Series:										
Apple Core—Spring	GEM	GEM	1989	LC	40 X 29	HMP	57	4	11000	12500
Apple Core—Summer	GEM	GEM	1989	LC	41 X 31	HMP	54	4	11000	12500
Apple Core—Autumn	GEM	GEM	1989	LC	41 X 31	HMP	58	4	11000	12500
Apple Core—Winter	GEM	GEM	1989	LC	40 X 30	HMP	59	3	11000	12500
Apple Core—State I	GEM	GEM	1989	LC	40 X 29	HMP	24	2	8500	9500
Extinguished Match	GEM	GEM	1989	LC	40 X 30	HMP	58	4	8500	9500
Extinguished Match, State I	GEM	GEM	1989	LC	40 X 31	HMP	24	1	6500	7500
Profiterole	GEM	GEM	1989	LC	31 X 41	HMP	57	5	8500	9500
Profiterole, Grey State	GEM	GEM	1989	LC	31 X 40	HMP	58	5	8500	9500
Sneaker Lace in Landscape Series:										
Sneaker Lace in Landscape with Palm Trees	GEM	GEM	1990	LC	57 X 43	HMP	55	4	9500	9500
Sneaker Lace in Landscape—Blue	GEM	GEM	1990	LC	57 X 43	HMP	55	4	9500	9500
Sneaker Lace in Landscape—Grey	GEM	GEM	1990	LC	57 X 43	HMP	55	4	9500	9500
Sneaker Lace in Landscape—Red	GEM	GEM	1990	LC	57 X 43	HMP	55	4	9500	9500
Sneaker Lace in Landscape—Line State	GEM	GEM	1990	LC	57 X 43	HMP	55	2	9500	9500
Thrown Ink Bottle with Fly and Dropped Quill	GEM	GEM	1990	LC	45 X 35	HMP	75	6	6000	6000
Study for Sneaker Lace—White	GEM	GEM	1990	LC	67 X 42	AC	35	3	9500	9500
Study for Sneaker Lace—Black	GEM	GEM	1990	LC	67 X 42	AC	35	3	9500	9500
Sneaker Lace	GEM	GEM	1990	SCULP/HC	52 X 25 X 45	Steel	16	Varies	125000	125000
Centennial Print for the Judson Memorial Church	BAI		1990	SP	44 X 30		100		3000	3000
Centennial Print for the Judson Memorial Church, State I	BAI		1990	SP	44 X 30		20		4500	4500
Centennial Print for the Judson Memorial Church, State II	BAI		1990	SP	44 X 30		20		4500	4500
Apple Core	BAI	MS/LG/JM/JP/DES	1991	LB	30 X 23	CotP/1971	26	1	1200	1200
Apple Core	BAI	MS/LG/JM/JP/DES	1991	LB	30 X 23	CotP/1971	45		2500	2500
Cherry	PE	AC/AtC	1991	WC	26 X 19		100		1500	1500
Proposed Colossal Monument for Mill Rock, East River, New York City: Slicing Strawberry Shortcake	AC	AC/AtC	1992	EC	23 X 30		60		4500	4500

The retail prices of the 100,000 limited edition prints quoted in this directory are subject to change. Print publishers, artists and galleries were the direct sources for these quotations. Prices in the secondary market listed as "Sold Out Editions (Rare)" indicate that the publisher has a limited supply of that print or that the print is difficult to locate in the galleries.

PATRICK OLIPHANT

BORN: Adelaide, Australia; July 24, 1935; U S Citizen
EDUCATION: Dartmouth Col, Hanover, NH, DHL
RECENT EXHIB: Nelson-Atkins Mus of Art, Kansas City, KS, 1992
PRINTERS: Judith Solodkin, NY (JS); Solo Press, NY (SP)
PUBLISHERS: Solo Press, NY (SP)
GALLERIES: Solo Gallery, New York, NY; Susan Conway Galleries, Wash, DC
MAILING ADDRESS: Universal Press Syndicate, 4900 Main St, 9th Fl, Kansas City, KS 64112

TITLE	PUBLISHER	PRINTER	DATE	MEDIUM	DIMENSION (PAPER SIZE) IN INCHES	TYPE OF PAPER	EDITION NUMBER	NO. OF COLORS	ORIGINAL OPENING PRICE	CURRENT RETAIL PRICE
CURRENT EDITIONS:										
I Have Returned	SP	JS/SP	1984	LB	18 X 23	AC	50	1	450	1000
I Shall Return	SP	JS/SP	1984	LC	15 X 22	AC	50		300	500
The Edge	SP	JS/SP	1984	LB	10 X 22	AC	50		200	250
The Naked Nixon	SP	JS/SP	1984	LC	12 X 22	AC	50		300	500

JULES OLITSKI

BORN: Snovsk, Russia; March 27, 1922
EDUCATION: Beaux Art Inst, NY, 1940–42; Acad Grande Chaumier, Paris, France, 1949–50; Nat Acad of Design, NY, 1939–42; New York Univ, BS, MA, 1952–54
TEACHING: Asst Prof, State Univ of New York, New Paltz, NY, 1954–55; Prof & Chmn, Dept of Fine Arts, C W Post Center, Long Island Univ, Greenvale, NY, 1956–63; Instr, Art Bennington Col, VT, 1963–67
AWARDS: Second Prize, Painting, Pittsburgh Int Painting & Sculpture Award, PA, 1961; Purchase Prize, Ford Found Award, 1964; First Prize, Painting, Corcoran Gallery of Art, Wash, DC, 1967
RECENT EXHIB: Knoedler Gallery, NY, 1987; Retrosp, Associated Am Artists, NY, 1989; Retrosp, Buschlen Mowatt Gallery, Vancouver BC, Canada, 1990; Retrosp, Francis Graham-Dixon Gallery, London, England, 1990; Retrosp, Galeria Almirante, Madrid, Spain, 1990; Retrosp, Galeria Afinsa, Madrid, Spain, 1990; Retrosp, Salander-O'Reilly Galleries, Inc, Beverly Hills, CA, 1990; Retrosp, Galerie Montaigne, Paris, France, 1990; Retrosp, Galerie Di Meo, Paris, France, 1990; Asheville Art Mus, NC, 1992; Brown Univ, David Winton Bell Gallery, Providence, RI, 1992
COLLECTIONS: Mus of Mod Art, NY; Metropolitan Mus of Art, NY; Whitney Mus of Am Art, NY; Guggenheim Mus, NY; Art Inst of Chicago, IL; Corcoran Gallery of Art, Wash, DC; Nat Gallery of Art, Wash, DC; Nat Gallery of Australia, Canberra, Australia; Israel Mus, Jerusalem, Israel; Art Coll of Nordrhein-Wastfallen, Dusseldorf, West Germany; Albright-Knox Art Gallery, Buffalo, NY; Cleveland Mus of Art, OH; Pasadena Art Mus, CA; Univ of Saskatchewan, Canada
PRINTERS: Catherine Mosley, NY (CM)
PUBLISHERS: Associated Am Artists, NY (AAA)
GALLERIES: Associated American Artists, New York, NY; Hokin Galleries, Bay Harbor Islands, FL & Palm Beach, FL; Riva Yares Gallery, Scottsdale, AZ; R H Love Galleries, Chicago, IL; Harcus Gallery, Boston, MA; Douglas Drake Gallery, New York, NY; Andre Emmerich Gallery, New York, NY; Meredith Long Gallery, Houston, TX; Knoedler Gallery, New York, NY; Francis Graham-Dixon Gallery, London, England; Galeria Almirante, Madrid, Spain; Galeria Atinsa, Madrid, Spain; Salander-O'Reilly Galleries, New York, NY; Galerie Montaigne, Paris, France; Galerie Di Meo, Paris, France; Gallery Camino Real, Boca Raton, FL; Helander Gallery, Palm Beach, FL; Salander-O'Reilly Galleries, New York, NY
MAILING ADDRESS: 22 E 80th St, New York, NY 10021

TITLE	PUBLISHER	PRINTER	DATE	MEDIUM	DIMENSION (PAPER SIZE) IN INCHES	TYPE OF PAPER	EDITION NUMBER	NO. OF COLORS	ORIGINAL OPENING PRICE	CURRENT RETAIL PRICE
CURRENT EDITIONS:										
Beauty of Angels	AAA	CM	1989	AC	22 X 28	GE	50	5	1800	2800

NATHAN OLIVEIRA

BORN: Oakland, CA; December 19, 1928
EDUCATION: Mills Col, Oakland, CA; California Col of Arts & Crafts, Oakland, CA, MFA, 1952
TEACHING: Prof, Art, San Francisco Art Inst, CA, 1955–56; Prof, Art, California Col of Arts & Crafts, Oakland, CA, 1955–56; Prof, Art, Univ of Illinois, Champaign, IL, 1961–62; Prof, Art, Univ of California, Los Angeles, CA, 1963–64; Prof, Art, Cornell Univ, Ithaca, NY, 1964; Prof, Art, Stanford Univ, CA, 1964–84; Prof, Art, Univ of Colorado, Boulder, CO, 1965; Prof, Art, Univ of Hawaii, Honolulu, HI, 1971; Prof, Art, Cranbrook Acad of Art, Bloomfield Hills, MI, 1972; Prof, Art, Baltimore Art Inst, MD, 1972; Prof, Art, John Herron Art Inst, Indianapolis, IN, 1972; Prof, Art, Kent State Univ, OH, 1973
AWARDS: Guggenheim Found Fel, NY, 1958; Norman Wait Harris Bronze Medal, Art Inst of Chicago, IL, 1960; Tamarind Fel, Albuquerque, NM, 1964
RECENT EXHIB: John Berggruen Gallery, San Francisco, CA, 1989; The Art Show, NY, 1989; Kansas City Art Inst, Charlotte Crosby Kemper Gallery, Kansas City, MO, 1989; G H Dalsheimer Gallery, Baltimore, MD, 1990; Salander-O'Reilly Galleries, NY, 1990; Palo Alto Cultural Center, CA, 1992; Rhode Island Sch of Design Mus, Providence, RI, 1992; Marsha Mateyka Gallery, Wash, DC, 1993
COLLECTIONS: Mus of Mod Art, NY; Guggenheim Mus of Art, NY; Hirshhorn Mus, Wash, DC; Smithsonian Inst, Wash, DC; San Francisco Mus of Mod Art, CA
PRINTERS: 3EP Ltd, Palo Alto, CA (3EP); Experimental Workshop, San Francisco, CA (EW); Wil Foo (WF); John Stemmer (JS); David Salgado, San Francisco, CA (DS); Eric Broege, San Francisco, CA (EB); Trillium Studios, San Francisco, CA (TS)
PUBLISHERS: 3EP Ltd, Palo Alto, CA (3EP); Experimental Workshop, San Francisco, CA (EW); Coplan/Dalsheimer Fine Art, Baltimore, MD (CDFA)
GALLERIES: John Berggruen Gallery, San Francisco, CA; Richard Gray Gallery, Chicago, IL; Charles Cowles Gallery, New York, NY; Smith Andersen Gallery, Palo Alto, CA; Experimental Workshop, San Francisco, CA; Dorothy Goldeen Gallery, Santa Monica, CA; Marsha Mateyka Gallery, Wash, DC; G H Dalsheimer Gallery, Baltimore, MD; Young Gallery, Los Gatos, CA; Robert Green Fine Arts, Mill Valley, CA; David Raymond, Ltd, San Francisco, CA; Salander-O'Reilly Gallery, New York, NY
MAILING ADDRESS: 785 Santa Maria Ave, Stanford, CA 94305

TITLE	PUBLISHER	PRINTER	DATE	MEDIUM	DIMENSION (PAPER SIZE) IN INCHES	TYPE OF PAPER	EDITION NUMBER	NO. OF COLORS	ORIGINAL OPENING PRICE	CURRENT RETAIL PRICE
SOLD OUT EDITIONS (RARE):										
Archive Site	3EP	3EP	1979	EB/A	22 X 31	AP	50		300	2500
Emerson Site I	3EP	3EP	1979	EB/A	22 X 15	AP	40		200	2000
Emerson Site II	3EP	3EP	1979	EB/A	22 X 15	AP	30		200	2000

NATHAN OLIVEIRA CONTINUED

TITLE	PUBLISHER	PRINTER	DATE	MEDIUM	DIMENSION (PAPER SIZE) IN INCHES	TYPE OF PAPER	EDITION NUMBER	NO. OF COLORS	ORIGINAL OPENING PRICE	CURRENT RETAIL PRICE
SOLD OUT EDITIONS (RARE):										
Kestrel Series	EW	WF/JS/EW	1985	MON	48 X 30	SS/B	21	MULTI	5000 EA	8000 EA
Pier Sites	EW	WF/JS/EW	1986	MON/HC	48 X 43	R/BFK	22	MULTI	9000	10000
CURRENT EDITIONS:										
Man	CDFA	DS/EB/TS	1989	LC	40 X 27	AC	45		3500	3500
Woman	CDFA	DS/EB/TS	1989	LC	40 X 27	AC	45		3500	3500
Monotypes (Series of 30)	CDFA	DS/EB/TS	1989	MON	47 X 32 EA	AC	1 EA		8000 EA	8000 EA

DENNIS A OPPENHEIM

BORN: Mason City, WA; September 6, 1938
EDUCATION: California Col of Arts & Crafts, Oakland, CA, BA, 1959–64; Stanford Univ, CA, MA, 1964–65
TEACHING: Vis Art, Sculpture, Yale Univ, New Haven, CT, 1969; Vis Art, Pratt Inst of Art, Brooklyn, NY, 1969; Vis Art, California Col of Arts & Crafts, Oakland, CA, 1970; Via Art, Rhode Island Sch of Design, Providence, RI, 1970; Vis Art, Univ of Wisconsin, Whitewater, WI, 1970; Vis Art, Sculpture, Art Inst of Chicago, IL, 1971–72; Vis Art, Sculpture, Nova Scotia Col of Art, Can, 1971–72
AWARDS: Newhouse Found Grant, Stanford Univ, CA, 1965; John Simon Guggenheim Found Fel, 1971–72; Nat Endowment for the Arts Fel, 1974,81
RECENT EXHIB: Laguna Gloria Art Mus, Austin, TX, 1987; Cleveland Mus of Art, OH, 1988; Queens Mus, NY, 1988; Grand Rapids Art Mus, MI, 1988; Anne Plume Gallery, NY, 1988; Alan Brown Gallery, Hartsdale, NY, 1988; Galleria Francoise Lambert, Milan, Italy, 1989; John Gibson Gallery, NY, 1989,90; Yvon Lambert Gallery, Paris, France, 1990; Pieredes Mus, Athens, Greece, 1990; Le Chanjour Gallery, Nice, France, 1990; Bernst & Krips Gallery, Cologne, Germany, 1990; Illinois State Univ Mus, Normal, IL, 1992; Cleveland Center for Contemp Art, OH, 1992; PS 1, NY, 1992; BlumHelman Gallery, NY, 1993
COLLECTIONS: Mus of Mod Art, NY; Baymans Mus, Rotterdam, The Netherlands; Centre Georges Pompideau, Paris, France; Kunsthaus, Zurich, Switzerland; Detroit Art Inst, MI; Hudson River Mus, NY; Queens Mus, Yonkers, NY; Nassau County Mus of Fine Art, Roslyn, NY; Rutgers Univ, Camden, NJ; Hobart Coll, Univ of Connecticut, Storrs, CT; Whitney Mus of Am Art, NY; Stedelijk Mus, Amsterdam, The Netherlands; Everson Mus of Art, Syracuse, NY; Cranbrook Acad of Art, Bloomfield Hills, MI
PRINTERS: John Campione, NY (JC); Patricia Branstead, NY (PB); Branstead Studios, NY (BS); Jack Lemon, Chicago, IL (JL); Landfall Press, Inc, Chicago, IL (LPI); Richard Finch, Normal, IL (RF); Veda Rives, Normal, IL (VR); Normal Editions Workshop, IL (NEW)
PUBLISHERS: Prestige Art Ltd, Mamaroneck, NY (PA); Multiples, Inc, NY (M); Landfall Press, Inc, Chicago, IL (LPI); Normal Editions Workshop, IL (NEW); University Galleries, Illinois State University, Normal, IL (ISU)
GALLERIES: Sonnabend Gallery, New York, NY; Marianne Deson Gallery, Chicago, IL; John Gibson, New York, NY; Sander Gallery, New York, NY; Vanderwoude/Tananbaum Gallery, New York, NY; Marian Goodman Gallery, New York, NY; Judith Posner Gallery, Milwaukee, WI; Helander Gallery, Palm Beach CA; Alan Brown Gallery, Hartsdale, NY; Anne Plumb Gallery, New York, NY; Galleria Francoise Lambert, Milan, Italy; Pascal de Sarthe Gallery, San Francisco, CA; Dart Gallery, Chicago, IL; Howard Yezerski Gallery, Boston, MA; Vared Gallery, East Hampton, NY; BlumHelman Gallery, New York, NY; Landfall Press, Inc, Chicago, IL; Sorrentino/Mayer Fine Art, New York, NY; Carla Stellweg Latin American & Contemporary Art, New York, NY; Ro Gallery Image Makers, Inc, New York, NY
MAILING ADDRESS: 54 Franklin St, New York, NY 10013

TITLE	PUBLISHER	PRINTER	DATE	MEDIUM	DIMENSION (PAPER SIZE) IN INCHES	TYPE OF PAPER	EDITION NUMBER	NO. OF COLORS	ORIGINAL OPENING PRICE	CURRENT RETAIL PRICE
CURRENT EDITIONS:										
Projects (Set of 10):	M	PB/BS	1973	LC	22 X 40	AP	81 EA		2500 SET	10000 SET
									275 EA	1100 EA
Mind Twist (Set of 8)	M	PB/BS	1977	PH/C	30 X 40 EA	AP	50 EA		2000 SET	8000 SET
									300 EA	1500 EA
Set of Four:										
Impulse Reactor	PA	JC	1980	SP	50 X 80	AP	100	4	450	4000
Station for Detaining	PA	JC	1980	SP	50 X 80	AP	100	4	450	4000
Magic Loom	PA	JC	1980	SP	50 X 80	AP	100	4	450	4000
Device to Convert	PA	JC	1980	SP	50 X 80	AP	100	4	450	4000
Ghost Toast	LPI	JL/LPI	1991	LC	34 X 48	AP	50		3000	3000
Kissing Racks	LPI	JL/LPI	1991	LC	34 X 48	AP	50		3000	3000
Study for Objects: Dreams of Flying	LPI	JL/LPI	1991	LC	34 X 48	AP	50		3000	3000
Untitled	NEW/ISU	RF/VR/NEW	1992	LC	35 X 29	R/BFK	50	4	1800	1800

DEBORAH OROPALLO

BORN: Hackensack, NJ; November 29, 1954
EDUCATION: Leo Marchutz Sch of Drawing & Painting, Aix-en-Provence, France, 1975; Alfred Univ, NY, BFA, 1979; Univ of California, Berkeley, CA, MA, 1982, MFA, 1983
TEACHING: Teaching Asst, Alfred Univ, NY, 1979; Lectr, Art History Dept, Alfred Univ, NY, 1979; Teaching Asst, Univ of California, Berkeley, CA, Drawing, 1982; San Francisco Art Inst, CA, Painting, 1984,85; San Francisco Art Acad Col, CA, Advanced Painting, 1986,87
AWARDS: FC-JC Fine Art Award, Alfred Univ, NY, 1977; Michael Cory Levins Sculpture Award, NY, 1978; Honorable Mention, California State Fair, Sacramento, CA, 1981; Second Place, California State Fair, Sacramento, CA, 1981; Richard Art Center Award, CA, 1982; Ann Bremer Award, Univ of California, Berkeley, CA, 1982; Second Place, HAFA, Hayward, CA, 1983; Engelhard Award, Inst of Contemp Art, Boston, MA, 1987; Support Grant, Art Space, San Francisco, CA, 1988,90; California Arts Council Grant, 1990; Nat Endowment for the Arts Award, 1991
RECENT EXHIB: Mem Union Art Gallery, Univ of California, Davis, CA, 1987; Stephen Wirtz Gallery, San Francisco, CA, 1988; Ann Jaffe Gallery, Bar Harbor Islands, FL, 1992; Susan Cummins Gallery, Mill Valley, CA, 1992; Krakow Gallery, Boston, MA, 1992; Katie Block Fine Arts, Boston, MA, 1992; Directions in Bay Area Printmaking, Palo Alto, CA, 1993
COLLECTIONS: Baltimore Mus of Art, MD; La Jolla Mus of Contemp Art, CA; Weatherspoon Art Gallery, Univ of North Carolina, Greensboro, NC

DEBORAH OROPALLO CONTINUED

PRINTERS: Will Foo, San Francisco, CA (WF); Charles Thomas, San Francisco, CA (CT); Experimental Workshop, San Francisco, CA (EW)
PUBLISHERS: Experimental Workshop, San Francisco, CA (EW)

GALLERIES: Betsy Senior Contemporary Prints, New York, NY; Experimental Workshop, San Francisco, CA; Stephen Wirtz Gallery, San Francisco, CA; Krakow Gallery, Boston, MA; Susan Cummins Gallery, Mill Valley, CA

TITLE	PUBLISHER	PRINTER	DATE	MEDIUM	DIMENSION (PAPER SIZE) IN INCHES	TYPE OF PAPER	EDITION NUMBER	NO. OF COLORS	ORIGINAL OPENING PRICE	CURRENT RETAIL PRICE
CURRENT EDITIONS:										
Rescue Device	EW	WF/CT/EW	1989	WC/A/ENG/SG 30 X 24	R/BFK	40	11	12000	12000

JOSÉ CLEMENTE OROZCO

BORN: Mexico; (1883–1949)
PRINTERS: Artist (ART)
PUBLISHERS: Artist (ART)
GALLERIES: Topaz Universal, Burbank, CA; B Lewin Galleries, Palm Springs, CA; George Belcher Gallery, San Francisco, CA; Harcourts Modern & Contemporary Art, San Francisco, CA; TwoSixtyOne Art, New York, NY

TITLE	PUBLISHER	PRINTER	DATE	MEDIUM	DIMENSION (PAPER SIZE) IN INCHES	TYPE OF PAPER	EDITION NUMBER	NO. OF COLORS	ORIGINAL OPENING PRICE	CURRENT RETAIL PRICE
SOLD OUT EDITIONS (RARE):										
Masked Dancers	ART	ART	1927	LB	13 X 16	WOVE	100	1	25	3000
Maquayes y Nopoles	ART	ART	1928	LB	12 X 17	WOVE	100	1	25	3200
La Pulquerra	ART	ART	1928	LB	13 X 16	WOVE	100	1	25	2500
Teatro de Variedades en . . .	ART	ART	1928	LB	12 X 16	WOVE	100	1	25	2000
Tourists	ART	ART	1928	LB	12 X 17	WOVE	100	1	25	2200
Pueblo Mexicano (H-20)	ART	ART	1930	LB	11 X 15	WOVE	100	1	25	1800
Manifestation	ART	ART	1935	LB	13 X 17	WOVE	120	1	50	3500
The Masses	ART	ART	1935	LB	13 X 17	WOVE	120	1	50	3800
Zapatistas	ART	ART	1936	LB	13 X 16	WOVE	120	1	50	4000

ERIC ORR

BORN: Covington, Kentucky
EDUCATION: Univ of California, Berkeley, CA; Univ of Mexico; New Sch for Social Research, NY; Ecole de Pataphysiques, Paris, France; Univ of Cincinnati, OH
RECENT EXHIB: Scott Hanson Gallery, NY, 1987; Adams-Middleton Gallery, Dallas, TX, 1988
PRINTERS: David Ordaz, CA, (DO); Cirrus Editions Workshop, Los Angeles, CA (CEW)
PUBLISHERS: Cirrus Editions, Los Angeles, CA (CE)
GALLERIES: Cirrus Editions, Ltd, Los Angeles, CA; Neil G. Ovsey Gallery, Los Angeles, CA; Angles Gallery, Santa Monica, CA; Scott Hanson Gallery, New York, NY; Adams-Middleton Gallery, Dallas, TX; James Corcoran Gallery, Santa Monica, CA; Tilden-Foley Gallery, New Orleans, LA; Thomas Babeor Gallery, La Jolla, CA; Charles Whitchurch Fine Art, Huntington Beach, CA; Acme Art, Santa Monica, CA; Works Gallery, Long Beach, CA; B Z Wagman Art, Inc, St Louis, MO; Sena Galleries, Santa Fe, NM; Karen Amiel & Contemporary Art, New York, NY

TITLE	PUBLISHER	PRINTER	DATE	MEDIUM	DIMENSION (PAPER SIZE) IN INCHES	TYPE OF PAPER	EDITION NUMBER	NO. OF COLORS	ORIGINAL OPENING PRICE	CURRENT RETAIL PRICE
CURRENT EDITIONS:										
Series of Lead Reliefs:										
Lead Window	CE	DO/CEW	1979	L/REL	24 X 17	LEAD	25		275	1200
Lead Window Gold X	CE	DO/CEW	1979	L/REL	24 X 17	LEAD	25		275	1200
Blue Door	CE	DO/CEW	1979	L/REL	24 X 17	LEAD	25		275	1200
Red Door	CE	DO/CEW	1979	L/REL	24 X 17	LEAD	25		275	1200
Lead Door	CE	DO/CEW	1979	L/REL	24 X 17	LEAD	25		275	950
Gold to Lead Strip	CE	DO/CEW	1979	L/REL	24 X 12	LEAD	30		275	750

ANDREW OSZE

BORN: Hungary; January 14, 1909
EDUCATION: Acad of Arts, Hungary, 1930–34 and Italy, 1947–48
TEACHING: Acad of Arts, Cuzco; Cat Univ, Lima, Peru
AWARDS: Ford Found Fel, Italy, 1946–48
COLLECTIONS: Hungary Nat Mus, Hungary; Polish Nat Mus, Poland; Modern Mus, Denver, CO; Baltimore Art Mus, MD; Springfield Art Mus, MA; Reading Art Mus, PA; Midland Art Mus, TX; The Young Mus, San Francisco, CA; McNey Art Inst; Nat Art Mus, NJ; Butler Inst of Am Art, Youngstown, OH
PRINTERS: Artist (ART)
PUBLISHERS: Artist (ART)
MAILING ADDRESS: 855 Doblia Lane, #7, Vero Beach, FL 32963

TITLE	PUBLISHER	PRINTER	DATE	MEDIUM	DIMENSION (PAPER SIZE) IN INCHES	TYPE OF PAPER	EDITION NUMBER	NO. OF COLORS	ORIGINAL OPENING PRICE	CURRENT RETAIL PRICE
SOLD OUT EDITIONS (RARE):										
Cluster of Stars	ART	ART	1979	LC	11 X 15	AP	10	3	200	450
Poetry, Come Your World	ART	ART	1979	MM	11 X 9	AP	10	4	200	400
Flowers of the Tale	ART	ART	1980	LC	11 X 9	AP	10	4	200	400
Love	ART	ART	1980	MM	15 X 22	AP	10	4	200	450
Dance	ART	ART	1980	MM	15 X 22	AP	10	3	200	450
Space and Form	ART	ART	1981	MM	11 X 15	AP	10	3	200	400

ELIZABETH OSBORNE

BORN: Philadelphia, PA; June 5, 1936
EDUCATION: Pennsylvania Acad of Fine Arts, Phila, PA, 1954–58; Univ of Pennsylvania, Phila, PA, BFA, 1959
TEACHING: Instr, Painting, Pennsylvania Acad of Fine Arts, Phila, PA, 1961 to present
AWARDS: Catherwood Travelling Fel, Pennsylvania Acad of Fine Arts, Phila, PA, 1955; Cresson Travelling Fel, Pennsylvania Acad of Fine Arts, Phila, PA, 1957; Scheidt Travelling Fel, Pennsylvania Acad of Fine Arts, Phila, PA, 1958; Fulbright Scholarship, Pais, Paris, France, 1963; Ford Found Purchase Prize, Pennsylvania Acad of Fine Arts, Phila, PA, 1964; Harrison Morris Prize, Pennsylvania Acad of Fine Arts, Phila, PA, 1971; Rosenthal Found Award, Am Acad & Inst of Arts & Letters, NY, 1976; McDowell Fel, Pennsylvania Acad of Fine Arts, Phila, PA, 1983; Art in Res, La Napoule Art Found, France, 1989; Percy Owens Mem Award, Pennsylvania Acad of the Fine Arts, Phila, PA, 1989
RECENT EXHIB: Butler Inst of Am Art, Youngstown, OH, 1987; Janss Coll, Boise Art Mus, ID, 1988; Mus of Mod Art, NY, 1988
COLLECTIONS: Philadelphia Mus, PA; Pennsylvania Acad of Fine Arts, Phila, PA, Delaware Art Mus, Wilmington, DE; Rahr-West Mus, Manitowoc, WI; Marion Koogler McNay Art Mus, San Antonio, TX; Print Club, Phila, PA
PRINTERS: John Bolles, Phila, PA (JB); Jack Lemon, Chicago, IL (JL); Landfall Press Inc, Chicago, IL (LPI); Orion Editions, NY (OE); Roni Henning, NY (RH); Tamarind Inst, Albuquerque, NM (TI); ChromComp, Inc, NY (CCI)
PUBLISHERS: Philadelphia Museum Fashion Group, PA (PMFG); Marian Locks Gallery, Phila, PA (ML); Orion Editions, NY (OE); Friends of the Philadelphia Mus of Art, PA (FPMA); Chalk & Vermilion Fine Art, Greenwich, CT (CVFA)
GALLERIES: Marian Locks Gallery, Phila, PA; Orion Editions, New York, NY
MAILING ADDRESS: 2125 Cypress St, Phila, PA 19103

TITLE	PUBLISHER	PRINTER	DATE	MEDIUM	DIMENSION (PAPER SIZE) IN INCHES	TYPE OF PAPER	EDITION NUMBER	NO. OF COLORS	ORIGINAL OPENING PRICE	CURRENT RETAIL PRICE
SOLD OUT EDITIONS (RARE):										
Passage	ML	JB	1971	SP	19 X 27	AP	50	10	200	600
Teriade	ML	JB	1972	SP	22 X 27	AP	50	12	200	600
Saba Bank	PMFG	JB	1973	SP	25 X 27	AP	200	15	200	600
Cirrha	ML	JB	1973	SP	25 X 27	AP	75	16	250	600
Hibiscus	ML	JB	1974	SP	22 X 30	AP	100	15	300	600
Still Life with Greek Vase	FPMA	JL/LPI	1979	LC	23 X 30	AP	125	6	275	550
Manchester	OE	RH	1979	PO	23 X 31	AP/WA	100	25	275	550
Winter Still Life	OE	RH	1982	PO	23 X 31	AP/WA	125	17	450	550
Nava in Flowered Dress	ML	TI	1983	LC	22 X 30	AP	75	6	400	600
CURRENT EDITIONS:										
Summer Still Life	CVFA	CCI	1986	SP	24 X 32	COV	352	40	500	550
Still Life with Cat	CVFA	RH	1986	SP	30 X 37	AC/W	352	22	500	550
Japanese Still Life	CVFA	RH	1986	SP	30 X 38	AC/W	352	31	500	550
Evening Still Life	CVFA	RH	1986	SP	30 X 38	AC/W	352	28	500	550
Rookwood Still Life II	CVFA	CCI	1987	SP	38 X 29	AC/W	352		550	625
Summer Lilies	CVFA	CCI	1987	SP	38 X 29	AC	422		550	650
Still Life with Floating Flowers	CVFA	CCI	1987	SP	30 X 37	AC	352	45	550	550
August Still Life	CVFA	CCI	1989	SP					550	550

ALFONSO A OSSORIO

PRINTERS: Judith Solodkin, NY (JS); Solo Press, NY (SP)
PUBLISHERS: Solo Press, NY (SP)
GALLERIES: Zabriskie Gallery, New York, NY; Hudson River Editions, South Nyack, NY; Vered Gallery, East Hampton, NY; Vanderwoude/Tananbaum Gallery, New York, NY; Solo Impressions, New York, NY

TITLE	PUBLISHER	PRINTER	DATE	MEDIUM	DIMENSION (PAPER SIZE) IN INCHES	TYPE OF PAPER	EDITION NUMBER	NO. OF COLORS	ORIGINAL OPENING PRICE	CURRENT RETAIL PRICE
CURRENT EDITIONS:										
Untitled	SP	JS/SP	1982	LB	32 X 24	AP	30		350	650

CARL OSTENDARP

PRINTERS: Brenda Zlamany, Brooklyn, NY (BZ); Erie-Lackawanna Press, Brooklyn, NY (E-LPr)
PUBLISHERS: Daniel Elias Editions, Lincoln, MA (DEEd)
GALLERIES: Graham Modern Galleries, New York, NY; John Post Lee Gallery, New York, NY; Jamie Wolff Fine Art, New York, NY

TITLE	PUBLISHER	PRINTER	DATE	MEDIUM	DIMENSION (PAPER SIZE) IN INCHES	TYPE OF PAPER	EDITION NUMBER	NO. OF COLORS	ORIGINAL OPENING PRICE	CURRENT RETAIL PRICE
CURRENT EDITIONS:										
Drip Print	DEEd	BZ/E-LPr	1992	PH/EB/A/SL	18 X 23	HMP	35	1	450	450
Pancake Print	DEEd	BZ/E-LPr	1992	PH/EB/A/SL	18 X 23	HMP	35	1	450	450

JERRY OTT

BORN: Albert Lee, MN; July 31, 1947
EDUCATION: Mankato State Col, MN, 1965–70; Univ of Minnesota, Minneapolis, MN, 1971
TEACHING: Art in Res, St Cloud State Univ, MN, 1979
COLLECTIONS: Mus of Contemporary Art, Tokyo, Japan; Minneapolis Inst of Art, MN, Univ of Kansas, Lawrence, KS; Univ of Georgia, Athens, GA; Smithsonian Inst, Wash, DC; Walker Art Ctr, Minneapolis, MN; Metropolitan Mus of Art, NY
PRINTERS: Styria Studio, NY (SS)
PUBLISHERS: Styria Studio, NY (SS)

JERRY OTT CONTINUED

GALLERIES: Styria Studio, New York, NY; R H Love Galleries, Chicago, IL; Brenda Kroos Gallery, Cleveland, OH; Thomson Gallery, Minneapolis, MN

MAILING ADDRESS: 1251 Barclay, St Paul, MN 55106

TITLE	PUBLISHER	PRINTER	DATE	MEDIUM	DIMENSION (PAPER SIZE) IN INCHES	TYPE OF PAPER	EDITION NUMBER	NO. OF COLORS	ORIGINAL OPENING PRICE	CURRENT RETAIL PRICE
CURRENT EDITIONS:										
Connie	SS	SS	1978	LC	23 X 31	HMP	90	5	250	400
Elaine/Mylar	SS	SS	1978	LC/SP/CD	30 X 38	AP88	100	11	550	700
Untitled	SS	SS	1980	LC	9 X 10	RNP/G	25	1	200	350
Susan	SS	SS	1981	LC	28 X 40	AP88	60	19	550	700

SABINA OTT

BORN: New York, NY; 1955
EDUCATION: San Francisco Art Inst, CA, BFA, 1979, MFA, 1981
RECENT EXHIB: Fresno Art Mus, CA, 1987; Los Angeles County Art Mus, CA, 1987; Galerie am Moritzplatz, Berlin, Germany, 1987; Betsy Rosenfield Gallery, Chicago, IL, 1987,88; Pence Gallery, Santa Monica, CA, 1988; Palo Alto Cultural Center, CA, 1992
COLLECTIONS: Metropolitan Mus of Art, NY; Los Angeles County Art Mus, CA; Dayton Hudson Found, Minneapolis, MN
PRINTERS: Cirrus Editions Workshop, Los Angeles, CA (CEW)
PUBLISHERS: Cirrus Editions, Ltd, Los Angeles, CA (CE)
GALLERIES: Cirrus Gallery, Los Angeles, CA; Charles Cowles Gallery, New York, NY; Experimental Workshop, San Francisco, CA; Vermillion Editions, Ltd, Minneapolis, MN; Betsy Rosenfield Gallery, Chicago, IL; Pence Gallery, Santa Monica, CA
MAILING ADDRESS: c/o Charles Cowles Gallery, Inc, 420 N. Broadway, New York, NY 10012

TITLE	PUBLISHER	PRINTER	DATE	MEDIUM	DIMENSION (PAPER SIZE) IN INCHES	TYPE OF PAPER	EDITION NUMBER	NO. OF COLORS	ORIGINAL OPENING PRICE	CURRENT RETAIL PRICE
CURRENT EDITIONS:										
Mater Rosa I–V	CE	CEW	1991	LC/SP	42 X 34 EA	FAB	40 EA		1200 EA	1200 EA

TOM OTTERNESS

BORN: Wichita, KS; 1952
EDUCATION: Arts Students League, NY, 1970; Whitney Mus of Am Art, NY, Independent Prog, 1973
COLLECTIONS: Brooklyn Mus, NY; Dallas Mus of Art, TX; San Francisco Mus of Mod Art, CA; Whitney Mus of Am Art, NY; Weatherspoon Art Gallery, Greensboro, NC; Museo Tamayo, Mexico City, Mexico; Lannan Found, Lake Worth, FL; Dannheisser Found, NY; Eli Broad Family Found, Los Angeles, CA
RECENT EXHIB: Mus of Mod Art, NY, 1987; Brooke Alexander Gallery, NY, 1987; Univ of Rhode Island, Kingston, RI, 1988; Bass Mus of Art, Miami Beach, FL, 1988; Anders Tornberg Gallery, Lund, Sweden, 1989; James Corcoran Gallery, Santa Monica, CA, 1990; Lannon Found, Los Angeles, CA, 1990–91
PRINTERS: Artist (ART)
PUBLISHERS: Brooke Alexander, Inc, NY (BAI)
GALLERIES: Brooke Alexander, Inc, New York, NY; Anders Tornberg Gallery, Lund, Sweden; John Berggruen Gallery, San Francisco, CA; James Corcoran Gallery, Santa Monica, CA; Nancy Drysdale Gallery, Wash, DC

TITLE	PUBLISHER	PRINTER	DATE	MEDIUM	DIMENSION (PAPER SIZE) IN INCHES	TYPE OF PAPER	EDITION NUMBER	NO. OF COLORS	ORIGINAL OPENING PRICE	CURRENT RETAIL PRICE
SOLD OUT EDITIONS (RARE):										
Sitting Man II	BAI	ART	1978	CP	4 X 2 X 12	HMP	250		90	100
Death Angel II	BAI	ART	1979	CP	8 X 2 X 2	HMP	250		100	150
Father/Daughter	BAI	ART	1979	CP	6 X 2 X 2	HMP	250		100	150
Lioness & Child	BAI	ART	1981	CP	11 X 3 X 3	HMP	250		100	180
Vertical Figures	BAI	ART	1981	CP	15 X 3 X 3	HMP	250		100	200
Couple II	BAI	ART	1978–82	CP	3 X 4 X 2	HMP	250		90	100
Death Dressed Up	BAI	ART	1982	CP	7 X 4 X 6	HMP	250		100	150
CURRENT EDITIONS:										
Flower Girl, Flower Boy (Cast Plaster) (Dipt)	BAI	ART	1989	C/PL	7 X 3 X 2	Plaster			200 SET	200 SET

JULIEN OUTIN

BORN: France
EDUCATION: Jesuit Sch, Brest, France
PRINTERS: American Atelier, NY (AA)
PUBLISHERS: Circle Fine Art, Chicago, IL (CFA)
GALLERIES: Circle Galleries, San Diego, CA & San Francisco, CA & Northbrook, IL & Pittsburgh, PA & Houston, TX & Soho, NY & Chicago, IL & Scottsdale, AZ & Beverly Hills, CA & Costa Mesa, CA & Sherman Oaks, CA & New Orleans, LA & Las Vegas, NV & Seattle, WA

TITLE	PUBLISHER	PRINTER	DATE	MEDIUM	DIMENSION (PAPER SIZE) IN INCHES	TYPE OF PAPER	EDITION NUMBER	NO. OF COLORS	ORIGINAL OPENING PRICE	CURRENT RETAIL PRICE
SOLD OUT EDITIONS (RARE):										
The Sitting	CFA	AA	1978	LC	29 X 21	AP	250		50	125

The retail prices of the 100,000 limited edition prints quoted in this directory are subject to change. Print publishers, artists and galleries were the direct sources for these quotations. Prices in the secondary market listed as "Sold Out Editions (Rare)" indicate that the publisher has a limited supply of that print or that the print is difficult to locate in the galleries.

The print market has become very selective. For the first time since we published the first edition of The Printworld Directory in 1982, the prices of prints have been greatly reduced and greatly increased for the same artists by the most reputable and established print publishers. Check the fifth edition to understand the movement.

FRANK OWEN (FRANKLIN CHARLES)

BORN: Kalispell, MT; May 13, 1939
EDUCATION: Antioch Col, Yellow Springs, OH; Univ of California, Davis, CA, BA, 1966, MA, 1968
TEACHING: Instr, Painting State Univ, Sacramento, CA, 1967–68; Instr, Fine Arts, Sch of Visual Arts, NY, 1970 to present
AWARDS: Univ of California Regent's Fel, 1967–68; Nat Endowment for the Arts Fel, 1978–79, 1989–90
RECENT EXHIB: Cook Company Gallery, Rancho Cordova, CA, 1987; Nancy Hoffman Gallery, NY, 1988; Iannetti Lanzone Gallery, San Francisco, CA, 1988
COLLECTIONS: Univ of North Carolina, Ackland Art Mus, Chapel Hill, NC; Albright-Knox Art Gallery, Buffalo, NY; Corcoran Gallery of Art, Wash, DC; Des Moines Art Center, IA; Elvehjem Mus of Art, Univ of Wisconsin, Madison, WI; Madison Art Center, WI; Univ of Massachusetts, Boston, MA; St Louis Art Mus, MO; Frederick R Weisman Found of Art, Los Angeles, CA
PRINTERS: Bill Weege, Madison, WI (BW); Andrew Rubin, Madison, WI (AR); Tandem Press, Univ of Wisconsin, Madison, WI (TanPr)
PUBLISHERS: Tandem Press, Univ of Wisconsin, Madison, WI (TanPr)
GALLERIES: Nancy Hoffman Gallery, New York, NY; Iannetti Lanzone Gallery, San Francisco, CA; Cook Company Gallery, Rancho Cordova, CA
MAILING ADDRESS: P O Box 703, Keene Valley, NY 12943

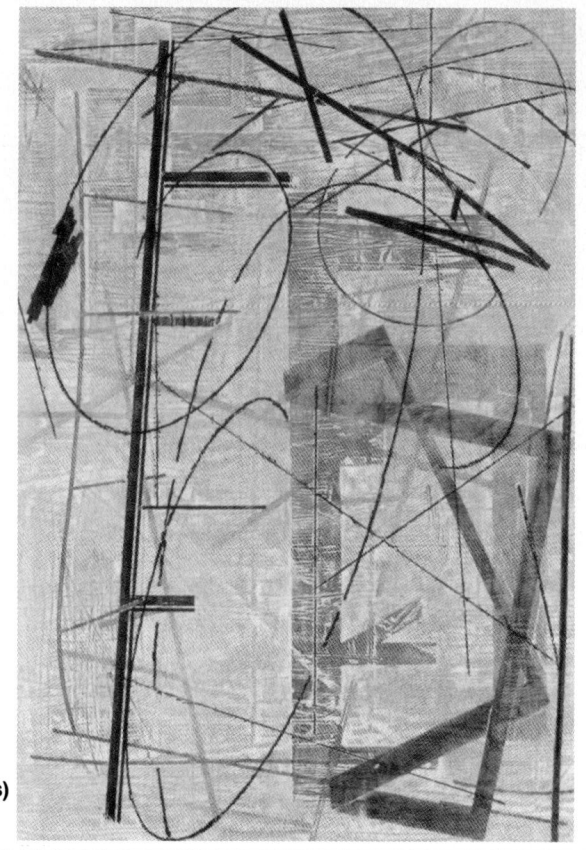

Frank Owen (Franklin Charles)
Vault
Courtesy Tandem Press

TITLE	PUBLISHER	PRINTER	DATE	MEDIUM	DIMENSION (PAPER SIZE) IN INCHES	TYPE OF PAPER	EDITION NUMBER	NO. OF COLORS	ORIGINAL OPENING PRICE	CURRENT RETAIL PRICE
SOLD OUT EDITIONS (RARE):										
Untitled (Dipt)	TanPr	BW/AR/TanPr	1989	MON	58 X 40 EA	AC/W	1 EA	Varies	2800 EA	3000 EA
CURRENT EDITIONS:										
Vault	TanPr	BW/AR/TanPr	1989	REL	58 X 40	HMP	12	8	2200	2200
Know the Elements	TanPr	BW/AR/TanPr	1989	LC	30 X 21	AC/BL	40	5	600	600

JACK OX

BORN: Denver, CO; February 4, 1948
EDUCATION: San Francisco Art Inst, CA, BFA, 1969; Univ of California, San Diego, CA, MFA, 1977
TEACHING: Vis Assoc Prof, Univ of California, Irvine, CA, 1986
AWARDS: Juror's Choice Award, CA, 1982
COLLECTIONS: Univ of Iowa, Iowa City, IA; Hood Mus of Art, Dartmouth Col, Hanover, NH
PRINTERS: Artist (ART); Gerson Photolithographic Press, NY (GPP)
PUBLISHERS: Artist (ART)
GALLERIES: Emily Harvey Gallery, New York, NY; Meyers/Bloom Gallery, Santa Monica, CA
MAILING ADDRESS: 712 Broadway, #5, New York, NY 10003–9707

TITLE	PUBLISHER	PRINTER	DATE	MEDIUM	DIMENSION (PAPER SIZE) IN INCHES	TYPE OF PAPER	EDITION NUMBER	NO. OF COLORS	ORIGINAL OPENING PRICE	CURRENT RETAIL PRICE
CURRENT EDITIONS:										
Edition Römerturm 4 (½') 33cm (Set of 3)	ART	ART/GPP	1987	PH/LB	24 X 24 EA	MOH/80	100 EA	1 EA	600 SET	600 SET
Edition Römerturm 4 (½') 33cm (Set of 3)	ART	ART/GPP	1987	PH/HC	24 X 24 EA	MOH/80	100 EA	Varies	1000 SET	1000 SET

KIRSTEN ORTWED

PRINTERS: Artist (ART)
PUBLISHERS: Fred Jahn, Munich, West Germany (FJ)
GALLERIES: David Nolan Gallery, New York, NY

TITLE	PUBLISHER	PRINTER	DATE	MEDIUM	DIMENSION (PAPER SIZE) IN INCHES	TYPE OF PAPER	EDITION NUMBER	NO. OF COLORS	ORIGINAL OPENING PRICE	CURRENT RETAIL PRICE
CURRENT EDITIONS:										
Werk-Statt-Foto (Set of 5)	FJ	ART	1986	PH/C	12 X 17 EA	PHP	10 EA	Multi	1000 SET	1800 SET

The retail prices of the 100,000 limited edition prints quoted in this directory are subject to change. Print publishers, artists and galleries were the direct sources for these quotations. Prices in the secondary market listed as "Sold Out Editions (Rare)" indicate that the publisher has a limited supply of that print or that the print is difficult to locate in the galleries.

KATJA OXMAN

BORN: Munich, Germany; August 2, 1942; US Citizen
EDUCATION: Pennsylvania Acad of Fine Arts, Phila, PA, 1962–65; Acad of Munich, Germany, 1965–66; Royal Col of Art, London, England, Research Certificate in Printmaking, Sch of Graphic Design, 1967
TEACHING: Art in Res, Bryn Mawr Col, PA, 1968–69; Dir, Ben Shahn Graphic Workshop, Skowhegan Sch, ME, 1972–73; Vis Lectr, Fine Art, Univ of Massachusetts, Amherst, MA 1975; Adj Prof, Art, American Univ, Wash, DC, 1976–85
AWARDS: Woodrow Prize, 1964; Pennsylvania Acad of Fine Arts, Phila, PA, Full Tuition Scholarship, 1963–65; Stauffer Prize, 1965; Friends Scholarship, Grad Study, 1966; New Jersey State Mus, Purchase Prize, 1969; Purchase Prize, Boston Printmakers, MA, 1982; Professional Prize, Print Club, Hunt Manuf Co, 1983; Purchase Award, Nat Print Annual, Moravian Col, PA, 1984; Print Club, Zelda & Josef Jaffe Award, 1984; Purchase Prize, Print & Drawing Soc, NC, 1985; Purchase Award, Univ of Delaware Biennial, Newark, DE, 1985; Purchase Prize, Auburn Works on Paper, AL, 1987; Juried Selection, Boston Printmakers Material Award, MA, 1987,88; Provost's Purchase Award, Bradley Nat Print & Drawing Exhib, Peoria, IL, 1989

RECENT EXHIB: Marcus Gordon Gallery, Pittsburgh, PA, 1989; David Adamson Gallery, Wash, DC, 1987,89; Randall Beck Gallery, Boston, MA, 1989,90,92
COLLECTIONS: Philadelphia Mus, PA; New Jersey State Mus, Trenton, NJ; Univ of Delaware, Newark, DE; Smithsonian Inst, Wash, DC; Pennsylvania Acad of Fine Arts, Phila, PA; Clemson Arch Found Coll, Clemson Univ, SC; American Univ Coll, Wash, DC; Univ of Scranton, PA; Roxbury Col, ID; Moravian Col, PA; U S Dept of State, Wash, DC; Hopkins Center, Dartmouth Col, NH; Nat Inst of Health, Bethesda, MD; Bradley Univ, Peoria, IL; Southern Alleghenies Mus, Loretto, PA; Federal Reserve Bank, Baltimore, MD; Tarble Art Center, Eastern Illinois Univ, Charleston, IL; Art complex Mus, Duxbury, MA; Univ of Maryland, College Park, MD
PRINTERS: Artist (ART); Tonia Matthews (TM); Ann Schlesinger (AS)
PUBLISHERS: Artist (ART); Orion Editions, NY (OE)
GALLERIES: Orion Editions, New York, NY; Gallery North, Setauket, NY; Cumberland Gallery, Nashville, TN; Bingham Gallery, Memphis, TN; Gallery 68, Belfast, MN; Print Club, Phila, PA; Stone Press Gallery, Seattle, WA; David Adamson Gallery, Wash, DC; Marcus Gordon Gallery, Pittsburgh, PA; Randall Beck Gallery, Boston, MA
MAILING ADDRESS: 620 Gist Ave, Silver Spring, MD 20910

TITLE	PUBLISHER	PRINTER	DATE	MEDIUM	DIMENSION (PAPER SIZE) IN INCHES	TYPE OF PAPER	EDITION NUMBER	NO. OF COLORS	ORIGINAL OPENING PRICE	CURRENT RETAIL PRICE
SOLD OUT EDITIONS (RARE):										
Familiar Patterns	ART	ART/TM/AS	1981	EB/A	29 X 22	GE	20	3	200	750
Caught Up in Details	ART	ART/TM/AS	1982	EC	30 X 22	GE	20	3	350	750
Collections of Fragments	OE	ART/TM/AS	1982	EC	30 X 22	GE	60	3	350	750
Normally Grown in Full Sun	OE	ART/TM/AS	1983	EB/A	31 X 27	GE	70	3	350	650
In the Dimness	OE	ART/TM/AS	1983	EB/A	30 X 42	GE	90	3	500	950
Unforeseen Directions	OE	ART/TM/AS	1984	EB/A	38 X 30	GE	90	3	450	1100
Passage of Time	OE	ART/TM/AS	1984	FR/A	38 X 30	GE	90	3	450	1100
Unsuspected Turns	OE	ART/TM/AS	1984	EB/A	30 X 34	GE	125	3	500	850
All the Gardens (Dipt)	OE	ART/TM/AS	1985	EB/A	26 X 45	GE	125	3	900	1500
The Next Moment	OE	ART/TM/AS	1985	EB/A	31 X 28	GE	125	3	350	750
Lands that Were	OE	ART/TM/AS	1986	EB/A	30 X 42	GE	125	3	750	950
The Other Side of the Air (Dipt)	OE	ART/TM/AS	1986	EB/A	35 X 47	GE	150	3	1500	2800
Silence Agreed	OE	ART/TM/AS	1987	EB/A	30 X 34	GE	175	3	650	950
What Solitude	OE	ART/TM/AS	1987	EB/A	25 X 54	GE	150	3	1500	2800
Passing Through	OE	ART/TM/AS	1987–88	EB/A	40 X 30	GE	150	4	850	1500
CURRENT EDITIONS:										
Night and Distant Rumbling (Dipt)	OE	ART/TM/AS	1988	EB/A	23 X 35	GE	150	3	950	1500
A House Within	OE	ART/TM/AS	1988	EB/A	42 X 30	GE	150	5	850	1100
Uncertain Sunlight	OE	ART/TM/AS	1988	EB/A	25 X 36	GE	75	3	1000	1200
Mid Solitude	OE	ART/TM/AS	1988	EC	20 X 18	GE		3	300	350
In the Chamber	OE	ART/TM/AS	1989	EB/A	26 X 29	GE	150	3	850	950
In the Wind	OE	ART/TM/AS	1989	EB/A	23 X 24	GE	150	3	350	500
Eventually to Embrace	OE	ART/TM/AS	1989	EC	22 X 30	GE	60	3	400	550
Quiet Transformations	OE	ART/TM/AS	1990	EC	26 X 29	GE	150	3	900	950
Most Practiced Distance	OE	TM	1990	EB/A	40 X 30	GE	150	4	950	950
Provenance Unknown	OE	TM	1991	EB/A	40 X 30	GE	150	4	850	850
Transparent Days	OE	TM	1991	EB/A	36 X 47	GE	150	4	2200	2200

PIERRE PAGÉS

BORN: Montreuil-sur-Mer, France; 1909
EDUCATION: L'Ecole d'Architecture, Paris, France; L'Académie de la Grande Chaumiére, Paris, France

PRINTERS: American Atelier, NY (AA)
PUBLISHERS: Circle Fine Art, Chicago, IL (CFA)
GALLERIES: Circle Galleries, San Diego, CA & San Francisco, CA & Northbrook, IL & Pittsburgh, PA & Houston, TX & Soho, NY & Chicago, IL & Scottsdale, AZ & Beverly Hills, CA & Costa Mesa, CA & Sherman Oaks, CA & Palm Beach, FL & Honolulu, HI & New Orleans, LA & Las Vegas, NV & Seattle, WA

TITLE	PUBLISHER	PRINTER	DATE	MEDIUM	DIMENSION (PAPER SIZE) IN INCHES	TYPE OF PAPER	EDITION NUMBER	NO. OF COLORS	ORIGINAL OPENING PRICE	CURRENT RETAIL PRICE
SOLD OUT EDITIONS (RARE):										
New York	CFA	AA	1980	LC	30 X 22	AP	300		75	525
New York (Roman Numerals)	CFA	AA	1980	LC	30 X 22	JP	60		100	625

ALAIN PAIEMENT

PRINTERS: Randy Hemminhaus, Vinalhaven, ME (RH); Vinalhaven Press, Vinalhaven, ME (VP)
PUBLISHERS: Vinalhaven Press, Vinalhaven, ME (VP)
GALLERIES: Vinalhaven Press, Vinalhaven, ME

TITLE	PUBLISHER	PRINTER	DATE	MEDIUM	DIMENSION (PAPER SIZE) IN INCHES	TYPE OF PAPER	EDITION NUMBER	NO. OF COLORS	ORIGINAL OPENING PRICE	CURRENT RETAIL PRICE
CURRENT EDITIONS:										
Grand Amphitheatre: According to Horizon	VP	RH/VP	1989	PH/EB/3-D	22 X 42 X 1	R/BFK	10	1	3200	4000

NAM JUNE PAIK

BORN: Seoul, Korea; 1932
EDUCATION: Univ of Tokyo, Japan, BFA, 1956
RECENT EXHIB: Univ of Missouri, Kansas City, MO, 1987; Contemp Arts Center, Cincinnati, OH, 1987; Everson Art Mus, Syracuse, NY, 1987; Whitney Mus of Am Art, NY, 1988; Holly Solomon Gallery, NY, 1988,89; Mus of Mod Art, NY, 1989; San Francisco Mus of Mod Art, CA, 1989; Retrosp, Carl Solway Gallery, Cincinnati, OH, 1991; Retrosp, Kunsthaus, Zurich, Switzerland, 1991; Retrosp, Kunsthalle, Basel, Switzerland, 1991; Retrosp, Kunsthalle, Dusseldorf, Germany, 1991
PRINTERS: Editions Schellmann & Klüser, Munich, Germany (SK); Mark Patsfall, Cincinnati, OH (MP); Deborah Steinkamp, Cincinnati, OH (DS); Artist (ART)
PUBLISHERS: Editions Schellmann & Klüser, Munich, West Germany (SK); Carl Solway Gallery, Cincinnati, OH (CS); Galerie Watari, Tokyo, Japan (GW); Editions Schellmann, Munich, Germany & NY (ES)
GALLERIES: Galeria Bonino Ltd, New York, NY; Carl Solway Gallery, Cincinnati, OH; Editions Schellmann, New York, NY; Galerie Watari, Tokyo, Japan; Holly Solomon Gallery, New York, NY; Dorothy Goldeen Gallery, Los Angeles, CA; Stein Bartlow Gallery, Ltd, Chicago, IL

Nam June Paik
Self Portrait
Courtesy Edition Schellmann

TITLE	PUBLISHER	PRINTER	DATE	MEDIUM	DIMENSION (PAPER SIZE) IN INCHES	TYPE OF PAPER	EDITION NUMBER	NO. OF COLORS	ORIGINAL OPENING PRICE	CURRENT RETAIL PRICE
CURRENT EDITIONS:										
A Tribute to John Cage	SK	ART	1978	SP	6 X 5 X 1	AP	250		350	1200
V-Idea (Set of 10)	CS/GW	MP/DS	1984	EB	19 X 22 EA	R/BFK	58 EA		6000 SET	10000 SET
Self Portrait	CS/ES	ART	1989	MULT	24 X 27 X 16	Metal	12		2500	15000
Sonatine for Goldfish (RCA Victor TV Casing—with Aquarium)	ES		1992	MULT	16 X 31 X 16		12		15000	15000
Before the Word, There was Light, After the Word . . . (Dumont TV Casing with Candle)	ES		1992	MULT	17 X 24 X 20		21		15000	15000

WOJCIECH PAKOWSKI

BORN: Poland

AWARDS: Artist in Residence, Bemis Found, Omaha, NE, 1989
PRINTERS: Artist (ART)
PUBLISHERS: Artist (ART)
GALLERIES: Greene Art Gallery, Guilford, CT

TITLE	PUBLISHER	PRINTER	DATE	MEDIUM	DIMENSION (PAPER SIZE) IN INCHES	TYPE OF PAPER	EDITION NUMBER	NO. OF COLORS	ORIGINAL OPENING PRICE	CURRENT RETAIL PRICE
CURRENT EDITIONS:										
Roots	ART	ART	1989	DPT	30 X 24	FAB	125	1	750	750

CHARLEMAGNE PALESTINE

PRINTERS: Centre Genevois de Gravure, Geneva, Switzerland (CGG)
PUBLISHERS: Galerie Eric Franck, Geneva, Switzerland (GEF)
GALLERIES: Galerie Eric Franck, Geneva, Switzerland; Zolla/Lieberman Gallery, Chicago, IL

TITLE	PUBLISHER	PRINTER	DATE	MEDIUM	DIMENSION (PAPER SIZE) IN INCHES	TYPE OF PAPER	EDITION NUMBER	NO. OF COLORS	ORIGINAL OPENING PRICE	CURRENT RETAIL PRICE
CURRENT EDITIONS:										
Set of 4:										
Mveshu	GEF	CGG	1983	PO/EMB/CO/ST	24 X 29	JP	25		500	750
Ozagnu	GEF	CGG	1983	PO/EMB/CO/ST	24 X 29	JP	25		500	750
Pnooz	GEF	CGG	1983	PO/EMB/CO/ST	24 X 29	JP	25		500	750
Yachtt	GEF	CGG	1983	PO/EMB/CO/ST	24 X 29	JP	25		500	750

KINGSLEY PARKER

PRINTERS: Nancy Brokopp, NY (NB)
PUBLISHERS: Artist (ART)
GALLERIES: Condeso/Lawler Gallery, New York, NY; A Clean, Well-Lighted Place, New York, NY

TITLE	PUBLISHER	PRINTER	DATE	MEDIUM	DIMENSION (PAPER SIZE) IN INCHES	TYPE OF PAPER	EDITION NUMBER	NO. OF COLORS	ORIGINAL OPENING PRICE	CURRENT RETAIL PRICE
CURRENT EDITIONS:										
Seafood	ART	NB	1984	EB/A	11 X 48	R/BFK	40	1	200	350

MIMMO PALADINO

BORN: Paduli, Benevento, Italy; 1948
EDUCATION: Liceo Artistico di Benevento, Italy, 1964–68
RECENT EXHIB: Waddington Gallery, London, England, 1988; Sperone Westwater Gallery, NY, 1989; Univ of Maine, Orono, ME, 1989,92
COLLECTIONS: Mus of Med Art, NY
PRINTERS: Patricia Branstead, NY (PB); Aeropress Inc, NY (A); Georgio Upiglio, Milan, Italy (GU); Grafica Uno, Milan, Italy (G-U); Artist (ART)
PUBLISHERS: Multiples Inc, NY (M); Waddington Graphics, London, England (WG); Schellman & Kluser, Munich, Germany (SK); Sperone Westwater, NY (SW); Edition Schellmann, Munich, Germany (ES)
GALLERIES: Marian Goodman, New York, NY; Annina Nosei Gallery, New York, NY; Sperone Westwater, New York, NY; Hillman Holland, Atlanta, GA; Editions Schellmann, New York, NY; Gian Enzo Sperone, Rome, Italy; Galerie Thomas, Munich, Germany; Galleria Toselli, Milan, Italy; Giselle Linder, Basel, Switzerland; Richard Gray Gallery, Chicago, IL; Waddington Gallery, London, England; Richard Gray Gallery, New York, NY; Nicola Jacobs Gallery, London, England; Galeria Quintana, Bogata, Columbia; Erika Meyerovich Gallery, San Francisco, CA; B R Kornblatt Gallery, Wash, DC; Dolly Fiterman Gallery, Minneapolis, MN; Rick Jones Modern Art, St. Louis, MO; Galeria Ramis F Barquet, Monterey, Mexico; J Noblett Gallery, Boyes Hot Springs, CA; Margaret Lipworth Fine Art, Boca Raton, FL; Nohra Haime Gallery, New York, NY Lillian Heidenberg Gallery, New York, NY; Meredith Long & Company, Houston, TX; Judy Youens Gallery, Houston, TX

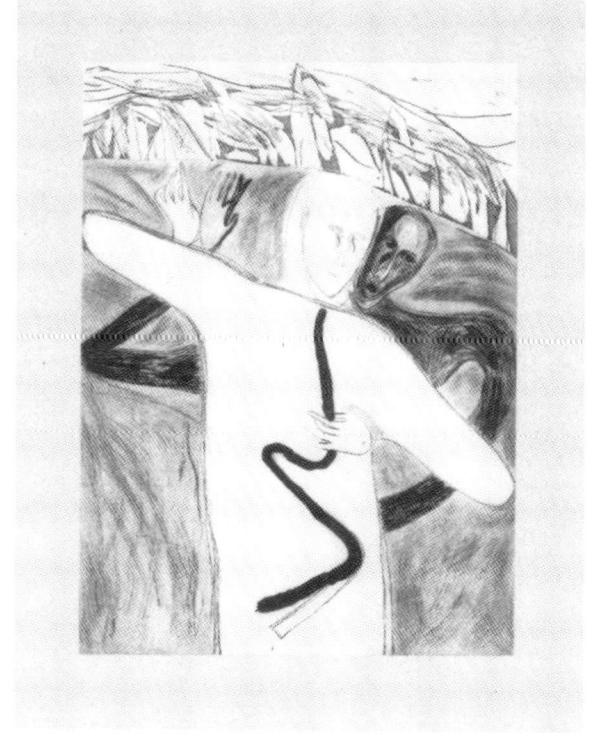

Mimmo Paladino
Untitled, 1982
Courtesy Edition Schellmann

TITLE	PUBLISHER	PRINTER	DATE	MEDIUM	DIMENSION (PAPER SIZE) IN INCHES	TYPE OF PAPER	EDITION NUMBER	NO. OF COLORS	ORIGINAL OPENING PRICE	CURRENT RETAIL PRICE
SOLD OUT EDITIONS (RARE):										
Con Musica	M	PB/A	1980	AB	25 X 22	AP	35	1	475	3000
Pietra di Pietro	M	PB/A	1980	DPT/HC	19 X 18	AP	35		350	2000
Tra Gli Ulivi	ES	ART	1984	ES/A/DPT	52 X 38	AC/DKP	35	7	1800	3500
Muto (with Fur Collage)	ES	ART	1985	EB/A/SL/CO	62 X 35	AC	35	1	2000	7500
CURRENT EDITIONS:										
Solo du Pesci	M	PB/A	1980	EB/A	32 X 23	AP	35		400	1200
Aqua di Ombra	M	PB/A	1980	EB/LI	24 X 32	AP	35	1	350	900
Fantasma	M	PB/A	1980	AC/SG/CC	24 X 30	AP	35		350	1200
Acqua di Stagno	M	PB/A	1980	EB/A/SB	23 X 25	AP	35		475	1500
Set of Four:									2600 SET	5500 SET
Tra Il Vento Fuoco	M	PB/A	1982	EB/LI	31 X 23	AP	35	1	650	1500
Guardar Misteri	M	PB/A	1982	EB/LI	31 X 23	AP	35	1	650	1500
Stelle Sulla Scena	M	PB/A	1982	EB/LI	31 X 23	AP	35	1	650	1500
Caverne Minacciose	M	PB/A	1982	EB/LI	31 X 23	AP	35	1	650	1500
Suite of 3 Lithographs (Untitled)	SK		1982	LB	24 X 32 EA	AP	75 EA	1 EA	1125 SET	2000 SET
Six Etchings (with Soft Ground)									500 EA	700 EA
(Set of 6):	SK	ART	1982	A/EMB/SL	32 X 26 EA	AP	60 EA		3000 SET	6000 SET
									600 EA	1000 EA
Tane di Napoli (Set of 4):	FE	GU/G-U	1983	DPT	20 X 23 EA	AP	33 EA	1 EA	1200 SET	3500 SET
Bosforo										
(Book with 6 Wood Engravings):	SW		1983	BOOK/WB	13 X 10 EA		60 EA		2500 SET	4500 SET
Portfolio of Four:									4125 SET	7500 SET
Ellpodbomool	WG	GU/G-U	1984	LI	38 X 53	FAB	65	1	1125	2000
Songo Umido	WG	GU/G-U	1984	LI	38 X 53	FAB	65	1	1125	2000
Dedalus	WG	GU/G-U	1984	LI	38 X 53	FAB	65	1	1125	2000
Introibo ad	WG	GU/G-U	1984	LI	38 X 53	FAB	65	1	1125	2000
Altare Dei	WG	GU/G-U	1984	LI	38 X 53	FAB	65	1	1125	2000
Lacrimosa I-VI (Set of 6)	WG	GU/G-U	1986	WC	30 X 42 EA	HAHN	42 EA		7500 SET	12000 SET
Untitled (Padoli Monotypes) (Series of 4)	WG	ART	1986	DPT/MON	29 X 20 EA	WOVE	1 EA	Varies	5000 EA	12500 EA

PABLO PALAZUELO

BORN: Madrid, Spain; 1916
AWARDS: Kandinsky Prize, 1952; Carnegie Prize, 1958
PRINTERS: Maeght Editeur, Paris, France (ME)
PUBLISHERS: Maeght Editions, Paris, France (ME)
GALLERIES: Galerie Lelong, New York, NY & Paris, France & Zürich, Switzerland; Spaightwood Galleries, Madison, WI

TITLE	PUBLISHER	PRINTER	DATE	MEDIUM	DIMENSION (PAPER SIZE) IN INCHES	TYPE OF PAPER	EDITION NUMBER	NO. OF COLORS	ORIGINAL OPENING PRICE	CURRENT RETAIL PRICE
CURRENT EDITIONS:										
Oval I	ME	ME	1975	EC	26 X 20	AP	75		100	200
Script IV	ME	ME	1975	EC	26 X 20	AP	50		100	200

PABLO PALAZUELO CONTINUED

TITLE	PUBLISHER	PRINTER	DATE	MEDIUM	DIMENSION (PAPER SIZE) IN INCHES	TYPE OF PAPER	EDITION NUMBER	NO. OF COLORS	ORIGINAL OPENING PRICE	CURRENT RETAIL PRICE
CURRENT EDITIONS:										
Script V	ME	ME	1975	EC	26 X 20	AP/CC	50		100	200
Nemo I	ME	ME	1975	EC	26 X 20	AP	75		100	200
Gotica I	ME	ME	1975	EC	27 X 21	SIR	50		100	200
Gotica I (Variation)	ME	ME	1975	EC	27 X 21	AP	50		100	250
Gotica III	ME	ME	1975	EC	31 X 23	AP	50		100	250
Gotica IV	ME	ME	1975	EC	23 X 31	AP	50		100	250
Sceaux V	ME	ME	1975	EC	20 X 16	AP	60		100	250
Sceaux VIII	ME	ME	1975	EC	26 X 20	AP	75		100	250
Rouge	ME	ME	1975	EC	26 X 20	AP	75		100	250
Oin I	ME	ME	1975	EC	26 X 36	AP	75		100	300
Sigilla I	ME	ME	1976	EC	36 X 25	AP	75		100	300
Sigilla II	ME	ME	1976	EC	36 X 25	AP	75		100	300
Sigilla III	ME	ME	1976	EC	36 X 25	AP	75		100	300
Sigilla V	ME	ME	1976	EC	36 X 25	AP	75		100	300
Sigilla VII	ME	ME	1976	EC	36 X 25	AP	75		100	300
Sigilla X	ME	ME	1976	EC	36 X 25	AP	75		100	300
Sigilla XI	ME	ME	1976	EC	36 X 25	AP	75		100	300
Parallelos	ME	ME	1976	LC	16 X 34	AP	120		100	200
Gotica-Variante	ME	ME	1976	LC	9 X 27	AP	75		100	200
Sing	ME	ME	1976	LC	27 X 20	JP	50		100	250
Barcelona 1977	ME	ME	1977	LC	34 X 25	AP	100		125	200
Invitacio	ME	ME	1977	LC	24 X 20	AP	100		125	200
En Verde	ME	ME	1977	LC	24 X 20	AP	100		125	200
De Musica II	ME	ME	1977	LC	31 X 31	AP	75		125	200
Lour	ME	ME	1977	LC	27 X 20	AP	50		125	200
Sceaux IV	ME	ME	1978	EC	56 X 41	AP	75		150	250
De Musica III	ME	ME	1978	LC	57 X 38 cm	AP	30		150	250
De Musica IV	ME	ME	1978	LC	86 X 64 cm	AP	30		150	250
De Musica V	ME	ME	1978	LC	86 X 64 cm	AP	30		150	250
De Musica VI	ME	ME	1978	LC	70 X 61 cm	AP	30		150	250
Emblema I	ME	ME	1980	LC	81 X 57 cm	AP	75		200	300
Emblema II	ME	ME	1980	LC	81 X 57 cm	AP	75		200	300
Emblema III	ME	ME	1980	LC	91 X 64 cm	AP	75		200	300
Temps Gris	ME	ME	1981	LC	56 X 38 cm	CM	75		200	300

JOAN R PALEY

BORN: Springfield, MA; May 4, 1943
EDUCATION: Connecticut Col for Women, New London, CT; Univ of Hartford, CT; Art Students League, NY
PRINTERS: American Atelier, NY (AA)
PUBLISHERS: Jackie Fine Arts, NY (JFA); New York Graphic Society, Greenwich, CT (NYGS)
MAILING ADDRESS: Winfield Ave, Harrison, NY 10528

TITLE	PUBLISHER	PRINTER	DATE	MEDIUM	DIMENSION (PAPER SIZE) IN INCHES	TYPE OF PAPER	EDITION NUMBER	NO. OF COLORS	ORIGINAL OPENING PRICE	CURRENT RETAIL PRICE
SOLD OUT EDITIONS (RARE):										
Daybreak	JFA	AA	1979	SP	19 X 28	AP	300	13	175	250
Early Spring	JFA	AA	1979	SP	20 X 28	AP	300	12	175	250
Iris	JFA	AA	1980	LC	18 X 27	AP	300	13	175	250
Ballet	JFA	AA	1981	LC	22 X 30	AP	300	10	175	250
Beau Belle	JFA	AA	1981	SP	19 X 27	AP	150	10	175	250
Tulip	JFA	AA	1981	SP	19 X 27	AP	150	11	175	250
Day Flowers	JFA	AA	1982	LC	19 X 27	AP	300	12	175	250
Allegro	JFA	AA	1982	LC	19 X 24	AP	300	11	175	250

PILAR PALOMER

BORN: Barcelona, Spain; April 13, 1945
EDUCATION: Escuela Superior de Bellas Artes, Barcelona, Spain, BFA
PRINTERS: La Poligrafa, SA, Barcelona, Spain (LP)
PUBLISHERS: Ediciones Poligrafa, SA, Barcelona, Spain (EdP)
GALLERIES: Galeria Joan Prats, Barcelona, Spain & New York, NY

TITLE	PUBLISHER	PRINTER	DATE	MEDIUM	DIMENSION (PAPER SIZE) IN INCHES	TYPE OF PAPER	EDITION NUMBER	NO. OF COLORS	ORIGINAL OPENING PRICE	CURRENT RETAIL PRICE
SOLD OUT EDITIONS (RARE):										
Cinc Alteracions del Paisatge									550 SET	1300 SET
(Series of 5 Etchings)	EdP	LP	1979	EC	22 X 30 EA	GP	75 EA		130 EA	280 EA
Lithograph AL Joan Prats	EdP	LP	1980	LC	22 X 30	GP	99		180	220

The Printworld Directory is accepting new applications for the seventh edition. Approximately 300 new artists will be accepted. Please use the two forms provided in the back section of this directory to submit biographical data and documentation of prints. Edition number of each print must not exceed 500 and the retail price must be $100 or more.

GIULIO PAOLINI

BORN: Genoa, Italy; 1940
PRINTERS: Artist (ART); Marco Noire, Turin, Italy (MN)
PUBLISHERS: AIEUO, Rome, Italy (AIEUO); Multiples, Inc, NY (M); Christian Stein, Turin, Italy & Milan, Italy (CS)
GALLERIES: Guiliana Setai Gallery, New York, NY; Marian Goodman Gallery, New York, NY; Rhona Hoffman Gallery, Chicago, IL

TITLE	PUBLISHER	PRINTER	DATE	MEDIUM	DIMENSION (PAPER SIZE) IN INCHES	TYPE OF PAPER	EDITION NUMBER	NO. OF COLORS	ORIGINAL OPENING PRICE	CURRENT RETAIL PRICE
SOLD OUT EDITIONS (RARE):										
Idea del Tempio della Pittura (4 Parts)	AIEUO	ART	1983	LC/PH	10 X 15 EA	R/100/W	100 EA		800 SET	2500 SET
CURRENT EDITIONS:										
The Triumph of Representation (Trip)	M/CS	MN	1986	LC/OFF	16 X 26 EA	Grap	90 EA		1400 SET	2000 SET

BILL PARKER

PUBLISHERS: Circle Fine Art, Chicago, IL (CFA)
GALLERIES: Circle Galleries, San Diego, CA & San Francisco, CA & Northbrook, IL & Pittsburgh, PA & Houston, TX & Soho, NY & Chicago, IL & Scottsdale, AZ & Beverly Hills, CA & Costa Mesa, CA & Sherman Oaks, CA & Palm Beach, FL & Honolulu, HI & New Orleans, LA & Las Vegas, NV & Seattle, WA

TITLE	PUBLISHER	PRINTER	DATE	MEDIUM	DIMENSION (PAPER SIZE) IN INCHES	TYPE OF PAPER	EDITION NUMBER	NO. OF COLORS	ORIGINAL OPENING PRICE	CURRENT RETAIL PRICE
SOLD OUT EDITIONS (RARE):										
Rites of Dawn	CFA	AA	1981	LSC	12"	AP	375		2000	3650
The Meaning of Radiance	CFA	AA	1981	LSC	12"	AP	325		2000	3150
Elegance of Becoming	CFA	AA	1981	LSC	12"	AP	375		2000	3950
Sleepless Nights	CFA	AA	1981	LSC	12"	AP	275		2000	3300
Ancient Frequencies	CFA	AA	1981	LSC	12"	AP	250		2000	2850
Ice Trees	CFA	AA	1982	LSC	12"	AP	275		2250	2950
Modern Frequencies	CFA	AA	1983	LSC	12"	AP	375		2250	2850
Fire Flower	CFA	AA	1983	LSC	12"	AP	375		2250	3150
October Sunrise	CFA	AA	1983	LSC	12"	AP	375		2250	13500
Elegance of Truth	CFA	AA	1985	LSC	12"	AP	375		2500	3200
Summer Celebrations	CFA	AA	1986	LSC	12"	AP	250		2750	3600
Desert Nights	CFA		1986	SCUL	21"		9			23500
Angry Whispers	CFA		1986	SCUL	21"		9			15800

J WHITEMAN PARKER

BORN: Long Beach, CA; October 8, 1945
EDUCATION: Acad of Art Col, San Francisco, CA, 1968–71; Art Inst, San Francisco, CA, 1971–72
AWARDS: Purchase Award, Univ of Texas, Austin, TX, 1972
PRINTERS: Artist (ART)
PUBLISHERS: Harleen & Allen Art Brokerage, San Francisco, CA (HA); Art Dimensions, Norcross, GA (AD)
GALLERIES: Hank Baum Gallery, San Francisco, CA; Choice, Inc, San Francisco, CA; Village Gallery, Maui, HI
MAILING ADDRESS: 3608 Taraval St, San Francisco, CA 94116

TITLE	PUBLISHER	PRINTER	DATE	MEDIUM	DIMENSION (PAPER SIZE) IN INCHES	TYPE OF PAPER	EDITION NUMBER	NO. OF COLORS	ORIGINAL OPENING PRICE	CURRENT RETAIL PRICE
CURRENT EDITIONS:										
Moon Marigold	AD	ART	1978	EC	22 X 30	AP	200	5	200	250
Tiger Lily	AD	ART	1978	EC	22 X 30	AP	200	2	200	250
CURRENT EDITIONS:										
Orchid Cactus	AD	ART	1979	EC	15 X 11	AP	200	2	100	150
Wax Plant	AD	ART	1979	EC	15 X 11	AP	200	3	100	150
Jade Plant	AD	ART	1979	EC	11 X 15	AP	200	2	100	150
Prickly Pear Cactus	AD	ART	1979	EC	11 X 15	AP	200	2	100	150
Hedgehog Cactus	AD	ART	1980	EC	30 X 22	AP	200	4	200	250
Dutch Iris	AD	ART	1981	EC	30 X 22	AP	200	4	200	250
Water Lily I, II	AD	ART	1982	EC	22 X 30 EA	AP	250 EA	3 EA	200 EA	250 EA

JÜRGEN PARTENHEIMER

PRINTERS: Artist (ART)
PUBLISHERS: Perma Press, NY (PerP)
GALLERIES: Perma Press, NY (PerP); Littlejohn-Smith Gallery, New York, NY

TITLE	PUBLISHER	PRINTER	DATE	MEDIUM	DIMENSION (PAPER SIZE) IN INCHES	TYPE OF PAPER	EDITION NUMBER	NO. OF COLORS	ORIGINAL OPENING PRICE	CURRENT RETAIL PRICE
CURRENT EDITIONS:										
Ying Yang (Passage)	PerP	ART	1984	LI	21 X 15	GE	25	1	500	900

The retail prices of the 100,000 limited edition prints quoted in this directory are subject to change. Print publishers, artists and galleries were the direct sources for these quotations. Prices in the secondary market listed as "Sold Out Editions (Rare)" indicate that the publisher has a limited supply of that print or that the print is difficult to locate in the galleries.

The Printworld Directory is accepting new applications for the seventh edition. Approximately 300 new artists will be accepted. Please use the two forms provided in the back section of this directory to submit biographical data and documentation of prints. Edition number of each print must not exceed 500 and the retail price must be $100 or more.

MAX PAPART

BORN: Marselle, France; December 14, 1911
RECENT EXHIB: Sheldon Swope Art Mus, Terre Haute, IN, 1989; Nahan Gallery, NY, 1990
COLLECTIONS: Brandeis Univ, Waltham, MA; Mus of San Diego, CA; Univ of Pennsylvania, Phila, PA; Yale Univ, New Haven, CT; Phoenix Art Mus, Phoenix, AZ; Peabody Col, Nashville, TN; Univ of Alabama, Birmingham, AL; New Orleans Mus, LA; Jacksonville Mus, FL; Syracuse Univ, NY; Franklin and Marshall Col, Lancaster, PA; La Jolla Art Center, CA; Fairleigh Dickenson Univ, Rutherford, NJ; Behaven Col, Jackson, MS; Lowe Art Ctr, NY; Lincoln Univ, Oxford, PA; Jamestown Col, Jamestown, ND; Mus of Mod Art, Miami, FL; Mus of Mod Art, Paris, France; Mus Cantini, Marseille, France; Israel Mus, Jerusalem, Israel; Kunst Mus, Boras, Sweden; Univ of Pennsylvania, Phila, PA; Mus of New Mexico, Albuquerque, NM; Mus of Mod Art, NY; New Orleans Mus of Art, LA
PRINTERS: Atelier Mourlot, Paris, France (AM); Fignier (FIG); Agnostini (AG); Pichard (PIC); M Felt (FG); Dutrou (DUT); Graphalith (GR); La Poligrafa, Barcelona, Spain (LP); Carrier (CR); Atelier Pasnic, Paris, France (APas); Atelier Joban, Paris, France (JOB)
PUBLISHERS: Nahan Editions, New Orleans, LA (NE); Ediciones Poligrafa, Barcelona, Spain (EdP); Martin Lawrence Limited Editions, Van Nuys, CA (MLLE)
GALLERIES: Nahan Galleries, New Orleans, LA & New York, NY & Tokyo, Japan; Galeria Joan Prats, Barcelona, Spain & New York, NY; Argus Fine Arts, Eugene, OR; Hahn Gallery, Phila, PA; Galerie Internationale, Bloomfield Hills, MI

Max Papart
Renaissance
Courtesy Nahan Editions

TITLE	PUBLISHER	PRINTER	DATE	MEDIUM	DIMENSION (PAPER SIZE) IN INCHES	TYPE OF PAPER	EDITION NUMBER	NO. OF COLORS	ORIGINAL OPENING PRICE	CURRENT RETAIL PRICE
SOLD OUT EDITIONS (RARE):										
The Wanderer	NE	DUT	1978	EB/CAR	27 X 37	AP	50	14	600	7500
Bird Under Red Moon	NE	DUT	1978	EB/A/CAR	54 X 37	AP	50	21	700	9000
Memory of the Future	NE	DUT	1979	EB/A/CAR	54 X 37	AP	50	20	700	8000
We Three	NE	DUT	1979	EB/A	37 X 54	AP	50	15	700	7500
O Douce Fantaisie	NE	DUT	1979	EB/A/CAR	47 X 29	AP	50	36	750	8000
Enchanted Bluebird	NE	DUT	1979	EB/A/CAR	37 X 54	AP	50	12	775	7500
Harlequin Bird	NE	DUT	1980	EB/A/CAR	37 X 54	AP	50	25	800	8000
Mr K	NE	DUT	1980	EB/A/CAR	30 X 22	AP	50	19	900	5500
Married Lady	NE	DUT	1980	EB/A/CAR	30 X 43	AP	50	28	1200	8500
April Romance	NE	DUT	1980	EB/A/CAR	39 X 39	AP	50	27	1500	9000
Accordian Player	NE	DUT	1980	EB/A/CAR	58 X 38	AP	50	32	2000	12000
Accordian Player (Deluxe)	NE	DUT	1980	EB/A/CAR/CO	58 X 38	AP	25	32	4000	14000
Petit Musique de Nuit	NE	FIG	1980	CAR/CO	24 X 18	HMP	60		450	3500
Blue/Brown/Bird	NE	PIC	1980	CAR/CO	24 X 30	HMP	60	14	450	3500
Multicolor Bird	NE	PIC	1980	CAR/CO	20 X 26	HMP	60		500	3500
Splendid Summer	NE	MF	1980	CAR/CO	22 X 36	HMP	60		450	3500
Songbird	NE	PIC	1980	CAR/CO	22 X 30	HMP	60	12	500	3500
Man with Mustache	NE	FIG	1980	CAR/CO	22 X 30	HMP	60	14	600	3500
Ideal Couple	NE	AG	1980	LC	32 X 24	AP	75	8	300	2000
Marianne	NE	AG	1980	LC	26 X 36	AP	85	12	350	2800
Personnages (Set of 6)	NE	AG	1980	LC/HWC	10 X 13 EA	AP	40 EA	18 EA	1500 SET	3000 SET
Beautiful Bird	NE	AM	1981	LC	30 X 23	AP	175	18	300	3000
Beautiful Bird (Deluxe)	NE	AM	1981	LC	30 X 23	JP	100	18	350	3500
Astronaut	NE	FIG	1981	CAR/CO	20 X 26	HMP	75	3	600	4000
Red Horse	NE	DUT	1981	EB/A/CAR	28 X 27	AP	50	25	700	5000
Red Horse (Deluxe)	NE	DUT	1981	EB/A/CAR/CO	28 X 27	AP	25	25	1800	5500
Red Harlequin	NE	DUT	1981	EB/A/CAR	54 X 41	AP	60	24	1800	6500
Red Harlequin (Deluxe)	NE	DUT	1981	EB/A/CAR	54 X 21	AP	25		2000	7000
Hello Broadway	NE	DUT	1981	EB/A/CAR	53 X 37	AP	60	19	1500	6500
Hello Broadway (Deluxe)	NE	DUT	1981	EB/A/CAR	53 X 37	AP	25	19	1800	7000
Indian Summer	NE	DUT	1981	EB/A/CAR	53 X 37	AP	60	26	2000	6500
Indian Summer (Deluxe)	NE	DUT	1981	EB/A/CAR	53 X 27	JP	25	26	3800	7000
Le Cirque (Trip)	NE	DUT	1981	EB/A/CAR	56 X 30	AP	50	32	5500 SET	14000 SET
					56 X 36	AP	50	19		
					56 X 25	AP	50	14		
Le Cirque (Trip) (Deluxe)	NE	DUT	1981	EB/A/CAR	56 X 30	AP	25	32	6500 SET	15000 SET
					56 X 36	AP	25	19		
					56 X 25	AP	25	14		
Trapeze	NE	GR	1981	LC/EMB	35 X 24	JP	135	12	375	2500
Blue Moon	NE	DUT	1981	EB/A/CAR	54 X 41	AP	60	21	1800	6500
Blue Moon (Deluxe)	NE	DUT	1981	EB/A/CAR	54 X 41	AP	25	21	2500	7000

MAX PAPART CONTINUED

TITLE	PUBLISHER	PRINTER	DATE	MEDIUM	DIMENSION (PAPER SIZE) IN INCHES	TYPE OF PAPER	EDITION NUMBER	NO. OF COLORS	ORIGINAL OPENING PRICE	CURRENT RETAIL PRICE
SOLD OUT EDITIONS (RARE):										
Profile	NE	FIG	1981	CAR/CO	23 X 30	HMP	75	14	600	3500
Clown Three	NE	AM	1981	LC	29 X 21	AP	135	18	300	1200
Carousel	NE	DUT	1982	EB/A/CAR	41 X 40	AP	65	17	1500	6000
Carousel (Deluxe)	NE	DUT	1982	EB/A/CAR	54 X 41	AP	25	17	1500	6500
Blue Harlequin	NE	DUT	1982	EB/A/CAR	54 X 41	AP	60	26	1400	6500
Circus Rider	NE	DUT	1982	EB/A/CAR	54 X 41	AP	60	22	1400	6500
Circus Rider (Deluxe)	NE	DUT	1982	EB/A/CAR	54 X 41	AP	25	22	1800	7000
Oval Bird	NE	M	1982	LC	30 X 22	AP	135	15	300	3200
Roman Circus	NE	APas	1982	CAR/CO	21 X 40	AP	75	7	400	3000
Roman Circus (Deluxe)	NE	APas	1982	CAR/CO	21 X 40	AP	25	7	1000	3500
Primavera	NE	DUT	1982	EB/A/CAR	41 X 39	AP	60	22	1250	5000
The Cyclist	NE	DUT	1982	EB/A/CAR	47 X 40	AP	60	24	1500	7000
The Cyclist (Deluxe)	NE	DUT	1982	EB/A/CAR	47 X 40	AP	25	24	2000	7500
Birds (Set of 4)	NE	APas	1982	CAR/CO	18 X 23 EA	AP	125 EA	7 EA	1000 SET	4000 SET
Combat Nocturne	NE	APas	1982	CAR/CO	38 X 40	AP	75	14	750	3500
Royal Bird	NE	DUT	1983	EB/A/CAR	38 X 54	AP	60	21	1500	5500
Condottiere	MLLE	LP	1983	CAR/CO	27 X 22	HMP	50	1	550	6000
Man of Venus	NE	DUT	1983	EB/A/CAR	59 X 38	AP	60	21	1800	9000
Man of Venus (Deluxe)	NE	DUT	1983	EB/A/CAR	59 X 38	AP	35	21	5000	10000
Sonata for a Bird	NE	FIG	1984	CAR/CO	25 X 42	HMP	85	38	1200	5500
Fantastic Voyage	NE	APas	1984	CAR/CO	21 X 30	HMP	85	18	650	3500
Enchanted Dream	NE	FIG	1984	CAR/CO	22 X 30	HMP	75	23	700	3500
Enchanted Dream (Deluxe)	NE	FIG	1984	CAR/CO	22 X 30	HMP	25	23	1200	4000
Streetwalker	NE	FG	1984	CAR/CO	22 X 30	HMP	75	14	650	3200
The Dancer	NE	DUT	1984	EB/A/CAR	55 X 44	AP	60	36	2100	9000
The Dancer (Deluxe)	NE	DUT	1984	EB/A/CAR	55 X 44	AP	25	36	2500	12000
Meloncholy Lady	NE	DUT	1984	EB/A/CAR	30 X 41	AP	60	22	1200	5500
Meloncholy Lady (Deluxe)	NE	DUT	1984	EB/A/CAR	30 X 41	AP	25	22	1500	6500
Electronic Man	NE	DUT	1984	EB/A/CAR	30 X 40	AP	60	28	1800	6000
Electronic Man (Deluxe)	NE	DUT	1984	EB/A/CAR	30 X 40	AP	25	28	2500	6500
Chromatic Composition	NE	DUT	1985	EB/A/CAR	30 X 40	AP	60	31	2000	6000
Chromatic Composition (Deluxe)	NE	DUT	1985	EB/A/CAR	30 X 40	AP	25	31	2500	6500
Silent Woman	NE	DUT	1985	EB/A/CAR	30 X 40	AP	60	31	2000	6000
Silent Woman (Deluxe)	NE	DUT	1985	EB/A/ CAR/CO	30 X 40	JP	25	31	2250	6500
Inca Bird	NE	APas	1985	CAR/CO	22 X 30	HMP	85	18	750	3500
Tomorrow's Children	NE	DUT	1985	EB/A/CAR	40 X 52	AP	75	28	3500	7500
Tomorrow's Children (Deluxe)	NE	DUT	1985	EB/A/ CAR/CO	40 X 52	JP	25	28	3700	8000
Romeo & Juliet	NE	DUT	1985	EB/A/CAR	33 X 60	AP	60		2000	7500
Romeo & Juliet (Deluxe)	NE	DUT	1985	EB/A/ CAR/CO	33 X 60	JP	25		2200	8000

Max Papart
Manhattan Transfer
Courtesy Nahan Editions

MAX PAPART CONTINUED

TITLE	PUBLISHER	PRINTER	DATE	MEDIUM	DIMENSION (PAPER SIZE) IN INCHES	TYPE OF PAPER	EDITION NUMBER	NO. OF COLORS	ORIGINAL OPENING PRICE	CURRENT RETAIL PRICE
SOLD OUT EDITIONS (RARE):										
Night & Day (Dipt)	NE	DUT	1986	EB/A/CAR	38 X 54	AP	35	24	6000	10000
Orange Sun	NE	APas	1986	CAR/CO	22 X 30	HMP	85		850	2800
Silver Bird	NE	DUT	1986	EB/A/CAR	35 X 30	AP	100		1800	4500
Kaleidoscope (Trip)	NE	DUT	1987	EB/A/CAR	20 X 19 EA	AP	60 EA		3000	5000
Moonlight	NE	DUT	1987	EB/A/CAR	27 X 24	AP	95		2200	4000
CURRENT EDITIONS:										
Trapeze Artist	NE	GR	1980	LC	35 X 24	AP	75	9	300	1600
Double Andante	NE	DUT	1981	EB/A/CAR	19 X 30	AP	75	32	650	3500
Italian Lady	NE	FIG	1981	CAR/CO	20 X 26	HMP	75	25	600	3000
Clown Three	NE	AM	1981	LC	29 X 21	JP	100	18	350	1500
Circle (with Engraving)	NE	M/PIC	1981	LC/ENG	30 X 21	AP	135	19	375	1600
Circus, Circus	NE	FIG	1981	DPT/HWC	15 X 22	R/BFK	45	1	450	1500
Mississippi River Romance	NE	FIG	1981	DPT/HWC	15 X 22	R/BFK	45	1	450	1400
Lovers III (Trip)	NE	PIC	1981	DPT/HWC	30 X 26 EA	AP	45 EA	1 EA	1200 SET	4000 SET
Liberte	NE	DUT	1982	EB/A/CAR	41 X 56	AP	60	16	1250	5500
Liberte (Deluxe)	NE	DUT	1982	EB/A/CAR	41 X 56	AP	25	16	1500	6000
Taxi America	NE	DUT	1982	EB/A/CAR	38 X 41	AP	60	26	1500	4500
Set of 5 Etchings with Carborundum (1–25):									3000 SET	5500 SET
#1, #4, #5	EdP	LP	1982	EB/CAR	30 X 22 EA	HMP	50 EA	1 EA	650 EA	1200 EA
#2, Profile	EdP	LP	1982	EB/CAR	30 X 22	HMP	50	1	650	1200
#3, Condottiere	EdP	LP	1982	EB/CAR	27 X 22	HMP	50	1	650	1200
Set of 5 Etchings with Carborundum (I–XXV):									3500 SET	6000 SET
#1, #4, #5	EdP	LP	1982	EB/CAR	30 X 22 EA	HMP	50 EA	1 EA	700 EA	1200 EA
#2, Profile	EdP	LP	1982	EB/CAR	30 X 22	HMP	50	1	700	1200
#3, Condottiere	EdP	LP	1982	EB/CAR	27 X 22	HMP	50	1	700	1200
Oval Bird Deluxe	NE	AM	1982	LC	30 X 22	HMP	85	15	350	2500
Blue Harlequin (Deluxe)	NE	DUT	1982	EB/A/CAR	54 X 41	AP	25	26	1800	7000
Primavera (Deluxe)	NE	DUT	1982	EB/A/CAR	41 X 39	AP	25	22	1500	5500
Birds (Set of 4) (Deluxe)	NE	APas	1982	CAR/CO	18 X 23 EA	JP	25 EA	7 EA	1200 SET	4500 SET
Combat Nocturne (Deluxe)	NE	APas	1982	CAR/CO	38 X 40	JP	25	14	850	4500
Spanish Bird	NE	AM/CR	1983	LC/EMB	22 X 30	HMP	120	8	300	2400
Le Guerrier	EdP	LP	1983	EB/A/CAR	30 X 22	HMP	50	1	550	2000
Rose and Green Bird	EdP	LP	1983	EB/A/CAR	22 X 30	HMP	50	1	550	2000
Andalousia	EdP	LP	1983	EB/A/CAR	30 X 22	HMP	50	1	550	2000
Royal Bird (Deluxe)	NE	DUT	1983	EB/A/CAR	38 X 54	AP	25	21	1800	6000
Profile	EdP	LP	1983	EB/A/CAR	30 X 22	HMP	50	1	550	1200
Dreams	NE	GR	1985	LC	40 X 30	AP	150	18	375	1500
Magic Man	NE	JOB	1985	LC	47 X 36	AP	150	11	500	1200
New Orleans Fantasy	NE	JOB	1985	LC	47 X 36	AP	150	11	500	1200
Oval Acrabat	NE	JOB	1986	LC	30 X 42	AP	125	11	650	1500
Bogie	NE	APas	1986	CAR/CO	20 X 36	HMP	85		850	2400
Seduction	NE	APas	1986	LC	34 X 24	AP	175		600	1600
Silver Bird (Deluxe)	NE	DUT	1986	EB/A/CAR	35 X 30	AP	85		2500	5000
Moonlight (Deluxe)	NE	DUT	1987	EB/A/CAR	27 X 24	AP	45		2500	4500
Into the Future	NE	APas	1987	CAR/CO	24 X 31	HMP	95		1000	2000
Le Voyageur	NE	APas	1987	CAR/CO	28 X 24	HMP	95		1250	2000
Janus	NE	APas	1987	CAR/CO	31 X 23	HMP	95		900	1800
American Ballet	NE	DUT	1987	EB/A/CAR	40 X 41	AP	75		5000	5500
Mirage	NE	DUT	1987	EB/A/CAR	21 X 39	AP	95		2500	3500
Equilibrist	NE	DUT	1988	EB/A/CAR	50 X 40	AP	85		4500	5500
Un Lot de Joyeuses (Set of 8):									12000 SET	18000 SET
L'Aristocrat	NE	DUT	1988	EB/A/CAR	23 X 18	AP	195		1500	2500
Le Rouge et le Gris	NE	DUT	1988	EB/A/CAR	23 X 18	AP	195		1500	2500
L'Enfant et le . . .	NE	DUT	1988	EB/A/CAR	23 X 18	AP	195		1500	2500
Bonne Nouvelle	NE	DUT	1988	EB/A/CAR	23 X 18	AP	195		1500	2500
Le Reflet au Chapeau	NE	DUT	1988	EB/A/CAR	23 X 18	AP	195		1500	2500
Jole d'Enfant	NE	DUT	1988	EB/A/CAR	23 X 18	AP	195		1500	2500
Parfum d'Ete	NE	DUT	1988	EB/A/CAR	23 X 18	AP	195		1500	2500
La Vie en Rose	NE	DUT	1988	EB/A/CAR	23 X 18	AP	195		1500	2500
Mrs S	NE	DUT	1988	EB/A/CAR	40 X 40	AP	95		3500	3500
Louisiana Springtime	NE	APas	1988	CAR/CO	23 X 29	HMP	95		1000	1600
Merry-Go-Round	NE	APas	1988	CAR/CO	23 X 29	HMP	95		1200	2000
Les Femmes d'Alger	NE	DUT	1989	EB/A/CAR	39 X 41	AP	85		4800	6500
Deux Musicians	NE	DUT	1989	EB/A/CAR	50 X 38	AP	85		5000	6500
Piano Blues	NE	APas	1989	CAR/CO	30 X 45	HMP	95		2500	3000
Banjo	NE	APas	1989	CAR/CO	30 X 35	HMP	125		1800	2600
Manhattan Transfer	NE	JOB	1990	CAR	31 X 58	HMP	75		4500	7500
Guitare	NE	JOB	1989	LC	30 X 21	AP	125		750	1800
Guitare (Deluxe)	NE	JOB	1989	LC	30 X 21	JP	75		850	2200
Guitare I	NE	JOB	1990	LC/CAR	21 X 30	AP	125		750	2000
Guitare II	NE	JOB	1990	LC/CAR	21 X 30	AP	125		750	2000

MAX PAPART CONTINUED

Max Papart
Japanese Birds
Courtesy Nahan Editions

TITLE	PUBLISHER	PRINTER	DATE	MEDIUM	DIMENSION (PAPER SIZE) IN INCHES	TYPE OF PAPER	EDITION NUMBER	NO. OF COLORS	ORIGINAL OPENING PRICE	CURRENT RETAIL PRICE
CURRENT EDITIONS:										
Concerto in Yellow	NE	JOB	1990	LC	21 X 30	AP	125		750	2000
Concerto in Yellow (Deluxe)	NE	JOB	1990	LC	21 X 30	JP	75		2500	2500
Japanese Birds	NE	JOB	1990	LC	24 X 45	AP	125		2000	2000
Renaissance	NE	DUT	1991	EB/A/CAR	34 X 28	AP	135		1750	2100
Magic Bird	NE	JOB	1992	CAR	29 X 42	HMP	75		4500	4500
Cubist Composition	NE	JOB	1992	CAR	31 X 25	HMP	75		3000	3000
Hommage a Picasso I	NE	JOB	1993	CAR	18 X 22	HMP	75		1400	1400
Hommage a Picasso II	NE	JOB	1993	CAR	18 X 22	HMP	75		1400	1400
Hommage a Braque I	NE	JOB	1993	CAR	18 X 22	HMP	75		1400	1400
Hommage a Braque II	NE	JOB	1993	CAR	18 X 22	HMP	75		1400	1400
Hommage a Juan Gris	NE	JOB	1993	CAR	18 X 22	HMP	75		1400	1400

OLIVIA PARKER

BORN: Boston, MA; June 10, 1941
EDUCATION: Wellesley Col, MA, BA, 1963
AWARDS: Artist's Found Fel, 1978; Cert of Excellence, Am Inst of Graphic Arts, Bk Show, 1979; Ferguson Grant, 1981
RECENT EXHIB: Univ of Minnesota, Tweed Mus of Art, Deluth, MN, 1989; Brent Sikkema Fine Art, NY, 1991
COLLECTIONS: Mus of Mod Art, NY; Mus of Fine Arts, Boston, MA; Metropolitan Mus of Art, NY; Art Inst of Chicago, IL; Victoria & Albert Mus, London, England; Int Nat Mus of Photography, Eastman House, Rochester, NY
PRINTERS: Artist (ART)
PUBLISHERS: Artist (ART)
GALLERIES: Marcuse Pfeifer Gallery, Ltd, New York, NY; Photography West Gallery, Carmel, CA; GH Dalsheimer Gallery, Baltimore, MD; Weston Gallery, Carmel, CA; Twining Gallery, New York, NY; Ginny Williams Gallery, Denver, CO; Sena International, Santa Fe, NM; Lieberman & Saul Gallery, New York, NY; Brent Sikkema Fine Arts, New York, NY
MAILING ADDRESS: Summer St, Manchester, MA 01944

TITLE	PUBLISHER	PRINTER	DATE	MEDIUM	DIMENSION (PAPER SIZE) IN INCHES	TYPE OF PAPER	EDITION NUMBER	NO. OF COLORS	ORIGINAL OPENING PRICE	CURRENT RETAIL PRICE
SOLD OUT EDITIONS (RARE):										
Lost Objects Portfolio	ART	ART	1977	PH			35		1500 SET	5000 SET
Ephemera Portfolio	ART	ART	1979	PH			25		2000 SET	5000 SET
Still Life with Peaches (Polaroid)	ART	ART	1981	PH	26 X 21		8		800	3000
CURRENT EDITIONS:										
From One to Another (Polaroid)	ART	ART	1987	PH	10 X 8		16		1000	1500
Sea Bowl (Framed)	ART	ART	1989	PH	16 X 20		6		1500	1500

MARIAN PARRY

BORN: San Francisco, CA; January 28, 1924
EDUCATION: Univ of California, Berkeley, CA, BA, 1946; Contemporaries Gallery, Etching & Lithography, with Michael Ponce de Leon, Stone Engraving, with Ben Shahn
TEACHING: Wellesley Col, MA; Massachusetts Col of Art, Boston, MA; Radcliffe Seminars Prog, Cambridge, MA, 1974 to present; Emmanuel Col, Boston, MA, 1974 to present
COLLECTIONS: Harvard Univ, Cambridge, MA; Smith Col, Northampton, MA; Wellesley Col, MA; Metropolitan Mus of Art, NY; Univ of Massachusetts, Northampton, MA
PRINTERS: Artist (ART)
PUBLISHERS: Runcible Press, Cambridge, MA (R)
GALLERIES: Van Buren/Brazelton/Cutting, Cambridge, MA; Galerie Caroline Corre, Paris, France
MAILING ADDRESS: 60 Martin St, Cambridge, MA 02138

MARIAN PARRY CONTINUED

TITLE	PUBLISHER	PRINTER	DATE	MEDIUM	DIMENSION (PAPER SIZE) IN INCHES	TYPE OF PAPER	EDITION NUMBER	NO. OF COLORS	ORIGINAL OPENING PRICE	CURRENT RETAIL PRICE
SOLD OUT EDITIONS (RARE):										
Harvard Square in 1970	R	ART	1970	W/ENG	3 X 4	RICE	200	1	10	125
Harvard Square in 1971	R	ART	1971	SP/PO	2 X 3	R/BFK	50	Multi	10	125
Harvard Square in 1972	R	ART	1972	SP/PO	2 X 3	R/BFK	50	Multi	12	125
CURRENT EDITIONS:										
Passions	R	ART	1979	HC/X/WA	6 X 5	R/BFK	60	Multi	100	125
8 Bostonians of the 1960's	R	ART	1979	HC/X/WA	3 X 4	AP	40	Multi	100	175
Characters From an English Novel	R	ART	1982	HC/X/WA	2 X 3	AP	30	Multi	100	125
Q for Quisby	R	ART	1982	LI/REL	11 X 18	RICE	90	2	120	150
W for Whigmaleery	R	ART	1982	LI/REL	11 X 18	RICE	90	3	120	150
D for Doversole	R	ART	1982	LI/REL	11 X 18	RICE	90	2	120	150

EDWARD F PASCHKE (ED)

BORN: Chicago, IL; June 22, 1939
EDUCATION: Art Inst of Chicago, BFA, 1961, MFA, 1970
TEACHING: Instr, Painting, Art Inst of Chicago, IL, 1974–76; Instr, Painting, Columbia Col, Chicago, IL, 1976–78; Prof, Drawing, Northwestern Univ, Evanston, IL, 1977 to present
AWARDS: Raymond Fel, Ponte del Arte Fel, Art Inst of Chicago, IL, 1961,70; Cassandra Grant, 1972; Logan Medal, Art Inst of Chicago, IL, 1973
RECENT EXHIB: The Renaissance Society, Chicago, IL, 1987; Retrosp, Art Inst of Chicago, IL, 1990; Print Retrosp, Dean Jensen Gallery, Milwaukee, WI, 1990; Phyllis Kind Galleries, Chicago, IL & NY, 1990; Dallas Mus, TX, 1990; Art Inst of Chicago, IL, 1991; Center for Visual Arts, IL, 1992; Col of DuPage, William E Gahlberg Arts Center Gallery, Glen Ellyn, IL, 1992
COLLECTIONS: Art Inst of Chicago, IL; Mus of the 20th Century, Vienna, Austria; Darthea Speyer Gallery, Paris, France; Mus of Contemp Art, Chicago, IL; Mus of Mod Art, Vienna, Austria; Mus Boymans, Rotterdam, Holland; Musee d'Art Moderne Nationale, Paris, France; Baltimore Art Mus, MD
PRINTERS: Landfall Press Inc, Chicago, IL (LPI); Jack Lemon, Chicago, IL (JL); Timothy Berry, Chicago, IL (TB); Jerry Raidiger, Chicago, IL (JR); T Morgan (TM); T Cvikota (TC)
PUBLISHERS: Abrams Original Editions, NY (AOE); Landfall Press Inc, Chicago, IL (LPI)
GALLERIES: Phyllis Kind Galleries, Chicago, IL & New York, NY; Landfall Press, Inc, Chicago, IL; Dean Jensen Gallery, Milwaukee, WI; Dorothy Goldeen Gallery, Santa Monica, CA; Remba Gallery/Mixografia Workshop, Santa Monica, CA; Quartet Editions, New York, NY
MAILING ADDRESS: 1629 N Killburn, Chicago, IL 60646

TITLE	PUBLISHER	PRINTER	DATE	MEDIUM	DIMENSION (PAPER SIZE) IN INCHES	TYPE OF PAPER	EDITION NUMBER	NO. OF COLORS	ORIGINAL OPENING PRICE	CURRENT RETAIL PRICE
SOLD OUT EDITIONS (RARE):										
Hairy Shoes	LPI	JR/LPI	1971	LC	18 X 24	R/BFK	30	3	350	1200
Hat	LPI	TB/LPI	1977	LC	16 X 14	TWP/AP	10	1	250	1000
Klaus	LPI	JL/TC/LPI	1977	LC	28 X 35	AC/W	35	5	250	1500
Klaus, State I	LPI	JL/TC/TM/LPI	1977	LC	28 X 35	AC/W	20	1	250	1200
Tudor	LPI	JL/TC/TM/LPI	1977	LC	29 X 23	AC/W	35	6	250	1500
Tudor, State I	LPI	JL/TC/TM/LPI	1977	LC	29 X 23	AC/W	20	1	250	1500
Hubert	AOE	JL/TC/LPI	1977	LC	28 X 35	AC/W	35	6	250	1500
Hubert, State I	LPI	JL/TC/TM/LPI	1977	LC	28 X 35	AC/W	20	1	250	1500
Bistro	LPI	JL/LPI	1981	LC	35 X 45	HMP	35	5	800	1500
Adatnok	LPI	JL/LPI	1984	LC	44 X 34	AP/W	15	6	1800	2400
Kontata	LPI	JL/LPI	1984	LC	36 X 24	AP/W	45	5	950	1500
Kontato	LPI	JL/LPI	1984	LC	36 X 24	AP/W	45	5	950	1500
Fem Rouge	LPI	JL/LPI	1987	LC	28 X 36	AP/W	50	5	1200	1500
Fem Verde	LPI	JL/LPI	1987	LC	28 X 36	AP/W	50	5	1200	1500
CURRENT EDITIONS:										
Pump	LPI	JL/LPI	1989	EB	30 X 22	SOM	50		1200	1500
Poderosa	LPI	JL/LPI	1990	LB	30 X 40	AC	60		1500	1800
Compassion	LPI	JL/LPI	1992	LB	18 X 20	AC	25	1	850	850

VICTOR PASMORE

BORN: Chelsham, England; December 3, 1908
EDUCATION: Central Sch of Arts & Crafts, London, England, 1927–31; Durham Univ, England, MA, 1954–61
TEACHING: Dir, Painting, Durham Univ, NC, 1954–61
AWARDS: International Painting Prize, Carnegie Inst, Pittsburgh, PA, 1964; Grand Prix d'Honneur, Llubljana, Czechoslovakia, 1977; Wollston Prize, Royal Academy, 1983
RECENT EXHIB: Yale Univ, Center for British Art, New Haven, CT, 1989,92; Center for Int Contemp Arts, NY, 1992
COLLECTIONS: Tate Gallery, London, England; Victoria and Albert Mus, London, England; Arts Council of Great Britain, London, England; British Council, London, England; Ulster Mus, Belfast, Ireland; Nat Mus of Wales, Cardiff, Wales; Scottish Nat Gallery of Mod Art, Edinburgh; Mus of Mod Art, NY; Mus d'Art Mod, Rome, Italy; Boymans Mus, Rotterdam, The Netherlands; Rijkmuseum Kroll-Muller, Otterlo, The Netherlands; Melbourne Mus, Adelaide, Australia
PRINTERS: 2 RC Editrice, Rome, Italy (2RCE)
PUBLISHERS: Marlborough Graphics, NY (MG); 2 RC Editrice, Rome, Italy (2RCE)
GALLERIES: Hirschl & Adler Modern, New York, NY; Lucy Berman Gallery, Palo Alto, CA; Marlborough Galleries, London, England & New York, NY; Robert Jackson Fine Art, Beaverton, OR; Ehrenkranz Fine Arts, Chevy Chase, MD
MAILING ADDRESS: Dar Gamri, Gudja, Malta; c/o Marlborough Fine Art, 6 Albemarle St, London, England WI, England

---

The retail prices of the 100,000 limited edition prints quoted in this directory are subject to change. Print publishers, artists and galleries were the direct sources for these quotations. Prices in the secondary market listed as "Sold Out Editions (Rare)" indicate that the publisher has a limited supply of that print or that the print is difficult to locate in the galleries.

VICTOR PASMORE CONTINUED

TITLE	PUBLISHER	PRINTER	DATE	MEDIUM	DIMENSION (PAPER SIZE) IN INCHES	TYPE OF PAPER	EDITION NUMBER	NO. OF COLORS	ORIGINAL OPENING PRICE	CURRENT RETAIL PRICE
SOLD OUT EDITIONS (RARE):										
Points of Contact #5	MG		1965	SP	84 X 20	AP	70		450	700
Points of Contact #6	MG		1965	LC	73 X 30	AP	70		475	700
Points of Contact #7	MG		1965	LC	18 X 18	AP	70		450	700
Points of Contact #8	MG		1966	SP	23 X 66	AP	70		450	700
Points of Contact #9	MG		1966	SP	60 X 50	AP	70		700	1200
Points of Contact #11	MG		1967	SP	24 X 54	AP	70		550	1200
Points of Contact #13	MG		1969	SP	22 X 52	AP	70		600	1200
Points of Contact #15	MG		1969	SP	55 X 22	AP	50		700	1200
Linear Development 2	MG		1970	SP	19 X 19	AP	60		500	1200
Transformation I, II, III, IV, V	MG		1970	SP	19 X 19 EA	AP	60 EA		350 EA	800 EA
Transformation VI	MG		1970	SP	19 X 19	AP	60		350	800
Points of Contact, Variation 4	MG		1971	SP	36 X 24	AP	60		450	500
By What Means (From Correspondences)	MG		1974	EC	28 X 24	AP	60		500	800
Linear Development in One Movement	MG		1974	EB/A	28 X 24	AP	60		500	1300
Linear Motif in Two Movements	MG		1974	EB/SP	28 X 24	AP	60		500	1300
Look into the Pool Narcissus Found!	MG		1974	SP	20 X 123	AP	30		2000	3000
Points of Contact #21	MG		1974	SP	34 X 24	AP	70		300	700
Turning and Turning	MG		1974	EC	24 X 28	AP	60		400	800
When the Curtain Falls	MG		1974	EC	28 X 24	AP	60		500	800
When the Lute is Broken	MG		1974	EC	28 X 24	AP	60		400	800
Hear the Sound of a Magic Tune	MG		1974	SP	96 X 26	AP	25		2000	3000
Two Images (Blue)	MG		1974	SP	25 X 25	AP	70		350	2000
Untitled	MG		1974–75	EB/A/SP	24 X 28	AP	55		350	1000
Earth and Sky	2RCE	2RCE	1975	EB/A	22 X 102	AP	80		1500	3500
Autunno	MG		1978	AC	28 X 39	AP	90		1000	1800
Un Bel di Vedremo (Puccini)	MG		1978	AC	118 X 25	AP	90		2000	3000
The Blue Between	MG		1978	AC	101 X 22	AP	90		1750	4000
Blue Mandala	MG		1978	AC	28 X 39	AP	90		1100	2800
Brown Imbage II	MG		1978	AC	63 X 44	AP	90		1400	2800
Cave of Calypso I, II	MG		1978	AC	44 X 63 EA	AP	90 EA		1400 EA	2700 EA
La Guerra	MG		1978	AC	44 X 87	AP	90		1700	3800
Owl of Minerva	MG		1978	AC	39 X 39	AP	90		1350	2500
Points of Contact #28	MG		1979	SP	28 X 21	AP	70		500	1200
Points of Contact #29	MG		1979	SP	28 X 21	AP	70		500	1200
Points of Contact #30	MG		1979	SP	28 X 21	AP	70		500	1200
Points of Contact #31	MG		1980	SP	28 X 21	AP	70		500	1200
Points of Contact #32	MG		1980	SP	28 X 21	AP	70		500	1200
Points of Contact #33	MG		1980	SP	34 X 26	AP	100		400	1200
Points of Contact #34	MG		1980	SP	28 X 21	AP	100		400	1200
Stromboli	MG		1980	AC	35 X 66	AP	90		1200	3000
Vigna Antoniniana	MG		1980	AC	48 X 73	AP	90		1800	3800
La Villa dei Misteri	MG		1980	AC	102 X 33	AP	90		2300	5000
Points of Contact #35	MG		1981	SP	34 X 21	AP	100		400	2000
Points of Contact #37	MG		1982	SP	35 X 19	AP	70		400	1400
Punto di Contatto I	MG		1982	AC	20 X 28	AP	90		750	1950
Punto di Contatto II	MG		1982	AC	30 X 43	AP	90		1050	2750
Punto di Contatto III	MG		1982	AC	13 X 10	AP	80		600	1100
Punto di Contatto IV	MG		1982	AC	29 X 99	AP	90		2100	4500
Punto di Contatto	MG		1982	AC	20 X 28	AP	85		750	3600
Il Risveglio della Pische	MG		1982	AC	37 X 27	AP	90		950	2500
Senza Titolo (Large Red)	MG		1982	AC	47 X 47	AP	90		1400	2200
Senza Titolo (Small Brown)	MG		1982	AC	14 X 37	AP	90		450	1600
The Space Within	MG		1982	AC	47 X 99	AP	90		2300	3600
Uomo e Donna	MG		1982	AC	30 X 79	AP	90		1150	2500
Burning Water	MG		1982	AC	51 X 99	AP	90		1700	5000
CURRENT EDITIONS:										
Points of Contact #38	MG		1984	SP	26 X 25	AP	70		300	600
Apollo I, II	MG		1985	SP	26 X 35 EA	AP	70 EA		800 EA	2200 EA
Blue Fantasy II	MG		1986	SP	35 X 30	AP	70		800	2400
Blue Image	MG		1986	EB/A	27 X 34	SOM	90		800	2700
Green Darkness	MG		1986	SP	26 X 37	AP	90		800	1200
Milky Way	MG		1986	SP	30 X 37	AP	70		800	2000
Untitled #1	MG		1987	SP	45 X 32	AP	70		1000	1400
Untitled #2	MG		1988	SP	33 X 24	AP	70		800	1000
Burning Waters/Visual & Poetic Images (Bound Book)	MG		1988	LC	12 X 10 EA	AP	195		100	100
Burning Waters/Visual & Poetic Images (Deluxe Edition Book)	MG		1988	LC	12 X 10 EA	AP	50		200	250
Senza Titolo #2	MG		1988	AC	38 X 39	AP	90		2250	2500
Senza Titolo #3	MG		1988	AC	38 X 39	AP	90		2000	2300
Senza Titolo #4	MG		1989	AC	27 X 55	AP	90		2300	2300
Senza Titolo #5	MG		1989	AC	28 X 54	AP	90		2300	2300

VICTOR PASMORE CONTINUED

TITLE	PUBLISHER	PRINTER	DATE	MEDIUM	DIMENSION (PAPER SIZE) IN INCHES	TYPE OF PAPER	EDITION NUMBER	NO. OF COLORS	ORIGINAL OPENING PRICE	CURRENT RETAIL PRICE
CURRENT EDITIONS:										
Senza Titolo #6	MG		1989	AC	191 X 98	AP	90		4100	4100
Senza Titolo #7	MG		1989	AC	24 X 99	AP	90		3400	3400
Senza Titolo #8	MG		1989	AC	17 X 48	AP	90		3600	3600
Senza Titolo #9	MG		1989	AC	85 X 49	AP	90		4700	4700
Senza Titolo #10	MG		1989	AC	36 X 10	AP	90		4700	4700
Senza Titolo #11	MG		1989	AC	15 X 22	AP	90		950	950

MAYEU PASSA

BORN: Provence, France; (1921–1991)
EDUCATION: Self-Taught
COLLECTIONS: Cultural Center Le Trouvet, Paris, France
PRINTERS: Atelier Joban, Paris, France (JOB)
GALLERIES: Nahan Galleries, New York, NY & New Orleans, LA & New York, NY

TITLE	PUBLISHER	PRINTER	DATE	MEDIUM	DIMENSION (PAPER SIZE) IN INCHES	TYPE OF PAPER	EDITION NUMBER	NO. OF COLORS	ORIGINAL OPENING PRICE	CURRENT RETAIL PRICE
CURRENT EDITIONS:										
Rue du Marche	NE	JOB	1989	LC	30 X 21	AP	175	10	500	500
Camouflage	NE	JOB	1989	LC	30 X 21	AP	175	8	500	500
Le 38	NE	JOB	1990	LC	30 X 22	AP	175	8	500	500
Clameur	NE	JOB	1990	LC	30 X 21	AP	175		500	500
Silent Drama	NE	JOB	1990	LC	30 X 21	AP	175		500	500
Les Mauresques	NE	JOB	1990	LC	20 X 35	AP	175	17	500	500
Abidos	NE	JOB	1990	LC	23 X 35	AP	175	17	750	750
Les Jongleurs	NE	JOB	1991	LC	23 X 35	AP	175	17	750	750

PETER ZACCARIA PASSUNTINO

BORN: Chicago, IL; February 18, 1936
EDUCATION: Sch of the Art Inst of Chicago, IL, 1954–58; Inst Des Artet Archeologie, Paris, France, 1963; S W Hayter Atelier, Paris, France, 1964
TEACHING: Livingston Col, East Brunswick, NJ; Great Neck Community Art Center, NY
AWARDS: Artist Guild of Chicago, IL, 1954; Fulbright Fel Painting, 1963–64; Guggenheim Fel Grant Graphics, 1971; Nat Endowment for the Arts Grant, 1984
COLLECTIONS: Hirshhorn Mus, Wash, DC; Henry Geld Zahler, NY; Walter P. Chrysler Mus, Norfolk, VA; Norfolk Mus of Art, VA
PRINTERS: Printmaking Workshop, NY (PW); Susan Kleinman, NY (SK)
PUBLISHERS: Seguy Gallery, New York, NY (SG)
GALLERIES: A Clean Well-Lighted Place Gallery, New York, NY; Nina Dausset Gallery, Paris, France; Gallery K, Wash, DC; The White Room Gallery, Winterslag-Genk, Belgium
MAILING ADDRESS: 530 La Guardia Place, New York, NY 10012

TITLE	PUBLISHER	PRINTER	DATE	MEDIUM	DIMENSION (PAPER SIZE) IN INCHES	TYPE OF PAPER	EDITION NUMBER	NO. OF COLORS	ORIGINAL OPENING PRICE	CURRENT RETAIL PRICE
SOLD OUT EDITIONS (RARE):										
Travelers	ART	PW	1976	A/COL	18 X 24	AP	35	5	100	350
Tower of Babel Head	ART	PW	1976	AB	24 X 18	AP	35	3	100	350
Lost Coke Bottle	ART	PW	1976	AB	24 X 18	AP	35	3	100	350
Trapeze over NYC	ART	PW	1976	AB	24 X 18	AP	35	4	100	350
Woman on a Balcony	ART	PW	1976	LC	22 X 31	AP	35	6	100	350
CURRENT EDITIONS:										
Baseball Players	ART	PW	1980	LC	19 X 25	R/BFK	35	4	100	400
Trapeze	SG	SK	1981	AB	9 X 9	R/BFK	100	1	100	150
Card House	ART	SK	1982	AB	9 X 12	AP	100	1	100	150
Hobby Horse	SG	SK	1982	AC	12 X 16	R/BFK	100	4	250	350
Explorers	SG	SK	1982	AB	12 X 15	R/BFK	150	5	150	200
Straw Hat	ART	SK	1982	AB	18 X 24	AP	100	1	200	250
Top Hat	ART	SK	1982	AB	18 X 24	AP	100	1	200	250
Large Carrousel	ART	SK	1982	AB	28 X 36	AP	100	1	250	300
Preformer #1, #2	ART	SK	1982	AB	12 X 9 EA	AP	100 EA	1 EA	100 EA	150 EA

JÜRGEN PETERS

PRINTERS: American Atelier, NY (AA)
PUBLISHERS: Circle Fine Art, Chicago, IL (CFA)
GALLERIES: Circle Galleries, San Diego, CA & San Francicsco, CA & Northbrook, IL & Pittsburgh, PA & Houston, TX & Soho, NY & Chicago, IL & Scottsdale, AZ & Beverly Hills, CA & Costa Mesa, CA & Sherman Oaks, CA & Palm Beach, FL & Honolulu, HI & New Orleans, LA & Las Vegas, NV & Seattle, WA

TITLE	PUBLISHER	PRINTER	DATE	MEDIUM	DIMENSION (PAPER SIZE) IN INCHES	TYPE OF PAPER	EDITION NUMBER	NO. OF COLORS	ORIGINAL OPENING PRICE	CURRENT RETAIL PRICE
CURRENT EDITIONS:										
Rainbow Waves	CFA	AA	1981	SP	23 X 38	AP	250		200	350

LORNA PATRICK

PUBLISHERS: Martin Lawrence Limited Editions, Van Nuys, CA (MLLE)
GALLERIES: Martin Lawrence Galleries, Escondido, CA & Newport Beach, CA & Palm Springs, CA & Redondo Beach, CA & Santa Clara, CA & Sherman Oaks, CA & Thousand Oaks, CA & Soho, NY

Lorna Patrick
Portal with a View
Courtesy Martin Lawrence Limited Editions

Lorna Patrick
Geraniums
Courtesy Martin Lawrence Limited Editions

TITLE	PUBLISHER	PRINTER	DATE	MEDIUM	DIMENSION (PAPER SIZE) IN INCHES	TYPE OF PAPER	EDITION NUMBER	NO. OF COLORS	ORIGINAL OPENING PRICE	CURRENT RETAIL PRICE
CURRENT EDITIONS:										
Cactus/Desert View Suite:									1000 SET	1650 SET
Cactus	MLLE		1988	SP	35 X 44	AP	595		650	1100
Desert View	MLLE		1988	SP	33 X 43	AP	595		650	1100
Kiva Wall	MLLE		1989	SP	42 X 31	AP	595		750	1100
Diamonds	MLLE		1989	SP	32 X 42	AP	595		750	1200
Gray Gate	MLLE		1989	SP	35 X 42	AP	595		750	1100
Courtyard Garden	MLLE		1990	SP	31 X 42	AP	595		750	1100
Approaching Strom over Taos Pueblo	MLLE		1990	SP	32 X 42	AP	595		750	1000
Taos Shops	MLLE		1990	SP	43 X 33	AP	595		750	900
Geraniums	MLLE		1990	SP	31 X 42	AP	595		750	900
Portal with a View	MLLE		1991	SP	31 X 42	AP	595		800	800
When the Sun is Low	MLLE		1991	SP	31 X 44	AP	595		650	800
Morning Light	MLLE		1992	SP	31 X 42	AP	226		650	650

CLAYTON PATTERSON

BORN: Calgary, Alta, Canada; October 9, 1948
EDUCATION: Univ of Alberta, Canada, BEd, 1973; Nova Scotia Col of Art, Canada, BFA, 1977
TEACHING: Instr, Art, Alberta Col of Art, Canada, 1978
AWARDS: Charles Brand Presses Award, Philadelphia Print Club, PA, 1984
COLLECTIONS: Brooklyn Mus, NY; New York Public Library, NY; Rutgers Mus, New Brunswick, NY; Flint Mus, MI
PRINTERS: Joe Petruzzelli, NY (JP); Sienna Studio, NY (SiS); Chip Elwell, NY (CE); Artist (ART)
PUBLISHERS: Diane Villani Editions, NY (DVE); Artist (ART)
GALLERIES: Pelavin Gallery, New York, NY; John Nichols Gallery, New York, NY; Diane Villani Editions, New York, NY; Arborite Art, New York, NY
MAILING ADDRESS: PO Box 103, Prince St, New York, NY 10012-0103

TITLE	PUBLISHER	PRINTER	DATE	MEDIUM	DIMENSION (PAPER SIZE) IN INCHES	TYPE OF PAPER	EDITION NUMBER	NO. OF COLORS	ORIGINAL OPENING PRICE	CURRENT RETAIL PRICE
CURRENT EDITIONS:										
Tooth Box	ART	ART	1979	LB	29 X 41	R/RBF	25	1	150	500
Only Taste Will Tell	ART	ART	1979	LB	29 X 41	R/BFK	25	1	150	500
Blah, Blah, Blah	ART	JP/SiS	1983/84	LI	29 X 41	R/BFK	35	1	350	500
Paradise Lost	ART	JP/SiS	1983/84	LI	29 X 41	R/BFK	35	1	350	500
Joe's Box	ART	JP/SiS	1983/84	LI	29 X 41	R/BFK	35	1	350	500
Suicide	ART	JP/SiS	1983/84	LI	29 X 41	R/BFK	35	1	350	500
Reaching Higher	ART	JP/SiS	1983/84	LI	29 X 41	R/BFK	35	1	350	500
Heart	ART	ART	1983/84	LI	29 X 41	R/BFK	35	1	350	500
Black Beauty	DVE	CE	1985	WC/HC	46 X 37	SUZ	15	Varies	700	750

WILLIAM JOSEPH PATTERSON

BORN: Albany, NY; March 16, 1941
EDUCATION: Hartford Art Sch, CT, BFA, 1965; Abbey Found Fel, Am Acad in Rome, Italy, 1965-67; Syracuse Univ, NY, MFA, 1969
TEACHING: Instr, Printmaking, Hartford Art Sch, CT, 1969-71; Assoc Prof, Printmaking & Drawing, Univ of Massachusetts, Amherst, MA, 1971 to present
AWARDS: Abbey Found Fel, Am Acad in Rome, Italy, 1966-67; Canon Prize, Nat Acad of Design, NY; Massachusetts Council of Arts Fel, 1975; Purdue Univ, Award, IN, 1980; New Britain Mus, CT, 1981

WILLIAM JOSEPH PATTERSON CONTINUED

COLLECTIONS: New Britain Mus, CT; Springfield Mus, MA; Honolulu Acad of Arts, HI; DeCordova Mus, Lincoln, MA; Arizona State Univ, Tempe, AZ; Purdue Univ, Lafayette, IN; Northern Illinois Univ, De Kalb, IL; Honolulu Acad of Art, HI; New York State Univ, Pottsdam, NY; Library of Congress, Wash, DC

PRINTERS: Artist (ART)
PUBLISHERS: Associated American Artists, NY (AAA)
GALLERIES: Associated American Artists, New York, NY; Thronja Gallery, Springfield, MA; Rolly Michelson Galleries, Amherst, MA
MAILING ADDRESS: 24 Applewood Lane, Amherst, MA 01002

TITLE	PUBLISHER	PRINTER	DATE	MEDIUM	DIMENSION (PAPER SIZE) IN INCHES	TYPE OF PAPER	EDITION NUMBER	NO. OF COLORS	ORIGINAL OPENING PRICE	CURRENT RETAIL PRICE
CURRENT EDITIONS:										
Daumier	AAA	ART	1972	AC	9 X 7	R/100	250		50	150
After Rembrandt	AAA	ART	1973	EB/AC	14 X 12	R/100	75		100	300
Sunday Morning	AAA	ART	1981	I	12 X 23	R/100	100	1	50	200
Twelve Apostles (Set of 13)	AAA	ART	1981	I	9 X 11	R/100	200	1	175	400
Alix (State I)	AAA	ART	1981	I	32 X 48	R/100	25	1	150	350

ABBOTT PATTISON

BORN: Chicago, IL; May 15, 1916
EDUCATION: Yale Col, New Haven, CT, BA, 1937; Yale Sch of Fine Arts, BFA, 1939
TEACHING: Instr, Sch of Art Inst, Chicago, IL, 1946,52; Art in Res, Univ of Georgia, Athens, GA, 1954; Instr, Sculpture, Skowhegan Art Sch, ME, 1955,56
AWARDS: Travelling Fel, Yale Univ, New Haven, CT, 1939; Logan Medal, Chicago, IL, 1942; Eisendrath Prize, Chicago, IL, 1946; Metropolitan Mus of Art, NY, Cash Award, 1951; Pauline Palmer Prize, Chicago, IL, 1950,53; Purchase Prize, Bundy Mus, VT, 1967; Clussman Prize, Chicago, IL, 1968
COLLECTIONS: Portland Mus, ME; Portland Art Mus, OR; Corcoran Mus, Wash, DC; Palm Springs Desert Mus, CA; Yorkshire Sculpture Park, England; Israeli State Mus, Jerusalem, Israel; Chrysler Mus, Norfolk, VA; Whitney Mus of Am Art, NY; Art Inst of Chicago, IL; San Francisco Mus of Mod Art, CA; Addison Gallery of Am Art, Andover, MA; California Palace of Legion of Honor, CA; St Louis Mus, MO; St Paul Art Center, MN; Wichita Mus, KS; Flint Inst of Arts, MI; Univ of Chicago, IL; Notre Dame, South Bend, IN; Bates Col, Lewiston, ME; Colby Col, Waterville, ME; Univ of Maine, Orono, ME; Syracuse Univ, NY: Holyoke Col, MA; Univ of Minnesota, Minneapolis, MN; Univ of Georgia, Athens, GA; Brandeis Univ, Waltham, MA; Stanford Univ, CA; St John's Univ, Jamaica, NY; Buckingham Palace, London, England
PRINTERS: Will Petersen, Evanston, IL (WP); Plucked Chicken Press, Evanston, IL (PCP); Artist (ART)
PUBLISHERS: Plucked Chicken Press, Evanston, IL (PCP)
GALLERIES: Fairweather Hardin Gallery, Chicago, IL
MAILING ADDRESS: RR #2, Box 12, Lincolnville, ME 04849-9601

TITLE	PUBLISHER	PRINTER	DATE	MEDIUM	DIMENSION (PAPER SIZE) IN INCHES	TYPE OF PAPER	EDITION NUMBER	NO. OF COLORS	ORIGINAL OPENING PRICE	CURRENT RETAIL PRICE
CURRENT EDITIONS:										
Bayscape, Winter	PCP	ART/WP/PCP	1985	LC	22 X 28	R/BFK			425	600

ELIZABETH JAYNE PEAK

BORN: Ft Belvoir, VA; May 19, 1952
EDUCATION: Univ of California, Santa Barbara, CA, BA, 1974; Brandeis Univ, Waltham, MA, with Michael Mazur, 1975; Yale Univ, New Haven, CT, with Gabor Peterdi, MFA, 1977
TEACHING: Asst Prof, Drawing, Kent State Univ, OH, 1979–80; Asst Prof, Bowdoin Col, Brunswick, ME, 1980–82; Col of Holy Cross, Worcester, MA, 1983 to present
AWARDS: Helen Wintnermitz Award, Yale Univ, New Haven, CT, 1977
RECENT EXHIB: Franz Bader Gallery, Wash, DC, 1989
COLLECTIONS: Yale Univ Mus, New Haven, CT; Kent State Univ, OH; Brigham Young Univ, Logan, UT; Smithsonian Inst, Wash, DC; Library of Congress, Wash, DC; Bowdoin Col, Brunswick, ME
PRINTERS: Artist (ART)
PUBLISHERS: Orion Editions, NY (OE)
GALLERIES: Franz Bader Gallery, Wash, DC; Jane Haslem Salon, Wash, DC
MAILING ADDRESS: c/o Dept of Visual Arts, College of Holy Cross, Worcester, MA 01610

TITLE	PUBLISHER	PRINTER	DATE	MEDIUM	DIMENSION (PAPER SIZE) IN INCHES	TYPE OF PAPER	EDITION NUMBER	NO. OF COLORS	ORIGINAL OPENING PRICE	CURRENT RETAIL PRICE
CURRENT EDITIONS:										
View of a City	OE	ART	1987	EB	30 X 46	AC	65	1	450	550
Night Garden	OE	ART	1987	EB	30 X 46	AC	65	1	350	375

PHILIP PEARLSTEIN

BORN: Pittsburgh, PA; May 24, 1924
EDUCATION: Carnegie Inst of Tech, Pittsburgh, PA, BFA, 1949; Inst of Fine Arts, New York Univ, NY, MA, 1955
TEACHING: Instr, Pratt Inst, Brooklyn, NY, 1959–63; Asst Prof, Art, Yale Univ, New Haven, CT, 1962–63; Prof, Art, Brooklyn Col, NY, 1963–87
AWARDS: Fulbright Fel, Italy 1958; Nat Endowment for the Arts Grant, 1969; Guggenheim Fel, 1971,72; Am Acad of Arts and Letters Prize, 1973; Am Acad in Rome Fel, Italy, 1982
RECENT EXHIB: Colby Col Mus, Waterville, ME, 1987; Univ of Northern Iowa Mus, Cedar Falls, IA, 1987; Williams Col Mus, Williamstown, MA, 1987; Southern Ohio Mus, Portsmouth, OH, 1987; Provincetown Art Mus, MA, 1987; Brooklyn Mus, NY, 1989; James Madison Univ, Sawhill Gallery, Harrisonburg, VA, 1989,92; Univ of South Florida, Tampa, FL, 1992; New Jersey State Mus, Trenton, NJ, 1992
COLLECTIONS: Mus of Mod Art, NY; Whitney Mus of Am Art, NY; Philadelphia Mus of Art, PA; Hirshhorn Mus, Wash, DC; Art Inst of Chicago, IL; Corcoran Gallery, Wash, DC; Allentown Art Mus, PA; Colorado Springs Fine Art Center; Des Moines Art Center, IA; Milwaukee Art Center, WI; New York Univ; Pennsylvania State Univ, University Park, PA; Indiana Univ; Reed Col, Portland, OR; Syracuse Univ, NY; Univ of Nebraska, Omaha, NE; Vassar Col, Poughkeepsie, NY; Univ of North Carolina, Greensboro, NC; Colgate Univ, NY
PRINTERS: Tamarind Inst, Albuquerque, NM (TI); Jack Lemon (JL); Landfall Press, Inc, Chicago, IL (LPI); Virginia Piersol (VP); Univ of Omaha, NE (UO); Fort Steilacoom Com Col (FSCC); Orlando Condeso, NY (OC); Nancy Brokopp, NY (B); Fred Gude, Chicago, IL (FG); Thomas Minkler, Chicago, IL (TM); Ron Wyffels, Chicago, IL (RW); Tamarind Inst, Albuquerque, NM (TI); Nancy Condeso, NY (NC)

PHILIP PEARLSTEIN CONTINUED

PUBLISHERS: Allan Frumkin Gallery, NY (AFG); Brooke Alexander, Inc, NY (BAI); 724 Prints, NY (724P); Landfall Press, Inc, Chicago, IL (LPI); Pyramid Arts, Ltd, Tampa, FL (PAL); American Friends of Israel, NY (AFI); Multi-Editions Press, Great Neck, NY (MEP); V & R Fine Arts, Temple Terrace, FL (VR); Tamarind Inst, Albuquerque, NM (TI); Graphicstudio, Tampa, FL (GS); Univ of South Florida, Tampa, FL; Artist (ART)

GALLERIES: Brooke Alexander, Inc, New York, NY; Associated American Artists, New York, NY; Graphics Gallery, San Francisco, CA; David Adamson Gallery, Wash, DC; Brody's Gallery, Wash, DC; Joan Hodgell Gallery, Sarasota, FL; Fay Gold Gallery, Atlanta, GA; Landfall Press, Inc, Chicago, IL; Harcus Gallery, Boston, MA; Donald Morris Gallery, Birmingham, MI; Signet Arts, St Louis, MO; Nancy Singer Gallery, St Louis, MO; Malcolm Brown Gallery, Shaker Heights, OH; Hirschl & Adler Modern, New York, NY; Sidney Rothman, The Gallery, Barnegat Light, NJ; Printworks, Chicago, IL; Tamarind Inst, Albuquerque, NM; Randall Beck Gallery, Boston, MA; Michael H Lord Gallery, Milwaukee, WI; Marianne Friedland Gallery, Naples, FL; CompassRose Gallery, Ltd, Chicago, IL; Bridgewater/Lustberg Gallery, New York, NY; Sorrentino/Mayer Fine Art, Great Neck, NY & New York, NY; Stiebel Modern, New York, NY

MAILING ADDRESS: 163 W 88th St, New York, NY 10024

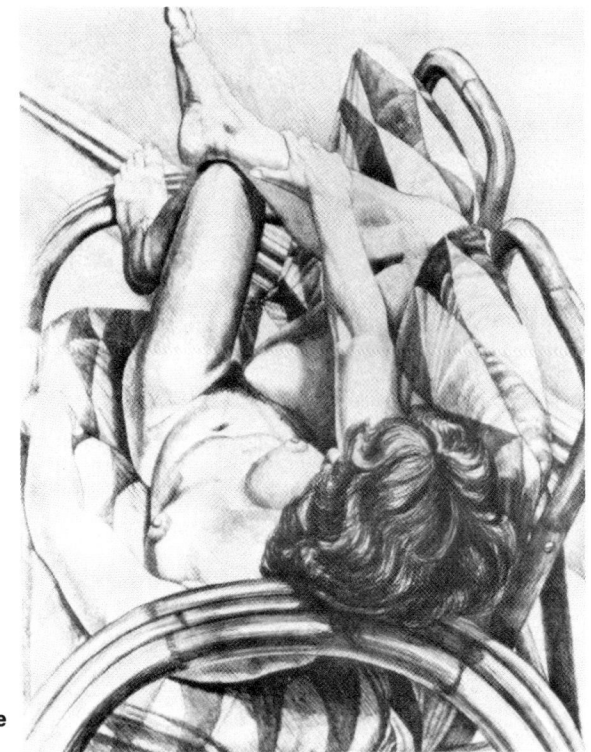

Philip Pearlstein
Nude on Summer Furniture
Courtesy the Artist

TITLE	PUBLISHER	PRINTER	DATE	MEDIUM	DIMENSION (PAPER SIZE) IN INCHES	TYPE OF PAPER	EDITION NUMBER	NO. OF COLORS	ORIGINAL OPENING PRICE	CURRENT RETAIL PRICE
SOLD OUT EDITIONS (RARE):										
Nude on Couch	BAI		1969	IG	22 X 30		100		225	3000
Six Lithographs Drawn from Life (Set of 6):										
Male and Female Figure	LPI	JR/LPI	1970	LB	22 X 30	AP/W	50	1	225	1000
Figure Lying on Rug	LPI	JR/LPI	1970	LC	22 X 30	AP/W	50	4	250	3000
Two Female Figures	LPI	JR/LPI	1970	LB	22 X 30	AP/W	50	1	200	1000
Figure Seated on Rug with Mirror	LPI	JR/LPI	1970	LB	22 X 30	AP/W	50	4	250	1000
Figure on Couch	LPI	JR/LPI	1970	LB	22 X 30	AP/W	50	1	200	1000
Figure on Folding Chair	LPI	JR/LPI	1970	LB	22 X 30	AP/W	50	1	200	1000
Reclining Nude on Green Couch	LPI	JL/LPI	1971	LC	27 X 22	AP/CR	72	4	250	2000
Nude on Silver Bench	ART	VP	1971	LC	30 X 36	AP	75	5	400	3000
Girl on Blue Coverlet	LPI	DK/LPI	1971	LC	22 X 27	AP/CR	50	2	400	1500
Girl on Stool	LPI	JL/LPI	1971	LB	18 X 24	AP/CR	150	1	200	1500
Male and Female on Spanish Rug	LPI	JL/LPI	1971	LC	22 X 30	AP	50	3	400	1500
Nude on Couch	LPI	JL/LPI	1971	LC	22 X 29	AP	50	3	400	1800
Girl on Striped Rug	LPI	JL/LPI	1972	LB	21 X 24	AP/CR	70	1	250	1500
Girl on Iron Bench	LPI	JR/LPI	1972	LB	24 X 32	AP/W	10	1	400	2000
Girl on Empire Sofa	LPI	JL/LPI	1972	LB	32 X 24	AP/W	75	1	250	1000
Nude on Navajo Rug	LPI	JR/LPI	1972	LC	25 X 34	AP/W	75	4	300	1200
Ellen in Tutu	LPI	JR/LPI	1972	LC	25 X 33	AP/W	75	2	300	800
Girl in Striped Robe	LPI	DK/LPI	1972	LC	27 X 22	AP/CR	50	4	400	1500
Girl on Orange and Black Mexican Rug	LPI	DK/LPI	1973	LC	25 X 34	AP/CR	100	5	450	4000
Model on Grey Patterned Rug	LPI	DK/LPI	1973	LB	23 X 33	AP/CR	90	1	400	1200
Nude Lying on Black and Red Blanket	LPI	JL/LPI	1974	EC	26 X 33	TWP	50		450	3000
Girl on Iron Bench	LPI	DK/TM/LPI	1974	LC	25 X 34	TWP	75	4	300	2500
Nude on Striped Hammock	LPI	JL/LPI	1974	EB/A	30 X 32	AP/CR			600	1500
Two Nudes with Hammock	LPI	DK/RW/LPI	1974	LC	25 X 36	AP/CR	100	5	700	2000
Nude Standing by Easel	LPI	DK/JL/LPI	1974	LC	30 X 22	AP/CR	50	4	700	1500
Two Female Nudes on Rocker and Stool	PAL		1975	LC	36 X 74	AP/W	20	5	1800	3500
Nude on Iron Bench	LPI	TB/LPI	1975	SGE/A	22 X 28	TWP	50	1	500	1200
Nude on Dahomey Stool	BAI		1976	EB	31 X 26	TWP	70	1	400	2000
Two Models in Studio	AFG		1976	EB/A	22 X 29	R/BFK	70		1200	2500
Female Nude with Legs Up	PAL		1976	LB	72 X 36	AP/W	10	1	800	3000
Two Nudes with Oak Stool and Canvas	LPI	JL/LPI	1976	LB	29 X 37	AP/W	100	1	500	2000
View over Soho-Lower Manhattan	BAI/ART		1977	AC	30 X 40	TWP	41	2	1800	6000
Two Nudes on Blue Coverlet	LPI	JL/LPI	1977	LC	28 X 39	HMP	65	5	900	3500
Nude with Rocker	LPI	JL/LPI	1977	LC	23 X 34	TWP	100	3	450	1200
Nude on Eames Stool	PMA	JL/FG	1977	LC	28 X 20	HMP	125	4	650	1200
Nude on Oak Chair	724P	OC/B	1978	EC	15 X 18	TW/HMP	50	2	375	1000
Legs	724P/SAM	JL/LPI	1978	LB	14 X 17	HMP	100	1	175	800

PHILIP PEARLSTEIN CONTINUED

TITLE	PUBLISHER	PRINTER	DATE	MEDIUM	DIMENSION (PAPER SIZE) IN INCHES	TYPE OF PAPER	EDITION NUMBER	NO. OF COLORS	ORIGINAL OPENING PRICE	CURRENT RETAIL PRICE
SOLD OUT EDITIONS (RARE):										
Nude on Chief's Blanket	724P	TI	1978	LC	28 X 40	R/BFK	50	6	850	4500
Nude on Director's Chair	724P	FSCC	1978	LB	20 X 17	R/BFK	30	1	270	1000
Ruins at Granquivira	724P	TI	1978	LC	19 X 30	R/BFK	27	2	420	1000
Nude with Iron Bench and Mirror	LPI	JL/LPI	1978	LC	30 X 23	AP/W	50	7	700	2000
Nude on Hammock	LPI	FG/LPI	1978	LC	30 X 23	AP/W	50	7	700	1500
Nude on Settee	724P	OC/B	1978	EB/AC	40 X 30	R/BFK	55	33	1200	2500
Machu Picchu	BAI		1978-79	AC	29 X 40	AP	41		1800	3500
Sphinx	BAI		1979	AC	29 X 40	AP	41		2000	4000
Canyon de Chelly	LPI	FG	1979	LC	28 X 23	AP/CR	100	3	350	900
Ruins and Landscapes (Set of 5):									12000 SET	20000 SET
Temple of Abusimbel	MEP/VR/724P	OC	1979	AC	30 X 40	R/BFK	55	5	2400	4000
Tintern Abbey	MEP/VR/724P	OC	1979	AC	30 X 40	R/BFK	55	3	2400	4000
Temple of Hatshepsut	MEP/VR/724P	OC	1979	AC	30 X 40	R/BFK	55	3	2400	4000
Stonehenge	MEP/VR/724P	OC	1979	AC	30 X 40	R/BFK	55	5	2400	4000
Sacsahuman	MEP/VR/724P	OC	1979	AC	30 X 40	R/BFK	55	5	2400	4000
Model with Green Kimono	724P	OC/B	1979	AC	41 X 27	R/BFK	41	5	2400	12000
Mummy Cave Ruins at Canyon de Chelly	BAI		1980	EB/A	41 X 29	AP	41		2000	2500
Two Nudes with Federal Sofa	724P	OC/B	1981	A/ENG/DPT	29 X 41	R/BFK	41	7	2000	3500
Monument Valley	BAI		1981	AC	29 X 40	AP	41		2000	3500
Two Models in Omaha	724P	UO	1981	LC	30 X 22	AP	60	4	950	1800
Nude in Hammock, 1982 (with Roulett Work)	724P	OC/B	1982	EB/AC	30 X 41	R/BFK	50	6	2200	5000
Model Sitting on African Stool	724P	LPI	1982	LB	30 X 21	AC/W	50	1	700	1000
Two Nudes with Andirondack Rocker	724P	LPI	1982	LB	22 X 30	AC/W	50	1	800	1000
Nude on Summer Furniture	724P	LPI	1982	LB	31 X 24	AC/W	50	1	700	1000
Temple at Paestum	724P	NB	1983	EB/A	31 X 41	R/BFK	50	3	2100	4000
Nude on Bamboo Sofa	724P	NB	1984	EB/A	31 X 40	R/BFK	50		2000	2500
Siesta Nude	724P	NB	1984	EB/A	25 X 21	R/BFK	50		950	1200
Models with Mirror (with Roulete Work)	GS/USF	NC	1985	A/EB	36 X 54	SP	60		5000	6000
View of Rome	724P	NB	1986	EB/A	30 X 42	R/BFK	50		2500	3000

HENRY C PEARSON

BORN: Kinston, NC; October 8, 1914
EDUCATION: Univ of North Carolina, Raleigh, NC, BA, 1935; Yale Univ, New Haven, CT, MFA, 1938; Art Students League, NY, 1953-56
TEACHING: Instr, Painting, New Sch of Social Research, NY; Instr, Pennsylvania Acad of Fine Arts, Phila, PA
AWARDS: Tamarind Lithography Workshop, Albuquerque, NM, 1964; Ford Found Fel, 1964; Keeger Purchase Prize, Corcoran Gallery of Art, Wash, DC, 1965; J Henry Scheidt Award, Pennsylvania Acad of Fine Art, Phila, PA, 1969
RECENT EXHIB: Retrosp, Columbia Mus of Art, SC, 1988
COLLECTIONS: Mus of Mod Art, NY; Metropolitan Mus, NY; Whitney Mus of Am Art, NY; Albright-Knox Art Gallery, Buffalo, NY; North Carolina Art Mus, Raleigh, NC
PRINTERS: American Atelier, NY (AA); Artist (ART)
PUBLISHERS: Circle Fine Art, Chicago, IL (CFA)
GALLERIES: Circle Galleries, San Diego, CA & San Francisco, CA & Northbrook, IL & Pittsburgh, PA & Houston, TX & Soho, NY, Chicago, IL & Scottsdale, AZ & Beverly Hills, CA & Costa Mesa, CA & Sherman Oaks, CA & Palm Beach, FL & Honolulu, HI & New Orleans, LA & Las Vegas, NV & Seattle, WA
MAILING ADDRESS: 58 W 58th St, New York, NY 10019

TITLE	PUBLISHER	PRINTER	DATE	MEDIUM	DIMENSION (PAPER SIZE) IN INCHES	TYPE OF PAPER	EDITION NUMBER	NO. OF COLORS	ORIGINAL OPENING PRICE	CURRENT RETAIL PRICE
SOLD OUT EDITIONS (RARE):										
Osiris	AAA	ART	1969	LC	23 X 25	AP	50		75	300
Westwind	CFA	AA	1979	LC	27 X 27	AP	175		150	300
128th Psalm	CFA	AA	1980	SP	39 X 30	R/BFK	200		100	350
Sacred River III	CFA	AA	1980	SP	47 X 47	R/BFK	200		250	450

MEL PEKARSKY (MELVIN HIRSCH)

BORN: Chicago, IL; September 18, 1934
EDUCATION: Sch, Art Inst of Chicago, IL; Northwestern Univ, BA, MA
TEACHING: Asst & Assoc Dean, Sch of Visual Arts, NY, 1967-69; Vis, Prof, Art, State Univ of New York, Stony Brook, NY, 1974,75; Prof, Art, State Univ of New York, Stony Brook, NY, 1975 to present; Chmn, Dept, State Univ of New York, Stony Brook, NY, 1977-78, 1984-89
AWARDS: Nat Endowment for the Arts Fel
RECENT EXHIB: Butler Inst of Am Art, Youngstown, OH, 1989; G W Einstein Company, Inc, NY, 1990,91
COLLECTIONS: Corcoran Gallery of Art, Wash, DC; Indianapolis Art Mus, IN; Weatherspoon Mus, Univ of North Carolina, Greensboro, NC; Cleveland Mus, OH; Yale Univ, New Haven, CT; Minneapolis Inst of the Arts, MN; Kendall Col, Evanston, IL; Marymount Col, Tarrytown, NY; Northwestern Univ, Evanston, IL; Univ of North Dakota, Grand Forks, ND; Ball State Univ, Muncie, IN
PRINTERS: Fine Creations, NY (FC); Mohammed Omer Khalil, NY (MOK); Solo Press, NY (SP); Artist (ART)
PUBLISHERS: Alecto International, NY (AI) (OB); G W Einstein, Inc, NY (GWE); Signet Arts, St Louis, MO (SA); Artist (ART)
GALLERIES: G W Einstein, Inc, New York, NY; Signet Arts, St Louis, MO
MAILING ADDRESS: PO Box CH, Stony Brook, NY 11790

MEL PEKARSKY (MELVIN HIRSCH) CONTINUED

TITLE	PUBLISHER	PRINTER	DATE	MEDIUM	DIMENSION (PAPER SIZE) IN INCHES	TYPE OF PAPER	EDITION NUMBER	NO. OF COLORS	ORIGINAL OPENING PRICE	CURRENT RETAIL PRICE
SOLD OUT EDITIONS (RARE):										
Places (Set of 3):									425 SET	3500 SET
Seven Places	GWE	MOK	1972–73	DPT/HC	15 X 23	AP	20		150	1200
Nine Places	GWE	MOK	1972–73	DPT/HC	15 X 23	AP	20		150	1200
Souvenir with Garden	GWE	MOK	1972–73	DPT/HC	15 X 23	AP	20		150	1200
Horizons	GWE/AI	FC	1973	SP	30 X 60	BRP	90	8	200	1800
Morning Garden with Line	GWE	MOK	1974	DPT/HC	28 X 23	ITAL	20	Varies	400	1200
Roundels	GWE	JC	1974	SP	24 X 36	BRP	90	20	300	800
Mojave I, II (Set of 2)	GWE	SP	1977	LC	29 X 41 EA	BRP	35 EA	2/3 EA	275 EA	800 EA
CURRENT EDITIONS:										
Western Place	ART	ART	1980	DPT/HC	10 X 14	AP	10	Varies	600	1200
Mojave	SA	SP	1985	LB	60 X 42	AP	26	1	1000	1500

MICHAEL JOSEPH PELLETTIERI

BORN: New York, NY; November 25, 1943
EDUCATION: Col of City of New York, Sch of Arts & Sciences, BFA, 1965; Art Students League, NY, 1963–67; Hunter Col, MA, 1969
TEACHING: Instr, Printmaking, Art Students League, NY, 1977 to present; Instr, Printmaking, Summit Art Center, NJ, 1982 to present
AWARDS: State Education Dept, Travel & Study Grant, India, 1969; Strathmore Award, Boston Printmakers, MA, 1979; Silver Medallion, Audubon Artists, 1982; Purchase Award, North Dakota Univ, Grand Forks, ND, 1984; MacDowell Colony Fel, 1988

RECENT EXHIB: Columbia Univ, NY, 1987; Landmark Gallery, Kingston, NY, 1988
COLLECTIONS: DeCordova Mus, Lincoln, MA; Univ of North Dakota, Grand Forks, ND; Newark Art Library, NJ; Columbia Univ Mus, NY
PRINTERS: Artist (ART)
PUBLISHERS: Artist (ART)
GALLERIES: Associated American Artists, New York, NY; Gallery of Graphic Art, New York, NY; Miriam Perlman, Chicago, IL; Morningstar Gallery, New York, NY; Pembroke Gallery, Houston, TX
MAILING ADDRESS: 325 W 77th St, #8-D, New York, NY 10024

TITLE	PUBLISHER	PRINTER	DATE	MEDIUM	DIMENSION (PAPER SIZE) IN INCHES	TYPE OF PAPER	EDITION NUMBER	NO. OF COLORS	ORIGINAL OPENING PRICE	CURRENT RETAIL PRICE
CURRENT EDITIONS:										
Poppies	ART	ART	1973	EC	22 X 30	AC	50	3	200	500
Winter	ART	ART	1978	EB	35 X 27	GE	80	1	110	500
Grand Central	ART	ART	1980	EB	22 X 30	AC/W	80	1	180	300
Goalie	ART	ART	1980	EC/COL	22 X 30	AC/W	100	8	275	500
Witness	ART	ART	1981	EB	30 X 42	GE	100	1		
Five Positions for an Open Heart (Set of 5)	ART	ART	1984	EC/CC	19 X 26 EA	AC/W-KIT	50	2	1200 SET	1500 SET
Interior	ART	ART	1985	EB	22 X 30	GE	80	1	200	300

FERNANDO PEREZNIETO

BORN: Mexico City, Mexico; August 12, 1938
EDUCATION: Nat Univ of Mexico; Villa Schifanoia, Florence, Italy
TEACHING: Nat University of Mexico
AWARDS: First Prize, Editorial Art, Mexico, 1980; First Nat Prize, Etching, Pelago, Italy, 1983; First Nat Prize, Painting, Lampedusa, Italy, 1984
RECENT EXHIB: Sala Gaudi, Barcelona, Spain, 1988; Segno Grafico, Venezia, Italy, 1989; Galeria Carani, Mexico City, Mexico, 1989; Galerie d'Art Fernando Pereznieto, Nice, France, 1991

PRINTERS: Lacouriere et Frelaut, Paris, France (LEF); Stamperia Pistelli, Florence, Italy (StPi); Stamperia Il Nascondiglio, Gaiole in Chianti, Italy (SIN)
PUBLISHERS: Pacifica Editions, Miami, FL (PacEd); Galeria Carani, Mexico City, Mexico (GC); Nat Univ of Mexico, University City, Mexico (NUM)
GALLERIES: Segno Grafico, Venezia, Italy; Galleria Mentana, Florence, Italy; Iturraude Gallery, La Jolla, CA; Sala Gaudi, Barcelona, Spain; Galeria Tlalpalli, Mexico City, Mexico; Galerie d'Art Fernando Pereznieto, Nice, France; Galeria Atenea, San Miguel de Allende, Mexico
MAILING ADDRESS: A P Post 41-897, Mexico DF, 11000, Mexico

TITLE	PUBLISHER	PRINTER	DATE	MEDIUM	DIMENSION (PAPER SIZE) IN INCHES	TYPE OF PAPER	EDITION NUMBER	NO. OF COLORS	ORIGINAL OPENING PRICE	CURRENT RETAIL PRICE
SOLD OUT EDITIONS (RARE):										
Los Requerimientos para la Politica (Set of 5)	GC	ALEF	1978	EB	65 X 50 cm EA	AP	50 EA	1 EA	500 SET	1500 SET
									100 EA	350 EA
Los Pecados Capitales y Como Ejercerlos con Propiedad (Set of 8)	GC	ALEF	1979	EC	50 X 65 EA	AP	50 EA	2 EA	800 SET	2500 SET
El Amor a la Musica	GC	ALEF	1980	EB	65 X 50 cm	AP	50	1	100 EA	350 EA
Duo de Malos Alientos	GC	ALEF	1980	EB	65 X 50 cm	AP	50	1	100	300
El Arte de la Fuga	GC	ALEF	1980	EB	65 X 50 cm	AP	50	1	100	300
El Trovador	GC	ALEF	1980	EB	65 X 50 cm	AP	50	1	100	300
El Encuentro con la Realidad	GC	ALEF	1980	EB	65 X 50 cm	AP	50	1	100	300
Divertimento Erotico (Set of 20)	ART	ART	1986	EB	35 X 25 cm	AP	100 EA	1 EA	1000 SET	5000 SET
									50 EA	250 EA
CURRENT EDITIONS:										
O/Maggio Musicale (Set of 10)	GC	IN	1983	EC	50 X 70 cm EA	MAG	99 EA	3–11 EA	1000 SET	2000 SET
									100 EA	200 EA

FERNANDO PEREZNIETO CONTINUED

TITLE	PUBLISHER	PRINTER	DATE	MEDIUM	DIMENSION (PAPER SIZE) IN INCHES	TYPE OF PAPER	EDITION NUMBER	NO. OF COLORS	ORIGINAL OPENING PRICE	CURRENT RETAIL PRICE
CURRENT EDITIONS:										
Il Carnevale (Set of 5)	GC	IN	1984	EC	35 X 50 cm EA	MAG	99 EA	3–4 EA	375 SET	750 SET
									75 EA	150 EA
Suite of Four:									600 SET	1000 SET
Gestacion	PacEd	LA	1985	LC	56 X 76 cm	AP	150	7	150	250
Viola, Violeta	PacEd	LA	1985	LC	56 X 76 cm	AP	150	7	150	250
La Grieta	PacEd	LA	1985	LC	56 X 76 cm	AP	150	13	150	250
Adan y Eva	PacEd	LA	1985	LC	56 X 76 cm	AP	150	13	150	250
Los Enanos Sarracenos	PacEd	LY	1985	EC	56 X 76 cm	AP	150	3	150	250
Coro	PacEd	LY	1985	EC	56 X 76 cm	AP	150	3	150	250
Capricho Florentino	GC	IN	1986	EC	50 X 70 cm	MAG	99	4	100	200
El Cuentahistorias	GC	ALEF	1988	EC	65 X 50 cm	AP	99	3	150	250
La Toma de la Reyna	GC	StP	1988	LC	25 X 70 cm	GRA	180	5	100	180
Jaque al Rey	GC	StP	1988	LC	25 X 70 cm	GRA	180	5	100	180
Bacco, Rosso di Montebello	GC	StP	1989	LC/PH	33 X 45 cm	FAB	250	4	100	150
Corazon a Duo	GC	StP	1989	LC/PH	33 X 45 cm	FAB	250	4	100	150
La Flauta Magica	GC	StP	1989	LC/PH	33 X 45 cm	FAB	250	4	100	150
Elogio de la Guitarra (Set of 40)	EMY	ART	1989	LB	22 X 22 cm EA	FAB	200 EA	1 EA	4000 SET	4000 SET
									100 EA	100 EA

A R PENCK (RALF WINKLER)

BORN: Dresden, Germany; 1939
RECENT EXHIB: Dolly Fiterman Gallery, Minneapolis, MN, 1987; Galeria Juana Mordo, Madrid, Spain, 1989; Mary Boone Gallery, NY, 1989; Goldman-Kraft Gallery, Chicago, IL, 1989; Michael Werner Gallery, NY, 1990; Univ of Maine Mus, Orono, ME, 1992
PRINTERS: Francois Lafrancs (FL); Burston Graphics Centre, Jerusalem, Israel (BGC); Aldo Crommelynck, Paris, France (C); Atelier Crommelynck, Paris, France (AC); Aldo Rossi, Rome, Italy (AR); 2RC, Rome, Italy (2RC); Patricia Branstead, NY (PB); Aeropress, NY (A); Jack Lemon, Chicago, IL (JL); Landfall Press, Inc, Chicago, IL (LPI)
PUBLISHERS: Peter Blum Edition, NY (PBE); Joshua Gessel, Tel Aviv, Israel (JG); Maximilian Verlag Sabine Knust, Munich, West Germany (MVSK); Multiples, NY (M); Landfall Press, Inc, Chicago, IL (LPI); Schellmann & Klüser, Münich, Germany & NY (SK); Achenbach Art Edition, Düsseldorf, Germany (AEE)
GALLERIES: Sonnabend Gallery, New York, NY; Steven Lieber, San Francisco, CA; Brody's Gallery, Wash, DC; Fay Gold Gallery, Atlanta, GA; Editions, Ilene Kurtz, Inc, New York, NY; Nicola Jacobs Gallery, London, England; Peter Blum Edition, New York, NY; Marian Goodman Gallery, New York, NY; Dolly Fiterman Gallery, Minneapolis, MN; Galerie Lelong, Paris, France & Zurich, Switzerland & New York, NY; Mary Boone Gallery, New York, NY; Galeria Juana Mordo, Madrid, Spain; Landfall Press, Inc, Chicago, IL & New York, NY; Michael Werner Gallery, New York, NY; Wenger Gallery, Los Angelas, CA; Fred Hoffman Gallery, Santa Monica, CA; Anthony Ralph Gallery, New York, NY;

A R Penck
#2 (from Berlin Suite)
Courtesy Achenbach Art Editions

Margarete Roeder Gallery, New York, NY; Eugene Binder Gallery, Dallas, TX; Thomas Erben Gallery, New York, NY; Figura, Inc, New York, NY
MAILING ADDRESS: Torre Gentile Di Todi, PG, Italy

TITLE	PUBLISHER	PRINTER	DATE	MEDIUM	DIMENSION (PAPER SIZE) IN INCHES	TYPE OF PAPER	EDITION NUMBER	NO. OF COLORS	ORIGINAL OPENING PRICE	CURRENT RETAIL PRICE
SOLD OUT EDITIONS (RARE):										
Abstract			1966	WC	26 X 20	AP	25		100	3000
Ich in England (mit Rotem Löwen)				WC	26 X 75	AP	10	2	200	8000
Ich in Western				AC/DPT	43 X 69	MAG	35	3	200	8000
8 Erfahrungen (Set of 8)	PBE	FL	1981	WB	32 X 24	HMP	50	1	3000 SET	10000 SET
Set of Six Lithographs	M	PB/A	1982	LB	32 X 24 EA	AP	25 EA		450 EA	1000 EA
Set of Six Lithographs	M	PB/A	1982	LB	32 X 24 EA	AP	30 EA		550 EA	1000 EA
Untitled	M	PB/A	1982	SP	40 X 55	AP	250		400	1200
Untitled (Set of 8)	M	PB/A	1983	DPT(1) AB(1) EB(6)	23 X 31 EA	R/BFK	35 EA		3000 SET	6000 SET
Expedition to the Holy Land (Set of 15)	JG	BGC	1983	LC(3) SP(3) ENG(3) AC(3)	30 X 41 EA	AP	50	Varies	9000 SET	20000 SET
Zumthema Verteidigung	MVSK	C/AC	1984	A/DPT	32 X 40	R/BFK	30		1200	3000
Three Etchings:										
Me in the West	MVSK	AR/2RC	1985	EB/A/DPT	43 X 68	MGA	35		4000	8500

A R PENCK (RALF WINKLER) CONTINUED

TITLE	PUBLISHER	PRINTER	DATE	MEDIUM	DIMENSION (PAPER SIZE) IN INCHES	TYPE OF PAPER	EDITION NUMBER	NO. OF COLORS	ORIGINAL OPENING PRICE	CURRENT RETAIL PRICE
SOLD OUT EDITIONS (RARE):										
Quo Vadis Germania	MVSK	AR/2RC	1985	EB/A/DPT	43 X 68	MAG	35		4000	8500
Me in the West	MVSK	AR/2RC	1985	EB/A/DPT	43 X 68	MAG	35		4000	8500
Strike	MVSK	AR/2RC	1985	EB/A	35 X 60	MAG	85		2500	5000
For Joseph Beuys: Untitled	SK		1986	LC	27 X 21	AC	90		1200	2000
Frau mit Kind	SEF	JB	1989	AC	30 X 40	R/BFK	35	4	2400	3800
Aufstand	SEF	JB	1990	AC	30 X 42	R/BFK	35	4	2400	3800
Veroleich (Blue-Yellow)	SEF	JB	1991–92	AC	42 X 30	R/BFK	50	3	2400	3500
Kontrolle (Red-Purple)	SEF	JB	1991–92	AC	42 X 30	R/BFK	50	3	2400	3500
CURRENT EDITIONS:										
Mul, Bul, Dang & Sentimentality (Series of 25)	LPI	JL/LPI	1988	WC	36 X 29 EA	AC	1 EA	3 EA	1500 EA	1500 EA
Quo Vadis gg			1989	AC	14 X 14	MAG	25	5	2500	3000
Lausanne Suite (Set of 6)	AAE		1990	LC	70 X 100 cm EA	AC	70 EA		24000 SET 4500 EA	24000 SET 4500 EA
Berlin Suite (Set of 10)	AAE		1990	AC	76.5 X 107 cm EA	AC	60 EA		30000 SET 3500 EA	30000 SET 3500 EA
Praxis (Blue-Purple)	SEF	JB	1991–93	AC	42 X 30		50	3	2400	2400
Vision (Green-Yellow)	SEF	JB	1991–93	AC	42 X 30		50	3	2400	2400
Wir (Green-Red)	SEF	JB	1991–93	AC	42 X 30		50	3	2400	2400
Ich (Green-Purple)	SEF	JB	1991–93	AC	42 X 30		50	3	2400	2400
Du (Purple-Yellow)	SEF	JB	1991–93	AC	42 X 30		50	3	2400	2400
Wächter (Blue-Red)	SEF	JB	1991–93	AC	42 X 30		50	3	2400	2400
Rächer (Yellow-Orange)	SEF	JB	1991–93	AC	42 X 30		50	3	2400	2400
Nacht (Blue-Red)	SEF	JB	1991–93	AC	42 X 30		50	3	2400	2400
Sie (Red-Yellow)	SEF	JB	1991–93	AC	42 X 30		50	3	2400	2400

BEVERLY PEPPER

BORN: New York, NY; December 20, 1924
EDUCATION: Pratt Inst, Brooklyn NY, 1939–41; Art Students League, NY, 1946; Studied with Leger & Lhote, Paris, France, 1948–49
AWARDS: Nat Endowment for the Arts Grants, 1975,79
RECENT EXHIB: Charles Cowles Gallery, NY, 1987,90; André Emmerich Gallery, NY, 1990; Kalamazoo Inst of Art, MI, 1992; Western Washington Univ, Bellingham, WA, 1992; Johnson Atelier Fine Arts, NY, 1992
COLLECTIONS: Albright-Knox Art Gallery, Buffalo, NY; Fogg Art Mus, Harvard Univ, Cambridge, MA; Massachusetts Inst of Technology, Cambridge, MA; Walker Art Inst, Minneapolis, MN; Indianapolis Mus, IN; Museo Civica d'Arte Moderna, Turin, Italy; Metropolitan Mus of Art, NY; Fogg Art Mus, Cambridge, MA
PRINTERS: 2 RC Workshop, Rome, Italy (2RC); Valter Rossi, Rome, Italy (VR); Atelier Vigna Antoniniana Stamperia d'Art, Rome, Italy (AVAS); Patricia Branstead, NY (PB); Riverhouse Editions Press, Clark, CO (REd)
PUBLISHERS: Marlborough Graphics, NY (MG); 2 RC Workshop, Rome, Italy (2RC); Riverhouse Editions, Chicago, IL (REd)
GALLERIES: Marlborough Gallery, New York, NY; André Emmerich Gallery, New York, NY; John Berggruen Gallery, San Francisco, CA; Makler Gallery, Phila, PA; Linda Farris Gallery, Seattle, WA; Yares Gallery, Seattle, WA; Jamie C Lee Gallery, Houston, TX & New York, NY; Huntington Galleries, Huntington, WVA; Garner Tullis Workshop, Santa Barbara, CA; Hokin Galleries, Bay Harbor Islands, FL & Palm Beach, FL; Charles Cowles Gallery, New York, NY; Adams-Middleton Gallery, Dallas, TX; Baumgartner Galleries, Inc, Wash, DC; Thomas Babeor Gallery, La Jolla, CA; Gerald Peters Gallery, Santa Fe, NM; James Corcoran Gallery, Santa Monica, CA; Van Straaten Gallery, Chicago, IL; Lemberg Gallery, Birmingham, MI; Nina Freudenheim Gallery, Buffalo, NY
MAILING ADDRESS: Torre Gentile, Di Todi, PG, Italy

TITLE	PUBLISHER	PRINTER	DATE	MEDIUM	DIMENSION (PAPER SIZE) IN INCHES	TYPE OF PAPER	EDITION NUMBER	NO. OF COLORS	ORIGINAL OPENING PRICE	CURRENT RETAIL PRICE
SOLD OUT EDITIONS (RARE):										
Black Virgo	MG		1968	CO	19 X 28	AP	60		75	1000
Blue and Black	MG		1968	CO	19 X 28	AP	60		75	1000
Blue and Black Frame	MG		1968	CO	19 X 28	AP	60		75	1000
Double Vertical Silver and Black	MG		1968	CO	19 X 28	AP	60		75	1000
Virgo Silver and Black	MG		1968	CO	19 X 28	AP	60		75	1000
White and Silver Frame	MG		1968	CO	19 X 28	AP	60		75	1000
Untitled	2RC	VR/AVAS	1973	EC	38 X 38	FAB	45		400	2000
CURRENT EDITIONS:										
Untitled	2RC	VR/AVAS	1988	EB/A/CAR	43 X 32	FAB	50		1800	2000
Finishing Beginning Now	REd	PB/REd	1991	EC	18 X 49	FAB	60		1200	1200
Fate Not the World's I-XX (Dipt)	REd	PB/REd	1991	MON	27 X 39 EA		1 EA	Varies	2000 EA	2000 EA
Untitled #1, #2, #3	REd	PB/REd	1992	MON	32 X 44 EA		1 EA	Varies	1800 EA	1800 EA

LINNEA PERGOLA

EDUCATION: California State Univ, Northridge, CA
PUBLISHERS: Martin Lawrence Limited Editions, Van Nuys, CA (MLLE)
GALLERIES: Martin Lawrence Galleries, Escondido, CA & Newport Beach, CA & Palm Springs, CA & Redondo Beach, CA & Santa Clara, CA & Sherman Oaks, CA & Thousand Oaks, Ca & West Los Angeles, CA & Los Angeles, CA & Short Hills, NJ & Soho, NY

The print market has become very selective. For the first time since we published the first edition of The Printworld Directory in 1982, the prices of prints have been greatly reduced and greatly increased for the same artists by the most reputable and established print publishers. Check the fifth edition to understand the movement.

LINNEA PERGOLA CONTINUED

TITLE	PUBLISHER	PRINTER	DATE	MEDIUM	DIMENSION (PAPER SIZE) IN INCHES	TYPE OF PAPER	EDITION NUMBER	NO. OF COLORS	ORIGINAL OPENING PRICE	CURRENT RETAIL PRICE
SOLD OUT EDITIONS (RARE):										
2 Piece Suite:									1250 SET	5000 SET
Giant	MLLE		1989	SP	39 X 42	AP	595		750	2800
One Summer Night	MLLE		1989	SP	34 X 42	AP	595		750	2800
Signs of the Times	MLLE		1989	SP	29 X 29	AP	595		750	3500
Hailing a Sky Cab	MLLE		1990	SP	34 X 43	AP	595		850	2575
London, 1943	MLLE		1990	SP	36 X 37	AP	595		850	2575
One World	MLLE		1990	SP	39 X 48	AP	595		850	3200
CURRENT EDITIONS:										
Casa Mila	MLLE		1989	SP	30 X 30	AP	595		750	1900
Wonder Wheel	MLLE		1990	SP	28 X 40	AP	595		850	2100
American Nostalgia Series:									1500 SET	3000 SET
Cruise Night	MLLE		1990	SP	35 X 42	AP	595		850	1825
Paradise Diner	MLLE		1990	SP	38 X 40	AP	595		850	1825
Mulberry Street	MLLE		1991	SP	39 X 38	AP	595		950	1825
London	MLLE		1991	SP	31 X 38	AP	595		950	1600
The Old Ball Game	MLLE		1991	SP	34 X 32	AP	595		950	1900
Seaside Nights—Northern Lights	MLLE		1991	SP	34 X 42	AP	595		950	1450
Rush Hour Suite:									975 SET	1550 SET
Rush Hour	MLLE		1991	SP	34 X 42	AP	595		xxx	xxx
Yellow Taxi	MLLE		1991	Acrylic	4 X 8 X 5	Wood	595		xxx	xxx
Pete's Burgers	MLLE		1992	SP	34 X 42	AP	595		875	1375
Four Seasons Suite (Set of 4):									2200 SET	3000 SET
Spring Boat Ride	MLLE		1992	SP	27 X 21	AP	595		600	825
Summer in the City	MLLE		1992	SP	27 X 21	AP	595		600	825
A Winter's Night	MLLE		1992	SP	27 X 21	AP	595		600	825
Center Avenue in Fall	MLLE		1992	SP	22 X 26	AP	595		600	825

JACK PERLMUTTER

BORN: New York, NY; January 23, 1920
TEACHING: Chmn, Graphics Dept, Corcoran Sch of Art, Wash, DC, 1960–82; Vis Prof, Univ of Costa Rica, 1983
AWARDS: Fulbright Fel, Art & Printmaking, Tokyo, Japan, 1959–60
COLLECTIONS: Metropolitan Mus of Art, NY; Nat Gallery of Art, Wash, DC; Library of Congress, Wash, DC; Nat Acad of Sciences, Wash, DC; Phillips Coll, Wash, DC; Corcoran Gallery of Art, Wash, DC; Nat Mus of Mod Art, Tokyo; Brooklyn Mus, NY; Carnegie Inst, Pittsburgh, PA
PRINTERS: Norma Mazo, Wash, DC (NM); Mazo Press, Wash, DC (MP)
PUBLISHERS: Am Society of Graphic Artists, NY; Mazo Press, Wash, DC
GALLERIES: Agra Gallery, Wash, DC (AG)
MAILING ADDRESS: 2511 Cliffbourne Pl NW, Wash, DC 20009

TITLE	PUBLISHER	PRINTER	DATE	MEDIUM	DIMENSION (PAPER SIZE) IN INCHES	TYPE OF PAPER	EDITION NUMBER	NO. OF COLORS	ORIGINAL OPENING PRICE	CURRENT RETAIL PRICE
CURRENT EDITIONS:										
Elevated Tracks	ART	ART	1969	LC	21 X 22	AP	50	3	75	700
Under the EL	MP	ART	1979	EB	12 X 10		75	1	75	450
To the Open Sea	MP	ART	1979	EB	12 X 11		75	1	75	450
The Other Side of the EL	ART	ART	1980	EB/ENG	17 X 12		75	1	75	450
Rainbow	MP	NM/MP	1980	EC/ENG	13 X 18	R/BFK	75	2	200	450
Umbrellas	MP	NM/MP	1981	EC/ENG	19 X 13	R/BFK	100	2	200	450
The End of the Tracks	MP	NM/MP	1981	EC/ENG	16 X 12	R/BFK	100	2	200	450
Towards the City	MP	NM/MP	1981	EC/ENG	22 X 14	R/BFK	100	2	200	450
Drizzle	MP	NM/MP	1981	EC/ENG	14 X 19	R/BFK	75	2	200	450
Rain	MP	NM/MP	1981	WC	10 X 16	R/BFK	100	2	100	450
Boardwalk	ASGA	ART	1982	SP	20 X 23	SOM	300	2	600	600
Lighthouse	ASGA	ART	1982	EC/ENG	17 X 24	SOM	300	2	600	600
Carousel	ASGA	ART	1982	EC/ENG	17 X 24	SOM	300	2	600	600
Adam & Eve	ASGA	ART	1982	EC/ENG	17 X 24	SOM	300	2	600	600
Justice	MP	NM/MP	1982	EC	14 X 19	SOM	75	2	100	450
Tunnel	MP	NM/MP	1985	EB/ENG	22 X 25	GE	75	1	300	300
Roots	MP	NM/MP	1985	EB/ENG	22 X 25	GE	75	1	300	300
Starfish	MP	NM/MP	1985	EB/ENG	22 X 25	GE	75	1	300	300
Turnpike	MP	NM/MP	1985	EB/ENG	22 X 25	GE	75	1	300	300
Fish and Crab	MP	NM/MP	1985	EB/ENG	22 X 22	GE	75	1	300	300
The End of the Walk	MP	NM/MP	1985	EB/ENG	22 X 25	GE	75	1	300	300
Bamboo	MP	NM/MP	1985	EB/ENG	22 X 25	GE	75	1	300	300
Full Moon	MP	NM/MP	1985	EB/ENG	19 X 22	R/BFK	75	1	300	300
Bridge with Flower	MP	NM/MP	1985	EB/ENG	22 X 25	GE	75	1	300	300
City Bird	MP	NM/MP	1985	EB/ENG	22 X 25	GE	75	1	300	300
Two Nudes	MP	NM/MP	1985	EB/ENG	22 X 25	GE	75	1	300	300
Schools of Fish	MP	NM/MP	1985	EB/ENG	22 X 25	GE	75	1	300	300
Sea Gulls	MP	NM/MP	1985	EB/ENG	22 X 25	GE	75	1	300	300
Temple Steps	MP	NM/MP	1985	EB/ENG	22 X 22	GE	75	1	300	300
Under the Bridge	MP	NM/MP	1985	EB/ENG	22 X 25	GE	75	1	300	300

The retail prices of the 100,000 limited edition prints quoted in this directory are subject to change. Print publishers, artists and galleries were the direct sources for these quotations. Prices in the secondary market listed as "Sold Out Editions (Rare)" indicate that the publisher has a limited supply of that print or that the print is difficult to locate in the galleries.

GABOR F PETERDI

BORN: Pestujhely, Hungary; September 17, 1915; US Citizen
EDUCATION: Hungarian Acad, Budapest, Hungary; Acad Julien, Paris, France; Atelier 17, Paris, France, with Stanley W Hayter
TEACHING: Instr, Brooklyn Mus Art Sch, NY, 1948–52; Assoc Prof, Hunter Col, NY, 1952–59; Prof, Art, Yale Univ, 1960 to present
AWARDS: Prix du Rome, Italy, 1930; Mus of Western Art Award, Tokyo, Japan, 1964; John Simon Guggenheim Fel, 1964–65
COLLECTIONS: Whitney Mus of Am Art, NY; Metropolitan Mus, NY; Mus of Mod Art, NY; Guggenheim Mus, NY; Art Inst of Chicago, IL; Mus of Fine Arts, Boston, MA
RECENT EXHIB: Coos Bay Art Mus, Coos Bay, OR, 1988; Borgenicht Gallery, NY, 1988; Borgenicht Gallery, NY, 1993
PRINTERS: Artist (ART)
PUBLISHERS: Artist (ART)
GALLERIES: Jane Haslem Gallery, Wash, DC; Glass Gallery, New York, NY; Connecticut Fine Arts, Westport, CT; Jacques Baruch Gallery, Chicago, IL; Borgenicht Gallery, New York, NY; Suzanne Brown Gallery, Scottsdale, AZ; Branchville Soho Gallery, Ridgefield, CT
MAILING ADDRESS: 108 Highland Ave, Rowayton, CT 06853

TITLE	PUBLISHER	PRINTER	DATE	MEDIUM	DIMENSION (PAPER SIZE) IN INCHES	TYPE OF PAPER	EDITION NUMBER	NO. OF COLORS	ORIGINAL OPENING PRICE	CURRENT RETAIL PRICE
SOLD OUT EDITIONS (RARE):										
The Hunter Hunted	ART	ART	1947	LI/ENG	15 X 14	COP	35	1	50	600
Dark Visit	ART	ART	1948	E/REL	16 X 20	ZINC	30	1	50	600
Alexander	ART	ART	1950	E/A/ENG	28 X 20	ZINC	15	1	50	800
The Vision of Fear	ART	ART	1953	EC/ENG	26 X 37	ZINC	20		75	1000
The Big Rock	ART	ART	1961	E/A/SG	34 X 22	ZINC	50	1	75	1000
Oregon Coast I	ART	ART	1962	EB	12 X 16	ZINC	50	1	75	600
The Big Norfolk	ART	ART	1963	ENG	22 X 36	ZINC	50	1	75	600
Floating (Vibrating Branches)		ART	1964	EB/SG	18 X 24	AP	100		100	900
Arctic Bird I	ART	ART	1964	MM	36 X 24		25	6	125	800
Arctic Night IV	ART	ART	1965	MM	25 X 36		25	4	125	1000
Angry Gulf	ART	ART	1970	DPT	24 X 36		25	1	125	800
The Big Red Eclipse	ART	ART	1971	MM	40 X 28		25	7	150	1000
Pacific	ART	ART	1971	DPT	30 X 40	ZINC	25	1	150	2500
Surging Wave	ART	ART	1972	DPTG	22 X 28		15	1	150	1000
Kavai Cactus I, II	ART	ART	1972	DPT	22 X 28 EA	MAG	15 EA	1 EA	150 EA	700 EA
Adam and Eve	ART	ART	1975	DPT	22 X 28		12	1	200	800
Self Portrait at 60	ART	ART	1975	DPT	28 X 22		8	1	200	800
Temptation of St Anthony	ART	ART	1981	DPT	40 X 30		20	1	800	1500

MARTIN PETERSEN

BORN: (1870–1956)
PRINTERS: American Atelier, NY (AA); Artist (ART)
PUBLISHERS: Reece Publishing, NY (RP); Artist (ART)

TITLE	PUBLISHER	PRINTER	DATE	MEDIUM	DIMENSION (PAPER SIZE) IN INCHES	TYPE OF PAPER	EDITION NUMBER	NO. OF COLORS	ORIGINAL OPENING PRICE	CURRENT RETAIL PRICE
SOLD OUT EDITIONS (RARE):										
Pile Drivers	ART	ART	1916	EB	7 X 6	WOVE	30	1	20	300
In the Elevated Train	ART	ART	1920	EB	7 X 6	WOVE	25	1	25	325
Factories at Weehawken	ART	ART	1926	EB	10 X 8	WOVE	35	1	30	450
In the Subway	ART	ART	1927	EB	8 X 7	WOVE	35	1	30	325
Sunset, New Hampshire	AAA	AA	1935	EB	9 X 8	WOVE	250	1	50	200
From Riverside Park	AAA	AA	1938	EB	8 X 10	AP	250	1	60	475
In the El	AAA	AA	1943	EB	8 X 10	AP	250	1	75	325
Summer Shower, Central...	RP		1944	EB	10 X 9	AP		1	85	600
Rush Hour (Estate Signed)	RP		1956	EB	10 X 12	AP		1	150	750

ROBERT PETERSEN

BORN: Le Mars, IA; 1945
RECENT EXHIB: Edison Com Col, Fort Meyers, FL, 1988; North Miami Center of Contemp Art, North Miami, FL, 1988,92
PRINTERS: Styria Studio, NY (SS); Palm Press, Tampa, FL (PalP); Brand X, NY (BX); Sette Publishing Company, Tempe AZ (SPC)
PUBLISHERS: Styria Studio, NY (SS); Palm Press, Tampa, FL (PalP); Castelli Gallery, NY (CG); Sette Publishing Company, Tempe, AZ (SPC); Artist (ART)
GALLERIES: Sonnabend Gallery, New York, NY; Hoshour Gallery, Albuquerque, NM; Shelly Guggenheim Gallery, Wash, DC; Barbara Greene Gallery, Miami, FL; Graham Gallery, Albuquerque, NM; Valley House Gallery, Dallas, TX; Lisa Sette Gallery, Scottsdale, AZ; Styria Studio, New York, NY

TITLE	PUBLISHER	PRINTER	DATE	MEDIUM	DIMENSION (PAPER SIZE) IN INCHES	TYPE OF PAPER	EDITION NUMBER	NO. OF COLORS	ORIGINAL OPENING PRICE	CURRENT RETAIL PRICE
CURRENT EDITIONS:										
Legend Series	SS	SS	1977	LC/SP/CO	32 X 42	AP88	77	13	250	700
Chart Series	SS	SS	1977	LC/EMB	30 X 42	AP88	50	4	250	700
Chart Series	SS	SS	1977	LC/CO	30 X 42	GE/BL	50	4	250	700
Chart Series	SS	SS	1977	LC/CO	42 X 30	AP88	50	3	250	700
Chart Series	SS	SS	1977	LC/CO	42 X 30	AP88	50	4	250	700
Chart Series	SS	SS	1977	LC/CO/EMB	30 X 42	AP88	50	3	250	700
Chart Series	SS	SS	1977	LC/CO	30 X 42	AP88	50	4	250	700
Stone Black	SS	SS	1981	LC/CO	50 X 36	AP/ROL	6		450	700
Vestige Series (Blue)	SS	SS	1983	LC/CO	30 X 42	AC/W	43	4	250	500
Vestige Series (Grey)	SS	SS	1983	LC/CO	30 X 42	AC/W	43	4	250	500

ROBERT PETERSEN CONTINUED

TITLE	PUBLISHER	PRINTER	DATE	MEDIUM	DIMENSION (PAPER SIZE) IN INCHES	TYPE OF PAPER	EDITION NUMBER	NO. OF COLORS	ORIGINAL OPENING PRICE	CURRENT RETAIL PRICE
CURRENT EDITIONS:										
Calendar Series: (January-December)	PP	PP	1980–82	EC	30 X 36 EA	AP	24 EA		300 EA	500 EA
Calendar Series (Special Edition): (January-December)	PP	PP	1980–82	EC	30 X 36 EA	AP	24 EA		800 EA	900 EA
Color Studies: April 1984	CG	BX	1984	SP/HC/CO	29 X 41	AP	40	Varies	850	900
Color Studies: Variant Months	ART	BX	1984	SP/HC/CO	29 X 41	AP	6	Varies	1200	1350

ROBERT PETERSON

BORN: Elmhurst, IL; 1943
RECENT EXHIB: Valley House Gallery, Dallas, TX, 1987; Graham Gallery, Albuquerque, NM, 1988
COLLECTIONS: Albuquerque Mus, NM; Amarillo Art Center, TX; Gallaudet Col, Wash, DC; Mus of New Mexico, Santa Fe, NM; Mus of New Mexico, Albuquerque, NM

PRINTERS: Heather Hoover, Albuquerque, NM (HH); Bill Lagattuta, Albuquerque, NM (BL); Tamarind Inst, Albuquerque, NM (TI); Artist (ART)
PUBLISHERS: Tamarind Inst, Albuquerque, NM (TI)
GALLERIES: Graham Gallery, Albuquerque, NM; Valley House Gallery, Dallas, TX; Shelly Guggenheim Gallery, Wash, DC; Tamarind Inst, Albuquerque, NM; I Wolk Gallery, St Helena, CA; CAFE, Albuquerque, NM; Munson Gallery, Santa Fe, NM; Jerald Melberg Gallery, Inc, Charlotte, NC

TITLE	PUBLISHER	PRINTER	DATE	MEDIUM	DIMENSION (PAPER SIZE) IN INCHES	TYPE OF PAPER	EDITION NUMBER	NO. OF COLORS	ORIGINAL OPENING PRICE	CURRENT RETAIL PRICE
SOLD OUT EDITIONS (RARE):										
Shop Towel over Block	TI	ART	1983	LC		R/BFK			250	800
Pepper on Dish	TI	HH/TI	1988	LC	16 X 26	MBDCP		4	400	450
Devil's Claw	TI	BL/TI	1988	LC	22 X 30	R/BFK/CR		1	300	375

BELA PETHEO

BORN: Budapest, Hungary; May 14, 1934; US Citizen
EDUCATION: Univ of Budapest, Hungary, MA, 1956; Univ of Vienna, Austria, 1957–59; Univ of Chicago, IL 1963
TEACHING: Instr, Art, Univ of Northern Iowa, Cedar Falls, IA, 1964–66; Assoc Prof & Art in Res, St John's Univ, Collegeville, MN, 1966–80, Prof, Art, 1980 to present
AWARDS: Belobende Anerkennung, Acad of Fine Arts, Vienna, Austria, 1958; Graphic Prize, Univ of Chicago, IL, 1962; Purchase Award, Pittsburgh Invitational, PA, 1981

COLLECTIONS: Hungarian State Mus of Fine Art, Budapest, Hungary; Kunstmuseum, Bern, Switzerland; Univ of New Mexico Art Mus, Albuquerque, NM; Tweed Mus, Duluth, MN; Rhodes Nat Gallery, Salisbury, Rhodesia, Zimbabwe, Africa; Boston Public Library, MA
PRINTERS: Artist (ART)
PUBLISHERS: Artist (ART)
GALLERIES: Groveland Gallery, Minneapolis, MN; Kenneth Probst Galleries, Inc, Chicago, IL
MAILING ADDRESS: 400 NE Riverside Dr, St Cloud, MN 56301

TITLE	PUBLISHER	PRINTER	DATE	MEDIUM	DIMENSION (PAPER SIZE) IN INCHES	TYPE OF PAPER	EDITION NUMBER	NO. OF COLORS	ORIGINAL OPENING PRICE	CURRENT RETAIL PRICE
SOLD OUT EDITIONS (RARE):										
Houses on Malia	ART	ART	1976	LC	30 X 22	AP/B	15	8	150	200
Red Ships in Duluth	ART	ART	1977	LC	30 X 22	AP/B	15	9	150	200
Venetian Horses on Canea	ART	ART	1978	LC	16 X 20	AP/B	15	6	100	120
Three Ages	ART	ART	1979	LC	16 X 20	AP/B	20	7	100	120
Two Girls at the Sea	ART	ART	1979	LC	16 X 20	AP/B	15	6	100	120
CURRENT EDITIONS:										
Studio Table at Night	ART	ART	1979	LC	16 X 20	AP/B	15	3	120	120
The Salute Venice	ART	ART	1980	LC	16 X 20	AP/B	23	7	150	150
San Geremia at Night Art	ART	ART	1981	LC	8 X 10	AP/B	15	2	100	100
Santa Maria della Salute	ART	ART	1981	LC	28 X 23	AP/B	30	7	250	300
On the Beach	ART	ART	1982	LC	22 X 29	AP/B	20	7	250	250
A Tribute	ART	ART	1982	LC	22 X 17	AP/B	14	4	175	175

ANTONIO PETICOV

BORN: Sao Paulo, Brazil; July 2, 1946
AWARDS: Silver Medal, Sao Paulo, Brazil, 1966
COLLECTIONS: Mus of Mod Art, Rio de Janiero, Brazil; The Pace Coll, Dallas, TX

PRINTERS: Twichell-Nichols Studio, NY (T-N); Arte 3, Italy (A-3); Seri Graphico, Italy (SER)
PUBLISHERS: Fred Dorfman, Inc, NY (FDI)
GALLERIES: Sachs Gallery, Los Angeles, CA; Fred Dorfman Gallery, New York, NY

TITLE	PUBLISHER	PRINTER	DATE	MEDIUM	DIMENSION (PAPER SIZE) IN INCHES	TYPE OF PAPER	EDITION NUMBER	NO. OF COLORS	ORIGINAL OPENING PRICE	CURRENT RETAIL PRICE
SOLD OUT EDITIONS (RARE):										
Benediction	FDI	A-3	1977	SP	20 X 29	FAB	135	46	150	400
Scala Chromation	FDI	A-3	1977	SP	35 X 27	FAB	150	23	250	400

ANTONIO PETICOV CONTINUED

TITLE	PUBLISHER	PRINTER	DATE	MEDIUM	DIMENSION (PAPER SIZE) IN INCHES	TYPE OF PAPER	EDITION NUMBER	NO. OF COLORS	ORIGINAL OPENING PRICE	CURRENT RETAIL PRICE
SOLD OUT EDITIONS (RARE):										
Jungfrau, Day & Night	FDI	A-3	1977	SP	27 X 31	FAB	150	16	250	400
Hommage to M C Escher	FDI	A-3	1978	SP	30 X 22	FAB	150	23	150	400
Mitocondria	FDI	A-3	1979	SP	28 X 32	FAB	150	23	250	400
Santa Elena Canyon	FDI	A-3	1979	SP	36 X 25	FAB	150	26	250	400
Amsterdam Rainbow	FDI	A-3	1979	SP	27 X 35	FAB	200	28	250	400
Interaction II	FDI	SER	1979	SP	35 X 17	AP	100	14	150	400
Natura	FDI	A-3	1980	SP	27 X 31	FAB	195	15	250	400
Working Fine	FDI	A-3	1983	SP	27 X 20	AF	195	28	300	400
CURRENT EDITIONS:										
Light Series Folio:									900 SET	1200 SET
Light Explosions	FDI	TN	1981	SP	45 X 37	AE	30	15	300	500
Light Texture	FDI	TN	1981	SP	45 X 37	AE	30	15	300	500
Passing By	FDI	TN	1981	SP	45 X 37	AE	30	15	300	500
The Great Circle	FDI	A-3	1983	SP	28 X 33	FAB	195	28	300	350
The Golden Room	FDI	A-3	1984	SP	27 X 39	FAB	195	46	300	350

SYLVIA SPENCER PETRIE

BORN: Wooster, OH; June 15, 1931
EDUCATION: Col of Wooster, OH, 1949–53, BA, Honors in Art; State Univ of Iowa, Iowa City, IA, 1954–57, with Mauricie LaSansky
COLLECTIONS: Wooster Col Art Mus, OH; Univ of Rhode Island, Kingston, RI
PRINTERS: Artist (ART)
PUBLISHERS: Biscuit City Press, Kingston, RI (BCP); Artist (ART)
GALLERIES: Brewster Gallery, New York, NY; Artists Guild & Gallery, Charlestown, RI
MAILING ADDRESS: 200 Pendron Rd, Peace Dale, RI 02879

TITLE	PUBLISHER	PRINTER	DATE	MEDIUM	DIMENSION (PAPER SIZE) IN INCHES	TYPE OF PAPER	EDITION NUMBER	NO. OF COLORS	ORIGINAL OPENING PRICE	CURRENT RETAIL PRICE
SOLD OUT EDITIONS (RARE):										
Burning Mosque	ART	ART	1970	I	14 X 20	AP	20	2	30	150
Piano Lesson	ART	ART	1972	EC	15 X 12	RP	25	4	50	150
Refuge I	ART	ART	1976	COL	19 X 25	RP	3	2	100	175
Oakwoods	ART	ART	1977	COL	17 X 22	RP	10	2	75	150
CURRENT EDITIONS:										
Doll House, Series IV	ART	ART	1977	COL	22 X 17	RP	30	1	60	150
The Emperor's New Clothes	ART	ART	1977	COL	28 X 21	AP	20	2	100	150
Refuge II	ART	ART	1977	COL	19 X 25	RP	15	3	100	150
Blackbird	ART	ART	1978	COL	26 X 20	RP	20	2	100	150
Hill Top	ART	ART	1979	COL	19 X 25	RP	30	2	110	150
Nocturne	ART	ART	1980	COL	20 X 25	RP	30	3	110	150
The Far Country	ART	ART	1980	I	13 X 9	AP	60	4	30	150
Lost Sun	ART	ART	1980	COL	17 X 22	AP	30	3	85	150

DIMITRE PETROV

BORN: Pennsylvania; June 13, 1919
EDUCATION: Pennsylvania Acad of Fine Arts, Phila, PA
PRINTERS: Artist (ART)
PUBLISHERS: Fred Dorfman, Inc, NY (FDI)
GALLERIES: Princeton Gallery of Fine Art, Princeton, NY; Fred Dorfman Gallery, New York, NY; Gremillion & Company Fine Art, Inc, Houston, TX

TITLE	PUBLISHER	PRINTER	DATE	MEDIUM	DIMENSION (PAPER SIZE) IN INCHES	TYPE OF PAPER	EDITION NUMBER	NO. OF COLORS	ORIGINAL OPENING PRICE	CURRENT RETAIL PRICE
CURRENT EDITIONS:										
Rehearsal #1, #2	FDI	ART	1978	LC	22 X 30 EA	AP	250 EA	4	200 EA	250 EA
Breeze Weigh	FDI	ART	1978	LC	22 X 30	AP	250	4	200	400
Man Blowing his Own Destiny	FDI	ART	1978	LC	22 X 30	AP	250	4	200	400

JOHN PFAHL

BORN: New York, NY; 1939
RECENT EXHIB: New Gallery of Contemp Art, Cleveland, OH, 1987; Sun Valley Art Center Gallery, ID, 1988; Florida Gulf Coast Art Center, Belleair, FL, 1989; Janet Borden Gallery, Inc, NY, 1990; Art Inst of Chicago, IL, 1991; Photographer's Gallery of Palo Alto, CA, 1992; Friends of Photography, Ansel Adams Center, San Francisco, CA, 1992
COLLECTIONS: Art Inst of Chicago, IL
PUBLISHERS: Robert Freidus Gallery, NY (RF); Visual Studies Workshop, NY (VSW); Artist (ART)
GALLERIES: Nina Freudenheim Gallery, Buffalo, NY; Tortue Gallery, Santa Monica, CA; Visual Studies Workshop, New York, NY; Jones Troyer Fitzpatrick Gallery, Wash, DC; Janet Borden Gallery, Inc, New York, NY

TITLE	PUBLISHER	PRINTER	DATE	MEDIUM	DIMENSION (PAPER SIZE) IN INCHES	TYPE OF PAPER	EDITION NUMBER	NO. OF COLORS	ORIGINAL OPENING PRICE	CURRENT RETAIL PRICE
CURRENT EDITIONS:										
Altered Landscapes (Set of 10)	VSW/RF/ART	ART	1981	PH	14 X 17 EA	AP	24 EA		5000 SET	6500 SET

JUDY PFAFF

BORN: London, England; 1946
EDUCATION: Wayne State Univ, Detroit, MI, 1965; Southern Illinois Univ, Edwardsville, IL, 1986; Washington Univ, St Louis, MO, BFA, 1971; Yale Univ, New Haven, CT, MFA, 1973
TEACHING: Instr, Sculpture, Yale Univ, New Haven, CT, currently; Instr, Skowhegan Sch of Painting & Sculpture, ME, currently
RECENT EXHIB: Carnegie-Mellon Univ Art Gallery, Pittsburgh, PA, 1989
AWARDS: Creative Artists Public Service Award, Sculpture, 1976; John Simon Guggenheim Fel, Sculpture, 1983; Bessie Award, 1984; Nat Endowment for the Arts Fels, 1979,86
COLLECTIONS: Whitney Mus of Am Art, NY; Albright-Knox Art Gallery, Buffalo, NY

PRINTERS: Tadashi-Toda Kyoto, Japan (TT); Shi-un-do Print Shop, Kyoto, Japan (SPS); Lawrence Hamlin, San Francisco, CA (LH); Renee Bott, San Francisco, CA (RB); Brian Shure, San Francisco, CA (BS); Crown Point Press, San Francisco, CA (CPP)
PUBLISHERS: Crown Point Press, San Francisco, CA (CPP)
GALLERIES: Crown Point Press, NY & San Francisco, CA ; Holly Solomon Gallery, New York, NY; Nancy Singer Gallery, St Louis, MO; Charles Cowles Gallery, New York, NY; John Weber Gallery, New York, NY; Hudson Center Galleries, New York, NY; Mary Singer Gallery, Wash, DC; Susanne Hilberry Gallery, Birmingham, MI; Max Protetch Gallery, New York, NY
MAILING ADDRESS: 310 Greenwich St, New York, NY 10013

TITLE	PUBLISHER	PRINTER	DATE	MEDIUM	DIMENSION (PAPER SIZE) IN INCHES	TYPE OF PAPER	EDITION NUMBER	NO. OF COLORS	ORIGINAL OPENING PRICE	CURRENT RETAIL PRICE
SOLD OUT EDITIONS (RARE):										
Six of One Series:										
Meloné	CPP	CPP	1987	WC	55 X 63	HMP	25		7500	7500
Las Margaritas	CPP	CPP	1987	WC/CO	41 X 69	HMP/HOSHO	15		2500	6500
Manzanas y Naranjas	CPP	CPP	1987	WC/CO	59 X 70	HMP/HOSHO	15		2500	7500
Nella Popilla (Single Sheet)	CPP	CPP	1992	DPT/AB/SB/HG 14 X 68		HMP	5	1	2000	2200
Nella Popilla (Divided Sheet) (Dipt)	CPP	CPP	1992	DPT/AB/SB/HG 14 X 68		HMP	5	1	2000	2200
CURRENT EDITIONS:										
Yoyogi I,II	CPP	TT/SPS/CPP	1985	WC	32 X 36 EA	HMP	75 EA	18 EA	1250 EA	3800 EA
Six of One Series:										
La Ceña	CPP	CPP	1987	WC/CO	52 X 65	HMP/HOSHO	15		2500	5500
Maize	CPP	CPP	1987	WC/CO	45 X 69	HMP/HOSHO	15		2500	5500
Tatoes	CPP	CPP	1987	WC/CO	43 X 63	HMP/HOSHO	15		2500	6500
Half a Dozen of the Other Series:										
Ogni Cosa So Fa Ogni Cosa	CPP	CPP	1992	DPT/AB/SB/HG 43 X 51		HMP	20	1	3500	3500
De Lumi e Obra	CPP	CPP	1992	DPT/AB/SB/HG 43 X 51		HMP	20	1	3500	3500
Del Fumio e Polvera	CPP	CPP	1992	DPT/AB/SB/HG 43 X 51		HMP	20	1	3500	3500
Che Cosa e Acqua	CPP	CPP	1992	DPT/AB/SB/HG 43 X 51		HMP	20	1	3500	3500
Del Flusso e Riflusso	CPP	CPP	1992	DPT/AB/SB/HG 43 X 51		HMP	20	1	3500	3500
Delli Spiriti	CPP	CPP	1992	DPT/AB/SB/HG 43 X 51		HMP	20	1	3500	3500

ERWIN PFRANG

PRINTERS: Karl Imhof, Zurich, Switzerland (KI)
PUBLISHERS: David Nolan Gallery, NY (DNG)
GALLERIES: David Nolan Gallery, New York, NY

TITLE	PUBLISHER	PRINTER	DATE	MEDIUM	DIMENSION (PAPER SIZE) IN INCHES	TYPE OF PAPER	EDITION NUMBER	NO. OF COLORS	ORIGINAL OPENING PRICE	CURRENT RETAIL PRICE
CURRENT EDITIONS:										
Untitled	DNG	KI	1990	LB	12 X 17	RdB	45	1	400	500

ELLEN DENISE PHELAN

BORN: Detroit, MI; November 3, 1943
EDUCATION: Wayne State Univ, BFA, 1969, MFA,1971
TEACHING: Instr, Painting, California Inst of Arts, Valencia, CA 1978,79,83; Instr, Painting & Drawing, Sch of Visual Arts, NY, 1981-83
AWARDS: Nat Endowment for the Arts Grant, 1978-79
RECENT EXHIB: Cleveland State Univ Art Gallery, OH, 1992

PRINTERS: Maurice Sanchez, NY (MS); Artist (ART); Derriére L'Etiole Studios, NY (DES); Betty Winkler, NY (BW); Yama Prints, NY (YP); Jennifer Melby, NY (JM)
PUBLISHERS: Artist (ART); Derriére L'Etoile Studios, NY (DES); Grenfell Press, NY (GPr)
GALLERIES: Barbara Toll Fine Arts, New York, NY; Susanne Hilberry Gallery, Birmingham, MI; Betsy Senior Contemporary Prints, New York, NY; Asher/Faure Gallery, Long Beach, CA
MAILING ADDRESS: 284 Lafayette St, New York, NY 10012

TITLE	PUBLISHER	PRINTER	DATE	MEDIUM	DIMENSION (PAPER SIZE) IN INCHES	TYPE OF PAPER	EDITION NUMBER	NO. OF COLORS	ORIGINAL OPENING PRICE	CURRENT RETAIL PRICE
CURRENT EDITIONS:										
Untitled (Series 02-I-XI)(Series of 11)	ART/DES	ART/MS/DES	1990	MON	22 X 30 EA	WatP	1 EA	Varies	2500 EA	2500 EA
Mother and Daught (Esmerelda)	GrenPr	BW/YP	1990	PH/B	28 X 15	HAHN	29		1500	1800

The retail prices of the 100,000 limited edition prints quoted in this directory are subject to change. Print publishers, artists and galleries were the direct sources for these quotations. Prices in the secondary market listed as "Sold Out Editions (Rare)" indicate that the publisher has a limited supply of that print or that the print is difficult to locate in the galleries.

The Printworld Directory is accepting new applications for the seventh edition. Approximately 300 new artists will be accepted. Please use the two forms provided in the back section of this directory to submit biographical data and documentation of prints. Edition number of each print must not exceed 500 and the retail price must be $100 or more.

The print market has become very selective. For the first time since we published the first edition of The Printworld Directory in 1982, the prices of prints have been greatly reduced and greatly increased for the same artists by the most reputable and established print publishers. Check the fifth edition to understand the movement.

ELLEN DENISE PHELAN CONTINUED

TITLE	PUBLISHER	PRINTER	DATE	MEDIUM	DIMENSION (PAPER SIZE) IN INCHES	TYPE OF PAPER	EDITION NUMBER	NO. OF COLORS	ORIGINAL OPENING PRICE	CURRENT RETAIL PRICE
CURRENT EDITIONS:										
Garden Amagansett (Set of 7):									3500 SET	3500 SET
Small Shrub	GrenPr	JM	1990	PH/G/CC	22 X 15	HAHN	18		600	600
Garden Scroll I	GrenPr	JM	1990	PH/G/CC	22 X 15	HAHN	18		600	600
Garden Scroll II	GrenPr	JM	1990	PH/G/CC	22 X 15	HAHN	18		600	600
Spring: First Drawing	GrenPr	JM	1990	PH/G/CC	22 X 15	HAHN	18		600	600
Summer, Light Morning	GrenPr	JM	1990	PH/G/CC	22 X 15	HAHN	18		600	600
Bright Sky	GrenPr	JM	1990	PH/G/CC	22 X 15	HAHN	18		600	600
Autumn Wind	GrenPr	JM	1990	PH/G/CC	22 X 15	HAHN	18		600	600

FREDERICK PHILLIPS

BORN: England
COLLECTIONS: Hara Mus, Japan; British Contemp Art, London, England; McMurdoe Coll, Sydney, Australia
PRINTERS: Artist (ART)
PUBLISHERS: John Szoke Graphics, NY (JSG)
GALLERIES: John Szoke Graphics, New York, NY; Summa Galleries, New York, NY & Brooklyn, NY; Atlas Galleries, Inc, Chicago, IL

Frederick Phillips
Enclave
Courtesy John Szoke Graphics

TITLE	PUBLISHER	PRINTER	DATE	MEDIUM	DIMENSION (PAPER SIZE) IN INCHES	TYPE OF PAPER	EDITION NUMBER	NO. OF COLORS	ORIGINAL OPENING PRICE	CURRENT RETAIL PRICE
CURRENT EDITIONS:										
Looking Glass	JSG	ART	1989	SP	34 X 27	SOM	345	8	1200	1400
Reverie	JSG	ART	1990	SP	35 X 35	SOM	345	8	1200	1400
Enclave	JSG	ART	1990	SP	26 X 36	SOM	345	6	1200	1400

JAY C PHILLIPS, III

BORN: Albuquerque, NM; (1954–1987)
EDUCATION: New Mexico State Univ, Las Cruces, NM, 1972–73; Univ of New Mexico, Albuquerque, NM, BFA, Painting & Printmaking, 1976; Printmaking Workshop, NY, Intaglio, 1977; Art, Paper & Technology Conf, World Print Council, San Francisco Mus of Art, 1978; Claremont Grad Sch, MFA, Printmaking & Painting, 1979
AWARDS: Young Talent Award, Los Angeles County Mus of Art, Arts Council, 1981

COLLECTIONS: Los Angeles County Mus of Art, CA
PRINTERS: Gary Reams (GR); Robert Knisel (RK); Smith/Andersen Gallery, Palo Alto, CA (SA); Lynne Allen, Albuquerque, NM (LA); Tamarind Inst Workshop, Albuquerque, NM (TI);
PUBLISHERS: Roy Boyd Gallery, Chicago, IL (RBG); Smith/ Andersen Gallery, Palo Alto, CA (SA); Tamarind Inst, Albuquerque, NM (TI)
GALLERIES: Roy Boyd Gallery, Chicago, IL & Los Angeles, CA; B Z Wagman Gallery, St Louis, MO; Smith/Andersen Gallery, Palo Alto, CA; Marlborough Gallery, New York, NY; Tamarind Inst, Albuquerque, NM; Dunlap-Freidenrich Fine Art, Newport Beach, CA

TITLE	PUBLISHER	PRINTER	DATE	MEDIUM	DIMENSION (PAPER SIZE) IN INCHES	TYPE OF PAPER	EDITION NUMBER	NO. OF COLORS	ORIGINAL OPENING PRICE	CURRENT RETAIL PRICE
SOLD OUT EDITIONS (RARE):										
Cardinal Series	SA	SA	1982	MON	34 X 42 EA	AP	1 EA	1 EA	500 EA	1000 EA
Serram Suite (Set of 5) (Diecut and Folded)	RBG	GR/RK	1981	SP	37 X 40 X 3	MRB	44		4275 SET	7500 SET
Untitled (JP-82-1)	SA	SA	1982	EB/A	22 X 28	AP	16		400	800
Untitled (JP-82-2)	SA	SA	1982	EB/A	23 X 30	AP	16		400	800
Untitled (JP-82-3)	SA	SA	1982	EB/A	23 X 30	AP	20		400	800
Untitled (JP-82-3B)	SA	SA	1982	EB/A	23 X 30	AP	16		400	800
Untitled (JP-82-4)	SA	SA	1982	EB/A	23 X 30	AP	16		400	800
Untitled (JP-82-4B)	SA	SA	1982	EB/A	23 X 30	AP	16		400	800
Beverly (JP-82-5)	SA	SA	1982	EB/A	19 X 23	AP	18		300	600
Beverly (JP-82-5B)	SA	SA	1982	EB/A	19 X 23	AP	22		300	600
Melrose (JP-82-6)	SA	SA	1982	EB/A	19 X 23	AP	20		300	600
Melrose (JP-82-6B)	SA	SA	1982	EB/A	19 X 23	AP	20		300	600
Untitled (JP-82-1B)	SA	SA	1982	EB	23 X 28	AP	6	1	400	800
Untitled (JP-82-2B)	SA	SA	1982	EB/A	23 X 30	AP	8		300	800

JAY C PHILLIPS, III CONTINUED

TITLE	PUBLISHER	PRINTER	DATE	MEDIUM	DIMENSION (PAPER SIZE) IN INCHES	TYPE OF PAPER	EDITION NUMBER	NO. OF COLORS	ORIGINAL OPENING PRICE	CURRENT RETAIL PRICE
CURRENT EDITIONS:										
Evening Arcade	TI	MB/TI	1984	LC/CO	26 X 32	GE/ARJ/JP	40	6	500	500
Summer Arcade	TI	MB/TI	1984	LC/CO	26 X 32	GE/ARJ/JP	40	7	500	500
Descent of Discord	TI	MB/TI	1984	LC	26 X 32	GE/ARJ/JP	40	6	500	500
Landscape	TI	LA/TI	1984	LC/MON	30 X 37	ARJ	12	Varies	950	950

MATT PHILLIPS

BORN: New York, NY
EDUCATION: Univ of Chicago, IL, MA; Standford Univ, CA; Barnes Found, Merion, PA
TEACHING: Prof, Head, Dept of Art, Bard Col, Annandale-on-Hudson, NY, 1964
RECENT EXHIB: Bannatyne Gallery, Santa Monica, CA, 1990
COLLECTIONS: Nat Coll of Fine Arts, Wash, DC; Whitney Mus of Am Art, NY; Metropolitan Mus of Art, NY; Nat Gallery of Art, Wash, DC; Philadelphia Mus of Art, PA

PRINTERS: Smith Andersen Gallery, Palo Alto, CA (3EP); Katherine Lincoln Press, San Francisco, CA (KLP); Pondside Press, Rhineback, NY
PUBLISHERS: Smith Andersen Gallery, Palo Alto, CA (3EP); Artist (ART)
GALLERIES: Donald Morris Gallery, Birmingham, MI; Dolly Fiterman Gallery, Minneapolis, MN; Marilyn Pearl Gallery, New York, NY; Keny & Johnson Gallery, Columbus, OH; Smith Andersen Gallery, Palo Alto, CA; Marsha Mateyka Gallery, Wash, DC; Wirtz Gallery, San Francisco, CA; Pondside Press, Rhinebeck, NY; Marilyn Pearl Gallery, New York, NY; Bannatyne Gallery, Santa Monica, CA
MAILING ADDRESS: c/o Forum Gallery, 1018 Madison Ave, New York, NY 10021

TITLE	PUBLISHER	PRINTER	DATE	MEDIUM	DIMENSION (PAPER SIZE) IN INCHES	TYPE OF PAPER	EDITION NUMBER	NO. OF COLORS	ORIGINAL OPENING PRICE	CURRENT RETAIL PRICE
CURRENT EDITIONS:										
New York Recalled	SA	SA	1979	MON	Varies		1 EA		900 EA	1000 EA
Morocco Remembered	SA	SA	1983	MON	43 X 52 EA		1 EA		2000 EA	5000 EA
Morocco Remembered	SA	SA	1983	MON	67 X 42 EA		1 EA		3000 EA	6000 EA
The Moroccans (Set of 6):									600 SET	1000 SET
Prelude	ART	KLP	1983	DPT	21 X 15	R/BFK	20	1	100	200
At the Cafe	ART	KLP	1983	DPT	21 X 15	R/BFK	20	1	100	200
Conversation	ART	KLP	1983	DPT	21 X 15	R/BFK	20	1	100	200
By the Sea	ART	KLP	1983	DPT	21 X 15	R/BFK	20	1	100	200
Crowded Souk	ART	KLP	1983	DPT	21 X 15	R/BFK	20	1	100	200
Mysterious Gathering	ART	KLP	1983	DPT	21 X 15	R/BFK	20	1	100	200
The Moroccans (Deluxe) (Set of 6):									1200 SET	2000 SET
Prelude	ART	KLP	1983	DPT	21 X 15	HMP	20	1	200	350
At the Cafe	ART	KLP	1983	DPT	21 X 15	HMP	20	1	200	350
Conversation	ART	KLP	1983	DPT	21 X 15	HMP	20	1	200	350
By the Sea	ART	KLP	1983	DPT	21 X 15	HMP	20	1	200	350
Crowded Souk	ART	KLP	1983	DPT	21 X 15	HMP	20	1	200	350
Mysterious Gathering	ART	KLP	1983	DPT	21 X 15	HMP	20	1	200	350

TOM PHILLIPS

BORN: London, England; 1937
EDUCATION: St Catherine's Col, London, England; Camberwell Sch of Art, London, England
TEACHING: Bath Academy of Art, London, England; Wolverhampton Col of Art, London, England
COLLECTIONS: Mus of Mod Art, NY; Philadelphia Mus of Art, Phila, PA; Nat Gallery of Australia, Sydney, Australia; Mus of Mod Art, New Delhi, India; Bibliotheque Nat, Paris, France; British Mus, London, England; Tate Gallery, London, England; Nat Mus of Art, Stockholm, Sweden; Gemeentemuseum, The Hague, Netherlands

PRINTERS: Chris Betambeau, London, England (CB); Advanced Graphics, London, England (AG); Brad Fane, London, England (BF); Coriander Press, London, England (CP); The Talfourd Press, London, England (TP); White Ink, London, England (WI); Dog's Ear Press, London, England (DEP); Nick Tite, London, England (NT); Nick Hunter, London, England (NH)
PUBLISHERS: Waddington Graphics, London, England (WG); Artist (ART)
GALLERIES: Waddington Graphics, London, England; Joy Moos Gallery, Miami, FL; Marita Gilliam Gallery, Raleigh, NC

TITLE	PUBLISHER	PRINTER	DATE	MEDIUM	DIMENSION (PAPER SIZE) IN INCHES	TYPE OF PAPER	EDITION NUMBER	NO. OF COLORS	ORIGINAL OPENING PRICE	CURRENT RETAIL PRICE
SOLD OUT EDITIONS (RARE):										
Walk to the Studio (Set of 6):										
Art on the Road	WG	WI	1976	SP	40 X 28	AC	50		220	1500
Eleven Emblems of Violence	WG	WI	1976	SP	40 X 28	AC	50		220	1500
A Grammar of Ornament	WG	WI	1976	SP	40 X 28	AC	50		220	1500
Linoleum	WG	WI	1976	SP	40 X 20	AC	50		220	1500
Matching Colours Struck by Heatwave	WG	WI	1976	SP	40 X 28	AC	50		220	1500
Sixty-Four Stopcock Box Lids	WG	WI	1976	SP	40 X 28	AC	50		220	1500

The Printworld Directory is accepting new applications for the seventh edition. Approximately 300 new artists will be accepted. Please use the two forms provided in the back section of this directory to submit biographical data and documentation of prints. Edition number of each print must not exceed 500 and the retail price must be $100 or more.

TOM PHILLIPS CONTINUED

TITLE	PUBLISHER	PRINTER	DATE	MEDIUM	DIMENSION (PAPER SIZE) IN INCHES	TYPE OF PAPER	EDITION NUMBER	NO. OF COLORS	ORIGINAL OPENING PRICE	CURRENT RETAIL PRICE
SOLD OUT EDITIONS (RARE):										
Composers (Set of 6):										
Debussy	WG	CB/AG	1979	SP	26 X 28	R/BFK	75		270	1800
Elgar	WG	CB/AG	1979	SP	26 X 28	R/BFK	75		270	1500
Mozart	WG	CB/AG	1979	SP	26 X 28	R/BFK	75		270	1500
Schönberg	WG	CB/AG	1979	SP	26 X 28	R/BFK	75		270	1500
Schumann	WG	CB/AG	1979	SP	26 X 28	R/BFK	75		270	1500
Wagner	WG	CB/AG	1979	SP	26 X 28	R/BFK	75		270	1500
Benches	WG	BF/CP	1982	SP	40 X 30	R/BFK	85		540	1500
CURRENT EDITIONS:										
Dante's Inferno (Set of 9):									2200 SET	12000 SET
Dante in his Study	WG	AG	1982	SP	30 X 22	R/BFK	75		450	1800
The Dark Wood	WG	AG	1982	SP	30 X 22	R/BFK	75		450	1500
Flying Man and the Ape of Nature	WG	AG	1982	SP	30 X 22	R/BFK	75		450	1500
A Folly for Wisdom	WG	AG	1982	SP	30 X 22	R/BFK	75		450	1500
Geryon, the Monster of Fraud	WG	AG	1982	SP	30 X 22	R/BFK	75		450	1500
Schismatics (the Skin Game and the Berlin Wall)	WG	AG	1982	SP	30 X 22	R/BFK	75		450	1500
Veltro	WG	AG	1982	SP	30 X 22	R/BFK	75		450	1500
Virgil in his Study	WG	AG	1982	SP	30 X 22	R/BFK	75		450	1500
The Wood of Suicides	WG	AG	1982	SP	30 X 22	R/BFK	75		450	1500
Dante's Inferno-the Artist's Illustrated Translation	WG	NT/TP/NH/ DEP/BF/CP/AG	1983	LC/SP/I	17 X 13	CRIS	185		12000	20000
Excerpts from the Dante Diary	ART	CB/AG	1983	SP/PH	28 X 41	CRIS	60		500	1200
Beckett	WG		1984	LB	28 X 17	CRIS	75		150	300
Beckett at Riverside	WG		1984	LB	15 X 11	CRIS	30		125	250

JOSEPH PICCILLO

BORN: Buffalo, NY; January 9, 1941
EDUCATION: State Univ of New York, Buffalo, NY, MFA, 1964
TEACHING: Prof, Art, State Univ of New York, Buffalo, NY, 1967 to present
AWARDS: Childe Hassam Purchase Award, Am Acad of Arts & Letters, NY, 1968; Nat Endowment for the Arts Fel, 1979
RECENT EXHIB: Betsy Rosenfield Gallery, Chicago, IL, 1988; Elliot Smith Gallery, St Louis, MO, 1988; Barbara Fendrick Gallery, NY, 1988; Brendan Walter Gallery, Santa Monica, CA, 1990
COLLECTIONS: Mus of Mod Art, NY; Brooklyn Mus, NY; Butler Inst of Am Art, Youngstown, OH; Southern Illinois Univ, Carbondale, IL; Minnesota Mus, Minneapolis, MN; Metropolitan Mus of Art, NY
PRINTERS: Jack Lemon, Chicago, IL (JL); Landfall Press, Inc, Chicago, IL (LPI)
PUBLISHERS: Landfall Press, Inc, Chicago, IL (LPI)
GALLERIES: Betsy Rosenfield Gallery, Inc, Chicago, IL; Signet Arts, St Louis, MO; Hadler/Rodriguez, Houston, TX; Landfall Press Inc, Chicago, IL; Elliot Smith Gallery, St Louis, MO; Barbara Fendrick Gallery, New York, NY; Brendan Walter Gallery, Santa Monica, CA; Iannuzzi Gallery, Scottsdale, AZ
MAILING ADDRESS: c/o State University of New York, Dept of Art, 1300 Elmwood Ave, Buffalo, NY 14222

TITLE	PUBLISHER	PRINTER	DATE	MEDIUM	DIMENSION (PAPER SIZE) IN INCHES	TYPE OF PAPER	EDITION NUMBER	NO. OF COLORS	ORIGINAL OPENING PRICE	CURRENT RETAIL PRICE
CURRENT EDITIONS:										
Edge Event I	LPI	JL/LPI	1981	LC	32 X 47	ARJ	45	3	750	1200
Edge Event II	LPI	JL/LPI	1981	LC	34 X 29	ARJ	25	2	750	1200
Edge Event III	LPI	JL/LPI	1981	LC	38 X 31	ARJ	16	2	750	1200
Head	LPI	JL/LPI	1982	LC	19 X 19	ARJ	20	2	200	250
EP I,II,III	LPI	JL/LPI	1992	EB	22 X 30 EA	R/BFK	25 EA	1 EA	700 EA	700 EA

PAUL PLETKA

BORN: San Diego, CA; 1946
EDUCATION: Arizona State Univ, Tempe, AZ; Colorado State Univ, Ft Collins, CO
AWARDS: Certificate of Excellence, Chicago Inst, IL, 1976; Nat Watercolor Society Award, 1977
RECENT EXHIB: Indianapolis Mus of Art, IN, 1987; Phoenix Art Mus, AZ, 1988
COLLECTIONS: Phoenix Art Mus, AZ; Minneapolis Inst of Art, MN; Milwaukee Fine Arts Center, WI; St Louis Art Mus, MO; San Antonio Mus of Art, TX
PRINTERS: Artist (ART)
PUBLISHERS: Artist (ART)
GALLERIES: ACA Galleries, New York, NY; Frameworks Gallery, Grand Junction, CO; Gallery 10, Inc, Phoenix, AZ & Scottsdale, AZ & New York, NY; Susan Duval Gallery, Aspen, CO; Naravisa Press, Santa Fe, NM
MAILING ADDRESS: c/o Western Colorado Art Center, 1803 N Seventh, Grand Junction, CO 81501

TITLE	PUBLISHER	PRINTER	DATE	MEDIUM	DIMENSION (PAPER SIZE) IN INCHES	TYPE OF PAPER	EDITION NUMBER	NO. OF COLORS	ORIGINAL OPENING PRICE	CURRENT RETAIL PRICE
CURRENT EDITIONS:										
There is No Center...	ART	ART	1975	LC	23 X 30	AP	50		500	3500
Ghost Dancer	ART	ART	1976	LC	22 X 30	AP	100		500	3500

The retail prices of the 100,000 limited edition prints quoted in this directory are subject to change. Print publishers, artists and galleries were the direct sources for these quotations. Prices in the secondary market listed as "Sold Out Editions (Rare)" indicate that the publisher has a limited supply of that print or that the print is difficult to locate in the galleries.

PABLO PICASSO

BORN: Málaga, Spain; (1881–1973)
RECENT EXHIB: Fisk Univ, Carl Van Vechten Gallery of Fine Arts, Nashville, TN, 1993; Solomon R Guggenheim Mus, NY, 1993; Phoenix Art Mus, AZ, 1993, Arkansas Arts Center, Little Rock, AR, 1993; Norton Simon Mus of Art, Pasadena, CA, 1993; Belian Art Center, Troy, MI, 1993; Univ of Missouri, Colombia, MO, 1993; St Louis Art Mus, MO, 1993; Albright-Knox Art Gallery, Buffalo, NY, 1993; Nassau County Mus of Fine Art, Roslyn Harbor, NY, 1993; Munson-Williams-Proctor Inst of Art Mus, Utica, NY, 1993; SCARABB Gallery, Cleveland, OH, 1993; Oberlin Col, Allen Mem Mus, OH, 1993; Philadelphia Art Mus, PA, 1993; Dallas Mus of Art, TX, 1993; Southern Methodist Univ, Meadows Mus, Dallas, TX, 1993; Kimball Art Mus, Fort Worth, TX, 1993; McNay Art Mus, San Antonio, TX, 1993; Galerie Gmurzynska, Cologne, Germany, 1993
PRINTERS: Atelier Frélaut, Paris, France (AF); Atelier Lacouriere, Paris, France (AL); Charlot Fréres, Paris, France (CF); Atelier Mourlot, Paris, France (AM); Atelier Arnera, Vallauris, France (AA); Delatré (DEL)
PUBLISHERS: Kahnweiler (KAHN); Vollard (VOL); Limited Edition Club, NY (LEC); Flammarion, Paris, France (FLAM); Galerie Louise Leiris, Paris, France (GLL); Atelier Mourlot, André Sauret, Monte Carlo, France (AS); George Braziller, NY (GB); Albert Skira, NY (ASK); Cercle d'Art, Paris, France (CDA); Marcel Guiot, Paris, France (MG)
GALLERIES: Bowles-Sorokko Galleries, Beverly Hills, CA & San Francisco, CA & New York, NY; Galerie Michael, Beverly Hills, CA; R K Goldman & Company, Los Angeles, CA; Louis Newman Gallery, Beverly Hills, CA; Charles Whitchurch Gallery, Huntington Beach, CA; Hanson Galleries, La Jolla, CA; Noble House, Los Angeles, CA; Herbert Palmer, Los Angeles, CA; Jack Rutberg Fine Arts, Los Angeles, CA; Edward Weston Fine Arts, Northridge, CA; Bond Street Gallery, Oakland, CA; Galerie Cujas, San Diego, CA; Eleanore Austerer Gallery, San Francisco, CA; Harcourts Modern & Contemporary, San Francisco, CA; Erika Meyerovich Gallery, San Francisco, CA; Walton-Gilbert Galleries, San Rafael, CA; Travelli Gallery, Aspen, CO; Georgetown Gallery of Art, Wash, DC; Galerie Lareuse, Wash, DC; Modernism Gallery, Coral Gables, FL; Apropos Art Gallery, Fort Lauderdale, FL; Barbara Scott Gallery, Bay Harbor Islands, FL; Atlanta Art Gallery, Atlanta, GA; Greggie Fine Art, Atlanta, GA; Richard Gray Gallery, Chicago, IL; R S Johnson Fine Art, Chicago, IL; Merrill Chase Galleries, Chicago, IL; Stein Bartlow Gallery, Ltd, Chicago, IL; Litwin Gallery, Wichita, KS; Rolly-Michaux Galleries, Ltd, Boston, MA; Eliza Spencer Gallery, Boston, MA; Gallery Internationale, Bloomfield Hills, MI; Donald Morris Gallery, Birmingham, MI; Kodner Gallery of the Masters, Inc, St Louis, MO; Galleria Maray, Allendale, NJ; Scherer Gallery, Marlboro, NJ; Claude Bernard Gallery, New York, NY; Hilde Gerst Gallery, New York, NY; Belgis-Freidel Gallery, New York, NY; Hirsch & Adler Galleries, New York, NY; Pasquale Iannetti Art Galleries, New York, NY & San Francisco, CA; Cohen Gallery, New York, NY; Elkon Gallery, Inc, New York, NY; Peter Findlay Gallery, New York, NY; Galleria Durini, Ltd, New York, NY; Isselbacher Gallery, New York, NY; Jane Kahan Gallery, New York, NY; Jan Krugier Gallery, New York, NY; Magidson Fine Art, New York, NY & Aspen, CO; Hammer Galleries, New York, NY; Hubert Gallery, New York, NY; Barbara Leibowits Graphics, New York, NY; Walter F Maibaum Fine Arts, Inc, New York, NY; Barbara Mathes Gallery, New York, NY; Pace Master Prints, New York, NY; Ro Gallery Image Makers, Inc, New York, NY; Michelle Rosenfeld Gallery, New York, NY; Susan Sheehan Gallery, Inc, New York, NY; Simon/Neuman Gallery, New York, NY; Sindin Galleries, New York, NY; Solomon & Company, New York, NY; Studio 53, New York, NY; Martin Sumers Graphics, New York, NY; Leila Taghinia-Milani, New York, NY; David Tunich, Inc, New York, NY; Yoshii Gallery, New York, NY; Uptown Gallery, New York, NY; Hartwick Col, Foreman Gallery, Oenonta, NY; Charles Foley Gallery, Columbus, OH; Nicolae Galerie, Columbus, OH; Jeffrey Fuller Fine Art, Ltd, Phila, PA; Contemporary Gallery, Dallas, TX; Neuhoff Galleries, Houston, TX; Broden Gallery, Ltd, Madison, WI; Posner Gallery, Milwaukee, WI; Galerie Gmurzynska, Cologne, Germany; Professional Fine Arts Services, Inc, New York, NY

Bloch (B); Geiser (G); Mourlot (M); Cramer (C); Baer (Baer)

Pablo Picasso
Le Repas Frugal
Courtesy Avantgarde Art Associates

Pablo Picasso
L'Homme a la Guitare
Courtesy Avantgarde Art Associates

PABLO PICASSO CONTINUED

Pablo Picasso
Femme au Chignon
Courtesy Avantgarde Art Associates

Pablo Picasso
Tete de Femme, No 6
Courtesy Atelièr Lacouriére

TITLE	PUBLISHER	PRINTER	DATE	MEDIUM	DIMENSION (PAPER SIZE) IN INCHES	TYPE OF PAPER	EDITION NUMBER	NO. OF COLORS	ORIGINAL OPENING PRICE	CURRENT RETAIL PRICE
SOLD OUT EDITIONS (RARE):										
Saltimbanques Suite:										
Le Repas Frugal (B-1) (G-2)	VOL		1904	EB	18 X 15	WOVE	250	1	30	190000
Tete de Femme (B-2) (G-3)	VOL		1905	EB	5 X 4	WOVE	250	1	10	10000
Les Saltimbanques (B-7) (G-9)	VOL		1905	DPT	11 X 13	WOVE	250	1	20	20000
L'Abreuvoir (B-8) (G-10)	VOL		1905	DPT	13 X 20	WOVE	250	1	30	5000
Le Bain (B-12) (G-14)	VOL		1905	DPT	14 X 11	WOVE	250	1	20	20000
La Tollette de la Mere (B-13) (G-15)	VOL		1905	EB	15 X 13	WOVE	250	1	20	12000
La Danse (B-15) (G-18)	VOL		1905	DPT	7 X 9	WOVE	250	1	10	8000
Deux Figures Nues (B-17) (G-21)			1909	DPT	5 X 4	LAID		1	10	13000
Nature Morte, Compotier (B-18) (G-22)	KAHN	DEL	1909	DPT	15 X 12	WOVE	100	1	35	16000
Nature Morte, á la Bouteille de Marc (B-24) (G-16) (Baer-33b)	KAHN	DEL	1912	DPT	20 X 12	AP	100	1	35	60000
Tete D'Homme (B-23) (G-32)	KAHN	DEL	1912	EB	5 X 4	WOVE	100	1	25	25000
L'Homme a la Guitare (B-30) (G-51)	MG		1915	ENG	6 X 5	JP	100	1	35	40000
Taureau Attaquant un Cheval (B-44) (G-60)		AF	1921	EB	7 X 9	WOVE	101	1	30	7000
Le Collier		AF	1922–23	DPT	7 X 5	AP	50	1	30	18000
Les Trois Baigneuses II		AF	1922–23	EB	7 X 5	AP	50	1	30	15000
Scéne d'Interieur (B-72)	GS	CF	1926	LB	9 X 11	VGP	100	1	40	15000
Le Modele Nu (B-78) (G-119)			1927	EB	11 X 8	JP	150	1	50	7000
Vollard Suite:										
Femme Nue Assise Devant un Rideau (B-137) (G-202)	VOL		1933	EB	12 X 9	WOVE	300	1	35	7000
Homme Devoilant une Femme (B-138) (G-203)	VOL		1933	EB	15 X 12	WOVE	300	1	35	7000
Sculpteur, Modele et Buste Sculpte (B-148) (G-300)	VOL		1933	EB	11 X 8	WOVE	300	1	35	7000
Modele Accoude Sur an Tableau (B-151) (G-303)	VOL		1933	EB	11 X 8	WOVE	300	1	35	14000
Le Repos du Sculpteur et le Modele au Masque (B-159) (G-312)	VOL		1933	EB	11 X 8	WOVE	300	1	35	10000
Le Repos du Sculpteur Devant le Petit Torse (B-162) (G-315)	VOL		1933	EB	8 X 11	WOVE	300	1	35	8000

PABLO PICASSO CONTINUED

TITLE	PUBLISHER	PRINTER	DATE	MEDIUM	DIMENSION (PAPER SIZE) IN INCHES	TYPE OF PAPER	EDITION NUMBER	NO. OF COLORS	ORIGINAL OPENING PRICE	CURRENT RETAIL PRICE
SOLD OUT EDITIONS (RARE):										
Repos du Sculpteur Devant le Jeune Cavalier (B-164) (G-317)	VOL		1933	EB	8 X 11	WOVE	300	1	35	11000
Repos du Sculpteur Devant des Chevaux et un Taureau (B-166) (G-319)	VOL		1933	EB	8 X 11	WOVE	300	1	35	6000
Repos du Sculpteur Devant un Centaure et une Femme (B-167) (G-320)	VOL		1933	EB	8 X 11	WOVE	300	1	35	10000
Modele et Grand Tete Sculptee (B-170) (G-323)	VOL		1933	EB	11 X 8	WOVE	300	1	35	7000
Le Repos de Sculpteur I, II, III (B-171) (G-324)	VOL		1933	EB	8 X 11 EA	WOVE	300 EA	1 EA	35 EA	10000 EA
Trois Femmes Nues Pres d'une Fenetre (B-176) (G-329)	VOL		1933	EB	15 X 12	WOVE	300	1	40	14000
Sculpteur et Modele Debout (B-177) (G-330)	VOL		1933	EB	14 X 12	WOVE	300	1	40	16000
Modele et Sculpture Surrealiste (B-187) (G-346)	VOL		1933	EB	11 X 8	WOVE	300	1	35	10000
Minotaure Caressant une Femme (B-191) (G-350)	VOL		1933	EB	12 X 15	WOVE	300	1	40	18000
Scene Bachique au Minotaure (B-192) (G-351)	VOL		1933	EB	12 X 15	WOVE	300	1	40	25000
Minotaure Vaineu (B-197) (G-365)	VOL		1933	EB	8 X 11	WOVE	300	1	35	7000
Minotaure Mourant (B-198) (G-366)	VOL		1933	EB	8 X 11	WOVE	300	1	35	6000
Minotaure, Buveur et Femmes (B-200) (G-368)	VOL		1934	EB	11 X 8	WOVE	300	1	35	18000
Rembrandt a la Palette (B-208) (G-406)	VOL		1933	EB	11 X 8	WOVE	300	1	35	6000
Femme Assise au Chapeau et Femme Debout Drapee (B-210) (G-408)	VOL		1933	EB	11 X 8	WOVE	300	1	35	12000
Quatre Femmes Nues et tete Sculptee (B-219) (G-424)	VOL		1934	EB	9 X 12	WOVE	300	1	40	40000
Minotaure Aveugle Guidé par une Fillette dans la Nuit (B-225) (G-437)	VOL		1934	AB	10 X 14	WOVE	300	1	45	75000
Taureau Aile Contemple par Quatre Enfants (B-229) (G-444)	VOL		1934	EB	9 X 12	WOVE	300	1	40	18000
Faune Dévoilant une Femme (B-230)	VOL		1936	EB/A	13 X 16	AP	300		40	60000
Portrait de Vollard II (B-231)	VOL		1937	EB	14 X 10	WOVE	300	1	35	5000
Femme Terero I (B-1329) (G-425)		AL	1934	EB	20 X 27	WOVE	50	1	40	8000
Lysistrata d'Aristophane (Set of 6) (B-267–274) (G-387–392)	LEC		1934	EB	15 X 11 EA	WOVE	150 EA	1 EA	300 SET	40000 SET
Trois Femmes: Les Trois Graces Couronnees de Fleurs (B-303)		AF	1938	EB	12 X 8	AP	50	1	50	13500
Femmes au Fauteuil: Dora Maar (B-318)			1939	AB/ENG	12 X 10	WOVE	50	1	50	8000
Tete de Femme, No 6 (Portrait of Dora Maar) (B-1338) (Baer-654/D)	AL		1939	AC	12 X 9	LAID	106	4	60	20000
Six Contes Fantasques: Nu au Collier (B-365)	FLAM	AL	1944	ENG	14 X 11	WOVE	30	1	75	11000
Femme Chevre et Nu: Faunesse et Femme			1945	EB	12 X 9	WOVE		1	60	10000
Tete de Jeune Fille (B-393) (M-9)	AM	AM	1946	LB	12 X 10	AP	50	1	75	9500
Composition au Vase de Fleurs (B-426) (M-74)	AM	AM	1947	LC	18 X 24	AP	50		125	16000
Jeunes Femmes Nues Reposant (B-453) (M-102)	AM	AM	1947	LB	19 X 24	AP	50	1	100	13000
Pan (B-518) (M-111)	AM	AM	1948	LB	30 X 22	AP	50	1	200	55000
Femme au Fauteuil No 1 (B-587) (M-134)	AM	AM	1949	LB	30 X 22	AP	50	1	250	75000
Le Chevalier et le Page (B-684) (M-200)	AM	AM	1951	LB	15 X 11	AP	50	1	150	3500
La Femme a' la Fenétre	GLL	AL	1952	AC	36 X 25	AP	50		600	160000
Tarse de Femme (B-746)	GLL	AL	1953	AB	24 X 36	AP	50		500	200000
Faun (B-793) (M-220)	AM	AM	1954	LC	11 X 10	AP	50		500	3000
Femme au Chignon (B-853) (M-310)	AM	AM	1957	LB	22 X 17	AP	50	1	400	50000
Buste au Corsage a Carreau (B-850) (M-308)	AM	AM	1958	LB	22 X 17	AP	50		60	60000
Buste de Femme d'Apres Cranach (B-859)			1958	LI	26 X 21	AP	50		600	275000

PABLO PICASSO CONTINUED

Pablo Picasso
Grande Tete de Femme au Chapeau
Courtesy Sotheby's

Pablo Picasso
Homme Barbu Couronne de Vigne
Courtesy Sotheby's

TITLE	PUBLISHER	PRINTER	DATE	MEDIUM	DIMENSION (PAPER SIZE) IN INCHES	TYPE OF PAPER	EDITION NUMBER	NO. OF COLORS	ORIGINAL OPENING PRICE	CURRENT RETAIL PRICE
SOLD OUT EDITIONS (RARE):										
Jacqueline au Mouchoir Noir (B-873) (M-316)			1958	LB	25 X 19	AP	50	1	600	40000
Bacchanale au Hibou (B-938)			1959	LI	21 X 25	AP	50		600	25000
Bacchanale au Taureau (B-933)			1959	LI	21 X 25	AP	50		600	60000
Pique (Noir et Beige)	GLL	AA	1959	LI	21 X 25	AP	50		750	25000
Le Picador (B-1013) (M-347)			1961	LB	7 X 9	AP	50	1	400	4000
La Pique (B-1014) (M-346)	AS		1961	LB		AP	50	1	400	4000
Jeu de Cape (B-1015) (M-348)	AS		1961	LB		AP	50	1	400	4000
Les Banderilles (B-1016) (M-349)	AS		1961	LB		AP	50	1	400	4000
Le Picador II (B-1017) (M-350)	AS		1961	LB		AP	50	1	400	4000
Football (B-1019) (M-356)			1961	LC	18 X 25	AP	200		500	5000
Le Petite Bacchanale (B-1020)			1959–61	LI	10 X 9	AP	50		500	3000
Madoura, 81, Rue d'Antibes, Cannes-AM, 1961 (B-1296)			1961	LI	25 X 21	AP	100		500	3000
Tete de Garcon (B-1025)			1962	LI	21 X 18	AP	50		500	3000
Déjuner sur L'Herbe (B-1027)			1962	LI	21 X 25	AP	50		500	160000
Grande Tete de Femme (B-1078)	GLL	AA	1962	LI	25 X 21	AP	50		600	50000
Jacqueline au Chapeau Noir (B-1028)			1962	LI	30 X 26	AP	50		600	95000
Danae (B-1084)			1962	LI	11 X 14	AP	50	5	500	60000
Buste de Femme au Chapeau (B-1072)			1962	LI	25 X 30	AP	50		750	250000
Femme au Bandeau (B-1081)			1962	LI	14 X 11	AP	50		500	40000
Homme Barbu Couronne de Vigne (B-1089) (Baer-1310)			1962	LI	14 X 11	AP	50		500	25000
Nature Morte a la Pasteque (B-1098)			1962	LI	23 X 30	AP	160		750	40000
Nature Morte sous la Lampe (B-1101)			1962	LI	25 X 30	AP	50		750	250000
Peintre au Travail (B-1121)			1963	EB/SG	12 X 17	AP	50		600	6000
L'Atelier du Peintre (B-1142)			1963	EB	9 X 13	AP	50		500	5000
Tete de Faune (B-1370)			1964	DPT	21 X 15	WOVE	50		600	12000
Nude Woman and Man with Stick (B-1464) (M-407)	CDA		1969	LB	11 X 9	AP	125		500	3000
La Chute d'Icare par Jean Leymarie (B-2016) (C-155)	ASK		1972	EB	14 X 19	R/BFK	125	1	800	12000

The print market has become very selective. For the first time since we published the first edition of The Printworld Directory in 1982, the prices of prints have been greatly reduced and greatly increased for the same artists by the most reputable and established print publishers. Check the fifth edition to understand the movement.

HOWARDENA DOREEN PINDELL

BORN: Phila, PA; April 14, 1943
EDUCATION: Boston Univ, Sch of Fine & Applied Arts, MA, BFA, 1965; Cumminton Sch of Art, 1963; Yale Univ, Sch of Art & Arch, New Haven, CT, MFA, 1967
TEACHING: Assoc Prof, State Univ of New York, Stony Brook, NY, 1979–84, Prof, 1984 to present
AWARDS: Distinguished Alumni Award, Boston Univ, MA, 1983; Nat Endowment of the Arts Fels, Painting, 1972–73, 1983–84; Guggenheim Fel, 1987–88; Col of Art Assn Award for Distinguished Body of Work, 1990
RECENT EXHIB: Wadsworth Atheneum, Hartford, CT, 1989; Gallery Liz Harris, Boston, MA, 1989; Cyrus Gallery, NY, 1989,90
COLLECTIONS: Mus of Mod Art, NY; Whitney Mus of Am Art, NY; Metropolitan Mus of Art, NY; Philadelphia Mus of Art, PA; Fogg Art Mus, Harvard Univ, Cambridge, MA; Nordjyllands Kunstmuseum, Aalborg, Denmark
PRINTERS: Peter Kruty, NY (PK); Solo Press, NY (SP)
PUBLISHERS: Ariana Found, NY (AF)
GALLERIES: Gallery Liz Harris, Boston, MA; Cyrus Gallery, New York, NY; Heath Gallery, Atlanta, GA; G R N'Namdi, Birmingham, MI
MAILING ADDRESS: c/o State Univ of New York, Dept of Art, Stony Brook, NY 11794

TITLE	PUBLISHER	PRINTER	DATE	MEDIUM	DIMENSION (PAPER SIZE) IN INCHES	TYPE OF PAPER	EDITION NUMBER	NO. OF COLORS	ORIGINAL OPENING PRICE	CURRENT RETAIL PRICE
CURRENT EDITIONS:										
Untitled	SP	JS/SP	1976	LC/CC	23 X 30	AP/JP	1		300	700
Kyoto Positive/Negative	SP	JS/SP	1980	LC	27 X 22	AP	1		500	1200
Peter Squares Waterfall, Johnson, Vermont	ART	PK/SP	1986	WC	26 X 36	JP	15		600	1500
Flight/Fields	SP	JS/SP	1989	LB/EB/CO	19 X 23	R/BFK	30	1	850	950

MICHELANGELO PISTOLETTO

BORN: Biella, Italy; 1933
EDUCATION: Mus of Mod Art, NY
PRINTERS: Artist (ART); American Atelier, NY (AA)
PUBLISHERS: V & R Fine Arts, Inc, Temple Terrace, FL (VR); Contemporary Art Publishing Consortium, Mineola, NY (CAP); Giorgio Persano, Italy (GP); Mulipli, Italy (MUL); Circle Fine Art, Chicago, IL (CFA)
GALLERIES: Salvatore Ala, New York, NY; Hokin Galleries Palm Beach, FL & Bay Harbor Islands, FL; Quartersaw Gallery, Portland, OR; Sorrentino/Mayer Fine Art, Great Neck, NY & New York, NY; V & R Fine Art, Great Neck, NY & New York, NY; Circle Galleries, New York, NY & Chicago, IL & Scottsdale, AZ & Beverly Hills, CA & Costa Mesa, CA & San Diego, CA & San Francisco, CA & Sherman Oaks, CA & Palm Beach, FL & Honolulu, HI & Northbrook, IL & New Orleans, LA & Las Vegas, NV & Pittsburgh, PA & Houston, TX & Seattle, WA

Michelangelo Pistoletto
Drape Suite: Cucitrice
Courtesy the Artist

TITLE	PUBLISHER	PRINTER	DATE	MEDIUM	DIMENSION (PAPER SIZE) IN INCHES	TYPE OF PAPER	EDITION NUMBER	NO. OF COLORS	ORIGINAL OPENING PRICE	CURRENT RETAIL PRICE
SOLD OUT EDITIONS (RARE):										
Pappagallo	MUL	ART	1971	SP	40 X 28	AP	99	10	900	4000
Self Portrait Through the Eyes of My Father	ART	ART	1978	SP	30 X 42	AP	125		500	1000
Furniture of My Father's Studio in My Studio	ART	ART	1978	SP	30 X 42	AP	125		500	1000
Art Assumes Religion	CFA	AA	1979	SP	41 X 30	AP	100		500	650
I am the Third	CFA	AA	1979	SP	41 X 30	AP	100		500	650
The Drape Suite (Trip);									12000 SET	20000 SET
Panni	CAP/VR/GP	ART	1982	SP/SS	40 X 48	Steel	60		4000	7000
La Rosa	CAP/VR/GP	ART	1982	SP/SS	40 X 48	Steel	60		4000	7000
La Cucitrice	CAP/VR/GP	ART	1982	SP/SS	40 X 48	Steel	60		4000	7000

LARI PITTMAN

BORN: Los Angeles, CA; 1952
EDUCATION: Univ of California, Los Angeles, CA, 1970–73; California Inst of Arts, Valencia, CA, BFA, 1974, MFA, 1976
AWARDS: Art Matters, Inc, Grant, 1986; Nat Endowment for the Arts Fel Grants, 1987,89; J Paul Getty Trust Fund for Visual Arts Fel Grant, 1989; Kuhlenschmidt-Simon Gallery, Los Angeles, CA, 1989; Newport Harbor Art Mus, Newport Beach, CA, 1990
RECENT EXHIB: Mus of Contemp Art, Los Angeles, CA, 1990; Rosamund Felsen Gallery, Los Angeles, CA, 1987,88,89,90,92

LARI PITTMAN CONTINUED

PRINTERS: Francesco Siqueiros, Los Angeles, CA (FS), Robert Dansby, Los Angeles, CA (RD); Cirrus Editions Workshop, Los Angeles, CA (CEW)

PUBLISHERS: Cirrus Editions, Ltd, Los Angeles, CA (CE)
GALLERIES: Cirrus Gallery, Los Angeles, CA; Rosamund Felsen Gallery, Los Angeles, CA; Jay Gorney Modern Art, New York, NY

TITLE	PUBLISHER	PRINTER	DATE	MEDIUM	DIMENSION (PAPER SIZE) IN INCHES	TYPE OF PAPER	EDITION NUMBER	NO. OF COLORS	ORIGINAL OPENING PRICE	CURRENT RETAIL PRICE
CURRENT EDITIONS:										
This Landscape, Beloved and Despised, Continues Regardless	CE	FS/RD/CEW	1989	LC/SP	44 X 38	AP88	45	9	1200	1200
This Recipe, Beloved and Despised, Continues Regardless	CE	FS/RD/CEW	1989	LC/SP	44 X 38	AP88	45	9	1200	1200
This Desire Beloved and Despise, Continues Regardless	CE	FS/RD/CEW	1989	LC/SP	44 X 38	AP88	45	9	1200	1200
Existential and Needy	CE	FS/RD/CEW	1991	LC/SP	49 X 38	R/BFK	40		1200	1200

PHYLLIS PLATTNER

BORN: New York, NY; April 25, 1940
EDUCATION: Bennington Col, VT, BA, 1960; Claremont Grad Sch, CA, MFA, 1962
TEACHING: Instr, Painting, Washington Univ of Fine Arts, St Louis, MO, 1985–87, Vis Assoc Prof, Watercolor, 1985–87; Maryland Inst of Art, Baltimore, MD, 1987 to present
COLLECTIONS: St Louis Art Mus, MO; Springfield Art Mus, MO
AWARDS: Mayor's Award for the Arts, St Louis, MO, 1984; Nat Endowment for the Arts Fel, 1988
RECENT EXHIB: Esther Saks Gallery, Chicago, IL, 1987; Fendrick Gallery, Wash, DC, 1989; Steven Scott Gallery, Baltimore, MD, 1989

PRINTERS: Jack Lemon, Chicago, IL (JL); Landfall Press, Inc, Chicago, IL (LPI); Four Brothers Press, Chicago, IL (FBP); Washington Univ Impressions, St Louis, MO (WUI)
PUBLISHERS: Landfall Press, Inc, Chicago, IL (LPI); Washington Univ Impressions, St Louis, MO (WUI); Artist (ART)
GALLERIES: Fendrick Gallery, Wash, DC; B Z Wagman Gallery, St Louis, MO; Struve Gallery, Chicago, IL; Landfall Press, Inc, Chicago, IL & New York, NY; Elaine Horwitz Gallery, Scottsdale, AZ; Steven Scott Gallery, Baltimore, MD; Gallery 10, Ltd, Wash, DC; Elliot Smith Gallery, St Louis, MO
MAILING ADDRESS: 6204 Redwing Rd, Bethesda, MD 20017

TITLE	PUBLISHER	PRINTER	DATE	MEDIUM	DIMENSION (PAPER SIZE) IN INCHES	TYPE OF PAPER	EDITION NUMBER	NO. OF COLORS	ORIGINAL OPENING PRICE	CURRENT RETAIL PRICE
SOLD OUT EDITIONS (RARE):										
Fern	LPI	JL/LPI	1984	LC	32 X 42	AP/W	30	6	350	500
Whiskey Begonias #1	WUI	WUI	1984	LC	26 X 23	AP/W	50	6	375	450
Whiskey Begonias #2	ART	FBP	1985	LC	26 X 23	AP/W	50	6	375	450

BERNARD PLOSSU

BORN: Dalat, South Vietnam; February 26, 1945
EDUCATION: Self-Taught
TEACHING: Photography Workshop, Oklahoma Summer Arts Inst, Oklahoma City, OK, 1983
COLLECTIONS: George Eastman House, Rochester, NY; San Francisco Mus of Mod Art, CA; Stedelijik Mus, Amsterdam, Holland; Amon Carter Mus, Fort Worth, TX; Bibliotheque Nat, Paris, France; Center for Creative Photography, Tucson, AZ; Niepce Mus, Chalon, France

PUBLISHERS: Eaton/Shoen Gallery, San Francisco, CA (ESG); Univ of New Mexico Press, Albuquerque, NM (UNM); Univ of Arizona Press, Tucson, AZ (UAP); Editions La Difference (ELD)
PRINTERS: Atelier Michel Fresson (AMF); Atelier Philippe Salaun (APS)
GALLERIES: Hoshour Gallery, Albuquerque, NM; Ernesto Mayans Gallery, Santa Fe, NM; Photo Forum, Pittsburgh, PA
MAILING ADDRESS: 21 rue Gazan, 75014 Paris, France

TITLE	PUBLISHER	PRINTER	DATE	MEDIUM	DIMENSION (PAPER SIZE) IN INCHES	TYPE OF PAPER	EDITION NUMBER	NO. OF COLORS	ORIGINAL OPENING PRICE	CURRENT RETAIL PRICE
CURRENT EDITIONS:										
Bernard Plossu: 1966–1981, Atelier Michel Fresson (10 Fresson Quadrichromie Photographic Prints)	ESG	AMF	1983	PH	10 X 14 EA	HMP	40 EA	4 EA	3000 SET 500 EA	5000 SET 600 EA

LINDA PLOTKIN

BORN: Milwaukee, WI; December 21, 1938
EDUCATION: Univ of Wisconsin, Milwaukee, WI, BA, 1961; Pratt Inst, Brooklyn, NY, MFA, 1962
TEACHING: Asst Prof, Art, Pennsylvania State Univ, State College, PA, 1962–77; Printmaker in Res, St Mary's Col, Notre Dame, IN, 1985; State Univ of New York, Purchase, NY, 1986 to present
AWARDS: Ossabow Island Project Fel, Savannah, GA, 1978; MacDowell Colony Fels, Peterborough, NH, 1976,78–79; Printmaker in Res, Univ of Nebraska, Omaha, NE, 1979; Painter in Resi, Camargo Found Fel, Cassis, France, 1981; Printmaker-in Res, St Mary's Col, Notre Dame, IN

COLLECTIONS: Mus of Mod Art, New York, NY; Metropolitan Mus of Art, New York, NY; Philadelphia Mus of Art, PA; Brooklyn Mus, NY; Cleveland Mus of Art, OH; Yale Univ Mus of Art, New Haven, CT; Rhode Island Sch of Design Mus, Providence, RI; Library of Congress, Wash, DC; Bibliotheque Nat, Paris, France; Chicago Art Inst, IL
PRINTERS: Mohammed Kahlil, NY (MK); Werner Graphics, NY (WG); Weston Press, NY (WP); R Cale (RC); M Lewis (ML); E Sorini (ES); Sienna Studio, NY (SiS); Le Blanc (LB); R Townsend (RT)
PUBLISHERS: Impressions Gallery, Boston, MA (IG) (OB); Artist (ART)
GALLERIES: GW Einstein Co, Inc, New York, NY; Mary Ryan Gallery, New York, NY; Fairweather-Hardin Gallery, Chicago, IL; Marilyn Pink Gallery, Los Angeles, CA; Randall Beck Gallery, Boston, MA; Peltz Gallery, Milwaukee, WI
MAILING ADDRESS: 55 Perry St, New York, NY 10014

LINDA PLOTKIN CONTINUED

TITLE	PUBLISHER	PRINTER	DATE	MEDIUM	DIMENSION (PAPER SIZE) IN INCHES	TYPE OF PAPER	EDITION NUMBER	NO. OF COLORS	ORIGINAL OPENING PRICE	CURRENT RETAIL PRICE
SOLD OUT EDITIONS (RARE):										
Bellefonte Courthouse	ART	LB	1974	EC	20 X 18	AP	150	4	150	350
Blue House	ART	MK	1975	EC	26 X 18	AP	100	3	200	350
Evening Light	ART	RT	1976	LC	28 X 20	AP	80	4	200	350
Two Houses	ART	RT	1976	EC	26 X 18	AP	100	4	200	350
Two Pines	IG	RT	1976	EC	12 X 10	AP	150	2	150	250
Morning Light	IG	RT	1976	I	24 X 22	R/BFK	150	1	150	350
CURRENT EDITIONS:										
Lemons	ART	ES	1978		10 X 10	AP	125	1	100	250
Morning Table	ART	ML	1978	AC/HC	18 X 18	AP	40	3	400	500
Lotus Bowl	ART	ML	1979	DPT/HC	18 X 18	AP	30	4	400	500
Ironstone Pitcher	ART	ML		1979	18 X 18	AP	30	4	400	500
Still Life with Coffee Pot	ART	SiS	1980	LC/HC	28 X 20	AP	50	3	400	500
Still Life with Apple & Limes	ART	SiS	1980	LC/HC	28 X 20	AP	75	4	400	500
Still Life with Tangerine	ART	RC	1982	I/HC	28 X 19	AP	50	3	450	500
French Breakfast	ART	RC	1982	I/HC	12 X 10	AP	50	3	250	350
Kimono & Coffee	ART	MK	1982	I/EC	28 X 19	AP	30	5	300	350
Fruit & Cups	ART	WG	1982	I/HC	18 X 16	AP	30	3	450	500
Zapotec Rug	ART	MK	1986	I	19 X 26	AP	25	5	350	400

EDWARD PLUNKETT

BORN: Highland Park, MI; 1922
EDUCATION: Univ of Chicago, IL; Sch of Art Inst of Chicago, IL; New York Inst of Fine Arts, NY; Sorbonne, Paris, France
TEACHING: Sch of Art Inst of Chicago, IL; City Col of New York, NY; Philadelphia Col of Art, PA
COLLECTIONS: Metropolitan Mus, NY; Baltimore Mus, MD; Univ of Colorado, Boulder, CO; Syracuse Univ, NY; Stempleplatz Gallery, Amsterdam, The Netherlands
PRINTERS: American Atelier, NY (AA)
PUBLISHERS: Circle Fine Art, Chicago, IL (CFA)
GALLERIES: Circle Galleries, San Diego, CA & San Francisco, CA & Northbrook, IL & Pittsburgh, PA & Houston, TX & Soho, NY & Chicago, IL & Scottsdale, AZ & Beverly Hills, CA & Costa Mesa, CA & Sherman Oaks, CA & Palm Beach, FL & Honolulu, HI & New Orleans, LA & Las Vegas, NV & Seattle, WA

TITLE	PUBLISHER	PRINTER	DATE	MEDIUM	DIMENSION (PAPER SIZE) IN INCHES	TYPE OF PAPER	EDITION NUMBER	NO. OF COLORS	ORIGINAL OPENING PRICE	CURRENT RETAIL PRICE
CURRENT EDITIONS:										
Eté 1914	CFA	AA	1980	LC	20 X 26	AP	300		150	200

JOANNA POEHLMANN

BORN: Milwaukee, WI; September 5, 1932
EDUCATION: Layton Sch of Art, Milwaukee, WI, 1950–54; Kansas City Art Inst, MO, Drawing, 1954; Marquette Univ, Milwaukee, WI, 1958; Univ of Wisconsin, Milwaukee, WI, European Study, Summer, 1965; Univ of Wisconsin, Milwaukee, WI, 1985; Milwaukee Art Mus, WI, Papermaking, 1985; Art Study Tour of London England, with Milwaukee Art Mus, WI, 1989–90
AWARDS: Second Award, Watercolor, Wisconsin-Wustum Mus of Fine Arts, Racine, WI, 1983; Purchase Award, Brad Nat Print & Drawing Exhib, Bradley Peoria, IL, 1985; Purchase Award, Univ of Dallas, Irving, TX, 1988; Sacajawea Award, Milwaukee, WI, 1991
RECENT EXHIB: Retrosp, Charles Allis Art Mus, Milwaukee, WI, 1991; Trenton State Col, NJ, 1991
COLLECTIONS: Milwaukee Art Mus, WI; Marquette Univ, Haggerty Mus, Milwaukee, WI; Charles A Wustum Mus, Racine, WI; Franklin Furnace Archives, NY; Embragel Int Print Coll, Cabo Frio, Brazil; Univ of Delaware, Newark, DE; Moravian Col, Bethlehem, PA; Univ of Wisconsin, Milwaukee, WI; Victoria & Albert Mus, London, England; New York Public Library, NY; Mus for Kunsthandwek, Frankfurt, Germany
PRINTERS: John Gruenwald, Milwaukee, WI (JG)
PUBLISHERS: Artist (ART); John Gruenwald, Milwaukee, WI (JG); Quad/Graphics, Inc, Pewaukee, WI (Q/G)
GALLERIES: Wenniger Graphics, Boston, MA; Miriam Perlman, Inc, Chicago, IL; Print Club, Phila, PA; Bradley Galleries, Milwaukee, WI; Grace Chosy Gallery, Madison, WI; David Barnett Gallery, Milwaukee, WI; Neville/Sargent Gallery, Chicago, IL; Tony Zwicker Gallery, New York, NY; Katie Gingrass Gallery, Milwaukee, WI
MAILING ADDRESS: 1231 N Prospect Ave, Milwaukee, WI 53202

TITLE	PUBLISHER	PRINTER	DATE	MEDIUM	DIMENSION (PAPER SIZE) IN INCHES	TYPE OF PAPER	EDITION NUMBER	NO. OF COLORS	ORIGINAL OPENING PRICE	CURRENT RETAIL PRICE
SOLD OUT EDITIONS:										
A Plate of Marcaroni	ART	JG	1980	LC/CO/HC	19 X 15	R/BFK	30	1	250	750
CURRENT EDITIONS:										
Christmas Stollen . . . and a Fruitful New Year	ART	JG	1981–82	LC/CO/HC	9 X 12	R/BFK	20	1	150	250
A Billboard Lovely as a Tree	ART	JG	1982	LC/CO/HC	12 X 13	R/BFK	100	2	110	275
Frame of Reference (After Dürer)	ART	JG	1982	LC/CO/HC/DR	24 X 19	R/BFK	10	1	500	650
I'm Just Wild about Hairy	ART	JG	1982	LC/HC/DR	11 X 10	R/BFK	60	1	150	350
A Toast Suite (Set of 2):										
A Toast (Raisin and Cinnamon)	ART	JG	1982	LC/AC	9 X 9	R/BFK	30	3	125	250
A Toast (Egg Twist with Sesame)	ART	JG	1982	LC/HC	9 X 9	R/BFK	30	3	125	250
Flight Patterns	ART	JG	1982–83	LC/HC/DR	10 X 40	R/BFK	25	1	600	900

JOANNA POEHLMANN CONTINUED

TITLE	PUBLISHER	PRINTER	DATE	MEDIUM	DIMENSION (PAPER SIZE) IN INCHES	TYPE OF PAPER	EDITION NUMBER	NO. OF COLORS	ORIGINAL OPENING PRICE	CURRENT RETAIL PRICE
CURRENT EDITIONS:										
Flight Patterns I, II, III (Trip)	ART	JG	1982–83	LC/HC/DR	11 X 14 EA	R/BFK	15 EA	1 EA	600 SET	1200 SET
									250 EA	400 EA
The Stamp Collection (Set of 8):									475 SET	1000 SET
Egg a'la Audubon	ART	JG	1983	LC/CO/HC	7 X 5	R/BFK	15	1	80	150
Orange a'la Albers	ART	JG	1983	LC/CO/HC	7 X 5	R/BFK	15	1	80	150
Scallops Florentine	ART	JG	1983	LC/CO/HC	7 X 5	R/BFK	15	1	80	150
Charlotte Rousseau	ART	JG	1983	LC/CO/HC	7 X 5	R/BFK	15	1	80	150
Toad Dancer	ART	JG	1983	LC/CO/HC	7 X 5	R/BFK	15	1	80	150
To Bee	ART	JG	1983	LC/CO/HC	7 X 5	R/BFK	15	1	80	150
Klimt Kiss (Stolen)	ART	JG	1983	LC/CO/HC	7 X 5	R/BFK	15	1	80	150
Carrots au Dürer	ART	JG	1983	LC/CO/HC	7 X 5	R/BFK	15	1	80	150
A Plate of Eggs	ART	JG	1984	LC/HC/DR	30 X 23	R/BFK	45	1	475	700
Eggs Under Glass (Set of 24 in Glass Covered Box)	ART	JG	1984	LC/HC	4 X 3 EA	R/BFK	15	1	300 SET	800 SET
Love and Kisses I–IV (Set of 4)	ART	JG	1984–85	LC/CO/HC	7 X 5 EA	R/BFK	30 EA	1 EA	300 SET	500 SET
Hawk Eyes (in Round Box)	ART	JG		LC/HC	2 X DIA EA	HMP	20 EA	1 EA	275 SET	500 SET
Hawk Eyes I	ART	JG	1985	LC/HC	9 X 23	R/BFK	10	1	250	500
Here's Looking at You (Bird's Eye Series)	ART	JG	1985	LC/HC	18 X 23	R/BFK	12	1	800	900
Drawings in a Nutshell (Artist's Book) (Accordion-folded into Walnut Shell)	ART	JG	1985	LC/HC	15 X 1	STR	50	1	175	300
Another Plate of Macaroni	ART	JG	1986–87	LC/CO/HD	30 X 22	R/BFK	10	1	500	600
Moult (with Graphite)	ART	JG	1986–87	LB/HC/CO	30 X 36	R/BFK	15	1	700	800
Quadratures of the Moon	Q/G	JG	1987	LB/HC/EMB	30 X 23	R/BFK	63	1	550	550
Dog Eared (Artist Book) (15 Hand Colored Lithographs Bound into Book Form)	ART	JG	1990	LB/HC	7 X 5 EA	R/BFK	35 EA	1 EA	600 SET	800 SET
Ringo, George and Paul	ART	JG	1990	EB/HC	6 X 8	R/BFK	10	1	100	100
The Reunion (Hand Colored)	JG	JG	1990	LB/EB/EMB/CO	11 X 15	R/BFK	60	1	250	350
Cornbelt for a Green Giant	JG	JG	1991	EB/HC/CO	9 X 12	R/BFK	24	1	200	200
The One That Got Away	ART	JG	1991	EB/HC	11 X 14	R/BFK	30	1	160	160
Doing the Tarantella	ART	JG	1991	EB/LB/HC	12 X 14	R/BFK	23	1	175	175
Old Hat (Two Views)	ART	JG	1991	EB/LB/HC	11 X 14	R/BFK	15	1	175	175
Cricket Anyone? (with Drawing)	ART	JG	1991	LB/HC/CO	9 X 20	R/BFK	20	1		

MIKLOS POGANY

BORN: Budapest, Hungary; February 4, 1945
EDUCATION: St Procopins Col, BA, 1965; Univ of Chicago, IL, MA, 1965, PhD, 1972
AWARDS: SECA award, Painting, San Francisco Mus of Mod Art, NY, 1977; Grant, Printmaking, Connecticut Comm of Art, 1980; Louis Comfort Tiffany Award, 1981
RECENT EXHIB: New Britain Mus of Am Art, CT, 1987; Spencer Mus, Lawrence, KS, 1987

COLLECTIONS: Metropolitan Mus of Art, NY; Philadelphia Art Mus, PA; Phillips Coll, Wash, DC; Victoria & Albert Mus, London, England; Nat Mus of Am Art, Wash, DC
PRINTERS: Smith Andersen Gallery, Palo Alto, CA (SA); Artist (ART)
PUBLISHERS: Smith Andersen Gallery, Palo Alto, CA (SA); Artist (ART)
GALLERIES: Smith Andersen Gallery, Palo Alto, CA; Victoria Munroe Gallery, New York, NY; Connecticut Gallery, Marlborough, CT; Marsha Mateyka Gallery, Wash, DC
MAILING ADDRESS: Four Roman Terrace, New Haven, CT 06511

TITLE	PUBLISHER	PRINTER	DATE	MEDIUM	DIMENSION (PAPER SIZE) IN INCHES	TYPE OF PAPER	EDITION NUMBER	NO. OF COLORS	ORIGINAL OPENING PRICE	CURRENT RETAIL PRICE
CURRENT EDITIONS:										
Three Florentine Tulips	ART	ART	1981	MON	18 X 28 EA	THS	1 EA	Varies	500 EA	2000 EA
Klarika, Presence	SA	SA	1982–83	MON/HC	60 X 43 EA	HMP	1 EA	Varies	2000 EA	4000 EA

SERGE POLIAKOFF

BORN: Russia; (1906–1969)
PRINTERS: Artist (ART)
PUBLISHERS: Artist (ART)

TITLE	PUBLISHER	PRINTER	DATE	MEDIUM	DIMENSION (PAPER SIZE) IN INCHES	TYPE OF PAPER	EDITION NUMBER	NO. OF COLORS	ORIGINAL OPENING PRICE	CURRENT RETAIL PRICE
SOLD OUT EDITIONS (RARE):										
Composition Jaune	ART	ART	1956	LC	13 X 20	R/BFK	200	6	60	5000
Composition Rouge	ART	ART	1956	LC	23 X 17	R/BFK	200	6	75	5000
Composition Bleue	ART	ART	1958	LC	20 X 26	WOVE	100	8	75	10000
Composition Orange	ART	ART	1959	LC	8 X 10	AP	65	5	60	4500
Composition Orange et Verte	ART	ART	1964	LC	24 X 18	WOVE	300	9	100	8000
Composition Verte, Rouge et . . .	ART	ART	1966	LC	19 X 25	AP	75	8	200	17000
Composition	ART	ART	1967	LB	23 X 17	AP	200	1	150	4000

SIGMAR POLKE

BORN: Germany; 1941
EDUCATION: Staatlichen Kunstakademie, Dusseldorf, Germany
RECENT EXHIB: Stadtische Kunstmuseum, Bonn, Germany, 1987; Mary Boone Gallery, NY, 1988
PRINTERS: Artist (ART)
PUBLISHERS: Artist (ART); Baron/Boisanté, NY (B/B)
GALLERIES: Mary Boone Gallery, New York, NY
MAILING ADDRESS: c/o Mary Boone Gallery, 417 W Broadway, New York, NY 10012

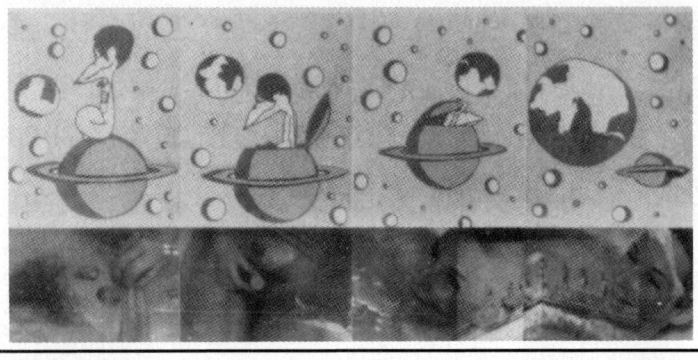

Sigmar Polke
Hallo Shiva
Courtesy Baron/Boisanté

TITLE	PUBLISHER	PRINTER	DATE	MEDIUM	DIMENSION (PAPER SIZE) IN INCHES	TYPE OF PAPER	EDITION NUMBER	NO. OF COLORS	ORIGINAL OPENING PRICE	CURRENT RETAIL PRICE
SOLD OUT EDITIONS (RARE):										
Hallo Shiva	B/B	ART	1974	LB/OFF	16 X 22	AP	80	1	400	3500
Untitled	ART	ART	1985	LB/OFF	20 X 27	AP	120	1	850	1500
Untitled	ART	ART	1985	LB/OFF	20 X 28	AP	120	1	850	1500
Untitled (on Velour)	ART	ART	1989	SP	39 X 26	AP			3500	4500

STEVE POLESKIE (STEPHEN FRANCIS)

BORN: Pringle, PA; June 3, 1938
EDUCATION: Wilkes Col, Wilkes-Barre, PA, BS, 1959; New Sch for Social Research, NY, 1960–81
TEACHING: Instr, Sch of Visual Arts, NY, 1966–68; Vis Prof, Univ of California, Bekeley, CA, 1976; Assoc Prof, Silkscreen, Cornell Univ, Ithaca, NY, 1968–81, Prof, 1981 to present
AWARDS: Am Federation of the Arts, NY, 1962; Rockefeller Prize, 1972; Creative Artists Public Service Award, 1978; Ohio Arts Council Grant, 1984; Best Found Grant, 1985
RECENT EXHIB: South Dakota State Univ, Art Mus, Brookings, SD, 1989
COLLECTIONS: Metropolitan Mus of Art, NY; Mus of Mod Art, NY; Nat Coll of Fine Art, Wash, DC; Walker Art Center, Minneapolis, MN; Fort Worth Art Center, TX; Johnson Mus Cornell Univ, Ithaca, NY; Massachusetts Inst of Technology, Cambridge, MA; Rochester Mem Art Gallery, NY; Victoria & Albert Mus, London, England; Tate Gallery of Art, London, England; Castlevecchio Mus, Verona, Italy; Whitney Mus of Am Art, NY; Everhart Mus, Scranton, PA; Mus of Mod Art, Mexico; Alternative Mus, Lido di Spina, Ferarra, Italy; Albert Einstein Medical Center, NY; Tweed Art Mus, Duluth, MN
PRINTERS: Frank Liu, Ithaca, NY (FL); Cornell Univ, Ithaca, NY (CU); Artist (ART)
PUBLISHERS: Apogee Airway, Ithaca, NY (ApA); Artist (ART)
GALLERIES: New Acquisitions, Syracuse, NY; Hank Baum Gallery, San Francisco, CA; Apogee Airway, Ithaca, NY
MAILING ADDRESS: 306 Stone Quarry Road, Ithaca, NY 14850

TITLE	PUBLISHER	PRINTER	DATE	MEDIUM	DIMENSION (PAPER SIZE) IN INCHES	TYPE OF PAPER	EDITION NUMBER	NO. OF COLORS	ORIGINAL OPENING PRICE	CURRENT RETAIL PRICE
SOLD OUT EDITIONS (RARE):										
Seawane	ART	ART	1967	SP	19 X 26	AP	35	5	65	600
Cades Cove	ART	ART	1968	SP	19 X 26	AP	40	6	65	550
Giswold	ART	ART	1969	SP	23 X 29	AP	30	6	65	600
Taughannock	ART	ART	1969	SP	23 X 29	AP	40	6	65	1000
Big Patchogue Bent	ART	ART	1969	SP	23 X 29	AP	50	5	65	1000
Poteet	ART	ART	1978	SP	22 X 90	AP	20	14	350	2800
CURRENT EDITIONS:										
Everhart	ART	ART	1976	SP	22 X 30	AP	35	12	100	300
Vega	ART	ART	1977	SP	22 X 30	AP	35	9	100	400
Orillia	ART	ART	1977	SP	22 X 30	AP	25	7	100	350
Donplumb	ART	ART	1978	SP	16 X 40	AP	10	5	125	450
Uvalde	ART	ART	1978	SP	16 X 40	AP	10	5	125	450
Helotes	ART	ART	1978	SP	20 X 30	AP	20	7	125	1000
Matagorda	ART	ART	1978	SP	20 X 30	AP	25	10	125	500
Aransas	ART	ART	1978	SP	20 X 30	AP	25	9	125	500
Wonder Wings	ART	ART	1980	SP	30 X 40	AP	50	1	300	600
Four Humpty Bumps Squared	ART	ART	1982	SP/CO	22 X 30	AP	20	15	350	600
Four Hammer Heads Squared	ART	ART	1982	SP/CO	22 X 30	AP	20	15	350	600
VFR	ART	ART	1983	SP/CO	7 X 7	AP	24	5	75	250
Solitaire	ART	ART	1983	SP/CO	7 X 7	AP	22	5	75	250
Cygnus	ART	ART	1983	SP/CO	7 X 7	AP	25	5	75	250
Loop of Top of Loop	ART	ART	1983	SP/CO	22 X 30	AP	22	15	350	600
Ad Astra	ART	ART	1983	SP/CO	7 X 7	AP	30	5	75	250
Ad Astra	ART	ART	1984	EC/HC	22 X 30	AP	25	5	500	600
Ad Astra	ApA	ART	1985	EC/SP	22 X 30	R/BFK	25	4	350	600
Solaris	ApA	ART	1985	EC/HC	22 X 30	R/BFK	25	5	350	600
Radial	ApA	FL/CU	1986	EC	22 X 30	R/BFK	25	2	500	600
Air-1-2-3	ApA	FL/CU	1986	LI	15 X 30	RICE	15	2	200	300
Air-3-2-1	ApA	FL/CU	1986	LI	15 X 30	RICE	15	2	200	300
Outer Marker	ApA	FL/CU	1986	EC	15 X 30	R/BFK	15	5	300	400
Scipio	ApA	FL/CU	1986	EC	15 X 30	R/BFK	15	4	300	400
Varna	ApA	FL/CU	1986	EC	15 X 30	R/BFK	15	5	300	400

The Printworld Directory is accepting new applications for the seventh edition. Approximately 300 new artists will be accepted. Please use the two forms provided in the back section of this directory to submit biographical data and documentation of prints. Edition number of each print must not exceed 500 and the retail price must be $100 or more.

OLGA POLOUKHINE

BORN: Paris, France
EDUCATION: Rutgers Univ, Newark, NY; Columbia Univ, Teachers Col, NY, MA

COLLECTIONS: Hecksher Mus, Huntington, NY
PRINTERS: Artist (ART)
PUBLISHERS: John Szoke Graphics, NY (JSG)
GALLERIES: John Szoke Graphics, New York, NY; Graphic Eye, Port Washington, NY

TITLE	PUBLISHER	PRINTER	DATE	MEDIUM	DIMENSION (PAPER SIZE) IN INCHES	TYPE OF PAPER	EDITION NUMBER	NO. OF COLORS	ORIGINAL OPENING PRICE	CURRENT RETAIL PRICE
CURRENT EDITIONS:										
Burning Sands	JSG	ART	1982	EC	24 X 35	R/BFK	100	10	250	450
Poppies	JSG	ART	1983	EC	24 X 35	R/BFK	175	10	250	400

MICHAEL PONCE DE LEON

BORN: Mexico City, Mexico; July 4, 1922
EDUCATION: Univ of Mexico, Mexico City, Mex, BA; Brooklyn Mus, NY; Art Students League, NY; Nat Acad of Design, NY
TEACHING: Hunter Col, NY, 1959–66; Univ of Pennsylvania, Phila, PA; Columbia Univ, NY, 1977; Pratt Inst, Brooklyn, NY, 1978; Art Students League, NY, 1978 to present
AWARDS: Tiffany Found Grant, 1954,55; Fulbright Grant 1956,57; Guggenheim Found Grant, 1967
COLLECTIONS: Mus of Mod Art, NY; Metropolitan Mus of Art, NY; Brooklyn Mus, NY; Oslo Art Mus, Norway; Corcoran Gallery of Art, Wash, DC; Nat Gallery, Wash, DC; Cincinnati Art Mus, OH; Chicago Art Inst, IL; Boston Mus of Fine Art, MA; Philadelphia Mus of Art, PA; Walker Art Ctr, Minneapolis, MN; Smithsonian Inst, Wash, DC; Library of Congress, Wash, DC; Stockholm Art Mus, Sweden; New York Univ, NY; Orlando Art Mus, FL; Victoria & Albert Mus, London, England; Auckland Art Mus, New Zealand
PRINTERS: Sienna Studio, NY (SiS); Artist (ART)
PUBLISHERS: Artist (ART)
GALLERIES: Associated American Artists, New York, NY; Jane Haslem Salon, Wash, DC; Asage Gallery, New York, NY; Fendrick Gallery, Wash, DC; New Gallery, Ft Worth, TX; Sienna Studio, New York, NY
MAILING ADDRESS: 463 West St, New York, NY 10014

TITLE	PUBLISHER	PRINTER	DATE	MEDIUM	DIMENSION (PAPER SIZE) IN INCHES	TYPE OF PAPER	EDITION NUMBER	NO. OF COLORS	ORIGINAL OPENING PRICE	CURRENT RETAIL PRICE
SOLD OUT EDITIONS (RARE):										
Entrapment	ART	ART	1975	CO/I	24 X 20	HMP	10	9	1000	1500
Omen	ART	ART	1975	CO/I	24 X 18	HMP	10	11	900	1350
Counter Trust	ART	ART	1976	CO/I	24 X 25	HMP	10	10	1000	1500
Terminus	ART	ART	1977	CO/I	23 X 17	HMP	10	10	900	1300
Samsara	ART	ART	1978	CO/I	27 X 18	HMP	10	9	850	1300
CURRENT EDITIONS:										
Spanish Impressions	ART	ART	1975	CO/I	38 X 21	HMP	18	24	600	700
The Recycling of Gran'ma	ART	ART	1978	CO/I	34 X 24	HMP	20	5	500	600
The Cat-A-Cization of the Circle	ART	ART	1979	I	19 X 18	HMP	30	3	450	500
Entrapment	ART	SiS	1980	LC	24 X 20	HMP	10	9	400	500
Heritage	ART	SiS	1980	LC	26 X 18	HMP	10	13	350	400
Succubus	ART	ART	1980	CO/I	22 X 24	HMP	10	5	1400	1500
Maelstrom	ART	SiS	1980	LC	24 X 19	HMP	10	12	350	400
Abduction of the Sun	ART	ART	1980	CO/I	27 X 22	HMP	25	15	800	900
Man Is the Measure of All Things—Love is the Measure of Man	ART	ART	1980	CO/I	20 X 30	HMP	25	1	600	700
Counter Trust	ART	ART	1980	LC	24 X 25	HMP	10	10	400	500
Anatomy of a Kiss	ART	ART	1981	CO/I	37 X 23	HMP	25	24	800	850
Kismet	ART	ART	1981	CO/I	21 X 22	HMP	15	15	800	850
Dialogue	ART	ART	1982	CO/I	15 X 25	HMP	18	6	550	600
Bessie's Dream	ART	ART	1982	CO/I	20 X 18	HMP	20	6	600	650
Midnite Watch (3D)	ART	ART	1982	CO/I	28 X 27	HMP	15	10	1000	1100
The Secret (3D)	ART	ART	1982	CO/I	20 X 18	HMP	15	12	800	850
OM (3D)	ART	ART	1982	CO/I	28 X 16	HMP	15	19	1200	1300
Birth of a Star	ART	ART	1983	I/CO	26 X 25	HMP	10	10	800	900
Birth of a Star	ART	ART	1985	I/CO	26 X 25	HMP	10	8	800	900
Contradictional Cultures	ART	ART	1985	I/CO	26 X 24	HMP	10	12	800	900
Once Upon a Ritual	ART	ART	1985	I/CO	25 X 23	HMP	10	10	800	900
Incantation	ART	ART	1985	I/CO	23 X 24	HMP	12	17	1600	1650
Cry in the Nite	ART	ART	1985	I/CO	24 X 24	HMP	10	10	800	900

CLAYTON POND

BORN: Bayside, NY; June 10, 1941
EDUCATION: Hiram Col, OH, 1959–61; Carnegie Inst, Pittsburgh, PA, BFA, 1964; Pratt Inst, NY, MFA, 1964–66
TEACHING: C W Post Col, Greenvale, NY, 1966–68; Sch of Visual Arts, NY, 1968–70; Instr, Photog & Printmaking, C W Post Col, Long Island Univ, NY, 1966–68; Adj Instr, Serigraphy, Sch of Visual Arts, NY, 1968–70; Vis Lectr, Univ of Wisconsin-Madison, WI, Spring, 1972
AWARDS: State Dept Grant, Smithsonian Inst, Wash, DC, 1967; Int Art Prog & Abby Gray Found, 1967; Purchase Award, Boston Printmakers, Boston Univ, MA, 1968

RECENT EXHIB: Sylvia Cordish Gallery, Baltimore, MD, 1988; St Mary's Col of Maryland, Dwight Frederic Boyden Gallery, St Mary's City, MD, 1992; Print Club of Albany, NY, 1992; State Mus of Pennsylvania, William Penn Mem Bldg, Harrisburg, PA, 1992
COLLECTIONS: State Univ of New York, Albany, NY; Boston Mus of Fine Arts, MA; Albright-Knox Art Gallery, Buffalo, NY; Amon Carter Mus, Fort Worth, TX; Art Inst of Chicago, IL; Colgate Univ, Hamilton, NY; Dartmouth Col, Hanover, NH; Indiana Univ, Bloomington, IN; Mus of Mod Art, NY; Los Angeles County Mus, CA; Philadelphia Mus, PA; Princeton Univ, NJ; Univ of Wisconsin, Madison, WI; Toledo Mus, OH; State Univ of New York, Pottsdam, NY; Western Michigan Univ, Kalamazoo, MI; Nat Coll of Fine Arts, Wash, DC; Art Inst of Chicago, IL

CLAYTON POND CONTINUED

PRINTERS: American Atelier, NY (AA)
PUBLISHERS: Circle Gallery, Chicago, IL (CG)
GALLERIES: DeGraaf Fine Art, Inc, Chicago, IL; Langman Gallery, Jenkintown, PA; David Anderson Gallery, Buffalo, NY; Circle Galleries, Houston, TX & Pittsburgh, PA & New York, NY & Chicago, IL & Beverly Hills, CA & San Diego, CA & Scottsdale, AZ & Beverly Hills, CA & Costa Mesa, CA & Sherman Oaks, CA & Palm Beach, FL & Honolulu, HI & New Orleans, LA & Las Vegas, NV & Seattle, WA
MAILING ADDRESS: 130 Greene St, New York, NY 10012

TITLE	PUBLISHER	PRINTER	DATE	MEDIUM	DIMENSION (PAPER SIZE) IN INCHES	TYPE OF PAPER	EDITION NUMBER	NO. OF COLORS	ORIGINAL OPENING PRICE	CURRENT RETAIL PRICE
SOLD OUT EDITIONS (RARE):										
American Leisure Series:										
Harley Davidson Motorcycle	CFA	AA	1980	SP	40 X 30	AP	300		300	750
Gyrocopter	CFA	AA	1980	SP	40 X 30	AP	300		300	750
Dirt Bike-Motocross	CFA	AA	1980	SP	40 X 30	AP	300		300	750
Ski Gondola	CFA	AA	1980	SP	40 X 30	AP	300		300	1050
Hanging Twenty	CFA	AA	1980	SP	30 X 40	AP	300		300	750
Fantasy	CFA	AA	1980	SP	30 X 40	AP	300		300	1750
End of the Trail	CFA	AA	1980	SP	30 X 40	AP	300		300	800
Snowmobile	CFA	AA	1980	SP	30 X 40	AP	300		300	750
Cessna Airplane	CFA	AA	1980	SP	30 X 40	AP	300		300	900
Hot Air Balloon	CFA	AA	1980	SP	40 X 30	AP	300		300	1150
Formula 5000	CFA	AA	1980	SP	30 X 40	AP	300		300	900
Camping American Style	CFA	AA	1980	SP	40 X 30	AP	300		300	750
Spinnaker and Blooper	CFA	AA	1980	SP	40 X 30	AP	300		300	1250
Vertigo	CFA	AA	1980	SP	40 X 30	AP	300		300	750
Dune Buggy	CFA	AA	1980	SP	30 X 40	AP	300		300	750
Parachute Tow	CFA	AA	1980	SP	30 X 40	AP	300		300	750
Drag Racer	CFA	AA	1980	SP	40 X 30	AP	300		300	750
Sail Plane	CFA	AA	1980	SP	30 X 40	AP	300		300	750

LAWRENCE POONS

BORN: Tokyo, Japan; October 1, 1937
EDUCATION: New England Conservatory of Music, Boston, MA, 1955–57; Boston Mus Sch, MA, 1958
TEACHING: Vis Faculty, New York Studio Sch, Bennington Col, VT, 1967
AWARDS: Francis J Greenburger Found Award, 1988
RECENT EXHIB: Hokin Gallery, Bay Harbor Islands, FL, 1987; Meadow Brook Art Gallery, Rochester, MI, 1988; Daniel Newburg Gallery, NY, 1989–90; Galerie Montaigne, Paris, France, 1989–90; Helander Gallery, NY, 1990; Salander-O'Reilly Gallery, NY, 1990
COLLECTIONS: Mus of Mod Art, NY; Whitney Mus of Am Art, NY; Tate Gallery of Art, London, England; Nassau County Mus of Fine Arts, NY; Univ of Connecticut, Storrs, CT; Brooklyn Mus, NY; New Sch for Social Research, NY; Am Fed of Art, NY; Albright-Knox Art Gallery, Buffalo, NY; Woodward Found, Wash, DC; Stedelijk Mus, Amsterdam, The Netherlands
PRINTERS: Larry B Wright, NY (LBW)
PUBLISHERS: Prestige Art Ltd, Mamaroneck, NY (PA)
GALLERIES: Douglas Drake Gallery, Kansas City, KS; André Emmerich Gallery, New York, NY; Hokin Galleries, Bay Harbor Islands, FL & Palm Beach, FL; Helander Gallery, Palm Beach, FL & New York, NY; Salander-O'Reilly Gallery, New York, NY; Meredith Long & Company, Houston, TX
MAILING ADDRESS: 831 Broadway, New York 10003

TITLE	PUBLISHER	PRINTER	DATE	MEDIUM	DIMENSION (PAPER SIZE) IN INCHES	TYPE OF PAPER	EDITION NUMBER	NO. OF COLORS	ORIGINAL OPENING PRICE	CURRENT RETAIL PRICE
CURRENT EDITIONS:										
Untitled Suite, A,B,C,D, (Set of 4)	PA	LBW	1980	SP	25 X 36 EA	AP	100 EA	3– 5 EA	600 EA	1000 EA

BERN PORTER

PRINTERS: Cincinnati Screen Process, Cincinnati, OH (CSP)
PUBLISHERS: Volatile, Cincinnati, OH (VOL)
GALLERIES: Volatile, Cincinnati, OH

TITLE	PUBLISHER	PRINTER	DATE	MEDIUM	DIMENSION (PAPER SIZE) IN INCHES	TYPE OF PAPER	EDITION NUMBER	NO. OF COLORS	ORIGINAL OPENING PRICE	CURRENT RETAIL PRICE
CURRENT EDITIONS:										
The Last Acts of Saint Fuck You (Window Shade Version)	VOL	CSP	1990	SP	52 X 36		20		500	500

DAVID PORTER

BORN: Chicago, IL; May 18, 1912
TEACHING: Artist in Res, Dartmouth Col, 1964–65; Cooper Union, NY, 1967–68; Lectr, Art, Corcoran Gallery of Art, Wash, DC, 1968,69; Instr, Painting, Guild Hall, East Hampton, NY, 1975–78
AWARDS: Gold Medal of President Gronchi of Italy, Sassoferrato, Italy, 1961; Beaux Arts Award, Paintings, Beaux Arts Club, 1969; Nat Inst of Arts & Letters Grant, 1970
COLLECTIONS: Whitney Mus of Am Art, NY; Miami Mus of Mod Art, FL; Chrysler Art Mus, Norfolk, VA; Norfolk Mus, VA; Parish Art Mus, Southampton, NY
PRINTERS: American Atelier, NY (AA)
PUBLISHERS: Circle Fine Art, Chicago, IL (CFA)
GALLERIES: Circle Galleries, San Diego, CA & San Francisco, CA & Northbrook, IL & Pittsburgh, PA & Houston, TX & Soho, NY & Chicago, IL
MAILING ADDRESS: Town Line Road, Wainscott, NY 11975

The retail prices of the 100,000 limited edition prints quoted in this directory are subject to change. Print publishers, artists and galleries were the direct sources for these quotations. Prices in the secondary market listed as "Sold Out Editions (Rare)" indicate that the publisher has a limited supply of that print or that the print is difficult to locate in the galleries.

DAVID PORTER CONTINUED

TITLE	PUBLISHER	PRINTER	DATE	MEDIUM	DIMENSION (PAPER SIZE) IN INCHES	TYPE OF PAPER	EDITION NUMBER	NO. OF COLORS	ORIGINAL OPENING PRICE	CURRENT RETAIL PRICE
SOLD OUT EDITIONS (RARE):										
Megacity IV	CFA	AA	1979	SP	50 X 60		250		250	600
CURRENT EDITIONS:										
Thru Peacock's Eye	CFA	AA	1978	SP	41 X 33		250		200	425
Megacity VI	CFA	AA	1980	SP	62 X 50		250		300	525

FAIRFIELD PORTER

BORN: Winnetka, IL; (1907–1975); US Citizen
EDUCATION: Harvard Univ, Cambridge, MA; Art Students League, NY
AWARDS: Longview Found, 1959; Purdue Univ, Print Prize, 1966; Nat Acad of Design, NY, Print Prize
RECENT EXHIB: Lauren Rogers Mus of Art, Laurel, MS, 1989,92; Albrecht-Kemper Mus, St Joseph, MO, 1992; Artists Mus, 1992; Heckscher Mus, Huntington, NY, 1992; Hunter Col, Leubsdorf Art Gallery, NY, 1992

COLLECTIONS: Brooklyn Mus of Art, NY; Cleveland Mus of Art, OH; Hirshhorn Mus of Art, Wash, DC; Whitney Mus of Am Art, NY; Santa Fe Mus of Art, NM
PRINTERS: Resam Press, NY (RP)
PUBLISHERS: Brooke Alexander, Inc, NY (BAI)
GALLERIES: Brooke Alexander, Inc, New York, NY; Hirschl & Adler Modern, New York, NY; Mary Ryan Gallery, New York, NY; Lopoukhine Gallery, Boston, MA; Susanne Hilberry Gallery, Birmingham, MI; Schultz & Co, New York, NY; Tibor de Nagy Gallery, New York, NY; CompassRose Gallery, Ltd, Chicago, IL; Alpha Gallery, Boston, MA; Michael Rosenfield Gallery, New York, NY

TITLE	PUBLISHER	PRINTER	DATE	MEDIUM	DIMENSION (PAPER SIZE) IN INCHES	TYPE OF PAPER	EDITION NUMBER	NO. OF COLORS	ORIGINAL OPENING PRICE	CURRENT RETAIL PRICE
SOLD OUT EDITIONS (RARE):										
Ocean, State I	BAI	RP	1973	LC	23 X 30	AP	85	4	250	3500
Sunrise	BAI	RP	1974	LC	35 X 24	AP	50		250	3500
Apple Blossoms I	BAI	RP	1974	LC	23 X 28	AP	50		250	2500
CURRENT EDITIONS:										
Sixth Avenue	BAI	RP	1971	LC	23 X 31	AP	60		200	3500
Broadway	BAI	RP	1972	LC	30 X 22	AP	125		250	3500
Ocean, State II	BAI	RP	1973	LC	22 X 32	AP	40		250	2000
Apple Blossoms II	BAI	RP	1974	LC	23 X 28	AP	50		250	2500
Girl in the Woods	BAI	RP	1971	LC	28 X 24	AP	100		100	4500
Isle au Haut	BAI	RP	1975	LC	29 X 24	AP	100		250	4500
Ocean II (the Gale)	BAI	RP	1974	LC	22 X 30	AP	70		250	3500

KATHERINE PORTER

RECENT EXHIB: André Emmerich Gallery, NY, 1990; Univ of Maryland, Baltimore, MD, 1992
PRINTERS: Robin Memlich, NY (RM); Experimental Workshop, San Francisco, CA (EW); Artist (ART)
PUBLISHERS: Fawbush Editions, NY (FE); Experimental Workshop, San Francisco, CA (EW); Artist (ART)
GALLERIES: Nielsen Gallery, Boston, MA; Hill Gallery, Birmingham, MI; Fawbush Editions, New York, NY; Experimental Workshop, San Francisco, CA; André Emmerich Gallery, New York, NY; Betsy Senior Contemporary Prints, New York, NY; Topaz Editions, Tampa, FL
MAILING ADDRESS: Brooksville, ME

Katherine Porter
The City
Courtesy Fawbush Editions

TITLE	PUBLISHER	PRINTER	DATE	MEDIUM	DIMENSION (PAPER SIZE) IN INCHES	TYPE OF PAPER	EDITION NUMBER	NO. OF COLORS	ORIGINAL OPENING PRICE	CURRENT RETAIL PRICE
CURRENT EDITIONS:										
A Sort of Biography (Set of 6)	ART	RM	1986	EB/DPT	21 X 16 EA	GE	27 EA	1 EA	2500 SET	5000 SET
Perpetuum Mobile: The City	FE	RM/ART	1987	WC/HC	22 X 35	GE	30		1500	1800

LILLIANA PORTER

BORN: Buenos Aires, Argentina; October 6, 1941; US Citizen
EDUCATION: Universidad Iberoamericana, Mexico City, Mexico; Sch of Fine Arts, Buenos Aires, Argentina; Iberoamerican Univ & La Ciudadela, Mexico City, Mex, Printmaking; Pratt Graphic Art Center, NY, Printmaking
TEACHING: Lectr, State Univ, Old Westbury Col, NY, 1974–76; Instr, Etching, New York Graphic Workshop, NY, 1965–68; Lectr, New York State Univ, Old Westbury Col, NY, 1974–76; Adj Lectr, Graphics, State Univ of New York, Purchase, NY, 1987; Instr, Printmaking Workshop, NY, 1988
AWARDS: Guggenheim Found Fel, NY, 1980; New York Found for the Arts Fel, NY, Graphics, 1985; John Simon Guggenheim Fel, 1980; New York Found for the Arts Fel, NY, Graphics, 1985; Grand Prix Prize, Cracow, Poland, 1986; First Prize, Latin Am Graphic Arts Biennial, NY, 1986; First Prize, Latin Am Print Biennial, San Juan, PR, 1986

LILLIANA PORTER CONTINUED

RECENT EXHIB: The Space, Boston, MA, 1988; Museo del Grabado, Latinoamericano, Inst of Puerto Rican Culture, Old San Juan, PR, 1989; Museo de Bellas Artes, Santiago, Chile, 1990–91; Steinbaum Krauss Gallery, NY, 1993
COLLECTIONS: Mus de Bellas Artes, Caracas, Venezuela; Mus of Mod Art, NY; Mus de Bellas Artes, Buenos Aires, Argentina; Bibliotheque Nat, Paris, France; New York Public Library, NY; Mus de Bellas Artes, Santiago, Chile; Mus de Arte Mod, Bogota, Colombia; Mus of Contemp Art, Montreal, Can; Mus of Contemp Art, Lodz, Poland; Univ Art Mus, Austin, TX; Mus de Arte Mod, Cali, Colombia; Hunter Mus, Chattanooga, TN; Pennsylvania Acad of Fine Arts, Phila, PA
PRINTERS: Al Weiner, NY (AW); Porter-Weiner Studio, NY (P-WS); Artist (ART)
PUBLISHERS: Barbara Toll Fine Arts, NY (BTFA); Artist (ART)
GALLERIES: Barbara Toll Fine Arts, New York, NY; Mary Ryan Gallery, New York, NY; Martina Hamilton & Associates, New York, NY; Associated American Artists, New York, NY; The Space, Boston, MA; Opus Art Studios, Miami, FL; Arch Gallery, New York, NY; Steinbaum Krauss Gallery, New York, NY
MAILING ADDRESS: 178 Franklin St, 5th Fl, New York, NY 10013

TITLE	PUBLISHER	PRINTER	DATE	MEDIUM	DIMENSION (PAPER SIZE) IN INCHES	TYPE OF PAPER	EDITION NUMBER	NO. OF COLORS	ORIGINAL OPENING PRICE	CURRENT RETAIL PRICE
SOLD OUT EDITIONS (RARE):										
Still Life with Apple	ART	P-WS	1983	SP/CO/HC	26 X 38	AC/B	35	6	500	800
CURRENT EDITIONS:										
The Open Box	ART	P-WS	1983	SP/CO	26 X 38	AC/B	35	3	550	650
Fragments with Open Book	ART	P-WS	1983	SP/CO	26 X 38	AC/B	35	4	500	600
The Blue Boat	ART	P-WS	1983	SP/CO	25 X 38	STP	35	3	550	650
The Post Card	BTFA	P-WS	1984	SP/CO	26 X 38	AC/B	35	7	500	600
Art Poetica	ART	P-WS	1985–86	SP/EB/A	43 X 31	GE	35	2	750	800
The Mirror	ART	P-WS	1986	EC	35 X 27	GE	35	2	750	800

MARJORIE ANNE PORTNOW

BORN: New York, NY; 1942
EDUCATION: Western Reserve Univ, Cleveland, OH, BA, Art History, 1964; Pratt Inst, NY, 1964–65; Skowhegan Sch of Painting & Sculpture, ME, with Lennart Anderson & Alex Katz, 1965; Art Students League, NY, 1970; Brooklyn Col, NY, Painting, with Philip Pearlstein, MFA, 1972
TEACHING: Instr, Skowhegan Sch, ME, 1989; Instr, Vermont Studio Sch, 1987–90; Univ of Pennsylvania, Grad Sch, Phila, PA, 1988–91; Pennsylvania Acad of Art, Phila, PA, 1988–91
AWARDS: Ingram Merrill Grant, 1976; Nat Endowment for the Arts Grant, 1980; New York State Creative Artists Public Service Grant, 1981–82; New York Found for the Arts Grant, 1986
RECENT EXHIB: Kalamazoo Art Inst, MI, 1987; Case-Western Reserve Univ, Cleveland, OH, 1988; East End Gallery, Provincetown, MA, 1989; Gibbs Mus, Charleston, SC, 1990
COLLECTIONS: Metropolitan Art Mus, NY; Sheldon Art Mus, Lincoln, NE
PRINTERS: Bill Weege, Madison, WI (BW); Andrew Rubin, Madison, WI (AR); Tandem Press, Univ of Wisconsin, Madison, WI (TanPr)
PUBLISHERS: Tandem Press, Univ of Wisconsin, Madison, WI (TanPr)
GALLERIES: Fischbach Gallery, New York, NY; East End Gallery, Provincetown, MA
MAILING ADDRESS: 67 Vestry St, New York, NY 10013

TITLE	PUBLISHER	PRINTER	DATE	MEDIUM	DIMENSION (PAPER SIZE) IN INCHES	TYPE OF PAPER	EDITION NUMBER	NO. OF COLORS	ORIGINAL OPENING PRICE	CURRENT RETAIL PRICE
CURRENT EDITIONS:										
Little Verona, Wisconsin	TanPr	BW/AR/TanPr	1988	LC	13 X 22	R/BFK/W	40	16	750	750

LEO POSILLICO

PUBLISHERS: Martin Lawrence Limited Editions, Van Nuys, CA (MLLE)
PRINTERS: Alexander Heinrici, NY (AH); Studio Heinrici, NY (SH); Impressions Limited (IL); Rosillo Studio (RS)
GALLERIES: Martin Lawrence Galleries, Sherman Oaks, CA & Los Angeles, CA & Newport Beach, CA & Short Hills, NJ & Palm Springs, CA & Redondo Beach, CA & Escondido, CA & Thousand Oaks, CA & West Los Angeles, CA & Santa Clara, CA; Florence Art Gallery, Dallas, TX; Emporium Enterprises, Inc, Dallas, TX

TITLE	PUBLISHER	PRINTER	DATE	MEDIUM	DIMENSION (PAPER SIZE) IN INCHES	TYPE OF PAPER	EDITION NUMBER	NO. OF COLORS	ORIGINAL OPENING PRICE	CURRENT RETAIL PRICE
CURRENT EDITIONS:										
Community Exhibit	MLLE	AH/SH	1986	SP	31 X 36	SOM	500		500	2350
Artists Have All the Fun	MLLE	AH/SH	1986	SP	38 X 33	SOM	500		500	1800
Break is Over	MLLE	RS	1986	SP	28 X 36	SOM	500		500	1800
Flasher's Convention	MLLE	AS	1987	SP	35 X 44	SOM	500		500	2000
Shoppers	MLLE	IL	1987	SP	33 X 42	SOM	500		500	1800
Guilty of Free Expression	MLLE	AS	1987	SP	33 X 42	SOM	500		500	1950
Uncontrollable Season	MLLE	AS	1987	SP	35 X 44	SOM	500		500	1750
Having a Mind of Your Own	MLLE	AS	1988	SP	39 X 30	SOM	500		550	1750
Life of a Cactus	MLLE	AS	1988	SP	37 X 30	SOM	500		550	1750
Shopper's Paradise	MLLE	AS	1989	SP	35 X 43	SOM	500		600	1750
Artist Crossing	MLLE	AS	1989	SP	34 X 43	SOM	500		600	1600
After the Rain	MLLE	AS	1989	SP	33 X 45	SOM	505		600	1650

The retail prices of the 100,000 limited edition prints quoted in this directory are subject to change. Print publishers, artists and galleries were the direct sources for these quotations. Prices in the secondary market listed as "Sold Out Editions (Rare)" indicate that the publisher has a limited supply of that print or that the print is difficult to locate in the galleries.

CONCETTO POSSATI

BORN: Vecchio, Padova, Italy; 1935
EDUCATION: L'Instituto de'Arte, Bologna, Italy
TEACHING: Prof, Art, Accademia de Belle Arti, Urbino, Italy
COLLECTIONS: Bronx Mus, NY; Pushkin Mus, Moscow, USSR; Museo de Sao Paulo, Brazil; Museo de Ixelles, Brussels, Belgium

PRINTERS: American Atelier, NY (AA)
PUBLISHERS: Circle Fine Art, Chicago, IL (CFA)
GALLERIES: Circle Galleries, San Diego, CA & San Francisco, CA & Northbrook, IL & Pittsburgh, PA & Houston, TX & Soho, NY & Chicago, IL & Scottsdale, AZ & Beverly Hills, CA & Costa Mesa, CA & Sherman Oaks, CA & Palm Beach, FL & Honolulu, HI & New Orleans, LA & Las Vegas, NV & Seattle, WA

TITLE	PUBLISHER	PRINTER	DATE	MEDIUM	DIMENSION (PAPER SIZE) IN INCHES	TYPE OF PAPER	EDITION NUMBER	NO. OF COLORS	ORIGINAL OPENING PRICE	CURRENT RETAIL PRICE
SOLD OUT EDITIONS (RARE):										
Pear is a Pear	CFA	AA	1980	SP	36 X 36		200		200	375
CURRENT EDITIONS:										
Tomato	CFA	AA	1980	SP	36 X 26		200		175	375

RUDY O POZZATTI

BORN: Telluride, CO; January 14, 1925
EDUCATION: Univ of Colorado, BFA, 1948, MFA, 1950, Hon PhD, 1973; Studied with Max Beckman & Ben Shahn
TEACHING: Asst Prof, Printmaking & Painting, Univ of Nebraska, Lincoln, NE, 1950–56; Prof, Printmaking, Indiana Univ, Bloomington, IN, 1956–72, Distinguished Prof, 1972 to present
AWARDS: Fulbright Fel, 1952–53, 1963–64; Ford Found Grant, Tamarind Lithography Workshop, Los Angeles, CA, 1963; Guggenheim Fel, Italy, 1963–64; Fine Arts Found Grant, Ft Wayne, IN, 1974; Nat Endowment for the Arts Fel, 1974
RECENT EXHIB: Sioux City Art Center, IA, 1989,92; Northern Kentucky Univ, Highland Heights, KY, 1992

COLLECTIONS: Mus of Mod Art, NY; Fogg Mus, Harvard Univ, Cambridge, MA; Philadelphia Mus of Art, PA; Pennsylvania Acad of Fine Art, Phila, PA; Boston Mus of Fine Arts, MA; Art Inst of Chicago, IL; Cleveland Mus of Art, OH; Los Angeles County Mus, CA; Dayton Art Inst, OH; Cincinnati Art Mus, OH; Honolulu Acad of Arts, HI; Yale Univ, New Haven, CT; J B Speed Mus, Louisville, KY; Pushkin Mus, Moscow, Russia; Toronto Mus of Art, Can; Malmo Mus, Malmo, Sweden; Mus of Art, Sydney, Australia
PRINTERS: David Kesiter, Bloomington, IN (DK); David Calkins, Bloomington, IN (DC); Echo Press, Bloomington, IN (EPr); Artist (ART)
PUBLISHERS: Echo Press, Bloomington, IN (EPr); Artist (ART)
GALLERIES: Jane Haslem Gallery, Wash, DC; Heath Gallery, Atlanta, GA; Graphics Gallery, San Francisco, CA; Neville-Sargent Gallery, Chicago, IL; Echo Press, Bloomington, IN
MAILING ADDRESS: 117 S Meadowbrook Ave, Bloomington, IN 47401

TITLE	PUBLISHER	PRINTER	DATE	MEDIUM	DIMENSION (PAPER SIZE) IN INCHES	TYPE OF PAPER	EDITION NUMBER	NO. OF COLORS	ORIGINAL OPENING PRICE	CURRENT RETAIL PRICE
SOLD OUT EDITIONS (RARE):										
Homage to Brunelleschi	ART	ART	1968	IB	37 X 25	R/100	35	1	350	1200
Homage to Vesalius	ART	ART	1968	IC	37 X 25	R/100	35	2	350	1200
Apollo	ART	ART	1970	IC	36 X 24	R/100	50	11	350	1200
Computer Person	ART	ART	1975	LC/AL/MY	13 X 17	R/100	45	3	250	750
To Outer Worlds	ART	ART	1976	LC/CO	20 X 14	R/100	22	4	250	750
Treaty at Vermillion	EPr	DK/DC/EPr	1979	LC	22 X 17	GOYA	30	3	175	500
Homage to Sharaku	EPr	DK/DC/EPr	1979	LC	30 X 21	GOYA	42	6	350	600
Eclipse	EPr	DK/DC/EPr	1979	EC	9 X 9	R/100	38	6	150	400
Blue Totem	EPr	DK/DC/EPr	1980	LC/W	24 X 18	R/100	18	11	350	600
Garden of Eden	EPr	DK/DC/EPr	1980	LC	17 X 24	R/100	20	6	350	600
Pecos Sky	EPr	DK/DC/EPr	1980	LC/W	27 X 21	R/100	28	9	375	600
Stag Petroglyph	EPr	DK/DC/EPr	1980	LC	12 X 14	R/100	15	5	200	400
Newspaper Rock	EPr	DK/DC/EPr	1980	LC	24 X 16	R/100	15	3	275	500
Desert Bloom	EPr	DK/DC/EPr	1980	LC	19 X 16	R/100	12	7	275	500
Petroglyphs of Today	EPr	DK/DC/EPr	1980	LC	15 X 22	R/100	18	4	250	500
Three Rivers Petroglyphs	EPr	DK/DC/EPr	1980	LC	16 X 12	R/100	20	4	250	500
Night of the Scorpion	EPr	DK/DC/EPr	1980	LC	16 X 12	R/100	18	5	250	500
CURRENT EDITIONS:										
The Raven	EPr	DK/DC/EPr	1981	LC	31 X 44	R/BFK/W	30	6	450	800
Enchanted Land/Seven Views	EPr	DK/DC/EPr	1984	LC	37 X 25	KAY/CR	30	38	500	800
Darwin's Bestiary (with Philip Appleman)	EPr	DK/DC/EPr	1986	LC/WC	19 X 14	KIT & R/BFK	175	6	750	1000
Israel: Words and Images	EPr	DK/DC/EPr	1990	LB	15 X 11	AC	35	1	1800	2000

LUCIO POZZI

BORN: Milano, Italy; November 29, 1935; US Citizen
EDUCATION: Studied with Michael Noble, Milan, Italy, 1955–59
TEACHING: Asst Prof, Art & Art History, Cooper Union, NY, 1969–75; Vis Prof, Art, Princeton Univ, NJ, 1975; Sr Critic, Grad Sculpture Prog, Yale Univ, New Haven, CT, 1990; Inst, Art, Sch of Visual Arts, NY, 1978 to present
AWARDS: Nat Endowment for the Arts Fel, 1983

RECENT EXHIB: Julian Pretto, NY, 1990; Univ of Maine Mus, Orono, ME, 1989,92
COLLECTIONS: Mus of Mod Art, NY; Mus of Contemp Art, Chicago, IL; Detroit Art Inst, MI
PRINTERS: Marjorie Van Dyke, NY (MVD); Printmaking Workshop, NY (PW)
GALLERIES: Alice Simsar Gallery, Ann Arbor, MI; John Weber Gallery, New York, NY; Hal Bromm Gallery, New York, NY
MAILING ADDRESS: 142 Greene St, New York, NY 10012

TITLE	PUBLISHER	PRINTER	DATE	MEDIUM	DIMENSION (PAPER SIZE) IN INCHES	TYPE OF PAPER	EDITION NUMBER	NO. OF COLORS	ORIGINAL OPENING PRICE	CURRENT RETAIL PRICE
CURRENT EDITIONS:										
Sen's Fence	ART	MVD/PW	1987	MON/CC	29 X 42 EA	AP/BL/JAP	1 EA		1400 EA	1800 EA

DAVID RAMAGE PRENTICE

BORN: Hartford, CT; December 22, 1943
EDUCATION: Hartford Art Sch, CT
TEACHING: Vis Instr, Painting, Hartford Art Sch, Univ of Hartford, CT, 1970
COLLECTIONS: Mus of Mod Art, NY; Yale Univ, New Haven, CT; Wadsworth Atheneum, Hartford, CT; Corcoran Gallery, Wash, DC; Nat Gallery of Art, Wash, DC; Aldrich Mus of Contemp Art, Ridgefield, CT
PRINTERS: Larry B Wright, NY (LBW); Styria Studio, NY (SS)
PUBLISHERS: Art Equity Inc, Toronto, ON, Canada (AEI); Prestige Art Ltd, Mamaroneck, NY (PA)
GALLERIES: Stephen Rosenberg, New York, NY; Alan Brown Gallery, Hartsdale, NY
MAILING ADDRESS: 654 Broadway, New York, NY 10012

TITLE	PUBLISHER	PRINTER	DATE	MEDIUM	DIMENSION (PAPER SIZE) IN INCHES	TYPE OF PAPER	EDITION NUMBER	NO. OF COLORS	ORIGINAL OPENING PRICE	CURRENT RETAIL PRICE
CURRENT EDITIONS:										
Untitled	PA	SS	1976	LC/SP/CO	24 X 35	R/BFK	110	HC	200	400
Ava	AEI	LBW	1981	SP	58 X 32	R/BFK	225	10	400	600
Kes An Ka	AEI	LBW	1981	SP	58 X 32	R/BFK	225	10	450	600

DAVID PRESTON

BORN: Sydney, Australia
EDUCATION: Nat Art Sch, Sydney, Australia
COLLECTIONS: Nat Gallery of Australia, Canberra, Australia; Art Gallery of Western Australia, Sydney, Australia; Nat Gallery, Lagos, Nigeria; Georges Pompidou Centre, Paris, France; Paliament House Coll, Canberra, Australia; Woolongong Gallery, Australia; World Trade Centre, Melbourne, Australia; Art Bank, Sydney, Australia; H R H Queen Elizabeth II, London, England
PRINTERS: Studio One, Inc, NY (SOI)
PUBLISHERS: John Szoke Graphics, Inc, NY (JSG)
GALLERIES: John Szoke Graphics, Inc, New York, NY

TITLE	PUBLISHER	PRINTER	DATE	MEDIUM	DIMENSION (PAPER SIZE) IN INCHES	TYPE OF PAPER	EDITION NUMBER	NO. OF COLORS	ORIGINAL OPENING PRICE	CURRENT RETAIL PRICE
CURRENT EDITIONS:										
Canna Lilies	JSG	SOI	1988	LI/HC	39 X 30	SOM	50	5	800	800
Strelizia	JSG	SOI	1989	LI/HC	40 X 30	SOM	50	8	800	800
Saddleback	JSG	SOI	1989	LI/HC	30 X 42	SOM	50	7	800	800

ROGER PREUSS

BORN: Waterville, MN; January 29, 1922
EDUCATION: Minneapolis Co of Art & Design, MN, BFA, 1945–47
TEACHING: Minneapolis Col of Art & Design, MN
AWARDS: Nat Audubon Art Award, 1959; Mead Graphics Award, 1963; Nat Wildlife Award, 1964; Explorers Club Fel, 1977; US Nat Mark Twain Award, 1978
RECENT EXHIB: Minnesota Art Mus, MN, 1990; Blauvelt Art Mus, Oradel, NJ, 1990
COLLECTIONS: Univ of Minnesota Art Mus, Minneapolis, MN; Blauvelt Art Mus, Oradel, NJ; Weisman Art Mus, Minneapolis, MN; Center for Western Studies, Sioux Falls, SD; Le Sueur Historical Soc Mus, Elysian, MN; Smithsonian Inst, Wash, DC; Nat Wildlife Fed Coll, Wash DC; Montana Historical Soc Mus, Helena, MT
PRINTERS: George C Miller & Son, NY (GCM); Phelps (P); Johnson (J); Colwell (C); Royal (R); McGill (M); Podany, (PO)
PUBLISHERS: Wildlife of America, Minneapolis, MN (WOA)
GALLERIES: Le Sueur Historical Society Mus, Elysian, MN; Wildlife of America, Minneapolis, MN; Cornell Norby, Newport Beach, CA
MAILING ADDRESS: Box 58004, Minneapolis, MN 55485/2224 Grand Ave, Minneapolis, MN 55405

Roger Preuss
Pheasants in Autumn Habitat
Courtesy Wildlife of America

TITLE	PUBLISHER	PRINTER	DATE	MEDIUM	DIMENSION (PAPER SIZE) IN INCHES	TYPE OF PAPER	EDITION NUMBER	NO. OF COLORS	ORIGINAL OPENING PRICE	CURRENT RETAIL PRICE
SOLD OUT EDITIONS (RARE):										
American Goldeneye	WOA	GCM	1949	LB	12 X 16	R/BFK	250	1	40	4200
Wood Ducks-Along the Creek	WOA	P	1953	ENG	9 X 11	STP	300	1	25	500
Woodies on a Spring Morn	WOA	J	1953	LC	16 X 20	RAP	400	4	25	800
Snow Geese	WOA	ART	1964	SP	8 X 9	STP	100	7	25	1500
Take a Boy Hunting	WOA	P	1967	ENG	10 X 8	STP	250	1	30	600
Sharp-Tailed Grouse	WOA	C	1968	LC	19 X 26	VEL	40	4	100	600
Canada Geese at Sunrise	WOA	R	1970	LC	22 X 28	RAP	400	4	25	1600
Largemouth Bass	WOA	J	1970	LC	16 X 20	VEL	40	4	125	500
Waiting for Mom	WOA	R	1970	LC	22 X 27	RAP	18	4	200	1700
CURRENT EDITIONS:										
Canvasbacks at Dawn	WOA	J	1971	LC	16 X 20	VEL	15	4	125	400
White-Tailed Deer	WOA	M	1973	LC	26 X 32	AND	20	4	150	450
Black Ducks Against Twilight V/VI	WOA	P	1974	LC	23 X 28	CAR	20	4	225	2200
First Flush-Bobwhite	WOA	I	1975	LC	16 X 20	VEL	50	4	200	500

ROGER PREUSS CONTINUED

TITLE	PUBLISHER	PRINTER	DATE	MEDIUM	DIMENSION (PAPER SIZE) IN INCHES	TYPE OF PAPER	EDITION NUMBER	NO. OF COLORS	ORIGINAL OPENING PRICE	CURRENT RETAIL PRICE
CURRENT EDITIONS:										
Canada Geese	WOA	J	1975	LC	16 X 20	VEL	20	4	150	400
Oolinka	WOA	PO	1975	LC	13 X 11	VEL	100	4	125	1100
Rutting Time	WOA	PO	1976	LC	16 X 20	AND	40	4	200	500
Cougar!	WOA	C	1977	C	19 X 26	VEL	60	4	175	600
Pheasants in Autumn Habit	WOA	RP	1981	LC	12 X 15	RAP	500	6	125	850
Out of the North Wind	WOA	RP	1982	LC	19 X 25	RAP	500	5	100	1250
Commemorative Federal Duck Print	WOA	RP	1989	EB	12 X 14	R/BFK	295	1	200	800

JOE PRICE

BORN: Ferriday, LA; February 6, 1935
EDUCATION: Northwestern Univ, Chicago, IL, BS, 1957; Art Center Col of Design, Los Angeles, CA, 1967–68; Stanford Univ, CA, MA, 1970
TEACHING: Prof, Studio Drawing, Col of San Mateo, CA, 1970 to present
AWARDS: Louis Lozowick Mem Award, Audubon Artists, NY, 1978; Lessing J Rosenwald Prize, Phila Print Club, PA, 1979; Kempshall Clark Award, Bradley, IL, 1981; Paul Lindsay Sample Mem Award, Chautauqua, NY, 1982; Stella Drabkin Mem Award, Am Color Print Soc, NY, 1986; Purchase Award, Ture Bengtz Mem Award, NY, 1986; Moses Lasky Award for Serigraphy, Palo Alto, CA, 1988
RECENT EXHIB: Huntsville Mus of Art, AL, 1987; Carnegie-Mellon Univ, Pittsburgh, PA, 1988; Wenniger Graphics, Boston, MA, 1988; Gallery 30, San Mateo, CA, 1988
COLLECTIONS: Huntsville Mus of Art, AL; Louisiana State Mus, New Orleans, LA; Midwest Mus of Am Art, Elkhart, IN; Nat Coll of Poland, Cracow, Poland; New Orleans Mus of Art, LA; Oakland Mus of Art, CA; Philadelphia Mus of Art, PA; Boise State Univ, ID; Bradley Univ, IL; California State Univ, Chico, CA; Univ of Chicago, IL; Texas Tech Mus, Lubbock, TX; Cabo Frio Mus, Rio de Janeiro, Brazil; Portland Mus of Art, ME; San Francisco Mus of Mod Art, CA; North Dakota State Col, Minot, ND; Santa Barbara Col, CA; Spencer Gallery, Univ of Arkansas, Little Rock, AR; State Univ of New York, Potsdamn, NY; Northwestern Univ, Chicago, IL; Miami Univ Mus, OH; Helen Euphrat Gallery, De Anza Col, CA; California Col of Arts & Crafts, Oakland, CA; Col of San Mateo, CA; Achenback Found for Graphic Arts, San Francisico, CA; Mus for Int Contemp Graphic Art, Fredrikstad, Norway; Mus of Int Contemp Art, Salvador, Brazil; Hunt Inst for Botanical Documentation, Carnegie-Mellon Univ, Pittsburgh, PA; Lufkin Historical & Creative Arts Mus, TX; Library of Congress, Wash, DC; Nat Mus of Am Art, Smithsonian Inst, Wash, DC; Worcester Art Mus, MA; Sheldon Mem Art Gallery, Univ of Nebraska, Lincoln, NE

Joe Price
Tulip
Courtesy Gallery 30

PRINTERS: Artist (ART)
PUBLISHERS: Artist (ART)
GALLERIES: Associated American Artists, New York, NY; Editions Galleries, S Melbourne, Australia; Gallery 30, Burlingame, CA; Jane Haslem Gallery, Wash, DC; Wenniger Graphics, Boston, MA; First Impressions/Barbara Linhard, Carmel, CA; Atlee & Atlee Fine Arts, Eureka, CA; Ballas Artes, Santa Fe, NM
MAILING ADDRESS: 2031 Belle Monti, Belmont, CA 94002

TITLE	PUBLISHER	PRINTER	DATE	MEDIUM	DIMENSION (PAPER SIZE) IN INCHES	TYPE OF PAPER	EDITION NUMBER	NO. OF COLORS	ORIGINAL OPENING PRICE	CURRENT RETAIL PRICE
SOLD OUT EDITIONS (RARE):										
Back Porch	ART	ART	1977	SP	16 X 21	RGPV	50	61	250	2000
Shadows	ART	ART	1977	SP	15 X 21	RGPV	50	42	200	1800
August Morning	ART	ART	1978	SP	16 X 21	RGPV	50	58	250	1800
Raincatcher	ART	ART	1979	SP	7 X 10	RGPS	75	82	175	800
December Gifts	ART	ART	1979	SP	14 X 20	RGPV	75	67	250	1800
Self Portrait	ART	ART	1981	SP	8 X 10	RMB	20	72	275	1200
California Morning	ART	ART	1981	SP	13 X 22	RMB	100	66	375	2000
Bing Cherries	ART	ART	1984	SP	14 X 16	RMB	100	67	300	1500
Red Ripe	ART	ART	1984	SP	16 X 22	RMB	100	74	350	1500
Bag of Candy	ART	ART	1984	SP	16 X 22	RMB	50	63	450	1500
CURRENT EDITIONS:										
Artist's Study	ART	ART	1981	SP	8 X 12	RMB	100	56	200	250
Marvel	ART	ART	1981	SP	14 X 16	RMB	100	54	300	350
Promise for Next Year	ART	ART	1982	SP	17 X 25	RMB	100	51	400	500
Afternoon Reflections	ART	ART	1982	SP	10 X 13	RMB	100	33	150	200
On a White Table	ART	ART	1983	SP	10 X 13	RMB	100	61	200	300
Cider Crock	ART	ART	1983	SP	14 X 16	RMB	100	43	250	300
Garlic	ART	ART	1983	SP	6 X 7	RMB	100	36	100	150
Fan with Feathers	ART	ART	1984	SP	10 X 11	RMB	100	44	200	275
Fan with Orange	ART	ART	1984	SP	10 X 11	RMB	100	47	200	275
Broken Blue	ART	ART	1984	SP	13 X 14	RMB	100	56	300	375
Trio	ART	ART	1985	SP	18 X 22	RMB	100	35	350	400
Homage: Studio Rackboard	ART	ART	1985	SP	15 X 18	RMB	100	72	350	350
For One	ART	ART	1985	SP	10 X 14	RMB	100	57	300	425

JOE PRICE CONTINUED

TITLE	PUBLISHER	PRINTER	DATE	MEDIUM	DIMENSION (PAPER SIZE) IN INCHES	TYPE OF PAPER	EDITION NUMBER	NO. OF COLORS	ORIGINAL OPENING PRICE	CURRENT RETAIL PRICE
CURRENT EDITIONS:										
New Growth	ART	ART	1985	SP	12 X 14	RMB	100	72	275	375
Belladonna	ART	ART	1986	SP	22 X 24	RMB	100	54	450	525
Egg Series I: Red Vise	ART	ART	1986	SP	7 X 9	RMB	100	51	150	275
Egg Series II: Cowskull	ART	ART	1986	SP	7 X 13	RMB	100	57	200	250
Soaring Thoughts	ART	ART	1986	SP	8 X 24	RMB	100	40	400	425
Iris in Brown Bottles	ART	ART	1987	SP	23 X 29	RMB	100	90	500	625
Egg Series III: Barbed Wire	ART	ART	1987	SP	9 X 10	RMB	100	46	200	275
Egg Series IV: String	ART	ART	1988	SP	9 X 10	RMB	100	57	200	250
Egg Series V: Manikin	ART	ART	1988	SP	12 X 17	RMB	100	47	350	350
Egg Series VI: Knife	ART	ART	1988	SP	12 X 17	RMB	100	47	350	350
A Single Yellow	ART	ART	1988	SP	17 X 20	RMB	100	75	500	500
Tulips	ART	ART	1988	SP	23 X 29	RMB	100	69	625	625

KEN PRICE

BORN: Los Angeles, CA; 1935
EDUCATION: Univ of California, Los Angeles, CA; Otis Art Inst, Los Angeles, CA; Chouinard Art Inst, CA; Univ of Southern California, BFA, 1956; State Univ of New York, Albany, NY, MFA, 1958
AWARDS: Tamarind Fel, Albuquerque, NM, 1968–69
RECENT EXHIB: James Corcoran Gallery, Santa Monica, CA, 1987; Contemp Mus, Honolulu, HI, 1989; Rena Bransten Gallery, San Francisco, CA, 1989; Menil Coll, Houston, TX, 1992; Walker Art Center, Minneapolis, MN, 1992; Charles Cowles Gallery, NY, 1992
COLLECTIONS: Los Angeles County Mus of Art, CA
PRINTERS: Cirrus Editions Workshop, Los Angeles, CA (CEW); Tamarind Inst, Albuquerque, NM (TI); Gemini GEL, Los Angeles, CA (GEM)
GALLERIES: Cirrus Editions Ltd, Los Angeles, CA; Hanson Fuller Gallery, San Francisco, CA; James Corcoran Gallery, Santa Monica, CA; Betsy Rosenfield Gallery, Chicago, IL; Soma Fine Art, San Francisco, CA; Thomas Segal Gallery, Boston, MA; Tally Richards Gallery, Taos, NM; Rena Bransten Gallery, San Francisco, CA; Gemini Gallery, Los Angeles, CA; Greenberg Gallery, St Louis, MO; Willard Gallery, New York, NY; Charles Cowles Gallery, New York, NY; Dunlap-Freidenrich Fine Art, Newport Beach, CA; CompassRose Gallery, Ltd, Chicago, IL; Moira James Gallery, Green Valley, NV
MAILING ADDRESS: Box 1356, Taos, NM 87571

TITLE	PUBLISHER	PRINTER	DATE	MEDIUM	DIMENSION (PAPER SIZE) IN INCHES	TYPE OF PAPER	EDITION NUMBER	NO. OF COLORS	ORIGINAL OPENING PRICE	CURRENT RETAIL PRICE
SOLD OUT EDITIONS (RARE):										
Figurine Cup Series (Set of 6):										
Figurine Cup I	GEM	GEM	1970	LC	22 X 18	ARJ	59	10	150	2000
Figurine Cup II	GEM	GEM	1970	LC	22 X 18	ARJ	60	10	150	2000
Figurine Cup III	GEM	GEM	1970	LC/SP	19 X 15	ARJ	63	7	150	2000
Figurine Cup IV	GEM	GEM	1970	LC/SP	22 X 18	ARJ	61	5	150	2000
Figurine Cup V	GEM	GEM	1970	LC	22 X 18	ARJ	60	10	150	2000
Figurine Cup VI	GEM	GEM	1970	LC/SP	22 X 18	ARJ	63	10	150	2000
Interior Series:										
Green Turtle Cup	GEM	GEM	1971	SP	57 X 40	ARJ	75	19	250	1500
Lizard Cup	GEM	GEM	1971	SP	30 X 40	ARJ	75	12	200	1800
French Figurine Cup	GEM	GEM	1971	SP	40 X 30	ARJ	75	8	200	900
Chairs, Table, Rug, Cup	GEM	GEM	1971	SP	52 X 42	ARJ	75	12	250	1250
Hermit Crab Cup	CE	CEW	1972	SP	28 X 22	HMP	60	14	150	1200
Kauai Crab Cup	CE	CEW	1972	SP	24 X 20	HMP	60	18	150	1200
Frog Cup	GEM	GEM	1975	SP	40 X 30	R/BFK	71	18	500	1500
Untitled	TI	TI	1977	LC	30 X 22	AP/W	70	35	500	1250
Club Flamingo	GEM	GEM	1989	LC/SP	24 X 17		28	5	800	800
At Club XX	GEM	GEM	1989	LC/SP	30 X 21		10	9	1200	1200
Club XX	GEM	GEM	1989	EC	18 X 15		30	4	600	600
Club Atomica	GEM	GEM	1989	PH/ENG	22 X 14		20	1	600	600
Club Romance	GEM	GEM	1989	PH/ENG	9 X 9		100	1	500	500
Don't Think about Her When You're Trying to Drive	GEM	GEM	1989	LC/SP	32 X 22		25	10	1200	1200

TERRI PRIEST

BORN: Worcester, MA; January 20, 1928
EDUCATION: Worcester Art Mus Sch, MA, 1947–48; Quinsigamond Comm Col, Worcester, MA, 1972,73; Univ of Massachusetts, Amherst, MA, BFA, Painting, 1975, MFA, Painting, 1977
TEACHING: Instr, Worcester Art Mus Sch, MA, 1967–70; Instr, DeCordova Mus Sch, Lincoln, MA, 1971–73; Instr, Framingham State Col, MA, 1977–78; Assoc Prof, Painting, Visual Design & Color, Holy Cross Col, Worcester, MA, 1978 to present
AWARDS: Worcester Art Mus, Frances Kinnicutt Travel Award, 1974; Mead Corp, Purchase Award, 1965; Holy Cross Col, Batchelor (Ford) Summer Fac Fel, 1981,84; Holy Cross Col, Research & Publication Awards, 1979,82,86; Dorland Mountain Colony, Temecula, CA, 1986
COLLECTIONS: DeCordova Mus, Lincoln, MA; Worcester Art Mus, MA; Brockton Art Mus, MA; Aldrich Mus of Contemp Art, Ridgefield, CT; Bundy Art Center, Waitsfield, VT
PRINTERS: Atelier Ettinger, NY (AE); Artist (ART)
PUBLISHERS: Holy Cross Col, Worcester, MA (HC); Mercantile Printing Co, Worcester, MA (MP); Ethel Putterman Gallery, Orleans, MA (EP); Gallery at OUI, Boston, MA (OUI); Thronja Art Gallery, Springfield, MA (TA); Eleanor Ettinger, Inc, NY (EEI); Artworks, Worcester, MA (AW); Artist (ART)
GALLERIES: Gallery at OUI, Boston, MA; Thronja Art Gallery, Springfield, MA; Artworks, Worcester, MA; Nuance Gallery, Tampa, FL; Signature Gallery, Canton, CT
MAILING ADDRESS: 5 Pratt St, Worcester, MA 01609

TERRI PRIEST CONTINUED

TITLE	PUBLISHER	PRINTER	DATE	MEDIUM	DIMENSION (PAPER SIZE) IN INCHES	TYPE OF PAPER	EDITION NUMBER	NO. OF COLORS	ORIGINAL OPENING PRICE	CURRENT RETAIL PRICE
SOLD OUT EDITIONS (RARE):										
Jericho, USA	EP	ART	1973	SP	30 X 22	R/100	50	2	150	500
Balcony at Nice	EP	ART	1976	SP	22 X 16	R/100	20	6	100	350
Stairway to the Stars	EP	ART	1980	SP	27 X 17	R/100	30	8	200	500
Night Passage	ART	ART	1980	SP	22 X 33	R/100	20	8	200	500
I Dreamed I Climbed a Rainbow	OUI	ART	1980	SP	22 X 33	R/100	20	8	200	500
Afternoon on Thera	ART	ART	1982	SP	30 X 22	FAB	25	13	250	500
CURRENT EDITIONS:										
Sous Le Pont	ART	ART	1974	SP	29 X 19	R/100	10	3	100	200
Three Towers	EP	ART	1977	SP	18 X 24	R/100	15	5	150	250
Duomo Day	EP	AKI	1978	SP	26 X 20	R/100	10	5	150	250
Moonlight Bridge	TA	ART	1979	SP	24 X 19	R/100	15	5	150	250
Walls and Doors	ART	ART	1979	SP	24 X 19	R/100	15	7	150	250
Passage to Beit-El	EP	ART	1979	SP	31 X 22	R/100	20	8	200	350
Blue Shadows in the Street	ART	ART	1979	SP	24 X 12	R/100	15	9	150	350
Night Light	OUI	ART	1980	SP	34 X 24	R/100	20	5	200	400
Pei in the Sky	OUI	ART	1980	SP	34 X 24	R/100	20	5	200	300
Summer Memory	OUI	ART	1980	SP	27 X 19	R/100	25	15	200	350
Entrance to the Night	EEI	AE	1984	LC	22 X 30	AP	275	12	200	250
Stepshadows	EEI	AE	1984	LC	30 X 22	AP	275	12	200	250
The Conversation	ART	ART	1984	SP	30 X 22	LEN	25	14	300	400
A Fair Wind	ART	ART	1984	SP	22 X 30	AP	25	14	300	400
Summer Shadows	ART	ART	1984	SP	22 X 30	FAB	20	23	300	400

RICHARD EDMUND PRINCE

BORN: Comox, BC, Canada; April 6, 1949
EDUCATION: Univ of British Columbia, Can, 3A, Art History, 1971, Study, 1972–73; Emma Lake Artists Workshop, Saskatewan, Can, with Ron Kitai, 1970
TEACHING: Instr, Sculpture, Vancouver Comm Col, BC, Can, 1974–75; Instr, Fine Arts & Sculpture, Univ of British Columbia, Can, 1975 to present
AWARDS: Award, Art Vancouver, Can, 1974; Canadian Council of the Arts Grant, Canadian Govt, 1975,1977–78
RECENT EXHIB: 49th Parallel Gallery, NY, 1989; Fundacion San German, PR, 1992; Whitney Mus of Am Art, NY, 1992
COLLECTIONS: Nat Gallery of Canada, Ottawa, Can; Vancouver Art Gallery, British Columbia, Can; Victoria Art Col, Govt of British Columbia, Can; Canadian Council Art Bank, Ottawa, Can; Vancouver Art Coll, Can
PRINTERS: Artist (ART); Arber & Son Editions, Alameda, NM (ASE); Aaron Klein, NY (AK); Ultimate, Inc, NY (UI)
PUBLISHERS: Tina Summerlin, NY (TS); I C Editions, NY (ICE); Painter Editions, Hong Kong (PaEd)
GALLERIES: Equinox Galleries, Vancouver, BC, Canada; Feature, Chicago, IL; Editions Ilene Kurtz, New York, NY; 303 Gallery, New York, NY; Kuhlenschmidt/Simon Gallery, Los Angeles, CA; Stuart Regen Gallery, Los Angeles, CA; Laura Carpenter Fine Art, Santa Fe, NM; Barbara Gladstone Gallery, New York, NY; Simon Watson Gallery, New York, NY
MAILING ADDRESS: 285 W 18th Ave, Vancouver, BC, Canada V5Y 2A8

TITLE	PUBLISHER	PRINTER	DATE	MEDIUM	DIMENSION (PAPER SIZE) IN INCHES	TYPE OF PAPER	EDITION NUMBER	NO. OF COLORS	ORIGINAL OPENING PRICE	CURRENT RETAIL PRICE
CURRENT EDITIONS:										
5 Polaroid Photographs:										
Angie	TS	ART	1986	PH	24 X 20	AP	5		1200	1500
Bunny Bleu	TS	ART	1986	PH	24 X 20	AP	5		1200	1500
Misty	TS	ART	1986	PH	24 X 20	AP	5		1200	1500
Misty Two	TS	ART	1986	PH	24 X 20	AP	5		1200	1500
Sissy Carrie	TS	ART	1986	PH	24 X 20	AP	5		1200	1500
(No Title) (Set of 12 Lithographs)	ICE	ASE	1991	LB	15 X 11 EA	AC	26		8000 SET	8000 SET
C & G (Set of 14 Ektacolor Prints)	PaEd	AK/UI	1992	PH	20 X 24 EA	Ekta	A-Z	Varies	15000 SET	15000 SET

CHARLES ROY PURCELL

BORN: Baltimore, MD; 1946
EDUCATION: Maryland Inst of Col of Art, Baltimore, MD, BFA, 1968
AWARDS: Ford Found Grants (2)
COLLECTIONS: Maryland Inst Col of Art, Baltimore, MD
PRINTERS: American Atelier, NY (AA)
PUBLISHERS: Circle Fine Art, Chicago, IL (CFA)
GALLERIES: Associated American Artists, New York, NY; Circle Galleries, San Diego, CA & San Francisco, CA & Northbrook, IL & Pittsburgh, PA & Houston, TX & Soho, NY & Chicago, IL & Scottsdale, AZ & Beverly Hills, CA & Costa Mesa, CA & Sherman Oaks, CA & Palm Beach, FL & Honolulu, HI & New Orleans, LA & Las Vegas, NV & Seattle, WA

TITLE	PUBLISHER	PRINTER	DATE	MEDIUM	DIMENSION (PAPER SIZE) IN INCHES	TYPE OF PAPER	EDITION NUMBER	NO. OF COLORS	ORIGINAL OPENING PRICE	CURRENT RETAIL PRICE
SOLD OUT EDITIONS (RARE):										
Knees	CFA	AA	1980	LC	27 X 41	AP	250		100	325
CURRENT EDITIONS:										
Girl on a Bench	CFA	AA	1980	LC	26 X 40	AP	250		100	325
February 14th	CFA	AA	1980	LC	22 X 30	AP	250		100	325

JANIS PROVISOR

BORN: Brooklyn, NY; 1946
EDUCATION: Univ of Michigan, Sch of Arch & Design, Ann Arbor, MI, 1964–66; Univ of Cincinnati, Col of Design, Art & Arch, OH, 1966–68; San Francisco, CA, BFA, 1969, MFA, 1971
TEACHING: Teaching Asst, Painting, San Francisco Art Inst, CA, 1971; Emmanuel Walter Gallery, San Francisco Art Inst, CA, 1971–73; Lectr, Art Dept, Humboldt State Univ, CA, 1973–75; Asst Prof, Art Dept, Univ of Texas, Austin, TX, 1975–78; Instr, Painting, San Francisco Art Inst, 1978; San Francisco Art Inst, CA, Summers, 1975,80,81; Vis Art, Tyler Sch of Art, Temple Univ, Phila, PA, 1982; Instr, Painting, Sch of Visual Arts, NY, 1982–83; Vis Art, Brown Univ, Providence, RI, 1983; Vis Art, Syracuse Univ, NY, 1983; Alfred C Glassell Sch of Art, Mus of Fine Arts, Houston, TX, 1983; Vis Art, Banff Arts Center, Alta, Canada, 1983; Vis Art, Anderson Ranch, Snowmass, CO, 1984
AWARDS: Ford Found Grant, with Univ of Texas, Austin, TX, 1978; Nat Endowment for the Arts, Fel, 1980,85; Colorado Council on the Arts & Humanities Fel, 1988
RECENT EXHIB: Eugene Binder Gallery, Dallas, TX, 1987; Dorothy Goldeen Gallery, Santa Monica, CA, 1988; New Jersey Center for the Visual Arts, Summit, NJ, 1988; Whitney Mus of Am Art, NY, 1988
PRINTERS: Bud Shark, Boulder, CO (BS); Ron Trujillo, Boulder, CO (RT); Artist (ART); Hiroki Morinoue, Honolulu, HI (HM); Shark's Inc, Boulder, CO (SI); Ji Quiz Heng, China (JQH); Jaing Ming, China (JM); Ku Jin Juen, China (KJJ); Fong Jiu Da, China (FJD); Crown Point Press, San Francisco, CA (CPP); Duo Yun Xuan Studio, Shanghai, China (DYX)
PUBLISHERS: Derriére L'Etoile Studios, NY (DES); Diane Villani Editions, NY (DVE); Shark's Inc, Boulder, CO (SI); Crown Point Press, San Francisco, CA (CPP)
GALLERIES: Tavelli Williams Gallery, Aspen, CO; Eugene Binder Gallery, Dallas, TX; Diane Villani Editions, New York, NY; Lisa Sette Gallery, Scottsdale, AZ; Fuller Cross Gallery, San Francisco, CA; Dorothy Goldeen Gallery, Santa Monica, CA; Shark's, Inc, Boulder, CO; Diane Villani Editions, New York, NY; Crown Point Press, San Francisco, CA & New York, NY; Quartet Editions, New York, NY

Janis Provisor
John's Place I
Courtesy Shark's, Inc

TITLE	PUBLISHER	PRINTER	DATE	MEDIUM	DIMENSION (PAPER SIZE) IN INCHES	TYPE OF PAPER	EDITION NUMBER	NO. OF COLORS	ORIGINAL OPENING PRICE	CURRENT RETAIL PRICE
SOLD OUT EDITIONS (RARE):										
Scattered Petals	CPP	KJJ/FJD/CPP	1989	WB/CC	24 X 31	SILK/RAG	35		850	1250
CURRENT EDITIONS:										
Parachute	DVE/DES	DES	1985	LC	45 X 28	AP/BL	24		800	80
Rifle	DVE/DES	DES	1985	LC	45 X 28	AP/BL	24		800	80
Near Home	SI	BS/RT/SI	1989	MON	45 X 30 EA	R/BFK	1 EA		3500 EA	5000 EA
About Face (Each Sheet Prepared with Print Composition, Copper & Aluminum Leaf Prior to Printing) (3 Panels)	SI	BS/RT/SI	1989	LC/WC/MON	25 X 59 TOT	R/BFK	25	6	3600	4250
Trophy	SI	BS/RT/SI	1989	MON	25 X 78 EA	R/BFK	1 EA		3500 EA	5000 EA
Eastern States	SI	BS/RT/SI	1989	MON	25 X 59 EA	R/BFK	1 EA		3500 EA	5000 EA
Long Fall	CPP	JQH/JM/CPP	1989	WB/CC	33 X 22	SILK/RAG	75		850	1250
Red Wood	CPP	KJJ/FJD/CPP	1989	WB/CC	22 X 31	SILK/RAG	35		850	1000
Bohemia	CPP	CPP	1991	AB/DPT/CC	44 X 38	R/BFK	10	1	1800	1800
Hinterland	CPP	CPP	1991	AB/DPT/CC	44 X 38	R/BFK	15	1	1800	1800
Philtre Red	CPP	CPP	1991	AB/DPT/CC	44 X 38	R/BFK	15	1	1800	1800
Philtre Black	CPP	CPP	1991	AB/DPT/CC	44 X 38	R/BFK	15	1	1800	1800
Star Throw	CPP	CPP	1991	AB/DPT/CC	21 X 17	R/BFK	15	1	850	850
Star Trap	CPP	CPP	1991	AB/DPT/CC	21 X 17	R/BFK	15	1	850	850
At the Ranch	SI	ART/BS/HM/SI	1992	MON	44 X 32	R/BFK	1 EA	Varies	5000 EA	5000 EA
Lotus Time I-IV (Set of 4)	SI	BS/RT/SI	1992	LC/WC/CC	19 X 16 EA	R/BFK	25 EA		3500 SET	3500 SET
Cross Walk	SI	ART/BS/HM/SI	1992	MON	31 X 28 EA	R/BFK	1 EA	Varies	3800 EA	3800 EA
Inferno	SI	ART/BS/HM/SI	1992	MON	31 X 28 EA	R/BFK	1 EA	Varies	3800 EA	3800 EA
Portrait	SI	ART/BS/HM/SI	1992	MON	31 X 28 EA	R/BFK	1 EA	Varies	3800 EA	3800 EA
Tie Me Up	SI	ART/BS/HM/SI	1992	MON	31 X 28 EA	R/BFK	1 EA	Varies	3800 EA	3800 EA
Chemical Wash	SI	ART/BS/HM/SI	1992	MON	31 X 28 EA	R/BFK	1 EA	Varies	3800 EA	3800 EA
Line Drive	SI	ART/BS/HM/SI	1992	MON	24 X 74 EA	R/BFK	1 EA	Varies	6000 EA	6000 EA
John's Place I (with Aluminum Leaf)	SI	ART/BS/HM/SI	1992	LC/WC	30 X 31	R/BFK	15	5	2000	2000
John's Place I (with Metalic Powder)	SI	ART/BS/HM/SI	1992	LC/WC/CC	29 X 27	R/BFK & SEK	15	5	2000	2000
Jelly (with Metalic Leaf & Metalic Powder)	SI	ART/BS/HM/SI	1992	LC/WC/CC	34 X 35	R/BFK & SEK	15	5	2200	2200
Flat Worm	SI	ART/BS/HM/SI	1992	MON/CC	16 X 13 EA	SLK	1 EA	Varies	800 EA	800 EA

MARTIN PURYEAR

BORN: Washington, DC; May 23, 1941
EDUCATION: Catholic Univ of America, Wash, DC; BFA, 1963; Swedish Royal Acad of Art, Printmaking & Sculpture, 1966–68; Yale Univ, Sch of Art, New Haven, CT, MFA, 1969–71

MARTIN PURYEAR CONTINUED

TEACHING: Asst Instr, Yale Univ, New Haven, CT, 1969–71; Asst Prof, Fish Univ, Nashville, TN, 1971–73; Asst Prof, Univ of Maryland, College Park, MD, 1974–78; Asst Prof, Univ of Illinois, Chicago, IL, 1978 to present
AWARDS: Purchase Prize, Baltimore Mus, MD, 1962; Scandinavian-American Found Study Fel, 1967; Yale Univ, New Haven, CT, Fel, 1969–71; Creative Artists Public Service Grant, 1976–77; Change, Inc, Robert Rauschenberg Found Grant, 1977; Creative & Performing Artists Grants, Univ of Maryland, College Park, MD, 1975, 78; Nat Endowment for the Arts Fel, 1977–78; Yaddo Fel, 1979; Louis Comfort Tiffany Grant, 1982; John Simon Guggenheim Mem Found Fel, 1982; Creative Arts Award, Sculpture, Brandeis Univ, Waltham, MA, 1989; Skowhegan Sch of Painting & Sculpture Award, ME, 1990

RECENT EXHIB: David McKee Gallery, NY, 1987; Whitney Mus of Am Art, NY, 1989; Carnegie Mellon Univ Mus, Pittsburgh, PA, 1989; Brooklyn Mus, NY, 1989; Donald Young Gallery, Chicago, IL, 1989; Governors State Univ, Nathan Mailow Gallery, University Park, IL, 1989,92; Univ of Massachusetts, Amherst, MA, 1992; Phillips Acad, Addison Gallery of Am Art, Andover, MA, 1992; Philadelphia Mus of Art, PA, 1992
PRINTERS: Barbara Spies, Chicago, IL (BS); Landfall Press, Inc, Chicago, IL (LPI)
PUBLISHERS: Landfall Press Inc, Chicago, IL (LPI)
GALLERIES: Nancy Drysdale Gallery, Wash, DC; Donald Young Gallery, Seattle, WA; Landfall Press Inc, Chicago, IL; Hill Gallery, Birmingham, MI; Margo Leavin Gallery, Los Angeles, CA; David McKee Gallery, New York, NY

TITLE	PUBLISHER	PRINTER	DATE	MEDIUM	DIMENSION (PAPER SIZE) IN INCHES	TYPE OF PAPER	EDITION NUMBER	NO. OF COLORS	ORIGINAL OPENING PRICE	CURRENT RETAIL PRICE
SOLD OUT EDITIONS (RARE):										
Dark Loop	LPI	BS/LPI	1982	WC	23 X 30	KOZO	35	1	500	1200

CAROL PYLANT

BORN: Louisville, KY; 1953
EDUCATION: Wayne State Univ, Detroit, MI, BFA, 1977, MFA, 1979
AWARDS: Milton & Sally Avery Award, Painting, 1985; Nat Endowment for the Arts Regional Visual Arts Fel, 1988; Faculty Research Fel, Univ of Wisconsin, Madison, WI, 1990
RECENT EXHIB: Rockefeller Found, Bellagio Study & Conference Center, Italy, 1987; Bowdoin Col Mus of Art, Brunswick, ME, 1989; Levinson Kane Gallery, Boston, MA, 1990; Hobe Sound Gallery, Brunswick, ME, 1990

COLLECTIONS: Bowdoin Col, Brunswick, ME; Oberpfalzer Kunstlerhaus, Schvandorf/Fromberg, Germany; Univ of Kansas, Lawrence, KS; Virginia Center for Creative Arts, Richmond, VA; Univ of Wisconsin, Grad Sch, Madison, WI
PRINTERS: Bill Weege, Madison, WI (BW); Andrew Rubin, Madison, WI (AR); Tandem Press, Univ of Wisconsin, Madison, WI (TanPr)
PUBLISHERS: Tandem Press, Univ of Wisconsin, Madison, WI (TanPr)
GALLERIES: Levinson Kane Gallery, Boston, MA; Hobe Sound Gallery, Brunswick, ME

Carol Pylant
The Secret Sharer
Courtesy Tandem Press

Carol Pylant
New York Writer
Courtesy Tandem Press

TITLE	PUBLISHER	PRINTER	DATE	MEDIUM	DIMENSION (PAPER SIZE) IN INCHES	TYPE OF PAPER	EDITION NUMBER	NO. OF COLORS	ORIGINAL OPENING PRICE	CURRENT RETAIL PRICE
CURRENT EDITIONS:										
New York Writer	TanPr	BW/AR/TanPr	1991	LC	21 X 15	R/BFK/W	40	6	500	500
The Secret Sharer	TanPr	BW/AR/TanPr	1991	LC	21 X 15	R/BFK/W	40	5	500	500

FLORENCE PUTTERMAN

BORN: Brooklyn, NY; April 14, 1927
EDUCATION: New York Univ, NY, BS; Grad Studies, Bucknell Univ, Lewisburg, PA, 1960–65; Pennsylvania State Univ, University City, PA, MFA, 1972
TEACHING: Art in Res, Fed Title III Prog, 1967–68; Demonstrating Artist, Title III Prog, 1969–70; Instr, Lycoming Col, Williamsport, PA, 1973–75; Instr, Susquehanna Univ, Selinsgrove, PA, 1984 to present
AWARDS: Silvermine Guild, New Canaan, CT, 1977; Gold Medal of Honor, Audubon Artists, NY, 1979; Nat Endowment for the Arts, 1979–80; Women in the Arts, Wm Penn Mus, Harrisburg, PA, 1981; Virginia Center for the Creative Arts, Fel, Sweet Briar, VA, 1983,84; Estelle Colwin Snellenberg Award, Artists Equity, Phila, PA, 1984; Chautauqua Nat, NY, 1980,85; Gold Medal of Honor, Audubon Artists, Nat Acad Galleries, NY, 1979,85; Laura Clary Mem Award, Buffalo, NY, 1985; Johnson & Johnson Purchase Prize, Printmaking Council of New Jersey, 1985; Purchase Prize, North Carolina P & D, Charlotte, NC, 1985; Andrew/Nelson/Whitehead Award, Boston Printmakers, DeCordova Mus, Lincoln, MA, 1985
RECENT EXHIB: Univ of Arizona Mus, Tucson, AZ, 1988; Mus of Fine Arts, Petersburg, FL, 1988; Moravian Col, Payne Gallery, Bethlehem, PA, 1992
COLLECTIONS: Metropolitan Art Mus, NY; Everson Mus, Syracuse NY; Grunewald Coll, Univ of California, Los Angeles, CA; Mus of Fine Art, Hagerstown, MD; Art Inst of Chicago, IL; Univ of South Florida, Tampa, FL; Univ of South Florida, Tampa, FL; New Jersey State Mus, Trenton, NJ; Jacksonville, FL
PRINTERS: Topaz Editions Inc, Tampa, FL (TE); Flatstone Studio, Tampa, FL (FS); Judith Solodkin, NY (JS); Solo Press, NY (SP)
PUBLISHERS: Ambur Art, Milton, PA (AA)
GALLERIES: Bergsma Gallery, Grand Rapids, MI; Mickelson Gallery, Wash, DC; Foster Harmon Gallery, Sarasota, FL; Dubins Gallery, Los Angeles, CA; Eve Mannes Gallery, Atlanta, GA; MacLaren/Markowitz Gallery, Boulder, CO; Edith Baker Fine Art, Dallas, TX; Gallery Contemporanea, Jacksonville, FL
MAILING ADDRESS: 3 Fairway Dr, Selinsgrove, PA 17870

TITLE	PUBLISHER	PRINTER	DATE	MEDIUM	DIMENSION (PAPER SIZE) IN INCHES	TYPE OF PAPER	EDITION NUMBER	NO. OF COLORS	ORIGINAL OPENING PRICE	CURRENT RETAIL PRICE
CURRENT EDITIONS:										
Lookout Mountain	AA	TE	1979	LC	22 X 30	AC	50	4	250	350
Petroglyph Series VI: China Lake	AA	TE	1980	LC	36 X 60	AP/ROL	50	3	400	1000
Petroglyph Series: China Lake III	AA	JS/SP	1980	LC	26 X 31	RP/CR	25	4	275	500
Looking Up	AA	TE	1981	LC	38 X 30	AP	75	4	375	500
Mucho Moki	AA	FS	1982	EC/HC	26 X 34	AP/B	50	7	300	500
Feathered Landsmen	AA	TE	1982	LC	22 X 30	AP/B	50	4	275	400
Homage a Dite	AA	JS/SP	1983	WC	26 X 37	SUZ	31	6	700	900
Midnight Rendezvous in the Catoctin Mountains	AA	FS	1984	WB	32 X 44	SUZ	25	1	500	750
Homage a Dite III	AA	FS	1985	WB	28 X 40	AP	25	1	500	750
Bongo, Bongo, Bongo, I Don't Want to Leave the Congo	AA	FS	1985	WB	30 X 42	SUZ	25	1	500	750
Bongo, Bongo, Bongo, I Don't Want to Leave the Congo IV	AA	FS	1985	EC/PO	28 X 40	AP	25	1	575	750

HARVEY QUAYTMAN

BORN: Far Rockaway, NY; April 20, 1937
EDUCATION: Syracuse Univ, NY, 1955–57; Boston Mus of Art Sch, MA, BFA, 1957–60; Tufts Univ, Boston, MA, MFA, 1957–60
TEACHING: Vis Lectr, Harvard Univ, Cambridge, MA, 1982,83; Adj Asst Prof, Hunter Col, NY, 1983
AWARDS: Creative Artists Public Service Prog Awards, 1972,75; Nat Endowment for the Arts Grant, 1983; Guggenheim Fels, 1979,84
RECENT EXHIB: McKee Gallery, NY, 1992
COLLECTIONS: Tate Gallery, London, England; Mus of Mod Art, NY; Whitney Mus of Am Art, NY; Israel Mus, Jerusalem, Israel; Carnegie Inst of Tech, Pittsburgh, PA
PRINTERS: Sheila Marbain, NY (SM); Jane Kent, NY (JK); Maurel Studios, NY (MS)
PUBLISHERS: Dolan/Maxwell Gallery, Phila, PA (DMG)
GALLERIES: Nielsen Gallery, Boston, MA; McKee Gallery, New York, NY
MAILING ADDRESS: 231 Bowery, New York, NY 10002

TITLE	PUBLISHER	PRINTER	DATE	MEDIUM	DIMENSION (PAPER SIZE) IN INCHES	TYPE OF PAPER	EDITION NUMBER	NO. OF COLORS	ORIGINAL OPENING PRICE	CURRENT RETAIL PRICE
CURRENT EDITIONS:										
Untitled (Set of 3):									7000 SET	10000 SET
Black and Red	DMG	SM/JK/MS	1988	A/SP/MEZ	34 X 34	AP/WA	20		2600	3500
Blue and Yellow	DMG	SM/JK/MS	1988	A/SP/MEZ	34 X 34	AP/WA	20		2600	3500
Diamond	DMG	SM/JK/MS	1988	A/SP/MEZ	34 X 34	AP/WA	20		2600	3500

ROBERT QUIJADA

BORN: Los Angeles, CA; 1935
EDUCATION: Otis Art Inst, Los Angeles, CA; Chouinard Inst, Los Angeles, CA
COLLECTIONS: Montclair Art Mus, NJ; Mus of Contemporary Art, Ibiza, Spain; Pace Univ, NY
PRINTERS: Sue Kleinman, NY (SK); Kathleen Caraccio, NY (KC)
PUBLISHERS: Orion Editions, NY (OE)
GALLERIES: Orion Editions, New York, NY; Dubins Gallery, Los Angeles, CA

TITLE	PUBLISHER	PRINTER	DATE	MEDIUM	DIMENSION (PAPER SIZE) IN INCHES	TYPE OF PAPER	EDITION NUMBER	NO. OF COLORS	ORIGINAL OPENING PRICE	CURRENT RETAIL PRICE
SOLD OUT EDITIONS (RARE):										
Baleares	OE	KC	1977	EC/HC	25 X 36	AP	40	HC	300	500
Horizons I, II	OE	KC	1978	EC/HC	35 X 30 EA	AP	40 EA	HC	300 EA	500 EA
Slate Screen	OE	KC	1980	EC/HC	30 X 34	AP	50	HC	300	500
Sienna Screen	OE	KC	1980	EC/HC	30 X 34	AP	50	HC	300	500
Rock Island I, II	OE	SK	1980	COL	22 X 30 EA	AP	40 EA	HC	200 EA	250 EA
Passages	OE	SK	1980	COL	22 X 30	AP	30	HC	200	250

ROBERT QUIJADA CONTINUED

TITLE	PUBLISHER	PRINTER	DATE	MEDIUM	DIMENSION (PAPER SIZE) IN INCHES	TYPE OF PAPER	EDITION NUMBER	NO. OF COLORS	ORIGINAL OPENING PRICE	CURRENT RETAIL PRICE
SOLD OUT EDITIONS (RARE):										
Southwest I, II	OE	KC	1981	EC/HC	30 X 36 EA	AP	65 EA	HC	325 EA	375 EA
Acoma	OE	KC	1981	AC	30 X 36	AP	65	17	325	375
Chimayo	OE	KC	1981	AC	30 X 36	AP	65	17	325	375
Chaco Sunrise (2 sheets)	OE	KC	1983	AC/HC	30 X 50	AP	85	HC	675	750
Chaco Sunset (2 sheets)	OC	KC	1983	AC/HC	30 X 50	AP	85	HC	675	750
Mesa Grande (2 sheets)	OE	KS	1983	AC/HC	30 X 50	AP	50	HC	700	800
Mesa Oscura I (2 sheets)	OE	KC	1983	AC/HC	30 X 50	AP	40	HC	700	800
Mesa Oscura II (2 sheets)	OE	KC	1983	AC/HC	30 X 50	AP	15	HC	700	800
CURRENT EDITIONS:										
Ancient Wall Series:										
Ancient Walls I (Blue)	OE	KC	1985	EC/HC	25 X 37	MOR	55	Varies	450	450
Ancient Walls II (Gray)	OE	KC	1985	EC/HC	25 X 37	MOR	55	Varies	450	450
Ancient Walls III (Red)	OE	KC	1985	EC/HC	25 X 37	MOR	30	Varies	450	450
Ancient Walls IV (Orange)	OE	KC	1985	EC/HC	25 X 37	MOR	30	Varies	450	450

WILLIAM QUINN

BORN: St Louis, MO; September 5, 1929
EDUCATION: Washington Univ, St Louis, MO, BFA, 1953; Univ of Illinois, Urbana, IL, MFA, 1957
TEACHING: Prof, Painting & Drawing, Washington Univ, St Louis, MO, 1958 to present
AWARDS: Millikin Travel Scholar, Washington Univ, St Louis, MO, 1958; Cité des Arts Fel, Paris, France, 1982; Nat Endowment for the Arts Fel, Painting, 1986
RECENT EXHIB: Northern Indiana Arts Assoc, Center for Visual & Performing Arts, Munster, IN, 1989
COLLECTIONS: Washington Univ Art Gallery, St Louis, MO; Butler Inst of Am Art, Youngstown, OH; Brooks Mem Art Gallery, Memphis, TN; Nelson-Atkins Gallery, Kansas City, MO; St Louis Art Mus, MO; Weatherspoon Art Gallery, Univ of North Carolina, Greensboro, NC; Univ of Illinois, Urbana, IL; Univ of Missouri, Columbia, MO; St Petersburg Mus, FL; Mexican-Am Cultural Inst, Mexico City, Mex; High Mus of Art, Atlanta, GA
PRINTERS: Artist (ART)
PUBLISHERS: Artist (ART)
GALLERIES: Martin Schwieg Gallery, St Louis, MO; Elliot Smith Gallery, St Louis, MO; John Davis Gallery, Akron, OH; Sazama/Brauer Gallery, Chicago, IL; Gallery 44, Boulder, CO
MAILING ADDRESS: Art Dept, Washington University, St Louis, MO 63130

TITLE	PUBLISHER	PRINTER	DATE	MEDIUM	DIMENSION (PAPER SIZE) IN INCHES	TYPE OF PAPER	EDITION NUMBER	NO. OF COLORS	ORIGINAL OPENING PRICE	CURRENT RETAIL PRICE
CURRENT EDITIONS:										
Modular Variation V	ART	ART	1977	SP	20 X 17	AP	25	5	200	250
White Sepertine	ART	ART	1977	SP	19 X 23	AP	25	3	200	250
Modular Variation XIV	ART	ART	1977	SP	19 X 23	AP	30	6	250	300
Blue Lady	ART	ART	1978	SP	18 X 18	AP	50	5	200	250

WILLIAM A RABINOVITCH

BORN: New London, CT; September 16, 1936
EDUCATION: Boston Mus Sch of Fine Arts, MA, 1963; San Francisco Art Inst, MFA, 1973; Whitney Mus, Independent Study, 1973
TEACHING: Instr, Gallatin Prog, New York Univ, NY, 1982
AWARDS: First Prize, Monterey Peninsula Art Mus, CA, 1965; Nat Endowment for the Arts, 1977; Grant, Artists Space, NY, 1983
RECENT EXHIB: San Francisco Art Inst, CA, 1987; Ingrid Cusson Gallery, NY, 1988; Barbara Mendes Gallery, Los Angeles, CA, 1990; Pacific Grove Art Center, CA, 1991
COLLECTIONS: Monterey Peninsula Col, CA
PRINTERS: Artist (ART)
PUBLISHERS: Jackie Fine Arts, Inc, NY (JKA); Circle Fine Arts (CFA); Counterweight Editions (CE); Rabinovitch Gallery (RG); John Nichols Studio, NY (JN); Evergreen Publishing, Inc (EPI); Artist (ART)
GALLERIES: Rabinovitch Gallery, New York, NY; Vorpal Gallery, New York, NY; Ingrid Cusson Gallery, New York, NY; Barbara Mendes Gallery, Los Angeles, CA
MAILING ADDRESS: 115 Mercer St, New York, NY 10012

TITLE	PUBLISHER	PRINTER	DATE	MEDIUM	DIMENSION (PAPER SIZE) IN INCHES	TYPE OF PAPER	EDITION NUMBER	NO. OF COLORS	ORIGINAL OPENING PRICE	CURRENT RETAIL PRICE
CURRENT EDITIONS:										
Unicorn	KA	ART	1980	SP	26 X 25	SOM	250	10	200	300
Fish of Life	KA	CFA	1980	SP	29 X 25	SOM	250	10	200	300
Lightwave	RG	ART	1980	SP	29 X 25	SOM	25	8	200	300
Free Shapes	RG	ART	1980	SP	26 X 25	SOM	25	8	200	300
Woman	RG	ART	1981	SP	20 X 19	SOM	40	1	200	300
Circumcision of Christ	KA	JN	1981	SP	26 X 30	SOM	250	14	200	300
Moose City	ART	ART	1983	SP/HC	22 X 26	SOM	40	Varies	200	300
Gringo	ART	ART	1983	SP	16 X 22	SOM	40	5	200	300
Runners	ART	ART	1983	SP	25 X 29	SOM	15	9	200	300

The retail prices of the 100,000 limited edition prints quoted in this directory are subject to change. Print publishers, artists and galleries were the direct sources for these quotations. Prices in the secondary market listed as "Sold Out Editions (Rare)" indicate that the publisher has a limited supply of that print or that the print is difficult to locate in the galleries.

The Printworld Directory is accepting new applications for the seventh edition. Approximately 300 new artists will be accepted. Please use the two forms provided in the back section of this directory to submit biographical data and documentation of prints. Edition number of each print must not exceed 500 and the retail price must be $100 or more.

MARKUS RAETZ

BORN: Zürich, Switzerland; 1941
COLLECTIONS: Mus of Mod Art, NY
PRINTERS: Bettina Lüscher, Zürich, Switzerland (BL); Lothar Osterburg, San Francisco, CA (LO); Pamela Paulson, San Francisco, CA (PP); Crown Point Press, San Francisco, CA (CPP); Peter Kneubühler, Zurich, Switzerland (PK)
PUBLISHERS: Editions Stähli, Zürich, Switzerland (EdSt); Crown Point Press, San Francisco, CA (CPP); Edition Cestio, Basel, Switzerland (EdCes)
GALLERIES: Margarete Roeder Gallery, New York, NY; Galerie Stähli, Zürich, Switzerland; Brooke Alexander, Inc, New York, NY; Farideh Cadot Gallery, New York, NY; Crown Point Press, San Francisco, CA & New York, NY

TITLE	PUBLISHER	PRINTER	DATE	MEDIUM	DIMENSION (PAPER SIZE) IN INCHES	TYPE OF PAPER	EDITION NUMBER	NO. OF COLORS	ORIGINAL OPENING PRICE	CURRENT RETAIL PRICE
CURRENT EDITIONS:										
Untitled (Set of 7)	EdSt	BL	1958–88	I	15 X 11 EA	Varies	33 EA	1 EA	3500 SET 500/ 900 EA	4000 SET 600/ 1000 EA
Schatten (16 Parts)	CPP	LO/PP/CPP	1991	PH/G	70 X 27	SOM	35		1800	2500
CURRENT EDITIONS:										
Views	CPP	LO/PP/CPP	1991	EB/So	24 X 22	SOM	15	1	1200	1200
Reflexion I, II, III (Set of 3)	CPP	LO/PP/CPP	1991	PH/EB/A	36 X 42 EA	SOM	35 EA	1 EA	3000 SET 1250 EA	3000 SET 1250 EA
Flusslandschaft (with Brushing)	EdCes	PK	1992	AB	23 X 31	RP	25		SF2500	SF2500

JOSEPH RAFFAEL

BORN: Brooklyn, NY; February 22, 1933
EDUCATION: Cooper Union, NY, 1954–55; Yale Univ Sch of Fine Arts, New Haven, CT, BFA, 1954–56
TEACHING: Instr, Art, Univ of California, Davis, CA, 1966; Instr, Art, Sch of Visual Art, NY, 1966–69; Assoc Prof, Art, Univ of California, Berkeley, CA, 1969; Prof, Art, Sacramento State Univ, CA, 1969–73
AWARDS: Fulbright Fel, Italy, 1958; Louis C Tiffany Fel, 1960; First Prize, Tokyo Int, Japan, 1974; Purchase Prize, Oakland Mus, CA, 1975
RECENT EXHIB: Davenport Mus of Art, IA, 1989; Nancy Hoffman Gallery, NY, 1989,90,92
COLLECTIONS: Mus of Mod Art, NY; Whitney Mus of Am Art, NY; Univ of Massachusetts, Amherst, MA; Brooklyn Mus, NY; Univ of New Mexico, Albuquerque, NM; Univ of California, Berkely, CA; Univ of Connecticut, Storrs, CT; Univ of Florida Gainesville, FL; Univ of Illinois, Chicago, IL; Long Beach Mus, CA; Los Angeles County Mus, CA; Joslyn Art Mus, Omaha, NE; San Francisco Mus of Mod Art, CA; Walker Mus, Fairlee, VT; Everson Mus, Syracuse, NY; Metropolitan Mus of Art, NY; Hirshhorn Mus, Wash, DC; Smithsonian Inst, Wash, DC
PRINTERS: Archer Press, CA (AP); Trillium Graphics, CA (TG); Experimental Workshop, San Francisco, CA (EW); Wil Foo, San Francisco, CA (WF); John Stemmer, San Francisco, CA (JS); Andrew Saftel, San Francisco, CA (AS); Karin Wikstrom, San Francisco, CA (KW)
PUBLISHERS: Experimental Workshop, San Francisco, CA (EW); Artist (ART)
GALLERIES: Nancy Hoffman Gallery, New York, NY; John Berggruen Gallery, San Francisco, CA; Suzanne Brown Gallery, Scottsdale, AZ; Fendrick Gallery, Wash, DC; Images Gallery, Toledo, OH; Michael H Lord Gallery, Milwaukee, WI; Richard Gray Gallery, Chicago, IL; Fernette's Gallery of Art, Des Moines, IA; Gallery 72, Omaha, NE; John Hodgell Gallery, Sarasota, FL; J Noblett Gallery, Boyes Hot Springs, CA; Art Source, Inc, Los Angeles, CA; Experimental Workshop, San Francisco, CA; Brett Mitchell Collection, Cleveland, OH; Elizabeth Leach, Portland, OR
MAILING ADDRESS: c/o Nancy Hoffman Gallery, 429 W Broadway, New York, NY 10012; c/o Site Charman, 6F Avenue des Pins, Cap d'Antibes, France 06600

TITLE	PUBLISHER	PRINTER	DATE	MEDIUM	DIMENSION (PAPER SIZE) IN INCHES	TYPE OF PAPER	EDITION NUMBER	NO. OF COLORS	ORIGINAL OPENING PRICE	CURRENT RETAIL PRICE
SOLD OUT EDITIONS (RARE):										
Eleven Fish	ART	AP	1978	LC	28 X 22	R/BFK	40	6	500	5000
Matthew's Lily	EW	WF/JS/EW	1984	WC	32 X 37	HMP	50	28	2100	5000
Luminous Journey	EW	WF/JS/EW	1985	WC	42 X 62	R/BFK	35	33	2100	7500
CURRENT EDITIONS:										
Island Magic	ART	TG	1975	LC	23 X 32	R/BFK	47		300	1500
Moonlight	ART	TG	1975	LC	22 X 30	R/BFK	75		200	1500
Mystic Lily	ART	TG	1976	LC	30 X 22	R/BFK	40		300	1500
Spirit Lily	ART	TG	1976	LC	24 X 29	R/BFK	50		300	1500
White Lily	ART	TG	1976	LC	42 X 30	R/BFK	50		300	1500
Autumn Fish	ART	TG	1978	LC	26 X 20	R/BFK	50		500	3000
Night Sky Fish	ART	TG	1978	LC	22 X 25	R/BFK	25		550	3000
Two Fish	ART	TG	1978	LC	22 X 25	R/BFK	50		500	3000
Bird	ART	TG	1979	LC	24 X 30	R/BFK	75		500	1000
Birds II	ART	TG	1979	LC	22 X 30	R/BFK	25		500	800
Haiku Fish I (White)	ART	TG	1979	LC	22 X 30	R/BFK	32		500	1500
Haiku Fish II (Black)	ART	TG	1979	LC	22 X 30	R/BFK	32		500	1500
Haiku Fish III (Gray)	ART	TG	1979	LC	22 X 30	R/BFK	34		500	1500
Haiku Fish IV (Beige)	ART	TG	1979	LC	22 X 30	R/BFK	30		500	2000
New Lily	ART	TG	1979	LC	24 X 30	R/BFK	75		500	4500
Winter Moon Lily	ART	TG	1979	LC	21 X 27	R/BFK	72		500	2500
Winter Fish-Silver	ART	TG	1980	LC	15 X 16	RP/NENS	40	3	350	1200
Winter Fish-Gold	ARt	TG	1980	LC	15 X 16	RP/TAN	40	3	350	1200
Lily for Matthew	ART	TG	1980	LC	30 X 41	AP	20		800	3500
Celebration	ART	TG	1980	LC	30 X 24	AP	44		550	3800
Returning	ART	TG	1980	LC	29 X 21	AP	50	9	525	1200
Luminous Lily Dream	ART	TG	1980	LC	30 X 40	AP	75		600	3200
Journey	ART	TG	1981	LC	39 X 17	AP	73	7	850	3500
Luce	ART	TG	1981	LC	26 X 20	AP	60	8	525	1200
Evening Lily	ART	TG	1981	LC	40 X 30	AP	75	11	950	4800

JOSEPH RAFFAEL CONTINUED

TITLE	PUBLISHER	PRINTER	DATE	MEDIUM	DIMENSION (PAPER SIZE) IN INCHES	TYPE OF PAPER	EDITION NUMBER	NO. OF COLORS	ORIGINAL OPENING PRICE	CURRENT RETAIL PRICE
CURRENT EDITIONS:										
Pink Lily with Dragonfly	ART	TG	1981	LC	41 X 30	AP	77	6	950	3200
Renewal	ART	TG	1981	LC	41 X 30	AP	44	9	1200	2250
Summer Passage	ART	TG	1981	LC	42 X 30	AP	32	7	1500	2800
Carol's Magic Garden	ART	TG	1982	LC	30 X 38	AP	110		1250	2000
The Wind on Water, Spring	ART	TG	1982	LC	38 X 28	AP	77	28	1250	4800
Luxembourg Gardens, Summer	ART	TG	1982	LC	41 X 30	AP	77		950	3500
Shadowlight	ART	TG	1984	LC	40 X 26	AP	89		1500	2500
Future Memory	EW	AS/KW/EW	1986	EC/A	32 X 23	R/BFK	46	12	1800	3000
Crystal Lily	EW	WF/JS/KW/EW	1987	WC/REL	25 X 32	R/BFK	75	30	2100	3000

ARNULF RAINER

BORN: Baden, Austria; 1924
EDUCATION: Self-Taught
RECENT EXHIB: Bucknell Univ, Lewisburg, PA, 1987; Simon/Neuman Gallery, NY, 1987; Florida Atlantic Univ, Ritter Art Gallery, Boca Raton, FL, 1987,89; Ulysses Gallery, NY, 1989; Galerie Krinzinger, Innsbruck, Austria, 1989; Solomon R Guggenheim Mus, NY, 1989; Maximilian Verlag Sabine Knust, Munich, West Germany, 1990; Gallery Heike, Munich, West Germany, 1990
PRINTERS: Robert Finger (RF); Peter Kneubühler, Zürich, Switzerland (PK); Karl Imhoff, Munich, West Germany (KI); Sigrid Friedrich (SF); Galerie Heike Curtze, Düsseldorf, West Germany & Vienna, Austria (GHC); Maximilian Verlag Sabine Knust, Munich, West Germany (MVSK); Kurt Zein, Vienna, Austria (KZ)
PUBLISHERS: Galerie Heike Curtze, Düsseldorf, West Germany (GHC); Maximilian Verlag Sabine Knust, Munich, West Germany (MVSK); Schellmann & Klüser, Munich, Germany & NY (SK)
GALLERIES: Editions Schellmann, New York, NY & Munich, West Germany; Margarete Roeder Fine Art, New York, NY; Galerie Lelong, Paris, France & Zürich, Switzerland & New York, NY; Editions Ilene Kurtz, New York, NY; Simon/Neuman Gallery, New York, NY; David Nolan Gallery, New York, NY; Alpha Gallery, Boston, MA; Ulysses Gallery, New York, NY; Schmidt/Dean Gallery, Phila, PA; Galerie Heike Curtze, Düsseldorf, West Germany; Galerie Krinzinger, Innsbruck, Austria; BlumHelman Gallery, New York, NY

TITLE	PUBLISHER	PRINTER	DATE	MEDIUM	DIMENSION (PAPER SIZE) IN INCHES	TYPE OF PAPER	EDITION NUMBER	NO. OF COLORS	ORIGINAL OPENING PRICE	CURRENT RETAIL PRICE
SOLD OUT EDITIONS (RARE):										
Anchbradiern (Blau)	SK		1965–68	DPT	20 X 25	AP	60	1	75	1500
Wasser, Wasser	SK		1970	DPT	19 X 25	AP	40	1	100	1500
Berliner Konzert (with Oil, Pencil & Black Chalk)			1974	PH	19 X 24	AP	40	1	150	6000
Breuz I (Set of 2):									1000 SET	2500 SET
Schwarz	SF/MVSK	RF	1980	DPT	53 X 24	BUT	35	1	500	1200
Blau	SF/MVSK	RF	1980	DPT	53 X 24	BUT	35	1	500	1200
CURRENT EDITIONS:										
Vertiefung durch Bewölkung (Set of 5)	HC/MVSK	PK	1985	EB	22 X 16 EA	AP/B	50 EA	1 EA	3000 SET	4000 SET
Green Cross	MVSK	KI	1986	EC	51 X 25	R/BFK	35		2400	2800
For Joseph Beuys: Oak Leaf	SK		1986	EC	14 X 10	R/BFK	90	1	500	1800
Untitled (Series of 5):									3000 SET	4000 SET
Rot-Wein (Red Wine)	MVSK/GHC	KZ	1987	EC	20 X 26	AP	40	1	700	900
Lilia (Lilac)	MVSK/GHC	KZ	1987	EC	20 X 26	AP	40	1	700	900
Blaue Nacht (Blue Night)	MVSK/GHC	KZ	1987	EC	20 X 26	AP	40	1	700	900
Rost (Rust)	MVSK/GHC	KZ	1987	EC	20 X 26	AP	40	1	700	900
Rohre (Pipe)	MVSK/GHC	KZ	1987	EC	20 X 26	AP	40	1	700	900
Marie Antoinette (Red & Gray)	GHC	KZ	1989	DPT	21 X 15	AP	20	2	600	600
Marie Antoinette (Brown & Black)	GHC	KZ	1989	DPT	21 X 15	AP	20	2	600	600
Tannenkreuz	MVSK	KZ	1989	DPT	31 X 27	R/BFK	50	1	1800	2000
Kreuze (Set of 11)	MVSK	KZ	1990	EC/DPT	26 X 20 EA	R/BFK	35 EA	2 EA	20000 SET 2000 EA	24000 SET 2200 EA

LAWRENCE FRANCIS RAKOVAN

BORN: Eleria, OH; October 26, 1939
EDUCATION: Detroit Soc of Arts & Crafts, MI; Wayne State Univ, Detroit, MI, BS, 1967; Rhode Island Sch of Design, Providence, RI, MA, 1969
TEACHING: Vis Prof, Art, Univ of Maine, Augusta, ME, 1979–80; Assoc Prof, Painting & Printmaking, Univ of Southern Maine, Gorham, ME, 1967 to present
AWARDS: Faculty Research Award, Univ of Maine, Augusta, ME, 1973
COLLECTIONS: Brooklyn Mus, NY; California Col of Arts & Crafts, Oakland, CA; Colby Col Mus, Waterville, ME; Bowdoin Col Mus of Art, Brunswick, ME; Univ of Maine, Orono, ME; Portland Mus of Art, ME
PRINTERS: Artist (ART)
PUBLISHERS: Artist (ART)
GALLERIES: Benbow Gallery, Newport, RI; Barridorf Galleries, Portland, ME; Maine Art Gallery, Wiscasset, ME
MAILING ADDRESS: 327 Maine St, Brunswick, ME 04011

TITLE	PUBLISHER	PRINTER	DATE	MEDIUM	DIMENSION (PAPER SIZE) IN INCHES	TYPE OF PAPER	EDITION NUMBER	NO. OF COLORS	ORIGINAL OPENING PRICE	CURRENT RETAIL PRICE
SOLD OUT EDITIONS (RARE):										
Quebec #1	ART	ART	1965	MEZ	5 X 9	R/BFK	20	1	25	300
Quebec #3	ART	ART	1967	WC	10 X 18	RICE	30	1	30	200
Soldier Series (Set of 6)	ART	ART	1969	LC	14 X 22 EA	R/BFK	20 EA	1 EA	200 SET	1000 SET
Chicago Under Seige of Mayor Daily	ART	ART	1969	LC	16 X 24	R/BFK	25	1	100	600
Japanese Dancer	ART	ART	1970	SP	18 X 24	BR	100	1	25	300

LAWRENCE FRANCIS RAKOVAN CONTINUED

TITLE	PUBLISHER	PRINTER	DATE	MEDIUM	DIMENSION (PAPER SIZE) IN INCHES	TYPE OF PAPER	EDITION NUMBER	NO. OF COLORS	ORIGINAL OPENING PRICE	CURRENT RETAIL PRICE
SOLD OUT EDITIONS (RARE):										
Maine Series #11	ART	ART	1977	LC	18 X 24	R/BFK	30	1	150	300
CURRENT EDITIONS:										
Maine Series #1	ART	ART	1973	LC	19 X 28	R/BFK	12	1	100	300
Movable Squares-Red	ART	ART	1975	SP	20 X 30	PAT	24	1	75	200
The Nursery	ART	ART	1976	SP	12 X 18		15	1	75	250
Movable Squares-Purple	ART	ART	1979	SP	20 X 30	JP	24	1	100	250
Maine Forest Series	ART	ART	1979-81	SP	12 X 28	HMP	24	1	400	500
Boris, The Wolfhound	ART	ART	1981	I	24 X 30	HMP	15	1	200	300
Russian Wolfhound Series	ART	ART	1981–82	CE	18 X 24	R/BFK	24	1	400	500
Eider Series (Set of 4)	ART	ART	1982	LC	17 X 24 EA	R/BFK	12 EA	1 EA	400 SET	800 SET
Vision Cities Series	ART	ART	1982	I	20 X 25	R/BFK	12	1	200	300
Maine Shore Landscape	ART	ART	1983	LC	17 X 22	R/BFK	22	5	300	400
Ice Series (Set of 4)	ART	ART	1983–84	LC	22 X 28 EA	R/BFK	15	4	800 SET	1000 SET
The Four Seasons	ART	ART	1984	LC	34 X 48	ZIKO/HMP	13	5	800	1000
The Fifth Season	ART	ART	1984	LC	22 X 28	R/BFK	12	3	250	400

RAMMELLZEE

BORN: Far Rockaway, NY; 1960
COLLECTIONS: Mus of Mod Art, NY
PRINTERS: Crown Point Press, San Francisco, CA (CPP)
PUBLISHERS: Crown Point Press, San Francisco, CA (CPP)
GALLERIES: Barbara Braathen Gallery, New York, NY; Gabrielle Bryers Gallery, New York, NY; Crown Point Press, New York, NY & San Francisco, CA

TITLE	PUBLISHER	PRINTER	DATE	MEDIUM	DIMENSION (PAPER SIZE) IN INCHES	TYPE OF PAPER	EDITION NUMBER	NO. OF COLORS	ORIGINAL OPENING PRICE	CURRENT RETAIL PRICE
SOLD OUT EDITIONS (RARE):										
Sirpier-E-Ule's Luxturnomere, Staff Landing (Future Futurism)	CPP	MB/PP/CPP	1984	EB/A/DPT	24 X 36	SOM/S	40		700	950
Palladium Protractor, Chase to Assassination (Gothic Futurism)	CPP	MB/PP/CPP	1984	EB/A/DPT	24 X 36	SOM/S	35		700	950

MELVIN JOHN RAMOS (MEL)

BORN: Sacramento, CA; July 24, 1935
EDUCATION: San Jose State Col, CA, 1955; Sacramento Jr Col, CA, with Wayne Thiebaud, 1954; Sacramento State Col, CA, BA, 1955–56, MFA, 1956–58
TEACHING: State Univ, Hayward, CA, 1966 to present; Assoc Prof, Painting, California State Univ, Hayward, CA, 1966–80, Prof, Art, 1980 to present
RECENT EXHIB: Tamara Bane Gallery, Los Angeles, CA, 1989
COLLECTIONS: Mus of Mod Art, NY; Kaiser Wilhelm Mus, Krefeld, Germany; San Francisco Mus of Mod Art, CA; Oakland Art Mus, CA; Indianapolis Mus of Art, IN; Univ Mus, Potsdam, NY; Neue Galerie Aachen, Germany; Chrysler Mus, Norfolk, VA; Solomon R Guggenheim Mus, NY; Neue Galerie, Aachen, Germany
PRINTERS: Univ of South Florida Graphics Workshop, Tampa, FL (USFGW); Lichtdruck, AG, Switzerland (LICH); Tamarind Inst, Albuquerque, NM (TI); American Atelier, NY (AA)
PUBLISHERS: Univ of South Florida Graphics Workshop, FL (USFGW); Collectors Press (CP); Master Editions (ME); Jackie Fine Arts, NY (JFA); Plura Edizioni (PE); London Arts, Inc, Detroit, MI (LAI); Tamarind Inst, Albuquerque, NM (TI); Circle Fine Art, Chicago, IL (CFA)
GALLERIES: Louis K Meisel Gallery, New York, NY; David Stuart Gallery, Los Angeles, CA; Galerie Rolfe Ricke, Cologne, Germany; Pace Prints, New York, NY; Graphics Gallery, San Francisco, CA; Modernism, San Francisco, CA; Taylor Gallery, Taos, NM; Freddie Fong Fine Arts, Los Angeles, CA; Steven Leiber Fine Art, San Francisco, CA; James Corcoran Gallery, Santa Monica, CA; Emporium Enterprises, Inc, Dallas, TX; Tamara Bane Gallery, Los Angeles, CA; Circle Galleries, Scottsdale, AZ & Chicago, IL & New York, NY & Beverly Hills, CA & Costa Mesa, CA & San Diego, CA & San Francisco, CA & Palm Beach, FL & Honolula, HI & Northbrook, IL & New Orleans, LA & Las Vegas, NV & Pittsburgh, PA & Houston, TX & Seattle, WA; Hank Baum Gallery, San Francisco, CA; David Raymond, Ltd, San Francisco, CA
MAILING ADDRESS: 5941 Ocean View Dr, Oakland, CA 94618

TITLE	PUBLISHER	PRINTER	DATE	MEDIUM	DIMENSION (PAPER SIZE) IN INCHES	TYPE OF PAPER	EDITION NUMBER	NO. OF COLORS	ORIGINAL OPENING PRICE	CURRENT RETAIL PRICE
SOLD OUT EDITIONS (RARE):										
Rhinocerous	USFGW	USFGW	1970	LC	22 X 30	AP	30	6	500	1200
Llama	USFGW	USSFGW	1970	LC	30 X 22	AP	30	6	500	1200
CURRENT EDITIONS:										
Manet's Olympia	LAI	LICH	1974	COL	20 X 27	R/BFK	150	20	500	800
Navajo Nudo	LAI	LICH	1974	COL	20 X 27	R/BFK	150	20	500	800
Touche Boucher	LAI	LICH	1974	COL	20 X 27	R/BFK	150	20	500	800
You Get more Salami with Modigliani	LAI	LICH	1974	COL	20 X 27	R/BFK	150	20	500	800
I Still Get a Thrill When I See Bill, #1, #2, #3,	LAI	LICH	1978	SP	29 X 21 EA	AP	500 EA	8/7/8	350 EA	500 EA
Bonnard's Bath	ME		1978	LC	21 X 29		500	7	350	500
Marquet's Mannequin	ME		1978	LC	29 X 21		500	7	350	500
Six Girls	PE		1979	C	36 X 27		60	8	500	750
Zebra	CFA	AA	1980	LC	21 X 25	AP	250		250	600

MELVIN JOHN RAMOS (MEL) CONTINUED

TITLE	PUBLISHER	PRINTER	DATE	MEDIUM	DIMENSION (PAPER SIZE) IN INCHES	TYPE OF PAPER	EDITION NUMBER	NO. OF COLORS	ORIGINAL OPENING PRICE	CURRENT RETAIL PRICE
CURRENT EDITIONS:										
Tenerife: Ode to Moe	TI	TI	1981	LC		R/BFK			1200	1750
Oakland: Ode to Moe	TI	TI	1981	LC		R/BFK			600	950
Salute to Art History (Set of 4)	LAI	LICH	1982	LC		AC			1500 SET	2400 SET

DANIEL RANALLI

BORN: New Haven, CT; October 17, 1946
EDUCATION: Clark Univ, Worcester, MA, BA, 1968; Boston Univ, MA, MA, 1971
AWARDS: Nat Endowment for the Arts Fel, 1978,80

COLLECTIONS: Boston Mus of Fine Arts, MA; Worcester Art Mus, MA; Minneapolis Inst of Art, MN; Mead Art Mus, Amherst Col, MA; Mus of Mod Art, NY; San Francisco Mus of Art, CA; Baltimore Mus of Fine Arts, MD; George Eastman House, Rochester, NY; Wellesley Col, MA
PRINTERS: Artist (ART)
PUBLISHERS: Artist (ART)
GALLERIES: Thomas Segal Gallery, Boston, MA
MAILING ADDRESS: 76 Sumner St, Newton, MA 02159

TITLE	PUBLISHER	PRINTER	DATE	MEDIUM	DIMENSION (PAPER SIZE) IN INCHES	TYPE OF PAPER	EDITION NUMBER	NO. OF COLORS	ORIGINAL OPENING PRICE	CURRENT RETAIL PRICE
SOLD OUT EDITIONS (RARE):										
Photism Series (15)	ART	ART	1976	PH/MON	16 X 20 EA	AP	1 EA	2 EA	250 EA	500 EA
#60–#70 (10)	ART	ART	1978	PH/MON	16 X 20 EA	AP	1 EA	2 EA	375 EA	600 EA
CURRENT EDITIONS:										
Vertical Division Series (15–20)	ART	ART	1979–80	PH/MON	16 X 20 EA	AP	1 EA	2 EA	500 EA	600 EA
Triad Division Series	ART	ART	1979–80	PH/MON	16 X 20 EA	AP	1 EA	2 EA	500 EA	600 EA
Light Line Bundles Series	ART	ART	1980	PH/MON	16 X 20 EA	AP	1 EA	2 EA	600 EA	700 EA
Studio Wall Series	ART	ART	1981	PH/CIBA	15 X 15 EA	AP	20 EA	Full EA	300 EA	400 EA

ARCHIE RAND

BORN: New York, NY; 1949
EDUCATION: City Col of New York, NY, 1965–66; Brooklyn Col, NY, 1967; Art Students League, NY, 1967–68; Pratt Inst, Brooklyn, NY, BFA, 1968–70
AWARDS: Creative Artists Public Service Award, NY, 1975; New York State Council of the Arts, 1975; Nat Endowment for the Arts Grant, Sculpture, 1983; Englehard Award, 1986; Award in the Visual Arts, 1987; New York Found Arts Fel, 1990
RECENT EXHIB: Galerie Evan, Toronto, Canada, 1987; Phyllis Kind Gallery, Chicago, IL, 1987; Phyllis Kind Gallery, NY, 1988; Cone Editions, NY, 1988; Mem Art Gallery, Rochester, NY, 1989; Schmidt/Dean Gallery, Phila, PA, 1989; Scott Hanson Gallery, NY, 1989,90; Bibliotheque Nat, Paris, France, 1990; Exit Art, NY, 1990; Contemp Arts Center, Cincinnati, OH, 1989,92

COLLECTIONS: Brooklyn Mus, NY; Pratt Inst, Brooklyn, NY; Israel Mus, Jerusalem, Israel; Mint Mus, Charlotte, NC; Art Inst of Chicago, IL; Elvehjem Mus, Jerusalem, Israel; Jewish Mus, NY; Palm Springs Desert Mus, CA; Univ of Chicago, Alfred Smart Gallery, IL; Carnegie Inst, Pittsburgh, PA; Copley Found; Michlaleh Jerusalem Col for Women, Israel
PRINTERS: Judith Solodkin, NY (JS); Solo Press, NY (SP); Jon Cone, East Topsham, VT (JC); Cone Editions, East Topsham, VT (CEd)
PUBLISHERS: Solo Press, NY (SP); Cone Editions, East Topsham, VT (CEd); Hadassah, Westfield, NJ (HAD)
GALLERIES: Dart Gallery, Chicago, IL; Phyllis Kind Galleries, Chicago, IL & New York, NY; Schmidt/Dean Gallery, Phila, PA; Feigenson/Preston Gallery, Birmingham, MI; Exit Art, New York, NY
MAILING ADDRESS: 326 55th St, Brooklyn, NY 11220

TITLE	PUBLISHER	PRINTER	DATE	MEDIUM	DIMENSION (PAPER SIZE) IN INCHES	TYPE OF PAPER	EDITION NUMBER	NO. OF COLORS	ORIGINAL OPENING PRICE	CURRENT RETAIL PRICE
CURRENT EDITIONS:										
Library	SP	JS/SP	1980		22 X 24	SOM	30		250	450
Lawn Furniture	SP	JS/SP	1980		24 X 31	SOM	30		300	600
Songs of the Death of Children	SP	SP	1981	LB	23 X 30	SOM/S	16		325	550
Stork Club	CEd	JC/CEd	1987	CR/PP	19 X 26	R/BFK	6		900	1250
Vines	CEd	JC/CEd	1987	REL/PP	35 X 25	SEK	6	1	1200	1250
Movie	CEd	JC/CEd	1987	CR/PP	25 X 35	JEP	0		1000	1600
The Nose	CEd	JC/CEd	1987	PP	19 X 26	RP/HWT	8	1	900	1000
Sailboat	CEd	JC/CEd	1987	CR/PP	19 X 26	JOH	6		900	1250
Satchmo	CEd	JC/CEd	1987	CR/PP	19 X 26	JOH	6		900	1250
Seagull with Mollusk	CEd	JC/CEd	1987	CR/PP	19 X 26	JOH	6		900	1250
Badmitton	CEd	JC/CEd	1987	CR/PP	19 X 26	JOH	6		900	1250
Assimilation	CEd	JC/CEd	1988	PP/C	50 X 75	JOH	5		3200	3500
Irises	HAD	JC/CEd	1988	SP	26 X 19	RP/HWT	200		150	500
Flower Heads	CEd	JC/CEd	1988	PP	26 X 26 EA	JOH	1 EA		900 EA	1000 EA
Guitarist	CEd	JC/CEd	1988	PP	17 X 14 EA	JOH	1 EA		800 EA	900 EA

KEITH RASMUSSEN

BORN: Madelia, MN; July 29, 1942
EDUCATION: Minneapolis Col of Art & Design, MN, BFA, 1966; Pennsylvania State Univ, University Part, PA, MFA, 1970
TEACHING: Univ of Wisconsin-Stout, Menomonie, WI; Atlanta Col of Art, GA, 1972 to present

COLLECTIONS: High Mus of Art, Atlanta, GA; Minneapolis Inst of Arts, MN; Brooklyn Mus, NY
PRINTERS: Artist (ART)
PUBLISHERS: Ronbie Editions, Bensalem, PA (RE)
GALLERIES: Portfolio Gallery, Atlanta, GA; Miriam Perlman Gallery, Chicago, IL; Wilhelm Gallery, Houston, TX; Monty Stabler Gallery, Birmingham, AL
MAILING ADDRESS: 1015 Rosedale Rd, NE, Atlanta, GA 30306

KEITH RASMUSSEN CONTINUED

TITLE	PUBLISHER	PRINTER	DATE	MEDIUM	DIMENSION (PAPER SIZE) IN INCHES	TYPE OF PAPER	EDITION NUMBER	NO. OF COLORS	ORIGINAL OPENING PRICE	CURRENT RETAIL PRICE
CURRENT EDITIONS:										
The Last Resort	RE	ART	1986	LC	30 X 42	R/BFK	100	5	375	500
They Called It Paradise	RE	ART	1986	LC	30 X 42	R/BFK	100	6	375	500
Greyfield Ghosts	RE	ART	1986	LC	30 X 42	R/BFK	100	6	375	500
Oyster Bay	RE	ART	1986	LC	30 X 42	R/BFK	100	6	375	500
Chincoteaque Bay	RE	ART	1986	LC	30 X 42	R/BFK	100	5	375	500
The Bunting	RE	ART	1986	LC	30 X 42	R/BFK	100	5	375	500
A Past Time	RE	ART	1986	LC	30 X 42	R/BFK	100	6	375	500
Assateaque Refuge	RE	ART	1986	LC	30 X 42	RBFK	100	6	375	500
Assateaque Light	RE	ART	1986	LC	30 X 42	R/BFK	100	4	375	500

ABRAHAM RATTNER

BORN: Poughkeepsie, NY; (1895–1978)
COLLECTIONS: Whitney Mus of Am Art, NY; Metropolitan Mus of Art, NY; Hirshhorn Mus, Wash, DC; Musee Jeu de Paume, Paris, France
PRINTERS: Atelier Desjobert, Paris, France (AD); Artist (ART)
PUBLISHERS: Kennedy Graphics, NY (KG); Circle Gallery, Ltd, Chicago, IL (CGL)
GALLERIES: Kennedy Graphics, New York, NY; Circle Galleries, San Diego, CA & San Francisco, CA & Northbrook, IL & Pittsburgh, PA & Houston, TX & Soho, NY & Chicago, IL & Scottsdale, AZ & Beverly Hills, CA & Costa Mesa, CA & Sherman Oaks, CA & Palm Beach, FL & Honolulu, HI & New Orleans, LA & Las Vegas, NV & Seattle, WA

TITLE	PUBLISHER	PRINTER	DATE	MEDIUM	DIMENSION (PAPER SIZE) IN INCHES	TYPE OF PAPER	EDITION NUMBER	NO. OF COLORS	ORIGINAL OPENING PRICE	CURRENT RETAIL PRICE
SOLD OUT EDITIONS (RARE):										
Feast of Candles			1960	LB	22 X 30	AP	25	1	100	800
Man	CGL	AD	1969	LB	26 X 19	AP	100	1	100	500
CURRENT EDITIONS:										
Dark Angel	KG	ART	1965	LC	21 X 29	AP	100	7	125	750
Blue and Purple	KG	ART	1966	LC	20 X 26	AP	100	4	125	750
Holocaust	KG	ART	1966	LC	23 X 31	AP	100	7	125	750
In the Valley	KG	ART	1966	LC	21 X 29	AP	100	5	125	750
Landscape with Figures	KG	ART	1966	LC	21 X 29	AP	100	7	125	750
Memorial to Israel	KG	ART	1966	LC	24 X 31	AP	100	8	125	750
Near the Sea of Galilee	KG	ART	1966	LC	23 X 30	AP	100	7	125	750
Why	KG	ART	1966	LC	20 X 26	AP	100	5	125	750
Boy with Turtle	KG	ART	1968	LC	36 X 24	AP	100	12	150	750
The Prophets	KG	ART	1969	LC	21 X 28	AP	100	9	150	750
Window Cleaner	KG	ART	1969	LC	30 X 22	AP	125	14	150	700
Feast of Lights	KG	ART	1971	LC	36 X 25	AP	120	17	200	700
The Beggar's Opera (Set of 20):									2500 SET	12000 SET
I Sipped	CGL	AD	1971	LC	20 X 26	AP	150	2	175	700
Alack	CGL	AD	1971	LC	20 X 26	AP	150	2	175	700
Man May Escape	CGL	AD	1971	LC	20 X 26	AP	150	2	175	700
I am Naturally	CGL	AD	1971	LC	20 X 26	AP	150	2	175	700
Money	CGL	AD	1971	LC	20 X 26	AP	150	2	175	700
Comfortable	CGL	AD	1971	LC	20 X 26	AP	150	2	175	700
MacHeath	CGL	AD	1971	LC	20 X 26	AP	150	2	175	700
O, What Pain	CGL	AD	1971	LC	20 X 26	AP	150	2	175	700
My Love	CGL	AD	1971	LC	20 X 26	AP	150	2	175	700
I'm Like a Skiff	CGL	AD	1971	LC	20 X 26	AP	150	2	175	700
Was e'er Such a	CGL	AD	1971	LC	20 X 26	AP	150	2	175	700
Be the Author	CGL	AD	1971	LC	20 X 26	AP	150	2	175	700
Since Laws	CGL	AD	1971	LC	20 X 26	AP	150	2	175	700
Is there any Man	CGL	AD	1971	LC	20 X 26	AP	150	2	175	700
I Go Undismayed	CGL	AD	1971	LC	20 X 26	AP	150	2	175	700
We Gentlemen	CGL	AD	1971	LC	20 X 26	AP	150	2	175	700
And the Shark	CGL	AD	1971	LC	20 X 26	AP	150	2	175	700
Not in that Time	CGL	AD	1971	LC	20 X 26	AP	150	2	175	700
Shut Not Your Eye	CGL	AD	1971	LC	20 X 26	AP	150	2	175	700
Of the Heart	CGL	AD	1971	LC	20 X 26	AP	150	2	175	700
Pretty Polly	CGL	AD	1971	LC	20 X 26	AP	150	2	175	700
Taking Count	KG	ART	1972	LC	37 X 25	AP	100	8	300	750
Generation	KG	ART	1975	LC	30 X 22	AP	100	10	400	750
Noah and the Dove	KG	ART	1975	LC	30 X 22	AP	100	10	400	750

HAVA RAUCHER

BORN: Ferdinand, Bulgaria; 1944
EDUCATION: Tel Aviv Univ, Israel, BA, 1971; Arni Inst of Art, Israel, 1976; Washington Univ, St Louis, MO, MFA, 1981
AWARDS: Israel Cultural Found, 1976,77; Bronstein Purchase Award, Evansville Mus of Arts, IN, 1981
COLLECTIONS: Evansville Mus of Art & Science, Evansville, IN
PRINTERS: Elexander Heinrici, NY (AH); Heinrici Studio, NY (HS)
PUBLISHERS: Jackie Fine Arts, Inc, NY (JFA)
GALLERIES: Ro Gallery Image Makers, Inc, New York, NY
MAILING ADDRESS: 1042 Willowbrook Dr, St Louis, MO 63141

HAVA RAUCHER CONTINUED

TITLE	PUBLISHER	PRINTER	DATE	MEDIUM	DIMENSION (PAPER SIZE) IN INCHES	TYPE OF PAPER	EDITION NUMBER	NO. OF COLORS	ORIGINAL OPENING PRICE	CURRENT RETAIL PRICE
CURRENT EDITIONS:										
On the Beach	JFA	AH/HS	1981	SP	32 X 24	LEN/100	300	250	250	300
Beach Group	JFA	AH/HS	1981	SP	24 X 32	LEN/100	300	250	250	300
Old Lady on the Beach	JFA	AH/HS	1981	SP	25 X 24	LEN/100	300	250	250	300

LILO RAYMOND

BORN: Frankfurt, Germany; June 23, 1922; US Citizen
EDUCATION: Photography Sem with David Vestal, 1961–63
TEACHING: Maine Photog Workshop, Rockport, ME, Summer, 1979; Int Center for Photog, NY, Winter, 1979; Mem Seminars, Photog, Sch of Visual Arts, NY, 1978 to present
AWARDS: Creative Artists Public Service Fel, 1978
COLLECTIONS: Mus of Mod Art, NY; Metropolitan Mus of Art, NY; New Orleans Mus of Art, LA; Sheldon Mem Art Mus, Lincoln, NE; Bibliotheque Nat, Paris, France; High Mus, Atlanta, GA; St Louis Mus of Art, MO
PRINTERS: Artist (ART)
PUBLISHERS: Marcuse Pfeifer Gallery, Ltd, NY (MP); Artist (ART)
GALLERIES: Marcuse Pfeifer Gallery, Ltd, New York, NY; Maine Photographic Workshops, Rockport, ME; Magenta Gallery, Rocky Hill, NJ
MAILING ADDRESS: 212 E 14th St, New York, NY 10003

TITLE	PUBLISHER	PRINTER	DATE	MEDIUM	DIMENSION (PAPER SIZE) IN INCHES	TYPE OF PAPER	EDITION NUMBER	NO. OF COLORS	ORIGINAL OPENING PRICE	CURRENT RETAIL PRICE
CURRENT EDITIONS:										
Portfolio of Six	ART	ART	1980	PH	11 X 14 EA		30 EA		1000 SET	3000 SET

GORDON RAYNER

BORN: Toronto, Canada; 1935
TEACHING: Painting, Three Schs of Art, Toronto, ON, Can, 1968–71; Instr, Painting (Founder), For Art's Sake, Inc, Toronto, ON, Can, 1977–80
AWARDS: First Prize, Graphics, Winnipeg Art Show, 1970; Canadian Council of Sr Arts Grants, 1973,75
COLLECTIONS: Mus of Mod Art, NY; Hirshhorn Coll, Wash, DC; Art Gallery of Ontario, Toronto, Can; Nat Gallery of Canada, Ottawa Can; Philadelphia Mus of Art, PA; Vancouver Art Gallery, Can; Montreal Mus of Fine Art, Can; Art Gallery of Windsor, Oshawa, Can
PRINTERS: Sword Street Press, Ltd, Toronto, ON, Can (SSP)
PUBLISHERS: Sword Street Press, Ltd, Toronto, ON, Can (SSP)
GALLERIES: The Isaacs Gallery, Ltd, Toronto, ON, Can
MAILING ADDRESS: 1493 Dupont St, Toronto, ON, Canada M6P 3S2

TITLE	PUBLISHER	PRINTER	DATE	MEDIUM	DIMENSION (PAPER SIZE) IN INCHES	TYPE OF PAPER	EDITION NUMBER	NO. OF COLORS	ORIGINAL OPENING PRICE	CURRENT RETAIL PRICE
SOLD OUT EDITIONS (RARE):										
Untitled	SSP	SSP	1979	LC	22 X 30	AP	22	6	250	900
Untitled	SSP	SSP	1979	LC	24 X 35	AP	27	5	300	900
Untitled	SSP	SSP	1979	LC	24 X 35	AP	27	5	300	900

LESTER JAMES REBBECK, JR

BORN: Chicago, IL; June 26, 1929
EDUCATION: Art Inst of Chicago, IL, BAEd 1953, MAEd, 1959; Univ of Chicago, IL, 1959
TEACHING: Asst Prof, Art Appreciation & Painting, Harper Junior Col, Palatine, IL, 1967–71
AWARDS: GI Show Medal Award, Art Inst of Chicago, IL, 1953
RECENT EXHIB: Fort Wayne Art Mus, IN, 1989–90
PRINTERS: Artist (ART)
PUBLISHERS: Artist (ART)
MAILING ADDRESS: 2041 Vermont, Rolling Meadows, IL 60008

TITLE	PUBLISHER	PRINTER	DATE	MEDIUM	DIMENSION (PAPER SIZE) IN INCHES	TYPE OF PAPER	EDITION NUMBER	NO. OF COLORS	ORIGINAL OPENING PRICE	CURRENT RETAIL PRICE
SOLD OUT EDITIONS (RARE):										
Classic Landscape	ART	ART	1978	LC	6 X 9	R/100	10	3	250	300
Cubist Knight	ART	ART	1979	LB	7 X 10	R/100	10	1	250	300
Jack of Diamonds II	ART	ART	1982	LB	6 X 9	R/100	10	1	250	300
CURRENT EDITIONS:										
Merlin	ART	ART	1978	LC	14 X 10	R/100	8	3	250	300
Jack of Diamonds	ART	ART	1978	LC	6 X 9	R/100	10	3	250	300
Spring In the Fox Country	ART	ART	1979	LC	10 X 14	R/100	15	3	250	300
CURRENT EDITIONS:										
Mid-Summers Nights Dream	ART	ART	1979	LB	9 X 7	R/100	10	1	250	300
Etching Medivel Modern	ART	ART	1980	EB	5 X 7	R/100	10	1	250	300
Landscape (Long Grove)	ART	ART	1980	EB	6 X 8	R/100	30	1	250	300
Landscape (Euclid Forest)	ART	ART	1980	EB	6 X 8	R/100	30	1	250	300
Landscape (Beaver Dam)	ART	ART	1980	EB	6 X 8	R/100	28	1	250	300
Le Lac Sombre	ART	ART	1982	LB	14 X 10	R/100	10	1	250	300
Hostages	ART	ART	1982	EB	10 X 14	R/100	30	1	250	300
Cheyenne Chief	ART	ART	1982	EB	7 X 10	R/100	30	1	250	300
Cheyenne Chief (Crazy Head)	ART	ART	1984	EB	6 X 8	R/100	30	1	150	200
Hostages #2 and #11	ART	ART	1984	EB	14 X 18	R/100	30	1	250	300
Landscape (Devil's Head)	ART	ART	1985	EB	6 X 8	AP/W	30	1	150	200

The retail prices of the 100,000 limited edition prints quoted in this directory are subject to change. Print publishers, artists and galleries were the direct sources for these quotations. Prices in the secondary market listed as "Sold Out Editions (Rare)" indicate that the publisher has a limited supply of that print or that the print is difficult to locate in the galleries.

ROBERT RAUSCHENBERG

BORN: Port Arthur, TX; October 22, 1925
EDUCATION: Kansas City Art Inst, KS, 1946–47; Acad Julian, Paris, France, 1947; Black Mountain Col, NC, 1948–49; Art Students League, NY, 1949–50
AWARDS: Corcoran Award, 1965; Chicago Inst of Art Award, 1966; Chicago Arts Award, 1978
RECENT EXHIB: BlumHelman Gallery, NY, 1987; Inst of Contemp Art, London, England, 1987; Los Angeles County Mus of Art, CA, 1987; Sogetsu Art Mus, Japan, 1988; Mus Ludwig, Cologne, West Germany, 1988; Heland Wetterling Gallery, Stockholm, Sweden, 1989; Fabian Carlsson Gallery, London, England, 1989; Ivory/Kimpton Gallery, San Francisco, CA, 1989; Arkansas State Univ, State University, AR, 1989; North Miami Center of Contemp Art, North Miami, FL, 1989; High Mus of Art, Atlanta, GA, 1989; Albright-Knox Art Gallery, Buffalo, NY, 1989; Coos Art Mus, Coos Bay, OR, 1989; Schwartz Cierlak Galery, Santa Monica, CA, 1989; Martina Hamilton Gallery, NY, 1989; Scott Hanson Gallery, NY, 1989,90; Lang & O'Hara Gallery, NY, 1990; M Knoedler & Company, NY, 1990; Bay Harbor Islands, FL, 1990; Le Marie Tranier Gallery, Wash, DC, 1991; M Knoedler & Company, Inc, NY, 1990,92
COLLECTIONS: Albright-Knox Art Gallery, Buffalo, NY; Tate Gallery, London, England; Mus of Mod Art, NY; Art Inst of Chicago, IL; Whitney Mus of Am Art, NY; Moderna Museet, Stockholm, Sweden; White Mus, Cornell Univ, Ithaca, NY; San Francisco Mus of Mod Art, CA; Whitney Mus of Am Art, NY; Neue Galerie, Aachen, Germany
PRINTERS: Universal Limited Art Editions, West Islip, NY (ULAE); Keith Brintzenhofe, NY (KB); Tyler Graphics, Mount Kisco, NY (TGL); Gemini GEL, Los Angeles, CA (GEM); Styria Studio, NY (SS); Iris Editions, NY (IE); Craig Sammiello, West Islip, NY (CZ); Larry Wright, NY (LW); American Atelier, NY (AA); Untitled Press Inc, Captiva, FL (UPI); Maeght Editeur, Paris, France (ME); Tanglewood Press, NY (TP); Patricia Branstead, NY (PB)
PUBLISHERS: Universal Limited Art Editions, West Islip, NY (ULAE); Tyler Graphics Ltd, Mount Kisco, Ltd, NY (TGL); Gemini GEL, Los Angeles, CA (GEM); Multiples, NY (M); Styria Studio, NY (SS); Iris Editions, NY (IE); Brooke Alexander, Inc, NY (BAI); Circle Fine Art, Chicago, IL (CFA); The Quary, Local One, Amalgamated Lithographers of America, and Color Lithographers Service, Inc (QLOALACLS); Castelli Graphics, NY (CG); Maeght Editions, Paris, France (ME); Democratic National Committee (DNC); Ruth Eckerd Hall, Clearwater, FL (REH); Dayton's Gallery 12, OH (OG12); Untitled Press, Inc, Captiva, FL (UPI); Tanglewood Press, NY (TP)
GALLERIES: Gemini GEL, Los Angeles, CA; R K Goldman Contemporary, Los Angeles, CA; Richard Green Galleries, Los Angeles, CA & New York, NY; Tokoro Gallery, Los Angeles, CA; Harcourts Contemporary, San Francisco, CA; Schwartz Ciertak Gallery, Santa Monica, CA; Xiliary Twil Fine Arts, Santa Monica, CA; Clark Cieriak Fine Arts, Valencia, CA; Ginny Williams Gallery, Denver, CO; Brody's Gallery, Wash, DC; Fendrick Gallery, Wash, DC; Mary Singer Gallery, Wash, DC; Gloria Luria Gallery, Bay Harbor Islands, FL; Art Collector Gallery, Gainesville, FL; Opus Art Studios, Miami, FL; Marvin Ross Friedman & Company, Miami, FL; Barbara Gellman Gallery, Miami, FL; Steiner Galleries, Miami, FL; Helander Gallery, Palm Beach, FL; R S Johnson Fine Art, Chicago, IL; Stephen A Solovy Fine Arts, Chicago, IL; G H Dalsheimer Gallery, Baltimore, MD; Nancy Singer Gallery, St Louis, MO; Leo Castelli Gallery, New York, NY; Gagosian Gallery, New York, NY; Gimpel & Weitzenhoffer Gallery, New York, NY; James Goodman Gallery, New York, NY; Martina Hamilton Gallery, New York, NY; M Knoedler & Company, New York, NY; Magidson Fine Arts, New York, NY; Marian Goodman Gallery, New York, NY; Styria Studio, New York, NY; Pace/MacGill Gallery, New York, NY; Elizabeth Paul Gallery, Cincinnati, OH & Columbus, OH; Posner Gallery, Milwaukee, WI; Richard Gray Gallery, Chicago, IL; van Straaten Gallery, Chicago, IL; Heland Wetterling Gallery, Stockholm, Sweden; Fabian Carlsson Gallery, London, England; Kimpton Gallery, San Francisco, CA; Feigen, Inc, Chicago, IL; Lang & O'Hara Gallery, New York, NY; Greene Gallery, Bay Harbor Islands, FL; Le Marie Tranier Gallery, Wash, DC

Robert Rauschenberg
Soviet American Array I
Courtesy Universal Limited Art Editions

Sparks (S)—Foster (F)—Brooklyn Museum (BM)

TITLE	PUBLISHER	PRINTER	DATE	MEDIUM	DIMENSION (PAPER SIZE) IN INCHES	TYPE OF PAPER	EDITION NUMBER	NO. OF COLORS	ORIGINAL OPENING PRICE	CURRENT RETAIL PRICE
SOLD OUT EDITIONS (RARE):										
Abbey's Bird (F-4)	ULAE	ULAE	1962	LC	20 X 14	STP	50		60	9000
Urban (F-6)(S-3)	ULAE	ULAE	1962	LB	41 X 30	R/BFK	38	1	75	6000
Suburban (F-7) (S-4)	ULAE	ULAE	1962	LB	41 X 29	R/BFK	25	1	75	20000
Stuntman Suite (Set of 3):									200 SET	50000 SET
Stuntman I (Blue) (F-9)	ULAE	ULAE	1962	LC	23 X 18	JP	37	1	75	18000
Stuntman II (Light Green) (F-10)	ULAE	ULAE	1962	LC	23 X 18	JP	35	1	75	18000
Stuntman III (Orange) (F-11)	ULAE	ULAE	1962	LC	23 X 18	JP	36	1	75	18000
Accident	ULAE	ULAE	1963	LB	41 X 30	R/BFK	29	1	100	80000
Dante's Inferno (1 Lithograph (Plank) with 34 Facsimile Drawings) (F-15) (S-11)	ULAE	ULAE	1964	LB	16 X 16	ALM	300		500	10500
Mark (F-16)	ULAE	ULAE	1964	LB	15 X 16	ALM	42	1	75	15000
Spot (F-24) (S-20)	ULAE	ULAE	1964	LB	41 X 30	R/BFK	37	1	100	40000
Front Roll (F-25) (S-21)	ULAE	ULAE	1964	LC	42 X 30	R/BFK	39	2	100	40000
Breakthrough I (F-26)	ULAE	ULAE	1964	LC	41 X 30	R/BFK	20	2	100	65000
Post Rally (F-28)	ULAE	ULAE	1965	LC	46 X 31	WOVE	42	2	150	40000

ROBERT RAUSHENBERG CONTINUED

TITLE	PUBLISHER	PRINTER	DATE	MEDIUM	DIMENSION (PAPER SIZE) IN INCHES	TYPE OF PAPER	EDITION NUMBER	NO. OF COLORS	ORIGINAL OPENING PRICE	CURRENT RETAIL PRICE
SOLD OUT EDITIONS (RARE):										
Visitation I (F-29) (S-25)	ULAE	ULAE	1965	LC	30 X 22	R/BFK	42	2	100	14000
Visitation II (F-30) (S-26)	ULAE	ULAE	1965	LC	30 X 22	R/BFK	44		100	16000
Dwan Gallery Poster			1965	LC/OFF	23 X 25	R/BFK			100	1500
Artist's Rights Now	DPHR	SS	1965	SP/CO	30 X 23	AP	50		150	2000
Lawn (F-31) (S-27)	ULAE	ULAE	1965	LC	35 X 26	R/BFK	41	2	150	8000
Passport (From Ten from Leo Castelli) (F-39)	TP	TP	1967	SP	20"	PLEX	200		100	3000
Test Stone Series:										
Test Stone #1 (F-40) (G-26)	TGL	TGL	1967	LC	18 X 14	R/BFK	77	1	100	6000
Test Stone #2 (F-41) (G-27)	GEM	GEM	1967	LC	41 X 30	R/BFK	76		100	6000
Test Stone #3 (F-42) (G-28)	TGL	TGL	1967	LC	23 X 31	R/BFK	71	2	100	6000
Test Stone #4 (F-43) (G-29)	TGL	TGL	1967	LC	24 X 34	R/BFK	46	1	100	6000
Test Stone #5 (Drills) (F-44) (G-30)	GEM	GEM	1967	LC	25 X 33	R/BFK	27		100	6000
Test Stone #5A (Green) (F-45) (G-31)	TGL	TGL	1967	LC	25 X 33	R/BFK	27	3	100	6000
Test Stone #6 (Drills) (F-46) (G-32)	TGL	TGL	1967	LC	47 X 35	DOM/E	44	3	100	7500
Test Stone #7 (F-47) (G-33)	TGL	TGL	1967	LC	34 X 48	DEP	38	1	100	9000
Booster (F-47) (G-32)	GEM	GEM	1967	LC/SP	72 X 36	R/BFK	38		100	95000
Still	GEM	GEM	1968	LC	30 X 22	R/BFK	34	4	100	17500
Promise (M-65)	ULAE	ULAE	1968	LC	31 X 23	ARJ	35	4	100	9000
Guardian (F-58)	ULAE	ULAE	1968	LC	43 X 30	GCP	44		100	8000
Landmark (F-59)	ULAE	ULAE	1968	LC	43 X 30	GCP	40		100	8000
Gamble (F-49) (S-31)	ULAE	ULAE	1968	LC/EMB	36 X 22	JWP	41		100	12000
Water Stop (F-50)			1968	LC/EMB	52 X 28	R/BFK	28		200	20000
Reels (B+C):										
Reels (B+C): Storyline I (F-52) (G-98)	GEM	GEM	1968	LC	22 X 17	R/BFK	62		100	7500
Reels (B+C): Storyline II (F-53) (G-99)	GEM	GEM	1968	LC	22 X 10	R/BFK	59	5	100	7500
Reels (B+C): Storyline III (F-54) (G-100)	GEM	GEM	1968	LC	22 X 18	R/BFK	72		100	7500
Reels (B+C): Still (F-57) (G-103)	GEM	GEM	1968	LC	30 X 22	R/BFK	34		100	8000
Untitled (F-63)	QLOALACLS		1968	LC/OFF	33 X 25	AP	300		100	3500
Pledge (F-64) (-35)	ULAE	ULAE	1968	LC	32 X 23	JWP	35		100	9000
Tides (F-68)	ULAE	ULAE	1969	LC	43 X 30	GCP	28		200	7000
Sky Garden (F-74)	GEM	GEM	1969	LC/SP	89 X 42	ARJ	35		250	75000
Stoned Moon Series:										
Ape	GEM	GEM	1969	LC	46 X 33	ARJ	46	3	150	22000
Trust Zone	GEM	GEM	1969	LC	40 X 33	R/BFK	65	3	150	22000
Horn (F-72) (G-162)	GEM	GEM	1969	LB	44 X 34	RP/SP	58	1	150	22000
Waves	GEM	GEM	1969	LC	89 X 42	ARJ	27	1	150	25000
Earth Tie	GEM	GEM	1969	LC	48 X 34	AC	48	2	150	22000
Marsh	GEM	GEM	1969	LC	36 X 25	AC	60		150	22000
Banner (F-77) (G-173)	GEM	GEM	1969	LC	54 X 36	AC	40	1	150	22000
Loop	GEM	GEM	1969	LC	33 X 28	R/BFK	79	1	150	22000
Brake	GEM	GEM	1969	LC	42 X 29	AC	60	1	150	22000
Moon Rose	GEM	GEM	1969	LC	51 X 35	AC	47	1	150	22000
Sky Hook	GEM	GEM	1969	LC	48 X 34	ARJ	52	1	150	22000
Score	GEM	GEM	1969	LC	26 X 20	R/BFK	75	3	150	22000
Post	GEM	GEM	1969	LC	34 X 26	AC	44	2	150	22000
Tracks	GEM	GEM	1969	LC	45 X 35	R/BFK	60	4	200	22000
Tilt (F-88) (G-188)	GEM	GEM	1969	LC	28 X 22	R/BFK	60	2	200	15000
Arena I, State I (F-91) (G-165)	GEM	GEM	1969	LC	47 X 32	AC	12	1	200	17500
Arena, II, State II (F-92) (G-167)	GEM	GEM	1969	LC	47 X 32	ARJ	50	1	200	17500
Marsh (F-76) (G-167)	GEM	GEM	1969	LC	45 X 30	AC	60	1	200	16500
Bait (F-96) (G-199)	GEM	GEM	1969	LC	36 X 26	ARJ	45	4	200	15000
Sky Rite	GEM	GEM	1969	LC	33 X 23	AC	56	1	200	5500
Rack	GEM	GEM	1969	LC	30 X 25	R/BFK	42	1	200	5500
Earth Crust	GEM	GEM	1969	LC	34 X 25	AC	42	2	200	15000
Shell	GEM	GEM	1969	LC	32 X 26	AP	70	2	200	6500
Sack	GEM	GEM	1969	LC	40 X 28	AP	60		200	7500
Medallion	GEM	GEM	1969	LC	32 X 26	ARJ	48		200	6000
Spore	GEM	GEM	1969	LC	34 X 24	AP	50		200	5500
Air Pocket	GEM	GEM	1969	LC	36 X 51	ARJ	47	1	200	8500
Fuse	GEM	GEM	1969	LC	38 X 36	AC	63	1	200	5500
Strawboss	GEM	GEM	1969	LC	30 X 22	ARJ	50	2	200	6000
Sub-Total	GEM	GEM	1970	LC	8 X 12	ARJ	500	3	50	3500
Earth Day	GEM	GEM	1970	LC/CO	53 X 38	R/BFK	50	7	250	5000
Hybrid (F-97) (G-205)	GEM	GEM	1970	LC	55 X 36	ARJ	52		250	6500
Currents: Surface Series (Set of 18)	CG/DG12		1970	SP	35 X 35EA	AB844	100 EA		4000 SET	35000 SET
Signs (F-155)	CG		1970	SP	43 X 34	ARJ	250		250	10000
White Walk	GEM	GEM	1970	LC	42 X 29	R/BFK	53		250	5000
Bait	GEM	GEM	1970	LC	35 X 26	R/BFK	45		250	4500

ROBERT RAUSCHENBERG CONTINUED

TITLE	PUBLISHER	PRINTER	DATE	MEDIUM	DIMENSION (PAPER SIZE) IN INCHES	TYPE OF PAPER	EDITION NUMBER	NO. OF COLORS	ORIGINAL OPENING PRICE	CURRENT RETAIL PRICE
SOLD OUT EDITIONS (RARE):										
Hybrid	GEM	GEM	1970	LC	54 X 36	R/BFK	52		250	5000
Hoe	GEM	GEM	1970	LC	46 X 33	R/BFK	46		250	5000
Tracks	GEM	GEM	1970	LC	44 X 35	ARJ	54	4	250	4000
General Delivery	M	PB	1971	SP/CO	49 X 34	ARJ	300		500	3000
Yellow Body	UPI	UPI	1971	SP/CO	48 X 62	ARJ	80		250	7500
General Delivery	UPI	UPI	1971	SP/CO	49 X 34	ARJ	300		250	4000
Cardbird Door Series:										
Cardbird Door I	GEM	GEM	1971	MM/SP	80 X 30 X 11	ARJ	25		300	9000
Cardbird Door II	GEM	GEM	1971	PH/SP/CO	54 X 34	ARJ	75		300	4500
Cardbird Door III	GEM	GEM	1971	PH/SP/CO	36 X 36	ARJ	75		300	4500
Cardbird Series:										
Cardbird I (G-262)	GEM	GEM	1971	PH/SP/CO	45 X 30	ARJ	75		300	4500
Cardbird IV	GEM	GEM	1971	PH/SP/CO	39 X 39	ARJ	75		300	4500
Cardbird V	GEM	GEM	1971	PH/SP/CO	34 X 40	ARJ	75		300	5000
Cardbird VI	GEM	GEM	1971	PH/SP/CO	26 X 28	ARJ	75		300	5000
Cardbird VII	GEM	GEM	1971	PH/SP/CO	33 X 33	ARJ	75		300	5000
Tampa Clay Piece 5	GS	GS	1972	MM	34 X 18 X 3	ARJ	10		300	20000
Untitled (from YIP)	M	PB	1972	SP	40 X 30	ARJ	150		500	6000
Horsefeathers Thirteen Series:										
Horsefeathers Thirteen I	GEM	GEM	1972	LC/SP/PO/CO/EMB	28 X 22	AMG	76		275	5000
Horsefeathers Thirteen III	GEM	GEM	1972	LC/SP/PO/CO/EMB	23 X 23	AMG	80		275	5000
Horsefeathers Thirteen IV	GEM	GEM	1972	LC/SP/PO/CO/EMB	28 X 23	AMG	89		275	5000
Horsefeathers Thirteen V (G-425)	GEM	GEM	1972	LC/SP/PO/CO/EMB	24 X 18	JGP	76		225	5000
Horsefeathers Thirteen XIV	GEM	GEM	1972	LC/SP/PO/CO/EMB	26 X 21	JGP	83		250	5000
Horsefeathers Thirteen XV	GEM	GEM	1972	LC/SP/PO/CO/EMB	26 X 21	JGP	80		250	5000
Horsefeathers Thirteen IX	GEM	GEM	1973	LC/SP/PO/CO/EMB	29 X 22	JGP	74		250	5000
Rays	SS	SS	1973	SP	53 X 39	ASHP	95		900	5000
Man Grove			1973	CO	60 X 38	HMP	20		900	7500
Peanuts			1973	CO	60 X 38	HMP	20		900	7500
Cactus			1973	CO	60 X 38	HMP	20		900	7500
Watermark	BAI		1973	SP	35 X 24	AP	250		300	4500
Veil Series:										
Veils I	ULAE	ULAE	1974	LB/LT	23 X 31	JWP	20	1	300	5000
Veils II	ULAE	ULAE	1974	LC/LT	23 X 31	JWP	21	2	300	5000
Veils III	ULAE	ULAE	1974	LC/LT	23 X 31	JWP	23	2	300	5000
Veils IV	ULAE	ULAE	1974	LC/LT	23 X 31	JWP	18	2	300	5000
Veils V	ULAE	ULAE	1974	LC/LT	23 X 31	JWP	21	2	300	5000
Hoarfrost Editions Series:										
Ringer (G-569)	GEM	GEM	1974	LC/OFF/CO	68 X 36	FABRIC	31		800	250000
Scent	GEM	GEM	1974	LC/OFF/CO	86 X 50	FABRIC	30		800	250000
Sand	GEM	GEM	1974	LC/OFF/CO	84 X 41	FABRIC	30		800	250000
Preview	GEM	GEM	1974	LC/OFF/SP/CO	46 X 79	FABRIC	32		800	35000
Scrape	GEM	GEM	1974		76 X 36	HMP	32		800	15000
Mule (with Newspaper Image Transfers on Cheesecloth, Muslin & Silk Satin with Collage of Paper Bag & Fabric) (G-571)	GEM	GEM	1974	LC/OFF	67 X 36	CLOTH	33	8	800	15000
Plus Fours (with Newspaper Transfer—Printed on Silk Satin & Silk Chiffon) (G-573)	GEM	GEM	1974	LC/OFF	67 X 95	HMP	28		800	18000
Pages and Fuses: Pages Series:										
Pages and Fuses: Page I (RAG) (G-514)	GEM	GEM	1974	MULT	21 X 27	HMP	27		900	15000
Pages and Fuses: Page II (G-515)	GEM	GEM	1974	MULT	21 X 27	HMP			900	15000
Pages and Fuses: Page III (RAG) (G-516)	GEM	GEM	1974	MULT	19 X 19	HMP	35		900	15000
Pages and Fuses: Page IV (Twine) (G-517)	GEM	GEM	1974	MULT	83 X 20	HMP	19		900	15000
Pages and Fuses: Page V (Cord) (G-518)	GEM	GEM	1974	MULT	21 X 27	HMP	23		900	15000
Pages and Fuses: Bit (Pigment, Laminated Paper Pulp) (G-522)	GEM	GEM	1974	MULT	19 X 17	HMP	33		800	15000
Pages and Fuses: Vale (G-524)	GEM	ART	1974	MULT	19 X 24	HMP	14		800	20000

ROBERT RAUSCHENBERG CONTINUED

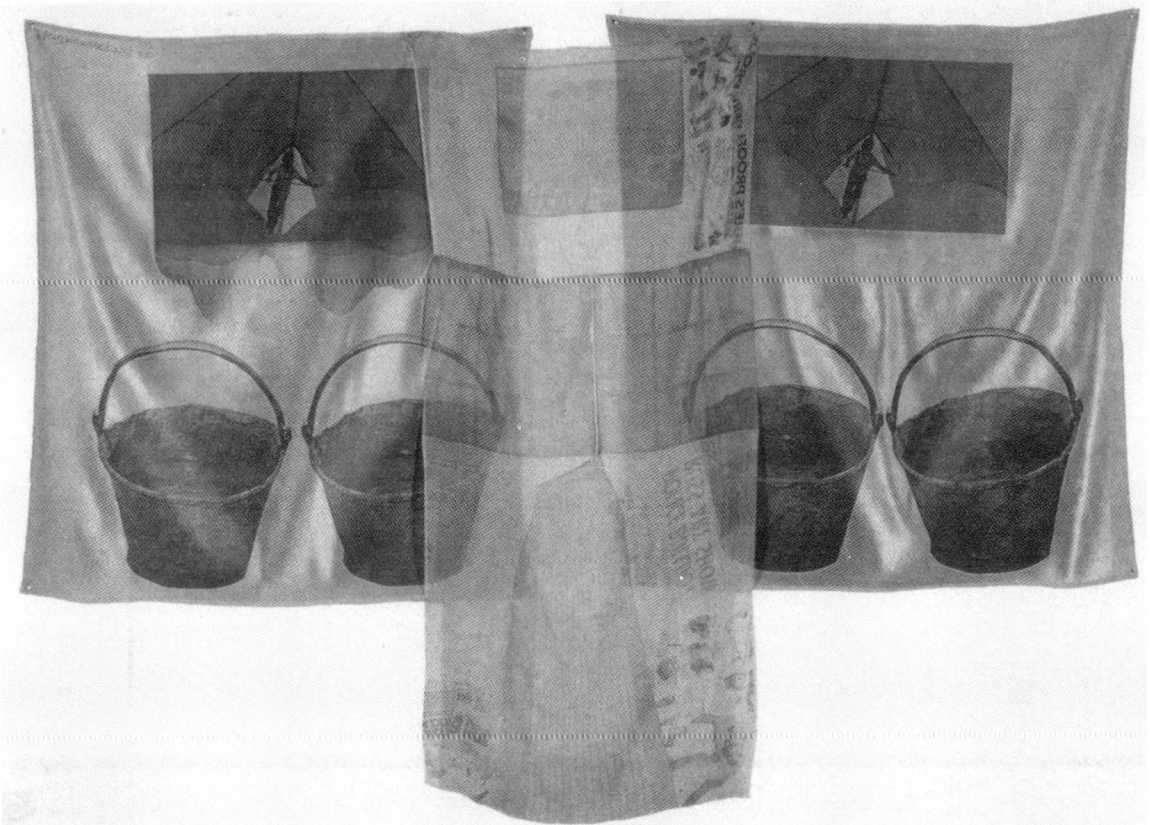

Robert Rauschenberg
Hoarfrost Editions: Plus Fours
Courtesy Gemini GEL

TITLE	PUBLISHER	PRINTER	DATE	MEDIUM	DIMENSION (PAPER SIZE) IN INCHES	TYPE OF PAPER	EDITION NUMBER	NO. OF COLORS	ORIGINAL OPENING PRICE	CURRENT RETAIL PRICE
SOLD OUT EDITIONS (RARE):										
Pages and Fuses: Hind	GEM	ART	1974	MULT	26 X 20	HMP	34		850	18000
Pages and Fuses: Link	GEM	ART	1974	MULT	25 X 20	HMP	29		900	18000
Pages and Fuses: Roan	GEM	ART	1974	MULT	20 X 25	HMP	36		850	18000
Pages and Fuses: Scow (Pigment, Laminated Paper Pulp)	GEM	GEM	1974	MULT/SP	19 X 18	HMP	34		900	18000
Tanya (S-45)	ULAE	ULAE	1974	LB	23 X 15	RdB	50	1	800	15000
Treaty (Dipt)	ULAE	ULAE	1974	LC	28 X 40	JWP	31		900	10000
Ringer State (Fabric)	GEM	GEM	1974	MULT/LC	70 X 36	HMP	31		900	12000
Airport Series:										
Airport Series: Room Service (White Cotton and Green Muslin) (BM-86)	GS/USF	GS/USF	1974	MM/CO	54 X 58		20		1500	7500
Airport Series: Sheephead (Cotton and Cheesecloth) (BM-07)	GS/USF	GS/USF	1974	MM/CO	34 X 51		20		1500	7500
Pull (with Newspaper Image Transfers) (Printed on Silk Tafeta, Cheesecloth, Paper Bag & Fabric Collage) (F-574)	GEM	GEM	1974	LC/OFF/CO	85 X 48	SILK	29	2	1500	25000
Killdevil Hill (Dipt) (S-52)	ULAE	ULAE	1974–75	LC	27 X 80	JWP	42	2	2000	40000
Re-Entry (from Mirrors of the Mind) (Dipt)	M	PB/A	1975	CO	15 X 22	AP	100		300	3500
Hard Eight (Bamboo, Fabric)	GEM	GEM	1975	MM	26 X 33 X 3	HMP	32		1000	12000
Box Cars	GEM	GEM	1975	MM	26 X 33 X 3	HMP	32		1000	12000
Bones & Unions (Handmade Paper with Bamboo & Fabric):										
Pit Boss	GEM	GEM	1975	MM	34 X 26 X 4	HMP	28		1000	10000
Snake Eyes	GEM	GEM	1975	MM	34 X 26 X 1	HMP	33		1000	10000
Hard Eight	GEM	GEM	1975	MM	26 X 33 X 3	HMP	32		1000	6000
Box Cars	GEM	GEM	1975	MM	34 X 26 X 3	HMP	31		1000	6000
Little Joe (G-637)	GEM	GEM	1975	MM	23 X 29 X 1	HMP	34		1000	6000
Ally (Rag-Mud/Bamboo/Rope/String)	GEM	GEM	1975	MM	45 X 49 X 3	HMP	13		1000	10000
Junction (Mud/Rope)	GEM	GEM	1975	MM	75 X 70 X 4	HMP	25		1000	6000

ROBERT RAUSCHENBERG CONTINUED

TITLE	PUBLISHER	PRINTER	DATE	MEDIUM	DIMENSION (PAPER SIZE) IN INCHES	TYPE OF PAPER	EDITION NUMBER	NO. OF COLORS	ORIGINAL OPENING PRICE	CURRENT RETAIL PRICE
SOLD OUT EDITIONS (RARE):										
Ballot (Rag-Mud/Rope)	GEM	GEM	1975	MM	72 X 28 X 1	HMP	15		1000	6000
Charter (Rag-Mud/Rope/Bamboo)	GEM	GEM	1975	MM	81 X 29 X 23	HMP	15		1000	10000
Quorum (Rag-Mud/Rope/Bamboo/Mud)	GEM	GEM	1975	MM	64 X 45 X 4	HMP	13		1000	15000
Horsefeathers Thirteen Series (Group II):										
Horsefeathers Thirteen VI	GEM	GEM	1976	LC/SP/PO/CO/EMB	27 X 20	HMP	82		750	5000
Horsefeathers Thirteen VII	GEM	GEM	1976	LC/SP/PO/CO/EMB	24 X 18		84		750	5000
Horsefeathers Thirteen VIII	GEM	GEM	1976	LC/SP/PO/CO/EMB	24 X 18	HMP	79		750	5000
Horsefeathers Thirteen XIII	GEM	GEM	1976	LC/SP/PO/CO/EMB	27 X 21	HMP	78		750	5000
Romances Series:										
Romances (Prophecy)	GEM	GEM	1977	LC	29 X 41	AMP	38	4	1250	10000
Romances (Yoke)	GEM	GEM	1977	LC	26 X 20	AMP	37	3	750	10000
Romances (Elopement)	GEM	GEM	1977	LC	42 X 30	AMP	39	5	1400	10000
Romances (Elysian)	GEM	GEM	1977	LC	39 X 30	AMP	38	4	1250	10000
Romances (Castles)	GEM	GEM	1977	LC	41 X 31	AMP	39	4	1250	10000
Romances (Epic) (G-764)	GEM	GEM	1977	LC	43 X 29	AMP	36	3	2000	12500
Romances (Myth)	GEM	GEM	1977	LC	23 X 31	AMP	39	4	850	10000
Romances (Pomegranate)	GEM	GEM	1977	LC	42 X 31	AMP	37	4	1000	10000
Chow Bags Series Suite (Set of 6):										
Calf	UPI	SS	1977	SP	36 X 48	AP	100	9	1250	4000
Rabbit	UPI	SS	1977	SP	36 X 48	AP	100	7	1250	4000
Hog	UPI	SS	1977	SP	36 X 48	AP	100	9	1250	4000
Monkey	UPI	SS	1977	SP	36 X 48	AP	100	6	1250	4000
Mink	UPI	SS	1977	SP	36 X 48	AP	100	10	1250	4000
Goat	UPI	SS	1977	SP	36 X 48	AP	100	9	1250	4000
Darkness Mother	ULAE	ULAE	1978	LC	31 X 23	HMP	42		750	5000
Picture Gallery	ULAE	ULAE	1978	LC	31 X 23	HMP	40		750	5500
Long Island Beach	ULAE	ULAE	1978	LC	31 X 23	HMP	39		750	6000
Echo When	ULAE	ULAE	1978	LC	31 X 23	HMP	41		750	5000
Publicons (Set of 6):									10000 SET	60000 SET
Publicon—Station I	GEM	GEM	1978	MS	59 X 30 X 12	HMP	30		1800	20000
Publicon—Station II	GEM	GEM	1978	MS	36 X 14 X 14	HMP	30		1800	10000
Publicon—Station III	GEM	GEM	1978	MS	37 X 31 X 15	HMP	30		1800	8000
Publicon—Station IV	GEM	GEM	1978	MS	28 X 36 X 13	HMP	30		1800	20000
Publicon—Station V	GEM	GEM	1978	MS	18 X 36 X 8	HMP	30		1800	10000
Publicon—Station VI	GEM	GEM	1978	MS	36 X 12 X 4	HMP	30		1800	10000
Rookery Mounds Series:										
Rookery Mounds—Night Tork	GEM	GEM	1979	LC	41 X 31	HMP	50		900	6000
Rookery Mounds—Steel Arbor	GEM	GEM	1979	LC	41 X 31	HMP	51		900	6000
Rookery Mounds—Grape Levee	GEM	GEM	1979	LC	41 X 31	HMP	52		900	6000
Rookery Mounds—Moon Melon	GEM	GEM	1979	LC	41 X 31	HMP	51		900	6000
Rookery Mounds—Mud Dauber	GEM	GEM	1979	LC	41 X 31	HMP	53		900	6000
Rookery Mounds—Masthead	GEM	GEM	1979	LC	41 X 31	HMP	53		900	6000
Rookery Mounds—Gray Garden	GEM	GEM	1979	LC	41 X 31	HMP	55		900	6000
Rookery Mounds—Yardarm	GEM	GEM	1979	LC	41 X 31	HMP	53		900	6000
Rookery Mounds—Crystal	GEM	GEM	1979	LC	41 X 31	HMP	55		900	6000
Rookery Mounds—Rose Bay	GEM	GEM	1979	LC	41 X 31	HMP	54		900	6000
Rookery Mounds—Level	GEM	GEM	1979	LC	41 X 31	HMP	50		900	6000
Suite of Nine Prints (Set of 9):									6000 SET	20000 SET
Two Reasons Birds Sing	M	SS	1979	SP	31 X 23	R/BFK	100		750	4500
Shoot from a Main Stream	M	SS	1979	SP	31 X 23	R/BFK	100		750	4500
From the Seat of Authority	M	SS	1979	SP	31 X 23	R/BFK	100		750	4500
People Have Enough Trouble Without being Intimidated by an Artichoke	M	SS	1979	SP	31 X 23	R/BFK	100		750	4500
Back Out	M	SS	1979	SP	31 X 23	R/BFK	100		750	4500
Most Distant Visible Part of the Sea	M	SS	1979	SP	31 X 23	R/BFK	100		750	4500
Most Visible Part of the Sea	M	SS	1979	LC/OFF/CO/TR	31 X 23	R/BFK	100		1000	5000
Why You Can't Tell #1	M	SS	1979	SP	31 X 23	R/BFK	100		750	4500
Why You Can't Tell #1	M	SS	1979	LC/OFF/CO/TR	31 X 23	R/BFK	100		1000	5000
Why You Can't Tell #2	M	SS	1979	SP	31 X 23	R/BFK	100		750	4500
Why You Can't Tell #2	M	SS	1979	LC/OFF/CO/TR	31 X 23	R/BFK	100		1000	5000

ROBERT RAUSCHENBERG CONTINUED

Robert Rauschenberg
Stoned Moon Series: Horn
Courtesy Gemini GEL

Robert Rauschenberg
Stoned Moon Series: Banner
Courtesy Gemini GEL

TITLE	PUBLISHER	PRINTER	DATE	MEDIUM	DIMENSION (PAPER SIZE) IN INCHES	TYPE OF PAPER	EDITION NUMBER	NO. OF COLORS	ORIGINAL OPENING PRICE	CURRENT RETAIL PRICE
SOLD OUT EDITIONS (RARE):										
One More and We Will be More than Half Way There	M	SS	1979	SP	31 X 23	R/BFK	100		750	4500
One More and We Will Be More than Half Way There	M	SS	1979	LC/OFF/CO/TR	31 X 23	R/BFK	100		1000	5000
Suite of Nine Prints (Set of 9):									8500 SET	35000 SET
Two Reasons Birds Sing	M	SS	1979	LC/OFF/CO/TR	31 X 23	R/BFK	100		1000	5000
Shoot from a Main Stem	M	SS	1979	LC/OFF/CO/TR	31 X 23	R/BFK	100		1000	5000
From the Seat of Authority	M	SS	1979	LC/OFF/CO/TR	31 X 23	R/BFK	100		1000	5000
People Have Enough Trouble without Being Intimidated by an Artichoke	M	SS	1979	LC/OFF/CO/TR	31 X 23	R/BFK	100		1000	5000
Back Out	M	SS	1979	LC/OFF/CO/TR	31 X 23	R/BFK	100		1000	5000
Mud Dauber	GEM	GEM	1979	LC	41 X 31	HMP	53		900	8500
Masthead	GEM	GEM	1979	LC	41 X 31	HMP	50		900	7500
Steel Arbor	GEM	GEM	1979	LC	41 X 31	HMP	51		900	8000
Level	GEM	GEM	1979	LC	41 X 31	HMP	50		900	7500
Etching II	ULAE	ULAE	1979	EB	25 X 17	HMP	24	1	750	7000
Etching III	ULAE	ULAE	1979	EB	25 X 17	HMP	22	1	750	7000
Etching IV	ULAE	ULAE	1979	EB	25 X 17	HMP	22	1	750	7000
Lithograph II	ULAE	ULAE	1980	LC	66 X 40	HMP	25		1500	10000
Lithograph III	ULAE	ULAE	1980	LC	25 X 36	HMP	22	1	1000	5000
Lithograph IV	ULAE	ULAE	1980	LC	60 X 44	HMP	25		1500	7500
White Pendulum	ULAE	ULAE	1980	LC	17 X 14	HMP	33		750	2500
Afte Homage to Picasso	DNC		1973–80	SP/TR	30 X 22	HMP	45		1000	5000
Glacial Decoy Series: Lithograph II (S-102)	ULAE	ULAE	1980	LC	60 X 40	AP	25	5	1500	15000
Aquafix	ULAE	ULAE	1981	LC/EB	40 X 29	HMP	25		2500	5000
The Razorback Bunch	ULAE	ULAE	1981	EB/CC	48 X 32	HMP	26		2500	5000
The Razorback Bunch: Etching II (3 Sheets)	ULAE	ULAE	1980	EC/CC	38 X 19	KIT/AP	24		2000	8500
5:29 Bayshore	ULAE	ULAE	1981	LC/CC	45 X 93	HMP	30		4500	10000

ROBERT RAUSCHENBERG CONTINUED

Robert Rauschenberg
Signs
Courtesy Castelli Editions

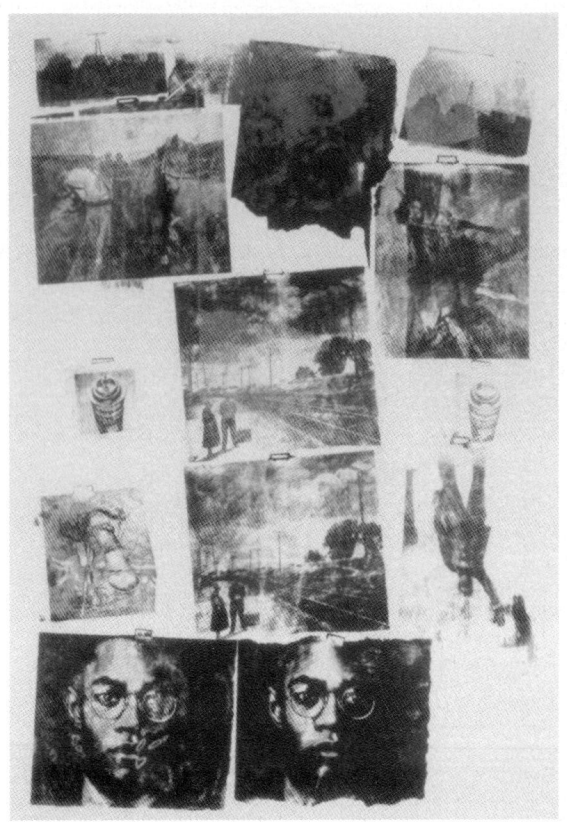

Robert Rauschenberg
Landmark
Courtesy Universal Limited Art Editions

TITLE	PUBLISHER	PRINTER	DATE	MEDIUM	DIMENSION (PAPER SIZE) IN INCHES	TYPE OF PAPER	EDITION NUMBER	NO. OF COLORS	ORIGINAL OPENING PRICE	CURRENT RETAIL PRICE
SOLD OUT EDITIONS (RARE):										
American Pewter with Burroughs (Set of 6):										
American Pewter with Burroughs I	GEM	GEM	1981	LC	32 X 24	HMP	34		1500	4500
American Pewter with Burroughs II	GEM	GEM	1981	LC	32 X 24	HMP	42		1500	4500
American Pewter with Burroughs III	GEM	GEM	1981	LC	32 X 24	HMP	34		1500	4500
American Pewter with Burroughs IV	GEM	GEM	1981	LC	32 X 24	HMP	45		1500	4500
American Pewter with Burroughs V	GEM	GEM	1981	LC	32 X 24	HMP	48		1500	4500
American Pewter with Burroughs VI	GEM	GEM	1981	LC	32 X 24	HMP	43		1500	4500
Arcanum (Set of 13)									13000 SET	75000 SET
Arcanum I	SS	SS	1981	SP/CO/HC	23 X 16	TWP/HMP	85	23	1200	6000
Arcanum II	SS	SS	1981	SP/CO	23 X 16	TWP/HMP	85	16	1200	6000
Arcanum III	SS	SS	1981	SP/CO/HC	23 X 16	TWP/HMP	85	14	1200	6000
Arcanum IV	SS	SS	1981	SP/CO/HC	23 X 16	TWP/HMP	85		1200	6000
Arcanum V	SS	SS	1981	SP/CO	23 X 16	TWP/HMP	85	12	1200	6000
Arcanum VI	SS	SS	1981	SP/CO/WA	23 X 16	TWP/HMP	85	10	1200	6000
Arcanum VII	SS	SS	1981	SP/CO/HST	23 X 16	TWP/HMP	85	8	1200	6000
Arcanum VIII	SS	SS	1981	SP/CO/HC	23 X 16	TWP/HMP	85	12	1200	6000
Arcanum IX	SS	SS	1981	SP/CO/WA	23 X 16	TWP/HMP	85	15	1200	6000
Arcanum X	SS	SS	1981	SP/CO/WA	23 X 16	TWP/HMP	85	7	1200	6000
Arcanum XI	SS	SS	1981	SP/CO/WA	23 X 16	TWP/HMP	85	16	1200	6000
Arcanum XII	SS	SS	1981	SP/CO/HC	23 X 16	TWP/HMP	85	12	1200	6000
Arcanum XIII	SS	SS	1981	SP/CO	23 X 16	TWP/HMP	85	23	1200	6000
7 Characters Series (Unique Paper & Fabric Collages Made in the People's Republic of China (Set of 7) (G-1033–G-1039):									10000 SET	95000 SET
Individual (G-1033)	GEM	GEM	1982	CO	38 X 27	HMP	1 EA		1500	15000
Change (G-1034)	GEM	GEM	1982	CO	38 X 27	HMP	1 EA		1500	15000
Howl (G-1035)	GEM	GEM	1982	CO	38 X 27	HMP	1 EA		1500	15000
Light (G-1036)	GEM	GEM	1982	CO	38 X 27	HMP	1 EA		1500	15000
Trunk (G-1037)	GEM	GEM	1982	CO	38 X 27	HMP	1 EA		1500	15000
Red Heart (G-1038)	GEM	GEM	1982	CO	38 X 27	HMP	1 EA		1500	15000
LA Flakes (Series of 8):										
LA Flakes—400; and Rising	GEM	GEM	1982	EB/EMB	31 X 23	HMP	40		600	2000
LA Flakes—400; and Falling	GEM	GEM	1982	EB/EMB	31 X 23	HMP	39		600	2000

ROBERT RAUSCHENBERG CONTINUED

TITLE	PUBLISHER	PRINTER	DATE	MEDIUM	DIMENSION (PAPER SIZE) IN INCHES	TYPE OF PAPER	EDITION NUMBER	NO. OF COLORS	ORIGINAL OPENING PRICE	CURRENT RETAIL PRICE
SOLD OUT EDITIONS (RARE):										
LA Flakes—2000; and Falling	GEM	GEM	1982	EB/EMB	31 X 23	HMP	37		600	2000
LA Flakes—10000; and Rising	GEM	GEM	1982	EB/EMB	31 X 23	HMP	37		600	2000
LA Flakes—11000; and Rising	GEM	GEM	1982	EB/EMB	31 X 23	HMP	42		600	2000
LA Flakes—13000; and Rising	GEM	GEM	1982	EB/EMB	31 X 23	HMP	36		600	2000
LA Flakes—19000; Still	GEM	GEM	1982	EB/EMB	31 X 23	HMP	39		600	2000
LA Flakes—22469; Still	GEM	GEM	1982	EB/EMB	31 X 23	HMP	44		600	2000
The Razorback Bunch	ULAE	ULAE	1982	EC	44 X 31	HMP	28		2000	5000
Cage	M/SS	SS	1983	SP/CO	41 X 30	AP	125		1500	5000
Photogravures (Set of 16)	IE	IE	1983	PH	20 X 26EA	HMP	40 EA		14000 SFT	35000 SFT
Untitled (Commemorative) (with Pencil Drawing, Embossing & Collage)	REH	LW	1983	LC/OFF/EMB/CO	29 X 21	AP	125		1100 EA 850	2500 EA 6000
Statue of Liberty	CFA	AA	1983	LC/SP	36 X 25	AP	250		1300	5000
Untitled	ART	ULAE	1984	LC/OFF	19 X 17	AP			500	5500
Untitled	ME	ME	1984	LC/OFF	22 X 18	AP	125		800	5500
Untitled	ULAE	KB/ULAE	1984	LC/OFF	14 X 17	JWP	40		900	5500
Studies for Chinese Summerhall (Series of 5) (G-1163–G-1167)										
Studies for Chinese Summerhall I	GEM	GEM	1984	PH/C	30 X 106	JWP	25		2000	5000
Studies for Chinese Summerhall II	GEM	GEM	1984	PH/C	30 X 88	JWP	25		1000	5000
Studies for Chinese Summerhall III	GEM	GEM	1984	PH/C	88 X 30	JWP	25		1000	5000
Studies for Chinese Summerhall IV	GEM	GEM	1984	PH/C	30 X 94	JWP	25		1200	5000
Studies for Chinese Summerhall V	GEM	GEM	1984	PH/C	30 X 100	JWP	25		1500	5000
Sling-Shots Lit (Light Box Assemblage with Lithography and Screen Printing) (Series of 11):										
Sling-Shots Lit #1 (G-1169)	GEM	GEM	1984	LC/SP/AS	85 X 36 X 12	HMP	25		5000	18000
Sling-Shots Lit #2 (G-1170)	GEM	GEM	1984	LC/SP/AS	85 X 48 X 12	HMP	25		5000	18000
Sling-Shots Lit #3 (G-1171)	GEM	GEM	1984	LC/SP/AS	85 X 48 X 12	HMP	25		5000	18000
Sling-Shots Lit #3 (Black State) (G-1172)	GEM	GEM	1984	LC/SP/AS	85 X 48 X 12	HMP	25		5000	18000
Sling-Shots Lit #4 (G-1173)	GEM	GEM	1984	LC/SP/AS	85 X 36 X 12	HMP	25		5000	18000
Sling-Shots Lit #5 (G-1174)	GEM	GEM	1984	LC/SP/AS	85 X 54 X 12	HMP	25		5000	15000
Sling-Shots Lit #6 (G-1175)	GEM	GEM	1984	LC/SP/AS	85 X 54 X 12	HMP	25		5000	22000
Sling-Shots Lit #6 (Black State) (G-1176)	GEM	GEM	1984	LC/SP/AS	85 X 54 X 12	HMP	25		5000	22000
Sling-Shots Lit #7 (G-1177)	GEM	GEM	1984	LC/SP/AS	85 X 54 X 36	HMP	25		5000	22000
Sling-Shots Lit #8 (G-1178)	GEM	GEM	1984	LC/SP/AS	85 X 54 X 12	HMP	25		5000	22000
Sling-Shots Lit #8 (Black State) (G-1179)	GEM	GEM	1984	LC/SP/AS	85 X 54 X 12	HMP	25		5000	18000
Bellini #1	ULAE	CZ/ULAE	1986	PH/G	58 X 38	AP	36		4000	18000
Fire Hydrant (on Aluminum)			1988	PH	53 X 44	AP/ALUM			5000	18000
Soviet American Array I	ULAE	ULAE	1988–89	I/CO	92 X 53	HMP	55		8000	15000
Soviet American Array II	ULAE	ULAE	1988–89	I/CO	88 X 52	HMP	55		8000	15000
Affiche pour Earth Day			1990	LC	60 X 40					
Blue Line Swinger	GEM	SB/KF/JR/GEM	1991	LC	30 X 67EA	DIEU	68	4	6800	7500

PAUL REBEYROLLE

BORN: Eymoutiers, France; November 3, 1926
PRINTERS: Maeght Editions, Paris, France (ME); Galerie Maeght Lelong, Paris, France (ML)
PUBLISHERS: Maeght Editions, Paris, France (ME); Galerie Maeght Lelong, Paris, France (ML)
GALLERIES: Galerie Lelong, Paris, France & Zürich, Switzerland & New York, NY

TITLE	PUBLISHER	PRINTER	DATE	MEDIUM	DIMENSION (PAPER SIZE) IN INCHES	TYPE OF PAPER	EDITION NUMBER	NO. OF COLORS	ORIGINAL OPENING PRICE	CURRENT RETAIL PRICE
CURRENT EDITIONS:										
Ca Ira Mieux Demain	ME	ME	1979	LC	32 X 23	AP	75		600 FF	1000 FF
Sondage d'Opinion II	ME	ME	1979	LC	32 X 23	AP	75		600 FF	1000 FF
Manipulation	ME	ME	1979	LC	24 X 32	AP	75		600 FF	1000 FF
A la Lumiere des Sondages	ME	ME	1979	LC	36 X 25	AP	65		900 FF	1500 FF
Enguete d'Opinion	ME	ME	1979	LC	35 X 25	AP	65		900 FF	1500 FF
Un Courant d'Opinion	ME	ME	1979	LC	34 X 23	AP	75		750 FF	1200 FF
L'Education des Masses	ME	ME	1979	LC	94 X 68 cm	AP	75		900 FF	1500 FF
Cloué au Sol	ME	ME	1981	LC	62 X 58 cm	AP	75	3	900 FF	1500 FF
La Fuite Impossible	ME	ME	1981	LC	71 X 49 cm	AP	75	3	900 FF	1500 FF
Le Dos au Mur	ME	ME	1981	LC	47 X 72 cm	AP	75	3	900 FF	1500 FF

GENEVIEVE RECKLING

BORN: St Louis, MO
EDUCATION: Univ of Texas, Austin, TX; Houston Mus of Fine Arts, TX; Arizona State Univ, Tempe, AZ
COLLECTIONS: Phoenix Art Mus, AZ; Arizona State Univ, Tempe, AZ
PRINTERS: Southwest Graphics, Scottsdale, AZ (SG); Sette Publishing Co, Tempe, AZ (SPC)
PUBLISHERS: C G Rein Publishers, St Paul, MN (CGR)
GALLERIES: C G Rein Galleries, St Paul, MN & Scottsdale, AZ & Los Angeles, CA & Denver, CO & Minneapolis, MN, & Santa Fe, NM & Houston, TX; Marilyn Butler Fine Art, Scottsdale, AZ; Elaine Starkman Fine Art, New York, NY

TITLE	PUBLISHER	PRINTER	DATE	MEDIUM	DIMENSION (PAPER SIZE) IN INCHES	TYPE OF PAPER	EDITION NUMBER	NO. OF COLORS	ORIGINAL OPENING PRICE	CURRENT RETAIL PRICE
CURRENT EDITIONS:										
Desert Flower I/Sandra Suite	CGR	SWG	1981	LC	22 X 20	AP	80	6	250	335
Desert Flower II/Sandra Suite	CGR	SWG	1981	LC	20 X 25	AP	80	6	250	335
Sanctuary	CGR	SWG	1982	LC	21 X 30	AP	80	4	250	475
City Flower Stand	CGR	SPC	1982	LC	32 X 24	AP	100	5	300	500
Summer Greenhouse	CGR	SPC	1985	SP	40 X 30	AP	200		300	420

STEVE REICH

BORN: New York, NY; October 3, 1936
EDUCATION: Cornell Univ, Ithaca, NY, 1957; Studied with Hall Overton, 1957–58; Julliard Sch of Music, NY, 1958–61; Mills Col, CA, MA in Music, 1963
PRINTERS: John Slivon (JS); Christine Bates (CB); Crown Point Press, San Francisco, CA (CPP)
PUBLISHERS: Crown Point Press, San Francisco, CA (CPP)
GALLERIES: Crown Point Press, San Francisco, CA & New York, NY

TITLE	PUBLISHER	PRINTER	DATE	MEDIUM	DIMENSION (PAPER SIZE) IN INCHES	TYPE OF PAPER	EDITION NUMBER	NO. OF COLORS	ORIGINAL OPENING PRICE	CURRENT RETAIL PRICE
CURRENT EDITIONS:										
Two Scores (Set of 2)	CPP	JS/CB/CPP	1978	EB	22 X 18 EA	GE/BL	35 EA	1 EA	450 SET / 250 EA	1000 SET / 650 EA
Four Freehand Watermark Tracings (Set of 4)	CPP	JS/CPP	1978	EB/SG	17 X 14 EA	GE/BL	25 EA	1 EA	450 SET / 250 EA	1000 SET / 650 EA

SAMUEL REINDORF

BORN: Warsaw, Poland; (1914–1988); US Citizen
EDUCATION: Cent Tech Sch, Toronto, Can; Am Artists Sch, NY
AWARDS: First Prize, Contemp Am Painting, Palm Beach, FL, 1964; First Prize, Connecticut Acad of Fine Arts, 1968
COLLECTIONS: Toronto Art Gallery, Can; Fairfield Univ, CT; Riverside Mus, NY; Tygeson Gallery, Toronto, Can; Collectors Gallery, New Orleans, LA
PRINTERS: Artist (ART)
PUBLISHERS: Artist (ART)
GALLERIES: Veerhoff Gallery, Washington, DC; La Galeria Proarte, Mexico City, Mexico
MAILING ADDRESS: c/o The Estate of Samuel Reindorf, Apartado Postal 285, San Miguel de Allende, Guanajuato, Mexico

TITLE	PUBLISHER	PRINTER	DATE	MEDIUM	DIMENSION (PAPER SIZE) IN INCHES	TYPE OF PAPER	EDITION NUMBER	NO. OF COLORS	ORIGINAL OPENING PRICE	CURRENT RETAIL PRICE
SOLD OUT EDITIONS (RARE):										
Sailing	ART	ART	1936	WB	5 X 5	AP	2	1	250	800
Harvest Time	ART	ART	1936	WB	5 X 5	AP	2	1	250	800
March Winds	ART	ART	1936	WB	5 X 5	AP	2	1	250	800
Beaver	ART	ART	1936	WB	5 X 5	AP	2	1	250	800
Skiing	ART	ART	1936	WB	5 X 5	AP	3	1	250	800
Spring	ART	ART	1936	WB	5 X 5	AP	15	1	250	800
Negro Spirituals	ART	ART	1936	WB	9 X 6	AP	10	1	300	1500
In the Subway	ART	ART	1936	WB	6 X 8	AP	10	1	300	1500
Mining Coal	ART	ART	1936	WB	9 X 7	AP	10	1	300	1500

CHARLOTTE REINE

BORN: Chambon Feugerolles, Loire, France; 1956
PRINTERS: Atelier Michel Bon, Paris, France (AMB)
PUBLISHERS: Lublin Graphics, Inc, Greenwich, CT (LG)
GALLERIES: J Todd Galleries, Wellesley, MA; Daruma Gallery, Cedarhurst, NY; Lublin Graphics, Greenwich, CT; Lublin Collection Fine Art Gallery, New York, NY; Daruma Gallery, Cedarhurst, NY

TITLE	PUBLISHER	PRINTER	DATE	MEDIUM	DIMENSION (PAPER SIZE) IN INCHES	TYPE OF PAPER	EDITION NUMBER	NO. OF COLORS	ORIGINAL OPENING PRICE	CURRENT RETAIL PRICE
SOLD OUT EDITIONS (RARE):										
Miroir d' Eau	LG	AMB	1978	EC	26 X 20	AP	140		150	300
Crocodile	LG	AMB	1978	EC	26 X 20	AP	140		150	300
L' Arbri de Ciel	LG	AMB	1978	EC	26 X 20	AP	140		150	300
Les Ruches	LG	AMB	1978	EC	26 X 20	AP	140		150	300
La Grosse Chouette	LG	AMB	1978	EC	26 X 20	AP	140		150	300
Partourelle	LG	AMB	1978	EC	26 X 20	AP	140		150	300

CHARLOTTE REINE CONTINUED

TITLE	PUBLISHER	PRINTER	DATE	MEDIUM	DIMENSION (PAPER SIZE) IN INCHES	TYPE OF PAPER	EDITION NUMBER	NO. OF COLORS	ORIGINAL OPENING PRICE	CURRENT RETAIL PRICE
SOLD OUT EDITIONS (RARE):										
Danse d' Automne	LG	AMB	1979	EC	26 X 20	AP	140		150	300
Horizon de l' Herisson	LG	AMB	1979	EC	26 X 20	AP	130		150	300
Enfant d' Elephant	LG	AMB	1979	EC	26 X 20	AP	140		150	300
Le Bouchon Bleu	LG	AMB	1979	EC	26 X 20	AP	140		150	300
Le Veilleur de Nuit	LG	AMB	1979	EC	26 X 20	AP	140		150	300
Danse du Vent	LG	AMB	1979	EC	26 X 20	AP	140		150	300
Elephant Chameleon	LG	AMB	1979	EC	26 X 20	AP	130		150	300
Perdu le Fil	LG	AMB	1979	EC	26 X 20	AP	130		150	300
Tender Flamingo	LG	AMB	1979	EC	26 X 20	AP	130		150	300
Rhino	LG	AMB	1979	EC	26 X 20	AP	140		150	300
Cache Cache	LG	AMB	1979	EC	26 X 20	AP	140		150	300
Accroche Fleurs	LG	AMB	1979	EC	26 X 20	AP	130		150	400
Accord Perdu	LG	AMB	1979	EC	26 X 20	AP	130		200	400
Jeu d' Escargot	LG	AMB	1980	EC	26 X 20	AP	140		150	300
Fleur de Lave	LG	AMB	1980	EC	26 X 20	AP	140		150	300
Jour Aven son Ombre	LG	AMB	1980	EC	26 X 20	AP	140		150	300
Habits de Fete	LG	AMB	1980	EC	26 X 20	AP	140		150	300
Les Amis de Vaches Tendres	LG	AMB	1980	EC	26 X 20	AP	140		150	300
Se Faire du Lait	LG	AMB	1981	EC	26 X 20	AP	140		150	300
Les Ruminants	LG	AMB	1981	EC	26 X 20	AP	130		150	300
Jardiner	LG	AMB	1981	EC	26 X 20	AP	130		150	300
Le Voleur de Mouton	LG	AMB	1981	EC	26 X 20	AP	130		200	300
J'ai des Ois	LG	AMB	1981	LC	26 X 20	AP	220		150	300
Retour du Pays	LG	AMB	1981	LC	26 X 20	AP	220		150	300
Rose	LG	AMB	1981	EC	26 X 20	AP	130		150	300
Silence	LG	AMB	1981	LC	26 X 20	AP	220		150	300
Canads Calins	LG	AMB	1982	LC	26 X 20	AP	220		150	300
La Merchande de Chapeaux	LG	AMB	1982	EC	26 X 20	AP	130		150	300
St Valentin	LG	AMB	1982	EC	26 X 20	AP	130		150	400
Un Jour sans Vent	LG	AMB	1982	EC	26 X 20	AP	130		200	300
Marchand de Pain	LG	AMB	1982	EC	26 X 20	AP	130		150	300
Sieste	LG	AMB	1982	LC	26 X 20	AP	210		150	300
Jazz	LG	AMB	1983	EC	26 X 20	AP	140		200	300
Le Piano a Bretelles	LG	AMB	1983	EC	26 X 20	AP	140		200	200
Violon d'Ingres	LG	AMB	1983	EC	26 X 20	AP	140		200	200
Rendez-Vous	LG	AMB	1983	EC	26 X 20	AP	130		200	300
Le Voyager	LG	AMB	1983	EC	26 X 20	AP	130		200	200
Les Sonnerus de Cloches	LG	AMB	1983	EC	26 X 20	AP	130		200	200
CURRENT EDITIONS:										
Bon Soir	LG	AMB	1983	EC	26 X 20	AP	130		200	200
Vent du Sud	LG	AMB	1983	EC	26 X 20	AP	130		200	200
Vent du Nord	LG	AMB	1983	EC	26 X 20	AP	130		200	200
Dormir dans sa Valise	LG	AMB	1983	EC	26 X 20	AP	130		200	200
Le Jongleur	LG	AMB	1983	EC	26 X 20	AP	130		200	200
Un Deux Trois	LG	AMB	1984	EC	26 X 20	AP	130		200	200
Pour Offrir	LG	AMB	1984	EC	26 X 20	AP	130		200	200
Piano Ivre	LG	AMB	1984	EC	26 X 20	AP	130		300	400
Retour au Pays	LG	AMB	1985	EC	19 X 26	AP	130		150	150
Outremer Blues	LG	AMB	1985	EC	26 X 20	AP	130		300	300
Chaussures de Jardin	LG	AMB	1985	EC	26 X 20	AP	130		300	300
Melomanie	LG	AMB	1985	EC	26 X 20	AP	130		300	300
Chanson d'Automne	LG	AMB	1985	EC	26 X 20	AP	130		300	300
Duo	LG	AMB	1986	EC	26 X 20	AP	130		300	300
La Trompette Rouge	LG	AMB	1986	EC	26 X 20	AP	120		300	300
Le Pianiste	LG	AMB	1986	EC	30 X 23	AP	120		300	300
Le Chanteur de Bleus	LG	AMB	1986	EC	16 X 12	AP	150		150	300
Paso Doble	LG	AMB	1987	EC	36 X 26	AP	150		450	450
Papillon de Nuit	LG	AMB	1987	EC	36 X 26	AP	150		450	450
Jours et Nuits (Set of 4):										
Coup de Théatre	LG	AMB	1987	EC	16 X 12	AP	150		150	150
Chanteur de Charme	LG	AMB	1987	EC	16 X 12	AP	150		150	150
Le Chant da Coquelicot	LG	AMB	1987	EC	16 X 12	AP	150		150	150
La Sieste	LG	AMB	1987	EC	16 X 12	AP	150		150	150
Rivage	LG	AMB	1988	EC	16 X 12	AP	150		300	350
Valse Bleue	LG	AMB	1988	EC	16 X 12	AP	150		300	350
L' Echo	LG	AMB	1988	EC	16 X 12	AP	150		300	350
Le Divan (Sculpture)	LG	AMB	1988	EC	7¼" HT	Bronze			750	750
Consonances	LG	AMB	1988	EC	30 X 23	AP	150		400	450
Quatuor	LG	AMB	1988	EC	30 X 23	AP	150		400	450

The retail prices of the 100,000 limited edition prints quoted in this directory are subject to change. Print publishers, artists and galleries were the direct sources for these quotations. Prices in the secondary market listed as "Sold Out Editions (Rare)" indicate that the publisher has a limited supply of that print or that the print is difficult to locate in the galleries.

CHARLOTTE REINE CONTINUED

TITLE	PUBLISHER	PRINTER	DATE	MEDIUM	DIMENSION (PAPER SIZE) IN INCHES	TYPE OF PAPER	EDITION NUMBER	NO. OF COLORS	ORIGINAL OPENING PRICE	CURRENT RETAIL PRICE
CURRENT EDITIONS:										
Les Portraits (Set of 5):									750 SET	750 SET
Le Portrait I (Trumpet)	LG	AMB	1989	EC	10 X 7	AP	150		150	150
Le Portrait II (Violin)	LG	AMB	1989	EC	10 X 7	AP	150		150	150
Le Portrait III (Camera)	LG	AMB	1989	EC	10 X 7	AP	150		150	150
Le Portrait IV (Cello)	LG	AMB	1989	EC	10 X 7	AP	150		150	150
Le Portrait V (Accordian)	LG	AMB	1989	EC	10 X 7	AP	150		150	150
Complice	LG	AMB	1990	EC	20 X 15	AP	150		250	250

AD F REINHARDT

BORN: New York, NY; (1913–1967)
EDUCATION: Columbia Univ, NY, 1936; Nat Acad of Design, NY
TEACHING: Instr, Brooklyn Col, NY, 1947–67
RECENT EXHIB: Montclair Art Mus, NJ, 1992

COLLECTIONS: Mus of Mod Art, NY; Whitney Mus of Am Art, NY; Metropolitan Mus of Art, NY; Brooklyn Mus, NY; Art Inst of Chicago, IL; Tate Gallery, London, England; Albright-Knox Art Gallery, Buffalo, NY; San Francisco Mus of Mod Art, CA
PRINTERS: Ives-Stillman, NY (IS)
PUBLISHERS: Wadsworth Atheneum, Hartford, CT (WA)
GALLERIES: Herbert Palmer Gallery, Los Angles, CA; Reger Galleries, Tinton Falls, NJ; Edward Tyler Nahem Fine Art, New York, NY; Simon/Neuman Gallery, New York, NY; Yoshii Gallery, New York, NY

TITLE	PUBLISHER	PRINTER	DATE	MEDIUM	DIMENSION (PAPER SIZE) IN INCHES	TYPE OF PAPER	EDITION NUMBER	NO. OF COLORS	ORIGINAL OPENING PRICE	CURRENT RETAIL PRICE
SOLD OUT EDITIONS (RARE):										
Ten Screenprints (Set of 10)	WA	I-S	1966	SP	22 X 17 EA	AP	250 EA		1000 SET	8000 SET
Untitled	WA	I-S	1967	SP	18 X 18	AP	100		100	1200

EDDA RENOUF

BORN: Mexico City, Mexico; June 17, 1943; US Citizen
EDUCATION: Sarah Lawrence Col, Bronxville, NY, BA, 1961–65; Acad Julian, Paris, France, 1963–64; Sorbonne, Paris, France, 1963–64; Inst D'Art et D'Arch, Paris, France, 1963–64; Art Students League, NY, 1966–67; Columbia Univ Sch of Art, NY, MFA, 1968–71
TEACHING: Instr, Drawing & Painting, Sarah Lawrence Col Prog, Paris, France, 1973–74
AWARDS: Nat Endowment for the Arts Grant, Printmaking, 1977; Grant, Pollock-Krasner Found, Inc, NY, 1990
RECENT EXHIB: Metropolitan Mus of Art, NY, 1987; Fridericianaum, Cassel, Germany, 1988; BlumHelman Gallery, NY, 1988; Mus of Mod Art, NY, 1990; Musee d'Art Mod de Lille, Ville Neuve D'Ascq, France, 1992

COLLECTIONS: Mus of Mod Art, NY; Metropolitan Mus of Art, NY; Whitney Mus of Am Art, NY; St Louis Mus of Art, MO; Yale Univ Art Gallery, New Haven, CT; Centre Georges Pompidou, Paris, France; Mus of Grenoble, France; Chicago Inst of Art, IL; Philadelphia Mus of Art, PA; Dallas Mus, TX; Neuberger Mus, Puchase, NY; Australian Nat Gallery, Canberra, Australia; Cincinnati Mus, OH; Detroit Mus, MI; New York Public Library, NY; Bibliotheque Nat, Paris, France
PRINTERS: John Slivon, Oakland, CA (JS); Doris Simmelink, Oakland, CA (DS); Crown Point Press, Oakland, CA (CPP); Carol Weaver, NY (CW); Felix Harlan, NY (FH); Harlan-Weaver Intaglio, NY (HWI)
PUBLISHERS: Parasol Press, NY (PaP);
GALLERIES: BlumHelman Gallery, New York, NY; Pace Prints, New York, NY; Margo Leavin Gallery, Los Angeles, CA; Martina Hamilton & Associates, Inc, Gallery, New York, NY; Parasol Press, Ltd, New York, NY; Parasol at Sag Harbor, Sag Harbor, NY; Yvon Lambert Gallery, Paris, France; J J Brookings & Company, San Jose, CA
MAILING ADDRESS: 37 rue Volta, 75003 Paris, France

TITLE	PUBLISHER	PRINTER	DATE	MEDIUM	DIMENSION (PAPER SIZE) IN INCHES	TYPE OF PAPER	EDITION NUMBER	NO. OF COLORS	ORIGINAL OPENING PRICE	CURRENT RETAIL PRICE
SOLD OUT EDITIONS (RARE):										
Traces (Set of 6)	PaP	JC/CPP	1974	EC/A	18 X 19 EA	R/BFK	25 EA	2 EA	2000 SET	3000 SET
Marks (Set of 6)	PaP	JS/CPP	1976	EC/A	23 X 22 EA	R/BFK	25 EA	3 EA	2000 SET	3000 SET
Clusters (Set of 8)	PaP	DS/CPP	1976	EC/A	9 X 9 EA	R/BFK	25 EA	5 EA	2000 SET	3000 SET
Overtones (Set of 5) (With Cassette of Electronic Music by Alain Middleton)	PaP	JS/CPP	1977	EC/A	20 X 20 EA	R/BFK	25 EA	5 EA	2000 SET	3000 SET
Resonances (Set of 8)	PaP	JS/CPP	1979	EC	20 X 20 EA	R/BFDK	25 EA	5 EA	2200 SET	3500 SET
Letters to Earth (Set of 7)	PaP	CW/FH/HWI	1991	EC/A	23 X 19 EA	SOM/S	25 EA	5 EA	2000 SET	2500 SET

ANNIE RETIVAT

PRINTERS: American Atelier, NY (AA)
PUBLISHERS: Circle Fine Art, Chicago, IL (CFA)

GALLERIES: Circle Galleries, San Diego, CA & San Francisco, CA & Northbrook, IL & Pittsburgh, PA & Houston, TX & Soho, NY & Chicago, IL & Scottsdale, AZ & Beverly Hills, CA & Costa Mesa, CA & Sherman Oaks, CA & Palm Beach, FL & Honolulu, HI & New Orleans, LA & Las Vegas, NV & Seattle, WA

TITLE	PUBLISHER	PRINTER	DATE	MEDIUM	DIMENSION (PAPER SIZE) IN INCHES	TYPE OF PAPER	EDITION NUMBER	NO. OF COLORS	ORIGINAL OPENING PRICE	CURRENT RETAIL PRICE
SOLD OUT EDITIONS (RARE):										
La Terrasse (The Terrace)	CFA	AA	1987	LC	36 X 26	AP	300		600	675
CURRENT EDITIONS:										
L'Air du Temps	CFA	AA	1986	LC	36 X 26	AP	300		600	625
Femme au Renard Argente (The Silver Fox)	CFA	AA	1987	LC	36 X 26	AP	300		600	625

ANNIE RETIVAT CONTINUED

TITLE	PUBLISHER	PRINTER	DATE	MEDIUM	DIMENSION (PAPER SIZE) IN INCHES	TYPE OF PAPER	EDITION NUMBER	NO. OF COLORS	ORIGINAL OPENING PRICE	CURRENT RETAIL PRICE
CURRENT EDITIONS:										
Nostalgie (Nostalgia)	CFA	AA	1987	LC	36 X 26	AP	300		600	675
Rendezvous	CFA	AA	1988	LC	28 X 21	AP	300		600	625
Reverie	CFA	AA	1988	LC/HC	35 X 26	AP	300		600	625
Opera	CFA	AA	1989	LC	35 X 26	AP	300		600	625
Apres L'Ete (After Summer)	CFA	AA	1989	LC	35 X 26	AP	300		600	600
Ville de Bellerive (City of Bellerive)	CFA	AA	1989	LC	35 X 26	AP	300		600	600
En Rive (Dreaming)	CFA	AA	1989	LC	36 X 26	AP	300		600	600

BRENT RICHARDSON

PRINTERS: Donna Shulman, Brooklyn, NY (DS); Downstairs Editions, Brooklyn, NY (DE)
PUBLISHERS: Downstairs Editions, Brooklyn, NY (DE)
GALLERIES: Castelli Graphics, New York, NY

TITLE	PUBLISHER	PRINTER	DATE	MEDIUM	DIMENSION (PAPER SIZE) IN INCHES	TYPE OF PAPER	EDITION NUMBER	NO. OF COLORS	ORIGINAL OPENING PRICE	CURRENT RETAIL PRICE
CURRENT EDITIONS:										
Entropy	DE	DS/DE	1986	LC/HC	30 X 36	AC	15	Varies	1200	1500
Entropy	DE	DS/DE	1986	LB	30 X 36	AC	5	1	800	1000

JEAN RICHARDSON

EDUCATION: Univ of Georgia, Athens, GA, BFA; Art Students League, NY
RECENT EXHIB: Syd Entel Galleries, Safety Harbor, FL, 1987; John A Boler, Indian & Western Art, Minneapolis, MN, 1988,92

PRINTERS: Cleveland Editions, Brooklyn, NY (CIEd); Sharon J Montgomery, NY (SJM); Artist (ART)
PUBLISHERS: John Szoke Graphics, Inc, NY (JSG)
GALLERIES: John Szoke Graphics, Inc, New York, NY; Joan Cawley Gallery, Scottsdale, AZ & Wichita, KS; Allard's Gallery, Fresco, CA; Joanne Chappell Gallery, San Francisco, CA; Cogswell Gallery, Vail, CO; Summa Gallery, New York, NY; Uptown Gallery, New York, NY; Southwest Gallery, Dallas, TX; Galerie Select, Ltd, New York, NY; Tercera Gallery, Los Gatos, CA

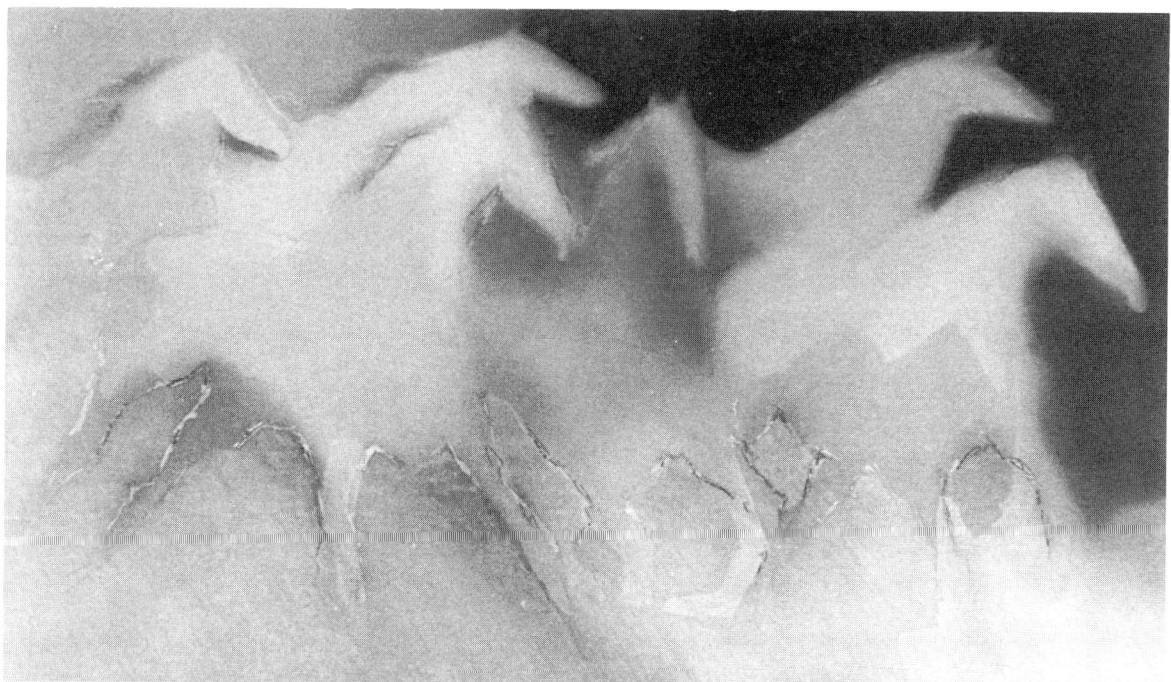

Jean Richardson
Skylark
Courtesy John Szoke Graphics, Inc

TITLE	PUBLISHER	PRINTER	DATE	MEDIUM	DIMENSION (PAPER SIZE) IN INCHES	TYPE OF PAPER	EDITION NUMBER	NO. OF COLORS	ORIGINAL OPENING PRICE	CURRENT RETAIL PRICE
SOLD OUT EDITIONS (RARE):										
Evening Benediction	JSG	CIEd	1985	EC	30 X 40	AP	100		300	750
Fallen Moon	JSG	CIEd	1985	EC	30 X 40	AP	100		300	800
Journey into Light	JSG	CIEd	1985	EC	24 X 33	AP	100		400	700
Mesa Journey	JSG	CIEd	1985	EC	42 X 30	AP	100		300	750
Red Chiefs	JSG	CIEd	1986	EC	42 X 30	AC	100		300	650

JEAN RICHARDSON CONTINUED

TITLE	PUBLISHER	PRINTER	DATE	MEDIUM	DIMENSION (PAPER SIZE) IN INCHES	TYPE OF PAPER	EDITION NUMBER	NO. OF COLORS	ORIGINAL OPENING PRICE	CURRENT RETAIL PRICE
SOLD OUT EDITIONS (RARE):										
Aura	JSG	CIEd	1986	EC	38 X 30	AC	100		325	650
Cloud Walk	JSG	CIEd	1986	EC	31 X 24	AC	100		400	800
Eternal Return	JSG	SJM	1986	COL	28 X 36	AC	60		400	700
Horizon Fires	JSG	CIEd	1986	EC	30 X 38	AC	100	8	325	650
Quiet Vigil	JSG	CIEd	1986	EC	38 X 30	AC	100		300	650
Rites of Spring	JSG	SJM	1986	COL	28 X 36	AC	60		400	750
Sojourners	JSG	CIEd	1986	EC	28 X 36	AC	100		400	750
Spirit Messenger	JGS	CIEd	1986	EC	30 X 38	AC	100		325	800
Hoofbeats	JSG	CIEd	1987	EC	28 X 36	AC	100		400	550
Moonlight Gathering	JSG	CIEd	1987	EC	28 X 36	AC	100		375	575
Peach Spring	JSG	CIEd	1987	EC	28 X 36	AC	100		400	700
Swift Cadence	JSG	CIEd	1987	EC	24 X 32	AC	100		350	600
Wildfire	JSG	CIEd	1987	EC	24 X 32	AC	100		425	650
Dream Shadow	JSG	CIEd	1988	EC	31 X 24	AC	100		400	625
Red Mesa	JSG	CIEd	1988	EC	9 X 12	AC	100		150	300
Untamed	JSG	CIEd	1988	EC	32 X 24	AC	100		400	650
CURRENT EDITIONS:										
Desert Prancers	JSG	CIEd	1987	EC	24 X 32	AC	100		375	500
Sky Herders	JSG	CIEd	1987	EC	24 X 32	AC	100		350	575
Long March	JSG	CIEd	1988	EC	24 X 32	AC	100		400	550
Morning Blaze	JSG	CIEd	1988	EC	14 X 10	AC	100		150	225
A Plain Myths—Book										
Book with Melodic Echos	JSG	CIEd	1988	EC	8 X 12	AC	100		200	300
Book with Moonlight Whispers	JSG	CIEd	1988	EC	12 X 9	AC	100		200	300
Book with Opalescence	JSG	CIEd	1988	EC	8 X 12	AC	100		200	300
Sky Spirits	JSG	CIEd	1988	EC	24 X 32	AC	100		400	650
Solitude	JSG	CIEd	1988	EC	14 X 10	AC	100		200	225
Dawn Shades	JSG	CIEd	1989	EC	24 X 35	AC	100		425	500
Duet	JSG	CIEd	1989	EC	18 X 12	AC	100		250	250
Free Spirit	JSG	CIEd	1989	EC	9 X 12	AC	100		200	250
Night Frolic	JSG	CIEd	1989	EC	9 X 12	AC	100		200	250
Pegasae	JSG	CIEd	1989	EC	24 X 31	AC	100		500	750
Skystreak	JSG	CIEd	1989	EC	24 X 32	AC	100		500	550
Sun Dance	JSG	CIEd	1989	EC	24 X 31	AC	100		400	475
Gemini	JSG	CIEd	1989	EC	17" High	Bronze			6900	6900
Genesis	JSG	CIEd	1989	EC	16" High	Bronze			5750	5750
Esprit	JSG	CIEd	1990	EC	26 X 29	AC	100		500	800
Incantation	JSG	ART	1990	EB/A/COL	34 X 24	AC	100		500	500
Moon Cycle (States I-V) (Set of 5)	JSG	ART	1990	EB/A/COL	40 X 24 EA	AC	50 EA		2000 SET 600 EA	2400 SET 650 EA
Rhythmic Fantasy (Set of 4):									1000 SET	1200 SET
Giselle	JSG	CIEd	1990	EC	18 X 12	AC	100		300	400
Moon Magic	JSG	CIEd	1990	EC	18 X 12	AC	100		300	350
Sprite	JSG	CIEd	1990	EC	18 X 12	AC	100		300	350
Tango	JSG	CIEd	1990	EC	18 X 12	AC	100		300	350
Ephemeral	JSG	CIEd	1991	EC	39 X 54	AC	100		1000	1400
Nocturne	JSG	ART	1991	COL	40 X 54	AC	60	10	1000	1300
Stargazers	JSG		1991	EC	34 X 27	AC			550	650
Whispers (States I-III) (Set of 3):									750 SET	1100 SET
States I,III	JSG	CIEd	1991	EC	12 X 12	AC	100 EA		300 EA	400 EA
States II	JSG	CIEd	1991	EC	12 X 12	AC	100		300	450
Equine Reverie (Set of 6):									1300 SET	1400 SET
Caprice	JSG	CIEd	1992	EC	16 X 8	AC	100		275	325
Huntresses	JSG	CIEd	1992	EC	9 X 9	AC	100		200	225
Out of the Blue	JSG	CIEd	1992	EC	6 X 16	AC	100		275	275
Rainbow Spirit	JSG	CIEd	1992	EC	6 X 16	AC	100		250	250
Sky Flung	JSG	CIEd	1992	EC	6 X 6	AC	100		150	150
Twilight Fantasy	JSG	CIEd	1992	EC	9 X 12	AC	100		300	325
Evensong	JSG	ART	1992	EC/COL	32 X 51	AP88	60	5	900	1000
Gestures (Set of 4):									725 SET	825 SET
Glad Heart	JSG	CIEd	1992	EC	6 X 4	AC	100		95	125
Light Fantastic	JSG	CIEd	1992	EC	8 X 16	AC	100		300	300
New Grace	JSG	CIEd	1992	EC	6 X 9	AC	100		125	175
Ode to Joy	JSG	CIEd	1992	EC	8 X 16	AC	100		275	300
Jubilation	JSG	CIEd	1992	EC	18 X 35	AC	100		475	525
Morning Glory	JSG	CIEd	1992	EC	18 X 35	AC	100		475	525
Skylark	JSG	CIEd	1992	EC	18 X 32	AC	100		300	350
Unbounded	JSG	CIEd	1992	EC	4 X 20	AC	100		275	300
Wild Wonder	JSG	CIEd	1992	EC	8 X 16	AC	100		275	300
Wonderleap	JSG	ART	1992	EC	32 X 53	AP88	60		900	1000

SAM RICHARDSON

BORN: Oakland, CA; July 19, 1934
EDUCATION: California Col of Arts & Crafts, Oakland, CA, BA, 1956, MA, 1960
TEACHING: Instr, Art, Oakland City Col, CA, 1960–61; Art Director, Mus of Contemp Crafts, NY, 1961–63; Asst Prof, Art, San Jose State Univ, CA, 1963–66, Assoc Prof, Art, 1972 to present
RECENT EXHIB: B Z Wagman Gallery, St Louis, MO, 1987; Allport Gallery, San Francisco, CA, 1989; Gwenda Jay Gallery, Chicago, IL, 1990

COLLECTIONS: Whitney Mus of Am Art, NY; San Francisco Mus of Mod Art, CA; M H De Young Mem Mus, San Francisco, CA; Hirshhorn Mus, Wash, DC; Nat Mus of Am Art, Smithsonian Inst, Wash, DC; Dallas Mus of Art, TX; Denver Art Mus, CO; Milwaukee Art Center, MN
PRINTERS: Bill Weege, Madison, WI (BW); Andrew Rubin, Madison, WI (AR); Tandem Press, Univ of Wisconsin, Madison, WI (TanPr)
PUBLISHERS: Tandem Press, Univ of Wisconsin, Madison, WI (TanPr)
GALLERIES: Gwenda Jay Gallery, Chicago, IL; Peter M David Gallery, Minneapolis, MN; Anderson Gallery, Buffalo, NY
MAILING ADDRESS: c/o San Jose State University, Art Department, San Jose, CA 95192

Sam Richardson
Working with the Prescence
Courtesy Tandem Press

Sam Richardson
The Sound When He was Younger
Courtesy Tandem Press

TITLE	PUBLISHER	PRINTER	DATE	MEDIUM	DIMENSION (PAPER SIZE) IN INCHES	TYPE OF PAPER	EDITION NUMBER	NO. OF COLORS	ORIGINAL OPENING PRICE	CURRENT RETAIL PRICE
SOLD OUT EDITIONS (RARE):										
Through the Oranged Into (with Hand-Drawn Additions in Colored Pencil)	TanPr	BW/AR/TanPr	1988	REL/CO CC/HC	38 X 30 EA	R/BFK-AC	1 EA	Varies	2000 EA	3000 EA
CURRENT EDITIONS:										
Through the Greened Into (with Hand-Drawn Additions in Colored Pencil)	TanPr	BW/AR/TanPr	1988	REL/CO CC/HC	26 X 36 EA	AC/W	16 EA	Varies	1350 EA	1500 EA
Through the Magenta'd Into (with Hand-Drawn Additions in Colored Pencil)	TanPr	BW/AR/TanPr	1988	REL/CO CC/HC	36 X 37 EA	AC/W	6 EA	Varies	2500 EA	2500 EA
Through the Chartreused Into (with Hand-Drawn Additions in Colored Pencil)	TanPr	BW/AR/TanPr	1988	REL/CO CC/HC	30 X 31	AC/W	7 EA	Varies	2500 EA	2500 EA
In the Fields of Unknown Time (with Hand-Drawn Additions in Colored Pencil)	TanPr	BW/AR/TanPr	1991	MON/CO/MM	23 X 30 EA	AP/W	7 EA	Varies	1500 EA	1500 EA
In this Field of Time	TanPr	BW/AR/TanPr	1990	CO/CC/HC	26 X 35 EA	AP/W	1 EA	Varies	2800 EA	2800 EA
This is the Shift	TanPr	BW/AR/TanPr	1990	CO/CC/HC	26 X 35 EA	AP/W	1 EA	Varies	2800 EA	2800 EA
The Sound when He was Younger (with Hand-Drawn Additions in Colored Pencil)	TanPr	BW/AR/TanPr	1991	MON/CO/HC	27 X 24	AP/W	8 EA	Varies	1800 EA	1800 EA
Working with the Presence (with Hand-Drawn Additions in Colored Pencil)	TanPr	BW/AR/TanPr	1991	MON/CO/HC	18 X 24 EA	AP	20 EA	Varies	1000 EA	1000 EA
This World of Pairs and Opposites	TanPr	BW/AR/TanPr	1991	MON/CO/HC	30 X 42 EA	AC/W	6 EA	Varies	2000 EA	2000 EA
The Power of Life Engaged	TanPr	BW/AR/TanPr	1991	MON/CO/HC	38 X 28 EA	HMP	12 EA	Varies	2000 EA	2000 EA

ROLAND RICHARDSON

BORN: St Martin, French West Indies; 1944
EDUCATION: Hartford Art Sch, Univ of Hartford, CT, BFA with Honors, 1967

PRINTERS: Atelier Ettinger, NY (AE)
PUBLISHERS: Transworld Art, Inc, NY (TAI)

ROLAND RICHARDSON CONTINUED

TITLE	PUBLISHER	PRINTER	DATE	MEDIUM	DIMENSION (PAPER SIZE) IN INCHES	TYPE OF PAPER	EDITION NUMBER	NO. OF COLORS	ORIGINAL OPENING PRICE	CURRENT RETAIL PRICE
CURRENT EDITIONS:										
The Sea	TAI	AE	1980	LC	21 X 29	AP	250		250	350
Interior View	TAI	AE	1980	LC	29 X 21	AP	250		250	350
Hybiscus	TAI	AE	1980	LC	29 X 22	AP	250		250	350

JIM RICHMOND

BORN: Geneva, IL; 1939
EDUCATION: Principia Col, Elsah, IL, BA, 1961; Art Center Col of Design, Los Angeles, CA, BFA, 1965; Sch of Visual Arts, NY, 1966
TEACHING: Univ of Southern Illinois, Carbondale, IL, 1968; Art Center College, Los Angeles, CA, 1964
PRINTERS: John Nichols, NY (JN)
PUBLISHERS: John Nichols, NY (JN)
GALLERIES: John Nichols Gallery, New York, NY; Olson-Larsen Gallery, Des Moines, IA

TITLE	PUBLISHER	PRINTER	DATE	MEDIUM	DIMENSION (PAPER SIZE) IN INCHES	TYPE OF PAPER	EDITION NUMBER	NO. OF COLORS	ORIGINAL OPENING PRICE	CURRENT RETAIL PRICE
CURRENT EDITIONS:										
Con & Landscape	JN	JN	1979	AP	22 X 29	AP88	80	6	400	500
Landscape (Set of 4)	JN	JN	1984	LC/SP	19 X 24 EA	AP88	80 EA	4 EA	1200 SET	2000 SET

REBEKAH RICHMOND

BORN: Ashland, KY
EDUCATION: Ringling Sch of Art, Sarasota, FL, 1960–61; Univ of Kentucky, Lexington, KY, 1961–62; Art Inst of Pittsburgh, PA, 1962–64
AWARDS: Gold Medals of Honor for Graphic Art, Acad Artists Assoc, 1978,79; Bronze, Medal, Anna Hyatt Huntington, CLWAC, NY, 1979; Annual Art Council & Telex Award, Tulsa, OK, 1984
COLLECTIONS: Coos Art Mus, Coos Bay, OR; Albany Inst of History & Art, NY; Nat Arts Club, NY
PRINTERS: Artist (ART)
PUBLISHERS: Artist (ART)
GALLERIES: Kerwin Galleries, Burlingame, CA
MAILING ADDRESS: P O Box 878, Estes Park, CO 80517

TITLE	PUBLISHER	PRINTER	DATE	MEDIUM	DIMENSION (PAPER SIZE) IN INCHES	TYPE OF PAPER	EDITION NUMBER	NO. OF COLORS	ORIGINAL OPENING PRICE	CURRENT RETAIL PRICE
CURRENT EDITIONS:										
Homemade Bread	ART	ART	1973	I	12 X 17	R/BFK	199	2	35	200
Near Hallett Park	ART	ART	1974	I	12 X 16	R/BFK	199	1	45	200
Primeval Domain	ART	ART	1975	I/REL	12 X 18	R/BFK	125	5	60	200
Woodland Tapestry	ART	ART	1976	I	17 X 12	R/BFK	120	3	60	175
Crescendo	ART	ART	1976	I	17 X 13	R/BFK	120	4	75	200
August Archaic	ART	ART	1977	I	16 X 10	R/BFK	120	2	70	175
In the Stillness	ART	ART	1978	I	12 X 17	SOM	120	3	95	200
Passage	ART	ART	1979	I	16 X 10	JOH	275	3	95	200
The Long Sleep	ART	ART	1979	I	10 X 16	JOH	120	4	95	200
Alpenglow	ART	ART	1979	I	14 X 11	AC	275	3	95	200
The Contention	ART	ART	1980	I	10 X 17	R/BFK	300	2	95	200
Veil of Dusk	ART	ART	1980	I	14 X 11	AC	300	4	95	200
A Timid Presence	ART	ART	1981	I	17 X 10	SOM	300	4	125	200
If You Just Close Your Eyes and Wish...	ART	ART	1982	I	14 X 11	SOM	300	5	120	200
Up, Up in the Air I Go Flying Again...	ART	ART	1982	I	14 X 11	SOM	300	5	120	200
Where Petals are Sails and Dreams Blossom...	ART	ART	1982	I	14 X 11	SOM	300	5	120	200
Just a Pinch of this and a Pinch of that...	ART	ART	1982	I	14 X 11	SOM	300	5	120	200
Reflecting	ART	ART	1982	I	11 X 17	JOH	300	5	125	200
Winter Prelude	ART	ART	1984	I	14 X 11	R/BFK	300	2	95	175
A Restless Quiet	ART	ART	1984	I	17 X 10	R/BFK	300	5	130	200
Aqueous Adiago	ART	ART	1984	I	15 X 11	AC	225	6	130	200

SCOTT RICHTER

BORN: Atlanta, GA, 1940
EDUCATION: Parsons Sch of Design, NY; New York Univ, NY, BFA; New Sch for Social Research, NY
TEACHING: Instr, State Univ of New York, NY, 1978–84; Instr, Cooper-Union Sch, NY, 1983–89
AWARDS: Nat Endowment for the Arts Grants, 1984,86; Englehard Grant, 1985; New York Found Arts, 1986
RECENT EXHIB: Los Angeles County Mus of Art, CA, 1987; Everson Mus of Art, CA, 1988; Univ of Massachusetts, Amherst, MA, 1988; Curt Marcus Gallery, NY, 1987,89; Nina Freudenheim Gallery, Buffalo, NY, 1989; Fuller Gross Gallery, San Francisco, CA, 1989; Beth Urdang Fine Art, Boston, MA, 1990; Ronald Greenberg Gallery, St Louis, MO, 1991; Carl Solway Gallery, Cincinnati, OH, 1991
PRINTERS: David Keister, Bloomington, IN (DK); David Calkins, Bloomington, IN (DC); Echo Press, Bloomington, IN (EPr)
PUBLISHERS: Echo Press, Bloomington, IN (EPr)
GALLERIES: Curt Marcus Gallery, New York, NY; Beth Urdang Fine Art, Boston, MA; Echo Press, Bloomington, IN; Ronald Greenberg Gallery, Cincinnati, OH
MAILING ADDRESS: c/o Curt Marcus Gallery, 758 Broadway, New York, NY 10012

SCOTT RICHTER CONTINUED

TITLE	PUBLISHER	PRINTER	DATE	MEDIUM	DIMENSION (PAPER SIZE) IN INCHES	TYPE OF PAPER	EDITION NUMBER	NO. OF COLORS	ORIGINAL OPENING PRICE	CURRENT RETAIL PRICE
CURRENT EDITIONS:										
Two of Ten Types I–V (2 Sheets Each)	EPr	DK/DC/EPr	1991	MON	30 X 45 EA	AC/W	1 EA	Varies	1200 EA	1200 EA
You Can't Get There From Here I–VII	EPr	DK/DC/EPr	1991	MON	26 X 18 EA	AC/W & JP	1 EA	Varies	800 EA	800 EA
You Can't Get There From Here VIII	EPr	DK/DC/EPr	1991	MON	36 X 25 EA	AC/W & JP	1 EA	Varies	1200 EA	1200 EA
Untitled (SR90–704)	EPr	DK/DC/EPr	1991	MON	37 X 25 EA	AC/W & JP	1 EA	Varies	1200 EA	1200 EA
Untitled (SR90–705)	EPr	DK/DC/EPr	1991	MON	36 X 25 EA	AC/W & JP	1 EA	Varies	1200 EA	1200 EA

GERHARD RICHTER

BORN: Waltersdorf, Germany; 1932
EDUCATION: Kunstakademie, Dresden, Germany, 1952–56; Staatliche Kunstakademie, Düsseldorf, West Germany, 1961–63
RECENT EXHIB: Art Gallery of Ontario, Toronto, Canada, 1988; Mus of Contemp Art, Chicago, IL, 1988; Goethe Inst of Chicago, IL, 1988; Hirshhorn Mus, Wash, DC, 1988–89; San Francisco Mus of Mod Art, CA, 1989; Kent Gallery, NY, 1989; Marian Goodman Gallery, NY, 1990; Lannan Found, Los Angeles, CA, 1990; Sperone Westwater Gallery, NY, 1990; Anthony d'Offay Gallery, London, England, 1991; St Louis Art Mus, MO, 1992
PRINTERS: Dunkes Studio, Munich, Germany (DS); Artist (ART)
PUBLISHERS: Galerie Heiner Friedrich, Munich, Germany (GHF); Kunstring Folkwang Essen, Germany (KFE); Griffel Kunst, Hamburg, Germany (GK); Jahresgabe des Kunsterein, Ghent, Belgium (JDK); Achenbach Art Edition, Düsseldorf, Germany (AAE); Artist (ART)
GALLERIES: Marian Goodman, New York, NY; Galerie Heiner Friedrich, Munich, Germany; Donald Young Gallery, Seattle, WA; David Nolan Gallery, New York, NY; Sperone Westwater Gallery, New York, NY; Deson Saunders Gallery, Chicago, IL, Thomas Babeor Gallery, La Jolla, CA; R K Goldman Contemporary Art, Los Angeles, CA; Goodman/Tinnon Fine Art, San Francisco, CA; Anthony Meier Fine Arts, San Francisco, CA; Baron/Boisante Gallery, New York, NY; Anthony d'Offay Gallery, London, England; Dranoff Fine Art, New york, NY; Thomas Erben Gallery, Inc, New York, NY; Gallery Urban, New York, NY; Jim Kempner Fine Art, Inc, New York, NY; Tomoko Liguori Gallery, New York, NY; Matthew Marks Gallery, New York, NY; Susan Sheehan Gallery, Inc, New York, NY; Galerie Fred Jahn, Cologne, Germany

Gerhard Richter
Meer
Courtesy the Artist

Block (B)

TITLE	PUBLISHER	PRINTER	DATE	MEDIUM	DIMENSION (PAPER SIZE) IN INCHES	TYPE OF PAPER	EDITION NUMBER	NO. OF COLORS	ORIGINAL OPENING PRICE	CURRENT RETAIL PRICE
SOLD OUT EDITIONS (RARE):										
Schweizer Alpen Motiv B-3 (B–R15a)	GK		1969	SP	27 X 27	AP	50		100	3000
Wolken			1969	LC/OFF	22 X 30	R/BFK	300		100	2000
Kugelobjekt II (Multiple Object, Painted Black Box with Glass, Photograph & 3 Steel Spheres (B–R21B)			1970	MULT					300	8500
Funken (B–R24)			1970	LC/OFF	13 X 18	R/BFK	200		150	2500
Cloud	KFE		1971	LC/OFF	25 X 24	R/BFK			150	3000
Canarian Islands (Set of 6)	GHF	DS	1971–72	AC/PH	16 X 20 EA	R/BFK	100 EA		900 SET	5500 SET
									175 EA	1000 EA
Meer (B–R36)	JDG		1972	LC/OFF			250		150	3000
Ohne Titel (with Pencil Drawing)	AAE		1987	LC/OFF/HC	50 X 58 cm	R/BFK	75		3500	7500
Sechs Fotos 2.5.89-7.5.89 (Set of 6)	ART	ART	1990	PH	14 X 20 EA		50 EA		5800 SET	6500 SET

BRIDGET RILEY

BORN: London, England; (1931–1984)
EDUCATION: Goldsmith's Sch of Art, 1949–52; Royal Col of Art, London, England, 1952–55
AWARDS: AICA Critics Prize, John Moores Liverpool Exhib, 1963; Peter Stuyvesant Foundation Prize, 1964; Major Painting Prize, Venice Biennale, Italy, 1968
RECENT EXHIB: Mayor Rowan Gallery, London, England, 1989
COLLECTIONS: Mus of Mod Art, NY; Tate Gallery of Art, London, England; Chicago Inst of Art, IL; Albright-Knox Art Gallery Buffalo, NY; Walker Art Gallery, Minneapolis, MN
PRINTERS: Graham Henderson, NY (GH); Kelpra Studios, London, England (KS)
PUBLISHERS: Pace Editions, NY (PE); Kelpra Studios, London, England (KS)
GALLERIES: Sidney Janis Gallery, NY; Nina Freudenheim Gallery, Buffalo, NY; Charles Cowles Gallery, New York, NY; Pace Prints, New York, NY; Mayor Rowan Gallery, London, England

BRIDGET RILEY CONTINUED

TITLE	PUBLISHER	PRINTER	DATE	MEDIUM	DIMENSION (PAPER SIZE) IN INCHES	TYPE OF PAPER	EDITION NUMBER	NO. OF COLORS	ORIGINAL OPENING PRICE	CURRENT RETAIL PRICE
SOLD OUT EDITIONS (RARE):										
Composition	KS	KS	1971	SP	38 X 11	WOVE	75		150	1000
Portfolio (Set of 3)	PE	GH	1977	SP	39 X 20 EA	R/BFK	100 EA	5 EA	750 SET	3000 SET
Blue, Green & Red Dominances									300 EA	1200 EA

JUDY RIFKA

BORN: New York, NY
EDUCATION: Hunter Col, NY, 1963–66; New York Studio Sch, NY, 1966; Skohegan Sch of Painting & Sculpture, ME, 1967
COLLECTIONS: Whitney Mus of Am Art, NY; Dallas Mus, TX; Huntington Art Gallery, Univ of Texas, Austin, TX; Mus of Fine Arts, Boston, MA; New York Public Library, NY; Newport Harbor Art Mus, Newport Beach, CA; Staatische Mus, Berlin, Germany; Toledo Mus, OH; Weatherspoon Art Gallery, Univ of North Carolina, Greenboro, NC
RECENT EXHIB: Saxon-Lee Gallery, Los Angeles, CA, 1987; Brooke Alexander, Inc, NY, 1987
PRINTERS: Barbara Telleen (BT); Wayne Kline (WK); Lynne Allen (LA); Tamarind Inst, Albuquerque, NM (TI); Joe Fawbush, NY (JF); Solo Press, NY (SP); Judith Solodkin, NY (JS); Experimental Workshop, San Francisco, CA (EW); Bill Weege, Madison, WI (BW); Andrew Rubin, Madison, WI (AR); Tandem Press, Univ of Wisconsin, Madison, WI (TanPr)
PUBLISHERS: Brooke Alexander, Inc, NY (BAI); Tamarind Inst, Albuquerque, NM (TI); Solo Press, NY (SP); Joe Fawbush Editions, NY (JFE); Art Issue Editions, Inc, NY (AEI); Tandem Press, Univ of Wisconsin, Madison, WI (TanPr)
GALLERIES: Brooke Alexander, Inc, New York, NY; Tamarind Inst, Albuquerque, NM; Holly Solomon Gallery, New York, NY; Nicola Jacobs Gallery, London, England; Fay Gold Gallery, Atlanta, GA; Fawbush Editions, New York, NY; Asher/Faure Gallery, Los Angeles, CA; Stephen Wirth Gallery, San Francisco, CA; Anna Friebe Galerie, Cologne, Germany; Daniel Saxon Gallery, Los Angeles, CA; Ann Jaffe Gallery, Bay Harbor Islands, FL

Judy Rifka
Facade
Courtesy Tandem Press

TITLE	PUBLISHER	PRINTER	DATE	MEDIUM	DIMENSION (PAPER SIZE) IN INCHES	TYPE OF PAPER	EDITION NUMBER	NO. OF COLORS	ORIGINAL OPENING PRICE	CURRENT RETAIL PRICE
CURRENT EDITIONS:										
A Museum	TI	WK/TI	1982	LC	23 X 30	AP/B	36	4	400	700
Off the Wall	TI	WK/TI	1982	SP	18 X 10	R/BFK	90		125	400
Portrait of Dracula	TI	LA/TI	1982	SP	40 X 30	GE	21	5	700	1200
Red, the Dog with Color Vision	TI	LA/TI	1982	LC	23 X 30	GE	40	4	400	700
Dancers I–IV (Set of 4):	SP	JF/SP	1984	LC	29 X 22 EA		35 EA	3 EA	1400 SET	35000 SET
									350 EA	850 EA
Modern Dance (Set of 4)	SP/FE	JF/SP	1984	LC	29 X 21 EA	R/BFK	35 EA		2000 SET	2000 SET
Opera of the Worms (Folio of Color Lithographs & Handset Letterpress)	SP/FE	JF/SP	1984	LC	9 X 12 EA	R/BFK	80 EA		600 SET	950 SET
On Acropolis	SP/FE	JF/SP	1985	LI/WC/EMB	17 X 25	R/BFK	25		500	900
Still Life	EW	EW	1986	WC	37 X 28	R/BFK	46	6	750	1200
San Francisco Still Life	EW	EW	1986	WC	24 X 22	R/BFK	40	8	650	1000
Thou Shalt Not Bear False Witness Against Thy Neighbor (from Ten Commandments Suite)	AJE	JS/SP	1987	LC	24 X 19	DIEU	84	5	500	1500
Apotheosis in Indigo	TanPr	BW/AR/TanPr	1991	LC/WC	29 X 41	GE	50	8	1000	1000
Facade	TanPr	BW/AR/TanPr	1991	LC/WC	43 X 21	GE	40	11	1200	1200

JEAN-PAUL RIOPELLE

BORN: Montreal, Canada; 1923
RECENT EXHIB: Pierre Matisse Gallery, NY, 1989; Galerie Claude Lafitte, Montreal, Canada, 1990
PRINTERS: Maeght Editeur, Paris, France (ME); Galerie Maeght Lelong, Paris, France (ML)
PUBLISHERS: Maeght Editions, Paris, France (ME); Galerie Maeght Lelong, Paris, France (ML)
GALLERIES: Galerie Lelong, Paris, France & New York, NY & Zürich, Switzerland; Pierre Matisse Gallery, New York, NY; Gallery Moos, Toronto, Canada; Claude Bernard Gallery, New York, NY; Alexander Kahan Fine Arts, New York, NY; Galerie Claude Lafitte, Montreal, Canada

JEAN-PAUL RIOPELLE CONTINUED

TITLE	PUBLISHER	PRINTER	DATE	MEDIUM	DIMENSION (PAPER SIZE) IN INCHES	TYPE OF PAPER	EDITION NUMBER	NO. OF COLORS	ORIGINAL OPENING PRICE	CURRENT RETAIL PRICE
SOLD OUT EDITIONS (RARE):										
Saint Paul VIII	ME	ME	1976	EC	26 X 28	AP	30		500 FF	2000 FF
Saint Paul IX	ME	ME	1976	EC	26 X 28	AP	30		500 FF	2000 FF
Triptyque Gris	ME	ME	1976	LC	47 X 30	AP	75		600 FF	2000 FF
Feuilles I	ME	ME	1976	LC	36 X 26	AP	75		600 FF	1800 FF
Feuilles II, III, IV	ME	ME	1976	LC	30 X 41 EA	AP	75 EA		600 FF	1800 FF EA
Jute I, II, III	ME	ME	1976	LC	30 X 41 EA	AP	75 EA		600 FF	1800 FF EA
Brisees	ME	ME	1977	LC	18 X 34	AP	75		500 FF	1800 FF
La Haie	ME	ME	1977	LC	16 X 32	AP	75		500 FF	1800 FF
L'Affut	ME	ME	1977	LC	29 X 34	AP	75		600 FF	1800 FF
Clairiere	MF	MF	1977	LC	47 X 63	AP	75		800 FF	3000 FF
Ete Indien	ME	ME	1977	LC	59 X 46	AP	75		800 FF	3000 FF
Automne	ME	ME	1977	LC	59 X 46	AP	75		800 FF	3000 FF
Poisson	ME	ME	1977	LC	19 X 13	AP	75		800 FF	1800 FF
Suite a l'Annee Verte	ME	ME	1977	LC	63 X 46	AP	30		800 FF	1800 FF
Suite Nounours	ME	ME	1977	LC	46 X 63	AP	30		800 FF	1800 FF
Suite Gaspesienne	ME	ME	1977	LC	63 X 46	AP	30		800 FF	1800 FF
Feutre	ME	ME	1977	LC	24 X 29	AP	75		600 FF	2000 FF
Treille	ME	ME	1977	LC	25 X 34	AP	75		600 FF	2000 FF
Apres la Lettre	ME	ME	1977	LC	29 X 22	AP	150		400 FF	1500 FF
Poursuite de Famille	ME	ME	1978	LC	63 X 46	AP	30		800 FF	1800 FF
Suite Teddy Bear	ME	ME	1978	LC	63 X 46	AP	30		800 FF	1800 FF
Suite Tabou	ME	ME	1978	LC	63 X 46	AP	30		800 FF	1800 FF
Suite Fancy	ME	ME	1978	LC	63 X 46	AP	30		800 FF	1800 FF
Suite Radison	ME	ME	1978	LC	63 X 46	AP	30		800 FF	1800 FF
Suite Caribou	ME	ME	1978	LC	63 X 46	AP	30		800 FF	1800 FF
Suite Guerriere	ME	ME	1978	LC	63 X 46	AP	30		800 FF	1800 FF
Suite Lachaudiere	ME	ME	1978	LC	63 X 46	AP	30		800 FF	1800 FF
Suite General	ME	ME	1978	LC	63 X 46	AP	30		800 FF	1800 FF
Suite Fortin	ME	ME	1978	LC	63 X 46	AP	30		800 FF	1800 FF
Suite Poursuite	ME	ME	1978	LC	63 X 46	AP	30		800 FF	1800 FF
Suite Lac Aux Puants	ME	ME	1978	LC	63 X 46	AP	30		800 FF	1800 FF
Suite Finale	ME	ME	1978	LC	63 X 46	AP	30		800 FF	1800 FF
Suite Montmorency	ME	ME	1978	LC	46 X 62	AP	30		800 FF	1800 FF
Chope	ME	ME	1978	LC	24 X 30	AP	75		700 FF	1800 FF
Lied a Emille Nilligan (Set of 16)	ME	ME	1979	LC	22 X 30 EA	AP	75 EA		700 FF	2000 FF SET
Le Sablier (Set of 6)	ME	ME	1979	LC	22 X 26 EA	AP	90 EA		700 FF	7500 FF SET
Oixeaux a la Fenetre	ME	ME	1980	LC	72 X 53 cm	AP	75		900 FF	1800 FF
Masques d'Hiver	ME	ME	1980	LC	72 X 53 cm	AP	75		900 FF	1800 FF
Deux Totems	ME	ME	1980	LC	72 X 53 cm	AP	75		900 FF	1800 FF
Gros Bec	ME	ME	1980	LC	72 X 53 cm	AP	75		900 FF	1800 FF
Masques et Oiseaux	ME	ME	1980	LC	72 X 53 cm	AP	75		900 FF	1800 FF
Grappes	ME	ME	1980	LC	72 X 53 cm	AP	75		900 FF	1800 FF
Visages Caches	ME	ME	1980	LC	71 X 53 cm	AP	75		900 FF	1800 FF
Aux Aguets	ME	ME	1980	LC	72 X 53 cm	AP	75		900 FF	1800 FF
Swoop	ME	ME	1980	LC	68 X 80 cm	AP	75		1000 FF	2000 FF
Scout	ME	ME	1981	LC	68 X 82 cm	AP	75		1000 FF	2000 FF
Le Guet	ME	ME	1981	LC	68 X 82 cm	AP	75		1000 FF	2000 FF
Sur L'etang	ME	ME	1981	LC	67 X 81 cm	AP	75	1	1800 FF	3000 FF
Au Repos	ME	ME	1981	LC	66 X 78 cm	AP	75	1	1800 FF	3000 FF
Touché	ME	ME	1981	LC	67 X 80 cm	AP	75	3	2000 FF	3500 FF
Touché	ME	ME	1981	LC	67 X 80 cm	JAP	30	3	2500 FF	4000 FF
Les Oies Bleue	ME	ME	1981	LC	66 X 76 cm	JAP	30	3	2500 FF	4000 FF
Leader	ME	ME	1981	LC	66 X 76 cm	AP	75	1	1800 FF	3500 FF
Les Oies Bleues	ME	ME	1981	LC	66 X 75.5m	AP	75	3	1800 FF	3000 FF
Echassiers	ML	ML	1902	LC	66 X 78 cm	AP	75	3	2000 FF	3500 FF
Echassiers	ML	ML	1902	LC	66 X 78 cm	JAP	30	3	2500 FF	4000 FF
Dans les Jones	ML	ML	1982	LC	67 X 79 cm	AP	75	3	1800 FF	3500 FF
Dans les Jones	ML	ML	1982	LC	67 X 79 cm	JAP	30	3	2500 FF	4000 FF
Tête Bêche	ML	ML	1983	LC	66 X 90 cm	AP	75	5	2000 FF	3500 FF

DAVID ROBBINS

PRINTERS: James J Kriegsmann, NY (JJK)
PUBLISHERS: Artist (ART)
GALLERIES: 303 Gallery, New York, NY; Metro Pictures, New York, NY; Jay Gorney Modern Art, New York, NY

TITLE	PUBLISHER	PRINTER	DATE	MEDIUM	DIMENSION (PAPER SIZE) IN INCHES	TYPE OF PAPER	EDITION NUMBER	NO. OF COLORS	ORIGINAL OPENING PRICE	CURRENT RETAIL PRICE
CURRENT EDITIONS:										
Talent (Set of 18)	ART	JJK	1986	PH	10 X 8 EA	PHP	100 EA		600 SET	1000 SET

The Printworld Directory is accepting new applications for the seventh edition. Approximately 300 new artists will be accepted. Please use the two forms provided in the back section of this directory to submit biographical data and documentation of prints. Edition number of each print must not exceed 500 and the retail price must be $100 or more.

SUSAN RIOS

BORN: Terre Haute, IN; February 16, 1950
EDUCATION: California State Univ, Northridge, CA
RECENT EXHIB: Martin Lawrence Gallery, Phila, PA, 1989
PRINTERS: Accent Studios, Canoga Park, CA (AS); Alexander Heinrici, NY (AH); Studio Heinrici, NY (SH)
PUBLISHERS: Martin Lawrence Limited Editions, Van Nuys, CA (MLLE)
GALLERIES: Martin Lawrence Galleries, Sherman Oaks, CA & West Los Angeles, CA & Newport Beach, CA & Palm Springs, CA & Santa Clara, CA & Redondo Beach, CA & Thousand Oaks, CA & Escondido, CA & Phila, PA & Short Hills, NJ & Los Angeles, CA; Art Brokerage, Ketchum, ID; Michelson Galleries, Northampton, MA; J Todd Galleries, Wellesley, MA; Artists Showcase International, Hartsdale, NY; Emporium Enterprises, Inc, Dallas, TX; Professional Fine Arts Services, Inc, New York, NY

Susan Rios
Aunt B's
Courtesy Martin Lawrence Limited Editions

TITLE	PUBLISHER	PRINTER	DATE	MEDIUM	DIMENSION (PAPER SIZE) IN INCHES	TYPE OF PAPER	EDITION NUMBER	NO. OF COLORS	ORIGINAL OPENING PRICE	CURRENT RETAIL PRICE
SOLD OUT EDITIONS (RARE):										
Amaryllis	MLLE	AS	1984	SP	30 X 35	SEK	545	70	550	4500
Fionas	MLLE	AS	1984	SP	35 X 30	SEK	505	70	550	4500
Phoebe's	MLLE	AS	1985	SP	32 X 30	SEK	500		500	4500
Afternoon Walk	MLLE	AH/SH	1985	SP	37 X 32	SEK	545		500	4500
Reunion	MLLE	AH/SH	1985	SP	34 X 37	SEK	545		500	4500
Lilacs and Lace	MLLE	AH/SH	1986	SP	37 X 42	SEK	524		550	4000
Planning the Future	MLLE	AH/SH	1986	SP	35 X 42	SEK	545		650	4500
After Breakfast	MLLE	AH/SH	1986	SP	35 X 29	SEK	545		650	4500
Coming Home	MLLE	AH/SH	1987	SP	38 X 40	SEK	545		650	4500
My Corner	MLLE	AH/SH	1987	SP	33 X 38	SEK	520		650	4500
Visiting	MLLE	AH/SH	1987	SP	34 X 35	SEK	570		650	4500
Our House	MLLE	AH/SH	1987	SP	38 X 44	SEK	545		650	4000
Emily's Inn	MLLE	AH/SH	1987	SP	40 X 32	SEK	545		650	4500
The Greeting	MLLE	AH/SH	1988	SP	40 X 33	SEK	545		700	5000
Fantasy	MLLE	AH/SH	1988	SP	39 X 35	SEK	545		700	4500
Blossoming	MLLE	AH/SH	1988	SP	36 X 39	SEK	545		700	4000
Black-Eyed Susans	MLLE	AH/SH	1990	SP	34 X 40	SEK	545		1000	4000
CURRENT EDITIONS:										
Peaceful Hours	MLLE	AS	1984	SP	35 X 36	SEK	540	70	550	3725
Sunday Morning	MLLE	AH/SH	1985	SP	35 X 33	SEK	545		500	3350
Special Visit	MLLE	AH/SH	1986	SP	37 X 48	SEK	541		500	3800
Main Street	MLLE	AS	1986	SP	30 X 36	SEK	540		550	4000
Granpa's House	MLLE	AH/SH	1987	SP	35 X 38	SEK	545		650	3000
Thoughts on a Happy Ending	MLLE	AH/SH	1987	SP	33 X 37	SEK	545		650	3500
Romance Suite (Set of 4):									1500 SET	4500 SET
Attic Memories	MLLE	AH/SH	1987	SP	20 X 18	SEK	1400		400	1150
First Love	MLLE	AH/SH	1987	SP	18 X 20	SEK	1400		400	1700
From this Day Forward	MLLE	AH/SH	1987	SP	18 X 20	SEK	1400		400	1025
The New Arrival	MLLE	AH/SH	1987	SP	20 X 18	SEK	1400		400	1200
With My Friends	MLLE	AH/SH	1988	SP	40 X 30	SEK	545		700	3000
A Visit with Susan	MLLE	AH/SH	1988	SP	29 X 31	SEK	545		700	2700
The Gardener	MLLE	AH/SH	1988	SP	37 X 38	SEK	545		700	2800
The New Arrangement	MLLE	AH/SH	1988	SP	37 X 34	SEK	545		700	2450
That One Afternoon	MLLE	AH/SH	1988	SP	39 X 34	SEK	545		700	2700
A Day with Friends	MLLE	AH/SH	1988	SP	41 X 34	SEK	545		700	2400
Retreat	MLLE	AH/SH	1989	SP	36 X 42	SEK	545		700	2275
Country House Suite (Set of 6):									2500 SET	3500 SET
Margaret's Hideaway	MLLE	AH/SH	1989	SP	16 X 20	SEK	545		450	800
The Collector	MLLE	AH/SH	1989	SP	20 X 16	SEK	545		450	800
Plant Tending Day	MLLE	AH/SH	1989	SP	20 X 16	SEK	545		450	800
Fiona's Collection	MLLE	AH/SH	1989	SP	20 X 16	SEK	545		450	800

SUSAN RIOS CONTINUED

TITLE	PUBLISHER	PRINTER	DATE	MEDIUM	DIMENSION (PAPER SIZE) IN INCHES	TYPE OF PAPER	EDITION NUMBER	NO. OF COLORS	ORIGINAL OPENING PRICE	CURRENT RETAIL PRICE
CURRENT EDITIONS:										
Gardener's Table	MLLE	AH/SH	1989	SP	16 X 20	SEK	545		450	800
The Side Garden	MLLE	AH/SH	1989	SP	20 X 16	SEK	545		450	800
Above the Garden	MLLE	AH/SH	1989	SP	42 X 36	SEK	545		1000	2250
Olivia's Place	MLLE	AH/SH	1990	SP	35 X 34	SEK	545		1000	2000
The New Place	MLLE	AH/SH	1990	SP	40 X 31	SEK	545		1000	2000
Creature Comforts	MLLE	AH/SH	1990	SP	39 X 32	SEK	545		1000	2300
Garden Memories	MLLE	AH/SH	1990	SP	34 X 39	SEK	545		1000	2400
The Dance	MLLE	AH/SH	1990	SP	42 X 34	SEK	555		1000	2400
Bouquet from the Side Garden	MLLE	AH/SH	1991	SP	46 X 26	SEK	545		1000	2000
Inner World	MLLE	AH/SH	1991	SP	40 X 35	SEK	545		1200	1750
Morning Garden	MLLE	AH/SH	1991	SP	47 X 36	SEK	545		1200	1925
The Path to Yourself	MLLE	AH/SH	1991	SP	40 X 33	SEK	555		1200	1750
Plant Shed	MLLE	AH/SH	1992	SP	38 X 44	SEK	555		900	1625
Friendship	MLLE	AH/SH	1992	SP	37 X 34	SEK	555		900	1350
Georgetown	MLLE	AH/SH	1992	SP	25 X 32	SEK	555		800	1250
Aunt B's	MLLE	AH/SH	1993	SP	41 X 34	SEK	545		900	1550
Blake & Alex	MLLE	AH/SH	1993	SP	29 X 34	SEK	555		900	1550

RODNEY RIPPS

BORN: New York, NY; December 6, 1950
EDUCATION: City Univ of New York, NY, BA, 1972; Hunter Col, NY, MA, 1973–74
TEACHING: Instr, Painting, Brooklyn Mus Art Sch, NY, 1974–76
AWARDS: Nat Endowment for the Arts Fel, 1979–80
RECENT EXHIB: Berkshire Mus, Pittsfield, MA, 1988
COLLECTIONS: Rhode Island Sch of Design, Providence, RI; Cincinnati Art Mus, OH; La Jolla Mus of Art, CA; Ludwig Coll, Aachen, Germany; Israeli Mus, Jerusalem, Israel
PRINTERS: Vermillion Editions Ltd, Minneapolis, MN (VEL)
PUBLISHERS: Vermillion Editions Ltd, Minneapolis, MN (VEL)
GALLERIES: Galerie Daniel Templon, Paris, France; Galerie Denise Rene-Hans Meyer, Düsseldorf, West Germany; Dart Gallery, Chicago, IL; Akira Ikeda Gallery, Tokyo, Japan; Vermillion Editions Ltd, Minneapolis, MN; Galerie Schema, Florence, Italy; Carl Solway, Cincinnati, OH; Marisa del Re Gallery, New York, NY
MAILING ADDRESS: Lenox, MA 01240; c/o Marisa del Re Gallery, 41 E 57th St, New York, NY 10022

TITLE	PUBLISHER	PRINTER	DATE	MEDIUM	DIMENSION (PAPER SIZE) IN INCHES	TYPE OF PAPER	EDITION NUMBER	NO. OF COLORS	ORIGINAL OPENING PRICE	CURRENT RETAIL PRICE
CURRENT EDITIONS:										
Centaur*	VEL	VEL	1982	ERC/AA	36 X 53 X 9				2800	3000
Athena*	VEL	VEL	1982	ERC/AA	40 X 40 X 18				2500	3000
The Triumph*	VEL	VEL	1982	ERC/AA	40 X 23 X 8				2500	3000

*Epoxy Resin Celastic with Walnut, Steel, and Assorted Attachments

MURRAY RISS

BORN: Poland; February 6, 1940; US Citizen
EDUCATION: City Col of Univ of New York, NY, BA, 1963; Cooper Union Art Sch, NY; Rhode Island Sch of Design, Providence, RI, with Harry Callahan, MFA
TEACHING: Penland Sch of Art, Penland, NC, Summers, 1970,78; Chmn, Dept of Photography, Memphis Col of Art, TN, 1968–86
AWARDS: Nat Endowment for the Arts, Photography Fel, 1979
COLLECTIONS: Mus of Mod Art, NY; Art Inst of Chicago, IL; Nat Gallery of Art, Ontario, Can; Atlanta Mus, GA; Minneapolis Mus, MN; New Orleans Mus, LA; Nat Bibliotheque, Paris, France
PRINTERS: Artist (ART)
PUBLISHERS: Center for Photographic Studies, Louisville, KY (CPS)
GALLERIES: Afterimage Gallery, Dallas, TX; Visual Studies Workshop, Rochester, NY
MAILING ADDRESS: 1306 Harbert Ave, Memphis, TN 38104

TITLE	PUBLISHER	PRINTER	DATE	MEDIUM	DIMENSION (PAPER SIZE) IN INCHES	TYPE OF PAPER	EDITION NUMBER	NO. OF COLORS	ORIGINAL OPENING PRICE	CURRENT RETAIL PRICE
CURRENT EDITIONS:										
Set of Ten Photographs:									400 SET	1500 SET
Man with Dark Face	CPS	ART	1976–86	PH	7 X 8		35	1	40	150
Car Ad	CPS	ART	1976–86	PH	7 X 8		35	1	40	150
Arms	CPS	ART	1976–86	PH	7 X 8		35	1	40	150
Child's Dress	CPS	ART	1976–86	PH	7 X 8		35	1	40	150
Elly & Shanna	CPS	ART	1976–86	PH	7 X 8		35	1	40	150
Shanna & Adya	CPS	ART	1976–86	PH	7 X 8		35	1	40	150
Shanna	CPS	ART	1976–86	PH	7 X 8		35	1	40	150
Adya	CPS	ART	1976–86	PH	7 X 8		35	1	40	150
Faces in the Tree	CPS	ART	1976–86	PH	7 X 8		35	1	40	150
Leaves	CPS	ART	1976–86	PH	7 X 8		35	1	40	150

The retail prices of the 100,000 limited edition prints quoted in this directory are subject to change. Print publishers, artists and galleries were the direct sources for these quotations. Prices in the secondary market listed as "Sold Out Editions (Rare)" indicate that the publisher has a limited supply of that print or that the print is difficult to locate in the galleries.

J B RIVARD

BORN: South Bend, IN; May 5, 1930
EDUCATION: Chicago Acad of Fine Art, IL; Univ of Florida, Gainesville, FL
AWARDS: Print Award, Salmagundi Club Open, NY, 1982; New Jersey Printmaking Council, 1983-84; Purchase Prize, Kansas Nat, 1986
COLLECTIONS: El Paso Mus, TX; Ft Hays State Univ, KS; Hammond Public Library, IN
PRINTERS: Jo Thompson, Palm Springs, CA (JT); Palo Verde Press, Palm Springs, CA (PVP); Artist (ART)
PUBLISHERS: High Plateau Etching Studio, Albuquerque, NM (HPES)
GALLERIES: High Plateau Gallery, Albuquerque, NM; Alpha Gallery, Denver, CO
MAILING ADDRESS: 6717 Lomas Blvd, NE, Albuquerque, NM 87110

TITLE	PUBLISHER	PRINTER	DATE	MEDIUM	DIMENSION (PAPER SIZE) IN INCHES	TYPE OF PAPER	EDITION NUMBER	NO. OF COLORS	ORIGINAL OPENING PRICE	CURRENT RETAIL PRICE
SOLD OUT EDITIONS (RARE):										
Night Mountain Fantasy	HPES	ART	1979	I	10 X 14	R/BFK	17	3	100	300
CURRENT EDITIONS:										
Fragmentary Man	HPES	ART	1981-82	I	22 X 15	R/BFK	40	5	125	300
A'Soldiering	HPES	ART	1982	I	10 X 11	R/BFK	10	4	125	200
Torsos	HPES	ART	1983	I/EMB	26 X 22	R/BFK	4	2	450	500
Counterplay	HPES	ART	1985	I	22 X 26	R/BFK	15	6	450	500
Night Vision	HPES	ART	1986	I	18 X 30	R/BFK	15	6	350	450
Mind Trap	HPES	JT/PVP	1986	I/EMB/REL	30 X 21	R/BFK	15	7	300	350
The Meeting	HPES	ART	1986	I	12 X 18	R/BFK	16	3	250	300
Disappearing Pasts	HPES	ART	1986	I/EMB	22 X 30	R/BFK	15	9	550	600
Condition Human I	HPES	ART	1986	I/EMB	26 X 19	R/BFK	18	5	350	400
Condition Human II	HPES	ART	1987	I/EMB	24 X 22	R/BFK	18	6	400	450

LARRY RIVERS

BORN: Bronx, NY; August 17, 1925
EDUCATION: Julliard Sch of Music, NY, 1944-45; Hans Hofmann Sch, NY, 1947-48; New York Univ, NY, 1948-51
TEACHING: Art in Res, Slade Sch of Fine Arts, London, England, 1964; Maryland Inst, Col of Art, Baltimore, MD
AWARDS: Third Prize, Corcoran Gallery of Art, Wash, DC, 1954
RECENT EXHIB: Simms Fine Art, New Orleans, LA, 1987; Marlborough Gallery, NY, 1988-89; Butler Inst of Am Art, Youngstown, OH, 1989; Coos Art Mus, Coos Bay, OR, 1989; Marlborough Fine Arts, Ltd, London, England, 1990; Elaine Horwitch Gallery, Scottsdale, AZ, 1991; Elaine Horwitch Gallery, Santa Fe, NM, 1991; Scottsdale Center for the Arts, AZ, 1992; Fort Wayne Mus, IN, 1992; Univ of Tennessee, UTC Art Gallery, Chattanooga, TN, 1989,92; Univ of Houston, Blaffer Gallery, TX, 1992; Sunrise Art Mus, Charleston, WV, 1992; Remba Gallery, Santa Monica, CA, 1992
COLLECTIONS: Mus of Mod Art, NY; Whitney Mus of Am Art, NY; Metropolitan Mus of Art, NY; Art Inst of Chicago, IL; Baltimore Mus of Art, MD; Corcoran Gallery of Art, Wash, DC; Tate Gallery, London, England; Nat Gallery of Art, Wash, DC; Hirshhorn Mus, Wash, DC; Brandeis Univ, Waltham, MA; Univ of North Carolina, Greensboro, NC; Fort Wayne Art Inst, IN; Mus of North Carolina, Raleigh, NC; Parrish Art Mus, Southampton, NY; Allentown Art Mus, PA; Chrysler Art Mus, Provincetown, MA; Kansas City Art Inst, MO; Rhode Island Sch of Design, Providence, RI; Munson-Williams-Proctor Inst, Utica, NY; Brooklyn Mus of Art, NY
PRINTERS: Styria Studio, NY (SS); Universal Limited Art Editions, West Islip, NY (ULAE); Mixografia Workshop, Los Angeles, CA (MIX); La Poligrafa, SA, Barcelona, Spain (LP)
PUBLISHERS: Transworld Art, Inc, NY (TAI); Marlborough Graphics, NY (MG); Abrams Original Editions, NY (AOE); Circle Gallery, Ltd, Chicago, IL (CGL); Styria Studio, NY (SS); Universal Limited Art Editions, West Islip, NY (ULAE); International Images, Inc, New York, NY (InIm); Clarkson N Potter, NY (CNP); Mixografia Workshop, Los Angeles, CA (MIX); GHJ Graphics, Inc, NY (GHJG); Ediciones Poligrafa, SA, Barcelona, Spain (EdP)
GALLERIES: Marlborough Graphics, New York, NY; Irving Galleries, Palm Beach, FL; van Straaten Gallery, Chicago, IL; Styria Studio, New York, NY; Michael H Lord Gallery, Milwaukee, WI; Gloria Luria Gallery, Bay Harbor Islands, FL; Elaine Benson Gallery, Bridgehampton, NY; International Images, Inc, New York, NY; Lillian Heidenberg Gallery, New York, NY; Michelle Rosenfeld Fine Arts, New York, NY; Styria Studios, New York, NY; Mixografia Gallery, Santa Monica, CA; Opus Art Studios, Miami, FL; Marvin Ross Friedman & Company, Miami, FL; Thomson Gallery, Minneapolis, MN; Margot Gallery, Inc, Larchmont, NY & Palm Beach, FL; Circle Galleries, San Diego, CA & San Francisco,

**Larry Rivers
Camel Quartet
Courtesy Marlborough Graphics, Ltd**

CA & Northbrook, IL & Pittsburgh, PA & Houston, TX & Soho, NY & Chicago, IL & Scottsdale, AZ & Beverly Hills, CA & Costa Mesa, CA & Sherman Oaks, CA & Palm Beach, FL & Honolulu, HI & New Orleans, LA & Las Vegas, NV & Seattle, WA; Argus Fine Arts, Eugene, OR; Elaine Horwitch Galleries, Scottsdale, AZ & Santa Fe, NM; Remba Gallery, Santa Monica, CA; Edward Tyler Nahem Fine Art, New York, NY; Galeria Joan Prats, New York, NY & Barcelona, Spain; Magidson Fine Art, Inc, Aspen, CO; Hokin Galleries, Palm Beach, FL & Bay Harbor Islands, FL; Hokin Kaufman Gallery, Chicago, IL; Stein Bartlow Gallery, Ltd, Chicago, IL; Golden Gallery, Boston, MA; Morgan Gallery, Boston, MA; Vered Gallery, East Hampton, NY; Alan Brown Gallery, Hartsdale, NY; Avanti Galleries, Inc, New York, NY; Dorsky Gallery, New York, NY
MAILING ADDRESS: 92 Little Plains Rd, Southampton, NY 11968

Sparks (S)

The print market has become very selective. For the first time since we published the first edition of The Printworld Directory in 1982, the prices of prints have been greatly reduced and greatly increased for the same artists by the most reputable and established print publishers. Check the fifth edition to understand the movement.

LARRY RIVERS CONTINUED

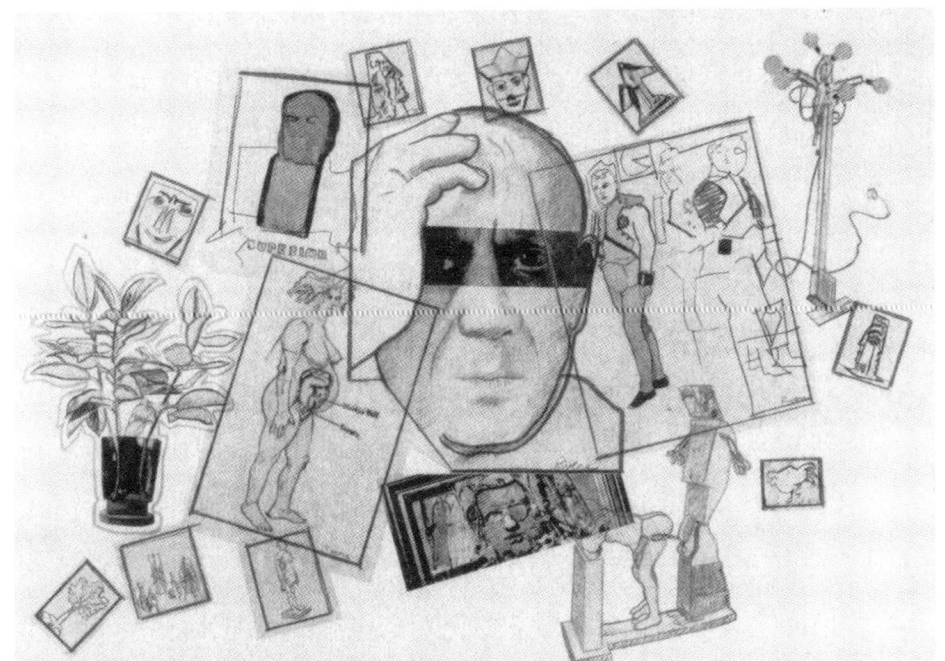

Larry Rivers
Homage to Picasso
Courtesy Propyläen-Verlag

TITLE	PUBLISHER	PRINTER	DATE	MEDIUM	DIMENSION (PAPER SIZE) IN INCHES	TYPE OF PAPER	EDITION NUMBER	NO. OF COLORS	ORIGINAL OPENING PRICE	CURRENT RETAIL PRICE
SOLD OUT EDITIONS (RARE):										
The Afternoon I–III (S-1)	ULAE	ULAE	1958	LB	14 X 17 EA	HMP	100 EA	1 EA	100 EA	4000 EA
The Afternoon IV (S-2)	ULAE	ULAE	1958	LB/HC	14 X 17	HMP	2	Varies	200	8000
The Bike Girl II	ULAE	ULAE	1958	LC	12 X 16	RP	30		100	8000
Stones (with Frank O'Hara) (Set of 12)	ULAE	ULAE	1958–59	LC	26 X 19 EA	AP	25 EA		600 SET	40000 SET
Marriage Photograph	ULAE	ULAE	1959	LB/HC	15 X 19	HMP	15	8	150	20000
Jack of Spades	ULAE	ULAE	1960	LC	43 X 30	HMP	35	7	200	2000
Daniel Webster	ULAE	ULAE	1961	LC	22 X 29	AP	80		100	5000
Portrait of Clarise	ULAE	ULAE	1961	LC	12 X 14	AP	15		100	3000
Nine Bank Notes (S-37)	ULAE	ULAE	1963–64	LC	23 X 31	CRIS	26	7	250	9000
Tanfastic			1966	LC/OFF			225		150	4000
Map with Frazier	MG	SS	1966	SP	25 X 20	AP	14		350	3000
Robert Frazier and the Underground	MG	SS	1966	SP	35 X 31	AP	25		350	3000
Underground with Two Fraziers	MG	SS	1966	SP	37 X 16	AP	15		350	3500
O'Hara Reading (S-46)	ULAE	ULAE	1967	LC	28 X 33	R/BFK	31		300	3000
Downtown Lion (S-47)	ULAE	ULAE	1967	EC	12 X 18	ALMP	24	1	300	3000
Boston Massacre (Set of 12) (Book)	MG	SS	1970	LC	28 X 19 EA	AP			1200	8000
Girlie	MG	SS	1970	SP/CO	28 X 18	AP	100		200	3000
Bread and Butter	MG	SS	1974	SP/EB	14 X 17	AP	25		250	2500
Patriotic Stamps	MG	SS	1976	LC/AirB	30 X 30	AP	30		450	2700
Big B Signs Up	TAI	SS	1976	LC/SP	20 X 26	AP	175	10	450	3500
Signing Up for the Big D	MG	SS	1976	LC/SP	20 X 26	AP88	125		350	1500
Madam Butterfly (Metropolitan Opera I)	CGL	SS	1978	LC/SP	23 X 31	AP88	250	11	600	2500
Bronx Zoo	CGL	SS	1978	LC/SP	26 X 34	AP88	250		650	1500
Blue Line Camel	MG	SS	1978	DR/PO	18 X 25	AP88	120		1200	3500
Camel Quartet	MG	SS	1978	SP/LC	22 X 21	AP88	120		1000	5000
Open Camel	MG	SS	1978	DR/PO	22 X 30	AP88	120		1000	5000
Acetate Camel	MG	SS	1978	STEN/HC	18 X 25	AP88	120		1000	2500
Stencilpack Camel	GHJG	SS	1978	STEN	23 X 30	AP88	120		800	3000
Four Camels	MG	SS	1978	SP	23 X 21	AP88	125		600	3500
Stencil Pack (2 Parts)	MG	SS	1978	DR/PO	25 X 22	AP	120		1300	5000
Webster (Pink)	MG	SS	1979	LC/HC	26 X 30	AP	75		900	5000
Webster (White)	MG	SS	1979	LC/HC	26 X 30	AP	75		900	5000
Last Civil War Veteran	MG	SS	1979	SP/PO	42 X 30	AP	125		1000	5000
Queen of Clubs	CNP		1979	LC/SP	30 X 23	AP	200		800	5000
Polish Rider	SS	SS	1983	LC/SP	31 X 39	AP	90	18	1200	5000
Blue Collar Holiday	MIX	MIX	1990	LC/REL	48 X 39 X 4	CAN	100	4	13500	13500
Matisse Opera (Graphic Relief on Canvas)			1992	LC/REL	47 X 38 X 4		50			

JAMES RIZZI

BORN: New York, NY; 1950
EDUCATION: Univ of Florida, Gainesville, FL, BA
RECENT EXHIB: Barrett Gallery, El Paso, TX, 1987; Enthios Gallery, Santa Fe, NM, 1987; Jeck Gallery, Scottsdale, AZ, 1987; Newbury Fine Art, Boston, MA, 1987; Brigham City Mus Gallery, UT, 1989; Martin Lawrence Galleries, Short Hills, NJ, 1993
COLLECTIONS: McNay Art Inst of Fine Arts, San Antonio, TX; Brooklyn Mus, NY
PRINTERS: Atelier Ettinger, NY (AE); B. T. Werkner, Los Angeles, CA (BTW); Galapagos Studio, Huntington Valley, PA (GS); Moshin Graphics, NY (MG)
PUBLISHERS: John Szoke Graphics, NY (JSG)
GALLERIES: Southwest Gallery, Dallas, TX; Graphic Art Collection, Hallandale, FL; David Gary, Ltd, Milburn, NJ; Morningstar Gallery, New York, NY; John Szoke Graphics, New York, NY; JRS Fine Art, Providence, RI; Bennett Galleries, Knoxville, TN; Atlas Galleries, Inc, Chicago, IL; The Gallery, Indianapolis, IN; Ventana Fine Art, Santa Fe, NM; A J Fine Arts, Ltd, Brooklyn, NY; Gallery 121 Internationale, New York, NY; Landing Gallery of Woodbury, Inc, New York, NY; Langman Gallery, Willow Grove, PA; American Art, Tacoma, WA

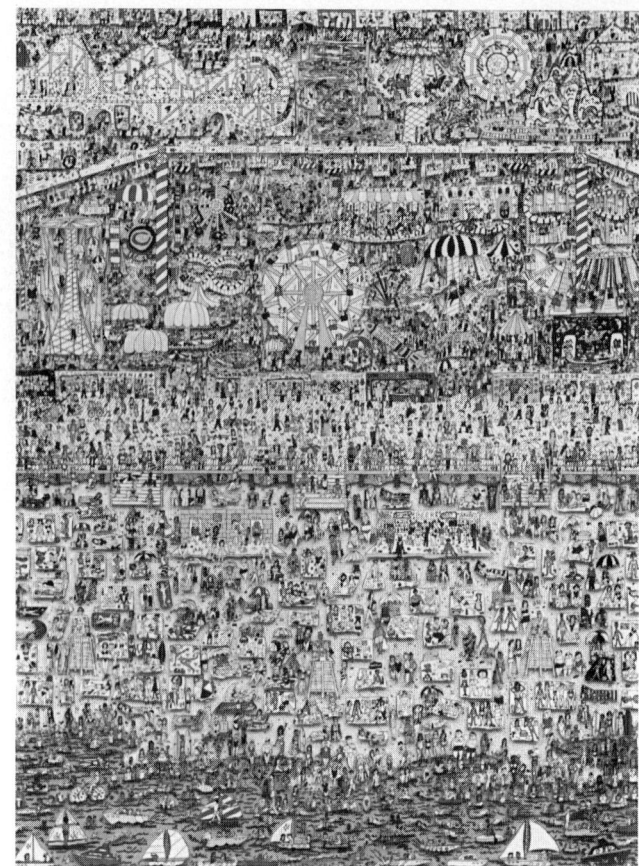

James Rizzi
Let's Get Lost at Coney Island
Courtesy John Szoke Graphics, Inc

TITLE	PUBLISHER	PRINTER	DATE	MEDIUM	DIMENSION (PAPER SIZE) IN INCHES	TYPE OF PAPER	EDITION NUMBER	NO. OF COLORS	ORIGINAL OPENING PRICE	CURRENT RETAIL PRICE
CURRENT EDITIONS:										
Great American Pastime	JSG	BTW	1981	LC/CON	18 X 24	AP	150		500	7500
Brooklyn Bridge	JSG	GS	1982	LC/CON	10 X 8	AP	125		250	2750
Coney Island	JSG	GS	1982	LC/CON	14 X 19	AP	125	15	550	6500
Glad, Sad, Mad, Bad	JSG	GS	1982	LC/CON	3 X 12	AP	150		125	850
Holiday on Ice	JSG	GS	1982	LC/CON	10 X 8	AP	150		250	1750
It's So Hard to be a Saint in the City	JSG	GS	1982	LC/CON	16 X 21	AP	150		500	8000
Painting the Town	JSG	GS	1982	LC/CON	4 X 6	AP	150		125	550
Skyline	JSG	GS	1982	LC/CON	5 X 4	AP	150		75	650
Table Life	JSG	GS	1982	LC/CON	5 X 4	AP	150		100	700
Main Street	JSG	GS	1982	LC/CON	10 X 8	AP	150		250	900
Fun in the Sun	JSG	GS	1982	LC/CON	10 X 8	AP	150		250	2750
Alley Cats	JSG	GS	1983	LC/CON	7 X 5	AP	125		150	550
Baseball	JSG	GS	1983	LC/CON	8 X 12	AP	125		275	2000
Crosstown Traffic	JSG	GS	1983	SP/CON	22 X 30	AP	99	16	800	5000
Golf	JSG	MG	1983	LC/CON	8 X 12	AP	125		275	2000
Grid Lock	JSG	BTW	1983	LC/CON	7 X 5	AP	150		150	800
Alligator Alley	JSG	AA	1984	LC/CON	5 X 7	AP	150		175	700
Basketball	JSG	AA	1984	LC/CON	8 X 12	AP	150		275	2000
Beach	JSG	AA	1984	LC/CON	4 X 3	AP	150		100	450
Big Apple	JSG	AA	1984	LC/CON	6 X 6	AP	150		170	1500
Breakin'	JSG	AA	1984	LC/CON	6 X 4	AP	150		75	400
Cat's Meow	JSG	AA	1984	LC/CON	4 X 4	AP	150		75	400
Circus	JSG	AA	1984	LC/CON	16 X 12	AP	150		400	2750
Football Frenzy	JSG	AA	1984	LC/CON	20 X 26	AP	150		900	2250
Night Out	JSG	AA	1984	LC/CON	4 X 4	AP	150		75	650
On the Town	JSG	BTW	1984	LC/CON	8 X 8	AP	150		225	550
Park Pond	JSG	BTW	1984	LC/CON	17 X 12	AP	150		400	1500
Party Time	JSG	BTW	1984	LC/CON	5 X 4	AP	150		75	500
Rainbow Regatta	JSG	BTW	1984	LC/CON	8 X 6	AP	150		275	650
Sundaze	JSG	MG	1984	LC/CON	4 X 6	AP	150		175	550
Sunset Sail	JSG	MG	1984	LC/CON	4 X 3	AP	150		75	600
Tennis	JSG	MG	1984	LC/CON	8 X 12	AP	125		275	2000
Birds Backyard	JSG	BTW	1985	LC/CON	9 X 7	AP	150		200	950
Cathouse	JSG	BTW	1985	LC/CON	4 X 4	AP	150		100	600
Crosswalk	JSG	BTW	1985	LC/CON	5 X 4	AP	150		150	600
Girl Next Door	JSG	BTW	1985	LC/CON	3 X 3	AP	150		50	300
Kiss Kiss	JSG	BTW	1985	LC/CON	5 X 4	AP	150		75	400
Kong	JSG	BTW	1985	LC/CON	7 X 3	AP	150		150	700

JAMES RIZZI CONTINUED

TITLE	PUBLISHER	PRINTER	DATE	MEDIUM	DIMENSION (PAPER SIZE) IN INCHES	TYPE OF PAPER	EDITION NUMBER	NO. OF COLORS	ORIGINAL OPENING PRICE	CURRENT RETAIL PRICE
CURRENT EDITIONS:										
Liberty	JSG	BTW	1985	LC/CON	6 X 4	AP	150		150	800
Neighborhood	JSG	BTW	1985	LC/CON	4 X 6	AP	150		125	500
On the Boardwalk	JSG	BTW	1985	LC/CON	23 X 24	AP	150		900	8000
Smell the Flowers	JSG	BTW	1985	LC/CON	9 X 7	AP	150		250	600
Trash Can School	JSG	BTW	1985	LC/CON	4 X 6	AP	150		150	550
Adam's Rib	JSG	BTW	1986	LC/CON	5 X 6	AP	150		175	500
City by the Bay	JSG	BTW	1986	LC/CON	14 X 20	AP	150		550	4000
Deja Vu	JSG	BTW	1986	LC/CON	3 X 2	AP	150		75	350
Fishin'	JSG	BTW	1986	LC/CON	6 X 3	AP	150		150	600
From Me to You	JSG	BTW	1986	LC/CON	4 X 4	AP	150		160	550
Good Times	JSG	BTW	1986	LC/CON	3 X 2	AP	150		75	350
Harbor	JSG	BTW	1986	LC/CON	5 X 4	AP	150		160	450
Help Yourself	JSG	BTW	1986	LC/CON	5 X 4	AP	150		125	350
It's a Jungle Out There	JSG	BTW	1986	LC/CON	19 X 26	AP	150		650	7000
Kiss	JSG	BTW	1986	LC/CON	4 X 3	AP	150		75	550
Kittys	JSG	BTW	1986	LC/CON	2 X 3	AP	150		50	350
Let's Do Lunch	JSG	BTW	1986	LC/CON	3 X 2	AP	150		75	325
Look of Love	JSG	BTW	1986	LC/CON	4 X 3	AP	150		35	600
Look Out	JSG	BTW	1986	LC/CON	3 X 3	AP	150		75	200
Meat Me at the Club	JSG	BTW	1986	LC/CON	20 X 11	AP	150		450	4000
My House	JSG	BTW	1986	LC/CON	4 X 4	AP	150		125	350
Night Club	JSG	BTW	1986	LC/CON	14 X 19	AP	150		450	3500
On the Beach	JSG	BTW	1986	LC/CON	5 X 4	AP	150		160	500
Oncoming Traffic	JSG	BTW	1986	LC/CON	4 X 4	AP	150		150	400
Outgoing Traffic	JSG	BTW	1986	LC/CON	3 X 4	AP	150		150	400
Peek a Boo	JSG	BTW	1986	LC/CON	4 X 3	AP	150		75	225
Proud Valley	JSG	BTW	1986	LC/CON	10 X 8	AP	150		300	800
Seven Beauties	JSG	BTW	1986	LC/CON	3 X 4	AP	150		75	400
Ski Weekend	JSG	BTW	1986	LC/CON	19 X 27	AP	150		750	4500
TGIF	JSG	BTW	1986	LC/CON	4 X 3	AP	150		125	450
Waiting on Line	JSG	BTW	1986	LC/CON	3 X 12	AP	150		300	800
Walk in the Park	JSG	BTW	1986	LC/CON	18 X 26	AP	150		575	3500
Water Under the Bridge	JSG	BTW	1986	LC/CON	8 X 11	AP	150		350	1500
A Big Apple	JSG	BTW	1987	LC/CON	3 X 2	AP	150		100	350
A Toast	JSG	BTW	1987	LC/CON	3 X 2	AP	150		100	500
Attitudes	JSG	BTW	1987	LC/CON	6 X 4	AP	150		200	500
Bad Times	JSG	BTW	1987	LC/CON	4 X 2	AP	150		75	250
Baseball as it Ought to Be	JSG	BTW	1987	LC/CON	12 X 9	AP	150		425	2000
Birds on a Wire	JSG	BTW	1987	LC/CON	3 X 4	AP	150		100	400
Cat Walk	JSG	BTW	1987	LC/CON	2 X 3	AP	150		100	300
Double Shift	JSG	BTW	1987	LC/CON	2 X 3	AP	150		100	350
Good Day	JSG	BTW	1987	LC/CON	4 X 5	AP	150		150	450
Good Wheels	JSG	BTW	1987	SP/OFF	20 X 6	R/BFK	150		450	1950
Halloween in the USA	JSG	BTW	1987	LC/CON	18 X 26	AP	150		850	5000
Hot Dog	JSG	BTW	1987	LC/CON	3 X 2	AP	150		100	325
It's Me	JSG	BTW	1987	LC/CON	3 X 3	AP	150		50	275
Letting Off Steam	JSG	BTW	1987	LC/CON	6 X 4	AP	150		150	400
Lift	JSG	BTW	1987	LC/CON	6 X 6	AP	150		250	550
Lucky in Love	JSG	BTW	1987	LC/CON	3 X 3	AP	150		50	400
Night Fishin'	JSG	BTW	1987	LC/CON	6 X 8	AP	150		300	850
On the Waterfront	JSG	BTW	1987	LC/CON	24 X 34	AP	150		1350	5500
One Man's Ceiling...	JSG	BTW	1987	LC/CON	36 X 26	AP	150		1575	5000
One Man's Floor....	JSG	BTW	1987	LC/CON	3 X 4	AP	150		1575	3150
Par 4	JSG	BTW	1987	LC/CON	4 X 5	AP	150		180	700
Room with a View	JSG	BTW	1987	LC/CON	12 X 9	AP	150		350	900
Running thru America	JSG	BTW	1987	LC/CON	6 X 20	AP	150		450	1950
Sidewalk Cafe	JSG	BTW	1987	LC/CON	9 X 12	AP	150		450	2500
Spacewar	JSG	BTW	1987	LC/CON	4 X 5	AP	150		150	400
Taxi	JSG	BTW	1987	LC/CON	6 X 8	AP	150		250	1000
To be a Kid Again	JSG	BTW	1987	LC/CON	9 X 8	AP	150		375	1500
Trash	JSG	BTW	1987	LC/CON	3 X 3	AP	150		50	300
Wall Flowers	JSG	BTW	1987	LC/CON	3 X 6	AP	150		125	250
When Living is Easy	JBG	BTW	1987	LC/CON	19 X 25	AP	150		900	3500
A Shore Thing	JSG	BTW	1988	LC/CON	7 X 12	AP	150		425	1000
Cat on a Can	JSG	BTW	1988	LC/CON	5 X 3	AP	150		150	450
Dreamland	JSG	BTW	1988	LC/CON	6 X 5	AP	150		225	550
Four Seasons Suite (with Book) (Set of 4):									1400 SET	4500 SET
Winter	JSG	BTW	1988	LC/CON	10 X 8	AP	150		450	700
Spring	JSG	BTW	1988	LC/CON	10 X 8	AP			450	1000
Summer	JSG	BTW	1988	LC/CON	10 X 8	AP	150		450	1250
Autumn	JSG	BTW	1988	LC/CON	10 X 8	AP	150		450	1250
Hookers	JSG	BTW	1988	LC/CON	5 X 7	AP	150		200	475

JAMES RIZZI CONTINUED

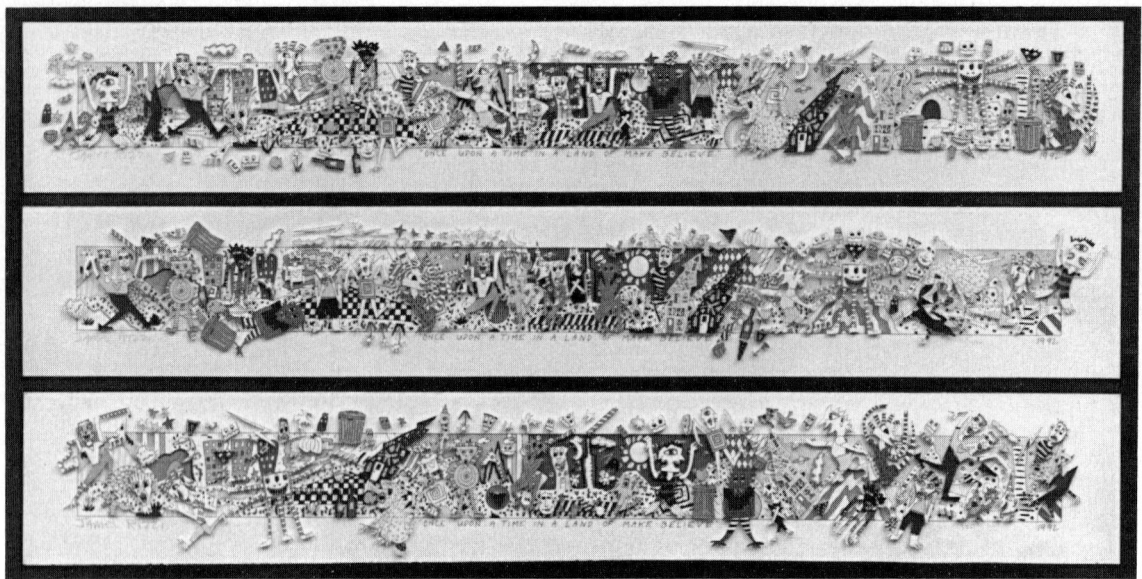

James Rizzi
Once Upon a Time in a Land of Make Believe
Courtesy John Szoke Graphics, Inc

TITLE	PUBLISHER	PRINTER	DATE	MEDIUM	DIMENSION (PAPER SIZE) IN INCHES	TYPE OF PAPER	EDITION NUMBER	NO. OF COLORS	ORIGINAL OPENING PRICE	CURRENT RETAIL PRICE
CURRENT EDITIONS:										
Iceday	JSG	BTW	1988	LC/CON	11 X 7	AP	150		400	750
In Line	JSG	BTW	1988	LC/CON	2 X 5	AP	150		125	450
It's the Altitude	JSG	BTW	1988	LC/CON	25 X 36	AP	150		2000	4500
King	JSG	BTW	1988	LC/CON	5 X 2	AP	150		150	450
Let the Good Times Roll	JSG	BTW	1988	LC/CON	26 X 36	AP	150		1600	4100
Lunch Break	JSG	BTW	1988	LC/CON	4 X 5	AP	150		175	400
Never Alone	JSG	BTW	1988	LC/CON	3 X 4	AP	150		175	500
Pals	JSG	BTW	1988	LC/CON	2 X 5	AP	150		100	400
People	JSG	BTW	1988	LC/CON	16 X 26	AP	150		1000	2750
Stickball	JSG	BTW	1988	LC/CON	4 X 4	AP	150		175	500
Team Photo	JSG	BTW	1988	LC/CON	3 X 4	AP	150		150	400
Tennis Anyone	JSG	BTW	1988	LC/CON	5 X 4	AP	150		200	425
Traffic	JSG	BTW	1988	LC/CON	16 X 26	AP	150		850	3500
When the Circus Comes to Town	JSG	BTW	1988	LC/CON	7 X 21	AP	150		675	3000
A Fish Called Swimo	JSG	BTW	1989	LC/CON	3 X 5	AP	150		100	200
Big Brother	JSG	BTW	1989	LC/CON	5 X 3	AP	150		150	400
Birthday Party	JSG	BTW	1989	LC/CON	3 X 4	AP	150		125	225
Bon Voyage	JSG	BTW	1989	LC/CON	14 X 26	AP	150		700	900
Boys	JSG	BTW	1989	LC/CON	4 X 5	AP	150		150	500
Cafe in Paris	JSG	BTW	1989	LC/CON	14 X 11	AP	150		500	850
City that Never Sleeps	JSG	BTW	1989	LC/CON	20 X 27	AP	150		650	3250
Country House	JSG	BTW	1989	LC/CON	4 X 5	AP	150		175	500
Crazy Cats	JSG	BTW	1989	LC/CON	5 X 4	AP	150		125	500
Daddy's Country Club	JSG	BTW	1989	LC/CON	15 X 21	AP	150		1100	3500
Girls	JSG	BTW	1989	LC/CON	3 X 5	AP	150		150	500
Flowers for My Love	JSG	BTW	1989	LC/CON	3 X 5	AP	150		125	400
Green House Effect	JSG	BTW	1989	LC/CON	8 X 3	AP	150		250	600
Hundertwasser's Neighborhood	JSG	BTW	1989	LC/CON	6 X 4	AP	150		200	600
I Can Row a Boat-Canoe?	JSG	BTW	1989	LC/CON	3 X 5	AP	150		150	200
It's Time to Buy a New TV	JSG	BTW	1989	LC/CON	26 X 36	AP	150		1200	2400
Jelly Bean	JSG	BTW	1989	LC/CON	3 X 5	AP	150		150	200
Jumping Rope	JSG	BTW	1989	LC/CON	5 X 4	AP	150		175	225
Junkyard Cats	JSG	BTW	1989	LC/CON	11 X 14	AP	150		450	850
Junkyard Dogs	JSG	BTW	1989	LC/CON	20 X 27	AP	150		850	1950
Liberty	JSG	BTW	1989	LC/CON	4 X 3	AP	150		125	550
Life Inside the Big Apple	JSG	BTW	1989	LC/CON	11 X 10	AP	150		500	1750
Lollypop Kids	JSG	BTW	1989	LC/CON	3 X 3	AP	150		100	150
Love is in the Air	JSG	BTW	1989	LC/CON	6 X 5	AP	150		250	800
Me at My Show	JSG	BTW	1989	LC/CON	7 X 4	AP	150		200	450
No Two Alike	JSG	BTW	1989	LC/CON	6 X 9	AP	150		300	550
Passion Fruit	JSG	BTW	1989	LC/CON	20 X 20	AP	150		600	1750
Passion Fruit Blue	JSG	BTW	1989	LC/CON	28 X 20	AP	150		600	1950
Passion Fruit Pink	JSG	BTW	1989	LC/CON	28 X 20	AP	150		600	1750
Playground	JSG	BTW	1989	LC/CON	6 X 5	AP	150		250	550

JAMES RIZZI CONTINUED

TITLE	PUBLISHER	PRINTER	DATE	MEDIUM	DIMENSION (PAPER SIZE) IN INCHES	TYPE OF PAPER	EDITION NUMBER	NO. OF COLORS	ORIGINAL OPENING PRICE	CURRENT RETAIL PRICE
CURRENT EDITIONS:										
Poker Face	JSG	BTW	1989	LC/CON	4 X 6	AP	150		225	450
Rain	JSG	BTW	1989	LC/CON	28 X 19	AP	150		800	1100
Send in the Clowns	JSG	BTW	1989	LC/CON	5 X 15	AP	150		300	800
Shortcut	JSG	BTW	1989	LC/CON	27 X 19	AP	150		850	2150
Simon Sez	JSG	BTW	1989	LC/CON	3 X 5	AP	150		175	250
Take the A Train	JSG	BTW	1989	LC/CON	20 X 26	AP	150		850	2300
That's Amore	JSG	BTW	1989	LC/CON	27 X 20	AP	150		700	2500
This Ain't No Lazy River	JSG	BTW	1989	LC/CON	7 X 18	AP	150		600	1500
Time Warp	JSG	BTW	1989	LC/CON	9 X 12	AP	150		500	900
Traffic & Noise	JSG	BTW	1989	LC/CON	5 X 8	AP	150		225	550
Triathlon	JSG	BTW	1989	LC/CON	4 X 5	AP	150		150	500
Trick or Treat	JSG	BTW	1989	LC/CON	5 X 9	AP	150		300	375
Twin Taxis	JSG	BTW	1989	LC/CON	3 X 3	AP	150		125	400
Waiting for the Sun	JSG	BTW	1989	LC/CON	8 X 6	AP	150		275	950
Waiting to Play Golf	JSG	BTW	1989	LC/CON	3 X 8	AP	150		200	550
Washington Ain't No Square Park	JSG	BTW	1989	LC/CON	26 X 36	AP	150		2750	4750
Which Way is Up?	JSG	BTW	1989	LC/CON	12 X 8	AP	150		500	1500
Women Who Work Out	JSG	BTW	1989	LC/CON	15 X 21	AP	150		1000	2400
A Lot of Fun for City Kids	JSG	BTW	1990	LC/CON	36 X 26	AP	150		2500	2750
Basketball Jones	JSG	BTW	1990	LC/CON	5 X 5	AP	150		175	275
Bottoms Up	JSG	BTW	1990	LC/CON	7 X 6	AP	150		300	850
Fabulous Foursome	JSG	BTW	1990	LC/CON	4 X 6	AP	150		225	550
Forty Days and Forty Nights	JSG	BTW	1990	LC/CON	26 X 16	AP	150		1350	2500
Girls on the Street	JSG	BTW	1990	LC/CON	4 X 9	AP	150		250	600
High Wire	JSG	BTW	1990	LC/CON	4 X 5	AP	150		200	500
Lost in a Concrete Jungle	JSG	BTW	1990	LC/CON	25 X 16	AP	150		1100	1250
Movin' In (Mobile Painting)	JSG	BTW	1990	LC/CON	36 X 24	AP	150		3500	3800
Movin' On (Mobile Painting)	JSG	BTW	1990	LC/CON	36 X 24	AP	150		3500	4000
Movin' Up (Mobile Painting)	JSG	BTW	1990	LC/CON	36 X 24	AP	150		3500	4000
Outside Looking In	JSG	BTW	1990	LC/CON	8 X 6	AP	150		275	325
Peek a Boo Eye See U	JSG	BTW	1990	LC/CON	6 X 8	AP	150		250	300
Take Me Out to the Ballgame	JSG	BTW	1990	LC/CON	26 X 36	AP	150		4000	5500
Tea Party	JSG	BTW	1990	LC/CON	7 X 9	AP	150		350	450
Too Many Boats in the Harbor	JSG	BTW	1990	LC/CON	10 X 8	AP	150		600	900
Too Many Cats in the Yard	JSG	BTW	1990	LC/CON	10 X 8	AP	150		600	900
Too Many Fish in the Sea	JSG	BTW	1990	LC/CON	10 X 8	AP	150		500	900
Too Many People Going Skiing	JSG	BTW	1990	LC/CON	10 X 8	AP	150		700	1350
Too Many People in the City	JSG	BTW	1990	LC/CON	10 X 8	AP	150		625	1250
Too Many People Playing Golf	JSG	BTW	1990	LC/CON	10 X 8	AP	150		625	1350
War Games	JSG	BTW	1990	LC/CON	6 X 8	AP	150		300	300
Welcome to the Big Apple	JSG	BTW	1990	LC/CON	8 X 9	AP	150		500	1250
Wishing Well	JSG	BTW	1990	LC/CON	4 X 3	AP	150		150	350
Let's Get Lost at Coney Island	JSG	BTW	1990	LC/CON	40 X 30	R/BFK	350		2950	5000
Adam's Nightmare III	JSG	BTW	1991	LC/CON	2 X 3	AP	150		150	375
All Fall Down II	JSG	BTW	1991	LC/CON	2 X 3	AP	150		100	125
Bed Rock I	JSG	BTW	1991	LC/CON	2 X 3	AP	150		100	150
Beep Beep I	JSG	BTW	1991	LC/CON	2 X 3	AP	150		100	250
Boys and their Boats I	JSG	BTW	1991	LC/CON	2 X 3	AP	150		150	250
Dog E Dog II	JSG	BTW	1991	LC/CON	2 X 3	AP	150		100	125
Don't Fence Me In I	JSG	BTW	1991	LC/CON	2 X 3	AP	150		100	125
Down and Out III	JSG	BTW	1991	LC/CON	2 X 3	AP	150		100	100
Early Bird III	JSG	BTW	1991	LC/CON	2 X 3	AP	150		100	125
Early to Rise II	JSG	BTW	1991	LC/CON	2 X 3	AP	150		100	150
Expecting Company III	JSG	BTW	1991	LC/CON	2 X 3	AP	150		150	200
Fly By I	JSG	BTW	1991	LC/CON	2 X 3	AP	150		125	300
Follow the Leader III	JSG	BTW	1991	LC/CON	2 X 3	AP	150		100	100
For Me I	JSG	BTW	1991	LC/CON	2 X 3	AP	150		150	350
Free as a Bird I	JSG	BTW	1991	LC/CON	2 X 3	AP	150		125	250
Good Kitty I	JSG	BTW	1991	LC/CON	2 X 3	AP	150		100	175
Hot Diggity Dog III	JSG	BTW	1991	LC/CON	2 X 3	AP	150		125	150
Hound Dog III	JSG	BTW	1991	LC/CON	2 X 3	AP	150		100	125
I Smell Something Burning I	JSG	BTW	1991	LC/CON	2 X 3	AP	150		150	200
I Wish I Had a Watermelon II	JSG	BTW	1991	LC/CON	2 X 3	AP	150		150	150
I'd Rather be in Philly I	JSG	BTW	1991	LC/CON	2 X 3	AP	150		100	100
It Ain't Easy Getting Rich III	JSG	BTW	1991	LC/CON	2 X 3	AP	150		150	200
Jail Ain't Happy III	JSG	BTW	1991	LC/CON	2 X 3	AP	150		100	100
Johnny on the Pony II	JSG	BTW	1991	LC/CON	2 X 3	AP	150		100	100
Jump in III	JSG	BTW	1991	LC/CON	2 X 3	AP	150		125	125
Last One Home is a Rotten Egg I (Dipt)	JSG	BTW	1991	LC/CON	2 X 7	AP	150		250	400
Lazy Day II	JSG	BTW	1991	LC/CON	2 X 3	AP	150		150	200
Let's Get Wet II	JSG	BTW	1991	LC/CON	2 X 3	AP	150		100	100

JAMES RIZZI CONTINUED

TITLE	PUBLISHER	PRINTER	DATE	MEDIUM	DIMENSION (PAPER SIZE) IN INCHES	TYPE OF PAPER	EDITION NUMBER	NO. OF COLORS	ORIGINAL OPENING PRICE	CURRENT RETAIL PRICE
CURRENT EDITIONS:										
London Bridges Falling Down II (Dipt)	JSG	BTW	1991	LC/CON	2 X 7	AP	150		250	375
Love and Marriage I	JSG	BTW	1991	LC/CON	2 X 3	AP	150		150	350
Love for Sale (Dipt) II	JSG	BTW	1991	LC/CON	2 X 7	AP	150		225	300
Love on Sail III	JSG	BTW	1991	LC/CON	2 X 3	AP	150		100	300
Marbles in your Head II	JSG	BTW	1991	LC/CON	2 X 3	AP	150		100	100
Meet Me at the Fair III	JSG	BTW	1991	LC/CON	2 X 3	AP	150		150	150
Middle of the Road II	JSG	BTW	1991	LC/CON	2 X 3	AP	150		125	225
Moon River I	JSG	BTW	1991	LC/CON	2 X 3	AP	150		150	300
My Mom Uses Tide III	JSG	BTW	1991	LC/CON	2 X 3	AP	150		100	125
My Turn Next II	JSG	BTW	1991	LC/CON	2 X 3	AP	150		100	100
No Two Ways About It II	JSG	BTW	1991	LC/CON	2 X 3	AP	150		100	125
Not Cloudy all Day III	JSG	BTW	1991	LC/CON	2 X 3	AP	150		100	125
Nothing Lasts Forever III	JSG	BTW	1991	LC/CON	2 X 3	AP	150		150	150
Old Friend I	JSG	BTW	1991	LC/CON	2 X 3	AP	150		100	275
On Line in Line in Russia III (Trip)	JSG	BTW	1991	LC/CON	2 X 11	AP	150		350	350
One Way Street I (Dipt)	JSG	BTW	1991	LC/CON	2 X 7	AP	150		250	300
Our Street II	JSG	BTW	1991	LC/CON	2 X 3	AP	150		125	200
Out of Shape II	JSG	BTW	1991	LC/CON	2 X 3	AP	150		100	125
Rain Rain Go Away I	JSG	BTW	1991	LC/CON	2 X 3	AP	150		125	225
Rolling on the River II	JSG	BTW	1991	LC/CON	2 X 3	AP	150		125	150
Rush Hour I	JSG	BTW	1991	LC/CON	2 X 3	AP	150		100	100
Smoke Gets in Your Eyes I	JSG	BTW	1991	LC/CON	2 X 3	AP	150		100	225
Stick Em Up II	JSG	BTW	1991	LC/CON	2 X 3	AP	150		125	125
Street Show II	JSG	BTW	1991	LC/CON	2 X 3	AP	150		150	150
Subway Rider I	JSG	BTW	1991	LC/CON	2 X 3	AP	150		125	150
Sugar, Baby, Cookie, Honey I	JSG	BTW	1991	LC/CON	2 X 3	AP	150		150	350
Sweeter than Wine II	JSG	BTW	1991	LC/CON	2 X 3	AP	150		150	300
Swinging on a Star III	JSG	BTW	1991	LC/CON	2 X 3	AP	150		100	125
Take Me to the River III	JSG	BTW	1991	LC/CON	2 X 3	AP	150		150	300
The New Kind in Town III	JSG	BTW	1991	LC/CON	2 X 3	AP	150		100	100
The Sky's the Limit I	JSG	BTW	1991	LC/CON	2 X 3	AP	150		100	125
Things are Looking Up II (Trip)	JSG	BTW	1991	LC/CON	8 X 3	AP	150		275	325
Too Close for Comfort II	JSG	BTW	1991	LC/CON	2 X 3	AP	150		100	100
Two's Company, Three's a Crowd II	JSG	BTW	1991	LC/CON	2 X 3	AP	150		100	100
Underground Connection III (Dipt)	JSG	BTW	1991	LC/CON	2 X 7	AP	150		250	275
Urban Terrain II	JSG	BTW	1991	LC/CON	2 X 3	AP	150		100	100
Wake Up Sleepy Heads I	JSG	BTW	1991	LC/CON	2 X 3	AP	150		150	375
What a Bummer I	JSG	BTW	1991	LC/CON	2 X 3	AP	150		125	125
Who's Got Winners III	JSG	BTW	1991	LC/CON	2 X 3	AP	150		125	125
Working for Peanuts III	JSG	BTW	1991	LC/CON	2 X 3	AP	150		125	125
You Get What You Need II	JSG	BTW	1991	LC/CON	2 X 3	AP	150		125	350
You're the Cats Meow III	JSG	BTW	1991	LC/CON	2 X 3	AP	150		125	325
Yummy III	JSG	BTW	1991	LC/CON	2 X 3	AP	150		100	100
Strokes of Genius	JSG	BTW	1991	LC/CON	10 X 7	AP	150		650	850
The City is My Castle (Sculpture)	JSG	BTW	1991	LC/CON	19 X 12 X 10				6000	6000
Once Upon a Time in a Land of Make Believe	JSG	BTW	1992	LC/CON	6 X 40	R/BFK	350	3	750	1000
Sports Prints (Set of 12):									8500 SET	8500 SET
Anyone for Tennis?	JSG	BTW	1992	LC/CON	9 X 9	AP	150		550	600
Are You Ready for Some Football?	JSG	BTW	1992	LC/CON	9 X 9	AP	150		650	650
Battle on the Ice	JSG	BTW	1992	LC/CON	9 X 9	AP	150		600	600
Champ	JSG	BTW	1992	LC/CON	9 X 9	AP	150		650	650
Come Ski with Me	JSG	BTW	1992	LC/CON	9 X 9	AP	150		650	650
Different Strokes for Different Folks	JSG	BTW	1992	LC/CON	9 X 9	AP	150		650	700
Everyone Wants to Win the World Cup	JSG	BTW	1992	LC/CON	9 X 9	AP	150		650	700
It Ain't Over Till It's Over	JSG	BTW	1992	LC/CON	9 X 9	AP	150		650	700
Not Just a Fish Tail	JSG	BTW	1992	LC/CON	9 X 9	AP	150		550	550
Shooting Like a Star	JSG	BTW	1992	LC/CON	9 X 9	AP	150		550	550
Striving for that Perfect Ten	JSG	BTW	1992	LC/CON	9 X 9	AP	150		550	550
Wings on My Feet	JSG	BTW	1992	LC/CON	9 X 9	AP	150		600	600

DAN RIZZIE

BORN: Poughkeepsie, NY; 1951
EDUCATION: Henrix Col, Conway, AR, BFA, 1973; Southern Methodist Univ, Dallas, TX, MFA, 1975
AWARDS: First Prize, Brooklyn Mus, NY, 1980

RECENT EXHIB: Gloria Luria Gallery, Bay Harbor Island, FL, 1987; Arthur Roger Gallery, New Orleans, LA, 1988; Ruth Siegel Gallery, NY, 1988; Eugene Binder Gallery, Dallas, TX, 1987,88; Allene Lapides Gallery, Santa Fe, NM, 1988
COLLECTIONS: Metropolitan Mus of Art, NY; Mus of Mod Art, NY; Dallas Mus of Art, TX; New York Public Library, NY; Laguna Gloria Art Mus, Austin, TX; Witte Mus, San Antonio, TX; Mus de Monterrey, Mexico; Wichita Falls Mus, TX

DAN RIZZIE CONTINUED

PRINTERS: Eileen Foti, Albuquerque, NM (EF); Bill Lagattuta, Albuquerque, NM (BL); Tamarind Inst, Albuquerque, NM (TI); Sette Publishing Co, Tempe, AZ (SPC); Maurice Payne, NY (MP); Artist (ART)
PUBLISHERS: Tamarind Inst, Albuquerque, NM (TI); Sette Publishing Co, Tempe, AZ (SPC); Maurice Payne, NY (MP); Artist (ART)
GALLERIES: Pace Prints, New York, NY; Eugene Binder Gallery, Dallas, TX; Sette Gallery, Scottsdale, AZ; Arthur Roger Gallery, New Orleans, LA; Peregrine Gallery, Dallas, TX; Allene Lapides Gallery, Santa Fe, NM; Thomson Gallery, Minneapolis, MN; Richard Levy Gallery, Albuquerque, NM
MAILING ADDRESS: c/o Sette Gallery, 4142 N Marshall Way, Scottsdale, AZ 85251

TITLE	PUBLISHER	PRINTER	DATE	MEDIUM	DIMENSION (PAPER SIZE) IN INCHES	TYPE OF PAPER	EDITION NUMBER	NO. OF COLORS	ORIGINAL OPENING PRICE	CURRENT RETAIL PRICE
SOLD OUT EDITIONS (RARE):										
Untitled (Series of 20)	ART/MP	ART/MP	1985	MON/CC	40 X 30 EA	R/BFK-JP	1 EA		1800 EA	2800 EA
CURRENT EDITIONS:										
Red Cross	TI	ART/BL/TI	1988	LC/CC	21 X 17	HAG/KIT	18		400	500
Case de Luce	SPC	SPC	1988	LC/CC	45 X 37	CHIRI/AP	40		900	1000
Kicking Man, State I	TI	ART/EF/BL/TI	1988	LB/CC	21 X 18	CO/ARS	10	1	300	350
Kicking Man State II	TI	ART/BL/TI	1988	LB/CC	21 X 18	KIT/ARS	10	1	300	350
Bernalillo I-VII	TI	ART/EF/BL/TI	1988	MON	39 X 32 EA	CHIRI/ARS	1 EA	Varies	1200 EA	1500 EA
Jardin de Bernalillo	TI	ART/EF/BL/TI	1988	LC/CC	40 X 30	GAS/ARS	20	6	500	750
Little Wing	SPC	SPC	1988	LC	30 X 22	CHIRI	40		500	600

MICHAEL ROBBINS

BORN: New York, NY; June 15, 1949
EDUCATION: Cooper Union Sch, NY, BFA, 1970; Syracuse Univ, Ithaca, NY, MFA, 1971
TEACHING: Asst Prof, Drawing, Syracuse Univ, NY, 1970–71; Prof, Painting, Sch of Visual Arts, NY, 1978–84
AWARDS: Creative Artists Public Service Grant, 1978; Nat Endowment for the Arts Grant, Painting, 1985
RECENT EXHIB: Montclair Mus of Art, NJ, 1987; Jane Voorhees Zimmerli Mus, Rutgers Univ, New Brunswick, NJ, 1988
COLLECTIONS: Univ of Kentucky, Lexington, KY; Mus of Liege, Belgium; Vassar Col, Poughkeepsie, NY; Weatherspoon Art Gallery, Greensboro, NC; Metropolitan Mus of Art, NY; Mus Boverie Park, Brussels, Belgium; Brooklyn Mus, NY; Mus of City of New York, NY
PRINTERS: Alan Koslin, NY (AK); X Press, NY (XP); Judith Solodkin, NY (JS); Solo Press, NY (SP); Artist (ART)
PUBLISHERS: Ellen Sragow Gallery, NY (ES); Solo Press, NY (SP); Artist (ART)
GALLERIES: Sragow Gallery, New York, NY
MAILING ADDRESS: c/o Sragow Gallery, 73 Spring St, New York, NY 10012

TITLE	PUBLISHER	PRINTER	DATE	MEDIUM	DIMENSION (PAPER SIZE) IN INCHES	TYPE OF PAPER	EDITION NUMBER	NO. OF COLORS	ORIGINAL OPENING PRICE	CURRENT RETAIL PRICE
CURRENT EDITIONS:										
Like Other Afternoons	ART	ART	1980	LI/HC	12 X 18	SB	50	Multi	300	500
Like Other Afternoons	ART	ART	1980	LI	12 X 18	SB	50	1	250	500
Sunset Street	ART	ART	1982	LI/HC	18 X 12	SB	30	Multi	350	500
Sunset Street	ART	ART	1982	LI	18 X 12	SB	30	1	300	500
Summer Solstice	ES	AK/XP	1984	LI/HC	30 X 44	R/BFK	15	Multi	750	900
Summer Solstice	ES	AK/XP	1984	LI	30 X 44	R/BFK	15	1	500	700
Ensueno de Mexico	SP	JS/SP	1989	LI/HC	31 X 42	SOM	50	Varies	800	900
Spirit of Speed I,II	SP	JS/SP	1989	LI/HC	15 X 14	SOM	50	Varies	850	850

CHARLOTTE ROBINSON

BORN: San Antonio, TX; November 1924
EDUCATION: Art Students League, NY, 1948; New York Univ, NY, 1948–49; Corcoran Sch of Art, Wash, DC, 1951–52
TEACHING: Instr, Art World Seminars, Washington Women's Art Center, Wash, DC, 1976–80; Instr, Drawing, Smithsonian Assoc Prog, Wash, DC, 1976 to present
AWARDS: Nat Endowment for the Arts Awards, 1977,78,81
RECENT EXHIB: Wallace/Wentworth Gallery, Wash, DC, 1988; Lowenstein Library Gallery, Fordham Univ, NY, 1990; San Antonio Art Inst, TX, 1991
COLLECTIONS: Museo Espanol de Arte Contemporaneo, Madrid, Spain; Museo de Arte Contemporanea, Lisbon, Portugal; New Sch for Social Research, NY; McNay Art Mus, San Antonio, TX
PRINTERS: Chromocomp Inc, New York, NY (CI); Dormuth Editions, New York, NY (DE)
PUBLISHERS: David Adamson Editions, Wash, DC (DAE); Artist (ART)
GALLERIES: Fendrick Gallery, Wash, DC; Gallery 4, Alexandria, VA; The Print Club, Phila, PA; Sol del Rio Gallery, San Antonio, TX; Mattingly-Baker Gallery, Dallas, TX; Wallace/Wentworth Gallery, Wash, DC; de Andino Fine Arts, Wash, DC
MAILING ADDRESS: 6324 Crosswoods Dr, Falls Church, VA 22044

TITLE	PUBLISHER	PRINTER	DATE	MEDIUM	DIMENSION (PAPER SIZE) IN INCHES	TYPE OF PAPER	EDITION NUMBER	NO. OF COLORS	ORIGINAL OPENING PRICE	CURRENT RETAIL PRICE
SOLD OUT EDITIONS (RARE):										
Crosswoods I	ART	CI	1979	SP	35 X 27	AP	100	22	100	400
White Nile	ART	DE	1980	SP	36 X 27	AP	75	28	100	450
CURRENT EDITIONS:										
Crosswoods II	ART	CI	1979	SP	36 X 28	AP	97	23	100	350
Crosswoods III	ART	CI	1979	SP	37 X 29	AP	97	23	100	350
Crosswoods IV	ART	CI	1979	SP	30 X 22	AP	90	23	100	350
Blue Nile	ART	DE	1980	SP	36 X 27	AP	100	27	100	400
Crosswoods XII, Hirosode	ART	DE	1983	SP/CO	32 X 39	AP	98	32	275	650
Crosswoods Series, Kul Kul Kau (with Pastels, Paint & Glitter)	DAE	DAE	1983	LC/HC	32 X 42	AP	40	31	300	650

JAUME ROCAMORA

BORN: Tortosa, Spain; July 6, 1946
EDUCATION: Escola Taller d'Arte de Tortosa, Spain, 1956–75
TEACHING: Cercle Artistic de Sant Luch de Barcelona, Spain
AWARDS: Medalla de Plata del Bilan de l'Art Contemporain, NY, 1983
RECENT EXHIB: Galeria Orfila, Madrid, Spain, 1992; Arte Xerea, Valencia, Spain, 1992; Galeria Susany, Vic, Spain, 1992; Galeria Velazquez, Valladolid, Spain, 1992
COLLECTIONS: Ohio Univ, Columbus, OH; Cultural Center, Bonn, Germany; Musée d'Art Contemporain des Pays Catalans de Banyoles, Spain; Musée Zabaleta de Quesada, Spain; Mus Vostell de Malpartida de Cáceres, Barcelona, Spain; Museo de Bellas Artes de Cholet, France; Museo Popular de Arte Contemporaneo de Villafames, Spain
PRINTERS: Filogràf Institute d'Art Gráfic, Barclona, Spain (FIA); Artist (ART); Contratalla/Obra Grafica, Tarragona, Spain (C/OG)
PUBLISHERS: Artist (ART)
GALLERIES: Galeria Cadques, Cadques, Spain; Galeria Canem, Castello, Spain; Arte Xerea, Valencia, Spain; Galeria Monells, Helsingborg, Sweden; Galeria A + B, Granollers, Spain; Galeria Wack, Kaiserslautern, Germany
MAILING ADDRESS: Argentina, 13,43500, Tortosa, Spain

TITLE	PUBLISHER	PRINTER	DATE	MEDIUM	DIMENSION (PAPER SIZE) IN INCHES	TYPE OF PAPER	EDITION NUMBER	NO. OF COLORS	ORIGINAL OPENING PRICE	CURRENT RETAIL PRICE
SOLD OUT EDITIONS (RARE):										
Materies Primeres	ART	JP/T	1980	LIN	50 X 65 cm	ING/GP	75	4	100	150
Mareries Primeres	ART	ART	1983	LIN	50 X 65 cm	POL	144	4	150	200
Elements Primaris	ART	FIA	1984	LIN	45 X 32 cm	ING/GP	300	4	100	150
Dialeg de Medis	ART	ART	1985	LIN	35 X 50 cm	M/VEL	8	4	200	250
Geminats Anaglifics	ART	C/OG	1991	EMB	50 X 65 cm	M/VEL	72	4	350	350

DOROTHEA ROCKBURNE

BORN: Verdun, PQ, Canada
EDUCATION: Ecole des Beaux-Arts, Montreal, Canada; Black Mountain Col, Black Mountain, NC
AWARDS: Painting Award, Art Inst of Chicago, IL, 1972; Guggenheim Fel, NY, 1972–73; Nat Endowment for the Arts, NY, 1974–75
RECENT EXHIB: Brandeis Univ, Waltham, MA, 1987; Corcoran Gallery of Art, Wash, DC, 1987; Haags Gemeentemuseum, The Hague, 1987; Mus of Contemp Art, Chicago, IL, 1987; Carnegie-Mellon Univ Art Gallery, Pittsburgh, PA, 1987; Arts Club of Chicago, IL, 1987; André Emmerich Gallery, NY, 1988,89,92; Guild Hall Mus, East Hampton, NY, 1992
COLLECTIONS: Albright-Knox Art Gallery, Buffalo, NY; Nordjyllands Kunstmuseum, Aalborg, Denmark; Metropolitan Mus, NY; Mus of Mod Art, NY; Brandeis Univ, Waltham, MA; Philadelphia Mus of Art, PA; Whitney Mus of Am Art, NY; Corcoran Gallery of Art, Wash, DC
PRINTERS: Gemini GEL, Los Angeles, CA (GEM)
PUBLISHERS: Parasol Press, Ltd, NY (PaP); Gemini GEL, Los Angeles, CA (GEM)
GALLERIES: André Emmerich Gallery, New York, NY; Gemini GEL Gallery, Los Angeles, CA; Garner Tullis, New York, NY
MAILING ADDRESS: 140 Grand St, New York, NY 10013

TITLE	PUBLISHER	PRINTER	DATE	MEDIUM	DIMENSION (PAPER SIZE) IN INCHES	TYPE OF PAPER	EDITION NUMBER	NO. OF COLORS	ORIGINAL OPENING PRICE	CURRENT RETAIL PRICE
SOLD OUT EDITIONS (RARE):										
Locus Series #1–#6 (Set of 6)	PaP		1972–75	EB/A	40 X 30 EA	STP	42 EA		1000 SET	7500 SET
Radiance (Printed on Both Sides)	GEM	GEM	1983	LC	40 X 32	TRANS	37	6	2500	5000
Melencolia	GEM	GEM	1983	LC	32 X 39	TRANS	40	6	2500	5000
Devine Ray	GEM	GEM	1983	LC	40 X 35	TRANS	44	9	2500	5000
Uriel	GEM	GEM	1983	LC	39 X 32	TRANS	34	7	2500	5000

NORMAN ROCKWELL

BORN: New York, NY; (1894–1978)
EDUCATION: Art Students League, NY; Univ of Vermont, Burlington, VT, DFA, 1949; Middlebury Col, VT, HHD, 1954; Univ of Massachusetts, Boston, MA, DFA, 1961
RECENT EXHIB: Midwest Mus of Am Art, Elkhart, IN, 1992; Daimaru Mus, Osaka, Japan, 1992; Matsuzakaya Art Mus, Nagoya, Japan, 1992; Judy Goffman Fine Art, NY, 1992
COLLECTIONS: Metropolitan Mus, NY; Smithsonian Inst, Wash, DC; Berkshire Mus, Pittsfield, MA; Columbus Mus of Fine Arts, OH; Bennington Mus, VT; Wadsworth Atheneum, Hartford, CT; Nat Portrait Gallery, Wash, DC
PRINTERS: Atelier Ettinger Inc, NY (AE); American Atelier, NY (AA)
PUBLISHERS: Eleanor Ettinger Inc, NY (EEI); Circle Fine Art, Chicago, IL (CFA)
GALLERIES: Studio 53, New York, NY; Eleanor Ettinger, Inc, New York, NY; Circle Galleries, Chicago, IL & Northbrook, IL & Pittsburgh, PA & New York, NY & Houston, TX & Scottsdale, AZ & Beverly Hills, CA & Costa Mesa, CA & Sherman Oaks, CA & Palm Beach, CA & Honolulu, HI & New Orleans, LA & Las Vegas, NV & Seattle, WA; Judy Goffman Fine Art, New York, NY; Adamson-Duvannes Gallery, Los Angeles, CA; R K Goldman & Company, Los Angeles, CA; John H Surovek Gallery, Palm Beach, FL; Art Brokerage, Ketchum, ID; David Raymond, Ltd, San Francisco, CA; Alan M Goffman Fine Art, New York, NY; Metropolitan Art Gallery, Los Angeles, CA; Professional Fine Arts Services, Inc, New York, NY

TITLE	PUBLISHER	PRINTER	DATE	MEDIUM	DIMENSION (PAPER SIZE) IN INCHES	TYPE OF PAPER	EDITION NUMBER	NO. OF COLORS	ORIGINAL OPENING PRICE	CURRENT RETAIL PRICE
SOLD OUT EDITIONS (RARE):										
Runaway	CFA	AA	1970	LC	26 X 20	AP	200		75	3800
The Artist at Work	CFA	AA	1970	EC	18 X 15	R/BFK	130		50	3500
Spelling Bee	CFA	AA	1971	LC	14 X 30	AP	200		75	6500
Circus	CFA	AA	1971	LC	20 X 26	AP	200		100	2650
Doctor and Boy	CFA	AA	1971	LC	30 X 24	AP	200		100	9400
Rocket Ship	CFA	AA	1971	LC	26 X 20	AP	200		100	3650

NORMAL ROCKWELL CONTINUED

TITLE	PUBLISHER	PRINTER	DATE	MEDIUM	DIMENSION (PAPER SIZE) IN INCHES	TYPE OF PAPER	EDITION NUMBER	NO. OF COLORS	ORIGINAL OPENING PRICE	CURRENT RETAIL PRICE
SOLD OUT EDITIONS (RARE):										
Welcome	CFA	AA	1971	LC	26 X 20	AP	200		100	3500
Blacksmith Shop	CFA	AA	1971	LC	14 X 30	AP	200		100	6300
Jerry	CFA	AA	1971	LC	26 X 20	AP	200		100	4700
Family Tree	CFA	AA	1971	LC	30 X 25	AP	200		100	5900
The House	CFA	AA	1971	LC	26 X 20	AP	200		100	3700
The Homecoming	CFA	AA	1971	LC	30 X 25	AP	200		100	3700
The Bridge	CFA	AA	1971	LC	20 X 26	AP	200		100	3100
Top of the World	CFA	AA	1971	LC	35 X 29	AP	200		100	4200
Aviary	CFA	AA	1971	LC	20 X 26	AP	200		100	4200
Barbershop Quartet	CFA	AA	1972	LC	30 X 24	AP	200		125	4200
Window Washer	CFA	AA	1972	LC	24 X 20	AP	200		125	4800
Outward Bound (Looking Out to Sea)	CFA	AA	1972	COL	35 X 29	AP	200		125	7900
Shuffelton's Barbershop	CFA	AA	1972	COL	35 X 28	AP	200		125	7400
Doctor and Doll	CFA	AA	1972	COL	35 X 29	AP	200		125	11900
Saying Grace	CFA	AA	1972	COL	35 X 29	AP	200		125	7400
Golden Rule	CFA	AA	1972	COL	35 X 29	AP	200			4400
Girl at Mirror	CFA	AA	1972	COL	33 X 27	AP	200		125	8400
Freedom from Fear	CFA	AA	1972	COL	35 X 29	AP	200		125	6400
Freedom from Want	CFA	AA	1972	COL	35 X 29	AP	200		125	6400
Freedom of Speech	CFA	AA	1972	COL	35 X 29	AP	200		125	6400
Freedom of Religion	CFA	AA	1972	COL	35 X 29	AP	200		125	6400
Spring Flowers	CFA	AA	1972	COL	33 X 27	AP	200		125	5200
Runaway	CFA	AA	1972	COL	32 X 28	AP	200		125	5700
The Critic	CFA	AA	1972	COL	32 X 28	AP	200		125	4650
Discovery	CFA	AA	1972	COL	32 X 28	AP	200		125	5900
Raleigh the Dog	CFA	AA	1972	COL	35 X 29	AP	200		125	3900
Marriage License	CFA	AA	1972	COL	32 X 28	AP	200		125	6900
Saturday People	CFA	AA	1972	COL	24 X 30	AP	200		125	3300
Moving Day	CFA	AA	1972	COL	24 X 30	AP	200		125	3900
County Agricultural Agent	CFA	AA	1973	COL	24 X 35	AP	200		150	3900
Gaiety Dance Team	CFA	AA	1973	COL	30 X 24	AP	200		150	4300
Music Hath Charms	CFA	AA	1973	COL	30 X 24	AP	200		150	4200
High Dive	CFA	AA	1973	COL	30 X 24	AP	200		150	3400
The Texan	CFA	AA	1973	COL	30 X 24	AP	200		150	3700
Wet Paint	CFA	AA	1973	COL	30 X 24	AP	200		150	3800
The Problem We All Live with	CFA	AA	1973	COL	31 X 44	AP	200		150	4500
Football Mascot	CFA	AA	1973	LC	26 X 20	AP	200		175	3700
Dressing Up (Pencil)	CFA	AA	1973	LC	26 X 20	AP	20		300	3700
Dressing Up (Ink)	CFA	AA	1973	LC	26 X 20	AP	60		350	4400
Children at Window	CFA	AA	1973	LC	26 X 20	AP	200		200	3600
Puppies	CFA	AA	1973	LC	20 X 26	AP	200		200	3700
Settling In	CFA	AA	1973	LC	20 X 26	AP	200		200	3600
The Inventor	CFA	AA	1973	LC	23 X 23	AP	200		200	4100
Three Farmers	CFA	AA	1973	LC	20 X 16	AP	200		200	3600
A Study for the Doctor's Office	CFA	AA	1974	LC	25 X 22	AP	200		200	6000
Lincoln	CFA	AA	1974	LC	26 X 20	AP	200		200	11400
Ichabod Crane	CFA	AA	1974	LC	20 X 26	AP	200		200	6700
At the Barber	CFA	AA	1974	LC	30 X 22	AP	200		200	4900
The Expected and Unexpected	CFA	AA	1974	LC	20 X 17	AP	200		200	3700
Safe and Sound	CFA	AA	1974	LC	17 X 20	AP	200		200	3800
Summer Stock	CFA	AA	1974	LC	27 X 21	AP	200		200	4900
Summer Stock/Japon	CFA	AA	1974	LC	27 X 21	JP	25		225	5000
Bookseller	CFA	AA	1974	LC	23 X 17	AP	200		200	2700
Bookseller/Japon	CFA	AA	1974	LC	23 X 17	JP	25		225	2750
The Teacher	CFA	AA	1974	LC	23 X 17	AP	200		200	3400
The Teacher/Japon	CFA	AA	1974	LC	23 X 17	JP	25		225	3500
A Day in the Life of a Boy	CFA	AA	1974	LC	25 X 22	AP	200		200	6200
A Day in the Life of a Boy/Japon	CFA	AA	1974	LC	25 X 22	JP	25		225	6500
The Big Top	CFA	AA	1973	LC	26 X 20	AP	198		200	2800
The Big Day	CFA	AA	1974	LC	29 X 21	AP	200		200	3400
Trumpeter	CFA	AA	1975	LC	27 X 21	AP	200		200	3900
Trumpeter/Japon	CFA	AA	1975	LC	27 X 21	JP	25		225	4100
Ticketseller	CFA	AA	1975	LC	27 X 21	AP	200		200	4200
Ticketseller/Japon	CFA	AA	1975	LC	27 X 21	JP	25		225	4400
Prescription	CFA	AA	1975	LC	26 X 21	AP	200		200	4900
Prescription/Japon	CFA	AA	1975	LC	26 X 21	JP	25		225	5000
See America First	CFA	AA	1975	LC	27 X 21	AP	200		200	5650
See America First/Japon	CFA	AA	1975	LC	27 X 21	AP	25		225	6100
The Schoolhouse	CFA	AA	1975	LC	15 X 18	AP	200		200	4500
The Schoolhouse/Japon	CFA	AA	1975	LC	15 X 18	JP	25		225	4650
Lobsterman	CFA	AA	1975	LC	28 X 21	AP	200		200	5500
Lobsterman/Japon	CFA	AA	1975	LC	28 X 21	JP	25		225	6000

NORMAN ROCKWELL CONTINUED

TITLE	PUBLISHER	PRINTER	DATE	MEDIUM	DIMENSION (PAPER SIZE) IN INCHES	TYPE OF PAPER	EDITION NUMBER	NO. OF COLORS	ORIGINAL OPENING PRICE	CURRENT RETAIL PRICE
SOLD OUT EDITIONS (RARE):										
Gossips	CFA	AA	1975	LC	25 X 22	AP	200		200	5000
Gossips/Japon	CFA	AA	1975	LC	25 X 22	JP	25		225	5100
Runaway	CFA	AA	1975	LC	26 X 20	AP	200		200	3650
The Big Day	CFA	AA	1975	LC	26 X 20	AP			200	3800
The Big Top	CFA	AA	1975	LC	26 X 20	AP	200		200	2800
Tom Sawyer Folio (Set of 8):									1500 SET	26500 SET
Church	CFA	AA	1976	LC	26 X 20	AP	200		200	3400
Smoking	CFA	AA	1976	LC	26 X 20	AP	200		200	3400
Cat	CFA	AA	1976	LC	26 X 20	AP	200		200	3400
Out of the Window	CFA	AA	1976	LC	26 X 20	AP	200		200	3400
White Washing	CFA	AA	1976	LC	26 X 20	AP	200		200	3400
Grotto	CFA	AA	1976	LC	26 X 20	AP	200		200	3400
Spanking	CFA	AA	1976	LC	26 X 20	AP	200		200	3400
Medicine	CFA	AA	1976	LC	26 X 20	AP	200		200	3400
Tom Sawyer Color Colotype Folio (Set of 8):									1000 SET	30000 SET
Church	CFA	AA	1976	LC/COL	26 X 20	AP	200		225	4000
Smoking	CFA	AA	1976	LC/COL	26 X 20	AP	200		225	4000
Cat	CFA	AA	1976	LC/COL	26 X 20	AP	200		225	4000
Out of the Window	CFA	AA	1976	LC/COL	26 X 20	AP	200		225	4000
White Washing	CFA	AA	1976	LC/COL	26 X 20	AP	200		225	4000
Grotto	CFA	AA	1976	LC/COL	26 X 20	AP	200		225	4000
Spanking	CFA	AA	1976	LC/COL	26 X 20	AP	200		225	4000
Medicine	CFA	AA	1976	LC/COL	26 X 20	AP	200		225	4000
Huck Finn Folio (Set of 8):										35000 SET
Then Miss Watson	CFA	AA	1976	LC	26 X 20	AP	200		250	4500
Jim Got Down on His Knees	CFA	AA	1976	LC	26 X 20	AP	200		250	4500
Miss Mary Jane	CFA	AA	1976	LC	26 X 20	AP	200		250	4500
My Hand Shook	CFA	AA	1976	LC	26 X 20	AP	200		250	4500
Your Eyes is Lookin'	CFA	AA	1976	LC	26 X 20	AP	200		250	4500
Then for Three Minutes	CFA	AA	1976	LC	26 X 20	AP	200		250	4500
There warn't No Harm	CFA	AA	1976	LC	26 X 20	AP	200		250	4500
When I Lit My Candle	CFA	AA	1976	LC	26 X 20	AP	200		250	4500
American Family Folio (Set of 5):										175000 SET
Teacher's Pet	CFA	AA	1976	LC	26 X 20	AP	200		300	3600
Fido's House	CFA	AA	1976	LC	26 X 20	AP	200		300	3600
Two O'Clock Feeding	CFA	AA	1976	LC	26 X 20	AP	200		300	3600
Debut	CFA	AA	1976	LC	26 X 20	AP	200		300	3600
Save Me	CFA	AA	1976	LC	26 X 20	AP	200		300	3600
Schools Days Folio (Set of 4):										14000 SET
Baseball	CFA	AA	1976	LC	26 X 20	AP	200			3600
Golf	CFA	AA	1976	LC	26 X 20	AP	200		300	3600
Studying	CFA	AA	1976	LC	26 X 20	AP	200		300	3600
Cheering	CFA	AA	1976	LC	26 X 20	AP	200		300	3600
Poor Richard's Almanac Folio (Set of 7):										24000 SET
Ben Franklin's Philadelphia	CFA	AA	1976	LC	20 X 26	AP	200		300	3600
The Drunkard	CFA	AA	1976	LC	26 X 20	AP	200		300	3600
Ben's Belles	CFA	AA	1976	LC	26 X 20	AP	200		300	3500
The Village Smithy	CFA	AA	1976	LC	26 X 20	AP	200		300	3500
Ye Old Print Shoppe	CFA	AA	1976	LC	26 X 20	AP	200		300	3500
The Golden Age	CFA	AA	1976	LC	26 X 20	AP	200		300	3500
The Royal Crown	CFA	AA	1976	LC	26 X 20	AP	200		300	3500
Four Season's Folio (Set of 4):									800 SET	13500 SET
Winter	CFA	AA	1976	LC	19 X 21	AP	200		225	3500
Spring	CFA	AA	1976	LC	19 X 21	AP	200		225	3500
Summer	CFA	AA	1976	LC	19 X 21	AP	200		225	3500
Autumn	CFA	AA	1976	LC	19 X 21	AP	200		225	3500
Four Seasons Folio/Japon (Set of 4):									850 SET	14000 SET
Winter/Japon	CFA	AA	1976	LC	19 X 21	AP	200		250	3600
Spring/Japon	CFA	AA	1976	LC	19 X 21	AP	200		250	3600
Summer/Japon	CFA	AA	1976	LC	19 X 21	AP	200		250	3600
Autumn/Japon	CFA	AA	1976	LC	19 X 21	AP	200		250	3600
American Marches Ahead	EEI	AE	1975	LC	20 X 36	AP	260		350	3200
Three Boys Fishing	EEI	AI	1975	COL	23 X 33	RP	260		350	5500
Colonial Sign Painter	FFI	AF	1975	LC	35 X 23	AP	260		700	6500
Rivals	EEI	AE	1975	LC	21 X 22	AP	260		375	6800
April Fool	EEI	AE	1976	COL	24 X 26	RP	260		400	8500
Buttercup	EEI	AE	1976	LC	21 X 24	JP	25		500	6500
Buttercup	EEI	AE	1976	LC	21 X 24	AP	260		450	6200
Puppy Love Portfolio	EEI	AE	1976	LC	20 X 22 EA	JP	26 EA		1700 SET	24000 SET
Puppy Love Portfolio	EEI	AE	1976	LC	20 X 22 EA	AP	260 EA		1500 SET	21000 SET
Charwomen	EEI	AE	1976	COL	25 X 32	RP	260		600	8500

NORMAN ROCKWELL CONTINUED

TITLE	PUBLISHER	PRINTER	DATE	MEDIUM	DIMENSION (PAPER SIZE) IN INCHES	TYPE OF PAPER	EDITION NUMBER	NO. OF COLORS	ORIGINAL OPENING PRICE	CURRENT RETAIL PRICE
SOLD OUT EDITIONS (RARE):										
Gilding the Eagle	EEI	AE	1976	LC	21 X 26	JP	25		650	5000
Gilding the Eagle	EEI	AE	1976	LC	21 X 26	AP	260		600	4800
Ben Franklin	EEI	AE	1976	LC	21 X 28	JP	25		850	5000
Ben Franklin	EEI	AE	1976	LC	21 X 28	AP	260		800	4800
Convention	EEI	AE	1976	COL	25 X 31	RP	260		600	4500
The Swing	EEI	AE	1976	LC	20 X 21	AP	260		650	6000
The Swing	EEI	AE	1976	COL	20 X 21	JP	25		600	5800
Top Hat and Tails	EEI	AE	1976	LC	28 X 34	AP	260		1000	9000
Racer	EEI	AE	1976	LC	24 X 30	JP	25		650	3500
Racer	EEI	AE	1976	LC	24 X 30	AP	260		600	3000
Football Hero	EEI	AE	1976	LC	21 X 27	JP	25		650	4000
Football Hero	EEI	AE	1976	LC	21 X 27	AP	260		600	3500
Extra Good Boys and Girls	EEI	AE	1976	LC	24 X 32	JP	25		1000	7000
Extra Good Boys and Girls	EEI	AE	1976	LC	24 X 32	AP	260		900	6800
She's My Baby	EEI	AE	1977	LC	23 X 31	JP	25		650	4000
She's My Baby	EEI	AE	1977	LC	23 X 31	AP	260		600	3500
Young Lincoln	EEI	AE	1977	LC	19 X 34	JP	14		1500	13000
Young Lincoln	EEI	AE	1977	LC	19 X 34	AP	260		1200	12000
Rejected Suitor	EEI	AE	1977	LC	21 X 26	JP	26		750	3800
Rejected Suitor	EEI	AE	1977	LC	21 X 26	AP	260		700	3500
Young Spooners	EEI	AE	1977	LC	21 X 28	JP	25		750	8000
Young Spooners	EEI	AE	1977	LC	21 X 28	AP	260		700	7500
Sports Portfolio	EEI	AE	1977	LC	20 X 25 EA	JP	25 EA		3200 SET	13000 SET
Sports Portfolio (Set 4)	EEI	AE	1977	LC	20 X 25 EA	AP	260 EA		3000 SET	12000 SET
Hayseed Critic	EEI	AE	1977	LC	24 X 27	JP	25		750	4800
Hayseed Critic	EEI	AE	1977	LC	24 X 27	AP	260		700	4500
Boy on Stilts	EEI	AE	1977	LC	24 X 31	JP	25		900	3800
Boy on Stilts	EEI	AE	1977	LC	24 X 31	AP	260		800	3500
Back from Camp	EEI	AE	1977	LC	21 X 27	JP	25		900	4000
Back from Camp	EEI	AE	1977	LC	21 X 27	AP	260		800	3500
Dreams of Long Ago	EEI	AE	1977	LC	24 X 32	JP	25		1100	8000
Dreams of Long Ago	EEI	AE	1977	LC	24 X 32	AP	260		1000	7500
Four Ages of Love	EEI	AE	1977	LC	21 X 22	JP	25		10200 SET	14500 SET
Four Ages of Love	EEI	AE	1977	LC	21 X 22	AP	260		10000 SET	13500 SET
Jester	EEI	AE	1977	LC	21 X 25	JP	25		900	3800
Jester	EEI	AE	1977	LC	21 X 25	AP	260		800	3600
After Christmas	EEI	AE	1977	LC	24 X 32	JP	25		900	5200
After Christmas	EEI	AE	1977	LC	24 X 22	AP	250		800	5000
Can't Wait	EEI	AE	1978	LC	24 X 22	JP	25		900	6000
Can't Wait	EEI	AE	1978	LC	24 X 30	AP	260		800	5500
Childs Surprise	EEI	AE	1978	LC	21 X 29	JP	25		1100	5000
Childs Surprise	EEI	AE	1978	LC	21 X 29	AP	260		1000	4800
Voyager	EEI	AE	1978	COL	25 X 33	RP	260		1000	9000
The Wind Up	EEI	AE	1978	LC	26 X 30	JP	25		1700	4500
The Wind Up	EEI	AE	1978	LC	26 X 30	AP	260		1500	4200
Catching the Big One	EEI	AE	1978	LC	27 X 35	JP	25		1200	4200
Catching the Big One	EEI	AE	1978	LC	27 X 35	AP	260		1000	4000
After the Prom	EEI	AE	1978	LC	24 X 27	JP	25		1700	5500
After the Prom	EEI	AE	1978	LC	24 X 27	AP	260		1500	5000
Horseshoe Forging Contest	EEI	AE	1978	COL	30 X 18	RP	260		3000	11000
Muggelton Stagecoach	EEI	AE	1978	LC	20 X 26	JP	25		2400	3800
Muggelton Stagecoach	EEI	AE	1978	LC	20 X 26	AP	260		2200	3500
First Airplane Ride	EEI	AE	1979	LC	21 X 26	JP	25		2400	5000
First Airplane Ride	EEI	AE	1979	LC	21 X 26	AP	260		2200	4700
Law Student	EEI	AE	1979	LC	24 X 33	JP	25		3400	6000
Law Student	EEI	AE	1979	LC	24 X 33	AP	260		3200	5700
Jazz It Up	EEI	AE	1979	LC	21 X 29	JP	25		2400	4000
Jazz It Up	EEI	AE	1979	LC	21 X 29	AP	260		2200	3700
School Walk	EEI	AE	1979	LC	25 X 21	JP	25		2200	5000
School Walk	EEI	AE	1979	LC	25 X 21	AP	260		2000	4500
Triple Self Portrait	EEI	AE	1979	LC	24 X 32	JP	25		5500	15000
Triple Self Portrait	EEI	AE	1979	LC	24 X 32	AP	260		5000	14500
Secrets	EEI	AE	1980	LC	21 X 27	JP	25		2200	4800
Secrets	EEI	AE	1980	LC	21 X 27	AP	260		2000	4500
The Connoisseur	EEI	AE	1980	COL	24 X 30	RP	260		6000	11000
Dreamboats	EEI	AE	1980	LC	24 X 30	JP	25		2200	4800
Dreamboats	EEI	AE	1980	LC	24 X 30	AP	260		2000	4400
Starstruck	EEI	AE	1980	LC	24 X 30	JP	25		2200	4800
Starstruck	EEI	AE	1980	LC	24 X 30	AP	260		2000	4600
Our Heritage	EEI	AE	1981	COL	25 X 33	RP	260		1500	5500
Under Sail	EEI	AE	1981	LC	19 X 25	JP	25		2200	3200
Under Sail	EEI	AE	1981	LC	19 X 25	AP	260		2000	3000

NORMAN ROCKWELL CONTINUED

TITLE	PUBLISHER	PRINTER	DATE	MEDIUM	DIMENSION (PAPER SIZE) IN INCHES	TYPE OF PAPER	EDITION NUMBER	NO. OF COLORS	ORIGINAL OPENING PRICE	CURRENT RETAIL PRICE
SOLD OUT EDITIONS (RARE):										
Fishing	EEI	AE	1981	LC	21 X 23	JP	25		2100	3800
Fishing	EEI	AE	1981	LC	21 X 23	AP	260		1900	3500
John Kennedy	EEI	AE	1982	LC	17 X 23	JP	25		2200	4000
John Kennedy	EEI	AE	1982	LC	17 X 23	AP	260		2000	3600
Stock Exchange	EEI	AE	1982	LC	21 X 29	JP	25		2500	3600
Stock Exchange	EEI	AE	1982	LC	21 X 29	AP	260		2200	3300
Ye Pipe & Bowl	EEI	AE	1983	LC	21 X 27	JP	25		2500	3300
Ye Pipe & Bowl	EEI	AE	1983	LC	21 X 27	AP	260		2300	3100

ANGEL PASCUAL RODRIGO (LA HERMANDAD PICTORICA)

BORN: Mallen, Spain; 1951
RECENT EXHIB: Salas del Palacio de Satago, Zaragoza, Spain, 1987
PRINTERS: La Poligrafa, SA, Barcelona, Spain (LP)
PUBLISHERS: Ediciones Poligrafa, SA, Barcelona, Spain (EdP)
GALLERIES: Galeria Joan Prats, New York, NY & Barcelona, Spain

TITLE	PUBLISHER	PRINTER	DATE	MEDIUM	DIMENSION (PAPER SIZE) IN INCHES	TYPE OF PAPER	EDITION NUMBER	NO. OF COLORS	ORIGINAL OPENING PRICE	CURRENT RETAIL PRICE
CURRENT EDITIONS:										
Los Largos Dias de Invierno	EdP	LP	1982	LC	22 X 30	GP	100	3	180	300
Lost Cause (Set of 3):									450 SET	800 SET
Una Cancion en el Regreso	EdP	LP	1985	LC	22 X 30	GP	100		180	300
Con la Serena Atencion de un Felino	EdP	LP	1985	LC	22 X 30	GP	100	5	180	300
Desde el Refugio Derrama Rayos de Victoria	EdP	LP	1985	LC	22 X 30	GP	100	4	180	300
Como un Eco (Like an Echo) (Set of 4):									800 SET	800 SET
The Memory Remains among the Indiana Woods	EdP	LP	1987	LC	11 X 29	GP	100	4	200	250
Manana Seguire Recordando	EdP	LP	1987	LC	11 X 29	GP	100	4	200	250
Sa Dona de S'Auba	EdP	LP	1987	LC	22 X 29	GP	100		250	300
. . . amb Flaires de Formentor	EdP	LP	1987	LC	22 X 29	GP	100	6	250	300
El Paso del Angel Pascual (Set of 7):									2000 SET	2000 SET
E Come la Mia Faccia si Distese	EdP	LP	1990	LC	21 X 28	GP	100	4	300	300
Un Splendor Mi Squarcio'l Velo del Senno	EdP	LP	1990	LC	21 X 28	GP	100	4	300	300
E Come arivi Grandi si Convenne ver lo Fiumerea	EdP	LP	1990	LC	21 X 28	GP	100	4	300	300
Quililay	EdP	LP	1990	LC	22 X 29	GP	100	3	300	300
Ezin dut Gehigo	EdP	LP	1990	LC	29 X 11	GP	100	5	250	250
. . . Zloela Zirudien	EdP	LP	1990	LC	29 X 11	GP	100	5	250	250
Bocklins Odysseus in der trapa	EdP	LP	1990	LC	28 X 39	GP	100	8	450	450

OSCAR RODRIGUEZ

BORN: Mexico; May 14, 1943
EDUCATION: Frente de Artes Plasticas de Mexico, 1957; La Esmeralda, Escurla Nacional de Pintura y Escultura, Inst de Bellas Artes, Mexico, 1965–67; Univ Benito Juarez, Oaxaca, Mexico, Engraving Workshop, 1972; Pratt Graphics Center, NY, Lithography, 1972
COLLECTIONS: Simon Fraser Univ, Vancouver, Canada; Casa de las Once Patios, Patzcuaro, Michoacan, Mexico; Univ Benito Juarez, Oaxaca, Mexico; La Casa del Lago, Univ Autonoma Nacional de Mexico; Vassar Col, Poughkeepsie, NY

PRINTERS: Artist (ART)
PUBLISHERS: EDAF Salas de Arte, Madrid, Spain (EDAF); Galeria ASKA, Mexico City, Mexico (ASKA); Originales Para Colectionistas, Mexico City, Mexico (OPC); Artist (ART)
GALLERIES: Galeria Uno, Puerto Vallarta, Jalisco, Mexico; EDAF Salas de Arte, Madrid, Spain; Originales Para Colectionistas, Mexico City, Mexico
MAILING ADDRESS: Edificio Condesa, Calle Matehuala, Entrada H, Depto 2, Mexico 11, DF, Mexico

TITLE	PUBLISHER	PRINTER	DATE	MEDIUM	DIMENSION (PAPER SIZE) IN INCHES	TYPE OF PAPER	EDITION NUMBER	NO. OF COLORS	ORIGINAL OPENING PRICE	CURRENT RETAIL PRICE
SOLD OUT EDITIONS (RARE):										
Espejismos: Camino Naciente	OPC	ART	1974	AC/ENG	25 X 18		50	3	100	600
Calbalgata: Entre Montes y Cielos	OPC	ART	1974	AC/ENG	25 X 18		50	3	100	600
Calbalgata: Te Regalo Mi Paisajes	OPC	ART	1974	AC/ENG	25 X 18		50	3	100	600
Espejismos: Pie de la Cuesta	OPC	ART	1975	SP	30 X 18		50	5	100	600
Espejismos: El Paso del Verde	OPC	ART	1975	SP	30 X 18		50	4	100	600
Espejismos: Vista Nocturna	OPC	ART	1975	SP	34 X 21		50	4	100	600
El Borracho	ART	ART	1976	MEZ	8 X 8		30	4	50	300
El Gran Cocinero	ART	ART	1976	AC/MEZ	11 X 8		30	3	50	300
Las Flores del Mal: XXIV	EDAF	ART	1979	SP	24 X 18		125	7	200	400

The print market has become very selective. For the first time since we published the first edition of The Printworld Directory in 1982, the prices of prints have been greatly reduced and greatly increased for the same artists by the most reputable and established print publishers. Check the fifth edition to understand the movement.

OSCAR RODRIGUEZ CONTINUED

TITLE	PUBLISHER	PRINTER	DATE	MEDIUM	DIMENSION (PAPER SIZE) IN INCHES	TYPE OF PAPER	EDITION NUMBER	NO. OF COLORS	ORIGINAL OPENING PRICE	CURRENT RETAIL PRICE
SOLD OUT EDITIONS (RARE):										
Las Flores del Mal: Un Fantasma	EDAF	ART	1979	SP	24 X 18		125	5	200	400
Las Flores del Mal: El Aparecido	EDAF	ART	1979	SP	24 X 18		125	6	200	400
Las Flores del Mal: XXIV	EDAF	ART	1979	SP/MM	24 X 18		25	12	400	800
Las Flores del Mal: Un Fantasma	EDAF	ART	1979	SP/MM	24 X 18		25	10	400	800
Las Flores del Mal: El Aparecido	EDAF	ART	1979	SP/MM	24 X 18		25	11	400	800
Necktie: The Flirt (2 Series)		ART	1979	SP	21 X 5		12	5	200	400
La Rosa es una Rosa	ASKA	ART	1979	AC/MEZ	14 X 18		50	5	200	400
Sin Limite	ASKA	ART	1979	AC/MEZ	14 X 18		50	4	200	400
La Lavandera	ASKA	ART	1980	AC/ENG/MEZ	12 X 16		30	5	200	400

P J ROGERS

BORN: Rochester, NY
EDUCATION: Wells Col, Aurora, NY, BA, 1947; Univ of Buffalo, NY, 1954; Studied with Robert Brackman, Art Students League, NY: Studied with Victor Hammer, Printer; Fine Art Acad, Vienna, Austria
TEACHING: Instr, Painting, Buffalo Mus of Science, NY, 1955; Instr, Arts & Crafts, Dept of Spec Programs, Univ of Akron, OH, 1958
AWARDS: Top Graphic Award, Cleveland Mus, OH, 1976; Boston Printmakers Award, Boston, MA, 1985–86; Ohio Arts Coun Fel, Ind Artists, 1979–80, 1986–87
RECENT EXHIB: Butler Inst of Am Art, Youngstown, OH, 1988
COLLECTIONS: Cleveland Art Mus, OH; Rockford Col, IL; Dulin Gallery of Art, Knoxville, TN; Butler Inst of Am Art, Youngstown, OH; Portland Art Mus, OR
PRINTERS: Artist (ART)
PUBLISHERS: Artist (ART)
GALLERIES: Toni Birkhead Gallery, Cincinnati, OH; Brenda Kroos Gallery, Columbus, OH; Miriam Perlman, Chicago, IL; Arnold Klein Gallery, Royal Oak, MI; Bonfoey Company, Cleveland, OH; Collectors Gallery, Columbus Mus of Art, OH
MAILING ADDRESS: 954 Hereford Dr, Akron, OH 44303

TITLE	PUBLISHER	PRINTER	DATE	MEDIUM	DIMENSION (PAPER SIZE) IN INCHES	TYPE OF PAPER	EDITION NUMBER	NO. OF COLORS	ORIGINAL OPENING PRICE	CURRENT RETAIL PRICE
CURRENT EDITIONS:										
Passage VIII	ART	ART	1984	EB/AC	22 X 30	DE	20	1	250	300
Waiting II	ART	ART	1985	EB/AC	22 X 30	DE	20	1	200	250
After Dinner Games IV	ART	ART	1985	EB/AC	22 X 30	DE	20	1	275	325

TIM ROLLINS + KOS*

BORN: Pittsfield, MA; 1955
EDUCATION: Sch of Visual Arts, NY, BFA, 1978; New York Univ, NY, MA, 1980
AWARDS: Expansion Arts Grant, 1985, 86; Nat Endowment for the Arts, Visual Arts Fel, 1986; Artists-In-Education Grant, 1983,84,86; Special Art Services Grant, 1988; New York State Council for the Arts, Joseph Beuys Prize, 1989
RECENT EXHIB: Dia Art found, NY, 1990; Wadsworth Atheneum, Hartford, CT, 1990; Mus fur Gegenwartskunst, Basel, Switzerland, 1990; Mus of Contemp Art, Los Angeles, CA, 1990; Cleveland Center for Contemp Art, OH, 1991; Bucknell Univ, Lewisburg, PA, 1991
COLLECTIONS: Mus of Mod Art, NY; Philadelphia Mus of Art, PA; Mint Mus of Art, Charlotte, NC
PRINTERS: Crown Point Press, San Francisco, CA (CPP)
PUBLISHERS: Crown Point Press, San Francisco, CA (CPP)
GALLERIES: Crown Point Press, New York, NY & San Francisco, CA; Barbara Krakow Gallery, Boston, MA; Richard/Bennett Gallery, Los Angeles, CA; Trans Avant-Garde Gallery, San Francisco, CA; Andrea Ruggieri Gallery, Wash, DC; Rhona Hoffman Gallery, Chicago, IL; Editions Schellmann, New York, NY; Jay Gorney Mod Art, New York, NY
MAILING ADDRESS: c/o Art & Knowledge Workshop, 890 Garrison Ave, Bronx, NY 10474

*KOS—Kids of Survival

TITLE	PUBLISHER	PRINTER	DATE	MEDIUM	DIMENSION (PAPER SIZE) IN INCHES	TYPE OF PAPER	EDITION NUMBER	NO. OF COLORS	ORIGINAL OPENING PRICE	CURRENT RETAIL PRICE
CURRENT EDITIONS:										
The Temptation of St. Antony I–XIV (Set of 14)	CPP	CPP	1989	EB/AB/SB	22 X 15 FA		30 EA	1 EA	18000 SET 1350 EA	18000 SET 1350 EA
The Temptation of St. Antony XXXV—The Queen of Sheba	CPP	CPP	1990	EB/SG/PHG/CC	50 X 30		16	1	2000	2000
The Temptation of St. Antony XV–XXXIV—The Solitaries (Series of 20)	CPP	CPP	1990	EB/A/SG/CC	16 X 12 EA		15 EA	1 EA	700 EA	700 EA
The Temptation of St. Antony XXXVI—The Sun (Series of 35 Xerographic Color Spitbite Aquatint Etchings with Blood & Vodka on Chiné Collé)	CPP	CPP	1990	EB/AC/CC	24 X 19 EA		35 EA		1500 EA	1500 EA

The retail prices of the 100,000 limited edition prints quoted in this directory are subject to change. Print publishers, artists and galleries were the direct sources for these quotations. Prices in the secondary market listed as "Sold Out Editions (Rare)" indicate that the publisher has a limited supply of that print or that the print is difficult to locate in the galleries.

The Printworld Directory is accepting new applications for the seventh edition. Approximately 300 new artists will be accepted. Please use the two forms provided in the back section of this directory to submit biographical data and documentation of prints. Edition number of each print must not exceed 500 and the retail price must be $100 or more.

CLARE CAMILLE ROMANO

BORN: Palisade, NJ; 1922
EDUCATION: Cooper Union Sch of Art, NY, 1939–43; Ecole Beaux-Arts, Fontainbleau, France, 1949; Inst Statale Arte, Florence, Italy
TEACHING: Instr, Printmaking, New Sch for Social Research, NY, 1960–73; Adj Assoc Prof, Printmaking, Pratt Graphic Arts Center, NY, 1963 to present
AWARDS: Louis Comfort Tiffany Grant, 1952; Fulbright Fel, 1958; Citation for Achievement, Cooper Union Sch of Art, NY, 1966; Distinguished Teacher Award, Pratt Inst, NY, 1979; New Jersey State Council on the Arts Grant, 1980
COLLECTIONS: Mus of Mod Art, NY; Metropolitan Mus of Art, NY; Whitney Mus of Am Art, NY; New Jersey State Mus, Trenton, NJ; Philadelphia Mus of Art, PA; Nat Coll of Fine Art, Wash, DC; Library of Congress, Wash, DC
PRINTERS: Katarina Izzo (KI); Clare Romano Studio (CRS)
PUBLISHERS: Artist (ART); Associated Am Artists, NY (AAA)
GALLERIES: Associated American Artists, New York, NY; Jane Haslem Gallery, Washington, DC; Malton Gallery, Cincinnati, OH; Benton Gallery, Southampton, NY
MAILING ADDRESS: PO Box 1122, Madison Square Station, New York, NY 10159; Dept of Visual Arts Pratt Inst, Brooklyn, NY 11205

TITLE	PUBLISHER	PRINTER	DATE	MEDIUM	DIMENSION (PAPER SIZE) IN INCHES	TYPE OF PAPER	EDITION NUMBER	NO. OF COLORS	ORIGINAL OPENING PRICE	CURRENT RETAIL PRICE
SOLD OUT EDITIONS (RARE):										
Grand Canyon	ART	CRS	1976	COLG	22 X 30	AP	50	10	200	600
Golden Canyon	MPC	CRS	1978	COLG	15 DIA	AP	100	8	250	450
CURRENT EDITIONS:										
Silver Canyon	ART	CRS	1976	COLG	22 X 30	AP	150	8	200	300
River Canyon	ART	CRS	1976	COLG	22 X 30	AP	150	4	200	300
Canyon Morning	ART	CRS	1980	COLG	25 X 30	AP	150	8	250	450
Desert Evening	ART	CRS	1981	COLG	22 X 30	AP	150	12	250	450
Red Canyon	AAA	KI/CRS	1982	COLG	22 X 30	AP/B	150	8	290	450
Tidal Patterns	ART	CRS	1986	COLG	30 X 22	AP	150	8	450	450
Tidal Ribbons	ART	CRS	1986	COLG	30 X 22	AP	100	11	450	450
Big Falls	ART	CRS	1986	COLG/WC	60 X 22	AP	150	8	950	950

FRANK ROMERO

RECENT EXHIB: Robert Berman Gallery, Santa Monica, CA, 1987; Lizardi-Harp Gallery, Pasadena, CA, 1988,89
PRINTERS: Bill Lagatutta, Albuquerque, NM (BL); Carolyn Muskat, Albuquerque, NM (CM); Tamarind Inst, Albuquerque, NM (TI)
PUBLISHERS: Tamarind Inst, Albuquerque, NM (TI)
GALLERIES: Robert Berman Gallery, Santa Monica, CA; Tamarind Institute, Albuquerque, NM; Lizardi-Harp Gallery, Pasadena, CA

Frank Romero
Chrysler
Courtesy Tamarind Institute

TITLE	PUBLISHER	PRINTER	DATE	MEDIUM	DIMENSION (PAPER SIZE) IN INCHES	TYPE OF PAPER	EDITION NUMBER	NO. OF COLORS	ORIGINAL OPENING PRICE	CURRENT RETAIL PRICE
CURRENT EDITIONS:										
Chevy	TI	ART/BL/TI	1988	LC					700	800
Calavera	TI	ART/BL/TI	1988	LC/CC	15 X 11	KIT/R-BER-T	20	3	250	400
My Dream of Reality	TI	ART/BL/TI	1988	LC	19 X 30	GE	30	5	350	800
Tierra Blanca	TI	ART/BL/TI	1988	LC	23 X 30	GE/AP- B	22	4	350	400
Carro de Muerte	TI	ART/CM/TI	1988	MON	30 X 38 EA	SOM/W	1 EA	Multi	800 EA	900 EA
Chrysler	TI	ART/CM/TI	1988	MON	30 X 44 EA	R/BFK/T	1 EA	Multi	700 EA	800 EA
Nudes	TI	ART/CM/TI	1988	MON	30 X 38 EA	SOM/W	1 EA	Multi	700 EA	800 EA
Run-around Sue	TI	ART/CM/TI	1988	MON	30 X 38 EA	SOM/W	1 EA	Multi	700 EA	800 EA
Still Life	TI	ART/CM/TI	1988	MON	30 X 38 EA	SOM/W	1 EA	Multi	1200 EA	1400 EA

JUAN ROMERO

BORN: Seville, Spain; 1932
EDUCATION: Seville Sch of Fine Arts, Spain, 1956
AWARDS: Prix de la Critique, Paris, France, 1967; Gold Medal, Graphic Art, Florence, Italy, 1972; Second Prize, Graphics, Alexandria, Egypt, 1976
COLLECTIONS: Mus of Contemp Art, Seville, Spain; Mus of Abstract Art, Cvenca, Spain; Mus de la Peau duLyon, Zurich, Switzerland; Baltimore Mus of Fine Arts, MD; Spanish Mus of Contemp Art, Madrid, Spain; Nat Ctr of Contemp Art, Paris, France; Uffizi Mus Library, Florence, Italy
PUBLISHERS: Edmund Newman, Inc, Swampscott, MA (EN)
GALLERIES: Gallery Studio 53, New York, NY; Galeria Rafael Ortiz, Seville, Spain

TITLE	PUBLISHER	PRINTER	DATE	MEDIUM	DIMENSION (PAPER SIZE) IN INCHES	TYPE OF PAPER	EDITION NUMBER	NO. OF COLORS	ORIGINAL OPENING PRICE	CURRENT RETAIL PRICE
SOLD OUT EDITIONS (RARE):										
Buenas Dias, Satellite Amigo Mio	EN	CC	1979	SP	38 X 29	AP	300		300	700
Thankful Blossom II	EN	CC	1979	SP	32 X 32	AP	300		300	700
Luna Park	EN	CC	1979	SP	39 X 29	AP	300		300	650

JUAN ROMERO CONTINUED

TITLE	PUBLISHER	PRINTER	DATE	MEDIUM	DIMENSION (PAPER SIZE) IN INCHES	TYPE OF PAPER	EDITION NUMBER	NO. OF COLORS	ORIGINAL OPENING PRICE	CURRENT RETAIL PRICE
SOLD OUT EDITIONS (RARE):										
Spring Tree	EN	CC	1980	SP	39 X 30	AP	300		300	650
CURRENT EDITIONS:										
Inhabited Tree	EN	AL	1980	LC	28 X 20	AP	275		340	400
Inhabited Tree	EN	AL	1980	LC	28 X 20	JP	75		370	425
The Enchanged Moon	EN	CC	1980	SP	31 X 31	AP	300		375	650
The Joyous Boat	EN	CC	1980	SP	26 X 32	AP	300		375	525
Le Grand Bouquet	EN	CC	1980	SP	27 X 22	AP	300		375	525
Summer Tree	EN	CC	1981	SP	39 X 29	AP	300		375	525
Le Corrida	EN	CC	1981	SP	33 X 27	AP	300		400	550
Conversation Sous un Noyer	EN	AL	1981	LC	20 X 26	AP	275		340	450
Conversation Sous un Noyer	EN	AL	1981	LC	20 X 26	JP	75		370	450
Alice in Wonderland	EN	CC	1982	SP		AP	300		450	525
The Birdkeeper	EN	CC	1982	SP		AP	300		425	500

BARBARA ROMNEY

BORN: Mill Valley, CA; January 4, 1926
EDUCATION: Pasadena Jr Col, CA
COLLECTIONS: Northern Virginia Community Col, Annandale, VA; US Dept of State, Wash, DC
PRINTERS: Artist (ART)
PUBLISHERS: Artist (ART)
GALLERIES: Hank Baum Graphics Gallery, San Francisco, CA; Printmakers Inc, Alexandria, VA
MAILING ADDRESS: 4105 Sulgrave Dr, Alexandria, VA 22309

TITLE	PUBLISHER	PRINTER	DATE	MEDIUM	DIMENSION (PAPER SIZE) IN INCHES	TYPE OF PAPER	EDITION NUMBER	NO. OF COLORS	ORIGINAL OPENING PRICE	CURRENT RETAIL PRICE
SOLD OUT EDITIONS (RARE):										
California Beach Rocks	ART	ART	1981	SP	22 X 30	AP	25	1	125	200
Pebbles	ART	ART	1981	SP	22 X 30	AP	25	1	125	200
Rocks and Reflections	ART	ART	1981	SP	18 X 26	AP	25	1	75	175
Pond Rocks I, II	ART	ART	1981	SP	18 X 26 EA	AP	25 EA	1 EA	75 EA	175 EA

WILLIAM RONALD

BORN: Stratford, Canada; August 13, 1926; US Citizen
EDUCATION: Ontario Col of Art, Can, 1951
TEACHING: York Univ, Toronto, ON, Can, 1966
AWARDS: Nat Award, Can Sect, Int Guggenheim Awards, 1956; Award, Nat Gallery, Can, 1957
COLLECTIONS: Mus of Mod Art, NY; Guggenheim Mus of Art, NY; Whitney Mus of Am Art, NY; Brooklyn Mus, NY; Hirshhorn Mus, Wash, DC; Nelson A Rockefeller Coll, NY; David Rockefeller Coll, NY; Art Inst of Chicago, IL; Albright-Knox Art Gallery, Buffalo, NY; Art Gallery of Ontario, Toronto, Can; Nat Gallery of Canada, Ottawa, Can; Carnegie Inst, Pittsburgh, PA; Montreal Mus of Fine Arts, Montreal, Can; Gallery of Mod Art, WA; Baltimore Mus, MD; Princeton Univ Mus, NJ
PRINTERS: Sword Street Press, Ltd, Toronto, Can (SSP)
PUBLISHERS: Sword Street Press Ltd, Toronto, Can (SSP)
GALLERIES: Isaacs Gallery, Toronto, Can

TITLE	PUBLISHER	PRINTER	DATE	MEDIUM	DIMENSION (PAPER SIZE) IN INCHES	TYPE OF PAPER	EDITION NUMBER	NO. OF COLORS	ORIGINAL OPENING PRICE	CURRENT RETAIL PRICE
SOLD OUT EDITIONS (RARE):										
Mrs Stickney's Orchard	SSP	SSP	1981	LC	34 X 30	HMP	75	2	600	900
Summer Holidays	SSP	SSP	1981	LC	34 X 30	HMP	75	3	600	900
Blues for Red	SSP	SSP	1981	LC	30 X 34	HMP	75	3	600	900
Garafraxa Tar Strip	SSP	SSP	1981	LC	34 X 30	HMP	75	2	600	900
St David's Bride	SSP	SSP	1981	LC	34 X 30	HMP	75	1	600	900

CHRISTINE ROSAMOND

BORN: Vallejo, CA; 1947
EDUCATION: Univ of California, Los Angeles, CA
PRINTERS: American Atelier, NY (AA)
PUBLISHERS: Circle Fine Art, Chicago, IL (CFA)
GALLERIES: Circle Galleries, Chicago, IL & New York, NY & San Diego, CA & San Francisco, CA & Northbrook, IL & Pittsburgh, PA & Houston, TX & Soho, NY & Chicago, IL & Scottsdale, AZ & Beverly Hills, CA & Costa Mesa, CA & Sherman Oaks, CA & Honolulu, HI & Palm Beach, FL & New Orleans, LA & Las Vegas, NV & Seattle, WA

TITLE	PUBLISHER	PRINTER	DATE	MEDIUM	DIMENSION (PAPER SIZE) IN INCHES	TYPE OF PAPER	EDITION NUMBER	NO. OF COLORS	ORIGINAL OPENING PRICE	CURRENT RETAIL PRICE
SOLD OUT EDITIONS (RARE):										
Autumn	CFA	AA	1974	LC	34 X 24	AP	275		150	950
Contemplation	CFA	AA	1974	LC	33 X 24	AP	300		150	700
Tristesse	CFA	AA	1974	LC/EMB	27 X 20	AP	300		150	750
Victoria	CFA	AA	1974	LC	33 X 24	AP	300		150	1050
Dawn	CFA	AA	1974	LC/EMB	34 X 24	AP	300		150	650
Dawn (Deluxe)	CFA	AA	1974	LC/EMB	34 X 24	RP	10		200	700

MEL ROSAS

BORN: Des Moines, IA; June 1, 1950
EDUCATION: Drake Univ, Des Moines, IA, BFA, 1972; Tyler Sch of Art, Temple Univ, Phila, PA, MFA, 1975
TEACHING: Univ of Calgary, Alta, Canada, 1975–76; Cranbrook Acad of Art, Bloomfield Hills, MI, 1981; Wayne State Univ, Detroit, MI, 1975 to present
AWARDS: Michigan Council for the Arts, Creative Artists Grants, 1981,84,87; Faculty Research Grants, Wayne State Univ, Detroit, MI, 1987,90
COLLECTIONS: Detroit Inst of Art, MI; Carnegie-Mellon Inst, Pittsburgh, PA; Cleveland County Council, Middlesbrough, England; Arkansas Art Center, Little Rock, AR; Col of the Siskiyous, Weed, CA; Henry Ford Com Col, Dearborn, MI; Univ of Iowa, Iowa City, IA; Nat Mus of Am Art, Smithsonian Inst, Wash, DC; Dulin Gallery of Art, Knoxville, TN; Alberta Art Found, Edmonton, Alta, Canada; Univ of Calgary, Alta, Canada
PRINTERS: Patrick Surgalski, Royal Oak, MI (PS); Norman Stewart, Bloomfield Hills, MI (NS); Mantissa Press, Royal Oak, MI (MP)
PUBLISHERS: Stewart & Stewart, Bloomfield Hills, MI (S-S)
GALLERIES: Maxwell Davidson Gallery, New York, NY
MAILING ADDRESS: 2515 Rochester Rd, Royal Oak, MI 48073

TITLE	PUBLISHER	PRINTER	DATE	MEDIUM	DIMENSION (PAPER SIZE) IN INCHES	TYPE OF PAPER	EDITION NUMBER	NO. OF COLORS	ORIGINAL OPENING PRICE	CURRENT RETAIL PRICE
CURRENT EDITIONS:										
Vanity	S-S	PS/NS/MP	1981	LB	22 X 30	AC/W	50	1	500	1000

KAY ROSEN

EDUCATION: Newcomb Col, Tulane Univ, New Orleans, LA, BA; Northwestern Univ, Evanston, IL
TEACHING: Vis Artist, Sch of Art Inst of Chicago, IL, 1988; Lectr, Inter-Arts, Columbia Col, Chicago, IL, 1989
AWARDS: Nat Endowment for the Arts, Visual Arts Grants, 1987,89; AVA Visual Arts Award, 1990
RECENT EXHIB: Cleveland Center of Contemp Art, OH, 1990; Milwaukee Art Mus, WI, 1990; Witte de With Center for Contemp Art, Rotterdam, The Netherlands, 1990; Victoria Miro Gallery, London, England, 1990; Hirshhorn Mus, Wash, DC, 1991; Feature Gallery, NY, 1987,88,89,90,91,92
PRINTERS: Julie Crossen, Cincinnati, OH (JC); Mark Cowgill, Cincinnati, OH (MC); Mark Patsfall Graphics, Cincinnati, OH (MPG); Cincinnati Screen Process, OH (CSP)
PUBLISHERS: Volatile, Cincinnati, OH (VOL); Feature, NY (FEA)
GALLERIES: Feature, New York, NY; Laura Carpenter Fine Art, New York, NY; Volatile, Cincinnati, OH
MAILING ADDRESS: 6926 Indian Boundary, Gary, IN 46403

TITLE	PUBLISHER	PRINTER	DATE	MEDIUM	DIMENSION (PAPER SIZE) IN INCHES	TYPE OF PAPER	EDITION NUMBER	NO. OF COLORS	ORIGINAL OPENING PRICE	CURRENT RETAIL PRICE
CURRENT EDITIONS:										
Lists (Set of 4)	VOL/FEA	CSP	1990	SP	30 X 23 EA	AP88	25 EA	1 EA	1250 SET	1500 SET
The Man	VOL	JC/MC/MPG	1991	PH/EB	26 X 20	R/BFK	32	1	600	600
The Ed Prints Portfolio	VOL	JC/MC/MPG	1992	LC/SP	14 X 10 EA	MAG	30 EA		2000 SET	2000 SET

JAY ROSENBLUM

BORN: New York, NY; October 12, 1933
EDUCATION: Pratt Inst, Brooklyn NY, with Richard Lindner; Bard Col, NY, BA, 1955, with Louis Schanke; Cranbrook Acad of Art, Bloomfield Hills, MI, MFA, 1956, with Fred Mitchell
TEACHING: Instr, Painting, YMHA, NY, 1965 to present; Adj Lectr, Painting, Queensboro Com Col, NY, 1969 to present; Adj Lectr, Painting, Lehman Col, NY, 1971 to present; Adj Lectr, Sch of Visual Arts, NY, 1978 to present
AWARDS: Carlos Lopez Mem Prize, Painting, Detroit Inst of Art, IL, 1956; Larry Aldrich Award, Painter of the year, 1970; City Walls, Inc Grant, 1972
COLLECTIONS: Whitney Mus of Am Art, NY; Corcoran Gallery, Wash, DC; Vassar Col Mus, Poughkeepsie, NY; Neuberger Mus Purchase, NY; Larry Aldrich Mus of Contemp Art, Ridgefield, CT; Univ of North Carolina, Greensboro, NC; Bard Col Mus, NY; Albright-Knox Art Gallery, Buffalo, NY
PRINTERS: John Nichols, NY (JN); Artist (ART)
PUBLISHERS: London Arts, Inc. Detroit, MI (LAI); Brooke Alexander, Inc, NY (BAI); John Nichols, NY (JN); Artist (ART)
GALLERIES: Brooke Alexander, Inc, New York, NY; Allan Stone Gallery, New York, NY; Jean Lumbard Fine Arts, New York, NY
MAILING ADDRESS: 502 E 11th St, New York, NY 10009

TITLE	PUBLISHER	PRINTER	DATE	MEDIUM	DIMENSION (PAPER SIZE) IN INCHES	TYPE OF PAPER	EDITION NUMBER	NO. OF COLORS	ORIGINAL OPENING PRICE	CURRENT RETAIL PRICE
SOLD OUT EDITIONS (RARE):										
Yellow's Choice	BAI	ART	1974	PO	25 X 37	STP	15	12	200	750
Aureola	BAI		1976	PO	8 X 10	STP	75		200	600
Ion II	BAI		1976	PO	8 X 10	STP	75		200	600
Red Top III	BAI		1976	PO	8 X 10	STP	75		200	600
Sherwood III	ART	ART	1978	PO	28 X 36	STP	43		200	350
Red Field	ART	ART	1978	PO	21 X 39	STP	42		200	350
Yellow Field	ART	ART	1978	PO	21 X 38	STP	42		200	350
Chorale III	ART	ART	1978	PO	20 X 30	STP	60		140	300
Aurora V	BAI	ART	1978	PO	34 X 62	STP	43		550	700
Tangent	BAI	ART	1978	PO	31 X 43	STP	43		350	500
Green Field	BAI	ART	1978	PO	21 X 39	STP	42		250	400
Seagirt	BAI	ART	1978	PO	21 X 39	STP	43		250	400
Cornith III	ART	ART	1978	PO	22 X 30	STP	43		150	300
Grove #1	LAI	ART	1979	HC/SP	24 X 42	STP	300	5	500	600

IRWIN ROSENHOUSE

BORN: Chicago, IL; March 1, 1929
EDUCATION: Cooper Union, NY, BFA, 1978
TEACHING: Mus of Mod Art Educ Ctr, NY, 1968–70; Brooklyn Col, NY, 1972; Nassau Community Col, NY, 1973 to present
AWARDS: Graphics Award, Louis Comfort Tiffany Found, 1957; Hartford Found, 1959–61

IRWIN ROSENHOUSE CONTINUED

COLLECTIONS: Metropolitan Mus of Art, New York, NY; Cooper Union Mus, NY; Brooklyn Col, NY; New York Public Library, NY; Everhart Mus, PA

PRINTERS: Desjobert, Paris, France (D); Artist (ART)
PUBLISHERS: New York Graphic Society, Greenwich, CT (NYG); Artist (ART)
MAILING ADDRESS: 256 Mott St, New York, NY 10012

TITLE	PUBLISHER	PRINTER	DATE	MEDIUM	DIMENSION (PAPER SIZE) IN INCHES	TYPE OF PAPER	EDITION NUMBER	NO. OF COLORS	ORIGINAL OPENING PRICE	CURRENT RETAIL PRICE
CURRENT EDITIONS:										
Music Lesson	ART	ART	1980	LC	16 X 22	STR	100	3	200	300
Manitou at Midnight	ART	ART	1980	SP	18 X 24	STR	100	7	200	300
Bird Watchers	ART	ART	1980	EC	16 X 20	STR	100	3	200	300
The Lake at Morning	ART	ART	1981	SP	18 X 26	STR	100	7	250	300
The Lake at Night	ART	ART	1981	SP	18 X 26	STR	100	7	250	300
To the Lake	ART	ART	1982	LC	18 X 26	STR	100	4	200	250
Music Lovers	ART	ART	1982	EC	16 X 20	AP	100	2	200	250

CHARLES ROSS

BORN: Philadelphia, PA; December 7, 1937
EDUCATION: Univ of California, Berkeley, CA, AB, 1960, MA, 1962
TEACHING: Instr, Univ of California, Berkeley, CA, 1962,65; Instr, Sch of Visual Arts, NY, 1967,70,71; Univ of Utah, Salt Lake City, UT, 1972-74
AWARDS: Am Inst of Graphic Arts Award, 1976
COLLECTIONS: Whitney Mus of Am Art, NY; Univ of California Art Mus, Berkeley, CA; Univ of Pennsylvania, Phila, PA; Indianapolis Mus of Art, IN; Nelson Art Gallery, Kansas City, MO
PRINTERS: John Nichols, NY (JN)
PUBLISHERS: Prestige Art Ltd, Mamaroneck, NY (PA); John Nichols, NY (JN)
GALLERIES: John Weber Gallery, New York, NY; Jayne Baum Gallery, New York, NY; John Nichols Gallery, New York, NY
MAILING ADDRESS: 383 W Broadway, New York, NY 10012

TITLE	PUBLISHER	PRINTER	DATE	MEDIUM	DIMENSION (PAPER SIZE) IN INCHES	TYPE OF PAPER	EDITION NUMBER	NO. OF COLORS	ORIGINAL OPENING PRICE	CURRENT RETAIL PRICE
CURRENT EDITIONS:										
Point Source Star Space, Day (Dipt)	PA	JN	1980	SP	85 X 36	R/BFK	100	15	1200	1500
Point Source Star Space, Night (Dipt)	PA	JN	1980	SP	85 X 36	R/BFK	100	15	1200	1500
Mansions of the Zodiac (Set of 12)	JN	JN	1980	SP	49 X 38	R/BFK	150	15	6000 SET	6500 SET

DAVID ROTH

BORN: New York, NY; June 7, 1942
EDUCATION: Illinois Inst of Tech, Chicago, IL, with Harry Callahan & Aaron Siskind
RECENT EXHIB: Bradford Col, 1988
COLLECTIONS: Albright-Knox Art Gallery, Buffalo, NY; Ball State Univ, Muncie, IN; Mus of Contemp Art, Tehran, Iran; Philadelphia Art Mus, PA; Rockefeller Inst, NY; Brooklyn Mus of Art, NY; Newark Mus of Art, NJ
PRINTERS: Artist (ART)
PUBLISHERS: Brooke Alexander, Inc, NY (BAI)
GALLERIES: Brooke Alexander Inc, New York, NY; Naples Art Gallery, Naples, FL; Jack Meier Gallery, Houston, TX; Elkon Gallery, New York, NY; Patricia Judith Art Gallery, Boca Raton, FL; Ro Gallery, Image Makers, Inc, New York, NY
MAILING ADDRESS: P O Box 731, Newtown, PA 18940

TITLE	PUBLISHER	PRINTER	DATE	MEDIUM	DIMENSION (PAPER SIZE) IN INCHES	TYPE OF PAPER	EDITION NUMBER	NO. OF COLORS	ORIGINAL OPENING PRICE	CURRENT RETAIL PRICE
SOLD OUT EDITIONS (RARE):										
Four Large Screenprints:										
Random Colors Woven with the Passage of the Spectrum	BAI	ART	1974	SP	23 X 54	R/100	20	7	225	900
Random Greys Woven with the Passage of the Spectrum	BAI	ART	1974	SP	23 X 54	R/100	20	7	250	900
Random Colors Woven with the Passage of White to Black	BAI	ART	1974	SP	23 X 54	R/100	20	7	250	900
Random Greys Woven with the Passage of White to Black	BAI	ART	1974	SP	23 X 54	R/100	20	7	225	900

JANET RUBY

BORN: Baltimore, MD; January 16, 1965
EDUCATION: Maryland Inst Col of Art, Baltimore, MD
PRINTERS: Artist (ART)
PUBLISHERS: Daedal Art Publishers, Fallston, MD (DAP)
GALLERIES: Daedal Fine Arts, Fallston, MD
MAILING ADDRESS: 2217 Stockton Rd, Joppa, MD 21085

TITLE	PUBLISHER	PRINTER	DATE	MEDIUM	DIMENSION (PAPER SIZE) IN INCHES	TYPE OF PAPER	EDITION NUMBER	NO. OF COLORS	ORIGINAL OPENING PRICE	CURRENT RETAIL PRICE
CURRENT EDITIONS:										
Disected Tomato	DAP	ART	1986	LC/HC	22 X 30	R/BFK	50	6	120	200
Jericho Covered Bridge	DAP	ART	1986	LC/HC	18 X 24	R/BFK	25	6	100	200
Prenatal Landscape	DAP	ART	1986	COL	22 X 30	R/BFK	20	3	120	200
Disected Artichoke	DAP	ART	1986	LC/HC	22 X 30	R/BFK	35	6	120	200

JAMES ROSENQUIST

BORN: Grand Forks, ND; November 29, 1933
EDUCATION: Univ of Minnesota, Minneapolis, MN, 1948; Art Students League, NY, 1954–55; Aspen Inst of Humanist Studies, CO, 1965
TEACHING: Vis Lectr, Yale Univ, New Haven, CT, 1964
AWARDS: Art Inst of Chicago, IL, Award, 1963; Torcuatodi Tella Int Prize, Buenos Aires, Argentina, 1965
RECENT EXHIB: Butler Inst of Am Art, Youngstown, OH, 1988; Mus of Fine Arts, Houston, TX, 1988; Pension Gallery, NY, 1988; Dolly Fiterman Gallery, Minneapolis, MN, 1988; Leo Castelli Gallery, NY, 1989; Heland Wetterling Gallery, Stockholm, Sweden, 1989; Richard L Feigen & Company, Chicago, IL, 1989; Arkansas State Univ, State University, AR, 1990; Florida State Univ, Tallahassee, FL, 1990; North Miami Center of Contemp Art, North Miami, FL, 1990; Leo Castelli Gallery, NY, 1990; North Miami Center of Contemp Art, North Miami, FL, 1992; Florida State Univ Mus, Tallahassee, FL, 1992; Tampa Mus of Art, FL, 1992; Univ of South Florida, Graphicstudio, Tampa, FL, 1992; Univ of South Florida, Contemp Art Mus, Tampa, FL, 1991; Univ of Missouri, Kansas City, MO, 1992; Southern Alleghenies Mus, Loretto, PA, 1992; Nassau County Mus of Fine Arts, Roslyn Harbor, NY, 1992; Gagosian Gallery, NY, 1992; Galerie Thadaeus Ropac, Paris, France, 1992; Leo Castelli Gallery, NY, 1993
COLLECTIONS: Art Gallery of Ontario, Toronto, Can; Stedelijk Mus, Amsterdam, The Netherlands; Mus of Mod Art, NY; Musee Nat d'Art, Moderne, Paris, France; Kaiser Wilhelm Mus, Krefeld, Germany; Metropolitan Mus of Art, NY
PRINTERS: Styria Studio, NY (SS); Dan Stack, NY (DS); Petersburg Press, London, England (PP); Bird Island Publishing, Minneapolis, MN (BI) (OB); American Atelier, NY (AA); James Petrocelli, NY (JP); Dwight Pogue, NY (DP); Maurice Sanchez, NY (MS); Derriére L'Etoile Studios, NY (DES); Alan Holoubeck, Tampa, FL (AH); Graphicstudio, Tampa, FL (GS); Univ of South Florida, Tampa, FL (USF); Universal Limited Art Editions, West Islip, NY (ULAE); Aripeka Press, FL (AP); Charles Ringness, Tampa, FL (CR); Patricia Branstead, NY (PB); Aeropress, NY (A); Brian Maxwell, NY (BM); Ken Tyler, NY (KT); Lee Funderberg, NY (LF); Paul Imboden, NY (PI); Tom Strianese, NY (TS); Kathy Cho, NY (KC); John Fulton, NY (JF); Doug Humes, NY (DH); Jim Lefkowitz, NY (JL); Tyler Graphics, Ltd, Mount Kisco, NY (TGL); Erickson, Delaney & M Sanches (E/D/S); Flagstone Studios, Tampa, FL (FS)
PUBLISHERS: Multiples, Inc, NY (M); Transworld Art, Inc, NY (TAI); Castelli Graphics, NY (CG); Universal Limited Art Editions, West Islip, NY (ULAE); Brooke Alexander, Inc, NY (BAI); Petersburg Press, London, England (PP); Circle Fine Art, Chicago, IL (CFA); Derriére L'Etoile Studios, NY (DES); Prestige Art Ltd, Mamaroneck, NY (PAL); Universal Limited Art Editions, West Islip, NY (ULAE); Irwin Hollander, NY (IH); Richard Feigen Graphics, NY (RFG); Aripeka Limited Editions FL (ALE); Pyramid Arts Ltd (OB) (PAL); Artist (ART); Flatstone Studios, Tampa, FL (FS); International Images, Inc, Putney VT (IIm); Tanglewood Editions (TE); Hollander Workshop (HW); Bird Island Publishing, Minneapolis, MN (BIP) (OB); Tyler Graphics, Ltd, Mount Kisco, NY (TGL); JR, Inc. (JRI)
GALLERIES: Marian Goodman Gallery, New York, NY; Brooke Alexander Inc, New York, NY; Thomas Babeor Gallery, La Jolla, CA; David Adamson Gallery, Wash, DC; Gloria Luria Gallery, Bay Harbor Islands, FL; Frances Aronson Gallery, Atlanta, GA; Marvin Ross Friedman & Co, Miami, FL; Dolly Fiterman Gallery, Minneapolis, MN; Vermillion Editions, Ltd, Minneapolis, MN; van Straaten Gallery, Chicago, IL; Castelli Graphics, New York, NY; Circle Galleries, New York, NY & Chicago, IL; Gemini GEL, Los Angeles, CA; Erika Meyerovich Gallery, San Francisco, CA; Opus Art Studios, Miami, FL; Helander Gallery, Palm Beach, FL; Benjamin-Beattie Fine Arts, Chicago, IL; Magnuson Gallery, Boston, MA; Laura Paul Galleries, Cincinnati, OH & Columbus, OH; International Images, Inc, New York, NY; Richard L Feigen & Company, New York, NY; Golden Gallery, Boston, MA; Greenberg Gallery, St Louis, MO; Arras Galleries, New York, NY; Heland Wetterling Gallery, Stockholm, Sweden; David Lawrence Editions, Beverly Hills, CA; David

James Rosenquist
Caught One, Lost One, For the Fast Student
Courtesy Tyler Graphics, Ltd

Stuart Galleries, Los Angeles, CA; Charles Whitchurch Gallery, Huntington Beach, CA; Jonathan Novak Contemporary Art, Los Angeles, CA; Dunlap-Freidenrich Fine Art, Newport Beach, CA; Harcourts Modern & Contemporary Art, San Francisco, CA; Janet Levitt Fine Arts, San Francisco, CA; Walton-Gilbert Galleries, San Francisco, CA; James Corcoran Gallery, Santa Monica, CA; Richard Green Gallery, Santa Monica, CA; Bobbie Greenfield Fine Art, Inc, Venice, CA; River Gallery, Westport, CT; Barbara Gillman Gallery, Miami, FL; Ochi Galleries, Boise, ID & Sun Valley, ID; J Rosenthal Fine Arts, Chicago, IL; Sylvia Cordish Fine Art, Baltimore, MD; Steven Scott Gallery, Baltimore, MD; William Shearburn Fine Art, St Louis, MO; Moira James Gallery, Green Valley, NV; Faber Fine Arts, Secaucus, NJ; Bowles-Sorokko Galleries, New York, NY & Beverly Hills, CA; Leslie Freely Fine Art, New York, NY; Thomas Erben Gallery, Inc, New York, NY; Enrico Navarra Gallery, New York, NY; Atsuko Murayama Fine Arts, New York, NY; Leslie Neumann Fine Art, New York, NY & Aripeka, FL; Oil & Steel Gallery, Long Island City, NY; Jeffrey Ruesch Fine Art, Ltd, New York, NY; David Barnett Gallery, Milwaukee, WI; Adams-Middleton Gallery, Dallas, TX; Argus Fine Art, Eugene, OR; Galerie Thadaeus Ropac, Paris, France; Ro Gallery Image Makers, Inc, New York, NY
MAILING ADDRESS: PO Box 4, 420 West Broadway, Aripeka, FL 33502

Sparks (S)—Varian (V)—Friedman/Krakow (F/K)—Brooklyn Museum, NY (BM)

TITLE	PUBLISHER	PRINTER	DATE	MEDIUM	DIMENSION (PAPER SIZE) IN INCHES	TYPE OF PAPER	EDITION NUMBER	NO. OF COLORS	ORIGINAL OPENING PRICE	CURRENT RETAIL PRICE
SOLD OUT EDITIONS (RARE):										
The Certificate (First Print)	ART	ART	1962	EB	5 X 6	R/BFK	60	1	350	3000
Dusting off Roses	ART	ART	1965	LB	26 X 22	AP	35	1	500	16500
John Adams	ULAE	ULAE	1965	LB	12 X 10	AP	28	1	250	1200
Circles of Confusion	ART	ART	1966	LC	20 X 20	AP	300		500	2500
Roll Down (S-8)	ULAE	ULAE	1964–66	LC	39 X 29	R/BFK	29		150	25500

JAMES ROSENQUIST CONTINUED

TITLE	PUBLISHER	PRINTER	DATE	MEDIUM	DIMENSION (PAPER SIZE) IN INCHES	TYPE OF PAPER	EDITION NUMBER	NO. OF COLORS	ORIGINAL OPENING PRICE	CURRENT RETAIL PRICE
SOLD OUT EDITIONS (RARE):										
Expo 67 Mural—Firepole			1967	LC	33 X 17	R/BFK	41		175	5000
Aspen Easter Jazz			1967	SP	25 X 25	AP	300		75	2500
Forehead I (V-6)	RFG		1968	LC	34 X 29	AP	121		100	7500
Forehead II (V-7)	RFG		1968	LC	34 X 29	AP	96		100	7500
See-Saw	RFG		1968	LC	24 X 35	AP	100		100	7500
For Love	TE		1968	SP	35 X 26	AP	200		100	5000
Horse Blinders	PP		1968	LC	28 X 40	AP	41		250	9000
Area Code (Dipt)	CG/HW	IH/HW	1969	LC	29 X 52	AP	86	10	300	12000
Horse Blinders Flash Card	ULAE	ULAE	1969	LC	24 X 28	AP	21		200	15000
Night Smoke	ULAE	ULAE	1969–70	LC	22 X 31	AP	18		350	10000
Tumbleweed	CG/HW	IH/HW	1970	LC	22 X 30	AP	68		200	6000
Silver Skies	CG/HW	IH/HW	1970	LC	34 X 30	AP	65		200	6000
Spaghetti (V-16)	CG/HW	IH/HW	1970	LC	31 X 42	CD	50		250	8500
Busy Signal	CG/HW	IH/HW	1970	LC/CO	16 X 21	AP	84		200	3500
Bun Raku	PP	PP	1970	LC	33 X 24	AP	60		200	4000
Moon Box	CG/PP	PP	1971	LC	16 X 19	AP	70		150	5000
Art Gallery	CG/PP	PP	1971	LC	30 X 22	AP	70		250	5000
Earth and Moon	CG/PP	PP	1971	LC	18 X 17	AP	70		150	6000
Moon Beam Mistaken for the News	CG/PP	PP	1971	LC	23 X 30	AP	70		100	4000
Fedora	CG/PP	PP	1971	LC	6 X 4	AP	70		100	3000
Music School (For Peter Schjeldahl) (V-23) (B-46)	GS/USF	GS/USF	1971	LC	35 X 30	AP	70		250	6000
Cold Light	CG/PP	PP	1971	LC	22 X 30	AP	70		250	6000
Mastaba	CG/PP	PP	1971	LC	30 X 22	AP	70		250	6000
Night Smoke II	ULAE	ULAE	1969–72	LC	22 X 31	AP	27		400	8000
Pulling Out	PP	PP	1972	LB	25 X 30	AP	40		200	6000
Zone (V-40)	PP	PP	1972	LB	28 X 28	HMP	66		200	7500
Horse Blinders, 1972 (Set of 4):									4800 SET	10000 SET
North	M	PB/A	1972	LC/SP/CO	36 X 64	AP	85		1200	2500
South	M	PB/A	1972	LC/SP/CO	36 X 64	AP	85		1200	2500
East	M	PB/A	1972	LC/SP/CO	36 X 68	AP	85		1200	3000
West	M	PB/A	1972	LC/SP/CO	36 X 68	AP	85		1200	2500
Sightseeing (V-33)	PP	PP	1972	LC	31 X 37	GE	75		200	6500
Universal Star Leg	M	PB/A	1972	LC	42 X 30	AC	80		750	2500
My Mind is a Glass of Water	BAI	PB/A	1972	LC	31 X 22	JBG	125		500	4000
Push Buttons	PP	PP	1972	LC	21 X 27	AC	75		400	2500
Toy Prison	CG/M	GS/USF	1972	SP	18 X 25	AP			350	1800
15 Years Magnified Through a Drop of Water (V-46) (S-16)	ULAE	ULAE	1972–73	LC	22 X 25	AP	50		600	6000
Short Schedule	CG/M		1973	LC	22 X 30	AP	75		500	2500
Hey, Let's Go for a Ride	PP	PP	1973	LC	32 X 31	AP	75		200	7500
The Light that Won't Fail	PP	PP	1973	LC	22 X 30	AP	75		200	8000
Brighter than the Sun	PP	PP	1973	LC	28 X 38	AP	60		200	5000
Rainbow	PP	PP	1973	LC	25 X 30	AP	75		200	5000
1-2-3 Outside (V-35)	PP	PP	1973	LC	40 X 31	GE	70		200	4500
Flower Garden (V-42)	PP	PP	1973	LC	31 X 36	AP	75		200	4500
Push Buttons	PP	PP	1973	LC	28 X 34	AP	75		200	4000
Flame Out—Homage to Picasso (V-47)	PP	PP	1973	LC	30 X 23	AP	120		175	5000
Tube	PP	SS	1973	LC	32 X 31	HMP	75	4	750	10000
First	BAI	DS	1973	LC/HC/A	23 X 31	JBG	32		750	5000
Off the Continental Divide (S-17)	ULAE	ULAE	1973–74	LC	43 X 79	IVORY	43		1500	55000
Flamingo Capsule (V-50)	CG/M	GS/USF	1974	LC/SP	36 X 76	AC	85		2400	20000
Spikes	CG/M	GS/USF	1974	LC/EMB	22 X 30	R/BFK	80		250	5000
Time Flowers	CG/M	GS/USF	1974	SP	22 X 30	R/BFK	80		250	5000
Untitled	CG/M	GS/USF	1974	EC	28 X 41	R/BFK	80		400	1500
Silkscreens	CG/M	GS/USF	1974	SP	22 X 31	R/BFK	80		250	5000
Charcoal Shed	CG/M	GS/USF	1974	SP	25 X 30	AP/ROL	80		500	7000
Tampa—New York 1188 (V-68) (BM-50)	GS/USF	GS/USF	1974	LC	36 X 74	AP/ROL	40	13	2000	25000
Mirage Morning	CG/M	GS/USF	1974	LC/PLEX	36 X 74	AP/ROL	40	13	2000	25000
Strawberry Sunglasses	CG/M	PB/A	1974	LC	37 X 75	AP/ROL	79		2000	9000
F-111 (North, East, South, West) (Four Panels)	PP	PP	1974	LC	37 X 70 (2) 36 X 75 (2)	AP	75 EA		1500 SET	35000 SET
Iris Lake (V-69)	GS/USF	GS/USF	1974	LC	36 X 74	AC	40		2000	12000
Paper Clip (V-60)	PP	PP	1974	LC	36 X 69	AP	75		500	9000
Yellow Landing	PP	PP	1974	LC	33 X 75	AP	86		350	8000
Geometrie			1975	LC	20 X 14	AP			250	1200
Miles	GS/USF	GS/USF	1975	SP/HC	30 X 23	AP	200			
Slip Stream	ULAE	ULAE	1975	COL/I	17 X 36	JBG	38		500	4000
Tampa—New York: Iris Lake	CG/M	CR/GS/USF	1975	LC	74 X 36	AP	40	2	2000	25000

JAMES ROSENQUIST CONTINUED

TITLE	PUBLISHER	PRINTER	DATE	MEDIUM	DIMENSION (PAPER SIZE) IN INCHES	TYPE OF PAPER	EDITION NUMBER	NO. OF COLORS	ORIGINAL OPENING PRICE	CURRENT RETAIL PRICE
SOLD OUT EDITIONS (RARE):										
Marilyn (V-59)	PP	PP	1975	LC	42 X 30	AP	75		350	35000
Echo Pale (with Mirror)	CG/M	CR/GS/USF	1975	LC/SP	24 X 31	AP	100		500	3500
Free for All (DE)	TAI	MS	1976	LC/CO	26 X 19	PL	50		500	4500
Free for All (DE)	TAI	MS	1976	LC/CO	26 X 19	PL	50		500	4500
Artist's Rights Today	TAI	SS	1976	SP	30 X 22	AP	125		500	4000
Artist's Rights Today (DF)	TAI	SS	1976	SP/CO	30 X 22	PL	50		500	4000
Bottomless House (V-77)	PAL		1976	EC	6 X 12	AP	41		300	1800
Flying Stone (Stone, String)	CG/M	GS	1974–76	LC/CO	36 X 74	AP/ROL	51	12	2000	10000
Cold Rolled	CG/M	GS	1974–76	LC	33 X 73	AP/ROL	60	14	2000	6000
Rails	CG/M	GS	1975–76	LC	35 X 71	AP/ROL	40	4	2000	6000
Toy on the Stairs	CG/M	GS	1976	LB	6 X 12	AP/ROL	40	1	300	1800
Star, Towel, Weather Vane	GEM	GEM	1977	LC/CO	22 X 44	AP88	42	19	850	5000
Head Stand	GEM	GEM	1977	LC	11 X 44	OKP	39	10	650	4500
Star Pointer	GEM	GEM	1977	LC/DC/CO	22 X 44	AP88	42	1	750	5000
Untitled (F/K)	ART	CE/DES	1977	MUR/CC/HC	12 X 16	R/BFK	18	Varies	500	42000
Elbow Lake (V-85)	ALE	AP	1977	LC	37 X 74	AP88	100	2	500	6000
More Points on a Bachelor's Tie (V-95)	M	PB/A	1977	EB/A	18 X 36	AP88	78		500	7500
More Points on a Bachelor's Tie (V-95)	M	PB/A	1977	EB/A/HC	23 X 40	AP88	78	Varies	1200	6000
Wall Street Journal, Dinner Triangle			1977	EB/A/HC	18 X 36	AP88	78		500	6000
Suite of Nine Hand-Colored Etchings (Set of 9):										
Wall Street Journal, Dinner Triangle	M	FS	1978	EB/A/HC	23 X 40	AP88	78	Varies	1200	6000
Tin Roof	M	FS	1978	EB/A/HC	23 X 40	AP88	78	Varies	1200	4000
The Book Disappears for the Fast Student	M	FS	1978	EB/A/HC	23 X 40	AP88	78	Varies	1200	4000
One Million Tops per Square Inch	M	FS	1978	EB/A/HC	23 X 40	AP88	78	Varies	1200	4000
Path from the Wall	M	FS	1978	EB/A/HC	23 X 40	AP88	78	Varies	1200	4000
Spokes	M	FS	1978	EB/A/HC	23 X 40	AP88	78	Varies	1200	4000
Nuclear Neighborhood	M	FS	1978	EB/A/HC	23 X 40	AP88	78	Varies	1200	4000
Towel, Star, Sunglasses	M	FS	1978	EB/A/HC	23 X 40	AP88	78	Varies	1200	4000
Red Highway Trust	ALE	AP	1978	LC	14 X 44	WOVE/CR	78		1200	4000
Other Great Cities	ALE	AP	1978	EB/A	18 X 36	AP	78		500	6000
Gravity Feed	ALE	AP	1978	EB/A	18 X 36	AP	78		500	5000
Black Star	ALE	AP	1978	EB/A	18 X 36	AP	24		500	5000
Black Tie	PAL	AP	1978	LC	74 X 36	AP	100	2	2000	8000
Red Pyramid	PAL	AP	1978	LB	22 X 44	AP	78	1	350	2000
Rinse	PAL	AP	1978	LC/EB	18 X 36	AP	78		500	2500
Terrarium	JRI	E/D/S	1978	LC	21 X 40	100			450	3000
Window Washer Glass House			1978	SP	18 X 36		78		500	2200
Spring Cheer	M	PB/A	1978	EB	23 X 40	AP	78	1	500	1500
One Million Tons	M	PB/A	1978	EB/I	22 X 40	AP	78	1	500	1500
Astronomical Backboard			1978	LC	18 X 36	AP	78		500	3000
Fourneaux	M	PB/A	1978	EB/A/HC	18 X 36	AP	78	1	500	4500
Coin Noir	PAL	AP	1978	LC	74 X 36	AP	100	2	2000	8000
Violent Turn	PAL	AP	1978	LC	74 X 36	AP	100	2	2000	8000
Derriére L'Etoile	PAL	AP	1978	LC	74 X 36	AP	100	2	2000	8000
Fast Feast	PAL	AP	1978	LC	74 X 36	AP	100	2	2000	8000
Rouge Pad	M	PB/A	1978	EB/A	18 X 36	AP	78		500	5000
Rouge Pad, State I	M	PB/A	1978	LC	18 X 36	AP	78		400	5000
Rouge Pad, State II	M	PB/A	1978	LC	18 X 36	AP	78	2	300	3500
Carousel	ALE		1978	EB/A	23 X 40	AP	78		500	3500
Carousel, State I	ALE		1978	LC	23 X 40	AP	78		400	5000
Carousel, State II	ALE		1978	LC	23 X 40	AP	78	1	300	3500
Alphabet Avalanche	BI	BI	1979	LC/DC	22 X 45	TR/HMP	85	Varies	1200	10000
Tide, State I			1979	EC		TR/HMP	78		1000	5000
Tide, State II (Blue)			1979	EC		TR/HMP	78	1	500	3500
Swingscreen, State I			1979	EC		TR/HMP	78		1000	5000
Swingscreen, State II (Brown-Black)			1979	EB		TR/HMP	78	1	400	3000
The Book Disappears for the Fast Student, State I			1979	EC		TR/HMP	78		1000	5000
The Book Disappears for the Fast Student, State II (Purple)			1979	EC		TR/HMP	78		500	3500
Tin Roof, State I			1979	EC		TR/HMP	78		1000	5000
Tin Roof, State II (Red)			1979	EC		TR/HMP	78	1	500	3500
Suite of Etchings (Set of 9):										
Sheer Line	M	PB/A	1979	LC	29 X 45	AP	100		1250	8500
Terrarium	M	PB/A	1979	LC	29 X 45	AP	100		1500	8000
Balcony	M	PB/A	1979	LC	23 X 31	AP	58		500	4000
Tide	M	PB/A	1979	EB/HC	23 X 40	AP	78		1500	4500

JAMES ROSENQUIST CONTINUED

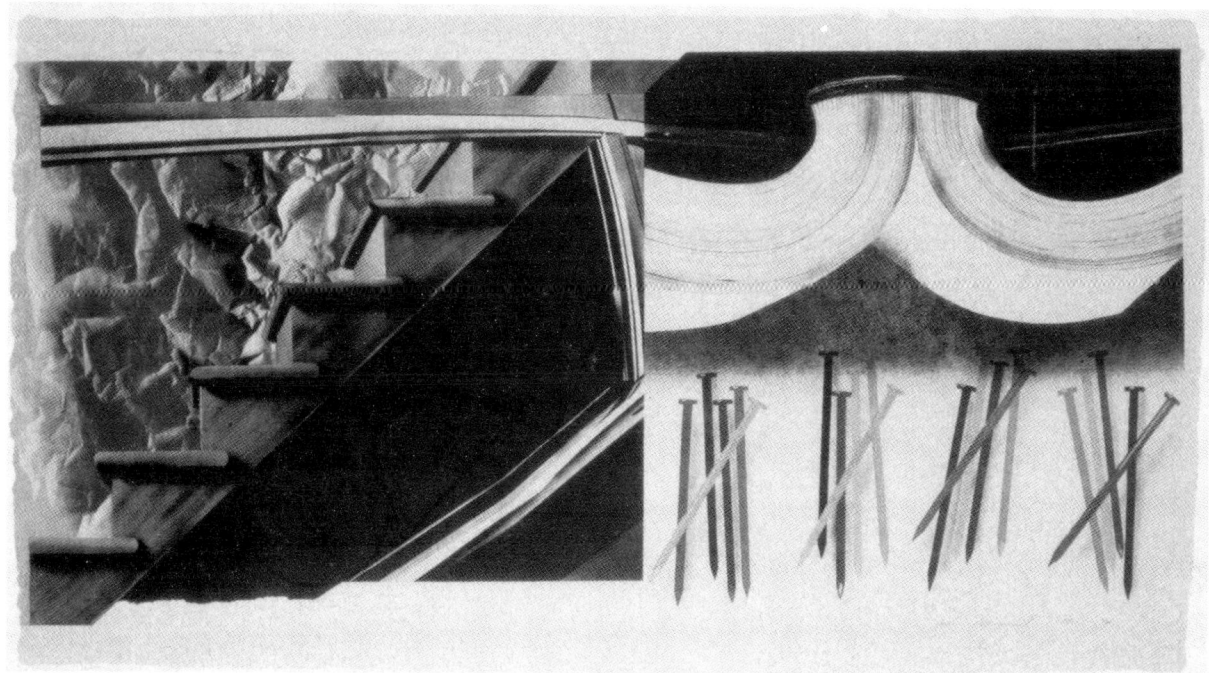

James Rosenquist
Off the Continental Divide
Courtesy Universal Limited Art Editions

TITLE	PUBLISHER	PRINTER	DATE	MEDIUM	DIMENSION (PAPER SIZE) IN INCHES	TYPE OF PAPER	EDITION NUMBER	NO. OF COLORS	ORIGINAL OPENING PRICE	CURRENT RETAIL PRICE
SOLD OUT EDITIONS (RARE):										
Idea Series:										
Idea I, II	M	PB/A	1979	LC	6 X 4 EA	AP	100 EA		150 EA	5000 EA
Star Ladder	M	PB/A	1978–80	EB/HC	23 X 40	AP88	78		1500	4000
Doorskin	M	PB/A	1978–80	EB/HC	28 X 38	AP88	78		1500	4000
Forneau	M	PB/A	1978–80	EB/HC	23 X 40	AP88	78		1500	4000
Wind and Lightning	M	PB/A	1978–80	EB/HC	23 X 40	AP88	78		1500	4000
Federal Spending	M	PB/A	1978–80	EB/HC	23 X 40	AP88	78		1500	4000
Black Triangle	M	PB/A	1978–80	EB/HC	23 X 40	AP88	78		1500	4000
Swing Screen	M	PB/A	1978–80	EB/HC	23 X 40	AP88	78		1500	4000
Hot Lake	M	PB/A	1978–80	EB/HC	23 X 40	AP88	78		1500	4000
Marco Polo Returns	M	PB/A	1978–80	EB/HC	23 X 40	AP88	78		1500	4000
Pyramid between Two Dry Lakes	M	PB/A	1978–80	EB/HC	23 X 40	AP88	78		1500	4000
Rouge Pad	M	PB/A	1978–80	EB/HC	23 X 40	AP88	78		1500	4000
Shallows	M	PB/A	1978–80	EB/HC	23 X 40	AP88	78		1500	4000
Spring Cheer	M	PB/A	1978–80	EB/HC	23 X 40	AP88	78		1500	4000
Star & Empty House	M	PB/A	1978–80	EB/HC	23 X 40	AP88	78		1500	4000
Star Proctor	M	PB/A	1978–80	EB/HC	23 X 40	AP88	78		1500	4000
Chambers	ULAE	ULAE	1980	LC	30 X 48	TRP	45	4	3500	17500
Red Highway Trust	CFA	AA	1980	LC/SP	23 X 47	AP	78		1500	4000
Highway Trust	CFA	AA	1980	LC/SP	23 X 47	AP	78		1500	4000
Divers Line	CFA	AA	1980	EC	23 X 47	AP	78		1500	4000
Star Leg	CFA	AA	1980	EC	23 X 47	AP	78		1500	4000
High Technology and . . .	ULAE	ULAE	1981	LC	34 X 33	AC	150		2500	9000
Dog Descending a Staircase	ULAE	ULAE	1980–82	LC/EB/A	42 X 70	AC	33		4500	35000
When a Leak . . .	GEM	GEM	1982	LC	43 X 54	AC	58	11	2500	9500
When a Leak . . . B&W	GEM	GEM	1982	LC	51 X 59	AC	25	7	2500	7500
The Glass Wishes Series:										
Leaky Neck	GEM	GEM	1982	AC	34 X 27	AC	59	2	650	5000
Beach	GEM	GEM	1982	EB/A	34 X 27	AC	59	1	650	5000
On Stage	GEM	GEM	1982	EB/DPT	34 X 27	AC	59	3	650	6000
Blood in Warm Water	GEM	GEM	1982	AC	34 X 27	AC	59	3	650	5000
Krapp's Banana	GEM	GEM	1982	EB/DPT	34 X 27	AC	59	1	650	5000
Appearance	GEM	GEM	1982	EB/A/DPT	34 X 27	AC	59	2	650	6000
L'Amour	GEM	GEM	1982	EB/A	34 X 27	AC	59	3	650	6000
Paper Head on a Nuclear Pillow	GEM	GEM	1982	AC	34 X 27	AC	59	5	650	5000
While the Earth Revolves at Night	GEM	GEM	1982	AC	34 X 27	AC	59	5	650	5000
Plume	GEM	GEM	1982	EB/A	34 X 27	AC	59	3	650	6000
Amusement Stops	GEM	GEM	1982	EB/A	34 X 27	AC	59	1	650	6000
While the Earth Revolves at Night	GEM	GEM	1982	AC	24 X 16	SOM/S	59		650	5000
New York Says It	CFA	AA	1983	SP	30 X 40	AP	250		750	1500
Ice Point	ART	FS	1983	LB	33 X 23	AP	150		750	8000

JAMES ROSENQUIST CONTINUED

James Rosenquist
The Bird of Paradise Approaches the Hot Water Planet
Courtesy Tyler Graphics, Ltd

James Rosenquist
Time Door Time D'or
Courtesy Tyler Graphics, Ltd

TITLE	PUBLISHER	PRINTER	DATE	MEDIUM	DIMENSION (PAPER SIZE) IN INCHES	TYPE OF PAPER	EDITION NUMBER	NO. OF COLORS	ORIGINAL OPENING PRICE	CURRENT RETAIL PRICE
CURRENT EDITIONS:										
Electrical Nymph on a Non-Objective Ground	ULAE	ULAE	1985	LC	42 X 42	PLAS/W	30	14	2800	10000
Night Transitions	ULAE	ULAE	1985	LC	53 X 44	AP	35	12	3500	12000
Flowers and Females	GS/USF	AH/GS/USF	1986	LC/MON	60 X 71	KOZO	75		15000	30000
Shriek (with Dry Mounted Elements)	GS/USF	AH/GS/USF	1986	LC/MON/CO	42 X 71	AP/W-AP88	29	13	7500	35000
Sister Shrieks	GS/USF	AH/GS/USF	1987	LC/MON/CO	48 X 80	AP/W-AP88	39		7500	30000
Star Thief	ART/DES	JP/DP/SC/DES	1986	LC	32 X 32	AC	25	2	1800	7500
Cross Hatch and Mutations	GS/USF	GS/USF	1986	MON/LC/CO	42 X 51	KOZO/SOM-S	29		7500	20000
The Persistence of Electrons in Space	ULAE	ULAE	1986	EB/A	32 X 32	KOZO	48		3000	7500
The Kubuki Bushes	GS/USF	GS/USF	1987	LC/MON/CO	39 X 41	KOZO/SOM-S	59		8500	20000
Starstrings			1988	SP	31 X 25	AC	100		1500	2500
Time Door Time D'Or (Dipt)	TGL	ART/BM/KT/ LMM/PI/TS/KC/JF/DH/JL/TGL	1988–89	LC/CO	98 X 120 EA	TGL/HMP/R-BFK	28	36	80000	80000
Bird of Paradise Approaches the Hot Water Planet	TGL	ART/BM/KT/ LMM/PI/TS/TGL	1989	LC/CO	97 X 85	TGL/HMP	28		75000	75000
Caught One, Lost One, for the Fast Student	TGL	ART/BM/KT/ LMM/PI/TS/TGL	1989	LC/CO	55 X 38	TGL/HMP	92		15000	20000
Sky Hole	TGL	ART/BM/KT/ LMM/PI/TS/TGL	1989	LC/CO	102 X 59	TGL/HMP	56		30000	50000
Space Dust	TGL	ART/BM/KT/ LMM/PI/TS/TGL	1989	LC/CO	67 X 105	TGL/HMP	56		50000	80000
Sun Sets on the Time Zone	TGL	ART/BM/KT/ LMM/PI/TS/TGL	1989	LC/CO	80 X 58	TGL/HMP	47		30000	50000
House of Fire	TGL	ART/BM/KT/ LMM/PI/TS/TGL	1989	LC/CO	50 X 120	TGL/HMP	54		90000	100000
Where the Water Goes	TGL	ART/BM/KT/ LMM/PI/TS/TGL	1989	LC/CO	103 X 58	TGL/HMP	32		60000	75000

DIETER ROTH

BORN: Hanover, Germany; 1930
EDUCATION: Studio Friedrich Wuthrich, Berne, Switzerland, 1947–51

COLLECTIONS: St Lawrence Univ, Richard F Brush Gallery, Canton, OH; Mus of Contemp Art, Chicago, IL
PRINTERS: Petersburg Press, London, England (PP)
PUBLISHERS: Petersburg Press, NY (PP)
GALLERIES: Anschel Gallery, London, England; Petersburg Press, New York, NY; Michael Lowe Gallery, Cincinnati, OH

The retail prices of the 100,000 limited edition prints quoted in this directory are subject to change. Print publishers, artists and galleries were the direct sources for these quotations. Prices in the secondary market listed as "Sold Out Editions (Rare)" indicate that the publisher has a limited supply of that print or that the print is difficult to locate in the galleries.

DIETER ROTH CONTINUED

TITLE	PUBLISHER	PRINTER	DATE	MEDIUM	DIMENSION (PAPER SIZE) IN INCHES	TYPE OF PAPER	EDITION NUMBER	NO. OF COLORS	ORIGINAL OPENING PRICE	CURRENT RETAIL PRICE
CURRENT EDITIONS:										
Relief Map	PP	PP	1970	SP	28 X 28	AP	40		300	2400
Seminar (with Richard Hamilton)	PP	PP	1971	LC	29 X 40	AP	96		300	1200
Icelandic Landscape	PP	PP	1971	EC	10 X 16	AP	25		200	600
Large Clouds (Feltpen & Mayonnaise on Paper)	PP	PP	1971	MM	30 X 40	AP	10		400	4500
A Little Tower	PP	PP	1971	EC	21 X 16	AP	30		300	1200

SYLVIA ROTH

BORN: New York, NY; 1934
EDUCATION: High Sch of Music & Art, NY, 1951; New York Univ, NY, BFA, 1954; Colorado Springs Sch of Fine Arts, CO; Art Students League, NY; Pratt Graphics Workshop, NY
AWARDS: CETA Grant, to Establish Etching Atelier, Rockland Center for the Arts, West Nyack, NY, 1977; Purchase Prize, Koenig Award, 1979; Subscription Prize, Rutgers Printmaking Archives, Jane Voorhees Zimmerli Mus, New Brunswick, NJ, 1983; Comm, Whitney Mus, Hand Printed Book, with Alfonso Ossorio & Dr. Lewis Thomas, 1984; Subscription Prize, Rutgers Printmaking Archives, Jane Voorhees Zimmerli Mus, New Brunswick, NJ, with April Gornik, 1985; Subscription Prize, Rutgers Printmaking Archives, Jane Voorhees Zimmerli Mus, New Brunswick, NJ, with John Beerman, 1986
RECENT EXHIB: Finkelstein Mem Library, Spring Valley, NY, 1992
COLLECTIONS: Jane Voorhees Zimmerli Art Mus, New Brunswick, NY
PRINTERS: Artist (ART); Mary Seibert, South Nyack, NY (MS); Hudson River Editions, South Nyack, NY (HRE)
PUBLISHERS: Hudson River Editions, South Nyack, NY (HRE)
GALLERIES: Kornbluth Gallery, Fairlawn, NJ; MiraMar Gallery, Sarasota, FL; Hudson River Editions, South Nyack, NY
MAILING ADDRESS: 288 Piermont Ave, South Nyack, NY 10960

TITLE	PUBLISHER	PRINTER	DATE	MEDIUM	DIMENSION (PAPER SIZE) IN INCHES	TYPE OF PAPER	EDITION NUMBER	NO. OF COLORS	ORIGINAL OPENING PRICE	CURRENT RETAIL PRICE
CURRENT EDITIONS:										
Endangered Species (Series of 12)	HRE	ART/MS/HRE	1991–92	MON	12 X 16 EA	GE	1 EA	1 EA	450 EA	500 EA
Young Speckeled Owl	HRE	ART/HRE	1992	EB	12 X 16	GE	36	1	350	350

PAUL ROTTERDAM

BORN: Wr Neustadt, Austria; Feb 12, 1939
EDUCATION: Univ of Vienna, Austria
TEACHING: Harvard Univ, Cambridge, MA; Cooper Union Sch of Art, NY
RECENT EXHIB: Arnold Herstand Gallery, NY, 1990,91; Storrer Gallery, Zürich, Switzerland, 1991; Denise Cadé Gallery, NY, 1991
COLLECTIONS: Mus of Mod Art, NY; Metropolitan Mus, NY; Brooklyn Mus, NY; Milwaukee Art Mus, WI; Guggenheim Mus, NY; Musee d'Art Moderne, Beaubourg, Paris, France; Busch-Reisinger Mus, Cambridge, MA; Albertina, Graphische Sammlung, Albertina, Vienna; Whitney Mus of Am Art, NY; Massachusetts Inst of Technology, Cambridge, MA; Nue Galleries Landesmuseum, Graz, Austria; Nat Mus of Art, Osaka, Japan
PRINTERS: Vermillion Editions Ltd, Minneapolis, MN (VEL); Maeght Editeur, Paris, France (ME); Robert Townsend, Georgetown, MA (RT); Herbert A Fox, Merrimac, MA (HF); Fox Graphics, Merrimac, MA (FG); Maeght Lelong, Paris, France (ML); Rolf Meier, Winterthur, Switzerland (RM); Frank Bordas, Paris, France (FB)
PUBLISHERS: Vermillion, Minneapolis, MN (VEL); Maeght Editions, Paris, France (ME); Impressions Gallery, Boston, MA (IG); Fox Graphics, Merrimac, MA (FG); Maeght Lelong, Paris, France (ML); Ed Storrer, Zürich, Switzerland (ES); Storrer Editions, Zürich, Switzerland (SEd); Limited Editions Club, NY (LEC); Artist (ART)
GALLERIES: Nielsen Gallery, Boston, MA; Galerie Bonnier, Geneva, Switzerland; Galerie Lelong, Paris, France & Zürich, Switzerland & New York, NY; Vermillion Editions Ltd, Minneapolis, MN; Luise Ross Gallery, New York, NY; Adams-Middleton Gallery, Dallas, TX; Nantenshi Gallery, Tokyo, Japan; Storrer Gallery, Zürich, Switzerland; Arnold Herstand Gallery, New York, NY; Denise Cade Gallery, New York, NY; Fox Graphics, Merrimac, MA; Ianuzzi Gallery, Scottsdale, AZ
MAILING ADDRESS: P O Box 952, North Blenheim, NY 12131

TITLE	PUBLISHER	PRINTER	DATE	MEDIUM	DIMENSION (PAPER SIZE) IN INCHES	TYPE OF PAPER	EDITION NUMBER	NO. OF COLORS	ORIGINAL OPENING PRICE	CURRENT RETAIL PRICE
SOLD OUT EDITIONS (RARE):										
Knight	ME	ME	1979	EB	18 X 13	R/BFK	50	1	500	1200
Staircase to Heaven	SEd	RM	1986	EB	15 X 11	HMP	5	1	800	4000
Illustration zu Rainer Maria Rilke "Die Aufzeichnungen des Malte Laurids Brigge" (Illustration of Rilke's "The Notebooks of Malte Laurids Brigge" Book with Texts Accompanying the Illustrations (Set of 12 Etchings)	SEd	RM	1988	EB	14 X 10 EA	HMP	33	1	3000 SET	9000 SET
CURRENT EDITIONS:										
Euphrat 975	ART/FG	HF/FG	1975	LC	29 X 41	R/BFK	60	4	250	1200
Kedemoth 974	ART/FG	HF/FG	1975	LC	29 X 41	R/BFK	60	2	250	1000
Mose 973	ART/FG	HF/FG	1975	LB	41 X 29	R/BFK	60	1	250	1000
Minnesota I	VEL	VEL	1980	LB	36 X 27	R/BFK	18	1	600	1000
Minnesota II	VEL	VEL	1981	E/I/SP	32 X 48	ACW	48	2	600	1000
Count of Burgundy	LEC	RM	1986	EB	15 X 11	R/BFK	30	1	400	800
Blenheim	SEd	RM	1991	DPT	16 X 12	R/BFK	33	1	600	800
Nest	SEd	RM	1991	EB	30 X 23	R/BFK	33	1	1200	1600
Nightbow	SEd	RM	1991	EB	30 X 23	R/BFK	33	1	1200	1600

The print market has become very selective. For the first time since we published the first edition of The Printworld Directory in 1982, the prices of prints have been greatly reduced and greatly increased for the same artists by the most reputable and established print publishers. Check the fifth edition to understand the movement.

G.H. Rothe
Gatja Helgart Rothe
Master of the Mezzotint

Being the master of the mezzotint in the 20th century I combine capability and knowledge. I was born in 1935 in Beuthen, (Poland after 1945). My studies in art history, human anatomy, goldsmithing and extensive drawing resulted in the discovery of the mezzotint technique ("There is not any living engraver or artist who could guess how this engraving has been executed", said Ludwig von Siegen 1642). In New York in 1972 I have felt impelled to dedicate my zeal work and time to revive this most difficult technique of printmaking.

I learned the technique by researching, studying hundreds of years old mezzotints, and practiced constantly to express my vast repertoire of images. My demand on skill manifested in perspicacity led to an invention never seen in mezzotint before: Transparency.

I carve my images into copperplates directly with a diamond. Then I pit the surface with a chisel like tool called a rocker. When the ground work is done I use a steel burnisher quite extensively to shape my images as one would do in a fine barr relief but working in reverse. After I pull a proof print from the copper plate I cover the surface anew with fine pitted holes using the rocker eliminating thought in action, practicing karma yoga. The experience of "layering", the transparent x-ray shapes which are guided by the mind's eye (I feel but cannot see the picture underneath the second layer of pits) culminates in enlightenment. The essence of life is an unknown force, seeing when I don't look.

After a mostly exclusive collaboration with several distributors for the past twenty years I have considered to take charge myself as it is my obligation for a method of work which is quite different from any of those in use for multiples.

G H ROTHE

BORN: Beuthen, Germany; 1935
EDUCATION: Acad of Design, Pforzheim, Germany, 1956; Art Students League, NY, Master, Mezzotint
AWARDS: Villa Romana Award, Germany, 1968; Honorary Citizen of Warwick Award, RI, 1986; Honorary Citizen of Wiedenbruck Award, Germany, 1988
RECENT EXHIB: Gallery at Cedar Kay, FL, 1987
COLLECTIONS: Kunsthalle, Dusseldorf, Germany; House of Parliament, Bonn, Germany; Bibliotheque Nat, Paris, France; Univ of Texas A & M, College Station, TX; Carnegie-Mellon Univ, Pittsburgh, PA; City Gallery, Stuttgart, Germany; Staatsgallerie Karlsruhe, Germany; Duke Univ, Durham, NC; Landesmuseum Muenster, Westfalen, Germany
PUBLISHERS: Hammer Publishing Co, NY (HP); Mezzotint, Ink, San Francisco, CA (MI); ArtIst (ART)
GALLERIES: Summa Galleries, New York, NY & Brooklyn, NY; Charles Barry International, Rockville, MD; Mussavi Gallery, New York, NY; Gallery One at Second Avenue, Denver CO; G H Rothe Galleries, Carmel, CA & Monterey, CA; Village Galleries, Lake Forest, CA & Santa Ana, CA & San Diego, CA & Irvine, CA & Mission Viejo, CA & Laguna Beach, CA
MAILING ADDRESS: 26364 Carmel Rancho Lane, Carmel, CA 93923

G H Rothe
Choice
Courtesy the Artist

TITLE	PUBLISHER	PRINTER	DATE	MEDIUM	DIMENSION (PAPER SIZE) IN INCHES	TYPE OF PAPER	EDITION NUMBER	NO. OF COLORS	ORIGINAL OPENING PRICE	CURRENT RETAIL PRICE
SOLD OUT EDITIONS (RARE):										
Busenbaum	HP	ART	1972	MEZ	6 X 4	AP88	99	1	40	2000
Dragonfly	HP	ART	1972	MEZ	4 X 3	AP88	10	1	300	3500
Telephone Connection	HP	ART	1972	MEZ	6 X 4	AP88	50	1	50	2000
Arabesque I	HP	ART	1973	MEZ	36 X 24	AP88	99	1	95	8000
Blue Shawl	HP	ART	1973	MEZ	24 X 18	AP88	120	1	250	4000
Bolshoi	HP	ART	1973	MEZ	35 X 24	AP88	99	1	60	10000
Dance (Blue Shawl)	HP	ART	1973	MEZ	24 X 18	AP88	120	1	250	4000
Dance Bejart	HP	ART	1973	MEZ	35 X 24	AP88	120	1	180	9000
Dancing Hands, State I	HP	ART	1973	MEZ	36 X 24	AP88	99	1	150	6000
Dancing Hands, State II	HP	ART	1973	MEZ	36 X 24	AP88	99	1	150	3000
Dome of the Butterflies (Color)	HP	ART	1973	MEZ	24 X 36	AP88	99	1	150	5000
Dome of the Butterflies (Black and White)	HP	ART	1973	MEZ	24 X 36	AP88	9 AP	1	150	5000
Les Eleves	HP	ART	1973	MEZ	24 X 18	AP88	200	1	90	8000
Small Arabesque I	HP	ART	1973	MEZ	23 X 17	AP88	120	1	120	5000
Small Arabesque II	HP	ART	1973	MEZ	23 X 17	AP88		1	120	7000
Glasstown	HP	ART	1973	MEZ	26 X 34	AP88	99	1	120	5000
Girl	HP	ART	1973	MEZ	25 X 8	AP88	60	1	100	3500
Alvin with the Dutch	HP	ART	1974	SP	43 X 31	AP88	300	1	200	4600
Butterflies Hall	HP	ART	1974	MEZ	4 X 3	AP88	50	1	60	1500
Dance	HP	ART	1974	MEZ	12 X 9	AP88	250	1	20	4000
Dance of Tom	HP	ART	1974	MEZ	12 X 9	AP88	250	1	80	2500
Downtown State I (Color)	HP	ART	1974	MEZ	35 X 24	AP88	99		150	6000
Downtown, State II (Color)	HP	ART	1974	MEZ	35 X 24	AP88	99		150	6000
For You	HP	ART	1974	MEZ	13 DIA	AP88	60	1	180	3300
Fruehling	HP	ART	1974	MEZ	18 X 12	AP88	260	1	52	4000
(Little) Glasstown	HP	ART	1974	MEZ	12 X 18	AP88	250	1	50	2500
Kristallball	HP	ART	1974	MEZ	5 X 3	AP88	75	1	50	1200
Dance on the Stairs	HP	ART	1975	MEZ	24 X 18	AP88	90	1	200	13000
Daphne	HP	ART	1975	MEZ	10 X 8	AP88	60	1	108	4500
Left Winding Shell	HP	ART	1975	MEZ	6 X 6	AP88	60	1	150	1500
Memory, State I	HP	ART	1975	MEZ	18 X 11	AP88	10 AP	1	100	4500
Memory, State II	HP	ART	1975	MEZ	18 X 11	AP88	250	1	250	4500
Memory (The Rose)	HP	ART	1975	MEZ	18 X 11	AP88	60	1	250	4500
Transparent Tulips	HP	ART	1975	MEZ	36 X 36	AP88	60	1	300	11000
Kirov	HP	ART	1975	SP	38 X 25	AP88	300		100	4000
Pas de Trois	HP	ART	1975	SP	38 X 25	AP88	300		100	2800
America's Pride	HP	ART	1976	MEZ	27 X 26	AP88	150		350	20000

G H ROTHE CONTINUED

TITLE	PUBLISHER	PRINTER	DATE	MEDIUM	DIMENSION (PAPER SIZE) IN INCHES	TYPE OF PAPER	EDITION NUMBER	NO. OF COLORS	ORIGINAL OPENING PRICE	CURRENT RETAIL PRICE
SOLD OUT EDITIONS (RARE):										
Audience Favorite	HP	ART	1976	MEZ	10 X 8	AP88	100		100	3500
Front View	HP	ART	1976	MEZ	17 DIA	AP88	100		100	4000
Glassrose	HP	ART	1976	MEZ	24 X 26	AP88	150		350	6000
Interlude	HP	ART	1976	MEZ	9 X 16	AP88	10		100	8000
Mollusk	HP	ART	1976	MEZ	36 X 24	AP88	150		300	3800
Moon Dance I	HP	ART	1976	MEZ	26 X 17	AP88	160		100	7000
Large Dance Suite:										
Grand Sauté	HP	ART	1976	MEZ	25 X 24	AP88	100		200	18000
Romeo and Giulietta	HP	ART	1976	MEZ	25 X 25	AP88	100		200	8000
School of Flight	HP	ART	1976	MEZ	24 X 26	AP88	100		200	10000
Romeo & Guilietta, State I	HP	ART	1976	MEZ	25 X 25	AP	10	1	200	8500
Romeo & Guilietta, State II	HP	ART	1976	MEZ	25 X 25	AP88	100	1	200	8500
On the Barre	HP	ART	1976	MEZ	9 X 16	AP88	10	1	100	3500
Shell	HP	ART	1976	MEZ	7 X 10	AP88	90		60	3200
Suzanne	HP	ART	1976	MEZ	24 X 26	AP88	100		1000	6000
Venetian Glass	HP	ART	1976	MEZ	12 X 9	AP88	100		100	3000
Arise Arose	HP	ART	1977	MEZ	32 X 24	AP88	150		300	25000
Ballet in New York	HP	ART	1977	MEZ	33 X 24	AP88	150		300	10000
Butterfly	HP	ART	1977	MEZ	24 X 24	AP88	150		300	6000
The Extra Effort	HP	ART	1977	MEZ	10 X 28	AP88	150		90	5400
Landmark	HP	ART	1977	MEZ	28 X 22	AP88	150		300	4400
Orchid	HP	ART	1977	MEZ	8 X 7	AP88	100		125	1800
Pas de Deux	HP	ART	1977	MEZ	24 X 24	AP88	150		300	2500
Red Shoes	HP	ART	1977	MEZ	33 X 24	AP88	150		300	6000
Thoroughbred (Running)	HP	ART	1977	MEZ	24 X 18	AP88	75/150		250	6500
Thoroughbred (Standing)	HP	ART	1977	MEZ	24 X 18	AP88	150		250	6500
Tulips	HP	ART	1977	MEZ	24 X 12	AP88	125		150	7000
The Horses, State I	HP	ART	1977	MEZ	6 X 8	AP88	5 AP	1	150	1000
The Horses, State II	HP	ART	1977	MEZ	6 X 8	AP88	5 AP	1	150	1800
The Horses, State III	HP	ART	1977	MEZ	6 X 8	AP88	100		125	2400
The Horses (Deluxe)	HP	ART	1977	MEZ	6 X 8	AP88	50		125	3000
Mindscape	HP	ART	1977	MEZ	6 X 8	AP88	150	1	125	3200
Secret Place	HP	ART	1978	MEZ	15 X 21	AP88	150	1	400	2800
Don Quixote	HP	ART	1978	MEZ	28 X 22	AP88	200	1	675	12000
Homecoming	HP	ART	1978	MEZ	15 X 21	AP88	150	1	400	8000
Myth	HP	ART	1978	MEZ	21 X 17	AP88	200	1	450	15000
Spanish Rose	HP	ART	1978	MEZ	8 X 6	AP88	100	1	300	3000
Sunday Roses (Green, Red or Brown)	HP	ART	1978	MEZ	6 X 8 EA	AP88	100 EA	1 EA	200 EA	2500 EA
The Way Out	HP	ART	1978	MEZ	10 X 28	AP88	60	1	90	8000
Joy	HP	ART	1978	MEZ	22 X 10	AP88	150	1	200	4000
Moon Dance II	HP	ART	1978	MEZ	26 X 16	AP88	100	1	500	6500
Horse Suite:										
Morning	HP	ART	1978	MEZ	9 X 22	AP88	150	1	266	3000
Night	HP	ART	1978	MEZ	9 X 22	AP88	150	1	300	3500
Shelter	HP	ART	1978	MEZ		AP88	150	1	300	2200
Breakfast	HP	ART	1978	MEZ		AP88	3 AP	1	300	1100
Sonata	HP	ART	1979	MEZ	6 X 4	AP88	200	1	300	1500
Small Dance Suite:										
Carousel	HP	ART	1979	MEZ	5 X 6	AP88	200		200	1800
Dance Together	HP	ART	1979	MEZ	6 X 5	AP88	200		200	1800
Performance	HP	ART	1979	MEZ	5 X 5	AP88	200		200	1800
Stage Debut	HP	ART	1979	MEZ	6 X 5	AP88	200		200	1800
Virtuosity	HP	ART	1979	MEZ	5 X 6	AP88	200		200	1800
Coral Corral	HP	ART	1979	MEZ	12 X 35	AP88	150		550	10000
Miniature Suite:										
Embryo	HP	ART	1979	MEZ	6 X 5	AP88	200		200	1800
Pinned Drop	HP	ART	1979	MEZ	6 X 4	AP88	200		200	2000
Road	HP	ART	1979	MEZ	6 X 4	AP88	200		200	1500
Twins	HP	ART	1979	MEZ	5 X 5	AP88	200		200	1800
Valley	HP	ART	1979	MEZ	5 X 6	AP88	200		200	1600
Peace	HP	ART	1979	MEZ	10 X 12	AP88	150		400	2500
The Poet	HP	ART	1979	MEZ	35 X 24	AP88	150		800	15000
Strength	HP	ART	1979	MEZ	28 X 16	AP88	200		650	18000
Ancestor	HP	ART	1979	MEZ	6 X 4	AP88	150		200	1200
Rosescape	HP	ART	1979	MEZ	22 X 28	AP88	200		660	5000
Solitude	HP	ART	1979	MEZ	21 X 15	AP88	150		500	7500
Herd	HP	ART	1979	MEZ	8 X 6	AP88	150		300	1500
Dawn	HP	ART	1979	MEZ	8 X 6	AP88	150		300	2800
Endurance	HP	ART	1979	MEZ	8 X 66	AP88	150		1000	3000
Grace and the Stallion	HP	ART	1979	MEZ	6 X 28	AP88	150		300	2800
Growth	HP	ART	1980	MEZ	16 X 22	AP88	150		650	6000
Ballet Picture I	HP	ART	1980	MEZ	28 X 22	AP88	150		1000	10000
Broadway Ambition	HP	ART	1980	MEZ	35 X 24	AP88	150		950	18000
The Fight	HP	ART	1980	MEZ	12 X 10	AP88	150	1	350	1600

G H ROTHE CONTINUED

G H Rothe
Ascending Pegasus
Courtesy the Artist

TITLE	PUBLISHER	PRINTER	DATE	MEDIUM	DIMENSION (PAPER SIZE) IN INCHES	TYPE OF PAPER	EDITION NUMBER	NO. OF COLORS	ORIGINAL OPENING PRICE	CURRENT RETAIL PRICE
SOLD OUT EDITIONS (RARE):										
Julie	HP	ART	1980	MEZ	7 X 4	AP88	100	1	300	1000
Pensive Motion	HP	ART	1980	MEZ	20 X 8	AP88	100	1	500	5500
Sonata	HP	ART	1980	MEZ	6 X 4	AP88	200	1	250	800
Harbor at Night	HP	ART	1980	MEZ	11 X 14	AP88	100	1	400	2500
Red Dress	HP	ART	1980	MEZ	22 X 16	AP88	150	1	650	6500
Flowerlife	HP	ART	1980	MEZ	8 X 6	AP88	150	1	300	1600
Bachelors	HP	ART	1981	MEZ	14 X 11	AP88	100	1	450	3000
Bougainvillea	HP	ART	1981	MEZ	16 X 11	AP88	150 1		550	3500
Chase	HP	ART	1981	MEZ	24 X 35	AP88	150	1	1200	20000
Dance for Pleasure	HP	ART	1981	MEZ	6 X 4	AP88	150	1	200	2500
Experiment	HP	ART	1981	MEZ	16 X 22	AP88	150	1	900	18000
Mosslanding	HP	ART	1981	MEZ	11 X 14	AP88	100	1	400	2800
Rhapsodic Committment	HP	ART	1981	MEZ	25 X 17	AP88	150	1	1100	10000
While They were Running	HP	ART	1981	MEZ	24 X 35	AP88	150	1	1500	25000
Junction	HP	ART	1981	MEZ	11 X 17	AP88	100	1	500	1500
Springrose	HP	ART	1981	MEZ	8 X 8	AP88	100	1	300	1800
Tassajar	HP	ART	1981	MEZ	14 X 11	AP88	150	1	500	1800
Penuel II (2 Plates)	HP	ART	1981	MEZ	7 X 10	AP88	96	1	450	1000
Recital	HP	ART	1982	MEZ	17 X 25	AP88	200	1	900	3900
Ball Dance	HP	ART	1982	MEZ	28 X 22	AP88	150	1	1200	2000
Conbrio	HP	ART	1982	MEZ	16 X 11	AP88	150	1	600	1800
Runners	HP	ART	1982	MEZ	9 X 12	AP88	150	2	500	2400
Salinas Hill	HP	ART	1982	MEZ	12 X 9	AP88	96	1	500	1500
Colts	HP	ART	1982	MEZ	24 X 36	AP88	150	1	1200	18000
Deprived Condition	HP	ART	1982	MEZ	24 X 18	AP88	96	1	850	5000
Electron (with Pastel)	HP	ART	1982	MEZ/PAS	12 X 8	AP88	96	1	450	3000
Emotional Intensity	HP	ART	1982	MEZ	28 X 22	AP88	150	1	1200	18000
Solo of Gemini	HP	ART	1982	MEZ	12 X 9	AP88	75	1	600	1500
Traditional Standard	HP	ART	1982	MEZ	16 X 11	AP88	150	1	500	2400
Trio	HP	ART	1982	MEZ	16 X 11	AP88	200	1	600	3000
Conquistador Cielo	HP	ART	1983	MEZ	24 X 36	AP88	150	1	1800	25000
San Bonancio Valley	HP	ART	1983	MEZ	24 X 36	AP88	150	1	1200	3400
Walnut	HP	ART	1983	MEZ	3 X 3	AP88	75	1	200	900
Arabian Nights I	HP	ART	1984	MEZ	6 X 14	AP88	150	1	550	2500
Californian Oak	HP	ART	1984	MEZ	9 X 6	AP88	100	1	400	1200
Attention	HP	ART	1984	MEZ	9 X 6	AP88	150	1	400	1200
Hibiscus	HP	ART	1984	MEZ	12 X 18	AP88	100		750	3400
Spectrum	HP	ART	1984	MEZ	24 X 18	AP88	200		1100	10000
Coyote	MI	ART	1985	MEZ	3 X 6	AP88	150		200	1200
Marvel	MI	ART	1985	MEZ	16 X 35	AP88	150		1400	10000
Beaconstars	MI	ART	1985	MEZ	10 X 8	AP88	150		450	1500
Big Creek (Color)	MI	ART	1985	MEZ	24 X 36	AP88	150		1200	4800
Big Creek (Black & White)	MI	ART	1985	MEZ	24 X 36	AP88	20		1200	4800
Sterling Silver	MI	ART	1985	MEZ	15 X 11	AP88	150		600	1600

G H ROTHE CONTINUED

TITLE	PUBLISHER	PRINTER	DATE	MEDIUM	DIMENSION (PAPER SIZE) IN INCHES	TYPE OF PAPER	EDITION NUMBER	NO. OF COLORS	ORIGINAL OPENING PRICE	CURRENT RETAIL PRICE
SOLD OUT EDITIONS (RARE):										
Threat Gesture	MI	ART	1985	MEZ	36 X 24	AP88	150		2000	12000
Dawning	MI	ART	1986	MEZ	36 X 24	AP88	150	1	1500	9000
Leaps and Bounds	MI	ART	1986	MEZ	35 X 24	AP88	150	1	1600	6000
Manitou	MI	ART	1986	MEZ	36 X 24	AP88	200	1	1800	15000
Manitou Deluxe (with Remarque)	MI	ART	1986	MEZ	36 X 24	AP88	50	1	1800	17000
Whimsy	MI	ART	1986	MEZ	36 X 24	AP88	150	1	1400	6000
Danby's Enchanted Island Revisited	MI	ART	1987	MEZ	35 X 24	AP88	100	1	3000	15000
Flowerstudy	MI	ART	1988	MEZ	14 X 6	AP88	150	1	1250	2100
Lake (Green)	MI	ART	1988	MEZ	5 X 7	AP88	75	1	800	900
Three Bees	MI	ART	1988	MEZ	3 X 3	AP88	150	1	750	900
Irene	ART	ART	1992	MEZ	5 X 7	AP88	150	1	900	900
CURRENT EDITIONS:										
Arabesque II	HP	ART	1973	MEZ	36 X 24	AP88	120		95	8000
The Heart	HP	ART	1975	MEZ	36 X 26	AP88	60		350	2500
Window	HP	ART	1978	MEZ	26 X 24	AP88	150		500	6000
Augusta (Blue, Red or Purple)	HP	ART	1978	MEZ	21 X 15 EA	AP88	150 EA	1 EA	400 EA	2400 EA
Augusta II (Purple)	HP	ART	1978	MEZ	21 X 15	AP88	150		400	2400
Competitors (2 Plates)	HP	ART	1980	MEZ	6 X 8	AP88	150		300	1800
Dance Picture I	HP	ART	1980	MEZ	28 X 22	AP88	150		900	3500
The Fight	HP	ART	1980	MEZ	12 X 10	AP88	150		550	1000
Flowerlife	HP	ART	1980	MEZ	8 X 6	AP88	150		350	850
Ballet Picture II	HP	ART	1980	MEZ	28 X 22	AP88	150		900	10000
Baby Ballerinas	HP	ART	1981	MEZ	28 X 22	AP88	150		1000	3000
Recurrent	HP	ART	1981	MEZ	10 X 7	AP88	96		350	2000
Wharf	HP	ART	1981	MEZ	17 X 25	AP88	150		850	2800
The Life Series Suite:										
Endeavers	HP	ART	1981	MEZ	22 X 28	AP88	150		1200	3500
Youth	HP	ART	1981	MEZ	28 X 22	AP88	150		1200	6500
Penuel I	HP	ART	1981	MEZ	7 X 10	AP88	96		450	1200
Beechlane	HP	ART	1982	MEZ	7 X 5	AP88	75		300	2400
Morgans (Half Edition—Blue)	HP	ART	1982	MEZ	9 X 12	AP88	150	2	500	1600
Pattern	HP	ART	1982	MEZ	36 X 24	AP88	96		400	4000
Almanac	HP	ART	1982	MEZ	28 X 22	AP88	150		1200	4500
Current	HP	ART	1982	MEZ	22 X 28	AP88	150		1200	4000
Roots in Love	HP	ART	1982	MEZ	25 X 17	AP88	96		950	2800
Arabians	HP	ART	1982	MEZ	25 X 17	AP88	200	1	800	2800
Practice	HP	ART	1982	MEZ		AP88	200	1	300	900
Schweigen ist Gold	HP	ART	1983	MEZ		AP88	10	1	300	800
Ben Rabba (Brown)	HP	ART	1983	MEZ	13 X 9	AP88	150	1	600	2000
Corn	HP	ART	1983	MEZ	12 X 18	AP88	150		600	1800
Grapes	HP	ART	1983	MEZ	9 X 12	AP88	150		600	1800
Nutbranch (Walnutbranch)	HP	ART	1983	MEZ	9 X 12	AP88	150		600	1800
Some of 48 Tulips	HP	ART	1983	MEZ	12 X 9	AP88	150		600	1800
Tassajara Stairs	HP	ART	1983	MEZ	12 X 18	AP88	96		600	2000
Arabian Colt	HP	ART	1984	MEZ	14 X 11	AP88	150		550	2500
Powerplay	HP	ART	1984	MEZ	24 X 36	AP88	200		2200	7800
Daphne's Transformation	MI	ART	1985	MEZ	36 X 24	AP88	150		1050	5800
Fourth of July	MI	ART	1985	MEZ	24 X 36	AP88	150		1500	6000
Friendliness	MI	ART	1985	MEZ	12 X 9	AP88	150		500	1500
Monarchs Journey	MI	ART	1985	MEZ	38 X 24	AP88	150		1200	4000
Strawberry Rose	MI	ART	1985	MEZ	6 X 9	AP88	150		425	1500
Violets	MI	ART	1985	MEZ	6 X 9	AP88	150		350	900
Sunrise Dahlia	MI	ART	1985	MEZ	18 X 12	AP88	150		600	2000
Cerimon	MI	ART	1985	MEZ	38 X 24	AP88	150	1	1200	4000
Deja Vu	MI	ART	1985	MEZ	6 X 9	AP88	150	1	425	1500
Beyond Reason (Watercolor)	MI	ART	1987	WA		AP88	1	1	5000	9750
Black Angel	MI	ART	1987	MEZ	24 X 18	AP88	150	1	1500	5000
Danby's Enchanted Island Revisited	MI	ART	1987	MEZ	35 X 24	AP88	100	1	5000	15000
Hidingplace	MI	ART	1987	MEZ	8 X 10	AP88	100	1	600	2100
Kiwis and their Leaves	MI	ART	1987	MEZ	6 X 9	AP88	150	1	500	1800
Oaktree (Black & White)	MI	ART	1987	MEZ	36 X 24	AP88	50	1	1800	3000
Arabian Nights II (Blue)	MI	ART	1988	MEZ	6 X 14	AP88	150	1	1250	2500
Arabian Nights III (Red)	MI	ART	1988	MEZ	6 X 14	AP88	150	1	1250	2500
Ben Rabba II (Red)	MI	ART	1988	MEZ	13 X 9	AP88	150	1	1250	2000
Big Sur	MI	ART	1988	MEZ	36 X 24	AP88	150		2000	6000
Burning Roses	MI	ART	1988	MEZ	12 X 11	AP88	200		1250	1800
Camelia	MI	ART	1988	MEZ	6 X 8	AP88	150		1000	1200
La Celestina	MI	ART	1988	MEZ	18 X 12	AP88	150		1500	2100
For Lee	MI	ART	1988	MEZ	5 X 4	AP88	150		500	500
Lake (Blue)	MI	ART	1988	MEZ	5 X 7	AP88	100		650	900
Lake (Plum Red)	MI	ART	1988	MEZ	5 X 7	AP88	75		750	900
Last Rose before the Gate Closes, A	MI	ART	1988	MEZ	36 X 24	AP88	150		2000	4000
Oakbranches	MI	ART	1988	MEZ	8 X 12	AP88	175	1	950	1200
Oaktree I (Color)	MI	ART	1988	MEZ	36 X 24	AP88	150		2000	3000

G H ROTHE CONTINUED

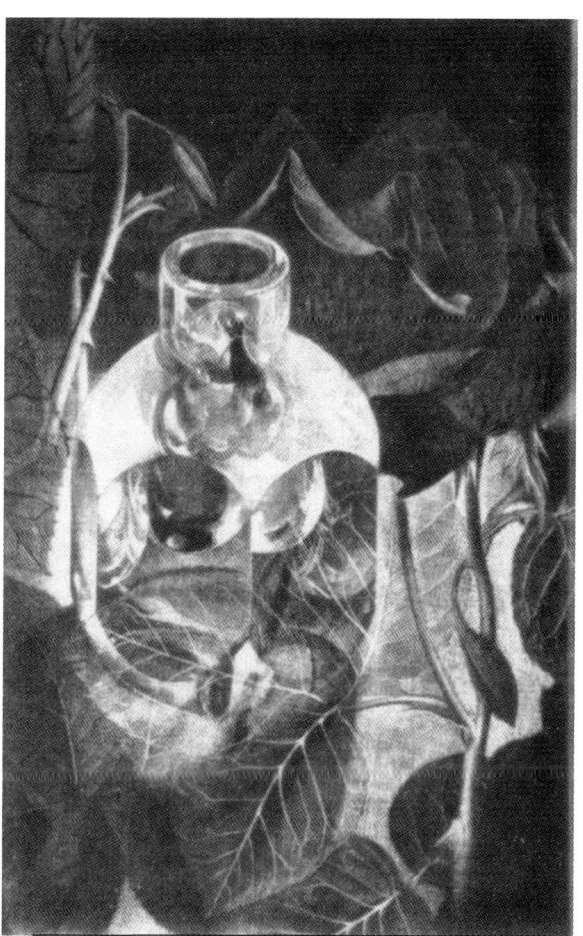

G H Rothe
Parfum I
Courtesy the Artist

G H Rothe
Senke Ikebana
Courtesy the Artist

TITLE	PUBLISHER	PRINTER	DATE	MEDIUM	DIMENSION (PAPER SIZE) IN INCHES	TYPE OF PAPER	EDITION NUMBER	NO. OF COLORS	ORIGINAL OPENING PRICE	CURRENT RETAIL PRICE
CURRENT EDITIONS:										
Parfum I	MI	ART	1988	MEZ	12 X 8	AP88	150	1	1250	1800
Poetic Motion (Olympic Edition)	MI	ART	1988	MEZ		AP88	250	1		POR
Rain and Sunshine over Seastone	MI	ART	1988	MEZ	12 X 18	AP88	150	1	2000	4500
Rebound I	MI	ART	1988	MEZ	8 X 7	AP88	96	1	950	1500
Rebound II	MI	ART	1988	MEZ	8 X 7	AP88	150	1	950	1500
Roots in Love II	MI	ART	1988	MEZ	25 X 17	AP88	150	1	1800	2800
Trapped	MI	ART	1988	MEZ	8 X 10	AP88	96	1	950	1200
Violets II	MI	ART	1988	MEZ	6 X 9	AP88	150	1	850	1000
Leaps and Bounds II (Blue)	MI	ART	1988	MEZ	36 X 24	AP88	150	1	2500	6000
Leaps and Bounds III (Red)	MI	ART	1988	MEZ	36 X 24	AP88	150	1	2500	6000
Choice	MI	ART	1989	MEZ	24 X 18	AP88	150	1	1600	4000
Grapes II	MI	ART	1989	MEZ	9 X 13	AP88	150	1	1200	2200
Grapes III (Violet)	MI	ART	1989	MEZ	9 X 13	AP88	150	1	1200	2200
Gold and Glass I	MI	ART	1989	MEZ	24 X 18	AP88	150	1	2000	3200
Legacy	MI	ART	1989	MEZ	11 X 8	AP88	150	1	1200	2500
Penuel III (Fuchsia)	MI	ART	1989	MEZ	7 X 10	AP88	150	1	950	1200
Princess	MI	ART	1989	MEZ	24 X 18	AP88	150	1	1600	3000
Stroll	MI	ART	1989	MEZ	18 X 24	AP88	150	1	1600	1600
The Transformation of the Unicorn	MI	ART	1989	MEZ	24 X 18	AP88	150	1	1600	2000
Sarafina	MI	ART	1989	MEZ	25 X 18	AP88	150	1	1800	3500
Cala Lily	MI	ART	1990	MEZ	18 X 12	AP88	150	1	1500	2000
Nightchase (Blue)	MI	ART	1990	MEZ	6 X 14	AP88	150	1	1250	1800
Nightchase (Red)	MI	ART	1990	MEZ	6 X 14	AP88	150	1	1250	1800
Province a'Côte te Serre (Watercolor)	MI	ART	1990	WA		AP88	1			30000
Students	MI	ART	1990	MEZ	7 X 5	AP88	200	1	750	900
Tender Strength	MI	ART	1990	MEZ	21 X 15	AP88	150	1	1800	2800
Two Red Roses (Watercolor)	MI	ART	1990	MEZ		AP88	1			16000
Scarlet	ART	ART	1991	MEZ	8 X 6	AP88	150	1	750	900
Anna	ART	ART	1991	MEZ	16 X 11	AP88	100	1	1800	2800
Blue Girl	ART	ART	1991	MEZ	14 X 12	AP88	150	1	1500	2200

G H ROTHE CONTINUED

TITLE	PUBLISHER	PRINTER	DATE	MEDIUM	DIMENSION (PAPER SIZE) IN INCHES	TYPE OF PAPER	EDITION NUMBER	NO. OF COLORS	ORIGINAL OPENING PRICE	CURRENT RETAIL PRICE
CURRENT EDITIONS:										
Brandy (Pastel)	ART	ART	1991	MEZ		AP88	1			25000
Carmel Valley	ART	ART	1991	MEZ	14 X 14	AP88	150	1	1600	2500
Colibri	ART	ART	1991	MEZ	8 X 13	AP88	200	1	950	1500
Color Magic	ART	ART	1991	MEZ	12 X 9	AP88	150	1	950	1800
Happy Horses	ART	ART	1991	MEZ	24 X 18	AP88	150	1	2500	4800
Insieme	ART	ART	1991	MEZ	10 X 12	AP88	150	1	1250	1900
Menage a Trois (Pastel)	ART	ART	1991	PAS	25 X 19	AP88	1			25000
Peach Roses in Glass (Pastel)	ART	ART	1991	PAS		AP88	1			25000
Summerglow	ART	ART	1991	MEZ	18 X 24	AP88	150		2500	2500
Tassajara II	ART	ART	1991	MEZ	14 X 11	AP88	150		1500	1800
Runners II	ART	ART	1991	MEZ	9 X 12	AP88	150	1	1800	1800
Allee	ART	ART	1992	MEZ	8 X 6	AP88	150	1	1300	1300
Amarilis Amour	ART	ART	1992	MEZ	35 X 24	AP88	150	1	4500	4500
California Bloom	ART	ART	1992	MEZ	6 X 8	AP88	150	1	900	900
Care	ART	ART	1992	MEZ	24 X 18	AP88	150	1	2200	2200
Congratulations	ART	ART	1992	MEZ	5 X 7	AP88	200	1	1000	1000
Dawning II	ART	ART	1992	MEZ	36 X 24	AP88	150	1	9000	9000
Roseman	ART	ART	1992	MEZ	19 X 16	AP88	150	1	2200	2200
Roses in Green Vase (Pastel)	ART	ART	1992	PAS		AP88	1		35000	35000
Schweigen ist Gold	ART	ART	1992	MEZ	5 X 7	AP88	60	1	800	800
Suzay's Flower	ART	ART	1992	MEZ	5 X 7	AP88	150	1	950	950
Junction II	ART	ART	1992	MEZ	11 X 17	AP88	150	1	1050	1050
Peace II	ART	ART	1992	MEZ	10 X 12	AP88	150	1	2500	2500
Senket Ikebana	ART	ART	1992	MEZ	14 X 8	AP88	150		1800	2000
Ikebana by Keishin	ART	ART	1992	MEZ	24 X 17	AP88	150		3000	4000
Pegasus	ART	ART	1992	MEZ	10 X 8	AP88	70		1400	1400
Care	ART	ART	1993	MEZ	24 X 18	AP88	150		2200	2200
Road II	ART	ART	1993	MEZ	6 X 5	AP88	150		950	1200

MICHAEL RUBIN

BORN: Quincy, IL; 1946
EDUCATION: Univ of Kansas, Lawrence, KS, BA, Educ, 1964–69; Eden Theological Seminary, St Louis, MO, 1970–71; Univ of Missouri, St Louis, MO, MA, Educ, 1971–72; Washington Univ, St Louis, MO, Grad Sch of Architecture, 1973–75; Southern Illinois Univ, Edwardsville, IL, MFA, 1977–79
RECENT EXHIB: Grae Gallery, St Louis, MO, 1987

COLLECTIONS: St Louis Univ, MO; Owensburo Art Mus, KY; Southern Illinois Univ, Edwardsville, IL
PRINTERS: Bud Shark, Boulder, CO (BS); Ron Trujillo, Boulder, CO (RT); Shark's, Inc, Boulder, CO (SI)
PUBLISHERS: Shark's, Inc, Boulder, CO (SI)
GALLERIES: Shark's, Inc, Boulder, CO; Philip Samuels Fine Art, St Louis, MO; Solomon Fima Fine Art, Sherman Oaks, CA; Charles Whitchurch Gallery, Huntington Beach, CA; Quartet Editions, New York, NY

TITLE	PUBLISHER	PRINTER	DATE	MEDIUM	DIMENSION (PAPER SIZE) IN INCHES	TYPE OF PAPER	EDITION NUMBER	NO. OF COLORS	ORIGINAL OPENING PRICE	CURRENT RETAIL PRICE
CURRENT EDITIONS:										
Tondo #1–#4	SI	BS/RT/SI	1984	MON	22 DIA EA	AC	1 EA		300 EA	400 EA
Rexene #2	SI	BS/RT/SI	1984	MON	32 X 48 EA	AC	1 EA		500 EA	1200 EA
Untitled (MR 85–#7)	SI	BS/RT/SI	1985	MON	21 X 30 EA	AC	1 EA		300 EA	400 EA
Untitled (MR 85–#8)	SI	BS/RT/SI	1985	MON	26 X 38 EA	AC	1 EA		300 EA	500 EA
L #5, #6	SI	BS/RT/SI	1986	MON	30 X 45 EA	AC	1 EA		800 EA	1400 EA
Y #4–#8	SI	BS/RT/SI	1986	MON	30 X 45 EA	AC	1 EA		800 EA	1400 EA
W #1–#5, #7, #8	SI	BS/RT/SI	1986	MON	30 X 45 EA	AC	1 EA		800 EA	1400 EA
Nile Green States I, II	SI	BS/RT/SI	1987	MON	30 X 30 EA	AC	1 EA		600 EA	1200 EA
Nile Green VI, VII	SI	BS/RT/SI	1987	MON	45 X 30 EA	AC	1 EA		800 EA	1400 EA
Nile Green H-I	SI	BS/RT/SI	1987	MON	30 X 45 EA	AC	1 EA		800 EA	1400 EA
Red, States I, II, III	SI	BS/RT/SI	1988	MON	30 X 30 EA	AC	1 EA		600 EA	1200 EA
Red H-I	SI	BS/RT/SI	1988	MON	30 X 45 EA	AC	1 EA		800 EA	1400 EA
Blue I, II	SI	BS/RT/SI	1988	MON	30 X 45 EA	AC	1 EA		800 EA	1400 EA
Bois I	SI	BS/RT/SI	1989	MON	30 X 45 EA	AC	1 EA		1000 EA	1400 EA
October	SI	BS/RT/SI	1989	MON	45 X 30 EA	AC	1 EA		1000 EA	1400 EA
FE II-VI, IX-XI	SI	BS/RT/SI	1989	MON	30 X 45 EA	AC	1 EA		1000 EA	1200 EA
Little Edge	SI	BS/RT/SI	1989	MON	22 X 30 EA	AC	1 EA		850 EA	1200 EA
PS-h I-X	SI	BS/RT/SI	1989	MON	26 X 48 EA	AC	1 EA	Varies	1200 EA	1600 EA
1990 Series (Vertical)	SI	BS/RT/SI	1990	MON	57 X 30 EA	AC	1 EA	Varies	2000 EA	2400 EA
1990 Series (Horizontal)	SI	BS/RT/SI	1990	MON	30 X 57 EA	AC	1 EA	Varies	2000 EA	2400 EA
1990 Series (Small)	SI	BS/RT/SI	1990	MON	29 X 40 EA	AC	1 EA	Varies	1400 EA	1600 EA
Red Weave (90-14)	SI	BS/RT/SI	1990	LC	48 X 25	R/BFK	25		1200	1400
90-15	SI	BS/RT/SI	1990	LB	25 X 48	R/BFK	12	1	800	1000
WCP Series	SI	BS/RT/SI	1992	MON/WA	14 X 39 EA	AC	1 EA	Varies	1400 EA	1400 EA
WCP Series	SI	BS/RT/SI	1992	MON/WA	20 X 30 EA	AC	1 EA	Varies	1400 EA	1400 EA
WCP Series	SI	BS/RT/SI	1992	MON/WA	22 X 30 EA	AC	1 EA	Varies	1400 EA	1400 EA
WCP Series	SI	BS/RT/SI	1992	MON/WA	28 X 34 EA	AC	1 EA	Varies	1600 EA	1600 EA

SUSAN ROTHENBERG

BORN: Buffalo, NY; Jan 20, 1945
EDUCATION: Cornell Univ, Ithaca, NY, BFA, 1966; George Washington Univ, Wash, DC, 1967; Corcoran Mus Sch, Wash, DC
AWARDS: Creative Artists Public Service Prog Grant, New York State Council on the Arts, NY, 1976–77; Guggenheim Fel, Painting, 1980; Am Acad of Arts & Letters Award, Painting, 1983
RECENT EXHIB: Munson-Williams-Proctor Inst, Utica, NY, 1989; Sonoma State Univ, Rohnert Park, CA, 1992; Hirshhorn Mus, Wash, DC, 1992; Munson-Williams-Proctor Inst Mus, Utica, NY, 1992; Sperone Westwater Gallery, NY, 1987,90,92; Albright-Knox Art Gallery, Buffalo, NY, 1992–93; Hirshhorn Mus, Wash, DC, 1993; St Louis Art Mus, MO, 1993; Chicago Mus of Contemp Art, IL, 1993; Seattle Art Mus, WA, 1993–94
COLLECTIONS: Mus of Mod Art, NY; Albright-Knox Art Gallery, Buffalo, NY; Whitney Mus of Am Art, NY; Walker Art Ctr, Minneapolis, MN; Mus of Fine Arts, Houston, TX
PRINTERS: Aeropress, NY (A); Patricia Branstead, NY (PB); Keith Brintzenhofe, NY (KB); Universal Limited Art Editions, West Islip, NY (ULAE); Mountain Shadow Studio, NY (MSS); Derriere L'Estoile Studios, NY (DES); Linda Larouche, NY (LL); James Miller, NY (JM); Maurice Sanchez, NY (MS); Douglas Scott Volle, NY (DSV); Gemini GEL, Los Angeles, CA (GEM); Artist (ART); Chris Erickson, NY (CE); Joanne Howad, NY (JH); Brenda Zlamany, NY (BZ); Jeryl Parker Editions, NY (JPE); Hitoshi Kido, NY (HK); Nancy Mesenbourg, NY (NM); Bruce Wankel, NY (BW); Ted Warner, Brooklyn, NY (TW); Damage Press, Brooklyn, NY (DP)
PUBLISHERS: Multiples, Inc, NY (M); Universal Limited Art Editions, West Islip, NY (ULAE); Derriere L'Etoile Studios, NY (DES); Maurice Sanchez, NY (MS); Gemini GEL, Los Angeles, CA (GEM); Friedman/Krakow, Boston, MA (FK); Artist (ART); Parasol Press, Ltd, NY (PaP); Brooke Alexander Editions, NY (BAI)
GALLERIES: Marian Goodman, New York, NY; Willard Gallery, New York, NY; Paula Cooper Gallery, New York, NY; Thomas Smith Fine Art, Fort Wayne, IN; Elizabeth Leach Gallery, Portland, OR; Barbara Krakow Gallery, Boston, MA; Flanders Contemporary Art, Minneapolis, MN; Greg Kucera Gallery, Seattle, WA; Nicola Jacobs Gallery, London, England; Sperone Westwater Gallery, New York, NY; Graystone Gallery, San Francisco, CA; John C Stoller & Company, Minneapolis, MN; Greenberg Gallery, St Louis, MO; A Clean, Well-Lighted Place, New York, NY; Charles Cowles Gallery, New York, NY; Maxwell Davidson Gallery, New York, NY; Elizabeth Paul Gallery, Cincinnati, OH; Pence Fine Art, Inc, Los Angeles, CA; Montgomery Glasoe Fine Art, Minneapolis, MN; Joseph Petrone Fine Arts, New York, NY; Brooke Alexander Editions, New York, NY
MAILING ADDRESS: c/o Sperone Westwater Gallery, 142 Green St, New York, NY 10012

Maxwell (M)—Friedman/Krakow (F/K)—Gemini GEL (G)—May (Ma)

Susan Rothenberg
Stumblebum
Courtesy Universal Limited Art Editions

TITLE	PUBLISHER	PRINTER	DATE	MEDIUM	DIMENSION (PAPER SIZE) IN INCHES	TYPE OF PAPER	EDITION NUMBER	NO. OF COLORS	ORIGINAL OPENING PRICE	CURRENT RETAIL PRICE
SOLD OUT EDITIONS (RARE):										
Winter Birch #2	ART	ART	1976	SP	17 X 24	AP	12	5	200	20000
Solitude	ART	ART	1977	SP	17 X 24	AP	5	5	200	20000
Dying Elm #0, #1	ART	ART	1977	SP	17 X 24 EA	AP	8 EA	5 EA	200 EA	20000 EA
Untitled	FK	CE/DES	1977	LC/CC/HC	12 X 16	R/BFK-MOR	18		200	42000
Carnival Trinidad #1, #2, #3	ART	ART	1978	SP	17 X 24 EA	AP	8 EA	6 EA	200 EA	20000 EA
Untitled (Ma-2) (with Scraping & Burnishing) (M-4) (F/K-3)	PaP	BZ/JH/JPE	1979	EB/A/SL/SG/SB	30 X 22	FAB	45	1	200	5500
Untitled (Ma-3) (with Scraping & Burnishing) (M-5) (F/K-4)	PaP	BZ/JH/JPE	1979	EB/A/SL/SG/SB	30 X 22	FAB	45	2	200	10000
Pinks (Ma-7) (F/K-6)	M		1980	WC	11 X 20	Umbria	20		500	10000
Doubles (M-11) (F/K-9)	M	PB/A	1980	WB	26 X 40	RP	20		800	15000
Head and Bones	M	PB/A	1980	WB	26 X 40	AP	20		500	20000
Head and Hands	M	PB/A	1980	WB	26 X 40	AP	15		400	20000
Algarve Orchard #1–#5 (Set of 5)	ART	ART	1982	SP	17 X 24 EA	AP	1 EA	5 EA	1250 SET	50000 SET
Algarve Variations:										
Algarve Variations #0	ART	ART	1983	SP	17 X 24	AP	12	4	200	10000
Algarve Variations #1	ART	ART	1983	SP	17 X 24	AP	5	5	200	10000
Algarve Variations #2	ART	ART	1983	SP	17 X 24	AP	12	5	200	10000
Geranium Stock	ART	ART	1983	SP	17 X 24	AP	12	5	200	10000
Puppet (M-16) (F/K-14)	M	PB/A	1983	WB	70 X 37	OKP	25		1350	40000
Untitled	M	PB/A	1983	EB	34 X 30	AP	35	1	1000	25000

SUSAN ROTHENBERG CONTINUED

TITLE	PUBLISHER	PRINTER	DATE	MEDIUM	DIMENSION (PAPER SIZE) IN INCHES	TYPE OF PAPER	EDITION NUMBER	NO. OF COLORS	ORIGINAL OPENING PRICE	CURRENT RETAIL PRICE
SOLD OUT EDITIONS (RARE):										
Plug	ULAE	KB/ULAE	1983	LC	30 X 22	HMP	29	2	650	30000
Untitled	ART/MS	LL/JM/MS/DES	1983	LB	21 X 24	HMP	34	1	750	15000
Untitled	ART	MSS	1983	AC/DPT	34 X 30	SOM	35		750	10000
Four Rays Horse (M-15)	ART/DES	MS/DES	1980–83	LB	21 X 24	JK/HMP	34	1	1000	10000
Boy/Girl (M-19)	ART/DES	MS/DES	1983–84	EB/DPT	22 X 18	R/BFK	35	1	400	3500
Girl/Boy (M-20)	ART/DES	MS/DES	1983–84	EB/DPT	26 X 22	R/BFK	35	1	400	3500
Four Green Lines (M-18) (F/K-16)	ULAE	ULAE	1984	LC	22 X 30	AP	30			7000
Between the Eyes	ULAE	KB/ULAE	1984	LC/WC/CO/HC	58 X 34	AP88	36	4	1200	25000
Missing Corner	ULAE	ULAE	1984	WC	22 X 15	PAP	18	2	2100	15000
Algarve Winter Variations #1–#4 (Set of 4)	ART	ART	1984	SP	17 X 24 EA	AP	5–13 EA	4–7 EA	800 SET	40000 SET
Black Water	ULAE	ULAE	1984–85	LB	60 X 40	DIEU/HMP	16	2	2500	18000
Untitled	LCPA		1985	SP	22 X 29	AP	72	1	300	2000
Swamp Grass #1, #2 (Set of 2)	ART	ART	1986	SP	17 X 24 EA	AP	4 EA	5 EA	500 SET	20000 SET
Stumblebum	ULAE	DSV/ULAE	1986	LC	87 X 43	AP	40		4500	15000
Neman (on Wood)	GEM	GEM	1986	MEZ	30 X 21	WOOD	40	12	1800	10000
Breath-Man	GEM	GEM	1986	J/REL	21 X 21	HMP	37	4	1250	8000
Red Dance (M-28)	GEM	GEM	1986	LC	20 X 15	LBP	31	1	900	10000
Tilting (M-30) (G-1282)	GEM	GEM	1986	LC/WC	54 X 57	S/100	46	4	3500	12000
Boneman (M-31) (G-1283)	GEM	GEM	1986	MEZ	30 X 20	R/BFK	42	1	1200	9000
Spinning	GEM	GEM	1986	LC	39 X 31	JK/HMP	38	7	1700	10000
Blue Violin	ULAE	KB/DSV/ULAE	1986	WC	65 X 43	TOY	37	6	4000	20000
Listening Bamboo	ULAE	BW/ULAE	1989–90	WB	54 X 84	MASHI	23	1	6500	6500
Mezzo Fist #2	ULAE	KB/HK/MM/ULAE	1990	MEZ	24 X 20	JWP/HMP	48	1	2500	2800
Untitled	BAI	TW/DP	1992–93	WB	11 X 12	KOZO	25	1	600	600

JEANNE ROVEGNO

BORN: Freeport, NY; 1957
EDUCATION: New York Inst of Tech, NY, BFA, 1979; Univ of Georgia, Summer Studies Abroad, Italy, 1981; Indiana Univ, Bloomington, IN, MFA, 1982
AWARDS: Honorable Mention, Univ of Massachusetts, Amherst, MA, 1983; Purchase Award, Nassau County Mus of Fine Art, Roslyn, NY, 1984
RECENT EXHIB: Sherry French Gallery, NY, 1988
COLLECTIONS: Nassau County of Fine Art, Roslyn, NY; Arkansas Art Center, Little Rock, AR
PRINTERS: David Keister, Bloomington, IN; David Calkins, Bloomington, IN (DC); Echo Press, Bloomington, IN (EPr)
PUBLISHERS: Echo Press, Bloomington, IN (EPr)
GALLERIES: Yvonne Rapp Gallery, Louisville, KY; Echo Press, Bloomington, IN

TITLE	PUBLISHER	PRINTER	DATE	MEDIUM	DIMENSION (PAPER SIZE) IN INCHES	TYPE OF PAPER	EDITION NUMBER	NO. OF COLORS	ORIGINAL OPENING PRICE	CURRENT RETAIL PRICE
CURRENT EDITIONS:										
Still Life With Pears	EPr	DK/DC/EPr	1985	LC	12 X 10	AC/S	26	11	200	250
Still Life with Crows	EPr	DK/DC/EPr	1985	LC	13 X 10	AC/5	26	12	200	250

FRANK ROWLAND

BORN: Altoona, PA; 1927
EDUCATION: Art Inst of Pittsburgh, PA; Acad of Art, Chicago, IL
PRINTERS: American Atelier, NY (AA); Artist (ART)
PUBLISHERS: Circle Fine Art, Chicago, IL (CFA)
GALLERIES: Circle Galleries, San Diego, CA & San Francisco, CA & Northbrook, IL & Pittsburgh, PA & Houston, TX & Soho, NY & Chicago, IL & Scottsdale, AZ & Beverly Hills, CA & Sherman Oaks, CA & Costa Mesa, CA & New Orleans, LA & Las Vegas, NV & Honolulu, HI & Palm Beach, FL & Seattle, WA

TITLE	PUBLISHER	PRINTER	DATE	MEDIUM	DIMENSION (PAPER SIZE) IN INCHES	TYPE OF PAPER	EDITION NUMBER	NO. OF COLORS	ORIGINAL OPENING PRICE	CURRENT RETAIL PRICE
SOLD OUT EDITIONS (RARE):										
Candid	CFA	ART	1978	SP	24 X 24	AP	75		75	250
Rally III	CFA	ART	1978	SP	24 X 24	AP	200		75	250
Moonglow	CFA	ART	1978	SP	24 X 24	AP	25		75	250
Cinders	CFA	ART	1978	SP	24 X 24	AP	100		75	250
Crosstown traffic	CFA	ART	1978	SP	24 X 24	AP	75		75	250
Blue Beaver	CFA	ART	1978	SP	24 X 24	AP	200		75	250
Sunset	CFA	ART	1978	SP	16 X 12	AP	75		75	250
Planet	CFA	ART	1978	SP	16 X 12	AP	75		75	250
Horizon	CFA	ART	1978	SP	16 X 12	AP	75		75	250
Mother Earth	CFA	ART	1978	SP	16 X 12	AP	75		75	250
Honey Pot	CFA	ART	1978	SP	36 X 36	AP	110		100	300
Fly Trap	CFA	ART	1978	SP	36 X 36	AP	100		100	300
Device III	CFA	ART	1979	SP	24 X 24	AP	200		75	250
Probe	CFA	ART	1979	SP	24 X 24	AP	200		75	250

FRANK ROWLAND CONTINUED

TITLE	PUBLISHER	PRINTER	DATE	MEDIUM	DIMENSION (PAPER SIZE) IN INCHES	TYPE OF PAPER	EDITION NUMBER	NO. OF COLORS	ORIGINAL OPENING PRICE	CURRENT RETAIL PRICE
SOLD OUT EDITIONS (RARE):										
Epitome	CFA	ART	1979	SP	36 X 36	AP	250		75	250
Sun God	CFA	ART	1980	SP	24 X 24	AP	250		75	250
Male Box	CFA	ART	1980	SP	24 X 24	AP	250		75	250
Act III	CFA	ART	1980	SP	24 X 24	AP	250		75	250
Fire Eye	CFA	ART	1980	SP	24 X 24	AP	250		50	250
Trix	CFA	ART	1980	SP	24 X 24	AP	250		50	250
Bounce	CFA	ART	1980	SP	24 X 24	AP	275		50	250
Score	CFA	ART	1980	SP	24 X 24	AP	275		50	225
Shaft	CFA	ART	1980	SP	24 X 24	AP	275		50	225
Pulse	CFA	ART	1980	SP	24 X 24	AP	275		50	250
CURRENT EDITIONS:										
Regatta	CFA	ART	1980	SP	24 X 24	AP	250		50	200
Love Nest	CFA	ART	1980	SP	24 X 24	AP	250		50	225
Foreplay	CFA	ART	1980	SP	36 X 36	AP	275		50	225
Race	CFA	ART	1980	SP	24 X 24	AP	275		50	225
Time	CFA	AA	1980	SP	36 X 36	AP	275		50	275
Fanfare	CFA	ART	1980	SP	24 X 24	AP	275		50	250

MARK ROWLAND

BORN: Chicago, IL; 1953
PUBLISHERS: Circle Fine Art, Chicago, IL (CFA)

GALLERIES: Circle Galleries, San Diego, CA & San Francisco, CA & Pittsburgh, PA & Northbrook, IL & Houston, TX & Soho, NY & Chicago, IL & Scottsdale, AZ & Beverly Hills, CA & Costa Mesa, CA & Sherman Oaks, CA & Palm Beach, FL & Honolulu, HI & New Orleans, LA & Las Vegas, NV & Seattle, WA

TITLE	PUBLISHER	PRINTER	DATE	MEDIUM	DIMENSION (PAPER SIZE) IN INCHES	TYPE OF PAPER	EDITION NUMBER	NO. OF COLORS	ORIGINAL OPENING PRICE	CURRENT RETAIL PRICE
SOLD OUT EDITIONS (RARE):										
Impact	CFA	ART	1978	SP	30 X 30	AP	200		100	250
Vista	CFA	ART	1980	SP	30 X 30	AP	300		125	350
CURRENT EDITIONS:										
Episode	CFA	ART	1979	SP	30 X 30	AP	300		100	250
Episode (Deluxe)	CFA	ART	1979	SP	30 X 30	JP	10		125	275
Gamut	CFA	ART	1979	SP	30 X 30	AP	300		100	250
Gamut (Deluxe)	CFA	ART	1979	SP	30 X 30	JP	15		125	275
Omega	CFA	ART	1979	SP	30 X 30	AP	300		100	250
Omega (Deluxe)	CFA	ART	1979	SP	30 X 30	JP	10		125	275
Impulse	CFA	ART	1979	SP	30 X 30	AP	300		100	250
Impulse (Deluxe)	CFA	ART	1979	SP	30 X 30	JP	10		125	275
Equity	CFA	ART	1979	SP	30 X 30	AP	300		100	250
Equity (Deluxe)	CFA	ART	1979	SP	30 X 30	JP	10		125	275
Whim	CFA	ART	1979	SP	30 X 30	AP	300		100	250
Whim (Deluxe)	CFA	ART	1979	SP	30 X 30	JP	10		125	275
Rapture	CFA	ART	1979	SP	30 X 30	AP	300		100	250
Rapture (Deluxe)	CFA	ART	1979	SP	30 X 30	JP	10		125	275
Motive	CFA	ART	1979	SP	30 X 30	AP	300		100	250
Motive (Deluxe)	CFA	ART	1979	SP	30 X 30	JP	15		125	275
Onset	CFA	ART	1979	SP	30 X 30	AP	300		100	250
Onset (Deluxe)	CFA	ART	1979	SP	30 X 30	JP	10		125	275
Tangent	CFA	ART	1979	SP	30 X 30	AP	300		100	250
Tangent (Deluxe)	CFA	ART	1979	SP	30 X 30	JP	10		125	275
Coarse	CFA	ART	1979	SP	30 X 30	AP	300		100	250
Coarse (Deluxe)	CFA	ART	1979	SP	30 X 30	JP	10		125	275
Tempo	CFA	ART	1979	SP	30 X 30	AP	300		100	250
Tempo (Deluxe)	CFA	ART	1979	SP	30 X 30	JP	10		125	275
Flags	CFA	ART	1979	SP	30 X 30	AP	300		100	275
Visage	CFA	ART	1980	SP	40 X 30	AP	300		125	275
Motive	CFA	ART	1980	SP	30 X 30	AP	300		100	250
Motive (Deluxe)	CFA	ART	1980	SP	30 X 30	JP	10		125	275

JOSEPH JOHN ROZMAN

BORN: Milwaukee, WI; December 26, 1944
EDUCATION: Univ of Wisconsin, WI, BFA with honors, 1967, MFA, 1969
TEACHING: Univ of Wisconsin, Milwaukee, WI, 1967–69,72–73; Carthage Col, Kenosha, WI, 1969–72; Univ of Wisconsin, Parkside, WI, 1970–71; Mount Mary Col, 1975 to present; Vis Lectr, Art, Univ of Wisconsin, Parkside, WI, 1970–71; Instr, Printmaking & Painting, Carthage Col, Kenosha, WI, 1969–72; Instr, Design & Printmaking, Univ of Wisconsin, Milwaukee, WI, 1967–69, 1972–73; Instr, Printmaking & Design, London, England, 1973–74; Milwaukee Art Mus, WI, 1968–76; Art in Res, Univ of Wisconsin, Platteville, WI, 1983; Prof, Printmaking, Painting, Photog & Film, Mt St Mary Col, Racine, WI, 1975 to present
AWARDS: Logan Medal & Prize, Art Inst of Chicago, IL, 1966; Purchase Prize, DeCordova Mus, Lincoln, MA, Nat Boston Printmakers Exhib, 1971; John G Curtis Award, Art Inst of Chicago, IL, 1981; Purchase Award, Nat Boston Printmakers Exhib, DeCordova Mus, Lincoln, MA, 1971; John G Curtis Award, Art Inst of Chicago, IL, 1981; Edgewood Col Award, Madison Nat Watercolor Exhib, WI, 1988; Janey & Carl Moebius Award for Excellence, Alumni Art Show, Univ of Wisconsin, Milwaukee Art Mus, WI, 1989

JOSEPH JOHN ROZMAN CONTINUED

RECENT EXHIB: Wustum Mus of Fine Arts, Racine, WI, 1989; Taipai Mus of Fine Arts Mus, Taiwan, 1990
COLLECTIONS: Milwaukee Art Mus, WI; DeCordova Mus, Lincoln, MA; Southwest Texas State Col, San Marcos, TX; Carroll Col, Waukesha, WI; Wisconsin State Univ, Stevens Point, WI; Univ of Wisconsin, Milwaukee, WI; Carthage Col, Kenosha, WI; Charles A Wustum Mus of Fine Arts, Racine, WI
PRINTERS: Artist (ART)
PUBLISHERS: Artist (ART)
GALLERIES: Joy Horwich Gallery, Chicago, IL; Cudahy Gallery, Wisconsin Art Mus, Milwaukee, WI
MAILING ADDRESS: 4935 N Fairway Drive, Racine, WI 53402

TITLE	PUBLISHER	PRINTER	DATE	MEDIUM	DIMENSION (PAPER SIZE) IN INCHES	TYPE OF PAPER	EDITION NUMBER	NO. OF COLORS	ORIGINAL OPENING PRICE	CURRENT RETAIL PRICE
SOLD OUT EDITIONS (RARE):										
A Cat Named Dog	ART	ART	1966	I/MM	12 X 8	AC	10	3	65	350
Nicolee's Rainbow	ART	ART	1970	I/EMB	7 X 6	AC	25	4	50	350
NRB	ART	ART	1971	I/EMB	2 X 2	AC	25	6	30	150
Mother's Rainbow	ART	ART	1971	I/EMB	18 X 11	AC	25	9	75	400
Nicolee's Jumbo	ART	ART	1971	SP/EMB	11 X 15	AC	30	10	50	250
Rainbow Vision Poster	ART	ART	1978	LC	24 X 18	STP	100	4	75	250
Before the Rainbow, in June	ART	ART	1979	E/WA	24 X 18	AC	1		425	800
Nicolee's Rainbow Machine	ART	ART	1972	I/MM/EMB	16 X 18	AC	7	8	125	550
CURRENT EDITIONS:										
Poached Coach at the Honky Grill	ART	ART	1971	SP/EMB	20 X 16	FP	30	1	65	250
Nicolee's Summer	ART	ART	1971	SP	11 X 18	AC	25	6	50	350
Rainbow Wall Mat	ART	ART	1972	I/SP/MM	12 X 17	AC	12	4	125	350
Hong Kong Kolors	ART	ART	1972	I/SP/MM	13 X 14	AC	14	5	65	300
TNTRBWB	ART	ART	1976	I/MM/EMB	11 X 10	AC	40	5	35	150
White Ridges	ART	ART	1977–78	E/EMB	14 X 11	AC		1	75	200
Rainbow Stars	ART	ART	1978	LC/MM/EMB	20 X 16 X 1	AC	45	4	175	400
Rainbow Roads	ART	ART	1980	E/EMB	14 X 11	AC	25	1	75	150
Before the Rainbow in June II	ART	ART	1979–81	E/WA	24 X 18	AC	1		450	650
Over the Hills	ART	ART	1981	E/WA	10 X 8	AC	1		275	350
LWB	ART	ART	1982–83	EB	8 X 6	R/BFK	50	1	25	150

LEO H RUBINFIEN

BORN: Chicago, IL; August 16, 1953
EDUCATION: California Inst of Arts, Valencia, CA, BFA, 1974; Yale Univ Art Sch, New Haven, CT, MFA, 1976
TEACHING: Instr, Photog, Swarthmore Col, PA, 1977; Vis Lectr, Cooper Union, NY, 1982; Sch of Visual Arts, 1978 to present; Assoc Prof, Art, Fordham Univ, 1981 to present
AWARDS: Guggenheim Fel, NY, 1982–83; Asian Cultural Council Fel, 1984
RECENT EXHIB: Mus of Mod Art, NY, 1989
COLLECTIONS: Mus of Mod Art, NY; Metropolitan Mus of Art, NY; Corcoran Gallery of Art, Wash, DC; San Francisco Mus of Mod Art, CA; Bibliotheque Nat, Paris, France
PRINTERS: Artist (ART)
PUBLISHERS: Artist (ART)
GALLERIES: Light Gallery, New York, NY; Fraenkel Gallery, San Francisco, CA
MAILING ADDRESS: 230 Riverside Dr #5L, New York, NY 10025

TITLE	PUBLISHER	PRINTER	DATE	MEDIUM	DIMENSION (PAPER SIZE) IN INCHES	TYPE OF PAPER	EDITION NUMBER	NO. OF COLORS	ORIGINAL OPENING PRICE	CURRENT RETAIL PRICE
CURRENT EDITIONS:										
Untitled Photographs	ART	ART	1979–82	PA	16 X 20 EA	DT	30 EA	FULL	500 EA	1000 EA

LAURA RUBY

BORN: Los Angeles, CA; December 7, 1945
EDUCATION: Univ of Southern California, Los Angeles, CA, BA, English, 1967; San Francisco State Col, CA, MA, English, 1969; Univ of Hawaii, Honolulu, HI, MFA, 1978
TEACHING: Instr, Art, Chaminade Univ, 1980–81; Instr, Art, Univ of Hawaii, Honolulu, HI, 1977 to present
AWARDS: Purchase Award, Erie Art Mus, PA, 1983; Award, Sculpture, Artquest, Los Angeles, CA, 1986
RECENT EXHIB: Honolulu Acad of Arts, HI, 1987; Cal-Poly State Univ, Union Gallery, San Luis Obispo, CA, 1988; Bishop Mus, Honolulu, HI, 1990
COLLECTIONS: Erie Art Mus, PA; Contemp Arts Center, Honolulu, HI
PRINTERS: Artist (ART)
PUBLISHERS: Artist (ART)
GALLERIES: Gallery EAS, Honolulu, HI
MAILING ADDRESS: 509 University Ave, #902, Honolulu, HI 92826

TITLE	PUBLISHER	PRINTER	DATE	MEDIUM	DIMENSION (PAPER SIZE) IN INCHES	TYPE OF PAPER	EDITION NUMBER	NO. OF COLORS	ORIGINAL OPENING PRICE	CURRENT RETAIL PRICE
SOLD OUT EDITIONS (RARE):										
The Edward Hopper Retrospective (1 Print in 5 Panels)	ART	ART	1979	SP	30 X 22	R/BFK	3	55	2000	2250
CURRENT EDITIONS:										
Cape Diamond Head	ART	ART	1985	SP	22 X 30	R/BFK	4	6	300	350
Buoy at Diamond Head	ART	ART	1986	SP	22 X 30	R/BFK	6	20	300	350

The Printworld Directory is accepting new applications for the seventh edition. Approximately 300 new artists will be accepted. Please use the two forms provided in the back section of this directory to submit biographical data and documentation of prints. Edition number of each print must not exceed 500 and the retail price must be $100 or more.

THOMAS RUFF

RECENT EXHIB: 303 Gallery, NY, 1991
PRINTERS: Edition Domberger, Stuttgart, Germany (DOM); Atelier Matthieu, Zürich, Switzerland (AM)
PUBLISHERS: Editions Schellmann, NY & Cologne, Germany (ES)
GALLERIES: Editions Schellmann, New York, NY & Munich, Germany; Stuart Regen Gallery, Los Angeles, CA; Ginny Williams Gallery, Denver, CO; 303 Gallery, New York, NY

TITLE	PUBLISHER	PRINTER	DATE	MEDIUM	DIMENSION (PAPER SIZE) IN INCHES	TYPE OF PAPER	EDITION NUMBER	NO. OF COLORS	ORIGINAL OPENING PRICE	CURRENT RETAIL PRICE
CURRENT EDITIONS:										
Stars (Set of 8)	ES	AMAT	1990	LC/GRANO	35 X 26 EA	IKON	40 EA		6000 SET 1000 EA	6000 SET 1000 EA
Zeitungsphotos (Set of 24 Offset Lithographs)	ES	DOM	1991	LC/OFF	20 X 16 EA	300gr/OFF	36 EA		3600 SET	3600 SET

ALLEN RUPPERSBERG

BORN: Cleveland, Ohio; January 5, 1944
EDUCATION: Chouinard Art Inst, CA, BFA
AWARDS: Endowment for the Arts Grant, 1976; Theodoron Award, Guggenheim Mus, NY, 1977,82
COLLECTIONS: Los Angeles County Mus of Art, CA; Guggenheim Mus of Art, NY; Pasadena Mus of Mod Art, CA; Stedelijk Mus, Amsterdam, Holland
PRINTERS: Patricia Bransted, NY (PB); Bransted Studio, NY (BS); Jack Lemon, Chicago, IL (JL); Landfall Press, Inc, Chicago, IL (LPI)
PUBLISHERS: Brooke Alexander, Inc, NY (BAI); Landfall Press, Inc, Chicago, IL (LPI)
GALLERIES: Brooke Alexander, Inc, New York, NY; Marian Goodman Gallery, New York, NY; Landfall Press, Inc, Chicago, IL; Linda Cathcart Gallery, Santa Monica, CA; Solo Gallery Press, New York, NY

TITLE	PUBLISHER	PRINTER	DATE	MEDIUM	DIMENSION (PAPER SIZE) IN INCHES	TYPE OF PAPER	EDITION NUMBER	NO. OF COLORS	ORIGINAL OPENING PRICE	CURRENT RETAIL PRICE
CURRENT EDITIONS:										
A Private Reading (3 Sheets)	BAI	PB/BS	1978	LC	21 X 29	AP	43		500	900
Tom Sawyer, Huck Finn, the Mississippi and Moonlight	BAI	PB/BS	1978	LC	26 X 20	AP	31		200	350
Untitled	BAI	PB/BS	1978	LC	21 X 29	AP	46		175	350
Preview (Set of 10)	LPI	JL/LPI	1988	LC	25 X 15 EA	SOM	30 EA		2500 SET	2500 SET

EDWARD RUSCHA

BORN: Omaha, NE; December 16, 1937
EDUCATION: Chouinard Art Inst, Los Angeles, CA, 1956–60
TEACHING: Lectr, Painting, Univ of California, Los Angeles, CA, 1969–70
AWARDS: Nat Council of the Arts Grant, 1967; Tamarind Lithography Workshop Fel, 1969; Guggenheim Fel, 1971; Skowhegan Sch of Painting & Sculpture Award, Graphics, 1974; Nat Endowment for the Arts Grant, 1969,78
RECENT EXHIB: Acme Art, San Francisco, CA, 1987; Robert Miller Gallery, NY, 1987; Whitney Mus of Am Art, NY, 1988; Los Angeles County Mus, CA, 1988; Contemp Arts Mus, Houston, TX; Vancouver Art Gallery, Canada, 1988; Inst of Contemp Art, Nagoya, Japan, 1988; Heland Wetterling Gallery, Stockholm, Sweden, 1989; Thomas Babeor Gallery, La Jolla, CA, 1989; Laguna Art Mus, Laguna Beach, CA, 1989; Serpentine Gallery, London, England, 1990; Boymans-van-Beuningen Mus, Rotterdam, the Netherlands, 1990; Pompidou Center, Paris, France, 1990; Los Angeles Mus of Contemp Art, CA, 1990-91; Springfield Art Mus, MO, 1992; Northern Kentucky Univ, Highland Heights, KY, 1992; Charles B Goddard Center for Visual & Performing Arts, Ardmore, OK, 1989,92; Newport Harbor Art Mus, Newport Beach, CA, 1992; Tony Shafrazi Gallery, NY, 1992; Robert Miller Gallery, NY, 1990,92; Gagosian Gallery, NY, 1993
COLLECTIONS: Mus of Mod Art, NY; Whitney Mus of Am Art, NY; Los Angeles County Mus of Art, CA; Joseph Hirshhorn Mus, Wash, DC; Oakland Mus of Art, CA; San Francisco Mus of Mod Art, CA
PRINTERS: Kanthos Press, Los Angeles CA (KP); Editions Alecto, London, England, (EA); Cirrus Editions Workshop, Los Angeles, CA (CEW); Ed Hamilton, Venice, CA (EH); Hamilton Press, Venice, CA (HP); Jane Aman, Los Angeles, CA (JA); Wasserman Silkscreen, Los Angeles, CA (WS); Advanced Graphics Print Workshop, London, England (AG); Alan Cox, London, England (AC); Univ of Hartford, CT (UH); Palm Tree Studios (PTS); Ian Lawson, London, England (IL); Timothy F Berry (TB); Centrum Press, Port Townsend, WA (CP); Styria Studios, NY (SS); Lynne Allen, Albuquerque, NM (LA); Tom Pruit, Albuquerque, NM (TP); Tamarind Inst, Albuquerque, NM (TI); Gemini GEL, Los Angeles, CA (GEM); Univ of South Florida, Tampa, FL (USF); Patricia Branstead, NY (PB); Aeropress, NY (A); Landfall Press, Inc, Chicago, IL (LPI); Peter Pettengill, San Francisco, CA (PP); Marcia Bartholme, San Francisco, CA (MB); Jume Lambia, San Francisco, CA (JL); Renée Bott, San Francisco, CA (RB); Mark Callan, San Francisco, CA (MD); Daria Swylak, San Francisco, CA (CPP); Crown Point Press, San Francisco, CA (CPP); Sam McKenne, Los Angeles, CA (SM); Brighter Image, Los Angeles, CA (BIm)

Edward Ruscha
Time is Up
Courtesy the Artist

EDWARD RUSCHA CONTINUED

PUBLISHERS: Kanthos Press, Los Angeles CA (KP); Editions Alecto, London, England (EA); Audrey Sabal, NY (AS); Cirrus Editions, Ltd, Los Angeles, CA (CE); Multiples, NY (M); Bernard Jacobson Ltd, London, England (BJL); Gemini GEL, Los Angeles, CA (GEM); Brooke Alexander, Inc, NY (BAI); Edizioni O, Milan, Italy (EO); Tamarind Institute, Albuquerque, NM (TI); Heavy Industry Publications (HIP); Styria Studios, NY (SS); Chicago International Art Expo, IL (CIAE); Centrum Press, Port Townsend, WA (CP); Crown Point Press, San Francisco, CA (CPP); Univ of South Florida, Tampa, FL (USF); Univ of Hartford, CT (UH); Hartford Art Sch, CT (HAS); Graphics Arts Council, Los Angeles, CA (GAC); Los Angeles County Mus of Art, CA (LACM); Artist (ART); Creative Workshop Editions, Osaka, Japan (CWE); Edition Julie Sylvester, NY (EJS)
GALLERIES: Cirrus Gallery, Los Angeles, CA; Manny Silverman Gallery, Los Angeles, CA; Thomas Babeor Gallery, La Jolla, CA; Crown Point Press, San Francisco, CA & New York, NY; Rhona Hoffman Gallery, Chicago, IL; Marian Goodman Gallery, New York, NY; Gemini GEL, Los Angeles, CA; James Corcoran Gallery, Santa Monica, CA; Barbara Krakow Gallery, Boston, MA; Thomson Gallery, Minneapolis, MN; Leo Castelli Gallery, New York, NY; Robert Miller Gallery, New York, NY; Tony Shafrazi Gallery, New York, NY; Heland Wetterling Gallery, Stockholm, Sweden; Thomas Segal Gallery, Boston, MA; Stux Modern, New York, NY; Hope Weiss Fine Art, Los Angeles, CA; Laura Carpenter Fine Art, Santa Fe, NM; Works Gallery, Long Beach, CA; Deanna Miller Fine Arts, Pacific Palisades, CA; Brian Gross Fine Art, San Francisco, CA; Janet Levitt Fine Arts, San Francisco, CA; Richard Green Gallery, Santa Monica, CA; Xiliary Twil Fine Arts, Santa Monica, CA; J Rosenthal Fine Arts, Chicago, IL; Beth Urdeng Fine Art, Boston, MA; Moira James Gallery, Green Valley, NV; Richard Levy Gallery, Albuquerque, NM; Carol Evans Fine Arts, Brooklyn, NY; Edition Julie Sylvester, New York, NY; Castelli Graphics, New York, NY; Joseph Petrone Fine Arts, New York, NY; Gagosian Gallery, New York, NY
MAILING ADDRESS: 1024¾ N Western Ave, Los Angeles, CA 90028

Minneapolis Institute of Art (MIA; Foster (F)

TITLE	PUBLISHER	PRINTER	DATE	MEDIUM	DIMENSION (PAPER SIZE) IN INCHES	TYPE OF PAPER	EDITION NUMBER	NO. OF COLORS	ORIGINAL OPENING PRICE	CURRENT RETAIL PRICE
SOLD OUT EDITIONS (RARE):										
Division ('39 Ford) (MIA-2)	KP	KP	1962	LB	13 X 10	RP	10	1	60	6000
Standard Station (MIA-4)	AS	ART	1966	SP	20 X 37	AP	50	6	75	50000
1984 (MIA-5)	GEM	GEM	1967	LB/HC	14 X 18	AP	60	Varies	75	5000
Hollywood (MIA-6)	ART	ART	1968	SP	13 X 41	AP	100	5	100	70000
Mocha Standard (MIA-29)	ART	ART	1969	SP	20 X 37	AP	100		100	50000
Stains	HIP		1969	MM/HC	12 X 13	AP	70		100	6500
Mint (MIA-8)	TI	TI	1969	LC	17 X 24	AP	20	2	100	8000
Hollywood with Observatory (Gray) (MIA-14)	TI	TI	1969	LB	7 X 29	AP	17	1	100	14000
Hey (MIA-27)	TI	TI	1969	LC	8 X 10	AP	20		100	4000
Nine Swimming Pools	USF/ART	USF	1970	LC	16 X 20	AP	30		150	8000
Twenty Six Gasoline Stations	USF/ART	USF	1970	LC	16 X 20	AP	30		150	8000
Various Small Fires	USF/ART	USF	1970	LC	16 X 20	AP	30		150	8000
Set of 6 Organic Silkscreens (Set of 6):									800 SET	16000 SET
News	EA	EA	1970	SP	23 X 32	AP	75		150	3000
Mews	EA	EA	1970	SP	23 X 32	AP	75		150	3000
Pews	EA	EA	1970	SP	23 X 32	AP	75		150	3000
Brews	EA	EA	1970	SP	23 X 32	AP	75		150	3000
Stews	EA	EA	1970	SP	23 X 32	AP	75		150	3000
Dues	EA	EA	1970	SP	23 X 32	AP	75		150	3000
Lisp	CE/BAI	CEW	1970	LC	20 X 28	AP/W	90	3	150	8500
OOO	CE/BAI	CEW	1971	LC	20 X 28	AP/W	90	3	150	8500
Fruit, Metrecal Hollywood (Three Colors Made from Grape & Apricot Jams & Metrecal) (MIA-51)	BJL/ART	CEW	1971	SP	15 X 42	AP	85	3	150	5000
I'm Amazed	BJL	AG	1971	SP	40 X 60	HOL	100	4	800	8000
Drops	CE/BAI	CEW	1971	LC	20 X 28	AP/W	90	3	150	7500
Raw (MIA-53)	BJL	CEW	1971	SP	16 X 26	JG	90	4	400	7500
Suds Series:										8500 SET
Blue Suds (MIA-55)	EO	CEW	1971	SP	18 X 24	AP	100		400	3500
Green Suds (MIA-56)	EO	CEW	1971	SP	18 X 24	AP	100		400	3500
Grey Suds (MIA-57)	EO	CEW	1971	SP	18 X 24	AP	100		400	3500
Insects (Set of 6) (MIA-58–MIA-63)	M	SS	1972	SP	20 X 27 EA	WOOD	100 EA		800 SET 200 EA	18000 SET 3000 EA
Documenta 5	SS	SS	1972	SP	33 X 24	AP	150		200	5000
Evil	CE	JA/CEW	1973	SP	20 X 30	WGV	50	3	225	15000
Hot Shot	BJL	IL	1973	LC	6 X 8	SP	100	3	200	6000
Vanish	CE	CEH/CEW	1973	LC	20 X 28	AP	50	3	250	8500
Domestic Tranquility (Set of 4):			LC						1000 SET	16000 SET
Clock	CG/M	SS	1974	LC	20 X 26	AP	65		300	4000
Bowl	CG/M	SS	1974	LC	18 X 22	AP	65		300	4000
Egg	CG/M	SS	1974	LC	17 X 26	AP	65		300	4000
Plate	CG/M	SS	1974	LC	18 X 26	AP	65		300	4000
Made in USA	ART	LPI	1974	LC	22 X 30	AP	125	5	300	6000
Tropical Fish Series (Set of 5):										
Open	GEM	GEM	1975	PH/SP	25 X 33	AP	56		300	5000
Closed	GEM	GEM	1975	PH/SP	25 X 33	AP	53		300	5000
Air, Water, Fire	GEM	GEM	1975	PH/SP	25 X 33	AP	57		300	5000
Music	GEM	GEM	1975	PH/SP	25 X 33	AP	58		300	5000
Sweets, Meats, Sheets	GEM	GEM	1975	PH/SP	33 X 25	AP	55		300	5000
You Know the Old Story	TI	TI	1975	LC	30 X 22	AP	20	2	300	5000
Thanks for Being with Us	TI	TI	1975	LC	30 X 22	AP	20		300	6000
There's no Job Too Small	TI	TI	1975	LC	30 X 22	AP	20		300	6000
Make-Up Department	M	SS	1975	DT/C	16 X 20	AP	60		300	4000

EDWARD RUSCHA CONTINUED

Edward Ruscha
Coyote
Courtesy Tamarind Institute

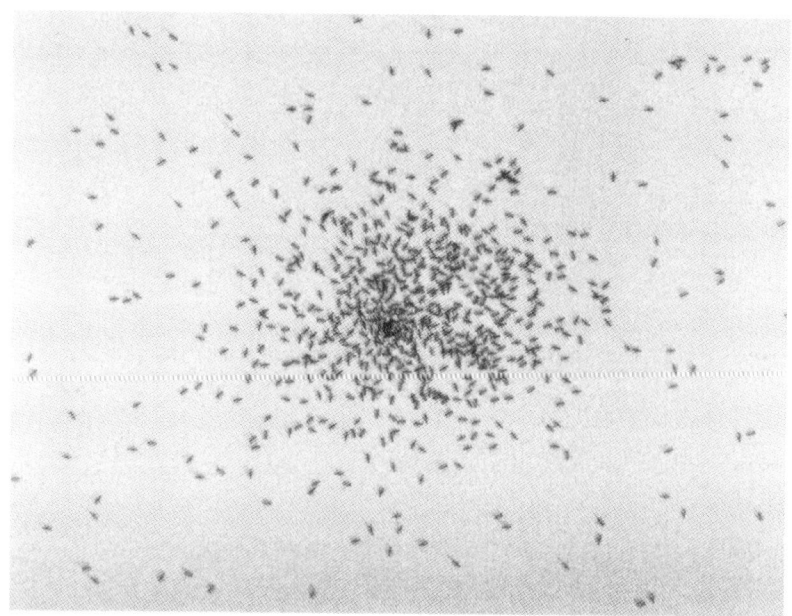

Edward Ruscha
From Insects Suite
Courtesy Multiples, Inc

TITLE	PUBLISHER	PRINTER	DATE	MEDIUM	DIMENSION (PAPER SIZE) IN INCHES	TYPE OF PAPER	EDITION NUMBER	NO. OF COLORS	ORIGINAL OPENING PRICE	CURRENT RETAIL PRICE
SOLD OUT EDITIONS (RARE):										
Various Cheeses (Series of 4):										
Eleven Pieces of Cheese	GEM	GEM	1976	LC	15 X 21	AP	50		275	5000
Exploding Cheese	GEM	GEM	1976	LC	15 X 21	AP	45		274	5000
Cheese Oval	GEM	GEM	1976	LC	15 X 21	AP	39		275	5000
Cheese Crescent	GEM	GEM	1976	LC	15 X 21	AP	21		275	5000
Miracle	GEM	GEM	1976	LC	22 X 31	AP	35		275	6500
Little Connecticut Sleeping House	UH	UH	1978	LC	15 X 22	AP	16		400	6500
Kansas, Oklahoma	UH	UH	1978	LC	22 X 30	AP	35		400	6500
I've Never Seen Two People Looking Healthier	M	PB/A	1978	SP	19 X 50	AP	45		650	10000
Kaye Eye Double S	HAS	PB/A	1978	LC	23 X 30	R/BFK	35		500	6500
Just an Average Guy	M	PB/A	1979	EC	15 X 44	R/BFK	45		500	6000
Two Happy People	BJL	PTS	1980	EC	20 X 39	R/BFK	55	4	750	9000
Two People Temporarily Separated	BJL	PTS	1980	EC	20 X 39	R/BFK	55	4	750	10000
Three Daughters	BJL	PTS	1980	EC	20 X 39	R/BFK	55	4	750	10000
Man Walking Away from It All	BJL	PTS	1980	EC	20 X 39	R/BFK	55	4	750	10000
Jumping Fish	BJL	PTS	1980	EC	20 X 39	R/BFK	55	4	750	10000
Two Jumping Fish	BJL	PTS	1980	EC	20 X 39	R/BFK	55	4	750	10000
Pick, Pan and Shovel	GAC/LACM		1980	LC	22 X 30	R/BFK	100		600	6000
Two Similar Cities	CE	CEW	1981	SP	22 X 60	AP88	35		2250	8500
Fan and Its Surroundings	BJL	AC	1982	LC	37 X 31	R/BFK	55		750	5000
The Globe and Its Surroundings	BJL	AC	1982	LC	41 X 31	R/BFK	55		750	5000
Fans of the World	BJL	AC	1982	LC	37 X 31	R/BFK	55		750	5000
World Series:										
It's Recreational	GEM	GEM	1982	LC	25 X 34	SOM	40		650	10000
Girls	GEM	GEM	1982	LC	25 X 34	SOM	40		650	10000
People Yawning	GEM	GEM	1982	LC	25 X 34	SOM	40		650	10000
Cities	GEM	GEM	1982	LC	25 X 34	SOM	40		650	10000
Thermometers	GEM	GEM	1982	LC	25 X 34	SOM	40		650	10000
Home with Complete Electronic Security System	ART	WS	1982	SP	19 X 48	RGPV	100		750	4500
Hot Air Being Blown	SS	SS	1982	LC	35 X 34	AP88	20	5	700	5000
Chicago Art Fair	BJL/CAE	CEW	1982	LC	33 X 29	AP	100	3	750	5000
Big Dipper	CPP	PP/MB/CPP	1982	AC	34 X 45	AP/SR	10	2	800	5000
Big Dipper over Desert	CPP	PP/JL/CPP	1982	AC	34 X 45	AP/SR	48	1	800	5000
Roughly 92% Angel, but about 8% Devil	CPP	PP/MB/CPP	1982	EC/SG	24 X 23	SOM	25	2	600	2500
Brave Men Run in My Family (Collaboration with Jim Ganzer)	CP	CP	1983	EB/A	22 X 30	R/BFK	40		600	4000
Sea of Desire (Collaboration with Jim Ganzer)	CP	TB/CP	1984	EB/A	23 X 30	R/BFK	40	3	500	15000
Brave Men Run in My Family (Collaboration with Jim Ganzer)	CP	TB/CP	1984	EB/A	23 X 30	R/BFK	40	5	500	15000
Sea of Desire	ART	TB/CP	1985	LC	18 X 26	R/BFK	25		450	15000
Western Vertical	CE/CG	CEW	1986	LC	54 X 37	AP88	36	4	1000	10000

EDWARD RUSCHA CONTINUED

Edward Ruscha
Rabbit
Courtesy Tamarind Institute

Edward Ruscha
Domestic Tranquility: Clock
Courtesy Castelli Graphics & Multiples, Inc

TITLE	PUBLISHER	PRINTER	DATE	MEDIUM	DIMENSION (PAPER SIZE) IN INCHES	TYPE OF PAPER	EDITION NUMBER	NO. OF COLORS	ORIGINAL OPENING PRICE	CURRENT RETAIL PRICE
SOLD OUT EDITIONS (RARE):										
Western Horizontal	CE/CG	CEW	1986	LC	38 X 56	AP88	36	4	1000	10000
Coyote	TI	LA/TP/TI	1986	LC	45 X 34	AP/ROL	30	1	450	8000
Rabbit	TI	LA/TP/TI	1986	LC	45 X 34	AP/ROL	30		450	8000
Dancer	TI	LA/TP/TI	1986	LC	45 X 34	AP/ROL	30	1	450	8000
Ship	TI	LA/TP/TI	1986	LC	45 X 34	AP/ROL	30	1	450	8000
Heaven	CPP	CPP	1988	AC	54 X 40	SOM	25		4000	7500
Hell	CPP	CPP	1988	AC	54 X 40	SOM	25		4000	7500
Rooster	CPP	RB/MC/DS/CPP	1988	AC/HG	26 X 22	SOM	50	5	9500	7500
Hourglass	CPP	CPP	1988	AC	53 X 37	WOVE	20		4000	7000
Jockey	CPP	CPP	1988	AB	30 X 18	SOM	20	1	5000	6500
Coyote	ART	ART	1989	LB	36 X 27	WOVE	50		7500	20000
Gasoline Stations (Set of 10)	ART	SM/BI	1989	LC	20 X 23 EA	WOVE	25 EA		20000 SET	25000 SET
Time Is Up	ART	EH/HP	1989	LB	36 X 27	WOVE	35	1	4500	6000
Sign	ART	EH/HP	1989	LB	27 X 36	WOVE	35	1	4500	6000
CURRENT EDITIONS:										
Indecision	CPP	PP/MB/CPP	1982	EC/SG	24 X 23	SOM	25	4	600	2500
Metro, Petro, Neuro, Psycho	CPP	PP/MB/CPP	1982	EC/SG	24 X 23	SOM	25	4	600	2500
Question and Answer	CWE	EH/HP	1991	LC	15 X 18	R/BFK	50	3	2500	3500
Cameo Cuts (Set of 6)	EJS	EH/HP	1992	LC	12 X 12 EA	R/BFK	28 EA	2 EA	12000 SET	12000 SET

PRINTERS: Donn Steward (Deceased), NY (DS)
PUBLISHERS: Artist (ART)
GALLERIES: Mary Ryan Gallery, New York, NY
MAILING ADDRESS: One Beekman Place, New York, NY 10022

JANET RUTTENBERG

TITLE	PUBLISHER	PRINTER	DATE	MEDIUM	DIMENSION (PAPER SIZE) IN INCHES	TYPE OF PAPER	EDITION NUMBER	NO. OF COLORS	ORIGINAL OPENING PRICE	CURRENT RETAIL PRICE
CURRENT EDITIONS:										
Kenneth's (Series of 22)	ART	DS	1984–86	I	12 X 15 to 20 X 40	TWP	10–25		400–700 EA	600–900 EA

ROBERT RYMAN

BORN: Nashville, TN; May 30, 1930
EDUCATION: Tennessee Polytechnic Inst, Cooksville, TN, 1948–49; George Peabody Col for Teachers, Baltimore, MD, 1949–50; Vanderbilt Univ, Nashville, TN
AWARDS: Skowhegan Sch of Painting, ME, 1987
RECENT EXHIB: DIA Art Found, NY, 1989; Sperone Westwater Gallery, NY, 1989; S Bitter-Larkin Gallery, NY, 1990; Pace Gallery, NY, 1990,92–93

COLLECTIONS: Mus of Mod Art, NY; British Mus, London, England; Whitney Mus of Am Art, NY; Georges Pompidou Center, Paris, France; Carnegie Inst, Pittsburgh, PA; Kunsthaus, Zurich, Switzerland
PRINTERS: Crown Point Press, San Francisco, CA (CPP); Editions Schellmann & Klüser, Munich, Germany (SK); Patrick Foy, San Francisco, CA (PF)
PUBLISHERS: Parasol Press, NY (PaP); Edition Domberger, KG, Germany (ED); I C Editions, Inc, NY (ICE); Nova Scotia Col of Art, Halifax, Canada (NSCA)

The retail prices of the 100,000 limited edition prints quoted in this directory are subject to change. Print publishers, artists and galleries were the direct sources for these quotations. Prices in the secondary market listed as "Sold Out Editions (Rare)" indicate that the publisher has a limited supply of that print or that the print is difficult to locate in the galleries.

ROBERT RYMAN CONTINUED

GALLERIES: Editions Schellmann, New York, NY & Munich, Germany; Rhona Hoffman Gallery, Chicago, IL; Donald Young Gallery, Seattle, WA; BlumHelman Gallery, New York, NY; Bonnier Gallery, New York, NY; Paula Cooper Gallery, New York, NY; Galerie Lelong, New York, NY; Sidney Janis Gallery, New York, NY; Crown Point Gallery, San Francisco, CA & New York, NY; Sperone Westwater Gallery, New York, NY; Pace Prints, New York, NY; S Bitter-Larkin Gallery, New York, NY; Jonathan Novak Contemporary, Los Angeles, CA; Garner Tullis, New York, NY; Nohra Haime Gallery, New York, NY; Laura Carpenter Fine Art, Santa Fe, NM; Maxwell Galleries, San Francisco, CA; Tomoko Liguori Gallery, New York, NY
MAILING ADDRESS: 17 W 16th St, New York, NY 10011

TITLE	PUBLISHER	PRINTER	DATE	MEDIUM	DIMENSION (PAPER SIZE) IN INCHES	TYPE OF PAPER	EDITION NUMBER	NO. OF COLORS	ORIGINAL OPENING PRICE	CURRENT RETAIL PRICE
SOLD OUT EDITIONS (RARE):										
On the Bowery: Untitled	ED		1969	SP	26 X 26	AP	100		250	6000
Circle Lithograph	NSCA		1971	LC	20 DIA	AP	50		350	3500
Untitled (Set of 7 Aquatints)	PaP	CPP	1972	AC	24 X 24 EA	R/BFK	50 EA		2500 SET	28000 SET
Six Aquatints (Set of 6)	PaP	PF/CPP	1975	AC	36 X 36 EA	LEN/100	50 EA		9000 SET	35000 SET
Untitled (4 Aquatints & 1 Etching) (Set of 5)	PaP		1990	AB(4) EB(1)	33 X 33 EA	R/BFK	80		15000 SET	25000 SET
Untitled (Set of 5)	ICE		1991	AC	36 X 36 EA	R/BFK	80 EA		35000 SET	35000 SET

BETYE SAAR

BORN: Los Angeles, CA; July 30, 1926
EDUCATION: Univ of California, Los Angeles, CA, BA; Univ of Southern California, Los Angeles, CA; Long Beach State Col, CA; San Fernando Valley State Col, CA
TEACHING: Vis Art, California State Univ, Hayward, CA, Fall, 1971; Prof, Art, California State Univ, Northridge, CA, 1973–75; Instr, Univ of Alaska, Anchorage, AK, 1979; Prof, Art, Otis Art Inst, Los Angeles, CA, 1976–84; Instr, Univ of California, Los Angeles, CA, 1984 to present
AWARDS: Purchase Award, California State Col, Los Angeles, CA, 1972; Nat Endowment for the Arts Award, 1974,84
RECENT EXHIB: Michigan State Univ, Kresge Art Mus, East Lansing, MI, 1992; Univ of Hartford, Joseloff Gallery, West Hartford, CT, 1992
COLLECTIONS: Univ of Massachusetts, Amherst, MA; Los Angeles County Mus, CA; Univ of California, Berkeley, CA
PRINTERS: Cirrus Editions Workshop, Los Angeles, CA (CEW)
PUBLISHERS: Cirrus Editions, Ltd, Los Angeles, CA (CE)
GALLERIES: Cirrus Editions Gallery, Los Angeles, CA; INTAR Gallery, New York, NY; Alitash Kebede Fine Arts, Los Angeles, CA
MAILING ADDRESS: 8074 Willow Glen Rd, Los Angeles, CA 90046

TITLE	PUBLISHER	PRINTER	DATE	MEDIUM	DIMENSION (PAPER SIZE) IN INCHES	TYPE OF PAPER	EDITION NUMBER	NO. OF COLORS	ORIGINAL OPENING PRICE	CURRENT RETAIL PRICE
CURRENT EDITIONS:										
Untitled (221c)	CE	CEW	1976	LB	15 X 19	SOM	250	1	250	250

PETER SAARI

PRINTERS: American Atelier, NY (AA)
PUBLISHERS: Circle Fine Art, Chicago, IL (CFA)
GALLERIES: Circle Galleries, Scottsdale, AZ & Chicago, IL & New York, NY & Beverly Hills, CA & Costa Mesa, CA & Sherman Oaks, CA & San Diego, CA & San Francisco, CA & Palm Beach, FL & Honolulu, HI & Northbrook, IL & New Orleans, LA, & Las Vegas, NV & Pittsburgh, PA & Houston, TX & Seattle, WA; Tortue Gallery, Santa Monica, CA; Helander Galleries, Palm Beach, FL & New York, NY

TITLE	PUBLISHER	PRINTER	DATE	MEDIUM	DIMENSION (PAPER SIZE) IN INCHES	TYPE OF PAPER	EDITION NUMBER	NO. OF COLORS	ORIGINAL OPENING PRICE	CURRENT RETAIL PRICE
CURRENT EDITIONS:										
Second Style Painting	CFA	AA	1980	SP	20 X 24	AP	175		150	200

HUIBERT SABELIS

BORN: Wageningen, The Netherlands; February 28, 1942
EDUCATION: Tech Sch, The Netherlands, 1957–60; Art Sch, Minneapolis, MN, 1964; Studied with Henk Krijger (Lino-Printing) & Rol Lampitoc (Serigraphy)
AWARDS: Gold Medal, Acad Italia dell Arti e del Lavoro
RECENT EXHIB: Aaron Gallery, Waterloo, Canada, 1987; Galerie Ram, Arnheim, The Netherlands, 1987; Rivercrest Gallery, Mississauga, Canada, 1987; Public Library & Gallery, Collingwood, Canada, 1988; Halton Hills Cult Center, Georgetown, Canada, 1988; The Gallery, Charlotte, NC, 1988; Kasteel Elsloo, The Netherlands, 1988; Galerie Jan J Albers, Apeldoorn, The Netherlands, 1989; Landhuis Galerie, Rotterdam, The Netherlands, 1990
COLLECTIONS: Royal Ontario Mus, Toronto, Can; Philippine Nat Mus, Manilla, PI; Los Angeles County Mus, CA; Niagara Falls Mus, NY; Municipal Arts Coll, Los Angeles, CA; UNESCO, Tokyo, Japan; Nat Library, Paris, France; The Vatican, Rome, Italy; Nat Library of Canada
PRINTERS: Arts Litho, Paris, France (AL); Rol Lampitoc, Agincourt, Can (RL); Pronovost (PRO); Artist (ART); Arts Graphics, Los Angeles, CA (AG)
PUBLISHERS: Art in Tapestry (AT); Atelier Symphony Streetsville, Canada (AS)
GALLERIES: Aaron Gallery, Waterloo, Canada; Nicholaas Gallery, Ottawa, Canada; Art Loft Gallery, Peterborough, Canada; Rain Dance Gallery, Portland, OR
MAILING ADDRESS: 1136 Bancroft Drive, Mississauga, ON, Canada L5V 1B9

TITLE	PUBLISHER	PRINTER	DATE	MEDIUM	DIMENSION (PAPER SIZE) IN INCHES	TYPE OF PAPER	EDITION NUMBER	NO. OF COLORS	ORIGINAL OPENING PRICE	CURRENT RETAIL PRICE
SOLD OUT EDITIONS (RARE):										
Seals	AS	ART	1976	LI	10 X 14	RICE	20	1	75	150
Papaya	AS	ART/AG	1977	SP	14 X 23	AP	100	8	100	250
Geese	AS	ART/AG	1977	SP	14 X 23	AP	100	7	100	250

HUIBERT SABELIS CONTINUED

TITLE	PUBLISHER	PRINTER	DATE	MEDIUM	DIMENSION (PAPER SIZE) IN INCHES	TYPE OF PAPER	EDITION NUMBER	NO. OF COLORS	ORIGINAL OPENING PRICE	CURRENT RETAIL PRICE
SOLD OUT EDITIONS (RARE):										
Appel en Tulip	AS	ART/AG	1978	SP	14 X 23	AP	100	8	100	250
Les Tulip	AS	ART/AG	1978	SP	14 X 23	AP	100	7	100	250
The Spectators	AS	ART/AG	1978	SP	14 X 23	AP	100	8	100	250
Leda and the Swan	AS	ART/AG	1978	SP	14 X 23	AP	100	8	100	250
The Travelers	AS	ART/AG	1978	SP	14 X 23	AP	100	7	100	250
The Lady and Her Suitor	AS	ART/AG	1979	SP	14 X 23	AP	100	7	100	250
Young Lovers	AS	ART/AG	1979	SP	14 X 23	AP	100	7	100	250
The Family	AS	ART/AG	1979	SP	14 X 23	AP	100	7	100	250
SOLD OUT EDITIONS (RARE):										
Evangelina	AS	ART/AG	1979	SP	14 X 23	AP	100	7	100	250
Evangelina and the Goose	AS	ART/AG	1979	SP	22 X 30	StP	100	10	150	700
Romeo and Juliet	AS	ART/RL	1980	SP	22 X 30	SP	75	9	200	600
Mother and Daughter	AS	ART/RL	1981	SP	22 X 30	SP	81	8	200	600
Bird of Paradise	AS	ART/RL	1982	AP	14 X 23	SP	75	8	100	300
Flower of Love	AS	ART/RL	1982	SP	14 X 23	AP	75	11	100	300
Together	AS	ART/RL	1982	SP	14 X 23	AP	75	9	100	300
The Minstrel	AS	ART/RL	1982	SP	17 X 23	AP	75	7	100	300
The Meeting	AS	ART	1986	SP	25 X 25 cm	AP	42	12	100	100
The Bride	AS	ART	1986	SP	25 X 25 cm	AP	42	11	100	150
Flower Girl	AS	ART	1986	SP	25 X 25 cm	AP	42	13	100	100
Huilers	MIT	MIT	1989	SP	22 X 30	VGP	60	9	500	600
Swan Dance	MIT	MIT	1989	SP	22 X 30	VGP	175	6	500	600
CURRENT EDITIONS:										
Woman Between Worlds	AS	PRO	1980	SP	22 X 30	AP	150	10	200	400
To be Courted	AS	PRO	1980	SP	22 X 30	AP	150	7	200	400
Lovers I, II	AS	PRO	1980	SP	22 X 30 EA	AP	150 EA	9 EA	200 EA	400 EA
Samson and Delila Suite (Set of 5):										
Samson and the Lion	AS	AL	1981	LC	22 X 30	AP	100	4	200	500
The Courtship	AS	AL	1981	LC	22 X 30	AP	100	4	200	500
The Wedding	AS	AL	1981	LC	22 X 30	AP	100	4	200	500
The Cutting of the Hair	AS	AL	1981	LC	22 X 30	AP	100	4	200	500
The Triumph	AS	AL	1981	LC	22 X 30	AP	100	4	200	500
Evangelina with the Goose	AS	ART/RL	1982	SP	14 X 17	AP	75	8	100	150
The Gate A, B (Dipt)	AS	ART/RL	1985	SP	22 X 30	VGP	100	13	500	500
Tree of Life	AS	ART/AL	1986	LC/SP	14 X 14	AP	100	10	100	100
Mother and Daughter	AS	ART/AL	1986	LC/SP	14 X 14	AP	100	10	100	100
A Man and a Woman	AS	ART/AL	1986	LC/SP	14 X 14	AP	100	10	100	100
Proud Parents	AS	ART/AL	1986	LC/SP	14 X 14	AP	100	10	100	100
The Family	AS	ART/AL	1986	LC/SP	14 X 14	AP	100	9	100	100
The Future Together	AS	ART/AL	1986	LC/SP	14 X 14	AP	100	9	100	100
Untitled	AS	ART	1986	SP	25 X 25 cm	AP	42	12	100	100
Lady at the Gate	AS	ART	1986	SP	20 X 14 cm	AP	42	20	100	100
Tomorrow's Bride	AS	ART	1986	SP	20 X 20 cm	AP	42	15	100	100
The Shy Girl	AS	ART	1986	SP	20 X 20 cm	AP	42	15	100	100
Together in the Garden	AS	ART	1986	SP	20 X 14 cm	AP	42	22	100	100
Canadian Autumn	AS	ART/RL	1987	SP	22 X 30	StP	115	9	300	400
Love Dance	AS	ART/RL	1987	SP	22 X 30	StP	112	5	300	400
Paradise Flowers	AS	ART	1988	SP	15 X 15 cm	AP	42	16	100	100
Flowers of Love	AS	ART	1988	SP	15 X 15 cm	AP	42	13	100	100
Flowers at Sunrise	AS	ART	1988	SP	12 X 15 cm	AP	42	15	100	100
O'Canada	AS	ART	1988	SP	15 X 22	StP	42	18	200	200
Love in Poetry and Image (Set of 6):										
The Kiss	AS	ART	1988	SP	15 X 22	StP	42	23	1000	1000
The Feeling of Love	AS	ART	1988	SP	15 X 22	StP	42	23	1000	1000
Raindrops	AS	ART	1988	SP	15 X 22	StP	42	23	1000	1000
Petit Fleur	AS	ART	1988	SP	15 X 22	StP	42	23	1000	1000
A Declaration	AS	ART	1988	SP	15 X 22	StP	42	23	1000	1000
My Haven	AS	ART	1988	SP	15 X 22	StP	42	23	1000	1000

DELI SACILOTTO

BORN: British Columbia, Canada; 1936
EDUCATION: Alberta Col of Art, Calgary, Canada, BA; Arts Student League, NY; Pratt Graphic Center, NY
TEACHING: Columbia Univ Teacher's Col, NY; Pratt Inst Grad Sch, NY; Sch of Visual Arts, NY; York Univ, Toronto, Canada
COLLECTIONS: Mus of Mod Art, NY; Nat Gallery of Canada, Ottawa, Can; Edmonton Art Gallery, Alberta, Canada
PRINTERS: American Atelier, NY (AA)
PUBLISHERS: Circle Fine Art, Chicago, IL (CFA)
GALLERIES: Circle Galleries, San Diego, CA & San Francisco, CA & Northbrook, IL & Pittsburgh, PA & Houston, TX & Soho, NY & Chicago, IL & Scottsdale, AZ & Beverly Hills, CA & Costa Mesa, CA & Sherman Oaks, CA & Palm Beach, LA & Honolulu, HI & New Orleans, LA & Las Vegas, NV & Seattle, WA

TITLE	PUBLISHER	PRINTER	DATE	MEDIUM	DIMENSION (PAPER SIZE) IN INCHES	TYPE OF PAPER	EDITION NUMBER	NO. OF COLORS	ORIGINAL OPENING PRICE	CURRENT RETAIL PRICE
CURRENT EDITIONS:										
McDowell Suite #2	CFA	AA	1982	LC	31 X 23	AP	250		125	175

DONALD JAY SAFF

BORN: Brooklyn, NY; December 12, 1937
EDUCATION: Pratt Graphic Art Workshop, NY, 1959–62; Queens Col, City Univ, NY, BA, 1959; Columbia Univ, NY, MA, 1960; Pratt Inst, NY, MFA, 1962; Teachers Col, Columbia Univ, NY, EdD, 1964
TEACHING: Instr, Printmaking & Drawing, Columbia Univ, NY, 1965, 66; Assoc Prof, Printmaking & Design, Univ of South Florida, Tampa, FL, 1965–67
AWARDS: Fulbright Fel, Italy, 1964–65; Patrick Gavin Mem Prize, MA, 1966; Nat Endowment for the Arts Fel, Univ of South Florida, Tampa, FL, 1973–77
COLLECTIONS: Mus of Mod Art, NY; Metropolitan Mus of Art, NY; Brooklyn Mus, NY; Philadelphia Mus of Art, PA; Fogg Art Mus, Harvard Univ, Cambridge, MA; Nat Gallery of Art, Wash, DC; Library of Congress, Wash, DC; Dartmouth Col, NH; Illinois State Univ, IL; La Salle Col, Phila, PA; Lessing Rosenwald Coll, Phila, PA; Mus of Fine Arts, Boston, MA; Southern Illinois Univ, IL; Florida Inst Univ, Miami, FL; Butler Inst of Am Art, Youngstown, OH
PRINTERS: Palm Press, Tampa, FL (PP); Betty Lenahan, Tampa, FL (BL); Gemini GEL, Los Angeles, CA (GEM)
PUBLISHERS: Getler/Pall Gallery, NY (G/P); Gemini GEL, Los Angeles, CA (GEM)
GALLERIES: I Irving Feldman Galleries, Sarasota, FL; Gemini GEL, Los Angeles, CA
MAILING ADDRESS: 1419 W Waters, #107, Tampa, FL 33604

TITLE	PUBLISHER	PRINTER	DATE	MEDIUM	DIMENSION (PAPER SIZE) IN INCHES	TYPE OF PAPER	EDITION NUMBER	NO. OF COLORS	ORIGINAL OPENING PRICE	CURRENT RETAIL PRICE
SOLD OUT EDITIONS (RARE):										
Tables (Set of 29)	G/P	BL/PP	1979	EC/HC	30 X 22 EA	FAB	50 EA		400 EA	1500 EA
Constellations (Set of 15)	G/P	BL/PP	1980	EC/HC	30 X 22 EA	FAB	12 EA		400 EA	1500 EA
Still Life with a Shell	GEM	GEM	1984	EC/HC	31 X 24	AC	15	2	500	1200
A Gift for RR	GEM	GEM	1984	EC/HC	31 X 24	AC	13	3	500	1200
L'Imagerie Parisienne	GEM	GEM	1984	EC/HC	31 X 24	AC	16	3	500	1200
Xian in the Evening	GEM	GEM	1984	EC/HC	31 X 24	AC	12	6	500	1000
CURRENT EDITIONS:										
The Horizon is a Biographical Line	GEM	GEM	1984	EC/HC	31 X 24	AC	14	5	500	800
Trophy for Chiang Yee	GEM	GEM	1984	EC/HC	31 X 24	AC	13	4	500	800
Lytton's Prologue	GEM	GEM	1984	EC/HC	31 X 24	AC	18	4	500	800
Morning in Jingxian	GEM	GEM	1984	EC/HC	31 X 24	AC	14	4	500	800

KAORU SAITO

BORN: Hayama Kanagawa, Japan; 1931
EDUCATION: The Academy 46 Art Sch, Japan
RECENT EXHIB: Newmark Gallery, NY, 1987; Robertson Gallery, Beverly Hills, CA, 1987
COLLECTIONS: Art Inst of Fine Arts, Chicago, IL; Portland Mus, OR; British Mus, London, England; Honolulu Art Mus, HI; Prefectural Art Mus, Aichi, Japan
PRINTERS: Artist (ART); Tsuneo Yamamura Studio, NY (TYS)
PUBLISHERS: John Szoke Graphics, NY (JSG)
GALLERIES: Newmark Gallery, New York, NY; Summa Gallery, Brooklyn, NY; Ronin Gallery, New York, NY; American Art, Tacoma, WA

TITLE	PUBLISHER	PRINTER	DATE	MEDIUM	DIMENSION (PAPER SIZE) IN INCHES	TYPE OF PAPER	EDITION NUMBER	NO. OF COLORS	ORIGINAL OPENING PRICE	CURRENT RETAIL PRICE
SOLD OUT EDITIONS (RARE):										
Red Illusion: Fluttering	JSG	ART	1986	MEZ	16 X 14	R/BFK	93	3	1700	2000
A Red Flower	JSG	ART	1986	MEZ	9 X 10	R/BFK	93	3	700	1000
Grow Wings	JSG	ART	1986	MEZ	14 X 17	R/BFK	93	3	700	1000
Sa Sangua	JSG	ART	1987	MEZ	15 X 18	R/BFK	93	3	1100	1500
CURRENT EDITIONS:										
A Pansy	JSG	TYS	1989	MEZ/A/HC	14 X 12	R/BFK	93	Varies	1800	2000
Manicure	JSG	TYS	1989	MEZ/HC	6 X 6	R/BFK	93	Varies	500	600
A Snowy Night	JSG	TYS	1989	MEZ/A/HC	9 X 10	R/BFK	93	Varies	900	1000

BARUJ SALINAS

BORN: Havana, Cuba; July 6, 1935; U S Citizen
EDUCATION: Kent State University, OH, Architecture Degree, 1958
AWARDS: Cintas Found Fel, 1970,71
COLLECTIONS: Inst Nacional de Bellas Artes, Mexico City, Mex; Beit Iri Mus, Kineret, Israel; Fine Arts Mus, Budapest, Hungary; Mus de Villafames, Castellon, Spain; McNay Art Inst, San Antonio, TX; Ft Lauderdale Mus, FL; San Antonio Mus, TX; Museo Arte Contemporaneo, Ibiza, Spain; Cabinet des Estampes, Mus of Art & History, Geneva, Switzerland
PRINTERS: La Poligrafa, SA, Barcelona Spain (LP); Taller Fort, Barcelona, Spain (TF); Masafumi Yamamoto, Barcelona, Spain (MY)
PUBLISHERS: Edicionese Poligrafa, SA, Barcelona, Spain (EdP) Editart Gallery, Geneva, Switzerland (EG); Schweyer-Galdo Gallery, Pontiac, MI (SGG); Ediciones Tabelaria, Barcelona, Spain (ET); Pacifica Editions, Miami, FL (PEd)
GALLERIES: Editart Gallery, Geneva, Switzerland; Galeria Joan Prats, New York, NY & Barcelona, Spain; Foster Harmon Galleries of America Art, Sarasota, FL & Sanibel Island, FL; Barbara Gillman Gallery, Miami, FL; Galerie Giesele Linder, Basel, Switzerland; Galeria Rayuela, Madrid, Spain; Franz Bader Gallery, Wash, DC; Erika Meyerovich Gallery, San Francisco, CA; River Gallery, Westport, CT; Phyllis Needlman Gallery, Chicago, IL
MAILING ADDRESS: 2740 SW 92nd Ave, Miami, FL 33165

TITLE	PUBLISHER	PRINTER	DATE	MEDIUM	DIMENSION (PAPER SIZE) IN INCHES	TYPE OF PAPER	EDITION NUMBER	NO. OF COLORS	ORIGINAL OPENING PRICE	CURRENT RETAIL PRICE
SOLD OUT EDITIONS (RARE):										
Series of 5:									500 SET	1800 SET
Le Disque d'Argent	EG	TF	1976	LC/EMB	20 X 26	R/BFK	125	5	125	450
Metamorphose	EG	TF	1976	LC/EMB	20 X 26	R/BFK	125	8	125	450
Alchemie	EG	TF	1976	LC/EMB	20 X 26	R/BFK	125	6	125	450
Signes dans la Lune	EG	TF	1976	LC/EMB	20 X 26	R/BFK	125	6	125	450
Universe	EG	TF	1976	LC/EMB	20 X 26	R/BFK	125	6	125	450

BARUJ SALINAS CONTINUED

TITLE	PUBLISHER	PRINTER	DATE	MEDIUM	DIMENSION (PAPER SIZE) IN INCHES	TYPE OF PAPER	EDITION NUMBER	NO. OF COLORS	ORIGINAL OPENING PRICE	CURRENT RETAIL PRICE
SOLD OUT EDITIONS (RARE):										
Series of 5:									750 SET	1400 SET
El Tercer Dia	EdP	LP	1977	LC	22 X 30	GP	75	6	170	300
Arcano	EdP	LP	1977	LC	22 X 30	GP	75	7	170	300
Nebula Incandescente	EdP	LP	1977	LC	22 X 30	GP	75	10	170	300
Insondable	EdP	LP	1977	LC	22 X 30	GP	75	6	170	300
Fuente Primigenia	EdP	LP	1977	LC	22 X 30	GP	75	6	170	300
Series of 10:									1650 SET	2800 SET
Delta	EdP	LP	1979	EC	22 X 30	GP	75	5	170	400
Hongo	EdP	LP	1979	EC	22 X 30	GP	75	5	170	400
Efluvia	EdP	LP	1979	EC	22 X 30	GP	75	6	170	400
Disco	EdP	LP	1979	EC	22 X 30	GP	75	6	170	400
Nuclea	EdP	LP	1979	EC	22 X 30	GP	75	5	170	400
Banda Blanca	EdP	LP	1979	EC	22 X 30	GP	75	6	170	400
Ictus	EdP	LP	1979	EC	22 X 30	GP	75	7	170	400
Rostro Petreo	EdP	LP	1979	EC	22 X 30	GP	75	5	170	400
Pepiferal	EdP	LP	1979	EC	22 X 30	GP	75	6	170	400
Espiral y Cinta	EdP	LP	1979	EC	22 X 30	GP	75	5	170	400
Homage to Miro	EG	TF	1981	LC	20 X 26	AP	125	6	150	400
Dintel Megalitico	EG	MY	1982	EC/EMB	17 X 20	AP	120	4	150	400
El Lenguaje de las Nubes	EG	MY	1982	EC	20 X 26	AP	60	4	200	400
Series of 5:									900 SET	1600 SET
White Pictogram	EdP	LP	1984	MM	30 X 22	GP	99	4	200	350
White Totem I	EdP	LP	1984	MM	30 X 22	GP	99	4	200	350
White Totem II	EdP	LP	1984	MM	30 X 22	GP	99	4	200	350
Vertebrated Kof, Inverted	EdP	LP	1984	MM	30 X 22	GP	99	4	200	350
Partial White Pictogram	EdP	LP	1984	MM	30 X 22	GP	99	4	200	350
Pink Bands	ET	MY	1985	EC	9 X 11	AP	75	6	100	250
Pictogram with Yellow Element	SGG	MY	1985	EC	20 X 26	AP	75	7	250	400
Series of 6:									1500 SET	2250 SET
Jai in Space	Ped	TF	1985	MM	30 X 22	AP	99	5	250	400
Brookline Sunset III	Ped	TF	1985	MM	30 X 22	AP	99	8	250	400
Vertebrated Channel	Ped	TF	1985	MM	30 X 22	AP	99	6	250	400
Doble Pictogram	Ped	TF	1985	MM	30 X 22	AP	99	6	250	400
Extended Pictogram	Ped	TF	1985	MM	30 X 22	AP	99	6	250	400
Lamed Sedente	Ped	TF	1985	MM	30 X 22	AP	99	5	250	400

DAVID SALLE

BORN: Norman, OK; September 28, 1952
EDUCATION: California Inst of Arts, Valencia, CA, BFA, 1973, MFA, 1975
AWARDS: Creative Artists Public Service Program Grant, 1979; Guggenheim Fel, NY, 1986
RECENT EXHIB: Galerie Bruno Bischotberger, Zürich, Switzerland, 1987; Daniel Templon Gallery, Paris, France, 1988; Mary Boone Gallery, NY, 1987–88; Parish Art Mus, Southampton, NY, 1988; Sara Hilden Art Mus, Finland, 1988; Tel Aviv Art Mus, Israel, 1989; Castelli Graphics, NY, 1990; Mario Diacono Gallery, Boston, MA, 1990; Tony Shafrazi Gallery, NY, 1990; Museo de Arte Contemp de Monterrey, Mexico, 1991; Robert Miller Gallery, NY, 1991; Gagosian Gallery, NY, 1991; Guild Hall Mus, East Hampton, NY, 1992
COLLECTIONS: Boymans Mus, Rotterdam, The Netherlands, Basel Kunst Mus, Switzerland; Whitney Mus of Am Art, NY; New York Public Library, NY
PRINTERS: Jeryl Park Editions, NY (JPE); Maurice Sanchez, NY (MS); Derrere L'Etoile, Studios, NY (DES); Brenda Zlamany, NY (BZ); Joanne Howard, NY (JH); Atelier Crommelynck, Paris, France (AC); Crown Point Press, San Francisco, CA (CPP); Till Verclas, Hamburg, Germany (TV)

PUBLISHERS: Parasol Press, NY (PaP); Editions Schellmann & Klüser, Munich, Germany (SK); Maximilian Verlag/Sabine Knust, Munich, Germany (MV/SK); Crown Point Press, San Francisco, CA (CPP); I C Editions, Inc, NY (ICE); Edition Julie Sylvester, NY (EJS)
GALLERIES: Mary Boone Gallery, New York, NY; Editions Schellmann, New York, NY & Munich, Germany; B R Kornblatt Gallery, Wash, DC; Magnuson Gallery, Boston, MA; Martina Hamilton Gallery, New York, NY; BlumHelman Gallery, New York, NY; Donald Young Gallery, Seattle, WA; Texas Gallery, Houston, TX; Editions Ilene Kurtz, New York, NY; Gallery Bruno Bischofberger, Zürich, Switzerland; Crown Point Press, New York, NY & San Francisco, CA; Daniel Templon Gallery, Paris, France; Fred Hoffman Gallery, Santa Monica, CA; Opus Art Studios, Miami, FL; Sylvia Cordish Fine Art, Baltimore, MO; Gagosian Gallery, New York, NY; Bowles-Sorokko Galleries, Beverly Hills, CA & New York, NY; Rubenstein/Siacono Gallery, New York, NY; Hine Editions/Limestone Press, Francisco, CA; Edition Julie Sylvester, New York, NY; Castelli Graphics, New York, NY; Robert Miller Gallery, New York, NY
MAILING ADDRESS: c/o Mary Boone Gallery, 420 West Broadway, New York, NY 10012

TITLE	PUBLISHER	PRINTER	DATE	MEDIUM	DIMENSION (PAPER SIZE) IN INCHES	TYPE OF PAPER	EDITION NUMBER	NO. OF COLORS	ORIGINAL OPENING PRICE	CURRENT RETAIL PRICE
CURRENT EDITIONS:										
Until Photographs Could Be Taken from Earth Satellites (Set of 8)	PaP	JPE	1981	AB	30 X 42 EA	R/BFK	10 EA		5500 SET	20000 SET
Theme for an Aztec Moralist (Set of 6)	SK	MS/DES	1983–84	LC	46 X 34 EA	AC	40 EA		4800 SET	10000 SET
Grandiose Synonyms for Church (Series of 8)	PaP	BZ/JH/JPE	1986	EB/A/SG/SB	60 X 48 EA	SOM	17 EA		900 EA / 2800 EA	1800 EA / 8000 EA
The Raffael (Set of 7)	MV/SK	AC	1986	EB/A/SG/SB/SL	25 X 30 EA	R/BFK	30 EA		7000 SET	15000 SET

DAVID SALLE CONTINUED

David Salle
#4 (from Lively Iris Suite)
Courtesy Achenbach Art Edition

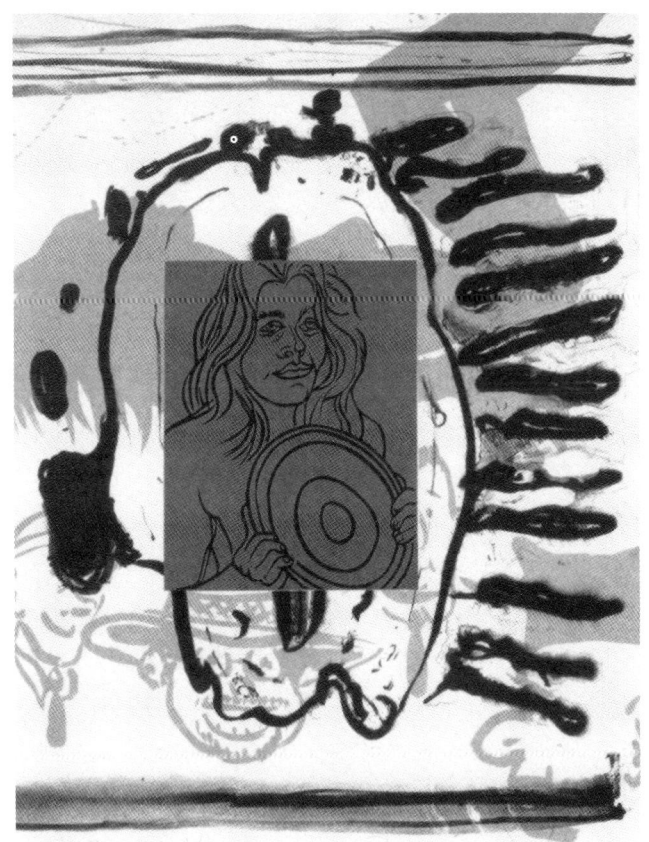

David Salle
#1 (from Lively Iris Suite)
Courtesy Achenbach Art Edition

TITLE	PUBLISHER	PRINTER	DATE	MEDIUM	DIMENSION (PAPER SIZE) IN INCHES	TYPE OF PAPER	EDITION NUMBER	NO. OF COLORS	ORIGINAL OPENING PRICE	CURRENT RETAIL PRICE
CURRENT EDITIONS:										
Portrait with Scissors and Nightclub	CPP	CPP	1987	WC	25 X 30	R/BFK	100	11	2000	2500
Untitled (from the Brooklyn Academy of Music Portfolio)	PaP	BZ/JH/JPE	1987	EB/A/SG	27 X 31	SOM	75		1500	3500
Canfield Hatfield (Set of 9)	ICE		1990	EB/A/SG/SB	30 X 44 EA	SOM	60 EA		30000 SET	30000 SET
The Universe Menders (Set of 5)	ICE		1991	EB/A	19 X 24 EA	SOM	50 EA		8000 SET	8500 SET
Lucky I-VI	EJS	TV	1992	Helio	30 X 22 EA	LANA	35 EA		6500 SET 1200 EA	6500 SET 1200 EA
Lively Iris (Set of 6)	AAE		1992	LC	69 X 54 cm EA		40 EA		20000 SET 3500 EA	20000 SET 3500 EA
Lively Iris (Set of 6)	AAE		1992	LC/HC	69 X 54 cm EA		x EA		30000 SET 5500 EA	30000 SET 5500 EA

TITO SALOMONI

BORN: Ferrara, Italy, 1928
COLLECTIONS: Centro d'Arte, Parma, Italy; The Convenant Club of Illinois, Chicago, IL

PRINTERS: Evergreen Publishing, Trenton, NJ (EP)
PUBLISHERS: Post Oak Fine Art Distributors, Houston, TX (POFA)
GALLERIES: Will Stone Collection, San Francisco, CA; London Arts Gallery, Detroit, MI; Ro Gallery Image Makers, Inc, New York, NY

TITLE	PUBLISHER	PRINTER	DATE	MEDIUM	DIMENSION (PAPER SIZE) IN INCHES	TYPE OF PAPER	EDITION NUMBER	NO. OF COLORS	ORIGINAL OPENING PRICE	CURRENT RETAIL PRICE
SOLD OUT EDITIONS (RARE):										
Rainbow Dream Weaver	POFA	EP	1981	LC	23 X 29	R/100	250	20	250	1000
Springtime	POFA	EP	1981	LC	23 X 29	R/100	250	20	250	1000
Catch a Falling Star	POFA	EP	1981	LC	23 X 29	R/100	250	20	250	1000
Past Romance	POFA	EP	1981	LC	23 X 29	R/100	250	21	250	1000
The Loving Prophesy	POFA	EP	1981	LC	23 X 29	R/100	250	21	250	1000
The Toy Boat	POFA	EP	1981	LC	23 X 29	R/100	250	21	250	1000
The Game of Life	POFA	EP	1981	LC	23 X 29	R/100	250	21	250	1000
The Wheel of Life	POFA	EP	1981	LC	23 X 29	R/100	250	21	250	1000
The Road to Knowledge	POFA	EP	1981	LC	23 X 29	R/100	250	21	250	1000
The Queen of Hearts	POFA	EP	1981	LC	23 X 29	R/100	250	21	250	1000
Dreamland	POFA	EP	1981	LC	23 X 29	R/100	250	21	250	1000

JEROME SALTZ

BORN: Chicago, IL; February 19, 1951
EDUCATION: Sch of Art, Art Inst of Chicago, IL, BFA, 1970–73
AWARDS: Nat Endowment for the Arts Grant, 1980
PRINTERS: Fred Gude, Chicago, IL (FG); Landfall Press, Inc, Chicago, IL (LPI)

PUBLISHERS: Landfall Press, Inc, Chicago, IL (LPI); NAME Gallery, Chicago, IL (NAME)
GALLERIES: Landfall Press, Inc, Chicago, IL; NAME Gallery, Chicago, IL; Quartet Editions, New York, NY
MAILING ADDRESS: 60 Avenue B, New York, NY 10009

TITLE	PUBLISHER	PRINTER	DATE	MEDIUM	DIMENSION (PAPER SIZE) IN INCHES	TYPE OF PAPER	EDITION NUMBER	NO. OF COLORS	ORIGINAL OPENING PRICE	CURRENT RETAIL PRICE
CURRENT EDITIONS:										
Canto III	LPI/NAME	FG/LPI	1980	LC	22 X 30	AP/W	100	2	150	250

LUCAS SAMARAS

BORN: Kastoria, Greece; (1936–1988); US Citizen
EDUCATION: Rutgers Univ, NJ, BA, 1959 with Alan Kaprow; Columbia Univ, NY, 1959–62, with Meyer Schapiro
TEACHING: Instr, Yale Univ, New Haven, CT, 1969; Instr, Brooklyn Col, NY, 1971–72
AWARDS: Woodrow Wilson Fel, Columbia Univ, NY, 1959
RECENT EXHIB: Pace Gallery, NY, 1987; Pace/McGill Gallery, NY, 1988; Smithsonian Inst, Wash, DC, 1988; Denver Art Mus, CO, 1988; Nat Mus of Am Art, Wash, DC, 1988; High Mus, Atlanta, GA, 1988,89; Center for Fine Arts, Miami, FL, 1989; Virginia Mus of Fine Arts, Richmond, VA, 1989; Mus of Fine Arts, Boston, MA, 1989; Univ of Missouri Art Gallery, Kansas City, MO, 1989; Tampa Mus of Art, FL, 1989; San Francisco Mus of Mod Art, CA, 1991

COLLECTIONS: Metropolitan Mus of Art, NY; Whitney Mus of Am Art, NY; Mus of Mod Art, NY; Albright-Knox Art Gallery, Buffalo, NY; Los Angeles County Mus of Art, CA; Walker Art Center, Minneapolis, MN; City Art Mus of St Louis, MO; Wadsworth Atheneum, Hartford, CT; Fort Worth Mus, TX; Chicago Inst of Art, IL; Aldrich Mus of Contemp Art, Ridgefield, CT; Smithsonian Inst, Wash, DC
PRINTERS: ChromaCorp Studio, NY (CS)
PUBLISHERS: Pace Editions, NY (PE); Abrams Original Editions, NY (AOE)
GALLERIES: Richard Gray Gallery, Chicago, IL; Pace/MacGill Gallery, New York, NY; Hokin Gallery, Palm Beach, FL & Bay Harbor Islands, FL; Pace Prints, New York, NY
MAILING ADDRESS: 52 W 71st St, New York, NY 10023

TITLE	PUBLISHER	PRINTER	DATE	MEDIUM	DIMENSION (PAPER SIZE) IN INCHES	TYPE OF PAPER	EDITION NUMBER	NO. OF COLORS	ORIGINAL OPENING PRICE	CURRENT RETAIL PRICE
SOLD OUT EDITIONS (RARE):										
Set of Five:									250 SET	7500 SET
Fork	PE	CS	1968	SP	6 X 5	AP	15		50	1500
Mat Knife	PE	CS	1968	SP	6 X 5	AP	15		50	1500
Thumb	PE	CS	1968	SP	6 X 5	AP	15		50	1500
Match	PE	CS	1968	SP	6 X 5	AP	15		50	1500
Brush	PE	CS	1968	SP	6 X 5	AP	15		50	1500
Book-Objects, Serigraphs, Paper Fold-Outs, Miniature Book, Six Stories (Serigraphy, Lithography, Embossing, Thermography and Diecutting) (18 Pages, Each Leaf, 3/16" Thick)	PE	CS	1968	SP/LC/EMB/ THER/DIE	10 X 10 X 3	AP	100		1200	20000
Album (Metallic Silver Cover with Signed, Numbered Polaroid Print) (104 Pages) (Deluxe Edition)	PE	CS	1971	PH	12 X 10	AP	100		100	1000
Hook	PE	CS	1972	SP	37 X 26	AP	150	10	150	3500
Ribbon	PE	CS	1972	SP	37 X 26	AP	150	9	150	3500
Photo-Transformations			1973-75	PH	3 X 3 EA				950 SET	20000 SET
Clenched Couple	PE	CS	1975	SP	40 X 32	AP	125	20	350	3500
Hand (on Plexiglas)	PE/HNA	CS	1975	SP	23 X 20	AP	100	2	500	3500
Bull-Pen	TGL	TGL	1984	EB/A/WC/CO	41 X 42	TGL/HMP	46	26	1800	3500
Gas-Up	TGL	TGL	1984	EB/A/WC/REL	57 X 41	TGL/HMP	46	33	1800	2500
Equatorial Route	TGL	TGL	1986	SP/CO/REL	47 DIA	TGL/HMP	20	34	2100	3500
Josh's Route	TGL	TGL	1986	SP/CO/REL	47 DIA	TGL/HMP	20	22	2100	3500
Rain Dance Route	TGL	TGL	1986	SP/CO/REL	47 DIA	TGL/HMP	20	38	2100	3500
Uncle Ferdinand's Route	TGL	TGL	1986	SP/CO/REL	47 DIA	TGL/HMP	20	20	2100	3500
Home Route	TGL	TGL	1986	SP/CO/REL	47 DIA	TGL/HMP	20	13	2100	3500
Trade Route (Roman)	TGL	TGL	1986	SP/CO/REL	47 DIA	TGL/HMP	20	16	2100	3500
CURRENT EDITIONS:										
Soft & Fluffy Gears Series (Assembled, Punched & Glued) (Set of 9):										
Synchromesh	SprSW/TP/ART	JW/RL/ART/ SprSW/BW/TP	1987	PW	21 X 19	HMP	15		1500	2500
Thinning Twin	SprSW/TP/ART	JW/RL/ART/ SprSW/BW/TP	1987	PW	19 X 19	HMP	15		1500	2500
King Sponge	SprSW/TP/ART	JW/RL/ART/ SprSW/BW/TP	1987	PW	18 X 18	HMP	15		1500	2500
West in the Breast	SprSW/TP/ART	JW/RL/ART/ SprSW/BW/TP	1987	PW	19 X 18	HMP	15		1500	2500
Sleeping Hair	SprSW/TP/ART	JW/RL/ART/ SprSW/BW/TP	1987	PW	18 X 18	HMP	15		1500	2500

LUCAS SAMARAS CONTINUED

TITLE	PUBLISHER	PRINTER	DATE	MEDIUM	DIMENSION (PAPER SIZE) IN INCHES	TYPE OF PAPER	EDITION NUMBER	NO. OF COLORS	ORIGINAL OPENING PRICE	CURRENT RETAIL PRICE
CURRENT EDITIONS:										
Wrack and Pin Whin	SprSW/TP/ART	JW/RL/ART/SprSW/BW/TP	1987	PW	19 X 19	HMP	15		1500	2500
Wets Yoog	SprSW/TP/ART	JW/RL/ART/SprSW/BW/TP	1987	PW	28 X 28	HMP	15		2000	3500
Worm with a Spur	SprSW/TP/ART	JW/RL/ART/SprSW/BW/TP	1987	PW	28 X 27	HMP	15		2000	3500
Bent Eggbeater	SprSW/TP/ART	JW/RL/ART/SprSW/BW/TP	1987	PW	36 X 35	HMP	15		2000	3500
Bent Eggbeater	SprSW/TP/ART	JW/RL/ART/SprSW/BW/TP	1987	PW	36 X 35	HMP	15		2000	3500
When Everyone Lost their Marbles(3 Sheets)	VAC	ART/KS/RK/VAC	1989	REL	19 X 19	HMP/KOZO	14		1400	1800
Kissing the Tundra	VAC	ART/KS/RK/VAC	1989	CO	28 X 28	HMP			2100	2500
Green Imperial, Blue Ice, Yellow Snow	VAC	ART/KS/RK/VAC	1989	CO	32 X 32	HMP			2100	2500

FRED SANDBACK

BORN: Bronxville, NY; August 29, 1943
EDUCATION: Yale Univ, New Haven, CT, BA, 1962–66; Yale Sch of Art and Architecture, BFA, MFA, 1966–69
AWARDS: Creative Artists Public Service Grant, 1972; Guggenheim Found Fel, 1975
RECENT EXHIB: Westfalian Kunstverein, Munster, Germany, 1987; Kestner-Gesellschaft, Hanover, Germany, 1987; David Nolan Gallery, NY, 1988; DIA Art Found, NY, 1988; Contemp Arts Mus, Houston, TX, 1989; Fred Sandback Mus, Winchendon, MA, 1989,92
COLLECTIONS: Mus of Mod Art, NY; Whitney Mus of Am Art, NY; Nat Gallery of Art, Ottawa, Can; Kunsthalle, Basel, Switzerland; Kaiser Wilhelm Mus, Krefeld, Germany; Rhode Island Sch of Design, Providence, RI
PRINTERS: Aeropress, NY (A); Patricia Branstead, NY (PB); C Mousley, NY (CM); Karl Imhof, Munich, West Germany (KI); Artist (ART)
PUBLISHERS: Brooke Alexander, Inc, NY (BAI); Fred Jahn, Munich, West Germany (FJ); Artist (ART)
GALLERIES: Brooke Alexander, Inc, New York, NY; John Weber Gallery, New York, NY; Marian Goodman, New York, NY; Margarete Roeder Fine Art, New York, NY; David Nolan Gallery, New York, NY; Burnett Miller Gallery, Los Angeles, CA; Cologne Kunstvercin, Cologne, West Germany; Barbara Krakow Gallery, Boston, MA; Nina Freudenheim Gallery, Buffalo, NY
MAILING ADDRESS: East Monomonac Rd, Rindge, NH 03461

TITLE	PUBLISHER	PRINTER	DATE	MEDIUM	DIMENSION (PAPER SIZE) IN INCHES	TYPE OF PAPER	EDITION NUMBER	NO. OF COLORS	ORIGINAL OPENING PRICE	CURRENT RETAIL PRICE
CURRENT EDITIONS:										
Four Variations of Two Diagonal Lines (Set of 4)	BAI	PB/A	1976	SG/E/A	22 X 30 EA		35 EA	1 EA	500 SET / 125 EA	2500 SET / 850 EA
Untitled I,II	BAI	PB/A	1976	W/ENG	14 X 19 EA		35 EA		125 EA	600 EA
Untitled (Black on Beige)	BAI	PB/A	1976	SG/E/A/CO	20 X 26		30		125	600
Untitled (Blue on White)	BAI	CM	1976	SG/E/A	21 X 35		40		150	600
Untitled (Red on White)	BAI	CM	1976	SG/E/A	22 X 26		35		150	600
Untitled (Set of 22)	FJ	KI	1982	PH	5 X 7 EA		7 EA	1 EA	4500 SET	7000 SET
Twenty-Two Constructions from 1967 (Set of 22):	FJ	KI	1986		14 X 11 EA (Mounted)				4500 SET	7000 SET
1-18—Black	FJ	KI	1986	LB/LC	9 X 11 EA	JP	35 EA		225 EA	500 EA
19-35—Blue	FJ	KI	1986	LB/LC	9 X 11 EA	JP	35 EA		225 EA	500 EA
Untitled	ART	ART	1989	PO	23 X 30	AP	15		800 DM	1200 DM

DAVID SANDLIN

BORN: Belfast, Ireland; November 9, 1956
EDUCATION: Univ of Alabama, Birmingham, AL, BA, 1979
TEACHING: Instr, Lithography, Sch of Visual Arts, NY, 1982 to present
AWARDS: Jurors Award, Birmingham Art Assn, Birmingham Mus, AL, 1979
RECENT EXHIB: Gracie Mansion Gallery, NY, 1987,92; James Madison Univ, Sawhill Gallery, Harrisonburg, VA, 1992
COLLECTIONS: Mercy Col, Dobbs Ferry, NY
PRINTERS: Bud Shark, Boulder, CO (BS); Ron Trujillo, Boulder, CO (RT); Roseanne Colachis, Boulder, CO (RC); Shark's Lithography, Ltd, Boulder, CO (SLL); Artist (ART)
PUBLISHERS: Shark's Lithography, Ltd, Boulder, CO (SLL); Artist (ART)
GALLERIES: Max Hutchinson Gallery, New York, NY; Stephen Rosenberg Gallery, New York, NY; Shark's, Inc, Boulder, CO; Carl Hammer Gallery, Chicago, IL
MAILING ADDRESS: 58 E First St, New York, NY 10003

TITLE	PUBLISHER	PRINTER	DATE	MEDIUM	DIMENSION (PAPER SIZE) IN INCHES	TYPE OF PAPER	EDITION NUMBER	NO. OF COLORS	ORIGINAL OPENING PRICE	CURRENT RETAIL PRICE
CURRENT EDITIONS:										
Beneath the Backyard of Earthly Delights (Series of 3):										
Fires are Raging	ART	ART	1986	SP	27 X 20	STP	15		150	400
Way to the Lord	ART	ART	1986	SP	27 X 20	STP	15		150	400
Torrid Death Dream	ART	ART	1986	SP	27 X 20	STP	15		150	400

SCOTT SANDELL

BORN: Minneapolis, MN; March 26, 1953
EDUCATION: Univ of Minnesota, Minneapolis, NM, BFA, 1975
AWARDS: Jerome Found Grant, 1983
COLLECTIONS: Walker Art Center, Minneapolis, MN; Library of Congress, Wash, DC; Minnesota Mus of Art, St Paul, MN; Univ of Minnesota, MN; Harvard Univ, Cambridge, MA; Minneapolis Inst of Arts, MN; Chrysler Mus of Art, Norfolk, VA
PRINTERS: Plum Island Press, Southampton, NY (PIP); Printmaking Workshop, Inc, New York, NY (PW); Artist (ART)
PUBLISHERS: C G Rein Publishers, St Paul, MN (CGR); Plum Island Press, Southampton, NY (PIP); Atlantic Canyon, Bedford, NY (AtC); John Szoke Graphics, NY (JSG)
GALLERIES: C G Rein Galleries, Scottsdale, AZ & Santa Fe, NM & Houston, TX & Minneapolis, MN & St Paul, MN; Somerstown Gallery, Somers, NY; Randall Beck Gallery, Boston, MA; John Szoke Graphics, New York, NY
MAILING ADDRESS: P O Box 901, Water Mill, NY 11976

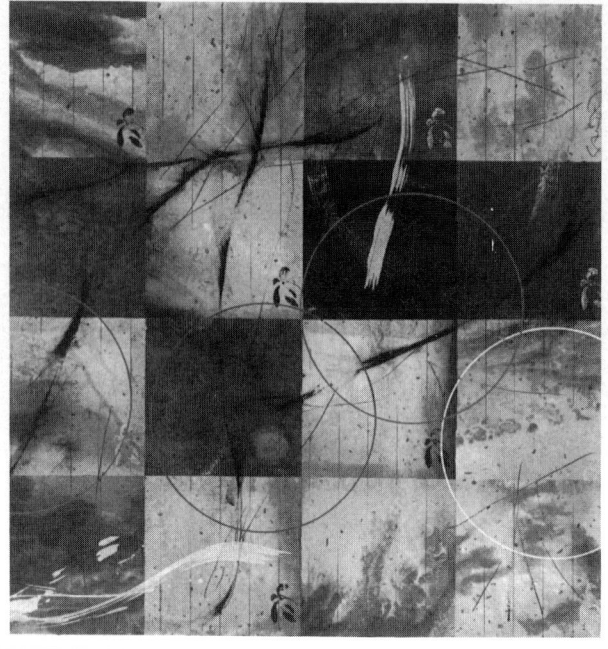

Scott Sandell
My Italian Dinghy
Courtesy John Szoke Graphics, Inc

TITLE	PUBLISHER	PRINTER	DATE	MEDIUM	DIMENSION (PAPER SIZE) IN INCHES	TYPE OF PAPER	EDITION NUMBER	NO. OF COLORS	ORIGINAL OPENING PRICE	CURRENT RETAIL PRICE
SOLD OUT EDITIONS (RARE):										
(Water) at 12000 Feet (with Painting)	CGR	PIP/PW	1982	WC/LI	54 X 26	AP	37	8	400	1800
(Surfing) A Typhoon	CGR	PIP/PW	1982	WC/LC/LI	54 X 26	AP	37	10	400	1500
(Surfing) A Hurricane (with Painting)	CGR	PIP/PW	1982	WC/LC/LI	54 X 26	AP	37	11	400	1800
Waterleaf (with Painting & Drawing)	CGR	PIP/PW	1982	WC/LC/LI	26 X 61	AP	37	7	400	2000
Island (Sheltered by Islands) (with Painting & Drawing)	CGR	PIP/PW	1982	WC/LI	52 X 27	AP	37	10	400	2000
Wild Gravity	CGR	PIP	1984	LC/CO	60 X 36	MUL/CHIRI	39		600	925
Club Montauk	CGR	PIP	1984	LC/CO	60 X 40	MUL/CHIRI	37		800	1100
Ditch Plains	CGR	PIP	1984	LC/CO	60 X 36	MUL/CHIRI	40		800	1025
New Rage	CGR	PIP	1984	LC/CO	50 X 40	MUL/CHIRI	36		600	925
Gansett Auto Works	CGR	PIP	1984	LC/CO	58 X 36	MUL/HOSHO	43		600	700
Tide Table	CGR	PIP	1984	LC/CO	58 X 26	MUL/OKP	31		500	865
Raisins	CGR	PIP	1985	LC/CO	27 X 60	MUL/HOSHO	44		550	805
Vitamin Sea	CGR	PIP	1985	LC/CO	55 X 40	MUL/CHIRI	30		700	975
Good Ground, State II	CGR	PIP	1985	MM	61 X 38	MUL/CHIRI	15		750	915
Darkness and Silence	CGR	PIP	1985	MM	62 X 38	MUL/CHIRI	19		750	915
Scene and Not Seen	CGR	PIP	1985	MM	61 X 36	MUL/CHIRI	20		750	925
Box 261, Bridgehampton	CGR	PIP	1985	MM	69 X 40	MUL/CHIRI	22		750	1115
Sea Through	CGR	PIP	1986	MM	66 X 36	MUL/CHIRI	17		750	990
From Memory	CGR	PIP	1986	MM	56 X 36	MUL/CHIRI	35		750	1150
Beach Architecture	CGR	PIP	1986	MM	66 X 36	MUL/CHIRI	36		750	915
Amagansett in Winter	CGR	PIP	1986	MM	68 X 38	MUL/CHIRI	20		750	875
Beach Frenzy	CGR	PIP	1986	MM	58 X 38	HMP	37		600	875
The Advantage of Sinking	CGR	PIP	1986	MM	58 X 38	MUL/HMP	36		750	915
Boy's Day Banner	CGR	PIP	1987	MM	76 X 26	MUL/HMP	18		750	865
Boat Loops	CGR	PIP	1987	MM	27 X 69	MUL/HMP	22		750	975
Eye of the Wind	CGR	PIP	1989	MM	20 X 80	MUL/HMP	25		750	700
Fluid Dynamics	CGR	PIP	1989	MM	17 X 24	MUL/HMP	38		350	350
Waves of Record	CGR	PIP	1989	MM	17 X 24	MUL/HMP	43		350	350
My Italian Dinghy	JSG	ART	1992	MM	44 X 44	KAS/HMP	25	Varies	750	750
CURRENT EDITIONS:										
Pail and Shovel	CGR	PIP	1984	LC/CO	46 X 38	MUL/HMP	44		600	805
Shark Bait	CGR	PIP	1985	LC/CO	27 X 70	MUL/CHIRI	39		600	925
Sharks!	CGR	PIP	1985	LC/CO	68 X 36	MUL/CHIRI	18		600	865
Slightly Sunken Memory	CGR	PIP	1985	LC/CO	58 X 38	MUL/CHIRI	21		600	815
Big Flamingo	CGR	PIP	1985	LC/CO	58 X 41	MUL/CHIRI	17		600	805
Good Ground, State I	CGR	PIP	1985	LC/CO	61 X 38	MUL/CHIRI	20		700	915
Not a Good Swimmer	CGR	PIP	1985	LC/CO	50 X 28	MUL/OKP	45		500	590
Millstone I (Printed on 2 Sheets of Chiri Paper & 3 Sheets of Mulberry Paper)	AtC	PIP	1986	LC/LI/WA	68 X 38	MUL/CHIRI	19	15	750	1500
Gage Roads	AtC	PIP	1986	LC/LI/WA	53 X 38	MUL/CHIRI	19	16	750	1500
Apparent Winds	AtC	PIP	1986	LC/LI/WA	68 X 38	MUL/CHIRI	19	19	750	1500
The Letter under the Door	AtC	PIP	1986	LC/LI/WA	68 X 38	MUL/CHIRI	19	19	750	1500
The Montauk School	CGR	PIP	1987	LC/SP/REL/HC	27 X 81	MUL/CHIRI	41	Varies	600	865
Equinox Farms	CGR	PIP	1987	LC/SP/REL/HC	77 X 26	MUL/CHIRI	37	Varies	750	915
The Boat House, State I	CGR	PIP	1987	LC/SP/REL/HC	68 X 24	MUL/CHIRI	20	Varies	750	875
Over the Falls	CGR	PIP	1988	LC/SP/REL/HC	24 X 69	MUL/CHIRI	76	Varies	600	650

SCOTT SANDELL CONTINUED

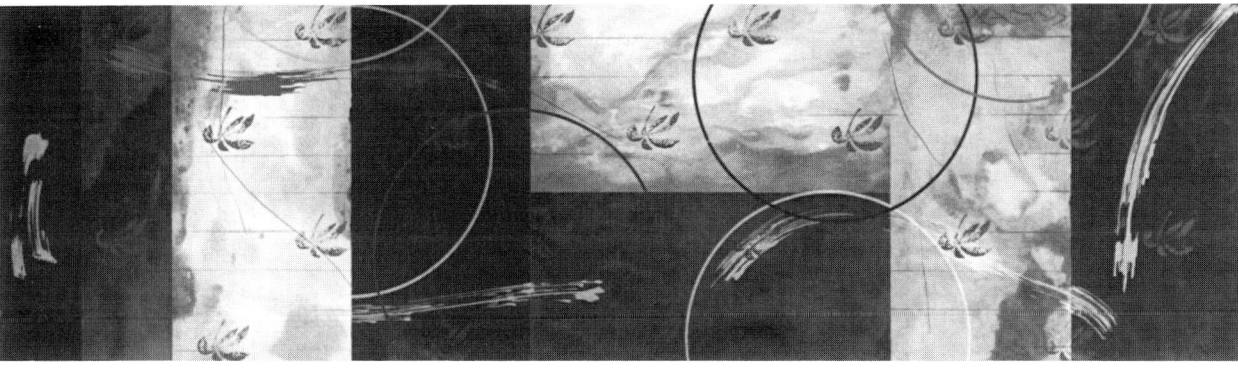

Scott Sandell
Clean Harbors
Courtesy John Szoke Graphics, Inc

TITLE	PUBLISHER	PRINTER	DATE	MEDIUM	DIMENSION (PAPER SIZE) IN INCHES	TYPE OF PAPER	EDITION NUMBER	NO. OF COLORS	ORIGINAL OPENING PRICE	CURRENT RETAIL PRICE
CURRENT EDITIONS:										
Ciphers (Red)	CGR	PIP	1988	LC/SP/REL/HC	32 X 24	MUL/CHIRI	77	Varies	350	400
Ciphers (Umber)	CGR	PIP	1988	LC/SP/REL/HC	32 X 24	MUL/CHIRI	76	Varies	350	400
Ciphers (Blue)	CGR	PIP	1988	LC/SP/REL/HC	32 X 24	MUL/CHIRI	70	Varies	350	400
Blue Sky Natural	CGR	PIP	1989	LC/SP/REL/HC	17 X 24	MUL/CHIRI	49	Varies	300	300
Hurricane Glassing	CGR	PIP	1989	LC/SP/REL/HC	17 X 24	MUL/CHIRI	50	Varies	300	300
Hurricane Specialists	CGR	PIP	1989	LC/SP/REL/HC	17 X 24	MUL/CHIRI	50	Varies	300	300
Lake Effect	CGR	PIP	1989	LC/SP/REL/HC	17 X 24	MUL/CHIRI	41	Varies	300	300
The Lemon Tarts	CGR	PIP	1990	LC/SP/REL/HC	21 X 56	MUL/CHIRI	44	Varies	600	650
Spiraling Ethics, State I	CGR	PIP	1990	LC/SP/REL/HC	27 X 78	MUL/CHIRI	28	Varies	750	900
Spiraling Ethics, State II	CGR	PIP	1990	LC/SP/REL/HC	26 X 87	MUL/CHIRI	35	Varies	750	1000
The X-Rays	CGR	PIP	1990	LC/SP/REL/HC	20 X 74	MUL/CHIRI	24	Varies	650	700
91.74	JSG	ART	1991	MM	33 X 33 EA	HMP	1 EA	Varies	1250 EA	1250 EA
91.75	JSG	ART	1991	MM	33 X 33 EA	HMP	1 EA	Varies	1250 EA	1250 EA
91.88	JSG	ART	1991	MM	33 X 33 EA	HMP	1 EA	Varies	1250 EA	1250 EA
Clean Harbors	JSG	ART	1992	MM	20 X 70	MUL/HMP	11	Varies	750	750

JONATHAN SANTLOFER

BORN: New York, NY; April 26, 1946
EDUCATION: Boston Univ, MA, BFA, Painting, 1967; Pratt Inst, Brooklyn, NY, MFA, Painting with George McNeil, 1969
TEACHING: Instr, Art History, Jersey City State Col, NJ, 1974 to present; Instr, Contemp Art, The New Sch, NY, 1976 to present; Columbia Univ, NY, currently
AWARDS: Skowhegan Sch, Summer Painting Grant, Skowheagan Sch of Painting & Sculpture, ME, 1966; Visual Arts Fel, Nat Endowment for the Arts, 1983,89
RECENT EXHIB: Galleria Peccolo, Livorno, Italy, 1988; Graham Modern Gallery, NY, 1988
COLLECTIONS: Art Inst of Chicago, IL; Grand Rapids Mus, MI; Norton Simon Mus, CA; Inst of Contemp Art, Tokyo, Japan; Indiana Mus of Art, IN; Miami-Dade Comm Col, FL
PRINTERS: Norman Stewart, Bloomfield Hills, MI (NS); Joe Keenan, Bloomfield Hills, MI (JK); Wing Lake Studio, Bloomfield Hills, MI (WLS); Stewart & Stewart, Bloomfield Hills, MI (S-S)
PUBLISHERS: Stewart & Stewart, Bloomfield Hills, MI (S-S)
GALLERIES: Stewart & Stewart, Bloomfield Hills, MI; Graham Modern Gallery, New York, NY; Nina Freundenheim Gallery, Buffalo, NY
MAILING ADDRESS: 151 West 28th St, New York, NY 10001

TITLE	PUBLISHER	PRINTER	DATE	MEDIUM	DIMENSION (PAPER SIZE) IN INCHES	TYPE OF PAPER	EDITION NUMBER	NO. OF COLORS	ORIGINAL OPENING PRICE	CURRENT RETAIL PRICE
CURRENT EDITIONS:										
Burning Bush	S-S	NS/JK/WLS	1990	SP	30 X 22	R/BFK/W	58	7	900	1250
Beyond the Forest	S-S	NS/JK/WLS	1990	SP	22 X 30	R/BFK/W	51	13	900	1250
Guardian	S-S	NS/JK/S-S	1991	SP	22 X 30	R/BFK/W	62	9	1250	1250
Human Nature	S-S	NS/JK/S-S	1991	SP	41 X 29	R/BFK/W	35	13	1500	1500

ALAN SARET

BORN: New York, NY; December 25, 1944
EDUCATION: Cornell Univ, Ithaca, NY, BA, Arch: Hunter Col, NY, with Robert Morris
TEACHING: Vis Art, Sculpture, Univ of California, Irvine, CA, 1978
AWARDS: Guggenheim Fel, NY, 1969; Nat Endowment for the Arts Fel, 1975; Creative Artist Public Service Grant, 1976
RECENT EXHIB: Daniel Weinberg Gallery, Los Angeles, CA, 1989; Retrosp, Inst of Art Urban Resources, PS 1, Long Island City, NY, 1992
COLLECTIONS: Mus of Mod Art, NY; Whitney Mus of Am Art, NY; Detroit Inst of Arts, MI; Nat Gallery of Toronto, Canada; Ft Worth Art Mus, TX; Dallas Art Mus, TX; Oberlin Col, Allen Art Mus, OH
PRINTERS: Diane Hunt, NY (DH)
PUBLISHERS: Mere Image, NY (MI)
GALLERIES: Charles Cowles Gallery, New York, NY; Margo Leavin Gallery, Los Angeles, CA; V & R Fine Arts, Temple Terrace, FL
MAILING ADDRESS: 65 S 11th St, Brooklyn, NY 11211

TITLE	PUBLISHER	PRINTER	DATE	MEDIUM	DIMENSION (PAPER SIZE) IN INCHES	TYPE OF PAPER	EDITION NUMBER	NO. OF COLORS	ORIGINAL OPENING PRICE	CURRENT RETAIL PRICE
CURRENT EDITIONS:										
Stars in the Sacred Ground (Set of 7)	MI	DH	1983	I	20 X 9 EA	R/BFK	25 EA	1 EA	675 SET	1200 SET

J MCNEIL SARGENT

BORN: Wilkesboro, NC; 1924
EDUCATION: Scholarship, Sch of Prof Art, 1942–45; Art Students League, NY, 1957; Independent Study, Guadalajara, Mexico, 1968; La Reparata Graphic Center, Florence, Italy, 1975; Pratt Graphic Center, NY, 1976; Univ of California, San Diego, CA, BA, Tutorial Degree, 1977; New York Univ, NY, 1982; Atelier 17, Paris, France, with William Hayter, 1980,81,83
TEACHING: Norfolk Mus, 1950–52; Corcoran Mus, Wash, DC, 1970; Community Col, San Diego, CA, 1971–83
AWARDS: San Diego Art Inst, CA, 1971,72,73; San Diego State Univ, CA, 1976,77; Pratt Graphic Purchase Prize, NY, 1982; Pratt Graphic Center, Purchase Award, NY, 1985; Statue of Liberty Award, Italy, 1990
RECENT EXHIB: Senior Eye Gallery, Long Beach, CA, 1990; Gallery 35, Nice, France, 1991
COLLECTIONS: New Zealand Embassy, Wash, DC; Nat Bibliotheque, Paris, France; Pratt Graphics, NY
PRINTERS: Bill Kelly, San Diego, CA (BK); Brighton Press, San Diego, CA (BP); Artist (ART)
PUBLISHERS: SD Graphics, San Diego, CA (SDG); Artist (ART)
GALLERIES: Kery Fine Arts, New York, NY; Tarbox Gallery, San Diego, CA; Art Nold, Nice, France
MAILING ADDRESS: 12245 Carmel Vista Rd, #193, San Diego, CA 92130

TITLE	PUBLISHER	PRINTER	DATE	MEDIUM	DIMENSION (PAPER SIZE) IN INCHES	TYPE OF PAPER	EDITION NUMBER	NO. OF COLORS	ORIGINAL OPENING PRICE	CURRENT RETAIL PRICE
SOLD OUT EDITIONS (RARE):										
Partners	ART	ART	1974	AB/I	9 X 12	R/BFK	20	1	25	300
Toni	ART	ART	1974	LB	13 X 19	R/BFK	15	1	75	500
Seated Nude	ART	ART	1975	AB/I	11 X 13	R/BFK	20	1	75	400
CURRENT EDITIONS:										
Seabird	ART	ART	1977	LB	14 X 23	R/BFK	50	1	100	300
Woodpecker	ART	ART	1977	LB	14 X 23	R/BFK	50	1	100	300
Landscape Nude	ART	ART	1978	EMB/I	26 X 16	R/BFK	50	3	125	500
Rooster #1	ART	ART	1980	EB/AC	10 X 10	R/BFK	46	5	150	250
Rooster #2	ART	ART	1980	EB/AC	10 X 10	R/BFK	38	4	150	250
Dialogue	ART	ART	1980	EB/AC	10 X 10	R/BFK	47	5	150	250
Dialogue	ART	ART	1982	EB/AC	15 X 22	R/BFK	18	7	250	500
Duet #1	ART	ART	1982	EB/AC	11 X 10	R/BFK	20	5	150	250
Duet #2	ART	ART	1982	EB/AC	11 X 10	R/BFK	30	5	150	250
Rain Drops	ART	BK/BP	1982	VIS/I	23 X 36	AP	90	5	200	450
Rainbow	ART	ART	1983	VIS/I	23 X 16	AP/W	90	5	200	450
Awakening	ART	ART	1983	EB/AC	11 X 10	R/BFK	20	8	150	250
Prelude	ART	ART	1983	EB/AC	11 X 10	R/BFK	20	9	150	250
Prelude	ART	ART	1985	DPT	15 X 20	R/BFK	10	2	300	350
Embrace	ART	ART	1985	DPT/CAR	15 X 20	R/BFK	10	2	300	350
Embrace	ART	ART	1985	DPT/A	15 X 20	R/BFK	10	2	300	350
Madrugada	ART	ART	1985	DPT/CAR	22 X 30	R/BFK	10	1	400	500
Recollection	ART	ART	1985	DPT/CAR	22 X 30	R/BFK	10	1	400	500
Encounter	ART	ART	1985	DPT/CAR	22 X 30	R/BFK	10	5	400	500
Encounter	ART	ART	1985	DPT	15 X 20	R/BFK	10	1	300	350
Messenger	ART	ART	1985	DPT/CAR	15 X 18	R/BFK	10	2	200	300
Barcelona	ART	ART	1986	DPT/AC	11 X 10	R/BFK	20	3	120	200
Rondo	ART	ART	1986	DPT/AC	11 X 10	R/BFK	15	3	120	200
Madrugada	ART	ART	1986	DPT/AC	11 X 10	R/BFK	15	3	120	200
Capriccio	ART	ART	1986	DPT/AC	11 X 10	R/BFK	15	2	120	200
Les Pins I	ART	ART	1991	VIS	17 X 20	R/BFK	50	4	250	350

ROBERT SARGENT

PRINTERS: American Atelier, NY (AA)
PUBLISHERS: Circle Fine Art, Chicago, IL (CFA)
GALLERIES: Circle Galleries, San Diego, CA & San Francisco, CA & Northbrook, IL & Pittsburgh, PA & Houston, TX & Soho, NY & Chicago, IL & Scottsdale, AZ & Beverly Hills, CA & Costa Mesa, CA & Sherman Oaks, CA & Palm Beach, FL & Honolulu, HI & New Orleans, CA & Las Vegas, NV & Seattle, WA

TITLE	PUBLISHER	PRINTER	DATE	MEDIUM	DIMENSION (PAPER SIZE) IN INCHES	TYPE OF PAPER	EDITION NUMBER	NO. OF COLORS	ORIGINAL OPENING PRICE	CURRENT RETAIL PRICE
SOLD OUT EDITIONS (RARE):										
Fish	CFA	AA	1978	LC	28 X 40	AP	70		50	200

MARCO M SASSONE

BORN: Florence, Italy; July 27, 1942
EDUCATION: Inst Gallileo Inst, Florence, Italy, 1959–62; Acad of Fine Arts, Florence, Italy, 1963
RECENT EXHIB: Gallery at Nichols Hills, Oklahoma City, OK, 1989; Fiordaliso, San Francisco, CA, 1987; Bernheim-Jeune Gallery, Paris, France, 1988; Buschlen-Mowatt Gallery, Vancouver, BC, Canada, 1990
PRINTERS: W W Graphics, Los Angeles, CA (WWG); Guy MacCoy Studios, Woodland Hills, CA (GMS); Rindom Studios, Hallandale, FL (RS); Soma Fine Art Press, San Francisco, CA (SOMA); Lev Moross Studios, Gardena, CA (LMS); Hinte/Santoyo Studio, Los Angeles, CA (H/SS)
PUBLISHERS: Bernard Galleries, Walnut Creek, CA (BG); Segal Fine Art, Woodland Hills, CA (SFA); Fiordaliso Editions, San Francisco, CA (FiEd)
GALLERIES: Diane Nelson Gallery, Laguna Beach, CA; Arti Grafiche, San Francisco, CA; Soma Fine Art, San Francisco, CA; Segal Fine Art, Woodland Hills, CA; Jean Stephen Galleries, Minneapolis, MN; Chetkin Gallery, Red Bank, NJ; New Riverside Gallery, Red Bank, NJ; Emporium Enterprises, Inc, Dallas, TX; Buschlen-Mowatt Gallery, Vancouver, BC, Canada; Bernheim-Jeune Gallery, Paris, France; Charles Barry International, Rockville, MD; P C Hart Gallery, Jupiter, FL; Post Gallery, Houston, TX; Professional Fine Arts Services, Inc, New York, NY
MAILING ADDRESS: 123 Townsend, #450, San Franciso, CA 94107

MARCO M SASSONE CONTINUED

TITLE	PUBLISHER	PRINTER	DATE	MEDIUM	DIMENSION (PAPER SIZE) IN INCHES	TYPE OF PAPER	EDITION NUMBER	NO. OF COLORS	ORIGINAL OPENING PRICE	CURRENT RETAIL PRICE
SOLD OUT EDITIONS (RARE):										
Laguna Terrace	FiEd	WWG	1975	SP	30 X 23	AP	100	34	110	2000
Sausalito Reflections	FiEd	GMS	1975	SP	30 X 24	AP	200	45	110	2000
Fisherman's Wharf	FiEd	WWG	1976	SP	30 X 33	AP	200	32	150	1700
Huntington Harbour	FiEd	WWG	1976	SP	30 X 36	AP	200	32	175	2700
Flood of Florence	FiEd	GMS	1976	SP	22 X 15	AP	200	42	100	1200
Nostalgia	FiEd	WWG	1976	SP	25 X 26	AP	200	30	135	1200
Japanese Garden	FiEd	GMS	1977	SP	34 X 30	AP	100	52	175	2700
Laguna	FiEd	GMS	1977	SP	44 X 38	STP	150	71	275	6500
Barche a Sera	FiEd	GMS	1977	SP	12 X 14	AP	150	34	100	550
Studio Vista	FiEd	WWG	1978	SP	30 X 37	AP	150	45	225	2700
Sausalito	FiEd	GMS	1978	SP	30 X 42	AP	150	84	250	5000
View from Victor Hugo	FiEd	GMS	1979	SP	27 X 22	AP	186	55	175	2000
View from Victor Hugo/ Festival of Arts Poster	FiEd	GMS	1979	SP	20 X 22	AP	30	57	175	2000
View from Victor Hugo/ Laguna Beach Museum of Arts Poster	FiEd	GMS	1979	SP	30 X 22	AP	50	57	175	2000
Santa Cruz Marina	FiEd	GMS	1979	SP	12 X 11	AP	150	51	100	550
Moss Point	FiEd	GMS	1979	SP	42 X 34	AP	100	64	350	6500
Venezia	FiEd	GMS	1980	SP	42 X 30	AP	100	91	350	5000
Saint Florent	FiEd	GMS	1980	SP	30 X 42	AP	100	102	450	5000
New Port	FiEd	GMS	1980	SP	27 X 29	AP	100	79	350	2200
Laguna Summer	FiEd	GMS	1981	SP	37 X 32	AP	125	106	500	5000
Las Brisas	FiEd	GMS	1981	SP	15 X 20	AP	100	53	250	1200
San Francisco Dusk	FiEd	GMS	1982	SP	30 X 32	AP	115	82	450	2200
San Francisco Dusk/Wally Findlay Galleries Poster	FiEd	GMS	1982	SP	30 X 26	AP	25	84	450	2200
Santa Cruz	FiEd	RS	1982	SP	30 X 34	R/100	200	81	500	3000
Santa Cruz/Oklahoma Poster	FiEd	SOMA	1982	SP	30 X 34	R/100	15	83	500	3000
San Francisco Day	FiEd	RS	1983	SP	37 X 30	R/100	175	69	500	4500
San Francisco Terrace	FiEd	SOMA	1983	SP	30 X 40	R/100	175	71	550	4500
Tiburon	FiEd	RS	1983	SP	39 X 30	R/100	175	68	500	5500
Vela a Tribuon	FiEd	RS	1983	SP	30 X 30	R/100	125	72	500	2800
Sausalito Marina	SFA	SOMA	1985	SP	30 X 40	R/100	250	78	700	4000
Colori di Portofini	SFA	SOMA	1985	SP	32 X 40	R/100	250	76	700	4500
Santa Margherita	SFA	H/SS	1985	SP	28 X 36	R/100	250	74	700	4500
Laguna Vista	SFA	SOMA	1986	SP	38 X 46	R/100	250	82	1000	6500
Portofino Reflections	SFA	SOMA	1986	SP	38 X 43	R/100	250	78	1500	4000
Chapel at Tiburon	SFA	LMS	1987	SP	38 X 31	R/100	250	112	1000	4000
Vernazza Rosa	SFA	LMS	1988	SP	32 X 40	R/100	275		1800	5000
Venice Canal	SFA	LMS	1988	SP	42 X 38	R/100	275		1800	6500
CURRENT EDITIONS:										
Sunset Cliffs	FiEd	GMS	1981	SP	15 X 19	AP	100	59	250	1000
Venetian Garden	FiEd	SOMA	1984	SP	32 X 37	R/100	175	72	600	4000
Campo San Giacomo da L'Orio	FiEd	SOMA	1984	SP	32 X 40	R/100	175	75	700	2000
San Francisco Marina Dusk	SFA	SOMA	1986	SP	32 X 40	R/100	250	79	900	2000
Hotel Gardena	SFA	LMS	1986	SP	40 X 49	R/100	250	126	1800	4000
Corniglia	SFA	LMS	1987	SP	28 X 28	R/100	250	119	1000	2000
Manarola	SFA	LMS	1987	SP	38 X 44	R/100	250	100	1200	2000
Pier Thirty Nine	SFA	LMS	1987	SP	26 X 32	R/100	275		1000	2000
View with Bay Bridge	SFA	LMS	1987	SP	23 X 24	R/100	275		1000	2000
Houseboat Flowers	SFA	LMS	1988	SP	23 X 24	R/100	275		1000	1800
Casamenti a Portofino	SFA	LMS	1988	SP	36 X 36	R/100	275		1000	1800
Le Balcon Bleu	SFA	LMS	1988	SP	32 X 33	R/100	275		1000	2200
Sausalito Houseboat	SFA	LMS	1989	SP	32 X 36	R/100	275		1200	2000
Coit Tower at Night	SFA	LMS	1989	SP	30 X 33	R/100	220		1200	2800
Bricole Rosse	SFA	LMS	1989	SP	24 X 24	R/100	295		1200	2800
Porto Roca	SFA	LMS	1989	SP	24 X 26	R/100	345		1200	1800
Venice	SFA	LMS	1989	SP	43 X 38	R/100	295		1200	1800
Tiburon Harbor	SFA	LMS	1990	SP	24 X 30	R/100	295		1500	4500
Santa Lucia	SFA	LMS	1990	SP	21 X 28	R/100	295		1500	2000
Rio Secondo	SFA	LMS	1990	SP	35 X 20	R/100	275		1000	1800
Vernazza	SFA	LMS	1990	SP	30 X 35	R/100	275		1000	1800
Vele a Portofino	SFA	LMS	1990	SP	33 X 30	R/100	315		1000	1800
24 Beach Road	SFA	LMS	1991	SP	26 X 31	R/100	375		1000	1200

PETER SAUL

BORN: San Francisco, CA; August 16, 1934
EDUCATION: Stanford Univ, Los Angeles, CA, 1950–52; California Sch of Fine Arts, Los Angeles, CA; Washington Univ, Seattle, WA, BFA, 1956
AWARDS: Wm & Norma Copley Found Fel, 1962
RECENT EXHIB: Allan Frumkin Gallery, NY, 1987; Whatcom Mus of History & Art, Bellingham, WA, 1988; Gracie Mansion Gallery, NY, 1988; Hillwood Art Gallery, Long Island Univ, S W Post, NY, 1988; Weatherspoon Art Gallery, Univ of North Carolina, Greensboro, NC, 1989; Bucknell Univ, Lewisburg, PA, 1989; Mus of Contemp Art, Chicago, IL, 1989–90; Contemp Arts Center, New Orleans, LA, 1989–90; Laguna Gloria Art Mus, Austin, TX, 1990; Mus of Contemp Arts, Houston, TX, 1990; Butler Inst of Am Art, Youngstown, OH, 1990;

PETER SAUL CONTINUED

RECENT EXHIB: Texas Gallery, Houston, TX, 1987,90; Florida Int Art Mus, Miami, FL, 1990; Miami-Dade Com Col, FL, 1992; Univ of Houston, Blaffer Gallery, TX, 1992; Frumkin/Adams Gallery, NY, 1990,92
COLLECTIONS: Art Inst of Chicago, IL; Whitney Mus of Am Art, NY; Mus of Mod Art, NY
PRINTERS: Landfall Press, Inc, Chicago, IL (LPI); David Keister, Chicago, IL (DK); David Panosh, Chicago, IL (DP); Jack Lemon, Chicago, IL (JL)
PUBLISHERS: Landfall Press, Inc, Chicago, IL (LPI)
GALLERIES: Landfall Press, Inc, Chicago, IL; Struve Gallery, Chicago, IL; Frumkin/Adams Gallery, New York, NY; Gallery Karl Oskar, Leawood, KS; John Natsoulas Gallery, Davis, CA; Galerie Thomas R Monahan, Chicago, IL
MAILING ADDRESS: 4416 N Paine, Chicago, IL 60640

TITLE	PUBLISHER	PRINTER	DATE	MEDIUM	DIMENSION (PAPER SIZE) IN INCHES	TYPE OF PAPER	EDITION NUMBER	NO. OF COLORS	ORIGINAL OPENING PRICE	CURRENT RETAIL PRICE
SOLD OUT EDITIONS (RARE):										
Angela Davis	LPI	DK/LPI	1972	LC	38 X 30	ARJ	100	5	100	800
Amboosh	LPI	DK/LPI	1975	LC	30 X 40	ARJ	50	5	150	800
CURRENT EDITIONS:										
Politics	LPI	JL/LPI	1985	LC	24 X 33	ARJ	25	3	450	600
Texas Artist	LPI	JL/LPI	1985	LC	30 X 30	ARJ	20	3	450	600
Daisy Crockett	LPI	JL/LPI	1985	LC	31 X 27	ARJ	20	3	450	600

DAVID C SAUNDERS

BORN: New York, NY; November 27, 1954
EDUCATION: Kansas City Art Inst, MO, BFA, 1975
TEACHING: Brooklyn Mus, NY, 1971; Metropolitan Mus of Art, NY, 1972
AWARDS: Garver Miller Award, Ossabow, GA, 1981; Nat Endowment for the Arts, 1983
RECENT EXHIB: Grace Borgenicht Gallery, NY, 1987; Center for Contemp Art, Chicago, IL, 1989
COLLECTIONS: Metropolitan Mus of Art, NY; Smithsonian Inst of Art, Wash, DC; Allen Mem Art Mus, Oberlin, OH
PRINTERS: Eldindean Press, NY (EP); Shark's, Inc, Boulder, CO (SLL); Bud Shark, Boulder, CO (BS); Ron Trujillo, Boulder, CO (RT); Artist (ART)
PUBLISHERS: Vermillion Editions Ltd, Minneapolis, MN (VEL); Shark's, Inc, Boulder, CO (SI)
GALLERIES: Grace Borgenicht Gallery, New York, NY; Vermillion Editions, Ltd, Minneapolis, MN; Shark's, Inc, Boulder, CO; CCA Gallery, Chicago, IL; Paul Drey Gallery, New York, NY; Quartet Editions, New York, NY

David C Saunders
Eve
Courtesy Shark's, Inc

TITLE	PUBLISHER	PRINTER	DATE	MEDIUM	DIMENSION (PAPER SIZE) IN INCHES	TYPE OF PAPER	EDITION NUMBER	NO. OF COLORS	ORIGINAL OPENING PRICE	CURRENT RETAIL PRICE
SOLD OUT EDITIONS (RARE):										
Planeta	SI	BS/SI	1987	LC/3D	30 X 22 X 3	PLEX	25		1000	1500
Apple I–XXI	SI	ART/BS/RT/SI	1990	LC/PH/MON/CO	27 X 24 EA	R/BFK	1 EA		1400 EA	1400 EA
CURRENT EDITIONS:										
Sea of Troubles	VEL	VEL	1983	LC/CO	30 X 22	AP	36	5	500	900
Saint Joan	VEL	VEL	1983	LC/CO	26 X 21	RP	36	4	450	800
Lear	VEL	VEL	1983	LC/CO	26 X 21	RP	36	3	450	800
Fame Comes to Boulder	SI	BS/SI	1987	LC	45 X 30	AC	30		500	850
Wild Turkey	SI	BS/SI	1988	LC	45 X 30	AC	30		750	900
Eve	SI	ART/BS/RT/SI	1990	LC	37 X 30	R/BFK	25		1800	1800

RAYMOND JENNINGS SAUNDERS

BORN: Pittsburgh, PA; October 28, 1934
EDUCATION: Pennsylvania Acad of Fine Arts, Phila, PA, 1953–57; Univ of Pennsylvania, Phila, PA, 1954–57; The Barnes Foundation, Merion, PA, 1953–55; Carnegie Inst, Pittsburgh, PA, BFA, 1959–60; California Col of Arts and Crafts, CA, MFA, 1960–61
TEACHING: Rhode Island Sch of Design, Providence, RI, 1968; Vis Art, Yale Univ, New Haven, CT, 1972; Prof, Painting, California State Univ, Hayward, CA, 1969 to present
AWARDS: Nat Inst of Arts and Letters Award, 1963; Ford Found Purchase Award, 1964; Prix de Rome, Italy, 1964–66; Atwater Kent Award, 1970; Society of Four Arts Award, Palm Beach, FL, 1972; Gregor Mem Award, Pennsylvania Acad of Fine Arts, Phila, PA, 1975; Guggenheim Found Fel, 1976; Nat Endowment for the Arts, Award 1977; Award, Visual Arts, New Orleans Mus, LA, 1990

The retail prices of the 100,000 limited edition prints quoted in this directory are subject to change. Print publishers, artists and galleries were the direct sources for these quotations. Prices in the secondary market listed as "Sold Out Editions (Rare)" indicate that the publisher has a limited supply of that print or that the print is difficult to locate in the galleries.

RAYMOND JENNINGS SAUNDERS CONTINUED

RECENT EXHIB: Hunsaker/Schlesinger Gallery, Los Angeles, CA, 1987; Addison Gallery of Am Art, Andover, MA, 1987; Sierra Nevada Art Mus, Reno, NV, 1988; Greenville County Mus, SC, 1989; Albright-Knox Art Gallery, Buffalo, NY, 1989; Cava Gallery, Phila, PA, 1987,89; California Crafts Mus, San Francisco, CA, 1990; Stephen Wirtz Gallery, NY, 1990; Oakland Mus, CA, 1992
COLLECTIONS: Whitney Mus of Am Art, NY; Mus of Mod Art, NY; Philadelphia Mus of Art, PA; Pennsylvania Acad of Fine Arts, Phila, PA; Univ of California, Berkeley, CA; Minneapolis Art Mus, MN; Carnegie Inst, Pittsburgh, PA; St Louis Mus of Art, MO; Dartmouth Col, Hanover, NH; Univ of Texas, Austin, TX; Nat Inst of Arts And Letters, NY; San Francisco Mus of Mod Art, CA; Univ of Wisconsin, Elvehjem Art Center, Madison, WI; Andover Coll of American Art, PA; Addison Gallery of Am Art, MA; Howard Univ, Wash, DC
PRINTERS: Cirrus Editions, Los Angeles, CA (CE); Trillium Graphics, San Francisco, CA (TG)
PUBLISHERS: Univ Art Mus, Univ of California, Berkeley, CA (UAM); Society of Fellows, Am Acad in Rome, NY (AAR); Cirrus Editions, Los Angeles, CA (CE)
GALLERIES: Stephen Wirtz Gallery, San Francisco, CA; Hunsaker/Schlesinger Gallery, Los Angeles, CA; Angeles Gallery, Santa Monica, CA; Cava Gallery, Phila, PA; Richard Green Gallery, Santa Monica, CA
MAILING ADDRESS: 6007 Rock Ridge Blvd, Oakland, CA 94618

TITLE	PUBLISHER	PRINTER	DATE	MEDIUM	DIMENSION (PAPER SIZE) IN INCHES	TYPE OF PAPER	EDITION NUMBER	NO. OF COLORS	ORIGINAL OPENING PRICE	CURRENT RETAIL PRICE
SOLD OUT EDITIONS (RARE):										
Watermelon Slice	CE	CE	1976	LC	21 X 23	R/BFK	50	4	200	750
CURRENT EDITIONS:										
Profile In Time	AAR	TG	1982	LC/SP/CO	29 X 23	AC	75	1	500	600

ANTONIO SAURA

BORN: Huesca, Spain; 1930
AWARDS: Guggenheim Fel, NY, 1960; Carnegie Mellon Prize, Pittsburgh, PA, 1964
RECENT EXHIB: Jason McCoy Gallery, NY, 1992
COLLECTIONS: Guggenheim Mus, NY; Carnegie-Mellon Inst, Pittsburgh, PA
PRINTERS: Maeght Editeur, Paris, France (ME); Maeght Lelong Editions, Paris, France (ML)
PUBLISHERS: Maeght Editions, Paris, France (ME); Maeght Lelong Editions, Paris, France (ML)
GALLERIES: Galerie Lelong, Paris, France & New York, NY; Galerie Stadler, Paris, France; Jason McCoy Gallery, New York, NY

TITLE	PUBLISHER	PRINTER	DATE	MEDIUM	DIMENSION (PAPER SIZE) IN INCHES	TYPE OF PAPER	EDITION NUMBER	NO. OF COLORS	ORIGINAL OPENING PRICE	CURRENT RETAIL PRICE
SOLD OUT EDITIONS (RARE):										
Cruces	ME	ME	1981	LC	26 X 40 cm	AP	125	3	900 FF	1500 FF
Diada 1,2,3 (set of 3)	ME	ME	1981	LC	59 X 88 cm EA	AP	125 EA	3 EA	1300 FF	2000 FF
Poste Centrale 1,2,3,4,5 (Set of 5)	ME	ME	1981	LC	59 X 79 cm EA	AP	125 EA	6 EA	1200 FF	2000 FF
Repetition/Sans Centre	ML	ML	1982	LC	60 X 88 cm	AP	125	4	1300 FF	2000 FF
Nocturne/Sans Centre	ML	ML	1982	LC	60 X 88 cm	AP	125	4	1300 FF	2000 FF
Cocktail Party 1	ML	ML	1982	LC	60 X 88 cm	AP	125	6	1300 FF	2000 FF
Cocktail Party 2	ML	ML	1982	LC	60 X 88 cm	AP	125	6	1300 FF	2000 FF
Les 4 Saisons (Printemps, Eté, Automne, Hiver) (Set of 4)	ML	ML	1982	LC	60 X 88 cm EA	AP	125 EA	2 EA	1200 FF	2000 FF
Jardin de Nations (Carmen, Gudule, Catherine, Cara, Xenia) (Set of 5)	ML	ML	1983	LC	75 X 56 cm EA	AP	125 EA	Multi	1200 FF	2000 FF

NAOMI SAVAGE

BORN: New Jersey; June 25, 1927
EDUCATION: Bennington Col, VT, with Man Ray
AWARDS: Cassandra Found, Photography, 1970; Nat Endowment for the Arts Fel, 1971
COLLECTIONS: Mus of Mod Art, NY; Univ of Kansas, IL; Princeton Univ, NJ; Fogg Mus, Boston, MA; New Jersey State Mus, Trenton, NJ
PRINTERS: Artist (ART)
PUBLISHERS: Princeton Gallery, NJ (PG); Ex Libris, NY (ExL)
GALLERIES: Princeton Gallery, Princeton, NJ; Laurence Miller Gallery, New York, NY; Witkin Gallery, New York, NY
MAILING ADDRESS: 41 Drakes Corner Rd, Princeton, NJ 08540

TITLE	PUBLISHER	PRINTER	DATE	MEDIUM	DIMENSION (PAPER SIZE) IN INCHES	TYPE OF PAPER	EDITION NUMBER	NO. OF COLORS	ORIGINAL OPENING PRICE	CURRENT RETAIL PRICE
SOLD OUT EDITIONS (RARE):										
Man Ray from Eight Sides (Set of 8):										
Man in Hollywood (1948)	ExL	ART	1975	PH	7 X 8		5		185	600
Man at the Beach (1948)	ExL	ART	1975	PH	8 X 9		5		185	600
Man and Nature (1951)	ExL	ART	1975	PH	9 X 7		5		175	600
The Parisian Man (1957)	ExL	ART	1975	PH	7 X 7		5		175	600
Marcel and Man (1963)	ExL	ART	1975	PH	7 X 7		5		185	600
Man and Wife (1964)	ExL	ART	1975	PH	7 X 7		5		175	600
Multiple Man (1965)	ExL	ART	1975	PH	10 X 5		5		175	600
Man Masquerading (1966)	ExL	ART	1975	PH	10 X 5		5		175	600
CURRENT EDITIONS:										
Portfolio	PG	ART	1981	PH	16 X 20 EA		20 EA		2700 SET	4500 SET

ROGER SAVAGE, RCA

BORN: Windsor, Canada; September 25, 1941
EDUCATION: Mt Allison Univ, Sackville, NB, Can, BFA, 1963
TEACHING: Serigraphic Workshop, Mt Saint Vincent Univ, Halifax, NS, Can, 1975; Canada Council, Vis Art Projects, 1977–79; Univ de Moncton, NB, Canada, 1979; Holland Col, Charlottestown, PEI, Canada, 1981; Watercolor Workshops, Bermuda, 1991,92

ROGER SAVAGE, RCA CONTINUED

AWARDS: Canada Council Grants, 1970, 1981; Prof Artists Award, 1975,79; Brucebo Grant, Gotland, Sweden, 1980; Nova Scotia Professional Artist Awards, 1975,79,89,91
RECENT EXHIB: Centre de Congres, Montreux, Switzerland, 1990; Palmengarten Gallery, Frankfurt, Germany, 1991; Galerie de Berliner Volksbank, Berlin, Germany, 1991
COLLECTIONS: Acadia Univ, Wolfville, Can; Univ of New Brunswick Art Centre, Fredericton, Can; Art Gallery of Nova Scotia, Halifax, Can; Athabasca Univ, Edmonton, Can; Canada Council Art Bank, Ottawa, Can; City of Dartmouth, Can; Confederation Centre Art Gallery, Charlottetown, Can; Dalhousie Univ, Halifax, Can; Foothill Coll, Calgary, Can; Glenbow Mus, Calgary, Can; Gotlands Kommun, Visby, Sweden; Mount Saint Vincent Univ, Halifax, Can; New Brunswick Mus, Saint John, Can; Municipality of Metropolitan Toronto, Can; Nova Scotia Art Bank, Halifax Can; Owens Art Gallery, Sackville, Can; St Mary's Univ, Halifax, Can; Seneca Col, Willowdale, Can; Univ of Waterloo, Can; Univ of Alberta, Calgary, Can; Owens Art Gallery, Sackville, NB, Canada; Tatamagouche Centre, NS, Canada
PRINTERS: John Neville, Nova Scotia, Can (JN); Susan Wakefield, Halifax, NS, Can (SW); Artist (ART); Judith Leidl, Halifax, Canada (JL)
PUBLISHERS: Atlantic Cultural Consulting Ltd, Halifax, Can (ACC); North Editions, Toronto, Can (NE); Artist (ART)
GALLERIES: Contemporary Fine Arts Services, Toronto, Canada; Gallery Mary McDonald Chandor, Basking Ridge, NJ; Eklektik Gallery, Toronto, Canada; North Editions, Toronto, Canada; Paperworks Gallery, Calgary, Canada; Atelier Gallery, Vancouver, Canada; Studio 21, Halifax, Canada; Miriam Perlman, Chicago, IL; Gallery 454, Winnipeg, Manitoba, Canada; Print Consortium, Kansas City, MO; Savage Gallery, Liverpool, NS, Canada
MAILING ADDRESS: 611 Mersey Point Road, Liverpool, Nova Scotia, Canada B0T 1K0

TITLE	PUBLISHER	PRINTER	DATE	MEDIUM	DIMENSION (PAPER SIZE) IN INCHES	TYPE OF PAPER	EDITION NUMBER	NO. OF COLORS	ORIGINAL OPENING PRICE	CURRENT RETAIL PRICE
SOLD OUT EDITIONS (RARE):										
Lifeboat	ART	ART	1971	SP	11 X 25	OFF	25	10	30	3000
Isolde and Cow	ART	ART	1972	SP	17 X 30	SCH	50	8	55	3000
Three O'Clock Tractor	ART	ART	1972	SP	20 DIA	SCH	52	3	45	3000
December Beach	ART	ART	1980	SP	22 X 30	R/BFK	15	7	300	1500
Cadden Bay	ART	ART	1980	SP	22 X 30	R/BFK	35	7	300	1000
Great Island	ART	ART	1982	SP	22 X 30	SOM	85	13	250	800
Cadden Bay	ART	ART	1982	SP	22 X 30	SOM	85	11	250	800
Cadden Bay II	ACC	SW	1983	SP	22 X 30	AP/W	100	8	250	800
Beach Meadows	ACC	ART	1983	SP	22 X 30	SOM	100	10	250	800
Liverpool Bay, NS	ART	ART	1984	SP	22 X 30	R/BFK	85	10	250	800
Low Tide, Beach Meadows	ART	SW	1985	SP	23 X 29	RG/100	100	9	300	900
Carter's Beach	ART	SW	1985	SP	29 X 22	RM	61	4	250	800
De Wolfe House	ART	JL	1989	EB	9 X 11	JOH	100	1	50	100
CURRENT EDITIONS:										
Ventilators	ART	ART	1971	SP	24 X 37	OFF	38	10	40	800
Sunday Morning Walk	ART	ART	1971	SP	20 X 31	BP	50	15	75	1000
English Part	ART	ART	1971	SP	18 X 31	SCH	25	3	40	400
Eastern Shore House	ART	ART	1971	SP	18 X 26	SCH	30	6	35	400
Four Nuns	ART	ART	1972	SP	18 X 30	SCH	51	2	40	300
Mobile Canteen	ART	ART	1973	SP	8 X 19	SCH	40	4	65	400
Diving Tower	ART	ART	1973	SP	18 X 26	SCH	54	10	55	400
Figure and Child	ART	ART	1974	SP	21 X 15	THS	50	8	65	400
Three Helicopters	ART	ART	1975	SP	20 DIA	SP	17	5	75	1000
Nude on the Dartmouth Ferry	ART	ART	1976	SP	17 X 17	SCH	50	10	200	1200
Dog and Pool	ART	ART	1977	LB	22 X 30	R/BFK	35	1	185	500
NS Landscape: November	ART	ART	1977	LB	22 X 30	R/BFK	35	1	185	400
PEI Diary	ART	ART	1978	SP	25 X 20	LEN	20	5	150	400
Ice Forms	ART	ART	1978	SP	19 X 25	AP	9	5	200	500
Baltic Shore, Gotland	ART	JN	1981	EB	12 X 17	AP	35	1	150	300
Sable River	ACC	SW	1983	SP	22 X 30	AP/W	100	9	250	500
Rock Forms	ART	SW	1985	SP	33 X 26	RG/100	100	8	300	500
Rock Forms	ART	SW	1985	SP	29 X 22	RM	62	4	250	400
Cadden Bay	ART	SW	1985	SP	22 X 29	RM	196	4	250	400
Summerville	ART	SW	1985	SP	22 X 29	RM	186	4	250	400
Carter's Beach	ART	SW	1985	SP	33 X 26	RG/100	50	4	250	400
Crows on the Medway	ART	ART	1987	SP	34 X 26	RG/245	100	14	385	585
Magpie & Crow	ART	ART	1988	SP	22 X 30	R/BFK	33	8	385	585
Rhododendron	ART	ART	1989	LC	27 X 34	AN/300	75	18	485	585
Berlin after 9th November	ART	ART	1989	LC/PENC	22 X 30	R/BFK	40	3	300	485
Frieda	ART	ART	1990	LC	34 X 25	AN/300	35	2	350	350
Otto Fiord	ART	ART	1991	LB	20 X 52	HMP	20	1	500	500

FRIEDA SAVITZ

BORN: New York, NY; December 3, 1931
EDUCATION: New York Univ, BS, Art, 1956, MA, 1957; Wisconsin Univ, 1950–51; Cooper Union, NY, 1953–54; Hans Hofmann Sch, NY, 1954,55
AWARDS: Ford Found Int Women's Award, 1975; Nat Endowment for the Arts Fel, 1979
COLLECTIONS: Syracuse Univ, NY; World Print Council, San Francisco, CA; San Francisco Mus of Mod Art, CA; Hudson River Mus, Yonkers, NY; Gesser Kibbutz D N, Nabel Anaylon, Israel; Smith Col, Northampton, MA; Carlsberg-Glystoteck Mus, Copenhagen, Denmark; Bibliotheque Nationale, Paris, France; Mus of Mod Art, Lujubljana, Yugoslavia; Kanagawa Galleries, Yokohama, Japan; Acad Italia, Parma, Italy; Philkia Mus, London, ON, Can; Chrysler Mus, Norfolk, VA; Smith Col, Sophia Smith Coll, Northampton, MA; Guild Hall, East Hampton
PRINTERS: Artist (ART)
PUBLISHERS: Artist (ART)
GALLERIES: Burgen/Treipel Gallery, Geneva, IL; David Anderson Gallery, Buffalo, NY
MAILING ADDRESS: 109 W Clarkstown Rd, New City, NY 10956

The Printworld Directory is accepting new applications for the seventh edition. Approximately 300 new artists will be accepted. Please use the two forms provided in the back section of this directory to submit biographical data and documentation of prints. Edition number of each print must not exceed 500 and the retail price must be $100 or more.

FRIEDA SAVITZ CONTINUED

TITLE	PUBLISHER	PRINTER	DATE	MEDIUM	DIMENSION (PAPER SIZE) IN INCHES	TYPE OF PAPER	EDITION NUMBER	NO. OF COLORS	ORIGINAL OPENING PRICE	CURRENT RETAIL PRICE
SOLD OUT EDITIONS (RARE):										
Love Again!	ART	ART	1974	SP	24 X 30	AP	50	10	100	750
Quiet Roams	ART	ART	1974	SP	24 X 36	AP	50	8	100	750

NOBORU SAWAI

BORN: Tamamatsu, Japan; February 18, 1931
EDUCATION: Augsburg Col, Minneapolis, MN, BA, 1966; Univ of Minnesota, Minneapolis, MN, MFA, 1969; Studied Woodcut Printmaking with Toshi Yoshida, Tokyo, Japan
TEACHING: Instr, Printmaking, Drawing & Art History, Berea Col, KY, 1970–71; Western Washington State Col, Bellingham, WA, 1971; Banff Center for the Arts, Banff, Alberta, Can, 1972; Assoc Prof, Printmaking, Univ of Calgary, Alberta, Can, 1971 to present
AWARDS: Purchase Award, Manisphere Grand Award, Winnipeg, Manitoba, Can, 1973; Purchase Award, London Mus, ON, Can, 1974
COLLECTIONS: Nat Gallery of Canada, Ottawa, Can; Glenbow Mus, Calgary, Alberta, Can; Nat Gallery of Canada, Ottawa, Can; Montreal Mus, Can; Winnipeg Art Gallery, Manitoba, Can
PRINTERS: Artist (ART)
PUBLISHERS: Sawai Atelier, Vancouver, BC, Can (SA)
GALLERIES: Windsors Gallery, Boca Raton, FL; Thomas Gallery, Winnipeg, Man, Canada; Shayne Gallery, Montreal, Quebec, Canada; Evelyn Aimis Gallery, Toronto, Ontario, Canada
MAILING ADDRESS: c/o Dept of Art, Univ of Calgary, 2500 University Drive, NW, Calgary, Alberta, Canada T2N 1N4

TITLE	PUBLISHER	PRINTER	DATE	MEDIUM	DIMENSION (PAPER SIZE) IN INCHES	TYPE OF PAPER	EDITION NUMBER	NO. OF COLORS	ORIGINAL OPENING PRICE	CURRENT RETAIL PRICE
SOLD OUT EDITIONS (RARE):										
Bayton Company (Set of 3):										
Left Wing	SA	ART	1983	WC/I	21 X 27	AC	75	7	275	400
Centre	SA	ART	1983	WC/I	21 X 27	AC	75	7	275	400
Right Wing	SA	ART	1983	WC/I	21 X 27	AC	75	7	275	400
Persimmons	SA	ART	1984	WC/I	22 X 28	GC	75	7	275	400
Samurai and Mrs. Gainsborugh	SA	ART	1984	WC/I	22 X 28	AC	75	8	300	450
Priest and Priestess	SA	ART	1985	WC/I	21 X 27	AC	75	10	300	450

ITALO SCANGA

BORN: Lago, Italy; June 6, 1932; US Citizen
EDUCATION: Michigan State Univ, East Lansing, MI, BA, 1955–58, MFA, 1958–61
TEACHING: Wisconsin Univ, Madison, WI, 1061–64; Rhode Island Sch Asst Prof, Sculpture, Rhode Island Sch of Design, Providence, RI, 1964–66; Assoc Prof, Sculpture, Tyler Sch of Art, Temple Univ, Phila, PA, 1967–78; Vis Assoc Prof, Visual Arts, Univ of California, San Diego, CA, 1976–66, Prof, 1978 to present
AWARDS: Howard Found Grant, Brown Univ, Providence, RI, 1970; Cassandra Found Grant, 1972; Copley Found Grant, Chicago, IL, 1972; Nat Endowment for the Arts Grant, Wash, DC, 1973,80
RECENT EXHIB: Cleveland Mus of Art, OH, 1987; Simon Neuman Gallery, NY, 1987–88; Everson Mus of Art, Syracuse, NY, 1988; Bates Col, Lewison, ME, 1988; Larry Becker Gallery, Phila, PA, 1988; Anders Tornberg Gallery, Lund, Sweden, 1988; Dorothy Goldeen Gallery, Santa Monica, CA, 1989; East Carolina Univ, Gray Art Gallery, Greenville, NC, 1989; Art Inst of Southern California, Laguna Beach, CA, 1989; Ewing Gallery of Art & Arch, Knoxville, TN, 1989; Betsy Rosenfield Gallery, Chicago, IL, 1990; Fairleigh Dickinson Univ, Phyllis Rothman Gallery, Madison, NJ, 1989,92; Helander Gallery, NY, 1992
COLLECTIONS: Metropolitan Mus of Art, NY; Philadelphia Art Mus, PA; Pennsylvania Acad of Fine Arts, Phila, PA; Rhode Island Sch of Design Art Mus, Providence, RI; Memorial Union, Univ of Wisconsin, WI; Fogg Mus, Cambridge, MA; Univ of California Art Mus, Berkeley, CA; Univ of Wisconsin, Madison, WI; Wright Art Center, Beloita, WI; J P Lannon Found, Palm Beach, FL; Mus of Mod Art, NY; Guggenheim Mus, NY; Albright-Knox Art Gallery, Buffalo, NY; Cincinnati Mus, OH; Newport Harbor Mus, CA; Los Angeles County Mus, CA; La Jolla Mus of Contemp Art, CA; Art Inst of Chicago, IL; Detroit Inst of Art, MI; Brooklyn Mus, NY; Toledo Mus, OH; Neuberger Mus, Purchase, NY; Walker Art Center, Minneapolis, MN; Hirshhorn Mus, Wash, DC; Smithsonian Inst, Wash, DC
PRINTERS: Crown Point Press, San Francisco, CA (CPP); Nancy Anello, CA (NA); Paul Singdahlsen, CA (PS); Chip Elwell, NY (CE); Garner Tullis, Santa Barbara, CA (GT); Garner Tullis Workshop, Santa Barbara, CA (GTW); Bud Shark, Boulder, CO (BS); Shark's Lithography, Ltd, Boulder, CO (SLL); Eric Katter (EK); Bill Lagattuta (BL); Anya Szykitka (AS); Jeffrey Sippel, Albuquerque, NM (JS); Tamarind Inst, Albuquerque, NM (TI); Bill Weege, Madison, WI (BW); Andrew Rubin, Madison, WI (AR); Tandem Press, Univ of Wisconsin, Madison, WI (TanPr); Matthew Christie, Boulder, CO (MC)

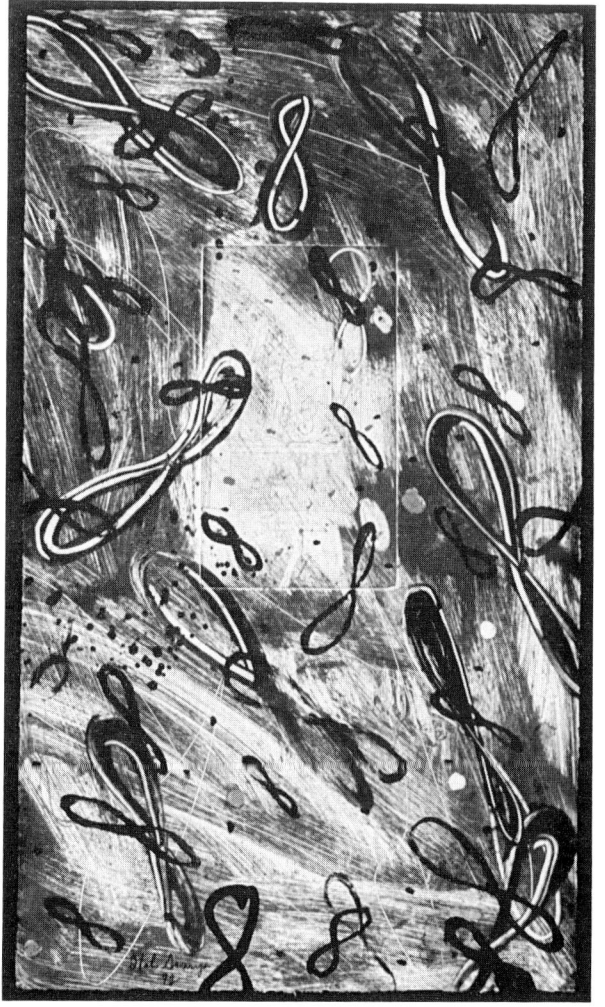

Italo Scanga
Infinity V
Courtesy Shark's, Inc

ITALO SCANGA CONTINUED

PUBLISHERS: Crown Point Press, San Francisco, CA (CPP); Diane Villani Editions, NY (DVE); Fabric Workshop, Phila, PA (FW); Garner Tullis Workshop, Santa Barbara, CA (GTW); Shark's Lithography, Ltd, Boulder, CO (SLL); Tandem Press, Univ of Wisconsin, Madison, WI (TanPr); David Lawrence Editions, Beverly Hills, CA (DLE)
GALLERIES: Charles Cowles Gallery, New York, NY; Roger Ramsay Gallery, Chicago, IL; Diane Villani Editions, New York, NY; Crown Point Press, New York, NY & San Francisco, CA; Susanne Hilberry Gallery, Birmingham, MI; Burnett Miller Gallery, Los Angeles, CA; John Berggruen Gallery, San Francisco, CA; Harcus Gallery, Boston, MA; Pamela Auchincloss Gallery, Santa Barbara, CA; Galeria Arte Contemporaneo, Mexico City, Mexico; Dorothy Goldeen Gallery, Santa Monica, CA; David Lawrence Editions, Beverly Hills, CA; Henri Gallery, Wash, DC; Betsy Rosenfield Gallery, Chicago, IL; Helander Galleries, Palm Beach, FL & Bay Harbor Islands, FL & New York, NY; Shark's, Inc, Boulder, CO; Nancy Singer Gallery, St Louis, MO; Smith Andersen Gallery, Palo Alto, CA; Susan Duval Gallery, Aspen, CO; Inkfish Gallery, Denver, CO; Quartet Editions, New York, NY
MAILING ADDRESS: 7127 Olivetas St, La Jolla, CA 92037

TITLE	PUBLISHER	PRINTER	DATE	MEDIUM	DIMENSION (PAPER SIZE) IN INCHES	TYPE OF PAPER	EDITION NUMBER	NO. OF COLORS	ORIGINAL OPENING PRICE	CURRENT RETAIL PRICE
SOLD OUT EDITIONS (RARE):										
Visiting with John Muir	CPP	NA/PS	1981	EC	42 X 30	AC/B	25	3	500	1000
Blue Glass	CPP	NA/PS	1981	EB/A	42 X 30	AC/B	25	3	500	1000
Sacrificial Lamb	CPP	NA/PS	1981	EB/A	42 X 30	AC/B	25	4	500	1000
Abundance	CPP	NA/PS	1981	EB/A	42 X 30	AC/B	25	2	500	1000
Toccata	CPP	NA/PS	1981	EC	42 X 30	AC/B	25	3	500	1000
Los Perdidos and Crying Woman	CPP	NA/PS	1981	EB	42 X 30	AC/B	10	1	400	850
Portrait of an Opera Singer	CPP	NA/PS	1981	EC	30 X 23	AC/B	25	2	400	850
Listening to T M	CPP	NA/PS	1981	EC	30 X 23	AC/B	25	2	400	850
Raven	CPP	NA/PS	1981	EC	30 X 23	AC/B	25	2	400	850
Bird and Snake	CPP	NA/PS	1981	EC	30 X 23	AC/B	25	2	400	850
Bad Habits	FW	FW	1981	SP	50 X 41	TAP	20		750	1500
The Revolt	DVE	CE	1982	WC	31 X 21	GTNP	20	3	450	1200
Musicians	DVE	CE	1982	WC	31 X 21	GTNP	20	3	450	1200
Gaspara Stampa	DVE	CE	1982	WC	31 X 21	GTNP	20	3	450	1000
The Bean Eater	DVE	CE	1982	WC	24 X 18	DOV	20	1	300	1200
Monte Cassino	DVE	CE	1984	WC	28 X 20	GTNP	25		450	1000
Monte Cassino	DVE	CE	1984	WB	28 X 20	TOR	10	1	400	1000
Metaphysical Beastiary	GTW	GT/GTW	1985	MON	32 X 23 EA	TUM	1 EA	Full	900 EA	1500 EA
Female Saint	SI	BS/SI	1987	LC/WC	45 X 30	R/BFK	20		800	1800
Greek Vase (with Wood Relief)	TanPr	BW/AR/TanPr	1989	LC/REL	42 X 30	AC/Wood	40		950	1500
CURRENT EDITIONS:										
Giorgione E; Giorgioneschi (with Acrylics & Ink)	DLE	RM/SB/KH/DL	1988	SP/HC	74 X 38	OKP/HMP	19	4	2500	3000
Tujunga (Series of 27 Unique Prints on Silk Plus 8 Unique Prints on Paper with Acrylics & Ink)	DLE	RM/SB/KH/DL	1988	SP/HC/CC	58 X 37 EA	S/325	1 EA	Varies	4000 EA	7500 EA

Italo Scanga
Figs, 1991
Courtesy Tandem Press

Italo Scanga
Pitcher, 1991
Courtesy Tandem Press

ITALO SCANGA CONTINUED

Italo Scanga
Ravenna I
Courtesy Shark's, Inc

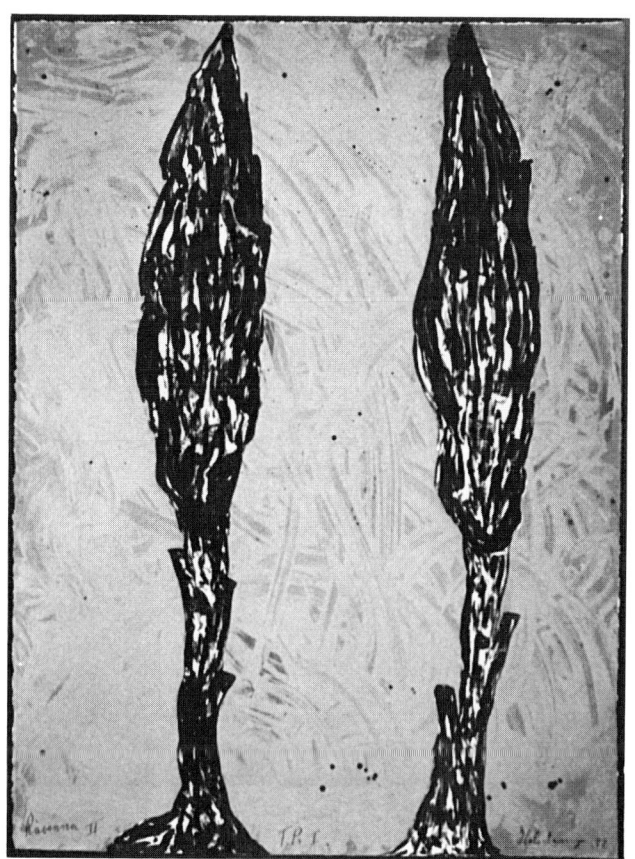

Italo Scanga
Ravenna II
Courtesy Shark's, Inc

TITLE	PUBLISHER	PRINTER	DATE	MEDIUM	DIMENSION (PAPER SIZE) IN INCHES	TYPE OF PAPER	EDITION NUMBER	NO. OF COLORS	ORIGINAL OPENING PRICE	CURRENT RETAIL PRICE
CURRENT EDITIONS:										
Sacro Speco (with Acrylics & Ink) Red Bunting (with Acrylic & Ink on Silk Laminated on Paper)	DLE	RM/SB/KH/DL	1988	SP/HC	38 X 71	OKP/HMP	19	4	2500	3000
(Series of 43 Unique Prints) A Tree in Rome (Series of 36 Unique Prints with Acrylics & Ink on Silk	DLE	RM/SB/KH/DL	1989	SP/HC	58 X 37 EA	S/325	1 EA	8 EA	5000 EA	5000 EA
Laminated on Paper)	DLE	RM/SB/KH/DL	1989	SP/HC	58 X 37 EA	S/325	1 EA	6 EA	5000 EA	5000 EA
Pot, Cherries and Retablo	TI	EK/BL/TI	1989	LB	45 X 30	R/BFK/CR	15	1	550	950
Abstraction and a Pot	TI	AS/BL/TI	1989	LC	30 X 22	AP	15	5	450	750
Rain in Sedona	TI	BL/TI	1989	LC		ARJ			450	850
To Max Ernst	TI	BL/TI	1989	LC		ARJ			450	850
Two Female Saints and a Skull	TI	BL/TI	1989	LC	16 X 45	ARJ	15	4	450	750
Two Male Saints and a Skull	TI	EK/BL/JS/TI	1989	LC	16 X 45	ARJ	15	4	450	750
Untitled (Small Monotypes)	TI	EK/BL/JS/TI	1989	MON	14 X 10 EA		1 EA	Varies	700 EA	900 EA
Untitled (Medium Monotypes)	TI	EK/BL/JS/TI	1989	MON	16 X 12 EA		1 EA	Varies	800 EA	1000 EA
Untitled (Large Monotypes)	TI	EK/BL/JS/TI	1989	MON	20 X 14 EA		1 EA	Varies	900 EA	1200 EA
Calabrian Jug I, II	SI	BS/MC/SI	1990	MON	48 X 32 EA	R/BFK	1 EA	Varies	2400 EA	2400 EA
Santa Lucia I, II	SI	BS/MC/SI	1990	MON	48 X 32 EA	R/BFK	1 EA	Varies	2400 EA	2400 EA
2 Birds I, II	SI	BS/MC/SI	1990	MON	48 X 32 EA	R/BFK	1 EA	Varies	2400 EA	2400 EA
Giallo	SI	BS/MC/SI	1990	MON	48 X 32 EA	R/BFK	1 EA	Varies	2400 EA	2400 EA
The Soul's Awakening	SI	BS/MC/SI	1990	MON	48 X 32 EA	R/BFK	1 EA	Varies 2400	EA 2400	EA
Untitled, 1990	SI	BS/MC/SI	1990	MON	48 X 32 EA	R/BFK	1 EA	Varies	2400 EA	2400 EA
The Temptation of St Anthony (Collaboration with Dale Chihuly)	SI	BS/MC/SI	1990	MON	48 X 32 EA	R/BFK	1 EA	Varies	2500 EA	2500 EA
Untitled (Collaboration with Dale Chihuly)	SI	BS/MC/SI	1990	MON	32 X 48 EA	R/BFK	1 EA	Varies	2500 EA	2500 EA
Beata	SI	ART/BS/MC/SI	1990	LC/HC	19 X 12 EA	R/BFK	1 EA	Varies	900 EA	900 EA
Sulvare	SI	ART/BS/MC/SI	1990	LC/HC	19 X 12 EA	R/BFK	1 EA	Varies	900 EA	900 EA
Virgo	SI	ART/BS/MC/SI	1990	LC/HC	19 X 12 EA	R/BFK	1 EA	Varies	900 EA	900 EA
Celeste	SI	ART/BS/MC/SI	1991	LC/HC	48 X 32 EA	R/BFK	1 EA	Varies	1800 EA	1800 EA
2 Cypress	TanPr	BW/AR/TanPr	1989	WC/LB	42 X 30	AC/W	40	6	1750	1750
Cubist	TanPr	BW/AR/TanPr	1989	WC/LB	42 X 30	AC/W	40	2	1200	1750
Landscape	TanPr	BW/AR/TanPr	1989	WC/LB	42 X 30	AC/W	40	7	1750	1750
Napoli	TanPr	BW/AR/TanPr	1989	WC/LB	42 X 30	AC/W	40	6	1750	1750

ITALO SCANGA CONTINUED

TITLE	PUBLISHER	PRINTER	DATE	MEDIUM	DIMENSION (PAPER SIZE) IN INCHES	TYPE OF PAPER	EDITION NUMBER	NO. OF COLORS	ORIGINAL OPENING PRICE	CURRENT RETAIL PRICE
CURRENT EDITIONS:										
Untitled (Series of 44)	TanPr	BW/AR/TanPr	1989	MON	23 X 20 EA	HMP	1 EA	Varies	1000 EA	1000 EA
Pitcher	TanPr	BW/AR/TanPr	1991	LC	29 X 22	AC/W	20	10	900	900
Figs	TanPr	BW/AR/TanPr	1991	LC	29 X 22	AC/W	20	8	900	900
Untitled (Series of 42)	TanPr	BW/AR/TanPr	1991	MON	Varies	HMP	1 EA	Varies	650/1500	650/1500
2 Trees	TanPr	BW/AR/TanPr	1992	WC	21 X 15	R/BFK	50	5	300	300
The Temptation of St Anthony (with Dale Chihuly)	SI	BS/MC/SI	1992	MON	48 X 32 EA	AC	1 EA	Varies	2500 EA	2500 EA
Untitled	SI	BS/MC/SI	1992	MON	32 X 48 EA	AC	1 EA	Varies	2500 EA	2500 EA
Ravenna I, II (Set of 2)	SI	BS/MC/SI	1993	LC	30 X 23 EA	R/BFK/W	25 EA	7 EA	1600 SET	1600 SET
									900 EA	900 EA
Alberti	SI	BS/MC/SI	1993	MON/CO	29 X 17 EA	R/BFK/W	10 EA	Varies	1200 EA	1200 EA
Infinity	SI	BS/MC/SI	1993	MON	29 X 17 EA	HMP	6 EA	Varies	1200 EA	1200 EA

MARCIA SCANLON

EDUCATION: Univ of Minnesota, BA, 1967, MFA, 1970
COLLECTIONS: Minneapolis Inst of Art, MN
PRINTERS: Vermillion Editions, Ltd, Minneapolis, MN (VEL)
PUBLISHERS: Vermillion Editions, Ltd, Minneapolis, MN (VEL)
GALLERIES: John C Stoller & Co, Minneapolis, MN

TITLE	PUBLISHER	PRINTER	DATE	MEDIUM	DIMENSION (PAPER SIZE) IN INCHES	TYPE OF PAPER	EDITION NUMBER	NO. OF COLORS	ORIGINAL OPENING PRICE	CURRENT RETAIL PRICE
SOLD OUT EDITIONS (RARE):										
Lispenard Street	VEL	VEL	1982	MON	12 X 42	ACW	5		450	900
Lispenard Street (State)	VEL	VEL	1982	MON	12 X 42	ACW	4		450	900
Prague Convent	VEL	VEL	1982	MON	12 X 42	ACW	5		450	900
Pine Hill	VEL	VEL	1983	MON	12 X 42	HMP	14	1	650	900
Pine Hill	VEL	VEL	1983	MON	13 X 42	HMP	10	1	650	900
Brownsville	VEL	VEL	1984	MON	31 X 40	HMP	4	1	900	1200

MIRIAM SCHAPIRO

BORN: Toronto, Canada; November 15, 1923; US Citizen
EDUCATION: Univ of Iowa, Iowa City, IA, BA, 1945 MA, 1946 MFA, 1949; Col of Wooster, OH, Hon DFA, 1983
TEACHING: Parsons Sch of Design, NY; Univ of California, San Diego, CA, 1967-71,75;
AWARDS: Ford Found Tamarind Fel, 1964; National Endowment for the Arts, 1976; Skowhegan Award, 1981; Guggenheim Fel Award, 1987
RECENT EXHIB: Simms Fine Art, New Orleans, LA, 1987; Cincinnati Art Mus, OH, 1989; Bernice Steinbaum Gallery, NY, 1988,90; Florida Int Univ Art Mus, Miami, FL, 1992; Guild Hall Mus, East Hampton, NY, 1992; Fairleigh Dickinson Mus, Phyllis Rothman Gallery, Madison, NJ, 1989,92; Miami Univ Art Mus, Oxford, OH, 1992
COLLECTIONS: Mus of Mod Art, NY; Whitney Mus of Am Art, NY; Stanford Univ, Palo Alto, CA; Hirshhorn Mus, Wash, DC; Allen Mem Art Mus, Oberlin Col, OH; Boston Mus of Fine Arts, MA; Massachusetts Mus of Contemp Art, Boston, MA
PRINTERS: Fabric Workshop, Phila, PA (FW); Bummy Huss, NY (BH); David Keister, Bloomington, IN (DK); David Calkins, Bloomington, IN (DC); Echo Press, Bloomington, IN (EPr); Eileen M Foti, New Brunswick, NJ (EMF); Rutgers Center for Innovative Printmaking, New Brunswick, NJ (RCIP)
PUBLISHERS: Barbara Gladstone Editions, NY (BGE); Abrams Original Editions, NY (AOE); Echo Press, Bloomington, IN (EPr); Rutgers Archive for Printmaking, Zimmerli Art Mus, New Brunswick, NJ (RAP/ZAM)
GALLERIES: Barbara Gladstone Gallery, New York, NY; Barbara Gillman Gallery, Miami, FL; Koplin Gallery, Los Angeles, CA; Douglas Drake Gallery, Kansas City, KS; Bernice Steinbaum Gallery, New York, NY; Vered Gallery, East Hampton, NY; LewAllen Gallery, Santa Fe, NM
MAILING ADDRESS: 393 W Broadway, New York, NY 10012

TITLE	PUBLISHER	PRINTER	DATE	MEDIUM	DIMENSION (PAPER SIZE) IN INCHES	TYPE OF PAPER	EDITION NUMBER	NO. OF COLORS	ORIGINAL OPENING PRICE	CURRENT RETAIL PRICE
SOLD OUT EDITIONS (RARE):										
Kimono	BGE	FW	1979	SP	54 X 35	SP	7	5	1400	2500
The Disguise (With Fabric, Glitter, Etc) (Hand Colored)	BGE	BH	1980	HACA/P	13 X 27	CP	20	Varies	1500	2500
CURRENT EDITIONS:										
Study for Costume for Robespierre's Niece	EPr	DK/DC/EPr	1985	MON/CO	60 X 44 EA	AC/W & AC/BL	1 EA	Varies	900 EA	1500 EA
String of Cats (with Lens Tissue)	EPr	DK/DC/EPr	1985	EB/REL/LI/CO	30 X 44	AC/W & AC/BL	4	3	900	1500
Dierdre's Dress	EPr	DK/DC/EPr	1985	MON/CO	60 X 44 EA	AC/W & AC/BL	1 EA	Varies	900 EA	1800 EA
Frida & Me	RAP/ZAM	EMF/RCIP	1990	LC/XER/FAB/CO	30 X 41	R/BFK	81	9	2200	2500

KENNY SCHARF

BORN: Los Angeles, CA; 1958
EDUCATION: Sch of Visual Arts, NY, BFA, 1980
RECENT EXHIB: Whitney Mus of Am Art, NY, 1988; California State Univ, Weisman Coll, Fullerton, CA, 1988; Akira Ikeda Gallery, Tokyo, Japan, 1988,89; Martin Lawrence Galleries, Phila, PA, 1990; Galerie Beaubourg, Paris, France, 1990; Hans Mayer Gallery, Dusseldorf, Germany, 1990; Tony Shafrazi Gallery, 1987,88,89,91
COLLECTIONS: Whitney Mus of Am Art, NY; Mus of Mod Art, Rio de Janiero, Brazil; Sammlung Ludwig Mus, Achen, Germany
PRINTERS: Maurice Sanchez, NY (MS); Derriere L'Etoile Studio, NY (DES)
PUBLISHERS: Art Issue Editions, Inc, NY (AIE); Lawrence Limited Editions, Van Nuys, CA (MLLE)

KENNY SCHARF CONTINUED

GALLERIES: Martin Lawrence Galleries, Escondido, CA & Newport Beach, CA & Palm Springs, CA & Redondo Beach, CA & Santa Clara, CA & Sherman Oaks, CA & Thousand Oaks, CA & West Los Angeles, CA & Los Angeles, CA & Short Hills, NJ & Soho, NY & Phila, PA; Galerie Bruno Bishofberger, Zürich, Switzerland; Akira Ikeda Gallery, Tokyo, Japan; Michael Kohn Gallery, Los Angeles, CA; Barbara Braathen Gallery, New York, NY; Tony Shafrazi Gallery, New York, NY

TITLE	PUBLISHER	PRINTER	DATE	MEDIUM	DIMENSION (PAPER SIZE) IN INCHES	TYPE OF PAPER	EDITION NUMBER	NO. OF COLORS	ORIGINAL OPENING PRICE	CURRENT RETAIL PRICE
CURRENT EDITIONS:										
Thou Shalt have No Other Gods before Me (from Ten Commandments Suite)	AIE	MS/DES	1987	LC	24 X 19	DIEU	84	5	500	2000
Space Balls	MLLE		1990	SP	32 X 40	AC	238		2000	2750

WILLIAM SCHARF

BORN: Calcutta, India; February 22, 1927
EDUCATION: Pennsylvania Acad of Fine Arts, Phila, PA; Barnes Found, Merion, PA
TEACHING: Instr, Sch of Visual Arts, NY, 1965–69; Instr, Painting, San Francisco Sch of Fine Arts, CA, 1963,66,69,74; Lectr, Art Students League, NY, 1987
COLLECTIONS: Nat Mus of Am Art, Smithsonian Inst, Wash, DC; Guggenheim Mus, NY; Inst of Contemp Art, Boston, MA; Newark Mus, NJ; Smith Col Mus, Northampton, MA; Neuberger Mus, Purchase, NY; Brooklyn Mus, NY
PRINTERS: John Campione, NY (JC)
PUBLISHERS: Prestige Art Ltd, Marmaroneck, NY (PA)
GALLERIES: Emily Harvey, New York, NY; Jayne Baum Gallery, New York, NY
MAILING ADDRESS: 75 Central Park, West, New York, NY 10023

TITLE	PUBLISHER	PRINTER	DATE	MEDIUM	DIMENSION (PAPER SIZE) IN INCHES	TYPE OF PAPER	EDITION NUMBER	NO. OF COLORS	ORIGINAL OPENING PRICE	CURRENT RETAIL PRICE
CURRENT EDITIONS:										
Golden Rope	PA	JC	1980	SP	28 X 23	AP	100	6	300	400
Menaced Tear	PA	JC	1980	SP	28 X 23	AP	100	6	300	400
Untitled	PA	JC	1980	SP	30 X 23	AP	100	6	300	400
Dove Leave	PA	JC	1980	SP	31 X 23	AP	100	6	300	400
Juggler	PA	JC	1980	SP	33 X 23	AP	100	6	300	400

EMANUEL SCHARY

BORN: Israel; February 27, 1924; US Citizen
EDUCATION: Carnegie Inst of Tech Sch of Fine Arts, Pittsburgh, PA; Art Students League, New York, NY; Pratt Graphics Center, Brooklyn, NY
TEACHING: Reali, Amani Sch, Israel
COLLECTIONS: Metropolitan Mus of Art, NY; Vatican Mus, Rome, Italy; Jewish Mus, NY; Brooklyn Mus, NY; Spertus Mus, Chicago, IL, Mus of Israel, Jerusalem, Israel; Mus of Haifa, Israel; Hebrew Univ, Tel Aviv Univ, Israel; Nat Coll of Fine Art, Smithsonian Inst, Wash, DC
PRINTERS: George C Miller, NY (GCM); American Atelier, NY (AA)
PUBLISHERS: JFM Publishers, Rock Hill, NY (JFM); Circle Fine Art, NY (CFA)
GALLERIES: Center Art Gallery, New York, NY; Moriah Gallery of Judaica, New York, NY; Solo Gallery, New York, NY; Sigma Gallery, New York, NY; Viridian Gallery, New York, NY
MAILING ADDRESS: 8 Nottingham Gate, Rock Hill, NY 12775

TITLE	PUBLISHER	PRINTER	DATE	MEDIUM	DIMENSION (PAPER SIZE) IN INCHES	TYPE OF PAPER	EDITION NUMBER	NO. OF COLORS	ORIGINAL OPENING PRICE	CURRENT RETAIL PRICE
SOLD OUT EDITIONS (RARE):										
Old Neighborhood	JEM	GCM	1968	LB	10 X 14	R/BFK	180	1	40	1200
Street of 100 Arches	JEM	GCM	1969	LB	14 X 18	R/BFK	180	1	60	1500
Coney Island	JEM	GCM	1970	LB	10 X 14	R/BFK	200	1	60	1200
Carnegie Hall	JEM	GCM	1972	LB	10 X 14	R/BFK	180	1	50	1200
Safad-In Galilee	JEM	GCM	1973	LB	14 X 18	R/BFK	180	1	75	1200
CURRENT EDITIONS:										
Tailoring	JEM	GCM	1980	LB	10 X 14	R/BFK	250	1	160	350
Memories	JEM	GCM	1980	LB	12 X 16	R/BFK	250	1	180	350
My Father's House	JEM	GCM	1980	LC	11 X 14	R/BFK	130	6	160	350
On Eagles Wings	JFM	GCM	1980	LC	9 X 12	R/BFK	175	2	150	350
Vender	JEM	GCM	1980	LB	11 X 14	R/BFK	250	1	160	350
Carousel	JEM	GCM	1981	LB	12 X 16	R/BFK	250	1	200	350
Plaza	JEM	GCM	1981	LB	12 X 16	R/BFK	250	1	200	350
Hills of Judea	JEM	GCM	1981	LB	12 X 16	R/BFK	250	1	180	350
Brass Band	JEM	GCM	1981	LB	14 X 18	R/BFK	250	1	180	350
Friends	JEM	GCM	1981	LB	12 X 16	R/BFK	250	1	200	350
Moriah	CFA	AA	1981	LB	18 X 23	AP	275	1	150	200

CAROL SCHIFFLEGER

BORN: Manitowoc, WI; November 3, 1937
EDUCATION: Univ of Wisconsin, Madison, WI, B Sc, Art, M Sc, Art
TEACHING: Sheridan Col, Oakville, ON, Can, 1969–86
COLLECTIONS: Nat Air & Space Mus, Wash, DC; Univ of Wisconsin, Madison, WI; Univ of Waterloo, ON, Can; Art Gallery of Brant, ON, Can; City of Toronto, ON, Can
PRINTERS: Presswerk Editions, Toronto, Can (PEd); Artist (ART)
PUBLISHERS: Artist (ART)
GALLERIES: Portfolio Gallery, Auckland, New Zealand; Deborah Grund, Toronto, Canada; Contemp Fine Art Services, Toronto, Canada
MAILING ADDRESS: 30 Reynard Terrace, Takanini, New Zealand

CAROL SCHIFFLEGER CONTINUED

TITLE	PUBLISHER	PRINTER	DATE	MEDIUM	DIMENSION (PAPER SIZE) IN INCHES	TYPE OF PAPER	EDITION NUMBER	NO. OF COLORS	ORIGINAL OPENING PRICE	CURRENT RETAIL PRICE
CURRENT EDITIONS:										
Process I	ART	ART	1976	WC	22 X 22	R/BFK	17	2	100	200
Process II	ART	ART	1977	WC	22 X 22	R/BFK	19	2	100	200
Process III	ART	ART	1977	WC	22 X 22	R/BFK	10	2	100	200
Process IV	ART	ART	1977	WC	22 X 22	R/BFK	38	2	100	200
Process V	ART	ART	1977	WC	22 X 22	R/BFK	35	2	100	200
Process VI	ART	ART	1977	WC	22 X 22	R/BFK	30	2	100	200
Process VII	ART	ART	1978	WC	22 X 22	R/BFK	31	2	100	200
Returning to the Source	ART	ART	1978	WC	22 X 27	R/BFK	25	2	125	200
Returning . . . II	ART	ART	1979	WC/PENC	22 X 30	R/BFK	20	4	150	200
Between Mali Halan and the Moon . . . in the place where,	ART	ART	1980	WC	30 X 30	STP	15	2	200	275
at the time when . . .	ART	ART	1981	WC	30 X 34	STP	19	2	225	275
Upcurrents	ART	PEd	1982	WC	30 X 32	SOM	25	2	225	275
Frontal Disturbance	ART	PEd	1983	WC	30 X 36	R/BFK	26	4	225	275
Lemon III	ART	ART	1985	WC	22 X 30	GOYU	6	1	175	225
Lemon-Lime	ART	ART	1985	WC	20 X 26	TROYA	9	2	175	225
Wind Shift	ART	PEd	1986	WC/LE	36 X 25	TOR	25	4	375	450

JOHN OTTO SCHLUMP

BORN: Monroe, MI; October 5, 1933
EDUCATION: Wittenberg Univ, Springfield, OH, BS, BFA, 1955; Michigan State Univ, Lansing, MI, MA, Art, 1957; Univ of Toledo, OH; Univ of Calgary, Alberta, Canada, with Toshida & Sadao Watanabe
TEACHING: Instr & Chmn, Art Dept, Printmaking, Frostburg State Col, MD, 1959–61; Chmn, Dept of Art, Wittenberg Univ, Springfield, OH, 1963–72; Prof, Art, Wittenberg Univ, Springfield, OH, 1961 to present
AWARDS: Int Dimensions Grant, Wittenberg Univ, Springfield, OH, 1975–76; Res & Creativity Grant, Lutheran Church in Am; Faculty Development Res Grant, 1979–80
COLLECTIONS: British Mus, London, England; Univ of Nebraska, Lincoln, NE; Weatherspoon Art Gallery, Univ of North Carolina, Greensboro, NC; Cleveland Mus of Art, OH; Univ of Iowa, Iowa City, IA; Nasson Col, Springvale, ME; Kalamazoo Inst of Art, MI; Ringling Mus, Sarasota, FL; E B Crocker Gallery of Art, Sacramento, CA; City of Sacramento Art Mus, CA; West Virginia Univ, Morgantown, WV; Boise Gallery of Art, ID; Milwaukee Art Center, WI; Kresge Art Center, Michigan State Univ, Lansing, MI; Indiana State Univ, Bloomington, IN; Smithsonian Mus, Wash, DC
PRINTERS: Wittenberg Univ, Springfield, OH (WU); Artist (ART)
PUBLISHERS: Wittenberg Univ, Springfield, OH (WU); Lakeside Studio, MI (LS); Artist (ART)
GALLERIES: Gallery G, Pittsburgh, PA

TITLE	PUBLISHER	PRINTER	DATE	MEDIUM	DIMENSION (PAPER SIZE) IN INCHES	TYPE OF PAPER	EDITION NUMBER	NO. OF COLORS	ORIGINAL OPENING PRICE	CURRENT RETAIL PRICE
SOLD OUT EDITIONS (RARE):										
Continental Terrain	ART	ART	1970	SP	24 X 96	T/MASON	6	7	600	1200
CURRENT EDITIONS:										
Seat of Consciousness	ART/LS	ART	1970	SP	7 X 24	BCS	50	5	100	200
Intimate Crevice	ART/LS	ART	1975	SP	22 X 28	BCS	50	6	100	200
Expose	ART	ART	1979	SP	13 X 21	BRC	20	7	100	175
The Other Side	ART	ART	1980	SP	15 X 42	BHC	10	7	125	400
Blue Orbit	ART	ART	1980	SP/STEN	24 X 24	T/MASON	10	8	125	450
Reflection	ART	ART	1985	SP	27 X 22	BRC	10	4	200	300
Lacus Magnus	ART	ART	1985	SP	21 X 26	TR/HMP	10	6	150	300
Blue Jubilee I,II,III	ART	ART	1985	SP	22 X 30 EA	BRC	7 EA	7 EA	280 EA	300 EA
Cliff Forms	ART	ART	1985	SP/STEN	48 X 60	T/MASON	6	8	600	850
Sea-Piece	ART	ART	1986	SP/CD	15 X 36	BRC/STP/HWT	12	3	240	300
Twinrocker III	ART	ART	1986	SP	13 X 34	COP/100	12	5	280	300
Confinement	ART	ART	1986	SP/CO	19 X 28	AP88	12	3	210	250
Lacus Magnus II	ART	ART	1986	SP	27 X 22	BRC	16	7	280	200
Simply Metallic	ART	ART	1985	SP/STEN	30 X 43	STP/HWT	10	6	400	600

GEORGE SCHNEEMAN

EDUCATION: Univ of Minnesota, Minneapolis, MN, BA, 1958
TEACHING: Skowhegan Sch of Painting and Sculpture, ME, Summer, 1979
AWARDS: Rosenthal Award, Am Acad of Arts and Letters, 1969
PRINTERS: Derriére l'Etoile Studios, NY (DES); Artist (ART)
PUBLISHERS: Holly Solomon Editions Ltd, NY (HSE); Artist (ART)
GALLERIES: Holly Solomon Editions, New York, NY

TITLE	PUBLISHER	PRINTER	DATE	MEDIUM	DIMENSION (PAPER SIZE) IN INCHES	TYPE OF PAPER	EDITION NUMBER	NO. OF COLORS	ORIGINAL OPENING PRICE	CURRENT RETAIL PRICE
SOLD OUT EDITIONS (RARE):										
Wristwatch	ART	ART	1968	SP	8 X 9	AP	70		100	300
Flannel Shirts	ART	ART	1977	SP	12 X 17	AP	70		200	400
Plaid Curtains	ART	ART	1978	SP	14 X 20	AP	70		200	400
Silk Stockings on Hanger (Red)	HSE	DES	1980	LC/OS	12 X 10	AP/W	40		100	300
Silk Stockings on Hanger (Green)	HSE	DES	1980	LC/OS	12 X 10	AP/W	40		100	300
Upside-Down Flannel Shirt	HSE	DES	1980	LC	25 X 19	AP/W	45	2	350	500

JULIAN SCHNABEL

BORN: New York, NY; 1951
EDUCATION: Univ of Houston, TX, BFA, 1972; Whitney Independent Study Prog, NY, 1973–74
RECENT EXHIB: Hoffman Borman Gallery, Santa Monica, CA, 1987; Städtische Künsthalle, Düsseldorf, West Germany, 1987; Centre Georges Pompidou, Paris, France, 1987; Whitney Mus of Am Art, NY, 1987–88; Milwaukee Art Mus, WI, 1988; San Francisco Mus of Mod Art, CA, 1989; Akira Ikeda Gallery, Tokyo, Japan, 1989; Museo d'Arte Contemporanea, Prate, 1989,90; Yvon Lambert Gallery, Paris, France, 1989–90; Duson Gallery, Seoul, Korea, 1990; Galerie Bruno Bischofberger, Zurich, Switzerland, 1988,92; Guild Hall Mus, East Hampton, NY, 1992; Univ of Houston, Blaffer Gallery, TX, 1992; Pace Gallery, HY, 1990,92
PRINTERS: Jeryl Parker Editions, New Paltz, NY (JPE), Jeryl Parker, New Paltz, NY (JP); Brenda Zlamany, NY (BZ); Parasol Press, NY (PaP); Tandem Press, Madison, WI (TPr); Vigna Antoniniana Stamperia D'Arte, Rome, Italy (VASDA)
PUBLISHERS: Parasol Press, Ltd, NY (PaP); Pace Editions, NY (PE); Editions 2 RC, Rome, Italy (2RC)
GALLERIES: Margo Leavin Gallery, Los Angeles, CA; Brody's Gallery, Wash, DC; Ochi Gallery, Boise, ID & San Valley, ID; Donald Young Gallery, Seattle, WA; Magnuson Gallery, Boston, MA; Galerie Daniel Templon, Paris, France; Martina Hamilton Gallery, New York, NY; Pace/MacGill Gallery, New York, NY; Pace Prints, New York, NY; Daniel Weinberg Gallery, New York, NY; Sylvia Cordish Fine Art, Baltimore, MD; Mario Diancono Gallery, Boston, MA; Fred Hoffman Gallery, Santa Monica, CA; Galerie Bruno Bischofberger, Zürich, Switzerland; Mary Boone Galley, New York, NY; Perry Rubenstein, New York, NY; Charles Foley Gallery, Columbus, OH; Duson Gallery, Seoul, Korea; Anthony Meier Fine Arts, San Francisco, CA; Fred Hoffman Gallery, Santa Monica, CA; Dorsky Gallery, New York, NY; Du Bois International, Ltd, New York, NY; Matthew Marks Gallery, New York, NY
MAILING ADDRESS: 24 E 20th St, New York, NY 10003

Julian Schnabel
For Anna Magnani
Courtesy Pace Editions, Inc

TITLE	PUBLISHER	PRINTER	DATE	MEDIUM	DIMENSION (PAPER SIZE) IN INCHES	TYPE OF PAPER	EDITION NUMBER	NO. OF COLORS	ORIGINAL OPENING PRICE	CURRENT RETAIL PRICE
SOLD OUT EDITIONS (RARE):										
Todd, Cage without Bars (Set of 9)	PaP	JP/PaP	1983	EB/A	30 X 24 EA	KOZO	50 EA	1	12500 SET	75000 SET
The Dream (2 Sheets)	PaP	JP/PaP	1983	AB	47 X 71	KOZO	30	1	3000	20000
Lola (Printed on Brown Velvet)	PaP	JP/BZ/JPE	1984	AC	115 X 67	Velvet	5		10000	50000
Brenda (Printed on Velvet and Framed without Glass)	PaP	JP/BZ/JPE	1984	EC	60 X 36	Velvet	5	1–2	8000	30000
Leaf (Unique Print—Printed on Purple Velvet)	PaP	JP/PaP	1984	AC	53 X 39	Velvet	1	1	12000	30000
Harp (Hand-Colored with Oil—Printed on Purple Velvet)	PaP	JP/PaP	1984	AB/HC	72 X 48	Velvet	5	4	9000	40000
Set of Four:									30000 SET	100000 SET
For Anna Magnani (Dipt)	PaP/PE	JP/PaP	1983–85	EB/LC	74 X 54	SOM	35	9	7500	25000
A Boy from Naples (Dipt)	PaP/PE	JP/PaP	1983–85	EB/LC	72 X 50	SOM	35	9	7500	25000
Mother (Dipt)	PaP/PE	JP/PaP	1983–85	EB/LC	72 X 49	SOM	35	9	9500	30000
Prison Rodeo (Dipt)	PaP/PE	JP/PaP	1983–85	EB/LC	86 X 36	SOM	35	9	9500	25000
For Anna Magnani, State I	PaP/PE	JP/PaP	1983–85	AC	71 X 47	SOM	15	2	3500	10000
CURRENT EDITIONS:										
Untitled (Collaborative Effort with Jean Kallina who Created the Original Photographic Image) (Set of 3):									30000 SET	30000 SET
Gothic Run Riot	PE	TPr	1990	PH/LB/WC/EB/SP	64 X 58	SWP	35		10000	12000
Billy's First Portrait of God	PE	TPr	1990	PH/LB/WC/EB/SP	66 X 56	SWP	35		10000	12000
Jean's First Trip to Versailles	PE	TPr	1990	PH/LB/WC/EB/SP	55 X 65	SWP	35		10000	12000
Untitled (Flamingo I,II)	2RC	VASDA	1991	EB/A/CAR/EMB/CO/CC	77 X 53 EA	Antiq/FAB	48 EA		12000 EA	12000 EA
Pandora and the Flying DutchmanI,II	2RC	VASDA	1991	EB/A/CAR/CO/CC	77 X 53 EA	Antiq/FAB	48 EA		12000 EA	12000 EA

CAROLEE SCHNEEMANN

BORN: Fox Chase, PA; October 12, 1939
EDUCATION: Univ of Illinois, Champaign-Urbana, IL, MFA; Bard Col, Annandale-on-Hudson, NY; Columbia Univ Sch of Painting & Sculpture, NY; New Sch for Social Research, NY; Univ de Puebla, Mexico

CAROLEE SCHNEEMANN CONTINUED

TEACHING: Instr, Art, Chicago Inst of Art, IL; Instr, Art, Rutgers Univ, Newark, NJ; Instr, Art, Univ of Colorado, Boulder, CO; Instr, Art, Univ of Ohio, Athens, OH; Instr, Art, Univ of California, Los Angeles, CA; Univ of Texas, Austin, TX; Hunter Col, NY; San Francisco Art Inst, CA
AWARDS: Nat Endowment for the Arts Grants, 1974–77; Creative Artists Public Service Grant, NY, 1978; Visual Artist Fel, Nat Endowment for the Arts Grants, 1983,85; Gottlieb Found, 1986
RECENT EXHIB: San Francisco Mus of Mod Art, CA, 1992; Pittsburgh Center for the Art, PA, 1992; Mus of Mod Art, NY, 1992; Walter/McBean Gallery San Francisco, CA, 1992
COLLECTIONS: Mus of Contemp Art, Chicago, IL; Mus of Mod Art, NY; Found Mudim, Milan, Italy; Ludwig Mus, Cologne, Germany; Collections Conz, Verona, Italy; Erotica Archives Mus, Zagreb, Croatia
PRINTERS: Women's Studio Workshop, Rosendale, NY (WSW); Artist (ART); Mark Patsfall Graphics, Inc, Cincinnati, OH (MPG); Heinrici Studio, NY (HS); Women's Studio Workshop, Rosendale, NY (WSW); Blast Editions, NY (BE); Editions Conz, Canoza Lake, NY (EC)
PUBLISHERS: Artist (ART); McPherson & Company, NY (MC); Reasearch, San Francisco, CA (RES); Max Hutchinson Gallery, Canoza Lake, NY (MHG)
GALLERIES: Emily Harvey Gallery, New York, NY; Max Hutchinson Gallery, Canoza Lake, NY
MAILING ADDRESS: 5126 Bur Oak Circle, P.O. Box 31226, Raleigh, NC 27622-1226

TITLE	PUBLISHER	PRINTER	DATE	MEDIUM	DIMENSION (PAPER SIZE) IN INCHES	TYPE OF PAPER	EDITION NUMBER	NO. OF COLORS	ORIGINAL OPENING PRICE	CURRENT RETAIL PRICE
SOLD OUT EDITIONS (RARE):										
Saw over Want (36 Prints Form an 88" X 216" Grid)	ART	ART	1980-82	PH	88 X 216	AP	4		6000	10000
Correspondence Course (Triptych)	ART	WSW	1983	PH/SP	30 X 54	AP	5		1000	1500
Cluny-Washing (10 Prints Form a Grid)	ART	ART	1983	PH/CON	36 X 116	AP	5		6000	7500
Vulva Prints (Set of 3)	ART	ART	1987	Acrylic	46 X 7	AP	40	2	2000 SET 750 EA	2000 SET 750 EA
Set of Two Silkscreens (Set of 2):									3000 SET	3000 SET
Vectors & Slice	ART	ART	1989	SP	30 X 42		20	4	1700	1700
Vectors-24 Sources	ART	ART	1989	SP	30 X 42		20	4	1700	1700

LYNN SCHNURNBERGER

BORN: New York, NY; 1949
EDUCATION: City Col of New York, NY, 1970; Pratt Graphics Center, NY, 1973
AWARDS: Virginia Center Creative Arts Fel, 1982
PRINTERS: Dieu Donne Press, NY (DDP)
PUBLISHERS: Diane Villani Editions, NY (DVE); Dieu Donne Press, NY (DDP)
GALLERIES: Magnunson Gallery, Boston, MA; Roger Ramsay, Chicago, IL; Diane Villani Editions, New York, NY
MAILING ADDRESS: 81 Grand St, New York, NY 10013

TITLE	PUBLISHER	PRINTER	DATE	MEDIUM	DIMENSION (PAPER SIZE) IN INCHES	TYPE OF PAPER	EDITION NUMBER	NO. OF COLORS	ORIGINAL OPENING PRICE	CURRENT RETAIL PRICE
CURRENT EDITIONS:										
Ribbons	DVE	DDP	1982	CP/HC	27 X 38	HMP	30	10–15	450	500

FRITZ SCHOLDER

BORN: Breckenridge, MN; Bismarck October 6, 1937
EDUCATION: Univ of Kansas, Lawrence, KS; Wisconsin State Univ, Milwaukee, WI; Sacramento State Univ, CA, with Wayne Thiebaud; Sacramento State Univ, CA, BA; Univ of Arizona, Tucson, AZ, MFA; Ripon Col, WI, Hon DFA, 1984; Univ of Arizona, Tucson, AZ, 1985; Concordia Col, Moorhead, MN, 1986
TEACHING: Univ of Arizona, Tucson, AZ; Dartmouth Col, Hanover, NH; Guest Artist, Oklahoma Summer Arts Inst, Quartz, MT
AWARDS: John Hay Whitney Found Fel, 1962–63; Ford Found Purchase Award, Houston Mus, 1962; Am Acad of Arts and Letters, 1977; Governor's Award, North Dakota, 1981; Governor's Award, New Mexico, 1983; Distinguished Achievement Award in the Arts, Arizona State Univ, Tempe, AZ, 1983; Int Prize, Lithography, Berlin, Germany, 1984; Societaire, Salon d'Automne, Paris, France, 1984
RECENT EXHIB: Albuquerque Mus of Art, History & Science, NM, 1989; Reading Public Mus of Art, PA, 1989; John A Boler, Indian & Western Art, Minneapolis, MN, 1989; Charlotte Jackson Fine Art, Santa Fe, NM 1989; Charles B Goddard Center for Visual & Performing Arts, Ardmore, OK, 1989,92; Southern Oregon State Col, Schneider Mus of Art, Ashland, OR, 1989,92; William Paterson Col, Ben Shahn Galleries, Wayne, NJ, 1992; Bismarck State Col, Gannon/Elsa Forde Galleries, ND, 1992; Univ of New Mexico, Jonson Gallery, Albuquerque, NM, 1992; Riva Yares Galleries, Scottsdale, AZ & Santa Fe, NM, 1992; Louis Newman Gallery, Beverly Hills, CA, 1993
COLLECTIONS: Mus of Mod Art, NY; San Francisco Mus of Art, CA; Nat Mus of Fine Art, Wash, DC; Los Angeles County Mus, CA; Boston Mus of Fine Arts, MA; Philadelphia Art Mus, PA; Hirshhorn Mus, Wash, DC; Chicago Art Inst, IL; Mus of Contemp Art, Chicago, IL; Albright-Knox Art Gallery, Buffalo, NY; Brooklyn Mus, NY; Dallas Mus of Fine Arts, TX; Houston Mus of Fine Arts, TX; High Mus of Art, Atlanta, GA; Detroit Inst of Art, MI; Cleveland Mus, OH; Boston Mus of Fine Arts, MA; Plains Art Mus, Moorhead, MN; Milwaukee Art Center, WI; Tucson Mus of Art, AZ
PRINTERS: La Poligrafa, Barcelona, Spain (LP); Tamarind Inst, Albuquerque, NM (TI); Editions Press, San Francisco, CA (EP); David Kelso, Oakland, CA (DK); Made in California, Oakland, CA (MIC)
PUBLISHERS: Tamarind Inst, Albuquerque, NM (TI); Transworld Art, Inc, NY (TAI); Editions Press, San Francisco, CA (EP); Houston Fine Arts Press, Houston, TX (HFAB); Sette Publishing Co, Tempe, AZ (SPC); Ediciones Poligrafa, SA, Barcelona, Spain (EP); Made in California, Oakland, CA (MIC)
GALLERIES: Weintraub Gallery, New York, NY; Bishop Gallery, Scottsdale, AZ; Elaine Horwitch Galleries, Scottsdale, AZ & Santa Fe, NM; Sette Publishing Co, Tempe, AZ; Tally Richards Gallery, Taos, NM; Annette Couch Fine Arts, South Pasadena, CA; ACA Galleries, New York, NY; Galeria Joan Prats, New York, NY & Barcelona, Spain; Malcolm Brown Gallery, Shaker Heights, OH; Kauffman Galleries, Houston, TX; Marilyn Butler Fine Art, Scottsdale, AZ & Santa Monica, CA; Martin Lawrence Galleries, Los Angeles, CA & Newport Beach, CA & Palm Springs, CA & Santa Clara, CA & Redondo Beach, CA & West Los Angeles, CA & Thousand Oaks, CA & Escondido, CA & Short Hills, NJ & Phila, PA; Donna Rose Galleries, Ketchum, ID; Joanne Lyon Gallery, Aspen, CO; Sena International Galleries, Santa Fe, NM; Charlotte Jackson Gallery, Santa Fe, NM; Riva Yares Galleries, Scottsdale, AZ & Santa Fe, NM; Louis Newman, Beverly Hills, CA; Susan Duval Gallery, Aspen, CO; John A Boler, Minneapolis, MN; Carolyn Ruff Gallery, Minneapolis, MN; Segal Fine Art, New York, NY; Ed Hill Gallery, El Paso, TX
MAILING ADDRESS: 118 Cattle Track Rd, Scottsdale, AZ 85253

FRITZ SCHOLDER CONTINUED

TITLE	PUBLISHER	PRINTER	DATE	MEDIUM	DIMENSION (PAPER SIZE) IN INCHES	TYPE OF PAPER	EDITION NUMBER	NO. OF COLORS	ORIGINAL OPENING PRICE	CURRENT RETAIL PRICE
SOLD OUT EDITIONS (RARE):										
Self Portrait with Dark Glasses	TI	TI	1971	LC	29 X 21	AP	50		100	5000
Indian at the Bar	TI	TI	1971	LC	30 X 22	AP	75	4	100	5000
Indians with Umbrellas	TI	TI	1971	LC	22 X 30	AP	75	4	100	5000
Bird Indian	EP	EP	1973	LC	22 X 30	AP/B	100		450	5000
Indian with Cat	EP	EP	1973	LC	30 X 22	CEP	100		450	5000
Portrait of Massacred Indian #3	EP	EP	1973	LC	40 X 30	R/BFK	100		750	5000
Indian With Flag	EP	EP	1973	LC	40 X 30	R/BFK	100		750	5000
Bicentennial Indian	TI	TI	1974	LC	22 X 30	AP	125	4	500	5000
Film Indian	TI	TI	1975	LB	22 X 30	AP	160	1	500	5000
Santo Domingo Bowl with Tomato Soup	TI	TI	1975	LC	19 X 25	AP	100	4	350	600
Sioux War Party	MIC	DK/MIC	1975	AC	22 X 30	AP/W	75		500	1200
Imaginary Buffalo	MIC	DK/MIC	1975	A/DPT/HG	17 X 15	AP/B	25		300	500
Buffalo Artist	MIC	DK/MIC	1975	AB	15 X 11	AP/B	25	1	300	500
Indian Cliché, State III	TI	TI	1978	LC						3000
Dancers at Zuni	TI	TI	1978	LC	22 X 30	AP	150	3	500	5000
Indian and Blue Window, State I	TAI	TI	1978	LC	30 X 22	AP	50	6	1200	2000
Indian with Blue Window, State II	TAI	TI	1978	LC	30 X 22	AP	50	6	1200	2000
Indian with Pistol	TAI	TI	1978	LC	22 X 30	AP	150		2000	5000
Matinee Cowboy and Horse	TAI	TI	1979	LC	30 X 22	AP	150	6	1000	1000
Butterfly Memories	TI	TI	1979	LC	25 X 19	AP	50	2	350	1000
Siren	TI	TI	1979	LC	25 X 19	AP	50	2	350	1200
Snake Dancer	TI	TI	1979	LC	30 X 22	AP	150	4	500	4000
The Sarcophagus, State I	TI	TI	1979	LC	30 X 22	AP	150	3	500	1200
Car	TI	TI	1979	LC	25 X 19	AP	100	4	500	1200
Sioux Burial at Mouse River	TI	TI	1980	LC	30 X 40	AP	100	2	800	3000
Artist at Opening	TI	TI	1980	LC	30 X 22	AP	50	2	500	500
The Rose	TI	TI	1981	LC	91 X 25	AP	150	5	450	500
American Warrior #2	TI	TI	1981	LB	30 X 22	AP	50	1	450	500
First Dream	TI	TI	1981	LC	30 X 22	AP	90	5	650	850
First Mystery	TI	TI	1982	LC	30 X 22	AP	50	3	350	500
Set of 5 Lithographs	EP	LP	1982	LC	30 X 22 EA	GP	120 EA		3000 SET	3000 SET
Set of 10 Etchings:									650 SET	650 SET
									6500 SET	6500 SET
#1, #2, #3, #8	EP	LP	1982	EC	30 X 22 EA	GP	120 EA		800 EA	800 EA
#7, #9, #10	EP	LP	1982	EC	30 X 22 EA	GP	120 EA		700 EA	700 EA
Lithograph Book (Text with Original Lithographs)	EP	LP	1984	LC	9 X 11				450	500
Dark Portrait	TI	TI	1984	LC		AP			250	350

LAURENCE SCHOLDER

BORN: Brooklyn, NY; November 23, 1942
EDUCATION: Carnegie Inst of Tech, Pittsburgh, PA, BFA; Univ of Iowa, Iowa City, IA, MA
TEACHING: Asst Prof, Printmaking, Southern Methodist Univ, Dallas, TX, 1968-73, Assoc Prof, 1973-81, Prof, 1981 to present
AWARDS: Purchase Awards, Young Printmakers, Heron Art Inst, Indianapolis, IN, 1967; Print & Drawing, Nat Oklahoma Art Center, 1968; Southwest Graphics, San Antonio, TX, Merit Award, 1972; Nat Endowment for the Arts Printmakers Fel, 1975
COLLECTIONS: Ft Worth Art Center, TX; Houston Mus of Fine Arts, TX; Brooklyn Mus, NY; Dallas Mus of Fine Arts, TX
PRINTERS: Artist (ART)
PUBLISHERS: Artist (ART)
GALLERIES: Gerald Peters Gallery, Dallas, TX
MAILING ADDRESS: 5239 Goodwin Ave, Dallas, TX 75206

TITLE	PUBLISHER	PRINTER	DATE	MEDIUM	DIMENSION (PAPER SIZE) IN INCHES	TYPE OF PAPER	EDITION NUMBER	NO. OF COLORS	ORIGINAL OPENING PRICE	CURRENT RETAIL PRICE
CURRENT EDITIONS:										
Bouquet	ART	ART	1989	EB/REL	16 X 13	AP/B	25	1	450	600

ILSE SCHREIBER

BORN: Germany
EDUCATION: State Univ of New York, Purchase, NY, BFA
TEACHING: State Univ of New York, Purchase, NY, Visual Arts Dept
AWARDS: Award of Excellence, Chappaqua Artists Guild, Juried Show, NY, 1984; Award, Nat Poster Comp, Artists in Solidarity with People of Central Am, NY, 1984
COLLECTIONS: Washington Irving Gallery, NY; Somerstown Gallery, Somers, NY
PRINTERS: State Univ of New York, Purchase, NY (SUNY); Artist (ART)
PUBLISHERS: Artist (ART)
GALLERIES: Associated American Artists, New York, NY
MAILING ADDRESS: 50 Gray Rock Lane, Chappaqua, NY 10514

TITLE	PUBLISHER	PRINTER	DATE	MEDIUM	DIMENSION (PAPER SIZE) IN INCHES	TYPE OF PAPER	EDITION NUMBER	NO. OF COLORS	ORIGINAL OPENING PRICE	CURRENT RETAIL PRICE
CURRENT EDITIONS:										
Pechstein Sleeping after Heckel	ART	ART/SUNY	1986	WC	38 X 25	JP		4	500	600

KARL SCHRAG

BORN: Karlsruhe, Germany; December 7, 1912
EDUCATION: Humanistisches Gymnasium, Karlsruhe, Germany, 1931; Ecole des Beaux-Arts, Geneva, Switzerland, 1932; Ecole Nat Superieure des Beaux-Arts, Paris, France; Acad Ranson, Paris, France, 1934; Acad de la Grande Chaumiere, Paris, France, 1935; Art Students League, NY, 1938; Atelier 17, with Stanley William Hayter, NY, 1945
TEACHING: Dir, Etching, Atelier 17, NY, 1950–51; Inst, Printmaking, Brooklyn Col, NY, 1953–54; Instr, Drawing & Printmaking, Cooper Union, NY, 1954–68
AWARDS: Purchase Awards, Brooklyn Mus Print Annual, 1947,50; Ford Found Grant, 1960; Ford Found Grant, Tamarind Lithograph Workshop, Los Angeles, CA, 1962; Cert of Merit, New Delhi, India, 1962; Am Acad of Arts & Letters Grant, 1966; Prize, Drawing, Ball State Univ, 1970; Trowbridge Wetter Mem Award, 1971; Soc of Am Graphic Arts, 1971; Childe Hassam Purchase Award, Am Acad & Inst of Arts & Letters, 1973; James R Marsh Mem Award, Soc of Am Graphics Artists, 1977
RECENT EXHIB: St Mary's Col of Maryland, Dwight Frederic Boyden Gallery, St Mary City, MD, 1992; Associated American Artists, NY, 1990,92; Kraushaar Gallery, NY, 1992
COLLECTIONS: Mus of Mod Art, NY; Metropolitan Mus of Art, NY; Whitney Mus of Am Art, NY; Guggenheim Mus, NY; Nat Gallery of Art, Wash, DC; Uffizi Gallery, Florence, Italy
PRINTERS: American Atelier, NY (AA); Stanley William Hayter, NY (SWH); Atelier 17, NY (A17); Elizabeth Eckbert, NY (EE); Printmaking Workshop, NY (PW)
PUBLISHERS: Artist (ART)
GALLERIES: Associated American Artists, New York, NY; Kornbluth Gallery, Fair Lawn, NJ; Kraushaar Galleries, New York, NY; Frost Fully Gallery, Portland, ME; Maine Coast Artists Gallery, Rockport, ME
MAILING ADDRESS: 127 East 95th St, New York, NY 10028

Karl Schrag
The Cliff
Courtesy Associated American Artists

TITLE	PUBLISHER	PRINTER	DATE	MEDIUM	DIMENSION (PAPER SIZE) IN INCHES	TYPE OF PAPER	EDITION NUMBER	NO. OF COLORS	ORIGINAL OPENING PRICE	CURRENT RETAIL PRICE
SOLD OUT EDITIONS (RARE):										
Rain & the Sea	ART	SWH/A17	1946	EB/ENG	15 X 11	R/100	30	1	50	2000
Evening Fragrance of Gardens	ART		1963	EB/A	11 X 15	R/100	50		150	1500
Evening Sun—Low Tide	ART	EC/PW	1976	EC	10 X 12	AP	50		150	1200
Color and Sound	ART		1985	LB	24 X 20	SOM	50		600	800
Yellow Roses in a Glass Vase	ART		1987	MON	24 X 18 EA	SOM		1 EA	1500 EA	1800 EA
Autumn Wind and Stars	ART	AA	1988	LC	20 X 24	SOM	60	4	800	1000

GEORGES SCHREIBER

BORN: Brussels, Belgium; (1904–1977)
EDUCATION: Arts & Crafts Sch, Elberfeld, West Germany, 1920
TEACHING: Northern Michigan Univ, Marquette, MI, 1964; New Sch For Social Research, NY, 1959–77
COLLECTIONS: Whitney Mus of Am Art, NY; Metropolitan Mus of Art, NY; Brookyn Mus, NY; Toledo Mus, OH
PRINTERS: Artist (ART)
PUBLISHERS: Kennedy Graphics Inc, NY (KG); Associated Am Artists, NY (AAA)
GALLERIES: Kennedy Galleries, New York, NY

TITLE	PUBLISHER	PRINTER	DATE	MEDIUM	DIMENSION (PAPER SIZE) IN INCHES	TYPE OF PAPER	EDITION NUMBER	NO. OF COLORS	ORIGINAL OPENING PRICE	CURRENT RETAIL PRICE
SOLD OUT EDITIONS (RARE):										
The Net	AAA	ART	1952	LC	11 X 14	AP	250		100	250
CURRENT EDITIONS										
The Bride and the Widow	KG	ART	1969	LC	19 X 25	AP	100	6	200	400
La Mer	KG	ART	1969	LC	20 X 27	AP	100	4	200	400
Sunrise	KG	ART	1969	LC	33 X 25	AP	150	6	200	400
The Thinker	KG	ART	1969	LC	23 X 33	AP	150	11	200	400
Thus It Came to Pass	KG	ART	1970	LC	20 X 26	AP	100	6	200	400
Balancing Act	KG	ART	1970	LC	32 X 22	AP	100	7	200	400
Trapeze	KG	ART	1970	LC	29 X 22	AP	100	6	200	400

JERRY SCHURR

BORN: Philadelphia, PA; May 4, 1940
EDUCATION: Univ of Pennsylvania, Phila, PA, 1958–59; Temple Univ, Phila, PA 1961–63; Pennsylvania Acad of Fine Arts, Phila, PA, 1958–60,65–69
TEACHING: Temple Univ, Phila, PA
AWARDS: Thouron Prize, Painting, 1966; Philadelphia Print Club, PA, Eugene Feldman Mem Prize, 1977
COLLECTIONS: Minneapolis Mus of Fine Art, MN; Philadelphia Mus of Art, PA; Portland Mus, OR; Herbert F Johnson Mus, Cornell Univ, Ithaca, NY; Delaware Art Mus, Wilmington, DE
PRINTERS: Galapagos Studio, Huntington Valley, PA (GS)
PUBLISHERS: John Szoke Graphics, NY (JSG)
GALLERIES: Now & Then Gallery, East Meadow, NY; IKS Fine Art, Providence, RI; Hensley Gallery, Alexandria, VA; Troy Art Gallery, Troy, NY; Allard's Gallery, Fresno, CA; Somerville Manning Gallery, Greenville, DE; Summa Galleries, Brooklyn, NY & New York, NY; John Szoke Graphics, New York, NY
MAILING ADDRESS: 1105 Melrose Ave, Melrose Park, PA 19126

JERRY SCHURR CONTINUED

TITLE	PUBLISHER	PRINTER	DATE	MEDIUM	DIMENSION (PAPER SIZE) IN INCHES	TYPE OF PAPER	EDITION NUMBER	NO. OF COLORS	ORIGINAL OPENING PRICE	CURRENT RETAIL PRICE
SOLD OUT EDITIONS (RARE):										
Mount McKinley	JSG	GS	1982	SP	29 X 35	AP88	290	48	600	1350
Carmel Cypress	JSG	GS	1984	SP	27 X 32	AP88	290	37	600	800
Tahoe	JSG	GS	1984	SP	21 X 36	AP88	290	62	500	1300
CURRENT EDITIONS:										
Beacon Rock	JSG	GS	1983	SP	19 X 18	AP88	290	21	375	500
Set of Two:									350 SET	500 SET
Sweet Briar Lake North	JSG	GS	1983	SP	13 X 18	AP88	290	21	200	300
Sweet Briar Lake Northwest	JSG	GS	1983	SP	13 X 18	AP88	290	21	200	300
Hidden Valley	JSG	GS	1983	SP	33 X 28	AP88	290	29	600	700
Cape Foulweather	JSG	GS	1983	SP	35 X 24	AP88	290	45	750	1350
Cape Shoalwater	JSG	GS	1984	SP	29 X 34	AP88	290	45	575	750

ELFI SCHUSELKA

BORN: Vienna, Austria; February 13, 1940
EDUCATION: Graphic and Experimental Inst of Vienna, Austria, 1958–59; Univ of Vienna 1958–59; Acad of Applied Arts, Vienna, Austria, 1959–61; Sch of Vision with Oskar Kokoschka, Summer 1960
TEACHING: Instr, Printmaking, Sch of Visual Arts, NY, 1970–73; Instr, Art, Ptratt/Phoenix Sch of Design, NY, 1974; Pratt Graphics Center, NY, 1978–80
AWARDS: Int Exhib, Graphic Art Medal, Frechen, Germany, 1978; Awards, Ibizagraphic, Spain, 1982; New York Found Arts Grant, 1986
RECENT EXHIB: Condeso/Lawler Gallery, NY, 1987; New York Univ, Broadway Windows, NY, 1988; Neue Galerie, Vienna, Austria, 1988
COLLECTIONS: Amon Carter Mus of Western Art, Fort Worth, TX; Mus of Mod Art, NY; Univ of Dallas, TX; California Col of Arts & Crafts, San Francisco, CA; Bibliotheque Nationale, Paris, France; Nat Mus of History, Taipei, Taiwan; Musee d'Art Contemporain, Skopje, Yugoslavia; Kunsan Univ, Korea; Mus for International Contemp Graphic Art, Fredrikstad, Norway; Mus d'Art Contemporain, Skopje, Yugoslavia, Rhode Island Univ Mus, Providence, RI; Albertina, Vienna, Austria; Mus of Contemp Art, Ibiza, Spain
PRINTERS: Hiroko Nagata, NY (HN); Artist (ART)
PUBLISHERS: Studio 13, NY (S-13)
GALLERIES: Pace, New York, NY; Condeso/Lawler, New York, NY; Studio 13, New York, NY; Emily Harvey Gallery, New York, NY; Sande Webster Gallery, Phila, PA
MAILING ADDRESS: 133 Eldridge St, New York, NY 10002

TITLE	PUBLISHER	PRINTER	DATE	MEDIUM	DIMENSION (PAPER SIZE) IN INCHES	TYPE OF PAPER	EDITION NUMBER	NO. OF COLORS	ORIGINAL OPENING PRICE	CURRENT RETAIL PRICE
SOLD OUT EDITIONS (RARE):										
Pieces of the Sky	S-13	ART	1970	SP	20 X 28	LEN	20	18	75	350
Porposal for the Bronx Zoo	S-13	ART	1974	LC/SP/HC	22 X 30	AP	30	11	200	350
Appearing-Disappearing	S-13	ART	1977	SC/HC	22 X 23	R/BFK	50	13	125	350
Fragments	S-13	ART	1978	SC/HC	22 X 30	R/BFK	50	18	150	375
Studio Still Life I	S-13	ART	1978	LC/HC	22 X 30	R/BFK	50	9	100	375
69 Strokes	S-13	ART	1979	LC	22 X 30	R/BFK	50	18	200	375
Studio Still Life II	S-13	ART	1979	LC/HC	22 X 30	R/BFK	50	9	100	375
Studio Still Life III	S-13	ART	1979	LC/HC	22 X 30	R/BFK	50	9	100	375
9 Variations on a Room	S-13	ART	1983	LB/HC	22 X 30	R/BFK	20	Multi	250	375
CURRENT EDITIONS:										
Strange Day at the Beach	S-13	ART	1975	LC/SC	22 X 30	AP	50	6	75	350
21 Passes, 13th odd	S-13	ART	1979	LC	22 X 30	R/BFK	50	18	225	375
Painting I	S-13	ART	1980	LC/HC	22 X 28	R/BFK	50	8	225	375
Painting II	S-13	ART	1980	LC/HC	22 X 30	R/BFK	50	13	225	375
22½ X 30, Cut & Represented in Reverse	S-13	ART	1980	LC/HC	22 X 30	R/BFK	50	11	250	375
29 Triangles	S-13	ART	1981	LC/SP/HC	22 X 30	R/BFK	50	24	250	375
Samen und Keime (Seeds & Sprouts) (Set of 5)	S-13	ART/HN	1986	SP	22 X 30 EA	AP	20 EA	13 EA	1100 SET / 250 EA	1500 SET / 375 EA
Kinderspiele (Games Children Play)	S-13	ART	1987	SP	22 X 30	R/BFK	20	12	250	375
Angles I,II	S-13	ART	1992	LC/SP/HC	22 X 30 EA	R/BFK	12 EA	12 EA	650 SET / 375 EA	650 SET / 375 EA

PETER SCHUYFF

RECENT EXHIB: Pat Hearn Gallery, NY, 1990,92
PRINTERS: New City Editions, Venice, CA (NCE); Jo Watanabe, NY (JW); Eric Ziemann, Brooklyn, NY (EZ); Watanabe Studios, NY (WS); Simca Print Artists, NY (SPA)
PUBLISHERS: New City Editions, Venice, CA (NCE); Kenneth Schacter Editions, NY (KS); Artist (ART); Watanabe Studios,NY (WS); Simca Print Artists, NY (SPA)
GALLERIES: Pat Hearn Gallery, New York, NY; Fred Hoffman Gallery, Santa Monica, CA; Tomoko Liquori Gallery, New York, NY; Simca Print Artists, New York, NY; Paul Kasmin Gallery, New York, NY; Watanabe Studios, New York, NY

TITLE	PUBLISHER	PRINTER	DATE	MEDIUM	DIMENSION (PAPER SIZE) IN INCHES	TYPE OF PAPER	EDITION NUMBER	NO. OF COLORS	ORIGINAL OPENING PRICE	CURRENT RETAIL PRICE
CURRENT EDITIONS:										
Untitled I, II	NCE	NCE	1986	SP	75 X 75 EA	SUP/100	20 EA	34 EA	3500 EA	4000 EA
Untitled	KSE	JW/WS	1990	SP	39 X 39	AP88	40	3	1200	1500
Untitled (Set of 6)	ART/WS	JM/EZ/WS	1990	SP	16 X 12 EA	MAG	50 EA		2000 SET	2500 SET
(....For Reference) (Set of 9)	ART/SPA	SPA	1990	SP	12 X 12 EA	STP	40 EA	23–26 EA	2800 SET	2800 SET

BARBARA ANN SCHWARTZ

BORN: Philadelphia, PA; August 23, 1948
EDUCATION: Carnegie-Mellon Univ, Pittsburgh, PA, BFA, 1970; Independent Study, Cite des Arts, Paris, France
TEACHING: Instr, Drawing, Brooklyn Mus Art Sch, NY, 1974–75; Instr, Drawing & Sculpture, Sch of Visual Art, NY, 1977–90
AWARDS: Creative Artists Public Service Prog, 1982–83
RECENT EXHIB: David Heath Gallery, Atlanta, GA, 1988; Pennsylvania Acad of Fine Arts, Morris Gallery, Phila, PA, 1988; Barbara Green Gallery, Miami, FL, 1990; Hirschl & Adler Modern, NY, 1991,92
COLLECTIONS: Mus of Contemp Art, Chicago, IL; Guggenheim Mus, NY; Albright-Knox Art Gallery, Buffalo, NY; Cincinnati Mus of Fine Arts, OH
PRINTERS: Artist (ART); Joe Wilfer, NY (JW); Ruth Lingen, NY (RL); Spring Street Workshop, NY (SprSW); Judith Solodkin, NY (JS); Solo Press, NY (SP)
PUBLISHERS: Barbara Gladstone Editions, NY (BGE); Spring Street Workshop, NY (SprSW); Solo Press, NY (SP)
GALLERIES: Barbara Gladstone Gallery, New York, NY; Willard Gallery, New York, NY; Dart Gallery, Chicago, IL; Hirschl & Adler Modern, New York, NY; Linda Farris Gallery, Seattle, WA; Solo Gallery, New York, NY
MAILING ADDRESS: 87 Crosby St, New York, NY 10012

TITLE	PUBLISHER	PRINTER	DATE	MEDIUM	DIMENSION (PAPER SIZE) IN INCHES	TYPE OF PAPER	EDITION NUMBER	NO. OF COLORS	ORIGINAL OPENING PRICE	CURRENT RETAIL PRICE
CURRENT EDITIONS:										
Quandorum	BGE	ART	1979	MULT/HC	48 X 35	CP	15	Varies	500	1200
Sabendahl (Hand Cast Paper on Wire Armature)	BGE	ART	1979	MULT/HC	37 X 14 X 7	CP	30	Varies	650	1500
Abalina (4 States)	BGE	ART	1980	MULT/HC	28 X 34 X 15	CP	20	Varies	1000	1800
Free Lancer	SprSW	JW/RL/SprSW	1991	WB	26 X 22	OKP	15	1	550	550
Fan Tale I	SprSW	JW/RL/SprSW	1991	WB	26 X 22	OKP	15	1	550	550
Fan Tale II (Reduction Block)	SprSW	JW/RL/SprSW	1991	WB	26 X 20	OKP	35	1	750	750
Free Wheeler (Reduction Block)	SprSW	JW/RL/SprSW	1991	WB	26 X 20	OKP	35	1	750	750
Presco Print	SP	JS/SP	1991	MON	27 X 27 EA	HMP	1 EA	Varies	1800 EA	1800 EA

DANIEL SCHWARTZ

EDUCATION: High Sch of Music & Art, NY; Art Students League, NY; Rhode Island Sch of Design, Providence, RI, BFA
AWARDS: Louis Comfort Tiffany Grants (2); Purchase Prize, Childe Hassam Fund, Am Acad of Arts & Letters, NY
COLLECTIONS: Boston Mus of Fine Art, MA; Corcoran Gallery of Art, Wash, DC; Whitney Mus of Am Art, NY; Pennsylvania Acad of Fine Arts, Phila, PA
PRINTERS: American Atelier, NY (AA)
PUBLISHERS: Circle Fine Art, Chicago, IL (CFA)
GALLERIES: Circle Galleries, San Diego, CA & San Francisco, CA & Northbrook, IL & Pittsburgh, PA & Houston, TX & Soho, NY & Chicago, IL & Scottsdale, AZ & Beverly Hills, CA & Costa Mesa, CA & Sherman Oaks, CA & Palm Beach, FL & Honolulu, HI & New Orleans, LA & Las Vegas, NV & Seattle, WA

TITLE	PUBLISHER	PRINTER	DATE	MEDIUM	DIMENSION (PAPER SIZE) IN INCHES	TYPE OF PAPER	EDITION NUMBER	NO. OF COLORS	ORIGINAL OPENING PRICE	CURRENT RETAIL PRICE
CURRENT EDITIONS:										
Two Girls	CFA	AA	1976	LC	24 X 31	AP	300		75	300

CONRAD SCHWIERING

BORN: Boulder, CO; (1916–1986)
EDUCATION: Univ of Wyoming, Laramie, WY; Art Student's League
COLLECTIONS: Univ of Wyoming, Laramie, WY; Sewell Gallery, Rice Univ, Houston, TX; Univ of Houston, University Park, TX; Alexandria Mus, LA; Long Beach Art Mus, CA; Whitney Gallery of Western Art, Cody, WY; Genessee County Mus, Rochester, NY; Nat Cowboy Hall of Fame, Oklahoma City, OK
PRINTERS: Makor Press, NY (MaP); Joseph Kleineman, NY (JK)
PUBLISHERS: Trussway, Inc (Trl); J C Publishing (JCP); NATO Interests (NATO); HJM Arts (HJM); Abstraction Partners, Ltd (APL)

TITLE	PUBLISHER	PRINTER	DATE	MEDIUM	DIMENSION (PAPER SIZE) IN INCHES	TYPE OF PAPER	EDITION NUMBER	NO. OF COLORS	ORIGINAL OPENING PRICE	CURRENT RETAIL PRICE
SOLD OUT EDITIONS (RARE):										
A Daily Roper	Trl	JK/MaP	1982	LC	22 X 30	AP	200	14	400	600
Singlin' Out	JCP	JK/MaP	1982	LC	22 X 28	SOM	200	12	400	600
Shoe Shop	Trl	JK/MaP	1982	LC	22 X 28	SOM	200	12	400	600
Tapestry of Spring	NATO	JK/MaP	1982	LC	22 X 28	AP	200	12	400	600
Burro Express	HJM	JK/MaP	1982	LC	22 X 28	AP	200	12	400	600
Easing 'Em Home	APL	JK/MaP	1984	LC	22 X 28	SOM	200	12	400	600

MICHAEL L SCOTT

BORN: Lawrence, KS; 1952
EDUCATION: Kansas City Art Inst, MO, MFA; Univ of Cincinnati, OH, MFA
COLLECTIONS: Cincinnati Art Mus, OH; New Orleans Mus of Art, LA; City of Covington, KY
PRINTERS: Jon Cone, East Topsham, VT (JC); Cone Editions, East Topsham, VT (CEd)
PUBLISHERS: John Szoke Graphics, Inc, NY (JSG)
GALLERIES: John Szoke Graphics, Inc, New York, NY; Tony Shafrazi Gallery, New York, NY; Sherry French Gallery, New York, NY; Cincinnati Art Galleries, Cincinnati, OH

TITLE	PUBLISHER	PRINTER	DATE	MEDIUM	DIMENSION (PAPER SIZE) IN INCHES	TYPE OF PAPER	EDITION NUMBER	NO. OF COLORS	ORIGINAL OPENING PRICE	CURRENT RETAIL PRICE
CURRENT EDITIONS:										
Fork at Black Creek	JSG	JC/CEd	1990	SP	30 X 42	AP88	85	6	800	800

SEAN SCULLY

BORN: Dublin, Ireland; 1945
EDUCATION: Croydon Col of Art, England, 1965-67
RECENT EXHIB: Pamela Auchincloss Gallery, Santa Barbara, CA, 1987; David McKee Gallery, NY, 1989; Major Rowan Gallery, London, England, 1989; Arnold Herstand Gallery, NY, 1990; Jamileh Weber Gallery, Zurich, Switzerland, 1991; Daniel Weinberg Gallery, Santa Monica, CA, 1992; Garner Tullis, NY, Santa Monica, CA & Pietrarubbia, Italy, 1991,92; Fort Worth Mus of Mod Art, 1993
COLLECTIONS: Mus of Fine Arts, Boston, MA; Bronx Mus, NY; Carnegie Inst, Pittsburgh, PA
PRINTERS: Chip Elwell, NY (CE); Andrew Bovell, NY (AB); Brian Shure, San Francisco, CA (BS); Pamela Paulson, San Francisco, CA (PP); Daria Sywulak, San Francisco, CA (DS); Crown Point Press, San Francisco, CA (CPP); Garner Tullis Workshop, Santa Barbara, CA & NY (GTW); Keiji Shinohara, NY (SH); Bruce Crownover, NY (BC); Emanuele Cacciatore, NY (EC); Benjamin Gervis, NY (BG)
PUBLISHERS: Diane Villani Editions, NY (DVE); Crown Point Press, San Francisco, CA (CPP); Garner Tullis, NY (GT); Brooke Alexander, Inc, NY (BAI); Artist (ART)
GALLERIES: David McKee Gallery, New York, NY; Charles Cowles Gallery, New York, NY; Barbara Krakow Gallery, Boston, MA; John Davis Gallery, Akron, OH; Pamela Auchincloss Gallery, Santa Barbara, CA; B R Kornblatt Gallery, Wash, DC; Goodman/Tinnon Fine Art, San Francisco, CA; A Clean, Well-Lighted Place, New York, NY; Diane Villani Editions, New York, NY; Garner Tullis Fine Art, New York, NY; Elizabeth Paul Galleries, Cincinnati, OH & Columbus, OH; Jan Pierce Fine Art, Fort Worth, TX; Crown Point Press, San Francisco, CA & New York, NY; Major Rowan Gallery, London, England; Brooke Alexander Gallery, New York, NY; Jamileh Weber Gallery, Zurich, Switzerland; Daniel Weinberg Gallery, Santa Monica, CA; Herbert Palmer Gallery, Los Angeles, CA; John Berggruen Gallery, San Francisco, CA; Stephen Solovy Fine Art, Chicago, IL; Golden Gallery, Boston, MA; McKee Gallery, New York, NY; Joseph Petrone Fine Arts, New York, NY

Sean Scully
Planes of Light
Courtesy Garner Tullis Fine Art

TITLE	PUBLISHER	PRINTER	DATE	MEDIUM	DIMENSION (PAPER SIZE) IN INCHES	TYPE OF PAPER	EDITION NUMBER	NO. OF COLORS	ORIGINAL OPENING PRICE	CURRENT RETAIL PRICE
SOLD OUT EDITIONS (RARE):										
The Fall	ART		1983	EB/A	22 X 14	AP	15	1	600	5000
Conversation	DVE	CD	1986	WC	37 X 54	OKP	40		1500	8000
Standing I	DVE	CE	1986	WC	52 X 36	OKP	35		1500	8000
Standing II	DVE	CE	1986	WC	52 X 36	OKP	35		1500	8000
Block	DVE	CE	1986	WC	37 X 44	OKP	30		1200	5500
The Stranger	DVE	AB	1987	WC	33 X 48	OKP	30	6	2500	8000
Sotto Voce	CPP	BS/PP/DS/CPP	1988	AC/SP	42 X 52	SOM/S	40		3500	9500
Wall	CPP	BS/PP/DS/CPP	1988	AC/SP	42 X 51	SOM/S	40		3500	9500
Room	CPP	BS/PP/DS/CPP	1988	AC/SP	42 X 51	SOM/S	40		3500	9500
Square Light 1,2	CPP	BS/PP/DS/CPP	1988	AC/SP	34 X 30 EA	SOM/S	25 EA		2500 EA	4500 EA
With	GT	GTW	1988	WC	40 X 48	SOM/S	8	8	6000	10000
CURRENT EDITIONS:										
Diptych	BAI		1991	SB/AB	19 X 22 EA	R/BFK	25	1	3000	3000
Triptych	BAI		1991	SB/AB	16 X 22 EA	R/BFK	25	1	3000	3000
Durango I	BAI		1991	SB/AB	19 X 21	R/BFK	25	1	3000	3000
Durango II	BAI		1991	SB/AB	17 X 22	R/BFK	25	1	3000	3000
Untitled	BAI		1991	SB/AB	18 X 20	R/BFK	21	1	3000	3000
Narcissus	GT	KS/BC/GTW	1991	WC	19 X 15	AWP	30		6000	6000
Planes of Light	GT	EC/BG/GTW	1991	WC	41 X 51	RBT/HMP	20		13000	13000

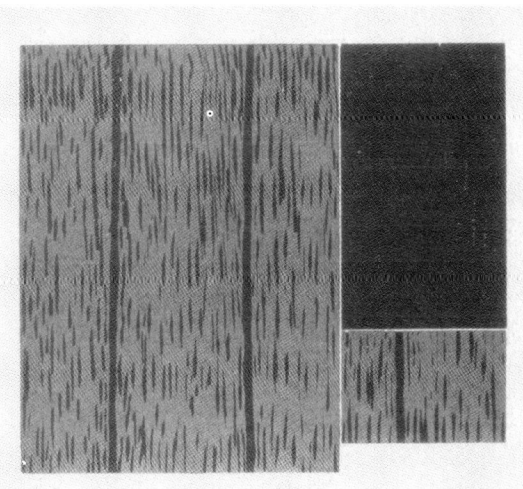

Sean Scully
Block
Courtesy Diane Villani Editions

Sean Scully
Standing II
Courtesy Diane Villani Editions

PETER SCULTHORPE

BORN: Toronto, Canada; July 23, 1948
EDUCATION: Pennsylvania Acad of Fine Arts, Phila, PA
AWARDS: Award, Artistic Excellence, Am Artists Professional League, 1984; Silver Medal, Philadelphia Sketch Club, PA, 1986; Albert Woofter Nat Realism Award, 1991; Watercolor USA Honor Society Award, 1992
RECENT EXHIB: Somerville/Manning Gallery, Greenville, DE, 1992; Woodmere Art Mus, Phila, PA, 1993; Saper Gallery, Lansing, MI, 1993
COLLECTIONS: Charles & Emma Frye Art Mus, Seattle, WA; Dunnegan Gallery of Art, Bolivan, MO; Parkersburg Art Center, WV; Springfield Art Mus, MO; Delaware Art Mus, Wilmington, DE; Brandywine River Mus, Chadds Ford, PA
PRINTERS: J K Fine Arts, NY (JKFA); Artist (ART)
PUBLISHERS: Bruce McGaw Graphics, NY (BMG); Artist (ART)
GALLERIES: Somerville/Manning Gallery, Greenville, DE; Saper Gallery, Lansing, MI; Sporting Gallery, Inc, Middleburg, VA
MAILING ADDRESS: RD 8, Box 353, Coatesville, PA 19320

Peter Sculthorpe
Old Stalls
Courtesy the Artist

Peter Sculthorpe
Silent Moon
Courtesy the Artist

TITLE	PUBLISHER	PRINTER	DATE	MEDIUM	DIMENSION (PAPER SIZE) IN INCHES	TYPE OF PAPER	EDITION NUMBER	NO. OF COLORS	ORIGINAL OPENING PRICE	CURRENT RETAIL PRICE
SOLD OUT EDITIONS (RARE):										
Heartland	BMG	JKFA	1989	LC	25 X 39	AC	350	18	550	1500
Domino	BMG	JKFA	1989	LC	26 X 40	AC	295	20	750	900
The Hilltopper	ART	JKFA	1989	LC	30 X 27	AC	275	20	750	1000
CURRENT EDITIONS:										
Littlewoods	ART	JKFA	1989	LC	37 X 39	AC	295	20	750	750
Buck Run Bridge	ART	JKFA	1990	LC	17 X 40	AC	295	20	750	750
Backland	ART	JKFA	1990	LC	18 X 41	AC	295	20	750	750
Old Stalls	ART	ART	1993	LC/HC	12 X 14	R/BFK	10	Varies	500	500
Lancaster Valley	ART	ART	1993	LC/HC	10 X 13	R/BFK	3	Varies	500	500
Silent Moon	ART	ART	1993	EB/A/HC	15 X 11	R/BFK	10	Varies	500	500

CAROLE SEBOROVSKI

BORN: San Diego, CA; 1960
EDUCATION: Grossmont Col, CA, 1977–79; San Francisco State Univ, CA, 1979; California Col of Arts & Crafts, Oakland, CA, BFA, 1982; New York Studio Sch, NY, 1982–83; Hunter Col, NY, MFA, 1987
AWARDS: Pollock-Krasner Found Grant, 1986
RECENT EXHIB: Virginia Commonwealth Univ, Anderson Gallery, Richmond, VA, 1988; Jon Cone Editions, NY, 1988; Lorence•Monk Gallery, NY, 1988,89
PRINTERS: Jon Cone, East Topsham, VT (JC); Cone Editions, East Topsham, VT (CEd)
PUBLISHERS: Cone Editions, East Topsham, VT (CEd)
GALLERIES: Cone Editions, East Topsham, VT; Angles Gallery, Santa Monica, CA; Betsy Senior Contemporary Prints, New York, NY

TITLE	PUBLISHER	PRINTER	DATE	MEDIUM	DIMENSION (PAPER SIZE) IN INCHES	TYPE OF PAPER	EDITION NUMBER	NO. OF COLORS	ORIGINAL OPENING PRICE	CURRENT RETAIL PRICE
CURRENT EDITIONS:										
Suite of 5 Etchings:									2745 SET	2745 SET
Landscape Diptych	CEd	JC/CEd	1986	AC/EB	20 X 25	LANA	30	2	700	700
Land over Water	CEd	JC/CEd	1986	AC/ED	16 X 13	LANA	30	3	550	550
Two 'T' Shapes	CEd	JC/CEd	1986	AB	17 X 16	LANA	30	2	550	550
Cast Shadows	CEd	JC/CEd	1986	AB	16 X 13	LANA	30	2	550	550
Three Black Bars	CEd	JC/CEd	1986	AB	16 X 33	LANA	30	3	700	700

SARAH SEAGER

RECENT EXHIB: Newport Harbor Art Mus, Newport Beach, CA, 1991; Los Angeles Municipal Art Gallery, CA, 1992; Gallery 1301, Santa Monica, CA, 1993
PRINTERS: Francesco Siqueiros, Los Angeles, CA (FS); Robert Dansby, Los Angeles, CA (RD); Cirrus Editions Workshop, Los Angeles, CA (CEW)
PUBLISHERS: Cirrus Editions, Ltd, Los Angeles, CA (CE)
GALLERIES: Cirrus Gallery, Los Angeles, CA; Burnett Miller Gallery, Los Angeles, CA; Hope Weiss Fine Art, Los Angeles, CA; Dennis Anderson Gallery, Los Angeles, CA; Massino Audiello Gallery, New York, NY; Gallery Schurr, Stuttgart, Germany

Sarah Seager
Untitled (Detail)
Catalogue with Exaggerated Gutter
Courtesy Cirrus Editions, Ltd

TITLE	PUBLISHER	PRINTER	DATE	MEDIUM	DIMENSION (PAPER SIZE) IN INCHES	TYPE OF PAPER	EDITION NUMBER	NO. OF COLORS	ORIGINAL OPENING PRICE	CURRENT RETAIL PRICE
CURRENT EDITIONS:										
Untitled (495c)	CE	FS/RD/CEW	1992	LC	38 X 50	COV	40	2	1200	1200
Untitled (496c)	CE	FS/RD/CEW	1992	LC	38 X 50	COV	40	2	1200	1200
Untitled (Catalogue with Exaggerated Gutter) (500c) (Set of 5)	CE	FS/RD/CEW	1992	LB/OFF	11 X 9 EA	COV	50 EA	1 EA	750 SET	750 SET

BERT D SEABOURN

BORN: Iraan, TX; July 9, 1931
EDUCATION: Oklahoma City Univ, OK, 1955–62; Famous Artist Sch, Westport, CT, 1965
TEACHING: Oklahoma City Univ, OK
AWARDS: First Place, Master Artist Show, Five Civilized Tribes Mus, Muskogee, OK, 1986, 88
COLLECTIONS: Heard Mus, Phoenix, AZ; Pacific Northwest, Indian Center, Gonzola Univ, OK; Vatican Mus, Vatican City, Italy; Five Civilized Tribes Mus, Muskogee, OK; Oklahoma Art Center, Oklahoma City, OK

PRINTERS: Artist (ART)
PUBLISHERS: Hand Graphics, Santa Fe, NM (HG); Origins Press (OP); El Cerro Graphics (ECG); Southwestern Terra (ST); Hodges Printing, Oklahoma City, OK (HP); Massive Graphics, Norman, OK (MG); Artist (ART)
GALLERIES: Moulton Gallery, Fort Smith, AR; Savage Galleries, Scottsdale, AZ & Santa Fe, NM; Gallery of American West, Sacramento, CA; Rosequist Galleries, Tucson, AZ; Painted Pony Gallery, Port Jefferson, NY; White Horse Gallery, Boulder, CO; Kimball Art Center, Park City, UT
MAILING ADDRESS: 6105 Covington Lane, Oklahoma City, OK 73132

TITLE	PUBLISHER	PRINTER	DATE	MEDIUM	DIMENSION (PAPER SIZE) IN INCHES	TYPE OF PAPER	EDITION NUMBER	NO. OF COLORS	ORIGINAL OPENING PRICE	CURRENT RETAIL PRICE
SOLD OUT EDITIONS (RARE):										
The Healer	ART	ART	1976	LC	30 X 22	AP	125	2	100	700
Owl Song	ART	ART	1977	LC	22 X 15	AP	40	2	150	500
Swift Dog, State I	ART	ART	1978	LC	29 X 22	AP	21	4	300	700
Medicine Bundle, State I	ART	ART	1979	LC	30 X 22	AP	28	5	300	700
Oklahoma Man, State I	ART	ART	1980	EB	30 X 22	AP	12	1	150	500
Hawk Brother	HG	HG	1981	EB	22 X 26	AP	25	2	300	700
CURRENT EDITIONS:										
Sun Hawk	ART	ART	1977	LC	22 X 30	AP	40	3	250	450
Swift Dog, State II	ART	ART	1978	LC	30 X 22	AP	50	3	250	450
Swift Dog, State III	ART	ART	1978	LC	29 X 22	AP	50	4	250	450
Morning Whispers, State I	ART	ART	1979	LC	22 X 30	AP	100	4	250	400
Morning Whispers, State III	ART	ART	1979	LB	22 X 30	AP	30	1	250	350
Medicine Bundle, State II	ART	ART	1979	LC	30 X 22	AP	75	5	250	350
Kingfisher Clan	ART	ART	1980	EB	24 X 22	AP	70	1	200	350
Skyhawk	ART	ART	1980	EB	13 X 11	AP	75	1	75	250
Oklahoma Man, State II	ART	ART	1980	EB	30 X 22	AP	75	1	75	250
Owl Medicine	ST	ST	1980	EB	15 X 11	AP	75	1	75	150
Hawk Man	ST	ST	1980	EB	15 X 11	AP	75	1	75	150
Summer Hawk	ART	HG	1981	LC	22 X 30	AP	100	4	400	450
Medicine Spirit	HG	HG	1981	LC	29 X 22	AP	75	15	450	500
Together We Can	ART	HG	1981	LC	30 X 22	AP	125	7	350	400
Hawk Brother	HG	HF	1981	EB	22 X 26	AP	25	2	400	450
Oklahoma Girl	ART	ART	1981	EB	22 X 15	RP	100	1	200	250

BERT D SEABOURN CONTINUED

TITLE	PUBLISHER	PRINTER	DATE	MEDIUM	DIMENSION (PAPER SIZE) IN INCHES	TYPE OF PAPER	EDITION NUMBER	NO. OF COLORS	ORIGINAL OPENING PRICE	CURRENT RETAIL PRICE
CURRENT EDITIONS:										
Swift Dog in Red	ECG	ECG	1981	SP	30 X 22	AP	100	5	400	450
Red Blanket	ECG	ECG	1981	SP	30 X 22	AP	100	5	400	550
Red Knight	ART	ART	1982	SP	30 X 22	RP	50	7	350	400
Black Hawk	HG	HG	1983	EB	22 X 26	AP	50	4	400	450
Night Visions	HG	HG	1983	LC	30 X 22	STP	75	6	400	450
Fritz	ART	HP	1985	SP	24 X 22	AP	100	9	250	300
Ghost Dance	ART	HP	1985	SP	19 X 6	AP	100	2	100	150
Apache Gallup	ART	HP	1985	SP	19 X 6	AP	100	3	125	175
Sioux Chief	ART	ART	1985	SP	15 X 11	STP	45	3	125	175
Sun Catcher	ART	ART	1985	SP	19 X 12	AP	40	3	250	300
Winter Walk	ART	HG	1985	SP	7 X 5	AP	200	5	75	150
Delegate	ART	ART	1985	EB	11 X 10	AP	100	1	100	150
Night Visions	ART	ART	1985	EB	15 X 11	RP	100	1	125	175
Racing The Wind	ART	ART	1986	EB	22 X 15	RP	100	1	125	175
Horse Feathers	ART	ART	1986	EB	22 X 15	RP	100	2	125	175
Warrior	ART	ART	1986	EB	11 X 8	RP	100	1	75	150
Night Spirits	ART	ART	1986	EB	11 X 15	RP	100	1	125	175
Buffalo Memories	MG	MG	1986	SP	7 X 5	AP	200	4	75	150
Southwest Love	MG	MG	1986	SP	7 X 5	AP	200	3	75	150

ARTHUR SECUNDA

BORN: Jersey City, NJ; November 12, 1927
EDUCATION: New York Univ, 1946,47; Art Students League, NY; 1947,48; Acad de la Grande Chaumiers, Paris, France, 1948–50; Acad Julian, Paris, France, 1948,50
TEACHING: Long Beach State Col, CA; Univ of California, Los Angeles, CA; Otis Art Inst, Los Angeles, CA
AWARDS: Tamarind Lithography Workshop Grants, CA, 1970, NM, 1972; Centre Genevois de Gravure Contemporain, Geneva, Switzerland
COLLECTIONS: Mus of Mod Art, NY; Nat Coll of Fine Arts, Wash, DC; Smithsonian Inst, Wash, DC; Library of Congress, Wash, DC; San Francisco Mus of Mod Art, CA; Los Angeles County Mus, CA; Nat Mus, Stockholm, Sweden; Honolulu Acad of Fine Arts, HI; Bibliotheque Nat, Paris, France; Art Inst, Chicago, IL; Brooklyn Mus, NY; Aldrich Mus of Contemp Art, Ridgefield, CT; Akron Art Inst, OH; Art Gallery of Windsor, ON, Can; California State Col, Los Angeles, CA; Colgate Univ, Hamilton, NY; Detroit Inst of Arts, MI; Herbert F. Johnson Mus, Cornell Univ, Ithaca, NY; Long Beach Mus, CA; Los Angeles Inst of Contemp Art, Los Angeles, CA; Malmo Mus, Sweden; Mills Col, Oakland, CA; Univ Art Mus, Berkeley, CA; Univ of Arkansas, Monticello, AR; Univ of Maine, Orono, ME; Univ of Michigan, Dearborn, MI; Univ of Minnesota, Minneapolis, MN; Univ of New Mexico, Albuquerque, NM; Utah Mus of Fine Arts, Salt Lake City, UT; St Louis Art Mus, MO; Palm Springs Desert Mus, CA; Santa Barbara Mus, CA; Stanford Univ, Palo Alto, CA; State Univ of New York, Buffalo, NY; Nat Gallery of Art, Wash, DC; Norton Simon Mus, Pasadena, CA; Oakland Mus, CA
PRINTERS: Jeff Wasserman (JW); Michael Caza (MC); Atelier Arcay, Paris, France (AA); American Atelier, NY (AA); Atelier Pasnic, Paris, France (APas); Artist (ART)
PUBLISHERS: Bolen Gallery, Santa Monica, CA (BG); T T Nieh, Inc, Falls Church, VA (TTNI); Peterson Fine Art, Dallas, TX (PFA); Galerie P Cramer, Geneva, Switzerland (GPC); Capra Press, London, England (CP); London Arts, Inc, Detroit, MI (LAI); Circle Fine Art, Chicago, IL (CFA); Robertson Publishing, Riverside, CA (RP); Artist (ART); Nahan Editions, New Orleans, LA (NE)
GALLERIES: Arras Gallery, New York, NY; Galerie P Cramer, Geneva, Switzerland; Owl 57 Galleries, Woodmere, NY; Dubins Gallery, Los Angeles, CA; Art Angles, Orange, CA; Now & Then Gallery, East Meadow, NY; J Richards Gallery, Englewood, NJ; Circle Galleries, San Diego, CA & San Francisco, CA & Northbrook, IL & Pittsburgh, PA & Houston, TX & Soho, NY & Chicago, IL & Scottsdale, AZ & Beverly Hills, CA & Sherman Oaks, CA & Palm Beach, FL & Honolulu, HI & New Orleans, LA & Las Vegas, NV & Seattle, WA; Tarbox Gallery, San Deigo, CA; Nahan Galleries, New York, NY & New Orleans, LA & Tokyo, Japan; Gallery International, Bloomfield Hills, MI
MAILING ADDRESS: P O Box 6363, Beverly Hills, CA 90212

TITLE	PUBLISHER	PRINTER	DATE	MEDIUM	DIMENSION (PAPER SIZE) IN INCHES	TYPE OF PAPER	EDITION NUMBER	NO. OF COLORS	ORIGINAL OPENING PRICE	CURRENT RETAIL PRICE
SOLD OUT EDITIONS (RARE):										
Vesuvius (Set of 14)	ART	ART	1977	EC	11 X 14 EA	R/BFK	26 EA	2 EA	250 SET	2000 SET
Acacia	RP		1978	SP	30 X 22	AP	150	3	150	800
Profusion Illusion	RP		1978	SP	42 X 24	AP	200	11	250	1200
Camarque	RP		1978	LB	30 X 22	AP	100	4	250	800
Gageron	RP		1978	LB	32 X 18	AP	100	11	250	800
Volcano	RP		1977–78	SP	71 X 39	AP	95	27	1000	2500
Sunrise	RP		1978	SP	38 X 30	AP	200	11	350	1500
New Dawn	TTNI		1979	EC	41 X 29	R/BFK	150	23	350	1800
Borealis	TTNI		1979	EC	38 X 30	R/BFK	99	16	350	800
Mirage	RP		1979	SP	30 X 22	AP	150	16	300	800
Rise and Shine	RP		1979	SP	32 X 27	AP	115	9	200	600
Shorelines	RP		1979	SP	38 X 38	AP	150	6	250	1000
Hello California	RP		1980	SP	71 X 39	AP	60	15	1200	2000
Space Curtains	RP		1980	SP	45 X 35	AP	250	16	250	1200
A Little Gem	RP		1980	EC	30 X 25	R/BFK	50	7	200	600
Black & Tan Fantasy	RP		1980	EC	34 X 25	R/BFK	20	9	600	1500
Heat Shivers	RP		1980	EC	31 X 22	R/BFK	50	5	150	600
Uprising	RP		1980	EC	30 X 22	R/BFK	75	7	200	900
Printemps	RP		1980	SP	33 X 24	AP	150	12	250	800
Hot Horizon	RP		1980	SP	30 X 40	AP	150	5	350	2500
Nido	RP		1981	EC	24 X 18	R/BFK	25	10	200	600
Namekagon	RP		1981	SP	32 X 28	STC	150	9	250	1000
Blue Ocean	RP		1981	SP	44 X 28	STC	250	12	500	1000
Long Distance Ocean	LAI	JW	1981	SP	40 X 23	STC	250	15	300	700

ARTHUR SECUNDA CONTINUED

TITLE	PUBLISHER	PRINTER	DATE	MEDIUM	DIMENSION (PAPER SIZE) IN INCHES	TYPE OF PAPER	EDITION NUMBER	NO. OF COLORS	ORIGINAL OPENING PRICE	CURRENT RETAIL PRICE
SOLD OUT EDITIONS (RARE):										
High Rise	LAI	JW	1981	SP	30 X 22	STC	250	3	300	700
Notte Luganese	RP	JW	1983	SP	33 X 26	MIR	100	10	450	1000
Au Revoir Corfu	RP	MC	1984	SP	26 X 36	MIR	10	10	450	1000
The Thunder Spoke Again	RP	JW	1984	SP	45 X 36	PAN	75	17	800	1500
Rodos	RP	AA	1984	SP	40 X 26	PAN	125	10	550	1000
Como	RP	JW	1984	SP	26 X 50	PAN	100	12	400	900
Hydra	RP	MC	1984	SP	26 X 20	PAN	125		400	900
CURRENT EDITIONS:										
Night Figure	CFA	AA	1980	LC	22 X 15	AP	200		50	350
Opening Space	CFA	AA	1986	LC	36 X 21	AP	300		400	500
Lugana Secunda	CFA	AA	1986	LC	26 X 34	AP	300		400	500
Moonlight	NE	APas	1989	LC/SP/ WC/CO	30 X 24	HMP	95		650	650
The Artist and His Palette	NE	APas	1989	SP	45 X 31	HMP	150		550	550
Night	NE	ART	1989	CON/LC/ WC/HC	30 X 24	MB	50		1800	1800
Four Seasons	NE	APas	1989	SP	31 X 39	HMP	150		550	550
Metamorphose des Fleurs	NE	APas	1989	SP	47 X 29	HMP	150		700	700
Paris is My World	NE	ART	1990	CON/HC	36 X 24		50		1500	1500

GEORGE SEGAL

BORN: New York, NY; November 26, 1924
EDUCATION: Cooper Union, NY, 1941; Rutgers Univ, Brunswick, NJ, 1941–46; Pratt Inst, NY, 1947; New York Univ, Purchase, NY, BS, 1948–50; Rutgers Univ, New Brunswick, NJ, MFA, 1963
AWARDS: Walter K Gutman Found Grant, 1962; First Prize, Art Inst of Chicago, IL, 1966; Governor's Walt Whitman Arts Award, 1989
RECENT EXHIB: Walker Art Center, Minneapolis, MN, 1987; Oregon Art Inst, Portland Art Mus, OR, 1990; Fairleigh Dickinson Univ, Phyllis Rothman Gallery, Madison, NJ, 1989,92; Hudson River Mus, Yonkers, NY, 1992; New Jersey State Mus, Trenton, NJ, 1992; Sidney Janis Gallery, NY, 1992
COLLECTIONS: Mus of Mod Art, NY; Mus of Mod Art, Stockholm, Sweden; Art Gallery of Ontario, Toronto, Can; Nat Gallery of Canada, Ottawa, Can; Art Inst of Chicago, IL; Art Inst of Ohio, Akron, OH; Stedelijk Mus, Amsterdam, Holland; Albright-Knox Gallery of Art, Buffalo, NY; Wadsworth Atheneum, Hartford, CT; Pennsylvania Acad of Fine Art, Phila, PA; San Francisco Mus of Fine Art, CA; Tamayo Mus, Mexico City, Mexico, Hirshhorn Mus, Wash, DC; Smithsonian Inst, Wash, DC
PRINTERS: Editions Alecto, Ltd, London, England (EAL); Consolidated Models, Cranbury, NJ (CM); La Poligrafa, SA, Barcelona, Spain (LP); Atelier Vigna Antoniniana Stamperia d'Arte, Rome, Italy (AVASA)
PUBLISHERS: Editions Alecto, Ltd, London, England (EAL); Metropolitan Mus of Art, NY (MMA); Transworld Art, Inc, NY (TAI); 2RC Editrice, Rome, Italy (2RCE); Ediciones Poligrafa, SA, Barcelona, Spain (EdP); Sidney Janis Editions, NY (SJE); International Images, Inc, Putney, VT (InIm)
GALLERIES: Sidney Janis Gallery, New York, NY; Galeria Joan Prats, New York, NY & Barcelona, Spain; Nina Freudenheim Gallery, Buffalo, NY; Galerie Lelong, New York, NY & Paris, France & Zürich, Switzerland; Evelyn Aimis Fine Art, Toronto, Canada; Mezzaine Gallery, Metropolitan Mus, New York, NY; L A Louver, Venice, CA; John C Stoller & Company, Minneapolis, MN; International Images, Inc, Putney, VT; Argus Fine Arts, Eugene, OR; Jan Krugier Gallery, New York, NY; Artes Magnus, New York, NY

George Segal
Redhaired Girl with Green Robe
Courtesy Ediciones Poligrafa

MAILING ADDRESS: Davidsons Mills Rd, South New Brunswick, NJ 08901

TITLE	PUBLISHER	PRINTER	DATE	MEDIUM	DIMENSION (PAPER SIZE) IN INCHES	TYPE OF PAPER	EDITION NUMBER	NO. OF COLORS	ORIGINAL OPENING PRICE	CURRENT RETAIL PRICE
SOLD OUT EDITIONS (RARE):										
Girl on a Chair	EAL	EAL	1970	MULT	36 X 24 X 11	CP	150	3	3500	22000
Hand on Buttock	MMA		1975	MULT	13 X 14 X 4	CP	50		1200	8000
Gazing Woman	TAI	CM	1976	MS	26 X 20 X 6	VFP	175	1	1500	6500
Set of 12 Lithographs:										
GS-1-6	EdP	LP	1978	LB	30 X 22 EA	GP	100 EA	1 EA	450 EA	1100 EA
GS-7	EdP	LP	1978	LC	30 X 22	GP	100		600	1500
GS-8-12	EdP	LP	1978	LB	30 X 22 EA	GP	100 EA		600 EA	1750 EA
Hand over Breast	SJE		1982	HC	14 X 10 X 7	HMP	75		1500	3500
Nude Torso	SJE		1982	HC	28 X 12 X 7	HMP	30		3500	6000
Oriental Woman against Tile Wall	SJE		1982		33 X 17 X 10	HMP	30		3500	6000

GEORGE SEGAL CONTINUED

TITLE	PUBLISHER	PRINTER	DATE	MEDIUM	DIMENSION (PAPER SIZE) IN INCHES	TYPE OF PAPER	EDITION NUMBER	NO. OF COLORS	ORIGINAL OPENING PRICE	CURRENT RETAIL PRICE
CURRENT EDITIONS:										
Redhaired Girl with Green Robe	EdP	LP	1986	SP	42 X 33	GP	85	8	3000	3300
Portraits (Set of 6):										
Helen I	2RC/SJE	AVASA	1986–87	A/DPT/SG	39 X 31	FAB	60		2000	3500
Helen II,III	2RC/SJE	AVASA	1986–87	A/DPT/SG	50 X 39 EA	FAB	60 EA		3000 EA	5000 EA
Rena	2RC/SJE	AVASA	1986–87	A/DPT/SG	39 X 31	FAB	60		2000	3500
Menasha	2RC/SJE	AVASA	1986–87	A/DPT/SG	50 X 39	FAB	60		3000	3500
Walter	2RC/SJE	AVASA	1986–87	A/DPT/SG	50 X 39	FAB	60		3000	3500

ADOLF SEHRING

BORN: Urupino, Russia; June 8, 1930; U S Citizen
EDUCATION: Berlin Acad of Arts, Germany, 1946–49
COLLECTIONS: Vatican Coll, Vatican City, Rome, Italy; Chrysler Mus, Norfolk, VA; Bayly Mus, Charlottesville, VA; Mellon Coll, Pittsburgh, PA
PRINTERS: Atelier Ettinger Inc, NY (AE)
PUBLISHERS: Eleanor Ettinger Inc., NY (EEI)
GALLERIES: Benjamin Art Gallery, Hagerstown, MD; Martin Lawrence Gallery, Phila, PA; Images International, Bethesda, MD; Eleanor Ettinger, Inc, New York, NY; Simic Galleries, La Jolla, CA; Lahaina Gallery, Maui, HI
MAILING ADDRESS: Tetley Plantation, Somerset, VA 22972

TITLE	PUBLISHER	PRINTER	DATE	MEDIUM	DIMENSION (PAPER SIZE) IN INCHES	TYPE OF PAPER	EDITION NUMBER	NO. OF COLORS	ORIGINAL OPENING PRICE	CURRENT RETAIL PRICE
CURRENT EDITIONS:										
Violets	EEI	AE	1980	LC	25 X 29	AP	300		275	600
Summer Woods	EEI	AE	1980	LC	24 X 29	AP	300		275	500
Pruning	EEI	AE	1980	LC	33 X 24	AP	300		275	600
Gathering Flowers	EEI	AE	1980	LC	25 X 28	AP	300		275	500
Golden Harvest	EEI	AE	1981	LC	29 X 24	AP	300		350	600
Snowdrift	EEI	AE	1981	LC	34 X 23	AP	300		350	500
End of Day	EEI	AE	1981	LC	25 X 29	AP	300		450	600
Summer by the Sea	EEI	AE	1983	LC	28 X 24	AP	300	17	400	500
Study for Leroy	EEI	AE	1985	LC	28 X 24	AP	110		425	600
Study for Leroy	EEI	AE	1985	LC	28 X 24	JP	50		475	600

JOANNE LYNN SELTZER

BORN: Philadelphia, PA; June 21, 1946
EDUCATION: Northwestern Univ, Chicago, IL, Cert, 1963; Univ of Michigan, Ann Arbor, MI, BFA, Painting, 1969; New York Univ, NY, MA, Photography, 1979; New Sch Social Research, NY, 1973; Pratt Inst, NY, 1973; Pratt Graphic Center, NY, 1974; Parsons Sch of Design, NY, Drawing, 1986–88
COLLECTIONS: Indianapolis Mus of Art, IN; Soc Friends Mus of Contemp Art, Ghent, Belgium; Brooklyn Mus, NY; Toledo Art Mus, OH; Worcester Art Mus, MA; Interlochen Arts Acad, MI
PRINTERS: Artist (ART)
PUBLISHERS: London Arts, Inc, Detroit, MI (LAI)
GALLERIES: Gallerie Yaki Kornblit, Amsterdam, The Netherlands; London Arts Gallery, Detroit, MI
MAILING ADDRESS: 210 Centre St, New York, NY 10013

TITLE	PUBLISHER	PRINTER	DATE	MEDIUM	DIMENSION (PAPER SIZE) IN INCHES	TYPE OF PAPER	EDITION NUMBER	NO. OF COLORS	ORIGINAL OPENING PRICE	CURRENT RETAIL PRICE
CURRENT EDITIONS:										
Dancing Lesson, I–VI	LAI	ART		LC	30 X 23 EA	AP	300 EA	3 EA	275 EA	350 EA

JAMES SEPYO

BORN: Hudson Co, NJ; June 29, 1933
EDUCATION: Weusi Acad of African Arts & Studies, NY, MA, 1970; Bob Blackburn's Sch of Printmaking, NY
AWARDS: New York City Council of the Arts AWG Award, NY, 1972
COLLECTIONS: Studio Mus, Harlem, NY; Hagg Gallery, Atlanta, GA; Origem Gallery, St Thomas, VI
PRINTERS: Bob Blackburn Printmaking Workshop, NY (BB); Artist (ART)
PUBLISHERS: Artist (ART)
GALLERIES: Treehouse Gallery, Brooklyn, NY
MAILING ADDRESS: 20 Henry St, Brooklyn, NY 11201

TITLE	PUBLISHER	PRINTER	DATE	MEDIUM	DIMENSION (PAPER SIZE) IN INCHES	TYPE OF PAPER	EDITION NUMBER	NO. OF COLORS	ORIGINAL OPENING PRICE	CURRENT RETAIL PRICE
SOLD OUT EDITIONS (RARE):										
Awaken	ART	ART	1964	WC	12 X 24	MAR	25	2	125	800
Sango	ART	ART	1967		9 X 12	MAR	25	2	60	600
Mother & Child	ART	ART	1968		9 X 12	MAR	25	2	60	600
Tropical Paradise	ART	ART	1971		6 X 8	MAR	150	2	45	400
Mother & Child #2	ART	ART	1973		6 X 8	MAR	150	2	50	400
Journey to See the Butterfly	ART	ART	1977		6 X 8	MAR	150	2	75	400
Journey to See the Moon	ART	ART	1977		6 X 8	MAR	150	2	75	400
Journey to See the Sun	ART	ART	1977		6 X 8	MAR	150	2	75	400
Ibeji (the Twins)	ART	ART	1979		6 X 8	MAR	150	2	95	400
Oba the King	ART	ART	1979		6 X 8	MAR	150	2	95	400
Journey to Tranquility	ART	ART	1981		6 X 8	MAR	150	2	150	400
Journey to Romance	ART	ART	1981		6 X 8	MAR	150	2	150	400
Princess	ART	ART	1981		6 X 8	MAR	150	2	150	400

PHYLLIS SELTZER

BORN: Detroit, MI; May 17, 1928
EDUCATION: Univ of Iowa, Iowa City, IA, BFA, 1949; MFA, 1952; Univ of Michigan, Ann Arbor, MI, 1953–55; Case Western Reserve Univ, Cleveland, OH, 1970
TEACHING: Univ of Iowa, Iowa City, IA, 1950–52; Univ of Michigan, Ann Arbor, MI, 1954–55; Cleveland State Univ, 1971; Case Western Reserve Univ, Cleveland, OH, 1966–70; Lake Erie Col, Painesville, OH 1971–72
AWARDS: Dayton Art Mus, OH, 1952; Purchase Prize, Cleveland Mus of Art, OH, 1952; Louis Comfort Tiffany Fel, 1952; Walker Mus Art Center, Minneapolis, MN, 1961; Minnesota Mus, St Paul, MN, 1975; Brooklyn Mus, NY, 1975; Canton Art Inst, OH, 1979; Printed Image Award, Hudson River Mus, Yonkers, NY, 1988; Printmaking Award, Nat Congress of Art & Design, Salt Lake City, UT, 1988; Print Publication, Print Club of Cleveland, OH & Cleveland Mus of Art, OH, 1989; Special Mention, Graphics, Cleveland, OH, 1990; Juror's Merit Award, Chattahoochee Valley Art Mus, LaGrange, GA, 1991
RECENT EXHIB: Associated Am Artists, NY, 1987; Cleveland Mus of Art, OH, 1987; Hudson River Mus, Yonkers, NY, 1987,88; Trenton State Col, NY, 1988; Cleveland Centre of Contemp Art, OH, 1988; Southwest Texas State Univ, San Marcos, TX, 1988; Bradley Univ, Peoria, IL, 1989; Butler Inst of Am Art, Youngstown, OH, 1989; Jane Haslem Gallery, Wash, DC, 1990; Bonfoey Gallery, Cleveland, OH, 1989,91
PRINTERS: Artist (ART)
PUBLISHERS: Artist (ART); John Szoke Graphics, NY (JSG)
COLLECTIONS: Brooklyn Mus, NY; Cleveland Mus of Art, OH; Butler Inst of Am Art, Youngstown, OH; Univ of California, Los Angeles, CA; Univ of Manitoba, Canada; Akron Art Inst, OH; Dayton Mus of Art, OH; Univ of Massachusetts, Boston, MA; Nat Gallery of Art, Ottawa, Canada; New Gallery, Cleveland, OH; Minnesota Mus of Art, Minneapolis, MN; London Ontario Library, Canada; Akron Art Inst, OH; Kentucky Mus, Louisville, KY; Center for Contemp Art, Cleveland, OH; H W Janson Coll, NY
GALLERIES: Bonfoey Gallery, Cleveland, OH; Center for Contempory Art, Cleveland, OH; Gallery G, Pittsburgh, PA; John Szoke Gallery, New York, NY; Jane Haslem Gallery, Wash, DC; Jan Cicero Gallery, Chicago, IL; Katie Gingrass Gallery, Milwaukee, WI; Art Exchange, Columbus, OH
MAILING ADDRESS: 1220 W 6th St, Cleveland, OH 44113

Phyllis Seltzer
Towerscape
Courtesy the Artist

TITLE	PUBLISHER	PRINTER	DATE	MEDIUM	DIMENSION (PAPER SIZE) IN INCHES	TYPE OF PAPER	EDITION NUMBER	NO. OF COLORS	ORIGINAL OPENING PRICE	CURRENT RETAIL PRICE
CURRENT EDITIONS										
Maseroti 450S	ART	ART	1980	PO	28 X 36	MUL	25		150	150
Ohio Hunter	ART	ART	1980	PO	24 X 29	MUL	20		150	150
Machu Pichu Meeting	ART	ART	1981	PO	24 X 30	MUL	5	15	300	300
Machu Pichu Journey	ART	ART	1981	PO	36 X 23	MUL	5	8	300	300
Machu Pichu Portrait	ART	ART	1981	PO	36 X 23	MUL	5	8	300	300
Tienanmen Square I,II	ART	ART	1981	PO	24 X 30 EA	MUL	10 EA	11 EA	300 EA	300 EA
Great Wall	ART	ART	1981	PO	24 X 30	MUL	10	8	300	300
Fayoum Sakarra	ART	ART	1982	PO	24 X 30	MUL	10	15	300	300
Coptic Fragment, Market	ART	ART	1983	HT	15 X 22	R/BFK	15	8	125	125
Meidum	ART	ART	1983	HT	15 X 22	R/BFK	15	8	125	125
Fayum Market	ART	ART	1983	HT	15 X 10	HMP	15	8	125	125
Wadsworth Horse	ART	ART	1984	HT	19 X 23	R/BFK	15	8	150	150
Erie Street Bridge	ART	ART	1985	HT	24 X 29	SEK	10		400	400
Bright Blue Cuyahoga	ART	ART	1985	HT	24 X 29	SEK	15		300	300
Challenger on the Cuyahoga	ART	ART	1985	HT	24 X 38	SEK	10		500	500
Stride	ART	ART	1986	HT	24 X 28	SEK	15		450	450
Bright Scape	ART	ART	1989	HTP	32 X 38	R/BFK	20	40	1045	1045
Palladio's Bridge (Dipt)	ART	ART	1989	HTP	52 X 40	R/BFK	20	72	1485	1485
Skyview Diptych	ART	ART	1989	HTP	44 X 49	R/BFK	10	40	1210	1210
Archway	ART	ART	1989	HTP	32 X 47	R/BFK	20	72	1350	1350
Other Complexities	ART	ART	1989	HTP	31 X 48	R/BFK	15	40	1450	1450
Pageantry	ART	ART	1989	HTP	31 X 48	R/BFK	20	72	1485	1485
A Sense of Place	JSG	ART	1989	HT	31 X 48	R/BFK	30	72	1250	1250
Towerscape	JSG	ART	1989	HT	31 X 48	R/BFK	30	72	1250	1250
Without Limits	JSG	ART	1989	HT	31 X 48	R/BFK	30	72	1250	1250
Archway	ART	ART	1989	HT	32 X 47	R/BFK	20	72	1350	1350
Bright Scape	ART	ART	1989	HT	32 X 38	SOM	20	72	1045	1045
East Passage	ART	ART	1990	HT	37 X 42	R/BFK	15	72	1350	1350
Steel Stressed	JSG	ART	1990	HT	54 X 42	R/BFK	30	72	1250	1250
Suspended	JSG	ART	1990	HT	50 X 42	R/BFK	30	72	1250	1250
Facade	ART	ART	1990	HT	42 X 50	R/BFK	15	72	1500	1500
Suspension View	ART	ART	1990	HT	42 X 55	R/BFK	30	72	2000	2000
Invention	ART	ART	1991	HT	32 X 42	R/BFK	15	72	1050	1050
The El	ART	ART	1991	HT	31 X 48	R/BFK	30	72	900	900
Sequence	ART	ART	1991	HT	21 X 50	R/BFK	30	72	800	800
Hovering	ART	ART	1991	HT	31 X 48	R/BFK	15	72	1150	1150
Piers	ART	ART	1991	HT	35 X 42	R/BFK	15	72	1150	1150
Multi-Tiered	ART	ART	1991	HT	32 X 48	R/BFK	15	72	900	900
Altered	ART	ART	1992	HT	32 X 48	R/BFK	15	72	1150	1150

RICHARD SERRA

BORN: San Francisco, CA; November 2, 1939
EDUCATION: Univ of California, Berkeley, CA; Univ of California, Santa Barbara, CA, MA Yale Univ, New Haven, CT, BA, MFA
AWARDS: Skowhegan Medal, ME, 1975; Carnegie Prize, Carnegie Inst, Pittsburgh, PA, 1985
RECENT EXHIB: Western Washington Univ, Bellingham, WA, 1992; Univ of Florida, Gainesville, FL, 1992; Pace Gallery, NY, 1987,89,92; Gagosian Gallery, NY, 1992
COLLECTIONS: Stedelijk Mus, Amsterdam, Netherlands; Nat Mus, Melbourne, Australia; Oberlin Col, OH; Pasadena Art Mus, CA; Aldrich Mus of Contemp Art, Ridgefield, CT; Guggenheim Mus, NY; Nat Mus of Art, Stockholm, Sweden; Whitney Mus of Am Art, NY; Allan Mem Art Mus, Oberlin, OH; Tate Gallery of Art, London, England; Yale Univ Art Gallery, New Haven, CT
PRINTERS: Gemini GEL, Los Angeles, CA (GEM); Tyler Graphics, Ltd, Mount Kisco, NY (TGL)
PUBLISHERS: Gemini GEL, Los Angeles, CA (GEM); Tyler Graphics, Ltd, Mount Kisco, NY (TGL)
GALLERIES: BlumHelman Gallery, New York, NY; William Beadleston Fine Art, New York, NY; Richard Hines Gallery, Seattle, WA; Hill Gallery, Birmingham, MI; Galerie Lelong, New York, NY & Paris, France; Pace Prints, New York, NY; Gemini GEL, Los Angeles, CA (G); Fred Hoffman Gallery, Santa Monica, CA; Tavelli Gallery, Aspen, CO; Hill Gallery, Birmingham, MI; Gottheiner Fine Arts, Ltd, St Louis, MO; Greenberg Gallery, St Louis, MO; Leo Castelli Gallery, New York, NY; Gagosian Gallery, New York, NY; Tony Shafrazi Gallery, New York, NY; Cynthia Drennon Fine Art, Los Angeles, CA; Pence Fine Art, Inc, Los Angeles, CA; Deanna Miller Fine Arts, Pacific Palisades, CA; Brian Gross Fine Art, San Francisco, CA; Janet Levitt Fine Arts, San Francisco, CA; G

Richard Serra
Spoleto Circle (G-401)
Courtesy Gemini GEL

Grimaldis Gallery, Baltimore, MD; Carol Evans Fine Arts, New York, NY; Figura, Inc, New York, NY; Matthew Marks Gallery, New York, NY; Atsuko Murayama Fine Art, New York, NY; Reinhold-Brown Gallery, New York, NY; TwoSixty-One Art, New York, NY; Lawrence Mangel Fine Art, Phila, PA Donald Young Gallery, Seattle, WA

Gemini (G)

TITLE	PUBLISHER	PRINTER	DATE	MEDIUM	DIMENSION (PAPER SIZE) IN INCHES	TYPE OF PAPER	EDITION NUMBER	NO. OF COLORS	ORIGINAL OPENING PRICE	CURRENT RETAIL PRICE
SOLD OUT EDITIONS (RARE):										
Balance Plate	GEM	GEM	1972	LC	32 X 45	ARJ	62		300	30000
Eight by Eight	GEM	GEM	1972	LC	52 X 41	ARJ	59		300	30000
183rd & Webster Avenue	GEM	GEM	1972	LC	32 X 45	ARJ	62	3	300	15000
Double Ring II	GEM	GEM	1972	LC	35 X 48	CUR	65	1	300	15000
Du Common	GEM	GEM	1972	LC	52 X 41	IT/W	59	2	300	15000
Spoleto Circle (G-401)	GEM	GEM	1972	LC	35 X 51	IT/W	65	2	300	15000
Out the Window at the Square Diner (G-960)	GEM	GEM	1981		14 X 11	AC	58	1	500	5000
Sketches I (G-961)	GEM	GEM	1981	LB	28 X 22	ARJ	30		450	1000
Sketches, 2-7 (G-962-967)	GEM	GEM	1981	LB	28 X 22 EA	ARJ	50 EA	1 EA	450 EA	10000 EA
Back to Black (G-969)	GEM	GEM	1981	LB	53 X 62	ARJ	20	1	1000	30000
Bad Water	GEM	GEM	1981	LB	53 X 62	ARJ	15	1	1000	30000
Malcolm X	GEM	GEM	1981	LB	62 X 53	ARJ	16	1	1100	30000
The Moral Majority Sucks (G-971)	GEM	GEM	1981	LB	53 X 61	ARJ	20	1	1200	30000
To Bobby Sands	GEM	GEM	1981	LB	60 X 40	ARJ	14	1	1000	30000
Left Square into Left Corner (Metal Wall Drawing: Paintstick on Aluminum)	GEM	GEM	1981	MM	107 X 104	Metal	6		15000	30000
Horizontal Rectangle to the Floor (Metal Wall Drawing: Paintstick on Aluminum)	GEM	GEM	1981	MM	41 X 204	Metal	6		15000	30000
Alemeda Black (Metal Wall Drawing: Paintstick on Alum)	GEM	GEM	1981	MM	72 X 72	Metal	6		12000	30000
Alameda Street (Paintstick on Handmade Paper)	GEM	GEM	1981	MM	20 FT X 21 FT	HMP	1 EA		25000	40000
St Louis (from Portfolio of Thirteen Prints) (Paintstick)	GEM	GEM	1982	MM	42 X 31	GE	75		1000	20000
Robeson (Paintstick on Silkscreen & Coated Paper) (G-1211)	GEM	GEM	1985	SP/PS	102 X 66	CP	15		2800	35000
Ernie's Mark (Paintstick on Silkscreen & Coated Paper)	GEM	GEM	1985	SP/PS	85 X 75	CP	15		2800	30000
Paris (Paintstick on Silkscreen & Coated Paper) (G-1212)	GEM	GEM	1985	SP/PS	85 X 53	CP	17	2	2500	30000
Alberta Hunter (Paintstick on Silkscreen & Coated Paper) (G-1214)	GEM	GEM	1985	SP/PS	53 X 60	CP	28		2000	30000
Glenda Lough (Paintstick on Silkscreen & Coated Paper)	GEM	GEM	1985	SP/PS	77 X 43	CP	19		2100	30000
Patience (Paintstick on Silkscreen & Coated Paper)	GEM	GEM	1985	SP/PS	62 X 53	CP	20		2100	30000
Tujunga Blacktop (Paintstick on Silkscreen & Coated Paper)	GEM	GEM	1985	SP/PS	60 X 53	CP	28		2100	30000

RICHARD SERRA CONTINUED

TITLE	PUBLISHER	PRINTER	DATE	MEDIUM	DIMENSION (PAPER SIZE) IN INCHES	TYPE OF PAPER	EDITION NUMBER	NO. OF COLORS	ORIGINAL OPENING PRICE	CURRENT RETAIL PRICE
SOLD OUT EDITIONS (RARE):										
Clara Clara I, II (Paintstick on Silkscreen & Coated Paper) (G-1219)	GEM	GEM	1985	SP/PS	37 X 72 EA	CP	28 EA	1	2000 EA	30000 EA
Rosa Parks (with Paintstik)	GEM	GEM	1987	SP	40 X 83	AC	30	1	2600 EA	30000 EA
My Curves are not Mod (with Paintstik) (G-1333)	GEM	GEM	1987	SP	50 X 77	AC	19	2	3500 EA	30000 EA
CURRENT EDITIONS:										
Ismael's Edge	GEM	GEM	1987	LC	70 X 46	AC	20	1	6000	7000
Rosa Parks (G-1330)	GEM	GEM	1987	SP/PS	40 X 83	AC	30	1	5000	10000
Paintstik Series:										
Double Black	GEM	GEM	1991	SP/PS	73 X 132	AC	20	1	22000	22000
Untitled	GEM	GEM	1991	SP/PS	79 X 152	AC	20	1	24000	24000
Esna	GEM	GEM	1991	SP/PS	77 X 77	AC	31	1	18000	18000
Spike	GEM	GEM	1991	SP/PS	138 X 96	AC	10	1	30000	30000
Reykjavik	GEM	GEM	1991	SP/PS	67 X 77	AC	46	1	14000	14000
Videy Afanger Series:										
Videy Afanger #1	GEM	GEM	1991	EC	10 X 12	FAB		1	1000	1000
Videy Afanger #2	GEM	GEM	1991	EC	10 X 12	FAB		1	1000	1000
Videy Afanger #3	GEM	GEM	1991	EC	10 X 12	FAB		1	1000	1000
Videy Afanger #4	GEM	GEM	1991	EC	10 X 12	FAB		1	1500	1500
Videy Afanger #5	GEM	GEM	1991	EC	10 X 12	FAB		1	1000	1000
Videy Afanger #6	GEM	GEM	1991	EC	10 X 12	FAB		1	1000	1000
Videy Afanger #7	GEM	GEM	1991	EC	10 X 12	FAB		1	1500	1500
Videy Afanger #8	GEM	GEM	1991	EC	12 X 14	FAB		1	1000	1000
Videy Afanger #9	GEM	GEM	1991	SP/PS	14 X 11	AC		1	1000	1500
Videy Afanger #10	GEM	GEM	1991	SP/PS	11 X 12	AC		1	1000	1500

SERRIER

BORN: Paris, France; 1929

PRINTERS: Accent Studio, Canoga Park, CA (AS)
PUBLISHERS: Martin Lawrence Limited Editions, Van Nuys, CA (MLLE)
GALLERIES: Martin Lawrence Galleries, Sherman Oaks, CA & Los Angeles, CA & Newport Beach, CA & West Los Angeles, CA & Phila, PA

TITLE	PUBLISHER	PRINTER	DATE	MEDIUM	DIMENSION (PAPER SIZE) IN INCHES	TYPE OF PAPER	EDITION NUMBER	NO. OF COLORS	ORIGINAL OPENING PRICE	CURRENT RETAIL PRICE
CURRENT EDITIONS:										
L'Envie	MLLE	AS	1982	SP	34 X 29	SE	200	80	600	850

RAYMUNDO SESMA

BORN: San Cristobal de las Chiapas, Mexico; June 26, 1954
EDUCATION: Cultural Center of Aquascalien, Mexico, 1973–74; American Univ, Puebla, Mexico, 1974–76; Open Studio Workshop, Toronto, Can, 1977
TEACHING: Cultural Center of Aquascalien, Mexico; American Univ, Puebla, Mexico

RECENT EXHIB: Galeria Ramis Barquet, Monterrey, Mexico, 1993
COLLECTIONS: Statische Gallery Schlob, Wolfsburg, Germany; Victoria and Albert Mus, London, England; Univ of the Americas, Mexico City, Mexico; Mus of Mexican Art, Plovdiv, Bulgaria; Bibliotheque Nat, Paris, France
PUBLISHERS: Figura Inc, NY (FI); Giorgio Upiglio, Milan, Italy (GU)
GALLERIES: Estela Shapiro, Mexico City, Mexico; Gallerita, Milan, Italy; Galeria Misrachi, Mexico City, Mexico; Mexican Cultural Center, Paris, France; Galeria Ramis Barquet, Monterrey, Mexico

TITLE	PUBLISHER	PRINTER	DATE	MEDIUM	DIMENSION (PAPER SIZE) IN INCHES	TYPE OF PAPER	EDITION NUMBER	NO. OF COLORS	ORIGINAL OPENING PRICE	CURRENT RETAIL PRICE
CURRENT EDITIONS:										
Advento (9 Sheets Each)	FI	GU	1983	COL/I II	19 X 27 EA / 58 X 82 TOT	AP	15 EA	7 EA	2100	4500
Settimo Sueno (Trip)	FI	GU	1983	COL/HI	48 X 31 EA	AP	7	7	2100	4800

DAVID SHARIR

BORN: Tel Aviv, Israel; 1938
EDUCATION: Tel Aviv, Israel; Acad di Belle Arti, Florence, Italy

COLLECTIONS: Fogg Mus, Cambridge, MA; Philadelphia Mus of Art, PA; Los Angeles County Mus, CA; Israel Mus, Jerusalem, Israel; Tel-Aviv Mus, Israel
PRINTERS: Screened Images, Port Washington, NY (SI)
PUBLISHERS: Transworld Art, Inc, NY (TAI)
GALLERIES: Pucker/Safrai Gallery, Boston, MA; New Acquisitions Gallery, Syracuse, NY

TITLE	PUBLISHER	PRINTER	DATE	MEDIUM	DIMENSION (PAPER SIZE) IN INCHES	TYPE OF PAPER	EDITION NUMBER	NO. OF COLORS	ORIGINAL OPENING PRICE	CURRENT RETAIL PRICE
CURRENT EDITIONS:										
A Gate for the City	TAI	SI	1979	SP	24 X 30	LEN	300	23	750	800
A Gate for the Righteous	TAI	SI	1979	SP	30 X 25	LEN	250	27	450	500
A Gate for the Angels	TAI	SI	1979	SP	32 X 25	LEN	250	24	450	500
A Gate for the Garden	TAI	SI	1980	SP	24 X 31	LEN	250	21	450	500
A Gate for the Birdhouse	TAI	SI	1980	SP	32 X 24	LEN	250	24	450	500

DANIEL SERRA-BADUE

BORN: Santiago de Cuba, Cuba; November 8, 1914
EDUCATION: Sch of Fine Arts, Santiago de Cuba, 1924–26; Sch of Fine Art, Barcelona, Spain, 1932–36; Art Students League, NY; Univ of Columbia, NY; Nat Acad of Design, NY, 1938–40; Sch of Fine Art, Havana, Cuba, 1943; Pratt Inst NY, 1964; Art Critics Workshop, NY, 1967
TEACHING: Columbia Univ, NY, 1962–63; Brooklyn Mus, NY, 1962–85; St Peters Col, Jersey City, NJ, 1967 to present
AWARDS: Guggenheim Fel, 1938,39; Lippincott Prize, Pennsylvania Acad of Fine Arts, Phila, PA, 1941; Purchase Prize, Hispano Am de Arte, Havana, Cuba, 1954; Cintas Found Fel, 1963,64; Graphic Award, Nat Acad of Design, NY, 1984
RECENT EXHIB: Jersey City Mus, NJ, 1988
COLLECTIONS: Mus of Mod Art, NY; Metropolitan Mus of Art, NY; Butler Inst of Am Art, Youngstown, OH; Musee d'Art et d'Histoire, Geneva Switzerland; Municipal Mus, Santiago de Cuba, Cuba; Museo Nacional, Havana, Cuba; Inst de Cultura Hispanica, Madrid, Spain; New York Public Library, NY; Mus of Contemp Latin Am Art, Wash, DC; Brooklyn Mus, NY; Cincinnati Art Mus, OH
PRINTERS: Burr Miller & Sons, NY (BM)
PUBLISHERS: Artist (ART)
GALLERIES: Susan Teller Gallery, New York, NY
MAILING ADDRESS: 15 W 72nd St, #10-T, New York, NY 10023

Daniel Serra-Badue
At the Beginning, 1492
Courtesy the Artist

TITLE	PUBLISHER	PRINTER	DATE	MEDIUM	DIMENSION (PAPER SIZE) IN INCHES	TYPE OF PAPER	EDITION NUMBER	NO. OF COLORS	ORIGINAL OPENING PRICE	CURRENT RETAIL PRICE
SOLD OUT EDITIONS (RARE):										
Self-Portrait in the Park	ART	BM	1979	LB	17 X 21	R/BFK	50	1	75	200
CURRENT EDITIONS:										
Imprisoned Shopping Bag	ART	BM	1982	LB	20 X 26	R/BFK	70	1	150	300
Exactitude I	ART	BM	1983	LB	20 X 26	R/BFK	40	1	200	300
Pineapple and Walnut	ART	BM	1984	LB	20 X 26	R/BFK	50	1	200	300
The Impossible Step	ART	BM	1985	LB	20 X 26	R/BFK	50	1	200	300
Musical Instrument in a Failing Attempt to Reach the Moon	ART	BM	1986	LB	20 X 26	R/BFK	40	1	250	300
Twenty Five Years as a Lithographer	ART	BM	1987	LB	20 X 26	R/BFK	50	1	250	300
Clamoring Newspaper	ART	BM	1988	LB	20 X 26	R/BFK	50	1	250	300
At the Beginning, 1492	ART	BM	1992	LB	18 X 22	R/BFK	125	1	200	250

RICHARD SHAFFER

BORN: Fresno, CA; March 17, 1947
EDUCATION: Univ of California, Santa Cruz, CA; New Sch for Social Research, NY; San Francisco Art Inst, CA, BFA, 1973; Stanford Univ, Palo Alto, CA, MFA, 1975
TEACHING: Instr, Printmaking, Univ of California, Santa Cruz, CA, Summer, 1975; Assoc Prof, Painting & Drawing, Univ of Texas, Arlington, TX, 1978–83
AWARDS: Roswell Mus Grant, 1975–76; Fulbright-Hays Fel, 1976–77; Nat Endowment for the Arts Fel, Painting, 1981; Visual Arts Award, Painting, 1982
RECENT EXHIB: Roswell Mus, NM, 1987; John Berggruen Gallery, San Francisco, CA, 1988; La Jolla Mus of Contemp Art, CA, 1988; L A Louver Gallery, Venice, CA, 1987,88,89
COLLECTIONS: Dallas Mus of Art, TX; Univ of Texas, Tyler, TX; Stanford Univ Art Sch, Palo Alto, CA; Santa Barbara Mus of Art, CA; La Jolla Mus of Contemp, San Diego, CA & Roswell Mus & Art Center, NM
PRINTERS: Leslie Sutcliffe, Los Angeles, CA (LS); Robert Aull, Los Angeles, CA (RA); Artist (ART)
PUBLISHERS: L A Louver Publications, Venice, CA (LAL); Artist (ART)
GALLERIES: L A Louver, Venice, CA; Moody Gallery, Houston, TX; Eugene Binder Fine Art, Dallas TX

TITLE	PUBLISHER	PRINTER	DATE	MEDIUM	DIMENSION (PAPER SIZE) IN INCHES	TYPE OF PAPER	EDITION NUMBER	NO. OF COLORS	ORIGINAL OPENING PRICE	CURRENT RETAIL PRICE
CURRENT EDITIONS:										
Sceens	LAL	LS/RA	1982	E/A/DPT	30 X 36	R/BFK/W	50	1	750	1000
Rooms	LAL	LS/RA	1982	E/A/DPT	30 X 36	R/BFK/W	50	1	750	1000

RICHARD SHAFFER CONTINUED

TITLE	PUBLISHER	PRINTER	DATE	MEDIUM	DIMENSION (PAPER SIZE) IN INCHES	TYPE OF PAPER	EDITION NUMBER	NO. OF COLORS	ORIGINAL OPENING PRICE	CURRENT RETAIL PRICE
CURRENT EDITIONS:										
Shelf of Correspondence	LAL	LS/RA	1982	E/A/DPT	30 X 36	R/BFK/W	50	1	750	1000
Still Life with Inro	LAL	LS/RA	1982	E/A/DPT	30 X 36	R/BFK/W	50	1	750	1000
Untitled (Series of 60 Monotypes)	ART	ART	1986	MON	30 X 42 EA	AP	1 EA	Varies	1800 EA	2500 EA

BEN SHAHN

BORN: Kovno, Lithuania, Russia; (1898–1969)
EDUCATION: New York Univ, NY; City Col of New York, NY, 1919–22; Nat Acad of Design, NY, 1922
TEACHING: Univ of Colorado, 1950; Brooklyn Mus, NY, 1951, Harvard Univ, Cambridge, MA, 1956–57
AWARDS: Alice McFadden Eyre Medal, 1952; Pennsylvania Acad of Fine Arts, Pennell Mem Medal, 1939,53; Purchase Prize, Sao Paulo Bienal, Brazil, 1953–54; Joseph E Temple Gold Award, 1956; Harvard Univ Medal, 1956; Am Inst of Graphic Art Medal, 1958
COLLECTIONS: Whitney Mus of Am Art, Ny; Mus of Mod Art, NY; Metropolitan Mus of Art, NY; Fogg Mus, Harvard Univ, Cambridge, MA; Smith Col, MA; Dartmouth Col, MA; Detroit Inst of Art, MI; Wadsworth Atheneum, Hartford, CT; Chicago Art Inst, IL; Brandeis Univ, Waltham, MA; Baltimore Mus, MD; Butler Inst of Am Art, Youngstown, OH; Jewish Mus, NY; Newark Mus, NJ; Carnegie-Mellon Mus, Pittsburgh, PA; Albright-Knox Art Gallery, Buffalo, NY; Walker Art Center, Minneapolis, MN; Univ of Wichita, KS; Arizona State Col, Tempe, AZ; Univ of Arizona, Tucson, AZ
PUBLISHERS: Kennedy Graphics, NY (KG)
GALLERIES: Kennedy Galleries, New York, NY; Hooks-Epstein Galleries, Houston, TX; Maxwell Davidson Gallery, New York, NY; Terry Dintenfass Gallery, New York, NY; Heritage Gallery, Los Angeles, CA; Sragow Gallery, New York, NY; Rosenfield Fine Arts, New York, NY

TITLE	PUBLISHER	PRINTER	DATE	MEDIUM	DIMENSION (PAPER SIZE) IN INCHES	TYPE OF PAPER	EDITION NUMBER	NO. OF COLORS	ORIGINAL OPENING PRICE	CURRENT RETAIL PRICE
SOLD OUT EDITIONS (RARE):										
Mine Building	KG		1956	SP	22 X 31	LIN	63	7	50	5000
Alphabet of Creation	KG		1957	SP	39 X 27	AM	80	1	50	5000
Imortal Words	KG		1958	SP	16 X 21	AM	29	1	50	3500
Lute and Molecule #2	KG		1958	SP	25 X 39	JP	100	4	50	5000
Pleiades	KG		1960	SP	21 X 27	JP	54	5	75	4000
Maximus of Tyre	KG		1963	SP	36 X 26	JP	34	2	100	6000
Warsaw	KG		1963	SP	37 X 28	JP	97	1	100	5000
Blind Botanist	KG		1963	LC	27 X 21	AP	200	5	100	3000
Mask	KG		1963	LC	30 X 21	AP	200	5	100	3000
Psalm 133	KG		1963	LC	21 X 27	AP	200	6	100	3000
All that is Beautiful	KG		1965	HC/SP	26 X 39	R/BFK	34	8	125	5000
Credo	KG		1966	SP	27 X 21	JP	48	2	200	4500
Byzantine Memory	KG		1966	SP	27 X 21	JP	33	7	200	4500
Haggadah (Frontispiece)	KG		1966	LC	15 X 23	RdB	300	6	150	3500
Flowering Brushes	KG		1968	LC	40 X 27	AP	100	5	500	8000
Flowering Brushes (Signed by Mrs Shahn)	KG		1968	LC	40 X 27	AP	100	5	500	3000
Screams of Women in Labor			1968	LC	22 X 17		950		150	1000

DAVID SHAPIRO

BORN: New York, NY; August 28, 1916
EDUCATION: Educ Alliance Art Sch, 1933–35; Am Artists Sch, 1936–39
TEACHING: Instr, Art, Smith Col, Northampton, MA, 1946–47; Asst Prof, Art & Design, Univ of British Columbia, Can, 1947–49; Prof, Hofstra Univ, Hempstead, NY, 1962–1981; Prof Emeritus, Hofstra Univ, 1981 to present
AWARDS: Fulbright Awards, Painting, Italy, 1951–52, 1952–53; MacDowell Colony Peterborough, NH, 1976; Tamarind Inst of Lithography, Univ of New Mexico, Albuquerque, NM, 1976; Nat Endowment for the Arts Grant, 1977–78; Fulbright Fel, Univ of Belgrade, Yugoslavia, 1981
COLLECTIONS: Metropolitan Mus, NY; Nat Mus of Fine Arts Smithsonian Inst, Wash, DC; Philadelphia Mus, PA; Brooklyn Mus, NY; Boise Gallery of Art, ID; Carroll Reece Mus, East Tennessee Univ, Johnson City, TN; Castellon Mem Coll, Teachers Col, Columbia Univ, NY; Creative Arts Center, West Virginia Univ, Morgantown, WV; Davidson Col, NC; Drake Univ, Des Moines, IA; Flint Art Inst, MI; Univ of Georgia, Athens, GA; Hackley Art Gallery, Muskegon Art Mus, MI; Hildreth Gallery, Nasson Col, Springvale, ME; Kalamazoo Inst of Art, MI; Hofstra Univ, Hempstead, NY; Indiana State Univ, Terre Haute, IN; Kresge Art Center Gallery, Michigan State Univ, Lansing, MI; Madison Art Center, WI; Mesa Comm Col, AZ; Minneapolis Inst of Art, MN; Univ of Oklahoma, Norman, OK; Univ of Iowa, Iowa City, IA; Mus of Fine Arts, Springfield, MA; New Britain Mus of Am Art, CT; New York Public Library, NY; North Carolina State Univ, Raleigh, NC; North Dakota State Univ, Fargo, ND; Rockford Col, IL; Sheldon Mem Gallery, Univ of Nebraska, Lincoln, NE; Slater Mem Mus, Norwich, CT; Southern Illinois Univ, Carbondale, IL; Southern Utah State Col, Cedar City, UT; Univ of British Columbia, Can; Univ of Kansas, Lawrence, KS; Univ of Maine, Augusta, ME; Univ of Missouri, Columbia, MO; Univ of Nevada, Las Vegas, NV; Univ of New Mexico, Albuquerque, NM; Univ of Wisconsin, Sheboygan, WI; Univ of Utah, Salt Lake City, UT; Walker Art Center, Minneapolis, MN
PRINTERS: Tamarind Inst of Lithography, Albuquerque, NM (TI); Sienna Studios, NY (SiS); Herb Fox Graphics, Boston, MA (HFG); Artist (ART)
PUBLISHERS: Associated Am Artists, NY (AAA); Original Print Collectors Group, NY (OPCG); Litografia Internazionale, Milan, Italy (LI); Ferdinand Roten Galleries, Baltimore, MD (FTG); Lakeside Studios, Lakeside, MI (LS); Artist (ART)
GALLERIES: Associated American Artists, New York, NY; Alice Simsar Gallery, Ann Arbor, MI; Tamarind Inst, Albuquerque, NM; Galleria Dell 'Orso, Milan, Italy; Lakeside Studios, Lakeside, MI
MAILING ADDRESS: RFD, PO Box 77, Cavendish, VT 05142

TITLE	PUBLISHER	PRINTER	DATE	MEDIUM	DIMENSION (PAPER SIZE) IN INCHES	TYPE OF PAPER	EDITION NUMBER	NO. OF COLORS	ORIGINAL OPENING PRICE	CURRENT RETAIL PRICE
SOLD OUT EDITIONS (RARE):										
The Mourners (of the Holocaust)	ART	ART	1956	WB	23 X 36	MUL	20	1	100	600
Non-Conformist	ART	ART	1962	WB	24 X 36	MUL	25	1	100	500

DAVID SHAPIRO CONTINUED

TITLE	PUBLISHER	PRINTER	DATE	MEDIUM	DIMENSION (PAPER SIZE) IN INCHES	TYPE OF PAPER	EDITION NUMBER	NO. OF COLORS	ORIGINAL OPENING PRICE	CURRENT RETAIL PRICE
SOLD OUT EDITIONS (RARE):										
Winter Walk #3	ART	ART	1968	I	24 X 36	R/BFK	25	1	100	400
Windy Sunset	OPCG	ART	1975	SP	20 X 30	DOM/E	90	5	150	400
The Waves	OPCG	ART	1977	LC	22 X 29	R/BFK	125	7	150	400
Landscape with Village	OPCG	ART	1982	SP	30 X 22	AP88	125	11	185	400
CURRENT EDITIONS:										
Red Landscape	LI	LI	1970	LC	28 X 19	FAB	90	6	100	300
The Moon Rises	LI	LI	1970	LC	19 X 28	FAB	90	6	100	300
Mountain Suite (Set of 5):										
Hot Afternoon	ART	TI	1976	LC	22 X 30	AP/W	20	4	150	400
Blue Shadows	ART	TI	1976	LC	22 X 30	AP/W	20	4	150	400
Golden Day	ART	TI	1976	LC	20 X 30	AP/W	20	4	150	400
Towards Evening	ART	TI	1976	LC	22 X 30	AP/W	20	3	150	400
Shadows on the Mountain	ART	TI	1976	LC	22 X 30	AP/W	20	1	100	350
Lakeside Mountain Suite (Set of 3):									300 SET	550 SET
Towards Evening	LS	HFG	1977	LC	15 X 22	R/BFK	50	4	100	250
Springreen	LS	HFG	1977	LC	15 X 22	R/BFK	50	4	100	250
Near Albuquerque	LS	HFG	1977	LC	15 X 22	R/BFK	50	4	100	250

DAVID SHAPIRO

BORN: Brooklyn, NY; June 26, 1944
EDUCATION: Skowhegan Sch of Art, ME, 1965; Pratt Inst, Brooklyn, NY, BFA, 1966; Indiana Univ, Bloomington, IN, MFA, 1968
TEACHING: Instr, Parsons Sch of Design, NY, 1974–80; Vis Art, Drake Univ, Des Moines, IA, 1981; Vis Art, State Univ of New York, Buffalo, NY, 1981
AWARDS: Creative Artists Public Service Grant
RECENT EXHIB: Turner Gallery, Los Angeles, CA, 1987; Dolan/Maxwell Gallery, Phila, PA, 1987,88; Gloria Luria Gallery, Bay Harbor Islands, FL, 1988; Fay Gold Gallery, Atlanta, GA, 1988; New Orleans Mus of Art, LA, 1989; Woodstock Gallery of Art & Design Center, VT, 1989; Delaware Art Mus, Wilmington, DE, 1989,92
COLLECTIONS: Mus of Mod Art, NY; San Francisco Mus of Mod Art, CA; Guggenheim Mus, NY; Fort Lauderdale Mus of Art, FL; Univ of Iowa Art, Mus, Iowa City, IA; Brooklyn Mus, NY

PRINTERS: Aeropress Inc, New York, NY (AI); X-Press, NY (XP); Styria Studio, NY (SS); Echo Press, David Keister, Bloomington, IN (DK); David Calkins, Bloomington, IN (DC); Echo Press, Bloomington, IN (EPr); Betty Winkler, NY (BW); Yama Press, NY (YP)
PUBLISHERS: Corinthian Editions, NY (COR); Styria Studio, NY (SS); Getler/Pall, NY (G/P); Orion Editions, NY (OE); Prestige Art Ltd, Mamaroneck, NY (PA); Echo Press, Bloomington, IN (EPr); Artist (ART); Dolan/Maxwell Gallery, Phila, PA (D/M)
GALLERIES: Vanderwoude/Tananbaum Gallery, New York, NY; van Straaten Gallery, Chicago, IL; Thomas Smith Fine Art, Fort Wayne, IN; Styria Studio, New York, NY; Gloria Luria Gallery, Bay Harbor Islands, FL; Orion Editions, New York, NY; Cumberland Gallery, Nashville, TN; Thomson Gallery, Minneapolis, MN; Fay Gold Gallery, Atlanta, GA; Echo Press, Bloomington, IN; Styria Studio, New York, NY; Woodstock Gallery of Art, Woodstock, NY; Betsy Senior Contemporary Prints, New York, NY
MAILING ADDRESS: 315 Riverside Drive, New York, NY 10025

TITLE	PUBLISHER	PRINTER	DATE	MEDIUM	DIMENSION (PAPER SIZE) IN INCHES	TYPE OF PAPER	EDITION NUMBER	NO. OF COLORS	ORIGINAL OPENING PRICE	CURRENT RETAIL PRICE
SOLD OUT EDITIONS (RARE):										
Birnham Wood V (Red)	G/P/OE	XP	1982	AC	35 X 30	SUZ/AE	30	16	500	750
Birnham Wood VI (White)	G/P/OE	XP	1982	AC	35 X 30	SUZ/AE	30	15	500	750
CURRENT EDITIONS:										
Biely	PA	SS	1978	LC	25 X 30	AP	65	5	275	450
Seven Centers	PA	SS	1978	LC	25 X 30	AP	65	5	275	450
Chapter and Verse	PA	SS	1978	LC	25 X 30	AP	65	5	275	450
Suki	PA	SS	1978	LC	25 X 30	AP	65	5	350	500
Suki II	SS	SS	1979	LC/SP/HC	25 X 20	CH/KO	35		250	500
Poignancy of Things	SS	SS	1979	LC/HS/HC	21 X 17	KIT	35		250	500
Bely II	SS	SS	1979	LC/SP	17 X 14	WHP	35		250	400
Birnham Wood	SS	SS	1979	LC/HS/HC	10 X 9	MB	35		350	600
Untitled	G/P	AI	1980	EC/A	20 X 16	HODG	50	16	200	450
Birnham Wood I	G/P	AI	1981	EC	17 X 22	SUZ	50	11	300	500
Birnham Wood II	G/P	AI	1981	EC	17 X 22	SUZ	50	12	300	500
Birnham Wood III	G/P	AI	1981	EC	17 X 22	SUZ	50	15	300	500
Birnham Wood IV	G/P	AI	1981	EC	17 X 22	SUZ	50	14	300	500
Subtle Body	SS	SS	1981	LC/SP/HC	26 X 21	KO/KO	35	12	300	500
Poignancy of Things II	SS	SS	1981	LC/HC/HS	21 X 18	KIT	18	28	600	900
Chapter & Verse II	SS	SS	1982	LC/SP	44 X 37	OKP	50		600	750
Pleasure of the Road	SS	SS	1982	LC/SP/HC/HS	21 X 45	OKP	24	37	600	900
Subtle Body I, II	COR	AI	1982	EC	31 X 23 EA	SUZ	20 EA	10 EA	500 EA	700 EA
Birnham Wood VII (Blue)	OE		1982	AC/PO	35 X 30	SUZ	30	2	500	700
Birnham Wood VIII (Diamond)	OE		1982	AC/PO	38 DIA	SUZ	60	2	400	600
Birnham Wood (with Bronze Powder & Hand Stippling)	EPr	DK/EPr	1983	LC	60 X 30	SEK	30	12	800	1500
Subtle Body (2 Laminated Sheets)	EPr	DK/DC/EPr	1983	LC	42 X 32	SEK	25	20	500	1000
Untitled (DS84–163)	EPr	MON	1984	MON	30 X 15 EA	OKP	1 EA	Varies	500 EA	2000 EA
Seven Centers	EPr	DK/DC/EPr	1984–85	LC/SP/LI/SP/PAS	55 X 20	KOZO	30	18	800	1500
Twice Told Tale #2	GPS/ART	AK/XP	1985	MON/HC/EMA	35 X 18	HMP	1 EA	Varies	1600	2000

DAVID SHAPIRO CONTINUED

TITLE	PUBLISHER	PRINTER	DATE	MEDIUM	DIMENSION (PAPER SIZE) IN INCHES	TYPE OF PAPER	EDITION NUMBER	NO. OF COLORS	ORIGINAL OPENING PRICE	CURRENT RETAIL PRICE
CURRENT EDITIONS:										
Singer and Song (Sadness) (with Bronzing Powder & Pearl Powder)	EPr	DK/DC/EPr	1987	LC/LI/CO/WA/PAS	65 X 24	MOMI	20	3	1000	1500
The Lady and the Samurai (on Indigo Momi Paper & Bleached Cheesecloth)	EPr	DK/DC/EPr	1987	LC/LI/CO/WA/PAS	65 X 34	MOMI	20	2	1000	1500
Clearing I										
Clearing II	EPr	DK/DC/EPr	1988–89	LC/I/CO	24 X 56	UNG/MOR	15	9	1500	2100
Clearing II	EPr	DK/DC/EPr	1988–89	LC/COL/REL/CO	24 X 56	MOMI/MISU/ODP	15	7	1500	2100
Kala (Set of 7)	D/M	BW/YP	1988–89	I	26 X 21 EA	Varies	20 EA		500 EA	600 EA
Kala II	EPr	DK/DC/EPr	1988–89	LC/WC/REL/CO/WA		TRP	15	4	800	1000
Clearing (MP-1)	EPr	DK/EPr	1989	MON	24 X 58 EA	HMP	1 EA	Varies	2800 EA	3000 EA
Savasan 3	D/M	BW/YP	1989	I	15 X 90	OKP	20		2500	2800
Seer, Actor, Knower, Doer, II	EPr	DK/DC/EPr	1990	MON/HC	44 X 57 EA	KOZO	1 EA	Varies	4500 EA	4500 EA
Seer, Actor, Knower, Doer, V	EPr	DK/DC/EPr	1990	MON/HC	44 X 57 EA	KOZO	1 EA	Varies	4500 EA	4500 EA
Seer, Actor, Knower, Doer, XVII	EPr	DK/DC/EPr	1990	MON/HC	27 X 31 EA	KOZO	1 EA	Varies	2500 EA	2500 EA
Seer, Actor, Knower, Doer, XVIII	EPr	DK/DC/EPr	1990	MON/HC	27 X 31 EA	KOZO	1 EA	Varies	2500 EA	2500 EA
Seer, Actor, Knower, Doer, XX	EPr	DK/DC/EPr	1990	MON/HC	27 X 31 EA	KOZO	1 EA	Varies	2500 EA	2500 EA
Mirror-MP (Unique)	EPr	DK/DC/EPr	1991	COL/LB	57 X 37 EA	OKP	1 EA	Varies	4000 EA	4000 EA
Mirror I	EPr	DK/DC/EPr	1991	LC/COL	33 X 26	SEICHO/KOZO	15	5	1200	1200
Mirror II	EPr	DK/DC/EPr	1991	LC/COL	33 X 26	SEICHO/KOZO	15	5	1200	1200
Mirror III	EPr	DK/DC/EPr	1991	LC/COL	33 X 26	SEICHO/KOZO	15	5	1200	1200
Savasan 5	EPr	DK/DC/EPr	1991	LC/COL	13 X 75	UDA	25	16	2500	2500
Savasan 6	EPr	DK/DC/EPr	1991	LC/COL	13 X 75	UDA	25	4	2500	2500
Savasan 24-MP	EPr	DK/DC/EPr	1991	MON/HC	10 X 60 EA	KOZO	1 EA	Varies	3500 EA	3500 EA
Anecdote and Parable #1–#20	EPr	DK/DC/EPr	1992	MON	44 X 18 EA	JK/HMP/UDA	1 EA	Varies	1800 EA	1800 EA
Savasan 4	ART	BW/YP	1992	EB/CAR	7 X 37	KOZO	25	9	1000	1000

DEE SHAPIRO

BORN: Brooklyn, NY; November 30, 1936
EDUCATION: Univ of Mexico, Mexico City, Mexico, 1956; Queens Col, Flushing, NY, BA, 1958; MA, 1960
TEACHING: Instr, Adelphi Univ, Garden City, NY, 1981; Empire State Col, Old Westbury, NY, 1983 to present
AWARDS: Nat Assn of Women Artists, 1973; Award of Excellence, Hecksher Mus, Huntington, NY, 1974; Video-Tex Grant, Nat Endowment for the Arts, 1986
RECENT EXHIB: Andre Zarre Gallery, NY, 1990,92
COLLECTIONS: Guggenheim Mus, NY; Albright-Knox Mus, Buffalo, NY; Everson Mus, Syracuse, NY; Neuberger Mus, Purchase, NY; Birmingham Mus, AL; Lehigh Univ, Bethlehem, PA; Grey Art Mus, NY; New York Univ, NY; Dayton Art Inst, OH; Newark Mus, NJ; Oklahoma Art Mus, Oklahoma City, OK
PRINTERS: John Nichols, NY (JN); Michael Domberger, West Germany (MD)
PUBLISHERS: Orion Editions, NY (OE); Prestige Art Ltd, Mamaroneck, NY (PA)
GALLERIES: Andre Zarre Gallery, New York, NY; John Nichols Gallery, New York, NY; Jayne Baum, New York, NY; Alan Brown Gallery, Hartsdale, NY
MAILING ADDRESS: 28 Clover Drive, Great Neck, NY 11021

TITLE	PUBLISHER	PRINTER	DATE	MEDIUM	DIMENSION (PAPER SIZE) IN INCHES	TYPE OF PAPER	EDITION NUMBER	NO. OF COLORS	ORIGINAL OPENING PRICE	CURRENT RETAIL PRICE
SOLD OUT EDITIONS (RARE):										
Cosmic Pond	OE	MD	1980	SP	25 X 25	FAB	65	16	200	550
CURRENT EDITIONS:										
Hejaz I,II,III,IV, (Set of 4)	PA	JN	1983	SP	30 X 21 EA	FAB	100 EA	8 EA	1600 SET / 400 EA	2000 SET / 500 EA

SHARON SHIRAGA

EDUCATION: Univ of Wisconsin, Madison, WI, BFA, 1975
PRINTERS: Alan Koslin, NY (AK); X Press, NY (XP); Artist (ART)
PUBLISHERS: Orion Editions, NY (OE)
GALLERIES: Orion Editions, New York, NY; van Straaten Gallery, Chicago, IL

TITLE	PUBLISHER	PRINTER	DATE	MEDIUM	DIMENSION (PAPER SIZE) IN INCHES	TYPE OF PAPER	EDITION NUMBER	NO. OF COLORS	ORIGINAL OPENING PRICE	CURRENT RETAIL PRICE
SOLD OUT EDITIONS (RARE):										
Collé	OE	ART	1980	EB/CC	30 X 22	AP	50	1	275	400
Aralia	OE	AK/XP	1983	COL	41 X 30	AP	25	6	450	500
CURRENT EDITIONS:										
Grand Army Plaza (Series of 50)	OE	ART	1980	EB/MON	22 X 30 EA	AP	1 EA	1 EA	250 EA	400 EA
Refractions	OE	AK/XP	1981	AC	30 X 22	AP	50	5	250	300

The Printworld Directory is accepting new applications for the seventh edition. Approximately 300 new artists will be accepted. Please use the two forms provided in the back section of this directory to submit biographical data and documentation of prints. Edition number of each print must not exceed 500 and the retail price must be $100 or more.

JOEL SHAPIRO

BORN: New York, NY; September 27, 1941
EDUCATION: New York Univ, NY, BA, MA, 1961–69
AWARDS: Brandeis Award, 1984; Skowhegan Medal for Sculpture, 1986; Am Acad & Inst of Arts & Letters Award, NY, 1990
RECENT EXHIB: Hirshhorn Mus, Wash, DC, 1987; Saatchi Coll, London, England, 1988; Paula Cooper Gallery, 1989; Baltimore Mus of Art, MD, 1990; Des Moines Art Center, IA, 1990-91; Miami Center for Fine Arts, FL, 1991; Governors State Univ, Nathan Manilow Gallery, University Park, IL, 1989,92; North Carolina Mus of Art, Raleigh, NC, 1992; Pace Gallery, NY, 1993
COLLECTIONS: Fogg Art Mus, Cambridge, MA; Metropolitan Mus of Art, NY; Whitney Mus of Am Art, NY; Albright-Knox Art Gallery, Buffalo, NY; Stedelijk Mus, Amsterdam, Netherlands; Israel Mus, Jerusalem, Israel; Philadelphia Mus of Art, PA; Moderna Museet, Stockholm, Sweden
PRINTERS: Universal Art Limited Editions, Inc, West Islip, NY (ULAE); Leslie Miller, NY (LM); Grenfell Press, NY (GPr); Artist (ART); Catherine Mousley, NY (CM); Patricia Branstead, NY (PB); Aeropress, NY (A); Aldo Crommelynck, NY (AC); Atelier Crommelynck, NY (AtC)
PUBLISHERS: Brooke Alexander, Inc, NY (BAI); Paula Cooper, NY (PC); Simca Print Artists, NY (SPA); Universal Limited Art Editions, Inc, West Islip, NY (ULAE); Grenfell Press, NY (GPr); Artist (ART); Aldo Crommelynck, NY (AC)
GALLERIES: Paula Cooper Gallery, New York, NY; Brooke Alexander, Inc, New York, NY; Asher/Faure Gallery, Los Angeles, CA; Donald Young Gallery, Seattle, WA; Susanne Hilberry Gallery, Birmingham, MI; Betsy Senior Contemporary Prints, New York, NY; John Berggruen Gallery, San Francisco, CA; John C Stoller & Company, Minneapolis, MN; Brett Mitchell Collection, Cleveland, OH; Pace Prints, New York, NY; Lemberg Gallery, Birmingham, MI

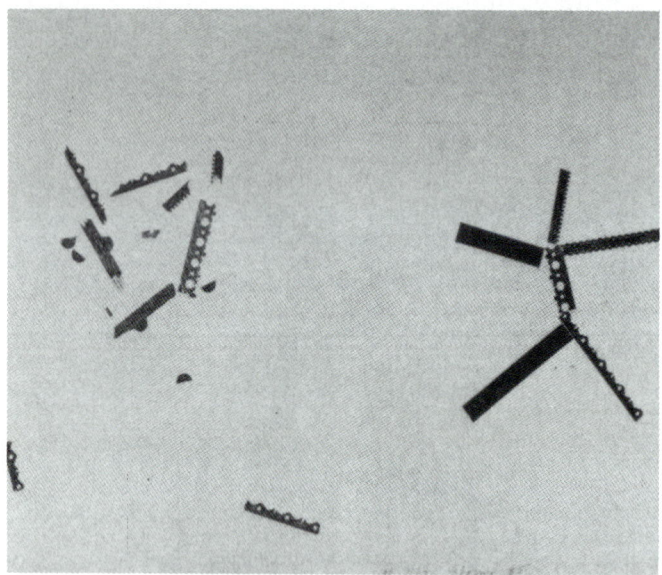

Joel Shapiro
Untitled
Courtesy Universal Limited Art Editions

Joel Shapiro
Untitled
Courtesy Grenfell Press

TITLE	PUBLISHER	PRINTER	DATE	MEDIUM	DIMENSION (PAPER SIZE) IN INCHES	TYPE OF PAPER	EDITION NUMBER	NO. OF COLORS	ORIGINAL OPENING PRICE	CURRENT RETAIL PRICE
SOLD OUT EDITIONS (RARE):										
Untitled (Set of 4)	ART	CM	1975	EC	13 X 18	FAB	7		800 SET	7500 SET
Untitled (Double Purple) (Catalogue #12)	PC/BAI	ART	1979–80	LC	29 X 41	HMP	30	2	750	3500
Untitled (Double Green) (Catalogue #8)	PC/BAI	ART	1979–80	LC	29 X 41	HMP	40	2	750	3500
Untitled (Double Red) (Catalogue #9)	PC/BAI	ART	1979–80	LC	29 X 41	HMP	30	2	750	3500
Untitled-First	ULAE	ULAE	1985	WC/CO	12 X 18	HMP	40		900	2000
Untitled-Second	ULAE	ULAE	1985	WC/CO	19 X 21	JWhat/1951	44		1200	2500
Untitled-Third	ULAE	ULAE	1985	WC/CO	17 X 14	JWhat/1956	41		1000	2000
Untitled	ULAE	ULAE	1985	LC/OFF/CO	17 X 14					
Untitled (Set of 3):										
Untitled I	GPr	LM/GPr	1987	WB	15 X 22	C-S	18	1	1000	2000
Untitled II	GPr	LM/GPr	1987	WB	15 X 22	C-S	26	1	900	2000
Untitled III	GPr	LM/GPr	1987	WB	15 X 22	C-S	27	1	1000	2000
CURRENT EDITIONS:										
Untitled (Black) (Catalogue #1)	PC/BAI	ART	1979	LB	36 X 30	HMP	40	1	750	1800
Untitled (Black) (Catalogue #2)	PC/BAI	ART	1979	LB	44 X 35	HMP	30	1	750	2000
Untitled (Black) (Catalogue #3)	PC/BAI	ART	1979	LB	37 X 43	HMP	30	1	650	2000
Untitled (Black) (Catalogue #4)	PC/BAI	ART	1979	LB	43 X 37	HMP	40	1	750	2500
Untitled (Black) (Catalogue #5)	PC/BAI	ART	1979	LB	37 X 42	HMP	30	1	750	2500
Untitled (Naples Yellow) (Catalogue #6)	PC/BAI	ART	1979–80	LC	22 X 30	HMP	36	2	600	1800
Untitled (Blue/Black) (Catalogue #7)	PC/BAI	ART	1979–80	LC	22 X 30	HMP	30	2	450	1500
Untitled (Black) (Catalogue #10)	PC/BAI	ART	1979–80	LB	22 X 30	HMP	30	1	450	1500
Untitled (Green) (Catalogue #11)	PC/BAI	ART	1979–80	LC	22 X 30	HMP	30	1	450	1500
Untitled 1980	SPA	ART	1980	SP	29 X 22	HMP	25		350	1500
Untitled	BAI	PB/A	1982	LC	37 X 54	HMP	15		600	3500
Untitled	BAI	PB/A	1982	LC	56 X 37	HMP	10		600	3500

JOEL SHAPIRO CONTINUED

TITLE	PUBLISHER	PRINTER	DATE	MEDIUM	DIMENSION (PAPER SIZE) IN INCHES	TYPE OF PAPER	EDITION NUMBER	NO. OF COLORS	ORIGINAL OPENING PRICE	CURRENT RETAIL PRICE
CURRENT EDITIONS:										
Untitled	GPr	LM/GPr	1989	LI	37 X 26	KOZO	28	3	2800	3000
Untitled	GPr	LM/GPr	1990	PO	44 X 31	SOM	36	2	3500	3800
Untitled (Set of 4)	AC	AC/AtC	1990	AB	37 X 28	HMP	60 EA	1 EA	25000 SET	25000 SET
									7500 EA	75 EA
Untitled	AC	AC/AtC	1992	EB/A	37 X 28	HAHN	60	1	3000	3000
Untitled	AC	AC/AtC	1992	EB	32 X 24	HAHN	60	1	3000	3000
Untitled	AC	AC/AtC	1992	EB	32 X 24	HAHN	60	1	3000	3000

ANNE SHARP

BORN: Red Bank, NJ; November 1, 1943
EDUCATION: Pratt Inst, Brooklyn, NY, BFA, 1965, with Richard Lindner; Brooklyn Col, NY, MFA, 1973, with Lee Bontecou
TEACHING: State Univ of New York, Purchase, NY, 1983; Sch of Visual Arts, NY, 1979 to present; Pratt Manhattan Center, NY, 1982 to present

RECENT EXHIB: Kendall Gallery, NY, 1988
COLLECTIONS: Albright-Knox Art Gallery, Buffalo, NY; Smithsonian Inst, Wash, DC
PRINTERS: Modern Classics Prints, NY (MCP); Screen Graphics, Maspeth, NY (SG); Artist (ART)
PUBLISHERS: Modern Classics Prints, NY (MCP); Artist (ART)
GALLERIES: Jack Tilton Gallery, New York, NY
MAILING ADDRESS: P O Box 100480, Anchorage, AK 99510-0480

TITLE	PUBLISHER	PRINTER	DATE	MEDIUM	DIMENSION (PAPER SIZE) IN INCHES	TYPE OF PAPER	EDITION NUMBER	NO. OF COLORS	ORIGINAL OPENING PRICE	CURRENT RETAIL PRICE
CURRENT EDITIONS:										
Marilyn Monroe I	ART	SG	1971	SP	30 X 30	VBP	150	5	75	375
The Dance	ART	ART	1964/74	WB	14 X 20	Rice	60	1	90	250
New York City Double Cloud	ART	ART	1974	CO	8 X 10	PLBP	10	4	90	800
Mrs America	ART	ART	1974	CO	8 X 10	PLBP	10	4	90	375
Double Surfer	ART	ART	1974	CO	24 X 36	AP	5	4	125	475
Life Guards	ART	ART	1974	MM	8 X 10	PLBP	10	4	90	270
USA Photo Dream	ART	ART	1974	MM	24 X 36	AP	5	4	125	450
Moon-Shot I, II	MCP	MCP/SG	1972/80	SP	24 X 24 EA	VBP	300 EA	5 EA	60 EA	350 EA
Artist's Hands	ART	ART	1980	MON	18 X 30	Rice	2	1	125	195

SUSAN SHATTER

BORN: New York, NY; January 17, 1943
EDUCATION: Skowhegan Sch of Painting and Sculpture, ME, 1964; Pratt Inst, NY, BFA, 1965; Boston Univ, MA, MFA, 1972
TEACHING: Univ of Pennsylvania, Phila, PA, 1974-75,79; Skowhegan Sch of Painting, ME, 1977,79; Bennington Col, VT, 1979; Sch of Visual Arts, NY, 1979; Parsons Sch of Design, NY, 1980; Tyler Sch of Art, Phila, PA, 1985; Univ of Pennsylvania, Phila, PA, 1983-85; San Francisco Art Inst, CA, 1989; Brooklyn Col, NY, 1991-92
AWARDS: Massachusetts Creative Artists Humanities Grant, 1975; Radcliffe Inst Fel, Boston, MA, 1975-76; Ingram-Merrill Found Grant, NY, 1976; New York State Found Grant, 1985; Nat Endowment for the Arts Grants, 1980,87
RECENT EXHIB: Aldrich Mus of Contemp Art, Ridgefield, CT, 1986-87; Heath Gallery, Atlanta, GA, 1987; Newport Art Mus, RI, 1987; Harcus Gallery, Boston, MA, 1987,89; Fischbach Gallery, NY, 1987,88,91,93
COLLECTIONS: Boston Mus of Fine Arts, MA; Univ of Utah Mus, Salt Lake City, UT; Philadelphia Art Mus, PA; Currier Mus, Manchester, NH; Dartmouth Col, Hanover, NH, Art Inst of Chicago, IL

PRINTERS: Judith Solodkin, NY (JS); Solo Press, NY (SP); Condeso & Brokopp Studio, NY (CBS); Nancy Brokopp, NY (NB); Chip Elwell, NY (CE); Wil Foo, San Francisco, CA (WF); John Stemmer, San Francisco, CA (JS); Experimental Workshop, San Francisco, CA (EW); Maurice Sanchez, NY (MS); Orlando Condeso, NY (OC); Bud Shark, Boulder, CO (BS); Shark's, Inc, Boulder, CO (SI)
PUBLISHERS: 724 Prints, NY (724P); Diane Villani Editions, NY (DVE); van Straaten Gallery, Chicago, IL (VS); Getler/Saper Gallery, NY (GS); Experimental Workshop, San Francisco, CA (EW); Mt Holyoke Col (MH); Smith Col (SC); Orlando Condeso, NY (OC); Artist (ART); Shark's, Inc, Boulder, CO (SI)
GALLERIES: Fischbach Gallery, New York, NY; Roger Ramsay, Chicago, IL; Diane Villani Editions, New York, NY; van Straaten Gallery, Chicago, IL; Harcus Gallery, Boston, MA; Betsy Senior Gallery, New York, NY; Maurice Sanchez, New York, NY; Condeso/Lawler Gallery, New York, NY; Shark's, Inc, Boulder, CO; Quartet Editions, New York, NY
MAILING ADDRESS: 26 W 20th St, New York, NY 10011

TITLE	PUBLISHER	PRINTER	DATE	MEDIUM	DIMENSION (PAPER SIZE) IN INCHES	TYPE OF PAPER	EDITION NUMBER	NO. OF COLORS	ORIGINAL OPENING PRICE	CURRENT RETAIL PRICE
SOLD OUT EDITIONS (RARE):										
Terrace Tilt	724P	NB	1980	A/EB	18 X 41	R/BFK	50	4	500	750
Prout's Neck	724P	NB	1981	A/EB	20 X 47	R/BFK	50	4	700	900
CURRENT EDITIONS:										
Rock Face/Zion Canyon	DVE	JS/SP	1981	LC	32 X 43	AGP	80	7	750	900
Vertigo	724P	NB/CBS	1983	A/EB	18 X 41	R/BFK	40	5	900	1000
Aquarhythms	VS/GS	CE	1984	PO	29 X 40	AP/300	40	14	500	750
Sea Arch	EW	WF/JS/EW	1986	WC	55 X 37	R/BFK	50	23	1500	1800
Canyon Rose	SI	BS/SI	1988	LC	23 X 45	AC	30	10	1200	1400
Suite of Four:									2000 SET	2000 SET
Canyon	MH/SC	MS	1989	LC/OFF	22 X 30	R/BFK	25	1	600	600
Desert	MH/SC	MS	1989	LC/OFF	22 X 30	R/BFK	25	1	600	600
Sea Coast	MH/SC	MS	1989	LC/OFF	22 X 30	R/BFK	25	1	600	600
Sculptured Land	MH/SC	MS	1989	LC/OFF	22 X 30	R/BFK	25	1	600	600
Glacial Light	OC/ART	OC	1991	A	23 X 27	LANA	35	5	900	900

CAMERON SHAW

PRINTERS: Mercantile Printing (MP); Robert Townsend, Georgetown, MA (RT)

PUBLISHERS: Daniel Elias, Lincoln, MA (DE)
GALLERIES: Barbara Krakow Gallery, Boston, MA

TITLE	PUBLISHER	PRINTER	DATE	MEDIUM	DIMENSION (PAPER SIZE) IN INCHES	TYPE OF PAPER	EDITION NUMBER	NO. OF COLORS	ORIGINAL OPENING PRICE	CURRENT RETAIL PRICE
CURRENT EDITIONS:										
Untitled with New York Times and Katzenjammer Page	DE	RT/MP	1992	LC/OFF/CO	21 X 16	CougP	35	4	550	550

RICHARD BLAKE SHAW

BORN: Hollywood, CA; September 12, 1941
EDUCATION: Orange Coast Col, Costa Mesa, CA, 1961–63; San Francisco Art Inst, BFA, 1965; State Univ of New York, Alfred, NY, 1965; Univ of California, Davis, CA, MFA, 1968
TEACHING: Chmn, Ceramics Dept, San Francisco Art Inst, CA, 1965 to present; Faculty, Univ of Wisconsin, WI, Summer, 1971
AWARDS: Nat Endowment for the Arts Fel, 1970; Nat Arts & Crafts Grant, 1974
RECENT EXHIB: Sun Valley Center Gallery, Boise, ID, 1988; Scottsdale, AZ, 1989; California State Univ, Chico Univ Art Gallery, CA, 1989; Frumkin/Adams Gallery, NY, 1990; Redding Mus, CA, 1992; Univ of Connecticut, Atrium Gallery, Storrs, CT, 1992; Southern Oregon State Col, Schneider Mus, Ashland, OR, 1992

COLLECTIONS: Oakland Mus, Oakland, CA; San Francisco Mus of Mod Art, CA; Nat Mus of Mod Art, Tokyo, Japan; Stedelijk Mus, Amsterdam, Holland; Whitney Mus of Am Art, NY; Smithsonian Inst, Wash, DC; Univ of New Mexico, Albuquerque, NM; Minneapolis Inst of Art, MN; Univ of Southern California, Los Angeles, CA; Honolulu Acad of Art, HI; Univ of Texas, Austin, TX
PUBLISHERS: Ernest De Soto Workshop, San Francisco, CA (EDSW)
PRINTERS: Ernest F De Soto, San Francisco, CA (EDS); Ernest De Soto Workshop, San Francisco, CA (EDSW)
GALLERIES: Ernest De Soto Workshop, San Francisco, CA; Braunstein-Quay Gallery, San Francisco, CA; Helander Gallery, Palm Beach, FL
MAILING ADDRESS: PO Box 88, Prince Street Station, New York, NY 10012

TITLE	PUBLISHER	PRINTER	DATE	MEDIUM	DIMENSION (PAPER SIZE) IN INCHES	TYPE OF PAPER	EDITION NUMBER	NO. OF COLORS	ORIGINAL OPENING PRICE	CURRENT RETAIL PRICE
CURRENT EDITIONS:										
Hard Luck	EDSW	EDS/EDSW	1983	LC	23 X 31	AP/W	100	7	500	800

JUDITH SHEA

BORN: Philadelphia, PA; November 13, 1948
EDUCATION: Parsons Sch of Design, NY, 1969; The New Sch for Social Research, Parson Sch, NY, BFA, 1975
TEACHING: Instr, Parsons Sch of Design, NY, 1979–86; Instr, New York Univ, NY, 1980–86
RECENT EXHIB: Albright-Knox Art Gallery, Buffalo, NY, 1987; Contemp Art Center, Cincinnati, OH, 1987; Barbara Krakow Gallery, Boston, MA, 1987; La Jolla Mus of Contemp Art, 1988; Nelson-Atkins Mus of Art, Kansas City, MO, 1989; Editions Ilene Kurtz, NY, 1989; Greenberg Gallery, St. Louis, MO, 1990; Univ of Massachusetts, Amherst, MA, 1992; John Berggruen Gallery, San Francisco, CA, 1992–93
COLLECTIONS: Neuberger Mus, State Univ of New York Col, Purchase, NY; Dallas Mus of Fine Art, TX; Walker Art Center, Minneapolis, MN; Hayden Gallery, Massachusetts Inst of Tech, Cambridge, MA; Pennsylvania Acad of Fine Arts, Phila, PA; Albright-Knox Gallery, Buffalo, NY
PRINTERS: Harlan & Weaver Intaglio, NY (H/WI)
PUBLISHERS: Editions Ilene Kurtz, NY (EIK); Betsy Senior Contemporary Prints, NY (BSCP)
GALLERIES: Barbara Krakow, Boston, MA; Editions Ilene Kurtz, New York, NY; Hank Baum Gallery, San Francisco, CA; Max Protetch Gallery, New York, NY; Betsy Senior Contemporary Prints, New York, NY; John Berggruen Gallery, San Francisco, CA
MAILING ADDRESS: 124 Chambers St, New York, NY 10007

Judith Shea
Venus
Courtesy Betsy Senior Contemporary Prints

TITLE	PUBLISHER	PRINTER	DATE	MEDIUM	DIMENSION (PAPER SIZE) IN INCHES	TYPE OF PAPER	EDITION NUMBER	NO. OF COLORS	ORIGINAL OPENING PRICE	CURRENT RETAIL PRICE
CURRENT EDITIONS:										
Torso (Composite Stone Multiple with Pedestal)	EIK		1986	MULT	52 X 15 X 12	STONE	12	6	6000	7500
Venus	BSCP	H/WI	1990	EB/SG	37 X 27	SOM	30	1	1500	1500

The retail prices of the 100,000 limited edition prints quoted in this directory are subject to change. Print publishers, artists and galleries were the direct sources for these quotations. Prices in the secondary market listed as "Sold Out Editions (Rare)" indicate that the publisher has a limited supply of that print or that the print is difficult to locate in the galleries.

LAURA J SHECHTER

BORN: Brooklyn, NY; August 25, 1944
EDUCATION: Brooklyn Col, NY, BFA, 1965
TEACHING: Instr, Parsons Sch of Design, NY, 1984; Inst, Nat Acad of Design, NY, 1985–88
AWARDS: Graphics Award, Brooklyn Col, NY, 1965; Creative Artists Public Service Fel, 1981–82
RECENT EXHIB: Rahr-West Art Mus, Manitowoc, WI, 1991; Univ of Richmond, VA, 1991; Katharina Rich Perlow Gallery, NY 1991
COLLECTIONS: Brooklyn Mus, NY; Boston Mus of Fine Arts, MA; Indianapolis Mus of Fine Art, IN; Carnegie Inst Art Mus, Pittsburgh, PA; Jewish Mus, NY; Art Inst of Chicago, IL; Albright-Knox Art Gallery, Buffalo, NY; Art Inst of Chicago, IL
PRINTERS: Echo Press, Bloomington, IN (EP); Solo Press, NY (SP); Burston Graphics Center, Jerusalem, Israel (BGC); Pratt Graphics Center, NY (PGC); Jim Martin, NY (JM); David Keister (DK); Christopher Lachy (CL); David Calkins (DC)
PUBLISHERS: GW Einstein Co, Inc, NY (GWE); Kathryn Markel, NY (KM); Forum Gallery Press, NY (FGP); Echo Press, Bloomington, IN (EP); Israel Mus, Jerusalem, Israel (IM); Pratt Graphics Center, NY (PGC)
GALLERIES: Katharina Rich Perlow Gallery, New York, NY
MAILING ADDRESS: 429 Fourth St, Brooklyn, NY 11215

TITLE	PUBLISHER	PRINTER	DATE	MEDIUM	DIMENSION (PAPER SIZE) IN INCHES	TYPE OF PAPER	EDITION NUMBER	NO. OF COLORS	ORIGINAL OPENING PRICE	CURRENT RETAIL PRICE
SOLD OUT EDITIONS (RARE):										
Still Life with Dried Flowers	IM	BGC	1982	LB	15 X 14	R/BFK	32	1	150	300
CURRENT EDITIONS:										
28 Objects	GWE	SP	1978	LB	22 X 30	R/BFK	50	1	175	400
Porcelain and Glass	KM	EP	1982	LC	22 X 30	R/BFK	50	5	350	500
Objects on Draped Cloths	FGP	SP	1982	LC	23 X 15	R/BFK	90	5	375	600
Still Life on a Fireplace	EP	DK/CL/DC	1983	LC/HC	22 X 29	AP/B	30	17	400	500
Still Life with a Broken Bottle	EP	EP	1983	LB	11 X 12	R/BFK	20	1	100	250
Still Life on a Red Velvet Cloth	PGC	JM/PGC	1984	LB	19 X 15	R/BFK	38	1	150	300

STUART SHEDLETSKY

BORN: New York, NY; May 19, 1944
EDUCATION: Parsons Sch of Design, NY, 1964–65; Univ of New Mexico, MFA, 1967; Yale Univ, New Haven, CT, BFA, 1969
TEACHING: Parsons Sch of Design, NY, 1969 to present; Pratt Inst, NY, 1969–71
COLLECTIONS: Whitney Mus of Am Art, NY
PRINTERS: Chip Elwell, NY (CE)
PUBLISHERS: Barbara Gladstone Editions, NY (BGE)
GALLERIES: Linda Durham Gallery, Santa Fe, NM; Michael Leonard & Associates, Inc, New York, NY

TITLE	PUBLISHER	PRINTER	DATE	MEDIUM	DIMENSION (PAPER SIZE) IN INCHES	TYPE OF PAPER	EDITION NUMBER	NO. OF COLORS	ORIGINAL OPENING PRICE	CURRENT RETAIL PRICE
CURRENT EDITIONS:										
Maritime I, II, III (Set of 3)	BGE	CE	1980	PO	48 X 36 EA	AC	40 EA	1 EA	1200 SET / 400 EA	1800 SET / 600 EA

MILLARD OWEN SHEETS

BORN: Pomona, CA; June 24, 1907
EDUCATION: Chouinard Art Inst, Los Angeles, CA, 1928; Otis Art Inst, Los Angeles, CA, Hon, MFA, 1963; Univ of Notre Dame, South Bend, IN, Hon LLD, 1964
TEACHING: Chouinard Art Inst, Los Angeles, CA, 1928–35; Head, Dept of Art, Scripps Col, Claremont, CA, 1932–55; Dir, Otis Art Inst, Los Angeles, CA, 1953–59; Prof, Scripps Col, Claremont, CA, 1931 to present
AWARDS: Purchase Prize, Art Inst of Chicago, IL; Purchase Prize, Nat Watercolor Soc; Purchase Prize, Philadelphia Watercolor Soc
COLLECTIONS: Metropolitan Mus, NY; Whitney Mus of Am Art, NY; Los Angeles Mus, CA; Nat Mus of Am Art, Wash, DC; Smithsonian Mus, Wash, DC
PRINTERS: Artist (ART)
PUBLISHERS: Circle Fine Art, Chicago, IL (CFA)
GALLERIES: Kennedy Gallery, New York, NY; Circle Galleries, San Diego, CA & San Francisco, CA & Northbrook, IL & Pittsburgh, PA & Houston, TX & Soho, NY & Chicago, IL & Scottsdale, AZ & Beverly Hills, CA & Costa Mesa, CA & Sherman Oaks, CA & Palm Beach, FL & Honolulu, HI & New Orleans, LA & Las Vegas, NV & Seattle, WA; Atelier Dore, Inc, San Francisco, CA; El Presidio Galleries, Sonoma, CA
MAILING ADDRESS: 34800 South Highway, One Barking Rocks, Gualala, CA 95445

TITLE	PUBLISHER	PRINTER	DATE	MEDIUM	DIMENSION (PAPER SIZE) IN INCHES	TYPE OF PAPER	EDITION NUMBER	NO. OF COLORS	ORIGINAL OPENING PRICE	CURRENT RETAIL PRICE
SOLD OUT EDITIONS (RARE):										
Shrimp Boats	CFA	ART	1979	SP	27 X 35	SOM	250		175	775
Going to Market	CFA	ART	1979	SP	24 X 36	SOM	250		175	900
Old Village France	CFA	ART	1980	LC	24 X 27	AP	250		200	775
Fields	CFA		1980	LC	23 X 35	AP	250		200	900
Brood Mare Pasture	CFA	ART	1980	LC	29 X 39	AP	250		200	775
Summer Gold	CFA	ART	1980	LC	35 X 24	AP	250		200	775

MORI SHIZUME

BORN: Tokyo, Japan; 1928
EDUCATION: Univ of San Francisco, CA; Stanford Univ, CA; California Sch of Fine Arts, Los Angeles, CA; Ecole des Beaux Arts, Paris, France, 1963
PRINTERS: Serigraphics, Houston, TX (S)
PUBLISHERS: Post Oak Fine Art Distributors, Houston, TX (POFA)

TITLE	PUBLISHER	PRINTER	DATE	MEDIUM	DIMENSION (PAPER SIZE) IN INCHES	TYPE OF PAPER	EDITION NUMBER	NO. OF COLORS	ORIGINAL OPENING PRICE	CURRENT RETAIL PRICE
SOLD OUT EDITIONS (RARE):										
Venice	POFA	S	1981	SP	22 X 30	AP	200	18	250	350
New York Scenes, #1–#6 (Set of 6)	POFA	S	1981	SP	30 X 18 EA	R/BFK	210 EA	20 EA	975 SET	1800 SET

CINDY SHERMAN

BORN: Glen Ridge, NJ; 1954
EDUCATION: New York State Univ, Buffalo, NY, BA, 1976
RECENT EXHIB: Whitney Mus of Am Art, NY, 1987; Inst of Contemp Art, Boston, MA, 1987; Dallas Mus of Fine Art, TX, 1987; HoffmanBorman Gallery, Los Angeles, CA, 1987; Provinciaal Mus, Hasselt, Belgium, 1987; La Maquina Española, Madrid, Spain, 1988; Lia Rumma Gallery, Naples, Italy, 1988; Monika Sprath Galerie, Cologne, West Germany, 1988; Studio Guenzani, Milan, Italy, 1988; Galerie Pierre Hubert, Geneva, Switzerland, 1989; Galerie der Wiener Secession, Vienna, Austria, 1989; Galerie Crousel-Robelin, Paris, France, 1989; Nat Art Gallery, Wellington, New Zealand, 1989; Kent Gallery, NY, 1989; Linda Cathcart Gallery, Santa Monica, CA, 1990; Metro Pictures, NY, 1987,88,90; San Jose Mus of Art, CA, 1992; Sonoma State Univ, Rohnert Park, CA, 1992; Contemp Arts Center, Cincinnati, OH, 1992; Metro Pictures, New York, NY, 1992
COLLECTIONS: Mus of Mod Art, NY; Brooklyn Mus, NY; Metropolitan Mus of Art, NY; Tate Gallery, London, England; Centre Georges Pompidou, Paris, France; Stedelijk Mus, Amsterdam, Netherlands; Australian Nat Gallery, Canberra, Australia; Baltimore Mus of Art, MD; San Francisco Mus of Mod Art, CA; Walker Art Center, Minneapolis, MN; Mus of Fine Arts, Houston, TX; Dallas Mus of Fine Arts, TX; Albright-Knox Art Gallery, Buffalo, NY; Mus Boymans-van-Beuningen, Rotterdam, Netherlands; Rijksmuseum Kroller-Muller, Otterlo, Netherlands; Akron Art Mus, OH; St Louis Art Mus, MO; Louisiana Mus, Humlebaek, Denmark; Allen Mem Art Mus, Oberlin, OH; Rose Art Mus, Brandeis Univ, Waltham, MA; Hayden Gallery, Massachusetts Inst of Tech, Cambridge, MA; George Eastman House, NY; Power Gallery of Contemporary Art, Univ of Sydney, Australia; High Mus, Atlanta, GA; Univ of Kentucky Art Mus, Lexington, KY; Mus Folkwang, Essen, West Germany; Philadelphia Art Mus, PA; Mus d'Art Contemporain, Montreal, Canada; Carnegie Inst, Pittsburgh, PA; Milwaukee Art Mus, WI; Contemp Arts Mus, Chicago, IL; Tamayo Mus, Mexico City, Mexico; Wadsworth Atheneum, Hartford, CT; Portland Art Mus, Portland, OR; Eli Broad Found, Los Angeles, CA; Saatchi Coll, London, England; Art Gallery of New South Wales, Australia; Art Inst of Chicago, IL; Victoria and Albert Mus, London, England; Mälmo Konsthall, Sweden; Art Gallery of Ontario, Ottawa, Canada; Burchfield Art Center, Buffalo, NY; Corcoran Gallery of Art, Wash, DC; International Center of Photography, NY; Moderna Museet, Stockholm, Sweden; Yale Univ Art Gallery, New Haven, CT; Kunsthaus, Zürich, Switzerland; Tampa Mus, Norfolk, VA; Everson Mus, Syracuse, NY
PRINTERS: Ultimate Image, NY (UIm); Foto-Labor Knoblich, Munich, Germany (FLK); Artist (ART)
PUBLISHERS: Editions Schellmann, Cologne, Germany & New York, NY (ES); Galerie Bernd Klüser, Munich, Germany (GBK);

Cindy Sherman
Untitled, 1989
Courtesy Edition Schellmann

Monika Spruth Galerie, Cologne, West Germany; Linda Cathcart Gallery, Santa Monica, CA; Galerie Pierre Hubert, Geneva, Switzerland; Galerie Crousel-Robelin, Paris, France; Thomas Erben Gallery, Inc, New York, NY; Artes Magnus, New York, NY; Rhona Hoffman Gallery, Chicago, IL
GALLERIES: Metro Pictures, New York, NY; Edition Schellmann, New York, NY & Cologne, Germany; Lia Rumma Gallery, Naples, Italy

TITLE	PUBLISHER	PRINTER	DATE	MEDIUM	DIMENSION (PAPER SIZE) IN INCHES	TYPE OF PAPER	EDITION NUMBER	NO. OF COLORS	ORIGINAL OPENING PRICE	CURRENT RETAIL PRICE
SOLD OUT EDITIONS (RARE):										
Untitled #123 (The Swimmer)			1983	PH/C	35 X 24	EKC	18		2500	10000
Untitled	ES/GBK	UIM	1986	PH/C	32 X 24	EKC	90		3000	5000
Untitled			1987	PH/C	72 X 48		6		3500	15000
CURRENT EDITIONS:										
Untitled (Electrical Light Box with Two Color Transparencies) (When Box is Not Lit, Only One Transparency is Seen; When Box is Lit, Both Transparencies are Seen)	ES	FLK	1989	MULT/PH	34 X 24 X 4		24		7500	15000

Z CHARLOTTE SHERMAN

BORN: Los Angeles, CA; June 18, 1924
EDUCATION: Kahn Art Inst; Univ of California, Los Angeles, CA; Otis Art Inst, Los Angeles, CA
TEACHING: Los Angeles Cultural Art Ctr, CA
AWARDS: Phelan Awards; Los Angeles Municipal Art Mus, CA; Beaux Arts Rome, Italy; Sao Paulo, Biennial; Pasadena Mus; Grand Pris Int, Paris, France
RECENT EXHIB: Heritage Gallery, Los Angeles, CA, 1987,88,89,90,91,91

COLLECTIONS: Palm Springs Mus, CA; Los Angeles Municipal Mus, CA; Brand Library Gallery, Glendale, CA; Riverside Mus of Art, CA; Laguna Art Mus, CA; Vincent Price Collection, Los Angeles, CA
PRINTERS: Artist (ART)
PUBLISHERS: Collier Fine Art (CFA); Heritage Gallery, Los Angeles, CA (HG)
GALLERIES: Heritage Gallery, Los Angeles, CA
MAILING ADDRESS: 1300 Chautauqua Blvd, Pacific Palisades, CA 90272

The print market has become very selective. For the first time since we published the first edition of The Printworld Directory in 1982, the prices of prints have been greatly reduced and greatly increased for the same artists by the most reputable and established print publishers. Check the fifth edition to understand the movement.

Z CHARLOTTE SHERMAN CONTINUED

TITLE	PUBLISHER	PRINTER	DATE	MEDIUM	DIMENSION (PAPER SIZE) IN INCHES	TYPE OF PAPER	EDITION NUMBER	NO. OF COLORS	ORIGINAL OPENING PRICE	CURRENT RETAIL PRICE
SOLD OUT EDITIONS (RARE):										
Three Images of Jacob	CFA	ART	1973	EB	12 X 18	AP	25	1	200	300
Cosmic Focus	CFA	ART	1973	COL	11 X 13	AP	20	1	175	275
Squared Earth	CFA	ART	1974	COL	10 X 6	AP	18	1	100	250
Jerusalem-triptych	CFA	ART	1974	EB	4 X 14	AP	25	1	100	275
Elijah Wrestling with Angels	CFA	ART	1977	EB	12 X 10	AP	25	1	100	350
A Just Balance and Scales	CFA	ART	1977	I	5 X 14	AP	25	1	100	500
Cosmos	CFA	ART	1978	COL	9 X 16	AP	30	1	150	400
Tide Pool	CFA	ART	1980	EC	9 X 12	AP	20	2	150	350
Ascent #1	CFA	ART	1980	SP	22 X 16	AP	20	8	200	400
Ascent #2	CFA	ART	1980	SP	18 X 23	AP	20	8	250	450
Jacob Wrestling with Angels	CFA	ART	1980	EC	18 X 12	AP	200	2	100	300
Stream Orchis Variation	CFA	ART	1980	SP	19 RD	AP	20	9	250	450
Great Horned Owl	CFA	ART	1980	LC	19 X 24	AP	325	10	300	500
CURRENT EDITIONS:										
Hills of Judeah	CFA	ART	1980	EC	9 X 12	AP	20	3	150	300
Eagle's Flight	CFA	ART	1980	EC	9 X 12	AP	15	1	100	200
Nocturne	CFA	ART	1980	LC	20 X 16	AP	325	2	150	200
Wave Motion, #1,#2	HG	ART	1982	CV	12 X 16 EA	AP	20 EA	5 EA	200 EA	300 EA
Inner Garden, #1,#2	HG	ART	1982	CV	12 X 16 EA	AC	20 EA	5 EA	200 EA	350 EA
Summer Pond	HG	ART	1983	CV	16 X 12	AP	20	5	200	300
Pond Lily	HG	ART	1983	CV	20 X 16	AP	25	5	200	300
Mountain on High	HG	ART	1984	EC	16 X 29	AP	20	4	150	200
Blue Flight (oval)	HG	ART	1985	SP	16 X 22	R/BFK	25	12	250	250
Morning's Flight	HG	ART	1988	SP	16 X 22	R/BFK	50	11	300	350
Passion Flower	HG	ART	1988	SP	24 X 19	AP	35	8	400	450
Mountain Pond	HG	ART	1989	SP	22 X 16	AP	35	10	300	350
Earth Focus #1, #2	HG	ART	1990	CV	20 X 16	AP	20	5	200	300
Mountains on High	HG	ART	1990	LC	20 X 24	R/BFK	100	10	300	450
Moving Coast	HG	ART	1991	SP	18 X 24	AP	75	10	300	350
Myth of the Mountain	HG	ART	1992	SP	20 X 24	AP	25	12	300	400

PHILIP LAWRENCE SHERROD

BORN: Pauls Valley, OK; October 12, 1935
EDUCATION: Oklahoma State Univ, OK, BS, 1957; BFA, 1959; Art Students League, NY, 1960–62
TEACHING: Instr, Color & Design, Oklahoma State Univ, Oklahoma City, OK, 1959; Asst Prof, Painting, Art Students League, NY, 1960; Instr, Morristown Art Assn, NJ, 1973–74; Instr, Painting, Art Students League, NY, 1984–86; Instr, New Jersey Center for the Visual Arts, NJ, 1977–90; Instr, Art Students League, NY, 1984–90
AWARDS: Art Students League, NY, 1960; Am Acad of Arts and Letters, Childe Hassam Purchase, 1967,69,74; Creative Artists Public Service Grant, 1980; Adolphe/Esther Gottlieb Found Grant, 1981,88; Pollock-Krasner Found Grant, NY, 1989
RECENT EXHIB: Nat Acad of Design, NY, 1988
COLLECTIONS: Tulane Univ Mus, New Orleans, LA; Everhart Mus, Scranton, PA; Almsford House, Fine Arts Center, Anderson, IN; Rose Art Mus, Brandeis Univ, Waltham, MA; Herbert Johnson Gallery, Cornell Univ, Ithaca, NY; Mus of Fine Art, Springfield, MA; Smithsonian Inst, Wash, DC; Hirshhorn Mus, Wash, DC
PRINTERS: Artist (ART)
PUBLISHERS: Artist (ART)
GALLERIES: Allan Stone Gallery, New York, NY; Susan Montezinos Gallery, Phila, PA
MAILING ADDRESS: 41 W 24th St, 4th Floor, New York, NY 10010

TITLE	PUBLISHER	PRINTER	DATE	MEDIUM	DIMENSION (PAPER SIZE) IN INCHES	TYPE OF PAPER	EDITION NUMBER	NO. OF COLORS	ORIGINAL OPENING PRICE	CURRENT RETAIL PRICE
CURRENT EDITIONS:										
Bona-Fide Death at U-Haul University	ART	ART	1974	EB	5 X 5	AP	50	1	300	350
Nixo Gene (War)	ART	ART	1974	EB	9 X 6	AP	50	1	400	450
Princess Oceana (East Hampton)	ART	ART	1974	EB	9 X 10	AP	50	1	800	850
Cigar-Christ at Absurd V Mass	ART	ART	1974	EB	3 X 18	AP	50	1	555	600
My Cowkiss!!	ART	ART	1974	EB	2 X 2	AP	50	1	100	200
Susan with Dress Up!	ART	ART	1975	EB	7 X 8	AP	50	1	400	450
Puntar's Payment (Set of 11)	ART	ART	1976	EB	7 X 8 EA	AP	50 EA	1 EA	400 EA	450 EA
Cat Woman of Houston St	ART	ART	1976	EB	5 X 5	AP	50	1	300	350
Coke-Cola Cigar-Christ	ART	ART	1977	EB	5 X 4	R/BFK	50	1	250	300
Helena of Pudena (Doing Palmas)	ART	ART	1977	EB	6 X 5	R/BFK	50	1	350	400
Monnie 50 Hea	ART	ART	1979	EB	5 X 8	R/BFK	50	1	475	500
Federer's 12 Gauge 6-½ Shot	ART	ART	1978	EB	5 X 5	R/BFK	50	1	250	300
Lemoa	ART	ART	1980	EB	2 X 2	R/BFK	50	1	225	250
Woman Squatting	ART	ART	1980	EB	2 X 2	R/BFK	50	1	100	150

The retail prices of the 100,000 limited edition prints quoted in this directory are subject to change. Print publishers, artists and galleries were the direct sources for these quotations. Prices in the secondary market listed as "Sold Out Editions (Rare)" indicate that the publisher has a limited supply of that print or that the print is difficult to locate in the galleries.

The Printworld Directory is accepting new applications for the seventh edition. Approximately 300 new artists will be accepted. Please use the two forms provided in the back section of this directory to submit biographical data and documentation of prints. Edition number of each print must not exceed 500 and the retail price must be $100 or more.

ALAN J SHIELDS

BORN: Harrington, KS; February 4, 1944
EDUCATION: Kansas State Univ, Manhattan, KS
AWARDS: Guggenheim Fel, 1973
RECENT EXHIB: Memphis Brooks Mus, TN, 1987; Paula Cooper Gallery, NY, 1987; Cleveland Center for Contemp Art, OH, Retrosp, 1988; Hartford Art Sch, CT, 1988; New Jersey Center for Visual Arts, Summit, NJ, 1988; Kalamazoo Inst of Arts, MI, 1988; James Madison Univ, Sawhill Gallery, Harrisonburg, VA, 1992; James Madison Univ, Sawhill Gallery, Harrisonburg, VA, 1988,92
COLLECTIONS: Mus of Mod Art, NY; Guggenheim Mus, NY; Whitney Mus of Am Art, NY; Chicago Art Inst, IL; Philadelphia Mus of Art, PA; Hirshhorn Mus, Wash, DC; Oberlin Col, OH; Aldrich Mus of Contemp Art, Ridgefield, CT; Art Inst of Akron, OH
PRINTERS: Tyler Graphics, Ltd, Mount Kisco, NY (TGL); Jones Road Print Shop & Stable (JRPS); Hartford Art Sch, CT (HAS); Shenanigan Press (SP); Joe Wilfer, NY (JW); Ruth Lingen, NY (RL); Spring Street Workshop, NY (SprSW); Bill Weege, Madison, WI (BW); Andrew Rubin, Madison, WI (AR); Tandem Press, Madison, WI (TanPr); Artist (ART); Karen Stahlecker, Anchorage, AK (KS); Rodney Konopaki, Anchorage, AK (RK); Artist (ART); Visual Arts Center, Anchorage, AK (VAC); Lee Funderburg, NY (LF); Scott Lewis, NY (SL); Michael Mueller, NY (MM)
PUBLISHERS: Tyler Graphics, Ltd, Mount Kisco, NY (TGL); Jones Road Print Shop & Stable Barneveld, WI (JRPS); Omar Space Corp, NY (OSC); Hartford Art Sch, CT (HAS); Lincoln Center, NY (LC); Spring Street Workshop, NY (SprSW); Tandem Press, Madison, WI (TanPr); Artist (ART); Visual Arts Center, Anchorage, AK (VAC)
GALLERIES: Paula Cooper Gallery, New York, NY; Thomas Segal Gallery, Boston, MA; Dorry Gates Gallery, Kansas City, MO; Heath Gallery, Atlanta, GA; I Irving Feldman Galleries, West Bloomfield, MI; New Jersey Center for Visual Arts, Summit, NJ; Cleveland Center for Contemporary Art, Cleveland, OH; Pace Prints, New York, NY; Sylvia Cordish Fine Art, Baltimore, MD; Alice Simsar Gallery, Ann Arbor, MI; Tyler Graphics, Mount Kisco, NY; Sigrid Freundorfer Fine Art, New York, NY
MAILING ADDRESS: PO Box 1554, Shelter Island, NY 11964

Tyler (T)

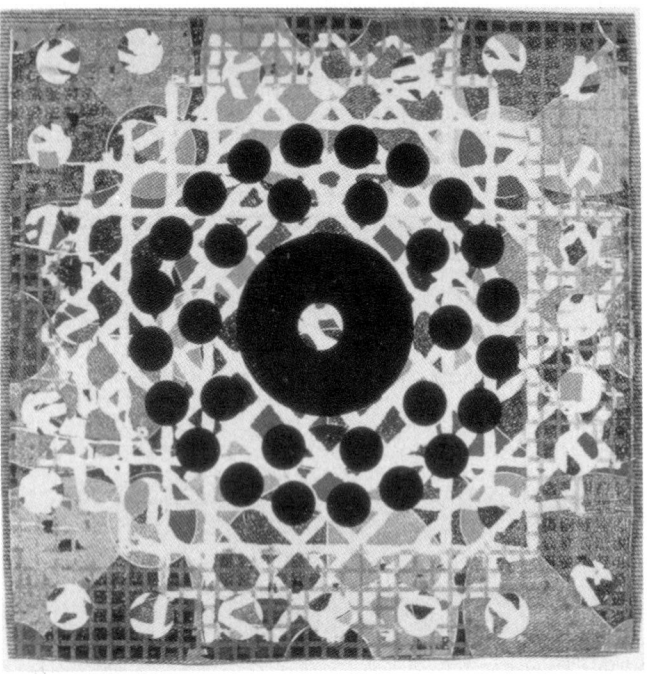

Alan J Shields
Dragonfly Chips Series: Edna
Courtesy Tandem Press

Alan J Shields
Soft and Fluffy Gears Series: Thinning Twin
Courtesy Tandem Press

TITLE	PUBLISHER	PRINTER	DATE	MEDIUM	DIMENSION (PAPER SIZE) IN INCHES	TYPE OF PAPER	EDITION NUMBER	NO. OF COLORS	ORIGINAL OPENING PRICE	CURRENT RETAIL PRICE
SOLD OUT EDITIONS (RARE):										
Sun Moon Title Page (2 Sided)	JRPS/OCS	JRPS	1971	SP/CO	26 X 26	HMP	100		300	3500
Dish #8	JRPS/OCS	JRPS	1974	SP	20 DIA	HMP	11		350	3000
Chicken Shit	JRPS/OCS	JRPS	1974	SP	14 X 14	HMP	20		350	3000
Spruce	JRPS/OCS	JRPS	1976	SP	10 X 10	HMP	20		250	2000
Fan Dance	JRPS/OCS	JRPS	1977	LC/SP	17 X 22	HMP	18	2	450	3000
Two Four Too (2 Sided)			1978	WB/EMB	21 X 20	HMP	20		800	2500
Sea City (2 Sided)	JRPS/OCS	JRPS	1978	SP/EMB	25 X 25	HMP	21		800	3000
Liquid Plumber's Revenge	JRPS/OCS	JRPS	1978	EMB	21 X 21	HMP	15		600	2000
TV Rerun-A (with Silverleaf)	TGL	TGL	1978	EMB/LI	10 DIA	TGL/HMP	10	8	400	2000
TV Rerun-B	TGL	TGL	1978	EMB/MEZ/DPT	10 DIA	TGL/HMP	10	10	400	2000
TV Rerun-C	TGL	TGL	1978	EMB/MEZ/DPT	10 DIA	TGL/HMP	10	17	400	2000
Armie's Tough Course	TGL	ART	1978	IC	22 X 21	TGL/HMP	8	22	600	3500
Rickshaw Radar (on Three Sheets)	TGL	TGL	1980	EB/A/REL	25 X 71	CHIRI	5		800	4000
Hazel's Witch Hat (Collage with Hand Stamping and Sewing)	TGL	TGL	1980	SP/EMB/REL	23 X 18	TGL/HMP	9		600	2500
Soft Action (Two Sheets with Sewing)	TGL	TGL	1980	REL	24 X 18	TGL/HMP	10		600	2500
Treasure Rute, I, II	TGL	TGL	1980	REL/CO	24 X 18 EA	TGL/HMP	11 EA		600 EA	2000
Color Radar Smile A, B, C	TGL	TGL	1980	EB/A	25 X 25 EA	TGL/HMP	8 EA		750 EA	3000

ALAN J SHIELDS CONTINUED

TITLE	PUBLISHER	PRINTER	DATE	MEDIUM	DIMENSION (PAPER SIZE) IN INCHES	TYPE OF PAPER	EDITION NUMBER	NO. OF COLORS	ORIGINAL OPENING PRICE	CURRENT RETAIL PRICE
SOLD OUT EDITIONS (RARE):										
Santa's Collar (with Stitching)	TGL	TGL	1981	EB/A	43 X 37	TGL/HMP	32		1500	3000
Polar Route (Four Layers of White Paper Pulp Configurations with Imbedded String Sewn by the Artist)	TGL	TGL	1986	SP/WC/REL	47 DIA	TGL/HMP	20	41	2100	4500
CURRENT EDITIONS:										
Rare Pyramid	TGL	TGL	1978	EB/A/SP/ENG	10 DIA	TGL/HMP	20	8	400	450
Guardian Mole	TGL	TGL	1978	EB/A/REL	10 DIA	TGL/HMP	34	4	400	400
Two Birds, Woodcock I, II	TGL	TGL	1978	LC	21 X 24 EA	TGL/HMP	11 EA	7 EA	450 EA	600 EA
Box Sweet Jane's Egg Triumvirate (Set of 3):										
Roosevelt Set	TGL	TGL	1978	LC/SP	19 X 23 X 19	TGL/HMP	18	Multi	600	2000
Kool Set	TGL	TGL	1978	LC/SP	25 X 25 X 3	TGL/HMP	18	Multi	600	2000
Moose Set	TGL	TGL	1978	LC/SP	21 X 46 X 3	TGL/HMP	18	Multi	600	2000
Alice in Grayland (with Hand Stamping and Sewing)	TGL	TGL	1980	EB/A/SP	24 X 20	TGL/HMP	13		600	2500
Treasure Map Light, 2 Sheets, Stitched with Thread	OSC	TGL	1980–81	WC	36 X 28	HMP	18		1000	2500
Treasure Map Dark, 2 Sheets, Stitched with Treasure Map Light, 2 Sheets, Stitched with Thread	OSC	JRPS	1980–81	WC	36 X 28	HMP	18		1000	2500
Sushi Bar, 2 Sheets Stitched with Thread	HAS/OSC	HAS	1981	LC/LI	18 X 18	HMP	35		700	2000
Santa's Collar (with Stitching)	TGL	TGL	1981	EC/A	43 X 37	TGL/HMP	32		1500	3500
The Castle Window Set: (Series of Multi-Colored Prints)										
Plastic Bucket (T-504)	TGL	TGL	1981	LI/EB/A/REL/CO	36 X 27	TGL/HMP	10	34	1500	2500
Chicago Tenement	TGL	TGL	1981	EB/A/REL	36 X 28	TGL/HMP	23		900	2500
Jason's Rabbit Holler with Flying Rabbits	TGL	TGL	1981	EB/A/REL	36 X 28	TGL/HMP	25		900	2500
Ahmadabad Silk	TGL	TGL	1981	EB/A/REL	36 X 28	TGL/HMP	33		900	2500
Fire Escape Plan	TGL	TGL	1981		36 X 28	TGL/HMP	23		900	2500
Fran Tarkington's Tie	TGL	TGL	1981	EB/A/REL	36 X 28	TGL/HMP	23		900	2500
Kite Riddle	TGL	TGL	1981	LI/WC/REL/CO	36 X 28	TGL/HMP	40		900	2000
Milan-Fog	TGL	TGL	1984	I/NB	40 X 32	TGL/HMP	46	24	1800	2500
Odd-Job	TGL	TGL	1984	EB/WC/REL/CO	42 X 42	TGL/HMP	46	24	1800	3500
Bull-Pen	TGL	TGL	1984	EB/A/WC/CO	41 X 42	TGL/HMP	46	26	1800	3500
Gas-Up	TGL	TGL	1984	EB/A/WC/REL	57 X 41	TGL/HMP	46	33	1800	2500
Equatorial Route	TGL	TGL	1986	SP/CO/REL	47 DIA	TGL/HMP	20	34	2100	3500
Josh's Route	TGL	TGL	1986	SP/CO/REL	47 DIA	TGL/HMP	20	22	2100	3500
Rain Dance Route	TGL	TGL	1986	SP/CO/REL	47 DIA	TGL/HMP	20	38	2100	3500
Uncle Ferdinand's Route	TGL	TGL	1986	SP/CO/REL	47 DIA	TGL/HMP	20	20	2100	3500
Home Route	TGL	TGL	1986	SP/CO/REL	47 DIA	TGL/HMP	20	13	2100	3500
Trade Route (Roman)	TGL	TGL	1986	SP/CO/REL	47 DIA	TGL/HMP	20	16	2100	3500
Soft & Fluffy Gears Series (Assembled, Punched & Glued) (Set of 9):										
Synchromesh	SprSW/TanPr/ART	JW/RL/ART/SprSW/BW/TanPr	1987	PW	21 X 19	HMP	15		1500	2200
Thinning Twin	SprSW/TanPr/ART	JW/RL/ART/SprSW/BW/TanPr	1987	PW	19 X 19	HMP	15		1500	2200
King Sponge	SprSW/TanPr/ART	JW/RL/ART/SprSW/BW/TanPr	1987	PW	18 X 19	HMP	15		1500	2200
West in the Breast	SprSW/TanPr/ART	JW/RL/ART/SprSW/BW/TanPr	1987	PW	19 X 18	HMP	15		1500	2200
Sleeping Hair	SprSW/TanPr/ART	JW/RL/ART/SprSW/BW/TanPr	1987	PW	18 X 18	HMP	15		1500	2200
Wrack and Pin Whin	SprSW/TanPr/ART	JW/RL/ART/SprSW/BW/TanPr	1987	PW	19 X 19	HMP	15		1500	2200
Wets Yoog	SprSW/TanPr/ART	JW/RL/ART/SprSW/BW/TanPr	1987	PW	28 X 28	HMP	15		2000	3200
Worm with a Spur	SprSW/TanPr/ART	JW/RL/ART/SprSW/BW/TanPr	1987	PW	28 X 27	HMP	15		2000	3500
Bent Eggbeater	SprSW/TanPr/ART	JW/RL/ART/SprSW/BW/TanPr	1987	PW	36 X 35	HMP	15		2000	3200
Dragon Chips Series:										
Edna's Balls	TanPr	BW/AR/TanPr	1988	PW/REL	24 X 24	HMP	10	Varies	2200	2800
Sylvia	TanPr	BW/AR/TanPr	1988	PW/REL	24 X 24	HMP	22	Varies	1500	1500
Marcus	TanPr	BW/AR/TanPr	1988	PW/REL	24 X 24	HMP	24	Varies	2000	2000
Edna	TanPr	BW/AR/TanPr	1988	PW/REL	24 X 24	HMP	20	Varies	1500	1500

ALAN J SHIELDS CONTINUED

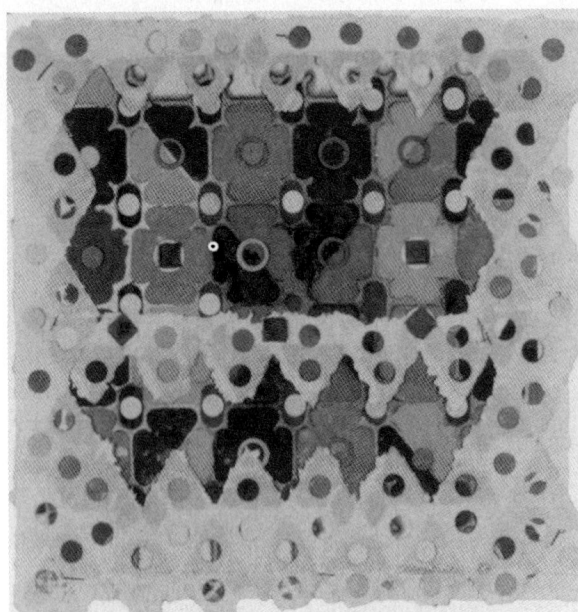

Alan J Shields
Soft and Fluffy Gears Series:
West in the Breast
Courtesy Tandem Press

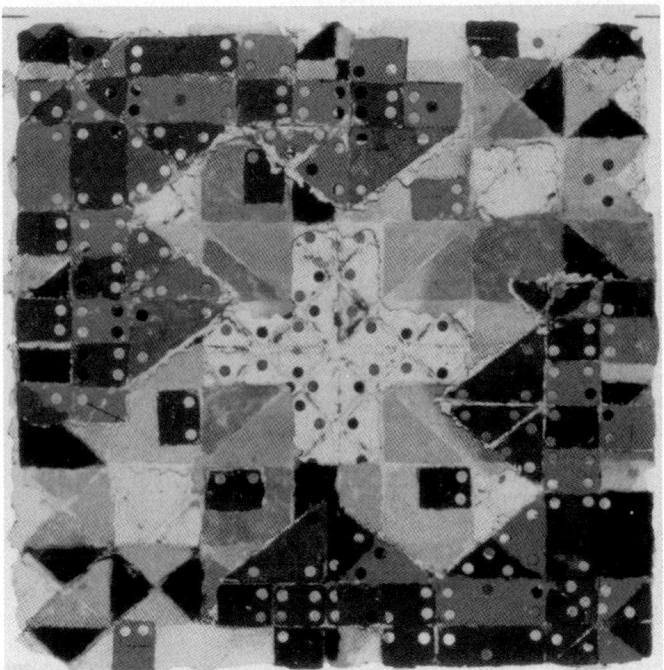

Alan J Shields
Soft and Fluffy Gears Series:
Wrack and Pin Whin
Courtesy Tandem Press

TITLE	PUBLISHER	PRINTER	DATE	MEDIUM	DIMENSION (PAPER SIZE) IN INCHES	TYPE OF PAPER	EDITION NUMBER	NO. OF COLORS	ORIGINAL OPENING PRICE	CURRENT RETAIL PRICE
CURRENT EDITIONS:										
When Everyone Lost their Marbles (3 Sheets)	VAC	ART/KS/RK/VAC	1989	REL	19 X 19	HMP/KOZO	14		1400	1800
Kissing the Tundra	VAC	ART/KS/RK/VAC	1989	CO	28 X 28	HMP			2100	2500
Green Imperial, Blue Ice, Yellow Snow	VAC	ART/KS/RK/VAC	1989	CO	32 X 32	HMP			2100	2500
Shorebirds Identification Chart Series:										
Curlew	TGL	LF/SL/MM/TGL	1992	WC/REL/LB/CO	26 X 26	HMP	23		1000	1000
Godwit	TGL	LF/SL/MM/TGL	1992	WC/REL/LB/CO	26 X 26	HMP	21		1000	1000
Ibis	TGL	LF/SL/MM/TGL	1992	WC/REL/LB/CO	26 X 26	HMP	20		1000	1000
Pharalope	TGL	LF/SL/MM/TGL	1992	WC/REL/LB/CO	26 X 26	HMP	23		1000	1000
Piping Plover	TGL	LF/SL/MM/TGL	1992	WC/REL/LB/CO	26 X 26	HMP	17		1000	1000
Sanderling	TGL	LF/SL/MM/TGL	1992	WC/REL/LB/CO	26 X 26	HMP	20		1000	1000
Yellowlegs	TGL	LF/SL/MM/TGL	1992	WC/REL/LB/CO	26 X 26	HMP	19		1000	1000
Wilson's Snipe	TGL	LF/SL/MM/TGL	1992	WC/REL/LB/CO	26 X 26	HMP	22		1000	1000

ZINOVY SHERSHER

BORN: Russia; April 12, 1947
EDUCATION: Sch of Fine Arts & Design, Kursk, Russia, 1962–65; M A Univ of Fine/Applied Arts, Kursk, Russia, 1965–70; Sch of Visual Arts, NY, 1981–82
TEACHING: Art Sch, Kuzsk, Russia, 1972–76; Regal Art Studio, NY, 1983–85
AWARDS: California Com Found, City Hall, Los Angeles, Mural, 1991; Award, Oil Pastel Assoc, NY, 1992
RECENT EXHIB: Installation One Gallery, Encino, CA, 1988; Mussavi Galleries, South Hampton, NY & Soho, NY, 1989; Sherberg Gallery, Univ of Judaism, Los Angeles, CA, 1987,89,90; Univ of Judaism, Bel Air, CA, 1990; Mussavi Gallery, Soho, NY & Southampton, NY, 1990; Window Gallery, Beverly Hills, CA, 1991; Salmagundi Club, NY, 1992
COLLECTIONS: Univ of Judaism, Bel Air, CA
PRINTERS: Master Art, Inc, Sun Valley, CA (MAI)
PUBLISHERS: Artist (ART)
GALLERIES: Window Gallery, Beverly Hills, CA; Beverly Connection, Beverly Hills, CA; Los Angeles Contemporary Museum of Art, Sales Gallery, Los Angeles, CA
MAILING ADDRESS: 6260 Morse Ave, North Hollywood, CA 91606

TITLE	PUBLISHER	PRINTER	DATE	MEDIUM	DIMENSION (PAPER SIZE) IN INCHES	TYPE OF PAPER	EDITION NUMBER	NO. OF COLORS	ORIGINAL OPENING PRICE	CURRENT RETAIL PRICE
CURRENT EDITIONS:										
The Muse	ART	MAI	1990	SP	30 X 40	WWP	200	66	1100	1400
The Mask	ART	MAI	1990	SP	40 X 30	WWP	200	74	750	1200
Music of Love	ART	ART	1992	I	6 X 5	AP	25	4	150	300
Dialogue (Hand Painted with Oil Pastel)	ART	ART	1992	I/HC	12 X 9	AP	25	Varies	200	300

The retail prices of the 100,000 limited edition prints quoted in this directory are subject to change. Print publishers, artists and galleries were the direct sources for these quotations. Prices in the secondary market listed as "Sold Out Editions (Rare)" indicate that the publisher has a limited supply of that print or that the print is difficult to locate in the galleries.

ROGER YUTAKA SHIMOMURA

BORN: Seattle, WA; June 26, 1939
EDUCATION: Univ of Washington, Seattle, WA, BA, 1961; Cornish Sch of Allied Arts, Seattle, WA, 1964; Stanford Univ, Palo Alto, CA, 1967; Cornell Univ, Ithaca, NY, 1968; Syracuse Univ, NY, MFA, 1969
TEACHING: Instr, Univ of Washington, Seattle, WA, 1966; Instr, Syracuse Univ, NY, 1967–69; Prof, Art, Univ of Kansas, Lawrence, KS, 1969 to present
AWARDS: Japan Found Grant, Tokyo, Japan, 1975; General Research Grants, Univ of Kansas, Lawrence, KS, 1970–72, 1975–76, 1979–82; Nat Endowment for the Arts Award, 1977,89
RECENT EXHIB: Elaine Horwitch Gallery, Scottsdale, AZ, 1989; Bernice Steinbaum Gallery, NY, 1989

COLLECTIONS: Metropolitan Mus, Miami, FL; Seattle Art Mus, WA; Denver Art Mus, CO; Syracuse Univ, NY; Ithaca Col, NY; California State Univ, San Diego, CA; Birmingham Mus, AL; Seattle Opera House, WA
PRINTERS: Artist (ART)
PUBLISHERS: Artist (ART)
GALLERIES: Osuna Gallery, Wash, DC; Gordon Woodside/Braseth Galleries, Seattle, WA; Elaine Horwitch Gallery, Scottsdale, AZ; Morgan Art Gallery, Kansas City, MO; Sebastian/Moore Gallery, Denver, CO; Davidson Galleries, Seattle, WA; Jan Weiner Gallery, Topeka, KS; Greg Kucera Gallery, Seattle, WA; Bernice Steinbaum Gallery, New York, NY
MAILING ADDRESS: 1019 Delaware, Lawrence, KS 66044

TITLE	PUBLISHER	PRINTER	DATE	MEDIUM	DIMENSION (PAPER SIZE) IN INCHES	TYPE OF PAPER	EDITION NUMBER	NO. OF COLORS	ORIGINAL OPENING PRICE	CURRENT RETAIL PRICE
SOLD OUT EDITIONS (RARE):										
Oriental Masterprint, #1, #4, #5	ART	ART	1975	SP	22 X 22 EA	AP	25 EA	15 EA	150 EA	400 EA
Oriental Masterprint, #2, #3	ART	ART	1975	SP	15 X 15 EA	AP	25 EA	15 EA	125 EA	350 EA
Oriental Masterprint, #13–#18	ART	ART	1975	SP	22 X 22 EA	AP	25 EA	12 EA	175 EA	250 EA
7 Views of a Japanese Restaurant, #1, #2	ART	ART	1977	SP	18 X 22 EA	AP	30 EA	12 EA	250 EA	350 EA
7 Views of a Japanese Restaurant, #3–#7	ART	ART	1978	SP	18 X 22 EA	AP	30 EA	12 EA	250 EA	350 EA

HARRIET SHORR

BORN: New York, NY; May 14, 1939
EDUCATION: Swarthmore Col, PA, BA, 1960; Yale Univ, New Haven, CT, BFA, 1962
TEACHING: Swarthmore Col, PA, 1963–74; Univ of Pennsylvania, Phila, PA, 1976; State Univ of New York, Purchase, NY, 1979 to present
AWARDS: Nat Endowment for the Arts Grant, 1980
RECENT EXHIB: Peter Tatistcheff Gallery, NY, 1987; Rahr-West Art Mus, Manitowoc, WI, 1992

COLLECTIONS: Utah Mus of Fine Art, Salt Lake City, UT; Rahr-West Mus, Manitowoc, WI
PRINTERS: K Carraccio, NY (KC); Bruce Cleveland, NY (BC)
PUBLISHERS: Orion Editions, NY (OE)
GALLERIES: Kimpton Gallery, San Francisco, CA; Fischbach Gallery, New York, NY; Editions Limited Gallery, Indianapolis, IN; Orion Editions, NY; Peter Tatistcheff Gallery, New York, NY; Cumberland Gallery, Nashville, TN; Hokin Gallery, Palm Beach, FL; Levinson Kane Gallery, Boston, MA
MAILING ADDRESS: State University of New York, Purchase, NY 10577; 117 Mercer St, New York, NY 10012

TITLE	PUBLISHER	PRINTER	DATE	MEDIUM	DIMENSION (PAPER SIZE) IN INCHES	TYPE OF PAPER	EDITION NUMBER	NO. OF COLORS	ORIGINAL OPENING PRICE	CURRENT RETAIL PRICE
SOLD OUT EDITIONS (RARE):										
Big Blue	OE	KC	1980	AC	30 X 40	AP	60	12	600	950
Blue Present	OE	KC	1983	AC	37 X 30	AP	65	9	500	750
CURRENT EDITIONS:										
Cattleyas for Odette	OE	KC	1981	AC	30 X 42	AP	85	27	600	850
Summer Pears	OE	BC	1985	EC	30 X 42	AP	125	14	650	750
Kimono and Kiwi	OE	BC	1986	EC	29 X 38	AP	125	13	575	650
Casablanca Lillies	OE	BC	1988	EC	30 X 39	AP	125	19	850	950

KENNETH SHOWELL

BORN: Huron, South Dakota; October 22, 1939
EDUCATION: Kansas City Art Inst, KS, BFA, 1963; Indiana Univ, Bloomington, IN, MFA, 1965

COLLECTIONS: Whitney Mus of Am Art, NY; Art Inst of Chicago, IL; Akron Mus, OH; Michener Coll, Univ of Texas, Austin, TX
PRINTERS: Landfall Press Inc, Chicago, IL (LPI); Jerry Raidiger, Chicago, IL (JR)
PUBLISHERS: Landfall Press Inc, Chicago, IL (LPI)
GALLERIES: Landfall Press, Chicago, IL; Quartet Editions, New York, NY
MAILING ADDRESS: 82 Forsyth, New York, NY 10002

TITLE	PUBLISHER	PRINTER	DATE	MEDIUM	DIMENSION (PAPER SIZE) IN INCHES	TYPE OF PAPER	EDITION NUMBER	NO. OF COLORS	ORIGINAL OPENING PRICE	CURRENT RETAIL PRICE
SOLD OUT EDITIONS (RARE):										
Aldan	LPI	JR/LPI	1970	LC	30 X 22	GE	50	4	150	450
Terni	LPI	JR/LPI	1970	LC	22 X 30	GE	50	4	150	450

SOLOMON SHUKMAN

BORN: Bobr, Province, Minsk, Russia; July 5, 1927, US Citizen
EDUCATION: Col of Fine Arts & Theatre Design, Moscow, Russia, 1946–49; Stroganov Inst of Art, Moscow, Russia, 1949–52
COLLECTIONS: Magnes Mus, Berkeley, CA; Union of Soviet Artists, Moscow, Russia; Art Found of USSR, Moscow, Russia

PRINTERS: Ernest F De Soto Workshop, San Francisco, CA (EDS); Artist (ART)
PUBLISHERS: Ernest F De Soto Workshop, San Francisco, CA (EDS); Artist (ART)
GALLERIES: Loeb Rhoades Gallery, San Francisco, CA; Magnes Museum, Berkeley, CA; Pantheon Gallery, San Francisco, CA; Nathan Gallery, San Francisco, CA
MAILING ADDRESS: 554 Beresford Ave, Redwood City, CA 94061

SOLOMON SHUKMAN CONTINUED

TITLE	PUBLISHER	PRINTER	DATE	MEDIUM	DIMENSION (PAPER SIZE) IN INCHES	TYPE OF PAPER	EDITION NUMBER	NO. OF COLORS	ORIGINAL OPENING PRICE	CURRENT RETAIL PRICE
SOLD OUT EDITIONS (RARE):										
Dark Shadows	ART	ART	1975	LB	16 X 20	AP	40	1	175	300
Gray Birds	ART	ART	1975	EC	20 X 16	R/BFK	25	3	320	400
SOLD OUT EDITIONS (RARE):										
Self Portrait	ART	ART	1975	EC	16 X 20	R/BFK	25	2	220	400
XXth Century Woman	ART	ART	1977	LB	23 X 31	AP	15	1	450	700
XXth Century Men	ART	ART	1977	LC	23 X 31	AP	15	1	450	700
Human Flow	ART	ART	1978	LC	22 X 30	AP	40	3	600	900
Little Birds	ART	ART	1978	EC	16 X 20	R/BFK	25	2	220	400
Flowing	ART	ART	1978	EC	16 X 20	R/BFK	25	2	220	400
Bottles in a Cap	ART	ART	1978	EC	16 X 20	R/BFK	25	2	220	400
Day Dreams	ART	ART	1978	LC	22 X 30	AP	40	3	600	900
The Work is Done	ART	ART	1979	EC	20 X 16	R/BFK	15	3	250	500
Sadness	ART	ART	1979	EC	20 X 16	R/BFK	20	3	275	500
Touching	ART	ART	1980	EC	16 X 20	R/BFK	25	3	275	500
Double Profile	ART	ART	1980	EC	16 X 20	R/BFK	25	3	275	500
People	ART	ART	1981	LB	18 X 25	AP	40	1	150	300
Time	ART	ART	1982	LB	22 X 30	AP	30	1	250	500
Hagleuin	ART	ART	1983	LB	30 X 22	AP	25	1	320	500
CURRENT EDITIONS:										
Set of Five:										
Impression of Red	EDS	EDS	1985	LC	24 X 32	AP/HW	75	12	275	400
Impression of Green	EDS	EDS	1985	LC	24 X 32	AP/HW	75	12	275	400
Impression of Violet	EDS	EDS	1985	LC	24 X 32	AP/HW	75	12	275	400
Impression of Orange	EDS	EDS	1985	LC	24 X 32	AP/HW	75	12	275	400
Impression of Yellow	EDS	EDS	1985	LC	24 X 32	AP/HW	75	12	275	400

HUBERT SHUPTRINE

BORN: Tennessee; 1940
RECENT EXHIB: Montgomery Gallery, San Francisco, CA, 1992
PRINTERS: Styria Studio, NY (SS)
PUBLISHERS: Hammer Publishing Co, NY (HP)
GALLERIES: Hammer Galleries, New York, NY; C G Rein Galleries, Scottsdale, AZ & Santa Fe, NM & Houston, TX & Minneapolis, MN; Montgomery Gallery, San Francisco, CA

TITLE	PUBLISHER	PRINTER	DATE	MEDIUM	DIMENSION (PAPER SIZE) IN INCHES	TYPE OF PAPER	EDITION NUMBER	NO. OF COLORS	ORIGINAL OPENING PRICE	CURRENT RETAIL PRICE
CURRENT EDITIONS:										
Plantation Tub	HP	SS	1977	EC	30 X 21	AP	300	7	500	700
Summer Again	HP	SS	1977	EC	28 X 40	AP	360	6	500	700

JOSE MARIA SICILIA

BORN: Spain
RECENT EXHIB: Runkel-Hue-Williams, Ltd, London, England, 1989; BlumHelman Gallery, NY, 1990,92
PRINTERS: Lawrence Hamlin, San Francisco, CA (LH); Paul Mullowney, San Francisco, CA (PM); Crown Point Press, San Francisco, CA (CPP); Magi-Baleta, Barcelona, Spain (MB)
PUBLISHERS: Crown Point Press, San Francisco, CA (CPP); Ediciones T, Barcelona, Spain (EdT)
GALLERIES: Crown Point Press, San Francisco, CA & New York, NY; Runkel-Hue-Williams, Ltd, London, England; BlumHelman Gallery, New York, NY; Janet Steinberg Fine Arts, San Francisco, CA; Thomas Segal Gallery, Boston, MA; Rick Jones Modern & Contemporary Art, St Louis, MO

TITLE	PUBLISHER	PRINTER	DATE	MEDIUM	DIMENSION (PAPER SIZE) IN INCHES	TYPE OF PAPER	EDITION NUMBER	NO. OF COLORS	ORIGINAL OPENING PRICE	CURRENT RETAIL PRICE
SOLD OUT EDITIONS (RARE):										
Fleur Rouge II, IV	CPP	CPP	1988	EC/CC	30 X 23 EA	HMP	25 EA		850 EA	1000 EA
CURRENT EDITIONS:										
Fleur Rouge I, II, III, V	CPP	CPP	1988	EC/CC	30 X 23 EA	HMP	25 EA		850 EA	1000 EA
Fleur Rouge VI	CPP	CPP	1988	EC/CC	55 X 24	HMP	24		2000	3000
Fleur Rouge VII	CPP	CPP	1988	EC/CC	55 X 23	HMP	25		2000	3000
Fleur Rouge VIII	CPP	CPP	1988	EC/CC	55 X 30	HMP	25		2000	3000
Untitled (Set of 5)			1989	EB	24 X 24 EA	HMP	60 EA	1 EA	10000 SET	10000 SET
Asebi, Shikibu (Set of 2)	CPP	CPP	1989	WC	26 X 30 EA	HMP	100 EA		1500 SET	1650 SET
									900 EA	950 EA
Series A (Framed) Each with Overlaid Sheet of Hosho Paper Coated in Beeswax) (Set of 7):									11000 SET	11000 SET
Rabbit Inside Pitcher	CPP	LH/PM/CPP	1990	EB/A	23 X 18	HOSHO	15		1800	1800
Skull Inside Teapot	CPP	LH/PM/CPP	1990	EB/A	18 X 17	HOSHO	15		1800	1800
Crescent Moon and Cat	CPP	LH/PM/CPP	1990	EB/A	20 X 18	HOSHO	15		1800	1800
Rooster and Skull	CPP	LH/PM/CPP	1990	EB/A	16 X 22	HOSHO	15		1800	1800
Bottle, Skull and Figure	CPP	LH/PM/CPP	1990	EB/A	19 X 28	HOSHO	15		1800	1800
Pipe, Ladle and Spoon	CPP	LH/PM/CPP	1990	EB/A	20 X 19	HOSHO	15		1800	1800
Figurine, Candle, Pitcher and Head of Fox Inside Jug	CPP	LH/PM/CPP	1990	EB/A	21 X 34	HOSHO	15		1800	1800

JOSE MARIA SICILIA CONTINUED

TITLE	PUBLISHER	PRINTER	DATE	MEDIUM	DIMENSION (PAPER SIZE) IN INCHES	TYPE OF PAPER	EDITION NUMBER	NO. OF COLORS	ORIGINAL OPENING PRICE	CURRENT RETAIL PRICE
CURRENT EDITIONS:										
Series B (Framed) (Each with Overlaid Sheet of Hosho Paper Coated in Beeswax) (Set of 5)	CPP	LH/PM/CPP	1990	EB/A/SB	14 X 16 EA to 13 X 25 EA	SOM/W/T	15 EA		6500 SET	6500 SET
Series C (Each Etching Printed on 2 Sides) (Set of 3):										
Pitcher and Candlestick	CPP	LH/PM/CPP	1990	EB/A	64 X 48	HOSHO	15		2000	2000
Chicken and Bowl	CPP	LH/PM/CPP	1990	EB/A	64 X 48	HOSHO	15		2000	2000
Jug and Spoon	CPP	LH/PM/CPP	1990	EB/A	64 X 48	HOSHO	15		2000	2000
Ohtomo #1-#7	EdT	MB	1991	SP	30 X 30 EA	AP	9 EA		Ptas 200000	Ptas 200000
Ohtomo #8 (Trip)	EdT	MB	1991	SP	43 X 16 EA	AP	9		Ptas 400000	Ptas 400000

HERBERT SIEBNER, RCA

BORN: Stettin, Germany; April 16, 1925; Canadian Citizen
EDUCATION: Atelier Richter, Stettin, Germany, 1941–43; Berlin Acad, Germany, 1946–49
TEACHING: Vis Prof, Painting, Univ of Washington, Seattle, WA, 1963; Vis Prof, Univ of British Columbia, Canada, 1964; Vis Prof, Univ of Alberta, Canada, 1965; Lectr, Painting, Univ of Victoria, Canada, 1967, 69
COLLECTIONS: Seattle Art Mus, WA; Confed Art Mus, PEI; Royal Canadian Acad, Ottawa, Can; Nat Gallery, Ottawa, Can; Mus of Inter Xilographia, Capri, Italy; Victoria Art Gallery, Can; Maltwood Mus, Victoria, Can; Univ of Victoria, Can; H H Princess Thurn and Taxis, Munich, Germany, Vancouver Art Gallery, Can

AWARDS: Reid Award, Graphics, 1956; Berlin Acad, Art in Res, 1963; Canadian Council Grants, 1962,86
PRINTERS: Artist (ART)
PUBLISHERS: Maltwood Mus, Univ of Victoria, Can (MM); Artist (ART)
GALLERIES: Elfriede Wirnitzger, Baden-Baden Germany; Shayne Gallery, Montreal, Canada; Horizon Gallery, Edmonton, Canada; Atelier Gallery, Vancouver, Canada; Winchester Gallery, Victoria, BC, Canada; Wallace Galleries, Calgary, Alta, Canada; Weisenstein Foundation of Expressionism, Victoria, BC, Canada
MAILING ADDRESS: 270 Meadowbrook Road, Victoria, BC, Canada, V8X 3X3

TITLE	PUBLISHER	PRINTER	DATE	MEDIUM	DIMENSION (PAPER SIZE) IN INCHES	TYPE OF PAPER	EDITION NUMBER	NO. OF COLORS	ORIGINAL OPENING PRICE	CURRENT RETAIL PRICE
SOLD OUT EDITIONS (RARE):										
Canal (Berlin)	ART	ART	1953	LI	14 X 20	FAB	30	3	30	900
Paris (Sacre Coeur)	ART	ART	1955	SP	22 X 15	CAN	24	2	25	600
Reclining Figure	ART	ART	1955	PE	22 X 17	ING	1	1	250	1500
Byzantine Knights	ART	ART	1963	LB	13 X 17	GE	30	1	50	600
Emerging Figures	ART	ART	1963	LB	11 X 17	GE	25	1	50	600
Sitting Woman	ART	ART	1965	MON	25 X 20 EA	WAP	1 EA	1 EA	200 EA	1200 EA
Woman Breeding Better Men	ART	ART	1967	SP	15 X 12	CAN	150	1	60	500
Amazone	ART	ART	1967	LB	11 X 12	CAN	50	1	75	500
On the Beach	ART	ART	1969	WC	14 X 21	HMP	12	3	90	800
Day of Arrival	ART	ART	1973	SP	15 X 25	CAN	75	3	150	500
Brother and Sister	ART	ART	1977	WC	12 X 21	CAN	75	2	175	600
Amazones and Flying Man	ART	ART	1981	WC	11 X 20	CAN	120	2	250	500
Via Appia Antiqua	ART	ART	1981	WC	11 X 17	CAN	100	3	300	600
Flower Girl and King	ART	ART	1981	LB/HC	14 X 18	WAP	17	1	450	600
Tender Care	ART	ART	1982	WB	12 X 12	RICE	15	1	450	600

ZDZISLAW R SIKORA

BORN: Mannheim, West Germany; September 10, 1952; US Citizen
EDUCATION: Univ of Illinois-Chicago, IL, BA, 1975; Univ of Wisconsin, Madison, WI, MFA, 1978
TEACHING: Asst Prof, Wesleyan Col, Macon, GA, 1979–82; Asst Prof, Montgomery Col, Rockville, MD, 1982–84; Assoc Prof, Univ of South Carolina, Coastal Carolina Col, Conway, SC, 1984 to present
COLLECTIONS: Dulin Gallery of Art, Knoxville, TN; Mus of Arts & Sciences, Macon, GA; Austin Peay State Univ, Clarksville, TN; Museo del Grabado, Buenos Aires, Argentina; Columbus Mus of Arts & Sciences, Columbus, GA; Honolulu Acad of Art, HI; Elvhejem Mus, Madison, WI; USIA, Wash, DC; Univ of Dallas, TX; Furman Univ, Greenville, SC; Univ of Hawaii, Hilo, HI; Rice Univ, Houston, TX; Univ of California, Los Angeles, CA; Univ of Maine, Orono, MA
RECENT EXHIB: Univ of North Carolina, Wilmington, NC, 1987; J Webb Gallery, Macon, GA, 1987; International Images, Ltd, Sewickley, PA, 1987
PRINTERS: K O Ray, Macon, GA (KOR); M Sikora, Myrtle Beach, SC (MS); Artist (ART)
PUBLISHERS: Artist (ART)
GALLERIES: Chicago Center for the Print, Chicago, IL; J Noblett Gallery, Sonoma, CA; Galerie Albrecht, The Netherlands; Fanny Garver Gallery, Madison, WI; Stanley & Schenck Gallery, Atlanta, GA

TITLE	PUBLISHER	PRINTER	DATE	MEDIUM	DIMENSION (PAPER SIZE) IN INCHES	TYPE OF PAPER	EDITION NUMBER	NO. OF COLORS	ORIGINAL OPENING PRICE	CURRENT RETAIL PRICE
SOLD OUT EDITIONS (RARE):										
The Martrydom Suite:										
St Lucy	ART	ART/KOR/MBS	1980	IC	24 X 36	MUR	20	18	150	550
St Julian	ART	ART/KOR/MBS	1980	IC	24 X 35	MUR	20	18	150	400
St Roch	ART	ART/KOR/MBS	1981	IC	24 X 36	MUR	20	12	150	350
St Bartholomew	ART	ART/KOR/MBS	1981	IC	24 X 36	MUR	20	14	150	350

ZDZISLAW R SIKORA CONTINUED

TITLE	PUBLISHER	PRINTER	DATE	MEDIUM	DIMENSION (PAPER SIZE) IN INCHES	TYPE OF PAPER	EDITION NUMBER	NO. OF COLORS	ORIGINAL OPENING PRICE	CURRENT RETAIL PRICE
SOLD OUT EDITIONS (RARE):										
The Temptations (Dipt)	ART	ART/KOR/MBS	1981	IC	36 X 48	MUR	20	15	350	800
Memento Mori I	ART	ART/MBS	1984	IC	15 X 20	MUR	55	8	200	300
CURRENT EDITIONS:										
The Temptations of St Anthony II (Dipt)	ART	ART/MBS	1984	IC	36 X 48	MUR	20	10	500	800
Adam and Eve Witness the Temptations of St Anthony (Dipt)	ART	ART/MBS	1984	IC	24 X 36	MUR	20	14	500	800
Momento Mori II	ART	ART	1985	IC	15 X 20	MUR	20	8	200	250
Conflicts #1 (Dipt)	ART	ART	1986	IC	24 X 36	MUR	20	12	600	650
Flora I, II, III	ART	ART/MBS	1986	IC	24 X 36 EA	MUR	15 EA	5/8/8	200 EA	250 EA

HOLLIS SIGLER

BORN: Gary, IN; March 2, 1948
EDUCATION: Moore Col of Art, Phila, PA, BFA, 1970; Art Sch, Art Inst of Chicago, IL, MFA, 1973
TEACHING: Instr, Painting & Drawing, Columbia Col, Chicago, IL, 1984 to present
AWARDS: Anne Louis Raymond Traveling Fel, Sch of Art, Inst of Chicago, IL, 1973; First Prize, Union League Club, Chicago, IL, Watercolor, 1976; Golden Heritage Award, Rocky Mountain Nat Watercolor Exhib, Foothills Art Center, Golden, CO, 1977; Emile L Weld Prize, Painting, Art Inst of Chicago, IL, 1980; Illinois Arts Council, Artist Grant & Chairman's Grant, Chicago, IL, 1986; Cash Award, Southeastern Center for Contemp Art, Winston-Salem, NC, 1987; Nat Endowment for the Arts, Visual Arts Fel Grant, 1987
RECENT EXHIB: State of Illinois, Art Gallery, Chicago, IL, 1989; Evanston Art Center, Center for the Visual Arts, IL, 1989; Munson-Williams-Proctor Inst, Mus of Art, Utica, NY, 1989; Dart Gallery, Chicago, IL, 1990; Nat Mus of Women Artists, Wash, DC, 1991; Susan Cummins Gallery, San Francisco, CA, 1992; State of Illinois Art Gallery, Chicago, IL, 1992; Univ of Maryland, Baltimore County Fine Arts Gallery, Catonsville, MD, 1992
PRINTERS: Vermillion Editions, Ltd, Minneapolis, MN (VEL); Julio Juristo, Tampa, FL (JJ); Graphicstudio II, Tampa, FL (GII); Topaz Editions, Tampa, FL (TE); Bud Shark, Boulder, CO (BS); Shark's, Inc, Boulder, CO (SI)
PUBLISHERS: Shark's, Inc, Boulder, CO (SI); Vermillion Editions, Ltd, Minneapolis, MN (VEL); Graphicstudio II, Tampa, FL (GII); Topaz Editions, Tampa, FL (TE)
GALLERIES: Stein Gladstone Gallery, New York, NY; Dart Gallery, Chicago, IL; Shark's, Inc, Boulder, CO; Printworks Gallery, Chicago, IL; Steven Scott Gallery, Baltimore, MD; Quartet Editions, New York, NY; Susan Cummins Gallery, Mill Valley, CA; Tamarind Inst, Albuquerque, NM; Topaz Editions, Inc, Tampa, FL
MAILING ADDRESS: 22663 N Prairie Rd, Prairie View, IL 60069

Hollis Sigler
From Me All Things Proceed and To Me They Must Return
Courtesy Shark's, Inc

TITLE	PUBLISHER	PRINTER	DATE	MEDIUM	DIMENSION (PAPER SIZE) IN INCHES	TYPE OF PAPER	EDITION NUMBER	NO. OF COLORS	ORIGINAL OPENING PRICE	CURRENT RETAIL PRICE
SOLD OUT EDITIONS (RARE):										
They were Right, They are Perfect	VEL	VEL	1982	LC	27 X 31	ACW	35	28	1200	4000
She was Tired of Filling Her Heart with Hopeless Dreams	VEL	VEL	1982	LC/CO/SP	27 X 31	ACW	35	24	1200	2500
There is a Doubt She Could be Right	VEL	VEL	1982	LC	27 X 31	ACW	35	32	1200	2500
She Always Thought She was Wrong	VEL	VEL	1982	LC	27 X 31	ACW	35	26	1200	2500
If She Could Free Her Heart to Her Wildest Desires	GII	JJ/GII	1982	MULT	12 X 15	n/or((	00		650	1200
There's No Future in it	TE	JJ/TE	1984	LC/HC	22 X 28	AC	47	10	800	1800
Letting Go of the Pain	SLL	BS/SLL	1985	LC/3D	19 X 27 X 3	HMP	15		1200	1400
Where Daughters Fear Becoming their Mothers	SLL	BS/SLL	1985	LC/3D	14 X 12 X 17	HMP	30		1500	2000
It is Your Friendship that has Fed My Soul (Painted Frame)	SLL	BS/SLL	1986	MON	32 X 48 EA	AC	1 EA		3500 EA	5000 EA

HOLLIS SIGLER CONTINUED

TITLE	PUBLISHER	PRINTER	DATE	MEDIUM	DIMENSION (PAPER SIZE) IN INCHES	TYPE OF PAPER	EDITION NUMBER	NO. OF COLORS	ORIGINAL OPENING PRICE	CURRENT RETAIL PRICE
SOLD OUT EDITIONS (RARE):										
What is Her True Nature? (Painted Frame)	SLL	BS/SLL	1986	MON	32 X 48 EA	AC	1 EA		3500 EA	5000 EA
A Slice of the Good Life (Painted Frame)	SLL	BS/SLL	1986	MON	32 X 48 EA	AC	1 EA		3500 EA	5000 EA
The Dance of Life (Painted Frame)	SLL	BS/SLL	1986	MON	32 X 48 EA	AC	1 EA		3500 EA	5000 EA
The Lady Learns the Limits of Love (Painted Frame)	SLL	BS/SLL	1986	MON	32 X 48 EA	AC	1 EA		3500 EA	5000 EA
CURRENT EDITIONS:										
From Me All Things Proceed and To Me They Must Return	SI	BS/SI	1992	LC	36 X 67	R/BFK	15		3000	3000
Dancing on the Edge (Painted Frame)	SI	BS/SI	1992	MON	22 X 30 EA	AC	1 EA	Varies	2000 EA	2000 EA

TODD SILER (LAEL)

BORN: Long Island, NY; August 21, 1953
EDUCATION: Smith Col, Northampton, MA, with Leonard Baskin, 1973–74; Bowdoin Col, Brunswick, ME, BA, 1975 (Cum Laude); Massachusetts Inst of Tech, Cambridge, MA, MS, Visual Studies, 1981, PhD, Interdisciplinary Studies, Psychology & Art, 1986
TEACHING: Instr, Visual Design, Massachusetts Inst of Technology, Cambridge, MA, 1982–83
AWARDS: Thomas J Watson Fel, Paris, France, 1975–76; Felbright Fel, India, 1985–86; Massachusetts Artists Found Fel, Painting, 1987; Meitec Fel, Nagoya, Japan, 1989

RECENT EXHIB: Ronald Feldman Fine Arts, NY, 1987; Saidye Bronfman Center, Montreal, Canada, 1987; New York Acad of Science, NY, 1988; Univ of Hartford, Art Sch, West Hartford, CT, 1992
COLLECTIONS: Solomon R Guggenheim Mus, NY; Metropolitan Mus of Art, NY; Mus of Mod Art, NY; Pushkin Mus, Moscow
PUBLISHERS: Ronald Feldman Fine Art, New York, NY (RFFA)
GALLERIES: Ronald Feldman Fine Art, New York, NY
MAILING ADDRESS: c/o Center for Advanced Visual Studies, Massachusetts Inst of Technology, Cambridge, MA 02139

TITLE	PUBLISHER	PRINTER	DATE	MEDIUM	DIMENSION (PAPER SIZE) IN INCHES	TYPE OF PAPER	EDITION NUMBER	NO. OF COLORS	ORIGINAL OPENING PRICE	CURRENT RETAIL PRICE
CURRENT EDITIONS:										
Metaphorms I, II	RFFA		1988	LB	30 X 45 EA	R/BFK	30 EA	1 EA	2500 SET 1500 EA	2500 SET 1500 EA
Metaprints: Forms of Metaphor (Series of 15)	RFFA		1988	MON/CO/HC	30 X 45 EA	Varies	1 EA	Varies	4500 EA	4500 EA
Metaphorming Minds (Unbound Book) (Boxed) (Set of 37)	RFFA		1991	SP/CO	16 X 24 EA	AP	130 EA		12000 SET	12000 SET
Metaphorming Minds (Bound Book) (Set of 37)	RFFA		1991	SP/CO	16 X 24 EA	AP	100 EA		12000 SET	12000 SET

NICOLA SIMBARI

BORN: Calabria, Italy; 1927
AWARDS: Gold Medal, Italian State Nat Consorso, Rome, Italy, 1954
PRINTERS: Corot Atelier, Paris, France (CA); Chromacomp, NY (CH); Sigart, Rome, Italy (SA); Bellini, Paris, France; Bottega Simbari, Rome, Italy (BS)

PUBLISHERS: Edmund Newman, Inc, Swampscott, MA (EN); Contemporary Art Masters, NY (CAM); Selene Ltd, Jersey, Channel Islands (SL); Phoebus, SA, MA (PH)
GALLERIES: Naples Art Gallery, Naples, FL; Patricia Judith Gallery, Boca Raton, FL; Graphic Art Collection, Hallandale, FL; Austin Galleries, Chicago, IL; Studio 53, New York, NY; Tamar Arts, New York, NY; Nan Miller Gallery, Rochester, NY; Florence Art Gallery, Dallas, TX; P C Hart Gallery, Jupiter, FL

TITLE	PUBLISHER	PRINTER	DATE	MEDIUM	DIMENSION (PAPER SIZE) IN INCHES	TYPE OF PAPER	EDITION NUMBER	NO. OF COLORS	ORIGINAL OPENING PRICE	CURRENT RETAIL PRICE
SOLD OUT EDITIONS (RARE):										
Target			1969	SP	18 X 25	AP	125		150	3000
Ischia	CAM	CA	1974	SP/WOOL	46 X 78	WOOL/SP	300		2000	20000
Fiddler on the Roof	CAM	CA	1974	SP/WOOL	46 X 78	WOOL/SP	300		2000	20000
Boy on a Beach Towel	PH	CH	1976	SP	33 X 25	AP	300		375	4500
Dressing Room	PH	CH	1976	SP	33 X 26	AP	300		375	4500
Nanette	PH	CH	1976	SP	27 X 39	AP	300		375	4500
Palisades	PH	CH	1977	SP	25 X 33	AP	300		375	4500
Boy on a Bicycle	PH	CH	1977	SP	28 X 33	AP	300		375	4500
Girl with Sailboats	PH	CH	1977	SP	33 X 25	AP	300		375	4500
Taormina	PH	CH	1977	SP	36 X 36	AP	300		375	9000
Girl on Balcony	PH	CH	1977	SP	27 X 38	AP	300		375	9000
L'Escalier	PH	CH	1977	SP	39 X 25	AP	300		375	9000
Paris at Six O'Clock Dawn/Dusk (the Pair)	PH	CH	1978	SP	20 X 27 EA	AP	300 EA		375 SET	5500 SET
Marco	PH	CH	1978	SP	29 X 32	AP	300		400	8000
Sorrento	PH	CH	1978	SP	32 X 32	AP	300		450	6500
Jennifer	PH	CH	1978	SP	29 X 32	AP	300		400	6500
Mykonos	PH	CH	1978	SP	28 X 39	AP	300		450	8000

NICOLA SIMBARI CONTINUED

TITLE	PUBLISHER	PRINTER	DATE	MEDIUM	DIMENSION (PAPER SIZE) IN INCHES	TYPE OF PAPER	EDITION NUMBER	NO. OF COLORS	ORIGINAL OPENING PRICE	CURRENT RETAIL PRICE
SOLD OUT EDITIONS (RARE):										
Ostia Beach	PH	CH	1978	SP	25 X 39	AP	300		525	8000
Girl on a Sea Wall	PH	CH	1978	SP	27 X 40	AP	300		550	6500
Cirque (Set of 5)									3000 SET	6000 SET
Clown a L'Ombelle	PH	CH	1978	SP	32 X 29	AP	300		600	1000
Le Cheval Blanc	PH	CH	1978	SP	28 X 33	AP	300		600	1000
La Famille	PH	CH	1978	SP	29 X 32	AP	300		600	1000
Vera	PH	CH	1978	SP	28 X 32	AP	300		600	1000
Deux Clowns	PH	CH	1978	SP	29 X 31	AP	300		600	3000
Panarea	SL	SA	1980	SP/RE	36 X 40	FAB	300	33	2350	9000
Les Paraluies	SL	SA	1980	SP/RE	22 X 30	FAB	100	10	1700	9000
Angela	SL	SA	1980	SP/RE	30 X 36	FAB	250	26	1375	7500
L'Ecuyere	SL	BE	1980	LC	40 X 28	AP	200	14	1050	4000
La Spiaggia	SL	BE	1980	LC	23 X 32	AP	200	14	950	4000
St. Germain	SL	BE	1980	LC	23 X 32	AP	200	14	950	4000
Acrobate	SL	SA	1980	AC	19 X 25	FAB	100	5	850	4000
Saltimbanchi	SL	SA	1980	AC	19 X 25	FAB	100	5	850	4000
White Beach	SL	SA	1980	SP/RE	24 X 34	FAB	200	26	845	10000
Maronti	SL	SA	1980	SP/RE	24 X 34	FAB	200	26	995	9000
Marinella	SL	SA	1980	SP/RE	24 X 34	FAB	250	28	875	9000
Summertime	EN	CH/JL	1980	SP	35 X 38	AP	300		850	8000
Il Patio	EN	CH/JL	1980	SP	34 X 36	AP	300		850	4000
La Plage	EN	CH/JL	1980	SP	26 X 33	AP	300		950	4000
Driftwood	EN	CH/JL	1980	SP	31 X 36	AP	300		950	4000
Il Giardino	EN	CH/JL	1980	SP	36 X 36	AP	300		1500	5000
Il Porto	SL	SA	1980	SP/RE	28 X 40	FAB	250	45	995	7500
Lavinio	EN	CH/JL	1981	SP	36 X 36	AP	300		1050	4000
Sylvie	SL	BS	1981	SP/RE	32 X 36	FAB/HMP	175	36	1750	13500
Sylvie (on Canvas)	SL	BS	1981	SP/RE	32 X 36	CANVAS	40	36	2250	18500
Astura	SL	BS	1981	SP/RE	35 X 40	S/FAB	180	32	1450	11500
Astura (Deluxe)	SL	BS	1981	SP/RE	35 X 40	CANVAS	40	32	3200	16500
Acrobats a Cheval	SL	BS	1981	SP/Q	33 X 36	FAB/S	110	4	350	4000
Clowns	SL	BS	1981	SP/Q	33 X 36	FAB/S	110	4	350	4000
Ionian	SL	BS	1981	SP/R	30 X 39	FAB/S	150	25	1500	10500
Ionian (Deluxe)	SL	BS	1981	SP/RE	30 X 39	CANVAS	40	25	3550	15500
Balcony in Amalfi	SL	BS	1981	SP/RE	36 X 40	FAB/S	200	25	1875	8500
Terracina	SL	BS	1981	SP/RE	24 X 36	MUR	175	25	695	6500
Terracina (Deluxe)	SL	BS	1981	SP/RE	24 X 36	CANVAS	35	25	2050	11500
Nettuno	SL	BS	1981	SP/RE	25 X 38	MUR	165	25	795	6500
Nettuno (Deluxe)	SL	BS	1981	SP/RE	25 X 38	CANVAS	35	25	1655	11500
Gold Interior (Deluxe)	SL	BS	1981	SP/RE	32 X 36	CANVAS	40	28	3400	11000
Mediterranee	SL	BS	1981	SP/RE	36 X 36	FAB/S	130	33	1625	11500
Mediterranee (Deluxe)	SL	BS	1981	SP/RE	36 X 36	CANVAS	40	33	3850	15500
Afternoon in Procida	SL	BS	1982	SP/RE	39 X 39	FAB/S	160	35	1800	12500
Afternoon in Procida (Deluxe)	SL	BS	1982	SP/RE	39 X 39	CANVAS	30	35	3950	18000
Circeo	SL	BS	1982	SP/RE	36 X 39	FAB/S	150	31	1725	8500
Circeo (Deluxe)	SL	BS	1982	SP/RE	36 X 39	CANVAS	35	31	3850	13000
Lipari	SL	BS	1982	SP/RE	32 X 39	FAB/S	160	46	1600	9000
Lipari (Deluxe)	SL	BS	1982	SP/RE	32 X 39	CANVAS	35	46	3750	15000
Serena	SL	BS	1983	SP/RE	31 X 35	S/FAB	200	37	1400	12500
Marche Aux Fleurs	SL	BS	1983	SP/RE	24 X 34	S/FAB	165	25	750	10000
Marche Aux Fleurs (Deluxe)	SL	BS	1983	SP/RE	24 X 34	CANVAS	35	25	1850	15000
Ischia	SL	BS	1983	SP/RE	32 X 40	S/FAB	150	35	1450	8500
Ischia (Deluxe)	SL	BS	1983	SP/RE	32 X 40	CANVAS	35	35	3000	13000
Diana	SL	BS	1983	SP/RE	36 X 36	S/FAB	150	33	1500	11000
Diana (Deluxe)	SL	BS	1983	SP/RE	36 X 36	CANVAS	40	33	3700	17500
Il Sogno	SL	BS	1985	SP/RE	37 X 38	S/FAB	120	23	1600	6500
Mimosa	SL	BS	1986	SP/RE	40 X 32	S/FAB	160	23	1500	7500
CURRENT EDITIONS:										
Capri	SL	SA	1980	SP/RE	24 X 36	FAB	300	35	1425	6500
Gold Interior	SL	BS	1981	SP/RE	32 X 36	FAB/S	100	28	1400	8000
Lily	SL	BS	1981	SP/RE	36 X 36	FAB/S	200	26	1150	6500
Nino	SL	BS	1981	SP/RE	32 X 40	FAB/S	200	30	1600	6500
Sha'nah	SL	BS	1982	SP/RE	33 X 40	FAB/S	190	42	1750	6500
Sha'nah (Deluxe)	SL	BS	1982	SP/RE	33 X 40	CANVAS	35	42	3850	10500
La Baigneuse	SL	BS	1983	SP/RE	34 X 38	S/FAB	120	47	1500	6500
Maria	SL	BS	1985	SP/RE	40 X 28	S/FAB	110	12	1100	6500
Praia a' Mare	SL	BS	1986	SP/RE	36 X 36	S/FAB	150	49	1300	6500
Praia a' Mare (Deluxe)	SL	BS	1986	SP/RE	36 X 36	CANVAS	35	49	3200	12000
Settembre	SL	BS	1986	SP/RE	32 X 40	S/FAB	160	16	1400	6500
Blue Marina	SL	BS	1986	SP/RE	28 X 39	S/FAB	150	23	1200	6500
Ornella	SL	BS	1987	SP/RE	28 X 36	S/FAB	120	21	1100	6500

LAURIE SIMMONS

BORN: New York, NY, October 3, 1949
EDUCATION: Tyler Sch of Art, Temple Univ, Phila, PA, BFA, 1971
AWARDS: Nat Endowment for the Arts Fel, 1984
RECENT EXHIB: Baltimore Mus of Art, MD, 1987, Mus of Contemp Art, Los Angeles, CA, 1989; Whitney Mus of Am Art, NY, 1989; Nat Mus of Am Art, Smithsonian Inst, Wash, DC, 1989; Corcoran Gallery of Art, Wash, DC, 1989; Daniel Weinberg Gallery, Los Angeles, CA, 1989; Galerie Jablonka, Cologne, Germany, 1989; Seibu Contemp Art Gallery, Tokyo, Japan, 1990; San Jose Mus of Art, CA, 1990,92; Metro Pictures, NY, 1992
COLLECTIONS: Univ of California, Santa Barbara, CA; Albright-Knox Art Gallery, Buffalo, NY; Fogg Mus of Art, Boston, MA; Philadelphia Mus of Art, PA; High Mus of Art, Atlanta, GA; Mus of Contemp Art, Montreal, Canada; Dallas Mus of Art, TX; Walker Art Center, Minneapolis, MN; St Louis Mus, MO; Musée d'Art Contemporain, Montreal, Canada
PRINTERS: Jon Goodman, NY (JG); Sally Sturman, NY (SS); Maurice Sanchez, NY (MS); Derriére L'Etoile Studios, NY (DES); ORT Druckstudio, Berlin, Germany (ORTD)
PUBLISHERS: Editions Ilene Kurtz, NY (EIK)
GALLERIES: Metro Pictures, New York, NY; Editions Ilene Kurtz, New York, NY; Heath Gallery, Atlanta, GA; Rhona Hoffman Gallery, Chicago, IL; Texas Gallery, Houston, TX; Josh Baer Gallery, New York, NY; Daniel Weinberg Gallery, Santa Monica, CA
MAILING ADDRESS: 547 Broadway, New York, NY 10012

TITLE	PUBLISHER	PRINTER	DATE	MEDIUM	DIMENSION (PAPER SIZE) IN INCHES	TYPE OF PAPER	EDITION NUMBER	NO. OF COLORS	ORIGINAL OPENING PRICE	CURRENT RETAIL PRICE
CURRENT EDITIONS:										
Ventriloquism (Set of 3)	EIK	JG/SS/MS/DES	1986	PH/LC	34 X 27 EA	AP	40 EA		1800 SET	3000 SET
Lying Objects (Set of 4)	EIK	ORTD	1992	PH/OFF	15 X 20 EA	SOM/S	50 EA	1 EA	2800 SET	2800 SET
									900 EA	900 EA

CLIFFORD SINGER

BORN: Great Neck, NY; May 19, 1955
EDUCATION: Alfred Univ, NY, BFA, 1973–77; Hunter Col, Grad Prog, NY, 1977–79; City Col of New York, NY, MFA, 1990; Baruch Col, City of New York, Department of Education, NY, 1992
TEACHING: Fiorello H LaGuardia, High Sch of Music & Art & Performing Arts, NY, 1991,92; High Sch of Art & Design, NY, 1990,91,92
AWARDS: Honorable Mention, Summit Art Center, NJ, Juried by Richard Anuszkiewicz, 1985; Change Found, Robert Rauschenberg, Founder, Grant, 1989
COLLECTIONS: Aldrich Mus of Contemp Art, Ridgefield, CT; Mus of Mod Art, NY; Gemeente Mus, Den Haag, The Netherlands; Rijksmuseum, Meermano, Den Haag, The Netherlands; Victoria & Albert Mus, London, England; Tate Gallery, London, England; British Mus, London, England; Metropolitan Mus of Art, NY; Stanford Univ, CA; Art Research Center, Kansas City, KS; Chelsea Sch of Art, London, England; Canterbury Sch of Art, London, England; Mus of Graphic Art, Tokyo, Japan; Bayerische Staatsbibliotek, Munchen, Germany; Book Mus, The Hague, The Netherlands; Armand Hammer Coll; Boca Raton Mus, FL
PRINTERS: Artist (ART)
PUBLISHERS: Artist (ART)
GALLERIES: Pace Editions, New York, NY; O K Harris Gallery, New York, NY; Lincoln Center Gallery, New York, NY
MAILING ADDRESS: 510 Broome St, New York, NY 10012

Clifford Singer
Jupiter
Courtesy the Artist

TITLE	PUBLISHER	PRINTER	DATE	MEDIUM	DIMENSION (PAPER SIZE) IN INCHES	TYPE OF PAPER	EDITION NUMBER	NO. OF COLORS	ORIGINAL OPENING PRICE	CURRENT RETAIL PRICE
CURRENT EDITIONS:										
Blue	ART	ART	1980	SP	34 X 34	R/100	30	1	150	400
Red	ART	ART	1980	SP	34 X 34	R/100	30	1	150	400
Black	ART	ART	1980	SP	34 X 34	R/100	30	1	150	400
Heptameter Suite (Set of 7)	ART	ART	1981	SP	24 X 24 EA	R/100	50 EA	1 EA	1200 SET	2100 SET
Pentameter Suite (Set of 5)	ART	ART	1982	SP	24 X 24 EA	R/100	50 EA	1 EA	1200 SET	1800 SET
Trimeter Suite (Set of 3)	ART	ART	1983	SP	32 X 32 EA	R/100	50 EA	1 EA	900 SET	1200 SET
Blue Pregression	ART	ART	1983	SP	14 X 25	R/100	100	1	200	250
Startfighter (Acrylic on Plexiglas)	ART	ART	1984	MULT	32 X 32	PLEX	30	8	650	3500
Phthalo (Acrylic on Plexiglas)	ART	ART	1984	PO	32 X 32	PLEX	200	8	500	3500
Magenta (Acrylic on Plexiglas)	ART	ART	1984	PO	32 X 32	PLEX	200	8	500	3500
Gray Composition (Acrylic on Plexiglas)	ART	ART	1984	PO	32 X 32	PLEX	200	8	500	3500
Infinity Suite (Set of 3) (Acrylic on Plexiglas)	ART	ART	1988	SP	20 DIA EA	PLEX	10 EA	2 EA	1500 SET	2100 SET
Jupiter	ART	ART	1991	SP	48 X 45	R/100	91	7	600	600
Jupiter (Sculpture)	ART	ART	1991	MULTI	16 X 17 X 3	WOOD	9	6	3000	3000

The retail prices of the 100,000 limited edition prints quoted in this directory are subject to change. Print publishers, artists and galleries were the direct sources for these quotations. Prices in the secondary market listed as "Sold Out Editions (Rare)" indicate that the publisher has a limited supply of that print or that the print is difficult to locate in the galleries.

MICHAEL SINGER

BORN: New York, NY; 1945
EDUCATION: Cornell Univ, Ithaca, NY; Rutgers Univ, New Brunswick, NJ 1963–68
COLLECTIONS: Wenkenpark Riehen, Basle, Switzerland, Guggenheim Mus, NY
PUBLISHERS: Palisades Press, Jersey City, NJ (PalP); Artist (ART)
PRINTERS: John Hutchinson, Jersey City, NJ, (JH); Palisades Press, Jersey City, NJ (PalP)
GALLERIES: Sperone Westwater Gallery, New York, NY; Fabric Workshop, New York, NY & Phila, PA

TITLE	PUBLISHER	PRINTER	DATE	MEDIUM	DIMENSION (PAPER SIZE) IN INCHES	TYPE OF PAPER	EDITION NUMBER	NO. OF COLORS	ORIGINAL OPENING PRICE	CURRENT RETAIL PRICE
CURRENT EDITIONS:										
7 Moon Ritual Series	ART/PalP	JH/PalP	1985	LC/CO	50 X 38 EA	AE/MUL/KIT	25 EA		2500 EA	3000 EA

JOHN CLEMENTE SIRICA

BORN: New Britain, CT; November 28, 1936
EDUCATION: The Citadel, Charleston, SC, BA; Georgetown Univ, Wash, DC, MFA
TEACHING: Smithsonian Associates Resident Program, Wash, DC; Printmakers Workshop, Wash, DC; Nat Coll of Fine Arts, Wash, DC
COLLECTIONS: Huntsville Art Mus, AL; George Washington Univ, Dimock Gallery, Wash, DC; Nat Coll of Fine Arts, Wash, DC; Phillips Mus, Wash, DC; Corcoran Gallery, Wash, DC; DeCordova Mus, Lincoln, MA
PRINTERS: Herbert A Fox, Merrimac, MA (HF); Fox Graphics, Merrimac, MA (FG)
PUBLISHERS: Fox Graphics, Merrimac, MA (FG); Washington Portfolio, Wash, DC (WP); Artist (ART)
GALLERIES: Fox Graphics, Merrimac, MA; Martha Tepper Contemporary Fine Arts, West Newton, MA

TITLE	PUBLISHER	PRINTER	DATE	MEDIUM	DIMENSION (PAPER SIZE) IN INCHES	TYPE OF PAPER	EDITION NUMBER	NO. OF COLORS	ORIGINAL OPENING PRICE	CURRENT RETAIL PRICE
SOLD OUT EDITIONS (RARE):										
View from the Shore	ART/FG	HG/FG	1983	LB	29 X 41	R/BFK	30	1	150	350
Small Horizontal Seascape	ART/FG	HG/FG	1983	LB	18 X 24	R/BFK	30	1	100	300
Winthrop Horizon Seascape	ART/FG	HG/FG	1983	LB	29 X 41	R/BFK	30	1	150	350
North Shore Seascape	ART/FG	HG/FG	1983	LB	29 X 41	R/BFK	30	1	150	350
Full Moon	ART/FG	HG/FG	1983	LB	29 X 41	R/BFK	30	1	150	350

ROBERT PAUL SIVARD

BORN: New York, NY; December 7, 1914
EDUCATION: Pratt Inst, NY; Nat Acad of Design; Acad Julian, Paris, France; New Sch for Social Research, NY
AWARDS: Thomas B Clarke Award Nat Acad of Design, NY, 1958; Gold Medal, Art Directors Club, 1958; Butler Mus Purchase Prize, 1970; Purchase Prize, Am Inst & Acad, 1980
COLLECTIONS: Library of Congress, Wash, DC; Butler Mus of Am Art, Youngstown, OH; Nat Mus of Am Art, Wash, DC; Newark Mus, NJ; New Jersey State Mus, Trenton, NJ; Gibbs Art Gallery, Charleston, SC
PRINTERS: Artist (ART)
PUBLISHERS: McBride Publishing (MP); NAIF International, Ltd, Los Angeles, CA (NAIF); Portfolio Prints (PP)
GALLERIES: Midtown Galleries, New York, NY; McBride Gallery, Annapolis, MD; Harison Soamer Gallery, Wash, DC
MAILING ADDRESS: 3013 Dumbarton Ave, NW, Washington, DC 20007

TITLE	PUBLISHER	PRINTER	DATE	MEDIUM	DIMENSION (PAPER SIZE) IN INCHES	TYPE OF PAPER	EDITION NUMBER	NO. OF COLORS	ORIGINAL OPENING PRICE	CURRENT RETAIL PRICE
SOLD OUT EDITIONS (RARE):										
Concierge Au Cour	PP	ART	1974	LC	14 X 20	R/100	50	1	70	300
L'Ame de France	PP	ART	1976	LC	17 X 24	R/100	50	1	70	300

ARLENE SLAVIN

BORN: New York, NY; October 26, 1942
EDUCATION: Cooper Union, NY, BFA, 1960–64; Pratt Inst, NY, MFA, 1965–67
TEACHING: Hofstra Univ, Long Island, NY, 1971–72; Pratt Inst, Brooklyn, NY, 1974; Skowhegan Art Sch, ME, 1975–76; Univ of Pennsylvania, Phila, PA, 1977; Syracuse Univ, NY, 1979
AWARDS: Nat Endowment for the Arts Fel, 1978; Winnipeg Art Gallery, Can, 1985; Madison Art Center, WI, 1985
RECENT EXHIB: Heckscher Mus, Huntington, NY, 1987; Katharina Rich Perlow Gallery, NY, 1988; Chauncey Gallery, Princeton, NJ, 1990
COLLECTIONS: Brooklyn Mus, NY; Berkeley Univ Mus, CA; Colby Col Mus, Waterville, ME; Metropolitan Mus, NY; Smithsonian Inst, Wash, DC; Allen Mem Mus, Oberlin Col, OH; Hudson River Mus, Yonkers, NY; Fogg Art Mus, Cambridge, MA; Portland Mus, OR; Norton Mus, West Palm Beach, FL; Neuberger Mus, Purchase NY; Orlando Mus of Art, FL; Heckscher Mus, Huntington, NY
PRINTERS: Jennifer Melby, NY (JM); Exeter Press, NY (EP); Styria Studio, NY (SS); Abigail J Brown, NY (AJB)
PUBLISHERS: 724 Prints (724P); Brooke Alexander, Inc, NY (BAI); Artist (ART)
GALLERIES: Brooke Alexander, Inc, New York, NY; Pace Editions, New York, NY; Elaine Benson Gallery, Bridgehampton, NY; Meredith Gallery, Baltimore, MD; Katharine Rich Perlow Gallery, New York, NY; Metropolitan Mus of Art, Mezzanine Gallery, New York, NY
MAILING ADDRESS: 119 E 18th St, New York, NY 10003

TITLE	PUBLISHER	PRINTER	DATE	MEDIUM	DIMENSION (PAPER SIZE) IN INCHES	TYPE OF PAPER	EDITION NUMBER	NO. OF COLORS	ORIGINAL OPENING PRICE	CURRENT RETAIL PRICE
SOLD OUT EDITIONS (RARE):										
Abnaki	BAI	SS	1975	MM	29 X 41	AP	30	10	300	850
Jackman	BAI	SS	1975	MM	29 X 41	AP	30	10	300	850
Sunset and Shooting Stars	BAI	SS	1977	MM	41 X 29	AP	15	7	350	750
Green Pastures in Golden Days	BAI	SS	1977	MM	29 X 41	AP	10	9	350	750
Butterflies and Little Fishes	BAI	SS	1977	MM	41 X 29	AP	15	8	350	750
Blue Skies and Sunny Days	BAI	SS	1977	MM	29 X 41	AP	15	7	350	750
Orange Sky Watching Night Arrive	BAI	SS	1977	MM	29 X 41	AP	10	8	350	750
Nightlights	BAI	SS	1977	MM	41 X 29	AP	10	8	350	750

ARLENE SLAVIN CONTINUED

TITLE	PUBLISHER	PRINTER	DATE	MEDIUM	DIMENSION (PAPER SIZE) IN INCHES	TYPE OF PAPER	EDITION NUMBER	NO. OF COLORS	ORIGINAL OPENING PRICE	CURRENT RETAIL PRICE
SOLD OUT EDITIONS (RARE):										
A Flag for Ree	BAI	SS	1977	MM	29 X 41	AP	15	9	350	750
Dawn Heron	724P	JM	1980	EB/A	27 X 38	SOM	40	7	650	850
Blue Mist	724P	JM	1980	EB/A	38 X 27	SOM	40	8	650	850
Twilight Cranes (Screen 4 Panel Folding)	724P	EP	1980	HMP	20 X 32	SOM	12	10	1200	1250
Twight Cranes (Flat)	724P	EP	1980	HMP	20 X 32	SOM	12	10	800	850
Foggy Dawn Geese (Folding Screen 4 Panel)	724P	EP	1980	HMP	20 X 32	SOM	12	10	1200	1250
Foggy Dawn Geese (Flat)	724P	EP	1980	HMP	20 X 32	SOM	12	10	800	850
CURRENT EDITIONS:										
American Narratives (Set of 4):									4800 SET	4800 SET
Ghost Tracks (with Gold Leaf)	ART	AJB	1989	PO/LIN/HC	30 X 41	AP/WA550	12	10	1200	1200
Spirits of the Night (with Gold Leaf)	ART	AJB	1989	PO/LIN/HC	30 X 41	AP/WA550	12	7	1200	1200
Alaskan Chronicles (with Gold Leaf)	ART	AJB	1989	PO/LIN/HC	30 X 41	AP/WA550	12	12	1200	1200
Still Point (with Gold Leaf)	ART	AJB	1989	PO/LIN/HC	30 X 41	AP/WA550	12	11	1200	1200

MARTHA SLAYMAKER

BORN: Saratoga, IN
EDUCATION: Ohio State Univ, Columbus, OH; Edinboro Col, PA; Baldwin Wallace Col, Berea, OH; John Herron Sch of Art, Indiana Univ, Bloomington, IN
TEACHING: Indiana Univ, Indianapolis, IN; Indianapolis Mus of Art, IN; Albuquerque Mus of Art, NM
RECENT EXHIB: Dubins Gallery, Los Angeles, CA, 1989; E M Donahue Gallery, NY, 1989; Dartmouth Street Gallery, Albuquerque, NM, 1990; Editions Limited, Indianapolis, IN, 1991
COLLECTIONS: Indianapolis Mus of Art, IN; New Mexico Mus of Fine Arts, Sante Fe, NM; Albuquerque Mus of Art, NM; Nat Mus of Jos, Nigeria; Univ of Northern Arizona, Flagstaff, AZ; Univ of Southern Illinois, Carbondale, IL; Columbia Univ, NY; Univ of Western Ontario, London, ON, Can; Jonson Gallery, Univ of New Mexico, Albuquerque, NM; Indiana Univ, Bloomington, IN; Ball State Univ, Muncie, IN; Mus of Art, History & Science, Albuquerque, NM; Univ of Illinois, Urbana, IL; Pennsylvania State Univ, State University Park, PA; Indiana State Univ, Terre Haute, IN; East Texas State Univ, Commerce, TX; Univ of Oklahoma, Norman, OK
PRINTERS: Tamarind Inst Albuquerque, NM (TI); William Haberman, Albuquerque, NM (WH); Jan Nelson (JN); Mark Berman (MB); Debbie Kirsch, Albuquerque, NM (DK); Ed Polack, Cape Girardeau, MO (EP); Tom Priut, Albuquerque, NM (TP); Deborah Kirsch-Hesse, Albuquerque, NM (DKH); Artist (ART)
PUBLISHERS: American Design, Denver, CO (AD); Jack O'Grady Galleries, Chicago, IL (OGGP); New York Graphic Society, Greenwich, CT (NYG); Artist (ART)
GALLERIES: Munson Gallery, Sante Fe, NM; Suzanne Brown Gallery, Scottsdale, AZ, Editions Limited Art Galleries, Indianapolis, IN & San Francisco, CA; Gallery A. Taos, NM; American Design, Denver, CO; Jack Meier Gallery, Houston, TX; Alpha Gallery, Denver, CO; Dubins Gallery, Los Angeles, CA; E M Donahue Gallery, New York, NY
MAILING ADDRESS: 451 Gavilan PL NW, ALbuquerque, NM 87107

TITLE	PUBLISHER	PRINTER	DATE	MEDIUM	DIMENSION (PAPER SIZE) IN INCHES	TYPE OF PAPER	EDITION NUMBER	NO. OF COLORS	ORIGINAL OPENING PRICE	CURRENT RETAIL PRICE
SOLD OUT EDITIONS (RARE):										
Canaanite Fragments	ART	ART	1978	COL	12 X 20	AP	20	6	60	600
Canaanite Woman	ART	ART	1978	COL	12 X 18	AP	20	3	40	700
Canaanite Woman, State 2	ART	ART	1979	COL	12 X 18	AP	40	3	80	600
Canaanite Woman State 3	ART	JN	1979	COL	12 X 18	AP	225	3	150	500
Pueblo Woman, State 1	AD	JN	1980	COL	30 X 22	AP	175	9	180	500
Pueblo Woman, State 2	ART	JN	1981	COL	22 X 30	AP	80	11	300	500
CURRENT EDITIONS:										
Anasazi the Ancient Ones	ART	MB	1980	COL	19 X 26	AP	175	9	200	350
The Ancient Ones V	ART	MB	1981	COL	24 X 36	AP	150	8	250	500
In the Beginning III	ART	MB	1981	COL	24 X 34	AP	175	5	200	350
*Full Moon in Aries	ART	DK	1982	COL	24 X 36	AP	150	6	250	400
*Full Moon in Aries	ART	DK	1982	COL	24 X 36	AP	150	6	250	400
*Moonlight Pagodas	ART	DK	1982	COL	24 X 36	AP	150	6	250	400
Pueblo Women	OGG	WH/TI	1982	LC	22 X 30	R/BFK	150	5	300	500
Night Skies I, II, III (Set of 3)	ART	TP/DKH	1982	SP/WC	24 X 36 EA	AP	80 EA	7 EA	600 SET	1000 SET
									250 EA	350 EA
Origins I	AD	EP	1983	SP/WC/ EMB/COL	25 X 36	AP	35	7	250	500
Counterpoint	ART	MB	1984	WC/EMB/ COL	25 X 40	AP	30	5	250	400

*The Above Three Prints Work as a Triptych

THOMAS CHESTER SLETTEHAUGH

BORN: Minneapolis, MN; May 8, 1925
EDUCATION: Univ of South Carolina; Univ of Georgia, 1943–45; Univ of Minnesota, Minneapolis, MN, BS, 1943–49; MEd, 1949–50; Williams Col, MA, Syracuse Univ, NY, 1954; Pennsylvania State Univ, PhD Ed, 1954–56
TEACHING: Pennsylvania State Univ, 1954–56; Univ of Minnesota, MN, 1970 to present
RECENT EXHIB: Minnesota Fine Arts, Minneapolis, MN, 1988; Centro Para Las Artes, Montevideo, Uruguay, 1990; Kossuth Univ, Debrecen, Hungary, 1990; Taller Gallery, Barcelona, Spain, 1987,88,89,90
COLLECTIONS: Dubrovnik Univ Center, Vienna; Art Univ Gallery, Madrid, Spain; Heidelberg Univ, Germany; Carnegie-Mellon Inst, Pittsburgh, PA; Philadelphia Mus of Art, PA; Baltimore Mus, MD; Univ of MInnesota, MN; Univ of Belgrade, Yugoslavia; Bucharest Univ, Romania; Cultural Center of Budapest, Hungary
PRINTERS: Artist (ART)
PUBLISHERS: Finsbury Press Pty, Ltd (FP); Adelaide, South Australia, Australia (A)

THOMAS CHESTER SLETTEHAUGH CONTINUED

GALLERIES: Lesch at Butler, Minneapolis, MN; Coffman Gallery, Univ of Minnesota, Minneapolis, MN

MAILING ADDRESS: 49 Southeast Williams Ave, Prospect Park, Minneapolis, MN 55414

TITLE	PUBLISHER	PRINTER	DATE	MEDIUM	DIMENSION (PAPER SIZE) IN INCHES	TYPE OF PAPER	EDITION NUMBER	NO. OF COLORS	ORIGINAL OPENING PRICE	CURRENT RETAIL PRICE
SOLD OUT EDITIONS (RARE):										
Portrait of an Artist	A	ART	1980	SP	12 X 14	R/100	35	3	250	500
People's Rupublic of China-1	A	ART	1981	SP	12 X 14	R/100	20	4	250	450
People's Republic of China-2	A	ART	1981	P	8 X 10	R/100	97		150	350
CURRENT EDITIONS:										
After Images of Emotion	FP	ART	1970	SP	20 X 30	R/100	35	9	125	500
Outer Space Concepts	FP	ART	1972	SP	20 X 30	R/100	30	6	145	500
Vine Variations	FP	ART	1972	SP	14 X 20	R/100	24	6	120	450
Nature Series	FP	ART	1975	P	8 X 10	R/100	18		75	250
Hungarian Series	A	ART	1977	P	8 X 10	R/100	12		85	250
England-Soviet Series	A	ART	1978	P	8 X 10	R/100	18		85	250
Materialdrucke	A	ART	1978	SP/M	20 X 30	R/100	30	7	175	450
See Peter Magrath	A	ART	1980	SP/MON	12 X 14	R/100	15	4	250	450

JEANETTE PASIN SLOAN

BORN: Chicago, IL; March 18, 1946
EDUCATION: Marymount Col, Tarrytown, NY, BFA, 1967; Art Inst of Chicago, IL, MFA, 1969
AWARDS: Purchase Award, Illinois State Mus, Springfield, IL, 1976; Galex Award, Galesburg Civic Center, IL, 1977; Watson F Blair Prize, Art Inst of Chicago, IL, 1981; Illinois Arts Coun Fel, 1986
RECENT EXHIB: Adams-Middleton Gallery, Dallas, TX, 1987; David Adamson Gallery, Wash, DC, 1987; Leedy-Voulkos Gallery, Kansas City, MO, 1987; Univ of Oklahoma, Norman, OK, 1987–88; Roger Ramsay Gallery, NY, 1987,92
COLLECTIONS: Cleveland Mus of Fine Arts, OH; Art Inst of Chicago, IL; Fogg Mus, Boston, MA; Metropolitan Mus, NY; Yale Univ, New Haven, CT; Minneapolis, Art Inst, MN; Nat Coll of Fine Art, Smithsonian Inst, Wash, DC

PRINTERS: Landfall Press Inc, Chicago, IL (LPI); Jack Lemon, Chicago, IL (JL); Brian Lynch (BL); Michael Berdan (MB); Barbara Spies, Chicago, IL (BS); Heidijo Lemon, Chicago, IL (HL); Four Brothers Press, Chicago, IL (FBP)
PUBLISHERS: Landfall Press Inc, Chicago, IL (LPI); John Szoke Graphics, Inc, NY (JSG); Artist (ART); Four Brothers Press, Chicago, IL (FBP)
GALLERIES: G W Einstein Gallery, New York, NY; David Adamson Gallery, Wash, DC; Landfall Press Inc, Chicago, IL; Adams–Middleton Gallery, Dallas, TX; Roger Ramsey Gallery, Chicago, IL; John Szoke Graphics, New York, NY; Leedy-Voulkos Gallery, Kansas City, MO; Tatistcheff Gallery, Inc, Santa Monica, CA; Steven Scott Gallery, Baltimore, MD; Peltz Gallery, Milwaukee, WI; Butters Gallery, Ltd, Portland, OR
MAILING ADDRESS: 535 Keystone River, Forest, IL 60305

Jeanette Pasin Sloan
Mercado Stripes
Courtesy John Szoke Graphics, Inc

Jeanette Pasin Sloan
La Terazza, State I
Courtesy Landfall Press, Inc

The retail prices of the 100,000 limited edition prints quoted in this directory are subject to change. Print publishers, artists and galleries were the direct sources for these quotations. Prices in the secondary market listed as "Sold Out Editions (Rare)" indicate that the publisher has a limited supply of that print or that the print is difficult to locate in the galleries.

JEANETTE PASIN SLOAN CONTINUED

TITLE	PUBLISHER	PRINTER	DATE	MEDIUM	DIMENSION (PAPER SIZE) IN INCHES	TYPE OF PAPER	EDITION NUMBER	NO. OF COLORS	ORIGINAL OPENING PRICE	CURRENT RETAIL PRICE
SOLD OUT EDITIONS (RARE):										
Silver Bowls	LPI	JL/LPI	1978	LC	32 X 43	R/BFK	50	9	300	1500
Silver Bowls, State I	LPI	JL/LPI	1978	LC	30 X 42	R/BFK	10	1	300	1800
Cup with Blue Rim	LPI	JL/LPI	1980	LC	25 X 34	R/BFK	60	6	400	900
Cup with Blue Rim, State I	LPI	JL/LPI	1980	LC	25 X 34	R/BFK	10	1	400	800
Cup with Blue Spoon	ART	JL/LPI	1980	LC	25 X 34	R/BFK	60	6	400	1200
Jeanette Pasin Sloan (Set of 4)							25		2400 SET	4000 SET
Binary	LPI	BL/LPI	1986	AB	24 X 22	JBG	45	1	650	850
Boston Red	LPI	MB/LPI	1986	WC	24 X 22	KIZ	45	15	950	1100
Sergeant First Class	LPI	JL/BS/HL/LPI	1986	LC	24 X 22	R/BFK	40	8	850	950
Sergeant First Class, State I	LPI	JL/BS/HL/LPI	1986	LC	24 X 22	R/BFK				
(Available Only as Part of Portfolio)	LPI	JL/BS/HL/LPI	1986	LB	24 X 22	R/BFK	25	1	xxx	xxx
Sears Tower	JSG	JL/LPI	1986	LC	49 X 31	R/BFK	85	10	1200	1800
Sears Tower	JSG	JL/LPI	1986	LB	49 X 31	R/BFK	20	1	800	1500
Notre Dame	LPI	JL/LPI	1986	LC	20 X 26	R/BFK	30	2	400	850
CURRENT EDITIONS:										
Red Shift	FBP	FBP	1983	LC	30 X 26	R/BFK	50	5	500	1000
Bassano Stripes	FBP	FBP	1984	LC	25 X 23	R/BFK	75	11	500	1000
La Terrazza	LPI	JL/LPI	1986	LC	27 X 22	SOM	125		650	900
La Terrazza, State I	LPI	JL/LPI	1986	LB	27 X 22	SOM	18	1	500	850
Notre Dame	LPI	JL/LPI	1986	LC	20 X 26	AC	30	2	450	750
Mexican Zebra	LPI	JL/LPI	1987	WC/MON	32 X 32	KIZ/BL	8	Varies	800	800
La Terrazza	LPI	JL/LPI	1988	LC	27 X 22	SOM	125	5	900	1200
Texas	LPI	JL/LPI	1989	LC	27 X 22	SOM	50	8	750	750
Trinity	LPI	JL/LPI	1989	LC	24 X 22	SOM	65	11	900	950
Untitled	LPI	JL/LPI	1989	MON/C	23 X 18 EA	SOM	1 EA	Varies	1200 EA	1500 EA
Emergence	LPI	JL/LPI	1990	EB/HC	30 X 22	SOM	10	Varies	1200	1500
Penumbra	LPI	JL/LPI	1991	LC/EB	23 X 22	SOM	25		750	750
Mercato Stripes	JSG	JL/LPI	1992-93	LC	36 X 40	R/BFK	75	6	1200	1200

CARY SMITH

BORN: Puerto Rico; 1955; US Citizen
EDUCATION: Sir John Cass Art Sch, London, England, 1976; Syracuse Abroad, Florence, Italy, 1976; Syracuse Univ Art Sch, NY, BFA, 1977
AWARDS: Art in Public Spaces Award, 1985; Connecticut Comm on the Art Grants, 1983,86
RECENT EXHIB: Koury Wingate Gallery, NY, 1990; Vrej Baghoomian Gallery, NY, 1990; Linda Cathcart Gallery, Santa Monica, CA, 1991; Fay Gold Gallery, Atlanta, GA, 1991; Stephen Wirtz Gallery, San Francisco, CA, 1991; Rubin Spangle Gallery, New York, NY, 1992

COLLECTIONS: Whitney Mus of Am Art, NY; Brooklyn Mus, NY; Osaka Art Mus, Japan; Wadsworth Atheneum, Hartford, CT
PRINTERS: Peter Pettengill, Hinsdale, NH (PP); Wingate Studio, Hinsdale, NH (WS)
PUBLISHERS: Edition Deger, Sag Harbor, NY (EdDeg)
GALLERIES: Linda Cathcart Gallery, Santa Monica, CA; Stephen Wirtz Gallery, San Francisco, CA; Koury Wingate Gallery, New York, NY; Rubin Spangle Gallery, New York, NY; Vrej Baghoomian Gallery, New York, NY; Adam Baumgold Fine Art, New York, NY
MAILING ADDRESS: P O Box 924, Farmington, CT 06034

TITLE	PUBLISHER	PRINTER	DATE	MEDIUM	DIMENSION (PAPER SIZE) IN INCHES	TYPE OF PAPER	EDITION NUMBER	NO. OF COLORS	ORIGINAL OPENING PRICE	CURRENT RETAIL PRICE
CURRENT EDITIONS:										
Views & Mirrors (Set of 3)	EdDeg	PP/WS	1992	EB/A	37 X 28 EA	SOM	35 EA	1 EA	2400 SET	2400 SET

GARY DOUGLAS SMITH

BORN: San Francisco, CA; July 29, 1948
EDUCATION: California Col of Arts & Crafts, Oakland, CA, BFA, 1971; Study with S W Hayter, Etching, Paris, France, 1979; Study with Yozo Hamaguchi, San Francisco, CA, 1982
TEACHING: Lectr, Fine Art Mus of San Francisco, Ca, 1985; Lectr, California Col of Arts & Crafts, Oakland, CA, 1987,88
AWARDS: Silver Prize, California Col of Arts & Crafts, Oakland, CA, 1969
RECENT EXHIB: Inverness Ridge Assoc, CA, 1987; San Francisco Arts Comm, CA, 1988; Concordia-Argonaut Club, San Francisco, CA, 1988,89; Inverness Studio, CA, 1987,88,89,90

COLLECTIONS: Palm Springs Desert Art Mus, CA; Achenbach Found, San Francisco, CA
PRINTERS: Richard Newlin, Berkeley, CA (RN); Hayoka Press, San Francisco, CA (HP); Richard Horn, San Francisco, CA (RH); Archer Press, Berkeley, CA (AP); Joan Doane, Berkeley, CA (JD); Ink Press, Daly City, CA (IP); Ikuru Kuwahara, Daly City, CA (IK); Marilyn O'Keeffe, San Francisco, CA (MO)
PUBLISHERS: M Elder, San Francisco, CA (ME)
GALLERIES: Vorpal Galleries, San Francisco, CA & New York, NY; Gallery 56, Salt Lake City, UT; Claudia Chapline Gallery, Stinson Beach, CA; PS Galleries, Ogunquit, ME
MAILING ADDRESS: PO Box 244, Inverness, CA 94937

TITLE	PUBLISHER	PRINTER	DATE	MEDIUM	DIMENSION (PAPER SIZE) IN INCHES	TYPE OF PAPER	EDITION NUMBER	NO. OF COLORS	ORIGINAL OPENING PRICE	CURRENT RETAIL PRICE
SOLD OUT EDITIONS (RARE):										
Dawn	VG	RN	1976	LC	10 X 14	GE	20	4	500	3500
Mountain Sound-Four Panels	VG	RN	1976	LC	16 X 62	AP	40	20	2200	3000
Winter Lake	VG	RN	1977	LC	22 X 18	AP	40	5	1200	6000

GARY DOUGLAS SMITH CONTINUED

TITLE	PUBLISHER	PRINTER	DATE	MEDIUM	DIMENSION (PAPER SIZE) IN INCHES	TYPE OF PAPER	EDITION NUMBER	NO. OF COLORS	ORIGINAL OPENING PRICE	CURRENT RETAIL PRICE
CURRENT EDITIONS:										
Ocean Passage	ME	RN	1977	LC	14 X 20	RP	48	4	700	1200
La Corriente	ME	RN	1978	LC	28 X 20	GE	40	10	1100	1800
Evening Rain III	ME	RH	1978	SP	24 X 39	AP	24	5	2200	3500
Ridge of Light	ME	JD	1980	LC	10 X 15	GE	30	4	1200	2000
Shadow of Dawn	ME	IK	1981	LC	15 X 20	AP	48	5	1800	2000
Red Forest	ME	IK	1981	LC	28 X 19	AP	30	4	2000	2200
Solar Wind	ME	RH	1981	SP	28 X 20	GE	37	3	2000	2200
Mountain Lake	ME	IK	1981	LC	17 X 14	IN	35	7	1500	1800
Sierra	ME	ME	1982	AC	10 X 6	GE	75	5	900	1000
Mist	ME	IK	1982	LC	10 X 6	GE	60	4	900	1000

KIKI SMITH

RECENT EXHIB: Illinois State Univ, Normal, IL, 1992; Wesleyan Univ, Ezra & Cecile Zilkha Gallery, Middletown, CT, 1992; Shoshana Wayne Gallery, Santa Monica, CA, 1992
PRINTERS: Judith Solodkin, NY (JS); Solo Press, NY (SP); Keith Brintzenhofe, NY (KB); Lorena Salcedo, NY (LS); Douglas Volle, NY (DV); Hitoshi Kido, West Islip, NY (HK); Bruce Wankel, West Islip, NY (BW); Craig Zammiello, West Islip, NY (CZ); Universal Limited Art Editions, West Islip, NY (ULAE); Richard Finch, Normal, IL (RF); Meda Rives, Normal, IL (MR); Veda Rives, Normal, IL (VR); Normal Editions Workshop, IL (NEW); John Lund, West Islip, NY (JL)
PUBLISHERS: Fawbush Editions, NY (FE); Universal Limited Art Editions, West Islip, NY (ULAE); Normal Editions Workshop, IL (NEW)
GALLERIES: Fawbush Editions, New York, NY; Solo Press Gallery, New York, NY; Shoshana Wayne Gallery, Santa Monica, CA; Thomas Smith Fine Art, Fort Wayne, IN; Thomas Segal Gallery, Boston, MA; Normal Editions Workshop, Illinois State Univ, Normal, IL; Brooke Alexander Editions, New York, NY

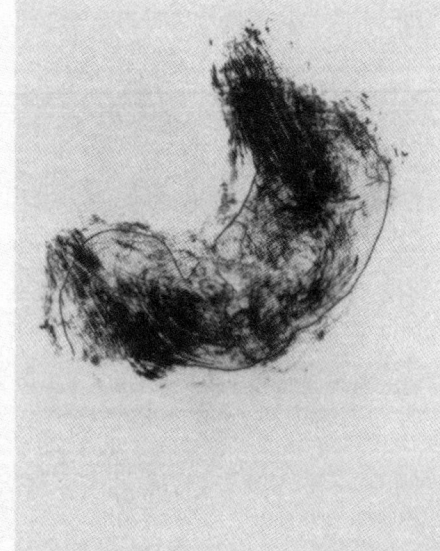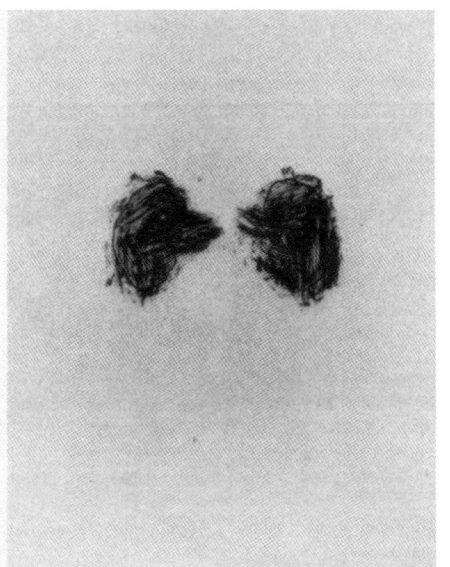

Kiki Smith
Heart, Stomach and Kidneys
(from Possession is Nine-Tenths of the Law)
Courtesy the Artist

TITLE	PUBLISHER	PRINTER	DATE	MEDIUM	DIMENSION (PAPER SIZE) IN INCHES	TYPE OF PAPER	EDITION NUMBER	NO. OF COLORS	ORIGINAL OPENING PRICE	CURRENT RETAIL PRICE
CURRENT EDITIONS:										
Possession is Nine-Tenths of the Law (Set of 9)	FE	JS/SP	1985	SP/WA/MON	21 X 17 EA	AC	15 EA		2000 SET	2400 SET
Untitled			1990	LC	36 X 36	AC	54	2		650
Banshee Pearls (12 Sheets)	ULAE	KB/LS/DV/ULAE	1991	LC	23 X 31	TOR	51	4	3600 SET	3600 SET
Untitled	ULAE	KB/HK/BW/CZ/ULAE	1992	I/CO	42 X 62	HMP	50		2500	2500
Untitled	NEW	RF/MR/VR/NEW	1992	LB	32 X 22	Nepal H4	30	1	800	800
Kiki Smith, 1993	ULAE	HK/JL/CZ/ULAE	1993	I	73 X 37	JP	33	1	2500	2500

LESLIE SMITH

BORN: Bromley, Kent, England; September 28, 1948
EDUCATION: Hornsley Col of Art, England, 1967–68; Maidstone Col of Art, England, Diploma, 1968–71; Royal Acad Sch, London, England, Grad Work, Painting, 1971–74
PRINTERS: Curwen Chilford, London, England (CC)
PUBLISHERS: John Szoke Graphics, NY (JSG)
GALLERIES: John Szoke Graphics, New York, NY; King Street Galleries, London, England

LESLIE SMITH CONTINUED

TITLE	PUBLISHER	PRINTER	DATE	MEDIUM	DIMENSION (PAPER SIZE) IN INCHES	TYPE OF PAPER	EDITION NUMBER	NO. OF COLORS	ORIGINAL OPENING PRICE	CURRENT RETAIL PRICE
CURRENT EDITIONS:										
Sheffield Park Garden in Autumn	JSG	CC	1991	SP	17 X 21	AP	300		400	400
Stourhead in Winter	JSG	CC	1991	SP	17 X 21	AP	300		400	400

JAUNE QUICK-TO-SEE SMITH

BORN: Flathead Reservation, MT; 1940
EDUCATION: Framingham State Col. MA, BA, 1976; Univ of New Mexico, Albuquerque, NM, MA, 1980
AWARDS: Purchase Award, Acad of Arts & Letters, NY, 1987; Fel Award, Western States Art Found, 1988; Honorary Prof, Beaumont Chair, Washington Univ, St Louis, MO, 1989
RECENT EXHIB: Custer County Art Center, Miles City, MT, 1987; Bernice Steinbaum Gallery, NY, 1987; Marilyn Butler Fine Art, Scottsdale, AZ, 1987,88,89; Portland Sch of Art, Baxter Gallery, ME, 1992
COLLECTIONS: Albuquerque Mus, NM; Denver Art Mus, CO; Thomas Gilcrease Mus, OK; Heard Mus, Phoenix, AZ; Minneapolis Art Inst, MN; Mus of Mankind, Vienna, Austria; Nat Mus of Am Art, Smithsonian Inst, Wash, DC; Newark Art Mus, NJ; Stamford Mus, CT; Univ of Regina, Canada; Albright-Knox Art Gallery, Buffalo, NY; Corcoran Gallery of Art, Wash, DC
PRINTERS: Barbara Telleen, Albuquerque, NM (BT); Carolyn Muskat, Albuquerque, NM (CM); Maria Schleiner, Albuquerque, NM (MS), Artist (ART); Bill Lagattuta, Albuquerque, NM (BL); Tamarind Inst, Albuquerque, NM (TI)
PUBLISHERS: Tamarind Inst, Albuquerque, NM (TI)
GALLERIES: Tamarind Inst, Albuquerque, NM; Lew Allen/Butler Fine Art, Santa Fe, NM; Bernice Steinbaum Gallery, New York, NY; Stremmel Galleries, Reno, NV; Hoshour Gallery, Albuquerque, NM; DEL Fine Art Galleries, Taos, NM; Jan Cicero Gallery, Chicago, IL

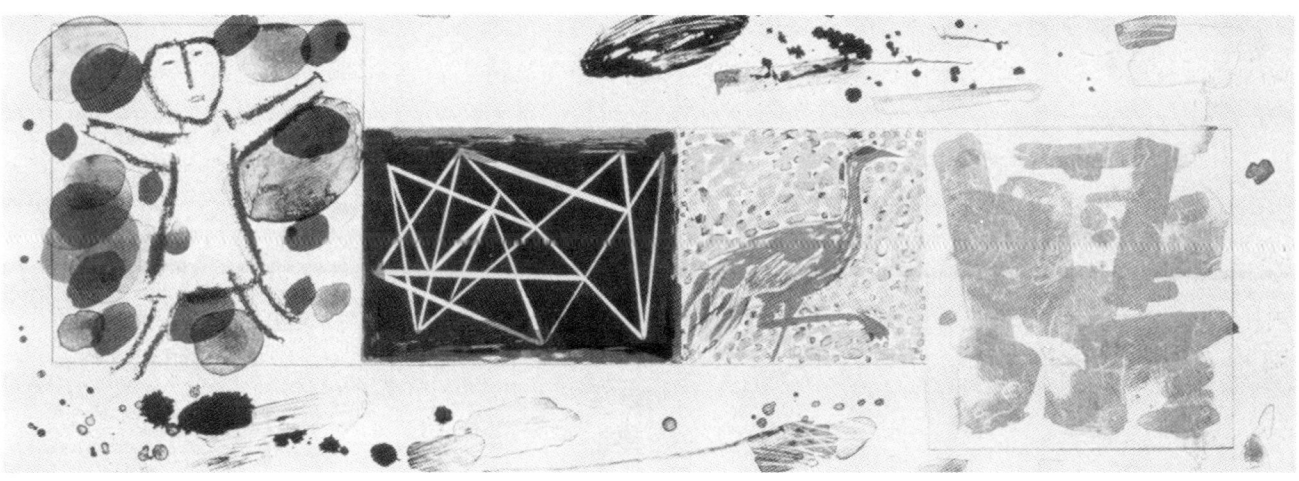

Juane Quick-To-See Smith
Sandhill North
Courtesy Tamarind Institute

TITLE	PUBLISHER	PRINTER	DATE	MEDIUM	DIMENSION (PAPER SIZE) IN INCHES	TYPE OF PAPER	EDITION NUMBER	NO. OF COLORS	ORIGINAL OPENING PRICE	CURRENT RETAIL PRICE
CURRENT EDITIONS:										
Sandhill North	TI	BT/TI	1982	LC/CC/HC	15 X 42	AP/W	40	3	250	385
Sandhill South	TI	BT/TI	1982	LC/HC	30 X 15	SOM/S	47	3	200	330
Fancy Dancer	TI	ART/CM/BL/TI	1988	LC/MON	30 X 42 EA	AP/W	12 EA	Varies	500	550
Salish Dancers, State I	TI	ART/CM/BL/TI	1988	LC/MON	26 X 23 EA	AP/W	11 EA	Varies	225	250
Salish Dancers, State II	TI	ART/MS/BL/TI	1988	LC/MON	26 X 23 EA	AP/W	5 EA	Varies	225	250

MICHAEL A SMITH

BORN: Philadelphia, PA; February 16, 1942
EDUCATION: Temple Univ, Phila, PA, BS, 1963
TEACHING: Vis Prof, Philadelphia Col of Art, PA, 1970–72; Bucks County Com Col, Newton, PA, 1971–73
AWARDS: Nat Endowment for the Arts Fel, Photography, 1977; Commission, Photography, Toledo Mus, OH, 1980; International Festival of Photography, Arles, France, Best Photographic Book of the Year, 1981; Commission, Historic New Orleans Collection, Photography, LA, 1985
RECENT EXHIB: Loyola Col, Baltimore MD, 1987; Retrosp, Photography, International Mus of Photography, George Eastman House, Rochester, NY, 1992
COLLECTIONS: Mus of Mod Art, NY; Art Inst of Chicago, IL; Center for Creative Photography, Tucson, AZ; Metropolitan Mus of Art, NY; Mus of Fine Arts, Boston, MA; Nat Gallery of Canada, Ottawa, Canada; Philadelphia Mus, PA; Stedelijk Mus, Amsterdam, Netherlands
PRINTERS: Artist (ART)
PUBLISHERS: Lodima Press, Revere, PA (LP); Regnis Press, Boynton Beach, FL (RP); Princeton Gallery of Fine Art, NJ (PGFA); Artist (ART)
GALLERIES: Paul Kopeiken Gallery, Los Angeles, CA; Scott Nichols Gallery, San Francisco, CA; Santa Fe Lightsource, Santa Fe, NM; Alinder Gallery, Gualala, CA
MAILING ADDRESS: PO Box 400, Bunker Hill Rd, Ottsville, PA 18942

TITLE	PUBLISHER	PRINTER	DATE	MEDIUM	DIMENSION (PAPER SIZE) IN INCHES	TYPE OF PAPER	EDITION NUMBER	NO. OF COLORS	ORIGINAL OPENING PRICE	CURRENT RETAIL PRICE
SOLD OUT EDITIONS (RARE):										
Twelve Photographs, 1967–69 (Set of 12)	ART	ART	1970	PH	13 X 15 EA		25 EA	1 EA	150	8000

MICHAEL A SMITH CONTINUED

TITLE	PUBLISHER	PRINTER	DATE	MEDIUM	DIMENSION (PAPER SIZE) IN INCHES	TYPE OF PAPER	EDITION NUMBER	NO. OF COLORS	ORIGINAL OPENING PRICE	CURRENT RETAIL PRICE
SOLD OUT EDITIONS (RARE):										
Eight Landscape Photographs	RP	ART	1983	PH	13 X 25 EA		20 EA	1 EA	2500	6000
Princeton: A Portfolio of 36 Black and White Photographs (Set of 36)	PGFA	ART	1986	PH	13 X 15 13 X 25 24 X 28		50 EA	1 EA	12500 SET	15000 SET

MOISHE SMITH

BORN: Chicago, IL; January 10, 1929
EDUCATION: New Sch of Social Research, NY, BA, 1950; Univ of Iowa, Iowa City, IA, MFA, 1953
TEACHING: Vis Art, Printmaking, Univ of Wisconsin, Milwaukee, WI, 1966–67; Vis Art, Ohio State Univ, Columbus, OH, Spring, 1971; Univ of Iowa, Iowa City, IA, Fall, 1971; Assoc Prof, Univ of Wisconsin, Parkside, WI, 1972–77; Prof, Utah State Univ, Logan, UT, 1977 to present
AWARDS: Four Seasons Res Grant, Southern Illinois Univ, Carbondale, IL, 1957; Fulbright Fel, 1959–61; Solomon R Guggenheim Fel, 1967–68; Eastern European Res Grant, Univ of Wisonsin, Parkside, WI, 1976; Mountain Landscapes & Nat Monuments Res Grants, Utah State Univ, Logan, UT, 1983; Utah Artist of the Year, 1988
RECENT EXHIB: Chase Home Mus of Utah Folk Art, Salt Lake City, UT, 1989; Utah Arts Council, Glendinning Gallery, Salt Lake City, UT, 1989
COLLECTIONS: Metropolitan Mus of Art, NY; Rijksmuseum, Amsterdam, Holland; Boymans Van Beuningen, Rotterdam, Holland; Mus of Mod Art, NY; Art Inst of Chicago, IL; Philadelphia Art Mus, PA; Nat Gallery of Art, Wash, DC; Galleria Degli Uffizi, Florence, Italy; Kestner Mus, Hannover, Germany; Library of Congress, Wash, DC
PRINTERS: Artist (ART)
PUBLISHERS: Artist (ART)
GALLERIES: Associated American Artists, New York, NY; Jane Haslem Salon, Wash, DC; van Straaten Gallery, Chicago, IL; Hank Baum Gallery, San Francisco, CA; Hahn Gallery, Phila, PA; Dolores Chase Fine Art, Salt Lake City, UT
MAILING ADDRESS: Department of Art, Utah State Unversity, Logan, UT 84322–4000

TITLE	PUBLISHER	PRINTER	DATE	MEDIUM	DIMENSION (PAPER SIZE) IN INCHES	TYPE OF PAPER	EDITION NUMBER	NO. OF COLORS	ORIGINAL OPENING PRICE	CURRENT RETAIL PRICE
CURRENT EDITIONS:										
The Point	ART	ART	1965	EB	14 X 19	R/BFK	50	1	75	300
Budapest	ART	ART	1977	I	20 X 27	GE	60	1	175	250
Juniper and Sage	ART	ART	1978	EC	20 X 26	GE	60	2	200	275
Blacksmith Fork	ART	ART	1979	I	24 X 34	GE	60	1	200	300
The Dugway	ART	ART	1980	I	24 X 34	GE	60	1	200	350
China Wall	ART	ART	1980	I	24 X 34	GE	60	1	200	300
Classic Landscape	ART	ART	1980	EC	18 X 22	GE	60	3	200	275
Left Hand Fork	ART	ART	1981	I	24 X 34	GE	60	1	250	300
The Benches	ART	ART	1981	EC	18 X 26	GE	60	3	200	275
Ivory Towers	ART	ART	1981	EC	18 X 26	GE	60	3	200	275
Wellsvilles	ART	ART	1982	EC	18 X 26	GE	60	2	225	275

RICHARD SMITH

BORN: Letchworth, Hertfordshire, England; 1931
EDUCATION: Luton Sch of Art, England, 1948–50; St Albans Sch of Art, London, England, 1952–54; Royal Col of Art, London, England, 1954–57
TEACHING: St Martin's Sch of Art, London, England, 1961–63; Univ of Virginia, Charlottesville, VA, 1967; Univ of California, Davis, CA, 1975
AWARDS: Royal Col of Art, Scholarship for Travel in Italy, 1957; Harkness Fel Travel in US, 1959–61; Scull Award, Venice Biennale, Italy, 1966; Grand Prize, Sao Paulo Bienal, Brazil, 1967
RECENT EXHIB: Richard L Feigen & Company, NY, 1992
PRINTERS: Advanced Graphics, London, England (AG); Cliff White, London, England (CW); Ian Lawson, London, England, (IL); Crown Point Press, San Francisco, CA (CPP); J C Editions, (JCE); Patricia Branstead, NY (PB); Aeropress, NY (A); Maurice Sanchez, NY (MS); Alan Cox (AC); Petersburg Press, London, England (PP); Artist (ART)
PUBLISHERS: Bernard Jacobson Ltd, London, England (BJL); Crown Point Press, San Francisco, CA (CPP); Petersburg Press, London, England (PP); Riverhouse Editions, Clark, CO (RHE)
GALLERIES: Bernard Jacobson Ltd, London, England; Irving Galleries, Palm Beach, FL; Crown Point Press, New York, NY & San Francisco, CA; Dolly Fiterman Gallery, Minneapolis, MN; Gallery One, Fort Worth, TX; Petersburg Press, London, England & New York, NY; Van Straaten Gallery, Chicago, IL; Tyler Graphics, Ltd, Mount Kisco, NY; Gallery C, Raleigh, NC; Gallery 10, Inc, Santa Fe, NM & North Scottsdale, AZ & Scottsdale, AZ

Richard Smith
Untitled #25
Courtesy Riverhouse Editions

RICHARD SMITH CONTINUED

TITLE	PUBLISHER	PRINTER	DATE	MEDIUM	DIMENSION (PAPER SIZE) IN INCHES	TYPE OF PAPER	EDITION NUMBER	NO. OF COLORS	ORIGINAL OPENING PRICE	CURRENT RETAIL PRICE
SOLD OUT EDITIONS (RARE):										
Sixteen Pieces of Paper	PP	PP	1969	LC	16 X 15	AP	75		500	5000
Bramble	PP	PP	1970	LC	30 X 22	AP	75		500	1500
Diary	BJL	AG	1975	SP	28 X 72	JG	25	2	1000	6000
Nosegay	BJL	AG	1975	SP	20 X 20	JG	25	4	500	3500
Parterre	BJL	AG	1975	SP	20 X 20	JG	75	3	300	1500
Russian I, II (Set of 2)	BJL	CW	1975	EC	20 X 20 EA	JG	50 EA	2–3 EA	500 EA	2000 EA
Four Knots	BJL	IL	1976	LC	30 X 30	SP	50	4	500	1500
Red Button	BJL	IL	1976	LC	27 X 30	SP	50	4	500	1500
Garden City	BJL	IL	1976	LC	30 X 30	SP	50	2	500	1500
Large Green	BJL	CPP	1976	A	39 X 39	AP	35	3	600	2500
CURRENT EDITIONS:										
Large Red	BJL	CPP	1976	A	39 X 39	AP	35	2	600	2200
Grey	BJL	JCE	1976	A	24 X 24	AP	50	2	600	1200
Yellow	BJL	JCE	1977	A	26 X 22	AP	50	2	600	1000
Blue	BJL	JCE	1977	A	26 X 22	AP	50	2	600	1000
Large Blue	BJL	JCE	1977	A	27 X 28	AP	60	2	600	1000
Orange	BJL	JCE	1977	A	28 X 27	AP	80	2	600	1000
Burgandy	BJL	JCE	1977	A	32 X 29	AP	50	2	500	1000
CRM	BJL	JCE	1977	A	27 X 10	AP	18	2	200	1000
Chocolate Boxes (Set of 2)	BJL	IL	1977	LC	27 X 27 EA	AP	90 EA	3 EA	800 SET	2500 SET
Pieces of Eight (Set of 3)	BJL	IL	1977	LC	19 X 39 EA	SP	35 EA	1–3 EA	1500 SET	3000 SET
Two of a Kind, Three of a Kind (Set of 15)	BJL	IL	1978	LC	28 X 29 EA	SP	50–90 EA	2–4 EA	300 EA	2000 EA
Drawing Boards (Color) (Set of 5)	BJL	PB/A	1980	EC	26 X 23 EA	R/BFK	60 EA	4 EA	3000 SET	6000 SET
Drawing Boards (Chine-Colle) (Set of 5)	BJL	PB/A	1981	EC	30 X 22 EA	R/BFK	30 EA	2 EA	4500 SET	6000 SET
Espalier (Dipt)	BJL	MS	1982	LC	44 X 61	AP	100	10	1800	2200
Chapbook	BJL	MS	1982	LC	22 X 30	AP	75	6	600	1000
Arbor	BJL	MS	1982	LC	41 X 37	AP	100		1200	1000
Card Enclosed (Set of 3)	BJL	ART/AC	1982	MON	46 X 31 EA	R/BFK	1 EA		2500 EA	3200 EA
Field and Streams Series:										
Ick	TGL	TGL	1982	I/LC	30 X 22	AP/WA	38	8	600	900
Pix	TGL	TGL	1982	I/LC	30 X 22	AP/WA	34	5	600	900
Pix I	TGL	TGL	1982	I/LC	30 X 22	AP/WA	20	2	600	750
Double Meadow	TGL	TGL	1982	I/LC	30 X 22	AP/WA	44	7	600	900
Ouse	TGL	TGL	1982	I/LC	30 X 22	AP/WA	44	5	600	900
Cam	TGL	TGL	1982	I/LC	30 X 22	AP/WA	34	5	600	900
Hiz	TGL	TGL	1982	I/LC	30 X 22	AP/WA	27	5	600	900
Wild Life (Green/Red)	CPP	CPP	1985	AC	29 X 39	R/BFK	35		1200	1200
First Dancer (Silver Fan)	CPP	CPP	1985	AC	30 X 23	R/BFK	35		900	900
Ensemble (Silver Ball)	CPP	CPP	1985	AC	23 X 30	R/BFK	35		1000	1000
Coup de Theatre (Magenta/Red)	CPP	CPP	1985	AC	40 X 30	R/BFK	15		900	900
Untitled (Triangle)	RHE		1989	MON	39 X 39 EA	R/BFK	1 EA	Varies		2500 EA
Untitled (Square)	RHE		1989	MON	34 X 22 EA	R/BFK	1 EA	Varies		2000 EA

RUPERT JASON SMITH

BORN: Trenton, NJ; (1954–1988)
EDUCATION: Pratt Inst, Brooklyn, NY
TEACHING: Sch of Visual Arts, NY
PRINTERS: 525 Editions, NY (525E); Artist (ART)
PUBLISHERS: Fred Dorfman, Inc, NY (FDI); Artist (ART)
GALLERIES: Fred Dorfman Gallery, New York, NY; Hokin Gallery, Palm Beach, FL & Bay Harbor Islands, FL; Langman Gallery, Jenkintown, PA; L'Imagerie, Encino, CA

TITLE	PUBLISHER	PRINTER	DATE	MEDIUM	DIMENSION (PAPER SIZE) IN INCHES	TYPE OF PAPER	EDITION NUMBER	NO. OF COLORS	ORIGINAL OPENING PRICE	CURRENT RETAIL PRICE
SOLD OUT EDITIONS (RARE):										
Water Sports I, II	FDI	525E	1979	SP	42 X 30 EA	AP	100 EA	29 EA	300 EA	1000 EA
Water Sports I, II (Deluxe)	FDI	525E	1979	SP	42 X 30 EA	AP	20 EA	31 EA	450 EA	1200 EA
Ski Resorts (with Hand Painting and Diamond Particles) (Series of 25)	FDI	525E	1981	SP/CO/HC	60 X 40 EA	AP	25 EA	19 EA	1200 EA	2000 EA
Pool Play (with Hand Painting and Diamond Particles) (Series of 25)	FDI	525E	1981	SP/CO/HC	40 X 60 EA	AP	25 EA	37 EA	1400 EA	2000 EA
Morso Torso	FDI	525E	1982	SP/HP	60 X 40	AP	20	26	1400	1800
Undercurrents	FDI	525E	1982	SP/HP	60 X 40	AP	20	32	1400	2000
Kick (Series of 25)	FDI	ART	1982–83	SP	40 X 60 EA	LEN	25 EA	27 EA	1600 EA	2000 EA
Torta	FDI/ART	ART	1984	SP/HP	44 X 32	AP/WA	30	30	500	800

The retail prices of the 100,000 limited edition prints quoted in this directory are subject to change. Print publishers, artists and galleries were the direct sources for these quotations. Prices in the secondary market listed as "Sold Out Editions (Rare)" indicate that the publisher has a limited supply of that print or that the print is difficult to locate in the galleries.

The Printworld Directory is accepting new applications for the seventh edition. Approximately 300 new artists will be accepted. Please use the two forms provided in the back section of this directory to submit biographical data and documentation of prints. Edition number of each print must not exceed 500 and the retail price must be $100 or more.

PHILIP SMITH

RECENT EXHIB: Millikin Univ, Perkinson Gallery, Decatur, IL, 1992
PRINTERS: Stephen Cadwalader, Somerville, MA (SC); Mixit Print Studio, Somerville, MA (MPS)
PUBLISHERS: Jason McCoy, Inc, NY (JMC)
GALLERIES: Barbara Gillman Gallery, Miami, FL; Jason McCoy, Inc, New York, NY

TITLE	PUBLISHER	PRINTER	DATE	MEDIUM	DIMENSION (PAPER SIZE) IN INCHES	TYPE OF PAPER	EDITION NUMBER	NO. OF COLORS	ORIGINAL OPENING PRICE	CURRENT RETAIL PRICE
CURRENT EDITIONS:										
Ranger	JMC	SC/MPS	1992	EB/A	30 X 22	R/BFK	30	1	900	900

NED SMYTHE

BORN: 1948
EDUCATION: Kenyon Col, Gambier, OH, 1970
TEACHING: Col of New Resources, Univ of Rochelle, NY, 1977
AWARDS: CAPS Grant, 1975–76; American the Beautiful Found, Harriman Award, NY, 1978
RECENT EXHIB: Univ of Nevada, Inst for Fine Art, Donna Beam Fine Art Gallery, Las Vegas, NV, 1989; E L Smythe, Inc, NY, 1991
PRINTERS: Solo Press, NY (SP); Fabric Workshop, Phila, PA (FW); Twichell-Nichols, NY (T–N)
PUBLISHERS: Holly Solomon Editions, Ltd, NY (HSE); Fabric Workshop, Phila, PA (FW)
GALLERIES: Holly Solomon Gallery, New York, NY; McIntosh/Drysdale Gallery, Houston, TX; E L Smythe, Inc, New York, NY

TITLE	PUBLISHER	PRINTER	DATE	MEDIUM	DIMENSION (PAPER SIZE) IN INCHES	TYPE OF PAPER	EDITION NUMBER	NO. OF COLORS	ORIGINAL OPENING PRICE	CURRENT RETAIL PRICE
SOLD OUT EDITIONS (RARE):										
Philadelphia Pattern Palms	FW	FW	1979	SP/F	101 X 45	AP	11		500	2000
Untitled (The Beast)	HSE	SP/T-N	1981	LC/SP	40 X 79	AP	25	7	1500	3500

JOAN SNYDER

BORN: Highland Park, NJ; April 16, 1940
EDUCATION: Douglas Col New Brunswick, NJ, BA, 1962; Rutgers Univ, New Brunswick, NJ, MFA, 1966
TEACHING: Yale Univ, New Haven, CT; State Univ of New York, Stonybrook, NY; Princeton Univ, NJ
AWARDS: Nat Endowment for the Arts Fel, 1974; Guggenheim Grant, 1983
RECENT EXHIB: Hirschl & Adler Modern, NY, 1988; Victoria Munroe Gallery, NY, 1990; Allentown Art Mus, PA, 1992
COLLECTIONS: Metropolitan Mus of Art, NY; Mus of Mod Art, NY; Whitney Mus of Am Art, NY; Dallas Mus of Contemp Art, TX; J B Speed Mus, Louisville, KY, High Mus of Art, Atlanta, GA, Mus of Fine Arts, Boston, MA; Fogg Mus, Boston, MA; Neuberger Mus, State Univ of New York, Purchase, NY
PRINTERS: Chip Elwell, NY (CE)
PUBLISHERS: Diane Villani Editions, NY (DVE)
GALLERIES: Hirschl & Adler Modern, New York, NY; Nielsen Gallery, Boston, MA; Diane Villani Editions, New York, NY; Victoria Munroe Gallery, New York, NY; CompassRose, Ltd, Chicago, IL
MAILING ADDRESS: P O Box 375, Eastport, NY 11941

TITLE	PUBLISHER	PRINTER	DATE	MEDIUM	DIMENSION (PAPER SIZE) IN INCHES	TYPE OF PAPER	EDITION NUMBER	NO. OF COLORS	ORIGINAL OPENING PRICE	CURRENT RETAIL PRICE
CURRENT EDITIONS:										
Dancing in the Dark	DVE	CE	1982–84	WB	29 X 26	SHO	15	1	900	900
Mommy Why?	DVE	CE	1983–84	WC	20 X 26	KOCHI	15	9	1500	2000
Things Have Tears and We Know Suffering	DVE	CE	1984	WC	26 X 25	YAM	9	9	1500	2000
Can We Turn Our Rage to Poetry	DVE	CE	1985	LC	30 X 44	R/BFK	20		900	900
For the Children	DVE		1988	WC/PO	38 X 25	SUZ	10		1800	2000

RANDALL SNYDER

BORN: Murray, UT; April 29, 1949
EDUCATION: Bellingham Tech Inst, Bellingham, WA
PRINTERS: Artist (ART)
PUBLISHERS: Ultra Limited Edition Graphics, Stockton, CA (ULTRA)
GALLERIES: Frameworks, Stockton, CA; Flowercraft, Stockton, CA
MAILING ADDRESS: PO Box 692273, Stockton, CA 95269

TITLE	PUBLISHER	PRINTER	DATE	MEDIUM	DIMENSION (PAPER SIZE) IN INCHES	TYPE OF PAPER	EDITION NUMBER	NO. OF COLORS	ORIGINAL OPENING PRICE	CURRENT RETAIL PRICE
CURRENT EDITIONS:										
Futures	ULTRA	ART	1986	SP	9 X 12	CAN	56	45	103	215
Elegant Answer Iris	ULTRA	ART	1988	SP	26 X 28	DUL	121	7	130	287
American Flags	ULTRA	ART	1993	SP	26 X 28	DUL	134	4	71	152
Victorian Valentine	ULTRA	ART	1993	SP	26 X 28	DUL	134	4	71	152

SUSANA SOLANO

BORN: Barcelona, Spain; 1946
RECENT EXHIB: Galeria Montenegro, Madrid, Spain, 1987; Galeria Maeght, Barcelona, Spain, 1987; Galerie Maeght-Montrouge, Paris, France, 1987; Galerie des Arenes-Chapelle des Jesuites, Nimes, France, 1987; Galleria Fiorgio Persona, Torino, Italy, 1987; Bonnefantenmuseum, Maastricht, The Netherlands, 1988; La Maquina Espagnola, Madrid, Spain, 1989; Galeria Oliva Arauna, Madrid, Spain, 1989; Donald Young Gallery, Chicago, IL, 1989; Hirshhorn Mus, Wash, DC, 1989; San Jose Mus of Art, CA, 1992
PRINTERS: Crown Point Gallery, San Francisco, CA (CPP)
PUBLISHERS: Crown Point Press, San Francisco, CA (CPP)
GALLERIES: Crown Point Press, San Francisco, CA & New York, NY

SUSANA SOLANO CONTINUED

TITLE	PUBLISHER	PRINTER	DATE	MEDIUM	DIMENSION (PAPER SIZE) IN INCHES	TYPE OF PAPER	EDITION NUMBER	NO. OF COLORS	ORIGINAL OPENING PRICE	CURRENT RETAIL PRICE
CURRENT EDITIONS:										
Ghardaia I	CPP	CPP	1991	EB/A/SG/SB	39 X 42	R/BFK	5	1	1000	1000
Ghardaia II	CPP	CPP	1991	EB/A/SB	39 X 42	R/BFK	5	1	1000	1000
Ghardaia III	CPP	CPP	1991	EB/A/SB	39 X 42	R/BFK	12	1	1000	1000
Ghardaia IV	CPP	CPP	1991	EB/A/SB	43 X 35	R/BFK	5	1	1000	1000
Impluvium	CPP	CPP	1991	EB/A/SB	43 X 36	R/BFK	5	1	1000	1000
Marinada I	CPP	CPP	1991	EB/A/SB	45 X 41	R/BFK	5	1	1000	1000
Marinada II,III	CPP	CPP	1991	EB/A/SG/SB	45 X 41 EA	R/BFK	5 EA	1 EA	1000 EA	1000 EA
Marades I,II	CPP	CPP	1991	EB/SG	39 X 42 EA	R/BFK	10 EA	1 EA	1000 EA	1000 EA

T L SOLIEN

BORN: Fargo, N Dakota; 1949
EDUCATION: Morehead State Univ, KY, 1973, BA; Univ of Nebraska, Lincoln, NE, MFA, 1977
AWARDS: Jerome Found Grant, 1980–81; Bush Found Fel, 1981
COLLECTIONS: Grey Art Gallery, New York Univ, NY
PRINTERS: Vermillion Editions, Ltd., Minneapolis, MN (VEL); Experimental Workshop, San Francisco, CA (EW); Hidekatsu Takada (HT); Crown Point Press, San Francisco, CA (CPP); Artist (ART); Jack Lemon, Chicago, IL (JL); Landfall Press, Inc, Chicago, IL (LPI); David Cawkins, Bloomington, IN (DC); David Keister, Bloomington, IN (DK); Echo Press, Bloomington, IN (EPr)
PUBLISHERS: Vermillion, Minneapolis, MN (VEL); Crown Point Press, San Francisco, CA (CPP); Artist (ART); Landfall Press, Inc, Chicago, IL (LPI); Univ of Nebraska, Omaha, NE (UN); Echo Press, Bloomington, IN (EPr)
GALLERIES: Glen Hanson Gallery, Minneapolis, NM; van Straaten Gallery, Chicago, IL; Vermillion Editions, Ltd, Minneapolis, MN; Lemberg Gallery, Birmingham, MI; John C Stoller Gallery, Minneapolis, MN; Landfall Press, Inc, Chicago, IL; Barbara Toll Fine Arts, New York, NY; Estelle Dodge, Inc, Bay Harbor Islands, FL

TITLE	PUBLISHER	PRINTER	DATE	MEDIUM	DIMENSION (PAPER SIZE) IN INCHES	TYPE OF PAPER	EDITION NUMBER	NO. OF COLORS	ORIGINAL OPENING PRICE	CURRENT RETAIL PRICE
SOLD OUT EDITIONS (RARE):										
Nightwatchman	VEL	VEL	1982	LD/SP/I	30 X 45	HMP	1	8	800	1800
Iron Shirt	VEL	VEL	1982	MON	13 X 17 EA	HMP	1 EA	5 EA	650 EA	650 EA
Cannibal	VEL	VEL	1982	MON	13 X 17 EA	HMP	1 EA	5 EA	650 EA	650 EA
Steer with Prizes	VEL	VEL	1982	MON	13 X 17 EA	HMP	1 EA	5 EA	650 EA	650 EA
Harvest of History	VEL	VEL	1982	MON	30 X 22 EA	ACW	1 EA	5 EA	900 EA	900 EA
Sailor with Life Preserver	VEL	VEL	1982	MON	30 X 22 EA	ACW	1 EA	5 EA	900 EA	900 EA
Neverland	VEL	VEL	1982	MON	22 X 30 EA	ACW	1 EA	5 EA	900 EA	900 EA
Three Sailors	VEL	VEL	1982	LC/SP/I	32 X 46	HMP	1	8	800	1200
Fragments of Hope	VEL	VEL	1982	LC/SP/I	14 X 17	HMP	1	1	1200	1200
Family Fire	VEL	VEL	1982	MON	17 X 38 EA	HMP	1 EA	5 EA	1000 EA	1800 EA
Boy with Pocket Knife	VEL	VEL	1982	MON	30 X 22 EA	ACW	1 EA	5 EA	900 EA	900 EA
The Wishing Well	VEL	VEL	1982	MON	22 X 30 EA	TRP	1 EA	1 EA	900 EA	900 EA
The Target Shooter	VEL	VEL	1982	MON	22 X 30 EA	AP	1 EA	1 EA	900 EA	900 EA
Imposter in the Rain	VEL	VEL	1982	MON	13 X 17 EA	JAP	1 EA	1 EA	700 EA	700 EA
The True Hoof	VEL	VEL	1983	MON	31 X 40 EA	HMP	1 EA	1 EA	1800 EA	1800 EA
The Tongue	VEL	VEL	1983	MON	31 X 41 EA	HMP	1 EA	1 EA	1800 EA	1800 EA
At the Foot of the Cross	VEL	VEL	1983	MON	31 X 40 EA	HMP	1 EA	1 EA	1800 EA	1800 EA
Victim of Doubt	VEL	VEL	1983	MON	31 X 40 EA	HMP	1 EA	1 EA	1800 EA	1800 EA
The Good Shepherd	VEL	VEL	1983	MON	31 X 40 EA	HMP	1 EA	1 EA	1800 EA	1800 EA
Acts	VEL	VEL	1983	MON	31 X 40 EA	HMP	1 EA	1 EA	1800 EA	1800 EA
History of Broken Arms	VEL	VEL	1983	MON	31 X 40 EA	HMP	1 EA	1 EA	1800 EA	1800 EA
The Tin Man	VEL	VEL	1984	MON	31 X 40 EA	HMP	1 EA	1 EA	2000 EA	2000 EA
Maker of Shame	VEL	VEL	1984	MON	31 X 40 EA	HMP	1 EA	1 EA	1800 EA	1800 EA
The Fall	VEL	VEL	1984	LI/MON	33 X 47 EA	HMP	42 EA	9 EA	1200 EA	1200 EA
Bad Blood	LPI	JL/LPI	1985	LC/WC	31 X 41	HMP	51	5	700	1200
Head of a King	EPr	DK/DC/EPr	1986	LC/WC/SP/EB/A	36 X 24	ACW	29	9	1000	1000
The Fountain (with Charcoal & Hand-Tinting)	ART/UN	DC/EPr	1987	PO/LC/LI/HC	23 X 15	MEX	30		950	1500
I Corpus	LPI	JL/LPI	1990	LC/EB	38 X 23	SOM	15		1800	1800
The All Bone	LPI	JL/LPI	1990	LC/EB	21 X 14	SOM	35		600	600
Good Place	LPI	JL/LPI	1990	LC/EB	21 X 14	SOM	35		600	600
Oath	LPI	JL/LPI	1990	LC/EB	21 X 14	SOM	35		600	600
Clarion Lung	LPI	JL/LPI	1990	LC/EB	21 X 14	SOM	35		600	600

JEAN SOLOMBRE

BORN: Paris, France, 1948
COLLECTIONS: Art Inst of Chicago, IL; Spencer Coll, NY; Musée d'Art Moderne, Paris, France; Bibliothesque Nationale, Paris, France
PRINTERS: Artist (ART)
PUBLISHERS: John Szoke Graphics, NY (JSG); Fred Dorfman, Inc, NY (FDI)
GALLERIES: Szoke Graphics, Inc, New York, NY; Frances Aronson Gallery, Atlanta, GA; Art Extension, Paris, France; Galerie Lahumier, Paris, France; Galerie Michele Broutta, Paris, France; Fernette's Gallery of Art, Des Moines, IA; Bruton Gallery, New York, NY; Fred Dorfman Gallery, New York, NY

The Printworld Directory is accepting new applications for the seventh edition. Approximately 300 new artists will be accepted. Please use the two forms provided in the back section of this directory to submit biographical data and documentation of prints. Edition number of each print must not exceed 500 and the retail price must be $100 or more.

JEAN SOLOMBRE CONTINUED

TITLE	PUBLISHER	PRINTER	DATE	MEDIUM	DIMENSION (PAPER SIZE) IN INCHES	TYPE OF PAPER	EDITION NUMBER	NO. OF COLORS	ORIGINAL OPENING PRICE	CURRENT RETAIL PRICE
SOLD OUT EDITIONS (RARE):										
Silence Attentif	JSG	ART	1983	EC	21 X 39	AP	110	4	300	400
Oiseaux du Monde	JSG	ART	1983	EC	21 X 39	AP	110	4	300	400
Untitled Series	FDI	ART	1984–86	EB/A	22 X 30 EA	R/BFK	Varies		250–400 EA	350–500 EA

ALAN SONFIST

BORN: New York, NY; March 26, 1946
AWARDS: Creative Artists Public Service Grant, 1977; Nat Endowment for the Arts Fel, 1978
RECENT EXHIB: Indianapolis Art League, IN, 1989; Butler Inst of Am Art, Youngstown, OH, 1989; Long Island Univ, Hillwood Art Mus, Brookville, NY, 1992; LedisFlam Gallery, NY, 1992
COLLECTIONS: Mus of Mod Art, NY; Boston Mus of Fine Arts, MA; Oberlin Art Mus, OH; Wallarf-Richartz Mus, Cologne, West Germany; Power Inst, Sydney, Australia; Queens Mus, Yonkers, NY; Brooklyn Mus, NY; Nassau County Mus of Fine Arts, Roslyn, NY; Univ of Bonn, West Germany; Rutgers Univ, Rutherford, NJ; New Sch for Social Research, NY; Hobart Col, Geneva, NY; Kingsborough Com Col, Brooklyn, NY
PRINTERS: Patricia Branstead, NY (PB); Aeropress, NY (A); B Miller, NY (BM)
PUBLISHERS: Multiples, Inc, NY (M); Prestige Art Ltd, Mamaroneck, NY (PA)
GALLERIES: Marian Goodman Gallery, New York, NY; Carl Solway Gallery, Cincinnati, OH; Max Protetch Gallery, New York, NY
MAILING ADDRESS: 833 Broadway, New York, NY 10003; 205 Mulberry St, New York, NY 10012

TITLE	PUBLISHER	PRINTER	DATE	MEDIUM	DIMENSION (PAPER SIZE) IN INCHES	TYPE OF PAPER	EDITION NUMBER	NO. OF COLORS	ORIGINAL OPENING PRICE	CURRENT RETAIL PRICE
SOLD OUT EDITIONS (RARE):										
Views of New York (Set of 12)	M	PB/A	1979	LC	22 X 22 EA	AP	100 EA		2500 SET	6000 SET
									250 EA	500 EA
Views of Manhattan (Set of 12)	PA	BM	1980	LC/PH/CO/HC	28 X 28 EA	AP	100 EA	5 EA	450 EA	500 EA

KEITH SONNIER

BORN: Mamou, LA; July 31, 1941
EDUCATION: Univ of Southwestern Louisiana, Lafayette, LA, BA, 1959–63; Rutgers Univ, New Brunswick, NJ, MFA, 1965–66
TEACHING: Instr, Art & Art History, Rutgers Univ, NJ, 1969–72; Sch of Visual Arts, NY, 1972–84; Bard Col, Rhinebeck, NY, 1984–86
AWARDS: Guggenheim Found Fel, 1974; First Prize, Tokyo Prints Biennale, Japan, 1974; New York State Council on the Arts Fel, 1985; Nat Endowment for the Arts Fel, 1986
RECENT EXHIB: Chrysler Mus of Art, Norfolk, VA, 1988; Alexandria Mus, LA, 1989; Barbara Gladstone Gallery, New York, NY, 1989; BlumHelman Gallery, Santa Monica, CA, 1990; Whitney Mus of Am Art, NY, 1990; Univ of South Florida, Graphicstudio, Tampa, FL, 1992; Capital Arts Center, Ervin G Houchens Gallery, Bowling Green, KY, 1992; Univ of Southwestern Louisiana, Lafayette, LA, 1992; Leo Castelli Gallery, NY, 1989,90,92; 65 Thompson Street Gallery, NY, 1992
COLLECTIONS: Harvard Univ, Cambridge, MA; Univ of North Carolina, Greensboro, NC; Whitney Mus of Am Art, NY; Nat Mus of Art, Stockholm, Sweden; Mus of Mod Art, NY; von Abbe Mus, Eindhoven, The Netherlands; Mus St Pierre, Lyons, France; Mus of Contemp Art, Tokyo, Japan; Tehran Mus of Contemp Art, Iran; Hara Mus of Contemp Art, Tokyo, Japan; Australian Nat Gallery, Canberra, Australia
PUBLISHERS: Gemini GEL, Los Angeles, CA (GEM)
GALLERIES: Rosamund Felson Gallery, Los Angeles, CA; Annina Nosei Gallery, New York, NY; Carol Taylor Art, Dallas, TX; Tilden-Foley Gallery, New Orleans, LA; Tony Shafrazi Gallery, New York, NY; Susanne Hilberry Gallery, Birmingham, MI; Stein Gladstone Gallery, New York, NY; Leo Castelli Gallery, New York, NY; BlumHelman Galleries, New York, NY & Santa Monica, CA; Editions Ilene Kurtz, New York, NY; Harcus Gallery, Boston, MA; 65 Thompson Street Gallery, New York, NY

TITLE	PUBLISHER	PRINTER	DATE	MEDIUM	DIMENSION (PAPER SIZE) IN INCHES	TYPE OF PAPER	EDITION NUMBER	NO. OF COLORS	ORIGINAL OPENING PRICE	CURRENT RETAIL PRICE
SOLD OUT EDITIONS (RARE):										
Video Still Screen Series, I-V	GEM	GEM	1973	SP	28 X 36 EA	HMP	50 EA		200 EA	800 EA
Control Scene	GEM	GEM	1975	SP/VD/WC	35 X 47	HMP	25		300	800
Air to Air (Album Cover with LP)	GEM	GEM	1975		12 DIA	HMP	50		150	500
Abaca Code Series:										
Abaca Code-Squares	GEM	GEM	1976	HCAP/HS	7' X 7'	HMP	10	1	2500	5000
Abaca Code-Circles	GEM	GEM	1976	HCAP/HS	7' DIA	HMP	10	2–3	2500	4500
Abaca Code-Rectangles	GEM	GEM	1978	HCAP/HS	6' X 8'	HMP	10	3	3500	5500
CURRENT EDITIONS:										
Wax-Wan Series:										
Toiny Orbit	GEM	GEM	1978	LC	40 X 60	HMP	25		500	900
Orbit I	GEM	GEM	1978	LC	42 X 38	HMP	25		450	1000
Orbit II	GEM	GEM	1978	LC	42 X 38	HMP	25		500	1000
Wax-Wan	GEM	GEM	1978	LC	40 X 30	HMP	26		450	800
Signal	GEM	GEM	1978	LC	36 X 74	HMP	25		500	900

STEVEN SORMAN

BORN: Minneapolis, MN; June 14, 1948
EDUCATION: Univ of Minnesota, MN, BFA, 1971
AWARDS: Bush Found Artist's Fel, 1979; Minnesota State Arts Fel, 1979; Merit Award, San Francisco Mus of Mod Art, CA, 1980
RECENT EXHIB: Heland Wetterling Gallery, Gothenburg, Sweden, 1989; New Harmony Gallery of Contemp Art, IN, 1988; Dolan/Maxwell Gallery, NY, 1989; Univ of Missouri, Kansas City, KS, 1992
COLLECTIONS: Mus of Mod Art, NY; Whitney Mus of Am Art, NY; Walker Art Center, Minneapolis, MN; Stedelijk Mus, Amsterdam, The Netherlands; St Louis Mus of Art, MO; Pennsylvania Acad of Fine Arts, Phila, PA; Art Inst of Chicago, IL; Nat Gallery of Art, Wash, DC; Australian Nat Gallery, Canberra Australia

STEVEN SORMAN CONTINUED

PRINTERS: Vermillion Editions, Ltd, Minneapolis, MN (VEL); Echo Press, Bloomington, IN (EP); David Keister (DK); Christopher Laehy (CL); David Calkins (DC); Tamarind Inst, Albuquerque, NM (TI); Catherine Kirsh Kuhn (CKK); William Haberman (WH); Lynne D Allen (LA); Tyler Graphics, Ltd, Mount Kisco, NY (TGL); Artist (ART); Tom Pruitt, Albuquerque, NM (TP); Molly Jo Souders, Albuquerque, NM (MJS); Bill Lagattuta (BL); Mark Attwood (MA); Julie Maher (JM); Cole Rogers (CR); Gary Denmark, Palo Alto, CA (GD); Smith Andersen Editions, Palo Alto, CA (SAE)

PUBLISHERS: Bird Island Publishing, Inc, Minneapolis, MN (BIPI); Echo Press, Bloomington, IN (EP); Tamarind Institute, Albuquerque, NM (TI); Vermillion Editions Ltd, Minneapolis, MN (VEL); American Center, Paris, France (AC); Tyler Graphics, Ltd, Mount Kisco, NY (TGL); Artist (ART); Smith Andersen Editions, Palo Alto, CA (SAE)

GALLERIES: Eve Mannes Gallery, Atlanta, GA; Thomas Smith Fine Art, Fort Wayne, IN; Thomson Gallery, Minneapolis, MN; Nancy Singer Gallery, St Louis, MO; Gallery 72, Omaha, NE; Smith Andersen Gallery, Palo Alto, CA; Echo Press, Bloomington, IN; Tamarind Inst, Albuquerque, NM; Pace Prints, New York, NY; Mary Singer Gallery, Wash, DC; Sylvia Cordish Fine Art, Baltimore, MD; Jan Turner Gallery, Los Angeles, CA; Michael Dunev Gallery, San Francisco, CA; Tyler Graphics, Mount Kisco, NY; Betsy Senior Contemporary Prints, New York, NY; Heland Wetterling Gallery, Gottenburg, Sweden; Lemberg Gallery, Birmingham, MI; Klein Art Works, Chicago, IL; R H Love Contemporary, Chicago, IL; Richard Levy Gallery, Albuquerque, NM

MAILING ADDRESS: P O Box 149, 400 Maple Marine on St Croix, MN 55047

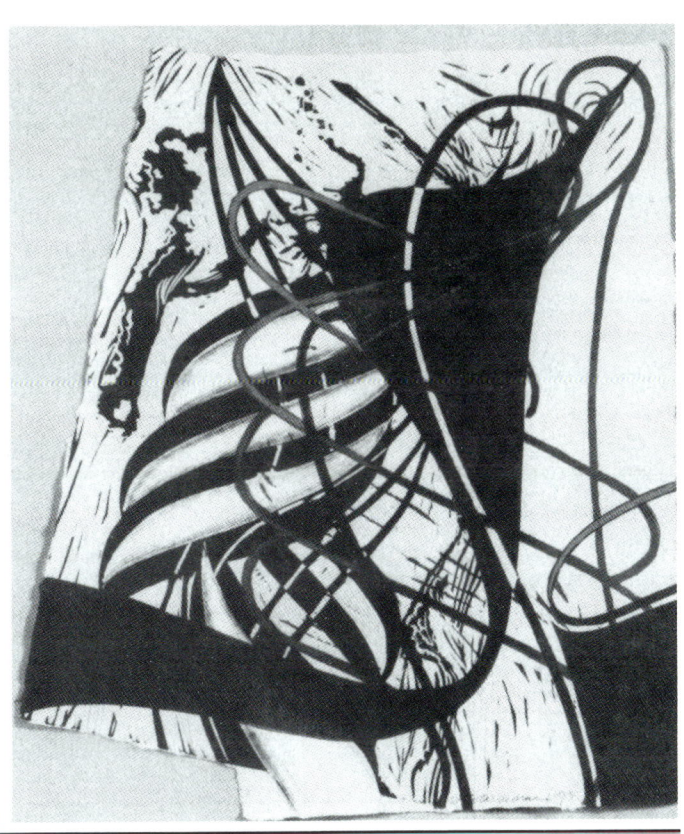

Steven Sorman
Those from Away IV
Courtesy Tyler Graphics, Ltd

TITLE	PUBLISHER	PRINTER	DATE	MEDIUM	DIMENSION (PAPER SIZE) IN INCHES	TYPE OF PAPER	EDITION NUMBER	NO. OF COLORS	ORIGINAL OPENING PRICE	CURRENT RETAIL PRICE
SOLD OUT EDITIONS (RARE):										
In No Given Place	BIPI	VEL	1978	LC/CO	25 X 52	HMP	15	1	800	3500
Not in any Given Place	BIPI	VEL	1978	LC/CO	25 X 65	HMP	16	1	800	3500
Spaces between Words	BIPI	VEL	1978	LC/CO	20 X 39	HMP	27	2	500	3000
A Deaf Man Sees	BIPI	VEL	1978	LC/CO	20 X 39	HMP	25	1	500	3000
The Letter to Matisse	BIPI	VEL	1978	LC/CO/HC	27 X 30	HMP	25	4	500	3000
Lewis and Clark	BIPI	VEL	1978	LC/SP/CO	38 X 38	HMP	50	2	500	3000
Explanation of this Which (Necessity)	BIPI	VEL	1979		40 X 32	HMP	25	1	600	3000
Going Back to Look in the Mirror	ART	VEL			24 X 36	HMP			600	2500
What This is (Set of 5)	ART	VEL	1980	EC/AC	17 X 20	HMP	28	3	2000	3000
The Singing Bridge	BIPI	VEL	1980		18 X 23	HMP	39	5	1800	2500
The Trick to being Recognized	ART	VEL	1980	LC/WC/EC	22 X 28	HMP	31	4	550	2000
Games the French Play (Set of 3)	ART	VEL	1980	LC/CO/WC	38 X 38 EA	HMP	28 EA	3 EA	3600 SET	7500 SET
Rax (Fault)	BIPI	VEL	1980	LC/L/SP/CO	26 X 75	HMP	33	5	2000	4000
Which (A Partial Memory)	ART	VEL	1981	LC/WC/CO	32 X 40	HMP	30	15	900	2500
CURRENT EDITIONS:										
Apparent Heir	ART	ART	1981	WC/Opt/CO	39 X 22	SP	9		850	1200
One (No Two) I	VEL	VEL	1981	LC/CL	19 X 24	HMP	15		600	1000
One (No Two) II	VEL	VEL	1981	LC/SP/W	19 X 24	HMP	32	4	600	1000
To (From)	TI	TI	1981	LC					250	1200
When Something is a Picture	VEL	VEL	1981	LC		HMP			900	1800
Going Back to Look in the Mirror	ART	VEL	1982	LC/SP/W/CO	22 X 36	HMP	23	4	850	1200
Practice Steps and Real Walking	ART	VEL	1982	LC/SP/W/CO	27 X 67	HMP	37	10	1050	3000
What's this-What's that	VEL	VEL	1982	LC/EC/WC	33 X 96	HMP	18	15	2500	3800
The Letter from Matisse	VEL/AC	VEL	1982	LC/SP/WC/PO/CO/MON	36 X 24	HMP	25	9	900	1500
Again: Said (Dipt)	EPr	DK/CL/EPr	1982	MULT	19 X 62	KAS	27	3	700	2500
West Union/Sabbathday Lake	TI	CKK/TI	1982	LC	24 X 52	TOS/CHIR	41	2	850	1800
The Meaning of the Conversation	TI	WH/TI	1982	LC	30 X 58	NISH	38	2	850	1500
Said in Part	TI	WH/TI	1982	LB	30 X 58	NISH	14	1	850	1500
What I Mean to Say	TI	LA/TI	1982	LB	26 X 72	KIT/CHIR/HMP	18	1	850	2000
Object (Which)	EPr	DK/CL/EPr	1982	LC/DPT/MON/CO	59 X 31	KAY/KUJ/KOZO	29	7	1250	1500
Pine: Necessity and Comfort	EPr	DK/CL/EPr	1983	MON/DPT/LB	36 X 25	JP	15	4	900	1800
My Brother and His Problems	EPr	DK/CL/EPr	1983	LC/MON/CO	37 X 25	KAY	33	6	1000	1500
Leaving the Room and Forgetting to Close the Door	EPr	DK/DC/EPr	1983	LC/BP	15 X 39	OKP	34	8	800	1200
Another Word (Yours)	EPr	DK/DC/EPr	1984	LC	58 X 25	K/BIT/DOM/MOR	25	5	1200	1200
A Given Name (Mine)	EPr	DK/DC/EPr	1984	LC/CO	62 X 28	SUZ/TOR/OKP	24	4	1200	1200

STEVEN SORMAN CONTINUED

Steven Sorman
Burden of Need
Courtesy Echo Press

TITLE	PUBLISHER	PRINTER	DATE	MEDIUM	DIMENSION (PAPER SIZE) IN INCHES	TYPE OF PAPER	EDITION NUMBER	NO. OF COLORS	ORIGINAL OPENING PRICE	CURRENT RETAIL PRICE
CURRENT EDITIONS:										
Monotypes	TGL	TGL	1985	MON/MM/CC	55 X 33 to 48 X 100	TGL/HMP	1 EA		1500/5000	2000/6000
Loggia Suite (Set of 4)	EPr	DK/DC/EPr	1985	LC	42 X 24 EA	SHIB	14 EA		7200 SET	10000 SET
In Residence (In the United States)	TGL	TGL	1985	WC/EB/LC/REL/CO	57 X 46	HMP	28	17	2000	6000
Years and When	TGL	TGL	1985	WC/EB/LC/REL/CO	58 X 38	HMP	28	12	2500	4500
Trees Blowing and Blowing Like Arms Akimbo	TGL	TGL	1985	LC/WC/EC/REL	59 X 37	TGL/HMP	42	6	2500	7500
Still Standing Still	TGL	TGL/ART	1985	LC/WC/REL/HC	66 X 43	TGL/HMP	20	9	3000	7500
Trees Like Men Walking	TGL	TGL/ART	1985	WC/EB/REL/CO	94 X 41	TGL/HMP	10	18	4500	7500
This: Stand Within Feet	TGL	TGL/ART	1985	WC/EC/REL/HC	66 X 49	TGL/HMP	18	10	3000	7500
I am Looking at You, I am Looking at You	TGL	TGL/ART	1985	LC/REL/HC	67 X 43	TGL/HMP	10	7	2800	6000
Now at First and When	TGL	TGL	1985	WC/EB/REL/CO	66 X 52	TGL/HMP	18	12	3500	5000
Forgetting and Forgetting	TGL	TGL/ART	1985	MON/EC/REL/HC	66 X 60	TGL/HMP	15	Varies	4200	8000
What It Seems You Look Like	TGL	ART/TGL	1985	MON/MM/CO/HC	70 X 40 EA	TGL/HMP	1 EA	Varies	5000 EA	10000 EA
Not Nearly (Before My Brothers) (Set of 6 with 16 variations in each)	EPr	DK/DC/EPr	1986	ENG	17 X 14 EA	JAP	1 EA		1800 EA	3000 EA
Why Because Goodnight	TI	TR/MJS/TI	1986	LC	23 X 62	CW/KIT/SEK	19	3	1500	1650
Why Why Because Because Goodnight Goodnight	TI	TP/MJS/TI	1986	LC	23 X 62	CW/KIT/SEK	18	3	1500	1650
At Least	EPr	DK/DC/EPr	1988	LC/WC/I/CO	37 X 91	KAY	22	10	3000	3700
From Away (Variant Edition of 12)	TGL	TGL	1988	WC/LC/SP/CO/HC	61 X 82 X 12 EA	OKP	1 EA		12000 EA	15000 EA
Those from Away Series:										
Those from Away III	TGL	TGL	1989	LI/C	21 X 15	FUGI	31		1200	1200
Those from Away IV	TGL	TGL	1989	LI/C	21 X 18	FUGI	26		2000	2000
Those from Away V	TGL	TGL	1989	LI/C	23 X 23	FUGI	24		2500	2500
Those from Away VI	TGL	TGL	1989	LI/C	30 X 29	FUGI	29		2000	2000
Those from Away VII	TGL	TGL	1989	LI/C	47 X 31	FUGI	30		2500	2500
If for Want, Not for Need	EPr	DK/DC/EPr	1989	LC/WC/LI/I/CO	47 X 45	KOZO/SEICHO/OKP	18	8	2500	2500
This Way Breathing	EPr	DK/DC/EPr	1989	LC/WC/LI/I/CO/GOU	55 X 40	SEICHO	18	7	2500	2500
Burden of Need	EPr	DK/DC/EPr	1989	LC/WC/LI/HC	62 X 36		16		2500	2500
With You	EPr	DK/DC/EPr	1990	LC/WC/CO	43 X 106	AC/W	35	6	4000	4000
Without You	EPr	DK/DC/EPr	1990	LC/WC/CO	42 X 87	TRP	35	6	3500	3500

STEVEN SORMAN CONTINUED

TITLE	PUBLISHER	PRINTER	DATE	MEDIUM	DIMENSION (PAPER SIZE) IN INCHES	TYPE OF PAPER	EDITION NUMBER	NO. OF COLORS	ORIGINAL OPENING PRICE	CURRENT RETAIL PRICE
CURRENT EDITIONS:										
These Stations (Next Page) (Set of 14)	TI	BL/MA/JM/C/TI	1990	LB	31 X 23 EA	NP/KP	33 EA	1 EA	6500 SET	6500 SET
Spine	EPr	DK/DC/EPr	1991	LI/LC/WC	35 X 61	KOZO/AC	34	7	3000	3000
Shoulder	EPr	DK/DC/EPr	1991	LC/WC	36 X 62	KOZO	31	6	2600	2600
Half Light Series: 6 + 13 States										
Dwarf of Itself	TGL	AK/PS/TGL	1991	EB/A/MEZ/DPT	40 X 33	R/BFK	18	1	1500	1500
Dwarf of Itself (Hand Colored)	TGL	AK/PS/TGL	1991	EB/A/MEZ/DPT	40 X 33	R/BFK	18	Varies	2000	2000
Stage (with Oilbar, Drawing, Assemblage) (Series of 19)	SAE	GD/SAE	1991	MON	58 X 23 EA	IVWP	1 EA	Varies	3800 EA	3800 EA
Women	EPr	DK/DC/EPr	1992	LC/I/PAS	73 X 30	AC/W	30	6	2200	2200

JANET SOROKIN

BORN: Hartford, CT; April 2, 1932
EDUCATION: Simmons Col; Hartford Art Sch, Univ of Hartford, CT; Trinity Col; Wesleyan Univ; Eastern Connecticut State Col
AWARDS: West Hartford Art League, CT, Honorable Mention, 1965, First Prize, 1966, West Hartford Art League, CT; First Prize, Connecticut Women Artists Annual, CT, 1966; Patron's Prize, Connecticut Women Artists Annual, CT, 1969; Goldie Paley Award, Nat Assn of Women Artists, 1970; Slater Mem Mus Award, Connecticut Women Artists, 1973; First Prize, Graphics, Stamford Art Show, CT, 1973; Irene Sickle Feist Mem Prize, Nat Assn of Women Artists, 1974; Honorable Mention, Connecticut Women Artists, CT, 1968,70,74; M Grumbacher Artists Material Prize & Cert of Merit, 1977; Ruth Walker Hasenfratz Mem Prize, Connecticut Women Artists, 1978; Northwestern Connecticut Com Col Purchase Award, 1979; Best in Show Award, West Hartford Art League, CT, 1980; Best in Show Award, Mus of Art, Science & Industry, 1981; Faber Birren Color Award, Citation, Stamford, CT, 1981,83; First Prize, Binney and Smith Award, Nat Arts Club, NY, 1983; Women's Committee Prize, New Britain Mus of Am Art, CT, 1986; M J Kaplan Award, Nat Arts Club, NY, 1986; Janet Turner Award, Nat Assn of Women Artists, 1985,87; Outstanding Merit Award, Dr Maury Liebowitz Art Awards Prog, NY, 1987; Elizabeth Morse Genius Found Award, NY, 1988; First Prize Awards, Slater Mem Mus, 1981,88
RECENT EXHIB: Atrium Gallery, St Louis, MO, 1987,88; Munson Gallery, New Haven, CT, 1988; Slater Mem Mus, Norwich, CT, 1989
COLLECTIONS: John Slade Ely House, New Haven, CT
PRINTERS: William L MacPherson, North Branford, CT (WLMP); Seraphim Screenprints, North Branford, CT (SerS)
PUBLISHERS: Artist (ART); Modernart Editions, NY (ModE)
GALLERIES: Morningstar Gallery, Ltd, New York, NY; Atrium Gallery, St Louis, MO
MAILING ADDRESS: 101 Mohawk Dr, West Hartford, CT 06117

TITLE	PUBLISHER	PRINTER	DATE	MEDIUM	DIMENSION (PAPER SIZE) IN INCHES	TYPE OF PAPER	EDITION NUMBER	NO. OF COLORS	ORIGINAL OPENING PRICE	CURRENT RETAIL PRICE
SOLD OUT EDITIONS (RARE):										
From the Center II	ART	WLMP/SerS	1980	SP	32 X 36	MOH	80	30	250	600
The Other Side II	ART	WLMP/SerS	1982	SP	30 X 38	MOH	50	39	250	600
Recent Interim	ART	WLMP/SerS	1982	SP	29 X 36	MOH	50	40	250	600
From Summer West	ART	WLMP/SerS	1983	SP	42 X 38	STP	30	54	500	700
Toward the Outside	ART	WLMP/SerS	1984	SP	30 X 35	STP	100	31	300	500
Under a Cloud	ART	WLMP/SerS	1984	SP	30 X 36	STP	100	38	300	400
And a Sea Beyond	ART	WLMP/SerS	1985	SP	30 X 35	STP	125	49	350	600
CURRENT EDITIONS:										
Patterns II	ART	WLMP/SerS	1981	SP	32 X 42	MOH	80	32	250	400
Inside/Outside	ART	WLMP/SerS	1984	SP	30 X 35	STP	125	44	300	400
Another Light	ART	WLMP/SerS	1985	SP	30 X 22	STP	150	41	280	300
Untold Stories	ART	WLMP/SerS	1985	SP	30 X 35	STP	125	51	300	400
A Distant Place	ART	WLMP/SerS	1986	SP	22 X 30	STP	100	55	280	300
Amid Ancient Walls	ART	WLMP/SerS	1986	SP	22 X 30	STP	100	49	280	300
Departure/Cornwall	ART	WLMP/SerS	1987	SP	38 X 46	STP	80	70	700	700
Distant Harmony/Provence	ART	WLMP/SerS	1988	SP	30 X 39	STP	125	77	400	400
Wanderlust	ART	WLMP/SerS	1989	SP	30 X 40	STP	80	94	400	400

JESUS RAPHAEL SOTO

BORN: Ciudad Bolivar, Venezuela; June 5, 1923
EDUCATION: Beaux Arts Acad, Caracas, Venezuela, 1942–47
RECENT EXHIB: Museo del Brabado Latinoamericano, Inst of Puerto Rican Culture, Old San Juan, PR, 1989; Galeria Oscar Ascanio, Caracas, Venezuela, 1990; Humphrey Gallery, NY, 1990,92
COLLECTIONS: Mus of Mod Art, NY; Tate Gallery, London, England; Victoria and Albert Mus, London, England; Stedelijk Mus, Amsterdam, the Netherlands; Albright-Knox Art Gallery, Buffalo, NY; Mus of Contemp Art, Sao Paulo, CA; Mus de Bellas Artes, Caracas, Venezuela; Kaiser Found, Argentina; Larry Aldrich Mus of Contemp Art, Ridgefield, CT; Mus of Mod Art, Jerusalem, Israel; Melbourne Mus, Australia; Boymans-Van-Beuningen Mus, Rotterdam, the Netherlands; Dayton Art Inst, OH; Dublin Mus, Ireland; Mus of Mod Art, Rome, Italy; Univ of Nebraska, Lincoln, NE; Contemp Soc of Mod Art, London; Kunst Mus, Basel, Switzerland; Kaiser Wilhelm Mus, Krefeld, Germany; Moderna Mus, Stockholm, Sweden; Kroller-Muller Mus, the Netherlands
PRINTERS: Atelier Tosi, Milan, Italy (AT)
PUBLISHERS: Edition MAT, Cologne, West Germany (MAT); Marlborough Graphics, NY (MG); Transworld Art, Inc, NY (TAI)
GALLERIES: Marlborough Graphics, New York, NY; Hokin Gallery, Bay Harbor Islands, FL; Charles Cowles Gallery, New York, NY; Gilbert Brownstone & Cie, Paris, France; Estudio I, Caracas, Venezuela; Marta Gutierrez Fine Arts, Key Biscayne, FL; Humphrey Fine Art, New York, NY

The print market has become very selective. For the first time since we published the first edition of The Printworld Directory in 1982, the prices of prints have been greatly reduced and greatly increased for the same artists by the most reputable and established print publishers. Check the fifth edition to understand the movement.

JESUS RAPHAEL SOTO CONTINUED

TITLE	PUBLISHER	PRINTER	DATE	MEDIUM	DIMENSION (PAPER SIZE) IN INCHES	TYPE OF PAPER	EDITION NUMBER	NO. OF COLORS	ORIGINAL OPENING PRICE	CURRENT RETAIL PRICE
SOLD OUT EDITIONS (RARE):										
Untitled (Box)	MAT		1965	MULT	19 X 11 X 5		100		800	2500
Jai-Alai: Multiple 3 (Perspex and Steel)	MG		1969	MULT	20" HT		300		1000	3000
CURRENT EDITIONS:										
Homenaje al Humane	TAI	AT	1976	MULT	20 X 26 X 6	SS/W	175	2	1800	3000

PIERRE SOULAGES

BORN: Rodez, France; December 24, 1919
EDUCATION: Fine Arts Col, Montpellier, France, 1941
COLLECTIONS: Mus of Mod Art, NY; Mus of Mod Art, Paris, France; Tate Gallery, London, England; Guggenheim Mus, NY; Phillips Gallery, Wash, DC; Rio de Janeiro Mus of Mod Art, Brazil
PRINTERS: Michel Caza, Paris, France (MC)
PUBLISHERS: Crown Publishers, NY (CP); Circle Fine Arts, Chicago, IL (CFA)
GALLERIES: Denise Cade/Art Prospect, New York, NY; Sigrid Freundorfer Fine Art, New York, NY; Gimpel & Weitzenhoffer Gallery, New York, NY; Glass Art Gallery, New York, NY; Arnold Herstand & Co, New York, NY; Circle Galleries, San Diego, CA & San Francisco, CA & Northbrook, IL & Pittsburgh, PA & Houston, TX & Soho, NY & Chicago, IL & Scottsdale, AZ & Beverly Hills, CA & Costa Mesa, CA & Sherman Oaks, CA & Palm Beach, FL & Honolulu, HI & New Orleans, LA & Las Vegas, NY & Seattle, WA; ACA Galleries, New York, NY

TITLE	PUBLISHER	PRINTER	DATE	MEDIUM	DIMENSION (PAPER SIZE) IN INCHES	TYPE OF PAPER	EDITION NUMBER	NO. OF COLORS	ORIGINAL OPENING PRICE	CURRENT RETAIL PRICE
SOLD OUT EDITIONS (RARE):										
Eauforte No 10a	CP	MC	1957	EB	24 X 20	RP	100	1	50	5000
Eauforte No 18	CP	MC	1962	EB	25 X 19	AP/T	100	1	75	4000
Eauforte No 21	CP	MC	1973	EB	10 X 8	AP	50	1	100	1800
Etching XXXV	CP	MC	1979	EB	19 X 21	RP	100	1	500	2500
CURRENT EDITIONS:										
Composition in Brown	CFA	MC	1981	SP	41 X 29	AP	250	2	1000	1600
Composition in Blue	CFA	MC	1981	SP	41 X 29	AP	250	2	1000	1600

HARRY SOVIAK

BORN: Lorain, OH; (1935–1984)
EDUCATION: Bowling Green State Univ, OH; Cranbrook Acad of Art, Bloomfield Hills, MI, BFA, MFA
TEACHING: Philadelphia Col of Art, PA, 1963 to present
AWARDS: Buenos Aires Convention Fel, 1958–59
COLLECTIONS: Philadelphia Mus of Art, PA; New Jersey State Mus, Trenton, NJ; New York Univ, NY; New Orleans Mus, LA
PRINTERS: Chip Elwell, NY (CE)
PUBLISHERS: Barbara Gladstone Editions, NY (BGE); Orion Editions, NY (OE); Marian Locks, Phila, PA (ML); Institute of Contemporary Art, Univ of Pennsylvania, Phila, PA (JCA)
GALLERIES: Marian Locks Gallery, Phila, PA; Roger Ramsay Gallery, Chicago, IL; Martha Tepper Contemporary Fine Arts, West Newton, MA; Orion Editions, New York, NY

TITLE	PUBLISHER	PRINTER	DATE	MEDIUM	DIMENSION (PAPER SIZE) IN INCHES	TYPE OF PAPER	EDITION NUMBER	NO. OF COLORS	ORIGINAL OPENING PRICE	CURRENT RETAIL PRICE
SOLD OUT EDITIONS (RARE):										
China III	BGE	CE	1979	PO	30 X 22	AP	60	16	250	1000
Japan III	OE/ML	CE	1979	PO	30 X 22	AP	50	16	275	1000
Japan IV	OE/ML	CE	1979	PO	30 X 22	AP	50	16	275	1500
Frieze	OE/ML	CE	1980	PO	30 X 42	AP	50	16	375	1500
The Empress	OE	OE	1981	AC	41 X 29	AP	68	7	325	1000
Sienna	OE	CE	1981	PO	22 X 30	AP	20	6	325	1000
Odalisque in Serpentine Robe	ICA	CE	1981	PO	22 X 30	AP	120	6	350	1000

RAPHAEL SOYER

BORN: Russia; (1899–1987); US Citizen
EDUCATION: Cooper Union, NY; Nat Acad of Design, NY; Art Students League, NY
TEACHING: Art Students League, NY; American Art Sch; New Sch For Social Research, NY
AWARDS: Carnegie Inst, Pittsburgh, PA; W A Clarke Prize, Corcoran Gallery, Wash, DC; Saltus Gold Medal, Beck Gold Medal, Nat Acad of Art, NY; Joseph H Temple Gold Medal, Pennsylvania Acad of Fine Arts, Phila, PA, 1943; Walter Lippincott Prize, 1946; Award of Merit, Acad of Arts and Letters, NY, 1977
RECENT EXHIB: Amherst Art Assoc, MA, 1988; Hebrew Union Col, Skirball Mus, Cincinnati, Oh, 1992
COLLECTIONS: Boston Mus of Fine Arts, MA; Albright-Knox Mus, Buffalo, NY; Mus of Mod Art, NY; Metropolitan Mus of Art, NY; Whitney Mus of Am Art, NY; Philadelphia Mus of Art, PA; Detroit Inst of Art, MI; Addison Mus of Art, Andover, MA
PRINTERS: Atelier Désjobert, Paris, France (AD); Artist (ART); Joseph Kleineman, NY (JK); The American Atelier, NY (AA)
PUBLISHERS: Touchstone Publishers, NY (TSP); Artist (ART); London Arts, Inc, Detroit, MI (LAI); Circle Fine Art Corp, Chicago, IL (CFA)
GALLERIES: Forum Gallery, New York, NY; Associated American Artists, New York, NY; A Clean Well-Lighted Place, New York, NY; Ella Lerner Gallery, Lenox, MA; Foster Harmon Galleries of American Art, Sarasota, FL; Circle Galleries, San Diego, CA & San Francisco, CA & Northbrook, IL & Pittsburgh, PA & Houston, TX & Soho, NY & Chicago, IL & Scottsdale, AZ & Beverly Hills, CA & Costa Mesa, CA & Sherman Oaks, CA & Palm Beach, FL & Honolulu, HI & New Orleans, LA & Las Vegas, NV & Seattle, WA; Heritage Gallery, Los Angeles, CA; American Scene Gallery, Sarasota, FL; Atlanta Art Gallery, Atlanta, GA; Centurion Galleries, Chicago, IL; David Gary, Ltd, Milburn, NJ; Glass Art Gallery, New York, NY; Rosenfeld Fine Arts, New York, NY; Michael Rosenfeld Gallery, New York, NY; Harcourts Modern & Contemporary Art, San Francisco, CA; Branchville Soho Gallery, Ridgefield, CT; David Gary, Ltd, Milburn, NJ; Owings-Dewey Fine Art, Santa Fe, NM; Ro Gallery Image Makers, Inc, New York, NY; Professional Fine Arts Services, Inc, New York, NY

RAPHAEL SOYER CONTINUED

TITLE	PUBLISHER	PRINTER	DATE	MEDIUM	DIMENSION (PAPER SIZE) IN INCHES	TYPE OF PAPER	EDITION NUMBER	NO. OF COLORS	ORIGINAL OPENING PRICE	CURRENT RETAIL PRICE
SOLD OUT EDITIONS (RARE):										
Self Portrait	ART	ART	1920	LB	9 X 6	WOVE	10	1	25	2500
East Side Street	ART	ART	1928	LB	8 X 10	WOVE	50	1	30	3000
Union Square	ART	ART	1929	LB	7 X 9	WOVE	10	1	30	2500
In Studio	ART	ART	1933	LB/HC	15 X 10	WOVE	25	Varies	35	2500
Waterfront	ART	ART	1934	LB	9 X 13	WOVE	300	1	25	3000
Girl at Window	ART	ART	1934	LB	15 X 13	WOVE	25	1	35	2500
In Studio	ART	ART	1935	LB	14 X 10	WOVE	100	1	30	1800
Entrance to Provincetown	ART	ART	1937	LB	10 X 14	AP		1	35	3000
Pugnacity	ART	ART	1937	LB	13 X 9	WOVE	4	1	75	3000
Protected	ART	ART	1938	LB	13 X 6	WOVE		1	35	1200
Springtime	ART	ART	1938	LB/HC	14 X 17	WOVE	25	Varies	35	6500
Young Model	ART	ART	1940	LB	12 X 10	WOVE	254	1	40	1800
Girl at Doorway	ART	ART	1941	EB	10 X 7	WOVE	250	1	40	2000
Farewell	AAA	AA	1943	LB	16 X 12	WOVE	100	1	60	2000
At the Mirror	AAA	AA	1943	LB		WOVE	250	1	50	1000
My Studio	AAA	AA	1944	LB	12 X 10	WOVE	250	1	50	1800
The Model	AAA	AA	1944	LB	12 X 8	WOVE	250	1	50	2000
Casting Office	AAA	AA	1945	LB	10 X 13	WOVE	250	1	50	2000
Railroad Waiting Room	AAA	AA	1954	LB	12 X 10	AP	250	1	100	1350
Boy and Girl	AAA	AA	1954	LB	12 X 8	AP	250	1	100	1000
Boy and Girl	AAA	AA	1954	LB	15 X 6	AP	30	1	100	700
Waitresses	AAA	AA	1954	LB	12 X 10	AP	250	1	100	1600
Self Portrait	AAA	AA	1954	LB	10 X 7	AP	250	1	100	700
Self Portrait	AAA	AA	1956	LB	8 X 6	AP	30	1	125	350
Self Portrait	AAA	AA	1956	LB	12 X 9	AP	250	1	125	400
Self Portrait	AAA	AA	1956	LB	12 X 9	AP	150	1	125	500
Self Portrait with Model	AAA	ART	1959	LB	14 X 12	AP	250	1	125	800
Mother Nursing Child	AAA	AA	1959	EB	14 X 11	AP	250	1	125	350
Mother Nursing Child	ART	AA	1959	LB	17 X 10	AP	30	1	125	700
Head of a Girl	AAA	AA	1960	LB	14 X 11	AP	250	1	135	800
Reflection	ART	ART	1962	LB	15 X 11	AP		1	135	800
Couple Embracing	AAA	AA	1963	EB	22 X 15	WOVE	85	1	150	450
Couple in Interior	AAA	AA	1963	EB	10 X 8	WOVE	85	1	150	600
Couple Walking	AAA	AA	1963	EB	14 X 11	WOVE	85	1	150	350
Four Nude Studies	ART	ART	1963	EB	8 X 10	WOVE	25	1	150	300
Lipstick	ART	ART	1963	EB	10 X 8	WOVE	25	1	150	400
Self Portrait (with Wife)	ART	ART	1964	EB	8 X 10	R/BFK	50	1	150	650
Greek Girl #2	ART	ART	1966	EB	11 X 9	R/BFK		1	150	500
Nudes	ART	ART	1966	LB	20 X 23	AP	100	1	175	1000
Young Dancers	ART	ART	1966	LB	17 X 13	AP	100	1	150	450
Are You Not As the Children	ART	ART	1967	LB	30 X 22	R/BFK	125	1	175	1000
Portrait of Joan	ART	ART	1967	LB	15 X 10	R/BFK		1	150	600
Woman Shading Her Eyes	ART	ART	1967	LB	15 X 11	AP	50	1	150	500
Street Scene	ART	ART	1968	LC	19 X 17	AP	275		200	1000
Bust of a Young Woman	ART	ART	1969	LB	14 X 12	AP	100	1	175	600
Artist's Drawing Board	ART	ART	1969	LC	17 X 12	AP	150		175	1000
Fannie	ART	ART	1969	LB	20 X 16	AP	150	1	175	300
Father	ART	ART	1969	LB	17 X 10	AP	150	1	175	300
Mother	ART	ART	1969	LB	18 X 12	AP	150	1	175	300
Memories	TSP	AD	1969	LB	26 X 20 EA	R/BFK	182 EA	1 EA		10000 SET
Girl Combing Her Hair	ART	ART	1970	LC	20 X 16	AP	150		200	800
Street Scene, #3	ART	ART	1970	LC	20 X 15	AP	300		175	500
Woman with Arms Folded	ART	ART	1970	LB	15 X 11	AP	100	1	200	600
Young Woman with Mirror	ART	ART	1972	EB	11 X 14	R/BFK	250	1	200	600
Young Mother	ART	ART	1973	EB	14 X 11	R/BFK	250	1	200	250
Friends	ART	ART	1973	EB	11 X 14	R/BFK	250	1	200	250
Studies	ART	ART	1974	EB	15 X 12	R/BFK	35	1	200	800
Nude	ART	ART	1975	LB	15 X 11	AP	100	1	250	600
Nude Seated in Chair	ART	ART	1975	LB	15 X 11	AP	100	1	250	400
Three Bathers	ART	ART	1975	EB	7 X 11	R/BFK	50	1	250	400
Eighth Avenue	CFA	AA	1978	LC/EMB	21 X 30	AP	300	11	200	850
Woman	LAI	JK	1979	LC	30 X 22	AP	300	7	500	1500
Woman	LAI	JK	1979	LB	30 X 22	AP	300	1	200	1000
Woman Nursing Child I	LAI	JK	1979	LC	30 X 22	AP	300	8	500	1500
Woman Nursing Child II	LAI	JK	1979	LB	30 X 22	AP	300	1	200	1000
Woman's Head II	LAI	JK	1979	LC	30 X 22	AP	300	10	500	1500
Woman's Head II	LAI	JK	1979	LB	30 X 22	AP	300	1	200	1000
Seamstress II	LAI	JK	1979	LC	30 X 22	AP	300	6	500	1500
Seamstress II	LAI	JK	1979	LB	30 X 22	AP	300	1	200	1000
Nude Woman	LAI	JK	1979	LC	30 X 22	AP	300	4	500	1500
Nude Woman	LAI	JK	1979	LB	30 X 22	AP	300	1	200	1000
Woman with Black Hair	LAI	JK	1979	LC	30 X 22	AP	300	4	500	1500
Woman with Black Hair	LAI	JK	1979	LB	30 X 22	AP	300	1	200	1000
Woman in Red Stockings	LAI	JK	1979	LC	30 X 22	AP	300	9	500	1500

RAPHAEL SOYER CONTINUED

TITLE	PUBLISHER	PRINTER	DATE	MEDIUM	DIMENSION (PAPER SIZE) IN INCHES	TYPE OF PAPER	EDITION NUMBER	NO. OF COLORS	ORIGINAL OPENING PRICE	CURRENT RETAIL PRICE
SOLD OUT EDITIONS (RARE):										
Woman in Red Stockings	LAI	JK	1979	LB	30 X 22	AP	300	1	200	1000
Woman's Head I	LAI	JK	1979	LC	30 X 22	AP	300	6	500	1500
Woman's Head I	LAI	JK	1979	LB	30 X 22	AP	300	1	200	1000
Woman Nursing Child II	LAI	JK	1979	LC	30 X 22	AP	300	7	500	1500
Woman Nursing Child II	LAI	JK	1979	LB	30 X 22	AP	300	1	200	1000
Woman Standing	LAI	JK	1979	LC	16 X 9	AP	275	6	500	750
Woman Seated	LAI	JK	1980	LC	17 X 14	AP	275	6	500	750
Self Portrait	LAI	JK	1980	LC	22 X 16	AP	250	6	500	1500
The Braid			1980	LC	17 X 12	AP	50		500	800
Nude Stretching			1982	EB	13 X 10	R/BFK	71		300	500

MERLE SUE SPANDORFER

BORN: Baltimore, MD; September 4, 1934
EDUCATION: Syracuse Univ, NY, 1952–54; Univ of Maryland, College Park, MD, BS, 1956
TEACHING: Instr, Printmaking, Tyler Sch of Art, Phila, PA, 1979–84; Instr, Printmaking, Pratt Inst, NY, 1985–86; Instr, Printmaking, Cheltenham Sch of Fine Arts, PA, 1965 to present
AWARDS: Governor's Prize & Purchase Award, Baltimore Mus of Art, MD, 1970; Maryland Inst of Art Award, 1971; Purchase Award, Cheltenham Sch of Fine Arts, PA, 1977; Am Color Print Soc, 1980,84; Outstanding Art Educators Award, Pennsylvania Art Education Assn, 1982

RECENT EXHIB: Governor's Residence, Harrisburg, PA, 1987
COLLECTIONS: Metropolitan Mus of Art, NY; Mus of Mod Art, NY; Philadelphia Mus, PA; Baltimore Mus, MD; Pennsylvania Acad of Fine Arts, Phila, PA; California Col of Arts & Crafts, San Francisco, CA; Albion Col, MI; Montclair Art Mus, NJ; Herbert F Johnson Mus, Cornell Univ, Ithaca, NY; Toyoh Bijutsu Gakko, Toyoh Art Inst, Tokyo, Japan; Israeli Mus, Jerusalem, Israel; Whitney Mus of Am Art, NY
PRINTERS: Artist (ART)
PUBLISHERS: Artist (ART)
GALLERIES: Marian Locks Gallery, Phila, PA; Soho South Contemporary Gallery, Safety Harbor, FL; Berghoff-Cowden Galleries, Tampa, FL
MAILING ADDRESS: 8012 Ellen Lane, Cheltenham, PA 19012

TITLE	PUBLISHER	PRINTER	DATE	MEDIUM	DIMENSION (PAPER SIZE) IN INCHES	TYPE OF PAPER	EDITION NUMBER	NO. OF COLORS	ORIGINAL OPENING PRICE	CURRENT RETAIL PRICE
SOLD OUT EDITIONS (RARE):										
Cobweb Array	ART	ART	1969	SP	43 X 31	AP	25	1	90	600
Algol Tranelator	ART	ART	1969	SP	36 X 27	AP	25	1	90	600
Memory Array	ART	ART	1979	SP	37 X 28	AP	25	1	300	400
Thumb Print	ART	ART	1979	SP	43 X 32	AP	20	2	400	500
Lacuna Eve	ART	ART	1981	GD/MON	32 X 27 EA	AP	1 EA	17 EA	500 EA	600 EA
Metal Element	ART	ART	1981	GD/MON	30 X 40 EA	AP	1 EA	14 EA	600 EA	700 EA
Fire Element	ART	ART	1981	GD/MON	30 X 40 EA	AP	1 EA	20 EA	600 EA	700 EA
Water Element	ART	ART	1981	GD/MON	30 X 40 EA	AP	1 EA	8 EA	500 EA	600 EA
Earth Element	ART	ART	1981	GD/MON	30 X 40 EA	AP	1 EA	15 EA	500 EA	600 EA
Wood Element	ART	ART	1981	GD/MON	30 X 40 EA	AP	1 EA	20 EA	500 EA	600 EA

JIM SPANFELLER

EDUCATION: Pennsylvania Acad of Fine Arts, Phila, PA, BFA, 1952
AWARDS: Artist of the Year Award, New York Artists, Guild, 1964
PRINTERS: American Atelier, NY (AA)
PUBLISHERS: Circle Fine Art, Chicago, IL (CFA)
GALLERIES: Circle Galleries, San Diego, CA & San Francisco, CA & Northbrook, IL & Pittsburgh, PA & Houston, TX & Soho, NY & Chicago, IL & Scottsdale, AZ & Beverly Hills, CA & Costa Mesa, CA & Sherman Oaks, CA & Palm Beach, FL & Honolulu, HI & New Orleans, LA & Las Vegas, NV & Seattle, WA

TITLE	PUBLISHER	PRINTER	DATE	MEDIUM	DIMENSION (PAPER SIZE) IN INCHES	TYPE OF PAPER	EDITION NUMBER	NO. OF COLORS	ORIGINAL OPENING PRICE	CURRENT RETAIL PRICE
SOLD OUT EDITIONS (RARE):										
Roadster	CFA	AA	1979	EC	20 X 28	AP	150		100	250
Bicycle	CFA	AA	1979	EC	22 X 30	AP	150		100	250
Broom	CFA	AA	1979	EC	13 X 20	AP	125		100	175
Self-Portrait	CFA	AA	1980	EC	22 X 30	AP	160		75	200
Auto	CFA	AA	1980	EC	20 X 28	AP	160		75	225

MICHELLE SPARK

PRINTERS: Anthony Kirk, East Topsham, VT (AK); Eldindean Press, East Topsham, VT (EldP)
PUBLISHERS: Artist (ART)
GALLERIES: Associated American Artists, New York, NY; Carol Getz Gallery, Coconut Grove, FL

TITLE	PUBLISHER	PRINTER	DATE	MEDIUM	DIMENSION (PAPER SIZE) IN INCHES	TYPE OF PAPER	EDITION NUMBER	NO. OF COLORS	ORIGINAL OPENING PRICE	CURRENT RETAIL PRICE
CURRENT EDITIONS:										
City Blizzard	ART	AK/EldP	1986	EC/A/DPT/HC	31 X 35	STP	30		750	900

CINDA SPARLING

BORN: Rochester, NY; February 27, 1953
EDUCATION: Moore Col of Art, BFA, 1971–75; Ohio Univ, Athens, OH, MFA, 1975–77
AWARDS: ARIANA Found for the Arts Grant, 1982; Mid-Atlantic Arts Consortium Grant, 1986; Special Project, Frankfurter Allemeine Seitung, Druckhaus AE Quensen, Lamspinge, Germany, 1987; Special Project, Vis Artist Research Inst, Arizona State Univ, Tempe, AZ, 1988
RECENT EXHIB: Anders Tornberg Gallery, Lund, Sweden, 1988; Greene Gallery, Coral Gables, FL, 1988
COLLECTIONS: Cleveland Center for the Arts, OH
PRINTERS: Artist (ART); Judith Solodkin, NY (JS); Solo Press, NY (SP); Sette Publishing Company, Tempe, AZ; Molly Jo Souders, Albuquerque, NM (MJS); Tamarind Inst, Albuquerque, NM (TI)
PUBLISHERS: Solo Press, NY (SP); Tamarind Inst, Albuquerque, NM (TI); Sette Publishing Company, Tempe, AZ (SPC); Artist (ART)
GALLERIES: Castelli Graphics, New York, NY; Greene Gallery, Coral Gables, FL; Anders Tornberg Gallery, Lund, Sweden; Lisa Sette Gallery, Scottsdale, AZ
MAILING ADDRESS: 66 Greene St, New York, NY 10012

TITLE	PUBLISHER	PRINTER	DATE	MEDIUM	DIMENSION (PAPER SIZE) IN INCHES	TYPE OF PAPER	EDITION NUMBER	NO. OF COLORS	ORIGINAL OPENING PRICE	CURRENT RETAIL PRICE
CURRENT EDITIONS:										
Bokeelia (Series of 5)	ART	ART/SP	1984	PH/LC/HC	48 X 32 EA	AP	1 EA	Varies	600 EA	750 EA
Bokeelia (Series of 26)	TI	MJS/TI	1986	LC/HC	46 X 29 EA	ARJ	1 EA	Varies	600 EA	600 EA

BUZZ SPECTOR (FRANKLIN MAC)

BORN: Chicago, IL; March 13, 1948
EDUCATION: Southern Illinois Univ, Carbondale, IL, BA, Studio Art, 1972; Univ of Chicago, IL, MFA, 1978
TEACHING: Vis Lectr, Art History & Criticism, Art Inst of Chicago, IL, 1983–88; Vis Artist, Univ of California, Santa Barbara, CA, 1988; Vis Lectr, Art Center Col of Design, Pasadena, CA, 1989 to present
AWARDS: Nat Endowment for the Arts Fel, 1988; Illinois Arts County Fel, 1988
RECENT EXHIB: Art Inst of Chicago, IL, 1988; Spertus Mus of Judaica, Chicago, IL, 1988; Los Angeles Municipal Art Gallery, CA, 1990; Newport Harbor Art Mus, Newport Beach, CA, 1990; Marsha Mateyka Gallery, Wash, DC, 1993
COLLECTIONS: Mus of Contemp Art, Chicago, IL; Getty Mus, Malibu, CA; Illinois State Mus, Springfield, IL; Univ of Alberta Art Mus, Edmonton, Canada; Art Inst of Chicago, IL; Lannan Found, Los Angeles, CA
PRINTERS: Daniel Freeman, Los Angeles, CA (DF); Susan Cornish, Los Angeles, CA (SC); Kyle Militzer, Los Angeles, CA (KM); Marco Salazar, Los Angeles, CA (MS); Freeman Editions, Los Angeles, CA (FreeEd)
PUBLISHERS: Freeman Editions, Los Angeles, CA (FreeEd)
GALLERIES: Roy Boyd Galleries, Santa Monica, CA & Chicago, IL; Mattress Factory, Pittsburgh, PA; Marsha Mateyka Gallery, Wash, DC
MAILING ADDRESS: c/o Roy Boyd Gallery, 1547 Tenth St, Santa Monica, CA 90401

TITLE	PUBLISHER	PRINTER	DATE	MEDIUM	DIMENSION (PAPER SIZE) IN INCHES	TYPE OF PAPER	EDITION NUMBER	NO. OF COLORS	ORIGINAL OPENING PRICE	CURRENT RETAIL PRICE
CURRENT EDITIONS:										
Malevich	FreeEd	DF/SC/KM/ MS/FreeEd	1992	SP/DEB	23 X 19	AC/B	20	4	750	750

NANCY SPERO

BORN: Cleveland, OH; August 24, 1926
EDUCATION: Art Inst of Chicago, IL, BFA, 1949; Atleier André L'Hote, Paris, France, 1949–50; Ecole des Beaux-Arts, Paris, France, 1949–50
TEACHING: Vis Art, State Univ of New York, Purchase, NY, 1981
AWARDS: Creative Artists Public Service Fel, New York State Council for the Arts, 1976–77; Nat Endowment for the Arts Grant, 1977–78
RECENT EXHIB: Josh Baer Gallery, NY, 1987; Lawrence Oliver Gallery, Phila, PA, 1987; S L Simpson Gallery, Toronto, Canada, 1987; Retrosp, Fruit Market Gallery, Edinburgh, Scotland, 1987; Retrosp, Orchard Gallery, Derry, Northern Ireland, 1987; Retrosp, Everson Mus, Syracuse, NY, 1987–88; Retrosp, New Mus of Contemp Art, NY, 1987–88; Barbara Gross Galerie, Munich, Germany, 1988; New Mus of Contemp Art, NY, 1989; New Mus of Contemp Art, Houston, TX, 1989; Mus of Hispanic Art, NY, 1990; Maryland Inst, Col of Art, Decker & Meyerhoff Galleries, Baltimore, MD, 1992
COLLECTIONS: Mus of Mod Art, NY; Ohio State Univ, Columbus, OH; Oberlin Col, OH; Ramapo Col, NJ; Greenville County Mus, SC; Australian Nat Gallery, Canberra, Australia; Massachusetts Inst of Tech, Boston, MA; Art Inst of Chicago, IL; Musee des Beaux-Arts de Montreal, Canada; New Sch for Social Res, NY; Philadelphia Mus of Art, PA; Toledo Mus of Art, OH; Art Gallery of Ontario, Toronto, Canada
PRINTERS: Judith Solodkin, NY (JS); Solo Press, NY (SP)
PUBLISHERS: Art Issue Editions, Inc, NY (AIE)
GALLERIES: Rhona Hoffman Gallery, Chicago, IL; Josh Baer Gallery, New York, NY; Lawrence Mangel Gallery, Phila, PA; Burnett Miller Gallery, Los Angeles, CA; Galerie Barbara Gross, Munich, Germany; S L Simpson Gallery, Toronto, Canada; Terrain Gallery, San Francisco, CA; Printworks Gallery, Chicago, IL
MAILING ADDRESS: 530 LaGuardia Place, New York, NY 10012

TITLE	PUBLISHER	PRINTER	DATE	MEDIUM	DIMENSION (PAPER SIZE) IN INCHES	TYPE OF PAPER	EDITION NUMBER	NO. OF COLORS	ORIGINAL OPENING PRICE	CURRENT RETAIL PRICE
CURRENT EDITIONS:										
Thou Shalt Not Kill (from Ten Commandments Suite)	AIE	JS/SP	1987	LC	24 X 19	DIEU	84	9	500	1500
Goddess	SP	JS/SP	1987	LB/SP/HC	22 X 30	SOM	100	Varies	900	1000
Kill Commies	SP	JS/SP	1988	LC/LP	30 X 22	SOM	45		900	1000
Ballade Von der . . . Judenh ure Marie Sanders	SP	JS/SP	1991	LC	21 X 48	SOM	50		1500	1500

The retail prices of the 100,000 limited edition prints quoted in this directory are subject to change. Print publishers, artists and galleries were the direct sources for these quotations. Prices in the secondary market listed as "Sold Out Editions (Rare)" indicate that the publisher has a limited supply of that print or that the print is difficult to locate in the galleries.

The Printworld Directory is accepting new applications for the seventh edition. Approximately 300 new artists will be accepted. Please use the two forms provided in the back section of this directory to submit biographical data and documentation of prints. Edition number of each print must not exceed 500 and the retail price must be $100 or more.

ANDREW SPENCE

BORN: Bryn Mawr, PA; October 4, 1947
EDUCATION: Tyler Sch of Art, Temple Univ, Phila, PA, BFA, 1969; Univ of California, Santa Barbara, CA, MFA, 1971
PRINTERS: Garner Tullis Workshop, Santa Monica, CA (GTW); Joe Wilfer, NY (JW); Ruth NY (RL); Spring Street Workshop, NY (SprSW)
PUBLISHERS: Garner Tullis Workshop, Santa Monica, CA (GTW); Spring Street Workshop, NY (SprSW)
GALLERIES: Garner Tullis, New York, NY; Barbara Toll Fine Arts, New York, NY; A Clean, Well-Lighted Place, New York, NY; Max Protetch Gallery, New York, NY; Margulies Taplin Gallery, Boca Raton, FL; L Bartman Fine Arts, Chicago, IL
MAILING ADDRESS: 6 Varick St, New York, NY 10013

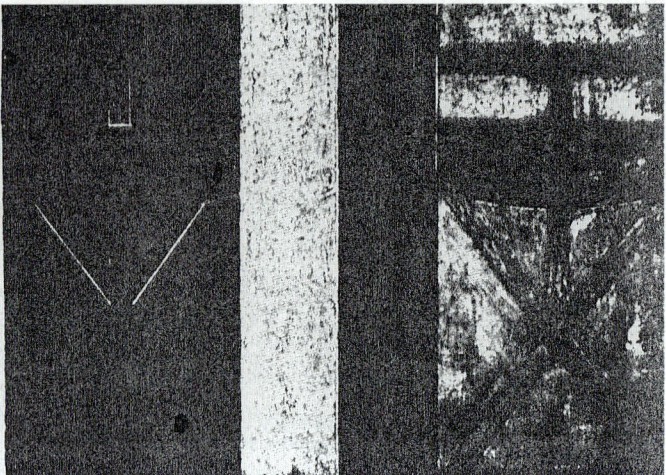

Andrew Spence
Untitled (Barbecue Grills)
Courtesy Barbara Toll Fine Arts

TITLE	PUBLISHER	PRINTER	DATE	MEDIUM	DIMENSION (PAPER SIZE) IN INCHES	TYPE OF PAPER	EDITION NUMBER	NO. OF COLORS	ORIGINAL OPENING PRICE	CURRENT RETAIL PRICE
CURRENT EDITIONS:										
Untitled (A-6)	GTW	GTW	1988	MON	40 X 31 EA	AC	1 EA		2000 EA	2500 EA
Untitled (A-12)	GTW	GTW	1988	MON	30 X 23 EA	AC	1 EA		1000 EA	1500 EA
Untitled (A-20)	GTW	GTW	1988	MON	63 X 43 EA	AC	1 EA		3000 EA	3500 EA
Untitled (Set of 5)	SprSW	JW/RL/SprSW	1990	WB/LI/SP	29 X 20 EA	AP88	35 EA	1 EA	3500 SET	3500 SET
									1000 EA	1000 EA
Untitled (Set of 5)	SprSW	JW/RL/SprSW	1991	WB/LI	29 X 20 EA	AC	35 EA	1 EA	3500 SET	3500 SET
									800 EA	800 EA
Untitled (Set of 3)	SprSW	JW/RL/SprSW	1992	WB/COL	33 X 24 EA	AC	33 EA	1 EA	2000 SET	2000 SET
									800 EA	800 EA

ART SPIEGELMAN

RECENT EXHIB: Fort Lauderdale Mus of Art, FL, 1993; Galerie St Etienne, NY, 1993
PRINTERS: Timothy Sheesley, Otego, NY (TS); Corridor Press, Otego, NY (CorPr)
PUBLISHERS: Raw Graphics, NY (RAW)
GALLERIES: Galerie St Etienne, New York, NY

TITLE	PUBLISHER	PRINTER	DATE	MEDIUM	DIMENSION (PAPER SIZE) IN INCHES	TYPE OF PAPER	EDITION NUMBER	NO. OF COLORS	ORIGINAL OPENING PRICE	CURRENT RETAIL PRICE
CURRENT EDITION:										
Mice Portfolio (Set of 4):									800 SET	800 SET
Mäuse & Mouse	RAW	TS/CorPr	1992	LC	8 X 6	R/BFK	30	3	225	225
Cat & Maus	RAW	TS/CorPr	1992	LC	8 X 6	R/BFK	30	3	225	225
Mickey, Maus & Mouse	RAW	TS/CorPr	1992	LC	8 X 6	R/BFK	30	3	225	225
Nadja, Mickey & Mäuse	RAW	TS/CorPr	1992	LC	8 X 6	R/BFK	30	3	225	225

BENTON MURDOCK SPRUANCE

BORN: Phila, PA; (1904–1967)
PRINTERS: Artist (ART)
PUBLISHERS: Artist (ART); American Artists Group, NY (AAG); Associated American Artists, NY (AAA); Philadelphia Print Club, PA (PPC)
GALLERIES: Hahn Gallery, Phila, PA; Sande Garcia Fine Arts, Miami, FL; Sylvan Cole Gallery, New York, NY

TITLE	PUBLISHER	PRINTER	DATE	MEDIUM	DIMENSION (PAPER SIZE) IN INCHES	TYPE OF PAPER	EDITION NUMBER	NO. OF COLORS	ORIGINAL OPENING PRICE	CURRENT RETAIL PRICE
SOLD OUT EDITIONS (RARE):										
Amusement Park, Vienna	ART	ART	1928	LC/CC	10 X 10	AP	22		35	1650
Landscape	ART	ART	1932	LB	11 X 8	AP			25	150
Church at Night	ART	ART	1932	LB	13 X 12	AP	40	1	25	800
Adolescent	ART	ART	1933	LB	13 X 11	AP	28	1	25	750
The Driving Tackle	ART	ART	1933	LB	11 X 15	AP	40	1	25	2000

BENTON MURDOCK SPRUANCE CONTINUED

TITLE	PUBLISHER	PRINTER	DATE	MEDIUM	DIMENSION (PAPER SIZE) IN INCHES	TYPE OF PAPER	EDITION NUMBER	NO. OF COLORS	ORIGINAL OPENING PRICE	CURRENT RETAIL PRICE
SOLD OUT EDITIONS (RARE):										
Entrance to Germantown	ART	ART	1933	LB	10 X 14	AP	35	1	25	1700
Late Departure	ART	ART	1933	LB	10 X 13	AP	40	1	25	3700
Touchdown Play	ART	ART	1933	LB	12 X 17	AP	40	1	25	1500
Introduction to Love	ART	ART	1935	LB	8 X 14	AP	40	1	35	2000
Philatelists	ART	ART	1935	LB	10 X 14	AP	25	1	35	1850
Shovel Pass	ART	ART	1935	LB	14 X 19	AP	40	1	35	1850
Design for America #2	ART	ART	1935	LB	16 X 10	AP	40	1	35	750
A Short Gain	AAG	ART	1936	LB	9 X 15	AP	40	1	30	250
Traffic Control	ART	ART	1936	LB	9 X 14	AP	35	1	30	15000
Caustic Comment	ART	ART	1936	LB	10 X 15	AP	30	1	30	1900
Fencers	AAG	ART	1937	LB	13 X 8	AP			35	400
Portrait of a Sullen Girl	ART	ART	1937	LB	11 X 9	AP	20	1	40	500
Supplies for Suburbia	ART	ART	1938	LB	10 X 15	AP	30	1	50	2300
The Vagrant	ART	ART	1938	LB	10 X 15	AP	35	1	50	1200
Figure of a Woman	ART	ART	1939	LB	9 X 17	AP	25	1	50	500
Portrait at Dusk	ART	ART	1939	LB	16 X 10	AP	20	1	50	500
Landscape with Figures	ART	ART	1940	LB	10 X 13	AP	30	1	75	1800
Arrangement for Drums	ART	ART	1941	LB	9 X 15	AP	30	1	85	16500
The Lovers	ART	ART	1942	LB	15 X 10	AP	40	1	85	1900
Riders of the Apocalypse	ART	ART	1943	LB	13 X 17	AP	35	1	100	19500
Nero	ART	ART	1944	LB		AP	30	1	100	2500
Forward Pass	ART	ART	1944	LC	20 X 13	AP	35	1	100	750
Ridge Valley Churches	ART	ART	1944	LB	13 X 19	AP	40	1	100	500
Soldier and Chaplain	ART	ART	1944	LB	12 X 18	AP	40	1	100	900
Sonia and Her Cello	ART	ART	1944	LB	19 X 14	AP	40	1	100	500
Ecclesiastes: Vanity, Striving	ART	ART	1945	LB	15 X 13	AP	30	1	100	650
Midsummer Spiel	ART	ART	1946	LB	14 X 17	AP	35	1	100	350
Ecclesiates: Essay Three	ART	ART	1946	LB	19 X 15	AP	40	1	100	750
Eyes for the Night	ART	ART	1947	LB	19 X 13	AP	35	1	125	1200
Newtown Towers	ART	ART	1948	LB	10 X 8	AP		1	75	200
Newtown, Bucks County, PA	ART	ART	1948	LB	10 X 8	AP		1	75	200
Head of a Drum Majorette	ART	ART	1951	WB	14 X 12	R/BFK		1	125	500
When I Laid the Earth's...	ART	ART	1951	LB	18 X 12	AP	30	1	125	200
Subway Playground	ART	ART	1951	LC	19 X 14	AP	40		125	1800
Fragment	ART	ART	1955	LC	17 X 11	AP	32	6	150	250
Paper Shapes	ART	ART	1955	LC	12 X 17	AP	30	7	150	350
Winter Portrait	ART	ART	1955	LC	21 X 14	AP	25		175	600
Skyhawk	ART	ART	1965	MON	18 X 14 EA	AP	1 EA	Varies	200 EA	600 EA

GAEL Z STACK

BORN: Chicago, IL; April 28, 1941
EDUCATION: Univ of Illinois, Champaign, IL, BFA, 1970; Univ of Southern Illinois Univ, IL, MFA, 1972
TEACHING: Instr, Univ of Wisconsin, La Crosse, WI, 1972–73; From Asst Prof to Assoc Prof, Univ of Houston, TX, 1974–85, Prof, 1985 to present
AWARDS: Univ of Houston, TX, Travel Grant; Cultural Arts Council of Houston, Visual Arts Award, TX, 1985; Louis Comfort Tiffany Found Grant, 1986; Nat Endowment for the Arts Grants, 1982,89
RECENT EXHIB: Beitzel Fine Arts, NY, 1988; Janie C Lee, Houston, TX, 1987,89; Diverse Works, Houston, TX, 1989; Univ of Arkansas, Little Rock, AR, 1989; Moody Gallery, Houston, TX, 1990; RGK Found Gallery, Austin, TX, 1990; Mus of Fine Arts, Houston, TX, 1990; Palm Springs Desert Mus, TX, 1990; Univ of Houston, Sarah Campbell Blaffer Gallery, Houston, TX, 1989,92
COLLECTIONS: Solomon R Guggenheim Mus, NY; Mus of Fine Art, Houston, TX; Dallas Mus of Art, TX; Menil Coll, Houston, TX
PRINTERS: Eileen Foti, Albuquerque, NM (EF); Artist (ART); Tamarind Inst, Albuquerque, NM (TI)
PUBLISHERS: Tamarind Inst, Albuquerque, NM (TI)
GALLERIES: Janie C Lee Galleries, Houston, TX & New York, NY; Tamarind Inst, Albuquerque, NM; Moody Gallery, Houston, TX; David Beitzel Gallery, New York, NY
MAILING ADDRESS: 3703 Granstark, Houston, TX 77006–4207

TITLE	PUBLISHER	PRINTER	DATE	MEDIUM	DIMENSION (PAPER SIZE) IN INCHES	TYPE OF PAPER	EDITION NUMBER	NO. OF COLORS	ORIGINAL OPENING PRICE	CURRENT RETAIL PRICE
CURRENT EDITIONS:										
Untitled (Series of 5)	TI	EF/ART/TI	1988	MON	22 X 30 EA	R/BFK	1 EA	Multi	1200 EA	1200 EA
Untitled	TI	EF/ART/TI	1988	LC	34 X 21	R/BFK/CR	20	6	400	400

CHIP SPEAR

PRINTERS: Diablo C-150 Printer (DC-150); Artist (ART)
PUBLISHERS: Artist (ART)
GALLERIES: Circlework Visions Gallery, New York, NY

TITLE	PUBLISHER	PRINTER	DATE	MEDIUM	DIMENSION (PAPER SIZE) IN INCHES	TYPE OF PAPER	EDITION NUMBER	NO. OF COLORS	ORIGINAL OPENING PRICE	CURRENT RETAIL PRICE
SOLD OUT EDITIONS (RARE):										
Bokeelia (Series of 5)	ART	ART/SP	1984	PH/LC/HC	48 X 32 EA	AP	1 EA	Varies	600 EA	800 EA

ROBERT STACKHOUSE

BORN: Bronxville, NY; 1942
EDUCATION: Univ of South Florida, Tampa, FL, BA, 1965; Univ of Maryland, College Park, MD, MA, 1967
TEACHING: Lectr, New Gallery of Contemp Art, Cleveland, OH, 1977; Lectr, Cleveland State Univ, OH, 1977; Lectr, Artpark, Lewiston, NY, 1977; Lectr, Cleveland Inst of Art, OH, 1977; Lectr, Cranbrook Acad of Art, Bloomfield Hills, MI, 1978; Lectr, Brown Univ, Providence, RI, 1978; Lectr, Tyler Sch of Art, Phila, PA, 1979; Lectr, Northwestern Univ, Evanston, IL, 1979; Lectr, Univ of Minnesota, Minneapolis, MN, 1979; Lectr, Univ of Wisconsin, Eau Claire, WI, 1979; Lectr, Pennsylvania State Univ, University Park, PA, 1979; Lectr, Kean Col, Newark, NJ, 1979; Lectr, Syracuse Univ, NY, 1979; Lectr, State Univ of New York, Fresonia, NY, 1980; Lectr, Ohio Univ, Athens, OH, 1980; Lectr, Nassau County Mus of Fine Art, Roslyn, NY, 1981; Lectr, Univ of South Florida, Tampa, FL, 1981; Lectr, Art Inst Sch of Art, Chicago, IL, 1982; Lectr, Art Gallery of Toronto, ON; Lectr, Portland Mus of Art, OR, 1982; Lectr, Illinois State Univ, Normal, IL, 1983; Lectr, Pennsylvania Acad of Fine Arts, Phila, PA, 1983; Lectr, Ohio State Univ, Columbus, OH, 1984; Lectr, Virginia Commonwealth Univ, Richmond, VA, 1984; Univ of Tennessee, Knoxville, TN, 1983,84; Lectr, Univ of Cincinnati, OH, 1985; Lectr, Birmingham Mus of Art, AL, 1985; Lectr, Univ of Wisconsin, Madison, WI, 1985; Lectr, Carnegie Mellon Univ, Pittsburgh, PA, 1985; Lectr, Gassell Sch of Art, Houston, TX, 1985; Lectr, Univ of Pennsylvania, Phila, PA, 1986; Lectr, San Antonio Art Inst, San Antonio, TX, 1987
RECENT EXHIB: Koplin Gallery, Los Angeles, CA, 1988; Kornblatt Gallery, Wash, DC, 1988; Dolan/Maxwell Gallery, Phila, PA, 1987,88,90; Virginia Mus of Fine Arts, Richmond, VA, 1990; Dolan/Maxwell Gallery, NY, 1990; Delaware Art Mus, Wilmington, DE, 1991; Univ of South Florida, Tampa, FL, 1991; Lumeier Sculpture Park, St Louis, MO, 1992; Univ of South Florida, Graphic Studio, Tampa, FL, 1992
COLLECTIONS: Indianapolis Mus of Art, IN; Mus of Contemp Art, Chicago, IL; Walker Art Center, Minneapolis, MN; Art Inst of Chicago, IL; Allen Mem Art Mus, Oberlin, Col, OH; Baltimore Mus of Art, MD; Corcoran Gallery of Art, Wash, DC; Philadelphia Art Mus, PA; Indianapolis Mus, IN; Madison Art Center, WI; Hunter Mus of Art, Chattanooga, TN; Australian Nat Gallery, Canberra Australia; Pennsylvania Acad of Fine Arts, Phila, PA; Delaware Art Mus, Wilmington, DE; Mus of Fine Arts, Boston, MA; Smith Col, Northampton, MA; Hirshhorn Mus, Wash, DC; Phillips Collections, Wash, DC; Sunrise Found, Inc, Charleston, WV
PRINTERS: Normal Editions Workshop, Illinois State Univ, Normal, IL (NEW); Artist (ART); Joe Wilfer, NY (JW); Ruth Lingen, NY (RL); Spring Street Workshop, NY (SprSW); Julie D'Amario, NY (JDA); Kathy Kuehn, NY (KK); Bill Weege, Madison, WI (BW); Andrew Rubin, Madison, WI (AR); Tandem Press, Univ of Wisconsin, Madison, WI (TanPr)
PUBLISHERS: Normal Editions Workshop, Illinois State Univ, Normal, IL (NEW); Pace Editions, NY (PE); Spring Street Workshop, NY (SprSW); Tandem Press, Univ of Wisconsin, Madison, WI (TanPr)
GALLERIES: Middendorf Gallery, Wash, DC; Leila Taghinia-Milani, New York, NY; Pace Prints, New York, NY; Landfall Press, Inc, Chicago, IL & New York, NY; Feigenson/Preston Gallery, Birmingham, MI; Margulies Taplin Gallery, Boca Raton, FL; Lemberg Gallery, Birmingham, MI; Morgan Gallery, Kansas City, MO

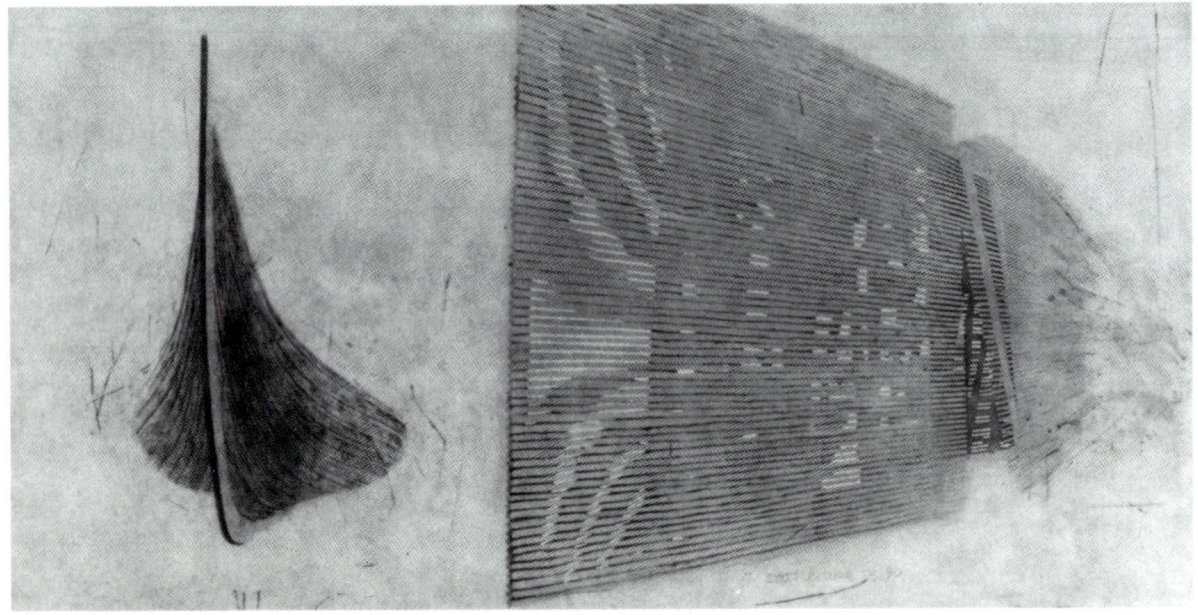

Robert Stackhouse
Untitled, 1990
Courtesy Spring Street Workshop
& Tandem Press

TITLE	PUBLISHER	PRINTER	DATE	MEDIUM	DIMENSION (PAPER SIZE) IN INCHES	TYPE OF PAPER	EDITION NUMBER	NO. OF COLORS	ORIGINAL OPENING PRICE	CURRENT RETAIL PRICE
CURRENT EDITIONS:										
Brooklyn Bridge	NEW	NEW	1983	LC	21 X 35	R/BFK	20	5	400	1200
Running Animals/Reindeer Way	PE	ART	1986	LC	43 X 30	R/BFK	45		600	1500
Niagara Dance	PE	ART	1986	LC	31 X 46	R/BFK	45		600	1500
Mountain Climbers and Ship Hull	PE	ART	1987	LC	31 X 45	R/BFK	35		600	1500
Red Deck and Passage Structure	PE	ART	1987	LC	43 X 31	R/BFK	45		600	1500
Sources and Structures (805-5) (Set of 6):									3600 SET	7500 SET
Naja (805-5-1)	SprSW	JDA/KK/SprSW	1988–89	EC/SB	31 X 21	HAHN	50		650	1700
Gokstad (805-5-2)	SprSW	JDA/KK/SprSW	1988–89	EC/SB	31 X 21	HAHN	50		650	2000
Shipwreck (805-5-3)	SprSW	JDA/KK/SprSW	1988–89	EC/SB	31 X 21	HAHN	50		650	1500
At Hudson River Museum (805-5-4)	SprSW	JDA/KK/SprSW	1988–89	EC/SB	31 X 21	HAHN	50		650	1700
At Eau Clair Wisconsin (805-5-5)	SprSW	JDA/KK/SprSW	1988–89	EC/SB	31 X 21	HAHN	50		650	1900
At Sculpture Now, NYC (805-5-6)	SprSW	JDA/KK/SprSW	1988–89	EC/SB	31 X 21	HAHN	50		650	1500
Untitled, 1990	SprSW/TanPr	AR/TanPr	1990	EB/A/SB/DPT	55 X 102	SOM/W	45	3	7500	7500

ROBERT STACKHOUSE CONTINUED

TITLE	PUBLISHER	PRINTER	DATE	MEDIUM	DIMENSION (PAPER SIZE) IN INCHES	TYPE OF PAPER	EDITION NUMBER	NO. OF COLORS	ORIGINAL OPENING PRICE	CURRENT RETAIL PRICE
CURRENT EDITIONS:										
Diviners	SprSW	JW/RL/SprSW	1990	EB/A	50 X 98	HAHN	45		7500	7500
Blue Diviners	SprSW	JW/RL/SprSW	1991	WC	27 X 18	HMP	75	24	1000	1000
Encounterings	SprSW	JW/RL/SprSW	1991	WC	18 X 26	HMP	75	21	1000	1000
Approaching Diviner	SprSW	JW/RL/SprSW	1992	EB/A	103 X 54	HAHN	45		5000	5000
Soundless	TanPr	BW/AR/TanPr	1992	EC/SB	38 X 58	R/BFK	45	3	3500	3500
Fragmentary Bones (Cast Bronze Sculpture)	TanPr		1992	Mult	46 X 27 X 11	Bronze	12		15000	15000

DONALD L STACY

BORN: West Paterson, NJ; September 3, 1925
EDUCATION: Newark Sch of Fine Arts, 1942–43; Art Students League, NY, 1946–53; Pratt Graphic Art Center, NY, 1956–57; Univ of Paris, Dept of Art and Archeology, 1953–54; Univ of Aix-Marseille, Provence, France, 1954–55
TEACHING: Mus of Mod Art, NY, 1957–69; Sch of Visual Arts, NY, 1969–70; New Sch for Social Research, 1967 to present
AWARDS: Fulbright Fel Grants, 1953–55
COLLECTIONS: Mus of Mod Art, NY; Birla Acad of Art, Calcutta, India
PRINTERS: Artist (ART)
PUBLISHERS: Stacy Studio Workshop, NY (SSW)
GALLERIES: Stacy Studio Workshop, New York, NY
MAILING ADDRESS: 17 E 16th St, New York, NY 10003

TITLE	PUBLISHER	PRINTER	DATE	MEDIUM	DIMENSION (PAPER SIZE) IN INCHES	TYPE OF PAPER	EDITION NUMBER	NO. OF COLORS	ORIGINAL OPENING PRICE	CURRENT RETAIL PRICE
SOLD OUT EDITIONS (RARE):										
Night Woman	SSW	ART	1970	WC	12 X 20	AP	25	2	150	650
Modern Vitruvian	SSW	ART	1972	WC	17 X 20	AP	12	3	150	650
Sea Offering	SSW	ART	1972	WC	11 X 18	AP	14	2	150	650
Creation Theme	SSW	ART	1974	WC	20 X 30	AP	14	3	300	650
Center Image	SSW	ART	1976	WC	12 X 17	AP	17	3	300	650
CURRENT EDITIONS:										
Sol	SSW	ART	1978	WB	8 X 10	AP	25	1	300	600
Luna	SSW	ART	1978	WB	8 X 10	AP	25	1	300	600
Nude Reaching Osiris	SSW	ART	1985	SP	7 X 16	AP	100	1	150	300

ANSELM STADLER

BORN: Magden AG, Switzerland; 1956
PRINTERS: Peter Kneubluhler, Zurich, Switzerland (PK)
PUBLISHERS: Peter Blum Edition, NY (PBE)
GALLERIES: Peter Blum Edition, New York, NY

TITLE	PUBLISHER	PRINTER	DATE	MEDIUM	DIMENSION (PAPER SIZE) IN INCHES	TYPE OF PAPER	EDITION NUMBER	NO. OF COLORS	ORIGINAL OPENING PRICE	CURRENT RETAIL PRICE
SOLD OUT EDITIONS (RARE):										
Der Umfang des Fassungsvermögens 1983/84 (the Limits of Perception) (Portfolio Includes Poem, Book & Monotype) (Set of 5)	PBE	PK	1983/84	WC	23 X 30 EA	R/BFK	35 EA		2000 SET	4500 SET

THEODOROS S STAMOS

BORN: New York, NY; December 31, 1922
EDUCATION: Am Artists Sch, NY, 1936
TEACHING: Instr, Art Students League, NY, 1956 to present; Lectr, Columbia Univ, NY; Prof, Art, Brandeis Univ, Waltham, MA
AWARDS: Brandeis Univ Creative Arts Award; Tiffany Foundation Fel; Nat Arts Grant
RECENT EXHIB: Midwest Mus of Am Art, Elkhart, IN, 1992; ACA Gallery, NY, 1992
COLLECTIONS: Mus of Mod Art, NY; Metropolitan Mus of Art, NY; Whitney Mus of Am Art, NY; Albright-Knox Art Gallery, Buffalo, NY; Walker Art Center, Minneapolis, MN; Munson-Williams-Proctor Inst, Utica, NY; Wadsworth Atheneum, Hartford, CT; Vassar Univ, Poughkeepsie, NY; Wellesley Col, MA; Univ of Iowa; Detroit Inst of Art, MI; Tel Aviv Mus, Israel; Duncan Phillips Gallery, Wash, DC; Art Inst of Chicago, IL; Baltimore Mus of Art, MD; Corcoran Gallery of Art, Wash, DC; Brandeis Univ, Waltham, MA; Addison Gallery of Am Art, Andover, MA; San Francisco Mus of Art, CA; Des Moines Art Center, IA; Art Gallery of Toronto, Can; Univ of California, Berkeley, CA; Nat Picture Gallery, Athens, Greece
PRINTERS: Artist (ART)
PUBLISHERS: Marlborough Graphics, NY (MG)
GALLERIES: Marlborough Graphics, New York, NY; Louis K Meisel Gallery, New York, NY; Knoedler Gallery, Zürich, Switzerland; Harcourts Modern & Contemporary Gallery, San Francisco, CA; Hokin Galleries, Palm Beach, FL & Bay Harbor Islands, FL; Louis Newman Gallery, Beverly Hills, CA; ACA Galleries, New York, NY; DuBois International, Ltd, New York, NY; Kouros Gallery, New York, NY; Snyder Fine Art, New York, NY
MAILING ADDRESS: 37 W 83rd St, New York, NY 10024

TITLE	PUBLISHER	PRINTER	DATE	MEDIUM	DIMENSION (PAPER SIZE) IN INCHES	TYPE OF PAPER	EDITION NUMBER	NO. OF COLORS	ORIGINAL OPENING PRICE	CURRENT RETAIL PRICE
CURRENT EDITIONS:										
Delphis Sun Box I	MG	ART	1971	SP	26 X 24	AP	75		150	1500
Green Sun Box	MG	ART	1971	SP	26 X 24	AP	75		150	1500
Infinity Field, Delphi I (Blue)	MG	ART	1971	SP	25 X 23	AP	75		150	1500
Infinity Field, Olympia I	MG	ART	1971	SP	25 X 23	AP	75		150	1500
Spartan Sun Box I	MG	ART	1971	SP	26 X 24	AP	75		150	1500

THEODOROS S STAMOS CONTINUED

TITLE	PUBLISHER	PRINTER	DATE	MEDIUM	DIMENSION (PAPER SIZE) IN INCHES	TYPE OF PAPER	EDITION NUMBER	NO. OF COLORS	ORIGINAL OPENING PRICE	CURRENT RETAIL PRICE
CURRENT EDITIONS:										
Infinity Field, Lefkada	MG	ART	1972	SP	30 X 22	AP	75		150	1500
Infinity Field, Lefkada II	MG	ART	1972	SP	30 X 22	AP	75		150	1500
Infinity Field, Lefkada III	MG	ART	1972	SP	30 X 22	AP	75		150	1500
Infinity Field, Olympia II	MG	ART	1972	SP	30 X 22	AP	75		150	1500
Infinity Field, Olympia III	MG	ART	1972	SP	30 X 22	AP	75		150	1500
Untitled Purple	MG	ART	1977	SP	30 X 22	AP	95		200	1200
Untitled Red	MG	ART	1977	PS	30 X 22	AP	95		200	1200

JULIAN STANCZAK

BORN: Borownica, P; Poland; November 5, 1928; US Citizen
EDUCATION: Cleveland Inst of Art, OH, BFA, 1954; Yale Univ, New Haven, CT, MFA, 1956 with Josef Albers & Conrad Marca-Relli
TEACHING: Instr, Art Acad of Cincinnati, OH, 1957–64; Artist in Res, Dartmouth Col, Hanover, NH, 1968; Prof, Painting, Cleveland Art Inst, OH, 1964 to present
AWARDS: Cleveland Fine Arts Award, 1970; Outstanding Am Educator Award, 1970; Ohio Arts Council Award, 1972
RECENT EXHIB: Cleveland Center for Contemp Art, OH, 1989
COLLECTIONS: Carnegie Inst, Pittsburgh, PA; Albright-Knox Art Gallery, Buffalo, NY; Aldrich Mus of Contemp Art, Ridgefield, CT; Corcoran Gallery of Art, Wash, DC; Hirshhorn Mus, Wash, DC
PRINTERS: Vistec Graphics, NY (VG)
PUBLISHERS: London Arts Inc, Detroit, MI (LAI)
GALLERIES: David Anderson Gallery, Buffalo, NY; Carl Solway Gallery, Cincinnati, OH; Images Gallery, Toledo, OH; Brubaker Gallery, Sarasota, FL; Alice Simsar Gallery, Ann Arbor, MI; Charles Foley Gallery, Columbus, OH
MAILING ADDRESS: 6229 Cabrini Lane, Seven Hill, OH 44131

TITLE	PUBLISHER	PRINTER	DATE	MEDIUM	DIMENSION (PAPER SIZE) IN INCHES	TYPE OF PAPER	EDITION NUMBER	NO. OF COLORS	ORIGINAL OPENING PRICE	CURRENT RETAIL PRICE
SOLD OUT EDITIONS (RARE):										
Trespass	LAI	VG	1979	SP	27 X 23	SOM	175	6	375	800
Sequential Chroma	LAI	VG	1979	SP	30 X 26	SOM	175	6	375	800
Continual	LAI	VG	1979	SP	26 X 26	SOM	175	6	375	800
Compound Red	LAI	VG	1979	SP	26 X 26	SOM	175	6	375	800
Conferring Blue	LAI	VG	1979	SP	25 X 25	SOM	175	6	375	800
Filtration	LAI	VG	1979	SP	26 X 26	SOM	175	6	375	800
Stratified	LAI	VG	1979	SP	26 X 39	SOM	175	6	375	600

ROBERT STANLEY

BORN: Yonkers, NY; January 3, 1932
EDUCATION: Oglethorpe Univ, Atlanta, GA, BA, 1953; High Mus of Art, Atlanta, GA, 1951–52; Columbia Univ, NY, 1953; Art Students League, NY, 1953; Brooklyn Mus Art Sch, Max Beckman Painting Scholar, 1955–56
TEACHING: Vis Art, Louisiana State Univ, Baton Rouge, LA, 1976; Vis Art, Syracuse Univ, NY, 1978; Vis Art, Princeton Univ, NJ, 1979–80; Vis Art, St Lawrence Univ, Canton, OH, 1978; Instr, Sch of Visual Arts, NY, 1970–72, 1984 to present
AWARDS: Max Beckman Fel, Brooklyn Mus Art Sch, Ny, 1955–56; Casandra Found Award, 1969; Igor Found Award, 1987
RECENT EXHIB: John Davis Gallery, NY, 1987; Galerie Georges Laurov, Paris, France, 1987; Galleri Johnny Ericsson, Stockholm, Sweden, 1988; Gallery Bebert, Rotterdam, The Netherlands, 1989; The Painted Bride Art Center, Phila, Pa, 1990; Greenville County Mus of Art, Greenville, SC, 1992
COLLECTIONS: Metropolitan Mus of Art, NY; Whitney Mus of Am Art, NY; Milwaukee Art Center, WI; Corcoran Gallery of Art, Wash, DC; Parrish Art Mus, Southampton, NY; Fogg Art Mus, Cambridge, MA; Minneapolis Mus of Art, MN; Corcoran Gallery, of Art, Wash, DC
PRINTERS: XPress, NY (XP); Chiron Press, NY (CP); Styria Studio, NY (SS); Larry B Wright, NY (LBW); John Nichols, NY (JN); Grenfell Press, NY (GP); Artist (ART)
PUBLISHERS: Brooke Alexander, Inc, NY (BAI); Paul Bianchini, NY (PB); Master Editions, NY (ME); John Nichols, NY (JN); Artist (ART)
GALLERIES: John Nichols Gallery, New York, NY; Holly Keenberg, Winnipeg, Canada; Brooke Alexander Inc, New York, NY; Davlyn Gallery, New York, NY; Galerie Georges Laurov, Paris, France; Galleri Johnny Ericsson, Stockholm, Sweden

TITLE	PUBLISHER	PRINTER	DATE	MEDIUM	DIMENSION (PAPER SIZE) IN INCHES	TYPE OF PAPER	EDITION NUMBER	NO. OF COLORS	ORIGINAL OPENING PRICE	CURRENT RETAIL PRICE
SOLD OUT EDITIONS (RARE):										
Rock Suite (Set Of 10)	PB	ART	1965	SP	18 X 24 EA	AP	95 EA	2 EA	1000 SET	8000 SET
Vitti	PB	ART	1967	SP	24 X 18	AP	200	2	100	900
Hockey Suite on Plexiglass (Set of 10)	ART	ART	1968	SP	25 X 36 EA	AP	5 EA	4–6 EA	2000 SET	15000 SET
Branches	BAI	CP	1970	LC	30 X 23	AP	60	3	150	1800
Runners-Trial Proofs	ART	SS	1974	SP	30 X 23	AP	11	12	250	900
CURRENT EDITIONS:										
Celery & Tomatoes	JN	JN	1978	SP	41 X 33	AP	75	5	400	600
Strawberries	ME	JN	1978	SP	36 X 33	AP	250	7	300	500
Strawberries	ME	JN	1978	SP	36 X 33	AP	60	7	400	600
Sunbather	ME	JN	1978	SP	37 X 34	AP	250	16	300	500
Sunbather	ME	JN	1978	SP	37 X 34	AP	60	16	400	600
Jello Mold	ART	SS	1978	LC	9 X 10		150	10	50	350
Drum-Majorette (3 Versions)	ME	LBW	1979	SP	30 X 31		175	3	275 EA	400 EA
Beets (3 Versions)	ME	JN	1979	SP	30 X 22		175	5	275 EA	400 EA
Rooster (3 Versions)	ME	SS	1979	LC	30 X 22		175	7	275 EA	400 EA
A Very Large Flying Boat	ME	SS	1979	LC	22 X 30		175	5	275 EA	400 EA
Castle (3 Versions)	ME	SS	1979	LC	30 X 22		175	11	275 EA	400 EA

ROBERT STANLEY CONTINUED

TITLE	PUBLISHER	PRINTER	DATE	MEDIUM	DIMENSION (PAPER SIZE) IN INCHES	TYPE OF PAPER	EDITION NUMBER	NO. OF COLORS	ORIGINAL OPENING PRICE	CURRENT RETAIL PRICE
CURRENT EDITIONS:										
Boston Baked Beans (5 Versions)	JN	JN	1980	SP	44 X 36 EA		40 EA	3-14 EA	400 EA	500 EA
Window Suite (Set of 4)	JN	JN	1980	PH	11 X 14 EA	AP	50 EA		350 SET	600 SET
Keylime Pie	JN	JN	1981	SP/LC	29 X 42	R/BFK/B	20	24	650	700
Marylin's Lament	JN	JN	1981	SP/LC	29 X 42	R/BFK	20	28	650	700
Magnetic Arms	JN	JN	1981	SP	19 X 20		40	2	150	350
Trains & Keylime Pie	JN	JN	1981	SP/LC	30 X 44		50	19	500	700
Lamont & The Universe	JN	JN	1982	SP/LC	30 X 44		50		500	700
Bowl of Cereal & Whale Kitt	JN	JN	1982	SP/LC	30 X 44		50	19	500	700
Tracks (Set of 9)	XP/GP	XP/GP	1982	FC	18 X 13		50	11	1500	1800
Avis of Symmetry	JN	JN	1983	SP/LC	29 X 42	R/BFK	40	25	650	700

TED STANUGA

PRINTERS: Fred Gude, Chicago, IL (FG); Four Brothers Press, Chicago, IL (FBP)

PUBLISHERS: Four Brothers Press, Chicago, IL (FBP); Artist (ART)
GALLERIES: Four Brothers Press, Chicago, IL; Karen Lennox Gallery, Chicago, IL; Lannon-Cole Gallery, Chicago, IL

TITLE	PUBLISHER	PRINTER	DATE	MEDIUM	DIMENSION (PAPER SIZE) IN INCHES	TYPE OF PAPER	EDITION NUMBER	NO. OF COLORS	ORIGINAL OPENING PRICE	CURRENT RETAIL PRICE
CURRENT EDITIONS:										
Killer	ART/FBP	FG/FBP	1982	LB	15 X 12	AP/B	50	1	200	500

LARRY STARK

BORN: 1941
RECENT EXHIB: Haydon Gallery, Nebraska Art Assoc, Lincoln, NE, 1992
COLLECTIONS: Detroit Inst of Arts, MI; Bowdoin Col Mus, Brunswick, ME; Washington Univ Mus, St Louis, MO; Minneapolis Inst of Art, MN; Allen Mus, Oberlin Col, OH; Albright-Knox Art Gallery, Buffalo, NY; State Univ of New York, Albany, NY; Yale Univ, New Haven, CT; William Col Mus, Williamstown, MA; Andrew Dickson White Mus, Cornell Univ, Ithaca, NY; Hopkins Art Center, Dartmouth Col, Hanover, NH; Currier Art Gallery, Manchester, NH; Rose Mus, Brandeis Univ, Waltham, MA; Tyron Art Gallery, Smith Col, Northampton, MA; Nat Coll of Fine Arts, Smithsonian Inst, Wash, DC; Mus of Mod Art, NY; Philadelphia Mus, PA; Addison Gallery of Am Art, Phillips Acad, Andover, MA; Sheldon Gallery, Univ of Nebraska, Lincoln, NE; Indianapolis Mus, IN; Davison Art Center, Wesleyan Univ, Middletown, CT; Univ of Kansas Mus, Lawrence, KS; Univ of Oklahoma Mus, Norman, OK; Mus of Fine Art, Houston, TX; Bluffton Col, OH; Univ of Wisconsin, Madison, WI; Univ of Texas, Austin, TX; Nat Gallery of Canada, Ottawa, Can; Eastman House Photography Mus, Rochester, NY; Art Inst of Chicago, IL; Notre Dame, South Bend, IN; Univ of New Hampshire, Durham, NH; Univ of Minnesota, Minneapolis, MN; East Central State Col, Ada, OK; Univ of Michigan, Ann Arbor, MI; Kresge Art Center, Michigan State Univ, East Lansing, MI; Flint Inst of Art, MI; Utah Mus of Fine Arts, Univ of Utah, Salt Lake City, UT; Portland Mus, OR; Wallraf Richartz Mus, Koln, Germany; Wichita Art Mus, KS
PRINTERS: Ron Wyffels, Chicago, IL (RW); Jack Lemon, Chicago, IL (JL); Landfall Press, Inc, Chicago, IL (LPI)
PUBLISHERS: Landfall Press, Inc, Chicago, IL (LPI)
GALLERIES: Landfall Press, Inc, Chicago, IL; Morgan Gallery, Kansas City, MO; Mona Berman Fine Arts, New Haven, CT

TITLE	PUBLISHER	PRINTER	DATE	MEDIUM	DIMENSION (PAPER SIZE) IN INCHES	TYPE OF PAPER	EDITION NUMBER	NO. OF COLORS	ORIGINAL OPENING PRICE	CURRENT RETAIL PRICE
SOLD OUT EDITIONS (RARE):										
The Best of Stark and the Best of Oilwell	LPI	RW/LPI	1975	LC	30 X 40	ARJ	35	4	200	500
On the Way to Bud's House in the Winter of '74	LPI	RW/LPI	1975	LC	30 X 40	ARJ	35	4	200	500

DOUG AND MIKE STARN

BORN: Absecon, NJ; 1961
EDUCATION: Sch of Mus of Fine Arts, Boston, MA, 1980-85
AWARDS: Travelling Scholarship Award, Mus of Fine Arts, Boston, MA, 1985; Nat Endowment for the Arts Grant, 1986; Massachusetts Council for the Arts Fel, Photography, 1986; Infinity Award, Int Center for Photography, NY, 1992
RECENT EXHIB: John & Mable Ringling Mus, Sarasota, FL, 1987; San Francisco Mus of Mod Art, CA, 1988; Wadsworth Atheneum, Hartford, CT, 1988; Mus of Contemp Art, Chicago, IL, 1988; Honolulu Acad of Art, HI, 1988; Univ of California, Berkeley, CA, 1988; Akira Ikeda Gallery, Tokyo, Japan; 1989; Baltimore Mus of Art, MD, 1990; Akron Mus, OH, 1990; Fred Hoffman Gallery, Santa Monica, CA, 1990; Stux Gallery, NY, 1987,88,89,90; Israel Mus, Jerusalem, Israel, 1990; Metropolis Int Art Exhib, Berlin, Germany, 1991; Karen Amiel Mod & Contemp Art, NY, 1992; Univ of Maryland, Baltimore County, Fine Arts Gallery, Catonsville, MD, 1992; Contemp Arts Center Cincinnati, OH, 1992; Sarah Campbell Blaffer Gallery, Univ of Houston, TX, 1990,92; Leo Castelli Gallery, NY, 1988,89,90,92
COLLECTIONS: Metropolitan Mus of Art, NY; Mus of Fine Arts, Boston, MA; Chicago Art Inst, IL; Baltimore Mus of Art, MD; Israel Mus, Jerusalem, Israel; Wadsworth Atheneum, Hartford, CT; Everson Mus of Art, Syracuse, NY; Los Angeles County Mus, Los Angeles, CA; Mito Arts Center, Mito, Japan; Ringling Mus of Art, Sarasota, FL; Bibliotheque Nat, Paris, France
PUBLISHERS: Inst of Contemp Art, Boston, MA (ICA)
GALLERIES: Stux Gallery, New York, NY; Akira Ikeda Gallery, Tokyo, Japan; Fred Hoffman Gallery, Santa Monica, CA; Leo Castelli Gallery, New York, NY; Pace/MacGill Gallery, New York, NY

The retail prices of the 100,000 limited edition prints quoted in this directory are subject to change. Print publishers, artists and galleries were the direct sources for these quotations. Prices in the secondary market listed as "Sold Out Editions (Rare)" indicate that the publisher has a limited supply of that print or that the print is difficult to locate in the galleries.

DOUG AND MIKE STARN CONTINUED

TITLE	PUBLISHER	PRINTER	DATE	MEDIUM	DIMENSION (PAPER SIZE) IN INCHES	TYPE OF PAPER	EDITION NUMBER	NO. OF COLORS	ORIGINAL OPENING PRICE	CURRENT RETAIL PRICE
SOLD OUT EDITIONS (RARE):										
Horses	ICA		1986	PH	45 X 34				350	30000
Louvre Floor			1985–1988	PH	84 X 99				5000	30000

JEFF STARR

BORN: Fort Dix, NJ; October 6, 1956
AWARDS: First Place; Western Colorado Center for the Arts, 1987; First Place, Emerging Regional Artist Comp, 1987; Comm on Cult Affairs, Denver, CO, Ind Artist Fel Grant, 1987; Nat Endowment for the Arts, Visual Artists Fel Grant, 1987; Colorado Council on the Arts & Humanities Fel Grant, 1988

RECENT EXHIB: Michael Leonard & Associates, NY, 1989
PRINTERS: Bud Shark, Boulder, CO (BS); Shark's, Inc, Boulder, CO (SLL)
PUBLISHERS: Shark's, Inc, Boulder, CO (SI)
GALLERIES: Shark's Inc, Boulder, CO; Robischon Gallery, Denver, CO; Payton/Rule Gallery, Denver, CO; Davidson Galleries, Seattle, WA; Quartet Editions, New York, NY

TITLE	PUBLISHER	PRINTER	DATE	MEDIUM	DIMENSION (PAPER SIZE) IN INCHES	TYPE OF PAPER	EDITION NUMBER	NO. OF COLORS	ORIGINAL OPENING PRICE	CURRENT RETAIL PRICE
CURRENT EDITIONS:										
Pariah	SI	BS/RT/SI	1989	LC	30 X 45	AC	25		750	850

JANET STAYTON

BORN: Natchez, MS; September 2, 1939
EDUCATION: Texas Christian Univ, Fort Worth, TX, BFA, 1961; Tulane Univ, New Orleans, LA, MFA, 1963
AWARDS: First Prize, Purchase Award, MacArthur Arts Center, Little Rock, AR, 1962
RECENT EXHIB: Patricia Heesy Gallery, NY, 1987; Raymond J Hage Gallery, Inc, Huntington, WV, 1988; Washington Arts Club, Wash, DC, 1989
COLLECTIONS: Brooklyn Mus, NY; MacArthur Arts Center, Little Rock, AR; Ministry d'Affaires Culturelles, Paris, France; Art Inst of Chicago, IL

PRINTERS: Aeropress, NY (A); Patricia Branstead, NY (PB); Jennifer Melby, NY (JM); Maurice Payne, NY (MP); Solo Press, NY (SP); Michel Durand, NY (MD); Pat Kaufman, NY (PK); Luke Sterling, NY (LS); Aldo Galleni, Pietrasanta, Italy (AG); Il Malbacco Press, Pietrasanta, Italy (IMP)
PUBLISHERS: van Straaten Gallery, Chicago, IL (VS); Bristol Art Editions, NY (BA); Veillet Press, NY (VP); Maurice Payne, NY (MP); Patricia Heesy Gallery, NY (PHG); Artist (ART)
GALLERIES: van Straaten Gallery, Chicago, IL; Michael Klein Gallery, New York, NY; Il Ponte, Rome, Italy; Nancy Singer Gallery, St Louis, MO; Associated American Artists, New York, NY; Raymond J Hage Gallery, Inc, Huntington, WV
MAILING ADDRESS: 216 Lafayette St, New York, NY 10012

TITLE	PUBLISHER	PRINTER	DATE	MEDIUM	DIMENSION (PAPER SIZE) IN INCHES	TYPE OF PAPER	EDITION NUMBER	NO. OF COLORS	ORIGINAL OPENING PRICE	CURRENT RETAIL PRICE
CURRENT EDITIONS:										
Fountain	VSG	JM/MP	1981	EC/AC	34 X 24	AC/W	50		750	850
Casa	VSG	PB/A	1981	AC/CO	29 X 43	OK/GE	60		750	850
Blue Columns	ART	AG/IMP	1982	EB	19 X 16	PM	40	1	250	450
Giardino I	ART	AG/IMP	1982	EB	24 X 20	PM	40	1	350	550
Loggia	ART	AG/IMP	1982	EB	20 X 20	PM	40	1	350	550
Through the Columns	ART	AG/IMP	1982	EB	20 X 24	PM	40	1	350	550
Through the Arch	ART	AG/IMP	1982	EB	18 X 19	PM	40	1	250	450
Red Columns	ART	AG/IMP	1982	EB	20 X 24	PM	40	1	350	550
From the Balcony	ART	AG/IMP	1982	EB	40 X 28	PM	40	1	600	800
Fontana	ART	AG/IMP	1982	EB	20 X 24	PM	40	1	350	550
Vesuvius I,II	ART	AG/IMP	1982	EB	24 X 20 EA	PM	40 EA	1 EA	350 EA	550 EA
Vesuvius III	ART	AG/IMP	1982	EB	19 X 15	PM	40	1	250	450
Vesuvius Erupting	ART	AG/IMP	1982	EB	39 X 28	PM	40	1	600	800
No I through No XXV (Set of 25)	ART/MP	MP	1983	MON	29 X 30 EA	STP	1 EA	Varies	800 EA	1000 EA
Claude Series (Set of 22)	ART	AG/IMP	1984	MON	28 X 39 EA	PM	1 EA	Varies	1200 EA	1350 EA
Waterfall	ART/MP	MP	1985	DPT	12 X 15	R/100	20	1	450	550
Flower Pieces (Series of 50)	PHG	MP	1985	MON	40 X 30 EA	R/BFK	1 EA	Varies	1650 EA	1800 EA
Red Balustrade (from Monostampa)	PHG	AG/IMP	1986	MON	30 X 23 EA	PESCIA	1 EA	Varies	1500 EA	1500 EA

HESTER A STINNETT

BORN: Baltimore, MD; June 29, 1956
EDUCATION: Univ of Hartford Art Sch, CT, BFA, 1978; Temple Univ, Tyler Sch of Art, Phila, PA, MFA, 1982
TEACHING: Adj Lectr, Printmaking, Philadelphia Col of Art, PA, 1982–86; Lectr, Printmaking, Bryn Mawr Col, PA, 1985–86; Asst Prof, Printmaking, Temple Univ, Tyler Sch of Art, Phila, PA, 1986 to present

RECENT EXHIB: Cassa de Risparmio di Biella, Biella, Italy, 1987
COLLECTIONS: Walker Art Center, Minneapolis, MN; West Chester Univ, PA; Philadelphia Mus of Art, PA
PRINTERS: Artist (ART)
PUBLISHERS: Artist (ART)
MAILING ADDRESS: 1110 S Franklin St, Phila, PA 19147

TITLE	PUBLISHER	PRINTER	DATE	MEDIUM	DIMENSION (PAPER SIZE) IN INCHES	TYPE OF PAPER	EDITION NUMBER	NO. OF COLORS	ORIGINAL OPENING PRICE	CURRENT RETAIL PRICE
CURRENT EDITIONS:										
Stake	ART	ART	1987	MON	72 X 30 EA	SUZ	1 EA	1 EA	1200 EA	1500 EA

ANITA STECKEL

BORN: New York, NY
EDUCATION: Cooper Union Music & Art High Sch, NY
TEACHING: Sch of Visual Arts, NY, presently; Parsons Sch of Design, 1979 to present
AWARDS: Nat Endowment for the Arts Grant, Painting, 1983
COLLECTIONS: Rochester Mus, NY; Portland Mus, ME; Brooklyn Mus, NY; Krannert Mus, IL; Elehjem Mus, Madison, WI; Bronx Mus, NY; Patrick Lannan Mus, Palm Beach, FL
PRINTERS: Editions Lassiter-Meisel, NY (ELM)
PUBLISHERS: Transworld Art Inc, NY (TAI)
GALLERIES: Hansen/Yeakel Fine Arts, New York, NY
MAILING ADDRESS: 463 West Street, New York, NY 10014

TITLE	PUBLISHER	PRINTER	DATE	MEDIUM	DIMENSION (PAPER SIZE) IN INCHES	TYPE OF PAPER	EDITION NUMBER	NO. OF COLORS	ORIGINAL OPENING PRICE	CURRENT RETAIL PRICE
SOLD OUT EDITIONS (RARE):										
Giant Animal Series:										
Giant Fox	TAI	ELM	1979	SP	32 X 38	LEN	275	6	300	450
Giant Horse	TAI	ELM	1979	SP	32 X 38	LEN	275	6	300	450
Giant Giraffe	TAI	ELM	1979	SP	32 X 38	LEN	275	6	300	450
Giant Lion	TAI	ELM	1979	SP	32 X 38	LEN	275	6	300	450

SAUL STEINBERG

BORN: Ramnicul-Sarat, Bucharest, Rumania; June 15, 1914; US Citizen
EDUCATION: Univ of Bucharest, Rumania, 1932; Univ of Milan, Italy, 1932
RECENT EXHIB: Galleria Seno, Milan, Italy, 1990; John Berggruen Gallery, San Francisco, CA, 1990; Pace Gallery, NY, 1992–93
COLLECTIONS: Metropolitan Art Mus, NY; Mus of Mod Art, NY; Albright-Knox Art Gallery, Buffalo, NY; Fogg Mus, Harvard Mus, Cambridge, MA; Victoria & Albert Mus, London, England
PUBLISHERS: Gemini GEL, Los Angeles, CA (GEM); Pace Editions, NY (PE)
PRINTERS: Gemini GEL, Los Angeles, CA (GEM)
GALLERIES: James Goodman Gallery, New York, NY; Richard Gray Gallery, Chicago, IL; Galerie Lelong, New York, NY; Marvin Ross Friedman & Co, New York, NY; Pace Gallery, New York, NY; Galleria Seno, Milan, Italy; John Berggruen Gallery, San Francisco, CA; BenedicteSaxe Gallery/Maeght Editions, Beverly Hills, CA; William R Davis Fine Arts, New York, NY
MAILING ADDRESS: c/o The New Yorker, 25 W 43rd St, New York, NY 10036

TITLE	PUBLISHER	PRINTER	DATE	MEDIUM	DIMENSION (PAPER SIZE) IN INCHES	TYPE OF PAPER	EDITION NUMBER	NO. OF COLORS	ORIGINAL OPENING PRICE	CURRENT RETAIL PRICE
SOLD OUT EDITIONS (RARE):										
Sphynx	GEM	GEM	1984	EC	22 X 25	HMP	50		800	2000
Provincetown	GEM	GEM	1984	EC	21 X 25	HMP	54		800	2000
North Dakota	GEM	GEM	1984	EC	24 X 28	HMP	54		800	2000
Rabbit	GEM	GEM	1984	EC/EMB	27 X 20	HMP	52		800	2000
Gogol I	GEM	GEM	1984	EC/EMB	27 X 20	HMP	51		800	2000
Gogol II	GEM	GEM	1984	EC/EMB	28 X 20	HMP	52		800	2000
Gogol IV	GEM	GEM	1984	EC/EMB	28 X 20	HMP	47		800	2000
Gogol V	GEM	GEM	1984	EC/EMB	27 X 20	HMP	50		800	2000

MICHAEL STEINER

BORN: New York, NY; 1945
TEACHING: Instr, Emma Lake Workshop, Univ of Saskatawan, Regina, Can, 1969; Vis Art, Cranbrook Art Inst, Bloomfield Heights, MI, 1969
AWARDS: Guggenheim Fel, NY, 1971
RECENT EXHIB: Bruce Mus, Greenwich, CT, 1989; Meredith Long & Co, Houston, TX, 1989; Univ of Michigan, Ann Arbor, MI, 1990; Steven Scott Gallery, Baltimore, MD, 1990; Salander-O'Reilly Galleries, NY, 1990; Helander Gallery, Palm Beach, FL, 1990,92; Andre Emmerich Gallery, Berlin, Germany, 1992; Andre Emmerich Gallery, NY, 1990,92
COLLECTIONS: Storm King Art Center, Mountainville, NY; Mus of Fine Arts, Boston, MA; Mus of Mod Art, NY; Solomon R Guggenheim Mus, NY; Walker Art Center, Minneapolis, MN; Denver Art Mus, CO; Massachusetts Inst of Technology, Cambridge, MA; Edmonton Art Gallery, Canada; Musee d'Art Moderne, Paris, France; Mus d'Art Contemporain, Paris, France; Art Gallery of Hamilton, Canada; Centre Georges Pompidou, Paris, France; Denver Art Mus, CO; Des Moines Art Center, IA; Edmonton Art Gallery, Canada; Everson Mus of Art, Syracuse, NY; Simon Fraser Univ, Burnaby, Canada; Wilhelm-Hack-Mus, Ludwigshafen, Germany; Hirshhorn Mus, Wash, DC; Huntington Galleries, WV; Kitchener-Waterloo Art Gallery, Canada; Kunsthalle, Bielefeld, Germany; J Patrick Lannan Found, Palm Beach, FL; Wilhelm-Lehmbruck-Mus, Duisburg, Germany; Massachusetts Inst of Tech, Cambridge, MA; Mus d'Art Mod, Nice, France; Mus of Fine Arts, Houston, TX; Power Gallery of Contemp Art, Sydney, Australia; J B Speed Art Mus, Louisville, TN; Sprengel Mus, Hanover, Germany; MacDonald Stewart Art Centre, Guelph, Canada; Von der Heydt-Mus, Wuppertal, Germany; Walker Art Center, Minneapolis, MN; Weatherspoon Art Gallery, Greensboro, NC; Wellesley Col, MA
PRINTERS: Lisa Mackie, NY (LM); Kathy Caraccio, NY (KC)
PUBLISHERS: Orion Editions, NY (OE)
GALLERIES: Irene Drori, Los Angeles, CA; Andre Emmerich Gallery, New York, NY; Pleiades Gallery, New York, NY; C S Schulte Galleries, South Orange, NJ; Udinotti Gallery, San Francisco, CA; Salander-O'Reilly Gallery, New York, NY; Meredith Long & Company, Houston, TX
MAILING ADDRESS: 704 Broadway, New York, NY 10003

TITLE	PUBLISHER	PRINTER	DATE	MEDIUM	DIMENSION (PAPER SIZE) IN INCHES	TYPE OF PAPER	EDITION NUMBER	NO. OF COLORS	ORIGINAL OPENING PRICE	CURRENT RETAIL PRICE
CURRENT EDITIONS										
Tapestry I	OE	LM/KC	1986	EC/CC	47 X 36	AP/ROL	65	14	1200	1200
Untitled	OE	LM/KC	1987	COL	43 X 34	SILK/HMP	46	10	900	900

The retail prices of the 100,000 limited edition prints quoted in this directory are subject to change. Print publishers, artists and galleries were the direct sources for these quotations. Prices in the secondary market listed as "Sold Out Editions (Rare)" indicate that the publisher has a limited supply of that print or that the print is difficult to locate in the galleries.

The Printworld Directory is accepting new applications for the seventh edition. Approximately 300 new artists will be accepted. Please use the two forms provided in the back section of this directory to submit biographical data and documentation of prints. Edition number of each print must not exceed 500 and the retail price must be $100 or more.

PAT STEIR

BORN: Newark, New Jersey; 1940
EDUCATION: Boston Univ, MA, 1960; Pratt Inst, NY 1962
AWARDS: Nat Endowment for the Arts Fel, 1974; Guggenheim Fel, 1982
RECENT EXHIB: Baltimore Mus, MD, 1987; New Mus, NY, 1987; Retrosp, Cabinet des Estampes, Mus d'Art et d'Histoire, Geneva, Switzerland, 1988; Retrosp, Tate Gallery, London, England, 1988; M Knoedler & Co, NY 1988; Walker Art Center, Minneapolis, MN, 1988-89; Massimo Audiello Gallery, NY, 1989; Nat Gallery of Art, Wash, DC, 1990; Louver Gallery, NY, 1990; Robert Miller Gallery, NY, 1990; Nohra Haime Gallery, NY, 1990; Musee d'Art Contemporain, Lyon, France, 1990; Crown Point Press, NY, & San Francisco, CA, 1988-89,91; Brooklyn Mus, NY, 1992; Univ of South Florida, Contemp Art Mus, Tampa, FL, 1992; Lincoln Center, Fine Arts Prints, Avery Fisher Hall, NY, 1992; Robert Miller Gallery, NY, 1990,92
COLLECTIONS: Mus of Mod Art, NY; Metropolitan Mus of Art, NY; Whitney Mus of Am Art, NY; Brooklyn Mus, NY; Tate Gallery, London, England; Walker Art Center, Minneapolis, MN
PRINTERS: Landfall Press Inc, Chicago, IL (LPI); Jack Lemon, Chicago, IL (JL); David Panosh (DP); Thomas Minkler (TM); Timothy Berry (TB); Crown Point Press, San Francisco, CA (CPP); Patrick Fay (PF); Doris Simmelink (DS); John Slivon (JS); Hidekatsu Takada (HT); Peter Pettengill (PP); Marcia Bartholme (MB); Paul Singdahlsen (PS); June Lambla (JL); Brian Shure (BS); Renée Bott (RB); Pamela Paulson, NY (PP); Hu Qinyun, Shanghai, China (HQ); Jiang Min, Shanghei, China (JM); Duo Yun Xuan Studio, Shanghei, China (YXS); Rong Bao Zhai Studio, Beijing, China (RBZS); Sun Shu Mei, Beijing, China (SSM); Brian Shure, San Francisco, CA (BS); Kathan Brown, San Francisco, CA (KB); Julie Goldman, San Francisco, CA (JG); Linda Geary, San Francisco, CA (LG); Mari Andrews, San Francisco, CA (MA)
PUBLISHERS: Crown Point Press, San Francisco, CA (CPP); Landfall Press, Inc, Chicago, IL (LPI)
GALLERIES: Deson/Saunders Gallery, Chicago, IL; Crown Point Press, New York, NY & San Francisco, CA; Douglas Drake Gallery, Kansas City, KS; Landfall Press, Inc, Chicago, IL; Barbara Krakow Gallery, Boston, MA; Harcus Gallery, Boston, MA; van Straaten Gallery, Chicago, IL; Gloria Luria Gallery, Bar Harbor Islands, FL; Flanders Contemp Art, Minneapolis, MN; Michael Klein, Inc, New York, NY; Castelli Graphics, New York, NY; John C Stoller & Co, Minneapolis, MN; M Knoedler & Co, New York, NY; L A Louver Gallery, Venice, CA; Louver Gallery, New York, NY; Robert Miller Gallery, New York, NY; Nohra Haime Gallery, New York, NY; Ochi Galleries, Boise, ID & Sun Valley, ID; Steven Scott Gallery, Baltimore, MD; Fabric Workshop, Phila, PA; Quartet Editions, New York, NY
MAILING ADDRESS: 81 Wooster St, New York, NY 10012

TITLE	PUBLISHER	PRINTER	DATE	MEDIUM	DIMENSION (PAPER SIZE) IN INCHES	TYPE OF PAPER	EDITION NUMBER	NO. OF COLORS	ORIGINAL OPENING PRICE	CURRENT RETAIL PRICE
SOLD OUT EDITIONS (RARE):										
Between the Lines	LPI	DP/LPI	1974	LC	27 X 32	AP/W	50	7	200	1200
Wish #2-Breadfruit	LPI	TM/LPI	1974	LC	32 X 32	AP/W	50	10	200	1200
Wish #3-Transformation	LPI	DP/LPI	1974	LC	32 X 31	AP/W	50	8	200	1200
Roll Me a Rainbow	LPI	DP/TM/LPI	1974	LC	22 X 29	AP/W	35	12	200	1500
Large Line	LPI	TB/LPI	1976	DPT/EB	20 X 20	TWP	15	1	300	1000
Series of 7: Little Line, Space Meaning, Identity, Being, I Don't Know, Introduction (Set of 7)	LPI	TB/LPI	1976	DPT/EB	10 X 10 EA	TWP	35 EA	1 EA	800 SET	2000 SET
Series of 5: Border Line, Line with Line, Dot Line, Written Line, Poem Line (Set of 5)	LPI	TB/LPI	1976	DPT/EB	4 X 4	TWP	10	1	300 SET	850 SET
Line/Frame	CPP	PF/DS/CPP	1977	EB	9 X 9	R/BFK	10		200	650
Word	CPP	PF/CPP	1977	EB/HC	6 X 6	AP/B	10		200	750
Marking Time	CPP	PE/DS/CPP	1977	DPT/E/A	30 X 42	R/BFK	35	2	400	1000
For RL	CPP	JS/HT/CPP	1978	AB	41 X 41	RO/BFK	25	1	650	3500
Drawing Lesson, Part II, Color (Set of 5)	CPP	JS/HT/CPP	1978	EB	16 X 16 EA	AP/S	25	1	1800 SET	7500 SET
When I Think of Venice (Two Images)	CPP	HT/PS/CPP	1980	AC	24 X 36 EA	R/BFK	35	1	2000 SET	7500 SET
Abstraction, Belief, Desire (Three Images)	CPP	HT/PP/CPP	1981	AC	18 X 36 EA	AP88	35	1	3000 SET	9000 SET
Self-Portrait with Toothache after Rembrandt (Series of 6 Monotypes)	CPP	JL/CPP	1982	MON	23 X 18	WP/ANT	1 EA	Varies	900 EA	2500 EA
The Tree after Hiroshige	CPP	MB/PP/CPP	1984	A/DPT/SB/HG	32 X 42	AC/B	30		1000	3500
Self Portraits (Series of 23)	CPP	HT/CPP	1985	MON	24 X 18 EA	FP/RdB	1 EA	Varies	950 EA	2500 EA
Self as Picasso as a Young Man #13	CPP	CPP	1985	MON	10 X 10 EA	HMP	1 EA	Varies	950 EA	2500 EA
Yellow Bridge in the Rain after Van Gogh after Hiroshige (Series of Monoprints with Etching)	CPP	CPP	1985	MON/EC	44 X 30		1 EA	Varies	2000 EA	3500 EA
The Wave-from the Sea-after Leonardo, Hokusai and Courbet	CPP	HT/CPP	1985	AC	43 X 54	HMP	50		3000	6500
PS after Turner (Series of 4 Monoprints)	CPP	CPP	1985	MON	18 X 24 EA	HMP	4 EA		1200 EA	2500 EA
Waterfall	CPP	BS/RB/PP/CPP	1988	AC/SB/SG/HG/DPT	54 X 42	SOM	60	7	3500	6000
Waterfall Night	CPP	BS/RB/PP/CPP	1988	EC	54 X 41	SOM	20	1	5000	6000
CURRENT EDITIONS:										
Wish #1	LPI	DP/LPI	1974	LC	32 X 32	AP/W	50	2	200	1200
Drawing Lesson, Part I, Line (Set of 7)	CPP	JS/HT/CPP	1978	AC	16 X 16 EA	AP/S	25	1	1800 SET	6500 SET
At Sea, after Turner & Rothko (Series of 13 Monotypes):										
#1-#4, #6-#8, #13	CPP	JS/CPP	1982	MON/DPT	31 X 44 EA	SOM	1 EA	1 EA	2500 EA	5000 EA
#5, #9-#12	CPP	JL/CPP	1982	MON/DPT	24 X 36 EA	GE/B	1 EA	1 EA	2500 EA	3500 EA
Set of 3 (Trip):										2000 SET	2800 SET
Form	LPI	JL/LPI	1982	LC	30 X 40	HMP	25	4	750	1000
Illusion	LPI	JL/LPI	1982	LC	30 X 40	HMP	25	4	750	1000
Myth	LPI	JL/LPI	1982	LC	30 X 40	HMP	25	3	750	1000

PAT STEIR CONTINUED

TITLE	PUBLISHER	PRINTER	DATE	MEDIUM	DIMENSION (PAPER SIZE) IN INCHES	TYPE OF PAPER	EDITION NUMBER	NO. OF COLORS	ORIGINAL OPENING PRICE	CURRENT RETAIL PRICE
CURRENT EDITIONS:										
Kyoto Chrysanthemum	CPP	TT/CPP	1982	WB	15 X 21	K/HMP	200	26	500	950
Self after Dürer as Christ	CPP	HT/CPP	1985	EB	26 X 20	AP88	5	1	600	950
Self after Rembrandt	CPP	HT/CPP	1985	EB	26 X 20	AP88	5	1	600	950
Self after Courbet Man in Terror	CPP	HT/CPP	1985	EB	26 X 20	AP88	5	1	600	950
Self after Courbet Man with Pipe	CPP	HT/CPP	1985	EB	26 X 20	AP88	5	1	600	950
Self after Self (Series of 49)	CPP	HT/CPP	1985	MON	26 X 20 EA	HMP	49 EA	Varies	950 EA	2500 EA
Self Portraits (Third Series) (Series of 46)	CPP	HT/CPP	1986	MON	26 X 20 EA	HMP	46 EA	Varies	1200 EA	2500 EA
Sunflowers	CPP	HT/CPP	1986	WC	27 X 40	HMP	100	16	1800	2500
Self after Rembrandt #1,2,3,4	CPP	BS/RB/PP/CPP	1987	ED	26 X 20 EA	SOM	5 EA	1 EA	600 EA	950 EA
Self after Dürer	CPP	BS/RB/PP/CPP	1987	EB	26 X 20	SOM	5	1	600 EA	950 EA
Waterfall Monoprints (Series of 37 Monoprints)	CPP	BS/RB/PP/CPP	1988	MON	51 X 40 EA	SOM/KOZO	37 EA		7500 EA	7500 EA
Seascape	CPP	HQ/JM/DYXS/ JG/BS/KB/CPP	1989	WC/HC	27 X 28	SILK-AP/B	65	Varies	750	750
Kweilin Dreaming, Part A, #1-#35 (Series of 35)	CPP	SSM/RBZS/ BS/KB/CPP	1989	WC/HC	38 X 43 EA	SOM	35 EA	Varies	3500 EA	4500 EA
Kweilin Dreaming, Part B, #36-#50 (Series of 16)	CPP	SSM/RBZS/ BS/KB/CPP	1989	WC/HC	38 X 43 EA	SOM	15 EA	Varies	3500 EA	4500 EA
Kweilin Dreaming, Part C, #51-66 (Series of 16)	CPP	SSM/RBZS/ BS/KB/CPP	1989	WC/HC	38 X 43 EA	SOM	16 EA	Varies	3500 EA	4500 EA
Kweilin Dreaming, Part D, #67-76 (Series of 10)	CPP	SSM/RBZS/ BS/KB/CPP	1989	WC/HC	38 X 43 EA	SOM	10 EA	Varies	3500 EA	4500 EA
Beloved Ghost Waterfall/Beijing (Chinese Watercolor Woodblock)	CPP	BS/LG/MA/CPP	1990	WB	48 X 33	MUL/SOM	75		1200	1200
Long Vertical Falls #1-#4	CPP	BS/LG/MA/CPP	1991	EB/A/SB	53 X 30 EA	SOM/W	20 EA	1 EA	1800 EA	1800 EA
Big Fall, Black and White	CPP	BS/LG/MA/CPP	1991	EB/A/SB	42 X 50	SOM	20	1	2000	3500
Big Fall, Color:										
1-15 Variants (Green)	CPP	BS/LG/MA/CPP	1991	EB/A/SB	42 X 50	SOM	15 EA		2500 EA	2800 EA
16-30 Variants (Blue)	CPP	BS/LG/MA/CPP	1991	EB/A/SB	42 X 50	SOM	15 EA		2500 EA	2800 EA
The Direction of Water	CPP	BS/LG/MA/CPP	1991	EB/A/DPT/SB	42 X 50	SOM	30	1	2800	3000
From the Boat	CPP	BS/LG/MA/CPP	1991	EB/A/SG	21 X 51	SOM/W	20	1	1000	2000
Long Horizontal (with Burnishing and Sanding)	CPP	BS/LG/MA/CPP	1991	EB/A/SG	30 X 51	SOM/W	20	1	2000	2500
Little Drip	CPP	BS/LG/MA/CPP	1991	EB/SB/SG	21 X 19	SOM/W	25		800	800
Big Drip	CPP	BS/LG/MA/CPP	1991	EB/A	25 X 19	SOM/W	25		800	800
Little Red Shapes	CPP	BS/LG/MA/CPP	1991	EB/A/SB/SL	25 X 19	SOM/W	25		800	800
Framed Waterfall	CPP	BS/LG/MA/CPP	1991	EB/SB/SL	25 X 19	SOM/W	25		800	800
Narrow Waterfall	CPP	BS/LG/MA/CPP	1991	EB/A/SB/SL	25 X 19	SOM/W	25		800	800
Sepia Rainclouds	CPP	BS/LG/MA/CPP	1991	EB/A	25 X 19	SOM/W	25		800	800
Raindrops	CPP	BS/LG/MA/CPP	1991	EB/A/SB/SL	25 X 19	SOM/W	25		800	800
Orange and Green	CPP	BS/LG/MA/CPP	1991	EB/A/SB/SL	25 X 19	SOM/W	25		800	800
Small Vertical Falls	CPP	BS/LG/MA/CPP	1991	EB/A/SG	25 X 19	SOM/W	25		800	1000
Small Horizontal Falls	CPP	BS/LG/MA/CPP	1991	EB/A/SG	25 X 19	SOM/W	25		800	1000
Rainclouds	CPP	BS/LG/MA/CPP	1991	EB/A/DPT/SB	25 X 19	SOM/W	25		800	800
Long Vertical Falls, #1-#4 (Set of 4)	CPP	BS/MA/LG/CPP	1991	EB/A/SG/SB	53 X 30 EA	SOM/W	20 EA	1 EA	1800 EA	3500 EA
Little Red Shapes	CPP	CPP	1991	EB/A/SG/SB	25 X 19	SOM/W	20	1	800	800

MAY STEVENS

BORN: Boston, MA; June 9, 1924
EDUCATION: Massachusetts Col of Art, Amherst, MA, BFA, 1946; Art Students League, NY, 1948; Acad Julian, Paris, France, 1949
TEACHING: Vis Artist, Cornell Univ, Ithaca, NY, 1973; Vis Artist, Rhode Island Sch of Design, Providence, RI, 1977; Vis Artist, California State Univ, Long Beach, CA, 1990; Instr, Painting, Sch of Visual Arts, NY, 1962 to present
AWARDS: Nat Endowment for the Arts Grant, Painting, 1983; Yaddo Artists Award, 1985; Guggenheim Found Fel, Painting, 1986

RECENT EXHIB: New Mus of Contemp Art, NY, 1988; Orchard Gallery, Derry, Northern Ireland, 1989; DeCordova Mus, Lincoln, NE, 1990; Herter Gallery, Univ of Massachusetts, Amherst, MA, 1991,92; Greenville County Mus of Art, SC, 1992
COLLECTIONS: Whitney Mus of Am Art, NY; Brooklyn Mus, NY; Herbert F Johnson Mus, Cornell Univ, Ithaca, NY
PRINTERS: Judith Solodkin, NY (JS); Solo Press, NY (SP)
PUBLISHERS: Solo Press, NY (SP)
GALLERIES: Orchard Gallery, Derry, Northern Ireland; Solo Gallery, New York, NY
MAILING ADDRESS: 97 Wooster St, New York, NY 10012

TITLE	PUBLISHER	PRINTER	DATE	MEDIUM	DIMENSION (PAPER SIZE) IN INCHES	TYPE OF PAPER	EDITION NUMBER	NO. OF COLORS	ORIGINAL OPENING PRICE	CURRENT RETAIL PRICE
CURRENT EDITIONS:										
Artemisio Gentilischi	SP	JS/SP	1979	LC	38 X 23	AP	50		450	650

The print market has become very selective. For the first time since we published the first edition of The Printworld Directory in 1982, the prices of prints have been greatly reduced and greatly increased for the same artists by the most reputable and established print publishers. Check the fifth edition to understand the movement.

FRANK STELLA

BORN: Malden, MA; 1936
EDUCATION: Phillips Acad, Andover, MA, 1950–54; Princeton Univ, NJ, 1954–58, with Stephen Greene, NY
AWARDS: Mayor's Award, Honor Arts & Culture, NY, 1982; Purchase Award, American Art, Pennsylvania Acad of Fine Arts, Phila, PA, 1985
RECENT EXHIB: Galerie Hans Streow, Düsseldorf, West Germany, 1987; Knoedler Gallery, London, England, 1987; Mus of Mod Art, NY, 1987–88; Stedelijk Mus, Amsterdam, Netherlands, 1988; Musee Nat d'Art Moderne/Centre Georges Pompidou, Paris, France, 1988; L A Louver, Venice, CA, 1988; Walker Art Center, Minneapolis, MN, 1988–89; Houston Contemp Arts Mus, TX, 1989; Los Angeles County Mus, CA, 1989; M Knoedler & Company, NY, 1989; Heland Wetterling Gallery, Stockholm, Sweden, 1989; Mus of Fine Arts, St Petersburg, FL, 1989; Carnegie Mellon Univ, Pittsburgh, PA, 1989; Gerald Peters Gallery, Santa Fe, NM, 1990; Marisa Del Re Gallery, NY, 1990; Hokin Gallery, Inc, Bay Harbor Islands, FL, 1990; Gagosian Gallery, NY, 1987,90; Robert Schoelkopf Gallery, NY, 1990; Galerie Daniel Templon, Paris, France, 1991; Galerie Beyeler, Basil, Switzerland, 1991; 65 Thompson Street Gallery, NY, 1991; Univ of Wisconsin, Allen R Priebe Gallery, Oshkosh, WI, 1992; Pennsylvania Acad of Fine Arts, Phila, PA, 1989,92; High Mus of Art, Atlanta, GA, 1989,92; Phillips Acad, Addison Gallery of Am Art, MA, 1989,92; Guild of Boston Artists, MA, 1992; Brown Univ, David Winton Bell Gallery, Providence, RI, 1992; Munson-Williams-Proctor Inst of Mus of Art, NY, 1992; Albright-Knox Art Gallery, Buffalo, NY, 1989,92; Erika Meyerovich Gallery, San Francisco, CA, 1992
COLLECTIONS: Mus of Mod Art, NY; Whitney Mus of Am Art, NY; Albright-Knox Gallery of Art, Buffalo, NY; Pasadena Mus of Art, CA; Pennsylvania Acad of Fine Arts, Phila, PA; San Francisco Mus of Mod Art, CA; Walker Art Center, Minneapolis, MN; Hirshhorn Mus, Wash, DC; Moderna Museet, Stockholm, Sweden; Kitakushu Municipal Mus, Tokyo, Japan; Galerie Hans Strelow, Dusseldorf, West Germany
PRINTERS: Styria Studio, NY (SS); Center for Constitutional Rights, NY (CCR); Gemini GEL, Los Angeles, CA (GEM); Tyler Graphics, Ltd, Mount Kisco, NY (TGL); Bruce Porter, NY (BP); Jim Welty, NY (JW); Spencer Tomkins, NY (ST); Bob Blanton, NY (BB); Bill Wygonik, NY (BW); Brand X, NY (X); James Welty, (JW); Trestle Editions, NY (TEd)
PUBLISHERS: Gemini GEL, Los Angeles, CA (GEM); Tyler Graphics, Ltd, Mount Kisco, NY (TGL); Petersburg Press, NY (PP); Transworld Art, Inc, NY (TAI); Metzenbaum for Senate Committee (MSC); Waddington Graphics, London, England (WG)
GALLERIES: Gemini GEL, Los Angeles, CA; Andrew Dierken Fine Art, Los Angeles, CA; R K Goldman Contemporary, Los Angeles, CA; John Berggruen Gallery, San Francisco, CA; Harcourts Modern & Contemporary, San Francisco, CA; Erika Meyerovich Gallery, San Francisco, CA; James Corcoran Gallery, Santa Monica, CA; Hokin Galleries, Bay Harbor Islands, FL & Palm Beach, FL; Kass/Meridian Gallery, Chicago, IL; Harcus Gallery, Boston, MA; Jan Weiner Gallery, Kansas City, MO; Tyler Graphics, Ltd, Mount Kisco, NY; Lillian Heidenberg Gallery, New York, NY; Jane Kahan Gallery, New York, NY; M Knoedler & Company, New York, NY; Contemporary Gallery, Dallas, TX; Fenton Fine Arts, Fort Worth, TX; Meredith Long Gallery, Houston, TX; Michael H Lord Gallery, Milwaukee, WI; Turske & Turske Gallery, Zurich, Switzerland; Irene Drori Graphics, Los Angeles, CA; Waddington Graphics, London, England; Nan Miller Gallery, Rochester, NY; L A Louver Gallery, Venice, CA; Gagosian Gallery, New York, NY; Schoelkopf Gallery, New York, NY; Galerie Daniel Templon, Paris, France; Galerie Beyeler, Basil, Switzerland; 65 Thompson Street Gallery, New York, NY; Allyson Louis Gallery, Bethesda, MD; Margo Gallery, Inc, Palm Beach, FL; Walton-Gilbert Galleries, San Francisco, CA; Richard Green Graphics, Santa Monica, CA; Gallery One at Second Avenue, Denver, CO; Collector Art Gallery, Wash, DC; Jupiter Fine Arts, Jupiter, FL; Thomas Babeor Gallery, La Jolla, CA; Noble House, Los Angeles, CA; Dunlop-Freidenrich Fine Art, Newport Beach, CA; Joanne Chappell Gallery, San Francisco, CA; Graystone, San Francisco, CA; Castelli Graphics, New York, NY; Nancy Singer Gallery, St Louis, MO; Scherer Gallery, Marlboro, NJ; DEL Fine Art Gallery, Santa Fe, NM; Golden Gallery, Boston, MA; Morgan Gallery, Boston, MA; Genovese Gallery, Boston, MA; Stux Modern, New York, NY; Nan Miller Gallery, Rochester, NY; Solo Gallery, New York, NY
MAILING ADDRESS: 17 Jones St, New York, NY 10021

Axson (A)—Gemini GEL (G)—Tyler Graphics, Ltd (T)—Waddington Graphics (W)

Frank Stella
Guifa e la Berrette Rossa
Courtesy Tyler Graphics, Ltd

Frank Stella
Bene Come Il Sale
Courtesy Tyler Graphics, Ltd

FRANK STELLA CONTINUED

TITLE	PUBLISHER	PRINTER	DATE	MEDIUM	DIMENSION (PAPER SIZE) IN INCHES	TYPE OF PAPER	EDITION NUMBER	NO. OF COLORS	ORIGINAL OPENING PRICE	CURRENT RETAIL PRICE
SOLD OUT EDITIONS (RARE):										
Star of Persia I (A-1) (G-46)	GEM	GEM	1967	LC	26 X 32	EVG	92	6	200	18000
Star of Persia II (A-2) (G-47)	GEM	GEM	1967	LC	26 X 32	EVG	92	6	200	18000
Irvina Blum Memorial Edition	GEM	GEM	1967	LC	26 X 31	AP	16		200	10000
Fortin de las Flores (with Pencil)	GEM	GEM	1967	SP/PENC	17 X 22	AP	200		200	8500
Black Series I (Set of 8):									12000 SET	75000 SET
Clinton Plaza	GEM	GEM	1967	LC	15 X 22	JBG	100	2	200	10000
Arundel Castle	GEM	GEM	1967	LC	15 X 22	JBG	100	2	200	10000
Die Fahne Hoch	GEM	GEM	1967	LC	15 X 22	JBG	100	2	200	10000
Tomlinson Court Park	GEM	GEM	1967	LC	15 X 22	JBG	100	2	200	10000
Getty Tomb	GEM	GEM	1967	LC	15 X 22	JBG	100	2	200	10000
Bethlehem's Hospital	GEM	GEM	1967	LC	15 X 22	JBG	100	2	200	10000
Arbeit Macht Frei	GEM	GEM	1967	LC	15 X 22	JBG	100	2	200	10000
Club Onyx-Seven Steps	GEM	GEM	1967	LC	15 X 22	JBG	100	2	200	10000
Black Series II (Set of 8) (A-13–A-20) (G-66–G-73)									12000 SET	45000 SET
Tuxedo Park	GEM	GEM	1967	LB	15 X 22	JBG	100	1	200	6000
Gezira	GEM	GEM	1967	LB	15 X 22	JBG	100	1	200	6000
Point of Pines	GEM	GEM	1967	LB	15 X 22	JBG	100	1	200	6000
Zambesi	GEM	GEM	1967	LB	15 X 22	JBG	100	1	200	6000
Jill	GEM	GEM	1967	LB	15 X 22	JBG	100	1	200	6000
Delphine and Hippolyte	GEM	GEM	1967	LB	15 X 22	JBG	100	1	200	6000
Gavotte	GEM	GEM	1967	LB	15 X 22	JBG	100	1	200	6000
Turkish Mambo	GEM	GEM	1967	LB	15 X 22	JBG	100	1	200	6000
V Series:										
V Series: Empress of India I (A-27) (G-81)	GEM	GEM	1968	LC	11 X 32	LP	100		250	8000
V Series: Empress of India (A-28) (G-82)	GEM	GEM	1968	LC	11 X 33	LP	100		250	8000
Ifala I, II	GEM	GEM	1968	LC	16 X 22 EA	AP	100 EA		200 EA	4500 EA
Pastel Stack (A-48) (G-227)	GEM	GEM	1970	SP	41 X 28	EVG	100		400	7500
Copper Series: Creed II	TGL	TGL	1970	LC/SP	16 X 22	AJP	70	3	200	5000
Referendum '70 (A-49) (G-229)	GEM	GEM	1970	SP	32 X 32	ARJ	200	8	300	17000
Stack Series:										
Grid Stack	GEM	GEM	1970	LC	46 X 35	ARJ	50	1	400	8000
Black Stack	GEM	GEM	1970	LC	41 X 29	ARJ	56	1	400	8000
Pastel Stack	GEM	GEM	1970	LC	41 X 28	ARJ	100	1	400	8000
Creed I, II	GEM	GEM	1970	LC/SP	16 X 22 EA	ARJ	70 EA	3 EA	300 EA	10000 EA
Ophir	GEM	GEM	1970	LC/SP	16 X 22	ARJ	70	3	300	10000
Metropolitan Museum of Art	GEM	GEM	1970	SP	31 X 29	ARJ	250		150	1500
Aluminum Series (Set of 9) (A-30–A-38) (G-213–G-221):									1500 SET	38000 SET
Newstand Abbey	GEM	GEM	1971	LC/SP	16 X 22	ARJ	75	3	300	5000
Marquis de Portago	GEM	GEM	1971	LC/SP	16 X 22	ARJ	75	3	300	5000
Union Pacific (A-32) (G-215)	GEM	GEM	1971	LC/SP	16 X 22	ARJ	75	3	300	5000
Six Mile Bottom (A-33) (G-216)	GEM	GEM	1971	LC/SP	16 X 22	ARJ	75	3	300	5000
Averroes (A-34) (G-217)	GEM	GEM	1971	LC/SP	16 X 22	ARJ	75	3	300	5000
Casa Corny	GEM	GEM	1971	LC/SP	16 X 22	ARJ	75	3	300	5000
Luis Miquel Dominquin	GEM	GEM	1971	LC/SP	16 X 22	ARJ	75	3	300	5000
Ayicenna	GEM	GEM	1971	LC/SP	16 X 22	ARJ	75	3	300	5000
Kingsbury Run	GEM	GEM	1971	LC/SP	16 X 22	ARJ	75	3	300	5000
Delaware Crossing	GEM	GEM	1971	LC	16 X 22	AP	100	1	300	4500
New Madrid	GEM	GEM	1971	LC	16 X 22	AP	100	1	300	4500
Island No 10	GEM	GEM	1971	LC	16 X 22	AP	100	1	300	4500
Hampton Roads	GEM	GEM	1971	LC	16 X 22	AP	100	1	300	4500
Angriff	CCR	SS	1971	SP	18 X 24	R/100	150	1	300	5000
Port aux Basques (G-274)	GEM	GEM	1971	LC	32 X 64	AP	58		800	9000
Benjamin Moore Series (Set of 6) (G-296–G-301):									1500 SET	15000 SET
Sabine Pass	GEM	GEM	1971	LC	16 X 22	AP	100	1	300	3000
Palmito Ranch (Yellow)	GEM	GEM	1971	LC	16 X 22	AP	100	1	300	3000
Delaware Crossing	GEM	GEM	1971	LC	16 X 22	AP	100	1	300	3000
York Factory I (A-63) (G-303)	GEM	GEM	1971	SP	14 X 40	ARJ	100	6	400	40000
Purple Series (Set of 9):										
Kay Bearman	GEM	GEM	1972	LC	16 X 22	CD	100	1	300	3500
Ileana Sonnabend	GEM	GEM	1972	LC	16 X 22	CD	100	1	300	3500
Henry Garden	GEM	GEM	1972	LC	16 X 22	CD	100	1	300	3500
D	GEM	GEM	1972	LC	16 X 22	CD	100	1	300	3500
Sidney Guberman	GEM	GEM	1972	LC	16 X 22	CD	100	1	300	3500
Charlotte Tokayer	GEM	GEM	1972	LC	16 X 22	CD	100	1	300	3500
Carl Andre	GEM	GEM	1972	LC	16 X 22	CD	100	1	300	3500
Hollis Frampton	GEM	GEM	1972	LC	16 X 22	CD	100	1	300	3500
Leo Castelli	GEM	GEM	1972	LC	16 X 22	CD	100	1	300	3500
Aqua Caliente	GEM	GEM	1972	SP	22 X 82	CD	75		1000	10000

FRANK STELLA CONTINUED

TITLE	PUBLISHER	PRINTER	DATE	MEDIUM	DIMENSION (PAPER SIZE) IN INCHES	TYPE OF PAPER	EDITION NUMBER	NO. OF COLORS	ORIGINAL OPENING PRICE	CURRENT RETAIL PRICE
SOLD OUT EDITIONS (RARE):										
Race Track Series:										
Del Mar (A-73) (G-377)	GEM	GEM	1972	SP	15 X 75	CD	75	6	800	8000
Jasper's Dilemma Suite (Set of 4):									1200 SET	20000 SET
Jasper's Dilemma	PP	PP	1973	LC	16 X 22	AP	100		300	5000
Hyena Stomp	PP	PP	1973	LC	16 X 22	AP	100		300	5000
Line-Up	PP	PP	1973	LC	16 X 22	AP	100		300	5000
Portin de las Flores	PP	PP	1973	LC	16 X 22	AP	100		300	5000
Multicolored Squares (Set of 6):									1800 SET	27000 SET
Honduras Lottery	PP	PP	1973	LC	16 X 20	AP	100		300	4500
Cato Manor	PP	PP	1973	LC	16 X 20	AP	100		300	4500
Louisiana Lottery	PP	PP	1973	LC	16 X 20	AP	100		300	4500
Cipango	PP	PP	1973	LC	16 X 20	AP	100		300	4500
Gran Cairo	PP	PP	1973	LC	16 X 20	AP	100		300	4500
Sharpsville	PP	PP	1973	LC	16 X 20	AP	100		300	4500
Les Indes Galantes (Set of 5) (A-86–A-90):									1500 SET	20000 SET
1 Grey Square	PP	PP	1973	LC/OFF	16 X 20	JBG	100		300	4000
1 Colour Square	PP	PP	1973	LC/OFF	16 X 20	JBG	100		300	4000
2 Grey Squares	PP	PP	1973	LC/OFF	16 X 20	JBG	100		300	4000
2 Colour Squares	PP	PP	1973	LC/OFF	16 X 20	JBG	100		300	4000
1 Colour Square and 1 Grey Square	PP	PP	1973	LC/OFF	16 X 20	JBG	100		300	4000
Double Gray, Scramble (A-93) (G-491)	GEM	GEM	1973	SP	29 X 50	AP88	100	8	150	60000
Sidi Ifni (A-91a)	PV/PaPr		1974	LC/OFF	22 X 30	CD	120	3	400	4500
Sidi Ifni (A-91A)	PP	PP	1974	LC	19 X 19	CD	42	3	400	6000
Eccentric Polygons (Set of 10):										
Sunapee	GEM	GEM	1974	LC/SP	22 X 17	AP	100	14	400	7500
Moultonville	GEM	GEM	1974	LC/SP	22 X 17	AP	100	12	400	7500
Wolfeboro	GEM	GEM	1974	LC/SP	22 X 17	AP	100	8	400	7500
Effingham (A-102) (G-549)	GEM	GEM	1974	LC/SP	18 X 22	AP	100	8	400	7500
Ossipee	GEM	GEM	1974	LC/SP	18 X 22	AP	100	9	400	7500
Sanbornville	GEM	GEM	1974	LC/SP	18 X 22	AP	100	12	400	7500
Union	GEM	GEM	1974	LC/SP	18 X 22	AP	100	9	400	7500
Conway (A-97) (G-553)	GEM	GEM	1974	LC/SP	18 X 22	AP	100	9	400	7500
Tuftonboro	GEM	GEM	1974	LC/SP	18 X 22	AP	100	8	400	7500
Chocorua (A-104) (G-555)	GEM	GEM	1974	LC/SP	18 X 22	AP	100	9	400	7500
York Factory II (A-94) (G-567)	GEM	GEM	1974	SP	14 X 40	AP/B	100	10	1000	55000
Grodno (I) (T-542) (FS-1)	TGL	TGL	1975	CO/HC	26 X 22	HMP	26	10	800	12000
Olyka (III) (T-544) (FS-3)	TGL	TGL	1975	CO/HC	25 X 21	HMP	26	8	800	18000
Lunna Wola (V) (T-546) (FS-5)	TGL	TGL	1975	CO/HC	24 X 21	HMP	26	6	800	25000
Exotic Bird Series:										
Inaccessible Island Rail (A-110) (T-551) (FS-10)	TGL	TGL	1977		32 X 43	AP88	50		2000	32000
Sinjerli Variations (Set of 6):									12000 SET	100000 SET
Sinjerli Variation #I (A-113)	PP	BP/JW	1977	LC/SP/OFF	32 X 42	AC	100	36	2000	20000
Sinjerli Variation #IA (A-114)	PP	BP/JW	1977	LC/SP/OFF	32 X 42	AC	100	36	2000	18000
Sinjerli Variation #II (A-115)	PP	BP/JW	1977	LC/SP/OFF	32 X 42	AC	100	42	2000	18000
Sinjerli Variation #IIA (A-116)	PP	BP/JW	1977	LC/SP/OFF	32 X 42	AC	100	42	2000	18000
Sinjerli Variation III (A-117)	PP	BP/JW	1977	LC/SP/OFF	32 X 42	AC	100	48	2000	18000
Sinjerli Variation IV (A-118)	PP	BP/JW	1977	LC/SP/OFF	32 X 42	AC	100	60	2000	18000
Inaccessible IslandRail	TGL	TGL	1977	LC/SP	34 X 46	AP88	50	47	2500	15000
Mysterious Bird of Ulieta	TGL	TGL	1977	LC/SP	34 X 46	AP88	50	30	2500	15000
Steller's Albatross	TGL	TGL	1977	LC/SP	34 X 46	AP88	50	57	2500	36000
Eskimo Curlew	TGL	TGL	1977	LC/SP	34 X 46	AP88	50	34	2500	12000
Puerto Rican Blue Pigeon	TGL	TGL	1977	LC/SP	34 X 46	AP88	50	52	2500	15000
Noguchi's Okinawa Woodpecker	TGL	TGL	1977	LC/SP/MM	34 X 46	AP88	50	27	2500	10000
Bermuda Petrel (Framed)	TGL	TGL	1979	SP/HC	5 X 7 X 1	TYP	10	32	18000	22000
Wake Island Rail (Framed)	TGL	TGL	1979	SP/HC	5 X 7 X 1	TYP	10	34	18000	22000
Green Solitaire (Framed)	TGL	TGL	1979	SP/HC	5 X 7 X 1	TYP	10	23	18000	22000
Polar Coordinates for Ronnie Peterson (Series of 8):									25000 SET	100000 SET
Polar Coordinates I (A-119)	PP	PP	1980	LC/OFF/SP	39 X 38	AC	100	12	3000	15000
Polar Coordinates II (A-120)	PP	PP	1980	LC/OFF/SP/LP	39 X 38	AC	100	12	3000	15000
Polar Coordinates IV (A-122)	PP	PP	1980	LC/OFF/SP	38 X 39	AC	100	12	3000	15000
Polar Coordinates VI (A-124)	PP	PP	1980	LC/OFF/SP	39 X 38	AC	100	12	3000	15000
Polar Coordinates VII (A-125)	PP	PP	1980	LC/OFF/SP	38 X 38	AC	100	12	3000	15000
Polar Coordinates VIII (A-126)	PP	PP	1980	LC/OFF/SP	39 X 38	AC	100	12	3000	15000
Polar Coordinates IIIA (A-128)	PP	PP	1980	LC/OFF/SP	39 X 38	AC	100	12	3000	15000
Sinjerli Variations Squared with Colored Grounds (Series of 6):										
SVSCG I (A-129)	PP	PP	1977–81	LC/OFF/SP	32 X 32	AC	38	12	3000	25000
SVSCG IA (A-130)	PP	PP	1977–81	LC/OFF/SP	32 X 32	AC	61	12	3000	25000

FRANK STELLA CONTINUED

Frank Stella
The Wave: Squid
Courtesy Waddington Graphics

Frank Stella
The Wave: The Counterpane
Courtesy Waddington Graphics

TITLE	PUBLISHER	PRINTER	DATE	MEDIUM	DIMENSION (PAPER SIZE) IN INCHES	TYPE OF PAPER	EDITION NUMBER	NO. OF COLORS	ORIGINAL OPENING PRICE	CURRENT RETAIL PRICE
SOLD OUT EDITIONS (RARE):										
SVSCG II (A-131)	PP	PP	1977–81	LC/OFF/SP	32 X 32	AC	50	12	3000	25000
SVSCG IIA (A-132)	PP	PP	1977–81	LC/OFF/SP	32 X 32	AC	29	12	3000	25000
SVSCG III (A-133)	PP	PP	1977–81	LC/OFF/SP	32 X 32	AC	32	12	3000	25000
SVSCG IV (A-134)	PP	PP	1977–81	LC/OFF/SP	32 X 32	AC	44	12	3000	25000
Swan Engraving Series:										
Swan Engraving I (A-155) (T-569) (FS-26)	TGL	TGL	1982	EC/ENG	66 X 52	TGL/HMP	30	1	3500	20000
Swan Engraving II (A-156) (T-570) (FS-27)	TGL	TGL	1982	EC/ENG	66 X 52	TGL/HMP	30	1	3500	20000
Swan Engraving III (A-157) (T-571) (FS-28)	TGL	TGL	1982	EC/REL	66 X 52	TGL/HMP	30	1	3500	20000
Swan Engraving IV (A-158) (T-572) (FS-29)	TGL	TGL	1982	EC/REL	66 X 52	TGl/HMP	30	1	3500	20000
Swan Engraving Square Series:										
Swan Engraving Square I	TGL	TGL	1982	EC	54 X 52	TGL/HMP	20	1	3000	12000
Swan Engraving Square II	TGL	TGL	1982	EC	54 X 52	TGL/HMP	20	1	3000	15000
Swan Engraving Square III	TGL	TGL	1982	EC	52 X 54	TGL/HMP	20	1	3000	12000
Swan Engraving Square IV	TGL	TGL	1982	EC	52 X 54	TGL/HMP	20	1	3000	12000
Circuits Series:										
Estoril Three II	TGL	TGl	1982	EC/WC/REL	66 X 51	TGL/HMP	30	6	10000	80000
Estoril Five I	TGL	TGL	1982	EC/WC/REL	66 X 51	TGL/HMP	30	10	7500	80000
Estoril Five II (A-141) (T-564) (FS-23)	TGL	TGL	1982	EB/ENG/REL	66 X 51	TGL/HMP	30	12	7500	100000
Talladega Three I	TGL	TGL	1982	EC	66 X 51	TGL/HMP	30	1	7500	40000
Talladega Three II (A-136) (T-554) (FS-18)	TGL	TGL	1982	EC/REL	67 X 52	TGL/HMP	30	21	7500	160000
Talladega Three III	TGL	TGL	1982	EC/REL	66 X 51	TGL/HMP	30	4	7500	40000
Talladega Five I	TGL	TGL	1982	WC/REL	66 X 51	TGL/HMP	30	9	7500	80000
Imola Three I	TGL	TGL	1984	EC/REL	66 X 51	TGL/HMP	30	5	7500	80000
Imola Three II	TGL	TGL	1984	EC/REL/WC	66 X 52	TGL/HMP	30	27	7500	80000
Imola Three II, State I	TGL	TGL	1984	EC/REL/WC/SP	66 X 52	TGL/HMP	10	36	7500	80000
Imola Three IV	TGL	TGL	1984	EC/SP/REL	66 X 52	TGL/HMP	30	20	7500	80000
Imola Five II	TGL	TGL	1984	EC/WC/REL	66 X 49	TGL/HMP	30	15	7500	80000
Imola Five II, State I	TGL	TGL	1984	WC/SP/REL	66 X 49	TGL/HMP	10	21	10000	80000

FRANK STELLA CONTINUED

TITLE	PUBLISHER	PRINTER	DATE	MEDIUM	DIMENSION (PAPER SIZE) IN INCHES	TYPE OF PAPER	EDITION NUMBER	NO. OF COLORS	ORIGINAL OPENING PRICE	CURRENT RETAIL PRICE
SOLD OUT EDITIONS (RARE):										
Pergusa Three	TGL	TGL	1982	EC/WC/REL	67 X 52	TGL/HMP	30	27	10000	80000
Pergusa Three, State I	TGL	TGL	1983	WC/REL	66 X 52	TGL/HMP	10	28	10000	80000
Pergusa Three Double	TGL	TGL	1984	EC/ENG/REL/SP	102 X 66	TGL/HMP	30	64	8000	80000
Shards Series:										
Shards I–V (Set of 5)	PP	PP	1982	LB/OFF/SP	45 X 40 EA	AC	100 EA	12 EA	15000 SET	75000 SET
Shards Variant I A	PP	PP	1982	LB/OFF/SP	45 X 40	AC	38	12	3000	15000
Shards Variant III (A-146)	PP	PP	1982	LB/OFF/SP	40 X 45	AC	100	12	3000	15000
Shards Variant III (A-150)	PP	PP	1982	LB/OFF/SP	45 X 40	AC	27	12	3000	15000
Shards Variant IV A	PP	PP	1982	LB/OFF/SP	40 X 45	AC	49	12	3000	15000
Shards Variant V A	PP	PP	1982	LB/OFF/SP	40 X 45	AC	30	12	3000	15000
Yellow Journal	MSC	TGL	1982	LC	53 X 39	AP	50	15	3000	15000
Swan Engraving Blue	TGL	TGL	1983	EC/ENG/WC/REL	39 X 32	TGL/HMP	20	2	2500	15000
Swan Engraving Circle I Series:										
Swan Engraving Circle I (T-589) (FS-49)	TGL	TGL	1983	EC/REL	52 DIA	TGL/HMP	5	1	3000	18000
Swan Engraving Circle I, State I (T-590) (FS-50)	TGL	TGL	1983	EC/REL	52 DIA	TGL/HMP	5	4	3500	22000
Swan Engraving Circle I, State II (T-591) (FS-51)	TGL	TGL	1983	EC/REL	52 DIA	TGL/HMP	5	5	3500	22000
Swan Engraving Circle I, State III (T-592) (FS-52)	TGL	TGL	1983	EC/REL	52 DIA	TGL/HMP	5	4	3500	22000
Swan Engraving Circle I, State IV (T-593) (FS-53)	TGL	TGL	1983	EC/REL	52 DIA	TGL/HMP	5	4	3500	22000
Swan Engraving Circle I, State V (T-594) (FS-54)	TGL	TGL	1983	EC/REL	52 DIA	TGL/HMP	5	4	3500	22000
Swan Engraving Circle II Series:										
Swan Engraving Circle II (T-596) (FS-55)	TGL	TGL	1983	EC/REL	52 DIA	TGL/HMP	5	4	3500	22000
Swan Engraving Circle II, State I (T-597) (FS-56)	TGL	TGL	1983	EC/REL	52 DIA	TGL/HMP	5	4	3500	22000
Swan Engraving Circle II, State II (T-598) (FS-57)	TGL	TGL	1983	EC/REL	52 DIA	TGL/HMP	5	6	3500	22000
Swan Engraving Circle II Continued:										
Swan Engraving Circle II, State III (T-599) (FS-58)	TGL	TGL	1983	EC/REL	52 DIA	TGL/HMP	5	5	3500	22000
Swan Engraving Circle II, State IV (T-600) (FS-59)	TGL	TGL	1983	EC/REL	52 DIA	TGL/HMP	5	5	3500	22000
Swan Engraving Circle II, State V (T-601) (FS-60)	TGL	TGL	1983	EC/REL	52 DIA	TGL/HMP	5	5	3500	22000
Illustrations after El Lissitzky's Had Gadya (Set of 12):									40000 SET	250000 SET
#A—Had Gadya: Front Cover	WG		1982–84	LC/SP/LI/CO/HC	54 X 52	WOVE	60		4500	18000
#1—One Small Goat Papa Brought for Two Zuzim	WG		1982–84	LC/SP/LI/CO/HC	54 X 52	WOVE	60		4500	25000
#2—A Hungry Cat Ate Up the Goat	WG		1982–84	LC/SP/LI/CO/HC	54 X 52	WOVE	60		4500	20000
#3—Then Came a Dog and Bit the Cat	WG		1982–84	LC/SP/LI/CO/HC	54 X 52	WOVE	60		4500	30000
#4—Then Came a Stick and Beat the Dog	WG		1982–84	LC/SP/LI/CO/HC	54 X 52	WOVE	60		4500	25000
#5—Then Came a Fire and Burnt the Stick	WG		1982–84	LC/SP/LI/CO/HC	54 X 52	WOVE	60		4500	25000
#6—Then Came Water and Quenched the Fire	WG		1982–84	LC/SP/LI/CO/HC	54 X 52	WOVE	60		4500	25000
#7—Then Came an Ox and Drank the Water	WG		1982–84	LC/SP/LI/CO/HC	54 X 52	WOVE	60		4500	25000
#8—The Butcher Came and Slew the Ox	WG		1982–84	LC/SP/LI/CO/HC	54 X 52	WOVE	60		4500	30000
#9—Then Came Death and Took the Butcher	WG		1982–84	LC/SP/LI/CO/HC	59 X 47	WOVE	60	12	4500	25000
#10—Then the Holy One, Blessed be He, Came and Smote the Angel of Death	WG		1982–84	LC/SP/LI/CO/HC	51 X 41	WOVE	60	12	4500	25000
#B—Had Gadya: Back Cover	WG		1982–84	LC/SP/LI/CO/HC	60 X 56	WOVE	60	8	4500	25000
Yellow Journal, State I	TGL	TGL	1984	LC	53 X 39	AC	16	20	3500	18000
Green Journal (T-606) (FS-65)	TGL	TGL	1985	EC/REL/SP	66 X 52	TGL/HMP	25	3	4500	30000
Swan Engraving Series (1985):										
Swan Engraving V (T-607) (FS-66)	TGL	TGL	1985	EC/REL	60 X 50	TGL/HMP	25	1	4500	20000

FRANK STELLA CONTINUED

TITLE	PUBLISHER	PRINTER	DATE	MEDIUM	DIMENSION (PAPER SIZE) IN INCHES	TYPE OF PAPER	EDITION NUMBER	NO. OF COLORS	ORIGINAL OPENING PRICE	CURRENT RETAIL PRICE
SOLD OUT EDITIONS (RARE):										
Swan Engraving Framed Series (1985):										
Swan Engraving Framed I (T-608) (FS-67)	TGL	TGL	1985	EC/REL	53 X 40	TGL/HMP	20	2	3500	20000
Swan Engraving Framed II (T-609) (FS-68)	TGL	TGL	1985	EC/REL	58 X 43	TGL/HMP	15	3	3500	20000
Swan Engraving Blue, Green, Grey (T-610) (FS-69)	TGL	TGL	1985	EC/REL	66 X 52	TGL/HMP	20	5	4500	36000
CURRENT EDITIONS:										
La Penna di Hu	TGL	TGL	1988	EC/REL/WC/ STEN/SP/HC	56 X 66	TGL/HMP	50	25	30000	60000
La Penna di Hu (Black & White)	TGL	TGL	1988	A/EB/REL	78 X 59	TGL/HMP	42	1	15000	35000
The Wave Series (Series of 13):										
The Wave: Hark!	WG	ST/JW/BP/TE/ BB/BW/BX	1985–88	LC/LI/SP/ HC/CO	74 X 53	THS	60	12	25000	45000
The Wave: The Pacific	WG	ST/JW/BP/TE/ BB/BW/BX	1985–88	LC/LI/SP/ HC/CO	75 X 55	THS	60	12	25000	45000
The Wave: Ahab	WG	ST/JW/BP/TE/ BB/BW/BX	1985–88	LC/LI/SP/ HC/CO	74 X 55	THS	60	12	25000	50000
The Wave: Squid (W-3)	WG	ST/JW/BP/TE/ BB/BW/BX	1985–88	LC/LI/SP/ HC/CO	74 X 55	THS	60	12	25000	40000
The Wave: A Squeeze of the Hand	WG	ST/JW/BP/TE/ BB/BW/BX	1985–88	LC/LI/SP/ HC/CO	55 X 73	THS	60	8	25000	50000
The Wave: The Great Heidelburgh Tun	WG	ST/JW/BP/TE/ BB/BW/BX	1985–88	LC/LI/SP/ HC/CO	75 X 55	THS	60	18	25000	45000
The Wave: The Whale as a Dish	WG	ST/JW/BP/TE/ BB/BW/BX	1985–88	LC/LI/SP/ HC/CO	68 X 54	THS	60		25000	35000
The Wave: The Counterpane (W-5)	WG	ST/JW/BP/TE/ BB/BW/BX	1985–88	LC/LI/SP/ HC/CO	71 X 51	THS	60		25000	35000
The Wave: Going Aboard	WG	ST/JW/BP/TE/ BB/BW/BX	1985–88	LC/LI/SP/ HC/CO	73 X 55	THS	60		25000	35000
The Wave: Moby Dick	WG	ST/JW/BP/TE/ BB/BW/BX	1985–88	LC/LI/SP/ HC/CO	67 X 55	THS	60		25000	45000
The Wave: The Quarter-Deck	WG	ST/JW/BP/TE/ BB/BW/BX	1985–88	LC/LI/SP/ HC/CO	75 X 56	THS	60		25000	35000
Bene Come il Sale Series:										
Bene Come il Sale	WG	ST/JW/BP/WG	1989	EB/A	80 X 59	THS	50	18	30000	45000
Bene Come il Sale, State I	WG	ST/JW/BP/WG	1989	EB/A	76 X 59	THS	9	12	30000	45000
Bene Come il Sale, State II	WG	ST/JW/BP/WG	1989	EB/A	76 X 59	THS	5	11	30000	45000
Bene Come il Sale, State III	WG	ST/JW/BP/WG	1989	EB/A	76 X 59	THS	6	10	30000	45000
Bene Come il Sale, State IV	WG	ST/JW/BP/WG	1989	EB/A	76 X 59	THS	9	12	30000	45000
Guifa e la Beretta Rossa	WG	ST/JW/BP/WG	1989	EB/A/ENG	78 X 59	THS	50	9	35000	75000

PETER STEVENS

PRINTERS: Kathy Carraccio, NY (KC); Sue Evans, NY (SE); Evans Editions, NY (EEd)

PUBLISHERS: Dumbarton Press, NY (DPr); Evans Edition, NY (EEd)
GALLERIES: Addison/Ripley Gallery, Wash, DC; Graham Modern Galleries, New York, NY; Dumbarton Press, New York, NY

TITLE	PUBLISHER	PRINTER	DATE	MEDIUM	DIMENSION (PAPER SIZE) IN INCHES	TYPE OF PAPER	EDITION NUMBER	NO. OF COLORS	ORIGINAL OPENING PRICE	CURRENT RETAIL PRICE
CURRENT EDITIONS:										
Effects (Set of 3):									2200 SET	2200 SET
Effect of Touch	DPr	KC	1992	EB	30 X 22	R/BFK	22	1	800	800
Effect of Memory	DPr	KC	1992	EB	30 X 22	R/BFK	22	1	800	800
Effect of Time	DPr	KC	1992	EB	30 X 22	R/BFK	22	1	800	800
Untitled	EEd	SE/EEd	1992	DPT	20 X 14	SOM/S	12	1	700	700

GARY STEPHAN

PRINTERS: Joe Wilfer, NY (JW); Harlan Weaver Intaglio, NY (HWI); Spring Street Workshop, NY (SprSW); Sheila Marbain, NY (SM); Maurel Studio, NY (MS)
PUBLISHERS: Brooke Alexander, Inc, NY (BAI); Spring Street Workshop, NY (SprSW); Crown Point Press, San Francisco, CA (CPP)
GALLERIES: Mary Boone Gallery, New York, NY; Margo Leavin Gallery, Los Angeles, CA; Texas Gallery, Houston, TX; Brooke Alexander Inc, New York, NY; Pace Prints, New York, NY; Harris Samuel & Co, Inc, Miami, FL; Baumgartner Galleries, Wash, DC; Lemberg Gallery, Birmingham, MI; Fenton Fine Arts, Ft Worth, TX; Richard Levy Gallery, Albuquerque, NM

Gary Stephan
Airbrush Aquatint IIII
Courtesy Crown Point Press

TITLE	PUBLISHER	PRINTER	DATE	MEDIUM	DIMENSION (PAPER SIZE) IN INCHES	TYPE OF PAPER	EDITION NUMBER	NO. OF COLORS	ORIGINAL OPENING PRICE	CURRENT RETAIL PRICE
SOLD OUT EDITIONS (RARE):										
If/then, A–F (Set of 6)	BAI	SM/MS	1974	AC	25 X 29 EA	AC	50 EA		600 SET	4500 SET
									100 EA	750 EA
CURRENT EDITIONS:										
Series of Three:									6500 SET	7500 SET
Untitled (836-1-1)	SprSW	JW/HWI/SprSW	1988	EC	23 X 18	SOM/S	35	4	2500	3500
Untitled (836-1-2)	SprSW	JW/HWI/SprSW	1988	EC	29 X 23	SOM/S	43	4	2500	2000
Untitled (836-1-3)	SprSW	JW/HWI/SprSW	1988	EC	35 X 28	SOM/S	48	4	2500	2500
Untitled (836-2) (Set of 3):									4000 SET	4000 SET
Untitled (836-2-1)	SprSW	JW/HWI/SprSW	1988	EC/CC	23 X 18	AC/CHIRI	15	1	2000	1200
Untitled (836-2-2)	SprSW	JW/HWI/SprSW	1988	EC/CC	29 X 23	AC/CHIRI	15	1	2000	1500
Untitled (836-2-3)	SprSW	JW/HWI/SprSW	1988	EC/CC	35 X 28	AC/CHIRI	15	1	2000	1500
Planets (Set of 6)			1989	LC			10 EA		10000 SET	10000 SET
1990 I,II,III,IV (with Airbrush) (Series of 4)	CPP	DS/RB/LG/ PP/CPP	1990	EB/A/SB	51 X 41 EA	SOM	30 EA		2800 EA	2800 EA
Untitled	SprSW	JW/RL/SprSW	1991	LI	19 X 15	HAHN	45	1	700	700

JAROMIR STEPHANY

BORN: Rochester, NY; March 23, 1930
EDUCATION: Rochester Inst of Tech, NY, 1956, BFA, 1958; Indiana Univ, Bloomington, IN, MFA, 1960
TEACHING: Lectr, History of Photography, Maryland Inst of Col Arts, Baltimore, MD, 1966–67; Assoc Prof, Dept of Visual Arts, Univ of Maryland, Baltimore, MD, 1972 to present
AWARDS: Univ of Maryland, Baltimore, MD, Summer Fel, 1983
COLLECTIONS: George Eastman House, Int Mus of Photography, Rochester, NY; Mus of Fine Arts, St Petersburg, FL; Univ of Maryland, Catonsville, MD; Detroit Inst of Art, MI; Baltimore Mus of Art, MD
MAILING ADDRESS: 786 Creekview Rd, Severna Park, MD 21146

TITLE	PUBLISHER	PRINTER	DATE	MEDIUM	DIMENSION (PAPER SIZE) IN INCHES	TYPE OF PAPER	EDITION NUMBER	NO. OF COLORS	ORIGINAL OPENING PRICE	CURRENT RETAIL PRICE
CURRENT EDITIONS:										
Landscapes of Outer Space (Set of 10)	ART	ART	1980	PH	16 X 20 EA		100 EA	1 EA	200 EA	350 EA
Radiant Day (Set of 7)	ART	ART	1980	PH	11 X 14 EA		100 EA	1 EA	125 EA	200 EA
Non-War Years (Set of 9)	ART	ART	1980	PH	11 X 14 EA		100 EA	1 EA	125 EA	200 EA
Psychosis (Set of 8)	ART	ART	1980	PH	16 X 20 EA		100 EA	1 EA	200 EA	350 EA
Children of the Lens (Set of 6)	ART	ART	1980	PH	16 X 20 EA		100 EA	4 EA	250 EA	550 EA

The retail prices of the 100,000 limited edition prints quoted in this directory are subject to change. Print publishers, artists and galleries were the direct sources for these quotations. Prices in the secondary market listed as "Sold Out Editions (Rare)" indicate that the publisher has a limited supply of that print or that the print is difficult to locate in the galleries.

BERT STERN

BORN: Brooklyn, NY; 1930
COLLECTIONS: Mus of Mod Art, NY
PRINTERS: American Atelier, NY (AA)
PUBLISHERS: Circle Fine Art, Chicago, IL (CFA)
GALLERIES: Circle Galleries, San Diego, CA & San Francisco, CA & Northbrook, IL & Pittsburgh, PA & Houston, TX & Soho, NY & Chicago, IL & Scottsdale, AZ & Beverly Hills, CA & Costa Mesa, CA & Sherman Oaks, CA & Palm Beach, FL & New Orleans, LA & Las Vegas, NV & Seattle WA & Honolulu, HI & Northbrook, IL; Edward Weston Fine Arts, Northridge, CA

TITLE	PUBLISHER	PRINTER	DATE	MEDIUM	DIMENSION (PAPER SIZE) IN INCHES	TYPE OF PAPER	EDITION NUMBER	NO. OF COLORS	ORIGINAL OPENING PRICE	CURRENT RETAIL PRICE
SOLD OUT EDITIONS (RARE):										
Marilyn Monroe Series:										
MM Brown/White	CFA	AA	1978	SP	36 X 36	AP	100		325	1050
MM Navy/Light Blue	CFA	AA	1978	SP	36 X 36	AP	100		300	1050
MM Blue/Dark Green	CFA	AA	1978	SP	36 X 36	AP	100		300	1050
MM Silver/Green	CFA	AA	1978	SP	36 X 36	AP	100		300	1050
MM Silver/Black	CFA	AA	1978	SP	36 X 36	AP	100		300	1050
MM Silver/Navy	CFA	AA	1978	SP	36 X 36	AP	100		325	1050
MM Gold/Champagne	CFA	AA	1978	SP	36 X 36	AP	100		325	1050
MM White/Orange	CFA	AA	1978	SP	36 X 36	AP	100		325	1050
MM Beige/Brown	CFA	AA	1978	SP	36 X 36	AP	100		325	1050
MM Yellow/Dark Green	CFA	AA	1978	SP	36 X 36	AP	100		300	1050
MM Body Gold/Blue	CFA	AA	1979	SP	40 X 32	AP	300		375	1050
MM Body Gold/Champaign	CFA	AA	1979	SP	40 X 32	AP	300		375	1050
MM Body Silver/Blue	CFA	AA	1979	SP	40 X 32	AP	300		375	1050
MM Body Dark and Light Blue	CFA	AA	1979	SP	40 X 32	AP	300		375	1050

ANDREW VLASTIMIR STEVOVICH

BORN: Salzburg, Austria; July 2, 1948; U S Citizen
EDUCATION: Rhode Island Sch of Design, Providence, RI, BFA, Painting, 1970; Massachusetts Col of Art, MFA, Painting, 1980
AWARDS: Sydney Richmond Burley Award, Painting, 1970; Presidential Fel, Traveling, Europe, 1970
RECENT EXHIB: Tatistcheff Gallery, Santa Monica, CA, 1989,92; Coe Kerr Gallery, NY, 1987,90,92
COLLECTIONS: Brockton Art Mus, MA; Danforth Mus, Framington, MA; New Britain of Am Art, CT
PRINTERS: Robert Townsend, Georgetown, MA (RT); Robert Townsend, Inc., Georgetown, MA (RTI)
PUBLISHERS: Artist (ART)
GALLERIES: Coe Kerr Gallery, New York, NY; Tatistcheff Gallery, Santa Monica, CA; Sarah E Mleczko Fine Arts, New York, NY
MAILING ADDRESS: 120 Sewall Ave, Brookline, MA 02140

TITLE	PUBLISHER	PRINTER	DATE	MEDIUM	DIMENSION (PAPER SIZE) IN INCHES	TYPE OF PAPER	EDITION NUMBER	NO. OF COLORS	ORIGINAL OPENING PRICE	CURRENT RETAIL PRICE
CURRENT EDITIONS:										
Twenty-One	ART	RT/RTI	1988	AC	22 X 30	AP	100	7	700	1000
The Dance	ART	RT/RTI	1989	AC	22 X 30	R/BFK	100	6	800	1000

NORMAN STEWART

BORN: Detroit, MI; March 31, 1947
EDUCATION: Univ of Michigan, Ann Arbor, MI, BFA, 1969, MA, 1972; Cranbrook Acad of Art, Bloomfield Hills, MI, MFA, 1977; Rochester Inst of Technology, NY, 1977
TEACHING: Parsons Sch of Design, NY, 1977; Cranbrook Acad of Art, Bloomfield Hills, MI, 1977–79; Wayne State Univ, Detroit, MI, 1977–79; Univ of Michigan, Ann Arbor, MI, 1979 to 1984
AWARDS: Michigan Council for the Arts, Creative Artists Grants, 1973,81; Detroit Inst of Arts, MI, Print Comm, 1982
RECENT EXHIB: Detroit Inst of Arts, MI, 1991; Kalamazoo Inst of Art, MI, 1991; Nelson-Atkins Mus of Art, Kansas City, MO, 1992; Cleveland Mus of Art, OH, 1992
COLLECTIONS: Brooklyn Mus, NY; Detroit Inst of Arts, MI; Kalamazoo Inst of Arts, MI; Mount Union Col, Alliance, OH; Muskegon Mus, MI; Cleveland Mus, OH; Cranbrook Acad of Art, Bloomfield Hills, MI; Flint Inst of Art, MI; Univ of Michigan, Ann Arbor, MI
PRINTERS: Wing Lake Studio, Bloomfield Hills, MI (WLS); Artist (ART); Peter Juneau (PJ); Tobin Smith (TS)
PUBLISHERS: Stewart & Stewart, Bloomfield Hills, MI (S-S); Detroit Inst of Art, Founders Soc, MI (DIA); Artist (ART)
GALLERIES: Stewart & Stewart, Bloomfield Hills, MI
MAILING ADDRESS: 5571 Wing Lake Rd, Bloomfield Hills, MI 48010

TITLE	PUBLISHER	PRINTER	DATE	MEDIUM	DIMENSION (PAPER SIZE) IN INCHES	TYPE OF PAPER	EDITION NUMBER	NO. OF COLORS	ORIGINAL OPENING PRICE	CURRENT RETAIL PRICE
SOLD OUT EDITIONS (RARE):										
Entre	ART	ART	1976	SP	26 X 19	AP	20	15	250	2000
Tutti-Frutti	ART	ART	1976	SP	26 X 19	AP	30	13	200	1500
Frutti-Tutti	ART	ART	1976	SP	26 X 19	AP	30	13	200	1500
Vertigo	ART	ART	1977	SP	26 X 19	AP	15	15	400	1500
Gossamer	ART	ART	1977	SP	26 X 20	AP	20	13	250	2000
Bias	ART	ART	1977	SP	26 X 20	AP	20	12	250	1500
Eddies	ART	ART	1978	SP	26 X 19	AP	35	13	300	1200
Tendril	ART	ART	1978	SP	26 X 20	AP	24	10	300	1200
Menonaqua (Proofs Only)	ART	ART	1979	SP	26 X 19	AP	20	15	300	1800
Trifles	S-S	ART/WLS	1980	SP	26 X 20	R/BFK/T	20	16	300	1800
Rhombus (Proofs Only)	S-S	ART/WLS	1981	SP	26 X 20	R/BFK/T	30	30	350	2200
Mirage	DIA	ART/WLS	1982	SP	26 X 20	R/BFK/G	40	21	400	1500
Serac	S-S	ART/WLS	1984	SP	26 X 20	R/BFK/G	35	22	500	1800
CURRENT EDITIONS:										
Onyx I,II	S-S	ART/WLS	1983	SP	26 X 20 EA	MUR/BL	38 EA	14 EA	400 EA	850 EA

NORMAN STEWART CONTINUED

TITLE	PUBLISHER	PRINTER	DATE	MEDIUM	DIMENSION (PAPER SIZE) IN INCHES	TYPE OF PAPER	EDITION NUMBER	NO. OF COLORS	ORIGINAL OPENING PRICE	CURRENT RETAIL PRICE
CURRENT EDITIONS:										
Tartan	S-S	ART/WLS	1984	SP	26 X 20	R/BFK	46	27	400	850
April	S-S	ART/TS/WLS	1985	SP	26 X 20	R/BFK/W	42	17	450	850
Sonata	S-S	ART/WLS	1987	SP	26 X 20	R/BFK/G	41	14	450	850
Echelon	S-S	ART/WLS	1987	SP	26 X 20	R/BFK/G	50	10	450	850
Simokon	S-S	ART/PJ/WLS	1988	SP	29 X 22	R/BFK/G	40	11	500	850
Nokomis	S-S	ART/PJ/WLS	1988	SP	29 X 22	R/BFK/G	40	11	500	850
Harbinger	S-S	ART/PJ/WLS	1989	SP	30 X 22	R/BFK/W	41	5	600	850
Hi-Flyer	S-S	ART/PJ/WLS	1990	SP	41 X 29	R/BFK/W	41	7	900	1000
Head to Head	S-S	ART/PJ/WLS	1992	SP	41 X 29	R/BFK/W	22	14	1250	1250

PAUL L STEWART

BORN: Cleveland, OH; June 28, 1928
EDUCATION: Cleveland Inst of Art, OH, 1946; Albion Col, MI, BA, 1953; New Sch for Social Research, NY, 1954; Univ of Michigan, Ann Arbor, MI, MA, 1959
TEACHING: Instr & Assoc Prof, Albion Col, MI, 1959–72; Prof, Univ of Michigan, Ann Arbor, MI, 1973 to present
AWARDS: Jurors Commendation, North Am Print Exhib, Boston Printmakers, MA, 1986; Marian Malina Purchase Award, Medalist, Print Biennale, Krakow, Poland, 1988; Purchase Award, Nat Print & Drawing Exhib, Bradley Univ, Peoria, IN, 1989; Award for Excellence, Midwest Print & Drawing Exhib, Northwestern Univ, Evanston, IL, 1989
RECENT EXHIB: Philadelphia Print Club, PA, 1987; China Fine Arts Mus, Taipei, China, 1988; Brockton Art Mus, MA, 1988
COLLECTIONS: Cleveland Mus of Art, OH; Metropolitan Mus of Art, NY; Nat Gallery of Art, Wash, DC; Brooklyn Mus, NY; Mus de Arte Contemp de Campinas, Brazil; Detroit Inst of Art, MI; Walker Art Center, Minneapolis, MN; Library of Congress, Wash, DC
PRINTERS: Eulalia Stewart, Ann Arbor, MI (ES); Artist (ART); Norman Steward, Bloomfield Hills, MI (NS); Wing Lake Studio, Bloomfield Hills, MI (WLS)
PUBLISHERS: Stewart & Stewart, Bloomfield Hills, MI (S-S)
GALLERIES: Szoke Graphics, New York, NY; Gallery G, Pittsburgh, PA; Hudson Fine Art, Santa Monica, CA; Editions Limited Galleries San Francisco, CA & Indianapolis, IN; Perimeter Gallery, Chicago, IL
MAILING ADDRESS: 2281 Ayreshire Rd, Ann Arbor, MI 48105

TITLE	PUBLISHER	PRINTER	DATE	MEDIUM	DIMENSION (PAPER SIZE) IN INCHES	TYPE OF PAPER	EDITION NUMBER	NO. OF COLORS	ORIGINAL OPENING PRICE	CURRENT RETAIL PRICE
CURRENT EDITIONS:										
Aerial	S-S	ART/ES	1988	I/REL	21 X 29	HMP	50	4	400	750

MARCELLE STOIANOVICH

BORN: Paris, France; May 8, 1936
EDUCATION: Col of Applied Art, Paris, France
COLLECTIONS: Rutgers Univ, New Brunswick, NJ
PUBLISHERS: Claude de Runde, Paris, France (CR); Original Print Collectors Group, NY (OPCG); Union des Arts et Traditions Lithographiques, Paris, France (UATL); Art 204, Paris, France (A204)
PRINTERS: Arts Litho, Paris, France (AL); Agostini, Paris, France (AG)
GALLERIES: Venable/Neslage Galleries, Wash, DC; Ulmarra Galleries, Ulmarra, Australia; France Garo, Tokyo, Japan; Art 204, Paris, France

TITLE	PUBLISHER	PRINTER	DATE	MEDIUM	DIMENSION (PAPER SIZE) IN INCHES	TYPE OF PAPER	EDITION NUMBER	NO. OF COLORS	ORIGINAL OPENING PRICE	CURRENT RETAIL PRICE
SOLD OUT EDITIONS (RARE):										
Honfleur	OPCG	AG	1978	LC	20 X 26	AP	225	12	195	600
A Domani	OPCG	AG	1978	LC	20 X 26	AP	225	12	125	500
St Jean-Cap-Ferrat	OPCG	AG	1979	LC	20 X 26	AP	225	12	165	600
Aimex-Vous Mozart	CR	AL	1979	LC	20 X 26	AP	175	12	130	700
First of May	UATL	AG	1980	LC	20 X 26	AP	125	10	140	500
CURRENT EDITIONS:										
Femme Au Coque Licot	JA	AG	1977	LC	20 X 26	AP	175	10	170	500
Deux Japonaises en Ile de France	OPCG	AL	1978	LC	20 X 26	AP	225	11	195	400
Plein ete	OPCG	AL	1980	LC	20 X 26	AP	225	13	235	400
Ma Prairie	OPCG	AG	1980	LC	20 X 26	AP	225	12	195	400
Vol de Nuit	ARTES	AG	1980	LC	20 X 26	AP	250	13	150	400
Kathy's Kitty	CR	AL	1981	LC	20 X 26	AP	275	15	200	400
Bord de Mer	OPCG	AL	1981	LC	20 X 26	AP	225	13	235	400
Vacances	OPCG	AL	1982	LC	20 X 26	AP	225	13	235	400
Grimaldi	A204	AL	1983	LC	20 X 26	AP	225	13	200	500
Les Désenchantées	CR	AL	1983	LC	20 X 26	AP	200	17	250	400

ARDY STRUWER

PRINTERS: American Atelier, NY (AA)
PUBLISHERS: Circle Fine Art, Chicago, IL (CFA)
GALLERIES: Circle Galleries, Chicago, IL & New York, NY & San Diego, CA & San Francisco, CA & Northbrook, IL & Pittsburgh, PA & Houston, TX & Scottsdale, AZ & Beverly Hills, CA & Costa Mesa, CA & Sherman Oaks, CA & Palm Beach, FL & Honolulu, HI & Lahaina, Maui, HI & New Orleans, LA & Las Vegas, NV & Seattle, WA

TITLE	PUBLISHER	PRINTER	DATE	MEDIUM	DIMENSION (PAPER SIZE) IN INCHES	TYPE OF PAPER	EDITION NUMBER	NO. OF COLORS	ORIGINAL OPENING PRICE	CURRENT RETAIL PRICE
CURRENT EDITIONS:										
Palette Music I	CFA	AA	1982	LC	34 X 25	AP	37		225	450
Palette Music II	CFA	AA	1982	LC	34 X 25	AP	63		250	450

DANIEL O STOLPE

BORN: Los Angeles, CA; November 14, 1939
EDUCATION: Pasadena City Col, CA, 1958–60; Los Angeles County Art Inst, CA, 1960
TEACHING: Univ of California Ext, Santa Cruz, CA, 1978 to present
AWARDS: Special Project Grant, California Arts Council Grant, 1978; First Place, Affaire in the Garden, Beverly Hills, CA, 1989,90; First Prize, Grand Prix D'Aquitaine, Bordeaux, France; 1990
RECENT EXHIB: Coyote Gallery, Idyllwild, CA, 1989–90; Huntington Mus, Univ of Texas, Austin, TX, 1990; New Mexico Mus of Fine Arts, Santa Fe, NM, 1990; Trojanowska Gallery, San Francisco, CA, 1991–92; Gallery Piazza, Ausalito, CA, 1992–93; Gallery Mayu, Tokyo, Japan, 1993
COLLECTIONS: Smithsonian Inst, Was, DC; Salt Lake Art Ctr, UT; Portland Art Mus, Gordon W Gilkey Coll, OR; C E Smith Mus, California State Univ, Hayward, CA; Univ of Texas, Austin, TX; Univ of New Mexico, Albuquerque, NM; Mint Mus, Charlotte, NC; Fogg Art Mus, Harvard Univ, Cambridge, MA; Univ of Arizona, Tempe, AZ; Grunwald Center for Graphics Arts, Los Angeles, CA; Boston Public Library, MA; Everson Mus, Syracuse, NY; Henry Art Gallery & Univ Library, Univ of Washington, Seattle, WA; Mus of New Mexico Mus, Santa Fe, NM; Oklahoma Art Center, Oklahoma City, OK; New York Public Library, NY
PRINTERS: Joseph Funk, Venice, CA (JF); Native Images, Santa Cruz, CA (NI); Herbert A Fox, Merrimac, MA (HF); Mark Tabler, Santa Cruz, CA (MT); Steve Cooper, Santa Cruz, CA (SC); Richard Williams, Santa Cruz, CA (RW); Lynn Miller, Santa Cruz, CA (LM); Juan Gonzalez, Santa Cruz, CA (JG); Manuel Montez, Santa Cruz, CA (MM); Israel Williams, Santa Cruz, CA (IW); Janet Seman, Santa Cruz, CA (JS); Jamie Olson, Santa Cruz, CA (JO); Xavier Pujol, Barcelona, Spain (XP); Kurt W Algayer, Santa Cruz, CA (KWA)
PUBLISHERS: Native Images Inc, Santa Cruz, CA (NI); Fox Graphics, Boston, MA (FG); A Associated Fine Art, Hayward, CA (AAFA)
GALLERIES: Bear Gallery, San Juan Bautista, CA; Coyote Gallery, Idyllwild, CA; Fox Graphics/Merrimac Editiion Editions, Merrimac, MA; Pulliman/Nugent Gallery, Portland, OR; Walton-Gilbert Gallery, San Rafael, CA; Trojanowska Gallery, San Francisco, CA; Gallery Piazza, Sausalito, CA
MAILING ADDRESS: 2539 Mission St, Santa Cruz, CA 95060

Daniel O Stolpe
Crowman Displays His Pain
Courtesy Native Images

TITLE	PUBLISHER	PRINTER	DATE	MEDIUM	DIMENSION (PAPER SIZE) IN INCHES	TYPE OF PAPER	EDITION NUMBER	NO. OF COLORS	ORIGINAL OPENING PRICE	CURRENT RETAIL PRICE
SOLD OUT EDITIONS (RARE):										
Icarian	NI	HF/FG	1963	WC	36 X 24	TROYA	20	2	200	400
Figures with Moon	NI	JF	1975	LC	14 X 12	R/BFK	12	3	125	350
American Avocet	NI	JF	1975	LC/HC	16 X 14	R/BFK	40	3	125	1200
Incatation	NI	JF	1975	LB	10 X 9	AP	80	2	90	2000
Transformation	NI	JF	1975	LB	13 X 10	R/BFK	40	2	90	1500
Elk Rite: Placing the Head	NI	RW	1975	WC	22 X 15	AP	20	3	225	450
Elk Rite: The Dancer	NI	RW	1975	EC	22 X 15	AP	20	3	225	450
Elk Rite: The Preparation	NI	RW	1975	EC	22 X 15	AP	20	3	225	450
Dancing Figure with Wing	NI	ART	1975	EC	12 X 8	AP	30	2	175	250
Grizzly	NI	MT	1977	EC	8 X 11	AP	30	1	90	325
Bittern	NI	NI	1977	EC	12 X 4	AP	30	1	90	325
Young Bitterns	NI	NI	1977	EC	4 X 12	AP	30	2	90	325
Winged Harbinger	NI	NI	1978	EC	13 X 8	R/BFK	30	2	90	850
Winged Beginning	NI	NI	1978	EC	13 X 10	STP	30	3	90	1500
Woman & Deer Spirit Dancing	NI	JF	1978	LC/HC	13 X 8	R/BFK	20	4	125	1200
Pelican	NI	SC	1979	EC	11 X 8	AP	30	3	90	325
Buffalo	NI	JF	1979	LB	22 X 18	AP	30	2	250	850
Unknown Image	NI	RW	1979	EC	13 X 10	R/BFK	30	4	225	350
Coyote Listening to Dragon Fly	NI	MT	1981	WC	24 X 28	TROYA	30	Multi	650	2000
Champagne with Red Tears	NI	ART/NI	1985	MON	22 X 30 EA	R/BFK	1 EA	Multi	650 EA	1500 EA
Touching His Wound, States I,II	NI	ART/NI	1989	MON	31 X 47 EA	AC/W	1 EA	Multi	1500 EA	2500 EA
Crow Man's Agony, States I,II	NI	ART/NI	1989	MON	30 X 44 EA	R/BFK/G	1 EA	Multi	1500 EA	2500 EA
CURRENT EDITIONS:										
Fallen Bird	NI	HF/FG	1964	WC	36 X 24	TROYA	40	3	150	525
Study for Icarus	NI	JF/NI	1966	LB	16 X 20	R/BFK	50	2	100	550
Tragic Vision	NI	JF/NI	1966	LB	21 X 7	AP	50	2	100	450
A Portrait	NI	JF/NI	1966	LB	21 X 7	AP	50	2	100	450
Boy Reaching, Bird Watching	NI	MT/NI	1968	EC	6 X 11	AP	30	3	90	150
Looking Behind	NI	ART/NI	1968	EC	6 X 11	AP	30	3	90	150
Mythic Web	NI	MT/NI	1969	EC	8 X 12	RP	30	2	90	150
Deer Skull #1	NI	MT/NI	1973	EC	11 X 7	AP	25	3	90	150
Deer Skull #2	NI	MT/NI	1973	EC	10 X 7	AP	25	3	90	150
Dancing Wolf Figures	NI	ART/NI	1974	LC	16 X 12	AP	20	2	90	350
Boy and Totem	NI	MT/NI	1975	EC	11 X 6	RP	25	3	90	150
Man and totem	NI	MT/NI	1975	EC	6 X 11	RP	30	2	90	150
October Vision from Northwest	NI	MT/NI	1975	EC	11 X 7	AP	30	3	90	150
Owl Triptych	NI	ART/NI	1975	EC	30 X 20	AP	20	2	450	650

DANIEL O STOLPE CONTINUED

TITLE	PUBLISHER	PRINTER	DATE	MEDIUM	DIMENSION (PAPER SIZE) IN INCHES	TYPE OF PAPER	EDITION NUMBER	NO. OF COLORS	ORIGINAL OPENING PRICE	CURRENT RETAIL PRICE
CURRENT EDITIONS:										
Winged Figure	NI	ART/NI	1975	EC	15 X 11	AP	30	2	225	325
Dancing Wolf Figures	NI	MT/NI	1975	EC	7 X 15	AP	30	2	225	325
Wolf Shaman of the Northwest	NI	MT/NI	1975	EC	15 X 8	AP	30	3	150	225
Northwest Interior	NI	MT/NI	1975	EC	7 X 12	AP	30	3	90	150
Inner Image of the Northwest	NI	MT/NI	1975	EC	7 X 11	AP	30	2	90	150
Wolf Dancer	NI	MT/NI	1975	EC	11 X 8	R/BFK	30	3	150	225
Figures with Moon	NI	JF/NI	1975	LC	14 X 12	R/BFK	12	3	125	350
Shaman, Man, Wolf, Fire	NI	JF/NI	1975	LC	14 X 11	R/BFK	20	3	125	350
Putting on the Deer	NI	JF/NI	1975	LC	14 X 10	R/BFK	20	3	125	225
Shaman Dream	NI	JF/NI	1975	LB	19 X 7	AP	80	2	125	650
Man-Wolf Spirit (Triptych)	NI	NI	1975	EC	7 X 4	AP	30	2	150	450
Woman-Deer Spirit (Triptych)	NI	NI	1975	EC	7 X 4	AP	30	2	150	450
Shaman Dancing I	NI	NI	1978	EC	11 X 8	R/BFK	30	3	125	350
Shaman Dancing II	NI	SC/NI	1978	EC	13 X 8	R/BFK	30	2	175	225
Coyote Dancer	NI	SC/NI	1978	EC	15 X 11	STP	15	3	225	275
Coyote Shield	NI	SC/NI	1978	EC	21 X 15	STP	30	3	225	375
Man & Bear Dancing	NI	NI	1979	EC	13 X 9	AP	30	2	90	350
Boy and Skull	NI	JF/NI	1979	LB	22 X 15	AP	30	4	150	350
A Rite of Passage	NI	JF/NI	1979	LC	20 X 15	AP	35	4	200	550
Elk Spirit Dance	NI	JF/NI	1979	LC	19 X 24	AP	35	4	200	550
Offering (State I)	NI	JF/NI	1979	LC	11 X 6	R/BFK	20	4	75	125
Offering (State II)	NI	JF/NI	1979	LC	12 X 5	R/BFK	20	3	75	125
Placement	NI	JF/NI	1979	LC	12 X 5	R/BFK	20	3	75	125
Eagle Dreams	NI	JF/NI	1979	LC	28 X 20	R/BFK	20	5	350	850
Woman and Coyote	NI	RW/NI	1979	EC	11 X 6	R/BFK	30	4	225	325
Mythic Figure	NI	RW/NI	1979	EC	10 X 8	R/BFK	30	4	150	225
A Man and His Shadow (Twilight)	NI	ART/NI	1980	LC	30 X 22	AP	30	6	450	1200
Boy and Tragic Bird	NI	MT/NI	1980	EC	11 X 6	AP	30	2	150	225
Eagle Catcher	NI	JF/NI	1980	LC	30 X 22	AP	30	4	350	1200
A Man and His Shadow I	NI	JF/NI	1980	LC	30 X 22	AP	30	6	450	1200
Coyote Suite I (Set of 10):									5500 SET	7500 SET
And there was Coyote Biting at the Moon	NI	MT/NI	1980	WC	24 X 28	TROYA	30	5	650	2000
Coyote Changing the Moon by Eating It	NI	ART/NI	1980	WC	24 X 28	TROYA		4	650	1500
Coyote by Flying Causes Great Waters	NI	MT/NI	1981	WC	24 X 28	TROYA	30	Multi	650	850
Coyote thinks the Morning Sun Is Chasing Him...	NI	MT/NI	1981	WC	24 X 28	TROYA	30	Multi	650	850
Coyote Changes the Color of the Sun	NI	MT/NI	1981	WC	24 X 28	TROYA	30	Multi	650	850
Coyote Digging for His Bones	NI	MT/NI	1981	WC	24 X 28	TROYA	30	6	650	850
Coyote Scratching His Fleas	NI	MT/NI	1981	WC	24 X 28	TROYA	30	Multi	650	1500
The Earth Shakes...	NI	MT/NI	1981	WC	24 X 28	TROYA	30	Multi	650	1500
When the Moon Fell...	NI	MT/NI	1981	WC	24 X 28	TROYA	30	5	650	1500
Coyote was there Helping Coyote Tries to Eat the Sun	NI	MT/NI	1981	WC	24 X 28	TROYA	30	Multi	650	850
Coyote Suite II (Set of 10):									5500 SET	7500 SET
Coyote as Chief	NI	MT/NI	1981	WC	28 X 25	UNRYU	30	Multi	650	850
Coyote Ready to Give Birth	NI	MT/NI	1981	WC	24 X 28	UNRYU	30	Multi	650	1500
Coyote Juggling His Eyes	NI	ART/NI	1981	WC	28 X 24	UNRYU	30	6	650	850
Coyote Spinning	NI	MT/NI	1981	WC	24 X 28	UNRYU	30	Multi	650	850
Coyote and His Woman	NI	ART/NI	1981	WC	28 X 24	UNYRU	30	3	650	1500
Woman Under Coyote's Spell	NI	ART/NI	1981	WC	28 X 24	UNRYU	30	7	650	850
Coyote is Intrigued	NI	ART/NI	1981	WC	28 X 24	UNYRU	30	5	650	850
Porcupine Surprises Coyote	NI	MT/NI	1981	WC	24 X 28	UNRYU	30	Multi	650	850
Coyote's Evening Approach	NI	ART/NI	1981	WC	28 X 24	UNYRU	30	3	650	1500
Leda and the Swan	NI	LM/NI	1981	EC	9 X 13	R/BFK	30	3	225	325
Wolf Dancer I	NI	ART/NI	1982	LC	30 X 22	R/BFK	10	3	350	450
Wolf Dancer II	NI	ART/NI	1982	LC	30 X 22	R/BFK	10	3	350	450
Shaman's Vision	NI	NI	1982	WC	29 X 78	MASA	50	14	1950	2950
Coyote Moons	NI	JG/NI	1982	EC	14 X 6	AP	40	Multi	225	225
Totemscape	NI	JG/NI	1982	EC	10 X 15	AP	40	3	225	225
Coyote Ritual	NI	NI	1982	EC	16 X 11	R/BFK	40	Multi	225	225
Past is the Future	NI	RW/NI	1983	WC	11 X 8	UNRYU	70	4	175	175
Ancient Voice	NI	RW/NI	1983	WC	15 X 12	UNRYU	70	3	225	225
Coyote Dancer and Conjured Image	NI	YA/NI	1984	EC	22 X 15	BFK/G	30	?	425	425
Elk	NI	YA/NI	1984	EC	8 X 11	AP	30	2	150	225
Coyote Now (Set of 6)	NI	NF/NI	1984	LC/LP	32 X 14 EA	AP/W	30 EA	Multi	2000 SET	4000 SET
Coyote Cycle (Set of 7):									5000 SET	5000 SET
I-Pointing	NI	JH/NI	1984	WC	31 X 24	UNRYU	35	Multi	750	750
II-The Shadow Ripens	NI	JH/NI	1984	SC	31 X 24	UNRYU	35	Multi	750	750
III-Planet of the Spider People	NI	JH/NI	1984	WC	31 X 24	UNRYU	35	Multi	750	750

DANIEL O STOLPE CONTINUED

TITLE	PUBLISHER	PRINTER	DATE	MEDIUM	DIMENSION (PAPER SIZE) IN INCHES	TYPE OF PAPER	EDITION NUMBER	NO. OF COLORS	ORIGINAL OPENING PRICE	CURRENT RETAIL PRICE
CURRENT EDITIONS:										
IV-Other Side Camp	NI	JH/NI	1984	WC	31 X 24	UNRYU	35	Multi	750	750
V-Listening to Old Nana	NI	JH/NI	1984	WC	31 X 24	UNRYU	35	Multi	750	750
VI-The Sacred Dump	NI	JH/NI	1984	WC	31 X 24	UNRYU	35	Multi	750	750
VII-He Brings the Waterfall	NI	JH/NI	1984	WC	31 X 24	UNRYU	35	Multi	750	750
Portrait Series (Series of 10)	NI	ART/NI	1985	MON	22 X 30 EA	UNRYU	1 EA	Multi	650	1500
Woman & Coyote Shadow Series	NI	ART/NI	1985	MON	22 X 30 EA	UNRYU	1 EA	Multi	650	1500
Spirit Dancer Series (Set of 10)	NI	ART/NI	1986	MON	22 X 30 EA	R/BFK	1 EA	Multi	850 EA	1500 EA
Coyote's Enchantment (Set of 10)	NI	MM/IW/JS/JO/NI	1987	EC	16 X 19 EA	AC/W	35 EA	2 EA	350 EA	450 EA
Getting their Attention	NI	NI	1987	EB	16 X 19	AC/W	35	1	350	450
Something They're Beginning	NI	NI	1987	EB	16 X 19	AC/W	35	1	350	450
Coyote Vesture	NI	IW/NI	1987	EB	16 X 19	AC/W	35	1	350	450
Interlude	NI	MM/NI	1987	EB	16 X 19	AC/W	35	1	350	450
Imitating Coyote Poses	NI	IW/NI	1987	EB	16 X 19	AC/W	35	1	350	450
Imitating Coyote	NI	MM/NI	1987	EB	16 X 19	AC/W	25	1	350	450
Coyote Makes Her Dance	NI	MM/NI	1987	EB	16 X 19	AC/W	35	1	350	450
They have their Own Way	NI	JS/NI	1987	EB	16 X 19	AC/W	35	1	350	450
They Act in their Own World	NI	JO/NI	1987	EB	16 X 19	AC/W	35	1	350	450
Resolution	NI	NI	1987	EB	16 X 19	AC/W	35	1	350	450
Coyote Sunrise	NI	MM/NI	1987	EC	16 X 19	AC/W	40	3	350	350
Coyote Peeking	NI	ART/NI	1987	MON	30 X 22	R/BFK/W	10	Multi	850	1500
Dreaming Coyote	NI	ART/NI	1987	MON	30 X 22	R/BFK/W	10	Multi	850	1500
Blindfold Vision	NI	ART/NI	1987	MON	30 X 22	R/BFK/W	10	Multi	850	1500
Dancing Wolf Spirit	NI	ART/NI	1987	MON	30 X 22	R/BFK/W	3	Multi	850	1500
Masked Judgement	NI	ART/NI	1988	MON	30 X 22	AP/B	10	Multi	850	1500
Blistering Coyote	NI	ART/NI	1988	MON	30 X 22	R/BFK/W	3	Multi	850	1500
Animal Spirit	NI	ART/NI	1988	MON	30 X 22	AC/W	1	Multi	850	1500
Sacred Embrace	NI	ART/NI	1988	MON	30 X 22	R/BFK/W	3	Multi	850	1500
I Turn My Back on You	NI	ART/NI	1988	MON	30 X 22	AP/B	1	Multi	1200	1500
He Leaves the Room Unresolved	NI	ART/NI	1988	MON	30 X 22	AP/B	1	Multi	1200	1500
Crow Man Displays His Pain	NI	ART/NI	1988	MON	30 X 22	AP/B	1	Multi	1200	1500
Man Talking Coyote	NI	ART/NI	1989	MON	30 X 22	AC/W	1	Multi	850	1500
Struck While Walking	NI	ART/NI	1989	MON	30 X 44	R/BFK/G	1	Multi	1500	2500
Crow Man Holding His Wound	NI	ART/NI	1989	MON	30 X 44	R/BFK/G	1	Multi	1500	2500
Just Struck	NI	ART/NI	1989	MON	30 X 44	R/BFK/G	1	Multi	1500	2500
Crow Man Impaled	NI	ART/NI	1989	MON	31 X 47	AC/W	1	Multi	1500	2500
Suturing the Wound	NI	ART/NI	1989	MON	30 X 44	R/BFK/G	1	Multi	1500	2500
Not Alone with His Pain	NI	ART/NI	1989	MON	30 X 44	R/BFK/G	1	Multi	1500	2500
Male God of Night (Aztec)	NI	JL/NI	1990	WC	22 X 30	MASA	50	Multi	350	450
Cat Colossus (Aztec)	NI	JL/NI	1990	WC	21 X 22	MASA	50	Multi	350	450
En Su Interior (Set of 10)	AAFA	XP/NI	1993	LC	24 X 32 EA	AL/BL	75 EA	9 EA	4000 SET	8000 SET
En Su Interior, State I	AAFA	XP/NI	1993	LC	24 X 32	AL/BL	75	9	450	900
En Su Interior, State II	AAFA	XP/NI	1993	LC	24 X 32	AL/BL	35	6	300	600

DONALD STOLTENBERG

BORN: Milwaukee, WI; October 15, 1927
EDUCATION: Inst of Design, Chicago, IL, BS, 1948–53
TEACHING: Inst of Design, Chicago, IL, 1952; Instr, Painting & Printmaking, DeCordova Mus Sch, Lincoln, MA, 1957–74; Vis Critic, Rhode Island Sch of Design, Providence, RI
AWARDS: Grand Prize, Boston Arts Inst, MA, 1957; First Prize, Printmaking, Am Watercolor Soc; Fel, Am Sch of Marine Arts; Award, New England Watercolor Sch
COLLECTIONS: Mus of Fine Arts, Boston, MA; Addison Gallery of Am Art, Andover, MA; DeCordova Mus, Lincoln, MA; Portland Mus of Art, ME
PRINTERS: Artist (ART)
PUBLISHERS: Ronbie, Inc, PA (R); Artist (ART)
GALLERIES: Associated American Artists, New York, NY
MAILING ADDRESS: 947 Satucket Rd, RD #1, Brewster, MA 02631

TITLE	PUBLISHER	PRINTER	DATE	MEDIUM	DIMENSION (PAPER SIZE) IN INCHES	TYPE OF PAPER	EDITION NUMBER	NO. OF COLORS	ORIGINAL OPENING PRICE	CURRENT RETAIL PRICE
SOLD OUT EDITIONS (RARE):										
Drawbridges	ART	ART	1977	COL	17 X 22	AP	100	4	150	450
Tall Ships	ART	ART	1977	COL	23 X 14	AP	150	4	150	400
Sails in the Wind	ART	ART	1978	COL	20 X 31	AP	100	3	250	500
Shipyard	ART	ART	1977	COL	18 X 22	AP	100	4	160	400
Central Station	ART	ART	1979	COL	14 X 24	AP	100	3	175	400
Rail Bridge	ART	ART	1979	COL	24 X 36	AP	100	4	300	500
Airliner	ART	ART	1979	COL	12 X 20	AP	150	3	150	400
Barn	ART	ART	1980	COL	14 X 18	AP	100	3	150	400

TODD STONE

BORN: New York, NY; 1951
EDUCATION: Wesleyan Univ, Macon, GA; Univ of New Mexico, Albuquerque, NM
TEACHING: Nat Endowment for the Arts Fel
PRINTERS: Atelier Ettinger, Inc, NY (AE); Chip Elwell, NY (CE)
PUBLISHERS: Fred Dorfman, Inc, NY (FDI)
GALLERIES: Fred Dorfman Gallery, New York, NY; Robinson Contemporary Arts, New York, NY

TODD STONE CONTINUED

TITLE	PUBLISHER	PRINTER	DATE	MEDIUM	DIMENSION (PAPER SIZE) IN INCHES	TYPE OF PAPER	EDITION NUMBER	NO. OF COLORS	ORIGINAL OPENING PRICE	CURRENT RETAIL PRICE
SOLD OUT EDITIONS (RARE):										
Passage I, II, III	FDI	AE	1979	LC	38 X 28 EA	AP	275 EA	5–9 EA	200 EA	500 EA
CURRENT EDITIONS:										
Shift I-VI (Set of 6)	FDI	CE	1980	PO	30 X 24 EA	AP	50 EA	7–8 EA	1400 SET	2200 SET
									300 EA	450 EA
Florida Series (Set of 4):									1000 SET	1500 SET
Butternut Banks	FDI	CE	1981	PO	22 X 30	AP	50		300	450
Coral Reef Wash	FDI	CE	1981	PO	22 X 30	AP	50		300	450
Blackwater Sound	FDI	CE	1981	PO	22 X 30	AP	50		300	450
Turtle Shoals	FDI	CE	1981	PO	22 X 30	AP	50		300	450

FRED STONEHOUSE

BORN: Milwaukee, WI; 1960
EDUCATION: Univ of Wisconsin, Milwaukee, WI, BFA, 1982
RECENT EXHIB: Artemisia Gallery, Chicago, IL, 1987; Michael H Lord Gallery, Milwaukee, WI, 1988; Thomas Barry Fine Art, Minneapolis, MN, 1989; Pence Gallery, Los Angeles, CA, 1990; Center for Contemp Art, Chicago, IL, 1988,90
PRINTERS: Bill Weege, Madison, WI (BW); Andrew Rubin, Madison, WI (AR); Tandem Press, Univ of Wisconsin, Madison, WI (TanPr)
PUBLISHERS: Tandem Press, Univ of Wisconsin, Madison, WI (TanPr)
GALLERIES: CCA Gallery, Chicago, IL; Dean Jensen Gallery, Minneapolis, MN; Artemisia Gallery, Chicago, IL; Michael H Lord Gallery, Milwaukee, WI; Pence Gallery, Los Angeles, CA; Thomas Barry Fine Art, Minneapolis, MN

Fred Stonehouse
Untitled (Red/Yellow Duck)
Courtesy Tandem Press

TITLE	PUBLISHER	PRINTER	DATE	MEDIUM	DIMENSION (PAPER SIZE) IN INCHES	TYPE OF PAPER	EDITION NUMBER	NO. OF COLORS	ORIGINAL OPENING PRICE	CURRENT RETAIL PRICE
CURRENT EDITIONS:										
Series of 47 Untitled Monoprints	TanPr	BW/AR/TanPr	1991	MON	Varies	AC/W	1 EA	Varies	300/600	300/600
Untitled (Red/Yellow Duck)	TanPr	BW/AR/TanPr	1991	WC/REL	24 X 23	TRP/AP-W	5	3	600	600
Untitled (Black Duck)	TanPr	BW/AR/TanPr	1991	WC/REL	24 X 23	AP/B	5	3	600	600

INEZ STORER

BORN: Santa Monica, CA; October 11, 1933
EDUCATION: San Francisco Col for Women, CA, AA, 1953; Univ of California, Berkeley, CA, 1953–54; San Francisco Art Inst, CA, 1955, with Nathan Oliviera; Dominican Col, San Rafael, CA, BA, 1970; California State Univ, San Francisco, CA, MA, 1971
TEACHING: Instr, Col of Martin, Kentfield, CA, 1969–79; Lectr, San Francisco State Univ, CA, 1970–72; Instr, Univ of California, Santa Cruz, CA, 1976; Vis Art, Univ of California, Davis, CA, 1980; Prof, Painting, California State Col, CA, 1976–82; San Francisco Art Inst, CA, 1983 to present

RECENT EXHIB: Olga Dollar Gallery, San Francisco, CA, 1992; Nina Frost Gallery, Santa Monica, CA, 1992
COLLECTIONS: Oakland Mus of Art, CA; Univ of California, Davis, CA
PRINTERS: Smith Andersen Gallery, Palo Alto, CA (SA)
PUBLISHERS: Smith Andersen Gallery, Palo Alto, CA (SA)
GALLERIES: Thomas Babeor Gallery, La Jolla, CA; William Sawyer Gallery, San Francisco, CA; Smith Andersen Gallery, Palo Alto, CA; Olga Dollar Gallery, San Francisco, CA; Nina Frost Gallery, Santa Monica, CA; San Francisco Museum of Modern Art, Rental Gallery, CA
MAILING ADDRESS: P O Box 117, Inverness, CA 94937

TITLE	PUBLISHER	PRINTER	DATE	MEDIUM	DIMENSION (PAPER SIZE) IN INCHES	TYPE OF PAPER	EDITION NUMBER	NO. OF COLORS	ORIGINAL OPENING PRICE	CURRENT RETAIL PRICE
SOLD OUT EDITIONS (RARE):										
Window Series	SA	SA	1982	MON	Varies	HMP	1 EA		450 EA	750 EA
Handerchief Series	SA	SA	1982	MON	Varies	HMP	1 EA		600 EA	900 EA
Series D^2	SA	SA	1982	MON	Varies	HMP	1 EA		700 EA	1000 EA
Lisa	SA	SA	1982	MON	30 X 38 EA	HMP	1 EA		800 EA	1200 EA

The retail prices of the 100,000 limited edition prints quoted in this directory are subject to change. Print publishers, artists and galleries were the direct sources for these quotations. Prices in the secondary market listed as "Sold Out Editions (Rare)" indicate that the publisher has a limited supply of that print or that the print is difficult to locate in the galleries.

DAVID STOREY

BORN: Madison, WI; 1948
EDUCATION: Univ of California, Berkeley, CA, 1966–68; Univ of California, Davis, CA, CA, BA, 1970, MFA, 1972
AWARDS: New York State Found Arts Grant, 1989; Nat Endowment for the Arts, 1991
RECENT EXHIB: Lino Silverstein Gallery, Barcelona, Spain, 1989; Davis/McClain Gallery, Houston, TX 1990; Zimmerli Art Mus, Rutgers Univ, NJ 1990; Mus of Fine Arts, Boston, MA, 1990; Betsy Senior Contemp Prints, NY, 1991; Paula Cooper Gallery, NY, 1991; Hirsch & Adler Modern, NY, 1987,91,92

PRINTERS: Jane Kent, NY (JK); Maurice Sanchez, NY (MS); Derriére L'Etoile Studios, NY (DES); Grenfell Press, NY (GrPr)
PUBLISHERS: Jane Kent, NY (JK); Derriére L'Etoile Studios, NY (DES); Artist (ART); Grenfell Press, NY (GrPr)
GALLERIES: Jay Gorney Modern Art, New York, NY; Hirschl & Adler Modern, New York, NY; Davis/McClain Gallery, Houston, TX; Echo Press, Bloomington, IN; Lino Silverstein Gallery, Barcelona, Spain; Betsy Senior Contemporary Prints, New York, NY; Jorge Albero Arte Contemporary, Madrid, Spain
MAILING ADDRESS: 134 W Broadway, New York, NY 10013

TITLE	PUBLISHER	PRINTER	DATE	MEDIUM	DIMENSION (PAPER SIZE) IN INCHES	TYPE OF PAPER	EDITION NUMBER	NO. OF COLORS	ORIGINAL OPENING PRICE	CURRENT RETAIL PRICE
CURRENT EDITIONS:										
Untitled	JK	JK	1985	DPT/ENG/MEZ	26 X 22	R/BFK	15	2	350	600
Untitled	JK/ART	JK	1985		15 X 11	R/BFK		4	300	600
Monotype Series:										
Black & White	DES/ART	MS/DES	1987	MON	32 X 24 EA	Varies	1 EA	Varies	1200 EA	1800 EA
Color	DES/ART	MS/DES	1987	MON	32 X 24 EA	Varies	1 EA	Varies	1500 EA	2000 EA
Series III, Proof II	DES/ART	MS/DES	1987	MON	37 X 24 EA	Varies	1 EA	Varies		
Mars & Mars	GrPr	GrPr	1989	LI	28 X 18					
Mars & Mars	GrPr	GrPr	1989	LI	28 X 18					

HAL STOWERS

BORN: Dallas, TX; February 13, 1944
EDUCATION: Univ of Florida, Gainesville, FL, BA, Landscape Architecture; Univ of California, Berkeley, CA, MA, Landscape Architecture; Printmaking Studies, Univ of South Florida, Tampa, FL
COLLECTIONS: Williams Col, Williamstown, MA; Millikin Univ, Decatur, IL; St Louis Com Col, MO; Grunwald Center for the Graphic Arts, Univ of California, Los Angeles, CA; Lemoyne Art Found, Tallahassee, FL; Marine Science Center Coll, Clearwater, FL

PUBLISHERS: Happy Bayou Editions, Crystal Beach, FL (HBE); Topaz Editions, Inc, Tampa, FL (TE)
PRINTERS: Julio Juristo, Tampa, FL (JJ); Topaz Editions, Inc, Tampa, FL (TE); Ernest DeSoto, San Francisco, CA (EDS); DeSoto Workshop, San Francisco, CA (DSW); Ron Kraver, Crystal Beach, FL (RK); Happy Bayou Press, Crystal Beach, FL (HBP)
GALLERIES: Walking Tree, Inc, Palm Harbor, FL; Happy Bayou Editions, Crystal Beach, FL
MAILING ADDRESS: P O Box 468, Crystal Beach, FL 34256

TITLE	PUBLISHER	PRINTER	DATE	MEDIUM	DIMENSION (PAPER SIZE) IN INCHES	TYPE OF PAPER	EDITION NUMBER	NO. OF COLORS	ORIGINAL OPENING PRICE	CURRENT RETAIL PRICE
SOLD OUT EDITIONS (RARE):										
Islands (Set of 3):										
Moonshine & Caladesi at Big Pass	HBE	JJ/TE	1985	LB/HC	23 X 30	AC/W	40	1	625	2000
Honeymoon, North Point	HBE	JJ/TE	1985	LB/HC	23 X 30	AC/W	40	1	625	2000
Anclote Key from Three Rookery	HBE	JJ/TE	1985	LB/HC	23 X 30	AC/W	40	1	625	2000
Sun Dance	HBE	JJ/TE	1985	LC/HC	15 X 19	AC/W	250	2	300	700
Sun Time	HBE	JJ/TE	1986	LC/HC	23 X 30	AC/W	75	2	1250	2800
CURRENT EDITIONS:										
Wild (Set of 6):										
Sea Oats Fulltide	HBE	EDS/DSW	1979	LC/HC	23 X 30	AC/W	60	6	325	1500
California Pacific	HBE	EDS/DSW	1979	LC/HC	23 X 30	AC/W	60	6	325	600
Grand Tetons at Jackson Hole	HBE	EDS/DSW	1979	LC/HC	23 X 30	AC/W	60	6	325	600
Sonoran Saguaro	HBE	EDS/DSW	1979	LC/HC	23 X 30	AC/W	60	6	325	600
Boulder Creek	HBE	EDS/DSW	1979	LC/HC	23 X 30	AC/W	60	6	325	600
Shangri-La	HBE	EDS/DSW	1979	LC/HC	23 X 30	AC/W	60	6	325	600
Flight after Glow	HBE	JJ/TE	1982	EB/A/HC	19 X 15	AC/W	60	1	350	700
Anchorages I (Set of 4):										
Anclote Key Anchorage	HBE	JJ/TE	1984	LB/HC	23 X 30	AC/W	40	1	625	2000
Point Ybel-Sanibel	HBE	JJ/TE	1984	LB/HC	23 X 30	AC/W	40	1	625	1800
Little Shark River	HBE	JJ/TE	1984	LB/HC	23 X 30	AC/W	40	1	625	1800
Big Spanish Channel-The Keys	HBE	JJ/TE	1984	LB/HC	23 X 30	AC/W	40	1	625	1800
View from My Window	HBE	RK/HBP	1986	EB/A/HC	30 X 23	AC/W	60	1	1250	1800
Boca Grande Pass	HBE	JJ/TE	1986	LC/HC	22 X 30	AC/W	60	6	1250	1800

PAUL STRAND

PRINTERS: Richard Benson, Newport, RI (RB)

PUBLISHERS: Michael Hoffman, NY (MH)
GALLERIES: Weston Gallery, Carmel, CA; Zabriskie Gallery, New York, NY; Allan Frumkin Gallery Photographs, Chicago, IL; Jill Quasha Gallery, New York, NY

TITLE	PUBLISHER	PRINTER	DATE	MEDIUM	DIMENSION (PAPER SIZE) IN INCHES	TYPE OF PAPER	EDITION NUMBER	NO. OF COLORS	ORIGINAL OPENING PRICE	CURRENT RETAIL PRICE
SOLD OUT EDITIONS (RARE):										
Portfolio I: On My Doorstep, 1914–1973 (Set of 11)	MH	RB	1976	PH		SGP	50 EA		10000 SET	25000 SET

PAUL STRAND CONTINUED

TITLE	PUBLISHER	PRINTER	DATE	MEDIUM	DIMENSION (PAPER SIZE) IN INCHES	TYPE OF PAPER	EDITION NUMBER	NO. OF COLORS	ORIGINAL OPENING PRICE	CURRENT RETAIL PRICE
SOLD OUT EDITIONS (RARE):										
Portfolio II: The Garden, 1957–1967 (Set of 6)	MH	RB	1976	PH		SGP	50 EA		6000 SET	15000 SET
Portfolio III (Set of 10)	MH	RB	1976–77	PH	Varies	SGP	100 EA		12500 SET	20000 SET
Portfolio IV (Set of 10)	MH	RB	1976–77	PH	Varies	SGP	100 EA		12500 SET	20000 SET

THOMAS J STRICKLAND

BORN: Keyport, NJ; December 28, 1932
EDUCATION: Newark Sch of Fine Arts, NJ; Am Art Sch, NY; Nat Acad of Fine Arts, NY
AWARDS: Blue Dome Art Fel, 1972; First Prize, Hollywood Art Mus, FL, 1973; Charles Hawthorne Mem Award, Nat Arts Club, 1977
COLLECTIONS: Hollywood Mus of Art, FL; Elliot Mus, Stuart, FL; Salem Col, NC; St Vincent Col, Latrobe, PA
PRINTERS: Artist (ART)
PUBLISHERS: Artist (ART)
MAILING ADDRESS: 2598 Taluga Drive, Miami, FL 33133

TITLE	PUBLISHER	PRINTER	DATE	MEDIUM	DIMENSION (PAPER SIZE) IN INCHES	TYPE OF PAPER	EDITION NUMBER	NO. OF COLORS	ORIGINAL OPENING PRICE	CURRENT RETAIL PRICE
SOLD OUT EDITIONS (RARE):										
Linda and Joshua	ART	ART	1978	LB	10 X 12		19	1	175	300
Deborah by the Pond	ART	ART	1978	LB	15 X 22		5	1	275	400
Girl by the Window	ART	ART	1978	LB	10 X 13		5	1	175	300
Cafe at Viscaya	ART	ART	1978	EB	9 X 12		30	1	125	200
Rendezvous	ART	ART	1978	LB	11 X 15		3	1	175	300
Cagnes Cafe	ART	ART	1978	EB	9 X 12		30	1	125	200
Mother and Child	ART	ART	1978	EB	6 X 8		30	1	100	200
Self Portrait	ART	ART	1981	EB	9 X 12		30	1	125	200
Nudes	ART	ART	1981	EB	9 X 12		30	1	125	200
Amsterdam Cafe	ART	ART	1981	EB	9 X 12		30	1	125	200

MARJORIE VIRGINIA STRIDER

BORN: Guthrie, OK
EDUCATION: Kansas City Art Int, MO; Oklahoma Univ, OK, BFA
TEACHING: Prof, Univ of Georgia, Athens, GA, 1972; Prof, Sculpture, Univ of Iowa, Iowa City, IA, 1972; Prof, Sculpture, Sch of Visual Arts, NY, 1968 to present
AWARDS: McDowell Colony Fel, 1973; Longview Found Grant, 1973; Nat Endowment for the Arts Fel, 1974,80–81; Pollock-Krasner Grant, 1990
COLLECTIONS: Albright-Knox Art Gallery, Buffalo, NY; Univ of Colorado, Boulder, CO; Wadsworth Atheneum, Hartford, CT; New York Univ, NY; Des Moines Art Ctr, IA; Hirshhorn Mus, Wash, DC; Guggenheim Mus, NY; Storm King Art Center, NY; Aldrich Mus of Contemp Art Mus, Ridgefield, CT
PRINTERS: Water Street Press, NY (WSP)
PUBLISHERS: Water Street Press, NY (WSP)
GALLERIES: Bernice Steinbaum Gallery, New York, NY
MAILING ADDRESS: 7 Worth St, New York, NY 10013

TITLE	PUBLISHER	PRINTER	DATE	MEDIUM	DIMENSION (PAPER SIZE) IN INCHES	TYPE OF PAPER	EDITION NUMBER	NO. OF COLORS	ORIGINAL OPENING PRICE	CURRENT RETAIL PRICE
SOLD OUT EDITIONS (RARE):										
Home of the Brave	WSP	WSP	1982	LC/SP/HC/CP/CO	22 X 30	ACP	150	Multi	450	600

EARL STROH

BORN: Buffalo, NY; 1924
EDUCATION: Art Inst of Buffalo, NY; Art Students League, NY; Univ of New Mexico, Albuquerque, NM; Atleier Friedlander, Paris, France; Worked with Andrew Dasburg & Tom Benrimo
TEACHING: Fort Worth Art Center; Univ of New Mexico, Albuquerque, NM
RECENT EXHIB: Univ of New Mexico, Harwood Found Mus, NY, 1992
COLLECTIONS: Metropolitan Mus of Art, NY; Art Inst of Chicago, IL; Dallas Art Mus, TX; Fort Worth Art Center, TX; Denver Art Mus, CO; Cincinnati Art Mus, OH; Minneapolis Art Inst, MN; Univ of New Mexico, Albuquerque, NM; Roswell Mus, NM
PRINTERS: Catherine Kuhn, Albuquerque, NM (CK); Tamarind Inst, Albuquerque, NM (TI)
PUBLISHERS: Tamarind Inst, Albuquerque, NM (TI)
GALLERIES: Mission Gallery, Taos, NM; Tamarind Inst, Albuquerque, NM; Valley House Gallery, Dallas, TX

Earl Stroh
Quiet Scherzo II
Courtesy Tamarind Institute

EARL STROH CONTINUED

TITLE	PUBLISHER	PRINTER	DATE	MEDIUM	DIMENSION (PAPER SIZE) IN INCHES	TYPE OF PAPER	EDITION NUMBER	NO. OF COLORS	ORIGINAL OPENING PRICE	CURRENT RETAIL PRICE
SOLD OUT EDITIONS (RARE):										
Edge of the Mesas I,II	TI	TI	1977	LC		SOM			250 EA	700 EA
Thracian Mode I	TI	TI	1979	LC					300	800
Thracian Mode II	TI	TI	1979	LC					250	400
Quiet Scherzo I	TI	CK/TI	1983	LC/CC	18 X 25	MASA/GE	40	5	400	900
Quiet Scherzo II	TI	CK/TI	1983	LC	18 X 25	SOM/CR	10	5	350	600

BRETT-LIVINGSTONE STRONG

BORN: Junee, Australia; October 31, 1953
PRINTERS: Moross Studio, Gardenia, CA (MSI); Weinman Hinte, Inc (WHI); Workshop Editions, Santa Monica, CA (WE); Arellanes Studios, Inc, San Rafael, CA (ASI)
PUBLISHERS: Gallery Rodeo, Inc, Beverly Hills, CA (GRI)
GALLERIES: Gallery Rodeo, Beverly Hills, CA & Lake Arrowhead, CA & Taos, NM
MAILING ADDRESS: c/o Gallery Rodeo, Inc, 421 North Rodeo Dr, Beverly Hills, CA 90210

TITLE	PUBLISHER	PRINTER	DATE	MEDIUM	DIMENSION (PAPER SIZE) IN INCHES	TYPE OF PAPER	EDITION NUMBER	NO. OF COLORS	ORIGINAL OPENING PRICE	CURRENT RETAIL PRICE
SOLD OUT EDITIONS (RARE):										
The World Friendship Collection (Set of 5):										
The Tree of Life	GRI	MSI	1988	SP	49 X 58	AP	300	155	1800	7500
Tranquility	GRI	WHI	1989	SP	36 X 48	AP	300	62	2300	6000
Emerald Rain Forest	GRI	WE	1990	SP	25 X 42	AP	300	90	2500	6000
Surreal Sea	GRI	WE	1990	SP	31 X 40	AP	300	60	2800	6000
Timeless	GRI	WE	1990	SP	31 X 40	AP	300	60	3000	5000
Seven Natural Wonders of the World (Set of 7):										
Guilin	GRI	ASI	1991	SP	32 X 30	AP	300	48	2150	4500
Niagara Falls	GRI	ASI	1992	SP	31 X 40	AP	300	40	2350	4500
Mt. Fuji	GRI	ASI	1992	SP	29 X 36	AP	300		4500	4500
Stonehenge	GRI	ASI	1992	SP	22 X 30	AP	300		4500	4500
CURRENT EDITIONS:										
Seven Natural Wonders of the World:										
Matterhorn	GRI	ASI		SP	25 X 40	AP	300		4500	4500
Victoria Falls	GRI	ASI	1993	SP	25 X 36	AP	300		4500	4500
Monument Valley	GRI	ASI	1993	SP	40 X 24	AP	300		4500	4500
Ayers Rock	GRI	ASI	1994	SP	24 X 30	AP	300		4500	4500

MICHELLE STUART

BORN: Borrego Springs, CA; February 10, 1940
EDUCATION: Chouinard Art Inst, Los Angeles, CA; Apprenticed to Diego Rivera, Mexico; New Sch for Social Research, NY
AWARDS: Guggenheim Found Fel, NY, 1975; Nat Endowment for the Arts, Ind Artist Awards, 1974,77,80; New York State Creative Artists Public Service Grants, 1975,86
RECENT EXHIB: van Straaten Gallery, Chicago, IL, 1988; Wadsworth Atheneum, Hartford, CT, 1988; Rose Art Mus, Brandeis Univ, Waltham, MA, 1988; Richmond Art Center, CA, 1989; Univ of Washington, Henry Art Gallery, Seattle, WA, 1989; Santa Barbara Contemp Arts Forum, CA, 1992; Long Island Univ, Hillwood Art Mus, Brookville, NY, 1992
COLLECTIONS: Allen Mem Art Mus, Oberlin Col, OH; Aldrich Mus of Contemp Art, Ridgefield, CT; Power Inst Mus, Sydney, Australia; Mus of Art, Univ of New Mexico, Albuquerque, NM; Landesmuseum, Graz, Austria; Mus of Mod Art, NY; Brooklyn Mus, NY; Walker Art Center, Minneapolis, MN; Nat Coll of Australia, Canberra, Australia; Moderna Museet, Stockholm, Sweden; Kaiser Wilhelm Mus, Krefeld, West Germany
PRINTERS: Printmaking Workshop, NY (PW); Pat Branstead, NY (PB); Sally Sturman, NY (ST); Aeropress, NY (A); Gary Day, Omaha, NE (GD); UNO Print Workshop, Omaha, NE (UNO)
PUBLISHERS: Diane Villani Editions, NY (DVE); Fawbush Editions, NY (FE); Artist (ART); Joslyn Art Mus, Omaha, NE (JAM); UNO Print Workshop, Omaha, NE (UNO)
GALLERIES: Printmaking Workshop, New York, NY; Max Protetch Gallery, New York, NY; David Saxon Gallery, Los Angeles, CA; Belles Artes, Santa Fe, NM; Diane Villani Editions, New York, NY
MAILING ADDRESS: 152 Wooster St, New York, NY 10012

TITLE	PUBLISHER	PRINTER	DATE	MEDIUM	DIMENSION (PAPER SIZE) IN INCHES	TYPE OF PAPER	EDITION NUMBER	NO. OF COLORS	ORIGINAL OPENING PRICE	CURRENT RETAIL PRICE
CURRENT EDITIONS:										
Correspondences Series:										
Correspondences: Time Connecticut, Fuchsia	ART/JAM/ UNO	GD/UNO	1983	LC	24 X 29	R/BFK/ROL	36	4	800	1000
Correspondences: Light Avebury, Wiltshire, England	ART/JAM/ UNO	GD/UNO	1983	LC	24 X 29	R/BFK/ROL	36	4	800	1000
Navigating Coincidence: Reflecting on the Voyages of Captain J S Cook (Set of 5)	ART	LR/JDA/PW	1987	I	22 X 30	R/BFK	33		3500 SET 800 EA	3500 SET 800 EA
Voyage to the South Seas (Set of 3):										5000 SET	6000 SET
Flora Australis	DVE	PB/SS/A	1989	EC/A/CC	26 X 33	FAB	40		1700	2000
Flora Iris	DVE	PB/SS/A	1989	EC/A/CC	26 X 33	FAB	40		1700	2000
Flora Otaheite	DVE	PB/SS/A	1989	EC/A/CC	26 X 33	FAB	40		1700	2000

JOCK STURGES

PRINTERS: David Hawes, Allentown, PA (DH)
PUBLISHERS: Paul Cava, Phila, PA (PC)

GALLERIES: Paul Cava Gallery, Phila, PA; Thomas V. Meyer Fine Art, San Francisco, CA; Camera Obscura Gallery, Denver, CO; Roger Ramsey Gallery, Chicago, IL; Robert Klein, Chicago, IL; Burden Gallery of Aperture, New York, NY; Charles Cowles Gallery, New York, NY; Butters Gallery, Ltd, Portland, OR

TITLE	PUBLISHER	PRINTER	DATE	MEDIUM	DIMENSION (PAPER SIZE) IN INCHES	TYPE OF PAPER	EDITION NUMBER	NO. OF COLORS	ORIGINAL OPENING PRICE	CURRENT RETAIL PRICE
CURRENT EDITIONS:										
Standing on Water (Set of 10)	PC	DH	1984–90	PH	24 X 20 EA		40 EA	1 EA	6500 SET	6500 SET

SALLY MARA STURMAN

BORN: Chicago, IL; September 2, 1953
EDUCATION: Univ of Hartford Art Sch, Hartford, CT, Painting, Drawing, 1971; Univ of Michigan Art Sch, Drawing, 1971–73; Ecole des Beaux Arts Superiore, Lithography, 1976; Atelier 17, Etching with S W Hayter, 1976; Rhode Island Sch of Design, Providence, RI, BFA, 1976

AWARDS: Creative Artists Public Service Grant, 1981–82
PRINTERS: Artist (ART)
PUBLISHERS: Diane Villani Editions, NY (DVE)
GALLERIES: Diane Villani Editions, New York, NY
MAILING ADDRESS: 200 W 16th St, Apt 8A, New York, NY 10011

TITLE	PUBLISHER	PRINTER	DATE	MEDIUM	DIMENSION (PAPER SIZE) IN INCHES	TYPE OF PAPER	EDITION NUMBER	NO. OF COLORS	ORIGINAL OPENING PRICE	CURRENT RETAIL PRICE
SOLD OUT EDITIONS (RARE):										
Tulips	DVE	ART	1981	AC	31 X 30	AP	35	4	400	500
Night Table	DVE	ART	1982	A/SG/SB	30 X 33	AC	25		400	500

EUGENE STURMAN

BORN: New York, NY; January 28, 1945
EDUCATION: Alfred Univ, BA, 1967; Univ of New Mexico, MA, 1969; Tamarind Lithograph Workshop, 1970
TEACHING: Instr, Printmaking, Painting & Drawing, Long Beach State Univ, 1972–74; Lectr, Univ of California, Los Angeles, CA, 1974; Inst, Otis-Parsons Sch of Design, CA, 1984
AWARDS: Michael Levins Award, Alfred Univ, 1966; New Talent Award, Los Angeles County Mus, CA, 1974; Nat Endowment for the Arts Grant, 1975

RECENT EXHIB: Mount St Mary's Col, Jose Drudis-Biada Art Gallery, Los Angeles, CA, 1989
COLLECTIONS: Newport Harbor Mus, CA; Los Angeles County Mus, CA
PRINTERS: Jean Milant, Los Angeles, CA (JM); James Allen, Los Angeles, CA (JA); Cirrus Editions Workshop, Los Angeles, CA (CEW)
PUBLISHERS: Cirrus Editions, Ltd, Los Angeles, CA (CE)
GALLERIES: Cirrus Editions, Ltd, Los Angeles, CA; Koplin Gallery, Los Angeles, CA
MAILING ADDRESS: Otis Parsons Sch of Design, 2401 Wilshire Blvd, Los Angeles, CA 90057

TITLE	PUBLISHER	PRINTER	DATE	MEDIUM	DIMENSION (PAPER SIZE) IN INCHES	TYPE OF PAPER	EDITION NUMBER	NO. OF COLORS	ORIGINAL OPENING PRICE	CURRENT RETAIL PRICE
SOLD OUT EDITIONS (RARE):										
Quadrant Series #I-IV	CE	JA/JM/CEW	1977	SP	23 X 30 EA	AC	50 EA	4/5 EA	800 SET	3000 SET
									200 EA	850 EA

GEORGE SUGARMAN

BORN: New York, NY; May 11, 1912
EDUCATION: City Univ of New York, NY, BA; Atelier Zadkine, Paris, France, 1951
TEACHING: Assoc Prof, Sculpture, Hunter Col, NY, 1960–70; Vis Prof, Sculpture, Yale Univ, New Haven, CT, 1967–68
AWARDS: Pittsburgh Inst, PA, 1961–62; Longview Found Grants, 1961–63; Nat Art Council Award, 1966

COLLECTIONS: Walker Art Center, Minneapolis, MN; Kunstmuseum, Zurich, Switzerland; Mus of Mod Art, NY; Whitney Mus of Am Art, NY; Chicago Art Inst, IL
PRINTERS: Exeter Press, NY (EP); 3EP Ltd, Palo Alto, CA (3EP); Berghoff-Cowden Studio, Tampa, FL (B-CS)
PUBLISHERS: 724 Prints, NY (724P); 3EP Ltd, Palo Alto, CA (3EP); Berghoff-Cowden Editions, Tampa, FL (B-CEd)
GALLERIES: Robert Miller, New York, NY; Ingber Gallery, New York, NY; Tavelli Gallery, Aspen, CO
MAILING ADDRESS: 21 Bond St, New York, NY 10012

TITLE	PUBLISHER	PRINTER	DATE	MEDIUM	DIMENSION (PAPER SIZE) IN INCHES	TYPE OF PAPER	EDITION NUMBER	NO. OF COLORS	ORIGINAL OPENING PRICE	CURRENT RETAIL PRICE
SOLD OUT EDITIONS (RARE):										
Yin Seed	SSW	SSW	1979	WC	13 X 17	SOM	20	4	250	600
Sky Spirit	SSW	SSW	1979	WC	8 X 19	SOM	20	3	300	600
Woman	SSW	SSW	1979	WC	9 X 11	SOM	25	3	250	600
Air Image	SSW	SSW	1979	WC	10 X 16	SOM	17	2	250	600
Pre Birth	SSW	SSW	1980	WC	15 X 18	SOM	30	2	300	600
Woman/Child	SSW	SSW	1980	WC	8 X 17	SOM	15	3	300	600
Blue Rock Figure	SSW	SSW	1980	WC	9 X 12	SOM	16	4	350	600
Woman/Children	SSW	SSW	1980	WC	8 X 15	SOM	17	3	300	600
Seated Man	SSW	SSW	1980	WB	12 X 16	SOM	25	1	250	600
Anima Mundi	SSW	SSW	1981	WC	12 X 16	SOM	25	3	450	600
Spark	724P	EP	1981	CP	33 X 61 X 7	R/100	15	9	3800	5000
CURRENT EDITIONS:										
Storm over Tampa, State I	B-CEd	B-CS	1992	SP	16 X 27	LEN	8	1	2500	2500
Storm over Tampa, State II (5 Sheets)	B-CEd	B-CS	1992	SP	16 X 82	LEN	8	1	9500	9500
The Sun Divides	B-CEd	B-CS	1992	SP	23 X 29	LEN	20	2	3500	3500

GEORGE SUGARMAN CONTINUED

TITLE	PUBLISHER	PRINTER	DATE	MEDIUM	DIMENSION (PAPER SIZE) IN INCHES	TYPE OF PAPER	EDITION NUMBER	NO. OF COLORS	ORIGINAL OPENING PRICE	CURRENT RETAIL PRICE
CURRENT EDITIONS:										
Flat over Fold (Unique Folded Diptych Series)	B-CEd	B-CS	1992	SP	25 X 38 EA	LEN	6 EA	5 EA	12000 EA	12000 EA
The Accident	B-CEd	B-CS	1992	SP	22 X 30	LEN	24	1	2000	2000
Double Dance (Dipt)	B-CEd	B-CS	1992	SP	24 X 55	LEN	15	4	9000	9000
The Vanishing Landscape (Dipt)	B-CEd	B-CS	1992	SP	27 X 56	MUL	30	4	9000	9000
The Box (with Folded Construction)	B-CEd	B-CS	1992	SP/HC	25 X 28 & 10 X 15	LEN	30	2	8500	8500
Purple & White (Wall Sculpture) (Polychromed Aluminum)	B-CEd	B-CS	1992	MULT	42 X 44 X 9	ALUM	6	2	20000	20000
Yellow & White (Wall Sculpture) (Polychromed Aluminum)	B-CEd	B-CS	1992	MULT	41 X 29 X 12	ALUM	6	2	20000	20000

BILL SULLIVAN

BORN: Hartford, CT; September 10, 1942
EDUCATION: Silvermine Col of Art, New Canaan, CT, with Josef & Anni Albers, 1960–65; Grad Sch of Fine Arts, Univ of Pennsylvania, Phila, PA, MFA, 1968
AWARDS: Quirama, Inst de Integracion Cultural Medellin, Colombia, 1979; Ingram Merrill Found Fel, NY, 1981; Nat Endowment for the Arts Fel, 1989
RECENT EXHIB: Delaware Art Mus, Wilmington, DE, 1987; Parrish Art Mus, Southhampton, NY, 1987; Arts & Science Center, Nashua, NH, 1987; State Univ of New York, Art Gallery, New Paltz, NY, 1987; Hudson River Mus, Yonkers, NY, 1987; Lafayette Col, The Gallery, Williams Center for the Arts, Easton, PA, 1989; G W Einstein Gallery, NY, 1987,89; Susan Schreiber Gallery, NY, 1990; Tatistcheff Gallery, Santa Monica, CA, 1990
COLLECTIONS: Smith Col, Northampton, MA; Cleveland Mus, OH; Reading Public Mus, PA; Hudson River Mus, Yonkers, NY; Mus de Artes Graficas, Maracaibo, Venezuela; Mus de Antioquia, Medellin, Colombia; Mus de Bellas Artes, Maracaibo, Venezuela; Mus de Arte Moderno, Bogata, Colombia; Metropolitan Mus of Art, NY
PRINTERS: Ed O'Connell, NY (EOC); O'Connell Graphics, NY (OCG); Sheila Marbain, NY (SM); Maurel Studios, NY (MS); Sirocco Screenprints, NY (SirSc); Gin Louis, NY (GL); Lower East Side Printshop, NY (LESP); Bruce Cleveland, NY (BC); Cleveland Press, NY (CP); Hitoshi Nakazato, NY (HN); Univ of Pennsylvania, Phila, PA (UP); Roni Henning, NY (RH); Larry B Wright, NY (LBW); Artist (ART); Jason Rodrigues, NY (JR)
PUBLISHERS: London Arts, Inc, Detroit, MI (LAI); G W Einstein Company, Inc, NY (GWE); Orion Editions, NY (OE); John Szoke Graphics, Inc, NY (JSG); Committee for International Poetry, NY (CIP); Susan Schreiber Gallery, NY (SSG); Artist (ART); Tatistcheff Gallery, Inc, Santa Monica, CA (TGI)
GALLERIES: John Szoke Gallery, New York, NY; Tatistcheff Gallery, Santa Monica, CA
MAILING ADDRESS: 687 Eighth Ave, New York, NY 10036

TITLE	PUBLISHER	PRINTER	DATE	MEDIUM	DIMENSION (PAPER SIZE) IN INCHES	TYPE OF PAPER	EDITION NUMBER	NO. OF COLORS	ORIGINAL OPENING PRICE	CURRENT RETAIL PRICE
SOLD OUT EDITIONS (RARE):										
Weehawken Milonga (57 Variations)	GWE	SM/MS	1977	SP/PAS/HC	32 X 42 EA	STP	1 EA	Varies	300 EA	1000 EA
Monserrate (50 Variations)	ART	SirSc	1978	SP/PAS/HC	22 X 36 EA	STP	1 EA	Varies	350 EA	1000 EA
Weehawken Variations (43 Variations)	OE	ART	1981	PO/PAS/HC	22 X 36 EA	AC/B	1 EA	Varies	500 EA	1000 EA
Santa Marta Variations (14 Variations)	OE	ART	1982	PO/PAS/HC	24 X 40 EA	AP/BAP/W	1 EA	Varies	600 EA	1000 EA
Liberty Variations (35 Variations)	OE	EOG/OCG	1983	SP/PAS/HC	44 X 31 EA	STP	1 EA	Varies	650 EA	1000 EA
Turkish Twilight	CIP	GL/LESP	1983	SP	20 X 26	LEN	20		500	750
Harbor Variations (35 Variations)	OE	EOC/OCG	1984	SP/PAS/HC	30 X 44 EA	STP	1 EA	Varies	50 EA	1000 EA
Palisades Variations (40 Variations)	OE	RH	1985	SP/PAS/HC	30 X 44 EA	STP	1 EA	Varies	750 EA	1000 EA
View from Olona	SSG	LBW	1989	SP/HC	14 X 28	STP/W	10		1500	1500
CURRENT EDITIONS:										
Flowers	LAI	EOC/OCG	1982	SP	30 X 22	SOM	250	7	150	175
Columbian Gold	LAI	EOC/OCG	1982	SP	22 X 20	SOM	250	7	150	175
Harbor of Hope I-VI	OE	BC/CP-HN/UP	1985	EC/A	20 X 44 EA	R/BFK-AP/B	16 EA		450 EA	500 EA
Hudson Pines	JSG	LBW	1986	SP	30 X 44	STP/G	85	11	400	400
Islands (46 Variations)	JSG	LBW	1986	SP/PAS/HC	26 X 44 EA	STP	1 EA		625 EA	750 EA
Stony Creek Sunset (30 Variations)	JSG	LBW	1987	SP/CRAY/HC	30 X 44 EA	STP	1 EA		750 EA	900 EA
Santa Marta	JSG	LBW	1987	SP/HC	24 X 40	STP/W	30		600	750
Low Tide Variations	JSG	LBW	1988	SP/HC	30 X 40	STP/W	30		1000	1250
Cove Variations	JSG	LBW	1989	SP/HC		STP/W	25		900	900
Santa Monica Bay	TGI	JR	1990	SP/HC	18 X 36	STP/W	12	Varies	1800	1800
Metropolitan Sunset	JSG	JR	1992	SP/HC	27 X 26	STP/W	40	Varies	1250	1250

JIM SULLIVAN

BORN: Providence, RI; April 1, 1939
EDUCATION: Rhode Island Sch of Design, Providence, RI, BFA, Stanford Univ, CT, 1962–63
TEACHING: Prof, Painting, Bard Col, NY, 1965 to present
AWARDS: Fulbright Fel, 1961; Guggenheim Foundation Grant, 1972; Nat Endowment for the Arts Grant, 1983
RECENT EXHIB: Nancy Hoffman Gallery, NY, 1988,90,92
COLLECTIONS: Whitney Mus of Am Art, NY; Worcester Art Mus, MA; Albany State Mus, NY; Wadsworth Atheneum, Hartford, CT; Metropolitan Mus of Art, NY
PRINTERS: Judith Solodkin, NY (JS); Solo Press, NY (SP)
PUBLISHERS: 724 Prints, NY (724P)
GALLERIES: Nancy Hoffman, New York, NY
MAILING ADDRESS: 59 Wooster St, New York, NY 10013

JIM SULLIVAN CONTINUED

TITLE	PUBLISHER	PRINTER	DATE	MEDIUM	DIMENSION (PAPER SIZE) IN INCHES	TYPE OF PAPER	EDITION NUMBER	NO. OF COLORS	ORIGINAL OPENING PRICE	CURRENT RETAIL PRICE
CURRENT EDITIONS:										
Waiting Room-State I	724P	JS/SP	1981	LC	30 X 23	AP/W	20	2	500	750
Waiting Room (Pink)	724P	JS/SP	1981	LC	30 X 23	AP/W	20	2	500	750
Waiting Room (Green)	724P	JS/SP	1981	LC	30 X 23	AP/W	20	2	500	750

ALTOON SULTAN

BORN: Brooklyn, NY; September 29, 1948
EDUCATION: Brooklyn Col, NY, BA, 1969; MFA, with Phillip Pearlstein, 1971; Boston Univ, MA, Tanglewood, MA, 1969; Skowhegan Art Sch, ME, 1970
TEACHING: Vis Critic, Univ of Pennsylvania, Phila, PA, 1985–88; Res Faculty, Skowhegan Sch of Painting & Sculpture, ME, 1988
AWARDS: MacDowell Colony Fel, 1972,74; Yaddo Fel, 1975,76; Nat Endowment for the Arts Fel, 1983,89
RECENT EXHIB: Marlborough Gallery, NY, 1990
COLLECTIONS: Yale Univ Art Gallery, New Haven, CT; Hunter Mus of Art, Chattanooga, TN; Boston Mus of Fine Arts, MA; The American Mus, Bath, England; Newark Public Library, NJ; Princeton Univ Library, NJ; New Jersey State Mus, Trenton, NJ
PRINTERS: Eldindean Press, NY (EP)
PUBLISHERS: Eldindean Press, NY (EP)
GALLERIES: Mary Ryan Gallery, New York, NY; Associated American Artists, New York, NY; Marlborough Gallery, New York, NY; Adams-Middleton Gallery, Dallas, TX; Art Source Gallery, Los Angeles, CA; Solo Gallery, New York, NY; Hokin Galleries, Palm Beach, FL & Bay Harbor Island, FL; Tyler Graphics, Ltd, Mount Kisco, NY

TITLE	PUBLISHER	PRINTER	DATE	MEDIUM	DIMENSION (PAPER SIZE) IN INCHES	TYPE OF PAPER	EDITION NUMBER	NO. OF COLORS	ORIGINAL OPENING PRICE	CURRENT RETAIL PRICE
SOLD OUT EDITIONS (RARE):										
DS 1–8 (Set of 8)	EP	EP	1979	EC	18 X 18 EA	SOM	45 EA		100 EA	600 EA
Two Houses, Lunenberg, Nova Scotia	EP	EP	1982	EB/A/DPT	14 X 11	SOM/W	30	1	100	500
Picking Grapes, Greenport, LI, NY	EP	EP	1983	DPT	11 X 14	SOM/CR	30	1	100	500
CURRENT EDITIONS:										
Arched Portico, Catskill, New York	MG		1981	LB	21 X 31	AC	45	1	200	900
Gingerbread Porch, Ocean Grove, NY	EP	EP	1982	DPT	11 X 14	SOM/CR	35	1	100	300
Porch & House, Catskill, New York	EP	EP	1982	DPT	14 X 11	SOM/CR	30	1	100	300
Back Door, New York, NY	EP	EP	1982	EB/A	14 X 11	SOM/W	30	1	100	300
Woman by a Wall, Eleuthera, Bahamas	EP	EP	1983	DPT	11 X 14	SOM/CR	30	1	100	300
Long Island Farm, Peconic, LI, NY	EP	EP	1983	DPT	11 X 14	SOM/CR	30	1	100	300
House & Yard, Cutchogue, LI, NY	EP	EP	1983	DPT/A	11 X 14	SOM/W	30	1	100	300
Still Life with Calipers	EP	EP	1983	DPT/A	14 X 11	SOM/W	30	1	100	300
Wisteria, Orient, LI, NY	EP	EP	1983	DPT	11 X 14	SOM/CR	75	1	100	300
Bird & Gourds	EP	EP	1983	DPT	14 X 11	SOM/W	30	1	100	300
The Small Veranda	EP	EP	1984	DPT	11 X 14	SOM/W	30	1	150	500
Artist on the Road, Tachanic, NY	MG		1984	DPT	15 X 16	SOM/W	40	1	150	350
The Draughtsman in Siena, Italy	MG		1985	DPT	10 X 15	SOM/W	30	1	150	300
Village Green, South Royalton	MG		1986	EB/HC	15 X 24	SOM/W	40	Varies	200	600
Black and White Cows, Majorca, Spain	MG		1986	DPT	14 X 17	SOM/W	40		150	400
Blue Boat, Eleuthera, Bahamas	MG		1986	DPT/HC	15 X 24	SOM/W	40	Varies	300	600
Sheep Farm, Yorkshire, England	MG		1986	DPT	15 X 24	SOM/W	30		200	500
Road Between Walls	MG		1987	DPT/HC	21 X 29	SOM/W	50	Varies	300	600
Laundry Day, Cambridge, New York	MG		1988	DPT/HC	15 X 24	SOM/W	40	Varies	350	600
Maine Farmhouse, Skowhegan, Maine	SP	JS/SP	1989	LC	11 X 40	SOM/W	50		950	950
Roadside Farm, Cambridge, New York	SP	JS/SP	1989	LC	11 X 40	SOM/W	50		950	950
Hills and Cows, Gippsland, Victoria, Australia	SP	JS/SP	1989	LC	20 X 72	SOM/W	30		2800	2800
House and Hill, North Island . . .			1990	DPT/HC	17 X 27	SOM/W	30	Varies	750	750
Red Roofs, North Island . . .			1990	DPT/HC	27 X 37	SOM/W	30	Varies	1000	1000

DONALD K SULTAN

BORN: Asheville, NC; May 5, 1951
EDUCATION: Univ of North Carolina, Chapel Hill, NC, BFA, 1973; Chicago Art Inst, Sch of Art, IL, MFA, 1975
TEACHING: Creative Artists Public Service Award, 1978–79; Nat Endowment for the Arts Fel, 1980–81
AWARDS: Creative Service Public Service Grant, 1978–79; Nat Endowment for the Arts Grant, 1980
RECENT EXHIB: Sonoma State Univ Art Gallery, Rohnert Park, CA, 1987; Chicago Mus of Contemp Art, IL, 1987; Los Angeles Mus of Contemp Art, CA, 1987–88; Fort Worth Art Mus, TX, 1988; Brooklyn Mus, NY, 1988; Greenberg Gallery, St Louis, MO, 1989; Guild Hall Mus, East Hampton, NY, 1992; Asheville Art Mus, NC, 1992; Knoedler & Co, NY, 1992,93; Mus of Fine Arts, Houston, TX, 1993; Retrosp, Butler Inst of Am Art, Youngstown, OH, 1993–94
COLLECTIONS: Metropolitan Mus of Art, NY; Mus of Mod Art, NY; Albright-Knox Art Gallery, Buffalo, NY; Addison Gallery, Andover, MA; Dallas Mus of Fine Art, TX; San Francisco Mus of Mod Art, CA; Neuberger Mus, State Univ of New York, Purchasee, NY; Art Inst of Chicago, IL; Des Moines Art Center, IA; High Mus, Atlanta, GA; La Jolla Mus of Contemp Art, CA; Toledo Mus, OH; Australian Nat Gallery, Canberra, Australia; Kitakyushu Municipal Mus, Tobataku Kitakyushu, Japan; Solomon R Guggenheim Mus, NY; Art Inst of Chicago, IL

DONALD K SULTAN CONTINUED

PRINTERS: Imprimeris Arnéra, Vallauris, France (IA); Maurice Payne, NY (MP); Brenda Zlamany, NY (BZ); Joanne Howard, NY (JH); Jeryl Parker Editions, NY (JPE); Jo Watanabe, NY (JW); Katsumi Suzuki, NY (KS); Robert Meyer, NY (RM); Watanabe Studio, Brooklyn, NY (WS); Aldo Crommelynck, Paris, France (AC); Atelier Crommelynck, Paris, France (AtC)
PUBLISHERS: BlumHelman Gallery, NY (BH); Carmen Gimenez, Madrid, Spain (CG); Fawbush Editions, NY (FEd); Parasol Press, NY (PaP); Metropolitan Mus of Art, NY (MMA); Aldo Crommelynck, Paris, France (AC); Friedman/Krakow, Boston, MA (F/K); Jewish Mus, NY (JM); Brooklyn Mus, NY (BM); Paris Review, Paris, France (PR); BlumHelman Gallery, NY (BHG); Lincoln Center/List Print Program, NY, NY (LC/LPP)
GALLERIES: BlumHelman Gallery, New York, NY; Donald Young Gallery, Seattle, WA; Hans Strelow Gallery, Düsseldorf, Germany; Akira Ikeda Gallery, Tokyo, Japan; Barbara Krakow Gallery, Boston, MA; Fawbush Editions, New York, NY; Martina Hamilton & Associates, Inc, New York, NY; A Clean, Well-Lighted Place, New York, NY; Greenberg Gallery, St Louis, MO; Magnuson Gallery, Boston, MA; Marvin Ross Friedman Gallery, Miami, FL; Irene Drori Fine Art, Los Angeles, CA; Paula Matisse Fine Arts, Los Angeles, CA; Jonathan Novak Contemporary Art, Los Angeles, CA; John Berggruen Gallery, San Francisco, CA; Goodman/Tinnon Fine Art, San Francisco, CA; Graystone, San Francisco, CA; J J Brooklings Gallery, San Jose, CA; Richard Green Gallery, Santa Monica, CA; Rick Jones Modern & Contemporary Art, St Louis, MO; Jan Weiner Galleries, Kansas City, MO & Topeka, KS; Greene Gallery, Miami, FL; Kass/Meridian Gallery, Chicago, IL; Peter M David Gallery, Minneapolis, MN; Flanders Contemporary Art, Minneapolis, MN; C G Rein Galleries, Minneapolis, MN; Paul Kasmin Gallery, New York, NY; Knoedler & Company, New York, NY; Tomoko Liguori Gallery, New York, NY; Solo Gallery, New York, NY; Greg Kucera Gallery, Seattle, WA; Meredith Long & Company, Houston, TX
MAILING ADDRESS: 54 N Moore St, New York, NY 10013

Friedman/Krakow (F/K)

Donald Sultan
Freesias
Courtesy Aldo Crommelynck

TITLE	PUBLISHER	PRINTER	DATE	MEDIUM	DIMENSION (PAPER SIZE) IN INCHES	TYPE OF PAPER	EDITION NUMBER	NO. OF COLORS	ORIGINAL OPENING PRICE	CURRENT RETAIL PRICE
SOLD OUT EDITIONS (RARE):										
Moon Beam (F/K-1)	PaP		1982	LC	14 X 19	AP	30		500	5500
Yellow Iris, June I (F/K-15)	BHG		1982	WC/LI	16 X 11	RiEG	45	2	500	5000
Tramp Pictures—French Irises (Set of 3) (F/K-21-23)	BA/CG	IA	1982	LI	22 X 15 EA	ACW	15 EA	1 EA	1800 SET	35000 SET
Tramp Pictures—Cypresses and Stacks (Set of 5) (F/K-16-20)	BH/CG	IA	1982	LI	22 X 15 EA	ACW	15 EA	1 EA	1800 SET	35000 SET
Black Tulips (Set of 4) (F/K-24-27)	BH	MP	1984	AB	20 X 13 EA	AP/SSS	20 EA	1 EA	2000 SET	35000 SET
Black Lemon Suite (Set of 2):									6000 SET	80000 SET
Black Lemon, Nov 29, 1984	PaP	BZ/JH/JPE	1984–85	A/SB	63 X 44	SOM/S	7		3000	40000
Black Lemon, Dec 1, 1984	PaP	BZ/JH/JPE	1984–85	A/SB	63 X 49	SOM/S	7		3000	40000
Black Lemon, Dec 14, 1984 (F/K-29)	PaP	BZ/JH/JPE	1984–85	A/SB	62 X 47	SOM/S	10		3000	30000
Black Lemon, Nov 28, 1984 (F/K-28)	PaP	BZ/JH/JPE	1984–85	A/SB	62 X 47	SOM/S	10		3000	30000
Black Tulips and Lemons	JM		1986	AC	21 X 15	WOVE	54		3000	500
Black Lemon	PaP		1986	SP	40 X 28	AP88	100	2	3000	25000
Still Life with Pears and Lemons (Set of 3)	PaP	BZ/JH/JPE	1986	AC/LC/OFF	25 X 21	WOVE	45		10000 SET	50000 SET
Apples & Oranges	MMA	JW/KS	1987	SP	21 X 20	AP88	100	63	600	20000
Black Lemons and Egg, April 14, 1987	PaP	BZ/JH/JPE	1987	A/SB	63 X 49	WOVE	14		500	40000
Freesias (Set of 6):									10000 SET	45000 SET
Freesia I (April 18)	AC	AC/AtC	1987	EB/A/SB	20 X 20	AP88	40		1000	8000
Freesia II (April 16)	AC	AC/AtC	1987	EB/A/SB	20 X 20	AP88	40		1000	8000
Freesia III (April 15)	AC	AC/AtC	1987	EB/A/SB	20 X 20	AP88	40		1000	8000
Freesia IV (April 7)	AC	AC/AtC	1987	EB/A/SB	20 X 20	AP88	40		1000	8000
Freesia V (April 10)	AC	AC/AtC	1987	EB/A/SB	20 X 20	AP88	40		1000	8000
Freesia VI (April 16)	AC	AC/AtC	1987	EB/A/SB	20 X 20	AP88	40		1000	8000
Still Life with Peach	BM	BZ/JH/JPE	1987	SP	12 X 12	AP88	100		3500	10000
Black Lemon	PaP		1987	AC	40 X 30		75		3000	16000
Three Black Lemons	PaP	BZ/JH/JPE	1987	AB	62 X 48	HMP	14	1	7500	50000
Black Lemon	PaP	BZ/JH/JPE	1987	AB	40 X 29	HMP	75	1	5000	20000
Black Lemon, June 3, 1988	PaP	BZ/JH/JPE	1988	AB	62 X 47	HMP	10	1	7500	40000
Morning Glories	PaP	BZ/JH/JPE	1988	SP	12 X 12	HMP	100		3500	8000
Quinces	MMA	JW/KS	1988	SP	12 X 12	HMP	100		3500	8000
Female Series (Set of 10)	PaP	BZ/JH/JPE	1988	EB/A	21 X 15 EA	AP88	15 EA		25000 SET	75000 SET
Cherries	MMA	BZ/JH/JPE	1988	SP	12 X 12	AP88	100		3500	10000
Four Pears	MMA	BZ/JH/JPE	1989	SP	12 X 12	AP88	100		3500	10000
Peppers	PaP	BZ/JH/JPE	1989	SP	12 X 12	HMP	100		3500	8500
CURRENT EDITIONS:										
Black Roses (Set of 3)	ICE	TE	1989	AB	32 X 40 EA	HMP	53 EA	1 EA	20000 SET	25000 SET
Fish			1990	SP	22 X 23	HMP	125		2500	4000
Morning Glory I, II, III (Set of 3)			1990	EB/A	59 X 47 EA	HMP	60 EA		25000 SET	30000 SET
									10000 EA	12000 EA

DONALD K SULTAN CONTINUED

TITLE	PUBLISHER	PRINTER	DATE	MEDIUM	DIMENSION (PAPER SIZE) IN INCHES	TYPE OF PAPER	EDITION NUMBER	NO. OF COLORS	ORIGINAL OPENING PRICE	CURRENT RETAIL PRICE
CURRENT EDITIONS:										
Pomegranate I, II, III (Set of 3)			1990	EB/A	40 X 30 EA	HMP	60 EA		20000 SET	25000 SET
Fruit & Flowers (Set of 8):									7000 EA	9000 EA
Apples	PaP	RM/KS/WS	1990–91	SP	23 X 22	HMP	125	55	3000	4000
Pears	PaP	RM/KS/WS	1990–91	SP	23 X 22	HMP	125	35	3000	4000
Fish	PaP	RM/KS/WS	1990–91	SP	23 X 22	HMP	125	10	3000	4000
Flower	PaP	RM/KS/WS	1990–91	SP	23 X 22	HMP	125	42	3000	4000
Red Pear	PaP	RM/KS/WS	1990–91	SP	23 X 22	HMP	125	43	3000	4000
Tulips	PaP	RM/KS/WS	1990–91	SP	23 X 22	HMP	125	27	3000	4000
Holly Hocks	PaP	RM/KS/WS	1990–91	SP	23 X 22	HMP	125		3000	4000
Playing Cards (Set of 54)	ICE	TE	1991	AB	21 X 15 EA	HMP	44 EA	1 EA	35000 SET	35000 SET
Dominoes (Set of 29)	ICE	TE	1991	AB	21 X 15 EA	HMP	53 EA	1 EA	28000 SET	28000 SET
Untitled	LC/LPP	WS	1993	SP	30 X 30	LEN	108	26	2200	2200

CAROL SUMMERS

BORN: Kingston, NY; December 26, 1925
EDUCATION: Bard Col, NY, BA, 1951, PhD, 1975
TEACHING: Instr, Brooklyn Mus, Sch of Art, NY, 1954; Instr, Pratt Graphic Art Center, NY, 1962; Instr, Hunter Col, NY, 1963; Instr, Sch of Visual Arts, NY, 1965; Instr, Pennsylvania State Univ, University Park, PA, 1968; Columbia Univ, NY, 1969; San Francisco Art Inst, CA, 1973; US Info Service, Tour of India, 1974,1979
AWARDS: Guggenheim Fel, 1959; Fulbright Fel, 1959; Louis Comfort Tiffany Found Fel, 1955,61
COLLECTIONS: Brooklyn Mus, NY; Metropolitan Mus, NY; Mus of Mod Art, NY; Victoria & Albert Mus, London, England; Cornell Univ, Ithaca, NY; Philadelphia Mus, PA; Baltimore Mus, MD; Bradley Univ, Peoria, IL; Art Inst of Chicago, IL; Univ of Kentucky, Lexington, KY; Cincinnati Mus, OH; Los Angeles County Mus, CA; Nat Gallery of Art, Wash, DC; Univ of Tennessee, Knoxville, TN, Univ of Utah, Salt Lake City, UT; Univ of Seattle, WA; Univ of Minnesota, Minneapolis, MN; Univ of Nebraska, Omaha, NE; Corcoran Gallery of Art, Wash, DC; Kunstmuseum Malmö, Sweden

PRINTERS: Tamarind Inst Workshop, Albuquerque, NM (TI); Harry Westlund (HW); John Butke (JB); Artist (ART)
PUBLISHERS: Tamarind Inst, Albuquerque, NM (TI); Associated American Artists, NY (AAA); Artist (ART)
GALLERIES: Associated American Artist, New York, Pace Prints, New York, NY; Benjamin-Beattie Gallery, Chicago, IL; Editions Limited Gallery, Indianapolis, IN; Fernette's Gallery of Art, Des Moines, IA; Malton Gallery, Cincinnati, OH; Images Gallery, Toledo, OH; Davidson Galleries, Seattle, WA; Tamarind Inst, Albuquerque, NM; Randall Beck Gallery, Boston, MA; CCA Galleries, New York, NY; David Barnett Gallery, Milwaukee, WI; Stein Bartlow Gallery, Ltd, Chicago, IL; Gallery 72, Omaha, NE; Cable Gallery, San Diego, CA; Concept Art Gallery, Pittsburgh, PA; Joanne Chappell Gallery, San Francisco, CA; First Impressions/Barbara Linhard Gallery, Carmel, CA; Davidson Galleries, Seattle, WA
MAILING ADDRESS: 133 Prospect Ct, Santa Cruz, CA 95065

TITLE	PUBLISHER	PRINTER	DATE	MEDIUM	DIMENSION (PAPER SIZE) IN INCHES	TYPE OF PAPER	EDITION NUMBER	NO. OF COLORS	ORIGINAL OPENING PRICE	CURRENT RETAIL PRICE
SOLD OUT EDITIONS (RARE):										
Cockfight	ART	ART	1956	WC	11 X 18	AP	50		35	2000
Bon Appetit	ART	ART	1966	WC	8 X 7	JP	50		40	1000
The Dream of Constantine	ART	ART	1969	WC	36 X 37	AP	75		150	4000
Comet Over the Lower Falls of the Yellowstone	TI	HW/TI	1970–71	LC	104 X 74 cm	CD	17	4	250	2000
Comet Over the Lower Falls of the Yellowstone	TI	JB/TI	1970–71	LC	194 X 74 cm	CD	33	5	250	2000
Little Wolf's Last Camp	ART	ART	1977	WC	37 X 37	AP	100		300	2000
Starry Night	ART	ART	1979	WC	20 X 16	AP	250		200	2000
The Libiang	AAA	ART	1980	WC	25 X 27	HMP	150		200	2500
Gobyo	AAA	ART	1980	WC	18 X 18	HMP	150		175	2000
Basholi	ART	ART	1980	WC	25 X 37	HMP	125		200	2500
Krishna Steal the Gopis Clothes	ART	ART	1981	WC	37 X 37	HMP	100		300	3000
Family Portrait by the Sea	ART	ART	1981	WC	37 X 37	JP	100		300	3000
Ravanna Palace Burning	AAA	ART	1981	WC		HMP	125		175	2000
Delta	AAA	ART	1982	WC	20 X 16	HMP	150		200	2000
Pass 5420	ART	ART	1982	WC	12 X 12	HMP	250	10	175	1500
Monsoon	ART	ART	1982	WC	37 X 37	JP	100		300	3000

ANNE TUNIS SUMMY

BORN: Baltimore, MD
EDUCATION: Pennsylvania Acad of Fine Arts, Phila, PA; Inst of Allende, Mexico; Millersville State Col, PA; Edison Com Col, FL

COLLECTIONS: William Penn Mem Mus, Harrisburg, PA; Bloomsburg Col, PA; Franklin and Marshall Col, Lancaster, PA; Millersville State Col, PA; Edison Com Col, FL
PRINTERS: Artist (ART)
PUBLISHERS: Artist (ART)
GALLERIES: Foster Harmon Galleries, Sarasota, FL; The Gallery, Naples, FL

The Printworld Directory is accepting new applications for the seventh edition. Approximately 300 new artists will be accepted. Please use the two forms provided in the back section of this directory to submit biographical data and documentation of prints. Edition number of each print must not exceed 500 and the retail price must be $100 or more.

ANNE TUNIS SUMMY CONTINUED

TITLE	PUBLISHER	PRINTER	DATE	MEDIUM	DIMENSION (PAPER SIZE) IN INCHES	TYPE OF PAPER	EDITION NUMBER	NO. OF COLORS	ORIGINAL OPENING PRICE	CURRENT RETAIL PRICE
SOLD OUT EDITIONS (RARE):										
African Woman	ART	ART	1978	EB/A	9 X 18	R/BFK	100	1	75	200
Looking Glass	ART	ART	1978	EB/A	9 X 18	E/BFK	100	2	75	200
Robin's Nest	ART	ART	1979	ENG	9 X 12	R/BFK	100	3	50	200
First Born	ART	ART	1979	EB/A	18 X 12	R/BFK	50	2	75	200
Inner Circle	ART	ART	1979	ENG	12 X 11	R/BFK	50	2	60	200
Peninsula	ART	ART	1979	EB/A	20 X 12	R/BFK	75	2	100	200
November Landscape	ART	ART	1980	ENG	18 X 14	R/BFK	50	3	75	200
Solitude	ART	ART	1980	ENG	14 X 18	R/BFK	75	5	75	250
Gift from the City	ART	ART	1980	EB/A	18 X 16	R/BFK	75	2	100	250
End and Beginning	AKI	AKI	1980	ENG	12 X 12	R/BFK	100	4	75	250
City at Dusk	ART	ART	1981	ENG	18 X 12	R/BFK	100	7	100	250
Golden Orb	ART	ART	1981	ENG	16 X 18	R/BFK	100	1	125	200
Fragments	ART	ART	1981	ENG	12 X 17	R/BFK	75	3	100	200

GEORGE SUMNER

BORN: San Francisco, CA; April 29, 1940
EDUCATION: City Col, San Francisco, CA, 1961; San Francisco Art Inst, CA, 1962–63; Skyline Col, San Mateo, CA, 1966; Self-Taught
COLLECTIONS: Whale Mus, Friday Harbor, WA; Cal Poly Univ, San Luis Obispo, CA; Univ of Hawaii, Honolulu, HI
PUBLISHERS: Sumner Studios, Sausalito, CA (GS); John Brown Publications, San Francisco, CA (JBP); Equity Artfund Ltd, Greenwich, CT (EAL); Swanson Gallery, San Francisco, CA (S); Impress Graphics, Stamford, CT (IG)
PRINTERS: Robert Collins Lithography, San Francisco, CA (RCL); Impress Graphics, Stamford, CT (IG); Artist (ART)
GALLERIES: Aad Van Der Heyde Gallery, Morea, Tahiti; Barrington Gallery, Auckland, New Zealand; Lahaina Gallery, Maui, Hawaii; Swanson Gallery, San Francisco, CA; Artboard Gallery, Honolulu, Hawaii; Burke Gallery, Rutherford, San Carlos, Mexico; Saratoga Gallery, Saratoga, NY; Artworld, Stamford, CT; Connoiseur's Gallery, Honolulu, HI; Kahn Gallery, Kapaa, Kauai, HI & Kauai, HI; Coast Galleries, Big Sur, CA & Maui, HI; Wildlife Gallery, Mendocino, CA; Gallery San Francisco, CA; Ward Center Gallery, Honolulu, HI; Ocean Gallery, San Francisco, CA; Principally Prints, Onedota, NY; Illuninarium Gallery, Corte Madera, CA & Santa Monica, CA; Ingrid's Gallery, Los Altos, CA; Aqua Classics, Laguna Beach, CA; Chinook Winds, Seattle, WA
MAILING ADDRESS: Industrial Center Bldg, I C B #325, Gate Five Rd, Sausalito, CA 94965

TITLE	PUBLISHER	PRINTER	DATE	MEDIUM	DIMENSION (PAPER SIZE) IN INCHES	TYPE OF PAPER	EDITION NUMBER	NO. OF COLORS	ORIGINAL OPENING PRICE	CURRENT RETAIL PRICE
SOLD OUT EDITIONS (RARE):										
Mother & Baby	EAL	ART	1982	LC	25 X 38	AP	275	5	225	400
Canyon Lands	EAL	ART	1982	LC	25 X 38	AP	275	5	225	400
Red Abstract	EAL	ART	1982	LC	25 X 38	AP	275	5	225	400
Blue Abstract	EAL	ART	1982	LC	25 X 38	AP	275	5	225	400
Misty Waters	EAL	ART	1982	LC	25 X 38	AP	275	5	225	400

BARBARA ZEIGLER SUNGUR

BORN: London, ON, Canada; October 1, 1949
EDUCATION: Univ of Illinois, Champaign-Urbana, IL; Printmaking, BFA, MFA, Acad der Bildenden Kunst, Munich, Germany, 1969–70, 1971–73; Universitat Munchen, Munich, Germany, 1972
TEACHING: Univ of Illinois, Champaign-Urbana, IL; 1974–75; Univ of Alberta, Can, 1975–78; Nova Scotia Col of Art & Design, Can, 1978; Queen's Univ, Kingston, ON, Can, 1978–79; Univ of British Columbia, Can, 1979 to present
AWARDS: Ontario Arts Council Award, Canada, 1974
COLLECTIONS: Art Gallery of Ontario, Toronto, Canada; Laurentian Univ, Sudbury, ON, Canada; Univ of Guelph, Canada; Ontario Arts Council, Toronto, Canada; Art Gallery of Brandt, Brantford, Canada; Art Bank, Ottawa, Canada; Red Deer Col, Red Deer, Canada; Burnaby Art Gallery, Burnaby, Canada
GALLERIES: Gallery Pascal Graphics, Toronto, Canada
MAILING ADDRESS: 2959 W 20th St, Vancouver, BC, Canada V6L 1H6

TITLE	PUBLISHER	PRINTER	DATE	MEDIUM	DIMENSION (PAPER SIZE) IN INCHES	TYPE OF PAPER	EDITION NUMBER	NO. OF COLORS	ORIGINAL OPENING PRICE	CURRENT RETAIL PRICE
CURRENT EDITIONS:										
First Day of Spring	ART	ART	1973	I	24 X 36	AP	30	1	100	400
Earth Knows No Desolation...	ART	ART	1975	I	23 DIA	AP	30	1	125	400
By their Fruits Yes Shall Know them...	ART	ART	1975	I	24 X 30	AP	30	2	125	400
Saturday's Child	ART	ART	1976	I	17 X 20	AP	20	1	125	400
Sun Bathers	ART	ART	1976	I	17 X 20	AP	20	1	125	400
Perspectives	ART	ART	1976	I	24 X 30	AP	20	1	150	400
Separation	ART	ART	1977	LB	13 X 23	AP	11	1	150	400
Perspective #2	ART	ART	1978	LB/SP	19 X 20	AP	14	1	150	400
Hostess	ART	ART	1978	I/LB/SP	14 X 25	AP	15	1	150	400
Sweet Misery	ART	ART	1978	I	22 X 33	AP	20	1	150	400
Between Two Waves	ART	ART	1978	I	23 X 36	AP	20	1	150	400
Focus	ART	ART	1980	I	24 X 36	AP	10	1	200	400
The Blaring Twist of Time	ART	ART	1980	I	23 X 37	AP	15	1	200	400
Seascape	ART	ART	1980	I	10 X 23	AP	50	2	175	400
Anticipations	ART	ART	1980	I	11 X 23	AP	50	1	175	400

SARAH SUPPLEE

BORN: Laurel, MD; 1941
EDUCATION: American Univ, Wash, DC, BA, 1963; Univ of Iowa, Iowa City, IA, MA
RECENT EXHIB: Tatistcheff & Company, Inc, NY, 1989; Louis Newman Galleries, Los Angeles, CA, 1989
COLLECTIONS: DeCordova Mus, Lincoln, MA; Addison Gallery of Am Art, Andover, MA
PRINTERS: Patricia Branstead, NY (PB); Riverhouse Editions, Clark, CO (REd)
PUBLISHERS: Riverhouse Editions, Clark, CO (REd)
GALLERIES: Louis Newman Gallery, Beverly Hills, CA; Tatistcheff & Company, New York, NY

TITLE	PUBLISHER	PRINTER	DATE	MEDIUM	DIMENSION (PAPER SIZE) IN INCHES	TYPE OF PAPER	EDITION NUMBER	NO. OF COLORS	ORIGINAL OPENING PRICE	CURRENT RETAIL PRICE
CURRENT EDITIONS:										
Christiana's Pond	REd	PB/REd	1990	EC	22 X 48	SOM	50	6	1000	1200
Christiana's Pond (Sepia)	REd	PB/REd	1991	EC	22 X 48	SOM	20	5	900	900

GRAHAM SUTHERLAND

BORN: London, England; (1903–1980)
PRINTERS: Artist (ART)
PUBLISHERS: Artist (ART)
GALLERIES: James Marony Fine Art, New York, NY

TITLE	PUBLISHER	PRINTER	DATE	MEDIUM	DIMENSION (PAPER SIZE) IN INCHES	TYPE OF PAPER	EDITION NUMBER	NO. OF COLORS	ORIGINAL OPENING PRICE	CURRENT RETAIL PRICE
SOLD OUT EDITIONS (RARE):										
Barn Interior II	ART	ART	1923	DPT	6 X 8	LAID	25	1	20	4000
Number Forty-Nine	ART	ART	1924	EB	7 X 10	LAID	5	1	25	3000
Pecken Wood	ART	ART	1925	EB	5 X 7	LAID	85	1	25	7500
The Village	ART	ART	1925	EB	7 X 9	LAID	85	1	25	10000
Lammes	ART	ART	1926	EB	5 X 7	ANT	85	1	30	3000
St. Mary's Hatch	ART	ART	1926	EB	5 X 7	LAID	26	1	30	4500
May Green	ART	ART	1927	EB	5 X 6	LAID	92	1	30	2500
The Meadow Chapel	ART	ART	1928	EB	4 X 6	LAID	83	1	30	3000
Michaelmas	ART	ART	1928	EB	3 X 3	LAID	109	1	25	2000
The Garden	ART	ART	1931	EB	9 X 6	LAID/Blue	30	1	30	8000
Welsh Landscape...	ART	ART	1938	EB	8 X 6	LAID	1	1	30	1000
Folded Hills-Francis Quarles (Set of 3)	ART	ART	1943	LC		AP	4 EA		50	3000 SET
Portrait Somerset Maugham	ART	ART	1953	LC	9 X 6	AP			80	4000
Bees	ART	ART	1963	LC	25 X 20	AP	65		125	1500
Portrait of Aloys Senefelder	ART	ART	1971	LB	19 X 19	AP		1	200	2500
Primitive Hive I	ART	ART	1977	EB/A	16 X 12	R/BFK	80		225	2500
Bestiaire by Apollinare...	ART	ART	1979	EB/A	25 X 33	R/BFK	75		250	5000

SHARON E SUTTON

EDUCATION: Manhattan Sch of Music, NY, 1959–62; Univ of Hartford, Hart Col of Music, Batchelor of Music, CT, 1962–63; Parsons Sch of Design, NY, 1967–69; Columbia Univ Sch of Fine Art, Printmaking Workshop, NY, 1970–76; City Univ of New York, Grad Center, Dept of Environmental Psychology, Master of Philosophy, 1976–78; Hunter Col, NY, MA, Psychology, 1978–80; City Univ of New York, Grad Center, NY, PhD, Psychology, 1980–82
AWARDS: Nat Endowment for the Arts, Travel Award, 1970; Am Inst of Architects, Minority Scholarship, 1970; Metropolitan Applied Research Center Fel, 1970–71; William K Fellows Fel, Undergrad Travel Award, 1971; William K Fellows Fel, Grad Telephone Award, 1973; City Univ Grad Center, Grad Award, 1976–81; Danforth Grad Fel, Post-Baccalaureate Award, 1977–81; Pamela Galiber Mem Award Scholarship, 1981
COLLECTIONS: Smithsonian Inst, Wash, DC; Millersville State Col, PA; Orleans Parish Sch Board, New Orleans, LA
PRINTERS: Artist (ART)
PUBLISHERS: London Arts, Inc, Detroit, MI (LAI)
GALLERIES: London Arts, Inc, Detroit, MI
MAILING ADDRESS: 8071 Main St, Dexter, MI 48130

TITLE	PUBLISHER	PRINTER	DATE	MEDIUM	DIMENSION (PAPER SIZE) IN INCHES	TYPE OF PAPER	EDITION NUMBER	NO. OF COLORS	ORIGINAL OPENING PRICE	CURRENT RETAIL PRICE
CURRENT EDITIONS:										
I am Here in the World	LAI	ART	1981	SP	29 X 29	SOM	200	3	400	600

ZOLITA SVERDLOVE

BORN: New York, NY; February 21, 1936
EDUCATION: Art Students League, NY, 1949–52; Cooper Union Art Sch, NY, Certificate, 1953–56; Pratt Graphic Arts Center, Brooklyn, NY, 1967; Cooper Union Art Sch, NY, BFA, 1977
AWARDS: Purchase Prize, Purdue Univ, West Lafayette, IN, 1970; Purchase Award, Dallas Mus of Fine Arts, TX, 1972; Purchase Award, Marymount Col, Tarrytown, NY, 1974
RECENT EXHIB: Masters Gallery, San Diego, CA, 1988; Int Graphic Society, Sigma Gallery, NY, 1990; Connecticut Art Mus, Stamford, CT, 1990; Valley House Gallery, Dallas, TX, 1992
COLLECTIONS: Dallas Mus of Fine Arts, TX; Marymount Col, Tarrytown, NY; Toledo Mus of Art, OH; Purdue Univ, West Lafayette, IN
PRINTERS: Artist (ART)
PUBLISHERS: Los Angeles Printmaking Society, CA (LAPS)
GALLERIES: Valley House Gallery, Dallas, TX; Hooks-Epstein Gallery, Houston, TX; Allan Stone Gallery, New York, NY; Los Angeles Printmaking Society, Los Angeles, CA
MAILING ADDRESS: 1445 Indiana Ave, South, Pasadena, CA 91030

The Printworld Directory is accepting new applications for the seventh edition. Approximately 300 new artists will be accepted. Please use the two forms provided in the back section of this directory to submit biographical data and documentation of prints. Edition number of each print must not exceed 500 and the retail price must be $100 or more.

ZOLITA SVERDLOVE CONTINUED

TITLE	PUBLISHER	PRINTER	DATE	MEDIUM	DIMENSION (PAPER SIZE) IN INCHES	TYPE OF PAPER	EDITION NUMBER	NO. OF COLORS	ORIGINAL OPENING PRICE	CURRENT RETAIL PRICE
CURRENT EDITIONS:										
Motorcycle Hill	LAPS	ART	1982	EC	12 X 14	R/BFK	50	2	75	250

ROBERT SWAIN

BORN: Austin, TX; December 7, 1940
EDUCATION: American Univ, Wash, DC, BA
TEACHING: Prof, Fine Arts, Hunter Col, NY
AWARDS: Guggenheim Fel, 1969; Nat Endowment for the Arts Fel, 1976
COLLECTIONS: Albright-Knox Art Gallery, Buffalo, NY; Corcoran Gallery of Art, Wash, DC; Detroit Inst of Art, MI; Walker Art Ctr, Minneapolis, MN; Denver Art Mus, CO
PRINTERS: Artist (ART)
PUBLISHERS: Brand X, NY (BX)
GALLERIES: Nina Freudenheim Gallery, Buffalo, NY; Toni Birckhead Gallery, Cincinnati, OH
MAILING ADDRESS: 57 Leonard St, New York, NY 10013

TITLE	PUBLISHER	PRINTER	DATE	MEDIUM	DIMENSION (PAPER SIZE) IN INCHES	TYPE OF PAPER	EDITION NUMBER	NO. OF COLORS	ORIGINAL OPENING PRICE	CURRENT RETAIL PRICE
CURRENT EDITIONS:										
5 X 5–1	BX	ART	1981	SP	22 X 30	HMP	250	25	500	750

MARIUS SZNAJDERMAN

BORN: Paris, France; July 18, 1926; US Citizen
EDUCATION: Escuela de Artes Plasticas, Caracas, Venezuela, 1947–48; Columbia Univ, NY, BS, 1956; Teachers Col, Columbia Univ, NY, MFA, 1958
TEACHING: Sch of Visual Arts, NY, 1965–71; New York Univ, NY; Fairleigh Dickinson Univ, Madison, NJ, 1969–73; AIM & FSAA Programs, New Jersey (HEW Grant), 1975–77
RECENT EXHIB: Metro of Caracas, Venezuela, 1988; Mus of Contemp Hispanic Arts, NY, 1989; Corinne Timsit International Galleries, San Juan, PR, 1990; Mus of Contemp Art, Sofia Imber of Caracas, Caracas, Venezuela, 1991–92
COLLECTIONS: Mus of Mod Art, NY; Mus of Mod Art, Merida, Venezuela; Columbia Univ, NY; Fine Arts Mus, Caracas, Venezuela; Mus of Contemp Art, Bogota, Colombia; Nat Inst of Fine Arts, Mexico City, Mex; Yad Vashem, Jerusalem, Israel; Morris Mus, Morristown, NJ; Rayo Mus, Roldanillo, Colombia; Cincinnati Art Mus, OH; Nat Gallery, Caracas, Venezuela; Municipal Mus of Graphic Arts, Maracaibo, Venezuela; Fine Arts Center, Maracaibo, Venezuela; Mus of Contemp Hispanic Arts, NY; Bibliotheque Nat, Paris, France; Smithsonian Inst, Wash, DC; Mus of Mod Art, Cali, Colombia; New York Public Library, NY; Mus of Mod Art, Cartagena, Colombia; Contemp Art, Sofia Imber of Caracus, Venezuela; Yeshiva Univ Mus, NY; New Jersey State Mus, Trenton, NJ; Library of Congress, Wash, DC; Univ of Tel Aviv, Ramat Aviv, Israel; Jewish Heritage Mus, NY; Inst de Cultura Puertoriqueña, San Juan, PR
PRINTERS: Rafael Bogarin, NY (RB); Jorge Dumas, NY (Deceased) (JD); Atelier Dumas, NY (AD) (OB); Claudio Juarez, NY (CJ); Printmaking Workshop, NY (PW); Joseph Kleineman, Union City, NJ (JK); JK Fine Art, Union City, NJ (JKFA); Miguel Herrera, NY (MH); Atelier 2/20, NY (A2/20); Mackie/Damast, NY (M/D); Tangent Graphics, Hackensack, NJ (TG)
PUBLISHERS: AGPA Group Chicago, IL (AGPA); Carton de Venezuela, Caracas, Venezuela, (CV); Artist (ART)
GALLERIES: Kerygma Gallery, Ridgewood, NJ
MAILING ADDRESS: 242 Summit Ave, Hackensack, NJ 07601

Marius Sznajderman
Magicismo del 90, #1
Courtesy the Artist

Marius Sznajderman
Wedding Scene
Courtesy the Artist

TITLE	PUBLISHER	PRINTER	DATE	MEDIUM	DIMENSION (PAPER SIZE) IN INCHES	TYPE OF PAPER	EDITION NUMBER	NO. OF COLORS	ORIGINAL OPENING PRICE	CURRENT RETAIL PRICE
SOLD OUT EDITIONS (RARE):										
Balzac by Rodin	ART	ART	1972	WC	15 X 12	RICE	25	4	45	250
Blue Witch	ART	ART	1976	WC/HC	22 X 15	AP	20	4	60	300
Recordando	AGPA	PW	1978	WC	22 X 30	AC	150	2	200	500
L'Invitation au Voyage	CV	JD/AD	1982	LC	22 X 30	LEN	150	7	300	500
El Taller de Artista	AGPA	M/D	1986	SP	22 X 30	AC	150	10	300	500
CURRENT EDITIONS:										
Small Rodin B	ART	ART	1971	SP	20 X 26	AP	60	2	65	250

MARIUS SZNAJDERMAN CONTINUED

Marius Sznajderman
Taller del Artista
Courtesy the Artist

Marius Sznajderman
Magicismo del 90, #2
Courtesy the Artist

TITLE	PUBLISHER	PRINTER	DATE	MEDIUM	DIMENSION (PAPER SIZE) IN INCHES	TYPE OF PAPER	EDITION NUMBER	NO. OF COLORS	ORIGINAL OPENING PRICE	CURRENT RETAIL PRICE
CURRENT EDITIONS:										
Dances & Masks	ART	RB	1976	SP	22 X 30	AP	100	3	90	350
Homage to Oswaldo, No 1	ART	RB	1976	SP	22 X 30	AP	80	5	110	400
Homage to Oswaldo, No 2	ART	RB	1976	SP	22 X 30	AP	80	6	110	400
Caracas-Guanare Series, No 2	ART	RB	1977	SP	30 X 22	AP	70	3	90	350
Shawanwunk Mts (Mohonk)	ART	CJ	1980	WB	30 X 22	R/BFK	45	1	180	300
Zooming Bird	ART	CJ	1981	WB	22 X 30	R/BFK	45	1	180	300
Mizrach of Many Symbols	ART	CJ	1981	EB/ENG	22 X 30	R/BFK	45	1	180	300
Mizrach 82, No 1	ART	JD/AD	1982	LC	20 X 22	LEN/100	200	7	200	350
Mizrach 82, No 2	ART	JD/AD	1982	LC	22 X 30	LEN/100	125	4	160	300
Mohonk	ART	JD/AD	1982	LC	30 X 22	LEN/100	125	4	160	300
Commedia Dell'Arte	ART	JD/AD	1983	LC	23 X 27	LEN/100	125	10	220	400
The Balcony, No 1	ART	JD/AD	1983	LC	21 X 27	LEN/100	125	10	220	350
The Balcony, No 2	ART	JD/AD	1983	LC	21 X 27	LEN/100	125	10	220	350
The Balcony, No 3	ART	JD/AD	1984	LC	21 X 27	LEN/100	75	3	180	250
Grand Canyon	ART	CJ	1984	EB/A/ENG	22 X 30	R/BFK	20	1	180	350
Icarus	ART	JK/JKFA	1986	LC	22 X 30	AP	125	4	200	300
Ofrenda (Offering)	ART	TG	1988	LC/HC	20 X 29	AP	16	12	400	400
Model with Amaryllis and Chinelo	ART	TG	1988	LC/HC	22 X 30	AP	25	15	350	350
Elegy for my "Shtetl"	ART	JK/JKFA	1988	LC	22 X 30	AP	100	2	250	350
Landscape of the Mind	ART	JK/JKFA	1989	LC/HC	26 X 36	AP	24	9	400	500
Magicista	ART	MH/A2/20	1989	EB	22 X 30	AP	25	1	200	300
Magicismo del 90, #1	ART	MH/A2/20	1991	EB/A	22 X 30	SOM	12	1	400	400
Magicismo del 90, #2	ART	MH/A2/20	1991	EB/A	22 X 30	SOM	12	1	400	400
Wedding Scene	ART	TG	1991	LC/HC	22 X 30	AP	25	12	450	450
Landscape of the Mind (Magicismo) Stage Setting #1, #2	ART	MH/A2/20	1992	EB/A/HC	22 X 30 EA	SOM	16 EA	8 EA	450 EA	450 EA

WILLIAM JOHN TAGGART

BORN: Buffalo, NY; August 8, 1940
EDUCATION: Art Inst of Chicago, BFA; Univ of New Mexico, Albuquerque, NM, MFA
TEACHING: Instr, Cooper Union, NY, 1968–71; Vis Artist, Sch of Art Inst, Chicago, IL, 1978 to present; Instr, Montclair State Col, NY, 1977 to present
COLLECTIONS: Univ of New Mexico, Albuquerque, NM; Mus of Contemp Art, Chicago, IL
PRINTERS: American Atelier, NY (AA)
PUBLISHERS: Circle Fine Art, Chicago, IL (CFA)
GALLERIES: Circle Fine Art Galleries, San Diego, CA & San Francisco, CA & Northbrook, IL & Pittsburgh, PA & Houston, TX & Soho, NY & Chicago, IL & Scottsdale, AZ & Beverly Hills, CA & Costa Mesa, CA & Sherman Oaks, CA & Palm Beach, FL & Honolulu, HI & New Orleans, LA & Las Vegas, NV & Seattle, WA
MAILING ADDRESS: 429 Broome St, New York, NY 10013

TITLE	PUBLISHER	PRINTER	DATE	MEDIUM	DIMENSION (PAPER SIZE) IN INCHES	TYPE OF PAPER	EDITION NUMBER	NO. OF COLORS	ORIGINAL OPENING PRICE	CURRENT RETAIL PRICE
CURRENT EDITIONS:										
Spiral	CFA	AA	1980	SP	24 X 32	R/BFK	200		200	300

ERNESTINE TAHEDL

BORN: Vienna, Austria; October 12, 1940; Canadian Citizen
EDUCATION: Acad for Applied Art, Vienna, Austria, BA, MA, 1955–61
TEACHING: Acad for Applied Art, Vienna, Austria, 1961–63; Edmonton Art Gallery, Univ of Alberta, Can 1963–65
AWARDS: Bronze Medal, Vienna Int Exhib, Austria, 1963; Allied Arts Medal, Royal Arch Inst of Canada, 1966; Canadian Council of the Arts Award, 1967; Royal Canadian Acad of Arts, 1977

ERNESTINE TAHEDL CONTINUED

RECENT EXHIB: Metropolitan Mus, Tokyo, Japan, 1987; J Arends Gallery, Edmonton, Canada, 1987,88; Shayne Gallery, Montreal, Canada, 1988,89; Gallery Quan, Toronto, Canada, 1987,88,89,90,92
COLLECTIONS: Mus du Quebec, Can; Mendel Art Gallery, Saskatoon, Can; Art Gallery of London, Can; Ecole dex Beaux Arts, Montpellier, France; Cultural Centre of Vienna, Austria; Public Gallery of El Salvador, San Salvador; Art Gallery of Hamilton, Ont, Can; Govt of Alberta, Edmonton, Can

PRINTERS: Artist (ART)
PUBLISHERS: Artworld Int, Victoria, BC, Can (AI); Artist (ART)
GALLERIES: Lefebvre Galleries, Edmonton, Canada; Artworld International, Victoria, Canada; Arends Galleries Ltd, Edmonton, Canada; Shayne Gallery, Montreal, Canada; Estampe Pluse, Quebec, Canada; Jean Lumbard Fine Arts, New York, NY; Gallery Quan, Toronto, Canada
MAILING ADDRESS: 79 Collard Dr, RR 1, King City, ON, Canada L0G IK0

TITLE	PUBLISHER	PRINTER	DATE	MEDIUM	DIMENSION (PAPER SIZE) IN INCHES	TYPE OF PAPER	EDITION NUMBER	NO. OF COLORS	ORIGINAL OPENING PRICE	CURRENT RETAIL PRICE
SOLD OUT EDITIONS (RARE):										
Fiord Panqnirtung	AI	ART	1980	EB/A/MON	30 X 22	AP	10	3	150	300
Baffin Island	AI	ART	1980	EB/A/MON	30 X 22	AP	20	3	150	300
Baffin Island II	AI	ART	1980	EB/A/MON	32 X 19	AP	5	3	180	300
Spring Breakup I	AI	ART	1982	EB/A/MON	26 X 19	AP	20	3	180	300
CURRENT EDITIONS:										
Circle of Energy (Set of 12)	AI	ART	1981	EB/A/MON	12 X 12 EA	AP	50 EA	3 EA	1000 SET	2000 SET
Reflection I	AI	ART	1982	EB/A/MON	30 X 22	AP	20	3	180	300
Reflection II	AI	ART	1982	EB/A/MON	39 X 28	FAB	10	3	220	300
Stone Glacier	AI	ART	1982	EB/A/MON	30 X 22	AP	20	3	180	300
Stone Glacier II	ART	ART	1982	EB/A/MON	39 X 28	FAB	10	3	220	300
Northern Cross	ART	ART	1983	EB/A/MON	39 X 28	FAB	10	3	260	300
Creek	ART	ART	1983	EB/A/MON	22 X 30	AP	25	3	220	300
Hilltops I	ART	ART	1983	EB/A/MON	22 X 30	AP	10	3	220	300

PETER TAKAL

BORN: Bucharest, Romania, December 8, 1905; US Citizen
TEACHING: Beloit Col, 1965; Central Col, Pella, IA, 1968
AWARDS: Print Club, Phila, PA, 1957; Yaddo Fel 1961; Purchase Award, Pasadena Art Mus, CA, 1962; Ford Found Fel, Tamarind Fel, Grant, 1963–64
RECENT EXHIB: Michigan State Univ, Kresge Art Mus, East Lansing, MI, 1989; Editart D Blanco, Geneva, Switzerland, 1990; Pfalzgalerie, Kaiserslautern, Germany, 1992
COLLECTIONS: Metropolitan Mus of Art, NY; Whitney Mus of Am Art, NY; Mus of Mod Art, NY; Art Inst of Chicago, IL; Cleveland Mus of Art, OH; Los Angeles County Mus, CA; Nat Gallery of Art, Wash, DC; Lessing J Rosenwald, Phila, PA; Victoria & Albert Mus, London, England; Mus de L'Art Moderne, Paris, France; Nat Gallery, Berlin, Germany; Kunsthalle Bremen, Germany; Kunsthalle Hamburg, Germany; Brooklyn Mus of Art, NY

PRINTERS: Tamarind Lithography Workshop, Albuquerque, NM (TI); Aris Koutroulis (AK); Robert Gardner (RG); Jason Leese (JL); Ken Tyler (KT); John Dowell (JD); Jurgen Fischer (JF); Pratt Graphic Workshop, NY (PGW); St Prex Lithography Workshop (SPLW); Michael Dupla (D); Edouard Quench (EQ)
PUBLISHERS: Tamarind Lithography Workshop (TI); Hollanders Workshop (H); Contemporaries (C); Pratt Graphic Arts Center, NY (PGAC); Associated American Artists, NY (AAA); St Prex Lithography (SPL); Artist (ART); Weber Editions, Geneva, Switzerland, (WE)
GALLERIES: Weber Gallery, Geneva, Switzerland; Editart, D Blanco, Geneva, Switzerland; Gallery de L'Hotel de Ville, Geneva, Switzerland
MAILING ADDRESS: 40, rue du Môle, CH 1201 Geneva, Switzerland

TITLE	PUBLISHER	PRINTER	DATE	MEDIUM	DIMENSION (PAPER SIZE) IN INCHES	TYPE OF PAPER	EDITION NUMBER	NO. OF COLORS	ORIGINAL OPENING PRICE	CURRENT RETAIL PRICE
SOLD OUT EDITIONS (RARE):										
From Tamarind Suite:										
Queen Anne's Lace	TI	AK/TI	1964	LB	30 X 22	AP	20	1	100	1500
Open Barn Door	TI	RG/TI	1964	LB	22 X 30	RP	20	1	100	1500
Kneeling Nude	TI	JL/TI	1964	LB	22 X 30	RP	20	1	100	1500
Head of a Woman	TI	KT/TI	1964	LC	22 X 30	RP	20	1	125	1500
Snow Fields	TI	AK/TI	1964	LB	22 X 30	RP	20	1	100	1500
From Tamarind Suite:										1800 SET	12000 SET
Of Nature, of Man	TI	KT/TI	1964	LC	22 X 30	AP	20	1	100	1000
Reclining Nude	TI	KT/TI	1964	LB	22 X 30	AP	20	1	80	1000
Wave	TI	JD/TI	1964	LC	22 X 30	AP	20	1	100	1000
Tree Opening	TI	JD/TI	1964	LB	30 X 22	RP	20	1	80	1000
Bougainvilla	TI	JD/TI	1964	LB	30 X 22	AP	20	1	80	1000
Wood	TI	KT/TI	1964	LC	30 X 22	RP	20	1	150	1000
Winter Weeds	TI	AK/TI	1964	LB	30 X 22	AP	20	1	80	1000
Birds	TI	RG/TI	1964	LC	18 X 22	RP	20	1	75	1000
City Window	TI	JD/TI	1964	LB	22 X 30	RP	20	1	80	1000
Autumn Lake	TI	AK/TI	1964	LC	22 X 30	RP	20	1	150	1000
Landscape	TI	AK/TI	1964	LC	22 X 30	RP	20	1	150	1000
Eclipse	TI	KT/TI	1964	LC	30 X 22	RP	20	1	150	1000
Jar, Clothespin & Flower	AAA		1967	ENG	12 X 6	RP	250	1	35	500
Silent Woman	PGAC	JF/PGW	1969	LC	30 X 22	RP	17	1	150	800
Field Trees	HW	FG	1969	LB	22 X 30	AP/GR	100	1	100	800
Clouds, Fields, Clouds	SPL	MD/SPLW	1975	ENG	12 X 16	AP	9	1	125	700
Dusk	SPL	EQ/SPLW	1978	LC	13 X 21	RP		1	300	800
Winter Landscape	ED/DB	GU	1981	LC	19 X 26	H	150	3	250	600
Leaf	ART	VOCAT	1985	SP	26 X 18	JO	20	1	300	500
City	ART	VOCAT	1985	SP	20 X 27	JO	20	1	300	500

SEIKICHI TAKARA

BORN: Honolulu, HI; 1929
EDUCATION: Honolulu Acad of Art, HI
RECENT EXHIB: Martin Lawrence Galleries, Phila, PA, 1987,88; Martin Lawrence Galleries, Sherman Oaks, CA, 1987,89; Martin Lawrence Galleries, West Los Angeles, CA, 1989; Martin Lawrence Galleries, Palm Desert, CA, 1989; Martin Lawrence Galleries, Newport Beach, CA, 1989; Martin Lawrence Galleries, Thousand Oaks, CA, 1989; Martin Lawrence Galleries, Redondo Beach, CA, 1987,89; Martin Lawrence Galleries, Escondido, CA, 1987,89; Martin Lawrence Galleries, Wash, DC, 1989; Martin Lawrence Galleries, Baltimore, MD, 1989; Martin Lawrence Galleries, Burlington, MA, 1989; Martin Lawrence Galleries, Woodland Hills, CA, 1990; Martin Lawrence Galleries, Santa Ana, CA, 1990; Martin Lawrence Galleries, Soho, NY, 1990; Martin Lawrence Galleries, McLean, VA, 1990
PRINTERS: Atelier Ettinger, NY (AE); Accent Studio, Canoga Park, CA (AC)
PUBLISHERS: Martin Lawrence Limited Editions, Van Nuys, CA (MLLE)
GALLERIES: Martin Lawrence Galleries, Sherman Oaks, CA & West Los Angeles, CA & Newport Beach, CA & Palm Springs, CA & Santa Clara, CA & Redondo Beach, CA & Thousand Oaks, CA & Escondido, CA & Short Hills, NJ & Los Angeles, CA

Seikichi Takara
Distant Moon
Courtesy Martin Lawrence Limited Editions

Seikichi Takara
Red Karma
Courtesy Martin Lawrence Limited Editions

TITLE	PUBLISHER	PRINTER	DATE	MEDIUM	DIMENSION (PAPER SIZE) IN INCHES	TYPE OF PAPER	EDITION NUMBER	NO. OF COLORS	ORIGINAL OPENING PRICE	CURRENT RETAIL PRICE
SOLD OUT EDITIONS (RARE):										
Lake Arakat	MLLE	AE	1983	LC	29 X 23	R/BFK	3	13	400	1950
Lake Arakat (Deluxe)	MLLE	AS	1984	LC	29 X 23	SE	45		450	2050
Nocturnal Image	MLLE	AS	1984	SP	30 X 36	SE	275	60	400	2050
CURRENT EDITIONS:										
Tranquility	MLLE	AS	1984	SP	35 X 28	SE	350	63	400	1825
Tranquility (Deluxe)	MLLE	AS	1984	SP	35 X 28	SE	75		450	1925
Five Horses	MLLE	AS	1985	SP	5 X 29	SE	128		500	1600
Encounter	MLLE	AS	1986	SP	36 X 42	SE	550		500	2225
Cosmic Energy	MLLE	AS	1987	SP	32 X 37	SE	550		550	1550
Samurai	MLLE	AS	1988	SP	40 X 32	SE	550		600	1650
Odyssey	MLLE	AS	1988	SP	43 X 36	SE	550		600	2050
Nightscape	MLLE	AS	1989	SP	45 X 37	SE	550		650	1750
Red Karma	MLLE	AS	1990	SP	35 X 43	SE	550		650	1650
Distant Moon	MLLE	AS	1991	SP	31 X 42	SE	550		650	1525
Taiko Odori	MLLE	AS	1991	SP	40 X 32	SE	550		650	1550

TAKIS

BORN: Athens, Greece; 1925
TEACHING: Center for Advanced Visual Studies, Massachusetts Inst of Technology, Cambridge, MA, 1968–69
PRINTERS: Maeght Editeur, Paris, France (ME); Maeght Lelong, Paris, France (ML)
PUBLISHERS: Maeght Editions, Paris, France (ME); Maeght Lelong Editions, Paris, France (ML)
GALLERIES: Galerie Lelong, Paris, France & Zürich, Switzerland & New York, NY

TITLE	PUBLISHER	PRINTER	DATE	MEDIUM	DIMENSION (PAPER SIZE) IN INCHES	TYPE OF PAPER	EDITION NUMBER	NO. OF COLORS	ORIGINAL OPENING PRICE	CURRENT RETAIL PRICE
CURRENT EDITIONS:										
Totem	ME	ME	1981	LC	53 X 66 cm	AP	75		900 FF	2000 FF
Insectes	ML	ML	1982	LC	56 X 76 cm	AP	75		900 FF	2000 FF

STEPHEN TALASNIK

BORN: Philadelphia, PA; November 21, 1954
EDUCATION: Rhode Island Sch of Design, Providence, RI, 1972–76; Syracuse Univ, NY, 1976–77; Tyler Sch of Art, Rome, Italy, 1977–78; Tyler Sch of Art, Phila, PA, MFA, 1979
TEACHING: Grad Asst, Design, Syracuse Univ, NY, 1976–77; Grad Asst, Drawing, Tyler Sch of Art, Rome, Italy, 1977–78; Grad Asst, Painting, Tyler Sch of Art, Phila, PA, 1978–79; Asst Prof, Drawing, Adjunct, Moore Col of Art, Phila, PA, 1984; Gallery Coordinator, Samuel S Fleisher Art Mem Col, Phila, PA, 1980–85; Instr, Drawing, Summer Sessions, Tyler Sch of Art, Phila, PA, 1983–86; adjunct Prof, Drawing, Tyler Sch of Art, Phila, PA, 1980 to present

STEPHEN TALASNIK CONTINUED

AWARDS: Artist in Res, Samuel S Fleisher Art Mem Col, Phila, PA, 1982–84; Vis Artist, Brandywine Graphics Workshop (Funded by Pennsylvania State Council for the Arts & Nat Endowment for the Arts), 1984; Nat Endowment for the Arts Fel, Drawing, 1985; MacDowell Colony Fel Res, Peterborough, NH, 1987
RECENT EXHIB: Pennsylvania Acad of Fine Art, Morris Gallery, Phila, PA, 1987; Dolan/Maxwell Gallery, Phila, PA, 1987,88; Dolan/Maxwell Gallery, NY, 1990

COLLECTIONS: Philadelphia Mus of Art, PA; Pennsylvania Acad of Fine Arts, Phila, PA; Univ of Delaware, Wilmington, DE/ Philadelphia Col of Art Print Coll, PA; Free Library of Philadelphia, PA
PRINTERS: David Keister, Bloomington, IN (DK); David Calkins, Bloomington, IN (DC); Echo Press, Bloomington, IN (EPr)
PUBLISHERS: Echo Press, Bloomington, IN (EPr)
GALLERIES: Echo Press, Bloomington, IN
MAILING ADDRESS: c/o Echo Press, 1901 E Tenth St, Bloomington, IN 47408

TITLE	PUBLISHER	PRINTER	DATE	MEDIUM	DIMENSION (PAPER SIZE) IN INCHES	TYPE OF PAPER	EDITION NUMBER	NO. OF COLORS	ORIGINAL OPENING PRICE	CURRENT RETAIL PRICE
SOLD OUT EDITIONS (RARE):										
Ockham's Razor	EPr	DK/DC/EPr	1987	LB	44 X 30	R/BFK/G	24	1	550	900
CURRENT EDITIONS:										
Isolate (with Graphite)	EPr	DK/DC/EPr	1990	LB	42 X 31 EA	GE	1 EA	Varies	1500 EA	1500 EA
Isolate	EPr	DK/DC/DPr	1991	COL	42 X 31	HAHN/CR	10	3	1400	1400
Skeletal	EPr	DK/DC/EPr	1991	COL	29 X 25	HAHN/CR	61	3	900	900

RAYA TALMOR

BORN: Tel Aviv, Israel; October 13, 1938
EDUCATION: Height Inst of Art, Oranim, Israel, 1956–61; Haifa Univ, Israel, BFA, 1972–75; with Honors; Haifa Univ, Israel, MFA, 1975–78
TEACHING: Instr, Haifa Univ, Israel; Instr, Studio Art, 1975 to present
AWARDS: United Nations Stamp, "Shelter for the Homeless"—Issued March 1987
RECENT EXHIB: IAPS, Jerusalem, Israel, 1990; IAPS, Forum, Herzlya, Israel, 1990
COLLECTIONS: IAPS, Jerusalem, Israel, IAPS, Haifa, Israel; Nechushtan Kibbutz, Israel; Museum Ashdot Yaacov, Israel; Haharia Municipal Museum, Israel
PRINTERS: Har-El Printers, Tel Aviv, Israel (Har-El)
PUBLISHERS: Artist (ART)
GALLERIES: Avantgarde Art Associates, West Chester, PA; Kibbutz Yagur, Israel
MAILING ADDRESS: c/o Raya Talmor, Kibbutz Yagur, 30065, Israel

Raya Talmor
Blues
Courtesy the Artist

TITLE	PUBLISHER	PRINTER	DATE	MEDIUM	DIMENSION (PAPER SIZE) IN INCHES	TYPE OF PAPER	EDITION NUMBER	NO. OF COLORS	ORIGINAL OPENING PRICE	CURRENT RETAIL PRICE
CURRENT EDITIONS:										
Blues	ART	Har-El	1990	SP	29 X 30	R/100	300	24	100	300

OTIS TAMASAUSKAS

BORN: Terschenreuth, Germany; July 11, 1947
EDUCATION: Univ of Windsor, Canada, BFA
TEACHING: McMaster Univ, Canada, 1977–79; Univ of Toronto, Canada, 1977–83; Queen's Univ, Canada, 1980–82 & 1984 to present
AWARDS: Purchase Award, British Biennale, Bradford, England, 1982; Ontario Arts Grant, Canada, 1983
COLLECTIONS: Univ of Windsor, Canada; McMaster Univ, Canada; Laurentian Univ, Canada; Univ of Guelph, Canada; Univ of Western Ontario, Canada; Art Gallery of Brant, Canada; Art Gallery of Ontario, Canada; Art Gallery of Hamilton, Canada; MacDonald Stewart Art Centre, York Univ, Canada; Carleton Univ, Canada; Seneca Col Gallery, Canada; Univ of Waterloo, Canada
PRINTERS: Artist (ART); Robert Achtemichuk, Toronto, Canada (RA); Alan Flint, Toronto, Canada, (AF)
PUBLISHERS: Open Studio, Toronto, Canada (OS); Saugeen Highland Impressions, Priceville, Canada (SHI); Artist (ART)
GALLERIES: Mira Godard Gallery, Toronto, Canada
MAILING ADDRESS: General Delivery, Priceville, ON, Canada N0C 1K0

TITLE	PUBLISHER	PRINTER	DATE	MEDIUM	DIMENSION (PAPER SIZE) IN INCHES	TYPE OF PAPER	EDITION NUMBER	NO. OF COLORS	ORIGINAL OPENING PRICE	CURRENT RETAIL PRICE
SOLD OUT EDITIONS (RARE):										
Tropical Flying Fan No 18	ART	ART	1981	LC/I/CO	40 X 30	R/BFK	1	22	400	750
From Fading Forest Series, Ancient Rituals	OS	RA/AF	1991	PH/EC/ENG	40 X 79	HMP	8	2	1700	1700

RUFINO TAMAYO

BORN: Oaxaco, Mexico; 1899
EDUCATION: Acad de Bellas Artes, Mexico City, Mexico, 1917–21
TEACHING: Dalton Sch, NY; Brooklyn Mus, NY
AWARDS: Carnegie Inst, Pittsburgh, PA, 1952,55; Guggenheim Int Found Award, 1960
RECENT EXHIB: Arizona State Univ, Tempe, AZ, 1992; Associated American Artists, NY, 1993
COLLECTIONS: Mus of Mod Art, NY; Art Inst of Chicago, IL; Philadelphia Mus of Art, PA; Albright-Knox Art Gallery, Buffalo, NY; Cincinnati Art Mus, OH; Dallas Mus of Fine Art, TX; Cleveland Mus of Art, OH; Milwaukee Art Center, WI; Phoenix Art Mus, AZ; Rhode Island Sch of Design, Providence, RI; St Louis Art Mus, MO; Washington Univ, St Louis, MO; Mus de Bellas Artes, Caracas, Venezuela; Mus of Fine Arts, Jerusalem, Israel; Mus of Mod Art, Tokyo, Japan; Mus of Mod Art, Rio de Janeiro, Brazil; Royal Mus, Brussels, Belgium; UNESCO, Paris, France; Kunsternes Hus, Oslo, Norway; Phillips Coll, Wash, DC
PRINTERS: Guilde de la Gravure, Paris, France (GG); Bank Street Atelier, NY (BSA); Taller de Grafica, Mexicana, Mexico City, Mexico (TGM); American Atelier, NY (AA); La Poligrafa, SA, Barcelona, Spain (LP); Quadrangle Press (QP); Atelier Desjobert, Paris, France (AD); Mixografa, Santa Monica, CA (MIX); Tamarind Inst, Albuquerque, NM (TI)
PUBLISHERS: Guilde de la Gravure, Paris, France (GG); Taller de Grafica Mexicana (TGM); Transworld Art, Inc, NY (TAI); Circle Fine Art, Chicago, IL (CFA); Ediciones Poligrafa, SA, Barcelona, Spain (EdP); Mixografa, Santa Monica, CA (MIX); Tamarind Inst, Albuquerque, NM (TI); Touchstone Studio (TS); Quadrangle Press (QP)

GALLERIES: Perls Gallery, New York, NY; River Gallery, Westport, CT; Marta Guitierrez Fine Arts, Key Biscayne, FL; Meridian Gallery, Chicago, IL; Fernette's Gallery of Art, Des Moines, IA; Joan Cawley Gallery, Wichita, KS; Phyllis Needlman Gallery, Winnetka, IL; I Irving Feldman Galleries, Sarasota, FL; Hanson Galleries, New Orleans, LA; Nahan Galleries, New Orleans, LA; Fingerhut Gallery, Minneapolis, MN; Lake Gallery, Incline Village, NV; Nathan Silberberg Fine Arts, New York, NY; Southwest Gallery, Dallas, TX; Gallery Mack NW, Seattle, WA; Rolly-Michaux, Boston, MA & New York, NY; Galeria Joan Prats, Barcelona, Spain & New York, NY; Circle Galleries, San Diego, CA & San Francisco, CA & Northbrook, IL & Pittsburgh, PA & Houston, TX & Soho, NY & Chicago, IL & Scottsdale, AZ & Beverly Hills, CA & Costa Mesa, CA & Sherman Oaks, CA & Palm Beach, FL & Honolulu, HI & New Orleans, LA & Las Vegas, NV & Seattle, WA; Charles Whitchurch Gallery, Huntington Beach, CA; Iturralde Gallery, Los Angeles, CA; Noble House, Los Angeles, CA; Bond Street Gallery, Oakland, CA; B Lewin Galleries, Palm Springs, CA; George Belcher Gallery, San Francisco, CA; DeSoto Workshop, San Francisco, CA; Harcourts Modern & Contemporary, San Francisco, CA; Remba Gallery/Mixografia Workshop, Santa Monica, CA; Israel Art Gallery, West Hills, CA; River Gallery, Westport, CT; Phyllis Needlman Gallery, Chicago, IL; Scherer Gallery, Marlboro, NJ; Dorsky Gallery, New York, NY; Mary-Anne Martin Fine Art, New York, NY; Nathan Silberberg Fine Arts, New York, NY; J Barrett Galleries, Toledo, OH; Argus Fine Arts, Eugene, OK; Southwest Gallery, Dallas, TX

TITLE	PUBLISHER	PRINTER	DATE	MEDIUM	DIMENSION (PAPER SIZE) IN INCHES	TYPE OF PAPER	EDITION NUMBER	NO. OF COLORS	ORIGINAL OPENING PRICE	CURRENT RETAIL PRICE
SOLD OUT EDITIONS (RARE):										
Mermaids	ART	ART	1930	WC	6 X 8	WOVE			25	5000
Standing Guard	ART	ART	1930	WC	8 X 6	WOVE/T			25	5000
Man and Woman	ART	ART	1930	WC	6 X 8	WOVE			25	5000
Woman Leaning on Table	ART	ART	1930	WC	6 X 8	WOVE			25	5000
Early Spring	ART	ART	1941	EC/A/EMB	14 X 11	WOVE	4		50	5000
Hombre Contemplando la Luna	QP	QP	1947	EB/A	8 X 6	AP	75		60	5000
Girl with Melon	GG	GG	1950	LC	26 X 20	AP	65		100	6000
Watermelon Eater	GG	GG	1950	LC	22 X 17	AP	200		50	6000
Aztec Landscape	GG	GG	1950	LC	13 X 20	AP	200		50	6000
Tete Indienne			1958	LC	13 X 10	AP			80	3500
Wolf Howling			1960	LC	20 X 26	AP	75		200	5500
Transparent Man	GG	GG	1964	LC	37 X 26	AP	200		300	6000
Head	TI	TI	1964	LB	10 X 11	AP	20		100	4500
Mujer			1965	LC	33 X 24	AP	XXV		300	6500
Femme Noiro			1969	LC	27 X 21	AP	150		300	3500
Mujeres Portfolio:										
Venus	TS	AD	1969	LC	28 X 21	GP	150		300	3500
Deux Tetes de Femmes	TS	AD	1969	LC	21 X 27	GP	150		300	4000
Femme aus Bas	TS	AD	1969	LC	27 X 21	GP	150		300	3500
Carnavalesque	TS	AD	1969	LC	27 X 21	GP	150		300	5000
Femme au Collant Noir	TS	AD	1969	LC	28 X 21	GP	150		300	3500
La Negresse	TS	AD	1969	LC	27 X 21	GP	150		300	3500
Torse de Femme	TS	AD	1969	LC	27 X 21	GP	150		300	3500
Untitled (Mujer)			1970	LC	26 X 20	AP	100		600	3500
Cabeza	MIX	MIX	1972	MIX	29 X 22	AP	75	1	500	1800
Man	TAI	BSA	1972	LC	37 X 26	AP	100		800	7000
Two Personages	TAI	BSA	1972	LC	26 X 36	AP	100		800	7000
Watermelons	TAI	BSA	1972	LC	36 X 24	AP	100		800	7000
Woman	TAI	BSA	1972	LC	36 X 26	AP	100		800	7000
Extasis Cosmico	TGM		1975	EC/EMB	29 X 21		80		800	5000
El Perro	TGM	MIX	1975	EC/EMB	22 X 30	AP	100		800	5000
Perro Aullando	TGM		1975	LC	22 X 30	AP	50		800	5000
The Obscure Man	TAI	BSA	1975	LC	26 X 20	AP	175		600	3000
Dos Figuras (Set of 8):									6000 SET	16000 SET
Dos Figuras	TAI	TG	1976	LC/ENG/ME	22 X 30	AP	175		800	10000
Hombre Blanco	TAI	TG	1976	LC/ENG/ME	30 X 22	AP	175		800	10000
Hombre Con Los Brazos En Alto	TAI	TG	1976	LC/ENG/ME	22 X 30	AP	175		800	10000
Hombre Negro	TAI	TG	1976	LC/ENG/ME	30 X 22	AP	175		800	10000
Hombre Rojo	TAI	TG	1976	LC/ENG/ME	30 X 22	AP	175		800	10000
Mascara Rojo	TAI	TG	1976	LC/ENG/ME	30 X 22	AP	175		800	10000
Mujer Con Los Brazos En Alto	TAI	TG	1976	LC/ENG/ME	30 X 22	AP	175		800	10000
Sol	TAI	TG	1976	LC/ENG/ME	22 X 30	AP	175		800	10000
Dos Figuras	EdP	LP	1976	MIX	22 X 29	GP	75		800	6000
Mujeres Azul	EdP	LP	1976	MIX	30 X 22	GP	75		800	7000
Cabeza en Violetta	EdP	LP	1976	EC	29 X 22	GP	75		800	6000
Figura en Rojo	MIX/TAI	MIX	1976	MIX	31 X 23	AP	140		800	6000

RUFINO TAMAYO CONTINUED

TITLE	PUBLISHER	PRINTER	DATE	MEDIUM	DIMENSION (PAPER SIZE) IN INCHES	TYPE OF PAPER	EDITION NUMBER	NO. OF COLORS	ORIGINAL OPENING PRICE	CURRENT RETAIL PRICE
SOLD OUT EDITIONS (RARE):										
Perfil	TGM	MIX	1977	EC/EMB	23 X 16	AP	100		800	5000
Perfil Sobre Estuco	TGM	MIX	1977	MIX	28 X 20	AP	100		800	4500
Estela	MIX	MIX	1977	MIX	29 X 23	AP	100		800	5000
Figura de Pie	MIX	MIX	1977	MIX	27 X 20	AP	100		800	5500
Figure Composition Hombre Rojo	MIX	MIX	1978	MIX	31 X 22	AP	140		800	4500
Mascaro Rojo	MIX	MIX	1978	MIX	31 X 23	AP	140		800	4500
Salome (Metropolitan Opera II)	CFA	AA	1978	LC	30 X 22	AP	250		350	2600
Hombre con Baston	EdP	LP	1979	EC/A	22 X 30	GP	99		800	10000
Cabeza en Rojo	EdP	LP	1979	FC/A	30 X 22	GP	99		800	10000
Cabeza en Rojo	EdP	LP	1979	LC	13 X 10	AP	300		300	5000
Cabeza en Fonda Verde Gris	EdP	LP	1979	EC/A	22 X 30	GP	99		800	10000
Manos en Rojos	EdP	LP	1979	EC	22 X 30	GP	99		800	10000
Manos Sobre Fondo Azul	EdP	LP	1979	EC	22 X 30	GP	99		800	7500
Personaje con Sombrero	EdP	LP	1979	MIX	30 X 22	GP	99		800	5000
Figura en Negra	EdP	LP	1980	EC	30 X 22	GP	99		800	6000
Personaje en Gris	EdP	LP	1980	EC	30 X 22	GP	99		800	5000
Portada Suite:										
Torso en Rosa	EdP	LP	1980	MIX	30 X 22	GP	99		800	7500
Figura en Jarras	EdP	LP	1981	MIX	30 X 22	GP	99		800	6000
La Cirquera	EdP	LP	1984	EC	30 X 22	GP	99		1500	17000

ERNESTO TATAFIORE

BORN: Marigliano, Italy; 1943
EDUCATION: Städtische Galerie im Lenbachhaus, Munich, Germany
PRINTERS: 3–K Workshop, Rome, Italy (3K)
PUBLISHERS: Edition Ressle, Stockholm, Sweden (ER); Il Ponte, Rome, Italy (IP)
GALLERIES: Annina Nosei Gallery, New York, NY; André Emmerich Gallery, New York, NY; Marianne Deson Gallery, Chicago, IL; Metropolitan Museum Mezzanine, New York; Tossan-Tossan Gallery, New York, NY

TITLE	PUBLISHER	PRINTER	DATE	MEDIUM	DIMENSION (PAPER SIZE) IN INCHES	TYPE OF PAPER	EDITION NUMBER	NO. OF COLORS	ORIGINAL OPENING PRICE	CURRENT RETAIL PRICE
SOLD OUT EDITIONS (RARE):										
Acquaforte Historico (Set of 3)	ER	3K	1983	EB/CO	28 X 20 EA	AP	60 EA	1 EA	1000 SET	2000 SET
La Vertu	IP	3K	1985	EB/HC	12 X 69	JP	34	Varies	500	750

PATRICIA TAVENNER

BORN: Michigan
EDUCATION: Michigan State Univ, East Lansing, MI, BFA, 1962; California Col of Arts & Crafts, Oakland, CA, MFA, 1965
TEACHING: Instr, Cornell Univ, Ithaca, NY, 1979; Instr, Univ of California, Davis, CA, 1987; Prof, Art, Univ of California, Berkeley, Ext, CA, 1967–92
RECENT EXHIB: Mus of Mod Kunst, Weddel, West Germany, 1987; Univ of California, San Francisco, CA, 1989
COLLECTIONS: Herbert F Johnson Art Mus, Cornell Univ, Ithaca, NY; Kansas City Art Inst, MO; Oakland Mus of Art, CA; Mills Col, Oakland, CA; Tyringham Inst of 20th Century Art, MA; Wichita Art Mus, KS; Smith Col, Amherst, MA; Simon Frazer Univ, Vancouver, Canada; Mus of Mod Art, NY; Royal Coll of Belgium, Antwerp, Belgium
PRINTERS: Artist (ART); Eternal Press, Oakland, CA (EtPr)
PUBLISHERS: Eternal Press, Oakland, CA (EtPr)
MAILING ADDRESS: P O Box 11102, Oakland, CA 94611

TITLE	PUBLISHER	PRINTER	DATE	MEDIUM	DIMENSION (PAPER SIZE) IN INCHES	TYPE OF PAPER	EDITION NUMBER	NO. OF COLORS	ORIGINAL OPENING PRICE	CURRENT RETAIL PRICE
CURRENT EDITIONS:										
Channel	EtPr	ART/EtPr	1988	PH/SP	15 X 22	AC/BL	55	3	150	225
Cosmic Horizons	EtPr	ART/EtPr	1988	PH/SP	15 X 22	AC/W	55	3	125	200
Square One	EtPr	ART/EtPr	1988	PH/SP	15 X 22	AC/BL	50	2	125	200

AL C TAYLOR

BORN: Springfield, MO; 1948
EDUCATION: Yale Norfolk Summer Session, 1969; Whitney Mus of Art, Resources Center, NY, 1969; Kansas City Art Inst, MO, 1970
AWARDS: Nat Endowment for the Arts Fel, 1988
RECENT EXHIB: Brooklyn Mus, NY, 1989; Europaische Acad fur Bildende Kunst, Trier, Germany, 1990; Mus of Fine Arts, Boston, MA, 1990; Morris Mus, Morristown, NJ, 1990; Galerie Alfred Kren, Cologne, Germany, 1990,92
COLLECTIONS: Mus of Fine Arts, Boston, MA; Mus of Mod Art, NY; Walker Art Center, Minneapolis, MN; New York Public Library, NY
PRINTERS: Artist (ART); Albert Benveniste, Copenhagen, Denmark (AB); Mette Ulstrup, Copenhagen, Denmark (MU); Niels Borch Jensen, Copenhagen, Denmark (NBJ)
PUBLISHERS: Artist (ART); Galerie Alfred Kren, NY (GAK)
GALLERIES: Galerie Alfred Kren, New York, NY & Cologne, Germany
MAILING ADDRESS: 72 Franklin St, New York, NY 10013

TITLE	PUBLISHER	PRINTER	DATE	MEDIUM	DIMENSION (PAPER SIZE) IN INCHES	TYPE OF PAPER	EDITION NUMBER	NO. OF COLORS	ORIGINAL OPENING PRICE	CURRENT RETAIL PRICE
CURRENT EDITIONS:										
Untitled (Large Tape)	ART	ART	1988	EB/A	34 X 20	R/BFK	20		750	750
Large Pet Stains	ART	ART	1989	EB	18 X 24	R/BFK	15	1	400	400
Ten Common (Hawaiian Household) Objects (Set of 10)	GAK	AB/MU/NBJ	1989	DPT/AC	20 X 14 EA	ZER	15 EA		4000 SET	5000 SET

ANTONI TAPIES

Antoni Tapies
La Grande Table
Courtesy Galerie Lelong

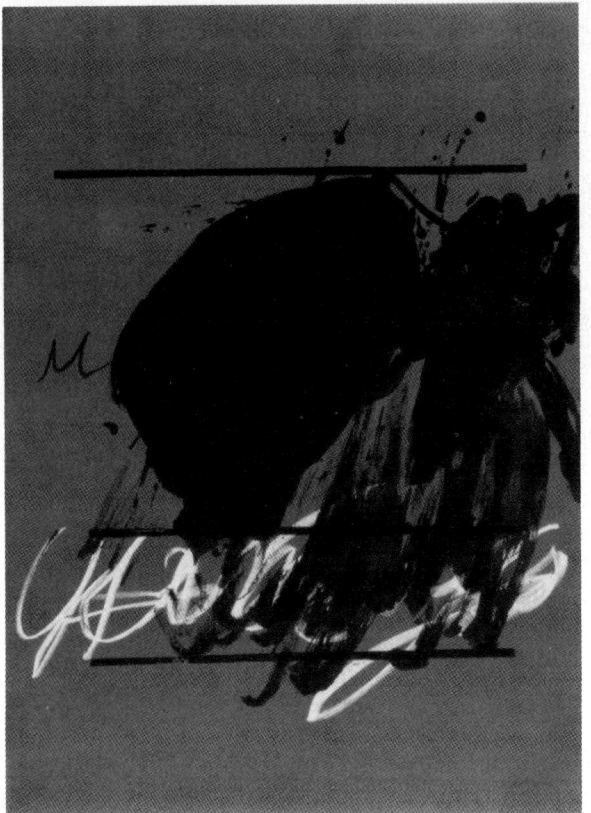

Antoni Tapies
U No Es Ningu
Courtesy Ediciones Poligrafa

BORN: Barcelona, Spain; Dec 13, 1923
AWARDS: Carnegie Prize, 1958; Int Biennale Prize, Etchings, Tokyo, Japan, 1960; Guggenheim Prize, NY, 1964; Rubens Prizez, 1972
RECENT EXHIB: Muhlenberg Col, Frank Martin Art Gallery, Allentown, PA, 1989; Virginia Commonwealth Univ, Anderson Gallery, Richmond, VA, 1989; Elkon Gallery, NY, 1989; Richard Gray Gallery, Chicago, IL, 1990; Galerie Lelong, NY, 1990; Galerie Lelong, Paris, France, 1990; BenedicteSaxe Gallery, Beverly Hills, CA, 1991; Virginia Commonwealth Univ, Anderson Gallery, Richmond, VA, 1992; Southern Methodist Univ, Meadows Mus, Dallas, TX, 1992; Muhlenberg Col, Frank Martin Art Gallery, Allentown, PA, 1992; Associated Am Artists, NY, 1992
PRINTERS: Maeght Editeur, Paris, France (ME); Galerie Maeght Lelong, Paris, France (ML); La Poligrafa, SA, Barcelona, Spain (LP); Ecker Presse, St Gallen, Switzerland (EckPr); Steindrucke Stoob, St Gallen, Switzerland (StS); Georges Fall (GF); Foto-Repro (FR)
PUBLISHERS: Maeght Editions, Paris, France (ME); Galerie Maeght Lelong, Paris, France (ML); Ediciones Poligrafa, SA, Barcelona, Spain (EdP); Editions Galilée (EdG); Galleria due Cui (GdC); Il Bulino de Sergio Pandolfini (BdSP); Sala Gaspar (SG); Kunstverein für die Rheinlande und Westphalen (KRW); Ecker Presse, St Gallen, Switzerland (EckPr); Editions F B (EFB); Arte Adrien Maeght, Paris, France (AAM); Aras Verlag, Saulgau, Switzerland (AV)
GALLERIES: Wenger Gallery, Los Angeles, CA; Michael Dunev Gallery, San Francisco, CA; River Gallery, Westport, CT; Marvin Ross Friedman & Company, Miami, FL; Elkon Gallery, Inc, New York, NY; Galeria Joan Prats, New York, NY & Barcelona, Spain; Galerie Lelong, Paris, France & Zürich, Switzerland & New York, NY; Tossan-Tossan Gallery, New York, NY; Brenda Kroos Gallery, Cleveland, OH; Spaightwood Galleries, Madison, WI; Richard Gray Gallery, Chicago, IL; Flanders Modern, Minneapolis, MN; Nancy Singer Gallery, St Louis, MO; Charlotte Jackson Fine Art, Santa Fe, NM; Anderson Gallery, New York, NY; Associated American Artists, New York, NY; Michael Deleccea Fine Art, New York, NY; Arnold Herstand & Company, New York, NY; Jan Krugier Gallery, New York, NY; BenedicteSaxe Gallery/Maeght Editions, Beverly Hills, CA; Lucy Berman Gallery, Palo Alto, CA; Art Search International, San Francisco, CA; Mary Singer Gallery, Wash, DC

Galfetti (G)

TITLE	PUBLISHER	PRINTER	DATE	MEDIUM	DIMENSION (PAPER SIZE) IN INCHES	TYPE OF PAPER	EDITION NUMBER	NO. OF COLORS	ORIGINAL OPENING PRICE	CURRENT RETAIL PRICE
SOLD OUT EDITIONS (RARE):										
Le Portail			1955	EB/HC	48 X 32	AP		Varies	30	30000
Untitled (G-20)	SG	FR	1959	LB	19 X 29	AP	50	1	20	3000
Sieben Lithographien (Set of 7) (G-30-6)	SG		1960	EMB		AP	50 EA		350 SET	18000 SET
Abstrakte Komposition (G-32)			1960	LC	25 X 19	AP	50		30	3000
Lithographie in Gary, Ocker, Schwarz, Rot und Zwei Beiges (G34)			1960	LC	19 X 25	AP	50		30	4500
Untitled Composition (G-42)	SG	FR	1962	LC	30 X 22	AP	50		50	2800
L in Zwei Schwarz, Rot und Grünlichgrau (G-74)			1962	LC	20 X 25	AP	300		40	1500
Quattre Traces Noires (G-46)			1963	LC	30 X 21	AP	75		45	1500
Ohne Titel (G-47)			1963	LC	20 X 26	AP	150		50	1200
Lithographie in Grau, Blau und Schwarz (G-127)			1965	LC	20 X 28	AP	75		75	2500
L in Schwarz und Braun (G-128)	EckPr	EckPr	1965	LC	21 X 26	AP	75		75	1500
L in Grau und Schwarz (G-130)	EckPr	EckPr	1965	LB	28 X 20	AP	75	1	75	1500
Ohne Titel (G-136)			1966	LC	20 X 26	AP	150		75	1200
Untitled (G-137)	KRW		1966	LC	31 X 22		150		75	1500
Les Banyes del Sol, 1947-48 (G-8)			1966	ENG	10 X 8	R/BFK	50		50	2000
Noir et Craie (G-154)	ME	ME	1968	LC	22 X 30	AP	75		75	3500
Marron Diagonal (G-156)	ME	ME	1968	LC	40 X 29	AP	75		150	5000
Ovale (G-158)	ME	ME	1968	LC	26 X 40	AP	75		150	2000
La Paille (G-195)	ME	ME	1969	AC	14 X 20	R/BFK	75		75	4500

ANTONI TAPIES CONTINUED

TITLE	PUBLISHER	PRINTER	DATE	MEDIUM	DIMENSION (PAPER SIZE) IN INCHES	TYPE OF PAPER	EDITION NUMBER	NO. OF COLORS	ORIGINAL OPENING PRICE	CURRENT RETAIL PRICE
SOLD OUT EDITIONS (RARE):										
Coup de Pinceau en Rouge (G-207)			1969	LB	12 X 10	AP	150	1	75	2500
Moustache de la Série Frégoli (G-214)			1969	LC/CO	14 X 11	AP	100		75	2000
Le Tamis	ME	ME	1969	EB/A/EMB	26 X 35	R/BFK	75		150	6500
Composition (G-I-235)			1970	LB	22 X 18	AP	125	1	100	800
L in Schwarz und Zwei Braun (G-237)			1970	LC	14 X 15	AP	100		100	1800
Nocturn Matinal			1970	LC		AP	100		100	2200
Komposition Blau-Scwarz (G-240a)			1970	LC	20 X 26	AP	100		125	3000
L in Gelb, Zwei Rosa und Schwarz (G-241)			1970	LC	18 X 37	AP	100		150	1800
L in Schwarz, Zwei Grau und Serigraphiertem Weiss (G-242)			1970	LC	11 X 15	AP	100		100	1500
Komposition (G-247)			1970	LC	20 X 26	AP	300		150	2000
L in Gelb, Rot, Grün, Blau, und Schwarz (G-249)			1971	LC	16 X 22	AP	100		150	2000
Ausstellungsplakat: Galerie Rössli, Balsthal (G-247)			1971	LC	24 X 20	AP	300		150	700
Trois Taches et Trois Lignes Noir sur Gris	ME	ME	1972	EC	14 X 20	R/BFK	75		175	2000
Pissarra (G-287)			1972	EB/ENG	23 X 31	R/BFK	75		200	3000
Roba Interior (G-294)			1972	LC/CAR	23 X 30	AP	75		200	3000
Deux Pieds sur Ocre (G-317)	ME	ME	1972	LC	15 X 22	AP	75		150	3000
La Grande Porte (G-323)			1972	EB/CO	35 X 27	R/BFK	75		250	5500
Matiére et Journal (G-325)			1972	EB	26 X 35	R/BFK	75	1	250	5000
Mois du Coeur (G-340)			1972	LC	30 X 21	AP	75		250	2000
Poem I-V			1973	LC	29 X 21 EA	AP	75 EA		250	2500 EA
Composition (G-II-348)	ME	GF	1973	LC	20 X 26	AP	100		250	2000
Fussabdruck			1973	LC	29 X 20	AP			250	2000
Esperit Catalá II (G-392)			1974	EC	17 X 25	R/BFK	75		250	2500
Cartes per la Teresa	ME	AAM	1974	LB		AP	150	1	250	15000
A Effacé (G-394)			1974	LC	25 X 35	AP	90		300	2000
Komposition mit Eingedrucktem Text von André du Bouchet (G-398)			1974	LC	22 X 30	AP	500		250	1800
Mains et Croix (G-495)			1975	AC	17 X 27	R/BFK	75		350	2000
Composition			1975	LB	30 X 22	AP	150	1	400	1500
Paper Cremet (G-501)	EdP	LP	1975	EB/I	17 X 25	GP	75		350	1500
Arc Negre amb Iletres (G-508)			1975	EB/ENG	17 X 24	R/BFK	75		350	4000
La Cama (G-510)			1975	EB/A/REL	17 X 25	R/BFK			350	2500
Llambrec Material Suite:										
#1, #3, #5, #8, #10, #12	EdP	LP	1975	LB	18 X 25 EA	GP	200 EA	1 EA	280 EA	2200 EA
#2, #7, #13, #14, #16, #17	EdP	LP	1975	LB	18 X 25 EA	GP	200 EA	1 EA	280 EA	3300 EA
#4, #6, #9	EdP	LP	1975	LB	18 X 25 EA	GP	200 EA	1 EA	280 EA	1700 EA
#11, #15, #18	EdP	LP	1975	LB	18 X 25 EA	GP	200 EA	1 EA	280 EA	2800 EA
Homentage a Joan Prats	EdP	LP	1975	LP		GP	100		700	3300
500 Anys del Libre Catala	EdP	LP	1975	LC		GP	99		250	1000
Dibujos Suite (Set of 10)	EdP	LP	1975	LC	22 X 30 EA	GP	150 EA		5000 SET	40000 SET
									530 EA	4400 EA
Les Voix Roses			1976	LC	8 X 17	AP			300	1750
Fora			1976	EC/HC	22 X 28	R/BFK	75	Varies	350	3500
Signed et Bras (G-597)	ME	ME	1976	EC/A/CAR	25 X 36	R/BFK	50		400	3000
Signes Negres			1976	EB	22 X 30	R/BFK	75	1	350	9000
Ecriture sur Collage (G-568)			1976	EC/CO	13 X 21	R/BFK	50		300	2800
L'Addition			1976	LC	13 X 12	AP	75		250	1900
Fenetre a Campins (G-571)	ME	ME	1976	EB/SG	7 X 17	R/BFK	50		250	2100
Deux et Trois (G-577)	ME	ME	1976	EB/A	20 X 13	R/BFK	50		300	1800
Jambe sur Ovale (G-584)	ME	ME	1976	EB/A	30 X 22	R/BFK	50		350	2000
Lletres I Gris			1976	EB	22 X 30	R/BFK		1	300	1800
Libertad (G-632)			1976	LC	32 X 22	AP	200		300	1500
Ailes (G-606)	ME	ME	1976	EB/A/CAR/CO	24 X 27	R/BFK	50		350	4500
Composition AT			1976	LC	8 X 17	AP			250	1800
Sans Titre (G-639)			1976	LC	22 X 30	AP			300	1750
Negre i Roig (Set of 15):									11000 SET	90000 SET
Lletres i Gris (1)	EdP	LP	1976	EC	22 X 30	GP	75		800	5500
Esgrafiats Sabre Negre (4)	EdP	LP	1976	EC	22 X 30	GP	75		800	7500
A Damunt Vermell (5)	EdP	LP	1976	EC	22 X 30	GP	75		800	7500
Gran x (7)	EdP	LP	1976	EC	22 X 30	GP	75		800	6500
Espai amb Signes (8)	EdP	LP	1976	EC	22 X 30	GP	75		800	6500
Visca Catalunya (10)	EdP	LP	1976	EC	22 X 30	GP	75		800	5500
Lletra O (12)	EdP	LP	1976	EC	22 X 30	GP	75		800	5500
Creu i S (13)	EdP	LP	1976	EC	22 X 30	GP	75		800	5500
Dues Mans (14)	EdP	LP	1976	EC	22 X 30	GP	75		800	6500
Espiral (15)	EdP	LP	1976	EC	22 X 30	GP	75		800	7500

ANTONI TAPIES CONTINUED

TITLE	PUBLISHER	PRINTER	DATE	MEDIUM	DIMENSION (PAPER SIZE) IN INCHES	TYPE OF PAPER	EDITION NUMBER	NO. OF COLORS	ORIGINAL OPENING PRICE	CURRENT RETAIL PRICE
SOLD OUT EDITIONS (RARE):										
Quatre Ditades	EdP	LP	1976	EC	22 X 30	GP	75		800	7500
Negri i Roig (G-617)	EdP	LP	1976	EC	22 X 30	GP	75		800	7500
Set of 5 Etchings:										
Etching #1	EdP	LP	1976	EC	22 X 30	GP	75		1100	5000
Etching #2	EdP	LP	1976	EC	22 X 30	GP	75		1000	5000
Etching #3	EdP	LP	1976	EC	22 X 30	GP	75		1000	5000
Etching #4	EdP	LP	1976	EC	22 X 30	GP	75		1000	5000
Etching #5	EdP	LP	1976	EC	22 X 26	GP	75		700	4500
Endarrera Aquesta Gent	EdP	LP	1977	LC/CO	28 X 40	GP	75		600	5000
Untitled			1978	LB	25 X 36	AP	50	1	600	3500
Komposition			1978	LC	32 X 36	AP			600	5000
Matiére-Mur	EdG		1978	ENG	9 X 7	R/BFK			400	1250
Petrificada Petrificante (Set of 8)	ME	ME	1978	EB/A	22 X 17 EA	R/BFK	175 EA		2500 SET	12500 SET
Tableau	ME	ME	1978	EC	23 X 31	AP	75		150	3000
Gravier	ME	ME	1978	EC	25 X 35	AP	75		225	3500
Le Clou	ME	ME	1978	EC	26 X 36	AP	75		150	3000
Traits et Points	ME	ME	1978	EC	41 X 36	AP	75		150	3000
Graphismes et Deux Croix	ME	ME	1978	EC	33 X 47	AP	75		150	3000
H Renverse	ME	ME	1978	EC	23 X 30	AP	75		150	3000
Les Quatre Coins	ME	ME	1978	EC	23 X 31	AP	75		150	3000
Visage	ME	ME	1978	EC	36 X 25	AP	50		200	3500
Cartographic	ME	ME	1978	EC	25 X 36	AP	50		200	3500
Numero 7	ME	ME	1978	EC	36 X 25	AP	50		200	3500
Ailes	ME	ME	1978	EC	28 X 40	AP	50		250	4000
Tissu Colle	ME	ME	1978	EC	25 X 36	AP	50		250	4000
Manuscrit	ME	ME	1978	EC	25 X 36	AP	50		250	4000
Huit Poinconne	ME	ME	1978	EC	25 X 36	AP	50		250	4000
Triptic	ME	ME	1978	EC	28 X 40	AP	50		250	4000
Taches et Chiffres	ME	ME	1978	EC	29 X 41	AP	75		250	4000
Tirets Superieurs	ME	ME	1979	LC	18 X 25	AP	75		100	3000
Deux Taches Symetriques	ME	ME	1979	LC	29 X 40	AP	75		100	3000
Pointilles	ME	ME	1979	LC	20 X 26	AP	75		100	3000
Ovale	ME	ME	1979	LC	27 X 47	AP	75		150	3500
Angle et Tache	ME	ME	1979	LC	22 X 30	AP	75		100	3000
Noir sur Fond Blanc	ME	ME	1979	LC	22 X 30	AP	150		100	3000
Les Trois Noirs	ME	ME	1979	LC	26 X 20	AP	75		100	3000
L'Etiquette	ME	ME	1979	LC	15 X 18	AP	75		100	3000
Sous Zero	ME	ME	1979	LC	21 X 28	AP	75		100	3000
U No es Ningu	EdP	LP	1979	LC	30 X 22	GP	99		240	3000
Silenci	EdP	LP	1979	LC	30 X 22	GP	100		200	2700
12 Etchings & 2 Lithographs:										
No I—Z	EdP	LP	1975–80	EC	22 X 29	GP	75		900	5000
No II—Estisores-2	EdP	LP	1975–80	EC	33 X 27	GP	75		1000	5000
No III—Creu i Equis	EdP	LP	1975–80	EC	22 X 29	GP	75		600	5000
No IV—Cinta Roja	EdP	LP	1975–80	EC	22 X 29	GP	82/75		750	5000
No V—Cerche	EdP	LP	1975–80	EC	22 X 29	GP	82/75		680	5000
No VI—Creu Deformada	EdP	LP	1975–80	EC	22 X 29	GP	75		750	5000
No VII—70	EdP	LP	1975–80	EC	22 X 29	GP	75		600	5000
No VIII—740	EdP	LP	1975–80	EC	22 X 29	GP	75		750	5000
No IX—Cinta Negra	EdP	LP	1975–80	EC	22 X 29	GP	82		750	5000
No X—Ratlles Vermelles	EdP	LP	1975–80	EC	22 X 29	GP	75		750	5000
No XI—Oval	EdP	LP	1975–80	EC	22 X 29	GP	82		800	5000
No XII—U No es Ningu	EdP	LP	1975–80	EC	22 X 29	GP	82/75		750	5000
Quatre Rectangles	EdP	LP	1975–80	LC	22 X 29	GP	82/75		370	2800
Paisatge	EdP	LP	1975–80	LC	22 X 29	GP	82/75		370	2800
Set of 7 Etchings	EdP	LP	1975–80	EC	22 X 30 EA	GP	99 EA		5000 SET 800 EA	30000 SET 5500 EA
Grand M avec Taches			1980	LC	29 X 37	AP	120		500	3600
Komposition			1980	EC/AC	31 X 42	R/BFK	50		800	8000
Panier et Signes Noirs	ME	ME	1980	LC	26 X 32	AP	75		300	3000
En Forme de Montagne	ME	ME	1980	LC	23 X 30	JP	75		250	2500
Lè Bocal	ME	ME	1980	LC	31 X 41	AP	75		250	2500
Vague d'Encre	ME	ME	1980	LC	31 X 39	AP	75		250	2500
Le Vase	ME	ME	1980	LC	17 X 26	AP	75		125	2000
Angle et Signes	ME	ME	1980	LC	14 X 22	AP	75		100	1500
N a L'Envers	ME	ME	1980	LC	28 X 35	AP	75		200	2000
Deux Taches Symetriques II	ME	ME	1980	LC	22 X 19	AP	77		150	1800
Dessin Biffe	ME	ME	1980	LC	39 X 24	AP	75		125	1500
Noir et Cartons	ME	ME	1980	LC	24 X 22	AP	75		150	1800
Noir et Blanc	ME	ME	1980	EC	63 X 90 cm	AP	50	1	400	4500
Tresse	ME	ME	1980	EC	80 X 107 cm	AP	50	2	1000	9500
Empreinte	ME	ME	1980	EC	63 X 90 cm	AP	50	3	900	8500
Voilé	ME	ME	1980	EC	63 X 91 cm	AP	50	3	650	6000

ANTONI TAPIES CONTINUED

TITLE	PUBLISHER	PRINTER	DATE	MEDIUM	DIMENSION (PAPER SIZE) IN INCHES	TYPE OF PAPER	EDITION NUMBER	NO. OF COLORS	ORIGINAL OPENING PRICE	CURRENT RETAIL PRICE
SOLD OUT EDITIONS (RARE):										
Glissement	ME	ME	1980	EC	81 X 121 cm	AP	50	3	650	6000
Feu II	ME	ME	1980	EC	78 X 107 cm	AP	50	2	850	7500
Horizontal	ME	ME	1980	EC	34 X 106 cm	AP	50	4	500	5000
Vertical	ME	ME	1980	EC	40 X 21 cm	AP	50	4	650	6000
Aus Suite	EckPr	EckPr	1980	LC	25 X 36	AP			700	2800
N A' L'Envers			1980	LC	22 X 30	AP			700	2500
Terrain Vague	ME	ME	1981	AC/CAR	17 X 25	R/BFK	75		800	2500
Trace	ME	ME	1981	AC/CAR	27 X 42	R/BFK	50		700	3000
Annular (Set of 4):			1981	EC		R/BFK	125 EA		1500 SET	3500 SET
Sofa	ME	ME	1981	EB/A/CAR	16 X 25	R/BFK	75	2	700	3500
Untitled (from L'Entaille)	EFB		1981	EC	16 X 13	R/BFK	75		700	2800
AM	ME	ME	1981	LB	21 X 28	AP	75	3	250	3500
Relief Sable	ME	ME	1981	EC	71 X 97 cm	AP	75	3	650	4000
Detritus	ME	ME	1981	EC	71 X 93 cm	AP	75	4	700	4500
Semelle	ME	ME	1981	EC	71 X 96 cm	AP	75	2	650	4000
Macule	ME	ME	1981	EC	63 X 90 cm	AP	75	2	650	4000
TA	ME	ME	1981	EC	71 X 97 cm	AP	75	2	650	4000
Relief et Vernis	ME	ME	1981	EC	63 X 91 cm	AP	75	2	700	4500
Cercle Croix et Collage	ME	ME	1981	EC	70 X 96 cm	AP	75	2	650	4000
M 1/2	ME	ME	1981	LC	70 X 100 cm	AP	75	2	500	3000
Cercle	ME	ME	1981	EC	81 X 122 cm	AP	50	3	900	7500
Paralléle	ME	ME	1981	LC	77 X 103 cm	AP	75	3	550	3500
Deux Volets	ME	ME	1981	LC	139 X 105 cm	AP	75	2	800	6000
Croix Carton	ME	ME	1981	LC	66 X 83 cm	AP	75	3	300	2000
Y	ML	ML	1982	LC	56 X 76 cm	AP	75	2	225	1800
Pied Marron	ML	ML	1982	LC	111 X 76 cm	AP	75	3	500	3000
Ovale Rouge et Noir	ML	ML	1982	LC	110 X 78 cm	AP	75	2	500	3000
Quatre Carrés	ML	ML	1982	EC	120 X 78 cm	AP	75	2	500	3000
Profil	ML	ML	1982	LC	81 X 61 cm	AP	75	?	225	1800
Dechirure	ML	ML	1982	LC	99 X 73 cm	AP	75	3	500	3000
Met Flèches	ML	ML	1982	LC	66 X 83 cm	AP	75	2	225	1800
Quatre Gestes Noirs	ML	ML	1982	LC	61 X 78 cm	AP	75	2	250	2000
Vague 1,2	ML	ML	1982	LC	66 X 100 cm	AP	75	2	225	1800
Deux Croix	ML	ML	1982	LC	61 X 77 cm	AP	75	3	225	1800
Empreinte Barré	ML	ML	1982	LC	66 X 95 cm	AP	75	2	350	2500
La Grande Table	ML	ML	1982	LC	155 X 107 cm	AP	75	3		
Aparicions (Set of 9):										
#1, #3, #6	EdP	LP	1982	EC	22 X 30 EA	GP	99 EA		650 EA	5500 EA
#4	EdP	LP	1982	EC	22 X 30	GP	99		500	4000
#2, #5	EdP	LP	1982	EC	22 X 30 EA	GP	99 EA		800 EA	6500 EA
#7, #8, #9	EdP	LP	1982	EC	22 X 30 EA	GP	99 EA		600 EA	5000 EA
Blanc Central			1982	EB	22 X 30	R/BFK	99	1	350	1500
Affiche avant Lettre			1982	LB	63 X 47	AP	40	1	650	10000
Catalina			1983	LB	20 X 26	AP	100	1	350	2500
Vernis Paysage	ML	ML	1983	LC	64 X 97 cm	AP	75	2	300	3500
AT	ML	ML	1983	LC	61 X 79 cm	AP	75	3	200	2500
Deux Trous	ML	ML	1983	LC	66 X 85 cm	AP	75	3	300	3500
Neuf Tirets	ML	ML	1983	LC	61 X 76 cm	AP	75	2	200	2500
Petit T	ML	ML	1983	LC	69 X 54 cm	AP	75	3	200	2500
Affiche Avant Lettre Chicago	ML	ML	1983	LC	76 X 50 cm	AP	100	3	200	2500
Affiche Avant Lettre N 207	ML	ML	1983	LC	96 X 64 cm	AP	75	3	225	3000
Cobert de Roig			1984	EB/A/CAR	30 X 29	R/BFK	99		500	5000
L'Oeil			1984	AC	11 X 16	R/BFK	50		400	2000
Yves Bonnefoy-un Fragment de Stature dans L'Herbe d'un Enclos										
Encore Desert (Set of 3):	EFB		1984	EB/A	26 X 20	R/BFK	75		1800 SET	9000 SET
CURRENT EDITIONS:										
Forma Ombrejada	EdP	LP	1987	EC/CAR	30 X 31	GP	99		1200	8500
Cap	EdP	LP	1987	EB/CAR	39 X 51	GP	99	1	1500	5500
Red Cross and Brown Foot			1987	LC	40 X 28	AP	50		1500	2000
Ein Spiel von Spiegeln (Set of 5)			1987	LC	10 X 8 EA	AP	230		2500 SET	4000 SET
Une Vase de Terre Crue et le T du Nom de Tapies (Set of 3)	EFB		1988	EB	20 X 26 EA	R/BFK	85 EA	1 EA	3000 SET	9000 SET
Serp i Creu			1989	EC	22 X 30	R/BFK	90		3000	9000
Komposition			1989	EC/HC	27 X 23	R/BFK	15	Varies	3500	5000
Maria Zambrano: El Arbol de la Vida (Set of 3)			1989	AB	19 X 23 EA	R/BFK	30 EA	Varies	6500 SET	8000 SET
Forms Vernis	EdP	LP	1990	EB/A/MM	38 X 50	HMP	99		12000	15000
Untitled	AV	StS	1991	LB/EMB	22 X 30	But/HMP	100	1	SF4500	SF4500

The print market has become very selective. For the first time since we published the first edition of The Printworld Directory in 1982, the prices of prints have been greatly reduced and greatly increased for the same artists by the most reputable and established print publishers. Check the fifth edition to understand the movement.

ITZCHAK TARKAY

BORN: Yugoslavia; 1935
EDUCATION: Avni Inst of Fine Art, Tel Aviv, Jerusalem, Israel; Bezadel Acad, Jerusalem, Israel
RECENT EXHIB: Windmill Gallery, Jerusalem, Israel, 1987; Gemoart Gallery, Tel Aviv, Israel, 1987; Weizman Gallery, Beer-Sheba, Israel, 1987; Chetkin Gallery, Red Bank, NJ, 1988; Ursus Press Gallery, Dusseldorf, Germany, 1988; Lovin Gallery, Long Island, NY, 1989; London Contemporary Art Gallery, London, England, 1989; Gallery 454, Detroit, MI, 1989; Bruno Gallery, Jerusalem, Israel, 1990; Dixon Bate Gallery, Manchester, England, 1990; Laurence Gallery, Santa Rosa, CA, 1990; CCA Galleries, Oxford, England, 1990; Ambassador Gallery, NJ, 1990; Art Spectrum Gallery, FL, 1990; Bell Gallery, Belfast, North Ireland, 1991; St Hellier Gallery, Jersey, England, 1991; Pictures Gallery, Birmingham, England, 1991; Renjeau Gallery, Boston, MA, 1989,91; World of Watercolours, London, England, 1991; Montpellier Gallery, Cheltenham, England, 1991
PRINTERS: Har-El Printers, Tel Aviv, Israel (HarEl)
PUBLISHERS: London Contemporary Art, Inc, London, England & Prospect, IL (LCA)
MAILING ADDRESS: c/o London Contemporary Art, Inc, 729 Pinecrest, Prospect Heights, IL 60070

Itzchak Tarkay
Springtime
Courtesy London Contemporary Art, Inc

TITLE	PUBLISHER	PRINTER	DATE	MEDIUM	DIMENSION (PAPER SIZE) IN INCHES	TYPE OF PAPER	EDITION NUMBER	NO. OF COLORS	ORIGINAL OPENING PRICE	CURRENT RETAIL PRICE
SOLD OUT EDITIONS (RARE):										
Interior	LCA	Har-El	1989	SP	19 X 27	COV	350		300	700
Landscape	LCA	Har-El	1989	SP	21 X 21	COV	350		300	800
Marianne	LCA	Har-El	1989	SP	27 X 27	COV	350		300	1000
Secrets I, II	LCA	Har-El	1989	SP	23 X 16 EA	COV	350		250 EA	600 EA
Women & Flowers	LCA	Har-El	1989	SP	27 X 34	COV	350		300	800
Behind the Curtain	LCA	Har-El	1989	SP	27 X 36	COV	350		300	1200
Spare Time	LCA	Har-El	1990	SP	36 X 27	COV	350		300	1200
Temptation	LCA	Har-El	1990	SP	27 X 36	COV	350		350	1400
High Tea	LCA	Har-El	1990	SP	31 X 44	COV	350		550	3000
Lady with a Fruit Basket	LCA	Har-El	1990	SP	27 X 27	COV	350		450	1200
Afternoon Chat	LCA	Har-El	1990	SP	32 X 44	COV	350		600	2500
Leila	LCA	Har-El	1990	SP	26 X 35	COV	350		400	2500
Second Thought	LCA	Har-El	1990	SP	27 X 36	COV	350		850	2000
Cafe de Paris	LCA	Har-El	1990	SP	31 X 44	COV	350		700	3000
Red Hats	LCA	Har-El	1990	SP	36 X 45	COV	350		600	1400
Femme Fatale	LCA	Har-El	1990	SP	34 X 27	COV	350		500	1400
Gossip	LCA	Har-El	1990	SP	25 X 32	COV	350		500	1400
Danniele's Corner	LCA	Har-El	1990	SP	33 X 44	COV	350		700	3000
Cosette	LCA	Har-El	1990	SP	33 X 26	COV	350		500	1000
Happy Memories I, II	LCA	Har-El	1990	SP	20 X 16 EA	COV	350 EA		400 EA	800 EA
On the Stage	LCA	Har-El	1990	SP	32 X 26	COV	350		500	2000
Party Time	LCA	Har-El	1990	SP	36 X 27	COV	350		500	1400
Nostalgia	LCA	Har-El	1990	SP	27 X 27	COV	350		500	1400
Confession	LCA	Har-El	1990	SP	27 X 27	COV	350		500	1200
Quiet Afternoon	LCA	Har-El	1990	SP	33 X 44	COV	350		700	1400
Intimacy	LCA	Har-El	1990	SP	32 X 32	COV	350		600	1400
Daydream	LCA	Har-El	1990	SP	35 X 26	COV	350		500	1200
Champs Elysee	LCA	Har-El	1990	SP	23 X 47	COV	350		1000	3000
Loneliness I, II	LCA	Har-El	1990	SP	21 X 17 EA	COV	350 EA		450 EA	800 EA
Leisure Time	LCA	Har-El	1990	SP	31 X 27	COV	350		500	1400
Matchmakers I, II	LCA	Har-El	1990	SP	22 X 17 EA	COV	350 EA		500 EA	800 EA
Nude I, II, II	LCA	Har-El	1990	SP	8 X 8 EA	COV	350 EA		150 EA	250 EA
Passage	LCA	Har-El	1990	SP	8 X 8	COV	350		150	250
Aperitif	LCA	Har-El	1990	SP	32 X 42	COV	350		1200	1600
Montparnasse I, II	LCA	Har-El	1990	SP	17 X 21 EA	COV	350 EA		500 EA	800 EA
Rendezvous	LCA	Har-El	1990	SP	27 X 27	COV	350		850	1400
Companion	LCA	Har-El	1991	SP	27 X 36	COV	350		850	1400
Friendship	LCA	Har-El	1991	SP	27 X 36	COV	350		850	1400
Anne Marie	LCA	Har-El	1991	SP	39 X 40	COV	350		1000	2000
Pink Shadows I, II	LCA	Har-El	1991	SP	21 X 21 EA	COV	350 EA		500 EA	800 EA
Bon Jour la Vie I, II	LCA	Har-El	1991	SP	21 X 22 EA	COV	350 EA		500 EA	800 EA
Eve	LCA	Har-El	1991	SP	38 X 27	COV	350		850	1200
Harmony	LCA	Har-El	1991	SP	27 X 27	COV	350		850	1200
Reflection	LCA	Har-El	1991	SP	39 X 39	COV	350		1200	2500
In the Garden	LCA	Har-El	1991	SP	28 X 44	COV	350		1200	1800

ITZCHAK TARKAY CONTINUED

TITLE	PUBLISHER	PRINTER	DATE	MEDIUM	DIMENSION (PAPER SIZE) IN INCHES	TYPE OF PAPER	EDITION NUMBER	NO. OF COLORS	ORIGINAL OPENING PRICE	CURRENT RETAIL PRICE
SOLD OUT EDITIONS (RARE):										
Tea Party	LCA	Har-El	1991	SP	27 X 35	COV	350		850	2000
Jaffa Port	LCA	Har-El	1991	SP	38 X 36	COV	350		1200	2000
Trio	LCA	Har-El	1991	SP	27 X 35	COV	350		900	1600
Sarah	LCA	Har-El	1991	SP	16 X 21	COV	350		525	900
Lilac Time	LCA	Har-El	1991	SP	16 X 21	COV	350		525	900
Jaffa Cafe	LCA	Har-El	1991	SP	26 X 35	COV	350		900	1400
Blue Hat	LCA	Har-El	1991	SP	26 X 34	COV	350		900	1600
Memories	LCA	Har-El	1992	SP	30 X 27	COV	350		900	1300
Elegance I, II, III, IV (Set of 4)	LCA	Har-El	1992	SP	25 X 20 EA	COV	350 EA		2000 SET	2800 SET
Paris Cafe	LCA	Har-El	1992	SP	28 X 53	COV	350		1500	3000
Summer's Day	LCA	Har-El	1992	SP	38 X 39	COV	350		1200	1500
Serenity I, II (Set of 2)	LCA	Har-El	1992	SP	21 X 21 EA	COV	350 EA		1100 SET	1400 SET
Cafe	LCA	Har-El	1992	SP	27 X 34	COV	350		900	1100
Society I, II, III, IV (Set of 4)	LCA	Har-El	1992	SP	20 X 26 EA	COV	350 EA		2200 SET	2800 SET
Sevillana	LCA	Har-El	1992	SP	34 X 26	COV	350		900	1400
St Germain	LCA	Har-El	1992	SP	23 X 44	COV	350		1200	1400
The Flower Market	LCA	Har-El	1992	SP	28 X 53	COV	350		1500	1800
CURRENT EDITIONS:										
Lady in Blue	LCA	Har-El	1993	SP	44 X 16	COV	350		700	800
Lady in Red	LCA	Har-El	1993	SP	44 X 16	COV	350		700	800
Reading	LCA	Har-El	1993	SP	27 X 35	COV	350		900	1100
Springtime	LCA	Har-El	1993	SP	29 X 29	COV	350		900	1100
Rive Gauche	LCA	Har-El	1993	SP	25 X 51	COV	350		1500	1800
Unspoken Thoughts I, II	LCA	Har-El	1993	SP	23 X 23 EA	COV	350 EA		750 EA	850 EA
Contemplation	LCA	Har-El	1993	SP	34 X 27	COV	350		900	1100
Cassis	LCA	Har-El	1993	SP	21 X 28	COV	350		700	800
Mademoiselle	LCA	Har-El	1993	SP	21 X 28	COV	350		700	800

JANET TREBY

BORN: London, England; 1955
EDUCATION: West Surrey Col of Art & Design, England; Slade Col of Art, London, England
TEACHING: West Surrey Col of Art, England; Ruskin Sch of Drawing, Oxford, England; Barnfield Col, Luton, England; Southill Park Col, Bracknell, England

RECENT EXHIB: Curwen Gallery, London, England, 1987; Royal Gallery, London, England, 1991; St Helier Gallery, London, England, 1992
PRINTERS: London Contemporary Art, Inc, London, England (LCA)
PUBLISHERS: London Contemporary Art, Inc, London, England (LCA)
GALLERIES: Royal Gallery, London, England; St Helier Gallery, London, England; London Contemporary Art Gallery, London, England
MAILING ADDRESS: c/o London Contemporary Art, Inc, 729 Pinecrest, Prospect Heights, IL 60070

TITLE	PUBLISHER	PRINTER	DATE	MEDIUM	DIMENSION (PAPER SIZE) IN INCHES	TYPE OF PAPER	EDITION NUMBER	NO. OF COLORS	ORIGINAL OPENING PRICE	CURRENT RETAIL PRICE
SOLD OUT EDITIONS (RARE):										
Reposant	LCA	LCA	1987	EC	25 X 19	AP	200	12	275	700
Practice Room I	LCA	LCA	1988	EC	18 X 16	AP	200	15	275	550
Practice Room II	LCA	LCA	1988	EC	18 X 16	AP	200	18	275	550
Rehearsal	LCA	LCA	1988	EC	18 X 16	AP	200	19	300	600
Tranquillity	LCA	LCA	1989	EC	22 X 19	AP	200	17	300	600
Soft Interlude	LCA	LCA	1989	EC	21 X 17	AP	200	21	250	600
Calm Seclusion	LCA	LCA	1990	EC	21 X 17	AP	200	21	250	600
Veiled Secrets	LCA	LCA	1990	LC	25 X 19	R/BFK	275	19	275	300
Wild Horses I	LCA	LCA	1990	LC	23 X 30	R/BFK	225	12	250	750
Wild Horses II	LCA	LCA	1990	LC	23 X 30	R/BFK	225	12	250	750
Adoration	LCA	LCA	1991	LC	29 X 21	R/BFK	275	13	350	700
Awakening	LCA	LCA	1991	LC	26 X 19	R/BFK	200	17	275	650
Circus	LCA	LCA	1991	LC	26 X 19	R/BFK	200	11	250	600
Danse de Printemps	LCA	LCA	1991	LC	25 X 19	R/BFK	250	11	275	600
Fleeting Movement	LCA	LCA	1991	LC	26 X 20	R/BFK	250	18	300	650
Intimate Retreat	LCA	LCA	1991	LC	37 X 27	R/BFK	150	12	375	800
Liberation	LCA	LCA	1991	LC	37 X 27	R/BFK	200	9	375	800
Tumbling	LCA	LCA	1991	LC	26 X 19	R/BFK	200	14	250	600
CURRENT EDITIONS:										
The Dream	LCA	LCA	1991	LC	29 X 21	R/BFK	275	13	300	500
Graces	LCA	LCA	1992	LC	23 X 16	R/BFK	275	19	300	550
Muse	LCA	LCA	1992	LC	23 X 17	R/BFK	275	15	300	550
Birth of Venus	LCA	LCA	1993	LC	26 X 35	R/BFK	225	19	400	600
Olympian Myth I	LCA	LCA	1993	SP	35 X 22	AP	385	51	600	600
Olympian Myth II	LCA	LCA	1993	SP	35 X 22	AP	385	51	600	600
Aegean Legend I	LCA	LCA	1993	SP	40 X 30	AP	385	53	700	700
Dreams of Thira	LCA	LCA	1993	SP	30 X 37	AP	385	63	700	700

ANN TAYLOR

BORN: Rochester, NY; March 23, 1941
EDUCATION: Vassar Col, Poughkeepsie, NY; New Sch for Social Research, NY, BA, 1962
RECENT EXHIB: Marilyn Butler Fine Art, Scottsdale, AZ, 1987; Oxford Gallery, Rochester, NY, 1987
COLLECTIONS: Indianapolis Mus of Art, IN; Arizona State Univ, Tempe, AZ; Saginaw Mus, MI; Scottsdale Center for the Arts, AZ; Rochester Mem Mus, NY; Palm Springs Desert Mus, CA

PRINTERS: Kimball Lithographic Co, Ltd, Mesa, AZ
PUBLISHERS: C G Rein Publishers, St Paul, MN (CGR)
GALLERIES: C G Rein Galleries, Scottsdale, AZ & Santa Fe, NM & Houston, TX & Minneapolis, MN; Oxford Gallery, Rochester, NY; Gallery Henoch, New York, NY; Kauffman Galleries, Houston, TX; Branner Spangenberg Contemporary Art, Davis, CA
MAILING ADDRESS: 145 Water St, Stonington, CT 06378

TITLE	PUBLISHER	PRINTER	DATE	MEDIUM	DIMENSION (PAPER SIZE) IN INCHES	TYPE OF PAPER	EDITION NUMBER	NO. OF COLORS	ORIGINAL OPENING PRICE	CURRENT RETAIL PRICE
SOLD OUT EDITIONS (RARE):										
Warp Speed	CGR	KLC	1982	LC	22 X 22	AP	100	11	300	750
Celerity	CGR	KLC	1982	LC	22 X 28	AP	75	10	300	750

ELYSE TAYLOR

RECENT EXHIB: Douglass Col, New Brunswick, NJ, 1992
PRINTERS: John Nichols, NY (JN)
PUBLISHERS: John Nichols, Printmakers & Publishers, NY (JN)

TITLE	PUBLISHER	PRINTER	DATE	MEDIUM	DIMENSION (PAPER SIZE) IN INCHES	TYPE OF PAPER	EDITION NUMBER	NO. OF COLORS	ORIGINAL OPENING PRICE	CURRENT RETAIL PRICE
CURRENT EDITIONS:										
What a Day!	JN	JN	1985	SP	22 X 30	RF/BFK/B	60	9	350	500

N WAYNE TAYLOR

BORN: Nampa, ID; January 13, 1931
EDUCATION: Sacramento State Col, CA, AB, 1957; Mills Col, Oakland, CA, MFA, 1959
TEACHING: Instr, Sacramento State Col, CA, Summer, 1961; Instr, Northern Illinois Univ, DeKalb, IL, 1962–63; Instr, Sculptor, Rutgers Univ, New Brunswick, NJ, 1968–69; Vis Prof, California State Univ, Sacramento, CA, Spring, 1974; Chmn, Art Dept, Univ of Wisconsin, Madison, WI, 1981–84; Prof, Univ of Wisconsin, Madison, WI, 1963 to present

COLLECTIONS: Whitney Mus of Am Art, NY; New Jersey State Mus, Trenton, NJ; Univ of North Dakota, Grand Forks, ND; Mills Col, Oakland, CA; Milton Col, WI; Milwaukee Art Center, WI
PRINTERS: Artist (ART)
PUBLISHERS: Artist (ART)
GALLERIES: Spaightwood Galleries, Madison, WI; Marita Gilliam Gallery, Raleigh, NC
MAILING ADDRESS: 2370 County Trail Highway, N, Stoughton, WI 53589

TITLE	PUBLISHER	PRINTER	DATE	MEDIUM	DIMENSION (PAPER SIZE) IN INCHES	TYPE OF PAPER	EDITION NUMBER	NO. OF COLORS	ORIGINAL OPENING PRICE	CURRENT RETAIL PRICE
CURRENT EDITIONS:										
Face Off	ART	ART	1984	MON	22 X 30 EA	R/BFK	1 EA	1 EA	800 EA	900 EA
Zapped Square	ART	ART	1984	MON	22 X 30 EA	R/BFK	1 EA	1 EA	800 EA	900 EA
Cochise	ART	ART	1984	MON	22 X 30 EA	R/BFK	1 EA	1 EA	800 EA	900 EA
Kegonsa Series: A/20	ART	ART	1984	MON	22 X 30 EA	R/BFK	1 EA	1 EA	500 EA	600 EA
The Kiss	ART	ART	1984	MON	22 X 30 EA	R/BFK	1 EA	1 EA	800 EA	900 EA
Lydian Bold	ART	ART	1984	MON	22 X 30 EA	R/BFK	1 EA	1 EA	800 EA	900 EA
Arapahoe	ART	ART	1984	MON	22 X 30 EA	R/BFK	1 EA	1 EA	800 EA	900 EA
Kegonsa Series: C/13	ART	ART	1984	MON	22 X 30 EA	R/BFK	1 EA	1 EA	800 EA	900 EA
Marked	ART	ART	1984	MON	22 X 30 EA	R/BFK	1 EA	1 EA	850 EA	950 EA
Blue Dun	ART	ART	1985	MON	22 X 30 EA	R/BFK	1 EA	1 EA	800 EA	900 EA
Opening Nite	ART	ART	1985	MON	22 X 30 EA	R/BFK	1 EA	1 EA	800 EA	900 EA
Martin's Maze	ART	ART	1985	MON	22 X 30 EA	R/BFK	1 EA	3 EA	600 EA	700 EA
Glitz	ART	ART	1985	MON	22 X 30 EA	R/BFK	1 EA	1 EA	800 EA	900 EA
Jungle Drums (Dipt)	ART	ART	1985	MON	22 X 30 EA	R/BFK	1 EA	1 EA	1000 SET	2000 SET
Ghost Riders	ART	ART	1985	MON	22 X 30 EA	R/BFK	1 EA	3 EA	850 EA	950 EA
Zonk	ART	ART	1985	MON	22 X 30 EA	R/BFK	1 EA	1 EA	800 EA	900 EA
Zippydoo	ART	ART	1985	MON	22 X 30 EA	R/BFK	1 EA	1 EA	800 EA	900 EA
Zap Zap	ART	ART	1985	MON	22 X 30 EA	R/BFK	1 EA	1 EA	800 EA	900 EA
Carnival	ART	ART	1985	MON	22 X 30 EA	R/BFK	1 EA	5 EA	850 EA	950 EA
Windward	ART	ART	1985	MON	22 X 30 EA	FAB	1 EA	2 EA	850 EA	950 EA
Deepdeen	ART	ART	1985	MON	22 X 30 EA	R/BFK	1 EA	1 EA	800 EA	900 EA
Granjon	ART	ART	1985	MON	22 X 30 EA	R/BFK	1 EA	1 EA	800 EA	900 EA
Crossbow	ART	ART	1985	MON	22 X 30 EA	R/BFK	1 EA	1 EA	800 EA	900 EA
Blue Dun Again	ART	ART	1985	MON	22 X 30 EA	R/BFK	1 EA	1 EA	800 EA	900 EA
Five Bandaleras	ART	ART	1986	MON	36 X 48 EA 40 X 52 EA	AP88	1 EA	3 EA	800 EA	900 EA
Five White Poles	ART	ART	1986	MON	36 X 48 EA 40 X 52 EA	AP88	1 EA	1 EA	750 EA	850 EA
Bandaleras	ART	ART	1986	MON	24 X 48 EA 24 X 48 EA	AP88	1 EA	3 EA	700 EA	800 EA
Snowdance	ART	ART	1986	MON	22 X 30 EA	AP88	1 EA	1 EA	800 EA	900 EA
Karnak Black	ART	ART	1986	MON	22 X 30 EA	R/BFK	1 EA	1 EA	800 EA	900 EA

PRENTISS TAYLOR

BORN: (1907–1991)
PRINTERS: Artist (ART)
PUBLISHERS: Artist (ART)

TITLE	PUBLISHER	PRINTER	DATE	MEDIUM	DIMENSION (PAPER SIZE) IN INCHES	TYPE OF PAPER	EDITION NUMBER	NO. OF COLORS	ORIGINAL OPENING PRICE	CURRENT RETAIL PRICE
SOLD OUT EDITIONS (RARE):										
Riding the Rail	ART	ART	1931	LB	12 X 9	WOVE	10	1	25	600
Christ in Alabama	ART	ART	1932	LB	9 X 6	WOVE	45	1	25	700
Scottsboro Limited	ART	ART	1932	LB	9 X 6	WOVE	80	1	25	700
Town of Scottsboro	ART	ART	1932	LB	8 X 6	WOVE	42	1	25	700
Horlbeck Alley	ART	ART	1934	LB	9 X 13	WOVE		1	25	1200
Jenkins Orphanage	ART	ART	1934	LB	12 X 10	WOVE		1	25	350
Assembly Church	ART	ART	1936	LB	10 X 14	WOVE	40	1	30	700
Myself as Mezzetint	ART	ART	1936	LB	13 X 9	WOVE	40	1	30	500
Christiansted Plaza	ART	ART	1939	LB	10 X 14	WOVE	35	1	30	300
The Service Club	ART	ART	1939	LB	11 X 14	WOVE	35	1	30	600
In Whom I am Well Pleased	ART	ART	1940	LB	11 X 15	WOVE	35	1	35	600
Uprooted Stalk	ART	ART	1940	LB	10 X 12	WOVE	35	1	35	500
Autumn Breakfast	ART	ART	1944	LB	10 X 9	AP	25	1	40	350
Watermelon Wagon	ART	ART	1947	LB	7 X 11	AP	30	1	50	300
Black on Black	ART	ART	1948	LB	10 X 14	AP	30	1	50	400
Morning Light-Telluride			1961	LB	12 X 16	AP			75	350
Pictograph Trail—Mesa...			1965	LC	13 X 17	AP			90	400
Cliff and Ruin-Canyon de Chell			1976	LB	15 X 10	AP	75		125	350

SYDNEY TAYLOR

BORN: London, England
COLLECTIONS: Wayne State Univ, NE; Univ of Houston, TX; Rice Univ, Sewell Art Gallery, Houston, TX; Mus of Printing History, Houston, TX; Arkansas Art Center, Little Rock, AR; Alexandria, Mus, LA
PRINTERS: Joseph Kleineman, NY (JK)
PUBLISHERS: Post Oak Fine Art Distributors, Houston, TX (POFA)

TITLE	PUBLISHER	PRINTER	DATE	MEDIUM	DIMENSION (PAPER SIZE) IN INCHES	TYPE OF PAPER	EDITION NUMBER	NO. OF COLORS	ORIGINAL OPENING PRICE	CURRENT RETAIL PRICE
SOLD OUT EDITIONS (RARE):										
Leopards, Out of Shadows	POFA	JK	1982	LC	22 X 30	SOM	200	10	250	300
Dusty Elephants	POFA	JK	1982	LC	22 X 30	SOM	200	10	250	300
Lion Portrait	POFA	JK	1982	LC	22 X 30	SOM	200	10	250	300
Siberian Tigers	POFA	JK	1982	LC	22 X 30	SOM	200	10	250	300

MARY TEICHMAN

BORN: Newark, NJ; September 8, 1954
EDUCATION: Cooper Union, NY, BFA, 1976
AWARDS: Nat Arts Club, Hon Mention, 1979; Purchase Prize, Nat Print Exhib, 1980; Otis Philbrook Award, Boston Printmakers Show, 1985; Arch Prize, Soc of Am Graphic Artists, NY, 1986; Purchase Award, Heart of Am Print Exhib, Univ of Missouri, Columbia, MO, 1986; Purchase Prize, Stella Drabkin Mem Award, Am Color Print Soc Exhib, 1986; Boston Printmakers Award, 1988
RECENT EXHIB: Univ of Minnesota, Morrin, MN, 1987; Ernesto Mayans Gallery, Santa Fe, NM, 1987; Mid-Hudson Art & Science Center, Poughkeepsie, NY, 1988; Nat Acad of Dessi Design, NY, 1988; Univ of New Brunswick, NJ, 1989
COLLECTIONS: Brooklyn Mus, NY; Trenton State Col, NJ; Carnegie Inst, Pittsburgh, PA; Columbus Mus of Art & Arch, Columbia, MO
PRINTERS: Artist (ART)
PUBLISHERS: Artist (ART)
GALLERIES: A Clean, Well Lighted Place, Inc, New York, NY; Mona Berman Gallery, New Haven, CT; Ernesto Mayans Gallery, Santa Fe, NM; Associated American Artists, New York, NY; Mary Ryan Gallery, New York, NY; van Straaten Gallery, Chicago, IL; Lumley Cazalet Ltd, London, England; Adamson Gallery, New York, NY; Jacob Fanning Gallery, Wellfleet, MA; Shoestring Gallery, Rochester, NY
MAILING ADDRESS: 453 15th St, Brooklyn, NY 11215

TITLE	PUBLISHER	PRINTER	DATE	MEDIUM	DIMENSION (PAPER SIZE) IN INCHES	TYPE OF PAPER	EDITION NUMBER	NO. OF COLORS	ORIGINAL OPENING PRICE	CURRENT RETAIL PRICE
SOLD OUT EDITIONS (RARE):										
Interior	ART	ART	1977	EC/AC	12 X 10	THS	30	4	65	200
Southern Exposure	ART	ART	1980	EC/AC	8 X 13	THS	50	4	80	200
Tools of the Trade	ART	ART	1981	EC/AC	7 X 9	THS	50	4	90	200
Token, et Cetera	ART	ART	1981	EC/AC	12 X 15	THS	50	4	150	200
Light Reading	ART	ART	1981	EC	18 X 24	THS	50	4	125	300
Vanity	ART	ART	1983	EC	19 X 23	R/BFK	50	4	125	300
CURRENT EDITIONS:										
Daydream	ART	ART	1980	C/AC	15 X 14	R/BFK	50	4	125	200
Waiting	ART	ART	1980	EC/AC	12 X 10	R/BFK	50	4	125	200
Les Oranges	ART	ART	1981	EC/AC	14 X 20	R/BFK	50	4	185	300
A Woman's Place	ART	ART	1982	EC/AC	16 X 20	THS	50	4	200	250
In Retrospect	ART	ART	1982	EC/AC	5 X 14	THS	50	4	125	200
Over the Edge	ART	ART	1983	EC	19 X 22	R/BFK	50	4	125	250
Broken Heart	ART	ART	1983	EC	14 X 18	THS	50	4	100	200
Rome Beauty	ART	ART	1984	EC	14 X 15	THS	50	4	100	200
Downtown	ART	ART	1984	EC	19 X 20	R/BFK	75	4	125	300
At Both Ends	ART	ART	1984	EC	15 X 19	R/BFK	50	4	100	200

MARY TEICHMAN CONTINUED

TITLE	PUBLISHER	PRINTER	DATE	MEDIUM	DIMENSION (PAPER SIZE) IN INCHES	TYPE OF PAPER	EDITION NUMBER	NO. OF COLORS	ORIGINAL OPENING PRICE	CURRENT RETAIL PRICE
CURRENT EDITIONS:										
Night Rates	ART	ART	1984	EC	17 X 24	THS	75	4	150	250
Sideways	ART	ART	1985	EC	13 X 24	R/BFK	50	4	100	200
Local Station	ART	ART	1985	EC	19 X 23	R/BFK	50	4	150	250
Glass Minute	ART	ART	1985	EC	15 X 16	THS	50	4	125	200
Permanent Wave	ART	ART	1985	EC	15 X 17	R/BFK	50	4	125	200
Tempus Fugit	ART	ART	1986	EC	11 X 14	THS	50	4	85	200

IRVIN TEPPER

RECENT EXHIB: Gallery Paule Anglim, San Francisco, CA, 1987
PRINTERS: Conrad Schwable, Medical Lake, WA (CS); Ocean Works, Medical Lake, WA (OW)
PUBLISHERS: Marc Freidus, NY (MF); Anderson Ranch Arts Center, Snowmass, CO (ARAC)
GALLERIES: Vanderwoude/Tananbaum Gallery, New York, NY; Morgan Gallery, Kansas City, MO; Gallery Paule Anglim, San Francisco, CA; Sander Gallery, New York, NY

TITLE	PUBLISHER	PRINTER	DATE	MEDIUM	DIMENSION (PAPER SIZE) IN INCHES	TYPE OF PAPER	EDITION NUMBER	NO. OF COLORS	ORIGINAL OPENING PRICE	CURRENT RETAIL PRICE
CURRENT EDITIONS:										
Big Ear/Big Mouth	MF	CS/OW	1984	LB	22 X 30	AP/BL	30	1	500	600
Happy Boy	MF/ARAC	CS/OW	1985	LC	41 X 30	AP/BL	50	14	950	1000

MASAMI TERAOKA

BORN: Onomichi, Japan; January 13, 1936
EDUCATION: Kwansei Gwakuin Univ, Kobe, Japan, BA, Aesthetics, 1959; Otis Art Inst, Los Angeles, CA, BA, MFA, 1968
AWARDS: Los Angeles County Mus, CA, 1978; Purchase Award, Kay Nielsen Mem Prize, Graphic Arts Council, Los Angeles, CA; Nat Endowment for the Arts Fel, 1980–81
RECENT EXHIB: Monterey Peninsula Mus, CA, 1987; Los Angeles County Mus, CA, 1987; Delaware Art Mus, Wilmington, DE, 1992; Jersey City Mus, NY, 1992; Univ of Washington, Henry Art Gallery, Seattle, WA, 1992; Pamela Auchincloss Gallery, NY, 1989,90,92
COLLECTIONS: Oakland Mus, CA; Achenbach Found of Graphic Arts, Fine Arts Mus, San Francisco, CA; Los Angeles County, CA; Newport Harbor Art Mus, Newport Beach, CA; Minneapolis Inst of Arts, MN; Monterey Peninsula Mus, CA; San Francisco Mus of Mod Art, CA; Nat Mus of Fine Arts, Wash, DC
PRINTERS: Editions Press, San Francisco, CA (EP); Smalltree Press, San Francisco, CA (SmP); Experimental Workshop, San Francisco, CA (EW); Vermillion Editions, Ltd, Minneapolis, MN (VEL)
PUBLISHERS: Editions Press, San Francisco, CA (EP); Smalltree Press, San Francisco, CA (SmP); Vermillion Editions, Ltd, Minneapolis, MN (VEL)
GALLERIES: Space Gallery, Los Angeles, CA; Walton-Gilbert Gallery, San Francisco, CA; Merging One Gallery, Santa Monica, CA; Experimental Workshop, San Francisco, CA; Betsy Senior Contemporary Prints, New York, NY; Pamela Auchincloss Gallery, New York, NY; Schmidt/Dean Gallery, Phila, PA; Vermillion Editions, Ltd, Minneapolis, MN; Tyler Graphics, Ltd, Mount Krisco, NY

TITLE	PUBLISHER	PRINTER	DATE	MEDIUM	DIMENSION (PAPER SIZE) IN INCHES	TYPE OF PAPER	EDITION NUMBER	NO. OF COLORS	ORIGINAL OPENING PRICE	CURRENT RETAIL PRICE
CURRENT EDITIONS:										
Woman/Ice Cream Cone	VEL	VEL	1980	LC		AP			300	1200
MHIJ/Tokyo Ginza & Broom	VEL	VEL	1980	LC		AP			500	2000
MHIJ/Tokyo Ginza Shuffle	VEL	VEL	1980	LC		AP			500	900
Spring Women I	VEL	VEL	1980	LC		AP			250	350
Spring Women II	VEL	VEL	1980	LC		AP			250	350
Namiyo at Hanauma Bay	EP	EP	1985	LC	25 X 36	AC/B	150	18	1700	3500
AIDS Series (Set of 4):									1700 SET	1700 SET
Artist and Canvas	SmP	SmP	1988	EB/CC	15 X 11	KIT/GEE	52	1	500	650
Condom Pillow Book	SmP	SmP	1988	EB/CC	15 X 11	KIT/GEE	52	1	500	650
Woman at Balcony	SmP	SmP	1988	EB/CC	15 X 11	KIT/GEE	52	1	500	650
Geisha and the Geigin	SmP	SmP	1988	EB/CC	15 X 11	KIT/GEE	52	1	500	650

MICHAEL TETHEROW

BORN: Tacoma, WA; 1942
EDUCATION: San Francisco Art Inst, CA, BFA, 1968
AWARDS: Engelhard Found Award, 1985; Nat Endowment for the Arts Fel Awards, 1979,87
RECENT EXHIB: Nina Freudenheim Gallery, Buffalo, NY, 1989– 90; Heckscher Mus, Huntington, NY, 1991; Albright-Knox Art Gallery, Buffalo, NY, 1991; Jason McCoy, Inc, NY, 1992
COLLECTIONS: Whitney Mus of Am Art, NY; Brooklyn Mus, NY; Dallas Mus of Art, TX; Seattle Mus of Contemp Art, WA; Syracuse Univ, NY; Neuberger Mus of Art, Southhampton, NY; New York Public Library, NY; Albright-Knox Art Gallery, Buffalo, NY; Heckscher Mus, Huntington, NY
PRINTERS: Stephen Cadwalder, Somerville, MA (SC); Mix-It, Somerville, MA (MI)
PUBLISHERS: Jason McCoy, Inc, NY (JMI)
GALLERIES: Jason McCoy, Inc, New York, NY
MAILING ADDRESS: c/o Jason McCoy, Inc, 41 E 57th St, New York, NY 10022

TITLE	PUBLISHER	PRINTER	DATE	MEDIUM	DIMENSION (PAPER SIZE) IN INCHES	TYPE OF PAPER	EDITION NUMBER	NO. OF COLORS	ORIGINAL OPENING PRICE	CURRENT RETAIL PRICE
CURRENT EDITIONS:										
Intaglio Suite (Set of 4)	JMI	SC/MI	1990	AB/SB	22 X 30 EA	R/BFK	15 EA	1 EA	2800 SET	2800 SET

IVAN THEIMER

BORN: Olomouc, Czechoslovakia; 1944
EDUCATION: Gottwaldor Sch of Arts & Crafts, Czechoslovakia

AWARDS: Prix I A T, Salon de la Jeune Sculpture, Paris, France, 1969–71
PRINTERS: Pierre Bada Lithographie, Paris, France (PBL)
PUBLISHERS: Post Oak Fine Art, Houston, TX (POFA)

TITLE	PUBLISHER	PRINTER	DATE	MEDIUM	DIMENSION (PAPER SIZE) IN INCHES	TYPE OF PAPER	EDITION NUMBER	NO. OF COLORS	ORIGINAL OPENING PRICE	CURRENT RETAIL PRICE
SOLD OUT EDITIONS (RARE):										
Le Leze 1973/74	POFA	PBL	1982	LC	21 X 30	AP	200	6	400	450
Le Leze 1979/80	POFA	PBL	1982	LC	21 X 30	AP	200	6	400	450
Le Leze II	POFA	PBL	1982	LC	21 X 30	AP	200	6	400	450
Passage	POFA	PBL	1982	LC	21 X 30	AP	200	6	400	450
St. Hubert	POFA	PBL	1982	LC	21 X 30	AP	200	6	400	450

PAUL THEK

PRINTERS: Patricia Branstead, NY (PB); Branstead Studio, NY (BS)
PUBLISHERS: Brooke Alexander, Inc, NY (BAI)
GALLERIES: Brooke Alexander Editions, New York, NY

TITLE	PUBLISHER	PRINTER	DATE	MEDIUM	DIMENSION (PAPER SIZE) IN INCHES	TYPE OF PAPER	EDITION NUMBER	NO. OF COLORS	ORIGINAL OPENING PRICE	CURRENT RETAIL PRICE
CURRENT EDITIONS:										
Untitled (Set of 28):		PB/BS	1975–92	EB	8 X 10 EA	R/BFK	12 EA	1 EA	7500 SET	7500 SET
Untitled	BAI	PB/BS	1975–92	EB	26 X 20	R/BFK	25	1	2500	2500
Untitled (Ave Eva)	BAI	PB/BS	1975–92	EB	8 X 11	R/BFK	25	1	300	300
Untitled (Balloon)	BAI	PB/BS	1975–92	EB	8 X 10	R/BFK	25	1	300	300
Untitled (Beau Jangles)	BAI	PB/BS	1975–92	EB	8 X 11	R/BFK	25	1	300	300
Untitled (Bouncing Earth 2nd Time)	BAI	PB/BS	1975–92	EB	8 X 11	R/BFK	25	1	300	300
Untitled (Broken Glass)	BAI	PB/BS	1975–92	EB	8 X 11	R/BFK	25	1	300	300
Untitled (Burning Brook)	BAI	PB/BS	1975–92	EB	8 X 10	R/BFK	25	1	300	300
Untitled (Campfire)	BAI	PB/BS	1975–92	EB	8 X 10	R/BFK	25	1	300	300
Untitled (Coming out of the Hills)	BAI	PB/BS	1975–92	EB	8 X 10	R/BFK	25	1	300	300
Untitled (Prunes)	BAI	PB/BS	1975–92	EB	8 X 10	R/BFK	25	1	300	300
Untitled (Eye)	BAI	PB/BS	1975–92	EB	8 X 10	R/BFK	25	1	300	300
Untitled (Fall the 3rd Time)	BAI	PB/BS	1975–92	EB	8 X 11	R/BFK	25	1	300	300
Untitled (Horned Cross)	BAI	PB/BS	1975–92	EB	8 X 11	R/BFK	25	1	300	300
Untitled (I Am, Am I?)	BAI	PB/BS	1975–92	EB	8 X 11	R/BFK	25	1	300	300
Untitled (Potato)	BAI	PB/BS	1975–92	EB	8 X 10	R/BFK	25	1	300	300
Untitled (Prune)	BAI	PB/BS	1975–92	EB	8 X 10	R/BFK	25	1	300	300
Untitled (Rising Heart, 1st Version)	BAI	PB/BS	1975–92	EB	8 X 10	R/BFK	25	1	300	300
Untitled (Rising Heart, 2nd Version)	BAI	PB/BS	1975–92	EB	8 X 10	R/BFK	25	1	300	300
Untitled (Rising Heart, 3rd Version)	BAI	PB/BS	1975–92	EB	8 X 10	R/BFK	25	1	300	300
Untitled (Scourging of Beau Jangles)	BAI	PB/BS	1975–92	EB	8 X 11	R/BFK	25	1	300	300
Untitled (Stars & Stripes)	BAI	PB/BS	1975–92	EB	8 X 11	R/BFK	25	1	300	300
Untitled (Swan)	BAI	PB/BS	1975–92	EB	8 X 10	R/BFK	25	1	300	300
Untitled (Sweet Corn)	BAI	PB/BS	1975–92	EB	8 X 10	R/BFK	25	1	300	300
Untitled (Tar Baby)	BAI	PB/BS	1975–92	EB	8 X 11	R/BFK	25	1	300	300
Untitled (The Cross of Polyana)	BAI	PB/BS	1975–92	EB	8 X 11	R/BFK	25	1	300	300
Untitled (The People of the Earth)	BAI	PB/BS	1975–92	EB	8 X 11	R/BFK	25	1	300	300
Untitled (This is My Body)	BAI	PB/BS	1975–92	EB	8 X 11	R/BFK	25	1	300	300
Untitled (Tower of Babel)	BAI	PB/BS	1975–92	EB	8 X 11	R/BFK	25	1	300	300
Untitled (Wild Oaf)	BAI	PB/BS	1975–92	EB	8 X 11	R/BFK	25	1	300	300

GILLIAN LEE THEOBALD

BORN: La Jolla, CA; November 17, 1944
EDUCATION: Studied with Byam Shaw, London, England, 1964–65; San Diego State Univ, CA, BA, 1967, MA, 1971
RECENT EXHIB: Fresno Mus of Art, CA, 1987; Patty Aande Gallery, San Diego, CA, 1987; Palomar Col, San Marcos, CA, 1988; Cirrus Gallery, Los Angeles, CA, 1988; Long Island Art Mus, NY, 1989; Palomar Col, San Marcos, CA, 1990; Occidental Col, Los Angeles, CA, 1990; Cirrus Gallery, Los Angeles, CA, 1989,90; Rose Art Gallery, Brandeis Mus, Waltham, Ma, 1991

PRINTERS: Richard Hammond, Los Angeles, CA (RH); Francesco Siqueiros, Los Angeles, CA (RS); Cirrus Editions Workshop, Los Angeles, CA (CEW)
PUBLISHERS: Cirrus Editions, Ltd, Los Angeles, CA (CE)
GALLERIES: Cirrus Gallery, Los Angeles, CA; David Lewinson Gallery, Del Mar, CA
MAILING ADDRESS: 7225 29th St, NE, Seattle, WA 98115

TITLE	PUBLISHER	PRINTER	DATE	MEDIUM	DIMENSION (PAPER SIZE) IN INCHES	TYPE OF PAPER	EDITION NUMBER	NO. OF COLORS	ORIGINAL OPENING PRICE	CURRENT RETAIL PRICE
CURRENT EDITIONS:										
Firestorm Series:										
Firestorm: Illuminated Site	CE	CEW	1984	LC	30 X 40	AP	30	4	500	850
Firestorm: Stolen Vision	CE	CEW	1984	LC	30 X 40	AP	30	5	500	850
Phenomena Series:										
Singular Phenomena	CE	RH/FS/CEW	1986	LC	30 X 40	AP88/W	35	7	500	850
Related Phenomena	CE	RH/FS/CEW	1986	LC	30 X 40	AP88/W	35	7	500	850

WAYNE THIEBAUD

BORN: Mesa, Arizona; November 15, 1920
EDUCATION: San Jose State Col, CA; Sacramento State Col, CA, BA, 1951, MA, 1952; California Sch of Arts & Crafts, Valencia, CA, Hon DFA, 1973; Dickinson Col, Carlisle, PA, Hon, DFA, 1983; San Francisco Art Inst, Hon DFA, 1987
TEACHING: Chmn, Art Dept, Sacramento City Col, CA, 1951; Guest Instr, San Francisco Art Inst, CA, 1958; Prof, Art, Uni Prof, Art & Artist in Res, Cornell Univ, Ithaca, NY, 1966; Artist in Res, Yale Univ, New Haven, CT, 1974; Artist in Res, Rice Univ, Houston, TX, 1975
AWARDS: Creative Research Found Grant, 1961; California Col of Arts & Crafts, Valencia, CA, 1974; College Art Assoc of Am, 1981
RECENT EXHIB: San Antonio Mus of Art, TX, 1987; Arts Club of Chicago, IL, 1987; Marilyn Butler Gallery, Santa Monica, CA, 1989; Fresno Metropolitan Mus, CA, 1992; Univ of California, Irvine, CA, 1992; Palo Alto Cultural Center, CA, 1987,92; Miami-Dade Com Col, FL, 1992; Albrecht-Kemper Mus of Art, St Joseph, MO, 1992; Fairleigh Dickinson Univ, Phyllis Rothman Gallery, Madison, WI, 1992; Heckscher Mus, Huntington, NY, 1992; Associated Am Artists, NY, 1993
COLLECTIONS: Mus of Mod Art, NY; Whitney Mus of Mod Art, NY; San Francisco Mus of Mod Art, CA; Metropolitan Mus of Art, NY; Brandeis Univ, Waltham, MA; Bryn Mawr Col, PA; Chicago Inst of Art, IL; Philadelphia Mus of Art, Phila, PA; Corcoran Art Gallery, Wash, DC; Rhode Island Sch of Design, Providence, RI; Albright-Knox Art Gallery, Buffalo, NY; Mus of Fine Arts, Dallas, TX; Univ of Miami, FL; Stanford Univ, CA; Newark Mus, NJ; Univ of Nebraska, Omaha, NE; Sacramento State Col, CA; San Jose State Col, CA; Southern Illinois Univ, Carbondale, IL
PRINTERS: Fleming Silkscreen Company, NY (FSC); Artist (ART); Crown Point Press, San Francisco, CA (CPP); Tadashi Toda, Kyoto, Japan (TT); Shiu-un-do Print Shop, Kyoto, Japan (SRS); Marcia Bartholme (MB); Peter Pettengill (PP); Hidekatsu Takada (HT); June Lambla (JL); Shunzo Matsuda, Kyoto, Japan (SM); Lawrence Hamlin, San Francisco, CA (LH); Mark Callen, San Francisco, CA (MC); Daria Sywulak, San Francisco, CA (DS); Katan Brown, San Francisco, CA (KB)
PUBLISHERS: Parasol Press, NY (PaP); Crown Point Press, San Francisco, CA (CPP); Artist (ART); Chicago Int Art Expo, IL (CIAE)
GALLERIES: John Berggruen Gallery, San Francisco, CA; Crown Point Press, New York, NY & San Francisco, CA; Martina Hamilton Gallery, New York, NY; Davidson Galleries, Seattle, WA; Greystone, San Francisco, CA; Magnuson Gallery, Boston, MA; Andrew Dierken Fine Art, Los Angeles, CA; John Natsoulas Gallery, Davis, CA; J Noblett Gallery, Boyes Hot Springs, CA; Irene Drori Fine Art, Los Angeles, CA; Jonathan Novak Contemporary Art, Los Angeles, CA; Herbert Palmer Gallery, Los Angeles, CA; Dunlop-Freidenrich Fine Art, Newport Beach, CA; Harcourts Modern & Contemporary Art, San Francisco, CA; Walton-Gilbert Galleries, San Francisco, CA; James Corcoran Gallery, Santa Monica, CA; Richard Green Graphics, Santa Monica, CA; Van Straaten Gallery, Chicago, IL; Golden Gallery, Boston, MA; Thomson Gallery, Minneapolis, MN; Nancy Singer Gallery, St Louis, MO; Associated American Artists, New York, NY; Foster Goldstrom, Inc, New York, NY; Nohra Haime Gallery, New York, NY; Linda Hyman Fine Arts, New York, NY; Posner Gallery, Milwaukee, WI; Gerald Peters Gallery, Dallas, TX
MAILING ADDRESS: Dept of Art, University of California, Davis, CA 95616

Wayne Theibaud
Valley Farm
Courtesy Crown Point Press

TITLE	PUBLISHER	PRINTER	DATE	MEDIUM	DIMENSION (PAPER SIZE) IN INCHES	TYPE OF PAPER	EDITION NUMBER	NO. OF COLORS	ORIGINAL OPENING PRICE	CURRENT RETAIL PRICE
SOLD OUT EDITIONS (RARE):										
Cut Melon	ART		1964	EB	6 X 7	R/BFK	15	1	100	8000
Pie Rows	CPP	CPP	1964	EB/A	4 X 5	R/BFK	100	1	100	5000
Nickle Machine			1964	EB	8 X 5	R/BFK	15	1	100	5000
Sucker Tree			1964	WC	8 X 7	R/BFK	8		125	12000
Untitled			1964	EB	20 X 26	R/BFK	15		250	24000
Delights Suite (Set of 17):									1500 SET	105000 SET
Lunch	CPP	CPP	1965	EC	15 X 11	R/BFK	100		100	6500
Fish	CPP	CPP	1965	DPT	15 X 11	R/BFK	100		100	6500
Banana Splits	CPP	CPP	1965	EC	15 X 11	R/BFK	100		100	6500
Cherry Stand	CPP	CPP	1965	EC	15 X 11	R/BFK	100		100	6500
Bacon & Eggs	CPP	CPP	1965	EC	15 X 11	R/BFK	100		100	6500
Double Deckers	CPP	CPP	1965	DPT	15 X 11	R/BFK	100		100	6500
Lunch Counter	CPP	CPP	1965	EC	15 X 11	R/BFK	100		100	6500
Dispensers	CPP	CPP	1965	DPT	15 X 11	R/BFK	100		100	6500
Gum Machine	CPP	CPP	1965	EC	15 X 11	R/BFK	100		100	6500
Lemon Meringue	CPP	CPP	1965	EC	15 X 11	R/BFK	100		100	6500
Suckers	CPP	CPP	1965	AC	15 X 11	R/BFK	100		100	6500
Candied Apples	CPP	CPP	1965	EC	15 X 11	R/BFK	100		100	6500
Cake Window	CPP	CPP	1965	EC	15 X 11	R/BFK	100		100	6500
Club Sandwich	CPP	CPP	1965	EC	15 X 11	R/BFK	100		100	6500
Pies	CPP	CPP	1965	EB/A	15 X 11	R/BFK	100		100	6500
Delicatessen	CPP	CPP	1965	AC	15 X 11	R/BFK	100		100	6500
Olives	CPP	CPP	1965	AC	15 X 11	R/BFK	100		100	6500
Suckers—Red, State II (G-86)	GEM	GEM	1968	LC	16 X 22	R/BFK	150	1	200	10500
Lipstick Row	PaP	FSC	1970	SP	22 X 30	R/BFK	50		200	26000

WAYNE THIEBAUD CONTINUED

TITLE	PUBLISHER	PRINTER	DATE	MEDIUM	DIMENSION (PAPER SIZE) IN INCHES	TYPE OF PAPER	EDITION NUMBER	NO. OF COLORS	ORIGINAL OPENING PRICE	CURRENT RETAIL PRICE
SOLD OUT EDITIONS (RARE):										
Seven Still Lifes & a Rabbit Series:										
Toy Counter	PaP		1970	SP	22 X 30	AP	50		200	9000
Candy Counter	PaP		1970	LI	22 X 30	AP	50	2	200	9000
Gum Ball Machine	PaP		1970	LI	30 X 22	AP	50	5	200	9000
Chocolate Cake	PaP		1971	LC	30 X 22	AP	50		250	9000
Big Suckers	PaP		1971	AC	22 X 30	R/BFK	50		200	15000
Black Suckers	PaP		1971	AB	22 X 28	R/BFK	50	1	200	12000
Triangle Thins	PaP		1971	EC	22 X 18	R/BFK	50		250	10000
Recent Etchings I Series:										
Shoe Rows	PaP	CPP	1979	EB/A/DPT	16 X 24	SOM	50	2	300	12000
Four Cakes	PaP	CPP	1979	EB/A/DPT	16 X 24	SOM	50	18	300	20000
Bird	PaP	CPP	1979	EB/A/DPT	16 X 24	SOM	50	2	300	12000
Recent Etchings II Series:										
Cigars	PaP	CPP	1979	EB/A/DPT	16 X 20	SOM	50		300	8000
Cherry Cakes	PaP	CPP	1979	EB/A/DPT	16 X 24	SOM	50		300	10000
Rose	PaP	CPP	1979	EB/A/DPT	24 X 18	SOM	50		300	9000
Boxed Balls	PaP	CPP	1979	EB/A/DPT	30 X 22	AP	50		400	12000
Recent Etchings III Series:										
Down Mariposa	PaP	CPP	1979	EB/A/DPT	30 X 22	AP	50		400	12000
Cake	ART	ART	1980	EB	10 X 8	AP	60	1	350	5000
Sardines	CPP	TT/SPS/CPP	1982	WBP	20 X 16	KOZO/HMP	50		850	6000
Dark Cake	CPP	TT/SPS/CPP	1983	AC/DPT	20 X 22	KOZO/HMP	200	18	1250	20000
Dark Cherries	CPP	CPP	1984	AC/DPT	16 X 19	AP88	25		1500	6000
Neighborhood Ridge	CPP	PP/HT/MB/JL/CPP	1984	AC/DPT/HG	23 X 18	AP88	50		1250	7000
Cherries	CPP	PP/HT/MB/JL/CPP	1984	EC/SB	16 X 19	SSP	25		1500	6000
Wide Downstreet	CPP	CPP	1985	AC/DPT	20 X 16	AP88	35		1800	7000
Apartment Hill	CPP	CPP	1985	AC/DPT	31 X 24	AP88	35		1800	8500
Candy Apples	CPP	CPP	1987	WC	24 X 24	KOZO	200	16	3500	20000
Lipsticks—Black	CPP	LH/MC/DS/CPP	1988	EC/DPT	14 X 12	SOM	15		5000	6500
Eight Lipsticks	CPP	LH/MC/DS/CPP	1988	EC/DPT	14 X 12	SOM	60		5000	12000
Dark Country City	CPP	LH/MC/DS/CPP	1988	AC/DPT/SG	31 X 40	SOM	25		7000	12000
Van (Color Drypoint)	CPP	CPP	1989	EC/DPT	17 X 19	SOM	50		5000	6000
Steep Street	CPP	CPP	1989	AC/DPT/SB	39 X 31	SOM	50		7500	25000
CURRENT EDITIONS:										
Hill Street	CPP	TT/SM/CPP	1987	WC	37 X 24	ECH	200	16	4000	15000
Country City	CPP	LH/MC/DS/CPP	1988	KOZO	31 X 40	SOM	60		5000	12000
City Edge	CPP	LH/MC/DS/CPP	1988	AC/DPT/SB	20 X 16	SOM	60		5500	6000
Steep Street—Black and Grey	CPP	CPP	1989	AC/DPT/SB	39 X 31	SOM	30		7500	12000
Steep Street	CPP	CPP	1989	EB/A/DPT/SB	39 X 31	SOM	50		16000	16000
Eight Dogs	CPP	CPP	1990	EB/HG	12 X 13	SOM	35		1200	2200
Paint Cans	CIAE		1990	LC	30 X 23	WOVE	100		10000	13500
Display Rows			1990	LC	29 X 23	SOM	60		22500	22500
Three Cows	CPP	CPP	1991	DPT	18 X 20	SOM	50	1	2000	3500
Valley Farm	CPP	CPP	1993	EB/A/SG/SB/DPT	30 X 23	SOM	50		3500	3500
Chocolates	CPP	CPP	1993	EC/DPT	15 X 16	SOM	50		2200	2200

Wayne Thiebaud
Recent Etchings II: Cherry Cakes
Courtesy Parasol Press, Ltd

Wayne Thiebaud
Black Suckers
Courtesy Parasol Press, Ltd

LARRY W THOMAS

BORN: Memphis, TN; October 29, 1943
EDUCATION: Memphis Acad of Art, TN, BFA; San Francisco Art Inst, CA, MFA, 1979
TEACHING: Instr, Memphis Col of Art, TN, 1966; Drawing & Printmaking, San Francisco Art Inst, CA, 1983; Instr, Drawing, Santa Rosa Junior Col, CA, 1981-84; Instr, Drawing & Printmaking, San Francisco Art Inst, CA, 1983 to present; Stanford Univ, Palo Alto, CA, Prof, 1989 to present & Chairman, Print Dept, 1992 to present
AWARDS: Nat Endowment for the Arts Fel, 1980; SECA Art Award, San Francisco Mus of Mod Art, CA, 1984; Djerassi Foundation, Woodside, CA, 1986; Nat Endowments for the Arts Fel, 1980-81,87-88
RECENT EXHIB: Brooklyn Mus, NY, 1986-87; Alvar Aalto Mus, Jyraskla, Finland, 1987; Santa Rosa Junior Col, CA, 1988; Univ Pacific, Stockton, CA, 1988; Converse Col, Millikin Gallery, Spartanburg, SC, 1992; Gallery Mill Valley, CA, 1992; Koplin Gallery, Santa Monica, CA, 1992; Susan Cummins Gallery, Mill Valley, CA, 1993
COLLECTIONS: San Francisco Mus of Mod Art, CA; Oakland Mus, CA; Achenbach Foundation of Graphic Arts, Palace Legion of Honor, San Francisco, CA; Nat Mus of Am Art, Wash, DC; Memphis Col of Arts, TN
PUBLISHERS: Experimental Workshop, San Francisco, CA (EW)
PRINTERS: Experimental Workshop, San Francisco, CA (EW)
GALLERIES: Mary Bell Galleries, Chicago, IL: Susan Cummins Gallery, Mill Valley, CA; Koplin Gallery, Santa Monica, CA; Experimental Workshop, San Francisco, CA; Chicago Street Gallery, Lincoln, IL; Gallery Mill Valley, Mill Valley, CA
MAILING ADDRESS: 601 Chenery St, San Francisco, CA 94131

TITLE	PUBLISHER	PRINTER	DATE	MEDIUM	DIMENSION (PAPER SIZE) IN INCHES	TYPE OF PAPER	EDITION NUMBER	NO. OF COLORS	ORIGINAL OPENING PRICE	CURRENT RETAIL PRICE
CURRENT EDITIONS:										
Nagheezi Series	EW	EW	1985	MON	16 X 31 EA	R/BFK	7 EA	MULTI	900 EA	1800 EA
Quapaw Vessel	EW	EW	1985	EC/MON/HC	31 X 43	R/BFK	15 EA	MULTI	750 EA	1200 EA
Nagheezi Entrance I	EW	EW	1986	MON	22 X 32 EA	GE	8 EA	MULTI	1200 EA	1800 EA

LEW THOMAS

BORN: San Francisco, CA; December 19, 1932
EDUCATION: Univ of San Francisco, CA, BA, 1960
TEACHING: Vis Art, San Francisco Art Inst, CA, 1977; Inst, Photog, San Francisco Art Inst, CA, 1981; San Francisco City Col, Art Inst, CA, 1982-83; Lectr, San Francisco State Col, CA, 1983; Center of Experimental & Interdisciplinary Arts, CA, 1983; Instr, Univ of Arizona, Tucson, AZ, 1983-84
AWARDS: Nat Endowment for the Arts Fel, 1975, 79–80
COLLECTIONS: Mus of Mod Art, NY; Mus of Fine Arts, Houston, TX; Princeton Univ Art Mus, NJ; Achenbach Found for Graphic Arts, San Francisco, CA; Univ of Santa Clara, CA; de Saisset Art Gallery, La Mamelle's Art Center, San Francisco, CA
PRINTERS: Artist (ART)
PUBLISHERS: NFS Press, San Francisco, CA (NFS); Artist (ART)
GALLERIES: Fraenkel Gallery, San Francisco, CA; Asher/Faure Gallery, Los Angeles, CA
MAILING ADDRESS: 243 Grand View Ave, San Francisco, CA 94114

TITLE	PUBLISHER	PRINTER	DATE	MEDIUM	DIMENSION (PAPER SIZE) IN INCHES	TYPE OF PAPER	EDITION NUMBER	NO. OF COLORS	ORIGINAL OPENING PRICE	CURRENT RETAIL PRICE
CURRENT EDITIONS:										
Time Equals 36 Exposures	ART	ART	1971	PH	48 X 96	KOD		1	500	2500
Sink: Filling/Filled/Draining	ART	ART	1972	PH	32 X 30	KOD		1	300	800
9 Perspectives	ART	ART	1972	PH	48 X 60	KOD		1	300	2500
Arithmetical	ART	ART	1972	PH	41 X 42	KOD		1	500	2500
Grass	ART	ART	1973	PH	48 X 60	KOD		1	500	2000
Ruler	ART	ART	1975	PH	5 X 48	KOD		1	350	900
Bibliography 3	ART	ART	1975	SP	22 X 30	R/BFK	75	1	75	350
Review	ART	ART	1978	PH	30 X 40	KOD		1	300	450
Bookspines	ART	ART	1980	PH	24 X 20	KOD		1	200	450
Bookspines	ART	ART	1981	PH/C	10 X 8	KOD		Full	200	350

STEFFEN WOLFGANG THOMAS

BORN: Fürth, Germany; (1906–1990)
EDUCATION: Sch of Applied Arts, Nürenberg, Germany; Royal Acad of Fine Arts, Munich, Germany
AWARDS: First Prize & Purchase Prize, City of Firth, Germany, 1925; Hon Mention, Fine Arts Acad of Munich, Germany, 1928; Governor's Award, GA, 1986
COLLECTIONS: High Mus, Atlanta, GA; St John's Mus, Wilmington, NC; Dalton Gallery, Agnes Scott Col, Decatur, GA; Macon Mus, GA; Univ of Georgia, Athens, GA; Univ of Edinborough, Scotland
PRINTERS: Artist (ART)
PUBLISHERS: Printmakers Press, Marietta, GA (PrP); Artist (ART)
GALLERIES: Bryant Galleries, New Orleans, LA & Jackson, MS; Shirley Fox Galleries, Atlanta, GA; Ann Jacob Gallery, Atlanta, GA; Oemulgee Arts, Macon, GA
MAILING ADDRESS: c/o Mrs Steffen Thomas, 848 Mentelle Dr, NE, Atlanta, GA 30308

TITLE	PUBLISHER	PRINTER	DATE	MEDIUM	DIMENSION (PAPER SIZE) IN INCHES	TYPE OF PAPER	EDITION NUMBER	NO. OF COLORS	ORIGINAL OPENING PRICE	CURRENT RETAIL PRICE
SOLD OUT EDITIONS (RARE):										
Persephone	ART	ART	1968	EB	11 X 14	AP	75	1	250	500
Sidewalk Philosophers	ART	ART	1970	WB	5 X 15	AP	75	1	90	200
Climbers	ART	ART	1972	EB	5 X 7	AP	75	1	125	250
Lady Godiva	ART	ART	1977	WB	18 X 26	AP	75	1	200	300
Forest Deer	ART	ART	1978	WB	18 X 28	AP	75	1	225	350
Eine Kleine Nachtmusik	ART	ART	1979	LI	16 X 25	R/BFK	75	1	200	350
Girl in Hammock	ART	ART	1979	WB	23 X 46	R/BFK	75	1	350	500
Sitters	ART	ART	1979	EB	5 X 7	R/BFK	75	1	125	200
Grace I	ART	ART	1980	LI	6 X 15	R/BFK	75	1	90	200
Grace II	ART	ART	1980	LI	4 X 16	R/BFK	75	1	90	200
Joy	ART	ART	1980	EB	2 X 7	R/BFK	75	1	90	200

STEFFEN WOLFGANG THOMAS CONTINUED

TITLE	PUBLISHER	PRINTER	DATE	MEDIUM	DIMENSION (PAPER SIZE) IN INCHES	TYPE OF PAPER	EDITION NUMBER	NO. OF COLORS	ORIGINAL OPENING PRICE	CURRENT RETAIL PRICE
SOLD OUT EDITIONS (RARE):										
Clowns	ART	ART	1980	EB	5 X 7	R/BFK	75	1	125	200
Care	ART	ART	1980	EB	4 X 10	R/BFK	75	1	135	200
Awakening	ART	ART	1980	EB	2 X 7	R/BFK	75	1	90	200
We	ART	ART	1980	EB	4 X 5	R/BFK	75	1	100	200

RICHARD EARL THOMPSON, SR

BORN: Oak Park, IL; September 26, 1914
EDUCATION: Chicago Acad of Fine Art, IL, 1931–32; American Acad of Fine Art, Chicago, IL 1932–33; Art Inst of Chicago, IL, 1944
TEACHING: Artist in Res, Univ of Wisconsin, Rhinelander, WI; Instr, American Acad of Fine Art, Chicago, IL, 1935–37
AWARDS: First Honorable Mention, Salmagundi Club, NY, 1980
COLLECTIONS: Brigham Young Univ, Salt Lake City, UT; Leigh Yawkey Woodson Art Mus, Wausau, WI; New Britain Mus of Am Art, CT; De Sasset Mus, Santa Clara, CA; Marquette Univ, Milwaukee, WI; Milwaukee Art Mus, WI; Naval Art Coll, Pentagon, Wash, DC; R W Norton Art Mus, Shreveport, LA
PRINTERS: Artist (ART)
PUBLISHERS: Artist (ART)
GALLERIES: Space Gallery, Los Angeles, CA; Elizabeth Leach Gallery, Portland, OR; Harris Gallery, Houston, TX; William Campbell Contemporary Art, Fort Worth, TX; Payton Rule Gallery, Denver, CO

TITLE	PUBLISHER	PRINTER	DATE	MEDIUM	DIMENSION (PAPER SIZE) IN INCHES	TYPE OF PAPER	EDITION NUMBER	NO. OF COLORS	ORIGINAL OPENING PRICE	CURRENT RETAIL PRICE
SOLD OUT EDITIONS (RARE):										
Lovely Day	ART	ART	1978	LC	24 X 18	AP	300	4	100	300
Autumn Day	ART	ART	1978	LC	18 X 24	AP	300	4	100	300
Moody Day	ART	ART	1978	LC	24 X 18	AP	300	4	100	300
In the Sumacs	ART	ART	1978	LC	18 X 24	AP	300	4	100	300
Impression in Springtime	ART	ART	1978	LC	27 X 18	AP	300	4	100	300

JOAN THORNE

BORN: 1943
EDUCATION: New York Univ, NY, BA, 1965; Hunter Col, NY, MFA, 1968
PRINTERS: Vinalhaven Press, Vinalhaven, ME (VP); Judith Solodkin, NY (JS); Solo Press, NY (SP)
PUBLISHERS: Graham Modern, NY (GM); Vinalhaven Press, Vinalhaven, ME (VP); Artist (ART)
GALLERIES: Graham Modern, New York, NY; Nina Freudenheim Gallery, Buffalo, NY; Sidney Janis Gallery, New York, NY; Ruth Bachofner Gallery, Santa Monica, CA; Gloria Luria Gallery, Bay Harbor Islands, FL

TITLE	PUBLISHER	PRINTER	DATE	MEDIUM	DIMENSION (PAPER SIZE) IN INCHES	TYPE OF PAPER	EDITION NUMBER	NO. OF COLORS	ORIGINAL OPENING PRICE	CURRENT RETAIL PRICE
SOLD OUT EDITIONS (RARE):										
Salu II	ART	JS/SP	1983	LC	29 X 41		30		750	1000
Fata Morgana	GM/VP	VP	1985	LC	23 X 20	R/BFK	31	7	800	1000

FREDERIC MATYS THURSZ

PRINTERS: Atelier Rene Taze, Paris, France (AtRT)
PUBLISHERS: Daniel Lelong Editeur, Paris, France (DLE)
GALLERIES: Galerie Lelong, Paris, France & New York, NY

TITLE	PUBLISHER	PRINTER	DATE	MEDIUM	DIMENSION (PAPER SIZE) IN INCHES	TYPE OF PAPER	EDITION NUMBER	NO. OF COLORS	ORIGINAL OPENING PRICE	CURRENT RETAIL PRICE
CURRENT EDITIONS:										
Elegia Judaica: Coda Oblada	DLE	AtRT	1992	EB	30 X 23	RP	9	1	900	900
Elegia Judaica: Psalmoldia Spectra	DLE	AtRT	1992	EC	30 X 23	RP	9	2	1300	1300

GEORGE ANDREW TICE

BORN: Newark, NJ; October 13, 1938
TEACHING: Instr, Photography, The New Sch, NY, 1970 to present
AWARDS: Nat Endowment for the Arts Fel, 1973; Grand Prix, Festival d'Arles, France, 1973; Guggenheim Fel, 1973–74; Fel, Nat Mus of Photography & Bradford & Ikley Col, Bradford, England, 1990–91
RECENT EXHIB: Witkin Gallery, NY, 1988–89
COLLECTIONS: Mus of Mod Art, NY; Metropolitan Mus of Art, NY; Art Inst of Art, Chicago, IL; Victoria & Albert Mus, London, England; Bibliotheque Nat, Paris, France
PRINTERS: Artist (ART)
PUBLISHERS: Artist (ART)
GALLERIES: Witkin Gallery, New York, NY; Maine Photographic Workshops, Rockford, ME; Afterimage Photograph Gallery, Dallas, TX; Halsted Gallery, Birmingham, MI; Hills Gallery, Denver, CO; Susan Spiritus Gallery, Costa Mesa, CA; Photographer's Gallery of Palo Alto, CA; Photo Forum, Pittsburgh, PA; Benteler-Morgan Galleries, Houston, TX; Magenta Gallery, Rocky Hill, NJ
MAILING ADDRESS: 323 Gill Lane, #9-B, Iselin, NJ 08830

TITLE	PUBLISHER	PRINTER	DATE	MEDIUM	DIMENSION (PAPER SIZE) IN INCHES	TYPE OF PAPER	EDITION NUMBER	NO. OF COLORS	ORIGINAL OPENING PRICE	CURRENT RETAIL PRICE
SOLD OUT EDITIONS (RARE):										
Peeka Moose (Set of 12)	ART	ART	1973	PH	11 X 14		50 EA		150 SET	2000 SET

WILLIAM TILLYER

BORN: 1938
EDUCATION: Middlesborough Col of Art, London, England, 1957–60; Slade Sch of Fine Art, London, England, 1960–63
TEACHING: Central Sch of Art, London, England, 1964–70; Bath Acad of Art, Corsham, Wiltshire, England, Etching, 1964–72; Watford Sch of Art, England, Etching, 1970–73; Prof, Art, Brown Univ, Providence, RI, 1975–76
COLLECTIONS: Tate Gallery, London, England; Mus of Mod Art, NY; Arts Council of Great Britain; Victoria and Albert Mus, London, England; Bibliotheque Nat, Paris, France; Boston Mus of Fine Arts, MA; Brooklyn Mus, NY; Mus of Contemp Art, Friedrickstad, Norway; Mus of Lodz, Poland; Mus of Varsoyie, Poland; Mus of Contemp Art, Utrecht, Holland; Fort Worth Art Mus, TX
PRINTERS: Cirrus Editions Workshop, Los Angeles, CA (CEW); Advanced Graphics Printshop, London, England (AG); Ian Lawson, London, England (IL); Robert Saich, London, England (RS); Homer Frankland, Glaidale, Yorkshire, England (HF); CTD, Glaidale, Yorkshire, England (CTD); Artist (ART); Mixografia Workship, Santa Monica, CA (MIX)
PUBLISHERS: Bernard Jacobson Ltd, London, England (BJL)
GALLERIES: Bernard Jacobson Ltd, London, England; Dolly Fiterman Gallery, Minneapolis, MN; Remba Gallery/Mixografia Workshop, Santa Monica, CA

William Tillyer
Lunsden Vase (from Courthope Collection)
Courtesy the Artist

TITLE	PUBLISHER	PRINTER	DATE	MEDIUM	DIMENSION (PAPER SIZE) IN INCHES	TYPE OF PAPER	EDITION NUMBER	NO. OF COLORS	ORIGINAL OPENING PRICE	CURRENT RETAIL PRICE
SOLD OUT EDITIONS (RARE):										
Shoji	BJL		1974	SP	41 X 60	AP	85	3	400	1500
A Furnished Landscape (Set of 25)	BJL	AG	1974	EB/SP/LC/W	36 X 27	JG	90	1–6	5000 SET	18000 SET
Vase Series (Set of 6)	BJL	AG	1975	SP	48 X 36 EA	JG	75 EA	6–15 EA	400 EA	1500 EA
Bel Air Series (Set of 3)	BJL	CEW	1975	LC	22 X 42 EA	CD	50 EA	4 EA	1200 SET	4500 SET
Still Life Set (Set of 4)	BJL		1975	LC	41 X 22 EA	AP	35 EA	4 EA	1500 SET	5000 SET
Wizard's Fall	BJL	AG	1976	SP	59 X 15	JG	250	7	100	1200
Black Venus	BJL	AG	1976	SP	45 X 14	JG	100	9	300	2000
Providence Suite (Set of 7)	BJL	RS	1976	WB/LI	50 X 17 EA	JAP	40 EA	1 EA	500 EA	1500 EA
Courthope Collection (Set of 10)	BJL		1977	EC	30 X 22 EA	AP	60 EA	2–3 EA	300 EA	2000 EA
Reflected Vases (Set of 5):	BJL	ART	1977	EC	27 X 8 EA	AP	35 EA	3 EA	800 SET	5500 SET
Florist Set: One Theme, Four Works (Set of 4)	BJL	AG	1978	SC	43 X 51 EA	JG	80 EA	6 EA	500 EA	1500 EA
Annex to Mrs. Lumdsden's Pool	BJL	ART	1979	EB	9 X 11	AP	25	1	200	800
Japanese Boxes (Set of 3)	BJL	ART	1980	EC	26 X 20 EA	AP	100 EA	2 EA	1000 SET	1800 SET
Interiors (Set of 3)	BJL	ART	1980	EC	26 X 20 EA	EMB	100 EA	6 EA	1000 SET	1800 SET
Huysmans Nudes (Set of 3)	BJL	ART	1981	EB	26 X 30 EA	JAP	100 EA	1 EA	1000 SET	1800 SET
York Vases (Set of 9)	BJL	ART	1981	WC	42 X 30 EA	AP	100 EA	5–8 EA	750 EA	1500 EA
Lake Coon Etchings (Set of 4)	BJL	ART	1982	EB	17 X 18 EA	AP	40 EA	1 EA	300 EA	1000 EA
Living by the Esk (Set of 20):										
I—Crunkly Gill	BJL	CTD/HF	1983	EB/A	28 X 32	AP	35	3	500	1000
II—Twizzy Gill	BJL	CTD/HF	1983	EB/A	28 X 32	AP	20	3	600	1200
III—Nicholson, the Half Vase	BJL	CTD/HF	1983	EC/REL	28 X 32	AP	35	5	500	1000
IV—Milly Mires	BJL	CTD/HF	1983	EC/REL	28 X 32	AP	35	4	500	1000
V—Murk Mire	BJL	CTD/HF	1983	AC/REL	28 X 32	AP	150	6	350	900
VI—De Stijl	BJL	CTD/HF	1983	WC/I/CO/HC	28 X 32	AP	60	5	500	1000
VII—Arnecliff	BJL	CTD/HF	1983	AC/CO/REL	28 X 32	AP	20	2	500	1000
VIII—Loggerhead Primaries	BJL	CTD/HF	1983	AC/CO/REL	28 X 32	AP	30	4	600	1200
IX—Finkel Bottoms	BJL	CTD/HF	1983	AC/CO/REL	28 X 32	AP	50	6	500	1000
X—The Black Vase	BJL	CTD/HF	1983	AC/CO/REL	28 X 32	AP	30	7	500	1000
XI—Thorneywaite	BJL	CTD/HF	1983	EC/CO/REL	28 X 32	AP	150	5	350	900
XII—Stoneygate	BJL	CTD/HF	1983	AC/CO/REL	28 X 32	AP	50	5	500	1000
XIII—The Square Vase	BJL	CTD/HF	1983	EB/A	28 X 32	AP	20	7	500	1000
XIV—The Black Bridge I	BJL	CTD/HF	1983	EB/A/CO/HC	28 X 32	AP	60	12	600	1200
XV—The Black Bridge II	BJL	CTD/HF	1983	EB/A/CO/HC	28 X 32	AP	60	12	500	1000
XVI—The Black Bridge III	BJL	CTD/HF	1983	EB/A/CO/HC	28 X 32	AP	150	16	350	900
XVII—The Medallion Vase I	BJL	CTD/HF	1983	WC/REL	28 X 32	AP	30	3	500	1000
XVIII—The Medallion Vase II	BJL	CTD/HF	1983	WC/REL	28 X 32	AP	30	3	500	1000
XIX—Red, White and Blue	BJL	CTD/HF	1983	EB/A/CO/WA	28 X 32	AP	70	9	600	1200
XX—Living by the Esk	BJL	CTD/HF	1983	EB/A/CO/WA	28 X 32	AP	70	9	600	1200

JOE TILSON

BORN: London, England; 1928
EDUCATION: St Martin's Sch of Art, London, England, 1949–52; Royal Col of Art, London, England, 1952–55
TEACHING: St Martin's Sch of Art, London, England
COLLECTIONS: Carnegie Inst, Pittsburgh, PA; Nat Gallery of Australia; Tate Gallery of Art, London, England; Mus of Mod Art, Rome, Italy; Boymans-Van-Beuningen Mus, Rotterdam, Holland; British Council, London, England

JOE TILSON CONTINUED

PRINTERS: Kelpro Studio, London, England (KS); Walter Rossi, Rome, Italy (WR); Studio 2RC, Rome, Italy (2RC); Jack Shirreff, Wiltshire, England (JS); 107 Workshop, Wiltshire, England (107W); Giorgio Upiglio, Milan, Italy (GU); Grafica Uno, Milan, Italy (G-UNO)
PUBLISHERS: Waddington Graphics, London, England (WG); David Krut Fine Art, London, England; Natalie Knight Gallery, London, England (NK); PMR International, London, England (PMR)
GALLERIES: Waddington Graphics, London, England; Dolly Fiterman Gallery, Minneapolis, MN; Fawbush Editions, New York, NY; Natalie Knight Gallery, London, England; David Krut Fine Art, London, England; Fisher Island Gallery, Fisher Island, FL

TITLE	PUBLISHER	PRINTER	DATE	MEDIUM	DIMENSION (PAPER SIZE) IN INCHES	TYPE OF PAPER	EDITION NUMBER	NO. OF COLORS	ORIGINAL OPENING PRICE	CURRENT RETAIL PRICE
SOLD OUT EDITIONS (RARE):										
Sky I,II,III		KS	1967	SP/PH/LB	47 X 26 EA		70 EA		100 EA	2500 EA
Clip-O-Matic		KS	1968	SP/PH/LB	38 X 26	AP	70		100	1800
Transparency Clip-O-Matic Eye			1969	SP	32 X 21	AP	200		100	1000
Ho Chi Minh			1970	SP/CO	40 X 24	HMP	70		100	2200
Namings and Origins			1973	SP	40 X 28	HMP	70		150	2000
Rope & Feather			1973–74	LC/CO	28 X 21	HMP	100		150	1500
Prorosia	WG	G-UNO/GU	1977	EB/A/SG	24 X 28	HMP	70		270	1350
Pool Mantra	WG	G-UNO/GU	1977	EB/A	34 X 26	HMP	71		270	2800
Earth Mantra	WG	G-UNO/GU	1977	EB/A	42 X 30	HMP	71		270	2800
Seed Mantra	WG	G-UNO/GU	1977	EB/A	42 X 30	HMP	71		270	2800
Proscinemi Dodona, Oracle of Zeus	WG	G-UNO/GU	1978	EB/A	36 X 26	HMP	71		225	1500
Moon Mantra	WG	G-UNO/GU	1978	EB/A	42 X 30	HMP	70		270	2800
Proscinemi, Tiryns	WG	G-UNO/GU	1978	EB/A	36 X 26	HMP	71		225	1500
Demeter and Persephone	WG	G-UNO/GU	1978	EB/A/SG	35 X 24	HMP	70		225	1500
Demeter's Ladder	WG	G-UNO/GU	1978	EB/A/SP/SG	32 X 23	HMP	71		225	1500
Proscinemi, Delphi	WG	G-UNO/GU	1979	EB/A/SG	32 X 23	HMP	30		290	1200
Proscinemi, Olympia	WG	G-UNO/GU	1979	EB/A/SG	32 X 23	HMP	30		290	1200
Air Mantra	WG	G-UNO/GU	1979	EB/A	32 X 40	HMP	75		360	2000
Sky Mantra	WG	G-UNO/GU	1979	EB/A	32 X 40	HMP	75		360	2000
Sun Mantra	WG	G-UNO/GU	1979	EB/A	32 X 40	HMP	75		360	2000
Eye Mantra	WG	G-UNO/GU	1979	EB/A	32 X 40	HMP	75		360	2800
Sea Mantra	WG	G-UNO/GU	1979	EB/A/SG	32 X 40	HMP	75		360	2200
Sea Mantra, State I	WG	G-UNO/GU	1979	EB/A/SG	32 X 40	HMP	5		400	1850
Earthearth I	WG	G-UNO/GU	1980	EB/A	41 X 41	HMP	80		540	2000
Earthearth II	WG	G-UNO/GU	1980	EB/HC	36 X 31	HMP	14	Varies	620	3200
Proscinemi, Eleiusis	WG	G-UNO/GU	1980	EB/A/SG	32 X 23	HMP	60		480	1200
Oak Oracle	WG	G-UNO/GU	1980	EB/A/SG	32 X 22	HMP	100		360	1200
Delphic Oracle	WG	G-UNO/GU	1980	SP/CO	29 X 25	HMP	150		320	1200
Earth Cube I	WG	G-UNO/GU	1980	EB/A/SG	51 X 43	HMP	80		540	2200
Oak Mantra	WG	G-UNO/GU	1981	EB/A/SG	33 X 25	HMP	100	13	480	1350
Earth Cube II	WG	G-UNO/GU	1981	EB/A	45 X 39	HMP	60		540	2200
Kore	WG	2RC/WR	1981	EB/A	71 X 17	HMP	50		800	2000
The Oracle of Zeus	WG	2RC/WR	1981	EB/A	47 X 54	HMP	80		1100	2800
Proscinemi for Demeter	WG	107W/JS	1981	EB/A/CO	32 X 48	HMP	50		450	1800
Proscinemi for Persephone	WG	107W/JS	1981	EB/A/CO	32 X 48	HMP	50		450	1800
Proscinemi for Dionysus	WG	2RC/WR	1982	EB/A	41 X 60	HMP	60		1100	2800
Proscinemi for Kore (4 parts)	WG	107W/JS	1982	EB/A/SG	63 X 52 EA	HMP	35 EA		900 EA	3500 EA
Demeter's Search	WG	107W/JS	1982	EB/A	15 X 15	HMP	25		190	1200
Dionysos/Hyron	WG	107W/JS	1982	EB/A	15 X 15	HMP	25		190	1200
Kore Lost	WG	107W/JS	1982	EB/A	15 X 15	HMP	25		190	1200
The Arrival of Demeter	WG	107W/JS	1982	EB/A	22 X 19	HMP	25		225	1200
The Arrival of Dionysos	WG	107W/JS	1982	EB/A	22 X 19	HMP	25		225	1200
The Arrival of Kore	WG	107W/JS	1982	EB/A	22 X 19	HMP	25		225	1200
Demeter, the Hidden Seed (4 parts)	WG	107W/JS	1982	EB/A	58 X 56	HMP	35		900	3500
Masks (Set of 3):									950 SET	3600 SET
Mask of Dionysos	WG	JS/107W	1984	EB/SG	45 X 41	R/BFK	40	1	380	1350
Mask of Okeanus	WG	JS/107W	1984	EB/SG	45 X 41	R/BFK	40	1	380	1350
Mask of Poseidon	WG	JS/107W	1984	EB/SG	45 X 41	R/BFK	40	1	380	1350
Set of Three Etchings:									1500 SET	5000 SET
Fruits of Dionysos	WG/DK/NK/PMR	JS/107W	1985	EB/A	34 X 30	R/BFK	60		400	1800
Liknon	WG/DK/NK/PMR	JS/107W	1985	EB/A/WC/SG	34 X 30	R/BFK	60		400	1800
Persephone	WG/DK/NK/PMR	JS/107W	1985	EB/A/SG	34 X 30	R/BFK	60		400	1800
CURRENT EDITIONS:										
Festival Suite (Set of 5):									3800 SET	5800 SET
Festival for Dionysos	WG/DK/NK/PMR	JS/107W	1987	EB	16 X 15	R/BFK	35	1	850	1250
Festival for Kore	WG/DK/NK/PMR	JS/107W	1987	EB	16 X 15	R/BFK	35	1	850	1250
Festival for Persephone	WG/DK/NK/PMR	JS/107W	1987	EB	16 X 15	R/BFK	35	1	850	1250
Festival of Anthesteria	WG/DK/NK/PMR	JS/107W	1987	EB	16 X 15	R/BFK	35	1	850	1250
Festival of Eiresione	WG/DK/NK/PMR	JS/107W	1987	EB	16 X 15	R/BFK	35	1	850	1250

JOE TILSON CONTINUED

TITLE	PUBLISHER	PRINTER	DATE	MEDIUM	DIMENSION (PAPER SIZE) IN INCHES	TYPE OF PAPER	EDITION NUMBER	NO. OF COLORS	ORIGINAL OPENING PRICE	CURRENT RETAIL PRICE
CURRENT EDITIONS:										
Liknon II	WG/DK/ NK/PMR	JS/107W	1987	EB	12 X 12	R/BFK	48	1	350	650
Liknon/Poseidon	WG		1987	SP	16 X 17	AP	250		350	650
Metamorphosis of Daphne	WG/DK/ NK/PMR	JS/107W	1987	EB/A	49 X 43	R/BFK	35		1200	1500
Metamorphosis of Dionysos	WG/DK/ NK/PMR	JS/107W	1987	EB/A	49 X 43	R/BFK	35		1200	1500
Signature Suite (Set of 6):									4500 SET	6000 SET
The Doctrine of Signatures	WG/DK/ NK/PMR	JS/107W	1987	EB/A/LB/CAR	22 X 15	R/BFK	40	1	850	1200
Signatures of Dionysos	WG/DK/ NK/PMR	JS/107W	1987	EB/A/LB/CAR	22 X 15	R/BFK	40	1	850	1200
Star Signature	WG/DK/ NK/PMR	JS/107W	1987	EB/A/LB/CAR	22 X 15	R/BFK	40	1	850	1200
Sun Signature	WG/DK/ NK/PMR	JS/107W	1987	EB/A/LB/CAR	22 X 15	R/BFK	40	1	850	1200
Signatures and . . .	WG/DK/ NK/PMR	JS/107W	1987	EB/A/LB/CAR	22 X 15	R/BFK	40	1	850	1200
Delian Apollo	WG		1989	SP/WC	48 X 37	AC	45		1800	2200
Dionysos Prassinos	WG		1989	EB/LB/CAR	42 X 44	R/BFK	35		1800	2200
Hephaistos	WG		1989	SP/WC	48 X 37	AC	45		1800	2200
Hephaistos	WG		1989	SP/WC	48 X 37	AC	45		1800	2200
Keramos I	WG		1989	SP	39 X 55	AC	100		1500	1800
Keramos II	WG		1989	SP	39 X 28	AC	100		1000	1350
Liknon for Poseidon	WG		1989	EB/LB/CAR	42 X 44	R/BFK	35		1800	2200
The Shield of Achilles	WG		1989	SP/WC	48 X 37	AC	45		1800	2200
Aphrodite	WG		1990	SP/WC	48 X 45	AC	45		1400	1600
Dionysos Anthios	WG		1990	SP/WC	75 X 49	AC	45		1600	2000
Dionysos Karpios	WG		1990	SP/WC	48 X 45	AC	45		1400	1600
The Muses and Apollo	WG		1990	SP/WC	48 X 45	AC	45		1400	1600

WALASSE TING

BORN: Shanghai, China; October 13, 1929
AWARDS: Guggenheim Fel, NY, 1970
COLLECTIONS: Stedelijk Mus, Amsterdam, Netherlands; Chicago Art Inst, IL; Musee Cernuschi, Paris, France; Mus of Mod Art, NY; Israel Nat Mus, Jerusalem, Israel; Mus of Fine Art, Boston, MA; Silkeborg Mus, Denmark; Chrysler Mus, Norfolk, VA; Detroit Inst of Art, MI; Guggenheim Mus, NY; Carnegie Inst, Pittsburgh, PA

PRINTERS: Atleier Clot, Paris, France (AtC); Bjorn Rosengreen (BR); Joseph Kleineman, NY (JK); Jorge Dumas, NY (JD); 2 RC, Rome, Italy (2RC)
PUBLISHERS: Cleveland Print Club, OH (CPC); Dobiaschofsky (DOB); La Bret Publishing Company (LBPC); Post Oak Fine Art Distributors, Houston, TX (POFA); London Arts Inc, Detroit, MI (LAI); 2 RC, Rome, Italy (2RC)
GALLERIES: Lemberg Gallery, Birmingham, MI
MAILING ADDRESS: 100 W 25th St, New York, NY, 10001

TITLE	PUBLISHER	PRINTER	DATE	MEDIUM	DIMENSION (PAPER SIZE) IN INCHES	TYPE OF PAPER	EDITION NUMBER	NO. OF COLORS	ORIGINAL OPENING PRICE	CURRENT RETAIL PRICE
SOLD OUT EDITIONS (RARE):										
Scéne Erotique			1968	DPT	10 X 13 EA	AP	20	1	100	500
Hot and Cold Soup (Set of 22)		BR	1969	LC	16 X 12 EA	AP	1050		500 SET	800 SET
Fireworks	CPC		1974	LC	15 X 22	AP			200	500
Flower			1974	LC	34 X 24	AP	75		250	650
Nogen Kvinde (Set of 2)			1974	LC		AP			350 SET	1000 SET
Ausstellungspla Kate (Set of 2)			1974	LC		AP			500 SET	800 SET
Hidden Smiles	LBPC	JD/AD	1979	LC	21 X 29	SOM	200	12	450	700
Busy Bodies	LAI	JK	1981	LC	21 X 29	SOM	200	5	500	700
Bird Talk	LAI	JK	1981	LC	22 X 30	SOM	200	8	500	700
Cat in the Garden	LAI	JK	1981	LC	21 X 29	SOM	200	13	500	700
Lady with a Vase	LAI	JK	1981	LC	21 X 29	SOM	200	12	500	700
Grape Flavor	LAI	JK	1981	LC	22 X 30	SOM	200	11	500	700
Geisha Girls #3	POFA	JK	1981	LC	18 X 24	SOM	200	10	450	700
Geisha Girls #5	POFA	JK	1981	LC	18 X 24	SOM	200	10	450	700
Geisha Girls #6	POFA	JK	1981	LC	18 X 24	SOM	200	10	450	700
Geisha Girls #7	POFA	JK	1981	LC	18 X 24	SOM	200	10	450	700
Geisha Girls #15	POFA	JK	1981	LC	18 X 24	SOM	200	11	450	700
Geisha Girls #18	POFA	JK	1981	LC	18 X 24	SOM	200	11	450	700
Two Red Parrots	POFA	JK	1981	LC	18 X 24	SOM	200	11	450	700
Green Horse	LAI	JK	1981	LC	18 X 24	SOM	200	4	500	700
Pink Horse	LAI	JK	1981	LC	18 X 23	SOM	200	4	500	700
Red Horse	LAI	JK	1981	LC	18 X 23	SOM	200	4	500	700
Woman in Flowers	POFA	JK	1981	LC	21 X 29	SOM	200	10	450	700
The Blue Table	2RC	2RC	1984	AC	37 X 57	MAG	50	24	2000	3000
Untitled		AtC	1984	LC	21 X 30	MAG	100		500	800
Negen Kvinde i det Gronne			1985	LC		MAG	200		400	600

WALASSE TING CONTINUED

TITLE	PUBLISHER	PRINTER	DATE	MEDIUM	DIMENSION (PAPER SIZE) IN INCHES	TYPE OF PAPER	EDITION NUMBER	NO. OF COLORS	ORIGINAL OPENING PRICE	CURRENT RETAIL PRICE
CURRENT EDITIONS:										
Still Life		AtC	1986	LC	21 X 29	SOM	125		500	850
Fische		AtC	1986	LC	21 X 29	SOM	125		500	850
Untitled			1987	LC	24 X 35	SOM	250		400	750
Springtime is Here	2RC	2RC	1989	LC	35 X 38	SOM	200		1200	1800

MURRAY TINKELMAN

EDUCATION: Cooper Union Sch, NY; Brooklyn Mus Art Sch, NY
TEACHING: Manhattanville Col, NY; Parsons Sch of Design, NY
AWARDS: Max Beckmann Scholarship Award, Brooklyn Mus, NY; Artist of the Year Award, 1970
COLLECTIONS: Brooklyn Mus, NY; Univ of Minnesota, Minneapolis, MN; Queens Col, Bronx, NY

PRINTERS: American Atelier, NY (AA)
PUBLISHERS: Circle Fine Art, Chicago, IL (CFA)
GALLERIES: Circle Galleries, San Diego, CA & San Francisco, CA & Northbrook, IL & Pittsburgh, PA & Houston, TX & Soho, NY & Chicago, IL & Scottsdale, AZ & Beverly Hills, CA & Costa Mesa, CA & Sherman Oaks, CA & Palm Beach, FL & Honolulu, HI & New Orleans, LA & Las Vegas, NV & Seattle, WA

TITLE	PUBLISHER	PRINTER	DATE	MEDIUM	DIMENSION (PAPER SIZE) IN INCHES	TYPE OF PAPER	EDITION NUMBER	NO. OF COLORS	ORIGINAL OPENING PRICE	CURRENT RETAIL PRICE
SOLD OUT EDITIONS (RARE):										
Birdee	CFA	AA	1979	SP	26 X 13	AP	200		150	300
CURRENT EDITIONS:										
Flea by Night	CFA	AA	1978	EB	30 X 22	R/BFK	150	1	75	200

GÉRARD TITUS-CARMEL

BORN: Paris, France: 1942
PRINTERS: Maeght Editions, Paris, France (ME); Maeght Lelong, Paris, France (ML)

PUBLISHERS: Maeght Editions, Paris, France (ME); Maeght Lelong, Paris, France (ML)
GALLERIES: Galerie Lelong, Paris, France & Zürich, Switzerland & New York, NY; Spaightwood Galleries, Madison, WI

TITLE	PUBLISHER	PRINTER	DATE	MEDIUM	DIMENSION (PAPER SIZE) IN INCHES	TYPE OF PAPER	EDITION NUMBER	NO. OF COLORS	ORIGINAL OPENING PRICE	CURRENT RETAIL PRICE
SOLD OUT EDITIONS (RARE):										
Suite Narwa (Set of 5):									5000 FF SET	10000 FF SET
Suite Narwa I	ME	ME	1980	EC	30 X 23	AP	100		1200 FF	2500 FF
Suite Narwa II	ME	ME	1980	EC	30 X 23	AP	100		1200 FF	2500 FF
Suite Narwa III	ME	ME	1980	EC	30 X 23	AP	100		1200 FF	2500 FF
Suite Narwa IV	ME	ME	1980	EC	30 X 23	AP	100		1200 FF	2500 FF
Suite Narwa V	ME	ME	1980	EC	30 X 23	AP	100		1200 FF	2500 FF
Abaques Series:									5000 SET	10000 FF SET
Abaques I	ME	ME	1980	EC	30 X 23	AP	100		1200 FF	2500 FF
Abaques II	ME	ME	1980	EC	30 X 23	AP	100		1200 FF	2500 FF
Abaques III	ME	ME	1980	EC	30 X 23	AP	100		1200 FF	2500 FF
Abaques IV	ME	ME	1980	EC	30 X 23	AP	100		1200 FF	2500 FF
Abaques V	ME	ME	1980	EC	30 X 23	AP	100		1200 FF	2500 FF
Caparacon Series:										
Caparacon I	MEC	MEC	1980	A	57 X 76 cm	R/BFK	100		1000 FF	2500 FF
Caparacon II	MEC	MEC	1980	EC	57 X 76 cm	R/BFK	100		1000 FF	2500 FF
Caparacon III	MEC	MEC	1980	EC	57 X 76 cm	AP	100	2	1300 FF	2500 FF
Caparacon IV	MEC	MEC	1980	EC	58 X 76 cm	AP	100	3	1300 FF	2500 FF
Caparacon V	MEC	MEC	1980	EC	57 X 76 cm	AP	100	2	1300 FF	2500 FF
Caparacon VI	MEC	MEC	1980	EC	57 X 76 cm	AP	100	3	1300 FF	2500 FF
Caparacon VII	MEC	MEC	1980	LC	57 X 76 cm	AP	75	6	1100 FF	2000 FF
Caparacon VIII	MEC	MEC	1980	LC	57 X 76 cm	AP	75	4	1100 FF	2000 FF
Caparacon X	MEC	MEC	1980	LC	76 X 57 cm	AP	75	5	800 FF	1500 FF
Caparacon IX	MEC	MEC	1980	LC	57 X 76 cm	AP	75	5	1100 FF	2000 FF
Construction Ephemere Series:										
Construction Ephemere I	MEC	MEC	1980	EC	80 X 60 cm	RP	100	4	1300 FF	3500 FF
Construction Ephemere II	MEC	MEC	1980	EC	60 X 45 cm	RP	100	4	1000 FF	2000 FF
Petit Eclat	MEC	MEC	1980	EC	32 X 22 cm	AP	100	4	1000 FF	2000 FF
Eclat Series:										
Eclat I	MEC	MEC	1981	EC	46 X 57 cm	AP	100	4	1500 FF	3000 FF
Eclat II	MEC	MEC	1981	EC	46 X 57 cm	AP	100	3	1300 FF	3000 FF
The Pocket Size Tlinglit Coffin I	MEC	MEC	1981	EC	68 X 98 cm	JP	100		1500 FF	3000 FF
Noren	MEC	MEC	1981	EC	30 X 23	JP	100		1200 FF	2500 FF

The retail prices of the 100,000 limited edition prints quoted in this directory are subject to change. Print publishers, artists and galleries were the direct sources for these quotations. Prices in the secondary market listed as "Sold Out Editions (Rare)" indicate that the publisher has a limited supply of that print or that the print is difficult to locate in the galleries.

TING SHAO KUANG

BORN: Shansi, China; 1939
EDUCATION: Univ of Education, Art Dept, Kumming, China
TEACHING: Prof, Art, Univ of California, Los Angeles, CA
RECENT EXHIB: Mercyhurst Col, Cummings Gallery, Erie, PA, 1990; Ginza Art Mus, Tokyo, Japan, 1988; Taiwan Fine Art Mus, China, 1991; Historia Mus of Art, Beijing, China, 1992; Shanghai Mus of Art, China, 1992

COLLECTIONS: Great Hall of the People, China; Univ of California, Los Angeles, CA
PUBLISHERS: Segal Fine Art, Woodland Hills, CA (SFA)
GALLERIES: Segal Fine Art, Woodland Hills, CA; Soma Fine Art, San Francisco, CA; Artists Showcase International, Hartsdale, NY; Allyson Louis Gallery, Bethesda, MD
MAILING ADDRESS: 707 North Alpine Dr, Beverly Hills, CA

Ting Shao Kuang
Morning Flowers
Segal Fine Art

Ting Shao Kuang
Dream
Segal Fine Art

TITLE	PUBLISHER	PRINTER	DATE	MEDIUM	DIMENSION (PAPER SIZE) IN INCHES	TYPE OF PAPER	EDITION NUMBER	NO. OF COLORS	ORIGINAL OPENING PRICE	CURRENT RETAIL PRICE
SOLD OUT EDITIONS (RARE):										
Harmony	SFA	SOMA	1986	SP	40 X 40	R/100	275	47	700	10000
Ashima at Sunrise	SFA	SOMA	1986	SP	40 X 40	R/100	275	47	700	5000
Ashima at Sunrise (Deluxe)	SFA	SOMA	1986	SP	40 X 40	RICE	275	47	800	7500
Mother & Child	SFA	SOMA	1986	SP	40 X 40	R/100	450		700	5000
Mother & Child (Deluxe)	SFA	SOMA	1986	SP	40 X 40	RICE	450		800	7500
Paradise	SFA	SOMA	1987	SP	34 X 33	R/100	450		700	8000
Paradise (Deluxe)	SFA	SOMA	1987	SP	34 X 33	RICE	450		800	12000
Breezes	SFA	SOMA	1987	SP	33 X 33	R/100	450		700	7000
Breezes (Deluxe)	SFA	SOMA	1987	SP	33 X 33	RICE	450		800	10500
Silk Road	SFA	SOMA	1987	SP	33 X 33	R/100	450		700	5000
Silk Road (Deluxe)	SFA	SOMA	1987	SP	33 X 33	RICE	450		800	7500
Friendship along the River	SFA	SOMA	1987	SP	33 X 33	R/100	450		700	5000
Friendship along the River (Deluxe)	SFA	SOMA	1987	SP	33 X 33	RICE	450		800	7500
Pisces	SFA	SOMA	1987	SP	33 X 33	R/100	450		700	7000
Pisces (Deluxe)	SFA	SOMA	1987	SP	33 X 33	RICE	450		800	10500
Ten Suns	SFA	SOMA	1987	SP	33 X 33	R/100	450		700	5000
Ten Suns (Deluxe)	SFA	SOMA	1987	SP	33 X 33	RICE	450		800	7500
Twins	SFA	SOMA	1988	SP	52 X 24	R/100	450		1000	10000
Twins (Deluxe)	SFA	SOMA	1988	SP	52 X 24	RICE	450		1200	15000
Night Rider	SFA	SOMA	1988	SP	36 X 28	R/100	450		800	8000
Night Rider (Deluxe)	SFA	SOMA	1988	SP	36 X 28	RICE	450		900	12000
The Hunters	SFA	SOMA	1988	SP	33 X 33	R/100	450		800	12000
The Hunters (Deluxe)	SFA	SOMA	1988	SP	33 X 33	RICE	450		900	18000
Distant Dreams	SFA	SOMA	1988	SP	32 X 33	R/100	450		800	8000
Distant Dreams (Deluxe)	SFA	SOMA	1988	SP	32 X 33	RICE	450		900	12000
Emerald Valley	SFA	SOMA	1988	SP	32 X 33	R/100	500		800	9000
Emerald Valley (Deluxe)	SFA	SOMA	1988	SP	32 X 33	RICE	500		900	13500
Dreaming of the Zoo	SFA	SOMA	1988	SP	34 X 33	R/100	500		800	5000
Dreaming of the Zoo (Deluxe)	SFA	SOMA	1988	SP	34 X 33	RICE	500		900	7500
Motherhood	SFA	SOMA	1988	SP	28 X 29	R/100	450		800	6000
Motherhood (Deluxe)	SFA	SOMA	1988	SP	28 X 29	RICE	450		900	9000
Patterns	SFA	SOMA	1988	SP	30 X 29	R/100	450		800	5000
Patterns (Deluxe)	SFA	SOMA	1988	SP	30 X 29	RICE	450		900	7500

TING SHAO KUANG CONTINUED

TITLE	PUBLISHER	PRINTER	DATE	MEDIUM	DIMENSION (PAPER SIZE) IN INCHES	TYPE OF PAPER	EDITION NUMBER	NO. OF COLORS	ORIGINAL OPENING PRICE	CURRENT RETAIL PRICE
SOLD OUT EDITIONS (RARE):										
Homage to Chikako	SFA	SOMA	1988	SP	30 X 29	R/100	500		800	5000
Homage to Chikako (Deluxe)	SFA	SOMA	1988	SP	30 X 29	RICE	500		900	7500
Eastern Song	SFA	SOMA	1989	SP	28 X 28	R/100	500		800	6000
Eastern Song (Deluxe)	SFA	SOMA	1989	SP	28 X 28	RICE	500		900	9000
Cradle Song	SFA	SOMA	1989	SP	28 X 28	R/100	500		800	5000
Cradle Song (Deluxe)	SFA	SOMA	1989	SP	28 X 28	RICE	500		900	7500
Cherry Blossom	SFA	SOMA	1989	SP	33 X 33	R/100	500		800	5000
Cherry Blossom (Deluxe)	SFA	SOMA	1989	SP	33 X 33	RICE	500		900	7500
The Huntress	SFA	SOMA	1989	SP	40 X 30	R/100	500		800	7000
The Huntress (Deluxe)	SFA	SOMA	1989	SP	40 X 30	RICE	500		900	10500
Wind and Sea	SFA	SOMA	1989	SP	33 X 33	R/100	500		3000	5000
Wind and Sea (Deluxe)	SFA	SOMA	1989	SP	33 X 33	RICE	500		4500	7500
Purple Dreams	SFA	SOMA	1986	SP	32 X 33	R/100	500		3000	7000
Purple Dreams (Deluxe)	SFA	SOMA	1986	SP	32 X 33	RICE	500		4500	10500
The Dance	SFA	SOMA	1989	SP	45 X 36	R/100	500		3000	9000
The Dance (Deluxe)	SFA	SOMA	1989	SP	45 X 36	RICE	500		4500	13500
Voyage on the Mei Kang	SFA	SOMA	1989	SP	38 X 30	R/100	500		800	5000
Voyage on the Mei Kang (Deluxe)	SFA	SOMA	1989	SP	38 X 30	RICE	500		900	7500
Return to Nature	SFA	SOMA	1990	SP	33 X 33	R/100	500		900	6000
Return to Nature (Deluxe)	SFA	SOMA	1990	SP	33 X 33	RICE	500		1000	9000
Messenger	SFA	SOMA	1990	SP	33 X 33	R/100	500		900	6000
Messenger (Deluxe)	SFA	SOMA	1990	SP	33 X 33	RICE	500		1000	9000
Lullabye	SFA	SOMA	1990	SP	28 X 29	R/100	500		900	5000
Lullabye (Deluxe)	SFA	SOMA	1990	SP	28 X 29	RICE	500		1000	7500
Reminiscence	SFA	SOMA	1990	SP	33 X 33	R/100	500		900	4000
Reminiscence (Deluxe)	SFA	SOMA	1990	SP	33 X 33	RICE	500		1000	6000
Hunting Ages	SFA	SOMA	1990	SP	33 X 33	R/100	500		900	5000
Hunting Ages (Deluxe)	SFA	SOMA	1990	SP	33 X 33	RICE	500		1000	7500
Eyes of Prey	SFA	SOMA	1990	SP	33 X 33	R/100	500		900	6000
Eyes of Prey (Deluxe)	SFA	SOMA	1990	SP	33 X 33	RICE	500		1000	9000
Song of Freedom	SFA	SOMA	1991	SP	33 X 33	R/100	500		1000	4000
Song of Freedom (Deluxe)	SFA	SOMA	1991	SP	33 X 33	RICE	500		1200	6000
Crane and Sunlight	SFA	SOMA	1991	SP	32 X 28	R/100	500		1000	6000
Crane and Sunlight (Deluxe)	SFA	SOMA	1991	SP	32 X 28	RICE	500		1200	9000
Phoenix Lady	SFA	SOMA	1991	SP	24 X 24	R/100	500		1800	3000
Illumination of Buddha	SFA	SOMA	1991	SP	24 X 24	R/100	500		1800	3000
Running Sand River	SFA	SOMA	1992	SP		R/100	500		3500	8000
Sacred Village	SFA	SOMA	1992	SP	24 X 24	R/100	500		3000	3500
Morning Flowers	SFA	SOMA	1992	SP	35 X 28	R/100	500		1800	3000
CURRENT EDITIONS:										
Golden Age in India	SFA	SOMA	1989	SP	33 X 33	R/100	500		800	4000
Golden Age in India (Deluxe)	SFA	SOMA	1989	SP	33 X 33	RICE	500		900	6000
Echoes	SFA	SOMA	1990	SP	33 X 33	R/100	500		900	4000
Echoes (Deluxe)	SFA	SOMA	1990	SP	33 X 33	RICE	500		1000	6000
The Bride	SFA	SOMA	1990	SP	33 X 33	R/100	500		900	4000
The Bride (Deluxe)	SFA	SOMA	1990	SP	33 X 33	RICE	500		1000	6000
Golden Empress	SFA	SOMA	1990	SP	33 X 33	R/100	500		900	4000
Golden Empress (Deluxe)	SFA	SOMA	1990	SP	33 X 33	RICE	500		1000	6000
Peaceful World	SFA	SOMA	1990	SP	33 X 33	R/100	500		1000	3000
Peaceful World (Deluxe)	SFA	SOMA	1990	SP	33 X 33	RICE	500		1200	4500
Dawn of the Yunnan School	SFA	SOMA	1991	SP	45 X 29	R/100	500		1000	4000
Dawn of the Yunnan School (Deluxe)	SFA	SOMA	1991	SP	45 X 29	RICE	500		1200	6000
Flowers of Paradise	SFA	SOMA	1992	SP		R/100	500		1800	1800
Shadow Play	SFA	SOMA	1992	SP		R/100	500		1800	1800
Morning Flowers (Deluxe)	SFA	SOMA	1992	SP	35 X 8	RICE	500		2700	4500
Sun of Phoenix	SFA	SOMA	1992	SP		R/100	500		1800	1800
Amorous Feelings of Xishuangbanna	SFA	SOMA	1993	SP		R/100	500		3500	3500
Aurora	SFA	SOMA	1993	SP		R/100	500		1800	2400
Aurora (Deluxe)	SFA	SOMA	1993	SP		RICE	500		2700	3600
Dream	SFA	SOMA	1993	SP	24 X 24	R/100	520		1500	1800
Keeping Peace	SFA	SOMA	1993	SP		R/100	520		1800	1800
Best Wishes	SFA	SOMA	1993	SP	33 X 33	R/100	520		1800	1800
Best Wishes (Deluxe)	SFA	SOMA	1993	SP	33 X 33	RICE	520		2700	2700

The retail prices of the 100,000 limited edition prints quoted in this directory are subject to change. Print publishers, artists and galleries were the direct sources for these quotations. Prices in the secondary market listed as "Sold Out Editions (Rare)" indicate that the publisher has a limited supply of that print or that the print is difficult to locate in the galleries.

The Printworld Directory is accepting new applications for the seventh edition. Approximately 300 new artists will be accepted. Please use the two forms provided in the back section of this directory to submit biographical data and documentation of prints. Edition number of each print must not exceed 500 and the retail price must be $100 or more.

MARK TOBEY

BORN: Centerville, Wisconsin; (1890–1976)
EDUCATION: Chicago Art Inst, IL, 1908
TEACHING: Cornish Sch, Seattle, WA, 1923–29; Darlington Hall, Devonshire, England, 1931–38
AWARDS: Seattle Art Mus, WA, Katherine Baker Award, 1940; Metropolitan Mus of Art, NY, 1942; Guggenheim Int Award, NY, 1956; Am Inst of Architects, Fine Arts Medal, 1957; Skowhegan Sch Painting Award, ME, 1971
RECENT EXHIB: Saint Martin's Abbey Col; Lacey, WA, 1989
COLLECTIONS: Metropolitan Mus of Art, NY; Mus of Mod Art, NY; Whitney Mus of Am Art, NY; San Francisco Mus of Art, CA; Brooklyn Mus of Art, NY; Boston Mus of Fine Arts, MA; Detroit Inst of Art, MI; Portland Mus of Art, OR; Baltimore Mus of Art, MD; Chicago Art Inst, IL; Wadsworth Atheneum, Hartford, CT; Phillips Mus, Andover, MA; Albright-Knox Art Gallery, Buffalo, NY; Seattle Mus of Art, WA; Norton Simon Mus, West Palm Beach, FL
PRINTERS: Petersburg Press, London, England (PP); Fred Genis, London, England (FG); Mourlot, Paris, France (M); Atelier Rigal, Fontenay-Aux-Roses, France (AR)
PUBLISHERS: Transworld Art, Inc, NY (TAI); Petersburg Press, London, England (PP)
GALLERIES: Wenger Gallery, Los Angeles, CA; Goldman Kraft Gallery, Chicago, IL; Willard Gallery, New York, NY; Gordon Woodside/John Braseth Galleries, Seattle, WA; Foster/White Gallery, Seattle, WA; Dorothy Rosenthal Art Gallery, Chicago, IL; David Anderson Gallery, Buffalo, NY; Claude Bernard Gallery, New York, NY; Phyllis Hattis Fine Arts, Inc, New York, NY; Makler Gallery, Phila, PA

TITLE	PUBLISHER	PRINTER	DATE	MEDIUM	DIMENSION (PAPER SIZE) IN INCHES	TYPE OF PAPER	EDITION NUMBER	NO. OF COLORS	ORIGINAL OPENING PRICE	CURRENT RETAIL PRICE
SOLD OUT EDITIONS (RARE):										
The Woven World	TAI	M	1973	LC	20 X 23	AP	175	7	750	2000
The Woven World (Deluxe)	TAI	M	1973	LC	20 X 23	AP	75	7	850	2500
The Scroll of Liberty	TAI	M	1973	LC	20 X 26	AP	175	7	750	1100
The Scroll of Liberty (Deluxe)	TAI	M	1973	LC	20 X 26	AP	75	7	850	1200
Fragment (Brown)	PP	PP	1973	LC	27 X 10	AP	45		100	1000
Underwater Fragment (Red)	PP	PP	1973	LB	17 X 15	AP	70	1	100	1000
Underwater Fragment (Black)	PP	PP	1973	LB	27 X 10	AP	35	1	100	1000
Mandarin	PP	PP	1973	LC	30 X 40	AP	95		200	2000
Ritual	PP	PP	1973	LC	17 X 15	AP	80		100	1000
Black by Yellow	PP	PP	1973	LC	17 X 15	AP	70		100	1000
Clarte I	PP	PP	1973	LC	17 X 15	AP	80		100	1000
Clarte II	PP	PP	1973	LC	17 X 15	AP	21		100	1000
Dialogue Between Ancients	PP	PP	1973	LB	26 X 20	AP	45	1	150	1000
Chinese Memories	PP	PP	1974	LB	36 X 15	AP	50	1	200	1000
The Awakening Dawn	TAI	AR	1974	EC	20 X 26	R/BFK	150		500	750
The Awakening Dawn (Deluxe)	TAI	AR	1974	EC	20 X 26	R/BFK	75		600	850
High Tide	TAI	M	1974	LC	20 X 26	AP	150	5	650	950
High Tide (Deluxe)	TAI	M	1974	LC	20 X 26	AP	75	5	750	1050
The Awakening Night	TAI	AR	1974	EC	20 X 26	R/BFK	150	4	500	750
The Awakening Night (Deluxe)	TAI	AR	1974	EC	20 X 26	R/BFK	75	4	600	850
To Life	TAI	AR	1974	EC	20 X 26	R/BFK	150		500	1100
To Life (Deluxe)	TAI	AR	1974	EC	20 X 26	R/BFK	75		600	1200
Winter Leaves	TAI	AR	1974	EC	20 X 26	R/BFK	150		500	1100
Winter Leaves (Deluxe)	TAI	AR	1974	EC	20 X 26	R/BFK	75		600	1200
Crowded City	TAI	M	1974	LC	20 X 26	AP	150		500	750
Crowded City (Deluxe)	TAI	M	1974	LC	20 X 26	AP	75		600	850
The Grand Parade	TAI	M	1974	LC	20 X 26	AP	150		500	900
The Grand Parade (Deluxe)	TAI	M	1974	LC	20 X 26	AP	75		600	1000
The Flame of Colors	TAI	M	1974	LC	26 X 20	AP	150		650	1500
The Flame of Colors (Deluxe)	TAI	M	1974	LC	26 X 20	AP	75		750	1750
Psaltery—First Form	TAI	AR	1974	EC	26 X 20	R/BFK	150	2	500	750
Psaltery—First Form (Deluxe)	TAI	AR	1974	EC	26 X 20	R/BFK	75	2	600	850
Psaltery—Second Form	TAI	AR	1974	EC	26 X 20	R/BFK	150	3	500	750
Psaltery—Second Form (Deluxe)	TAI	AR	1974	EC	26 X 20	R/BFK	75	3	600	850
Stained Glass	TAI	M	1974	LC	26 X 20	AP	150	7	650	950
Stained Glass (Deluxe)	TAI	M	1974	LC	26 X 20	AP	75	7	750	1050
Vibrating Surface	TAI	AR	1974	EC	26 X 20	R/BFK	150	5	650	800
Vibrating Surface (Deluxe)	TAI	AR	1974	EC	26 X 20	R/BFK	75	5	750	900
Confusion	TAI	M	1975	LC	26 X 20	AP	150	7	800	1150
Confusion (Deluxe)	TAI	M	1975	LC	26 X 20	AP	75	7	900	1250
The Harvest's Gleaning	TAI	AR	1975	EB/A	20 X 26	R/BFK	150	5	500	750
The Harvest's Gleaning (Deluxe)	TAI	AR	1975	EB/A	20 X 26	R/BFK	75	5	600	850
Morning Grass	TAI	AR	1975	EC	26 X 20	R/BFK	150	4	400	750
Morning Grass (Deluxe)	TAI	AR	1975	EC	26 X 20	R/BFK	75	4	500	850
Of Time and Age	TAI	AR	1975	EC	26 X 20	R/BFK	150	5	550	750
Of Time and Age (Deluxe)	TAI	AR	1975	EC	26 X 20	R/BFK	75	5	650	850
Paean	TAI	AR	1975	EC	20 X 26	R/BFK	150	5	550	750
Paean (Deluxe)	TAI	AR	1975	EC	20 X 26	R/BFK	75	5	650	850
Raissance of a Flower	TAI	M	1975	LC	26 X 20	AP	150	7	650	900
Raissance of a Flower (Deluxe)	TAI	M	1975	LC	26 X 20	AP	75	7	750	1000
Homage a Mourlot	TAI	M	1975	LC	26 X 20	AP	200		450	750
Homage a Mourlot (Deluxe)	TAI	M	1975	LC	26 X 20	AP	75		550	850

ROBERT PAUL TOBIAS

BORN: Reading, PA; December 14, 1933
EDUCATION: Arizona State Univ, Tempe, AZ, BS, Applied Arts & Ceramics, 1964, MFA, Sculpture, 1969
AWARDS: Purchase Award, Sculpture, Wisconsin State Univ, Platteville, WI, 1967; Painting Award, Arizona Western Col, Yuma, AZ, 1972; Sculpo Sculptrue Sculpture Award, Tucson Art Mus, AZ, 1974
RECENT EXHIB: Brooke Alexander, Inc, NY, 1987
COLLECTIONS: Matthews Center, Arizona State Univ, Tempe, AZ; Univ of Arizona, Tucson, AZ; Arizona Western Col, Yuma, AZ; Phoenix Art Mus, AZ

ROBERT PAUL TOBIAS CONTINUED

PRINTERS: Andrea Callard, Lexington, NY (AC); Jolie Stahl, Lexington, NY (JS); Sparrow Press, Lexington, NY (SpPr)
PUBLISHERS: Sparrow Press, Lexington, NY (SpPr); Avocet, NY (AV)
GALLERIES: Asher/Faure Gallery, Los Angeles, CA; Brooke Alexander, Inc, New York, NY; Gekas/Nicholas Gallery, Tucson, AZ
MAILING ADDRESS: Dept of Art, University of Arizona, Tucson, AZ 85721

TITLE	PUBLISHER	PRINTER	DATE	MEDIUM	DIMENSION (PAPER SIZE) IN INCHES	TYPE OF PAPER	EDITION NUMBER	NO. OF COLORS	ORIGINAL OPENING PRICE	CURRENT RETAIL PRICE
CURRENT EDITIONS:										
Thursday I,II,III (Set of 3)	SpPr	AC/JS/SpPr	1986	SP	30 X 22 EA	AP	10 EA	5 EA	750 SET 300 EA	750 SET 300 EA
Lexington	AV	AC/ART/SpPr	1987	SP	11 X 14	R/BFK	8	2	150	150

THEO TOBIASSE

BORN: Jaffa, Israel; 1926
EDUCATION: Arts Decoratifs, Paris, France
RECENT EXHIB: Nahan Galleries, NY, 1990
PRINTERS: Giraudon, Paris, France (GIR); Remusat, Paris, France (REM); Dutrou, Paris, France (DUT); Chave, Paris, France (CH)
PUBLISHERS: Nahan Editions, New Orleans, LA (NE); Galleri Kunst-Invest Salg A/S, Oslo, Norway (GKIS)
GALLERIES: Nahan Galleries, New York, NY & New Orleans, LA & Tokyo, Japan; Argus Fine Arts, Eugene, OR; Peterson Fine Art, Minneapolis, MN; Ja'Ney's Galerie d'Art, Corpus Christi, TX; Galleri Kunst-Invest Salg A/S, Oslo, Norway; Graphic Art Collection, Hallandale, FL; Gallery 22, Bloomfield Hills, MI; Fingerhut Gallery, Minneapolis, MN; Art Gallery-Studio 53, New York, NY; Saper Galleries, East Lansing, MI

Theo Tobiasse
Venise est un Bateau qui Creuse le Temps
Courtesy Nahan Editions

TITLE	PUBLISHER	PRINTER	DATE	MEDIUM	DIMENSION (PAPER SIZE) IN INCHES	TYPE OF PAPER	EDITION NUMBER	NO. OF COLORS	ORIGINAL OPENING PRICE	CURRENT RETAIL PRICE
SOLD OUT EDITIONS (RARE):										
Cantinique de Deborah	NE	GIR	1980	EB/CAR	36 X 25	AP	75		425	4500
Cantinique de Deborah (Deluxe)	NE	GIR	1980	EB/CAR	36 X 25	JP	25		475	5500
Duomo de Firenze	NE	GIR	1980	EB/CAR	26 X 21	AP	75		275	3500
Duomo de Firenze (Deluxe)	NE	GIR	1980	EB/CAR	26 X 21	JP	25		300	4500
Sur les Rives de Babylon	NE	GIR	1980	EB/CAR	22 X 26	AP	75		275	3500
Sur les Rives de Babylon (Deluxe)	NE	GIR	1980	EB/CAR	22 X 26	JP	25		300	4500
Le Train Rouge	NE	GIR	1980	EB/CAR	27 X 19	AP	75		325	4000
Le Train Rouge (Deluxe)	NE	GIR	1980	EB/CAR	27 X 19	JP	25		350	5000
Les Fruits de la Thora	NE	GIR	1980	EB/CAR	13 X 12	AP	75		225	3500
Les Fruits de la Thora (Deluxe)	NE	GIR	1980	EB/CAR	13 X 12	JP	25		250	4000
La Dame aux Cheveux Rouge	NE	GIR	1980	EB/CAR	9 X 7	AP	75		175	2500
Le Dame aux Cheveux Rouge (Deluxe)	NE	GIR	1980	EB/CAR	9 X 7	JP	25		200	3500
Aujourd 'hue je t'ai Engendrer	NE	GIR	1980	EB/CAR	17 X 16	AP	75		250	3500
Aujourd 'hue je t'ai Engendrer (Deluxe)	NE	GIR	1980	EB/CAR	17 X 16	JP	25		275	4000
Le Rendez-Vous	NE	GIR	1980	EB/CAR	27 X 16	AP	75		275	5000
Le Rendez-Vous (Deluxe)	NE	GIR	1980	EB/CAR	27 X 16	JP	25		300	6000
Fruits of Jerusalem	NE	GIR	1980	EB/CAR	29 X 21	HMP	99		400	5000
Fleur de Cantique	NE	CH	1980	LC	41 X 28	AP	175		600	2000
Let my People Go Suite (Set of 4)	NE	REM	1981	EB/CAR	38 X 28 EA	HMP	75 EA		3000 SET	20000 SET
Let my People Go Suite (Deluxe) (Set of 4)	NE	REM	1981	EB/CAR	38 X 28 EA	HMP	25 EA		3500 SET	24000 SET
Le Roi la Pomme Rouge	NE	REM	1981	EB/CAR	34 X 25	HMP	75		450	4500
Le Roi la Pomme Rouge (Deluxe)	NE	REM	1981	EB/CAR	34 X 25	HMP	25		500	5000
Le Acrobat	NE	GIR	1981	EB/CAR	34 X 25	HMP	75		450	5000
Le Acrobat (Deluxe)	NE	GIR	1981	EB/CAR	34 X 25	HMP	25		500	6000
Purim	NE	REM	1981	EB/CAR	33 X 26	HMP	75		375	5000
Purim (Deluxe)	NE	REM	1981	EB/CAR	33 X 26	HMP	25		400	6000
Femme Fleur avec Bicyclette	NE	REM	1981	EB/CAR	34 X 25	HMP	75		450	4500
Femme Fleur avec Bicyclette (Deluxe)	NE	REM	1981	EB/CAR	34 X 25	HMP	25		500	5000
Homme Assis sur Vagues	NE	REM	1981	EB/CAR	38 X 28	HMP	75		750	5000
Homme Assis sur Vagues (Deluxe)	NE	REM	1981	EB/CAR	38 X 28	HMP	25		800	6000
La Danse Deux Bougies	NE	REM	1981	EB/CAR	34 X 25	HMP	75		450	4000
La Danse Deux Bougies (Deluxe)	NE	REM	1981	EB/CAR	34 X 25	HMP	25		500	4500
Le Guitariste	NE	REM	1981	EB/CAR	14 X 16	HMP	75		325	2500
Le Guitariste (Deluxe)	NE	REM	1981	EB/CAR	14 X 16	HMP	25		350	3000
La Dame a la Theiere Bleue	NE	REM	1981	EB/CAR	38 X 28	HMP	75		750	6000
La Dame a la Theiere Bleue (Deluxe)	NE	REM	1981	EB/CAR	38 X 28	HMP	25		800	7500

THEO TOBIASSE CONTINUED

TITLE	PUBLISHER	PRINTER	DATE	MEDIUM	DIMENSION (PAPER SIZE) IN INCHES	TYPE OF PAPER	EDITION NUMBER	NO. OF COLORS	ORIGINAL OPENING PRICE	CURRENT RETAIL PRICE
SOLD OUT EDITIONS (RARE):										
La Femme et le Pantin (Deluxe)	NE	REM	1981	EB/CAR	25 X 19	HMP	25		500	3500
Dame aux Grand Chapeaux	NE	REM	1981	EB/CAR	38 X 28	HMP	75		750	8000
Dame aux Grand Chapeaux (Deluxe)	NE	REM	1981	EB/CAR	38 X 28	HMP	25		850	9000
L'Homme a l'Habit Rouge	NE	REM	1981	EB/CAR	38 X 28	HMP	75		750	5000
L'Homme a l'Habit Rouge (Deluxe)	NE	REM	1981	EB/CAR	38 X 28	HMP	25		850	5500
Femme Totem	NE	REM	1981	EB/CAR	38 X 28	HMP	75		750	5000
Femme Totem (Deluxe)	NE	REM	1981	EB/CAR	38 X 28	HMP	25		850	6000
Femme Foraine	NE	REM	1981	EB/CAR	38 X 28	HMP	75		750	5000
Femme Foraine (Deluxe)	NE	REM	1981	EB/CAR	38 X 28	HMP	25		850	5500
Portrait de Dame avec Cerise	NE	REM	1981	EB/CAR	34 X 25	HMP	75		450	4000
Portrait de Dame avec Cerise (Deluxe)	NE	REM	1981	EB/CAR	34 X 25	HMP	25		850	4500
Le Chant du Silence Devant L'Imaginaire		CH	1981	LC	27 X 23	JP	150		350	4000
Je me Souviens Seulement de son Sourire		CH	1981	LC	27 X 23	JP	150		350	4000
Une Femme est Venue a' moi depuis les Bords d'une Autre Vie		CH	1981	LC	27 X 23	JP	150		350	4000
Un Souvenir Opaque		CH	1981	LC	27 X 23	JP	150		350	4000
Laissé entre les Mots		CH	1981	LC	27 X 23	JP	150		350	4000
Image pour un Homme de Couvrant sa Propre Éstrangeté		CH	1981	LC	27 X 23	JP	150		350	4000
Melopée de Venise qui Sonne Comme un Psaume		CH	1981	LC	27 X 23	JP	150		350	4000
Vers quel Monde suis je Entrainé		CH	1981	LC	27 X 23	JP	150		350	4000
Femme aux Violoncelle	NE	REM	1982	EB/A/CAR	28 X 27	HMP	75		450	3000
Une Fleur Pour Meardochee	NE	REM	1982	EB/A/CAR	28 X 27	HMP	75		450	3000
La Grappe de Cannon	NE	REM	1982	EB/CAR	19 X 14	HMP	75		300	2000
Balaam	NE	REM	1982	EB/CAR	19 X 14	HMP	75		300	2000
L'Poupee et Pomme Rouge	NE	REM	1982	EB/CAR	19 X 14	HMP	75		300	2000
I'l N'Y'A plus J'Etincelles	NE	DUT	1982	EB/A/CAR	39 X 29	AP	50		975	6500
I'L N'Y'A plus J'Etincelles (with Original Drawing)	NE	DUT	1982	EB/A/CAR	39 X 29	AP	25		1050	9500
Le Fruit qui Retient les Songs	NE	REM	1982	EB/A/CAR	25 X 20	AP	50		500	4500
Le Fruit qui Retient les Songs (with Original Drawing)	NE	REM	1982	EB/A/CAR	25 X 20	AP	25		1200	6800
Poupee Gigogne	NE	REM	1982	EB/CAR	38 X 28	HMP	75		750	5000
Poupee Gigogne (Deluxe)	NE	REM	1982	EB/CAR	38 X 28	HMP	25		850	6000
Le Roi Mage aux Raisins	NE	REM	1982	EB/CAR	32 X 25	HMP	75		450	4500
Le Roi Mage aux Raisins (Deluxe)	NE	REM	1982	EB/CAR	32 X 25	HMP	25		500	5500
Une Odeur de Pomme	NE	DUT	1982	EB/A/CAR	51 X 35	AP	50		1200	7500
Une Odeur de Pomme (with Original Drawing)	NE	DUT	1982	EB/A/CAR	51 X 35	AP	25		1500	10500
Jacob, Rachel and Lea	NE	CH	1983	LC	22 X 30	AP	175		250	1200
Femme qui Danse ses Legendes dans la Fumee des Bouges	NE	DUT	1983	EB/A/CAR	53 X 37	AP	50		1250	6500
Femme qui Danse ses Legendes dans la Fumee des Bouges (with Original Drawing)	NE	DUT	1983	EB/A/CAR	53 X 37	AP	25		1500	9500
Lorsque le Jour Entier Devient Fruit	NE	DUT	1983	EB/A/CAR	53 X 37	AP	50		1250	7500
Lorsque le Jour Entier Devient Fruit (with Original Drawing)	NE	DUT	1983	EB/A/CAR	53 X 37	AP	25		1500	12000
Couleur Voyage pour Attraper les Mots avec les Mains	NE	DUT	1983	EB/A/CAR	53 X 37	AP	50		1400	6000
Couleur Voyage pour Attraper les Mots avec les Mains (with Original Drawing)	NE	DUT	1983	EB/A/CAR	53 X 37	AP	25		1500	9000
Chaque Homme est un Prophete qui Voit avec Tout Son Corps (with Original Drawing)	NE	DUT	1983	EB/A/CAR	53 X 37	AP	25		1500	8000
Danse de Myriam	NE	REM	1983	EB/CAR	36 X 23	HMP	75		375	4000
Bellerophon	NE	REM	1983	EB/CAR	25 X 20	HMP	75		400	4000
Bellerophon (Deluxe)	NE	REM	1983	EB/CAR	25 X 20	HMP	25		500	5000
La Femme Errante	NE	REM	1983	EB/CAR	31 X 28	HMP	75		425	4500
Le Femme Errante (Deluxe)	NE	REM	1983	EB/CAR	31 X 28	HMP	25		500	5000
L'Amazone	NE	REM	1983	EB/CAR	31 X 28	HMP	75		400	4500
L'Amazone (Deluxe)	NE	REM	1983	EB/CAR	31 X 28	HMP	25		475	5000
Femme a la Lyre	NE	REM	1983	EB/CAR	23 X 23	HMP	75		400	4000
Femme a la Lyre (Deluxe)	NE	REM	1983	EB/CAR	23 X 23	HMP	25		475	4500
David and Bathsheba	NE	REM	1983	EB/CAR	26 X 23	HMP	75		400	4000
David and Bathsheba (Deluxe)	NE	REM	1983	EB/CAR	26 X 23	HMP	25		475	4500
Lumiere d'Acrobate	NE	REM	1983	EB/CAR	32 X 28	HMP	75		400	4000

THEO TOBIASSE CONTINUED

Theo Tobiasse
Fruits of Jerusalem
Courtesy Nahan Editions

Theo Tobiasse
Le Reve de Jacob
Courtesy Nahan Editions

TITLE	PUBLISHER	PRINTER	DATE	MEDIUM	DIMENSION (PAPER SIZE) IN INCHES	TYPE OF PAPER	EDITION NUMBER	NO. OF COLORS	ORIGINAL OPENING PRICE	CURRENT RETAIL PRICE
SOLD OUT EDITIONS (RARE):										
Lumiere d'Acrobate (Deluxe)	NE	REM	1983	EB/CAR	32 X 28	HMP	25		500	4500
Parfum d'Odalisque Chair de L'Exile Suite (Set of 4)	NE	CH	1983	LC	22 X 30 EA	AP	175 EA		850 SET 250 EA	5000 SET 850 EA
Je Vous Enverrai le Prophite Elie	NE	CH	1983	LC	22 X 30	AP	175		250	1200
Shavuot Suite (Set of 4)	NE	CH/REM	1984	LC/CAR	23 X 30 EA	ECRU	125 EA		1500 SET 450 EA	12000 SET 3200 EA
Shavuot Suite (Deluxe) (Set of 4)	NE	CH/REM	1984	LC/CAR	23 X 30 EA	ECRU	85 EA		1800 SET 500 EA	15000 SET 10000 EA
Les Meres Biblique Suite (Set of 3):										
Sarah	NE	REM	1984	LC/CAR	41 X 28	AP	125		600	4000
Rebecca	NE	REM	1984	LC/CAR	41 X 28	AP	125		600	4000
Rachel	NE	REM	1984	LC/CAR	41 X 28	AP	125		600	4000
Fleurs Sechees pour . . .	NE	REM	1985	LC/CAR	22 X 30	ECRU	85		325	3500
Venise est un Bateau	NE	REM	1985	LC/CAR	22 X 30	ECRU	85		325	3500
Leda et le Cygne	NE	REM	1985	LC/CAR	22 X 30	ECRU	85		325	3500
La Rue est un Monde Ouvert aux Deeses	NE	REM	1985	LC/CAR	30 X 22	ECRU	85		325	3500
L'Oiseleur	NE	REM	1986	EB/CAR	38 X 27	HMP	75		450	5000
L'Oiseleur (Deluxe)	NE	REM	1986	EB/CAR	38 X 27	HMP	25		500	6000
America	NE	REM	1986	LC	48 X 43	AP	175		1500	4000
Le Reve de Jacob	NE	REM	1986	EB/A/CAR	38 X 30	AP	75		1500	6000
Le Reve de Jacob (with Original Drawing)	NE	REM	1986	EB/A/CAR	38 X 30	JP	25		1800	8000
Le Desir (with Original Drawing)	NE	REM	1986	EB/A/CAR	34 X 25	JP	25		1500	8000
Le Pichet	NE	REM	1986	CAR/OP	19 X 16	AP	75		400	3500
Le Pichet (Deluxe)	NE	REM	1986	CAR/OP	19 X 16	ECRU	25		500	4000
La Reine Esther	NE	REM	1986	CAR/OP	22 X 19	HMP	75		400	3800
La Reine Esther (Deluxe)	NE	REM	1986	CAR/OP	22 X 19		25		500	4500
Sarah	NE	REM	1986	CAR/OP	38 X 27	HMP	30		1400	6000
Rebecca	NE	REM	1986	CAR/OP	38 X 27	HMP	30		1400	6000
Leah	NE	REM	1986	CAR/OP	38 X 27	HMP	30		1400	6000
Rachel	NE	REM	1986	CAR/OP	38 X 27	HMP	30		1400	6000
Le Desir	NE	REM	1986	EB/A/CAR	34 X 25	AP	75		1250	4000
La Colombe	NE	REM	1986	CAR/OP	27 X 20	HMP	75		400	4500
La Colombe (Deluxe)	NE	REM	1986	CAR/OP	27 X 20	HMP	25		500	5500
Les Personages I Suite (Set of 4)	NE	REM	1986	LC	12 X 12 EA	AP	175 EA		450 SET	1800 SET
Les Personages I Suite (Deluxe) (Set of 4)	NE	REM	1986	LC	12 X 12 EA	JP	135 EA		500 SET	2400 SET
Les Personages II Suite (Set of 4)	NE	REM	1987	LC	12 X 12 EA	AP	175 EA		450 SET	1800 SET
Les Personages II Suite (Set of 4) (Deluxe)	NE	REM	1987	LC	12 X 12 EA	JP	135 EA		500 SET	2400 SET
Quand le Soleil . . .	NE	REM	1987	LC/CAR	15 X 13	AP	175		275	1000
Quand le Soleil . . . (Deluxe)	NE	REM	1987	LC/CAR	15 X 13	JP	135		350	1200

THEO TOBIASSE CONTINUED

TITLE	PUBLISHER	PRINTER	DATE	MEDIUM	DIMENSION (PAPER SIZE) IN INCHES	TYPE OF PAPER	EDITION NUMBER	NO. OF COLORS	ORIGINAL OPENING PRICE	CURRENT RETAIL PRICE
SOLD OUT EDITIONS (RARE):										
L'Enfant Habille de ...	NE	REM	1987	LC/CAR	23 X 30	AP	175		450	1500
J'ai Retrouve mon Pere ...	NE	REM	1987	LC/CAR	30 X 22	AP	175		450	1200
CURRENT EDITIONS:										
Grand Parade 'Jazz	NE	CH	1980	LC	30 X 22	AP	150		300	1000
Quels Sont-ils ces Rivages au Meurt la Memorie	NE	CH	1980	LC	41 X 28	AP	175		500	1200
Quels Sont-ils ces Rivages au Meurt la Memorie (Deluxe)	NE	CH	1980	LC	41 X 28	AP	135		550	1400
Histoire Graves dans L'Encorce des Vies	NE	CH	1980	LC	41 X 28	AP	175		500	1200
Histoire Graves dans L'Encorce des Vies (Deluxe)	NE	CH	1980	LC	41 X 28	AP	135		550	1400
Fleur de Cantique	NE	CH	1980	LC	41 X 28	AP	135		600	2000
Man Who Walks on the Ramparts	NE	REM	1981	EB/CAR	25 X 19	HMP	99		400	3500
Rachel	NE	REM	1981	EB/CAR	24 X 25	HMP	75		450	3500
Rachel (Deluxe)	NE	REM	1981	EB/CAR	24 X 25	HMP	25		850	4000
Les Fleurs Geantes	NE	REM	1981	EB/CAR	31 X 22	HMP	75		375	2500
Les Fleurs Geantes (Deluxe)	NE	REM	1981	EB/CAR	31 X 22	HMP	25		400	3000
Bucolique aux Fleurs Bleus	NE	REM	1981	EB/CAR	34 X 26	HMP	75		450	3500
Bucolique aux Fleurs Bleus (Deluxe)	NE	REM	1981	EB/CAR	34 X 26	HMP	25		850	4000
La Femme et le Pantin	NE	REM	1981	EB/CAR	25 X 19	HMP	75		450	3000
Melodie pour une Oiseau	NE	REM	1982	EB/CAR	34 X 26	HMP	75		450	3500
Melodie pour une Oiseau (Deluxe)	NE	REM	1982	EB/CAR	34 X 26	HMP	25		500	4500
Chaque Homme est un Prophete qui Voit avec Tout Son Corps	NE	DUT	1983	EB/A/CAR	53 X 37	AP	50		1400	5000
Danse de Myriam (Deluxe)	NE	REM	1983	EB/CAR	36 X 23	HMP	25		450	5000
Parfum d'Odalisque Chair de L'Exile Suite (Deluxe) (Set of 4)	NE	CH	1983	LC	22 X 30 EA	AP	150 EA		950 SET / 300 EA	6000 SET / 1800 EA
Je Vois Enverrai le Prophite Elie (Deluxe)	NE	CH	1983	LC	22 X 30	AP	150		300	1500
Jacob, Rachel and Lea (Deluxe)	NE	CH	1983	LC	22 X 30	ECRU	150		350	1500
Autobus pour une Fête Estrange	GKIS	CH	1983	LC	23 X 16	JP	120	17	275	2000
Le Musicien de Firenze	GKIS	CH	1983	LC	23 X 16	JP	120	17	275	2000
Ou' Donc est Resté mon Roiberger	GKIS	CH	1983	LC	23 X 16	JP	120	17	275	2000
Sourire Habité sur de Cordes de Violon	GKIS	CH	1983	LC	23 X 16	JP	120	18	275	2000
Petite Fille de Cirque qui est ma Lumiére	GKIS	CH	1983	LC	23 X 16	JP	120	17	275	2000
Misique Vagabonde pour Femme avec Grand Chapeau	GKIS	CH	1983	LC	23 X 16	JP	120	18	275	2000
La Colombe et le Roi-Mage	GKIS	CH	1983	LC	23 X 16	JP	120	18	275	2000
Cette Femme qui N'Etait que Songe on Voudrait quela Vie Soil la Douceur d'un Chant	GKIS	CH	1983	LC	23 X 16	JP	120	19	275	2000
Fleur de Roulotte mon Grand Théâtre	GKIS	CH	1983	LC	23 X 16	JP	120	18	275	2000
David et Bethsabee	NE	CH/REM	1984	LC/CAR	41 X 28	AP	125		675	2000
David et Bethsabee (Deluxe)	NE	CH/REM	1984	LC/CAR	41 X 28	AP	85		875	2500
Les Meres Biblique Suite (Deluxe) (Set of 3):									1800 SET	12000 SET
Sarah	NE	REM	1984	LC/CAR	41 X 28	AP	85		700	4500
Rebecca	NE	REM	1984	LC/CAR	41 X 28	AP	85		700	4500
Rachel	NE	REM	1984	LC/CAR	41 X 28	AP	85		700	4500
America (Deluxe)	NE	REM	1986	LC	48 X 43	JP	135		1800	5000
L'Enfant Habille de ... (Deluxe)	NE	REM	1987	LC/CAR	23 X 30	JP	135		550	1800
J'ai Retrouve mon Pere ... (Deluxe)	NE	REM	1987	LC/CAR	30 X 22	JP	135		550	1500
Poeme a Trois Voix au Pied ... (Trip)	NE	REM	1988	LC	28 X 24 EA	AP	125 EA		2500 SET	5500 SET
Le Ciel est Etroit Entroit entre les Vagues et la Nuit	NE	CH	1990	LC	30 X 22	AP	200		1400	1400
Un Peuple Assis Dans ...	NE	CH	1990	LC	22 X 30	AP	200		1400	1400
Enfant Venus du Palais de la Memoire	NE	CH	1991	LC	30 X 22	AP	200		1400	1400
La-Bas Vers Canaan	NE	CH	1991	LC	30 X 22	AP	200		1400	1400
Les Premiers Matins du Monde	NE	CH	1992	LC	23 X 30	AP	200		1400	1400
Des Fruits pour Bethsabee	NE	CH	1992	LC	23 X 30	AP	200		1400	1400

The retail prices of the 100,000 limited edition prints quoted in this directory are subject to change. Print publishers, artists and galleries were the direct sources for these quotations. Prices in the secondary market listed as "Sold Out Editions (Rare)" indicate that the publisher has a limited supply of that print or that the print is difficult to locate in the galleries.

The print market has become very selective. For the first time since we published the first edition of The Printworld Directory in 1982, the prices of prints have been greatly reduced and greatly increased for the same artists by the most reputable and established print publishers. Check the fifth edition to understand the movement.

MARJORIE TOMCHUK

BORN: Canada; October 16, 1933
EDUCATION: Univ of Michigan, BA, MA; Sophia Univ, Tokyo; Pratt Inst, NY; Univ of California, Long Beach, CA
RECENT EXHIB: Fayette Mus of Art, NC, 1989; White Gallery, Franklin Lakes, NJ, 1989; Silvermine Arts Center, New Canaan, CT, 1991; Castle Art Gallery, Col of New Rochelle, NY 1991
AWARDS: Nat Arts Club, NY, 1972; DeCordova Mus, Lincoln, MA, 1971,73; Dartmouth Col, Hanover, NH, 1981; Am Diabetes Assn, Graphic Award, 1982
COLLECTIONS: Smithsonian Inst, Wash, DC; Nelson Gallery, Kansas City, MO; Newark Mus, NJ; Butler Inst of Am Art, Youngstown, OH; Denver Art Mus, CO; DeCordova Mus, MA; Davison Art Center, CT; Tacoma Mus of Art, WA; Mus of Native Am Culture, Spokane, WA; Midwest Mus of Am Art, Elkart, IN; City Mus of New York, NY
PRINTERS: Artist (ART)
PUBLISHERS: Lublin Graphics, Greenwich, CT (LG); Artist (ART)
GALLERIES: Isetan Art Gallery, Tokyo, Japan; Galerie Roucka, Munich, Germany; White Gallery, Franklin Lakes, NJ
MAILING ADDRESS: 44 Horton Lane, New Canaan, CT 06840

Marjorie Tomchuk
Crystal Creek
Courtesy the Artist

TITLE	PUBLISHER	PRINTER	DATE	MEDIUM	DIMENSION (PAPER SIZE) IN INCHES	TYPE OF PAPER	EDITION NUMBER	NO. OF COLORS	ORIGINAL OPENING PRICE	CURRENT RETAIL PRICE
SOLD OUT EDITIONS (RARE):										
Arabian Horse	ART	ART	1965	EC	12 X 12	IT	75	4	75	800
Icarus	LG	ART	1969	EC	18 X 18	IT	100	3	75	800
One Giant Leap	LG	ART	1970	EC	16 X 20	IT	100	5	100	700
Divine Sarah	LG	ART	1971	EC	16 X 20	IT	100	5	100	700
Peanut Cart	LG	ART	1972	EC	16 X 20	IT	100	5	100	700
CURRENT EDITIONS:										
Grand Victorian	LG	ART	1975	EC	18 X 24	AP	100	5	100	700
Unicorn	ART	ART	1979	EC	20 X 24	AP	150	6	150	600
Dawn	ART	ART	1979	EC	20 X 24	AP	150	4	150	600
Sky Symphony	ART	ART	1979	EC	20 X 24	AP	150	5	150	600
Aleutian Island	ART	ART	1980	EC	20 X 24	GE	150	6	250	600
Sandhills	ART	ART	1980	EC	20 X 24	AP	150	5	200	600
Sierra (Quartet)	ART	ART	1980	EC	22 X 31 EA	GE	150	5	1000	2400
Pacific Storm (Dipt)	ART	ART	1980	EC	22 X 31 EA	GE	150	5	500	1200
North Ridge (Tript)	ART	ART	1981	EC	20 X 24 EA	GE	150	6	750	1800
Star Cluster	ART	ART	1982	EC	20 X 24	GE	150	5	250	600
Span	ART	ART	1984	EMB	25 X 36	HMP	100	4	400	700
Sonic Stream	ART	ART	1984	EMB	25 X 36	HMP	100	4	400	700
Blue Ridge	ART	ART	1984	EMB	25 X 36	HMP	100	4	400	700
Mirage	ART	ART	1984	EMB	25 X 36	HMP	100	4	400	700
Morning Glow	ART	ART	1984	EMB	14 X 19	HMP	75	4	175	350
Contrails	ART	ART	1985	EMB	25 X 36	HMP	100	8	900	1400
Eclipse	ART	ART	1985	EMB	25 X 36	HMP	100	4	900	1400
Coral Reef	ART	ART	1986	EMB	25 X 36	HMP	100	5	450	700
Eterna I, II	ART	ART	1986	EMB	25 X 36 EA	HMP	100 EA	5 EA	1200 SET	1400 SET
Summer Breeze	ART	ART	1987	EMB	14 X 19	HMP	75	6	300	350
Fronds	ART	ART	1987	EMB	14 X 19	HMP	75	6	300	350
Galley	ART	ART	1987	EMB	14 X 19	HMP	75	5	300	350
Solar Winds I, II	ART	ART	1988	EMB	25 X 36 EA	HMP	100	5	1000	1400
Spiral	ART	ART	1988	EMB	25 X 36	HMP	100	5	500	700
Red Planet	ART	ART	1988	EMB	25 X 36	HMP	100	6	500	700
Marquee	ART	ART	1988	EMB	25 X 36	HMP	100	6	500	700
North Range I, II	ART	ART	1989	EMB	25 X 36 EA	HMP	100 EA	6 EA	1200 SET	1400 SET
City Island I, II	ART	ART	1989	EMB	25 X 36 EA	HMP	100 EA	7 EA	1200 SET	1400 SET
Sounding	ART	ART	1989	EMB	25 X 36	HMP	100	5	600	700
Echo Fields	ART	ART	1989	EMB	25 X 36	HMP	100	5	600	700
Shield	ART	ART	1989	EMB	25 X 36	HMP	100	5	600	700
Vines	ART	ART	1989	EMB	25 X 36	HMP	100	4	600	700
Transept	ART	ART	1989	EMB	25 X 36	HMP	100	4	600	700
Sea Grass I, II, III	ART	ART	1990	EMB	36 X 25 EA	HMP	100 EA	8 EA	1800 SET	2100 SET
Window	ART	ART	1990	EMB	36 X 25	HMP	100	5	600	700
Romanesque	ART	ART	1990	EMB	36 X 25	HMP	100	5	600	700
Basilica	ART	ART	1990	EMB	36 X 25	HMP	100	5	600	700
Edan Flow	ART	ART	1991	EMB	36 X 25	HMP	50	6	2800	2800
Tri-Point	ART	ART	1991	EMB	36 X 25	HMP	50	6	2800	2800
Auburn Valley	ART	ART	1992	EMB	36 X 25	HMP	50	8	2800	2800
Monotypes	ART	ART	1992	MON	36 X 25 EA	HMP	1 EA	10	3600	3600
Monotypes	ART	ART	1992	MON	15 X 19 EA	HMP	1 EA	10	900	900

BETTY TOMPKINS

BORN: Washington, DC; June 20, 1945
EDUCATION: Syracuse Univ, NY, BFA, 1966; Central Washington State Col, Ellensburg, WA BEd, MA, 1969
TEACHING: Central Washington State Col, Ellensburg, WA, 1967–68; Bentley Sch, NY, 1969–71; Montgomery Col, MD, 1972–73; Univ of Wisconsin, Eau Claire, WI, 1973–74; New York Univ, NY, 1975–76; Memphis Acad of Fine Arts, TN, 1979
AWARDS: Fel, Ossabow Island Project, 1979; Creative Artists Public Service Grant, New York Council of the Arts, 1983; MacDowell Colony Fel, 1982,83,88; New York Found for the Arts Grant, 1988; Yaddo Fel, 1990
RECENT EXHIB: Hallwalls, Buffalo, NY, 1987; Fairleigh Dickinson Univ, NJ, 1987; Sensory Evolution Gallery, NY, 1987; PS 1, NY, 1987; Richard Green Gallery, NY, 1988; Trabia MacAfee Gallery, NY, 1988; Stamford Mus, CT, 1988; White Columns, NY, 1991; Alan Brown Gallery, Hartsdale, NY, 1991; Margulies Taplin Gallery, Boca Raton, FL, 1991; Fridholm Fine Arts, Asheville, NC, 1991
COLLECTIONS: Aldrich Mus of Contemp Art, Ridgefield, CT; Oberlin Col, OH; Rutgers Univ, Newark, NJ; Stamford Mus, CT; Zimmerli Mus, NJ; Patterson Mus, NJ
PRINTERS: Water Street Press, Brooklyn, NY (WSP); K Caraccio, NY (KC)
PUBLISHERS: Orion Editions, NY (OE); Bernice Steinbaum Gallery, NY (BSG)
GALLERIES: Bernice Steinbaum Gallery, New York, NY; Orion Editions, New York, NY; Fridholm Fine Arts, Asheville, NC; Alan Brown Gallery, Hartsdale, NY; Margulies Taplin Gallery, Boca Raton, FL
MAILING ADDRESS: 101 Prince St, New York, NY 10012

TITLE	PUBLISHER	PRINTER	DATE	MEDIUM	DIMENSION (PAPER SIZE) IN INCHES	TYPE OF PAPER	EDITION NUMBER	NO. OF COLORS	ORIGINAL OPENING PRICE	CURRENT RETAIL PRICE
SOLD OUT EDITIONS (RARE):										
Celeste	OE	KC	1980	EC	30 X 23	HML	35	4	275	500
Black Shouldered African Kite	OE	KC	1982	EC	37 X 30	RWSP	40	2	275	350
Black Shouldered African Kite, State II	OE	KC	1982	EC	22 X 30	RWSP	15	3	275	350
Anna's Hummingbird	OE	KC	1982	AC	22 X 30	GE	85	11	325	450
Broad-Tailed Hummingbird	BSG	WSP	1983	EC/HG/A/PH	17 X 19	GE	10	15	350	450

GEORGE CLAIR TOOKER, JR.

BORN: Brooklyn, New York; August 5, 1920
EDUCATION: Phillips Acad, Andover, MA, 1936–38; Harvard Univ, Cambridge, MA, AB, 1942, Art Students League, NY, 1943–45, with Reginald Marsh, Kenneth Hayes Miller, Harry Sternberg; Studied privately with Paul Cadmus, 1946
TEACHING: Art Students League, NY, 1965–68
AWARDS: Nat Inst of Arts and Letters Grant, 1960; Governor's Award for Excellence in Arts, Montpelier, VT, 1983
RECENT EXHIB: Fine Art Mus of San Francisco, California Palace of the Legion of Honor, CA, 1987; Berry-Hill Galleries, Inc, NY, 1987; Midtown Galleries, NY, 1990
COLLECTIONS: Whitney Mus of Am Art, NY; Metropolitan Mus of Art, NY; Mus of Mod Art, NY; Dartmouth Col, Hanover, NH; Nat Coll of Fine Arts, Wash, DC; Walker Art Center, Minneapolis, MN; Sara Roby
PRINTERS: Editions Press, San Francisco, CA (EP); American Atelier, NY (AA); George C Miller & Sons, NY (GCM)
PUBLISHERS: Editions Press, San Francisco, CA (EP); Frank Rehn Gallery, NY (FR); Circle Fine Art, Chicago, IL (CFA); Marisa del Re, NY (MDR); Artist (ART)
GALLERIES: Walton-Gilbert Galleries, San Francisco, CA; Marisa del Re Gallery, New York, NY; Circle Galleries, San Diego, CA & San Francisco, CA & Northbrook, IL & Clayton, MO & Pittsburgh, PA & Houston, TX & Soho, NY & Chicago, IL & Scottsdale, AZ & Beverly Hills, CA & Costa Mesa, CA & Sherman Oaks, CA & Palm Beach, FL & Honolulu, HI & Las Vegas, NV & New Orleans, LA & Seattle, WA; Midtown Galleries, New York, NY; Berry-Hill Galleries, Inc, New York, NY

TITLE	PUBLISHER	PRINTER	DATE	MEDIUM	DIMENSION (PAPER SIZE) IN INCHES	TYPE OF PAPER	EDITION NUMBER	NO. OF COLORS	ORIGINAL OPENING PRICE	CURRENT RETAIL PRICE
SOLD OUT EDITIONS (RARE):										
Voice	EP	EP	1977	LB	22 X 18	R/BFK	125	1	400	2500
Sleepers	FR	EP	1977	I	8 X 10	R/BFK	125		400	2500
Mirror	EP	EP	1978	LB	27 X 22	AC/W	125	1	600	2500
Dreamers	FR	EP	1979	I	9 X 11	AC/W	125		400	2500
Un Ballo in Maschera (A Masked Ball) (Metropolitan Suite II)	CFA	AA	1983	LB	22 X 30	AC/W	250	1	800	2300
Embrace II	ART/MDR	GCM	1984	LB	14 X 18	R/BFK	175	1	900	2000

ROLAND TOPOR

BORN: Paris, France; 1938
EDUCATION: Ecole des Beaux-Arts, Paris, France
COLLECTIONS: Centre Nat Georges Pompidou, Paris, France; Israeli Mus, Jerusalem, Israel
PRINTERS: American Atelier, NY (AA)
PUBLISHERS: Circle Fine Art, Chicago, IL (CFA)
GALLERIES: Circle Galleries, San Diego, CA & San Francisco, CA & Northbrook, IL & Pittsburgh, PA & Houston, TX & Soho, NY & Chicago, IL & Scottsdale, AZ & Beverly Hills, CA & Costa Mesa, CA & Sherman Oaks, CA & Palm Beach, FL & Honolulu, HI & New Orleans, LA & Las Vegas, NV & Seattle, WA

TITLE	PUBLISHER	PRINTER	DATE	MEDIUM	DIMENSION (PAPER SIZE) IN INCHES	TYPE OF PAPER	EDITION NUMBER	NO. OF COLORS	ORIGINAL OPENING PRICE	CURRENT RETAIL PRICE
SOLD OUT EDITIONS (RARE):										
L'Homme Deracine	CFA	AA	1980	LC	12 X 16	AP	150		125	750
L'Homme aux Valises	CFA	AA	1980	LC	12 X 16	AP	150		125	750
Les Quatre Jambes	CFA	AA	1980	LC	12 X 16	AP	150		125	750
L'Homme a la Cape	CFA	AA	1980	LC	12 X 16	AP	150		125	750
L'Escalier	CFA	AA	1980	LC	12 X 16	AP	150		125	750
Le Lapin	CFA	AA	1980	LC	12 X 16	AP	150		125	750
La Bascule	CFA	AA	1980	LC	12 X 16	AP	150		125	750
Les Boules	CFA	AA	1980	LC	12 X 16	AP	150		125	750

MICHAEL ARNOLD TORLEN

BORN: San Diego, CA; February 28, 1940
EDUCATION: Cranbrook Acad of Art, Bloomfield Hills, MI, BFA, 1962; Ohio State Univ, Columbus, OH, MFA, 1965
TEACHING: Asst Prof, Drawing & Painting, Univ of Georgia, Athens, GA, 1965–70; Assoc Prof & Dept Head, Painting & Drawing, State Univ of New York, Purchase, NY, 1972 to present
AWARDS: Fel, Ohio State Univ, Columbus, OH, 1963–64; Res Fel, State Univ of New York, Purchase, NY, 1978; Vis Artist Traveling Fel, Australian Council, 1982
RECENT EXHIB: Luise Ross Gallery, NY, 1989
COLLECTIONS: Aldrich Mus of Contemp Art, Ridgefield, CT; Neuberger Mus, Purchase, NY
PRINTERS: James Frank, NY (JF); Kendra Carlson, NY (KC)
PUBLISHERS: Artist (ART)
GALLERIES: Luise Ross Gallery, New York, NY; Windmueller Fine Arts, Scarsdale, NY
MAILING ADDRESS: Division of Visual Arts, State University of New York College, Purchase, NY 10577

TITLE	PUBLISHER	PRINTER	DATE	MEDIUM	DIMENSION (PAPER SIZE) IN INCHES	TYPE OF PAPER	EDITION NUMBER	NO. OF COLORS	ORIGINAL OPENING PRICE	CURRENT RETAIL PRICE
CURRENT EDITIONS:										
Revolations (Set of 7 Collotypes and 7 Signed Text Pages)	ART	JF/KC	1983	COL	30 X 22 EA	AP			950 SET	1500 SET

JOHN TORREANO

BORN: Flint, MI; August 17, 1941
EDUCATION: Cranbrook Acad of Art, Bloomfield Hills, MI, BFA, 1963; Ohio State Univ, Columbus, OH, MFA, 1967; Studied with Robert King & Hoyt L Sherman
TEACHING: Asst Prof, Painting, Univ of South Dakota, Vermillion, SD, 1967–68; Instr, Painting, Sch of Visual Arts, NY, 1969–70; Vis Art, Art Inst of Chicago, IL, 1972; Nova Scotia Col of Art & Design, Halifax, Canada, 1975; Vis Lectr, Ohio State Univ, Columbus, OH, 1975; State Univ of New York, Goddard Col, Purchase, NY, 1973–75; Vis Art, Univ of New Mexico, Las Cruces, NM, 1976–80; Rhode Island Sch of Design, Providence, RI, 1982–83; Banff Sch of Art, AB, Canada, 1985; Tyler Sch of Art, Temple Univ, Phila, PA, 1986
AWARDS: Creative Artists Public Service Prog Grant, 1978–79; Nat Endowment for the Arts Grants, 1978–79, 1982–83
RECENT EXHIB: Elizabeth McDonald Gallery, NY, 1987; Corcoran Gallery of Art, Wash, DC, 1989
COLLECTIONS: Whitney Mus of Am Art, NY; Aldrich Mus of Contemp Art, Ridgefield, CT; Rhode Island Sch of Design, Art Mus, Providence, RI; Michener Coll, Univ of Texas, Austin, TX; Corcoran Gallery of Art, Wash, DC
PRINTERS: Judith Solodkin, NY (JS); Solo Press, NY (SP)
PUBLISHERS: Solo Press, NY (SP)
GALLERIES: Margo Leavin Gallery, Los Angeles, CA; Susanne Hilberry Gallery, Birmingham, MI; Adair Margo Gallery, El Paso, TX; Dart Gallery, Chicago, IL; Helander Gallery, Palm Beach, FL; Solo Press Gallery, New York, NY; Genovese Gallery, Boston, MA; Janet Marqusee Fine Arts, New York, NY; Carl Solway Gallery, Cincinati, OH
MAILING ADDRESS: 103 Franklin St, New York, NY 10013

TITLE	PUBLISHER	PRINTER	DATE	MEDIUM	DIMENSION (PAPER SIZE) IN INCHES	TYPE OF PAPER	EDITION NUMBER	NO. OF COLORS	ORIGINAL OPENING PRICE	CURRENT RETAIL PRICE
CURRENT EDITIONS:										
Oxygems (Set of 5):									8000 SET	8500 SET
Oxygems: Amethyst	SP	JS/SP	1989	WC/EMB	30 X 36	AP	50		1700	1800
Oxygems: Emerald	SP	JS/SP	1989	WC/EMB	30 X 36	AP	50		1700	1800
Oxygems: Ruby	SP	JS/SP	1989	WC/EMB	30 X 36	AP	50		1700	1800
Oxygems: Sapphire	SP	JS/SP	1989	WC/EMB	30 X 36	AP	50		1700	1800
Oxygems: Topaz	SP	JS/SP	1989	WC/EMB	30 X 36	AP	50		1700	1800

FRANCESC TORRES

BORN: Barcelona, Spain; August 8, 1948
EDUCATION: Massana Art Inst, Barcelona, Spain, 1964,67; Fine Arts Sch, Etching, Cert, Paris, France, 1967–68
TEACHING: Instr, Mixed Media & Installation, Sch of Visual Arts, NY, 1986
AWARDS: New York State Council on the Arts, 1983–84; Ind Art Fel, DAAD Berliner Kinstleprogramm, 1986; Spanish-Am Joint Committee of Cult & Educ Coop, 1985–89
RECENT EXHIB: State Univ of New York, Stony Brook, NY, 1987; Virginia Commonwealth Univ, Anderson Gallery, Richmond, VA, 1987; Nat Galerie, Berlin, West Germany, 1988; Contemp Arts Mus, Houston, TX, 1989; Whitney Mus of Am Art, NY, 1989; Indianapolis Center for Contemp Art, Herron Gallery, Indianapolis, IN, 1987,92; Capp Street Project, San Francisco, CA, 1989,92; Univ of Massachusetts, Amherst, MA, 1992
COLLECTIONS: Mus of Mod Art, NY; Cooper-Hewitt Mus, NY; Alternative Mus, NY; Everson Mus of Art, Syracuse, NY; Carnegie Inst of Art, Pittsburgh, PA
PRINTERS: Pelavin Editions, NY (PelEd)
PUBLISHERS: Pelavin Editions, NY (PelEd); Artist (ART)
GALLERIES: Pelavin Editions, New York, NY
MAILING ADDRESS: 38 N Moore St, New York, NY 10013

TITLE	PUBLISHER	PRINTER	DATE	MEDIUM	DIMENSION (PAPER SIZE) IN INCHES	TYPE OF PAPER	EDITION NUMBER	NO. OF COLORS	ORIGINAL OPENING PRICE	CURRENT RETAIL PRICE
CURRENT EDITIONS:										
Nature Morte/Dead Nature	ART	PelEd	1986	MON/HC/CC	34 X 23 EA	AP/CC	1 EA	Varies	1900 EA	2500 EA
A–B (Jean Moulin as San Sebastian)	PelEd	PelEd	1986	CAR/MON/HC	44 X 30 EA	AP	1 EA	Varies	1500 EA	2000 EA

RICHARD A TREASTER

BORN: Lorain, OH; July 14, 1932
EDUCATION: Cleveland Inst of Art, OH, BFA
TEACHING: Instr, Painting, Cooper Sch of Art, Cleveland, OH, 1966–67; Assoc Prof, Cleveland, Inst of Art, OH, 1966–80; Adj Prof, Ursuline Col, 1976–81
AWARDS: Mainstreams Award of Excellence, Marietta Col, OH, 1969; Emily Goldsmith Award, Am Watercolor Soc, 1969; Third Butler Medal, Butler Inst of Am Art, Youngstown, OH 1976
COLLECTIONS: Butler Inst of Am Art, Youngstown, OH; Nat Acad of Design, NY; Cleveland Mus of Art, OH; Southern Alleghenies Mus of Art, Loretto, PA; Wittenberg Univ, Springfield, OH
PUBLISHERS: Stewart & Stewart, Bloomfield Hills, MI (S-S)
PRINTERS: Norman Stewart, Bloomfield Hills, MI (NS); Wing Lake Studio, Bloomfield Hills, MI (WLS)
GALLERIES: Stewart & Stewart, Bloomfield Hills, MI; Images Gallery, Toledo, OH; A B Closson Gallery, Cincinnati, OH; Alan Gallery, Berea, OH; Bonfoey Company, Cleveland, OH
MAILING ADDRESS: 1228 Virginia Ave, Lakewood, OH 44107

RICHARD A TREASTER CONTINUED

TITLE	PUBLISHER	PRINTER	DATE	MEDIUM	DIMENSION (PAPER SIZE) IN INCHES	TYPE OF PAPER	EDITION NUMBER	NO. OF COLORS	ORIGINAL OPENING PRICE	CURRENT RETAIL PRICE
CURRENT EDITIONS:										
Vermeer and Times	S-S	NS/WLS	1984	SP	22 X 30	R/BFK	50	29	500	750

JAN PETER TRIPP

BORN: Oberstorf, Germany; 1945
EDUCATION: Stuttgart Art Acad, Germany; Vienna Art Acad, Austria
RECENT EXHIB: John Szoke Graphics, Inc, NY, 1987
COLLECTIONS: Montreal Mus, Canada; Mus Amersfort, Netherlands; Mus of Warsaw, Poland; State Gallery of Biberach, West Germany
PRINTERS: Kuit Zein Gallery, Vienna, Austria (KZS); Sabina Klein Studio, NY (SKS)
PUBLISHERS: Artist (ART); John Szoke Graphics, Inc, NY (JSG)
GALLERIES: John Szoke Graphics, Inc, New York, NY

Jan Peter Tripp
Kinsey Meets Man Ray
Courtesy John Szoke Graphics, Inc

Jan Peter Tripp
American Dream
Courtesy John Szoke Graphics, Inc

TITLE	PUBLISHER	PRINTER	DATE	MEDIUM	DIMENSION (PAPER SIZE) IN INCHES	TYPE OF PAPER	EDITION NUMBER	NO. OF COLORS	ORIGINAL OPENING PRICE	CURRENT RETAIL PRICE
SOLD OUT EDITIONS (RARE):										
Ulrikes Fenster	ART	KZ	1980	EB/MEZ	20 X 24	AP	100	1	400	1500
Im Blauen Zimmer	ART	KZ	1980	EB/MEZ	20 X 24	AP	100	1	400	1500
CURRENT EDITIONS:										
Kinsey Meets Man Ray (50 Hand-Colored)	JSG	SKS	1989	DPT/ROU	21 X 27	R/BFK	95	Varies	1000	1250
American Dream	JSG	KZS	1991	EB/ENG	37 X 28	R/BFK	100	1	1750	1750

ERNEST TINO TROVA

BORN: St Louis, Missouri, February 19, 1927
AWARDS: Nat Humanitarian Award, Nat Recreation & Park Assn, 1979; Utsukushi-ga-hara Open Air Mus Award, 1983
RECENT EXHIB: Hokin Gallery, Palm Beach, FL, 1987; Anchorage Mus of History & Art, AK, 1987–88; Hokin Gallery, Bay Harbor Islands, FL, 1988; Wichita State Univ, Edwin A Ulrich Mus, KS, 1989; Trova Found, Clayton, MO, 1989; Philharmonic Center for the Arts, Naples, FL, 1991
COLLECTIONS: Mus of Mod Art, NY; Guggenheim Mus, NY; Whitney Mus of Am Art, NY; Brandeis Mus, Waltham, MA; Hirshhorn Mus of Art, Wash, DC; Nelson Mus, Kansas City, KS; Aldrich Mus of Contemp Art, Ridgefield, CT; Phoenix Mus, AZ; Tate Gallery, London, England; Walker Art Center, Minneapolis, MN; Worcester Art Mus, MA; Wichita State Mus, KS; Everson Mus, Syracuse, NY; Los Angeles County Mus of Art, CA; Metropolitan Mus of Art, NY
PRINTERS: K Carraccio, NY (KC); Fine Creations, NY (FC)
PUBLISHERS: Pace Editions, NY (PE); Abrams Original Editions, NY (AOE); Multiples, Inc, NY (M); 2:30 Productions, St Louis, MO (2:30P)
GALLERIES: Pace Prints, New York, NY; Hokin Gallery, Palm Beach, FL & Bay Harbor Islands, FL; Greenberg Gallery, St Louis, MO; Hanson Galleries, Beverly Hills, CA; R H Love Galleries, Chicago, IL; Samuel Stein Fine Arts, Ltd, Chicago, IL; Images Gallery, Toledo, OH; Mangel Gallery, Phila, PA
MAILING ADDRESS: c/o Trova Foundation, 8112 Maryland Ave, St Louis, MO 63105

TITLE	PUBLISHER	PRINTER	DATE	MEDIUM	DIMENSION (PAPER SIZE) IN INCHES	TYPE OF PAPER	EDITION NUMBER	NO. OF COLORS	ORIGINAL OPENING PRICE	CURRENT RETAIL PRICE
SOLD OUT EDITIONS (RARE):										
Mickey Mouse World	PE		1968	SP	23 X 29	WSP	100	5	100	1000
Falling Man Suspended Relief	PE		1969	MULT	13 X 11 X 3	PLEX/BR	175	1	650	3500

ERNEST TINO TROVA CONTINUED

TITLE	PUBLISHER	PRINTER	DATE	MEDIUM	DIMENSION (PAPER SIZE) IN INCHES	TYPE OF PAPER	EDITION NUMBER	NO. OF COLORS	ORIGINAL OPENING PRICE	CURRENT RETAIL PRICE
SOLD OUT EDITIONS (RARE):										
Falling Man Manscapes (Set of 10)	PE		1969	SP	28 X 28 EA	RAG/H	175 EA	6 EA	1500 SET 150 EA	8000 SET 1000 EA
Banner #1 (Canvas & Felt Appliqué)	M		1970	MULT	70 X 72	Felt	20		350	2500
Falling Man Variant	PE		1970	SP	36 X 36	SP/H	200	8		2000
Falling Man Shadow Figure	PE		1971	MULT	7 X 11 X 7	PLEX/BR	150	6	1200	6000
Falling Man Perspective Shadow Man	PE		1972	SP	35 X 35		150	11	250	1800
Shadows, Planes, and Targets (Set of 4)	PE	KC	1972	SP	24 X 24	COR	150	6	750 SET	4000 SET
Four Foot Falling Man	PE	KC	1973	SP	70 X 38	BECK	150			4500
Falling Man Profile Canto	PE	KC	1974	MULT	11 X 15 X 4	ST/PLEX/BR	125	1	1500	
Series 75 (Set of 4)	PE	KC	1975	SP	42 X 35	ST/FAIR	150	6	2000 SET	7500 SET
Falling Man Gox	PE	KC	1976	MULT	11 X 8 X 2	MET/BL	125	1	2000	4500
Falling Man/Study "A" (with Signed Book)	AOE	LEN	1977	SP	35 X 35	SP	100	12	600	1200
Green Sun	PE	KC	1978	EB/A	30 X 34	AP/W	90	4	500	2000
Study/Falling Man (Walking Jackman) (Stainless Steel)	2:30P		1986	MULT	10 X 10 X 10	Steel	99		4500	15000

DAVID TRUE

BORN: Marietta, OH; February 24, 1942
EDUCATION: Ohio Univ, Athens, OH, BFA, MFA, 1967
RECENT EXHIB: Crown Point Press, Oakland, CA & New York, NY, 1987; BlumHelman Gallery, NY, 1988–89,90
PRINTERS: Marcia Bartholme (MB); Lilah Toland (LT); Crown Point Press, San Francisco, CA (CPP); Renée Bott (RB); Lawrence Hamlin (LH); Brian Shure (BS); Jeryl Parker Editions, NY (JPE)
PUBLISHERS: Crown Point Press, San Francisco, CA (CPP)
GALLERIES: Edward Thorp Gallery, New York, NY; Crown Point Press, San Francisco, CA & New York, NY; Barbara Krakow Gallery, Boston, MA; BlumHelman Gallery, New York, NY

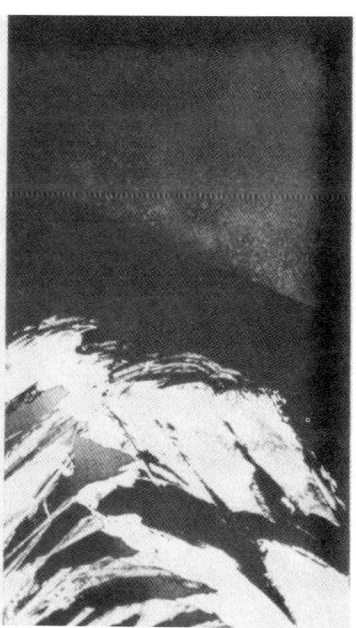

David True
Cold Romance
Courtesy Crown Point Press

TITLE	PUBLISHER	PRINTER	DATE	MEDIUM	DIMENSION (PAPER SIZE) IN INCHES	TYPE OF PAPER	EDITION NUMBER	NO. OF COLORS	ORIGINAL OPENING PRICE	CURRENT RETAIL PRICE
SOLD OUT EDITIONS (RARE):										
Late	CPP	MB/LT/CPP	1983	AC	30 X 45	R/BFK	25	7	850	2000
Savannah Sea	CPP	MB/LT/CPP	1983	AC	26 X 33	FAB	35	3	650	2000
Day without Words	CPP	CPP	1985	AC	49 X 66	R/BFK	10		3000	6000
Cold Romance	CPP	CPP	1985	AC	36 X 48	FAB	10		3000	4500
Roaming Swiftly, Knowing Quickly	CPP	CPP	1985	EC	65 X 48	FAB	10		3000	5000
Open Channel	CPP	RB/LH/BS/CPP	1987	AC	30 X 52	SOM	50		1500	4500
CURRENT EDITIONS:										
Lifting Descent	CPP	MB/LT/CPP	1983	EC/HG	16 X 12	WP/ANT	25	4	350	350
Sour Mistress	CPP	MB/LT/CPP	1983	AC/SG	26 X 33	R/BFK	15	3	750	1000
Doggone	CPP	CPP	1985	EC/CLOTH	62 X 48	CLOTH	5		3000	4000
Dark Song	CPP	CPP	1985	EC/CLOTH	62 X 48	CLOTH	5		3000	4000
Father and Son	CPP	CPP	1985	EC	65 X 48	FAB	5		3000	3500
Woodland	CPP	JPE	1985	EB/A/SB	60 X 44	SOM	10	1	2000	3500
Back Around	CPP	RB/LH/BS/CPP	1987	AC	41 X 31	SOM/S	50	1	800	2000
Cut Secure (Dipt)	CPP	RB/LH/BS/CPP	1987	AC/SL/SOG	34 X 46	SOM/S	25	1	900	2200
Cut Flowers, Unexpected	CPP	CPP	1989	WC	30 X 43	SUZ	150	16	2000	2000
Fragile Wings	CPP	CPP	1989	WC	21 X 25	SUZ	100	14	1200	2000

The print market has become very selective. For the first time since we published the first edition of The Printworld Directory in 1982, the prices of prints have been greatly reduced and greatly increased for the same artists by the most reputable and established print publishers. Check the fifth edition to understand the movement.

DAVID TROWBRIDGE

PRINTERS: Cirrus Editions Workshop, Los Angeles, CA (CEW)
PUBLISHERS: Cirrus Editions Ltd, Los Angeles, CA (CE)
GALLERIES: Cirrus Editions Ltd, Los Angeles, CA; Thomas Babeor Gallery, La Jolla, CA; Modernism, San Francisco, CA

TITLE	PUBLISHER	PRINTER	DATE	MEDIUM	DIMENSION (PAPER SIZE) IN INCHES	TYPE OF PAPER	EDITION NUMBER	NO. OF COLORS	ORIGINAL OPENING PRICE	CURRENT RETAIL PRICE
SOLD OUT EDITIONS (RARE):										
Untitled (#67 cs)	CE	CEW	1972	SP/MY	24 X 18	Mylar	45		200	350
Untitled (#157 c)	CE	CEW	1974	LC	24 X 20	AP	50		200	450

BARBARA LEE TRUPP

BORN: Scott's Bluff, NE; November 17, 1950
EDUCATION: Banff Center Sch of Fine Arts, Alberta, Canada, 1968–70; Univ of Puget Sound, Tacoma, WA, 1969–70; Univ of MIchigan, Ann Arbor, MI, BFA, Cumbiude, 1971–74
TEACHING: Instr, Ceramics, Evanston Arts Center, IN, 1987 to present; Instr, Painting, Noyes Cultural Art Center, IL, 1988 to present
RECENT EXHIB: Illinois Street Gallery, Chicago, IL, 1988; Illinois State Mus, Springfield, IL, 1988–89,91
COLLECTIONS: Illinois State Mus, Springfield, IL; Oregon State Mus, Portland, OR; American Mus, Bath, England; Banff Center of Arts, Canada; Mary & Leigh Block Gallery, Northwestern Univ, Evanston, IL; Krannert Mus, Univ of Illinois, Champaign, IL; Ruttenberg Art Found, Chicago, IL; Univ of Nevada, Reno, NV
PUBLISHERS: Plucked Chicken Press, Evanston, IL (PCP)
PRINTERS: Will Petersen, Evanston, IL (WP); Plucked Chicken Press, Evanston, IL (PCP); Artist (ART)
GALLERIES: Plucked Chicken Press, Evanston, IL; Citywoods, Highland Park, IL; Illinois Artisans Shop, Chicago, IL
MAILING ADDRESS: 636 Hinman, #3-E, Evanston, IL 60202

TITLE	PUBLISHER	PRINTER	DATE	MEDIUM	DIMENSION (PAPER SIZE) IN INCHES	TYPE OF PAPER	EDITION NUMBER	NO. OF COLORS	ORIGINAL OPENING PRICE	CURRENT RETAIL PRICE
CURRENT EDITIONS:										
Theban Archaeopteryx Lithographica	PCP	ART/WP/PCP	1985	LC	40 X 30	R/BFK/T	30	4	350	600

PHILIP TSIARAS

PRINTERS: Bobbi Berkman, Coconut Grove, FL (BB); Figura, Inc, NY (FI)
PUBLISHERS: Grafico Uno, Milan, Italy (GU)
GALLERIES: Figura, Inc, New York, NY; Inkfish Gallery, Denver, CO

TITLE	PUBLISHER	PRINTER	DATE	MEDIUM	DIMENSION (PAPER SIZE) IN INCHES	TYPE OF PAPER	EDITION NUMBER	NO. OF COLORS	ORIGINAL OPENING PRICE	CURRENT RETAIL PRICE
CURRENT EDITIONS:										
Target Horse	BB/FI	GU	1987–88	EB	23 X 16	TorP	23		200	300
Target Horse	BB/FI	GU	1987–88	EB/HC	23 X 16	TorP	23		440	550
Target Horse Diagonal	BB/FI	GU	1987–88	EB	22 X 30	R/BFK	20		390	475
Target Horse Spiral	BB/FI	GU	1987–88	EB	29 X 20	R/BFK	20		390	475

SEYMOUR TUBIS

BORN: Philadelphia, PA; September 20, 1919
EDUCATION: Temple Univ, Phila, PA, 1937–39; Philadelphia Mus Sch, PA, 1941–42; Art Students League, NY, 1946–49; Acad Grande-Chaumiere, Paris, France, 1949–50; Inst d'Arte, Florence, Italy, 1950; Hans Hofmann Sch, 1950–51
TEACHING: Brooklyn Mus Sch, NY, 1950–51; Inst, Am Indian Arts, Santa Fe, NM, 1962, Chmn, Dept of Fine Arts, 1965–80
AWARDS: First Prize, Soc of Am Graphic Artists, NY, 1948; Purchase Award, Lowe Found, NY, 1950; First Prize, Newspaper Guild of NY, 1952; Purchase Award, Mus of New Mexico, 1975; Nat Endowment for the Arts, 1980
RECENT EXHIB: Bluecreek/West Gallery, Denver, CO, 1989; Retrosp, Pacific Grove Art Center, CA, 1990; Retrosp, Associated American Artists, NY, 1990; Masterpiece Gallery, Carmel, CA, 1992
COLLECTIONS: Metropolitan Mus of Art, NY; Mus of New Mexico, Santa Fe, NM; Univ of Calgary, Can; Georgetown Univ, Wash, DC
PRINTERS: Tamarind Inst, Albuquerque, NM (TI); Artist (ART)
PUBLISHERS: Tamarind Inst, Albuquerque, NM (TI); Artist (ART)
GALLERIES: Tobey C Moss Gallery, Los Angeles, CA; Associated American Artists, New York, NY; Bluecreek/West Gallery, Denver, CO
MAILING ADDRESS: 1531 S Flamingo Way, Denver, CO 80222

TITLE	PUBLISHER	PRINTER	DATE	MEDIUM	DIMENSION (PAPER SIZE) IN INCHES	TYPE OF PAPER	EDITION NUMBER	NO. OF COLORS	ORIGINAL OPENING PRICE	CURRENT RETAIL PRICE
SOLD OUT EDITIONS (RARE):										
Lackawanna Ferry	ART	ART	1947	EC	5 X 7		6		50	600
Woman in Striped Dress	ART	ART	1949	EB/A/SG	9 X 6		12		75	700
The Wave	ART	ART	1965	COL	11 X 14	CD	14	4	125	600
Stonehenge I	ART	ART	1966	WC	15 X 24	CD	14	4	150	700
Seascape	ART	ART	1966	I	16 X 16	CD	15	2	150	600
Owl	ART	ART	1968	WC	30 X 17	CD	12	3	175	800
CURRENT EDITIONS:										
Two Men at a Table	ART	ART	1947	EB	9 X 12	AP	26	1	50	500
House on the Beach	ART	ART	1948	DPT	9 X 12	DE	24	1	60	400
Miriam Asleep	ART	ART	1949	LB/EB	9 X 12	BH	24	1	60	400
Moon of Three Directions	ART	ART	1968	EMB	20 X 18	CD	14	0	175	500
Moon of Peace	ART	ART	1968	EMB	24 X 14	CD	20	0	175	500
Moon of Attraction	ART	ART	1968	EMB	24 X 14	CD	20	0	175	500
The Scavengers	TI	TI	1968	LC	24 X 20	RP	12	2	175	500
Sarah and Gene	TI	TI	1969	LB	20 X 22	RP	20	1	175	500
Inscrutability	ART	ART	1970	I/MED/GR	26 X 14	KOZO	12	3	300	700

SEYMOUR TUBIS CONTINUED

TITLE	PUBLISHER	PRINTER	DATE	MEDIUM	DIMENSION (PAPER SIZE) IN INCHES	TYPE OF PAPER	EDITION NUMBER	NO. OF COLORS	ORIGINAL OPENING PRICE	CURRENT RETAIL PRICE
CURRENT EDITIONS:										
Flight of Birds around a Dark Sun	ART	ART	1972	I	17 X 23	GE	23	2	200	500
Propaganda Machine	ART	ART	1972	SP	26 X 20	Italia	36	3	200	300
Man's Double-Cross	ART	ART	1973	MM	30 X 22	CD	10	7	250	800
Pueblo Ceremonial Trio	ART	ART	1975	WO	21 X 28	IN	25	1	225	600
Bryce Canyon Suite (Cov, Intro, 9 pr.)	ART	ART	1979	I	27 X 16	GE/DE/RB	25	2	900 SET	1400 SET
Central Park II	ART	ART	1981	I	14 X 18	CD	25	1	300	500
Flight of the Female Chauvinist	ART	ART	1981	I	18 X 18	CD	25	3	225	800
Old Musician	ART	ART	1981	I	22 X 16	DE/I	25	1	325	800
Antarctica Metamorphosis	ART	ART	1981	COL	20 X 40	CD	12	2	400	1000
Face in the Window	ART	ART	1982	I	22 X 18	DE	25	1	300	800
Dawn of Birds	ART	ART	1982	I	14 X 12	GE	25	1	175	400
Dream of My Lie	ART	ART	1983	COL/DPT	16 X 16	M-T	AP-12	2-3	175	400
The Jungle	ART	ART	1982-92	COL	28 X 40	CPDL	AP-12	2-3	1000	1000

ELLEN FRANCIS TUCHMAN

BORN: Los Angeles, CA; October 16, 1954
EDUCATION: Univ of California, Los Angeles, CA, 1972-74; California Col of Arts & Crafts, Valencia, CA, BFA, 1976
AWARDS: Creative Artists Public Service Award, New York State Council on the Arts Grant, Graphics, 1981; Arian Found Arts Grant, Mixed Media, 1982
COLLECTIONS: Metropolitan Mus of Art, NY
PRINTERS: Bristol Art Editions, Ltd, NY (BA); Capezio, NY (CAP)
PUBLISHERS: Doris Weintraub, NY (DW); Bristol Art Editions, Ltd, NY (BA)
GALLERIES: Baker Gallery, Dallas, TX; Markel/Sears Fine Art, New York, NY

TITLE	PUBLISHER	PRINTER	DATE	MEDIUM	DIMENSION (PAPER SIZE) IN INCHES	TYPE OF PAPER	EDITION NUMBER	NO. OF COLORS	ORIGINAL OPENING PRICE	CURRENT RETAIL PRICE
SOLD OUT EDITIONS (RARE):										
Aurora's Dream I (Beads, Fabric, etc)	BA	CAP	1982	CO		AP	30	Multi	350	500
Aurora's Dream II (Beads, Fabric, etc)	BA	CAP	1982	CO		AP	30	Multi	350	500

WILLIAM G TUCKER

BORN: Cairo, Egypt; February 28, 1935
EDUCATION: Oxford Univ, England, BA, 1955-58; Martin's Sch of Art, London, 1959-62
AWARDS: Guggenheim Fel, NY, 1980-81
RECENT EXHIB: Florida International Univ Art Mus, Miami, FL, 1989,92; Storm King Art Center, Mountainville, NY, 1989,92; Lafayette Col, Easton, PA, 1992
COLLECTIONS: Tate Gallery, London, England; Mus of Mod Art, NY; Arts Council of Great Britain, London, England; Walker Art Center, Minneapolis, MN; British Mus, London, England; Guggenheim Mus, NY; Victoria & Albert Mus, London, England; Metropolitan Mus of Art, NY; Louisiana Mus, Denmark; Univ of California, Los Angeles, CA; Kroller-Muller Mus, The Netherlands
PRINTERS: Solo Press, NY (SP); Artist (ART)
PUBLISHERS: Bernard Jacobson Ltd, London, England (BJL); Artist (ART)
GALLERIES: Bernard Jacobson Ltd, London, England; McKee Gallery, New York, NY; Pamela Auchincloss Gallery, Santa Barbara, CA; Panicali Fine Art, New York, NY; Garner Tullis Fine Art, New York, NY; Philippe Staib Gallery, New York, NY; Gallery Paule Anglim, San Francisco, CA
MAILING ADDRESS: 99 Commercial St, Brooklyn, NY 11222

TITLE	PUBLISHER	PRINTER	DATE	MEDIUM	DIMENSION (PAPER SIZE) IN INCHES	TYPE OF PAPER	EDITION NUMBER	NO. OF COLORS	ORIGINAL OPENING PRICE	CURRENT RETAIL PRICE
SOLD OUT EDITIONS (RARE):										
Prisoner	BJL	SP	1982	LC	30 X 42	AP	20	2	600	1000
Sun	BJL	SP	1982	LC	30 X 42	AP	20	2	600	1000
Victory	BJL	SP	1982	LC	30 X 42	AP	20	2	600	1000
The Law	BJL	SP	1982	LC	30 X 42	AP	20	2	600	1000
Promise	BJL	SP	1982	LC	30 X 42	AP	20	2	600	1000
Turning	BJL	SP	1982	LC	30 X 42	AP	20	2	600	1000
Untitled	ART	ART	1985	MON	60 X 44 EA	HMP	1 EA	Varies	1500 EA	2000 EA

ALAN TURNER

BORN: New York, NY; July 6, 1943
EDUCATION: City Col of New York, NY, BA, 1965; Univ of California, Berkeley, CA, MA, 1967
AWARDS: Univ of California Alumni Assn Fel, 1967; Eisner Award, Univ of California, 1967; Nat Endowment for the Arts Fel, 1977,81,87; Guggenheim Mem Found Fel, 1988
RECENT EXHIB: Jason McCoy, Inc, NY, 1987; Everson Mus, Syracuse, NY, 1988; Lorence•Monk Gallery, NY, 1988; Wingate Gallery, NY, 1988
PRINTERS: Maurice Sanchez, NY (MS); Derriére L'Etoile Studio, NY (DES); Artist (ART); Harlan & Weaver Intaglio, NY (HW)
PUBLISHERS: Brooke Alexander, Inc, NY (BAI); Derriére L'Etoile Studio, NY (DES); Artist (ART); Editions Ilene Kurtz, NY (EIK)
GALLERIES: Brooke Alexander, Inc, New York, NY; Jason McCoy, Inc, New York, NY; Editions Ilene Kurtz, New York, NY
MAILING ADDRESS: 114 Franklin St, New York, NY 10013

TITLE	PUBLISHER	PRINTER	DATE	MEDIUM	DIMENSION (PAPER SIZE) IN INCHES	TYPE OF PAPER	EDITION NUMBER	NO. OF COLORS	ORIGINAL OPENING PRICE	CURRENT RETAIL PRICE
SOLD OUT EDITIONS (RARE):										
Three Seasoned Wooded Scene	BAI	MS	1980	EB	27 X 52	AC	21	1	300	1200

ALAN TURNER CONTINUED

TITLE	PUBLISHER	PRINTER	DATE	MEDIUM	DIMENSION (PAPER SIZE) IN INCHES	TYPE OF PAPER	EDITION NUMBER	NO. OF COLORS	ORIGINAL OPENING PRICE	CURRENT RETAIL PRICE
SOLD OUT EDITIONS (RARE):										
Three Seasoned Wooded Scene	BAI	MS	1980	EC	27 X 52	AC	59		450	1800
Pine Cut Down (3 Sheets) A–C	BAI	MS	1981	LC	22 X 51 EA	AP/ROL	40 EA	2 EA	750 EA	900 EA
Tree Felled by Swirl I, II, III (3 Sheets)	BAI	MS	1981	LC	47 X 34 EA	AP/ROL	45 EA		1800 SET 650 EA	2400 SET 900 EA
Botanical Garden	DES/ART	MS/ART	1983	LC/HC	26 X 20	AP	14		650	800
Jardin Botanico	DES	MS/DES	1983	LC	24 X 16	AC	40	3	500	700
CURRENT EDITIONS:										
Hook & Eye (Series of 3)	EIK	HW	1990	EB	21 X 18 EA	AP	30 EA	1 EA	1500 SET 650 EA	1800 SET 750 EA

JANET E TURNER

BORN: Kansas City, MO; (1914–1988)
EDUCATION: Stanford Univ, CA, BA, 1932–36; Kansas City Art Inst, MO, 1936–41; Claremont Grad Sch, CA, MFA, 1942–47; Columbia Univ, NY, 1956–59
TEACHING: Austin State Col, Nacogdoches, TX; California State Univ, Chico, CA

AWARDS: Guggenheim Fel, 1953; Audubon Award, NY, 1981; Am Color Print Soc, 1981; Nat Assn of Women Artists, NY, 1981
COLLECTIONS: Philadelphia Mus, PA; Cleveland Mus, OH; Smithsonian Inst, Wash, DC; Metropolitan Art Mus, NY
PRINTERS: Artist (ART)
PUBLISHERS: Artist (ART)
GALLERIES: Associated American Artists, New York, NY; Arts & Crafts, Chico, CA; Valley House Gallery, Dallas, TX; Bay Window Gallery, Mendocino, CA; Kabutoya Galleries, San Francisco, CA

TITLE	PUBLISHER	PRINTER	DATE	MEDIUM	DIMENSION (PAPER SIZE) IN INCHES	TYPE OF PAPER	EDITION NUMBER	NO. OF COLORS	ORIGINAL OPENING PRICE	CURRENT RETAIL PRICE
SOLD OUT EDITIONS (RARE):										
Imature Golden Eagle	ART	ART	1974–75	LI/SP	25 X 35	TOR	140	10	350	800
Quail Amid Wild Grapes	ART	ART	1975	LI/SP	17 X 38	AP	150	10	90	2100
Wintering Snow Geese	ART	ART	1976	LI/SP/EMB	17 X 38	AP	175	8	125	2100
Koi	ART	ART	1977	LI/SP	8 X 30	AP	185	20	200	700
CURRENT EDITIONS:										
Tundra Series: Raven	ART	ART	1980	LI/SP	13 X 24	TOR	80	10	200	450
Tundra Series: Snowy Owls	ART	ART	1980–81	LI/SP/WC	36 X 27	TOR	185	15	300	500
Pin Tails	ART	ART	1981–82	LI/SP	21 X 28	TOR	185	15	400	550
Pin Tails	ART	ART	1982	LI/SP	28 X 36	TOR/HODO	185	20	400	650
Roots and Ducks	ART	ART	1983	LI/SP	15 X 36	HODO	185	25	350	400
Red Shouldered Hawk Family	ART	ART	1984–85	LI/SP	36 X 26	TOR	155	20	450	500

JAMES TURRELL

BORN: Los Angeles, CA; May 6, 1943
EDUCATION: Pomona Col, CA, BA, Psychology, 1965; Grad Studies, Art, Univ of California, Irvine, CA, 1965–66; Claremont Sch, CA, MA, 1973
AWARDS: Nat Endowment for the Arts, 1968; Guggenheim Fel, 1974; Nat Endowment for the Arts, Matching Grant, 1975; Arizona Comm for the Arts & Humanities, Visual Arts Fel, 1980; Lumen Award, Int Assoc of Lighting Engineers, 1981; MacArthur Found Fel, 1984,85
RECENT EXHIB: Phoenix Art Mus, AZ, 1987; Univ of Arizona Mus, Tucson, AZ, 1987; Capp Street Project, San Francisco, CA, 1987; St Louis Art Mus, MO, 1988; Walker Art Center, Minneapolis, MN, 1987,89; Guggenheim Mus, NY, 1989; Nat Gallery of Art, Wash, DC, 1989–90; Le Musee d'Art Contemporain de Montreal, Canada, 1990; Chateau de Rochechouart, France, 1990; Mus of Mod Art, NY, 1990; SteinGladstone Gallery, NY, 1990; Turske & Turske Gallery, Zurich, Switzerland, 1990; La Jolla Mus of Contemp Art, CA, 1990; Karl Bornstein Gallery, Santa Monica, CA, 1990; Williams Col of Art, Williamstown, MA, 1991; Anthony d'Offay Gallery, London, England, 1991; Florida State Univ, Tallahasse, FL, 1989,92; Henry Art Gallery, Seattle, WA, 1992–93; Inst of Contemp Art, Univ of Pennsylvania, Phila, PA, 1993; Locks Gallery, Phila, PA, 1993
COLLECTIONS: Art Inst of Chicago, IL; DIA Art Found, NY; Mus of Contemp Art, Los Angeles, CA; Seattle Art Mus, WA; Whitney Mus of Am Art, NY; Stedelijk Mus, Amsterdam, The Netherlands
PRINTERS: Peter Kneubücuhler, Zürich, Switzerland (PK)
PUBLISHERS: Peter Blum Edition, NY (PBE); Turske & Turske, Zürich, Switzerland (TT)
GALLERIES: Marian Goodman, New York, NY; Karl Bornstein Gallery, New Santa Monica, CA; Barbara Krakow Gallery, Boston, MA; Gemini GEL, Los Angeles, CA; Mattress Factory, Pittsburgh, PA; Lisa Sette Gallery, Scottsdale, AZ; Sette & Segura Publishing Company, Tempe, AZ; Tavelli Williams Gallery, Aspen, CO; Montgomery Glascoe Fine Art, Minneapolis, MN; Susan Caldwell & Company, New York, NY; SteinGladstone Gallery, New York, NY; Wilkey Fine Arts, Seattle, WA; Locks Gallery, Phila, PA
MAILING ADDRESS: Rte 7, Hanger 1, Flagstaff, AZ 86001

James Turrell
Alta and Gard
Courtesy Turske & Turske

The retail prices of the 100,000 limited edition prints quoted in this directory are subject to change. Print publishers, artists and galleries were the direct sources for these quotations. Prices in the secondary market listed as "Sold Out Editions (Rare)" indicate that the publisher has a limited supply of that print or that the print is difficult to locate in the galleries.

JAMES TURRELL CONTINUED

TITLE	PUBLISHER	PRINTER	DATE	MEDIUM	DIMENSION (PAPER SIZE) IN INCHES	TYPE OF PAPER	EDITION NUMBER	NO. OF COLORS	ORIGINAL OPENING PRICE	CURRENT RETAIL PRICE
SOLD OUT EDITIONS (RARE):										
Untitled	PBE	PK	1984	AC	13 X 17	R/BFK	50		500	2000
Deep Sky (Portfolio of Seven Aquatints) (Set of 7)	PBE	PK	1984	AC	21 X 27	R/BFK	45		3000 SET	6500 SET
CURRENT EDITIONS:										
Matching Spaces Suite (Set of 3):									4500 SET	10000 SET
Matching Spaces, Fumarole	PBE	PK	1987	EB/A/PH	22 X 31	HAHN	35		1000	3500
Matching Spaces, North Chamber	PBE	PK	1987	EB/A/PH	22 X 31	HAHN	35		1000	3500
Matching Spaces, West Chamber	PBE	PK	1987	EB/A/PH	22 X 31	HAHN	35		1000	3500
Mapping Spaces: East	PBE	PK	1988	EB	23 X 31	HAHN	35	1	1500	2500
Mapping Spaces: West	PBE	PK	1988	EB	23 X 31	HAHN	35	1	1500	2500
Crating Bowl: Cross Section	PBE	PK	1988	EB	23 X 31	HAHN	35	1	1500	2500
First Light (Set of 20)	PBE	PK	1988	EB/A	23 X 31 EA	HAHN	35 EA		60000 SET	65000 SET
Still Light (Alta, Gard, Enzu, Tollyn, Munson, Squat, Juke, Carn) (Set of 8)	TT	PK	1990–91	AC	42 X 30 EA	ZER	30 EA		22000 SET	30000 SET

RICHARD TUTTLE

BORN: Rahway, New Jersey; 1941
EDUCATION: Trinity Col, Hartford, CT, 1959–63; Cooper Union Art Sch, NY
RECENT EXHIB: BlumHelman Gallery, NY, 1987; Thomas Segal Gallery, Boston, MA, 1988; Sperone Westwater Gallery, NY, 1989; Brooke Alexander, Inc, NY, 1990; Galerie Schmela, Dusseldorf, Germany, 1988,90; Galerie Hubert Winter, Vienna, Austria, 1989,90; Sprengel Mus, Hanover, Germany, 1990; Galerie Yvon Lambert, Paris, France, 1990; Galerie Anne Marie Verna, Switzerland, 1990; Andrea Rosen Gallery, NY, 1990; Anders Tornborg Gallery, Sweden, 1990; A/D Gallery, NY, 1990; Mary Boone Gallery, NY, 1992; Lawrence Markey Gallery, NY, 1992
COLLECTIONS: Corcoran Gallery of Art, Wash, DC; Kaiser-Wilhelm Mus, Krefeld, Germany; James A Michener Found, Nat Gallery of Can, Ottawa, Can; City Mus, St Louis, MO
PRINTERS: Sheila Marbain, NY (SM); Maurel Studio, NY (MS); Patricia Branstead, NY (PB); Aeropress, Inc, NY (A); Maurice Sanchez, NY (MS); Linda Gray, NY (LG); James Miller, NY (JM); Joe Petruzelli, NY (JP); Derriere L'Etoile Studios, NY (DES); Limestone Press, San Francisco, CA (LP)
PUBLISHERS: Brooke Alexander, Inc, NY (BAI); Multiples, Inc, NY (M); Galerie Heiner Friedrich (GHF); Hine Editions, San Francisco, CA (HE); Limestone Press, San Francisco, CA (LP)
GALLERIES: Brooke Alexander Gallery, New York, NY; Marian Goodman, New York, NY; Donald Young Gallery, Seattle, WA; Jack Tilton Gallery, New York, NY; BlumHelman Gallery, New York, NY; Arnold Herstand & Company, New York, NY; Steven Leiber Gallery, San Francisco, CA; Thomas Segal Gallery, Boston, MA; Sperone Westwater Gallery, New York, NY; Mary Boone Gallery, New York, NY; Lawrence Markey Gallery, New York, NY; Rhona Hoffman, Chicago, IL; Hine Editions/Limestone Press, San Francisco, CA; Laura Carpenter Fine Art, Santa Fe, NM; Naravisa Press, Santa Fe, NM

TITLE	PUBLISHER	PRINTER	DATE	MEDIUM	DIMENSION (PAPER SIZE) IN INCHES	TYPE OF PAPER	EDITION NUMBER	NO. OF COLORS	ORIGINAL OPENING PRICE	CURRENT RETAIL PRICE
SOLD OUT EDITIONS (RARE):										
In Praise of Historical Determinism, I, II, III (Set of 3)	BAI	SM/MS	1974	LC	30 X 22 EA	HMP	50 EA		750 SET	4500 SET
Print (Dipt)	BAI	SM/MS	1976	SP	30 X 23 EA	HMP	31	1	450	6000
Stacked Color Drawing (Set of 4)	GHF	SM/MS	1976	LC/OFF	30 X 45 EA	NEWS	100 EA		200 SET	1500 SET
Two with Any Two (3 Sheets, Printed Front and Back)	BAI/GHF	SM/MS	1977	EB/LC/SP	28 X 19 EA	HMP	50 EA		750 SET	1500 SET
Paris 1966/ New York 1982 (Waxed Styro Foam Multiple)	M	PB/A	1982	MULT	8 X 21 X 13	HMP	18		1800	3000
Suite I, II, III (Set of 3):									1800 SET	4500 SET
Suite I (Gigue)	M	PB/A	1983	SB/SL	30 X 42	HMP	15		700	1800
Suite II (Gavotte)	M	PB/A	1983	SB/SL	30 X 42	HMP	15		700	1800
Suite III (Sarabende)	M	PB/A	1983	SB/SL	30 X 42	HMP	15		700	1800
CURRENT EDITIONS:										
Perceived Obstacle (Set of 5)	BAI	MS/LG/JM/JP/DES	1991	LC	13 X 36 EA	SOM/S	45 EA		2500 SET	3000 SET
Untitled (with Mei-Mei Berssenbrugge)	BAI	MS/LG/JM/JP/DES	1991	LC/SP	15 X 39	SOM/S	75		750	750
Treatise in Intaglio (Framed)	HE/LP	LP	1991	EB	37 X 29	AP	7	1	7000	7000

RANDY TWADDLE

BORN: Elmo, MO; 1957
EDUCATION: Northwest Missouri State Univ, Maryville, MO, BFA, 1980
AWARDS: Nat Endowment for the Arts Fel, 1987; Visual Arts Award, New Orleans Mus, LA, 1990; Visual Arts Award, SECCA, Winston-Salem, NC, 1990
RECENT EXHIB: D W Gallery, Dallas, TX, 1988; Damon Brandt Gallery, NY, 1989; Southwest Craft Center, San Antonio, TX, 1989; Barry Whistler Gallery, Dallas, TX, 1989; Mus of Fine Arts, Houston, TX, 1990; BMW Gallery, NY, 1990
COLLECTIONS: Mus of Fine Arts, Houston, TX; Dallas Mus of Art, TX; Tyler Mus of Art, TX; Huntington Art Gallery, Univ of Texas, Austin, TX
PRINTERS: Jack Lemon, Chicago, IL (JL); Landfall Press, Inc, Chicago, IL (LPI)
PUBLISHERS: Landfall Press, Inc, Chicago, IL (LPI)
GALLERIES: Landfall Press, Inc, Chicago, IL; Moody Gallery, Houston, TX; Barry Whistler Gallery, Dallas, TX

RANDY TWADDLE CONTINUED

TITLE	PUBLISHER	PRINTER	DATE	MEDIUM	DIMENSION (PAPER SIZE) IN INCHES	TYPE OF PAPER	EDITION NUMBER	NO. OF COLORS	ORIGINAL OPENING PRICE	CURRENT RETAIL PRICE
CURRENT EDITIONS:										
Rocket/Crutch (Black on White)	LPI	JL/LPI	1985	LB	20 X 26	AC	20	1	150	300
Untitled	LPI	JL/LPI	1985	LB	30 X 40	AC	20	3	250	350
Patriotic Appropriation: Three Eagles (Trip) (Set of 3)	LPI	JL/LPI	1987	LC	20 X 26	AP	15	2	250	250
Extended Orbits	LPI	JL/LPI	1989	LB	30 X 30	AP	20	1	1200	1200
Untitled	LPI	JL/LPI	1990	EB/A	30 X 40	AP	20		1200	1200
UPC Print	LPI	JL/LPI	1992	EB/A	40 X 30	AP	50	1	1200	1200

CY TWOMBLY

BORN: Lexington, VA; April 25, 1928
EDUCATION: Boston Mus Sch of Fine Arts, MA, 1948–49; Washington & Lee Univ, Lexington, VA, 1950; Art Students League, NY, 1951; Black Mountain Col, NC, 1951–52, with Franz Kline & Robert Motherwell
TEACHING: Head, Art Dept, Southern Seminary & Junior Col, Buena Vista, VA, 1955–56
AWARDS: Virginia Mus of Fine Arts Fel, Travel, Europe & Africa, 1952–53; Skowhegan Sch of Painting & Sculpture Award, ME, 1990
RECENT EXHIB: Anthony d'Offay Gallery, London, England, 1987; Sperone Westwater Gallery, NY, 1989; Karsten Greve Gallery, Cologne, West Germany, 1990
COLLECTIONS: Rhode Island Sch of Design, Providence, RI; Mus of Mod Art, NY; Whitney Mus of Am Art, NY
PRINTERS: Black Mountain Graphics Workshop, NC (BMGW); Universal Limited Art Editions, West Islip, NY (ULAE); Electa Editrice, Venice, Italy, (EEd); Edition Domberger, KG, Stuttgart, Germany (DOM)
PUBLISHERS: Nicola Cernovich, Black Mountain Graphics Workshop, Black Mountain Col, NC (NC/BMGW); Edition Schellmann & Klüser, Cologne, Germany; Universal Limited Art Editions, West Islip, NY (ULAE); Neuendorf Verlag, Hamburg, Germany (NV); Propläen Verlag, West Berlin, Germany (PV); Edition Domberger, KG, Stuttgart, Germany (DOM); Visconti Art Spectrum, Wien, Germany (VAS)
GALLERIES: Editions Schellmann, New York, NY & Cologne, Germany; Sonnabend Gallery, New York, NY; Sperone Westwater Gallery, New York, NY; L A Louver Gallery, Venice, CA; Marisa del Re Gallery, New York, NY; Hirschl & Adler Modern, New York, NY; Charles Cowles Gallery, New York, NY; Anthony d'Offay Gallery, London, England; Thomas Segal Gallery, Boston, MA; John C Stoller & Co, Minneapolis, MN; Greenberg Gallery, St Louis, MO; Gagosian Gallery, New York, NY; Judith Goldberg Fine Arts, New York, NY; Phyllis Kind Galleries, New York, NY & Chicago, IL; Karsten Greve Gallery, Cologne, West Germany; J Noblett Gallery, Boyes Hot Springs, CA; Anthony Meier Fine Arts, San Francisco, CA; James Corcoran Gallery, Santa Monica, CA; L Bartman Fine Arts, Chicago, IL; Laura Carpenter Fine Art, Santa Fe, NM; Dranoff Fine Art, New York, NY; Thomas Erben Gallery, Inc, New York, NY; Figura, Inc, New York, NY; Matthew Marks Gallery, New York, NY; Atsuko Murayama Fine Art, New York, NY; Rubenstein/Diacono, New York, NY; Scharf Fine Art, New York, NY; Susan Sheehan Gallery, Inc, New York, NY; Stux Modern, New York, NY; TwoSixtyArt, New York, NY; Owl 57 Galleries, Woodmere, NY

Bastian (B); Sparks (S)

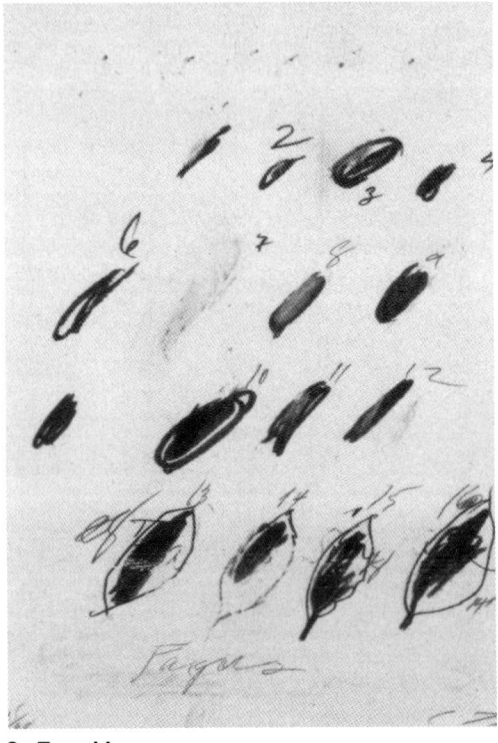

Cy Twombly
Natural History, Part II
(Some Trees of Italy)
Courtesy Edition Schellmann

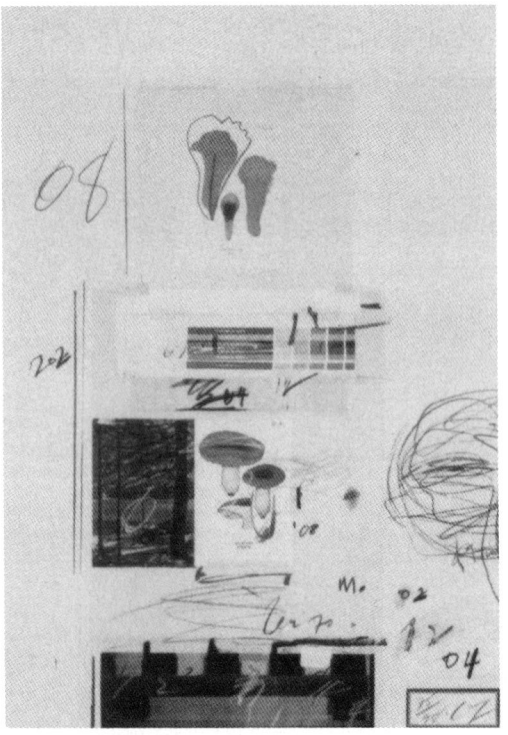

Cy Twombly
Natural History, Part I (Mushrooms)
Courtesy Edition Schellmann

The print market has become very selective. For the first time since we published the first edition of The Printworld Directory in 1982, the prices of prints have been greatly reduced and greatly increased for the same artists by the most reputable and established print publishers. Check the fifth edition to understand the movement.

CY TWOMBLY CONTINUED

TITLE	PUBLISHER	PRINTER	DATE	MEDIUM	DIMENSION (PAPER SIZE) IN INCHES	TYPE OF PAPER	EDITION NUMBER	NO. OF COLORS	ORIGINAL OPENING PRICE	CURRENT RETAIL PRICE
SOLD OUT EDITIONS (RARE):										
The Song of the Border-Guard:										
Untitled	NC/BMGW	BMGW	1952	LI	13 X 20	WOVE	200		100	8000 SET
Roman Notes I, II, III	ULAE	ULAE	1967	EB	26 X 21 EA	AUV	14 EA	1 EA	300 SET	70000 SET
Notes I, II, III	NV	NV	1967	LC/OFF	34 X 28 EA	AP	100 EA		150 SET	20000 SET
8 Oden von Horaz (Set of 8)	ESK	DOM	1968	SP	16 X 24	AP	30		1000 SET	50000 SET
2 Kassette (Set of 8)	ESK	DOM	1968	SP	16 X 24	AP	100		500 SET	25000 SET
Aquatina-Radierung	ESK	DOM	1968	EB/A	20 X 16	AP	12		100	6000
Untitled (B-19) (S-1)	ULAE	ULAE	1968	MEZ/DPT	9 X 6	AUV	12		100	125000
On the Bowery; Untitled (B-27)	DOM	DOM	1969	SP	26 X 26	AP	100		100	22000
Roman Notes (Set of 6) (B-21–B-26)	NV	EEd	1970	LC/OFF	34 X 28 EA	AP	100 EA		1000 SET	75000 SET
Farblithographie aus Mappe										
Hommage à Picasso	ESK	DOM	1973	LC	30 X 22	AP	90		150	4000
Lithographie/Lichtdruck	ESK	DOM	1973	LB	30 X 22	AP	150		100	3500
Natural History, Part I (Mushrooms) (Set of 10) (B-42–B-53)	PV		1974	LC/OFF/CO	30 X 22	AP	98		2000 SET 200 EA	65000 SET 7000 EA
Natural History, Part II (Some Trees of Italy) (Set of 8)	ESK	DOM	1976	LC	30 X 22	AP	98		2000 SET 250 EA	75000 SET 5000 EA
Some Trees of Italy	ESK	DOM	1975–76	LC	30 X 22	AP	98		300	10000
Quercus Ilex	ESK	DOM	1975–76	LC	30 X 22	AP	98		300	10000
Quercus Robur (B-54)	ESK	DOM	1975–76	LC	30 X 22	AP	98		300	10000
Fagus Silvatica	ESK	DOM	1975–76	LC	30 X 22	AP	98		300	10000
Laurus Nobilis	ESK	DOM	1975–76	LC	30 X 22	AP	98		300	10000
Six Latin Writers and Poets (Set of 7)	ESK	DOM	1976	LC	26 X 20 EA	AP	60 EA		4000 SET 600 EA	40000 SET 6000 EA
Five Greek Poets and a Philosopher (Set of 7) (B-67-B-73)	ESK/PV	DOM	1978	LC	32 X 26 EA	RdB	40 EA		4000 SET 600 EA	50000 SET 7500 EA
Untitled (B-76)	VAS		1983	LC/EB/A	30 X 22	AP	150		2000	10000

JACK TWORKOV

BORN: Biala, Poland; (1900–1982)
EDUCATION: Columbia Univ, NY, 1920-23; Nat Acad of Design, NY, 1923–25; Art Students League, NY, 1925–26
TEACHING: Yale Univ, New Haven, CT, 1963–69; Cooper Union, NY, 1970–72; Columbia Univ, NY, 1973
AWARDS: William A Clark Prize & Corcoran Gold Metal, Corcoran Art Gallery, Wash, DC, 1963; Guggenheim Fel, NY, 1971
RECENT EXHIB: Retrosp, Pennsylvania Acad of Fine Arts, Phila, PA, 1987
COLLECTIONS: Albright-Knox Art Gallery, Buffalo, NY; Cleveland Mus of Fine Art, OH; Mus of Mod Art, NY; Nat Coll of Fine Art, Wash, DC; Whitney Mus of Am Art, NY
PRINTERS: Landfall Press Inc, Chicago, IL (LPI); Jack Lemon, Chicago, IL (JL); Timothy Berry, Chicago, IL (TB); Lowell Farlow, Chicago, IL (LF); Tamarind Institute, Albuquerque, NM (TI); Tyler Graphics, Ltd, Mount Kisco, NY (TGL); S Britko (SB); Richard Hamilton (RH); W Masi (WM)
PUBLISHERS: Landfall Press, Inc, Chicago, IL (LPI); NAME Gallery, Chicago, IL (NG); Tyler Graphics, Ltd, Mount Kisco, NY (TGL); Nancy Hoffman Gallery, NY (NHG)
GALLERIES: Nancy Hoffman Gallery, New York, NY; Landfall Press, Inc, Chicago, IL; Manny Silverman Gallery, Los Angeles, CA; Andre Emmerich Gallery, New York, NY; Brett Mitchell Collection, Cleveland, OH

TITLE	PUBLISHER	PRINTER	DATE	MEDIUM	DIMENSION (PAPER SIZE) IN INCHES	TYPE OF PAPER	EDITION NUMBER	NO. OF COLORS	ORIGINAL OPENING PRICE	CURRENT RETAIL PRICE
SOLD OUT EDITIONS (RARE):										
LP–Q2 Series:										
LP #1–Q2–75	LPI/NHG	JL/LF/LPI	1975	LC	30 X 30	RP	20	3	300	1000
LP #2–Q2–75	LPI/NHG	JL/LF/LPI	1975	LC	30 X 34	RP	20	3	300	1000
LP #3–Q2–75	LPI/NHG	JL/LF/LPI	1975	LC	37 X 37	RP	30	5	300	1000
Intaglio Print #1	LPI	TB/LPI	1976	EB/HG	16 X 20	AP/W	15	1	150	800
TL Series:										
TR #I	TI	SB/TI	1977	LC	66 X 66 cm	AP/W	35	6	400	1200
TR #II	TI	SB/TI	1977	LC	66 X 66 cm	AP/W	17	6	400	1200
TR #III	TI	SB/TI	1977	LC	66 X 66 cm	AP/W	10	6	400	1200
TR #IV	TI	SB/TI	1977	LC	66 X 66 cm	AP/W	27	4	400	1200
TR #V	TI	WM/TI	1977	LB	41 X 56 cm	R/BFK	20	1	300	1000
Tworkov Suite (Set of 3):										900 SET	2400 SET
L–SF–ES #1	LPI	TB/LPI	1979	AC	17 X 17	R/BFK	25	2	300	800
L–SF–ES #2	LPI	TB/LPI	1979	AC	17 X 17	R/BFK	25	3	300	800
L–SF–ES #3	LPI	TB/LPI	1979	AC	17 X 17	R/BFK	25	2	300	800
CURRENT EDITIONS:										
Untitled	LPI/NG	TB/LPI	1980	EB/A/HG	22 X 30	R/BFK	100	1	300	1200
KTL #1	TGL	TGL	1982	LC	27 X 28	AP	150	4	500	900
Commissioned by Chicago Exposition										

The retail prices of the 100,000 limited edition prints quoted in this directory are subject to change. Print publishers, artists and galleries were the direct sources for these quotations. Prices in the secondary market listed as "Sold Out Editions (Rare)" indicate that the publisher has a limited supply of that print or that the print is difficult to locate in the galleries.

RAOUL UBAC

BORN: Malmedy, Belgium; 1910
RECENT EXHIB: Robert Miller Gallery, NY, 1987
PRINTERS: Maeght Editeur, Paris, France (ME); Maeght Lelong, Paris, France (ML)
PUBLISHERS: Maeght Editions, Paris, France (ME); Maeght Lelong Editions, Paris, France (ML)
GALLERIES: Galerie Lelong, Paris, France & Zürich, Switzerland & New York, NY; Robert Miller Gallery, New York, NY; BenedicteSaxe Gallery, Beverly Hills, CA; Res Nova, New York, NY

TITLE	PUBLISHER	PRINTER	DATE	MEDIUM	DIMENSION (PAPER SIZE) IN INCHES	TYPE OF PAPER	EDITION NUMBER	NO. OF COLORS	ORIGINAL OPENING PRICE	CURRENT RETAIL PRICE
SOLD OUT EDITIONS (RARE):										
Silex I	ME	ME	1981	LC	54 X 56 cm	AP	75	1	600 FF	1200 FF
Silex II	ME	ME	1981	LC	50 X 65 cm	AP	75	1	600 FF	1200 FF
Pierre Taillée	ME	ME	1981	LC	50 X 65 cm	AP	75	3	900 FF	1800 FF
Tete Levee	ME	ME	1981	LC	66 X 48 cm	AP	75	1	900 FF	1800 FF
Empreinte	ME	ME	1981	LC	54 X 44 cm	AP	75	2	900 FF	1800 FF
Stéle Tete Levée	ME	ME	1981	LC	66 X 48 cm	AP	75	1	900 FF	1800 FF

GÜNTHER UECKER

BORN: Wendorf, Germany; March 13, 1930
EDUCATION: Art Acad, Berlin Weissensee, Germany, 1949–53; Wismar, 1949–53; Art Acad, Düsseldorf, Germany, 1955–58
TEACHING: Instr, Art Acad, Düsseldorf, Germany
AWARDS: Bienale, San Marino, 1971; Bienale, Sao Paulo, Brazil, 1971; Kaiserring Goslar, 1983
RECENT EXHIB: Wesleyan Univ, Ezra & Cecile Zilkha Gallery, Middletown, CT, 1993
PRINTERS: Erker Presse, St Gallen, Switzerland (Erk); Steindrucke Stobb, St Gallen, Switzerland (StSt)
PUBLISHERS: Schumacher Edition Fils, Düsseldorf, Germany (SEF); Aras Verlag, Saulgau, Switzerland (AV)
GALLERIES: Galerie Heseler, Munich, Germany; Galerie Hans Mayer, Dusseldorf, Germany; Galerie Reckermann, Cologne, Germany; Galerie Schoreller, Dusseldorf, Germany; Galerie Streblow, Dusseldorf, Germany; Galerie Wassermann, Munich, Germany

TITLE	PUBLISHER	PRINTER	DATE	MEDIUM	DIMENSION (PAPER SIZE) IN INCHES	TYPE OF PAPER	EDITION NUMBER	NO. OF COLORS	ORIGINAL OPENING PRICE	CURRENT RETAIL PRICE
SOLD OUT EDITIONS (RARE):										
Brett I, II	SEF	Erk	1991	LC	28 X 20 EA	But	90 EA	3 EA	560 EA	750 EA
CURRENT EDITIONS:										
Untitled (Set of 6)	AV	StSt	1992	LC/HC/WC/EMB	13 X 9 EA	But	10 EA	Varies	SF4600 SET	SF4600 SET

ALAN UGLOW

BORN: Luton, England; 1941
EDUCATION: Center Sch of Art, London, England, BA, 1964
RECENT EXHIB: Galerie Rolf Ricke, Cologne, Germany, 1987; Une Austere Affaire, Le Consortium, Dijon, France, 1989; Galerie Onrust, Amsterdam, The Netherlands, 1990; Red Show, Brussels, Belgium, 1990; Galerie Christine, Brussels, Belgium, 1990; Galerie Isy Brachot, Brussels, Belgium, 1990
COLLECTIONS: Fundacion Cultural Televisa, Mexico City, Mexico
PRINTERS: Genovese Graphics, Boston, MA (GG)
PUBLISHERS: Genovese Graphics, Boston, MA (GG)
GALLERIES: Siegel Contemporary Art, New York, NY; Genovese Graphics, Boston, MA
MAILING ADDRESS: 103 Bowery, New York, NY 10002

TITLE	PUBLISHER	PRINTER	DATE	MEDIUM	DIMENSION (PAPER SIZE) IN INCHES	TYPE OF PAPER	EDITION NUMBER	NO. OF COLORS	ORIGINAL OPENING PRICE	CURRENT RETAIL PRICE
CURRENT EDITIONS:										
Persecution, Torture, and Power (Set of 5)	GG	GG	1984	SP	31 X 22 EA	AP88	20 EA	Multi	1200 SET	2500 SET

RICHARD THOMAS UPTON

BORN: Hartford, CT; May 26, 1931
EDUCATION: Univ of Connecticut, Storrs, CT, BFA, 1960; Indiana Univ, Bloomington, IN, MFA, 1963; Ecole des Beaux-Arts, Paris, France
AWARDS: Fulbright Fel Nat Education Assn Grant; Interlaken Corp Designer Award, Providence, RI, 1967
COLLECTIONS: Smithsonian Inst, Nat Coll of Fine Arts, Wash, DC; Mus of Mod Art, NY; Victoria and Albert Mus, London, Eng; Bibleotheque Nat, Paris, France; Montreal Mus of Fine Art, Canada
PRINTERS: Gehenna Press, North Hampton, MA (GP)
PUBLISHERS: Interlocken Corp, RI (IC); Gehenna Press, North Hampton, MA (CP); Salmagundi, Skidmore College, NY (SC); Artist (ART)
GALLERIES: Salmagundi, Skidmore Col, Saratoga Springs, NY
MAILING ADDRESS: 113 Regent St, Saratoga Springs, NY 12866

TITLE	PUBLISHER	PRINTER	DATE	MEDIUM	DIMENSION (PAPER SIZE) IN INCHES	TYPE OF PAPER	EDITION NUMBER	NO. OF COLORS	ORIGINAL OPENING PRICE	CURRENT RETAIL PRICE
SOLD OUT EDITIONS (RARE):										
Figures	ART	GP	1975	LB	30 X 40	AP	4	1	300	900
CURRENT EDITIONS:										
Impressions: A Paris Suite (Set of 8)	ART	GP	1965	LB	23 X 30 EA	AP	50 EA	1 EA	300 SET	1500 SET
Eros Thanatos (Set of 8)	IC	GP	1968	WC	12 X 15 EA	AP	150 EA	2 EA	150 SET	1000 SET
Credo (Set of 12)	GP/ART	GP	1969	LC	22 X 30 EA	AP	20 EA	2 EA	400 SET	1000 SET
Models (Set of 8)	ART	GP	1971	EB	20 X 28 EA	AP	20 EA	1 EA	300 SET	1500 SET
River Road (Set of 4)	SC	GP	1975	LC	22 X 30 EA	AP	75 EA	3 EA	350 SET	1500 SET

KARL UMLAUF

BORN: Chicago, IL; May 16, 1939
EDUCATION: Univ of Texas, Austin, TX, BFA, 1957–61; Yale Univ, New Haven, CT, Fel, 1960; Cornell Univ, Ithaca, NY, MFA, 1962
TEACHING: Cornell Univ, Ithaca, NY, 1961–63; Univ of Pennsylvania, Phila, PA, 1963–66; Univ of Northern Iowa, Cedar Falls, IA, 1966–67; Prof, Indiana Univ, Bloomington, IN, 1974–75,80; Prof, Art, East Texas State Univ, Commerce, TX, 1967–89; Artist in Res, Baylor, Waco, TX, 1989 to present
AWARDS: First Prize, Oklahoma Art Center, Oklahoma City, OK, 1970; First Prize, Evansville Mus of Art, IN, 1975; First Prize, Longview Mus of Art, TX, 1987; Merit Award, Amarillo Competition, TX, 1987
RECENT EXHIB: Missouri State Univ, Kirksville, MO, 1990; Lamar Univ, Dishman Art Gallery, Beaumont, TX, 1992
COLLECTIONS: Dallas Mus of Art, TX; Joslyn Mus of Art, Omaha, NE; Everson Mus of Art, Syracuse, NY; Barnwell Art Center, Shreveport, LA; White Art Mus, Ithaca, NY; Masur Mus, Monroe, LA; New Orleans Mus of Art, LA; Longview Mus of Art, TX; Silvermine Guild, New Canaan, CT; Evansville Mus of Science & Industry, IN; Cornell Univ, Ithaca, NY; Oklahoma Art Center, Oklahoma City, OK; Evansville Mus, IN
PRINTERS: Echo Press, Bloomington, IN (EPr); Artist (ART)
PUBLISHERS: Echo Press, Bloomington, IN (EPr); Artist (ART)
GALLERIES: Eve Mannes Gallery, Atlanta, GA; Miriam Perlman, Chicago, IL; William Campbell Contemporary Art, Fort Worth, TX
MAILING ADDRESS: 109 Royal Lane, Commerce, TX 75428

TITLE	PUBLISHER	PRINTER	DATE	MEDIUM	DIMENSION (PAPER SIZE) IN INCHES	TYPE OF PAPER	EDITION NUMBER	NO. OF COLORS	ORIGINAL OPENING PRICE	CURRENT RETAIL PRICE
SOLD OUT EDITIONS (RARE):										
Formation #14	EPr	ART/EPr	1980	LC	16 X 20	AP	4		450	1000
Formation CP-016	ART	ART	1981	CPM	25 X 20	AP	4		450	1000
Formation EM005	ART	ART	1981	CPM	25 X 20	AP	4		450	1000
Formation EM007	ART	ART	1981	CPM	25 X 20	AP	4		450	1000
Formation CM012	ART	ART	1981	CPM	25 X 20	AP	4		450	1000
Legend Series XVI	ART	ART	1984	CPM	28 X 27	AP	5		450	1000
Legend Series XVII	ART	ART	1985	CPM	28 X 27	AP	5		450	1000
RimLine IX	ART	ART	1985	CPM	28 X 27	AP	5		450	1000

TONY URQUHART

BORN: Niagara Falls, ON, Canada; (1934–1989)
EDUCATION: Yale Univ, New Haven, CT, 1955; Albright Art Sch, Buffalo, NY, 1956; Univ of Buffalo, NY, BFA, 1958
TEACHING: Univ of Western Ontario, London, Can, 1960–63, 64–65, 67–72; Univ of Waterloo, Can, 1972 to present
AWARDS: Canada Council, Senior Fel, 1979–80
RECENT EXHIB: Baldwin-Wallace Col, Fawick Gallery, Berea, OH, 1992
COLLECTIONS: Nat Gallery of Can, Ottawa, Can; Art Gallery of Ontario, Toronto, Can; Montreal Mus of Fine Art, Can; Mus of Mod Art, NY; Victoria and Albert Mus, London, England; Phoenix Art Gallery, AZ; Vancouver Art Gallery, Can; Norman Mackenzie Gallery, Regina, Can; London Art Gallery, London, Can; Hamilton Art Gallery, Can; Art Gallery of Stratford, Can; Hirshhorn Mus, Wash, DC
PRINTERS: Artist (ART)
PUBLISHERS: Artist (ART)
GALLERIES: Bau-Xi Galleries, Toronto, Canada; Meridian Gallery, San Francisco, CA

TITLE	PUBLISHER	PRINTER	DATE	MEDIUM	DIMENSION (PAPER SIZE) IN INCHES	TYPE OF PAPER	EDITION NUMBER	NO. OF COLORS	ORIGINAL OPENING PRICE	CURRENT RETAIL PRICE
SOLD OUT EDITIONS (RARE):										
The Urquhart Sampler	ART	ART	1974	LB	18 X 24	AP	25	1	175	500
La Nasse	ART	ART	1975	LC	16 X 22	AP	10	7	250	500
CURRENT EDITIONS:										
Three Skulls	ART	ART	1974	EB	4 X 6	AP	25	1	150	300
La Scala di Sta Regina	ART	ART	1974	EB	4 X 6	AP	25	1	150	300
Three Feathers	ART	ART	1974	EB	4 X 6	AP	25	1	150	300
Sampler with Elephants Foot	ART	ART	1975	EB	7 X 12	AP	20	1	150	300
Nostalgia Print-2 variations	ART	ART	1976	EB	8 X 9 EA	AP	10 EA	2 EA	175 EA	300 EA
Landscape with Elephants Foot	ART	ART	1976	EB/A	4 X 6	AP	20	1	150	300
Allegory of the Animals	ART	ART	1980	EB	8 X 11	AP	20	2	175	300
Garden	ART	ART	1981	EB	4 X 16	AP	15	1	175	300
The Poetics of the Microscope	ART	ART	1982	EB	5 X 4	AP	10	1	150	300
Ornament I, II, III	ART	ART	1983	EB	5 X 5 EA	R/BFK	20 EA	1 EA	150 EA	300 EA
Double threshold	ART	ART	1983	EB	4 X 5	R/BFK	25	1	100	200
Ontario Bridge Box	ART	ART	1983	PLEX/ENG	4 X 3	R/BFK	10	1	150	300
Time Machine	ART	ART	1984	PLEX/ENG	8 X 6	R/BFK	20	2	200	300
Project For an Opening Box Sculpture	ART	ART	1985	PLEX/ENG	10 X 7	R/BFK	20	2	250	350
Four Floral Tributes I	ART	ART	1985	PLEX/ENG	6 X 4	R/BFK	20	2	150	300
Four Floral Tributes II	ART	ART	1985	PLEX/ENG	5 X 4	R/BFK	20	2	150	300
Four Floral Tributes III	ART	ART	1985	PLEX/ENG	4 X 5	R/BFK	20	2	150	300

DEMIAN UTENKOV

BORN: Moscow, Russia; 1948
EDUCATION: Moscow Sch for Theatrical Art, Russia USSR
TEACHING: Art Inst, Moscow, Russia
PRINTERS: Artist (ART)
PUBLISHERS: Artist (ART)
AWARDS: Int Youth Exhib Award, 1974
GALLERIES: Union of Artists, Moscow, Russia; International Images, Ltd, Sewickley, PA

TITLE	PUBLISHER	PRINTER	DATE	MEDIUM	DIMENSION (PAPER SIZE) IN INCHES	TYPE OF PAPER	EDITION NUMBER	NO. OF COLORS	ORIGINAL OPENING PRICE	CURRENT RETAIL PRICE
SOLD OUT EDITIONS (RARE):										
Father Zosima (From the Brothers Karamazov)	ART	ART	1972	EB	9 X 19	LP	15	1	325	500
Self-Portrait with Wife and Cats	ART	ART	1972	EB	9 X 14	LP	15	1	300	500

DEMIAN UTENKOV CONTINUED

TITLE	PUBLISHER	PRINTER	DATE	MEDIUM	DIMENSION (PAPER SIZE) IN INCHES	TYPE OF PAPER	EDITION NUMBER	NO. OF COLORS	ORIGINAL OPENING PRICE	CURRENT RETAIL PRICE
SOLD OUT EDITIONS (RARE):										
Raskolnikov (From Crime and Punishment)	ART	ART	1974	EB	10 X 20	LP	15	1	380	600
N W Gogol	ART	ART	1974	EB	5 X 8	LP	10	1	220	500
Hieronymus Bosch	ART	ART	1975	EB	12 X 12	LP	15	1	300	500
Byliny	ART	ART	1975	EB	9 X 16	LP	10	1	370	600
The Adventurer	ART	ART	1975	EB	16 X 11	LP	10	1	325	500
The Fall of the Tungus Meteorite	ART	ART	1977	EB	10 X 16	LP	15	1	300	500

THOMAS UTTECH

BORN: Merrill, WI; October 27, 1942
EDUCATION: Layton Sch of Art, BFA, 1965; Univ of Cincinnati, OH, MFA, 1967
TEACHING: Prof, Painting, Drawing & Photography, Univ of Wisconsin, Milwaukee, WI, 1968 to present
AWARDS: Top Award, Wisconsin Painters & Sculptors, Milwaukee Art Center, WI, 1973; Grant, Penninsula Sch of Art, Fish Creek, WI, 1973; Res Grant Univ of Wisconsin, Madison, WI, 1975,79; Nat Endowment for the Arts, 1988; Wisconsin Arts Board, 1989
RECENT EXHIB: Maxwell Davidson Gallery, NY, 1988; Schmidt-Bingham Gallery, NY, 1988; Sherry French Gallery, NY, 1988; Arthur Rogers Gallery, New Orleans, LA, 1988; Struve Gallery, Chicago, IL, 1987,90; Univ of Illinois, A Montgomery Ward Gallery, Chicago, IL, 1992; Univ of Wisconsin, Carlsten Art Gallery, Stevens Point, WI, 1992
COLLECTIONS: Milwaukee Art Mus, WI; Univ of Wisconsin, Madison, WI
PRINTERS: Artist (ART); Jack Lemon, Chicago, IL (JL); Landfall Press, Inc, Chicago, IL (LPI)
PUBLISHERS: Cream City Graphics, Milwaukee, WI (CCG; Landfall Press, Inc, Chicago, IL (LPI))
GALLERIES: Dorothy Bradley Gallery, Milwaukee, WI; Friends Gallery, Minneapolis Art Inst, MN; Carl Solway, Cincinnati, OH; Struve Gallery, Chicago, IL; M C Gallery, Minneapolis, MN; Schmidt-Bingham Gallery, New York, NY; Sherry French Gallery, New York, NY; Maxwell Davidson Gallery, New York, NY; Stremmel Gallery, Reno, NV; Tory Folliard Gallery, Milwaukee, WI; Landfall Press, Inc, Chicago, IL
MAILING ADDRESS: 4305 Highway O, Saukville, WI 53080

TITLE	PUBLISHER	PRINTER	DATE	MEDIUM	DIMENSION (PAPER SIZE) IN INCHES	TYPE OF PAPER	EDITION NUMBER	NO. OF COLORS	ORIGINAL OPENING PRICE	CURRENT RETAIL PRICE
SOLD OUT EDITIONS (RARE):										
Lynx Dance/Hodag Rock	CCG	ART	1981	LC	14 X 18	AP	25	4	125	450
Wolf Dance/Widow Maker	CCG	ART	1981	LC	14 X 18	AP	25	4	125	450
Owl Dance/Narhwall	CCG	ART	1981	LC	14 X 18	AP	25	4	125	450
CURRENT EDITIONS:										
Kasakogwog	LPI	JL/LPI	1990	LC	36 X 41	AP	25		1500	1500

MARCUS UZILEVSKY

BORN: New York, NY; April 10, 1937
EDUCATION: Pratt Inst, NY; Sch of Industrial Art, NY
AWARDS: Purchase Award, Bradley Univ, Peoria, IL, 1989; Purchase Award, Edinboro State Col, PA, 1989; Purchase Award, San Bernadino County Mus, Redlands, CA, 1989; Hill Purchase Award, Hill County Arts Found, CA, 1989; Merit Award, Minot Art Assoc, ND, 1990
COLLECTIONS: Israel Mus, Jerusalem, Israel; Portland Art Mus, OR; Tucson Mus of Fine Arts, AZ; Washington County Mus, Hagerstown, MD; California Inst of the Arts, Valencia, CA; Los Angeles County Mus, CA; Univ of Wyoming, Laramie, WY; Mus Nacional, Rio de Janiero, Brazil; Arkansas Art Center, Little Rock, AR; Brooks Mem Art Gallery, Memphis, TN; New Center for Contemp Art, Brooklyn, NY; Hood Art Mus, Dartmouth Col, Hanover, NH; New Britain Art Mus, CT; Memphis Mus of Art, TN; El Paso Mus, TX; Erie Art Mus, PA; Fine Arts Center of the South, Mobile, AL; Greenville Mus, NC; Hunter Mus, Chattanooga, TN; Judah L Magnes Mus, Berkeley, CA; Mead Art Mus, Amherst Col, MA; Missoula Mus of the Arts, MT; Monterey Peninsula Mus, CA; Mus of Arts & Sciences, Daytona Beach, FL; New England Center for Contemp Art, New Britain, CT; Smithsonian Inst, Wash, DC; Triton Mus, Santa Clara, CA; Jane Voorhees Zimmerli Art Mus, Rutgers Univ, New Brunswick, NJ
RECENT EXHIB: Wesleyan Col, Macon, GA, 1987; Meadowlark Gallery, Corte Madera, CA, 1987; Rosequist Gallery, Tucson, AZ, 1987; Chemers Gallery, Tustin, CA, 1988; Kenneth Alan Fine Art, San Francisco, CA, 1988; Gallerie Julian, Alexandria, VA, 1988; Lawrence Gallery, Santa Rosa, CA, 1987,89; Gallerie Julian of Georgetown, Wash, DC, 1990; San Geranimo Cultural Center, CA, 1991; San Francisco Fine Art Center, CA, 1990,91
PRINTERS: Al Khouri, San Francisco, CA (AK); Peter Caxton, Fairfax, CA (PC); Chromacomp, Inc, NY (CI); Serigraphics, Indianapolis, IN (SER); Westwood Graphics, San Francisco, CA (WG); Vistec Graphics, Rochester, NY (VG); Bluestone Editions, Los Angeles, CA (BE); Blackbox, Chicago, IL (BB); Atelier Unlimited, NY (AU); Sunshine Graphics, FL (SG); P S Press, Oakland, CA (PSP); Atelier Julian, Rochester, NY (AJ); Grapholith, Paris, France (GR); Har-El Printers, Israel (Har-El); Arellanes & Co, Inc, San Rafael, CA (ACI); Atelier Julian, Rochester, NY (AJ); San Francisco Atelier, CA (SFA)
PUBLISHERS: John Szoke Graphics, NY (JSG); Editions Ltd, Indianapolis, IN (EL); Source Gallery, San Francisco, CA (SG); Prestige Art (PA); ADI Gallery, San Francisco, CA (ADI); Bowles-Hopkins Gallery, San Francisco, CA (BH); T T Nieh & Associates, Falls Church, VA (TTN); Oaksprings Impressions, Fairfax, CA (OI); Prestige Art, Ltd, Mamaroneck, NY (PA); Artist (ART); San Francisco Fine Art Publishers, CA (SFFAP)
GALLERIES: van Straaten Galleries, Chicago, IL; Kaufmann Galleries, Houston, TX; Galerie Michael, Los Angeles, CA; Galerie Julian, Alexandria, VA; Young Gallery, San Jose, CA; Kenneth Behm Galleries, Seattle, WA; Judith Posner Gallery, Milwaukee WI; Avantgarde Art Associates, West Chester, PA
MAILING ADDRESS: P O Box 166, Woodacre, CA 94973

TITLE	PUBLISHER	PRINTER	DATE	MEDIUM	DIMENSION (PAPER SIZE) IN INCHES	TYPE OF PAPER	EDITION NUMBER	NO. OF COLORS	ORIGINAL OPENING PRICE	CURRENT RETAIL PRICE
SOLD OUT EDITIONS (RARE):										
Sundance	ADI	AK	1974	SP	18 X 30	BV	80	8	100	375
Moonsong	ADI	AK	1974	SP	18 X 30	BV	80	8	100	250
Jericho	ART	AK	1975		17 X 22	BV	25	5	125	350
Sheckinah	ART	AK	1975	SP	17 X 22	LEN/100	100	9	125	300
Living Waters	ART/SG	PC	1975	SP	18 X 38	R/BFK	100	13	100	350
Thyatira	SG	PC	1976	SP	24 X 38	LEN/100	50	8	135	300

MARCUS UZILEVSKY CONTINUED

TITLE	PUBLISHER	PRINTER	DATE	MEDIUM	DIMENSION (PAPER SIZE) IN INCHES	TYPE OF PAPER	EDITION NUMBER	NO. OF COLORS	ORIGINAL OPENING PRICE	CURRENT RETAIL PRICE
SOLD OUT EDITIONS (RARE):										
Genesis	ART	ART	1976	LB/HC	18 DIA	LEN/100	75	1	150	250
Genesis II	ART	ART	1976	SP	18 DIA	LEN/100	15	3	150	250
Solitary Places	JSG	CI	1977	SP	16 X 23	LEN/100	250	19	150	300
Let the Sea Resound	JSG	CI	1977	SP	19 X 38	LEN/100	250	21	150	300
Blossom as the Rose (Dipt)	EL	CI	1979	SP	52 X 76	LEN/100	300	22	275	600
Onias	ART	AK	1979	SP	16 X 30	BV	100	12	150	600
Kedar	EL	CI	1979	SP	26 X 30	R/100	300	19	175	500
Mt Zion	EL	SER	1980	SP	30 X 30	R/100	300	20	175	400
Rose of Sharon	BH	AC	1980	SP	19 X 33	AP	250	12	225	750
Morning Star	EL	AC	1980	SP	25 X 39	M/100	300	15	175	250
Morning Koinonia	BH	SER	1980	SP	18 DIA	M/100	275	14	175	400
Tiberius	PA	PSP	1980	LC/HC	12 X 19	M/100	100	4	200	400
Gilead	OI	PSP	1980	LC	12 X 19	M/100	140	3	150	250
Tiberius	PA	PSP	1980	LC	26 X 20	STP	100	3	200	400
Song of Ruth	OI	SER	1981	SP	18 DIA	M/100	290	13	175	750
Onias II	OI	AK	1981	SP	16 X 30	BV	100	12	250	600
Key of David	OI	SER	1981	SP	25 X 38	RG100	295	24	325	1000
Rachel's Song	OI	BE	1981	SP	17 X 39	MV	290	20	275	400
River of Chebar	OI	WG	1981	LC	30 X 19	ML/R	100	15	150	600
Kedar	OI	SER	1981	SP	23 X 35	M/100	300	28	325	700
Rose of Sharon	OI	AC	1981	SP	26 X 40	M/100	290	18	250	1500
Samaria (Dipt)	BH	SER	1981	SP	40 X 52	ML/R	285	22	525	900
Judah	OI	SER	1981	SP	25 X 38	ML/R	300	24	275	900
Cyrene	OI	AC	1981	SP	24 X 38	ML/R	250	15	250	900
Bronze Concerto No 1	OI	AC	1982	SP/HC	23 X 31	DBC/W/R	75	11	500	1500
Magrigal for Maryann	OI	AC	1982	SP	16 X 34	SP/R	175	13	425	1500
Seven Stars	OI	SER	1982	SP	21 X 35	SP/R	250	17	325	1100
Flora Musica	OI	AC	1982	SP/HC	31 X 23	DBIF	90	15	600	1500
Reflections of Monet	OI	BB/SG	1982	LC/SP	14 X 19	MLR/R	328	16	250	1250
Lilly of the Valley	OI	SER	1982	SP	21 X 38	MLR/R	300	32	350	1750
Symphony for Sara	OI	AC	1982	SP/HC	30 X 44	AP/BL	150	14	400	1750
Symphony for Sara, 1st Movement	OI	AC	1982	SP/HC	30 X 44	AP/BL	11	14	600	2000
Duet for Dulcimer & Cello	OI	AC	1982	SP/HC	26 X 40	MLR/R	34	8	300	800
Crystal Gates	TTN/OI	VG	1982	SP	24 X 36	MLR/R	300	21	325	850
Eden	TTN/OI	VG	1982	SP	23 X 35	MLR/R	300	22	325	1000
Linear Mode Symphony #1	OI	BB/AC	1982	LC/SP	16 X 22	MLR/R	150	11	400	750
Springtime Sonata	OI	VG	1982	SP	36 X 20	MLR/R	150	20	500	1300
Water Lillies	OI	AU	1982	LC	13 X 19	R/BFK	150	10	250	450
Jacob's Dream	BH	SER	1982	SP	22 X 36	MLR/R	300	22	350	500
Aquarelle	OI	AC	1983	SP/HC	32 X 24	MLR/R	40	10	600	950
The Wayfarer	OI	AC	1983	SP	45 X 30	AC/BL	160	15	600	1000
Macedonia	OI	AJ	1983	SP	21 X 35	IE/R	290	27	325	600
Hosanna	OI	SER	1983	SP	32 X 20	SP/R	250	23	375	1300
Symphony for Cyrene	OI	AJ	1983	SP/HC	21 X 31	DBIF	115	17	600	1300
Bread Upon the Water	OI	AJ	1984	SP	26 X 40	COV	95	18	500	900
Giverny	OI	GR	1984	LC	24 X 30	AP/R	150	15	375	1100
Morning on the Seine	OI	AJ	1984	SP	26 X 32	SP/R	290	20	325	650
Gideon's Song	OI	AJ	1984	SP/HC	23 X 31	DBIF	150	19	600	1200
Damascus (Dipt)	OI	SER	1984	SP	38 X 25 EA	SP/R	250	27	650	750
Song of Solomon	OI	AJ	1984	SP	26 X 40	SP/R	300	21	350	800
Bluegrass Sonata in C	OI	AJ	1985	SP/HC	23 X 31	RdB	125	17	600	1200
Son of David	OI	AJ	1985	SP	19 X 40	M/100	290	24	325	500
Eventide	OI	SER	1985	SP	26 X 40	STP/100	290	25	375	1250
Carnelian	OI	AC	1985	SP	26 X 40	M/100	150	21	550	1250
Daystar	OI	AC	1985	SP	20 X 35	STP/100	240	13	300	400
Exodus	OI	AJ	1985	SP	24 X 33	M/100	290	20	325	550
First Epistle	OI	SER	1985		50 X 34	STP/100	135	28	700	1100
Jeremiah	OI	AJ	1985	SP	14 X 40	M/100	290	24	275	475
Aqua Verde	OI	AP	1985	LC	23 X 30	AP/W	90	6	300	450
Sketches for Sara	OI	EDSW	1985	LC	25 X 25	AP/W	100	4	450	550
Dancing in the Dark	OI	SER	1985	SP	20 X 15	AP/BL	200	7	150	300
San Francisco Bay Blues	OI	SER	1985	SP	20 X 15	AP/BL	200	7	150	300
Song of Ascents	OI	AC	1985	LB	14 X 22	R/100		1	250	250
South of France	OI	AC	1985	SP	20 X 15	AP			275	450
Sunrise Sonata	OI	AC	1986	SP	26 X 40	R/100		18	550	550
California Zephyr	OI	AC	1986	SP	26 X 40	R/100	185	20	550	950
Shalimar Sonata	OI	AJ	1986	SP	31 X 23	RdB	150	21	600	1200
Jordan River	OI	HE	1986	SP	23 X 38	LEN/100	300	45	350	450
Memphis Jazz in California	OI	AC	1986	SP	30 X 45	R/100	130	7	1100	1400
Memphis Jazz Suite	OI	AC	1986	SP	14 X 22	R/100	40	6	400	450
Nuevo—October	OI	AC	1986	SP	24 X 23	R/100	200	12	250	325
Nuevo—September	OI	AC	1986	SP	24 X 23	R/100	200	12	250	325
Scarborough Fair	OI	AC	1986	SP	18 X 26			16	300	600
Scroll of Nehemiah	OI	AJ	1986	SP	23 X 30	HMP	135	28	600	800
Shenandoah	OI	GR	1986	SP	27 X 25	AC/W	150	18	375	1200

MARCUS UZILEVSKY CONTINUED

TITLE	PUBLISHER	PRINTER	DATE	MEDIUM	DIMENSION (PAPER SIZE) IN INCHES	TYPE OF PAPER	EDITION NUMBER	NO. OF COLORS	ORIGINAL OPENING PRICE	CURRENT RETAIL PRICE
SOLD OUT EDITIONS (RARE):										
Blue Skies Sonata	OI	GR	1987	SP	31 X 23		150	25	650	800
Evening Shadows	OI	AJ	1987	SP	24 X 37	COV	290	29	400	450
G Minor Sonata	OI	AJ	1987	SP	22 X 30		150	30	600	700
Moriah	OI	AC	1987	SP	28 X 42	R/100	96	16	400	500
Morning Star	OI	SER	1987	SP	26 X 40		300	28	400	500
New World Symphony	OI	AC	1987	SP	26 X 40	R/100		15	600	650
New York City Midnight	OI	AC	1987	SP	30 X 45	AP/BL	130	5	375	450
Pachelbell Kanon	OI	AJ	1987	SP	23 X 31	HMP	250	29	700	1100
San Geronimo Valley	OI	HarEl	1987	SP	26 X 40		300	40	375	450
Violet Dawn	OI	HarEl	1987	SP	30 X 44		38	15	600	900
Woodacre	OI	SER	1987	SP	26 X 40		300	40	375	450
Brandenburg Concerto	OI	AJ	1988	SP	31 X 23		150	28	650	1000
Central Park	OI	AC	1988	SP	23 X 36	R/100	40	42	350	450
Four Seasons (Set of 4)	OI	AC	1988	SP	16 X 22		90	30	2000	2000
Sedona	OI	GR	1988	SP	24 X 38	AP/W	40	18	550	900
Snowdance	OI	AJ	1988	SP	26 X 40		300	40	350	450
Ravel's Bolero	OI	SER	1988	SP	39 X 58	R/100	200	30	1100	1400
CURRENT EDITIONS:										
Jagger	SFFAP	ACI	1991	SP	48 X 60	COV	450	15	700	700
Elvis	SFFAP	ACI	1991	SP	19 X 28	COV	450	20	400	400
Dylan	SFFAP	ACI	1991	SP	18 X 29	COV	450	15	400	400
Morrison	SFFAP	ACI	1991	SP	18 X 29	COV	450	15	400	400
Lennon	SFFAP	ACI	1991	SP	18 X 29	COV	450	15	400	400
Ancient Future	SFFAP	SFA	1991	EC	13 X 16	COV	250	15	900	900
Rainbow Rhapsody	SFFAP	AJ	1991	SP	23 X 31	HMP	175	23	900	900
Dear America	SFFAP	AJ	1991	SP	20 X 25	COV	95	40	800	800
Loretta	SFFAP	AJ	1991	SP	20 X 25	COV	95	40	800	800
Noya	SFFAP	AJ	1991	SP	20 X 25	COV	95	40	800	800

ANGELO VADALA

BORN: Florence, Italy; December 11, 1940
EDUCATION: Univ of Florence, Italy
COLLECTIONS: Inst of Artistic Editions, Florence, Italy; Civic Gallery of Mod Art, Palermo, Italy
PRINTERS: Atelier Ettinger Inc, NY (AE)
PUBLISHERS: Eleanor Ettinger Inc, NY (EEI)
GALLERIES: La Roninia, Palermo, Italy; Galerie Vecu, Anver, Belgium

TITLE	PUBLISHER	PRINTER	DATE	MEDIUM	DIMENSION (PAPER SIZE) IN INCHES	TYPE OF PAPER	EDITION NUMBER	NO. OF COLORS	ORIGINAL OPENING PRICE	CURRENT RETAIL PRICE
CURRENT EDITIONS:										
New Odalisque	EEI	AE	1984	LC	26 X 31	AP	275	13	450	600
Two Roses	EEI	AE	1984	LC	26 X 38	AP	275	14	450	600
Monumento Alla Natura Morta	EEI	AE	1984	LC	27 X 34	AP	275	14	450	600

MEYER VAISMAN

BORN: Caracas, Venezuela; 1960
EDUCATION: Parsons Sch of Design, NY
RECENT EXHIB: Univ of California Art Mus, Berkeley, CA, 1988; La Jolla Mus of Contemp Art, CA, 1988; Daniel Weinberg Gallery, Los Angeles, CA, 1988; Beaver Col, Glenside, PA, 1989; Jay Gorney Modern, NY, 1987,91; Univ of Maryland, Catonsville, MD; Beaver Col, Glenside, PA, 1992; Leo Castelli Gallery, NY, 1987,89,92–93
COLLECTIONS: Boston Mus of Fine Arts, MA
PRINTERS: Joe Wilfer, NY (JW); Ruth Lingen, NY (RL); Spring Street Workshop, NY (SprSW)
PUBLISHERS: Spring Street Workshop, NY (SprSW)
GALLERIES: Pace Prints, New York, NY; Daniel Weinberg Gallery, Santa Monica, CA; Jay Gorney Modern Art, New York, NY; Editions Ilene Kurtz, New York, NY; Cable Gallery, New York, NY; Leo Castelli Gallery, New York, NY; Edition Julie Sylvester, New York, NY

TITLE	PUBLISHER	PRINTER	DATE	MEDIUM	DIMENSION (PAPER SIZE) IN INCHES	TYPE OF PAPER	EDITION NUMBER	NO. OF COLORS	ORIGINAL OPENING PRICE	CURRENT RETAIL PRICE
CURRENT EDITIONS:										
Summer Suite (Set of 6)	SprSW	JW/RL/SprSW	1989	SP	49 X 34 EA	AC	75 EA		6000 SET / 1200 EA	6000 SET / 1200 EA

MANOLO VALDES

BORN: Valencia, Spain; March 8, 1942
EDUCATION: House of the Dominicans, Spain, 1948–52; Ecole des Beaux-Arts "San Carlos", Valencia, Spain, 1957–59
AWARDS: Silver Medal, II Int Biennal of Grabados, Tokyo, Japan, 1979; Purchase Prize, Bridgestone Mus of Art, Lisbon, Portugal, 1979; Purchase Prize, Nacional de Bellas Artes, Spain, 1984; National Medal, Painting, Bellas Artes, Spain, 1985; Medal, Int Festival, Plastic Arts, Bagdad, Iraq, 1986
RECENT EXHIB: Galeria 4, Valencia, Spain, 1987; Galeria Val i 30, Valencia, Spain, 1987; Galerie Adrien Maeght, Paris, France, 1988; Museo de Bellas Artes, Bilbao, Spain, 1988; Galeria El Coleccionista, Madrid, Spain, 1988; Galeria Luis Adelantodo, Valencia, Spain, 1988; Chateau de Tarascon, Tarascon, France, 1988; Galeria Maeght, Madrid, Spain, 1988; Inst Valenciano de Arte Moderno, Valencia, Spain, 1989; Galeria de Arte Soledad Lorenzo, Madrid, Spain, 1989; Casa de la Caritat, Barcelona, Spain, 1989; Galeria Maeght, Barcelona, Spain, 1989; Centre Arte Reina Sofia, Madrid, Spain, 1989; Galeria Sen, Madrid, Spain, 1989; Museo de Bellas Artes, Oviedo, Spain, 1989;

MANOLO VALDES CONTINUED

RECENT EXHIB:
Palacio de Almudi, Murcia, Spain, 1990; Col de Arquitectos, Canary Islands, Spain, 1990; Palacio Condes de Gaira, Granada, Spain, 1990; Caja de Ahorros, Brugos, Spain, 1990; Cultural Rioja, Logrono, Spain, 1990; Galeria Freites, Caracas, Venezuela, 1988,90; Marlborough Gallery, NY, 1991; Galeria Guereta, Madrid, Spain, 1991; Galerie Sonia Zannettacci, Geneva, Switzerland, 1989,92; Galeria Trama, Barcelona, Spain, 1992; Galeria Fandos, Valencia, Spain, 1991,92
COLLECTIONS: Metropolitan Mus of Art, NY; Solomon R Guggenheim Mus, NY; J B Speed Art Mus, Louisville, KY; Nacional Centro de Arte Reina Sotia, Madrid, Spain; Ayuntamiento de Madrid, Spain; Ayuntamiento de Valencia, Spain; Diputacion de Valencia, Spain; Fonds Mat d'Arts Plastiques, Paris, France; Fundacion Caia de Pensiones, Barcelona, Spain; Fundacion Juan March, Madrid, Spain; Gemeidnde Mus & Univ, Bremen, Germany; Hamburger Kunsthalle, Hamburg, Germany; Inst Valenciano de Arte Mod, Valencia, Spain; Kunsthalle, Kiel, Germany; Kunstmuseum, Berlin, Germany; Kunsthmuseum, Dusseldorf, Germany; Levenszeichen, Botschaft der Bilder, Kunstmuseum, Hannover, Germany; Menil Found, Houston, TX; Milwaukee Art Mus, WI; Moderna Museet, Norrkoping, Sweden; Moderna Museet, Stockholm, Sweden; Musee Cantini, Marseille, France; Musee des Beaux Arts, Grenoble, France; Musee Nat de'Art Mod, Centre Georges Pompidou, Paris, France; Musee Picasso, Antibes, France; Museo de Albacete, Spain; Museo de Arte Contemp, Caccres, Spain; Museo de Arte Contemp, Seville, Spain; Museo de Arte Contemp, Int Rufino Tamayo, Mexico City, Mexico; Museo de Arte Mod, Medellin, Colombia; Museo de Bellas Artes, Bilbao, Spain; Museo de Bellas Artes, Victoria, Spain; Museo de Bellas Artes, Caracas, Venezuela; Museo de la Asegurada, Alcante, Spain; Museo de la Solidaridad a Salvador Allende, Spain; Museo Nacional Centro de arte Reina Soria, Madrid, Spain; Museo Pio V, Valencia, Spain; Museo Rufino Tamayo, Mexico City, Mexico Senado Espanol, Madrid, Spain
PRINTERS: Artist (ART)
PUBLISHERS: Marlborough Graphics, NY (MG)
GALLERIES: Marlborough Graphics, New York, NY; BenedicteSaxe Gallery, Beverly Hills, CA; Galeria Fondos, Valencia, Spain; Galeria Guerta, Madrid, Spain; Galerie Sonia Zannettacci, Geneva, Switzerland; Galeria Trama, Barcelona, Spain

TITLE	PUBLISHER	PRINTER	DATE	MEDIUM	DIMENSION (PAPER SIZE) IN INCHES	TYPE OF PAPER	EDITION NUMBER	NO. OF COLORS	ORIGINAL OPENING PRICE	CURRENT RETAIL PRICE
CURRENT EDITIONS:										
La Infanta Margarita	MG	ART	1991	EB/SP/CO	68 X 38	R/BFK	52		4500	4500
Cabeza	MG	ART	1991	EB/SP/CO	35 X 40	R/BFK	52		2800	2800
Eva I, II	MG	ART	1991	EP/SP/CO	67 X 26 EA	R/BFK	51 EA		3200 EA	3200 EA
Infanta	MG	ART	1991	EB/SP/CO	52 X 38	R/BFK	51		3000	3000
Retrato de una Dama	MG	ART	1991	EB/SP/CO	66 X 38	R/BFK	51		3500	3500

JAMES ROBERT VALERIO

BORN: Chicago, IL; December 2, 1938
EDUCATION: Art Inst of Chicago, IL, BFA, 1966; MFA, 1968
TEACHING: Asst Prof, Art, Rock Valley, Col, Rockford, IL, 1968–70; Assoc Prof, Art, Univ of California, Los Angeles, CA, 1970–79; Assoc Prof, Cornell Univ, Ithaca, NY, 1979–82; Prof, Art, Northwestern Univ, Evanston, IL
AWARDS: Anne Louis Raymond Fel, 1968; Purchase Award, Long Beach Mus, CA, 1970; Creative Arts Award Fel, Univ of CA, Los Angeles, CA, 1976; Nat Endowment for the Arts Grant, 1986
RECENT EXHIB: Allan Frumkin Gallery, NY, 1987; Florida State Univ Gallery Mus, Talahassee, FL, 1989,92; Evanston Art Center for Visual Arts, IL, 1992
COLLECTIONS: Long Beach Mus of Art, CA; Univ of Iowa Mus, Iowa City, IA; Albuquerque Mus of Art, NM; Metropolitan Mus of Art, NY; Solomon R Guggenheim Mus, NY
PUBLISHERS: 724 Prints, NY (724P)
GALLERIES: Struve Gallery, Chicago, IL
MAILING ADDRESS: 1308 Gregory, Willmette, IL 60091

TITLE	PUBLISHER	PRINTER	DATE	MEDIUM	DIMENSION (PAPER SIZE) IN INCHES	TYPE OF PAPER	EDITION NUMBER	NO. OF COLORS	ORIGINAL OPENING PRICE	CURRENT RETAIL PRICE
CURRENT EDITIONS:										
Still Life on Chenile Spread	724P		1984	LB	20 X 24	R/BFK	40	1	500	750
Still Life on Chenile Spread	724P		1984	LC	20 X 24	R/BFK	40		700	1200

FRANCES VALESCO

BORN: Los Angeles, CA; August 3, 1941
EDUCATION: Univ of California, Los Angeles, CA, BA, 1963; California State Univ, Long Beach, CA, MA, 1972
TEACHING: Lcctr, Etching & Screen Printing, Univ of California, Berkeley, CA, 1975–76,79; Lectr, Screen Printing & Drawing, Sonoma State Univ, Rohnert Park, CA, 1977–80; Instr, Printmaking, San Francisco Acad of Art, CA, 1982 to present
AWARDS: Univ of California Art Council Award, Los Angeles, CA, 1963; Kingley Arts Club, Sacramento, CA, 1965; USIA Print Purchase for Embassies, 1967; California Arts Council Grants, 1980–85; Neighborhood Initiated Improvement Grants, Fed Housing & Urban Development, Mural Grants, 1981,82,86; Cert of Honor, San Francisco City, CA, 1987; Art Comm, City of Oakland, CA, 1988
RECENT EXHIB: Grande Halle de la Vilette, Paris, France, 1988; Univ of New Mexico, Albuquerque, NM, 1988; Bronx Mus, NY, 1988; Hartley Martin Gallery, San Francisco, CA, 1989; Computer Mus, Boston, MA, 1989
COLLECTIONS: Mus of Mod Art, NY; San Francisco Art Comm, CA; Oakland Mus, CA; Drawing Center, NY; Nat Mus of Women in the Arts, Wash, DC; California Soc of Printmakers; Bronx Mus, NY
PUBLISHERS: Avocet Print Editions, NY (APE); Artist (ART)
PRINTERS: Artist (ART)
GALLERIES: Szoke Gallery, New York, NY; Jayne Baum Gallery, New York, NY; Pasquale Iannetti, Inc, San Francisco, CA
MAILING ADDRESS: 135 Jersey St, San Francisco, CA 94114

TITLE	PUBLISHER	PRINTER	DATE	MEDIUM	DIMENSION (PAPER SIZE) IN INCHES	TYPE OF PAPER	EDITION NUMBER	NO. OF COLORS	ORIGINAL OPENING PRICE	CURRENT RETAIL PRICE
SOLD OUT EDITIONS (RARE):										
Cow #2	ART	ART	1976	EC/SP	24 X 18	R/BFK	50	5	40	200
Flying Fish #2 (Monotype with Etching, Silk Screen & Xerox)	ART	ART	1983	MM	22 X 30 EA	LANA	1 EA	MULTI	225 EA	350 EA
Flying Fish #15	ART	ART	1983	MM	15 X 22 EA	LANA	1 EA	MULTI	125 EA	225 EA

FRANCES VALESCO CONTINUED

TITLE	PUBLISHER	PRINTER	DATE	MEDIUM	DIMENSION (PAPER SIZE) IN INCHES	TYPE OF PAPER	EDITION NUMBER	NO. OF COLORS	ORIGINAL OPENING PRICE	CURRENT RETAIL PRICE
CURRENT EDITIONS:										
(Monotype with Etching, Silk Screen, Xerox & Acrylic)										
Eastern Fish	ART	ART	1984	MM	32 X 32 EA	CD	1 EA	MULTI	2500 EA	3500 EA
(Monotype with Silk Screen, Xerox, Acrylic, Chiné Collé & Marbling)										
Birthday Greetings #2	ART	ART	1984	MM	22 X 30 EA	LANA	1 EA	MULTI	225 EA	350 EA
(Monotype with Etching, Silk Screen Chiné Collé & Xerox)										
Deep Water II	ART	ART	1985	MM	30 X 40 EA	CD	1 EA	MULTI	300 EA	550 EA
(Monotype with Silk Screen, Collage, Xerox, Marbling & Acrylic)										
Dancing Litely #6	ART	ART	1986	MM	31 X 44 STP	LANA	1 EA	MULTI	500 EA	600 EA
(Monotype with Silk Screen Marbling, Acrylic, India Ink Collage & Computer)										
Sir Flaco in Spain #2	ART	ART	1986	MM	22 X 30 EA	LANA	1 EA	MULTI	300 EA	350 EA
(Monotype with Etching, Silk Screen, Collage & Acrylic)										
Flight Down Highway 5-#6	ART	ART	1986	MM	26 X 40 EA	STP	1 EA	MULTI	450 EA	550 EA
(Monotype with Silk Screen, Acrylic, Marbling & Computer)										
Fish Fly South for the Summer #3	ART	ART	1986	MM	30 X 42 EA	CD	1 EA	MULTI	500 EA	600 EA
Monotype with Silk Screen Xerox, Collage, Acrylic & India ink)										
Deep Sea Diving #6	ART	ART	1986	MM	15 X 22 EA	AP/B	1 EA	MULTI	175 EA	200 EA
Mixed Message #5	ART	ART	1986	MON	22 X 30	LANA	1 EA	MULTI	250	300
Southern Sea #22	ART	ART	1988	MON	30 X 44	STP	1 EA	MULTI	600	600
Lexington Suite (Set of 4):									1200 SET	1200 SET
Lexington #1,#2	APE	ART	1989	SP	30 X 22 EA	R/BFK	10 EA	7 EA	400 EA	400 EA
Lexington #3	APE	ART	1989	SP	30 X 22	R/BFK	10	10	400	400
Lexington #4	APE	ART	1989	SP	30 X 22	R/BFK	8	9	400	400

BIRON VALIER

BORN: West Palm Beach, FL; March 13, 1943
EDUCATION: Cranbrook Acad of Art, Bloomfield Hills, MI, BFA, 1965–67; Yale Univ Sch of Art & Arch, New Haven, CT, MFA, 1967–69
TEACHING: Wheelock Col, Boston, MA, 1969–72; DeCordova Mus Sch, Lincoln, MA, 1974–77; Prahran Col of Adv Ed, Melbourne, Australia, 1977–79
COLLECTIONS: Achenbach Found, California Palace of the Legion of Honor, San Francisco, CA; Art Gallery of New South Wales, Sydney, Australia; Butler Inst of Am Art, Youngstown, OH; City of Boston, City Hall, MA; DeCordova Mus, Lincoln, MA; Lehigh Univ, Bethlehem, PA; Los Angeles County Mus, CA; Metropolitan Mus of Art, NY; Mus of Fine Arts, Boston, MA; Milton Acad, MA; Univ of Sydney, Australia; Weber State Col, Ogden, UT; Artbank, Sydney, Australia; Univ of Queensland Art Mus, Australia; Boston Public Library, MA
PRINTERS: Theo Tremblay, Canberra, Australia (TT); Basil Hall, Canberra, Australia (BH); Artist (ART)
PUBLISHERS: Associated American Artists, NY (AAA); Toren Galleries, Baltimore, MD (RG); Artist (ART)
GALLERIES: Associated American Artists, New York, NY; Wenniger Graphics, Boston, MA; Artbiz Pty Ltd, Potts Point, Australia
MAILING ADDRESS: 8A/70 Terrace Rd, East Perth, WA 6004, Australia

TITLE	PUBLISHER	PRINTER	DATE	MEDIUM	DIMENSION (PAPER SIZE) IN INCHES	TYPE OF PAPER	EDITION NUMBER	NO. OF COLORS	ORIGINAL OPENING PRICE	CURRENT RETAIL PRICE
SOLD OUT EDITIONS (RARE):										
RPM	ART	ART	1970	SP	20 X 26	R/BFK	30	10	50	250
Switch Engine	ART	ART	1970	SP	18 X 24	R/BFK	30	13	50	250
Silver Top Diner	ART	ART	1973	SP	20 X 26	R/BFK	50	17	50	300
Sea Gull Diner	ART	ART	1973	SP	20 X 26	R/BFK	25	9	50	300
Fenway Flyer	ART	ART	1973	SP	20 X 26	R/BFK	100	10	50	200
CURRENT EDITIONS:										
Celestial Star Express	ART	ART	1966	SP	18 X 24	R/BFK	15	6	50	275
Route 133	ART	ART	1974	SP	26 X 20	AP	100	12	50	200
Practice	ART	BH	1986	EB	22 X 24	HAHN	75	1	90	125
Old Boy Network	ART	TT	1986	LB	20 X 28	MAG/CR	20	1	100	125
Red Ship	ART	TT	1986	Lc	22 X 30	FAB	18	2	120	150

JOHN VAN ALSTINE

BORN: Johnstown, New York; August 14, 1952
EDUCATION: St Lawrence Univ, Canton, NY, 1970–72; Blossom Festival Sch, Cleveland, OH, 1973; Kent State Univ, OH, BFA, 1974; Cornell Univ, Ithaca, NY, MFA, 1976
TEACHING: Colorado Col, Colorado Springs, CO, 1979; Univ of Colorado, Boulder, CO, 1980; Eastern Montana Col, Billings, MT, 1980; Vis Prof, Maryland Art Inst, Baltimore, MD, 1988

The Printworld Directory is accepting new applications for the seventh edition. Approximately 300 new artists will be accepted. Please use the two forms provided in the back section of this directory to submit biographical data and documentation of prints. Edition number of each print must not exceed 500 and the retail price must be $100 or more.

JOHN VAN ALSTINE CONTINUED

AWARDS: Blossom Festival Sch of Art, Kent-Cleveland, OH, Scholarship, 1973; Cornell Grad Fel, 1974–75; Juror's Award, Univ of Wyoming, 1977; Arts and Sciences Creative Research Grant, Univ of Wyoming, 1977; Nat Endowment for the Arts Award, 1977; Finalist, Rome Prize, Fel, 1978–79; Juror's Award, Kansas City Art Inst, Kansas City, MO, 1979; Best in Show/Color, Annual Allied Arts Assn, Nat Photo Show, Richland, WA, 1979; Nat Finalist, Comp, Outdoor Sculpture, City of Columbus, OH, Funded by NEA, Greater Columbus Arts Council, & City of Columbus, 1979; Louis C Tiffany Foundation Grant, 1980; Wash DC Comm of Art Fel, 1982; Art Fel, New Jersey Art Council, 1984; Nat Endowment for the Arts Fel, 1986; Ind Artist Fel, New Jersey State Council Fel, 1988
RECENT EXHIB: Sible Larney Gallery, Chicago, IL, 1987; Nohra Haime Gallery, NY, 1987; Nat Acad of Sciences, Wash, DC, 1992; Gerald Peters Gallery, Santa Fe, NM, 1991,92
COLLECTIONS: Denver Art Mus, CO; Hirshhorn Mus, Wash, DC; McKissick Mus, Univ of South Carolina, Columbia, SC; Mus of Mod Art, NY; Gulpenkian Found, Lisbon, Portugal; Nat Mus of Am Art, Smithsonian Inst, Wash, DC; Carnegie Inst Mus, Pittsburgh, PA
PRINTERS: Artist (ART)
PUBLISHERS: Artist (ART)
GALLERIES: Marlborough Graphics, New York, NY; Henri Gallery, Washington, DC; Osuna Gallery, Washington, DC; Diane Brown Gallery, New York, NY; Gerald Peters Gallery, Santa Fe, NM; Nohra Haime Gallery, New York, NY; Franz Bader Gallery, Wash, DC; C Grimaldis Gallery, Baltimore, MD

TITLE	PUBLISHER	PRINTER	DATE	MEDIUM	DIMENSION (PAPER SIZE) IN INCHES	TYPE OF PAPER	EDITION NUMBER	NO. OF COLORS	ORIGINAL OPENING PRICE	CURRENT RETAIL PRICE
CURRENT EDITIONS:										
Color Prints/Easel Landscape Series	ART	ART	1979–80	PH/C	16 X 20 EA	AP	10 EA		300 EA	550 EA

GER VAN ELK

BORN: Amsterdam, Holland; 1941
EDUCATION: Applied Arts Sch, Amsterdam, Holland, 1959–61; Immaculate Heart Col, Los Angeles, CA, 1961–63; State Univ, Groningen, 1965–66
TEACHING: Ateliers 63, Haarlem, Netherlands, 1972 to present
COLLECTIONS: Stedelijk Mus, Amsterdam, Holland; Tate Gallery, London, England; Mus Bormans van Beuingen, Rotterdam, Holland
PRINTERS: Aeropress, NY (A); Patricia Branstead, NY (PB); Zeger Reyers, Amsterdam, The Netherlands (ZR)
PUBLISHERS: Multiples, NY (M); Art & Project, Amsterdam, The Netherlands (AP); Artist (ART)
GALLERIES: Marian Goodman Gallery, New York, NY

TITLE	PUBLISHER	PRINTER	DATE	MEDIUM	DIMENSION (PAPER SIZE) IN INCHES	TYPE OF PAPER	EDITION NUMBER	NO. OF COLORS	ORIGINAL OPENING PRICE	CURRENT RETAIL PRICE
SOLD OUT EDITIONS (RARE):										
Symmetry of Diplomacy (Composite Color Photo with two Silkscreen Printings & Airbrushing) (From Portfolio of Photos by Seven Artists)	M	ART	1975	PH/SP/AirBr	20 X 24	FAB	60	Varies	500	900
Conversation Piece from Missing Persons (Set of 2)	M	PB/A	1976	PH/C	23 X 33 EA	FAB	40 EA		750 SET	1800 SET
Pulling Babies from Heaven	M	PB/A	1980	SP	30 X 40	FAB			750	1500
Roquebrune	M	PB/A	1980	PH/C/SP	36 X 67	FAB	30		1500	2500
Roquebrune II	M	PB/A	1981	SP	20 X 39	FAB	20		1100	2500
Three Pets	M	PB/A	1981	SP	11 X 20	FAB	40		750	750
Pets	ART	ZR	1981	SP	20 X 38	FAB	40		750	1200
Bouquet Anvers	ART	ZR	1982	SP/EN	34 X 33	FAB	20		900	1800
Bouquet Altmaer	ART/AP/M	ZR	1983	SP/PH	36 X 34	PHP	20		900	1800

BETH VAN HOESEN

BORN: Boise, ID; June 27, 1926
EDUCATION: San Francisco Art Inst, CA, 1946–47,51–52; Stanford Univ, CA, BA, 1948; Ecole Arts, Fountainbleau, France, 1948–51; Acad Julian, Paris, France, 1948–51; Acad Grande Chaumier, Paris, France, 1948–51; San Francisco State Univ, CA, 1957–58
COLLECTIONS: Brooklyn Mus, NY; Mus of Mod Art, NY; San Francisco Mus of Mod Art, CA; Victoria & Albert Mus, London, England; Art Inst of Chicago, IL
PRINTERS: Crown Point Press, San Francisco, CA (CPP); Katherine Lincoln Press, San Francisco, CA (KLP); Kay Bradner, San Francisco, CA (KB); R E Townsend, Boston, MA (RT); Teaberry Press, Oakland, CA (TP); Timothy Berry, Oakland, CA (TB); David Kelso, Oakland, CA (DK); Made in California, Oakland, CA (MIC)
PUBLISHERS: John Berggruen Gallery, San Francisco, CA (JB); Ed Hill Editions, El Paso, TX (EHE); Made in California, Oakland, CA (MIC); Artist (ART)
GALLERIES: John Berggruen Gallery, San Francisco, CA; Ed Hill Editions, El Paso, TX; India Ink Gallery, Santa Monica, CA; Nancy Singer Gallery, St. Louis, MO; Susan Blanchard Gallery, New York, NY; First Impressions Gallery, Carmel, CA; Made in California, Oakland, CA; Young Gallery, Los Gatos, CA; Photography West Gallery, Carmel, CA; Himovitz Miller Gallery, Sacramento, CA
MAILING ADDRESS: 3816 22nd St, San Francisco, CA 94114

TITLE	PUBLISHER	PRINTER	DATE	MEDIUM	DIMENSION (PAPER SIZE) IN INCHES	TYPE OF PAPER	EDITION NUMBER	NO. OF COLORS	ORIGINAL OPENING PRICE	CURRENT RETAIL PRICE
SOLD OUT EDITIONS (RARE):										
Matilija Poppy	EHE	CPP	1975	A/EB	24 X 20	R/BFK	40	4	225	1000
CURRENT EDITIONS:										
Corsage	MIC	DK/MIC	1978	AB/DPT/HC	15 X 15	R/BFK/W	50		200	450
Peony	EHE	KB/KLP	1978	A/EB	24 X 20	R/BFK	40	4	225	900
Poppy in Hand	EHE	KB/KLP	1978	A/EB	24 X 20	R/BFK	40	4	225	900
Aegean Poppies	EHE	KB/KLP	1978	A/EB	24 X 20	R/BFK	40	4	225	900
Bowl of Roses	EHE	KB/KLP	1979	A/EB/DPT	17 X 15	R/BFK	100	4	225	900
Bowl of Hydrangeas	EHE	KB/KLP	1979	A/EB/DPT	20 X 17	R/BFK	100	7	225	900
Annie	MIC	DK/MIC	1978–80	AC/DPT	24 X 19	R/BFK/W	25		250	800
Fungi	MIC	DK/MIC	1981–82	AC/DPT/HC	19 X 17	R/BFK/W	30		225	600
Suffolk Sheep	ART	RT/TP	1982	EB/A/DPT	23 X 23	R/BFK	100		700	900

BETH VAN HOESEN CONTINUED

TITLE	PUBLISHER	PRINTER	DATE	MEDIUM	DIMENSION (PAPER SIZE) IN INCHES	TYPE OF PAPER	EDITION NUMBER	NO. OF COLORS	ORIGINAL OPENING PRICE	CURRENT RETAIL PRICE
CURRENT EDITIONS:										
Newborns Volume I (Set of 8)	ART	TB/TP	1983	DPT	14 X 11 EA	AC/W	15 EA	1 EA	1200 SET	2500 SET
Newborns Volume II (Set of 8)	ART	TB/TP	1983	DPT	14 X 11 EA	AC/W	15 EA	1 EA	1200 SET	2500 SET
Rhino	MIC	DK/MIC	1985	DPT	23 X 26	R/BFK/W	20	1	350	500
Monterey Otter	MIC	DK/MIC	1987	AC/DPT	16 X 15	R/BFK/W	40	2	300	350
Manatee	MIC	DK/MIC	1988	AC/DPT	17 X 19	R/BFK/W	50	2	475	500
Wallflower	MIC	DK/MIC	1988	AC/SG/DPT/HC	16 X 15	R/BFK/W	50	5	550	575
Traci	MIC	DK/MIC	1990	AC/HG/DPT/HC	18 X 15	R/BFK/W	50	5	500	500
Steve	MIC	DK/MIC	1990	AC/HG/DPT	18 X 15	R/BFK/W	50	3	500	500
Edible Roots	MIC	DK/MIC	1990	EB/HG/DPT/HC	16 X 15	R/BFK/W	25	1	300	300
Nose Toy	MIC	DK/MIC	1990	AB/HG	16 X 15	R/BFK/W	26	1	300	300
Haitian Dolls	MIC	DK/MIC	1991	AC/SG/DPT	18 X 15	R/BFK/W	50	4	500	500

PAUL VAN HOEYDONCK

BORN: Antwerp, Belgium; Oct 8, 1925
EDUCATION: Inst of Art History & Architecture, Antwerp, Belgium
COLLECTIONS: Mus of Fine Arts, Middelheim, Antwerp, Belgium; Mus Plantin-Moretus, Antwerp, Belgium; Univ of Georgia, Athens, GA; Mus of Fine Art, Brussels, Belgium; Van Abbe State Mus, Eindhoven, Netherlands; Albertina Mus, Brussels, Belgium; Wallraf-Richartz Mus, Cologne, Germany; Mus of Contemp Art, Houston, TX; Israel Mus, Jerusalem, Israel; Mus of Mod Art, NY; Guggenheim Mus, NY; New York Univ, NY; Joslyn Mus of Mod Art, Omaha, NE; John F Kennedy Univ, Orinda, CA; Vatican Mus of Mod Art, Rome Italy; Mus of Mod Art, Stockholm, Sweden; Brandeis Univ, Billy Rose Coll, Waltham, MA
PRINTERS: Atelier Ettinger, NY (AE)
PUBLISHERS: Transworld Art Inc, NY (TAI); Stux Gallery, Boston, MA (S)

TITLE	PUBLISHER	PRINTER	DATE	MEDIUM	DIMENSION (PAPER SIZE) IN INCHES	TYPE OF PAPER	EDITION NUMBER	NO. OF COLORS	ORIGINAL OPENING PRICE	CURRENT RETAIL PRICE
SOLD OUT EDITIONS (RARE):										
Blue Rose & Red Sky	TAI	AE	1981	LC	27 X 33	AP	150		350	450
Twilight Dream	TAI	AE	1981	LC	27 X 33	AP	150		350	450
Roses and Bionic Bees	TAI	AE	1981	LC	27 X 33	AP	150		350	450
Pamela's Dream and Red Rose	TAI	AE	1981	LC	27 X 33	AP	150		350	450

LLOYD VAN-PITTERSON

BORN: Kingston, Jamaica, WI; 1926
EDUCATION: Inst of Jamaica, WI
AWARDS: First Prize, Print Exhib, Leonardo DaVinci Exhib, Paramus, NJ
PRINTERS: Serigraphics Ltd, Inc, Elizabeth, NJ (SLI)
PUBLISHERS: Jackie Fine Art, NY (JFA)
GALLERIES: Edward S Frisch Gallery, New York, NY; Ro Gallery Image Makers, Inc, New York, NY
MAILING ADDRESS: 624 Myrtle St, Elizabeth, NJ 07202

TITLE	PUBLISHER	PRINTER	DATE	MEDIUM	DIMENSION (PAPER SIZE) IN INCHES	TYPE OF PAPER	EDITION NUMBER	NO. OF COLORS	ORIGINAL OPENING PRICE	CURRENT RETAIL PRICE
SOLD OUT EDITIONS (RARE):										
Boats on the Beach	JFA	SLI	1981	SP	22 X 30	STP/100R	300	9	80	200
The Sun Shines Bright	JFA	SLI	1981	SP	23 X 29	STP/100R	200	17	100	250
The Higgler	JFA	SLI	1982	SP	22 X 28	STP/100R	150	21	100	200

DANA CARL VAN HORN

BORN: San Diego, CA; 1950
EDUCATION: San Diego State Univ, CA, BFA, 1972; Yale Univ, New Haven, CT, MFA, 1974; Studied with Jack Beal
RECENT EXHIB: Sherry French Gallery, NY, 1987,92
AWARDS: Whitney Mus of Am Art Scholarship, NY, 1971
COLLECTIONS: Metropolitan Mus of Art, NY; Madison Art Center, WI; Univ of Illinois Medical Center Hospital Chicago, IL
PRINTERS: Jennifer Melby, NY (JM); Chip Elwell, NY (CE)
PUBLISHERS: Orion Editions, NY (OE)
GALLERIES: Orion Editions, New York, NY; Sherry French Gallery, New York, NY

TITLE	PUBLISHER	PRINTER	DATE	MEDIUM	DIMENSION (PAPER SIZE) IN INCHES	TYPE OF PAPER	EDITION NUMBER	NO. OF COLORS	ORIGINAL OPENING PRICE	CURRENT RETAIL PRICE
SOLD OUT EDITIONS (RARE):										
Treadwell Valley	OE	JM	1980	EC	30 X 29	AP	30	1	225	350
Franklin Mountain	OE	CE	1980	PO	24 X 34	AP	60	18	275	450

BRAM VAN VELDE

BORN: Zoeterwoude, Holland; 1895
PRINTERS: Maeght Editeur, Paris, France (ME); Maeght Lelong, Paris, France (ML)
PUBLISHERS: Maeght Editions, Paris, France (ME); Maeght Lelong, Paris, France (ML)
GALLERIES: Galerie Lelong, New York, NY & Paris, France & Zürich, Switzerland; Spaightwood Galleries, Madison, WI

BRAM VAN VELDE CONTINUED

TITLE	PUBLISHER	PRINTER	DATE	MEDIUM	DIMENSION (PAPER SIZE) IN INCHES	TYPE OF PAPER	EDITION NUMBER	NO. OF COLORS	ORIGINAL OPENING PRICE	CURRENT RETAIL PRICE
SOLD OUT EDITIONS (RARE):										
Fond Blanc	ME	ME	1975	LC	27 X 25	AP	100		800 FF	3000 FF
Ecoute	ME	ME	1975	LC	38 X 24	AP	100		1000 FF	3500 FF
Changement	ME	ME	1975	LC	38 X 25	AP	100		1000 FF	3500 FF
Recul	ME	ME	1975	LC	37 X 25	AP	100		1000 FF	3500 FF
Apparition	ME	ME	1975	LC	38 X 25	AP	75		1000 FF	3500 FF
Combat	ME	ME	1975	LC	35 X 25	AP	100		800 FF	3000 FF
Impulsion	ME	ME	1975	LC	39 X 25	AP	100		1000 FF	3500 FF
La Jaune	ME	ME	1975	LC	33 X 25	AP	100		800 FF	3500 FF
Glauque	ME	ME	1975	LC	37 X 25	AP	90		1200 FF	4000 FF
Clarte	ME	ME	1975	LC	36 X 25	AP	100		1200 FF	4000 FF
Liberation	ME	ME	1975	LC	38 X 25	AP	100		1200 FF	4000 FF
Venin	ME	ME	1975	LC	15 X 12	AP	110		400 FF	1200 FF
Quel Visage	ME	ME	1975	LC	22 X 17	AP	120		600 FF	2000 FF
Souvenir Duthuit	ME	ME	1975	LC	18 X 26	AP	90		600 FF	1800 FF
Paysage	ME	ME	1975	LC	18 X 26	AP	90		600 FF	1800 FF
Vif	ME	ME	1975	LC	20 X 15	AP	90		400 FF	1500 FF
Centree	ME	ME	1975	LC	19 X 18	AP	90		600 FF	2000 FF
Eclat	ME	ME	1976	LC	19 X 26	AP	100		600 FF	2000 FF
Grise Nuit	ME	ME	1976	LC	19 X 26	AP	100		600 FF	2000 FF
Vieil Or	ME	ME	1976	LC	26 X 18	AP	100		600 FF	2000 FF
Laque Rouge	ME	ME	1976	LC	26 X 18	AP	100		600 FF	2000 FF
Apaisement	ME	ME	1977	LC	19 X 26	AP	100		600 FF	2000 FF
Gaite	ME	ME	1977	LC	19 X 27	AP	100		600 FF	2000 FF
Oubli	ME	ME	1977	LC	14 X 22	AP	100		600 FF	2000 FF
Ensemble	ME	ME	1977	LC	24 X 31	AP	100		600 FF	2000 FF
En Dedans	ME	ME	1977	LC	29 X 22	AP	100		600 FF	2000 FF
Espace	ME	ME	1977	LC	25 X 31	AP	100		600 FF	2000 FF
Decantement	ME	ME	1977	LC	26 X 21	AP	100		500 FF	1800 FF
Dechirure	ME	ME	1977	LC	29 X 22	AP	100		600 FF	2000 FF
Hantise	ME	ME	1977	LC	19 X 25	AP	100		600 FF	1800 FF
Dans Le Filet	ME	ME	1977	LC	19 X 26	AP	100		600 FF	1500 FF
Inquietude	ME	ME	1978	LC	13 X 20	AP	100		600 FF	1500 FF
Automne	ME	ME	1978	LC	19 X 18	AP	100		600 FF	1500 FF
La Chose	ME	ME	1978	LC	19 X 24	AP	100		600 FF	1500 FF
Devant	ME	ME	1978	LC	19 X 26	AP	100		600 FF	1800 FF
Eclatement	ME	ME	1978	LC	35 X 24	AP	100		1000 FF	3500 FF
Eloignement	ME	ME	1978	LC	34 X 24	AP	100		1000 FF	3500 FF
En Deux	ME	ME	1979	LC	37 X 25	AP	100		1000 FF	3500 FF
Le Tout	ME	ME	1979	LC	24 X 27	AP	100		1000 FF	3000 FF
Ciseaux	ME	ME	1980	LC	16 X 12	AP	100		400 FF	1500 FF
Emergence	ME	ME	1980	LC	39 X 25	AP	100		1200 FF	4000 FF
Exhalaison	ME	ME	1980	LC	24 X 35	AP	100		1200 FF	4000 FF
Spleen	ME	ME	1980	LC	25 X 37	AP	100		1200 FF	4000 FF
Le Feu	ME	ME	1980	LC	18 X 26	AP	100		600 FF	2000 FF
Braises	ME	ME	1980	LC	18 X 26	AP	100		600 FF	2000 FF
Greffe	ME	ME	1980	LC	14 X 12	AP	100		400 FF	1200 FF
Penombre	ME	ME	1980	LC	14 X 12	AP	100		400 FF	1200 FF
Sans Mot	ME	ME	1980	LC	14 X 12	AP	100		400 FF	1200 FF
Le Sauve	ME	ME	1980	LC	59 X 80 cm	AP	100		600 FF	2000 FF
Partage	ME	ME	1980	LC	42 X 57 cm	AP	100		400 FF	1200 FF
Ce Qui Reste	ME	ME	1980	LC	65 X 48 cm	AP	100		600 FF	2000 FF
La Jeune Fille	ME	ME	1980	LC	65 X 49 cm	AP	100		600 FF	2000 FF
Victoire Du Blanc	ME	ME	1980	LC	39 X 59 cm	AP	100		600 FF	2000 FF
Hantise I	ME	ME	1980	EB	50 X 34 cm	CHIF	45	1	600 FF	1500 FF
Hantise II	ME	ME	1980	EB	50 X 34 cm	CHIF	45	1	600 FF	1500 FF
Hantise III	ME	ME	1980	EB	50 X 34 cm	CHIF	45	1	600 FF	1500 FF
Hantise IV	ME	ME	1980	EB	50 X 34 cm	CHIF	45	1	600 FF	1500 FF
Hantise V	ME	ME	1980	EB	50 X 34 cm	CHIF	45	1	600 FF	1500 FF
Hantise VI	ME	ME	1980	EB	50 X 34 cm	CHIF	45	1	600 FF	1500 FF
Hantise VII	ME	ME	1980	EB	50 X 34 cm	CHIF	45	1	600 FF	1500 FF
Hantise VIII	ME	ME	1980	EB	50 X 34 cm	CHIF	45	1	600 FF	1500 FF
Enseveli	ME	ME	1980	LC	65 X 97 cm	AP	100	7	1200 FF	5500 FF
Embrasement	ME	ME	1980	LC	65 X 83 cm	AP	100	Multi	1200 FF	4000 FF
Equilibre	ME	ME	1980	LC	48 X 68 cm	AP	90	6	800 FF	3000 FF
Limpide	ME	ME	1980	LC	62 X 83 cm	AP	100	Multi	1200 FF	4000 FF
La Bonheur de Matisse	ME	ME	1980	LC	65 X 98 cm	AP	100	Multi	1200 FF	5500 FF
Ecolosion	ME	ME	1980	LC	64 X 96 cm	AP	100	Multi	1200 FF	5500 FF
Exubérance	ME	ME	1980	LC	64 X 96 cm	AP	100	7	1200 FF	5500 FF
Derniere Inquietude	ME	ME	1980	LC	64 X 64 cm	AP	100	Multi	800 FF	3500 FF
Nord	ME	ME	1980	LC	100 X 57 cm	AP	100	7	1200 FF	5500 FF
Desertique	ME	ME	1980	LC	65 X 66 cm	AP	100	6	800 FF	3500 FF
Croisee	ME	ME	1980	LC	70 X 63 cm	AP	100	6	800 FF	3500 FF
Acte Sadique	ME	ME	1980	LC	100 X 65 cm	AP	100	6	1200 FF	5500 FF
Separation	ME	ME	1980	LC	63 X 72 cm	AP	100	6	800 FF	3500 FF

BRAM VAN VELDE CONTINUED

TITLE	PUBLISHER	PRINTER	DATE	MEDIUM	DIMENSION (PAPER SIZE) IN INCHES	TYPE OF PAPER	EDITION NUMBER	NO. OF COLORS	ORIGINAL OPENING PRICE	CURRENT RETAIL PRICE
SOLD OUT EDITIONS (RARE):										
Appel	ME	ME	1980	LC	63 X 68 cm	AP	100	6	800 FF	3500 FF
Enigme	ME	ME	1981	LC	64 X 98 cm	AP	100	Multi	1200 FF	5500 FF
Vent des Sables	ME	ME	1981	LC	65 X 99 cm	AP	100	Multi	1200 FF	5500 FF
Partage du Rouge	ME	ME	1981	LC	64 X 48 cm	AP	100	3	800 FF	3000 FF
Fenêtre	ME	ME	1981	LC	64 X 48 cm	AP	100	4	800 FF	3000 FF
Nocturne	ME	ME	1981	LC	61 X 88 cm	AP	100	4	1200 FF	4000 FF
Elément	ME	ME	1981	LC	65 X 99 cm	AP	100	Multi	1200 FF	5500 FF

CLAIRE VAN VLIET

BORN: Ottawa, ON, Canada; August 9, 1933
EDUCATION: San Diego State Univ, CA, AB, 1952; Claremont Grad Sch, CA, MFA, 1954
TEACHING: Asst Prof, Printmaking, Philadelphia Col of Art, PA, 1959–65; Vis Lectr, Univ of Wisconsin, Madison, WI, 1965–66; Vis Lectr, Univ of Vermont, Burlington, VT, 1974–75; Vis Lectr, Univ of Alabama, Huntsville, AL, 1983
AWARDS: VCA Grant, 1975–77; Nat Endowment for the Arts Grants, 1976–78,80; MacArthur Grant, 1989
RECENT EXHIB: Centre Culturel de Pointe-Claire, Canada, 1992
COLLECTIONS: Nat Gallery of Art, Wash, DC; Philadelphia Mus, PA; Montreal Mus of Fine Arts, Can; Cleveland Mus, OH; Victoria & Albert Mus, London, England
PRINTERS: George Lockwood, Boston, MA (GL); Impressions Workshop, Boston, MA (IW) (OB); Carl Urwald, Copenhagen, Denmark (CU); Kai Milsted, Copenhagen, Denmark (KM); U M Grafik, Copenhagen, Denmark (UMG); SKHS, Oslo, Norway (SKHS); Jon Clemens, Lakeside, MI (JC); Lakeside Studio, Lakeside, MI (LS); Artist (ART); Bill Weege, Madison, WI (BW); Andrew Rubin, Madison, WI (AR); Tandem Press, Univ of Wisconsin, Madison, WI (TanPr); Jack Damer (JD)
PUBLISHERS: Impressions Gallery, Boston, MA (IG) (OB); U M Grafik, Copenhagen, Denmark (UMG); Lakeside Studio, Lakeside, MI (LS); Philadelphia Print Club, PA (PPC); Aktuelt Kunst, Oslo, Norway (AK); Artist (ART); Tandem Press, Univ of Wisconsin, Madison, WI (TanPr)

Claire Van Vliet
from Wheeler Rock Series
Courtesy Tandem Press

GALLERIES: Mary Ryan Gallery, New York, NY
MAILING ADDRESS: RD #1, West Burke, VT 05871

TITLE	PUBLISHER	PRINTER	DATE	MEDIUM	DIMENSION (PAPER SIZE) IN INCHES	TYPE OF PAPER	EDITION NUMBER	NO. OF COLORS	ORIGINAL OPENING PRICE	CURRENT RETAIL PRICE
SOLD OUT EDITIONS (RARE):										
Aftensol	UMG	CU/KM/UMG	1962	LC	22 X 30	ZER	50	6	50	400
Bois du Boulogne	UMG	CU/KM/UMG	1962	LB	22 X 28	R/BFK	40	1	40	300
Only a Doctor	UMG	CU/KM/UMG	1962	LB	20 X 26	R/BFK	40	1	40	300
The Country Doctor	UMG	CU/KM/UMG	1962	LB	16 X 21	R/BFK	40	1	40	300
Lupins	UMG	CU/KM/UMG	1963	LB	22 X 30	AP	25	1	50	300
Sailor's Delight	UMG	CU/KM/UMG	1963	LC	22 X 30	R/BFK	50	10	50	600
The Sea	UMG	CU/KM/UMG	1963	LC	22 X 30	R/BFK	30	4	50	400
The Wave	IG	GL/IW	1965	LC	22 X 26	RP/195	50	2	50	400
Horbylunde Storm	UMG	CU/KM/UMG	1965	LB	22 X 30	R/BFK	30	1	50	400
Poppyfield	UMG	CU/KM/UMG	1965	LC	22 X 26	R/BFK	50	6	50	400
Trolde	UMG	CU/KM/UMG	1965	LB	22 X 26	R/BFK	30	1	50	350
Midsummer Night	PPC	CU/KM/UMG	1965	LC	22 X 24	R/BFK	40	5	50	400
CURRENT EDITIONS:										
The Hunter Gracchus	UMG	CU/KM/UMG	1962	LB	22 X 27	AP	40	1	50	250
Summer Storm	UMG	CU/KM/UMG	1971	LB	22 X 25	AP	50	1	50	250
Northern Sea (Second State)	UMG	CU/KM/UMG	1971	LC	22 X 30	AP	75	5	75	300
Cumulus	UMG	CU/KM/UMG	1971	LC	22 X 24	AP	170	4	60	300
Autumn Storm	ART	SKHS	1971	LC	24 X 30	ZER	100	6	75	300
Winter	UMG	CU/KM/UMG	1971	LC	22 X 30	AP	160	4	75	300
After Rain	UMG	CU/KM/UMG	1973	LC	22 X 25	AP	100	6	75	300
Breakthrough	AK	SKHS	1973	LC	22 X 24	AP	275	6	75	300
Before Rain	UMG	CU/KM/UMG	1973	LC	22 X 25	AP	210	6	75	300
Snow Cloud	ART	SKHS	1973	LC	18 X 22	AP	160	5	60	250
June	UMG	CU/KM/UMG	1973	LC	22 X 26	AP/250	160	6	75	300
Grey Cloud	LS	JC/LS	1974	LC	22 X 30	AP	50	3	75	250
Tower of Babel	LS	JC/LS	1974	LB	22 X 30	AP	50	1	75	250
Stormlight	LS	JC/LS	1974	LB	22 X 25	AP	50	1	75	250
Wheeler Rocks (Series of 32)	TanPr	BW/AR/TanPr	1989	MON/EB	33 X 45 EA	HMP	1 EA	4 EA	2000 EA	2000 EA
Wheel Mountain Bowl (Trip)	TanPr	BW/AR/TanPr	1989	LB	3 X 23 X 31	BG/MC	40	1	1500	1800
Sonoran Outcrop (Dipt)	ART	JD	1992	LB	23 X 31 EA	Varies	20	1	900	900

IAN PIETER VAN WIERINGEN

BORN: Amsterdam, The Netherlands; January 11, 1943
EDUCATION: Univ of Sydney, Australia
TEACHING: Univ of Sydney, Australia
AWARDS: Grant, Government of Australia, 1961
COLLECTIONS: Nat Mus of Australia, Sydney, Australia
PRINTERS: Art Atelier, Santa Monica, CA (ArtAt)
PUBLISHERS: Iris Fine Arts, Santa Monica, CA (IFA)
MAILING ADDRESS: c/o Iris Fine Arts, 2450 Broadway, #550, Santa Monica, CA 90404

TITLE	PUBLISHER	PRINTER	DATE	MEDIUM	DIMENSION (PAPER SIZE) IN INCHES	TYPE OF PAPER	EDITION NUMBER	NO. OF COLORS	ORIGINAL OPENING PRICE	CURRENT RETAIL PRICE
CURRENT EDITIONS:										
Dolphin Dreams	IFA	ArtAt	1993	ARTA	27 X 36	CAN	250		1000	1000

VICTOR VASARELY

BORN: Pecs, Hungary; April 9, 1908
EDUCATION: Poldini-Volkmann Acad, Budapest, Hungary, 1925–27; Muhely Acad, Budapest, Hungary, 1928–29; Bauhaus, Budapest, Hungary, 1929
AWARDS: Guggenheim Fel, NY
RECENT EXHIB: Vasarely Center, NY, 1989; Univ of Minnesota, Minneapolis, MN, 1989; Belian Art Center, Troy, MI, 1989; Walton Street Gallery, Chicago, IL, 1989
COLLECTIONS: Mus of Mod Art, Paris, France; Guggenheim Mus, NY; Mus of Mod Art, NY; Harvard Univ, Cambridge, MA; Art Inst of Chicago, IL; Mus of Contemp Art, Montreal, Can; Royal Mus of Fine Art, Brussels, Belgium; Art Mus, Copenhagen, Denmark; Tel-Aviv Mus, Israel; Mus of Fine Art, Budapest, Hungary; Univ of Sydney, Australia
PRINTERS: Editions Denise René, Paris, France (EDR); Atelier Arcay, Paris, France (AAR); Nicholas Serdar, Paris, France (NS); George Fall (GF); American Atelier, NY (AA)
PUBLISHERS: Editions Denise René, Paris, France (EDR); Kennedy Gallery, NY (KG); Transworld Art Inc, NY (IAI); Martin Lawrence Limited Editions, Van Nuy, CA (MLLE); Contemporary Art Masters, NY (CAM); Edward Weston Graphics, Northridge, CA (EWG); Georges Fall (GF); Circle Fine Art, Chicago, IL (CFA)
GALLERIES: Edward Weston Graphics, New York, NY; Kennedy Galleries, New York, NY; Fernette's Gallery, Des Moines, IA; D Erlein Fine Arts, Milwaukee, WI; Park West Galleries, Southfield, MI; Scherer Gallery, Marlboro, NJ; Petan Art Gallery, Short Hills, NJ; Meridian Galleries, Chicago, IL & New York, NY; Glass Art Gallery, New York, NY; Martin Lawrence Galleries, Sherman Oaks, CA & Los Angeles, CA & West Los Angeles, CA & Newport Beach, CA & Palm Springs, CA & Santa Clara, CA & Redondo Beach, CA & Thousand Oaks, CA & Escondido, CA & Short Hills, NJ & New York, NY; Circle Galleries, San Diego, CA & San Francisco, CA & Northridge, CA & Pittsburgh, PA & Houston, TX & Soho, NY & Chicago, IL & Scottsdale, AZ & Beverly Hills, CA & Costa Mesa, CA & Sherman Oaks, CA & Palm Beach, FL & Honolulu, HI & New Orleans, LA & Las Vegas, NV & Seattle, WA; Owl Gallery, San Francisco, CA; Graphic Art Collection, Hallandale, FL; Jupiter Fine Arts, Jupiter, FL; The Hang-Up, Sarasota, FL; R H Love Gallery, Chicago, IL & Scottsdale, AZ & Beverly Hills, CA & Costa Mesa, CA & Sherman Oaks, CA & Palm Beach, FL & Honolulu, HI & New Orleans, LA & Las Vegas, NV & Seattle, WA; Walton Street Gallery, Chicago, IL; Arras Galleries, New York, NY; T R's Gallery, New York, NY; Langman Gallery, Willow Grove, PA

Victor Vasarely
Hang
Courtesy Georges Fall

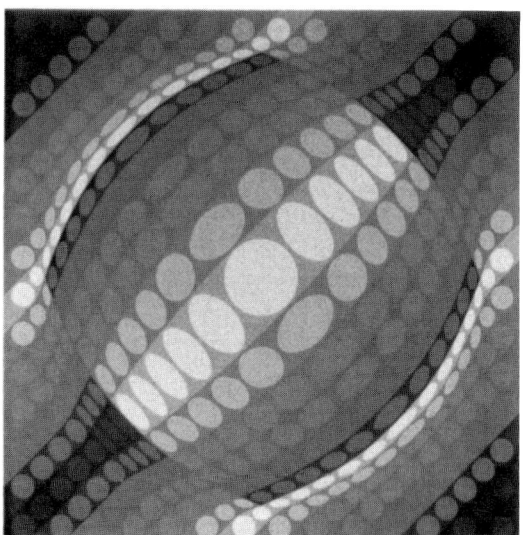

Victor Vasarely
Planeta
Courtesy Georges Fall

TITLE	PUBLISHER	PRINTER	DATE	MEDIUM	DIMENSION (PAPER SIZE) IN INCHES	TYPE OF PAPER	EDITION NUMBER	NO. OF COLORS	ORIGINAL OPENING PRICE	CURRENT RETAIL PRICE
SOLD OUT EDITIONS (RARE):										
Lapidare (from Suite of 8)	EDR	EDR	1966	SP	27 X 26	AP	150	3	200	2500
Dyevat	CFA	AA	1973	SP	44 X 44	AP	300		300	3175
Tettye	CFA	AA	1973	SP	36 X 30	AP	250		300	1700
Teke	CFA	AA	1973	SP	36 X 30	AP	250		300	1650
Semiha	CFA	AA	1973	SP	28 X 43	AP	250		300	4300
Nora-Dell	CFA	AA	1973	SP	35 X 31	AP	250		300	4700
Thez-II	CFA	AA	1973	SP	24 X 19	AP	250		300	4100
Denise Rene Edition (Quadrangles)	AP	AAR	1974	SP	26 X 33	AP	250		450	3500
Zebre Rouge	CFA	AA	1974	SP	26 X 21	AP	75		300	3950
Zebre Vert	CFA	AA	1974	SP	26 X 21	AP	75		300	4000

VICTOR VASARELY CONTINUED

TITLE	PUBLISHER	PRINTER	DATE	MEDIUM	DIMENSION (PAPER SIZE) IN INCHES	TYPE OF PAPER	EDITION NUMBER	NO. OF COLORS	ORIGINAL OPENING PRICE	CURRENT RETAIL PRICE
SOLD OUT EDITIONS (RARE):										
Coelum	CFA	AA	1974	SP	12 X 10	AP	350		100	1200
Or-vit	CFA	AA	1974	SP	12 X 10	AP	350		100	1200
Ive	CFA	AA	1974	SP	12 X 10	AP	350		100	1200
Tetcie	CFA	AA	1974	SP	36 X 30	AP	250		300	4600
Kaldor	CFA	AA	1974	SP	36 X 30	AP	250		300	4400
Trivega	CFA	AA	1974	SP	36 X 30	AP	250		300	4000
Galaxy	CFA	AA	1974	SP	36 X 30	AP	250		300	4600
Zeng	CFA	AA	1974	SP	36 X 30	AP	250		300	4000
Basse-Cour	CFA	AA	1974	LC	19 X 20	AP	135		300	4200
Etude-Bleue	CFA	AA	1975	LC	23 X 22	AP	135		300	4200
Etude-Jaune	CFA	AA	1975	LC	23 X 22	AP	250		300	4200
Chat (Etude de Lumieres)	CFA	AA	1975	LC	21 X 23	AP	180		300	4400
Kiddo	CFA	AA	1976	LC	28 X 21	AP	200		300	900
Vonal	CFA	AA	1976	SP	24 X 24	AP	248		300	975
Attirà Tours	CFA	AA	1976	SP	27 X 23	AP			300	1700
Gestalt Gris	CFA	AA	1976	SP	32 X 32	AP	200		300	1200
Gestalt Mauve	CFA	AA	1976	SP	32 X 32	AP	200		300	1200
Orvar	CFA	AA	1976	SP	36 X 28	AP	250		300	1700
Quivar-Na	CFA	AA	1976	SP	30 X 28	AP	250		300	1200
Neptune-E	CFA	AA	1976	SP	24 X 19	AP	250		300	850
Zebre Zambo	CFA	AA	1976	SP	28 X 24	AP	250		300	4300
Tecture	CFA	AA	1976	SP	40 X 46	AP	250		300	4100
Self Portrait	CFA	AA	1976	LC	35 X 25	AP	250		300	4600
Lador	CFA	AA	1976	SP	14 X 12	AP	400		100	1050
Papillon	CFA	AA	1976	SP	30 X 37	AP	250		500	4300
Penzo-Z	TAI	NS	1976	SP	26 X 20	AP	175	18	500	2000
Zuska	CFA	AA	1976	SP	30 X 31	AP	300		500	2550
Tsoda (Miracle)	CFA	AA	1977	SP	18 X 18	AP	150		350	2350
Remek (Marvel)	CFA	AA	1977	SP	18 X 18	AP	150		350	2400
Album Melodies (Set of 19):									2800 SET	17600 SET
Luth	CFA	AA	1977	SP	23 X 15	AP	135		350	2100
Trumpette	CFA	AA	1977	SP	23 X 15	AP	135		350	2100
Harpe	CFA	AA	1977	SP	23 X 15	AP	135		350	2000
Violin	CFA	AA	1977	SP	23 X 15	AP	135		350	2000
Flute	CFA	AA	1977	SP	23 X 15	AP	135		350	2050
Mandoline	CFA	AA	1977	SP	23 X 15	AP	135		350	2000
Cithar	CFA	AA	1977	SP	23 X 15	AP	135		350	2000
Guitare	CFA	AA	1977	SP	23 X 15	AP	135		350	2000
Horn	CFA	AA	1977	SP	23 X 15	AP	135		350	2000
Viva	MLLE	AAR	1978	SP	31 X 31	AP	275	16	900	1800
Verchte	MLLE	AAR	1978	SP	25 X 25	AP	250	18	900	1800
Delocta	MLLE	AAR	1978	SP	30 X 32	AP	275		900	1800
Bi-Dagg	CAM	AAR	1981	SP	25 X 31	AP	250	12	575	1800
Battor	CAM	AAR	1981	SP	25 X 43	AP	250	7	575	1800
VP 100	MLLE	A/P/FR	1982	SP	43 X 24	AP	325	18	550	1800
Door	MLLE	A/P/FR	1982	SP	43 X 24	AP	325	16	700	1500
Reflections	MLLE	A/P/FR	1982	SP	44 X 27	SE	325		600	1500
Makk-S	MLLE	A/P/FR	1982	SP	36 X 30	AP	250		500	1500
Bouloss	MLLE	A/P/FR	1982	SP	32 X 28	AP	300		500	1200
Gestalt MC	CFA	AA	1985	MULT	17 X 16		100		1500	8000
Gestalt RJ	CFA	AA	1985	MULT	17 X 16		100		1500	7200
Axo-M3	CFA	AA	1985	MULT	12 X 7		100		900	4000
Zebre I-Droit	CFA	AA	1985	MULT	12 X 7		100		900	3700
Zebre-B	CFA	AA	1985	MULT	26 X 21		100		900	3700
Felhoe	CFA	AA	1985	MULT	26 X 21	Wood	100		900	92500
Torony II	CFA	AA	1985	MULT	25 X 15		275		900	13500
Kettes	CFA	AA	1986	MULT	27 X 16		175		900	7500
Tridos	CFA	AA	1987	SP	28 X 33	AP	300		900	6300
Zebra	CFA	AA	1987	SP	31 X 39	CP	200		2500	5000
Ionau	CFA	AA	1987	SP	40 X 72	AP	300		1400	3850
Raura	CFA	AA	1987	SP	34 X 32	AP	300		800	4600
Kartsou (formerly Torony-Black)	CFA	AA	1987	CP	37 X 25	AP	200		2000	3900
Paris-Tokyo Folio (Set of 6):									2500 SET	7200 SET
Audard	CFA	AA	1987	SP	23 X 22	AP	75		450	1300
Bi-Octans	CFA	AA	1987	SP	23 X 22	AP	75		450	1300
Silva	CFA	AA	1987	SP	23 X 22	AP	75		450	1300
Takat	CFA	AA	1987	SP	23 X 22	AP	75		450	1250
Triboss	CFA	AA	1987	SP	23 X 22	AP	75		450	1300
Tupa Tu	CFA	AA	1987	SP	23 X 22	AP	75		450	1300
Vancouver Folio (Set of 8):									3500 SET	9100 SET
Terroide	CFA	AA	1987	SP	30 X 30	AP	75		450	1300
Virgo	CFA	AA	1987	SP	30 X 30	AP	75		450	1300
Dumb "B"	CFA	AA	1987	SP	30 X 30	AP	75		450	1250
Lum	CFA	AA	1987	SP	30 X 30	AP	75		450	1250

VICTOR VASARELY CONTINUED

TITLE	PUBLISHER	PRINTER	DATE	MEDIUM	DIMENSION (PAPER SIZE) IN INCHES	TYPE OF PAPER	EDITION NUMBER	NO. OF COLORS	ORIGINAL OPENING PRICE	CURRENT RETAIL PRICE
SOLD OUT EDITIONS (RARE):										
Stridim	CFA	AA	1987	SP	30 X 30	AP	75		450	1200
Haynal	CFA	AA	1987	SP	30 X 30	AP	75		450	1250
Letz	CFA	AA	1987	SP	30 X 30	AP	75		450	1300
Vallas	CFA	AA	1987	SP	30 X 30	AP	75		450	1200
CURRENT EDITIONS:										
Golda	AP	AAR	1976	SP	30 X 33	AP	250		575	2500
KST	GF	GF	1976	SP	30 X 28	AP	250		600	2000
Kerek	GF	GF	1976	SP	44 X 26	AP	250		600	2000
Hang	GF	GF	1976	SP	33 X 30	AP	250		600	2000
Planeta	GF	GF	1976	SP	31 X 31	AP	250		600	2000
Homage to Uneven Numbers	KG		1976	LC	23 X 22	AP/W	150	11	600	1800
Oltar	KG		1976	SP		AP/W	150		600	2500
Togonne	CFA	AA	1976	SP	39 X 29	AP	300		500	2200
Zilver	CFA	AA	1976	SP	33 X 30	AP	300		875	1950
Vega Kocka (Chrome)	CFA	AA	1976	SP	24 X 38	AP	150		875	2200
Vega Kocka (Gold)	CFA	AA	1976	SP	24 X 38	AP	150		875	2300
Axo 77	CFA	AA	1977	SP	23 X 39	AP	300		750	2500
Geometry in Color	CFA	AA	1977	SP	43 X 34	HMP	200		1200	4450
Jeu D'Echecs (Game of Chess)	CFA	AA	1977	SP	30 X 32	AP	300		500	1100
Torony III	CFA	AA	1977	SP	40 X 40	AP	300		975	2450
Dyss	CFA	AA	1977	SP	34 X 32	AP	300		875	2300
Fenyes (Luminosity)	CFA	AA	1977	SP	18 X 18	AP	175		500	2300
Pontos (Pointed)	CFA	AA	1977	SP	18 X 18	AP	150		500	2300
Vegogta	AP	AAR	1977	SP	26 X 43	AP	250		575	2500
Pava	AP	AAR	1978	SP	26 X 43	AP	250		575	2500
Sirtme	EWG		1978	LC	26 X 34	AP	250		600	2000
Nadir	EWG		1978	LC	17 X 34	AP	250		600	2000
Ta-Ma-Fa	EWG		1978	LC	22 X 20	AP	250		600	2000
Sinpo	MLLE	AAR	1978	SP	30 X 31	AP	275	18	900	2000
Quadrature	MLLE	AAR	1978	SP	32 X 30	AP	275	12	550	2000
Fondau	MLLE	AAR	1978	SP	30 X 31	AP	275	14	900	2000
Vilag	MLLE	AAR	1978	SP	30 X 32	AP	275	14	900	2000
Homage to Vasarely I (Set of 3):									900 SET	3500 SET
Callisto	MLLE	AAR	1979	SP	15 X 17	AP	250		300	1300
Deimos	MLLE	AAR	1979	SP	15 X 17	AP	250		300	1300
Volans	MLLE	AAR	1979	SP	15 X 17	AP	250		300	1300
Homage to Vasarely II (Set of 3):	MLLE	AAR	1979	SP	15 X 17	AP	75		900 SET	3500 SET
Sancton	MLLE	AAR	1979	SP	15 X 17	SP	250	12	300	1300
Pixis	MLLE	AAR	1979	SP	15 X 17	AP	250	12	200	1300
Xanor	MLLE	AAR	1979	SP	15 X 17	AP	250	12	300	1300
Kas-Kas	AP	AAR	1979	SP	30 X 34	AP	200		450	2000
Peer-Rough	AP	AAR	1980	SP	28 X 43	AP	250		575	2000
Cubic Relationship Serigraph	MLLE	A/P/FR	1982	SP	27 X 23	AP	325		400	1800
Paper Relief	MLLE	A/P/FR	1982	REL	27 X 24	HMP	150		450	2000
Cosca										
Serigraph	MLLE	A/P/FR	1982	SP	27 X 24	AP	325		400	1800
Paper Relief	MLLE	A/P/FR	1982	REL	27 X 24	HMP	150		450	1800
Album GAIA (Set of 8)	EDR	Sil	1986	SP	33 X 33 EA	AP	250 EA		1400 SET	3000 SET
Museum Portfolio (Set of 5)	EDR	Sil	1986	SP	29 X 42 EA	AP	295 EA		1400 SET	3000 SET
Zett (Dipt)	CFA	AA	1989	SP	20 X 40	AC	300		1500	2900
Penta Job	CFA	AA	1989	SP/EMB	18 X 18	AC	300		700	1500
Zebra (White on Black)	CFA	AA	1989	CP	39 X 31	HMP	200		2500	3600
Zebra (Violet on Silver)	CFA	AA	1989	CP	39 X 31	HMP	100		1850	3000
Zebra (Purple with Beige)	CFA	AA	1989	CP	39 X 31	HMP	100		1850	3000
Zebra (Beige with Purple Lines)	CFA	AA	1989	CP	39 X 31	HMP	100		1850	3000
Zebra (Blue with Gold Lines)	CFA	AA	1989	CP	39 X 31	HMP	100		1850	3000
Leopard (Pink on Green)	CFA	AA	1989	CP	40 X 31	HMP	100		1850	3750
Leopard (White on Blue)	CFA	AA	1989	CP	40 X 31	HMP	100		1850	3750
Leopard (Yellow on Black)	CFA	AA	1989	CP	40 X 31	HMP	100		1850	5000
Leopard (White on Black)	CFA	AA	1989	CP	40 X 31	HMP	100		1850	3750
Leopard (Magenta, Blue-Green on Gray)	CFA	AA	1990	CP	32 X 40	HMP	100		1500	3450
Leopard (White, Black on Blue)	CFA	AA	1990	CP	32 X 39	HMP	100		1500	3450
Zebra (Violet with Silver)	CFA	AA	1990	CP	39 X 31	HMP	100		1500	3000
Zebra (Purple with Beige)	CFA	AA	1990	CP	39 X 31	HMP	100		1500	3000
Zebra (Beige with Purple Lines)	CFA	AA	1990	CP	39 X 31	HMP	100		1500	3000
Tsikos-A (Black/Blue on Black)	CFA	AA	1990	CP	39 X 31	HMP	150		1550	3050
Tsikos-B (Blue/Green/Off-White)	CFA	AA	1990	CP	39 X 31	HMP	150		1550	3400
Tsikos-C (White on Black)	CFA	AA	1990	CP	39 X 31	HMP	150		1550	4900
Tsikos-D (Black on White)	CFA	AA	1990	CP	39 X 31	HMP	150		1550	3650
Tsikos-E (Bronze on White)	CFA	AA	1990	CP	39 X 31	HMP	150		1550	3500
Geometry in Color	CFA	AA	1991	CP	43 X 34	HMP	200		2200	4450
Attika	CFA	AA	1992	SP	23 X 22	HMP	300		1550	2000
Tsiga & Biga (Set of 6)	CFA	AA	1992	SP	15 X 15 EA	HMP	100		7000 SET	7550 SET

ROBERT VAVRA

BORN: California, USA
EDUCATION: Univ of Southern California, Los Angeles, CA
PRINTERS: American Atelier, NY (AA)
PUBLISHERS: Circle Fine Art, Chicago, IL (CFA)

GALLERIES: Circle Galleries, San Diego, CA & San Francisco, CA & Northbrook, IL & Pittsburgh, PA & Houston, TX & Soho, NY & Chicago, IL & Scottsdale, AZ & Beverly Hills, CA & Costa Mesa, CA & Sherman Oaks, CA & Palm Beach, FL & Honolulu, HI & New Orleans, LA & Las Vegas, NV & Seattle, WA

TITLE	PUBLISHER	PRINTER	DATE	MEDIUM	DIMENSION (PAPER SIZE) IN INCHES	TYPE OF PAPER	EDITION NUMBER	NO. OF COLORS	ORIGINAL OPENING PRICE	CURRENT RETAIL PRICE
SOLD OUT EDITIONS (RARE):										
By Reason of His Elegance	CFA	AA	1979	PH/C	19 X 26	AP	300		200	500
Horses of the Waves	CFA	AA	1979	PH/C	15 X 18	AP	300		200	500
Pegasus	CFA	AA	1979	PH/C	20 X 28	AP	300		300	675
Spanish Stallion	CFA	AA	1979	PH/B	7 X 14	AP	300		125	350
Foal in Fall Field	CFA	AA	1979	PH/C	9 X 13	AP	300		125	400
Oriental Stampede	CFA	AA	1980	PH/C	13 X 19	AP	300		150	475
CURRENT EDITIONS:										
Toros de Iberia	CFA	AA	1979	PH/B	10 X 14	AP	300		125	350
Comic Bullfighters	CFA	AA	1979	PH/B	11 X 14	AP	300		125	300
Boy of the Marshes	CFA	AA	1979	PH/B	14 X 12	AP	300		125	300
After the Fair	CFA	AA	1979	PH/B	14 X 14	AP	300		125	300
At the Bullring	CFA	AA	1979	PH/B	14 X 11	AP	300		125	300
A Dream of Horses	CFA	AA	1979	PH/B	15 X 15	AP	300		125	300
The Wounds of Hunger	CFA	AA	1979	PH/B	12 X 17	AP	300		125	300
Matador Dressing	CFA	AA	1979	PH/B	20 X 15	AP	300		150	425
Mantilla at the Feria	CFA	AA	1979	PH/B	14 X 20	AP	300		150	400
The Real Nature of Horses	CFA	AA	1979	PH/C	9 X 13	AP	300		125	375
Feathered Wings	CFA	AA	1980	PH/C	10 X 13	AP	300		125	400
Freedom of Movement	CFA	AA	1980	PH/C	13 X 19	AP	300		125	450
The Drowsy Year	CFA	AA	1980	PH/C	20 X 28	AP	300		150	475
Flow of Nectar	CFA	AA	1980	PH/C	15 X 18	AP	300		150	450
Pageant of Proud Horses	CFA	AA	1980	PH/C	16 X 29	AP	300		150	575
The Distant Fight	CFA	AA	1980	PH/C	30 X 17	AP	300		150	475
Horses of Thunder	CFA	AA	1980	PH/C	12 X 19	AP	300		150	400
Hot Courage & High Desire	CFA	AA	1980	PH/C	15 X 18	AP	300		150	400
Around and Around He Galloped	CFA	AA	1980	PH/C	20 X 28	AP	300		150	575
Flight without Wings	CFA	AA	1980	PH/C	19 X 27	AP	300		150	475
Xenophon's Horse	CFA	AA	1980	PH/C	19 X 23	AP	300		150	550
Some Horses are Coming	CFA	AA	1980	PH/C	19 X 28	AP	300		150	550
Stallion of a Dream	CFA	AA	1980	PH/C	9 X 13	AP	300		125	375
Together	CFA	AA	1980	PH/C	9 X 14	AP	300		125	375
Drinker of the Wind	CFA	AA	1980	PH/C	9 X 13	AP	300		125	375
To be a Horse	CFA	AA	1980	PH/C	13 X 20	AP	300		125	425
My Hand Forever in Your Mane	CFA	AA	1980	PH/C	9 X 13	AP	300		125	325
Farewell	CFA	AA	1981	PH/C	9 X 13	AP	300		125	325
The Golden Dust	CFA	AA	1981	PH/C	9 X 13	AP	300		125	325
As I Become One	CFA	AA	1981	PH/C	9 X 13	AP	300		125	375
Stand for My Horse	CFA	AA	1981	PH/C	20 X 29	AP	300		125	475
Crossing the Dunes	CFA	AA	1981	PH/C	11 X 19	AP	300		125	400
Horse of the Quiet Clouds	CFA	AA	1981	PH/C	15 X 20	AP	300		125	400
A Golden Pat for Him	CFA	AA	1981	PH/C	20 X 28	AP	300		125	475
My Bed of Roses, Steed of Fire	CFA	AA	1981	PH/C	11 X 18	AP	300		125	450
He Lacks a Proud Rider on His Back	CFA	AA	1981	PH/C	15 X 19	AP	300		125	400
How Could I Live without You?	CFA	AA	1981	PH/C	13 X 20	AP	300		125	450
I Love Nature More	CFA	AA	1981	PH/C	19 X 27	AP	300		125	550
My Horse of Flowers	CFA	AA	1981	PH/C	20 X 29	AP	300		125	475
Deep Draughted Wines of Memory	CFA	AA	1981	PH/C	20 X 27	AP	300		125	475
Morning in Jerez	CFA	AA	1981	PH/C	9 X 14	AP	300		125	375
Flight	CFA	AA	1981	PH/C	13 X 20	AP	300		150	400
I am Alive, I am Alive	CFA	AA	1981	PH/C	15 X 19	AP	300		150	575

EMILIO VEDOVA

BORN: Venice, Italy; 1919
EDUCATION: Self-Taught
TEACHING: Lectr, Acad of Fine Arts, Venice, Italy, 1968; Lectr, Rhode Island Sch of Design, Providence, RI, 1965,67,70; Lectr, Chicago Univ, IL, 1965,67,70; Lectr, Inst of Contemp Art, Cleveland, OH, 1965,67,70; Lectr, Wayne Univ, Detroit, MI, 1965,67,70; Lectr, Wisconsin Univ, Madison, WI, 1965,67,70; Lectr, Boston Univ, MA, 1965,67,70; Lectr, Carnegie Inst, Pittsburgh, PA, 1965,67,70; Lectr, Univ of California, Berkeley, CA, 1967,70; Lectr, Monmouth Oregon Univ, OR, 1967,70; Lectr, Smith Col, Northampton, MA, 1970; Lectr, Cooper Union Univ, NY, 1970; Prof, Salzburg Int Sommerakademie, Switzerland, 1965–70; Lectr, Nat Univ, Mexico City, Mexico, 1980; Prof, Painting, Venice Acad of Fine Arts, Italy, 1975–87

AWARDS: Cini Found Prize, Venice, Italy, 1950; Young Artist Prize, Sao Paulo, Brazil, 1951; Morganti Found Prize, Sao Paulo, Brazil, 1953; Solomon Guggenheim Found Award, Italy, 1956; First Prize, Lissone Award, Italy, 1958; Grand Prix Award, Painting, Juried by Herbert Read, Venice, Italy, 1960; First Prize, Graphic Art, Venice, Italy, 1962; Graphic Art Award, Ljubljana, Poland, 1978; Graphic Art Award, Warsaw, Poland, 1978; First Prize, Drawing, Rijeka, Poland, 1978
PRINTERS: Garner Tullis Workshop, Santa Barbara, CA (GTW)
PUBLISHERS: Garner Tullis, NY (GT); Eineaudi, Italy (EiN)
GALLERIES: Garner Tullis, New York, NY & Santa Barbara, CA

EMILIO VEDOVA CONTINUED

TITLE	PUBLISHER	PRINTER	DATE	MEDIUM	DIMENSION (PAPER SIZE) IN INCHES	TYPE OF PAPER	EDITION NUMBER	NO. OF COLORS	ORIGINAL OPENING PRICE	CURRENT RETAIL PRICE
SOLD OUT EDITIONS (RARE):										
Immagine del Tempo			1959	LB	14 X 21	AP	99	1	60	750
No la Sopraffazione 2			1969	LB	23 X 31	AP	25	1	125	1200
Spagna Oggi (Set of 10)	EiN		1975	LB	17 X 24 EA		100 EA	1 EA		3000 SET
CURRENT EDITIONS:										
Untitled	GT	GTW	1989	MON	76 X 43 EA	R/BFK	1 EA	Varies	28000 EA	28000 EA

VLADIMIR VELICKOVIC

BORN: Belgrade; 1935
RECENT EXHIB: Mayer-Schwarz Gallery, Beverly Hills, CA, 1989
PRINTERS: Maeght Editeur, Paris, France (ME); Galerie Maeght Lelong, Paris, France (ML)
PUBLISHERS: Maeght Editions, Paris, France (ME); Galerie Maeght Lelong, Paris, France (ML); 3 Continents Editions, NY (3CE)
GALLERIES: Galerie Lelong, Paris, France & Zürich, Switzerland & New York, NY

TITLE	PUBLISHER	PRINTER	DATE	MEDIUM	DIMENSION (PAPER SIZE) IN INCHES	TYPE OF PAPER	EDITION NUMBER	NO. OF COLORS	ORIGINAL OPENING PRICE	CURRENT RETAIL PRICE
CURRENT EDITIONS:										
Mouvement Fig M/I	ME	ME	1981	LC	39 X 55	AP	100		2500 FF	3500 FF
Mouvement Fig M/II	ME	ME	1981	LC	39 X 55	AP	100		2500 FF	3500 FF

BERNAR P VENET

BORN: Saint Auban, France; April 20, 1941
EDUCATION: Sch of Villa Thiole, Nice, France, 1957–58
TEACHING: Lectured: New York Univ, NY, 1969,79, Northwestern Univ, Evanston, IL, 1970, Art Inst of Chicago, IL, 1970; California Inst of Art, Valencia, CA, 1976; Sch of Visual Arts, NY, 1968,76
AWARDS: Nat Endowment for the Arts Award; Design Award, Norfolk Design Review Committee, 1988
RECENT EXHIB: Univ of Tennessee Art Gallery, Chattanooga, TN, 1989; Greenberg Gallery, St Louis, MO, 1989; Brent Sikkema Fine Art, NY, 1992
COLLECTIONS: Mus of Mod Art, NY; Kaiser Wilhelm Mus, Krefeld, Germany; Akron Art Inst, OH; Santa Barbara Mus of Art, CA; New York Univ, NY; Mus Sztuky W Lodzi, Lodz, Poland; Centre Nat d'Art Contemp, Paris, France; Wadsworth Atheneum, Hartford, CT; Musee d'Art Mod et d'Industrie, Saint Etienne, France; La Jolla Mus of Contemp Art, CA; Dartmouth Col Mus, Hanover, NH; Solomon R Guggenheim Mus, NY; Centre Georges Pompidou, Paris, France; Neue Galerie Alten Kurhaus, Aachen, West Germany
PRINTERS: Landfall Press Inc, Chicago, IL (LPI); Multiples Fine Art Printing, Los Angeles, CA (MFAP); Raul Castello (RC); Monika Mallewicz (MM)
PUBLISHERS: Landfall Press Inc, Chicago, IL (LPI); David Lawrence Editions, Beverly Hills, CA (DLE)
GALLERIES: Landfall Press Inc, Chicago, IL; Wenger Gallery, Los Angeles, CA; Deson Saunders Gallery, Chicago, IL; Zack/Shuster Gallery, Boca Raton, FL; Lemberg Gallery, Birmingham, MI; Greenberg Gallery, St Louis, MO; Fred Hoffman Gallery, Santa Monica, CA; David Lawrence Editions, Beverly Hills, CA; Margaret Lipworth Fine Art, Boca Raton, FL; Enrico Navarra Gallery, New York, NY; Brent Sikkema Fine Art, New York, NY
MAILING ADDRESS: 533 Canal St, New York, NY 10013

TITLE	PUBLISHER	PRINTER	DATE	MEDIUM	DIMENSION (PAPER SIZE) IN INCHES	TYPE OF PAPER	EDITION NUMBER	NO. OF COLORS	ORIGINAL OPENING PRICE	CURRENT RETAIL PRICE
SOLD OUT EDITIONS (RARE):										
Angles	LPI	MM/LPI	1981	LC/CO	20 X 26	AP/W	35	3	175	800
Arc	LPI	MM/LPI	1981	LC/CO	20 X 26	AP/W	35	3	175	800
Line	LPI	MM/LPI	1981	LC/CO	20 X 26	AP/W	35	3	175	800
CURRENT EDITIONS:										
Two Undetermined Lines	DLE	RC/MM/MFAP	1990	SP/HC	54 X 41	WesVel	88	32	4500	450

MICHAEL VENTRESCA

BORN: Portland, ME; February 19, 1952
EDUCATION: Buddhist Monastery, Korea
RECENT EXHIB: Screening Room, Newburyport, MA, 1987; Portsmouth Gallery, NH, 1987
PUBLISHERS: Fox Graphics, Boston, MA (FG); Merrimac Editions, Merrimac, MA (MerEd); Artist (ART)
PRINTERS: Herbert Fox, Merrimac, MA (HF); Fox Graphics, Merrimac, MA (FG); Artist (ART)
GALLERIES: Fox Graphics, Merrimac, MA

TITLE	PUBLISHER	PRINTER	DATE	MEDIUM	DIMENSION (PAPER SIZE) IN INCHES	TYPE OF PAPER	EDITION NUMBER	NO. OF COLORS	ORIGINAL OPENING PRICE	CURRENT RETAIL PRICE
CURRENT EDITIONS:										
Marilyn Monroe	ART/FG/MerEd	HF/FG	1986	LC	22 X 22	AP	60	2	250	600
Untitled	ART/FG/MerEd	HF/FG	1987	WC	42 X 96	AP	5	2	1500	1800

The retail prices of the 100,000 limited edition prints quoted in this directory are subject to change. Print publishers, artists and galleries were the direct sources for these quotations. Prices in the secondary market listed as "Sold Out Editions (Rare)" indicate that the publisher has a limited supply of that print or that the print is difficult to locate in the galleries.

The Printworld Directory is accepting new applications for the seventh edition. Approximately 300 new artists will be accepted. Please use the two forms provided in the back section of this directory to submit biographical data and documentation of prints. Edition number of each print must not exceed 500 and the retail price must be $100 or more.

ESTEBAN VICENTE

BORN: Turegano, Spain; January 20, 1903; US Citizen
EDUCATION: Real Acad de Ballas Artes de San Fernando, Madrid, Spain, 1922
TEACHING: Univ of Puerto Rico; Univ of California, Berkeley, CA; Univ of California, Los Angeles, CA; Yale Univ, New Haven, CT; American Univ, Wash, DC; Princeton Univ, NJ; Columbia Univ, NY; New York Univ, NY
AWARDS: Ford Found Fel (2); Tamarind Lithography Workshop Fel, Albuquerque, NM; Nat Acad of Design Fel; Acad Belles Artes, Madrid, Spain; Parsons Sch of Design, Hon Degree, 1984
RECENT EXHIB: Berry-Hill Galleries, Inc, NY, 1989; Louis Newman Gallery, Beverly Hills, CA, 1992
COLLECTIONS: Albright-Knox Mus, Buffalo, NY; Baltimore Mus of Art, MD; Brandeis Mus, Waltham, MA; Chicago Art Inst, IL; Dartmouth Col, Hanover, NH; Fogg Art Mus, Cambridge, MA; Hirshhorn Mus, Wash, DC; Honolulu Acad of Fine Arts, HI; Iowa State Univ, Ames, IA; Los Angeles County Mus, CA; Metropolitan Mus, NY; Mus of Mod Art, NY; Nat Coll of Fine Arts, Wash, DC; Newark Mus, NJ; Princeton Univ Art Mus, NJ; San Francisco Mus of Fine Arts, CA; Smithsonian Inst, Wash, DC; Syracuse Univ Coll, NY; Guggenheim Mus, NY; Tate Gallery, London, England; Trenton State Mus, NJ; Univ of California, Berkeley, CA; Univ of New Mexico, Albuquerque, NM; Univ of North Carolina, Greensboro, NC; Wadsworth Atheneum, Hartford, CT; Whitney Mus of Am Art, NY; Yale Univ, New Haven, CT
PRINTERS: American Atelier, NY (AA); Sylvia Roth, South Nyack, NY (SR); Hudson River Editions, South Nyack, NY (HRE)
PUBLISHERS: Transworld Art Inc, NY (TAI); Tom Gruenbaum, NY (TG)
GALLERIES: Riva Yares Gallery, Scottsdale, AZ; Berry-Hill Gallery, Inc, New York, NY; Hudson River Editions, South Nyack, NY; Louis Newman Gallery, Beverly Hills, CA
MAILING ADDRESS: 1 W 67th St, New York, NY 10023

TITLE	PUBLISHER	PRINTER	DATE	MEDIUM	DIMENSION (PAPER SIZE) IN INCHES	TYPE OF PAPER	EDITION NUMBER	NO. OF COLORS	ORIGINAL OPENING PRICE	CURRENT RETAIL PRICE
CURRENT EDITIONS:										
Noon	TAI	AA	1982	LC	22 X 30	SOM	150		350	600
Madrigal II	TAI	AA	1982	LC	26 X 35	SOM	150		350	600
Point to Point	TG	SR/HRE	1984	EC	26 X 40	GE	50		900	1500

ROBERT REMSEN VICKREY

BORN: New York, NY; August 20, 1926
EDUCATION: Yale Univ, New Haven, CT, BA; Yale Sch of Fine Arts, New Haven, CT, MFA; Art Students League, NY
AWARDS: Am Audubon Artists Award; Newton Mem Award
COLLECTIONS: Brooklyn Mus, NY; Metropolitan Mus, NY; Whitney Mus of Am Art, NY; Corcoran Art Gallery, Wash, DC; Butler Inst of Am Art, Youngstown, OH; Mus Arte Mod, Rio de Janeiro, Brazil; Nat Mus of Am Art, Wash, DC
PRINTERS: Marcia Brown, Albuquerque, NM (MB); Tamarind Inst, Albuquerque, NM (TI)
PUBLISHERS: Tamarind Inst, Albuquerque, NM (TI)
GALLERIES: Hirschl & Adler Gallery, New York, NY; Tamarind Inst, Albuquerque, NM; Harmon-Meek Gallery, Naples, FL; PS Galleries, Dallas, TX & Ogunquit, ME; ACA Galleries, New York, NY; Midtown Galleries, New York, NY; Kennedy Gallery, New York, NY; Munson Galleries, Chatham, MA & Santa Fe, NM; Foster Harmon Galleries of American Art, Sarasota, FL; Harmon-Meek Third Street Gallery, Harbor Springs, MI
MAILING ADDRESS: Box 445, Orleans, MA 02653

Robert Remsen Vickrey
Wooden Ponies
Courtesy Tamarind Institute

TITLE	PUBLISHER	PRINTER	DATE	MEDIUM	DIMENSION (PAPER SIZE) IN INCHES	TYPE OF PAPER	EDITION NUMBER	NO. OF COLORS	ORIGINAL OPENING PRICE	CURRENT RETAIL PRICE
SOLD OUT EDITIONS (RARE):										
Sister Mariposa	TI	MB/TI	1983	LC	25 X 19	R/BFK	40	6	500	500
Wooden Ponies	TI	MB/TI	1983	LC	22 X 28	R/BFK	40	4	500	500

RICARDO VIERA

BORN: Ciego de Avila, Cuba; December 15, 1945; US Citizen
EDUCATION: Boston Mus Sch, MA, 1972; Tufts Univ, Boston, MA, BFA, 1973; Rhode Island Sch of Design, Providence, RI, MFA, 1974
TEACHING: Lehigh Univ, Bethlehem, PA, 1974 to present
AWARDS: Cintas Fel, NY, 1974; Lehigh Univ, Noble Robison Award, 1978; Mellon Grant for Faculty Development, Lehigh Univ, 1980,81, Governor's Award for Excellence in the Arts, PA, 1981
COLLECTIONS: Allentown Mus of Art, PA; Cleveland Mus, OH; Canton Art Inst, OH; Lehigh Univ, Bethlehem, PA; Tel Aviv Mus, Israel
PRINTERS: Gary Maurer, Slatington, PA (GM); Maurer Print Shop, Slatington, PA (MPS)
PUBLISHERS: Polmita Enterprises, Bethlehem, PA (PE); Maurer Printmaking Workshop, Slatington, PA (M); Artist (ART)
GALLERIES: Miriam Perlman, Inc, Chicago, IL
MAILING ADDRESS: c/o Dept of Art, Lehigh University, Chandler #17, Bethlehem, PA 18015

TITLE	PUBLISHER	PRINTER	DATE	MEDIUM	DIMENSION (PAPER SIZE) IN INCHES	TYPE OF PAPER	EDITION NUMBER	NO. OF COLORS	ORIGINAL OPENING PRICE	CURRENT RETAIL PRICE
SOLD OUT EDITIONS (RARE):										
The Bale Series, I–X	ART	GM/MPS	1972	LB	22 X 30 EA	AP	50 EA	1 EA	100 EA	800 EA
The Islas Series, I–VIII	ART	GM/MPS	1973	LC/MON	22 X 30 EA	AP	31 EA	8 EA	250 EA	1000 EA
Wallpaper Series, I–VI	ART	GM/MPS	1974	LC	19 X 24 EA	AP	25 EA	7 EA	150 EA	800 EA
Discovery of America, I	ART	GM/MPS	1975	LC/MON	22 X 30	AP	13	10	350 EA	1000 EA

RICARDO VIERA CONTINUED

TITLE	PUBLISHER	PRINTER	DATE	MEDIUM	DIMENSION (PAPER SIZE) IN INCHES	TYPE OF PAPER	EDITION NUMBER	NO. OF COLORS	ORIGINAL OPENING PRICE	CURRENT RETAIL PRICE
SOLD OUT EDITIONS (RARE):										
Rediscovery of America, I–VI	ART	GM/MPS	1976	LC/MON	22 X 30 EA	AP	12 EA	11 EA	300 EA	1000 EA
Palma en Azul	ART	GM/MPS	1980	SP	19 X 25	AP	15	4	175	500
Palma en Rojo	ART	GM/MPS	1980	SP	19 X 25	AP	13	6	185	500
Seis Palmeras en Rojo	ART	GM/MPS	1980	SP	19 X 25	AP	10	8	200	500
Seis Palmeras en Verde	ART	GM/MPS	1980	SP	19 X 25	AP	6	7	175	500
Garabatos	ART	GM/MPS	1981	SP	19 X 25	AP	6	10	275	600
Dos Palmeras en Verde	ART	GM/MPS	1981	SP	19 X 25	AP	13	4	150	450
Dos Palmeras en Azul	ART	GM/MPS	1981	SP	19 X 25	AP	9	4	150	450
Seis Palmas	ART	GM/MPS	1981	SP/MON	19 X 25	AP	9	10	300	600
Palmeras 6	ART	GM/MPS	1981	SP/MON	19 X 25	AP	26	6–12	300	600
Mis Palmas Llevan el Azul en Su Vende (HC)	ART	GM/MPS	1981	SP/MON	20 X 26	AP	2	1–6	200	500

VELOY VIGIL

BORN: Denver, CO; March 5, 1931
EDUCATION: Colorado Inst of Art, Denver, CO; Denver Art Acad, CO
AWARDS: Winslow Homer Mem Award, Springfield Art Mus, MO, 1970; Franklin Murphy Award, Ankrum Gallery, Los Angeles, CA, 1972; Avery Mem Award, Heard Mus, Phoenix, AZ, 1976; Texas Fine Arts Assn Award, Laguna Gloria Mus, Austin, TX
RECENT EXHIB: Retrosp, Millicent Rogers Mus, Taos, NM, 1988; Ontario Mus of Art, CA, 1989; Smithsonian Inst, Wash, DC, 1990
COLLECTIONS: Colorado Springs Fine Arts Center, CA; Heard Mus, Phoenix, AZ; Mus of the American Indian, NY
PRINTERS: Michael Vigil, Taos, NM (MV); Daniel J Vigil, Taos, NM (DJV); Ricardo C Ximenes, Taos, NM (RCX); John Bates, Taos, NM (NB); William Lynn Coffin, Taos, NM (WLC); Peter Igo, Taos, NM (PI); Wally Young, Taos, NM (WY); Elven Harvey, Jr, Taos, NM (EH); Jeanne E Noordsy, Taos, NM (JEN); Graphics Impressions, Taos, NM (GImp); El Cerro Graphics, Los Lunas, NM (ECG)
PUBLISHERS: Vigil Graphics, Taos, NM (VG)
GALLERIES: Gallery Elena, Taos, NM; Suzanne Brown Gallery, Scottsdale, AZ; Gallery Ellington, Wichita, KS; M R Schweitzer Fine Art, New York, NY; JRS Fine Art, Providence, RI; Spaightwood Gallery, Madison, WI
MAILING ADDRESS: P O Box 2934, Taos, NM 87571

Veloy Vigil
Caballo Dos
Courtesy the Artist

TITLE	PUBLISHER	PRINTER	DATE	MEDIUM	DIMENSION (PAPER SIZE) IN INCHES	TYPE OF PAPER	EDITION NUMBER	NO. OF COLORS	ORIGINAL OPENING PRICE	CURRENT RETAIL PRICE
CURRENT EDITIONS:										
Red Sour	VG	MV/DJV/VG	1986	COL	32 X 27	AP/W	65	11	550	550
Kiva Prayer, State I	VG	RCX/VG	1986	EB/MON	23 X 25	AP/W	30	10	600	600
First Candle, State II	VG	RCX/VG	1986	EB/MON	30 X 24	AP/W	20	8	600	1200
Entering Hunt	VG	JB/WLC/VG	1987	LC	22 X 15	AP/W	125	12	600	600
Big Hunt	VG	JB/WLC/VG	1987	LC	22 X 18	AP	125	7	500	500
Good Medicine	VG	JB/WLC/VG	1987	LC/EMB	17 X 24	R/BFK	125	7	600	600
Yellow Path, State I	VG	PI/VG	1987	SP	22 X 30	MAG	65	9	950	950
Fossil	VG	DJV/WY/VG	1987	LC	30 X 22	AP/B	30	6	550	550
Bird Dance	VG	DJV/EH/VG	1988	LC	22 X 30	AP/W	80	12	600	600
Wind Spirit Wind	VG	DJV/EH/VG	1988	LC	15 X 22	AP/B	65	12	500	500
Mujeres de Talpa	VG	DJV/VG	1989	LC/WC	13 X 30	AP/W	65	10	1200	1200
Strings of Color	VG	DJV/VG	1989	LC	26 X 19	HMP	10	7	1000	1000
Paloma India	VG	EH/JEN/VG	1989	EB/MON	14 X 42	AP/W	10	10	1200	1200
Dos Cruces	VG	JB/WLC/VG	1989	LC/EMB	18 X 24	AP/W	125	8	600	600
Fire Wind	VG	DJV/EH/JEN/VG	1989	LC/WC	22 X 28	AP/W	65	14	600	600
Caballo Dos	VG	EH/JEN/VG	1989	COL/HC	46 X 32	AP/W	65	20	2500	2800

The retail prices of the 100,000 limited edition prints quoted in this directory are subject to change. Print publishers, artists and galleries were the direct sources for these quotations. Prices in the secondary market listed as "Sold Out Editions (Rare)" indicate that the publisher has a limited supply of that print or that the print is difficult to locate in the galleries.

The Printworld Directory is accepting new applications for the seventh edition. Approximately 300 new artists will be accepted. Please use the two forms provided in the back section of this directory to submit biographical data and documentation of prints. Edition number of each print must not exceed 500 and the retail price must be $100 or more.

VELLO VINN

BORN: Estonia, USSR; 1939
EDUCATION: Tallinn Art Inst, USSR, 1963–68
COLLECTIONS: Cremona Foundation, Wash, DC
PRINTERS: Artist (ART)
PUBLISHERS: Artist (ART)
GALLERIES: International Images, Ltd, Sewickley, PA

TITLE	PUBLISHER	PRINTER	DATE	MEDIUM	DIMENSION (PAPER SIZE) IN INCHES	TYPE OF PAPER	EDITION NUMBER	NO. OF COLORS	ORIGINAL OPENING PRICE	CURRENT RETAIL PRICE
CURRENT EDITIONS:										
Time I	ART	ART	1972	EB	19 X 25	LP	20	1	380	600
Forest I	ART	ART	1975	EB	20 X 19	LP	20	1	275	450
Tubes I, II	ART	ART	1975	EB	19 X 25 EA	LP	20 EA	1 EA	325 EA	550 EA
Clock III	ART	ART	1976	EB	19 X 19	LP	20	1	275	450
Album	ART	ART	1976	EB	19 X 25	LP	20	1	325	550
Flight	ART	ART	1977	EB	19 X 19	LP	20	1	275	450
The Shift	ART	ART	1977	EB	19 X 25	LP	20	1	380	600
Shift II	ART	ART	1978	EB	19 X 25	LP	55	1	380	600

NOT VITAL

BORN: Sent, Switzerland; 1948
EDUCATION: Centre Universitaire Experimental de Vincennes, Paris, France, 1968–71
RECENT EXHIB: Kunstmuseum, Luzern, Switzerland, 1988; Swiss Inst, NY, 1988; Centre of Arts in Zamalek, Cairo, Egypt, 1989; Galerie Montenay, Paris, France, 1989; Baron/Boisante, NY, 1989; Musée Rath, Geneva, Switzerland, 1989; Rudolph Zwirner, Cologne, West Germany, 1987,90; P S Gallery, Tokyo, Japan, 1990; Ascan Crone Gallery, NY, 1988,90; Curt Marcus Gallery, NY, 1992; Galerie Lehman, Lausanne, Switzerland, 1993
COLLECTIONS: Mus of Mod Art, NY; Brooklyn Mus, NY; Carnegie Inst, Pittsburgh, PA; Guggenheim Mus, NY; Israel Mus, Tele Tel Aviv, Israel; Kunstmuseum, Glarus, Switzerland; Kunstmuseum, St Gallen, Switzerland; Buedner Kunstmuseum, Chur, Switzerland
PRINTERS: Donna Shulman, Brooklyn, NY (DS); Downstairs Editions, Brooklyn, NY (DE); Harlan & Weaver Intaglio, NY (HWI)
PUBLISHERS: Mark Baron, NY (MB); Baron/Boisante Editions, NY (B/BE); Piero Crommelynck, Paris, France (PC)
GALLERIES: Curt Marcus Gallery, New York, NY; Rick Jones Modern & Contemporary Art, St Louis, MO; Mendelson Gallery, Pittsburgh, PA

Not Vital
Snowblind
Courtesy Baron/Boisanté Editions

TITLE	PUBLISHER	PRINTER	DATE	MEDIUM	DIMENSION (PAPER SIZE) IN INCHES	TYPE OF PAPER	EDITION NUMBER	NO. OF COLORS	ORIGINAL OPENING PRICE	CURRENT RETAIL PRICE
CURRENT EDITIONS:										
Notes (Set of 7)	MB	DS/DE	1986	EB/A/DPT	18 X 15 EA	FAB	19 EA			
Snowblind (7 Parts):					12 X 132 total				5000 SET	7500 SET
A	B/BE	DS/DE	1987	A/REL/ PHE/MON	34 X 27	FAB	23	1	XXX	XXX
B	B/BE	DS/DE	1987	A/REL/ PHE/MON	18 X 14	FAB	23	1	XXX	XXX
C	B/BE	DS/DE	1987	A/REL/ PHE/MON	18 X 14	FAB	23	1	XXX	XXX
D	B/BE	DS/DE	1987	A/REL/ PHE/MON	18 X 14	FAB	23	1	XXX	XXX
E	B/BE	DS/DE	1987	A/REL/ PHE/MON	18 X 14	FAB	23	1	XXX	XXX
F	B/BE	DS/DE	1987	A/REL/ PHE/MON	8 X 6	FAB	23	1	XXX	XXX
G	B/BE	DS/DE	1987	A/REL/ PHE/MON	24 X 12	FAB	23	1	XXX	XXX
Tongue (Signed in 4 Tongues- Swiss, Hebrew, Arabic & Thai)	B/BE	HWI	1990	A/LG	43 X 43	SOM/S	18		1000	1200
El Maktoub Maktoub (What is Written is Written) (5 Parts)	B/BE-PC	PC/AtPC	1990	EB/A	14 X 13 EA 87 X 15 TOT	R/BFK	48		5000	5000

MAI VO-DINH

BORN: Hue, Vietnam; November 14, 1933; U S Citizen
EDUCATION: Sorbonne, Paris, France, 1956; Acad de La Grande Chaumiere, Paris, France; Ecole Nat Superieure des Beaux-Arts, Paris, France, 1959
TEACHING: Instr, Watercolor, Painting, Hood Col, MD, 1978–79; Art in Res, Maryland State Council on the Arts, 1985,86,87,90,92
AWARDS: Christopher Award, NY, 1975; Nat Endowment for the Arts Fel, 1984
RECENT EXHIB: George Mason Univ, Fairfax, VA, 1987; Les Jardina du Boisé, Montreal, Canada, 1992
COLLECTIONS: Mus de Rouen, Rouen, France; Milwaukee Art Center, WI; Nashville Mus, TN; Univ of Hue, Vietnam; Fairleigh Dickinson Univ, Rutherford, NJ; Washington County Mus of Fine Arts, MD; The Art Coll of Auroville, Pondicherry, India; Mus d'Art Mod de la Ville, Paris, France; Schiedam Mus, The Netherlands
PRINTERS: Artist (ART)
PUBLISHERS: Artist (ART)
MAILING ADDRESS: Stonevale, Box 425, Burkittsville, MD 21718

TITLE	PUBLISHER	PRINTER	DATE	MEDIUM	DIMENSION (PAPER SIZE) IN INCHES	TYPE OF PAPER	EDITION NUMBER	NO. OF COLORS	ORIGINAL OPENING PRICE	CURRENT RETAIL PRICE
CURRENT EDITIONS:										
Stonevale, Snowy Evening	ART	ART	1980	WB	11 X 20	AP	75	1	100	250
Bird & Image	ART	ART	1980–81	WC	11 X 20	AP	100	2	125	300
The Yellow Mountain	ART	ART	1981	WC	11 X 20	AP	125	4	150	300
A Tree in the Night	ART	ART	1981	WC	9 X 18	AP	100	3	125	250
Clouds over Mountain	ART	ART	1984	WC	14 DIA	AP	100	1	150	250

HILDA APPEL VOLKIN

BORN: Boston, MA; September 24, 1933
EDUCATION: Massachusetts Col of Art, BS, 1954; Radcliffe Col, Cambridge, MA, MA, 1956
TEACHING: Univ of New Mexico, Los Alamos, NM, 1974 to present
COLLECTIONS: Cleveland Mus of Art, OH; Albuquerque Mus, NM; Univ of New Mexico Mus, Albuquerque, NM; Massillon Mus, OH
PRINTERS: Artist (ART)
PUBLISHERS: Artist (ART)
GALLERIES: Munson Gallery, Santa Fe, NM; Gallery A, Taos, NM; Conway Art Gallery, Albuquerque, NM; Wenniger Graphics Gallery, Boston, MA
MAILING ADDRESS: 8421 Aztec Rd, NE, Albuquerque, NM 87111

TITLE	PUBLISHER	PRINTER	DATE	MEDIUM	DIMENSION (PAPER SIZE) IN INCHES	TYPE OF PAPER	EDITION NUMBER	NO. OF COLORS	ORIGINAL OPENING PRICE	CURRENT RETAIL PRICE
SOLD OUT EDITIONS (RARE):										
Three Views of Pedernal	ART	ART	1977	SP	20 X 25	R/BFK	14	5	150	300
Moon Lit Rio	ART	ART	1980	SP	29 X 30	R/BFK	5	5	300	400
Road to Espanola	ART	ART	1980	SP	14 X 50	R/BFK	18	5	200	300
CURRENT EDITIONS:										
Mesa Shapes	ART	ART	1977	SP	20 X 20	R/BFK	20	5	150	250
Truchas Peaks	ART	ART	1977	SP	21 X 32	AP	20	5	200	300
Early Morning Mesa	ART	ART	1977	SP	21 X 28	R/BFK	50	6	200	300
Truchas Peaks—Near & Far	ART	ART	1978	SP	20 X 32	R/BFK	20	4	200	300
Three Views of Landscape I	ART	ART	1979	SP	31 X 21	R/BFK	25	4	200	300
White Rock Canyon	ART	ART	1980	SP	20 X 27	R/BFK	12	4	200	300
Rio Sand Bars—Albuquerque Bosque	ART	ART	1980	SP	24 X 30	R/BFK	15	6	200	300
River and Road to Taos	ART	ART	1980	SP	28 X 16	R/BFK	14	4	200	300
Chamlzai—The Shifting Rio	ART	ART	1980	SP	37 X 16	R/BFK	13	8	300	400
Elephant Butte	ART	ART	1982	SP	18 X 18	R/BFK	8	6	350	400

STEPHAN VON HUENE

BORN: Los Angeles, CA; September 15, 1932
EDUCATION: Pasadena City Col, 1950–52; Univ of California, Los Angeles, CA, MA, 1952–53; 1963–65; Chouinard Art Inst, BFA, 1955–59
TEACHING: California Inst of Art, Valencia, CA, 1971, Assoc Dean, 1972–76; Acting Dean, 1976–77
AWARDS: Nat Endowment Grant, 1974; Deutscher Akad Austauschdienst, Berlin Grant, 1976; Media Arts Award, Center for Art & Media Tech, Karlsruhe, Germany, 1992
RECENT EXHIB: Künstlerhaus Wien, Vienna, Austria, 1987; Kölnischer Kunstverein, Cologne, West Germany, 1987; Galerie Alfred Kren, Cologne, West Germany & NY, 1987
COLLECTIONS: Los Angeles County Mus of Art, CA; Pasadena Art Mus, CA; Southwestern Col, Chula Vista, CA; Whitney Mus of Am Art, NY; Exploratorium, San Francisco, CA
PRINTERS: Cirrus Editions Workshop, Los Angeles, CA (CEW)
PUBLISHERS: Cirrus Editions, Los Angeles, CA (CE)
GALLERIES: Cirrus Editions, Ltd, Los Angeles, CA
MAILING ADDRESS: California Inst of Arts, 24700 McBean Parkway, Valencia, CA 91355

TITLE	PUBLISHER	PRINTER	DATE	MEDIUM	DIMENSION (PAPER SIZE) IN INCHES	TYPE OF PAPER	EDITION NUMBER	NO. OF COLORS	ORIGINAL OPENING PRICE	CURRENT RETAIL PRICE
SOLD OUT EDITIONS (RARE):										
Untitled (#27)	CE	CEW	1972	LC	24 X 30	CP/D	45	1	250	500
Untitled (#29)	CE	CEW	1972	LC	24 X 30	CP/D	45	1	250	500
Untitled (#75)	CE	CEW	1972	LC	22 X 30	AP	40	3	300	500

FRANK WAHLE

PRINTERS: Matthias Kleindienst, Leipzig, Germany (MK)
PUBLISHERS: Edition M, Leipzig, Germany (EdM)

TITLE	PUBLISHER	PRINTER	DATE	MEDIUM	DIMENSION (PAPER SIZE) IN INCHES	TYPE OF PAPER	EDITION NUMBER	NO. OF COLORS	ORIGINAL OPENING PRICE	CURRENT RETAIL PRICE
CURRENT EDITIONS:										
Papagallos I-IV (Set of 4)	EdM	MK	1992	LI	34 X 43 EA	LANA	20 EA	1 EA	DM 700 SET	DM 700 SET

THEODORE WADDELL

BORN: Billings, MT; October 6, 1941
EDUCATION: Brooklyn Mus Art Sch, NY, 1962; Eastern Montana Col, Billings, MT; BS, 1966; Wayne State Univ, Detroit, MI, MFA, 1968
RECENT EXHIB: Hockaday Center of the Arts, Kalispell, MT, 1989,92
COLLECTIONS: Sheldon Mem Art Gallery, Univ of Nebraska, Lincoln, NE; Eastern Mount Col, Billings, MT; Yellowstone Art Center, Billings, MT, City of Great Falls, MT
PRINTERS: Andrew Saftel, San Francisco, CA (AS); John Stemmer, San Francisco, CA (JS); Experimental Workshop, San Francisco, CA (EW); Cirrus Editions Workshop, Los Angeles, CA (CEW); Richard Hammond, Los Angeles, CA (RH)
PUBLISHERS: Experimental Workshop, San Francisco, CA (EW); Cirrus Editions, Ltd, Los Angeles, CA (CE)
GALLERIES: Stephen Wirtz Gallery, San Francisco, CA; Cantor Lemberg Gallery, Birmingham, MI; Cirrus Gallery, Los Angeles, CA; Munson Gallery, Santa Fe, NM & Vero Beach, FL; Stremmel Gallery, Reno, NV; Experimental Workshop, San Francisco, CA; Young Gallery, Los Gatos, CA; Images . . . a Gallery, San Francisco, CA; Gallery 44, Boulder, CO; Anne Reed Gallery, Ketchum, ID; Jan Cicero Gallery, Chicago, IL; Leedy-Voulkos Gallery, Kansas City, MO; Bernice Steinbaum Gallery, New York, NY; Linda Hodges Gallery, Seattle, WA

TITLE	PUBLISHER	PRINTER	DATE	MEDIUM	DIMENSION (PAPER SIZE) IN INCHES	TYPE OF PAPER	EDITION NUMBER	NO. OF COLORS	ORIGINAL OPENING PRICE	CURRENT RETAIL PRICE
CURRENT EDITIONS:										
Angus I, State I	CE	RH/CEW	1985	LC	22 X 28	AC/W	45	4	450	500
Angus I, State II	CE	RH/CEW	1985	LC	22 X 28	AC/W	20	3	500	550
Longhorn, State I	CE	RH/CEW	1985	LC	22 X 28	AC/W	45	4	400	500
Longhorn, State II	CE	RH/CEW	1985	LC	22 X 28	AC/W	20	3	450	550
Untitled (Series of 8)	EW	EW	1985	MON	25 X 30 EA	R/BFK	1 EA	MULTI	650 EA	700 EA
Beresford I, II, III	EW	AS/EW	1986	DPT/HC	16 X 13 EA	R/BFK	13 EA	MULTI	450 EA	500 EA
Wind Series	EW	AS/JS/EW	1986	MON	25 X 31 EA	R/BFK	1 EA	MULTI	750 EA	800 EA

PAUL WALDMAN

BORN: Erie, PA; August 1, 1936
EDUCATION: Brooklyn Mus Art Sch, NY; Pratt Inst, NY
TEACHING: Instr, Greenwich Art Center, CT, Spring, 1963; Instr, New York Community Col, NY, 1963–64; Instr, Brooklyn Mus Art Sch, NY, 1963–67; Instr, Sch of Visual Arts, NY, 1966 to present
AWARDS: Ford Found Fel, Artist in residence, 1965
RECENT EXHIB: Farideh Cadot Gallery, Paris, France, 1987,88; Phyllis Kind Gallery, Chicago, IL, 1988; Leo Castelli Gallery, NY, 1988
COLLECTIONS: Mus of Mod Art, NY; Brooklyn Mus, NY; Los Angeles County Mus of Mod Art, CA; Hirshhorn Mus, Wash, DC; Smithsonian Inst, Wash, DC; Rhode Island Sch of Design, Providence, RI; Rutgers Univ, New Brunswick, NJ; State Univ of New York, Stony Brook, NY; Mount Holyoke Col, South Hadley, MA; Univ of Massachusetts, Amherst, MA; Massachusetts Inst of Technology, Cambridge, MA; John Hopkins Univ, Baltimore, MD; Colgate Univ, Hamilton, NY; Colby Col, Waterville, ME; Fairleigh Dickinson Col, Rutherford, NJ; Newark Mus, NJ; Solomon R Guggenheim Mus, NY; Tomasulo Gallery, Union Col, NY; White Mus, Ithaca, NY; Finch Col Mus; Fairleigh Dickinson Univ, Rutherford, NJ; Fogg Art Mus, Harvard Univ, Cambridge, MA; Palace of the Legion of Honor, Achenbach Found, CA; Nelson Gallery of Art, Atkins Mus, Kansas City, MO; Univ of Rochester, Mem Art Gallery, NY; Rose Art Mus, Brandeis Univ, Waltham, MA; Storm King Art Center, Mountainville, NY; Des Moines Mus, IA; Pasadena Mus, CA; Russell Sage Col, Troy, NY; Yale Univ Art Gallery, New Haven, CT; Mus of Fine Arts, Houston, TX; La Jolla Art Mus, CA; Dartmouth Col, Hanover, NH; Toledo Mus, OH; Jewitt Art Center, Wellesley Col, WA; Denver Art Mus, CO; Louisiana Mus, Copenhagen, Denmark; Allen Mem Art Mus, Oberlin Col, OH; Baltimore Mus of Art, MD; Norbyllands Kunstmuseum, Aalborg, Denmark; Fort Lauderdale Mus, FL; Carnegie Mus, Pittsburgh, PA; Mem Art Gallery, Univ of Rochester, NY; DeCordova Mus, Lincoln, MA; Dallas Mus of Fine Arts, TX; Vassar Col, Poughkeepsie, NY; Weatherspoon Art Gallery, Univ of North Carolina, Greensboro, NC
PRINTERS: Styria Studio, NY (SS)
PUBLISHERS: Castelli Graphics, NY (CG); Multiples, NY (M); Styria Studio, NY (SS)
GALLERIES: Styria Studio, New York, NY; Marian Goodman, New York, NY; Phyllis Kind Gallery, Chicago, IL & New York, NY; Leo Castelli Gallery, New York, NY
MAILING ADDRESS: Dept of Fine Arts, School of Visual Arts, 209–213 E 23rd St, New York, NY 10010

TITLE	PUBLISHER	PRINTER	DATE	MEDIUM	DIMENSION (PAPER SIZE) IN INCHES	TYPE OF PAPER	EDITION NUMBER	NO. OF COLORS	ORIGINAL OPENING PRICE	CURRENT RETAIL PRICE
CURRENT EDITIONS:										
Ballatine	CG		1975	LC	30 X 23	AP	50		450	800
Toiny's Lunch	CG		1975	LC	22 X 30	AP	52		450	800
Diane's Sit-up	M		1979	LC	25 X 40	AP	20		650	900
Sectional II	SS	SS	1984	SP	37 X 51	AP	50	11	1200	1500

PAUL WALDUM

BORN: Livingston, MT
EDUCATION: Montana State Univ, Boseman, MT
COLLECTIONS: Kensington Fine Art Galleries, Calgary, Alberta, Canada
PUBLISHERS: C G Rein Publishers, St Paul, MN (CGR)
GALLERIES: C G Rein Galleries, Scottsdale, AZ & Santa Fe, NM & Houston, TX & Minneapolis, MN

TITLE	PUBLISHER	PRINTER	DATE	MEDIUM	DIMENSION (PAPER SIZE) IN INCHES	TYPE OF PAPER	EDITION NUMBER	NO. OF COLORS	ORIGINAL OPENING PRICE	CURRENT RETAIL PRICE
SOLD OUT EDITIONS (RARE):										
Waterton Lake	CGR	ART	1985	SP	30 X 43	AP88	95	18	400	575
Deep Creek Evening	CGR	ART	1985	SP	30 X 43	AP88	95	12	400	575
Evening Light—St Mary Lake	CGR	ART	1986	SP	30 X 43	AP88	95	12	400	575
CURRENT EDITIONS:										
Sheep Mountain	CGR	ART	1985	SP	22 X 30	AP88	110		250	440
Gallatin River	CGR	ART	1985	SP	22 X 30	AP88	95	14	350	520
Lake McDonald	CGR	ART	1985	SP	22 X 30	AP88	115	15	350	400
Snake River	CGR	ART	1986	SP	30 X 43	AP88	95	13	400	475
Emigrant and Chico Peaks	CGR	ART	1986	SP	30 X 43	AP88	95	19	400	575
Mallard's Rest	CGR	ART	1987	SP	30 X 43	AP88	95		400	450

CLAY WALKER

BORN: Middlesboro, KY; July 28, 1924
EDUCATION: Ecole des Beaux Artes, Paris, France, 1946; Univ of Toledo, OH, BA, 1947–50; Kent State Univ, OH, MA, 1958–60; Ohio Univ, Athens, OH, 1964
TEACHING: Sam Houston State Univ, Huntsville, TX, 1960–61; Art Dir, San Antonio Art Inst, TX, 1962–63; Long Beach State Col, CA, 1963; Teaching Fel, Ohio Univ, Athens, OH, 1964; Chouinard Art Inst, Los Angeles, CA, 1965,67,68
AWARDS: Purchase Award, Library of Congress, Wash, DC; Mildred Boericke Award, Nat Print Exhib, Phila, PA; Thomas Flaxman Award, Dayton Art Mus, OH; Graphic Arts Award, Philbrook Mus, Tulsa, OK; Purchase Award, Butler Inst of Am Art, Youngstown, OH
COLLECTIONS: Toledo Mus, OH; Philadelphia Mus, PA; Houston Mus of Fine Arts, TX; Detroit Inst, MI; Butler Inst of Am Art, Youngstown, OH; San Francisco Mus of Mod Art, CA; J B Speed Mus, Louisville, KY; Philbrook Mus, Tulsa, OK; Jerusalem Art Mus, Israel; Library of Congress, Wash, DC
PUBLISHERS: Lone Oak Press, Escondido, CA (LOP)
PRINTERS: Lone Oak Press, Escondido, CA (LOP)
GALLERIES: Art Center Gallery, Des Moines, IA; Dana Gallery, San Diego, CA
MAILING ADDRESS: 11660 Turner Heights Drive, Escondido, CA 92025

TITLE	PUBLISHER	PRINTER	DATE	MEDIUM	DIMENSION (PAPER SIZE) IN INCHES	TYPE OF PAPER	EDITION NUMBER	NO. OF COLORS	ORIGINAL OPENING PRICE	CURRENT RETAIL PRICE
SOLD OUT EDITIONS (RARE):										
Agony on the Border	LOP	LOP	1962	WC	34 X 25	MUL	10	5	90	2000
CURRENT EDITIONS:										
Colored Head Wearing Horses Scull	LOP	LOP	1977	COL/I	21 X 25	ROSA	30	6	100	300
Lola as Lola	LOP	LOP	1977	COL	37 X 26	R/BFK	20	4	150	450
St Sebastian	LOP	LOP	1978	LIN	22 X 30	TIEP	20	7	125	350
Birds	LOP	LOP	1978	WC	25 X 32	MUL	15	5	100	300
One is Enough	LOP	LOP	1978	WC	22 X 30	MUL	100	7	100	350
Cayote	LOP	LOP	1986	WC	25 X 35	KOZO	50	1	350	400
Aldebaran	LOP	LOP	1986	WC	36 X 25	OKP	20	6	350	400

WILLIAM AUBREY WALMSLEY

BORN: Tuscumbia, AL; October 9, 1923
EDUCATION: Univ of Alabama, Birmingham, AL, BFA, 1951, MFA, 1953; Art Students League, NY; Acad Julian, Paris, France; Tamarind Lithography Workshop, Los Angeles, CA
TEACHING: Prof, Lithog, Florida State Univ, Tallahassee, FL, 1962; Visiting Artist, Lithog, Northern Illinois Univ, Dekalb, IL, Summer, 1973; Visiting Artist, Lithog, Penland Sch for Crafts, Spruce Pine, NC, Summers, 1975,77
AWARDS: Purchase Award, Colorprint USA, Texas Tech, Lubbock, TX, 1972; Purchase Award, Potsdam Prints, NY, 1972; Purchase Award, Annual Calgary Graphic Exhib, Canada, 1972
COLLECTIONS: Mus of Mod Art, NY; Tate Gallery, London, England; Hawaii Acad of Art, Honolulu, HI; Ohio State Univ, Columbus, OH; Library of Congress, Wash, DC
PRINTERS: Wayne Kline, Atlanta, GA (WK); Sarah Shortt, Atlanta, GA (SS); William Holton, Atlanta, GA (WH); Rolling Stone Press, Atlanta, GA (RSP)
PUBLISHERS: Rolling Stone Press, Atlanta, GA (RSP)
MAILING ADDRESS: c/o Art Department, Studio Art, Florida State University, Tallahassee, FL 32306

TITLE	PUBLISHER	PRINTER	DATE	MEDIUM	DIMENSION (PAPER SIZE) IN INCHES	TYPE OF PAPER	EDITION NUMBER	NO. OF COLORS	ORIGINAL OPENING PRICE	CURRENT RETAIL PRICE
CURRENT EDITIONS:										
Ding Dong Daddy Half & Half	RSP	WK/SS/WH/RSP	1990	LC	30 X 38	R/BFK	53	7	1250	1250

ERNEST WALTERS

BORN: Elizabethtown, KY; November 11, 1927
EDUCATION: Univ of Louisville, KY; Univ of Miami, FL; Towson State Univ, Towson, MD; Studio Art Sch, Paris, France
COLLECTIONS: Mus of Mod Art, NY; Israel Mus, Jerusalem, Israel; Kunstmuseum, Bern, Switzerland; Kunsthaus, Zurich, Switzerland; Stedelijk Mus, Amsterdam, Netherlands; Albertina Mus, Vienna, Austria; Mus d'Art Mod, Brussels, Belgium; Cabinet des Estampes, Brussels, Belgium; Siemens-Overbeck Mus, Lubeck, Germany
PRINTERS: Atelier North Star, Burlington, VT (ANS); Artist (ART)
PUBLISHERS: Glaerie Indiat Vienna, Austria (GI); Daedal Art Publishers, Baltimore, MD (DAP); Artist (ART)
GALLERIES: IFA Galleries, Wash, DC; Galerie Richter, Wiesbaden, Germany; Daedal Fine Arts, Baltimore, MD
MAILING ADDRESS: 257 Foster Knoll Drive, Joppa, MD 21085

TITLE	PUBLISHER	PRINTER	DATE	MEDIUM	DIMENSION (PAPER SIZE) IN INCHES	TYPE OF PAPER	EDITION NUMBER	NO. OF COLORS	ORIGINAL OPENING PRICE	CURRENT RETAIL PRICE
SOLD OUT EDITIONS (RARE):										
Twilight	GI	ART	1966	LB	22 X 30	AP	50	1	100	350
Starflake, I–VIII	ART	ART	1971–76	ENG	6 X 5 EA	STR	175 EA	1 EA	175 SET	500 SET
Imagero	ART	ART	1982	M/HC	18 X 24	AP	25	1	350	400
CURRENT EDITIONS:										
Upswing Screen	ART	ART	1972	SP	20 X 16	STR	20	7	75	200
Floating Screen	ART	ART	1972	SP	16 X 20	STR	20	7	75	200
Post Primary	DAP	ART	1975	SP	20 X 26	STR	20	6	90	200
Blue Screen	DAP	ART	1975	SP	20 X 26	STR	20	7	90	200
Anti-Depth	DAP	ART	1975	SP/HC	20 X 26	STR	40	9	100	200
Les Onze Mille Verges	DAP	ART	1980	MULT/HC	18 X 24	AP	25	7	200	400
Les Douze Mille Verges	DAP	ART	1980	MULT/HC	18 X 24	AP	25	7	200	400
Les Trois Mille Verges	DAP	ART	1982	MULT/HC	18 X 24	AP	25	7	350	400
Angelgate	DAP	ANS	1985	LC/HC	22 X 30	R/BFK	100	6	275	350
Stargate	DAP	ANS	1985	LB	22 X 30	R/BFK	100	1	175	250

ANDY WARHOL

BORN: Cleveland, OH; (1931–1987)
EDUCATION: Carnegie Inst of Technology, Pittsburgh, PA, 1945–49
RECENT EXHIB: Robert Miller Gallery, NY, 1988; Gallery Bruno Bischofberger, Zürich, Switzerland, 1988; Fay Gold Gallery, Atlanta, GA, 1988; Kent Gallery, NY, 1989; Univ of Maine, Orono, ME, 1989; Martin Lawrence Galleries, Phila, PA, 1990; Gagosian Gallery, NY, 1988, 92–93; Gallery Bruno Bischofberger, Zürich, Switzerland, 1993
COLLECTIONS: Mus of Mod Art, NY; Whitney Mus of Am Art, NY; Walker Art Inst, Minneapolis, MN; Albright-Knox Art Gallery, Buffalo, NY; Los Angeles County Mus, CA; Brandeis Univ, Waltham, MA; Nelson Mus, Kansas City, KS
PRINTERS: Total Color, NY (TC); Factory Additions, NY (FA); Racolin Press, Inc, Briarcliff Manor (RPI); ChromaComp, Inc, NY (CCI); Tanglewood Press, Inc, NY (TPr); Editions Bischofberger, Zürich, Switzerland (EdB); Rupert J Smith, NY (RJS); Joe Grippi, NY (JG); Styria Studio, NY (SS)
PUBLISHERS: Wadsworth Atheneum, Hartford, CT (WA); Galerie Börjeson, Malmö, Sweden (GB); Moderna Museet, Stockholm, Sweden (MM/S); Racolin Press, Inc, Briarcliff Manor (RPI); Factory Additions, NY (FA); Castelli Gallery, NY (CG); Multiples, Inc, NY (M); Kass/Meridian Gallery, Chicago, IL (K/M); Peter M Brandt, NY (PMB); Tanglewood Press, Inc, NY (TP); Axel Springer Verlag, Hamburg, Germany (ASV); William Hechter, Toronto, Canada (WH); Gandai Hanga Center, Tokyo, Japan (GHC); George C Mulder, Amsterdam, The Netherlands & NY (GCM); Bruno Bischofberger, Zürich, Switzerland (BB); Inst of Contemp Art, Univ of Pennsylvania, Phila, PA (ICA/UP); Schellmann & Kluser, Munich, Germany & NY (SK); Editions Schellmann, NY (ES); Martha Graham Center of Contemp Dance, Inc, NY (MGCCD); Gaultney-Klineman Art, NY (GKA); Andy Warhol, NY (AW); Ronald Feldman Fine Arts, NY (RFFA); Jonathan A Editions, Tel Aviv, Israel (JAE); Inst of Contemp Art, Boston, MA (ICA/B); Colorado State University (CSU); Luciano Anselmino, Milan, Italy (LA); Friends of Tom Hayden (FTH); Seabird Editions, London, England (SeaEd); Andy Warhol Enterprises, NY (AWE); Michael Zivian, NY (MZ); Denise Rene, Paris, France (DR); Hans Meyer, Paris, France (HM); Fondazione Amelio, Naples, Italy (FAm); Inst of Contemp Art, Naples, Italy (ICA/N); Lucio Amelio, Naples, Italy (LA)
GALLERIES: Andrew Dierken Fine Art, Los Angeles, CA; Michael Kohn Gallery, Los Angeles, CA; Harcourts Contemporary Art, San Francisco, CA; Xiliary Twil Fine Arts, Santa Monica, CA & Venice, CA; Hokin Gallery, Bay Harbor Islands, FL & Palm Beach, FL; Gloria Luria Gallery, Bay Harbor Islands, FL; Marvin Ross Friedman, Miami, FL; Barbara Gillman Gallery, Miami, FL; Kass/Meridian Gallery, Chicago, IL; O'Farrell Gallery, Brunswick, ME; Castelli Graphics, New York, NY; Editions Ilene Kurtz, New York, NY; Martina Hamilton Gallery, New York, NY; Martin Lawrence Galleries, Newport Beach, CA & Palm Springs, CA & Redondo Beach, CA & Santa Clara, CA & Santa Monica, CA & Sherman Oaks, CA & West Los Angeles, CA & Short Hills, NJ & Soho, NY & Phila, PA; Gallery Bruno Bischofberger, Zürich, Switzerland; Fay Gold Gallery, Atlanta, GA; Joy Tash Gallery, Scottsdale, AZ; Charles Whitchurch Fine Arts, Huntington Beach, CA; R K Goldman Contemporary, Los Angeles, CA; Graystone Gallery, San Francisco, CA; Erika Meyerovich Gallery, San Francisco, CA; Acme Art, Santa Monica, CA; Petrini Art Gallery, Rocky Hill, CT; Jupiter Fine Arts, Jupiter, FL; Opus Art Studios, Miami, FL; Donna Rose Galleries, Ketchum, ID; R S Johnson Fine Art, Chicago, IL; Morgan Gallery, Boston, MA

Feldman-Schellmann (F/S)

Andy Warhol
Grace Kelly
Courtesy Institute of Contemporary Art

Andy Warhol
Moon Walk
Courtesy Ronald Feldman Fine Arts, Inc

TITLE	PUBLISHER	PRINTER	DATE	MEDIUM	DIMENSION (PAPER SIZE) IN INCHES	TYPE OF PAPER	EDITION NUMBER	NO. OF COLORS	ORIGINAL OPENING PRICE	CURRENT RETAIL PRICE
SOLD OUT EDITIONS (RARE):										
Love is a Pink Cake (Book)			1953	PH/LC	11 X 9	AP	100		100	3000
Cats Name Sam and One Blue Pussy			1954	LC	9 X 6	AP	190		50	6000
Flash—November 22, 1963 (Set of 11)	RPI	RPI	1963	SP	22 X 21 EA	AP	200		3000 SET	20000 SET
Birmingham Race Riot (F/S-3)	WA		1964	SP	20 X 24	AP	500	1	200	2500
Cagney	CG		1964	SP	30 X 40	AP	5		300	50000
Flowers (Blue)	CG		1964	SP	8 X 8	AP	35		300	6000
Flower (F/S-6)	CG		1964	LC/OFF	22 X 22	AP	300		100	6000
Liz (F/S-7)	CG		1964	LC/OFF	23 X 23	WOVE	300		100	9000
Flowers (Unnumbered Edition) (Fushia & Violet) (Unnumbered Edition)	CG		1964	SP	18 X 24	AP		2	100	6000

ANDY WARHOL CONTINUED

TITLE	PUBLISHER	PRINTER	DATE	MEDIUM	DIMENSION (PAPER SIZE) IN INCHES	TYPE OF PAPER	EDITION NUMBER	NO. OF COLORS	ORIGINAL OPENING PRICE	CURRENT RETAIL PRICE
SOLD OUT EDITIONS (RARE):										
Marilyn Monroe, I Love Your... (2 Sheets)	CG		1964	LC	16 X 23	AP	100		100	6500
S & H Green Stamps (F/S-9)	IC/UP		1965	LC/OFF	23 X 23	AP	300		100	7500
Jackie II (from 11 Pop Artists II) (F/S-14)	OEd	OEd	1966	SP	24 X 30	AP	200		100	10000
Jackie III (Blue & Black)	OEd	OEd	1966	SP	40 X 30	AP	200	2	100	14000
Campbell's Soup Can Shopping Bag (F/S-4a)	ICA/B		1966	SP	24 X 17	AP			100	5000
Kiss (from Seven Objects in a Box)	TPr	TPr	1966	SP	12 X 8 X 6	AP	75		100	7500
Marilyn Monroe (Set of 10)	FA	FA	1967	SP	36 X 36 EA	WOVE	250 EA	5 EA	3500 SET	250000
Stamped Indelibly: Little Cow (Printed in Light Purple)	CG	CCI	1967	SP	10 X 7	AP			100	4500
Self Portrait	CG	CCI	1967	SP	46 X 30	AP	100	3	100	8000
Self Portrait (F/S-16)	CG	TC	1967	SP	22 X 21	SCP	300	1	100	5000
Self Portrait (Yellow)	CG	CCI	1967	SP	10 X 7	AP	300	1	100	10000
Ten from Castelli: Portraits of the Artist (F/S-17) (Set of 10)	CG	TPr	1967	SP	20 X 20 X 1	AP	200		250	35000
Flash-November 22, 1963 (Set of 11) (F/S-32-F/S-42)	RPI	RPI	1968	SP	21 X 21 EA	AP	200 EA		1500 SET	40000 SET
SAS Passenger Ticket (F/S-20)	MM/S		1968	SP	27 X 49	AP	250		200	4500
Campbell's Soup I (Set of 5):									1000 SET	30000 SET
Pepper Pot	RFFA/ES		1968	SP	35 X 23	AP	250		250	6000
Black Bean	RFFA/ES		1968	SP	35 X 23	AP	250		250	6000
Onion	RFFA/ES		1968	SP	35 X 23	AP	250		250	6000
Chicken Noodle	RFFA/ES		1968	SP	35 X 23	AP	250		250	6000
Cream of Mushroom	RFFA/ES		1968	SP	35 X 23	AP	250		250	6000
Campbell's Soup II (Set of 5):									1000 SET	30000 SET
Beef with Vegetables and Barley	RFFA/ES		1968	SP	35 X 23	AP	250		250	6000
Chicken and Dumplings	RFFA/ES		1968	SP	35 X 23	AP	250		250	6000
Cheddar Cheese	RFFA/ES		1968	SP	35 X 23	AP	250		250	6000
Vegetarian Vegetable	RFFA/ES		1968	SP	35 X 23	AP	250		250	6000
Oyster Stew	RFFA/ES		1968	SP	35 X 23	AP	250		250	6000
Flowers (Set of 10) (F/S-64–F/S-73)	FA	FA	1970	SP	36 X 36 EA	AP	250 EA		3000 SET	130000 SET
Brillo (Poster)	ESK		1970	SP	26 X 25	AP		3	100	3000
Electric Chairs (Set of 10)	BB	FA/EdB	1971	SP	36 X 48 EA	WOVE	250 EA	2 EA	4000 SET	45000 SET
Cow (Printed in Blue & Yellow) (F/S-12)	FA	FA	1971	SP	46 X 30	AP	150	2	350	3000
Sunset	FA	FA	1972	SP	34 X 34	AP	632	5	300	10000
Vote McGovern (F/S-84) (G-396)	GEM	GEM	1972	SP	42 X 42	AP	250	16	350	8000
Mao Tse-Tung (Set of 10) (F/S-90–F/S-99)	CG/M	SS	1972	SP	36 X 36 EA	AP	250 EA	5 EA	5000 SET	100000 SET
Mao	CG/M	SS	1974	SP	40 X 30	AP	100	3	350	5000
Flowers (Black & White) (Set of 10)	CG/M/PMB	CCI	1974	SP	41 X 27 EA	AP	100 EA	1 EA	3000 SET	25000 SET
Flowers (Hand Colored) (Set of 10)	CG/M/PMB	CCI	1974	SP/HC	41 X 27 EA	AP	250 EA		5000 SET	60000 SET
Mick Jagger (Set of 10) (F/S-139)	CG/M/PMB	CCI	1975	SP	44 X 29 EA	AP/ROL	250 EA	3 EA	5000 SET	120000 SET
Jimmy Carter (F/S-150) DNC	ASV		1976	SP	39 X 29	STP	50		450	5000
Skulls (Set of 4)	AWE		1976	SP	30 X 40 EA	AP	50 EA		1800 SET	30000 SET
Hammer and Sickle (Set of 4)	AWE		1977	SP	30 X 40 EA	STP	50 EA		2000 SET	12000 SET
Torsos-Ace Gallery Poster	AWE		1977	LC	61 X 42	AP			500	1650
Mohammed Ali (Set of 4)	AWE		1978	SP	40 X 30 EA	STP	150 EA		2400 SET	25000 SET
Gems	AWE		1978	SP	30 X 40	AP	20		500	5000
Merce Cunningham	M		1978	SP	30 X 20	AP	25		750	9500
Grapes (Set of 6)	AWE		1979	SP	40 X 30 EA	AP	50 EA		2500 SET	30000 SET
Space Fruit: Still Lifes (Set of 6)	MZ	RJS/JG	1979	SP	30 X 40 EA	LEN/MB	150 EA		2500 SET	30000 SET
Fiesta Pig (F18-184)	ASV		1979	SP	22 X 31	AP	200		500	8000
Shadows I (with Diamond Dust) (Set of 6)	AWE		1979	SP	43 X 31 EA	AP88	15 EA		2500 SET	15000 SET
Judy Garland & Liza Minelli			1979	SP	49 X 49	AP88			300	8000
Shoes (Set of 5)	AWE		1980	SP	40 X 60 EA	AP	60 EA		4500 SET	75000 SET
Joseph Beuys (Set of 3)	SK		1980	SP/DD	44 X 30 EA	AP	90 EA		4800 SET	45000 SET
Ten Portraits of the Twentieth Century (Set of 10):									12000 SET	45000 SET
Sarah Bernhardt	RFFA/JAE	RJS	1980	SP	40 X 32	LEN/MB	200	12	1350	10000
Louis Brandeis (F/S-230)	RFFA/JAE	RJS	1980	SP	40 X 32	LEN/MB	200	11	1350	6000
Martin Buber (F/s-228)	RFFA/JAE	RJS	1980	SP	40 X 32	LEN/MB	200	10	1350	7000
Albert Einstein	RFFA/JAE	RJS	1980	SP	40 X 32	LEN/MB	200	9	1350	13000
Sigmund Freud (F/S-235)	RFFA/JAE	RJS	1980	SP	40 X 32	LEN/MB	200	11	1350	10000
George Gershwin	RFFA/JAE	RJS	1980	SP	40 X 32	LEN/MB	200	13	1350	8000
Franz Kafka	RFFA/JAE	RJS	1980	SP	40 X 32	LEN/MB	200	11	1350	15000
The Marx Brothers	RFFA/JAE	RJS	1980	SP	40 X 32	LEN/MB	200	21	1350	11000
Golda Meir (F/S-233)	RFFA/JAE	RJS	1980	SP	40 X 32	LEN/MB	200	10	1350	9000
Gertrude Stein (F/S-227)	RFFA/JAE	RJS	1980	SP	40 X 32	LEN/MB	200	12	1350	7000
Still Life after the Party	M		1980	SP	22 X 31	LEN/MB	1000		350	2500

1993/94 PRINTWORLD DIRECTORY OF CONTEMPORARY PRINTS & PRICES

ANDY WARHOL CONTINUED

Andy Warhol
Endangered Species: Bald Eagle
Courtesy Ronald Feldman Fine Arts, Inc

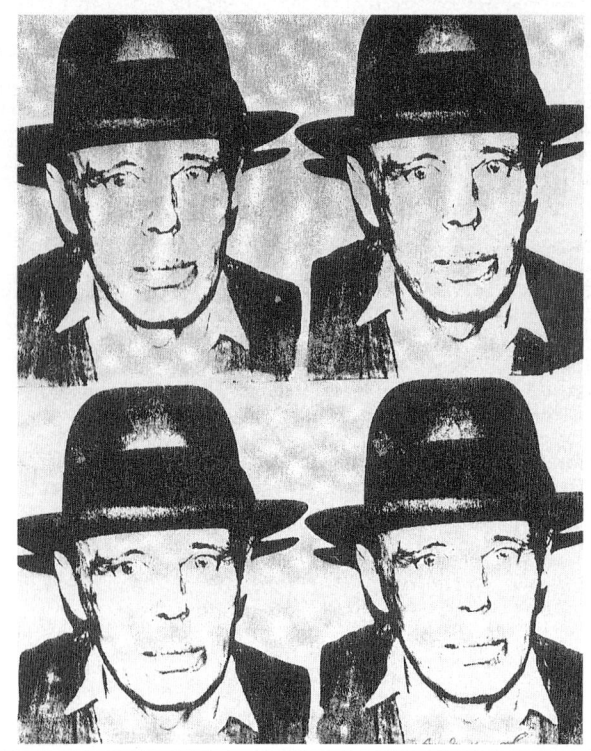

Andy Warhol
from Joseph Beuys Suite
Courtesy Edition Schellmann

TITLE	PUBLISHER	PRINTER	DATE	MEDIUM	DIMENSION (PAPER SIZE) IN INCHES	TYPE OF PAPER	EDITION NUMBER	NO. OF COLORS	ORIGINAL OPENING PRICE	CURRENT RETAIL PRICE
SOLD OUT EDITIONS (RARE):										
Karen Kain (with Diamond Dust) (F/S-236)	WH		1980	SP	40 X 32	LEN/MB	200		1350	8000
Double Mickey Mouse (25 Unique Series)			1981	MON		LEN/MB	1 EA		2000 EA	50000 EA
Myths (with Diamond Dust) (Set of 10):									15000 SET	100000 SET
The Star	RFFA	RJS	1981	SP	38 X 38	LEN/MB	200	10	1500	18000
Uncle Sam (F/S-259)	RFFA	RJS	1981	SP	38 X 38	LEN/MB	200	7	1500	16000
Superman	RFFA	RJS	1981	SP	38 X 38	LEN/MB	200	8	1500	20000
The Witch	RFFA	RJS	1981	SP	38 X 38	LEN/MB	200	8	1500	16000
Mammy	RFFA	RJS	1981	SP	38 X 38	LEN/MB	200	11	1500	16000
Howdy Doody	RFFA	RJS	1981	SP	38 X 38	LEN/MB	200	11	1500	18000
Dracula (F/S-264)	RFFA	RJS	1981	SP	38 X 38	LEN/MB	200	3	1500	16000
Mickey Mouse	RFFA	RJS	1981	SP	38 X 38	LEN/MB	200	8	1500	35000
Santa Claus (F/S-266)	RFFA	RJS	1981	SP	38 X 38	LEN/MB	200	6	1500	12000
The Shadow	RFFA	RJS	1981	SP	38 X 38	LEN/MB	200	3	1500	18000
Marilyn Monroe Poster (Day-Glo)	ESK		1981	LC/OFF	12 X 12	AP	250	5	150	3000
Marilyn	CG	CCI	1981	SP	12 X 12	LEN/MB	500		1000	10000
Ladies and Gentlemen Suite (Set of 10)	LA		1981	SP	44 X 29 EA	AP	125 EA		15000 SET	75000 SET
Kimiko (Portrait of Kimono Powers)	CSU	CSU	1981	SP	36 X 36	STP	250		1000	8000
Jane Fonda	FTH		1982	SP			100		1000	10000
Goethe (Set of 4)	SK/DR/HM		1982	SP	40 X 32 EA	LEN/MB	90 EA		15000 SET	50000 SET
Goethe (Trial Proof)	SK/DR/HM		1982	SP	38 X 38	LEN/MB	1	8	350	25000
Committee 2000	MLLE		1982	SP	30 X 20	AC	2280		300	3500
Brooklyn Bridge	MLLE		1982	SP	39 X 39	AC	265		500	6000
Watercolor Paint Kit with Brushes	MLLE		1982	LC	9 X 12	AC	580		500	3000
$4 (Set of 2)	SK		1982	SP	40 X 32 EA	AC	70 EA	8 EA	500 EA	10000 EA
Alexander the Great	SK		1982	SP	40 X 40	AC		2	500	20000
Chelsea Girls (Eric Emerson)	SK		1982	SP	22 X 30	AC			300	3000
Magazine and History	SK		1983	SP/OFF	34 X 28	AC	500		500	8000
Joseph Beuys Suite (Set of 3):									3500 SET	75000 SET
Black Print on Turquoise Velvet	SK		1980–83	SP	44 X 30	VEL	50	1	1200	25000
Four Colors on Turquoise Velvet	SK		1980–83	SP	44 X 30	VEL	50	4	1200	25000
Rainbow Colors on Turquoise Velvet	SK		1980–83	SP	44 X 30	VEL	50	Multi	1200	25000
Endangered Species (Set of 10):									15000 SET	125000 SET
African Elephant	RFFA	RJS	1983	SP	38 X 38 EA	LEN	150 EA	Multi	2200	10000
Pine Barrens Tree Frog (F/S-294)	RFFA	RJS	1983	SP	38 X 38 EA	LEN	150 EA	Multi	2200	10000
Giant Panda	RFFA	RJS	1983	SP	38 X 38 EA	LEN	150 EA	Multi	2200	12000
Bald Eagle	RFFA	RJS	1983	SP	38 X 38 EA	LEN	150 EA	Multi	2200	12000
Siberian Tiger	RFFA	RJS	1983	SP	38 X 38 EA	LEN	150 EA	Multi	2200	16000

ANDY WARHOL CONTINUED

TITLE	PUBLISHER	PRINTER	DATE	MEDIUM	DIMENSION (PAPER SIZE) IN INCHES	TYPE OF PAPER	EDITION NUMBER	NO. OF COLORS	ORIGINAL OPENING PRICE	CURRENT RETAIL PRICE
SOLD OUT EDITIONS (RARE):										
San Francisco Silverpot (F/S-298)	RFFA	RJS	1983	SP	38 X 38 EA	LEN	150 EA	Multi	2200	10000
Orangutan	RFFA	RJS	1983	SP	38 X 38 EA	LEN	150 EA	Multi	2200	10000
Grevy's Zebra	RFFA	RJS	1983	SP	38 X 38 EA	LEN	150 EA	Multi	2200	14000
Black Rhinoceros	RFFA	RJS	1983	SP	38 X 38 EA	LEN	150 EA	Multi	2200	10000
Bighorn Ram (F/S-302)	RFFA	RJS	1983	SP	38 X 38 EA	LEN	150 EA	Multi	2200	10000
Speed Skater			1983	SP					1000	6000
Kiku (F/S-308)	GHC		1983	SP	20 X 26	LEN	300		1000	4500
Love Suite (Set of 3):									4500 SET	30000 SET
Herself			1983	SP		AP			1500	10000
The Nun			1983	SP		AP			1500	10000
With Hat			1983	SP		AP			1500	10000
Ingrid Bergman Portraits (Set of 3)	GB		1983	SP	38 X 38 EA	AP	250 EA		7500 SET	35000 SET
Grace Kelly (F/S-305)	ICA/UP		1984	SP	40 X 32	LEN/MB	235	Multi	1000	15000
Wayne Gretsky, #99	ICA/UP		1984	SP		LEN/MB	300	Multi	1000	8000
Details of Rennaisance Paintings (3 Portfolios):										
Botticelli: The Birth of Venus (Set of 4)	SK	RJS	1984	SP	33 X 44 EA	AP	60 EA		7000 SET	60000 SET
									2000 EA	15000 EA
Paolo Uccello, St George and the Dragon (Set of 4)	SK	RJS	1984	SP	33 X 44 EA	AP	60 EA	10 EA	7000 SET	28000 SET
									2000 EA	7000 EA
Leonardo da Vince: The Annunciation of the Virgin (Set of 4)	SK	RJS	1984	SP	33 X 44 EA	AP	60 EA	8 EA	7000 SET	32000 SET
									2000 EA	8000 EA
The Only Way Out . . . is In!			1984	SP		SILK			2000	5000
Ads (Set of 10):									15000 SET	75000 SET
Mobil (F/S-350)	RFFA/ES	RJS	1985	SP	38 X 38	LEN/MB	190		2200	7500
Blackgamma (F/S-351)	RFFA/ES	RJS	1985	SP	38 X 38	LEN/MB	190		2200	8500
Paramount (F/S-352)	RFFA/ES	RJS	1985	SP	38 X 38	LEN/MB	190		2200	7500
Life Savers (F/S-353)	RFFA/ES	RJS	1985	SP	38 X 38	LEN/MB	190		2200	7500
Chanel (F/S-354)	RFFA/ES	RJS	1985	SP	38 X 38	LEN/MB	190		2200	10500
Rebel without a Cause (James Dean) (F/S-355)	RFFA/ES	RJS	1985	SP	38 X 38	LEN/MB	190	7	2200	15000
Van Heusen (Ronald Reagan) (F/S-356)	RFFA/ES	RJS	1985	SP	38 X 38	LEN/MB	190		2200	7500
The New Spirit (Donald Duck) (F/S-357)	RFFA/ES	RJS	1985	SP	38 X 38	LEN/MB	190		2200	7500
Volkswagon (F/S-358)	RFFA/ES	RJS	1985	SP	38 X 38	LEN/MB	190		2200	7500
Apple (F/S-359)	RFFA/ES	RJS	1985	SP	38 X 38	LEN/MB	190		2200	7500

Andy Warhol
Cagney
Courtesy Castelli Graphics, Inc

ANDY WARHOL CONTINUED

Andy Warhol
Endangered Species: San Francisco Silverspot
Courtesy Ronald Feldman Fine Arts, Inc

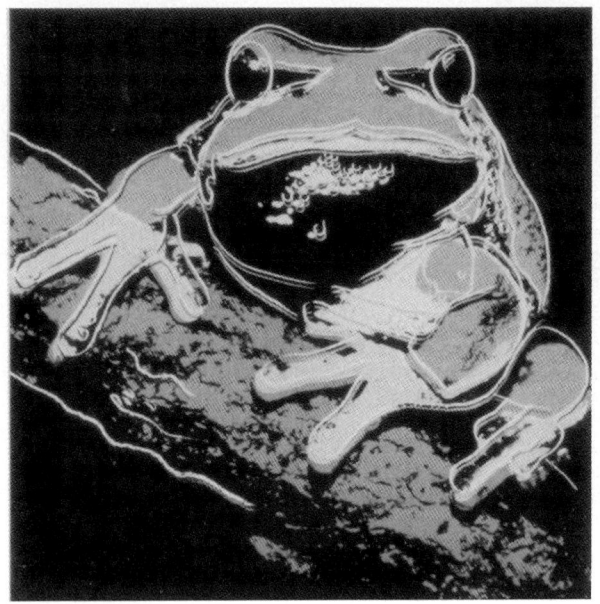

Andy Warhol
Endangered Species: Pine Barrens Tree Frog
Courtesy Ronald Feldman Fine Arts, Inc

TITLE	PUBLISHER	PRINTER	DATE	MEDIUM	DIMENSION (PAPER SIZE) IN INCHES	TYPE OF PAPER	EDITION NUMBER	NO. OF COLORS	ORIGINAL OPENING PRICE	CURRENT RETAIL PRICE
SOLD OUT EDITIONS (RARE):										
Reigning Queens Suite (Set of 16):									15000 SET	50000 SET
Queen Elizabeth II (4 Images)	GCM	RJS	1985	SP	40 X 32	LEN	40 EA		1800 EA	6000 EA
Queen Beatrix (4 Images)	GCM	RJS	1985	SP	40 X 32	LEN	40 EA		1800 EA	6000 EA
Queen Margarethe II of Denmark										
(4 Images)	GCM	RJS	1985	SP	40 X 32	LEN	40 EA		1800 EA	6000 EA
Queen Ntombi Twala of Swaziland										
(4 Images)	GCM	RJS	1985	SP	40 X 32	LEN	40 EA		1800 EA	6000 EA
Vesuvius (Set of 10)	LA	RJS	1985	SP	32 X 40 EA	R/100	250 EA	7 EA	18000 SET	60000 SET
Vesuvius (F/S-365)	FAM/ICA/M	RJS	1985	SP	32 X 40 EA	R/100	250	7	1800	6000
Cowboys and Indians (Portfolio of										
One Unique Screenprint Plus										
Nine Screenprints):									15000 SET	100000 SET
John Wayne	GKS	RJS	1986	SP	36 X 36	LEN/MB	250		2300	20000
1913 Indian Head Nickel	GKS	RJS	1986	SP	36 X 36	LEN/MB	250		2300	10000
General George Armstrong Custer	GKS	RJS	1986	SP	36 X 36	LEN/MB	250		2300	12000
Teddy Roosevelt	GKS	RJS	1986	SP	36 X 36	LEN/MB	250		2300	12000
Kachina Dolls	GKS	RJS	1986	SP	36 X 36	LEN/MB	250		2300	10000
Northwest Coast Totem	GKS	RJS	1986	SP	36 X 36	LEN/MB	250		2300	10000
Plains Indian Shield	GKS	RJS	1986	SP	36 X 36	LEN/MB	250		2300	12000
Annie Oakley	GKS	RJS	1986	SP	36 X 36	LEN/MB	250		2300	12000
Geronimo	GKS	RJS	1986	SP	36 X 36	LEN/MB	250		2300	10000
Indian Mother and Child	GKS	RJS	1986	SP	36 X 36	LEN/MB	250		2300	10000
Martha Graham Portfolio (Set of 3):									6000 SET	22000 SET
Satyric Festival Song	MGCCD	RJS	1986	SP	36 X 36	LEN/MB	100	6	2500	7500
Lamentation	MGCCD	RJS	1986	SP	36 X 36	LEN/MB	100	6	2500	7500
Letter to the World (the Kick)	MGCCD	RJS	1986	SP	36 X 36	LEN/MB	100	6	3000	9000
Milton Berle										
(6 Sheets Stitched Together)										
(Set of 6)			1986	PH	27 X 32 EA	LEN		1	3000 SET	15000 SET
Beethoven	KM		1987	SP	40 X 40	LEN		6	2500	14000
Neuschwanstein (F/S-372)	ES		1987	SP	43 X 30	LEN	100	6	2500	20000
Neuschwanstein Poster	ES		1987	SP/OFF	36 X 25	AP	1200	6	750	1500
Red Lenin	ES		1987	SP	40 X 30	LEN	120	4	2500	11000
Moonwalk Suite (Set of 2)	RFFA		1987	SP	38 X 38 EA	LEN	160 EA		5000	15000 SET

BURTON WASSERMAN

BORN: Brooklyn, NY; March 10, 1929
EDUCATION: Brooklyn Col, NY, BA, with Ad Reinhardt; Columbia Univ, NY, MA, EdD
TEACHING: Glassboro State Col, NY, 1960 to present
COLLECTIONS: Philadelphia Mus of Art, PA; Allentown Art Mus, PA; Montreal Mus of Fine Arts, Can; New Jersey State Mus, Trenton, NJ; Stedelijk Mus, Amsterdam, Netherlands; Wallrat-Richartz-Ludwig Mus, Cologne, Germany; Die Neue Sammlung, Munich, Germany; Dickenson Col, Carlisle, PA; Munson-Williams-Proctor Inst, Utica, NY; Delaware Art Center, Wilmington, DE
PRINTERS: Artist (ART)
PUBLISHERS: Artist (ART)
GALLERIES: Benjamin Mangel Gallery, Phila, PA; International Print Society, New Hope, PA
MAILING ADDRESS: 204 DuBois Rd, Glassboro, NJ 08028

BURTON WASSERMAN CONTINUED

TITLE	PUBLISHER	PRINTER	DATE	MEDIUM	DIMENSION (PAPER SIZE) IN INCHES	TYPE OF PAPER	EDITION NUMBER	NO. OF COLORS	ORIGINAL OPENING PRICE	CURRENT RETAIL PRICE
SOLD OUT EDTIONS (RARE):										
The Royal Purple Passage	ART	ART	1977	SP/MON	17 X 22 EA	R/100	1 EA	8 EA	125 EA	150 EA
1982—D	ART	ART	1982	SP/MON	13 X 14 EA	R/100	1 EA	8 EA	125 EA	150 EA
1982—J	ART	ART	1982	SP/MON	13 X 14 EA	R/100	1 EA	8 EA	125 EA	150 EA
1982—K	ART	ART	1982	SP/MON	14 X 14 EA	R/100	1 EA	8 EA	125 EA	150 EA
1982—L	ART	ART	1982	SP/MON	13 X 14 EA	R/100	1 EA	8 EA	150 EA	175 EA
1982—M	ART	ART	1982	SP/MON	14 X 16 EA	R/100	1 EA	8 EA	150 EA	175 EA

RYO WATANABE

BORN: Tokyo, Japan; September 12, 1936
EDUCATION: Art Sch, Bunka-Gakuin Col, Tokyo, Japan, 1958–61; Art Students League, NY, 1965–67; Pratt Inst, NY, 1968–70
TEACHING: Instr, Rutgers Univ, Newark, NJ, 1976–78,1982–83; Instr, Pratt Graphics Center, Pratt Inst, NY, 1975–85
AWARDS: William H Walker Award, Philadelphia Int, PA, 1977
COLLECTIONS: Mus of Mod Art, NY; Brooklyn Mus, NY; Philadelphia Mus, PA; Rutgers Univ, Newark, NJ; Mus of Mod Art, Haifa, Israel; Wadsworth Atheneum, Hartford, CT; Pratt Inst, NY; Long Island Univ, NY; Bibliotheque Nat, Paris, France; White House, Wash, DC
PUBLISHERS: Sande Webster Gallery, Phila, PA (SWG); Boar Press, NY (BP)
PRINTERS: Roger Winters, NY (RW); David Awoki, NY (DA); Boar Press, NY (BP)
GALLERIES: Sande Webster Gallery, Phila, PA
MAILING ADDRESS: 117 Hester St, New York, NY 10002

TITLE	PUBLISHER	PRINTER	DATE	MEDIUM	DIMENSION (PAPER SIZE) IN INCHES	TYPE OF PAPER	EDITION NUMBER	NO. OF COLORS	ORIGINAL OPENING PRICE	CURRENT RETAIL PRICE
CURRENT EDITIONS:										
OneHundredUndressing	BP	RW/DA/BP	1986	LC	14 X 14	R/BFK	18	4	300	400

SOL WATANABE

PUBLISHERS: Multiples, NY (M)
PRINTERS: Jennifer Melby, NY (JM); Jo Watanabe, NY (JW)
GALLERIES: Marian Goodman, New York, NY; Sande Webster Gallery, Phila, PA

TITLE	PUBLISHER	PRINTER	DATE	MEDIUM	DIMENSION (PAPER SIZE) IN INCHES	TYPE OF PAPER	EDITION NUMBER	NO. OF COLORS	ORIGINAL OPENING PRICE	CURRENT RETAIL PRICE
SOLD OUT EDITIONS (RARE):										
Isometric Form and Isometric Cube (Set of 2)	M	JW	1983	SP	42 X 42 EA		20 EA	4 EA	900 EA	1200 EA
Doubles in Black and Grey (Set of 10)	M	JM	1984	AB			10 EA	2 EA	750 EA	1000 EA

JUNE WAYNE

BORN: Chicago, IL
AWARDS: For Film, Golden Eagle, Cine, Acad Award Nomination; Nat Endowment for the Arts, Visual Arts Fel, 1980; Lulu Award, 1983; Honorary Doctorate Degrees: Atlanta Col of Art, California Col of Arts & Crafts, And Int Col of Los Angeles/London, England
RECENT EXHIB: Fresno Art Mus, CA, 1988; Australian Nat Gallery, Canberra, Australia, 1989; Graham Gallery, Brisbane, Australia, 1989; Macquarie Gallery, Sydney, Australia, 1989; Associated Am Artists, NY, 1989; Benton Gallery, Southampton, NY, 1989
COLLECTIONS: Mus of Mod Art, NY; San Diego Mus, CA; Art Inst of Chicago, IL
PRINTERS: Ed Hamilton (EH); Tamarind Inst, Albuquerque, NM (TI); Toby Michel, Los Angeles, CA (TM); Angeles Press, Los Angeles, CA (AP)
PUBLISHERS: Tamarind Inst, Albuquerque, NM (TI); Angeles Press, Los Angeles, CA (AP); Artist (ART)
GALLERIES: Associated American Artists, New York, NY; Macquarie Galleries, Sydney, Australia; Benton Gallery, Southampton, NY
MAILING ADDRESS: 1108 N Tamarind Ave, Los Angeles, CA 90038

TITLE	PUBLISHER	PRINTER	DATE	MEDIUM	DIMENSION (PAPER SIZE) IN INCHES	TYPE OF PAPER	EDITION NUMBER	NO. OF COLORS	ORIGINAL OPENING PRICE	CURRENT RETAIL PRICE
CURRENT EDITIONS:										
Chinook	ART	EH	1976	LC	22 X 24	R/BFK	20	9	500	3500
Sea Change	ART	EH	1976	LC	21 X 26	R/BFK	20	7	400	2750
Visa Series:										
Visa/Sunday	TI	EH/TI	1976	LC	30 X 22	AP/W	20	6	600	2000
Visa/Monday	TI	EH/TI	1976	LC	30 X 22	AP/W	70	7	600	2000
Visa/Tuesday	TI	EH/TI	1976	LC	30 X 22	AP/W	20	8	600	2000
Visa/Wednesday	TI	EH/TI	1976	LC	30 X 22	AP/W	20	3	600	2000
Visa/Friday	ART	EH	1976	LC	30 X 22	R/BFK	25	2	600	2000
Visa II	ART	EH	1976	LC	34 X 25	R/BFK	18	4	600	2000
Fly-by, States I,II	ART	EH	1976	LC	27 X 21 EA	R/BFK	10 EA	2 EA	400 EA	2500 EA
Dorothy Series:										5000 SET	35000 SET
Arriving 1909	ART	EH	1976	LC	17 X 21	R/BFK	20	7	400	2750
Twenty Five Years with the Firm	ART	EH	1976	LC	21 X 17	R/BFK	20	9	400	2750
Write a Lonely Soldier	ART	EH	1976	LC	21 X 17	R/BFK	25	16	400	2750
Dorothy 1957	ART	EH	1976	LC	21 X 17	R/BFK	4	8	400	2750
The Desire to Write	ART	EH	1976	LC	21 X 17	R/BFK	25	11	400	2750

JUNE WAYNE CONTINUED

TITLE	PUBLISHER	PRINTER	DATE	MEDIUM	DIMENSION (PAPER SIZE) IN INCHES	TYPE OF PAPER	EDITION NUMBER	NO. OF COLORS	ORIGINAL OPENING PRICE	CURRENT RETAIL PRICE
CURRENT EDITIONS:										
Secretary to a Publisher	ART	EH	1976	LC	21 X 17	R/BFK	25	8	400	2750
Dorothy, 1914, Palmer Method	ART	EH	1976	LC	17 X 21	R/BFK	25	10	400	2750
I'm Sorry I Made You Cry	ART	EH	1976	LC	17 X 21	R/BFK	20	7	400	2750
Leaving, 1909, State II	ART	EH	1976	LC	17 X 21	RdB	12	6	400	2750
Leaving, 1909, State III	ART	EH	1976	LC	17 X 21	HMP/GR	10	6	400	2750
The Chicago Territory	ART	EH	1976	LC	21 X 17	R/BFK	16	17	400	2750
Delegate Dorothy	ART	EH	1976	LC	21 X 17	R/BFK	20	19	400	2750
Dorothy and the Paris Garter Company	ART	EH	1976	LC	17 X 21	R/BFK	15	20	400	2750
Power Net	ART	EH	1976	LC	17 X 21	R/BFK	20	5	400	2750
White Knight	ART	EH	1976	LC	21 X 17	R/BFK	20	16	400	2750
Dorothy, 1912	ART	EH	1976	LC	21 X 17	R/BFK	20	16	400	2750
Whose White Knight Was He?	ART	EH	1976	LC	21 X 17	R/BFK	20	16	400	2750
Dorothy and the IRS	ART	EH	1976	LC	21 X 17	R/BFK	20	19	400	2750
Goodbye	ART	EH	1976	LC	21 X 17	R/BFK	20	13	400	2750
Last Time	ART	EH	1976	LC	17 X 21	R/BFK	25	7	400	2750
Coming Out	ART	EH	1976	LC	17 X 21	IND	20	6	400	2750
Winter of '37	ART	EH	1976	LC	17 X 21	R/BFK	25	5	400	2750
Stellar Winds Suite:										
Astral Wave, State I	ART	EH	1978	LC	19 X 15	R/BFK	15	3		2750
Astral Wave, White, State II	ART	EH	1978	LC	19 X 15	R/BFK	15	2		2750
Stellar Roil	ART	EH	1978	LB	19 X 15	R/BFK	15	1		2750
Wind Veil	ART	EH	1978	LB	19 X 15	R/BFK	15	1		2750
Star Dust, State I	ART	EH	1978	LB	19 X 15	R/BFK	15	1		2750
Magnawind	ART	EH	1979	LC	19 X 15	R/BFK	15	3		2750
Debristream	ART	EH	1979	LC	19 X 15	R/BFK	15	3		2750
Scintillae	ART	EH	1979	LC	19 X 15	R/BFK	15	2		2750
Star Shower	ART	EH	1979	LC	19 X 15	R/BFK	15	7		2750
Double Current	ART	EH	1979	LC	19 X 15	R/BFK	15	3		2750
Capella Wind	ART	EH	1979	LC	19 X 15	R/BFK	10	5		2750
Stellar Edge, State I	ART	EH	1979	LC	19 X 15	R/BFK	10	8		2750
Stellar Edge, State II	ART	EH	1979	LC	19 X 15	R/BFK	10	8		2750
White Noise	ART	EH	1979	LC	22 X 22	R/BFK	10	3		2250
Star Fringe, State I	ART	EH	1979	LC	16 X 9	R/BFK	9	4		1500
Star Fringe, State II	ART	EH	1979	LC	16 X 9	R/BFK	8	4		1500
Star Leap	ART	EH	1979	LC	11 X 13	R/BFK	12	5		1500
Velowind	ART	EH	1980	LC	19 X 15	R/BFK	16	2		2500
Frothing	ART	EH	1980	LC	19 X 15	R/BFK	15	4		2500
Plumelet	ART	EH	1980	LC	19 X 15	R/BFK	15	12		1500
Aigrette	ART	EH	1980	LC	19 X 15	R/BFK	15	8		1500
Ruth Weisberg	ART	EH	1980	LC	19 X 15	R/BFK	15	9		1500
Judy Chicago	ART	EH	1980	LC	19 X 15	R/BFK	15	10		1500
Nevelson	ART	EH	1980	LC	19 X 15	R/BFK	15	4		1500
Tabak	ART	EH	1980	LC	19 X 15	R/BFK	15	5		1500
Jock for Coctails	ART	EH	1980	LC	17 X 17	R/BFK	15	6		1750
Jock for Sport	ART	EH	1980	LC	17 X 17	R/BFK	15	9		1750
Robin's Lock	ART	EH	1980	LC	19 X 15	R/BFK	15	2		1500
Asawa	ART	EH	1980	LC	15 X 18	R/BFK	14	4		1500
Two Way Stretch	ART	EH	1980	LC	24 X 19	R/BFK	15	4		1750
Merry Widow, State I	ART	EH	1980	LC	22 X 30	R/BFK	15	5		2750
Merry Widow, State II	ART	EH	1980	LC	22 X 30	R/BFK	15	3		2750
A Little Nothing	ART	EH	1980	LC	14 X 28	RdB	15	4		2750
Strapless	ART	EH	1980	LC	13 X 23	R/BFK	15	6		2750
Stop and Go Fuzz	ART	EH	1981	LC	18 X 18	R/BFK	15	19		1500
Glitterwind	ART	EH	1981	LC	23 X 18	R/BFK	10	7		2500
Lodestar	ART	EH	1981	LC	24 X 18	R/BFK	15	3		2500
A Day Off Suite (Set of 6):										4000 SET
Feather I	ART	EH	1981	LC	13 X 10	R/BFK	15	6		850
Feather II, State II	ART	EH	1981	LC	13 X 10	R/BFK	10	4		850
Dusk	ART	EH	1981	LC	13 X 10	R/BFK	15	9		850
High Noon	ART	EH	1981	LC	13 X 10	R/BFK	15	8		850
Studio Keys	ART	EH	1981	LC	13 X 10	R/BFK	15	7		850
Xacto	ART	EH	1981	LC	13 X 10	R/BFK	15	8		850
Tapestry Needle	ART	EH	1981	LC	13 X 10	R/BFK	15	5		850
Tapestry Needle II, State II	ART	EH	1981	LC	13 X 10	R/BFK	15	4		850
Viridian	ART	EH	1982	LC	20 X 25	R/BFK	15	4		2250
Four Stream	ART	EH	1982	LC	18 X 15	R/BFK	15	9		1200
Fizz	ART	EH	1982	LC	15 X 11	R/BFK	15	4		850
Static	ART	EH	1982	LC	14 X 11	R/BFK	15	4		1200
Solar Flares Suite (Set of 5):										10000 SET
Solar Refraction	ART	EH	1982	LC	17 X 17	R/BFK	15	30		2250
Solar Refraction, State II	ART	EH	1982	LC	17 X 17	R/BFK	15	23		2250
Solar Wave	ART	EH	1982	LC	17 X 17	R/BFK	15	16		2250

JUNE WAYNE CONTINUED

TITLE	PUBLISHER	PRINTER	DATE	MEDIUM	DIMENSION (PAPER SIZE) IN INCHES	TYPE OF PAPER	EDITION NUMBER	NO. OF COLORS	ORIGINAL OPENING PRICE	CURRENT RETAIL PRICE
CURRENT EDITIONS:										
Solar Flash	ART	EH	1982	LC	17 X 17	R/BFK	15	17		2250
Solar Burst	ART	EH	1982	LC	17 X 17	R/BFK	15	11		2250
Solar Flares	ART	EH	1982	LC	17 X 17	R/BFK	15	17		2250
Code I	ART	EH	1982	LB	20 X 21	R/BFK	15	1		1750
Code II, State II	ART	EH	1982	LB	20 X 21	BOX/B	5	1		1750
Jumar	ART	EH	1983	LC	17 X 22	R/BFK	20	15		2000
Between	ART	EH	1983	LC	18 X 21	R/BFK	10	11		2000
Between State II	ART	EH	1983	LC	18 X 21	R/BFK	10	17		2000
My Palomar Suite (Set of 9):										22500 SET
Ablaze	ART	EH	1984	LC	18 X 16	R/BFK	15	13		2750
Ablaze II, State II	ART	EH	1984	LC	18 X 16	R/BFK	15	13		2750
Cool Take	ART	EH	1984	LC	18 X 16	R/BFK	15	6		2750
Meridian, State II	ART	EH	1984	LC	18 X 16	R/BFK	15	8		2750
Over & Out	ART	EH	1984	LC	18 X 16	R/BFK	15	6		2750
Solstice	ART	EH	1984	LC	18 X 16	R/BFK	15	8		2750
Night Field	ART	EH	1984	LC	18 X 16	R/BFK	15	8		2750
Earthscan	ART	EH	1984	LC	18 X 16	R/BFK	15	8		2750
Twinight	ART	EH	1984	LC	18 X 16	R/BFK	15	4		2750
Setsun	ART	EH	1984	LC	18 X 16	R/BFK	15	8		2750
My Self	ART	EH	1985	LC	22 X 21	R/BFK	15	4	650	2500
Marie Dedieu	ART	EH	1985	LC	36 X 26	R/BFK	15	1	750	2500
Robagen	ART	EH	1986	LC	29 X 21	R/BFK	15	6	750	2750
Escalade	ART	EH	1986	LC	25 X 35	R/BFK	15	1	750	3000
Makari	ART	EH	1986	LC	25 X 21	R/BFK	15	6	750	2500
No Sun	ART	EH	1986	LC	26 X 21	R/BFK	20	5	750	2750
Vio	ART	EH	1986	LC	20 X 15	R/BFK	20	10	750	2250
Stare	ART	EH	1986	LC	24 X 22	R/BFK	15	3	750	2000
Two Blacks	ART	EH	1987	LC	30 X 22	R/BFK	15	4	2750	2750
Sophex, States I,II	ART	EH	1907	LC	36 X 27 EA	R/BFK	12 EA	7 EA	2750 EA	2750 EA
Sagh Eye, States I,II	ART	EH	1987	LC	36 X 27 EA	R/BFK	15 EA	2 EA	2750 EA	2750 EA
Saghee	ART	EH	1987	LC	35 X 27	R/BFK	15	7	2750	2750
Echo, States I,II	ART	EH	1987	LC	31 X 25 EA	R/BFK	12 EA	2 EA	2750 EA	2750 EA
Exoh	ART	EH	1987	LC/CO	36 X 26	R/BFK	13	2	2750	2750
Ankidor	ART	EH	1987	LC	36 X 27	R/BFK	15	2	3000	3000
Djunaway	ART	EH	1987	LB	36 X 27	R/BFK	15	2	3000	3000
Goodbye Louise (on the Death of Louise Nevelson)	ART	EH	1988	LC	21 X 16	R/BFK	15	2	2750	2750
Robagen Agen	ART	EH	1988	LC	32 X 24	R/BFK	15	3	2750	2750
Rhed Kiss	ART	EH	1988	LC	25 X 19	R/BFK	15	3	2750	2750
Tiger Mean	ART	EH	1988	LC	31 X 25	R/BFK	15 EA		2750 SET 400 EA	2750 SET 400 EA
Eight Nippers (Set of 8):									2500 SET	2500 SET
Dozo	ART	EH	1989	LB	9 X 6	R/BFK	50 EA	1	400 EA	400 EA
Lash	ART	EH	1989	LC	7 X 7	R/BFK	50 EA	2	400 EA	400 EA
Mystere	ART	EH	1989	LC	7 X 6	R/BFK	50 EA	3	400 EA	400 EA
Planet	ART	EH	1989	LC	8 X 7	R/BFK	50 EA	3	400 EA	400 EA
Trace	ART	EH	1989	LB	6 X 7	R/BFK	50 EA	1	400 EA	400 EA
Event	ART	EH	1989	LB	7 X 7	R/BFK	50 EA	1	400 EA	400 EA
Ohio	ART	EH	1989	LC	8 X 6	R/BFK	50 EA	3	400 EA	400 EA
Query	ART	EH	1989	LC	7 X 6	R/BFK	50 EA	2	400 EA	400 EA

ROBERT WEAVER (JOHN)

BORN: Stillwell, KS; September 9, 1935
EDUCATION: Kansas City Art Inst, KS, BFA, 1965; Univ of New Mexico, Albuquerque, NM, 1966; Univ of Nebraska, Lincoln, NE, MFA, 1968
AWARDS: Tamarind Fel, 1966; William Vreeland Award, Univ of Nebraska, 1967; Governors Arts Awards, 1978
COLLECTIONS: Albrecht Art Gallery, St Joseph, MO; Sheldon Mem Art Gallery, Lincoln, NE; Illinois State Univ, Bloomington-Normal, IL; Univ of Wisconsin Mus, Green Bay, WI; Oklahoma Arts Ctr, Oklahoma City, OK
PRINTERS: Landfall Press, Inc, Chicago, IL (LPI); Jack Lemon, Chicago, IL (JL); Jerry Raidiger, Chicago, IL (JR); Timothy Berry, Chicago, IL (TB)
PUBLISHERS: Landfall Press, Inc, Chicago, IL (LPI)
GALLERIES: Landfall Press, Inc, Chicago, Il

TITLE	PUBLISHER	PRINTER	DATE	MEDIUM	DIMENSION (PAPER SIZE) IN INCHES	TYPE OF PAPER	EDITION NUMBER	NO. OF COLORS	ORIGINAL OPENING PRICE	CURRENT RETAIL PRICE
SOLD OUT EDITIONS (RARE):										
Wee Willie Wilson	LPI	JR/JL/LPI	1973	LC	46 X 32	ARJ	35	4	100	350
Toy Tank II	LPI	TB/LPI	1978	SG/A	22 X 28	AP/EP	20	1	100	300
E-12	LPI	JL/LPI	1981	LC	26 X 36	AP/CR	30	5	250	400

The retail prices of the 100,000 limited edition prints quoted in this directory are subject to change. Print publishers, artists and galleries were the direct sources for these quotations. Prices in the secondary market listed as "Sold Out Editions (Rare)" indicate that the publisher has a limited supply of that print or that the print is difficult to locate in the galleries.

MARY WEATHERFORD

BORN: Ojai, CA; 1963
EDUCATION: Princeton Univ, NJ, BA, 1984; Whitney Independent Study Program, 1984–85
RECENT EXHIB: PS 1 Museum, Inst for Art & Urban Resources, Long Island City, NY, 1989; Diane Brown Gallery, NY, 1990; Galerie Marc Jancou, Zurich, Switzerland, 1991; BlumHelman Warehouse, NY, 1992
PRINTERS: Joseph Montague, NY (JM); Riverhouse Editions, Clark, CO (REd)
PUBLISHERS: Riverhouse Editions, Clark, CO (REd)
GALLERIES: Van Straaten Gallery, Chicago, IL; BlumHelman Gallery, New York, NY; Margulies Taplin Gallery, Boca Raton, FL

**Mary Weatherford
Violetta #2
Courtesy Van Straaten Gallery**

TITLE	PUBLISHER	PRINTER	DATE	MEDIUM	DIMENSION (PAPER SIZE) IN INCHES	TYPE OF PAPER	EDITION NUMBER	NO. OF COLORS	ORIGINAL OPENING PRICE	CURRENT RETAIL PRICE
CURRENT EDITIONS:										
Odile #5	REd	JM/REd	1991	EC	27 X 29	R/BFK	35	3	600	600
Violetta #2, #3, #4	REd	JM/REd	1991	EC	27 X 29 EA	R/BFK	35 EA	4/7/4	600 EA	600 EA

DOUG WEBB

RECENT EXHIB: Martin Lawrence Galleries, Phila, PA, 1987
PRINTERS: Atelier Arcay, Paris, France (AA); Alexander Heinrici, NY (AH); Studio Heinrici, NY (SH); Jaffe Atelier, Vienna, Austria (JA); Moross Studio, Los Angeles, CA (MS); Black Box Collotype, Chicago, IL (BBC); Arion Press, Carson, CA (AP)
PUBLISHERS: Martin Lawrence Limited Editions, Van Nuys, CA (MLLE); Gregory Editions, CA (GEd); Ronmar Limited Editions, CA (RLE)
GALLERIES: Molly Barnes Gallery, Los Angeles, CA; Gallery Yves Arman, New York, NY; Martin Lawrence Galleries, Sherman Oaks, CA & West Los Angeles, CA & Newport Beach, CA & Palm Springs, CA & Santa Clara, CA & Redondo Beach, CA & Thousand Oaks, CA & Escondido, CA & Phila, PA & Short Hills, NJ & Los Angeles, CA; Professional Fine Arts Services, Inc, New York, NY

TITLE	PUBLISHER	PRINTER	DATE	MEDIUM	DIMENSION (PAPER SIZE) IN INCHES	TYPE OF PAPER	EDITION NUMBER	NO. OF COLORS	ORIGINAL OPENING PRICE	CURRENT RETAIL PRICE
SOLD OUT EDITIONS (RARE):										
Urban Daydream	MLLE	AH/SH	1984	SP	29 X 34	SOM	275		500	2400
CURRENT EDITIONS:										
Urban Daydream II	MLLE	AH/SH	1985	SP	29 X 35	SOM	275		500	1250
Life Raft	MLLE	AH/SH	1985	SP	37 X 30	SOM	275		500	1100
Kitchenetic Energy	MLLE	AH/SH	1985	SP	30 X 36	SOM	275		500	1250
Wash and Where	MLLE	AH/SH	1985	SP	38 X 30	SOM	275		500	1100
Liberty Renewed	MLLE	AH/SH	1985	SP	30 X 37	SOM	275		500	1100
Cleanliness is Next to Godliness	MLLE	AH/SH	1985	SP	30 X 36	SOM	275		500	1100
American Dream	MLLE	AH/SH	1986	SP	29 X 35	SOM	275		500	1100
Nightfall	MLLE	AH/SH	1987	SP	36 X 29	SOM	275		500	1400
Face Value	MLLE	AH/SH	1988	SP	30 X 37	SOM	275		600	1400
Reconstruction	MLLE	AH/SH	1989	SP	42 X 32	SOM	275		600	1100
Lost in the Shuffle	GEd	JA/MS	1989	SP/MM/HC	24 X 30	R/100	375	Varies	800	1000
Yacht in Cold Running Water	RLE	BBC/AP	1990	SP	22 X 27	OK/100	375		600	800
Yacht in Cold Running Water Signed by Christopher Forbes	RLE	BBC/AP	1990	SP/MM	22 X 27	OK/100	375		1000	1200

STOKELY WEBSTER

BORN: Evanston, IL; August 23, 1912
EDUCATION: Art Students League, NY; Nat Acad of Design, NY; Yale Univ, New Haven, CT
TEACHING: Instr, Winter Part Park Artists Workshop, Stetson Univ, Deland, FL
AWARDS: First Halgarten Prize, Nat Acad of Design, NY
RECENT EXHIB: Lyman Allyn Mus, New London, CT, 1989; State Univ of New York Mus, Stony Brook, NY, 1990
COLLECTIONS: Phillips Coll, Wash, DC; Smithsonian Inst, Wash, DC; Newark Mus, NJ; Indianapolis Mus, IN; Heckscher Mus, Huntington, NY; Parrish Mus, Southhampton, NY; Nat Mus of Am Art, Wash, DC; High Mus, Atlanta, GA; Fine Art Mus, St Petersburg, FL; Newark Mus, NJ; Albright-Knox Art Gallery, Buffalo, NY
PRINTERS: Artist (ART)
PUBLISHERS: Artist (ART)
GALLERIES: Eric Galleries, New York, NY; Chapellier Gallery, New York, NY; Susan Conway Galleries, Wash, DC
MAILING ADDRESS: 10 Harbor Rd, Southport, CT 06490

The retail prices of the 100,000 limited edition prints quoted in this directory are subject to change. Print publishers, artists and galleries were the direct sources for these quotations. Prices in the secondary market listed as "Sold Out Editions (Rare)" indicate that the publisher has a limited supply of that print or that the print is difficult to locate in the galleries.

The Printworld Directory is accepting new applications for the seventh edition. Approximately 300 new artists will be accepted. Please use the two forms provided in the back section of this directory to submit biographical data and documentation of prints. Edition number of each print must not exceed 500 and the retail price must be $100 or more.

STOKELY WEBSTER CONTINUED

TITLE	PUBLISHER	PRINTER	DATE	MEDIUM	DIMENSION (PAPER SIZE) IN INCHES	TYPE OF PAPER	EDITION NUMBER	NO. OF COLORS	ORIGINAL OPENING PRICE	CURRENT RETAIL PRICE
SOLD OUT EDITIONS (RARE):										
Dancer	ART	ART	1980	EB	8 X 10	DE	80	1	150	300
Nude with Halo,	ART	ART	1980	EB	8 X 4	DE	80	1	125	250
Park Bench	ART	ART	1980	EB	6 X 8	DE	80	1	150	300

EMIL WEDDIGE

BORN: Canada; December 23, 1907
EDUCATION: Eastern Michigan Univ, Ysilanti, MI, BS; Univ of Michigan, Ann Arbor, MI, MA; Eastern Michigan Univ, Ysilanti, MI, Hon PhD; Art Students League, NY; Acad Julian, Paris, France
AWARDS: First Prize, State of Michigan, 1933; Purchase Award, Michigan Watercolor Soc, 1945; Best Print Award, Detroit Inst of Art, MI, 1950
RECENT EXHIB: Creative Arts Gallery, Central Michigan Univ, Mt Pleasant, MI, 1989; Le Minotaure Gallery, Ann Arbor, MI, 1989; Saper Galleries, East Lansing, MI 1989
COLLECTIONS: Metropolitan Mus of Art, NY; Nat Gallery of Art, Wash, DC; Bibliotheque Nat, Paris, France; Library of Congress, Wash, DC

PRINTERS: Guy Field, London, England (GF); Curwen Studio, London, England (CS); Jacques Desjobert, Paris, France (JD); Edmond Desjobert, Paris, France (ED); Fishy Whale Studio, Rockport, IL (FWS); Hanke-Hans Muller, Mattieu, Switzerland Dusseldorf Deilsdorf, Switzerland (HHM); Matteau Matteau Studio, Deilsdorf, Switzerland (MS); Artist (ART); Jean Michael Machet, Paris, France (JMM); Roland Paska, Rockford, IL (RP); Fishy Whale Studio, Rockport, IL (FWS)
PUBLISHERS: Alex Kraski, Royal Oak, MI (AK); Univ of Michigan, Ann Arbor, MI (UM); Michael Mitchel, Bayside, NY (MM)
GALLERIES: Saper Galleries, East Lansing, MI; Hunt-Wulkowicz Graphics, Chicago, IL; Le Minotaure Gallery, Ann Arbor, MI; Michael Mitchel Fine Art, Bayside, NY; David Kalb Fine Art, Redford, MI
MAILING ADDRESS: 870 Stein Rd, Ann Arbor, MI 48105

TITLE	PUBLISHER	PRINTER	DATE	MEDIUM	DIMENSION (PAPER SIZE) IN INCHES	TYPE OF PAPER	EDITION NUMBER	NO. OF COLORS	ORIGINAL OPENING PRICE	CURRENT RETAIL PRICE
SOLD OUT EDITIONS (RARE):										
Farleys Road	ART	ART	1931	EB/LC	14 X 18	AP	20	1	18	1500
Sachmo and the Saints	ART	ED	1953	LC	19 X 26	RP	50	7	35	2550
St Francis	ART		1956	LC	19 X 26	AP	50	7	50	2500
University of Michigan Suite (Set of 11)	UM	JD/ED	1964–67	LC	22 X 18 EA	AP	125 EA	7 EA	POR	POR
Americana Suite (Set of 9)	ART	HHM	1972	LC	22 X 30 EA	AP	50 EA	7–11 EA	450 SET	7600 SET
									50 EA	850 EA
Bicentennial Suite (Set of 7)	LC/JF	AE	1975–76	LC		AP		7 EA	1200 SET	3600 SET
RFD Jennings Road	ART	ART	1976	LC	22 X 30	AP	40	7	100	800
Bouquet	ART	GF/CS		LC	22 X 30	AP	45	14	125	400
Front Garden	ART	AE	1978	LC	19 X 26	AP	50	12	100	550
Legend	AK	AE	1979	LC	22 X 30	AP	80	12	125	450
Legend	AK	AE	1979	LC	22 X 30	AP	80	12	125	450
Give Us This Day	MM	JMM	1986	LC		AP		17	150	350
Sunday Afternoon	ART	AC/Gerard	1986	LC	22 X 28	AP	60	7	150	300
Early Spring	ART	JM/AE	1987	LC	24 X 34	AP	70	17	200	550
Papillon	DK	AE	1987	LC	24 X 36	AP	80	7	200	400
Rocks and Goatsbeard	ART	AE		LC	22 X 30	AP	80	16	150	350
My Cat Speedy	AK	AE	1988	LC	22 X 30	AP	60	7	250	400
CURRENT EDITIONS:										
Les Families	ART	AE	1988	LC	22 X 30	AP	60	16	350	450
Shore	ART	AE	1988	LC	19 X 24	AP	95	7	200	400
Off the Cape	AK	AE	1989	LC	22 X 30	AP	60	14	450	450

NEIL WEDMAN

PRINTERS: Torrie Groening, Vancouver, BC, Canada (TG); Prior Editions, Vancouver, BC, Canada (PEd)
PUBLISHERS: Diane Farris Gallery, Vancouver, BC, Canada (DFG)
GALLERIES: Diane Farris Gallery, Vancouver, BC, Canada

TITLE	PUBLISHER	PRINTER	DATE	MEDIUM	DIMENSION (PAPER SIZE) IN INCHES	TYPE OF PAPER	EDITION NUMBER	NO. OF COLORS	ORIGINAL OPENING PRICE	CURRENT RETAIL PRICE
CURRENT EDITIONS:										
Landscapes (Set of 4):									1200 SET	1200 SET
Gate	DFG	TG/PEd	1990	LB	15 X 22	AC	30	1	425	425
Grave	DFG	TG/PEd	1990	LB	15 X 22	AC	30	1	425	425
1991	DFG	TG/PEd	1990	LB	15 X 22	AC	30	1	425	425
Wind	DFG	TG/PEd	1990	LB	15 X 22	AC	30	1	425	425

KENNETH RUSSELL WEEDMAN

BORN: Little Rock, AR; September 26, 1939
EDUCATION: Memphis Acad of Art, TN; Univ of Tulsa, OK, BA, 1961–64, MA, 1964–68
TEACHING: Philbrook Mus, Tulsa, OK, 1963–64; Instr, Sculpture, Sul Ross State Col, Alpine, TX, 1965–66; Vis Artist, Nicolls State Univ, Thiobodaux, LA, 1970–71; Prof, Sculpture, Cumberland Col, Williamsburg, KY, 1968 to present

AWARDS: Purchase Award, Arkansas Univ, State University, AR, 1963; Award of Merit, Sculpture, Univ of Tulsa, OK, 1964; Award, Nebraska Wesleyan Univ, Lincoln, NE, 1966; Andrew Mellon Found Grant, 1981; Andrew Mellon Grant, 1988; Lilly Found Grant, 1989
RECENT EXHIB: Water Tower Gallery, Louisville, KY, 1987
COLLECTIONS: Cincinnati Mus of Art, OH; Arkansas Arts Center Little Rock, AR; Masur Mus of Art, Monroe, LA; Baldwin-Wallace Art & Drama Center, Berea, OH; Univ of Tulsa, OK, Mus de Arte Contemp International, Salvador, Brazil

KENNETH RUSSELL WEEDMAN CONTINUED

PRINTERS: Artist (ART)
PUBLISHERS: Artist (ART)
GALLERIES: Lakeside Studio, Lakeside, MI; Pinkerton House Portfolio, Louisville, KY; A Clean, Well-Lighted Place, New York, NY; Marilyn Pink Gallery, Los Angeles, CA
MAILING ADDRESS: 191 Florence, Williamsburg, KY 40769

TITLE	PUBLISHER	PRINTER	DATE	MEDIUM	DIMENSION (PAPER SIZE) IN INCHES	TYPE OF PAPER	EDITION NUMBER	NO. OF COLORS	ORIGINAL OPENING PRICE	CURRENT RETAIL PRICE
SOLD OUT EDITIONS (RARE):										
G-Gasm-AO	ART	ART	1968	SP	16 X 9	R/BFK	18	4	35	1200
−15 +14 Star	ART	ART	1970	LC/SP	9 X 12	R/BFK	17	4	35	600
CURRENT EDITIONS:										
3 Star	ART	ART	1971	LC	12 X 9	R/BFK	20	2	40	200
AB, JK, ST; 12	ART	ART	1971	LC	14 X 10	R/BFK	20	3	45	200
1 + 2½	ART	ART	1971	LB	12 X 9	R/BFK	18	1	35	200
Blood Canto	ART	ART	1972	LC	14 X 10	R/BFK	27	1	35	200
Small Canto	ART	ART	1972	SP	18 X 24	RICE	12	9	50	300
Elan Vital	ART	ART	1981	COL	9 X 12	R/BFK	12	1	100	300
Vision	ART	ART	1981	MM	15 X 24	IN	10	4	300	400
Red Garden	ART	ART	1982	I	6 X 6	IN	30	1	150	200
Red Hand	ART	ART	1982	I	8 X 10	IN	10	2	200	300
Autumn	ART	ART	1982	I	3 X 3	IN	40	2	100	200
Remembrances	ART	ART	1983	I	24 X 18	R/BFK	45	1	100	250
Sky After Sky	ART	ART	1983	EB/A	5 X 7	R/BFK	25	2	100	200
Early April	ART	ART	1984	AB	7 X 7	R/BFK	25	1	100	200
Wall	ART	ART	1985	LC	17 X 10	R/BFK	11	5	300	350
Sampler	ART	ART	1985	COLL	4 X 4	R/BFK	10	2	200	250
Comet	ART	ART	1985	LC	9 X 7	MAG	22	2	200	250
England	ART	ART	1985	LC	4 X 5	MAG	11	3	200	250
Sketch	ART	ART	1985	LC	4 X 4	MAG	8	2	200	250
Alpine	ART	ART	1985	L	17 X 12	MAG	15	1	300	350
Closed	ART	ART	1985	COLL	2 X 2	LEN	10	1	100	150
Acupuncture	ART	ART	1986	EB	12 X 18	LANA	10	1	350	400
Africa	ART	ART	1986	EB/A	9 X 2	R/BFK	10	1	200	250
Africa II	ART	ART	1986	EC/A	12 X 9	R/BFK	11	2	500	550
Outside	ART	ART	1986	EC/A	6 X 9	MAG	14	2	250	300
Outside II	ART	ART	1986	EB/A	6 X 9	R/BFK	10	1	200	250

WILLIAM WEEGE

BORN: Milwaukee, WI; 1935
EDUCATION: Univ of Wisconsin, Milwaukee, WI, BA, 1965; Univ of Wisconsin, Madison, WI, MA, 1967, MFA, 1968
TEACHING: Prof, Univ of Wisconsin, Madison, WI, 1967–1980
COLLECTIONS: Mus of Mod Art, NY; Brooklyn Mus, NY; Art Inst of Chicago, IL; Akron Art Inst, OH; Frankfurt Library, Germany
PRINTERS: Artist (ART)
PUBLISHERS: Jones Road Print Shop & Stable (JRPS) (OB); Lakeside Studio, MI (LS); Associated American Artists, NY (AAA)
GALLERIES: Ellen Sragow Gallery, New York, NY; Richard Gray Gallery, Chicago, IL; Peter M David Gallery, Minneapolis, MN; Joan Hodgell Gallery, Sarasota, FL; Alice Simsar Gallery, Ann Arbor, MI; Nina Freudenheim Gallery, Buffalo, NY; Grace Chosy Gallery, Madison, WI; Katie Gingrass Gallery, Milwaukee, WI; Photographic Image Gallery, Portland, OR; Ledel Gallery, New York, NY
MAILING ADDRESS: P O Box 185, Barneveld, WI 53507

TITLE	PUBLISHER	PRINTER	DATE	MEDIUM	DIMENSION (PAPER SIZE) IN INCHES	TYPE OF PAPER	EDITION NUMBER	NO. OF COLORS	ORIGINAL OPENING PRICE	CURRENT RETAIL PRICE
SOLD OUT EDITIONS (RARE):										
Home, Home on the Range Played	AAA	ART	1970	EC/Flock	33 X 25	AP	24		100	750
Heavenly Bodies	JRPS	ART	1976	SP	Varies	Varies	250	Multi	125/600	500/1000

ROBERT WEIL

BORN: St Louis, MO; 1945
EDUCATION: Santa Barbara City Col, CA; San Francisco Art Inst, CA
PRINTERS: American Atelier, NY (AA)
PUBLISHERS: Circle Fine Art, Chicago, IL (CFA)
GALLERIES: Circle Galleries, San Diego, CA & San Francisco, CA & Northbrook, IL & Pittsburgh, PA & Houston, TX & Soho, NY & Chicago, IL & Scottsdale, AZ & Beverly Hills, CA & Costa Mesa, CA & Sherman Oaks, CA & Honolulu, HI & Palm Beach, FL & New Orleans, LA & Las Vegas, NV & Seattle, WA

TITLE	PUBLISHER	PRINTER	DATE	MEDIUM	DIMENSION (PAPER SIZE) IN INCHES	TYPE OF PAPER	EDITION NUMBER	NO. OF COLORS	ORIGINAL OPENING PRICE	CURRENT RETAIL PRICE
SOLD OUT EDITIONS (RARE):										
City Scene	CFA	AA	1976	EB/LC	18 X 25	AP	200		75	175
After All	CFA	AA	1976	LC	30 X 22	AP	100		125	300
Man with Papers	CFA	AA	1976	LC	21 X 16	AP	150		75	175
Cello	CFA	AA	1977	LC	22 X 30	AP	350		75	125
Conductor	CFA	AA	1977	LC	10 X 14	AP	350		75	125
Flute	CFA	AA	1977	LC	10 X 14	AP	350		75	125
Piano	CFA	AA	1977	LC	10 X 14	AP	350		75	125
CURRENT EDITIONS:										
What Next?	CFA	AA	1976	LC	29 X 21	AP	300		75	150

WILLIAM WEGMAN

BORN: Holyoke, MA; December 2, 1943
EDUCATION: Massachusetts Col of Art, Boston, MA, BFA, 1965; Univ of Illinois, Urbana-Champaign, IL, MFA, 1967
TEACHING: Univ of Wisconsin, Madison, WI, 1968–70; California State Univ, Long Beach, CA, 1970
AWARDS: Creative Artists Public Service Prog Grant, 1979; Nat Endowment for the Arts Grants, 1975–76,82; Guggenheim Fel, 1975,86
RECENT EXHIB: Contemp Arts Center, Cincinnati, OH, 1987; Honolulu Acad of Arts, HI, 1987; Solo Gallery, NY, 1988; Gallery Durrand, Dessert, Paris, France, 1989; Kunstmuseum, Lucerne, Switzerland, 1990; Sonoma State Univ, Rohnert Park, CA, 1992; Univ of Florida, Gainesville, FL, 1992; Miami-Dade Com Col, FL, 1992; Col of DuPage, William E Gahlborg Arts Center, Glen Ellyn, IL, 1992; Springfield Art Mus, MO, 1992; Contemp Arts Mus, Houston, TX, 1992; Whitney Mus of Am Art, NY, 1992; Holly Solomon Gallery, NY, 1990,92; Pace/MacGill Gallery, NY, 1990,92; Olga Dollar Gallery, San Francisco, CA, 1992; John Berggruen Gallery, San Francisco, CA, 1992; Sperone Westwater Gallery, NY, 1992; Gerald Peters Gallery, Dallas, TX, 1992
COLLECTIONS: Whitney Mus of Am Art, NY; Mus of Mod Art, NY; Mus of Mod Art, Paris, France; Los Angeles County Art Mus, CA; Inst of Photography Mus, Rochester, NY; Brooklyn Mus, NY; Corcoran Gallery of Art, Wash, DC; Walker Art Center, Minneapolis, MN
PRINTERS: Jeff Botz, NY (JB); Judith Solodkin, NY (JS); Solo Press, NY (SP); Artist (ART); Sette Publishing Company, Tempe, AZ (SPC); Max Lanier, Tempe, AZ (ML); Mary Statzer, Tempe, AZ (MS); Sette & Segura Publishing Company, Tempe, AZ (Set-Seg); Steven Anderson, Minneapolis, MN (SA); Philip Barber, Minneapolis, MN (PB); Vermillion Editions, Ltd, Minneapolis, MN (VEL); Bill Weege, Madison, WI (BW); Andrew Rubin, Madison, WI (AR); Tandem Press, Univ of Wisconsin, Madison, WI (TanPr); Joe Wilfer, NY (JW); Spring Street Workshop, NY (SprSW)
PUBLISHERS: Holly Solomon Editions, NY (HSE); Jones Road Stable, NY (JRS); Solo Press, NY (SP); Artist (ART); Sette Publishing Company, Tempe, AZ (SPC); Sette & Segura, Tempe, AZ (Set-Seg); Vermillion Editons, Ltd, Minneapolis, MN (VEL); Tandem Press, Univ of Wisconsin, Madison, WI (TanPr); Spring Street Workshop, NY (SprSW)
GALLERIES: Pace Prints, New York, NY; Holly Solomon Gallery, New York, NY; Dart Gallery, Chicago, IL; Brentwood Gallery, St Louis, MO; Marian Goodman Gallery, New York, NY; Texas Gallery, Houston, TX; Pace/MacGill Gallery, New York, NY; Betsy Senior Contemporary Prints, New York, NY; Solo Gallery, New York, NY; Sette Gallery, Scottsdale, AZ; John Berggruen Gallery, San Francisco, CA; Olga Dollar Gallery, San Francisco, CA, Sperone Westwater Gallery, New York, NY; Gerald Peters Gallery, Dallas, TX; Sette & Segura Publishing Company, Tempe, AZ; Dunlap-Freidenrich Fine Art, Newport Beach, CA; Fraenkel Gallery, San Francisco, CA; Linda Cathcart Gallery, Santa Monica, CA; James Corcoran Gallery, Santa Monica, CA; Nancy Drysdale Gallery, Wash, DC; Fay Gold Gallery, Atlanta, GA; Vermillion Editions, Ltd, Milwaukee, WI; Carol Evans Fine Arts, Brooklyn, NY

William Wegman
Endless Column
Courtesy Tandem Press

TITLE	PUBLISHER	PRINTER	DATE	MEDIUM	DIMENSION (PAPER SIZE) IN INCHES	TYPE OF PAPER	EDITION NUMBER	NO. OF COLORS	ORIGINAL OPENING PRICE	CURRENT RETAIL PRICE
SOLD OUT EDITIONS (RARE):										
Before/On/After Permutations	ART	ART	1974	PH	41 X 35				600	35000
Man Ray Black and White and 2 Dye Transfer Prints (Plus Drawing) (Set of 10):									3500 SET	20000 SET
Modeling School	HSE	ART/JB	1974	PH	14 X 11	AC	20		350	2000
Three Dolls	HSE	ART/JB	1976	PH	14 X 11	AC	20		350	2000
Of the Lake	HSE	ART/JB	1976	PH	14 X 11	AC	20		350	2000
Contemplating the Bust of Man Ray	HSE	ART/JB	1978	PH	14 X 11	AC	20		350	2000
Dog Cabin	HSE	ART/JB	1979	PH	14 X 11	AC	20		350	2000
Double Portrait	HSE	ART/JB	1973,81	PH	14 X 11	AC	20		350	2000
Dog House	HSE	ART/JB	1981	PH	14 X 11	AC	20		350	2000
Red Dog on Mrs. Wegman's Couch after Courbet	HSE	ART/JB	1982	PH	14 X 11	AC	20		350	2000
Monument	HSE	ART/JB	1982	PH	14 X 11	AC	20		350	2000
Out of State, State I	HSE	ART	1983	EB	14 X 20	AC	17	1	700	1200
Out of State, State II	HSE	ART	1983	EC	14 X 20	AC	7	2	700	1200
Missing Dog	HSE	ART	1983	LC	20 X 16	AC	22		800	1350
Card with Flowers	HSE	ART	1983	LC	25 X 35	AC	28		750	1200
Boulder (C-Print Trip)	HSE	ART	1983	CP	8 X 10	AC	15		850	1400
Menu	HSE	ART	1983	LC	31 X 24	AC	24		750	1300
Untitled (Series of 18)	ART/SVC	ART	1985	MON	30 X 22 EA	Varies	1 EA	Varies	600 EA	1800 EA
CURRENT EDITIONS:										
Untitled (Series of Paper Constructions)	JRS	ART	1981	PH/C	30 X 40 EA	AC	1 EA	Varies	800 EA	1800 EA
A Good Plumber	SP	JS/SP	1987	MON	27 X 36 EA	AC	1 EA	Varies	1200 EA	1500 EA
Carlin	SP	JS/SP	1987	MON	22 X 30 EA	AC	1 EA	Varies	800 EA	800 EA
Kind of Dive	SP	JS/SP	1987	MON	22 X 30 EA	AC	1 EA	Varies	800 EA	800 EA
Last Resort	SP	JS/SP	1987	MON	30 X 22 EA	AC	1 EA	Varies	800 EA	800 EA
Monogramed Lake	SP	JS/SP	1987	MON	30 X 22 EA	AC	1 EA	Varies	800 EA	1000 EA

WILLIAM WEGMAN CONTINUED

TITLE	PUBLISHER	PRINTER	DATE	MEDIUM	DIMENSION (PAPER SIZE) IN INCHES	TYPE OF PAPER	EDITION NUMBER	NO. OF COLORS	ORIGINAL OPENING PRICE	CURRENT RETAIL PRICE
CURRENT EDITIONS:										
Rich Neighbors	SP	JS/SP	1987	MON	30 X 22 EA	AC	1 EA	Varies	800 EA	800 EA
Handcolored Lithographs (Series of 10 Unique Images)	SP	JS/SP	1987	LC/HC	24 X 35 EA	HMP	1 EA	Varies	1200 EA	1500 EA
Doguerreotype	SP	JS/SP	1987	LC	27 X 24	HMP	55		1000	1200
Ray Beard	SP	JS/SP	1987	LC	34 X 28	HMP	55		1000	1200
Ye Olde Bootery/Ye Olde Winery (with Letterpress)	SP	JS/SP	1987	LC	35 X 29	HMP	55		900	1000
Dog Motel	SP	JS/SP	1987	LC	31 X 25	HMP	55		1000	1200
Ray Cat	SP	JS/SP	1988	LC	35 X 24	R/BFK	55		700	1400
Busy Week	TanPr	BW/AR/TanPr	1989	LB	18 X 24	AC	30	1	1200	1500
Museum	TanPr	BW/AR/TanPr	1989	LB	23 X 32	AC	20	1	450	500
Nature Song	TanPr	BW/AR/TanPr	1989	LB	18 X 23	AC	30	1	700	800
Bat Bite	TanPr	BW/AR/TanPr	1990	PH/LB/OFF	27 X 23	AC	40	1	1200	2500
Bees and Bombs	TanPr	BW/AR/TanPr	1990	LB	26 X 25	AC	50	1	1200	1500
Charitable	TanPr	BW/AR/TanPr	1990	PH/LB/OFF	27 X 23	AC	50	1	600	750
Rainy Day Oxen	TanPr	BW/AR/TanPr	1990	EB	13 X 17	AC/W	8	1	500	600
FDS	TanPr	BW/AR/TanPr	1990	EB	14 X 11	AC/W	10	1	400	400
Endless Column	TanPr	BW/AR/TanPr	1990	WC	25 X 18	SUZ	40	14	900	900
Dragonflies and Others (Series of 12)	SprSW	JW/SprSW	1990	MON/HC	22 X 30 EA		1 EA	Varies	3200 EA	3200 EA
Dusted Transcription	TanPr	BW/AR/TanPr	1991	EB	17 X 13	AC/W	50	1	750	750
Armed Chair	VEL	SA/PB/TN/VEL	1992	LC/OFF/STAMP	50 X 37	SOM/S	48		4500	4500
Seven Sisters (Two Sheets)	Set-Seg	ML/MS/Set-Seg	1992	PH/LC/OFF	32 X 88	AC	40	3	3000	3000

REYNOLD HENRY WEIDENAAR

BORN: Grand Rapids, MI (1915–1985)
EDUCATION: Kendall Sch of Design, Grand Rapids, MI, 1935–36; Kansas City Art Inst, Scholar, MO, 1938–40
TEACHING: Instr, Life Drawing & Painting, Kendall Sch of Design, Grand Rapids, MI, 1956–74
AWARDS: Guggenheim Found Award, 1944; Tiffany Found, Scholar, 1948; Hefner Galleries, Grand Rapids, MI, 1950

RECENT EXHIB: Hefner Galleries, Grand Rapids, MI, 1988,90
COLLECTIONS: Detroit Inst of Art, MI; Honolulu Acad of Fine Arts, HI; Hackley Art Gallery, Muskegon, MI; Nat Gallery, South Wales, Liverpool, England; Library of Congress, Wash, DC
PRINTERS: American Atelier, NY (AA); Artist (ART)
PUBLISHERS: Associated American Artists, NY (AAA); Artist (ART)
GALLERIES: Hefner Galleries, Grand Rapids, MI; Associated American Artists, New York, NY

TITLE	PUBLISHER	PRINTER	DATE	MEDIUM	DIMENSION (PAPER SIZE) IN INCHES	TYPE OF PAPER	EDITION NUMBER	NO. OF COLORS	ORIGINAL OPENING PRICE	CURRENT RETAIL PRICE
SOLD OUT EDITIONS (RARE):										
Fantasy	ART	ART	1940	MEZ	10 X 6	WOVE		1	35	350
Glory to God	ART	ART	1941	EB/A	13 X 8	WOVE			50	275
The Road is Rough	ART	ART	1944	EB	7 X 9	WOVE		1	35	700
Alabama	ART	ART	1945	EB	11 X 13	WOVE		1	35	600
The Dozing Tippler	ART	ART	1945	EB	11 X 9	WOVE		1	35	550
Streets of Goats, Taxco	ART	ART	1948	MEZ	10 X 15	WOVE	150	1	50	700
Grain Thrashers, Old	ART	ART	1948	EP/A	8 X 16	WOVE	150		60	700
Grain Thrashers, Old Mexico	ART	ART	1949	EB/A	10 X 15	WOVE	150		60	950
Cathedral Repairs, Mexico	ART	ART	1949	MEZ	9 X 7	WOVE	180	1	50	700
Cathedral Repairs, Mexico	ART	ART	1949	EB	9 X 7	WOVE	180		50	450
Demolition in the Plaza			1950	MEZ	13 X 9	RP	121	1	75	750
Last Run	AAA	AA	1950	EB/A	8 X 11	AP	250		85	700
Reverie (Nude)	AAA	AA	1950	MEZ	13 X 11	AP	50	1	75	600
Solitude	AAA	AA	1950	MEZ	13 X 11	HMP	50	1	75	900
Valley of Wrath	AAA	AA	1951	MEZ	11 X 13	HMP	50	1	75	500
Building the Bridge	ART	ART	1953	EB	13 X 17	AP	100	1	100	4500
Case of the People	ART	ART	1953	DPT	13 X 17	AP	100	1	100	600
Eyes of the City	ART	ART	1953	EB	13 X 17	RP	200	1	100	800
Still Life of Wilted Celery	ART	ART	1954	EB	13 X 17	HMP	200	1	125	1100
Bridge Builders	ART	ART	1956	MEZ	13 X 7	WOVE	243	1	150	1350
Venice-Piazza San Marco	ART	ART	1962	EB	13 X 7	AP	199		200	600
Yacht Club	ART	ART	1964	EB/DPT	13 X 17	WOVE	100		250	1500

SUSAN WEIL

EDUCATION: Acad Julian, Paris, France; Black Mountain Col, NC; Art Students League, NY

AWARDS: Nat Endowment for the Arts Fel, 1976; Guggenheim Fel, NY, 1977
PRINTERS: Styria Studio, NY (SS)
PUBLISHERS: Styria Studio, NY (SS)
GALLERIES: Styria Studio, New York, NY; Somerstown Gallery, Somers, NY

The Printworld Directory is accepting new applications for the seventh edition. Approximately 300 new artists will be accepted. Please use the two forms provided in the back section of this directory to submit biographical data and documentation of prints. Edition number of each print must not exceed 500 and the retail price must be $100 or more.

SUSAN WEIL CONTINUED

TITLE	PUBLISHER	PRINTER	DATE	MEDIUM	DIMENSION (PAPER SIZE) IN INCHES	TYPE OF PAPER	EDITION NUMBER	NO. OF COLORS	ORIGINAL OPENING PRICE	CURRENT RETAIL PRICE
SOLD OUT EDITOINS (RARE):										
Siena	SS	SS	1981	LC/SP	45 X 30	RP/ROL	14	12	600	800
Handprint Right	SS	SS	1983	LC/SP	54 X 34	R/BFK	14	8	600	800
Handprint Left	SS	SS	1983	LC/SP	54 X 34	R/BFK	14	8	600	800
Copper Moon	SS	SS	1983	LC/SP	54 X 34	R/BFK	15	10	600	800
Paper Moon	SS	SS	1983	LC/SP	54 X 34	R/BFK	15	10	600	800

LAWRENCE CHARLES WEINER

BORN: Bronx, NY; February 10, 1942
AWARDS: Deutscher Akademischer Austauschdienst Fel, 1975; Nat Endowment for the Arts Fel, 1976–77, 1985–86
RECENT EXHIB: Univ of Chicago, Renaissance Society, Chicago, IL, 1989,92; Marian Goodman Gallery, NY, 1993
COLLECTIONS: Mus of Mod Art, NY; Vanable Mus, Eindhoven, The Netherlands; Staatisches Mus Monchengladbach, Germany; Centre Georges Pompidou, Paris, France; Nat Gallery of Australia, Canberra, Australia
PRINTERS: Patricia Branstead, NY (PB); Branstead Studios, NY (BS); Erie Ceramic Arts Company, Erie, PA (ECAC); Sally Mara Sturman, NY (SMS)
PUBLISHERS: Multiples, Inc, NY (M); Brooke Alexander, Inc, NY (BAI)
GALLERIES: Marian Goodman Gallery, New York, NY; Hayward Gallery, London, England; Leo Castelli Gallery, New York, NY; Matthew Marks Gallery, New York, NY; Stuart Regen Gallery, Los Angeles, CA; Brooke Alexander Gallery, New York, NY
MAILING ADDRESS: 13 Bleecker St, New York, NY 10012

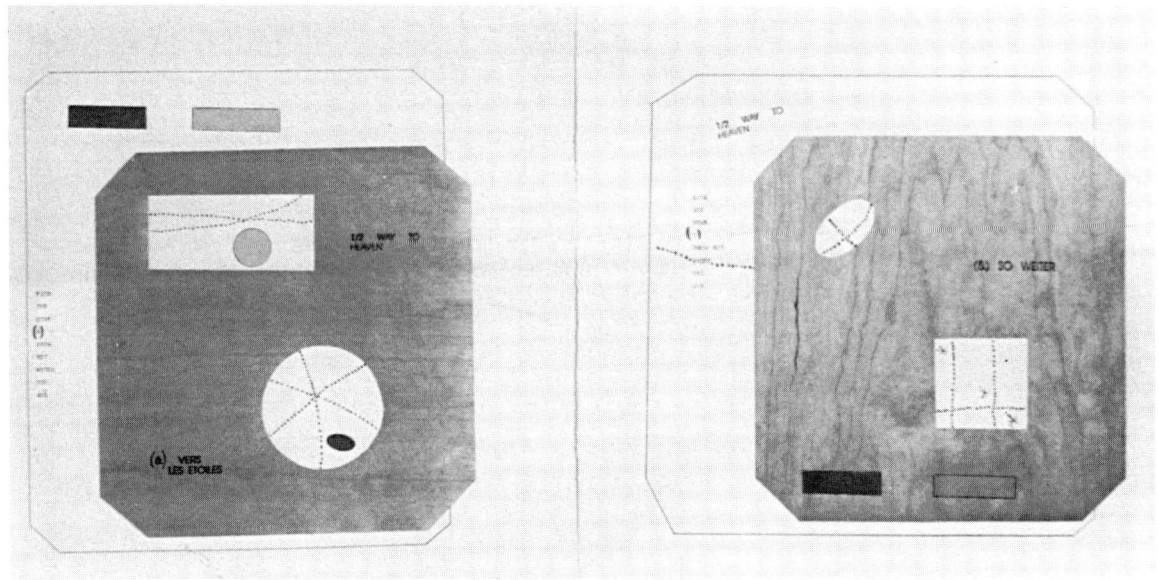

Lawrence Charles Weiner
Half Way to Heaven: Know & Know Not
Courtesy Marian Goodman Gallery

TITLE	PUBLISHER	PRINTER	DATE	MEDIUM	DIMENSION (PAPER SIZE) IN INCHES	TYPE OF PAPER	EDITION NUMBER	NO. OF COLORS	ORIGINAL OPENING PRICE	CURRENT RETAIL PRICE
CURRENT EDITIONS:										
Islands in the Storm (Series of 4) & Across the Great Divide (Baked Porcelain Enamel Screenprinted in Color onto 3 Steel Plates) (Enameled Screenprints) (Set of 3)	M	PB/BS	1990	EB/A/SG/CC	17 X 23 EA	SOM	35 EA		5000 SET	5500 SET
									4000 SET	4000 SET
1 if by Land	BAI	ECAC	1991	SP	12 X 36	Steel	45		XXXX	XXXX
2 if by Sea	BAI	ECAC	1991	SP	12 X 12	Steel	45		XXXX	XXXX
& Across the Great Divide	BAI	ECAC	1991	SP	12 X 12	Steel	45		XXXX	XXXX
Half Way to Heaven (Set of 2):									2500 SET	2500 SET
Know	M	SMS/BS	1992	PH/EB/RS/CC	16 X 16	AP/R-BFK	25		1250	1250
Know Not	M	SMS/BS	1992	PH/EB/RS/CC	16 X 16	AP/R-BFK	25		1250	1250

RUTH ELLEN WEISBERG

BORN: Chicago, IL; July 31, 1942
EDUCATION: Acad di Belli Arte, Perugia, Italy; Univ of Michigan, Ann Arbor, MI, BS, MA; Atelier 17, Paris, France, with Stanley William Hayter
TEACHING: Asst Prof, Fine Arts, Eastern Michigan Univ, Ypsilanti, MI, 1966–67; Asst Prof, Univ of Southern California, Los Angeles, CA, 1970–75, Prof, Fine Arts, 1976 to present
AWARDS: Vesta Award, Visual Arts, Women's Bldg, Los Angeles, CA, 1984
RECENT EXHIB: Claremont Grad Sch, CA, 1992; Spertus Mus of Judaica, Chicago, IL, 1992
COLLECTIONS: Chicago Art Inst, IL; Los Angeles County Mus, CA; New York Public Library, NY; Norwegian Nat Coll; Bibliotheque Nat, Paris, France
PRINTERS: Bill Weege, Madison, WI (BW); Andrew Rubin, Madison, WI (AR); Tandem Press, Univ of Wisconsin, Madison, WI (TanPr)
PUBLISHERS: Tandem Press, Univ of Wisconsin, Madison, WI (TanPr)

RUTH ELLEN WEISBERG CONTINUED

GALLERIES: Jack Rutberg Fine Arts, Los Angeles, CA; Alice Simsar Gallery, Ann Arbor, MI

MAILING ADDRESS: c/o University of Southern California, Art Department, Los Angeles, CA 90089

TITLE	PUBLISHER	PRINTER	DATE	MEDIUM	DIMENSION (PAPER SIZE) IN INCHES	TYPE OF PAPER	EDITION NUMBER	NO. OF COLORS	ORIGINAL OPENING PRICE	CURRENT RETAIL PRICE
SOLD OUT EDITIONS (RARE):										
The Artist	TanPr	BW/AR/TanPr	1989	MON	49 X 29 EA	TAB	1 EA	Varies	2000 EA	3000 EA
CURRENT EDITIONS:										
The Good Daughter	TanPr	BW/AR/TanPr	1989	LC	40 X 30	AC/W	40	3	1000	1000

CLEMENS WEISS

BORN: Dusseldorf, Germany; September 26, 1955
RECENT EXHIB: Forderkoje Galerie Lohrl, Cologne, Germany, 1989; Joseph Haubrich Kunsthalle, Cologne, Germany, 1989; Neuer Aachener Kunstverein, Aachen, Germany, 1990; Delta Galerie, Dusseldorf, Germany, 1990; Andrea Ruggieri Gallery, Wash, DC, 1990; Ronald Feldman Fine Arts, NY, 1989,91; Galerie Lohrl, Monchengladbach, Germany, 1989,90,91,92; Galerie Bernd Lutze, Friedrichshafen, Germany, 1990,92; Virginia Commonwealth Univ, Anderson Gallery, Richmond, VA, 1992

COLLECTIONS: Mus of Mod Art, NY; Wadsworth Atheneum, Hartford, CT; Commonwealth Univ, Anderson Gallery, Richmond, VA; New York Public Library, NY; Pushkin Mus, Moscow, Russia; June Zimmerli Art Mus, Rutgers Univ, New Brunswick, NJ: Folckwang Mus, Essen, Germany
PUBLISHERS: Ronald Feldman Fine Arts, NY (RFFA)
GALLERIES: Ronald Feldman Fine Arts, New York, NY; Galerie Lohr, Cologne, Germany & Monchengladbach, Germany; Galerie Bernd Lutze, Friedrichshafen, Germany; Andrea Ruggieri Gallery, Wash, DC
MAILING ADDRESS: c/o Ronald Feldman Fine Arts, 31 Mercer St., New York, NY 10013

TITLE	PUBLISHER	PRINTER	DATE	MEDIUM	DIMENSION (PAPER SIZE) IN INCHES	TYPE OF PAPER	EDITION NUMBER	NO. OF COLORS	ORIGINAL OPENING PRICE	CURRENT RETAIL PRICE
CURRENT EDITIONS:										
Poems and Drawings (Book with 12 Watercolors—Poems by Albert Vigoleis Thelen) (Set of 12)	RFFA		1989	WA	13 X 10 EA	AP	100 EA		1500 SET	1500 SET
Objectfragmente (Object, Glass and Fragment of Book)	RFFA		1990	MM	14 X 9 X 2		100		1500	1500
Installation of No. 3 Multiple (English Edition)	RFFA		1990	WA	4 X 12	AP	30		2500	2500
Installation No. 3 Multiple (German Edition)	RFFA		1990	WA	4 X 12	AP	30		2500	2500
Fragments (Set of 12)	RFFA		1990	EB	15 X 11 EA	Nouchi	30 EA		1800 SET	1800 SET

DANIEL W WELDEN

BORN: New York, NY; October 22, 1941
TEACHING: Prof, Art, State Univ of New York, Stony Brook, NY, 1977–85
EDUCATION: Adelphi Univ Printmaking, MA, 1967; Garden City, NY, BA, 1964, Acad of Fine Art, Munich, Germany, 1969–71; State Univ of New York, Stony Brook, NY
AWARDS: Soc of Am Graphic Artists, Nat Exhib Award, 1980; Printmaking Council of NJ, 1981; State Univ of New York Research Found Travel Grant, Germany, 1982; Nat Endowment for the Arts, Wilkes Col, Wilkes-Barre, PA, Artist in Res, 1985

RECENT EXHIB: Anthony Giordano Gallery & Visual Arts Center, NY, 1988
COLLECTIONS: Long Beach Mus, Long Beach, NY; Frans Masereel Mus, Kasterlee, Belgium; Inez Whipple Coll, Guilde Hall Mus, East Hampton, NY; Clatsop Cumm Col, Astoria OR; Kunsthochschule, Kassel, Germany; Great Mus of Art, Alice Baber Mem, Lafayette, IN
PUBLISHERS: Hampton Editions, Ltd, Sag Harbor, NY (HE); Rijkscentrum Frans Masereel, Belgium (RFM)
GALLERIES: Felice Cole Gallery, Setauket, NY; Loft Gallery, Southampton, NY; Gallery North, Setauket, NY; Fridholm Fine Arts Gallery, Asheville, NC
MAILING ADDRESS: P O Box 520, Sag Harbor, NY 11963

TITLE	PUBLISHER	PRINTER	DATE	MEDIUM	DIMENSION (PAPER SIZE) IN INCHES	TYPE OF PAPER	EDITION NUMBER	NO. OF COLORS	ORIGINAL OPENING PRICE	CURRENT RETAIL PRICE
SOLD OUT EDITIONS (RARE):										
Brown Line	HE	ART	1978	LC	20 X 16	SOM	13	4	140	400
Promethius	HE	ART	1979	LC	30 X 23	SOM	40	3	125	350
Straight & Narrow	HE	ART	1979	LB	17 X 16	SOM	20	1	75	300
US Lines	HE	ART	1979	LB	47 X 36	SOM	6	1	200	600
AAA Trucking	HE	ART	1980	LB	47 X 36	SOM	6	1	400	950
CURRENT EDITIONS:										
Belgium Plate	HE	ART	1979	LC	19 X 26	SOM	8	3	140	300
NY Worlds Fair	HE	ART	1979	LC	26 X 30	SOM	6	3	140	450
Florida Plate	HE	ART	1980	LC	17 X 23	SOM	10	3	175	350
Subaru	HE	ART	1980	LC	17 X 23	SOM	6	2	185	350
Mud Flap	HE	ART	1980	LB	41 X 29	SOM	6	1	200	450
Subaru Landscape	HE	ART	1980	LC	19 X 24	SOM	12	4	140	450
GMC	HE	ART	1980	LC	22 X 16	SOM	10	3	125	300
IL9274	HE	ART	1980	AB	15 X 18	SOM	10	1	125	350
Texas Truck	HE	ART	1981	LC	29 X 25	SOM	45	4	175	400
Missouri Plate	HE	ART	1981	LC	20 X 25	SOM	12	4	140	350
Tennessee	HE	ART	1981	LC	10 X 18	SOM	8	2	125	300
Connecticut Plate	HE	ART	1981	LC	17 X 24	SOM	12	4	140	350

JAMES WELLING

BORN: Hartford, CT; 1951
EDUCATION: Carnegie-Mellon Univ, Pittsburgh, PA, Studio Art, 1969–71; California Col of Arts, Valencia, CA, BFA, 1972, MFA, 1974
AWARDS: New York Found Arts Fel, 1986; Art in Res, Lightworks, Syracuse, NY, 1986
RECENT EXHIB: Jay Gorney Mod Art, NY, 1989; Kunsthalle, Bern, Switzerland, 1990; Sous Sol, Geneva, Switzerland, 1990

COLLECTIONS: Mus of Mod Art, Vienna, Austria
PRINTERS: Artist (ART)
PUBLISHERS: Artist (ART)
GALLERIES: Cash/Newhouse Gallery, New York, NY; Jay Gorney Modern Art, New York, NY
MAILING ADDRESS: 135 Grand St, New York, NY 10013

TITLE	PUBLISHER	PRINTER	DATE	MEDIUM	DIMENSION (PAPER SIZE) IN INCHES	TYPE OF PAPER	EDITION NUMBER	NO. OF COLORS	ORIGINAL OPENING PRICE	CURRENT RETAIL PRICE
CURRENT EDITIONS:										
Bigelow House, Newton, MA, 1986–87	ART	ART	1988	PH	22 X 18		4		1500	1500
III (Framed)	ART	ART	1988	PH/POL	24 X 20		1 EA		3500	3500

NEIL G WELLIVER

BORN: Millville, PA; July 22, 1929
EDUCATION: Philadelphia Mus Col of Art, PA, BFA, 1953; Yale Univ, New Haven, CT, MFA, 1955
TEACHING: Cooper Union Sch, NY, 1953–57; Yale Univ, New Haven, CT, 1955–65; Univ of Pennsylvania, Phila, PA, 1966 to present
AWARDS: Morse Fel, 1960–61; Skowhegan Award, ME, 1975
RECENT EXHIB: Univ of Hartford, Joseloff Gallery, West Hartford, CT, 1992; Colby Col, Waterville, ME, 1992; Lincoln Center Fine Art Prints, Avery Fisher Hall, NY, 1992; Knight Gallery, Spirit Square Art Center, Charlotte, NC, 1992
COLLECTIONS: Brandeis Mus, Waltham, MA; New York Univ, NY; North Carolina Mus of Art, Raleigh, NC; Pennsylvania Acad of Fine Arts, Phila, PA; Hirshhorn Mus, Wash, DC; Philadelphia Mus of Art, PA; Whitney Mus of Am Art, NY; Smith Col, Northampton, MA; Vassar Col, Poughkeepsie, NY; Colby Col, ME, Utah Mus of Fine Arts, Salt Lake City, UT; Boston Mus of Fine Arts, MA; Metropolitan Mus of Art, NY
PRINTERS: Shigemitsu Tsukaguchi, Phila, PA (ST); Tsuka-Guchi Atelier, Phila, PA (TGA); Arlene Gostin (AG)
PUBLISHERS: Harcus-Krakow, Ltd, Boston, MA (HKL); Brooke Alexander, Inc, NY (BAI)
GALLERIES: Brooke Alexander, Inc, New York, NY; Fischbach Gallery, New York, NY; Brody's Gallery, Wash, DC; Marsha Mateyka Gallery, Wash, DC; Harcus Gallery, Boston, MA; Adams-Middleton Gallery, Dallas, TX; Flanders Contemporary Art, Minneapolis, MN; Marlborough Gallery, New York, NY; O'Farrell Gallery, Brunswick, ME; Randell Beck Gallery, Boston, MA; Images Gallery, Toledo, OH; Bayview Gallery, Camden, ME
MAILING ADDRESS: RD 2, Lincolnville, ME 04849

TITLE	PUBLISHER	PRINTER	DATE	MEDIUM	DIMENSION (PAPER SIZE) IN INCHES	TYPE OF PAPER	EDITION NUMBER	NO. OF COLORS	ORIGINAL OPENING PRICE	CURRENT RETAIL PRICE
SOLD OUT EDITIONS (RARE):										
Landscapes (Set of 6)	HKL		1973	SP	40 X 40 EA	BCP/80			2000 SET	12000 SET
Trout II	BAI		1973	EB/HC	22 X 23	R/BFK	14	Varies	350	3500
Nude	BAI		1974	EB/HC	15 X 11	R/BFK	28	Varies	225	1800
Brown Trout	BAI		1975	EB/HC	27 X 36	AP	37	Varies	500	4000
Maine Landscape	BAI		1976	LC	22 X 30	AP	150	Varies	200	1000
Salmon	BAI		1977	EB/HC	27 X 36	AP	40	Varies	750	4000
Smelts	BAI		1977	EB/HC	23 X 25	AP	40	Varies	650	4000
Cedar Water Pool	BAI		1977	LC	22 X 31	AP	36		250	900
Brown Trout State II	BAI		1978	EB/HC	28 X 37	AP	50	Varies	450	900
Immature Great	BAI		1978	EB/A	31 X 28	AP	60		650	4000
Canadian Geese	BAI		1978–79	EB/WA/HC	33 X 28	AP	40	Varies	900	4000
Big Flowage	BAI		1979	WB	24 X 26	KNP	20		250	800
Big Flowage	BAI	ST/TGA	1979	WC	21 X 24	KNP	80		400	1500
Osprey's Nest	BAI	ST/TGA	1979–80	WC	36 X 36	KNP	80		800	3500
Trout and Reflection	BAI	ST/TGA	1980	WC	36 X 36	KNP	60		1000	4000
Moose	BAI	ST/TGA	1981	AC	18 X 15	KNP	79		400	700
Trout	BAI	ST/TGA	1981	WC	18 X 15	KNP	130		350	1500
Night Scene	BAI	ST/TGA	1982	WC	14 X 16	AP	90		750	1800
Deer	BAI	AG	1983	A/EC	29 X 33	AC/W	68	11	1500	2500
Birches	BAI	ST/TGA	1983	WC	35 X 34	KNP	100	15	1800	3500
Wood Duck	BAI		1985	EB/HC	24 X 26	AC/W	90	Varies	1800	3000

LYNTON WELLS

BORN: Baltimore, Maryland; October 21, 1940
EDUCATION: Rhode Island Sch of Design, Providence, RI, BFA, 1962; Cranbrook Acad of Art, Bloomfield Hills, MI, MFA, 1965

AWARDS: Nat Endowment for the Arts Grant, 1975
COLLECTIONS: Mus of Mod Art, NY; Dallas Mus of Fine Art, TX
PRINTERS: Sienna Studios, NY (SiS)
PUBLISHERS: 724 Prints, NY (724P)
GALLERIES: Holly Solomon Gallery, New York, NY; Lawrence Mangel Gallery, Phila, PA

TITLE	PUBLISHER	PRINTER	DATE	MEDIUM	DIMENSION (PAPER SIZE) IN INCHES	TYPE OF PAPER	EDITION NUMBER	NO. OF COLORS	ORIGINAL OPENING PRICE	CURRENT RETAIL PRICE
SOLD OUT EDITIONS (RARE):										
Untitled	724P	SiS	1978	LC	30 X 21	AC/W	50	4	225	400

The print market has become very selective. For the first time since we published the first edition of The Printworld Directory in 1982, the prices of prints have been greatly reduced and greatly increased for the same artists by the most reputable and established print publishers. Check the fifth edition to understand the movement.

C J WELLS

BORN: Santa Fe, NM; 1952
EDUCATION: Univ of California, Los Angeles, CA; Eastern Col Billings, MT
RECENT EXHIB: Lakota Gallery, Santa Monica, CA, 1989
COLLECTIONS: Univ of New Mexico, Albuquerque, NM; Inst of Am Indian Art, Santa Fe, NM
PRINTERS: Southwest Graphics, Scottsdale, AZ (SG); Hand Graphics, Ltd, Santa Fe, NM (HG)
PUBLISHERS: C G Rein Publishers, St Paul, NM (CGR)
GALLERIES: C G Rein Galleries, Scottsdale, AZ & Santa Fe, NM & Houston, TX & Minneapolis, MN
MAILING ADDRESS: 222 Polaco St, Santa Fe, NM 87501

TITLE	PUBLISHER	PRINTER	DATE	MEDIUM	DIMENSION (PAPER SIZE) IN INCHES	TYPE OF PAPER	EDITION NUMBER	NO. OF COLORS	ORIGINAL OPENING PRICE	CURRENT RETAIL PRICE
SOLD OUT EDITIONS (RARE):										
The Chief's Son	CGR	SG	1981	LC	30 X 22	AC/B	100	7	250	350
Ii Hawiik, State I (Lavender)	CGR	SG	1982	LC	22 X 30	AC/B	50	7	250	350
Ii Hawiik, State II (Turquoise)	CGR	SG	1982	LC	22 X 30	AC/B	50	7	250	350
Red Crow	CGR	SG	1982	LC	30 X 22	AC/B	100	7	300	360
Cold Snow Moon	CGR	HG	1982	LC	27 X 28	AC/W	100	5	250	450
Horse Canyon	CGR	HG	1982	LC	34 X 24	AC/B	100	6	250	450
Journey Through the Ten Sleeps	CGR	HG	1983	LC	40 X 30	AC/B	100		250	450

MARY ANN WENNIGER

BORN: Berlin, Germany; October 12, 1931
EDUCATION: Inst of Fine Arts, New York Univ, NY; Boston Univ, MA; Harvard Univ, Cambridge, MA, MA
TEACHING: New England Sch of Art & Design, Boston, MA
COLLECTIONS: DeCordova Mus, Boston, MA
PRINTERS: Chamelon Press, El Paso, TX (CP); Wenniger Graphics, Boston, MA (WG)
PUBLISHERS: Wenniger Graphics, Boston, MA (WG)
GALLERIES: Windsor Gallery, Miami, FL; Paige Gallery, Dallas, TX; Alice Bingham Gallery, Memphis, TN; The Print Mint Gallery, Wilmette, IL; Alice Deming Gallery, New London, NH; Wenniger Graphics, Boston, MA
MAILING ADDRESS: 174 Newbury St, Boston, MA 02116

TITLE	PUBLISHER	PRINTER	DATE	MEDIUM	DIMENSION (PAPER SIZE) IN INCHES	TYPE OF PAPER	EDITION NUMBER	NO. OF COLORS	ORIGINAL OPENING PRICE	CURRENT RETAIL PRICE
SOLD OUT EDITIONS (RARE):										
Afternoon Shadows	WG	WG	1980	COL	16 X 30	GE	50	8	125	250
CURRENT EDITIONS:										
New England Churches	WG	WG	1982	COL	18 X 30	GE	50	6	200	250
Summer Conversations	WG	CP	1983	COL	18 X 30	GE	50	9	150	250
Morning Market	WG	OCS	1983	COL	18 X 30	GE	50	7	200	250
A Time to Think	WG	CP	1984	COL	18 X 24	GE	50	3	150	250
Rain Clouds	WG	WG	1984	COL	48 X 60	HMP	10	5	700	750
Bacon Bits (5 pcs)	WG	WG	1984	COL	18 X 30 EA	HMP	10	4	1200	1300
The Tailor Shop	WG	WG	1984	COL	18 X 30	GE	50	8	200	250
The Boat Yard	WG	WG	1985	COl	18 X 30	GE	50	10	200	250
Sandcastles	WG	WG	1985	COl	48 X 96	HMP	10	7	1200	1300

FRED W WESSEL

BORN: Amityville, NY; June 14, 1946
EDUCATION: Syracuse Univ, NY, BFA, 1968; Pratt Graphics Center, NY, 1968–71; Univ of Massachusetts, Amherst, MA, MFA, 1976
TEACHING: Univ of Massachusetts, Amherst, MA, 1974–76; Instr, Hartford Art Sch, Univ of Hartford, West Hartford, CT, 1977; Asst Prof, Hartford Art Sch, Univ of Hartford, West Hartford, CT, 1979 to present
AWARDS: Vincent B Coffin Grant for Faculty Research, Univ of Hartford, West Hartford, CT, 1979,81
RECENT EXHIB: Philadelphia Mus of Art, PA, 1987; Schneider Mus of Art, Ashland, OR, 1987; Printworks Gallery, Chicago, IL, 1988; Stone Press Gallery, Seattle, WA, 1988
COLLECTIONS: Mus of Mod Art, NY; Brooklyn Mus, NY; Art Inst of Chicago, IL; De Cordova Mus, Lincoln, MA; Wichita Mus of Art, KS; Miami Univ, OH; Edinboro Col, PA; Westfield State Col, MA; Art Inst of Chicago, IL; Univ of Hartford, West Hartford, CT; State Univ of New York, Potsdam, NY; Ft Hays State Univ, KS; Univ of Dallas, TX; Dulin Gallery, Univ of Connecticut, Storrs, CT; State Univ of New York, Albany, NY; Univ of Rhode Island, Providence, RI; Univ of Vermont, Burlington, VT; Philadelphia Mus of Art, PA
PRINTERS: Barbara Telleen (BT); Susan Brown (SB); Old Lyme Art Works, CT (OLAW)
PUBLISHERS: Old Lyme Art Works, CT (OLAW)
GALLERIES: Old Lyme Art Works, Old Lyme, CT; Sun Valley Center Gallery, ID; Printworks, Ltd, Chicago, IL; Stone Press Editions, Seattle, WA; Dorsky Gallery, New York, NY; Jerald Melberg Gallery, Inc, Charlotte, NC
MAILING ADDRESS: 4 Edgewood Terrace, Northampton, MA 01060

TITLE	PUBLISHER	PRINTER	DATE	MEDIUM	DIMENSION (PAPER SIZE) IN INCHES	TYPE OF PAPER	EDITION NUMBER	NO. OF COLORS	ORIGINAL OPENING PRICE	CURRENT RETAIL PRICE
SOLD OUT EDITIONS (RARE):										
Aquarium (Old Lyme)	OLAW	BT/SB	1984	LC/GL/HC	22 X 30	AP88	48	5	425	600
Aquarium Rennaissance	OLAW	BT/SB	1984	LC	22 X 30	AP88		4	275	400

H C WESTERMANN

BORN: Los Angeles, CA (1922–1981)
EDUCATION: Art Inst of Chicago, IL, BFA, 1947–54; Hon DFA, 1979
AWARDS: Nat Arts Council, NY, 1967
RECENT EXHIB: Lennon, Weinberg Gallery, NY, 1988; Univ of Wisconsin, Carlsten Art Gallery, Stevens Point, WI, 1992
COLLECTIONS: Mus of Contemp Art, Chicago, IL; Whitney Mus of Am Art, NY; San Diego Mus of Art, CA; Seattle Art Mus, WA; Des Moines Art Center, IA
PRINTERS: Jerry Raidiger, Chicago, IL (JR); Landfall Press, Inc, Chicago, IL (LPI); Tamarind Inst, Albuquerque, NM (TI)
PUBLISHERS: Allan Frumkin Inc, NY (AFI); Tamarind Inst, Albuquerque, NM (TI)
GALLERIES: John Berggruen Gallery, San Francisco, CA; Lennon, Weinberg Gallery, New York, NY; James Corcoran Gallery, Santa Monica, CA; Hank Baum Gallery, San Francisco, CA

H C WESTERMANN CONTINUED

TITLE	PUBLISHER	PRINTER	DATE	MEDIUM	DIMENSION (PAPER SIZE) IN INCHES	TYPE OF PAPER	EDITION NUMBER	NO. OF COLORS	ORIGINAL OPENING PRICE	CURRENT RETAIL PRICE
SOLD OUT EDITIONS (RARE):										
See America First (Set of 18)	TI	TI	1968	LC	22 X 30 EA	AP	20 EA		1500 SET	12000 SET
Six Lithographs: (Set of 6):									1250 SET	11000 SET
Death Ship in Port	AFI	JR/LPI	1972	LC	25 X 33	R/BFK	60	6	250	2000
Green River	AFI	JR/LPI	1972	LC	25 X 33	AP	60	8	250	2000
The Lost Planet	AFI	JR/LPI	1972	LC	25 X 33	R/BFK	60	7	250	2000
J Print	AFI	JR/LPI	1972	LC	25 X 33	R/BFK	60	9	250	2000
An Affair in the Islands	AFI	JR/LPI	1972	LC	25 X 33	R/BFK	60	9	250	2000
Holiday Inn	AFI	JR/LPI	1972	LC	25 X 33	R/BFK	60	8	250	2000

DOUG WEST

BORN: Riverside, CA; May 29, 1947
EDUCATION: Univ of Southern California, Los Angeles, CA, BFA, 1966–70; Brigham Young Univ, Honolulu, HI, 1971–72; California Western Univ, CA, 1965–66

RECENT EXHIB: Barrett Gallery, El Paso, TX, 1987
PRINTERS: Artist (ART)
PUBLISHERS: Bowles-Hopkins Gallery, San Francisco, CA (BHG); John Szoke Graphics, Inc, NY (JSG)
GALLERIES: Munson Gallery, Sante Fe, NM; MacLaren/Markowitz Gallery, Boulder, CO; Leslie Levy Fine Art, Scottsdale, AZ; Big Sky Gallery, Lenox, MA; Post Gallery, Houston, TX

TITLE	PUBLISHER	PRINTER	DATE	MEDIUM	DIMENSION (PAPER SIZE) IN INCHES	TYPE OF PAPER	EDITION NUMBER	NO. OF COLORS	ORIGINAL OPENING PRICE	CURRENT RETAIL PRICE
SOLD OUT EDITIONS (RARE):										
Grace	BHG	ART	1981	SP	36 X 23	FAB	70	51	275	800
Dreams of the Dawn	BHG	ART	1981	SP	39 X 27	FAB	62	62	350	800
Keeping Still	BHG	ART	1981	SP	19 X 49	GE	50	49	300	800
La Tetilla Peak	BHG	ART	1981	P	21 X 29	AP	90	74	300	450
Southern Vision	BHG	ART	1981	SP	22 X 30	SOM	62	21	300	450
Storm over the Sangres	BHG	ART	1981	SP	22 X 30	AP	100	48	300	450
Sky Poem	BHG	ART	1981	SP	29 X 21	AP	100	21	300	450
To Stand Alone	BHG	ART	1982	SP	22 X 30	SOM	100	25	300	450
Cielo	JSG	ART	1983	SP	30 X 22	STP	100	58	375	550
Mesa Verde	JSG	ART	1984	SP	29 X 22	STP	110	58	350	500
The Wanderer's Call	JSG	ART	1984	SP	30 X 22	STP	110	58	400	750
In the Afterglow	JSG	ART	1985	SP	33 X 22	STP	110		400	750
A String of Pearls	JSG	ART	1985	SP	39 X 28	STP	120		550	800
Sandias	JSG	ART	1985	SP	23 X 30	STP	100		425	650
CURRENT EDITIONS:										
Southern Spur	JSG	ART	1985	SP	30 X 44	STP	110		525	650
Shacoan Sun Stride	JSG	ART	1986	SP	16 X 30	STP	120		350	500
Her Every Ward	JSG	ART	1986	SP	30 X 22	STP	120		400	450
Tranquility	JSG	ART	1986	SP	22 X 15	STP	120		300	400
Where Waters Meet	JSG	ART	1986	SP	22 X 15	STP	120		300	400
Mountains and Seas (Set of 4)	JSG	ART	1986	SP	15 X 11 EA	STP	120 EA		600 SET	900 SET

EILEEN MONAGHAN WHITAKER

BORN: Holyoke, MA; November 22, 1911
EDUCATION: Massachusetts Col of Art, Boston, MA
AWARDS: Silver Medal, Am Watercolor Soc, NY, 1965
COLLECTIONS: High Art Mus, Atlanta, GA; Charles & Emma Frye Mus, Seattle, WA; Hispanic Mus, NY; Nat Acad of Design, NY; Oklahoma Art Mus, Oklahoma City, OK

PRINTERS: American Atelier, NY (AA)
PUBLISHERS: Circle Fine Art, Chicago, IL (CFA)
GALLERIES: Jones Gallery, La Jolla, CA; Circle Galleries, San Diego, CA & San Francisco, CA & Northbrook, IL & Houston, TX & Pittsburgh, PA & Soho, NY & Chicago, IL & Scottsdale, AZ & Beverly Hills, CA & Sherman Oaks, CA & Costa Mesa, CA & Palm Beach, FL & Honolulu, HI & Las Vegas, NV & New Orleans, LA & Seattle, WA; Riggs Galleries, La Jolla, CA
MAILING ADDRESS: 1579 Alta La Jolla Drive, La Jolla, CA 92037

TITLE	PUBLISHER	PRINTER	DATE	MEDIUM	DIMENSION (PAPER SIZE) IN INCHES	TYPE OF PAPER	EDITION NUMBER	NO. OF COLORS	ORIGINAL OPENING PRICE	CURRENT RETAIL PRICE
SOLD OUT EDITIONS (RARE):										
Elena	CGL	AA	1971	SP	35 X 23	AP	300		100	625

GUY WHITNEY

PRINTERS: Mary McDonald, Chicago, IL (MM); Landfall Press Inc, Chicago, IL (LPI)
PUBLISHERS: Landfall Press, Chicago, IL (LPI); NAME Gallery, Chicago, IL (NAME)
GALLERIES: Landfall Press, Inc, Chicago, IL; NAME Gallery, Chicago, IL

TITLE	PUBLISHER	PRINTER	DATE	MEDIUM	DIMENSION (PAPER SIZE) IN INCHES	TYPE OF PAPER	EDITION NUMBER	NO. OF COLORS	ORIGINAL OPENING PRICE	CURRENT RETAIL PRICE
SOLD OUT EDITIONS (RARE):										
Grid	LPI/NAME	MM/LPI	1980	LC	30 X 22	AP/W	100	4	150	350

TOM WESSELMANN

BORN: Cincinnati, Ohio; February 23, 1931
EDUCATION: Hiram Col, OH; Univ of Cincinnati, OH, BA; Art Acad of Cincinnati, OH; Cooper Union Art Sch, NY
RECENT EXHIB: Art Design Col of Design, Pasadena, CA, 1987; Lennon/Weinberg Gallery, NY, 1988; Nan Miller Gallery, Rochester, NY, 1989; Jonathan Novak Contemp Art, Los Angeles, CA, 1990; Hara Mus of Contemp Art, Tokyo, Japan, 1990; Hokin Gallery, Palm Beach, FL, 1990; Avanti Galleries, NY, 1990; Wilkey Modern & Contemporary, Seattle, WA, 1990; Morgan Gallery, Boston, MA, 1990
COLLECTIONS: Mus of Mod Art, NY; Whitney Mus of Am Art, NY; Dallas Mus of Fine Arts, TX; Albright-Knox Art Gallery, Buffalo, NY; Brandeis Univ, Waltham, MA; Cincinnati Mus of Art, OH; Walker Art Inst, Minneapolis, MN; Philadelphia Mus of Art, PA; Princeton Univ, NJ; Univ of Nebraska; Rice Univ, Houston, TX; Univ of Texas; Washington Univ, St Louis, MO; Atkins Mus of Fine Arts, Kansas City, MO; Suermondt Mus, Aachen, Germany; Worcester Art Mus, MA; Nasjonalgalleriet, Oslo, Norway; Hirshhorn Mus, Wash, DC
PRINTERS: Original Editions, NT (OEd); Styria Studio, NY (SS); Chiron Press, NY (CP); Norman Lassiter, NY (NL); Editions Lassiter-Meisel, NY (ELM); Maurel Studio, NY (MS); Steve Maiorano, Port Washington, NY (SM); Screened Images, Port Washington, NY (SI); Bummy Huss, NY (BH); Tom Wesselman Studio (TWS); Michael Berdan, NY (MB); American Atelier, NY (AA); Abbeville Press (AbPr); Artist (ART)

PUBLISHERS: Multiples, NY (M); Transworld Arts, Inc, NY (TAI); Sidney Janis Editions, NY (SJE); Circle Fine Art, Chicago, IL (CFA); Original Editions, NY (OEd); Patricia Branstead, NY (PB); Aeropress, NY (A); Metropolitan Opera Assn, NY (MOA); Styria Studio, NY (SS); Abbeville Press, (AbPr); International Images, Inc, Putney, VT (InIm); Rosenthal China, Germany (RC); Artist (ART)
GALLERIES: Charles Whitchurch Fine Arts, Huntington Beach, CA; Hokin Galleries, Palm Beach, FL & Bay Harbor Islands, FL; Stein Bartlow Gallery, Ltd, Chicago, IL; Golden Gallery, Boston, MA; Maxwell Davidson Gallery, New York; Sidney Janis Gallery, New York, NY; Mary Ryan Gallery, New York, NY; Marian Goodman Gallery, New York, NY; Morningstar Gallery, New York, NY; Charles Foley Gallery, Columbus, OH; Argus Fine Arts, Eugene, OR; Martin Lawrence Galleries, Phila, PA & Soho, NY; Michael H Lord Gallery, Milwaukee, WI; International Images, Inc, New York, NY; Morgan Gallery, Boston, MA; L'Imagerie, Encino, CA; Paul Matisse Fine Arts, Los Angeles, CA; Caldwell-Snyder Gallery, San Francisco, CA; Walton-Gilbert Gallery, San Francisco, CA; Jaffe Baker Gallery, Boca Raton, FL; Ann Jaffe Gallery, Bay Harbor Islands, FL; Margaret Lipworth Fine Art, Boca Raton, FL; Margot Gallery, Inc, Palm Beach, FL; Kass/Meridian Gallery, Chicago, IL; Alan Brown Gallery, Hartsdale, NY; Thomas Erben Gallery, Inc, New York, NY; Posner Gallery, Milwaukee, WI; Nan Miller Gallery, Rochester, NY; Adams-Middleton Gallery, Dallas, TX
MAILING ADDRESS: RD 1, Box 36, Long Eddy, NY 12760

Institute of Contemporary Art (ICA); International Images, Inc (II)

Tom Wesselmann
Blonde Vivienne
Courtesy International Images, Inc

Tom Wesselmann
Big Blonde
Courtesy International Images, Inc

TITLE	PUBLISHER	PRINTER	DATE	MEDIUM	DIMENSION (PAPER SIZE) IN INCHES	TYPE OF PAPER	EDITION NUMBER	NO. OF COLORS	ORIGINAL OPENING PRICE	CURRENT RETAIL PRICE
SOLD OUT EDITIONS (RARE):										
Cut Out Nude (from 11 Pop Artists I) (ICA-4)	OEd	OEd	1965	SP	20 X 24 EA	VINYL	200 EA		300 EA	8500 EA
TV Still Life (from 11 Pop Artists III)	OEd	OEd	1963	SP	29 X 38 EA		200 EA		300 EA	8500 EA
Great American Nude Cut Out (Watercolor with Lithographic Outline on Paper and Acrylic)			1970		13 X 17		100		500	18000
Nude Banner, Brown Version	M	PB/A	1971	MULT	60 X 70	FELT	10		2500	10000
Claire's Valentine	M	PB/A	1973	MULT	78 X 72	VINYL			4000	10000
Nude Banner, Pink Version	M	PB/A	1976	MULT	50 X 66	VINYL	20		2500	10000
Smoker (ICA-23)	M	SS	1976	LC/EMB	22 X 30	AP	75	20	750	9000
Nude (ICA-24)	M	SS	1976	LC/SP/EMB	22 X 30	R/BFK	75	34	900	9000
Smoker	TAI	CP	1976	SP	26 X 20	R/100	175	27	600	5500
Bedroom Face (ICA-26)	M	SS	1977	AC	24 X 20	R/100	75	29	1000	5500
Seascape Portfolio (Set of 5):									5000 SET	28000 SET
Seascape Face	ART	ART	1978	PEN/LIQ	11 X 11	AP/EMB	20	10	1200	6000
Seascape Tit	ART	ART	1978	PEN/LIQ	11 X 10	AP/EMB	20	10	1200	6000
Seascape Nude	ART	ART	1978	PEN/LIQ	10 X 11	AP/EMB	20	10	1200	6000

TOM WESSELMANN CONTINUED

TITLE	PUBLISHER	PRINTER	DATE	MEDIUM	DIMENSION (PAPER SIZE) IN INCHES	TYPE OF PAPER	EDITION NUMBER	NO. OF COLORS	ORIGINAL OPENING PRICE	CURRENT RETAIL PRICE
SOLD OUT EDITIONS (RARE):										
Bedroom Portfolio (Set of 5):									5000 SET	30000 SET
Bedroom Face (with Pencil and Thinned Liquitex)	ART	ART	1978	PEN/LIQ	10 X 11	AP/EMB	20	10	1200	6000
Bedroom Tit	ART	ART	1978	PEN/LIQ	11 X 10	AP/EMB	20	10	1200	6500
Nude Painting Print	SJE	TWS	1979	OIL/CAN	24 X 26	HMP	28		800	7500
Tiny Shoes & Tulips	SJE	ART	1980	LIQ	2 X 2 X 1	BB	24		1000	7500
Tiny Dropped Bra	SJE	ART	1980	LIQ	3 X 5 X 2	BB	21	6	1000	7500
Nude	AbPr	AbPr	1980	AC	28 X 31	R/BFK	100		750	6000
Stockinged Nude Edition (Brunette, Blond, Redhead)	SJE	ART	1980	LIQ	0 X 19	R/100	25		1000	10000
Claire Nude (Seated Nude Edition)	SJE	MS	1980	SP/LC	31 X 30	AP88	200	30	1000	5000
Nude Aquatint	M	PB/A	1980	EB/A	35 X 38	AP88	100		2000	5000
Smoker Sculpture	M	PB/A	1980	MULT/M	33 X 21 X 15		15		5500	10000
Beautiful Kate	SJE/M	ART	1981	PEN/LIQ	3 X 9	R/100/B	14			7500
Smoker Sculpture Edition	SJE/M	ART	1981	PA/ALUM	12 X 32 X 14		15		6000	10000
Lulu	CFA/MOA	AA	1982	LC	22 X 30	HMP	250		1000	8000
Tulip & Smoker	SJE/M	MB	1982	PA/ALUM	33 X 21 X 15	HMP	15		6500	8000
Cynthia Nude	M	MB	1982	SP/LC	29 X 40	HMP	100		1250	8000
Cynthia in the Bedroom	TAI	SI	1982	SP	33 X 37	R/100	100		1250	8000
Helen Nude	TAI	ELM/NL	1982	SP	36 X 36	R/100	150	26	1250	8000
Seascape Dropout	M	MB	1982	WC	22 X 25	HMP	50	23	1250	6000
Bedroom Dropout	M	MB	1983	WC	25 X 29	HMP	50	21	1500	8500
Reclining Nude/Steel Drawing	SJE	ART	1985	MULT	33 X 12	Steel	50		7500	18000
CURRENT EDITIONS:										
Bedroom Face Print	Inlm	SM/SI	1987	SP	47 X 53	MB/4 Ply	100	16	8500	12000
Blonde Vivienne (II-5)	Inlm	SM/SI	1988	SP	56 X 57	MB/4-Ply	100		8500	12000
Big Blonde (II-6)	Inlm	SM/SI	1988	SP	58 X 77	MB/4-Ply	100		8000	12000
Bedroom Blond Doodle	Inlm	SM/SI	1988	SP	58 X 68	MB/4-Ply	100	10	8000	15000
Woman with Green Blouse	Inlm	SM/SI	1988	SP	56 X 70	MB/4-Ply	100		8000	12000
Still Life with Petunias	Inlm	SM/SI	1988	SP	48 X 62	MB/4-Ply	100	17	4500	12000
Still Life with Fruit, Petunias and Claire (Glazed Porcelain)	RC		1988	MULT	19 X 20		299		3500	5000
Monica Lying on Blanket (Black)/Steel Drawing	SJE	ART	1988	MULT	19 X 41		25		15000	15000
Country Bouquet/Steel Drawing (Steel Laser Cut Painted in Colored Enamel)	ART	ART	1989	MULT	38 X 30		25	10	15000	20000
Vivienne	Inlm	ART	1989	MULT	60 DIA		100	14	8000	12000
Monica Sitting with Mondrian	Inlm	SM/SI	1989	SP	16 X 37		100	10	8500	12000
Steel Drawing Edition: Rosemary Lying on One Elbow	ART/SJE	ART	1989	MULT	8 X 15	Steel	45		5000	12000
Steel Drawing Edition: Monica Lying Down on Robe	ART/SJE	ART	1986–90	MULT	14 X 6	Steel	25		7500	12000
Steel Drawing Edition: Rosemary with Socks, Arms Outstretched	ART/SJE	ART	1989–90	MULT	10 X 12	Steel	25		7500	12000
Untitled	Inlm	ART	1990	LB	50 X 39	R/BFK	26			
Thames Scene, with Power Station	Inlm	SM/SI	1990	SP	59 X 96	MB/4P	100	19		

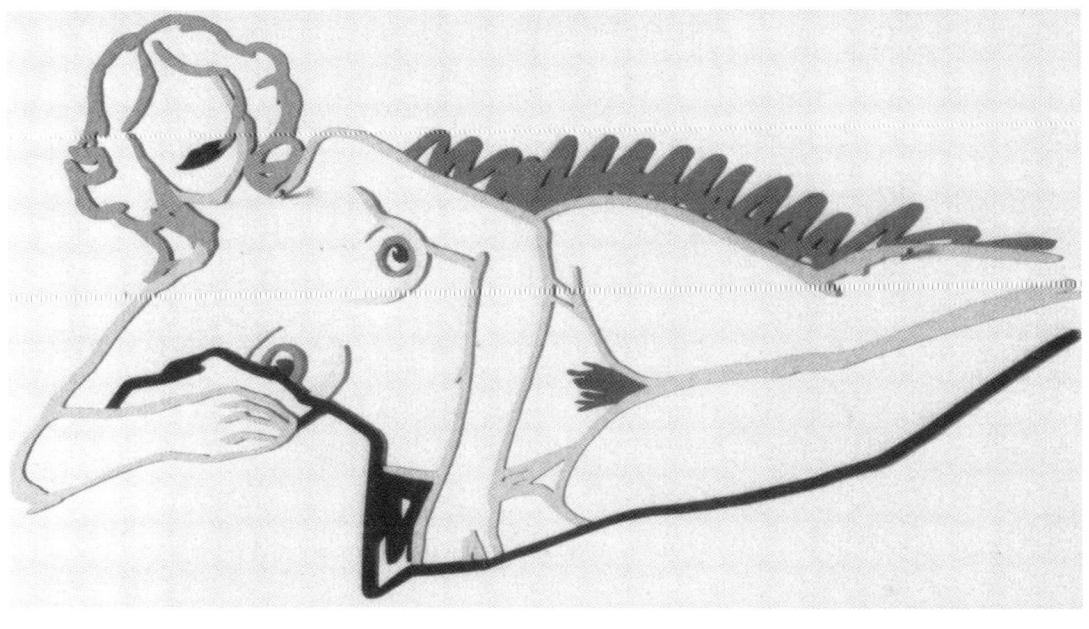

Tom Wesselmann
Rosemary Lying on One Elbow
Courtesy Sidney Janis Gallery
& the Artist

DAVID W WHARTON

BORN: Wichitaw Falls, TX; November 19, 1951
EDUCATION: Univ of Oklahoma, Norman, OK, BFA, 1974; Cranbrook Acad of Art, Bloomfield Hills, MI, MFA, 1978; Univ of Oklahoma City, OK, BFA, 1979
TEACHING: Univ of Washington, Seattle, WA, Spring, 1981; Humboldt State Univ, Arcata, CA, Fall, 1982; Fine Arts Dir, Sun Valley Center for the Arts & Humanities, ID, 1978–86
AWARDS: Litzier Achievement Award, Univ of Oklahoma, Norman, OK, 1974; Ten Western Printmakers Fel, Western States Arts Found, 1979; Dade Book Award, 1982
RECENT EXHIB: South Dakota State Univ, Brookings, SD, 1989
COLLECTIONS: Univ of Lethbridge, Lethbridge, Alberta, Can; Cranbrook Acad Art Mus, Bloomfield Hills, MI; Boise Gallery of Art, ID; Humboldt State Univ, Arcata, CA; Montana State Univ, Bozeman, MT; Oklahoma Center for the Arts, Oklahoma City, OK; Inst of North America, West, Boise, ID; Col of Southern Idaho, Caldwell, ID
PRINTERS: Matthew Sugarman (MS); Alaska Center for the Arts, Anchorage, AK (ACA); Melissa Hall, Seattle, WA (MH); Michael Corney, Seattle, WA (MC); Fran Noel, Bozeman, MI (FN); Artist (ART); Preston Lawing, CT (PL)
PUBLISHERS: Univ of Washington, Seattle, WA (UW); Sun Valley Center for the Arts, ID (SVC); Montana State Univ, Bozeman, MT (MSU); Humboldt State Univ, Arcata, CA (HSU); Cranbrook Acad of Art, Bloomfield Hills, MI (CAA); Artist (ART); Littleton Company, Inc, Spruce Pine, NC (LCI)
GALLERIES: Images Gallery, Ketchum, ID; Mariane Partlou Gallery, Olympia, WA; Harvey K Littleton, Spruce Pine, NC; Little Company, Spruce Pine, NC; Rutgers Barclay Gallery, Santa Fe, NM; Twining Gallery, New York, NY; Robinschon Gallery, Denver, CO; Gail Severn Gallery, Ketchum, ID; Waterworks, Ruth Pearson, Friday Harbor, WA; Susan Duvall Fine Art, Aspen, CO; Kneeland Gallery, Sun Valley, ID; Ellison Gallery, Telluride, CO
MAILING ADDRESS: P O Box 185, Little Switzerland, NC 28749

TITLE	PUBLISHER	PRINTER	DATE	MEDIUM	DIMENSION (PAPER SIZE) IN INCHES	TYPE OF PAPER	EDITION NUMBER	NO. OF COLORS	ORIGINAL OPENING PRICE	CURRENT RETAIL PRICE
SOLD OUT EDITIONS (RARE):										
Souther Prints of Flannery O'Connor Suite (Set of 10)	CAA	ART	1976	LB/I/REL/DPT	11 X 15 EA	GE	10 EA	1 EA	500 SET	2000 SET
Who Said I was Drunk?	SVC	ART	1979	LB	22 X 30	AC	20	1	350	600
Idanha Hotel Suite (Set of 5)	SVC	ART	1980	LB	22 X 30 EA	RP/G	10 EA	1 EA	1200 SET	2500 SET
The Rain Baby Suite (Bound Set of 6)	UW	ART	1981	LB	20 X 26 EA	AP	8 EA	1 EA	800 SET	2500 SET
Set of 2:									3000 SET	5000 SET
Steelhead	LCI	PL	1988	VIT/HC	36 X 36	RICE	50		1500	2500
Salmo Nebulea	LCI	PL	1988	VIT/HC	36 X 36	RICE	50		1500	2500
CURRENT EDITIONS:										
Push Don't Shove It	SVC	ART	1978	LB	22 X 30	AC	20	1	250	500
Frenchmen's Bend	SVC	ART	1980	LB	22 X 30	AC	20	1	300	500
The New Manhattan Cafe	SVC	ART	1980	LB	22 X 30	AC	20	1	300	500
Il Sacraficio d'Trout	HSU	ART	1981	LB	22 X 30	AP	20	1	350	450
A Used Wet Heart	HUS	ART	1981	LB	22 X 30	AP	20	1	350	550
A Simple Big Bang Theory	HSU	ART	1981	LB	22 X 30	AC	20	1	250	400
A Neo Tex-Mex Amphora	HSU	ART	1981	LB	22 X 30	AP	20	1	350	550
Pshaw the Shaw	SVC	ART	1982	ENG/REL	22 X 30	MUR	30	1	350	500
The Blue Room at Gophers Gulch	SVC	ART	1982	LB	22 X 30	AC	20	1	350	500
Attempting to Remove the Bias from the Basic Question. Is it Art?	SVC	ART	1983	ENG/REL	22 X 30	MUR	25	1	350	450
Tell a Vision Tales for Richard Braughtigan	MSU	FN	1983	LB	22 X 30	AP	30	1	300	450
Out of Africa, Out of Mind	SVC	ART	1984	LB	22 X 30	RP/T	20	1	350	500
Wave Goodbye	SVC	ART	1984	LB	22 X 30	MUR	20	1	350	650
Brooks Heaven	SVC	ART	1984	LB	22 X 30	AC	20	1	350	500
Lady Caroline	SVC	ART	1986	I/WA/HC	22 X 30	AP	50	1	350	750
German Brown Trout	SVC	ART	1986	I/WA/HC	22 X 30	AP	50	1	350	750

BARBARA WHIPPLE

BORN: San Francisco, CA
EDUCATION: Swarthmore Col, PA, BA, 1943; Rochester Inst of Technology, NY, 1956; Tyler Sch of Art, Temple Univ, Phila, PA, BFA, 1961; Inst Allende, Mexico, 1968; Hanga Workshop, with Toshi Yoshida, Japan, 1984
TEACHING: Mem Art Gallery, Rochester Sch for the Deaf, NY, 1954–56; Asst Prof, Art, Geneseo State Univ of New York, NY, 1958–59; Grad Asst, Tyler Sch of Art, Phila, PA, 1961; Lectr, Graphics, Elizabethtown Col, PA 1973–76; Prof, Drawing, Franklin & Marshall Col, Lancaster, PA, 1974–75; Colorado Graphic Arts Workshop, CO, 1980,82; Adams State Col Workshop, Alamose, CO, 1982,83,85; Sangre de Cristo Art Center, Pueblo, CO, 1985
AWARDS: First Prize, Drawing, Philadelphia Art Alliance, PA, 1980; Third Prize, White Bear Gallery, Denver, CO, 1982
RECENT EXHIB: Adams State Col, Alamasa, CO, 1988; Retrosp, North Mus, F&M Col, Lancaster, PA, 1988; Western Colorado Center for the Arts, Grande Junction, CO, 1989
COLLECTIONS: Swarthmore Col, PA; Washington County Mus, Hagerstown, MD; Elizabethtown Col, PA
PRINTERS: Artist (ART)
PUBLISHERS: Artist (ART)
GALLERIES: Chestnut Street Gallery, Lancaster, PA; Off Broadway Gallery, Pueblo, CO; Antero Arts, Buena Vista, CO; Art Brokers, Colorado Springs, CO

Barbara Whipple
Return of the Kachinas
Courtesy the Artist

MAILING ADDRESS: 429 E Main St, P O Box 609, Buena Vista, CO 81211

BARBARA WHIPPLE CONTINUED

TITLE	PUBLISHER	PRINTER	DATE	MEDIUM	DIMENSION (PAPER SIZE) IN INCHES	TYPE OF PAPER	EDITION NUMBER	NO. OF COLORS	ORIGINAL OPENING PRICE	CURRENT RETAIL PRICE
SOLD OUT EDITIONS (RARE):										
Tiger	ART	ART	1962	WC	20 X 24	TROYA	12	3	50	300
Zebras	ART	ART	1965	WC	29 X 18	3M	12	3	35	200
The Procession	ART	ART	1968	WC	23 X 18	TROYA	20	1	50	200
Magician's Daughter	ART	ART	1976	WC	18 X 23	TROYA	25	3	35	250
CURRENT EDITIONS:										
Fallen Eagle	ART	ART	1979	WC	36 X 28	TAB	45	1	75	200
Spirit Bird	ART	ART	1981	WC	29 X 15	TAB	18	4	85	250
Dawn (Talátowi)	ART	ART	1983	I	15 X 12	R/BFK	45	1	135	150
Return of the Kachinas	ART	ART	1983	I	15 X 22	R/BFK	45	1	65	175
Miasa Rainbird	ART	ART	1984	WC/WA	17 X 11	HOSHO	12	5	100	175
Fourth World of the Hopi	ART	ART	1984	WC	19 X 24	HOSHO	11	4	100	175

FREDERIC WHITAKER

BORN: Providence, RI; (1891–1980)
EDUCATION: Rhode Island Sch of Design, Providence, RI
COLLECTIONS: Metropolitan Mus, NY; Nat Acad of Design, NY; Boston Mus of Fine Arts, MA; Charles and Emma Frye Art Mus, Seattle, WA
PRINTERS: American Atelier, NY (AA)
PUBLISHERS: Circle Fine Art, Chicago, IL (CFA)
GALLERIES: Circle Galleries, San Diego, CA & San Francisco, CA & Pittsburgh, PA & Northbrook, IL & Houston, TX & Soho, NY & Chicago, IL & Scottsdale, AZ & Beverly Hills, CA & Costa Mesa, CA & San Diego, CA & Sherman Oaks, CA & Palm Beach, FL & Honolulu, HI & New Orleans, LA & Las Vegas, NV & Seattle, WA

TITLE	PUBLISHER	PRINTER	DATE	MEDIUM	DIMENSION (PAPER SIZE) IN INCHES	TYPE OF PAPER	EDITION NUMBER	NO. OF COLORS	ORIGINAL OPENING PRICE	CURRENT RETAIL PRICE
SOLD OUT EDITIONS (RARE):										
The Parrot	CFA	AA	1974	LC	35 X 24	AP	250		100	500
CURRENT EDITIONS:										
Cactus Cowboy	CFA	AA	1975	LC	24 X 36	AP	275		100	350

C J WHITE

BORN: Pine Hill, NJ; February 2, 1925
RECENT EXHIB: Gallery 68, New York, NY, 1986–87
PRINTERS: Atelier Ettinger, NY (AE)
PUBLISHERS: White Collection Ltd, Skippack, PA (WCL)
GALLERIES: Collectors Delight, Lahaska, PA; Gentleman Framer, Allentown, PA; Fergus-Jean Gallery, Harbor Springs, MI; Gallery of the Palm Beaches, Tequesta, FL; Modern Art Collectors, Ltd, New York, NY
MAILING ADDRESS: 1673 Route 309, Quakertown, PA 18951

TITLE	PUBLISHER	PRINTER	DATE	MEDIUM	DIMENSION (PAPER SIZE) IN INCHES	TYPE OF PAPER	EDITION NUMBER	NO. OF COLORS	ORIGINAL OPENING PRICE	CURRENT RETAIL PRICE
SOLD OUT EDITIONS (RARE):										
Cherry Blossoms	WCL	AE	1985	LC	24 X 33	AP	275	13	200	550
Cherry Blossoms	WCL	AE	1985	LC	24 X 33	AP	25	13	250	650
Cherry Blossoms (Deluxe Edition)	WCL	AE	1985	LC	24 X 33	JP	25	13	300	750

JOHN WILDE

BORN: Milwaukee, WI; December 12, 1919
EDUCATION: Univ of Wisconsin, Madison, WI, BS, MS
TEACHING: Prof, Univ of Wisconsin, Madison, WI, 1969–82, Prof Emeritus, 1982 to present
AWARDS: Lambert Prize, Pennsylvania Acad of Fine Art, Phila, PA, 1960; Childe Hassam Purchase Award, Am Acad, 1965,80
RECENT EXHIB: Schmidt-Bingham Gallery, NY, 1990,92; Perimeter Gallery, Chicago, IL, 1990,92
COLLECTIONS: Whitney Mus of Am Art, NY; Nat Mus of Am Art, Smithsonian Mus, Wash, DC; Art Inst of Chicago, IL; Pennsylvania Acad of Fine Arts, Phila, PA; Detroit Inst of Art, MI; Wadsworth Atheneum, Hartford, CT
PRINTERS: Perishable Press, Ltd, Mt Horeb, WI (PePr); Imago Imprint, Inc, NY (III); Jack Damer, Madison, WI (JD); Univ of Wisconsin, Madison, WI (UW); Warrington Colescott, Hollandale, WI (WC); Mantegna Press, Hollandale, WI (MP)
PUBLISHERS: Perishable Press, Ltd, Mt Horeb, WI (PePr); Imago Imprint, Inc, NY (III); Marshall Erdman & Associates, Madison, WI (MEA)
GALLERIES: Haslem Gallery, Wash, DC; Fanny Garver Gallery, Madison, WI; Perimeter Gallery, Chicago, IL; Schmidt-Bingham Gallery, New York, NY
MAILING ADDRESS: RFD 1, P.O. Box 480, Evansville, WI 53536

TITLE	PUBLISHER	PRINTER	DATE	MEDIUM	DIMENSION (PAPER SIZE) IN INCHES	TYPE OF PAPER	EDITION NUMBER	NO. OF COLORS	ORIGINAL OPENING PRICE	CURRENT RETAIL PRICE
SOLD OUT EDITIONS (RARE):										
A Portfolio of Mostly Good Things (Set of 10 with Titled Page, Boxed)	PePr	PePr	1974	LC/HC	14 X 19 EA	AP	20 EA		750 SET	3500 SET
British Soldiers	PePr	PePr	1977	LB	14 X 10	AP	21	1	150	600
Story of Jane & Joan (Set of 12, Titled Pages, Book, Boxed)	PePr	PePr	1977	EC/HC	4 X 6 EA 6 X 4 EA	AP	25 EA	1 EA	1200 SET	4500 SET
Wildeview	III	JD/UW	1985	LB	24 X 36	AP88	LXXXV	1	500	500
Wildeview	III	JD/UW	1985	LB	24 X 36	GE	90	1	500	500
7 Kiefers	MEA	WC/MP	1987	EC	22 X 30	R/BFK	100	3	600	600
8 Russets	MEA	WC/MP	1987	EC	22 X 30	R/BFK	100	3	600	600

SUSAN DOROTHEA WHITE

BORN: Adelaide, Australia; August 10, 1941
EDUCATION: Julian Ashton Art Sch, Sydney, Australia, 1960–61; South Australian Sch of Art, Adelaide, Australia, 1959–65
AWARDS: Sands & McDougall Prize, Drawing, South Australian Sch of Art, Australia, 1959; Rowney Prize, Fine Art, South Australian Sch of Art, Australia, 1959; Commonwealth Scholarship, South Australian Sch of Art, Australia, 1960; J Gero Prize, Painting, Macquarie Univ, Sydney, Australia, 1975; Mornington Peninsula Print Purchase Award, Victoria, 1978
RECENT EXHIB: Galerie Art & Architecture, Amsterdam, The Netherlands, 1990; Galerie am Buttermarkt, Cologne, Germany, 1991
COLLECTIONS: Australian Nat Gallery, Canberra, Australia; Majdanek State Mus, Lublin, Poland; Mus of Int Contemp Graphic Art, Fredrikstad, Norway; Volkshochscule, Munich, Germany; Australian Embassy, Bonn, Germany; FMK Gallery, Budapest, Hungary; Mornington Peninsula Arts Centre, Mornington, Victoria, Australia; Westmead Centre, Sydney, Australia
PRINTERS: Artist (ART)
PUBLISHERS: Artist (ART)
GALLERIES: Artlease +, Vollenhove, The Netherlands
MAILING ADDRESS: 278 Annandale St, Annandale, NSW, Australia 2038

Susan Dorothea White
Blind
Courtesy the Artist

TITLE	PUBLISHER	PRINTER	DATE	MEDIUM	DIMENSION (PAPER SIZE) IN INCHES	TYPE OF PAPER	EDITION NUMBER	NO. OF COLORS	ORIGINAL OPENING PRICE	CURRENT RETAIL PRICE
SOLD OUT EDITIONS (RARE):										
Desert Bush	ART	ART	1960	DPT	6 X 9	R/100	5	1	50	150
Monkey	ART	ART	1960	DPT	10 X 7	R/100	5	1	50	150
Emu	ART	ART	1960	DPT	10 X 8	R/100	2	1	50	150
Emu Chicks	ART	ART	1960	DPT	10 X 7	R/100	3	1	50	150
Drummers	ART	ART	1960	DPT	14 X 10	Ingres	5	1	50	200
Sydney: Construction City	ART	ART	1972	LI	20 X 13	Ingres	2	1	75	250
Winter Walk	ART	ART	1972	LB	30 X 22	R/100	4	1	75	275
Ochre Glade	ART	ART	1972	LC	15 X 22	R/100	5	5	75	300
Evening: Factory Valley No 1	ART	ART	1975	LB	22 X 27	R/100	5	1	100	300
Cattai Ridge	ART	ART	1975	LC	22 X 30	Ingres	5	4	100	300
Cattai Ridge (3rd State)	ART	ART	1975	LC	22 X 30	Ingres	3	3	100	300
Banksias after Bushfire	ART	ART	1975	LC	22 X 30	Kent	2	6	100	400
Gardner's Dream No 1	ART	ART	1976	LC	22 X 30	RP	14	10	100	400
Casualty: Children's Hospital, 3 am	ART	ART	1978	LC	24 X 32	AP/W	18	6	125	300
Where Children Play: No 2	ART	ART	1978	LB	30 X 20	RP	4	1	125	350
Two: Sepia	ART	ART	1978	LB	31 X 24	MUL	12	1	125	280
The 470 at 6 PM	ART	ART	1978	LC	22 X 16	RP	18	6	125	200
Marienplatz No 1	ART	ART	1980	LC	15 X 23	RP	4	7	150	400
Olympiazentrum	ART	ART	1980	LC	17 X 25	MUL	30	2	150	200
Lederhosen	ART	ART	1980	LB	18 X 23	AP/W	10	1	150	200
Chess	ART	ART	1982	LB	30 X 23	RP	20	1	150	280
Made in Australia	ART	ART	1982	LB	10 X 10	AP/W	5	1	150	100
A Month in the Life of a Sydney Schoolboy	ART	ART	1983	LB	20 X 28	RP	5	1	200	300
The Story: II	ART	ART	1985	LB	23 X 30	Varies	4	1	200	200
Genesis: II	ART	ART	1986	LC	30 X 23	RP/G	5	4	200	280
Genesis: III	ART	ART	1986	LB	30 X 23	RP/G	4	1	200	250
To Let: No 1	ART	ART	1990	LB	23 X 15	RP	4	1	250	250
CURRENT EDITIONS:										
Sister & Brother: City Winter	ART	ART	1972	LB	22 X 15	R/100	3	1	75	250
Three-Quarter Birthday	ART	ART	1972	LC	22 X 30	R/100	6	6	75	300
Maitland Ghost Gums	ART	ART	1975	WB	30 X 22	Kent	6	1	100	280
Sunlit Gully	ART	ART	1975	LB	22 X 30	Kent	5	1	100	300
Byzantine Birthday	ART	ART	1975	LC	15 X 21	RP	7	3	100	280
Silent River	ART	ART	1975	LB	15 X 22	R/100	8	1	100	300
Tea-Tree & Gum	ART	ART	1975	LC	22 X 30	Kent	10	3	100	250
Haze	ART	ART	1975	LB	20 X 30	Ingres	14	1	100	200
Slingshot	ART	ART	1975	WB	24 X 19	MUL	30	1	100	200
Coast Banksias	ART	ART	1976	LC	22 X 30	Kent	9	4	125	300
Blackened Banksias	ART	ART	1977	LB	8 X 10	MUL	12	1	75	120
Colo Plateau: Grey	ART	ART	1977	LC	16 X 39	RP	7	2	150	210
Colo Plateau: Brown	ART	ART	1977	LC	16 X 39	RP	8	2	150	210
Pedestrian Crossing	ART	ART	1977	LC	21 X 32	RP	11		125	300
At Home: No 278	ART	ART	1978	EB	16 X 20	RP	30	1	125	220
At Home: No 278	ART	ART	1978	EC	16 X 23	AP/W	40	6	125	200
The Retired Mechanic	ART	ART	1978	LC	24 X 32	RP	20	2	150	280
Flooded Mongarlowe-River (Upstream & Downstream (Dipt)	ART	ART	1978	LC	22 X 32	AP/W	12	8	150	750

SUSAN DOROTHEA WHITE CONTINUED

TITLE	PUBLISHER	PRINTER	DATE	MEDIUM	DIMENSION (PAPER SIZE) IN INCHES	TYPE OF PAPER	EDITION NUMBER	NO. OF COLORS	ORIGINAL OPENING PRICE	CURRENT RETAIL PRICE
CURRENT EDITIONS:										
Mongarlowe River	ART	ART	1978	LC	25 X 34	MUL	8	3	150	250
The Magic Pudding	ART	ART	1978	LC	32 X 24	AP/W	35	9	150	300
Evening: Factory Valley No 2	ART	ART	1978	LB	24 X 32	RP	30	1	150	150
Two	ART	ART	1978	EB	12 X 9	RP	30	1	100	200
Children Playing in Car Park	ART	ART	1978	DPT	9 X 10	RP	20	1	100	250
Stonefish			1978	EB	11 X 9	RP	30	1	100	200
Stephen & Tigger	ART	ART	1978	EB/SG	16 X 24	RP	30	1	150	250
Noah's Rocket	ART	ART	1978	LC	31 X 23	RP	33	5	150	180
Two: Black	ART	ART	1978	LD	31 X 24	RP	20	1	150	280
Two: Coloured	ART	ART	1978	LC	32 X 22	RP	11	10	150	320
The Wishful Fisherman	ART	ART	1980	LC	16 X 24	AP/W	35	8	150	220
The Fisherman's Dream	ART	ART	1980	LC	16 X 24	AP/W	18	8	150	250
Munich Shoppers	ART	ART	1980	LC	15 X 23	RP	20	13	150	220
Lederhosen	ART	ART	1980	LB	18 X 23	AP/W	10	1	150	200
Religious Woman of Bavaria	ART	ART	1980	LB	24 X 32	RP	37	1	150	180
The Empty Chair	ART	ART	1980	LC	16 X 24	AP/W	30	9	150	220
Gardener's Dream No 2	ART	ART	1980	LC	24 X 32	RP	30	12	175	300
The Death of St Francis of Australia	ART	ART	1982	LC	30 X 22	RP	12	6	200	320
Octopus	ART	ART	1982	LB	10 X 10	AP/W	20	1	75	100
Macaroni Face: Ochre	ART	ART	1982	LB	10 X 10	AP/W	30	1	75	100
Macaroni Face: Black	ART	ART	1982	LB	10 X 10	RP	25	1	75	100
Thelma of Wilcannia	ART	ART	1983	WB	24 X 31	MUL	30	1	200	240
The Ghost of Kabbarlia	ART	ART	1983	LC	24 X 32	AP/W	12	3	150	280
To Cut Both Ways	ART	ART	1983	LB	7 X 7	RP/W	30	1	75	100
Spaghetti Legs	ART	ART	1983	LB	7 X 7	RP	45	1	75	100
A Storm in a Tea-Cup	ART	ART	1983	LB	7 X 7	RP/G	45	1	75	100
Mise-en-Scène	ART	ART	1984	LB	30 X 22	RP	20	1	150	200
The Story: I	ART	ART	1985	LD	30 X 23	RP/G	12	1	150	200
Genesis: Miniature	ART	ART	1985	LB	7 X 7	RP	25	1	75	100
Genesis: I	ART	ART	1986	LB	30 X 23	RP/G	20	5	150	280
Ward 4	ART	ART	1986	LB	30 X 22	RP	14	1	150	220
Cornered	ART	ART	1986	LB	7 X 7	RP	25	1	75	100
The Front Verandah	ART	ART	1986	LC	24 X 32	RP	20	15	150	300
Fenced-In	ART	ART	1988	LB	11 X 10	AP/W	20	1	110	110
Cliff-Hanger	ART	ART	1988	LB	7 X 7	RP	25	1	100	100
Cry Freedom	ART	ART	1989	LC	23 X 15	RP	40	3	180	180
Massacre	ART	ART	1989	WB	23 X 15	AP/W	20	1	220	220
To Let: No 2	ART	ART	1990	LC	23 X 15	RP	30	12	250	250
Man Creating the Hole in the Ozone Layer	ART	ART	1990	WC/HC	11 X 15	AP/W	16	5	220	220
Cry Freedom	ART	ART	1990	WB	23 X 15	AP/W	20	1	220	220
Blind	ART	ART	1991	LB	16 X 24	RP	25	1	220	220
Ms Atlass	ART	ART	1991	LB	24 X 16	RP	20	1	220	220
Choosing a Mask	ART	ART	1992	LC	15 X 23	AP/W	20	3	250	250

CHRIS WILDER

BORN: Long Beach, CA
EDUCATION: San Francisco Art Inst, CA, 1985; California Inst of the Arts, Valencia, CA, 1988
RECENT EXHIB: California Inst of the Arts, Valencia, CA, 1987; Dennis Anderson Gallery, Los Angeles, CA, 1988,89,90; Petersburg Gallery, NY, 1990,91; Linda Cathcart Gallery, Santa Monica, CA, 1991

PRINTERS: Cirrus Editions Workshop, Los Angeles, CA (CEW)
PUBLISHERS: Cirrus Editions, Ltd, Los Angeles, CA (CE)
GALLERIES: Cirrus Editions Gallery, Los Angeles, CA; Linda Cathcart Gallery, Los Angeles, CA; Dennis Anderson Gallery, Los Angeles, CA; Thomas Solomon's Garage, Los Angeles, CA

TITLE	PUBLISHER	PRINTER	DATE	MEDIUM	DIMENSION (PAPER SIZE) IN INCHES	TYPE OF PAPER	EDITION NUMBER	NO. OF COLORS	ORIGINAL OPENING PRICE	CURRENT RETAIL PRICE
CURRENT EDITIONS										
Set of Three Lithographs (Set of 3):									1855 SET	1855 SET
Fabricated UFO Sighting at Monte Carlo with Jewels from Hong Kong (in Your Dreams) (489c)	CE	CEW	1991	LC	24 X 51	R/BFK	45		950	950
Dead Old Men and Dead Fish in the Land of the Rising Sun	CE	CEW	1991	LC	24 X 53	R/BFK	45		950	950
Flying High in the Sky with Peyote in Your Eye (Crest)	CE	CEW	1991	LC	42 X 22	R/BFK	45		750	750

The Printworld Directory is accepting new applications for the seventh edition. Approximately 300 new artists will be accepted. Please use the two forms provided in the back section of this directory to submit biographical data and documentation of prints. Edition number of each print must not exceed 500 and the retail price must be $100 or more.

RAY CHARLES WHITE

PRINTERS: Jean-Paul Russell, Durham, PA (JPR); Durham Press, Durham, PA (DURPr)
PUBLISHERS: Durham Press, Durham, PA (DURPr)
GALLERIES: Reider-Caribe, Inc, New York, NY

TITLE	PUBLISHER	PRINTER	DATE	MEDIUM	DIMENSION (PAPER SIZE) IN INCHES	TYPE OF PAPER	EDITION NUMBER	NO. OF COLORS	ORIGINAL OPENING PRICE	CURRENT RETAIL PRICE
CURRENT EDITIONS:										
Set of Five Screenprints:									2500 SET	2500 SET
Geldzahler (Gold)	DurPR	JPR/DurPr	1991	SP	22 X 22	COV	35		550	550
Lichtenstein (Blue)	DurPR	JPR/DurPr	1991	SP	22 X 22	COV	35		550	550
Burroughs (Lavender)	DurPR	JPR/DurPr	1991	SP	22 X 22	COV	35		550	550
Hopper (Cobalt)	DurPR	JPR/DurPr	1991	SP	22 X 22	COV	35		550	550
Castelli (Silver)	DurPR	JPR/DurPr	1991	SP	22 X 22	COV	35		550	550

MARK WHOLEY

EDUCATION: Butera Sch of Art, Boston, MA, 1962–65; California Col of Arts & Crafts, Oakland, CA, 1981–82; Studied in Italy & France, Drawing, 1982,83; Studied Pietrasanta, Italy, Sculpture, 1984; Studied in Mexico, Drawing, 1984,85; Univ of California, Berkeley, CA, 1983–84,86
PRINTERS: David Kelso, Oakland, CA (DK); Made in California, Oakland, CA (MIC)
PUBLISHERS: Made in California, Oakland, CA (MIC)
MAILING ADDRESS: 2512 9th St, Berkeley, CA 94710

TITLE	PUBLISHER	PRINTER	DATE	MEDIUM	DIMENSION (PAPER SIZE) IN INCHES	TYPE OF PAPER	EDITION NUMBER	NO. OF COLORS	ORIGINAL OPENING PRICE	CURRENT RETAIL PRICE
SOLD OUT EDITIONS (RARE):										
Red on Black	MIC	DK/MIC	1984	AC/SL	15 X 11	GE	30		150	350
Love from Paris	MIC	DK/MIC	1984	AB/SL/CC	15 X 11	AP/B-KIT	30		150	350

WILLIAM T WILEY

BORN: Bedford, IN; October 21, 1937
EDUCATION: San Francisco Art Inst, CA, BFA, 1960; MFA, 1962
TEACHING: Prof, Art, Univ of California, Davis, CA, 1962 to present
AWARDS: Purchase Prize, Whitney Mus of Am Art, NY, 1968; Traveling Grant, Australian Arts Council, 1980
RECENT EXHIB: Frankfurter Kunstverein, Frankfurt, West Germany, 1987; Marsha Mateyka Gallery, Wash, DC, 1987; Galerie Grita Insam, Vienna, Austria, 1987; Richard L. Nelson Gallery, Davis, CA, 1988; James Corcoran Gallery, Santa Monica, CA, 1988; Indianapolis Center for Contemp Art, IN, 1988; Milwaukee Art Mus, WI, 1988; Arkansas Art Center, Little Rock, AR, 1988; Indianapolis Center for Contemp Art, Herron Gallery, IN, 1989; Struve Gallery, Chicago, IL, 1989; Springfield Art Mus, MA, 1992; Redding Mus, CA, 1992; Palm Spring Desert Mus, CA, 1989,92; Cuesta Col, San Luis Obispo, CA, 1989,92; Gallery Paule Anglim, San Francisco, CA, 1992; Rena Bransten Gallery, San Francisco, CA, 1993
COLLECTIONS: San Francisco Mus of Mod Art, CA; Mus of Mod Art, NY; Whitney Mus of Am Art, NY; Los Angeles County Mus, CA; Art Inst of Chicago, IL; Univ of California Mus, Berkeley, CA; Univ of Kansas Mus, Lawrence, KS; Stedelijk van Abbemuseum, Eindhoven, The Netherlands; Oakland Mus, CA; Denver Mus, CO; Dallas Mus, TX
PRINTERS: Landfall Press Inc, Chicago, IL (LPI); Jack Lemon, Chicago, IL (JL); Timothy Berry, Chicago, IL (TB); Cirrus Editions Workshop, Los Angeles, CA (CEW); Lloyd Baggs, Los Angeles, CA (LB); Teaberry Press, Oakland, CA (TP); Hidekatsu Takada (HT); Marcia Bartholme (MB); Crown Point Press, San Francisco, CA (CPP); Tadashi Toda (TT); Reinzo Monjyu (RM); Shunzo Matsuda (SM); Sun Valley Center for the Arts, ID (SVCA); David Wharton (DW); Experimental Printmaking, San Francisco, CA (ExP); Univ of Illinois, Urbana-Champaign, IL (UI); Univ of California, Berkeley, CA (UCB); Lawrence Hamlin, San Francisco, CA (LH); Daria Sywulak, San Francisco, CA (DS); Ted Skanuga (TS); Bud Shark, Boulder, CO (BS); Shark's, Inc. Boulder, CO (SI)
PUBLISHERS: Landfall Press Inc, Chicago, IL (LPI); Crown Point Press, San Francisco, CA (CPP); NAME Gallery, Chicago, IL (NAME); Wizdumbridge, CA (W); Experimental Printmaking, San Francisco,CA (ExP); Nelson Atkins Mus, Kansas City, KS (NAM); Univ of Illinois, Urbana-Champaign, IL (UI); Univ of California, Berkeley, CA (UCB); Paul Facchetti (PF); Sun Valley Center for the Arts, ID (SVCA); Los Angeles County Mus of Art, CA (LACMA); Shark's, Inc, Boulder, CO (SI)
GALLERIES: Graphics Gallery, San Francisco, CA; Morgan Gallery, Boston, MA; David Adamson Gallery, Wash, DC; Marsha Mateyka Gallery, Wash, DC; Landfall Press Inc, Chicago, IL; Signet Arts, St Louis, MO; Elizabeth Leach Gallery, Portland, OR; Struve Gallery, Chicago, IL; L A Louver Gallery, Los Angeles, CA; Crown Point Gallery, New York, NY & San Francisco, CA; Experimental Workshop, San Francisco, CA (EW); Ellen Erpf Miller, Fine Art, Newton, MA; Max Protetch Gallery, New York, NY; Betsy Senior Contemporary Prints, New York, NY; Magnuson Gallery, Boston, MA; MIA Gallery, Seattle, WA; Gallery Paule Anglim, San Francisco,CA; Rena Bransten Gallery, San Francisco, CA; John Natsoulas Gallery, Davis, CA; Shark's, Inc, Boulder, CO; Locks Gallery, Phila, PA; Brian Gross Fine Art, San Francisco, CA; Quartet Editions, New York, NY
MAILING ADDRESS: c/o Wanda Hansen, 615 Main St, Sausalito, CA 94965

TITLE	PUBLISHER	PRINTER	DATE	MEDIUM	DIMENSION (PAPER SIZE) IN INCHES	TYPE OF PAPER	EDITION NUMBER	NO. OF COLORS	ORIGINAL OPENING PRICE	CURRENT RETAIL PRICE
SOLD OUT EDITIONS (RARE):										
Thank You Hide	LPI	JR/LPI	1972	LC	35 X 48	AP	65	5	500	3500
Coast Reverse (Chamois Object)	LPI	JL/LPI	1972	LC	35 X 46	ARJ/CH	35	2	500	3500
Little Hide	LPI	JR/LPI	1972	LC	5 X 5	CH	30	1	600	3000
Lessen Plans	LPI	JR/LPI	1973	LC	25 X 37	AP/W	200	4	90	200
Mask	LPI	JR/LPI	1973	LC	32 DIA	TWP	10	5	600	4000
Ecnud	LPI	JM/LPI	1973	LC	23 X 29	AP/CR	10	3	500	2500
Seasonall Gate	LPI	JL/TB/LPI	1974	LC/LE	28 X 22	TWP	50	3	500	2000
Scarecrow	LPI	TB/LPI	1974	AC	22 X 18	AP/W	50	3	400	2000
I Hope You Learned Your Lesson	LPI	TB/LPI	1974	A/LE	28 X 22	JBG	50	3	300	2500
It's Only a Paper Moon	UCB	UCB	1974	A/LE		JBG			600	4500
CD	LPI	TB/TS/LPI	1975	EC	22 X 20	UP	10	1	300	2000
Mr Unatural	LPI	JL/LPI	1976	LC	36 X 25	AP/CR	65	4	500	3000
Erie Cafe	LPI	JL/LPI	1976	LC	30 X 22	AP/CR	10	1	500	2500
Hanging Up the Frame	LPI	TB/LPI	1976	EB/SG	18 X 14	AP/CR	25	1	300	1200
Beginning Passes	LPI	TB/LPI	1976	A/HG	18 X 14	AP/CR	25	1	300	1200

WILLIAM T WILEY CONTINUED

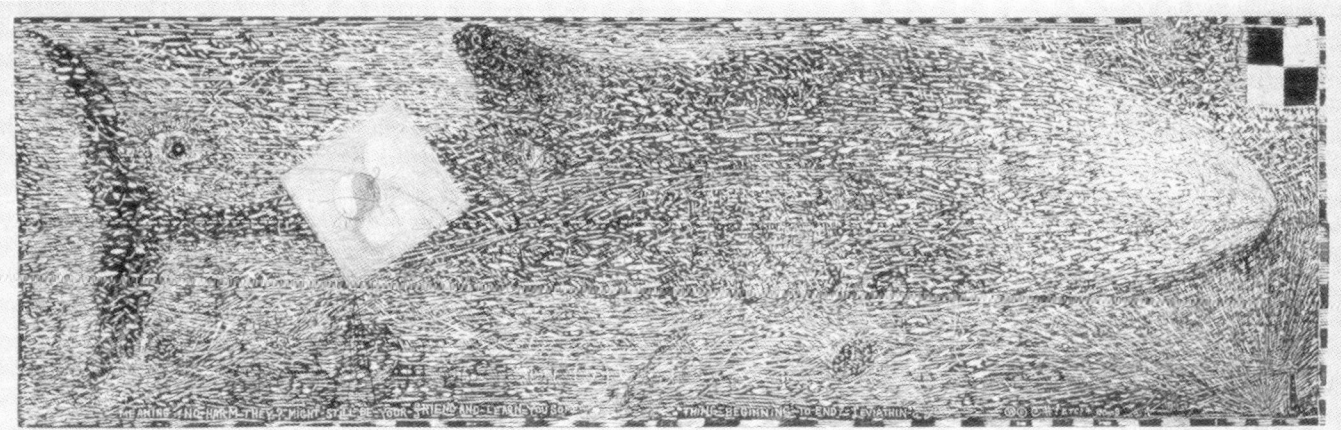

William T Wiley
Leviathin II
Courtesy Shark's, Inc

TITLE	PUBLISHER	PRINTER	DATE	MEDIUM	DIMENSION (PAPER SIZE) IN INCHES	TYPE OF PAPER	EDITION NUMBER	NO. OF COLORS	ORIGINAL OPENING PRICE	CURRENT RETAIL PRICE
SOLD OUT EDITIONS (RARE):										
Down the Line	LPI	TB/LPI	1976	EB/HG	18 X 14	AP/CR	25	1	300	1200
The Glittering Remains	LPI	TB/LPI	1976	EB/SG	18 X 14	AP/CR	25	1	300	1200
Green Shoes	LPI	TB/LPI	1976–77	EB/A/SG	22 X 30	AP/CR	25	2	500	3000
Green Shoes, State I	LPI	TB/LPI	1977	EB/A/SG	22 X 30	AP/CR	18	2	500	3000
Ooh La La	PF		1977	LC		AP/CR			500	2000
Jolly Regret	PF		1977	LC		AP/CR			300	1200
Working at CPP	CPP	CPP	1978	EB/SG	15 X 13	R/BFK	15	1	300	1200
OTPAG Fishing	CPP	CPP	1978	EB/SG	26 X 32	R/BFK	10	1	500	2000
Line Fever	CPP	CPP	1978	EB/SG	33 X 26	R/BFK	25	1	500	1800
OTPAG (16 Monotypes)	CPP	CPP	1978	MON	30 X 39 EA	AP	16 EA	1	600 EA	3000 EA
OTPAG (16 Monotypes)	CPP	CPP	1978	MON	30 X 39 EA	CHAMOIS	16 EA	1	600 EA	3000 EA
Nowhere's That Blame Treaty	CPP	ST	1979	EB/A	49 X 40	R/BFK	15	1	600	4000
Nowhere's That Blame Treaty, State I	CPP	HT/CPP	1979	A/SG/DPT	49 X 40	AP/ROL	15		2000	4000
Spooky on the Line	LPI/NAME	JL/LPI	1979	LC	30 X 22	R/BFK	100	1	450	1200
Mr Unpopular	LPI	JL/LPI	1980	LC	38 X 38	RWP	35	4	600	2500
Three Mile Island	LPI	JL/LPI	1980	LC	38 X 26	AP/W	20	3	500	1200
Studio Light	W	TP	1980	EB	11 X 11	AP	20	1	200	500
OTPAG for PG	W	TP	1981	EB/A	22 X 30	STP	35	3	700	900
Too Many Sides	W	TP	1981	EB	17 X 15	AP	35	1	300	500
Keep Foolin' Around	W/CPP	TP/CPP	1981	EC	26 X 26	AP	50	3	450	1200
Planks Pool	NAM	TP	1981	EB/SG	22 X 23	STP	50	1	450	1200
Eerie Grotto? Okini	CPP	TT/RM/SM/CPP	1982	WC	22 X 30	KOZO	200	85	750	5000
Now Here's That Blame Treaty, State II	CPP	HT/CPP	1983	A/SG/DPT	52 X 42	AP/ROL	50	1	1800	4500
Agent Orange	ExP	ExP	1983	WC	53 X 27	R/BFK	11	1	750	900
El Salvador	ExP	ExP	1983	WC	53 X 27	R/BFK	20	1	750	900
Muddy Waters	ExP	ExP	1983	WC	54 X 42	R/BFK	20	1	750	900
Three Mile Island, Three Years Later	LPI	JL/LPI	1983	LC	38 X 27	R/BFK	40	4	850	1000
MX	ExP	ExP	1983	WC	53 X 27	R/BFK	10	1	750	900
Cute Rules	ExP	ExP	1983	WC	53 X 27	R/BFK	10	1	750	900
Quint Rules	SVCA	SVCA	1983–84	MON	Varies	R/BFK	29 EA		2500 EA	3000 EA
Marvin Gaye	ExP	ExP	1983–86	WC	5 X 42	R/BFK	10	1	750	900
Pallate Monoprints		TP	1986	MON	22 X 30 EA	R/BFK	1 EA		2500 EA	3000 EA
Break the Rule	W	TP	1986	EB/SG/HC	27 X 22	AP	25		600	900
Environment I	W	TP	1986	DPT/HG	15 X 22	AP	13	1	400	600
Environment II	W	TP	1986	DPT/HG	15 X 22	AP	12	1	400	600
Count Nowhere	W	TP	1986	EB/HG	22 X 15	AP	20	1	400	600
Dr King	W	TP	1986	EB/HG	15 X 22	AP	20	1	400	600
Where's the Beef	W	TP	1986	EB/A	15 X 26	R/BFK	25		450	600
Nothing . . . is as it Seems	LACMA	TP	1986	EB/A	22 X 27	R/BFK	50		750	900
Now Here's That Blame Treaty (State B)	CPP	CPP	1989	AC/SG/BUR	54 X 41	AC	6		4000	4500
CURRENT EDITIONS:										
Moon Mullings	LPI	JR/LPI	1972	LC	22 X 22	AP/W	80	5	300	750
Wash Doubt	LPI	JL/LPI	1972	LC	22 X 30	R/BFK	80	4	300	750
Checking It all Out	LPI	DK/LP	1972	LC	22 X 30	R/BFK	35	3	300	850

The print market has become very selective. For the first time since we published the first edition of The Printworld Directory in 1982, the prices of prints have been greatly reduced and greatly increased for the same artists by the most reputable and established print publishers. Check the fifth edition to understand the movement.

WILLIAM T WILEY CONTINUED

TITLE	PUBLISHER	PRINTER	DATE	MEDIUM	DIMENSION (PAPER SIZE) IN INCHES	TYPE OF PAPER	EDITION NUMBER	NO. OF COLORS	ORIGINAL OPENING PRICE	CURRENT RETAIL PRICE
CURRENT EDITIONS:										
Thank Yute Rubble	LPI	JR/LPI	1972	LC	22 X 30	R/BFK	80	2	300	750
Set of Three:									200 SET	1200 SET
Field Stone	LPI	JL/LPI	1973	LC	22 X 30	R/BFK	20	1	XXX	XXX
Feels Tone	LPI	JR/LPI	1973	LC	22 X 30	R/BFK	20	2	XXX	XXX
Feel Stoned	LPI	JR/LPI	1973	LC	22 X 30	R/BFK	20	2	XXX	XXX
Yea Boss	UI	UI	1973	LC		R/BFK			300	400
Untitled (#173c) (Mr Nobody)	CE/HF	CEW	1975	LC	43 X 31	TWP/HMP	25	4	325	1500
Untitled (#186c) (Mr Nobody)	CE/HF	CEW	1975	LC	43 X 31	RP/ROL	45	6	425	1200
Mask	LPI	JL/LPI	1975	LC	32 DIA	R/BFK	10	5	400	3000
Mask	LPI	JL/LPI	1975	MON/C	32 DIA	HMP	1 EA	Varies	600 EA	4000 EA
Monoprint #5	LPI	JL/LPI	1976	MON/C	22 X 30 EA	AP	1 EA	Varies	500 EA	3000 EA
Monoprint #10 (On Chamois)	LPI	JL/LPI	1976	MON/C	22 X 30 EA	Chamois		Varies	600 EA	4000 EA
Suite of Daze (Set of 14)	LPI	TB/LPI	1976	EC	17 X 13 EA	AP	50 EA	12 EA	2400 SET	5000 SET
In Transit	LPI	JL/LPI	1982	LB	18 X 23	TWP/HMP	20	1	450	700
Once Upon a Time When all was Flawless (Printed on 4 Scarves)	LPI	JL/LPI	1982	LP	33 X 32	FABRIC	15	1	1800	2500
Who the Alien?	CPP	HT/MB/CPP	1983	DPT/SG	37 X 29	CHAM	10	2	800	1500
Set of Three Prints:									1000 SET	1500 SET
Digging Implement	CPP	HT/MB/CPP	1983	EB/HG	39 X 8	R/BFK	35	1	400	550
Show Me the Line Between, State I (Only Available in Set)	CPP	HT/MB/CPP	1983	EB/HG	10 X 39	RP/W/HW	10	1	400	550
Show Me the Line Between, State II	CPP	HT/MB/CPP	1983	EB/HG	10 X 39	R/BFK	35	1	400	550
Rhoom for Error (Series of 46 Monotypes)	CPP	HT/MB/CPP	1983	EC/HG/HC	27 X 37 EA	RP/W/HW	46 EA	7 EA	2500 EA	3500 EA
Ol Unkl Scam	LPI	JL/LPI	1987	LC	39 X 26	AC	60		1000	1500
Mr Bones	CPP	LH/DS/CPP	1989	WC/HC	76 X 25	RICE	25	Varies	4500	5000
Now Here's That Blame Treaty (State A)	CPP	CPP	1989	AC/SG/BUR	54 X 40	AC	10		4000	4500
Now Here's That Blame Treaty, Hand-Worked Proofs	CPP	CPP	1989	AC/SG/BUR/HC	53 X 41	AC	19		6000	6000
Now Who's Got the Blue Prints	CPP	CPP	1989	AC/SG/BUR/DPT	52 X 42	AC	25		4500	5000
Torturer	CPP	CPP	1989	EC/SG	19 X 15	AC	25		750	850
Thickening Heir	LPI	JL/LPI	1989	LB	50 X 36	SOM	20	1	2000	2000
Untitled	LPI	JL/LPI	1990	MON	50 X 36 EA	AC	1 EA	Varies	4500 EA	4500 EA
Heads Lips across the Near Frontier (with Terry Allen)	SI	BS/SI	1991	LC	30 X 45	R/BFK	21		3000	3500
Various Monotypes, 1991 (With Terry Allen)	SI	BS/SI	1991	MON	45 X 30 EA	AC	1 EA	Varies	4500 EA	4500 EA
Leviathin II	SI	BS/SI	1992	WC/HC	26 X 78	R/BFK/ROL	10	Varies	6500	7500
Palette	SI	BS/SI	1992	LC/HC	30 X 22	R/BFK/W	10	Varies	2500	2500

HANNAH WILKE

BORN: New York, NY; March 7, 1940
EDUCATION: Temple Univ, Phila, PA, BFA, 1961, BS, 1962
TEACHING: Instr, Sculpture, Sch of Visual Arts, NY, 1974 to present
AWARDS: Nat Endowment for the Arts Grants, 1976,79,80; Alaska Council of the Arts Award, 1980; Guggenheim Fel, 1982; Pollock-Krasner Grant, 1987–88
RECENT EXHIB: Whitney Mus of Am Art, NY, 1989; Ludwig Mus, Germany, 1989
COLLECTIONS: Metropolitan Mus of Art, NY; Brooklyn Mus, NY; Albright-Knox Art Gallery, Buffalo, NY; Allen Art Mus, Oberlin, OH; Power Inst, Sydney, Australia
PUBLISHERS: Ronald Feldman Fine Arts, NY (RFFA)
GALLERIES: Ronald Feldman Fine Arts, New York, NY; Genovese Gallery, Boston, MA; Volatile Gallery, Cincinnati, OH
MAILING ADDRESS: 62 Green St, New York, NY 10012

TITLE	PUBLISHER	PRINTER	DATE	MEDIUM	DIMENSION (PAPER SIZE) IN INCHES	TYPE OF PAPER	EDITION NUMBER	NO. OF COLORS	ORIGINAL OPENING PRICE	CURRENT RETAIL PRICE
CURRENT EDITIONS:										
Roy Rogers (Trip)	RFFA		1974	LB/OFF	12 X 26	AP	100	1	200	500
Untitled (Dog)	RFFA		1974	SP	18 X 24	AP	50	11	150	300
Hannah Can (Photo Reproduction on Coin-Collection Can)	RFFA		1978	MM	6 X 3 DIA		365		300	500
Untitled (Series of 11)	RFFA		1987	MON	44 X 30 EA	AC	1 EA	Varies	8000 EA	9000 EA
EVEN-TU-ALLY	RFFA		1969–91	PH/SP	21 X 21	AC			1500	1500
Hername	RFFA		1978–91	EB	36 X 26	R/BFK	30		1500	1500
Handle with Care (Thermometer, Black & White Photo & Rubber-Stamped Acrostic)	RFFA		1987	MM	15 X 5		250		500	750

The retail prices of the 100,000 limited edition prints quoted in this directory are subject to change. Print publishers, artists and galleries were the direct sources for these quotations. Prices in the secondary market listed as "Sold Out Editions (Rare)" indicate that the publisher has a limited supply of that print or that the print is difficult to locate in the galleries.

ULFERT WILKE

BORN: Bad Tolz, Germany; July 14, 1907
EDUCATION: Acad Chaumier, Paris, France, 1927–28; Harvard Univ, Cambridge, MA, 1940–41; Iowa State Univ, Ames, IA, MA, 1947
TEACHING: Asst Prof, Art, Univ of Louisville, KY, 1948–55; Visiting Grad Prof, Painting, Univ of Georgia, Athens, GA, 1955–56; Assoc Prof, Art, Rutgers Univ, New Brunswick, NJ, 1962–68
AWARDS: Albrecht Durer Prize, Germany, 1927; Guggenheim Found Fel, 1959–60, 60–61; Am Acad Award, 1978; Inst of Arts & Letter, 1978
COLLECTIONS: Philadelphia Mus, PA; Guggenheim Mus, NY; Whitney Mus of Am Art, NY; Cleveland Mus, OH; Tel Aviv Mus, Israel
PRINTERS: Tamarind Inst Workshop, Albuquerque, NM (TI)
PUBLISHERS: Tamarind Inst, Albuquerque, NM (TI)
GALLERIES: Tamarind Institute, Albuquerque, NM
MAILING ADDRESS: Box 211, Rt 3, Solon, IA 52333

TITLE	PUBLISHER	PRINTER	DATE	MEDIUM	DIMENSION (PAPER SIZE) IN INCHES	TYPE OF PAPER	EDITION NUMBER	NO. OF COLORS	ORIGINAL OPENING PRICE	CURRENT RETAIL PRICE
SOLD OUT EDITIONS (RARE):										
Without Words (Series of 10)	TI	TI	1977–81	LC	18 X 13 EA	HMP	20 EA		450 EA	750 EA

JOHN A WILL

BORN: Waterloo, Iowa; June 30, 1939
EDUCATION: Univ of Northern Iowa, BA, 1961; Univ of Iowa, MFA, 1964; Tamarind Inst, Albuquerque, NM, 1970, 71
TEACHING: Univ of Wisconsin, Stout, WI, 1965–70; Univ of Calgary, Canada, 1971 to present; Nova Scotia Col of Art & Design, Canada, Summers, 1973–75, 77, 79, 84
AWARDS: Fulbright Fel; Ford Found Grant, 1970–71
RECENT EXHIB: Glenbow Mus, Calgary, Canada, 1992
COLLECTIONS: Art Inst of Chicago, IL; Art Gallery of Ontario, Toronto, Canada; Glenbow Mus, Calgary, Canada; Mus of New Mexico, Santa Fe, NM; New York Public Library, NY; Nat Gallery of Canada
PRINTERS: Artist (ART)
PUBLISHERS: Artist (ART)
MAILING ADDRESS: Art Dept, Univ of Calgary, Calgary, AB, T2N 1N4 Canada

TITLE	PUBLISHER	PRINTER	DATE	MEDIUM	DIMENSION (PAPER SIZE) IN INCHES	TYPE OF PAPER	EDITION NUMBER	NO. OF COLORS	ORIGINAL OPENING PRICE	CURRENT RETAIL PRICE
SOLD OUT EDITIONS (RARE):										
Exshaw	ART	ART	1978	LC	30 X 22	AP/W	15	16	200	300
Naive Letters	ART	ART	1979	LC	15 X 22	AP/W	15	14	200	300
The Hillbilly	ART	ART	1979	EB	22 X 30	AP/W	20	1	200	300
Great Moments in Sport, I–VIII	ART	ART	1980	LB	22 X 30 EA	AP/W	10 EA	1 EA	200 EA	300 EA
The Night Hawk	ART	ART	1981	LC	15 X 22	AP/W	12	4	200	300

DIANE WILLIAMS

PRINTERS: American Atelier, NY (AA)
PUBLISHERS: Circle Fine Art, Chicago, IL (CFA)
GALLERIES: Circle Galleries, San Diego, CA & San Francisco, CA & Northbrook, IL & Pittsburgh, PA & Houston, TX & Soho, NY & Chicago, IL & Scottsdale, AZ & Beverly Hills, CA & Costa Mesa, CA & Sherman Oaks, CA & Palm Beach, FL & Honolulu, HI & New Orleans, LA & Las Vegas, NV & Seattle, WA

TITLE	PUBLISHER	PRINTER	DATE	MEDIUM	DIMENSION (PAPER SIZE) IN INCHES	TYPE OF PAPER	EDITION NUMBER	NO. OF COLORS	ORIGINAL OPENING PRICE	CURRENT RETAIL PRICE
SOLD OUT EDITIONS (RARE):										
The Captive and the Treasure	CFA	AA	1981	SP	26 X 20	AP	140		200	300
Afternoon Treasures	CFA	AA	1981	SP	26 X 32	AP	150		200	300
Feminine Presence	CFA	AA	1981	SP	32 X 26	AP	150		200	300
Dinner for Charcot	CFA	AA	1981	SP	26 X 20	AP	140		200	300

GUY WILLIAMS

TEACHING: Univ of California, Santa Barbara, CA, currently
AWARDS: Nat Endowment for the Arts Fel; Ford Found Grant
COLLECTIONS: La Jolla Mus, CA; Los Angeles Inst of Contemp Art, CA
PRINTERS: Marcia Brown, Albuquerque, NM (MB); Lynne Allen, Albuquerque, NM (LA); Tamarind Inst, Albuquerque, NM (TI)
PUBLISHERS: Tamarind Inst, Albuquerque, NM (TI)
GALLERIES: Kiyo Higashi Gallery, Los Angeles, CA; Tamarind Inst, Albuquerque, NM; Frost Gully Gallery, Portland, ME

TITLE	PUBLISHER	PRINTER	DATE	MEDIUM	DIMENSION (PAPER SIZE) IN INCHES	TYPE OF PAPER	EDITION NUMBER	NO. OF COLORS	ORIGINAL OPENING PRICE	CURRENT RETAIL PRICE
SOLD OUT EDITIONS (RARE):										
Tao/Dow	TI	MB/TI	1983	LC	26 X 18	AP/B	30	4	450	600
Central Avenue Breakdown	TI	LA/TI	1983	LC	24 X 33	CHIRI/CD	35	2	450	600

PETER WIRTH

PRINTERS: Untitled Press, Captiva Island, FL (UP)
PUBLISHERS: Untitled Press, Captiva Island, FL (UP)

TITLE	PUBLISHER	PRINTER	DATE	MEDIUM	DIMENSION (PAPER SIZE) IN INCHES	TYPE OF PAPER	EDITION NUMBER	NO. OF COLORS	ORIGINAL OPENING PRICE	CURRENT RETAIL PRICE
CURRENT EDITIONS:										
Onionsets (Series of 15 Paper Laminations in Plexiglas Box)	UP	UP	1976		13 X 13 X 2 EA		20 EA		500 SET	7500 SET

The retail prices of the 100,000 limited edition prints quoted in this directory are subject to change. Print publishers, artists and galleries were the direct sources for these quotations. Prices in the secondary market listed as "Sold Out Editions (Rare)" indicate that the publisher has a limited supply of that print or that the print is difficult to locate in the galleries.

VICTOR WILLING

BORN: Alexandria, Egypt; 1928
EDUCATION: Slade Sch of Fine Art, London, England
PRINTERS: Sky Editions, London, England (SE)
PUBLISHERS: Bernard Jacobson Ltd, London, England (BJL)
GALLERIES: Bernard Jacobson Ltd, London, England; Blond Fine Art Gallery, London, England; House Gallery, London, England

TITLE	PUBLISHER	PRINTER	DATE	MEDIUM	DIMENSION (PAPER SIZE) IN INCHES	TYPE OF PAPER	EDITION NUMBER	NO. OF COLORS	ORIGINAL OPENING PRICE	CURRENT RETAIL PRICE
SOLD OUT EDITIONS (RARE):										
Drum	BJL	SE	1982		20 X 38	AP	70		600	1000

JAY STEWART WILLIS

BORN: Fort Wayne, IN; October 22, 1940
EDUCATION: Western Illinois Univ, Macomb, IL, 1958–61; Univ of Illinois, Urbana-Champaign, IL, BFA, 1961–64; Univ of California, Berkeley, CA, MFA, 1964–66
TEACHING: Instr, Univ of Arizona, Tucson, AZ, 1966–69; Assoc Prof, Univ of Southern California, Los Angeles, CA, 1969 to present
AWARDS: Purchase Award, Drawing, Moore Col of Art, Phila, PA, 1968
COLLECTIONS: Metropolitan Museum of Art, NY; California State Univ, Fullerton, CA; Moore Col of Art, Phila, PA; Del Mar Col Corpus Christi, TX
PRINTERS: Cirrus Editions Workshop, Los Angeles, CA (CEW)
PUBLISHERS: Cirrus Editions Ltd, Los Angeles, CA (CE)
GALLERIES: Cirrus Gallery, Los Angeles, CA
MAILING ADDRESS: c/o University of Southern California, Los Angeles, CA 90089

TITLE	PUBLISHER	PRINTER	DATE	MEDIUM	DIMENSION (PAPER SIZE) IN INCHES	TYPE OF PAPER	EDITION NUMBER	NO. OF COLORS	ORIGINAL OPENING PRICE	CURRENT RETAIL PRICE
SOLD OUT EDITIONS (RARE):										
A – 1½	CE	CEW	1973	SS/MS	22 X 41	Metal	30		175	500

THORNTON WILLIS

BORN: Pensacola, FL; May 25, 1936
EDUCATION: Univ of Southern Mississippi, Hattiesburg, MS, BA, 1962; Univ of Alabama, Birmingham, AL, MFA, 1964
TEACHING: Wagner Col, Staten Island, NY, 1967–69; Louisiana State Univ, New Orleans, LA, 1971–72
AWARDS: John Simon Guggenheim Fel, 1979; Nat Endowment for the Arts Fel, Painting, 1979; Nat Endowment for the Arts Fel, Printmaking, 1984; Adolph & Esther Gottlieb Fel, 1991
COLLECTIONS: Whitney Mus of Am Art, NY; Aldrich Mus of Contemp Art, Ridgefield, CT; Wagner Col, Staten Island, NY; Univ of Alabama, Birmingham, AL; New Orleans Mus of Art, LA; Sidney Lewis Found, Richmond, VA; Herbert F Johnson Mus, Cornell Univ, Ithaca, NY; Rochester Mem Gallery, NY; Denver Mus of Fine Art, CO; Carnegie Mellon Mus, Pittsburgh, PA; Mus of Mod Art, NY; Phillips Coll, Wash, DC; Albright-Knox Art Gallery, Buffalo, NY; Guggenheim Mus, NY
PRINTERS: Maurice Sanchez, NY (MS); Gary Day, Omaha, NE (GD); Univ of Nebraska, Omaha, NE (UON)
PUBLISHERS: Oscarsson Hood Gallery, NY (OH); Univ of Nebraska, Omaha, NE (UON)
GALLERIES: Nina Freudenheim Gallery, New York, NY; Deson-Saunders Gallery, Chicago, IL; Barbara Krakow Gallery, Boston, MA; Siegeltuch Gallery, New York, NY; Claes Nordenhake, Malmo, Sweden; Twining Gallery, New York, NY; Andre Zarre Gallery, New York, NY
MAILING ADDRESS: 85 Mercer St, New York, NY 10012

TITLE	PUBLISHER	PRINTER	DATE	MEDIUM	DIMENSION (PAPER SIZE) IN INCHES	TYPE OF PAPER	EDITION NUMBER	NO. OF COLORS	ORIGINAL OPENING PRICE	CURRENT RETAIL PRICE
SOLD OUT EDITIONS (RARE):										
Omaha Flash (Set)	UON	GD/UON	1985	MON/EC	22 X 30 EA	R/BFK/AP	10 EA	6 EA	17000 SET	20000 SET
CURRENT EDITIONS:									2000 EA	3000 EA
Red Hook Series	OH	MS	1981	LC	22 X 34 EA	AP	40 EA	5 EA	650 EA	1800 EA
Omaha Flash	UON	GD/UON	1985	LC	22 X 30	R/BFK	30	3	1500	2000

CHARLES BANKS WILSON

BORN: Springdale, AR; August 6, 1918
EDUCATION: Art Inst of Chicago, IL, Lithography & Watercolor, 1937–41; Univ of Oklahoma, Oklahoma City, OK, 1976
TEACHING: Head, Dept of Art, Northeastern Oklahoma A&M Col, Miami, OK, 1947–60
AWARDS: Covernor's Art Award, 1976; Distinguished Service Citation, Univ of Oklahoma; Oklahoma Hall of Fame, 1977
COLLECTIONS: Metropolitan Mus of Art, NY; Corcoran Gallery, Wash, DC; Library of Congress, Wash, DC; Smithsonian Mus, Wash, DC; Cowboy Hall of Fame, Oklahoma City, OK; Nat Capitol, Speakers Gallery, Wash, DC; Gilcrease Mus, Tulsa, OK; Nat Portrait Gallery, Wash, DC
PRINTERS: Artist (ART)
PUBLISHERS: Artist (ART)
GALLERIES: Deson-Saunders Gallery, Chicago, IL; Dart Gallery, New York, NY
MAILING ADDRESS: 100 N Main St, Miami, OK 74354

TITLE	PUBLISHER	PRINTER	DATE	MEDIUM	DIMENSION (PAPER SIZE) IN INCHES	TYPE OF PAPER	EDITION NUMBER	NO. OF COLORS	ORIGINAL OPENING PRICE	CURRENT RETAIL PRICE
SOLD OUT EDITIONS (RARE):										
Swimmin' Hole	AAA	ART	1942	LB	14 X 10	R/100	200	1	5	2500
Judge Roy Bean	ART	ART	1942	LB	13 X 10	R/100	25	1	15	3500
Sugar in the G	ART	ART	1968	LB	17 X 13	R/100	45	1	50	1000
Indian Profile	ART	ART	1969	LB	16 X 10	R/100	75	1	45	1000
Plains Madonna	ART	ART	1977	LB	17 X 12	R/100	300	1	65	1500
CURRENT EDITIONS:										
Pigeons	ART	ART	1954	LB	12 X 6	R/100	50	1	25	300
Sorghum Time	ART	ART	1975	LB	17 X 11	R/100	75	1	45	300
Enter Coronado	ART	ART	1976	LB	18 X 11	R/100	100	1	45	300
The Race	ART	ART	1976	LB	15 X 11	R/100	200	1	45	500
Osage Trade	ART	ART	1977	LB	16 X 13	R/100	250	1	65	500

CHARLES BANKS WILSON CONTINUED

TITLE	PUBLISHER	PRINTER	DATE	MEDIUM	DIMENSION (PAPER SIZE) IN INCHES	TYPE OF PAPER	EDITION NUMBER	NO. OF COLORS	ORIGINAL OPENING PRICE	CURRENT RETAIL PRICE
CURRENT EDITIONS:										
Race to the Barn	ART	ART	1978	LB	17 X 12	R/100	75	1	45	500
White Hats	ART	ART	1978	LB	17 X 7	R/100	200	1	45	300
War Dancer's Camp	ART	ART	1980	LB	16 X 13	R/100	150	1	100	300
Sequoyah, Great Cherokee	ART	ART	1981	LB	12 X 15	R/100	200	1	45	300

DONALD ROLLER WILSON

BORN: Houston, TX; 1938
EDUCATION: Kansas State Univ, Manhattan, KS, MFA
TEACHING: Nebraska State Col, Peru, NE, 1966–67; Asst Prof, Univ of Arkansas, Fayetteville, AR, 1967–74
RECENT EXHIB: Florida State Univ, Tallahassee, FL, 1989,92
COLLECTIONS: Florida State Univ Fine Arts Gallery, Tallahassee, FL; Univ of Arkansas, Fayetteville, AR; Univ of North Dakota, Grand Forks, ND; Univ of Tulsa, OK; Phillips Univ, Enid, OK; La Jolla Mus of Contemp Art, CA; Virginia Commonwealth Univ, Richmond, VA; Northwest Missouri State Univ, Maryville, MO
PRINTERS: Editions Press, San Francisco, CA (EP)
PUBLISHERS: Editions Press, San Francisco, CA (EP)
GALLERIES: Moody Gallery, Houston, TX; John Berggruen Gallery, San Francisco, CA; Holly Solomon Editions, New York, NY; Jan Turner Gallery, Los Angeles, CA; Coe Kerr Gallery, New York, NY; LewAllen Gallery, Santa Fe, NM

TITLE	PUBLISHER	PRINTER	DATE	MEDIUM	DIMENSION (PAPER SIZE) IN INCHES	TYPE OF PAPER	EDITION NUMBER	NO. OF COLORS	ORIGINAL OPENING PRICE	CURRENT RETAIL PRICE
CURRENT EDITIONS:										
Patricia in the Temple	EP	EP	1984	LC	30 X 22	AC/W	60	12	800	900
Girls who Have Helped Me and One was Very Hot, and One was Very Not	EP	EP	1984	LC	22 X 30	AC/W	60	12	800	900
The Shadow of Mrs Jenkins	EP	EP	1984	LC	10 X 10	AC/W	50	14	350	500
Match on Her Melon	EP	EP	1984	LC	12 X 17	AC/B	50	10	400	600
Jewels In Her Eyes	EP	EP	1984	LC	15 X 11	TR/WF	50	15	500	750

GAHAN WILSON

BORN: Evanston, IL; February 18, 1930
EDUCATION: Art Inst of Chicago, IL, 1948–52
PRINTERS: Editions Press, San Francisco, CA (EP); American Atelier, NY (AA)
PUBLISHERS: Editions Press, San Francisco, CA (EP); Circle Fine Art, Chicago, IL (CFA)
GALLERIES: Walton-Gilbert Galleries, San Francisco, CA; Louis K Meisel Gallery, New York, NY; Circle Fine Art, Chicago, Il & New York, NY & San Diego, CA & San Francisco, CA & Beverly Hills, CA & Sherman Oaks, CA & Costa Mesa, CA & Honolulu, HI & Scottsdale, AZ; Palm Beach, FL & Northbrook, IL & New Orleans, LA & Las Vegas, NV & Pittsburgh, PA & Houston, TX & Seattle, WA

TITLE	PUBLISHER	PRINTER	DATE	MEDIUM	DIMENSION (PAPER SIZE) IN INCHES	TYPE OF PAPER	EDITION NUMBER	NO. OF COLORS	ORIGINAL OPENING PRICE	CURRENT RETAIL PRICE
SOLD OUT EDITIONS (RARE):										
Slide	EP	EP	1978	LB	23 X 18	AC/W	100	1	90	400
Pleasant Dreams	EP	EP	1979	LC	30 X 22	AC/W	150	4	200	400
Lobster Dinner	EP	EP	1979	LC	30 X 22	AC/W	150	8	200	400
Chicken Spook	EP	EP	1979	LC	30 X 22	AC/W	150	5	200	400
Breakfast	EP	EP	1979	LC	30 X 22	AC/W	150	6	200	400
Park Bench	EP	EP	1979	LC	22 X 30	AC/W	150	8	200	400
Uneasy Diagnosis	CFA	AA	1980	LC	22 X 30	AP	300		150	250

ROBERT WILSON

BORN: Waco, TX
EDUCATION: Studied with George NcNeil, Paris, France, 1962; Pratt Inst, Brooklyn, NY, BFA, 1965
AWARDS: Guggenheim Fel, 1980; Skowhegan Medal for Drawing, ME, 1987
RECENT EXHIB: Galerie Fred Jahn, Gutersloh, Germany, 1987; Stedelijk Mus, Amsterdam, The Netherlands, 1989; Galerie Yvon Lambert, Paris, France, 1989; Anne Marie Verna Galerie, Zurich, Switzerland, 1989; Feigen Gallery, Chicago, IL, 1989; Virginia Lynch Gallery, Tiverton, RI, 1990; John Berggruen Gallery, San Francisco, CA, 1991; Bank of America World Headquarters Galleries, San Francisco, CA, 1992; Contemp Arts Mus, Houston, TX, 1992; Contemp Arts Center, Cincinnati, OH, 1989,92; Laura Carpenter Fine Art, Santa Fe, NM, 1992; Paula Copper Gallery, NY, 1992
COLLECTIONS: Mus of Mod Art, NY; Mus of Mod Art, Paris, France; Australian Nat Gallery, Canberra, Australia; Stedelijk Mus, Amsterdam, The Netherlands; Menil Coll, Houston, TX
PRINTERS: Aeropress, NY (A); Patricia Branstead, NY (PB); Urdla Atelier Litho, NY (UAL); Ken Hale, Austin, TX (KH); Univ of Texas, Austin, TX (UT); Karl Imhof, Munich, West Germany (KI)
PUBLISHERS: Multiples, NY (M); Patricia Forest, NY (PF); Univ of Texas, Austin, TX (UT); Fred Jahn, Munich, West Germany (FJ); Artist (ART); David Nolan, NY (DN)
GALLERIES: Marian Goodman Gallery, New York, NY; Paula Cooper Gallery, New York, NY; David Nolan Gallery, New York, NY; Alpha Gallery, Boston, MA; Feigen Gallery, Chicago, IL; Laura Carpenter Fine Art, Santa Fe, NM
MAILING ADDRESS: c/o Paula Cooper Gallery, 155 Wooster St, New York, NY 10012

The retail prices of the 100,000 limited edition prints quoted in this directory are subject to change. Print publishers, artists and galleries were the direct sources for these quotations. Prices in the secondary market listed as "Sold Out Editions (Rare)" indicate that the publisher has a limited supply of that print or that the print is difficult to locate in the galleries.

ROBERT WILSON CONTINUED

TITLE	PUBLISHER	PRINTER	DATE	MEDIUM	DIMENSION (PAPER SIZE) IN INCHES	TYPE OF PAPER	EDITION NUMBER	NO. OF COLORS	ORIGINAL OPENING PRICE	CURRENT RETAIL PRICE
CURRENT EDITIONS:										
Set of Ten Etchings:									3000 SET	15000 SET
Patio Sofa	M	A/PB	1977	EB	29 X 22	HMP	20	1	300	1500
Louis XV	M	A/PB	1977	EB	29 X 22	HMP	20	1	300	1500
Hanging Chair	M	A/PB	1977	EB	29 X 22	HMP	20	1	300	1500
Cafe Chair	M	A/PB	1977	EB	29 X 22	HMP	20	1	300	1500
Einstein Chairs	M	A/PB	1977	EB	29 X 22	HMP	20	1	300	1500
Stalin Chairs	M	A/PB	1977	EB	29 X 22	HMP	20	1	300	1500
Overture Chair	M	A/PB	1977	EB	29 X 22	HMP	20	1	300	1500
Flying Bench	M	A/PB	1977	EB	29 X 22	HMP	20	1	300	1500
Cafe Table	M	A/PB	1977	EB	29 X 22	HMP	20	1	300	1500
Queen Victoria Chairs	M	A/PB	1977	EB	29 X 22	HMP	20	1	300	2000
Medea (Set of 20)	ART/PF	UAL	1984	LC	13 X 18 EA	AP/JP	Varies	Multi	600 EA	1000 EA
Medea (Set of 20)	ART/PF	UAL	1984	LB	13 X 18 EA	AP/JP	Varies	1 EA	300/500	600 EA
Persifal (Set of 19)	FJ	KI	1985	LC	Varies	Varies	35 EA	Varies	7000 SET	10000 SET
Alceste (Series of 10)	UT	KH/UT	1986	LC	Varies	Varies	20 EA	Varies	400/450	750 EA

YORK WILSON

BORN: Toronto, Canada; December 6, 1907
EDUCATION: Ontario Col of Art, Can; Detroit Inst of Art, MI
TEACHING: Instr, Painting & Drawing, Artist Workshop, Art Gallery, ON, Canada, 1944–45; Ontario Col of Art, Canada, 1944–45; Doon Sch of Fine Arts, Summer, 1949–54
AWARDS: JWL Forster Award, 1945,50; McGill Comp, 1954; Winnipeg Exhib, 1956; Baxter Award, 1959; Centennial Medal, 1967; Print Award, Montreal, Can, 1979; Ontario Soc of Artists Award, Canada, 1983; Italian Acad Award, 1984
RECENT EXHIB: Art Gallery of Ontario/ The Station Gallery, Whitby, ON, Canada, 1991; The Gallery, Stratford, ON, Canada; Art Gallery of Windsor, Canada; Museo Casa de Allende, San Miguel de Allende, Mexico, 1991; Kennedy Gallery, North Bay, ON, Canada, 1991; Moore Gallery, Ltd, Hamilton, ON, Canada, 1992
COLLECTIONS: Nat Gallery of Canada, Ottawa, Can; Art Gallery of Ontario, Toronto, Can; Mus of Mod Art, Paris, France; Mus de Dijon, France; Mus de Eduardo Westerdahl, Spain; Birla Acad Mus, Calcutta, India; Mus de Arte Moderna, Mexico; Montreal Mus Des Beaux-Arts, Can; Mus D'Art Contemporain, Montreal, Can; Art Gallery of Windsor, Canada; Art Gallery of Hamilton, Canada; Sarnia Art Gallery, Canada; Uffizi Gallery, Florence, Italy; Tanaka Mus, Japan
PRINTERS: Open Studios, Toronto, Canada (OS); Artist (ART)
PUBLISHERS: Wallack Gallery, Ottawa, Canada (WG); Artist (ART)
GALLERIES: Wallack Galleries, Ottawa, Canada; Moore Galleries, Hamilton, Canada
MAILING ADDRESS: 41 Alcina Ave, Toronto, ON Canada M6G 2E7

TITLE	PUBLISHER	PRINTER	DATE	MEDIUM	DIMENSION (PAPER SIZE) IN INCHES	TYPE OF PAPER	EDITION NUMBER	NO. OF COLORS	ORIGINAL OPENING PRICE	CURRENT RETAIL PRICE
CURRENT EDITIONS:										
New York (France)	ART	ART	1963	SP	19 X 26	AP	50	5	60	650
Bleu (France)	ART	ART	1963	SP	19 X 26	AP	50	5	60	650
Cities of the World Suite (Set of 7):	ART	ART	1967	SP	23 X 28	AP	60	5	350 SET	5000 SET
Cairo	ART	ART	1967	SP	23 X 28	AP	60	5	60	800
Kuala Lumpur	ART	ART	1967	SP	23 X 28	AP	60	5	60	800
Marrekesch	ART	ART	1967	SP	23 X 28	AP	60	5	60	800
Jaipur	ART	ART	1967	SP	23 X 28	AP	60	5	60	800
Srinagar	ART	ART	1967	SP	23 X 28	AP	60	5	60	800
Isfahan	ART	ART	1967	SP	23 X 28	AP	60	5	60	800
Kuching	ART	ART	1967	SP	23 X 28	AP	60	5	60	800
Ngaio	ART	ART	1976	LC	19 X 11	AP	20	2	50	450
Donotis	ART	ART	1976	LC	22 X 30	AP	48	4	200	850
Mayan	ART	ART	1976	LC	21 X 25	AP	50	4	250	850
Blue Opus, with Limited Edition Biography Only	WG	ART	1977	LC	21 X 24	AP	300	4	300	1000

ROLF WINNEWISSER

BORN: Niederfosgen, Switzerland; 1949
EDUCATION: Sch of Graphic Design, Lucerne, Switzerland, 1972
PRINTERS: Solo Press, Inc, NY (SP)
PUBLISHERS: Judith Solodkin, NY (JS); Peter Blum Edition, NY (PBE)
GALLERIES: Marian Goodman Gallery, New York, NY; Peter Blum Edition, New York, NY

TITLE	PUBLISHER	PRINTER	DATE	MEDIUM	DIMENSION (PAPER SIZE) IN INCHES	TYPE OF PAPER	EDITION NUMBER	NO. OF COLORS	ORIGINAL OPENING PRICE	CURRENT RETAIL PRICE
SOLD OUT EDITIONS (RARE):										
Non-Territory Maps of a Strange Loop Between Visiting and Staying in a Picture, 1981 (4 color, 7 Black & White) (Set of 11 Linocuts)	PBE	JS/SP	1981	LI	25 X 38 EA	YAM	25 EA		2500 SET	5000 SET

The retail prices of the 100,000 limited edition prints quoted in this directory are subject to change. Print publishers, artists and galleries were the direct sources for these quotations. Prices in the secondary market listed as "Sold Out Editions (Rare)" indicate that the publisher has a limited supply of that print or that the print is difficult to locate in the galleries.

ROBIN WINTERS

BORN: Benicia, CA; 1950
RECENT EXHIB: Luhring, Augustine & Hodes Gallery, NY, 1987; Experimental Workshop, San Francisco, CA; San Francisco Art Inst, Emanuel Walter & Atholl McBean Galleries, San Francisco, CA, 1989; Temple Univ, Tyler Sch of Art, Tyler Gallery, Phila, PA, 1989
PRINTERS: John Stemmer, San Francisco, CA (JS); David Crook, San Francisco, Ca (DC); Experimental Workshop, San Francisco, CA (EW); David Calkins, Bloomington, IN (DCa); David Keister, Bloomington, IN (DK); Echo Press, Bloomington, IN (EPr)
PUBLISHERS: Experimental Workshop, San Francisco, CA (EW); Echo Press, Bloomington, IN (EPr)
GALLERIES: Lawrence Mangel Gallery, Phila, PA; Rosa Esman Gallery, New York, NY; Luhring, Augustine Gallery, New York, NY; Brooke Alexander, Inc, New York, NY; Michael Klein, Inc, New York, NY; Betsy Senior Contemporary Prints, New York, NY

TITLE	PUBLISHER	PRINTER	DATE	MEDIUM	DIMENSION (PAPER SIZE) IN INCHES	TYPE OF PAPER	EDITION NUMBER	NO. OF COLORS	ORIGINAL OPENING PRICE	CURRENT RETAIL PRICE
CURRENT EDITIONS:										
Ghost Story (Series of 25)	EW	JS/DC/EW	1986	MON	54 X 43 EA	R/BFK/ROL	1 EA	Varies	3000 EA	3500 EA
Fiddleback Flea Market (Set of 16)	EW	JS/DC/EW	1987			Wood	5 EA		3700 SET	5000 SET
The Seed Multipliers (3 Panels)	EPr	DK/DCa/EPr	1988	EB/LC/WC/LI	57 X 59	MUL	25	26	5500	6000
Cutaway	TH	RL/MF	1989	LI/C	38 X 26	AP/MOR/MIT	22		1500	1800
Mandible	TH	RL/MF	1989	LI/C	38 X 26	AP/MOR/MIT	22		1500	1800

TERRY WINTERS

BORN: 1949
EDUCATION: Pratt Inst, NY
RECENT EXHIB: Editions Ilene Kurtz, NY, 1989; Fawbush Gallery, NY, 1989; Van Straaten Gallery, Chicago, IL, 1991; Sonoma State Univ, Rohnert Park, CA, 1992
COLLECTIONS: Reed Col of Art, Portland, OR; Mus of Fine Arts, Boston, MA; St Louis Art Mus, MO
PRINTERS: Thomas Cox (TC); Keith Brintzenhofe (KB); Hitoshi Kido (HK); John Lund (JL); Tina Diggs (TD); Doug Volle (DV); Bill Goldston (BG); Univeral Limited Art Editions, West Islip, NY (ULAE); Aldo Crommelynck, Paris, France (AC); Atelier Crommelynck, Paris, France (AtC); Francois Lafrance, NY (FL); Judith Solodkin, NY (JS); Solo Gallery, NY (SG)
PUBLISHERS: Universal Limited Art Editions, West Islip, NY (ULAE); Editions Ilene Kurtz, NY (EIK); Peter Blum Editions, NY (PLE); Parasol Press, Ltd, NY (PaP); Solo Press, NY (SP); Aldo Crommelynck, Paris, France (AC)
GALLERIES: Sonnabend Gallery, New York, NY; Paula Cooper Gallery, New York, NY; Universal Limited Art Editions, New York, NY; Barbara Krakow Gallery, Boston, MA; Edition Ilene Kurtz, New York, NY; Peter Blum Edition, New York, NY; Fawbush Gallery, New York, NY; Van Straaten Gallery, Chicago, IL; Margo Leavin Gallery, Los Angeles, CA; Pence Fine Art, Inc, Los Angeles, CA; Goodman/Tinnon Fine Art, San Francisco, CA; Graystone, San Francisco, CA; Daniel Weinberg Gallery, Santa Monica, CA; Thomas Smith Fine Art, Fort Wayne, IN; Magnuson Gallery, Boston, MA; Bobbie Greenfield Fine Art, Inc, Venice, CA; John C Stoller & Company, Minneapolis, MN; Martina Hamilton & Associates, Inc, New York, NY; Jim Kempner Fine Art, Inc, New York, NY; Pietrasanta Fine Arts, New York, NY; Elizabeth Paul Gallery, Cincinnati, OH; Greg Kucera Gallery, Seattle, WA; Brooke Alexander Editions, New York, NY; Pace Editions, New York, NY
MAILING ADDRESS: c/o Sonnabend Gallery, 420 West Broadway, New York, NY 10012

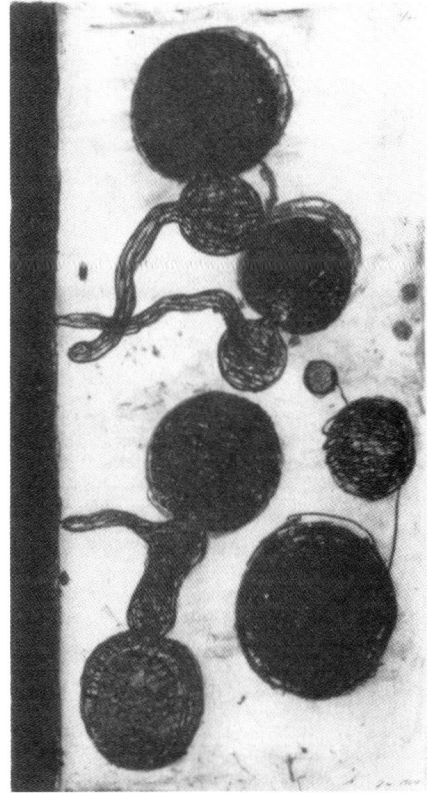

Terry Winters
Double Standard
Courtesy Universal Limited Art Editions

TITLE	PUBLISHER	PRINTER	DATE	MEDIUM	DIMENSION (PAPER SIZE) IN INCHES	TYPE OF PAPER	EDITION NUMBER	NO. OF COLORS	ORIGINAL OPENING PRICE	CURRENT RETAIL PRICE
SOLD OUT EDITIONS (RARE):										
Ova	ULAE	TC/KB/ULAE	1982	LB	30 X 22	MdV	2	1	800	17500
Factors of Increase	ULAE	TC/KB/ULAE	1983	LB	31 X 23	MdV	30	1	600	12000
Novalis	ULAE	TC/KB/ULAE	1983	LC	43 X 31	MdV	50		800	8000
Morula Series:										
Morula I	ULAE	TC/KB/ULAE	1983–84	LC	42 X 32	TOY/HMP	38	2	700	30000
Morula II	ULAE	TC/KB/ULAE	1983–84	LC	42 X 32	TOY/HMP	37	3	700	30000
Morula III	ULAE	TC/KB/ULAE	1983–84	LC	42 X 32	TOY/HMP	36	3	700	30000
Double Standard	ULAE	TC/KB/ULAE	1984	LC	78 X 43	AP/ROL	40		1800	28000
Primer	ULAE	TC/KB/ULAE	1985	LC	31 X 23	JWP/1961	66	8	1350	16000
Folio (Box Designed by Frank D'Agostino) (Set of 11)	ULAE	ULAE	1985–86	LC	32 X 23 EA	JWP/JKP	39 EA		20000 SET	18000 SET
CURRENT EDITIONS:										
Untitled	PaP	KB/DV/ULAE	1986	LC	30 X 26	JBG	75		1500	12000
Untitled	ULAE	KB/DV/ULAE	1987	LC	32 X 23	JBG	71	11	3000	9000
Album (Fabric Box) (Set of 9)	EIK	AC/AtC	1988	EC	27 X 21 EA	HAHN	50 EA		20000 SET	85000 SET

TERRY WINTERS CONTINUED

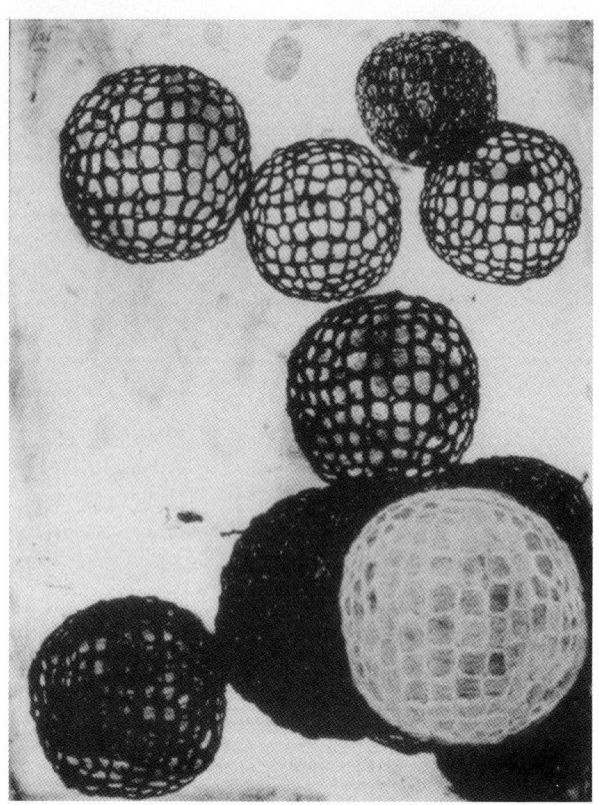

Terry Winters
Morula III
Courtesy Universal Limited Art Editions

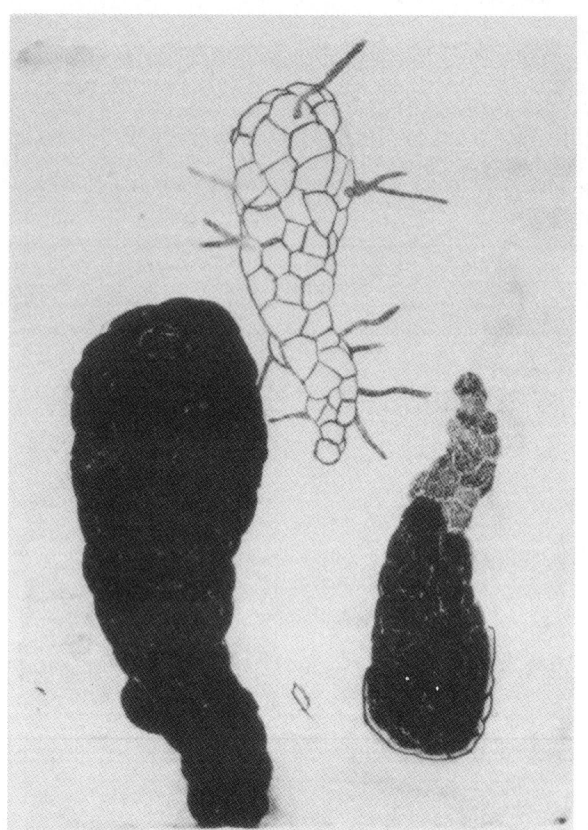

Terry Winters
Factors of Increase
Courtesy Universal Limited Art Editions

TITLE	PUBLISHER	PRINTER	DATE	MEDIUM	DIMENSION (PAPER SIZE) IN INCHES	TYPE OF PAPER	EDITION NUMBER	NO. OF COLORS	ORIGINAL OPENING PRICE	CURRENT RETAIL PRICE
CURRENT EDITIONS:										
Untitled	EIK	AC/AtC	1988	EC	36 X 29	HAHN	50		4500	15000
Marginalia	ULAE	KB/DV/ULAE	1988	LC	48 X 32	AP	66		7500	15000
Section			1988	I/CC	30 X 35	HAHN	50	1	6000	7000
Station	ULAE	KB/KH/ULAE	1988	I/CC	30 X 35	HAHN	55	1	6000	7000
Untitled			1988	EB	30 X 35	HAHN	50	1	6000	8000
Untitled			1988	EB	36 X 29	HAHN	50	1	6000	7500
Untitled			1988	EB	27 X 35	HAHN	50	1	6000	6500
Furrows (Set of 5)	PBE	FL	1989	WB	27 X 21 EA	HMP	45 EA	1 EA	12000 SET	20000 SET
Furrows (Set of 5)	PBE	FL	1989	WB	27 X 21 EA	HMP	XII EA	1 EA	12000 SET	20000 SET
Fourteen Etchings (Set of 14)	ULAE	KB/KH/JL/TD/ULAE	1989	EB	19 X 14 EA	Amalfi	65 EA		20000 SET	25000 SET
Theorem	ULAE	BG/ULAE	1992	LC	32 X 48	AP	41	18	3500	3500
Field Notes (Set of 25)	AC	AC/AtC	1992	EB	13 X 10	HAHN	75 EA	1 EA	15000 SET	15000 SET

KARL WIRSUM

BORN: Chicago, IL; September 27, 1939
EDUCATION: Art Inst of Chicago, Sch, IL, BFA, 1961–65
TEACHING: Instr, Painting & Drawing, Art Inst of Chicago, Art Sch, IL, 1974 to present
AWARDS: Logan Medal, Art Inst of Chicago, IL, 1969; Nat Endowment for the Arts Fel, 1971–77–83; Illinois Arts Council Fel, 1986
RECENT EXHIB: Col of DuPage, William E Gahlberg Arts Center Gallery, Glen Ellyn, IL, 1992

COLLECTIONS: Art Inst of Chicago, IL; Mus of Contemp Art, Chicago, IL; Whitney Mus of Am Art, NY; Univ of Chicago, IL; Nat Mus of Am Art, Wash, DC
PRINTERS: Jerry Raidiger, Chicago, IL (JR); Jack Lemon, Chicago, IL (JL); Landfall Press, Inc, Chicago, IL (LPI)
PUBLISHERS: Landfall Press, Inc, Chicago, IL (LPI)
GALLERIES: Landfall Press, Inc, Chicago, IL; Phyllis Kind Galleries, New York, NY & Chicago, IL; Quartet Editions, New York, NY
MAILING ADDRESS: c/o Art Inst of Chicago, Columbus Dr, Jackson, Chicago, IL 60603

TITLE	PUBLISHER	PRINTER	DATE	MEDIUM	DIMENSION (PAPER SIZE) IN INCHES	TYPE OF PAPER	EDITION NUMBER	NO. OF COLORS	ORIGINAL OPENING PRICE	CURRENT RETAIL PRICE
SOLD OUT EDITIONS (RARE):										
Skull Daze	LPI	JR/LPI	1971	LC	24 X 34	GE	50	4	150	750
CURRENT EDITIONS:										
Jello Joel	LPI	JL/LPI	1989	LC	30 X 22	SOM	50		600	600

NANCY CAMDEN WITT

BORN: Richmond, VA; October 24, 1930
EDUCATION: Randolph-Macon Women's Col, 1948–50; Old Dominion Univ, Norfolk, VA, BA, 1965; Virginia Commonwealth Univ, Richmond, VA, MFA, 1967
TEACHING: Acting Chmn, Art Department, Bland Col, William & Mary Col, Williamsburg, VA, 1961,63,64,65
AWARDS: Purchase Prize, Virginia Comn on Arts & Humanities, 1975; Award, Int Woman Artists Exhib, 1976; Purchase Prize, Henrico Library, Richmond, VA
RECENT EXHIB: Cudahy's Galleries, New York, NY & Richmond, VA, 1990
COLLECTIONS: Univ of North Carolina, Chrysler Mus, Norfolk, VA; Mississippi Mus of Art; Univ of Virginia, Charlottesville, VA, Richmond, VA; Randolph Macon Col, Lynchburg, VA
PRINTERS: Richmond Printmaking Workshop, Richmond, VA (RPW); Atlantic Editions, Richmond, VA (AE)
PUBLISHERS: Richmond Printmaking Workshop, Richmond, VA (RPW); Atlantic Editions, Richmond, VA (AE)
GALLERIES: Reynolds Gallery, Richmond, VA; Cudahy's Gallery, Richmond, VA & New York, NY
MAILING ADDRESS: Rt 3 Box 3115, Ashland, VA 23005

TITLE	PUBLISHER	PRINTER	DATE	MEDIUM	DIMENSION (PAPER SIZE) IN INCHES	TYPE OF PAPER	EDITION NUMBER	NO. OF COLORS	ORIGINAL OPENING PRICE	CURRENT RETAIL PRICE
SOLD OUT EDITIONS (RARE):										
Window I	RPW	RPW	1980	LC	16 X 26	AP	25	2	125	250
CURRENT EDITIONS:										
Break	AE	AE	1980	LB	15 X 19	AP	50	1	125	150
Blocks	AE	AE	1980	LB	16 X 21	AP	50	1	125	150
Psyche	AE	AE	1980	LB	17 X 22	AP	25	1	150	175
Sand Dollar	AE	AE	1980	LB	17 X 21	AP	40	1	150	175
Key	AE	AE	1980	LB	17 X 23	AP	50	1	125	150

EMERSON WOELFFER

BORN: Chicago, IL; July 27, 1914
EDUCATION: Art Inst of Chicago, IL, BA; Inst of Design, Chicago, IL, Hon DFA
TEACHING: Instr, Sch of Design, Chicago, IL, 1942; Colorado Springs Fine Arts Center, Boulder, CO, 1950; Instr, Chouinard Art Inst, CA, 1959; Vis Prof, Black Mountain Col, 1949; Vis Prof, Painting, Univ of Southern California, CA, Summer, 1962; Otis Art Inst, Los Angeles, CA, 1974 to present
RECENT EXHIB: Gruenebaum Gallery, NY, 1987; Manny Silverman Gallery, Los Angeles, CA, 1990
AWARDS: Guggenheim Found Fel, 1967–68; Raymond A Speiser Mem Prize, Pennsylvania Acad of Fine Arts, Phila, PA, 1968; Nat Endowment for the Arts Grant, 1973; Pollock-Krasner Grant, 1985–86; Francis J Greenburger Award, NY, 1988
COLLECTIONS: Whitney Mus of Am Art, NY; Mus of Mod Art, NY; Art Inst of Chicago, IL; Univ of Illinois, Urbana-Champaign, IL; Los Angeles County Art Mus, CA; Seattle Art Mus, WA; Santa Fe Mus of Art, NM; Bibliotheque Nat, Paris, France
PRINTERS: Marcia Brown, Albuquerque, NM (MB); Tamarind Inst, Albuquerque, NM (TI)
PUBLISHERS: Tamarind Institute, Albuquerque, NM (TI)
GALLERIES: Graphics Gallery, San Francisco, CA; Wenger Gallery, Los Angeles, CA; David Stuart Gallery, Los Angeles, CA; Manny Silverman Gallery, Los Angeles, CA; Harcourts Modern & Contemporary Art, San Francisco, CA
MAILING ADDRESS: 475 Dustin Dr, Los Angeles, CA 90065

TITLE	PUBLISHER	PRINTER	DATE	MEDIUM	DIMENSION (PAPER SIZE) IN INCHES	TYPE OF PAPER	EDITION NUMBER	NO. OF COLORS	ORIGINAL OPENING PRICE	CURRENT RETAIL PRICE
SOLD OUT EDITIONS (RARE):										
Untitled	TI	RB/TI	1977	LC	76 X 56 cm	AP/W	70	3	400	750
Blue Lake	TI	MB/TI	1983	LC	30 X 22	R/BFK	30	4	450	600
Red Moon, White Sun	TI	MB/TI	1983	LC	30 X 22	R/BFK	30	4	450	600

PAUL WONNER (JOHN)

BORN: Tucson, AZ; April 24, 1920
EDUCATION: California Col of Arts & Crafts, Oakland, CA, BA, 1937–41; Art Students League, NY, 1946–50; Univ of California, Berkeley, CA, BFA, 1952, MFA, 1953, MA, 1955
TEACHING: Instr, Painting, Univ of California, Los Angeles, CA, 1963–64; Instr, Otis Art Inst, Los Angeles, CA, 1965–66; Instr, Col of Creative Studies, Santa Barbara, CA, 1968–71; Instr, Univ of California, Davis, CA, 1975–76; Instr, Univ of California State Univ, Long Beach, CA, 1981
AWARDS: Anne Bremer Mem Scholarship, CA, 1953
RECENT EXHIB: Hirschl & Adler Modern, NY, 1987
COLLECTIONS: Mus of Mod Art, NY; Guggenheim Mus, NY; Hirshhorn Mus, Wash, DC; Smithsonian Inst, Wash, DC; Oakland Mus, CA; San Francisco Mus of Mod Art, CA; Minneapolis Inst of Arts, MN; Sheldon Mem Art Gallery, Univ of Nebraska, Lincoln, NE; Mus of Fine Arts, Boston, MA; Charles A Wustum Mus of Fine Arts, Racine, WI; Nat Coll of Fine Arts, Smithsonian Inst, Wash, DC
PRINTERS: Editions Press, San Francisco, CA (EP)
PUBLISHERS: Editions Press, San Francisco, CA (EP)
GALLERIES: Hirschl & Adler Modern Art, New York, NY; John Berggruen Gallery, San Francisco, CA; James Corcoran Gallery, Santa Monica, CA; David Raymond, Ltd, San Francisco, CA; Coe Kerr Gallery, New York, NY
MAILING ADDRESS: 468 Jersey St, San Francisco, CA 94994

TITLE	PUBLISHER	PRINTER	DATE	MEDIUM	DIMENSION (PAPER SIZE) IN INCHES	TYPE OF PAPER	EDITION NUMBER	NO. OF COLORS	ORIGINAL OPENING PRICE	CURRENT RETAIL PRICE
SOLD OUT EDITIONS (RARE):										
Basket of Plums	EP	EP	1982	LC	30 X 23	AC/W	75	18	675	2000
Tulips in a Milk Carton	EP	EP	1983	LC	25 X 18	AC/B	60	11	750	1500

The retail prices of the 100,000 limited edition prints quoted in this directory are subject to change. Print publishers, artists and galleries were the direct sources for these quotations. Prices in the secondary market listed as "Sold Out Editions (Rare)" indicate that the publisher has a limited supply of that print or that the print is difficult to locate in the galleries.

The Printworld Directory is accepting new applications for the seventh edition. Approximately 300 new artists will be accepted. Please use the two forms provided in the back section of this directory to submit biographical data and documentation of prints. Edition number of each print must not exceed 500 and the retail price must be $100 or more.

DAVID WOJNAROWICZ

BORN: New Jersey; (1954–1992)
RECENT EXHIB: Ground Zero, NY, 1987; Gracie Mansion Gallery, NY, 1987; Bucknell Univ Center, Lewisburg, PA, 1987; Galerie Buades, Madrid, Spain; Fort Madison Art Center, IA, 1989; Milwaukee Art Mus, WI, 1990; Wadsworth Atheneum, Hartford, CT, 1990; Real Art Ways, Hartford, CT, 1990; Dorothy Goldeen Gallery, Santa Monica, CA, 1990; Wessel O'Connor Gallery, NY, 1990; Mus of Contemp Art, Los Angeles, CA, 1992; Retrosp, Illinois State Univ, Normal, IL, 1992; Bridge Center for Contemp Art, El Paso, TX, 1992; Tony Shafrazi Gallery, NY, 1990,92; PPOW, NY, 1989,90,92
COLLECTIONS: Metropolitan Mus of Art, NY
PRINTERS: Keith Davis, NY (KD); Artist (ART); Normal Editions Workshop, IL (NEW)
PUBLISHERS: Artist (ART); Normal Editions Workshop, IL (NEW); Illinois State Univ, Normal, IL (ISU)
GALLERIES: Peter Miller Gallery, Chicago, IL; Hal Bromm Gallery, New York, NY; Gracie Mansion Gallery, New York, NY; PPOW Gallery, New York, NY; Exit Art, New York, NY; John Post Lee Gallery, New York, NY
MAILING ADDRESS: c/o Gracie Mansion Gallery, 442 E 9th St, New York, NY 10009

David Wojnarowicz
Earth & Wind
Courtesy Normal Editions Workshop

David Wojnarowicz
Fire & Water
Courtesy Normal Editions Workshop

TITLE	PUBLISHER	PRINTER	DATE	MEDIUM	DIMENSION (PAPER SIZE) IN INCHES	TYPE OF PAPER	EDITION NUMBER	NO. OF COLORS	ORIGINAL OPENING PRICE	CURRENT RETAIL PRICE
SOLD OUT EDITIONS (RARE):										
The Myth (on Domino Sugar Poster)	ART	KD	1983	SP	34 X 24	AP	50		150	300
The Myth (on Domino Sugar Poster)	ART	KD	1983	SP	34 X 24	AP	45		150	300
In Genet Masterbating in Mattery Bison	ART	KD	1983	SP	34 X 24	AP	50		150	300
In Genet Masterbating in Mattery Bison	ART	KD	1983	SP	34 X 24	AP	45		150	300
CURRENT EDITIONS:										
Untitled (From Art Series)	ART	ART	1988-89	PH	16 X 20					
Earth & Wind	NEW/ISU	NEW	1990-91	LC	23 X 30	R/BFK	24	9	1600	1600
Fire & Water	NEW/ISU	NEW	1990-91	LC	23 X 30	R/BFK	24	10	1600	1600

WONG MOO-CHEW

BORN: Selangor, Malaysia; 1942
EDUCATION: L'Ecole Nat Supérieure des Beaux Arts, Paris, France; Atelier Lacouriére, Montmartre, France
TEACHING: Prof, Printmaking, L'Ecole Nat des Arts Decoratifs, Nice, France, 1974 to present
AWARDS: Gold Medal, Printmaking, Epinal, 1973; Int Grand Prize, Printmaking, Premio Biella, Italy, 1976
PRINTERS: American Atelier, NY (AA)
PUBLISHERS: Circle Fine Art, Chicago, IL (CFA)
GALLERIES: Circle Galleries, San Diego, CA & San Francisco, CA & Northbrook, IL & Pittsburgh, PA & Houston, TX & Soho, NY & Chicago, IL & Scottsdale, AZ & Beverly Hills, CA & Costa Mesa, CA & Sherman Oaks, CA & Palm Beach, FL & Honolulu, HI & New Orleans, LA & Las Vegas, NV & Seattle, WA

TITLE	PUBLISHER	PRINTER	DATE	MEDIUM	DIMENSION (PAPER SIZE) IN INCHES	TYPE OF PAPER	EDITION NUMBER	NO. OF COLORS	ORIGINAL OPENING PRICE	CURRENT RETAIL PRICE
SOLD OUT EDITIONS (RARE):										
Ecriture No 121	CFA	AA	1972	EC	22 X 30	R/BFK	75		50	300

CHRISTOPHER WOOL

AWARDS: Nat Endowment for the Arts Fel, 1987
RECENT EXHIB: Kansas City Art Inst, MO, 1987; Luhring, Augustine & Hodes Gallery, NY, 1987,88; Jean Bernier Gallery, Athens, Greece, 1988; Galerie Gisela Capitain, Cologne, Germany, 1988
PUBLISHERS: Edition Julie Sylvester, NY (EJS)
GALLERIES: Edition Julie Sylvester, New York, NY; Jack Hanley Gallery, San Francisco, CA; Luhring, Augustine Gallery, New York, NY; Thea Westrich Fine Art, New York, NY

The Printworld Directory is accepting new applications for the seventh edition. Approximately 300 new artists will be accepted. Please use the two forms provided in the back section of this directory to submit biographical data and documentation of prints. Edition number of each print must not exceed 500 and the retail price must be $100 or more.

CHRISTOPHER WOOL CONTINUED

TITLE	PUBLISHER	PRINTER	DATE	MEDIUM	DIMENSION (PAPER SIZE) IN INCHES	TYPE OF PAPER	EDITION NUMBER	NO. OF COLORS	ORIGINAL OPENING PRICE	CURRENT RETAIL PRICE
CURRENT EDITIONS:										
Black Monotype on Suzuki	EJS		1989	MON	74 X 37 EA	SUZ	1 EA	1	3500 EA	5000 EA

FRANK WOOTTON

BORN: England; 1914
EDUCATION: Eastbourne Col of Art, England
COLLECTIONS: Arkansas Arts Center Found, Little Rock, AR; Smithsonian Inst, Wash, DC; Imperial War Mus, England; Alexandria Mus, LA
PRINTERS: Werkner-Momii Studios, Gretna, LA (WMS); James Haworth Ltd, Leicester, England (JH); Marie Dormuth, NY (MD)
PUBLISHERS: TINK Art Trading Company (TINK); Options Unlimited (OU); Gallery Productions (GP); HJM Arts (HJM); Abstraction Partners, Ltd (APL); C A Saunders (CAS); Peterson Publishing (PPC)
GALLERIES: Ro Gallery, Image Makers, Inc, New York, NY

TITLE	PUBLISHER	PRINTER	DATE	MEDIUM	DIMENSION (PAPER SIZE) IN INCHES	TYPE OF PAPER	EDITION NUMBER	NO. OF COLORS	ORIGINAL OPENING PRICE	CURRENT RETAIL PRICE
SOLD OUT EDITIONS (RARE):										
Huntsman Crossing a Stream	TINK	MD	1982	SP	22 X 30	R/100	200	22	350	500
Drawing the Wood	OU	MD	1982	SP	22 X 30	R/100	200	22	350	500
Going Out with the Hounds	GP	MD	1982	SP	22 X 30	R/100	200	22	350	500
Saddle Bronc Rider	HJM	WMS	1982	SP	22 X 30	AP	200	54	350	500
Horse Show	APL	JHL	1983	LC/OFF	22 X 30	SOM	250	6	150	300
Going to the Start	CAS	JHL	1983	LC/OFF	22 X 30	SOM	250	6	150	300
At the Start	PPC	JHL	1983	LC/OFF	22 X 30	SOM	250	6	150	300

AMY N WORTHEN

BORN: New York, NY, August 13, 1946
EDUCATION: High Sch of Music & Art, NY, 1963; Smith Col, Northampton, MA, BA, 1967, with Leonard Baskin; Univ of Iowa, Iowa City, IA, MA, 1969, with Mauricio Lasansky
TEACHING: Instr, Printmaking, Des Moines Art Center, IA, 1971–81; Drake Univ, Des Moines, IA, 1972–74,81,83,85
AWARDS: Phi Beta Kappa, 1967; Stoekel Fel, Yale Univ, New Haven, CT, 1966; Iowa Arts Council Touring Exhib Grant, 1978; Hon Mention, Am Color Print Soc, 1984
RECENT EXHIB: C W Post Col, NY, 1988; Beaver Col, Jenkintown, PA, 1988; Univ of California, Irvine, CA, 1988; Grinell Col, IA, 1992
COLLECTIONS: Metropolitan Mus, NY; Iowa State Univ, Ames, IA; Univ of Arizona, Tucson, AZ; Albrecht Gallery Mus, St Joseph, MO; Arkansas Arts Center, Little Rock, AR; Cedar Rapids Art Center, IA; Des Moines Art Center, IA; Keokek Art Mus, IA; Univ of Arizona, Tucson, AZ; Univ of Iowa Mus of Art, Iowa City, IA, Cooper-Hewitt Mus, NY; Sioux City Art, Center, IA; Iowa State Univ, Ames, IA; Nat Mus of Am Art, Wash, DC
PRINTERS: Santa Reparta Graphic Workshop, Florence, Italy (SRGW); Lakeside Studio, Lakeside, MI (LS); Bill Sandusky (BS); Tom Blackman (TB); Artist (ART)
PUBLISHERS: Lakeside Studio, Lakeside, MI (LS); Des Moines Opera, Indianola, IA (DMO); Terrace Hill Soc, Des Moines, IA (THS); Friends of Univ of Iowa Mus, Iowa City, IA (F/IUM); Artist (ART)
GALLERIES: van Straaten Gallery, Chicago, IL; Wenniger Graphics, Boston, MA
MAILING ADDRESS: 5130 Shriver Ave, Des Moines, IA 50312

TITLE	PUBLISHER	PRINTER	DATE	MEDIUM	DIMENSION (PAPER SIZE) IN INCHES	TYPE OF PAPER	EDITION NUMBER	NO. OF COLORS	ORIGINAL OPENING PRICE	CURRENT RETAIL PRICE
SOLD OUT EDITIONS (RARE):										
Stairway with Skeleton	ART	ART	1977	ENG	23 X 20	R/BFK	50	1	100	300
The Supreme Court	ART	ART	1978	I	20 X 23	R/BFK	50	1	100	300
Department of Agriculture	ART	ART	1978	EB	23 X 20	R/BFK	50	1	75	250
Homage to an Unknown Draughtman	ART	ART	1978	DPT/CO	18 X 51	R/BFK	25	1	100	300
Terrace Hill with Bengal Tiger and Raccoons	THS	BS/SRGW	1979	ENG	23 X 20	MAG	100	1	100	250
Terrace Hill with Moose	THS	BS/SRGW	1979	ENG	23 X 20	MAG	100	1	100	250
CURRENT EDITIONS:										
The Governor's Office	ART	ART	1978	ENG	23 X 20	R/BFK	50	1	100	200
50319	ART	ART	1980	ENG	12 X 9	R/BFK	50	1	150	200
Androne, Lecce	ART	ART	1980	ENG	10 X 13	R/BFK	40	1	150	200
Architecture in Apulia, Androne, Lecce, #2	ART	ART	1981	ENG	23 X 20	R/BFK	40	1	175	250
Terrace Hill with Engraving of Sankt Gottard, Mainz	LS	TB	1981	ENG	10 X 13	R/BFK	50	2	100	150
Barn Interior-LHF	ART	ART	1982	ENG	19 X 11	R/BFK	40	1	250	300
Duck Print and Duck Stamp	ART	ART	1983	ENG/HC	18 X 20	MUR	60	1	105	150
Duck Print #2-Mall Landscape	ART	ART	1984	ENG/MEZ	12 X 18	R/BFK	25	1	100	150
Wild Duck Dinner	ART	ART	1984	ENG/MEZ	20 X 27	R/BFK	25	1	125	200
Aida in Des Moines	DMO	ART	1984	ENG/MEZ	20 X 23	R/BFK	125	1	100	150
Five Gothic Churches	ART	ART	1984	ENG	6 X 20	R/BFK	20	1	250	300
Edgehill: After the Fire	ART	ART	1985	ENG	23 X 20	R/BFK	30	1	300	350
House Destroyed by Fire	ART	ART	1985	ENG	23 X 20	R/BFK	30	1	300	350
Fire Damage-Living Room	ART	ART	1986	ENG	23 X 20	R/BFK	30	1	300	350

The retail prices of the 100,000 limited edition prints quoted in this directory are subject to change. Print publishers, artists and galleries were the direct sources for these quotations. Prices in the secondary market listed as "Sold Out Editions (Rare)" indicate that the publisher has a limited supply of that print or that the print is difficult to locate in the galleries.

BETTY WOODMAN

BORN: Norwalk, CT; May 14, 1930
EDUCATION: Alfred Univ, Sch of Am Craftsman, NY, 1948–50
TEACHING: Vis Art, Alfred Univ, New York State Col, Ceramics, 1975; Assoc Prof, Fine Arts, Scripps Col, CA, 1977; Asst Prof, Fine Arts Dept, Univ of Colorado, Boulder, CO, 1976–79, Assoc Prof, 1979 to present
AWARDS: Nat Endowment for the Arts Fel, 1986
RECENT EXHIB: Boulder Center of Visual Arts, CO, 1987; Nat Mus of Mod Art, Seoul, Korea, 1987; Seattle Art Mus, WA, 1987; Denver Art Mus, CO, 1988; Kansas City Contemp Art Center, MO, 1989; Fort Wayne Mus of Art, IN, 1989; Musee des Arts Decoratifs, Paris, France, 1989; Max Protetch Gallery, NY, 1989,90; Douglas Drake Gallery, NY, 1990; Bemis Found/Alternative Worksite, Omaha, NE, 1992

PRINTERS: Judith Solodkin, NY (JS); Solo Press, NY (SP); Bud Shark, Boulder, CO (BS); Shark's, Inc, Boulder, CO (SI)
PUBLISHERS: Solo Press, NY (SP); Shark's, Inc, Boulder, CO (SI); Artist (ART)
GALLERIES: Greenberg Gallery, St Louis, MO; Max Protetch Gallery, New York, NY; Solo Gallery, New York, NY; Anderson O'Brien Gallery, Omaha, NE; Shark's, Inc, Boulder, CO; Quartet Editions, New York, NY
MAILING ADDRESS: c/o Shark's Inc, 2020 9th St, Boulder, CO 80302

Betty Woodman
Kimono Still Life Vase
Courtesy Shark's, Inc

Betty Woodman
Oribe Tray/Classical Pitchers, #10
Courtesy Shark's, Inc

TITLE	PUBLISHER	PRINTER	DATE	MEDIUM	DIMENSION (PAPER SIZE) IN INCHES	TYPE OF PAPER	EDITION NUMBER	NO. OF COLORS	ORIGINAL OPENING PRICE	CURRENT RETAIL PRICE
CURRENT EDITIONS:										
Alberello #1, #6	SI	BS/SI	1988	MON/CO	45 X 30 EA	SUZ	1 EA	Varies	3600 EA	3600 EA
Etruscan Pot in the Window	SI	BS/SI	1988	MON/CO	30 X 22 EA	SUZ	1 EA	Varies	2000 EA	2000 EA
Turkish Delight	SI	BS/SI	1988	MON/CO	45 X 30 EA	SUZ	1 EA	Varies	2000 EA	2000 EA
A Potter's Dream	SI	BS/SI	1988	MON	30 X 45 EA	SUZ	1 EA	Varies	3600 EA	3600 EA
Memory of a Spanish Kitchen	SI	BS/SI	1988	MON	45 X 30 EA	SUZ	1 EA	Varies	3600 EA	3600 EA
Museum Sketches #5–#9	SI	BS/SI	1988	MON	30 X 45 EA	SUZ	1 EA	Varies	2200 EA	2200 EA
Attic Confusion	SI	BS/SI	1988	MON/CO	32 X 48 EA	SUZ	1 EA	Varies	3600 EA	3600 EA
Pals	SI	BS/SI	1988	MON/CO	32 X 48 EA	SUZ	1 EA	Varies	3600 EA	3600 EA
Cool Symmetry	SI	BS/SI	1988	MON/CO	32 X 48 EA	SUZ	1 EA	Varies	3600 EA	3600 EA
Shadow	SI	BS/SI	1988	MON/CO	32 X 48 EA	SUZ	1 EA	Varies	3600 EA	3600 EA
Oribe Tray/Classical Pitchers #1–15	SI	BS/SI	1989	MON/CO	30 X 35 EA	SUZ	1 EA	Varies	3600 EA	3600 EA
Minoan Pitchers/Oribe Tray	SI	BS/SI	1989	LC	30 X 33		16		850	850
Vases & Lattice #2–#8	SI/ART	BS/SI	1989	MON/CO	16 X 48 EA	R/BFK	1 EA	Varies	3600 EA	3600 EA
Vases, Handles & Lattice #1	SI	BS/SI	1989	MON/CO	18 X 16 EA	SUZ	1 EA	Varies	2000 EA	2000 EA
Vases, Handles & Lattice #2	SI	BS/SI	1989	MON/CO	13 X 16 EA	SUZ	1 EA	Varies	2000 EA	2000 EA
On the Way to India	SP	JS/SP	1988	LC	28 X 55	AP	65	7	2800	2800
Porcelain Cups (with Embossing & Gold Leaf) (Set of Four Monotypes)	SP	JS/SP	1989	MON	11 X 15 EA	SUZ	10 EA	Varies	3600 EA	3600 EA
Porcelain Cups (Color Monotypes) (Gold Leaf & Embossing) (Set of 4)	SP	JS/SP	1990	MON/EMB/GL	11 X 15 EA	AP/S	10 EA		3200 SET 800 EA	3200 SET 800 EA
Porcelain Vessels (Gold Leaf & Embossing)	SP	JS/SP	1990	MON/EMB/GL	11 X 30	HMP	30		1800	1800
Pompeian Garden	SI	BS/SI	1992	WC	29 X 35	R/BFK	15	11	1400	1400

ADRIANNE WORTZEL

BORN: Brooklyn, NY; October 7, 1941
EDUCATION: Brooklyn Mus Art Sch, NY, 1957–65; Brooklyn Col, with Ad Reinhardt, Burgoyne Diller & Louise Bourgeois, BA, with Honors, Fine Art, 1963; Hunter Col, NY, with Mark Rothko, MA, 1969
TEACHING: Lectr, Contemp Art, Great Neck Adult Ed Prog, NY, 1970–73; Guest Artist, Printmaking Workshop, NY, 1989
AWARDS: Creative Artists Public Service Grant, New York State Council of the Arts, 1981
RECENT EXHIB: Stamford Mus, CT, 1989
COLLECTIONS: Moderna Museet, Stockholm, Sweden; City of Lund, Sweden
PRINTERS: Marjorie Van Dyck, NY (MVD); Printmaking Workshop, NY (PW)
PUBLISHERS: Artist (ART)
GALLERIES: Bernice Steinbaum Gallery, New York, NY; Andrea Marquit Fine Arts, Boston, MA; Peter Drew Gallery, Boca Raton, FL
MAILING ADDRESS: 19 E 7th St, New York, NY 10003

ADRIANNE WORTZEL CONTINUED

TITLE	PUBLISHER	PRINTER	DATE	MEDIUM	DIMENSION (PAPER SIZE) IN INCHES	TYPE OF PAPER	EDITION NUMBER	NO. OF COLORS	ORIGINAL OPENING PRICE	CURRENT RETAIL PRICE
CURRENT EDITIONS:										
Untitled (Series of 3)	ART	MVD/PW	1989	EC	9 X 12 EA	R/BFK	15 EA		800 EA	900 EA

TROELS WÖRSEL

BORN: Aarhus, Denmark; 1950
COLLECTIONS: Stadtmuseum, Munich, West Germany

PRINTERS: Niels Borch Jensen, Copenhagen, Denmark (NBJ); Jorgen Hansen, Copenhagen, Denmark (JH)
PUBLISHERS: Fred Jahn, Munich, West Germany (FJ); Suzanne Ottensen, Copenhagen, Denmark (SO)

TITLE	PUBLISHER	PRINTER	DATE	MEDIUM	DIMENSION (PAPER SIZE) IN INCHES	TYPE OF PAPER	EDITION NUMBER	NO. OF COLORS	ORIGINAL OPENING PRICE	CURRENT RETAIL PRICE
CURRENT EDITIONS:										
Untitled (Series of 3)	FJ	NBJ	1986	AC	15 X 18 EA	WP	24 EA		250 EA	600 EA
Untitled	SO	JH	1989	SP	79 X 33	AP/W	50		800	1000

ZAO WOU-KI

BORN: Peking, China; 1921
EDUCATION: Nat Sch of Art, Hong Tcheou, China
TEACHING: Nat Sch of Art, Hong Tcheou, China, 1945–8
COLLECTIONS: Cincinnati Art Mus, OH; Tate Gallery, London, England; Victoria and Albert Mus, London, England; Musée Nat d'Art Moderne, Paris, France; Guggenheim Mus, NY; Walker Art Center, Minneapolis, MN; Fogg Art Mus, Harvard Mus, Cambridge, MA, Wadsworth Atheneum, Hartford, CT; Mus of Mod Art, Brazil; Art Inst of Chicago, IL

PRINTERS: J Desjobert, Paris, France (JD); E Desjobert, Paris, France (ED); Atelier Desjobert, Paris, France (AD); Artist (ART); Lacouriere et Frelaunt, Paris, France (L/F); Bellini (Bel); Maeght Editions, Paris, France (ME); American Atelier, NY (AA)
PUBLISHERS: La Guilde International de la Gravure, Paris, France (GdGr); Editeur Klipstein, Paris, France (EdK); L'Oeuvre Gravee, Paris, France (LOG); Galerie de France, Paris, France (GdF); Editeur de Francony, Paris, France (EdFran); Maeght Editions, Paris, France (ME); Circle Fine Art, Chicago, IL (CFA)
GALLERIES: Circle Galleries, San Diego, CA & San Francisco, CA & Scottsdale, AZ & Beverly Hills, CA & Costa Mesa, CA & Sherman Oaks, CA & Palm Beach, FL & Honolulu, HI & New Orleans, LA & Seattle, WA & Northbrook, IL & Pittsburgh, PA & Houston, TX & Soho, NY & Chicago, IL

TITLE	PUBLISHER	PRINTER	DATE	MEDIUM	DIMENSION (PAPER SIZE) IN INCHES	TYPE OF PAPER	EDITION NUMBER	NO. OF COLORS	ORIGINAL OPENING PRICE	CURRENT RETAIL PRICE
SOLD OUT EDITIONS (RARE):										
Landscape with Trees, Small Animals and Woodchopper	ART	ART	1949	LB	10 X 8	WOVE	30			1000
Les Loup	ART	ART	1950	EB	13 X 16	WOVE	50	1	35	800
La Mare aux Canards	ART	ART	1950	EB	13 X 16	WOVE	50	1	35	800
Montagnes et Soleil (R-61)	GdGr	ART	1951	LC	12 X 18	WOVE	200		25	900
Flore et Faune (R-66)	GdGr	ED/JD/AD	1951	EB	12 X 19	WOVE	200	1	35	1800
Les Maisonnettes (R-70)	GdGr	ART	1951	EC	13 X 16	WOVE	65		50	1250
Cathedral	EdK	ED/JD/AD	1953	LC	17 X 23	AP	95		50	1800
La Vielle Ville (R-82)	EdK	ED/JD/AD	1953	LC	20 X 26	AP	95		60	1200
Composition in Blues	EdK	ED/JD/AD	1954	LC	17 X 23	AP	95		75	1800
Nocturne (R-96)	EdK	ED/JD/AD	1954	LC	20 X 26	AP	150		60	1000
Two Trees (R-99)	EdK	ED/JD/AD	1955	LC	20 X 28	AP	95		75	1200
Untitled			1960	EB/A	9 X 12	AP	10		75	1350
Sans Titre (R-129)	LoGr	ED/JD/AD	1960	LC	26 X 20	AP	140		60	600
Composition (R-130)	LoGr	ED/JD/AD	1960	LC	26 X 20	AP	100		75	850
Untitled	LoGr	ED/JD/AD	1960	LC	22 X 14	AP	125		60	600
LX	LoGr	ED/JD/AD	1962	LC		AP	125		75	600
Composition in Browns, Black and White			1963	AC	19 X 17	AP	90	3	100	1800
LXI	LoGr		1963–64	LC		AP	125		75	600
Composition			1967	AC	15 X 21	AP			100	1250
Composition Bleue			1967	LB	12 X 9	AP	1		75	600
Les Compagnons du Jardin (Set of 4)			1967	AC		AP	140 EA		350 SET	3000 SET
Untitled (R-172)	L/F	L/F	1969	AC	11 X 21	R/BFK	99		125	1200
Abstract	CFA	AA	1970	LC	22 X 30	AP	99		200	450
Church in Walled City			1970	LC		AP	95		125	800
Two Figures in Landscape			1970	LC		AP	50	1		1000
Six Boats			1970	LC		AP	90		125	800
San Titre (R-213)	GdF	L/F	1971	EC	23 X 17	R/BFK	99		125	800
Sans Titre (R-215)	GdF	L/F	1971	EB/A	30 X 22	R/BFK	99		125	800
Abstrakie Komposition			1973	LC	24 X 19	AP	120		150	1150
Composition (R-256)	EdFran	Bel	1974	LC	30 X 21	AP	120		150	600
Grande Composition Bleue			1975	LC	35 X 24	AP	95		250	750
Composition			1975	LC	19 X 14	AP	75		200	600
Composition			1975	LC	14 X 10	AP	75		150	500
Composition			1975	LC	35 X 24	AP	95		250	800
Composition			1976	LC	20 X 30	AP	99		200	800
Composition in Blue and Purple			1976	LC		AP	120		200	600
Composition Abstract			1978	LC	21 X 15	AP	60		200	1200

ZAO WOU-KI CONTINUED

TITLE	PUBLISHER	PRINTER	DATE	MEDIUM	DIMENSION (PAPER SIZE) IN INCHES	TYPE OF PAPER	EDITION NUMBER	NO. OF COLORS	ORIGINAL OPENING PRICE	CURRENT RETAIL PRICE
SOLD OUT EDITIONS (RARE):										
Paysage Soleil Rouge			1978	EC	20 X 26	R/BFK			250	800
Sans Titre			1979	LC	15 X 19	AP			200	600
Composition			1981	AC	30 X 23	R/BFK	99		300	800
Beauregard (Text by Philippe Jacottet)	ME	ME	1981	ENG		R/BFK	40		850	15000
CURRENT EDITIONS:										
Composition			1989	LC	26 X 20	AP	75		350	800

DICK WRAY

BORN: Houston, TX; December 5, 1933
EDUCATION: Univ of Houston, TX, Sch of Arch, TX, 1955–58; Kunstakademie, Dusseldorf, Germany, 1958
AWARDS: Purchase Prize, Ford Found, 1962; Purchase Prize, Mus of Fine Arts, Houston, TX, 1963; Nat Endowment for the Arts Fel Grant, 1978
TEACHING: Art in Res, Texas A & M Univ, College Station, TX, 1974; Vis Artist, Southern Methodist Univ, Dallas, TX, 1975; Vis Artist, Anderson Ranch Arts Center, Aspen, CO, Painting, 1983; Instr, Mus of Fine Arts, Sch of Art, Houston, TX, 1968–82
COLLECTIONS: Albright-Knox Art Gallery, Buffalo, NY; Southern Methodist Univ, Dallas, TX; Contemp Arts Mus, Houston, TX; Mus of Fine Arts, Houston, TX; Univ of Oklahoma, Norman, OK; Mus of Mod Art, NY; Witte Mem Mus, San Antonio, TX; Nat Gallery of Art, Wash, DC; San Antonio Mus of Art, TX
PRINTERS: Bud Shark, Boulder, CO (BS); Ron Trujillo, Boulder, CO (RT); Shark's, Inc, Boulder, CO (SI)
PUBLISHERS: Shark's, Inc, Boulder, CO (SI)
GALLERIES: Moody Gallery, Houston, TX; Shark's, Inc, Boulder, CO; Quartet Editions, New York, NY
MAILING ADDRESS: c/o Moody Gallery, 2815 Colquitt, Houston, TX 77098

Dick Wray
92-4
Courtesy Shark's, Inc

TITLE	PUBLISHER	PRINTER	DATE	MEDIUM	DIMENSION (PAPER SIZE) IN INCHES	TYPE OF PAPER	EDITION NUMBER	NO. OF COLORS	ORIGINAL OPENING PRICE	CURRENT RETAIL PRICE
CURRENT EDITIONS:										
100 Ways to Draw a Crow	SI	BS/RT/SI	1985	LC	24 X 30	AC	40		200	250
Untitled, 85–86	SI	BS/RT/SI	1985–86	MON	43 X 30 EA	HMP	1 EA	Varies	800 EA	1200 EA
A Series	SI	BS/RT/SI	1987	MON	45 X 30 EA	HMP	1 EA	Varies	800 EA	1200 EA
B Series	SI	BS/RT/SI	1987	MON	45 X 30 EA	HMP	1 EA	Varies	800 EA	1200 EA
C Series	SI	BS/RT/SI	1987	MON	45 X 30 EA	HMP	1 EA	Varies	800 EA	1200 EA
Untitled, 88	SI	BS/RT/SI	1988	MON	43 X 30 EA	HMP	1 EA	Varies	1000 EA	1200 EA
Untitled, 89	SI	BS/RT/SI	1989	MON	48 X 32 EA	HMP	1 EA	Varies	1200 EA	1400 EA
Untitled, 92	SI	BS/RT/SI	1992	MON	45 X 30 EA	HMP	1 EA	Varies	1400 EA	1400 EA

DAVID ORR WRIGHT

BORN: Orlando, FL; July 20, 1948
EDUCATION: Ringling Sch of Art, Sarasota, FL, 1969–71
PRINTERS: Artist (ART)
PUBLISHERS: Gallery One, Lake Park, FL (GO); Pleiades Press, Bradenton, FL (PL)
GALLERIES: Gallery One, Lake Park, FL; Pleiades Press Gallery, Bradenton, FL
MAILING ADDRESS: 1331 3rd Ave, W, Bradenton, FL 33506

TITLE	PUBLISHER	PRINTER	DATE	MEDIUM	DIMENSION (PAPER SIZE) IN INCHES	TYPE OF PAPER	EDITION NUMBER	NO. OF COLORS	ORIGINAL OPENING PRICE	CURRENT RETAIL PRICE
SOLD OUT EDITIONS (RARE):										
Emaciating Child on Atomic Powered Crucification Crib, State I	GO	ART	1983	EB	14 X 16	IT/E	16	1	150	200
CURRENT EDITIONS:										
Flesh Thief on Atomic Powered Pollution Couch, with Urination	PL	ART	1984	EB/A	16 X 18	GE	25	1	170	200
Rape of the Unborn	PL	ART	1984	EB/A/HC	15 X 19	R/BFK	10	6	225	300
Dichildal (Death)	PL	ART	1984	EB/A/HC	15 X 18	AP	25	2	200	250

DAVID ORR WRIGHT CONTINUED

TITLE	PUBLISHER	PRINTER	DATE	MEDIUM	DIMENSION (PAPER SIZE) IN INCHES	TYPE OF PAPER	EDITION NUMBER	NO. OF COLORS	ORIGINAL OPENING PRICE	CURRENT RETAIL PRICE
CURRENT EDITIONS:										
Dead Child Under Important										
Astronomical Equation	PL	ART	1984	EB	17 X 16	AP	20	1	175	200
Blind Nude	PL	ART	1984	EB/A	15 X 18	MAG/IB	35	1	175	200
All Flesh	PL	ART	1984	EB/A	18 X 15	RP/HW	18	1	160	200
Blind Madonna and Child, #1	PL	ART	1984	EB	15 X 18	MAG/IB	18	1	160	200
Blind Madonna and Child, #2	PL	ART	1984	EB	15 X 19	R/BRK	40	1	200	250
Madonna and Child	PL	ART	1984	EB/A	16 X 18	GE	15	1	200	250
Blind Head Study	PL	ART	1984	EB	18 X 14	AP/B	25	1	200	250
Flesh Thief on Atomic Powered	PL	ART	1984	EB/A/DPT	15 X 18	AC/B	25	1	200	250
Yellow Sylvette, Color Study	GO	ART	1983	LI	15 X 11	AP	18	8	300	350
Flesh Thief on Atomic Powered										
Intellectualization Couch	PL	ART	1983	EB/A	12 X 16	AP	30	1	150	200
Atomic Feeding Enema Couch Study	PL	ART	1983	EB/A/LG	12 X 16	AP	30	1	125	200
Flesh Thief of Atomic Powered										
Luxury Couch with Fallout	PL	ART	1983–84	EB/A	15 X 18	CP	30	1	175	200
Blind Child on Atomic										
Emaciation Crib	PL	ART	1984	EB/A	18 X 15	CP	20	1	175	200
Scientific Drawing of the High										
Speed Crucifixion	PL	ART	1984	EB	15 X 18	R/BFK	35	1	140	200
Rain Eater (Child)	PL	ART	1984	EB	13 X 16	AC/B	20	1	160	200
Emaciating Child on Atomic	PL	ART	1984	EB	16 X 18	GE	25	1	160	200

THEO WUJCIK

BORN: Detroit, MI; January 29, 1936
EDUCATION: Center for Creative Studies, Detroit, MI, 1958–62; Creative Graphic Workshop, NY, 1959; Univ of New Mexico, Albuquerque, NM, 1967; Tamarind Workshop, Los Angeles, CA, 1967–68
TEACHING: Instr, Graphics, Center for Creative Studies, Detroit, MI, 1965–70; Univ of South Florida, Tampa, FL, 1970–71; Assoc Prof, Printmaking & Drawing, Univ of South Florida, Tampa, FL, 1971 to present
AWARDS: Louis Comfort Tiffany Found Award, 1964; Ford Found Grant, Tamarind Lithography Workshop, 1967,68; Research Grant, Graphics, Univ of South Florida, FL, 1974; Nat Endowment for the Arts Fel, Drawing, 1977–78
COLLECTIONS: Brooklyn Mus, NY; Art Inst of Chicago, IL; Detroit Inst of Arts, MI; Mus of Mod Art, NY; Mus of Fine Arts, Boston, MA; Whitney Mus of Am Art, NY; Yale Univ of Art, New Haven, CT; Pennsylvania Acad of Fine Art, Phila, PA; Walker Art Gallery, Liverpool, England; Pasadena Art Mus, CA; San Francisco Mus of Mod Art, CA; Library of Congress, Wash, DC; Los Angeles County Mus, Los Angeles, CA; Carnegie Inst, Pittsburgh, PA
PUBLISHERS: Brooke Alexander Editions, NY (BAI)
GALLERIES: Brooke Alexander, Inc, New York, NY
MAILING ADDRESS: c/o College of Fine Arts, Fah 229, Tampa, FL 33620–7350

TITLE	PUBLISHER	PRINTER	DATE	MEDIUM	DIMENSION (PAPER SIZE) IN INCHES	TYPE OF PAPER	EDITION NUMBER	NO. OF COLORS	ORIGINAL OPENING PRICE	CURRENT RETAIL PRICE
SOLD OUT EDITIONS (RARE):										
New Portraits (Set of 7):										
Bell	BAI	ART	1972	LB	9 X 10	AP	20	1	200	500
Bengston	BAI	ART	1972	LB	9 X 10	AP	20	1	200	500
Irwin	BAI	ART	1972	LB	9 X 10	AP	20	1	200	500
Kauffman	BAI	ART	1972	LB	9 X 10	AP	20	1	200	500
Moses	BAI	ART	1972	LB	9 X 10	AP	20	1	200	500
Price	BAI	ART	1972	LB	9 X 10	AP	20	1	200	500
Ruscha	BAI	ART	1972	LB	9 X 10	AP	20	1	200	500
Portrait of June Wayne	BAI	ART	1973	HC/LC	22 X 21	AP	25		175	600
Robert Rauschenberg	BAI	ART	1977	EB/STIP	31 X 42	AP	42		375	600
Alex Katz	BAI	ART	1978	EB/STIP	31 X 42	AP	42		375	600
Tatyana Grosman	BAI	ART	1979	ENG	23 X 31	AP	30		300	650
Self-Portrait	BAI	ART	1979	EB/ENG/STIP	22 X 31	AP	20		300	600

PAUL WUNDERLICH

PRINTERS: (MAG); American Atelier, NY (AA); Hanke, Switzerland (Ha)
PUBLISHERS: Kennedy Galleries, NY (KG); (VH); Castelli Graphics Ltd, NY (CGL); Associated American Artists, NY (AAA); Artist (ART)
GALLERIES: John Szoke Graphics, New York, NY; Ianuzzi Gallery, Phoenix, AZ; Staempfli Gallery, New York, NY; Worthington Gallery, Chicago, IL; Red Fern Gallery, London, England; Kass/Meridian Gallery, Chicago, IL; Triangle Gallery, Lexington, KY; Brenda Kroos Gallery, Columbus, OH; Heike Pickett Gallery, Lexington, KY

TITLE	PUBLISHER	PRINTER	DATE	MEDIUM	DIMENSION (PAPER SIZE) IN INCHES	TYPE OF PAPER	EDITION NUMBER	NO. OF COLORS	ORIGINAL OPENING PRICE	CURRENT RETAIL PRICE
SOLD OUT EDITIONS (RARE):										
Elle Attend Fernand	KG		1971	LC	29 X 22	AP	75	7	300	2500
Twilight Portfolio (Set of 12):										2500 SET	15000 SET
Photo Lithos (4)	AAA	AA	1973	LC/PH	23 X 30 EA	AP	125 EA		100 EA	800 EA
Color Lithos (8)	AAA	AA	1973	LC	23 X 30 EA	AP	125 EA		300 EA	1500 EA
Aida (Metropolitan Opera I)	CGL	MAG	1976	LC	30 X 22	R/BFK	250		600	2400
Sphinx mit Pyramide	VH		1978	LC	33 X 25	R/BFK	50		500	3500

PAUL WUNDERLICH CONTINUED

TITLE	PUBLISHER	PRINTER	DATE	MEDIUM	DIMENSION (PAPER SIZE) IN INCHES	TYPE OF PAPER	EDITION NUMBER	NO. OF COLORS	ORIGINAL OPENING PRICE	CURRENT RETAIL PRICE
SOLD OUT EDITIONS (RARE):										
Bacchus und Adriadne	VH		1978	LC	33 X 25	R/BFK	200		750	3500
Campagna bei Rom	VH		1978	LC	33 X 25	R/BFK	200		750	3500
Ein Kleid	VH		1978	LC	33 X 25	R/BFK	100		650	3000
Begegnung	VH		1979	LC	33 X 25	R/BFK	110		750	3000
Selbst mit Maske, Anton und Maus	VH		1979	LC	33 X 25	R/BFK	100		550	3000
Sphinx vor Landschaft	VH		1979	LC	33 X 25	R/BFK	100		650	3000
Skizzenblatt mit Roten Kopf	VH		1979	LC	33 X 25	R/BFK	100		750	3500
Epitaph auf den Hund Anton	VH		1979	LC	33 X 25	R/BFK	90		750	4000
Kleiner Kopf mit Mutz	VH		1979	LC	15 X 12	R/BFK	35		350	4000
Familienbild	VH		1980	LC	33 X 25	R/BFK	100		750	3500
Dame mit Hut und Hund bei Tisch	VH		1980	LC	33 X 25	R/BFK	100		850	3000
Familie W bei Tisch	VH		1980	LC	33 X 25	R/BFK	90		750	4000
Karin im Schneckenkleid	VH		1980	LC	33 X 25	R/BFK	125		750	3000
Schone Photographin	VH		1980	LC	33 X 25	R/BFK	100		750	3000
Amaryllis	VH		1980	LC	33 X 25	R/BFK	100		650	3000
CURRENT EDITIONS:										
Still Life with Melon	ART	Ha	1988	LC	26 X 38	ZER	30	6	3200	3500

HENRIETTE WYETH

BORN: Wilmington, DE; October 22, 1907
EDUCATION: Pennsylvania Acad of Fine Arts, Phila, PA
AWARDS: Governor's Awards, Santa Fe, NM, 1981
RECENT EXHIB: Albuquerque Mus of Art, NM, 1988,92; Roswell Mus, NM, 1988,92; Charles B Goddard, Center for Visual & Performing Arts, Ardmore, OK, 1988,92

COLLECTIONS: New Britain Art Mus, CT; Lubbock Art Mus, TX; Roswell Mus, NM
PRINTERS: Rowland Workshop, Park Ridge, IL (RW); Frank Rowland, Park Ridge, IL (FR)
PUBLISHERS: Circle Gallery, Ltd, Chicago, IL (CGL)
GALLERIES: Fenn Galleries, Santa Fe, NM
MAILING ADDRESS: Sentinel Ranch, San Patricio, NM 88348

TITLE	PUBLISHER	PRINTER	DATE	MEDIUM	DIMENSION (PAPER SIZE) IN INCHES	TYPE OF PAPER	EDITION NUMBER	NO. OF COLORS	ORIGINAL OPENING PRICE	CURRENT RETAIL PRICE
SOLD OUT EDITIONS (RARE):										
Green Apple, Purple Shell	CGL	FR/RW	1973	SP	15 X 14	VV	300	3	250	1700

JAMIE WYETH

BORN: Wilmington, DE; July 6, 1946
RECENT EXHIB: Brandywine River Mus, Chadds Ford, PA, 1987; Parkersburg Art Center, Parkersburg, WVA, 1987; Coe Kerr Gallery, NY, 1990; William A Farnsworth Art Mus, Rockland, ME, 1992; Brandywine River Mus, Chadds Ford, PA, 1988,92
COLLECTIONS: Mus of Mod Art, NY; Nat Gallery of Art, Washington, DC; Joslyn Art Mus, Omaha, NE; Delaware Art Mus, Wilmington, DE; Brandywine River Mus, Chadds Ford, PA; Nat Portrait Gallery, Smithsonian Inst, Wash, DC

PRINTERS: American Atelier, NY (AA)
PUBLISHERS: Circle Fine Arts, Chicago, IL (CFA); Adelson Graphics, NY (AG); Werner Graphics, NY (WG)
GALLERIES: Coe Kerr Gallery, New York, NY; Gallery at Greenville, DE; Fernette's Gallery of Art, Des Moines, IA; Charles Barry International, Bethesda, MD; Foster Harmon Galleries of American Art, Sarasota, FL; Ron Hall Galleries, Dallas, TX; Somerville Manning Gallery, Greenville, DE
MAILING ADDRESS: c/o Sarah E Mleczko, 211 E 73rd St, #4-G, New York, NY 10021

TITLE	PUBLISHER	PRINTER	DATE	MEDIUM	DIMENSION (PAPER SIZE) IN INCHES	TYPE OF PAPER	EDITION NUMBER	NO. OF COLORS	ORIGINAL OPENING PRICE	CURRENT RETAIL PRICE
SOLD OUT EDITIONS (RARE):										
La Boheme (Metropolitan Opera I)	CFA	AA	1978	LC	30 X 22	AP/W	250	16	700	3500
Nureyev	CFA	AA	1978	LC	34 X 24	AP/W	300	6	1000	5000
Nureyev (State II)	CFA	AA	1978	LC	34 X 24	AP/BL	300	3	1000	3500
Moon and the Horse	CFA	AA	1978	LC	24 X 33	SOM	300	3	900	3500
CURRENT EDITIONS:										
Herring Gulls	CFA	AA	1978	LC	25 X 28	SOM	300	3	950	5750
The Wicker Chair	CFA	AA	1979	LC	21 X 28	AP	300	5	975	4750
A Sea Pumpkin	CFA	AA	1980	LC	26 X 29	SOM	300	3	850	5750
Weathervane	CFA	AA	1980	LC	34 X 24	SOM	300	3	850	5750
The Farm (Set of 4)	AG	WG	1980	EB/DPT	25 X 20 EA	GE	150 EA	2 EA	3000 SET	7000 SET
SOS	AG	WG	1981	EC	27 X 30	R/BFK	150	4	2250	3200
White Leghorns	AG	WG	1981	EC	27 X 30	R/BFK/W	150	3	2250	3200
Atlantic City Rolling Chair	AG	WG	1983	EC	22 X 30	SOM/W	150	5	950	1450

HIRO YAMAGATA

BORN: Maibara, Japan; 1948
EDUCATION: Ecole de Beaux Arts, Paris, France

COLLECTIONS: Dietz Mus, Wassenberg, West Germany
PRINTERS: Accent Design, NY (AD); Accent Studio, Canoga Park, CA (AS); Alexander Heinrici, NY (AH); Studio Heinrici, NY (SH); Aurora Serigraphics (ASer)
PUBLISHERS: Martin Lawrence Limited Editions, Van Nuys, CA (MLLE)

HIRO YAMAGATA CONTINUED

GALLERIES: Martin Lawrence Galleries, Sherman Oaks, CA & Los Angeles, CA & Newport Beach, CA & Short Hills, NJ & Phila, PA & Palm Springs, CA & Redondo Beach, CA & Escondido, CA & Thousand Oaks, CA & West Los Angeles, CA & Santa Clara, CA; Swahn Fine Arts, San Diego, CA; Petrini Art Gallery, Rocky Hill, CT; Art Brokerage, Ketchum, ID; Allyson Louis Gallery, Bethesda, MD; Artists Showcase International, Hartsdale, NY; Emporium, Inc, Dallas, TX

TITLE	PUBLISHER	PRINTER	DATE	MEDIUM	DIMENSION (PAPER SIZE) IN INCHES	TYPE OF PAPER	EDITION NUMBER	NO. OF COLORS	ORIGINAL OPENING PRICE	CURRENT RETAIL PRICE
SOLD OUT EDITIONS (RARE):										
Perrier Tour de Paris	MLLE	AD	1982	SP	30 X 44	STP	430	136	600	15000
Concert in the Park	MLLE	AD	1982	SP	30 X 44	STP	445	121	600	15000
Sky Cycles	MLLE	AD	1982	SP	30 X 37	STP	485	132	600	9500
Air Show	MLLE	AD	1982	SP	36 X 30	STP	445	114	600	10000
Sunday Sundae	MLLE	AD	1982	SP	36 X 30	STP	445	112	600	10000
Robbers	MLLE	AD	1982	SP	31 X 30	STP	460	96	600	15000
Aquarium	MLLE	AD	1982	SP	30 X 36	STP	445	110	600	0000
Fallen Leaves	MLLE	AS	1983	SP	28 X 29	AP	465	98	600	12500
Tour de France	MLLE	AS	1983	SP	30 X 37	AP	470	86	750	8500
Celebration	MLLE	AS	1983	SP	35 X 30	AP	470	94	900	10000
Rainbow	MLLE	AS	1984	SP	37 X 30	SE	470	95	900	10000
Snow Caastle	MLLE	AS	1984	SP	40 X 29	SP	425	103	900	15000
Dolphins	MLLE	AS	1984	SP	31 X 30	AP	490	120	1050	8500
Museum	MLLE	AS	1984	SP	30 X 36	AP	480	75	1050	10000
Bubbles	MLLE	AS	1984	SP	23 X 42	AP	490	90	1050	9500
The Impressionists	MLLE	AH/SH	1984	SP	28 X 37	AP	480		1050	10000
Robbers II	MLLE	AH/SH	1984	SP	31 X 31	AP	480		1050	9500
The Poet	MLLE	AH/SH	1984	SP	31 X 31	AP	490		1050	9500
Stained Glass Studio	MLLE	AH/SH	1985	SP	31 X 31	AP	480		1050	8000
Picnic	MLLE	AS	1985	SP	32 X 30	AP	480	168	1050	8500
Chateau Rouge	MLLE	AS	1985	SP	30 X 37	AP	505		1050	7500
Concert in the City	MLLE	ASer	1985	SP	29 X 32	AP	505		1250	9500
Marriage	MLLE	AH/SH	1985	SP	30 X 34	AP	505		1450	12000
Toys	MLLE	AH/SH	1985	SP	32 X 31	AP	505		1450	8500
Polo	MLLE	AH/SH	1985	SP	28 X 40	AP	505		1450	9500
Once Upon a Time	MLLE	AH/SH	1986	SP	35 X 28	AP	505		1450	8000
Four Cities Suite (Set of 4):									3000 SET	11500 SET
Los Angeles	MLLE	AH/SH	1986	SP	15 X 17	AP	1255		800	3000
Tokyo	MLLE	AH/SH	1986	SP	15 X 17	AP	1255		800	3000
New York	MLLE	AH/SH	1986	SP	17 X 15	AP	1255		800	3000
Paris	MLLE	AH/SH	1986	SP	17 X 15	AP	1255		800	3000
American in Paris	MLLE	AH/SH	1986	SP	35 X 28	AP	507		1250	8500
Carousel	MLLE	AH/SH	1986	SP	35 X 28	AP	505		1650	8000
Parade of Angels	MLLE	AS	1986	SP	36 X 30	AP	505		1650	8500
Gare St Lazare	MLLE	AH/SH	1986	SP	37 X 36	AP	505		1800	7000
Snowline	MLLE	AH/SH	1986	SP	30 X 38	AP	505		1650	12000
Finish Line	MLLE	AH/SH	1986	SP	28 X 32	AP	505		1800	7500
Rainy Day	MLLE	AH/SH	1986	SP	30 X 40	AP	505		1800	15000
Neon	MLLE	AH/SH	1986	SP	35 X 28	AP	505		1850	7500
Raindrops	MLLE	AH/SH	1987	SP	37 X 29	AP	505		1850	9500
Telephone	MLLE	AH/SH	1987	SP	24 X 48	AP	505		2000	9000
Country Club	MLLE	AH/SH	1987	SP	40 X 27	AP	505		2000	7500
Park Monceau	MLLE	AH/SH	1987	SP	42 X 30	AP	506		2000	8500
Fathers & Son	MLLE	AH/SH	1987	SP	23 X 42	AP	505		2000	9500
The Hill	MLLE	AH/SH	1987	SP	23 X 26	AP	505		1800	7000
Starlight Express	MLLE	AH/SH	1987	SP	33 X 34	AP	505		2000	9500
Four Seasons Suite (Set of 4):										11500 SET
Winter	MLLE	AH/SH	1987	SP	20 X 17	AP	530		1500	3000
Spring	MLLE	AH/SH	1987	SP	20 X 17	AP	530		1500	3000
Summer	MLLE	AH/SH	1987	SP	20 X 17	AP	530		1500	3000
Fall	MLLE	AH/SH	1987	SP	20 X 17	AP	530		1500	3000
City Lights	MLLE	AH/SH	1987	SP	35 X 28	AP	505		2000	8000
Circus in the Square	MLLE	AH/SH	1987	SP	30 X 35	AP	505		2000	7500
Balloon Wedding	MLLE	AH/SH	1988	SP	41 X 33	AP	565		2250	7500
Express	MLLE	AH/SH	1988	SP	25 X 38	AP	505		2000	7000
La Louvre	MLLE	AH/SH	1988	SP	32 X 38	AP	565		2250	7500
A View from the Top	MLLE	AH/SH	1988	SP	30 X 42	AP	565		2250	7500
1988 Winter Olympic Games	MLLE	AH/SH	1988	SP	45 X 33	AP	580		2250	7000
US Constitution (with Book)	MLLE	AH/SH	1988	SP	23 X 16	AP	830		1800	3500
Accordion Player	MLLE	AH/SH	1988	SP	32 X 38	AP	565		2250	6500
Metro	MLLE	AH/SH	1988	SP	23 X 26	AP	505		2000	7000
Happy Birthday Liberty 1886–1986	MLLE	AH/SH	1988	SP	36 X 46	AP	555		2500	15000
Summer Olympics Suite (Set of 2):									3500 SET	10000 SET
Summer Olympics	MLLE	AH/SH	1988	SP	27 X 37	AP	580		1850	4500
Summer Olympics Museum	MLLE	AH/SH	1988	SP	27 X 37	AP	580		1850	7500
Autumn Afternoon	MLLE	AH/SH	1988	SP	34 X 42	AP	566		2250	6500
Snowy Night	MLLE	AH/SH	1988	SP	28 X 44	AP	567		2250	6000
Full Moon	MLLE	AH/SH	1989	SP	35 X 41	AP	505		2500	8500
Club Bahama (with Catalog)	MLLE	AH/SH	1989	SP	21 X 25	AP	1212		1800	3800
Milky Way	MLLE	AH/SH	1989	SP	21 X 32	AP	680		2250	5000

HIRO YAMAGATA CONTINUED

TITLE	PUBLISHER	PRINTER	DATE	MEDIUM	DIMENSION (PAPER SIZE) IN INCHES	TYPE OF PAPER	EDITION NUMBER	NO. OF COLORS	ORIGINAL OPENING PRICE	CURRENT RETAIL PRICE
SOLD OUT EDITIONS (RARE):										
July 14th	MLLE	AH/SH	1989	SP	29 X 34	AP	680		2250	5000
Castle Festival	MLLE	AH/SH	1989	SP	42 X 33	AP	557		2500	5000
Very Special Celebration	MLLE	AH/SH	1989	SP	39 X 48	AP	557		2500	6000
Galerie Suite (Set of 3):									4500 SET	9500 SET
Galerie Van Gogh	MLLE	AH/SH	1989	SP	16 X 21	AP	557		1200	2150
Galerie Moderne	MLLE	AH/SH	1989	SP	16 X 21	AP	557		1200	2500
La Galerie	MLLE	AH/SH	1989	SP	21 X 16	AP	557		1200	2500
Joan of Arc	MLLE	AH/SH	1989	SP	21 X 32	AP	557		1200	6000
Last Day of Summer	MLLE	AH/SH	1990	SP	36 X 27	AP	557		2000	6000
First Day of Fall	MLLE	AH/SH	1990	SP	33 X 38	AP	557		2000	6000
Museum Suite (Set of 3):									4000 SET	6250 SET
Monsieur Seurat	MLLE	AH/SH	1990	SP	16 X 21	AP	557		1500	2450
Exhibition	MLLE	AH/SH	1990	SP	21 X 16	AP	557		1500	2450
Rembrandt	MLLE	AH/SH	1990	SP	21 X 16	AP	557		1500	2450
Stargazer	MLLE	AH/SH	1990	SP	60 X 31	AP	557		2400	7500
Winter Day	MLLE	AH/SH	1990	SP	26 X 42	AP	557		2000	7000
Riviera	MLLE	AH/SH	1990	SP	38 X 26	AP	557		2000	6000
King Kong	MLLE	AH/SH	1990	SP	38 X 30	AP	557		2000	6000
Van Gogh Collector	MLLE	AH/SH	1990	SP	37 X 36	AP	565		2000	6500
Balloon Race	MLLE	AH/SH	1990	SP	34 X 33	AP	555		2000	6000
Two Graphic Release:									3500 SET	11000 SET
Foggy Day	MLLE	AH/SH	1990	SP	34 X 31	AP	567		2000	6000
Courtyard Fountain	MLLE	AH/SH	1990	SP	33 X 40	AP	555		2000	5500
CURRENT EDITIONS:										
Banner Day	MLLE	AH/SH	1990	SP	29 X 40	AP	555		2000	6500
Pool Party	MLLE	AH/SH	1991	SP	35 X 35	AP	555		2250	5500
Snowy Night Swing	MLLE	AH/SH	1991	SP	26 X 46	AP	557		2500	5500
Northwind	MLLE	AH/SH	1991	SP	44 X 32	AP	555		2500	4500
Sculpture Garden	MLLE	AH/SH	1991	SP	33 X 30	AP	555		2250	4500

C J YAO

BORN: Taiwan, China; September 16, 1941
EDUCATION: Nat Taiwan Normal Univ, Fine Arts Dept, Taiwan, China, 1965
TEACHING: Honorary Prof, Central Inst of Fine Arts & Crafts, Beijing, China
COLLECTIONS: China Nat Mus of History, Taipei, Taiwan; J B Speed Art Mus, Louisville, KY; Huntsville Mus of Art, AL; Hong Kong Mus of Art; Antonio Mus, TX; Mus of Art, Costa Rica

PRINTERS: Alexander Heinrici, NY (AH); Studio Heinrici, NY (SH); Styria Studio, NY (SS); Norman Lassiter, NY (NL); Editions Lassiter-Meisel, NY (ELM)
PUBLISHERS: London Arts Inc, Detroit, MI (LAI); Christie's Art Inc, NY (C); Styria Studio, NY (SS); Barry Ross (BR); Allen Kline Investments (AKI); Pollock Publishing Company (PPC)
GALLERIES: Louis K Meisel Gallery, New York, NY; Styria Studio, New York, NY
MAILING ADDRESS: 393 West Broadway, 4th Floor, New York, NY 10012

TITLE	PUBLISHER	PRINTER	DATE	MEDIUM	DIMENSION (PAPER SIZE) IN INCHES	TYPE OF PAPER	EDITION NUMBER	NO. OF COLORS	ORIGINAL OPENING PRICE	CURRENT RETAIL PRICE
SOLD OUT EDITIONS (RARE):										
Bus	SS	SS	1978	LC/CO	30 X 42	AP88	95	5	500	1000
Times Square Window #2	PPC	SS	1979	SP	22 X 30	SOM	250	17	500	750
Coca Cola #3	LAI	NL/ELM	1981	SP	23 X 22	SOM	250	17	500	750
Coca Cola #4	LAI	NL/ELM	1981	SP	22 X 30	SOM	250	17	500	750
Entex Building	BR	AH/SH	1982	SP	22 X 30	SOM	250	80	400	750
Downtown Houston, Milam at Polk	AKI	AH/SH	1982	SP	22 X 30	SOM	250	82	400	750
Untitled	SS	SS	1982	LC	19 X 22	JBG	60	1	250	600

ROBERT YARBER

BORN: Dallas, TX; 1948
EDUCATION: Cooper Union Col, NY, BFA, 1967–70; Louisiana State Univ, Baton Rouge, LA, MFA, 1971
TEACHING: Vis Lectr, Univ California, Berkeley, CA, 1982,83; Vis Instr, Univ of Texas, Austin, TX, 1982,84
AWARDS: Nat Endowment for the Arts Fel Grant, 1983
RECENT EXHIB: Asher Faure Gallery, Los Angeles, CA, 1987; Greene Gallery, Coconut Grove, FL, 1987; Thomas Cohn Arte Contemporanea, Rio de Janiero, Brazil, 1987; Pennsylvania State Univ, Palmer Mus of Art, University Park, PA, 1989; Gallery Paule Anglim, San Francisco, CA, 1989; Muhlenberg Col, Frank Martin Art Gallery, Allentown, PA, 1992
COLLECTIONS: Pennsylvania State Univ, University Park, PA
PRINTERS: Jack Lemon, Chicago, IL (JL); Landfall Press, Chicago, IL (LPI)
PUBLISHERS: Landfall Press, Inc, Chicago, IL (LPI)
GALLERIES: Landfall Press, Inc, Chicago, IL; Asher/Faure Gallery, Los Angeles, CA; Greene Gallery, Miami, FL; Gallery Paule Anglim, San Francisco, CA; Thomas Cohn Arte Contemporanea, Rio de Janiero, Brazil; Dorsky Gallery, New York, NY; Lieberman & Saul Gallery, New York, NY; Quartet Editions, New York, NY

TITLE	PUBLISHER	PRINTER	DATE	MEDIUM	DIMENSION (PAPER SIZE) IN INCHES	TYPE OF PAPER	EDITION NUMBER	NO. OF COLORS	ORIGINAL OPENING PRICE	CURRENT RETAIL PRICE
CURRENT EDITIONS:										
The Corruption of Ecstasy	LPI	JL/LPI	1989	LC	30 X 44	AP/BL	25	7	1200	1200

LEILA KEPERT YARBROUGH

BORN: Katoomba, NSW, Australia; March 23, 1932; US Citizen
EDUCATION: Univ of Florida, Gainesville, FL, 1950–51,1952; Atlanta Sch of Art, GA, 1963–71
AWARDS: Purchase Awards, Georgia Commission of Visual Art Project, 1967,71; Purchase Award, Norfolk Mus of Arts & Sciences, VA, 1971; First Prize, Nat Monoprint Comp, Oglethorpe Univ, Atlanta, GA, 1973; Purchase Prize, Great Smoky Mountains Nat Park, Gatlinburg, TN, 1974
RECENT EXHIB: Miriam Perlman Gallery, Chicago, IL, 1990,91
COLLECTIONS: Chrysler Mus, Norfolk, VA; Augusta Mus of Art, GA; Piedmont Col, Demorest, GA; Dekalb Col, Clarkston, GA; Loch Haven Art Center, Orlando, FL; Agnes Scott Col, Decatur, GA; Great Smoky Mountains Nat Park, Gatlinburg, TN

PRINTERS: Phil Elie, Atlanta, GA (PE); Suzanne Garsten, Atlanta, GA (SG); Yarbrough Graphics, Atlanta, GA (YG); Kathy Caraccio, NY (KC); Carol Heffer, NY (CH); Artist (ART); Michael Crouse (MC); Impressions Workshop (IW)
PUBLISHERS: Ronbie Editions, Yardley, PA (RE); Artist (ART); Atlantic Arts, Annapolis, MD (AA)
GALLERIES: Artist's Associates, Gallery, Atlanta, GA; Miriam Perlman Gallery, Chicago, IL; Monty Stabler Gallery, Birmingham, AL; State of the Art, Marietta, GA; Global Arts, Atlanta, GA; Windsor's Gallery, Dania, FL; Winn/Regency Gallery, Decatur, GA; Contempo Arts, Ltd, Clemons, NC; Pinkerton House Portfolio, Louisville, KY; Bell-Ross Gallery, Memphis, TN
MAILING ADDRESS: 4061 Arden Way, NE, Atlanta, GA 30342

TITLE	PUBLISHER	PRINTER	DATE	MEDIUM	DIMENSION (PAPER SIZE) IN INCHES	TYPE OF PAPER	EDITION NUMBER	NO. OF COLORS	ORIGINAL OPENING PRICE	CURRENT RETAIL PRICE
SOLD OUT EDITIONS: (RARE)										
Early Morning I-VI	ART	ART	1972	EC	24 X 37	AC	5 EA	2 EA	250 EA	500 EA
Tree Trunk with Vines	ART	ART	1972	EC	32 X 44	AC	10	6	300	700
Beech Tree	RE	ART	1973	EB/I	29 X 36	AC	50	3	200	500
Ice Storm	ART	SG	1973	I	28 X 33	R/BFK	50	1	100	350
Invitation	ART	ART	1975	EC	33 X 28	AC	50	2	175	450
Tree Lover	ART	ART	1976	EB/I	16 X 22	R/BFK	85	3	100	150
The Lake & the Tree	ART/RE	ART	1976	EC/A/OB	30 X 22	AC	50	5	150	300
A Wide Place in the River	ART/RE	IW/ART	1976	EC	28 X 40	R/BFK	60	6	200	500
Guardian of the Lake	ART/RE	ART	1977	EC	30 X 22	AC	75	5	180	300
Sentry	ART/RE	IW/ART	1977	EC	30 X 22	AC	85	3	150	300
Royal Invitation	ART/RE	PE	1977	VE	28 X 33	AC	100	Multi	200	400
Lake Sentinels	ART	ART/SG	1978	I	28 X 33	AC	85	1	250	350
Autumn Breezes	ART	SG	1978	VE	27 X 34	AC	100	Multi	225	400
Banks of the River	RE	MC	1978	EC	18 X 24	R/BFK	100	4	130	130
Chattahoochee	ART	ART	1978	EC	18 X 30	R/BFK	74	4	115	250
Family of Five	ART/RE	MC/ART	1978	EC	29 X 40	R/BFK	80	5	200	400
View from the Terrace	ART/RE	SG/ART	1979	EC	26 X 35	R/BFK	100	4	180	400
View of the River	ART/RE	ART	1979	EC	38 X 48	AC	100	4	400	700
Far Side of the River	ART/RE	KC/PE/ART	1981	VE	35 X 28	R/BFK	150	Multi	275	500
Early Morning by the River	ART/RE	KC/PE/ART	1981	VE	28 X 35	R/BFK	150	Multi	275	500
Song of the Trees	ART/RE	PE/ART	1982	EC	36 X 46	R/BFK	150	6	400	900
Distant Hills	RE	PE/KC	1982	VE	28 X 34	AC	150	Multi	300	400
River Grasses	RE	CH	1982	VE	36 X 46	AC	100	Multi	500	600
Spring Medley	RE	KC	1983	VE	28 X 35	AC	150	Multi	300	400
Prelude to Fall	RE	PE	1984	VE	28 X 35	R/BFK	200	Multi	300	400
Suite of Two:									500 SET	POR
Southern Mist	ART/RE	PE/ART	1984	EC	29 X 29	R/BFK	150	4	275	POR
Mountain Moods	ART/RE	PE/ART	1984	EC	29 X 29	R/BFK	150	4	275	POR
Spring Medley, Version Two	RE	SG	1985	VE	28 X 35	R/BFK	50	Multi	350	450
Autumn Serenade	RE	PE	1985	VE	28 X 35	R/BFK	200	Multi	350	450
Evensong	ART/AA	SG/ART	1988	VE	30 X 38	R/BFK	200	Multi	400	500
Eventide	ART/AA	SG/ART	1988	VE	30 X 38	R/BFK	200	Multi	400	500
CURRENT EDITIONS:										
Dunes	ART	ART	1973	EB/I	8 X 20	AC	50	1	40	125
Wild River	ART	ART	1973	EB/I	22 X 28	AC	20	1	150	300
Tree Forms I,II	ART	ART	1973	EB/EMB/I/REL	22 X 28	R/BFK	50	5	300	400
October Leaves	ART	ART	1975	EC/I/REL	26 X 32	AC	50	5	225	400
Sacrosanct	ART	ART	1975	EC/I/REL		AC	50	5	225	400
The Wood Between the Worlds	ART	SG/PE	1977	I/REL	36 X 46	AC	100	2	300	500
Winter Beech	ART	SG	1977	I	24 X 30	R/BFK	50	1	130	300
Winter Woods I, II	ART	SG/PE	1978	I/REL	24 X 30 EA	AC	100 EA	3 EA	150 EA	250 EA
Autumn Tapestry	ART	SG/PE	1979	VE	27 X 34	R/BFK	100	Multi	150	250
The Hedgerow	ART	SG/PE	1979	VE	27 X 34	R/BFK	100	Multi	150	250
Poplars Across the Way	ART/RE	SG/KC	1980	VE	36 X 46	AC	125	Multi	300	550
Water's Edge	ART	ART/PE	1980	VE	26 X 36	R/BFK	150	Multi	275	400
Colleagues of the River	ART/RE	PE	1981	VE	28 X 35	R/BFK	125	Multi	275	400
Cattails	ART	SG/PE	1982	VE	14 X 28	AC	150	Multi	150	200
Beech Tree in the Snow	ART	PE	1983	VE	28 X 34	AC/R-BFK	150	3	300	350
Still Waters	RE	CH	1983	VE	36 X 46	AC	100	Multi	500	600
The River	RE	PE	1983	VE	28 X 35	R/BFK	150	4	300	350
A Secret Place	ART	SG/PE	1985	VE	28 X 35	R/BFK	150	Multi	300	350
River Breezes	RE	SG	1985	VE	28 X 35	R/BFK	200	Multi	350	400
A Place by the River I, II	RE	SG/PE	1985	VE	29 X 43 EA	R/BFK	200 EA	Multi	450 EA	500 EA
Late Day by the River	RE	SG/PE	1986	VE	28 X 35	R/BFK	200	Multi	400	450
River Shallows	RE	SG	1986	VE	28 X 35	R/BFK	200	Multi	400	450
Big Creek	RE	PE	1986	VE	28 X 35	R/BFK	200	Multi	400	450
Bend in the River	RE	SG	1987	VE	28 X 36	R/BFK	200	Multi	400	450
River Suite (Set of 2):									950 SET	1000 SET
River to the Sea I,II	ART/AA	SG/ART	1987	VE	43 X 31 EA	R/BFK	200 EA	Multi	475 EA	500 EA
Woodland Mosaic	ART	SG/ART	1988	VE	30 X 38	R/BFK	225	Multi	400	400

LEILA KEPERT YARBROUGH CONTINUED

TITLE	PUBLISHER	PRINTER	DATE	MEDIUM	DIMENSION (PAPER SIZE) IN INCHES	TYPE OF PAPER	EDITION NUMBER	NO. OF COLORS	ORIGINAL OPENING PRICE	CURRENT RETAIL PRICE
CURRENT EDITIONS:										
Lake Country	ART	ART	1988	VE	12 X 18	R/BFK	200	Multi	110	125
Lake's Edge	ART	ART	1988	VE	12 X 18	R/BFK	200	Multi	110	125
Twilight	ART	ART	1988	EC	18 X 12	R/BFK	200	5	110	125
Cloudy Day	ART	ART	1989	EC	18 X 12	R/BFK	200	4	110	125
Lillies and Light	ART	ART	1989	EC	12 X 18	R/BFK	200	4	110	125
Lakeside	ART	ART	1989	VE	12 X 18	R/BFK	200	Multi	110	125
Lake Suite (Set of 2)										
Lake Flowers	ART	SG/ART	1989	VE	38 X 26	R/BFK	200	Multi	400	400
Lake Breezes	ART	SG/ART	1989	VE	38 X 26	R/BFK	200	Multi	400	400
Summer Suite (Set of 3)										1200 SET	1200 SET
Summer Skies	ART/AA	SG/ART	1990	VE	30 X 38	R/BFK	225	Multi	400	400
Summer Breezes	ART/AA	SG/ART	1990	VE	30 X 38	R/BFK	225	Multi	400	400
Summer Sentinel	ART/AA	SG/ART	1990	VE	30 X 38	R/BFK	225	Multi	400	400
Shimmering Waters	ART	SG/ART	1990	VE	30 X 38	R/BFK	200	Multi	400	400
River Reflections	ART	ART	1990	EC	12 X 18	R/BFK	200	4	110	125
Cloud Reflections Suite (Set of 3):										300 SET	375 SET
Cloud Reflections I,II,III	ART	ART	1990	VE	13 X 19 EA	R/BFK	200 EA	Multi	100 EA	125 EA
Water's Edge	ART	SG/ART	1991	VE	30 X 38	R/BFK	225	Multi	400	400
Distant Shore Suite (Set of 2):										450 SET	500 SET
Distant Shore I,II	ART	SG/ART	1991	VE	30 X 23 EA	R/BFK	225 EA	Multi	225 EA	250 EA
Nature Trail I,II	ART	ART	1991	I/REL//HC	25 X 18 EA	R/BFK	75 EA	5 EA	200 EA	200 EA
Island Path I,II	ART	ART	1991	I/REL//HC	25 X 18 EA	R/BFK	75 EA	5 EA	200 EA	200 EA
River Pebbles	ART	ART	1991	VE	32 X 26	R/BFK	225	Multi	300	320
River Mosaic	ART	ART	1991	VE	32 X 26	R/BFK	225	Multi	300	320

AMOS YASKIL

BORN: Haifa, Israel; August 24, 1935
EDUCATION: Self-Taught
RECENT EXHIB: Universal Prints, Hamburg, Germany, 1990; Alon Gallery, Boston, MA, 1990; Amza Gallery, Hamburg, West Germany, 1990; Galerie St Germain-Stavit, Paris, France, 1990; Jan Mark Laic Gallery, Koblenz, Germany, 1993
PRINTERS: Har-El Printers, Israel (Har-El); Salman El Kara, Dalia, Mt Carmel, Israel (SalEk)
PUBLISHERS: Artist (ART); Jan Mark Laic, Koblenz, Germany (JML)
GALLERIES: Alon Gallery, Boston, MA; Kromholtz, Cologne, Germany; Pierres Gate, VT; Jan Mark Laic Gallery, Koblenz, Germany; Stavit Gallery, Paris, France
MAILING ADDRESS: 7, Hashomer St, Tiberias, Israel

TITLE	PUBLISHER	PRINTER	DATE	MEDIUM	DIMENSION (PAPER SIZE) IN INCHES	TYPE OF PAPER	EDITION NUMBER	NO. OF COLORS	ORIGINAL OPENING PRICE	CURRENT RETAIL PRICE
CURRENT EDITIONS:										
Sea of Galilee	ART	Har-El	1990	SP	24 X 25	COV	250	28	450	750
Village Landscape	ART	Har-El	1990	SP	37 X 35	COV	250	30	600	1000
Orchards	ART	Har-El	1990	SP	37 X 36	COV	250	35	600	1000
Rothchild's Garden	ART	Har-El	1990	SP	26 X 24	COV	250	32	450	750
Spring Blossoms	ART	Har-El	1990	SP	37 X 35	COV	250	18	600	900
Cactus Fruit	ART	SalEK	1990	LC	26 X 22	AP	100	6	450	750
Mt Fuji	ART	Har-El	1990	SP	36 X 36	COV	250	28	600	900
Mt Fuji (Set of 3)	ART	Har-El	1990	SP	15 X 12 EA	COV	250 EA	28 EA	600 SET	900 SET
Homage to the Galilee (Set of 12)	ART	Har-El	1990	SP	11 X 10 EA	COV	250 EA	28 EA	900 SET	1600 SET
									125 EA	300 EA
Sea of Galilee	LAIC	Har-El	1991	SP	13 X 13	COV	150	18	300 EA	400 EA
Village in Galilee	LAIC	Har-El	1992	SP	28 X 28	COV	250	18	800	900
Mt. Hermon	LAIC	Har-El	1992	SP	11 X 11	COV	250	18	225	250
Garden	LAIC	Har-El	1992	SP	11 X 11	COV	250	18	225	250
Garden Wall	LAIC	Har-El	1992	SP	11 X 11	COV	250	18	225	250
Village Landscape	LAIC	Har-El	1993	SP	8 X 8	COV	250	22	175	175
Lavender Held	LAIC	Har-El	1993	SP	11 X 11	COV	250	12	250	250
Cactus	LAIC	Har-El	1993	SP	11 X 11	COV	250	22	250	250
Sea of Galilee Mont Beatitude	LAIC	Har-El	1993	SP	11 X 11	COV	250	22	250	250
Yellow Mountain	LAIC	Har-El	1993	SP	11 X 9	COV	250	22	250	250
Yellow Field	LAIC	Har-El	1993	SP	17 X 13	COV	250	22	400	400
Sea of Galilee	LAIC	Har-El	1993	SP	13 X 17	COV	250	28	400	400
Olive Trees	LAIC	Har-El	1993	SP	20 X 23	COV	250	28	450	450

DIMITRIS YEROS

BORN: Levadia, Greece; December 6, 1948
COLLECTIONS: Ball State Univ, Muncie, IN; Oxford Univ, England; Bochum Mus, Germany; Athens Nat Gallery, Greece; Goethe Inst, Thessaloniki, Greece; Vorres Mus, Athens, Greece; British Mus, London, England; Nat Portrait Gallery, London, England
PRINTERS: Elias Kouvelis, Athens, Greece (EK); G Kotsaitis, Athens, Greece (GK); Thanasis Kimakarakos, Athens, Greece (TK); Kentro Tehnis/Artigraf, Athens, Greece (KT/A)
PUBLISHERS: Argo Gallery, Athens, Greece (AG); Collections Helleniques, Athens, Greece (CH); Kouvelis Fine Art, Athens, Greece (KFA); Thanasis Dimakarakos, Athens, Greece; Alex Bolotas, Athens, Greece (AB); Kentro Tehnis/Artigraf, Athens, Greece (KT/A); Artist (ART)
GALLERIES: Scoeller Galerie, Düsseldorf, Germany; Skoufa Gallery, Athens, Greece; Lumley Cazalet Gallery, London, England; Gloria Gallery, Nicosia, Cyprus; Iakinthos Gallery, Kifisia, Greece; Kentro Tehnis/Artigraf, Athens, Greece
MAILING ADDRESS: Karamanlaki 2, 112 53, Athens, Greece

DIMITRIS YEROS CONTINUED

TITLE	PUBLISHER	PRINTER	DATE	MEDIUM	DIMENSION (PAPER SIZE) IN INCHES	TYPE OF PAPER	EDITION NUMBER	NO. OF COLORS	ORIGINAL OPENING PRICE	CURRENT RETAIL PRICE
CURRENT EDITIONS:										
Fruit in Exile	KT/A	KT/A	1980	LC	50 X 70 cm	AP	200	14	100	200
Secretive Dawn	TD	TD	1980	LC	50 X 70 cm	AP	100	7	100	200
Innocent Prisoner	KFA	KFA	1980	SP	50 X 70 cm	AP	70	16	160	250
Apple-Apple Tree	KFA	KFA	1982	EB	50 X 70 cm	R/BFK	50	1	100	200
Platform	ART	TD	1982	EB	50 X 70 cm	R/BFK	50	1	100	200
Springtime Impulse	ART	TD	1983	EC	50 X 70 cm	R/BFK	50	9	200	300
Game for Tow	ART	TD	1984	EC	50 X 70 cm	R/BFK	100	6	200	300
The Authentic Bird of Peace	TD	TD	1984	EC	35 X 50 cm	R/BFK	50	3	150	250
Time Out	IK	IK	1985	SP	70 X 100 cm	AP	180	15	100	200
Tree	KT/A	KT/A	1986	EC	35 X 50 cm	R/BFK	50	6	150	250

TOMOE YOKOI

BORN: Tokyo, Japan; 1943
EDUCATION: Bunka-Gakuin, Tokyo, Japan; S W Hayter, Atelier, 17, Paris, France
AWARDS: Pratt Graphics Annual Prize, 1975; First Prize, Nat Arts Club Print Exhib, 1976
COLLECTIONS: Achenbach Found, Univ of Fine Arts, San Francisco, CA; Brooklyn Mus, NY; Nat Gallery of Art, Oslo, Norway; Mus d'Art Mod, Paris, France; Honolulu Acad of Art, HI

PRINTERS: Artist (ART)
PUBLISHERS: John Szoke Graphics, NY (JSG)
GALLERIES: Galerie Grafica, Tokyo, Japan; Galerie Lorizon, Nagoya, Japan; Gallery Hachibankan, Osaka, Japan; Augen Galleries, Portland, OR; Portfolio Gallery, Stamford, CT; Christie's Contemporary Art, New York, NY; Newmark Gallery, New York, NY; John Szoke Graphics, New York, NY; Saper Gallery, East Lansing, MI; Ro Gallery Image Makers, Inc, New York, NY

TITLE	PUBLISHER	PRINTER	DATE	MEDIUM	DIMENSION (PAPER SIZE) IN INCHES	TYPE OF PAPER	EDITION NUMBER	NO. OF COLORS	ORIGINAL OPENING PRICE	CURRENT RETAIL PRICE
SOLD OUT EDITIONS (RARE):										
Bowl & Peach	JSG	ART	1982	MEZ	25 X 20	R/BFK	130	5	400	600
Strawberries & Apple	JSG	ART	1983	MEZ	25 X 20	R/BFK	185	5	400	600
Watermelons in Bowl	JSG	ART	1983	MEZ	19 X 26	R/BFK	100	5	400	600
Cherry & Peach	JSG	ART	1983	MEZ	20 X 26	R/BFK	100	5	400	600
Orange & Apple	JSG	ART	1983	MEZ	19 X 26	R/BFK	100	5	400	600
Vase & Cherries	JBG	ART	1984	MEZ	26 X 20	R/BFK	100	5	400	600
Flower in the Basket	JBG	ART	1984	MEZ	20 X 13	R/BFK	100	5	200	400
Cherry & Lily	JBG	ART	1984	MEZ	13 X 20	R/BFK	100	5	200	400

ANNE YOUKELES

BORN: Bad Ischl, Austria; US Citizen
EDUCATION: Kunstgewerbe Schule, Vienna, Austria; Acad de la Grande Chaumiere, Paris, France; Ohio State Univ; New Sch & Educational Alliance, NY; Studied with Alexander Dobkin, Rudolf Baranik, Sidney Chafetz & Carol Summers
TEACHING: Ohio State Univ, Columbus, OH; New Sch for Social Research, NY; Educational Alliance, NY
AWARDS: Pratt Miniature Show, 1971; Philadelphia Print Club, PA, 1975; SAGA, 1977; Boston Printmakers, MA, 1974,78

COLLECTIONS: Philadelphia Art Mus, PA; Rosenwald Coll, Phila, PA; Olivet Col, MI; Austin Col, TX; Bibliotheque Nat, Paris, France; Ball State Univ, Muncie, IN; DeCordova Mus, Lincoln, MA; Williams Col, Williamstown, MA; Minneapolis Mus of Art, MN; Columbus Mus, GA
PRINTERS: Maurel Studios, NY (MS); Derriere l'Etoile Studio, NY (DES); Artist (ART)
PUBLISHERS: Judith L Posner & Assoc, Inc, Milwaukee, WI (JPA); Artist (ART)
GALLERIES: Posner Gallery, Milwaukee, WI; Dubins Gallery, Los Angeles, CA; Benjamin Mangel Gallery, Phila, PA; Reece Gallery, New York, NY
MAILING ADDRESS: 81–42 193rd St, Jamaica, NY 11423

TITLE	PUBLISHER	PRINTER	DATE	MEDIUM	DIMENSION (PAPER SIZE) IN INCHES	TYPE OF PAPER	EDITION NUMBER	NO. OF COLORS	ORIGINAL OPENING PRICE	CURRENT RETAIL PRICE
SOLD OUT EDITIONS (RARE):										
Grand Turnabout	IPA	ART	1973	SP	36 X 36	HMP	50		300	500
CURRENT EDITIONS:										
Silver Lining	ART	MS	1980	SP/CO	29 X 26	AP/WA	100	14	250	500
Mon Plaisir	ART	MS	1981	SP	29 X 27	AC	100	16	250	500
Sequence	ART	ART	1981	LC/HC	21 X 54	AP	50	32	350	600
Ways & Means	ART	ART	1982	SP	31 X 32	AP	100	6	300	500
Turning Point	ART	MS	1982	SP	31 X 32	AP	100	100	300	500
Evensong	ART	MS/ART	1984	SP/PO	29 X 36	LANA/W	100	3	300	500
Inside-Out	ART	MS/DES	1985	SP/LC	22 X 30	HMP	100	13	350	500
Shadowplay	ART	ART	1986	STEN/CP	27 X 34	HMP	20	10	500	600

MICHAEL YOUNG

BORN: Houston, TX; 1952
EDUCATION: Univ of Texas, Austin, TX, BFA, 1971–75; Skowhegan Sch of Sculpture & Painting, ME, 1974; Whitney Mus of Am Art, Independent Study Prog, NY, 1975; Yale Univ Sch of Art, New Haven, CT, 1975–77

RECENT EXHIB: Mus of Mod Art, NY; 1987; Rose Art Mus, Brandeis Univ, Waltham, MA, 1987
PRINTERS: Joe Wilfer, NY (JW); Ruth Lingen, NY (RL); Spring Street Workshop, NY (SprSW)
PUBLISHERS: Spring Street Workshop, NY (SprSW); Dyansen Corp, NY (DC)
GALLERIES: Pace Prints, New York, NY; BlumHelman Gallery, New York, NY; Dyansen Eclipse Gallery, New York, NY; Professional Fine Arts Services, Inc, New York, NY

MICHAEL YOUNG CONTINUED

TITLE	PUBLISHER	PRINTER	DATE	MEDIUM	DIMENSION (PAPER SIZE) IN INCHES	TYPE OF PAPER	EDITION NUMBER	NO. OF COLORS	ORIGINAL OPENING PRICE	CURRENT RETAIL PRICE
CURRENT EDITIONS:										
Six Crosses: Sign + Matter (Set of 6)	SprSW	JW/RL/SprSW	1989	MM/REL	19 X 24 EA	AC	35 EA		5000 SET 900 EA	8000 SET 1500 EA
Tripping the Light Fantastic	DC		1990	SP	32 X 35	AC	300		1600	2000
Ladies Ready-to-Wear	DC		1990	SP	23 X 42	AC	300		1600	2000
White Cross with Red Wedge	SprSW	JW/RL/SprSW	1990	REL/SP	38 X 51	AC	50		1000	1000
The Impossibility of Perpetual Motion (Set of 3)	SprSW	JW/RL/SprSW	1990	REL/CC/Sand	30 X 27 EA	HAHN	35 EA	1 EA	2500 SET 1000 EA	2500 SET 1000 EA
The Impossibility of Perpetual Motion (Set of 3)	SprSW	JW/RL/SprSW	1991	REL	20 X 17 EA	HAHN	25 EA	1 EA	1000 SET 400 EA	1000 SET 400 EA

NANCY J YOUNG

BORN: Evergreen Park, IL; November 7, 1939
EDUCATION: Univ of Illinois, Champaign-Urbana, IL, 1958–59; Univ of Arizona, Tucson, AZ, BS, 1961
AWARDS: First Prize, Albuquerque Arts Festival, New Mexico Art League, 1975; Award, Merit, Public Service Council, Albuquerque, NM, 1982; Best of Show, Nat League of Am Penwomen, NM, 1985; Purchase Award, Sperry Corp, 1985
RECENT EXHIB: Univ of Arizona, Tucson, AZ, 1990; Eastern New Mexico Univ, 1990; Univ of New Mexico, Albuquerque, NM, 1990–91; John A Boler, Indian & Western Art, Minneapolis, MN, 1989,92

COLLECTIONS: Univ of New Mexico, Thompson Gallery, Albuquerque, NM; Univ of Arizona, Tucson, AZ; Univ of Northern Arizona, Flagstaff, AZ; Sun Valley Center for the Arts, ID; New Mexico Inst of Mining & Tech, Socorro, NM; Albuquerque Tech Vocational Inst, NM
PRINTERS: Artist (ART)
PUBLISHERS: Artist (ART)
GALLERIES: Gallery 3, Phoenix, AZ; Tarbox Gallery, San Diego, CA; Magic Mountain Gallery, Taos, NM, Nan Miller Gallery, Rochester, NY
MAILING ADDRESS: 11416 Brussels, NE, Albuquerque, NM 87111

TITLE	PUBLISHER	PRINTER	DATE	MEDIUM	DIMENSION (PAPER SIZE) IN INCHES	TYPE OF PAPER	EDITION NUMBER	NO. OF COLORS	ORIGINAL OPENING PRICE	CURRENT RETAIL PRICE
SOLD OUT EDITIONS (RARE):										
Pedernal Cloudrise	ART	ART	1981	REL/EC	30 X 22	STP	50	10	200	350
Canyon Country	ART	ART	1981	REL/EC	30 X 22	STP	70	12	225	350
Blue Divide	ART	ART	1981	REL/EC	22 X 30	STP	50	10	200	350
Wilderness Canyon	ART	ART	1982	REL/EC	32 X 22	STP	20	18	225	350
Dark Ice	ART	ART	1982	REL/EC	23 X 31	HMP	25	3	225	350
Lost River	ART	ART	1982	REL/EC	22 X 32	STP	30	20	275	450
North Fork	ART	ART	1982	REL/EC	22 X 30	STP	40	15	225	350
Cielo Grande	ART	ART	1983	REL/EC	30 X 22	HMP	40	18	225	350
Canyon Gateway Diptych, States I, II (Set of 2)	ART	ART	1984	REL/EC	22 X 30 EA	STP	25 EA	15 EA	450 SET	900 SET
Ghost Mountain	ART	ART	1984	REL/EC	23 X 31	HMP	28	8	240	400
Anasazi Moon	ART	ART	1984	REL/EC	22 X 30	STP	50	14	240	400
Cliff Passage	ART	ART	1984	REL/EC	31 X 23	HMP	40	11	225	350

ROBERT YOUNG

BORN: Vancouver, BC, Canada; August 8, 1938
EDUCATION: Univ of British Columbia, BA, Honors, Art History Dept, 1962; City & Guilds, London Art Sch of Art, Can, 1962–64; Vancouver Sch of Art, Can, 1964–66
TEACHING: Assoc Prof, Univ of British Columbia, Canada, 1982 to present
COLLECTIONS: Montreal Mus of Fine Arts, Can; Art Gallery of Ontario, Toronto, Can; Canada Council Art Bank, Ottawa, Can

PRINTERS: Artist (ART)
PUBLISHERS: Christie's Contemporary Art, London England (CCA); J C Editions, London, England (JCE); Artist (ART)
GALLERIES: Redfern Gallery, London, England; Mira Godard Gallery, Toronto, Canada; Queen Emma Gallery, Honolulu, HI; Charles H Scott Gallery, Vancouver, BC, Canada; Bau Xi Galleries, Vancouver, Canada & Toronto, Canada
MAILING ADDRESS: 3940 Quebec St, Vancouver, BC, Canada V5U 3K8

TITLE	PUBLISHER	PRINTER	DATE	MEDIUM	DIMENSION (PAPER SIZE) IN INCHES	TYPE OF PAPER	EDITION NUMBER	NO. OF COLORS	ORIGINAL OPENING PRICE	CURRENT RETAIL PRICE
SOLD OUT EDITIONS (RARE):										
Sounds Inside	ART	ART	1973	SP	27 X 22	AP	150	15	50	1500
Synchronicity	ART	ART	1975	EC	31 X 24	AP	70	2	150	1000
Chromatic Aberration	ART	ART	1976	EC	30 X 22	AP	60	5	150	1000
Chiccyclist	ART	ART	1977	EC	30 X 22	AP	22	2	150	600
The Suprematist	ART	ART	1979	SP	28 X 19	AP	36	6	200	600
CURRENT EDITIONS:										
Floating	ART	ART	1975	SP	30 X 22	AP	50	7	125	400
A is For	ART	ART	1977	EC	30 X 22	AP	22	2	125	500
Sax and Reality	ART	ART	1979	EB	20 X 23	AP	22	1	125	400
Wardell Cuts Out	ART	ART	1979	EC	27 X 22	AP	35	5	150	450
Jongleur	ART	ART	1980	EC	12 X 11	AP	28	4	75	350
Musiker	ART	ART	1980	EC	12 X 11	AP	28	4	75	350

ROBERT YOUNG CONTINUED

TITLE	PUBLISHER	PRINTER	DATE	MEDIUM	DIMENSION (PAPER SIZE) IN INCHES	TYPE OF PAPER	EDITION NUMBER	NO. OF COLORS	ORIGINAL OPENING PRICE	CURRENT RETAIL PRICE
CURRENT EDITIONS:										
The Juggler's Map	ART	ART	1980	EB	29 X 37	AP	20	1	150	450
The Juggler's Rehearsal	ART	ART	1980	EC	29 X 37	AP	37	4	200	500
Dream of Dionysus	ART	ART	1981	SP	23 X 22	AP	70	7	250	450
Oleo	ART	ART	1983	EC	30 X 21	AP	28	1	300	500

JACK YOUNGERMAN

BORN: Louisville, KY; March 25, 1926
EDUCATION: Univ of North Carolina, Chapel Hill, NC, 1944–46; Univ of Missouri, Columbia, MO, BA, 1947; Ecole des Beaux-Arts, Paris, France, 1947–48
TEACHING: Instr, Yale Univ, New Haven, CT, 1974–75; Instr, Hunter Col, NY, 1981–82; Instr, School of Visual Arts, NY, 1982 to present
AWARDS: New Talent Award, Art in America Mag, 1959; Nat Council Arts & Sciences Award, 1966; Nat Endowment Arts Award, 1972,84; Guggenheim Found Fel, 1976; Nat Acad of Design, NY, 1992
RECENT EXHIB: Washburn Gallery, NY, 1987; Arkansas State Univ Art Gallery, State University, AR, 1989; Heland Wetterling Gallery, Stockholm, Sweden, 1989
COLLECTIONS: Mus of Mod Art, NY; Whitney Mus of Am Art, NY; Corcoran Gallery of Art, Wash, DC; Albright-Knox Art Gallery, Buffalo, NY; Univ of California, Berkeley, CA; Carnegie Inst, Pittsburgh, PA; Chicago Art Inst, IL; Hirshhorn Mus, Wash, DC; Wadsworth Atheneum, Hartford, CT; Virginia Mus of Fine Arts, Richmond, VA; Yale Univ, New Haven, CT; Wichita Mus of Art, KS; Phillips Coll, Wash, DC; Nat Coll of Fine Arts, Wash, DC; Worcester Art Mus, Worcester, MA; Meade Art Mus, Amherst, MA; Guggenheim Mus, NY; Milwaukee Art Center, WI; Mus of Fine Art, Houston, TX; Mus of Fine Arts, Baltimore, MD
PRINTERS: Roni Henning, NY (RH); New York Institute of Technology, Old Westbury, Long Island, NY (NYI)
PUBLISHERS: Pace Editions, NY (PE); Transworld Art, Inc, NY (TAI); Prestige Art Ltd, Mamaroneck, NY (PA)
GALLERIES: Pace Prints, New York, NY; Washburn Gallery, New York, NY; Heath Gallery, Atlanta, GA; Jayne Baum Gallery, New York, NY; Alan Brown Gallery, Hartsdale, NY; Osuna Gallery, Wash, DC; Heland Wetterling Gallery, Stockholm, Sweden
MAILING ADDRESS: 130 W Third St, New York, NY 10012

TITLE	PUBLISHER	PRINTER	DATE	MEDIUM	DIMENSION (PAPER SIZE) IN INCHES	TYPE OF PAPER	EDITION NUMBER	NO. OF COLORS	ORIGINAL OPENING PRICE	CURRENT RETAIL PRICE
SOLD OUT EDITIONS (RARE):										
Changes Portfolio (Set of 8)	PE		1970	SP	43 X 33	AP	175	4	1200 SET	4000 SET
White Portfolio (Set of 6)	PE		1972	I	36 X 27	AP	150	4	1000 SET	2500 SET
Images Portfolio (Set of 6)	PE		1974	SP	32 X 32	AP	150	4	750 SET	3000 SET
Ukiyo-E Portfolio (Set of 4)	PE		1976	LC/SP	33 X 39	RAG	150	4	800 SET	2000 SET
Untitled Suite, I-VI (Set of 6)	PA	RH	1978	SP	45 X 52 EA	STP	100 EA	5	750 EA	1000 EA
Untitled Suite, A-H (Set of 8)	PA	RH/NYI	1980	SP/WC	29 X 28 EA	STP	50 EA	4	400 EA	500 EA
Yantra Series (Set of 6):										
Swirl (Maroon, Lt Blue, Aquamarine, Pale Gray)	TAI	RH/NYI	1978–82	SP/PO/I	37 X 36	AP	75	4	500	700
Orbit (Gray, Tan, Yellow, Orange)	TAI	RH/NYI	1978–82	SP/PO/I	37 X 36	AP	75	4	500	750
Galaxy (Yellow Orange, Apple Green, Sienna, Blue Green)	TAI	RH/NYI	1978–82	SP/PO/I	37 X 36	AP	75	3	500	750
Mandala (Green, Blue, Black, Pink)	TAI	RH/NYI	1978–82	SP/PO/I	37 X 36	AP	75	4	500	750
Nimbus (Gray Blue, Vermillion, Pale Yellow, Ochre Orange)	TAI	RH/NYI	1978–82	SP/PO/I	37 X 36	AP	75	4	500	750
Involute (Chinese Orange, Umber, Pale Ochre, Gray Green)	TAI	RH/NYI	1978–82	SP/PO/I	37 X 36	AP	75	4	500	750

MARIO YRISARRY

BORN: Manila, Philippines; March 29, 1933; US Citizen
EDUCATION: Queens Col, NY, BA; Cooper Union, NY
AWARDS: Ford Found Grant, Tamarind Inst, Albuquerque, NM, 1973
COLLECTIONS: Whitney Mus of Am Art, NY; Baltimore Mus of Art, MD; Indianapolis Mus of Art, IN; Rose Art Mus, Brandeis Univ, Waltham, MA; Carnegie Inst, Pittsburgh, PA
PRINTERS: Tamarind Inst, Albuquerque, NM (TI)
PUBLISHERS: Tamarind Inst, Albuquerque, NM (TI)
GALLERIES: Tamarind Inst, Albuquerque, NM
MAILING ADDRESS: 297 Third Ave, New York, NY 10010

TITLE	PUBLISHER	PRINTER	DATE	MEDIUM	DIMENSION (PAPER SIZE) IN INCHES	TYPE OF PAPER	EDITION NUMBER	NO. OF COLORS	ORIGINAL OPENING PRICE	CURRENT RETAIL PRICE
SOLD OUT EDITIONS (RARE):										
Pale Space	TI	TI	1973	LC	23 X 22		20	1	100	600

ADJA YUNKERS

BORN: Riga, Latvia; (1900–1983)
TEACHING: New Sch for Soc Res, NY, 1947–56; Cooper Union, NY, 1956–67; Columbia Univ, NY, 1967–69; Barnard Col, NY, 1969–78
AWARDS: Guggenheim Fel, 1949–50, 1954–55; Ford Found, 1960; Tamarind Workshop, Los Angeles, CA, 1960; Bronze Medal, Chicago Inst of Art, IL; Gold Medal, Int Graphics Show, Oslo, Norway, 1974
RECENT EXHIB: Print Retrosp, Associated Am Artists, NY, 1988; Fine Arts Mus of Long Island, NY, 1992
COLLECTIONS: Mus of Mod Art, NY; Guggenheim Mus, NY; Whitney Mus of Am Art, NY; Metropolitan Mus of Art, NY; Albright-Knox Art Gallery, Buffalo, NY
PRINTERS: Maurel Studio, NY (MS); Styria Studio, NY (SS); Vermillion Editions Ltd, Minneapolis, MN (VEL); Ernest F De Soto, San Francisco, CA (EDS); Ernest De Soto Workshop, San Francisco, CA (EDSW)
PUBLISHERS: C & D Editions, NY (C/D); Styria Studio, NY (SS); Vermillion Editions Ltd, Minneapolis, MN (VEL); Ernest De Soto Workshop, San Francisco, CA (EDSW)

ADJA YUNKERS CONTINUED

GALLERIES: Estudio Actual, Caracas, Venezuela; CDS Gallery, New York, NY; Alice Simsar, Ann Arbor, MI; Nielsen Gallery, Boston, MA; Galeria Juan Martin, Mexico City, Mexico; John C Stroller & Co, Minneapolis, MN; Allrich Gallery, San Francisco, CA; Graphics Gallery, San Francisco, CA; Vermillion Editions, Minneapolis, MN; Styria Studio, New York, NY; Associated American Arts, New York, NY

TITLE	PUBLISHER	PRINTER	DATE	MEDIUM	DIMENSION (PAPER SIZE) IN INCHES	TYPE OF PAPER	EDITION NUMBER	NO. OF COLORS	ORIGINAL OPENING PRICE	CURRENT RETAIL PRICE
SOLD OUT EDITIONS (RARE):										
Arabesque	ART	ART	1952	WC	31 X 45	JP	7		50	8000
The Gathering of the Clans	ART	ART	1952	WB	22 X 27	R/100	14		50	5000
The Gathering of the Clans	ART	ART	1953	WC	19 X 14	R/100	95		75	7500
Composition	ART	ART	1955	WC	21 X 14	R/100	200		60	5000
Nature Monte	ART	ART	1955	WC	21 X 36	R/100	5		75	10000
Second Dream of Infanta Isabel II	C/D	MS	1973	SP	41 X 28	JBG	90	2	175	8000
Composition XIII	SS	SS	1974	SP/EMB	46 X 37	CD	100	2	450	7000
Sun Drops Petrefied Black	SS	SS	1975	SP/HC	46 X 37	AP/ROL	50	1	450	7000
Sky Hides Birds at Night	SS	SS	1976	EC	42 X 30	CD	50	1	450	7000
Red Echo	SS	SS	1976	EC	40 X 30	CD	40	1	450	7000
Echo II in Pink	SS	SS	1977	EC	42 X 30	CD	50	1	450	7000
Echo II in Gray	SS	SS	1977	EC	42 X 30	CD	25	1	450	7000
Echo II in Black	SS	SS	1977	EB	42 X 30	CD	25	1	450	7000
Pink One #1	SS	SS	1977	EC/CO	42 X 30	CD	50	1	450	7000
Pink One #2 in Gray	SS	SS	1977	EC/CO	42 X 30	CD	25	1	450	7000
Pueblo	EDSW	EDS/EDSW	1977	LC	34 X 25	GE	70	4	500	7000
The Sky Hides All Its Birds (Black)	ART	MS	1977	EC	42 X 30	JBG	50	1	450	7000
The Sky Hides All Its Birds (White)	ART	MS	1977	EC	42 X 30	JBG	50	1	450	7000
The Sky Hides All Its Birds (Beige)	ART	MS	1977	EC	42 X 30	JBG	50	1	450	7000
The King in Pink	SS	SS	1977	EC	42 X 30	CD	50	1	450	7000
The King in Black	SS	SS	1977	EC	42 X 30	CD	50	1	450	7000
The King in Gray	ART	MS	1977	EC	42 X 30	JBG	50	1	450	7000
The King in White	ART	MS	1977	EC	42 X 30	JBG	50	1	450	7000
Requiem for a Virgin King	ART	MS	1977	SP	42 X 30	JBG	50	3	450	7000
Composition XIII E	ART	MS	1977	SP	44 X 36	JBG	50	2	450	7000
Echo in Gray II	ART	MS	1977	I	40 X 29	JBG	25	1	450	7000
Veronica II	EDSW	EDS/EDSW	1977	LC	34 X 26	GE	70	4	500	2000
Icon I	VEL	VEL	1978	LC/EMB	25 X 19	R/BFK	100	3	350	2000
Untitled I	VEL	VEL	1978	I/NI	30 X 22	AP	40	0	250	2000
Untitled II	VEl	VEL	1978	I/NI	30 X 22	AP	40	0	250	2000
Untitled III	VEL	VEL	1978	I/SP	30 X 22	AP	40	2	350	2400
Falling Birds	VEL	VEL	1978	LC/SP	32 X 24	HMP	100	5	350	3200
Falling Birds	ART	MS	1980	LC	44 X 36	JBG	50	3	350	3200
Immobile Sun	ART	MS	1980	LC	44 X 36	JBG	30	4	450	5000
Les Pendus	VEL	VEL	1980	I/SP	30 X 42	AP	42	4	350	2800
Les Pendus II	VEL	VEL	1980	I	30 X 22	AP	40	1	350	2400
Icon II	VEL	VEL	1980	I/SP	30 X 22	AP	40	3	350	2500
Untitled IV	VEL	VEL	1980	I/SP	30 X 22	AP	30	2	350	2200
Untitled V	VEL	VEL	1980	I	30 X 22	AP	40	1	250	2200
Untitled VI	VEL	VEL	1980	I/SP	30 X 22	AP	40	2	250	2200
A Moment into Eternity II	VEL	VEL	1982	I/LC/SP	39 X 28	AP	42	5	350	3500
Immobile Sun XXI-B	VEL	VEL	1982	I/SP	37 X 28	AP	7	3	250	5000
Immobile Sun XXI	VEL	VEL	1982	I/LC/SP	37 X 28	AP	39	4	350	5000
Immobile Sun XXI-A	VEL	VEL	1982	I/LC/SP/EMB	37 X 28	AP	20	6	350	5000
Immobile Sun XXI-C	VEL	VEL	1983	I/SP	36 X 28	AP	17	3	450	5000
*Icon III	VEL	VEL	1983	I/LC/EMB	25 X 19	AP/B	23	4	450	4000

*Artist's Last Print

DAVID E YUST

BORN: Wichita, KS; April 3, 1939
EDUCATION: Wichita State Univ, KS, 1957–59; Kansas State Univ, Manhattan, KS, 1959–61; Univ of Kansas, Lawrence, KS, BFA, 1961–63; Univ of Oregon, Eugene, OR, MFA, 1966–69
TEACHING: Assoc Prof, Colorado State Univ, Ft Collins, CO, Painting & Drawing, 1965 to present
AWARDS: US State Dept, Am Embassy Arts Program, 1966–68; Purchase Award, Mulvane Art Center, Topeka, KS, 1970; Purchase Award, Oklahoma Art Center, Oklahoma City, OK, 1973
RECENT EXHIB: Wyoming Art Mus, Laramie, WY, 1987; Boulder Visual Arts Center, CO, 1988; St Paul Gallery, MN, 1989,92; Rourke Art Gallery, Moorhead, MN, 1992
COLLECTIONS: Denver Art Mus, CO; Wichita Art Mus, KS; Sheldon Mem Art Ctr, Topeka, KS; North Dakota State Univ, Fargo, ND; Colorado Springs Fine Arts Center, CO; Salina Mus, KS; Sierra Nevada Art Mus, Reno, NV; Oklahoma Art Center, Oklahoma City, OK; Mulvane Art Center, Topeka, KS; Kansas State Univ, Manhattan, KS; Colorado State Univ, Ft Collins, CO; Univ of Oregon, Eugene, OR; Univ of Kansas, Lawrence, KS; Wichita State Univ, KS; Indianapolis Mus of Art, IN; Rockford Art Mus, IL; Minnesota Mus of Art, St Paul, MN; Butler Mus of Am Art, Youngstown, OH
PRINTERS: Fred Jurado Graphics, Denver, CO (FJG); Bud Shark, Boulder, CO (BS); Shark's Lithography Ltd, Boulder, CO (SLL); Gene Licht, Denver, CO (GL); Licht Editions Ltd, Denver, CO (LEL)
PUBLISHERS: Yust Studio, Ft Collins, CO (YS); Inkfish Gallery, Denver, CO (IG); Licht Editions Ltd, Denver, CO (LEL)
GALLERIES: Inkfish Gallery, Denver, CO; Sol Del Rio, San Antonio, TX; Rourke Gallery, Moorhead, MN; Laura Erlich Fine Arts, Bedford, MA
MAILING ADDRESS: 1301 Patton St, Fort Collins, CO 80524

The retail prices of the 100,000 limited edition prints quoted in this directory are subject to change. Print publishers, artists and galleries were the direct sources for these quotations. Prices in the secondary market listed as "Sold Out Editions (Rare)" indicate that the publisher has a limited supply of that print or that the print is difficult to locate in the galleries.

DAVID E YUST CONTINUED

TITLE	PUBLISHER	PRINTER	DATE	MEDIUM	DIMENSION (PAPER SIZE) IN INCHES	TYPE OF PAPER	EDITION NUMBER	NO. OF COLORS	ORIGINAL OPENING PRICE	CURRENT RETAIL PRICE
SOLD OUT EDITIONS (RARE):										
Circular Composition #97A (Change in Scale #81)	YS	FJ/G	1976	SP	21 X 20	AP88/W	18	3	150	400
CC #109A (CIS #93) Intense Blue	YS	BS/SLL	1977	LC	21 X 20	AP/BL	13	1	120	350
CC #129A (CIS #113)	IG/LEL	GL	1979	SP	12 X 12	LEN/W	24	3	60	200
CC #129B (CIS #113)	IG/LEL	GL	1979	SP	12 X 12	LEN/W	37	3	50	200
CC #130A (CIS #114) Trial Proof	IG	GL	1980	SP	21 X 20	R/BFK	10	6	200	350
CC #130B (CIS #114) Trial Proof	IG	GL	1980	SP	21 X 20	R/BFK	10	6	200	350
CC #130b (CIS #114)	IG	GL	1980	SP	29 X 28	R/BFK	80	6	300	400
CURRENT EDITIONS:										
Circular Composition #91 (Change in Scale #75)	YS	FJ/G	1975	SP	21 X 20	CUR	100	3	50	200
CC #92 (CIS #76)	YS	FJ/G	1975	SP	21 X 20	CUR	100	3	50	200
CC #93 (CIS #77)	YS	FJ/G	1975	SP	21 X 20	CUR	100	3	50	200
CC #94 (CIS #78)	YS	FJ/G	1975	SP	21 X 20	CUR	100	3	50	200
CC #95 (CIS #79)	YS	FJ/G	1975	SP	21 X 20	CUR	100	3	50	200
CC #96 (CIS #80)	YS	FJ/G	1975	SP	21 X 20	CUR	100	3	50	200
CC #101 (CIS #85)(Dipt)	YS	BS/SLL	1977	LC/EMB	21 X 20	R/BFK	100	4	150	300
CC #102 (CIS #86)	YS	BS/SLL	1977	LC/EMB	20 X 20	R/BFK	100	4	150	350
CC #109 (CIS #93) Intense Blue	YS	BS/SLL	1977	LC	21 X 20	R/BFK	50	1	100	250
CC #110 (CIS #94)	YS	BS/SLL	1977	LC	29 X 28	R/BFK	100	4	200	300
CC #120 (CIS #104)	YS	BS/SLL	1978	LC	29 X 28	R/BFK	60	3	200	400
CC #121 (CIS #105)	YS	BS/SLL	1978	LC	29 X 28	AP/BL	60	3	200	400
CC #130 (CIS #114)	IG	GL	1980	SP	29 X 28	R/BFK	80	6	200	350
Alpha Inclusion (warm) after RV (with 4 Bronze Powders)	YS	BS/SLL	1982	LC/BP	30 X 30	AP/BL & R/BFK	30	6	325	550
Alpha Inclusion (cool) after RV (with 3 Bronze Powders)	YS	BS/SLL	1982	LC/BP	30 X 30	AP/BL & R/BFK	30	7	325	550

YVARAL

BORN: Paris, France; January 25, 1934
EDUCATION: Applied Arts Sch, Paris, France, 1953
COLLECTIONS: Mus of Mod Art, NY; Newark Mus, NJ; Philadelphia Mus, PA; Albright-Knox Art Gallery, Buffalo, NY; Tate Gallery, London, England; Mus of Mod Art, Paris, France; Mus of Contemp Art, Zagreb, Yugoslavia

PRINTERS: Arcay Atelier, Paris, France (AA)
PUBLISHERS: Martin Lawrence Limited Editions, Van Nuys, CA (MLLE)
GALLERIES: Gallery Denise Rene, Saint Germain, Paris, France; Martin Lawrence Galleries, Sherman Oaks, CA & Los Angeles, CA & Newport Beach, CA & Short Hills, NJ & Phila PA & Palm Springs, CA & Redondo Beach, CA & Escondido, CA & Thousand Oaks, CA & West Los Angeles, CA & Santa Clara, CA

TITLE	PUBLISHER	PRINTER	DATE	MEDIUM	DIMENSION (PAPER SIZE) IN INCHES	TYPE OF PAPER	EDITION NUMBER	NO. OF COLORS	ORIGINAL OPENING PRICE	CURRENT RETAIL PRICE
SOLD OUT EDITIONS (RARE):										
Star Suite (Set of 3):									650 SET	6100 SET
Star I (Violet)	CFA	AA	1976	LC	30 X 30	AP	100		250	2200
Star II (Beige)	CFA	AA	1976	LC	30 X 30	AP	100		250	2200
Star III (Blue)	CFA	AA	1976	LC	30 X 30	AP	100		250	2400
Mona Lisa Suite—La Joconde (Set of 3):									650 SET	4000 SET
Mona Lisa—Green/Blue La Joconde	CFA	AA	1976	SP	37 X 25	AP	100		250	1700
Mona Lisa—Blue La Joconde	CFA	AA	1976	SP	37 X 25	AP	100		250	1400
Mona Lisa—Red La Joconde	CFA	AA	1976	SP	37 X 25	AP	100		250	1400
Splendeur I, II (Set of 2)	CFA	AA	1977	SP	37 X 29 EA	AP	100 EA		450 SET	2600 SET
									275 EA	1400 EA
Splendeur Ile Legend (Set of 4)	CFA	AA	1977	SP	37 X 29 EA	AP	100 EA		950 SET	5000 SET
CURRENT EDITIONS:										
Faces of Dali (Set of 6):									2400 SET	4250 SET
Dali Image #1	MLLE	AA	1979	SP	25 X 36	AP	200	20	400	900
Dali Image #2	MLLE	AA	1979	SP	25 X 36	AP	200	21	400	900
Dali Image #3	MLLE	AA	1979	SP	25 X 36	AP	200	22	400	900
Dali Image #4	MLLE	AA	1979	SP	25 X 36	AP	200	21	400	900
Dali Image #5	MLLE	AA	1979	SP	25 X 36	AP	200	23	400	900
Dali Image #6	MLLE	AA	1979	SP	25 X 36	AP	200	21	400	900
George Washington	MLLE	AA	1980	SP	28 X 41	AP	200	18	600	950
Abraham Lincoln	MLLE	AA	1980	SP	28 X 41	AP	200		600	950
Kennedy	MLLE	AA	1980	SP	28 X 41	AP	200	18	600	950
Kennedy-Lincoln	MLLE	AA	1980	SP	28 X 41	AP	200	16	600	950
Star	MLLE	AA	1981	SP	24 X 26	AP	225		450	800
Horizon	MLLE	AA	1981	SP	24 X 26	AP	225	16	450	800
Pyramid	MLLE	AA	1981	SP	24 X 26	AP	225		450	800
Form Ronde	MLLE	AA	1981	SP	24 X 26	AP	225	14	450	800
Sphere	MLLE	AA	1981	SP	24 X 26	AP	225	14	450	800
Purple Horizon	MLLE	AA	1981	SP	24 X 26	AP	225	14	450	800

ATHOS ZACHARIAS

BORN: Marlborough, MA; June 17, 1927
EDUCATION: Rhode Island Sch of Design, Providence, RI, BFA, 1952; Art Students League, NY, 1952; Cranbrook Acad of Arts, Bloomfield Hills, MI, MFA, 1953
TEACHING: Brown Univ, Providence, RI, 1953–55; Parsons Sch of Design, NY, 1963–65; Cooper Union Art Sch, NY; Wagner Col, Staten Island, NY, 1969 to present
RECENT EXHIB: Laforet Mus, Tokyo, Japan, 1987
COLLECTIONS: Providence Mus of Art, RI; Inst of Contemp Art, Boston, MA; Phoenix Mus of Art, AZ; Weatherspoon Art Gallery, Univ of North Carolina; Kalamazoo Inst of Art, MI; Corcoran Gallery of Art, Wash, DC
PRINTERS: Artist (ART)
PUBLISHERS: Fred Dorfman, Inc, NY (FDI)
GALLERIES: Fred Dorfman Gallery, New York, NY; Westbeth Gallery, New York, NY; Owl 57 Galleries, Woodmere, NY
MAILING ADDRESS: 463 West St, Apt B-946, New York, NY 10014

TITLE	PUBLISHER	PRINTER	DATE	MEDIUM	DIMENSION (PAPER SIZE) IN INCHES	TYPE OF PAPER	EDITION NUMBER	NO. OF COLORS	ORIGINAL OPENING PRICE	CURRENT RETAIL PRICE
CURRENT EDITIONS:										
Early Fortune	FDI	ART	1979	LC	26 X 35	AP	275	6	150	300
Easy Money	FDI	ART	1979	LC	24 X 31	AP	275	7	150	300

TINO ZAGO (AGOSTINO C)

BORN: Crespano del Grappa, Italy; 1937; US Citizen
EDUCATION: Lawrence Inst of Technology, MI, BS, Arch, 1960; Cranbook Acad of Art, Bloomfield Hills, MI, MFA, Painting, 1966; Yale Univ, New Haven, CT 1969
TEACHING: Vis Artist, Michigan State Univ, East Lansing, MI; Vis Artist, Yale Univ, New Haven, CT
AWARDS: Nat Endowment for the Arts Emerging Artist Grant, 1982, Individual Artist Grant, 1985
RECENT EXHIB: Tortue Gallery, Santa Monica, CA, 1988; OK Harris Works of Art, NY, 1987,89; McIntosh Gallery, Atlanta, GA, 1989
COLLECTIONS: Sidney Lewis Coll, Richmond, VA
PRINTERS: Editions Sheridan/Bardin, Brooklyn, NY (ES/B)
PUBLISHERS: Fred Dorfman, Inc, NY (FDI)
GALLERIES: Fred Dorfman Gallery, New York, NY; OK Harris Works of Art, New York, NY; Tortue Gallery, Santa Monica, CA
MAILING ADDRESS: 376 Broome St, 2nd Fl, New York, NY 10013

TITLE	PUBLISHER	PRINTER	DATE	MEDIUM	DIMENSION (PAPER SIZE) IN INCHES	TYPE OF PAPER	EDITION NUMBER	NO. OF COLORS	ORIGINAL OPENING PRICE	CURRENT RETAIL PRICE
CURRENT EDITIONS:										
Variations of Dolores	FDI	ES/B	1985	SP/HC	38 X 50 EA	STP	65 EA	23–26 EA	1000 EA	1500 EA

ROBERT S ZAKANITCH

BORN: Elizabeth, NJ; May 24, 1935
EDUCATION: Newark Sch of Fine & Industrial Art, NJ, 1954–57
TEACHING: Univ of California, San Diego, CA, 1974; Art Inst of Chicago, IL, 1976; Instr, Drawing & Painting, OK Summer Arts Inst, 1989,90,91
RECENT EXHIB: Yares Gallery, Scottsdale, AZ, 1987; Inst of contemp Art, Univ of Pennsylvania, Phila, PA, 1988; Helander Gallery, Palm Beach, FL, 1989; Sidney Janis Gallery, NY, 1990
COLLECTIONS: Philadelphia Mus of Art, PA; Whitney Mus of Am Art, NY; Munich Mus of Mod Art, Munich, West Germany; Mus of Fine Arts, Richmond, VA; Phoenix Mus, AZ; Vassar Col Mus, Poughkeepsie, NY; Wadsworth Atheneum, Hartford, CT; Larry Aldrich Mus of Contemp Art, Ridgefield, CT; Hirshhorn Mus, Wash, DC; High Mus of Art, Atlanta, GA; Milwaukee Art Mus, WI
PRINTERS: Handworks (HAN); Tyler Graphics, Ltd, Mount Kisco, NY (TGL); Tamarind Inst, Albuquerque, NM (TI); Lynne Allen, Albuquerque, NM (LA); Molly Jo Souders, Albuquerque, NM (MJS); Artist (ART); Berghoff-Cowden Studio, Tampa, FL (B-CS)
PUBLISHERS: Barbara Gladstone Editions, NY (BGE); Tyler Graphics, Ltd, Mount Kisco, NY (TGL); Diane Villani Editions, NY (DVE); Brooke Alexander, Inc, NY (BAI); Tamarind Inst, Albuquerque, NM (TI); Berghoff-Cowden Editions, Tampa, FL (B-CEd)
GALLERIES: Robert Miller Gallery, New York, NY; Asher/Faure Gallery, Los Angeles, CA; McIntosh/Drysdale Gallery, Wash, DC; Greenberg Gallery of Contemp Art, St Louis, MO; Michael H Lord Gallery, Milwaukee, WI; Helander Gallery, Palm Beach, FL; Harcus Gallery, Boston, MA; Tamarind Inst, Albuquerque, NM; Sidney Janis Gallery, New York, NY; Topaz Editions, Inc, Tampa, FL; Vinalhaven Press, Vinalhaven, ME; Tyler Graphics, Ltd, Mount Kisco, NY; Berghoff-Cowden Editions, Tampa, FL
MAILING ADDRESS: 119 N 11th St, Brooklyn, NY 11211

TITLE	PUBLISHER	PRINTER	DATE	MEDIUM	DIMENSION (PAPER SIZE) IN INCHES	TYPE OF PAPER	EDITION NUMBER	NO. OF COLORS	ORIGINAL OPENING PRICE	CURRENT RETAIL PRICE
SOLD OUT EDITIONS (RARE):										
Old World Series	BGE/DVE	HAN	1979	LC/SP/PO	30 X 50	R/BFK	49	12	550	3000
How I Love Ya, How I Love Ya	TGL	TGL	1981	LC/SP/PO	42 X 120	R/BFK	43	21	3000	6000
Hearts of Swan (Black)	TGL	TGL	1981	LC/SP/PO	28 X 23	TGL/HMP	75	13	750	1000
Hearts of Swan (Red)	TGL	TGL	1981	LC/SP/PO	28 X 23	TGL/HMP	75	17	750	900
Double Geese Mountain	TGL	TGL	1981	LC/SP/PO	28 X 23	TGL/HMP	75	15	750	900
Colored 7 Pressed Paper Pulp Pieces (One-of-a-Kind Works-Framed):										
Sapphire (6 Panels)	TGL	TGL	1981	MON	85 X 103 EA	HMP	1 EA	Varies	2500	18000
Hussy	TGL	TGL	1981	MON	86 X 103 EA	HMP	1 EA	Varies	2500	18000
Hearts of Swan (Marooned) (4 Panels)	TGL	TGL	1981	MON	85 X 68 EA	HMP	1 EA	Varies	2000	16000
Hearts of Swan (Black Bottom) (4 Panels)	TGL	TGL	1981	MON	84 X 69 EA	HMP	1 EA	Varies	2000	16000
Hearts of Swan (Bottom Lined) (4 Panels)	TGL	TGL	1981	MON	85 X 70 EA	HMP	1 EA	Varies	2000	16000
Straightback Swans I (4 Panels)	TGL	TGL	1981	MON	87 X 71 EA	HMP	1 EA	Varies	2000	16000
Straightback Swans II (4 Panels)	TGL	TGL	1981	MON	87 X 71 EA	HMP	1 EA	Varies	2000	16000
Swan Mallow (4 Panels)	TGL	TGL	1981	MON	44 X 127 EA	HMP	1 EA	Varies	3000	12000
Longwater Lilies (3 Panels)	TGL	TGL	1981	MON	35 X 124 EA	HMP	1 EA	Varies	3000	12000
Double Green Geese (Dark Braid) (3 Panels)	TGL	TGL	1981	MON	64 X 48 EA	HMP	1 EA	Varies	2000	14000
Double Green Geese (Palmed) (3 Panels)	TGL	TGL	1981	MON	65 X 48 EA	HMP	1 EA	Varies	2000	14000

ROBERT ZAKANITCH CONTINUED

TITLE	PUBLISHER	PRINTER	DATE	MEDIUM	DIMENSION (PAPER SIZE) IN INCHES	TYPE OF PAPER	EDITION NUMBER	NO. OF COLORS	ORIGINAL OPENING PRICE	CURRENT RETAIL PRICE
SOLD OUT EDITIONS (RARE):										
Double Green Geese (Braided) (3 Panels)	TGL	TGL	1981	MON	64 X 48 EA	HMP	1 EA	Varies	2000	14000
Night Stepper I (3 Panels)	TGL	TGL	1981	MON	71 X 49 EA	HMP	1 EA	Varies	2000	12000
Night Stepper II (3 Panels)	TGL	TGL	1981	MON	69 X 48 EA	HMP	1 EA	Varies	2000	12000
Double Geese Gourds (3 Panels)	TGL	TGL	1981	MON	69 X 48 EA	HMP	1 EA	Varies	2000	12000
Veranda (3 Panels)	TGL	TGL	1981	MON	64 X 48 EA	HMP	1 EA	Varies	2000	12000
Shadrack (3 Panels)	TGL	TGL	1981	MON	72 X 51 EA	HMP	1 EA	Varies	2000	8000
Red Thunder (3 Panels)	TGL	TGL	1981	MON	72 X 51 EA	HMP	1 EA	Varies	2000	8000
Frog Lilies Sofa (2 Panels)	TGL	TGL	1981	MON	34 X 86 EA	HMP	1 EA	Varies	3000	8000
Pickled Mallows	TGL	TGL	1981	MON	44 X 34 EA	HMP	1 EA	Varies	2000	8000
Glories of Morning	TGL	TGL	1981	MON	49 X 39 EA	HMP	1 EA	Varies	2000	8000
Thrush	TGL	TGL	1981	MON	37 X 50 EA	HMP	1 EA	Varies	2000	8000
Cameo Basket	TGL	TGL	1981	MON	43 X 48 EA	HMP	1 EA	Varies	2000	8000
Double Peacock (Colored and Pressed Paper Pulp) (Series of 21)	TGL	TGL	1981	MON	48 X 36 EA	HMP	1 EA		2000	7500 EA
Angel Food	TI	ART/LA/MJS/TI	1986		63 X 32	MUL/AP-ROL	39	6	600	1300
White Feet	TI	TI	1986						500	950
CURRENT EDITIONS:										
Tampa Yellow Series	B-CEd	B-CS	1992	SP/MON/HC	23 X 30 EA	LEN	8 EA	Multi	2000 EA	2000 EA
Sportsman Series (Dipt)	B-CEd	B-CS	1992	SP/MON/HC	22 X 56 EA	LEN	1 EA	Multi	3500 EA	3500 EA
Sportsman Series	B-CEd	B-CS	1992	SP/MON/HC	22 X 30 EA	LEN	5 EA	Multi	2000 EA	2000 EA
Fly Fishing Series	B-CEd	B-CS	1992	SP/MON/HC	22 X 30 EA	LEN	11 EA	Multi	2000 EA	2000 EA
Fly Fishing Series	B-CEd	B-CS	1992	SP/MON/HC	38 X 50 EA	LEN	37 EA	Multi	5000 EA	5000 EA

DUANE ZALOUDEK

BORN: Enid, OK; January 15, 1931
EDUCATION: Portland Mus Art Sch, OR, Certificate, 1956
TEACHING: Artist in Res, Portland Univ, OR, 1962–65; Vis Artist, Univ of California, Davis, CA, 1970–73
AWARDS: Adolph Gottleib Found Award, 1978; Mark Rothko Found Award, 1986; Nat Endowment for the Arts Fel, 1987
PRINTERS: Jack Lemon, Chicago, IL (JL); Landfall Press, Inc., Chicago, IL (LPI)
PUBLISHERS: Landfall Press, Inc, Chicago, IL (LPI)
GALLERIES: Landfall Press, Inc, Chicago, IL; Mark Muller Gallery Zurich, Switzerland; Quartet Editions, New York, NY
MAILING ADDRESS: 431 E 12th St, New York, NY 10009

TITLE	PUBLISHER	PRINTER	DATE	MEDIUM	DIMENSION (PAPER SIZE) IN INCHES	TYPE OF PAPER	EDITION NUMBER	NO. OF COLORS	ORIGINAL OPENING PRICE	CURRENT RETAIL PRICE
CURRENT EDITIONS:										
Untitled	LPI	JL/LPI	1991	EB/CC	30 X 28	R/BFK	20	1	600	600
Untitled	LPI	JL/LPI	1991	EMB	30 X 28	R/BFK	20	1	600	600

MARTHA ZELT

BORN: Washington, PA; November 16, 1930
EDUCATION: Connecticut Col, New London, CT, 1948–50; Pennsylvania Acad of Fine Arts, Phila, PA, 1950–55; New Sch for Social Research, NY; Mus of Mod Art, Brazil; Univ of New Mexico, Albuquerque, NM; Temple Univ, Tyler Sch of Art, Phila, PA, BA, 1968
TEACHING: Res Printmaker, Virginia Mus of Fine Arts, Richmond, VA, 1975; Instr, Printmaking, Pennsylvania Acad of Fine Arts, Phila, PA, 1968–82; Instr, Printmaking, Philadelphia Col of Art, PA, 1969–82; Res Printmaker, Univ of North Carolina, Chapel Hill, NC, 1981; Distinguished Vis Prof, Univ of Delaware, Newark, DE, 1988–89
AWARDS: Cresson Traveling Award, Pennsylvania Acad of Fine Arts, Phila, PA, 1954; Scheidt Mem Traveling Award, Pennsylvania Acad of Fine Arts, Phila, PA, 1954; Philadelphia Print Club, PA, Fel, 1965; Roswell Mus Grant, NM, 1982; Purchase Award, Colorprint, USA, Texas Tech Univ, Lubbock, TX, 1982; Percy Owens Award, Pennsylvania Acad of Fine Arts, Phila, PA, 1983; Roswell Mus, Artist-in-Residence, NM, 1989
RECENT EXHIB: Univ of Dallas, Irving, TX, 1991
COLLECTIONS: Carnegie Inst, Pittsburgh, PA; Pennsylvania Acad of Fine Arts, Phila, PA; Philadelphia Art Mus, PA; Brooklyn Mus, NY; Princeton Univ, NJ; Rhode Island Sch of Design, Providence, RI; Yale Univ, New Haven, CT
PRINTERS: Pyramid Press, Baltimore, MD (PyrP); Catherine Kuhn, Albuquerque, NM (CK); Wayne Kline, Albuquerque, NM (WK); Lynne Allen, Albuquerque, NM (LA); Molly Jo Sounders, Albuquerque, NM (MJS); Tom Pruitt, Albuquerque, NM (TP); Artist (ART); Tamarind Inst, Albuquerque, NM (TI)
PUBLISHERS: Tamarind Inst, Albuquerque, NM (TI); Dolan/Maxwell Gallery, Phila, PA (DMG)
GALLERIES: Tamarind Inst, Albuquerque, NM; Hodges Taylor Gallery, Charlotte, NC; Campbell Gallery, Greenville, SC
MAILING ADDRESS: 1301 North Montana Ave, Roswell, NM 88201

TITLE	PUBLISHER	PRINTER	DATE	MEDIUM	DIMENSION (PAPER SIZE) IN INCHES	TYPE OF PAPER	EDITION NUMBER	NO. OF COLORS	ORIGINAL OPENING PRICE	CURRENT RETAIL PRICE
SOLD OUT EDITIONS (RARE):										
Return to A-qq (Set of 3):									1200 SET	3000 SET
Return to A-qq #1	TI	WK/TI	1983	LC	26 X 22	HMP/R-BFK	25	7	500	1200
Return to A-qq #2	TI	LA/TI	1983	LC	26 X 31	AP/BL-R-BFK	25	7	500	1200
Return to A-qq #3	TI	CK/TI	1983	LC	21 X 27	R/BFK	20	6	500	1200
Another Time	DMG	PyrP	1985	ASSEM	40 X 30	HMP	20	Varies	900	1500
CURRENT EDITIONS:										
Grey Cat	TI	ART/MJS/TI	1986	LC/CO	38 X 30 X 1	R-BFK/JP	24	7	600	900
Milagro para Angela	TI	ART/TP/TI	1986	LC/CO	38 X 30 X 1	RP/T	22	5	600	900

MARCO ZAMBRELLI

PRINTERS: Artist (ART)
PUBLISHERS: John Szoke Graphics, Inc, NY (JSG)
GALLERIES: John Szoke Graphics, Inc, New York, NY

TITLE	PUBLISHER	PRINTER	DATE	MEDIUM	DIMENSION (PAPER SIZE) IN INCHES	TYPE OF PAPER	EDITION NUMBER	NO. OF COLORS	ORIGINAL OPENING PRICE	CURRENT RETAIL PRICE
CURRENT EDITIONS:										
Summertime I,II	JSG	ART	1990	EC	23 X 20 EA	R/BFK/CO	100 EA	6 EA	300 EA	300 EA

JOSEPH ZIRKER

BORN: Los Angeles, CA; August 13, 1924
EDUCATION: Univ of California, Los Angeles, CA, 1943–44, 1946–47; Univ of Denver, CO, BFA, 1948–49, with Jules Heller; Univ of Southern California, Los Angeles, CA, MFA, 1949–51
TEACHING: Lect, Printmaking Univ of Southern California, Los Angeles, CA, 1951,63; Los Angeles County Art Inst, Otis, CA, 1963–64; Instr, Drawing, San Jose City Col, CA, 1966–82; Lectr, Standford Univ, CA, 1981–83,86
AWARDS: Tamarind Fel, Albuquerque, NM, 1962,63,64
RECENT EXHIB: Quincy Col, Gray Gallery, Quincy, IL 1992
COLLECTIONS: Arizona State Univ, Tempe, AZ; Achenbach Found for the Graphic Arts, San Francisco, CA; San Diego Mus, CA; DaSaisset Art Mus, Univ of Santa Clara, CA; Idaho Col, Caldwell, ID; Los Angeles County Mus, CA; Brooklyn Mus, NY
PRINTERS: Smith Andersen Gallery, Palo Alto, CA (SA)
PUBLISHERS: Smith Andersen Gallery, Palo Alto, CA (SA)
GALLERIES: Klein Gallery, Chicago, IL; Alice Simsar Gallery, Ann Arbor, MI; Smith Andersen Gallery, Palo Alto, CA; Perimeter Gallery, Chicago, IL
MAILING ADDRESS: 451 O'Connor St, Menlo Park, CA 94025

TITLE	PUBLISHER	PRINTER	DATE	MEDIUM	DIMENSION (PAPER SIZE) IN INCHES	TYPE OF PAPER	EDITION NUMBER	NO. OF COLORS	ORIGINAL OPENING PRICE	CURRENT RETAIL PRICE
SOLD OUT EDITIONS (RARE):										
Cosmic Landscape	SA	SA	1981	MON	11 X 11 EA	R/BFK	1 EA	Varies	300 EA	500 EA
CURRENT EDITIONS:										
Cosmic Entity	SA	SA	1981	MON	30 X 22 EA	R/BFK	1 EA	Varies	500 EA	1200 EA
Cosmic Entity	SA	SA	1981	EB	15 X 11	R/BFK	26	1	150	300
Cosmic Entity States I–IV	SA	SA	1982	EB	Varies	R/BFK		1	250 EA	600 EA
Cosmic Landscapes	SA	SA	1982	MON	21 X 21 EA	R/BFK	1 EA	Varies	400 EA	1200 EA
Cosmic Fragments	SA	SA	1982	MON	30 X 30 EA	R/BFK	1 EA	Varies	500 EA	1500 EA
Cosmic Window	SA	SA	1982	MON	42 X 30 EA	R/BFK	1 EA	Varies	600 EA	2000 EA

ANDERS LEONARD ZORN

BORN: Sweden; (1860–1920)
PRINTERS: Artist (ART)
PUBLISHERS: Artist (ART)

TITLE	PUBLISHER	PRINTER	DATE	MEDIUM	DIMENSION (PAPER SIZE) IN INCHES	TYPE OF PAPER	EDITION NUMBER	NO. OF COLORS	ORIGINAL OPENING PRICE	CURRENT RETAIL PRICE
SOLD OUT EDITIONS (RARE):										
The Waltz	ART	ART	1891	EB	13 X 9	LAID	40	1	20	4500
Ernest Renan	ART	ART	1892	EB	9 X 13	LAID		1	20	3800
The Toast	ART	ART	1893	PH/G	12 X 10	LAID		1	15	600
Henry Marquand	ART	ART	1893	EB	11 X 8	LAID	35	1	30	5500
Paul Verlaine	ART	ART	1895	EB	10 X 6	LAID		1	20	900
Portrait of Edward Bacon	ART	ART	1897	EB	9 X 6	LAID			25	1000
Billiards	ART	ART	1898	EB	7 X 5	LAID		1	30	2200
President Grover Cleveland	ART	ART	1899	EB	9 X 7	LAID		1	35	5000
Billy Bacon, Sénateur . . .	ART	ART	1900	EB	8 X 6	LAID	350	1	30	800
Self Portrait I	ART	ART	1904	EB	7 X 5	WOVE		1	20	850
Dance at Gopsmor	ART	ART	1906	EB	11 X 8	WOVE		1	40	2000
Le Musicien de Village	ART	ART	1907	EB	6 X 5	WOVE		1	30	500
Summer	ART	ART	1907	EB	7 X 5	WOVE		1	30	500
The Village Violinist	ART	ART	1907	EB	6 X 5	WOVE		1	30	450
Queen Sophia	ART	ART	1909	EB	10 X 7	WOVE		1	40	1800
Mona	ART	ART	1911	EB	10 X 7	WOVE		1	40	800
Frightened	ART	ART	1912	EB	8 X 6	WOVE		1	50	2000
The Letter	ART	ART	1913	EB	6 X 5	WOVE		1	50	1800
Crown Princess Margaret . . .	ART	ART	1914	EB	10 X 7	WOVE		1	60	2500
The Swan	ART	ART	1915	EB	10 X 8	WOVE		1	60	2500
The Two	ART	ART	1916	EB	8 X 6	WOVE		1	75	2500
Self Portrait in Fur Coat	ART	ART	1916	EB	7 X 5	WOVE		1	75	1500
On Hemslo Island	ART	ART	1917	EB	8 X 6	WOVE		1	75	1800
Dal River	ART	ART	1919	EB	7 X 5	WOVE		1	85	1500

LARRY ZOX

BORN: Des Moines, IA, May 31, 1936
EDUCATION: Univ of Oklahoma, Norman, OK; Drake Univ, Des Moines, IA; Des Moines Art Center, IA, with George Grosz
TEACHING: Artist in Res, Juniata Col, Huntington, PA, 1964; Cornell Univ, Ithaca, NY, 1967; Univ of North Carolina, Greensboro, NC, 1967; Dartmouth Col, Hanover, NH, 1969; Sch of Visual Arts, NY, 1967–70; Yale Univ, New Haven, CT, 1972
AWARDS: Guggenheim Fel, 1967; Nat Council of Arts Award, 1969; Esther and Adolph Gottlieb Found Grant, 1985
RECENT EXHIB: Univ of Richmond, Marsh Gallery, VA, 1992
COLLECTIONS: Metropolitan Mus of Art, NY; Mus of Mod Art, NY; Whitney Mus of Am Art, NY; Mus of Fine Arts, Houston, TX; Tate Gallery, London, England; Cornell Univ, Ithaca, NY; Hirshhorn Mus, Wash, DC; Dallas Mus of Fine Arts, TX; Indianapolis Mus of Art, IN; Oberlin Col, OH; Solomon R Guggenheim Mus, NY; Philip Johnson Coll; Mus of Fine Arts, Boston, MA; Art Inst of Chicago, IL

LARRY ZOX CONTINUED

PRINTERS: Chip Elwell, NY (CE); Joseph Kleineman, NY (JK) Alpha Omega (AO); Larry B Wright, NY (LBW); Sabina Klein Studio, NY (SKS); Roni Henning, NY (RH); NYIT Screen Print Workshop, Old Westbury, NY (NYIT/SPW)
PUBLISHERS: Barbara Gladstone Editions, NY (BGE); London Arts, Inc, Detroit, MI (LAI); Post Oak Fine Art Distributors, Houston, TX, (POFA); John Szoke Graphics, Inc, NY (JSG); Images Gallery, Toledo, OH (IG)

GALLERIES: André Emmerich, New York, NY; Douglas Drake Gallery, New York, NY; Rubiner Gallery, West Bloomfield, MI; Salander-O'Reilly Galleries, New York, NY & Beverly Hills, CA; Images Gallery, Toledo, OH; Ann Jaffe Gallery, Bay Harbor Islands, FL; Percival Galleries, Des Moines, IA; John Szoke Graphics, New York, NY; Faber Fine Arts, Secaucus, NY; Brooke Alexander Editions, New York, NY

TITLE	PUBLISHER	PRINTER	DATE	MEDIUM	DIMENSION (PAPER SIZE) IN INCHES	TYPE OF PAPER	EDITION NUMBER	NO. OF COLORS	ORIGINAL OPENING PRICE	CURRENT RETAIL PRICE
SOLD OUT EDITIONS (RARE):										
Stencil Series	BGE	CE	1977	PO	23 X 22	AP	20	12	550	1200
Prussian Blue	BGE	CE	1978	PO	31 X 26	AP	35	19	350	1200
Untitled	BGE	CE	1978	PO	30 X 22	AP	11	11	550	1200
Untitled, a, b, c, d	BGE	CE	1979	PO	34 X 27	AP	40	22	550	1200
Untitled	BGE	CE	1980	PO	34 X 37	AP	30	16	650	1200
CURRENT EDITIONS:										
Untitled 1981 (3 States):										
Grey	BGE	CE	1981	PO	29 X 40	AP	30	14	600	1500
Yellow	BGE	CE	1981	PO	29 X 40	AP	30	14	600	1200
Rose	BGE	CE	1981	PO	29 X 40	AP	30	14	600	1200
Niagara Series:										
Niagara Series #1	LAI	JK	1981	LI	26 X 35	AP	175	8	325	750
Niagara Series #2	POFA	AD	1981	LI	40 X 20	AP	175	11	325	750
Niagara Series #3 (Gray-Orange)	LAI	JK	1981	LI	43 X 30	AP	88	4	325	750
Niagara Series #3 (Orange-Gray)	LAI	JK	1981	LI	43 X 30	AP	88	4	325	750
Niagara Series #4	LAI	JK	1981	LI	26 X 35	AP	175	5	325	750
Niagara Series #5	POFA	AD	1981	LI	42 X 30	AP	175	5	325	750
Bostwick Crown, State I (#1–#22)	JSG	CE	1986	PO	42 X 36	AC	22	15	1000	1500
Bostwick Crown, State II (#23–#45)	JSG	CE	1986	PO	42 X 36	AC	23	15	1000	1500
Cotulla, State I (#1–#22)	JSG	CE/LBW	1986	PO	38 X 45	AC	22	15	1000	1500
Cotulla, State II (#23–#45)	JSG	CE/LBW	1986	PO	38 X 45	AC	23	15	1000	1500
Grand Codroy, State I (#1–#22)	JSG	LBW	1988	PO	40 X 60	AP/WA	22	15	1200	1800
Grand Codroy, State II (#23–#45)	JSG	LBW	1988	PO	40 X 60	AP/WA	23	15	1200	1800
Chiyuga, States I,II,III	JSG	SKS	1990	PO	18 X 20 EA	AP/WA	23 EA	10 EA	750 EA	750 EA
Dexter's Choice I,II	IG	RH/NYIT/SPW	1993	PO	40 X 60 EA	AC	30 EA		2600	2600
Nazca Ridge I	JSG	SKS	1993	PO	40 X 60	AP/WA	35	12	1800	1800
Nazca Ridge II	JSG	SKS	1993	PO	40 X 60	AP/WA	35	13	1800	1800

ZU MING HO

BORN: Shanghai, China; August 26, 1949
EDUCATION: Shanghai Drama Inst, Dept of Fine Arts, Painting, BFA 1978; California State Univ, Los Angeles, CA, MFA, 1988
TEACHING: Vice-Chancellor, JiaZhou Painting Acad, Shanghai, China, 1985

RECENT EXHIB: Pacific Rim Fine Art, Los Angeles, CA, 1988; Promenade Gallery, Santa Monica, CA, 1989
PRINTERS: Hue Art Studio, Gardena, CA (HAS); Kato Art Studio, Torrance, CA (KAS)
PUBLISHERS: Pacific Rim Fine Art, Los Angeles, CA (PRFA); Blinder Fine Arts, Inc, Santa Monica, CA (BFA)
GALLERIES: Silver K Gallery, Melbourne, Australia; Nan Miller Gallery, Rochester, NY; Studio 53, New York, NY; Emporium Enterprises, Dallas, TX

TITLE	PUBLISHER	PRINTER	DATE	MEDIUM	DIMENSION (PAPER SIZE) IN INCHES	TYPE OF PAPER	EDITION NUMBER	NO. OF COLORS	ORIGINAL OPENING PRICE	CURRENT RETAIL PRICE
CURRENT EDITIONS:										
Ma Qui Polo		HAS	1990	SP	31 X 30	WWP	450	35	550	750
Beneath the Waterfall		HAS	1990	SP	31 X 30	WWP	450	35	550	750
Freedom to Fly		KAS	1990	SP	35 X 34	WWP	450	35	700	850

TERRI ZUPANC

PRINTERS: Jack Lemon, Chicago, IL (JL); Landfall Press, Inc, Chicago, IL (LPI)
PUBLISHERS: Landfall Press, Inc, Chicago, IL (LPI)
GALLERIES: Landfall Press, Inc, Chicago, IL; Quartet Editions, New York, NY

TITLE	PUBLISHER	PRINTER	DATE	MEDIUM	DIMENSION (PAPER SIZE) IN INCHES	TYPE OF PAPER	EDITION NUMBER	NO. OF COLORS	ORIGINAL OPENING PRICE	CURRENT RETAIL PRICE
CURRENT EDITIONS:										
Untitled-A	LPI	JL/LPI	1990	MON	33 X 42 EA	SOM	1 EA	Varies	1200	1200
Untitled-B	LPI	JL/LPI	1990	MON	33 X 42 EA	SOM	1 EA	Varies	1200	1200
Untitled-C	LPI	JL/LPI	1990	MON	33 X 42 EA	SOM	1 EA	Varies	1200	1200
Untitled-D	LPI	JL/LPI	1990	MON	22 X 30 EA	SOM	1 EA	Varies	700	700
Untitled-E	LPI	JL/LPI	1990	MON	22 X 30 EA	SOM	1 EA	Varies	700	700
Untitled-F	LPI	JL/LPI	1990	MON	24 X 40 EA	SOM	1 EA	Varies	700	700

The retail prices of the 100,000 limited edition prints quoted in this directory are subject to change. Print publishers, artists and galleries were the direct sources for these quotations. Prices in the secondary market listed as "Sold Out Editions (Rare)" indicate that the publisher has a limited supply of that print or that the print is difficult to locate in the galleries.

JOSEPH ZUCKER

BORN: Chicago, IL; May 21, 1941
EDUCATION: Miami Univ, FL, 1959–60; Art Inst of Chicago, IL, BFA, 1964; MFA, 1966
TEACHING: Instr, Painting, Minneapolis Sch of Art, MN, 1966–68; Sch of Visual Arts, NY, 1968–71; New York Univ, 1971–74
AWARDS: First Prize & Special Jury Awards, Minneapolis inst of Art Biennial, MN, 1965; Second Prize & Purchase Award, Walker Art Center Biennial, Minneapolis, MN, 1966
RECENT EXHIB: Arts Club of Chicago, IL, 1988; Texas Gallery, Houston, TX, 1988; Carol Getz Gallery, Coconut Grove, FL, 1988; Hirsch & Adler Modern, NY, 1989
COLLECTIONS: Metropolitan Mus of Art, NY; Mus of Mod Art, NY; Whitney Mus of Am Art, NY; Albright-Knox Art Gallery, Buffalo, NY; Addison Gallery of Am Art, Phillips Acad, Andover, MA; Australian Nat Gallery, Canberra, Australia; Contemp Arts Center, Honolulu, HI; Denver Art Mus, CO; Mod Art Mus of Fort Worth, TX; High Mus of Art, Atlanta, GA; Inst for Experimental Printmaking, San Francisco, CA; Mem Art Gallery, Univ of Rochester, NY; Mus Mod Kunst, Palais Liechtenstein, Vienna, Austria; Art Gallery of Ontario, Toronto, Canada; Nat Gallery of Victoria, Melbourne, Australia; Neue Galerie Sammlung Ludwig, Aachen, West Germany; Mus of Contemp Art, La Jolla, CA; Sydney & Frances Lewis Collection, Richmond, VA; Treat Gallery, Bates Col, Lewiston, ME; Walker Art Center, Minneapolis, MN; Philadelphia Mus of Art, PA
PRINTERS: Experimental Printmaking, NY (EP); Judith Solodkin, NY (JS); Solo Press, NY (SP); Joe Wilfer, NY (JW); Ruth Lingen, NY (RL); Bill Hall, NY (BH); Spring Street Workshop, NY (SprSW); Patricia Branstead, NY (PB); Riverhouse Editions, Clark, CO (REd)
PUBLISHERS: Holly Solomon Editions, Ltd, NY (HSE); Pace Editions, NY (PE); Solo Press, NY (SP); Spring Street Workshop, NY (SprSW); Riverhouse Editions, Clark, CO (REd)
GALLERIES: Holly Solomon Editions, Ltd, New York, NY; Pace Prints, New York, NY; McIntosh/Drysdale Gallery, Wash, DC; Dart Gallery, Chicago, IL; Nina Freudenheim Gallery, Buffalo, NY; Texas Gallery, Houston, TX; Brentwood Gallery, St Louis, MO; Fay Gold Gallery, Atlanta, GA; Susanne Hilberry Gallery, Birmingham, MI; Hirschl & Adler Modern, New York, NY; Solo Press, New York, NY; Van Straaten Gallery, Chicago, IL
MAILING ADDRESS: PO Box 553, Wainscott, NY 11975

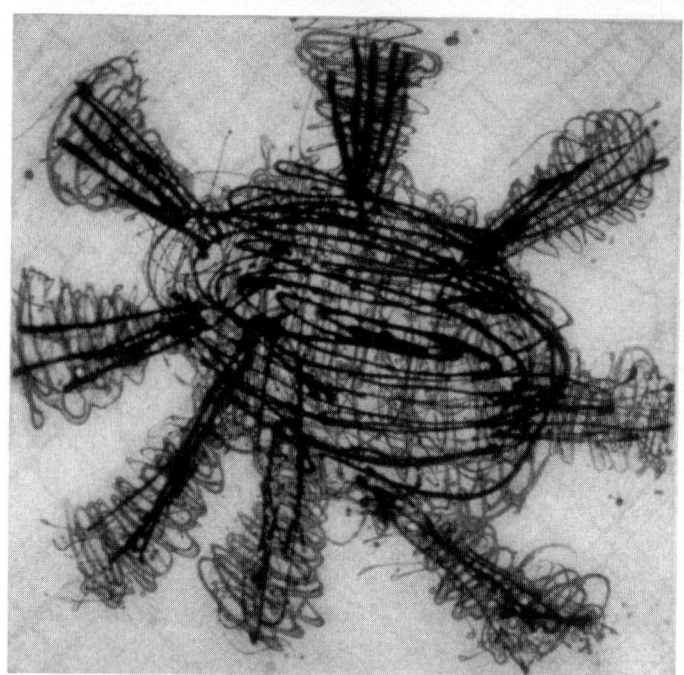

Joseph Zucker
Nephilia
Courtesy Van Straaten Gallery

TITLE	PUBLISHER	PRINTER	DATE	MEDIUM	DIMENSION (PAPER SIZE) IN INCHES	TYPE OF PAPER	EDITION NUMBER	NO. OF COLORS	ORIGINAL OPENING PRICE	CURRENT RETAIL PRICE
SOLD OUT EDITIONS (RARE):										
Toucan	PE	EP	1980	SP	36 X 36	RAG	36		3500	12000
Candles	PE	EP	1980	SP	36 X 36	RAG	36		2500	8000
Ponce de Leon Series (Set of 5):									8500 SET	8500 SET
Ponce de Leon's Flagship	SP	JS/SP	1984	LC/FOIL	36 X 48	THS	18		2000	2200
Ponce Duels Seminole Chief Misha Gosh	SP	JS/SP	1984	LC/FOIL	36 X 48	THS	18		2000	2200
Death of the Conquistador	SP	JS/SP	1984	LC/FOIL	36 X 48	THS	18		2000	2200
The Awful Heat Wastes Man and Beast	SP	JS/SP	1984	LC/FOIL	36 X 48	THS	18		2000	2200
Deadly Anapholes	SP	JS/SP	1984	LC/FOIL	36 X 48	THS	18		2000	2200
CURRENT EDITIONS:										
Dap	SprSW	JS/RL/SprSW	1989	EB/A/SB	23 X 22	SOM	35		700	700
Cryro-genics	SprSW	JS/RL/SprSW	1989	EB/A/SB	23 X 22	SOM	35		700	700
Cochise Series (Set of 3):									1500 SET	1500 SET
Arrow	SprSW	BH/JS/RL/SprSW	1989	EB/SB	16 X 30	SOM	30		700	700
Scalp	SprSW	BH/JS/RL/SprSW	1989	EB/SB	16 X 30	SOM	30		700	700
Mr Cochise	SprSW	BH/JS/RL/SprSW	1989	EB/SB	16 X 30	SOM	30		700	700
Spider	REd	PB/REd	1991	EC	24 X 22	AP	20	1	250	250
Spider Chronicles	REd	PB/REd	1991	EC	36 X 36	UNRYU/W	40	1	600	600
Black Morse Code Web	REd	PB/REd	1991	EC	36 X 36	UNRYU/BL	40	2	600	600
White Morse Code Web	REd	PB/REd	1991	EC	36 X 36	UNRYU/W	40	2	600	600
Nephilia	REd	PB/REd	1991	EC	36 X 36	UNRYU/W	40	3	600	600
Tarantula	REd	PB/REd	1991	EC	36 X 36	UNRYU/W	40	3	600	600
Life and Times of an Orb Weaver	REd	PB/REd	1991	EC	36 X 36	UNRYU/W	40	1	600	600

MURRAY HARVEY ZUCKER

BORN: New York, NY; December 14, 1920
EDUCATION: AM Soc of Contemp Artists, Heydenryk Award, 1976; Kulicke Award, Graphics, 1978; Feigin Award, Graphics, 1981
AWARDS: First Prize, Graphics, Am Soc of Contemp Art, 1976; Kulicke Award for Graphics, 1978; Feigin Award for Graphics, 1981
COLLECTIONS: Butler Inst of Am Art, Youngstown, OH; Slater Mem Mus, CT
PRINTERS: Artist (ART)
PUBLISHERS: Grippi Gallery, NY (GG)
GALLERIES: Roads Art Gallery, New York, NY
MAILING ADDRESS: 54 Cosdrew Lane, East Hampton, NY 11937

The print market has become very selective. For the first time since we published the first edition of The Printworld Directory in 1982, the prices of prints have been greatly reduced and greatly increased for the same artists by the most reputable and established print publishers. Check the fifth edition to understand the movement.

MURRAY HARVEY ZUCKER CONTINUED

TITLE	PUBLISHER	PRINTER	DATE	MEDIUM	DIMENSION (PAPER SIZE) IN INCHES	TYPE OF PAPER	EDITION NUMBER	NO. OF COLORS	ORIGINAL OPENING PRICE	CURRENT RETAIL PRICE
SOLD OUT EDITIONS (RARE):										
Ionization	GG	ART	1975	SP	27 X 36	AP	200	1	75	150
Laser II	GG	ART	1975	SP	24 X 24	AP	175	5	75	150
Windows On Red	GG	ART	1978	CO/M	18 X 24	AP	25	7	175	250
Corn Dancer	GG	ART	1979	CO/M	17 X 24	AP	25	7	175	250
Frisbee	GG	ART	1979	CO/M	17 X 24	AP	25	3	150	250
Interlude	GG	ART	1979	CO/M	17 X 24	AP	25	5	175	250
Sound Track	GG	ART	1979	CO/M	17 X 24	AP	25	4	175	250
Marina	GG	ART	1979	CO/M	17 X 24	AP	25	3	150	225
Shattered Image	GG	ART	1979	CO/M	17 X 24	AP	25	4	175	250
Glyph I	GG	ART	1979	CO/M	18 X 24	AP	25	5	150	225
Glyph IV	GG	ART	1979	CO/M	10 X 24	AP	25		150	225
Graffiti IV	GG	ART	1979	CO/M	17 X 24	AP	25	5	150	225
Graffiti III	GG	ART	1979	CO/M	17 X 24	AP	25	2	150	225
Crocus	GG	ART	1979	CO/M	18 X 24	AP	25	5	100	175
Corona	GG	ART	1980	CO/M	18 X 24	AP	25	3	100	175

MICHAEL ZWACK

BORN: Buffalo, NY; 1949
EDUCATION: State Univ of New York, Buffalo, NY, BA, 1970
RECENT EXHIB: Curt Marcus Gallery, NY, 1987
PRINTERS: Judith Solodkin, NY (JS); Solo Press, NY (SP); Dan Stack, NY (DS)
PUBLISHERS: Solo Press, NY (SP)
GALLERIES: Michael Kohn Gallery, Santa Monica, CA; Curt Marcus Gallery, New York, NY; Joe Fawbush Editions, New York, NY; Solo Gallery, New York, NY; Betsy Rosenfield Gallery, Chicago, IL

TITLE	PUBLISHER	PRINTER	DATE	MEDIUM	DIMENSION (PAPER SIZE) IN INCHES	TYPE OF PAPER	EDITION NUMBER	NO. OF COLORS	ORIGINAL OPENING PRICE	CURRENT RETAIL PRICE
CURRENT EDITIONS:										
History of the World	SP	JS/DS/SP	1986	LC/HC	22 X 28	R/BFK/CR	20	Varies	900	1200

ROSEMARY ZWICK

BORN: Chicago, IL; July 13, 1925
EDUCATION: State Univ of Iowa, Iowa City, IA, BFA, 1945, with Phillip Guston; Sch of Art Inst of Chicago, IL, Lithography, 1946–47; De Paul Univ, Chicago, IL, 1946–47
RECENT EXHIB: Triangle Gallery, Chicago, IL, 1990
COLLECTIONS: Antioch Col, Yellow Springs, OH; Albion Col, MI; Art Inst of Chicago, IL
PRINTERS: Artist (ART)
PUBLISHERS: Artist (ART)
GALLERIES: Four Arts Gallery, Evanston, IL
MAILING ADDRESS: 1720 Washington St, Evanston, IL 60202

TITLE	PUBLISHER	PRINTER	DATE	MEDIUM	DIMENSION (PAPER SIZE) IN INCHES	TYPE OF PAPER	EDITION NUMBER	NO. OF COLORS	ORIGINAL OPENING PRICE	CURRENT RETAIL PRICE
CURRENT EDITIONS:										
Pale Moon	ART	ART	1974	WC	18 X 23	HOSHO	23	3	100	150
Riders	ART	ART	1974	WC	18 X 23	HOSHO	23	3	100	150
Tiki and Sunshine	ART	ART	1974	WC	19 X 25	KOZO	50	3	100	150
Dunes and Sandpipers (Engraving on Plastic Plate)	ART	ART	1976	ENG/HC	19 X 25	R/BFK	25	Varies	100	150
Pebble Beach Seals	ART	ART	1978	EB/HC	15 X 22	R/BFK	25	Varies	85	150
Balancing	ART	ART	1978	EC	10 X 22	R/BFK	30	2	75	125
In Line	ART	ART	1980	EC	12 X 26	R/BFK	15	5	85	125
I-80	ART	ART	1980	EC	18 X 27	R/BFK	25	5	150	175
Dusk	ART	ART	1986	EC	19 X 27	R/BFK	20	3	200	225
Empire Beach at 4	ART	ART	1986	EC	19 X 27	R/BFK	20	3	200	225
Autumn Trees	ART	ART	1990	WC	19 X 24	HOSHO	20	5	225	225
Lincoln Park Zoo	ART	ART	1991	WC	19 X 24	HOSHO	20	4	200	200
Wind	ART	ART	1991–92	WC	19 X 24	HOSHO	25	5	250	250
City & Lake	ART	ART	1992	WC	19 X 24	HOSHO	25	5	250	250
Jaz I, II	ART	ART	1992	WC	16 X 20	KOZO	25	4	200	200

FRANCISCO ZUÑIGA

BORN: San Jose, Costa Rica; December 27, 1912
EDUCATION: La Esmerald Sch of Painting & Sculpture, Mexico City, Mexico, 1936
TEACHING: La Esmeralda Sch of Painting & Sculpture, Mexico City, Mexico, 1938–70
AWARDS: First Prize, Salon of Mexican Plastic Arts, Mexico, 1957; Aquisition Prize, Middelheim Open Air Mus, Antwerp, Belgium, 1971; Nat Prize, Costa Rica, 1979; Nomina di Accademico con Medaglia d'Oro, Parma, Italy, 1981
RECENT EXHIB: Univ of California, Los Angeles, CA, 1989
COLLECTIONS: Fogg Art Mus, Univ of Harvard Univ, Cambridge, MA; Hirshhorn Mus, Wash, DC; Nat Inst of Fine Arts, Mexico City, Mexico; Los Angeles County Mus, CA; Metropolitan Mus, NY; Musee Middelheim, Antwerp, Belgium; Mus of Mod Art, NY; Univ of Haifa, Israel; Yale Univ, New Haven, CT
PRINTERS: Kyron Press, Mexico City, Mexico (KP); Mourlot Atelier, Paris, France (MA); Gasper (GAS); La Poligrafa, SA, Barcelona, Spain (LP); Mixografia Workshop, Los Angeles, CA (MIX)
PUBLISHERS: Ediciones Poligrafa, SA, Barcelona, Spain (EdP); Brewster Editions, NY (BE); Contemporary Art Masters, NY (CAM); Mixografia Workshop, Los Angeles, CA (MIX)

FRANCISCO ZUÑIGA CONTINUED

PRINTERS: Editions Press, San Francisco, CA (EP); Taller de Grafica Mexicana, SA, Mexico (TdG); Kyron, SA, Mexico (Ky); Mourlot Atelier, Paris, France (MAt); La Poligrafa, SA, Barcelona, Spain (LP); Wolfensberger, Zürich, Switzerland (Wolf); Amerian Atelier, NY (AA); Eldindean Press, NY (EldPr) (OB); Artist (ART)

PUBLISHERS: Editions Press, San Francisco, CA (EP); Carton y Papel de Mexico, SA, Mexico (C/P); J M Tasende, Mexico (JMT); Mourlot Atelier, Paris, France (MAt); Fibracél, SA, Mexico (Fib); Graphic Arts Council of Los Angeles County Mus of Art, CA (GAC/LACMA); Brewster Editions, NY (BEd); Ediciones Poligrafa, SA, Barcelona, Spain (EdP); Mixografia Workshop, Santa Monica, CA (MIX); Gallery Börjeson, Malmö, Sweden (GB); Artist (ART)

GALLERIES: Brewster Galleries, New York, NY; B Lewin Gallery, Palm Spring, CA; DeVorzon Gallery, Los Angeles, CA; Harcourts Modern & Contemporary, San Francisco, CA; Marta Gutierrez Fine Arts, Inc, Key Biscayne, FL; River Gallery, Irvington-on-Hudson, NY; Galeria Joan Prats, New York, NY & Barcelona, Spain; Nathan Silberberg Fine Arts, New York, NY; Sindin Gallery, New York, NY; Adams-Middleton Gallery, Dallas, TX; Southwest Gallery, Dallas, TX; Gallery Mack, NW, Seattle, WA; Wolf Schulz Gallery, San Francisco, CA; Charles Whitchurch Fine Arts, Huntington Beach, CA; Mixografia Workshop Gallery, Santa Monica, CA; Pasquale Iannetti Art Galleries, San Francisco, CA; Joanne Lyon Gallery, Aspen, CO; Connecticut Fine Arts, Westport, CT; Phyllis Needlman Gallery, Chicago, IL; Joan Cawley Gallery, Wichita, KS; Carmen Llewellyn Graphics, New Orleans, LA; Adobe Gallery, Albuquerque, NM; Nedra Matteucci's Fenn Galleries, Santa Fe, NM; Mussavi Gallery, New York, NY; Weintraub Gallery, New York, NY; TwoSixtyOne Arts, New York, NY; J Barrett Galleries, Toledo, OH; Ravel Fine Art Association, Austin, TX; Santa Fe Gallery, Madison, WI; Louis Newman Gallery, Beverly Hills, CA; Art Collector, San Diego, CA

Brewster (B); Zuñiga (Z)

Francisco Zuñiga
El Rebozo Blanco
Courtesy Brewster Editions

TITLE	PUBLISHER	PRINTER	DATE	MEDIUM	DIMENSION (PAPER SIZE) IN INCHES	TYPE OF PAPER	EDITION NUMBER	NO. OF COLORS	ORIGINAL OPENING PRICE	CURRENT RETAIL PRICE
SOLD OUT EDITIONS (RARE):										
La Juchiteca (Juchitecan Woman (B-1)	EP	EP	1972	LC	22 X 15	AP	5	3	250	5000
Tres Mujeres Sentadas (Three Seated Women (B-2)	EP	EP	1972	LC	15 X 22	AP	5	3	250	5000
Cuatro Figures (Four Figures) (B-3)	EP	EP	1972	LC	16 X 22	AP	100	2	200	3000
La Espera (the Waiting (B-4)	EP	EP	1973	LC	22 X 30	AP	100	4	250	4500
Mujeres de Mexico (Women of Mexico) (S-5)	EP	EP	1973	LC	22 X 30	AP	100	3	250	4500
Soledad Acostada (Solitude Lying Down) (S-6)	EP	EP	1973	LC	22 X 30	AP	100	4	250	4500
Dos Mujeres con Rebozos, Sentados (Two Women with Shawls, Seated) (B-7)	EP	EP	1973	LC	22 X 30	AP	100	6	250	4500
Mujer de Yucatán con Naranjas (Woman from Yucatan with Oranges) (B-8)	EP	EP	1973	LC	30 X 22	AP	100	8	250	4500
Madre Juchiteca (Juchitecan Mother) (B-9)	EP	EP	1973	LC	22 X 30	AP	100	6	250	4000
Mujer con Rebozo (Woman with Shawl) (B-9)	C/P	TdG	1973	LC	30 X 23	R/BFK	150	2	250	4000
Madre con Niño (Mother & Boy) (B-11)	Ky/JMT	Ky	1973	LC	20 X 25	AP	58	2	300	5000
Grupo de Mujeres Sentadas I (Group of Seated Women I) (B-12)	Ky/JMT	Ky	1974	LC	21 X 27	AP	92	6	250	4500
Juchitecas I (Juchitean Women I) (B-13)	Ky/JMT	Ky	1974	LC	21 X 28	AP	91	8	250	4500
Madre e Hija (Mother & Daughter) (B-14)	Ky/JMT	Ky	1974	LC/SP	21 X 27	FAB	99	7	250	4500
Mujer Sentada con Rebozo (Seated Woman with Shawl) (B-15)	Ky/JMT	Ky	1974	LB	27 X 19	AP	83	3-BL	200	4000
La Visita (The Visit) (B-16)	Ky/JMT	Ky	1974	LB	22 X 28	AP	60	3-BL	250	4500
Tres Mujeres de Pie I (Three Standing Women I) (B-17)	Ky/JMT	Ky	1974	LB	27 X 22	AP	83	2-BL	250	3500
El Umbral (The Threshold) (B-18)	Ky/JMT	Ky	1974	LB/SP	17 X 24	Amate	47	2	300	3500
Mujer con Naranja (Woman with Orange) (B-19)	Ky	Ky	1974	SP	27 X 19	R/BFK	300	4	200	2500

FRANCISCO ZUÑIGA CONTINUED

TITLE	PUBLISHER	PRINTER	DATE	MEDIUM	DIMENSION (PAPER SIZE) IN INCHES	TYPE OF PAPER	EDITION NUMBER	NO. OF COLORS	ORIGINAL OPENING PRICE	CURRENT RETAIL PRICE
SOLD OUT EDITIONS (RARE):										
Dos Juchitecas Sentadas (Two Seated Juchitecas Women) (B-20)	Fib	Ky	1974	LC/SP	21 X 27	AP	100	8	350	4000
Juchiteca Sentada (Seated Juchiteca Woman) (B-21)	Ky	Ky	1976	LB	15 X 21	AP	30	1	275	3000
Cabeza de Muchacha (Head of a Girl) (B-22)	Ky	Ky	1976	LB	18 X 12	AP	16	1	275	3500
Rostro con Manos (Face with Hands) (B-23)	Ky	Ky	1976	LB	17 X 13	AP	16	1	300	4000
Tres Cabezas con Rebozos (Three Heads with Shawl) (B-24)	Ky	Ky	1976	LB	12 X 17	AP	40	1	300	4000
Dos Mujeres Sentadas con Rebozos (Two Seated Women with Shawls) (B-25)	Ky	Ky	1976	LC	16 X 20	CD	72	3	500	5000
Familia Indigena I (Country Family I) (B-26)	GAC/LACMA	Ky	1976	LC	25 X 36	AP	125	6	600	7000
Grupo de Mujeres Sentadas II (Group of Seated Women II) (B-27)	Ky	Ky	1976	LC	25 X 36	AP	125	5	600	7000
La Sembradora (The Sower) (B-28)	Ky	Ky	1976	LC	25 X 35	AP	40	2	600	8500
Mujeres ante el Fuego (Women by the Fire) (B-29)	Ky	Ky	1977	LC	22 X 30	CD	100	3	600	5000
Grupo de Mujeres (Group of Women) (B-30)	BEd	Ky	1977	LC	22 X 30	R/BFK	100	6	600	7000
Mujeres en la Ventana (Women in the Window) (B-31)	BEd	Ky	1977	LB	21 X 30	CD	50	1	300	3500
Mujer Reclinada (Reclining Woman) (B-32)	BEd	Ky	1977	LC	22 X 30	AP	100	3	450	5000
El Sueño (The Dream) (B-33)	BEd	Ky	1977	LB	22 X 30	AP	25	1	300	3500
La Calera (The Lime Seller) (B-34)	BEd	Ky	1977	LC	20 X 15	CD	46	3	400	7500
Dolores Sentada (Dolores Seated) (B-35)	BEd	Ky	1977	LC	30 X 22	CD	50	3	600	8500
Mujeres al Mar (Woman by the Sea) (B-36)	BEd	Ky	1977	LC/SP	23 X 31	GE	80	3	600	7000
Mujeres con Niño en la Puerta (Woman with Child in the Doorway) (B-37)	BEd	Ky	1977	LC	32 X 24	GE	100	2	700	5000
Mujeres Frente al Mar (Women Facing the Sea) (B-38)	BEd	Ky	1978	LC	21 X 26	GE	70	2	700	4500
Mujeres Frente al Mar, Noche (Women Facing the Sea, Night) (B-39)	BEd	Ky	1978	LB	20 X 26	CD	21	1	750	3500
La Vela (The Candle) (B-40)	BEd	Ky	1978	LB	24 X 17	AP	50	1	750	3500
Dos Mujeres Sentadas (Two Seated Women) (B-41)	BEd	Ky	1978	LB	22 X 31	CD	100	3-BL	650	4500
Mujer de Oaxaca (Woman from Oaxaca) (B-42)	BEd	Ky	1978	LB	24 X 20	CD	80	1	600	3000
Desnudo (Nude) (B-43)	BEd	Ky	1978	LB	20 X 25	RdB	22	1	650	2500
La Novia (The Bride) (B-44)	BEd	Ky	1978	LC	17 X 23	AP	70	2	750	3000
El Peinado (The Combing) (B-45)	BEd	Ky	1978	LB	19 X 24	JBG/T	70	1	750	3000
Muchacha en la Silla (Girl in the Chair) (B-46)	BEd	Ky	1978	LC	23 X 31	JBG	100	2	700	3000
Coloquio (Conversation) (B-47)	BEd	Ky	1979	LC	23 X 31	JBG	63	5	850	5000
Mujer con Canasto (Woman with Basket) (B-48)	BEd	Ky	1979	LC	21 X 26	JBG	125	8	800	3000
Cuatro Figuras de Pie (Four Standing Figures) (B-49)	BEd	Ky	1979	LC	17 X 24	RdB	25	2	800	3000
El Niño y la Vela (The Boy and the Candle) (B-50)	BEd	Ky	1980	LC	19 X 23	TRP/HMP	125	2	800	2500
La Comida (The Meal) (B-51)	BEd	Ky	1980	LC	24 X 35	AP	125	6	1000	5000
Silvia (B-52)	BEd	Ky	1980	LB	33 X 24	CD	125	2-BL	1000	4500
Campesinos (Country People) (B-53)	BEd	Ky	1980	LC	27 X 20	AP	125	6	1000	3500
Niñas con Panes (Girls with Bread) (B-54)	BEd	Ky	1980	LC	22 X 32	AP	125	8	1000	4000
Mujer en el Mercado I (Woman in the Market) (B-55)	BEd	Ky	1980	LB	27 X 23	Dewint/T	93	1	800	2500
Domitila (Domitila) (B-56)	BEd	Ky	1980	LC	23 X 18	CD	93	2	800	3000
Familia Indigena II (Country Family IV) (B-57)	BEd	Ky	1980	LC	22 X 32	AP	125	8	1250	4500
Mujer con Pescados (Woman with Fish) (B-58)	BEd	MAt	1980	LC	22 X 30	AP	135	9	1200	5000
Chamulas Rojo (Chamulas Red) (B-59)	BEd	MAt	1981	LC	22 X 30	AP	75	3	1200	3500
Chamulas Azul (Chamulas Blue) (B-60)	BEd	MAt	1981	LC	22 X 30	AP	75	3	1200	4000
Figuras Sentadas (Seated Figures) (B-61)	BEd	MAt	1981	LC	22 X 30	AP	135	6	1200	4000
El Canasto (The Basket) (B-62)	BEd	MAt	1981	LC	30 X 23	AP	135	6	1200	4000
La Abuela (The Grandmother) (B-63)	EdP	LP	1981	LC	30 X 22	GP	100	2	850	3500
Pescadoras (Fisherwomen) (B-64)	EdP	LP	1981	LC	29 X 22	GP	100	5	850	3500

FRANCISCO ZUÑIGA CONTINUED

Francisco Zuñiga
Madre Dormida
Courtesy Brewster Editions

Francisco Zuñiga
El Rebozo
Courtesy Brewster Editions

TITLE	PUBLISHER	PRINTER	DATE	MEDIUM	DIMENSION (PAPER SIZE) IN INCHES	TYPE OF PAPER	EDITION NUMBER	NO. OF COLORS	ORIGINAL OPENING PRICE	CURRENT RETAIL PRICE
SOLD OUT EDITIONS (RARE):										
Juchitecas II (Juchitecan Women II) (B-65)	EdP	LP	1981	LC	22 X 29	GP	100	6	850	3500
Grupo de Mujeres Sentadas III (Group of Seated Women III (B-66)	EdP	LP	1981	LC	22 X 29	GP	100	6	850	3500
La Fonda (The Inn) (B-67)	EdP	LP	1981	LC	22 X 29	GP	100	5	850	3500
La Mecedora (The Rocking Chair) (B-68)	BEd	Ky	1982	LC	23 X 31	AP	135	6	1250	4000
Madre Dormida (Sleeping Mother) (B-69)	BEd	Ky	1982	LC	18 X 25	AP	135	3	1000	3500
Mujeres Caminando I (Walking Women I) (B-70)	BEd	Ky	1982	LC	25 X 36	AP	135	6	1350	5000
Mujeres Caminado II (Walking Women II) (B-71)	BEd	Ky	1982	LC	25 X 36	AP	45	2	1350	4500
El Rebozo (The Shawl) (B-72)	BEd	MAt	1982	LC	22 X 30	AP	135	5	1200	3000
La Señal (The Sign) (B-73)	BEd	MAt	1982	LC	22 X 30	AP	135	5	1200	2500
Impresiónes de Egipto, Plancha 1 (Impressions of Egypt, Plate 1) (B-74)	BEd	MAt	1982	LC	20 X 14	AP	90	3	450	950
Impresiónes de Egipto, Plancha 2 (Impressions of Egypt, Plate 2) (B-75)	BEd	MAt	1982	LC	20 X 14	AP	90	3	450	950
Impresiónes de Egipto, Plancha 3 (Impressions of Egypt, Plate 3) (B-76)	BEd	MAt	1982	LC	14 X 20	AP	90	3	450	950
Impresiónes de Egipto, Plancha 4 (Impressions of Egypt, Plate 4) (B-77)	BEd	MAt	1982	LC	14 X 20	AP	90	5	450	950
Impresiónes de Egipto, Plancha 5 (Impressions of Egypt, Plate 5) (B-78)	BEd	MAt	1982	LC	14 X 20	AP	90	5	450	950
Impresiónes de Egipto, Plancha 6 (Impressions of Egypt, Plate 6) (B-79)	BEd	MAt	1982	LC	14 X 20	AP	90	4	450	950
Impresiónes de Egipto, Plancha 7 (Impressions of Egypt, Plate 7) (B-80)	BEd	MAt	1982	LC	14 X 20	AP	90	5	450	950
Impresiónes de Egipto, Plancha 8 (Impressions of Egypt, Plate 8) (B-81)	BEd	MAt	1982	LC	14 X 20	AP	90	4	450	950
Impresiónes de Egipto, Plancha 9 (Impressions of Egypt, Plate 9) (B-82)	BEd	MAt	1982	LC	14 X 20	AP	90	3	450	950
Impresiónes de Egipto, Plancha 10 (Impressions of Egypt, Plate 10) (B-83)	BEd	MAt	1982	LC	14 X 20	AP	90	3	450	950
Mujer con Niño (Woman with Child) (B-84)	BEd	Ky	1982	LC	23 X 19	AP	45	2	1200	3000
Muchacha en una Silla (Girl in a Chair) (B-85)	BEd	Ky	1982	LC	23 X 17	AP	135	5	1200	2500
Dos Mujeres con Niños (Two Women with Children) (B-86)	BEd	Ky	1982	LC	24 X 35	AP	135	6	1350	4500
Muchacha con Limones (Girl with Lemons) (B-87)	BEd	Ky	1982	LC	34 X 23	AP	135	6	1350	6500
Grupo (The Group) (B-88)	MIX	TdG	1982	MIX	12 X 17	HMP	100	Varies	1500	5000
Dos Mujeres Mayas (Two Mayan Women) (B-89)	MIX	TdG	1983	MIX	21 X 30	HMP	100	Varies	1800	5000
Mujer con Olla (Woman with Bowl) (B-90)	GB	Wolf	1983	LC	23 X 30	R/BFK	100	6	1000	4000

FRANCISCO ZUÑIGA CONTINUED

TITLE	PUBLISHER	PRINTER	DATE	MEDIUM	DIMENSION (PAPER SIZE) IN INCHES	TYPE OF PAPER	EDITION NUMBER	NO. OF COLORS	ORIGINAL OPENING PRICE	CURRENT RETAIL PRICE
SOLD OUT EDITIONS (RARE):										
Virginia (Virginia) (B-91)	EdP	LP	1983	LC	30 X 22	GP	100	4	900	4000
Mujer en el Mercado II (Woman in the Market) (B-92)	EdP	LP	1983	LC	22 X 30	GP	100	6	900	2500
Familia Indigena III (Country Family III) (B-93)	EdP	LP	1983	LC	22 X 30	GP	100	8	900	2500
Tres Mujeres de Pie II (Three Standing Women II) (B-94)	BEd	Ky	1983	LC	23 X 18	JBG	135	2	900	2500
Rosa Sentada (Rosa Seated) (B-95)	BEd	Ky	1983	LC	32 X 24	JP	135	2	1200	6500
Doncella (Maiden) (B-96)	BEd	AA	1984	LC	30 X 22	SOM	135	8	1200	5000
Ritual (Ritual) (B-97)	BEd	AA	1984	LB	19 X 15	SOM	250	2-BL	650	1000
Mujer Bebiendo (Woman Drinking) (B-98)	BEd	AA	1984	LC	19 X 15	SOM	250	3	650	1000
Hombres con Barca I (Men with Boat I) (B-99)	BEd	AA	1984	LB	24 X 34	SOM	50	2-BL	850	2000
Hombres con Barca II (Men with Boat II) (B-100)	BEd	AA	1984	LB	24 X 34	SOM	40	2-BL	850	2000
Pilar en la Ventana (Pilar at the Window) (B-101)	BEd	EldPr	1984	EB/A/DPT	21 X 19	SOM	50	1	1000	3500
CURRENT EDITIONS:										
Juchiteca Platicando (Women Chatting) (Z-202)	BEd	Ky	1985	LC	23 X 30	SOM	150	7	1000	4500
El Rebozo Blanco (The White Shawl) (Z-198)	BEd	Ky	1986	LC	21 X 30	SOM	135	8	1200	2500
Yucetecas en el Parque (Yucatecan Women in the Park) (Z-200)	BEd	Ky	1986	LC	22 X 30	SOM	150	6	1200	3000
La Escalera (The Stairway) (Z-201)	BEd	Ky	1986	LC	21 X 30	SOM	135	5	1200	3500

Francisco Zuñiga
La Señal
Courtesy Brewster Editions

Francisco Zuñiga
Yucatecas en el Parque
Courtesy Brewster Editions

Francisco Zuñiga
Juchitecas Platicando
Courtesy Brewster Editions

PRINT PUBLISHERS INDEX

AMX Art International
37 West 65th Street
New York, NY 10023
TEL (212) 874-6700
FAX (212) 877-1146

Brooke Alexander Editions, Inc
476 Broome Street
New York, NY 10013
Attn: Carolina Nitsch-Jones, Director
TEL (212) 925-2070

Art Affair
3871 Valley View, #9
Las Vegas, NV 89103
Attn: Ron Martin
TEL (702) 368-7888
FAX (702) 368-0220
Publisher of A Sehring & Roy Purcell

Art West Collections
8306 Wilshire Blvd, #1081
Beverly Hills, CA 90211
Attn: Alexandre Mahban
TEL (800) 441-0455

Associated American Artists
20 West 57th Street
New York, NY 10019
TEL (212) 399-5510

Austin Publishing Co
P O Box 929
Palatine, IL 60067
TEL (312) 358-8750

B & R International Art, Ltd
5641 Circle View Drive
Bonsall, CA 92003
Attn: Judy Bishop
TEL (619) 945-5581
FAX (619) 945-7827

BLD Limited
118 East 25th Street
New York, NY 10010
TEL (212) 460-8700
TEL (800) 847-4207

Robert Bane Editions
8025 Melrose Avenue
Los Angeles, CA 90046
Attn: Chris Kelly
TEL (213) 205-0555
TEL (800) 325-2765

Baron/Boisante Editions
50 West 57th Street, 5th Floor
New York, NY 10019
Attn: Mark Baron
TEL (212) 581-9191
FAX (212) 581-9291

Belgravia Contemporary Arts Limited
8 Frederic Mews
London SW1X 8 EQ, England
Attn: Jeffrey Sion
TEL (01) 245-6131

John Berggruen Gallery
228 Grant Avenue
San Francisco, CA 94108
TEL (415) 781-4629

Berghoff-Cowden Editions, Inc
3209 Bay to Bay Blvd
Tampa, FL 33629
Attn: Lois Berghoff
TEL (813) 835-5019
FAX (813) 835-5019

Black Dolphin Workshop
California State University
1250 North Bellflower Boulevard
Long Beach, CA 90840

Blinder Fine Arts
3435 Ocean Park Blvd, #103
Santa Monica, CA 90405
TEL (213) 396-3766
FAX (213) 452-0771

Blue Heron Press
RD #3, P O Box 198
Greenwich, NY 12834
TEL (518) 692-9116

Peter Blum Edition
14 West 10th Street
New York, NY 10011
TEL (212) 475-0227

BlumHelman Gallery
20 West 57th Street
New York, NY 10019
TEL (212) 245-2888

Brana Publishing, Inc
525 Palisades Drive
Pacific Palisades, CA 90272
Attn: Bruce Hochman
TEL (310) 459-8883
TEL (800) 776-3254
FAX (310) 454-2090

Castelli Graphics
578 Broadway
New York, NY 10012
Attn: Pat Marie Caporaso
TEL (212) 941-9855

Enrique Cattaneo
Avena 102
Mexico DF, Mexico
TEL-581-3753
FAX-581-7362

Chalk & Vermilion Fine Arts, Ltd
200 Greenwich Avenue
Attn: Ellen Venable
Greenwich, CT 06830
TEL (203) 869-9500
FAX (203) 869-9520

Circle Fine Art
232 East Ohio
Chicago, IL 60611
TEL (312) 943-0664

Cirrus Editions, Ltd
542 South Alemeda Street
Los Angeles, CA 90013
TEL (213) 680-3473

Cleveland Museum of Art
11150 East Boulevard
Cleveland, OH 44106
Attn: Evan Turner
TEL (216) 421-7340

Cleveland Editions
195 Plymouth Street
Brooklyn, NY 11201
Attn: Bruce Cleveland
TEL (718) 643-9007

Coast Publishing
P O Box 223519
Carmel, CA 93922
Attn: Deborah Johansen
TEL (408) 625-4145
TEL (800) 842-6278
FAX (408) 625-3575

Cone Editions
P O Box 51
East Topsham, VT 05076
Attn: Jon Cone
TEL (802) 439-5751

Paula Cooper Gallery
155 Wooster Street
New York, NY 10012
TEL (212) 674-0766

Corridor Press
6139 North 7th Street
Philadelphia, PA 19120
Attn: Tim Sheesley
TEL (215) 924-4715

Aldo Crommelynck
72 Spring Street
New York, NY 10012
TEL (212) 22601355

Crown Point Press
657 Howard Street
San Francisco, CA 94105
Attn: Kathan Brown
TEL (415) 974-6273
FAX (415) 495-4220

Crown Point Press
568 Broadway
New York, NY 10012
Attn: Karen McCready
TEL (212) 226-5476
FAX (212) 966-7042

DeSoto Workshop
319 11th Street
San Franciso, CA 94103
Attn: Ernest F DeSoto
Mariane Zanetti
TEL (415) 863-3232
FAX (415) 863-1595

Diverse Dimensions Art, Ltd
P O Box 88-H
Scarsdale, NY 10583
TEL (914) 636-6012
FAX (914) 636-8978

Fred Dorfman, Inc
123 Watts Street
New York, NY 10013
TEL (212) 966-4611

Irene Drori, Inc
138 North Orange Drive
Los Angeles, CA 90036
TEL (213) 931-1779

Echo Press
1901 East 10th Street
Bloomington, IN 47408
Attn: Rudy Pozzatti
TEL (812) 855-0476
FAX (812) 855-0477

Brenda Edelson, Inc
P O 268
Brooklandville, MD 47408
TEL (410) 823-0030
FAX (410) 823-0031

Edition Julie Sylvester
10 White Street
New York, NY 10013
TEL (212) 941-0398
FAX (212) 226-3914

Edition Schellmann
50 Greene Street
New York, NY 10013
Attn: Meg Malloy
TEL (212) 219-1821
FAX (212) 941-9206
Publishers of Multiples & Prints by Contemporary Artists

Editions T
Consell de Cent 290
08007 Barcelona, Spain
TEL (343) 487-6402
FAX (343) 488-2495

El Cerro Graphics
26 Airport Road
Los Lunas, NM 87031
Attn: Ricardo C Zimenes
TEL (505) 865-5602

Eldindean Press
83-45 Broadway, #507
Elmhurst, NY 11373
Attn: Anthony Kirk
TEL (718) 592-2660

Daniel Elias Editions
27 Tower Road
Lincoln, MA 01773
TEL (617) 259-1102

Engman Limited
23182 Alcalde Drive, #J
Laguna Hills, CA 92653
Attn: Glenn Engman
TEL (714) 588-5494
FAX (714) 588-7568

Erie-Lackawanna Editions
119 North 11th Street, #3C
Brooklyn, NY 11211
Attn: Brenda Zlamany
TEL (718) 387-3905.

Etching Studio
1121 East Freeway
Houston, TX 77002
Attn: Penelope Cerling
TEL (713) 228-4116

Eleanor Ettinger, Inc
155 Avenue of the Americas
New York, NY 10013
Attn: Fran Bradshaw
TEL (212) 807-7607
FAX (212) 691-3508

Cindi Ettinger Studio
144 Vine Street
Philadelphia, PA 19016
TEL (215) 928-9897

Evans Editions, Inc
140 Watts Street
New York, NY 10013
Attn: Sue Ann Evans
TEL (212) 274-1128
FAX (212) 274-1215

Exeter Press
168 Mercer Street, #4
New York, NY 10012
Attn: A Lynn Forgach
TEL (212) 966-4125
FAX (212) 966-5678

PRINT PUBLISHERS INDEX CONTINUED

Experimental Workshop
P O Box 77504
Pier 46-B, Door 13
San Francisco, CA 94107
Attn: Ann Mclaughlin
TEL (415) 957-0148
FAX (415) 957-9309

Experimental Etching Studio, Inc
EES Arts
34 Plympton Street
Boston, MA 02118
Attn: Deborah Cornell
TEL (617) 482-9646

Fawbush Editions
578 Broadway, 5th Floor
New York, NY 10012
Attn: Joe Fawbush
TEL (212) 966-6650

Ronald Feldman Fine Arts, Inc
31 Mercer Street
New York, NY 10013
TEL (212) 226-3232
FAX (212) 941-1536

Figura, Inc
53 East 75th Street
New York, NY 10021
TEL (212) 772-6627

Fiordaliso
125 Townsend Street
San Francisco, CA 97107
Attn: Carolyn Klaner
TEL (415) 543-6333

Flanagan Graphics, Inc
506 West Patcong Avenue
Linwood, NJ 08221
TEL (609) 926-1040
FAX (609) 926-1036

Flatbed Press
912 West 3rd Street
Austin, TX 78703
Attn: Mark L. Smith
TEL (512) 477-9328
FAX (512) 477-1799

Raymond Foye Editions
Chelsea Hotel, #807
222 West 23rd Street
New York, NY 10011
TEL (212) 645-1840

Freeman Editions
742 North Haysworth
Los Angeles, CA 90046
TEL (213) 651-5361

Gallery Rodeo, Inc
421 North Rodeo Drive
Beverly Hills, CA 90210
TEL (213) 273-6615

Gaultney-Klineman Art
1345 Avenue of the Americas
New York, NY 10105
Attn: Kent Kleinman
TEL (212) 586-2525
FAX (212) 582-6382

Galerie Eric Franck
15 Route de Florissant
1206 Geneva, Switzerland
TEL (22) 47-08-09

Galerie Lelong
20 West 57th Street, 15th Floor
New York, NY 10019
TEL (212) 315-0470

Galerie Lelong
13 Rue de Teheran
75008 Paris, France
TEL (1) 563-13-19

Galerie Sho Contemporary Art
3-2-9 Nihonbashi
Chuo-ku, Tokyo, Japan
Attn: Sho Satake
TEL 32, 75, 10, 08
FAX 32, 73, 93, 09
Specializing in Contemporary Art

Galleri Kunst-Invest
Dronning Maudsgt 1-3
0250 Oslo 2, Norway
TEL (02) 42-41

Gallerie Joan Prats
568 Broadway, #501
New York, NY 10012
Attn: Juan de Muga
TEL (212) 219-0510
FAX (212) 219-0495

Gemini GEL
8365 Melrose Avenue
Los Angeles, CA 90069
Attn: Sidney Felsen
   Stanley Grinstein
TEL (213) 651-1513

Genovese Graphics
535 Albany Street
Boston, Camellia Genovese
TEL (617) 426-9738
TEL (617) 426-2062

Barbara Gladstone Editions, Ltd
99 Green Street
New York, NY 10012
Attn: Richard Flood
TEL (212) 431-3334

Graphic Arts Unlimited
225 Fifth Avenue
New York, NY 10010
TEL (212) 255-4805

Graphics Workshop
632 Agua Fria
Santa Fe, NM 87501
Attn: Ron Pokrasso
TEL (505) 984-0827

Graphicstudio
3702 Spectrum Blvd, #100
Tampa, FL 33612
Attn: Alan Eaker
TEK (813) 974-3503
FAX (813) 974-2579

Greenfell Press
116 West 29th Street
New York, NY 10001
Attn: Leslie Miller
TEL (212) 947-8846

Grin Graphics
465 West 46th Street, #5
New York, NY 10036
Attn: Rand Russell
TEL (212) 307-5405

I C Editions, Inc
21 East 22nd Street
New York, NY 10010
TEL (212) 475-6990
FAX (212) 475-6563

Iris Editions
399 Washington Street
New York, NY 10013
Attn: Deli Sacilotto
TEL (212) 966-7274
FAX (212) 431-3471

Iris Fine Arts
2450 Broadway, #550
Santa Monica, CA 90404
Attn: David Paget
TEL (310) 392-2222

Sidney Janis Gallery Editions
110 West 57th Street
New York, NY 10019
TEL (212) 586-0110

Kennedy Galleries, Inc
40 West 57th Street, 5th Floor
New York, NY 10019
TEL (212) 541-9600

Bernd Kluser Edition
Georgenstrasse 15
Munich 40, Germany
TEL (49) (40) 33.21.79
FAX (40) (40) 39.25.41

Knoedler Publishing, Inc
19 East 70th Street
New York, NY 10021
TEL (212) 794-0674

Kunstverlag Schumacher Edition Fils
Eduardo-Schloemannstrasse 47-49
P O Box 230147
40087 Düsseldorf, Germany
Attn: Dr. Alexander Fils
TEL - 011-211-67.20.63
FAX 011-211-76.20.65

La Paloma
10308 Glenoaks Blvd
Pacoima, CA 91331
Attn: Ron McPherson
TEL (818) 890-2216
FAX (818) 890-4371

Lakeside Studio
15263 South Lakeshore Road
Lakeside, MI 49116
TEL (616) 469-1377

Land Mark Editions
700 Washington Avenue, North, #419
Minneapolis, MN 55401
Attn: Jon M Swenson
TEL (612) 375-1690

Landfall Press, Inc
329 West 18th Street, #601
Chicago, IL 60616
Attn: Jack Lemon
TEL (312) 666-6709
FAX (312) 666-1486

Lapis Press
589 North Venice Blvd
Venice, CA 90291
TEL (310) 396-4152

Martin Lawrence Limited Editions
16250 Stagg Street
Van Nuys, CA 91406
TEL (818) 988-0630

The Litho Shop, Inc
2058 Broadway
Santa Monica, CA 90404
Attn: Beth Silverman
TEL (310) 828-0792
FAX (310) 829-6842

Lococo-Mulder, Inc
9104 Clayton Road
St Louis, MO 63124
Attn: Robert Lococo
TEL (314) 994-0240
FAX (314) 994-0545

Lococo-Mulder, Inc
106 Central Park South, #24-F
New York, NY 10019
Attn: George Mulder
TEL (212) 246-6040

London Arts, Inc
321 Fisher Building
Detroit, MI 48202
Attn: David Zelman
TEL (313) 871-2411

L A Louver
55 North Venice Boulevard
Venice, CA 90291
TEL (213) 392-8695

Magnolia Editions
2527 Magnolia Street
Oakland, CA 94607
Attn: Don Farnsworth
   David Kimball
TEL (510) 834-2527
FAX (510) 893-8334

Made in California
3246 Ettie Street
Oakland, CA 94608
TEL (415) 428-2699

Marco Fine Arts, Inc
1633 West 135th Street
Gardena, CA 90249
Attn: John Marco
TEL (310) 719-1818
FAX (310) 719-1125

Marlborough Graphics
40 West 57th Street
New York, NY 10019
Attn: Pierre Leval
TEL (212) 541-4900

Maurel Studios
12 Warren Street
New York, NY 10007
Attn: Sheila Marbain
TEL (212) 513-7435

Maximilian Verlag/Sabine Knust
Maximilianstrasse 36
8 Munich, Germany

Maxwell-Nova Fine Arts, Inc
111 Cedar Street
New Rochelle, NY 10801
Attn: William C Maxwell
TEL (914) 633-3314

PRINT PUBLISHERS INDEX CONTINUED

Merrimac Editions
4 Mechanic Street
Merrimac, MA 01860
Attn: Herb Fox
TEL (617) 346-8859

Mixografia Workshop, Inc
1419 East Adams Blvd
Los Angeles, CA 90011
Attn: Luis Ramba
TEL (213) 232-1158
FAX (213) 232-1655

Multiples, Inc
24 West 57th Street
New York, NY 10019
Attn: Jill Walla-Sussman
    Nan Tooker
TEL (212) 977-7160

Nahan Editions
450 Royal Street
New Orleans, LA 70130
Attn: Ken Naham
TEL (504) 524-8696

Nash Editions
1201 Oak Avenue
Manhattan Beach, CA 90266
Attn: R Mac Holbert
TEL (310) 545-4352
FAX (310) 545-8565

Navavisa Press
Rte 2, Box 280
Santa Fe, NM 87505
Attn: Stephen Britko
TEL (505) 473-2684

New City Editions
525 Venezia Avenue
Venice, CA 90291
Attn: Joel Stearns
TEL (310) 822-0818
FAX (310) 822-0971

Newbury Fine Arts
29 Newbury Street
Boston, MA 02116
Attn: Anthony Parrella
TEL (617 536-0210
FAX (617) 536-0517

T T Nieh, Inc
506 King Street
Alexandria, VA 22314
TEL (703) 548-6203

Noblet Serigraphie, Inc
425 West 13th Street
New York, NY 10014
Attn: Jean-Yves Noblet
TEL (212) 243-0439
FAX (212) 243-0503

Normal Editions Workshop
c/o Art Department 5620
Illinois State University
Normal, IL 61761
Attn: Richard Finch
TEL (309) 438-7530
FAX (309) 438-8318

Orion Editions
270 Lafayette Street
New York, NY 10012
Attn: Robert Kimbril
TEL (212) 226-2766

PCAD Printmaking Workshop
Borowsky Center for Publication
Arts University of the Arts
Philadelphia College of Art &
Design Printmaking
320 South Broad Street
Philadelphia, PA 19102
Attn: Lois M Johnson
TEL (215) 875-1119
FAX (215) 875-5467

Pace Editions
32 East 57th Street
New York, NY 10022
TEL (212) 421-3237

**Pacifica Editions Corporations
Editors and Publishers**
P O Box 558474
Miami, FL 33255
Attn: Maria Espinosa
TEL (305) 662-8690

Palm Press, Ltd
2015 15th Street
Tampa, FL 33605
TEL (813) 248-3959

Parasol Press, Ltd
289 Church Street
New York, NY 10013
TEL (212) 431-9387

Mark Patsfall Graphics, Inc
1312 Clay Street
Cincinnati, OH 45210
TEL (513) 241-3232
FAX (513) 241-3029

Pelavin Editions
13 Jay Street
New York, NY 10013
Attn: Cheryl Pelavin
TEL (212) 925-9424

Peregrine Gallery
P O Box 671046
Dallas, TX 75367-8046
Attn: Michael Hart
Jo Ann Hart
TEL (214) 871-3770

Perimeter Press
356 West Huron
Chicago, IL 60610
Attn: Frank Paluch
TEL (312) 266-9473

Petersburg Press
380 Lafayette Street
New York, NY 10003
TEL (212) 420-0890

Petersburg Press
59A Portobello Road
London, W1, England
TEL (01) 229-0105

Pleiades Press
Studio Graphic Workshop
3014 Avenue C, #1
Holmes Beach, FL 34217
Attn: Barbara Neustadt
TEL (813) 778-2466
Representing Printmaker B Neustadt
& Others

Plucked Chicken Press
1604 Greenleaf
Evanston, IL 60202
Attn: Will Petersen
TEL (708) 475-0530

Pondside Press
4 Bollenbecker Road
Rhinebeck, NY 12572
Attn: Melissa Katzman Braggins
    Ted Braggins

Joan Prats Gallery
568 Broadway, #501
New York, NY 10012
Attn: Juan de Maga
TEL (212) 219-0510
FAX (212) 219-0495

Preston Graphics
44 Currierville Road
Newton, NH 03858
Attn: Robert Preston
TEL (603) 382-3077
FAX (603) 382-3077

Print Editions, Ltd
156 Haven Avenue
Port Washington, NY 11050
Attn: K C Wilsey, Jr
TEL (516) 883-5678

Printmaking Workshop
55 West 17th Street
New York, NY 10011
Attn: Robert Blackburn
TEL (212) 989-6125

Prints in Progress
54 North 3rd Street
Philadelphia, PA 19106
Attn: Michele D Grant
TEL (215) 928-0206
FAX (215) 925-3856

Prior Editions
1028 Hamilton Street #303
Vancouver, BC
Canada V6A 2R9
Attn: Nigel Harrison
TEL (604) 685-0535

Pyramid Atlantic
6001 66th Avenue, #103
Riverdale, MD 20737
Attn: Helen Frederick
TEL (301) 459-7154
TEL (301) 577-3424
FAX (301) 459-7629

C G Rein Publishers
949 Sibley Memorial Highway
St Paul, MN 55118
Attn: Sterling Blumstein
TEL (612) 328-3158
TEL (800) 328-3158

Riverhouse Editions
31055 County Road, #64
P O Box 669
Clark, CO 80428
Attn: William Van Straaten
TEL (303) 879-6394
FAX (312) 642-5693

Margarete Roeder Editions
545 Broadway
New York, NY 10012
TEL (212) 925-6098

Ronbie Editions, Inc
1970 Timber Lakes Drive
Yardley, PA 19067
Attn: Bob Phillips
TEL (215) 968-7711

Andrea Ruoff Art Associates, Ltd
2050 Center Avenue
Fort Lee, NJ 07024
TEL (201) 592-0820
FAX (201) 592-1520

**Rutgers Center for Innovative
Printmaking**
Department of Visual Arts
Mason Gross School of the Arts
New Brunswick, NJ 08901
Attn: Judith K Brodsky
TEL (908) 932-8449
TEL (908) 932-9499
FAX (908) 932-1343

San Francisco Fine Art Publishing
1500 Howard Street
San Francisco, CA 94103
Attn: Ray Madeiros
TEL (415) 255-1992
FAX (415) 255-2049

Segura Publishing Company, Inc
688 West First, #6
Tempe, AZ 85281
Attn: Joe Segura
TEL (602) 894-0551
FAX (602) 921-4310

Sette Publishing Co
688 West First Street, #4
Tempe, AZ 85281
Attn: Kristi Warren
TEL (602) 894-0551

Shark's Incorporated
2020 Ninth Street
Boulder, CO 80302
Attn: Bud Shark
TEL (303) 443-4601
FAX (303) 443-1245

Donald Sheridan Fine Arts
350 Manhattan Avenue
Brooklyn, NY 11211
TEL (718) 383-4924
FAX (718) 383-4924

Simca Print Artists, Inc
5-5-11 Ginza
Chuo-Ku
Tokyo, Japan

Simca Print Artists, Inc
27 Howard Street
New York, NY 10013
Attn: Hiroshi Kawanishi
TEL (212) 431-5848

Simmelink/Sukimoto Editions
13327 Beach Avenue
Marina Del Rey, CA 90292
Attn: Doris Simmelink
Chris Sukimoto
TEL (310) 301-3330

Solo Impressions, Inc
520 Broadway
New York, NY 10012
Attn: Judith Solodkin
TEL (212) 925-3315
TEL (212) 925-3316
TEL (212) 925-3599
FAX (212) 226-3251

PRINT PUBLISHERS INDEX CONTINUED

Split Fountain
141 - Suite A, South Crescent Drive
Beverly Hills, CA 90212
Attn: Anthony Ditton
TEL (310) 273-7770
FAX (310) 273-7771

Holly Solomon Editions
724 Fifth Avenue
New York, NY 10019
TEL (212) 757-7777

Spring Street Workshop
72 Spring Street
New York, NY 10012
Attn: Joe Wilfer
TEL (212) 226-1577
FAX (212) 431-5825

Stewart & Stewart
5571 Wing Lake Road
Birmingham, MI 48010
Attn: Norman Stewart
TEL (313) 626-5248

Stone Press Editions
3815 4th Avenue, NE
Seattle, WA 98105
Attn: Kent Lovelace
TEL (206) 633-1160

Styria Studio, Inc
126 Broome Street
New York, NY 10013
Attn: Adi Rischner
TEL (212) 226-1373

John Szoke Graphics
164 Mercer Street
New York, NY 10012
TEL (212) 219-8300

Raya Talmor Gallery
Kibbutz Yagur
30065 Israel
TEL 972-4-848271
FAX 972-4-848686

Tamarind Institute
108 Cornell Avenue, SE
Albuquerque, NM 87106
Attn: Marjorie Devon
TEL (515) 277-3901

Tandem Press
201 South Dickinson Street
Madison, WI 53703
Attn: Paula McCarthy Panczenko
TEL (608) 263-3437
FAX (608) 265-2356

Tangent Graphics
162 Lodi Street
Hackensack, NJ 07601

Elizabeth Tapper Intaglio Printing
307 3rd Avenue, South, #203
Seattle, WA 98104
TEL (206) 623-8824

Teaberry Press
347 Dolores, #105
San Francisco, CA 94110
Attn: Timothy Berry
TEL (415) 552-6363

Tiger Lily Press
1125 Saint Gregory Street
Cincinnati, OH 45202
Attn: Steve Clark
Louann Elliott
TEL (513) 562-8759

Barbara Toll Fine Arts, Inc
146 Greene Street
New York, NY 10012
TEL (212) 431-1785

Tomoko Liguori Gallery
93 Grand Street
New York, NY 10013
TEL (212) 315-0470
FAX (212) 274-8641

Topaz Editions, Inc
13305 Cain Road
Tampa, FL 33625
Attn: Julio Juristo
TEL (813) 961-3137

Trestle Editions, Ltd
75 Varick Street
New York, NY 10013
Attn: Bruce Porter
TEL (212) 226-8111

Trillium Graphics
91 Park Lane
Brisbane, CA 94005
Attn: David M Salgado
TEL (415) 468-8166
FAX (415) 468-8166

Tullis Workshop
1 North Salsipuedes Street, #9
Santa Barbara, CA 93103
Attn: Richard B Tullis II
TEL (805) 965-1091
FAX (805) 965-1093

Garner Tullis
10 White Street
New York, NY 10013
TEL (212) 226-6665
FAX (212) 941-0678

2/20 Workshop
220 West 16th Street
New York, NY 10011
Attn: M Herrera
TEL (212) 807-8348

21 Steps
413 2nd Street, SW
Albuquerque, NM 87102
Attn: Richard Levy
Jeffrey Ryan
TEL (505) 242-1115

Turske & Turske, AG
Seefeldstrasse 227/229
CH 8008, Zurich,
Switzerland
Attn: Veight Turske
Irene Preiswerk Turske
TEL 41.1.55.97.70
FAX 41.1.53.71.49

Tyler Graphics, Ltd
250 Kisco Avenue
Mount Kisco, NY 10549
Attn: Ken Tyler
TEL (914) 241-2707

USF Graphicstudio II
College of Fine Arts
University of South Florida
Tampa, FL 33620
TEL (813) 974-2360

Universal Limited Art Editions, Inc.
5 Skidmore Place
West Islip, NY 11795
Attn: Bill Goldston
TEL (516) 669-7484
FAX (516) 669-7338

Vinalhaven Press
P O Box 464
Vinalhaven, ME 04863
Attn: Patricia Nick
TEL (207) 863-4937
FAX (212) 219-1561

Vermillion Editions, Ltd
420 East Wisconsin Avenue
Milwaukee, WI 53202
Attn: Michael Lord

Diane Villani Editions
271 Mulberry Street, #3-D
New York, NY 10012
TEL (212) 925-1075

Waddington Graphics
16 Clifford Street
London, W1, England
TEL (01) 439-1866

Water Street Press, Ltd
223 Water Street
Brooklyn, NY 11201
TEL (212) 522-5983

Watermark Editions
SE 3591 Old Olympic Highway
Shelton, WA 98584
Attn: Mahri Breenan
TEL (206) 427-1717
TEL (206) 427-1313

Edward Weston Graphics
P O Box 655
6th Avenue
Carmel, CA 93921
TEL (408) 624-4453

Larry B Wright Productions
164 Mulberry Street
New York, NY 10013
TEL (212) 925-3047

X Press
116 West 29th Street
New York, NY 10001
Attn: Alan Koslin
TEL (212) 947-9214

Yama Prints
140 West 30th Street, #4-E
New York, NY 10001
Attn: Betty Winkler
TEL (212) 594-1771

Zimmerman Editions
875 Hollins Street
Baltimore, MD 21201
TEL (301) 659-0066

PRINTERS/PRINT WORKSHOPS INDEX

AGB Graphics Workshop
1021 South Park Street
Madison, WI 53715
Attn: Andrew G Balkin
TEL (608) 251-7277

Accent Studios, Inc
9666 Owensmouth Avenue
Chatsworth, CA 91311
Attn: LeRoy Olson
TEL (818) 700-0550
FAX (818) 700-2655

David Adamson Editions
406 7th Street, NW
Washington, DC 20024
TEL (202) 628-0257

Angeles Press
800 Traction Avenue
Angeles, CA 90013
TEL (213) 620-0615

Anchor Graphics
935 North Damen
Chicago, IL 60622
Attn: David R Jones
TEL (312) 252-4669

Arabesque Studio
59 Amory Street
Boston, MA 02119
Attn: Jonathan Moore
       Shahriar Samani
TEL (617) 442-8928

Arber & Son Editions
P O Box 10121
Alameda, NM 87184
Attn: Robert H Arber
TEL (505) 898-7436
FAX (505) 344-7581

Arch Press
1702 Adams
Steilacoom, WA 98388
Attn: Paul Clinton
TEL (206) 582-9116

Archer Press
6139 Wood Drive
Oakland, CA 94611
TEL (415) 547-3465

Arellanes, Inc
3095-D Kerner Blvd.
San Rafael, CA 94901

Arion Press
460 Bryant Street
San Francisco, CA 94107
Attn: Andre Hoyem
TEL (415) 777-9651
FAX (415) 777-2730

Arte Dos Grafico Print Shop
Carrera 14, No 75-35
Bogota, Colombia
Attn: Luis Angel Parra, Director
TEL 212-8781
FAX 211-9358

Artist's Proof Graphics Workshop
469-A Magnolia Avenue
Larkspur, CA 94939
Attn: Harriette Frances
TEL (415) 924-6690

Asheville Working Press
Zone One Contemporary Gallery
37 Biltmore Avenue
Asheville, NC 28730
Attn: Kevin Hogan
TEL (704) 258-3088
TEL (704) 254-4055

Atelier Aldo Crommelynck
72 Spring Street
New York, NY 10012
Attn: Aldo Crommelynck
TEL (212) 226-1355

Atelier Ettinger, Inc
155 Avenue of the Americas
New York, NY 10013
Attn: Eleanor Ettinger
       Fran Bradford
TEL (212) 759-7074
FAX (212) 691-3508

Atelier Royce
57 Grove Street
Salem, MA 01970
Attn: Richard Royce
TEL (508) 741-1798
FAX (508) 744-8697

Aurobora Press
P O Box 626
Sausalito, CA 94966
Attn: Michael Dunev
TEL (415) 398-7300
FAX (415) 398-7680

Avocet
P O Box 37
New York, NY 10013
Attn: Andrea Callard
TEL (212) 925-8974

Aztlan Multiples
1745 East 7th Street, 7th Floor
Los Angeles, CA 90021
TEL (213) 622-5482

Below the Surface Printmakers Atelier
27 North 4th Street, #301
Minneapolis, MN 55401
Attn: Denise Sanders
TEL (612) 340-1001
FAX (612) 644-7221

Michael Berdan Woodblock Printing, Cutting
31 Jackson Street
Cambridge, MA 02140
TEL (617) 547-2546

Beta Press
130 Elliott Avenue, West
Seattle, WA 98119
Attn: Marcia Bartholme
TEL (206) 281-9323

Black Swann Editions
98 Newberry Street, Lot 2A
Danvers, MA 01923
TEL (617) 777-1891

Brand X Editions
75 Varick Street
New York, NY 10013
Attn: Robert Blanton
TEL (212) 925-6490
FAX (212) 925-6561

Brandywine Workshop
1520-22 Kater Street
Philadlephia, PA 19146
Attn: Allan Edmunds
TEL (215) 546-3657
FAX (215) 545-0932

Brighton Press
320 G Street
San Diego, CA 92101
Attn: Michele Burgess
       Bill Kelly
TEL (619) 234-1179
FAX (619) 232-4884

Kathleen Caraccio, Printer
270 Bowery
New York, NY 10012
TEL (212) 966-9730

Enrique Cattaneo
Avena 102
Mexico DF, Mexico
TEL 581-3753
FAX 581-7362

Center Street Studio
516 East 2nd Street
Boston, MA 02127
TEL (617) 268-1254

Centrum Press
PO Box 1158
Port Townsend, WA 98368
TEL (206) 385-3102

Cherry Press
452 Pleasant Street
Malden, MA 02148
Attn: Keiji Shinohara
TEL (617) 397-0345

Chestnut Street Press
150 Chestnut Street
Providence, RI 02903
Attn: Clary Nelson
TEL (401) 421-0588

Chicago Printmakers Collaborative
1101 North Paulina
Chicago, IL 60622
Attn: Deborah Maris Lader
TEL (311) 235-3712

Cirrus Editions, Ltd
542 South Alameda Street
Los Angeles, CA 90013
Attn: Jean Milant
TEL (213) 680-3473
FAX (213) 680-0930

Clary Lake Farm/Studio
RFD 1, Box 1250
North Whitefield, ME 04353
Attn: Frances Hodsdon
TEL (207) 549-7087

Cleveland Editions
195 Plymouth Street
Brooklyn, NY 11201
Attn: Bruce Cleveland
TEL (718) 643-9007

Dwight Coburn Press
2623 3rd Avenue, North
Seattle, WA 98109
TEL (206) 285-6344

Colombia Graphic Arts, Ltd
20 West 22,d Street
New York, NY 10010
Attn: Alan Granat
TEL (212) 242-8168
FAX (212) 691-7489

Color West Lithography, Inc
2228 North Hollywood Way
Burbank, CA 91505
Attn: Randy Quiring
TEL (818) 840-8881

Cone Editions
P O Box 51
East Topsham, VT 05076
Attn: Jon Cone
TEL (802) 439-5751

Frank Copello Printshop
20 Lexington Avenue
Brooklyn, NY 11238
TEL (718) 857-8032
TEL (212) 967-9640

Corridor Press
Bert Washburn Road
RR2, Box 191
Otego, NY 13825
Attn: Timothy P Sheesley
TEL (607) 432-7605

Creative Arts Workshop
80 Audubon Street
New Haven, CT 06511
TEL (203) 562-4927

Custom Etching Studio
3727 La Plaza Drive, NW
Albuquerque, NM 87107
Attn: Robert Blanchard
TEL (505) 345-8556

Damage Press
55 Washington Street, 9th Floor
Brooklyn, NY 11201
Attn: Ted Warner
TEL (718) 852-3702

Del Bello Editions
363 Queen Street, West
Toronto, ON
Canada M5V 2A4
Attn: Eglidio Del Bello
TEL (416) 593-0884

PRINTERS/PRINT WORKSHOPS INDEX CONTINUED

DeSoto Workshop
319 11th Street
San Francisco, CA 94103
Attn: Ernest F DeSoto
   Mariane Zanetti
TEL (415) 863-3232
FAX (415) 863-1595

Derriére L'Etoile Studios
12 Warren Street
New York, NY 10007
Attn: Maurice Sánchez
TEL (212) 227-3795

Diverse Dimensions Art, Ltd
P.O. Box 88-H
Scarsdale, NY 10583
TEL (914) 636-6012
FAX (914) 636-8978

Drake Prints
2809 Forest Avenue
Des Moines, IA 50311
Attn: Richard Black
TEL (515) 271-3160
FAX (515) 271-3977

Durham Press, Inc
892 Durham Road
P O Box 159
Durham, PA 18039
Attn: Jean-Paul Russell
TEL (215) 346-6133
FAX (215) 346-8504

Echo Press
1901 East 10th Street
Bloomington, IN 47408
Attn: Rudy Pozzatti
TEL (812) 855-0476
FAX (812) 855-0477

Egan/Reams Silkscreen
219 West 24th Street
Los Angeles, CA 90007
TEL (213) 749-8800

El Cerro Graphics
26 Airport Road
Los Lunas, NM 87031
Attn: Ricardo C Zimenes
TEL (505) 865-5602

Eldindean Press
83-45 Broadway, #507
Elmhurst, NY 11373
Attn: Anthony Kirk
TEL (718) 592-2660

Erie-Lackawanna Editions
119 North 11th Street, #3C
Brooklyn, NY 11211
Attn: Brenda Zlamany
TEL (718) 387-3905

Etching Studio
1121 East Freeway
Houston, TX 77002
Attn: Penelope Cerling
TEL (713) 228-4116

Cindi Ettinger Studio
144 Vine Street
Philadelphia, PA 19106
TEL (215) 928-9897

Evans Editions, Inc
140 Watts Street
New York, NY 10013
Attn: Sue Ann Evans
TEL (212) 274-1128
FAX (212) 274-1215

Exeter Press & Paper
168 Mercer Street, #4
New York, NY 10012
Attn: A Lynn Forgach
TEL (212) 966-4125
FAX (212) 966-5678

Experimental Etching Studio, Inc
EES Arts
34 Plympton Street
Boston, MA 02118
Attn: Deborah Cornell
TEL (617) 482-9646

Experimental Workshop
P O Box 77504
Pier 46-B, Door 13
San Francisco, CA 94107
Attn: Ann Mclaughlin
TEL (415) 957-0148
FAX (415) 957-9309

Fabric Workshop
1100 Vine Street
Philadelphia, PA 19107
Attn: Nancy Miller Batty
   Marion Boulton Stroud
TEL (215) 922-7303
FAX (215) 922-3791

Fishy Whale Press
411 Lincoln Avenue
Rockford, IL 61102
Attn: Roland Poska
TEL (815) 964-0016

Flatbed Press
912 West 3rd Street
Austin, TX 78703
Attn: Mark L Smith
TEL (512) 477-9328
FAX (512) 474-1799

Flatstone Studio
201 West Comanche Avenue
Tampa, FL 33604
TEL (813) 237-8707

Four Brothers Press
1312 West North Avenue
Chicago, IL 60622
TEL (312) 486-0130

4th Street Printshop
219 East 4th Street, #3-B
New York, NY 10009
Attn: William Jung
   Susan Rostow
TEL (212) 473-4670

Fox Graphics Editions, Ltd
4 Mechanic Street
Merrimac, MA
Attn: Herb Fox
TEL (617) 346-8859

Freeman Editions
742 North Hayworth Avenue
Los Angeles, CA 90046
Attn: Daniel B Freeman
TEL (213) 651-5361
FAX (213) 658-6822

Full Court Press
8917 Meade
Morton Grove, IL 60053
Attn: Eric Robbins
TEL (708) 966-3623

Gehenna Press
P O Box 687
Rockport, ME 04856
Attn: Leonard Baskin
TEL (207) 236-8665
FAX (207) 236-8670

Gemini GEL
8365 Melrose Avenue
Los Angeles, CA 90069
TEL (213) 651-0513

Genovese Graphics
535 Albany Street
Boston, MA 02118
Attn: Camellia Genovese
TEL (617) 426-9738
TEL (617) 426-2062

Randy Gibbs, Lithography
4523 East Sunland Avenue
Phoenix, AZ 85040
TEL (602) 829-1025

Graphics Workshop
632 Agua Fria
Santa Fe, NM 87501
Attn: Ron Pokrasso
TEL (505) 984-0827

Graphicstudio
3702 Spectrum Blvd, #100
Tampa, FL 33612
Attn: Alan Eaker
TEK (813) 974-3503
FAX (813) 974-2579

Graphicstudio II
College of Fine Arts
Univ of South Florida
Tampa, FL 33620
TEL (813) 247-5173

Grenfell Press
116 West 29th Street
New York, NY 10001
Attn: Leslie Miller
TEL (212) 947-8846

Grin Graphics
465 West 46th Street, #5
New York, NY 10036
Attn: Rand Russell
TEL (212) 307-5405

John Gruenwald, Printmaker
341 North Milwaukee Street
Milwaukee, WI 53202
TEL (414) 276-7484

H E I
P.O. Box 370
Nevada City, CA 95959
Attn: Morgan Fox
TEL (800) 869-0658
FAX (916) 432-1810

HMK Fine Arts, Inc
15 Gramercy Park, South
New York, NY 10003
TEL (212) 982-4800

Hamilton Press
5340 Hamilton Avenue
Cleveland, OH 44114
Attn: Barry Hoffman
TEL (216) 431-9001
FAX (216) 431-0008

Hampton Editions, Ltd
P O Box 520
Sag Harbor, NY 11963
Attn: Dan Welden
TEL (516) 725-3990

Hand Graphics
418 Montezuma
Santa Fe, NM 87501
Attn: Michael Costello
   Robert Brady
TEL (505) 988-1241
TEL (505) 988-2350

Hand Print Workshop
210 West Windsor Avenue
Alexandria, VA 22301
Attn: Dennis O'Neil
TEL (703) 549-3988

Hard Press Editions
1101 North Paulina
Chicago, IL 60622
TEL (312) 235-3712

Har-El Printers
Jaffa Port
P O Box 8053
Jaffa 61081 Israel
TEL (972-3) 81.68.34
FAX (972-3) 81.35.63

Harlan & Weaver Intaglio
83 Canal Street
New York, NY 10002
Attn: Felix Harlan
   Carol Weaver
TEL (212) 925-5421

Heliochrome Press
P O Box 214
Dalton, MA 01226
Attn: Thomas Reardon
TEL (413) 684-2200
FAX (413) 684-0220

Henning Studio
120 95th Street
Brooklyn, NY 11209
TEL (212) 745-1335

Miguel Herrer
Atelier 2/20
220 West 16th Street
New York, NY 10011

Edna Hibel Corporation
P O Box 9967
Riviera Beach, FL 33419
Attn: Cheryll R Plotkin
TEL (407) 848-9633

PRINTERS/PRINT WORKSHOPS INDEX CONTINUED

Hine Editions/Limestone Press
357 Tehama Street
San Francisco, CA 94103
Attn: Hank Hine
TEL (415) 777-2214
FAX (415) 495-2665

Hollaender Press
52 Beach Street
New York, NY 10013
Attn: Sherri Hollaender
TEL (212) 431-8529

Honolulu Printmaking Workshop
1111 Victoria Street
Honolulu, HI 96814
Attn: Laura Smith
TEL (808) 536-5507

Horton Tank Graphics
47 East Street
Hadley, MA 01035
Attn: Arthur Larson
TEL (513) 584-0783
FAX (413) 586-2415

Susan Hover Editions
119 North 11th Street
Brooklyn, NY 11211
TEL (718) 388-1864

Hudson River Editions
288 Piermont Avenue
South Nyack, NY 10960
Attn: Sylvia Roth
TEL (914) 358-2399

Hudson Street Press
100 Hudson Street, #2-E
New York, NY 10013
Attn: Peter Yamaoka
TEL (212) 334-9325
FAX (212) 334-1214

I/RS Press
309 Portman Villa Road
Black Mountain, NC 28711
Attn: Porge Buck
TEL (704) 669-1939

Il Pointe Editrice d'Arte
Via S Ignazio 6
Rome, Italy 00186

Images Limited Edition Press
912 124th Avenue
Shelbyville, MI 49344
Attn: Jonathan B Clemens
TEL (616) 672-7213

Imprint Fine Art
100 Hudson Street, #2-E
New York, NY 10013
Attn: Karl Godber
        Peter Yamaoka
TEL (212) 226-4750
FAX (212) 334-1214

Iris Editions
399 Washington Street
New York, NY 10013
Attn: Deli Sacilotto
TEL (212) 966-7274
FAX (212) 431-3471

K5
179 DeKalb Avenue
Brooklyn, NY 11205
Attn: Karl Hecksher
TEL (718) 330-0425

KJH Press
1009 Dove Drive
Manchaca, TX 78652
Attn: Ken Hale
TEL (512) 282-4552

Kala Institute
1060 Heinz Avenue
Berkeley, CA 94710
Attn: Archana Horsting
TEL (510) 549-2977
FAX (510) 549-2984

Karl & Gail, Inc
338 Berry Street
Brooklyn, NY 11211
Attn: Karl Godber
TEL (718) 338-3568
FAX (718) 388-0661

Kelyn Press
254 Hampton
Venice, CA 90291
TEL (213) 396-6524

Kimball Lithograph Co, Ltd
1328 East Harvest Street
Mesa, AZ 85203
TEL (602) 964-5208

Michael Klein
250 West 104th Street
New York, NY 10025
TEL (212) 749-3837

Sabina Klein Studios
S K Fine Arts
245 West 29th Street
New York, NY 10001
TEL (212) 695-5293

Joseph Kleineman
J K Fine Arts
600 Palisades Avenue
New York, NY 10011
Attn: Joseph Kleineman
        Maureen A Turci
TEL (212) 947-0501
Established in 1975

Peter Koch, Printer
2203 4th Street
Berkeley, CA 94710
TEL (510) 849-0673

Koda Lithographik
PO Box 30
Springville, UT 84663-0030
Attn: Todd Frye, Director
TEL (801) 489-8427

La Paloma
10308 Glenoaks Blvd
Pacoima, CA 91331
Attn: Ron McPherson
TEL (818) 890-2216
FAX (818) 890-4371

Lakeside Studio
15263 Lakeshore Road
Lakeside, MI 49116
TEL (616) 469-1377

Land Mark Editions
700 Washington Avenue, North, #419
Minneapolis, MN 55401
Attn: Jon M Swenson
TEL (612) 375-1690

Landfall Press, Inc
329 West 18th Street, #601
Chicago, IL 60616
Attn: Jack Lemon
TEL (312) 666-6709
FAX (312) 666-1486

Lawrence Lithography Workshop
7 East 7th Street
Lawrence, KS 66044
Attn: Michael Sims
TEL (913) 843-8375

David Lawrence Editions
P O Box 3702
Beverly Hills, CA 90212
TEL (310) 278-0882
FAX (310) 278-0883

Ruth Leaf Studio
40-30 235th Street
Douglaston, NY 11363
TEL (718) 225-4734

Lee Center Studios & Print Shop
5722 Lee Highway
Arlington, VA 22207
Attn: Sandra Wasko-Flood
TEL (703) 358-5256

Limestone Press
357 Tehama Street
San Francisco, CA 94103
TEL (415) 777-2214

Katherine Lincoln Press
4253 21st Street
San Francisco, CA 94114
Attn: Kay Bradner
TEL (415) 282-7196

The Litho Shop, Inc
2058 Broadway
Santa Monica, CA 90404
Attn: Beth Silverman
TEL (310) 828-0792
FAX (310) 829-6842

Logan Elm Press
Ohio State Univ
340 Hopkins Hall
Columbus, OH 43210
TEL (614) 422-0421

Lonetown Press
P O Box 62
Redding, CT 06875
Attn: Randall Folkman
TEL (203) 938-9921

Lower East Side Printshop
59-61 East 4th Street
New York, NY 10009
Attn: Sara Pasti
TEL (212) 673-5390

M O K
68 Day Street
Brooklyn, NY 11201
Attn: Mohammad O Khalil
TEL (212) 255-9429

Mackie/Damast
450 West 31st Street
New York, NY 10001
TEL (212) 564-8532

Made in California
3246 Ettie Street, #16
Oakland, CA 94608-4016
Attn: David Kelso
TEL (415) 428-2699

Magnolia Editions
2527 Magnolia Street
Oakland, CA 94607
Attn: Don Farnsworth
        David Kimball
TEL (510) 834-2527
FAX (510) 893-8334

Mahaffey Fine Arts
328 NW Broadway, #238
Portland, OR 97209
Attn: Mark Mahaffey
        Rae Mahaffey
TEL (503) 295-6666

Maine Printmaking Workshop
Westbrook Col, Stevens Avenue
Portland, ME 04103
TEL (207) 797-7261

Maurel Studios
12 Warren Street
New York, NY 10007
Attn: Sheila Marbain
TEL (212) 513-7435

Maxwell-Nova Fine Arts, Inc
111 Cedar Street
New Rochelle, NY 10801
Attn: William C Maxwell

Jennifer Melby, Printer
356 Bowery
New York, NY 10012
TEL (212) 477-3891

Burr Miller & Sons
20 West 22nd Street
New York, NY 10010

Mirror Image Press
148 North Dey Street
Virden, IL 62690
Attn: Meda R Rives
        Veda M Rives
TEL (217) 965-5311

Mixit Print Studio
32 Clifton Street
Somerville, MA 02144
Attn: Jane E Goldman
        Catherine Kerman
TEL (617) 628-8014
TEL (617) 629-2568

PRINTERS/PRINT WORKSHOPS INDEX CONTINUED

Mixografia Workshop, Inc
1419 East Adams Blvd
Los Angeles, CA 90011
Attn: Luis Ramba
TEL (213) 232-1158
FAX (213) 232-1655

Catherine Mosley Workshop
Art Press
458 Broome Street
New York, NY 10012
TEL (212) 431-4826

Naravisa Press
128 Naravisa Road, NW
Albuquerque, NM 87107
TEL (505) 344-7312

Nash Editions
1201 Oak Avenue
Manhattan Beach, CA 90266
Attn: R Mac Holbert
TEL (310) 545-4352
FAX (310) 545-8565

Navavisa Press
Rte 2, Box 280
Santa Fe, NM 87505
Attn: Stephen Britko
TEL (505) 473-2684

New City Editions
525 Venezia Avenue
Venice, CA 90291
Attn: Joel Stearns
TEL (310) 822-0818
FAX (310) 822-0971

New Harmony Print Workshop
P O Box 551
New Harmony, IN 47631
TEL (812) 682-4855

Noblet Serigraphie, Inc
425 West 13th Street
New York, NY 10014
Attn: Jean-Yves Noblet
TEL (212) 243-0439
FAX (212) 243-0503

Normal Editions Workshop
c/o Art Department 5620
Illinois State University
Normal, IL 61761
Attn: Richard Finch
TEL (309) 438-7530
FAX (309) 438-8318

North Light Editions
1624 NW Lovejoy
Portland, OR 97209
TEL (503) 241-2200

NYIT Screen Print Workshop
New York Institute of Technology
Wheatley Road
Old Westbury, NY 11568
Attn: Roni Henning
TEL (516) 686-7611

Oberon Press
480 Canal Street
New York, NY 10013
Attn: Raymond Bligh
        Malcolm MacNeill
TEL (212) 274-0560
FAX (212) 274-0562

Occasional Works
P O Box 620588
Woodside, CA 94062
Attn: Ann Rosener
TEL (415) 322-6350

Off Jones Road Prints
7046 Reimann Road
Arena, WI 53503
Attn: Bill Weege
TEL (608) 753-2332
FAX (608) 753-2590

Okeanos Press
2808 San Pablo Avenue
Berkeley, CA 94702
Attn: Eric Johnson
TEL (510) 858-4114
FAX (510) 848-4141

Olive Press
100 Olive Tjaden Hall
Department of Art
Cornell University
Ithaca, NY 14853
Attn: Victor Kord
        Greg Page
TEL (607) 255-3558
FAX (607) 255-1900

Osiris Screen
480 Canal Street
New York, NY 10013
Attn: George Drexel
TEL (212) 226-5729
FAX (212) 941-6714

Oxbow Press
65 University Drive
Amherst, MA 01002
TEL (413) 549-6506

PCAD Printmaking Workshop
Borowsky Center for Publication Arts
University of the Arts
Philadelphia College of Art &
Design Printmaking
320 South Broad Street
Philadelphia, PA 19102
Attn: Lois M Johnson
TEL (215) 875-1119
FAX (215) 875-5467

Palm Press, Ltd
2015 15th Street
Tampa, FL 33605
TEL (813) 248-3959

Mark Patsfall Graphics, Inc
1312 Clay Street
Cincinnati, OH 45210
TEL (513) 241-3232
FAX (513) 241-3029

Pelavin Editions Press
13 Jay Street
New York, NY 10013
Etching Workshop
TEL (212) 925-9424

Peregrine Press, Inc
P O Box 671046
Dallas, TX 75367-8046
TEL (214) 939-9050

Petersburg Press
380 Lafayette Street
New York, NY 10003
TEL (212) 420-0890

Pleiades Press
Studio Graphic Workshop
3014 Avenue C, #1
Holmes Beach, FL 34217
Attn: Barbara Neustadt
TEL (813) 778-2466
Representing Printmaker B
Neustadt & Others

Plucked Chicken Press
1604 Greenleaf
Evanston, IL 60202
Attn: Will Petersen
TEL (708) 475-0530

Pondside Press
4 Bollenbecker Road
Rhinebeck, NY 12572
Attn: Melissa Katzman Braggins
        Ted Braggins

Prasada-Press, Inc
4303 Hamilton Avenue
Cincinnati, OH 45223
TEL (513) 542-0350

Preston Graphics
44 Currierville Road
Newton, NH 03858
Attn: Robert Preston
TEL (603) 382-3077
FAX (603) 382-3077

Print Editions, Ltd
156 Haven Avenue
Port Washington, NY 11050
Attn: K C Wilsey, Jr
TEL (516) 883-5678

Printmaking Workshop
55 West 17th Street
New York, NY 10011
Attn: Robert Blackburn
TEL (212) 989-6125

Prints in Progress
54 North 3rd Street
Philadelphia, PA 19106
Attn: Michele D Grant
TEL (215) 928-0206
FAX (215) 925-3856

Prior Editions
1028 Hamilton Street #303
Vancouver, BC
Canada V6A 2R9
Attn: Nigel Harrison
TEL (604) 685-0535

Public Image Prints
Fine Art Silkscreen Printing
Newton Road—P O Box 158
Stephenson, NY 12168
Attn: Nick Farina
TEL (519) 733-6080

Pyramid Atlantic
6001 66th Avenue, #103
Riverdale, MD 20737
Attn: Helen Frederick
TEL (301) 459-7154
TEL (301) 577-3424
FAX (301) 459-7629

Quiet Sun Press
2351 Sonoma
Torrance, CA 90501
Attn: Connor Everts
TEL (310) 320-1624

Renaissance Press
P O Box 774
8 Snow Avenue
Hinsdale, NH 03451
Attn: Paul M Taylor
TEL (603) 336-7411
FAX (603) 382-3077

Riverhouse Editions
31055 County Road, #64
P O Box 669
Clark, CO 80428
Attn: William Van Straaten
TEL (303) 879-6394
FAX (312) 642-5693

Rolling Stone Press
432 Calhoun Street, NW
Atlanta, GA 30318
Attn: Wayne Kline
TEL (404) 873-3322

Rutgers Center for Innovative Printmaking
Department of Visual Arts
Mason Gross School of the Arts
New Brunswick, NJ 08901
Attn: Judith K Brodsky
TEL (908) 932-8449
TEL (908) 932-9499
FAX (908) 932-1343

Screen Print Workshop
New York Inst of Tech
Media/Art Center
Wheatley Road
Old Westbury, NY 11568
TEL (516) 686-7611

Screen Print Workshop
924 Fireplace Road
East Hampton, NY 11937
TEL (516) 324-5391

Screened Images, Inc
156 Haven Avenue
Port Washington, NY 11050
Attn: Steven Maiorano
TEL (516) 883-1343
Specializing in Fine Art Screen Printing

Segura Publishing Company, Inc
688 West First, #6
Tempe, AZ 85281
Attn: Joe Segura
TEL (602) 894-0551
FAX (602) 921-4310

Self-Help Graphics
3802 Brooklyn Avenue
Los Angeles, CA 90063
Attn: Sister Karen Boccalero
TEL (213) 264-1259

PRINTERS/PRINT WORKSHOPS INDEX CONTINUED

Serigraphics
1029 San Mateo, SE
Albuquerque, NM 87108
TEL (505) 265-0071

Sette Publishing Co
688 West First Street, #4
Tempe, AZ 85281
Attn: Kristi Warren
TEL (602) 894-0551

Shark's, Inc
2020 9th Street
Boulder, CO 80302
Attn: Bud Shark
TEL (303) 443-4601
FAX (303) 443-1245

Donald Sheridan Fine Arts
350 Manhattan Avenue
Brooklyn, NY 11211
TEL (718) 383-4924
FAX (718) 383-4924

Simca Print Artists, Inc
27 Howard Street
New York, NY 10013
Attn: Hiroshi Kawanishi
TEL (212) 431-5848

Simmelink/Sukimoto Editions
13327 Beach Avenue
Marina Del Rey, CA 90292
Attn: Doris Simmelink
    Chris Sukimoto
TEL (310) 301-3330

Soho Graphic Arts Workshop
433 West Broadway, #5
New York, NY 10012
Attn: Mr. Rivera
Etching, Lithography, Silkscreen
TEL (212) 966-7292

Solo Press, Inc
520 Broadway
New York, NY 10012
Attn: Judith Solodkin
TEL (212) 925-3315
TEL (212) 925-3316
TEL (212) 925-3599
FAX (212) 226-3251

Soma Fine Art Press
665 Third Street, #225
San Francisco, CA 94107
Attn: Sarah Henderson
TEL (415) 495-7997

Small Tree Press
1402 18th Street
San Francisco, CA 94107
Attn: Evie Lincoln
    Brian Shure
TEL (415) 431-0676

Spring Press
524 Broadway, Room 207
New York, NY 10012
Attn: Orlando Condeso
TEL (212) 226-7430

Spring Street Workshop
72 Sprint Street
New York, NY 10012
Attn: Joe Wilfer
TEL (212) 226-1577
FAX (212) 431-5825

St Jives Intaglio Workshop
254 Hampton Drive
Venice, CA 90291
Attn: Annette Bird
TEL (310) 399-3987

St Michael's Printshop
St Michael's Southern Shore
Newfoundland
Canada AOA 4A0
Attn: Agnes Morry Williams
TEL (709) 334-2931

Stewart & Stewart
5571 Wing Lake Road
Birmingham, MI 58010
Attn: Norman Stewart
TEL (313) 626-5248

C Stone Press
80 Wooster Street
New York, NY 10012
Attn: Carolyn Stone
TEL (212) 226-2932

Stone Press Editions
3815 4th Avenue, NE
Seattle, WA 98105
Attn: Kent Lovelace
TEL (206) 633-1160

Studio Heinrici, Ltd
163 Varick Street
New York, NY 10013
Attn: Alexander Heinrici
TEL (212) 989-1717

Survival Graphics
853 Williamson Street
Madison, WI 53703
Attn: Patrick J B Flynn
    Dorla Mayer
TEL (608) 251-2440

Styria Studio, Inc
426 Broome Street
New York, NY 10013
Attn: Adi Rischner
TEL (212) 226-1373

Tamarind Institute
108 Cornell Avenue SE,
Albuquerque, NM 87106
Attn: Marjorie Devon
Tel (505) 277-3901

Tandem Press
201 South Dickinson Street
Madison, WI 53703
Attn: Paula McCarthy Panczenko
TEL (608) 263-3437
FAX (608) 265-2356

Tangent Graphics
162 Lodi Street
Hackensack, NJ 07601

Elizabeth Tapper Intaglio Printing
307 3rd Avenue, South, #203
Seattle, WA 98104
TEL (206) 623-8824

Teaberry Press
347 Dolores, #105
San Francisco, CA 94110
Attn: Timothy Berry
TEL (415) 552-6363

Tiger Lily Press
1125 Saint Gregory Street
Cincinnati, OH 45202
Attn: Steve clark
    Louann Elliott
TEL (513) 562-8759

Topaz Editions, Inc
13305 Cain Road
Tampa, FL 33625
Attn: Julio Juristo
TEL (813) 961-3137

R E Townsend Studio
18 Andover Street
Georgetown, MA 01833
Attn: Robert E Townsend
TEL (508) 352-2174

Trestle Editions, Ltd
75 Varick Street
New York, NY 10013
Attn: Bruce Porter
TEL (212) 226-8111

Trillium Graphics
91 Park Lane
Brisbane, CA 94005
Attn: David M Salgado
TEL (415) 468-8166
FAX (415) 468-8166

Triton Collection
104 West 27th Street
New York, NY 10001
Attn: Derek L Limbocker
TEL (212) 255-3703
TEL (800) 847-4198
FAX (212) 691-0543

Tsuka-Guchi Atelier
2704 Poplar Street
Philadelphia, PA 19130
Attn: Shigemitsu Tsukaguchi
TEL (215) 236-9097

Tullis Workshop
1 North Salsipuedes Street, #9
Santa Barbara, CA 93103
Attn: Richard B Tullis II
TEL (805) 965-1091
FAX (805) 965-1093

Garner Tullis
10 White Street
New York, NY 10013
TEL (212) 226-6665
FAX (212) 941-0678

2/20 Workshop
220 West 16th Street
New York, NY 10011
Attn: M Herrera
TEL (212) 807-8348

21 Steps
413 2nd Street, SW
Albuquerque, NM 87102
Attn: Jeffrey Ryan
TEL (505) 242-1115

Tyler Graphics, Ltd
250 Kisco Avenue
Mount Kisco, NY 10549
Attn: Ken Tyler
TEL (914) 241-2707

Unified Arts
1212 Lovato, SW
Albuquerque, NM 87105
Attn: Judy Booth
    Jim Kraft
TEL (505) 842-6301

Union Printmakers
Room 712—1900 L Street, NW
Washington, DC 20037
Attn: Scip Barnhart
TEL (202) 296-5857

Universal Limited Art Editions, Inc
5 Skidmore Place
West Islip, NY 11795
Attn: Bill Goldston
TEL (516) 669-7484
FAX (516) 669-7338

University of Hartford Print Workshop
University of Hartford
Hartford Art School
200 Bloomfield Avenue
West Hartford, CT
Attn: Fred Wessel
TEL (203) 243-4393

UNO Print Workshop
Art & Art History Department
University of Nebraska
Omaha, NE 68114
Attn: Gary Day
    Thomas Majeski
TEL (402) 554-3757
FAX (402) 554-3436

UW Printworkshop
Univ of Wisconsin
455 Park Street
Madison, WI 53706
TEL (608) 263-2246

Vermillion Editions, Ltd
2919 Como Avenue
Minneapolis, MN 55414
TEL (612) 338-6808

Vinalhaven Press
P O Box 464
Vinalhaven, ME 04863
Attn: Patricia Nick
TEL (207) 863-4937
FAX (212) 219-1561

PRINTERS/PRINT WORKSHOPS INDEX CONTINUED

Visual Studies Workshop
31 Prince Street
Rochester, NY 14607
Attn: Nathan Lyons
TEL (716) 442-8676

Wasserman Silk Screen Company
1664 12th Street
Santa Monica, CA 90404
Attn: Jeffrey A Wasserman
TEL (310) 450-6777

Washington University Printmaking Workshop
Univ Sch of Fine Arts
Bixby Hall, PO Box 1031
St Louis, MO 63130
TEL (314) 889-5490

Watanabe Studio, Ltd
341 Scholes Street
Brooklyn, NY 11206
Attn: Jo Watanabe
TEL (718) 456-6894
FAX (718) 386-8709

Water Street Press, Ltd
223 Water Street, 1st & 2nd Floors
Brooklyn, NY 11201
TEL (212) 522-5983

Watermark Editions
SE 3591 Old Olympic Highway
Shelton, WA 98584
Attn: Mahri Breenan
TEL (206) 427-1717
TEL (206) 427-1313

Western Illinois Folio Press
c/o Art Department
Western Illinois University
Macomb, IL 61455
Attn: Frederick Jones
TEL (309) 298-1768

Wild Carrot Letterpress
47 East Street
Hadley, MA 01035
Attn: Daniel Keleher
TEL (413) 586-2648
FAX (413) 586-9844

Wingate Studio
RFD 2, Rte 63
Hinsdale, NH 03451
Attn: Peter Pettengill
TEL (603) 239-6725

Winstone Press, Inc
Rte 2, Box 118
Mocksville, NC 27028
Attn: Cappy Kuhn
TEL (919) 998-3330
FAX (919) 766-9661

Efram Wolff Studio
14535 Arminta Street, East
Van Nuys, CA 91402
TEL (213) 780-0893

Women's Studio Workshop
P O Box 489
Rosendale, NY 12472
Attn: Ann Kalmbach
TEL (914) 658-9133

Workshop, Inc
3145 Newark Street, NW
Washington, DC 20008
Attn: Lou Stovall
TEL (202) 966-4202
FAX (202) 362-0116

Larry B Wright Art Productions
164 Mulberry Street
New York, NY 10013
TEL (212) 925-3047

Wycross Press
P O Box 2311
Auburn, AL 36830
Attn: Conrad Ross
TEL (205) 887-6836

X Press
116 West 29th Street
New York, NY 10001
Attn: Alan Koslin
TEL (212) 947-9214

Yama Prints
140 West 30th Street, #4-E
New York, NY 10001
Attn: Betty Winkler
TEL (212) 594-1771

FINE ART APPRAISERS INDEX

Anderson Gallery
Martha Jackson Place
Buffalo, NY 14214
Attn: Anne Wayson
TEL (716) 834-2579
FAX (716) 834-7789
Specializing in Contemporary
Paintings, Sculptures & Prints

Appraisers International, Inc
3729 South Dixie Highway
West Palm Beach, FL 33405
Attn: Mary Lou Nicholas
TEL (407) 832-0099

Juanita C Brown, Ltd
4401 NE 36th Street
Oklahoma City, OK 73121-6502
Fine Art Appraiser
TEL (405) 424-3795

Gilda Ellis Beane Fine Art
P O Box 1026
Palm Beach, FL 33480
TEL (407) 655-2346
FAX (407) 655-2346
Member of Appraisers Association
of America
Appraiser & Consultant Since 1971
By Appt

Edelstein & Associates
Fine Art Appraisers
2650 Lakeview, Suite 1202
Chicago, IL 60614
Attn: Carrie Edelstein
TEL (312) 665-4744
FAX (312) 665-4744

Edrich Fine Arts, Ltd
208 Wheatley Road
Old Westbury, NY 11568
Attn: Hal Edrich
Hildy Travis
Specializing in Contemporary Prints
TEL (516) 626-7903

Evelio Art Studio
401 South Clinton Avenue
Trenton, NJ 08609
Attn: Prof. Sigmund J. Kardas, Jr
TEL (609) 695-ARTS

Fine Arts Appraisers
180 North Michigan Avenue,
Suite #305
Chicago, IL 60601
Attn: Barbara K. Schnitzer
Sarah M. Potter
TEL (312) 782-6650

Glass Art Gallery
315 Central Park, West, Suite 8-W
New York, NY 10025
Attn: Wendy D Glass
TEL (212) 787-4704
Member: Appraisers Association
of America

National Arts Services
88 University Avenue, #707
Toronto, ON
M5J 1T6 Canada
Attn: Martin M Carmelly, ASA
Fine Art/Antiques/Decorative Art
TEL (416) 340-8000
FAX (416) 340-0129

National Institute of Appraisers
P O Box 69301
Los Angeles, CA 90069
Attn: Ed Okil
    Craig McMichael
    Ed Albaugh
    Ann Solomon
TEL (213) 289-1148
TEL (800) 676-2148
FAX (213) 289-1148

PRINT ASSOCIATIONS INDEX

Los Angeles Printmaking Society & Foundation
3666 Longridge Avenue
Sherman Oaks, CA 91423
Attn: Jean Burg, President
350 Artist Members
Exhibitions/Seminars
Slide Register: Toby Willner
TEL (818) 788-3319 (Burg)
TEL (213) 931-6298 (Willner)

PRINT CLUB INDEX

Print Club of Albany, Inc
P.O. Box 6578
Albany, NY 12019
Attn: Charles Semowich
TEL (518) 432-9514

AUCTION INDEX

Santa Monica Auctions
2044 Broadway
Santa Monica, CA 90404
Attn: Robert Berman
    Gabriela Trench
TEL (310) 453-9196
Specializing in Contemporary Art

GALLERY INDEX

A Associated Fine Art
22458 Mission Blvd
Hayward, CA 94541
Attn: Bill R Neads
TEL (510) 886-6700

ACA Galleries
41 East 57th Street
New York, NY 10021
Attn: Sidney Bergen
　　　Jeffrey Bergen
TEL (212) 644-8300

AIR Gallery
63 Crosby Street
New York, NY 10012
Attn: Sarah Savidge
TEL (212) 966-0799

AOI Gallery
634 Canyon Road
Santa Fe, NM 87501
Attn: Frank Aoi
TEL (505) 982-3456
FAX (505) 982-2040

ARC Gallery
1040 West Huron Street
Chicago, IL 60622
Attn: Janet Stevens
TEL (312) 733-2787

A T Galleries
255 North Lake Blvd
P O Box 95
Tahoe City, CA 96145
Attn: Peter Torres
TEL (916) 583-1635

Aaron Galleries
620 North Michigan Avenue
Chicago, IL 60611
Attn: Patrick Albano
TEL (312) 943-0660

Aaron Gallery
1717 Connecticut, NW
Washington, DC 20009
Attn: Consuelo C Aaron
TEL (202) 234-3311

Didier Aaron Gallery
32 East 67th Street
New York, NY 10021
Attn: Herve Aaron
TEL (212) 988-5248
FAX (212) 737-3513

Abacus Gallery
44 Exchange Street
Portland, ME 04101
TEL (207) 772-4880

Abanté Fine Art
204 SW Yamhill
Portland, OR 97204
Attn: Rudi Milpacher
　　　Tom Milpacher
TEL (503) 295-2508

Aberbach Fine Art
675 Third Avenue
New York, NY 10017-5704
Attn: Joachim Aberbach
TEL (212) 988-1100

Abney Gallery
591 Broadway, 3rd Floor
New York, NY 10012
Attn: O'Delle Abney
TEL (212) 941-8602
FAX (212) 941-8602

Abstein Gallery of Art
558 14th Street, NW
Atlanta, GA 30318
Attn: Maralice Kiernan
TEL (404) 872-8020

Acquavella Contemporary Art
10 East 79th Street
New York, NY 10021
Attn: William R. Acquavella
TEL (212) 734-6300

Adams Davidson Galleries
3233 P Street, NW
Washington, DC 20007
Attn: Theodore Cooper
　　　Kristin Johnson
TEL (202) 965-3800

Adams/Middleton Gallery
3000 Maple Avenue
Dallas, TX 75201
Attn: Anita Middleton
　　　Holly Johnson
TEL (214) 871-7080
FAX (214) 871-7084

David Adamson Gallery
406 Seventh Street, NW
Washington, DC 20004
TEL (202) 628-0257

Adamson-Duvannes Galleries
484 South San Vicente Blvd
Los Angeles, CA 90048
Attn: Jerome D Adamson, Jr
TEL (213) 653-1015

Addison/Ripley Gallery, Ltd
9 Hillyer Court, NW
Washington, DC 20008
Attn: Christopher Addison
　　　Sylvia Ripley
TEL (202) 328-2332

Adele M Gallery
3317 McKinney Avenue
Dallas, TX 75204
Attn: Adelle M Taylor
TEL (214) 220-0300

Rachel Adler Gallery
41 East 57th Street, #1300
New York, NY 10022
TEL (212) 308-0511
FAX (212) 308-0516

Adobe Gallery
413 Romero, NW
Albuquerque, NM 87104
Attn: Alexander E Anthony, Jr
TEL (505) 243-8485

Aetna Gallery
205 Farmington Avenue
Hartford, CT 66156
TEL (203) 727-4286

Affrica
2010 R Street, NW
Lower Level
Washington, DC 20009
Attn: Mona Gavigan
TEL (202) 745-7272

Afterimage Photograph Gallery
Quadrangle #115
2828 Routh Street
Dallas, TX 75201
Attn: Ben Breard
TEL (214) 871-9140

Akin Gallery
207 South Street
Boston, MA 02111
Attn: Alison Akin Righter
TEL (617) 266-3535

Salvatore Ala
560 Broadway, 3rd Floor
New York, NY 10012
Attn: Caroline Martin
TEL (212) 941-1990
FAX (212) 334-6439

Scott Alan Gallery
524 Broadway, 6th Floor
New York, NY 10012
Attn: Scott Krawitz
TEL (212) 226-5145

Jean Albano Gallery
311 Superior Street
Chicago, IL 60610
Attn: Jean Albano Broday
TEL (312) 440-0770
FAX (312) 440-3103

Albers Fine Art Gallery
1102 Brookfield Road
Memphis, TN 38119
Attn: Kathy Albers
TEL (901) 683-2256

Albertson-Peterson Gallery
329 Park Avenue, South
Winter Park, FL 32789
Attn: Judy Albertson
　　　Louise Peterson
TEL (407) 628-1258

Alex Gallery
2106 R Street, NW
Washington, DC 20008
Attn: Victor Gaetan
TEL (212) 667-2599

Brooke Alexander, Inc.
59 Wooster Street, 2nd Floor
New York, NY 10012-4349
Attn: Ted Bonin
TEL (212) 925-4338
FAX (212) 941-9565

Brooke Alexander Editions, Inc
476 Broome Street
New York, NY 10013
Attn: Carolina Nitsch-Jones, Director
TEL (212) 925-2070
FAX (212) 941-9565

Alianza Gallery
154 Newbury Street
Boston, MA 02116
Attn: Karen Rotenberg
TEL (617) 262-2385

Allard's Gallery
2225 West Shaw, #117
Fresno, CA 93711
Attn: Gladia Sethre
TEL (209) 225-7000

Allegra Gallery
1604 Sparkling Way
San Jose, CA 95125
Attn: Russell Moore
TEL (408) 265-7289

Allrich Gallery
251 Post Street
San Francisco, CA 94108
Attn: Louise Allrich
TEL (415) 398-8896
FAX (415) 398-0401

Allyson Louis Gallery
7200 Wisconsin Avenue
Bethesda, MD 20814
Attn: Robyn A Kluger
TEL (301) 656-2877

Alpha Gallery
121 Newbury Street
Boston, MA 02116
Attn: Alan Fink
　　　Joanna E Fink
TEL (617) 536-4465
FAX (617) 536-5695

Alpha Gallery
959 Broadway
Denver, CO 80203
Attn: Hilary DePolo-Ayers
TEL (303) 623-3577

Ambassador Galleries
137 Spring Street
New York, NY 10012
TEL (212) 431-9431
FAX (212) 431-8123

American Art
1126 Broadway Plaza
Tacoma, WA 98402
Attn: Rick Gottas
TEL (206) 272-4327

American Hand
2906 M Street, NW
Washington, DC 20007
Attn: Ken Deavers
TEL (202) 965-3273

Americana West Gallery
1630 Connecticut Avenue, NW
Washington, DC 20009
Attn: Leslie Stone
TEL (202) 265-1630

Will Ameringer Fine Art, Inc
350 East 79th Street, #6-B
New York, NY 10021
Attn: Gordon Avard
TEL (212) 452-0484
FAX (212) 452-0284

David Anderson Gallery
One Barcher Place
Buffalo, NY 14214
Attn: Carl Hecker
TEL (716) 834-2579
FAX (716) 834-7783

GALLERY INDEX CONTINUED

Anderson & Anderson Gallery
414 First Avenue, North, #240
Minneapolis, MN 55401
Attn: John Anderson
  Sue Anderson
TEL (612) 332-4889

Andres Art Gallery
219-225 West 25th Street, #2-B
New York, NY 10001
Attn: Jonathan A Benavides
TEL (212) 691-6739
FAX (212) 691-6739

Angles Gallery
2230 Main Street
Santa Monica, CA 90405
Attn: David McAuliffe
TEL (310) 396-5019
FAX (310) 396-3797

Joan Ankrum Fine Arts
327 North Orange Drive
Los Angeles, CA 90036
TEL (213) 857-5657

Annex Gallery
453 Sixth Avenue
San Diego, CA 92101
Attn: Joan Warren
TEL (619) 531-0888

Anton Gallery
2108 R Street, NW
Washington, DC 20008
Attn: Gail Enns
  John Figura
TEL (202) 328-0828

Apropos Art Gallery
701 East Las Olas Blvd
Fort Lauderdale, FL 33301
Attn: Laurie Lee Clark
TEL (305) 524-2100
FAX (305) 524-1817

W Graham Arader III Gallery
29 East 72nd Street
New York, NY 10021
Attn: Tom McLaughlin
TEL (212) 628-3668
FAX (212) 879-8714

W Graham Arader III Gallery
620 North Michigan
Chicago, IL 60611
Attn: Esther Sparks
TEL (312) 337-6033

Arch Gallery
644 Broadway, #2-E
New York, NY 10012
Attn: Daniela Montana
TEL (212) 260-5847
FAX (212) 260-5847

Archway Gallery
2600 Montrose Blvd.
Houston, TX 77006
Attn: Marcie Masterson
  Pat Moberley Moore
TEL (713) 522-2409

Arden Gallery
129 Newbury Street
Boston, MA 02116
Attn: Hope Turner
TEL (617) 247-0610

Area X Gallery
251 East 32nd Street, #16-H
New York, NY 10016
Attn: Bobbie Sioux Xuereb
TEL (212) 779-9360

Arras Gallery East
725 Fifth Avenue
New York, NY 10022
Attn: Adele Siegel
TEL (212) 751-0080

Art Angles Gallery
3411 East Chapman
Orange, CA 92669
Attn: Gerrie Schusterman
TEL (714) 639-8310

The Art Collector
4151 Taylor Street
San Diego, CA 92110
Attn: Janet Disraeli
TEL (619) 299-3232

Art Collector Gallery
802 West University Avenue
Gainesville, FL 32601
Attn: Eleanor Schmidt
TEL (904) 377-4211

The Art Gallery at Corvette Mike's
407 N Anheim Blvd
Orange, CA 92668
Attn: Mike Vietro
TEL (714) 978-1234
Specializing in Prints by Asaro,
Authouart, Behrens, Neiman,
Pergola & Others

Art Expressions
1006 East New Haven Avenue
Melbourne, FL 32901
Attn: Joseph L Conneen, Jr
TEL (407) 728-7053

Art Space
10550 Santa Monica Boulevard
Los Angeles, CA 90025
Attn: Lucy Adelman
TEL (310) 474-9813

Art Spectrum
425 East 59th Street, #32-C
New York, NY 10022
Attn: Mitch Morse
TEL (212) 593-1812

Artemisia Gallery
700 North Carpenter
Chicago, IL 60622
Attn: Michelle Constance-Boley
TEL (312) 226-7323

Artifacts Galleries
308 East Main
Bozeman, MT 59715
Attn: Kathryn Helzer
  Dianne Kommers
TEL (406) 586-3755

Artigliography
415 Massachusetts Avenue
Indianapolis, IN 46204
Attn: Kerry J Brown
TEL (317) 684-9855

Artique, Ltd
314 G Street
Anchorage, AK 99501
Attn: Tennys Owens
TEL (907) 277-1663

Artists' Den
203 Jefferson Street
Valparaiso, IN 46383
Attn: Dennis Miller
  Patricia Miller
TEL (219) 462-3883

Artists Space
223 West Broadway
New York, NY 10013
Attn: Susan Wyatt
TEL (212) 226-3970

Artmain
13 South Main
Minot, ND 58701
Attn: Beth Kjelson
  Becky Piehl
TEL (701) 838-4747

Artmakers, Inc
280 Broadway, #412
New York, NY 10007
TEL (212) 374-1461

Artspace
534 North Woodward
Birmingham, MI 48009
Attn: Lois P Pincus
TEL (313) 258-1540

Artworks Gallery
30 Arbor Street, South
Hartford, CT 06106
Attn: Judith Green
TEL (203) 231-9323

Artyard Gallery
1251 South Pearl Street
Denver, CO 80210
Attn: Peggy Mangold
TEL (303) 777-3219

Asher/Faure Gallery
612 North Almont Drive
Los Angeles, CA 90069
Attn: Patricia Faure
  Kyria Sabin
TEL (213) 271-3665

Asora Gallery
560 Broadway, #502
New York, NY 10013
TEL (212) 966-1937

Associated American Artists
20 West 57th Street
New York, NY 10019
Attn: Lillian Berkman
TEL (212) 399-5510

Atherton Gallery
219 West San Francisco Street
Santa Fe, NM 87501
Attn: Pamela Hagan
TEL (505) 986-8390

Atlanta Art Gallery
262 East Paces Ferry Road, NE
Atlanta, GA 30305
Attn: Edward Fritzie
TEL (404) 261-1233

Atlantic Gallery
164 Mercer Street
New York, NY 10012
Attn: Kate Rabinowitz
TEL (212) 219-3183

Atlantic Gallery
1055 Thomas Jefferson Street, NW
Washington, DC 20007
Attn: Virginia Smith
TEL (202) 337-2299

Atlas Galleries, Inc
549 North Michigan Avenue
Chicago, IL 60611
TEL (312) 329-9330
TEL (800) 423-7635
FAX (312) 329-9436

Attic Gallery
206 SW First Avenue
Portland, OR 97204
Attn: Diana Faville
TEL (503) 228-7830

Pamela Auchincloss Gallery
558 Broadway, 2nd Floor
New York, NY 10012
TEL (212) 966-7753
FAX (212) 431-3763

Eleanore Austerer Gallery
540 Sutter Street
San Francisco, CA 94102
TEL (415) 986-2244
FAX (415) 986-2281

Austral Gallery
2115 Park Avenue
St Louis, MO 63104
Attn: Mary Reid Brunstrom
TEL (314) 776-0300

Avery Gallery
390 Roswell Street
Marietta, GA 30060
Attn: Shae Avery
TEL (404) 427-2459

Axis Twenty, Inc
200 Peachtree Hills Avenue, NE
Atlanta, GA 30305
Attn: Joseph R Langford
  Renee C Gaston
TEL (404) 261-4022

BFL Gallery
42 Owenoke Park
Westport, CT 06880
Attn: Barbara E Lans
TEL (203) 227-9215

Babcock Galleries
724 Fifth Avenue
New York, NY 10019
Attn: Michael St Clair
  John Driscoll
TEL (212) 767-1852
FAX (212) 767-1857

GALLERY INDEX CONTINUED

Thomas Babeor Gallery
7470 Girard Avenue
La Jolla, CA 92037
TEL (619) 454-0345
FAX (619) 454-8722

Bacardi Art Gallery
2100 Biscayne Boulevard
Miami, FL 33137
Attn: Juan Espinosa
TEL (305) 573-8511

Bill Bace Gallery
2 Bond Street
New York, NY 10012
TEL (212) 388-9755

Ruth Bachofner Gallery
926 Colorado Avenue
Santa Monica, CA 90401
TEL (310) 458-8007
FAX (310) 458-9087

Franz Bader Gallery
1500 K Street
Washington, DC 20005
Attn: Wretha Hanson
TEL (202) 393-6111

Joshua Baer Gallery
476 Broome Street
New York, NY 10013
TEL (212) 431-4774
FAX (212) 431-3631

Joshua Baer & Company
116½ East Palace Avenue
Santa Fe, MN 87501
Attn: Michael Freiberg
TEL (505) 988-8944
FAX (505) 988-4621

Paolo Baldacci Gallery
41 East 41st Street, 5th Floor
New York, NY 10022
Attn: Philip Ottenbrite
TEL (212) 826-4210
FAX (212) 826-4292

Tamara Bane Gallery
8025 Melrose Avenue
Los Angeles, CA 90046
TEL (213) 651-1400
FAX (310) 205-0794

Bannatyne Gallery
604 Colorado Avenue
Santa Monica, CA 90401
Attn: Bryce Bannatyne, Jr.
TEL (310) 396-9668

Barclay Simpson, Inc
3669 Mt Diablo Blvd
Lafayette, CA 94549
Attn: Sharon Simpson
TEL (510) 284-7048

Barclay Fine Art, Inc.
424 Canyon Road
Santa Fe, NM 87501
Attn: Rutgers Barclay
TEL (505) 986-1400
FAX (505) 984-3007

David Barnett Gallery
1024 East State Street
Milwaukee, WI 53202
TEL (414) 271-5058

Baron/Boisante Gallery
50 West 57th Street
New York, NY 10019
TEL (212) 581-9191
FAX (212) 581-9291

J Barrett Galleries
4840 Monroe Street
Toledo, OH 43623
Attn: Jim Barrett
TEL (419) 471-1243

Thomas Barry Fine Arts
400 First Avenue, North, #304
Minneapolis, MN 55401
TEL (612) 338-3656

Jacques Baruch Gallery
40 East Delaware Place
Chicago, IL 60611
Attn: Anne Baruch
TEL (312) 944-3377

Jan Baum Gallery
170 South Le Brea Avenue
Los Angles, CA 90036
Attn: Daniel Stearns
TEL (213) 932-0170
FAX (213) 932-0245

Jayne H Baum Gallery, Inc
588 Broadway
New York, NY 10012
TEL (212) 219-9854

Baumgartner Galleries
2016 R Street, NW
Washington, DC 20009
Attn: Manfred Baumgartner
TEL (202) 232-6320

William Beadleston Fine Art
60 East 91st Street
New York, NY 10128
TEL (212) 348-7234

Randall Beck Gallery
225 Newbury Street
Boston, MA 02116
Attn: E Davis
K Barrette
J Barrette
TEL (617) 266-2475

Larry Becker Gallery
43 North Second Street
Philadelphia, PA 19106
TEL (215) 925-5389

David Beitzel Gallery
102 Prince Street, 2nd Floor
New York, NY 10012
TEL (212) 219-2863
FAX (212) 941-7158

Belanthi Gallery
142 Court Street
Brooklyn, NY 11201
Attn: James G DeMartini
TEL (718) 855-2769

George Belcher Gallery
340 Townsend, #407
San Francisco, CA 94107
TEL (415) 543-1908

Kyle Belding Gallery
1110 17th Street
Denver, CO 80202
TEL (303) 825-2555

Belgis-Freidel Gallery
77 Mercer Street
New York, NY 10011
Attn: S Freidel
TEL (212) 941-8715

Mary Bell Galleries
215 West Superior Street
Chicago, IL 60610
TEL (312) 642-0202

Bellas Artes
653 Canyon Road
Santa Fe, NM 87501
Attn: Charlotte Kornstein
Bob Kornstein
TEL (505) 983-2745

Belles Artes
584 Broadway
New York, NY 10012
Attn: Barbara Rosenthal Juster
TEL (212) 274-1116

Belstone Gallery
321 East Front Street
Traverse City, MI 49684
Attn: Marcia Bellinger
TEL (616) 946-0610

Benedetti Gallery
52 Prince Street
New York, NY 10012
Attn: Charles Huller
Bettina Caiola
TEL (212) 226-2238
FAX (212) 431-8106

Benjamin Art Gallery
1303 Pennsylvania Avenue
Hagerstown, MD 21740
Attn: Benjamin Green
TEL (301) 797-4775

Benjamin-Beattie Fine Arts
1000 Lake Shore Drive
Chicago, IL 60611
Attn: Orville C Beattie
TEL (312) 337-1343

Elaine Benson Gallery
Montauk Highway
Bridgehampton, NY 11932
TEL (516) 537-3233

Benteler-Morgan Galleries
4100 Montrose, #D
Houston, TX 77006
Attn: Susan R Morgan
TEL (713) 522-8228

John Berggruen Gallery
228 Grant Avenue, 3rd Floor
San Francisco, CA 94108
TEL (415) 781-4629
FAX (415) 781-0126

Bergsma Gallery
Amway Grand Plaza Hotel
Grand Rapids, MI 49503
Attn: Kenneth Bergsma
TEL (616) 458-1776

Berman/Daferner
568 Broadway
New York, NY 10012
TEL (212) 226-8330

Lucy Berman Gallery
534 Ramona Street
Palo Alto, CA 94301
TEL (415) 322-2533
FAX (415) 322-2460

Robert Berman/B-1 Gallery
2730 Main Street
Santa Monica, CA 90405
Attn: Jeffrey Poe
TEL (213) 392-9625
FAX (213) 450-6516

Claude Bernard Gallery, Ltd
33 East 74th Street
New York, NY 10021
Attn: Michel Soskine
TEL (212) 988-2050
FAX (212) 737-2290

David Bernstein Fine Art
737 Park Avenue
New York, NY 10021
TEL (212) 794-0389

Berry-Hill Galleries, Inc
11 East 70th Street
New York, NY 10021
TEL (212) 744-2300
FAX (212) 744-2838

Jessica Berwind Gallery
301 Cherry Street, 2nd Floor
Philadelphia, PA 19106
TEL (215) 574-1645
FAX (215) 574-1646

Eugene Binder Gallery
840 Exposition
Dallas, TX 75226-0305
Attn: Gene Binder
TEL (214) 821-5864

Bingham Kurts Gallery
766 South White Station Road
Memphis, TN 38117
Attn: Lisa Kurts
TEL (901) 683-6200
FAX (901) 683-6265

GALLERY INDEX CONTINUED

Biota Gallery
15233 Ventura Blvd, #611
Sherman Oaks, CA 91403-2201
Attn: Donna Kobrin
TEL (213) 289-0979

Toni Birckhead Gallery
342 West 4th Street
Cincinnati, OH 45202
TEL (513) 241-0212
FAX (513) 723-8060

Bishop Gallery
7164 Main Street
Scottsdale, AZ 85251
Attn: W P Bishop
TEL (602) 949-9062

D & J Bittker Gallery, Ltd
536 North Woodward
Birmingham, MI 48009
Attn: Deanna I Bittker
TEL (313) 258-1670
FAX (313) 258-0216

Blackfish Gallery
420 NW 9th Avenue
Portland, OR 97209-3820
Attn: Cheryl Glazer Snow
TEL (503) 224-2634

Blondies Contemporary Art
72 Thompson Street
New York, NY 10012
Attn: Jill Castlelove
TEL (212) 431-8601

Blue Heron Gallery
Bank Street
Wellfleet, MA 02667
Attn: Harriet Rubin
TEL (508) 349-6724

Blue Mountain Gallery
121 Wooster Street
New York, NY 10012
Attn: Jackie Lima
TEL (212) 226-9402

Blue Sky Art Consultants
5401 Kentucky Avenue
Pittsburgh, PA 15232
Attn: Mimsie Stuhldreher
TEL (412) 682-7050

BlumHelman Gallery
20 West 57th Street, 2nd Floor
New York, NY 10019
Attn: Christine Wachter
TEL (212) 245-2888

BlumHelman Warehouse
80 Greene Street
New York, NY 10012
TEL (212) 226-8770
FAX (212) 334-3148

Blumka II Gallery
101 East 81st Street
New York, NY 10028
Attn: Anthony Blumka
TEL (212) 879-5611
FAX (212) 249-1087

Bockley Gallery
400 First Avenue, North
Minneapolis, MN 55401
Attn: Todd Bockley
      Mark Bockley
TEL (612) 339-3139

La Boetie, Inc
9 East 82nd Street
New York, NY 10028
TEL (212) 535-4865
FAX (212) 650-9561

Bonfoey Company
1710 Euclid Avenue
Cleveland, OH 44115
Attn: Marcia Hall
      Laura Sherman
TEL (216) 621-0178

Bonnier Gallery
419 West Broadway
New York, NY 10012
Attn: Frits de Knegt
TEL (212) 431-8909

Mary Boone Gallery
417 West Broadway
New York, NY 10012
TEL (212) 431-1818

Janet Borden, Inc
560 Broadway
New York, NY 10012
TEL (212) 431-0166

Grace Borgenicht Gallery
724 Fifth Avenue
New York, NY 10019
TEL (212) 247-2111
FAX (212) 247-2119

Bowles-Sorokko Galleries
765 Beach Street
San Francisco, CA 94109
Attn: Jean Audigier
TEL (415) 441-8008

Bowles-Sorokko Galleries
314 North Rodeo Drive
Beverly Hills, CA 90210
Attn: Tim Yarger
TEL (310) 278-4400
FAX (310) 278-6771

Bowles-Sorokko Galleries
447 West Broadway
New York, NY 10012
Attn: Valerie Dillon
TEL (212) 228-4200
FAX (212) 228-4900

Roy Boyd Gallery
739 North Wells
Chicago, IL 60610
Attn: Roy Boyd
      Ann Boyd
TEL (312) 642-1606
FAX (312) 642-2143

Roy Boyd Gallery
1547 10th Street
Santa Monica, CA 90401
Attn: Richard Telles
TEL (310) 394-1210

Fred Boyle Fine Arts
181 Duane Street
New York, NY 10013
TEL (212) 966-0168

Barbara Braathen Gallery
33 Bleeker Street
New York, NY 10012
TEL (212) 777-1161
FAX (212) 777-3729

John Bradley Gallery
RR #3-PO Box 502
Burlingham Road
Pine Bush, NY 12566-0502
TEL (914) 744-3642

Bradley Galleries
2639 North Downer Avenue
Milwaukee, WI 53211
Attn: Ellen T. Clark
      J W Kohler
TEL (414) 332-9500

Brandywine Fantasy Gallery
750 North Orleans Street
Chicago, IL 60610
TEL (312) 951-8466

Rena Bransten Gallery
77 Geary Street
San Francisco, CA 94108
TEL (415) 982-3292
FAX (415) 982-1807

Braunstein Quay Gallery
250 Sutter Street
San Francisco, CA 94108
Attn: Ruth Braunstein
TEL (415) 392-5532

Breckenridge Gallery
124 South Main Street
Breckenridge, CO 80424
Attn: Gary Freese
TEL (303) 453-2592

Brewster Gallery
41 West 57th Street
New York, NY 10019
Attn: Amy Beth Fischoff
TEL (212) 980-1975
FAX (212) 754-6651

I Brewster & Company Gallery
1742 Sansom Street
Philadelphia, PA 19103
Attn: Nicky Brewster
      Darrell Hookway
TEL (215) 864-9222
FAX (215) 972-1410

Brian Art Galleries
717 Elmwood Avenue
Buffalo, NY 14222
Attn: Brian Cheman
TEL (716) 883-7599

Bridgewater/Lustberg Gallery
529 Broadway
New York, NY 10012
Attn: Paul Bridgewater
      Jamie Lustberg
TEL (212) 941-6355

Broadway Windows
80 Washington Square, East
New York, NY 10003
Attn: M Karp
      R D Newman
TEL (212) 998-5751

Brody's Gallery
1706 21st Street, NW
Washington, DC 20009
Attn: Tom Brody
TEL (202) 462-4747

Broken Diamond
201 Grand Street
Billings, MT 59101
Attn: Frederick R Logan
TEL (406) 259-3440

Bromfield Gallery
107 South Street
Boston, MA 02111
TEL (617) 451-3605

Hal Bromm Gallery
90 West Broadway
New York, NY 10007
TEL (212) 732-6196

Broome Street Gallery
498 Broome Street
New York, NY 10013
TEL (212) 226-6085

Alan Brown Gallery
210 East Hartsdale Street
Hartsdale, NY 10530
TEL (914) 723-0040

Diane Brown Gallery
620 Broadway
New York, NY 10012
TEL (212) 260-8797
FAX (212) 260-8798

Malcolm Brown Gallery
20100 Chagrin Boulevard
Shaker, Heights, OH 44122
Attn: Ernestine T Brown
TEL (216) 751-2955

Robert Brown Contemporary Art
2030 R Street, NW
Washington, DC 20009
TEL (202) 483-4383
FAX (202) 483-4288

Suzanne Brown Gallery
7160 Main Street
Scottsdale, AZ 85251
TEL (602) 945-8475

Browning Arts
22 North 4th Street
Grand Forks, ND 58201
Attn: Mark Browning
TEL (701) 746-5090

Brubaker Gallery
415 St Armands Circle
St Armands Key
Sarasota, FL 34236
Attn: John Dineen
TEL (813) 388-2992

GALLERY INDEX CONTINUED

Bruton Gallery
40 East 61st Street
New York, NY 10021
Attn: Michael Le Marchant
TEL (212) 980-1640

Bryans Gallery
121-C North Plaza
Taos, NM 87571
Attn: Michael McCormick
TEL (505) 758-9407

Bryant Galleries
524 Royal Street
New Orleans, LA 70133
Attn: Cole Pratt
TEL (504) 525-5584

Bryant Galleries
2845 Lakeland Drive
Jackson, MS 39208
Attn: Jennifer Packer
TEL (601) 932-1993

Bunnell Gallery
166 Newbury Street
Boston, MA 02116
Attn: Deborah Brown
TEL (617) 266-6193

Burden Gallery at Aperture
20 East 23rd Street
New York, NY 10010
Attn: Michael Hoffman
    Sara Echaniz
TEL (212) 475-8790
FAX (212) 979-7759

Frank Bustamente Gallery
560 Broadway
New York, NY 10012
TEL (212) 226-2108

Hiram Butler Gallery
4520 Blossom
Houston, TX 77007
TEL (713) 863-7097
FAX (713) 863-7130

Butters Gallery, Ltd
313 NW 10th Avenue
Portland, OR 97209
Attn: J Butters
    C Butters
    K Butters
TEL (503) 248-9378

C & A Gallery
96 Spring Street
New York, NY 10012
Attn: Christina Grassi
TEL (212) 431-8664

CAFE
516 Central Avenue, SW
Albuquerque, NM 87102
Attn: Bonnie Verardo
TEL (505) 242-8244

CCA Gallery
325 West Huron Street
Chicago, IL 60610
Attn: Howard B Capponi
TEL (312) 944-0094

CDS Gallery
76 East 79th Street
New York, NY 10021
Attn: Clara D Sujo
TEL (212) 772-9555
FAX (212) 772-9542

CFM
112 Greene Street
New York, NY 10012
Attn: Neil Zukerman
TEL (212) 966-3864
FAX (212) 691-5453

J Cacciola Galleries
125 Wooster Street
New York, NY 10012
Attn: John Cacciola
    Carol Craven
TEL (212) 966-9177
FAX (212) 274-1745

Denise Cade Gallery
1045 Madison Avenue
New York, NY 10021
TEL (212) 734-3670
FAX (212) 737-7206

Edith Caldwell Gallery
251 Post Street, 2nd Floor
San Francisco, CA 94108
TEL (415) 989-5414

Susan Caldwell & Company
27 East 22nd Street
New York, NY 10010
TEL (212) 505-5212
FAX (212) 941-0083

Caldwell-Snyder Gallery
228 Grant Avenue, 5th Floor
San Francisco, CA 94108
Attn: Oliver Caldwell
    Susan Snyder
TEL (415) 296-7896

Calnan Gallery
105 4th Street, NW
Albuquerque, NM 87102
Attn: K Calnan
TEL (505) 764-8545

Camera Obscura Gallery
1309 Bannock Street
Denver, CO 80204
Attn: Hal Gould
TEL (303) 623-4059

Campanile Gallery
200 South Michigan Avenue
Chicago, IL 60604
Attn: Howard B Capponi
TEL (312) 663-3885
FAX (312) 642-3869

Campbell-Thiebaud Gallery
645-647 Chestnut Street
San Francisco, CA 94133
Attn: Charles Campbell
TEL (415) 441-8680

Cape Impressions Gallery I/II
Main Street
Wellfleet, MA 02667
Attn: Betti Williams
TEL (508) 349-6479

Capricorn Galleries
4849 Rugby Avenue
Bethesda, MD 20814
Attn: Philip Desind
TEL (301) 657-3477
TEL (301) 654-3880

Carega Foxley Leach Gallery
2543 Waterside Drive, NW
Washington, DC 20008
Attn: Patricia Carega
    Elisabeth Foxley Leach
TEL (202) 843-0530

Carey-Mangum Gallery
2182 Lawndale Drive
Greensboro, NC 27408
Attn: William Mangum
TEL (919) 379-9200

Carib Art Gallery
584 Broadway
New York, NY 10012
Attn: Veronica Ortiz
TEL (212) 343-2539
FAX (212) 343-2659

Carlson Gallery
2443 Fillmore Street, #114
San Francisco, CA 94109
Attn: Jeanne Carlson
TEL (415) 982-2882

Frank Caro Gallery
41 East 57th Street
New York, NY 10022
TEL (212) 753-2166
FAX (212) 888-1510

Carone Gallery
600 SE Second Court
Fort Lauderdale, FL 33301
Attn: Matthew Carone
    Jodie Carone
TEL (305) 463-8833

Laura L Carpenter Gallery
3009 Maple Avenue, #212
Dallas, TX 75201
Attn: James Kelly
TEL (214) 922-9090
FAX (214) 922-9093

Sandy Carson Gallery
1734 Wazee Street
Denver, CO 80202
Attn: Jodi Carson
TEL (303) 297-8585

Carus Gallery
872 Madison Avenue
New York, NY 10021
Attn: Dorothea Carus
TEL (212) 879-4660
FAX (212) 879-4660

Casell Galleries
818 Royal Street
New Orleans, LA 70116
Attn: Joaquin Casellas
TEL (504) 524-0671

Leo Castelli Graphics
578 Broadway, 3rd Floor
New York, NY 10012
Attn: Jodi Scherer
TEL (212) 941-9855
FAX (212) 941-0093
Contemporary American Prints

Linda Cathcart Gallery
924 Colorado Avenue
Santa Monica, CA 90401
TEL (310) 451-1121
FAX (213) 451-2781

Cava Gallery
22 North 3rd Street
Philadelphia, PA 19106
Attn: Paul Cava
TEL (215) 627-1172

Cavalier Galleries
One Landmark Square
Stamford, CT 06901
Attn: Ron Cavalier, Jr
TEL (203) 325-8444

Cavin-Morris Gallery
560 Broadway, 2nd Floor
New York, NY 10012
TEL (212) 226-3768
FAX (212) 226-0155

Joan Cawley Gallery
7137 East Main Street
Scottsdale, AZ 85251
TEL (602) 947-3548

Joan Cawley Gallery
15500 College Blvd
Lenexa, KS 66219
TEL (913) 599-2442
TEL (800) 835-0075

Ceres Gallery
584 Broadway, #306
New York, NY 10012
TEL (212) 226-4725

Central Bank Gallery
Kincaid Towers
300 West Vine Street
Lexington, KY 40507
Attn: John G Irvin
TEL (606) 253-6135

Centurion Art
540 North Michigan, #112-A
Chicago, IL 60611
Attn: Vam Lember
TEL (312) 661-0220

Jackie Chalkley Gallery
5301 Wisconsin Avenue, NW
Washington, DC 20015
TEL (202) 537-6100

Channing Gallery
53 Old Santa Fe Trail
Santa Fe, NM 87501
Attn: Allen Harrill
TEL (505) 988-1078
FAX (505) 988-3879

Claudia Chapline Gallery
3445 Shoreline Highway
Stinson Beach, CA 94970-0946
TEL (415) 868-2308
FAX (415) 868-1239

Joanne Chappell Gallery
625 2nd Street
Studio 400
San Francisco, CA 94107
TEL (415) 777-5711
FAX (415) 777-1390

GALLERY INDEX CONTINUED

Chetkin Gallery
9 Wharf Avenue
Red Bank, NJ 07701
Attn: Donald Chetkin
Carol Lynn Chetkin
TEL (201) 741-6116
FAX (908) 741-1380

Chiaroscuro
Chicago Place
700 North Michigan Ave. 4th Floor
Chicago, IL 60611
Attn: Peggy Wolf
Ronna Isaacs
TEL (312) 988-9253
FAX (312) 988-9254

Chicago Center for the Print
1509 West Fullerton Avenue
Chicago, IL 60614
Attn: Richard Kasuin
David Grossfeld
TEL (312) 477-1585

Childs Gallery
169 Newbury Street
Boston, MA 02116
Attn: D Roger Howlett
TEL (617) 266-1108

Chosy Gallery
218 North Henry Street
Madison, WI 53703
Attn: Grace Chosy
TEL (608) 255-1211

Joseph Chowning Gallery
1717 17th Street
San Francisco, CA 94103
TEL (415) 626-7496
FAX (415) 863-5471

Lori Ciancaglini Fine Art
328 West 76th Street
New York, NY 10023
TEL (212) 724-3145

Jan Cicero Gallery
221 West Erie
Chicago, IL 60610
TEL (312) 440-1904

Cielo Gallery
East Main Street
Wellfleet, MA 02667
Attn: Hayes O Black
Richard Pullak
TEL (508) 349-2108

Cincinnati Art Galleries
635 Main Street
Cincinnati, OH 45202
Attn: Riley Humler
TEL (513) 381-2128

Cinque Gallery
560 Broadway
New York, NY 10012
TEL (212) 966-3464

Circle Gallery
468 West Broadway
New York, NY 10012
TEL (212) 677-5100
FAX (212) 533-8531

Circle Gallery
Northbrook Court
Northbrook, IL 60062
Attn: Nancy Grill
TEL (708) 564-5860

Circle Gallery
2895 The Galleria 2
Houston, TX 77056
Attn: Jessie Skates
Mary Prado
TEL (713) 961-7241

Circle Gallery
5416 Walnut Street
Pittsburgh, PA 15232
Attn: Beth Evans
TEL (412) 687-1336

Circle Gallery
Frank Lloyd Wright Bldg
140 Maiden Lane
San Francisco, CA 94108
Attn: Karen Anderson
TEL (415) 989-2100

Circle Gallery
2501 San Diego Avenue
San Diego, CA 92110
Attn: Barbara Cox
TEL (619) 296-2596

Circle Gallery
205-207 Front Street
South Street Seaport
New York, NY 10038
Attn: Jessica Bush
TEL (212) 732-5625

Circle Gallery
Ghirordelli Square
900 North Point
San Francisco, CA 94109
TEL (415) 776-2370
FAX (415) 776-1786

Circle Gallery
Frank Lloyd Wright Bldg
140 Maiden Lane
San Francisco, CA 94108
TEL (415) 989-2100
FAX (415) 989-2066

Circle Fine Art, Ltd
303 East Wacker Drive, #830
Chicago, IL 60601
TEL (312) 616-1300
FAX (312) 616-9170

Cirrus Gallery
542 South Alameda Street
Los Angeles, CA 90013
Attn: Jean R Milant
TEL (213) 680-3473

City Gallery
2 Columbus Circle
New York, NY 10019
Attn: Elyse Reissman
TEL (212) 974-1150

Civilisation
78 2nd Avenue
New York, NY 10003
Attn: Mitchell Soble
Evie McKenna
TEL (212) 254-3788

J Claramunt Gallery
375 West Broadway, 3rd Floor
New York, NY 10012
TEL (212) 431-3456
FAX (212) 431-3485

C L Clark Galleries
1818 V Street
Bakersfield, CA 93301
Attn: C L Clark
T Allen
TEL (805) 325-7094

Garth Clark Gallery
170 South La Brea Avenue
Los Angeles, CA 90036
Attn: Wayne Kuwade
TEL (213) 939-2189
FAX (213) 939-6069

Garth Clark Gallery
24 West 57th Street
New York, NY 10019
Attn: Mark Del Vecchio
TEL (212) 246-2205
FAX (212) 489-5168

Claypoole-Freese Gallery
216 Grand Avenue
Pacific Grove, CA 93950
Attn: Lisa M Parker
TEL (408) 373-7179

Clayton Galleries
4105 South MacDill Avenue
Tampa, FL 33611
Attn: Cathleen Clayton
TEL (813) 831-3753

A Clean Well-Lighted Place
363 Bleeker Street
New York, NY 10014
Attn: Thomas Martinelli
Marjorie Martinelli
TEL (212) 255-3656

Cline Fine Art Gallery
526 Canyon Road
Santa Fe, NM 87501
Attn: Geoff Cline
Helen Cline
TEL (505) 982-5328
FAX (505) 986-0880

A B Closson Gallery
401 Race Street
Cincinnati, OH 45202
Attn: Phyllis J Weston
TEL (513) 762-5500

Coast Gallery—Pebble Beach
P O Box 1501
Pebble Beach, CA 93953
Attn: Emma Koeppel
TEL (408) 624-2002
FAX (408) 624-2909

Cobra Fine Art
580 Sutter Street
San Francisco, CA 94102-1102
TEL (415) 397-2195
FAX (415) 397-5113

Cogswell Gallery
223 East Gore Creek Drive
Vail, CO 81657
TEL (303) 476-1769

Cohen Gallery
1018 Madison Avenue
New York, NY 10021
Attn: Michael Cohen
Tanya Bonakdar
TEL (212) 628-0303
FAX (212) 628-9560

Eva Cohon Gallery, Ltd
301 West Superior
Chicago, IL 60610
TEL (312) 644-3669
FAX (312) 664-8573

Sylvan Cole Gallery
101 West 57th Street
New York, NY 10019
Attn: Sylvan Cole
TEL (212) 333-7760

The Collector Art Gallery
1505 19th Street, NW
Washington, D 20036
TEL (202) 797-0160

Lowell Collins Gallery
2903 Saint Street
Houston, TX 77027
TEL (713) 622-6962

Colnaghi USA, Ltd
21 East 67th Street
New York, NY 10021
Attn: Nicholas Hall
Alan P Wintermute
TEL (212) 772-2266
FAX (212) 737-8325

Compton Art Gallery
409 West Fisher Avenue
Greensboro, NC 27401
Attn: Ann A Compton
TEL (919) 370-9147

Conacher Galleries
134 Maiden Avenue
San Francisco, CA 94108
Attn: Don Conacher
TEL (415) 392-5447

Concept Art Gallery
1031 South Braddock Avenue
Pittsburgh, PA 15218
Attn: Sam Berkowitz
TEL (412) 242-9200

Condeso/Lawler Gallery
524 Broadway, 2nd Floor
New York, NY 10012
Attn: Sue Lawler
TEL (212) 219-1283
FAX (212) 226-7430

Conduit Gallery
3200 Main Street, 2nd Floor
Dallas, TX 75226
Attn: Nancy Whitenack
TEL (214) 939-0064

Congress Square Gallery
42 Exchange Street
Portland, ME 04101
TEL (207) 774-3369

GALLERY INDEX CONTINUED

Conlon Gallery
125 North Guadalupe
Santa Fe, NM 87501
Attn: Sunny Zohn Conlon
TEL (505) 984-1877

Connecticut Fine Arts
2 Gorham Avenue
Westport, CT 06880
Attn: Bert Chernow
TEL (203) 227-8016

Contemporary Art Workshop
542 West Grant Place
Chicago, IL 60614
Attn: Lynn Kearney
TEL (312) 472-4004

Contemporary Gallery
4152 Shady Bend Drive
Dallas, TX 75244
Attn: Patsy C Kahn
TEL (214) 247-5246

Contemporary Realist Gallery
23 Grant Avenue, 6th Floor
San Francisco, CA 94108
Attn: Michael R Hackett
    Tracy Freedman
TEL (415) 362-7152

Susan Conway Carroll Gallery
1058 Thomas Jefferson Street, NW
Washington, DC 20007
TEL (202) 333-4082

Brad Cooper Gallery
1712–14 East 7th Street
Tampa, FL 33605
TEL (813) 248-6098

Paula Cooper Gallery
155 Wooster Street
New York, NY 10012
Attn: Julie Graham
TEL (212) 674-0766
FAX (212) 674-1938

Cooper-Seeman Fine Art
126 East 12th Street
New York, NY 10003
Attn: Wendy Cooper
    Laurie Seeman
TEL (212) 475-2174

Corbino Galleries
1472 Main Street
Sarasota, FL 34236
Attn: Michael Corbino
TEL (813) 955-8845

James Corcoran Gallery
1327 5th Street
Santa Monica, CA 90401
Attn: Sandra Starr
TEL (213) 451-4666
FAX (213) 451-0950

Cordier & Ekstrom Gallery
417 East 75th Street
New York, NY 10021
Attn: Arne H Ekstrom
TEL (212) 988-8857

Sylvia Cordish Fine Art
5701 Oakshire Road
Baltimore, MD 21209
TEL (410) 542-7418

Cornerhouse Gallery & Frame
2753 First Avenue, SE
Cedar Rapids, IA 52402
Attn: Janelle V McClain
TEL (319) 365-4348
FAX (319) 365-1707
Specializing in Grant Wood &
Contemporary Regional Works

Cortland-Leyton Gallery
815 North Milwaukee Street
Chicago, IL 60622
TEL (312) 733-2781

Coty Gallery
Tuna Wharf
PO Box #2334
Rockport, MA 01966
Attn: Sophina G Coty
TEL (508) 546-6231
FAX (508) 546-3979

Couturier Gallery
166 North La Brea Avenue
Los Angeles, CA 90036
Attn: Darrel Couturier
TEL (213) 933-5557
FAX (213) 933-2357

Cove Gallery
Commercial Street
Wellfleet, MA 02667
Attn: Larry Diron
    LiAnn Diron
TEL (207) 349-2530

Charles Cowles Gallery
420 West Broadway
New York, NY 10012
TEL (212) 925-3500
FAX (212) 925-3501

Crane Collection
218 Newbury Street
Boston, MA 02166
Attn: Bonnie Crane
TEL (617) 262-4080

Cross Gate Gallery
219 East High Street
Lexington, KY 40507
Attn: Greg Ladd
TEL (606) 233-3856

Crown Point Press
657 Howard Street
San Francisco, CA 94105
Attn: Kathan Brown
TEL (415) 974-6273

Crown Point Press
568 Broadway
New York, NY 10012
Attn: Karen McCready
TEL (212) 226-5476

Crux Gallery
20 West Hubbard Street
Chicago, IL 60610
TEL (312) 527-1002

Cudahy's Gallery
1314 East Cary Street
Richmond, VA 23219
Attn: Helen G Levinson
TEL (804) 782-1776

Cumberland Gallery
4107 Hillsboro Circle
Nashville, TN 37215
Attn: Carol Stein
TEL (615) 297-0296

Cummer Gallery of Art
829 Riverside Avenue
Jacksonville, FL 32204
Attn: Robert Schlageter
TEL (904) 356-6857

Susan Cummins Gallery
12 Miller Avenue
Mill Valley, CA 94941
TEL (415) 383-1512

Currier Gallery of Art
192 Orange Street
Manchester, NH 03104
Attn: Marilyn F Hoffman
TEL (603) 699-6144

Bess Cutler Gallery
379 West Broadway
New York, NY 10012
TEL (212) 219-1577
FAX (212) 941-8150

Robert Dana Gallery
1849 Union Street
San Francisco, CA 94123
Attn: Bernadette Mendoza
TEL (415) 749-1849
FAX (415) 749-1850

Danforth Street Gallery
34 Danforth Street
Portland, ME 04101
TEL (207) 775-6245

Dart Gallery
712 North Carpenter
Chicago, IL 60610
Attn: Andree Stone
TEL (312) 733-7864
FAX (312) 733-7892

Dartmouth Street Gallery
3011 Monte Visa, NE
Albuquerque, NM 87106
TEL (505) 226-7751
FAX (505) 266-0006

David Gary, Ltd
391 Milburn Avenue
Milburn, NJ 07041
Attn: Steve Saukauer
TEL (201) 467-9240

Peter M David Gallery
3351 St Louis Avenue
Minneapolis, MN 55403
Attn: Bonnie K Sussman
TEL (612) 926-7637

Davidson Galleries
313 Occidental Avenue, South
Seattle, WA 98104
Attn: Sam Davidson
    Isabel Borland
TEL (206) 624-1324

Maxwell Davidson Gallery
41 East 57th Street
New York, NY 10022
TEL (212) 759-7555

Davis Gallery
3964 Magazine Street
New Orleans, LA 70115
Attn: Candy Davis
TEL (504) 897-0780
FAX (504) 897-0248

Davis Gallery
6812 North Oracle Road
Tucson, AZ 85704
Attn: Candy Davis
    Mike Dominguez
TEL (602) 297-1427

John Davis Contemporary Art
59 Walker Street
New York, NY 10013
TEL (212) 334-4834
FAX (212) 334-6195

Davis & Langdale Company
231 East 60th Street
New York, NY 10022
TEL (212) 838-0333

Davis/McClain Galleries
2627 Colquitt
Houston, TX 77098
Attn: Barbara Davis
    Bob McClain
TEL (713) 520-9200

Davlyn Gallery
975 Madison Avenue
New York, NY 10021
Attn: Berta Katz
TEL (212) 879-2075

Douglas Dawson Gallery
814 North Franklin
Chicago, IL 60610
TEL (312) 751-1961

Dawson Gallery
349 East Avenue
Rochester, NY 14604
Attn: Shirley Dawson
    B McInerny
TEL (716) 454-6609

De Graaf Fine Art
9 East Superior Street
Chicago, IL 60611
Attn: Daniel De Graaf
TEL (312) 951-5180

DeLigny Art Galleries
709 East Las Olas Blvd.
Fort Lauderdale, FL 33301
Attn: Lee DeLigny
TEL (305) 467-9303

GALLERY INDEX CONTINUED

Tibor de Nagy Gallery
41 West 57th Street
New York, NY 10019
Attn: Andrew H Arnot
TEL (212) 421-3780

De Ru's Fine Art Gallery
9100 East Artesia Blvd
Bellflower, CA 90706
Attn: Dewitt C McCall, III
TEL (310) 920-1312
FAX (310) 920-3077

Pascal de Sarthe Gallery
640 North La Peer Drive
Los Angeles, CA 90069
TEL (310) 289-1012
FAX (310) 289-0542

De Ville Galleries
8751 Melrose Avenue
Los Angeles, CA 90069
Attn: Lyn Lincoln
TEL (213) 652-0525
FAX (213) 652-5180

DeVorzon Gallery, Inc
8687 Melrose Avenue, #188
Los Angeles, CA 90069
Attn: Karen Dotrice
TEL (310) 659-0555
FAX (310) 659-2838

DEL Fine Art Galleries
109 East Kit Carson Road
Taos, NM 87571-2243
Attn: Dana R Lesnett
TEL (505) 982-9127
FAX (505) 758-1131

Del Bello Gallery
363 Queen Street
Toronto, ON
Canada M5V 2A4
Attn: Egidio Del Bello
TEL (416) 593-0884

Del Mano Gallery
11981 San Vicente Blvd
Los Angeles, CA 90049
Attn: Raymond G Leier
Jan Peters
TEL (213) 476-8508

Del Mano Gallery
33 East Colorado Blvd
Pasadena, CA 91105
Attn: Raymond G Leier
Jan Peters
TEL (818) 793-6648

Marisa del Re Gallery
41 East 57th Street
New York, NY 10022
Attn: Bill Maynes
Andrew Ruth
TEL (212) 688-1843
FAX (212) 688-7019

Delphine Gallery
1324 State Street
Santa Barbara, CA 93101
Attn: Letty Rossbach
TEL (805) 962-6625

Deson-Saunders Gallery
230 West Chicago Street
Chicago, IL 60610
Attn: Ken Saunders
TEL (312) 787-0005

DeSoto Workshop
319 11th Street
San Francisco, CA, 94103
Attn: Ernest DeSoto
TEL (415) 863-3232

Sid Deutsch Gallery
305 East 61st Street
New York, NY 10021
TEL (212) 754-6660
FAX (212) 754-6662

Dewey Gallery
74 East San Francisco Street
Santa Fe, NM 87501
Attn: Nancy Ellis
James Conian
TEL (505) 982-8632

Leonarda Di Mauro Gallery
49 East 96th Street
New York, NY 10128
TEL (212) 360-5049

David Dike Fine Art
2613 Fairmount
Dallas, TX 75201
TEL (214) 720-4044

Geoffrey Diner Gallery
1730 21st Street, NW
Washington, DC 20009
TEL (202) 483-5005

Terry Dintenfass Gallery
50 West 57th Street
New York, NY 10019
TEL (212) 581-2268
FAX (212) 307-1443

Diverse Works
1117 East Freeway
Houston, TX 77002
Attn: Caroline Huber
Michael Peranteau
TEL (713) 223-8346

Dixon Gallery
4339 Park Avenue
Memphis, TN 38117
Attn: John E Buchanan, Jr
TEL (901) 761-5250

George J Doizaki Gallery
244 South San Pedro Street, #505
Los Angeles, CA 90012
Attn: Robert Hori
TEL (213) 628-2725
FAX (213) 617-8576

Olga Dollar Gallery
210 Post Street, 2nd Floor
San Francisco, CA 94108
TEL (415) 398-2297

Dominion Gallery
1438 Sherbrooke, West
Montreal, Canada H3G 1H4
TEL (514) 845-7471

E M Donahue Gallery
560 Broadway, #304
New York, NY 10012
Attn: Ronald Sosinski
TEL (212) 226-1111
FAX (212) 982-5579

M A Doran Gallery
3509 South Peoria
Tulsa, OK 74105
Attn: Mary Ann Foran
TEL (918) 748-8700

Fred Dorfman Gallery
123 Watts Street
New York, NY 10013
TEL (212) 966-4611
FAX (212) 941-7515

Dorsky Galleries
379 West Broadway
New York, NY 10012
Attn: Karen Dorsky
TEL (212) 966-6170
FAX (212) 966-9724

Downtown Gallery
1330 St Charles Avenue
New Orleans, LA 70130
Attn: Naomi D Marshall
TEL (504) 527-7757

Douglas Drake Gallery
50 West 57th Street
New York, NY 10019
Attn: Elisabeth Kirsch
TEL (212) 582-5930

Dranoff Fine Art
588 Broadway, #305
New York, NY 10012
TEL (212) 966-0153
FAX (212) 941-1646

The Drawing Center
35 Wooster Street
New York, NY 10013
Attn: Ann Philbin
TEL (212) 219-2166

Paul Drey Gallery
11 East 57th Street
New York, NY 10022
Attn: Margo Drey Catherwood
John A Catherwood
TEL (212) 753-2551

Irene Drori Fine Art
138 North Orange Drive
Los Angeles, CA 90036
TEL (213) 931-1779
FAX (213) 931-4642

Dubins Gallery
11948 San Vincente Boulevard
Los Angeles, CA 90049
Attn: Lisa Dubins
TEL (310) 820-1409

Michael Dunev Gallery
77 Geary Street
San Francisco, CA 94108
TEL (415) 398-7300

Linda Durham Gallery
400 Canyon Road
Santa Fe, NM 87501
TEL (505) 988-1313
FAX (505) 983-1347

Dyansen Eclipse Gallery
157 Spring Street
New York, NY 10012
Attn: Betty Greenberg
TEL (212) 925-6203

Eaton Gallery
968 June Road
Memphis, TN 38119
Attn: Sandra Saunders
TEL (901) 767-0690

Ebert Gallery
49 Geary Street
San Francisco, CA 94108
Attn: Richard Ebert
TEL (415) 296-8405

Edelman Fine Arts, Ltd
386 West Broadway, 3rd Floor
New York, NY 10012-4302
Attn: H Heather Edelman
TEL (212) 226-1198
FAX (212) 226-4422

Paul Edelstein Gallery
519 North Highland Avenue
Memphis, TN 38117
TEL (901) 767-0425

Edition Schellmann
50 Greene Street
New York, NY 10013
Attn: Meg Malloy
TEL (212) 219-1821
FAX (212) 941-9206

Edition Julie Sylvester
10 Leonard Street
New York, NY 10013
Attn: Jade R Dellinger
TEL (212) 941-0074
FAX (212) 941-0108

Editions Ilene Kurtz
591 Broadway
New York, NY 10012
TEL (212) 226-2771

Editions Limited Gallery
2727 East 86th Street, #208
Woodfield Centre
Indianapolis, IN 46240
Attn: Bridget Webster
TEL (317) 253-7800

Ehlers Caudill Gallery
750 North Orleans, #203
Chicago, IL 60610
Attn: Carol Ehlers
Shashi Caudill
TEL (312) 642-8611
FAX (312) 642-9151

871 Fine Arts
250 Sutter Street, #450
San Francisco, CA 94108
Attn: Adrienne Fish
TEL (415) 543-5155
FAX (415) 398-9388

1800 Gallery
1800 North Clybourn
Chicago, IL 60614
Attn: Haley Cohen
TEL (312) 951-1855

GALLERY INDEX CONTINUED

G W Einstein Company
591 Broadway
New York, NY 10012
TEL (212) 226-1414
FAX (212) 941-9561

El Prado/Santa Fe
112 West San Francisco Street
Santa Fe, NM 87501
Attn: Don Pierson
      Elyse Pierson
TEL (505) 988-2906

El Presidio Gallery
120 North Main Avenue
Tucson, AZ 85701
Attn: H Rentschler
TEL (602) 884-7379

El Taller Gallery
1221 West 6th Street
Austin, TX 78703
Attn: Olga O Pena
TEL (512) 480-0100

El Taller de Taos Gallery
119-A Kit Carson Road
Taos, NM 87571
Attn: Judith Gesell-Jones
TEL (505) 758-4887

Elkon Gallery
18 East 81st Street
New York, NY 10028
Attn: Dorothea Elkon
TEL (212) 535-3940

Peter Eller Gallery
206 Darmouth, NE
Albuquerque, NM 87106
TEL (505) 268-7437
FAX (505) 266-0005

Phyllis Elliot Gallery
524 East 20th Street
New York, NY 10009
TEL (212) 260-4576

Francine Ellman Gallery
671 North La Cienega Blvd
Los Angeles, CA 90069
TEL (310) 917-6688
FAX (310) 652-0336

Elysium Arts
28 East 78th Street
New York, NY 10028
TEL (212) 628-3828
FAX (212) 628-3852

Joy Emery Gallery
84 Moross Avenue
Grosse Point Farms, MI 48236
TEL (313) 886-9663

Andre Emmerich Gallery
41 East 57th Street
New York, NY 10022
Attn: James Yohe
TEL (212) 752-0124

William Engle Gallery
415 Massachusetts Avenue
Indianapolis, IN 46204
TEL (317) 632-1391

English Gallery
6 Old Street Road
Peterborough, NH 03458
Attn: Marylin Ash
TEL (603) 924-9044

Engman International
326 Glenneyre Street
Laguna Beach, CA 92651
Attn: Glenn Engman
TEL (714) 497-7135
FAX (714) 497-0595

Erickson & Elins Gallery
345 Sutter Street
San Francisco, CA 94108
Attn: Sandra Erickson
      Mel Elins
TEL (415) 981-1080
FAX (415) 981-1206

Rosa Esman Gallery
575 Broadway
New York, NY 10012
TEL (212) 219-3044
FAX (212) 941-5921

Esti-Arte Print Gallery
Almagro 44
28010 Madrid, Spain
Attn: Gonzalo Cabo De La Sierra
TEL (91) 419 76 69

Etherton/Stern Gallery
135 South Sixth Avenue
Tucson, AZ 85701
Attn: Terry Etherton
      Michael Stern
TEL (602) 624-7370

Eleanor Ettinger, Inc
155 Sixth Avenue
New York, NY 10013
TEL (212) 691-3508
    (800) 776-7077

Carol Evans Fine Arts
107 Wychoff Street
Brooklyn, NY 11201
TEL (718) 852-6691

Jerome Evans Gallery
21 Round Hill Mall
P O Box 527
Zephyr Cove
Lake Tahoe, NV 89448
TEL (702) 588-6468

Larry Evans Fine Art
731 Sansome Street
San Francisco, CA 94111
TEL (415) 627-4635

Kathleen Ewing Gallery
1609 Connecticut Avenue
Washington, DC 20009
TEL (202) 328-0955

Exit Art
548 Broadway, 2nd Floor
New York, NY 10012
TEL (212) 966-7745
FAX (212) 925-2928

Experimental Workshop
Pier 46-B
San Francisco, CA 94107
TEL (415) 957-9309
FAX (415) 957-0148

FDR Gallery
670 Broadway, 5th Floor
New York, NY 10012
Attn: Rose A Deutsch
      Jay R Deutsch
TEL (212) 777-3051
FAX (212) 777-6960

Fagen-Peterson Fine Art
7077 Main Street
Scottsdale, AZ 85251
Attn: G Fagen
      E Fagen
TEL (602) 941-0089

Fahey/Klein Gallery
148 North La Brea Avenue
Los Angeles, CA 90036
Attn: David Fahey
      Randee Klein
TEL (213) 934-2250
FAX (213) 934-4243

Barton Faist Gallery
Tree Studio Bldg
4 East Ohio Street
Chicago, IL 60611
TEL (312) 664-8182

Linda Farris Gallery
322 Second Avenue, South
Seattle, WA 98104
TEL (206) 623-1110

Feigen, Incorporated
325 West Huron Street
Chicago, IL 60610
Attn: Lance Kinz
      Moira du Brul
TEL (312) 787-0500

Richard L Feigen & Company
49 East 68th Street
New York, NY 10021
TEL (212) 628-0700

Feigenson/Preston Gallery
796 North Woodward
Birmingham, MI 48009
Attn: Mary Preston
TEL (313) 644-3955

Ronald Feldman Fine Arts
31–33 Mercer Street
New York, NY 10013
TEL (212) 226-3232
FAX (212) 941-1536

Rosamund Felsen Gallery
8525 Santa Monica Blvd
Los Angeles, CA 90069
TEL (310) 652-9172
FAX (310) 652-2618

Fenix Gallery
228-B North Pueblo Road
Taos, NM 87571
Attn: Judith Eyre
TEL (505) 758-9120

Fergus-Jean Gallery
280 Cozzins Street
Columbus, OH 43215
Attn: Elizabeth Fergus-Jean
TEL (614) 464-4696

Fifty-50
793 Broadway
New York, NY 10003
Attn: Mark Isaacson
TEL (212) 777-3208

55 Mercer Street Gallery
55 Mercer Street
New York, NY 10013
Attn: Nancy Oliver
TEL (212) 226-8513

David Findlay, Jr Fine Art
41 East 57th Street, Room 308
New York, NY 10022
Attn: Bernay Schwartz
      Reagan Upshaw
TEL (212) 486-7660
FAX (212) 486-7674

David Findlay Jr, Fine Art
Cherokee Station
P O Box 20080
New York, NY 10028-0050
TEL (212) 486-7660

Peter Findlay
1001 Madison Avenue
New York, NY 10021
TEL (212) 772-8660

Wally Findlay Galleries
17 East 57th Street
New York, NY 10022
Attn: Simon Karoff
TEL (212) 421-5390

Wally Findlay Galleries
814 North Michigan Avenue
Chicago, IL 60611
Attn: Helen T Findlay
TEL (312) 649-1500

Fine Art & Artists, Inc
1710 Connecticut Avenue, NW
Washington, DC 20009
Attn: Judy duBerrier
TEL (202) 462-2787
FAX (202) 462-3128
Specializing in Contemporary/
Pop Art

Fine Arts Gallery of New Orleans
614 Canal Street
New Orleans, LA 70130
Attn: Thomas Bayer
      Robert McHarg
TEL (504) 522-0691

First Street Gallery
560 Broadway
New York, NY 10012
TEL (212) 226-9127

GALLERY INDEX CONTINUED

Fischbach Gallery
24 West 57th Street
New York, NY 10019
Attn: Lawrence L DiCarlo
TEL (212) 759-2345

Victor Fischer Galleries
Oakland City Center
1300 Clay Street
Oakland, CA 94612
TEL (510) 464-8044

Victor Fischer Galleries
Hills Plaza
350 Steuart Street
San Francisco, CA 94119
Attn: Linda Fischer
TEL (415) 982-1616

Five Points Gallery
Route 295 Sheridan House
East Chatham, NY 12060
Attn: Frank Peseckis
      Lynn Peseckis
TEL (518) 392-5205

Fitch-Febvrel Gallery
5 East 57th Street
New York, NY 10022
Attn: Andrew Fitch
TEL (212) 688-8522
FAX (212) 207-8065

Flanders Modern
400 First Avenue, North
Minneapolis, MN 55401
Attn: Douglas Flanders
TEL (612) 344-1700

Fletcher Gallery
668 Canyon Road
Santa Fe, NM 87501
Attn: Jay Fletcher

Florence Art Gallery
2500 Cedar Springs
Dallas, TX 75201
Attn: Estelle Shwiff
TEL (214) 748-6463

Flury & Company
322 First Avenue, South
Seattle, WA 98104
Attn: Lois Flury
TEL (206) 587-0260

Focal Point Gallery
321 City Island Avenue
Bronx, NY 10464
Attn: Ron Terner
TEL (212) 885-1403

Charles Foley Gallery
973 East Broad Street
Columbus, OH 43205
TEL (614) 253-7921

Tory Folliard Gallery
233 North Milwaukee Street
Milwaukee, WI 53202
Attn: Katherine Schwab
TEL (414) 273-7311

Fort Worth Gallery
901 Boland Street
Fort Worth, TX 76107
Attn: Dutch Phillips
TEL (817) 332-5603

Forum Gallery
745 Fifth Avenue
New York, NY 10151
Attn: Robert Fishko
TEL (212) 355-4545

Foster-White Gallery
3112 Occidental Street
Seattle, WA 98104
Attn: Donald Foster
TEL (206) 622-2833

Foundry Gallery
9 Hillyer Court, NW
Washington, DC 20008
Attn: Jenny Burden
TEL (202) 387-0203

Fox Graphics
4 Mechanic Street
Merrimac, MA 01860
Attn: Herb Fox
TEL (617) 346-8859

Shirley Fox Galleries
1500 Piedmont Avenue, NE
Atlanta, GA 30324
TEL (404) 874-7294

Foxhall Gallery
3301 New Mexico Avenue, NW
Washington, DC 20016
Attn: Jerry Eisley
      Caryl Brody
TEL (202) 966-7144

Fraenkel Gallery
49 Geary Street
San Francisco, CA 94108
Attn: Jeffrey Fraenkel
      Frish Brandt
TEL (415) 981-2661
FAX (415) 981-4014

Franklin Square Gallery
900 North Franklin Street
Chicago, IL 60610
Attn: Laurence Conn
TEL (312) 751-1300
FAX (312) 751-1331

Frederick Galleries
1234 East Juneau Avenue
Milwaukee, WI 53202
Attn: Paul A Frederick
TEL (414) 271-1500

Sherry French Gallery
24 West 57th Street
New York, NY 10019
TEL (212) 247-2457

Nina Freudenheim Gallery
300 Delaware Avenue
Buffalo, NY 14202
TEL (716) 856-4444
FAX (716) 856-4445

Sigrid Freundorfer Fine Art
790 Madison Avenue, #402
New York, NY 10021
TEL (212) 517-9700
FAX (212) 744-5982

Fridholm Fine Arts Gallery
Broadway Arts Building
49 Broadway
Asheville, NC 28801
Attn: Bonnie Fridholm Hobbs
TEL (704) 258-9206

Oskar Friedl Gallery
750 North Orleans, #302
Chicago, IL 60610
TEL (312) 337-7550
FAX (312) 337-2466

Anita Friedman Fine Arts
980 Madison Avenue
New York, NY 10021
TEL (212) 472-1527

Barry Friedman, Ltd
851 Madison Avenue
New York, NY 10021
Attn: Jonathan Hallam
TEL (212) 794-8950
FAX (212) 794-8889

Fulcrum Gallery
144 Mercer Street
New York, NY 10012
TEL (212) 226-3109

Jeffrey Fuller Fine Art, Ltd
132 South 17th Street
Philadelphia, PA 19103
TEL (215) 564-9977
FAX (215) 564-9792

FUEL Gallery
316 Occidental Avenue, South
Seattle, WA 98104
Attn: Sean Elwood
      Carole Fuller
TEL (206) 625-0890

Gage Gallery
9621 Verdict Drive
Vienna, VA 22181
Attn: Gary Evans
TEL (703) 242-0343

Galeria Bonino
48 Great Joones Street
New York, NY 10012
Attn: Fernanda Bonino
TEL (212) 598-4262
FAX (212) 982-2842

Galeria Botello I
208 Christo Street
San Juan, Puerto Rico 00901
TEL (809) 723-9987
TEL (809) 723-2879

Galeria Botello II
Plaza Las Americas, #143
Hato Rey, PR 00919
TEL (809) 754-7430
FAX (809) 250-8274

Galeria Capistrano
409 Canyon Road
Santa Fe, NM 87501
Attn: Randall Sanderson
TEL (505) 984-3024

Galeria Mesa
155 North Center
Mesa, AZ 85211-1466
TEL (602) 644-2242

Galeria Palomas
207 Cristo Street
Old San Juan, PR 00901
Attn: Sharon Cooper
TEL (809) 724-8904

Galeria Seztante
Carrerall, No 67 86
Bogota, Colombia
Attn: Maria Eugenia Nino, Director
TEL 249-0461
FAX 217-5214

Galerie Baks
Bobelstraat 1, Den-Haag
The Netherlands
TEL 31.70.345.6604
FAX 31.70.392.4992

Galerie Beyeler
Baumlungasse 9
4001 Basle
Switzerland
TEL (61) 23-54-12

Galerie Isy Brachot
35 Rue Guenegaud
Paris, France 75006
TEL (1) 354-22-40

Galerie Cujas
2424 San Diego Avenue
San Diego, CA 92110
Attn: Gary Hansmann
      Lilly Rosa
TEL (619) 491-0166

Galerie Galerie
8182 Sunset Blvd, #205
Los Angeles, CA 90046
Attn: Junko Takano
TEL (213) 650-7949
FAX (213) 650-8523

Galerie Maurice Keitelman
Crearte 9
Rue de la Paille Sablon
1000 Brussels, Belgium,
TEL (2) 511-35-80

Galerie Lareuse
2820 Pennsylvania Avenue, NW
Washington, DC 20007
Attn: J Michel Lareuse
TEL (202) 333-5704

Galerie Lelong
20 West 57th Street
New York, NY 10019
Attn: Mary Sabbatino
TEL (212) 315-0470
FAX (212) 262-0624

Galerie Lelong
13 Rue de Teheran
75008 Paris, France
TEL (1) 563-13-19

GALLERY INDEX CONTINUED

Galerie Lelong
Predigerplatz 10-12
8025 Zurich
Switzerland
TEL (1) 251-11-20

Galerie Martin
417 Town Center
Boca Raton, FL 33432
Attn: Edith V Mallinger
TEL (407) 395-3050

Galerie Michael
430 North Rodeo Drive
Beverly Hills, CA 90210
Attn: Michael Schwartz
TEL (310) 273-3377
TEL (800) PICASSO

Galerie Thomas R Monahan
1038 North La Salle
Chicago, IL 60610
TEL (312) 266-7530
FAX (312) 266-8726

Galerie Ravel
1210 West 5th Street
Austin, TX 78703
Attn: Dana Ravel
TEL (512) 474-2628

Galerie Rienzo
922 Madison Avenue
New York, NY 10021
Attn: Robert Rienzo
TEL (212) 288-2226

Galerie Thaddeus Ropac
Kaigasse 40
A-5020 Salzburg, Austria
TEL (0662) 84 97 31

Galerie St Etienne
24 West 57th Street
New York, NY 10019
Attn: Hildegard Bachert
Jane Kallir
TEL (212) 245-6734

Galerie Sho Contemporary Art
3-2-9 Nihonbashi
Chuo-ku, Tokyo, Japan
Attn: Sho Satake
TEL 3275-1008
FAX 3273-9309
Specializing in Contemporary Art

Galerie Simonne Stern
518 Julis Street
New Orleans, LA 70130
Attn: Donna C Perret
TEL (504) 529-1118
FAX (504) 525-7030

Galerie Stendhal
622–626 Broadway
New York, NY 10012
Attn: Harry W Stendhal
TEL (212) 505-1201
FAX (212) 505-1201

Galerie Vega
5 Rue de Strivay
4051 Neupre
Belgium
TEL 041-80-22-70

Galerie Waldvogel
Avenue de la Gare 22
1860 Aigle, Switzerland
Attn: Philippe Waldvogel
TEL (025) 26-20-78

Gallerie International
1170 Valley View Center
Dallas, TX 75240
Attn: Kenneth Winkler
TEL (214) 661-8778

Galleries Maurice Sternberg
North Michigan Avenue
at Walton Street
Chicago, IL 60611
TEL (312) 642-1700

Gallery One at Second Avenue
2940 East Second Avenue
Denver, CO 80206
Attn: Jeannie Denholm
TEL (303) 393-0460

Gallery 3
3819 North Third Street
Phoenix, AZ 85012
Attn: Sherry Manoukian
TEL (602) 277-9540

Gallery Eight
7464 Girard Avenue
La Jolla, CA 92037
Attn: Ruth Newmark
TEL (619) 454-9781

Gallery 9
215 Main Street
Chatam, NJ 07928
Attn: Randy M Dembo
TEL (201) 635-6505

Gallery 10
7 Greenwich Avenue
New York, NY 10014
Attn: Marcia Smith
TEL (212) 206-1058

Gallery 10, Inc
225 Canyon Road
Santa Fe, NM 87501
Attn: Phillip Cohen
TEL (505) 983-9707

Gallery 10
7045 Third Avenue
Scottsdale, AZ 85251
Attn: Lee Cohen
TEL (602) 994-0405

Gallery 10, Ltd
1519 Connecticut Avenue, NW
Washington, DC 20036
Attn: Nancy Susick
TEL (202) 232-3326

Gallery 10, Inc
34505 North Scottsdale Road, #33
North Scottsdale, AZ 85262
Attn: David Stock
TEL (602) 945-3385
TEL (602) 488-1292

Gallery X
800 West Madison
P O Box 56942
Phoenix, AZ 85079
Attn: Peter Petrisko, Jr
TEL (602) 420-9390

Gallery XII
412 East Douglas Avenue
Wichita, KS 67202
Attn: Betty Sieler
TEL (316) 267-5915

Gallery 16
608 Central Avenue
Great Falls, MT 59401
Attn: Judith Ericksen
TEL (406) 453-6103

Gallery 20
800 East Diamond Boulevard
Anchorage, AK 99504
Attn: Mary Ann Perkins
TEL (907) 344-2712

Gallery 44
1916 13th Street
Boulder, CO 80302
Attn: Kitty Edward
TEL (303) 444-4490

Gallery 53 Artworks
118 Main Street
Cooperstown, NY 13326
Attn: Sydney Lancaster Waller
TEL (607) 547-5655

Gallery 56
56 West 400, South
Salt Lake City, UT 84101
Attn: David Ericson
TEL (801) 533-8245

Gallery 57
204 North Harbor Blvd
Fullerton, CA 92632
TEL (714) 870-9194

Gallery 72
2709 Leavenworth
Omaha, NE 68105
Attn: Robert D Rogers
TEL (402) 345-3347

Gallery 84
50 West 57th Street
New York, NY 10019
Attn: Joe Bascom
TEL (212) 581-6000

Gallery 200
200 West Mound Street
Columbus, OH 43215
Attn: Renee Steidle
TEL (614) 224-1259

Gallery 292
120 Wooster Street, 2nd Floor
New York, NY 10012
TEL (212) 431-0292
FAX (212) 941-7479

Gallery 500
Church & Old York Roads
Elkins Park, PA 19117
Attn: Gary Pilkey
TEL (215) 572-1203

Gallery 539
539 Bienville Street
New Orleans, LA 70130
Attn: Jim Lamantia
TEL (504) 522-0695

Gallery 600
600 Broadway
Paducah, KY 42001
Attn: Nancy Flowers
TEL (502) 442-1985

Gallery 1616
1616 North Damen Street
Chicago, IL 60647
TEL (312) 489-5492
FAX (312) 489-5266

Gallery 1633
1633 North Damen Street
Chicago, IL 60647
Attn: Montana Morrison
TEL (312) 384-4441

Gallery A
300 Superior Street
Chicago, IL 60610
TEL (312) 280-4500
FAX (312) 280-4968

Gallery A
105–107 Kit Carson Road
Taos, NM 87571
Attn: Mary Lowe Sanchez
TEL (505) 758-2343

Gallery Paule Anglim
14 Geary Street
San Francisco, CA 94108
TEL (415) 433-2710
FAX (415) 433-1501

Gallery Antiqua
5138 Biscayne Blvd
Miami, FL 33137
Attn: Caleb A Davis
TEL (305) 759-5355

Gallery C
3532 Wade Avenue
Cameron Village
Raleigh, NC 27607
Attn: Charlene Newsom
TEL (919) 828-3165

Gallery Camino Real
608 Banyon trail
Boca Raton, FL 33431
Attn: Marjorie Margolis
Bill Biety
TEL (407) 241-1606

Gallery Contemporanea
526 Lancaster Street
Jacksonville, FL 32204
Attn: Sally Ann Freeman
TEL (904) 359-0016

GALLERY INDEX CONTINUED

Gallery East
247 Pantigo Road
East Hampton, NY 19937
Attn: Rose Millevolte
 Rosemary Terribile
TEL (516) 324-9393

Gallery Elena
119-C Bent Street
Taos, NM 87571
TEL (505) 758-9094

A Gallery for Fine Photography
323 Royal Street
New Orleans, LA 70130
Attn: Joshua Mann Pailet
TEL (504) 568-1313

Carol Getz Gallery
2843 South Bayshore Drive
Coconut Grove, FL 33133
TEL (305) 448-3243

Gallery Henoch
80 Wooster Street
New York, NY 10012
Attn: George Henoch Schechtman
TEL (212) 966-6360

Gallery Jupiter
25 Church Street
Little Silver, NJ 07739
Attn: Brian Reddy
TEL (908) 530-8035
FAX (908) 758-1871

Gallery K
2010 R Street, NW
Washington, DC 20009
Attn: Komei Wachi
TEL (202) 234-0339
FAX (202) 234-0605

Gallery Mack NW
2001 Western Avenue
Seattle, WA 98121
Attn: Barbara Mack
TEL (206) 448-1616

Gallery Moos
133 Greene Street, 2nd Floor
New York, NY 10012
Attn: David Moos
TEL (212) 982-0411

Gallery NAGA
67 Newbury Street
Boston, MA 02116
Attn: Arthur Dion
TEL (617) 267-9060

Kodner Gallery of the Masters, Inc
9918 Clayton Road
St Louis, MO 63124
Attn: Martin Kodner
TEL (314) 993-4477
FAX (314) 993-4478

Gallery on the Green
1837 Massachusetts Avenue
Lexington, MA 02173
Attn: Molly H Nye
TEL (617) 861-6044

Gallery Piazza
819 Bridgeway
Sausalito, CA 94965
Attn: Yoshihisa Aso
TEL (415) 331-6711
FAX (415) 331-7064

Gallery Revel
96 Spring Street
New York, NY 10012
TEL (212) 925-0600

Gallery Rodeo, Inc
421 North Rodeo Drive
Beverly Hills, CA 90210
TEL (310) 273-2105

Gallery Show
3-2-9 Nihonbashi, Chuo-ku
Tokyo 103, Japan
Attn: Sho Satake
TEL (275) 1008

Gallery Vienna
750 North Orleans
Chicago, IL 60610
Attn: Norbert Gleicher
TEL (312) 951-0300

Gallery West
107 South Robertson Blvd
Los Angeles, CA 90010
Attn: Roberta Feuerstein
TEL (310) 271-1145

Guillaume Gallozzi Gallery
203 West Houston Street
New York, NY 10014
TEL (212) 645-9306
FAX (212) 691-1982

Galuchat Gallery
182 Avenue Louise
1050 Brussels
Belgium
TEL (02) 647-45-40

Garzoli Gallery
930 B Street
San Rafael, CA 94901
Attn: John H Garzoli
TEL (415) 459-4321

Gasperi Gallery
320 Julia Street
New Orleans, LA 70130
Attn: Richard D Gasperi
TEL (504) 524-9373

Georgeart
1510 North Wells Street
Chicago, IL 60610
Attn: Giulia Sindler
TEL (312) 751-9277
FAX (312) 751-8137

Sandra Gering Gallery
476 Broome Street, 2nd Floor
New York, NY 10013
TEL (212) 226-8195
FAX (212) 226-7186

Germans Van Eck
420 West Broadway
New York, NY 10012
TEL (212) 219-0717
FAX (212) 219-0728

Hilde Gerst Gallery
685 Madison Avenue
New York, NY 10021
TEL (212) 751-5655
FAX (212) 751-0886

John Gibson Gallery
568 Broadway
New York, NY 10012
TEL (212) 925-1192
FAX (212) 925-1274

Stephen Gill Gallery
135 East 55th Street
New York, NY 10022
TEL (212) 832-0800

Marita Gilliam Gallery
126 Glenwood Avenue
Raleigh, NC 27603-1704
TEL (919) 834-5800

Gillman/Gruen Galleries
226 West Superior
Chicago, IL 61610
Attn: Bradley Lincoln
 Renee Sax
TEL (312) 337-6262

Gimpel & Weitzenhoffer Gallery
415 West Broadway
New York, NY 10012
Attn: Joseph Rickards
TEL (212) 925-6090

Katie Gingrass Gallery
241 North Broadway
Milwaukee, WI 53202
Attn: Pat Brophy
TEL (414) 289-0855

Glacier Gallery
1498 Old Scenic Highway 2-E
Kalispell, MT 59901-1054
Attn: V K Nelson
TEL (406) 752-4742

Barbara Gladstone Gallery
99 Greene Street
New York, NY 10012
Attn: Richard Flood
TEL (212) 431-3334
FAX (212) 966-9310

Glass Art Gallery, Inc
315 Central Park West, #8-W
New York, NY 10025
Attn: Wendy Glass
TEL (212) 787-4704

Fay Gold Gallery
247 Buckhead Avenue
Atlanta, GA 30305
TEL (404) 233-3843
FAX (404) 365-8633

Dorothy Goldeen Gallery
1547 9th Street
Santa Monica, CA 90401
TEL (310) 395-0222
FAX (213) 458-3368

Goldfield Galleries
8380 Melrose Avenue
Los Angeles, CA 90069
Attn: Ed Goldfield
TEL (213) 651-1122

R K Goldman Contemporary
10850 Wilshire Blvd
Los Angeles, CA 90024
Attn: Mary-Ann Rosendale
TEL (310) 824-5800
FAX (310) 824-5615

John Good Gallery
532 Broadway
New York, NY 10012
TEL (212) 941-8066
FAX (212) 274-0124

Lynn Goode Gallery
2719 Colquitt
Houston, TX 77098
Attn: Ben Crump
TEL (713) 526-5966
FAX (713) 527-9461

James Goodman Gallery
41 East 57th Street
New York, NY 10022
TEL (212) 593-3737
FAX (212) 980-0195

Marian Goodman Gallery
24 West 57th Street
New York, NY 10019
Attn: Jill Sussman
TEL (212) 977-7160
FAX (212) 581-5187

Gordon Gallery
1311 Montana Avenue
Santa Monica, CA 90403
Attn: Barry Gordon
TEL (310) 394-6545
FAX (310) 576-2453

Beverly Gordon Gallery
2404 Cedar Springs Road, #100
Dallas, TX 75201
TEL (214) 880-9600

Jay Gorney Modern Art
100 Greene Street
New York, NY 10012
TEL (212) 966-4480
FAX (212) 925-1239

Gottheiner Fine Arts, Ltd
219 Plant Avenue
St Louis, MO 63119
Attn: Gary S Godwin
TEL (314) 961-6175

Graham Gallery
521 Central Avenue, NW
Albuquerque, NM 87103
TEL (505) 764-9939

W A Graham Gallery
1431 West Alabama
Houston, TX 77006
TEL (713) 528-4957

Graham Modern
1014 Madison Avenue
New York, NY 10021
Attn: Lisa Travers
TEL (212) 535-5767

GALLERY INDEX CONTINUED

Grand Central Art Galleries
24 West 57th Street
New York, NY 10019
Attn: John Evans
TEL (212) 867-3344

Graphic Art Collection
133 NE 1st Avenue
Hallendale, FL 33009
Attn: Bruce Sher
       Dorothy Schaffer
TEL (305) 454-8806

Graphics House Gallery
702 Canyon Road
Santa Fe, NM 87501
Attn: Anne Sawyer
TEL (505) 983-2654

Richard Gray Gallery
620 North Michigan Avenue
Chicago, IL 60611
Attn: Paul L Gray
TEL (312) 642-8877
FAX (312) 642-8488

Graystone Gallery
250 Sutter Street, 3rd Floor
San Francisco, CA 94108
Attn: Edmund Russell
       Freddie Fong
TEL (415) 956-7693

Glenn Green Galleries
50 East San Francisco Street
Santa Fe, NM 87501
Attn: Glenn Green
       Sandy Green
TEL (505) 998-4168

Richard Green Graphics
2036 Broadway
Santa Monica, CA 90404
Attn: Irit Krygier
TEL (310) 828-6666

Greenberg Gallery
44 Maryland Plaza
St Louis, MO 63108
Attn: Ronald K Greenberg
       Sissy Thomas
TEL (314) 361-7600
FAX (314) 361-7743

Howard Greenberg Gallery
120 Wooster Street, 2nd Floor
New York, NY 10012
TEL (212) 334-0010
FAX (212) 941-7479

Greene Gallery
1541 Brickell Avenue
Miami, FL 33129
Attn: Barbara Greene
TEL (305) 858-7868

Ralph Greene Gallery
208 Dartmouth Drive, NE
Albuquerque, NM 87106
TEL (505) 266-1414

Greenhut Galleries
146 Middle Street
Portland, ME 04101
Attn: Peg Golden
TEL (207) 772-2693

Greggie Fine Art
12 Piedmont Center, #329
Atlanta, GA 30305
TEL (404) 261-3961
FAX (404) 261-3962

Griffith Gallery
337 Beaver Street
Sewickley, PA 15143
Attn: J Blaine
TEL (412) 741-3276

C Grimaldis Gallery
1006 Morton Street
Baltimore, MD 21201
TEL (301) 539-1080

Gremillion & Company Fine Art, Inc
2501 Sunset
Houston, TX 77005
Attn: Christopher Skidmore
TEL (713) 522-2701
FAX (713) 522-3712

Christopher Grimes Gallery
1644 17th Street
Santa Monica, CA 90404
TEL (310) 450-5962
FAX (213) 450-7882

Groveland Gallery
25 Groveland Terrace
Minneapolis, MN 55403
Attn: Sally Johnson
TEL (612) 377-7800

Gruen Galleries
226 West Superior
Chicago, IL 60610
Attn: Bradley Lincoln
       Renee Sax
TEL (312) 337-6262

Guarisco Gallery
2828 Pennsylvania Avenue, NW
Washington, DC 20007
Attn: Jane Studabaker
TEL (202) 333-8533
FAX (202) 625-0834

Gwenda Joy Gallery
301 West Superior Street, 2nd Floor
Chicago, IL 60610
TEL (312) 664-3406

Hahn Gallery
8439 Germantown Avenue
Philadelphia, PA 19118
Attn: Roslyn S Hahn
TEL (215) 247-8439
FAX (215) 247-8849

Nohra Haime Gallery
41 East 57th Street, 6th Floor
New York, NY 10022
TEL (212) 888-3550
FAX (212) 888-7869

Haines Gallery
49 Geary Street, 5th Floor
San Francisco, CA 94108
Attn: Cheryl Haines
TEL (415) 397-8114

Juliette Halioua Editions
20 East 67th Street
New York, NY 10021
TEL (212) 794-2757

Ron Hall Gallery
500 Crescent Court
Dallas, TX 75201
Attn: Kristy Stubbs
       John Runyon
TEL (214) 871-3400
FAX (214) 871-3401

Stephen Haller Fine Art
560 Broadway, #609
New York, NY 10012
TEL (212) 219-2500
FAX (212) 219-3246

Matina Hamilton & Associates
1623 Third Avenue, #3KW
New York, NY 10128
TEL (212) 722-3311
FAX (212) 996-3198

Carl Hammer Gallery
200 West Superior Street
Chicago, IL 60610
TEL (312) 266-8512

Hammer Galleries
33 West 57th Street
New York, NY 10019
Attn: Richard Lynch
TEL (212) 644-4400
FAX (212) 832-3763

Hammerquist/Facs Gallery
419 Third Avenue
New York, NY 10016
Attn: Robert Hammerquist
       Sam Smith
TEL (212) 889-8173
FAX (212) 683-1550

The Hang-Up
45 South Palm Avenue, #100
Sarasota, FL 34236
Attn: Frank Troncale
TEL (813) 953-5757

Hangar-Galeria de Arte
Arroyo 889-CP
Buenos Aires, Argentina
Attn: Marta Guerra-Alem
TEL (240) 3533

Jack Hanley Gallery
41 Grant Street, 3rd Floor
San Francisco, CA 94108
TEL (415) 291-8911
FAX (415) 291-8940

Hanson Galleries
229 Royal Street
New Orleans, LA 70130
Attn: Angela King
TEL (504) 566-0816

Hanson Galleries
839 Front Street
Maui, HI 96761
Attn: John Kenney
TEL (808) 661-0764

Hanson Galleries
839 North Rodeo Drive
Beverly Hills, CA 90210
Attn: Dennis Rae
TEL (310) 205-3922
FAX (310) 205-0652

Hanson Galleries
1227 Prospect Place
La Jolla, CA 92037
Attn: Mark Miles
       Tom Noel
TEL (619) 454-9799

Hanson Galleries
465 West Broadway
New York, NY 10012
Attn: Mary Felton
TEL (212) 353-2080

Hanson Galleries
669 Bridgeway
Sausalito, CA 94965
Attn: Rebecca Faiola
TEL (415) 332-3078
FAX (415) 331-6134

Hanson Galleries
153 Maiden Lane
San Francisco, CA 94108
Attn: Nancy Toomey
TEL (415) 956-4338

Hanson Gallery Northeast
Main Street
Northeast Harbor, ME 04662
Attn: Jeannine Hanson
TEL (207) 276-5323

Hanson Howard Galleries
82 North Main Street
Ashland, OR 97520
Attn: Judy Howard
       Marie Baxter
TEL (503) 488-2562

Harbor Gallery
24 West 57th Street
New York, NY 10019
TEL (212) 307-6667
FAX (212) 307-6748

Harcourts Modern & Contemporary Art
460 Bush Street
San Francisco, CA 94108
Attn: James P. Healy
TEL (415) 421-3428
FAX (415) 421-7842

Harcus Gallery
6 Melrose Street
Boston, MA 02111
Attn: Portia Harcus
TEL (617) 262-4445
FAX (617) 451-3221

The Harmon-Meek Gallery
386 Broad Avenue, South
Naples, FL 33940
Attn: J William Meek, III
TEL (813) 261-2637
FAX (813) 261-3804

Harris Gallery
1100 Bissonnet
Houston, TX 77005
Attn: Harrison Itz
TEL (713) 552-9116

Elizabeth Harris Gallery
524 Broadway, 3rd Floor
New York, NY 10012
TEL (212) 941-9895
FAX (212) 941-7495

GALLERY INDEX CONTINUED

Ellen Harris Gallery
355 Commercial Street
Provincetown, MA 02657
Attn: Elsbeth Hino
TEL (508) 487-1414
TEL (508) 487-0065

Lisa Harris Gallery
1922 Pike Place
Seattle, WA 98101
TEL (206) 443-3315

O K Harris/Works of Art
383 West Broadway
New York, NY 10012
Attn: Ivan C Karp
TEL (212) 431-3600

P C Hart Gallery
337 East Indiantown Road, #16
Jupiter, FL 33477
Attn: Pamela C Hart
TEL (407) 747-7094

Harley-Madigan Gallery
156 West 86th Street, #4A
New York, NY 10024
Attn: D Harley
    T Madigan
TEL (212) 580-8446

Emily Harvey Gallery
537 Broadway & Spring Street
New York, NY 10012
TEL (212) 925-7651
FAX (212) 966-0439

Jane Haslem Gallery
2025 Hillger Place, NW
Washington, DC 20009
Attn: Jeffrey A Haslem
TEL (202) 232-4644

Sally Hawkins Gallery
448 West Broadway, 2nd Floor
New York, NY 10012
TEL (212) 477-5699

Linda Hayman Gallery
32500 Northwestern Highway
Farmington Hills, MI 48334
Attn: Linda Hayman
TEL (312) 932-0080
FAX (312) 923-0861

Pat Hearn Gallery
39 Wooster Street
New York, NY 10013
TEL (212) 941-7055

Heath Gallery
416 East Paces Ferry Road, NE
Atlanta, GA 30305
TEL (404) 262-6407

Charles Hecht Galleries
1855 Ventura Blvd
Tarzana, CA 91356
TEL (818) 881-3218

Hefner Galleries
1440 Wealthy, SE
Grand Rapids, MI 49506
Attn: Jacob Hefner
    Amy L Braun
    James Myers
TEL (616) 458-1715

Lillian Heidenberg Gallery
50 West 57th Street
New York, NY 10019
Attn: Philip Tifft
TEL (212) 586-3808

Helander Gallery
415 West Broadway
New York, NY 10012
AttN; Neil Watson
TEL (212) 966-9797

Helander Gallery
350 South County Road
Palm Beach, FL 33480
Attn: Bruce Helander
    Wendy Helander
TEL (407) 659-1711
FAX (407) 659-4023

Heller Gallery
71 Greene Street
New York, NY 10012
Attn: Douglas Heller
TEL (212) 966-5948

Henri Gallery
1500 21st Street NW
Washington, DC 20036
TEL (202) 659-9313

Heritage Gallery
718 North La Cienega Blvd
Los Angeles, CA 90069
Attn: Charlotte Sherman
TEL (213) 652-7738
Specializing in American &
International Prints

Kiyo Higashi Gallery
8332 Melrose Avenue
Los Angeles, CA 90069
TEL (213) 655-2482
FAX (213) 655-7016

Susanne Hilberry Gallery
555 South Woodward
Birmingham, MI 48009
TEL (313) 642-8250
FAX (313) 642-9039

Hildt Galleries
6 West Hubbard Street
Chicago, IL 60610
TEL (312) 527-3525

Hill Gallery
163 Townsend
Birmingham, MI 48009
Attn: Pamela Hill
    Timothy Hill
TEL (313) 540-9288

Carolyn Hill Gallery
60 Gramercy Park, North, #7-A
New York, NY 10010
TEL (212) 903-4216

Michael Himovitz Gallery
1020 10th Street
Sacramento, CA 95814
Attn: Charles Miller
TEL (916) 448-8723
FAX (916) 448-7481

Hine Gallery
357 Tehama
San Francisco, CA 94103
Attn: Hank Hine
TEL (415) 777-2214
FAX (415) 495-2665

Hirschl & Adler Galleries
21 East 70th Street
New York, NY 10021
Attn: Stuart Feld
TEL (212) 535-8810

Hirschl & Adler Modern
420 West Broadway
New York, NY 10012
Attn: Donald McKinney
TEL (212) 966-6211
FAX (212) 966-6331

Linda Hodges Gallery
410 Occidental Avenue
Seattle, WA 98104
TEL (206) 624-3034

Joan Hodgell Gallery
46 South Palm Avenue
Sarasota, FL 34236
Attn: Kate Hansen
TEL (813) 336-1146

Fred Hoffman Gallery
912 Colorado Avenue
Santa Monica, CA 90401
TEL (310) 394-4199

Nancy Hoffman Gallery
429 West Broadway
New York, NY 10012
TEL (212) 966-6676
FAX (212) 334-5078

Rhona Hoffman Gallery
215 West Superior Street
Chicago, IL 60610
Attn: Susan Reynolds
TEL (312) 951-8828
FAX (312) 951-5274

Hokin Gallery, Inc
1086 Kane Concourse
Bay Harbor Islands, FL 33154
Attn: Grace Hokin
    Dorothy Berenson Blau
TEL (305) 861-5700

Hokin Gallery
245 Worth Avenue
Palm Beach, FL 33480
Attn: Grace Hokin
TEL (407) 655-5177
FAX (407) 655-6315

B C Holland, Inc
222 West Superior
Chicago, IL 60610
TEL (312) 664-5000

Hooks-Epstein Galleries
2623 Jipling
Houston, TX 77098
Attn: Charles V Hooks
TEL (713) 522-0718

Hoorn-Ashby Gallery
766 Madison Avenue
New York, NY 10021
Attn: Mary-Claire Barton
TEL (212) 628-3199

Vivian Horan Fine Art
35 East 67th Street
New York, NY 10021
TEL (212) 517-9410
FAX (212) 772-6107

Joy Horwich Gallery
226 East Ontario Avenue
Chicago, IL 60611
TEL (312) 787-0171

Elaine Horwitch Gallery
4211 North Marshall Way
Scottsdale, AZ 85251
Attn: Victoria Boyce
TEL (602) 945-0791

Elaine Horwitch Gallery
129 West Palace Avenue
Sante Fe, NM 87501
Attn: Abby Braun
TEL (505) 988-8997

Hoshour Gallery
417 Second Street, SW
Albuquerque, NM 87102
Attn: Lise Hoshour
TEL (505) 842-5332

Edwynn Houk Gallery
200 West Superior Street
Chicago, IL 60610
TEL (312) 943-0698
FAX (312) 943-6494

Hourian Fine Art Gallery
1843 Union Street
San Francisco, CA 94123
Attn: Caroline Moassessi
    Mohammad Hourian
TEL (415) 346-6400

Henry Howells Gallery
137 Thompson Street
New York, NY 10012
Attn: Gary Zarchy
TEL (212) 533-7994

Hubert Gallery
1046 Madison Avenue
New York, NY 10021
TEL (212) 628-2922
FAX (212) 794-3889

Leonard Hutton Galleries
33 East 74th Street
New York, NY 10021
Attn: L Hutton
    I Hutton
TEL (212) 249-9700
FAX (212) 772-9439

GALLERY INDEX CONTINUED

Pasquale Iannetti Art Galleries
522 Sutter Street
San Francisco, CA 94102
TEL (415) 433-2771

Ianuzzi Gallery
34505 North Scottsdale Road
Scottsdale, AZ 85262
Attn: Mara Ianuzzi
Nick Ianuzzi
TEL (602) 488-3737
TEL (602) 991-4679

Images . . . A Gallery
372 Hayes Street
San Francisco, CA 94102
TEL (415) 626-2284

Images Gallery
3154 Markway Drive
Toledo, OH 43606
Attn: Frederick D Cohn
TEL (419) 537-1400

Impulse
188 Commerical Street
Provincetown, MA 02657
Attn: Frederick Bayer
TEL (508) 487-1154

Ingbar Gallery
568 Broadway
New York, NY 10012
Attn: Michael Ingbar
TEL (212) 334-1100

Inkfish Gallery
949 Broadway
Denver, CO 80203
Attn: Paul Hughes
Nancy Hughes
TEL (303) 825-6727

International Gallery
643 G Street
San Diego, CA 92101
Attn: Stephen Ross
TEL (619) 235-8255

International Images
514 Beaver Street
Sewickley, PA 15143
Attn: Elena Kornetchuk
TEL (412) 741-3036

Irving Galleries
332 Worth Avenue
Palm Beach, FL 33480
Attn: Holden Luntz
TEL (407) 659-6221

Ismael Gallery
221 Centre Street
New York, NY 10013
TEL (212) 431-7860

Isselbacher Gallery
41 East 78th Street
New York, NY 10021
Attn: Alfred Isselbacher
TEL (212) 472-1766

Iturralde Gallery
154 North La Brea Avenue
Los Angeles, CA 90036
TEL (213) 937-4269
FAX (213) 937-4269

Ana Izax Galleries
Empyrean Way 10116, #101
Century City
Los Angeles, CA 90667
Attn: Anna Isaacs-Bersano
TEL (310) 271-6660
FAX (310) 271-9901

Ann Jacob Gallery
3500 Peachtree Street
Phipps Plaza
Atlanta, GA 30326
Attn: Yvonne Spiotta
TEL (404) 262-3399

Yvette Jacob Gallery
760 Madison Avenue, 2nd Floor
New York, NY 10021
TEL (212) 717-5162

Donna Jacobs Gallery
574 North Woodward Avenue
Brimingham, MI 48011
TEL (313) 540-1600

Jadite Galleries
415 West 50th Street
New York, NY 10019
Attn: Roland Sainz
TEL (212) 315-2740

James Gallery
2930 Revere, #200
Houston, TX 77081
Attn: Kathleen James
Helen Robertson
TEL (713) 942-7035
FAX (713) 942-7038

Jamison Galleries
560 Monezuma Avenue, #103
Santa Fe, NM 87501
Attn: Zeb B Conley, Jr
TEL (505) 982-3666

Jamison/Thomas Gallery
1313 NW Giisan Street
Portland, OR 97209
Attn: William Jamison
TEL (503) 222-0063

Sidney Janis Gallery
110 West 57th Street
New York, NY 10019
Attn: Carroll Janis
TEL (212) 586-0110

Janus Gallery
225 Canyon Road
Santa Fe, NM 87501
Attn: Joan Clark
Nancy Strell
TEL (505) 983-1590

Jaro Art Galleries
955 Madison Avenue
New York, NY 10021
Attn: Jaro Parizek
TEL (212) 734-5475

Jean Stephen Galleries
800 Niccollet Mall, #401
Minneapolis, MN 55402
Attn: Jean Danko
Steve Danko
TEL (612) 338-4333

Jeb Gallery
295 Albany Street
Fall River, MA 02720
Attn: Ronald Caplain
TEL (508) 673-8010

Dean Jensen Gallery
217 North Broadway
Milwaukee, WI 53202
TEL (414) 278-7100

R S Johnson Fine Art
645 North Michigan Avenue
Chicago, IL 60611
Attn: R Stanley Johnson
Ursula Johnson
TEL (312) 943-1661
FAX (312) 943-4450

Carole Jones Gallery
300 West Superior Street
Chicago, IL 60610
TEL (312) 587-8820
FAX (312) 587-9859

The Jones Gallery
1264 Prospect Street
La Jolla, CA 92037
Attn: Douglas M Jones
TEL (619) 459-1370

Jones Troyer Fitzpatrick Gallery
1614 20th Street, NW
Washington, DC 20009
Attn: Sally Troyer
Sandra Fitzpatrick
TEL (202) 328-7189

Jordan-Volpe Gallery
958 Madison Avenue
New York, NY 10021
Attn: V Jordan
T Volpe
TEL (212) 570-9500

Peter Joseph Gallery
745 Fifth Avenue, 4th Floor
New York, NY 10151
Attn: Larry Parks Dudley
Cardell Oliphant
TEL (212) 751-5500
FAX (212) 751-0213

Julie: Artisans' Gallery
687 Madison Avenue
New York, NY 10021
Attn: Julie Schafler Dale
TEL (212) 688-2345

Jupiter Fine Arts
111 Spinnaker Lane
Jupiter, FL 33477
Attn: Steve Garshell
TEL (407) 575-1549

Alexander Kahan Fine Arts
40 East 76th Street
New York, NY 10021
TEL (212) 737-4230

Jane Kahan Gallery
922 Madison Avenue
New York, NY 10021-3511
TEL (212) 744-1490
FAX (212) 744-1598

Constance Kamens Fine Art, Inc
405 East 54th Street
New York, NY 10022
TEL (212) 953-6710
FAX (212) 753-1465

Ulrike Kantor Gallery
9143 St Ives Drive
Los Angeles, CA 90069
TEL (310) 272-5650
FAX (310) 275-3893

Rodi Karkazis Gallery
168 North Michigan Avenue, #300
Chicago, IL 60601
TEL (312) 346-5050

Paul Kasmin Gallery
74 Grand Street
New York, NY 10013
Attn: Michelle Rogan Heinrici
TEL (212) 219-3219
FAX (212) 219-2385

Kass/Meridian Gallery
215 West Superior Street
Chicago, IL 60610
Attn: Alan Kass
Grace Kass
TEL (312) 266-5999

Hal Katzen Gallery
345 West Broadway
New York, NY 10013
TEL (212) 219-0165

Keen Gallery
423 Broome Street
New York, NY
Attn: Lisa Wong
TEL (212) 966-2216

June Kelly Gallery
591 Broadway, 3rd Floor
New York, NY 10012
TEL (212) 226-1660

Kelmscott Gallery
4611 North Lincoln Street
Chicago, IL 60625
TEL (312) 784-2559

Kenkeleha Gallery
214 East 2nd Street
New York, NY 10009
Attn: Corine Jennings
TEL (212) 674-3939
FAX (212) 505-5080

Kennedy Graphics, Inc
40 West 57th Street, 5th Floor
New York, NY 10019
Attn: Lawrence Fleischman
TEL (212) 541-9600
FAX (212) 333-7451

GALLERY INDEX CONTINUED

Kent Fine Art
47 East 63rd Street
New York, NY 10021
Attn: D Walla
A Lundgren
E Costello
TEL (212) 980-9696
FAX (212) 421-5368

Keny Galleries, Inc
300 East Beck Street
Columbus, OH 43206
Attn: Timothy Keny
James Keny
TEL (614) 464-1228

Douglas Kenyon, Inc
1357 North Wells Street
Chicago, IL 60610
Attn: Joel Oppenheimer
TEL (312) 642-5300

Jan Kesner Gallery
164 North La Brea Avenue
Los Angeles, CA 90036
TEL (213) 938-6834
FAX (213) 938-1106

Ray Ketchum Gallery
540 Forestdale Drive, NE
Atlanta, GA 30342-2307
TEL (404) 255-8745

Robert L Kidd Galleries
107 Townsend Street
Birmingham, MI 48011
Attn: Ray Frost Fleming
TEL (313) 642-3909

Kim Light Gallery
126 North La Brea
Los Angeles, CA 90036
TEL (213) 933-9816
FAX (213) 933-9921

Kimberly Gallery
1621 21st Street, NW
Washington, DC 20009
Attn: Elena G Kimberly
TEL (202) 234-1988

Kimmel/Cohn Photography Arts
1 West 64th Street
New York, NY 10023
Attn: Roberta Kimmel Cohn
TEL (212) 799-6675
FAX (212) 787-1722

Kimzey Miller Gallery
1225 Second Avenue
Seattle, WA 98101
Attn: Terry Miller
TEL (206) 682-2339

Phyllis Kind Gallery
136 Greene Street
New York, NY 10012
TEL (212) 925-1200

Phyllis Kind Gallery
313 West Superior Street
Chicago, IL 60610
Attn: William H Bengston
TEL (312) 642-6302

Patrick King Contemporary Art
427 Massachusetts Avenue
Indianapolis, IN 46204
TEL (317) 634-4101

Kingston Gallery
129 Kingston Street
Boston, MA 02116
Attn: Rob Todd
TEL (617) 423-4113

Kirsten Gallery
5320 Roosevelt Way, NE
Seattle, WA 98105
Attn: Nicholas Kirsten
Richard Kirsten
TEL (206) 522-2011

The Kitchen Gallery
512 West 19th Street
New York, NY 10011-2807
Attn: Bobbi Tsumagari
TEL (212) 255-5793

Klarfeld Perry Gallery
472 Broome Street
New York, NY 10013
TEL (212) 941-0303
FAX (212) 925-0849

Klein Art Works
400 North Morgan
Chicago, IL 60622
Attn: Paul Klein
Judith Simon
TEL (312) 243-0400
FAX (312) 243-6782

Arnold Klein Gallery
4520 North Woodward Avenue
Royal Oak, MI 48073
TEL (313) 647-7709

Michael Klien, Inc
594 Broadway, Room #302
New York, NY 10012
Attn: David Gray
TEL (212) 505-1980
FAX (212) 431-1985

Robert Klein Gallery
207 South Street, #6
Boston, MA 02111
TEL (617) 482-8818

Kline Gallery
1000 Hillcrest Drive
Santa Fe, NM 87501
Attn: Fred Kline
Jann Kline
TEL (505) 988-1103

Kneeland Gallery
271 First Avenue, North
P O Box 2070
Sun Valley, ID 83353
Attn: Char Thompson
TEL (208) 726-5512

Knoedler & Company
19 East 70th Street
New York, NY 10021
Attn: Lawrence Rubin
TEL (212) 794-0550
FAX (212) 772-6932

Robert Koch Gallery
49 Geary Street
San Francisco, CA 94108
Attn: Ada Takahashi
TEL (415) 421-0122
FAX (415) 421-6306

Koehler Galleries, Ltd
175 Franklin Street
Chicago, IL 60606
TEL (312) 332-7185

Michael Kohn Gallery
920 Colorado Avenue
Santa Monica, CA 90401
TEL (310) 393-7713
FAX (310) 393-1554

Koplin Gallery
1438 9th Street
Santa Monica, CA 90405
Attn: Marti Koplin
TEL (310) 319-9956
FAX (310) 319-9959

Korby Gallery
479 Pompton Avenue
Cedar Grove, NJ 07009
Attn: Alfred Korby
TEL (201) 239-6789

Kornbluth Gallery, Inc
7-21 Fair Lawn Avenue
Fair Lawn, NJ 07410
Attn: Sally Fowler
TEL (201) 791-3374
TEL (201) 857-0457

Kouros Gallery
23 East 73rd Street
New York, NY 10021
Attn: Angelos E Camillos
TEL (212) 288-5888

Barbara Krakow Gallery
10 Newbury Street
Boston, MA 02116
TEL (617) 262-4490
FAX (617) 262-8971

Kraushaar Galleries
724 Fifth Avenue
New York, NY 10019
Attn: Carole M Pesner
TEL (212) 307-5730

George Krevsky Fine Art
77 Geary Street
San Francisco, CA 94108
TEL (415) 397-9740
FAX (415) 398-7680

Jan Krugier Gallery/Graphics
41 East 57th Street, 6th Floor
New York, NY 10022
Attn: Emmanuel Benador
Director of Graphics
TEL (212) 755-7288
FAX (212) 980-6079
Original Graphics by Picasso from
Marina Picasso Collection

Greg Kucera Gallery
626 Second Avenue
Seattle, WA 98104
TEL (206) 624-0770
FAX (206) 624-4031

Richard Kuhlenschmidt Gallery
1630 17th Street
Santa Monica, CA 90404
Attn: Barbara Steffen
TEL (310) 450-2010
FAX (310) 450-0872

Kurland/Summers Gallery
8742-A Melrose Avenue
Los Angeles, CA 90069
Attn: Ruth T Summers
TEL (213) 659-7098

L'Ibis Gallery, Ltd
20 East 67th Street
New York, NY 10021
Attn: Lucien Viola
TEL (212) 734-9229
FAX (212) 734-9230

L A Artcore Center
652 Mateo Street
Los Angeles, CA 90021
Attn: Lydia Takeshita
TEL (213) 617-3274

LACE
1804 Industrial Street
Los Angeles, CA 90021
Attn: Gwen Darien
TEL (213) 624-5650

Lafayette Parke Gallery
58 East 79th Street
New York, NY 10021
Attn: Susan Peers
TEL (212) 517-5550
FAX (212) 734-2791

Lafayette Parke Gallery
250 Sutter Street
San Francisco, CA 94108
Attn: Roy Karlen
TEL (415) 788-5050
FAX (415) 788-5052

Lagerquist Gallery
3235 Paces Ferry Place, NW
Atlanta, GA 30305
Attn: Evelyn J Lagerquist
TEL (404) 261-8273

Lahaina Gallery
181-C Lahainaluna Road
Lahaina, HI 96761
Attn: Jim Killett
TEL (808) 661-0839

Lahaina Gallery
728 Front Street
Lahaina, HI 96761
Attn: Jim Killett
TEL (808) 667-2152
TEL (800) 445-7026

Edith Lambert Gallery
707 Canyon Road
Sante Fe, NM 87501
TEL (505) 984-2783
TEL (800) 594-9667
FAX (505) 988-4494

Landfall Press, Inc
329 West 18th Street, #601
Chicago, IL 60616
Attn: Jack Lemon
TEL (312) 666-6709

GALLERY INDEX CONTINUED

Martin Lawrence Galleries
Mission Valley Center
1640 Camino Del Rio, North
San Diego, CA 91208
Attn: Jack Bosman
TEL (619) 295-4646

Martin Lawrence Galleries
Main Place
2800 North Main Street
Santa Ana, CA 92701
Attn: Kelly Poisson
TEL (714) 834-0414

Martin Lawrence Galleries
The Gallery at Harborplace
200 East Pratt Street
Baltimore, MD 21202
Attn: Brian Silver
TEL (301) 332-1003

Martin Lawrence Galleries
Palm Desert Town Center
72-840 Highway 111
Palm Desert, CA 92260
Attn: Bunnie Gerstel
TEL (619) 341-3778

Martin Lawrence Galleries
Georgetown Park
3222 M Street, NW
Washington, DC 20007
Attn: Shirley Goldberg
TEL (202) 965-4811

Martin Lawrence Galleries
Soho-457 West Broadway
New York, NY 10012
TEL (212) 995-8865
FAX (212) 353-3650

Martin Lawrence Modern
426-428 West Broadway
New York, NY 10012
Attn: Thomas O'Brien
TEL (212) 941-5665
FAX (212) 353-3650

Martin Lawrence Galleries
865 Market Street
San Francisco, CA 94103
Attn: Karen Berkovitz
TEL (415) 512-8480
FAX (415) 512-8482

Martin Lawrence Galleries
North County Fair Mall
200 East Via Rando Parkway
Escondido, CA 92025
Attn: Jack Bosma
TEL (619) 489-7011

Martin Lawrence Galleries
Lido Marina Village
3439 Via Oporto
Newport Beach, CA 92663
Attn; Diana Fisher
TEL (714) 673-0171

Martin Lawrence Galleries
Desert Fashion Plaza
123 North Palm Canyon Drive
Palm Springs, CA 92262
Attn: Bonnie Gerstel
TEL (619) 320-2728

Martin Lawrence Galleries
The Galleria at South Bay
1815 Hawthorne Blvd
Redondo Beach, CA 90278
Attn: Carol Carp
TEL (213) 375-3788

Martin Lawrence Galleries
Valley Fair
2855 Stevens Creek Blvd
Santa Clara, CA 95050
Attn: Kay Zwickert
TEL (408) 985-8885

Martin Lawrence Galleries
Sherman Oaks Galleria
15301 Ventura Blvd
Sherman Oaks, CA 91403
Attn: Alan Fleishman
TEL (818) 783-2410

Martin Lawrence Galleries
Westside Pavilion
10800 West Pico Blvd
West Los Angeles, CA 90064
Attn: Stuart Thompson
TEL (213) 475-3497

Martin Lawrence Galleries
The Mall at Short Hills
Route 24, JFK Parkway
Short Hills, NJ 07078
Attn: Daniel Crosby
TEL (201) 467-5535

Martin Lawrence Galleries
The Bourse
21 South 5th Street
Philadelphia, PA 19106
Attn: Rick Rounick
TEL (215) 627-0794

Martin Lawrence Galleries
Chicago Place
700 North Michigan Avenue
Chicago, IL 60611
TEL (312) 335-0053
FAX (312) 335-0055

Langman Gallery
Willow Grove Park
Willow Grove, PA 19090
Attn: Richard Langman
TEL (610) 657-8333

Lanning Gallery
Hozho Center
413 Highway 179
Sedona, AZ 86336
Attn: Peggy Lanning
       Airen Sapp
TEL (602) 282-6865

Allene LaPides Gallery
217 Johnson Street
Santa Fe, NM 87501
Attn: Mary Pat Butler
TEL (505) 984-0191
FAX (505) 982-5351

K C Larson Galleries
500 North Wells Street
Chicago, IL 60610
TEL (312) 645-0900
FAX (312) 645-1234

Larson Art Gallery
790 North Jackson Street
Milwaukee, WI 53202
Attn: Scott F Larson
TEL (414) 277-9797
FAX (414) 277-0909

Le Cappellaine Gallery
252 Lafayette Street
New York, NY 10012
Attn: Dooley Le Cappellaine
TEL (212) 274-9383

Elizabeth Leach Gallery
207 SW Pine Street
Portland, OR 97204
TEL (503) 224-0521
FAX (503) 224-0844

Leaping Lizard Gallery
708 Canyon Road, #1
Santa Fe, NM 87501
Attn: Tom Ross
      Lily Waters
TEL (505) 984-8434

Margo Leavin Gallery
812 North Roberston Blvd
Los Angeles, Ca 90069
Attn: Wendy Brandow
TEL (310) 273-0603
FAX (310) 273-9131

LedisFlam
130 Prince Street, 3rd Floor
New York, NY 10012
Attn: Lori S Ledis
      Robert E Flam
TEL (212) 925-2806
FAX (212) 925-2971

Janie C Lee Gallery
1209 Berthea
Houston, TX 77006
TEL (713) 523-7306
FAX (713) 523-0462

John Post Lee Gallery
588 Broadway, 10th Floor
New York, NY 10012
TEL (212) 966-2676
FAX (212) 966-2585

Barbara Leibowits Graphics
80 Central Park West
New York, NY 10023
TEL (212) 769-0105
FAX (212) 769-0058

Leighton Gallery
Parker Point Road
Blue Hill, ME 04614
TEL (207) 374-5001

Lennon, Weinberg
580 Broadway, 2nd Floor
New York, NY 10012
Attn: Bernard Lennon
      Jill Weinberg Adams
TEL (212) 941-0012
FAX (212) 966-2585

Ella Lerner Gallery
17 Franklin Street
Lenox, MA 01240
TEL (413) 637-3315

Levinson Kane Gallery
14 Newbury Street
Boston, MA 02116
Attn: June Levinson
      Barbara Kane
      Rob Levinson
TEL (617) 247-0545
FAX (617) 247-3096

Janet Levitt Fine Arts
850 Powell Street, #901
San Francisco, CA 94108
TEL (415) 421-1407
FAX (415) 296-0493

Richard Levy Gallery
514 Central, SW
Albuquerque, NM 87102
TEL (505) 766-9888
FAX (505) 242-4279

Leslie Levy Gallery
7141 Main Street
Scottsdale, AZ 85251
TEL (602) 947-0937
TEL (800) 283-ARTS

Stuart Levy Gallery
588 Broadway
New York, NY 10012
TEL (212) 941-0009
FAX (212) 941-7987

LewAllen/Butler Fine Art
225 Galesto
Santa Fe, NM 87501
Attn: Arlene Lewallen
TEL (505) 988-5387

B Lewin Galleries
210 South Palm Canyon Drive
Palm Springs, CA 92262
Attn: Bernard Lewin
TEL (619) 325-7611
TEL (619) 322-2525

Daniel E Lewitt Fine Art
16 East 79th Street
New York, NY 10021
TEL (212) 628-0918

Light Gallery
135 East 74th Street, #10-B
New York, NY 10021
Attn: Fern Schad
TEL (212) 249-5653
FAX (212) 447-5006

Lightside Gallery
225 Canyon Road
Santa Fe, NM 87501
Attn: Patricia Smith
TEL (505) 982-5501

Tomoko Liguori Gallery
93 Grand Street
New York, NY 10013
TEL (212) 334-0190
FAX (212) 431-6693

Limner Gallery
598 Broadway
New York, NY 10012
Attn: Tim Slowinski
TEL (212) 431-1190
FAX (212) 431-1190

Lite Rail Gallery
912 12th Street
Sacramento, CA 95814
Attn: Mike Xepoleas
TEL (916) 441-1013

Littlejohn-Smith Fine Art
245 East 72nd Street
New York, NY 10021
Attn: Jacquie Littlejohn-Smith
TEL (212) 744-4360

GALLERY INDEX CONTINUED

Littlejohn/Sternau Gallery
41 East 57th Street
New York, NY 10022
Attn: Jacquie Littlejohn
TEL (212) 980-2323

Liros Gallery
Main Street
Blue Hill, ME 04614
Attn: Serge Liros
TEL (207) 374-5370

Marian Locks Gallery
600 Washington Square, South
Philadelphia, PA 19106
Attn: Sueyun Locks
 Marian Locks
TEL (215) 629-1000
FAX (215) 629-3868

Lococo-Mulder
106 Central Park South, #24-F
New York, NY 10019
TEL (212) 246-6040
FAX (212) 246-6040

Locus Gallery
710 North Tucker, #315
St. Louis, MO 63101
Attn: Kate Anderson
TEL (314) 231-2515

London Arts, Inc
321 Fisher Building
Detroit, MI 48202
Attn: David Zelmon
TEL (313) 871-2411
FAX (313) 873-4935

Long Point Gallery, Inc
492 Commercial Street
Provincetown, MA 02657
Attn: Mary Abell
TEL (508) 487-1795

Lopoukhine Gallery
198 Marlborough Street
Boston, MA 02116
Attn: Andre Lopoukhine
TEL (617) 262-4211

Michael H Lord Gallery
420 East Wisconsin Avenue
Milwaukee, WI 53202
TEL (414) 272-1007
FAX (414) 272-1450

Loring Art Gallery
661 Central Avenue
Cedarhurst, NY 11516
Attn: Rosemary Uffner
TEL (516) 295-1919

L A Louver Gallery
55 North Venice Blvd
Venica, CA 90291
Attn: P Goulds
 Kimberly Davis
TEL (310) 822-4955
FAX (310) 821-7529

R H Love Galleries
100 East Ohio Street
Chicago, IL 60611
Attn: Richard H Love
TEL (312) 664-9620

Michael Lowe Gallery
338 West 4th Street
Cincinnati, OH 45202
TEL (513) 651-4445

Lucia Gallery
150 Spring Street
New York, NY 10012
Attn: Lucia Chen
TEL (212) 473-6393

Luhring Augustine Gallery
130 Prince Street
New York, NY 10012
Attn: Claudia Carson
TEL (212) 219-9600
FAX (212) 966-1891

Gloria Luria Gallery
1033 Kane Concourse
Bay Harbor Islands
Miami, FL 33154
TEL (305) 865-3060

Nancy Lurie Gallery
1632 North La Salle Street
Chicago, IL 60614
TEL (312) 337-2883

Virginia Lust Gallery
61 Sullivan Street
New York, NY 10012
TEL (212) 941-9220

Lydon Fine Art, Inc
203, West Superior Street
Chicago, IL 60610
TEL (312) 943-1143
FAX (312) 943-8090

Virginia Lynch Gallery
3883 Main Road
Tiverton, RI 02878
TEL (401) 624-3392
TEL (401) 635-4456

M-13 Gallery
72 Greene Street, 2nd Floor
New York, NY 10012
Attn: Howard Scott
TEL (212) 925-3007

M C Gallery
400 First Avenue, North, #336
Minneapolis, MN 55401
Attn: M C Anderson
TEL (612) 339-1480
FAX (612) 339-1480

The Magenta Gallery
131 Washington Street
PO Box 55
Rocky Hill, NJ 08553
Attn: Alicia Nieves
TEL (609) 924-3513

Magic Mountain Gallery
107-A North Plaza
Taos, NM 87571
Attn: Kay Decker
TEL (505) 758-9604

Magidson Fine Art
1070 Madison Avenue
New York, NY 10028
Attn: Melton Magidson
 Carol Caldwell
TEL (212) 288-0666
FAX (212) 288-6050

Magnuson Gallery
286 Commonwealth Avenue
Boston, MA 02115
Attn: Betsy Magnuson
TFI (617) 262-5252

Mallet Fine Art
141 Prince Street
New York, NY 10012
Attn: Jacques Mallet
TEL (212) 477-8291
FAX (212) 673-1051

Malton Gallery
2709 Observatory Avenue
Cincinnati, OH 45208
Attn: Donald F Malton
TEL (513) 321-8614

Mangel Gallery
1714 Rittenhouse Square
Philadelphia, PA 19103
Attn: Benjamin Mangel
 Deborah Mangel
TEL (215) 545-9343

Manley-Riback, Inc
201 East 79th Street, #19-D
New York, NY 10021
Attn: Marianne Manley
 Estelle Riback
TEL (212) 861-0001

Eve Mannes Gallery
116 Bennett Street
Atlanta, GA 30309
Attn: Kathleen Cody Guy
TEL (404) 351-6651

Gracie Mansion Fine Art
54 St Marks Place
New York, NY 10009
TEL (212) 505-7055

Marbella Gallery
28 East 72nd Street
New York, NY 10021
Attn: Mildred G Thaler
TEL (212) 288-7809

Curt Marcus Gallery
578 Broadway, 10th Floor
New York, NY 10012
TEL (212) 226-3200

Adair Margo Gallery
415 East Yandell, #10-B
El Paso, TX 79902
TEL (915) 533-0048
FAX (915) 532-9182

Margulies Taplin Gallery
1401 Brickell Avenue
Miami, FL 33131
Attn: Dwight Santiago
TEL (305) 372-1031
FAX (407) 997-9703

Mariposa Gallery
113 Romero Street, NW
Old Town
Albuquerque, NM 87104
Attn: Fay Abrams
 Peg Cronin
TEL (505) 842-9097

Markel/Sears Fine Arts, Inc
560 Broadway
New York, NY 10012
Attn: Kathryn Markel
 Marcie Sears
TEL (212) 966-7469

Matthew Marks Gallery
1018 Madison Avenue
New York, NY 10021
TEL (212) 861-9455
FAX (212) 861-9382

Marlborough Gallery
40 West 57th Street
New York, NY 10019
Attn: Pierre Levai
TEL (212) 541-4900
FAX (212) 861-9382

Mars Gallery
1139 West Fulton Market
Chicago, IL 60607
Attn: Barbara Bancroft
TEL (312) 226-7808

Mary-Anne Martin Fine Art
23 East 73rd Street
New York, NY 10021
TEL (212) 288-2213
FAX (212) 861-7656

Andrea Marquit Fine Arts
207 Newbury Street
Boston, MA 02116
Attn: Andrea Marquit Clagett
TEL (617) 859-0190

Marx Gallery
230 West Superior Street
Chicago, IL 60610
TEL (312) 573-1400

Marsha Mateyka Gallery
2012 R Street, NW
Washington, DC 20009
TEL (202) 328-0088
FAX (202) 328-0088

Barbara Mathes Gallery
41 East 57th Street
New York, NY 10022
Attn: Laurence Shopmaker
TEL (212) 752-5135
FAX (212) 752-5145

Paula Matisse Fine Arts
1618 South Sherbourne Drive
Los Angeles, CA 90035
TEL (310) 273-3317
FAX (310) 273-8735

Matrix Gallery, Ltd
1255 South Wabash, 4th Floor, North
Chicago, IL 60605
Attn: Althea Stevens
TEL (312) 554-8868

GALLERY INDEX CONTINUED

Nedra Matteucci Fine Art
555 Canyon Road
Santa Fe, NM 87501
Attn: Roberta Brashears
TEL (505) 983-2731
FAX (505) 983-3170

Maveety Gallery
Portland Annex
1314 NW Irving, #508
Portland, OR 97209
Attn: Billye Turner
TEL (503) 224-9442

Maxwell Galleries, Ltd
551 Sutter Street
San Francisco, CA 94102
Attn: Mark Hoffman
TEL (415) 421-5193

Ernesto Mayans Gallery
601 Canyon Road
Santa Fe, NM 87501
Attn: Leonor Mayans
TEL (505) 983-8008
FAX (505) 982-1999

Linda McAdoo Galleries
503 Canyon Road
Sante Fe, NM 87501
TEL (505) 983-7182

Lynn McAllister Gallery
416 University
Seattle, WA 89104
TEL (206) 624-6864

Jason McCoy Gallery
41 East 57th Street
New York, NY 10022
TEL (212) 379-1996
FAX (212) 319-4799

Earl McGrath Gallery
454 North Robertson Blvd
Los Angeles, CA 90048
TEL (310) 652-9850
FAX (310) 652-0140

McIntosh Gallery
One Virginia Hill
587 Virginia Avenue
Atlanta, GA 30306
Attn: Louisa McIntosh
TEL (404) 892-4023

David McKee Gallery
745 Fifth Avenue
New York, NY 10151
TEL (212) 688-5951
FAX (212) 752-5638

McMann Fine Arts
364 Walnut Avenue, SW
Roanoke, VA 24016
Attn: W D McMann
TEL (703) 345-5123

McMurtrey Gallery
3508 Lake Street
Houston, TX 77098
Attn: Eleanor McMurtrey
TEL (713) 523-8238

Anthony Meier Fine Arts
726 El Camino del Mar
San Francisco, CA 94121
TEL (415) 751-7080
FAX (415) 751-7083

Galerie Anton Meier
8, rue St Leger
CH-1205 Geneva
Switzerland
TEL 022.29.14.50

Jack Meier Gallery
2310 Bissonnet
Houston, TX 77005
Attn: Martha Meier
TEL (713) 526-2983

Louis K Meisel Gallery
141 Prince Street
New York, NY 10012
Attn: Aaron Miller
Diane Sena
TEL (212) 677-1340
FAX (212) 533-7340

Jerald Melberg Gallery, Inc
119 East 7th Street
Charlotte, NC 28202
Attn: Jerald Melberg
TEL (704) 333-8601
FAX (704) 333-8607

Mendelson Gallery
Titus Square
Washington Depot, CT 06794
Attn: Carol Mendelson
TEL (203) 868-0307

Meredith Gallery
805 North Charles Street
Baltimore, MD 21201
Attn: Judith Lippman
TEL (301) 837-3575

Merging One Gallery
1547 6th Street
Santa Monica, CA 90401
Attn: Diana Wong
Cecilia Davidson
TEL (310) 395-0033

Merida Rapp Graphics
Artspace
2007 Frankfort Avenue
Louisville, KY 40206
Attn: Yvonne Rapp
TEL (502) 896-2331

Merrill Chase Galleries
Water Tower Place
835 North Michigan Avenue
Chicago, IL 60611
Attn: Albert Sanford
TEL (312) 337-6600

Merrin Gallery
724 Fifth Avenue
New York, NY 10019
Attn: Edward H Merrin
TEL (212) 757-2884

Metro Pictures
150 Greene Street
New York, NY 10012
Attn: Janelle Reiring
Helen Winer
TEL (212) 925-8335

Thomas V Meyer Fine Art
169 25th Avenue
San Francisco, CA 94121
TEL (215) 386-1225
FAX (215) 386-1634

Erika Meyerovich Gallery
231 Grant Avenue
San Francisco, CA 94108
Attn: Alex Meyerovich
TEL (415) 421-9997
FAX (415) 421-2775
Specializing in 20th Century Masters

Meyers/Bloom Gallery
2112 Broadway
Santa Monica, CA 90404
Attn: Mary Artino
TEL (310) 829-0062
FAX (213) 828-2624

Cliff Michel Gallery
520 Second Avenue
Seattle, WA 98104
TEL (206) 623-4484

Middendorf Gallery
20009 Columbia Road, NW
Washington, DC 20009
Attn: Christopher S Middendorf
TEL (202) 462-2009
FAX (202) 462-9059

Midtown-Payson Galleries
745 Fifth Avenue
New York, NY 10151
Attn: Bridget Moore
TEL (212) 758-1900
FAX (212) 832-2226

Mill Street Gallery, Inc
112 South Mill
Aspen, CO 81611
Attn: Barbara Bussell
TEL (303) 925-4988

Miller Gallery
2715 Erie Avenue
Cincinnati, OH 45208
Attn: Barbara Miller
Norman Miller
TEL (513) 871-4420
FAX (513) 871-4429

Burnett Miller Gallery
964 North La Brea Avenue
Los Angeles, CA 90038
Attn: Burnett Miller
TEL (213) 874-4757
FAX (213) 874-7478

Laurence Miller Gallery
138 Spring Street
New York, NY 10012
TEL (212) 226-1220

Nan Miller Gallery
3450 Winton Place
Rochester, NY 14623
TEL (716) 292-1430
FAX (716) 292-1253

Peter Miller Gallery
401 West Superior Street
Chicago, IL 60610
Attn: Natalie R Domchencko
TEL (312) 951-0252

Robert Miller Gallery
41 East 57th Street
New York, NY 10022
Attn: John Cheim
TEL (212) 980-5454
FAX (212) 935-3350

Miller & Main Street Galleries
500 South Main Street
Blacksburg, VA 24060
Attn: Robert A Miller
TEL (703) 552-6969

Mincher/Wilcox Gallery
228 Grant Avenue, 6th Floor
San Francisco, CA 94108
Attn: Michele Mincher
Tessa Wilcox
TEL (415) 433-4660
FAX (415) 433-6818

Mindscape Gallery
1506 Sherman Avenue
Evanston, IL 60201
Attn: Ronald G Isaacson
Deborah Farber
TEL (708) 864-2660

Mineta Move
43 Rue Ernest Allard
1000 Brussels, Belgium
TEL (02) 513-0360

Minot Art Gallery
PO Box 325
Minot, ND 58702
Attn: Judith Allen
TEL (701) 838-4445

Mission Gallery
138 East Kit Carson Road
Taos, NM 87571
Attn: Rena Rosequist
TEL (505) 758-2861
FAX (505) 758-2861

Mitchell, Brown, Duncan Gallery
301 Garcia at Kenyon Road
Santa Fe, NM 87501
Attn: Jeffrey Mitchell
TEL (505) 988-4708

Mobilia Gallery
348 Huron Avenue
Cambridge, MA 02138
Attn: Libby Cooper
TEL (617) 876-2109

Mock Studios
112 Sackett Street
Brooklyn, NY 11231
Attn: Richard Mock
TEL (718) 643-1309

Modern Realism
1903 MacMillan Avenue, Room #1
Dallas, TX 75206
Attn: Jonathan Held, Jr
TEL (214) 553-1116

Modernism
685 Market, #290
San Francisco, CA 94105
Attn: Martin Muller
TEL (415) 541-0461
FAX (415) 541-0425

GALLERY INDEX CONTINUED

Achim Moeller Fine Fine Art
52 East 76th Street
New York, NY 10021
TEL (212) 988-8483
FAX (212) 439-6663

Mongerson-Wunderlich
704 North Wells Street
Chicago, IL 60610
Attn: Rudy Wunderlich
TEL (312) 943-2354

Montgomery Gallery
250 Sutter Street
San Francisco, CA 94108
Attn: Peter Fairbanks
TEL (415) 788-8300

Montgomery-Taylor
7100 Main Street
Scottsdale, AZ 85251
Attn: Randy Venable
TEL (602) 945-0111

Montserrat Gallery
584 Broadway
New York, NY 10012
Attn: Marie Montserrat
TEL (212) 941-8899

Moody Gallery
2815 Colquitt
Houston, TX 77098
Attn: Betty Moody
TEL (713) 526-9911

Joy Moos Gallery
355 NE 59th Terrace
Miami, FL 33137
TEL (305) 754-9373
FAX (305) 757-2124

Morning Star Gallery
513 Canyon Road
Santa Fe, NM 87501
Attn: Joe Rivera
TEL (505) 982-8187
FAX (505) 984-2368

Morningstar Gallery
164 Mercer Street
New York, NY 10012
Attn: Jack Krumholz
TFL (212) 334-9330

Morphos Gallery
544 Hayes Street
San Francisco, CA 94102
Attn: Catherine Clark
TEL (415) 626-1936
FAX (415) 626-0368

Donald Morris Gallery
105 Townsend Street
Birmingham, MI 48011
TEL (313) 642-8812

Robert Morrison Gallery
59 Thompson Street
New York, NY 10012
TEL (212) 274-9059
FAX (212) 986-9373

Moss Gallery
214 Grant Avenue, #325
San Francisco, CA 94108
Attn: Marvin Moss
TEL (415) 433-7224

Tobey C Moss Gallery
7321 Beverly Boulevard
Los Angeles, CA 90036
TEL (213) 933-5523
FAX (213) 933-7618

P Buckley Moss Gallery
190 Fourth Avenue, NE
St Petersburg, FL 33701
TEL (813) 894-2899

Multiples Impressions
128 Spring Street
New York, NY 10012
Attn: Stephen Feinman
TEL (212) 925-1313

Multiples, Inc
24 West 57th Street
New York, NY 10019
Attn: Jill Sussman
TEL (212) 977-7160
FAX (212) 581-5187

Victoria Munroe Fine Art
9 East 84th Street, #1-D
New York, NY 10028
TEL (212) 249-5480
FAX (212) 249-5883

Munson Gallery
33 Whitney Avenue
New Haven, CT 06511
Attn: Jennifer Dennison
TEL (203) 865-2121

Munson Gallery
225 Canyon Road
Santa Fe, NM 87501
Attn: Jo Chapman
TEL (505) 983-1657
FAX (505) 988-9867

Munson Gallery
800 Main Street
Chatham, MA 02633
Attn: Sally Munson
TEL (508) 945-2888

Michael Murphy Gallery
3011 Aquila Street
Tampa, FL 33629
TEL (813) 254-1414

NAB Gallery
1117 West Lake Drive
Chicago, IL 60607
Attn: Bob Horn
    Craig Anderson
TEL (312) 525-5418
FAX (312) 226-3887

Nahan Galleries
381 West Broadway
New York, NY 10012
Attn: Kenneth Nahan
TEL (212) 966-9313
FAX (212) 966-9316

Nahan Galleries
450 Royal Street
New Orleans, LA 70130
Attn: Kenneth Nahan
TEL (504) 524-8696

Edward Tyler Nahem Fine Art
56 East 66th Street
New York, NY 10021
TEL (212) 571-2453
FAX (212) 861-3566

NAME
700 North Carpenter Street
Chicago, IL 60622
Attn: Irene Tsatsos
TEL (312) 226-0671

Nantenshi Gallery
3-6-5 Kyobashi
Cheo-Ku
Tokyo, Japan
TEL (03) 563-3511

Naples Art Gallery
275 Broad Avenue, South
Naples, FL 33940
Attn: Warren C Nelson
    William B Spink
    Ronald C Reblin
TEL (813) 262-4551

Naravisa Press
Route 2, Box 280
Santa Fe, NM 87505
Attn: Stephen Britko
    Geralyn Britko
TEL (505) 473-2684

Ann Nathan Gallery
210 West Superior Street
Chicago, IL 60610
TEL (312) 664-6622
FAX (312) 664-9392

Nathans Gallery
1205 McBride Avenue
West Patterson, NJ 07424
Attn: Rita Nathans
TEL (201) 785-9119

Native American Images
98 San Jacinto Blvd
P O Box 746
Austin, TX 78767
Attn: Gill Pearsall
TEL (512) 472-3049
TEL (800) 531-5008

John Natsoulas Gallery
140 F Street
Davis, CA 95616
TEL (916) 756-3938

Navajo Gallery
210 Ledoux Street
P O Box 1756
Taos, NM 87571
Attn: Virginia Dooley
TEL (505) 758-3250

Enrico Navarra Gallery
41 East 57th Street, #1301
New York, NY 10022
Attn: John Cavaliero
TEL (212) 223-2828
FAX (212) 223-7111

Isobel Neal Gallery, Ltd
200 West Superior Street
Chicago, IL 60610
TEL (312) 944-1570

Phyllis Needlman Gallery
1515 North Astor Street
Chicago, IL 60610
TEL (312) 642-7929

Diane Nelson Fine Art
P O Box 216
Laguna Beach, CA 92652
Attn: Stephen Gillette
TEL (714) 494-2440

Neo Persona Gallery
178 Duane Street
New York, NY 10013
Attn: Helen Strau
TEL (212) 966-5101
FAX (212) 732-1467

Heidi Neuhoff Gallery
999 Madison Avenue
New York, NY 10021
TEL (212) 879-8890
FAX (212) 861-4921

Neville-Sargent Gallery
215 West Huron Street
Chicago, IL 60610
Attn: Jane Neville
TEL (312) 664-2787
FAX (312) 664-5989

New Acquisitions Gallery
120 East Washington Avenue, #1004
Syracuse, NY 13202
Attn: Celia Skoler
TEL (315) 422-2320

New Directions Gallery
107-B North Plaza
Taos, NM 87571
Attn: Cecilia Torres
TEL (505) 758-2771
TEL (800) 658-6903

New Gallery
2639 Colquitt
Houston, TX 77098
Attn: T Andriola
    A Andriola
TEL (713) 520-7053

New Langton Arts
1246 Folsom Street
San Francisco, CA 94103
Attn: Nancy Gonchar
TEL (415) 626-5416
FAX (415) 255-1453

New Renaissance
1205 Prospect D
La Jolla, CA 92037
Attn: Stefan Radovich
TEL (619) 456-4076

GALLERY INDEX CONTINUED

New Visions Gallery
1000 North Oak Avenue
Marshfield Clinic
Marshfield, WI 54449
Attn: Ann Waisbrot
TEL (715) 387-3046

New Zone Gallery
411 High Street
Eugene, OR 97401
Attn: Mike E Walsh
TEL (503) 485-2278

Newbury Fine Arts
29 Newbury Street
Boston, MA 02116
Attn: Elizabeth Alch
TEL (617) 536-0210
FAX (617) 536-0517

Newhouse Galleries, Inc
19 East 66th Street
New York, NY 10021
Attn: Meg Newhouse
      Adam Williams
TEL (212) 879-2700

Newman Galleries
850 West Lancaster Avenue
Bryn Mawr, PA 19010
Attn: India Dello-Strologo
TEL (215) 525-0625

Newman Galleries
1625 Walnut Street
Philadelphia, PA 19103
Attn: Walter Newman
      Andrew Newman
      Terrence Newman
TEL (215) 563-1779

Newmark Gallery
1194 Third Avenue
New York, NY 10021
Attn: Alfred Gonzalez
TEL (212) 744-7779

Newspace
5241 Melrose Avenue
Los Angeles, CA 90038
Attn: Joni Gordon
TEL (213) 469-9353
FAX (213) 469-1120

Nicolae Galerie
641 High Street
Columbus, OH 43215
Attn: Nicolae Halmaghi
TEL (614) 461-9111
FAX (614) 461-9112

Nicole Gallery
734 North Wells Street
Chicago, IL 60610
TEL (312) 787-7716

Nielsen Gallery
179 Newbury Street
Boston, MA 02116
Attn: Nina Nielsen
TEL (617) 266-4835
FAX (617) 266-0480

J Noblett Gallery
22 Boyes Blvd
P O Box 1777
Boyes Hot Springs, CA 95416
Attn: R Schwartz
TEL (707) 996-2416

Noho Gallery
168 Mercer Street
New York, NY 10012
Attn: Stephanie Rauschenbusch
TEL (212) 219-2210

G R N'Namdi Gallery
161 Townsend
Birmingham, MI 48009
Attn: Martine Wiener
      George N'Nandi
TEL (313) 642-2700

David Nolan Gallery
560 Broadway, 6th FL
New York, NY 10012
Attn: David Nolan
      Carol Eckman
TEL (212) 925-6190

Northport Galleries, Inc
B J Spoke Gallery
299 Main Street
Huntington, NY 11743
Attn: Bernice Taplitz
TEL (516) 549-5106

Annina Nosei Gallery
100 Prince Street
New York, NY 10012
TEL (212) 431-9253

Jonathan Novak Contemporary Art
10350 Wilshire Blvd, #1802
Los Angeles, CA 90024
TEL (310) 858-2918

Now & Then Gallery
797 Merrick Avenue
East Meadow, NY 11554
Attn: Aphrodite Zules
TEL (516) 481-1447

Nuance Galleries
720 South Dale Mabry
Tampa, FL 33609
Attn: Robert A Rowen
TEL (813) 875-7885

O'Farrell Gallery
46 Maine Street
Brunswick, ME 04011
Attn: Ray Farrell
TEL (207) 729-8228

O'Hara Gallery
41 East 57th Street, #1302
New York, NY 10022
Attn: Steven O'Hara
      Ruth O'Hara
TEL (212) 355-3330
FAX (212) 355-3361

Oates Gallery
2775 Lombardy
Memphis, TN 38111
Attn: Rena Dewey
TEL (901) 452-9986

Objects Gallery
230 West Huron Street
Chicago, IL 60610
Attn: Ann Nathan
      Mary Donaldson
TEL (312) 664-6622
FAX (312) 664-9392

October Art
120 Park Avenue
Philip Morris Bldg
New York, NY 10017
Attn: Delores Brown Abelson
TEL (212) 986-3680

Oehischlaeger Gallery
28 Boulevard of the Presidents
St Armands Key
Sarasota, FL 34236
Attn: Frank J Oehischlaeger
TEL (813) 388-3312

Okun Gallery
301 North Guadalupe
Santa Fe, NM 87501
Attn: Barbara Okun
      Ed Okun
TEL (505) 982-4531
FAX (505) 989-1646

Old State House
800 Main Street
Hartford, CT 06103
Attn: Wilson H Faude
TEL (203) 522-6766

Oneiros Gallery
711 Eighth Avenue, Studio A
San Diego, CA 92101
Attn: Bill Beck
      Kathleen Benton
TEL (619) 696-0882
FAX (619) 696-0833

Opus Art Studios
1810 Ponce de Leon
Miami, FL 33134
Attn: Fredric B Snitzer
TEL (305) 448-8976
FAX (305) 448-0711

Orca Aart Gallery
300 West Grand Street
Chicago, IL 60610
TEL (312) 245-5245
FAX (312) 245-5245

Orion Editions
270 Lafayette Street
New York, NY 10012
Attn: Robert Kimbril
TEL (212) 226-2766

Orlando Gallery
14553 Ventura Blvd
Sherman Oaks, CA 91403
Attn: Philip Orlando
      Robert Gino R
TEL (818) 789-6012

Osuna Gallery
1919 Q Street, NW
Washington, DC 20009
Attn: Ramon Osuna
      Andrew Cullinan
TEL (202) 296-1963
FAX (202) 296-1965

Jon Oulman Gallery
400 First Avenue, North, #706
Minneapolis, MN 55401
TEL (612) 333-2386

Outside-In
6909 Melrose Avenue
Los Angeles, CA 90038
Attn: Liz Blackman
TEL (213) 933-4096

Ovsey Gallery
170 South La Brea Avenue
Los Angeles, CA 90036
Attn: Neil G Ovsey
TEL (213) 935-1883
FAX (213) 935-9589

Owl Gallery
465 Powell Street
San Francisco, CA 94102
Attn: Keith Yoder
      Barbara Nadolna
TEL (415) 781-5464

Owl 57 Galleries
1074 Broadway
Woodmere, NY 11598
TEL (516) 374-5707
FAX (516) 374-5757

Owings-Dewey Fine Art
74 East San Francisco
Santa Fe, NM 87501
Attn: Nathaniel O Owings
      Mary Pat Day
TEL (505) 982-6244
FAX (505) 982-4803

Oxford Gallery
267 Oxford Street
Rochester, NY 14607
Attn: Nancy Buckett
TEL (716) 271-5885

P P O W
532 Broadway, 3rd Floor
New York, NY 10012
Attn: Penny Pilkington
      Wendy Olsoff
      Scott Catto
TEL (212) 941-8642
FAX (212) 274-8339

Pace Prints
32 East 57th Street, 3rd Floor
New York, NY 10022
Attn: Kristin Heming
TEL (212) 421-3237
FAX (212) 751-7280

Pace/MacGill Gallery
32 East 57th Street, 9th Floor
New York, NY 10022
Attn: Peter MacGill
TEL (212) 759-7999

Paideia Gallery
765 North La Cienega Blvd
Los Angeles, CA 90069
Attn: Stevan Kissel
TEL (310) 652-8224

Palladio Gallery
Wilshire Courtyard
5750 Wilshire Blvd, #180
Los Angeles, CA 90036
Attn: Sofia Gonzolez Perez
TEL (213) 933-4025
FAX (213) 933-8670

Herbert Palmer Gallery
802 North La Cienega Blvd
Los Angeles, CA 90069
TEL (310) 854-0096
FAX (310) 659-8545

GALLERY INDEX CONTINUED

Paper Press Gallery
1017 West Jackson Street
Chicago, IL 60607
Attn: Linda Sorkin-Eisenberg
  Marilyn Sward
TEL (312) 226-6300

Park Gallery
174 North Hurstborne
Louisville, KY 40207
Attn: Ellen Guthrie
  Martha Juckett
TEL (502) 425-4029

Park Shore Gallery II
3333 Tamiami Trail, North
Naples, FL 33940
Attn: Evan J Obrentz
TEL (813) 434-0833
FAX (813) 434-8471

Park West Gallery
29469 Northwestern
Southfield, MI 48034
Attn: Nancy Neubauer
TEL (313) 354-2343
FAX (313) 354-0387
TEL (800) 521-9654
Specializing in Old Masters,
Modern Masters & Contemporary
Paintings, Drawings & Prints

Parkerson Gallery
3510 Lake Street
Houston, TX 77098
Attn: John E Parkerson (Sandy)
TEL (713) 524-4945

Franklin Parrasch Gallery
588 Broadway
New York, NY 10012
Attn: James Leventhal
TEL (212) 925-7090

Patricia Judith Art Gallery
720 East Palmetto Park Road
Boca Raton, FL 33432
Attn: Patricia Cohn
TEL (407) 368-3316
FAX (407) 393-7006

Elizabeth Paul Gallery
1854 Keys Crescent
Cincinnati, OH 45206
Attn: Paul G Sittenfeld
TEL (513) 751-4944
TEL (800) 869-5666

Laura Paul Gallery
49 East 4th Street, #109
Cincinnati, OH 45202
TEL (513) 651-5885

Laura Paul Gallery
600 South Lazelle Street
Columbus, OH 43206
Attn: Cynthia Paine
TEL (614) 224-8808

Jennifer Pauls Gallery
1825 Q Street
Sacramento, CA 95814
Attn: Dean Moniz
TEL (916) 448-4039

Payton Rule Gallery
1736 Wazee Street
Denver CO 80202
Attn: Cydney Payton
  Robin Rule
TEL (303) 293-9080

Mary Peachin's Art Company
3955 East Speedway, #109
Tucson, AZ 85712
Attn: Mary Peachin
TEL (602) 881-1311

Peachtree Gallery
2277 Peachtree Road, NE
Atlanta, GA 30309
TEL (404) 355-0511

Marilyn Pearl Gallery
420 Broadway
New York, NY 10012
Attn: Birgit Spears
TEL (212) 734-7421

Pelavin Editions
13 Jay Street
New York, NY 10013
Attn: Cheryl Pelavin
TEL (212) 925-9424

Pence Fine Art, Inc
8491 Sunset Blvd
Los Angeles, CA 90069
Attn: Putter Pence
TEL (310) 271-0367
FAX (310) 271-0258

John Pence Gallery
750 Post Street
San Francisco, CA 94109
TEL (415) 441-1138
FAX (415) 771-4069

Percival Galleries
6th and Walnut Streets
Des Moines, IA 50309
Attn: Bonnie Percival
TEL (515) 243-4893

Peregrine Gallery
PO Box 671046
Dallas, TX 75367-8046
Attn: Michael Hart
  Jo Ann Hart
TEL (214) 871-3770

Perimeter Gallery
750 North Orleans
Chicago, IL 60610
Attn: Frank Paluch
TEL (312) 266-9473

Katharina Rich Perlow Gallery
560 Broadway, 3rd Floor
New York, NY 10012
TEL (212) 941-1220

Gerald Peters Gallery
439 Camino del Monte Sol
Santa Fe, NM 87504-0908
TEL (505) 988-8961
FAX (505) 983-2481

Gerald Peters Gallery
2913 Fairmount
Dallas, TX 75201
Attn: Marguerite Steed
TEL (214) 969-9410
FAX (214) 969-9023

Petersburg Press
380 Lafayette Street, #6
New York, NY 10003
Attn: Tamie Swett
TEL (212) 420-0890
FAX (212) 420-1617

Greta Peterson Galerie
7696 Camargo Road, Madeira
Cincinnati, OH 45243
TEL (513) 561-6785

Phillips Gallery
444 East 200, South
Salt Lake City, UT 84111
Attn: Renee Fitzpatrick
TEL (801) 364-8284

Phoenix Gallery
568 Broadway, #607
New York, NY 10012
Attn: Linda Handler
TEL (212) 226-8711

Photography West Gallery
Dolores at Ocean Avenue
Carmel, CA 93921-4829
Attn: Carol Williams
TEL (408) 625-1587

Pierce Galleries, Inc
721 Main Street—Route 228
Hingham, MA 02043
Attn: Patricia J Pierce
TEL (617) 749-6023
FAX (617) 749-6685

Pierce Street Gallery
217 Pierce Street
Birmingham, MI 48009
Attn: N Carnick
  M Boxman
  E Yaker
TEL (313) 646-6950

I Pinckney Simons Gallery
926 Gervais Street
Columbia, SC 29201
Attn: Richard Simons, Jr
TEL (803) 771-8815

Pleiades Gallery
164 Mercer Street
New York, NY 10012
TEL (212) 274-8825

Anne Plumb Gallery, Inc
393 Greenwich Street
New York, NY 10013-2323
TEL (212) 219-2007

Maya Polsky Gallery
311 West Superior Street, 2nd Floor
Chicago, IL 60610
TEL (312) 440-0055
FAX (312) 440-0501

Portals, Ltd
230 West Huron
Chicago, IL 60610
Attn: William McIlvaine
  Nancy McIlvaine
TEL (312) 642-1066
FAX (312) 642-2991

Portfolio Gallery
2007 Devine Street
Columbia, SC 29205
Attn: Judith K Roberts
TEL (803) 256-2434

Posner Gallery
207 Milwaukee Street
Milwaukee, WI 53202
Attn: Judith L Posner
TEL (414) 273-3097
TEL (800) 227-3097
FAX (414) 273-1436

Post Road Gallery
2128 Boston Post Road
Larchmont, NY 10538
Attn: Robert Bahssin
TEL (914) 834-7568

Postmasters Gallery
80 Greene Street, 2nd Floor
New York, NY 10012
Attn: Magdalena Sawon
TEL (212) 941-5711
FAX (212) 431-4679

Joan Prats Gallery
568 Broadway, #501
New York, NY 10012
Attn: Juan de Muga
TEL (212) 219-0510
FAX (212) 219-0495

Mary Praytor Gallery
26 South Main Street
Greenville, SC 29601
TEL (803) 235-1800

Fran Preisman Fine Art
1626 Buckingham Drive
La Jolla, CA 92037
TEL (619) 459-2684
TEL (619) 456-3557
FAX (619) 459-0980

Premier Gallery
803 Caroline Street
Fredericksburg, VA 22401
Attn: Jack Garver
TEL (703) 899-3100

Previti Gallery
110 Riverside Drive, #12-B
New York, NY 10024
Attn: Marie Previti
TEL (212) 724-1826
FAX (212) 724-1826

Ellen Price Gallery
26 West 75th Street
New York, NY 10023
TEL (212) 580-9734

Prince Street Gallery
121 Wooster Street
New York, NY 10012
Attn: Iona Fromboluti
TEL (212) 226-9402

Print Gallery
29203 Northwestern Highway
Southfield, MI 48034
Attn: Diane Shipley
(TEL) 356-5454

Printworks Gallery
311 West Superior Street, #105
Chicago, IL 60610
Attn: Sidney Block
  Robert Hiebert
TEL (312) 664-9407
FAX (312) 664-8823

GALLERY INDEX CONTINUED

Pro-Art
1214 Washington Avenue
St Louis, MO 63103
Attn: H Shieber
TEL (314) 231-5848

Professional Fine Arts Services, Inc
386 West Broadway, 3rd Floor
New York, NY 10012-4302
Attn: Walter Edelman
TEL (212) 226-2247
FAX (212) 226-4422

Max Protetch Gallery
560 Broadway
New York, NY 10012
Attn: Jeffrey Hoffeld
TEL (212) 966-5454

Puchong Gallery
36-A Third Avenue
New York, NY 10003
Attn: Melvin Dennis
      David Schlessinger
      Tom Stetz
TEL (212) 982-1811

Pucker-Safrai Gallery
171 Newbury Street
Boston, MA 02116
Attn: Bernard H Pucker
TEL (617) 267-9473
FAX (617) 424-9759

Quartet Editions
568 Broadway, Room 104-A
New York, NY 10012
Attn: Riva Blumenfeld
TEL (212) 219-2819
FAX (212) 219-2875

Quartersaw Gallery
528 NW 12th
Portland, OR 97209
Attn: Victoria Frey
TEL (503) 223-2264

Queen Emma Gallery
1301 Punchbowl Street
Honolulu, HI 96813
Attn: Masa Taira
TEL (808) 547-4397

Quint Krichman Projects
7447 Girard Avenue
La Jolla, CA 92037
Attn: Mark Quint
      Michael Krichman
TEL (619) 454-3409

Raydon Gallery
1091 Madison Avenue
New York, NY 10028
Attn: Alexander R Raydon
TEL (212) 288-3555

Rabbet Gallery
120 Georges Road
New Brunswick, NJ 08901
Attn: Dot Paolo
TEL (908) 828-5150

Ramsay Chinatown Gallery
1128 Smith Street
Honolulu, HI 96817
TEL (808) 537-ARTS
TEL (808) 537-2787

Roger Ramsay Gallery
325 West Huron Street, #207
Chicago, IL 60610
TEL (312) 337-4678

Randolph Street Gallery
756 North Milwaukee Avenue
Chicago, IL 60622
Attn: Peter Taub
TEL (312) 666-7737

Red Piano Art Gallery
220 Cordillo Parkway
Hilton Head Island, SC 29928
Attn: Louanne C LaRoche
TEL (803) 785-2318

Reece Galleries
24 West 57th Street
New York, NY 10019
Attn: Shirley Reece
TEL (212) 333-5830
FAX (212) 333-7366

Stuart Regen Gallery
619 North Almont Drive
Los Angeles, CA 90069
Attn: Shaun Caley
TEL (310) 276-5424
FAX (310) 276-7430

Rehs Galleries, Inc
305 East 63rd Street
New York, NY 10021
Attn: Joseph Rehs
      Howard Rehs
TEL (212) 355-5710
FAX (212) 355-5742

C G Rein Galleries
1700 Bissonet Street
Houston, TX 77005
Attn: Gena Alderman
TEL (713) 526-4916
FAX (713) 526-4918

C G Rein Galleries
4235 North Marshall Way
Scottsdale, AZ 85251
Attn: Constance Calhoun
TEL (602) 941-0900
FAX (602) 941-0814

C G Rein Galleries
203 West Water Street
Santa Fe, NM 87501
Attn: Joseph Gierek
TEL (505) 982-6226
FAX (505) 982-8364

Reinhold-Brown Gallery
26 East 78th Street
New York, NY 10021
Attn: Susan Reinhold
      Robert K Brown
TEL (212) 734-7999

Reinike Gallery
2300 Peachtree Road, NW, #B-201
Atlanta, GA 30309
Attn: Edna Reinike
TEL (404) 352-5269

Reiss Gallery
429 Acoma Street
Denver, CO 80204
Attn: Rhoda Reiss
TEL (303) 778-6924

Renaissance Galleria
1500 Washington Road, #2801
Mount Lebanon, PA 15228
Attn: Ann Wallace
TEL (412) 341-3222

Renaissance Gallery
550 Wood Street
Pittsburgh, PA 15222
Attn: Ann Wallace
TEL (412) 391-3199

Ricky Renier Gallery
1550 North Milwaukee
Chicago, IL 60622
TEL (312) 227-3090

Shahin Requicha Gallery
3301 Crest Drive
Manhattan Beach, CA 90266
TEL (213) 545-8549

Rettig y Martinez Gallery
901 San Mateo
Santa Fe, NM 87501
Attn: David Rettig
      Sandra Martinez
TEL (505) 983-4640

Reynolds Gallery
1514 West Main Street
Richmond, VA 23220
Attn: Beverly W Reynolds
TEL (804) 355-6553

Robert Rice Gallery
2627 Kipling, #107
Houston, TX 77098
Attn: Barbara Menen
TEL (713) 528-0741

J Richards Gallery
64 East Palisade Avenue
Englewood, NJ 07631
Attn: Jeanne Richards
TEL (201) 871-1050

Riggs Galleries
7463 Girard
La Jolla, CA 92037
Attn: Mary Kathryn Riggs
TEL (619) 454-3070

River Gallery
20 Ridge Drive
Westport, CT 06880
Attn: Cecelia J Scher
TEL (203) 227-3583

River Gallery
49 Main Street
Irvington-On-Hudson, NY 10533
Attn: A G Matero
TEL (914) 591-6208

Ro Gallery Image Makers, Inc
300 East 74th Street, #15-C
New York, NY 10021
Attn: Robert Rogal
TEL (718) 937-0901
FAX (718) 937-1206

Bennett Roberts Fine Art
10711 Ashton Avenue
Los Angeles, CA 90024
TEL (310) 474-7184
FAX (310) 474-7184

Douglas Roberts Gallery
979½ Hancock Avenue
Los Angeles, CA 90069
TEL (310) 652-8270
TEL (310) 652-0357

Joan Robey Gallery
939 Broadway
Denver, CO 80203
TEL (303) 892-9600

Robinson Galleries
3514 Lake Street
Houston, TX 77098
Attn: Thomas V Robinson
TEL (713) 526-0761
FAX (713) 526-0763

Robischon Gallery
1740 Wazee
Denver, CO 80202
Attn: James Robischon
TEL (303) 298-7788

Robley Gallery
1356 Old Northern Blvd
Roslyn, NY 11576
Attn: Roberta Frank
      Shirley Janowitz
TEL (516) 484-5960

Rockefeller Town House Gallery
20 West 55th Street
New York, NY 10022
TEL (212) 265-8643

Lorenzo Rodriguez Gallery
1178 North Milwaukee Street
Chicago, IL 60622
TEL (312) 342-5156

Margaret Roeder Fine Art/Editions
545 Broadway
New York, NY 10012
TEL (212) 925-6098

Arthur Roger Gallery
432 Julia Street
New Orleans, LA 70130
TEL (504) 522-1999

Rogue Gallery
40 South Bartlett
Medford, OR 97501
Attn: D Elizabeth Withers
TEL (503) 772-8118

Rolly-Michaux Galleries, Ltd
290 Dartmouth Street
Boston, MA 02116
Attn: Ronald Rolly
      Ronald Michaux
TEL (617) 536-9898

Ronin Gallery
605 Madison Avenue
New York, NY 10022
Attn: Roni Neuer
TEL (212) 688-0188

GALLERY INDEX CONTINUED

Donna Rose Art Brokerage, Inc
544 East Fork Road
P O Box 3730
Ketchum, ID 83340
TEL (208) 788-9300
FAX (208) 788-9337

Peter Rose Gallery
200 East 58th Street
New York, NY 10022
TEL (212) 759-8173

Andrea Rosen Gallery
130 Prince Street, 3rd Floor
New York, NY 10012
TEL (212) 941-0203
FAX (212) 941-0327

Stephen Rosenberg Gallery
115 Wooster Street
New York, NY 10012
Attn: Fran Kaufman
TEL (212) 431-4838

Rosenfeld Fine Arts
44 East 82nd Street
New York, NY 10028
Attn: Samuel L Rosenfeld
TEL (212) 734-3284
FAX (212) 734-3322

Michael Rosenfeld Gallery
24 West 57th Street
New York, NY 10019-3914
TEL (212) 247-0082
FAX (212) 247-0402

Michelle Rosenfeld Gallery
16 East 79th Street
New York, NY 10021
TEL (212) 734-0900
FAX (201) 327-1794

Rosenfeld Gallery
113 Arch Street
Philadelphia, PA 19106
Attn: Barbara Rosenfeld
    Richard Rosenfeld
TEL (215) 922-1376

Betsy Rosenfield Gallery
212 West Superior Street
Chicago, IL 60610
TEL (312) 787-8020

Rosenstock Arts
1228 East Colfax Avenue
Denver, CO 80218
Attn: Stephen L Good
TEL (303) 832-7190

Dorothy Rosenthal Art
1000 Lake Shore Plaza
Chicago, IL 60611
TEL (312) 943-2523

J Rosenthal Fine Arts
212 West Superior Street
Chicago, IL 60610
Attn: Dennis Rosenthal
TEL (312) 642-2966
FAX (312) 642-5169

Luise Ross Gallery
50 West 57th Street, 11th FL
New York, NY 10019
TEL (212) 307-0400

Sheldon Ross Gallery
250 Martin Street
Birmingham, MI 48011
TEL (313) 258-9550

Ross-Constantine Gallery
65 Prince Street
New York, NY 10012
Attn: Stuart Ross
TEL (212) 226-0391

Judi Rotenberg Gallery
130 Newbury Street
Boston, MA 02116
Attn: Amnon Goldman
TEL (617) 437-1518

G H Rothe Gallery
26364 Carmel Rancho Lane
Carmel, CA 93923
Attn: Elke A Fields
TEL (800) 824-7254

G H Rothe Gallery
Lincoln Between Ocean & 7th
Carmel, CA 93921
TEL (408) 624-9377

G H Rothe Gallery
2 Portola Plaza
Doubletree Hotel
Monterey, CA 93940
TEL (408) 655-1313

Rothschild Fine Arts
205 West End Avenue
New York, NY 10023
Attn: John D Rothschild
TEL (212) 873-9142

Carolyn J Roy Gallery
128 Wooster Street
New York, NY 10012
Attn: Joy Roy
TEL (212) 343-2337
FAX (212) 490-3316

Royal Art Gallery
537 Rue Royal
New Orleans, LA 70130
Attn: Yves Langlet
    Marsha Ercegovic
    William L Jones, III
TEL (504) 524-6070

Royal Athena Galleries
153 East 57th Street
New York, NY 10022
Attn: Jerome M Eisenberg
TEL (212) 355-2034

Rubenstein/Diacono Gallery
130 Prince Street
New York, NY 10012
Attn: Perry Rubenstein
    Mario Diacono
TEL (212) 431-4221
FAX (212) 431-4369

Rubiner Gallery
7001 Orchard Lake Road, #430-A
West Bloomfield, MI 48322
Attn: Allen Rubiner
TEL (313) 626-3111

RubinSpangle Gallery
420 East 72nd Street
New York, NY 10021
Attn: Morgan Spangle
    Laurie Rubin
    Lynn Rubin
TEL (212) 226-2161
FAX (212) 879 1852

Jeffrey Ruesch Fine Art, Ltd
134 Spring Street
New York, NY 10012
TEL (212) 925-1137
FAX (212) 226-8070

Running Ridge Gallery
640 Canyon Road
Santa Fe, NM 87501
Attn: Chuck Waldeck
    Dan Appleby
TEL (505) 988-2515
TEL (800) 584-6830

Laura Russo Gallery
805 NW 21st Avenue
Portland, OR 97209
TEL (503) 226-2754

Jack Rutberg Fine Arts
357 North La Brea Blvd
Los Angeles, CA 90036-2577
TEL (213) 938-5222
FAX (213) 938-0577

Mary Ryan Gallery
24 West 57th Street
New York, NY 10019
TEL (212) 397-0669
FAX (212) 397-0766

Sacred Circle Gallery of American Indian Art
P O Box 99100
Seattle, WA 98199
Attn: Steven Charles
TEL (206) 285-4425
FAX (206) 285-4427

Salander-O'Reilly Galleries
20 East 79th Street
New York, NY 10021
Attn: Lori Bookstein
TEL (212) 879-6606
FAX (212) 744-0655

Sander Gallery, Inc
19 East 76th Street
New York, NY 10021
TEL (212) 794-4500
FAX (212) 794-8600

Sangamon Gallery
1549 North Wells Street
Chicago, IL 60610
Attn: Francesca Sparacino
TEL (312) 587-7500
FAX (312) 751-8137

Santa Fe East Gallery
200 Old Santa Fe Trail
Santa Fe, NM 87501
Attn: Alma S King
TEL (505) 988-3103

Santa Fe Lightsource Gallery
100 East San Francisco Street
Santa Fe, NM 87501
Attn: Joette T O'Connor
TEL (505) 989-9540

Julie Saul Gallery
560 Broadway, #503
New York, NY 10012
TEL (212) 431-0747
FAX (212) 925-3491

Savage Galleries
7112 Main Street
Scottsdale, AZ 85251
Attn: Gwen Meisner
TEL (602) 945-7114

Savage Gallery
102 East Water Street
Santa Fe, NM 87501
Attn: James H Bottorff
TEL (505) 982-1640

William Sawyer Gallery
3045 Clay Street
San Francisco, CA 94115
Attn: David Busham
TEL (415) 921-1600

Saxon Mountain Gallery
406 6th Avenue
Georgetown, CO 80444-0112
Attn: Bill Alexander
TEL (303) 569-3186
TEL (303) 674-0353

Daniel Saxon Gallery
7525 Beverly Blvd
Los Angeles, CA 90036
TEL (213) 933-5282
FAX (213) 933-8105

Carol Sayre Gallery
Red Hills Road
Thoreau NM 87323
TEL (505) 862-7550

Sazama Gallery
300 West Superior Street
Chicago, IL 60610
Attn: Susan Sazama
TEL (312) 951-0004
FAX (312) 951-9356

William H Schab Gallery
24 West 57th Street, #301
New York, NY 10019
TEL (212) 974-0337

Kenneth Anthony Schachter Editions
111 Third Avenue, 15th Floor
New York, NY 10003
TEL (212) 777-0420

Scheinbaum & Russek, Ltd
328 Guadaloupe Street, #M
Santa Fe, NM 87501
Attn: David Scheinbaum
    Janet Russek
TEL (505) 988-5116

GALLERY INDEX CONTINUED

Scherer Gallery
93 School Road
Marlboro, NJ 07746
Attn: Charlotte Scherer
TEL (201) 536-9465

Schiller & Bodo
19 East 74th Street
New York, NY 10021
TEL (212) 772-8527
FAX (212) 535-5943

Schlesinger Gallery
24 East 73rd Street
New York, NY 10021
Attn: Stephen L Schlesinger
TEL (212) 734-3600

Brigitte Schluger Gallery
929 Broadway
Denver, CO 80203
TEL (303) 825-8555

Schmidt Bingham Gallery
41 East 57 Street
New York, NY 10022
Attn: Penelope Schmidt
TEL (212) 888-1122
FAX (212) 754-1863

Schmidt/Dean Gallery
1636 Walnut Street
Philadelphia, PA 19103
Attn: Christopher Schmidt
       Ilana Dean
TEL (215) 546-7212

Schneider-Bluhm-Loeb Gallery, Inc
230 West Superior Street
Chicago, IL 60610
TEL (312) 988-4033

Kurt E Schon Gallery
510 St Louis & Royal Street
New Orleans, LA 70130
TEL (504) 524-5462
FAX (504) 524-6233

C S Schulte Galleries
315 Valley Street
South Orange, NJ 07079
Attn: Carol Schulte
       Stephen Schulte
TEL (201) 762-4409

Andrea Schwartz Gallery
333 Bryant Street, #180
San Francisco, CA 94107
TEL (415) 495-2090

Martin Schwieg Gallery
4658 Maryland Avenue
St Louis, MO 63108
Attn: Cena Pohl
TEL (314) 361-3000

Steven Scott Gallery
515 North Charles Street
Baltimore, MD 21201
TEL (301) 752-6218

Francine Seders Gallery
6701 Greenwood Avenue, North
Seattle, WA 98103
TEL (206) 782-0355
FAX (206) 783-6593

Ron Segal Gallery
Brentwood Gardens
11677 San Vincente Blvd
Los Angeles, CA 90049
TEL (310) 447-8334
FAX (310) 826-5266

Segal Fine Art
21220 Erwin Street
Woodland Hills, CA 91367
Attn: Jill H Muller
       Mark D Muller
TEL (818) 713-0250
TEL (800) 999-1297

Thomas Segal Gallery
207 South Street
Boston, MA 02111
TEL (617) 292-0789

Marvin Seline Gallery
3510 Lake Street
Fort Worth, TX 77098
TEL (713) 520-5550

Charles Semowich Fine Arts
168 North Allen Street
Albany, NY 12206
TEL (518) 459-2674

Sena Galleries West
Plaza Mercado, Upper Level
112 West San Francisco Street
Santa Fe, NM 87501
Attn: Mary Thompson
TEL (505) 982-8808
FAX (505) 982-0878

Betsy Senior Contemporary Prints
375 West Broadway
New York, NY 10012
TEL (212) 941-0960
FAX (212) 334-3109

Kathryn Sermas Gallery
19 Green Street, 4th Floor
New York, NY 10013
TEL (212) 431-5743

Lisa Sette Gallery
4142 North Marshall Way
Scottsdale, AZ 85251
Attn: Peter Wirmusky
TEL (602) 990-7342

750 Gallery
1727 I Street
Sacramento, CA 95814
Attn: Scott Wilson
TEL (916) 923-6393

Gail Severn Gallery
620 Sun Valley Road
P O Box 1679
Ketchum, ID 83340
TEL (208) 726-5079

Tony Shafrazi Gallery
199 Wooster Street
New York, NY 10012
TEL (212) 274-9300

Jack Shainman Gallery
560 Broadway, 2nd Floor
New York, NY 10012
TEL (212) 966-3866
FAX (212) 334-8453

Anita Shapolsky Gallery
99 Spring Street
New York, NY 10012
TEL (212) 334-9755

Leslie Ava Shaw Fine Art
110 West 87th Street
New York, NY 10024
TEL (212) 724-4053
FAX (212) 334-9755

Susan Sheehan Gallery, Inc
41 East 57th Street, 11th Floor
New York, NY 10022
TEL (212) 888-4220

Shepherd Gallery
21 East 84th Street
New York, NY 10028
Attn: R Kashey
TEL (212) 861-4050
FAX (212) 772-1314

H Shickman Gallery
980 Madison Avenue, 3rd Floor
New York, NY 10021
TEL (212) 249-3800
FAX (212) 472-1178

Shoestring Gallery
1855 Monroe Avenue
Rochester, NY 14618
Attn: Ellen Brown
       Nancy Esmay
TEL (716) 271-3886

Shogun Gallery
1083 Wisconsin Avenue
Washington, DC 20007
Attn: Gary Gestson
TEL (202) 965-5454

Shorney Gallery of Fine Art
6616 North Olie Avenue
Oklahoma City, OK 73116
Attn: Margo Kay Shorney
TEL (405) 842-6175

Shoshana Wayne Gallery
1454 5th Street
Santa Monica, CA 90401
TEL (213) 451-3733

Shriver Gallery
401 Passeo del Pueblo Norte
Taos, NM 87571
Attn: Marge Harrison
       Bill Harrison
TEL (505) 758-4994

Evelyn Siegel Gallery
3612 West 7th Street
Fort Worth, TX 76107
TEL (817) 731-6412

Sigma Gallery
379 West Broadway
New York, NY 10012
Attn: Dolores An
TEL (212) 941-0014
TEL (212) 941-0015
FAX (212) 941-0016

Signature Gallery
1 Dock Square
North Street
Boston, MA 02109
Attn: Erin Huggard
TEL (617) 227-4885

Nathan Silberberg Fine Arts
301 East 63rd Street, #7-G
New York, NY 10012
TEL (212) 980-2353

Silver Cloud Galleries
734 North Wells
Chicago, IL 60610
Attn: Herbert Goode
TEL (312) 664-9356

Silver Image Gallery
318 Occidental Avenue, South
Seatte, WA 98104
Attn: Dan Fear
TEL (206) 623-8116

Silver Sun Gallery
656 Canyon Road
Santa Fe, NM 87501
Attn: Neil Winterbottom
TEL (505) 983-8743

Linda R Silverman Fine Art
160 East 65th Street
New York, NY 10021
TEL (212) 794-1352
FAX (212) 249-0271

Manny Silverman Gallery
619 North Almont Drive
Los Angeles, CA 90069
Attn: Linda Hooper-Kawakami
TEL (310) 659-8256
FAX (310) 659-1001

Simic Galleries
San Carlos & 6th Street
P O Box 5687
Carmel, CA 93921
TEL (408) 624-7522

Simon/Neuman Gallery
42 East 76th Street
New York, NY 10021
Attn: A Simon
       D Neuman
TEL (212) 744-8460
FAX (212) 744-0576

Barclay Simpson Fine Arts
3669 Mount Diablo Blvd
Lafayette, CA 94549
TEL (510) 284-7048

GALLERY INDEX CONTINUED

Merton Simpson Gallery
1063 Madison Avenue
New York, NY 10028
TEL (212) 988-6290

Alice Simsar Gallery
301 North Main Street
Ann Arbor, MI 48104
TEL (313) 665-4883

Sindin Galleries
956 Madison Avenue
New York, NY 10021
Attn: Karen Sindin
    Bernita Mirisola
TEL (212) 288-7902

Mary Singer Gallery
2920 44th Place, NW
Washington, DC 20016
TEL (202) 363-6785

Nancy Singer Gallery
31 Crestwood Drive
St Louis, MO 63105
TEL (314) 727-1830

Sloane Gallery of Art
Oxford Office Bldg
1612 17th Street
Denver, CO 80202
Attn: Mina Litinsky
TEL (303) 595-4230

Andrew Smith Gallery
76 East San Francisco Street
Santa Fe, NM 87501
TEL (505) 984-1234
FAX (505) 983-2428

Smith Andersen Gallery
200 Homer Street
Palo Alto, CA 94301
Attn: Paula Kirkeby
    Ruth Benson
TEL (415) 327-7762
FAX (415) 327-8737

Smith Gallery
1045 Madison Avenue
New York, NY 10021
Attn: Patricia Smith
TEL (212) 744-6171

Elliot Smith Gallery
4727 McPherson Avenue
St Louis, MO 63108
TEL (314) 361-4800

Thomas Smith Fine Art
615 South Harrison Street
Fort Wayne, IN 46802
TEL (219) 422-1307

Snyderman Gallery
317 South Street
Philadelphia, PA 19147
Attn: Rick Snyderman
TEL (215) 238-9576

Soho Graphic Arts Workshop
433 West Broadway
New York, NY 10012
Attn: Xavier H Rivera
TEL (212) 966-7292

Soho Photo
15 White Street
New York, NY 10013
Attn: David Chalk
TEL (212) 226-8571

SoHo 20
469 Broome Street
New York, NY 10013
Attn: Eugenia C Foxworth
TEL (212) 226-4167

Soker Gallery
251 Post Street
San Francisco, CA 94108
Attn: Don Soker
TEL (415) 291-0966
FAX (415) 291-0962

Solo Impressions, Inc
520 Broadway, 8th Floor
New York, NY 10012
Attn: Eliza Beghe
TEL (212) 925-3599
FAX (212) 226-3251

Solomon & Company Fine Art
959 Madison Avenue
New York, NY 10021
Attn: Gerald Solomon
    Sally Solomon
TEL (212) 737-8200

Holly Solomon Gallery
172 Mercer Street
New York, NY 10012
Attn: Lance Fung
TEL (212) 941-5777
FAX (212) 226-4990

Thomas Solomon's Garage
928 North Fairfax Avenue
Los Angeles, CA 90046
Attn: Douglas Roberts
TEL (213) 654-4731
FAX (213) 654-4759

Stephen Solovy Fine Art
620 North Michigan Avenue
Chicago, IL 60611
TEL (312) 664-4860
FAX (312) 664-6726

Carl E Solway Gallery
314 West Fourth Street
Cincinnati, OH 45202
TEL (513) 621-0069

Soma Fine Art Press
665 Third, #225
San Francisco, CA 94107
Attn: Sarah Henderson
TEL (415) 495-7997

Sonnabend Gallery
420 West Broadway
New York, NY 10012
Attn: Antonio Homem
TEL (212) 966-6160
FAX (212) 941-9218

Soufer Gallery
1015 Madison Avenue
New York, NY 10021
TEL (212) 628-3225
FAX (212) 628-3752

Southern Exposure Gallery
401 Alabama Street
San Francisco, CA 94110
Attn: Jon Winet
TEL (415) 863-2141

Southwest Gallery
737 Preston Forest S/C
Dallas, TX 75230
Attn: E C Carmock
TEL (214) 696-0182

Space Gallery
1945 West North Avenue
Chicago, IL 60605
TEL (312) 276-5146

Space Gallery
6015 Santa Monica Blvd
Los Angeles, CA 90038
Attn: Edward Den Lau
TEL (213) 461-8166

Spaces
2220 Superior Viaduct
Cleveland, OH 44113
Attn: Susan R Channing
TEL (216) 621-2314

Spaightwood Galleries
1150 Spaight Street
Madison, WI 53703
Attn: Andre D Weiner
TEL (608) 255-3043
FAX (608) 257-4559

Ira Spanlerman Gallery
50 East 78th Street
New York, NY 10021
Attn: David C Henry
TEL (212) 879-7085
FAX (212) 249-5227

Spark Gallery
3300 Osage
Denver, CO 80211
Attn: David Sharpe
TEL (303) 477-6782

Spectrum Gallery
5111 Harrison Street
San Francisco, CA 94105
TEL (415) 495-1113

Spectrum Gallery
1132 29th Street, NW
Washington, DC 20007
Attn: Anna G Practor
TEL (202) 333-0954

Sperone Westwater Gallery
142 Greene Street
New York, NY 10012
Attn: David Lieber
TEL (212) 431-3685
FAX (212) 941-1030

Spirit Gallery
215 West San Francisco Street
Santa Fe, NM 87501
Attn: Neil Winterbottom
TEL (505) 983-1104
FAX (505) 986-1228

Susan Spiritus Gallery
3333 Bear Street, #30
Costa Mesa, CA 92626
TEL (714) 549-7550

Clare Spitler Works of Art
2007 Pauline Court
Ann Arbor, MI 48103
TEL (313) 662-8914

Split Fountain
141 Suite A, South Crescent Drive
Beverly Hills, CA 90212
Attn: Anthony Ditton
TEL (310) 273-7770
FAX (310) 273-7771

Sragow Gallery
73 Spring Street
New York, NY 10012
Attn: Ellen Sragow
TEL (212) 219-1793
Specializing in American Prints
from the 1920's, 30's & 40's

St Albus Fine Arts
225 Scott Street
San Francisco, CA 94117
Attn: Lynn St Albus
TEL (415) 861-4458

Monty Stabler Galleries
1811 29th Avenue, South
Birmingham, AL 35209
TEL (205) 978-9888

Stair-Sainty Fine Art
42 East 74th Street
New York, NY 10021
Attn: Guy Stair-Sainty
TEL (212) 288-1088

Carolyn Staley Fine Prints
313 1st Avenue, South
Seattle, WA 98104
TEL (206) 621-1888

Staley-Wise Gallery
560 Broadway
New York, NY 10012
Attn: Etheleen Staley
    Takouhy Wise
TEL (212) 966-6223
FAX (212) 966-6293

Stark Gallery
594 Broadway, #301
New York, NY 10012
Attn: Eric Stark
    Margaret Thatcher
TEL (212) 925-4484
FAX (212) 274-9525

Stein-Bartlow Gallery, Ltd
620 North Michigan Avenue, #340
Chicago, IL 60611
Attn: Peter E Bartlow
TEL (312) 337-1782
FAX (312) 337-2516

GALLERY INDEX CONTINUED

Steinbaum Krauss Gallery
132 Green Street
New York, NY 10012
Attn: Bernice Steinbaum
TEL (212) 431-4224
FAX (212) 431-3252

Janes Steinberg Fine Arts
909 Montgomery Street, #600
San Francisco, CA 94133
TEL (415) 397-3266

Paul Steinhacker Gallery
151 East 71st Street
New York, NY 10021
TEL (212) 879-1245

Greig Steiner Gallery
Stanley Hotel
333 Wonderview Drive
P O Box 1671
Estes Park, CO 80517
TEL (303) 586-3358

Stephan Fine Arts Gallery
600 West 6th Avenue
Anchorage, AK 99501
Attn: Dawn Kelly
TEL (907) 278-9555

Stewart & Stewart Gallery
5571 Wing Lake Road
Bloomfield Hills, MI 48301
Attn: Norman Stewart
TEL (313) 626-5248

Stiebel Modern
32 East 57th Street
New York, NY 10022
Attn: Deven Golden
TEL (212) 759-5536
FAX (212) 935-5735

Stiha Gallery
La Fonda Hotel
Santa Fe, NM 98501
Attn: Elena Stiha
      Vladan Stiha
TEL (505) 983-6145

Still-Zinsel Contemporary Fine Art
328 Julia Street
New Orleans, LA 70130
Attn: Sam Still
      Suzanne Zinsel
TEL (504) 588-9999
TEL (504) 588-9900

John C Stoller & Company
81 South 9th Street
Minneapolis, MN 55402
TEL (612) 339-7060
FAX (612) 349-2850

Stones at Kilohana
3-2087 Kaumualii Hwy
Lihue, Kauai, HI 96766
Attn: Kenne Brittain
TEL (808) 245-6684

Stonington Gallery
415 F Street
Anchorage, Alaska 995
Attn: Jane Purinton
TEL (907) 272-1489

Strecker Gallery
332 Poyntz Street
Manhattan, KS 66502
Attn: Julie Strecker
TEL (913) 539-2139

Stremmel Gallery
1400 South Virginia Street
Reno, NV 89502
Attn: Peter Stremmel
TEL (702) 786-0558
FAX (702) 786-0311

Struve Gallery
309 West Superior Street
Chicago, IL 60610-3515
Attn: Keith Struve
TEL (312) 787-0563
FAX (312) 787-7268

David Stuart Galleries
748 1/2 North La Cienega Blvd
Los Angeles, CA 90069
TEL (213) 652-7422

Studio 53
424 Park Avenue
New York, NY 10022
Attn: Ellen Silverberg
TEL (212) 755-6650
TEL (800) 237-5353

Studio Raid Gallery
7378 Beverly Blvd
Los Angeles, CA 90036
Attn: Claudette M Lussier
TEL (213) 939-8084
FAX (213) 939-8925

Studio Sixteen-Seventeen
1617 Silverlake Blvd
Los Angeles, CA 90026
Attn: Bill Wheeler
TEL (213) 660-7991

Stux Gallery
163 Mercer Street
New York, NY 10012
Attn: Stefan Stux
TEL (212) 219-0010
FAX (212) 219-2243

Styria Studio
419 Broome Street
New York, NY 10013
Attn: Adi Rischner
TEL (212) 226-1373
FAX (212) 226-1072

Martin Sumers Graphics
50 West 57th Street
New York, NY 10019
TEL (212) 541-8334

Summa Gallery
527 Amsterdam Avenue
New York, NY 10024
Attn: Donald Pandina
      Sal Cigna
TEL (212) 787-8533

Summa Gallery
152 Montague Street
Brooklyn, NY 11201
Attn: Donald Pandina
      Sal Cigna
TEL (718) 875-1647

Sunnen Gallery
49 Prince Street
New York, NY 10012
TEL (212) 679-0679

John H Surovek Gallery
349 Worth Avenue
Palm Beach, FL 33480
Attn: Janice E Caiazzo
TEL (407) 832-0422

Swan Coach House Gallery
3130 Slaton Drive, NW
Atlanta, GA 30305
Attn: Rebecca Warner
TEL (404) 266-2636

Swearington Gallery
110 Tribal Road
Louisville, KY 40207-1515
TEL (502) 893-5209

Sonia Szabados Fine Art
261 Leopold Crescent
Regina, SASK
Canada S4T 6N8

John Szoke Graphics, Inc
164 Mercer Street
New York, NY 10012
TEL (212) 219-8300
FAX (212) 966-3064

John Szoke Graphics, Inc
591 Broadway
New York, NY 10012
Attn: John Szoke
TEL (212) 217-8300
FAX (212) 966-3064

Taggart & Jorgensen Gallery
3241 P Street, NW
Washington, DC 20007
Attn: Hillis Taggart
      Carl Jorgensen
TEL (202) 298-7676

Leila Taghainia-Milani
1080 Madison Avenue
New York, NY 10028
TEL (212) 570-6173
FAX (212) 744-6523

Takada Fine Arts
251 Post Street, 6th Floor
San Francisco, CA 94108
Attn: Hidekatsu Takada
TEL (415) 956-5288
FAX (415) 956-5409

Talma Gallery
27 Gordon Street
Tel Aviv, Israel
Attn: Talma, Zarai
TEL USA (212) 288-3932

Tamenaga Gallery
982 Madison Avenue
New York, NY 10021
Attn: Kotaro Inagaki
      Patrick O'Connor
TEL (212) 734-6789
FAX (212) 734-9413

Kornelia Tamm, Ltd
560 West 43rd Street, #42-A
New York, NY 10026
TEL (212) 967-7315
FAX (212) 268-0198

Jon Taner Gallery
183 Westwood, NJ 07675
Attn: Jon Taner
      Ellen Taner
TEL (201) 664-5858

Tanton Gallery
699 Marginal Road
West Palm Beach, FL 33411
Attn: Richard L Tanton
TEL (407) 793-8160

Taos Fine Art Gallery
208 Ranchitos Road
Taos, NM 87571
Attn: Rita Perna
      Chuck Perna
TEL (505) 751-1295

Tartt Gallery
2017 Q Street
Washington, DC 20009
Attn: Jo C Tartt, Jr
      Sara Hutchinson
TEL (202) 332-5652
FAX (202) 462-1019

Tasende Gallery
820 Prospect Street
La Jolla, CA 92037
Attn: Jose M Tasende
      Mary Beth Hynes
TEL (619) 454-3691

Joy Tash Gallery
4142 North Marshall Way
Scottsdale, AZ 85251
TEL (602) 945-0195

Tatistcheff & Company
50 West 57th Street, 8th Floor
New York, NY 10019
Attn: Frank Bernaducci
TEL (212) 664-0907
FAX (212) 541-8814

Tatyana Gallery
145 East 27th Street
New York, NY 10016
Attn: Tatyana Gribanova
TEL (212) 683-2387
FAX (212) 683-9147

Tavelli Williams Gallery
620 East Hyman Avenue
Aspen, CO 81611
Attn: Thomas Tavelli
      Ginny Williams
TEL (303) 920-3071

Susan Teller Gallery
568 Broadway, Room 405-A
New York, NY 10012
TEL (212) 941-7335

Ten Arrow Gallery
10 Arrow Street
Cambridge, MA 02138
Attn: Elizabeth Tinlot
TEL (617) 876-1117

GALLERY INDEX CONTINUED

Martha Tepper Fine Arts
The Park Square Bldg
31 St James Avenue, #901
Boston, MA 02116
Attn: Martha Tepper
   Atsuyoshi Takayama
TEL (617) 542-0557
FAX (617) 542-0607
Specializing in Contemporary & Emerging Artists

Texas Gallery
2012 Peden
Houston, TX 77019
Attn: Fredericka Hunter
TEL (713) 524-1593

Thackrey & Robertson
2266 Union Street
San Francisco, CA 94123
Attn: Sean Thackrey
   Sally Robertson
TEL (415) 567-4842

THE Gallery Three Zero
30 Bond Street
New York, NY 10012-2406
Attn: Emily Sorkin
   Thomas Zoliner
TEL (212) 505-9668
FAX (212) 505-9679

Things Japanese
127 East 60th Street
New York, NY 10022
Attn: Sally Pleet
TEL (212) 371-4661

Frederick Thom Gallery
194 Bloor Street, West
Toronto, ON
Canada M5S 1T8
TEL (416) 921-3522

Thomson Gallery
321 Second Avenue, North
Minneapolis, MN 55401
Attn: Robert Thomson
   Leah Stoddard
TEL (612) 338-7734
FAX (612) 337-5293

Edward Thorp Gallery
103 Prince Street, 2nd Floor
New York, NY 10012
Attn:
TEL (212) 431-6880
FAX (212) 219-0081

Thronja Original Art
260 Worthington Street
Springfield, MA 01103
Attn: Janice S Throne
TEL (413) 732-0260

Tilden-Foley Gallery
4119 Magazine Street
New Orleans, LA 70115
Attn: Timothy A Foley
TEL (504) 897-5300

Jack Tilton Gallery
47–49 Greene Street
New York, NY 10013
Attn: Janine Cirincione
TEL (212) 941-1775
FAX (212) 941-1812

Barbara Toll Fine Arts
146 Greene Street
New York, NY 10012
TEL (212) 431-1788
FAX (212) 431-0183

Tompkins Square Gallery
331 East 10th Street
New York, NY 10009
Attn: Hara Seltzer
TEL (212) 228-4747

Tortue Gallery
2917 Santa Monica Blvd
Santa Monica, CA 90404
Attn: Mallory Freeman
TEL (310) 828-8878
FAX (310) 828-3763

Tossan-Tossan Gallery
305 East 50th Street
New York, NY 10022
Attn: Marta-Lourdes Santos
TEL (212) 688-1574

Touchstone Gallery
2009 R Street, NW
Washington, DC 20009
Attn: Mary Sawchenko
TEL (202) 223-6683

Tower Park Gallery
4709 North Prospect Road
Peoria Heights, IL 61614
Attn: David Brown
TEL (309) 682-8932

Trans Avant-Garde Gallery
1000 West 31st Street, #202
Austin, TX 78705
TEL (512) 454-9050

Transamerica Pyramid Gallery
600 Montgomery Street
San Francisco, CA 94111
Attn: Corinne Beauvais
TEL (415) 983-4088

William Traver Gallery
110 Union Street, #200
Seattle, WA 98101
TEL (206) 587-6501
FAX (206) 587-6502

Triangle Gallery
165 Post Street, 4th Floor
San Francisco, CA 94108
Attn: Jack Van Hiele
TEL (415) 392-1686

Tribeca 148 Gallery
148-B Duane Street
New York, NY 10013
Attn: Edward Enck
   Gail Swithenbank
TEL (212) 406-4073

Tribeca Gallery
51-A Hudson Street
New York, NY 10013
Attn: Madelyn Jordon
TEL (212) 233-5858

Trumbull Gallery
Trumbull Center, North
2 Daniels Farm Road
Trumbull, CT 06611
TEL (203) 268-9243

Garner Tullis
10 White Street
New York, NY 10013
TEL (212) 226-6665
FAX (212) 941-0678

David Tunick, Inc
12 East 81st Street
New York, NY 10028
Attn: Elizabeth Tunick
   Walton Boring
TEL (212) 570-0090

James Turcotte Gallery
8128 Tiana Road
Los Angeles, CA 90046
TEL (213) 385-2260

Turner Carroll Gallery
725 Canyon Road
Santa Fe, NM 87501
Attn: Tonya Turner Carroll
   Michael Carroll
TEL (505) 986-9800
FAX (505) 986-9800

Turner/Krull Gallery
9006 Melrose Avenue
Los Angeles, CA 90069
Attn: Craig Krull
TEL (310) 271-1536
FAX (310) 271-3469

Turner Fine Art
185 East 85th Street
New York, NY 10028
Attn: Kim Turner
TEL (212) 427-5173
FAX (212) 996-3231

Steve Turner Gallery
7220 Beverly Blvd
Los Angeles, CA 90036
TEL (213) 931-1185
FAX (213) 931-1187

Turske & Turske, AG
Seefeldstrasse 227/229
CH 8008, Zurich,
Switzerland
Attn: Veith Turske
   Irene Preiswerk Turske
TEL 41.1.55.97.70
FAX 41.1.53.71.49

TwoSixtyOne Arts
261 Broadway, #8-A
New York, NY 10007
Attn: Richard Gardner
TEL (212) 619-0869

Two Street Studio
126 South Second Street
Paducah, KY 42001
Attn: Sarah Roush
TEL (502) 443-2582

Udinotti Gallery
3525 Sacramento Street
San Francisco, CA 94118
Attn: Agnese Udinotti
TEL (415) 929-1193

Ulysses Gallery
41 East 57th Street
New York, NY 10022
TEL (212) 754-4666
FAX (212) 754-4469

Uptown Gallery
1194 Madison Avenue
New York, NY 10028
Attn: Philip M Williams
   Steve Williams
TEL (212) 722-3677
FAX (212) 410-2097

Bertha Urdang Gallery
23 East 74th Street
New York, NY 10021
TEL (212) 288-7004

Ursus Prints
981 Madison Avenue
New York, NY 10021
Attn: Evelyn Kraus
TEL (212) 722-8787

Valperine Gallery
1791 Monroe Street
Madison, WI 53711
Attn: Valerie Kazamias
   Petie Rudy
TEL (608) 256-4090

Van Straaten Gallery
742 North Wells Street
Chicago, IL 60610
Attn: William van Straaten
TEL (312) 642-2900

Vanderwoude/Tananbaum Gallery
24 East 81st Street
New York, NY 10028
Attn: S Vanderwoude
   D Tananbaum
TEL (212) 879-8200
FAX (212) 879-0785

Veerhoff Galleries
1604 17th Street
Washington, DC 20009
Attn: Margaret Veerhoff
TEL (202) 357-2322

Venable Neslage Galleries
1803 Connecticut Avenue, NW
Washington, DC 20009
Attn: Oliver J Neslage
TEL (202) 462-1800

Ventana Fine Art
Inn at Loreto
211 Old Santa Fe Trail
Santa Fe, NM 87501
Attn: Connie Axton
TEL (505) 983-8815
FAX (505) 988-4780

Vered Gallery
68 Park Place
East Hampton, NY 11937
Attn: Ruth Vered
TEL (516) 324-3303
TEL (212) 288-6234

Althea Viafora Gallery
203 East 72nd Street
New York, NY 10017
TEL (212) 628-2402
FAX (212) 628-2402

GALLERY INDEX CONTINUED

Mario Villa Gallery
500 North Wells Street
Chicago, IL 60610
TEL (312) 923-0993
FAX (312) 923-0977

Mario Villa Gallery
3908 Magazine Street
New Orleans, LA 70115
TEL (504) 895-8731

Village Art Gallery
7 Pondfield Road
Bronxville, NY 10708
Attn: Mary LaGreca
TEL (914) 337-7711

Village Galleries
22651 Lambert Street, #103
Lake Forest, CA 92630
Other Locations: Laguna Beach,
Santa Ana, San Diego, Irvine &
Mission Viejo
Attn: Martin Brown
    Pamela Brown
TEL (714) 768-8421
FAX (714) 768-1565
TEL (800) 546-5233
Representing: Delacroix, R C Gorman,
Maimon, Neiman, G H Rothe, Ting &
Many Others

Diane Villani Editions
271 Mulberry Street, #3D
New York, NY 10012
TEL (212) 925-1075
FAX (212) 966-8411

Vinalhaven Press
565 Broadway
New York, NY 10012
TEL (212) 219-1561

Viridian Gallery
24 West 57th Street
New York, NY 10019
Attn: Kari Staubo
TEL (212) 245-2882

Vorpal Gallery, Soho
411 West Broadway
New York, NY 10012
Attn: Muldoon Elder
TEL (212) 334-3939
FAX (212) 941-8350

Vorpal Gallery
393 Grove Street
San Francisco, CA 94102
Attn: David Love
TEL (415) 397-9200

Vose Galleries of Boston
238 Newbury Street
Boston, MA 94102
Attn: Abbot W Vose
    Robert C Vose, Jr
TEL (617) 536-6176

Wade Gallery
308 North Sycamore Avenue, #208
Los Angeles, CA 90069
Attn: John W Long
TEL (213) 931-7516

Wadle Galleries, Ltd
128 West Palace
Santa Fe, NM 87501
Attn: Albert Wadle
TEL (505) 983-9219

B Z Wagman Art, Inc
9783 Clayton Road
St Louis, MO 63124
Attn: Barbara Z Wagman
TEL (314) 997-7273

Walker, Ursitti & McGinness Gallery
500 Greenwich Street
New York, NY 10013
Attn: Christopher F Ursitti
TEL (212) 966-7543
FAX (212) 431-9087

Kevin V Wallace Gallery
10580 Wellworth Avenue
Los Angeles, CA 90024
TEL (213) 470-1306

Michael Walls Gallery
156 Wooster Street
New York, NY 10012
TEL (212) 982-9800

Brendan Walter Gallery
1001 Colorado Avenue
Santa Monica, CA 90401
TEL (310) 395-1155

Eileen Walters Gallery
654 Madison Avenue, #1702
New York, NY 10021
TEL (212) 644-1414

Walton-Gilbert Galleries
50 La Crescenta Way
San Rafael, CA 94901
Attn: Harris Stewart
TEL (415) 391-8185
FAX (415) 457-0104

Ward-Nasse Gallery
178 Prince Street
New York, NY 10012
Attn: Robert Curcio
TEL (212) 925-6951

Washburn Gallery
20 West 57th Street, 8th Floor
New York, NY 10019
TEL (212) 397-6780
FAX (212) 397-4853

Wave Gallery
263 College Street
New Haven, CT 06510
Attn: Phyllis Satin
TEL (203) 782-6212

Waxlander Gallery
622 Canyon Road
Santa Fe, NM 87501
Attn: Robert Brody
TEL (505) 984-2202

John Weber Gallery
142 Greene Street
New York, NY 10012
TEL (212) 966-6115
FAX (212) 941-8727

Phyllis Weil & Company
1065 Park Avenue
New York, NY 10028
TEL (212) 369-0255

Daniel Weinberg Gallery
2032 Broadway
Santa Monica, CA 90404
TEL (310) 453-0180
FAX (310) 453-0177

Jan Weiner Gallery
3014 Eveningside Drive
Topeka, KS 66614
TEL (913) 272-5535

Weintraub Gallery
988 Madison Avenue
New York, NY 10021
Attn: Jacob D Weintraub
TEL (212) 879-1132
FAX (212) 570-4192

Dorothy Weiss Gallery
256 Sutter Street
San Francisco, CA 94108
TEL (415) 397-3611
FAX (415) 397-2141

Hope Weiss Fine Art
2436 Halm Avenue
Los Angeles, CA 90034
TEL (310) 841-2608
FAX (310) 841-2931

Jan Weiss Gallery
68 Laight Street
New York, NY 10013
TEL (212) 925-7313

L J Wender Gallery
3 East 80th Street
New York, NY 10021
Attn: Leon Wender
TEL (212) 734-4360

Wenger Gallery
638 1/2 North Robertson Blvd
Los Angeles, CA 90069
TEL (310) 657-9069
FAX (310) 657-1185

Wenniger Graphics
174-A Newbury Street
Boston, MA 02116
Attn: Mary Ann Wenniger
TEL (617) 536-4688

Michael Werner
21 East 67th Street
New York, NY 10021
Attn: Gordon Veneklasen
TEL (212) 988-1623
FAX (212) 988-1774

Wessel O'Connor Gallery
60 Thomas Street
New York, NY 10013
Attn: John C Wessel
    William C O'Connor
TEL (212) 406-0040
FAX (212) 406-0141

Weston Gallery
6th Avenue
P O Box 655
Carmel, CA 93921
Attn: Margaret W Weston
    Matthew Weston
TEL (408) 624-4453
FAX (408) 624-7190

Thea Westreich Associates
114 Greene Street
New York, NY 10012
TEL (212) 941-9449
FAX (212) 966-0174

Barry Whistler Gallery
2909-A Canton Street
Dallas, TX 75226
TEL (214) 939-0242

Whistler Gallery
P O Box 362
Basking Ridge, NJ 07920-0362
Attn: Douglas Krienke
TEL (908) 766-6222

White Columns
154 Christopher Street
New York, NY 10011
Attn: Bill Arning
TEL (212) 924-4212

Whitehall
12 White Street
New York, NY 10013
Attn: Louis Branco
    Richard W Berger
TEL (212) 941-8138
FAX (212) 941-8815

Wiesner Gallery, Ltd
425 West 13th Street
New York, NY 10014
Attn: Craig Killy
TEL (212) 675-8722

Wilde-Meyer Gallery
4142 North Marshall Way
Scottsdale, AZ 85251
Attn: Betty Wilde
    Mark Meyer
TEL (602) 945-2323

Wildenstein & Company
19 East 64th Street
New York, NY 10021
Attn: Harry A Brooks
TEL (212) 879-0500

Wilhelmi-Holland Gallery
300 South Chaparral
Corpus Christi, TX 78401
Attn: Ben Holland
TEL (512) 882-3523

Wilkes Art Gallery
800 Elizabeth Street
North Wilkesboro, NC 28657
Attn: Frank Thompson
TEL (919) 667-2841

GALLERY INDEX CONTINUED

Willard Gallery
12 East 12th Street
New York, NY 10021
Attn: Miani Johnson
TEL (212) 255-8581

Ginny Williams Gallery
299 Fillmore Street
Denver, CO 80206
TEL (303) 321-4077
FAX (303) 394-2060

James Willis Gallery
1637 Taylor Street
San Francisco, CA 94133
TEL (415) 885-6737

Willis Gallery
422 West Willis
Detroit, MI 48202
Attn: Gilda Snowden
TEL (313) 871-1913

Winters Gallery
St Francis Plaza
Ranchos de Taos
Taos, NM 87557
Attn: Lisa S Winters
TEL (505) 758-0323
TEL (800) 736-4313

Stephen Wirtz Gallery
49 Geary Street
San Francisco, CA 94108
Attn: Connie Writz
TEL (415) 433-6879

Witkin Gallery, Inc
415 West Broadway
New York, NY 10012
Attn: Evelyne Z Daitz
TEL (212) 925-5510
FAX (212) 925-5648

Wylie Wong Asian Art
21 Scott Street
San Francisco, CA 94117
TEL (415) 626-1014

Wood Street Gallery
1239 West Wood
Chicago, IL 60622
TEL (312) 227-3306

Woodhull Gallery
743 Fifth Avenue, 8th Floor
New York, NY 10022
Attn: Helen Woodhull
    Linda Graham
TEL (212) 826-1212

Woodside Braseth Galleries
1533 Ninth Avenue
Seattle, WA 98101
Attn: Gordon Woodside
    John Braseth
TEL (206) 622-7243

Wooster Garden
40 Wooster Street
New York, NY 10013
TEL (212) 941-6210
FAX (212) 941-5480

Worthington Gallery
620 North Michigan Avenue
Chicago, IL 60611
Attn: Eva-Maria Worthington
TEL (312) 266-2424
FAX (312) 266-2461

Gerold Wunderlich & Company
50 West 57th Street, 12th Floor
New York, NY 10019
TEL (212) 974-8444
FAX (212) 956-0553

Gerhard Wurzer Gallery
5701 Memorial Drive
Houston, TX 77056
TEL (713) 863-1933
FAX (713) 869-9466

Wychoff Gallery
648 Wyckoff Street
Wyckoff, NJ 07481
Attn: Sherry Cosloy
TEL (201) 891-7436

Riva Yares Gallery
231 Washington Avenue
Santa Fe, NM 87501
Attn: Dennis Yares
TEL (505) 984-0330
FAX (505) 986-8661

Riva Yares Gallery
3625 Bishop Lane
Scottsdale, AZ 85251
Attn: Douglas Webster
TEL (602) 947-3251
FAX (602) 947-4251

Richard York Gallery
21 East 65th Street
New York, NY 10021
Attn: Eric P Widing
TEL (212) 772-9155
FAX (212) 288-0410

Yoseido Gallery
5-5-15 Ginza
Chuo-Ku 104
Tokyo, Japan
TEL (03) 571-1312

Yoshii Gallery
20 West 57th Street, 8th Floor
New York, NY 10019
Attn: Kazuhito Yoshii
    Ted Greenwald
TEL (212) 265-8876
FAX (212) 265-8893

Donald Young Gallery
2107 Third Avenue
Seattle, WA 98121
TEL (206) 448-9484
FAX (206) 448-8661

Zabriskie Gallery
724 Fifth Avenue
New York, NY 10019
Attn: Virginia M Zabriskie
    Leslie Tonkonow
TEL (212) 307-7430

Zaks Gallery
620 Michigan Avenue, #305
Chicago, IL 60611
Attn: Sonia Zaks
TEL (312) 943-8440

Andre Zarre Gallery
48 Greene Street
New York, NY 10013
Attn: Roberta Johrmarkt
TEL (212) 966-2222

Zenith Gallery
413 7th Street, NW
Washington, DC 20004
Attn: Margery Goldberg
TEL (202) 783-2963

Zephyr Gallery
637 West Main Street
Louisville, KY 40202
Attn: Mario M Muller
    Pat Donley
TEL (502) 585-5646

Zolla/Lieberman Gallery
325 West Huron Street
Chicago, IL 60610-3617
Attn: Robert Zolla
    Roberta Lieberman
TEL (312) 944-1990
FAX (312) 944-8967

Zeus
1820 West Webster, 3rd Floor
Chicago, IL 60622
TEL (312) 384-1355

GENERAL ABBREVIATIONS

A - Aquatint
AB - Black Aquatint
AC - Color Aquatint
Acad - Academy
ad - advertisement
adj - adjunct
Adm - Admiral
admin - administration
adv - adviser-advisory
affil - affiliation
agr - agriculture
AirB - Airbrush
AL - Alabama, Aluminum
Alta - Alberta
Am - American
Ann - annual
AP - Artist Proof
app - appointed
appl - applied
appt - appointed, appointment
Apr - April
Apt - Apartment(s)
AR - Arkansas
Arch - Architecture
ARG - Argentina
ART - Artist
Assoc - Associate
Assn - Association
Asst - Assistant
atty - attorney
Aug - August
auth - author
AV - Audio-Visual
Ave - Avenue
AZ - Arizona

B - Buff
BAM - Bamboo
BC - British Columbia
BD - board
Belg - Belgium
BFA - Bachelor of Fine Arts
Bibliog - bibliography
biog - biography
BL - Black, Blue Line
Bldg - Building
Blvd - Boulevard
BP - Bronze Powder
BR - Brass, Brown
BRON - Bronze
br - branch(es)
Brit - Britain, British
BU - Burnishing
BUR - Burnishing, Bureau
BW - Black & White
BWI - British West Indies

C - Color
CA - California, Cast Aluminum
C/CA - Cast Acrylic
Can - Canada
CP - Cast Paper
CPM - Cast Paper Multiple
CAPS - Creative Artists Public Service
Capt - Captain
CAR - Carborundum
CBS - Columbia Broadcasting System
cc - chine collé
CCT - colorcopy transfer
cent - central
cert - certificate
chap - chapter
chmn - chairman
CIR - Circular
CL - Copper Leaf
CO - collage; Colorado
Co - County, Company

C-O - Cut-Out
c/o - in care of
COL - Collotype, College, Collograph
Coll - Collection
com - community
Comp - Competition
CON - Construction
conf - conference
conv - convention
COP - Copper, Coated Paper
Corp - Corporation
COT - Cotton
Coun - Council, County
CPI - Cast Plaster
CR - Crayon, Cream, Color Reduction
Ctr - Center
CS - Canal Zone; Chinese Silk
CT - Color Transfer
CV - Clicke Verre
Czech - Czechoslovakia

D - dyed
DB - Direct Bite
DC - District of Columbia, Die Cut
DE - Deluxe Edition, Delaware
DEB - Debossing
Dec - December
deleg - delegate, delegation
Dept - Department
DIA - Diameter
DIAG - Diagonal
dict - dictionary
DIE - Diecutting
DIG - Digigraph (Computer Originated)
Dipt - Diptych
Dir - Director
dist - district
div - division
DM - Deutsch Marks
DrT - Dremel Tool
DPT - Drypoint
DR - Drawing; Doctor; Drive
DT - Dye Transfer

E - East, Etching
econ - economy, economist
ed - edition
educ - education
EIP - Editions in Progress
elem - elementary
EMB - Embossed, Embossing
EN - Enamel
ENG - Engraving
Eng - England
Equiv - Equivalency, Equivolent
ERC - Epoxy Resin Celastic
estab - established
Eur - European
Ex - Examples
exhib - exhibit, exhibition
EXP - Expanded
Expo - Exposition
exten - extension

F - Foil
FA - Fabric
Fac - Faculty
FC - Full Color
FE - Felt
Fed - Federal, Federation
FF - French Francs
Fel - Fellowship
FL - Florida, Flocking
for - foreign
FOR - Formica
FP - Freepoint

G - Gold, Gouache, Gray
GA - Georgia
gen - general
GER - German, Germany
GL - Gold Leaf
GO - Gouache
Gov - Governor
Govt - Government
GR - Green
GRA - Gravure
GRS - Graphisculptures
GS - Gunshot
GT/Brit - Great Britain
Gym - Gymnasium

HC - Hand Colored; Hors de Commerce
HG - Hardground, Heliogravure
Helio - Heliogravure
hist - historical
HI - Hand-Inked
HL - Hand-Leaf
HM - Her Majesty; Handmade
HMP - Handmade Paper
hon - honorable, honorary
Hosp - Hospital
Hq - Headquarters
HS - Hot-Stamping
HST - Hand Set Type
HT - Heat Transfer, Height
HTP - Heat Transfer Print
Hwy - Highway

I - Intaglio, Ivory
IB - Black & White Intaglio
IC - Color Intaglio
IJ - Ink Jet
IL - Illuminated, Illinois
IL/BK - Illustrated Book
illum - illuminated
illus - illustrated, illustration
IN - Indiana
Inc - Incorporated
incl - include, includes, included, including
IND - Independent, India
info - Information
Inst - Institution
Instr - Instructor
Int - International
intro - introduction
IS - Image Size
Ital - Italian

Jr - Junior
Juv - juvenile

KS - Kansas, Kinetic Sculpture
KY - Kentucky

LA - Louisiana
lab - laboratory, laboratories
LAM - Lamination, Laminated
lang - language
LB - Black & White Lithograph
LC - Color Lithograph
LD - Lead
LEA - Leather
Lect - Lecturer
LG - Lift Ground
lib - liberal
Libr - Library
Librn - Librarian
LI - Line Etching
L/REL - Lead Relief
LIN - Linoleum
LP - Letterpress
Lt - Lieutenant

GENERAL ABBREVIATIONS CONTINUED

Ltd - Limited
LUMA - Lumagraph
LUS - Luster

M - Metal
MA - Massachusetts, Metal Applique
mag - magazine
maj - maj
MC - Microcast
MD - Maryland
ME - Mixografia Etching
Med - Medical
Mem - Memorial, member
MEI - metal
Metrop - Metropolitan
MEX - Mexico
MFA - Master of Fine Arts
MM - Mixed Media
MN - Minnesota
MO - Missouri; Mounted
Mod - Modern, Moderna, Moderne, Moderno
MON - Monoprint
M/REL - Metal Relief
MS - Multiple Sculpture, Mississippi
MSC - Metal Sculpture
Mt - Mount, Mountain
MT - Montage
MULT - Multiple
Mus - Musee, Museo, Museums(s)
Mgt - Management
MI - Michigan
MY - Mylar

N - North
Nat - National, Nationale
NB - New Brunswick
NC - North Carolina
ND - North Dakota
NE - Nebraska, Neon
NH - New Hampshire
NJ - New Jersey
NM - New Mexico
NO - Not Optional
Nov - November
NS - Nova Scotia
NV - Nevada
NY - New York, New York City
NZ - New Zealand

O - Other
OB - Out of Business, Open Bite
Oct - October
OFF - offset
off - office, official
OK - Oklahoma
ON - Ontario
OP - Oil Pastel
OR - Oregon
Orgn - Organization

P - Polymorph
PA - Pennsylvania, Painted
Pac - Pacific
PAL - Paladium
Pan-Am - Pan American
PAS - Pastel
PAT - Patton
PE - Pewter
PEI - Prince Edward Island
PENC - Pencil Lines
Ptas - Pesetas

P/FR - Paris, France
PH - Photograph
PH/GRA - Photogravure
PHC - Color Photograph
Photog - Photography
PI - Printer's Ink
PIG - Pigment
Pkwy - Parkway
PLEX - Plexiglass
PMO - Photo Mechanical Offset
PO - Pochoir
PO Box - Post Office Box
POL - Polyester, Policrom
POLAR - Polaroid
POR - Price on Request, Porcelain
PORT - Portugal, Portugese
PP - Pages, Potato Print
PQ - Province of Quebec
Pr - Proof
PR - Puerto Rico, Printed
Pres - President
Prof - Professor
Prog - Program
Prov - Province
PS - Paint Stik
PSc - Paper Sculptures
Pub - Public
pvt - private
PW - Paper Works

Q - Quarterly
Que - Quebec

R - Rubber, Rag
RD - Rural Delivery
Rd - Road
RE - Retablo
REL - Relief
rep - representative
Res - Research
rev - review
RFD - Rural Free Delivery
RH - Rhinestones
RI - Rhode Island
RL - Remarked Lithograph
RR - Rural Route, Relief Rolling
RS - Rubber Stamp
Rte - Route

S - South, Sandblasting
Sask - Saskatchewan
SB - Speedball; Spit Bite
SC - South Carolina, Sculpture
Scand - Scandanavia, Scandanavian
Sci - Science
SCUL - Sculpture
SD - South Dakota
SE - Sewing
Sec - Secondary
sect - section
Secy - Secretary
Sen - Senator, Senatorial
Sept - September
Serv - Service
SF - Swiss Francs
SG - Softground, Stonegravure
SI - Silk
SL - Sugarlift
Soc - Society
SOG - Soapground
SP - Sceenprint, Silkscreen

Span - Spanish
SPG - Sand Paper Ground
Sq - Square
Sr - Senior
SS - Stainless Steel
St - Saint, Street
Ste - Suite
STEN - Stenciled
STIT - Stitchery
STIP - Stipple
STR - Stratograph
Supt - Superintendent
Swed - Swedish
Switz - Switzerland

TAB - Tableau
TAP - Tapestry
tech - technical
Tel - Telephone
3D - Three Dimensional
THER - Thermography
TN - Tennessee
TR - Trials
Treas - Treasury, Treasurer
Trip - Triptych
Twp - Township
TX - Texas

UN - United Nations
UNESCO - United States Educational, Scientific & Cultural Organization
UNIQ - Unique
Univ - University, universidad
US - United States
USA - United States of America, United States Army
USAF - United States Air Force
USMC - United States Marine Corp
USN - United States Navy
USSR - Union of Soviet Socialist Republic

V - Vinyl
VA - Virginia
VAR - Varnished
Var - Various, Variety
VEL - Velvet
Vet - Veteran(s)
Vis - Visiting
VIS - Viscosity
VIT - Vitreograph
VP - Vice President
VT - Vermont

W - White, Woodcut, West
WA - Washington, Watercolor
WAL - Walnut
WB - Woodblock
WB/C - Woodblock Color Print
WBP - Woodblock Print
WC - Wax Coated, Color Woodcut
WD - Wood
WE - Wood Engraving, Wax Encaustic
WI - Wisconsin
wk - week
Wksp - Workshop
WVA - West Virginia
WY - Wyoming

X - Xerox
XC - Color Xerox

PAPER ABBREVIATIONS

AAP - Amatruda Amalfi Paper
AB-844 - Aqua B-844 Paper
AC/BL - Arches Cover, Black
AC - Arches Cover
ACET - Acetate
AE - American Etching
AE/R - American Etching Rag
AgB - Agfa Brovira
AgP/R118 - Agfa Portiga Rapid 118
AGP - Arches Garmari Paper
AHMP - Auvergne Handmade Paper
ALEX - Alexandra Paper
AM - A Milborn Paper
AMEP - American Etching Paper
AMG - Angoumois a la Main Paper
AMP - Angoumois a la Main Paper
AN/300 - Alt Nurnberg/300 lbs
AND - Andora
Antiq - Antique
AP - Arches Paper
AP/B - Arches Paper, Buff
AP/88 - Arches Paper, 88
AP/HS - Arches Paper, Heavy Satin
AP/260 - Arches Paper, 260
AP/S - Arches Paper, Satine
AP/SR - Arches Silkscreen Roll
AP/W - Arches Paper, White
AP/WA - Arches Paper, Watercolor
AQUA - Aquarelle Paper
ARJ - Arjamari Paper
ARM - Armand Paper
AS - Astralux; Arches Satine
ASHP - Arches Special Hot Press
AT - Atlantis Paper
AUV - Auvergne Paper
AWCP - Arches Watercolor Coldpress
AWP - Arches Watercolor Paper
AWP - A Wagami Paper

B - Buff, Board
BAP - Arches Paper, Buff
BAR - Barrier Paper
BAS - Basin Paper
BB - Bristol Board
BBR - British Barcham Regent, Green
BCP/80 - Buckeye Cover Paper - 80 pounds
BECK - Becket Paper
BEM - Bemboka Paper
BG/MC - Barcham Green/Michelle Cover
BHP - Basingwerk Heavy Paper
B/HMP - Bodleian Handmade Paper
BIT - Bitchutorinoko
BOD - Bodelian Mold Paper
BOX - Boxley Paper
BP - Bronze Powder
BP/BUP - Bütten Paper
BR - Brown
BrB - Bristol Board
BU - Butten Karton
BUT - Butcher Paper
BV - Buckeye Vellum

C/425 - Cansom 425
C/PL - Cast Plaster
C-S - Crown & Septre Paper
CAM/D - Cameo Dull
CAN - Canson Paper
CANV - Canvas
CARD - Cardboard
CB - Conqueror Bleu Paper
CC - Cailara Cover
CD - Copperplate Paper Deluxe
CFB - Cotton Fiber Board
CGP - Cedar Gasen Paper, Canson Gris Paper
CH - Chamois, Chiri Paper
CHP - Chatham Paper
CHI - Chijumatsu Paper
CHIF - Chiffon
CHIR - Chiri

CH/MAN - Chiffon de Mandeure
CHP - Chanke Paper
CIBA - Ciba Chrome
COL - Collombe Duchen, France
COLP - Colombe Paper
ColP - Colombre Paper
COR - Coranado
CotP/1927 - Cotman Paper/1927
CougP - Cougar Paper
COV - Coventry Paper
COV/R - Coventry Paper
CP - Copperplate Paper, Cast Paper
CP - Cast Paper
CP/100 - Cotton Pulp 100
CPP - Colored Pressed Paper Pulp
CPP - Copper Print Paper
CR - Carton, Crestwood Paper
CR/HMP - Crisbrook Handmade Paper
CRIS - Crisbrook Paper
CRP - Crestwood Paper
CRP - Chinese Rattan Paper
CUR - Curtis Rag Paper
CW - Crisbrook Waterleaf paper
CWCP - Commercial Wrapping Cartridge Paper
CYP - Cygne Paper

DB - Dewint Batil
DBC/W/R - DeBas Chamois Blanc 100 Oraz
DBIF - DeBas Inclusion Florales
DCBP - Duchene Colombe Black Paper
DD - Diamond Dust
DD/DPA - David David DPA Paper
DE - Dutch Etching Paper
DEP - Domestic Etching Paper
DIEU - Dieu Donne 100% Rag
DOM - Dominion, Domukuhanga
DOM/E - Domestic Etching Paper
DOV/DP - Dover Paper
DP - Dansk Paper
DPA - David Davis Japanese Rice Paper
Dul - Dulcite (80 pounds)
DV - Dupont Veralure

EKC - Ekta Color Photograph Paper
EKTA - Ekta Color Photograph Paper
ENG - English Paper
ENG/HMP - English Handmade Paper
EP - Essex Paper
EX/100 - Exeter
EVG - English Vellum Graph Paper
EXP - Exeter Paper
EXV - Exeter Vellum

F/HM - Don Farnsworth Handmade Paper
FAB - Fabriano Rosapina
FLP - French Lana Paper
FolAn - Folio Antique Paper
4/MM - 4 Mil Mylar
FP - Foil Paper
FrP - Frankfurt Paper
FRP - French Recycling Paper

G - Gray, Grey, Gold
G/100 - Gallery Paper 100
GAAP - G Amatruda Amalfi Paper
GAS - Gasenshi Echizen Paper
GB/V - Gum Bichromate on Vinyl
GC - German Copperplate
GCD - German Copperplate Deluxe Paper
GCP - German Copperplate Paper
GE - German Etching
GM/W - Grand Mogul/White
GMP - Grand Mogul Paper
GO - Glosskote Overscreen
GP - Guarro Paper
GPap - Glass Paper
GPP - Gallery Print Paper
GRA - Graphia Paper
GTNP - Gampi Torinoko Natural Paper

GUT - Gutenberg Laid Paper

H - Hahnemuhle Paper
H/HMP - Hodgkins Handmade Paper
HAHN - Hahnemühle Paper
HAM - Hammermill Index Paper
HAP - Happer White Graphic Weave Cover
HAW - Hawthorne Paper
HC - Hammermill Cover Paper
Heizo - Heizoburo Paper
HCP - Hand-Cast Paper
HEN - Henley Paper
HER - Heritage Paper
HIR - Hiroshi Paper
HMB - Handmade Board
HLP - Hawthorne of Larroque Paper
HMP - Handmade Paper
HMCP - Handmade Castle Paper
HMKP - Handmade Kozo Paper
HML - Hayle Mill Linen
HOD - Hodomura
HODG - Hodgkinson
HOL - Hollingsworth
HP/CP/A - Hand-Painted Cast Paper, Acrylic
HP/Cr - Holland Paper, Cream
HS - Hand-Stamped
HST - Hand-Stitched
HW, HWT - Heavy Weight

IE/R - Inveresk Exeter Paper
IKON - Ikonorex White Board
IN - Inveresk Paper
INC - Incisioni Paper
INCI - Incisioni Paper
ING - Ingres Paper
ING/C - Ingres Color Paper
INO - Inomachi Paper
INV - Inverest Paper
IP - Ivorex Paper
ITAL - Italia Paper
ITALIA - Italia Paper
IV - Inomachi Vellum Paper
IVWP - Indian Village Watercolor Paper
IWANO - Iwano Heizoburo

J - Japon Paper
JAP/E - Japanese Etching Paper
JAP/T - Japanese Tissue
JBG - J Barcham Green Paper
JBG/BOX - J Barcham Green Boxley Paper
JC - Japan Collé Paper
JEP - Japanese Etching Paper
JGP - Jeff Goodman Paper
JGW - J Green Waterleaf Paper
JK/HMP - John Koller Handmade Paper
JLP/R - Jack Lemon Paper
JM - Japanese Moriki Paper
JMP - Japanese Mulberry Paper
JO - Johanot Paper
JOH - Johannot Paper
JP - Japanese Paper
JRP - Japon Rice Paper
JSP - Japanese Suzuki Paper
J/Vel - Japanese Vellum
JW/HMP - I Whatman Handmade Paper
JWP - Joe Wilfer Paper

K - Kayasuki Paper
K/C - Kochi Paper tipped on Canson Paper
KAS - Kasuiri Paper
KASU - Kasugami Paper
KATH - Kathmandu Paper
KAY - Kayasuki Paper
KBR - Kupferdruck-Bütten-Romerturm Paper
KC/80 - Karma Cover, 80 pounds
KCJP - Kinwashi Japanese Paper, Cream
KEP - Kodak Ectocolor Paper
K/80 - Karma/80 lb. Paper
KHMP - Kozo Handmade Paper

PAPER ABBREVIATIONS CONTINUED

KHOP - Kisuki Hanga Dosa Paper
KHP - Kurotani Paper
KIN/ROL - Kinwashi Roll Paper
KIT - Kitakata Paper
KIZ - Kizuki Hanga Paper
KNP - Kizuki Nishinouchi Paper
KO - Kochi Paper
KOD - Kodak Paper
KOZO - Kozo Paper
KRP - Kozo Rice Paper
KUJ - Kujaku Paper
KUM - Kumoi Paper
KUR - Kurotani Paper

L/100 - Lenox 100
LAID - Laid Paper
LANA - Lana Paper
LarP - Larroque Paper
LAV - Lavis a Grains
LBP - Lawrence Barker Paper
LEN - Lenox Paper
LEN/MB - Lenox Museum Board
LFP - La France Paper
LIN - Linen, Linden Paper
LNP - Laga Narcissi Paper
LP - Lenox Paper, Lowell Paper, Linorg Paper
L/2P - 2-Ply Lenox Paper
LINR - Linen Rag Paper

M/100 - Mirage 100% Rag Paper
M/ROW - Metalic Rowlex
M/VEL - Meirat Vellum Paper
MAG - Magnani Incisioni Paper
MAG/IT - Magnani Italia
MAR - Mareki Paper
MASA - Masa Paper
MAY - Mayfair Paper
MB - Moulin des Berger Paper
MB/100 - Museum Board 100% Rag Paper
MDL/ML - Moulin de Larroque Paper
MdV - Moulin du Verger Paper
MEX - Mexican Bark Paper
MF - Metallic Foil
MG - Moulin du Gue Paper
MING/BL - Mingel Blue Paper
MINO - Mino Paper
MIR - Mirage Paper
MLP - Monteval Laid Paper
MMB - Museum Mounting Board
MM/HMP - Mingei Momo Handmade Paper
MO, MOH - Mohawk Paper
MO/S - Mohawk Superfine
MOR - Japanese Moriki Paper
MOR/BL - Moriki Paper, Black
MOR/G - Moriki Paper, Grey
MP - Marsa Paper, Metallic Powder, Muslin Paper, Mirage Plate Paper
MUL - Mulberry Paper
MUR - Murillo Paper
MV - Mirage Vellum Paper
MVP - Moulin de Verge Paper
MY - Mylar

NAJ - Najaho Cover Paper
NAT, NP - Natsume Paper
NB - Nelson Bristol Paper
Nepal/H4 - Nepal H4 Papers
NEWS - Newsprint
NG - Natural Gasen Paper
NI - No Ink (Inkless)
NISH - Nishinouchi Gasen
Nouchi - Nouchi Paper
NP - Nacre Paper

OKP - Okawara Paper
OP - Oatmeal Paper, Oriental Paper

PAN - Pangeae Paper
PAP - Papel de Amate Paper

PaP - Painte Papers
PAT - Pattan Paper
PCP - Pressed Cedarbark Paper
PdL - Papier du Lin
Pes Mag - Pescia Magnani
PHP - Photographic Paper
PL - Papier du Lin
PLEX - Plexiglass
PLBP - Plate Bristol Paper
PM - Pescia Malaspina
PN - Papier Noir
POLAR - Polaroid
PP - Printmaster Paper, Paper Pulp
PT - Papier de Taiwan
PU - Pulp
PW - Paper Work

Q/100 - Quintessence/100 lb

R/BFK - Rives BFK
R/100 - 100% Rag Paper
RAG/B - Rag Board
RAG/H - Heavy Rag
RAK - Rakusau Paper
RB - Rives Bütten Paper
RBP, RdB - Richard de Bas Paper
RBT/HMP - Richard B Tullis II/Handmade Paper
RcP - Ragcoat Paper
RG, RGP - Rising Gallery Paper
RG/100 - Rising Gallery 100 Paper
RG/245 - Rising Gallery - 245 lbs
RGPS - Rising Gallery Print Smooth
RGPV - Rising Gallery Print Vellum 100% Rag
RHW/B - Rives Heavyweight Paper, Buff
RIP - Rives Infine Paper
RKB - R K Burt Paper
RLP - Roleaf Paper
RMB - Rising Museum Board 100% Rag Paper
RO - Rose Oatmeal Paper
ROL - Roll Paper
ROMA - Roma Paper
ROP - Roulette Paper
ROS - Rosapina Paper
ROU - Roulette Paper
RP - Rives Paper, Rice Paper
RP/BUT - River Butten Paper
RP/G - Rives Paper, Grey
RP/HWT - Rives Paper, Heavy Weight
RP/MdG - Rives Paper, Moulin du Gue
RP/NEWS - Rives Paper/Newsprint
RP/SP - Special Rives Paper
RT - Ripple Tone Paper
RWP - Rosapina Paper, White
RWSP - Royal Watercolor Society Paper

S - Satine Paper
S/100 - Supra 100 Paper
SA - St Armands Paper
SAK - Sakamoto Paper
SB - Speedball Paper
SCH - Schoellerhammer Paper
SchD - Schoeller Durex Paper
SchP - Schoeller Hammer Paper
SchPar - Schoeller Parole Paper
SCP - Silver Coated Paper
SE - Stone Edge Paper
SEK - Sekishu Paper
SEN - Sennelier Paper
SFP - Standard Form Paper
SHO - Shoin Paper, Shojigami Paper
SHP - Schoeller Hammer Paper
SIC - Sicars Paper
SIR - Sirene Paper
SKP - Seichosen Kozo Paper
SL - Silver Leaf
SNP - Sekishu Natural Paper
SOM - Somerset Paper
SOM/SAT - Somerset Satin Paper
SOM/T - Somerset Textured Paper

SP - Silver Paper
SP/H - Heavy Stock Paper
SRP/W - Sekishi Rice Paper, White
SS/W - Somerset Satin Paper, White
STAR - Starwhite (Weyerhauser) Paper
ST/100 - Strathmore 100% Rag Paper
STR - Strathmore Paper
STR/IM - Strathmore Impress
STP/C - Stonehenge Paper, Cream
STP/100 - Stonehenge 100% Rag Paper
SUG - Suginkawa Paper
SUGI - Sugi Veneer
SUP - Superior Training Paper
SUP/100 - Supra 100
SUZ - Suzuki Paper
SWHP - Saunders Wooky Hale Paper
SWP - Saunders Waterford Paper

T - Tan, Textured Paper
TAB - Tableau Paper
TC - Torinoko Paper, Cream
3DC - Three Dimensional Cutout Construction Paper
THS - TH Saunders Paper
THS/W - TH Saunders Paper, White
TI - Taiten Indigo Paper
TIEM - Tiempolo Paper
TOR - Torinoko Paper
TorP - Torchon Paper
TOS - Toshi Paper
TOSA - Tosa Hanga Paper
TOY - Toyoshi Paper
TR/HMP - Twin Rocker Handmade Paper
TR/WF - Twin Rocker, White Feather Paper
TRANS - Transpagra Paper
TUS - Tuscan Paper
TWC - Twisiso Weave Cover Paper
TYP - Tycore Panel Paper

UDA - Uda Thin Paper
UMB - Umbria Paper
UNRYU - Unryu Paper
UP - Uriuchi Paper
UT - Utrecht Paper

VBP - Vellum Bristol Paper
VC - Velin Chiffon Paper
VD - Vat-Dyed
VEL - Vellum
VF - Vacuum-Formed
VFP - Vacuum-Formed Plastic
VGP - Van Gelderen Paper
VGZ - Van Gelder Zonex Paper
VG/DE - Van Gelder Dutch Etching Paper

W/AP/CC - White Arches Paper
WAP - Watercolor Paper
WASH - Washi Paper
WatP - Waterford Paper
WatPr - Waterford Paper
WEST - Westwinds Paper
WesVel - Westwinds Vellum Paper
WHMP - Wookery Hole Mauve Paper
WHP - Whatman Paper
WJP - Jersey Plate Paper, White
WLP - Water leaf Paper
WP - Watercolor Paper
WP/ANT - Whatman Antique Paper
WP/BB - Waterproof Billboard Paper
WP/80 - Weyerhauser Paper, 80 lbs
WR/BFK - Rives BFK Paper, White
WSHP - WS Hodgkinson
WSP - White Stock Paper
WWP - Westwind Paper

YAM - Yamato Paper
YO - Yoseido Paper

ZER - Zerkall Paper

ARTIST APPLICATION FOR THE PRINTWORLD DIRECTORY

BIOGRAPHICAL DATA

All information must be typed! Please give complete mailing addresses for all galleries, museums, universities, printers, and publishers. Do not abbreviate (except city & state). All applicants must include print listings (use the documentation form provided on the opposite page). All print/price listings must be original signed, numbered, limited editions with a retail value of $100 or more.

NAME _____ DATE _____

ADDRESS _____

_____ PHONE _____

PLACE OF BIRTH: _____ DATE OF BIRTH: _____

EDUCATION:

TEACHING EXPERIENCE:

AWARDS (Precise) (Year)

RECENT SHOWS (Solo or Group) (Complete Addresses) (Year)

REPRESENTATION IN MUSEUMS, UNIVERSITIES, INSTITUTIONS:

PUBLISHERS (Complete Addresses):

PRINTERS (Complete Addresses):

GALLERIES: (Complete Address):

PRINTWORLD INTERNATIONAL, INC. • Publisher of The Printworld Directory of Contemporary Prints & Prices
Post Office Box 1957 • West Chester, Pennsylvania 19380 • (215) 649-5140 • (215) 431-6654

SAMPLE DOCUMENTATION FORM FOR THE PRINTWORLD DIRECTORY

Please use this format for each print you submit. Be explicit and complete. Please type.

ARTIST:

ADDRESS:

COMPLETE PRINT TITLE (Suites may be listed together):

PUBLISHER:

PRINTER:

DATE (PUBLICATION):

MEDIUM:

EDITION NUMBER:

PRINT SIZE (PAPER SIZE):   **PAPER STOCK:**

NUMBER OF COLORS:

RELEASE PRICE (OPENING):   **SET:**   **EACH:**

CURRENT RETAIL PRICE: **SET:**   **EACH:**

SOLD OUT EDITION (RARE):   **CURRENT EDITION:**
                                   (Please check one)

GALLERIES WHO SELL THIS PRINT: **COMPLETE ADDRESS:**

Artists, galleries and print publishers may submit artist biographical and print documentation forms for The Printworld Directory. All information must be approved by the Selection Committee. There is a small fee to process each artist's file. Inclusion of all materials will be at the discretion of the editor.

PRINTWORLD INTERNATIONAL, INC. • Publisher of The Printworld Directory of Contemporary Prints & Prices
Post Office Box 1957 • West Chester, Pennsylvania 19380 • (215) 649-5140 • (215) 431-6654

GLOSSARY OF PRINT TERMINOLOGY

Acid Bath—A tray containing acid mixed with water in which the plate is immersed to be bitten. See Bite.

A la Poupee—A method of applying multi-color inks by rollers or other tools, to one plate in different areas for a single impression.

Aluminum—Metal used in connection with hand printed lithography as an alternative to stone.

Aquatint—An etching process in which the tonality is achieved by dusting powdered resin onto a plate, heating it, when the resin has adhered to the plate, the plate is etched.

Artist's Proof—Artist's Proof should be exactly the same as the edition in quality and image though they are outside the numbered edition. They are identified with "A.P." or "Artist's Proof" on the impression. They are often retained by the artist or publisher.

Asphaltum—A bituminous substance used in intaglio as an acid resist. In lithography it may be used for drawing or rolling up stones or plates.

Baren—A padded tool used for rubbing the back of paper in relief printing from blocks.

Bite—Term is used for the action of acid on the plate in the acid bath.

Blankets—Pads used between the paper and roller on an etching press to prevent movement of paper during printing. Also to provide cushioning and aid in pressing paper into the lines of the plates, etc.

Blind Stamp—The same as chop but stamped with ink on verso of the print. See also Chop.

Bon a Tirer—A literal translation from the French meaning "good to pull" and refers to the first print the artist decides to use for editioning. This print is then used as a guide for printer of the edition. This print is annotated Bon a Tirer, B.A.T. or R.T.P. (Right to Print), and is outside the edition.

Burin—A tool with a steel shaft used for engraving metal plates or wood blocks.

Burr—The ridge left in the metal plate on both sides of the needle-cut line. A ridge of metal created as the needle cuts into the metal plate. In printing creates a soft fuzzy line, instead of a clean sharp line as in engraving.

Cancellation Proof—A proof pulled from defaced plate, screen or block, to guarantee that no other prints may be made from that edition, thus insuring a limited edition.

Chine Colle/Chine Applique—A process in which one sheet of paper is adhered to another by pressure, usually a thin paper laminated to backing during the printing process.

Chop—An identifying mark embossed on a print to identify the workshop, printer or publisher of the print.

Collagraph—A print of a collage which may consist of a variety of materials glued to a rigid plate. The plate is then inked and printed usually on an etching press.

Color Separations—Proofs of each separate color of a multicolor print.

Color Trial Proof—This term may be used to annotate Trial Proofs, these proofs may be done using the same plates as in the edition but the color varies from that used in the edition.

Couching—The process of transferring a wet just formed sheet of paper from mold to a wet felt. Two or more sheets may be couched together to form one sheet. This can be used as a means of making limited editions of cast paper.

Deckle Edge—The uneven edge on handmade paper or mould made paper.

Drypoint—Drawing on a metal plate with a needle of hard steel, often with a diamond point. The "burr" that is formed along the edge of the line traps the ink for a soft rich effect.

Dustbox—A box in which a plate is coated with powdered rosin for aquatint processing.

Edition—Total number of prints pulled from one image and represents the largest body of work for sale from that image. These prints are consecutively numbered to show that the edition is limited by publisher or artist.

Embossment/Debossment—The effect attained by a specially cut plate or block printed inkless. This results in the image on paper having a raised or lowered effect.

Engraving—A method of drawing that employs a burin or graver to cut or incise on a metal plate.

Etching—An intaglio process in which the lowered printing areas are bitten and etched by acid. The drawing and preparation of the plate can be accomplished with a variety of techniques dealt with elsewhere in this glossary. See Hardground, Sugar Lift and Softground.

Felts—The woven fabrics, such as wool, on which the made papers are placed when wet. See Couching.

Fibers—Threadlike structures, often cellulose, that make up papermaking pulp.

Handmade Paper—Paper formed by a hand held mould or matrix.

Hardground—A waxy varnish or ground applied to a plate to prepare it for drawing. The ground masks out areas not to be bitten in the acid bath, it acts as a resist. This technique is commonly used to produce fine line drawings.